Notable Names in the American THEATRE

Notable Names in the American THEATRE

James T. White & Company
Clifton, New Jersey
1976

First edition (*The Biographical Encyclopaedia and Who's Who of the American Theatre*) 1966

New and revised edition (*Notable Names in the American Theatre*)

For information address: James T. White & Company,
1700 State Highway Three, Clifton, N.J. 07013

Printed and bound in the United States of America

Library of Congress Cataloging in Publication Data

Main entry under title:

Notable names in the American theatre.

First ed. (1966) edited by W. Rigdon.
Bibliography: p.
1. Theater—United States—Biography. I. Rigdon, Walter. The biographical encyclopedia & who's who of the American theatre.
PN2285.N6 1976 790.2/0973 76-27356
ISBN 0-88371-018-8

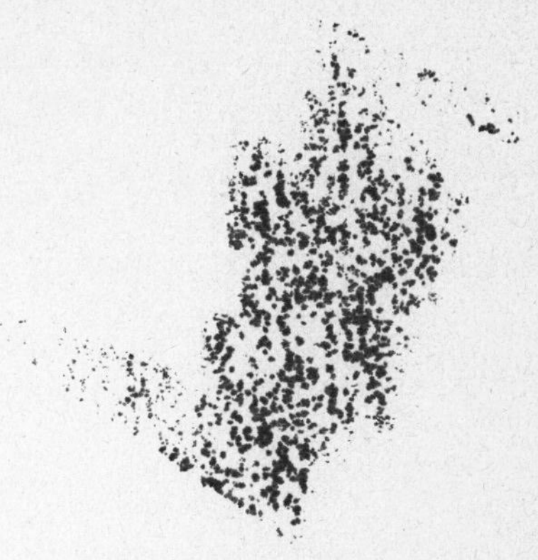

Foreword

In many ways it seems impossible that a decade has passed since the publication of the First Edition of this work, at that time called THE BIOGRAPHICAL ENCYCLOPAEDIA AND WHO'S WHO OF THE AMERICAN THEATRE *and now retitled* NOTABLE NAMES IN THE AMERICAN THEATRE. *When I turn to consult the original edition, however, I realize acutely how much the present revision is needed. So many of the newer figures are not included in the earlier edition, so many of the personages have passed from the main body of the book to the necrology, new theatre groups have been born and some of the older ones have passed into history. Some pages of the copy I constantly use are crisscrossed with additions, death dates, and notes that this dramatist or that actor is not listed.*

During the pre-austerity days in Great Britain, the WHO'S WHO IN THE THEATRE *(the* BIOGRAPHICAL ENCYCLOPAEDIA'S *English counter-companion) was published every three years. This seems about right when one considers how quickly events take place, how many productions open and close, how many awards are bestowed in the space of three years. Present economic conditions, I realize, make this schedule fairly impossible. One hopes, however, that it will not be another decade before a successor volume to this second edition appears and that the audience for this book will welcome it with both kudos and with dollars so that we may look forward to what George Freedley envisioned in the introduction to the First Edition—"that it may bring home many future editions through the coming years!"*

PAUL MYERS
Curator, Theatre Collection
THE NEW YORK PUBLIC LIBRARY

Preface

Every publishing venture, needless to say, has a beginning and an end. Contradictorily, however, only when the end is in view does the editor prepare to unburden himself of a few *prefatory* remarks. In the case of a theatre book, he may be said to set the stage, block the action, adjust the sightlines, and give the historical background in program notes: to drop the metaphor, he writes a preface. This volume will not break the tradition. Herewith, then, is the information the researcher needs to know about the book and its genesis, its uses and form, and acknowledgment of and thanks to several individuals who contributed significantly to its successful fruition.

More than a decade ago James H. Heineman issued the first major one-volume biographical reference work devoted exclusively to the American theatre, its personalities, and a record of its and their activities. The inclusion of individuals from other countries who had played an important part in theatre in this country made the volume truly reflective of the thespian art in the United States.

Called *The Biographical Encyclopaedia and Who's Who of the American Theatre*, the volume, under the editorship of Walter Rigdon, was greeted with rapturous reviews and a multitude of compliments, and very quickly secured an important place on library reference shelves and in professional offices throughout the world. No other volume previous or current brought together such a large quantity of diverse information vital to the theatrical researcher's needs. No wonder, then, that John Mason Brown called the First Edition "not a book but a library" and the *Saturday Review* referred to it as "the biggest thing in drama."

Another significant accomplishment of this volume, one widely hailed by reviewers and users alike, was that at last the American theatre had been provided with its own reference work and was no longer dependent on a British-oriented *Who's Who*. Generously enough, it was a London newspaper that paid the book one of its most appropriate commendations by dubbing it the bible of Broadway.

Therefore, when the present editor almost two years ago inquired of an experienced theatre librarian what service a publishing house could best give in the performing arts area, it was not surprising that the answer came back immediately, "Update the theatre *Who's Who*—we need current information." This rejoinder marks the beginning of the road that ends with the publication of what in a real way is the Second Edition of *The Biographical Encyclopaedia and Who's Who of the American Theatre*. It has been decided, however, to retitle the work *Notable Names in the American Theatre* so that it will conform with other titles in a series of reference works inaugurated by this company with *Notable Names in American History* and planned to cover other aspects of America's social and cultural history—today and yesterday.

Notable Names in the American Theatre was prepared with a twofold object. Our first task was to provide a ten-year update of the already existing material, and where fitting, to introduce new material and increase the scope of previously established "chapters." Secondly, our particular aim, of course, has been to continue the availability of a one-volume reference work containing the answers to the professional and casual researcher's and the student's basic queries about the theatre in this country. Immediately below are brief explanatory notes on the parts making up this work. The reader should know that, although the major portion of the book is devoted to biographies, several supportive sections greatly enhance its usefulness and contain a considerable amount of independent data.

New York Productions

This section, one of the most frequently consulted of the First Edition, provides a veritable index to the New York theatre from 1900 to the present. In one alphabetical listing by title, the user will find all New York productions with the following data: type of production, name of theatre, date of opening, and number of performances. Frequently this section provides the starting point for research into the American theatre. It has been prepared by Maxwell Silverman, long a staff member of the New York Public Library's Theatre Collection at Lincoln Center.

Premieres in America

This entirely new section offers a listing of play premieres throughout America, giving title, author, date of first performance, and names of producing groups and theatres. Although more proscribed by time limits, this compendium represents, as does the New York Productions section, an index to plays produced in the United States since 1968. The lists have been compiled by Donald W. Fowle, also of the Theatre Collection, for publication in *Plays and Players*. The alphabetically arranged titles are augmented by an author index.

Premieres of American Plays Abroad

Foreign interest in American plays is attested to by this list of premieres abroad. Entries supply such data as name of play, author, director, producer and theatre, location, and date of premiere.

Theatre Group Biographies

In this edition, emphasis has been placed on enlarging the scope of the coverage of this section. Noteworthy defunct organizations have been retained for historical reasons; more recently established groups and producing organizations have been added. Otherwise, the previously published entries have been brought up to date to illustrate the groups' activities during the past decade.

Theatre Building Biographies

Here is a continuation of a similar section of the First Edition to which have been added entries concerning playhouses of various kinds that have been opened since 1964. The theatres at Lincoln Center, the new office building theatres, and a number of off-Broadway houses are among the new buildings treated. Here in brief and alphabetically arranged and cross-indexed, the New York theatres are delineated.

In this connection, we might with understandable pride point out a source for further research in this subject published by James T. White and Company: Dr. Mary C. Henderson's *The City and the Theatre*, which sets forth in fascinating detail the history of the New York playhouses from the earliest years to 1934.

Awards

The list of awards includes those significant prizes which are presented to theatre professionals or groups, or awards in other media for which theatrical persons may be eligible. Current awards have been continued and brought up to date or added to the lists in the First Edition, while notable discontinued prizes have been retained for reference purposes. Names of recipients are given from the inception of each award, and where it has seemed helpful, a brief description of the award has been appended.

Biographical Bibliography

This reference list of books by and about significant personalities of the theatre represents a major enlargement of a section of the First Edition. There are over 900 names listed and nearly 2900 titles—surely a liberal introduction to the literature of theatrical biography and a checklist of books about the people of the theatre. If not American, all cited persons are relevant to a study of the theatre in this country.

The bibliography was prepared by Dorothy L. Swerdlove, First Assistant, the Theatre Collection at Lincoln Center, and she has prepared the following notes about her list:

> Some of these titles are straight-forward accounts, some are more highly-colored biographies, and others are scholarly, critical works. Some biographies cover only a portion of the subject's life, or consist mainly of reminiscences or diary excerpts or correspondence. They are all published monographs in English, and in one way or another are worthy of the researcher's attention.
>
> When an author chose to write under an assumed name, the pseudonym has generally been used in the bibliography. Wherever possible, the original date of publication is used even though a reprint may exist, because the original date gives a better picture of the information available when the book was written.
>
> Most of the titles in this section are available in The New York Public Library, either in the Branch Libraries System or in the Research Department, and will be found in other large public libraries.
>
> If there are several entries under a subject's name, the titles are alphabetized by author; where one of these authors has written several works, individual titles are listed in chronological order.

Special attention should be given to the essay on the history of theatre magazines under the heading "Stage Periodicals" in the Theatre Group Biographies section.

Necrology

The original necrology is herewith continued with the addition of (1) names of theatre persons deceased since the previous edition, (2) names of others who were missed in that edition, and (3) further statistics to complete entries already published. In any listing of this sort, missing statistics present an on-going challenge; as data is subsequently uncovered, it will be added in future editions.

Notable Names in the American Theatre

Here is a biographical directory of today's leading theatrical figures, most of them Americans but some of other nationalities who have made important contributions to the American stage. Initially, names of persons deceased since the publication of the First Edition have been eliminated; these are being preserved for a subsequent historical volume. On the other hand, names have been added of persons who have come to prominence during the past decade.

The biographies in the First Edition were so widely hailed that the present editors opted to continue the same style with regard to manner of presentation of factual data. Already printed biographies were sent to the subjects themselves for updating, and specially prepared questionnaires went to new subjects. When biographies were returned, they were checked against reliable sources by a staff of researchers; when information was not received, the biographies were researched and carefully checked against authoritative sources. All basic source material is on hand in the publisher's files.

One overriding principle has governed the selection of names of persons to be included in this section: that the subject has made a notable contribution in one or more of several ways to the American theatre. The "several ways" include more than twenty categories, among them performer, producer, playwright, stage and costume designer, choreographer, composer, lyricist, conductor, casting director, teacher, critic, educator, author, historian, archivist, administrator, representative, publicist . . . and the individuals who have been selected are the practitioners of these arts. The statistics of their lives and their professional credits offer a panorama of the American stage and the basis for contemporary theatre research. Their achievements recommend them to this volume and qualify them as research subjects.

While *Notable Names in the American Theatre* is based in large part on the work of the editors of the First Edition, the present editors must assume complete responsibility for this edition. We have reviewed the previously published text and exercised our own judgment on what material should be included, keeping in mind always that our objective was to create a one-volume theatrical reference library. Certain deletions were made in the biographical section to insure the pertinency of all subjects to the area of today's theatrical arts; and because it is our aim to follow this volume with others in a series pertaining to the performing arts, biographies of individuals whose careers are more closely connected with other fields will subsequently be found in works dealing with film, television, music and dance, thus permitting fuller coverage in each instance.

Although many individuals and organizations have been helpful in our task, acknowledgment must be made primarily to the Theatre Collection, New York Public Library, at Lincoln Center, to the institution as an entity and to its dedicated and obliging staff. Paul Myers presides paternalistically over this collection, without whose munificent files the satisfactory compilation of this book would have been all but impossible, and he graciously assisted our researchers in many practical ways. The completion of the project must in large part be credited to the splendid efforts of a dedicated editorial staff. And a special word of thanks must be expressed to James H. Heineman, whose foresight made possible the original volume and whose faith in our sincerity guaranteed the second.

To the student, to the researcher, to the browser and buff, to the theatre professional—herewith is your book about the theatre in the United States told in terms of the individual. We already dare to see the need for another edition and welcome your comments.

The curtain is up!

William H. White
Publisher

Raymond D. McGill
Editor

Table of Contents

New York Productions

A

A for Adult (p), 2/17/64, Sheridan Square Playhouse
A la Broadway / Hello, Paris (r), 9/22/11, Folies Bergère, 8
A la Carte (r), 8/17/27, Martin Beck Theatre, 46
A Media Luz Los Tres (p), 10/25/70, Greenwich Mews Theatre, 17
Abbey Theatre Players, 10/18/32, Martin Beck Theatre, 31
Abbey Theatre Players, 11/12/34, John Golden Theatre, 14
Abe and Mawruss (p), 10/21/15, Lyric Theatre, 196
Abe Lincoln in Illinois (p), 10/15/38, Plymouth Theatre, 472
Abe Lincoln in Illinois (p), 1/21/63, Anderson Theatre, 40
Abelard and Heloise (p), 3/10/71, Brooks Atkinson Theatre, 53
Abide with Me (p), 11/21/35, Ritz Theatre, 36
Abie's Irish Rose (p), 5/23/22, Fulton Theatre, 2,327
Abie's Irish Rose (p), 5/12/37, Little Theatre, 46
Abie's Irish Rose (p), 11/18/54, Holiday Theatre, 20
Abigail (p), 2/21/05, Savoy Theatre, 47
About Town (p), 8/30/06, Herald Square Theatre, 138
Abraham Cochrane (p), 2/17/64, Belasco Theatre, 1
Abraham Lincoln (p), 12/15/19, Cort Theatre, 244
Abraham Lincoln (p), 10/21/29, Forrest Theatre, 8
Absence of a Cello (p), 9/21/64, Ambassador Theatre, 120
Absent Father (p), 10/17/32, Vanderbilt Theatre, 88
Absolutely Freeee (r), 5/24/67, Garrick Theatre, 206
Abyssinia (m), 2/20/06, Majestic Theatre, 31
Accent on Youth (p), 12/25/34, Plymouth Theatre, 229
Accent on Youth (p), 5/16/69, Master Theatre, 9, (Equity Library Theatre)
According to Law / A Strange Play (p), 6/1/44, Mansfield Theatre, 4
According to Law / The Devil Is a Good Man / What D'You Call It (p), 3/19/40, Provincetown Playhouse, 38
Accused (p), 9/29/25, Belasco Theatre, 95
AC/DC (p), 2/23/71, Brooklyn Academy of Music, 28, (Chelsea Theatre Center)
Achilles Had a Heel (p), 10/13/35, 44th St. Theatre, 8
Acid Wine / Frugal Noon (p), 5/22/64, Theatre East, 3
Acquisition, The. See Trainer, Dean, Liepolt and Company
Acquittal, The (p), 1/5/20, Cohan and Harris Theatre, 138
Acrobats / Line (p), 2/15/71, Theatre de Lys, 31
Acropolis (p), 11/4/69, Washington Square Methodist Church, 12, (Polish Laboratory Theatre)
Across the Board on Tomorrow Morning / Talking to You (p), 8/17/42, Belasco Theatre, 8
Across the Board on Tomorrow Morning / Talking to You (p) (Two by Saroyan), 10/22/61, East End Theatre, 96
Across the Street (p), 3/24/24, Hudson Theatre, 32
Act without Words I / Happy Days (p), 11/20/72, Forum Theatre, 16
Actorines and Actorettes (p), 6/7/73, Hudson Guild Theatre, 11
Actors' and Authors' Theatre, Inc. (Rep.), 6/10/18, Fulton Theatre
Actors / At Home (p), 5/16/74, Ensemble Studio Theatre
Ada Beats the Drum (p), 5/8/30, John Golden Theatre, 46
Ada Rehan Repertory (p), 1/18/04, Lyric Theatre, 24
Ada Rehan Repertory, 2/6/05, Liberty Theatre, 16
Adam and Eva (p), 9/13/19, Longacre Theatre, 312
Adam Had Two Sons (p), 1/20/32, Alvin Theatre, 5
Adam's Apple (p), 6/10/29, Princess Theatre, 16
Adam Solitaire (p), 11/6/25, Provincetown Playhouse, 17
Adams' Wife (p), 12/28/31, Ritz Theatre, 8
Adaptation / Next (p), 2/10/69, Greenwich Mews Theatre, 707
Adding Machine, The (p), 3/19/23, Garrick Theatre, 72
Adding Machine, The (p), 2/9/56, Phoenix Theatre, 6
Adding Machine, The (p), 11/19/70, WPA Theatre
Adele (m), 8/28/13, Longacre Theatre, 196
Adler, Larry and Draper, Paul, 12/31/43, New York City Center, 4
Admirable Bashville, The / The Dark Lady of the Sonnets (p), 2/20/56, Cherry Lane Theatre, 98
Admirable Crichton, The (p), 11/17/03, Lyceum Theatre, 144
Admirable Crichton, The (p), 3/9/31, New Amsterdam Theatre, 56
Admiral, The (p), 4/24/24, 48th St. Theatre, 6
Adora. See Playwrights Cooperative Festival
Adorable Liar, The (p), 8/30/26, 49th St. Theatre, 33
Adrea (p), 1/11/05, Belasco Theatre, 123
Adrienne (m), 5/28/23, George M. Cohan Theatre, 235
Adventure (p), 9/25/28, Republic Theatre, 22
Adventure of Lady Ursula, The (p), 3/1/15, Maxine Elliott's Theatre, 32
Adventurous Age, The (p), 2/7/27, Mansfield Theatre, 16
Advertising of Kate, The (p), 5/8/22, Ritz Theatre, 24
Advise and Consent (p), 11/17/60, Cort Theatre, 212
Advocate, The (p), 10/14/63, ANTA Theatre, 8
Aero Club, The (p), 1/28/07, Criterion Theatre, 22
Aesop's Fables (r), 8/17/72, Mercer / Brecht Theatre, 58
Affair of Honor (p), 4/6/56, Ethel Barrymore Theatre, 27
Affair of State, An (p), 11/19/30, Broadhurst Theatre, 24
Affair, The (p), 9/20/62, Henry Miller's Theatre, 116
Affairs of Anatol, The (p), 10/14/12, Little Theatre, 72
Affairs of Anatol, The. See also Anatol
Affairs of State (p), 9/25/50, Royale Theatre, 610
Affinity, The (p), 1/3/10, Comedy Theatre, 24
Affinity, The. See also Incubus
Afgar (m), 11/8/20, Central Theatre, 168
African Millionaire, An (p), 4/4/04, Princess Theatre, 8
Africana (r), 7/11/27, Daly's Theatre, 77
Africana (m), 11/26/34, Venice Theatre, 3
After All (p), 12/3/31, Booth Theatre, 20
After Five (p), 10/29/13, Fulton Theatre, 13
After Liverpool / Games (p), 1/22/73, Bijou Theatre, 1, (New Phoenix Repertory Sideshow)
After Magritte / The Real Inspector Hound (p), 4/23/72, Theatre Four, 465
After Such Pleasures (r), 2/7/34, Bijou Theatre, 23
After the Fall (p), 1/23/64, ANTA—Washington Square Theatre, 208
After the Rain (p), 10/9/67, John Golden Theatre, 64

Note: The letters following titles of production indicate: play (p), musical (m), and revue (r). Performers' names are given after the titles of many classics to identify a particular revival. The date indicates the opening performance of a run, and the final figure represents the total number of performances.

After Tomorrow (p), 8/26/31, John Golden Theatre, 78
After-Dinner Evening with Oskar Werner, An, 3/25/67, Town Hall, 1
Afternoon of Dance, An, 1/8/28, Cosmopolitan Theatre, 1
Afternoon Storm / Hope Is the Thing with Feathers / Celebration (p) (The Six O'Clock Theatre's Studio Productions), 4/11/48, Maxine Elliott's Theatre, 8
Agatha Sue, I love you (p), 12/14/66, Henry Miller's Theatre, 5
Age of Anxiety, The (p), 3/18/54, Living Theatre Studio
Age of Innocence, The (p), 11/27/28, Empire Theatre, 209
Aged 26 (p), 12/21/36, Lyceum Theatre, 32
Agee, 2/10/69, Theatre de Lys, 2, (ANTA Matinee)
Ages of Man (Gielgud), 12/28/58, 46th St. Theatre, 40
Ages of Man (Gielgud), 4/14/63, Lyceum Theatre, 9
Aglavaine and Selysette, 1/3/22, Maxine Elliott's Theatre
Agnes (p), 10/5/08, Majestic Theatre, 16
Ah, Wilderness! (p), 10/2/33, Guild Theatre, 285
Ah, Wilderness! (p), 10/2/41, Guild Theatre, 29
Ah! Wine! (p), 1/14/74, New York Theatre Ensemble Arena, 18
Aiglon, L' (p) (Sarah Bernhardt), 4/8/01, Metropolitan Opera House, 8
Aiglon, L' (p), 10/20/24, Henry Miller's Theatre, 8
Aiglon, L' (p), 12/26/27, Cosmopolitan Theatre, 8
Aiglon, L' (p), 11/3/34, Broadhurst Theatre, 58
Ain't It the Truth (r), 12/19/21, Manhattan Opera House, 17
Ain't Supposed To Die a Natural Death (m), 10/20/71, Ethel Barrymore Theatre, 325
Air-Minded (p), 2/10/32, Ritz Theatre, 13
Airways, Inc., 2/20/29, Grove St. Theatre, 27
Akokawe (r), 6/4/70, St. Marks Playhouse, 30
Akokawe (Initiation) (r), 5/19/69, St. Marks Playhouse, 44
Alarm Clock, The (p), 12/24/23, 39th St. Theatre, 32
Alarums and Excursions (r), 5/29/62, Second City at Square East, 450
Alaskan, The (m), 8/12/07, Knickerbocker Theatre, 29
Alcestis Comes Back / At Sea (p), 4/23/62, Mermaid Theatre, 8
Alchemist, The (p) (Jose Ferrer), 5/6/48, New York City Center, 14
Alchemist, The (p), 9/14/64, Gate Theatre, 46
Alchemist, The (p), 10/13/66, Vivian Beaumont Theatre, 56
Alfie! (p), 12/17/64, Morosco Theatre, 21
Algeria (m), 8/31/08, Broadway Theatre, 48
Ali Baba and the 40 Thieves (m), 12/26/70, Bil Baird Theatre, 91
Alias Jimmy Valentine (p), 1/21/10, Wallack Theatre, 155
Alias Jimmy Valentine (p), 12/8/21, Gaiety Theatre, 46
Alias the Deacon (p), 11/24/25, Sam H. Harris Theatre, 277
Alibi Bill (p), 12/31/12, Weber Theatre, 3
Alice in Arms (p), 1/31/45, National Theatre, 5
Alice in Wonderland (p), 3/23/15, Booth Theatre, 20
Alice in Wonderland (p), 4/20, Little Theatre
Alice In Wonderland (p), 4/5/47, International Theatre, 100
Alice in Wonderland (p), 10/8/70, The Extension, 122, (Manhattan Project)
Alice in Wonderland (p), 3/1/72, Performing Garage, 50
Alice in Wonderland (p), 4/6/73, New York University Theatre
Alice in Wonderland (p), 3/7/74, Performing Garage, 20, (Manhattan Project)
Alice in Wonderland / Through the Looking Glass (p), 12/12/32, Civic Repertory Theatre, 119
Alice of Old Vincennes (p), 12/2/01, Garden Theatre, 64
Alice Sit-by-the-Fire / Pantaloon (p), 12/25/05, Criterion Theatre, 81
Alice Sit-by-the-Fire / The Old Lady Shows Her Medals (p), 3/7/32, Playhouse, 40
Alice Sit-by-the-Fire / The Twelve Pound Look (p), 2/13/11, Empire Theatre, 32
Alice Takat (p), 2/10/36, John Golden Theatre, 8
Alice with Kisses, 5/7/64, 41st St. Theatre
Alien Corn (p), 2/20/33, Belasco Theatre, 98
Alison's House (p), 12/1/30, Civic Repertory Theatre, 42
Alive and Kicking (r), 1/17/50, Winter Garden Theatre, 46
Alive and Well in Argentina (p), 3/21/74, Theatre at St. Clement's, 14
All Aboard (m), 6/5/13, 44th St. Roof Garden Theatre, 108
All American (m), 3/19/62, Winter Garden Theatre, 86
All by Myself (r), 6/15/64, 41st St. Theatre, 40
All Dressed Up (p), 9/9/25, Eltinge Theatre, 13
All Editions (p), 12/22/36, Longacre Theatre, 23
All for a Girl (p), 8/22/08, Bijou Theatre, 33
All for All (p), 9/29/43, Bijou Theatre, 85
All for Love (r), 1/22/49, Mark Hellinger Theatre, 121
All for the Ladies (p), 12/30/12, Lyric Theatre, 112
All God's Chillun Got Wings (p), 5/15/24, Provincetown Playhouse, 43
All God's Chillun Got Wings (p), 8/18/24, Greenwich Village Theatre, 62
All Good Americans (p), 12/5/33, Henry Miller's Theatre, 39
All in Favor (p), 1/20/42, Henry Miller's Theatre, 7
All in Fun (r), 12/27/40, Majestic Theatre, 3
All in Good Time (p), 2/18/65, Royale Theatre, 44
All in Love (m), 11/10/61, Martinique Theatre, 141
All in Love (m), 12/2/66, Master Theatre, 15, (Equity Library Theatre)
All in One, Trouble in Tahiti opera / Paul Draper, dance / 27 Wagons Full of Cotton (p), 4/19/55, Playhouse, 47
All Kinds of Giants (m), 12/18/61, Cricket Theatre, 16
All Men Are Alike (p), 10/6/41, Hudson Theatre, 32
All My Pretty Little Ones / Damn You, Scarlett O'Hara. See Riverside Drive
All My Sons (p), 1/29/47, Coronet Theatre, 328
All My Sons (p), 11/15/68, Master Theatre, 9, (Equity Library Theatre)
All on Account of Eliza (p), 9/3/00, Garrick Theatre, 32
All on Account of Eliza (p), 2/25/01, Wallack Theatre, 24
All Over (p), 3/27/71, Martin Beck Theatre, 40
All Rights Reserved (p), 11/6/34, Ritz Theatre, 31
All's Well That Ends Well (p), 6/15/66, Delacorte Theatre, 16
All Soul's Eve (p), 5/12/20, Maxine Elliott's Theatre, 21
All Star Idlers of 1921 (r), 7/14/21, Shubert Theatre, 1
All Star Jamboree (r), 7/13/21, Cort Theatre, 13
All Star Variety Jubilee (r), 12/29/13, Casino Theatre, 8
All Summer Long (p), 9/23/54, Coronet Theatre, 60
All That Glitters (p), 1/19/38, Biltmore Theatre, 69
All the Comforts of Home (p), 5/25/42, Longacre Theatre, 8
All the Girls Came Out To Play (p), 4/20/72, Cort Theatre, 4
All the King's Horses (m), 1/30/34, Shubert Theatre, 120
All the King's Men (p), 2/4/29, Fulton Theatre, 33
All the King's Men (p), 1/14/48, President Theatre, 21
All the King's Men (p), 10/16/59, East 74th St. Theatre, 51
All the King's Men (p), 11/11/66, Master Theatre, 9, (Equity Library Theatre)
All the King's Men (p), 5/14/74, Urban Arts Corps Theatre, 16
All the Living (p), 3/24/38, Fulton Theatre, 53
All the Way Home (p), 11/30/60, Belasco Theatre, 333
All Wet (p), 7/6/25, Wallack Theatre, 8
All Women Are One (p), 1/7/65, Gate Theatre, 6
All You Need Is One Good Break (p), 2/9/50, Mansfield Theatre, 4
All You Need Is One Good Break (p), 2/20/50, Mansfield Theatre, 32
Allah Be Praised! (m), 4/20/44, Adelphi Theatre, 20
Allegiance (p), 8/1/18, Maxine Elliott's Theatre, 44
Allegro (m), 10/10/47, Majestic Theatre, 315
Allergy / The Cretan Bull (p), 1/24/74, Manhattan Theatre Club, 17
Alley Cat (p), 9/17/34, 48th St. Theatre, 8
Alley of the Sunset (p), 12/30/59, Jan Hus House, 7
Allez-Oop (r), 8/2/27, Earl Carroll Theatre, 119
Alligation, The. See Three by Ferlinghetti
Alligators, The / Rosemary (p), 11/15/60, York Playhouse, 40
All-of-a-Sudden Peggy (p), 2/11/07, Bijou Theatre, 34
Alloy (p), 10/27/24, Princess Theatre, 16
Allure (p), 10/29/34, Empire Theatre, 8
Alma, Where Do You Live? (m), 9/26/10, Weber Theatre, 232
Almanac. See John Murray Anderson's Almanac
Almost Crazy (r), 6/20/55, Longacre Theatre, 16
Aloma of the South Seas (p), 4/20/25, Lyric Theatre, 163
Alone at Last (m), 10/14/15, Shubert Theatre, 180
Along Came a Spider (p), 5/27/63, Mermaid Theatre, 21
Along Came Ruth (p), 2/23/14, Gaiety Theatre, 56
Along Fifth Avenue (r), 1/13/49, Broadhurst Theatre, 180
Alpha Beta (p), 5/3/73, Eastside Playhouse, 14
Altar of Friendship, The (p), 12/1/02, Knickerbocker Theatre, 50
Always You (m), 1/5/20, Central Theatre, 66
Amante Anglaise, L' (p), 4/14/71, Barbizon-Plaza Theatre, 16, (Le Treteau de Paris)
Amazing Activity of Charlie Contrare and the 98th Street Gang, The (p), 1/20/74, Circle Repertory Theatre, 19
Amazing Dr. Clitterhouse, The (p), 3/2/37, Hudson Theatre, 80
Amazons, The (p), 4/28/13, Empire Theatre, 48
Ambassador (m), 11/19/72, Lunt-Fontanne Theatre, 8
Ambassador, The (p), 2/5/00, Daly's Theatre, 51
Amber Express, The (m), 9/19/16, Globe Theatre, 15
Ambitious Mrs. Alcott, The (p), 4/1/07, Astor Theatre, 24
Ambush (p), 10/10/21, Garrick Theatre, 98
Amedee; or How To Disentangle Yourself (p), 10/31/55, Tempo Playhouse
Amen Corner, The (p), 4/15/65, Ethel Barrymore Theatre, 84
America (r), 8/30/13, New York Hippodrome, 360
America Hurrah (Interview/TV/Motel) (p), 11/6/66, Pocket Theatre, 634
America's Sweetheart (m), 2/10/31, Broadhurst Theatre, 135
American Ace, An (p), 4/2/18, Casino Theatre, 32
American Ballad Singers, The, 2/6/44, New York City Center, 2
American Ballet, 3/1/35, Adelphi Theatre
American Born (p), 10/5/25, Hudson Theatre, 88
American Conservatory Theatre (Tiny Alice; A Flea in Her Ear; The Three Sisters) (p), 9/29/69, ANTA Theatre, 32
American Dream (p), 2/21/33, Guild Theatre, 39
American Dream, The / Bartleby (p), 1/24/61, York Theatre, 16
American Dream, The / Domino Furioso (p), 2/7/61, York Theatre, 16
American Dream, The / Dutchman (p), 4/21/64, Cherry Lane Theatre, 232
American Dream, The / The Death of Bessie Smith (p), 10/2/68, Billy Rose Theatre, 10, (Theatre 1969 Playwrights Repertory)
American Dream, The / The Death of Bessie Smith / See Happy Days, 2/28/61, York Theatre, 328

American Dream, The / The Zoo Story (p), 5/28/63, Cherry Lane Theatre, 143
American Gothics (A Piece of Fog / Modern Statuary / Filling the Hole / Strangulation) (p), 11/19/72, Roundabout Theatre, 15
American Grand Guignol Players, 1/12/27, Grove St. Theatre, 69
American Hamburger League, The (r), 9/16/69, New Theatre, 1
American Holiday (p), 2/21/36, Manhattan Theatre, 20
American Idea, The (m), 10/5/08, New York Theatre, 64
American Invasion, An (p), 10/20/02, Bijou Theatre, 24
American Landscape (p), 12/3/38, Cort Theatre, 43
American Lord, The (p), 4/16/06, Hudson Theatre, 32
American Lyric Theatre, The, 5/18/39, Martin Beck Theatre, 12
American Maid, The (m), 3/3/13, Broadway Theatre, 16
American Millionaire, An (p), 4/20/74, Circle in the Square / Joseph E. Levine Theatre, 17
American Night Cry (Thunder in the Index / This Bird of Dawning Singeth All Night Long / The Minstrel Boy) (p), 3/7/74, Actors Studio, 12
American Place Theatre (The Cannibals; Trainer, Dean, Liepolt and Company; Boy on the Straight-Back Chair; Papp) (p), 10/17/68, St. Clement's Church, 164
American Savoyards, The, 2/26/57, Shakespearewrights Theatre, 40
American Savoyards, The, 4/27/61, Greenwich Mews Theatre
American Savoyards, The, 10/26/61, Jan Hus House, 56
American Savoyards, The, 6/4/63, Jan Hus House, 112
American Savoyards, The (m), 5/18/65, Jan Hus House, 263
American Savoyards, The, 5/23/66, Jan Hus Playhouse, 114
American Savoyards, The (m), 10/12/67, Jan Hus Playhouse, 88
American Tragedy, An (p), 10/11/26, Longacre Theatre, 216
American Tragedy, An (p), 2/20/31, Waldorf Theatre, 118
American— Very Early (p), 1/30/34, Vanderbilt Theatre, 7
American War Mothers / Fifth of July (p), 5/24/74, Theatre in Space
American Way, The (p), 1/21/39, Center Theatre, 164
American Way, The (p), 7/17/39, Center Theatre, 80
American Widow, An (p), 9/6/09, Hudson Theatre, 32
Americana (r), 7/26/26, Belmont Theatre, 224
Americana (r), 10/30/28, Lew Fields' Theatre, 12
Americana (r), 10/5/32, Shubert Theatre, 76
Americana Pastoral (p), 12/10/68, Greenwich Mews Theatre, 8
Americans in France, The (p), 8/3/20, Comedy Theatre, 23
Americans, The (p), 8/27/69, La Mama Experimental Theatre Club
Among the Married (p), 10/3/29, Bijou Theatre, 44
Among Those Present (p), 11/10/02, Garden Theatre, 22
Among Those Sailing (p), 2/11/36, Longacre Theatre, 7
Amorous Antic, The (p), 12/2/29, Theatre Masque, 8
Amorous Flea, The (m), 2/17/64, East 78th St. Playhouse, 32
Amorous Flea, The (m), 3/20/64, York Theatre, 61
Amourette (p), 9/27/33, Henry Miller's Theatre, 21
Amphitryon (p), 5/28/70, Forum Theatre, 28
Amphitryon (p), 11/17/70, Barbizon-Plaza Theatre, 8, (Die Brücke)
Amphitryon / La Troupe du Roi (p), 2/3/70, New York City Center, 6, (ComéFrançaise)
Amphitryon / Les Fourberies de Scapin (p), 11/20/52, Ziegfeld Theatre, 12
Amphitryon 38 (p), 11/1/37, Shubert Theatre, 152
Anastasia (p), 12/29/54, Lyceum Theatre, 272
Anathema (p), 4/10/23, 48th St. Theatre, 23
Anatol (p), 1/16/31, Lyceum Theatre, 43
Anatol. See also The Affairs of Anatol
Anatomist, The (p), 10/24/32, Bijou Theatre, 8
Ancient Mariner, The / George Dandin (p), 4/6/24, Provincetown Playhouse, 33
And Be My Love (p), 1/18/34, Ritz Theatre, 4
And Be My Love (p), 2/21/45, National Theatre, 14
And He Never Knew, 1/29/21, Princess Theatre, 33
And I Met a Man (p), 4/10/70, Lincoln Square Theatre Cabaret, 4
And Mama Makes Three (p), 7/3/62, Actors Playhouse, 8
And Miss Reardon Drinks a Little (p), 2/25/71, Morosco Theatre, 108
And Now Goodbye (p), 2/2/37, John Golden Theatre, 26
And Puppy Dog Tails (p), 10/19/69, Bouwerie Lane Theatre, 141
And So To Bed (p), 11/9/27, Shubert Theatre, 175
And Stars Remain (p), 10/12/36, Guild Theatre, 57
And the Devil Makes Five (p), 2/25/71, Blackfriars' Guild, 39
And the Rains Came (p), 10/13/73, Downstairs City Center Theatre
And the Wind Blows (p), 4/28/59, St. Marks Playhouse, 32
And They Put Handcuffs on the Flowers (p), 10/14/71, The Extension
And They Put Handcuffs on the Flowers (p), 4/21/72, Mercer-O'Casey Theatre, 172
And Things That Go Bump in the Night (p), 4/26/65, Royale Theatre, 16
And Whose Little Boy Are You? (p), 5/3/71, McAlpin Rooftop Theatre, 1
Andersonville Trail, The (p), 12/29/59, Henry Miller's Theatre, 179
Andorra (p), 2/9/63, Biltmore Theatre, 9
Andrew. See The Corner
Androcles and the Lion (p), 12/16/38, Lafayette Theatre, 104
Androcles and the Lion / Pound on Demand (p), 12/19/46, International Theatre, 40
Androcles and the Lion / The Dark Lady of the Sonnets (p), 12/14/61, Phoenix Theatre, 23
Androcles and the Lion / The Man of Destiny (p), 11/23/25, Klaw Theatre, 68
Androcles and the Lion / The Man Who Married a Dumb Wife (p), 1/27/15, Wallack Theatre
Androcles and the Lion / The Policeman (p), 11/21/61, Phoenix Theatre, 49
Andromache (p) (Théâtre de France, Renaud-Barrault Company), 2/28/64, New York City Center, 5
Andromache (p), 4/27/73, WPA Theatre, 12
Angel Face (m), 12/29/19, Knickerbocker Theatre, 57
Angel in the House, The (p), 11/8/15, Fulton Theatre, 8
Angel in the Pawnshop (p), 1/18/51, Booth Theatre, 84
Angel in the Wings (r), 12/11/47, Coronet Theatre, 308
Angel Island (p), 10/20/37, National Theatre, 21
Angel Street (p), 12/5/41, John Golden Theatre, 1,293
Angel Street (p) (Hagen-Ferrer), 1/22/48, New York City Center, 14
Angela (p), 12/3/28, Ambassador Theatre, 40
Angela (p), 10/30/69, Music Box, 4
Angeline Moves In (p), 4/19/32, Forrest Theatre, 7
Angels Are Exhausted, The / At the End of the Street (p), 2/14/74, Puerto Rican Traveling Theatre, 16
Angels Don't Kiss (p), 4/5/32, Belmont Theatre, 7
Angels Kiss Me (p), 4/17/51, National Theatre, 2
Angels of Anadarko (p), 10/10/62, York Theatre, 15
Animal Crackers (m), 10/23/28, 44th St. Theatre, 213
Animal Kingdom, The (p), 1/12/32, Broadhurst Theatre, 171
Ankles Aweigh (m), 4/18/55, Mark Hellinger Theatre, 176
Ann Boyd (p), 3/31/13, Wallack Theatre, 8
Anna (p), 5/15/28, Lyceum Theatre, 31
Anna Ascends (p), 9/22/20, Playhouse, 63
Anna Christie (p), 11/2/21, Vanderbilt Theatre, 177
Anna Christie (p), 1/9/52, New York City Center, 28
Anna K. (p), 5/7/72, Actors Playhouse, 196
Anna Karenina (p), 9/2/07, Herald Square Theatre, 47
Anna Kleiber / Masks of Angels (p), 1/19/65, Provincetown Playhouse, 14
Anna Lucasta (p), 6/8/44, 135th St. Library Theatre, 19
Anna Lucasta (p), 8/30/44, Mansfield Theatre, 957
Anna Lucasta (p), 9/22/47, National Theatre, 32
Anna Russell's Little Show (r), 9/7/53, Vanderbilt Theatre, 16
Anna-Luse, 11/30/72, CSC Repertory Theatre
Anne of England (p), 10/7/41, St. James Theatre, 7
Anne of Green Gables (m), 12/21/71, New York City Center, 16
Anne of the Thousand Days (p), 12/8/48, Shubert Theatre, 288
Annie Dear (m), 11/4/24, Times Square Theatre, 103
Annie Get Your Gun (m), 5/16/46, Imperial Theatre, 1,147
Annie Get Your Gun (m), 2/19/58, New York City Center, 16
Annie Get Your Gun (m), 5/31/66, State Theatre, 47
Annie Get Your Gun (m), 9/21/66, Broadway Theatre, 77
Anniversary, The (p), 8/1/73, U.R.G.E.N.T. Theatre, 11
Anniversary, The / On the High Road / The Wedding. See Evenings with Chekhov, 4/20/61, Key Theatre, 61
Anniversary Waltz (p), 4/7/54, Broadhurst Theatre, 615
Annonce Faite à Marie, L' (p), 4/5/65, Barbizon-Plaza Theatre, 18
Another Chance. See The World of Mrs. Solomon
Another City, Another Land (p), 10/8/68, Gramercy Arts Theatre, 8
Another Evening with Harry Stoones (r), 10/21/61, Gramercy Arts Theatre, 1
Another Language (p), 4/25/32, Booth Theatre, 348
Another Language (p), 5/8/33, Waldorf Theatre, 80
Another Love (p), 3/19/34, Vanderbilt Theatre, 16
Another Love Story (p), 10/12/43, Fulton Theatre, 104
Another Man's Shoes (p), 9/12/18, 39th St. Theatre, 20
Another Part of the Forest (p), 11/20/46, Fulton Theatre, 182
Another Sun (p), 2/23/40, National Theatre, 11
Anrana Review, 8/19/01, Academy of Music, 105
Answered the Flute (p), 3/9/60, Finch Theatre, 6
Answers (p), 6/8/72, WPA Theatre
Anthony in Wonderland (p), 10/23/17, Criterion Theatre, 7
Antigone (p) (Anouilh), 2/18/46, Cort Theatre, 64
Antigone (p) (Anouilh), 10/21/56, Carnegie Hall Playhouse
Antigone (p), 1/12/67, Sheridan Square Playhouse, 4
Antigone (p), 5/13/71, Vivian Beaumont Theatre, 46
Antigone of Sophokles, The (p), 10/10/68, Brooklyn Academy of Music, 4, (Living Theatre)
Antigone, The (p), 5/24/23, 48th St. Theatre, 3
Anti-Matrimony (p), 9/22/10, Garrick Theatre, 20
Antiques (r), 6/19/73, Mercer-O'Casey Theatre, 8
Anton Chekhov's Garden, 11/22/72, Roundabout Theatre, 22
Antonia (p), 10/20/25, Empire Theatre, 55
Antony and Cleopatra (p), 11/6/09, New Theatre
Antony and Cleopatra (p), 2/19/24, Lyceum Theatre, 32
Antony and Cleopatra (p), 11/10/37, Mansfield Theatre, 5

Antony and Cleopatra (p) (Godfrey Tearle-Katharine Cornell), 11/26/47, Martin Beck Theatre, 126
Antony and Cleopatra (p) (Laurence Olivier-Vivien Leigh), 12/20/51, Ziegfeld Theatre, 66
Antony and Cleopatra (p) (Michael Higgins-Colleen Dewhurst), 6/20/63, Delacorte Theatre, 15
Anvil, The (The Trial of John Brown) (p), 10/30/62, Maidman Playhouse, 16
Any Day Now (p), 6/9/41, Studio Theatre, New School for Social Research
Any House (p), 2/14/16, Cort Theatre, 16
Any Resemblance to Persons Living or Dead. . . (p), 5/24/71, Gate Theatre, 8
Any Wednesday (p), 2/18/64, Music Box Theatre, 983
Anya (m), 11/29/65, Ziegfeld Theatre, 16
Anybody Home (p), 2/25/49, John Golden Theatre, 5
Anybody's Game (p), 12/21/32, Bijou Theatre, 31
Anyone Can Whistle (m), 4/4/64, Majestic Theatre, 9
Anything Goes (m), 11/21/34, Alvin Theatre, 415
Anything Goes (m), 5/15/62, Orpheum Theatre, 239
Anything Might Happen (p), 2/20/23, Comedy Theatre, 64
Aoi-No-Ue. See National Theatres of Japan
APA Repertory Co., 3/4/64, Phoenix Theatre, 120
Apache, The (p), 5/7/23, Punch and Judy Theatre, 16
APA-Phoenix Repertory Co. (Pantagleize; The Show-Off) (p), 9/3/68, Lyceum Theatre, 29
APA-Phoenix Repertory Co. (Pantagleize; The Show-Off; Exit the King; The Cherry Orchard) (p), 11/30/67, Lyceum Theatre, 225
APA-Phoenix Repertory Co. (The Cocktail Party; The Misanthrope; Cock-a-Doodle Dandy; Hamlet) (p), 10/7/68, Lyceum Theatre, 215
Apartment 12-K (p), 7/20/14, Maxine Elliott's Theatre, 16
Aphrodite (p), 11/24/19, Century Theatre, 148
Apocalypsis cum Figuris (p), 11/18/69, Washington Square Methodist Church, 15, (Polish Laboratory Theatre)
Apology (p), 3/22/43, Mansfield Theatre, 8
Apothecary, The / Kuan Yin / A Burmese Pwe (p), 3/16/26, Neighborhood Playhouse, 27
Apparition Theatre of Prague, The, 11/16/66, Cort Theatre, 21
Appearances (p), 10/13/25, Frolic Theatre, 23
Appearances (p), 4/1/29, Hudson Theatre, 64
Applause (m), 3/30/70, Palace Theatre, 896
Apple Blossoms (m), 10/7/19, Globe Theatre, 256
Apple Cart, The (p), 2/24/30, Martin Beck Theatre, 88
Apple Cart, The (p) (Maurice Evans), 10/18/56, Plymouth Theatre, 124
Apple of His Eye (p), 2/5/46, Biltmore Theatre, 118
Apple, The (p), 12/7/61, Living Theatre, 69
Apple Tree, The (The Diary of Adam and Eve / The Lady or the Tiger? / Passionella) (m), 10/18/66, Sam S. Shubert Theatre, 463
Applesauce (p), 9/28/25, Ambassador Theatre, 90
Approaching Simone (p), 3/4/70, La Mama Repertory Theatre, 5
April (p), 4/6/18, Punch and Judy Theatre, 31
Apron Strings (p), 2/17/30, Bijou Theatre, 226
Arab, The (p), 9/20/11, Lyceum Theatre, 53
Arabesque (p), 10/20/25, National Theatre, 23
Arabian Nightmare ("The Galloping Sheik") (p), 1/10/27, Cort Theatre, 24
Arabian, The (p), 10/31/27, Eltinge Theatre, 32
Arcadians, The (m), 1/17/10, Liberty Theatre, 136
Architect and the Emperor of Assyria, The (p), 6/12/72, St. Clement's Church Theatre, 6
Architruc / Lettre Morte (p), 4/15/70, Barbizon-Plaza Theatre, 10, (Le Treteau de Paris)
Ardele (p), 4/8/58, Cricket Theatre, 48
Arden of Faversham / UBU (p), 2/70, La Mama Experimental Theatre Club
Are You a Crook? (p), 5/1/13, Longacre Theatre, 12
Are You a Mason? (p), 4/1/01, Wallack Theatre, 32
Are You a Mason? (p), 8/19/01, Garrick Theatre, 32
Are You a Mason? (p), 9/5/04, Garrick Theatre, 16
Are You Decent? (p), 4/19/34, Ambassador Theatre, 188
Are You My Father? (p), 10/8/03, Bijou Theatre, 11
Are You Now or Have You Ever Been (p), 11/27/73, Theatre of Riverside Church, 22
Are You with It? (m), 11/10/45, Century Theatre, 266
Aren't We All? (p), 5/21/23, Gaiety Theatre, 284
Aren't We All? (p), 4/13/25, Globe Theatre, 16
Arena Conta Zumbi (m), 8/18/69, St. Clement's Church, 13, (Arena Theatre of Sao Paulo)
Arf / The Great Airplane Snatch (p), 5/27/69, Stage 73, 5
Argyle Case, The (p), 12/24/12, Criterion Theatre, 191
Ari (m), 1/15/71, Mark Hellinger Theatre, 19
Aria da Capo / Guests of the Nation (p), 6/26/58, Theatre Marquee, 102
Aria da Capo / The Widow Veil / Autumn Fires (p), 6/10/21, Provincetown Playhouse, 11
Ariadne (p), 2/23/25, Garrick Theatre, 48
Aries Is Rising (p), 11/21/39, Golden Theatre, 7
Arise, Arise (p), 8/19/65, Cinematheque Theatre, 3
Arizona (p), 9/10/00, Herald Square Theatre, 140
Arizona (p), 4/28/13, Lyric Theatre, 40
Arlecchino, Servitore di due Padroni (p) (Piccolo Teatro di Milano), 2/23/60, New York City Center, 16
Arlequin Poli par l'Amour / Le Barbier de Seville (Comé die Française), 11/8/55, Broadway Theatre, 8
Arms and the Girl (p), 9/27/16, Fulton Theatre, 77
Arms and the Girl (m), 2/2/50, 46th St. Theatre, 134
Arms and the Man (p) (Arnold Daly), 4/16/06, Lyric Theatre, 48
Arms and the Man (p), 5/3/15, Garrick Theatre
Arms and the Man (p), 9/14/25, Guild Theatre, 181
Arms and the Man (p), 10/19/50, Arena, 108
Arms and the Man (p), 4/27/64, East End Theatre, 23
Arms and the Man (p), 1/14/66, Master Theatre, 9, (Equity Library Theatre)
Arms and the Man (p), 6/22/67, Sheridan Square Playhouse, 189
Arms and the Man / How He Lied to Her Husband (p) (Arnold Daly), 5/14/06, Lyric Theatre, 16
Arms for Venus (p), 3/11/37, John Golden Theatre, 12
Army Play-by-Play, The (p), 8/2/43, Martin Beck Theatre, 40
Army with Banners, The, 4/9/18, Vieux Colombier Theatre, 17
Arnold Daly Players, 4/30/07, Lyceum Theatre, 3
Arnold Daly Repertory, 9/11/05, Garrick Theatre, 72
Arnold Daly Repertory, 10/15/07
Around the Corner (p), 12/28/36, 48th St. Theatre, 16
Around the Map (r), 11/1/15, New Amsterdam Theatre, 104
Around the World (r), 9/2/11, New York Hippodrome, 445
Around the World in Eighty Days (m), 5/31/46, Adelphi Theatre, 75
Arrah-Na-Pogue (p), 9/7/03, 14th St. Theatre, 65
Arrest That Woman (p), 9/18/36, National Theatre, 7
Arrow Maker, The, 2/27/11, New Theatre
Arsene Lupin (p), 8/26/09, Lyceum Theatre, 144
Arsenic and Old Lace (p), 1/10/41, Fulton Theatre, 1,444
Art and Mrs. Bottle, 11/18/30, Maxine Elliott's Theatre, 51
Art and Opportunity (p), 11/26/17, Knickerbocker Theatre, 32
Artef Players Repertory, 4/18/35, Artef Theatre, 132
Artie (p), 10/28/07, Garrick Theatre, 22
Artistic Temperament (p), 12/9/24, Wallack Theatre, 7
Artists and Models (r), 8/20/23, Shubert Theatre, 312
Artists and Models (r), 10/15/24, Astor Theatre, 258
Artists and Models (r), 6/24/25, Winter Garden Theatre, 416
Artists and Models (r), 11/15/27, Winter Garden Theatre, 151
Artists and Models (r), 6/10/30, Majestic Theatre, 55
Artists and Models (r), 11/5/43, Broadway Theatre, 27
Arturo Ui (p), 11/11/63, Lunt-Fontanne Theatre, 8
As a Man Thinks (p), 3/13/11, Nazimova's 39th St. Theatre, 128
As Good As New (p), 11/3/30, Times Square Theatre, 56
As Husbands Go (p), 3/5/31, John Golden Theatre, 148
As Husbands Go (p), 1/19/33, Forrest Theatre, 144
As the Girls Go (m), 11/13/48, Winter Garden Theatre, 414
As the Girls Go (m), 9/14/49, Broadway Theatre, 141
As Thousands Cheer (r), 9/30/33, Music Box Theatre, 390
As We Forgive Our Debtors (p), 3/9/47, Princess Theatre, 5
As Ye Mould (p), 10/19/21, 15th St. Theatre, 11
As Ye Sow (p), 12/25/05, Garden Theatre, 34
As You Desire Me (p), 1/28/31, Maxine Elliott's Theatre, 142
As You Like It (p) (Henrietta Crosman), 2/27/02, Republic Theatre, 60
As You Like It (p) (Edith Wynne Matthison), 2/8/18, Cort Theatre, 2
As You Like It (p) (Elsie Mackay), 1/21/19, Plymouth Theatre, 1
As You Like It (p), 4/23/23, 44th St. Theatre, 8
As You Like It (p) (Fritz Leiber), 4/2/30, Shubert Theatre, 2
As You Like It (p), 12/31/30, Ambassador Theatre, 3
As You Like It (p), 11/26/32, Shakespeare Theatre, 15
As You Like It (p), 10/30/37, Ritz Theatre, 17
As You Like It (p) (Helen Craig-Alfred Drake), 10/20/41, Mansfield Theatre, 8
As You Like It (p), 7/3/45, President Theatre, 7
As You Like It (p), 2/20/47, Century Theatre, 4
As You Like It (p) (Katherine Hepburn), 1/26/50, Cort Theatre, 144
As You Like It (p), 2/1/58, Heckscher Theater, 45
As You Like It (p), 7/11/63, Delacorte Theatre, 20
As You Like It (m), 10/27/64, Theatre de Lys, 1, (ANTA Matinee)
As You Like It (p), 12/6/68, Master Theatre, 9, (Equity Library Theatre)
As You Like It (p), 6/21/73, Delacorte Theatre, 28
As You Were (r), 1/27/20, Central Theatre, 143
Ashes (p), 10/20/24, National Theatre, 24
Ashes of Love (p), 3/22/26, National Theatre, 8
Ask My Friend Sandy (p), 2/4/43, Biltmore Theatre, 12
Asmodee (p), 3/25/58, Theatre 74, 23
Aspern Papers, The (p), 2/7/62, Playhouse, 93
Assassin, The (p), 10/17/45, National Theatre, 13
Assumption of Hannele, The (p), 2/15/24, Cort Theatre, 3
Astrakhan Coat, The (p), 1/12/67, Helen Hayes Theatre, 20
At Bay (p), 10/7/13, 39th St. Theatre, 119
At Home Abroad (r), 9/19/35, Winter Garden Theatre, 198
At Home / Actors (p), 5/16/74, Ensemble Studio Theatre

At Home with Ethel Waters (r), 9/22/53, 48th St. Theatre, 23
At Mrs. Beam's (p), 4/26/26, Guild Theatre, 222
At Sea / Alcestis Comes Back (p), 4/23/62, Mermaid Theatre, 8
At the Barn (p), 11/30/14, Comedy Theatre, 24
At the Bottom (p), 1/9/30, Waldorf Theatre, 71
At the Drop of a Hat (r), 10/8/59, John Golden Theatre, 215
At the Drop of Another Hat (r), 12/27/66, Booth Theatre, 105
At the End of the Street / The Angels Are Exhausted (p), 2/14/74, Puerto Rican Traveling Theatre, 16
At the Gate of the Kingdom (p), 12/8/27, American Laboratory Theatre, 23
At the Stroke of Eight (p), 5/20/40, Belasco Theatre, 8
At the Telephone / There's Many a Slip (p), 10/2/02, Garrick Theatre, 20
At War with the Army (p), 3/8/49, Booth Theatre, 151
At 1:45, 6/28/19, Playhouse, 139
Atelje 212 (Who's Afraid of Virginia Woolf?; The Progress of Bora, the Tailor; Victor, or The Children Take Over; Ubu Roi) (p), 6/26/68, Forum Theatre, 24
Athenian Touch, The (m), 1/14/64, Jan Hus House, 1
Atlas and Eva (p), 2/6/28, Mansfield Theatre, 24
Atta Boy (m), 12/23/18, Lexington Theatre, 24
Attack, The (p), 9/19/12, Garrick Theatre, 100
Au Pair Man, The (p), 12/27/73, Vivian Beaumont Theatre, 37
Aucassin and Nicolette (p), 12/23/23, Garrick Theatre, 4
Auctioneer, The (p), 9/23/01, Bijou Theatre, 105
Auctioneer, The (p), 5/4/03, Hammerstein's Victoria Theatre, 32
Auctioneer, The (p), 9/30/13, Belasco Theatre, 95
Auctioneer, The (p), 11/4/18, Manhattan Opera House, 56
Audrey (p), 11/24/02, Madison Square Theatre, 44
Augustus Does His Bit / Toby's Bow (p), 3/12/19, Comedy Theatre, 5
Augustus in Search of a Father / It's the Poor as 'Elps the Poor / Muddle Anna (p), 3/15/21, Little Theatre, 1
Aunt Hannah (m), 2/22/00, Bijou Theatre, 21
Aunt Jeannie (p), 9/16/02, Garden Theatre, 21
Auntie Mame (p), 10/31/56, Broadhurst Theatre, 639
Auntie Mame (p), 8/11/58, New York City Center, 24
Auto Race, The / The Four Seasons / Circus Events (r), 11/25/07, New York Hippodrome, 312
Autobiography (p), 10/2/56, Booth Theatre, 6
Autograph Hound, The / Lemonade (p), 12/13/68, Jan Hus Playhouse, 28
Automobile Graveyard, The (p), 11/13/61, 41st St. Theatre, 8
Autumn Crocus (p), 11/19/32, Morosco Theatre, 212
Autumn Fire (p), 10/26/26, Klaw Theatre, 71
Autumn Fire (p), 12/28/32, Martin Beck Theatre, 2
Autumn Fires / Aria da Capo / The Widow Veil (p), 6/10/21, Provincetown Playhouse, 11
Autumn Fires / The Eternal Judith / The Pot Boiler (p), 11/7/21, Princess Theatre, 8
Autumn Garden, The (p), 3/7/51, Coronet Theatre, 101
Autumn Hill (p), 4/13/42, Booth Theatre, 8
Autumn's Here (r), 10/25/66, Bert Wheeler Theatre, 80
Avanti! (p), 1/31/68, Booth Theatre, 21
Avare, L' (p), 2/8/66, New York City Center, 8, (Comédie Française)
Aventurière, L' (p), 11/13/22, 39th St. Theatre, 16
Aventurière, L', 11/30/26, Cosmopolitan Theatre, 3
Aviator, The, 12/6/10, Astor Theatre, 44
Awaji Puppet Theater, 2/6/74, Carnegie Hall, 2
Awake and Sing (p), 2/19/35, Belasco Theatre, 184
Awake and Sing (p), 3/7/39, Windsor Theatre, 45
Awake and Sing! (p), 5/27/70, Bijou Theatre, 40
Awake and Sing / Waiting for Lefty (p), 9/9/35, Belasco Theatre, 24
Awakening of Helena Richie, The (p), 9/20/09, Savoy Theatre, 120
Awakening of Spring, The (p), 5/12/64, Pocket Theatre, 8
Awakening of Spring, The. See also Spring's Awakening
Awakening, The (p), 10/1/18, Criterion Theatre, 29
Awful Truth, The (p), 9/18/22, Henry Miller's Theatre, 146
Aztec Romance, The (p), 9/16/12, Manhattan Theatre, 8
Azuma Kabuki Dancers and Musicians, 12/26/55, Broadway Theatre, 32

B

Baal (p), 5/6/65, Martinique Theatre, 58
Bab (p), 10/18/20, Park Theatre, 88
Baba Goya (p), 5/21/73, American Place Theatre, 26
Babbling Brookes (p), 2/25/27, Edyth Totten Theatre, 3
Babes and the Baron, The (m), 12/25/05, Lyric Theatre, 45
Babes Don't Cry Anymore (p), 2/20/68, Blackfriars' Guild, 70
Babes in Arms (m), 4/14/37, Shubert Theatre, 289
Babes in Arms (m), 10/20/67, Master Theatre, 15, (Equity Library Theatre)
Babes in the Wood (m), 12/28/64, Orpheum Theatre, 45
Babes in Toyland (m), 10/13/03, Majestic Theatre, 192
Babes in Toyland (m), 1/5/05, Majestic Theatre, 16
Babes in Toyland (m), 12/23/29, Jolson Theatre, 32
Babes in Toyland (m), 12/20/30, Imperial Theatre, 29
Babette (m), 1/16/03, Broadway Theatre, 59
Babies a la Carte (p), 8/15/27, Wallack Theatre, 24
Baby Cyclone, The (p), 9/12/27, Henry Miller's Theatre, 187
Baby Mine (p), 8/23/10, Daly's Theatre, 287
Baby Mine (p), 6/9/27, Chanin's 46th St. Theatre, 12
Baby Pompadour (p), 12/27/34, Vanderbilt Theatre, 4
Baby Want a Kiss (p), 4/19/64, Little Theatre, 148
Baby with a Knife. See Pets
Bachelor Belles, The (m), 11/7/10, Globe Theatre, 32
Bachelor Born (p), 1/25/38, Morosco Theatre, 400
Bachelor Father, The (p), 2/13/28, Belasco Theatre, 264
Bachelor's Baby, The (p), 12/27/09, Criterion Theatre, 192
Bachelor's Brides (p), 5/28/25, Cort Theatre, 28
Bachelor's Night, A (p), 10/17/21, Park Theatre, 8
Bachelor, The (p), 3/15/09, Maxine Elliott's Theatre, 56
Bachelors and Benedicts (p), 11/2/12, Criterion Theatre, 9
Back Bog Beast Bait (p), 4/29/71, St. Clement's Church, 39
Back Bog Beast Bait (p), 12/6/73, Exchange for the Arts, 12
Back Fire (p), 6/13/32, Vanderbilt Theatre, 8
Back Here (p), 11/26/28, Klaw Theatre, 8
Back Home (p), 11/15/15, Cohan Theatre, 16
Back Pay (p), 8/30/21, Eltinge Theatre, 79
Back Seat Drivers (p), 12/25/28, Wallack Theatre, 16
Back to Earth (p), 12/23/18, Henry Miller's Theatre, 16
Back to Methuselah (p) (in three divisions), 2/27/22, Garrick Theatre, 25
Back to Methuselah (p), 3/26/58, Ambassador Theatre, 29
Backfire (p), 10/2/16, 39th St. Theatre, 64
Backslapper, The (p), 4/11/25, Hudson Theatre, 33
Bad Bad Jo-Jo. See Stop, You're Killing Me
Bad Girl (p), 10/2/30, Hoduson Theatre, 85
Bad Habits of 1926 (r), 4/30/26, Greenwich Village Theatre, 19
Bad Habits (Ravenswood / Dunelawn) (p), 2/4/74, Astor Place Theatre, 126
Bad Man, The (p), 8/30/20, Comedy Theatre, 320
Bad Manners (p), 1/30/33, Playhouse, 8
Bad Place To Get Your Head, A (p), 7/14/70, St. Peter's Church, (Dove Company)
Bad Samaritan, The (p), 9/12/05, Garden Theatre, 15
Bad Seed (p), 12/8/54, 46th St. Theatre, 334
Badges (p), 12/3/24, 49th St. Theatre, 104
Bagels and Yox (r), 9/12/51, Holiday Theatre, 204
Bagels and Yox of '67 (r), 4/26/67, Anderson Theatre, 15
Baird, Dorothea. See Dorothea Baird
Bajour (m), 11/23/64, Shubert Theatre, 232
Baker, Josephine. See Josephine Baker and Her Company
Baker Street (m), 2/16/65, Broadway Theatre, 313
Bal des Voleurs, Le (p), 11/28/38, Barbizon-Plaza Theatre
Bal Negre (r), 11/7/46, Belasco Theatre, 52
Balcony, The (p), 2/29/60, Circle in the Square, 672
Bald Soprano, The / Jack (p), 6/3/58, Sullivan St. Playhouse, 184
Bald Soprano, The / The Great Man (p), 5/28/63, Judson Hall
Bald Soprano, The / The Lesson (p), 9/17/63, Gate Theatre, 48
Balieff's Chauve-Souris (r), 1/22/29, Jolson Theatre, 47
Balkan Princess, The (m), 2/9/11, Herald Square Theatre, 108
Ball in Old Vienna, A / The Big City / The Mikado (m), 2/3/42. St. James Theatre, 19
Ballad for a Firing Squad (m), 12/11/68, Theatre de Lys, 7
Ballad for Bimshire (m), 10/15/63, Mayfair Theatre, 72
Ballad of Boris, The (p), 5/28/74, Cricket Theatre
Ballad of Jazz Street, The (p), 11/11/59, Greenwich Mews Theatre, 22
Ballad of John Ogilvie, The (p), 10/8/68, Blackfriars' Guild, 48
Ballad of Johnny Pot, The (m), 4/26/71, Theatre Four, 16
Ballad of the Sad Cafe, The (p), 10/30/63, Martin Beck Theatre, 123
Ballet Ballads (m), 5/9/48, Maxine Elliott's Theatre, 69
Ballet Ballads (m), 1/3/61, East 74th St. Theatre, 37
Ballet Behind the Bridge, A (p), 3/14/72, St. Marks Playhouse, 40
Ballet Folklorico of Mexico, The, 9/11/62, New York City Center, 16
Ballet Moderene (r), 4/8/28, Gallo Theatre, 14
Ballet of Niagara, The / The Earthquake / The International Cup (r), 9/3/10, New York Hippodrome, 333
Ballet Russe de Monte Carlo, 4/9/44, New York City Center, 27
Ballets Africains de Keita Fodeba, Les, 2/16/59, Martin Beck Theatre, 48
Ballets de Paris, Les, 4/7/58, Broadway Theatre, 32
Ballets: U.S.A. See Jerome Robbins' Ballets: U.S.A.
Balls / Up to Thursday / Home Free! (p) (New Playwrights Series, Evening I), 2/10/65, Cherry Lane Theatre, 23
Ballyhoo (p), 1/4/27, 49th St. Theatre, 7
Ballyhoo (m), 12/22/30, Hammerstein Theatre, 68
Ballyhoo of 1932 (m), 9/6/32, 44th St. Theatre, 94
Bamboola (m), 6/26/29, Royale Theatre, 27
Bananas (p), 12/5/68, Forum Theatre, 42
Banco (p), 9/20/22, Ritz Theatre, 70
Band Box Follies, The (r), 9/5/27, Daly's Theatre, 8

Band Wagon, The (r), 6/3/31, New Amsterdam Theatre, 262
Bandanna Land (m), 2/3/08, Majestic Theatre, 89
Bandwagon (r), 3/17/73, Bil Baird Theatre, 75
Banjo Eyes (m), 12/25/41, Hollywood Theatre, 126
Banker's Daughter, The (m), 1/22/62, Jan Hus House, 64
Banquet for the Moon, A (p), 1/19/61, Theatre Marquee, 22
Banshee, The (p), 12/5/27, Daly's Theatre, 49
Baptiste / Les Fausses Confidences (p), 11/12/52, Ziegfeld Theatre, 13
Bar That Never Closes, The (m), 12/3/72, Astor Place Theatre, 33
Barbara (p), 11/5/17, Plymouth Theatre, 16
Barbara's Millions (p), 10/8/06, Savoy Theatre, 14
Barbara's Wedding / The Father (p), 10/8/31, 49th St. Theatre, 27
Barbary Shore (p), 12/18/74, Public / Anspacher Theatre, 48
Barber Had Two Sons, The (p), 2/1/43, Playhouse, 24
Barber of New Orleans, The (p), 1/15/09, Daly's Theatre, 27
Barbier de Seville, Le (p) (Comédie Française), 11/8/55, Broadway Theatre, 8
Barchester Towers (p), 11/30/37, Martin Beck Theatre, 37
Bare Facts of 1926 (r), 7/16/26, Triangle Theatre, 107
Barefoot (p), 10/19/25, Princess Theatre, 37
Barefoot Boy with Cheek (m), 4/3/47, Martin Beck Theatre, 108
Barefoot in Athens (p), 10/31/51, Martin Beck Theatre, 29
Barefoot in the Park (p), 10/23/63, Biltmore Theatre, 1,532
Barefoot in the Park (p), 3/12/70, Master Theatre, 12, (Equity Library Theatre)
Bargain, The (p), 10/6/15, Comedy Theatre, 13
Barker, The (p), 1/18/27, Biltmore Theatre, 225
Barnum Was Right (p), 3/12/23, Frazee Theatre, 88
Baron Trenck (m), 3/11/12, Casino Theatre, 40
Baroness Fiddlesticks, The (m), 11/21/04, Casino Theatre, 25
Barrault, Jean-Louis. See Renaud-Barrault
Barretts of Wimpole Street, The (p), 2/9/31, Empire Theatre, 372
Barretts of Wimpole Street, The (p), 2/25/35, Martin Beck Theatre, 24
Barretts of Wimpole Street, The (p), 3/26/45, Ethel Barrymore Theatre, 87
Barrier, The (p), 1/10/10, New Amsterdam Theatre, 24
Barrier, The (m), 11/2/50, Broadhurst Theatre, 4
Barrister, The (p), 11/21/42, Masque Theatre, 8
Barroom Monks, The / Portrait of the Artist as a Young Man (p), 5/28/62, Martinique Theatre, 300
Bartleby / The American Dream (p), 1/24/61, York Theatre, 16
Barton Mystery, The (p), 10/13/17, Comedy Theatre, 20
Basement, The / Fragments (p), 10/2/67, Cherry Lane Theatre, 24
Basement, The / Tea Party (p), 10/15/68, Eastside Playhouse, 176
Basic Training of Pavlo Hummel, The (p), 5/20/71, Public/Newman Theatre, 363
Basker, The (p), 10/30/16, Empire Theatre, 40
Bat, The (p), 8/23/20, Morosco Theatre, 878
Bat, The (p), 5/31/37, Majestic Theatre, 18
Bat, The (p), 1/20/53, National Theatre, 23
Bathsheba (p), 3/26/47, Ethel Barrymore Theatre, 29
Battle Cry, The (p), 10/31/14, Lyric Theatre, 17
Battle for Heaven (p), 5/18/48, Educational Alliance, 3
Battle Hymn (p), 5/22/36, Experimental Theatre
Battle of Port Arthur, The / The Auto Race / The Four Seasons / Circus Events (r), 1/13/08, New York Hippodrome
Battle, The (p), 12/21/08, Savoy Theatre, 144
Battleship Gertie (p), 1/18/35, Lyceum Theatre, 2
Battling Buckler (m), 10/8/23, Selwyn Theatre
Bavarian State Theatre, The (Die Mitschuldigen / Woyzeck; Die Ratten) (p), 4/5/66, New York City Center, 16
Bavu (p), 2/25/22, Earl Carroll Theatre, 25
Baxter's Partner (p), 6/27/11, Bijou Theatre, 7
Be Calm, Camilla (p), 10/31/18, Booth Theatre, 84
Be So Kindly (p), 2/8/37, Little Theatre, 8
Be Your Age (p), 2/4/29, Belmont Theatre, 32
Be Your Age (p), 1/14/53, 48th St. Theatre, 5
Be Yourself (p), 9/3/24, Sam H. Harris Theatre, 93
Bear, The / On the Harmfulness of Tobacco / The Wedding / A Tragedian in Spite of Himself (p), 2/5/48, New York City Center, 14
Beard, The (p), 10/24/67, Evergreen Theatre, 100
Beard, The (p), 10/25/73, Performing Garage
Beast in Me, The (r), 5/16/63, Plymouth Theatre, 4
Beast's Story, A. See Cities in Bezique
Beat the Band (m), 10/14/42, 46th St. Theatre, 67
Beaten Track, The (p), 2/8/26, Frolic Theatre, 19
Beau Brummel (p), 4/24/16, Cort Theatre, 24
Beau Gallant (p), 4/5/26, Ritz Theatre, 24
Beaucaire (p), 12/2/01, Herald Square Theatre, 64
Beau-Strings (p), 4/26/26, Mansfield Theatre, 24
Beautiful! (p), 5/16/74, Theatre For The New City
Beautiful Adventure, The (p), 9/5/14, Lyceum Theatre, 41
Beautiful People, The (p), 4/21/41, Lyceum Theatre, 120
Beautiful People, The (p), 4/5/56, Theatre East, 20
Beauty and the Barge (p), 9/6/05, Lyceum Theatre, 12
Beauty and the Barge / The Ghost of Jerry Bundler (p), 11/13/13, Wallack Theatre, 6
Beauty and the Beast / A Servant of Two Masters (p), 1/23/65, Master Theatre, 6, (Equity Library Theatre)
Beauty and the Jacobin / Poetasters of Ispahan, The (p), 11/29/12, Comedy Theatre, 1
Beauty Part, The (p), 12/26/62, Music Box Theatre, 85
Beauty Shop, The (m), 4/13/14, Astor Theatre, 88
Beauty Spot, The (m), 4/10/09, Herald Square Theatre, 137
Beaux' Stratagem, The (p), 6/4/28, Hampden Theatre, 8
Beaux' Stratagem, The (p), 2/24/59, Phoenix Theatre, 16
Beaux' Stratagem, The (p), 3/25/66, Master Theatre, 9, (Equity Library Theatre)
Becket (p), 10/5/60, St. James Theatre, 193
Becky Sharp (p), 9/14/04, Manhattan Theatre, 70
Becky Sharp (p), 3/20/11, Lyceum Theatre, 16
Becky Sharp (p), 6/3/29, Knickerbocker Theatre, 8
Beclch (p), 12/16/68, Gate Theatre, 48
Bed Bug, The, 3/19/31, Provincetown Playhouse, 28
Bed-Fellows (p), 7/2/29, Waldorf Theatre, 47
Bedford's Hope (p), 1/29/06, 14th St. Theatre, 56
Beekman Place (p), 10/7/64, Morosco Theatre, 29
Bees and the Flowers, The (p), 9/26/46, Cort Theatre, 28
Beethoven (p), 4/11/10, New Theatre, 24
Before and After (p), 12/12/05, Manhattan Theatre, 72
Before and After (p), 4/25/07, Astor Theatre, 32
Before Breakfast / The Earth Between (p), 3/5/29, Provincetown Playhouse, 30
Before I Wake (p), 10/13/68, Greenwich Mews Theatre, 17
Before Morning (p), 2/9/33, Ritz Theatre, 28
Before You Go (p), 1/11/68, Henry Miller's Theatre, 29
Before You're 25 (p), 4/16/29, Maxine Elliott's Theatre, 23
Beg, Borrow or Steal (m), 2/10/60, Martin Beck Theatre, 5
Beggar on Horseback (p), 2/12/24, Broadhurst Theatre, 224
Beggar on Horseback (p), 3/23/25, Shubert Theatre, 16
Beggar on Horseback (p), 5/14/70, Vivian Beaumont Theatre, 52
Beggar's Holiday (m), 12/26/46, Broadway Theatre, 108
Beggar's Opera, The (m), 12/29/20, Greenwich Village Theatre, 37
Beggar's Opera, The (m), 3/28/28, 48th St. Theatre, 37
Beggar's Opera, The (m), 3/13/57, New York City Center, 15
Beggar's Opera, The (m), 10/9/64, Master Theatre, 9, (Equity Library Theatre)
Beggar's Opera, The (m), 3/29/72, Brooklyn Academy of Music, 253, (Chelsea Theatre Center)
Beggar's Opera, The (m), 12/22/73, Billy Rose Theatre, 6, (City Center Acting Co.)
Beggar Student, The (m), 3/22/13, Casino Theatre, 33
Beggars Are Coming to Town (p), 10/27/45, Coronet Theatre, 25
Behavior of Mrs. Crane, The (p), 3/20/28, Erlanger Theatre, 31
Behind Red Lights (p), 1/13/37, Mansfield Theatre, 176
Behind the Wall (p), 11/1/60, Jan Hus House, 8
Behold! Cometh the Vanderkellans (p), 3/31/71, Theatre de Lys, 23
Behold the Bridegroom (p), 12/26/27, Cort Theatre, 88
Behold This Dreamer (p), 10/31/27, Cort Theatre, 58
Being Old and Full of Days (p), 7/28/66, 2nd Story Players, 14
Believe Me Xantippe (p), 8/19/13, 39th St. Theatre, 79
Believers, The (r), 5/9/68, Garrick Theatre, 300
Belinda / The New World (p), 5/6/18, Empire Theatre, 32
Bell, Book and Candle (p), 11/14/50, Ethel Barrymore Theatre, 233
Bell for Adano, A (p), 12/6/44, Cort Theatre, 296
Bella (m), 11/16/61, Gramercy Arts Theatre, 6
Bella Donna (p), 11/11/12, Empire Theatre, 72
Bellamy Trial, The (p), 4/22/31, 48th St. Theatre, 17
Belle Marseillaise, La (p), 11/27/05, Knickerbocker Theatre, 29
Belle of Bohemia, The (m), 9/24/00, Casino Theatre, 55
Belle of Bond Street, The (m), 3/30/14, Shubert Theatre, 48
Belle of Bridgeport, The (p), 10/29/00, Bijou Theatre, 45
Belle of Brittany, The (m), 11/8/09, Daly's Theatre, 72
Belle of Broadway, The (m), 3/17/02, Winter Garden Theatre, 24
Belle of London Town, The (m), 1/28/07, Lincoln Square Theatre, 16
Belle of Mayfair, The (m), 12/3/06, Daly's Theatre, 140
Belle Paree, La (m), 3/11, 104
Bells Are Ringing (m), 11/29/56, Shubert Theatre, 924
Bells, The (p), 4/13/26, Nora Bayes Theatre, 15
Belmont Varieties (r), 9/26/32, Belmont Theatre, 4
Below the Belt (r), 6/21/66, Downstairs at the Upstairs, 186
Belt, The (p), 10/19/27, New Playwrights Theatre, 48
Ben Bagley's New Cole Porter Revue (r), 12/22/65, Square East Cabaret Theatre, 76
Ben Bagley's Shoestring Revues (r), 10/15/70, Master Theatre, 19, (Equity Library Theatre)
Ben Franklin in Paris (m), 10/27/64, Lunt-Fontanne Theatre, 215
Ben Greet Repertory, 3/4/07, Garden Theatre
Ben Greet Repertory, 1/17/10, Garden Theatre, 104
Ben Hur (p) (William Farnum), 9/3/00, Broadway Theatre, 40

Ben Hur (p) (Henry Woodruff), 9/21/03, New York Theatre, 96
Ben Hur (p) (A. H. Van Buren), 2/25/07, Academy of Music, 64
Ben Hur (p) (Richard Buhler), 12/23/11, New Amsterdam Theatre, 41
Ben Hur (p) (A. H. Van Buren), 11/6/16, Manhattan Opera House, 88
Bench, The (p), 3/4/68, Gramercy Arts Theatre, 1
Benito Cereno / My Kinsman, Major Molineaux (p) (The Old Glory), 11/1/64, St. Clement's Church, 122
Berenice (Marie Bell and Her Company), 10/20/63, Brooks Atkinson Theatre, 16
Berkeley Square (p), 11/4/29, Lyceum Theatre, 227
Berlin (p), 12/30/31, George M. Cohan Theatre, 25
Berlin to Broadway with Kurt Weill (r), 10/1/72, Theatre de Lys, 153
Bernadine (p), 10/16/52, Playhouse, 157
Bernard Shaw Story, The, 10/26/65, Theatre de Lys, 1, (ANTA Matinee)
Bernard Shaw Story, The, 11/18/65, East 74th Street Theatre, 52
Bernhardt, Sarah. See Sarah Bernhardt
Bernhardt-Coquelin Repertory, 11/26/00, Garden Theatre, 40
Bertha the Sewing Machine Girl (p), 11/5/35, Fifth Avenue Theatre, 33
Beryozka Russian Dance Company, 11/4/58, Broadway Theatre, 34
Best Foot Forward (m), 10/1/41, Ethel Barrymore Theatre, 326
Best Foot Forward (m), 4/2/63, Stage 73, 224
Best House in Naples, The (p), 10/26/56, Lyceum Theatre, 3
Best Laid Plans, The (p), 3/25/66, Brooks Atkinson Theatre, 3
Best Man, The (p), 3/31/60, Morosco Theatre, 520
Best of Burlesque (r), 9/29/57, Carnegie Hall Playhouse
Best of Friends, The (p), 10/19/03, Academy of Music, 65
Best People, The (p), 8/19/24, Lyceum Theatre, 144
Best People, The (p), 3/15/33, Waldorf Theatre, 67
Best Sellers (p), 5/3/33, Morosco Theatre, 53
Best Years (p), 9/7/32, Bijou Theatre, 45
Bet Your Life (p), 4/5/37, John Golden Theatre, 8
Betrothal, The (p), 11/18/18, Shubert Theatre, 120
Betsy (m), 12/11/11, Herald Square Theatre, 32
Betsy (m), 12/28/26, New Amsterdam Theatre, 39
Better Luck Next Time. See Rooms
Better 'Ole, The (p), 10/19/18, Greenwich Village Theatre, 353
Better Times (r), 9/2/22, Hippodrome, 405
Betty (m), 10/3/16, Globe Theatre, 63
Betty at Bay (p), 12/2/18, 39th St. Theatre, 16
Betty, Be Careful (p), 5/4/31, Liberty Theatre, 8
Betty Be Good (m), 5/4/20, Casino Theatre, 31
Betty Lee (m), 12/25/24, 44th St. Theatre, 98
Betty. See Four on a Garden
Between the Devil (m), 12/23/37, Imperial Theatre, 93
Between Two Thieves (p), 2/11/60, York Playhouse, 254
Between Two Worlds (p), 10/25/34, Belasco Theatre, 32
Beverley Hills (p), 11/7/40, Fulton Theatre, 28
Beverly's Balance (p), 4/12/15, Lyceum Theatre, 40
Beware of Dogs (p), 10/3/21, Broadhurst Theatre, 88
Beware of Widows (p), 12/1/25, Maxine Elliott's Theatre, 57
Bewitched (p), 10/1/24, National Theatre, 29
Beyond (p), 1/26/25, Provincetown Playhouse, 14
Beyond Desire (p), 10/10/67, Theatre Four, 7
Beyond Evil (p), 6/7/26, Cort Theatre, 1
Beyond the Fringe (r), 10/27/62, John Golden Theatre, 673
Beyond the Fringe '65 (r), 12/15/64, Ethel Barrymore Theatre, 30
Beyond the Horizon (p), 2/2/20, Morosco Theatre, 111
Beyond the Horizon (p), 11/30/26, Mansfield Theatre, 79
Beyond the Mountains, 12/30/51, Cherry Lane Theatre
Bible Salesman, The (m), 2/21/60, Broadway Congregational Church, 9
Bible Salesman, The / The Oldest Trick in the World. See Double Entry, 2/20/61, Martinique Theatre, 56
Bicycle Ride to Nevada (p), 9/24/63, Cort Theatre, 1
Bidding High (p), 9/28/32, Vanderbilt Theatre, 23
Biff! Bang! (r), 5/30/18, Century Theatre, 16
Biff! Bing! Bang! (r), 5/9/21, Ambassador Theatre
Big Blow, The (p), 10/1/38, Maxine Elliott's Theatre, 157
Big Boy (m), 1/7/25, Winter Garden Theatre, 48
Big Boy (m), 8/24/25, 44th St. Theatre, 120
Big Chance, The (p), 10/28/18, 48th St. Theatre, 120
Big City, The / The Mikado / Ball in Old Vienna (m), 2/3/42, St. James Theatre, 19
Big Fight, The (p), 9/18/28, Majestic Theatre, 31
Big Fish, Little Fish (p), 3/15/61, ANTA Theatre, 101
Big Game (p), 1/2/20, Fulton Theatre, 21
Big Hearted Herbert (p), 1/1/34, Biltmore Theatre, 154
Big House, The (p), 1/4/33, Martin Beck Theatre, 1
Big Idea, The (p), 11/16/14, Hudson Theatre, 24
Big Jim Garrity (p), 10/16/14, New York Theatre, 27
Big Knife, The (p), 2/24/49, National Theatre, 109
Big Knife, The (p), 11/12/59, Seven Arts Playhouse, 62
Big Lake, 4/11/27, American Laboratory Theatre, 11
Big Man / Duet for Three (p), 5/19/66, Cherry Lane Theatre, 14
Big Mogul, The (p), 5/11/25, Daly's Theatre, 24
Big Night (p), 1/17/33, Maxine Elliott's Theatre, 7
Big Pond, The (p), 8/21/28, Bijou Theatre, 47
Big Scene, The / 'Ile / The Maid of France (p), 4/18/18, Greenwich Village Theatre, 52
Big Shot, The. See Nigger Rich
Big Show of 1936, The (r), 5/30/72, Felt Forum, 8
Big Show, The (r), 8/31/16, New York Hippodrome, 425
Big Time Buck White (p), 12/8/68, Village South Theatre, 124
Big Two, The (p), 1/8/47, Booth Theatre, 21
Big White Fog (p), 10/22/40, Lincoln Theatre, 64
Bigfoot (p), 11/3/72, Theatre Genesis, 16
Biggest Thief in Town, The (p), 3/30/49, Mansfield Theatre, 13
Bill of Divorcement, A (p), 10/10/21, George M. Cohan Theatre, 173
Billeted (p), 12/25/17, Playhouse, 79
Billeted (p), 5/9/22, Greenwich Village Theatre, 23
Billie (m), 10/1/28, Erlanger Theatre, 112
Billion Dollar Baby (m), 12/21/45, Alvin Theatre, 220
Billionaire, The (m), 12/29/02, Daly's Theatre, 104
Billy (p), 8/2/09, Daly's Theatre, 64
Billy (m), 3/22/69, Billy Rose Theatre, 1
Billy Barnes People, The (r), 6/13/61, Royale Theatre, 7
Billy Barnes Revue, The (r), 6/9/59, York Playhouse, 199
Billy Barnes Revue, The (r), 8/4/59, John Golden Theatre, 87
Billy Budd (p), 2/10/51, Biltmore Theatre, 105
Billy Budd (p), 5/2/55, The Masquers, 23
Billy Draws a Horse (p), 12/21/39, Playhouse, 13
Billy Liar (p), 3/17/65, Gate Theatre, 30
Billy Noname (m), 3/2/70, Truck and Warehouse Theatre, 48
Billy Rose's Crazy Quilt (r), 5/19/31, 44th St. Theatre, 67
Billygoat Eddie (p), 4/20/64, Writers' Stage Theatre, 2
Bio in Song, A, 12/6/71, Theatre de Lys, 2, (ANTA Matinee)
Biography (p), 12/12/32, Guild Theatre, 210
Biography (p), 2/5/34, Ambassador Theatre, 17
Bird Cage, The (p), 6/2/25, 52nd St. Theatre, 4
Bird Cage, The (p), 2/22/50, Coronet Theatre, 21
Bird Center (p), 11/3/04, Majestic Theatre, 13
Bird in Hand (p), 4/4/29, Booth Theatre, 500
Bird in Hand (p), 11/10/30, 49th St. Theatre, 64
Bird in Hand (p), 10/19/42, Morosco Theatre, 8
Bird in the Cage, The (p), 1/12/03, Bijou Theatre, 40
Bird of Paradise, The (p), 1/8/12, Daly's Theatre, 112
Birdbath. See Six from La Mama (1st Program)
Birds, The (p), 10/19/72, Actors Studio Theatre, 8
Birthday (p), 12/26/34, 49th St. Theatre, 13
Birthday Party, The (p), 10/3/67, Booth Theatre, 126
Birthday Party, The (p), 2/5/71, Forum Theatre, 39
Birthright (p), 11/21/33, 49th St. Theatre, 7
Birthright / Crabbed Youth and Age / The Shadow of the Glen (p), 11/3/32, Martin Beck Theatre, 1
Biscuit / Fritz (p), 5/16/66, Circle in the Square, 8
Bishop Misbehaves, The (p), 2/20/35, Cort Theatre, 120
Bishop's Move, The (p), 3/2/03, Manhattan Theatre, 24
Bishop's Move, The (p), 3/30/03, Mrs. Osborn's Theatre, 8
Bishop, The (The Bishop's Move) / For Love's Sweet Sake (p), 2/12/06, Princess Theatre, 8
Bit of Love, A (p), 5/12/25, 48th St. Theatre, 4
Bitch of Waverly Place, The / The Blind Angel (p) (Two by Sainer), 4/1/65, Bridge Theatre, 50
Bits and Pieces, XIV (r), 10/6/64, Plaza 9 Room, 426
Bitter Oleander (p), 2/11/35, Lyceum Theatre, 24
Bitter Stream (p), 3/30/36, Civic Repertory Theatre, 61
Bitter Sweet (m), 11/5/29, Ziegfeld Theatre, 159
Bitter Sweet (m), 5/7/34, 44th St. Theatre, 16
Black Boy (p), 10/6/26, Comedy Theatre, 39
Black Chiffon (p), 9/27/50, 48th St. Theatre, 12
Black Chiffon (p), 10/23/50, 48th St. Theatre, 107
Black Cockatoo, The (p), 12/30/26, Comedy Theatre, 4
Black Comedy (White Lies / Black Comedy) (p), 2/12/67, Ethel Barrymore Theatre, 337
Black Diamond (p), 2/24/33, Provincetown Playhouse, 9
Black Girl (p), 6/16/71, Theatre de Lys, 247
Black Light Theatre of Prague (r), 9/27/71, New York City Center, 10
Black Limelight (p), 11/9/36, Mansfield Theatre, 64
Black Mass / Mad Heart (p), 9/28/72, Afro-American Studio
Black Monday (p), 3/6/62, Vandam Theatre, 16
Black Nativity (p), 12/11/61, 41st St. Theatre, 57
Black Pit (p), 3/20/35, Civic Repertory Theatre, 86
Black Quartet, A (Prayer Meeting or the First Militant Minister / The Warning—A Theme for Linda / The Gentleman Caller / Great Goodness of Life A Coon Show) (p), 4/25/69, Brooklyn Academy of Music (Chelsea Theatre Center)
Black Quartet, A (Prayer Meeting or the First Militant Minister / The Warning—A Theme for Linda / The Gentleman Caller / Great Goodness of Life A Coon Show (p), 7/30/69, Tambellini's Gate Theatre, 111
Black Rhythm (r), 12/19/36, Comedy Theatre, 6

Black Sheep (p), 10/13/32, Morosco Theatre, 4
Black Souls (p), 3/30/32, Provincetown Playhouse, 13
Black Sunlight (p), 3/19/74, St. Marks Playhouse, 8
Black Terror, The (p), 11/10/71, Public/Other Stage, 180
Black Tower, The (p), 1/11/32, Sam H. Harris Theatre, 73
Black Velvet (p), 9/27/27, Liberty Theatre, 15
Black Visions (Sister Son/Ji / Players Inn / Cop and Blow / Gettin' It Together) (p), 4/4/72, Public Theatre Annex, 64
Black Widow (p), 2/12/36, Mansfield Theatre, 7
Blackberries of 1932 (r), 4/4/32, Liberty Theatre, 24
Blackbirds (p), 1/6/13, Lyceum Theatre, 16
Blackbirds (r), 12/2/33, Apollo Theatre, 25
Blackbirds of 1928 (r), 5/9/28, Liberty Theatre, 519
Blackbirds of 1930 (r), 10/22/30, Royale Theatre, 61
Black-Eyed Susan (p), 12/23/54, Playhouse, 4
Blacks, The (p), 5/4/61, St. Marks Playhouse, 1,408
Blancs, Les (p), 11/15/70, Longacre Theatre, 40
Bless You All (r), 12/14/50, Mark Hellinger Theatre, 84
Bless You, Sister (p), 12/26/27, Forrest Theatre, 24
Blessed Are the Debonair (p), 1/22/38, Barbizon-Plaza Hotel, 1
Blessed Event (p), 2/12/32, Longacre Theatre, 124
Blind Alley (p), 9/24/35, Booth Theatre, 118
Blind Alley (p), 10/15/40, Windsor Theatre, 63
Blind Alleys (p), 11/17/24, Punch and Judy Theatre, 8
Blind Angel, The / The Bitch of Waverly Place (p) (Two by Sainer), 4/1/65, Bridge Theatre, 50
Blind Heart, The (p), 5/7/27, Forrest Theatre, 2
Blind Mice (p), 10/15/30, Times Square Theatre, 13
Blind Youth (p), 12/3/17, Republic Theatre, 96
Blindness of Virtue, The (p), 10/28/12, 39th St. Theatre, 16
Blithe Spirit (p), 11/5/41, Morosco Theatre, 650
Blithe Spirit (p), 9/6/43, Morosco Theatre, 32
Blitzstein! (r), 11/30/66, Provincetown Playhouse, 7
Blond Beast, The, 3/2/23, Plymouth Theatre, 1
Blonde in Black, The (m), 6/8/03, Knickerbocker Theatre, 35
Blonde Sinner, The (m), 7/14/26, Cort Theatre, 179
Blood (m), 3/7/71, Public/Martinson Theatre, 17
Blood and Sand (p), 9/20/21, Empire Theatre, 71
Blood Bugle, The / West of the Moon (p), 6/28/61, New Playwrights Theatre, 6
Blood Knot, The (p), 3/2/64, Cricket Theatre, 240
Blood Money (p), 8/22/27, Hudson Theatre, 64
Blood Red Roses (m), 3/22/70, John Golden Theatre, 1
Blood, Sweat and Stanley Poole (p), 10/5/61, Morosco Theatre, 84
Blood Wedding (p), 2/6/49, New Stages Theatre, 35
Blood Wedding (p), 3/31/58, Actors Playhouse, 275
Blood Wedding (p), 3/11/73, Gramercy Arts Theatre, (Spanish Theatre Repertory Co.)
Bloodstream (p), 3/30/32, Times Square Theatre, 28
Bloody Laughter (p), 12/4/31, 49th St. Theatre, 35
Bloomer Girl (m), 10/5/44, Shubert Theatre, 657
Bloomer Girl (m), 1/6/47, New York City Center, 48
Bloomers (p), 4/18/74, Master Theatre, 12, (Equity Library Theatre)
Blossom Time (m), 9/28/21, Ambassador Theatre, 516
Blossom Time (m), 5/21/23, Shubert Theatre, 24
Blossom Time (m), 5/19/24, Jolson Theatre, 24
Blossom Time (m), 3/8/26, Jolson Theatre, 16
Blossom Time (m), 3/4/31, Ambassador Theatre, 29
Blossom Time (m), 12/26/38, 46th St. Theatre, 19
Blossom Time (m), 9/4/43, Ambassador Theatre, 47
Blot in the 'Scutcheon, A (p), 4/7/05, Hudson Theatre, 5
Blow Ye Winds (p), 9/23/37, 46th St. Theatre, 36
Bludgeon, The (p), 9/7/14, Maxine Elliott's Theatre, 16
Blue Bandanna, The (p), 6/23/24, Vanderbilt Theatre, 16
Blue Bird, The (p), 12/25/23, Jolson Theatre, 29
Blue Bird, The (m) (Yushny's), 1/28/25, Frolic Theatre, 82
Blue Bird, The (r), 4/21/32, Cort Theatre, 23
Blue Bonnet (p), 8/28/20, Princess Theatre, 81
Blue Boy in Black, The (p), 4/30/63, Masque Theatre, 23
Blue Boys (p), 11/29/72, Martinique Theatre, 1
Blue Denim (p), 2/27/58, Playhouse, 166
Blue Envelope, The (p), 3/13/16, Cort Theatre, 48
Blue Eyes (m), 2/21/21, Casino Theatre, 48
Blue Flame, The (p), 3/15/20, Shubert Theatre, 48
Blue Ghost, The (p), 3/10/30, Forrest Theatre, 112
Blue Grass (p), 11/9/08, Majestic Theatre, 24
Blue Holiday (r), 5/21/45, Belasco Theatre, 8
Blue Kitten, The (m), 1/13/22, Selwyn Theatre, 140
Blue Lagoon, The (p), 9/14/21, Astor Theatre, 21
Blue Monday, 6/2/32, Provincetown Playhouse, 10
Blue Moon, The (m), 1/3/06, Casino Theatre, 76
Blue Mouse, The (p), 11/30/08, Lyric Theatre, 232
Blue Paradise, The (m), 8/5/15, Casino Theatre, 356
Blue Pearl, The (p), 8/8/18, Longacre Theatre, 36
Blue Peter, The (p), 3/24/25, 52nd St. Theatre, 39
Blue Pierrots, The, 1/3/16, Liberty Theatre, 8
Blue Widow, The (p), 8/30/33, Morosco Theatre, 30
Bluebeard (p), 3/24/70, La Mama Experimental Theatre Club
Bluebeard's Eighth Wife (p), 9/19/21, Ritz Theatre, 155
Bluebird, The (p), 10/1/10, New Theatre
Bluebird, The (p), 9/15/11, Century Theatre, 19
Blueprints: Projections and Perspectives. See The National Theatre of the Deaf
Blues for Mr. Charlie (p), 4/23/64, ANTA Theatre, 150
Bluffing Bluffers (p), 12/22/24, Ambassador Theatre, 24
Bluffs (p), 3/19/08, Bijou Theatre, 12
Bluffs. Also called Sham Battles
Blushing Bride, The (m), 2/6/22, Astor Theatre, 144
Bob and Ray—The Two and Only (r), 9/24/70, John Golden Theatre, 158
Bobby Burnit (p), 8/22/10, Republic Theatre, 32
Boccaccio (m), 11/17/31, New Yorker Theatre, 21
Body Beautiful, The (p), 10/31/35, Plymouth Theatre, 4
Body Beautiful, The (m), 1/23/58, Broadway Theatre, 60
Body Indian (p), 10/25/72, La Mama Experimental Theatre Club
Boeing-Boeing (p), 2/2/65, Cort Theatre, 23
Boesman and Lena (p), 6/22/70, Circle in the Square, 205
Bohemian Girl, The (m), 7/27/33, Majestic Theatre, 11
Bohikee Creek (p), 4/28/66, Stage 73, 30
Bold Sojer Boy, The (p), 2/9/03, 14th St. Theatre, 16
Bolshoi Ballet, The, 9/6/62, Metropolitan Opera House, 29
Bombo (r), 10/6/21, Jolson's 59th St. Theatre, 218
Bombo (m), 5/14/23, Winter Garden Theatre, 32
Bond, The / Waiting for Lefty (p), 12/13/67, Masque Theatre, 41
Bonds of Interest (p), 4/19/19, Garrick Theatre, 32
Bonds of Interest (p), 10/14/29, Hampden Theatre, 24
Bonds of Interest (p), 5/6/58, Sheridan Square Playhouse, 24
Bonehead, The (p), 4/12/20, Fulton Theatre, 24
Bonnie Brier Bush, The (p), 9/23/01, Republic Theatre, 56
Book of Charm, The (p), 9/3/25, Comedy Theatre, 34
Book of Job, The (p), 10/30/22, Cort Theatre, 5
Book of Job, The (p), 2/9/62, Christ Church Methodist, 16
Boom Boom (m), 1/28/29, Casino Theatre, 72
Boom Boom Room (p), 11/8/73, Vivian Beaumont Theatre, 37
Boomerang, The (p), 8/10/15, Belasco Theatre, 522
Boomerang, The (p), 5/10/27, Garrick Theatre, 3
Booster, The (p), 10/24/29, Nora Bayes Theatre, 12
Bootleggers, The (p), 11/27/22, 39th St. Theatre, 32
Borak (p), 12/13/60, Martinique Theatre, 31
Border-Land (p), 3/29/32, Biltmore Theatre, 23
Borderside (p), 4/30/00, Lyceum Theatre, 16
Borge, Victor. See Comedy in Music
Born Yesterday (p), 2/4/46, Lyceum Theatre, 1,642
Born Yesterday (p), 2/14/74, Manhattan Theatre Club, 14
Borned in Texas (p), 8/21/50, Fulton Theatre, 8
Borrowed Love (p), 6/17/29, Times Square Theatre, 16
Borscht Capades (r), 9/17/51, Royale Theatre, 90
Borstal Boy (p), 3/31/70, Lyceum Theatre, 143
Boshibari. See National Theatres of Japan
Bosom Friends (p), 4/9/17, Liberty Theatre, 48
Boss, The (p), 1/30/11, Astor Theatre, 88
Bostonians Repertory, The, 4/30/00, Knickerbocker Theatre, 24
Botany Lesson, The. See Please Don't Cry and Say No
Both Your Houses (p), 3/6/33, Royale Theatre, 72
Both Your Houses (p), 6/12/33, Ethel Barrymore Theatre, 48
Bottled (p), 4/10/28, Booth Theatre, 63
Bottled Room, The (p), 8/65, 41st Street Theatre
Bottom of the Cup, The (p), 1/31/27, Mayfair Theatre, 16
Boubouroche (p), 6/9/71, Theatre-in-the-Courthouse, 10
Boubouroche / The Wife with a Smile (p), 11/28/21, Garrick Theatre, 41
Boudoir (p), 2/7/41, Golden Theatre, 11
Bough Breaks, The (p), 11/19/37, Little Theatre, 3
Bought and Paid For (p), 9/26/11, Playhouse, 431
Bought and Paid For (p), 12/7/21, Playhouse, 30
Bound East for Cardiff / The Long Voyage Home / Moon of the Caribbees / In the Zone (p), 10/29/37, Lafayette Theatre, 68
Bound East for Cardiff / The Moon of the Caribbees / In the Zone / The Long Voyage Home (p), 5/20/48, New York City Center, 14
Boundary Line, The (p), 2/5/30, 48th St. Theatre, 37
Bourgeois Gentilhomme, Le (p) (Comédie Française), 10/25/55, Broadway Theatre, 16
Box of Watercolors, A (p), 2/17/57, Broadway Congregational Church, 10
Box Seats (p), 4/19/28, Little Theatre, 28
Box/Quotations from Chairman Mao Tse-Tung (p), 9/30/68, Billy Rose Theatre, 12, (Theatre 1969 Playwrights Repertory)
Boy and the Girl, The (m), 5/31/09, Aerial Gardens, 24
Boy Friend, The (p), 6/7/32, Morosco Theatre, 15
Boy Friend, The (m), 9/30/54, Royale Theatre, 485
Boy Friend, The (m), 1/25/58, Downtown Theatre, 763
Boy Friend, The (m), 2/4/66, Master Theatre, 17, (Equity Library Theatre)
Boy Friend, The (m), 4/14/70, Ambassador Theatre, 111

Boy Growing Up, A, 10/7/57, Longacre Theatre, 17
Boy Meets Girl (p), 11/27/35, Cort Theatre, 669
Boy Meets Girl (p), 6/22/43, Windsor Theatre, 15
Boy on the Straight-Back Chair (p), 2/14/69, St. Clement's Church, 38, (American Place Theatre)
Boy on the Straight-Back Chair (p), 10/28/71, Theatre of the Lost Continent
Boy Who Came To Leave, The (p), 6/6/73, Astor Place Theatre, 1
Boy Who Lived Twice, A (p), 9/11/45, Biltmore Theatre, 15
Boy with a Cart, 4/4/54, Broadway Tabernacle Church, 1
Boyd's Daughter (p), 10/11/40, Booth Theatre, 3
Boys and Betty, The (m), 11/2/08, Wallack Theatre, 112
Boys and Girls Together (r), 10/1/40, Broadhurst Theatre, 191
Boys from Syracuse, The (m), 11/23/38, Alvin Theatre, 235
Boys from Syracuse, The (m), 4/15/63, Theatre Four, 500
Boys in the Band, The (p), 4/14/68, Theatre Four, 1,001
Boys of Company "B," The (p), 4/8/07, Lyceum Theatre, 96
Boys Will Be Boys (p), 10/13/19, Belmont Theatre, 45
Brücke, Die (Amphitryon; Die Kurve / Die Kleinburgerhochzeit) (p), 11/17/70, Barbizon-Plaza Theatre, 18
Brücke, Die (Minna von Barnheim; Das Schloss) (p), 11/12/68, Barbizon-Plaza Theatre, 14
Brücke, Die (Nathan der Weise; Bürger Schippel; Kennen Sie die Milchstrasse?) (p), 12/8/66, Barbizon-Plaza Theatre
Brain Sweat (p), 4/4/34, Longacre Theatre, 5
Braisley Diamond, The / A Case of Arson (p), 1/9/06, Madison Square Theatre, 32
Bramhall Players, The, 11/17/15, Bramhall Playhouse
Brand (p), 3/21/74, Nighthouse Theatre, 21
Brand / Sister Beatrice (p), 3/14/10, New Theatre
Branded (p), 9/24/17, Fulton Theatre, 8
Brass Ankle (p), 4/23/31, Masque Theatre, 42
Brass Bottle, The (p), 8/11/10, Lyceum Theatre, 44
Brass Butterfly, The (p), 1/30/70, Brooklyn Academy of Music, 7, (Chelsea Theatre Center)
Brass Buttons (p), 12/5/27, Bijou Theatre, 8
Brass Ring, The (p), 4/10/52, Lyceum Theatre, 4
Brat, The (p), 3/5/17, Harris Theatre, 136
Bravo! (p), 11/11/48, Lyceum Theatre, 44
Bravo Giovanni (m), 5/19/62, Broadhurst Theatre, 76
Bread (p), 1/12/74, American Place Theatre, 32
Breadwinner, The (p), 9/22/31, Booth Theatre, 56
Break a Leg (p), 5/13/74, U.R.G.E.N.T. Theatre, 12
Break in the Skin, A (p), 5/28/73, Actors Studio Theatre, 9
Breakfast in Bed (p), 2/3/20, Eltinge Theatre, 75
Breaking Point, The (p), 8/16/23, Klaw Theatre, 68
Breaking Wall, The (p), 1/25/60, St. Marks Playhouse, 50
Breaks, The (p), 4/16/28, Klaw Theatre, 8
Brecht on Brecht, 1/3/62, Theatre de Lys, 440
Brecht on Brecht, 7/9/63, Sheridan Square Playhouse, 55
Breeze from the Golf, A (p), 10/15/73, Eastside Playhouse, 48
Brewster's Millions (p), 12/31/06, New Amsterdam Theatre, 163
Bridal Crown, The (p), Vanderbilt Theatre, 1
Bridal Night, The. See Three Hand Reel
Bridal Path, The (p), 2/18/13, 39th St. Theatre, 16
Bridal Quilt (p), 10/10/34, Biltmore Theatre, 5
Bridal Veil, The (p), 1/26/28, American Laboratory Theatre, 38
Bridal Wise (p), 5/30/32, Cort Theatre, 128
Bride Got Farblondjet, The (m), 11/4/67, Yiddish Anderson Theatre, 84
Bride in the Morning, A (p), 5/25/60, Maidman Playhouse, 2
Bride of the Lamb (p), 3/30/26, Greenwich Village Theatre, 103
Bride of Torozko, The (p), 9/13/34, Henry Miller's Theatre, 12
Bride Retires, The (p), 5/16/25, National Theatre, 146
Bride, the (p), 5/5/24, 39th St. Theatre, 70
Bride the Sun Shines On, The (p), 12/26/31, Fulton Theatre, 79
Bridge of Distances, The (p), 9/28/25, Morosco Theatre, 16
Bridge, The (p), 9/4/09, Majestic Theatre, 33
Bridge, The. See The Friday Bench
Bridges (p) / The Choir Rehearsal (m) / The Robbery (p) / Chinese Love (m), 2/28/21, Punch and Judy Theatre, 12
Brief Lives (p), 12/18/67, John Golden Theatre, 16
Brief Moment (p), 11/9/31, Belasco Theatre, 129
Brig, The (p), 5/15/63, The Living Theatre, 177
Brig, The (p), 12/19/63, Midway Theatre, 68
Brigadier Gerard (p), 11/5/06, Savoy Theatre, 16
Brigadoon (m), 3/13/47, Ziegfeld Theatre, 581
Brigadoon (m), 5/2/50, New York City Center, 24
Brigadoon (m), 3/27/57, New York City Center, 47
Brigadoon (m), 5/30/62, New York City Center, 16
Brigadoon (m), 1/30/63, New York City Center, 15
Brigadoon (m), 12/23/64, New York City Center, 17
Brigadoon (m), 12/13/67, New York City Center, 23
Bright Boy (p), 3/2/44, Playhouse, 16
Bright Eyes (m), 2/28/10, New York Theatre, 40
Bright Honor (p), 9/27/36, 48th St. Theatre, 17
Bright Lights of 1944 (r), 9/16/43, Forrest Theatre, 4
Bright Rebel (p), 12/27/38, Lyceum Theatre, 7
Bright Star (p), 10/15/35, Empire Theatre, 7
Brighten the Corner (p), 12/12/45, Lyceum Theatre, 29
Brightower (p), 1/28/70, John Golden Theatre, 1
Bring Me a Warm Body (p), 4/16/62, Martinque Theatre, 16
Bringing Up Father (m), 3/30/25, Lyric Theatre, 24
Bringing Up Father at the Seashore (m), 4/21/21, Manhattan Opera House, 18
Brisburial (p), 2/15/74, New Federal Theatre, 7
Britannicus (p), 11/28/58, Phoenix Theatre, 4
Brittle Heaven (p), 11/13/34, Vanderbilt Theatre, 23
Brixton Burglary, The (p), 5/20/01, Herald Square Theatre, 48
Broadway (p), 9/16/26, Broadhurst Theatre, 603
Broadway (p), 10/18/73, Master Theatre, 12, (Equity Library Theatre)
Broadway and Buttermilk (p), 8/15/16, Maxine Elliott's Theatre, 23
Broadway Boy (p), 5/3/32, 48th St. Theatre, 7
Broadway Brevities 1920 (r), 9/29/20, Winter Garden Theatre, 105
Broadway Interlude (p), 4/19/34, Forrest Theatre, 12
Broadway Jones (p), 9/23/12, George M. Cohan Theatre, 176
Broadway Nights (r), 7/15/29, 44th St. Theatre, 40
Broadway Shadows (p), 3/31/30, Belmont Theatre, 16
Broadway Sho-Window, 4/12/36, Broadway Theatre
Broadway to Paris (r), 11/20/12, Winter Garden Theatre, 77
Broadway to Tokio (r), 1/23/00, New York Theatre, 88
Broadway Whirl, The (r), 6/8/21, Times Square Theatre, 85
Broken Branches (p), 3/6/22, 39th St. Theatre, 16
Broken Chain, The (p), 2/19/29, Maxine Elliott's Theatre, 30
Broken Dishes (p), 11/5/29, Ritz Theatre, 165
Broken Hearts of Broadway (p), 6/12/44, New York Music Hall, 14
Broken Idol, A (m), 8/16/09, Herald Square Theatre, 40
Broken Journey (p), 6/23/42, Henry Miller's Theatre, 23
Broken Jug, The (p), 4/1/58, Phoenix Theatre, 12
Broken Threads (p), 10/29/17, Fulton Theatre, 56
Broken Wing, The (p), 11/29/20, 48th St. Theatre, 248
Broken Wings (p), 12/8/27, Manhattan Opera House, 17
Brontes, The (p), 10/29/63, Theatre de Lys, 2
Brontes, The (p), 12/20/63, Phoenix Theatre, 21
Bronx Express, The (p), 4/26/22, Astor Theatre, 61
Bronx Express, 1968 (p), 11/15/68, Folksbiene Theatre
Brook (p), 8/20/23, Greenwich Village Theatre, 16
Brooklyn Biarritz (p), 2/27/41, Royale Theatre, 4
Brooklyn, U.S.A. (p), 12/21/41, Forrest Theatre, 57
Broomsticks, Amen! (p), 2/9/34, Little Theatre, 41
Broomsticks. See Broomsticks, Amen!
Brothel, The. See The Friday Bench
Brother Cain (p), 9/12/41, Golden Theater, 19
Brother Elks (p), 9/14/25, Princess Theatre, 16
Brother Gorski (p), 3/15/73, Astor Place Theatre, 6
Brother Jacques (p), 12/5/04, Garrick Theatre, 40
Brother Officers (p), 1/16/00, Empire Theatre, 88
Brother Officers (p), 8/27/00, Empire Theatre, 16
Brother Officers (p), 4/8/01, Empire Theatre, 8
Brother Rat (p), 12/16/36, Biltmore Theatre, 575
Brotherhood / Day of Absence (p), 3/10/70, St. Marks Playhouse, 64
Brothers (p), 12/25/28, 48th St. Theatre, 255
Brothers (p), 2/13/72, Theatre Four, 1
Brothers Ashkenazi, The (p), 10/31/70, Folksbiene Playhouse
Brothers Karamazov, The (p), 1/3/27, Guild Theatre, 56
Brothers Karamazov, The (p), 12/6/57, Gate Theatre, 65
Brothers Menaechmus, The (p), 6/8/25, Provincetown Playhouse, 8
Brouhaha (p), 4/26/60, 175 East Broadway Playhouse, 2
Brown Buddies (m), 10/7/30, Liberty Theatre, 113
Brown Danube (p), 5/17/39, Lyceum Theatre, 21
Brown of Harvard, 2/26/06, Princess Theatre, 101
Brown of Harvard (p), 12/24/06, Majestic Theatre, 48
Brown Overcoat, The. See Please Don't Cry and Say No
Brown Sugar (p), 12/2/37, Biltmore Theatre, 4
Browning Version, The / Harlequinade (p), 10/12/49, Coronet Theatre, 69
Brownings in the Foot on the Stairs, The (p), 11/10/64, Theatre de Lys, 1, (ANTA Matinee)
Brownstone Urge, The (p), 12/17/69, Actors' Playhouse, 7
Bruno and Sidney (p), 5/3/49, New Stages Theatre, 6
Brute, The (p), 10/8/12, 39th St. Theatre, 22
Bubble, The (p), 4/5/15, Booth Theatre, 176
Buccaneer, The (p), 10/2/25, Plymouth Theatre, 20
Buck White (m), 12/2/69, George Abbott Theatre, 7
Buddies (m), 10/27/19, Selwyn Theatre, 259
Budget, The (p), 9/20/32, Hudson Theatre, 7
Buffalo Skinner, The (p), 2/19/59, Theatre Marquee, 28
Bugle Call, The / A Man and His Wife (p), 4/2/00, Empire Theatre, 24
Bugs / Veronica (p), 11/17/65, Pocket Theatre, 82
Builder of Bridges, The (p), 10/26/09, Hudson Theatre, 47
Builders, The (p), 5/20/07, Astor Theatre, 16
Bull Dog Drummond (p), 12/26/21, Knickerbocker Theatre, 162

Bulls, Bears and Asses (p), 5/6/32, Playhouse, 2
Bully, The (p), 12/25/24, Hudson Theatre, 36
Bunch and Judy, The (m), 11/28/22, Globe Theatre, 65
Bunk of 1926 (r), 2/16/26, Heckscher Theatre, 104
Bunny (p), 1/4/16, Hudson Theatre, 16
Bunraku Puppet Theatre, 3/15/66, New York City Center, 16
Bunraku, The National Puppet Theatre of Japan, 4/3/73, New York City Center, 16
Bunty, Bulls, and Strings / Hokey-Pokey, 2/8/12, Broadway Theatre, 108
Bunty Pulls the Strings (p), 10/10/11, Comedy Theatre, 391
Buoyant Billions / Cast Overruled / Getting Married. See A Shaw Festival, 5/26/59, Provincetown Playhouse, 155
Bürger Schippel (p), 12/11/66, Barbizon-Plaza Theatre, 2, (Die Brücke)
Burgomaster of Belgium, A (p), 3/24/19, Belmont Theatre, 32
Burgomaster of Stilemonde, The (p), 11/15/23, Century Theatre, 4
Burgomaster, The (m), 12/31/00, Manhattan Theatre, 33
Burial Committee, The (p), 4/4/66, New Theatre Workshop, 3
Buriai of Esposito, The. See Passing Through from Exotic Places
Burkaroo (p), 3/16/29, Erlanger Theatre, 9
Burlesque (p), 9/1/27, Plymouth Theatre, 372
Burlesque (p), 12/25/46, Belasco Theatre, 439
Burlesque on Parade (r), 12/10/63, Village Theatre, 33
Burmese Pwe, A / The Apothecary / Kuan Yin (p), 3/16/26, Neighborhood Playhouse, 27
Burn Me to Ashes! (p), 11/19/63, Jan Hus House, 23
Burning Bright (p), 10/18/50, Broadhurst Theatre, 13
Burning Bright (p), 9/25/51, Loft Players
Burning Bright (p), 10/16/59, Theatre East, 13
Burning Deck, The (p), 3/1/40, Maxine Elliott's Theatre, 3
Burning Glass, The (p), 3/4/54, Longacre Theatre, 28
Burning, The (p), 12/3/63, York Theatre, 31
Bury the Dead / Prelude (p), 4/18/36, Ethel Barrymore Theatre, 97
Bus Stop (p), 3/2/55, Music Box Theatre, 478
Business Before Pleasure (p), 8/15/17, Eltinge Theatre, 357
Business Is Business (p), 9/19/04, Criterion Theatre, 57
Business Widow, The (p), 12/10/23, Ritz Theatre, 32
Buskers, The (p), 10/30/61, Cricket Theatre, 6
Buster Brown (p), 1/24/05, Majestic Theatre, 95
Busybody, The (p), 9/29/24, Bijou Theatre, 65
But for the Grace of God (p), 1/12/37, Guild Theatre, 42
But for Whom Charlie (p), 3/12/64, ANTA-Washington Square Theatre, 47
But Never Jam Today (m), 4/23/69, New York City Center, 1
But Not for Love (p), 11/26/34, Empire Theatre, 8
—But Not Goodbye (p), 4/11/44, 48th St. Theatre, 23
But Seriously. . . (p), 2/27/69, Henry Miller's Theatre, 4
Butley (p), 10/31/72, Morosco Theatre, 135
Butter and Egg Man, The (p), 9/23/25, Longacre Theatre, 241
Butter and Egg Man, The (p), 10/17/66, Cherry Lane Theatre, 32
Butterflies Are Free (p), 10/21/69, Booth Theatre, 1,133
Butterfly Dream, The (p), 5/19/66, Greenwich Mews Theatre, 10
Butterfly McQueen and Friends (r), 8/4/69, Bert Wheeler Theatre, 7
Butterfly on the Wheel, A (p), 1/9/12, 39th St. Theatre, 191
Button, Button (p), 10/22/29, Bijou Theatre, 5
Button, Button (p), 10/19/70, Hunter College Playhouse, 7, (Theatre on the Balustrade of Prague)
Buttrio Square (m), 10/14/52, New Century Theatre, 7
Buy Bonds, Buster! (m), 6/4/72, Theatre de Lys, 1
Buy, Buy, Baby (p), 10/7/26, Princess Theatre, 12
Buy Me Blue Ribbons (p), 10/17/51, Empire Theatre, 13
Buzzard, The (p), 3/14/28, Broadhurst Theatre, 13
Buzzin' Around (r), 7/6/20, Casino Theatre, 23
By George, 10/12/67, Lyceum Theatre, 13
By Hex (m), 6/18/56, Tempo Playhouse, 40
By Jupiter (m), 6/3/42, Shubert Theatre, 421
By Jupiter (m), 2/16/65, Master Theatre, 15, (Equity Library Theatre)
By Jupiter (m), 1/19/67, Theatre Four, 118
By Pigeon Post (p), 11/25/18, George M. Cohan Theatre, 24
By Request (p), 9/27/28, Hudson Theatre, 28
By the Beautiful Sea (m), 4/8/54, Majestic Theatre, 268
By The Way (r), 12/28/25, Gaiety Theatre, 177
By Your Leave (p), 1/24/34, Morosco Theatre, 37
Bye, Bye, Barbara (m), 8/25/24, National Theatre, 16
Bye, Bye, Birdie (m), 4/14/60, Martin Beck Theatre, 607
Bye, Bye, Bonnie (m), 1/13/27, Ritz Theatre, 125

C

Cabalgata (m), 7/7/49, Broadway Theatre, 76
Cabaret (m), 11/20/66, Broadhurst Theatre, 1,166
Cabin in the Sky (m), 10/25/40, Martin Beck Theatre, 156
Cabin in the Sky (m), 1/21/64, Greenwich Mews Theatre, 47
Cactus Flower (p), 12/8/65, Royale Theatre, 1,234
Cadet Girl, The (m), 7/25/00, Herald Square Theatre, 48
Caesar and Cleopatra (p), 10/30/06, New Amsterdam Theatre, 49
Caesar and Cleopatra (p), 4/13/25, Guild Theatre, 128
Caesar and Cleopatra (p), 12/21/49, National Theatre, 151
Caesar and Cleopatra (Laurence Olivier-Vivien Leigh) (p), 12/20/51, Ziegfeld Theatre, 67
Caesar's Wife (p), 11/24/19, Liberty Theatre, 81
Cafe (p), 8/28/30, Ritz Theatre, 4
Cafe Crown (p), 1/23/42, Cort Theatre, 141
Cafe Crown (m), 4/17/64, Martin Beck Theatre, 3
Cafe de Danse (p), 1/15/29, Forrest Theatre, 31
Cage, The (p), 6/18/70, Playhouse Theatre, 126
Cages (p), 6/13/63, York Playhouse, 176
Cain (p), 4/8/25, Lenox Little Theatre, 12
Caine Mutiny Court-Martial, The (p), 1/20/54, Plymouth Theatre, 405
Calculated Risk (p), 10/31/62, Ambassador Theatre, 221
Caleb West (p), 9/17/00, Manhattan Theatre, 32
Caliban of the Yellow Sands, 5/24/16, Stadium of City College, 10
Calico Wedding (p), 3/7/45, National Theatre, 5
Caligula (p), 2/16/60, 54th St. Theatre, 38
Call It a Day (p), 1/28/36, Morosco Theatre, 195
Call It Virtue (p), 3/26/63, Astor Place Playhouse, 24
Call Me by My Rightful Name (p), 1/31/61, One Sheridan Square, 127
Call Me Charlie (m), 3/20/74, Performing Garage
Call Me Madam (m), 10/12/50, Imperial Theatre, 644
Call Me Madam (m), 11/8/73, Master Theatre, 19, (Equity Library Theatre)
Call Me Mister (m), 4/18/46, National Theatre, 734
Call Me Ziggy (p), 2/12/37, Longacre Theatre, 3
Call of Life, The (p), 10/9/25, Comedy Theatre, 19
Call of the Cricket, The (p), 4/19/10, Belasco Theatre, 17
Call of the North, The (p), 8/24/08, Hudson Theatre, 32
Call on Kuprin, A (p), 5/25/61, Broadhurst Theatre, 12
Call the Doctor (p), 8/31/20, Empire Theatre, 129
Calling All Stars (r), 12/13/34, Hollywood Theatre, 35
Calling in Crazy (p), 10/6/69, Fortune Theatre, 15
Calvary / Escurial / Santa Claus (p), 7/21/60, Gate Theatre, 14
Calvary. See Moon Mysteries
Cambridge Circus (r), 10/6/64, Plymouth Theatre, 23, reopened 10/28/64, Square East, 90
Camel's Back, The (p), 11/13/23, Vanderbilt Theatre, 15
Camel Through the Needle's Eye, The (p), 4/15/29, Martin Beck Theatre, 196
Camel Through the Needle's Eye, The (p), 5/27/29, Guild Theatre, 195
Camelot (m), 12/3/60, Majestic Theatre, 873
Camels Are Coming, The (p), 10/2/31, President Theatre, 11
Cameo Kirby (p), 12/20/09, Hacket Theatre, 24
Camera Obscura. See Collision Course
Camille (p) (Virginia Harned), 4/18/04, Harlem Opera House, 8
Camille (p) (Margaret Anglin), 4/18/04, Hudson Theatre, 16
Camille (p) (Virginia Harned), 5/9/04, Garrick Theatre, 8
Camille (p) (Mildred Holland), 4/24/11, Garden Theatre, 8
Camille (p), 1/26/31, Civic Repertory Theatre, 57
Camille (p), 10/27/32, Civic Repertory Theatre, 17
Camille (p), 11/1/32, Morosco Theatre, 15
Camille (p), 12/4/35, Sam S. Shubert Theatre, 7
Camille (p), 5/2/73, 13th Street Theatre
Camille (p), 5/13/74, Evergreen Theatre, 20
Camille. See also The Lady of the Camellias
Camino Real (p), 3/19/53, National Theatre, 60
Camino Real (p), 5/16/60, St. Marks Playhouse, 89
Camino Real (p), 1/8/70, Vivian Beaumont Theatre, 52
Campbell, Mrs. Patrick. See Mrs. Patrick Campbell
Can and the Canary (p), 4/23/23, National Theatre, 40
Canaries Sometimes Sing (p), 10/20/30, Fulton Theatre, 32
Canary Cottage (m), 2/5/17, Morosco Theatre, 112
Canary Dutch (p), 9/8/25, Lyceum Theatre, 39
Canary, The (m), 11/4/18, Globe Theatre, 152
Can-Can (m), 5/7/53, Shubert Theatre, 892
Can-Can (m), 8/25/59, Theatre-in-the-Park, 6
Can-Can (m), 5/16/62, New York City Center, 15
Candaules, Commissioner (p), 2/6/70, Brooklyn Academy of Music, 4
Candaules, Commissioner (p), 5/28/70, Mercer-Hansberry Theatre, 5
Candida (p) (Dorothy Donnelly), 12/9/03, Princess Theatre, 133
Candida (p), 10/11/07, Daly's Theatre, 30
Candida (p), 5/18/15, Garrick Theatre
Candida (p), 3/22/22, Greenwich Village Theatre, 43
Candida (p), 12/12/24, 48th St. Theatre, 148
Candida (p), 11/9/25, Comedy Theatre, 24
Candida (p), 3/10/37, Empire Theatre, 49
Candida (p), 4/27/42, Shubert Theatre, 27
Candida (p), 4/3/46, Cort Theatre, 24
Candida (p), 4/22/52, National Theatre, 31
Candida (p), 12/6/63, Master Theatre—Equity Library Theatre, 10
Candida (p), 2/2/69, Roundabout Theatre, 91
Candida (p), 4/6/70, Longacre Theatre, 8

Candida / The Man of Destiny (p), 2/11/04, Vaudville Theatre, 48
Candidate (p), 3/14/74, New Federal Theatre
Candide (m), 5/15/33, Booth Theatre, 7
Candide (m), 12/1/56, Martin Beck Theatre, 73
Candide (p), 4/14/71, Public/South Hall Theatre, 14
Candide (m), 12/11/73, Brooklyn Academy of Music, 48, (Chelsea Theatre Center)
Candide (m), 3/10/74, Broadway Theatre, 94, (Chelsea Theatre Center)
Candle in the Wind (p), 10/22/41, Shubert Theatre, 95
Candle-Light (p), 9/30/29, Empire Theatre, 129
Candy Shop, The (m), 4/27/09, Knickerbocker Theatre, 56
Candyapple, The (p), 11/23/70, Edison Theatre, 1
Cannibals, The (p), 10/17/68, St. Clement's Church, 38, (American Place Theatre)
Canterbury Tales (m), 2/3/69, Eugene O'Neill Theatre, 121
Cantilevered Terrace, The (p), 1/17/62, 41st St. Theatre, 39
Cape Cod Folks (p), 10/15/06, Academy of Music, 24
Cape Cod Follies (r), 9/18/29, Bijou Theatre, 29
Cape Smoke (p), 2/16/25, Martin Beck Theatre, 105
Caponsacchi (p), 10/26/26, Hampden Theatre, 271
Caponsacchi (p), 1/24/28, Hampden Theatre, 58
Caponsacchi (p), 11/19/28, Hampden Theatre, 16
Caponsacchi (p), 11/5/29, Hampden Theatre, 39
Cappy Ricks (p), 1/13/19, Morosco Theatre, 128
Caprice (p), 12/31/28, Guild Theatre, 178
Captain Applejack (p), 12/30/21, Cort Theatre, 366
Captain Barrington (p), 11/23/03, Manhattan Theatre, 51
Captain Brassbound's Conversion (p), 3/29/16, Playhouse
Captain Brassbound's Conversion (p), 12/27/50, New York City Center, 16
Captain Brassbound's Conversion (p), 4/17/72, Ethel Barrymore Theatre, 16
Captain Dieppe (p), 9/14/03, Herald Square Theatre, 60
Captain Fantastic Meets the Ectomorph / A Subject of Scandal and Concern (p), 3/7/66, New Theatre Workshop, 3
Captain Jinks (m), 9/8/25, Martin Beck Theatre, 167
Captain Jinks of the Horse Marines (p), 2/4/01, Garrick Theatre, 168
Captain Jinks of the Horse Marines (p), 9/16/01, Garrick Theatre, 24
Captain Jinks of the Horse Marines (p), 2/18/07, Empire Theatre, 33
Captain Jinks of the Horse Marines (p), 1/25/38, Maxine Elliott's Theatre, 2
Captain Kidd, Jr. (p), 11/13/16, Cohan and Harris Theatre, 128
Captain Molly (p), 9/8/02, Manhattan Theatre, 21
Captain of Koepenick, The (p), 12/1/64, New York State Theatre, 8, (Schiller Theatre)
Captains and the Kings, The (p), 1/2/62, Playhouse, 7
Captive, The (p), 9/29/26, Empire Theatre, 160
Caravan (p), 8/29/28, Klaw Theatre, 21
Career (p), 4/30/57, Seventh Avenue South Playhouse, 232
Career Angel (p), 11/8/43, Blackfriars' Theatre, 28
Career Angel (p), 5/23/44, National Theatre, 22
Carefree Tree, The (p), 10/11/55, Phoenix Theatre, 24
Caretaker, The (p), 10/4/61, Lyceum Theatre, 165
Caretaker, The (p), 1/30/64, Players Theatre, 94
Caretaker, The (p), 6/23/73, Roundabout Theatre, 36
Carib Song (m), 9/27/45, Adelphi Theatre, 36
Caribbean Carnival (r), 12/5/47, International Theatre, 11
Carmen (p) (Olga Nethersole), 12/18/05, Herald Square Theatre, 16
Carmen Jones (m), 12/2/43, Broadway Theatre, 502
Carmen Jones (m), 5/2/45, New York City Center, 21
Carmen Jones (m), 4/7/46, New York City Center, 32
Carmen Jones (m), 5/31/56, New York City Center, 24
Carmen Jones (m), 8/17/59, Theatre-in-the-Park, 7
Carmencita and the Soldier (p), 12/14/25, Jolson Theatre, 58
Carmencita and the Soldier (m), 5/1/26, Cosmopolitan Theatre, 18
Carmilla (m), 11/25/70, La Mama Experimental Theatre Club
Carmilla (m), 1/16/72, La Mama Experimental Theatre Club, 15
Carnival (p), 12/24/19, 44th St. Theatre, 13
Carnival (p), 12/29/24, Cort Theatre, 32
Carnival (p), 4/24/29, Forrest Theatre, 20
Carnival! (m), 4/13/61, Imperial Theatre, 719
Carnival! (m), 12/12/68, New York City Center, 30
Carnival in Flanders (m), 9/8/53, New Century Theatre, 6
Caroline (p), 9/20/16, Empire Theatre, 45
Caroline (m), 1/31/23, Ambassador Theatre, 151
Carolinian, The (p), 11/2/25, Sam H. Harris Theatre, 24
Carousel (m), 4/19/45, Majestic Theatre, 890
Carousel (m), 1/25/49, New York City Center, 48
Carousel (m), 6/2/54, New York City Center, 79
Carousel (m), 9/11/57, New York City Center, 24
Carousel (m), 8/10/65, New York State Theatre, 47
Carousel (m), 12/15/66, New York City Center, 22
Carousel (m), 2/7/74, Master Theatre, 19, (Equity Library Theatre)
Carpa de los Rasquachis, La. See El Teatro Campesino
Carpenters, The (p), 12/10/70, St. Clement's Church, 39, (American Place Theatre)
Carpetbagger, The (p), 3/5/00, 14th St. Theatre, 14
Carpetbagger, The (p), 4/9/00, Bijou Theatre, 20
Carricknabauna, 3/30/67, Greenwich Mews Theatre, 21
Carrots / A Country Mouse (p), 10/6/02, Savoy Theatre, 89
Carry Me Back to Morningside Heights (p), 2/27/68, John Golden Theatre, 7
Carry Nation (p), 10/29/32, Biltmore Theatre, 31
Carry On (p), 1/23/28, Masque Theatre, 8
Carter, Mrs. Leslie. See Mrs. Leslie Carter
Cartoon (p), 10/14/71, Theatre Genesis
Carving a Statue (p), 4/30/68, Gramercy Arts Theatre, 16
Casanova (p), 9/26/23, Empire Theatre, 78
Case History (p), 10/21/38, Lyceum Theatre, 11
Case of Arson, A / The Braisley Diamond (p), 1/9/06, Madison Square Theatre, 32
Case of Becky, The (p), 10/1/12, Belasco Theatre, 95
Case of Clyde Griffiths (p), 3/13/36, Ethel Barrymore Theatre, 19
Case of Frenzied Finance, A (p), 4/3/05, Savoy Theatre, 8
Case of Lady Camber, The (p), 3/26/17, Lyceum Theatre, 48
Case of Libel, A (p), 10/10/63, Longacre Theatre, 242
Case of Phillip Lawrence, The (p), 6/7/37, Lafayette Theatre, 55
Case of Rebellious Susan, The (p), 1/9/05, Lyceum Theatre, 16
Case of Youth, A (p), 3/23/40, National Theatre, 5
Casey Jones (p), 2/19/38, Fulton Theatre, 25
Cashel Byron (p) (Harrison J. Wolfe), 12/27/00, Herald Square Theatre, 1
Cashel Byron (p) (James J. Corbett), 1/8/06, Daly's Theatre, 16
Cashmere Love (p), 12/7/73, Fortune Theatre
Casino Girl, The (m), 3/19/00, Casino Theatre, 91
Casino Girl, The (m), 8/6/00, Casino Theatre, 40
Casino Girl, The (m), 4/8/01, Knickerbocker Theatre, 32
Cast Overruled / Buoyant Billions / Getting Married. See A Shaw Festival, 5/26/59, Provincetown Playhouse, 155
Caste (p), 4/25/10, Empire Theatre, 48
Caste (p), 12/23/27, Mansfield Theatre, 16
Castles in the Air (m), 9/6/26, Selwyn Theatre, 162
Castro Complex, The (p), 11/18/70, Stairway Theatre, 7
Cat and the Canary, The (p), 2/7/22, National Theatre, 349
Cat and the Canary, The (p), 6/14/37, Majestic Theatre, 9
Cat and the Canary, The (p), 1/4/65, Stage 3, 143
Cat and the Fiddle, The (m), 10/15/31, Globe Theatre, 395
Cat and the Moon, The. See Moon Mysteries
Cat on a Hot Tin Roof (p), 3/24/55, Morosco Theatre, 694
Cat Screams, The (p), 6/16/42, Martin Beck Theatre, 7
Cat-Bird, The (p), 2/16/20, Maxine Elliott's Theatre, 33
Catch a Star! (r), 9/6/55, Plymouth Theatre, 23
Catch Me If You Can (p), 3/9/65, Morosco Theatre, 103
Catch of the Season, The (m), 8/28/05, Daly's Theatre, 104
Catherine Was Great (p), 8/2/44, Shubert Theatre, 191
Cathleen Ni Houlahan, 12/14/34, John Golden Theatre, 1
Cats' Pajamas, The (r), 5/31/62, Sheridan Square Playhouse, 34
Catskill Dutch (p), 5/6/24, Belmont Theatre, 7
Caucasian Chalk Circle, The (p), 3/24/66, Vivian Beaumont Theatre, 94
Caught (p), 10/5/25, 39th St. Theatre, 32
Caught in the Rain (p), 12/31/06, Garrick Theatre, 161
Caught Wet (p), 11/4/31, John Golden Theatre, 13
Caukey (p), 2/17/44, Blackfriar's Theatre, 22
Caution: A Love Story (m), 4/2/69, La Mama Experimental Theatre Club
Cavalier, The (p), 12/8/02, Criterion Theatre, 70
Cave at Machpelah, The (p), 6/30/59, Living Theatre, 8
Cave Dwellers, The (p), 10/19/57, Bijou Theatre, 97
Cave Dwellers, The (p), 10/15/61, Greenwich Mews Theatre, 6
Cave Girl, The (p), 8/18/20, Longacre Theatre, 40
Cave Man, The (p), 10/30/11, Fulton Theatre, 16
Caviar (m), 6/7/34, Forrest Theatre, 20
Ceiling Zero (p), 4/10/35, Music Box Theatre, 102
Celebrated Case, A (p), 4/7/15, Empire Theatre, 70
Celebration (m), 1/22/69, Ambassador Theatre, 110
Celebration / Afternoon Storm / Hope Is the Thing with Feathers (p) (The Six O'Clock Theatre's Studio Productions), 4/11/48, Maxine Elliott's Theatre, 8
Celebrity (p), 12/26/27, Lyceum Theatre, 24
Celestina, La (The Spanish Bawd) (p), 2/27/74, Gramercy Arts Theatre
Cellar and the Well, The (p), 12/10/50, ANTA Playhouse, 9
Cenci, The (p), 12/30/70, La Mama Experimental Theatre
Censor and the Dramatists, The / The Doll Girl (p), 10/14/13, Globe Theatre, 33
Censored (p), 2/26/38, 46th St. Theatre, 9
Centuries, The (p), 11/29/27, New Playwrights Theatre, 33
Century Girl, The (m), 11/6/16, Century Theatre, 200
Century Revue, The (r), 7/12/20, Century Promenade Theatre, 150
'Ception Shoals (p), 1/10/17, Princess Theatre, 37
Ceremonies in Dark Old Men (p), 2/5/69, St. Marks Playhouse, 39
Ceremonies in Dark Old Men (p), 4/28/69, Pocket Theatre, 320
Ceremony of Innocence, The (p), 12/26/67, American Place Theatre, 36
Certain Party, A (m), 4/24/11, Wallack Theatre, 24
Certain Quiet, A. See Festival of New Italian Plays

Certain Young Man, A (p), 12/26/67, Stage 73, 8
Chéri (p), 10/12/59, Morosco Theatre, 56
Chad Mitchell's Counterpoint, 11/25/68, Bitter End, 12
Chaff (p), 3/17/48, President Theatre, 10
Chains (p), 12/16/12, Criterion Theatre, 1
Chains (p), 9/19/23, Playhouse, 131
Chains of Dew (p), 4/28/22, Provincetown Playhouse, 16
Chair Endowed / The No 'Count Boy / Supper for the Dead. See Salvation on a String, 7/6/54, Theatre de Lys, 8
Chairs, The / The Lesson (p), 1/19/58, Phoenix Theatre, 22
Chaises, Les / La Jeune Fille a Marier / La Lacune (p), 5/5/70, Barbizon-Plaza Theatre, 8, (Le Treteau de Paris)
Chalk Circle, The (p), 8/22/33, Playmillers Theatre, West 48th St., 8
Chalk Dust (p), 3/4/36, Experimental Theatre, 51
Chalk Garden, The (p), 10/26/55, Ethel Barrymore Theatre, 182
Chalk Marks on the Wall (p), 7/15/61, Take Three
Chalked Out (p), 3/25/37, Morosco Theatre, 12
Challenge of Youth, The (p), 1/20/30, 49th St. Theatre, 24
Challenge, The (p), 8/5/19, Selwyn Theatre, 72
Chamberlain Brown's Scrap Book (r), 8/1/32, Ambassador Theatre, 10
Chameleon, The (p), 7/18/32, Masque Theatre, 8
Champagne Complex (p), 4/12/55, Cort Theatre, 23
Champagne Sec (m), 10/14/33, Morosco Theatre, 113
Champion, The (p), 1/3/21, Longacre Theatre, 176
Change (p), 1/27/14, Booth Theatre, 11
Change Your Luck (m), 6/6/30, George M. Cohan Theatre, 16
Changeling, The (p), 10/29/64, ANTA Washington Square Theatre, 32
Changelings, The (p), 9/17/23, Henry Miller's Theatre, 139
Changing Room, The (p), 3/6/73, Morosco Theatre, 191
Channel Road, The (p), 10/17/29, Plymouth Theatre, 60
Chantecler (p), 1/23/11, Knickerbocker Theatre, 96
Chaparral (p), 9/9/58, Sheridan Square Playhouse, 14
Chaperon, The (p), 12/30/08, Maxine Elliott's Theatre, 62
Chaperons, The (m), 6/5/02, New York Theatre, 49
Character Intrudes, The (p), 12/11/34, Sutton Theatre, 23
Charity Girl, The (m), 10/2/12, Globe Theatre, 21
Charlatan, The (p), 4/24/22, Times Square Theatre, 64
Charlatans / Deuces Wild. See A Pair of Pairs, 4/24/62, Vandam Theatre, 16
Charles Aznavour, 2/4/70, Music Box, 23
Charley's Aunt (p), 3/19/06, Manhattan Theatre, 80
Charley's Aunt (p), 6/1/25, Daly' s Theatre, 24
Charley's Aunt (p), 10/17/40, Cort Theatre, 233
Charley's Aunt (p), 12/22/53, New York City Center, 16
Charley's Aunt (p), 7/4/70, Brooks Atkinson Theatre, 9
Charlie Was Here and Now He's Gone (p), 6/6/71, Eastside Playhouse, 17
Charlot Revue of 1926, The (r), 11/10/25, Selwyn Theatre, 140
Charlot's Revue of 1924, Andre (r), 1/9/24, Times Square Theatre, 298
Charm (p), 11/28/29, Wallack Theatre, 4
Charm of Isabel, The (p), 5/5/14, Maxine Elliott's Theatre, 7
Charm School, The (p), 8/2/20, Bijou Theatre, 87
Chartock's S. M., Gilbert and Sullivan Company, 10/20/52, Mark Hellinger Theatre, 32
Chas. Abbott & Son (p), 3/12/71, Roundabout Theatre, 24
Chase, The (p), 4/15/52, Playhouse, 31
Chastening, The (p), 3/16/23, 48th St. Theatre, 22
Chauve-Souris (m), 2/1/22, 49th St. Theatre, 544
Chauve-Souris (m), 10/10/27, Cosmopolitan Theatre, 80
Chauve-Souris, Balieff's (m), 9/3/23, Jolson Theatre, 32
Chauve-Souris, Balieff's (m), 1/14/25, 49th St. Theatre, 69
Chauve-Souris 1943 (r), 8/12/43, Royale Theatre, 12
Che! (p), 3/22/69, Free Store Theatre, 4
Cheaper to Marry (p), 4/15/24, 49th St. Theatre, 87
Cheater, The (p), 6/29/10, Lyric Theatre, 78
Cheating Cheaters (p), 8/9/16, Eltinge Theatre, 286
Checkerboard, The (p), 8/19/20, 39th St. Theatre, 13
Checkers (p), 9/28/03, American Theatre, 48
Checkers (p), 1/25/04, Academy of Music, 32
Checkers (p), 8/2/04, Academy of Music, 14
Chee-Chee (m), 9/25/28, Mansfield Theatre, 32
Cheer Up (p), 12/30/12, Harris Theatre, 24
Cheer Up (p), 8/23/17, New York Hippodrome, 456
Chekhov on the Lawn, 10/24/73, The Players, 1
Chekhov Sketchbook, A / The Vagrant / The Witch / The Music Shop (p), 2/15/62, Gramercy Arts Theatre, 94
Chemin de Fer (p), 11/26/73, Ethel Barrymore Theatre, 42, (New Phoenix Repertory Co.)
Cherry Blossoms (m), 3/28/27, 44th St. Theatre, 56
Cherry Orchard, The (p), 3/5/28, Bijou Theatre, 6
Cherry Orchard, The (p), 10/15/28, Civic Repertory Theatre, 63
Cherry Orchard, The (p), 9/23/29, Civic Repertory Theatre, 14
Cherry Orchard, The (p), 5/4/31, Civic Repertory Theatre, 2
Cherry Orchard, The (p), 3/6/33, New Amsterdam Theatre, 27
Cherry Orchard, The (p), 1/25/44, National Theatre, 96
Cherry Orchard, The (p), 1/1/45, New York City Center, 8
Cherry Orchard, The (p), 10/18/55, 4th St. Theatre, 96
Cherry Orchard, The (p), 11/14/62, Theatre Four, 61
Cherry Orchard, The (p), 2/9/65, New York City Center, 11, (Moscow Art Theatre)
Cherry Orchard, The (p), 3/19/68, Lyceum Theatre, 38, (APA-Phoenix)
Cherry Orchard, The (p), 5/6/70, ANTA Theatre, 5
Cherry Orchard, The (p), 12/7/73, Public / Anspacher Theatre, 86
Cherry Pie, 4/14/26, Cherry Lane Theatre, 37
Chester Mysteries (p), 12/24/23, Greenwich Village Theatre, 3
Chevalier, Maurice. See Maurice Chevalier
Chiaroscuro (p), 6/5/63, Gate Theatre, 5
Chic (r), 5/19/59, Orpheum Theatre, 6
Chicago (p), 12/30/26, Music Box Theatre, 173
Chicago 70 (p), 5/25/70, Martinique Theatre, 24
Chicken Every Sunday (p), 4/5/44, Henry Miller's Theatre, 317
Chicken Feed (p), 9/24/23, Little Theatre, 146
Chickencoop Chinaman, The (p), 5/27/72, American Place Theatre, 33
Chief, The (p), 11/22/15, Empire Theatre, 40
Chief Thing, The (p), 3/22/26, Guild Theatre, 40
Chief Thing, The (p), 4/29/63, Greenwich Mews Theatre, 24
Chien du Jardinier, Le (p) (Renaud-Barrault Repertory Co.), 2/18/57, Winter Garden Theatre, 8
Chiffon Girl, The (m), 2/19/24, Lyric Theatre, 103
Child and the Dragon, The. See Command Performance
Child Buyer, The (p), 12/21/64, Garrick Theatre, 32
Child of Fortune (p), 11/13/56, Royale Theatre, 23
Child of Manhattan (p), 3/1/32, Fulton Theatre, 86
Child's Play (p), 2/17/70, Royale Theatre, 343
Childhood / Someone from Assisi / Infancy. See Plays for Bleecker Street, 1/11/62, Circle in the Square, 349
Children (p), 10/4/15, Bandox Theatre
Children! Children! (p), 3/7/72, Ritz Theatre, 1
Children from Their Games (p), 4/11/63, Morosco Theatre, 4
Children in the Rain (p), 10/2/70, Cherry Lane Theatre, 1
Children of Darkness (p), 1/7/30, Biltmore Theatre, 79
Children of Darkness (p), 2/28/58, Circle in the Square, 301
Children of Destiny (p), 2/21/10, Savoy Theatre, 24
Children of Earth (p), 1/12/15, Booth Theatre, 39
Children of Kings, The (p), 11/3/02, Herald Square Theatre, 14
Children of the Gods (p), 5/15/73, New York University Theatre, 10
Children of the Moon (p), 8/17/23, Comedy Theatre, 109
Children of the Shadows (p), 2/26/64, Little Theatre, 16
Children of the Wind (p), 10/24/73, Belasco Theatre, 5
Children of Today (p), 12/1/13, Harris Theatre, 24
Children's Army Is Late, The (p), 3/8/74, Theatre for the New City
Children's Hour, The (p), 11/20/34, Maxine Elliott's Theatre, 691
Children's Hour, The (p), 12/18/52, Coronet Theatre, 189
Children's Mass, The (p), 5/16/73, Theatre de Lys, 7
Children's Tragedy, The / The Van Dych (p), 10/10/21, Greenwich Village Theatre, 8
Children, The (p), 11/28/72, Public / Other Stage Theatre, 64
Chimes of Normandy, The (m), 11/2/31, Erlanger Theatre, 16
Chimes of Normandy, The. See Les Cloches de Corneville
China Doll, A (m), 11/19/04, Majestic Theatre, 18
China Rose (m), 1/19/25, Martin Beck Theatre, 126
Chin-Chin (m), 10/20/14, Globe Theatre, 295
Chinese and Dr. Fish, The (The Chinese / Dr. Fish) (p), 3/10/70, Ethel Barrymore Theatre, 15
Chinese Honeymoon, A (m), 6/2/02, Casino Theatre, 376
Chinese Honeymoon, A (m), 3/28/04, Academy of Music, 31
Chinese Love (m) / Bridges (p) / The Choir Rehearsal (m) / The Robbery (p), 2/28/21, Punch and Judy Theatre, 12
Chinese Nightingale, The (p), 10/5/34, Theatre of Young America, 7
Chinese O'Neill (p), 5/22/29, Forrest Theatre, 12
Chinese Prime Minister, The (p), 1/2/64, Royale Theatre, 108
Chinese, The. See The Chinese and Dr. Fish
Chip Woman's Fortune, The / Salome (p), 5/7/23, Frazee Theatre, 8
Chip Woman's Fortune, The / The Comedy of Errors (A la Jazz), 5/15/23, Frazee Theatre, 7
Chippies (p), 5/29/29, Belmont Theatre, 22
Chips with Everything (p), 10/1/63, Plymouth Theatre, 151
Chivalry (p), 12/15/25, Wallack Theatre, 23
Chocolate Dandies, The (m), 9/1/24, Colonial Theatre, 96
Chocolate Soldier, The (m), 9/13/09, Lyric Theatre, 296
Chocolate Soldier, The (m), 12/12/21, Century Theatre, 83
Chocolate Soldier, The (m), 1/27/30, Jolson Theatre, 25
Chocolate Soldier, The (m), 9/21/31, Erlanger Theatre, 16
Chocolate Soldier, The (m), 5/2/34, St. James Theatre, 13
Chocolate Soldier, The (m), 6/23/42, Carnegie Hall, 24
Chocolate Soldier, The (m), 3/12/47, Century Theatre, 70
Chocolates (p), 4/10/67, Gramercy Arts Theatre, 8
Choephori, The / The Eumenides (p) (Greek Tragedy Theatre), 9/26/61, New York City Center, 8
Choir Rehearsal, The (m) / The Robbery (p) / Chinese Love (m) / Bridges (p), 2/28/21, Punch and Judy Theatre, 12

Choister, The (p), 6/5/21, Garrick Theatre, 2
Chorus Lady, The (p), 9/1/06, Savoy Theatre, 315
Chorus Lady, The (p), 11/25/07, Hudson Theatre, 33
Chosen People, The (p), 3/21/12, Garrick Theatre, 2
Chris and the Wonderful Lamp (m), 1/1/00, Victoria Theatre, 58
Christian Pilgrim, The (p), 11/11/07, Liberty Theatre, 14
Christine (m), 4/28/60, 46th St. Theatre, 12
Christmas Eve (p), 12/27/39, Henry Miller's Theatre, 6
Christophe (p), 12/68, Brooklyn Academy of Music (Chelsea Theatre Center), 3
Christophe Colomb (p) (Renaud-Barrault Repertory Co.), 1/30/57, Winter Garden Theatre, 6
Christopher Blake (p), 11/30/46, Music Box Theatre, 114
Christopher Comes Across (p), 5/31/32, Royale Theatre, 15
Chronicles of King Henry VI, Part 1, The (p), 6/23/70, Delacorte Theatre, 18, (The Wars of the Roses)
Chronicles of King Henry VI, Part 2, The (p), 6/24/70, Delacorte Theatre, 17, (The Wars of the Roses)
Chrysalis (p), 11/15/32, Martin Beck Theatre, 23
Chu Chin Chow (m), 10/22/17, Manhattan Opera House, 208
Chuck. See Collision Course
Church Mouse, A (p), 10/12/31, Playhouse, 162
Church Mouse, A (p), 6/26/33, Mansfield Theatre, 8
Church Street / The Respectful Prostitute (p), 2/9/48, New Stages Theatre, 40
Church Street / The Resurrection (p), 11/19/34, John Golden Theatre, 2
Chushingura. See The Grand Kabuki
Cicero (p), 2/8/61, St. Marks Playhouse, 15
Cicero (p), 2/22/61, East 74th St. Theatre, 8
Cid, Le (p), 2/11/66/, New York City Center, 5, (Comédie Française)
Cigarette Maker's Romance, A / Rouget de l'Isle (p), 11/12/02, Herald Square Theatre, 14
Cinderelative (p), 9/18/30, Comedy Theatre, 4
Cinderella Man, The (p), 1/17/16, Hudson Theatre, 192
Cinderella on Broadway (m), 6/24/20, Winter Garden Theatre, 126
Cinders (m), 4/3/23, Dresden Theatre, 31
Cindy (m), 3/19/64, Gate Theatre, 318
Cingalee, The (m), 10/24/04, Daly's Theatre, 33
Cipher Code, The (p), 9/30/01, 14th St. Theatre, 24
Circle in the Water (p), 4/22/70, Garrick Theatre, 85 prevs.
Circle, The (p), 9/12/21, Selwyn Theatre, 175
Circle, The (p), 4/18/38, Playhouse, 72
Circle, The (p), 4/17/74, Roundabout Theatre, 71
Circus Events / Neptune's Daughter / Pioneer Days (r), 11/28/06, New York Hippodrome, 288
Circus Events / The Auto Race / The Four Seasons (r), 11/25/07, New York Hippodrome, 312
Circus Princess, The (m), 4/25/27, Winter Garden Theatre, 192
Cities in Bezique (The Owl Answers / A Beast's Story) (p), 1/12/69, Public Theatre, 67
Citizen's Home, A (p), 10/1/09, Majestic Theatre, 19
City Chap, The (m), 10/26/25, Liberty Theatre, 72
City Haul (p), 12/30/29, Hudson Theatre, 77
City, The (p), 12/21/09, Lyric Theatre, 190
Civilian Clothes (p), 9/12/19, Morosco Theatre, 150
Claim, The (p), 10/9/17, Fulton Theatre, 24
Clair de Lune (p), 4/18/21, Empire Theatre, 64
Claire Adams (p), 11/19/29, Biltmore Theatre, 7
Clandestine Marriage, The (p), 10/2/54, Provincetown Playhouse, 48
Clandestine on the Morning Line (p), 10/30/61, Actors Playhouse, 24
Clansman, The (p), 1/8/06, Liberty Theatre, 51
Clara's Man. See The Electronic Nigger and Others
Clarence (p), 9/20/19, Hudson Theatre, 300
Clarence Darrow (p), 3/26/74, Helen Hayes Theatre, 22
Clarice (p), 10/16/06, Garrick Theatre, 79
Clash by Night (p), 12/27/41, Belasco Theatre, 49
Class of '29 (p), 5/15/36, Manhattan Theatre
Classmates, 8/29/07, Hudson Theatre, 102
Claudia (p), 2/12/41, Booth Theatre, 453
Claudia (p), 5/24/42, Booth Theatre, 24
Claw, The (p), 10/17/21, Broadhurst Theatre, 115
Clean Beds (p), 5/25/39, John Golden Theatre, 4
Clean Slate, A (p), 11/3/03, Madison Square Theatre, 31
Clear All Wires (p), 9/14/32, Times Square Theatre, 91
Clearing in the Woods, A (p), 1/10/51, Belasco Theatre, 36
Clearing in the Woods, A (p), 2/12/59, Sheridan Square Playhouse, 102
Clerambard (p), 11/7/57, Rooftop Theatre, 194
Clerambard (p), 3/14/64, Master Institute—Equity Library Theatre, 10
Clever Ones, The (p), 1/28/15, Punch and Judy Theatre, 100
Climate of Eden, The (p), 11/13/52, Martin Beck Theatre, 20
Climax, The (p), 4/12/09, Weber Theatre, 240
Climax, The (p), 4/30/10, Weber Theatre, 33
Climax, The (p), 1/16/19, Comedy Theatre, 28
Climax, The (p), 5/17/26, 48th St. Theatre, 8
Climax, The (p), 6/13/33, Bijou Theatre, 15
Climbers, The (p), 1/21/01, Bijou Theatre, 163
Clinging Vine, The (m), 12/25/22, Knickerbocker Theatre, 188
Close Harmony (p), 12/1/24, Gaiety Theatre, 24
Close Quarters (p), 3/6/39, John Golden Theatre, 8
Closing Door, The (p), 12/1/49, Empire Theatre, 22
Clothes (p), 9/11/06, Manhattan Theatre, 113
Cloud 7 (p), 2/14/58, Golden Theatre, 11
Clouds (p), 9/2/25, Cort Theatre, 22
Clouds (p), 1/25/26, Cort Theatre, 16
Clouds, The (p), 5/15/11, Bijou Theatre, 7
Cloudy with Showers (p), 9/1/31, Morosco Theatre, 63
Club Bedroom, The / Postcards (p), 12/4/67, Theatre de Lys, 2
Clubs Are Trumps (p), 10/14/24, Bijou Theatre, 7
Clutching Claw, The (p), 2/14/28, Forrest Theatre, 23
Clutterbuck (p), 12/3/49, Biltmore Theatre, 218
Coach with the Six Insides, The (p), 11/26/62, Village South Theatre, 114
Coach with the Six Insides, The (p), 5/11/67, East 74th St. Theatre, 53
Coastwise (p), 11/25/31, Provincetown Playhouse, 5
Coastwise Annie, 12/7/31, Belmont Theatre, 32
Coat-Tails (p), 7/31/16, Cort Theatre, 32
Cobra (p), 4/22/24, Hudson Theatre, 240
Coca-Cola Grande, El. See El Grande de Coca-Cola
Cock O'the Roost (p), 10/13/24, Liberty Theatre, 24
Cock O'the Walk (p), 12/27/15, Cohan Theatre, 72
Cock Robin (p), 1/12/28, 48th St. Theatre, 100
Cock-a-Doodle Dandy (p), 11/12/58, Carnegie Hall Playhouse, 31
Cock-a-Doodle Dandy (p), 1/20/69, Lyceum Theatre, 40, (APA-Phoenix)
Cock-a-Doodle-Doo (p), 2/26/49, Lenox Hill Playhouse, 4
Cockeyed Kite (p), 9/13/61, Actors Playhouse, 7
Cocktail Party, The (p), 1/21/50, Henry Miller'S Theatre, 409
Cocktail Party, The (p), 10/7/68, Lyceum Theatre, 44, (APA-Phoenix)
Coco (m), 12/18/69, Mark Hellinger Theatre, 332
Cocoanuts, The (m), 12/8/25, Lyric Theatre, 375
Cocoanuts, The (m), 5/16/27, Century Theatre, 16
C.O.D. (p), 11/11/12, Gaiety Theatre, 16
Coffee Lace, The. See Little Boxes
Coggerers, The / The Red Velvet Coat / Mr. Banks of Birmingham (p), 1/20/39, Hudson Theatre, 3
Cohan and Harris Minstrels (r), 8/3/08, New York Theatre, 24
Cohan and Harris Minstrels (r), 8/16/09, New York Theatre, 16
Cohan Revue of 1916, The (r), 2/9/16, Astor Theatre, 165
Cohan Revue of 1918, The (r), 12/31/17, New Amsterdam Theatre, 96
Coiner, The (p), 11/21/34, John Golden Theatre, 3
Cold Feet (p), 5/21/23, Fulton Theatre, 24
Cold Feet (p), 4/24/72, Players Theatre, 1
Cold in Sables (p), 12/23/31, Cort Theatre, 14
Cold Wind and the Warm, The (p), 12/8/58, Morosco Theatre, 120
Coldest War of All, The (m), 4/29/69, City Island Theatre, 16
Colette (p), 5/6/70, Ellen Stewart Theatre, 101
Colette (p), 10/14/70, Ellen Stewart Theatre, 7
Collection, The / The Dumbwaiter (Pinter Plays) (p), 11/26/62, Cherry Lane Theatre, 578
Collector's Item (p), 2/8/52, Booth Theatre, 3
College Sinners. See First Episode
College Widow, The (p), 9/20/04, Garden Theatre, 278
Collision (p), 2/16/32, Gaiety Theatre, 7
Collision Course (Wandering / Stars and Stripes / Chuck / Skywriting / Jew! / Thoughts on the Instant of Greeting a Friend on the Street / Tour / Camera Obscura / Metaphors / The Unexpurgated Memoirs of Bernard Mergendeiler / Rats) (p), 5/8/68, Cafe au Go-Go, 79
Colombe (p), 2/23/65, Garrick Theatre, 13
Colonel Newcome (p), 4/10/17, New Amsterdam Theatre, 31
Colonel Satan (p), 1/10/31, Fulton Theatre, 17
Color of Darkness / Cracks (p), 9/30/63, Writers' Stage Theatre, 31
Colorado (p), 11/18/01, Wallack Theatre, 48
Colt, Ethel. See Curtains Up
Comédie Française, 10/25/55, Broadway Theatre, 32, Le Bourgeois Gentilhomme; Arlequin Poli par l'Amour; Le Barbier de Seville; Le Jeu de L'Amour et du Hasard; Un Caprice
Comédie Française, 2/21/61, New York City Center, 24, L'Impromptu de Versailles; Les Fourberies de Scapin; Tartuffe; Britannicus; Le Dindon
Comèdie Française (L'Avare; Le Cid; Un Fil a la Patte; La Reine Morte) (p), 2/8/66, New York City Center, 25
Comèdie Française (La Troupe du Roi / Amphitryon; Le Malade Imaginaire; Dom Juan; Les Femmes Savantes) (p), 2/3/70, New York City Center, 24
Comédie Française Repertory, 11/10/22, 39th St. Theatre, 12
Come Across (p), 9/14/38, Playhouse, 13
Come Along (m), 4/8/19, Nora Bayes Theatre, 47
Come Angel Band (p), 2/18/36, 46th St. Theatre, 2
Come Back, Little Sheba (p), 2/15/50, Booth Theatre, 190
Come Back, Little Sheba (p), 10/22/65, Master Theatre, 10, (Equity Library Theatre)
Come Blow Your Horn (p), 2/22/61, Brooks Atkinson Theatre, 677
Come Easy (p), 8/29/33, Belasco Theatre, 23

Come Into the Garden, Maud. See Noel Coward in Two Keys
Come Live with Me (p), 1/26/67, Billy Rose Theatre, 4
Come Marching Home (p), 5/18/46, Blackfriars' Guild
Come Next Tuesday. See Present Tense
Come of Age (p), 1/12/34, Maxine Elliott's Theatre, 35
Come of Age (p), 1/23/52, New York City Center, 30
Come on Strong (p), 10/4/62, Morosco Theatre, 36
Come Out, Carol! / In the Penal Colony (p), 5/3/62, 41st St. Theatre, 6
Come Out of the Kitchen (p), 10/23/16, Cohan Theatre, 224
Come Play with Me (p), 4/30/59, York Playhouse, 4
Come Seven (p), 7/19/20, Broadhurst Theatre, 72
Come Share My House (p), 2/18/60, Actors Playhouse, 70
Come Slowly, Eden, 12/5/66, Theatre de Lys, 2, (ANTA Matinee)
Come Summer (m), 3/18/69, Lunt-Fontanne Theatre, 7
Come to Bohemia (m), 4/27/16, Maxine Elliott's Theatre, 20
Come What May (p), 5/15/34, Plymouth Theatre, 24
Comedian, The (p), 3/13/23, Lyceum Theatre, 87
Comedienne, The (p), 10/21/24, Bijou Theatre, 16
Comedy in Music (Victor Borge), 10/2/53, Golden Theatre, 849
Comedy in Music, Opus 2 (r), 11/9/64, John Golden Theatre, 192
Comedy of Errors, The (p), 11/21/32, Shakespeare Theatre, 6
Comedy of Errors, The (p), 5/20/64, New York State Theatre, 12
Comedy of Errors, The (p), 6/7/67, Delacorte Theatre, 22
Comedy of Errors, The (A la Jazz) / The Chip Woman's Fortune (p), 5/15/23, Frazee Theatre, 7
Comedy of Women, A (p), 9/13/29, Craig Theatre, 5
Come-on Charlie (p), 4/8/19, 48th St. Theatre, 55
Come-on Man, The, 4/22/29, 49th St. Theatre, 24
Comes a Day (p), 11/6/58, Ambassador Theatre, 28
Comes the Revelation (p), 5/26/42, Jolson Theatre, 2
Comet, The (p), 12/30/07, Bijou Theatre, 56
Comforter, The (p), 10/21/64, Blackfriars' Guild, 62
Comforts of Ignorance, The (p), 11/6/18, Bramhall Theatre, 13
Comic Artist, The (p), 4/19/33, Morosco Theatre, 21
Comic Strip (p), 5/14/58, Barbizon-Plaza Theatre, 156
Comic, The (p), 4/19/27, Masque Theatre, 15
Comin' Thro' the Rye (m), 1/9/06, Herald Square Theatre, 34
Coming of Mrs. Patrick, The (p), 11/6/07, Madison Square Theatre, 13
Coming Out (p), 9/7/72, Washington Square Methodist Church, 10
Command Decision (p), 10/1/47, Fulton Theatre, 409
Command Performance (Pin Up / Venus-Shot / The Child and The Dragon / Miracle in Brooklyn) (p), 6/23/66, Maidman Playhouse, 12
Command Performance, The (p), 10/3/28, Klaw Theatre, 29
Command to Love, The (p), 9/20/27, Longacre Theatre, 236
Commanding Officer, The (p), 12/27/09, Savoy Theatre, 24
Commedia dell' Arte, 4/5/27, Neighborhood Playhouse
Commedia World of Lafcadio Beau, The. See In the Voodoo Parlour of Marie Leveau
Committee, The (r), 9/16/64, Henry Miller's Theatre, 61
Commodore Marries, The (p), 9/4/29, Plymouth Theatre, 37
Common Clay (p), 8/26/15, Republic Theatre, 316
Common Ground (p), 4/25/45, Fulton Theatre, 69
Common Sense Bracket (p), 12/26/04, 14th St. Theatre, 24
Common Sin, The (p), 10/15/28, Forrest Theatre, 24
Commune (p), 12/20/70, Performance Garage, 64
Commuters, The (p), 8/15/10, Criterion Theatre, 160
Compagnie du Théâtre de la Cité de Villeurbanne (George Dandin; Tartuffe; The Three Musketeers) (p), 6/25/68, Vivian Beaumont Theatre, 24
Compania Dramatica Española, La, 4/1/32, New Yorker Theatre, 40
Company (m), 4/26/70, Alvin Theatre, 706
Company's Coming (p), 4/20/31, Lyceum Theatre, 8
Complaisant Lover, The (p), 11/1/61, Ethel Barrymore Theatre, 101
Complex, The (p), 3/3/25, Booth Theatre, 47
Compulsion (p), 10/24/57, Ambassador Theatre, 140
Comte Obligado, 3/11/29, Jolson Theatre, 4
Comtesse Coquette (p), 4/12/07, Bijou Theatre, 101
Con & Co. (p), 9/20/10, Nazimova's 39th St. Theatre, 23
Concept, The (p), 5/6/68, Sheridan Square Playhouse, 216
Concept, The (p), 8/21/69, Gramercy Arts Theatre, 268
Concert, The (p), 10/4/10, Belasco Theatre, 264
Concert Varieties (r), 6/1/45, Ziegfeld Theatre, 36
Condemned of Altona, The (p), 2/3/66, Vivian Beaumont Theatre, 46
Condition of Shadow, A, 10/28/73, Alice Tully Hall
Conditioned Reflex / The Viewing (p), 1/9/67, Theatre de Lys, 2, (ANTA Matinee)
Conditions of Agreement (p), 5/29/72, Roundabout Theatre, 1
Conduct Unbecoming (p), 10/12/70, Ethel Barrymore Theatre, 144
Conerico Was Here To Stay / Pigeons (p) (New Playwrights Series, Evening II), 3/3/65, Cherry Lane Theatre, 21
Conerico Was Here To Stay. See Frank Gagliano's City Scene
Coney Island Cycle, A (Revenge of the Law / Harvey McLeod / Hallelujah or St. George and the Dragon or Laos) (p), 9/7/72, Public / Martinson Theatre, 14, (Bread and Puppet Theatre)
Coney Island Play (r), 10/28/70, La Mama Experimental Theatre, 5
Confederates, The (p), 9/28/59, Theatre Marquee, 23
Confession, The (p), 3/13/11, Bijou Theatre, 56
Confessions of a Spent Youth (p), 1/15/72, Cubiculo Theatre, 10
Confidential Clerk, The (p), 2/11/54, Morosco Theatre, 116
Confirmation. See Festival of New Italian Plays
Conflict (p), 3/6/29, Fulton Theatre, 52
Conflict of Interest, A (p), 8/13/73, U.R.G.E.N.T. Theatre, 12
Conflict, The (p), 3/29/09, Garden Theatre, 16
Congai (p), 11/27/28, Harris Theatre, 137
Congratulations (p), 4/30/29, National Theatre, 39
Conjur Man Dies (p), 3/11/36, Lafayette Theatre, 24
Connecticut Yankee, A (m), 11/3/27, Vanderbilt Theatre, 421
Connecticut Yankee, A (m), 11/17/43, Martin Beck Theatre, 135
Connection, The (p), 7/15/59, Living Theatre, 678
Connection, The (p), 1/12/63, Living Theatre, 40
Connie Goes Home (p), 9/6/23, 49th St. Theatre, 19
Connie's Hot Chocolates. See Hot Chocolates
Conquering Hero, The (m), 1/16/61, ANTA Theatre, 8
Conquest (p), 2/17/33, Plymouth Theatre, 10
Conquest of Everest, The See Playwrights Cooperative Festival
Conscience (p), 9/11/24, Belmont Theatre, 132
Conscience (p), 5/15/52, Booth Theatre, 4
Consequences (p), 10/1/14, Comedy Theatre, 36
Consider the Lilies (p), 2/10/66, Blackfriars' Theatre, 82
Conspiracy, The (p), 12/21/12, Garrick Theatre, 153
Constant Love, The / Creditors (p), 5/2/22, Greenwich Village Theatre, 8
Constant Nymph, The (p), 12/9/26, Selwyn Theatre, 148
Constant Prince, The (p), 10/16/69, Washington Square Methodist Church, 24, (Polish Laboratory Theatre)
Constant Sinner, The (p), 9/14/31, Royale Theatre, 64
Constant Wife, The (p), 11/29/26, Maxine Elliott's Theatre, 295
Constant Wife, The (p), 12/8/51, National Theatre, 139
Consul, The (p), 1/19/03, Princess Theatre, 24
Consul, The (opera), 3/15/50, Ethel Barrymore Theatre, 269
Continental Varieties (r), 10/3/34, Little Theatre, 78
Continental Varieties (r), 12/26/35, Masque Theatre, 9
Contractor, The (p), 10/9/73, Chelsea Theatre Center-Manhattan, 72
Contrast, The (m), 11/27/72, Eastside Playhouse, 24
Contribution. See An Evening of One Acts
Contributions (Shoes / Plantation / Contribution) (p), 3/9/70, Tambellini's Gate Theatre, 16
Conversation at Midnight (p), 11/12/64, Billy Rose Theatre, 4
Conversation Piece (m), 10/23/34, 44th St. Theatre, 55
Conversation Piece (p), 11/18/57, Barbizon-Plaza Theatre, 29
Cook for Mr. General, A (p), 10/19/61, Playhouse, 28
Cool World, The (p), 2/22/60, Eugene O'Neill Theatre, 2
Cooler Near the Lake (r), 2/7/71, Plaza 9 Music Hall, 22
Coop, The (p), 3/1/66, Actors Playhouse, 24
Co-op, The (p), 6/1/72, Theatre for the New City, 20
Cop and Blow. See Black Visions
Cop-Out (Cop-Out/Home Fires) (p), 4/7/69, Cort Theatre, 8
Copper and Brass (m), 10/17/57, Martin Beck Theatre, 36
Copperhead, The (p), 2/18/18, Shubert Theatre, 120
Coquelin-Bernhardt Repertory, 11/26/00, Garden Theatre, 40
Coquette (p), 11/8/27, Maxine Elliott's Theatre, 366
Coralie and Company, Dressmakers (p), 2/5/00, Madison Square Theatre, 57
Cordelia Blossom (p), 8/31/14, Gaiety Theatre, 16
Co-Respondent, The (p), 4/10/16, Booth Theatre, 48
Co-Respondent Unknown (p), 2/11/36, Ritz Theatre, 121
C.O.R.F.A.X. (Don't Ask) (m), 1/18/74, La Mama Experimental Theatre Club
Coriolanus (p), 1/25/38, Maxine Elliott's Theatre, 6
Coriolanus (p), 1/19/54, Phoenix Theatre, 47
Coriolanus (p), 7/7/65, Delacorte Theatre, 16
Corn (m), 11/20/72, 13th Street Theatre
Corn Is Green, The (p) (Ethel Barrymore), 11/26/40, National Theatre, 477
Corn Is Green, The (p) (Ethel Barrymore), 5/3/43, Martin Beck Theatre, 56
Corn Is Green, The (p), 1/11/50, New York City Center, 15
Cornelia Otis Skinner, 11/22/32, Lyceum Theatre, 24
Cornelius' Jewels / Nerves / Thursday Evening, 12/6/21, 15th St. Theatre, 2
Corner of the Bed, A (p), 2/26/69, Gramercy Arts Theatre, 7
Corner, The (Andrew / His First Step Part 1 / The Corner) (p), 6/22/72, Public / Other Stage Theatre, 46
Cornered (p), 12/8/20, Astor Theatre, 141
Coronet of the Duchess, The, 9/21/04, Garrick Theatre, 19
Corruption in the Palace of Justice (p), 10/8/63, Cherry Lane Theatre, 103
Cortez (p), 11/4/29, Mansfield Theatre, 8
Cosmonaute Agricole, Le / Le Grand Vizir (p), 4/7/70, Barbizon-Plaza Theatre, 9, (Le Treteau de Paris)
Cottage in the Air, The (p), 11/11/09, New Theatre
Counsel's Opinion / Saturday It Rained / The White Dress / The Way Out / The March Heir / The Family Exit (p), 12/13/32, Chanin Auditorium, 5
Counsellor-at-Law (p), 11/6/31, Plymouth Theatre, 293

Counsellor-at-Law (p), 9/12/32, Plymouth Theatre, 104
Counsellor-at-Law (p), 5/15/33, 46th St. Theatre, 16
Counsellor-at-Law (p), 11/24/42, Royale Theatre, 258
Count Me In (m), 10/8/42, Ethel Barrymore Theatre, 61
Count of Luxembourg, The (m), 9/16/12, New Amsterdam Theatre, 120
Count of Luxembourg, The (m), 2/17/30, Jolson Theatre, 16
Counterattack (p), 3/3/43, Windsor Theatre, 84
Counterpoint. See Chad Mitchell's Counterpoint
Countess Cathleen, The (p), 3/28/05, Madison Square Theatre, 2
Countess Chiffon, The (p), 2/6/00, 5th Avenue Theatre, 8
Countess Julia (p), 4/28/13, 48th St. Theatre, 3
Countess Maritza (m), 9/18/26, Shubert Theatre, 321
Countess Maritza (m), 4/9/28, Century Theatre, 16
Country Boy, The (p), 8/30/10, Liberty Theatre, 143
Country Cousin, The (p), 9/3/17, Gaiety Theatre, 128
Country Girl, A (m), 9/22/02, Daly's Theatre, 112
Country Girl, A (m), 5/29/11, Herald Square Theatre, 32
Country Girl, The (p), 11/10/50, Lyceum Theatre, 235
Country Girl, The (p), 9/29/66, New York City Center, 22
Country Girl, The (p), 3/15/72, Billy Rose Theatre, 61
Country Mouse, A / Carrots (p), 10/6/02, Savoy Theatre, 89
Country Scandal, A (p), 5/5/60, Greenwich Mews Theatre, 203
Country Wife, The (p), 12/1/36, Henry Miller's Theatre, 88
Country Wife, The (p), 6/26/57, Renata Theatre
Country Wife, The (p), 11/27/57, Adelphi Theatre, 45
Country Wife, The (p), 12/9/65, Vivian Beaumont Theatre, 52
County Chairman, The (p), 11/24/03, Wallack Theatre, 222
County Chairman, The (p), 5/25/36, National Theatre, 8
Courage (p), 1/19/27, Princess Theatre, 10
Courage (p), 10/8/28, Ritz Theatre, 283
Courageous One, The (p), 1/20/58, Greenwich Mews Theatre, 104
Courtesan (p), 4/29/30, President Theatre, 7
Courtin' Time (m), 6/13/51, National Theatre, 37
Courting (p), 9/12/25, 49th St. Theatre, 41
Courtship of Kevin and Roxanne, The. See Things That Almost Happen
Courtyard (p), 2/29/60, Gramercy Arts Theatre, 32
Cousin Billy (p), 1/2/05, Criterion Theatre, 76
Cousin Kate (p), 10/19/03, Hudson Theatre, 44
Cousin Kate (p), 4/4/04, Hudson Theatre, 16
Cousin Kate (p), 5/6/07, Empire Theatre, 16
Cousin Kate / A Slice of Life (p), 1/29/12, Empire Theatre, 48
Cousin Louisa (p), 4/30/06, Daly's Theatre, 8
Cousin Lucy (p), 8/27/15, Cohan Theatre, 43
Cousin Sonia (p), 12/7/25, Central Park Theatre, 24
Coutouriere de Luneville, La, 3/21/24, Gaiety Theatre, 6
Cox and Box / H.M.S. Pinafore (m), 9/28/36, Martin Beck Theatre, 16
Cox and Box / H.M.S. Pinafore (m), 1/19/48, Century Theatre, 16, (D'Oyly Carte Opera Co.)
Cox and Box / The Pirates of Penzance (m), 9/6/34, Martin Beck Theatre, 14
Cox and Box / The Pirates of Penzance (m), 2/17/44, Ambassador Theatre, 8
Cox and Box / The Pirates of Penzance (m), 2/19/51, St. James Theatre, 8
Crabbed Youth and Age / The Shadow of the Glen / Birthright (p), 11/3/32, Martin Beck Theatre, 1
Cracks / Color of Darkness (p), 9/30/63, Writers' Stage Theatre, 31
Cradle Snatchers (p), 9/7/25, Music Box Theatre, 485
Cradle Snatchers (p), 5/2/27, Music Box Theatre, 16
Cradle Snatchers (p), 11/16/32, Liberty Theatre, 5
Cradle Song (p), 2/28/21, Times Square Theatre, 4
Cradle Song, The (p), 1/24/27, Civic Repertory Theatre, 52
Cradle Song, The (p), 10/19/27, Civic Repertory Theatre, 79
Cradle Song, The (p), 10/2/28, Civic Repertory Theatre, 13
Cradle Song, The (p), 9/17/29, Civic Repertory Theatre, 18
Cradle Song, The (p), 10/7/30, Civic Repertory Theatre, 16
Cradle Song, The (p), 11/9/32, Civic Repertory Theatre, 2
Cradle Song, The (p), 12/10/34, Broadhurst Theatre, 4
Cradle Song, The (p), 12/1/55, Circle in the Square, 175
Cradle Song, The / Fragila Rosina (p), 5/9/27, Forrest Theatre, 4
Cradle Will Rock, The (m), 6/16/37, Venice Theatre
Cradle Will Rock, The (m), 1/3/38, Windsor Theatre, 104
Cradle Will Rock, The (m), 12/26/47, Mansfield Theatre, 21
Cradle Will Rock, The (m), 11/8/64, Theatre Four, 82
Craig's Wife (p), 10/12/25, Morosco Theatre, 360
Craig's Wife (p), 2/12/47, Playhouse, 69
Cranks (r), 11/26/56, Bijou Theatre, 40
Crashing Through (p), 10/29/28, Republic Theatre, 40
Crazy Now (r), 9/10/72, Eden Theatre, 1
Crazy with the Heat (r), 1/14/41, 44th St. Theatre, 7
Crazy with the Heat (r), 1/30/41, 44th St. Theatre, 92
Creaking Chair, The (p), 2/22/26, Lyceum Theatre, 80
Cream Cheese. See A Festival of Short Plays
Cream in the Well, The (p), 1/20/41, Booth Theatre, 24
Creation of the World and Other Business, The (p), 11/30/72, Shubert Theatre, 20
Creditors (p), 1/25/62, Mermaid Theatre, 46
Creditors / The Constant Lover (p), 5/2/22, Grennwich Village Theatre, 8
Creeping Fire (p), 1/16/35, Vanderbilt Theatre, 23
Creeps (p), 12/4/73, Playhouse 2, 15
Creoles (p), 9/22/27, Klaw Theatre, 28
Cretan Bull, The / Allergy (p), 1/24/74, Manhattan Theatre Club, 17
Cretan Woman, The (p), 7/7/54, Provincetown Playhouse, 94
Crime (p), 2/2/27, Eltinge Theatre, 186
Crime and Crime (p), 12/16/63, Cricket Theatre, 1
Crime and Punishment (p), 1/22/35, Biltmore Theatre, 15
Crime and Punishment (p), 12/22/47, National Theatre, 64
Crime in the Whistler Room, The (p), 10/12/24, Provincetown Playhouse, 23
Crime Marches On (p), 10/23/35, Morosco Theatre, 46
Crimes of Passion (The Ruffian on the Stair / The Erpingham Camp) (p), 10/26/69, Astor Place Theatre, 9
Criminal at Large (p), 10/10/32, Belasco Theatre, 162
Criminal Code, The (p), 10/2/29, National Theatre, 174
Criminals, The (p), 2/25/70, Sheridan Square Playhouse, 15, (Phoenix Theatre)
Crimson Alibi, The (p), 7/17/19, Broadhurst Theatre, 51
Crinoline Girl, The (p), 3/16/14, Knickerbocker Theatre, 88
Crisis, The (p), 11/17/02, Wallack Theatre, 50
Crisis, The (p), 10/12/08, Hackett Theatre, 4
Criss Cross (m), 10/12/26, Globe Theatre, 210
Criss-Crossing / Watercolor (p), 1/21/70, ANTA Theatre, 5
Critic's Choice (p), 12/14/60, Ethel Barrymore Theatre, 189
Critic, The (p), 1/25/15, Princess Theatre, 16
Critic, The (p), 5/8/25, Neighborhood Playhouse, 38
Critic, The / Oedipus (p), 5/20/46, Century Theatre, 8
Critic, The. See A Tragedy Rehearsed
Critic, The. See The National Theatre of the Deaf
Critics, The, 1/9/22, Belmont Theatre, 24
Croesus and the Witch (m), 8/24/71, Urban Arts Corps Theatre
Croesus and the Witch / Step Lively Boy (m), 3/15/73, Urban Arts Corps Theatre
Crooked Friday, The (p), 10/8/25, Bijou Theatre, 21
Crooked Gamblers (p), 7/31/20, Hudson Theatre, 81
Crooked Square, The (p), 9/10/23, Hudson Theatre, 88
Crooks' Convention, The (p), 9/18/29, Forrest Theatre, 13
Crops and Croppers (p), 9/12/18, Belmont Theatre, 20
Cross My Heart (m), 9/17/28, Knickerbocker Theatre, 64
Cross Roads (p), 11/11/29, Morosco Theatre, 28
Cross Ruff (p), 2/19/35, Masque Theatre, 7
Crossing, The (p), 1/1/06, Daly's Theatre, 8
Crossing the Gap. See Sold to the Movies
Crossroads (p), 8/5/69, Riverside Park, 23, (Puerto Rican Traveling Theatre Co.)
Cross-Town (p), 3/17/37, 48th St. Theatre, 5
Cross-ways, The (p), 12/29/02, Garrick Theatre, 24
Crowded Hour, The (p), 11/22/18, Selwyn Theatre, 139
Crown Matrimonial (p), 10/2/73, Helen Hayes Theatre, 79
Crown Prince, The (p), 4/30/04, Daly's Theatre, 17
Crown Prince, The (p), 3/23/27, Forrest Theatre, 45
Crown, the Ring and the Roses, The (p), 1/3/63, Theatre de Lys, 1
Crowns (p), 11/11/22, Provincetown Playhouse, 8
Cruce de Vias. See Difunta, La
Cruce de Vias. See Program of 3 One-Acters
Crucible, The (p), 9/4/33, Forrest Theatre, 8
Crucible, The (p), 1/22/53, Martin Beck Theatre, 197
Crucible, The (p), 3/11/58, Martinique Theatre, 633
Crucible, The (p), 4/6/64, Belasco Theatre, 32
Crucible, The (p), 4/27/72, Vivian Beaumont Theatre, 44
Cruising Speed 600 M.P.H. / Mrs. Snow (p), 1/5/70, Theatre de Lys, 2, (ANTA Matinee)
Cry for Us All (m), 4/8/70, Broadhurst Theatre, 9
Cry Havoc. Also known as Proof through the Night (p), 12/25/42, Morosco Theatre, 11
Cry of Players, A (p), 11/14/68, Vivian Beaumont Theatre, 58
Cry of the Peacock (p), 4/11/50, Mansfield Theatre, 2
Cry of the People for Meat, The (p), 12/5/69, St. Peter's Church, 3, (Bread and Puppet Theatre)
Cry of the Raindrop (p), 3/7/61, St. Marks Playhouse, 40
Crystal and Fox (p), 4/23/73, McAlpin Rooftop Theatre, 24
Crystal Heart, The, 2/15/60, East 74th St. Theatre, 9
Cub, The (p), 11/1/10, Comedy Theatre, 32
Cuba Si / The Guns of Carrar (p), 12/9/68, Theatre de Lys, 2, (ANTA Matinee)
Cuban Thing, The (p), 9/24/68, Henry Miller's Theatre, 1
Cuckoos on the Hearth (p), 9/16/41, Morosco Theatre, 129
Cue for Passion (p), 12/19/40, Royale Theatre, 12
Cue for Passion (p), 11/25/58, Henry Miller's Theatre, 39
Cup of Trembling, The (p), 4/20/48, Music Box Theatre, 31
Cup, The (p), 11/12/23, Fulton Theatre, 16
Cupid Outwits Adam (p), 9/10/00, Bijou Theatre, 8

Cure for Curables, A (p), 2/25/18, 39th St. Theatre, 112
Cure for Matrimony (p), 10/25/39, Provincetown Playhouse, 27
Curiosity (p), 12/18/19, Greenwich Village Theatre, 28
Curious Evening with Gypsy Rose Lee, A, 5/9/61, Mayfair Theatre, 27
Curious Fern, The / Voices for a Mirror (p), 6/5/51, Master Institute
Curious Savage, The (p), 10/24/50, Martin Beck Theatre, 31
Curley McDimple (m), 11/22/67, Bert Wheeler Theatre, 931
Curley McDimple (m), 6/26/72, Plaza 9 Music Hall
Curtain Call (p), 4/22/37, John Golden Theatre, 4
Curtain Rises, The (p), 10/19/33, Vanderbilt Theatre, 61
Curtains Up! (Ethel Colt), 12/16/58, Theatre de Lys, 1
Curtains Up! (Ethel Colt), 11/2/59, East 74th St. Theatre, 6
Cut of the Axe (p), 2/1/60, Ambassador Theatre, 2
Cybele (m), 10/26/71, W.P.A. Theatre, 10
Cyclone Lover, The (p), 6/5/28, Frolic Theatre, 31
Cymbeline (p), 10/22/06, Astor Theatre, 32
Cymbeline (p), 10/2/23, Jolson Theatre, 15
Cymbeline (p), 8/12/71, Delacorte Theatre, 15
Cynara (p), 11/2/31, Morosco Theatre, 210
Cynthia (p), 3/16/03, Madison Square Theatre, 32
Cyrano (m), 5/13/73, Palace Theatre, 49
Cyrano de Bergerac (p), 11/1/23, National Theatre, 250
Cyrano de Bergerac (p), 12/22/24, Century Theatre
Cyrano de Bergerac (p), 2/18/26, Hampden Theatre, 97
Cyrano de Bergerac (p), 12/25/28, Hampden Theatre, 143
Cyrano de Bergerac (p), 12/26/32, New Amsterdam Theatre, 16
Cyrano de Bergerac (p), 4/27/36, New Amsterdam Theatre, 40
Cyrano de Bergerac (p), 10/8/46, Alvin Theatre, 193
Cyrano de Bergerac (p), 11/11/53, New York City Center, 16
Cyrano de Bergerac (p), 11/19/53, Broadhurst Theatre, 27
Cyrano de Bergerac (p), 4/25/68, Vivian Beaumont Theatre, 52
Czar Paul I (p), 3/18/12, Garrick Theatre, 8
Czarina, The (p), 1/31/22, Empire Theatre, 136

D

Daddies (p), 9/5/18, Belasco Theatre, 340
Daddy Come Home (p), 4/16/63, Blackfriars' Theatre, 42
Daddy Dufard (p), 12/6/10, Hackett Theatre, 31
Daddy Dumplins (p), 11/22/20, Republic Theatre, 64
Daddy Goodness (p), 6/4/68, St. Marks Playhouse, 64, (Negro Ensemble Co.)
Daddy Long-Legs (p), 9/28/14, Gaiety Theatre, 264
Daddy Long-Legs (p), 11/16/18, Henry Miller's Theatre, 17
Daddy's Gone A-Hunting (p), 8/31/21, Plymouth Theatre, 129
Daffy Dill (m), 8/22/22, Apollo Theatre, 69
Dagger, The (p), 9/9/25, Longacre Theatre, 5
Dagmar (p), 1/22/23, Selwyn Theatre, 65
Dairy of a Madman, The (p), 3/23/67, Orpheum Theatre, 4
Dairymaids, The (m), 8/26/07, Criterion Theatre, 86
Daisy Mayme (p), 10/25/26, Playhouse, 113
Daly, Arnold. See Arnold Daly
Dama Duende, La (p), 6/6/68, Greenwich Mews Theatre, 32
Damaged Goods (p), 3/14/13, Fulton Theatre, 66
Damaged Goods (p), 5/17/37, 48th St. Theatre, 8
Damask Cheek, The (p), 10/22/42, Playhouse, 93
Damask Drum, The / Sotoba Komachi / Han's Crime (p) (Three Modern Japanese Plays), 2/3/61, Players' Theatre, 45
Dame aux Camélias, La (p), 11/30/26, Cosmopolitan Theatre, 11
Dame Nature (p), 9/26/38, Booth Theatre, 48
Dames at Sea (m), 12/20/68, Bouwerie Lane Theatre, 575
Dames at Sea (m), 9/22/70, Plaza 9 Music Hall, 170
Damn the Tears (p), 1/21/27, Garrick Theatre, 11
Damn Yankees (m), 5/5/55, 46th St. Theatre, 1,019
Damn Yankees (m), 4/14/67, Master Theatre, 14
Damn You, Scarlett O'Hara / All My Pretty Little Ones. See Riverside Drive
Damn Your Honor (p), 12/30/29, Cosmopolitan Theatre, 8
Dance Me a Song (r), 1/20/50, Royale Theatre, 35
Dance Night (p), 10/14/38, Belasco Theatre, 3
Dance of Death, The (p), 12/16/23, Princess Theatre, 6
Dance of Death, The (p), 9/13/60, Key Theatre, 112
Dance of Death, The (p), 5/25/68, Roundabout Theatre, 55
Dance of Death, The (p), 4/28/71, Ritz Theatre, 5
Dance of Death, The (p), 4/4/74, Vivian Beaumont Theatre, 37
Dance wi' Me (m), 6/10/71, Public/Anspacher Theatre, 53
Dance with Your Gods (p), 10/6/34, Mansfield Theatre, 9
Dancer, The (p), 9/29/19, Harris Theatre, 61
Dancer, The (p), 6/5/46, Biltmore Theatre, 5
Dancers, The, 10/17/23, Broadhurst Theatre, 133
Dances Before a Wall (p), 3/30/58, Henry St. Playhouse
Dancing Around (m), 10/10/14, Winter Garden Theatre, 145
Dancing Duchess, The (m), 8/19/14, Casino Theatre, 13
Dancing Girl, The (m), 1/24/23, Winter Garden Theatre, 142
Dancing Mothers (p), 8/11/24, Booth Theatre, 311
Dancing Partner (p), 8/5/30, Belasco Theatre, 119
Dandelion (m), 12/20/69, Alice Tully Hall, 14, (Paper Bag Players)
Dandelion. See The Paper Bag Players
Dandy Dick (p), 1/10/56, Cherry Lane Theatre, 14
Danger (p), 12/22/21, 39th St. Theatre, 79
Dangerous Corner (p), 10/27/32, Empire Theatre, 210
Dangerous Corner (p), 7/17/33, Waldorf Theatre, 93
Danny Kaye, 4/10/63, Ziegfeld Theatre, 47
Danny Larkin (p), 5/24/48, Lenox Hill Playhouse, 3
Dante (p), 10/26/03, Broadway Theatre, 14
Danton's Death (p), 11/2/38, Mercury Theatre, 21
Danton's Death (p), 10/21/65, Vivian Beaumont Theatre, 46
Danton's Tod (p), 12/20/27, Century Theatre, 16
Daphne in Cottage D (p), 10/15/67, Longacre Theatre, 41
Daphne Laureola (p), 9/18/50, Music Box Theatre, 56
D'Arcy of the Guards (p), 12/16/01, Savoy Theatre, 48
Dark Angel, The (p), 2/10/25, Longacre Theatre, 64
Dark at the Top of the Stairs, The (p), 12/5/57, Music Box Theatre, 468
Dark Corner / Mr. Grossman (p), 5/5/64, Actors Playhouse, 7
Dark Eyes (p), 1/14/43, Belasco Theatre, 230
Dark Fire / The Owl Answers (p), 12/14/65, Theatre de Lys, 1, (ANTA Matinee)
Dark Hammock (p), 12/11/44, Forrest Theatre, 2
Dark Hours, The (p), 11/14/32, New Amsterdam Theatre, 8
Dark Is Light Enough, The (p), 2/23/55, ANTA Theatre, 69
Dark Lady of the Sonnets, The / Androcles and the Lion (p), 12/14/61, Phoenix Theatre, 23
Dark Lady of the Sonnets, The / The Admirable Bashville (p), 2/20/56, Cherry Lane Theatre, 98
Dark Legend (p), 3/24/52, President Theatre, 8
Dark Mirror, The (p), 11/9/28, Cherry Lane Theatre, 32
Dark of the Moon (p), 3/14/45, 46th St. Theatre, 318
Dark of the Moon (p), 2/26/58, Carnegie Hall Playhouse, 85
Dark of the Moon (p), 4/3/70, Mercer-Shaw Arena Theatre, 86
Dark Rosaleen (p), 4/22/19, Belasco Theatre, 87
Dark, The, 2/1/27, Lyceum Theatre, 13
Dark Tower, The (p), 11/25/33, Morosco Theatre, 57
Dark Victory (p), 11/7/34, Plymouth Theatre, 55
Darker Flower, A (p), 3/8/63, Pocket Theatre, 5
Darkness at Noon (p), 1/13/51, Alvin Theatre, 186
Darling of the Day (m), 1/27/68, George Abbott Theatre, 32
Darling of the Gallery Gods, The / The Dress Parade (r), 6/22/03, Crystal Gardens, 30
Darling of the Gods, The (p), 12/3/02, Belasco Theatre, 182
Darwin's Theories (r), 10/18/60, Madison Avenue Playhouse, 3
Date with April, A (p), 4/15/53, Royale Theatre, 13
Daughter of Heaven, The (p), 10/12/12, Century Theatre, 98
Daughter of Madame Angot, The (m), 12/14/25, Jolson Theatre, 8
Daughter of Silence (p), 11/30/61, Music Box Theatre, 36
Daughter of the Tumbrils, The / Lucky Miss Dean (p), 2/5/06, Madison Square Theatre, 8
Daughters of Atreus (p), 10/14/36, 44th St. Theatre, 13
Daughters of Men, The (p), 11/19/06, Astor Theatre, 59
David Garrick (p) (Charles Wyndham), 11/14/04, Lyceum Theatre, 24
David Garrick (p), 1/6/16, Booth Theatre, 20
David Garrick / The Man on the Box (p) (Henry E. Dixey), 11/27/05, Madison Square Theatre, 48
David Harum (p), 10/1/00, Garrick Theatre, 148
David Harum (p), 9/8/02, Criterion Theatre, 16
David Harum (p), 4/4/04, Academy of Music, 32
David's Crown (p) (Habimah), 5/8/48, Broadway Theatre, 8
David Show, The (p), 10/31/68, Players Theatre, 1
David Show, The. See Tonight in Living Color
Davy Jones Locker (m), 12/24/72, Bil Baird Theatre, 79
Davy Jones's Locker (m), 12/24/66, Bil Baird Theatre, 34
Dawn (p), 11/24/24, Sam H. Harris Theatre, 48
Dawn of a Tomorrow, The (p), 1/25/09, Lyceum Theatre, 152
Day After Tomorrow, The (p), 10/26/50, Booth Theatre, 12
Day Before Spring, The (m), 11/22/45, National Theatre, 165
Day Before, The / Mamzelle Champagne (p), 10/24/06, Berkeley Lyceum Theatre, 4
Day by the Sea, A (p), 9/26/55, ANTA Theatre, 24
Day in the Death of Joe Egg, A (p), 2/1/68, Brooks Atkinson Theatre, 154
Day in the Life of Just About Everyone, A (m), 3/9/71, Bijou Theatre, 7
Day in the Sun (p), 5/16/39, Biltmore Theatre, 6
Day of Absence / Brotherhood (p), 3/10/70, St. Marks Playhouse, 64
Day of Absence / Happy Ending (p), 11/15/65, St. Marks Playhouse, 504
Day of Dupes, The / Just as Well / The Forbidden Guests / Happiness (p), 3/6/14, Cort Theatre, 5
Day of the Serpent, 12/8/71, American Museum of Natural History, 6
Day the Money Stopped, The (p), 2/20/58, Belasco Theatre, 4

Day the Whores Came Out To Play Tennis, The / Sing to Me Through Open Windows (p), 3/15/65, Players Theatre, 24
Day Will Come, The (p), 9/7/44, National Theatre, 20
Daybreak (p), 8/14/17, Harris Theatre, 71
Days and Nights of Beebee Fenstermaker, The (p), 9/17/62, Sheridan Square Playhouse, 304
Days to Come (p), 12/15/36, Vanderbilt Theatre, 7
Days without End (p), 1/8/34, Henry Miller's Theatre, 57
De Feraudy, M. Maurice. See M. Maurice de Feraudy
De Lancey (p), 9/4/05, Empire Theatre, 68
De Luxe (p), 3/5/35, Booth Theatre, 15
De Luxe Annie (p), 9/14/17, Booth Theatre, 119
De Sade Illustrated (p), 5/12/69, Bouwerie Lane Theatre, 117
Deacon and the Lady, The (m), 10/4/10, New York Theatre, 16
Deacon, The. See Alias the Deacon
Dead City, The (p), 11/27/23, Century Theatre, 2
Dead End (p), 10/28/35, Belasco Theatre, 684
Dead Pigeon (p), 12/23/53, Vanderbilt Theatre, 21
Dead Souls (p), 2/4/65, New York City Center, 10, (Moscow Art Theatre)
Deadfall (p), 10/27/55, Holiday Theatre, 20
Deadlock, The (p), 1/20/14, Maxine Elliott's Theatre, 23
Deadly Art, The, 12/12/66, Theatre de Lys, 2, (ANTA Matinee)
Deadly Game, The (p), 2/2/60, Longacre Theatre, 39
Deadly Game, The (p), 2/13/66, Provincetown Playhouse, 105
Deafman Glance, 2/25/71, Brooklyn Academy of Music, 2
Dear Barbarians (p), 2/21/52, Royale Theatre, 4
Dear Brutus (p), 12/23/18, Empire Theatre, 184
Dear Charles (p), 9/15/54, Morosco Theatre, 157
Dear Fool, The (p), 1/26/14, Garrick Theatre, 24
Dear Jane (p), 11/14/32, Civic Repertory Theatre, 12
Dear Janet Rosenberg, Dear Mr. Kooning / Jakey Fat Boy (p), 4/5/70, Gramercy Arts Theatre, 48
Dear Judas (p), 10/5/47, Mansfield Theatre, 16
Dear Liar (p), 3/17/60, Billy Rose Theatre, 52
Dear Liar (p), 3/17/62, Theatre Marquee, 40
Dear Liar (p) (German language), 5/3/63, Barbizon-Plaza Theatre, 8
Dear Me (p), 1/17/21, Republic Theatre, 144
Dear Me, the Sky Is Falling (p), 3/2/63, Music Box Theatre, 145
Dear Nobody (p), 6/24/68, Actors Playhouse, 19
Dear Nobody (p), 2/19/74, Cherry Lane Theatre, 71
Dear Octopus (p), 1/11/39, Broadhurst Theatre, 53
Dear Old Charlie (p), 4/15/12, Maxine Elliott's Theatre, 32
Dear Old Darling (p), 3/4/36, Alvin Theatre, 16
Dear Old England (p), 3/25/30, Ritz Theatre, 23
Dear Oscar (m), 11/16/72, Playhouse Theatre, 5
Dear Ruth (p), 12/13/44, Henry Miller's Theatre, 683
Dear Sir (m), 9/23/24, Times Square Theatre, 15
Dear Unfair Sex, The (p), 9/10/06, Liberty Theatre, 21
Dear World (m), 2/6/69, Mark Hellinger Theatre, 132
Dearest Enemy (m), 9/18/25, Knickerbocker Theatre, 286
Death of a Salesman (p), 2/10/49, Morosco Theatre, 742
Death of Bessie Smith, The / The American Dream (p), 10/2/68, Billy Rose Theatre, 10, (Theatre 1969 Playwrights Repertory)
Death of Bessie Smith, The / The American Dream / Happy Days (p), 2/28/61, York Theatre, 328
Death of Lord Chatterly, The / Miss Julie (p), 7/31/73, Roundabout Theatre, 16
Death of Satan, The (p), 4/5/60, St. Marks Playhouse, 32
Death of the Well-Loved Boy, The (p), 5/15/67, St. Marks Playhouse, 8
Death Takes a Holiday (p), 12/26/29, Ethel Barrymore Theatre, 181
Death Takes a Holiday (p), 2/16/31, Ambassador Theatre, 32
Deathwatch (p), 10/9/58, Theatre East, 70
Debtors, The (p), 10/12/09, Bijou Theatre, 15
Deburau (p), 12/23/20, Belasco Theatre, 189
Deburau / Mozart (p), 12/27/26, Chanin's 46th St. Theatre, 32
Debut (p), 2/22/56, Holiday Theatre, 5
Debutante, The (m), 12/7/14, Knickerbocker Theatre, 48
Decameron, The (m), 4/12/61, East 74th St. Theatre, 39
Deceased, The / The Grand Vizier / Edward and Agrippina (p) (The French Way), 3/20/62, East End Theatre, 1
Decision (p), 5/27/29, 49th St. Theatre, 56
Decision (p), 2/2/44, Belasco Theatre, 158
Decision at Tongo (p), 2/5/63, Blackfriars' Theatre, 42
Declassee (p), 10/6/19, Empire Theatre, 257
Decline and Fall of the Entire World as Seen Through the Eyes of Cole Porter, Revisited, The (r), 3/30/65, Square East, 273
Decorating Clementine (p), 9/19/10, Lyceum Theatre, 48
Decoy, The (p), 4/1/32, Royale Theatre, 8
Deed from the King of Spain, A (p), 1/31/74, Greenwich Mews Theatre
Deep Are the Roots (p), 9/26/45, Fulton Theatre, 477
Deep Are the Roots (p), 10/3/60, St. Marks Playhouse, 65
Deep Blue Sea, The (p), 11/5/52, Morosco Theatre, 132
Deep Channels (p), 10/18/29, Waldorf Theatre, 4
Deep Harlem (m), 1/7/29, Biltmore Theatre, 8
Deep Mrs. Sykes, The (p), 3/19/45, Booth Theatre, 72
Deep Purple, The (p), 1/9/11, Lyric Theatre, 152
Deep River, 10/4/26, Imperial Theatre, 32
Deep Tangled Wildwood, The (p), 11/5/23, Frazee Theatre, 16
Deer Park, The (p), 1/31/67, Theatre de Lys, 128
Defender of the Faith. See Unlikely Heroes
Defender, The (m), 7/3/02, Herald Square Theatre, 60
Degenerates, The, 1/15/00, Garden Theatre, 36
Deirdre of the Sorrows, 9/20/20, Bramhall Playhouse, 16
Deirdre of the Sorrows (p), 10/14/59, Gate Theatre, 61
Delicate Balance, A (p), 9/22/66, Martin Beck Theatre, 132
Delicate Champions (p), 12/29/71, Forum Theatre, 6
Delicate Story (p), 12/4/40, Henry Miller's Theatre, 29
Deluge, The (p), 8/20/17, Hudson Theatre, 16
Deluge, The (p), 1/27/22, Plymouth Theatre, 45
Deluge, The (p), 12/13/26, Mansfield Theatre, 6
Deluge, The (p), 3/25/35, Majestic Theatre, 3
Demi Monde, Le, 11/30/26, Cosmopolitan Theatre, 3
Demi-Dozen (r), 10/11/58, Upstairs at the Downstairs
Demi-Virgin, The (p), 10/18/21, Times Square Theatre, 268
Democracy's King / The Master (p), 2/19/18, Hudson Theatre, 15
Demon / Gertrude (p), 1/9/72, La Mama Experimental Theatre Club, 13
Demonstration, The. See The Niggerlovers
Depths, The (p), 1/27/25, Broadhurst Theatre, 31
Deputy of Paris, The (p), 3/21/47, Henry St. Playhouse, 8
Deputy, The (p), 2/26/64, Brooks Atkinson Theatre, 318
Der Lebende Leichnam (The Living Corpse), 1/23/28, Cosmopolitan Theatre, 8
Derryowen (p), 10/28/46, Blackfriars' Theatre, 24
Desert Flower, The (p), 11/18/24, Longacre Theatre, 31
Desert Incident, A (p), 3/24/59, Golden Theatre, 7
Desert Sands (p), 2/13/22, Princess Theatre, 16
Desert Song, The (m), 11/30/26, Casino Theatre, 465
Desert Song, The (m), 1/8/46, New York City Center, 45
Desert Song, The (m), 9/5/74, Uris Theatre, 15
Deserters, The (p), 9/20/10, Hudson Theatre, 63
Design for a Stained Glass Window (p), 1/23/50, Mansfield Theatre, 8
Design for Living (p), 1/24/33, Ethel Barrymore Theatre, 135
Design for Living (p), 1/31/74, Manhattan Theatre Club, 8
Desire Caught by the Tail (p), 10/17/69, Theatre East
Desire Under the Elms (p), 11/11/24, Greenwich Village Theatre, 208
Desire Under the Elms (p), 1/16/52, ANTA Playhouse, 48
Desire Under the Elms (p), 1/8/63, Circle in the Square, 384
Desire Under the Elms (p), 3/14/74, Queensborough Community College, 7
Desk Set, The (p), 10/24/55, Broadhurst Theatre, 296
Desperate Hours, The (p), 2/10/55, Ethel Barrymore Theatre, 212
Destruction (p), 6/30/32, Chanin Auditorium, 1
Destry Rides Again (m), 4/23/59, Imperial Theatre, 472
Detective Sparks (p), 8/23/09, Garrick Theatre, 64
Detective Story (p), 3/23/49, Hudson Theatre, 581
Detour, The (p), 8/23/21, Astor Theatre, 48
Deuces Wild / Charlatans. See A Pair of Pairs, 4/24/62, Vandam Theatre, 16
Devil in the Cheese, The (p), 12/29/26, Charles Hopkins Theatre, 165
Devil in the Mind (p), 5/1/31, Fulton Theatre, 11
Devil Is a Good Man, The / What D'You Call It / According to Law (p), 3/19/40, Provincetown Playhouse, 38
Devil of Pie-ling, The (p), 2/20/36, Adelphi Theatre, 12
Devil Passes, The (p), 1/4/32, Selwyn Theatre, 97
Devil Peter, The. See Festival of New Italian Plays
Devil's Advocate, The (p), 3/9/61, Billy Rose Theatre, 116
Devil's Disciple, The (p), 4/23/23, Garrick Theatre, 192
Devil's Disciple, The (p), 1/25/50, New York City Center, 16
Devil's Disciple, The (p), 2/21/50, Royale Theatre, 111
Devil's Garden, The (p), 12/28/15, Harris Theatre, 23
Devil's Host, The (p), 11/19/31, Forrest Theatre, 36
Devil's Little Game, The (p), 8/1/32, Provincetown Playhouse, 3
Devil Takes a Bride, The (p), 10/7/38, Cort Theatre, 11
Devil, The (p) (George Arliss), 8/18/08, Garden Theatre, 87
Devil, The (p) (Edwin Stevens), 8/18/08, Belasco Theatre, 175
Devil to Pay, The (p), 12/3/25, 52nd St. Theatre, 12
Devil Within, The (p), 3/16/25, Hudson Theatre, 24
Devils (p), 3/17/26, Maxine Elliott's Theatre, 29
Devils Galore (p), 9/12/45, Royale Theatre, 5
Devils, The (p), 11/16/65, Broadway Theatre, 63
Devils, The (p), 1/11/73, CSC Repertory Theatre
Dew Drop Inn (m), 5/17/23, Astor Theatre, 52
Dew Drop Inn (m), 7/30/23, Astor Theatre, 31
Dial 'M' for Murder (p), 10/29/52, Plymouth Theatre, 552
Dialect Determinism. See Short Bullins
Diamond Lil (p), 4/9/28, Royale Theatre, 323
Diamond Lil (p), 2/5/49, Coronet Theatre, 181
Diamond Lil (p), 9/14/51, Broadway Theatre, 67
Diamond Orchid (p), 2/10/65, Henry Miller's Theatre, 5
Diana (p), 12/9/29, Longacre Theatre, 8
Diana of Dobson's (p), 9/5/08, Savoy Theatre, 17

Diary of a Madman (p), 4/16/64, Gramercy Arts Theatre, 14
Diary of a Scoundrel (p), 11/4/56, Phoenix Theatre, 25
Diary of Adam and Eve. See The Apple Tree
Diary of Anne Frank, The (p), 10/5/55, Cort Theatre, 717
Dice of the Gods, The (p), 4/5/23, National Theatre, 20
Dickey Bird, The / Polygamy (p), 2/22/15, Park Theatre, 64
Dictator, The (p), 4/4/04, Criterion Theatre, 64
Dictator, The (p), 8/24/04, Criterion Theatre, 25
Dictator, The (p), 4/13/11, Comedy Theatre, 44
Did I Say No? (p), 9/22/31, 48th St. Theatre, 15
Diener an Zweier Herrens / Er ist an Allem Schuld (p) (Servant of Two Masters / He Is to Blame for Everything), 1/9/28, Cosmopolitan Theatre, 8
Diff'rent (p), 12/27/20, Provincetown Playhouse, 74
Diff'rent (p), 1/25/38, Maxine Elliott's Theatre, 4
Diff'rent (p), 10/17/61, Mermaid Theatre, 88
Difference in Gods (p), 4/9/17, Bramhall Playhouse, 32
Difference in Gods (p), 2/6/18, Bramhall Playhouse, 8
Difference in Gods (p), 11/28/18, Bramhall Playhouse, 68
Difference in Gods (p), 10/27/21, Bramhall Play, 28
Difference in Gods (p), 3/4/26, Bramhall Playhouse, 70
Different Times (m), 5/1/72, ANTA Theatre, 24
Difficult Borning, A, 1/10/73, Brooklyn Academy of Music
Difficult Woman, The (m), 4/25/62, Barbizon-Plaza Theatre, 1
Difunta, La. See Program of 3 One-Acters
Difunta, La (The Dead Wife) / Cruce de Vias (The Railroad Crossing) / Pericas, La (The Parrots) (p), 11/19/70, Greenwich Mews Theatre, 26
Dime a Dozen (r), 10/18/62, Plaza 9, Plaza Hotel
Dinner at Eight (p), 10/22/32, Music Box Theatre, 243
Dinner at Eight (p), 9/27/66, Alvin Theatre, 127
Dinner Is Served (p), 8/15/29, Cort Theatre, 4
Dinny and the Witches (p), 12/9/59, Cherry Lane Theatre, 23
Dinosaur Wharf (p), 11/8/51, National Theatre, 4
Dionysus in 69 (p), 6/6/68, Performing Garage
Diplomacy (p), 4/15/01, Empire Theatre, 56
Diplomacy (p), 9/13/10, Maxine Elliott's Theatre, 33
Diplomacy (p), 10/20/14, Empire Theatre, 63
Diplomacy (p), 5/28/28, Erlanger Theatre, 32
Diplomat, The (p), 3/20/02, Madison Square Theatre, 76
Dirtiest Show in Town, The (p), 4/4/70, La Mama Experimental Theatre Club
Dirtiest Show in Town, The (p), 6/27/70, Astor Place Theatre, 509
Dirty Old Man, The / Sarah and the Sax (p), 5/4/64, Theatre de Lys, 16
Discovering America (p), 9/7/12, Daly's Theatre, 17
Disenchanted, The (p), 12/3/58, Coronet Theatre, 189
Disengaged (p), 3/11/09, Hudson Theatre, 1
Dishonored Lady (p), 2/4/30, Empire Theatre, 127
Disintegration of James Cherry, The (p), 1/29/70, Forum Theatre, 28
Disney on Parade (r), 8/1/72, Madison Square Garden, 40
Displaced Person, The (p), 12/29/66, St. Clement's Church, 18, (American Place Theatre)
Disposal, The (p), 9/22/73, Greenwich Mews Theatre
Disquieting Muses, 2/11/74, Theatre at St. Clement's, 16
Disraeli (p), 9/18/11, Wallack Theatre, 280
Disraeli (p), 4/9/17, Knickerbocker Theatre, 48
Distaff Side, The (p), 9/25/34, Booth Theatre, 154
Distaff Side, The (p), 3/5/35, Ethel Barrymore Theatre, 24
Distant Bell, A (p), 1/13/60, Eugene O'Neill Theatre, 5
Distant City, The (p), 9/22/41, Longacre Theatre, 2
Distant Drum, A (p), 1/20/28, Hudson Theatre, 11
Distant Drums (p), 1/18/32, Belasco Theatre, 40
Distant Shore, The (p), 2/21/35, Morosco Theatre, 12
District Leader, The (m), 4/30/06, Wallack Theatre, 8
Diverions (r), 11/7/58, Downtown Theatre, 85
Diversion, 1/11/28, 49th St. Theatre, 61
Divertissement / The Nightcap / Gutta Iconoclast / Pearls / The Good Women / Squaring the Triangle, 6/13/21, Apollo Theatre, 8
Divided by Three (p), 10/2/34, Ethel Barrymore Theatre, 31
Divided Honors (p), 9/30/29, Forrest Theatre, 40
Divine Drudge (p), 10/26/33, Royale Theatre, 12
Divine Moment, A (p), 1/6/34, Vanderbilt Theatre, 9
Divorce (p), 11/29/09, Lyric Theatre, 8
Divorce a la Carte (p), 3/26/28, Biltmore Theatre, 8
Divorce Me, Dear (p), 10/6/31, Avon Theatre, 6
Divorce of Judy and Jane, The (p), 4/26/72, Bijou Theatre, 7
Divorcons (p), 4/15/07, Wallack Theatre, 54
Divorcons (p), 8/15/07, Lyceum Theatre, 29
Divorcons (p) (Grace George), 2/25/09, Hackett Theatre, 1
Divorcons (p), 4/1/13, Playhouse, 55
Divorcons / Little Italy (p) (Mrs. Fiske), 5/26/02, Manhattan Theatre, 24
Dixey, Henry E. See Henry E. Dixey
Dixie to Broadway (r), 10/29/24, Broadhurst Theatre, 77
DMZ, The (r), 10/10/68, Village Vanguard, 57
Doña Rosita la Soltera (p), 3/20/70, Village South Theatre, 33, (Greenwich Mews Spanish Theatre)
Do I Hear a Waltz? (m), 3/18/65, 46th St. Theatre, 220
Do It Again! (r), 2/18/71, Promenade Theatre, 14
Do Not Pass Go (p), 4/19/65, Cherry Lane Theatre, 16
Do Re Mi (m), 12/26/60, St. James Theatre, 400
Do You Know the Koran? See What! And Leave Bloomingdales?
Do You Know the Milky Way? (p), 10/16/61, Billy Rose Theatre, 16
Do You Know the Milky Way? (p), 3/14/63, Gramercy Arts Theatre, 94
Dock Brief, The / What Shall We Tell Caroline? (p), 11/14/61, Midway Theatre, 6
Dockstader's Minstrels (r), 1/4/04, Victoria Theatre, 32
Dockstader's Minstrels (r), 10/31/04, Herald Square Theatre, 24
Doctor Faustus Lights the Lights, 12/2/51, Cherry Lane Theatre
Doctor in Spite of Himself, The (p), 7/5/73, Puerto Rican Traveling Theatre
Doctor in Spite of Himself, The. See El Medico a Palos
Doctor Monica (p), 11/6/33, Playhouse, 16
Doctor's Dilemma, The (p), 3/26/15, Wallack Theatre
Doctor's Dilemma, The (p), 11/21/27, Guild Theatre, 115
Doctor's Dilemma, The (p), 3/11/41, Shubert Theatre, 112
Doctor's Dilemma, The (p), 1/11/55, Phoenix Theatre, 48
Doctor Selavy's Magic Theatre (m), 11/23/72, Mercer-O'Casey Theatre, 144
Doctor Social (p), 2/11/48, Booth Theatre, 5
Doctor X, 2/9/31, Hudson Theatre, 80
Doctors Disagree (p), 12/28/43, Bijou Theatre, 23
Dodo Bird, The / The Peddler (p), 12/8/67, Martinique Theatre, 29
Dodsworth (p), 2/24/34, Shubert Theatre, 147
Dodsworth (p), 8/20/34, Shubert Theatre, 170
Does a Tiger Wear a Necktie? (p), 2/25/69, Belasco Theatre, 39
Dog Beneath the Skin, The (p), 7/21/47, Cherry Lane Theatre, 27
Dogs of Pavlov, The (p), 4/11/74, Cubiculo, 16
Doing Our Bit (r), 10/18/17, Winter Garden Theatre, 130
Dolce / The Eyes of the Heart / The Light from St. Agnes (p), 4/24/06, Manhattan Theatre, 3
Doll Girl, The (m), 8/25/13, Globe Theatre, 88
Doll Girl, The / The Censor and the Dramatists (p), 10/14/13, Globe Theatre, 33
Doll's House, A (p) (Mrs. Fiske), 5/21/02, Manhattan Theatre, 1
Doll's House, A (p) (Mrs. Fiske), 5/30/02, Manhattan Theatre, 1
Doll's House, A (p) (Ethel Barrymore), 5/2/05, Lyceum Theatre, 15
Doll's House, A (p), 1/18/07, Bijou Theatre, 28
Doll's House, A (p), 11/18/07, Bijou Theatre, 49
Doll's House, A (p) (Alla Nazimova), 4/29/18, Plymouth Theatre, 32
Doll's House, A (p), 2/21/24, Vanderbilt Theatre, 1
Doll's House, A (p) (Ruth Gordon), 12/27/37, Morosco Theatre, 142
Doll's House, A (p), 2/2/63, Theatre Four, 66
Doll's House, A (p), 1/13/71, Playhouse Theatre, 111
Dollar Mark, The (p), 8/23/09, Wallack Theatre, 48
Dollar Princess, The (m), 9/6/09, Knickerbocker Theatre, 288
Dolly Jordan (p), 10/3/22, Daly's Theatre, 7
Dolly Varden (m), 1/27/02, Herald Square Theatre, 154
Dolly Varden (m), 9/22/02, Hammerstein's Victoria Theatre, 24
Dom Juan (p), 2/6/70, New York City Center, 5, (Comédie Française)
Dominant Sex, The (p), 4/1/35, Cort Theatre, 16
Dominic's Lover. See Things That Almost Happen
Domino (p), 8/16/32, Playhouse, 7
Domino Furioso / The American Dream (p), 2/7/61, York Theatre, 16
Don (p), 12/30/09, New Theatre
Don Caesar's Return (p), 9/3/01, Wallack Theatre, 87
Don Carlos (p), 2/27/62, Masque Theatre, 26
Don Carlos (p), 11/24/64, N.Y. State Theatre, 8, (Schiller Theatre)
Don Juan (p), 9/5/21, Garrick Theatre, 14
Don Juan (p), 12/11/72, Lyceum Theatre, 22, (New Phoenix Repertory Co.)
Don Juan in Hell (p), 10/22/51, Carnegie Hall, 1
Don Juan in Hell (p), 11/29/51, Century Theatre, 39
Don Juan in Hell (p), 4/6/52, Plymouth Theatre, 64
Don Juan in Hell (p), 6/19/62, Actors Playhouse, 8
Don Juan in Hell, 1/15/73, Palace Theatre, 24
Don Juan Tenorio (p), 11/15/72, Gramercy Arts Theatre, 41, (Spanish Theatre Repertory Co.)
Don Juan Tenorio (Don Juan the Lover), 11/19/53, Broadhurst Theatre, 27
Don / Liz the Mother (p), 1/3/10, New Theatre, 1
Don Q., Jr., 1/27/26, 49th St. Theatre, 14
Don't Bother Me, I Can't Cope (r), 10/8/70, Lincoln Center Library Auditorium, 2
Don't Bother Me, I Can't Cope (r), 4/19/72, Playhouse Theatre, 914
Don't Bother Mother (p), 2/3/25, Little Theatre, 3
Don't Drink the Water (p), 11/17/66, Morosco Theatre, 588
Don't George (p), 11/2/44, Blackfriar's Theatre, 22
Don't Go Away Mad (p), 5/9/49, Master Institute Theatre, 2
Don't Let It Go to Your Head (p), 1/20/72, Henry St. Playhouse, 7
Don't Listen, Ladies (p), 12/28/48, Booth Theatre, 15
Don't Look Now! (p), 11/2/36, Nora Bayes Theatre, 16
Don't Play Us Cheap (m), 5/16/72, Ethel Barrymore Theatre, 164
Don't Shoot Mable, It's Your Husband (p), 10/22/68, Bouwerie Lane Theatre, 1

Don't Tell (p), 9/27/20, Nora Bayes Theatre, 16
Don't Throw Glass Houses (p), 12/27/38, Vanderbilt Theatre, 15
Don't Walk on the Clouds (m), 11/5/71, St. Clement's Church, 21
Don't Weaken (p), 1/14/14, Maxine Elliott's Theatre, 5
Donnybrook! (m), 5/18/61, 46th St. Theatre, 68
Donogoo (p), 1/18/61, Greenwich Mews Theatre, 35
Donovan Affairs, The (p), 8/30/26, Fulton Theatre, 128
Doormat, The (p), 12/7/22, Punch and Judy Theatre, 5
Dope (p), 1/4/26, 48th St. Theatre, 2
Dora Mobridge (p), 4/19/30, Little Theatre, 9
Dorian Gray (p), 5/21/28, Biltmore Theatre, 16
Dorian Gray (p), 7/20/36, Comedy Theatre, 16
Dorothea Baird—H. B. Irving Repertory, 10/1/06, New Amsterdam Theatre, 32
Dorothy Sands, 1/29/33, Booth Theatre, 2
Dorothy Sands, 11/11/33, Little Theatre, 6
Dorothy Vernon of Haddon Hall (p), 12/14/03, New York Theatre, 40
Dorothy Vernon of Haddon Hall (p), 12/12/04, Majestic Theatre, 16
Double Bill of Jean Giraudoux's Plays, A (The Virtuous Island) / The Apollo of Bellac (p), Carnegie Hall Playhouse, 22
Double Door (p), 9/21/33, Ritz Theatre, 138
Double Dublin (r), 12/26/63, Little Theatre, 4
Double Dummy (p), 11/11/36, John Golden Theatre, 21
Double Entry (m) (The Bible Salesman / The Oldest Trick in the World), 2/20/61, Martinique Theatre, 56
Double Exposure (p), 8/27/18, Bijou Theatre, 15
Double in Hearts (p), 10/16/56, Golden Theatre, 7
Double Life, The (p), 12/24/06, Bijou Theatre, 12
Double Play (Limb of Snow / The Meeting) (p), 12/11/67, Theatre de Lys, 2
Double Solitaire / Solitaire (p), 9/30/71, John Golden Theatre, 36
Doubletalk. See Sarah and the Sax / The Dirty Old Man
Doughgirls, The (p), 12/30/42, Lyceum Theatre, 671
Dove of Peace, The (m), 11/4/12, Broadway Theatre, 16
Dove, The (p), 2/11/25, Empire Theatre, 159
Dove, The (p), 8/24/25, Empire Theatre, 48
Dover Road, The (p), 12/23/21, Bijou Theatre, 324
Down in the Valley (m), 7/7/48, Lemonade Opera Company
Down in the Valley / Trouble in Tahiti (m), 4/23/65, Master Theatre, 14, (Equity Library Theatre)
Down Stream (p), 1/11/26, 48th St. Theatre, 16
Down to Miami (p), 9/11/44, Ambassador Theatre, 8
Downtown Holy Lady, The (p), 9/28/72, Greenwich Mews Theatre, 12
D'Oyly Carte Company, 1/5/39, Martin Beck Theatre, 77
D'Oyly Carte Opera Company, 12/29/47, Century Theatre, 136
D'Oyly Carte Opera Company, 9/27/55, Shubert Theatre, 72
D'Oyly Carte Opera Company, 11/13/62, New York City Center, 32
D'Oyly Carte Opera Company, 11/17/64, New York City Center, 40
D'Oyly Carte Opera Company (m), 11/15/66, New York City Center, 32
D'Oyly Carte Opera Company (m), 10/29/68, New York City Center, 24
Dozens, The (p), 3/13/69, Booth Theatre, 4
Dr. Cook's Garden (p), 9/25/67, Belasco Theatre, 8
Dr. David's Dad (p), 8/13/24, Vanderbilt Theatre, 5
Dr. De Luxe (m), 4/17/11, Knickerbocker Theatre, 32
Dr. Faustus (p), 1/8/37, Maxine Elliott's Theatre, 128
Dr. Fish. See The Chinese and Dr. Fish
Dr. Galley. See Transfers
Dr. Hero (p), 3/19/73, Shade Company Theatre
Dr. Kheal. See A Festival of Short Plays
Dr. Knock (p), 2/23/28, American Laboratory Theatre, 23
Dr. Wake's Patient (p), 11/19/07, Garrick Theatre, 1
Dr. Willy Nilly, 6/4/59, Barbizon-Plaza Theatre, 12
Dracula (p), 10/5/27, Fulton Theatre, 265
Dracula (p), 4/13/31, Royale Theatre, 8
Dracula (p), 9/10/73, Royal Playhouse, 60
Dracula Sabbat (p), 9/11/70, Judson Memorial Church, 12
Dragon Lady's Revenge, The (m), 11/24/72, Washington Square Methodist Church
Dragon's Claw, The (p), 9/14/14, New Amsterdam Theatre, 8
Dragon's Mouth (p), 11/16/55, Cherry Lane Theatre, 34
Dragon, The (p), 12/26/22, Earl Carroll Theatre, 6
Dragon, The (p), 3/25/29, Cherry Lane Theatre, 5
Dragon, The (p), 4/9/63, Phoenix Theatre, 32
Drama at Inish (p), 12/13/27, Ambassador Theatre, 4
Drama at Inish (p), 11/14/34, John Golden Theatre, 3
Drama at Inish (p), 10/13/37, Ambassador Theatre, 4
Dramatized Anthology of Puerto Rican Short Stories, A (p), 8/10/71, N.Y.C. Parks & Streets, 39
Draper, Paul. See Paul Draper
Draper, Paul / 27 Wagons Full of Cotton / Trouble in Tahiti. See All in One
Draper, Ruth. See Ruth Draper
Drat! (m), 10/18/71, McAlpin Rooftop Theatre, 1
Drat! The Cat! (m), 10/10/65, Martin Beck Theatre, 8
Dream Child (p), 9/27/34, Vanderbilt Theatre, 24
Dream City (p), 12/24/06, Weber Theatre, 102
Dream Girl (m), 8/20/24, Ambassador Theatre, 118
Dream Girl (p), 12/14/45, Coronet Theatre, 348
Dream Girl (p), 5/9/51, N.Y. City Center, 15
Dream Maker, The (p), 11/21/21, Empire Theatre, 82
Dream of a Blacklisted Actor (p), 12/15/69, Theatre de Lys, 2, (ANTA Matinee)
Dream of Swallows, A (p), 4/14/64, Jan Hus House, 1
Dream on Monkey Mountain, The (p), 3/9/71, St. Marks Playhouse, 48
Dream Out of Time, A (p), 11/8/70, Promenade Theatre, 49
Dream Play (p), 11/22/60, Theatre East, 44
Dream Play, The (p), 1/20/26, Provincetown Playhouse, 26
Dream with Music (m), 5/18/44, Majestic Theatre, 28
Dreams for Sale (p), 9/13/22, Playhouse, 13
Dreamy Kid, The / Emperor Jones (p), 2/11/25, 52nd St. Theatre, 24
Dress Parade, The / The Darling of the Gallery Gods (r), 6/22/03, Crystal Gardens, 30
Dressler's All Star Gambol, Marie. See Marie Dressler's etc.
Dreyfus on Devil's Island. See Tel Aviv Drama Company
Drift (p), 11/24/25, Cherry Lane Theatre, 13
Drifting, 12/21/10, Nazimova's 39th St. Theatre, 10
Drifting (p), 1/2/22, Playhouse, 63
Drink (p), 9/14/03, Academy of Music, 40
Drink to Me Only (p), 10/8/58, 54th St. Theatre, 77
Driven (p), 12/14/14, Empire Theatre, 24
Drone, The (p), 12/30/12, Daly's Theatre, 2
Druid Circle, The (p), 10/22/47, Morosco Theatre, 69
Drums Begin, The (p), 11/24/33, Shubert Theatre, 11
Drums in the Night (p), 5/17/67, Circle in the Square, 69
Drums of Jeopardy, The (p), 5/29/22, Gaiety Theatre, 8
Drums Under the Windows (p), 10/13/60, Cherry Lane Theatre, 109
Drunkard, The (p), 3/10/34, American Music Hall, 277
Drunkard, The (m), 4/13/70, 13th Street Theatre, 48
Du Barry (p), 12/25/01, Criterion Theatre, 165
Du Barry (p), 9/29/02, Belasco Theatre, 63
Du Barry Was a Lady (m), 12/6/39, 46th St. Theatre, 408
Du Barry Was a Lady (m), 5/4/72, Master Theatre, 19, (Equity Library Theatre)
DuBarry, The (m), 11/22/32, George M. Cohan Theatre, 86
Duchess Misbehaves, The (m), 2/13/46, Adelphi Theatre, 5
Duchess of Dantzic, The (m), 1/16/05, Daly's Theatre, 93
Duchess of Malfi, The (p), 10/15/46, Ethel Barrymore Theatre, 38
Duchess of Malfi, The (p), 3/19/57, Phoenix Theatre, 24
Duchess of Malfi, The (p), 4/6/66, I.A.S.T.A. Theatre, 12
Duchess, The (m), 10/16/11, Lyric Theatre, 24
Dude (m), 10/9/72, Broadway Theatre, 16
Duel of Angels (p), 4/19/60, Helen Hayes Theatre, 51
Duel, The (p), 2/12/06, Hudson Theatre, 73
Duet for Solo Voice. See Two Times One
Duet for Three / Big Man (p), 5/19/66, Cherry Lane Theatre, 14
Duet for Two Hands (p), 10/7/47, Booth Theatre, 7
Duke in Darkness, The (p), 1/24/44, Playhouse, 24
Duke of Duluth, The (m), 9/11/05, Majestic Theatre, 24
Duke of Duluth, The (m), 12/4/05, American Theatre, 8
Duke of Killicrankie, The (p), 9/5/04, Empire Theatre, 128
Duke of Killicrankie, The / Rosalind (p), 9/6/15, Lyceum Theatre, 48
Dulcy (p), 8/13/21, Frazee Theatre, 246
Dumb and the Blind, The / The Marriage of Kitty (p), 12/18/14, Comedy Theatre, 27
Dumb-Bell (p), 11/26/23, Belmont Theatre, 2
Dumbell People in a Barbell World (p) (The Immovable Gordons / The Little Lady of Friday Night / The Man with the Tranquil Mind), 2/14/62, Cricket Theatre
Dumbwaiter, The / The Collection (p) (Pinter Plays), 11/26/62, Cherry Lane Theatre, 578
Dumbwaiter, The / The Dwarfs (p), 5/3/74, Abbey Theatre, 11, (CSC Repertory)
Dummy, The (p), 4/13/14, Hudson Theatre, 200
Dunce Boy, The (p), 4/1/25, Daly's Theatre, 43
Dunelawn. See Bad Habits
Dunnigan's Daughter (p), 12/26/45, John Golden Theatre, 38
Duplex, The (p), 3/9/72, Forum Theatre, 28
Duse, Eleonora. See Eleonora Duse
Dust Heap, The (p), 4/24/24, Vanderbilt Theatre, 20
Dutchman (p) (opened with Two Executioners and Play, as Three at the Cherry Lane; continued with American Dream), 3/24/64, Cherry Lane Theatre, 366
Dwarfs, The / The Dumbwaiter (p), 5/3/74, Abbey Theatre, 11, (CAC Repertory)
Dybbuk, The (p), 12/15/25, Neighborhood Playhouse, 120
Dybbuk, The (p), 12/13/26, Mansfield Theatre, 24, (Moscow Habimah)
Dybbuk, The (p), 12/16/26, Neighborhood Playhouse, 41
Dybbuk, The (p), 10/26/54, Fourth St. Theatre, 112
Dybbuk, The (p) (Habimah), 2/3/64, Little Theatre, 25

Dybbuk, The (p), 9/19/72, Brooklyn Academy of Music, 8, (Jewish State Theatre of Bucharest)
Dylan (p), 1/18/64, Plymouth Theatre, 273
Dylan (p), 2/7/72, Mercer-O'Casey Theatre, 48
Dylan Thomas Growing Up, 10/31/72, Theresa L. Kaufman Concert Hall, 3.
Dynamite Tonight (m), 3/15/64, York Playhouse, 1
Dynamite Tonight (m), 3/15/67, Martinique Theatre, 9
Dynamo (p), 2/11/29, Martin Beck Theatre, 66

E

E. H. Sothern Repertory, 1/27/08, Lyric Theatre
E. H. Sothern Repertory, 5/18/08, Academy of Music
E. H. Sothern Repertory, 3/29/09, Daly's Theatre
E & O E / Something More Important / The Old Women (p), 7/11/35, Chanin Auditorium, 12
E. S. Willard Repertory, 12/31/00, Garden Theatre, 32
E. S. Willard Repertory, 12/2/02, Garden Theatre, 32
E. S. Willard Repertory, 12/11/05, New Amsterdam Theatre, 24
E. S. Willard Repertory, 1/23/05, Knickerbocker Theatre, 32
Each Had Six Wings (p), 3/11/64, Little Theatre, 16
Eagle Has Two Heads, The (p), 3/19/47, Plymouth Theatre, 29
Eagle Has Two Heads, The (p), 12/13/56, Actors Playhouse, 38
Earl and the Girl, The (m), 11/4/05, Casino Theatre, 148
Earl Carroll's Sketch Book (r), 7/1/29, Earl Carroll Theatre, 392
Earl Carroll's Sketch Book (r), 6/4/35, Winter Garden Theatre, 207
Earl Carroll's Vanities (r), 7/5/23, Earl Carroll Theatre, 204
Earl Carroll's Vanities (r), 9/10/24, Music Box Theatre, 134
Earl Carroll's Vanities (r), 7/6/25, Earl Carroll Theatre, 440
Earl Carroll's Vanities (r), 8/24/26, Earl Carroll Theatre, 154
Earl Carroll's Vanities (r), 1/4/27, Earl Carroll Theatre, 151
Earl Carroll's Vanities (r), 8/6/28, Earl Carroll Theatre, 200
Earl Carroll's Vanities (r), 7/1/30, New Amsterdam Theatre, 215
Earl Carroll's Vanities (r), 8/27/31, Earl Carroll Theatre, 300
Earl Carroll's Vanities (r), 9/27/32, Broadway Theatre, 87
Earl Carroll's Vanities (r), 1/13/40, St. James Theatre, 25
Earl of Pawtucket, The (p), 3/23/03, Manhattan Theatre, 191
Earl of Ruston (m), 5/5/71, Billy Rose Theatre, 5
Early Morning (p), 11/18/70, La Mama Experimental Theatre, 5
Early to Bed (m), 6/17/43, Broadhurst Theatre, 380
Earth (p), 3/9/27, 52nd St. Theatre, 26
Earth Between, The / Before Breakfast (p), 3/5/29, Provincetown Playhouse, 30
Earth Journey (p), 4/27/44, Blackfriars' Theatre, 16
Earth, The (p), 2/15/16, Playhouse
Earthlight (r), 1/17/71, Garrick Theatre, 56
Earthlight Theatre (r), 10/27/70, Gracie Square Theatre, 56
Earthquake, The / The International Cup / The Ballet of Niagara (r), 9/3/10, New York Hippodrome, 333
Easiest Way, The (p), 1/19/09, Belasco Stuyvesant Theatre, 157
Easiest Way, The (p), 9/6/21, Lyceum Theatre, 63
East Is West (p), 12/25/18, Astor Theatre, 680
East Lynne (p), 3/10/26, Greenwich Village Theatre, 38
East Lynne (p), 2/3/32, John Golden Theatre, 4
East of Broadway (p), 1/26/32, Belmont Theatre, 39
East of Suez (p), 9/21/22, Eltinge Theatre, 102
East Side—West Side. See Manhattan
East Wind (m), 10/27/31, Manhattan Theatre, 23
East Wind, The (p), 2/9/67, Vivian Baumont Theatre, 60
Easter (p), 3/18/26, Princess Theatre, 28
Easter (p), 1/16/57, Fourth St. Theatre, 47
Easterner, The (p), 3/2/08, Garrick Theatre, 16
Eastward–in Eden (p), 11/18/47, Royale Theatre, 15
Easy Come, Easy Go (p), 10/26/25, George M. Cohan Theatre, 180
Easy Dawson (p), 8/22/05, Wallack Theatre, 56
Easy Mark, The (p), 8/26/24, 39th St. Theatre, 104
Easy Street (p), 8/14/24, 39th St. Theatre, 12
Easy Terms (p), 9/22/25, National Theatre, 15
Easy Virtue (p), 12/7/25, Empire Theatre, 146
Ebb Tide (p), 6/8/31, New Yorker Theatre, 16
Eben Holden (p), 10/28/01, Savoy Theatre, 49
Echo, The (m), 8/17/10, Globe Theatre, 53
Echoes (p), 3/26/73, Bijou Theatre, 1
Ecole des Femmes, L' (p), 3/18/51, ANTA Playhouse, 22
Ed Wynn Carnival (r), 4/5/20, New Amsterdam Theatre, 150
Eddie Fisher and Buddy Hackett, 8/28/67, Palace Theatre, 42
Eddie Fisher at the Winter Garden (r), 10/2/62, Winter Garden Theatre, 40
Eden End (p), 10/21/35, Masque Theatre, 24
Edgar Allan Poe (p), 10/5/25, Liberty Theatre, 8
Edgar Allan Poe, 10/28/73, Alice Tully Hall, 1
Edith Piaf, 10/30/47, Playhouse, 49
Editha's Burglar / The Travelling Man / Merry Christmas, Daddy! (p), 12/26/16, Cohan and Harris Theatre, 2
Edmund Burke (p), 10/2/05, Majestic Theatre, 28
Edna His Wife (p), 12/7/37, Little Theatre, 32
Education of H*Y*M*A*N K*A*P*L*A*N, The (m), 4/4/68, Alvin Theatre, 28
Education of Mr. Pipp, The (p), 2/20/05, Liberty Theatre, 78
Edward and Agrippina / The Deceased / The Grand Vizier (p) (The French Way), 3/20/62, East End Theatre, 1
Edward, My Son (p), 9/30/48, Martin Beck Theatre, 260
Edward Terry Repertory, 12/26/04, Princess Theatre
Edwin Booth (p), 11/24/58, 46th St. Theatre, 24
Edwina Black (p), 11/21/50, Booth Theatre, 15
Effect of Gamma Rays on Man-in-the-Moon Marigolds, The (p), 4/7/70, Mercer-O'Casey Theatre, 819
Effect of Gamma Rays on Man-in-the-Moon Marigolds, The (p), 2/18/73, Actors Studio Theatre, 2
Effect of Gamma Rays on Man-in-the-Moon Marigolds, The (p), 5/12/73, Gramercy Arts Theatre, 13, (Spanish Theatre Repertory Co.)
Egg, The (p), 1/8/62, Cort Theatre, 8
Egghead, The (p), 10/9/57, Ethel Barrymore Theatre, 21
Egotist, The (p), 12/25/22, 39th St. Theatre, 49
Eh? (p), 10/16/66, Circle in the Square, 232
Eight Bells (p), 10/28/33, Hudson Theatre, 17
Eight O'Clock Tuesday (p), 1/6/41, Henry Miller's Theatre, 16
Eileen (m), 3/19/17, Shubert Theatre, 64
Eileen Asthore (p), 10/22/06, New York Theatre, 16
Einen Jux Will Er Sich Machen (p), 4/2/68, New York City Center, 6, (Vienna Burgtheater)
El Alcalde de Zalamea (The Mayor of Zalamea) (p), 11/17/53, Broadhurst Theatre, 27
El Cardenal (p), 11/19/53, Broadhurst Theatre, 27
Elder Son, The (p), 9/15/14, Playhouse, 23
Eldest, The (p), 2/11/35, Ritz Theatre, 24
Electra (p) (Margaret Anglin), 2/6/18, Carnegie Hall, 1
Electra (p), 5/3/27, Metropolitan Opera House, 2
Electra (p) (Margaret Anglin), 12/1/27, Gallo Theatre, 13
Electra (p), 12/26/30, New Yorker Theatre, 8
Electra (p), 1/8/32, Selwyn Theatre, 6
Electra (p) (Katina Paxinou), 11/19/52, Mark Hellinger Theatre, 6
Electra (p), 5/9/58, Jan Hus House, 26
Electra (p), 3/22/61, IASTA Theatre
Electra (p) (Greek Tragedy Theatre), 9/19/61, New York City Center, 8
Electra (p), 9/7/64, New York City Center, 8, (Greek Tragedy Theatre of Athens: Piraikon Theatron of Athens)
Electra (p) (Lee Grant), 8/11/64, Delacorte Theatre, 17
Electra (p), 7/29/69, New York Shakespeare Festival Mobile Theatre, 24
Electra (p), 5/27/74, Theatre at St. Clement's, 8
Electra / Harlequinade (p), 2/13/59, Rita Allen Theatre, 19
Electra / Marriage Game (p), 12/29/13, Comedy Theatre, 8
Electra / The Flower of Yamato (p), 2/11/08, Garden Theatre, 9
Electric Map, The. See The Memory Bank
Electricity (p), 10/31/10, Lyceum Theatre, 16
Electronic Nigger and Others, The (A Son, Come Home / The Electronic Nigger / Clara's Ole Man) (p), 2/21/68, American Place Theatre, 96
Electronic Nigger, The. See The Electronic Nigger and Others
Eleonora Duse Repertory, 11/4/02, Hammerstein's Victoria Theatre, 10
Eleonora Duse Repertory, 11/30/23, Century Theatre, 9
Elephant in the House, The (p), 2/20/72, Circle Theatre
Elevating a Husband (p), 1/22/12, Liberty Theatre, 120
Elevation, L', 11/14/17, Playhouse, 38
Elevator, The. See The Last Sweet Days of Isaac
Eli, the Fanatic. See Unlikely Heroes
Eliza Comes to Stay (p), 1/7/14, Garrick Theatre, 13
Elizabeth I (p), 4/5/72, Lyceum Theatre, 5
Elizabeth Sleeps Out (p), 4/20/36, Comedy Theatre, 44
Elizabeth the Queen (p), 11/3/30, Guild Theatre, 145
Elizabeth the Queen (p), 11/3/66, N.Y. City Center, 14
Ellen Terry Repertory, 1/28/07, Empire Theatre, 22
Ellen Terry-Henry Irving Repertory, 10/21/01, Knickerbocker Theatre, 16
Ellis Takes His Life Again. See What! And Leave Bloomingdales?
Elmer Gantry (p), 8/9/28, Playhouse, 44
Elmer the Great (p), 9/24/28, Lyceum Theatre, 40
Elsa Lanchester—Herself, 2/4/61, 41st St. Theatre, 75
Elsie (m), 4/2/23, Vanderbilt Theatre, 40
Elsie Janis and Her Gang (r), 12/1/19, George M. Cohan Theatre, 55
Elsie Janis and Her Gang (r), 1/16/22, Gaiety Theatre, 56
Elton Case, The (p), 9/10/21, Playhouse, 17
Embarrassment of Riches, The (p), 5/14/06, Wallack Theatre, 16
Embassy Ball, The (p), 3/5/06, Daly's Theatre, 48
Embers (p), 2/1/26, Henry Miller's Theatre, 33
Embezzled Heaven (p), 10/31/44, National Theatre, 52
Emerald Isle, The (m), 9/1/02, Herald Square Theatre, 50
Emerald Slippers, The (p), 9/1/70, Gramercy Arts Theatre, 10
Emlyn Williams as Charles Dickens, 2/4/52, John Golden Theatre, 48

Emlyn Williams as Charles Dickens, 4/20/53, Bijou Theatre, 24
Emlyn Williams as Charles Dickens, 11/3/70, Alice Tully Hall, 5
Emmanuel (p), 12/4/60, Gate Theatre, 25
Emperor Henry IV (p), 3/28/73, Ethel Barrymore Theatre, 38
Emperor Jones, The (p), 11/1/20, Provincetown Playhouse, 192
Emperor Jones, The (p), 5/6/24, Provincetown Playhouse, 21
Emperor Jones, The (p), 12/15/24, Provincetown Playhouse, 14
Emperor Jones, The (p), 1/12/25, Punch and Judy Theatre, 20
Emperor Jones, The (p), 2/16/26, Provincetown Playhouse, 35
Emperor Jones, The (p), 11/10/26, Mayfair Theatre, 81
Emperor Jones, The / The Dreamy Kid (p), 2/11/25, 52nd St. Theatre, 24
Emperor of Late Night Radio, The (p), 3/2/74, Public / Other Stage, 10
Emperor's Clothes, The (p), 2/9/53, Ethel Barrymore Theatre, 16
Emperor, The (p), 4/16/63, Maidman Playhouse, 24
Empire Builders, The (p), 10/1/68, Astor Place Theatre, 6
Empress Eugenie, The, 11/22/32, Lyceum Theatre, 24
Empress of Destiny (p), 3/9/38, St. James Theatre, 5
En Attendant Godot (Waiting for Godot) (p), 4/22/68, Barbizon-Plaza Theatre, 12, (Le Treteau de Paris)
Enchanted April, The (p), 8/24/25, Morosco Theatre, 32
Enchanted Cottage, The (p), 3/31/23, Ritz Theatre, 64
Enchanted Isle (m), 9/19/27, Lyric Theatre, 32
Enchanted, The (p), 1/18/50, Lyceum Theatre, 45
Enchanted, The (p), 4/22/58, Renata Theatre, 32
Enchanting Melody (m), 11/24/64, Folksbiene Playhouse, 84
Enchantment (p), 4/27/27, Edyth Totten Theatre, 9
Enchantress, The (m), 10/19/11, New York Theatre, 72
Enclave, The (p), 11/15/73, Theatre Four, 22
End as a Man (p), 9/15/53, Theatre de Lys, 137
End of All Things Natural, The (p), 9/11/69, Village South Theatre, 6
End of Summer (p), 2/17/36, 152
Endecott and the Red Cross (p), 4/18/68, American Place Theatre, 36
Endgame (p), 1/28/59, Cherry Lane Theatre, 104
Endgame (p), 5/30/70, Washington Square Methodist Church, 6, (Open Theatre)
Endgame (p), 4/11/74, Manhattan Project, 12
Endless Chain, The (p), 9/4/22, George M. Cohan Theatre, 40
Enemies (p), 3/18/35, Majestic Theatre, 2
Enemies (p), 11/9/72, Vivian Beaumont Theatre, 44
Enemies Don't Send Flowers / A God Slept Here (p), 2/19/57, Provincetown Playhouse, 16
Enemies / Friends (p), 9/16/65, Theatre East, 139
Enemy Is Dead, The (p), 1/14/73, Bijou Theatre, 1
Enemy of the People, An (p), 10/3/27, Hampden Theatre, 127
Enemy of the People, An (p), 11/5/28, Hampden Theatre, 24
Enemy of the People, An (p), 2/15/37, Hudson Theatre, 16
Enemy of the People, An (p), 12/28/50, Broadhurst Theatre, 36
Enemy of the People, An (p), 2/4/59, Actors Playhouse
Enemy of the People, An (p), 2/9/68, Master Theatre, 9, (Equity Library Theatre)
Enemy of the People, An (p), 3/11/71, Vivian Beaumont Theatre, 54
Enemy, The (p), 10/20/25, Times Square Theatre, 202
Enemy Within (p), 10/5/31, Hudson Theatre, 8
Engaged (m), 6/18/25, 52nd St. Theatre, 44
Engagement Baby, The (p), 5/21/70, Helen Hayes Theatre, 4
English Daisy, An (m), 1/18/04, Casino Theatre, 41
Englishman's Home, An (p), 3/22/09, Criterion Theatre, 40
Enter Laughing (p), 3/13/63, Henry Miller's Theatre, 419
Enter Madame (p), 8/16/20, Garrick Theatre, 366
Entertain a Ghost (p), 4/9/62, Actors Playhouse, 9
Entertainer, The (p), 2/12/58, Royale Theatre, 97
Entertaining Mr. Sloane (p), 10/12/65, Lyceum Theatre, 13
Entertaining Mr. Sloane (p), 3/27/74, U.R.G.E.N.T. Theatre, 12
Epic of Buster Friend, The / The Interview (p), 12/3/73, Theatre de Lys, 2, (Matinee Theatre)
Episode (p), 2/4/25, Bijou Theatre, 21
Epitaph for George Dillon (p), 11/4/58, Golden Theatre, 23
Epitaph for George Dillon (p), 1/12/59, Henry Miller's Theatre, 48
Epitaph for George Dillon (p), 12/28/60, Actors Playhouse, 84
Epstein. See Unlikely Heroes
Er ist an Allem Schuld / Diener an Zweier Herrens (p) (He Is to Blame for Everything / Servant of Two Masters), 1/9/28, Cosmopolitan Theatre, 8
Ergo (p), 3/13/68, Public Theatre, 49
Ermete Novelli Repertory, 3/18/07, Lyric Theatre
Ermete Novelli Repertory, 12/2/07, Lyric Theatre
Erminie (m), 10/19/03, Casino Theatre, 42
Erminie (m), 1/3/21, Park Theatre, 108
Ernest in Love (m), 5/4/60, Gramercy Arts Theatre, 111
Ernest in Love (m), 11/20/64, Master Theatre, 14, (Equity Library Theatre)
Eros and Psyche (p), 4/26/72, Brooklyn Academy of Music, 18, (Chelsea Theatre Center)
Erpingham Camp, The. See Crimes of Passion
Errant Lady (p), 9/17/34, Fulton Theatre, 40
Erstwhile Susan (p), 1/18/16, Gaiety Theatre, 167
Escapade (p), 11/18/53, 48th St. Theatre, 13
Escape (p), 10/26/27, Booth Theatre, 176
Escape Me Never (p), 1/21/35, Shubert Theatre, 96
Escape, The (p), 9/20/13, Lyric Theatre, 17
Escape This Night (p), 4/22/38, 44th St. Theatre, 11
Escurial / Santa Claus / Calvary (p), 7/21/60, Gate Theatre, 14
Escurial. See The Victims
Ete, L' (p), 4/9/73, Cherry Lane Theatre, 10
Eternal Cage (p), 3/21/45, Barbizon-Plaza Theatre
Eternal City, The (p), 11/17/02, Hammerstein's Victoria Theatre, 92
Eternal Jew, The (p) (Moscow Habimah), 12/13/26, Mansfield Theatre, 9
Eternal Judith, The / The Pot Boiler / Autumn Fires (p), 11/7/21, Princess Theatre, 8
Eternal Magdalene, The (p), 11/1/15, 48th St. Theatre, 88
Eternal Road, The (p), 1/7/37, Manhattan Opera House, 152
Eternal Triangle. See Three Hand Reel
Ethan Frome (p), 1/21/36, National Theatre, 119
Ethel Colt in Curtains Up, 12/16/58, Theatre de Lys, 1
Ethel Colt. See Curtains Up
Eugenia (p), 1/30/57, Ambassador Theatre, 12
Eumenides, The / The Choephori (p) (Greek Tragedy Theatre), 9/26/61, New York City Center, 8
Eunuchs of the Forbidden City (p), 4/5/72, Theatre for the New City, 11
Eva (m), 12/30/12, New Amsterdam Theatre, 24
Eva the Fifth (p), 8/28/28, Little Theatre, 63
Evangeline (p), 10/4/13, Park Theatre, 17
Evangelist, The (p), 9/30/07, Knickerbocker Theatre, 19
Eve of St. Mark, The (p), 10/7/42, Cort Theatre, 306
Eve's Daughter (p), 10/11/17, Playhouse, 36
Eve's Leaves (p), 3/26/25, Wallack Theatre, 12
Evening for Merlin Finch, An / A Great Career (p), 12/29/58, Forum Theatre, 35
Evening in Story and Song, An. See People of the Shadows
Evening of Bohemian Theatre, An, 3/2/52, Cherry Lane Theatre
Evening of One Acts, An (String / Contribution / Malcochon) (p), 3/25/69, St. Marks Playhouse, 32
Evening of Original Musical Satire, An, 3/7/64, Carnegie Hall, 1
Evening of Russian Theatre, An (Tales of Odessa / On the Harmfulness of Tobacco / The Proposal) (p), 12/20/71, Roundabout Theatre, 9
Evening of 3 Farces, An. See Le Mariage Forcé / Sganarelle / La Jalousie du Barbouille, 5/6/58, Phoenix Theatre, 8
Evening's Frost, An (p), 10/11/65, Theatre de Lys, 132
Evening with Beatrice Lillie, An (r), 10/2/52, Booth Theatre, 278
Evening with Chekhov, An (p) (The Anniversary / On the High Road / The Wedding), 4/20/61, Key Theatre, 61
Evening with Jake LaMotta, An, 11/15/63, Barbizon-Plaza Theatre, 1
Evening with Josephine Baker, An (r), 12/31/73, Palace Theatre, 7
Evening with Max Morath at the Turn of the Century, An, 2/17/69, Jan Hus Playhouse, 140
Evening with Mike Nichols and Elaine May, An (r), 10/8/60, John Golden Theatre, 306
Evening with Richard Nixon and . . ., An (p), 4/30/72, Shubert Theatre, 16
Evening with the Poet-Senator, An (p), 3/21/73, Playhouse 2, 14
Evening with the Times Square Two, An (r), 5/19/67, Gramercy Arts Theatre, 10
Evening with the Urban Arts Corps, An (Old Judge Mose Is Dead / Moon on a Rainbow Shawl) (p), 8/27/69, Hudson Guild Theatre, 6
Evening with Yves Montand, An, 10/24/61, John Golden Theatre, 55
Evensong (p), 1/31/33, Selwyn Theatre, 15
Ever Green Lady, The (p), 10/11/22, Punch and Judy Theatre, 14
Every Man for Himself (p), 12/9/40, Guild Theatre, 3
Every Other Evil (p), 1/22/61, Key Theatre
Every Thursday (p), 5/10/34, Royale Theatre, 60
Everybody Loves Opal (p), 10/11/61, Longacre Theatre, 21
Everybody's Welcome (m), 10/13/31, Shubert Theatre, 127
Everyday (p), 11/16/21, Bijou Theatre, 30
Everyman (p), 10/12/02, Mendelssohn Hall, 75
Everyman (p), 3/30/03, Garden Theatre, 56
Everyman (p), 3/10/13, Children's Theatre, 24
Everyman (p), 1/18/18, Cort Theatre, 2
Everyman and Roach (m), 10/4/71, Society for Ethical Culture Auditorium, 26
Everything (m), 8/22/18, New York Hippodrome, 461
Everything for Anybody (m), 9/9/72, La Mama Experimental Theatre Club
Everything in the Garden (p), 11/29/67, Plymouth Theatre, 84
Everything's Jake (p), 1/16/30, Assembly Theatre, 76
Everywhere I Roam (p), 12/29/38, National Theatre, 13
Everywoman (p), 2/27/11, Herald Square Theatre, 144
Evidence (p), 10/7/14, Lyric Theatre, 21
Exceeding Small (p), 10/22/28, Playhouse, 72
Exception and the Rule, The / The Prodigal Son (p, m) (Twin Bill), 5/20/65, Greenwich Mews Theatre, 141
Excess Baggage (p), 12/26/27, Ritz Theatre, 216
Exchange (r), 2/8/70, Mercer-O'Casey Theatre, 1
Exchange of Wives, An (p), 9/26/19, New Bijou Theatre, 19

Exciters, The (p), 9/22/22, Times Square Theatre, 35
Excursion (p), 4/9/37, Vanderbilt Theatre, 114
Excuse Me (p), 2/13/11, Gaiety Theatre, 160
Exercise, The (p), 4/24/68, John Golden Theatre, 5
Exhaustion of Our Son's Love, The / Good Day (p), 10/18/65, Cherry Lane Theatre, 64
Exhibition (p), 5/15/69, Actors Playhouse, 6
Exile, The (p), 4/9/23, George M. Cohan Theatre, 32
Exiles (p), 2/19/25, Neighborhood Playhouse, 29
Exiles (p), 3/12/57, Renata Theatre, 40
Exit the King (p), 1/9/68, Lyceum Theatre, 47, (APA-Phoenix)
Exit the King. See also Le Roi se Meurt
Ex-Miss Copper Queen on a Set of Pills (p), 3/22/74, Open Mind Theatre
Experience (p), 10/27/14, Booth Theatre, 255
Experience (p), 1/22/18, Manhattan Opera House, 23
Experience Unnecessary (m), 12/30/31, Longacre Theatre, 46
Experience Unnecessary (m), 3/26/32, National Theatre, 24
Experiment, The (p), 5/8/67, Orpheum Theatre, 16
Experimental Death Unit #1 / Junkies Are Full of (Sh...) / Great Goodness of Life (p), 9/18/72, Afro-American Studio
Explorer, The (p), 5/7/12, Daly's Theatre, 23
Expressing Willie (p), 4/16/24, 48th St. Theatre, 293
Extra (p), 1/23/23, Longacre Theatre, 23
Eye on the Sparrow (p), 5/3/38, Vanderbilt Theatre, 6
Eyes of Chalk (p), 6/7/72, Theatre at St. Clement's Church, 15
Eyes of the Heart, The / A Light from St. Agnes / Dolce (p), 4/24/06, Manhattan Theatre, 3
Eyes of the Heart, The / The Rose / A Light from St. Agnes (p), 3/27/05, Manhattan Theatre, 3
Eyes of Youth (p), 8/22/17, Maxine Elliott's Theatre, 414
Eyvind of the Hills (p), 2/1/21, Greenwich Village Theatre, 22

F

F. Jasmine Addams (m), 10/27/71, Circle in the Square, 6
Fabulous Invalid, The (p), 10/8/38, Broadhurst Theatre, 65
Fabulous Miss Marie, The (p), 3/5/71, New Lafayette Theatre
Face of a Hero (p), 10/20/60, Eugene O'Neill Theatre, 36
Face the Music (m), 2/17/32, New Amsterdam Theatre, 166
Face the Music (m), 1/31/33, 44th St. Theatre, 31
Face Value (p), 12/26/21, 49th St. Theatre, 41
Facing the Music / Over a Welsh Rarebit (p), 5/21/03, Garrick Theatre, 44
Fad and Folly (m), 11/27/02, Mrs. Osborn's Playhouse, 34
Fade Out—Fade In (m), 5/26/64, Mark Hellinger Theatre, 271
Fads and Fancies (m), 3/8/15, Knickerbocker Theatre, 48
Faggot, The, 4/13/73, Judson Memorial Church, 16
Faggot, The (r), 6/18/73, Truck and Warehouse Theatre, 182
Failures, The (p), 11/19/23, Garrick Theatre, 40
Failures, The (p), 1/5/59, Fourth St. Theatre, 9
Fair and Warmer (p), 11/6/15, Eltinge Theatre, 377
Fair Circassian, The (p), 12/6/21, Republic Theatre, 7
Fair Co-ed, The (m), 2/1/09, Knickerbocker Theatre, 136
Fair Exchange, A (p), 12/4/05, Liberty Theatre, 21
Fair Game (p), 11/2/57, Longacre Theatre, 217
Fair Game for Lovers (p), 2/10/64, Cort Theatre, 8
Faith Healer, The (p), 1/19/10, Savoy Theatre, 6
Faithful Heart, The (p), 10/10/22, Broadhurst Theatre, 31
Faithful, The (p), 10/13/19, Garrick Theatre, 49
Faithfully Yours (p), 10/18/51, Coronet Theatre, 68
Fake, The (p), 10/6/24, Hudson Theatre, 89
Fakir Rahman Bey, 5/25/26, Selwyn Theatre, 24
Fall and Rise of Susan Lenox (p), 6/9/20, 44th St. Theatre
Fall Guy, The (p), 3/10/25, Eltinge Theatre, 177
Fall of Eve, The (p), 8/31/25, Booth Theatre, 48
Fallen Angels (p), 12/1/27, 49th St. Theatre, 36
Fallen Angels (p), 1/17/56, Playhouse, 239
Fallen Idol, The (p), 1/23/15, Comedy Theatre, 9
Fallout (r), 5/20/59, Renata Theatre, 31
False Confessions, The (p), 4/1/71, Master Theatre, 14, (Equity Library Theatre)
False Dreams, Farewell (p), 1/15/34, Little Theatre, 25
Falstaff (p) (Charles Coburn), 12/25/28, Coburn Theatre, 15
Family Affair, A (p), 11/27/46, Playhouse, 6
Family Affair, A (m), 1/27/62, Billy Rose Theatre, 65
Family Affairs (p), 12/10/29, Maxine Elliott's Theatre, 7
Family Continues, The / The Great Nebula in Orion / Ikke, Ikke, Nye, Nye, Nye (p), 5/21/72, Circle Theatre
Family Cupboard, The (p), 8/21/13, Playhouse, 140
Family Exit, The (p), 9/19/17, Comedy Theatre, 21
Family Exit, The / Counsel's Opinion / Saturday It Rained / The White Dress / The Way Out / The March Heir (p), 12/13/32, Chanin Auditorium, 5
Family Failing, The (p), 6/9/25, Princess Theatre, 1
Family Portrait (p), 3/8/39, Morosco Theatre, 111
Family Reunion, The (p), 10/20/58, Phoenix Theatre, 32
Family, The (p), 10/11/10, Comedy Theatre, 7
Family, The (p), 3/30/43, Windsor Theatre, 7
Family Upstairs, The (p), 8/17/25, Gaiety Theatre, 72
Family Upstairs, The (p), 10/27/33, Biltmore Theatre, 3
Family Way, The (p), 1/13/65, Lyceum Theatre, 5
Famous Mrs. Fair, The (p), 12/22/19, Henry Miller's Theatre, 343
Fan, The (p), 10/3/21, Punch and Judy Theatre, 32
Fanatics, The (p), 11/7/27, 49th St. Theatre, 16
Fancy Free (m), 4/11/18, Astor Theatre, 116
Fancy Meeting You Again (p), 1/14/52, Royale Theatre, 8
Fanny (p), 9/21/26, Lyceum Theatre, 63
Fanny (m), 11/4/54, Majestic Theatre, 888
Fanny Hawthorn (p), 5/11/22, Vanderbilt Theatre, 36
Fanny's First Play (p), 9/16/12, Comedy Theatre, 256
Fanshastics. See Merry Wives of Gotham
Fantana (m), 1/14/05, Lyric Theatre, 298
Fantasia (p), 1/3/33, Provincetown Playhouse, 3
Fantastic Fricassee, A (r), 9/11/22, Greenwich Village Theatre, 111
Fantasticks, The (m), 5/3/60, Sullivan St. Playhouse, 1,703
Far Country, A (p), 4/4/61, Music Box Theatre, 271
Far Cry, The (p), 9/30/24, Cort Theatre, 31
Far-Away Horses (p), 3/21/33, Martin Beck Theatre, 4
Farewell, Farewell Eugene (p), 9/27/60, Helen Hayes Theatre, 7
Farewell Summer (p), 3/29/37, Fulton Theatre, 8
Farewell to Arms, A (p), 9/22/30, National Theatre, 24
Farm of Three Echoes (p), 11/28/39, Cort Theatre, 48
Farmer's Wife, The (p), 10/9/24, Comedy Theatre, 100
Farmer Takes a Wife, The (p), 10/30/34, 46th St. Theatre, 104
Far-Off Hills, The (p), 10/18/32, Martin Beck Theatre, 4
Far-Off Hills, The (p), 11/14/34, John Golden Theatre, 1
Far-Off Hills, The (p), 10/11/37, Ambassador Theatre, 51
Fascinating Flora (m), 5/20/07, Casino Theatre, 113
Fascinating Mr. Vanderveldt, The (p), 1/22/06, Daly's Theatre, 44
Fascinating Widow, The (m), 9/11/11, Liberty Theatre, 56
Fashion (p), 2/3/24, Provincetown Playhouse, 240
Fashion (m), 1/20/59, Royal Playhouse, 48
Fashion (m), 12/6/73, Greenwich Mews Theatre, 8
Fashion (m), 2/18/74, McAlpin Rooftop Theatre, 94
Fashions for Men (p), 12/5/22, National Theatre, 89
Fashions of 1924 (r), 7/18/23, Lyceum Theatre, 13
Fast and Furious (r), 9/15/31, New Yorker Theatre, 6
Fast and Grow Fat (p), 9/1/16, Globe Theatre, 11
Fast Life (p), 9/26/28, Ambassador Theatre, 20
Fast Service (p), 11/17/31, Selwyn Theatre, 7
Fata Morgana (p), 3/3/24, Garrick Theatre, 254
Fata Morgana (p), 12/25/31, Royale Theatre, 29
Fatal Alibi, The (p), 2/8/32, Booth Theatre, 24
Fatal Weakness, The (p), 11/19/46, Royale Theatre, 119
Fatal Wedding, The (p), 10/28/01, Grand Opera House, 8
Fatal Wedding, The (p), 6/2/24, Ritz Theatre, 16
Father and Son (p), 9/24/08, Majestic Theatre, 12
Father and the Boys (p), 3/2/08, Empire Theatre, 88
Father Malachy's Miracle (p), 11/17/37, St. James Theatre, 125
Father's Day (p), 3/16/71, John Golden Theatre, 1
Father, The (p), 4/9/12, Barkeley Lyceum Theatre, 31
Father, The (p), 5/11/28, Belmont Theatre, 11
Father, The (p), 7/19/49, Provincetown Playhouse, 95
Father, The (p), 11/16/49, Cort Theatre, 69
Father, The (p) (Royal Dramatic Th. of Sweden), 5/14/62, Cort Theatre, 3
Father, The (p), 11/24/66, Roundabout Theatre
Father, The (p), 10/16/73, Roundabout Theatre, 97
Father, The / Barbara's Wedding (p), 10/8/31, 49th St. Theatre, 27
Father Uxbridge Wants to Marry (p), 10/23/67, American Place Theatre, 27
Fatted Calf, The (p), 2/10/12, Daly's Theatre, 8
Faun, The (p), 1/16/11, Daly's Theatre, 48
Faust (p), 1/3/27, Edyth Totten Theatre, 24
Faust (p), 10/8/28, Guild Theatre, 48
Faust (p), 10/5/45, New York City Center, 4
Faust, Part I (p), 2/7/61, New York City Center, 16
Faustina (p), 5/25/52, Cherry Lane Theatre
Fear Market, The (p), 1/26/16, Booth Theatre, 118
Feast of Panthers (p), 3/20/61, East 74th St. Theatre, 3
Feathers in a Gale (p), 12/21/43, Music Box Theatre, 7
Fedora (p), 5/22/05, American Theatre, 8
Fedora (p), 2/10/22, Hudson Theatre, 12
Fedora (p), 1/23/24, Frazee Theatre, 5
Feiffer's People (r), 6/22/73, Lolly's Theatre Club, 15
Felix (p), 2/24/72, Actors Studio, 12
Felix (p), 1/17/74, Cherry Lane Theatre, 6
Femmes Noires, Les (p), 2/21/74, Other Stage / Public Theatre, 55
Femmes Savantes, Les (p), 2/6/67, Barbizon-Plaza Theatre, 21

Femmes Savantes, Les (p), 2/13/70, New York City Center, 5, (Comédie Française)
Festival (p), 1/18/55, Longacre Theatre, 23
Festival of New Italian Plays (He Says, She Says, They Say / Nuremburg Two / The Gasman; Three Monkeys in a Glass; The Seducers; Siegfried at Stalingrad; Confirmation; A Certain Quiet; The Devil Peter; The Masquerade; Il Manifesto) (p), 4/26/74, Provincetown Playhouse, 109
Festival of Short Plays, A (Shearwater / Cream Cheese / Dr. Kheal / Love Scene) (p), 3/6/74, American Place Theatre, 29
Feu la Mère de Madame / Les Nuits de la Colère (p) (Renaud-Barrault Repertory Co.), 2/11/57, Winter Garden Theatre, 4
Few Are Chosen (p), 9/17/35, 58th St. Theatre, 15
Few Wild Oats, A (p), 3/24/32, Forrest Theatre, 4
Fickle Women (p), 12/15/37, Nora Bayes Theatre, 1
Fiddle-dee-dee (r), 9/6/00, Weber and Fields Music Hall, 262
Fiddler on the Roof (m), 9/22/64, Imperial Theatre, 3,242
Fiddlers Three (m), 9/3/18, Cort Theatre, 87
Field God, The (p), 4/21/27, Greenwich Village Theatre, 45
Field of Ermine (p), 2/8/35, Mansfield Theatre, 11
Fields Beyond, The (p), 3/6/36, Mansfield Theatre, 3
Fiesta (p), 9/17/29, Garrick Theatre, 39
Fiesta in Madrid (m), 5/28/69, New York City Center, 23
Fifth Column, The (p), 3/6/40, Alvin Theatre, 87
Fifth Commandment, The (p), 11/12/65, Folksbiene Playhouse, 60
Fifth of July / American War Mothers (p), 5/24/74, Theatre in Space
Fifth Season, The (p), 1/23/53, Cort Theatre, 654
Fifty Miles from Boston (p), 2/3/08, Garrick Theatre, 32
Fifty Million Frenchmen (m), 11/27/29, Lyric Theatre, 254
Fifty-Fifty, Ltd. (m), 10/27/19, Comedy Theatre, 40
Fifty-seven Bowery (p), 1/26/28, Wallack Theatre, 28
Fig Leaf in Her Bonnet, A (p), 6/14/61, Gramercy Arts Theatre, 23
Fig Leaves Are Falling, The (m), 1/2/69, Broadhurst Theatre, 4
Fight, The (p), 10/31/12, Fulton Theatre, 4
Fight, The (p), 9/2/13, Hudson Theatre, 80
Fighting Cock, The (p), 12/8/59, ANTA Theatre, 87
Fighting Hope, The (p), 9/22/08, Belasco's Stuyvesant Theatre, 231
Figurè in the Night / Moon Shines on Kylenamoe (p), 11/30/63, Theatre de Lys, 1
Fille de Madame Angot, La (m), 12/30/27, Jolson Theatre, 7
Filling the Hole. See American Gothics
Fils a la Patte, Un (p), 2/17/66, New York City Center, 8, (Comédie Française)
Final Balance, The, 10/30/28, Provincetown Playhouse, 28
Find Daddy (p), 3/8/26, Ritz Theatre, 8
Find the Fox (p), 6/20/30, Wallack Theatre, 3
Find Your Way Home (p), 1/2/74, Brooks Atkinson Theatre, 133
Fine and Dandy (m), 9/23/30, Erlanger Theatre, 246
Fine Feathers (p), 1/7/13, Astor Theatre, 79
Fingernails Blue as Flowers / Lake of the Woods (p), 12/6/71, American Place Theatre, 33
Finian's Rainbow (m), 1/10/47, 46th St. Theatre, 725
Finian's Rainbow (m), 5/18/55, New York City Center, 15
Finian's Rainbow (m), 4/27/60, New York City Center, 15
Finian's Rainbow (m), 5/23/60, 46th St. Theatre, 12
Finian's Rainbow (r), 4/5/67, New York City Center, 23
Finis for Oscar Wilde (p), 2/14/64, Blackfriars' Theatre, 50
Finishing Touches (p), 2/8/73, Plymouth Theatre, 164
Finta Giardiniera, La (m), 1/17/27, Mayfair Theatre
Fiorello! (m), 11/23/59, Broadhurst Theatre, 796
Fiorello! (m), 6/13/62, New York City Center, 16
Fioretta (m), 2/5/29, Earl Carroll Theatre, 111
Fire! (p), 1/28/69, Longacre Theatre, 6
Firebird (p), 11/21/32, Empire Theatre, 42
Firebrand of Florence, The (m), 3/22/45, Alvin Theatre, 43
Firebrand, The (p), 10/15/24, Morosco Theatre, 287
Firebrand, The (p), 12/10/65, Master Theatre, 9, (Equity Library Theatre)
Firebugs, The (p), 2/11/63, Maidman Playhouse, 8
Firebugs, The (p), 7/1/68, Martinique Theatre, 8
Firebugs, The / Philipp Hotz (p), 11/26/69, Barbizon-Plaza Theatre, 6, (Schauspieltruppe Zurich)
Firefly, The (m), 12/2/12, Lyric, 120
Firefly, The (m), 11/30/31, Erlanger Theatre, 16
Fireman's Flame, The (m), 10/9/37, American Music Hall, 204
Fires of Fate, The (p), 12/28/09, Liberty Theatre, 23
Fires of St. John, The (p), 11/28/04, Daly's Theatre, 8
Fireworks for a Hot Fourth. See Fireworks
Fireworks (The Report / Football / Fireworks for a Hot Fourth) (p), 6/11/69, Village South Theatre, 4
Firm of Cunningham, The (p), 4/18/05, Madison Square Theatre, 31
Firmin Gemier Repertory, 11/17/24, Jolson Theatre, 24
First American Dictator (p), 3/14/39, Nora Bayes Theatre, 9
First Apple, The (p), 12/27/33, Booth Theatre, 52
First Crocus, The (p), 1/2/42, Longacre Theatre, 5
First Episode (p), 9/17/34, Ritz Theatre, 40
First Fifty Years, The (p), 3/13/22, Princess Theatre, 48
First Flight (p), 9/17/25, Plymouth Theatre, 11
First Gentleman, The (p), 4/25/57, Belasco Theatre, 28
First Impressions (m), 3/19/59, Alvin Theatre, 92
First Is Last (p), 9/17/19, Maxine Elliott's Theatre, 62
First Lady (p), 11/26/35, Music Box Theatre, 244
First Lady (p), 5/28/52, New York City Center, 16
First Lady in the Land, The (p), 12/4/11, Gaiety Theatre, 64
First Law, The (p), 5/6/29, Masque Theatre, 8
First Legion, The (p), 10/1/34, 46th St. Theatre, 112
First Love (p), 11/8/26, Booth Theatre, 50
First Love (p), 12/25/61, Morosco Theatre, 24
First Man, The, 3/4/22, Neighborhood Playhouse, 27
First Million, The (p), 4/28/43, Ritz Theatre, 5
First Mortgage (p), 10/10/29, Royale Theatre, 4
First Mrs. Fraser, The (p), 12/28/29, Playhouse, 352
First Mrs. Fraser, The (p), 11/5/47, Shubert Theatre, 38
First Night (p), 11/26/30, Eltinge Theatre, 86
First One Asleep, Whistle (p), 2/26/66, Belasco Theatre, 1
First Stone, The (p), 1/13/28, Civic Repertory Theatre, 19
First Stop to Heaven (p), 1/5/41, Windsor Theatre, 8
First, The / Five A.M. Jazz (m) (That Five A.M. Jazz), 10/19/64, Astor Place Playhouse, 94
First Year, The (p), 10/20/20, Little Theatre, 725
Firstborn, The, 4/30/58, Coronet Theatre, 38
Fisher Maiden, The (m), 10/5/03, Victoria Theatre, 32
Fisherman, The / The Fourth Pig (p), 1/26/65, Maidman Playhouse, 2
Fitz / Biscuit (p), 5/16/66, Circle in the Square, 8
Five Acts from Five Plays (p), 1/2/22, Lexington Theatre, 1
Five Alarm Waltz (p), 3/13/41, Playhouse, 4
Five A.M. Jazz / The First (m) (That Five A.M. Jazz), 10/19/64, Astor Place Playhouse, 94
Five Evenings (p), 5/9/63, Village South Theatre, 6
Five Finger Exercise (p), 12/2/59, Music Box Theatre, 337
Five Finger Exercise (p), 1/10/69, Master Theatre, 9, (Equity Library Theatre)
Five Frankforters, The (p), 3/3/13, 39th St. Theatre, 88
Five Million, The (p), 7/8/19, Lyric Theatre, 91
Five O'Clock (p), 10/13/19, Fulton Theatre, 41
Five O'Clock Girl, The (m), 10/10/27, 44th St. Theatre, 278
Five on the Black Hand Side (p), 12/10/69, St. Clement's Church Theatre, 54, (American Place Theatre)
Five Posts in the Market Place (p), 3/5/61, Gate Theatre, 9
Five Queens (p), 9/10/63, Judson Hall, 8
Five Star Final (p), 12/30/30, Cort Theatre, 176
Five Star Saint (p), 2/10/70, Blackfriars' Theatre, 41
Five Stars***** (p), 12/22/71, WPA Theatre
Five Visits. See Playwrights Cooperative Festival
Fixing Sister (p), 10/4/16, Maxine Elliott's Theatre, 85
Flag Is Born, A (m), 9/5/46, Alvin Theatre, 120
Flag Lieutenant, The (p), 8/30/09, Criterion Theatre, 24
Flahooley (m), 5/14/51, Broadhurst Theatre, 40
Flame of Love (p), 4/21/24, Morosco Theatre, 32
Flame, The (p), 9/4/16, Lyric Theatre, 96
Flamingo Road (p), 3/19/46, Belasco Theatre, 7
Flamme, La, 2/11/23, Playhouse, 1
Flare Path (p), 12/23/42, Henry Miller's Theatre, 14
Flashing Stream, The (p), 4/10/39, Biltmore Theatre, 8
Flea in Her Ear, A (p), 10/3/69, ANTA Theatre, 11, (American Conservatory Theatre)
Fledermaus (m), 5/19/54, New York City Center, 15
Fledgling (p), 11/27/40, Hudson Theatre, 13
Flesh (p), 5/7/25, Princess Theatre, 4
Flies, The (p), 4/17/47, President Theatre, 21
Flight (p), 2/18/29, Longacre Theatre, 41
Flight into Egypt (p), 3/18/52, Music Box Theatre, 46
Flight to the West (p), 12/30/40, Guild Theatre, 136
Flip Side, The (p), 10/10/68, Booth Theatre, 4
Flo-Flo (m), 12/20/17, Cort Theatre, 220
Flora Bella (m), 9/11/16, Casino Theatre, 112
Flora, the Red Menace (m), 5/11/65, Alvin Theatre, 87
Floriani's Wife (p), 10/1/23, Greenwich Village Theatre, 16
Florida Girl (m), 11/2/25, Lyric Theatre, 40
Florist Shop, The (p), 8/9/09, Liberty Theatre, 40
Florodora (m), 11/10/00, Casino Theatre, 505
Florodora (m), 1/27/02, Winter Garden Theatre, 48
Florodora (m), 3/27/05, Broadway Theatre, 32
Florodora (m), 4/5/20, Century Theatre, 150
Flossie (m), 6/3/24, Lyric Theatre
Flower Drum Song (m), 12/1/58, St. James Theatre, 600
Flower of the Palace of Han, The / The Terrible Meek (p), 3/19/12, Little Theatre, 39
Flower of the Ranch, The (m), 4/20/08, Majestic Theatre, 16
Flower of Yamato, The / Electra (p), 2/11/08, Garden Theatre, 9
Flowering Cherry (p), 10/21/59, Lyceum Theatre, 5
Flowering Peach, The (p), 12/28/54, Belasco Theatre, 135

Flowers of the Forest (p), 4/8/35, Martin Beck Theatre, 40
Flowers of Virtue, The (p), 2/5/42, Royale Theatre, 4
Fluffy Ruffles (m), 9/7/08, Criterion Theatre, 48
Fly Away Home (p), 1/15/35, 48th St. Theatre, 202
Fly Blackbird (m), 2/5/62, Mayfair Theatre, 127
Fly by Night (p), 6/2/33, Belmont Theatre, 4
Flying Colors (r), 9/15/32, Imperial Theatre, 181
Flying Gerardos, The (p), 12/29/40, Playhouse, 24
Flying High (m), 3/3/30, Apollo Theatre, 355
F.O.B. (p), 11/24/72, Mercer / Brecht Theatre, 3
Fog (p), 2/7/27, National Theatre, 97
Fog-Bound (p), 4/1/27, Belmont Theatre, 27
Folies Bergère (r), 12/25/39, Broadway Theatre, 121
Folies Bergère (r), 6/2/64, Broadway Theatre, 191
Follies (m), 4/4/71, Winter Garden, 522
Follies Burlesque '67 (r), 5/3/67, Players Theatre, 15
Follies of 1910, The (r), 1/12/60, Carnegie Hall Playhouse, 14
Follow Me (m), 11/29/16, Casino Theatre, 78
Follow the Girl (m), 3/2/18, 44th St. Roof Theatre, 25
Follow the Girls (m), 4/8/44, Century Theatre, 882
Follow Thru (m), 1/9/29, 46th St. Theatre, 401
Foo Hsing Theatre, 11/12/62, Longacre Theatre, 24
Fool and His Money, A (m), 4/14/03, Madison Square Theatre, 47
Fool and His Money, A (m), 10/26/04, Bijou Theatre, 24
Fool of Fortune, A (p), 1/12/12, Garrick Theatre, 1
Fool's Bells (p), 12/23/25, Criterion Theatre, 5
Fool, The (p), 10/23/22, Times Square Theatre
Fool There Was, A (p), 3/24/09, Liberty Theatre, 93
Foolish Notion (p), 3/13/45, Martin Beck Theatre, 103
Foolish Virgin, The (p), 12/19/10, Knickerbocker Theatre, 24
Fools Errant (p), 8/21/22, Maxine Elliott's Theatre, 64
Fools Rush In (r), 12/25/34, Playhouse, 14
Foolscap (p), 1/11/33, Times Square Theatre, 13
Foot Loose (p), 5/10/20, Greenwich Village Theatre, 162
Football. See Fireworks
Footlights (m), 8/19/27, Lyric Theatre, 43
Footsteps / A Little Act of Justice / The Stickup (p), 1/9/22, Provincetown Playhouse, 21
Footsteps of Doves, The. See You Know I Can't Hear You When the Water's Running
For All of Us (p), 10/15/23, 49th St. Theatre, 216
For Better or Worse (p), 1/31/27, Mansfield Theatre, 16
For Goodness Sake (m), 2/20/22, Lyric Theatre, 103
For Heaven's Sake, Mother! (p), 11/16/48, Belasco Theatre, 7
For Keeps (p), 6/14/44, Henry Miller's Theatre, 29
For Love or Money (p), 11/4/47, Henry Miller's Theatre, 263
For Love's Sweet Sake / The Bishop (The Bishop's Move) (p), 2/12/06, Princess Theatre, 7
For Services Rendered (p), 4/12/33, Booth Theatre, 21
For the Defense (p), 12/19/19, Playhouse, 77
For Valor (p), 11/18/35, Empire Theatre, 8
For Value Received (p), 5/7/23, Longacre Theatre, 48
For Your Pleasure (r), 2/5/43, Mansfield Theatre, 11
Forbes-Robertson Repertory, 9/29/13, Shubert Theatre
Forbidden (p), 12/20/19, Manhattan Opera House, 18
Forbidden (p), 10/1/23, Daly's Theatre, 8
Forbidden Guests, The / Happiness / The Day of Dupes / Just As Well (p), 3/6/14, Cort Theatre, 5
Forbidden Melody (m), 11/2/36, New Amsterdam Theatre, 32
Forbidden Roads (p), 4/16/28, Liberty Theatre, 16
Foreign Affairs (p), 4/13/32, Avon Theatre, 21
Foreigners (p), 12/5/39, Belasco Theatre, 7
Forensic and the Navigators / The Unseen Hand (p), 4/1/70, Astor Place Theatre, 21
Foreplay (p), 12/10/70, Bijou Theatre, 38
Forest Lovers, The (p), 9/10/01, Lyceum Theatre, 47
Forever After (p), 9/9/18, Central Theatre, 312
Forsaking All Others, 3/1/33, Times Square Theatre, 101
Fortuna (m), 1/3/62, Maidman Playhouse, 5
Fortune and Men's Eyes (p), 2/23/67, Actors Playhouse, 382
Fortune and Men's Eyes (p), 10/22/69, Stage 73, 231
Fortune Hunter, The (p), 9/4/09, Gaiety Theatre, 345
Fortune Teller, The (p), 2/27/19, Republic Theatre, 68
Fortune Teller, The (m), 11/4/29, Jolson Theatre, 16
Fortunes of the King, The (p), 12/6/04, Lyric Theatre, 38
Forty (p), 1/10/74, Cubiculo Theatre, 9
Forty Carats (p), 12/26/68, Morosco Theatre, 780
Forty-five Minutes from Broadway (m), 1/1/06, New Amsterdam Theatre, 90
Forty-five Minutes from Broadway (m), 11/5/06, New York Theatre, 32
Forty-five Minutes from Broadway (m), 3/14/12, George M. Cohan Theatre, 36
Forty-nine West 87th / Cabin 12 (p), 1/31/74, T. Schreiber Studio, 20
Forty-Niners, The (p), 11/7/22, Punch and Judy Theatre, 15
Forty-Ninth Cousin, The (p), 10/27/60, Ambassador Theatre, 100
Forty-one in a Sack (r), 3/25/60, 41st St. Theatre, 45
Forty-two Seconds from Broadway (p), 3/11/72, Playhouse Theatre, 1
Forward the Heart (p), 1/28/49, 48th St. Theatre, 19
Fountain of Youth, The (p), 4/1/18, Henry Miller's Theatre, 32
Fountain, The (p), 12/10/25, Greenwich Village Theatre, 24
Fountain, The (p), Jolson Theatre, 28
Four Americans (Now There's Just the Three of Us / The Reliquary of Mr. and Mrs. Potterfield) (p), 10/19/71, Brooklyn Academy of Music, 6, (Chelsea Theatre Center)
Four Americans (Tall and Rex / Things) (p), 10/26/71, Brooklyn Academy of Music, 6, (Chelsea Theatre Center)
Four in Hand, 9/6/23, Greenwich Village Theatre, 4
Four O'Clock (p), 2/13/33, Biltmore Theatre, 16
Four on a Garden (House of Dunkelmayer / Betty / Toreador / The Swingers) (p), 1/30/71, Broadhurst Theatre, 57
Four Saints in Three Acts (m), 2/20/34, 44th St. Theatre, 32
Four Saints in Three Acts (m), 4/2/34, Empire Theatre, 18
Four Saints in Three Acts (m), 4/16/52, Broadway Theatre, 15
Four Seasons, The (p), 3/14/68, Theatre Four, 6
Four Seasons, The / Circus Events / The Auto Race (r), 11/25/07, New York Hippodrome, 312
Four Twelves Are 48 (p), 1/17/51, 48th St. Theatre, 2
Four Walls (p), 9/19/27, John Golden Theatre, 144
Four Winds (p), 9/25/57, Cort Theatre, 21
Fourberies de Scapin, Les (p), 5/7/67, Hunter College Playhouse, 4
Four-Flusher, The (p), 4/13/25, Apollo Theatre, 65
Fourletterword for Boat (p), 2/2/62, 78th St. Playhouse, 4
Fourposter, The (p), 10/24/51, Ethel Barrymore Theatre, 632
Fourposter, The (p), 1/5/55, New York City Center, 15
Foursome, The (p), 11/12/73, Astor Place Theatre, 24
Fourth Avenue North (r), 9/27/61, Madison Avenue Playhouse, 2
Fourth Estate, The (p), 10/6/09, Wallack Theatre, 93
Fourth Pig, The / The Fisherman (p), 1/26/65, Maidman Playhouse, 2
Fourth Wall, The (r), 9/4/68, Theatre East, 141
Foxhole in the Parlor (p), 5/23/45, Booth Theatre, 45
Foxy (m), 2/16/64, Ziegfeld Theatre, 72
Foxy Grandpa (m), 2/17/02, 14th St. Theatre, 120
Foxy Quiller (In Corsica) (m), 11/5/00, Broadway Theatre, 50
Fragila Rosina / The Cradle Song (p), 5/9/27, Forrest Theatre, 4
Fragile Fox (p), 10/12/54, Belasco Theatre, 55
Fragments / The Basement (p), 10/2/67, Cherry Lane Theatre, 24
Francesca da Rimini (p), 12/31/01, Hammerstein's Victoria Theatre, 56
Francesca da Rimini (p), 1/6/03, Metropolitan Opera House, 3
Frank Fay's Fables (r), 2/6/22, Park Theatre, 32
Frank Gagliano's City Scene (Paradise Gardens East / Conerico Was Here to Stay) (p), 3/10/69, Fortune Theatre, 16
Frank Keenan Players, The, 2/27/05, Berkeley Lyceum Theatre
Frank Merriwell (m), 4/24/71, Longacre Theatre, 1
Frankenstein (p), 10/2/68, Brooklyn Academy of Music, 6, (Living Theatre)
Frankie and Johnnie (p), 9/25/30, Republic Theatre, 61
Freckles (p), 12/16/12, Grand Opera House, 8
Freddy (p), 7/16/29, Lyceum Theatre, 63
Frederick Douglass . . . Through His Own Words, 5/9/72, St. Marks Playhouse, 32
Frederika (m), 2/4/37, Imperial Theatre, 94
Free Fall (r), 3/20/69, Upstairs at the Downstairs
Free for All (m), 9/8/31, Manhattan Theatre, 15
Free Lance, The (m), 4/16/06, New Amsterdam Theatre, 35
Free Soul, A (p), 1/12/28, Playhouse, 100
Freedom (p), 10/19/18, Century Theatre, 33
Freedom of Suzanne, The (p), 4/19/05, Empire Theatre, 26
Freedom of the City, The (p), 2/17/74, Alvin Theatre, 9
Freeman (p), 1/25/73, American Place Theatre, 37
Freiburg Passion Play, 4/29/29, Hippodrome, 48
Freight / A Phoenix Too Frequent (p), 4/26/50, Fulton Theatre, 5
French Doll, The (p), 2/20/22, Lyceum Theatre, 120
French Dressing (r), 1/24/74, Top of the Gate
French Leave (p), 11/8/20, Belmont Theatre, 56
French Model, The (m), 6/14/26, Grove St. Theatre, 104
French Touch, The (p), 12/8/45, Cort Theatre, 33
French Way, The (p) (The Deceased / The Grand Vizier / Edward and Agrippina), 3/20/62, East End Theatre, 1
French without Tears (p), 9/28/37, Henry Miller's Theatre, 111
French without Tears (p), 3/16/74, Brooklyn Academy of Music, 8, (Young Vic Co.)
Frere Jacques (m), 6/6/68, Theatre 802, 9
Fresh Fields (p), 2/10/36, Empire Theatre, 80
Friday Bench, The / The Bridge / The Brothel (p), 2/11/72, Bastiano's Studio for the Arts
Friday Night (p) (The River / Passport / Mary Agnes Is Thirty-Five), 2/8/65, Pocket Theatre, 24
Frieden, Der (p), 11/28/72, Barbizon-Plaza Theatre, 7, (Die Brücke)
Friend Indeed, A (p), 4/26/26, Central Park Theatre, 16
Friend Martha (p), 8/7/17, Booth Theatre, 15
Friendly Enemies (p), 7/22/18, Hudson Theatre, 440

Friends and Relations (Friends / Relations) (p), 10/14/71, Provincetown Playhouse, 5
Friends / Enemies (p), 9/16/65, Theatre East, 139
Friends. See Friends and Relations
Friendship (p), 8/31/31, Fulton Theatre, 24
Friquet (p), 1/31/05, Savoy Theatre, 23
Frisky Mrs. Johnson, The (p), 2/9/03, Princess Theatre, 80
Frisky Mrs. Johnson, The (p), 5/16/04, Garrick Theatre, 8
Fritz in Tammany Hall (m), 10/16/05, Herald Square Theatre, 48
Fritz Leiber Repertory, 12/25/30, Ambassador Theatre
Fritz Leiber Shakespeare Repertory, 1/16/22, 48th St. Theatre, 13
Fritzi Scheff Repertory, 12/26/04, Broadway Theatre
Frivolities of 1920 (r), 1/8/20, 44th St. Theatre, 61
Frocks and Frills, 1/7/02, Daly's Theatre, 64
Frogs of Spring, The (p), 10/20/53, Broadhurst Theatre, 15
From A to Z (r), 4/20/60, Plymouth Theatre, 21
From Israel with Laughter (r), 10/16/69, Barbizon-Plaza Theatre, 20
From Israel with Love (r), 10/2/72, Palace Theatre, 10
From Morn to Midnight (p), 6/5/22, Garrick Theatre, 56
From the Second City (r), 9/26/61, Royale Theatre, 87
From the Second City (r), 10/14/69, Eastside Playhouse, 31
From Vienna (r), 6/20/39, Music Box Theatre, 79
Front Page, The (p), 8/14/28, Times Square Theatre, 281
Front Page, The (p), 9/4/46, Royale Theatre, 79
Front Page, The (p), 5/10/69, Ethel Barrymore Theatre, 64
Front Page, The (p), 10/18/69, Ethel Barrymore Theatre, 158
Frou-Frou (p), 6/5/02, Garrick Theatre, 4
Frou-Frou (p), 3/18/12, Hudson Theatre, 8
Frugal Noon / Acid Wine (p), 5/22/64, Theatre East, 3
Frying Pan, The. See Three Hand Reel
F.T.A. Show, The (r), 11/21/71, Philharmonic Hall, Lincoln Center, 1
Fugitive, The (p), 3/19/17, 39th St. Theatre, 56
Fugue for Three Marys / The Women at the Tomb (p), 3/22/59, Broadway Congregational Church, 8
Full Circle (p), 11/7/73, ANTA Theatre, 21
Full House, A (p), 5/10/15, Longacre Theatre, 112
Full Moon in March, A. See Moon Mysteries
Fulton of Oak Falls (p), 2/10/37, Morosco Theatre, 37
Fumed Oak. See Tonight at 8:30
Fun City (r), 3/6/68, Jan Hus Playhouse, 31
Fun City (p), 1/2/72, Morosco Theatre, 9
Fun Couple, The (p), 10/26/62, Lyceum Theatre, 3
Funabashi (m), 1/6/08, Casino Theatre, 32
Funa-Benkei. See National Theatres of Japan
Funny Face (m), 11/22/27, Alvin Theatre, 250
Funny Girl (m), 3/26/64, Winter Garden, 1,348
Funny Kind of Evening with David Kossoff, A, 1/30/67, Theatre de Lys, 3
Funny Thing Happened on the Way to the Forum, A (m), 5/8/62, Alvin Theatre, 966
Funny Thing Happened on the Way to the Forum, A (m), 3/30/70, Lunt-Fontanne Theatre, 156
Funnyhouse of a Negro, The (p), 1/14/64, East End Theatre, 48
Furies, The (p), 3/7/28, Shubert Theatre, 41
Furnished Rooms (p), 5/29/34, Ritz Theatre, 15
Furs and Frills (m), 10/9/17, Casino Theatre, 32
Future, The (m), 3/22/74, Judson Memorial Church, 16
Futz! (p), 6/13/68, Theatre de Lys, 233

G

G. B. Essence of Women, The (p), 12/8/64, Theatre de Lys, 1, (ANTA Matinee)
Gabrielle (p), 3/25/41, Maxine Elliott's Theatre, 2
Gabrielle Rejane Repertory, 11/7/04, Lyric Theatre, 32
Gaby / Hell / Temptation (r), 4/27/11, Follies Bergere Theatre, 92
Gala Night (p), 2/25/30, Erlanger Theatre, 15
Galileo (p), 12/7/47, Maxine Elliott's Theatre, 6
Galileo (p), 4/13/67, Vivian Beaumont Theatre, 76
Gallant Cassian, The / The Maids (p), 5/18/56, Tempo Playhouse
Galloper, The (p), 1/22/06, Garden Theatre, 76
Gallops (p), 2/12/06, Garrick Theatre, 65
Gallows Humor (p), 4/18/61, Gramercy Arts Theatre, 40
Gambler's All (p), 1/1/17, Maxine Elliott's Theatre, 8
Gambler, The (p), 10/13/52, Lyceum Theatre, 24
Gambler, The (p), 8/23/73, Shade Company Theatre
Gamblers, The (p), 10/31/10, Maxine Elliott's Theatre, 192
Gambling (p), 8/26/29, Fulton Theatre, 155
Game Is Up, The (1st Ed.) (r), 9/29/64, Upstairs at the Downstairs, 260
Game Is Up, The (2nd Ed.) (r), 3/11/65, Upstairs at the Downstairs, 132
Game Is Up, The (3rd Ed.) (r), 6/15/65, Upstairs at the Downstairs, 228
Game of Heroes, The, 2/21/66, Hunter College Assembly Hall, 3
Game of Love and Death, The (p), 11/25/29, Guild Theatre, 48
Game of Love, The (p), 5/24/09, Wallack Theatre, 16
Games / After Liverpool (p), 1/22/73, Bijou Theatre, 1, (New Phoenix Repertory Sideshow)
Gandhi (p), 10/20/70, Playhouse Theatre, 1
Gang's All Here, The (m), 2/18/31, Imperial Theatre, 23
Gang's All Here, The (p), 10/1/59, Ambassador Theatre, 132
Gang War (p), 8/20/28, Morosco Theatre, 77
Gantry (m), 2/14/70, George Abbott Theatre, 1
Garden District (p), 1/7/58, York Playhouse, 216
Garden of Allah, The (p), 10/21/11, Century Theatre, 241
Garden of Allah, The (p), 2/25/18, Manhattan Opera House, 24
Garden of Eden, The (p), 9/27/27, Selwyn Theatre, 23
Garden of Paradise, The (p), 11/28/14, Park Theatre, 17
Garden of Sweets, The (p), 10/31/61, ANTA Theatre, 1
Garden of Time (p), 3/7/45, 135th St. Library Theatre, 30
Garden of Weeds (p), 4/28/24, Gaiety Theatre, 16
Garrett O'Magh (p), 1/7/01, 14th St. Theatre, 81
Garrett O'Magh (p), 1/27/02, 14th St. Theatre, 24
Garrick Gaieties (r), 6/8/25, Garrick Theatre, 231
Garrick Gaieties (r), 5/10/26, Garrick Theatre, 174
Garrick Gaieties (r), 6/14/30, Guild Theatre, 155
Garrick Gaieties (2nd Edition) (r), 10/16/30, Guild Theatre, 12
Gasman, The. See Festival of New Italian Plays
Gasoline Gypsies (p), 6/6/31, Lyric Theatre, 3
Gay Divorce (m), 11/29/32, Ethel Barrymore Theatre, 248
Gay Divorce (m), 4/3/60, Cherry Lane Theatre, 25
Gay Hussars, The (m), 7/29/09, Knickerbocker Theatre, 44
Gay Life, The (m), 4/19/09, Daly's Theatre, 8
Gay Life, The (m), 11/18/61, Sam S. Shubert Theatre, 113
Gay Lord Quex, The (p), 11/12/00, Criterion Theatre, 67
Gay Lord Quex, The (p), 11/12/17, 48th St. Theatre, 40
Gay Musician, The (m), 5/18/08, Wallack Theatre, 21
Gay Paree (r), 8/18/25, Shubert Theatre, 181
Gay Paree (r), 11/9/26, Winter Garden Theatre, 175
Gay White Way, The (r), 10/7/07, Casino Theatre, 105
Gayden (p), 5/10/49, Plymouth Theatre, 7
Gazebo, The (p), 12/12/58, Lyceum Theatre, 218
Geese (Parents and Children / Geese) (p), 1/12/69, Players Theatre, 336
Geisha, The (m), 3/27/13, 44th St. Theatre, 52
Geisha, The (m), 10/5/31, Erlanger Theatre, 16
General John Regan (p), 11/10/13, Hudson Theatre, 72
General John Regan (p), 1/29/30, Irish Theatre, 28
General Post (p), 12/24/17, Gaiety Theatre, 72
General Seeger (p), 2/28/62, Lyceum Theatre, 2
Generation (p), 10/6/65, Morosco Theatre, 300
Genesee of the Hills (p), 2/11/07, Astor Theatre, 26
Geneva (p), 1/30/40, Henry Miller's Theatre, 15
Genius and the Crowd (p), 9/6/20, George M. Cohan Theatre, 24
Genius and the Goddess, The (p), 12/10/57, Henry Miller's Theatre, 7
Genius, The (p), 10/3/06, Bijou Theatre, 35
Gentile Wife, The (p), 12/24/18, Vanderbilt Theatre, 31
Gentle Grafters (p), 10/27/26, Music Box Theatre, 13
Gentle People, The (p), 1/5/39, Belasco Theatre, 141
Gentleman Caller, The. See A Black Quartet
Gentleman from Athens, The (p), 12/9/47, Mansfield Theatre, 7
Gentleman from Mississippi, A (p), 9/29/08, Bijou Theatre, 407
Gentleman from Number 19, The (p), 5/1/13, Comedy Theatre, 4
Gentleman of France, A (p), 12/30/01, Wallack's Theatre, 120
Gentleman of Leisure, A (p), 8/24/11, Playhouse, 76
Gentlemen of the Press (p), 8/27/28, Henry Miller's Theatre, 128
Gentlemen Prefer Blondes (p), 9/28/26, Times Square Theatre, 201
Gentlemen Prefer Blondes (m), 12/8/49, Ziegfeld Theatre, 740
Gentlewoman (p), 3/22/34, Cort Theatre, 12
Gently Does It (p), 10/28/53, Playhouse, 37
George and Margaret (p), 9/22/37, Morosco Theatre, 85
George Barnell / The Harlequinade / When Crummles Played (p), 10/1/28, Garrick Theatre, 40
George Bernard Shaw Series (p) (You Never Can Tell / The Philanderer), 5/12/58, Downtown Theatre, 32
George Dandin (p), 6/27/68, Vivian Beaumont Theatre, 5, (Compagnie du Théâtre de la Cité de Villeurbanne)
George Dandin / The Ancient Mariner (p), 4/6/24, Provincetown Playhouse, 33
George M! (m), 4/10/68, Palace Theatre, 433
George Washington (p), 3/1/20, Lyric Theatre, 16
George Washington Crossing the Delaware / Not Enough Rope / The Twenty-five Cent White Cap. See 3 x 3 (p), 3/1/62, Maidman Theatre, 5
George Washington, Jr. (m), 2/12/06, Herald Square Theatre, 81
George Washington, Jr. (m), 2/11/07, New York Theatre, 32
George Washington Slept Here (p), 10/18/40, Lyceum Theatre, 173
George White's Music Hall Varieties (r), 11/22/32, Casino Theatre, 71
George White's Scandals (r) (1st Edition), 6/2/19, Liberty Theatre, 128
George White's Scandals (r) (2nd Edition)
George White's Scandals (r), 7/11/21, Liberty Theatre, 97
George White's Scandals (r) (4th Edition), 8/28/22, Globe Theatre, 89

George White's Scandals (r) (5th Edition), 6/18/23, Globe Theatre, 168
George White's Scandals (r) (6th Edition), 6/30/24, Apollo Theatre, 196
George White's Scandals (r) (7th Edition), 6/22/25, Apollo Theatre, 169
George White's Scandals (r) (8th Edition), 6/14/26, Apollo Theatre, 432
George White's Scandals (r) (9th Edition), 7/2/28, Apollo Theatre, 240
George White's Scandals (r) (10th Edition), 9/23/29, Apollo Theatre, 159
George White's Scandals (r) (11th Edition), 9/14/31, Apollo Theatre, 204
George White's Scandals (r) (12th Edition), 12/25/35, New Amsterdam Theatre, 110
George White's Scandals (r), 8/28/39, Alvin Theatre, 120
Georgie Porgie (p), 8/10/71, Village Arena Theatre, 72
Georgy (m), 2/26/70, Winter Garden, 4
Geranium Hat, The (m), 3/17/59, Orpheum Theatre, 32
Geraniums in My Window (p), 10/26/34, Longacre Theatre, 27
Gertie (p), 11/15/26, Nora Bayes Theatre, 248
Gertie (p), 1/30/52, Plymouth Theatre, 5
Gertrude / Demon (p), 1/9/72, La Mama Experimental Theatre Club, 13
Gertrude Kingston Repertory, 12/18/16, Maxine Elliott's Theatre
Gertrude Stein's First Reader (r), 12/15/69, Astor Place Theatre, 40
Get Away Old Man (p), 11/24/43, Cort Theatre, 13
Get Me in the Movies (p), 5/21/28, Earl Carroll Theatre, 32
Get Thee to Canterbury (m), 1/25/69, Sheridan Square Playhouse, 20
Get Together (r), 9/3/21, New York Hippodrome, 397
Getout! (m), 2/14/74, La Mama Experimental Theatre Club
Get-Rich-Quick Wallingford (p), 9/19/10, Gaiety Theatre, 424
Get-Rich-Quick Wallingford (p), 5/7/17, Cohan Theatre, 16
Gettin' It Together. See Black Visions
Getting a Polish (p), 11/7/10, Wallack Theatre, 48
Getting Even (p), 8/19/29, Biltmore Theatre, 4
Getting Gertie's Garter (p), 8/1/21, Republic Theatre, 120
Getting Married (p), 11/6/16, Booth Theatre, 112
Getting Married (p), 3/30/31, Guild Theatre, 48
Getting Married (p), 5/7/51, ANTA Playhouse, 16
Getting Married (p), 1/15/70, Master Theatre, 12, (Equity Library Theatre)
Getting Married / Overruled / Buovant Billions. See A Shaw Festival, 5/26/59, Provincetown Playhouse, 155
Getting Together (p), 3/18/18, Lyric Theatre, 8
Getting Together (p), 6/3/18, Shubert Theatre, 104
Ghost Between, The (p), 3/22/21, 39th St. Theatre, 128
Ghost Breaker, The (p), 3/3/13, Lyceum Theatre, 72
Ghost for Sale (p), 9/29/41, Daly's Theatre, 6
Ghost of Jerry Bundler, The / Beauty and the Barge (p), 11/13/13, Wallack Theatre, 6
Ghost of Yankee Doodle, The (p), 11/22/37, Guild Theatre, 48
Ghost Parade, The (p), 10/30/29, Lyric Theatre, 13
Ghost Sonata, The (p), 11/11/71, Circle Theatre
Ghost Train, The (p), 8/25/26, Eltinge Theatre, 62
Ghost Writer, The (p), 6/19/33, Masque Theatre, 24
Ghosts (p), 3/3/03, Mrs. Osborn's Playhouse, 16
Ghosts (p), 3/14/12, Garrick Theatre, 4
Ghosts (p), 4/20/15, Longacre Theatre, 2
Ghosts (p), 2/7/19, Longacre Theatre, 1
Ghosts (p), 1/27/22, Broadhurst Theatre, 21
Ghosts (p), 11/6/23, Century Theatre, 2
Ghosts (p), 12/1/25, Princess Theatre, 2
Ghosts (p), 3/16/26, Comedy Theatre, 29
Ghosts (p), 10/10/27, Mansfield Theatre, 24
Ghosts (p), 2/4/29, Forrest Theatre, 5
Ghosts (p), 5/23/33, Sutton Theatre, 6
Ghosts (p), 12/12/35, Empire Theatre, 44
Ghosts (p), 5/11/36, John Golden Theatre, 32
Ghosts (p), 2/16/48, Cort Theatre, 9
Ghosts (p), 9/21/61, Fourth St. Theatre, 216
Ghosts (p), 4/3/73, Roundabout Theatre, 88
Gianni Schicci. See The National Theatre of the Deaf
Giant's Dance, The (p), 11/16/64, Cherry Lane Theatre, 6
Giants, Sons of Giants (p), 1/6/62, Alvin Theatre, 9
Giddy Throng, The (r), 12/24/00, New York Theatre, 164
Gideon (p), 11/9/61, Plymouth Theatre, 236
Gift of Time, A (p), 2/22/62, Ethel Barrymore Theatre, 92
Gift, The (p), 1/22/24, Greenwich Village Theatre, 7
Gigi (p), 11/24/51, Fulton Theatre, 217
Gigi (m), 11/13/73, Uris Theatre, 103
Gilbert and Sullivan Opera Company, 4/19/15, 48th St. Theatre
Gilbert Becaud on Broadway, 10/31/66, Longacre Theatre, 19
Gilbert Becaud Sings Love, 10/6/68, Cort Theatre, 17
Gilbert's Engaged (m), 6/18/25, 52nd St. Theatre
Gilbert & Sullivan Repertory, 10/4/49, Mark Hellinger Theatre, 23
Gillette, William. See William Gillette
Ginger (m), 10/16/23, Daly's Theatre, 30
Ginger Man, The (p), 11/21/63, Orpheum Theatre, 52
Ginger Snaps (r), 12/31/29, Belmont Theatre, 7
Gingerbread Lady, The (p), 12/13/70, Plymouth Theatre, 193
Gingerbread Man, The (m), 12/25/05, Liberty Theatre, 16
Gingerbread Man, The (m), 5/21/06, New York Theatre, 16
Gingham Dog, The (p), 4/23/69, John Golden Theatre, 5
Gingham Girl, The (m), 8/28/22, Earl Carroll Theatre, 322
Gioconda Smile, The (p), 10/7/50, Lyceum Theatre, 41
Gipsy Trail, The (p), 12/4/17, Plymouth Theatre, 111
Gipsy Trail, The / A Trench Fantasy (p), 1/24/18, Plymouth Theatre, 19
Girl and the Cat, The (p), 5/5/27, Forrest Theatre, 3
Girl and the Governor, The (m), 2/4/07, Manhattan Theatre, 26
Girl and the Judge, The (p), 12/4/01, Lyceum Theatre, 125
Girl and the Kaiser, The (m), 11/22/10, Herald Square Theatre, 64
Girl and the Pennant, The (p), 10/23/13, Lyric Theatre, 20
Girl and the Wizard, The (p), 9/27/09, Casino Theatre, 96
Girl Behind the Counter, The (m), 10/1/07, Herald Square Theatre, 260
Girl Behind the Gun, The (m), 9/16/18, New Amsterdam Theatre, 160
Girl Can Tell, A (p), 10/29/53, Royale Theatre, 60
Girl Could Get Lucky, A (p), 9/20/64, Cort Theatre, 8
Girl Crazy (m), 10/14/30, Alvin Theatre, 272
Girl Friend, The (m), 3/17/26, Vanderbilt Theatre, 301
Girl from Brazil, The (m), 8/30/16, 44th St. Theatre, 61
Girl from Brighton, The (r), 8/31/12, Academy of Music, 49
Girl from Dixie, The (m), 12/14/03, Madison Square Theatre, 26
Girl from Home, The (m), 5/3/20, Globe Theatre, 24
Girl from Kay's, The (m), 11/2/03, Herald Square Theatre, 223
Girl from Montmartre, The (m), 8/5/12, Criterion Theatre, 64
Girl from Nantucket, The (m), 11/8/45, Adelphi Theatre, 12
Girl from Rector's, The (p), 2/1/09, Weber Theatre, 184
Girl from Up There, The (m), 1/7/01, Herald Square Theatre, 96
Girl from Utah, The (m), 8/24/14, Knickerbocker Theatre, 120
Girl from Wyoming, The (p), 10/29/38, American Music Hall, 86
Girl He Couldn't Leave Behind Him, The (p), 3/9/10, Garrick Theatre, 37
Girl in Pink Tights, The (m), 3/5/54, Mark Hellinger Theatre, 115
Girl in the Freudian Slip, The (p), 5/18/67, Booth Theatre, 4
Girl in the Limousine, The (p), 10/6/19, Eltinge Theatre, 137
Girl in the Spotlight, The (m), 7/12/20, Knickerbocker Theatre, 54
Girl in the Taxi, The (m), 10/24/10, Astor Theatre, 48
Girl in the Train, The (m), 10/3/10, Globe Theatre, 40
Girl o' Mine (m), 1/28/18, Bijou Theatre, 48
Girl of My Dreams, The (m), 8/7/11, Criterion Theatre, 40
Girl of the Golden West, The (p), 11/14/05, Belasco Theatre, 224
Girl of the Golden West, The (p), 11/11/07, Belasco Theatre, 22
Girl of the Golden West, The (p), 1/27/08, Academy of Music, 24
Girl of the Golden West, The (p), 11/5/57, Phyllis Anderson Theatre, 8
Girl on the Film, The (m), 12/29/13, 44th St. Theatre, 64
Girl on the Via Flaminia, The (p), 2/9/54, Circle in the Square, 111
Girl Outside, The (p), 10/24/32, Little Theatre, 8
Girl Patsy, The (p), 5/26/06, Savoy Theatre, 17
Girl Question, The (m), 8/3/08, Wallack Theatre, 32
Girl Quiet, Man Out Loud / The Spanish Armada (p), 4/3/62, Cricket Theatre, 16
Girl Trouble (p), 10/25/28, Belmont Theatre, 22
Girl Who Came to Supper, The (m), 12/8/63, Broadway Theatre, 112
Girl Who Has Everything, The (p), 12/4/06, Liberty Theatre, 48
Girl Who Smiles, The (m), 8/9/15, Lyric Theatre, 104
Girl with the Carmine Lips, The (p), 8/9/20, Punch and Judy Theatre, 16
Girl with the Green Eyes, The (p), 12/25/02, Savoy Theatre, 108
Girl with the Whooping Cough, The (p), 4/25/10, New York Theatre, 24
Girlies (m), 6/13/10, New Amsterdam Theatre, 88
Girls (p) (Laura Nelson Hall), 3/23/08, Daly's Theatre, 64
Girls (p) (Florence Reed), 2/8/09, Hackett Theatre, 8
Girls Against the Boys, The (r), 11/2/59, Alvin Theatre, 16
Girls in Uniform (p), 12/30/32, Booth Theatre, 12
Girls in 509, The (p), 10/15/58, Belasco Theatre, 117
Girls of Gottenburg, The (m), 9/2/08, Knickerbocker Theatre, 103
Girls of Holland, The (m), 11/18/07, Lyric Theatre, 15
Girls of Summer (p), 11/19/56, Longacre Theatre, 56
Girls Will Be Girls (p), 8/29/04, 14th St. Theatre, 34
Girofle-Girofla (r), 11/22/26, Jolson Theatre, 10
Give and Take (p), 1/15/23, 49th St. Theatre, 188
Give Me Yesterday (p), 3/4/31, Charles Hopkins Theatre, 69
Give Us This Day (p), 10/27/33, Booth Theatre, 3
Glad of It (p), 12/28/03, Savoy Theatre, 32
Glad Tidings (p), 10/11/51, Lyceum Theatre, 100
Glamour, Glory and Gold (p), 3/22/74, Fortune Theatre
Glamour Preferred (p), 11/15/40, Booth Theatre, 11
Glass Menagerie, The (p), 3/31/45, Playhouse, 561
Glass Menagerie, The (p), 11/21/56, New York City Center, 15
Glass Menagerie, The (p), 5/4/65, Brooks Atkinson Theatre, 176
Glass of Water, A (p), 3/5/30, Laboratory Theatre, 9
Glass Slipper, The (p), 10/19/25, Guild Theatre, 65
Glickl Hameln Demands Justice (p), 2/13/72, Colden Center, Queens College, 32
Glimpse of the Great White Way, A / The Modiste Shop (m), 10/27/13, 44th St. Theatre, 12
Glittering Gloria (m), 2/15/04, Daly's Theatre, 22
Gloria and Esperanza (p), 4/3/69, La Mama Experimental Theatre Club, 6
Gloria and Esperanza (p), 2/4/70, ANTA Theatre, 13

Gloriana (p), 11/25/38, Little Theatre, 5
Glorianna (m), 10/28/18, Liberty Theatre, 96
Glorious Betsy (p), 9/7/08, Lyric Theatre, 24
Glorious Morning (p), 11/26/38, Mansfield Theatre, 9
Glorious Ruler, The (p), 6/30/69, Jan Hus Theatre, 8
Glory (m), 12/25/22, Vanderbilt Theatre, 74
Glory Hallelujah (p), 4/6/26, Broadhurst Theatre, 15
Gnadiges Fraulein, The. See Slapstick Tragedy
Go Children Slowly. See Playwrights Cooperative Festival
Go Easy, Mabel (m), 5/8/22, Longacre Theatre, 16
Go Fight City Hall (m), 11/2/61, Mayfair Theatre, 77
Go Fly a Kite! , 10/19/69, Tambellini's Gate Theatre, 8
Go, Go, Go, God Is Dead! (p), 10/11/66, Blackfriars' Guild, 61
Go Show Me a Dragon (p), 10/27/61, Midway Theatre, 3
Go to It (p), 12/24/16, Princess Theatre, 23
Go West, Young Man (p), 11/12/23, Punch and Judy Theatre, 48
Goa (p), 2/22/68, Martinique Theatre, 28
Goat Alley (p), 6/20/21, Bijou Theatre, 8
Goat Alley (p), 4/20/27, Princess Theatre, 13
Goat Song, The (p), 1/25/26, Guild Theatre, 58
God and Kate Murphy (p), 2/26/59, 54th St. Theatre, 12
God Bless Coney (m), 5/3/72, Orpheum Theatre, 3
God Bless You, Harold Fineberg (p), 3/30/69, Actors Playhouse, 9
God Is a (Guess What?) (p), 12/17/68, St. Marks Playhouse, 32, (Negro Ensemble Co.)
God Loves Us (p), 10/18/26, Maxine Elliott's Theatre, 32
God, Man and You, Baby (r), 10/29/63, Midway Theatre, 2
God of Vengeance, The (p), 12/20/22, Provincetown Playhouse, 137
God's Trombones / Shakespeare in Harlem, 2/9/60, 41st St. Theatre, 32
God Says There Is No Peter Ott (p), 4/17/72, McAlpin Rooftop Theatre, 8
God Slept Here, A / Enemies Don't Send Flowers (p), 2/19/57, Provincetown Playhouse, 16
Goddess of Liberty, The (m), 12/22/09, Weber Theatre, 29
Goddess of Reason, The (p), 2/15/09, Daly's Theatre, 48
Gods of the Lightning (p), 10/24/28, Little Theatre, 29
Gods of the Lightning (p), 2/18/31, Provincetown Playhouse, 22
Gods We Make, The (p), 1/3/34, Mansfield Theatre, 12
Godspell (m), 5/17/71, Cherry Lane Theatre, 1,270
Go-Go (m), 3/12/23, Daly's Theatre, 138
Gogo Loves You (m), 10/9/64, Theatre de Lys, 2
Goin' a Buffalo (p), 2/11/72, WPA Theatre
Goin' Home (p), 8/23/28, Hudson Theatre, 77
Going Gay (p), 8/3/33, Morosco Theatre, 24
Going Some (p), 4/12/09, Belasco Theatre, 96
Going Thru Changes / The Past Is the Past (p), 12/29/73, Billie Holiday Theatre
Going Up (m), 12/25/17, Liberty Theatre, 351
Gold (p), 6/1/21, Frazee Theatre, 13
Gold Braid (p), 5/13/30, Theatre Masque, 7
Gold Diggers, The (p), 9/30/19, Lyceum Theatre, 720
Gold Eagle Guy (p), 11/28/34, Morosco Theatre, 66
Golden Age, The (p), 4/24/28, Longacre Theatre, 6
Golden Age, The (p), 11/18/63, Lyceum Theatre, 7
Golden Apple, The (m), 3/11/54, Phoenix Theatre, 46
Golden Apple, The (m), 4/20/54, Alvin Theatre, 127
Golden Apple, The (m), 2/12/62, York Playhouse, 112
Golden Bat (m), 7/21/71, Sheridan Square Theatre, 152
Golden Boy (p), 11/4/37, Belasco Theatre, 248
Golden Boy (p), 3/12/52, ANTA Playhouse, 55
Golden Boy (m), 10/20/64, Majestic Theatre, 569
Golden Butterfly, The (m), 10/12/08, Broadway Theatre, 48
Golden Dawn (m), 11/30/27, Hammerstein Theatre, 200
Golden Days (p), 11/1/21, Gaiety Theatre, 40
Golden Falcon, The (p), 3/25/48, Henry Street Playhouse, 11
Golden Fleece, The. See Tonight in Living Color
Golden Fleecing (p), 10/15/59, Henry Miller's Theatre, 84
Golden Rainbow (m), 2/4/68, Shubert Theatre, 383
Golden Screw, The (m), 1/30/67, Provincetown Playhouse, 40
Golden Six, The (p), 10/25/58, York Playhouse, 16
Golden State, The (p), 11/25/50, Fulton Theatre, 25
Golden Streets, The (p), 8/12/70, Riverside Park, 14, (Puerto Rican Traveling Theatre)
Golden Wings (p), 12/8/41, Cort Theatre, 6
Goldfish, The (p), 4/17/22, Maxine Elliott's Theatre, 169
Goldilocks (m), 10/11/58, Lunt-Fontanne Theatre, 161
Golem, The (p) (Habimah), 5/15/48, Broadway Theatre, 16
Golem, The (p) (Habimah), 6/5/48, Broadway Theatre
Golem, The (p), 2/25/59, St. Marks Playhouse, 54
Gondoliers, The (m), 6/1/31, Erlanger Theatre, 16
Gondoliers, The (m), 1/11/32, Erlanger Theatre, 8
Gondoliers, The (m), 9/3/34, Martin Beck Theatre, 119
Gondoliers, The (m), 8/5/35, Adelphi Theatre, 8
Gondoliers, The (m), 8/29/35, Adelphi Theatre, 4
Gondoliers, The (m), 9/7/36, Martin Beck Theatre, 20
Gondoliers, The (m), 9/30/40, 44th St. Theatre, 7
Gondoliers, The (m), 3/3/42, St. James Theatre, 3
Gondoliers, The (m), 2/21/44, Ambassador Theatre, 4
Gondoliers, The (m), 1/26/48, Century Theatre, 16
Gondoliers, The (m), 2/12/51, St. James Theatre, 4
Gondoliers, The (m), 5/28/57, Shakespearewrights Theatre, 8
Gondoliers, The (m), 2/4/60, Jan Hus House
Gondoliers, The (m), 12/7/61, Jan Hus House, 6
Gondoliers, The (m), 4/11/62, New York City Center, 15
Gondoliers, The (m), 11/15/62, New York City Center, 5
Gondoliers, The (m), 3/27/64, New York City Center, 2
Gondoliers, The (m), 5/23/65, Jan Hus House, 15, (American Savoyards)
Gondoliers, The (m), 10/19/67, Jan Hus Playhouse, 16, (American Savoyards)
Gone Tommorrow / Home Life of a Buffalo / Hope Is the Thing with Feathers. See Hope's the Thing, 5/11/48, Playhouse, 7
Good as Gold (p), 3/7/57, Belasco Theatre, 4
Good Bad Woman, A (p), 4/8/19, Harris Theatre, 31
Good Bad Woman, A (p), 2/9/25, Comedy Theatre, 17
Good Bad Woman, A (p), 6/22/25, Playhouse, 64
Good Boy (m), 9/5/28, Hammerstein Theatre, 253
Good Companions, The (m), 10/1/31, 44th St. Theatre, 68
Good Day / The Exhaustion of Our Son's Love (p), 10/18/65, Cherry Lane Theatre, 64
Good Doctor, The (p), 11/27/73, Eugene O'Neill Theatre, 208
Good Earth, The (p), 10/17/32, Guild Theatre, 56
Good Evening (r), 11/14/73, Plymouth Theatre, 228
Good Fairy, The (p), 11/24/31, Henry Miller's Theatre, 154
Good Fairy, The (p), 11/17/32, Forrest Theatre, 72
Good Fellow, The (p), 10/5/26, Playhouse, 8
Good Gracious Annabelle (p), 10/31/16, Republic Theatre, 111
Good Hope, The (p), 10/18/27, Civic Repertory Theatre, 49
Good Hope, The (p), 12/15/28, Civic Repertory Theatre, 7
Good Hope, The (p), 12/17/30, Civic Repertory Theatre, 4
Good Hunting (p), 11/21/38, Hudson Theatre, 2
Good Little Devil, A (p), 1/18/13, Republic Theatre, 133
Good Luck (m), 10/17/64, Yiddish Anderson Theatre, 117
Good Men and True (p), 10/25/35, Biltmore Theatre, 11
Good Men Do, The / Her Honor, the Mayor (p), 5/20/18, Fulton Theatre, 16
Good Morning Corporal (p), 8/8/44, Playhouse, 13
Good Morning, Dearie (m), 11/1/21, Globe Theatre, 347
Good Morning, Judge (m), 2/6/19, Shubert Theatre, 140
Good Morning, Rosamond (p), 12/10/17, 48th St. Theatre, 8
Good Neighbor (p), 10/21/41, Windsor Theatre, 1
Good News (m), 9/6/27, Chanin's 46th St. Theatre, 551
Good Night, Ladies (p), 1/17/45, Royale Theatre, 78
Good Night, Paul (m), 9/3/17, Hudson Theatre, 40
Good Old Days (p), 8/14/23, Broadhurst Theatre, 71
Good Soldier Schweik, The (p), 4/8/63, Gate Theatre, 20
Good Soup, The (p), 3/2/60, Plymouth Theatre, 21
Good, The (p), 10/5/38, Windsor Theatre, 9
Good Times (m), 8/9/20, New York Hippodrome Theatre, 455
Good Woman of Setzuan, The (p), 12/18/56, Phoenix Theatre, 24
Good Woman of Setzuan, The (p), 11/5/70, Vivian Beaumont Theatre, 46
Good Woman, Poor Thing, A (p), 1/9/33, Avon Theatre, 8
Good Women, The / Squaring the Triangle / Divertissement / The Nightcap / Gutta Iconoclast / Pearls, 6/13/21, Apollo Theatre, 8
Goodbye Again (p), 12/28/32, Masque Theatre, 212
Goodbye Again (p), 11/9/43, New Amsterdam Roof, 8
Goodbye Again (p), 4/24/56, Helen Hayes Theatre, 7
Goodbye, Charlie (p), 12/16/59, Lyceum Theatre, 109
Goodbye in the Night (p), 3/18/40, Biltmore Theatre, 8
Goodbye, My Fancy (p), 11/17/48, Morosco Theatre, 446
Goodbye People, The (p), 12/3/68, Ethel Barrymore Theatre, 7
Good-Bye Please (p), 10/24/34, Ritz Theatre, 2
Goose for the Gander, A (p), 1/23/45, Playhouse, 15
Goose Hangs High, The (p), 1/29/24, Bijou Theatre, 186
Goose, The (p), 3/15/60, Sullivan St. Playhouse, 32
Gorilla Queen (p), 4/24/67, Martinique Theatre, 63
Gorilla, The (p), 4/28/25, Selwyn Theatre, 257
Gossipy Sex, The (p), 4/19/27, Mansfield Theatre, 23
Governor's Boss, The (p), 4/13/14, Garrick Theatre, 16
Governor's Lady, The (p), 9/10/12, Republic Theatre, 135
Governor's Son, The (m), 2/25/01, Savoy Theatre, 32
Governor's Son, The (m), 6/4/06, Aerial Gardens Theatre, 75
Grab Bag, The (r), 10/6/24, Globe Theatre, 184
Grab Bag, The (The Subscriber / Susie Is a Good Girl / The Grab Bag) (p), 11/4/68, Astor Place Theatre, 32
Graduation (p), 1/5/65, Theatre de Lys, 1, (ANTA Matinee)
Grail Green. See Kool Aid
Grain of Dust, The (p), 1/1/12, Criterion Theatre, 24
Gramercy Ghost (p), 4/26/51, Morosco Theatre, 100
Grand Army Man, A (p), 10/16/07, Stuyvesant Theatre, 149
Grand Duchess and the Waiter, The (p), 10/13/25, Lyceum Theatre, 31
Grand Duke, The (p), 11/1/21, Lyceum Theatre, 131

Grand Duke, The (m), 5/11/61, Greenwich Mews Theatre, 12
Grand Guignol Players, The, 10/15/23, Frolic Theatre, 56
Grand Hotel (p), 11/13/30, National Theatre, 444
Grand Kabuki, The (Chushingura / Kagami-Jishi; Kumagai Jinya / Momiji-Gari) (p), 9/10/69, New York City Center, 18
Grand Mal Crick (p), 1/7/71, Theatre Genesis
Grand Mogul, The (m), 3/25/07, New Amsterdam Theatre, 40
Grand Music Hall of Israel, The (r), 2/6/68, Palace Theatre, 64
Grand Music Hall of Israel, The (r), 1/4/73, Felt Forum, 15
Grand Prize, The (p), 1/26/55, Plymouth Theatre, 21
Grand Street Follies (r), 5/20/24, Neighborhood Playhouse, 172
Grand Street Follies (r), 6/18/25, Neighborhood Playhouse, 166
Grand Street Follies (r), 6/15/26, Neighborhood Playhouse, 55
Grand Street Follies (r), 5/19/27, Neighborhood Playhouse, 148
Grand Street Follies (r), 5/28/28, Booth Theatre, 144
Grand Street Follies (r), 5/1/29, Booth Theatre, 85
Grand Tour, The (p), 12/10/51, Martin Beck Theatre, 8
Grand Vizier, The / Edward and Agrippina / The Deceased (p) (The French Way), 3/20/62, East End Theatre, 1
Grand Vizir, Le / Le Cosmonaute Agricole (p), 4/7/70, Barbizon-Plaza Theatre, 9, (Le Treteau de Paris)
Grande de Coca-Cola, El (r), 2/13/73, Mercer / Oscar Wilde Room, 668
Grandma's Diary (p), 9/22/48, Henry Miller's Theatre, 6
Granite (p), 2/11/27, American Laboratory Theatre, 70
Granite (p), 11/29/27, American Laboratory Theatre, 26
Granite (p), 1/13/36, Vanderbilt Theatre, 8
Granny (p), 10/24/04, Lyceum Theatre, 24
Granny Maumee / A Woman Killed with Kindness (p), 3/30/14, Lyceum Theatre, 1
Granny Maumee / Simon the Cyrenian / The Rider of Dreams (p), 4/5/17, Garden Theatre
Grass Harp, The (p), 3/27/52, Martin Beck Theatre, 36
Grass Harp, The (p), 4/27/53, Circle in the Square Theatre
Grass Harp, The (m), 11/2/71, Martin Beck Theatre, 7
Grass Is Always Greener, The (p), 2/15/55, Downtown National Theatre, 40
Grass Widow, The (m), 12/3/17, Liberty Theatre, 48
Grasshopper (p), 4/7/17, Maxine Elliott's Theatre, 3
Gray Shadow (p), 3/10/31, New Yorker Theatre, 39
Grease (m), 2/14/72, Eden Theatre, 957
Great Adventure, The (p), 10/16/13, Booth Theatre, 52
Great Adventure, The (p), 12/22/26, Princess Theatre, 30
Great Adventure, The (p), 1/24/27, Edyth Totten Theatre, 16
Great Airplane Snatch, The / Arf (p), 5/27/69, Stage 73, 5
Great Barrington, The (p), 2/19/31, Avon Theatre, 15
Great Big Doorstep, The (p), 11/26/42, Morosco Theatre, 28
Great Broxopp, The (p), 11/15/21, Punch and Judy Theatre, 66
Great Campaign, The (m), 3/30/47, Princess Theatre, 5
Great Career, A / An Evening for Merlin Finch (p), 12/29/68, Forum Theatre, 35
Great Catherine, The / The Miser / Snickering Horses (p), 5/13/36, Experimental Theatre, 3
Great Day (m), 10/17/29, Cosmopolitan Theatre, 37
Great Day in the Morning (p), 3/28/62, Henry Miller's Theatre, 13
Great Divide, The (p), 10/3/06, Princess Theatre, 238
Great Divide, The (p), 2/7/17, Lyceum Theatre, 53
Great Gatsby, The (p), 2/2/26, Ambassador Theatre, 113
Great God Brown, The (p), 1/23/26, Greenwich Village Theatre, 271
Great God Brown, The (p), 10/6/59, Coronet Theatre, 32
Great God Brown, The (p), 12/10/72, Lyceum Theatre, 19, (New Phoenix Repertory Co.)
Great Goodness of Life (A Coon Show). See A Black Quartet
Great Goodness of Life. See Experimental Death Unit #1
Great Hoss Pistol, A, 5/16/73, New York University Theatre
Great Indoors, The (p), 2/1/66, Eugene O'Neill Theatre, 7
Great John Ganton, The (p), 5/3/09, Lyric Theatre, 40
Great Lady (m), 12/1/38, Majestic Theatre, 20
Great Lover, The (p), 11/10/15, Longacre Theatre, 245
Great Lover, The (p), 10/11/32, Waldorf Theatre, 23
Great MacDaddy, The (m), 2/12/74, St. Marks Playhouse, 72
Great Magoo, The (m), 12/2/32, Selwyn Theatre, 11
Great Man, The (p), 4/7/31, Ritz Theatre, 7
Great Man, The / The Bald Soprano (p), 5/28/63, Judson Hall
Great Music (p), 10/4/24, Earl Carroll Theatre, 44
Great Name, The (p), 10/4/11, Lyric Theatre, 21
Great Nebula in Orion, The. See The Family Continues
Great Necker, The (p), 3/6/28, Ambassador Theatre, 39
Great Power, The (p), 9/11/28, Ritz Theatre, 22
Great Pursuit, The (p), 3/22/16, Shubert Theatre, 29
Great Question, The (p), 10/26/08, Majestic Theatre, 16
Great Scot! (m), 11/10/65, Theatre Four, 38
Great Scott (p), 9/2/29, 49th St. Theatre, 16
Great Sebastians, The (p), 1/4/56, ANTA Theatre, 174
Great Temptations (r), 5/18/26, Winter Garden Theatre, 197
Great To Be Alive! (m), 3/23/50, Winter Garden Theatre, 52
Great Waltz, The (m), 9/22/34, Center Theatre, 297
Great Waltz, The (m), 8/5/35, Center Theatre, 48
Great Way, The (p), 11/7/21, Park Theatre, 8
Great Western Union, The (p), 2/9/65, Bouwerie Lane Theatre, 5
Great White Hope, The (p), 10/3/68, Alvin Theatre, 557
Greater Love, The (p), 3/2/31, Liberty Theatre, 8
Greater Love, The (p), 3/19/06, Madison Square Theatre, 32
Greatest Fairy Story Ever Told, The (m), 11/28/73, Theatre at St. Clement's, 14
Greatest Man Alive!, The (p), 5/8/57, Ethel Barrymore Theatre, 5
Greatest Nation, The (p), 2/28/16, Booth Theatre, 16
Greatest Show on Earth, The (p), 1/5/38, Playhouse, 29
Greatest Thing in the World, The (p), 10/8/00, Wallack's Theatre, 41
Greatest Thing in the World, The / The Moment of Death (p), 10/23/00, Wallack's Theatre, 24
Greco, Jose. See Jose Greco
Greek Tragedy Theatre (Electra, The Choephori, The Eumenides), 9/19/61, New York City Center, 16
Greek Tragedy Theatre of Athens (Medea; Electra) (p), 8/31/64, New York City Center, 16
Greeks Had a Word for It, The (p), 9/25/30, Sam H. Harris Theatre, 224
Green Bay Tree, The (p), 10/20/33, Cort Theatre, 163
Green Bay Tree, The (p), 2/1/51, Golden Theatre, 26
Green Beetle, The (p), 9/2/24, Klaw Theatre, 63
Green Cockatoo, The (p), 10/9/30, Civic Repertory Theatre, 9
Green Cockatoo, The / Hannele (p), 4/11/10, Lyceum Theatre, 16
Green Goddess, The (p), 1/18/21, Booth Theatre, 440
Green Grow the Lilacs (p), 1/26/31, Guild Theatre, 64
Green Hat, The (p), 9/15/25, Broadhurst Theatre, 237
Green Julia (p), 11/16/72, Sheridan Square Playhouse, 147
Green Pastures, The (p), 2/26/30, Mansfield Theatre, 640
Green Pastures, The (p), 2/26/35, 44th St. Theatre, 71
Green Pastures, The (p), 3/15/51, Broadway Theatre, 44
Green Ring, The (p), 4/4/22, Neighborhood Playhouse, 30
Green Stick (p), 10/9/34, Provincetown Playhouse, 20
Green Stockings (p), 10/2/11, 39th St. Theatre, 48
Green Table, The / H.M.S. Pinafore (m), 1/21/42, St. James Theatre, 18
Green Waters (p), 11/4/36, Masque Theatre, 5
Greenwich Village Follies (r), 7/15/19, Greenwich Village Theatre, 232
Greenwich Village Follies (r), 8/30/20, Greenwich Village Theatre, 217
Greenwich Village Follies (r), 8/31/21, Shubert Theatre, 167
Greenwich Village Follies (r), 9/12/22, Shubert Theatre, 209
Greenwich Village Follies (r), 9/20/23, Winter Garden Theatre, 131
Greenwich Village Follies (r), 9/16/24, Shubert Theatre, 131
Greenwich Village Follies (r), 12/24/25, Chanin's 46th St. Theatre, 180
Greenwich Village Follies (r), 3/15/26, Shubert Theatre, 180
Greenwich Village Follies (r), 4/9/28, Winter Garden Theatre, 128
Greenwich Village, U.S.A. (r), 9/28/60, One Sheridan Square, 87
Greenwich Villagers, The (r), 8/18/27, Grove St. Theatre, 5
Greenwillow (m), 3/8/60, Alvin Theatre, 97
Greenwillow (m), 12/3/70, Master Theatre, 22, (Equity Library Theatre)
Greet, Ben. See Ben Greet
Grenfell, Joyce. See Joyce Grenfell Requests the Pleasure. . .
Greta Keller, 4/13/64, Stage 73, 4
Gretna Green (p), 1/5/03, Madison Square Theatre, 28
Grey Farm (p), 5/3/40, Hudson Theatre, 35
Grey Fox, The (p), 10/22/28, Playhouse, 88
Grey Shadow (p), 3/10/31, New Yorker Theatre, 49
Grey-Eyed People, The (p), 12/17/52, Martin Beck Theatre, 5
Greyhound, The (p), 2/29/12, Astor Theatre, 108
Grierson's Way (p), 1/18/06, Princess Theatre, 12
Grin and Bare It! / Postcards (p), 3/16/70, Belasco Theatre, 16
Gringa, La (p), 2/1/28, Little Theatre, 21
Gringo (p), 12/14/22, Comedy Theatre, 29
Gris-Gris. See In the Voodoo Parlour of Marie Leveau
Grosse Valise, La (m), 12/14/65, 54th Street Theatre, 7
Grotesques / The Moon of the Caribbees / Trifles (p), 4/25/21, Provincetown Playhouse, 21
Grounds for Divorce (p), 9/23/24, Empire Theatre, 130
Group Soup (r), 12/28/69, Alice Tully Hall, 12, (Paper Bag Players)
Group Soup. See The Paper Bag Players
Growing Pains (p), 11/23/33, Ambassador Theatre, 28
Grumpy (p), 11/19/13, Wallack Theatre, 181
Guardsman, The (p), 10/13/24, Garrick Theatre, 274
Guernica / Pique-Nique en Campagne (p), 4/30/69, Barbizon-Plaza Theatre, 16, (Le Treteau de Paris)
Guest in the House (p), 2/24/42, Plymouth Theatre, 153
Guest of Honor, The (p), 9/20/20, Broadhurst Theatre, 75
Guest Room, The, 10/6/31, Biltmore Theatre, 65
Guests of the Nation / Aria da Capo (p), 6/26/58, Theatre Marquee, 102
Guibour (p), 3/1/22, 39th St. Theatre, 5
Guide, The (p), 3/6/68, Hudson Theatre, 5
Guilty Conscience, The / The Necken (p), 4/15/13, Lyceum Theatre, 1
Guilty Man, The (p), 8/17/16, Astor Theatre, 52
Guilty One, The (p), 3/20/23, Selwyn Theatre, 31

Guimpes and Saddles (p), 10/10/67, Blackfriars' Guild, 46
Guinea Pig, The (p), 1/7/29, President Theatre, 64
Guitar (p), 11/10/59, Jan Hus House, 2
Gun Play, A (p), 10/24/71, Cherry Lane Theatre, 23
Guns (p), 8/6/28, Wallack Theatre, 48
Guns of Carrar, The / Cuba Si (p), 12/9/68, Theatre de Lys, 2, (ANTA Matinee)
Gutta Iconoclast / Pearls / The Good Women / Squaring the Triangle / Divertissement / The Nightcap (p), 6/13/21, Apollo Theatre, 8
Guys and Dolls (m), 11/24/50, 46th St. Theatre, 1,194
Guys and Dolls (m), 4/20/55, New York City Center, 31
Guys and Dolls (m), 7/21/59, Theatre-in-the-Park, 14
Guys and Dolls (m), 4/28/65, New York City Center, 15
Guys and Dolls (m), 6/8/66, New York City Center, 23
Gypsy (p), 12/30/03, Garrick Theatre, 1
Gypsy (p), 1/14/29, Klaw Theatre, 64
Gypsy (m), 5/21/59, Broadway Theatre, 702
Gypsy Blonde (m), 6/25/34, Lyric Theatre, 24
Gypsy Fires (p), 12/7/25, George M. Cohan Theatre, 16
Gypsy Jim (p), 1/14/24, 49th St. Theatre, 48
Gypsy Lady (m), 9/17/46, Century Theatre, 79
Gypsy Love (m), 10/17/11, Globe Theatre, 31
Gypsy, The (m), 11/14/12, Park Theatre, 12
g-11 (p), 5/27/48, Henry Street Playhouse, 8

H

H. B. Irving-Dorothea Baird Repertory, 10/1/06, New Amsterdam Theatre, 32
H. R. Pufnstuf's Hollywood Revue (r), 2/12/74, Felt Forum, 30
H. R. Pufnstuf Show, The (r), 2/12/73, Felt Forum, 27
Habimah Theatre Repertory, 2/1/64, Little Theatre, 56
Habimah Theatre Repertory. See The Dybbuk; David's Crown; The Golem; Oedipus Rex
Habitual Husband, The (p), 12/24/24, 48th St. Theatre, 11
Hadame Hanako Repertory, 10/15/07
Hadrian VII (p), 1/8/69, Helen Hayes Theatre, 359
Hail and Farewell (p), 2/19/23, Morosco Theatre, 41
Hail Scrawdyke! (p), 11/28/66, Booth Theatre, 8
Hair (m), 10/29/67, Florence Sutro Anspacher Theatre, 65
Hair (m), 12/22/67, Cheetah, 45
Hair (m), 4/29/68, Biltmore Theatre, 1,750
Hairpin Harmony (m), 10/1/43, National Theatre, 3
Hairy Ape, The (p), 3/9/22, Provincetown Playhouse, 120
Haiti (p), 3/2/38, Lafayette Theatre, 168
Hajj Malik, El (p), 9/18/70, Afro-American Studio
Hajj Malik, El (p), 11/29/71, Martinique Theatre, 40
Half a Sixpence (m), 4/25/65, Broadhurst Theatre, 512
Half a Widow (m), 9/12/27, Waldorf Theatre, 16
Half an Hour / The Younger Generation (p), 9/25/13, Lyceum Theatre, 60
Half Gods (p), 12/21/29, Plymouth Theatre, 17
Half Horse, Half Alligator, 3/13/66, Players Theatre, 32
Half Moon, The (m), 11/1/20, Liberty Theatre, 48
Half Naked Truth, The (p), 6/7/26, Mayfair Theatre, 41
Half-Caste, The (p), 3/29/26, National Theatre, 63
Half-Past Wednesday (m), 4/6/62, Orpheum Theatre, 2
Half-Past Wednesday (m), 4/28/62, Orpheum Theatre, 4
Halfway to Hell (p), 1/2/34, Fulton Theatre, 7
Halfway Up the Tree (p), 11/7/67, Brooks Atkinson Theatre, 64
Hall of Fame, The (m), 1/30/02, New York Theatre, 152
Hallams, The (p), 3/4/48, Booth Theatre, 12
Hallelujah! (p), 11/29/73, Central Arts Theatre, 12
Hallelujah, Baby! (m), 4/26/67, Martin Beck Theatre, 293
Hallelujah or St. George and the Dragon or Laos. See A Coney Island Cycle
Hallowe'en (p), 2/20/36, Vanderbilt Theatre, 12
Ham Tree, The (r), 8/28/05, New York Theatre, 90
Hamilton (p), 9/17/17, Knickerbocker Theatre, 80
Hamlet (p) (E.H. Sothern), 9/17/00, Garden Theatre, 16
Hamlet (p) (E. H. Sothern), 12/30/02, Garden Theatre, 32
Hamlet (p) (E. H. Sothern), 3/23/03, Garden Theatre, 8
Hamlet (p) (Edmund Russell), 4/28/03, Wallack Theatre, 1
Hamlet (p) (Edmund Russell), 5/1/03, Wallack Theatre, 1
Hamlet (p) (Johnston Forbes-Robertson), 3/8/04, Knickerbocker Theatre, 28
Hamlet (p) (Aldora Shem), 2/14/05, New York Theatre, 1
Hamlet (p) (Johnston Forbes-Robertson), 3/13/05, Knickerbocker Theatre, 7
Hamlet (p) (Ian Maclaren), 4/23/12, Wallack Theatre, 1
Hamlet (p) (John E. Kellerd), 11/18/12, Garden Theatre, 102
Hamlet (p) (Walter Hampden), 11/22/18, Plymouth Theatre
Hamlet (p) (Walter Hampden), 5/20/19, 39th St. Theatre, 23
Hamlet (p), 12/6/20, Manhattan Opera House, 4
Hamlet (p), 12/27/20, Lexington Theatre, 8
Hamlet (p), 5/4/21, Broadhurst Theatre, 8
Hamlet (p) (Sothern-Marlowe Shakespeare Repertory), 11/7/21, Century Theatre, 11
Hamlet (p), 12/26/21, Lexington Theatre, 2
Hamlet (p) (Fritz Leiber), 1/23/22, 48th St. Theatre, 2
Hamlet (p) (John Barrymore), 11/16/22, Sam H. Harris Theatre, 101
Hamlet (p) (Sothern-Marlowe), 10/29/23, Jolson Theatre, 7
Hamlet (p) (Sir John Martin-Harvey), 11/19/23, Century Theatre, 8
Hamlet (p) (John Barrymore), 11/26/23, Manhattan Opera House, 24
Hamlet (p) (Walter Hampden), 10/10/25, Hampden Theatre, 68
Hamlet (p) (Basil Sydney), 11/9/25, Booth Theatre, 88
Hamlet (p), 1/4/28, Hampden Theatre, 13
Hamlet (p) (Fritz Leiber), 3/24/30, Shubert Theatre, 5
Hamlet (p), 12/26/30, Ambassador Theatre, 5
Hamlet (p) (Raymond Massey), 11/5/31, Broadhurst Theatre, 28
Hamlet (p) (Fritz Leiber), 11/18/31, Royale Theatre, 6
Hamlet (p) (Ian Maclaren), 12/22/32, Shakespeare Theatre, 24
Hamlet (p) (Walter Hampden), 12/25/34, 44th St. Theatre, 10
Hamlet (p) (John Gielgud), 10/8/36, Empire Theatre, 132
Hamlet (p) (Leslie Howard), 11/10/36, Imperial Theatre, 39
Hamlet (p) (Maurice Evans), 10/12/38, St. James Theatre, 96
Hamlet (p) (Maurice Evans), 12/4/39, 44th St. Theatre, 40
Hamlet (p) (Maurice Evans), 12/13/45, Columbus Circle Theatre, 131
Hamlet (p) (Maurice Evans), 6/4/46, New York City Center, 16
Hamlet (p) (Donald Wolfit), 2/26/47, Century Theatre, 2
Hamlet (p) (Jean-Louis Barrault), 12/1/52, Ziegfeld Theatre, 8
Hamlet (p), 10/27/56, Shakespearewrights Theatre, 75
Hamlet (p), 1/28/57, Theatre de Lys, 2
Hamlet (p) (Old Vic Company), 12/16/58, Broadway Theatre, 14
Hamlet (p) (Donald Madden), 3/16/61, Phoenix Theatre, 102
Hamlet (p) (Richard Burton), 4/9/64, Lunt-Fontanne Theatre, 137
Hamlet (p) (Alfred Ryder, Robert Burr), 6/16/64, Delacorte Theatre, 18
Hamlet (p), 2/16/67, New York City Center, 9, (Bristol Old Vic)
Hamlet (p), 12/26/67, Public Theatre, 56
Hamlet (p), 6/25/68, New York Shakespeare Festival Mobile Theatre
Hamlet (p), 3/3/69, Lyceum Theatre, 45, (APA-Phoenix)
Hamlet (p) (Nicol Williamson), 5/1/69, Lunt-Fontanne Theatre, 50
Hamlet (p), 12/26/70, Hunter College Playhouse, 7
Hamlet (p), 9/10/70, CSC Repertory Theatre, 18
Hamlet (p), 10/18/70, Roundabout Theatre, 37
Hamlet (p), 1/14/71, Carnegie Hall, 2
Hamlet (p), 12/4/72, Town Hall, 16, (Roundabout Theatre Co.)
Hamlet of Stepney Green (m), 11/13/58, Cricket Theatre, 165
Hamlet (Stacy Keach) (p), 6/28/72, Delacorte Theatre, 20
Hammerstein's 9 O'Clock Revue (r), 10/4/23, Century Roof, 12
Hamp (p), 3/9/67, Renata Theatre, 101
Han's Crime / The Damask Drum / Sotoba Komachi (p) (Three Modern Japanese Plays), 2/3/61, Players' Theatre, 45
Hanako, Madame. See Madame Hanako
Hand in Glove (p), 12/4/44, Playhouse, 40
Hand Is on the Gate, A, 9/21/66, Longacre Theatre, 20
Hand of the Potter, The (p), 12/5/21, Provincetown Playhouse, 21
Handful of Fire (p), 10/1/58, Martin Beck Theatre, 5
Hands Up (m), 7/22/15, 44th St. Theatre, 52
Handy Man, The (p), 3/9/25, 39th St. Theatre, 48
Hang Down Your Head and Die (r), 10/18/64, Mayfair Theatre, 1
Hangman's House (p), 12/16/26, Forrest Theatre, 4
Hangman's Whip (p), 2/24/33, St. James Theatre, 11
Hanky Panky (m), 8/5/12, Broadway Theatre, 104
Hanky Panky Land (r), 12/26/21, Century Roof, 10
Hannele / The Green Cockatoo (p), 4/11/10, Lyceum Theatre, 16
Hans the Flute Player (m), 9/20/10, Manhattan Opera House, 79
Happiest Days, The (p), 4/11/39, Vanderbilt Theatre, 7
Happiest Girl in the World, The (m), 4/3/61, Martin Beck Theatre, 96
Happiest Millionaire, The (p), 11/20/56, Lyceum Theatre, 271
Happiest Night of His Life, The (p), 2/20/11, Criterion Theatre, 24
Happiest Years, The (p), 4/25/49, Lyceum Theatre, 8
Happily Ever After (p), 3/15/45, Biltmore Theatre, 12
Happily Never After (p), 3/10/66, Eugene O'Neill Theatre, 4
Happiness (p), 12/31/17, Criterion Theatre, 136
Happiness Cage, The (p), 10/4/70, Public/Newman Theatre, 32
Happiness Is Just a Little Thing Called a Rolls Royce (p), 5/11/68, Ethel Barrymore Theatre, 1
Happiness / The Day of Dupes / Just As Well / The Forbidden Guests (p), 3/6/14, Cort Theatre, 5
Happiness / Walking to Waldheim (p), 11/10/67, Forum Theatre, 43
Happy (m), 12/5/27, Earl Carroll Theatre, 82
Happy as Larry (p), 1/6/50, Coronet Theatre, 3
Happy as Larry (p), 4/25/61, Martinique Theatre, 7
Happy Birthday (m), 10/31/46, Broadhurst Theatre, 564
Happy Birthday, Wanda June (p), 10/7/70, Theatre de Lys, 143
Happy Days (p), 10/12/68, Billy Rose Theatre, 4, (Theatre 1969 Playwrights Repertory)

Happy Days (r), 8/23/19, New York Hippodrome, 452
Happy Days (p), 9/14/65, Cherry Lane Theatre, 14, (Renaud-Barrault)
Happy Days / Act without Words I (p), 11/20/72, Forum Theatre, 16
Happy Days, The (p), 5/13/41, Henry Miller's Theatre, 23
Happy Days / The Death of Bessie Smith / The American Dream (p), 9/17/61, Cherry Lane Theatre, 29
Happy Days (White-Becher) (p), 9/28/65, Cherry Lane Theatre, 16
Happy Ending, The (p), 8/21/16, Shubert Theatre, 16
Happy Ending, The / Day of Absence (p), 11/15/65, St. Marks Playhouse, 540
Happy Faculty, The (p), 4/18/67, Blackfriars' Guild, 34
Happy Hunting (m), 12/6/56, Majestic Theatre, 412
Happy Husband, The (p), 5/7/28, Empire Theatre, 72
Happy Hypocrite, The (m), 9/5/68, Bouwerie Lane Theatre, 17
Happy Journey to Trenton and Camden. See Thornton Wilder's Triple Bill
Happy Journey to Trenton and Camden, The / The Respectful Prostitute (p), 2/9/48, Cort Theatre, 318
Happy Landing (p), 3/26/32, 46th St. Theatre, 25
Happy Marriage, The (p), 4/12/09, Garrick Theatre, 24
Happy Time, The (p), 1/24/50, Plymouth Theatre, 614
Happy Time, The (m), 1/18/68, Broadway Theatre, 286
Happy Town (m), 10/7/59, 54th St. Theatre, 5
Happy-Go-Lucky (p), 8/24/20, Booth Theatre, 79
Happy-Go-Lucky (m), 9/30/26, Liberty Theatre, 52
Happyland (m), 10/2/05, Lyric Theatre, 82
Happyland (m), 3/12/06, Casino Theatre, 54
Harangues, The (p), 1/13/70, St. Marks Playhouse, 56
Harbor Lights (p), 10/4/56, Playhouse, 4
Hard Job Being God (m), 5/15/72, Edison Theatre, 6
Hard To Be a Jew (m), 10/28/73, Eden Theatre, 156
Harem, The (p), 12/2/24, Belasco Theatre, 183
Hark! (r), 5/22/72, Mercer-O'Casey Theatre, 152
Harlem (p), 2/20/29, Apollo Theatre, 94
Harlem (p), 10/21/29, Eltinge Theatre, 16
Harlem Cavalcade (r), 5/1/42, Ritz Theatre, 49
Harlequinade / Electra (p), 2/13/59, Rita Allen Theatre, 19
Harlequinade, The (p), 5/10/21, Neighborhood Playhouse, 25
Harlequinade, The / A Night at an Inn (p), 6/14/21, Punch and Judy Theatre, 15
Harlequinade, The / When Crummles Played / George Barnell (p), 10/1/28, Garrick Theatre, 40
Harmony. See Three at Judson
Harold (p), 11/29/62, Cort Theatre, 20
Harold Arlen Songbook, The (r), 2/28/67, Stage 73, 41
Harold Pinter's Sketches / The Local Stigmatic (p), 11/3/69, Actors Playhouse, 8
Harold/Sondra (p), 5/9/67, Provincetown Playhouse, 8
Harp of Life, The (p), 11/27/16, Globe Theatre, 136
Harriet (p), 3/3/43, Henry Miller's Theatre, 377
Harriet (p), 9/27/44, New York City Center, 11
Harriet's Honeymoon (p), 1/4/04, Garrick Theatre, 24
Harry Delmar's Revels (r), 11/28/27, Shubert Theatre, 114
Harry, Noon and Night (p), 3/17/65, St. Clement's Church, 16, (American Place Theatre)
Harry, Noon and Night (p), 5/5/65, Pocket Theatre, 6
Harvest (p), 9/19/25, Belmont Theatre, 17
Harvest Moon, The (p), 10/15/09, Garrick Theatre, 91
Harvest of Years (p), 1/12/48, Hudson Theatre, 16
Harvester, The (p), 10/10/04, Lyric Theatre, 32
Harvey (p), 11/1/44, 48th St. Theatre, 1,775
Harvey (p), 2/24/70, ANTA Theatre, 80
Harvey McLeod. See A Coney Island Cycle
Hassan (p), 9/22/24, Knickerbocker Theatre, 16
Hassard Short's Ritz Revue (r), 9/17/24, Ritz Theatre, 109
Hassard Short's Ritz Revue (r), 2/2/25, Winter Garden Theatre, 8
Hasty Heart, The (p), 1/3/45, Hudson Theatre, 204
Hasty Heart, The (p), 9/14/59, Orpheum Theatre, 24
Hat, a Coat, a Glove, A (p), 1/31/34, Selwyn Theatre, 14
Hatful of Rain, A (p), 11/9/55, Lyceum Theatre, 398
Hatful of Rain, A (p), 4/9/70, Master Theatre, 12, (Equity Library Theatre)
Hats Off to Ice, 6/22/44, Center Theatre, 890
Haunted Host, The (p), 10/27/69, Castle Theatre, 8
Haunted House, The (p), 9/2/24, George M. Cohan Theatre, 103
Havana (m), 2/11/09, Casino Theatre, 272
Have a Heart (m), 1/11/17, Liberty Theatre, 76
Have I Got a Girl for You! (p), 12/2/63, Music Box Theatre, 1
Have I Got One for You (m), 1/7/68, Theatre Four, 1
Haven, The (p), 11/13/46, Playhouse, 5
Having Wonderful Time (p), 2/20/37, Lyceum Theatre, 310
Havoc (r), 9/1/24, Maxine Elliott's Theatre, 48
Havoc, The (p), 1/9/11, Bijou Theatre, 72
Hawk Island (p), 9/16/29, Longacre Theatre, 24
Hawk, The (p), 9/28/14, Shubert Theatre, 136
Hawk, The (p), 4/17/68, Actors Playhouse, 15
Hawthorne of the U.S.A. (p), 11/4/12, Astor Theatre, 72
Hay Fever (p), 10/5/25, Maxine Elliott's Theatre, 49
Hay Fever (p), 12/29/31, Avon Theatre, 98
Hay Fever (p), 11/9/70, Helen Hayes Theatre, 24
Hayride (m), 9/13/54, 48th St. Theatre, 24
Hazel Flagg (m), 2/11/53, Mark Hellinger Theatre, 190
He (p), 9/21/31, Guild Theatre, 40
He and She (p), 2/12/20, Little Theatre, 28
He Came from Milwaukee (m), 9/21/10, Casino Theatre, 117
He Comes Up Smiling (p), 9/16/14, Liberty Theatre, 61
He Didn't Want to Do It (m), 8/20/18, Broadhurst Theatre, 23
He Is To Blame / Servant of Two Masters (p), 1/9/28, Cosmopolitan Theatre, 16
He Loved the Ladies (p), 5/10/27, Frolic Theatre, 7
He Says, She Says, They Say. See Festival of New Italian Plays
He Understood Women (p), 8/15/28, Belmont Theatre, 37
He Walked in Her Sleep (p), 4/4/29, Princess Theatre, 20
He Who Gets Slapped (p), 1/9/22, Garrick Theatre, 308
He Who Gets Slapped (p), 3/20/46, Booth Theatre, 46
He Who Gets Slapped (p), 1/20/56, Actors Playhouse, 79
He Who Gets Slapped (p), 11/17/67, Master Theatre, 9, (Equity Library Theatre)
Head First (p), 1/6/26, Greenwich Village Theatre, 5
Head or Tail (p), 11/9/26, Waldorf Theatre, 7
Head Over Heels (m), 8/29/18, Cohan Theatre, 100
Headquarters (p), 12/4/29, Forrest Theatre, 13
Heads or Tails (p), 5/2/47, Cort Theatre, 35
Heads Up (m), 11/11/29, Alvin Theatre, 144
Hear That Trumpet (p), 10/7/46, Playhouse, 8
Heart of a City (p), 2/12/42, Henry Miller's Theatre, 28
Heart of a Thief, The (p), 10/5/14, Hudson Theatre, 8
Heart of Wetona, The (p), 2/29/16, Lyceum Theatre, 95
Heartbreak House (p) (Albert Perry), 11/10/20, Garrick Theatre, 128
Heartbreak House (p), 4/29/38, Mercury Theatre, 48
Heartbreak House (p) (Maurice Evans), 10/18/59, Billy Rose Theatre, 112
Hearts Aflame (p), 5/12/02, Garrick Theatre, 8
Hearts Aflame (p), 9/8/02, Bijou Theatre, 48
Hearts Are Trumps (p), 2/21/00, Garden Theatre, 93
Hearts Are Trumps (p), 4/7/27, Morosco Theatre, 20
Hearts Courageous (p), 10/5/03, Broadway Theatre, 24
Heat Lightning (p), 9/15/33, Booth Theatre, 43
Heat Wave (p), 2/17/31, Fulton Theatre, 15
Heathen! (m), 5/21/72, Billy Rose Theatre, 1
Heather Field, The / A Troubadour (p), 4/19/00, Carnegie Lyceum Theatre, 1
Heaven and Hell's Agreement (p), 4/9/74, St. Marks Playhouse, 8
Heaven Grand in Amber Orbit (m), 10/9/69, Gotham Art Theatre
Heaven on Earth (m), 9/16/48, New Century Theatre, 12
Heaven Tappers, The (p), 3/8/27, Forrest Theatre, 9
Heavenly Express (p), 4/18/40, National Theatre, 20
Heavenly Twins, The (p), 11/4/55, Booth Theatre, 35
Heavy Traffic (p), 9/5/28, Empire Theatre, 61
Hedda Gabler (p) (Mrs. Fiske), 10/5/03, Manhattan Theatre, 8
Hedda Gabler (p) (Mrs. Fiske), 11/19/04, Manhattan Theatre, 24
Hedda Gabler (p) (Nance O'Neill), 11/24/04, Daly's Theatre, 4
Hedda Gabler (p) (Alla Nazimova), 11/13/06, Princess Theatre, 40
Hedda Gabler (p) (Alla Nazimova), 3/11/07, Bijou Theatre, 32
Hedda Gabler (p) (Alla Nazimova), 4/8/18, Plymouth Theatre, 24
Hedda Gabler (p), 10/4/20, Little Theatre, 4
Hedda Gabler (p), 3/6/24, Vanderbilt Theatre, 1
Hedda Gabler (p), 5/16/24, 48th St. Theatre, 6
Hedda Gabler (p) (Emily Stevens), 1/26/26, Comedy Theatre, 59
Hedda Gabler (p) (Eva Le Gallienne), 3/26/28, Civic Repertory Theatre, 15
Hedda Gabler (p), 10/3/28, Civic Repertory Theatre, 11
Hedda Gabler (p) (Blanche Yurka), 2/2/29, 49th St. Theatre, 25
Hedda Gabler (p), 2/6/30, Civic Repertory Theatre, 3
Hedda Gabler (p), 12/6/30, Civic Repertory Theatre, 6
Hedda Gabler (p) (Eva Le Gallienne), 12/3/34, Broadhurst Theatre, 4
Hedda Gabler (p) (Mme. Nazimova), 11/16/36, Longacre Theatre, 32
Hedda Gabler (p) (Katina Paxinou), 2/29/42, Longacre Theatre, 12
Hedda Gabler (p) (Eva Le Gallienne), 2/24/48, Cort Theatre, 15
Hedda Gabler (p), 11/9/60, Fourth St. Theatre, 340
Hedda Gabler (p), 1/16/70, Actors Playhouse, 81
Hedda Gabler (p), 2/17/71, Playhouse Theatre, 56
Hedda Gabler (p), 2/14/74, Cubiculo Theatre, 15
Hedda Gabler (p), 3/23/74, Abbey Theatre, 20, (CSC Repertory)
Heeple Steeple, The (p), 11/10/49, Master Institute Theatre, 2
Heidelberg (p), 12/15/02, Princess Theatre, 40
Heigh-Ho, Everybody (p), 5/25/32, Fulton Theatre, 5
Heights, The (p), 1/31/10, Savoy Theatre, 16
Heir to the Hoorah, The (p), 4/10/05, Hudson Theatre, 59
Heir to the Hoorah, The (p), 9/3/06, Academy of Music, 24
Heiress, The (p), 9/29/47, Biltmore Theatre, 410
Heiress, The (p), 2/8/50, New York City Center, 16
Helen (p), 12/10/64, Bouwerie Lane Theatre, 22
Helen Goes to Troy (m), 4/24/44, Alvin Theatre, 96

Helen of Troy, New York, 6/19/23, Selwyn Theatre, 193
Helena Modjeska Repertory, 2/26/00, Fifth Avenue Theatre
Helena's Boys (p), 4/7/24, Henry Miller's Theatre, 40
Hell Freezes Over (p), 12/28/35, Ritz Theatre, 25
Hell's Balls (p), 1/26/25, Wallack Theatre, 139
Hell / Temptation / Gaby (r), 4/27/11, Folies Bergère Theatre, 92
Hell-Bent Fer Heaven (p), 12/30/23, Klaw Theatre, 128
Hello, Alexander (m), 10/7/19, 44th St. Theatre, 56
Hello and Goodbye (p), 11/11/68, Theatre de Lys, 2, (ANTA Matinee)
Hello and Goodbye (p), 9/18/69, Sheridan Square Playhouse, 45
Hello Broadway (m), 12/25/14, Astor Theatre, 123
Hello Charlie (m), 10/21/65, Yiddish Anderson Theatre
Hello, Daddy! (m), 12/26/28, Mansfield Theatre, 196
Hello, Dolly! (m), 1/16/64, St. James Theatre, 2,844
Hello, Dolly! (m), 11/12/67, St. James Theatre, 2,844
Hello, Lola (m), 1/12/26, Eltinge Theatre, 47
Hello, Out There / Magic (p), 9/29/42, Belasco Theatre, 47
Hello, Paris (r), 8/19/11, Folies Bergère Theatre, 30
Hello, Paris (m), 11/15/30, Shubert Theatre, 33
Hello, Paris / A la Broadway (r), 9/22/11, Folies Bergère Theatre, 8
Hello, Solly (r), 4/4/67, Henry Miller' s Theatre, 68
Hello Yourself (m), 10/30/28, Casino Theatre, 87
Hellzapoppin (r), 9/22/38, 46th St. Theatre, 1,404
Helmet of Navarre, The (p), 12/2/01, Criterion Theatre, 24
Heloise (p), 9/24/58, Gate Theatre, 256
Heloise (p), 2/4/71, Master Theatre, 14, (Equity Library Theatre)
Help Stamp Out Marriage! (p), 9/29/66, Booth Theatre, 20
Help Wanted (p), 2/11/14, Maxine Elliott's Theatre, 92
Help Yourself (p), 7/14/36, Manhattan Theatre, 82
Hen-Pecks, The (m), 2/4/11, Broadway Theatre, 137
Henri Christophe (p), 6/6/45, Library Theatre, Harlem, 25
Henry—Behave (p), 8/23/26, Nora Bayes Theatre, 96
Henry E. Dixey Repertory, 10/17/04, Berkeley Lyceum Theatre, 8
Henry Irving Repertory, 11/9/03, Broadway Theatre, 8
Henry Irving-Ellen Terry Repertory, 11/21/01, Knickerbocker Theatre, 16
Henry IV (p) (Maurice Evans), 1/30/39, St. James Theatre, 74
Henry IV, Part 1 (p), 5/31/26, Knickerbocker Theatre, 8
Henry IV, Part 1 (p), 5/6/46, Century Theatre, 14
Henry IV, Part 1 (p) (Thayer David), 9/21/55, New York City Center, 15
Henry IV, Part 1 (p) (Fritz Weaver), 3/1/60, Phoenix Theatre, 48
Henry IV, Part 1 (p) (Fritz Weaver), 5/7/60, Phoenix Theatre, 17
Henry IV, Part 2 (p), 5/13/46, Century Theatre, 6
Henry IV, Part 2 (p) (Fritz Weaver), 4/18/60, Phoenix Theatre, 31
Henry IV (Pirandello) (p), 12/10/47, Cherry Lane Theatre
Henry Ludlowe Repertory, 2/17/08, Bijou Theatre, 16
Henry of Navarre (p), 11/28/10, Knickerbocker Theatre, 24
Henry's Harem (p), 9/13/26, Greenwich Village Theatre, 8
Henry, Sweet Henry (m), 10/23/67, Palace Theatre, 80
Henry V (p) (Richard Mansfield), 10/3/00, Garden Theatre, 54
Henry V (p) (Lewis Waller), 9/30/12, Daly's Theatre, 16
Henry V (p) (Old Vic Company), 12/25/58, Broadway Theatre, 11
Henry VIII (p) (Herbert Tree-Lyn Harding), 3/14/16, New Amsterdam Theatre, 63
Henry VIII (p), 11/6/46, International Theatre, 40
Her Cardboard Lover (p), 3/21/27, Empire Theatre, 152
Her Country (p), 2/21/18, Punch and Judy Theatre, 76
Her Family Tree (m), 12/27/20, Lyric Theatre, 90
Her First Affaire (p), 8/22/27, Nora Bayes Theatre, 138
Her First Divorce (p), 5/5/13, Comedy Theatre, 8
Her First Roman (m), 10/20/68, Lunt-Fontanne Theatre, 17
Her Friend the King (p), 10/7/29, Longacre Theatre, 24
Her Great Match (p), 9/4/05, Criterion Theatre, 93
Her Honor, The Mayor / The Good Men Do (p), 5/20/18, Fulton Theatre, 16
Her Husband's Wife (p), 5/9/10, Garrick Theatre, 48
Her Husband's Wife (p), 1/8/17, Lyceum Theatre, 32
Her Little Highness (m), 10/13/13, Liberty Theatre, 16
Her Lord and Master (p), 2/24/02, Manhattan Theatre, 69
Her Majesty, the Girl Queen of Nordenmark (p), 10/15/00, Manhattan Theatre, 58
Her Majesty, the Widow (p), 6/18/34, Ritz Theatre, 32
Her Man of Wax (p), 10/11/33, Sam S. Shubert Theatre, 14
Her Master's Voice (p), 10/23/33, Plymouth Theatre, 220
Her Master's Voice (p), 12/26/64, 41st St. Theatre, 18
Her Own Money (p), 9/1/13, Comedy Theatre, 55
Her Own Way (p), 9/28/03, Garrick Theatre, 107
Her Regiment (m), 11/12/17, Broadhurst Theatre, 40
Her Salary Man (p), 11/28/21, Cort Theatre, 32
Her Sister (p), 12/25/07, Hudson Theatre, 61
Her Soldier Boy (m), 12/6/16, Astor Theatre, 198
Her Supporting Cast (p), 5/4/31, Biltmore Theatre, 32
Her Temporary Husband (p), 8/31/22, Frazee Theatre, 95
Her Tin Soldier (p), 4/6/33, Playhouse, 2
Her Unborn Child (p), 3/5/28, Eltinge Theatre, 52
Her Unborn Child (p), 6/11/28, 48th St. Theatre, 24
Her Way Out (p), 6/23/24, Gaiety Theatre, 24
Here Are Ladies, 2/22/71, Public/Newman Theatre, 67
Here Are Ladies, 3/29/73, Circle in the Square/Joseph E. Levine Theatre, 47
Here Be Dragons / A Knack with Horses (p), 12/5/70, St. Clement's Church
Here Come the Clowns (p), 12/7/38, Booth Theatre, 88
Here Come the Clowns (p), 9/19/60, Actors Playhouse, 72
Here Come the Clowns (p), 5/13/66, Master Theatre, 9, (Equity Library Theatre)
Here Comes the Bride (p), 9/25/17, Cohan Theatre, 63
Here Comes the Groom (m), 10/8/73, Mayfair Theatre, 202
Here Goes the Bride (m), 11/3/31, Chanin's 46th St. Theatre, 7
Here's Howe (m), 5/1/28, Broadhurst Theatre, 71
Here's Josephine Premice!, 4/25/66, East 74th St. Theatre, 2
Here's Love (m), 10/3/63, Shubert Theatre, 334
Here's Where I Belong (m), 3/3/68, Billy Rose Theatre, 1
Here Today (p), 9/6/32, Ethel Barrymore Theatre, 39
Heritage (p), 1/25/71, Theatre de Lys, 2, (ANTA Matinee)
Heritage, The (p), 1/14/18, Playhouse, 16
Hero Is Born, A (m), 10/1/37, Adelphi Theatre, 50
Hero, The (p), 3/14/21, Longacre Theatre, 4
Hero, The (p), 9/5/21, Belmont Theatre, 80
Hero, The. See Playwrights Cooperative Festival
Herod (p), 10/26/09, Lyric Theatre, 31
Heroes, The / Red Riding Hood (p), 5/18/52, Comedy Club
Heroes, The / Ubu Roi (p), 8/5/52, Cherry Lane Theatre
Heroine, The (p), 2/19/63, Lyceum Theatre, 23
Hey Nonny Nonny! (r), 6/6/32, Shubert Theatre, 38
Hey You, Light Man! (p), 3/1/63, Mayfair Theatre, 52
Hi, Paisano! (m), 9/30/61, York Playhouse, 3
Hickory Stick (p), 5/8/44, Mansfield Theatre, 8
Hidden (p), 10/4/27, Lyceum Theatre, 80
Hidden Horizon (p), 9/19/46, Plymouth Theatre, 12
Hidden River, The (p), 1/23/57, Playhouse, 61
Hidden Stranger (p), 1/8/63, Longacre Theatre, 7
Hide and Seek (p), 4/2/57, Ethel Barrymore Theatre, 7
Higgledy-Piggledy (r), 10/20/04, Weber Music Hall, 185
Higgledy-Piggledy (r), 8/26/05, Weber Musical Hall, 17
High Button Shoes (m), 10/9/47, Century Theatre, 727
High Cost of Loving, The (p), 8/25/14, Republic Theatre, 75
High Gear (p), 10/6/27, Wallack Theatre, 20
High Ground, The (p), 2/20/51, 48th St. Theatre, 23
High Hatters, The (p), 5/10/28, Klaw Theatre, 10
High Jinks (m), 12/10/13, Lyric Theatre, 213
High Kickers (m), 10/31/41, Broadhurst Theatre, 171
High Named Today (p), 12/10/54, Theatre de Lys, 13
High Road, The (p), 11/19/12, Hudson Theatre, 71
High Road, The (p), 9/10/28, Fulton Theatre, 144
High Spirits (m), 4/7/64, Alvin Theatre, 376
High Stakes (p), 9/9/24, Hudson Theatre, 120
High Tor (p), 1/8/37, Martin Beck Theatre, 171
Higher and Higher (m), 4/4/40, Shubert Theatre, 84
Higher and Higher (m), 8/5/40, Shubert Theatre, 24
Highest Tree, The (p), 11/4/59, Longacre Theatre, 21
Highland Fling, A (p), 4/28/44, Plymouth Theatre, 27
Highlights of the Empire, 5/24/53, Empire Theatre
Highway of Life, The (p), 10/26/14, Wallack Theatre, 24
Highwayman, The (m), 5/2/17, 44th St. Theatre, 22
Hilarities (r), 9/9/48, Adelphi Theatre, 14
Hilda Cassidy (p), 5/4/33, Martin Beck Theatre, 4
Hilda Crane (p), 11/1/50, Coronet Theatre, 70
Hill Between, The (p), 3/11/38, Little Theatre, 11
Him (p), 4/18/28, Provincetown Playhouse, 21
him (p), 4/14/74, Circle Repertory Theatre, 19
Hindle Wakes (p), 12/9/12, Maxine Elliott's Theatre, 32
Hindu, The (p), 3/21/22, Comedy Theatre, 71
Hip! Hip! Hooray! (r), 10/10/07, Weber's Theatre, 64
Hip-Hip-Hooray (r), 9/30/15, New York Hippodrome, 425
Hipper's Holiday (p), 10/18/34, Maxine Elliott's Theatre, 4
Hippolytus (p), 11/20/48, Lenox Hill Playhouse, 4
Hippolytus (p), 11/19/68, Felt Forum, 8, (Piraikon Theatron)
Hippy As a Lark. See Playwrights Cooperative Festival
Hired Husband (p), 6/3/32, Bijou Theatre, 19
His and Hers (p), 1/7/54, 48th St. Theatre, 77
His Bridal Night (p), 8/16/16, Republic Theatre, 77
His Chinese Wife (p), 5/17/20, Belmont Theatre, 16
His Excellency the Governor (p), 10/20/02, Garrick Theatre, 16
His Excellency the Governor (p), 4/4/07, Empire Theatre, 36
His First Step Part 1. See The Corner
His Honor, Abe Potash (p), 10/14/19, Bijou Theatre, 215
His Honor, the Barber (m), 5/8/11, Majestic Theatre, 16
His Honor, the Mayor (m) (Blanche Ring), 5/28/06, New York Theatre, 104
His Honor, the Mayor (m) (Claire Maentz), 9/17/06, Wallack Theatre, 16

His Honor, the Mayor (m) (Claire Maentz), 6/3/07, Wallack Theatre, 16
His Honor, the Mayor (p), 11/25/07, Circle Theatre, 17
His House in Order (p), 9/3/06, Empire Theatre, 127
His Little Widows (m), 4/30/17, Astor Theatre, 72
His Majesty (m), 3/19/06, Majestic Theatre, 24
His Majesty Bunker Bean (p), 10/2/16, Astor Theatre, 72
His Majesty's Car (p), 10/23/30, Ethel Barrymore Theatre, 12
His Name on the Door (p), 11/22/09, Bijou Theatre, 16
His Queen (p), 5/11/25, Hudson Theatre, 11
His Wife by His Side (p), 12/30/12, Berkeley Theatre, 16
His Wife's Family (p), 10/6/08, Wallack Theatre, 15
Hit the Deck (m), 4/25/27, Belasco Theatre, 352
Hit the Trail (m), 12/2/54, Mark Hellinger Theatre, 4
Hitch Your Wagon (p), 4/8/37, 48th St. Theatre, 28
Hitchy-Koo (r), 6/7/17, Cohan and Harris Theatre, 220
Hitchy-Koo of 1918 (r), 6/6/18, Globe Theatre, 68
Hitchy-Koo of 1919 (r), 10/6/19, Liberty Theatre, 56
Hitchy-Koo of 1920 (r), 10/19/20, New Amsterdam Theatre, 71
Hit-the-Trail Holiday (p), 9/13/15, Astor Theatre, 336
H.M.S. Pinafore (m), 5/29/11, Casino Theatre, 48
H.M.S. Pinafore (m), 6/27/12, Casino Theatre, 2
H.M.S. Pinafore (m), 5/5/13, Casino Theatre, 8
H.M.S. Pinafore (m), 4/9/14, New York Hippodrome, 89
H.M.S. Pinafore (m), 4/6/26, Century Theatre, 56
H.M.S. Pinafore (m), 5/18/31, Erlanger Theatre, 16
H.M.S. Pinafore (m), 3/3/60, Jan Hus House
H.M.S. Pinafore (m), 9/7/60, Phoenix Theatre, 55
H.M.S. Pinafore (m), 6/8/61, Greenwich Mews Theatre, 12
H.M.S. Pinafore (m), 11/13/62, New York City Center, 32
H.M.S. Pinafore (m), 3/20/64, New York City Center, 5
H.M.S. Pinafore (m), 5/20/65, Jan Hus House, 70, (American Savoyards)
H.M.S. Pinafore (m), 11/23/66, New York City Center, 8, (D'Oyly Carte Opera Co.)
H.M.S. Pinafore (m), 10/31/67, Jan Hus Playhouse, 16, (American Savoyards)
H.M.S. Pinafore (m), 4/27/68, New York City Center, 8
H.M.S. Pinafore (m), 10/29/68, New York City Center, 4, (D'Oyly Carte Opera Co.)
H.M.S. Pinafore / Cox and Box (m), 9/28/36, Martin Beck Theatre, 16
H.M.S. Pinafore / Cox and Box (m) (D'Oyly Carte Opera Co.), 1/19/48, Century Theatre, 16
H.M.S. Pinafore / Cox and Box (m), 2/23/48, Century Theatre, 1
H.M.S. Pinafore. See American Savoyards, 4/30/57, Shakespearewrights Theatre, 8
H.M.S. Pinafore. See Gilbert and Sullivan Rep., 10/4/49, Mark Hellinger Theatre, 23
H.M.S. Pinafore / The Green Table (m), 1/21/42, St. James Theatre, 18
H.M.S. Pinafore / Trial by Jury (m), 7/27/31, Erlanger Theatre, 16
H.M.S. Pinafore / Trial by Jury (m), 5/8/33, St. James Theatre, 16
H.M.S. Pinafore / Trial by Jury (m), 4/16/34, Majestic Theatre, 16
H.M.S. Pinafore / Trial by Jury (m), 9/13/34, Martin Beck Theatre, 15
H.M.S. Pinafore / Trial by Jury (m), 8/12/35, Adelphi Theatre, 12
H.M.S. Pinafore / Trial by Jury (m), 4/27/36, Majestic Theatre, 16
H.M.S. Pinafore / Trial by Jury (m), 2/14/44, Ambassador Theatre, 7
H.M.S. Pinafore / Trial by Jury (m), 10/17/55, Shubert Theatre, 13
H.M.S. Pinafore / Trial by Jury (m), 11/19/64, New York City Center, 10, (D'Oyly Carte Opera Co.)
H.M.S. Pinafore / Trial by Jury (m), 6/7/66, Jan Hus Playhouse, 28, (American Savoyards)
Hobo (p), 2/11/31, Morosco Theatre, 5
Hobo (m), 4/10/61, Gate Theatre, 32
Hobohemia (p), 2/8/19, Greenwich Village Theatre, 89
Hoboken Blues (p), 2/17/28, New Playwrights Theatre, 16
Hobson's Choice (p), 11/2/15, Princess Theatre, 135
Hodge, Podge & Co. (m), 10/23/00, Madison Square Theatre, 73
Hogan's Goat (p), 11/11/65, American Place Theatre, 607
Hoity Toity (r), 9/5/01, Weber and Fields Music Hall, 225
Hokey-Pokey / Bunty, Bulls and Strings (r), 2/8/12, Broadway Theatre, 108
Hold Everything (m), 10/10/28, Broadhurst Theatre, 413
Hold It! (m), 5/5/48, National Theatre, 46
Hold on to Your Hats (m), 9/11/40, Shubert Theatre, 158
Hold Your Horses (m), 9/25/33, Winter Garden Theatre, 88
Hole in the Head, A (p), 2/28/57, Plymouth Theatre, 156
Hole in the Wall, The (p), 3/26/20, Punch and Judy Theatre, 73
Holiday (p), 11/26/28, Plymouth Theatre, 230
Holiday (p), 12/26/73, Ethel Barrymore Theatre, 28, (New Phoenix Repertory Co.)
Holiday for Lovers (p), 2/14/57, Longacre Theatre, 100
Holka Polka (m), 10/14/25, Lyric Theatre, 21
Hollow Crown, The (p), 1/29/63, Henry Miller's Theatre, 46
Hollow Crown, The, 4/18/74, Brooklyn Academy of Music, 7, (Royal Shakespeare Co.)
Hollywood Pinafore (m), 5/31/45, Alvin Theatre, 52
Holmses of Baker Street, The (p), 12/9/36, Masque Theatre, 54
Holy Terror, A (p), 9/28/25, George M. Cohan Theatre, 32
Homage to Shakespeare, 3/15/64, Philharmonic Hall, Lincoln Center
Home (p), 11/17/70, Morosco Theatre, 110
Home Again (p), 11/11/18, Playhouse, 40
Home Away From, A (p), 4/28/69, Village South Theatre, 8
Home Fires (p), 8/20/23, 39th St. Theatre, 48
Home Fires. See Cop-Out
Home Folks (p), 12/26/04, New York Theatre, 34
Home Free! / Balls / Up to Thursday (p) (New Playwrights Series, Evening I), 2/10/65, Cherry Lane Theatre, 23
Home Is the Hero (p), 9/22/54, Booth Theatre, 30
Home Is the Hunter (p), 12/20/45, ANT Playhouse, Harlem, 18
Home Life of a Buffalo / Hope Is the Thing with Feathers / Gone Tomorrow. See Hope's the Thing, 5/11/48, Playhouse, 7
Home Movies (m), 5/11/64, Provincetown Playhouse, 72
Home of the Brave (p), 12/27/45, Belasco Theatre, 69
Home Towners, The (p), 8/23/26, Hudson Theatre, 64
Homecoming, The (p), 1/5/67, Music Box Theatre, 324
Homecoming, The (p), 5/18/71, Bijou Theatre, 32
Homecoming, The (p), 9/7/72, CSC Repertory Theatre
Homecoming, The (p), 12/5/73, Abbey Theatre, 21, (CSC Repertory)
Homme qui Assassin, L' (p), 11/10/24, Jolson Theatre, 24
Homo / The Queen of Greece (p), 4/11/69, La Mama Experimental Theatre Club
Hon. John Grigsby (p), 1/28/02, Manhattan Theatre, 27
Honest Jim Blunt (p), 9/16/12, Hudson Theatre, 16
Honest Liars (p), 7/19/26, Sam H. Harris Theatre, 97
Honest-to-God Schnozzola, The (The Honest-to-God Schnozzola / Leader) (p), 4/21/69, Gramercy Arts Theatre, 8
Honey Girl (m), 5/3/20, Cohan and Harris Theatre, 142
Honeydew (m), 9/6/20, Casino Theatre, 200
Honeydew (m), 5/16/21, Casino Theatre, 49
Honeymoon (p), 12/23/32, Little Theatre, 73
Honeymoon Express, The (m), 2/6/13, Winter Garden Theatre, 156
Honeymoon Lane (m), 9/20/26, Knickerbocker Theatre, 353
Honeymoon, The (p), 2/24/13, Lyceum Theatre, 1
Honeymooners, The (m), 6/3/07, Aerial Gardens, 72
Honeymooning (p), 3/17/27, Bijou Theatre, 20
Honeys, The (p), 4/28/55, Longacre Theatre, 36
Honor Be Damned (p), 1/26/27, Morosco Theatre, 45
Honor Code, The (p), 5/18/31, Vanderbilt Theatre, 16
Honor of the Family, The (p), 2/17/08, Hudson Theatre, 104
Honor of the Family, The (p), 3/17/19, Globe Theatre, 56
Honor of the Family, The (p), 12/25/26, Booth Theatre, 33
Honor. See Playwrights Cooperative Festival
Honors Are Even (p), 8/10/21, Times Theatre, 70
Hoofers, The (r), 7/29/69, Mercury Theatre, 88
Hook 'n' Ladder (p), 4/29/52, Royale Theatre, 1
Hook-Up, The (p), 5/8/35, Cort Theatre, 21
Hooray for What! (m), 12/1/37, Winter Garden Theatre, 199
Hooray! It's a Glorious Day. . .And All That (m), 3/9/66, Theatre Four, 15
Hop o' My Thumb (p), 11/26/13, Manhattan Opera House, 46
Hop, Signor! (p), 5/7/62, Cricket Theatre, 8
Hope for a Harvest (p), 11/26/41, Guild Theatre, 38
Hope for the Best (p), 2/7/45, Fulton Theatre, 117
Hope Is the Thing with Feathers / Celebration / Afternoon Storm. See Six O'Clock Theatre, 4/11/48, Maxine Elliott's Theatre, 8
Hope Is the Thing with Feathers / Gone Tomorrow / Home Life of a Buffalo. See Hope's the Thing, 5/11/48, Playhouse, 7
Hope's the Thing (p) (Gone Tomorrow / Home Life of a Buffalo / Hope Is the Thing with Feathers), 5/11/48, Playhouse Theatre, 7
Horse Eats Hat (p), 9/22/36, Maxine Elliott's Theatre, 61
Horse Fever (p), 11/23/40, Mansfield Theatre, 25
Horseman, Pass By (m), 1/15/69, Fortune Theatre, 39
Horses in Midstream (p), 4/2/53, Royale Theatre, 4
Hospitality (p), 11/13/22, 48th St. Theatre, 46
Hostage, The (p), 9/20/60, Cort Theatre, 127
Hostage, The (p), 12/12/61, One Sheridan Square, 545
Hostage, The (p), 3/24/67, Master Theatre, 9, (Equity Library Theatre)
Hostage, The (p), 10/10/72, Good Shepherd-Faith Church, 7, (City Center Acting Co.)
Hostile Witness (p), 2/17/66, Music Box Theatre, 157
Hot and Cold Heros (r), 5/9/73, 13th St. Theatre, 16
Hot Chocolates (r), 6/20/29, Hudson Theatre, 228
Hot Corner, The (p), 1/25/56, Golden Theatre, 5
Hot Feet (r), 12/19/70, Hunter College Playhouse, 10, (Paper Bag Players)
Hot Feet (r), 2/12/72, Brooklyn Academy of Music, 12
Hot Ice (p), 2/7/74, Evergreen Theatre, 71
Hot l Baltimore, The (p), 3/22/73, Circle in the Square, 499
Hot Mikado, The (m), 3/23/39, Broadhurst Theatre, 85
Hot Money (p), 11/7/31, George M. Cohan Theatre, 9
Hot Pan (p), 2/15/28, Provincetown Playhouse, 28
Hot Rhythm (r), 8/21/30, Times Square Theatre, 68
Hot Spot (m), 4/19/63, Majestic Theatre, 43
Hot Water (p), 1/21/29, Lucille La Verne Theatre, 32

Hotbed (p), 11/8/28, Klaw Theatre, 19
Hot-Cha! (m), 3/8/32, Ziegfeld Theatre, 118
Hotel Alimony (p), 1/29/34, Royale Theatre, 16
Hotel Mouse, The (m), 3/13/22, Shubert Theatre, 88
Hotel Paradiso (p), 4/11/57, Henry Miller's Theatre, 108
Hotel Passionato (m), 10/22/65, East 74th St. Theatre, 11
Hotel Universe (p), 4/14/30, Martin Beck Theatre, 81
Hothouse (p), 2/13/74, Circle Repertory Theatre, 6
Hottentot, The (p), 3/1/20, George M. Cohan Theatre, 113
Hour Glass, The / My Milliner's Bill / Marietta (p), 4/7/04, Garrick Theatre, 1
Hour Glass, The / The Land of Heart's Desire / Kathleen ni Houlihan (p), 2/21/05, Hudson Theatre, 1
Hour-Glass, The (p), 10/9/55, Broadway Congregational Church, 10
House Afire (p), 3/31/30, Little Theatre, 16
House Beautiful, The (p), 3/12/31, Apollo Theatre, 108
House Divided, The (p), 11/11/23, Punch and Judy Theatre, 1
House in Paris, The (p), 3/20/44, Fulton Theatre, 16
House in the Country, A (p), 1/11/37, Vanderbilt Theatre, 32
House Next Door, The (p), 4/12/09, Gaiety Theatre, 88
House of a Thousand Candles, The (p), 1/6/08, Daly's Theatre, 14
House of Atreus, The (p), 12/17/68, Billy Rose Theatre, 11, (Minnesota Theatre Co.)
House of Bernarda Alba, The (p), 1/7/51, ANTA Playhouse, 16
House of Blue Leaves, The (p), 2/10/71, Truck and Warehouse Theatre, 337
House of Bondage, The (p), 1/19/14, Longacre Theatre, 8
House of Connelly, The (p), 9/28/31, Martin Beck Theatre, 72
House of Connelly, The (p), 12/25/31, Mansfield Theatre, 11
House of Doom, The (p), 1/25/32, Masque Theatre, 8
House of Dunkelmayer. See Four on a Garden
House of Fear, The (p), 10/7/29, Republic Theatre, 48
House of Flowers (m), 12/30/54, Alvin Theatre, 165
House of Flowers (m), 1/28/68, Theatre de Lys, 57
House of Fools (p), 3/19/72, Greenwich Mews Theatre
House of Glass, The (p), 9/1/15, Candler Theatre, 245
House of Leather, The (m), 3/18/70, Ellen Stewart Theatre, 1
House of Mirth (p), 10/22/06, Savoy Theatre, 14
House of Remsen, The (p), 4/2/34, Henry Miller's Theatre, 34
House of Shadows, The, 4/21/27, Longacre Theatre, 29
House of Silence, The (p), 1/23/06, Savoy Theatre, 7
House of Usher, The (p), 1/13/26, Fifth Avenue Theatre, 20
House of Usher, The (p), 6/7/26, 49th St. Theatre, 205
House of Women, The (p), 10/3/27, Maxine Elliott's Theatre, 40
House Party (p), 10/16/73, American Place Theatre, 42
House Possessed, A (p), 11/21/47, Henry Street Playhouse, 10
House That Jack Built, The (p), 12/24/00, Madison Square Theatre, 18
House Unguarded (p), 1/15/29, Little Theatre, 39
Houseboat on the Styx, The (p), 12/25/28, Liberty Theatre, 103
Houseparty (p), 9/9/29, Knickerbocker Theatre, 178
Houses of Sand (p), 2/17/25, Hudson Theatre, 31
Housewarming (p), 4/7/32, Charles Hopkins Theatre, 4
How a Nice Girl Named Janet Contracted Syphilis. See Three. . .with Women in Mind
How Beautiful with Shoes (p), 11/28/35, Booth Theatre, 8
How Come? (m), 4/16/23, Apollo Theatre, 40
How Come, Lawd? (p), 9/30/37, 49th St. Theatre, 2
How Do You Do— See Short Bullins
How He Lied to Her Husband / Arms and the Man (p), 5/14/06, Lyric Theatre, 16
How He Lied to Her Husband / MATES (p), 10/18/73, Lolly's Theatre Club
How He Lied to Her Husband / The Man of Destiny (p), 9/26/04, Berkeley Lyceum Theatre, 8
How I Wonder (p), 9/30/47, Hudson Theatre, 63
How Long Till Summer (p), 12/27/49, Playhouse, 7
How Much, How Much? (p), 4/20/70, Provincetown Playhouse, 24
How Now, Dow Jones (m), 12/7/67, Lunt-Fontanne Theatre, 221
How's the World Treating You? (p), 10/24/66, Music Box Theatre, 40
How's Your Health (p), 11/26/29, Vanderbilt Theatre, 46
How the Other Half Loves (p), 3/29/71, Royale Theatre, 104
How To Be a Jewish Mother (r), 12/28/67, Hudson Theatre, 21
How To Get Tough About It (p), 2/8/38, Martin Beck Theatre, 23
How To Make a Man (p), 2/2/61, Brooks Atkinson Theatre, 12
How To Steal an Election (m), 10/13/68, Pocket Theatre, 80
How To Succeed in Business without Really Trying (m), 10/14/61, 46th St. Theatre, 1,417
How To Succeed in Business without Really Trying (m), 4/20/66, New York City Center, 23
How To Succeed in Business without Really Trying (m), 11/9/72, Master Theatre, 19, (Equity Library Theatre)
Howdy, King (p), 12/13/26, Morosco Theatre, 48
Howdy Mr. Ice of 1950 (r), 5/26/49, Center Theatre, 430
Howdy, Mrs. Ice! (r), 6/24/48, Center Theatre, 406
Howdy Stranger (p), 1/14/37, Longacre Theatre, 77
Howie (p), 9/17/58, 46th St. Theatre, 5
Hoyden, The (m), 10/19/07, Knickerbocker Theatre, 58
Hubbies in Distress / Revue of the Classics, 4/12/21, Greenwich Village Theatre, 8
Hughie (p), 12/22/64, Royale Theatre, 51
Human Nature (p), 9/24/25, Liberty Theatre, 4
Humble, The (p), 10/13/26, Greenwich Village Theatre, 21
Humbug, The (p), 11/27/29, Ambassador Theatre, 13
Humming Bird, The (p), 1/15/23, Ritz Theatre, 40
Humming Sam (m), 4/8/33, New Yorker Theatre, 1
Humoresque (p), 2/27/23, Vanderbilt Theatre, 31
Humpty Dumpty (m), 11/14/04, New Amsterdam Theatre, 132
Humpty Dumpty (m), 3/19/06, New York Theatre
Humpty Dumpty (p), 9/16/18, Lyceum Theatre, 40
Hunchback, The (p), 6/2/02, Garrick Theatre, 4
Hundred Years Old, A (p), 10/1/29, Lyceum Theatre, 39
Hundredth Man, The (p), 2/8/13, Wallack Theatre, 1
Hunky Dory (p), 9/4/22, Klaw Theatre, 49
Hunter, The (p), 5/23/72, Public Theatre Annex, 64
Hunting the Jingo Bird / Lovey (p) (New Playwrights Series, Evening III), 3/25/65, Cherry Lane Theatre, 6
Hurdy-Gurdy Girl, The (m), 9/23/07, Wallack Theatre, 24
Hurricane (p), 12/25/23, Frolic Theatre, 125
Hurry, Harry (m), 10/12/72, Ritz Theatre, 2
Husband and Wife (p), 9/21/15, 48th St. Theatre, 15
Husbands of Leontine, The / Ib and Little Christina (p), 9/8/00, Madison Square Theatre, 29
Hush! (p), 10/3/16, Little Theatre, 39
Hush Money (p), 3/15/26, 49th St. Theatre, 56
Hut a Yid a Landele (r), 10/18/68, Barbizon-Plaza Theatre, 48
Huui, Huui (p), 11/16/68, Public Theatre, 51
Hyphen, The (p), 4/19/15, Knickerbocker Theatre, 16
Hypocrites, The (p), 8/30/06, Hudson Theatre, 209

I

I Am a Camera (p), 11/28/51, Empire Theatre, 262
I Am a Camera (p), 10/9/56, Actors Playhouse, 48
I Am a Woman, 1/9/74, Theatre in Space, 54
I Am My Youth (p), 3/7/38, Playhouse, 8
I Can Get It for You Wholesale (m), 3/22/62, Shubert Theatre, 300
I'd Rather Be Right (m), 11/2/37, Alvin Theatre, 289
I Do! I Do! (m), 12/5/66, 46th St. Theatre, 584
I Dreamt I Dwelt in Bloomingdale's (m), 2/12/70, Provincetown Playhouse, 6
I Feel Wonderful (r), 10/18/54, Theatre de Lys, 49
I Forgot / Marriage (p), 3/11/35, Majestic Theatre, 2
I Got Shoes (p), 1/23/63, Cricket Theatre, 21
I Gotta Get Out (p), 9/25/47, Cort Theatre, 4
I Had a Ball (m), 12/15/64, Martin Beck Theatre, 199
I Have Been Here Before (p), 10/13/38, Guild Theatre, 20
I Hear It Kissing Me Ladies. See Three. . .with Women in Mind
I Killed the Count (p), 8/31/42, Cort Theatre, 29
I Knock at the Door, 9/29/57, Belasco Theatre, 48
I Knock at the Door (p), 11/25/64, Theatre de Lys, 23
I Know My Love (p), 11/2/49, Shubert Theatre, 246
I Know What I Like (p), 11/24/39, Hudson Theatre, 11
I Like It Here (p), 3/22/46, John Golden Theatre, 52
I'll Be Hanged If I Do (p), 11/28/10, Comedy Theatre, 80
I'll Be Home for Christmas. See You Know I Can't Hear You When the Water's Running
I'll Say She Is (m), 5/19/24, Casino Theatre, 313
I'll Take the High Road (p), 11/9/43, Ritz Theatre, 7
I Love an Actress (p), 9/17/31, Times Square Theatre, 20
I Love Thee Freely (p), 9/17/73, Astor Place Theatre, 23
I Love You (p), 4/28/19, Booth Theatre, 56
I Loved You Wednesday (p), 10/11/32, Sam H. Harris Theatre, 63
I'm Chelsea, Fly Me (r), 3/20/73, Brooklyn Academy of Music, 16, (Chelsea Theatre Center)
I'm Herbert. See You Know I Can't Hear You When the Water's Running
I'm Solomon (m), 4/23/68, Mark Hellinger Theatre, 7
I Married an Angel (m), 5/11/38, Sam S. Shubert Theatre, 338
I Must Be Talking to My Friends, 11/16/67, Orpheum Theatre, 27
I Must Love Someone (p), 2/7/39, Longacre Theatre, 191
I, Myself (p), 5/9/34, Mansfield Theatre, 7
I Never Sang for My Father (p), 1/25/68, Longacre Theatre, 124
I Only Want an Answer (p), 2/5/68, Stage 73, 8
I Remember Mama (p), 10/19/44, Music Box Theatre, 714
I Rise in Flame, Cried the Phoenix / Sweet Confusion (p), 4/14/59, Theatre de Lys, 1
I Saw a Monkey. See Triple Play
I've Got Sixpence (p), 12/2/52, Ethel Barrymore Theatre, 23

I Want a Policeman (p), 1/14/36, Lyceum Theatre, 47
I Want My Wife (p), 3/20/30, Liberty Theatre, 12
I Want To Walk to San Francisco. See The Last Sweet Days of Isaac
I Want You (m), 9/14/61, Maidman Playhouse, 4
I Was Dancing (p), 11/8/64, Lyceum Theatre, 16
I Was Waiting for You (p), 11/13/33, Booth Theatre, 8
I Will If You Will (p), 8/29/22, Comedy Theatre, 15
Ib and Little Christina / The Husbands of Leontine (p), 9/8/00, Madison Square Theatre, 29
Icebound (p), 2/10/23, Sam H. Harris Theatre, 170
Iceman Cometh, The (p), 10/9/46, Martin Beck Theatre, 136
Iceman Cometh, The (p), 5/8/56, Circle in the Square, 565
Iceman Cometh, The (p), 12/13/73, Circle in the Square / Joseph E. Levine Theatre, 85
Icetime (r), 6/20/46, Center Theatre, 405
Icetime of 1948 (r), 5/28/47, Center Theatre, 422
Ideal Husband, An (p), 9/16/18, Comedy Theatre, 80
Ideal Husband, An (p), 4/27/24, Hudson Theatre, 1
Idiot King, The (p), 12/2/54, Living Theatre Studio
Idiot's Delight (p), 3/24/36, Shubert Theatre, 120
Idiot's Delight (p), 8/31/36, Shubert Theatre, 179
Idiot's Delight (p), 5/23/51, New York City Center, 15
Idiot's Delight (p), 4/25/74, Vandam Theatre
Idiot, The (p), 4/7/22, Little Theatre, 2
Idiot, The (p), 9/25/60, Gate Theatre, 41
Idle Inn, The (p), 12/20/21, Plymouth Theatre, 25
Idols (p), 11/1/09, Bijou Theatre, 16
If (p), 2/7/17, Fulton Theatre, 13
If (p), 10/25/27, Little Theatre, 23
If a Body (p), 4/30/35, Biltmore Theatre, 46
If Booth Had Missed (p), 2/4/32, Maxine Elliott's Theatre, 20
If Five Years Pass (p), 5/10/62, Stage 73, 22
If I Was Rich (p), 9/2/26, Mansfield Theatre, 92
If I Were King (p), 10/14/01, Garden Theatre, 56
If I Were King (p), 4/29/16, Shubert Theatre, 33
If I Were You (p), 9/23/31, Ambassador Theatre, 76
If I Were You (p), 1/24/38, Mansfield Theatre, 8
If in the Greenwood (p), 1/16/47, Blackfriars' Guild, 28
If Love Were All (p), 11/13/31, Booth Theatre, 11
If the Shoe Fits (m), 12/5/46, Century Theatre, 21
If This Be Treason (p), 9/23/35, Music Box Theatre, 40
If Winter Comes (p), 4/2/23, Gaiety Theatre, 40
Ikkaku Sennin (p), 11/15/64, IASTA Institute, 12
Ikke, Ikke, Nye, Nye, Nye. See The Family Continues
'Ile / The Maid of France / The Big Scene (p), 4/18/18, Greenwich Village Theatre, 52
Illusioniste, L' (p), 1/10/27, Chanin's 46th St. Theatre, 16
Illustrators' Show, The (r), 1/22/36, 48th St. Theatre, 5
Illya Darling (m), 4/11/67, Mark Hellinger Theatre, 319
Imaginary Invalid, The (p), 3/19/17, Liberty Theatre, 8
Imaginary Invalid, The (p), 5/1/67, ANTA Theatre, 6
Immaculate Misconception, The (p), 10/27/70, Cherry Lane Theatre, 1
Immodest Violet (p), 8/24/20, 48th St. Theatre, 1
Immoral Isabella? (p), 10/27/27, Bijou Theatre, 60
Immoralist, The (p), 2/8/54, Royale Theatre, 104
Immoralist, The (p), 11/7/63, Bouwerie Lane Theatre, 210
Immortal Husband, The (p), 2/14/55, Theatre de Lys, 48
Immortal Thief, The (p), 10/2/26, Hampden Theatre, 25
Immortal Thief, The (p), 10/28/26, Hampden Theatre, 1
Immovable Gordons, The / The Little Lady of Friday Night / The Man with the Tranquil Mind. See Dumbell People in a Barbell World, 2/14/62, Cricket Theatre, 13
Importance of Being Earnest, The (p), 4/14/02, Empire Theatre, 49
Importance of Being Earnest, The (p), 11/14/10, Lyceum Theatre, 48
Importance of Being Earnest, The (p), 1/20/21, Bramhall Playhouse, 45
Importance of Being Earnest, The (p), 5/3/26, Comedy Theatre, 64
Importance of Being Earnest, The (p), 1/12/39, Vanderbilt Theatre, 61
Importance of Being Earnest, The (p), 3/3/47, Royale Theatre, 81
Importance of Being Earnest, The (p), 2/25/63, Madison Avenue Playhouse, 164
Importance of Being Ernest, The (p), 6/19/68, Roundabout Theatre, 61
Importance of Being Ernest, The (p), 5/17/74, New York Arts Theatre
Importance of Being Oscar, The (p), 3/14/61, Lyceum Theatre, 31
Importance of Coming and Going, The (p), 4/1/15, Bramhall Playhouse, 28
Impossible Years, The (p), 10/13/65, Playhouse, 670
Impostor, The (p), 12/20/10, Garrick Theatre, 31
Impromptu at Versailles / Scapin (p), 3/9/64, Phoenix Theatre, 18
Improvisations in June (p), 2/26/28, Civic Repertory Theatre, 14
Improvisations in June (p), 11/10/28, Civic Repertory Theatre
Imprudence (p), 11/17/02, Empire Theatre, 66
Impudent Wolf, An (p), 11/19/65, Theatre'62, 13
In a Balcony / The Land of Heart's Desire (p), 10/26/00, Wallack Theatre, 1
In a Balcony / The Land of Heart's Desire (p), 5/6/01, Knickerbocker Theatre, 1
In a Garden (p), 11/16/25, Plymouth Theatre, 73
In a Garden, 9/7/48, Jan Hus House
In a Garden / Three Sisters Who Are Not Sisters / The Maids (p), 5/6/55, Tempo Playhouse, 63
In Abraham's Bosom (p), 12/30/26, Provincetown Playhouse, 200
In Abraham's Bosom (p), 9/6/27, Provincetown Playhouse, 77
In Any Language (p), 10/7/52, Cort Theatre, 45
In April Once (p), 3/13/55, Broadway Tabernacle Church, 9
In Bed We Cry (p), 11/14/44, Belasco Theatre, 47
In Case of Accident (p), 3/27/72, Eastside Playhouse, 8
In Circles (p), 10/6/67, Judson Memorial Church, 10
In Circles (p), 11/5/67, Cherry Lane Theatre, 222
In Circles (m), 6/25/68, Gramercy Arts Theatre, 56
In Clover (p), 10/13/37, Vanderbilt Theatre, 3
In Dahomey (m), 2/18/03, New York Theatre, 53
In for the Night (p), 1/11/17, Fulton Theatre, 28
In Good King Charles's Golden Days (p), 1/24/57, Downtown Theatre
In Hayti (m), 8/30/09, Circle Theatre, 56
In Heaven and Earth (p), 3/26/36, Willis Theatre, 38
In His Arms (p), 10/13/24, Fulton Theatre, 40
In Love with Love (p), 8/6/23, Ritz Theatre, 122
In Love with Love (p), 5/14/28, Cosmopolitan Theatre, 8
In My Father's Court (p), 11/10/71, Folksbiene Playhouse
In New England Winter (p), 1/26/71, Henry Street Playhouse, 13
In Newport (m), 12/26/04, Liberty Theatre, 24
In Old Kentucky, 1/2/22, Manhattan Opera House, 1
In the Bag (p), 12/17/36, Belmont Theatre, 4
In the Bar of a Tokyo Hotel (p), 5/11/69, Eastside Playhouse, 25
In the Best of Families (p), 2/2/31, Bijou Theatre, 141
In the Bishop's Carriage (p), 2/25/07, Grand Opera House, 8
In the Counting House (p), 12/13/62, Biltmore Theatre, 4
In the Jungle of Cities (p), 12/20/60, Living Theatre, 117
In the Long Run (p), 12/3/09, Comedy Theatre, 1
In the Matter of J. Robert Oppenheimer (p), 3/6/69, Vivian Beaumont Theatre, 54
In the Matter of J. Robert Oppenheimer (p), 6/26/69, Vivian Beaumont Theatre
In the Near Future (p), 3/10/25, Wallack Theatre, 3
In the Next Room (p), 11/27/23, Vanderbilt Theatre, 164
In the Nick of Time (r), 6/1/67, Stage 73, 22
In the Night Watch (p), 1/29/21, Century Theatre, 113
In the Palace of the King (p), 12/31/00, Republic Theatre, 138
In the Penal Colony / Come Out, Carlo! (p), 5/3/62, 41st St. Theatre, 6
In the Shadow of the Glen / The Tinkers Wedding / Riders to the Sea. See Three Plays by Synge, 3/6/57, Theatre East
In the Summer House (p), 12/29/53, Playhouse, 55
In the Summer House (p), 3/25/64, Little Fox Theatre, 15
In the Time of Harry Harass (p), 10/25/71, Players Theatre, 1
In the Train / The Playboy of the Western World (p), 11/20/37, Ambassador Theatre, 9
In the Voodoo Parlour of Marie Leveau (Gris-Gris / The Commedia World of Lafcadio Beau (p), 4/19/74, Playhouse 2, 5, (New Phoenix Repertory Co.)
In the Wine Time (p), 12/10/68, New Lafayette Theatre, 36
In the Zone / The Moon of the Caribbees / Bound East for Cardiff / Long Voyage Home (p), 5/20/48, New York City Center, 14
In Time to Come (p), 12/28/41, Mansfield Theatre, 40
In Times Square (p), 11/23/31, Longacre Theatre, 8
In White America, 10/31/63, Sheridan Square Playhouse, 447
In White America (p), 5/18/65, Players Theatre, 32
In White America (p), 12/7/72, Master Theatre, 12, (Equity Library Theatre)
Inadmissible Evidence (p), 11/30/65, Belasco Theatre, 167
Incident at Vichy (p), 12/3/64, ANTA Washington Square Theatre, 99
Incomparable Max, The (p), 10/19/71, Royale Theatre, 23
Inconstant George (p), 9/29/09, Empire Theatre, 85
Increased Difficulty of Concentration, The (p), 12/4/69, Forum Theatre, 28
Incubator (p), 11/1/32, Avon Theatre, 7
Incubus (p), 4/27/09, Hackett Theatre, 2
Indestructible Wife (p), 1/30/18, Hudson Theatre, 22
Indian Experience, The (r), 10/23/73, Playhouse 2, 1
Indian Summer (p), 10/27/13, Criterion Theatre, 24
Indian Wants the Bronx, The / It's Called the Sugar Plum (p), 1/17/68, Astor Place Theatre, 171
Indians (p), 10/13/69, Brooks Atkinson Theatre, 96
Indiscretion (p), 3/4/29, Mansfield Theatre, 40
Indiscretion of Truth, The (p), 12/3/12, Harris Theatre, 7
Infancy / Childhood / Someone from Assisi. See Plays for Bleecker Street, 1/11/62, Circle in the Square, 349
Infantry, The (p), 11/14/66, 81st St. Theatre, 8
Inferior Sex, The (p), 1/24/10, Daly's Theatre, 64
Infernal Machine, The (p), 2/3/58, Phoenix Theatre, 40
Infinite Shoeblack, The (p), 2/17/30, Maxine Elliott's Theatre, 80
Information Please (p), 10/2/18, Selwyn Theatre, 46

Information, The / The Keyhole / The Lovers in the Metro (p), 1/30/62, Van Dam Theatre, 19
Ingomar (p), 5/16/04, Empire Theatre, 1
Inherit the Wind (p), 4/21/55, National Theatre, 806
Inheritors (p), 3/21/21, Provincetown Playhouse, 26
Inheritors (p), 5/21/21, Provincetown Playhouse, 17
Inheritors (p), 3/7/27, Civic Repertory Theatre, 21
Inheritors (p), 2/11/28, Civic Repertory Theatre, 7
Inheritors (p), 10/26/29, Civic Repertory Theatre, 6
Inheritors (p), 3/26/31, Civic Repertory Theatre, 3
Ink (p), 11/1/27, Biltmore Theatre, 15
Inner City (m), 12/19/71, Ethel Barrymore Theatre, 97
Inner Journey, The (p), 3/20/69, Forum Theatre, 36
Inner Man, The (p), 8/13/17, Lyric Theatre, 48
Innkeepers, The (p), 2/2/56, Golden Theatre, 4
Innocent (p), 9/9/14, Eltinge Theatre, 109
Innocent and Annabel (p), 5/10/21, Neighborhood Playhouse, 25
Innocent Eyes (r), 5/20/24, Winter Garden Theatre, 119
Innocent Idea, An (p), 5/25/20, Fulton Theatre, 7
Innocent Party, The / The Wax Museum (p), 4/4/69, Brooklyn Academy of Music, 3, (Chelsea Theatre Center)
Innocent Voyage, The (p), 11/15/43, Belasco Theatre, 40
Innocents, The (p), 2/1/50, Playhouse, 141
Inquest (p), 4/23/70, Music Box Theatre, 28
Insect Comedy, The (p), 6/3/48, New York City Center, 14
Inside Story, The (p), 2/22/32, National Theatre, 24
Inside the Lines (p), 2/9/15, Longacre Theatre, 103
Inside U.S.A. (r), 4/30/48, Century Theatre, 339
Inspector Calls, An (p), 10/21/47, Booth Theatre, 95
Inspector General, The (p), 4/30/23, 48th St. Theatre, 8
Inspector General, The (p), 12/23/30, Hudson Theatre, 6
Inspector General, The (p), 4/7/72, CSC Repertory Theatre
Inspector Kennedy (p), 12/20/29, Bijou Theatre, 43
Instant Replay (r), 8/6/68, Upstairs at the Downstairs
Instructions for the Running of Trains, Etc., on the Erie Railway, To Go into Effect January 1, 1862 (r), 1/6/70, Sheridan Square Playhouse, 7
Insult (p), 9/15/30, 49th St. Theatre, 24
Interference (p), 10/18/27, Empire Theatre, 226
Interference (p), 5/7/28, Cosmopolitan Theatre, 8
Interlock (p), 2/6/58, ANTA Theatre, 4
Intermezzo (p) (Renaud-Barrault Repertory Co.), 2/14/57, Winter Garden Theatre, 4
International Cup, The / The Ballet of Niagara / The Earthquake (r), 9/3/10, New York Hippodrome, 333
International Incident, An (p), 4/2/40, Ethel Barrymore Theatre, 15
International Marriage, An (p), 1/4/09, Weber Theatre, 16
International Playgirls '64 (r), 5/21/64, Village Theatre, 4
International Review, The (r), 2/25/30, Majestic Theatre, 95
International, The (p), 1/14/28, New Playwrights Theatre, 27
Interrogation of Havana, The (p), 12/27/71, Brooklyn Academy of Music, 14, (Chelsea Theatre Center)
Interrupted Honeymoon, The (p), 3/20/00, Daly's Theatre, 23
Interview. See America Hurrah
Interview, The / The Epic of Buster Friend (p), 12/3/73, Theatre de Lys, 2, (Matinee Theatre)
Intimate Relations (p), 3/28/32, Ambassador Theatre, 24
Intimate Relations (p), 11/1/62, Mermaid Theatre, 76
Intimate Strangers, The (p), 11/7/21, Henry Miller's Theatre, 91
Intruder, The (p), 9/22/09, Bijou Theatre, 13
Intruder, The (p), 9/26/16, Cohan and Harris Theatre, 31
Intruder, The (p), 7/25/28, Biltmore Theatre, 5
Investigation, The (p), 10/4/66, Ambassador Theatre, 103
Invisible Foe, The (p), 12/30/18, Harris Theatre, 112
Invitation au Voyage, L' (p), 10/4/28, Civic Repertory Theatre, 19
Invitation au Voyage, L' (p), 1/31/30, Civic Repertory Theatre, 1
Invitation to a Beheading (p), 3/8/69, Public Theatre, 67
Invitation to a March (p), 10/29/60, Music Box Theatre, 113
Invitation to a March (p), 5/12/67, Master Theatre, 9
Invitation to a Murder (p), 5/17/34, Masque Theatre, 52
Iolanthe (m), 5/12/13, Casino Theatre, 40
Iolanthe (m), 4/19/26, Plymouth Theatre, 255
Iolanthe (m), 11/14/27, Royale Theatre, 12
Iolanthe (m), 1/4/31, Erlanger Theatre, 8
Iolanthe (m), 7/13/31, Erlanger Theatre, 24
Iolanthe (m), 4/30/34, Majestic Theatre, 8
Iolanthe (m), 9/10/34, Martin Beck Theatre, 15
Iolanthe (m), 5/4/36, Majestic Theatre, 8
Iolanthe (m), 9/21/36, Martin Beck Theatre, 20
Iolanthe (m), 2/23/42, St. James Theatre, 5
Iolanthe (m), 2/22/44, Ambassador Theatre, 6
Iolanthe (m), 1/12/48, Century Theatre, 16, (D'Oyly Carte Opera Co.)
Iolanthe (m), 2/15/51, St. James Theatre, 4
Iolanthe (m) (S. M. Chartock), 11/10/52, Mark Hellinger Theatre, 8
Iolanthe (m) (D'Oyly Carte Opera Co.), 10/24/55, Shubert Theatre, 10
Iolanthe (m), 3/10/60, Jan Hus House
Iolanthe (m), 5/25/61, Greenwich Mews Theatre, 12
Iolanthe (m), 11/27/62, New York City Center, 4, (D'Oyly Carte Opera Co.)
Iolanthe (m), 4/3/64, New York City Center, 3
Iolanthe (m), 11/17/64, New York City Center, 7, (D'Oyly Carte Co.)
Iolanthe (m), 5/18/65, Jan Hus Playhouse, 58, (American Savoyards)
Iolanthe (m), 10/17/67, Jan Hus Playhouse, 18, (American Savoyards)
Iolanthe (m), 11/8/68, New York City Center, 4, (D'Oyly Carte Opera Company)
Iolanthe (m), 12/8/71, Jan Hus Playhouse
Iolanthe / The Gondoliers / The Mikado / H.M.S. Pinafore (m), 4/11/62, New York City Center, 15
Iole (m), 12/29/13, Longacre Theatre, 24
Ionescopade (r), 4/25/74, Theatre Four, 13
Ionescopade / Picnic on the Battlefield (p), 1/12/73, Gotham Art Theatre
I.O.U. (p), 10/5/18, Belmont Theatre, 10
Iphigenia in Aulis (p), 4/7/21, Manhattan Opera House, 2
Iphigenia in Aulis (p), 11/21/67, Circle in the Square, 232
Iphigenia in Aulis (p), 11/12/68, Felt Forum, 8, (Piraikon Theatron)
Iphigenia in Concert / The Wedding of Iphigenia (m), 12/16/71, Public/Martinson Hall, 139
Iphigenia in Tauris (p), 11/30/69, Barbizon-Plaza Theatre, 1, (Schauspieltruppe Zurich)
Irene (m), 11/1/19, Vanderbilt Theatre, 675
Irene (m), 4/2/23, Jolson Theatre, 16
Irene (m), 3/13/73, Minskoff Theatre, 590
Irene Wycherley, 1/20/08, Astor Theatre, 39
Iris (p), 9/23/02, Criterion Theatre, 77
Irish National Theatre Company, The (A Pot of Broth, 2/18/08, 7; The Rising of the Moon, 2/24/08, 24), Savoy Theatre
Irish Players Repertory, 11/20/11, Maxine Elliott's Theatre
Irish Players Repertory, 2/4/13, Wallack Theatre
Irma La Douce (m), 9/29/60, Plymouth Theatre, 524
Iron Cross, The (p), 2/13/17, Comedy Theatre
Iron Men (p), 10/19/36, Longacre Theatre, 16
Irregular Verb To Love, The (p), 9/18/63, Ethel Barrymore Theatre, 115
Irving, H. B. See H. B. Irving
Irving, Henry. See Henry Irving
Is Life Worth Living? (p), 11/9/33, Masque Theatre, 12
Is Matrimony a Failure? (p), 8/24/09, Belasco Theatre, 183
Is Zat So? (p), 1/5/25, 39th St. Theatre, 634
Isabel / Shall We Join the Ladies? (p), 1/13/25, Empire Theatre, 31
Island of Goats (p), 10/4/55, Fulton Theatre, 7
Isle O' Dreams, The (p), 1/27/13, Grand Opera House, 32
Isle of Children (p), 3/16/62, Cort Theatre, 11
Isle of Spice, The (p), 8/23/04, Majestic Theatre, 80
Israel (p), 10/25/09, Criterion Theatre, 72
Israeli Mime Theatre, 9/6/66, Theatre de Lys, 63
Istanboul (p), 9/17/65, Judson Poets' Theatre, 9
Istanboul (p), 2/8/71, Actors Playhouse, 8
It All Depends (p), 8/10/25, Vanderbilt Theatre, 16
It Can't Happen Here (p), 10/26/36, Adelphi Theatre, 95
It Happened in Nordland (m), 12/5/04, Lew Fields Theatre, 154
It Happened in Nordland (m), 8/31/05, Lew Fields Theatre, 100
It Happened Tomorrow (p), 5/5/33, Ritz Theatre, 11
It Happens on Ice (r), 10/10/40, Center Theatre, 180
It Happens on Ice (r), 4/4/41, Center Theatre, 96
It Happens on Ice (r), 7/15/41, Center Theatre, 386
It Happens to Everybody (p), 5/9/19, Park Theatre, 8
It Has No Choice. See Short Bullins
It Is the Law (p), 11/29/22, Ritz Theatre, 121
It Is To Laugh (p), 12/26/27, Eltinge Theatre, 37
It Never Rains (p), 11/19/29, Republic Theatre, 178
It Never Rains (p), 12/24/31, New Yorker Theatre, 23
It Pays To Advertise (p), 9/8/14, Cohan Theatre, 399
It Pays To Sin (p), 11/3/33, Morosco Theatre, 3
It's a Bird. . .It's a Plane. . .It's Superman (m), 3/29/66, Alvin Theatre, 129
It's a Boy! (p), 9/19/22, Sam H. Harris Theatre, 64
It's a Gift (p), 3/12/45, Playhouse, 47
It's a Grand Life (p), 2/10/30, Cort Theatre, 25
It's a Wise Child (p), 8/6/29, Belasco Theatre, 378
It's a Wise Child (p), 5/16/33, Hudson Theatre, 34
It's All Your Fault (p), 4/2/06, Savoy Theatre, 32
It's Called the Sugar Plum / The Indian Wants the Bronx (p), 1/17/68, Astor Place Theatre, 171
It's Hard To Be a Jew. See Hard To Be a Jew
It's Lynne Carter, 1/20/70, Carnegie Hall, 1
It's Never Too Late for Happiness (m), 10/19/68, Yiddish Anderson Theatre, 89
It's the Poor as 'Elps the Poor / Muddle Anna / Augustus in Search of a Father (p), 3/15/21, Little Theatre, 1
It's Up to You (m), 3/28/21, Casino Theatre, 24
It's You I Want (p), 2/5/35, Cort Theatre, 15
It Takes Two (p), 2/3/47, Biltmore Theatre, 8

Italian Straw Hat, The (m), 9/30/57, Fourth St. Theatre, 7
ITUCH Anthology, 2/4/68, Barbizon-Plaza Theatre, 2, (ITUCH Repertory Theatre of Chile)
ITUCH Repertory Theatre of Chile (La Remolienda; ITUCH Anthology) (p), 2/2/68, Barbizon-Plaza Theatre, 8
Ivan the Terrible (p), 3/1/04, New Amsterdam Theatre, 15
Ivanov (p), 5/3/66, Shubert Theatre, 47
Ivanov (p), 10/7/58, Renata Theatre, 184
Ivory Door, The (p), 10/18/27, Charles Hopkins Theatre, 312
Ivy Green, The (p), 4/5/49, Lyceum Theatre, 7
Izzy (p), 9/16/24, Broadhurst Theatre, 71

J

J. B. (p), 12/11/58, ANTA Theatre, 364
Jack and Jill (m), 3/22/23, Globe Theatre, 92
Jack and the Beanstalk (m), 12/21/31, 44th St. Theatre, 18
Jack Benny, 2/27/63, Ziegfeld Theatre, 50
Jack in the Pulpit (p), 1/6/25, Princess Theatre, 7
Jack MacGowran in the Works of Samuel Beckett, 11/19/70, Public/Newman Theatre, 67
Jack O'Lantern (m), 10/16/17, Globe Theatre, 265
Jack's Little Surprise (p), 8/25/04, Princess Theatre, 21
Jack Straw (p), 9/14/08, Empire Theatre, 112
Jack / The Bald Soprano (p), 6/3/58, Sullivan St. Playhouse, 184
Jackass, The (p), 3/23/60, Barbizon-Plaza Theatre, 2
Jackhammer, The (p), 2/5/62, Theatre Marquee, 2
Jackknife (p), 4/22/58, Royale Playhouse, 15
Jackpot (m), 1/13/44, Alvin Theatre, 67
Jackson White (p), 4/20/35, Provincetown Playhouse, 17
Jacob's Dream, 12/13/26, Mansfield Theatre, 16
Jacob Slovak, 10/5/27, Greenwich Village Theatre, 21
Jacobowsky and the Colonel (p), 3/14/44, Martin Beck Theatre, 415
Jacques Brel Is Alive and Well and Living in Paris (r), 1/22/68, Village Gate, 1,847
Jacques Brel Is Alive and Well and Living in Paris (r), 9/15/72, Royale Theatre, 51
Jacques Brel Is Alive and Well and Living in Paris (r), 5/17/74, Astor Place Theatre, 22
Jade God, The (p), 5/13/29, Cort Theatre, 105
Jakey Fat Boy / Dear Janet Rosenberg, Dear Mr. Kooning (p), 4/5/70, Gramercy Arts Theatre, 48
Jalousie du Barbouille, La / Le Mariage Forcé / Sganarelle. See An Evening of 3 Farces, 5/6/58, Phoenix Theatre, 8, Jalousie du Barbouille, La /Le
Jamaica (m), 10/31/57, Imperial Theatre, 555
Jamboree (p), 11/24/32, Vanderbilt Theatre, 28
James Joyce Memorial Liquid Theatre, 10/11/71, Solomon R. Guggenheim Museum, 189
James Joyce's A Portrait of the Artist as a Young Man / The Barroom Monks (p), 5/28/62, Martinique Theatre, 300
Jamimma (p), 3/16/72, Henry Street Playhouse, 56
Jane (p), 2/1/52, Coronet Theatre, 100
Jane Clegg (p), 2/23/20, Garrick Theatre, 112
Jane Eyre (p), 5/1/58, Belasco Theatre, 52
Jane, Our Stranger (p), 10/8/25, Cort Theatre, 4
Janice Meredith (p), 12/10/00, Wallack Theatre, 92
Janie (p), 9/10/42, Henry Miller's Theatre, 642
January Thaw (p), 2/4/46, John Golden Theatre, 48
Janus (p), 11/24/55, Plymouth Theatre, 251
Japanese Nightingale, A (p), 11/19/03, Daly's Theatre, 46
Jar, The. See The Man with the Flower in His Mouth
Jarnegan (p), 9/24/28, Longacre Theatre, 138
Jason (p), 1/21/42, Hudson Theatre, 125
Javelin (p), 11/9/66, Actors Playhouse, 14
Jay Walker, The (p), 2/8/26, Klaw Theatre, 17
Jayhawker (p), 11/5/34, Cort Theatre, 24
Jazz Singer, The (p), 9/14/25, Fulton Theatre, 315
Jazz Singer, The (p), 4/18/27, Century Theatre, 16
Jazznite. See Underground
Jealous Moon, The (p), 11/20/28, Majestic Theatre, 72
Jealousy (p), 10/22/28, Maxine Elliott's Theatre, 136
Jeannette (p), 3/24/60, Maidman Playhouse, 4
Jeb (p), 2/21/46, Martin Beck Theatre, 9
Jedermann (Everyman) (p), 12/7/27, Century Theatre, 14
Jeff Chandler. See Three. . .with Women in Mind
Jefferson Davis (p), 2/18/36, Biltmore Theatre, 3
Jennie (m), 10/17/63, Majestic Theatre, 82
Jenny (p), 10/8/29, Booth Theatre, 111
Jenny Kissed Me (p), 12/23/48, Hudson Theatre, 20
Jeremiah (p), 2/3/39, Guild Theatre, 35
Jerico-Jim Crow (p), 3/9/68, Greenwich Mews Theatre, 5
Jerico-Jim Crow (m), 1/12/64, The Sanctuary (Greenwich Mews), 32
Jerome Robbins' Ballets: U.S.A., 9/4/58, Alvin Theatre, 44
Jerome Robbins' Ballets: U.S.A., 10/8/61, ANTA Theatre, 24
Jerry (p), 3/28/14, Lyceum Theatre, 41
Jerry for Short (p), 8/12/29, Waldorf Theatre, 64
Jersey Lily, The (m), 9/14/03, Victoria Theatre, 24
Jest, The (p), 4/9/19, Plymouth Theatre, 77
Jest, The (p), 9/19/19, Plymouth Theatre, 179
Jest, The (p), 2/4/26, Plymouth Theatre, 78
Jesters, The (p), 1/15/08, Empire Theatre, 53
Jesus Christ Superstar (m), 10/12/71, Mark Hellinger Theatre, 720
Jeu de l'Amour et du Hasard, Le / Un Caprice (p) (Comédie Française), 11/15/55, Broadway Theatre, 8
Jeune Fille a Marier, La / La Lacune / Les Chaises (p), 5/5/70, Barbizon-Plaza Theatre, 8, (Le Treteau de Paris)
Jew!. See Collision Course
Jewel of Asia, The (m), 2/16/03, Criterion Theatre, 64
Jewel Robbery (p), 1/13/32, Booth Theatre, 53
Jeweled Tree, The, 10/7/26, 48th St. Theatre, 36
Jewish State Theatre of Bucharest (The Dybruk; The Pearl Necklace), 9/19/72, Brooklyn Academy of Music, 16
Jewish State Theatre of Poland, The (Mirele Efros; Mother Courage and Her Children) (p), 10/19/67, Billy Rose Theatre, 53
Jezebel (p), 12/19/33, Ethel Barrymore Theatre, 32
JFK, 11/21/71, Circle in the Square Theatre, 9
Jig Saw (p), 4/30/34, Ethel Barrymore Theatre, 49
Jim Bludso of the Prairie Belle (p), 1/5/03, 14th St. Theatre, 40
Jim Jam Jems (m), 10/4/20, Cort Theatre, 105
Jim the Penman (p), 5/10/10, Lyric Theatre, 31
Jimmie (p), 11/17/20, Apollo Theatre, 69
Jimmie's Women (p), 9/26/27, Biltmore Theatre, 217
Jimmy (m), 10/23/69, Winter Garden, 84
Jimmy Roselli Show, The, 5/2/69, Palace Theatre, 13
Jimmy Shine (p), 12/5/68, Brooks Atkinson Theatre, 153
Jinny / The Carrier (p), 4/10/05, Criterion Theatre, 21
Jitta's Atonement (p), 1/17/23, Comedy Theatre, 38
Jo (m), 2/12/64, Orpheum Theatre, 63
Joan (m), 6/19/72, Circle in the Square, 64
Joan o' the Shoals (p), 2/3/02, Republic Theatre, 8
Joan of Arc (p), 4/14/27, Edyth Totten Theatre, 9
Joan of Lorraine (p), 11/18/46, Alvin Theatre, 199
Joan of Lorraine (p), 3/13/74, Good Shepherd-Faith Church, 12
Jockey Club Stakes, The (p), 1/24/73, Cort Theatre, 69
Johannes Kreisler (p), 12/20/22, Apollo Theatre, 65
John (p), 11/4/27, Klaw Theatre, 11
John Brown (p), 1/22/34, Ethel Barrymore Theatre, 2
John Brown's Body, 2/14/53, New Century Theatre, 65
John Brown's Body, 6/21/60, Martinique Theatre, 76
John Bull's Other Island (p), 2/10/48, Mansfield Theatre, 8
John E. Kellerd Repertory, 8/24/11, Irving Place Theatre
John Ermine of the Yellowstone (p), 11/2/03, Manhattan Theatre, 24
John Ferguson (p), 5/13/19, Garrick Theatre, 177
John Ferguson (p), 5/23/21, Garrick Theatre, 24
John Ferguson (p), 6/20/21, Belmont Theatre, 10
John Ferguson (p), 1/17/28, Theatre Masque, 9
John Ferguson (p), 7/10/33, Belmont Theatre, 48
John Gabriel Borkman (p), 4/1/15, Lyceum Theatre, 3
John Gabriel Borkman (p), 1/29/26, Booth Theatre, 7
John Gabriel Borkman (p), 11/9/26, Civic Repertory Theatre, 15
John Gabriel Borkman (p), 1/28/28, Civic Repertory Theatre, 7
John Gabriel Borkman (p), 1/28/29, Civic Repertory Theatre, 2
John Gabriel Borkman (p), 3/28/30, Civic Repertory Theatre, 1
John Gabriel Borkman (p), 11/12/46, International Theatre, 21
John Gladye's Honour (p), 12/23/07, Daly's Theatre, 16
John Hawthorne (p), 1/24/21, Garrick Theatre, 4
John Henry (m), 5/25/03, Herald Square Theatre, 21
John Henry (m), 1/10/40, 44th St. Theatre, 7
John Hudson's Wife (p), 9/20/06, Weber Theatre, 27
John Loves Mary (p), 2/4/47, Booth Theatre, 423
John Murray Anderson's Almanac (r), 12/10/53, Imperial Theatre, 227
John Turner Davis / The Midnight Caller. See Two Plays by Horton Foote, 7/1/58, Sheridan Square Playhouse, 17
Johnny Belinda (p), 9/18/40, Belasco Theatre, 321
Johnny, Get Your Gun (p), 2/12/17, Criterion Theatre, 80
Johnny Johnson (m), 11/19/36, 44th St. Theatre, 68
Johnny Johnson (m), 10/21/56, Carnegie Hall Playhouse, 17
Johnny Johnson (m), 4/11/71, Edison Theatre, 1
Johnny No-Trump (p), 10/8/67, Cort Theatre, 1
Johnny No-Trump (p), 11/12/70, Master Theatre, 14, (Equity Library Theatre)
Johnny on a Spot (p), 1/8/42, Plymouth Theatre, 4
Johnny 2 × 4 (p), 3/16/42, Plymouth Theatre, 4
Joker, The (p), 11/16/25, Maxine Elliott's Theatre
Jolly Bachelors, The (m), 1/6/10, Broadway Theatre, 84
Jolly Roger, The (p), 8/30/23, National Theatre, 52
Jolly's Progress (p), 12/5/59, Longacre Theatre, 9

Jonah (p), 2/15/66, St. Clement's Church Theatre, 13, (American Place Theatre)
Jonah! (p), 9/21/67, Stage 73, 22
Jonathan Makes a Wish (p), 9/10/18, Princess Theatre, 23
Jonesy (p), 4/9/29, Bijou Theatre, 96
Jonica (m), 4/7/30, Craig Theatre, 40
José Greco, 10/1/51, Shubert Theatre, 65
José Greco, 1/12/53, New Century Theatre, 16
Josef Suss (p), 1/20/30, Erlanger's Theatre, 40
Joseph (p), 2/12/30, Liberty Theatre, 13
Joseph and His Brethren (p), 1/11/13, Century Theatre, 121
Joseph Entangled (p), 10/10/04, Garrick Theatre, 65
Josephine (p), 1/28/18, Knickerbocker Theatre, 24
Josephine Baker, 12/31/73, Palace Theatre, 4
Josephine Baker and Her Company, 2/4/64, Brooks Atkinson Theatre, 16
Josephine Baker and Her Company, 3/31/64, Henry Miller's Theatre, 24
Journey by Night, A (p), 4/16/35, Sam S. Shubert Theatre, 7
Journey of Snow White, The (m), 2/26/71, Judson Memorial Church, 10
Journey of the Fifth Horse, The (p), 4/21/66, St. Clement's Church Theatre, 12, (American Place Theatre)
Journey's End (p), 3/22/29, Henry Miller's Theatre, 485
Journey's End (p), 9/18/39, Empire Theatre, 16
Journey's End (p), 10/4/68, Roundabout Theatre, 32
Journey, The (p), 11/4/71, Theatre for the New City, 12
Journey to Jerusalem (p), 10/5/40, National Theatre, 17
Journey to the Day (p), 11/11/63, Theatre de Lys, 29
Journeyman (p), 1/29/38, Fulton Theatre, 41
Joy (r), 1/27/70, New Theatre, 208
Joy Forever, A (p), 1/7/46, Biltmore Theatre, 16
Joy of Living (p), 10/23/02, Garden Theatre, 19
Joy of Living (p), 4/6/31, Masque Theatre, 16
Joy to the World (p), 3/18/48, Plymouth Theatre, 124
Joyce Grenfell, 4/7/58, Lyceum Theatre, 24
Joyce Grenfell Requests the Pleasure . . ., 10/10/55, Bijou Theatre, 65
Joyful Noise, A (m), 12/15/66, Mark Hellinger Theatre, 12
Joyous Season, The (p), 1/29/34, Belasco Theatre, 16
Juana La Loca (p), 6/14/64, St. Clement's Church, 1, (American Place Theatre)
Juarez and Maximillian (p), 10/11/26, Guild Theatre, 42
Jubilee (m), 10/12/35, Imperial Theatre, 169
Judas (p), 1/24/29, Longacre Theatre, 12
Judge and the Jury, The (p), 9/1/06, Wallack Theatre, 17
Judge's Husband, The (p), 9/27/26, 49th St. Theatre, 112
Judgment Day (p), 9/12/34, Belasco Theatre, 94
Judith (p), 3/24/65, Phoenix Theatre, 79
Judith of Bethulia (p), 12/5/04, Daly's Theatre, 16
Judith Zaraine (p), 1/16/11, Astor Theatre, 16
Judy (m), 2/7/27, Royale Theatre, 104
Judy Drops In (p), 10/4/24, Punch and Judy Theatre, 43
Judy Forgot (m), 10/6/10, Broadway Theatre, 44
Judy Garland (r), 12/25/67, Felt Forum, 3
Judy Garland at Home at the Palace (r), 7/31/67, Palace Theatre, 24
Julia, Jake and Uncle Joe (p), 1/28/61, Booth Theatre, 1
Julie (p), 5/9/27, Lyceum Theatre, 8
Julie Bonbon (p), 1/1/06, Fields Theatre, 98
Julie Bonbon (p), 4/9/06, Lyric Theatre, 8
Julius Caesar (p), 12/1/02, Herald Square Theatre, 50
Julius Caesar (p) (William Faversham), 11/4/12, Lyric Theatre, 32
Julius Caesar (p), 2/16/14, Lyric Theatre
Julius Caesar (p) (Howard Kyle), 3/15/18, Cort Theatre, 1
Julius Caesar (p), 12/16/20, Manhattan Opera House, 4
Julius Caesar (p), 1/6/21, Lexington Theatre, 3
Julius Caesar (p), 12/26/21, Lexington Theatre, 2
Julius Caesar (p) (Fritz Leiber), 1/19/22, 48th St. Theatre, 3
Julius Caesar (p) (William Courtleigh), 6/6/27, New Amsterdam Theatre, 8
Julius Caesar (p), 4/3/30, Shubert Theatre, 2
Julius Caesar (p), 12/29/30, Ambassador Theatre, 4
Julius Caesar (p) (Fritz Leiber), 11/17/31, Royale Theatre, 4
Julius Caesar (p) (Harry Joyner), 12/14/32, Shakespeare Theatre, 24
Julius Caesar (p), 11/11/37, Mercury Theatre, 157
Julius Caesar (p) (Horace Braham), 6/20/50, Arena, Edison Hotel, 31
Julius Caesar (p) (Alfred Sandor), 10/23/57, Shakespearewrights Theatre
Julius Caesar (p) (Staats Cotsworth), 8/3/59, Belvedere Lake Theatre, 24
Julius Caesar (p), 1/7/72, Wollman Auditorium, Columbia U., (Oxford-Cambridge Shakespeare Co.)
Jumbo (m), 11/16/35, New York Hippodrome, 221
Jumpers (p), 4/22/74, Billy Rose Theatre, 46
Jumping Fool, The (p), 2/9/70, Fortune Theatre, 16
Jumping Jupiter (m), 3/6/11, New York Theatre, 24
June Days (m), 8/6/25, Astor Theatre, 85
June Love (m), 4/25/21, Knickerbocker Theatre, 48
June Madness (p), 9/25/12, Fulton Theater, 13
June Moon (p), 10/9/29, Broadhurst Theatre, 272
June Moon (p), 5/15/33, Ambassador Theatre, 49
June Moon (p), 10/21/71, Master Theatre, 12, (Equity Library Theatre)
Junebug Graduates Tonight! (m), 2/23/67, Chelsea Theatre Center, 6
Junior Miss (p), 11/18/41, Lyceum Theatre, 710
Junk, 1/5/27, Garrick Theatre, 9
Junkies Are Full of (Sh...). See Experimental Death Unit #1
Juno (m), 3/9/59, Winter Garden Theatre, 16
Juno and the Paycock (p), 3/15/26, Mayfair Theatre, 72
Juno and the Paycock (p), 12/19/27, Gallo Theatre, 25
Juno and the Paycock (p), 10/19/32, Martin Beck Theatre, 6
Juno and the Paycock (p), 11/23/34, John Golden Theatre, 9
Juno and the Paycock (p), 12/6/37, Ambassador Theatre, 8
Juno and the Paycock (p), 1/16/40, Mansfield Theatre, 105
Jupiter Laughs (p), 9/9/40, Biltmore Theatre, 24
Just a Minute (m), 10/27/19, Cort Theatre, 40
Just a Minute (m), 10/8/28, Ambassador Theatre, 80
Just a Wife (p), 2/1/10, Belasco Theatre, 79
Just a Woman (p), 1/17/16, 48th St. Theatre, 136
Just Around the Corner (p), 2/5/19, Longacre Theatre, 13
Just as Well / The Forbidden Guests / Happiness / The Day of Dupes (p), 3/6/14, Cort Theatre, 5
Just Because (m), 3/22/22, Earl Carroll Theatre, 46
Just Beyond (p), 12/1/25, National Theatre, 7
Just Boys (p), 9/13/15, Comedy Theatre, 16
Just Fancy (m), 10/11/27, Casino Theatre, 79
Just for Love (m), 10/17/68, Provincetown Playhouse, 6
Just for Openers (r), 11/3/65, Upstairs at the Downstairs, 395
Just Herself (p), 12/23/14, Playhouse, 13
Just Life (p), 9/14/26, Henry Miller's Theatre, 80
Just Like John (p), 8/12/12, 48th St. Theatre, 16
Just Married (p), 4/26/21, Comedy Theatre, 307
Just Out of College (p), 9/27/05, Lyceum Theatre, 61
Just Outside the Door (p), 8/30/15, Gaiety Theatre, 8
Just Suppose (p), 11/1/20, Henry Miller's Theatre, 88
Just To Get Married (p), 1/1/12, Maxine Elliott's Theatre, 24
Just To Remind You (p), 9/7/31, Broadhurst Theatre, 16
Justice (p), 4/3/16, Candler Theatre, 104
Justice Box, The (p), 6/2/71, Theatre de Lys, 7

K

K Guy, The (p), 10/15/28, Biltmore Theatre, 8
Ka Mountain and Guardenia Terrace, 4/24/72, Byrd Hoffman School of Byrds, 6
Kabale Und Liebe (p), 1/16/28, Cosmopolitan Theatre, 8
Kabale und Liebe (p), 11/2/71, Barbizon-Plaza Theatre, 7, (Szene 71)
Kaboom! (m), 5/1/74, Bottom Line Theatre, 1
Kaddish (p), 2/11/72, Brooklyn Academy of Music, 101, (Chelsea Theatre Center)
Kagami-Jishi. See The Grand Kabuki
Kaleidoscope (r), 6/13/57, Provincetown Playhouse
Kansas City Kitty (p), 9/25/29, Gansevoort Theatre, 2
Karen (p), 1/7/18, Greenwich Village Theatre, 80
Karl and Anna (p), 10/7/29, Guild Theatre, 49
Karl Marx Play, The (p), 3/16/73, American Place Theatre, 31
Kaspar (p), 2/6/73, Brooklyn Academy of Music, 48, (Chelsea Theatre Center)
Kassa (p), 1/23/09, Liberty Theatre, 65
Kataki (p), 4/9/59, Ambassador Theatre, 20
Kataki (p), 12/15/59, St. Marks Playhouse, 21
Katerina (p), 2/25/29, Civic Repertory Theatre, 19
Katherine Dunham (r), 4/19/50, Broadway Theatre, 37
Katherine Dunham and Her Company (r), 11/22/55, Broadway Theatre, 32
Kathleen (p), 2/3/48, Mansfield Theatre, 2
Kathleen ni Houlihan (p), 10/29/32, Martin Beck Theatre, 1
Kathleen ni Houlihan / The Land of Heart's Desire / A Pot of Broth. See Irish National Theatre Co., 6/3/03, Carnegie Lyceum Theatre, 2
Kathleen ni Houlihan / The Land of Heart's Desire / The Hour Glass (p), 2/21/05, Hudson Theatre, 1
Katie Roche (p), 10/2/37, Ambassador Theatre, 5
Katinka (m), 12/23/15, 44th St. Theatre, 220
Katja (m), 10/18/26, 44th St. Theatre, 113
Katy Did (p), 5/9/27, Daly's Theatre, 8
Katy's Kisses (p), 9/24/19, Greenwich Village Theatre, 13
Kean (m), 11/2/61, Broadway Theatre, 92
Keep 'Em Laughing (r), 4/24/42, 44th St. Theatre, 77
Keep Her Smiling, 8/5/18, Astor Theatre, 104
Keep It Clean (r), 6/24/29, Selwyn Theatre, 16
Keep It in the Family (p), 9/27/67, Plymouth Theatre, 5
Keep It to Yourself (p), 12/30/18, 39th St. Theatre, 128
Keep Kool (r), 5/22/24, Morosco Theatre, 148
Keep Moving (p), 8/23/34, Forrest Theatre, 21
Keep Off the Grass (m), 5/23/40, Broadhurst Theatre, 44
Keep Shufflin' (m), 2/27/28, Daly's Theatre, 104

Keeper of the Keys (p), 10/18/33, Fulton Theatre, 24
Keeping Expenses Down (p), 10/20/32, National Theatre, 12
Keeping Up Appearances (p), 10/19/10, Comedy Theatre, 9
Keeping Up Appearances (p), 11/8/16, Bramhall Playhouse, 173
Keeping Up Appearances (p), 1/17/18, Bramhall Playhouse, 4
Kelly (m), 2/6/65, Broadhurst Theatre, 1
Kempy (p), 5/15/22, Belmont Theatre, 212
Kempy (p), 5/11/27, Hudson Theatre, 48
Ken Murray's Blackouts of 1949 (r), 9/6/49, Ziegfeld Theatre, 51
Ken Murray's Hollywood (r), 5/10/65, John Golden Theatre, 18
Kennen Sie die Milchstrasse? (p), 12/13/66, Barbizon-Plaza Theatre, 2, (Die Brücke)
Kept (p), 9/17/26, Comedy Theatre, 11
Key Largo (p), 11/27/39, Ethel Barrymore Theatre, 105
Keyhole, The / The Lovers in the Metro / The Information (p), 1/30/62, Van Dam Theatre, 19
Khaki Blue / Lime Green (p), 3/26/69, Provincetown Playhouse, 13
Kibitzer (p), 2/18/29, Royale Theatre, 127
Kick Back, The (p), 6/22/36, Ritz Theatre, 16
Kick In (p), 10/15/14, Longacre Theatre, 188
Kicking the Castle Down (p), 1/18/67, Gramercy Arts Theatre, 21
Kid Boots (m), 12/31/23, Earl Carroll Theatre, 479
Kid, The (p), 11/2/72, American Place Theatre, 32
Kidding Kidders (p), 4/23/28, Bijou Theatre, 8
Kiki (p), 11/29/21, Belasco Theatre, 580
Kill That Story (p), 8/29/34, Booth Theatre, 15
Kill That Story (p), 9/17/34, Ambassador Theatre, 104
Kill the One-eyed Man (p), 10/20/65, Provincetown Playhouse, 8
Killdeer, The (p), 3/12/74, Newman / Public Theatre, 48
Killer, The (p), 3/22/60, Seven Arts Theatre, 16
Killers (p), 3/13/28, 49th St. Theatre, 23
Killing of Sister George, The (p), 10/5/66, Belasco Theatre, 205
Kilpatrick's Minstrels (r), 4/19/30, Royale Theatre, 8
Kind Lady (p), 4/23/35, Booth Theatre, 79
Kind Lady (p), 9/9/35, Longacre Theatre, 20
Kind Lady (p), 9/3/40, Playhouse, 107
Kind Sir (p), 11/4/53, Alvin Theatre, 165
Kindling (p), 12/5/11, Daly's Theatre, 39
Kindred (p), 12/26/39, Maxine Elliott's Theatre, 16
King and I, The (m), 3/29/51, St. James Theatre, 1,246
King and I, The (m), 4/18/56, N.Y. City Center, 23
King and I, The (m), 5/11/60, New York City Center, 23
King and I, The (m), 6/12/63, New York City Center, 15
King and I, The (m), 7/6/64, New York State Theatre, 40
King and I, The (m), 5/23/68, New York City Center, 23
King Can Do No Wrong, The (p), 11/16/27, Masque Theatre, 13
King Dodo (m), 5/12/02, Daly's Theatre, 64
King for All Ages, A (p), 10/9/71, Grace Rainey Rogers Auditorium, 3
King Henry IV, Part One (p), 6/11/68, Delacorte Theatre, 23
King Henry IV, Part Two (p), 6/30/68, Delacorte Theatre, 18
King Henry V (p), 3/15/28, Hampden Theatre, 51
King Henry V (p), 6/26/65, Delacorte Mobile Theatre, 25
King Henry V (p), 11/10/69, ANTA Theatre, 16, (American Shakespeare Festival)
King Henry V. See Henry V
King Herdin (p), 3/17/71, St. Philip's Community Theatre, 30
King Highball (m), 9/6/02, New York Theatre, 33
King John (p), 7/5/67, Delacorte Theatre, 19
King Lear (p) (Reginald Pole), 3/9/23, Earl Carroll Theatre, 2
King Lear (p), 3/31/30, Shubert Theatre, 3
King Lear (p) (Fritz Leiber), 12/25/30, Ambassador Theatre, 4
King Lear (p), 5/4/33, Shakespeare Theatre, 5
King Lear (p) (Donald Wolfit), 2/18/47, Century Theatre, 8
King Lear (p) (Louis Calhern), 12/25/50, National Theatre, 48
King Lear (p) (Orson Welles), 1/12/56, New York City Center, 21
King Lear (p) (Sidney Walker), 1/2/59, Players Theatre, 13
King Lear (p), 8/13/62, Delacorte Theatre, 59
King Lear (p) (Paul Scofield, Royal Shakespeare Co.), 5/18/64, New York State Theatre, 12
King Lear (p), 11/7/68, Vivian Beaumont Theatre, 57
King Lear (p), 7/31/73, Delacorte Theatre, 28, (James Earl Jones)
King Lear (p), 2/3/74, Brooklyn Academy of Music, 10, (Robert Eddison & The Actors Company)
King of Cadonia, The (m), 1/10/10, Daly's Theatre, 16
King of Friday's Men, The (p), 2/21/51, Playhouse, 4
King of Hearts (p), 4/1/54, Lyceum Theatre, 268
King of Nowhere, A (p), 3/20/16, Maxine Elliott's Theatre, 58
King of the Dark Chamber, The (p), 2/9/61, Jan Hus House, 255
King of the United States, The (p), 5/15/72, Theatre for the New City
King of the Whole Damn World! (m), 4/12/62, Jan Hus House, 43
King Richard II (p) (Ben Hayes), 8/28/61, Wollman Memorial Skating Rink, 12
King Richard II (p), 1/9/74, Brooklyn Academy of Music, 23, (Ian Richardson / Richard Pasco & Royal Shakespeare Co.)
King Richard II. See Richard II
King Richard III (p) (Joseph Bova), 8/9/66, Delacorte Theatre, 17
King Richard III (p), 6/25/70, Delacorte Theatre, 20, (The Wars of the Roses)
King Richard III. See Richard III
King's Carnival, The (m), 5/13/01, New York Theatre, 80
King, The (p), 11/20/17, Cohan Theatre, 127
King Washington (p), 4/26/01, Wallack Theatre, 1
Kingdom of God, The (p), 12/20/28, Ethel Barrymore Theatre, 93
Kingston, Gertrude, Repertory. See Gertrude Kingston Repertory
Kirokuda. See National Theatres of Japan
Kismet (p), 12/25/11, Knickerbocker Theatre, 184
Kismet (m), 12/3/53, Ziegfeld Theatre, 583
Kismet (m), 11/16/63, Master Institute—Equity Library Theatre, 9
Kismet (m), 6/22/65, N.Y. State Theatre, 47
Kiss and Tell (p), 3/17/43, Biltmore Theatre, 962
Kiss Burglar, The (m), 5/9/18, Cohan Theatre, 100
Kiss Burglar, The (m), 3/17/19, Broadhurst Theatre, 24
Kiss for Cinderella, A (p), 12/25/16, Empire Theatre, 152
Kiss for Cinderella, A (p), 3/10/42, Music Box Theatre, 48
Kiss in a Taxi, The (p), 8/25/25, Ritz Theatre, 103
Kiss Mama (p), 10/1/64, Actors Playhouse, 142
Kiss Me (m), 7/21/27, Lyric Theatre, 28
Kiss Me, Kate (m), 12/30/48, New Century Theatre, 1,077
Kiss Me, Kate (m), 1/8/52, Broadway Theatre, 8
Kiss Me, Kate (m), 5/9/56, New York City Center, 23
Kiss Me, Kate (m), 5/12/65, New York City Center, 23
Kiss Me Quick (p), 8/26/13, 48th St. Theatre, 31
Kiss Now (m), 4/20/71, Martinique Theatre, 3
Kiss of Importance, A (p), 12/1/30, Fulton Theatre, 24
Kiss the Boys Good-bye (p), 9/28/38, Henry Miller's Theatre, 286
Kiss Them for Me (p), 3/20/45, Belasco Theatre, 110
Kiss Waltz, The (m), 9/18/11, Casino Theatre, 88
Kissing Time (m), 10/11/20, Lyric Theatre, 65
Kitchen, The (p), 5/9/66, New Theatre Workshop, 3
Kitchen, The (p), 6/13/66, New 81st St. Theatre, 137
Kittiwake Island (m), 10/12/60, Martinique Theatre, 7
Kitty Darlin' (m), 11/7/17, Casino Theatre, 14
Kitty Grey (m), 1/25/09, New Amsterdam Theatre, 48
Kitty Mackay (p), 1/7/14, Comedy Theatre, 278
Kitty's Kisses (m), 5/6/26, Playhouse, 170
Kleinburgerhochzeit, Die / Die Kurve (p), 11/24/70, Barbizon-Plaza Theatre, 10, (Die Brücke)
Knack, The (p), 5/27/64, New Theatre, 685
Knack with Horses, A / Here Be Dragons (p), 12/5/70, St. Clement's Church
Knickerbocker Girl, The (m), 6/15/00, Herald Square Theatre, 14
Knickerbocker Holiday (m), 10/19/38, Ethel Barrymore Theatre, 168
Knife, The (p), 4/12/17, Bijou Theatre, 84
Knight for a Day, A (m), 12/16/07, Wallack Theatre, 176
Knight of the Burning Pestle, The (p), 10/23/53, Theatre de Lys, 5
Knights of Song (m), 10/17/38, 51st St. Theatre, 16
Knock on Wood (p), 5/28/35, Cort Theatre, 11
Knots (r), 1/30/74, Brooklyn Academy of Music, 5, (The Actors Company)
Know Thyself (p), 12/27/09, Berkeley Theatre, 1
Komisarzhevsky, Mme. Vera F. See Mme. Vera F. Komisarzhevsky
Kongi's Harvest (p), 4/14/68, St. Marks Playhouse, 33
Kongo (p), 3/30/26, Biltmore Theatre, 135
Konzert, Das (p), 3/23/68, New York City Center, 6, (Vienna Burgtheater)
Kool Aid (Grail Green / Three Street Koans) (p), 11/3/71, Forum Theatre, 5
Kosher Kitty Kelly (p), 6/15/25, Times Square Theatre, 105
Kosher Kitty Kelly (p), 10/21/25, Daly's 63rd St. Theatre, 61
Kosher Widow, The (m), 10/31/59, Anderson Theatre, 87
Krapp's Last Tape / Not I (p), 11/22/72, Forum Theatre, 15
Krapp's Last Tape / The Zoo Story (p), 1/14/60, Provincetown Playhouse, 582
Krapp's Last Tape / The Zoo Story (p), 6/8/65, Cherry Lane Theatre, 168
Krapp's Last Tape/The Zoo Story (p), 10/9/68, Billy Rose Theatre, 6, (Theatre 1969 Playwrights Repertory)
Kremlin Chimes (p), 2/24/65, New York City Center, 2, (Moscow Art Theatre)
Kreutzer Sonata, The (p) (Jacob Gordin version), 8/13/06, Manhattan Theatre, 29
Kreutzer Sonata, The (p) (Langdon Mitchell version), 9/10/06, Lyric Theatre, 19
Kreutzer Sonata, The (p), 5/14/24, Frazee Theatre, 61
Kuan Yin / A Burmese Pwe / The Apothecary (p), 3/16/26, Neighborhood Playhouse, 27
Kultur (p), 9/26/33, Mansfield Theatre, 9
Kumagai Jinya. See The Grand Kabuki
Kumquats (r), 11/15/71, Village Gate, 54
Kuriakos Theatre (Pelleas and Melisande / Metamorphosis) (p), 2/19/57, Theatre de Lys, 1
Kurve, Die / Die Kleinburgerhochzeit (p), 11/24/70, Barbizon-Plaza Theatre, 10, (Die Brücke)

Kwamina (m), 10/23/61, 54th St. Theatre, 32
Kykundor, 6/10/34, Little Theatre, 65

L

La, La, Lucille (m), 5/26/19, Henry Miller's Theatre, 104
La Repetition ou l'Amour Puni (p), 11/27/52, Ziegfeld Theatre, 4
Laburnum Grove (p), 1/14/35, Booth Theatre, 130
Labyrinth, The (p), 11/27/05, Herald Square Theatre, 16
Lace on Her Petticoat (p), 9/4/51, Booth Theatre, 79
Lace Petticoat (m), 1/4/27, Forrest Theatre, 15
Lacune, La / La Jeune Fille a Marier / Les Chaises (p), 5/5/70, Barbizon-Plaza Theatre, 8, (Le Treteau de Paris)
Ladder, The (p), 10/22/26, Mansfield Theatre, 794
Ladies All (p), 7/28/30, Morosco Theatre, 163
Ladies and Gentlemen (p), 10/17/39, Martin Beck Theatre, 105
Ladies Don't Lie (p), 10/10/29, Gallo Theatre, 12
Ladies First (m), 10/24/18, Broadhurst Theatre, 164
Ladies in Retirement (p), 3/26/40, Henry Miller's Theatre, 151
Ladies in Waiting (p), 10/15/73, New Federal Theatre
Ladies Leave (p), 10/1/29, Charles Hopkins Theatre, 15
Ladies' Money (p), 11/1/34, Ethel Barrymore Theatre, 36
Ladies Night (p), 8/9/20, Eltinge Theatre, 375
Ladies Night in a Turkish Bath (p), 3/21/61, Eleanor Gould Theatre, 40
Ladies of Creation (p), 9/8/31, Cort Theatre, 71
Ladies of the Corridor, The (p), 10/21/53, Longacre Theatre, 45
Ladies of the Evening (p), 12/23/24, Lyceum Theatre, 159
Ladies of the Evening (p), 8/17/25, Lyceum Theatre, 24
Ladies of the Jury (p), 10/21/29, Erlanger Theatre, 80
Ladies Paradise, The (m), 9/16/01, Metropolitan Opera House, 24
Lady Alone (p), 1/20/27, Forrest Theatre, 45
Lady Audley's Secret (m), 10/3/72, Eastside Playhouse, 7
Lady, Be Good (m), 12/1/24, Liberty Theatre, 330
Lady, Behave (p), 11/16/43, Cort Theatre, 23
Lady Beyond the Moon (p), 3/31/31, Bijou Theatre, 15
Lady Billy (m), 12/14/20, Liberty Theatre, 188
Lady Bug (p), 4/17/22, Apollo Theatre, 5
Lady Butterfly (m), 1/22/23, Globe Theatre, 128
Lady Clara (p), 4/17/30, Booth Theatre, 28
Lady Comes Across, The (m), 1/9/42, 44th St. Theatre, 3
Lady Cristilinda, The (p), 12/25/22, Broadhurst Theatre, 24
Lady Day—A Musical Tragedy (m), 10/17/72, Brooklyn Academy of Music, 24, (Chelsea Theatre Center)
Lady Dedlock (p), 12/31/28, Ambassador Theatre, 50
Lady Detained, A (p), 1/9/35, Ambassador Theatre, 13
Lady Do (r), 4/18/27, Liberty Theatre, 56
Lady Fingers (m), 1/31/29, Vanderbilt Theatre, 132
Lady for a Night, A (p), 4/16/28, 49th St. Theatre, 8
Lady Frederick (p), 11/9/08, Hudson Theatre, 96
Lady from Alfaqueque, The (p), 1/14/29, Civic Repertory Theatre, 17
Lady from Alfaqueque, The (p), 9/30/29, Civic Repertory Theatre, 8
Lady from Alfaqueque, The (p), 10/9/30, Civic Repertory Theatre, 9
Lady from Lane's, The, 8/19/07, Lyric Theatre, 47
Lady from Lobster Square, The (p), 4/4/10, Weber Theatre, 24
Lady from Maxims, The (p), 5/3/70, Roundabout Theatre, 40
Lady from Oklahoma, The (p), 4/2/13, 48th St. Theatre, 13
Lady from the Sea, The (p), 11/6/11, Lyric Theatre
Lady from the Sea, The (p) (Eleonora Duse), 11/29/23, Metropolitan Opera House, 1
Lady from the Sea, The (p), 3/18/29, Bijou Theatre, 24
Lady from the Sea, The (p), 5/1/34, Little Theatre, 15
Lady from the Sea, The (p), 8/7/50, Fulton Theatre, 16
Lady from the Sea, The (p), 9/20/73, Gotham Art Theatre
Lady Gay's Garden Party / The Four Seasons / Circus Events (r), 2/17/08, New York Hippodrome
Lady Has a Heart, The (p), 9/25/37, Longacre Theatre, 90
Lady Huntworth's Experiment (p), 12/21/00, Daly's Theatre, 86
Lady in Danger (p), 3/29/45, Broadhurst Theatre, 12
Lady in Ermine, The (m), 10/2/22, Ambassador Theatre, 238
Lady in Love, A (p), 2/21/27, Lyceum Theatre, 17
Lady in Red, The (m), 5/12/19, Lyric Theatre, 48
Lady in the Dark (m), 1/23/41, Alvin Theatre, 162
Lady in the Dark (m), 9/1/41, Alvin Theatre, 305
Lady in the Dark (m), 2/27/43, Broadway Theatre, 83
Lady in Waiting (p), 3/27/40, Martin Beck Theatre, 87
Lady Jane (p), 9/10/34, Plymouth Theatre, 40
Lady Jim (p), 8/28/06, Joe Weber Music Hall, 23
Lady Killer, The (p), 3/12/24, Morosco Theatre, 13
Lady Lies, The (p), 11/26/28, Little Theatre, 24
Lady Luck (p), 4/13/36, Adelphi Theatre, 8
Lady Luxury (m), 12/25/14, Casino Theatre, 35
Lady Margaret (p), 1/27/02, Bijou Theatre, 32
Lady of Coventry, The (p), 11/21/11, Daly's Theatre, 16
Lady of Dreams, The (p), 2/28/12, Hudson Theatre, 21
Lady of Letters (p), 3/28/35, Mansfield Theatre, 20
Lady of Lyons, The (p), 5/19/02, Garrick Theatre, 8
Lady of Mexico (m), 10/9/62, Blackfriars' Theatre, 56
Lady of the Camellias, The (p), 12/24/17, Empire Theatre, 56
Lady of the Camellias, The (p), 3/20/63, Winter Garden Theatre, 13
Lady of the Lamp, The (p), 8/17/20, Republic Theatre, 111
Lady of the Orchids, The (p), 12/13/28, Henry Miller's Theatre, 20
Lady of the Rose (p), 5/19/25, 49th St. Theatre, 8
Lady of the Slipper, The (m), 10/28/12, Globe Theatre, 232
Lady or the Tiger?, The. See The Apple Tree
Lady Patricia (p), 2/26/12, Empire Theatre, 32
Lady Precious Stream (p), 1/27/36, Booth Theatre, 104
Lady Refuses, The (p), 3/7/33, Bijou Theatre, 7
Lady Remembers, The (p), 5/10/32, Provincetown Playhouse, 10
Lady Rose's Daughter (p), 11/16/03, Garrick Theatre, 16
Lady's Name, A (p), 5/15/16, Maxine Elliott's Theatre, 56
Lady's Not for Burning, The (p), 11/8/50, Royale Theatre, 151
Lady's Not for Burning, The (p), 2/21/57, Carnegie Hall Playhouse, 46
Lady's Virtue, A (p), 11/23/25, Bijou Theatre, 147
Lady Says Yes, A (m), 1/10/45, Broadhurst Theatre, 87
Lady Screams, The (p), 5/2/27, Selwyn Theatre, 8
Lady Shore, The (p), 3/27/05, Hudson Theatre, 16
Lady Teazle (m), 12/24/04, Casino Theatre, 57
Lady, The (p), 12/4/23, Empire Theatre, 85
Lady Who Came To Stay, The (p), 1/2/41, Maxine Elliott's Theatre, 4
Lady Windermere's Fan (p), 3/30/14, Hudson Theatre, 72
Lady Windermere's Fan (p), 1/26/32, Recital Theatre, 2
Lady Windermere's Fan (p), 10/14/46, Cort Theatre, 228
Lady with a Lamp, The (p), 11/19/31, Maxine Elliott's Theatre, 12
Laff That Off (p), 11/2/25, Wallack Theatre, 390
Laffing Room Only (r), 12/33/44, Winter Garden Theatre, 232
L'Aiglon (p), 10/22/00, Knickerbocker Theatre, 73
Lake of the Woods / Fingernails Blue as Flowers (p), 12/6/71, American Place Theatre, 33
Lake, The (p), 12/26/33, Martin Beck Theatre, 55
Lally (p), 2/8/27, Greenwich Village Theatre, 60
Lamp at Midnight (p), 12/21/47, New Stages Theatre, 51
Lancashire Lass, The (p), 12/30/31, President Theatre, 36
Lancers, The (p), 12/3/07, Daly's Theatre, 12
Land Beyond the River, A (p), 3/28/57, Greenwich Mews Theatre, 96
Land Is Bright, The (p), 10/28/41, Music Box Theatre, 79
Land of Bells, The (in Italian) (m), 5/9/35, Majestic Theatre, 4
Land of Fame (p), 9/21/43, Belasco Theatre, 6
Land of Heart's Desire, The / A Pot of Broth / Kathleen ni Houlihan (p), 6/3/03, Carnegie Lyceum Theatre, 2
Land of Heart's Desire, The / In a Balcony (p), 10/26/00, Wallack Theatre, 1
Land of Heart's Desire, The / In a Balcony (p), 5/6/01, Knickerbocker Theatre, 1
Land of Heart's Desire, The / Kathleen ni Houlihan / The Hour Glass (p), 2/21/05, Hudson Theatre, 1
Land of Joy, The (m), 10/31/17, Park Theatre, 86
Land of Nod, The (r), 4/1/07, New York Theatre, 17
Land of Promise, The (p), 12/25/13, Lyceum Theatre, 76
Land of the Free, The (p), 10/2/17, 48th St. Theatre, 32
Land's End (p), 12/11/46, Playhouse, 5
Landscape / Silence (p), 4/2/70, Forum Theatre, 53
Landscape / Silence (p), 2/9/71, Forum Theatre, 6
Lark, The (p), 11/17/55, Longacre Theatre, 229
Lash of a Whip, The / The Shades of Night (p), 2/25/01, Lyceum Theatre, 40
Lass O'Laughter (p), 1/8/25, Comedy Theatre, 28
Lassie (m), 4/6/20, Nora Bayes Theatre, 159
Lassoo, The (p), 8/13/17, Lyceum Theatre, 56
Last Analysis, The (p), 10/1/64, Belasco, 28
Last Analysis, The (p), 6/23/71, Circle in the Square, 46
Last Appeal, The (p), 4/14/02, Wallack Theatre, 24
Last Dance, The (p), 1/27/48, Belasco Theatre, 7
Last Days of Lincoln, The (p), 4/20/65, Theatre de Lys, 1, (ANTA Matinee)
Last Enemy, The (p), 10/30/30, Shubert Theatre, 4
Last Laugh, The (p), 7/29/15, 39th St. Theatre, 52
Last Love of Don Juan, The, 11/23/55, Rooftop Theatre, 13
Last Mile, The (p), 2/13/30, Sam H. Harris Theatre, 285
Last Minstrel, The / Save Me a Place at Forest Lawn (p), 5/8/63, Pocket Theatre, 38
Last Night of Don Juan, The / The Pilgrimage (p), 11/9/25, Greenwich Village Theatre, 16
Last of Mrs. Cheyney, The (p), 11/9/25, Fulton Theatre, 283
Last of Mrs. Lincoln, The (p), 12/12/72, ANTA Theatre, 63
Last of the Red Hot Lovers (p), 12/28/69, Eugene O'Neill Theatre, 706
Last Pad, The (p), 12/7/70, 13th Street Theatre
Last Resort, The (p), 3/2/14, Longacre Theatre, 16

Last Stand. See One Night Stands of a Noisy Passenger
Last Stop (p), 9/5/44, Ethel Barrymore Theatre, 23
Last Straw, The. See Two Times One
Last Sweet Days of Isaac, The (The Elevator / I Want to Walk to San Francisco) (m), 1/26/70, Eastside Playhouse, 485
Last Toast, The / Uncle Sam's Money / The Worth of a Man / Lonesome Like (p), 4/27/14, 48th St. Theatre, 1
Last Triangle, The. See Two Camps by Koutoukas
Last Waltz, The (m), 5/10/21, Century Theatre, 185
Last Warning, The (p), 10/24/22, Klaw Theatre, 236
Late Christopher Bean, The (p), 10/31/32, Henry Miller's Theatre, 211
Late George Apley, The (p), 11/21/44, Lyceum Theatre, 384
Late Late Show, The. See Triple Play
Late Love (p), 10/13/53, National Theatre, 95
Late One Evening (p), 1/9/33, Plymouth Theatre, 8
Late Wisdom (p), 4/23/34, Mansfield Theatre, 2
Laterna Magika, 8/3/64, Carnegie Hall, 27
Latter Days of a Celebrated Soubrette, The (p), 5/16/74, Central Arts Theatre, 12
Laugh, Clown, Laugh! (p), 11/28/23, Belasco Theatre, 136
Laugh Parade, The (m), 11/2/31, Imperial Theatre, 243
Laugh Time (r), 9/8/43, Shubert Theatre, 126
Laugh, Town, Laugh! (r), 6/22/42, Alvin Theatre, 65
Laughing Husband, The (m), 2/2/14, Knickerbocker Theatre, 48
Laughing Lady, The (p), 2/12/23, Longacre Theatre, 97
Laughing Woman, The (p), 10/13/36, John Golden Theatre, 23
Laughs and Other Events (r), 10/10/60, Ethel Barrymore Theatre, 8
Laughs, Etc. See Stop, You're Killing Me
Laughwind (p), 3/2/66, Bouwerie Lane Theatre, 5
Launcelot and Elaine (p), 9/12/21, Greenwich Village Theatre, 32
Launcelot and Elaine (p), 3/8/30, President Theatre, 25
Laundry, The (p), 2/13/63, Gate Theatre, 30
Launzi (p), 10/10/23, Plymouth Theatre, 13
Laura (p), 6/26/47, Cort Theatre, 44
Laurette Taylor in Scenes from Shakespeare, 4/5/18, Criterion Theatre
Law and the Man, The (p), 12/20/06, Manhattan Theatre, 54
Law Breaker, The (p), 2/1/22, Booth Theatre, 90
Law of the Land, The (p), 9/30/14, 48th St. Theatre, 221
Lawful Larceny (p), 1/2/22, Republic Theatre, 225
Lawyer's Dilemma, The (p), 7/9/28, Belmont Theatre, 24
Lazarus Laughed (p), 4/8/48, Collins Auditorium, 8
Lazybones (p), 9/22/24, Vanderbilt Theatre, 72
Leader. See The Honest-to-God Schnozzola
Leading Lady, The (p), 10/18/48, National Theatre, 8
Leaf and Bough (p), 1/21/49, Cort Theatre, 3
Leah Kleschna (p), 12/12/04, Manhattan Theatre, 131
Leah Kleschna (p), 4/21/24, Lyric Theatre, 32
Lean Harvest (p), 10/13/31, Forrest Theatre, 31
Leap, The (p), 5/22/24, Cherry Lane Theatre, 12
Lear. See King Lear
Learned Ladies, The (p), 11/9/11, Lyric Theatre
Leave Her to Heaven (p), 2/27/40, Longacre Theatre, 15
Leave It to Jane (m), 8/28/17, Longacre Theatre, 167
Leave It to Jane (m), 5/25/59, Sheridan Square Playhouse, 928
Leave It to Me (m), 11/9/38, Imperial Theatre, 291
Leave It to Me (m), 9/4/39, Imperial Theatre, 16
Leaves of Grass (r), 9/12/71, Theatre Four, 49
Ledge, A (p), 11/18/29, Assembly Theatre, 16
Left Bank, The (p), 10/5/31, Little Theatre, 241
Left of Broadway, 3/12/39, Keynote Theatre
Legal Murder (p), 2/15/34, President Theatre, 7
Legend of Leonora, The (p), 1/5/14, Empire Theatre, 136
Legend of Leonora, The (p), 3/29/27, Ritz Theatre, 16
Legend of Lizzie, The (p), 2/9/59, 54th St. Theatre, 2
Legend of Lovers (p), 12/26/51, Plymouth Theatre, 22
Legend of Lovers (p), 10/27/59, 41st St. Theatre, 32
Legend of Sarah (p), 10/11/50, Fulton Theatre, 29
Legend of the Dance, The / Sooner and Later, 3/31/25, Neighborhood Playhouse, 28
Lemon Sky (p), 5/17/70, Playhouse, 16
Lemonade / The Autograph Hound (p), 12/13/68, Jan Hus Playhouse, 28
Lend an Ear (r), 12/16/48, National Theatre, 460
Lend an Ear (r), 9/24/59, Renata Theatre, 94
Lend an Ear (r), 10/16/69, Master Theatre, 19, (Equity Library Theatre)
Lend Me Your Ears! (p), 10/5/36, Mansfield Theatre, 8
Lenin's Dowry (p), 5/12/32, Chanin Auditorium, 2
Lenny (p), 5/26/71, Brooks Atkinson Theatre, 453
Leonard Bernstein's Theatre Songs (r), 6/28/65, Theatre de Lys, 88
Leonce and Lena (p), 12/9/65, Clark Center YWCA, 8
Les Cloches de Corneville (Chimes of Normandy) (m), 12/13/26, Jolson Theatre, 7
Les Fausses Confidences / Baptiste (p), 11/12/52, Ziegfeld Theatre, 13
Les Fourberies de Scapin / Amphitryon (p), 11/20/52, Ziegfeld Theatre, 12
Lesson in Love, A (p), 9/24/23, 39th St. Theatre, 75
Lesson, The / The Bald Soprano (p), 9/17/63, Gate Theatre, 48
Lesson, The / The Chairs (p), 1/9/58, Phoenix Theatre, 22
Lesson, The / The New Tenant (p), 3/9/60, Royal Playhouse, 333
Let and Sublet (p), 5/19/30, Biltmore Theatre, 40
Let 'Em Eat Cake (m), 10/21/33, Imperial Theatre, 89
Let Freedom Ring (p), 11/6/35, Broadhurst Theatre, 30
Let Freedom Ring (p), 12/17/35, Civic Repertory Theatre, 79
Let Freedom Sing (r), 10/5/42, Longacre Theatre, 8
Let It Ride! (m), 10/12/61, Eugene O'Neill Theatre, 68
Let Me Hear You Smile (p), 1/16/73, Biltmore Theatre, 1
Let My People Come (r), 1/8/74, Village Gate, 194
Let's Face It (m), 10/29/41, Imperial Theatre, 303
Let's Face It (m), 8/17/42, Imperial Theatre, 547
Let's Go (r), 3/9/18, Fulton Theatre, 25
Let's Make an Opera (m), 12/13/50, Golden Theatre, 5
Let's Sing Yiddish (r), 11/9/66, Brooks Atkinson Theatre, 107
Let Them Down, Gently (Our Man in Madras / On Vacation) (p), 1/8/68, Theatre de Lys, 2, (ANTA Matinee)
Let Us Be Gay (p), 2/21/29, Little Theatre, 132
Letter of the Law, The (p), 2/23/20, Criterion Theatre, 89
Letter, The (p), 9/26/27, Morosco Theatre, 105
Letters to Lucerne (p), 12/23/41, Cort Theatre, 23
Lettre Morte / Architruc (p), 4/15/70, Barbizon-Plaza Theatre, 10, (Le Treteau de Paris)
Letty (p), 9/12/04, Hudson Theatre, 64
Letty Pepper (m), 4/10/22, Vanderbilt Theatre, 32
Lew Dockstadter's Minstrels. See Dockstadter's Minstrels
Lew Leslie's Blackbirds of 1939 (r), 2/11/39, Hudson Theatre, 9
Li'l Abner (m), 11/15/56, St. James Theatre, 693
Liar, The (m), 5/18/50, Broadhurst Theatre, 12
Liars, The, 11/9/15, Playhouse Theatre
Lib Comes High (p), 10/14/71, Blackfriars' Guild Theatre, 40
Libby Holman's "Blues, Ballads and Sin-Songs," , 10/4/54, Bijou Theatre, 12
Libel (p), 12/20/35, Henry Miller's Theatre, 156
Liberty Belles, The (m), 9/30/01, Madison Square Theatre, 104
Liberty Hall (p), 3/11/13, Empire Theatre, 39
Liberty Jones (p), 2/5/41, Shubert Theatre, 22
License, The. See The Man with the Flower in His Mouth
Lido Girl, The (p), 8/23/28, Edyth Totten Theatre, 60
Lie, The (p), 12/24/14, Harris Theatre, 172
Lieber Augustin (m), 9/3/13, Casino Theatre, 37
Life (p), 3/31/02, Garden Theatre, 7
Life (p), 10/24/14, Manhattan Opera House, 161
Life and Death of An American (p), 5/19/39, Maxine Elliott's Theatre, 38
Life and Loves of Dorian Gray, The (p), 8/17/36, Comedy Theatre, 32
Life and Times of J. Walter Smintheus, The (p), 12/7/70, Theatre de Lys, 2, (ANTA Matinee)
Life and Times of J. Walter Smintheus, The. See Underground
Life and Times of Joseph Stalin, The, 12/14/73, Brooklyn Academy of Music, 4
Life Begins (p), 3/28/32, Selwyn Theatre, 8
Life Begins at 8:40 (r), 8/27/34, Winter Garden Theatre, 238
Life in Bed (p), 4/1/71, Theatre 80 St. Marks Playhouse, 78
Life Is a Dream (p), 3/19/64, Astor Place Playhouse, 40
Life Is a Dream (p), 12/2/72, Gramercy Arts Theatre, 3, (Spanish Theatre Repertory Co.)
Life Is Like That (p), 12/22/30, Little Theatre, 32
Life Line, The (p), 12/27/30, Vanderbilt Theatre, 17
Life of a Man, The (m), 9/29/72, Judson Poet's Theatre, 16
Life of Man, The (p), 1/14/17, Comedy Theatre, 1
Life of Reilly, The (p), 4/29/42, Broadhurst Theatre, 5
Life's Too Short (p), 9/20/35, Broadhurst Theatre, 11
Life Size. See Sold to the Movies
Life with Father (p), 11/8/39, Empire Theatre, 3,224
Life with Father (p), 10/19/67, New York City Center, 22
Life with Mother (p), 10/20/48, Empire Theatre, 265
Lifeline (p), 11/30/42, Belasco Theatre, 8
Lifting the Lid (m), 6/5/05, New Amsterdam Theatre, 112
Light Eternal, The (p), 12/10/06, Majestic Theatre, 16
Light from St. Agnes, The / Dolce / The Eyes of the Heart (p), 4/24/06, Manhattan Theatre, 3
Light from St. Agnes, The / The Eyes of the Heart / The Rose (p), 3/27/05, Manhattan Theatre, 3
Light, Lively and Yiddish (m), 10/27/70, Belasco Theatre, 88
Light of Asia, The (p), 10/9/28, Hampden's Theatre, 23
Light of the World, The (p), 1/6/20, Lyric Theatre, 31
Light That Failed, The (p), 11/9/03, Knickerbocker Theatre, 32
Light That Lies in Woman's Eyes, The (p), 1/25/04, Criterion Theatre, 23
Light Up the Sky (p), 11/18/48, Royale Theatre, 214
Light Wine and Beer (p), 11/10/30, Waldorf Theatre, 40
Lightnin' (p), 8/26/18, Gaiety Theatre, 1,291
Lightnin' (p), 9/15/38, John Golden Theatre, 54
Lights o' London, The (p), 5/1/11, Lyric Theatre, 32
Lights o' London, The (p), 6/23/36, Palm Garden Theatre, 11
Lights Out (p), 8/16/22, Vanderbilt Theatre, 12

Like a King (p), 10/3/21, 39th St. Theatre, 16
Like Other People (p), 3/29/63, Village South Theatre, 4
Likes o' Me, The / The Mollusc (p), 9/1/08, Garrick Theatre, 33
Lilac Domino, The (p), 10/28/14, 44th St. Theatre, 109
Lilac Room, The (p), 4/3/07, Weber Theatre, 4
Lilac Time (p), 2/6/17, Republic Theatre, 176
Lilies of the Field (p), 10/4/21, Klaw Theatre, 169
Liliom (p), 4/20/21, Garrick Theatre, 300
Liliom (p), 3/20/22, 44th St. Theatre, 16
Liliom (p), 10/26/32, Civic Repertory Theatre, 34
Liliom (p), 3/25/40, 44th St. Theatre, 56
Lillian Owen's Marionettes, 12/22/21, Shubert Theatre, 21
Lilly Turner (p), 9/19/32, Morosco Theatre, 24
Lily and the Prince, The (p), 4/17/11, Garden Theatre, 8
Lily of the Valley (p), 2/26/42, Windsor Theatre, 8
Lily Sue (p), 11/16/26, Lyceum Theatre, 47
Lily, The (p), 12/23/09, Stuyvesant Theatre, 164
Limb of Snow. See Double Play
Lime Green / Khaki Blue (p), 3/26/69, Provincetown Playhouse, 13
Lincoln (p), 3/26/06, Liberty Theatre, 21
Lincoln Center Community / Street Theatre Festival, 8/21/72, Lincoln Center Plaza, 33
Lincoln Mask, The (p), 10/30/72, Plymouth Theatre, 8
Lincoln (new version) (p), 2/5/09, Garden Theatre, 17
Linden Tree, The (p), 3/2/48, Music Box Theatre, 7
Line / Acrobats (p), 2/15/71, Theatre de Lys, 31
Linger Longer Letty, 11/20/19, Fulton Theatre, 69
Lingering Past, The (p), 6/29/32, Provincetown Playhouse, 4
Lion and the Mouse, The (p), 11/20/05, Lyceum Theatre, 686
Lion in Love, The (p), 4/25/63, One Sheridan Square, 6
Lion in Winter, The (p), 3/3/66, Ambassador Theatre, 92
Lion Tamer, The (p), 10/7/26, Neighborhood Playhouse, 33
Listen Lester (m), 12/23/18, Knickerbocker Theatre, 272
Listen, Professor! (p), 12/22/43, Forrest Theatre, 29
Listening In (p), 12/4/22, Bijou Theatre, 91
Literary Sense, The / The Reckoning (p), 1/13/08, Madison Square Theatre, 24
Little A (p), 1/15/47, Henry Miller's Theatre, 21
Little Accident (p), 10/9/28, Morosco Theatre, 304
Little Act of Justice, A / The Stickup / Footsteps (p), 1/9/22, Provincetown Playhouse, 21
Little Angel, The (p), 9/27/24, Frazee Theatre, 49
Little Bit of Everything, A (r), 6/6/04, New Amsterdam Theatre, 120
Little Bit of Fluff, A (p), 8/26/16, 39th St. Theatre, 17
Little Black Book, The (p), 12/26/32, Selwyn Theatre, 8
Little Black Book, The (p), 4/25/72, Helen Hayes Theatre, 7
Little Blue Devil, The (m), 11/3/19, Central Theatre, 75
Little Blue Light, The (p), 4/29/51, ANTA Playhouse, 16
Little Boxes (The Coffee Lace / Trevor) (p), 12/3/69, New Theatre, 15
Little Boy Blue (m), 11/27/11, Lyric Theatre, 176
Little Brother of the Rich, A (p), 12/27/09, Wallack Theatre, 24
Little Brother, The (p), 11/25/18, Belmont Theatre, 120
Little Brown Jug (p), 3/6/46, Martin Beck Theatre, 5
Little Cafe, The (m), 11/10/13, New Amsterdam Theatre, 144
Little Cherub, The (m), 8/6/06, Criterion Theatre, 155
Little Cherub, The (m), 8/6/07, Criterion Theatre, 21
Little Clay Cart, The (p), 12/5/24, Neighborhood Playhouse, 69
Little Clay Cart, The (p), 11/4/26, Neighborhood Playhouse, 39
Little Clay Cart, The (p), 6/30/53, Theatre de Lys
Little Damozel, The (p), 9/24/10, Comedy Theatre, 49
Little Dark Horse (p), 11/16/41, Golden Theatre, 9
Little Darling (p), 10/27/42, Biltmore Theatre, 23
Little Duchess, The (m), 10/14/01, Casino Theatre, 136
Little Eyolf (p), 4/18/10, Nazimova Theatre, 48
Little Eyolf (p), 2/2/26, Guild Theatre, 7
Little Eyolf (p), 3/16/64, Actors Playhouse, 33
Little Eyolf (p), 2/9/74, Manhattan Theatre Club, 14
Little Father of the Wilderness, The / Milestones (p), 6/2/30, Empire Theatre, 8
Little Father of the Wilderness, The / The Mountain Climber (p), 4/23/06, Criterion Theatre, 24
Little Foxes, The (p), 2/15/39, National Theatre, 410
Little Foxes, The (p), 10/26/67, Vivian Beaumont Theatre, 100
Little Glass Clock (p), 3/26/56, Golden Theatre, 8
Little Gray Lady, The (p), 1/22/06, Garrick Theatre, 32
Little Hut, The (p), 10/7/53, Coronet Theatre, 29
Little Hut, The (p), 7/25/61, 41st St. Theatre, 16
Little Italy / Divorçons (p), 5/26/02, Manhattan Theatre, 24
Little Jessie James (m), 8/15/23, Longacre Theatre, 385
Little Johnny Jones (m), 11/7/04, Liberty Theatre, 52
Little Johnny Jones (p), 5/8/05, New York Theatre, 128
Little Johnny Jones (m), 11/03/05, New York Theatre
Little Johnny Jones (m), 4/22/07, Academy of Music, 16
Little Journey, A (p), 12/26/18, Little Theatre, 252
Little Lady in Blue (p), 12/21/16, Belasco Theatre, 100
Little Lady of Friday Night, The / The Man with the Tranquil Mind / The Immovable Gordons (p) (Dumbbell People in a Barbell World), 2/14/62, Cricket Theatre, 13
Little Lord Fauntleroy (p), 4/13/03, Casino Theatre, 12
Little Man, The / Magic (p), 2/12/17, Maxine Elliott's Theatre, 56
Little Mary (p), 1/5/04, Empire Theatre, 24
Little Mary Sunshine (m), 11/18/59, Orpheum Theatre, 1,143
Little Mary Sunshine (m), 2/12/70, Master Theatre, 19, (Equity Library Theatre)
Little Me (m), 11/17/62, Lunt-Fontanne Theatre, 257
Little Michus, The (m), 1/31/07, Garden Theatre, 29
Little Millionaire, The (m), 9/25/11, Cohan Theatre, 192
Little Minister, The (p), 12/26/04, Empire Theatre, 73
Little Minister, The (p), 1/11/16, Empire Theatre, 79
Little Minister, The (p), 3/23/25, Globe Theatre, 16
Little Minister, The / Op o' Me Thumb (p), 2/6/05, Empire Theatre
Little Miss Bluebeard (m), 8/28/23, Lyceum Theatre, 175
Little Miss Brown (p), 8/29/12, 48th St. Theatre, 84
Little Miss Charity (m), 9/2/20, Belmont Theatre, 76
Little Miss Fix-It (m), 4/3/11, Globe Theatre, 56
Little Moon of Alban (p), 12/1/60, Longacre Theatre, 20
Little Murders (p), 4/25/67, Broadhurst Theatre, 7
Little Murders (p), 1/5/69, Circle in the Square, 400
Little Nell and the Marchioness (p), 3/26/00, Herald Square Theatre, 16
Little Nellie Kelly (m), 11/13/22, Liberty Theatre, 276
Little Nemo (m), 10/20/08, New Amsterdam Theatre, 111
Little Night Music, A (m), 2/25/73, Shubert Theatre, 527
Little Ol' Boy (p), 4/24/33, Playhouse, 11
Little Old New York (p), 9/8/20, Plymouth Theatre, 311
Little Orchid Annie (p), 4/21/30, Eltinge Theatre, 16
Little Poor Man, The (p), 8/5/25, Princess Theatre, 35
Little Princess, The (p), 1/14/03, Criterion Theatre, 33
Little Princess, The (p), 12/1/03, Madison Square Theatre, 15
Little Private World of Arthur Morton Fenwick, The / No Exit (p), 10/30/67, Bouwerie Lane Theatre, 8
Little Racketeer, A (m), 1/18/32, 44th St. Theatre, 48
Little Red Riding Hood (r), 1/8/00, Casino Theatre, 24
Little Red Riding Hood (p), 12/26/21, Manhattan Opera House, 3
Little Shot (p), 1/17/35, Playhouse, 4
Little Show, The (r), 4/30/29, Music Box Theatre, 321
Little Simplicity (m), 11/4/18, Astor Theatre, 112
Little Spitfire, The (p), 8/16/26, Cort Theatre, 201
Little Stranger, The (p), 8/27/05, Hackett Theatre, 25
Little Teacher, The (p), 2/4/18, Playhouse, 128
Little Theatre of the Deaf, The (r), 12/26/72, American Place Theatre, 12
Little Theatre Tournament, 5/7/23, Nora Bayes Theatre, 8
Little Theatre Tournament, 5/5/24, Belasco Theatre, 8
Little Theatre Tournament, 5/4/25, Wallack Theatre, 8
Little Theatre Tournament, 5/3/26, Nora Bayes Theatre, 5
Little Theatre Tournament, 5/2/27, Frolic Theatre, 7
Little Theatre Tournament, 5/7/28, Frolic Theatre, 7
Little Theatre Tournament, 5/6/29, Waldorf Theatre, 7
Little Theatre Tournament, 5/5/30, Waldorf Theatre, 14
Little Water on the Side, A (p), 1/6/14, Hudson Theatre, 63
Little Whopper, The (m), 10/13/19, Casino Theatre, 224
Little Women (p), 10/14/12, Playhouse, 184
Little Women (p), 12/18/16, Park Theatre, 24
Little Women (p), 12/7/31, Playhouse, 16
Little Women (p), 12/23/32, Playhouse, 14
Little Women (p), 12/12/44, New York City Center, 23
Little Women (p), 12/23/45, New York City Center, 16
Littlest Rebel, The (p), 11/14/11, Liberty Theatre, 55
Littlest Revue, The (r), 5/22/56, Phoenix Theatre, 32
Live and Learn (p), 4/9/30, Wallack Theatre, 5
Live Life Again (p), 9/29/45, Belasco Theatre, 2
Live Like Pigs (p), 6/7/65, Actors Playhouse, 128
Live Wire, The (p), 8/17/50, Playhouse, 28
Livin' the Life (m), 4/27/57, Phoenix Theatre, 25
Living Corpse, The (p), 12/6/29, Civic Repertory Theatre, 33
Living Dangerously (p), 1/12/35, Morosco Theatre, 9
Living Mask, The (p), 1/21/24, 44th St. Theatre, 36
Living Premise, The (r), 6/13/63, Premise Theatre, 192
Living Room, The (p), 11/17/54, Henry Miller's Theatre, 22
Living Room, The (p), 11/21/62, Gramercy Arts Theatre, 23
Living Theatre, The (Frankenstein / Mysteries and Smaller Pieces / The Antigone of Sophokles / Paradise Now) (p), 10/2/68, Brooklyn Academy of Music, 21
Liz the Mother / Don (p), 1/3/10, New Theatre, 1
Liza (m), 11/27/22, Daly's Theatre, 172
Liza, 1/6/74, Winter Garden Theatre, 23
Lo and Behold (p), 12/12/51, Booth Theatre, 38
Local Stigmatic, The / Harold Pinter's Sketches (Applicant / Interview / Last to Go / Request Stop / That's All / That's Your Trouble / Trouble in the Works) (p), 11/3/69, Actors Playhouse, 8
Locandiera, La (p), 12/6/26, Civic Repertory Theatre, 32

Locandiera, La, 10/21/27, Civic Repertory Theatre, 11
Locandiera, La (p), 10/12/28, Civic Repertory Theatre, 4
Locandiera, La (p), 1/4/30, Civic Repertory Theatre, 4
Locandiera, La (p), 4/25/31, Civic Repertory Theatre, 2
Locked Door, The (p), 6/19/24, Cort Theatre, 20
Locked Room, The (p), 12/25/33, Ambassador Theatre, 8
Loco (p), 10/16/46, Biltmore Theatre, 37
Lodger, The (p), 1/18/17, Maxine Elliott' s Theatre, 56
Loggerheads (p), 2/9/25, Cherry Lane Theatre, 70
Lola from Berlin (m), 9/16/07, Liberty Theatre, 35
Lollipop (m), 1/21/24, Knickerbocker Theatre, 145
Lolly (p), 10/16/29, Assembly Theatre, 29
Lombardi, Ltd. (p), 9/24/17, Morosco Theatre, 296
Lombardi, Ltd. (p), 6/6/27, George M. Cohan Theatre, 24
London Assurance (p), 4/3/05, Knickerbocker Theatre, 32
London Assurance (p), 2/18/37, Vanderbilt Theatre, 4
London Calling (p), 10/18/30, Little Theatre, 11
London Follies (r), 4/17/11, Weber Theatre, 11
London Intimate Opera Company, 1/4/38, Little Theatre
Lone Valley (p), 3/10/33, Plymouth Theatre, 3
Lonely Romeo, A (m), 6/10/19, Shubert Theatre, 87
Lonesome Like / The Last Toast / Uncle Sam's Money / The Worth of a Man (p), 4/27/14, 48th St. Theatre, 1
Lonesome Town (m), 1/20/08, New Circle Theatre, 88
Long and the Short and the Tall, The (p), 3/29/62, Maidman Playhouse, 22
Long Christmas Dinner, The. See Thornton Wilder's Triple Bill
Long Dash, The (p), 11/5/18, 39th St. Theatre, 31
Long Day's Journey into Night (p), 11/7/56, Helen Hayes Theatre, 390
Long Day's Journey into Night (p) (Royal Dramatic Theatre of Sweden), 5/15/62, Cort Theatre, 2
Long Day's Journey into Night (p), 4/21/71, Promenade Theatre, 121
Long Day's Journey into Night (p), 12/10/73, Actors Studio, 9
Long Days, The (p), 4/20/51, Empire Theatre, 3
Long Dream, The (p), 2/17/60, Ambassador Theatre, 5
Long Gallery, The (p), 3/6/58, RNA Theatre, 14
Long Play Tournament, 5/11/31, Craig Theatre, 5
Long Road, The (p), 9/9/30, Longacre Theatre, 23
Long Voyage Home The (p), 12/4/61, Mermaid Theatre, 32
Long Voyage Home, The / The Moon of the Caribbees / In the Zone / Bound East for Cardiff (p), 10/29/37, Lafayette Theatre, 68
Long Voyage Home, The / The Moon of the Caribbees / In the Zone / Bound East for Cardiff (p), 5/20/48, N.Y. City Center, 14
Long Watch, The (p), 3/20/52, Lyceum Theatre, 12
Long Way from Home, A (p), 2/8/48, Maxine Elliott's Theatre, 6
Look After Lulu (p), 3/3/59, Henry Miller's Theatre, 39
Look After Lulu (p), 4/2/65, Master Theatre, 9, (Equity Library Theatre)
Look at the Fifties, A (m), 4/14/72, Judson Memorial Church Theatre, 12
Look at the Heffernans (p), 11/16/34, John Golden Theatre, 1
Look Away (p), 1/7/73, Playhouse Theatre, 1
Look Back at Each Other, A (p), 5/21/74, Masque Theatre, 2
Look Back in Anger (p), 10/1/57, Lyceum Theatre, 407
Look Back in Anger (p), 11/11/58, 41st St. Theatre, 116
Look Homeward, Angel (p), 11/28/57, Ethel Barrymore Theatre, 564
Look, Ma, I'm Dancin' (m), 1/29/48, Adelphi Theatre, 188
Look Me Up (r), 10/6/71, Plaza 9 Music Hall, 406
Look to the Lillies (m), 3/29/70, Lunt-Fontanne Theatre, 25
Look: We've Come Through (p), 10/25/61, Hudson Theatre, 5
Look: We've Come Through (p), 1/10/74, Master Theatre, 12, (Equity Library Theatre)
Look Where I'm At (m), 3/5/71, Theatre Four, 5
Look Who's Here (m), 3/2/20, 44th St. Theatre, 87
Loose Ankles, 8/16/26, Biltmore Theatre, 161
Loose Ends (p), 11/1/26, Ritz Theatre, 40
Loose Moments (p), 2/4/35, Vanderbilt Theatre, 8
Loot (p), 3/18/68, Biltmore Theatre, 22
Loot (p), 5/12/73, CSC Repertory Theatre, 6
Lord and Lady Algy (p), 12/14/03, Criterion Theatre, 16
Lord and Lady Algy (p), 12/22/17, Broadhurst Theatre, 41
Lord Blesses the Bishop, The (p), 11/27/34, Adelphi Theatre, 7
Lord Pengo (p), 11/19/62, Royale Theatre, 175
Lorelei (p), 11/29/38, Longacre Theatre, 7
Lorelei (m), 1/27/74, Palace Theatre, 143
Lorenzaccid (p), 3/12/65, Master Theatre, 9, (Equity Library Theatre)
Lorenzo (p), 2/14/63, Plymouth Theatre, 4
Los Angeles (p), 12/19/27, Hudson Theatre, 16
Losers. See Lovers
Losing Eloise (p), 11/17/17, Harris Theatre, 72
Loss of Roses, A (p), 11/28/59, Eugene O'Neill Theatre, 25
Lost (p), 3/28/27, Mansfield Theatre, 8
Lost Boy (p), 1/5/32, Mansfield Theatre, 15
Lost Co-respondent, The (p), 5/3/15, Bramhall Playhouse, 8
Lost Horizons (p), 10/15/34, St. James Theatre, 56
Lost in the Stars (m), 10/30/49, Music Box Theatre, 281
Lost in the Stars (m), 3/22/68, Master Theatre, 15, (Equity Library Theatre)
Lost in the Stars (m), 4/18/72, Imperial Theatre, 39
Lost Leader, The (p), 11/11/19, Greenwich Village Theatre, 31
Lost River (p), 10/3/00, 14th St. Theatre, 95
Lost Sheep (p), 5/5/30, Selwyn Theatre, 96
Lost Sheep (p), 8/18/30, Selwyn Theatre, 16
Lotta, or The Best Thing Evolution's Ever Come Up With (m), 10/18/73, Anspacher / Public Theatre, 54
Lottery Man, The (p), 12/6/09, Bijou Theatre, 200
Loud Red Patrick, The (p), 10/3/56, Ambassador Theatre, 93
Loud Speaker (p), 3/2/27, 52nd St. Theatre, 29
Louder, Please (p), 11/12/31, Masque Theatre, 68
Louie the 14th (m), 3/3/25, Cosmopolitan Theatre, 319
Louisiana (p), 2/27/33, 48th St. Theatre, 8
Louisiana Lady (m), 6/2/47, Century Theatre, 4
Louisiana Purchase (m), 5/28/40, Imperial Theatre, 444
Love (p), 2/19/21, Provincetown Playhouse, 14
Love Among the Lions (p), 8/8/10, Garrick Theatre, 48
Love and Babies (p), 8/22/33, Cort Theatre, 7
Love and Death (p), 12/14/25, Jolson Theatre, 8
Love and Kisses (p), 12/18/63, Music Box Theatre, 13
Love and Let Love (p), 10/19/51, Plymouth Theatre, 56
Love and Let Love (m), 1/2/68, Sheridan Square Playhouse, 14
Love and Libel, or, The Ogre of the Provincial World (p), 12/7/60, Martin Beck Theatre, 5
Love and Maple Syrup (r), 1/7/70, Mercer-Hansbury Theatre, 15
Love and the Man (p), 2/20/05, Knickerbocker Theatre, 22
Love Birds (p), 3/15/21, Apollo Theatre, 103
Love Call, The (m), 10/24/27, Majestic Theatre, 81
Love Child, The (p), 11/14/22, George M. Cohan Theatre, 169
Love City, The (p), 1/25/26, Little Theatre, 24
Love Cure, The (m), 9/1/09, New Amsterdam Theatre, 35
Love Dreams (m), 10/10/21, Times Square Theatre, 40
Love Drive, The (p), 10/30/17, Criterion Theatre, 15
Love Duel, The (p), 4/15/29, Ethel Barrymore Theatre, 88
Love 'Em and Leave 'Em (p), 2/3/26, Sam H. Harris Theatre, 152
Love Expert, The (p), 9/23/29, Wallack Theatre, 16
Love for Love (p), 3/31/25, Greenwich Village Theatre, 47
Love for Love (p), 9/14/25, Daly's Theatre, 16
Love for Love (p), 6/3/40, Hudson Theatre, 8
Love for Love (p), 5/26/47, Royale Theatre, 48
Love from a Stranger (p), 9/29/36, Fulton Theatre, 31
Love Goes to Press (p), 1/1/47, Biltmore Theatre, 5
Love Gotta Come by Saturday Night / Orrin (p), 1/8/73, Theatre de Lys, 2, (ANTA Matinee)
Love Habit, The (p), 3/14/23, Bijou Theatre, 69
Love, Honor and Betray (p), 3/12/30, Eltinge Theatre, 45
Love in a Garden, 6/15/26, Garrick Theatre, 6
Love in a Mist (p), 4/12/26, Gaiety Theatre, 120
Love in a Pub. See What! And Leave Bloomingdales?
Love in E-Flat (p), 2/13/67, Brooks Atkinson Theatre, 24
Love in My Fashion (p), 12/3/37, Ritz Theatre, 2
Love in the Tropics (p), 10/18/27, Daly's Theatre, 15
Love Is a Time of Day (p), 12/22/69, Music Box Theatre, 8
Love Is Like That (p), 4/18/27, Cort Theatre, 24
Love Kills (p), 5/1/34, Forrest Theatre, 15
Love Laughs (p), 5/20/19, Bijou Theatre, 31
Love Leash, The (p), 10/20/13, Harris Theatre, 16
Love Letter, The (p), 10/9/06, Lyric Theatre, 23
Love Letter, The (m), 10/4/21, Globe Theatre, 31
Love Life (m), 10/7/48, 46th St. Theatre, 252
Love Match, The (p), 10/12/01, Lyceum Theatre, 57
Love Me Little (p), 4/14/58, Helen Hayes Theatre, 8
Love Me Long (p), 11/7/49, 48th St. Theatre, 16
Love Me, Love My Children (m), 11/3/71, Mercer-O'Casey Theatre, 187
Love Mill, The (m), 2/7/18, 48th St. Theatre, 52
Love Nest, The (p), 12/22/27, Comedy Theatre, 25
Love Nest, The (p), 1/25/63, Writers' Stage, 12
Love o' Mike (m), 1/15/17, Shubert Theatre, 192
Love of Four Colonels, The (p), 1/15/53, Shubert Theatre, 141
Love of Two Hours, The (p), 10/26/62, Actors Playhouse, 5
Love of Women (p), 12/13/37, John Golden Theatre, 8
Love on Leave (p), 6/20/44, Hudson Theatre, 7
Love on the Dole (p), 2/24/36, Sam S. Shubert Theatre, 145
Love Route, The (p), 10/30/06, Lincoln Square Theatre, 47
Love's Call (p), 9/10/25, 39th St. Theatre, 20
Love's Labour's Lost (p), 2/4/53, N.Y. City Center, 16
Love's Labour' s Lost (p), 6/15/65, Delacorte Theatre, 18
Love's Lightning (p), 3/25/18, Lexington Theatre
Love's Lottery (m), 10/3/04, Broadway Theatre, 50
Love's Old Sweet Song (p), 5/2/40, Plymouth Theatre, 44
Love's Pilgrimage (p), 4/14/04, Wallack Theatre, 1
Love Scandal, A (p), 11/5/23, Ambassador Theatre, 32
Love Scene. See A Festival of Short Plays
Love Set, The (p), 3/19/23, Punch and Judy Theatre, 8
Love Song, The (m), 1/13/25, Century Theatre, 167

Love Suicide at Schofield Barracks, The (p), 2/9/72, ANTA Theatre, 5
Love Thief, The ("Praying Curve"), 1/24/27, Eltinge Theatre, 32
Love Watches (p), 8/27/08, Lyceum Theatre, 172
Love Your Crooked Neighbor (p), 12/29/69, Cherry Lane Theatre, 8
Lovely Ladies, Kind Gentlemen (m), 12/28/70, Majestic Theatre, 16
Lovely Lady (p), 10/14/25, Belmont Theatre, 21
Lovely Lady (m), 12/29/27, Sam H. Harris Theatre, 164
Lovely Light, A, 2/8/60, Hudson Theatre, 17
Lovely Light, A, 1/20/64, Mayfair Theatre, 32
Lovely Me (p), 12/25/46, Adelphi Theatre, 37
Lover, The / Play (p), 1/4/64, Cherry Lane Theatre, 89
Lovers and Enemies (p), 9/20/27, Little Theatre, 2
Lovers and Friends (p), 11/29/43, Plymouth Theatre, 168
Lovers and Other Strangers (p), 9/18/68, Brooks Atkinson Theatre, 70
Lovers in the Metro, The / The Information / The Keyhole (p), 1/30/62, Van Dam Theatre, 19
Lovers' Lane (p), 2/6/01, Manhattan Theatre, 127
Lovers of Cass McGuire, The (p), 10/6/66, Helen Hayes Theatre, 20
Lovers, The (p), 5/10/56, Martin Beck Theatre, 4
Lovers (Winners/Losers) (p), 7/25/68, Vivian Beaumont Theatre, 149
Loves of Alonzo Fitz Clarence and Rosannah Ethelton, The / White Nights (m), 2/6/74, Theatre of Riverside Church, 23
Loves of Charles II, The (p), 12/27/33, 48th St. Theatre, 22
Loves of Lulu, The (p), 5/11/25, 49th St. Theatre, 16
Lovey / Hunting the Jingo Bird (p) (New Playwrights Series, Evening III), 3/25/65, Cherry Lane Theatre, 6
Low Bridge (p), 2/9/33, 57th St. Playhouse, 3
Lower Depths, The (p), 3/5/64, Phoenix Theatre, 38
Lower Depths, The (p), 11/13/69, Master Theatre, 12, (Equity Library Theatre)
Lower Depths, The (p), 10/24/72, Good Shepherd-Faith Church, 6, (City Center Acting Co.)
Lower North (p), 8/24/44, Belasco Theatre, 11
Lower Than the Angels (p), 1/30/65, St. Clement's Church, 2, (American Place Theatre)
Loyalties (p), 9/27/22, Gaiety Theatre, 220
Luana (m), 9/17/30, Hammerstein Theatre, 21
Luck in Pawn (p), 3/24/19, 48th St. Theatre, 8
Luck of MacGregor, The (p), 4/20/08, Garden Theatre, 16
Luck of the Navy, The, 10/14/19, Manhattan Opera House, 32
Luckee Girl (m), 9/15/28, Casino Theatre, 81
Lucky (m), 3/22/27, New Amsterdam Theatre, 71
Lucky Break, A (p), 8/11/25, Cort Theatre, 23
Lucky Miss Dean (p), 2/5/06, Madison Square Theatre, 16
Lucky O'Shea (p), 9/3/17, 39th St. Theatre, 32
Lucky One, The (p), 11/20/22, Garrick Theatre, 32
Lucky Sam McCarver (p), 10/21/25, Playhouse, 30
Lucky Sambo (m), 6/6/25, Colonial Theatre, 9
Lucky Star, A (p), 1/18/10, Hudson Theatre, 95
Lucrece (p), 12/20/32, Belasco Theatre, 31
Ludlow Fair / The Madness of Lady Bright (p), 3/22/66, Theatre East, 15
Lullaby (p), 2/3/54, Lyceum Theatre, 45
Lullaby, The, 9/17/23, Knickerbocker Theatre, 148
Lulu (p), 9/29/58, Fourth St. Theatre, 12
Lulu (p), 3/27/70, Sheridan Square Playhouse, 1
Lulu Belle (p), 2/9/26, Belasco Theatre, 461
Lulu's Husbands, 4/14/10, Maxine Elliott's Theatre, 42
Lunatic View, The (p), 11/27/62, Theatre de Lys, 1
Lunatics and Lovers (p), 12/13/54, Broadhurst Theatre, 336
Lure, The (p), 8/14/13, Maxine Elliott's Theatre, 132
Lusmore (p), 9/9/19, Henry Miller's Theatre, 23
Lute Song (m), 2/6/46, Plymouth Theatre, 142
Lute Song (m), 3/12/59, New York City Center, 14
Luther (p), 9/25/63, St. James Theatre, 212
Luv (p), 11/11/64, Booth Theatre, 902
Lydia Gilmore (p), 2/1/12, Lyceum Theatre, 12
Lyle (m), 3/20/70, McAlpin Rooftop Theatre, 3
Lyric Drama, 4/5/27, Neighborhood Playhouse, 31
Lyric Opera Company, 10/3/40, 44th St. Theatre, 24
Lysistrata (m), 12/14/25, Jolson Theatre, 10
Lysistrata (p), 6/5/30, 44th St. Theatre, 252
Lysistrata (p), 10/17/46, Belasco Theatre, 4
Lysistrata (p), 5/19/59, East 74th St. Theatre, 8
Lysistrata (p), 11/24/59, Phoenix Theatre, 24
Lysistrata (p), 10/23/70, New York Theatre Ensemble, 16
Lysistrata (p), 11/13/72, Brooks Atkinson Theatre, 8

M

M. Maurice de Feraudy Repertory, 3/10/24, Fulton Theatre, 16
Macbeth (p) (James K. Hackett), 2/7/16, Criterion Theatre, 40
Macbeth (p) (Walter Hampden), 12/7/18, Plymouth Theatre, 1
Macbeth (p), 12/9/20, Manhattan Opera House, 4
Macbeth (p), 1/4/21, Lexington Theatre, 3
Macbeth (p) (Lionel Barrymore), 2/17/21, Apollo Theatre, 28
Macbeth (p) (Walter Hampden), 4/19/21, Broadhurst Theatre, 6
Macbeth (p), 12/26/21, Lexington Theatre, 2
Macbeth (p) (Fritz Leiber), 1/16/22, 48th St. Theatre, 4
Macbeth (p) (James K. Hackett), 3/15/24, 48th St. Theatre, 33
Macbeth (p) (Lyn Harding), 11/19/28, Knickerbocker Theatre, 64
Macbeth (p) (Fritz Leiber), 3/25/30, Shubert Theatre, 4
Macbeth (p) (Fritz Leiber), 12/30/30, Ambassador Theatre, 3
Macbeth (p), 1/5/33, Shakespeare Theatre, 26
Macbeth (p) (Walter Hampden), 12/29/34, 44th St. Theatre, 5
Macbeth (p) (Philip Merivale-Gladys Cooper), 10/7/35, Ethel Barrymore Theatre, 8
Macbeth (p), 4/9/36, Lafayette Theatre
Macbeth (p) (Maurice Evans), 11/11/41, National Theatre, 131
Macbeth (p) (Michael Redgrave), 3/31/48, National Theatre, 29
Macbeth (p), 10/7/55, Rooftop Theatre
Macbeth (p) (Shakespearewrights), 10/19/55, Jan Hus House, 85
Macbeth (p) (Paul Rogers—Old Vic Co.), 10/29/56, Winter Garden Theatre, 25
Macbeth (p), 2/6/62, New York City Center, 21, (Old Vic Co.)
Macbeth (p), 11/15/62, Heckscher Theatre
Macbeth (p), 6/28/66, Mobile Theatre, 47
Macbeth (p), 12/21/69, Roundabout Theatre, 37
Macbeth (p), 1/4/71, Mercer-O'Casey Theatre, 132
Macbeth (p), 3/16/73, CSC Repertory Theatre, 5
Macbeth (p), 4/13/74, Mitzi E. Newhouse Theatre, 54
Macbeth (Spanish) (p), 8/26/66, Mobile Theatre, 9
MacBird! (p), 2/22/67, Village Gate Theatre, 385
Machinal (p), 9/7/28, Plymouth Theatre, 93
Machinal (p), 4/7/60, Gate Theatre, 79
Mackerel Skies (p), 1/23/34, Playhouse, 23
Mackey of Appalachia (m), 10/6/65, Blackfriars' Guild, 54
Mad Dog Blues (p), 3/4/71, Theatre Genesis
Mad Dog, The (p), 11/8/21, Comedy Theatre, 15
Mad Heart / Black Mass (p), 9/28/72, Afro-American Studio
Mad Honeymoon, The, 8/7/23, Playhouse, 14
Mad Hopes, The (p), 12/1/32, Broadhurst Theatre, 12
Mad Show, The (r), 1/9/66, New Theatre, 871
Madam President (p), 9/15/13, Garrick Theatre, 128
Madam, Will You Walk (p), 12/1/53, Phoenix Theatre, 48
Madame Aphrodite (m), 12/29/61, Orpheum Theatre, 13
Madame Bovary (p), 11/16/37, Broadhurst Theatre, 39
Madame Capet (p), 10/25/38, Cort Theatre, 7
Madame de Sade (p), 10/30/72, Theatre de Lys, 2, (ANTA Matinee)
Madame Lafayette (p), 3/1/60, Blackfriars' Theatre, 50
Madame Moselle (m), 5/23/14, Shubert Theatre, 9
Madame Pepita (p), 5/15/27, Forrest Theatre, 2
Madame Pierre (p), 2/15/22, Ritz Theatre, 37
Madame Sand (p), 11/19/17, Criterion Theatre, 64
Madame Sans Gêne (p), 11/3/24, Henry Miller's Theatre, 24
Madame Sherry (m), 8/30/10, New Amsterdam Theatre, 231
Madame Troubadour (m), 10/10/10, Lyric Theatre, 80
Madame X (p), 2/2/10, New Amsterdam Theatre, 125
Madame X (p), 7/6/27, Earl Carroll Theatre, 23
Madcap Duchess, The (m), 11/11/13, Globe Theatre, 71
Madcap Princess, A (m), 9/5/04, Knickerbocker Theatre, 48
Madcap, The (m), 1/31/28, Royale Theatre, 103
Made for Each Other (p), 9/29/24, 52nd St. Theatre, 16
Made in America (p), 10/14/25, Cort Theatre, 71
Made in France (p), 11/11/30, Cort Theatre, 8
Made in Heaven! (p), 10/24/46, Henry Miller's Theatre, 92
Madeleine and the Movies (p), 3/6/22, Gaiety Theatre, 80
Madeleine Renaud—Jean-Louis Barrault Repertory Company, 1/30/57, Winter Garden Theatre, 30
Madeline / Mary, Mary, Quite Contrary (p), 1/5/06, Garrick Theatre, 16
Mademoiselle (p), 10/18/32, Playhouse, 103
Mademoiselle Bourrat (p), 10/7/29, Civic Repertory Theatre, 26
Mademoiselle Colombe (p), 1/6/54, Longacre Theatre, 61
Mademoiselle Marni (p), 3/6/05, Wallack Theatre, 32
Madge Smith, Attorney (p), 12/10/00, Bijou Theatre, 38
Madness of Lady Bright, The / Ludlow Fair (p), 3/22/66, Theatre East, 15
Madonna in the Orchard, The (p), 11/23/65, La Mama Experimental Theatre Club, 6
Madonna of the Future, The (p), 1/28/18, Broadhurst Theatre, 56
Madras House, The (p), 10/29/21, Neighborhood Playhouse, 80
Madrigal of Shakespeare, A, 2/12/68, Theatre de Lys, 2, (ANTA Matinee)
Madwoman of Chaillot, The (p), 12/27/48, Belasco Theatre, 368
Madwoman of Chaillot, The (p), 6/13/50, New York City Center, 17
Madwoman of Chaillot, The (p), 3/22/70, Sokol Hall, 7
Magda (p), 11/21/04, Daly's Theatre, 5
Magda (p), 1/26/26, Maxine Elliott's Theatre, 24
Magdalena (m), 9/20/48, Ziegfeld Theatre, 88
Maggie (m), 2/18/53, National Theatre, 5

Maggie Flynn (m), 10/23/68, ANTA Theatre, 82
Maggie Pepper (p), 8/31/11, Harris Theatre, 147
Maggie the Magnificent (p), 10/21/29, Cort Theatre, 32
Magic (p), 12/16/29, Gansevoort Theatre, 7
Magic and the Loss, The (p), 4/9/54, Booth Theatre, 27
Magic / Hello, Out There (p), 9/29/42, Belasco Theatre, 47
Magic Melody, The (m), 11/11/19, Shubert Theatre, 143
Magic Onion, The (r), 7/11/72, Bil Baird Theatre, 18
Magic Ring, The (m), 10/1/23, Liberty Theatre, 96
Magic Show, The (m), 5/28/74, Cort Theatre, 5
Magic / The Little Man (p), 2/12/17, Maxine Elliott's Theatre, 56
Magic Time. See Playwrights Cooperative Festival
Magic Touch, The (p), 9/3/47, International Theatre, 12
Magnificent Hugo, The (p), 4/7/61, Comedy Theatre, 3
Magnificent Yankee, The (p), 1/22/46, Royale Theatre, 160
Magnolia (p), 8/27/23, Liberty Theatre, 40
Magnolia Alley (p), 4/18/49, Mansfield Theatre, 8
Magnolia Lady, The (m), 11/25/24, Shubert Theatre, 49
Mahagonny (m), 4/28/70, Anderson Theatre, 8
Mahogany Hall (p), 1/17/34, Bijou Theatre, 22
Maid and the Millionaire, The (m), 6/22/07, Madison Square Garden Roof, 72
Maid and the Mummy, The (m), 7/25/04, New York Theatre, 42
Maid as Mistress, The / The Secret of Suzanne (m), 5/14/44, Alvin Theatre, 2
Maid in America (r), 2/18/15, Winter Garden Theatre, 108
Maid in the Ozarks (p), 7/15/46, Belasco Theatre, 103
Maid Marian (m), 1/27/02, Garden Theatre, 64
Maid of France, The / The Big Scene / 'Ile (p), 4/18/18, Greenwich Village Theatre, 52
Maid of the Mountains, The (m), 9/11/18, Casino Theatre, 37
Maid's Tragedy, The (p), 10/19/72, Master Theatre, 12, (Equity Library Theatre)
Maidens and Mistresses at Home at the Zoo / Song of Songs. See Mistresses and Maidens, 1/21/59, Orpheum Theatre, 23
Maids of Athens (m), 3/18/14, New Amsterdam Theatre, 22
Maids, The (p), 11/14/63, One Sheridan Square, 62
Maids, The / In a Garden / Three Sisters Who Are Not Sisters (p), 5/6/55, Tempo Playhouse, 63
Maids, The / The Gallent Cassian (p), 5/18/56, Tempo Playhouse
Main Line, The (p), 3/25/24, Klaw Theatre, 27
Main Street (p), 10/5/21, National Theatre, 86
Mainly for Lovers (p), 2/21/36, 48th St. Theatre, 8
Maitresse De Roi (p), 11/30/26, Cosmopolitan Theatre, 17
Major Andre (p), 11/11/03, Savoy Theatre, 12
Major Barbara (p), 12/9/15, Playhouse
Major Barbara (p), 11/19/28, Guild Theatre, 73
Major Barbara (p), 10/30/56, Martin Beck Theatre, 232
Major Pendennis (p), 10/26/16, Criterion Theatre, 76
Majority of One, A (p), 2/16/59, Shubert Theatre, 556
Makbeth (p), 11/20/69, Performance Garage
Make a Million (p), 10/23/58, Playhouse, 308
Make a Wish (m), 4/18/51, Winter Garden Theatre, 102
Make It Snappy (m), 4/13/22, Winter Garden Theatre, 96
Make Like a Dog. See Monopoly
Make Me Disappear (p), 5/13/69, Mercury Theatre, 8
Make Me Know It (p), 11/4/29, Wallack Theatre, 4
Make Mine Manhattan (r), 1/15/48, Broadhurst Theatre, 429
Make Way for Lucia (p), 12/22/48, Cort Theatre, 29
Make Yourself at Home (p), 9/13/45, Ethel Barrymore Theatre, 4
Maker of Dreams, The / Tethered Sheep (p), 3/3/15, Neighborhood Playhouse
Maker of Men, A / Mrs. Leffingwell's Boots (p), 8/21/05, Lyceum Theatre, 14
Makers of Light (p), 5/23/22, Neighborhood Playhouse, 21
Making Good (p), 2/5/12, Fulton Theatre, 8
Making of Americans, The (m), 11/10/72, Judson Poet's Theatre, 16
Making of Moo, The (p), 6/11/58, Rita Allen Theatre, 29
Makropoulos Secret, The (p), 1/21/26, Charles Hopkins Theatre, 108
Makropoulos Secret, The (p), 12/3/57, Phoenix Theatre, 33
Malade Imaginaire, Le (p) (Le Théâtre du Nouveau Monde), 4/29/58, Phoenix Theatre, 8
Malade Imaginaire, Le (p), 2/17/70, New York City Center, 8, (Comédie Française)
Malcochon. See An Evening of One Acts
Malcolm (p), 1/11/66, Shubert Theatre, 7
Male Animal, The (p), 1/9/40, Cort Theatre, 243
Male Animal, The, 4/30/52, New York City Center, 317, (After two weeks moved to Music Box Theatre)
Maleficio de la Mariposa, El (p), 8/14/70, New York City Parks, 9, (Puerto Rican Traveling Theatre)
Malvaloca (p), 10/2/22, 48th St. Theatre, 48
Mam'selle 'Awkins (m), 2/26/00, Victoria Theatre, 35
Mam'selle Napoleon (m), 12/8/03, Knickerbocker Theatre, 43
Mama Loves Papa (p), 2/22/26, Forrest Theatre, 25
Mama's Baby Boy (m), 5/25/12, Broadway Theatre, 9
Mamba's Daughters (p), 1/3/39, Empire Theatre, 162
Mamba's Daughters (p), 3/23/40, Broadway Theatre, 17
Mame (m), 5/24/66, Winter Garden, 1508
Mamiko San (m), 6/6/27, Selwyn Theatre, 16
Mamma's Affair (p), 1/19/20, Little Theatre, 98
Mamselle Sallie (m), 11/26/06, Grand Opera House, 24
Mamzelle Champagne (r), 6/25/06, Madison Square Garden Roof, 60
Mamzelle Champagne (r) / The Day Before (p), 10/24/06, Berkeley Lyceum Theatre, 4
Man About Town, A / Mary Stuart (p), 3/21/21, Ritz Theatre, 40
Man and Boy (p), 11/12/63, Brooks Atkinson Theatre, 54
Man and Dog. See The Niggerlovers
Man and His Angel (p), 9/18/06, Hackett Theatre, 7
Man and His Wife, A / The Bugle Call (p), 4/2/00, Empire Theatre, 24
Man and John, 9/11/05, Manhattan Theatre, 12
Man and Superman (p), 9/05/05, Hudson Theatre, 192
Man and Superman (p), 9/30/12, Hudson Theatre, 32
Man and Superman (p) (Maurice Evans), 10/8/47, Alvin Theatre, 294
Man and Superman (p) (Maurice Evans), 5/16/49, New York City Center, 16
Man and Superman (p), 11/6/60, Gate Theatre, 23
Man and Superman (p), 12/6/64, Phoenix Theatre, 100
Man and the Masses (p), 4/14/24, Garrick Theatre, 32
Man Better Man (m), 7/2/69, St. Marks Playhouse, 23
Man Bites Dog (p), 4/25/33, Lyceum Theatre, 7
Man Crazy (p), 6/18/32, Cherry Lane Theatre, 8
Man for All Seasons, A (p), 11/22/61, ANTA Theatre, 640
Man for All Seasons, A (p), 1/27/64, New York City Center, 16
Man from Blankley's, The (p), 9/16/03, Criterion Theatre, 79
Man from Cairo, The (p), 5/4/38, Broadhurst Theatre, 21
Man from China, The (m), 5/2/04, Majestic Theatre, 41
Man from Cook's, The (m), 3/25/12, New Amsterdam Theatre, 32
Man from Home, The (p), 8/17/08, Astor Theatre, 496
Man from Mexico, The (p), 5/10/09, Garrick Theatre, 64
Man from Now, The, 9/3/06, New Amsterdam Theatre, 28
Man from the East, The (m), 10/23/73, Brooklyn Academy of Music, 8
Man from Toronto, The (p), 6/17/26, Selwyn Theatre, 28
Man in Evening Clothes, The (p), 12/5/24, Henry Miller's Theatre, 11
Man in Possession, The (p), 11/3/30, Booth Theatre, 97
Man in the Dog Suit, The (p), 10/30/58, Coronet Theatre, 36
Man in the Glass Booth, The (p), 9/26/68, Royale Theatre, 269
Man in the Making, The (p), 9/20/21, Hudson Theatre, 22
Man Inside, The (p), 11/11/13, Criterion Theatre, 63
Man Is Man (p), 9/18/62, Living Theatre, 166
Man of Destiny, The / Androcles and the Lion (p), 11/23/25, Klaw Theatre, 68
Man of Destiny, The / Candida (p), 2/11/04, Vaudeville Theatre, 48
Man of Destiny, The / How He Lied to Her Husband (p), 9/26/04, Berkeley Lyceum Theatre, 8
Man of Forty, The (p), 11/26/00, Daly's Theatre, 29
Man of Honor, A (p), 9/14/11, Weber Theatre, 36
Man of La Mancha (m), 11/22/65, ANTA Washington Square Theatre, 2328
Man of La Mancha (m), 6/22/72, Vivian Beaumont Theatre, 140
Man of the Hour, The (p), 12/4/06, Savoy Theatre, 479
Man of the People, A (p), 9/7/20, Bijou Theatre, 15
Man on Stilts, The (p), 9/9/31, Plymouth Theatre, 6
Man on the Box, The (p), 10/3/05, Madison Square Theatre, 111
Man on the Box, The / David Garrick (p), 11/27/05, Madison Square Theatre, 48
Man on the Case, The (p), 9/4/07, Madison Square Theatre, 21
Man or Devil (p), 5/21/25, Broadhurst Theatre, 20
Man Out Loud, Girl Quiet / The Spanish Armada (p), 4/3/62, Cricket Theatre, 16
Man Proposes (p), 3/11/04, Hudson Theatre, 24
Man's a Man, A (p), 9/19/62, Masque Theatre, 175
Man's Estate (p), 4/1/29, Biltmore Theatre, 55
Man's Friends, A (p), 3/24/13, Astor Theatre, 32
Man's Man, A (p), 10/13/25, 52nd St. Theatre, 120
Man's Name, The (p), 11/15/21, Republic Theatre, 24
Man's World, A (p), 2/8/10, Comedy Theatre, 71
Man, The (p), 1/19/50, Fulton Theatre, 92
Man Who Ate the Popomack, The (p), 3/24/24, Cherry Lane Theatre, 52
Man Who Came Back, The (p), 9/2/16, Playhouse, 457
Man Who Came to Dinner, The (p), 10/16/39, Music Box Theatre, 739
Man Who Changed His Name, The (p), 5/2/32, Broadhurst Theatre, 56
Man Who Had All the Luck, The (p), 11/23/44, Forrest Theatre, 4
Man Who Killed Lincoln, The (p), 1/17/40, Longacre Theatre, 5
Man Who Married a Dumb Wife, The / Androcles and the Lion (p), 1/27/15, Wallack Theatre
Man Who Never Died, The (p), 12/12/25, Provincetown Playhouse, 23
Man Who Never Died, The (p), 11/21/58, Jan Hus House, 125
Man Who Owns Broadway, The (m), 10/11/09, New York Theatre, 128
Man Who Reclaimed His Head, The (p), 9/8/32, Broadhurst Theatre, 28

Man Who Stayed at Home, The (p), 4/3/18, 48th St. Theatre, 109
Man Who Stole the Castle, The / There and Back (p), 4/20/03, Princess Theatre
Man Who Stood Still, The (p), 10/15/08, Circle Theatre, 61
Man Who Washed His Hands, The (p), 2/15/67, Blackfriars' Guild, 33
Man with a Load of Mischief (p), 10/26/25, Ritz Theatre, 16
Man with a Load of Mischief (m), 11/6/66, Jan Hus Playhouse, 240
Man with a Load of Mischief (m), 5/9/74, Master Theatre, 19, (Equity Library Theatre)
Man with a Load of Mischief (m), 5/9/74, Master Theatre, 19, (Equity Library Theatre)
Man with Blond Hair, The (p), 11/4/41, Belasco Theatre, 7
Man with Red Hair, A (p), 11/8/28, Garrick Theatre, 19
Man with the Flower in His Mouth, The (The Man with the Flower in His Mouth / The License / The Jar) (p), 4/22/69, Sheridan Square Playhouse, 80
Man with the Golden Arm, The (p), 5/21/56, Cherry Lane Theatre, 73
Man with the Tranquil Mind, The / The Immovable Gordons / The Little Lady of Friday Night (p) (Dumbell People in a Barbell World), 2/14/62, Cricket Theatre, 13
Man with Three Wives, The (m), 1/23/13, Weber and Fields Theatre, 52
Mandarin, The (p), 11/9/20, Princess Theatre, 16
Mandingo (p), 5/22/61, Lyceum Theatre, 8
Manhattan (p), 8/15/22, Playhouse, 89
Manhattan Mary (m), 9/26/27, Apollo Theatre, 264
Manhattan Nocturne (p), 10/26/43, Forrest Theatre, 23
Manhatters, The (r), 8/3/27, Selwyn Theatre, 77
Manifesto, Il. See Festival of New Italian Plays
Manon Lescaut (p), 3/19/01, Wallack Theatre, 15
Mansion on the Hudson (p), 4/2/35, Booth Theatre, 16
Many a Slip, 2/3/30, Little Theatre, 56
Many Happy Returns (p), 1/5/45, Playhouse, 3
Many Loves (p), 1/13/59, Living Theatre, 216
Many Loves (p), 5/15/61, Living Theatre, 4
Many Mansions (p), 10/27/37, Biltmore Theatre, 157
Many Waters (p), 9/25/29, Maxine Elliott's Theatre, 119
Marathon (p), 1/27/33, Mansfield Theatre, 11
Marathon '33 (p), 12/22/63, ANTA Theatre, 48
Marat/Sade. See The Persecution and Assassination of Marat as Performed by the Inmates of the Asylum at Charenton Under the Direction of the Marquis de Sade.
Marceau, Marcel. See Marcel Marceau
Marcel Marceau, 9/20/55, Phoenix Theatre (moved to Ethel Barrymore Theatre 10/4/44), 32
Marcel Marceau, 2/1/56, New York City Center, 15
Marcel Marceau, 1/21/58, New York City Center, 32
Marcel Marceau, 9/6/60, New York City Center, 24
Marcel Marceau, 1/1/63, New York City Center, 32
Marcel Marceau, 11/17/65, New York City Center, 31
Marcel Marceau, 4/7/70, New York City Center, 24
Marcel Marceau, 4/18/73, New York City Center, 23
Marcelle (p), 10/8/00, Broadway Theatre, 24
Marcelle (m), 10/1/08, Casino Theatre, 68
March Hares (p), 8/11/21, Bijou Theatre, 60
March Hares (p), 3/11/23, Little Theatre, 4
March Hares (p), 4/2/28, Little Theatre, 20
March Heir, The / The Family Exit / Counsel's Opinion / Saturday It Rained / The White Dress / The Way Out (p), 12/13/32, Chanin Auditorium, 5
March March, The / The Neighbors (p), 11/6/66, Theatre 62, 17
Marching By (m), 3/3/32, Chanin's 46th Street Theatre, 12
Marching Song (p), 2/17/37, Nora Bayes Theatre, 61
Marching Song (p), 12/28/59, Gate Theatre, 33
Marco Millions (p), 1/9/28, Guild Theatre, 102
Marco Millions (p), 3/3/30, Liberty Theatre, 8
Marco Millions (p), 2/20/64, ANTA—Washington Square Theatre, 49
Marcus in the High Grass (p), 11/21/60, Greenwich Mews Theatre, 16
Margaret Schiller (p), 1/31/16, New Amsterdam Theatre, 72
Margery Daw (p), 12/4/16, Princess Theatre, 8
Margin for Error (p), 11/3/39, Plymouth Theatre, 264
Maria Bazie Repertory Company, 9/26/25, Manhattan Opera House, 11
Maria Golovin (m), 11/5/58, Martin Beck Theatre, 5
Maria Rose (p), 1/19/14, 39th St. Theatre, 48
Maria Stuart (p), 3/26/68, New York City Center, 6, (Vienna Burgtheater)
Mariage de Figaro, Le (p) (Théâtre de France, Renaud-Barrault Co.), 2/25/64, New York City Center, 3
Mariage Forcé , Le / Sganarelle / La Jalousie du Barbouille (p) (An Evening of 3 Farces), 5/6/58, Phoenix Theatre, 8
Marie Antoinette (p), 11/22/21, Playhouse, 16
Marie Bell and Her Company (Phedra, Berenice), 10/20/63, Brooks Atkinson Theatre, 16
Marie Dressler's All Star Gambol, 3/10/13, Weber and Fields Theatre, 8
Marie Vison, La (p), 7/8/70, La Mama Experimental Theatre Club, 10
Marie-Odile (p), 1/26/15, Belasco Theatre, 119
Marietta / The Hour Glass / My Milliner' s Bill (p), 4/7/04, Garrick Theatre, 1
Marigold (p), 10/8/30, 49th St. Theatre, 13
Marilyn's Affairs (p), 3/15/33, Mansfield Theatre, 1
Mariners (p), 3/28/27, Plymouth Theatre, 16
Marinka (m), 7/18/45, Winter Garden Theatre, 165
Marionette Players, The (Teatro dei Piccoli di Roma), 9/10/23, Frolic Theatre, 16
Marionettes, The (p), 12/5/11, Lyceum Theatre, 63
Marjolaine (m), 1/24/22, Broadhurst Theatre, 136
Marjorie (m), 8/11/24, Shubert Theatre, 144
Mark of the Beast, The (Potash and Perlmutter in Society) (p), 10/20/15, Princess Theatre, 13
Mark Twain Tonight, 4/6/59, 41st St. Theatre, 172
Mark Twain Tonight, 3/23/66, Longacre Theatre, 85
Marlene Dietrich, 10/9/67, Lunt-Fontanne Theatre, 48
Marlene Dietrich, 10/3/68, Mark Hellinger, 68
Marlowe, Julia. See Sothern-Marlowe
Marquis de Priola, The (p), 1/20/19, Liberty Theatre, 70
Marquise, The (p), 11/14/28, Biltmore Theatre, 82
Marriage a la Carte (m), 1/2/11, Casino Theatre, 64
Marriage Bed, The (p), 1/7/29, Booth Theatre, 72
Marriage for Three (p), 11/11/31, Bijou Theatre, 5
Marriage Game, The (p), 12/10/01, Hammerstein's Victoria Theatre, 20
Marriage Game, The / Electra, 12/29/13, Comedy Theatre, 7
Marriage Game, The / Salome, 12/20/13, Comedy Theatre, 7
Marriage Game, The. See Salome / The Marriage Game; Electra / The Marriage Game, 10/29/13, Comedy Theatre, 78
Marriage / I Forgot (p), 3/11/35, Majestic Theatre, 2
Marriage Is for Single People (p), 11/21/45, Cort Theatre, 6
Marriage Market, The (m), 9/22/13, Knickerbocker Theatre, 80
Marriage of a Star, The (p), 8/15/10, Hackett Theatre, 40
Marriage of Cana, The (p), 2/2/32, Provincetown Playhouse, 4
Marriage of Columbine, The (p), 11/10/14, Punch and Judy Theatre, 31
Marriage of Convenience, A (p), 5/1/18, Henry Miller's Theatre, 53
Marriage of Kitty, The (p), 11/30/03, Hudson Theatre, 51
Marriage of Kitty, The / The Dumb and the Blind (p), 12/18/14, Comedy Theatre, 27
Marriage of Mr. Mississippi, The (p), 11/19/69, Barbizon-Plaza Theatre, 6, (Schauspieltruppe Zurich)
Marriage of Mr. Mississippi, The (p), 2/2/74, Shade Company Theatre
Marriage of Reason, A (p), 4/1/07, Wallack Theatre, 14
Marriage of the Telephone Company Man, The / Out of Control (p), 9/9/71, Actors Playhouse, 5
Marriage of William Ashe, The (p), 11/20/05, Garrick's Theatre, 40
Marriage on Approval (p), 3/1/28, Wallack Theatre, 182
Marriage-Go-Round, The (p), 10/29/58, Plymouth Theatre, 431
Marriage-Not, The (p), 5/13/12, Maxine Elliott's Theatre, 8
Married— And How! (p), 6/14/28, Little Theatre, 36
Married Woman, The (p), 12/16/16, Neighborhood Playhouse
Married Woman, The (p), 12/24/21, Princess Theatre, 51
Marry the Man (p), 4/22/29, Fulton Theatre, 8
Marry the Poor Girl (p), 9/23/20, Little Theatre, 18
Marrying Maiden, The / Women of Trachis (p), 6/22/60, Living Theatre, 50
Marrying Mary (m), 8/27/06, Daly's Theatre, 43
Marrying Money (p), 3/18/14, Princess Theatre, 45
Marseilles (p), 11/17/30, Henry Miller's Theatre, 16
Marta of the Lowlands (p), 10/13/03, Manhattan Theatre, 23
Marta of the Lowlands (p), 3/24/08, Garden Theatre, 13
Martine (p), 4/4/28, American Laboratory Theatre, 16
Martinique (p), 4/26/20, Eltinge Theatre, 40
Marvelous History of Saint Bernard, The (p), 2/23/58, Broadway Congregational Church, 5
Mary (m), 10/18/20, Knickerbocker Theatre, 220
Mary Agnes Is Thirty-Five. See Friday Night
Mary Anthony Dance Theatre, The, 12/2/58, Theatre de Lys, 1
Mary Goes First (p), 11/2/14, Comedy Theatre, 32
Mary Jane McKane (m), 12/25/23, Imperial Theatre, 151
Mary Jane's Pa (p), 12/3/08, Garden Theatre, 89
Mary Magdalene (p), 12/5/10, New Theatre, 16
Mary, Mary (p), 3/8/61, Helen Hayes Theatre, 1,572
Mary, Mary, Quite Contrary (p), 12/25/05, Garrick Theatre, 30
Mary, Mary, Quite Contrary (p), 9/11/23, Belasco Theatre, 86
Mary, Mary, Quite Contrary / Madeline (p), 1/5/06, Garrick Theatre, 16
Mary of Magdala (p), 11/12/02, Manhattan Theatre, 105
Mary of Magdala (p), 9/14/03, Manhattan Theatre
Mary of Magdala (p), 3/25/46, Blackfriars' Theatre, 25
Mary of Scotland (p), 11/27/33, Alvin Theatre, 236
Mary Rose (p), 12/22/20, Empire Theatre, 128
Mary Rose (p), 5/4/51, ANTA Playhouse, 16
Mary's Ankle (p), 8/6/17, Bijou Theatre, 80
Mary's Lamb (m), 5/25/08, New York Theatre, 16
Mary's Manoeuvres / Revenge, or The Pride of Lillian le Mar (p), 2/25/13, Lyceum Theatre, 1

Mary Stuart (p), 10/8/57, Phoenix Theatre, 56
Mary Stuart (p), 11/12/71, Vivian Beaumont Theatre
Mary Stuart / Man About Town, A (p), 3/21/21, Ritz Theatre, 40
Mary the 3rd, 2/5/23, 39th St. Theatre, 163
Mascot, The (m), 4/12/09, New Amsterdam Theatre, 32
Mascotte, La, 12/1/26, Jolson Theatre, 14
Mask and Gown (r), 9/10/57, Golden Theatre, 39
Mask and the Face, The (p), 9/10/24, Bijou Theatre, 13
Mask and the Face, The (p), 5/8/33, Guild Theatre, 40
Mask of Hamlet, The (p), 8/22/21, Princess Theatre, 8
Masked Woman, The (p), 12/22/22, Eltinge Theatre, 117
Masks and Faces (p), 3/18/33, Liberty Theatre, 1
Masks of Angels / Anna Kleiber (p), 1/19/65, Provincetown Playhouse, 14
Masque of Kings, The (p), 2/8/37, Shubert Theatre, 89
Masque of St. George and the Dragon, The, 12/15/72, Actors Studio Theatre, 10
Masque of St. George and the Dragon, The, 12/20/73, Actors Studio Theatre, 20
Masque of Venice, The (p), 3/2/26, Mansfield Theatre, 15
Masquerade (p), 3/16/59, Golden Theatre, 1
Masquerade (p), 11/28/71, Theatre Four, 1
Masquerade, The. See Festival of New Italian Plays
Masquerader, The (p), 9/3/17, Lyric Theatre, 160
Master Builder, The (p) (William H. Pascoe), 1/17/00, Carnegie Lyceum Theatre, 1
Master Builder, The (p) (William Hazeltine), 5/12/05, Carnegie Lyceum Theatre, 1
Master Builder, The (p), 9/23/07, Bijou Theatre, 65
Master Builder, The (p), 11/10/25, Maxine Elliott's Theatre, 78
Master Builder, The (p), 11/1/26, Civic Repertory Theatre, 29
Master Builder, The (p), 11/1/27, Civic Repertory Theatre, 14
Master Builder, The (p), 10/31/28, Civic Repertory Theatre, 6
Master Builder, The (p), 9/19/29, Civic Repertory Theatre, 5
Master Builder, The (p), 2/18/31, Civic Repertory Theatre, 3
Master Builder, The (p), 3/1/55, Phoenix Theatre, 38
Master Builder, The (p), 10/17/71, Roundabout Theatre, 74
Master Key, The (p), 10/4/09, Bijou Theatre, 16
Master Mind, The (p), 2/17/13, Harris Theatre, 128
Master of the House, The (p), 8/22/12, 39th St. Theatre, 84
Master of the Inn, The (p), 12/22/25, Little Theatre, 41
Master, The (p), 12/5/16, Fulton Theatre, 47
Master, The / Democracy's King (p), 2/19/18, Hudson Theatre, 39
Matchmaker, The (p), 12/5/55, Royale Theatre, 486
Match-Play / A Party for Divorce (p), 10/11/66, Provincetown Playhouse, 8
Mater (p), 9/25/08, Savoy Theatre, 27
Maternity (p), 1/6/15, Princess Theatre, 21
MATES / How He Lied to Her Husband (p), 10/18/73, Lolly's Theatre Club
Matilda (m), 12/31/06, Lincoln Square Theatre, 17
Matinée Hero, The (p), 10/7/18, Vanderbilt Theatre, 64
Matinata (p), 11/1/20, Provincetown Playhouse
Matinee Girl, The (m), 2/1/26, Forrest Theatre, 25
Matinee Idol, A (m), 4/28/10, Daly's Theatre, 68
Mating Dance, The (p), 11/3/65, Eugene O'Neill Theatre, 1
Mating Season, The (p), 7/18/27, Selwyn Theatre, 24
Matriarch, The (p), 3/18/30, Longacre Theatre, 15
Matrimonial Bed, The (p), 10/12/27, Ambassador Theatre, 15
Matter of Like Life and Death, A / Opening Night (p), 10/2/63, East End Theatre, 47
Matty and the Moron and Madonna (p), 3/29/65, Orpheum Theatre, 32
Maurice Chevalier, 3/30/30, Fulton Theatre, 18
Maurice Chevalier, 2/9/32, Fulton Theatre, 20
Maurice Chevalier, 3/10/47, Henry Miller's Theatre, 46
Maurice Chevalier, 2/29/48, John Golden Theatre, 33
Maurice Chevalier, 9/28/55, Lyceum Theatre, 46
Maurice Chevalier, 1/28/63, Ziegfeld Theatre, 27
Maurice Chevalier at 77, 4/1/65, Alvin Theatre, 32
May Wine (m), 12/5/35, St. James Theatre, 212
Maya (p), 2/21/28, Comedy Theatre, 15
Maya (p), 6/9/53, Theatre de Lys
Maybe Tuesday (p), 1/29/58, Playhouse, 5
Mayfair (p), 3/17/30, Belmont Theatre, 8
Mayflowers (m), 11/24/25, Forrest Theatre, 81
Mayor of Tokio, The (m), 12/4/05, New York Theatre, 50
Mayor of Zalemea, The, 1/27/46, Majestic Theatre, 2
Maytime (m), 8/16/17, Shubert Theatre, 492
Mazowsze Polish Song and Dance Company, 10/15/61, New York City Center, 24
Me, 11/23/25, Princess Theatre, 32
Me and Juliet (m), 5/28/53, Majestic Theatre, 358
Me and Juliet (m), 5/7/70, Master Theatre, 19, (Equity Library Theatre)
Me and Molly (p), 2/26/48, Belasco Theatre, 156
Me and Thee (p), 12/7/65, John Golden Theatre, 1
Me, Candido! (p), 10/15/56, Greenwich Mews Theatre, 159
Me Nobody Knows, The (m), 5/18/70, Orpheum Theatre, 587
Me, the Sleeper (p), 5/14/49, Lenox Hill Playhouse, 4
Meanest Man in the World, The (p), 10/12/20, Hudson Theatre, 204
Measure for Measure (p), 7/12/66, Delacorte Theatre, 17
Measure for Measure (p), 2/14/67, New York City Center, 7, (Bristol Old Vic)
Measure for Measure (p), 1/22/57, Phoenix Theatre, 32
Measure for Measure (p), 12/26/73, Billy Rose Theatre, 7, (City Center Acting Co.)
Measure for Measure (p), 2/12/73, CSC Repertory Theatre
Measure of a Man, The (p), 10/20/06, Weber Theatre, 15
Mecca (m), 10/4/20, Century Theatre, 130
Medal and the Maid, The (m), 1/11/04, Broadway Theatre, 49
Medea (p), 11/28/65, Martinique Theatre, 77, (Gloria Foster)
Medea (p), 3/22/20, Garrick Theatre, 14
Medea (p) (Judith Anderson), 10/20/47, National Theatre, 214
Medea (p) (Judith Anderson), 5/2/49, New York City Center, 16
Medea (p), 8/31/64, New York City Center, 8, (Greek Tragedy Theatre of Athens: Piraikon Theatron of Athens)
Medea (p), 1/21/72, La Mama Experimental Theatre Club
Medea (p), 1/17/73, Circle in the Square / Joseph E. Levine Theatre, 69
Medea (p), 10/30/73, Players Theatre, 40
Médecin Malgré Lui, Le (p), 4/16/73, American Place Theatre, 7, (Le Jeune Théâtre National)
Medicine Show (p), 4/12/40, New Yorker Theatre, 35
Medico a Palos, El (p), 6/21/73, Puerto Rican Traveling Theatre, 16
Medium, The (m), 5/8/47, Brander Mathews Theatre
Medium, The (m), 4/20/58, New York City Center
Medium, The (m), 4/16/59, New York City Center
Medium, The / The Telephone (m), 5/1/47, Ethel Barrymore Theatre, 212
Medium, The / The Telephone (m), 12/7/48, New York City Center, 40
Medium, The / The Telephone, 7/19/50, Arena, Edison Hotel, 110
Meek Mose (p), 2/6/28, Princess Theatre, 32
Meeow!! (m), 3/2/71, Cabaret Theatre, 48
Meet a Body (p), 10/16/44, Forrest Theatre, 24
Meet My Sister (m), 12/30/30, Shubert Theatre, 165
Meet the People (r), 12/25/40, Mansfield Theatre, 160
Meet the Prince (p), 2/25/29, Lyceum Theatre, 96
Meet the Wife (p), 11/26/23, Klaw Theatre, 261
Meeting by the River, A (p), 12/18/72, Edison Theatre, 1, (New Phoenix Repertory Co. Sideshow)
Meeting, The. See Double Play
Megilla of Itzik Manger, The (m), 10/9/68, John Golden Theatre, 78
Megilla of Itzik Manger, The (m), 4/19/69, Longacre Theatre, 12
Mei Lan-Fang, 2/17/30, 49th St. Theatre, 41
Meller, Raquel. See Raquel Meller
Melo (p), 4/16/31, Ethel Barrymore Theatre, 68
Melo (p), 10/19/31, Maxine Elliott's Theatre, 8
Melodrama Play (p), 6/16/71, La Mama Experimental Theatre Club
Melody (m), 2/14/33, Casino Theatre, 80
Melody Lingers On, The (m), 11/14/69, Folksbiene Playhouse
Melody Man, The (p), 5/13/24, Ritz Theatre, 61
Melody of Youth, The (p), 8/15/16, Fulton Theatre, 111
Melting of Molly, The (m), 12/30/18, Broadhurst Theatre, 88
Melting Pot, The (p), 9/6/09, Comedy Theatre, 136
Member of the Wedding, The (p), 1/5/50, Empire Theatre, 501
Memorandum, The (p), 5/5/68, Public Theatre, 49
Memory Bank, The (The Recorder / The Electric Map) (p), 1/11/70, Tambellini's Gate Theatre, 25
Memory of Two Mondays / Suddenly Last Summer (p), 10/30/64, Master Theatre, 9, (Equity Library Theatre)
Memphis Bound! (m), 5/24/45, Broadway Theatre, 36
Memphis Store-Bought Teeth (m), 12/29/71, Orpheum Theatre, 1
Men in Shadow (p), 3/10/43, Morosco Theatre, 21
Men in White (p), 9/26/33, Broadhurst Theatre, 357
Men Must Fight (p), 10/14/32, Lyceum Theatre, 35
Men of Distinction (p), 4/30/53, 48th St. Theatre, 4
Men to the Sea (p), 10/3/44, National Theatre, 23
Men We Marry, The (p), 1/16/48, Mansfield Theatre, 3
Menace (p), 3/14/27, 49th St. Theatre, 24
Mendel, Inc. (p), 11/25/29, Sam H. Harris Theatre, 216
Mercenary Mary (m), 4/13/25, Longacre Theatre, 136
Merchant of Glory (p), 12/14/25, Guild Theatre, 41
Merchant of Venice, The (p) (Nat C. Goodwin), 5/24/01, Knickerbocker Theatre, 3
Merchant of Venice, The (p) (John E. Kellerd— Shylock), 1/20/13, Harris Theatre
Merchant of Venice, The (p) (Sir Herbert Tree— Shylock), 5/8/16, New Amsterdam Theatre, 20
Merchant of Venice, The (p) (Albert Bruning), 1/25/18, Cort Theatre, 2
Merchant of Venice, The (p), 12/2/20, Manhattan Opera House, 4
Merchant of Venice, The (p), 1/6/21, Lexington Theatre, 3
Merchant of Venice, The (p), 4/26/21, Longacre Theatre, 6
Merchant of Venice, The (p), 5/13/21, Broadhurst Theatre, 7

Merchant of Venice, The (p), 11/21/21, Century Theatre, 8, (Sothern-Marlowe Shakespeare Repertory)
Merchant of Venice, The (p), 12/26/21, Lexington Theatre, 2
Merchant of Venice, The (p) (David Warfield), 12/21/22, Lyceum Theatre, 92
Merchant of Venice, The (p) (Sothern-Marlowe), 11/5/23, Jolson Theatre, 7
Merchant of Venice, The (p) (Firmin Gemier), 11/17/24, Jolson Theatre
Merchant of Venice, The (p) (Walter Hampden), 12/26/25, Hampden Theatre, 56
Merchant of Venice, The (p) (George Arliss), 1/16/28, Broadhurst Theatre, 72
Merchant of Venice, The (p) (Fritz Leiber), 3/27/30, Shubert Theatre, 3
Merchant of Venice, The (p) (Maurice Moscovitch), 12/2/30, Times Square Theatre, 24
Merchant of Venice, The (p) (Fritz Leiber), 12/27/30, Ambassador Theatre, 3
Merchant of Venice, The (p) (Fritz Leiber), 11/16/31, Royale Theatre, 6
Merchant of Venice, The (p) (Ian Maclaren), 11/23/32, Shakespeare Theatre, 30
Merchant of Venice, The (p) (Donald Wolfit), 2/22/47, Century Theatre, 6
Merchant of Venice, The (p) (Luther Adler), 3/4/53, New York City Center, 16
Merchant of Venice, The (p) (Clarence Derwent), 1/7/55, Club Theatre, 20
Merchant of Venice, The (p) (Thomas Barbour), 2/22/55, Jan Hus House, 63
Merchant of Venice, The (p) (Thomas Barbour), 5/3/55, Jan Hus House, 14
Merchant of Venice, The (p) (Boris Tumarin), 2/2/62, Gate Theatre, 37
Merchant of Venice, The (p), 6/14/62, Delacorte Theatre, 19
Merchant of Venice, The (p), 3/4/73, Vivian Beaumont Theatre, 44
Merchant of Yonkers, The (p), 12/28/38, Guild Theatre, 39
Merchants of Venus (p), 9/27/20, Punch and Judy Theatre, 65
Mercy Street (p), 10/11/69, St. Clement's Church Theatre, 41, (American Place Theatre)
Mere Man (p), 11/25/12, Harris Theatre, 8
Merely Mary Ann (p), 12/28/03, Garden Theatre, 148
Merely Mary Ann (p), 2/27/07, Liberty Theatre
Merely Murder (p), 12/3/37, Playhouse, 3
Mermaids Singing, The (p), 11/28/45, Empire Theatre, 53
Merrily We Roll Along (p), 9/29/34, Music Box Theatre, 155
Merry Andrew (p), 1/21/29, Henry Miller's Theatre, 24
Merry Christmas, Daddy! / Editha's Burglar / The Travelling Man (p), 12/26/16, Cohan and Harris Theatre, 2
Merry Countess, The (p), 8/20/12, Casino Theatre, 135
Merry Death, A (p), 11/9/59, St. Marks Playhouse, 1
Merry Malones (m), 9/26/27, Erlanger Theatre, 216
Merry, Merry (m), 9/24/25, Vanderbilt Theatre, 197
Merry Whirl, The (m), 5/30/10, New York Theatre, 24
Merry Widow Burlesque, The (m), 1/2/08, Weber Music Hall, 156
Merry Widow, The (m) (Ethel Jackson), 10/21/07, New Amsterdam Theatre, 416
Merry Widow, The (m), 9/5/21, Knickerbocker Theatre, 56
Merry Widow, The (m), 12/2/29, Jolson Theatre, 16
Merry Widow, The (m), 9/7/31, Erlanger Theatre, 16
Merry Widow, The (m), 7/15/42, Carnegie Hall, 39
Merry Widow, The (m), 8/4/43, Majestic Theatre, 321
Merry Widow, The (m), 10/7/44, New York City Center, 32
Merry Widow, The (m), 4/10/57, New York City Center, 15
Merry Widow, The (m), 10/26/61, Jan Hus House, 12
Merry Widow, The (m), 8/17/64, New York State Theatre, 40
Merry Wives of Gotham (p), 1/16/24, Henry Miller's Theatre, 96
Merry Wives of Windsor, The (p), 11/7/10, New Theatre
Merry Wives of Windsor, The (p), 5/25/16, New Amsterdam Theatre, 12
Merry Wives of Windsor, The (p) (Herbert Tree-Constance Collier), 1/8/17, Park Theatre, 24
Merry Wives of Windsor, The (p), 3/19/28, Knickerbocker Theatre, 24
Merry Wives of Windsor, The (p), 2/17/33, Shakespeare Theatre, 16
Merry Wives of Windsor, The (p), 4/14/38, Empire Theatre, 4
Merry World, The (r) (retitled Passions of 1926), 6/8/26, Imperial Theatre, 87
Merry-Go-Round (m), 4/25/08, Circle Theatre, 97
Merry-Go-Round (m), 5/31/27, Klaw Theatre, 135
Merry-Go-Round (p), 4/22/32, Provincetown Playhouse, 56
Merton of the Movies (p), 11/13/22, Cort Theatre, 398
Message for Margaret (p), 4/16/47, Plymouth Theatre, 5
Message from Mars, A (p), 10/7/01, Garrick Theatre, 184
Message from Mars, A (p), 3/30/03, Criterion Theatre, 56
Message from Mars, A (p), 10/17/04, Princess Theatre, 32
Messenger Boy, The (m), 9/16/01, Daly's Theatre, 128
Messin' 'Round (m), 4/22/29, Hudson Theatre, 33
Metamorphosis (r), 4/22/71, Ambassador Theatre, 35
Metamorphosis (p), 4/8/72, American Place Theatre, 29
Metamorphosis / Pelleas and Melisande (p) (Kuriakos Theatre), 2/19/57, Theatre de Lys, 1
Metaphors. See Collision Course
Meteor (p), 12/23/29, Guild Theatre, 92
Metropole (p), 12/6/49, Lyceum Theatre, 2
Metropolitan Players, The, 12/13/32, Chanin Auditorium, 5
Mexican Hayride (m), 1/28/44, Winter Garden Theatre, 479
Mexicana (m), 4/21/39, 46th St. Theatre, 35
Mexicanal (m), 1/29/06, Lyric Theatre, 82
Meyer & Son (p), 3/1/09, Garden Theatre, 16
Mice and Men (p), 1/19/03, Garrick Theatre, 120
Mice and Men (p), 2/29/04, Garrick Theatre, 16
Michael and Mary (p), 12/13/29, Charles Hopkins Theatre, 246
Michael Drops In (p), 12/27/38, Golden Theatre, 8
Michael Todd's Peep Show (r), 6/28/50, Winter Garden Theatre, 278
Michel Auclair (p), 3/4/25, Provincetown Playhouse, 20
Mid-Channel (p), 1/31/10, Empire Theatre, 96
Middle of the Night (p), 2/8/56, ANTA Theatre, 477
Middle of the Night (p), 12/9/71, Master Theatre, 12, (Equity Library Theatre)
Middle Watch, The (p), 10/16/29, Times Square Theatre, 29
Midgie Purvis (p), 2/1/61, Martin Beck Theatre, 21
Midnight (p), 12/29/30, Guild Theatre, 48
Midnight Caller, The / John Turner Davis. See Two Plays by Horton Foote, 7/1/58, Sheridan Square Playhouse, 17
Midnight Girl, The (m), 2/23/14, 44th St. Theatre, 104
Midnight Rounders of 1921, The (m), 2/7/21, Century Promenade Theatre, 49
Midnight Rounders, The (r), 7/12/20, Century Promenade Theatre, 120
Midnight Sons, The (m), 5/22/09, Broadway Theatre, 257
Mid-Summer (p), 1/21/53, Vanderbilt Theatre, 109
Midsummer Night's Dream, A (p) (Margaret Crawford-Kathryn Hutchinson), 11/2/03, New Amsterdam Theatre, 24
Midsummer Night's Dream, A (p) (James Young-Ina Brooks), 9/21/06, Astor Theatre, 34
Midsummer Night's Dream, A (p), 2/16/15, Wallack Theatre
Midsummer Night's Dream, A (p), 11/17/27, Century Theatre, 23
Midsummer Night's Dream, A (p), 11/17/32, Shakespeare Theatre, 26
Midsummer Night's Dream, A (p), 9/21/54, Metropolitan Opera House, 29
Midsummer Night's Dream, A (p), 1/13/56, Jan Hus House, 37
Midsummer Night's Dream, A (p), 8/2/61, Wollman Memorial Skating Rink, 17
Midsummer Night's Dream, A (p), 6/29/64, Delacorte Mobile Theatre, 39
Midsummer Night's Dream, A (p), 6/29/67, Theatre de Lys, 28
Midsummer Night's Dream, A (p), 12/7/68, Hunter College Auditorium, 14, (Oxford & Cambridge Shakespeare Co.)
Midsummer Night's Dream, A (p), 1/20/71, Billy Rose Theatre, 77, (Royal Shakespeare Co.)
Midsummer Night's Dream, A (p), 6/28/73, Shade Company Theatre, 23
Midweek Interludes, The (p), 1/10/22, Neighborhood Playhouse, 16
Mid-West (p), 1/7/36, Booth Theatre, 22
Mighty Man Is He, A (p), 1/6/60, Cort Theatre, 5
Mikado, The (m), 7/14/02, Madison Square Roof Garden, 70
Mikado, The (m), 5/30/10, Casino Theatre, 48
Mikado, The (m), 6/29/12, Casino Theatre, 2
Mikado, The (m), 4/21/13, Casino Theatre, 16
Mikado, The (m), 4/11/25, 44th St. Theatre, 65
Mikado, The (m), 9/17/27, Royale Theatre, 110
Mikado, The (m), 5/4/31, Erlanger Theatre, 16
Mikado, The (m), 8/24/31, Erlanger Theatre, 36
Mikado, The (m), 4/17/33, St. James Theatre, 16
Mikado, The (m), 4/2/34, Majestic Theatre, 8
Mikado, The (m), 4/22/34, Majestic Theatre, 8
Mikado, The (m), 5/21/34, Majestic Theatre, 8
Mikado, The (m), 9/17/34, Martin Beck Theatre, 20
Mikado, The (m), 7/15/35, Adelphi Theatre, 8
Mikado, The (m), 8/19/35, Adelphi Theatre, 8
Mikado, The (m), 4/10/36, Majestic Theatre, 16
Mikado, The (m), 8/20/36, Martin Beck Theatre, 28
Mikado, The (m), 10/3/40, 44th St. Theatre, 11
Mikado, The (m), 2/11/44, Ambassador Theatre, 6
Mikado, The (m), 12/29/47, Century Theatre, 40
Mikado, The (m), 10/4/49, Mark Hellinger Theatre, 24
Mikado, The (m), 1/29/51, St. James Theatre, 8
Mikado, The (m), 10/20/52, Mark Hellinger Theatre, 8
Mikado, The (m), 10/10/55, Shubert Theatre, 17
Mikado, The, 4/23/57, Shakespearewrights Theatre, 8, (American Savoyards)
Mikado, The (m), 5/4/61, Greenwich Mews Theatre, 12
Mikado, The (m), 4/11/62, New York City Center, 15
Mikado, The (m), 3/22/64, New York City Center, 6
Mikado, The (m), 11/26/64, New York City Center, 10, (D'Oyly Carte Opera Co.)
Mikado, The (m), 5/22/65, Jan Hus Playhouse, 70, (American Savoyards)
Mikado, The (m), 6/1/66, Jan Hus Playhouse, 28, (American Savoyards)
Mikado, The (m), 11/18/66, New York City Center, 9, (D'Oyly Carte Opera Co.)
Mikado, The (m), 10/24/67, Jan Hus Playhouse, 18, (American Savoyards)
Mikado, The (m), 5/1/68, New York City Center, 8

Mikado, The (m), 11/1/68, New York City Center, 8, (D'Oyly Carte Opera Co.)
Mikado, The / The Big City / A Ball in Old Vienna (m), 2/3/42, St. James Theatre, 19
Mike Angelo (p), 1/8/23, Morosco Theatre, 48
Mike Downstairs (p), 4/18/68, Hudson Theatre, 4
Milady's Boudoir (p), 10/29/14, Garrick Theatre, 12
Mile-a-Minute Kendall (p), 11/28/16, Lyceum Theatre, 47
Milestones (p), 9/17/12, Liberty Theatre, 215
Milestones / The Little Father of the Wilderness (p), 6/2/30, Empire Theatre, 8
Milgrim's Progress (r), 12/22/24, Wallack Theatre, 66
Military Mad (p), 8/22/04, Garrick Theatre, 16
Military Maid, The (m), 10/8/00, Savoy Theatre, 8
Milk and Honey (m), 10/10/61, Martin Beck Theatre, 543
Milk Train Doesn't Stop Here Anymore, The (p), 1/16/63, Morosco Theatre, 69
Milk Train Doesn't Stop Here Anymore, The (p), 1/1/64, Brooks Atkinson Theatre, 5
Milky Way, The (p), 5/8/34, Cort Theatre, 63
Milky Way, The (p), 6/9/43, Windsor Theatre, 16
Million Dollars, A (m), 9/27/00, New York Theatre, 28
Million, The (p), 10/23/11, 39th St. Theatre, 126
Millionairess, The (p), 4/6/49, President Theatre, 13
Millionairess, The (p), 10/17/52, Shubert Theatre, 84
Millionairess, The (p), 3/2/69, Sheridan Square Playhouse, 17
Mills of the Gods, The (p), 3/4/07, Astor Theatre, 48
Mima (p), 12/12/28, Belasco Theatre, 180
Mime Theatre of Etienne Decroux, The, 12/23/59, Cricket Theatre, 37
Mimic and the Maid, The (m), 1/11/07, Bijou Theatre, 2
Mimic World of 1921, The (r), 8/15/21, Century Roof, 27
Mimic World, The (r), 7/9/08, Casino Theatre, 92
Mimie Scheller (p), 9/30/36, Ritz Theatre, 29
"Mind-the-Paint" Girl, The (p), 9/9/12, Lyceum Theatre, 136
Minick (p), 9/24/24, Booth Theatre, 154
Minna von Barnheim (p), 11/12/68, Barbizon-Plaza Theatre, 8, (Die Brücke)
Minnesota Theatre Co. (The House of Atreus; The Resistible Rise of Arturo VI) (p), 12/17/68, Billy Rose Theatre, 26
Minnie and Mr. Williams (p), 10/27/48, Morosco Theatre, 5
Minnie's Boys (m), 3/26/70, Imperial Theatre, 76
Minor Adjustment, A (p), 10/6/67, Brooks Atkinson Theatre, 3
Minor Miracle (p), 10/7/65, Henry Miller's Theatre, 4
Minor Scene, A. See Short Bullins
Minstrel Boy, The. See American Night Cry
Mira (p), 5/20/70, La Mama Experimental Theatre Club
Miracle at Verdun (p), 3/16/31, Martin Beck Theatre, 48
Miracle in Brooklyn. See Command Performance
Miracle in the Mountains (p), 4/25/47, Playhouse, 3
Miracle Man, The (p), 9/21/14, Astor Theatre, 97
Miracle Play (p), 12/30/73, Playhouse 2 Theatre, 5, (New Phoenix Repertory Co.)
Miracle, The (p), 1/16/24, Century Theatre, 300
Miracle, The (p), 2/4/60, Broadway Congregational Church, 10
Miracle Worker, The (p), 10/19/59, Playhouse Theatre, 719
Mirage, The (p), 9/30/20, Times Square Theatre, 190
Miranda of the Balcony (p), 9/24/01, Manhattan Theatre, 62
Mirele Efros (p), 10/19/67, Billy Rose Theatre, 42, (Jewish State Theatre of Poland)
Mirele Efros (p), 12/25/69, Roosevelt Theatre, 15
Mirrors (p), 1/18/28, Forrest Theatre, 13
Mis' Nelly of N'Orleans (p), 2/4/19, Henry Miller's Theatre, 127
Misalliance (p), 9/27/17, Broadhurst Theatre, 52
Misalliance (p), 2/18/53, New York City Center, 146
Misalliance (p), 9/25/61, Sheridan Square Playhouse, 158
Misalliance (p), 3/28/72, Roundabout Theatre, 46
Misanthrope, Le (p), 11/30/26, Cosmopolitan Theatre, 7
Misanthrope, Le (p) (Renaud-Barrault Repertory Co.), 2/7/57, Winter Garden Theatre, 4
Misanthrope, The (p), 11/12/56, Theatre East, 114
Misanthrope, The (p), 10/9/68, Lyceum Theatre, 86, (APA-Phoenix)
Misanthrope, The (p), 11/6/73, Abbey Theatre, 27, (CSC Repertory)
Miser, The (p), 3/17/55, Downtown National Theatre, 6
Miser, The (p), 5/8/69, Vivian Beaumont Theatre, 52
Miser, The (p), 2/1/67, Roundabout Theatre
Miser, The. See Avare, L'
Miser, The / Snickering Horses / The Great Catherine (p), 5/13/36, Experimental Theatre, 3
Mis-Guided Tour (m), 10/12/59, Downtown Theatre, 56
Misleading Lady, The (p), 11/25/13, Fulton Theatre, 72
Mismates (p), 4/13/25, Times Square Theatre, 72
Miss Americana (r), 11/29/28, Liberty Theatre, 12
Miss Daisy (p), 9/9/14, Shubert Theatre, 29
Miss Dolly Dollars (m), 9/4/05, Knickerbocker Theatre, 56
Miss Dolly Dollars (m), 10/8/06, New York Theatre, 16
Miss Elizabeth's Prisoner (p), 11/23/03, Criterion Theatre, 32
Miss Emily Adam (m), 3/29/60, Theatre Marquee, 21
Miss Gulliver Travels (p), 11/25/31, Hudson Theatre, 22
Miss Hook of Holland (m), 12/31/07, Criterion Theatre, 119
Miss Information (m), 10/5/15, Cohan Theatre, 47
Miss Innocence (m), 11/30/08, New York Theatre, 176
Miss Isobel (p), 12/26/57, Royale Theatre, 53
Miss Jack (m), 9/4/11, Herald Square Theatre, 16
Miss Julie (p) (Royal Dramatic Th. of Sweden), 5/16/62, Cort Theatre, 3
Miss Julie (p), 11/20/73, Abbey Theatre, 27, (CSC Repertory)
Miss Julie / The Death of Lord Chatterly (p), 7/31/73, Roundabout Theatre, 16
Miss Julie / The Stronger (p), 11/10/65, Provincetown Playhouse, 11
Miss Julie / The Stronger (p), 2/21/56, Phoenix Theatre, 32
Miss Liberty (m), 7/15/49, Imperial Theatre, 308
Miss Lonelyhearts (p), 10/3/57, Music Box Theatre, 12
Miss Lulu Bett (p), 12/27/20, Belmont Theatre, 201
Miss Millions (m), 12/9/19, Punch and Judy Theatre, 47
Miss Patsy (p), 8/29/10, Nazimova Theatre, 24
Miss Phoenix (p), 11/3/13, Harris Theatre, 8
Miss Pocahontas (m), 10/28/07, Lyric Theatre, 16
Miss Princess (m), 12/23/12, Park Theatre, 16
Miss Prinnt (m), 12/25/00, Victoria Theatre, 28
Miss Quis (p), 4/7/37, Henry Miller's Theatre, 37
Miss Simplicity (m), 2/10/02, Casino Theatre, 56
Miss Springtime (m), 9/25/16, New Amsterdam Theatre, 224
Miss Swan Expects (p), 2/20/39, Cort Theatre, 8
Miss 1917 (r), 11/5/17, Century Theatre, 48
Missouri Legend (p), 9/19/38, Empire Theatre, 48
Mistakes Will Happen (p), 5/14/06, Garrick Theatre, 8
Mister Antonio (p), 9/18/16, Lyceum Theatre, 48
Mister Johnson (p), 3/29/56, Martin Beck Theatre, 44
Mister Malatesta (p), 2/26/23, Princess Theatre, 96
Mister Pitt (p), 1/22/25, 39th St. Theatre, 87
Mister Roberts (p), 2/18/48, Alvin Theatre, 1,157
Mister Roberts (p), 12/5/56, New York City Center, 15
Mister Romeo (p), 9/5/27, Wallack Theatre, 16
Mistress Nell (p), 10/9/00, Bijou Theatre, 104
Mistress Nell (p), 4/29/01, Wallack Theatre, 40
Mistress Nell (p), 2/11/02, Republic Theatre, 24
Mistress of the Inn, The. See La Locandiera
Mistresses and Maidens (Song of Songs / Maidens and Mistresses at Home at the Zoo) (p), 1/21/59, Orpheum Theatre, 23
Mitschuldigen, Die / Woyzeck (p), 4/5/66, New York City Center, 8, (The Bavarian State Theatre)
Mixed Doubles (r), 10/19/66, Upstairs at the Downstairs, 428
Mixed Doubles (p), 4/26/27, Bijou Theatre, 12
Mixed Marriage (p), 12/14/20, Bramhall Playhouse, 107
Mix-up, A (p), 12/28/14, 39th St. Theatre, 88
Mizpah (p), 9/24/06, Academy of Music, 24
Mlle. Mischief (m), 9/28/08, Lyric Theatre, 96
Mlle. Modiste (m), 12/25/05, Knickerbocker Theatre, 202
Mlle. Modiste (m), 9/1/06, Knickerbocker Theatre, 22
Mlle. Modiste (m), 5/20/07, Academy of Music, 29
Mlle. Modiste (m), 9/9/07, Knickerbocker Theatre, 21
Mlle. Modiste (m), 5/26/13, Globe Theatre, 24
Mlle. Modiste (m), 10/7/29, Jolson Theatre, 48
Mme. Pompadour (m), 11/11/24, Martin Beck Theatre, 79
Mme. Simone Repertory, 3/21/24, Gaiety Theatre
Mme. Vera F. Komisarzhevsky Repertory, 3/2/08, Daly's Theatre, 24
Mob, The (p), 10/9/20, Neighborhood Playhouse, 95
Moby Dick (p), 4/25/55, Phoenix Theatre, 1
Moby Dick (p), 4/10/61, Madison Avenue Playhouse, 7
Moby Dick (p), 11/28/62, Ethel Barrymore Theatre, 13
Moby Dick (p), 10/1/70, CSC Repertory Theatre, 8
Moby Dick (p), 9/12/73, Abbey Theatre, 11, (CSC Repertory)
Mocking Bird, The (m), 11/10/02, Bijou Theatre, 64
Mocking Bird, The (m), 5/25/03, Bijou Theatre, 14
Mod Donna (m), 5/3/70, Public Theatre, 56
Model, The (p), 8/31/12, Harris Theatre, 17
Modern Eve, A (m), 5/3/15, Casino Theatre, 56
Modern Girl, A (p), 9/12/14, Comedy Theatre, 17
Modern Magdalen, A (p), 3/29/02, Bijou Theatre, 73
Modern Marriage (p), 9/16/11, Bijou Theatre, 17
Modern Statuary. See American Gothics
Modern Virgin, A (p), 5/20/31, Booth Theatre, 45
Modest Suzanne (m), 1/1/12, Liberty Theatre, 24
Modiste Shop, The / A Glimpse of the Great White Way (m), 10/27/13, 44th St. Theatre, 12
Moiseyev Dance Company, 4/14/58, Metropolitan Opera House, 24
Moke-Eater, The (p), 9/19/68, Max's Kansas City
Moliere (p), 3/17/19, Liberty Theatre, 64
Mollusc, The, 6/7/09, Empire Theatre, 14
Mollusc, The / Mrs. Peckham's Carouse (p), 9/29/08, Garrick Theatre, 63
Mollusc, The / The Likes o' Me (p), 9/1/08, Garrick Theatre, 33

Molly (m), 11/1/73, Alvin Theatre, 68
Molly Darling (m), 9/1/22, Liberty Theatre, 101
Molly May (m), 4/8/10, Hackett Theatre, 27
Molly O' (m), 5/17/16, Cort Theatre, 45
Moloch (p), 9/20/15, New Amsterdam Theatre, 32
Moment of Death, The / The Greatest Thing in the World (p), 10/23/00, Wallack's Theatre, 24
Momiji-Gari. See The Grand Kabuki
Money Business (p), 1/20/26, National Theatre, 13
Money from Home (p), 2/28/27, Fulton Theatre, 32
Money in the Air (p), 3/7/32, Ritz Theatre, 48
Money Lender, The (p), 8/27/28, Ambassador Theatre, 16
Money Mad (p), 5/24/37, 49th St. Theatre, 1
Money Makers, The (p), 1/16/05, Liberty Theatre, 16
Money Makers, The (p), 10/5/14, Booth Theatre, 24
Mongolia (p), 12/26/27, Greenwich Village Theatre, 48
Mongrel, The (p), 12/15/24, Longacre Theatre, 34
Monique (p), 10/22/57, John Golden Theatre, 63
Monkey (p), 2/11/32, Mansfield Theatre, 29
Monkey's Paw, The (p), 1/30/22, Belmont Theatre, 32
Monkey Talks, The (p), 12/28/45, Sam H. Harris Theatre, 98
Monks of Malabar, The (m), 9/14/00, Knickerbocker Theatre, 39
Monna Vanna (p), 10/23/05, Manhattan Theatre, 50
Monopoly (Make Like a Dog / Suburban Tragedy / Princess Rebecca Birnbaum / Young Marrieds Play Monopoly) (p), 3/5/66, Stage 73, 49
Monsieur Artaud. See Tel Aviv Drama Company
Monsieur Beaucaire (p), 3/11/12, Daly's Theatre, 64
Monsieur Beaucaire (p), 12/11/19, New Amsterdam Theatre, 143
Monster, The (p), 8/9/22, 39th St. Theatre, 112
Monster, The (p), 2/10/33, Waldorf Theatre, 38
Monte Cristo (p), 10/23/00, Academy of Music, 80
Monte Cristo (p), 10/7/07, Lyric Theatre, 14
Monte Cristo, Jr., 2/12/19, Winter Garden, 254
Month in the Country, A (p), 3/17/30, Guild Theatre, 72
Month in the Country, A (p), 4/3/56, Phoenix Theatre, 48
Month in the Country, A (p), 5/28/63, Maidman Playhouse, 48
Month of Sundays (m), 9/16/68, Theatre de Lys, 8
Montmartre (p), 2/13/22, Belmont Theatre, 112
Montserrat (p), 10/29/49, Fulton Theatre, 65
Montserrat (p), 1/8/61, Gate Theatre, 49
Moon Besieged, The (p), 12/5/62, Lyceum Theatre, 1
Moon Dreamers, The (m), 12/8/69, Ellen Stewart Theatre, 24
Moon for the Misbegotten, A (p), 5/2/57, Bijou Theatre, 68
Moon for the Misbegotten, A (p), 6/12/68, Circle in the Square, 199
Moon for the Misbegotten, A (p), 12/29/73, Morosco Theatre, 175
Moon in the Yellow River, The (p), 2/29/32, Guild Theatre, 40
Moon in the Yellow River, The (p), 2/6/61, East End Theatre, 32
Moon in the Yellow River, The (p), 3/14/61, East End Theatre, 16
Moon Is a Gong, The (p), 3/12/26, Cherry Lane Theatre, 19
Moon Is Blue, The (p), 3/8/51, Henry Miller's Theatre, 924
Moon Is Blue, The (p), 8/8/61, 41st St. Theatre, 16
Moon Is Down, The (p), 4/7/42, Martin Beck Theatre, 71
Moon Mysteries (A Full Moon in March / The Cat and the Moon / Calvary) (p), 11/17/72, St. Clement's Church, 12
Moon of the Caribbees, The / In the Zone / Bound East for Cardiff / The Long Voyage Home (p), 10/29/37, Lafayette Theatre, 68
Moon of the Caribbees, The / In the Zone / Bound East for Cardiff / The Long Voyage Home (p), 5/20/48, New York City Center, 14
Moon of the Caribbees, The / Trifles / Grotesques (p), 4/25/21, Provincetown Playhouse, 21
Moon on a Rainbow Shawl (p), 1/15/62, East 11th St. Theatre, 105
Moon on a Rainbow Shawl (m), 12/17/70, Urban Arts Corps Theatre
Moon on a Rainbow Shawl. See An Evening with the Urban Arts Corps
Moon Over Mulberry Street (p), 9/4/35, Lyceum Theatre, 140
Moon Over Mulberry Street (p), 1/13/36, 44th St. Theatre, 160
Moon Shines on Kylenamoe / Figure in the Night (p), 11/30/63, Theatre de Lys, 1
Moon Vine, The (p), 2/11/43, Morosco Theatre, 21
Moon Walk (m), 11/28/70, New York City Center, 8
Moonbirds (p), 10/9/59, Cort Theatre, 3
Moonchildren (p), 2/21/72, Royale Theatre, 16
Moonchildren (p), 11/4/73, Theatre de Lys, 237
Moon-Flower, The (p), 2/25/24, Astor Theatre, 48
Moonlight (m), 1/30/24, Longacre Theatre, 174
Moonlight and Honeysuckle (p), 9/29/19, Henry Miller's Theatre, 97
Moonlight Mary (p), 1/27/16, Fulton Theatre, 20
Moonshine (m), 10/30/05, Liberty Theatre, 53
Moor Born (p), 4/3/34, Playhouse, 63
Moorborn, 10/4/50, Hotel Sutton Theatre
Moral Fabric (p), 11/21/32, Provincetown Playhouse, 32
Morals (p), 11/30/25, Comedy Theatre, 41
Morals of Marcus, The (p), 11/18/07, Criterion Theatre, 44
More Stately Mansions (p), 10/31/67, Broadhurst Theatre, 142
More Than Queen (p), 10/30/00, Broadway Theatre, 7
More Than You Deserve (m), 11/21/74, Newman / Public Theatre, 63
More the Merrier, The (p), 9/15/41, Cort Theatre, 16
Mormon Wife, The (p), 8/19/01, 14th St. Theatre, 32
Morning After, The (p), 7/27/25, Hudson Theatre, 24
Morning, Noon and Night (Morning/Noon/Night) (p), 11/28/68, Henry Miller's Theatre, 52
Morning. See Morning, Noon and Night
Morning Star (p), 4/16/40, Longacre Theatre, 63
Morning Star (p), 9/14/42, Morosco Theatre, 24
Morning Sun (m), 10/6/63, Phoenix Theatre, 9
Mornings at Seven (p), 11/30/39, Longacre Theatre, 44
Mornings at Seven (p), 6/22/55, Cherry Lane Theatre, 125
Morphia (p), 3/6/23, Eltinge Theatre, 57
Morris Dance, The (p), 2/13/17, Little Theatre, 23
Morris Gest's Midnight Whirl (r), 12/27/19, Century Grove Theatre
Morton: The Patient. See Things That Almost Happen
Moscow Art Players, 2/16/35, Majestic Theatre, 52
Moscow Art Theatre Musical Studio, 12/14/25, Jolson Theatre, 96
Moscow Art Theatre Musical Studio, 5/1/26, Cosmopolitan Theatre, 18
Moscow Art Theatre, The (p), 1/8/23, Jolson Theatre, 113
Moscow Art Theatre, The (p), 11/19/23, Jolson Theatre, 113
Moscow Art Theatre, The (p), 2/4/65, New York City Center, 31
Moscow Theatre Habima in Repertoire, 12/13/26, Mansfield Theatre, 55
Most Happy Fella, The (m), 5/3/56, Imperial Theatre, 676
Most Happy Fella, The (m), 2/10/59, New York City Center, 16
Most Happy Fella, The (m), 5/11/66, New York City Center, 15
Most Immoral Lady, A (p), 11/26/28, Cort Theatre, 160
Most of the Game (p), 10/1/35, Cort Theatre, 23
Motel. See America Hurrah
Mother (p), 9/7/10, Hackett Theatre, 133
Mother (p), 11/19/35, Civic Repertory Theatre, 31
Mother Carey's Chickens (p), 9/25/17, Cort Theatre, 39
Mother Courage and Her Children (p), 3/28/63, Martin Beck Theatre, 52
Mother Courage and Her Children (p), 11/16/67, Billy Rose Theatre, 11, (Jewish State Theatre of Poland)
Mother Earth (r), 10/19/72, Belasco Theatre, 12
Mother Goose (m), 12/2/03, New Amsterdam Theatre, 105
Mother Lode (p), 12/22/34, Cort Theatre, 9
Mother Lover, The (p), 2/1/69, Booth Theatre, 1
Mother of Us All, The (m), 11/26/72, Guggenheim Museum Theatre, 16
Mother's Day. See Playwrights Cooperative Festival
Mother's Liberty Bond (p), 8/7/18, Park Theatre, 13
Mother Sings (p), 11/12/35, 58th St. Theatre, 7
Mother, The (p), 4/25/39, Lyceum Theatre, 4
Moths, The (p), 5/11/70, Mercury Theatre, 1
Motor Girl, The (m), 6/15/09, Lyric Theatre, 95
Mountain Climber, The (p), 3/5/06, Criterion Theatre, 79
Mountain Climber, The / Little Father of the Wilderness (p), 4/23/06, Criterion Theatre, 24
Mountain Fury (p), 9/25/29, President Theatre, 13
Mountain Man, The (p), 12/12/21, Maxine Elliott's Theatre, 163
Mountain, The (p), 9/11/33, Provincetown Playhouse, 8
Mountebank, The (p), 5/7/23, Lyceum Theatre, 32
Mourning Becomes Electra (p), 10/26/31, Guild Theatre, 158
Mourning Becomes Electra (p), 5/9/32, Alvin Theatre, 12
Mourning Becomes Electra (p), 11/15/72, Circle in the Square / Joseph E. Levine Theatre, 53
Mousetrap, The (p), 4/8/59, 16th St. Theatre
Mousetrap, The (p), 11/5/60, Maidman Playhouse, 192
Move On (p), 1/18/26, Daly's Theatre, 8
Move On, Sister (p), 10/24/33, Playhouse, 7
Movers, The (p), 9/3/07, Hackett Theatre, 23
Mozart (p), 11/22/26, Music Box Theatre, 33
Mozart / Deburau (p), 12/27/26, Chanin's 46th St. Theatre, 32
Mr. Adam (p), 5/25/49, Royale Theatre, 5
Mr. and Mrs. Daventry (p), 2/23/10, Hackett Theatre, 4
Mr. and Mrs. Lyman (p), 3/4/68, Theatre de Lys, 2, (ANTA Matinee)
Mr. and Mrs. North (p), 1/12/41, Belasco Theatre, 163
Mr. Banks of Birmingham / The Coggerers / The Red Velvet Coat (p), 1/20/39, Hudson Theatre, 3
Mr. Barnum (p), 9/9/18, Criterion Theatre, 24
Mr. Barry's Etchings (p), 1/31/50, 48th St. Theatre, 31
Mr. Battling Buttler (m), 10/8/23, Selwyn Theatre, 313
Mr. Big (p), 9/30/41, Lyceum Theatre, 7
Mr. Bluebeard (r), 1/21/03, Knickerbocker Theatre, 134
Mr. Butles (p), 1/20/10, Weber Theatre, 12
Mr. Faust (p), 1/30/22, Provincetown Playhouse, 15
Mr. Gilhooley (p), 9/30/30, Broadhurst Theatre, 31
Mr. Grossman / Dark Corners (p), 5/5/64, Actors Playhouse, 7
Mr. Hamlet of Broadway (m), 12/23/08, Casino Theatre, 54
Mr. Hopkinson (p), 2/12/06, Savoy Theatre, 113
Mr. Hopkinson (p), 10/8/06, Savoy Theatre, 8
Mr. Lazarus (p), 9/5/16, Shubert Theatre, 39
Mr. Lode of Koal (m), 11/1/09, Majestic Theatre, 40
Mr. Moneypenny (p), 10/16/28, Liberty Theatre, 62
Mr. Myd's Mystery (p), 8/16/15, Comedy Theatre, 16

Mr. Papavert (p), 1/22/32, Vanderbilt Theatre, 11
Mr. Peebles and Mr. Hooker (p), 10/10/46, Music Box Theatre, 4
Mr. Pickwick (m), 1/19/03, Herald Square Theatre, 32
Mr. Pickwick (p), 9/17/52, Plymouth Theatre, 61
Mr. Pim Passes By (p), 2/28/21, Garrick Theatre, 210
Mr. Pim Passes By (p), 4/18/27, Garrick Theatre, 36
Mr. Preedy and the Countess (p), 11/7/10, 39th St. Theatre, 24
Mr. President (m), 10/20/62, St. James Theatre, 265
Mr. Samuel (p), 11/10/30, Little Theatre, 8
Mr. Simian (p), 10/21/63, Astor Place Playhouse, 22
Mr. Strauss Goes to Boston (m), 9/6/45, Century Theatre, 12
Mr. Sycamore (p), 11/13/42, Guild Theatre, 19
Mr. Wix of Wickham (m), 9/19/04, Bijou Theatre, 41
Mr. Wonderful (m), 3/22/56, Broadway Theatre, 383
Mr. Wu (p), 10/14/14, Maxine Elliott's Theatre, 53
Mrs. Avery (p), 10/23/11, Weber Theatre, 8
Mrs. Battle's Bath / The Firm of Cunningham (p), 5/05, Madison Square Theatre, 8
Mrs. Black Is Back (p), 11/7/04, Bijou Theatre, 71
Mrs. Black Is Back (p), 3/27/05, New York Theatre, 8
Mrs. Boltay's Daughters (p), 10/23/15, Comedy Theatre, 17
Mrs. Bumpstead-Leigh (p), 4/3/11, Lyceum Theatre, 64
Mrs. Bumpstead-Leigh (p), 4/1/29, Klaw Theatre, 72
Mrs. Christmas Angel (p), 11/19/12, Harris Theatre, 3
Mrs. Dakon (p), 12/14/09, Hackett Theatre, 2
Mrs. Dally (p), 9/22/65, John Golden Theatre, 53
Mrs. Dally Has a Lover / Whisper into My Good Ear (p), 10/1/62, Cherry Lane Theatre, 48
Mrs. Dane' s Defense (p), 12/31/00, Empire Theatre, 107
Mrs. Dane's Defense (p), 2/6/28, Cosmopolitan Theatre, 16
Mrs. Deering's Divorce (p), 9/7/03, Savoy Theatre, 28
Mrs. Dot (p), 1/24/10, Lyceum Theatre, 72
Mrs. Gibbons' Boys (p), 5/4/49, Music Box Theatre, 5
Mrs. Gorringe's Necklace (p), 12/7/04, Lyceum Theatre, 39
Mrs. Jack (p), 9/2/02, Wallack Theatre, 72
Mrs. January and Mr. X (p), 3/31/44, Belasco Theatre, 43
Mrs. Jimmie Thompson (p), 3/29/20, Princess Theatre, 64
Mrs. Kimball Presents (p), 2/29/44, 48th St. Theatre, 7
Mrs. Leffingwell's Boots (p), 1/11/05, Savoy Theatre, 123
Mrs. Leffingwell's Boots / A Maker of Men (p), 8/21/05, Lyceum Theatre, 14
Mrs. Leslie Carter Repertory, 9/20/05, Belasco Theatre, 61
Mrs. McThing (p), 2/20/52, ANTA Playhouse, 350
Mrs. Minter. See People of the Shadows
Mrs. Minter. See Playwrights Cooperative Festival
Mrs. Moonlight (p), 9/29/30, Charles Hopkins Theatre, 294
Mrs. O'Brien Entertains (p), 2/8/39, Lyceum Theatre, 37
Mrs. Partridge Presents (p), 1/5/25, Belmont Theatre, 146
Mrs. Patrick Campbell Repertory, 1/13/02, Republic Theatre, 24
Mrs. Patrick Campbell Repertory, 11/11/07, Lyric Theatre, 8
Mrs. Patterson (p), 12/1/54, National Theatre, 101
Mrs. Peckham's Carouse / The Mollusc (p), 9/29/08, Garrick Theatre, 63
Mrs. Peckham's Carouse / Widow by Proxy (p), 4/21/13, Cohan Theatre, 24
Mrs. Snow / Cruising Speed 600 M.P.H. (p), 1/5/70, Theatre de Lys, 2, (ANTA Matinee)
Mrs. Temple's Telegram (p), 2/1/05, Madison Square Theatre, 86
Mrs. Temple's Telegram (p), 4/16/06, Madison Square Theatre, 16
Mrs. Warren's Profession (p) (Mary Shaw), 3/9/07, Manhattan Theatre, 25
Mrs. Warren's Profession (p) (Mary Shaw), 3/11/18, Comedy Theatre, 48
Mrs. Warren's Profession (p), 2/22/22, Punch and Judy Theatre, 25
Mrs. Warren's Profession (p), 10/25/50, Bleecker St. Playhouse, 28
Mrs. Warren's Profession (p), 6/25/58, Gate Theatre, 5
Mrs. Warren's Profession (p), 4/24/63, Showboat Theatre, 15
Mrs. Wiggs of the Cabbage Patch (p), 9/3/04, Savoy Theatre, 150
Mrs. Wiggs of the Cabbage Patch (p), 9/17/06, New York Theatre, 24
Mrs. Wilson, That's All (p), 11/5/06, Bijou Theatre, 51
Much Ado About Nothing (p) (William Morris-Jessie Millward), 3/14/04, Princess Theatre, 16
Much Ado About Nothing (p), 11/25/12, 39th St. Theatre
Much Ado About Nothing (p) (Frank Reicher - Annie Russell), 9/1/13, Empire Theatre, 24
Much Ado About Nothing (p), 11/18/27, American Laboratory Theatre, 25
Much Ado About Nothing (p), 12/3/32, Shakespeare Theatre, 9
Much Ado About Nothing (p), 5/1/52, Music Box Theatre, 4
Much Ado About Nothing (p) (John Gielgud - Margaret Leighton), 9/17/59, Lunt-Fontanne Theatre, 58
Much Ado About Nothing (p), 7/5/61, Wollman Memorial Skating Rink, 17
Much Ado About Nothing (p), 8/10/72, Delacorte Theatre, 20
Much Ado About Nothing (p), 11/11/72, Winter Garden, 105
Mud (p), 7/3/24, Cherry Lane Theatre, 6
Mud Turtle, The (p), 8/20/25, Bijou Theatre, 52
Muddle Anna / Augustus in Search of a Father / It's the Poor as 'Elps the Poor (p), 3/15/21, Little Theatre, 1
Mulatto (p), 10/24/35, Vanderbilt Theatre, 373
Mulberry Bush, The (p), 10/26/27, Republic Theatre, 29
Multilated, The. See Slapstick Tragedy
Mum's the Word (r), 12/5/40, Belmont Theatre, 12
Mummenschanz, 10/27/73, Alice Tully Hall, 1
Mummenschanz, 11/29/74, Alice Tully Hall, 4
Mummers and Men (p), 3/26/62, Provincetown Playhouse, 6
Mummy and the Humming Bird, The (p), 9/4/02, Empire Theatre, 85
Mummy and the Humming Bird, The (p), 4/30/03, Empire Theatre, 16
Mundy Scheme, The (p), 12/11/69, Royale Theatre, 4
Murder at the Vanities (m), 9/12/33, New Amsterdam Theatre, 298
Murder in the Cathedral (p), 3/20/36, Manhattan Theatre, 38
Murder in the Cathedral (p), 2/16/38, Ritz Theatre, 21
Murder in the Cathedral (p), 3/17/71, Central Presbyterian Church, 8
Murder on the Second Floor (p), 9/11/29, Eltinge Theatre, 45
Murder without Crime (p), 8/18/43, Cort Theatre, 37
Murderer Among Us, A (p), 3/25/64, Morosco Theatre, 1
Murderous Angels (p), 12/20/71, Playhouse Theatre, 24
Murray Anderson's Almanac (r), 8/14/29, Erlanger Theatre, 69
Murray Hill (p), 9/29/27, Bijou Theatre, 28
Music Box Revue, The (r), 9/22/21, Music Box Theatre, 440
Music Box Revue, The (r), 10/23/22, Music Box Theatre, 330
Music Box Revue, The (r), 9/22/23, Music Box Theatre, 277
Music Box Revue, The (r), 12/1/24, Music Box Theatre, 184
Music Hath Charms (r), 12/29/34, Majestic Theatre, 25
Music in May (m), 4/1/29, Casino Theatre, 80
Music in My Heart (m), 10/2/47, Adelphi Theatre, 124
Music in the Air (m), 11/8/32, Alvin Theatre, 146
Music in the Air (m), 3/1/33, 44th St. Theatre, 196
Music in the Air (m), 10/8/51, Ziegfeld Theatre, 56
Music Man, The (m), 12/19/57, Majestic Theatre, 1,375
Music Man, The (m), 6/16/65, New York City Center, 15
Music Master, The (p), 9/26/04, Belasco Theatre, 288
Music Master, The (p), 9/2/05, Bijou Theatre, 306
Music Master, The (p), 9/1/06, Bijou Theatre, 33
Music Master, The (p), 2/24/08, Stuyvesant Theatre, 70
Music Master, The (p), 10/10/16, Knickerbocker Theatre, 159
Music! Music! (r), 4/11/74, New York City Center, 37
Music Shop, The / The Vagrant / The Witch (p) (A Chekhov Sketchbook), 2/15/62, Gramercy Arts Theatre, 94
Musical Timepiece, A (m), 10/19/70, Lincoln Center Library Auditorium, 3, (Equity Library Theatre)
Musk (p), 3/13/20, Punch and Judy Theatre, 9
Mutation Show, The, 3/17/73, Space for Innovative Development, 10, (Open Theatre)
Mutation Show, The, 9/19/73, St. Clement's Church Theatre, 6, (Open Theatre)
Mutilation (p), 5/18/72, Theatre Genesis
Muzeeka / Red Cross (p), 4/28/68, Provincetown Playhouse, 65
My Aunt from Ypsilanti (p), 5/1/23, Earl Carroll Theatre, 7
My Best Girl (m), 9/12/12, Park Theatre, 68
My Country (p), 8/9/26, Chanin's 46th St. Theatre, 49
My Darlin' Aida (m), 10/27/52, Winter Garden Theatre, 89
My Daughter, Your Son (p), 5/13/69, Booth Theatre, 47
My Daughter-in-Law (p), 2/26/00, Lyceum Theatre, 72
My Dear Children (p), 1/31/40, Belasco Theatre, 117
My Dear Public (r), 9/9/43, 46th St. Theatre, 44
My Fair Ladies (p), 3/23/41, Hudson Theatre, 32
My Fair Lady (m), 3/15/56, Mark Hellinger Theatre, 2,717
My Fair Lady (m), 5/20/64, New York City Center, 15
My Fair Lady (m), 6/13/68, New York City Center, 22
My Fat Friend (p), 3/31/74, Brooks Atkinson Theatre, 70
My Foot My Tutor / Self-Accusation (p), 4/27/71, Brooklyn Academy of Music, 7, (Chelsea Theatre Center)
My Girl (m), 11/24/24, Vanderbilt Theatre, 201
My Girl Friday (p), 2/12/29, Republic Theatre, 253
My Golden Girl (m), 2/2/20, Nora Bayes Theatre, 105
My Heart's in the Highlands (p), 4/13/39, Guild Theatre, 44
My House Is Your House (p), 10/15/70, Players Theatre, 1
My Kinsman, Major Molineaux / Benito Cereno (p) (The Old Glory), 11/1/64, St. Clement's Church, 122, (American Place Theatre)
My Lady (p), 2/11/01, Victoria Theatre, 93
My Lady Dainty (p), 1/8/01, Madison Square Theatre, 39
My Lady Friends (m), 12/3/19, Comedy Theatre, 214
My Lady Molly (m), 1/5/04, Daly's Theatre, 15
My Lady Peggy Goes to Town (p), 5/4/03, Daly's Theatre, 24
My Lady's Dress (p), 10/10/14, Playhouse, 57
My Lady's Garter (p), 9/9/15, Booth Theatre, 4
My Lady's Glove (m), 6/18/17, Lyric Theatre, 16
My Lady's Maid (m), 9/20/06, Casino Theatre, 44
My Little Friend (m), 5/19/13, New Amsterdam Theatre, 24
My Magnolia (m), 7/12/26, Mansfield Theatre, 4
My Mama the General (m), 10/17/73, Burstein Theatre, 95
My Man (p), 9/27/10, Bijou Theatre, 15
My Maryland (m), 9/12/27, Jolson Theatre, 312

My Milliner's Bill / Marietta / The Hour Glass (p), 4/7/04, Garrick Theatre, 1
My Mother, My Father and Me (p), 3/23/63, Plymouth Theatre, 17
My Name Is Aquilon (p), 2/9/49, Lyceum Theatre, 31
My Princess (m), 10/6/27, Shubert Theatre, 20
My Romance (m), 10/19/48, Shubert Theatre, 95
My Sister Eileen (p), 12/26/40, Biltmore Theatre, 866
My Sister, My Sister (p), 4/30/74, Little Theatre, 36
My Son (p), 9/17/24, Princess Theatre, 275
My Sweet Charlie (p), 12/6/66, Longacre Theatre, 31
My Wife (p), 8/31/07, Empire Theatre, 129
My Wife and I (m), 10/10/66, Theatre Four, 16
My Wife's Husbands (p), 8/24/03, Madison Square Theatre, 41
My Wife Won't Let Me (m), 8/14/06, Berkeley Lyceum Theatre, 1
My 3 Angels (p), 3/11/53, Morosco Theatre, 344
Myrtie (p), 2/4/24, 52nd St. Theatre, 24
Myself-Bettina (p), 10/5/08, Daly's Theatre, 32
Mysteries and Smaller Pieces, 10/9/68, Brooklyn Academy of Music, 5, (Living Theatre)
Mystery Man, The (p), 1/26/28, Nora Bayes Theatre, 100
Mystery Moon (m), 6/23/30, Royale Theatre, 1
Mystery Play (p), 1/3/73, Cherry Lane Theatre, 14
Mystery Program of Gilbert & Sullivan Numbers (r), 11/17/68, New York City Center, 1, (D'Oyly Carte Opera Co.)
Mystery Ship, The (p), 3/14/27, Garrick Theatre, 121
Mystery Square (p), 4/4/29, Longacre Theatre, 44

N

Nada Que Ver (p), 12/5/73, Gramercy Arts Theatre, 7
Nada Que Ver (p), 4/29/73, Gramercy Arts Theatre, 9, (Spanish Theatre Rep. Co.)
Naked (p), 10/27/24, Henry Miller's Theatre, 8
Naked (p), 11/8/26, Princess Theatre, 32
Naked Genius, The (p), 10/21/43, Plymouth Theatre, 36
Nala and Damayanti (p), 1/4/24, Garrick Theatre, 2
Naming, The, 4/3/73, Brooklyn Academy of Music, 18, (Chelsea Theatre Center-Iowa Theatre Lab)
Nan (p), 1/13/13, Hudson Theatre, 1
Nancy Ann (p), 3/31/24, 49th St. Theatre, 40
Nancy Brown (m), 2/16/03, Bijou Theatre, 104
Nancy Lee (p), 4/9/18, Hudson Theatre, 63
Nancy's Private Affair (p), 1/13/30, Vanderbilt Theatre, 136
Nancy Stair (p), 3/15/05, Criterion Theatre, 29
Naomi Court (p), 5/29/74, Manhattan Theatre Club, 10
Napi (p), 3/11/31, Longacre Theatre, 21
Napoleon (p), 3/8/28, Empire Theatre, 12
Narrow Path, The (p), 5/31/09, Hackett Theatre, 8
Narrow Road to the Deep North (p), 1/6/72, Vivian Beaumont Theatre, 44
Nash at Nine (r), 5/17/73, Helen Hayes Theatre
Nat Turner (p), 10/4/60, Casa Galicia, 7
Nathan de Weise (p), 12/8/66, Barbizon-Plaza Theatre, 3, (Die Brücke)
Nathan the Wise (p), 4/3/42, Belasco Theatre, 28
Nathan the Wise (p), 3/22/62, 78th St. Theatre, 14
Nathan Weinstein, Mystic, Connecticut (p), 2/25/66, Brooks Atkinson Theatre, 3
National Anthem, The (p), 1/23/22, Henry Miller's Theatre, 114
National Lampoon's Lemmings (r), 1/25/73, Village Gate, 350
National Repertory Company, 4/5/64, Belasco Theatre, 32
National Theatre of the Deaf (Sganarelle / Songs from Milkwood) (p), 1/12/70, ANTA Theatre, 8
National Theatre of the Deaf (The Tale of Kasane/Blueprints: Projections and Perspectives/Gianni Schicchi; On the Harmfulness of Tobacco/The Critic/Tyger! Tyger! and Other Burnings) (p), 2/27/69, Longacre Theatre, 16
National Theatres of Japan (Kirokuda / Funa-Benkei; Boshibari / Aoi-No-Ue; Shidohogaku / Sumidagawa) (p), 3/24/71, Carnegie Hall, 3
Native Ground (p), 3/23/37, Venice Theatre, 17
Native Son (p), 3/24/41, St. James Theatre, 114
Native Son (p), 10/23/42, Majestic Theatre, 84
Nativité, La (p), 2/5/33, Guild Theatre, 2
Natja (m), 2/16/25, Knickerbocker Theatre, 32
Natural Affection (p), 1/31/63, Booth Theatre, 36
Natural Affection (p), 5/30/73, 15th Floor Theatre, 12
Natural Affection (p), 6/7/73, U.R.G.E.N.T. Theatre, 27
Natural Law, The (p), 4/3/15, Republic Theatre, 81
Natural Look, The (p), 3/11/67, Longacre Theatre, 1
Nature of the Crime (p), 3/23/70, Bouwerie Lane Theatre, 24
Nature's Nobleman (p), 11/14/21, Apollo Theatre, 74
Nature's Way (p), 10/16/57, Coronet Theatre, 61
Naughty Anthony (p), 1/8/00, Herald Square Theatre, 90
Naughty Cinderella (p), 11/9/25, Lyceum Theatre, 121
Naughty Marietta (m), 11/7/10, New York Theatre, 136
Naughty Marietta (m), 10/21/29, Jolson Theatre, 16
Naughty Marietta (m), 11/16/31, Erlanger Theatre, 8
Naughty Marietta (m), 4/16/64, Dutch Coffee House, Astor Hotel, 17
Naughty Naught '00 (m), 1/23/37, American Music Hall, 173
Naughty Naught '00 (m), 10/19/46, Old Knickerbocker Music Hall, 21
Naughty Riquette (m), 9/13/26, Cosmopolitan Theatre, 88
Ne'er-Do-Well, The (p), 9/2/12, Lyric Theatre, 40
Near Santa Barbara (p), 1/31/21, Greenwich Village Theatre, 24
Near to the Stars (p), 2/22/32, Recital Theatre, 1
Nearly a Hero (m), 2/24/08, Casino Theatre, 116
Nearly Married (p), 9/5/13, Gaiety Theatre, 123
Necken, The / The Guilty Conscience (p), 4/15/13, Lyceum Theatre, 1
Ned McCobb's Daughter (p), 11/29/26, John Golden Theatre, 144
Ned Wayburn's Gambols (r), 1/15/29, Knickerbocker Theatre, 31
Ned Wayburn's Town Topics (r), 9/23/15, Century Theatre, 68
Neighbors (p), 12/26/23, 48th St. Theatre, 46
Neighbors / The Projection Room (p), 1/13/69, Theatre de Lys, 2, (ANTA Matinee)
Neighbors, The / The March March (p), 11/6/66, Theatre 62, 17
Nell Go In (m), 10/31/00, New York Theatre, 25
Nellie Bly (m), 1/21/46, Adelphi Theatre, 16
Nellie Toole & Co. (p), 9/24/73, Theatre Four, 32
Nemesis (p), 4/4/21, Hudson Theatre, 56
Neptune's Daughter / Pioneer Days / Circus Events (r), 11/28/06, New York Hippodrome, 288
Nerves (p), 9/1/24, Comedy Theatre, 16
Nerves / Thursday Evening / Cornelius' Jewels (p), 12/6/21, 15th St. Theatre, 2
Nervous Set, The (m), 5/12/59, Henry Miller's Theatre, 23
Nervous Wreck, The (p), 10/9/23, Sam H. Harris Theatre, 271
Nest Egg, The (p), 11/22/10, Bijou Theatre, 55
Nest, The, 1/28/22, 48th St. Theatre, 161
Nest, The (p), 4/9/70, Mercury Theatre, 6
Net, The (p), 2/10/19, 48th St. Theatre, 8
Nethersole, Olga. See Olga Nethersole
Never Homes, The (m), 10/5/11, Broadway Theatre, 92
Never Live Over a Pretzel Factory (p), 3/28/64, Eugene O'Neill Theatre, 9
Never No More (p), 1/7/32, Hudson Theatre, 12
Never Say Die (p), 11/12/12, 48th St. Theatre, 151
Never Say Never (p), 11/20/51, Booth Theatre, 7
Never Too Late (p), 11/27/62, Playhouse, 1,007
Nevertheless They Laugh (m), 3/24/71, Lambs Club Theatre, 5
New Brooms (p), 11/17/24, Fulton Theatre, 88
New Cambridge Circus, The (r), 1/14/65, Square East, 78
New Clown, The (p), 8/25/02, Garrick Theatre, 40
New Dominion, The (p), 11/5/06, Garden Theatre, 8
New England Folks (p), 10/21/01, 14th St. Theatre, 64
New Englander, The (p), 2/7/24, 48th St. Theatre, 36
New Faces (r), 3/15/34, Fulton Theatre, 148
New Faces of 1936 (r), 5/19/36, Vanderbilt Theatre, 192
New Faces of 1943 (r), 12/22/42, Ritz Theatre, 94
New Faces of 1952 (r), 5/16/52, Royale Theatre, 365
New Faces of 1962 (r), 2/1/62, Alvin Theatre, 28
New Faces of 1968 (r), 5/2/68, Booth Theatre, 52
New Faces of '56 (r), 6/14/56, Ethel Barrymore Theatre, 220
New Gallantry, The (p), 9/24/25, Cort Theatre, 20
New Girl in Town (m), 5/14/57, 46th St. Theatre, 431
New Gossoon, The (p), 10/21/32, Martin Beck Theatre, 6
New Gossoon, The (p), 11/13/34, John Golden Theatre, 2
New Gossoon, The (p), 11/29/37, Ambassador Theatre, 8
New Henrietta, The (p), 12/22/13, Knickerbocker Theatre, 48
New Lady Bantock, The (p), 2/8/09, Wallack Theatre, 40
New Life, A (p), 9/15/43, Royale Theatre, 69
New Moon, The (m), 9/19/28, Imperial Theatre, 519
New Moon, The (m), 8/18/42, Carnegie Hall, 24
New Moon, The (m), 5/17/44, New York City Center, 45
New Morality, The (p), 1/30/21, Playhouse, 9
New Music Hall of Israel, The (r), 10/2/69, Lunt-Fontanne Theatre, 68
New Playwrights Series, Evening I (Balls / Up to Thursday / Home Free!) (p), 2/10/65, Cherry Lane Theatre, 23
New Playwrights Series, Evening II (Pigeons / Conerico Was Here to Stay) (p), 3/3/65, Cherry Lane Theatre, 21
New Playwrights Series, Evening III (Hunting the Jingo Bird / Lovey) (p), 3/25/65, Cherry Lane Theatre, 6
New Poor, The (p), 1/7/24, Playhouse, 32
New Priorities of 1943 (r), 9/15/42, 46th St. Theatre, 54
New Secretary, The (p), 1/23/13, Lyceum Theatre, 44
New Sin, The (p), 10/16/12, Wallack Theatre, 22
New Sink, The (p), 5/27/23, Belasco Theatre, 1
New Tenant, The / The Lesson (p), 3/9/60, Royale Playhouse, 333
New Tenant, The / Victims of Duty (p), 5/24/64, Writers' Stage Theatre, 25
New Toys (p), 2/18/24, Fulton Theatre, 25
New Way, The (p), 12/4/23, Longacre Theatre, 2

New Word, The / Belinda (p), 5/6/18, Empire Theatre, 32
New Word, The / Old Friends / The Old Lady Shows Her Medals (p), 5/14/17, Empire Theatre, 48
New York (p), 10/17/10, Bijou Theatre, 16
New York (p), 11/14/27, Mansfield Theatre, 16
New York Exchange (p), 12/30/26, Klaw Theatre, 82
New York Idea, The (p), 11/19/06, Lyric Theatre, 66
New York Idea, The (p), 9/28/15, Playhouse
New York Idea, The (p), 3/22/33, Heckscher Theatre, 3
New York to Cherbourg (p), 2/19/32, Forrest Theatre, 3
New Yorkers, The (m), 10/7/01, Herald Square Theatre, 64
New Yorkers, The (r), 3/10/27, Edyth Totten Theatre, 52
New Yorkers, The (r), 12/8/30, Broadway Theatre, 158
Newcomers, The (r), 8/8/23, Ambassador Theatre, 20
Newlyweds and Their Baby, The (m), 3/22/09, Majestic Theatre, 40
Next (p), 9/28/11, Daly's Theatre, 18
Next / Adaptation (p), 2/10/69, Greenwich Mews Theatre, 707
Next Half Hour, The (p), 10/29/45, Empire Theatre, 8
Next of Kin, The (p), 12/27/09, Hudson Theatre, 24
Next President, The (m), 3/9/58, Bijou Theatre, 13
Next Time I'll Sing to You (p), 11/27/63, Phoenix Theatre, 23
Next Time I'll Sing to You (p), 3/1/68, Master Theatre, 9, (Equity Library Theatre)
Next Time I'll Sing to You (p), 10/25/72, Good Shepherd-Faith Church, 2, (City Center Acting Co.)
Next Time I'll Sing to You (p), 1/2/74, Billy Rose Theatre, 2, (City Center Acting Co.)
Nic Nax of 1926 (r), 8/2/26, Cort Theatre, 13
Nica (p), 1/25/26, Central Park Theatre, 16
Nice People (p), 3/2/21, Klaw Theatre, 247
Nice Place You Got Here. See Three at Judson
Nice Wanton / Noah's Flood (p), 3/27/11, New Theatre, 1
Nice Women (p), 6/10/29, Longacre Theatre, 64
Nicol Williamson's Late Show, 6/26/73, Eastside Playhouse, 30
Nifties of 1923 (Bernard & Collier's) (r), 9/25/23, Fulton Theatre, 47
Nigger Nightmare (p), 6/24/71, Public/Other Stage, 4
Nigger Rich (p), 9/20/29, Royale Theatre, 11
Nigger, The (p), 12/4/09, New Theatre
Niggerlovers, The (The Demonstration / Man and Dog) (p), 10/1/67, Orpheum Theatre, 25
Night at an Inn, A / Service (p), 4/15/18, Cohan Theatre, 16
Night at the Inn, A / The Harlequinade (p), 6/14/21, Punch and Judy Theatre, 15
Night Before Christmas, The (p), 4/10/41, Morosco Theatre, 22
Night Boat, The (m), 2/2/20, Liberty Theatre, 318
Night Call, The (p), 4/26/22, Frazee Theatre, 29
Night Circus, The (p), 12/2/58, Golden Theatre, 7
Night Duel, The (p), 2/15/26, Mansfield Theatre, 17
Night Hawk (p), 2/24/25, Bijou Theatre, 120
Night Hawk (p), 12/25/26, Frolic Theatre, 144
Night Hostess (p), 9/12/28, Martin Beck Theatre, 119
Night in Paris, A (r), 1/5/26, Casino de Paris, 335
Night in Spain (r), 12/6/17, Century Theatre, 33
Night in Spain, A (r), 5/3/27, 44th St. Theatre, 174
Night in the House (p), 11/7/35, Booth Theatre, 12
Night in Venice, A (r), 5/21/29, Shubert Theatre, 175
Night Is Black Bottles, The (p), 12/4/62, Cricket Theatre, 4
Night Life (p), 10/23/62, Brooks Atkinson Theatre, 63
Night Lodging (p), 12/22/19, Plymouth Theatre, 14
Night Music (p), 2/22/40, Broadhurst Theatre, 20
Night Music (p), 4/8/51, ANTA Playhouse, 9
Night Must Fall (p), 9/28/36, Ethel Barrymore Theatre, 64
Night Must Fall (p), 3/28/69, Master Theatre, 9, (Equity Library Theatre)
Night of January 16, The (p), 9/16/35, Ambassador Theatre, 232
Night of Love (p), 1/7/41, Hudson Theatre, 7
Night of Love, A (m), 4/30/23, Jolson Theatre, 8
Night of the Auk (p), 12/3/56, Playhouse, 8
Night of the Auk (p), 5/21/63, Cricket Theatre, 3
Night of the Dunce (p), 12/28/66, Cherry Lane Theatre, 47
Night of the Fourth, The (m), 1/21/01, Victoria Theatre, 14
Night of the Iguana, The (p), 12/28/61, Royale Theatre, 316
Night of the Iguana, The (p), 1/13/67, Master Theatre, 9
Night of the Party, The (p), 10/6/02, Princess Theatre, 80
Night Over Taos (p), 3/9/32, 48th St. Theatre, 13
Night Remembers, The (p), 11/27/34, Playhouse, 23
Night. See Morning, Noon and Night
Night Watch (p), 2/28/72, Morosco Theatre, 121
Nightcap, The (p), 8/15/21, 39th St. Theatre, 96
Nightcap, The / Gutta Iconoclast / Pearls / The Good Women / Squaring the Triangle / Divertissement (p), 6/13/21, Apollo Theatre, 8
Nighthawks (p), 12/29/67, Mermaid Theatre, 52
Nightingale, The (m), 1/3/27, Jolson Theatre, 96
Nightride (p), 12/9/71, Vandam Theatre, 94
Nights of Wrath (p), 11/26/47, President Theatre, 26
Nightstick (p), 11/10/27, Selwyn Theatre, 85
Nightwalk, 9/8/73, St. Clement's Church Theatre, 15, (Open Theatre)
Nighty-Night (p), 9/9/19, Princess Theatre, 154
Nikita Balieff's New Chauve-Souris (r), 10/21/31, Ambassador Theatre, 28
Nikki (m), 9/29/31, Longacre Theatre, 40
Nina (p), 12/5/51, Royale Theatre, 45
Nina Rosa (m), 9/20/30, Majestic Theatre, 129
Nine Girls (p), 1/13/43, Longacre Theatre, 5
Nine Pine Street (p), 4/27/33, Longacre Theatre, 29
Nine Till Six (p), 9/27/30, Ritz Theatre, 25
Nine-Fifteen Revue, 2/11/30, George M. Cohan Theatre, 7
Nineteen Thirty-Five—(The Living Newspaper), 5/12/36, Biltmore Theatre, 34
Nineteen Thirty-One— (p), 12/10/31, Mansfield Theatre, 12
Nineteenth Hole of Europe, The (p), 3/26/49, Lenox Hill Playhouse, 4
Nineteenth Hole, The (p), 10/11/27, George M. Cohan Theatre, 119
Ninety and Nine, The (p), 10/7/02, Academy of Music, 128
Ninety Horse Power (p), 3/15/26, Ritz Theatre, 24
Ninety in the Shade (m), 1/25/15, Knickerbocker Theatre, 40
Ninety-Day Mistress, The (p), 11/6/67, Biltmore Theatre, 24
Ninth Guest, The, 8/25/30, Eltinge Theatre, 72
Nirvana (p), 3/3/26, Greenwich Village Theatre, 5
Nju (p), 3/22/17, Bandbox Theatre, 44
No 'Count Boy, The / Supper for the Dead / Chair Endowed. See Salvation on a String
No Exit (p), 11/26/46, Biltmore Theatre, 31
No Exit (p), 8/14/56, Theatre East, 89
No Exit (p), 1/18/64, Royal Playhouse
No Exit / The Little Private World of Arthur Morton Fenwick (p), 10/30/67, Bouwerie Lane Theatre, 8
No Foolin' (r), 6/24/26, Globe Theatre, 108
No for an Answer, 1/5/41, Mecca Temple, 3
No Hard Feelings (p), 4/8/73, Martin Beck Theatre, 1
No More Blondes (p), 1/7/20, Maxine Elliott's Theatre, 29
No More Frontier (p), 10/21/31, Provincetown Playhouse, 28
No More Ladies (p), 1/23/34, Booth Theatre, 162
No More Ladies (p), 9/3/34, Morosco Theatre, 16
No More Peace (p), 1/25/38, Maxine Elliott's Theatre, 4
No More Women (p), 8/3/26, Ambassador Theatre, 7
No Mother To Guide Her (p), 12/25/33, President Theatre, 10
No Mother To Guide Her (p), 6/4/36, Cherry Lane Theatre
No, No, Nanette (m), 9/16/25, Globe Theatre, 329
No, No, Nanette (m), 1/19/71, 46th St. Theatre, 861
No Other Girl (m), 8/13/24, Morosco Theatre, 56
No Place To Be Somebody (p), 5/4/69, Public Theatre, 576
No Place To Be Somebody (p), 12/30/69, ANTA Theatre, 15
No Place To Be Somebody (p), 1/20/70, Promenade Theatre, 312
No Place To Be Somebody (p), 9/9/71, Morosco Theatre, 37
No Questions Asked (p), 2/5/34, Masque Theatre, 16
No Sex Please, We're British (p), 2/20/73, Ritz Theatre, 16
No So Fast (p), 5/22/23, Morosco Theatre, 102
No Strings (m), 3/15/62, 54th St. Theatre, 580
No Strings (m), 3/9/72, Master Theatre, 22, (Equity Library Theatre)
No Time for Comedy (p), 4/17/39, Ethel Barrymore Theatre, 185
No Time for Sergeants (p), 10/20/55, Alvin Theatre, 796
No Trespassing (p), 9/7/26, Sam H. Harris Theatre, 23
No Trifling with Love (p), 11/9/59, St. Marks Playhouse, 15
No Way Out (p), 10/30/44, Cort Theatre, 8
No. 13 Washington Square (p), 8/23/15, Park Theatre, 56
No. 33 Washington Square. See No. 13 Washington Square
Noah (p), 2/13/35, Longacre Theatre, 46
Noah (p), 10/10/54, Broadway Tabernacle Church, 14
Noah's Flood / Nice Wanton (p), 3/27/11, New Theatre, 1
Noble Experiment, The (p), 10/27/30, Waldorf Theatre, 8
Noble Rogue, A (m), 7/19/29, Gansevoort Theatre, 9
Noble Spaniard, The (p), 9/20/09, Criterion Theatre, 40
Nobody Hears a Broken Drum (p), 3/19/70, Fortune Theatre, 6
Nobody Home (p), 4/20/15, Princess Theatre, 135
Nobody Loves an Albatross (p), 12/19/63, Lyceum Theatre, 213
Nobody's Business (p), 10/22/23, Klaw Theatre, 40
Nobody's Daughter (p), 2/13/11, New Theatre
Nobody's Money (p), 8/17/21, Longacre Theatre, 29
Nobody's Widow (p), 11/15/10, Hudson Theatre, 215
Nocturne (p), 2/16/25, Punch and Judy Theatre, 12
Noel Coward in Two Keys (p), 2/28/74, Ethel Barrymore Theatre
Noel Coward in Two Keys (Come into the Garden, Maud / A Song at Twilight) (p), 2/28/74, Ethel Barrymore Theatre
Noel Coward's Sweet Potato (r), 9/29/68, Ethel Barrymore Theatre, 43
Noisy Passenger, The. See One Night Stands of a Noisy Passenger
Nona (p), 10/4/32, Avon Theatre, 31
None So Blind (p), 2/3/10, Hackett Theatre, 20
Noon. See Morning, Noon and Night
Noontide (p), 6/1/61, Theatre Marquee, 37
Noose, The (p), 10/20/26, Hudson Theatre, 197
Norman, Is That You? (p), 2/19/70, Lyceum Theatre, 12
Not a Way of Life (p), 3/22/67, Sheridan Square Playhouse, 7

Not Enough Rope / The Twenty-Five Cent White Cap / George Washington Crossing the Delaware (p) (3 × 3), 3/1/62, Maidman Playhouse, 5
Not for Children (p), 2/13/51, Coronet Theatre, 7
Not Herbert (p), 1/26/26, 52nd St. Theatre, 145
Not I / Krapp's Last Tape (p), 11/22/72, Forum Theatre, 15
Not Now, Darling (p), 10/29/70, Brooks Atkinson Theatre, 21
Not So Long Ago (p), 5/4/20, Booth Theatre, 137
Not While I'm Eating (r), 12/19/61, Madison Avenue Playhouse, 2
Not with My Money (p), 10/25/18, 39th St. Theatre, 11
Nothing But Lies (p), 10/8/18, Longacre Theatre, 135
Nothing But Love (m), 10/14/19, Lyric Theatre, 39
Nothing But the Truth (p), 9/14/16, Longacre Theatre, 332
Notre Dame (p), 2/26/02, Daly's Theatre, 45
Nourish the Beast (p), 10/3/73, Cherry Lane Theatre, 54, (formerly titled Baba Goya)
Novice and the Duke, The (p), 12/9/29, Assembly Theatre, 28
Now (r), 6/5/68, Cherry Lane Theatre, 23
Now I Lay Me Down to Sleep (r), 3/2/50, Broadhurst Theatre, 44
Now Is the Time for All Good Men (m), 9/26/67, Theatre de Lys, 112
Now Is the Time for All Good Men (m), 4/29/71, Master Theatre, 19, (Equity Library Theatre)
Now There's Just the Three of Us. See Four Americans
Now You've Done It (p), 3/5/37, Henry Miller's Theatre, 43
Now-A-Days (p), 8/5/29, Forrest Theatre, 8
Nowhere Bound (p), 1/22/35, Imperial Theatre, 15
Nowhere To Go But Up (m), 11/10/62, Winter Garden Theatre, 9
Nowhere To Run, Nowhere To Hide (p), 3/26/74, St. Marks Playhouse, 8
Nude with Violin (p), 11/14/57, Belasco Theatre, 86
Nude with Violin (p), 5/18/73, Lolly's Theatre Club, 12
Nuits de la Colère, Les / Feu la Mère de Madame (p) (Renaud-Barrault Repertory Company), 2/11/57, Winter Garden Theatre, 4
Number, The (p), 10/30/51, Biltmore Theatre, 88
Number 7 (p), 9/8/26, Times Sq. Theatre, 38
Nuns, The (p), 6/1/70, Cherry Lane Theatre, 1
Nuremburg Two. See Festival of New Italian Plays
Nurse Marjorie (p), 10/3/06, Liberty Theatre, 49
Nut Farm, The (p), 10/14/29, Biltmore Theatre, 41

O

O Evening Star! (p), 1/8/36, Empire Theatre, 5
O Marry Me! (m), 10/27/61, Gate Theatre, 21
O Mistress Mine (p), 1/23/46, Empire Theatre, 452
O, Nightingale (p), 4/15/25, 49th St. Theatre, 29
O Say Can You See (m), 10/8/62, Provincetown Playhouse, 32
Object — Matrimony (p), 10/25/16, Cohan and Harris Theatre, 30
Obratsov Russian Puppet Theatre, 10/2/63, Broadway Theatre, 76
O'Brien Girl, The (m), 10/3/21, Liberty Theatre, 164
Obsession (p), 10/1/46, Plymouth Theatre, 31
Occupe-Toi d'Amélie (p), 11/24/52, Ziegfeld Theatre, 4
Octoroon, or Life in Louisiana, The (p), 1/27/61, Phoenix Theatre, 45
Octoroon, The (p), 3/12/29, Maxine Elliott's Theatre, 7
O'Daniel (p), 2/23/47, Princess Theatre, 5
Odd Couple, The (p), 3/10/65, Plymouth Theatre, 965
Odd Man Out (p), 5/25/25, Booth Theatre, 16
Odds and Ends of 1917 (r), Bijou Theatre, 112
Odds on Mrs. Oakley, The (p), 10/2/44, Cort Theatre, 24
Ode to Liberty (p), 12/21/34, Lyceum Theatre, 66
Ododo (m), 11/24/70, St. Marks Playhouse, 48
Oedipus (p), 2/3/13, Garden Theatre
Oedipus (p), 2/15/70, Roundabout Theatre, 52
Oedipus at Colonus (p), 2/10/72, Master Theatre, 12, (Equity Library Theatre)
Oedipus Rex (p), 8/21/11, Irving Place Theatre
Oedipus Rex (p), 10/25/23, Century Theatre, 20
Oedipus Rex (p), 12/16/45, Majestic Theatre, 2
Oedipus Rex (p), 5/22/48, Broadway Theatre, 8, (Habimah)
Oedipus / The Critic (p), 5/20/46, Century Theatre, 8, (Old Vic Co.)
Oedipus Tyrannus (p), 11/24/52, Mark Hellinger Theatre, 10, (National Theatre of Greece)
Of Love Remembered (p), 2/18/67, ANTA Theatre, 9
O'Flynn, The (m), 12/27/34, Broadway Theatre, 11
Of Mice and Men (p), 11/23/37, Music Box Theatre, 207
Of Mice and Men (m), 12/4/58, Provincetown Playhouse, 37
Of Thee I Sing (m), 12/26/31, Music Box Theatre, 446
Of Thee I Sing (m), 5/15/33, Imperial Theatre, 32
Of Thee I Sing (m), 5/5/52, Ziegfeld Theatre, 72
Of Thee I Sing (m), 10/18/68, Master Theatre, 15, (Equity Library Theatre)
Of Thee I Sing (m), 3/7/69, New Anderson Theatre, 21
Of V We Sing (r), 2/11/42, Concert Theatre, 76
Ofay Watcher, The (p), 9/15/69, Stage 73, 40
Off Chance, The (p), 2/14/18, Empire Theatre, 92
Off to Buffalo (p), 2/21/39, Ethel Barrymore Theatre, 7
Offenders, The (p), 9/23/08, Hudson Theatre, 22
Offense, The (p), 11/16/25, Ritz Theatre, 4
Office Boy, The (m), 11/2/03, Victoria Theatre, 66
Officer 666 (p), 1/29/12, Gaiety Theatre, 192
Officer 666 (p), 5/29/23, Selwyn Theatre, 3
Off-Key (p), 2/8/27, Belmont Theatre, 15
Oh, Boy (m), 2/20/17, Princess Theatre, 463
Oh, Brother! (p), 6/19/45, Royale Theatre, 23
Oh, Calcutta! (r), 6/17/69, Eden Theatre, 1,314
Oh Captain! (m), 2/4/58, Alvin Theatre, 192
Oh Coward! (r), 10/4/72, New Theatre, 294
Oh Dad, Poor Dad, Mamma's Hung You in the Closet and I'm Feelin' So Sad (p), 2/26/62, Phoenix Theatre, 454
Oh Dad, Poor Dad, Mamma's Hung You in the Closet and I'm Feelin' So Sad (p), 8/27/63, Morosco Theatre, 47
Oh, Ernest! (m), 5/9/27, Royale Theatre, 56
Oh Glorious Tintinnabulation (m), 5/23/74, Actors Studio, 12
Oh, Henry (p), 5/5/20, Fulton Theatre, 21
Oh, I Say! (m), 10/30/13, Casino Theatre, 68
Oh, Kay! (m), 11/8/26, Imperial Theatre, 257
Oh, Kay! (m), 1/2/28, Century Theatre, 16
Oh, Kay! (m), 4/16/60, East 74th St. Theatre, 89
Oh, Lady! Lady! (m), 2/1/18, Princess Theatre, 219
Oh, Lady! Lady! (m), 3/14/74, Master Theatre, 19, (Equity Library Theatre)
Oh! Les Beaux Jours (p), 4/24/70, Barbizon-Plaza Theatre, 10, (Le Treteau de Paris)
Oh, Look! (m), 3/7/18, Vanderbilt Theatre, 68
Oh! Mama (p), 8/19/25, Playhouse, 70
Oh, Men! Oh, Women! (p), 12/17/53, Henry Miller's Theatre, 382
Oh, Mr. Meadowbrook! (p), 12/26/48, John Golden Theatre, 40
Oh, My Dear! (m), 11/27/18, Princess Theatre, 189
Oh! Oh! Delphine (m), 9/30/12, Knickerbocker Theatre, 248
Oh! Oh! Nurse (m), 12/7/25, Cosmopolitan Theatre, 32
Oh, Pioneers (p), 11/10/69, Theatre de Lys, 2, (ANTA Matinee)
Oh, Please (m), 12/17/26, Fulton Theatre, 79
Oh, Professor! (p), 5/1/30, Belmont Theatre, 4
Oh, Promise Me (p), 11/24/30, Morosco Theatre, 135
Oh, Say Can You See L.A. / The Other Man (p), 2/8/68, Actors Playhouse, 14
Oh, What a Girl (m), 7/28/19, Shubert Theatre, 68
Oh What a Lovely War (r), 9/30/64, Broadhurst Theatre, 125
Oh What a Wedding! (m), 10/18/69, Anderson Yiddish Theatre, 79
Oklahoma! (m), 3/31/43, St. James Theatre, 2,248
Oklahoma! (m), 5/29/51, Broadway Theatre, 72
Oklahoma! (m), 8/31/53, New York City Center, 40
Oklahoma! (m), 3/19/58, New York City Center, 16
Oklahoma! (m), 2/27/63, New York City Center, 15
Oklahoma! (m), 5/15/63, New York City Center, 15
Oklahoma! (m), 12/15/65, New York City Center, 24
Oklahoma! (m), 6/23/69, New York State Theatre, 88
Ol' Man Satan (p), 10/3/32, Forrest Theatre, 24
Olathe Response, The (p), 4/5/71, Actors Playhouse, 6
Old Acquaintance (p), 12/23/40, Morosco Theatre, 170
Old Bill, M. P. (p), 11/10/26, Biltmore Theatre, 23
Old Bucks and New Wings (r), 11/5/62, Mayfair Theatre, 8
Old Country, The (p), 10/30/17, 39th St. Theatre, 15
Old Dutch (m), 11/22/09, Herald Square Theatre, 88
Old English (p), 12/23/24, Ritz Theatre, 187
Old Firm, The (p), 2/3/13, Harris Theatre, 16
Old Foolishness, The (p), 12/20/40, Windsor Theatre, 3
Old Friends / The Old Lady Shows Her Medals / The New Word (p), 5/14/17, Empire Theatre, 48
Old Glory, The (My Kinsman, Major Molineaux / Benito Cereno) (p), 11/1/64, St. Clement's Church, 122, (American Place Theatre)
Old Heidelberg (p), 10/12/03, Lyric Theatre, 32
Old Heidelberg (p), 12/19/10, New Theatre
Old Homestead, The (p), 9/12/04, New York Theatre, 61
Old Homestead, The (p), 10/5/08, Academy of Music, 24
Old Judge Mose Is Dead. See An Evening with the Urban Arts Corps
Old Lady Says "No!", The (p), 2/17/48, Mansfield Theatre, 8
Old Lady Shows Her Medals, The / Alice Sit-by-the-Fire (p), 3/7/32, Playhouse, 40
Old Lady Shows Her Medals, The / The New Word / Old Friends (p), 5/14/17, Empire Theatre, 48
Old Lady 31 (p), 10/30/16, 39th St. Theatre, 160
Old Limerick Town (p), 10/27/02, 14th St. Theatre, 56
Old Maid, The (p), 1/7/35, Empire Theatre, 298
Old Man Murphy (p), 5/16/31, Royale Theatre, 64
Old Man Murphy (p), 9/14/31, Hudson Theatre, 48
Old New Yorker, An (p), 4/3/11, Daly's Theatre, 16
Old Rascal, The (p), 3/24/30, Bijou Theatre, 72

Old Soak, The (p), 8/22/22, Plymouth Theatre, 325
Old Times (p), 11/16/71, Billy Rose Theatre, 119
Old Town, The (m), 1/10/10, Globe Theatre, 171
Old Vic Company, The, 10/23/56, Winter Garden Theatre, 95
Old Vic Company, The, 12/9/58, Broadway Theatre, 40
Old Vic Company, The, 2/6/62, New York City Center, 48
Old Women, The / E & O E / Something More Important (p), 7/11/35, Chanin Auditorium, 12
Older People (p), 5/14/72, Public/Anspacher Theatre, 49
Oldest Trick in the World, The / The Bible Salesman. See Double Entry, 2/20/61, Martinique Theatre, 56
Ole! (m), 3/18/59, Greenwich Mews Theatre, 35
Ole! Ole! (r), 12/16/63, Mermaid Theatre, 176
Olga Nethersole Repertory, 2/8/08, Daly's Theatre
Olive Latimer's Husband (p), 1/7/10, Hackett Theatre, 1
Oliver! (m), 1/6/63, Imperial Theatre, 774
Oliver! (m), 8/2/65, Martin Beck Theatre, 64
Oliver Goldsmith (p), 3/19/00, Fifth Ave. Theatre, 33
Oliver Oliver (p), 1/5/34, Playhouse, 11
Oliver Twist (p), 2/26/12, New Amsterdam Theatre, 80
Olympe (p), 1/18/04, Knickerbocker Theatre, 21
Olympia (p), 10/16/28, Empire Theatre, 47
Omar, the Tentmaker (p), 1/13/14, Lyric Theatre, 103
On a Clear Day You Can See Forever (m), 10/17/65, Mark Hellinger Theatre, 273
On an Open Roof (p), 1/28/63, Cort Theatre, 1
On and Off / The Shades of Night (p), 4/1/01, Lyceum Theatre, 16
On Approval (p), 10/18/26, Gaiety Theatre, 99
On Borrowed Time (p), 2/3/38, Longacre Theatre, 321
On Borrowed Time (p), 2/10/53, 48th St. Theatre, 78
On Call (p), 11/9/28, Waldorf Theatre, 60
On Location (p), 9/27/37, Ritz Theatre, 8
On Ne Badine Pas avec l' Amour (p), 3/3/68, Hunter College Playhouse, 4
On Parole (p), 2/25/07, Majestic Theatre, 32
On Stage (p), 10/29/35, Mansfield Theatre, 47
On Strivers' Row (p), 2/28/46, ANT Playhouse, Harlem, 26
On the Eve (p), 10/4/09, Hudson Theatre, 24
On the Harmfulness of Tobacco. See The National Theatre of the Deaf
On the Harmfulness of Tobacco / The Wedding / A Tragedian in Spite of Himself / The Bear (p), 2/5/48, N.Y. City Center, 14
On the Hazards of Smoking Tobacco. See The Victims
On the High Road (p), 1/14/29, Civic Repertory Theatre, 15
On the High Road / The Wedding / The Anniversary. See An Evening with Chekhov, 4/20/61, Key Theatre, 61
On the Hiring Line (p), 10/20/19, Criterion Theatre, 48
On the Make (p), 5/23/32, 48th St. Theatre, 33
On the Necessity of Being Polygamous (p), 12/8/64, Gramercy Arts Theatre, 31
On the Quiet (p), 2/11/01, Madison Square Theatre, 160
On the Quiet (p), 2/10/02, Madison Square Theatre, 40
On the Quiet (p), 12/11/05, Criterion Theatre, 16
On the Rocks (p), 6/15/38, Daly's Theatre, 66
On the Seventh Day (p), 3/6/47, Blackfriars' Theatre, 25
On the Spot (p), 10/29/30, Wallace's Forrest Theatre, 167
On the Stairs (p), 9/25/22, Playhouse, 72
On the Town (m), 12/28/44, Adelphi Theatre, 462
On the Town (m), 1/15/59, Carnegie Hall Playhouse, 70
On the Town (m), 10/31/71, Imperial Theatre, 73
On to Fortune (p), 2/4/35, Fulton Theatre, 8
On Trial (p), 8/9/14, Candler Theatre, 365
On Vacation. See Let Them Down, Gently
On Whitman Avenue (p), 5/8/46, Cort Theatre, 150
On with the Dance (p), 10/29/17, Republic Theatre, 56
On Your Toes (m), 4/11/36, Imperial Theatre, 318
On Your Toes (m), 10/11/54, 46th St. Theatre, 64
Once for the Asking (p), 11/20/63, Booth Theatre, 1
Once I Saw a Boy Laughing... (p), 2/21/74, Westside Theatre, 5
Once in a Lifetime (p), 9/24/30, Music Box Theatre, 401
Once in a Lifetime (p), 1/28/64, York Playhouse, 1
Once Is Enough (p), 2/15/38, Henry Miller's Theatre, 105
Once More, with Feeling (p), 10/21/58, National Theatre, 263
Once Over Lightly (m), 11/19/42, Alvin Theatre, 6
Once There Was a Russian (p), 2/18/61, Music Box Theatre, 1
Once Upon a Mattress (m), 5/11/59, Phoenix Theatre, 460
Once upon a Mattress (m), 2/3/67, Master Theatre, 14
Once Upon a Tailor (p), 5/23/55, Cort Theatre, 8
Once Upon a Time (p), 1/2/05, Berkeley Lyceum Theatre, 8
Once Upon a Time (p), 4/15/18, Fulton Theatre, 24
Once Upon a Time (p), 12/20/39, Labor Stage Theatre, 1
Ondine (p), 2/18/54, 46th St. Theatre, 156
One (p), 9/14/20, Belasco Theatre, 111
One Bright Day (p), 3/19/52, Royale Theatre, 29
One by One (p), 12/1/64, Belasco Theatre, 7
One Eye Closed (p), 11/24/54, Bijou Theatre, 3
One Flew Over the Cuckoo's Nest (p), 11/13/63, Cort Theatre, 82
One Flew Over the Cuckoo's Nest (p), 3/23/71, Mercer-O' Casey Theatre, 1,025
One for All (p), 5/13/27, Greenwich Village Theatre, 3
One for All (p), 6/6/27, Princess Theatre, 48
One for the Money (r), 2/4/39, Booth Theatre, 132
One for the Money (r), 1/13/72, Master Theatre, 19, (Equity Library Theatre)
One for the Money, Etc. (r), 5/24/72, Eastside Playhouse, 23
One Glorious Hour (p), 4/14/27, Selwyn Theatre, 20
One Good Year (p), 11/27/35, Lyceum Theatre, 223
One Helluva Night (p), 6/4/24, Sam H. Harris Theatre, 1
One Hundred Ten in the Shade (m), 10/24/63, Broadhurst Theatre, 331
One Is a Lonely Number (p), 6/18/64, Mermaid Theatre, 6
One Kiss (p), 11/27/23, Fulton Theatre, 95
One Man's Woman, 5/25/26, 48th St. Theatre, 156
One More Honeymoon (p), 3/31/34, Little Theatre, 17
One More River (p), 3/18/60, Ambassador Theatre, 3
One Night in Rome (p), 12/2/19, Criterion Theatre, 107
One Night Stands of a Noisy Passenger (The Noisy Passenger / Un Passage / Last Stand) (p), 12/30/70, Actors Playhouse, 7
One of the Family (p), 12/21/25, 49th St. Theatre, 230
One of Us (p), 9/9/18, Bijou Theatre, 24
One Shot Fired (p), 11/7/27, Mayfair Theatre, 7
One Sunday Afternoon (p), 2/15/33, Little Theatre, 338
One Thing After Another (p), 12/28/37, Fulton Theatre, 15
One Touch of Venus (m), 10/7/43, Imperial Theatre, 567
One, Two, Three / The Violet (p), 9/29/30, Henry Miller's Theatre, 40
One Way Pendulum (p), 9/18/61, East 74th St. Theatre, 40
One Wife or Another (p), 2/6/33, Provincetown Playhouse, 14
One-Act Variety Theatre, 2/2/40, Provincetown Playhouse
O'Neill of Derry (p), 11/25/07, Liberty Theatre, 33
One-Man Show (p), 2/8/45, Ethel Barrymore Theatre, 36
One-Third of a Nation (p), 1/17/38, Adelphi Theatre, 237
One-Way Street (p), 12/24/28, George M. Cohan Theatre, 56
Only a Countess May Dance When She's Crazy. See Two Camps by Koutoukas
Only Fools Are Sad (r), 11/22/71, Edison Theatre, 144
Only Game in Town, The (p), 5/20/68, Broadhurst Theatre, 16
Only Girl, The (m), 11/2/14, 39th St. Theatre, 240
Only Girl, The (m), 5/21/34, 44th St. Theatre, 16
Only in America (p), 11/19/59, Cort Theatre, 28
Only Jealousy of Emer, The / Renard (m), 1/23/72, La Mama Experimental Theatre, 11
Only Law, The (p), 8/2/09, Hackett Theatre, 48
Only Son, The (p), 10/16/11, Gaiety Theatre, 32
Only the Heart (p), 4/4/44, Bijou Theatre, 47
Only the Young (p), 9/21/32, Sutton Show Shop, 4
Only Way, The (p), 10/20/02, Herald Square Theatre, 14
Only 38 (p), 9/13/21, Cort Theatre, 88
Ontological Proof of My Existence (p), 2/10/72, Cubiculo Theatre, 12
Op o' Me Thumb / The Little Minister (p), 2/6/05, Empire Theatre
Open and Shut Magic Company, The / Undercover Cop (p), 8/4/73, various street locations
Open Door, The / The Women Have Their Way (p), 1/27/30, Civic Repertory Theatre, 25
Open House (p), 12/14/25, Daly's Theatre, 73
Open House (p), 6/3/47, Cort Theatre, 7
Open Season at Second City (r), 1/22/64, Square East Theatre, 156
Open Theatre Company (Terminal; The Serpent: A Ceremony; Endgame) (p), 5/26/70, Washington Square Methodist Church, 18
Open Theatre (Nightwalk; Terminal; The Mutation Show), 9/8/73, St. Clement's Church Theatre, 26
Open Theatre (The Serpent: A Ceremony; Endgame; Terminal) (p), 5/26/70, Washington Square Methodist Church, 18
Open 24 Hours / Satisfaction Guaranteed (p), 2/11/69, Actors Playhouse, 22
Opening Night / A Matter of Like Life and Death (p), 10/2/63, East End Theatre, 47
Opening of a Window, The (p), 9/25/61, Theatre Marquee, 24
Opera Ball, The (m), 2/12/12, Liberty Theatre, 32
Operation Sidewinder (p), 3/12/70, Vivian Beaumont Theatre, 52
Opium (p), 10/5/70, Edison Theatre, 8
Opportunity (p), 7/30/20, 48th St. Theatre, 135
Optimist, The (p), 4/23/06, Daly's Theatre, 8
Optimists, The (m), 1/30/28, Casino de Paris, 24
Orange Blossoms (m), 9/19/22, Fulton Theatre, 95
Orange Souffle. See Under the Weather
Orchestral Drama Program, 5/4/28, Manhattan Opera House, 3
Orchid, The (m), 4/8/07, Herald Square Theatre, 178
Orchid, The (m), 3/2/08, Academy of Music, 16
Orchids Preferred (m), 5/11/37, Imperial Theatre, 7
Order Please (p), 10/9/34, Playhouse, 23
Ordinary Man, An (p), 9/9/68, Cherry Lane Theatre, 24
Originale (p), 9/8/64, Judson Hall, 5
Orlando Furioso, 11/4/70, Bryant Park Bubble Theatre, 27
Orphan, The (p), 3/30/73, Public / Anspacher Theatre, 53

Orpheus (m), 4/20/26, Provincetown Playhouse, 20
Orpheus (p), 9/30/54, Living Theatre Studio
Orpheus Descending (p), 3/21/57, Martin Beck Theatre, 68
Orpheus Descending (p), 10/5/59, Gramercy Arts Theatre, 230
Orrin / Love Gotta Come by Saturday Night (p), 1/8/73, Theatre de Lys, 2, (ANTA Matinee)
Oscar Wilde (p), 10/10/38, Fulton Theatre, 247
Oscar Wilde (p), 3/16/57, 41st St. Theatre, 40
Ostriches (p), 3/30/25, Comedy Theatre, 8
Otage, L' (p), 10/26/59, Phoenix Theatre, 2
Othello (p), 2/9/14, Lyric Theatre, 16
Othello (p), 12/13/20, Manhattan Opera House, 4
Othello (p), 1/3/21, Lexington Theatre, 1
Othello (p), 12/26/21, Lexington Theatre, 2
Othello (p) (Fritz Leiber), 1/23/22, 48th St. Theatre, 2
Othello (p), 1/10/25, Shubert Theatre, 51
Othello (p), 3/31/33, Shakespeare Theatre, 12
Othello (p) (Philip Merivale), 9/27/35, Ethel Barrymore Theatre, 11
Othello (p) (Walter Huston), 1/6/37, New Amsterdam Theatre, 21
Othello (p) (Paul Robeson), 10/19/43, Shubert Theatre, 295
Othello (p), 5/22/45, New York City Center, 24
Othello (p) (William Marshall), 9/7/55, New York City Center, 15
Othello (p) (William Marshall), 7/2/58, Belvedere Lake Theatre, 20
Othello (p) (James Earl Jones), 7/14/64, Delacorte Theatre, 19
Othello (p) (James Earl Jones), 10/12/64, Martinique Theatre, 224
Othello (p), 9/14/70, ANTA Theatre, 16, (American Shakespeare Festival)
Othello (p), 2/8/73, Actors Studio Theatre, 10
Other Fellow, The (p), 10/31/10, Bijou Theatre, 24
Other Girl, The (p), 12/29/03, Criterion Theatre, 160
Other House, The (p), 8/30/07, Majestic Theatre, 20
Other Man, The / Oh, Say Can You See L.A. (p), 2/8/68, Actors Playhouse, 14
Other Men's Wives (p), 11/12/29, Times Square Theatre, 23
Other One, The (p), 10/3/32, Biltmore Theatre, 16
Other Rose, The (p), 12/20/23, Morosco Theatre, 84
Otra Honra, La (The Other Honor) (p), 11/19/53, Broadhurst Theatre, 27
Ouija Board, The (p), 3/29/20, Bijou Theatre, 64
Our American Cousin (p), 11/29/15, Booth Theatre, 40
Our Betters (p), 3/12/17, Hudson Theatre, 112
Our Betters (p), 2/20/28, Henry Miller's Theatre, 128
Our Children (p), 9/10/15, Maxine Elliott's Theatre, 18
Our Lan' (m), 4/18/47, Henry Street Playhouse, 12
Our Lan' (m), 9/27/47, Royale Theatre, 41
Our Little Wife (p), 11/18/16, Harris Theatre, 41
Our Man in Madras. See Let Them Down, Gently
Our Miss Gibbs (m), 8/29/10, Knickerbocker Theatre, 64
Our Mrs. McChesney (p), 10/19/15, Lyceum Theatre, 151
Our Nell (m), 12/4/22, Nora Bayes Theatre, 40
Our Pleasant Sins (p), 4/21/19, Belmont Theatre, 32
Our Stage and Stars, 11/11/33, Little Theatre, 6
Our Town (p), 2/4/38, Henry Miller's Theatre, 336
Our Town (p), 1/10/44, New York City Center, 24
Our Town (p), 3/23/59, Circle in the Square, 385
Our Town (p), 11/27/69, ANTA Theatre, 36
Our Wife (p), 3/2/33, Booth Theatre, 20
Our Wives (p), 11/4/12, Wallack Theatre, 40
Our World (p), 2/6/11, Garrick Theatre, 8
Ourselves (p), 11/12/13, Lyric Theatre, 29
Out Cry (p), 3/1/73, Lyceum Theatre, 12
Out from Under (p), 5/4/40, Biltmore Theatre, 9
Out from Under. See Under the Weather
Out of a Blue Sky (p), 2/8/30, Booth Theatre, 17
Out of Control / The Marriage of the Telephone Company Man (p), 9/9/71, Actors Playhouse, 5
Out of Step (p), 1/29/25, Hudson Theatre, 21
Out of the Frying Pan (p), 2/11/41, Windsor Theatre, 104
Out of the Night (p), 10/17/27, Lyric Theatre, 56
Out of the Sea (p), 12/5/27, Eltinge Theatre, 16
Out of the Seven Seas (p), 11/19/23, Frazee Theatre, 16
Out of This World (m), 12/21/50, New Century Theatre, 157
Out of This World (m), 10/30/57, Actors Playhouse
Out of This World (m), 3/8/73, Master Theatre, 19, (Equity Library Theatre)
Out There (p), 5/17/18, Century Theatre, 8
Out There (p), 3/27/17, Globe Theatre, 80
Out There by Your Lonesome, 2/14/73, Women's House of Detention, 2
Out West of Eighth (p), 9/20/51, Ethel Barrymore Theatre, 4
Outcast (p), 11/2/14, Lyceum Theatre, 168
Outrageous Fortune (p), 11/3/43, 48th St. Theatre, 77
Outrageous Mrs. Palmer, The (p), 10/12/20, 39th St. Theatre, 58
Outside Looking In (p), 9/7/25, Greenwich Village Theatre, 113
Outside Man, The (p), 12/16/64, St. Clement's Church, 5, (American Place Theatre)
Outsider, The (p), 3/3/24, 49th St. Theatre, 91
Outsider, The (p), 4/9/28, Ambassador Theatre, 56
Outward Bound (p), 1/7/24, Ritz Theatre, 145
Outward Bound (p), 12/22/38, Playhouse, 255
Over a Welsh Rarebit / Facing the Music (p), 5/21/03, Garrick Theatre, 44
Over Here (p), 9/10/18, Fulton Theatre, 23
Over Here! (m), 3/6/74, Shubert Theatre, 100
Over Night (p), 1/2/11, Hackett Theatre, 160
Over the 'Phone (p), 9/12/17, 48th St. Theatre, 21
Over the River (m), 1/8/12, Globe Theatre, 120
Over the Top (r), 11/28/17, 44th St. Theatre, 78
Over 21 (p), 1/3/44, Music Box Theatre, 221
Overtons, The (p), 2/6/45, Booth Theatre, 175
Overture (p), 12/6/30, Longacre Theatre, 41
Owl and the Pussycat, The (p), 11/18/64, ANTA Theatre, 421
Owl Answers, The / Dark Fire (p), 12/14/65, Theatre de Lys, 1, (ANTA Matinee)
Owl Answers, The. See Cities in Bezique
Owners (p), 5/14/73, Mercer / Shaw Theatre, 2
Ox Cart, The (p), 12/19/66, Greenwich Mews Theatre, 83
Oy Is Dus a Leben! (m), 10/12/42, Molly Picon Theatre, 139

P

P. S. 193 (p), 10/30/62, Writers' Stage, 48
Pacific Paradise (r), 10/16/72, Palace Theatre, 8
Paddy the Next Best Thing (p), 8/27/20, Shubert Theatre, 51
Padlocks of 1927 (r), 7/5/27, Shubert Theatre, 95
Padre, The (r), 12/27/26, Ritz Theatre, 32
Pagan Lady (p), 10/20/30, 48th St. Theatre, 153
Paganini (p), 9/11/16, Criterion Theatre, 48
Pagans (p), 1/4/21, Princess Theatre, 15
Page Miss Glory (p), 11/27/34, Mansfield Theatre, 63
Page Pygmalion (p), 8/3/32, Bijou Theatre, 5
Paging Danger (p), 2/26/31, Booth Theatre, 4
Paid (p), 11/25/25, Booth Theatre, 22
Paid Companions (p), 6/22/31, Masque Theatre, 8
Paid in Full (p), 2/25/08, Astor Theatre, 167
Paint Your Wagon (m), 11/12/51, Shubert Theatre, 289
Painted Days, The (p), 4/6/61, Theatre Marquee, 28
Painted Woman, The (p), 3/5/13, Playhouse, 2
Pair of Pairs, A (Deuces Wild / Charlatans) (p), 4/24/62, Vandam Theatre, 16
Pair of Petticoats, A (p), 3/18/18, 44th St. Roof Theatre, 80
Pair of Queens, A (p), 8/29/16, Longacre Theatre, 15
Pair of Silk Stockings, A (p), 10/20/14, Little Theatre, 223
Pair of Sixes, A (p), 3/17/14, Longacre Theatre, 207
Paisley Convertible, The (p), 2/11/67, Henry Miller's Theatre, 9
Pajama Game, The (m), 5/13/54, St. James Theatre, 1,061
Pajama Game, The (m), 5/15/57, New York City Center, 23
Pajama Game, The (m), 12/9/73, Lunt-Fontanne Theatre, 65
Pal Joey (m), 12/25/40, Ethel Barrymore Theatre, 270
Pal Joey (m), 9/1/41, Shubert Theatre, 104
Pal Joey (m), 1/3/52, Broadhurst Theatre, 540
Pal Joey (m), 5/31/61, New York City Center, 31
Pal Joey (m), 5/29/63, New York City Center, 15
Pale Horse, Pale Rider (p), 12/9/57, Jan Hus House, 40
Palm Tree in a Rose Garden, A (p), 11/26/57, Cricket Theatre, 84
Palmy Days (p), 10/27/19, Playhouse, 50
Pals First (p), 2/26/17, Fulton Theatre, 152
Pan and the Young Shepherd (p), 3/18/18, Greenwich Village Theatre, 32
Panama Hattie (m), 10/30/40, 46th St. Theatre, 501
Panic (p), 3/14/35, Imperial Theatre, 3
Pansy (m), 5/14/29, Belmont Theatre, 3
Pantagleize (p), 11/30/67, Lyceum Theatre, 59, (APA-Phoenix)
Pantagleize (p), 9/3/68, Lyceum Theatre, 10, (APA-Phoenix)
Pantaloon / Alice Sit-by-the-Fire (p), 12/25/05, Criterion Theatre, 81
Panthea (p), 3/23/14, Booth Theatre, 80
Pantomime and Harlequinade, 12/26/23, Greenwich Village Theatre, 6
Paolo and Francesca (p), 12/2/24, Booth Theatre, 6
Paolo and Francesca (p), 4/1/29, Forrest Theatre, 17
Papa (p), 4/10/19, Little Theatre, 12
Papa Is All (p), 1/6/42, Guild Theatre, 63
Papa Lebonnard (p), 4/28/08, Bijou Theatre, 31
Papa's Darling (m), 11/2/14, New Amsterdam Theatre, 40
Papavert. See Mr. Papavert
Paper Bag Players, The (Group Soup; Dandelion; To the Rescue), 1/20/73, Hunter College Playhouse, 48
Paper Bag Players, The (Scraps; Guffawhaw; Dandelion) (p), 8/29/68, Henry Street Settlement Playhouse, 104
Paper Chase, The, 11/25/12, Wallack Theatre, 24
Papers (p), 12/2/68, Provincetown Playhouse, 2
Papp (p), 4/17/69, St. Clement's Church, 44, (American Place Theatre)
Parade (r), 5/20/35, Guild Theatre, 40

Parade (r), 1/20/60, Players Theatre, 95
Paradise (p), 12/26/27, 48th St. Theatre, 8
Paradise Alley (m), 3/31/24, Casino Theatre, 64
Paradise Gardens East. See Frank Gagliano's City Scene
Paradise Lost (p), 12/9/35, Longacre Theatre, 72
Paradise Now, 10/14/68, Brooklyn Academy of Music, 6, (Living Theatre)
Paradise of Mahomet, The (m), 1/17/11, Herald Square Theatre, 23
Parasite, The (p), 12/16/65, Renata Theatre, 2
Parasites (p), 11/19/24, 39th St. Theatre, 53
Pardon My English (m), 1/20/33, Majestic Theatre, 43
Pardon Our French (r), 10/5/50, Broadway Theatre, 100
Parents and Children. See Geese
Pariah / The Stronger (p), 3/18/13, 48th St. Theatre, 1
Paris (p), 10/8/28, Music Box Theatre, 194
Paris Bound (p), 12/27/27, Music Box Theatre, 234
Paris by Night (r), 7/2/04, Madison Square Roof Garden, 50
Paris Is Out! (p), 1/19/70, Brooks Atkinson Theatre, 104
Paris '90, 3/4/52, Booth Theatre, 87
Parish Priest, The (p), 8/30/00, 14th St. Theatre, 37
Parisian Model, The (m), 11/27/06, Broadway Theatre, 179
Parisian Model, The (m), 1/6/08, Broadway Theatre, 21
Parisiana (r), 2/9/28, Edyth Totten Theatre, 28
Parisienne (p), 7/24/50, Fulton Theatre, 16
Parisienne, La / Un Caprice (p), 11/24/24, Henry Miller's Theatre, 8
Park (m), 4/22/70, John Golden Theatre, 5
Park (m), 11/11/71, Master Theatre, 19, (Equity Library Theatre)
Park Avenue (m), 11/4/46, Shubert Theatre, 72
Park Avenue, Ltd. (p), 3/3/32, Provincetown Playhouse, 12
Parlor, Bedroom and Bath (p), 12/24/17, Republic Theatre, 232
Parlor Story (p), 3/4/47, Biltmore Theatre, 23
Parnell (p), 11/11/35, Ethel Barrymore Theatre, 98
Parnell (p), 5/4/36, 48th St. Theatre, 32
Parson's Bride, The (p), 1/21/29, Belmont Theatre, 8
Partners Again (p), 5/1/22, Selwyn Theatre, 250
Party, A (p), 8/23/33, Playhouse, 45
Party for Divorce, A / Match-Play (p), 10/11/66, Provincetown Playhouse, 8
Party on Greenwich Avenue, The (p), 5/10/67, Cherry Lane Theatre, 7
Party's Over, The (p), 3/27/33, Vanderbilt Theatre, 48
Party with Betty Comden and Adolph Green, A, 12/23/58, John Golden Theatre, 38
Party with Betty Comden and Adolph Green, A, 4/16/59, John Golden Theatre, 44
Pas sur la Bouche, 3/25/29, Jolson Theatre, 4
Pasquale Never Knew (p), 3/30/38, Nora Bayes Theatre, 3
Passage to E. M. Forster, A, 10/26/70, Theatre de Lys, 2, (ANTA Matinee)
Passage to India, A (p), 1/31/62, Ambassador Theatre, 109
Passage, Un. See One Night Stands of a Noisy Passenger
Passe, La / La Vierge Folle / La Coutouriere de Luneville (p), 3/21/24, Gaiety Theatre, 6
Passenger to Bali, A (p), 3/14/40, Ethel Barrymore Theatre, 4
Passers-by (p), 9/14/11, Empire Theatre, 124
Passing of the Idle Rich, The (p), 5/1/13, Garden Theatre, 4
Passing of the Third Floor Back, The (p), 10/4/09, Maxine Elliott's Theatre, 216
Passing Present, The (p), 12/7/31, Ethel Barrymore Theatre, 16
Passing Show of 1912, The (r), 7/22/12, Winter Garden Theatre, 136
Passing Show of 1913, The (r), 7/24/13, Winter Garden Theatre, 116
Passing Show of 1914, The (r), 6/10/14, Winter Garden Theatre, 133
Passing Show of 1915, The (r), 5/29/15, Winter Garden Theatre, 145
Passing Show of 1916, The (r), 6/22/16, Winter Garden Theatre, 140
Passing Show of 1917, The (r), 4/26/17, Winter Garden Theatre, 196
Passing Show of 1918, The (r), 7/25/18, Winter Garden Theatre, 124
Passing Show of 1919, The (r), 10/23/19, Winter Garden Theatre, 280
Passing Show of 1921, The (r), 12/29/20, Winter Garden Theatre, 191
Passing Show of 1922, The (r), 9/20/22, Winter Garden Theatre, 95
Passing Show of 1923, The (r), 6/14/23, Winter Garden Theatre, 118
Passing Show of 1924, The (r), 9/3/24, Winter Garden Theatre, 106
Passing Through from Exotic Places (The Son who Hunted Tigers in Jakarta / Sunstroke / The Burial of Esposito) (p), 12/7/69, Sheridan Square Playhouse, 25
Passion Flower, The (p), 1/13/20, Greenwich Village Theatre, 144
Passion of Antigona Perez, The (p), 5/17/72, Cathedral of St. John the Divine, 18
Passion of Antigonia Perez, The (p), 8/7/72, New York City Parks & Playgrounds, 20
Passion of Josef D., The (p), 2/11/64, Ethel Barrymore Theatre, 15
Passionate Pilgrim, The (p), 10/19/32, 48th St. Theatre, 5
Passionella. See The Apple Tree
Passionnement, 3/2/29, Jolson Theatre, 8
Passions of 1926 (r), 6/8/26, Imperial Theatre, 87
Passport. See Friday Night
Past Is the Past, The / Going Thru Changes (p), 12/29/73, Billie Holiday Theatre (Brooklyn)
Pasteur (p), 3/12/23, Empire Theatre, 16
Pastoral (p), 11/1/39, Henry Miller's Theatre, 14
Pastry Shop, The / The Young Among Themselves (p), 6/10/70, The Extension, 10
Patate (p), 10/28/58, Henry Miller's Theatre, 7
Paths of Glory (p), 9/26/35, Plymouth Theatre, 24
Patience (m), 5/6/12, Lyric Theatre, 32
patience (m), 12/29/24, Provincetown Playhouse, 104
Patience (m), 5/23/27, Masque Theatre, 16
Patience (m), 6/25/28, Masque Theatre, 24
Patience (m), 6/15/31, Erlanger Theatre, 16
Patience (m), 5/22/33, St. James Theatre, 8
Patience (m), 10/11/34, Martin Beck Theatre, 10
Patience (m), 10/5/36, Martin Beck Theatre, 12
Patience (m), 2/25/44, Ambassador Theatre, 4
Patience (m), 2/9/48, Century Theatre, 16, (D'Oyly Carte Opera Co.)
Patience (m), 3/25/64, New York City Center, 4
Patience (m), 11/29/66, New York City Center, 4, (D'Oyly Carte Opera Co.)
Patience (m), 10/12/67, Jan Hus Playhouse, 20, (American Savoyards)
Patience (m), 5/15/68, New York City Center, 3
Patience (m), 10/31/68, New York City Center, 4, (D'Oyly Carte Opera Co.)
Patriarch, The (p), 11/25/29, 49th St. Theatre, 13
Patrick —the First (p), 2/18/65, Blackfriars' Guild, 90
Patrimony Pfd. (p), 11/12/36, Playhouse, 61
Patriot for Me, A (p), 10/5/69, Imperial Theatre, 49
Patriot, The (p), 11/23/08, Garrick Theatre, 160
Patriot, The (p), 1/19/28, Majestic Theatre, 12
Patriots, The (p), 1/29/43, National Theatre, 172
Patriots, The (p), 12/20/43, New York City Center, 8
Patsy, The (p), 12/23/25, Booth Theatre, 242
Paul Draper and Larry Adler, 12/31/43, New York City Center, 1
Paul Draper and Larry Adler, 2/3/44, New York City Center, 3
Paul Draper / 27 Wagons Full of Cotton / Trouble in Haiti. See All in One
Paul Sills' Story Theatre. See Story Theatre
Pawn, The (p), 9/8/17, Fulton Theatre, 17
Pay-day (p), 2/26/16, Cort Theatre, 49
Payment Deferred (p), 9/30/31, Lyceum Theatre, 70
Peace (m), 1/27/69, Astor Place Theatre, 192
Peace on Earth (p), 11/29/33, Civic Repertory Theatre, 125
Peace on Earth (p), 3/31/34, 44th St. Theatre, 17
Peacemaker, The (p), 11/25/46, ANT Playhouse, Harlem, 21
Peacock (p), 10/11/32, 49th St. Theatre, 6
Peanut Butter and Jelly (p), 5/9/70, University of the Streets Theatre, 10
Pearl and the Pumpkin, The (m), 8/21/05, Broadway Theatre, 72
Pearl Maiden, The (m), 1/22/12, New York Theatre, 24
Pearl Necklace, The (r), 9/21/72, Brooklyn Academy of Music, 8, (Jewish State Theatre of Bucharest)
Pearl of Great Price, The, 11/1/26, Century Theatre, 33
Pearls / The Good Woman / Squaring the Triangle / Divertissement / The Nightcap / Gutta Iconoclast (p), 6/13/21, Apollo Theatre, 8
Peasant Girl, The (m), 3/2/15, 44th St. Theatre, 111
Peddler, The / The Dodo Bird (p), 12/8/67, Martinique Theatre, 29
Pedestrian, The. See World of Ray Bradbury, The
Peepshow (p), 2/3/44, Fulton Theatre, 28
Peer Gynt (p), 2/5/23, Garrick Theatre, 122
Peer Gynt (p), 3/24/47, Greenwich Mews Playhouse
Peer Gynt (p), 1/28/51, ANTA Playhouse, 32
Peer Gynt (p), 1/12/60, Phoenix Theatre, 32
Peer Gynt (p), 7/8/69, Delacorte Theatre, 19
Peg O' My Heart (p), 12/20/12, Cort Theatre, 603
Peg O' My Heart (p), 2/14/21, Cort Theatre, 88
Peggy (m), 12/7/11, Casino Theatre, 36
Peggy from Paris, 9/10/03, Wallack Theatre, 85
Peggy Machree (p), 12/21/08, Broadway Theatre, 40
Peggy-Ann (m), 12/27/26, Vanderbilt Theatre, 354
Peg-O'-My-Dreams (m), 5/5/24, Jolson Theatre, 32
Peh Shuh Tchuwan, or The White Snake, 1/2/63, Morosco Theatre, 8, (Foo Hsing Theatre)
Pelican, The (p), 9/21/25, Times Square Theatre, 65
Pelléas and Mélisande (p), 1/28/02, Hammerstein's Victoria Theatre, 2
Pelléas and Mélisande (p), 12/4/23, Times Square Theatre, 13
Pelléas and Mélisande / Metamorphosis (p), 2/19/57, Theatre de Lys, 1, (Kuriakos Theatre)
Penal Law 2010 (p), 4/18/30, Biltmore Theatre, 19
Penelope (p), 12/13/09, Lyceum Theatre, 48
Penguin, The (p), 6/15/53, Current Stages Theatre
Penny Arcade (p), 3/10/30, Fulton Theatre, 24
Penny Change (p), 10/24/63, Players Theatre, 1
Penny Friend, The (m), 12/26/66, Stage 73, 32
Penny Wars, The (p), 10/15/69, Royale Theatre, 5
Penny Wise (p), 3/10/19, Belmont Theatre, 40
Penny Wise (p), 4/19/37, Morosco Theatre, 64
Penrod (p), 9/2/18, Globe Theatre, 48

Penthouse Legend (p), 2/22/73, McAlpin Rooftop Theatre, 30
People Are Living There (p), 11/18/71, Forum Theatre, 20
People Don't Do Such Things (p), 11/23/27, 48th St. Theatre, 13
People Is the Thing That the World Is Fullest Of (r), 2/20/67, Bil Baird Theatre, 116
People of the Shadows (Mrs. Minter / An Evening in Story and Song) (p), 4/18/74, Actors Studio, 12
People on the Hill (p), 9/25/31, Princess Theatre, 5
People vs. Ranchman, The (p), 10/27/68, Fortune Theatre, 41
Pepper Mill (r), 1/5/37, Chanin Auditorium, 6
Pequod (p), 6/29/69, Mercury Theatre, 1
Perfect Alibi, The (p), 11/27/28, Charles Hopkins Theatre, 283
Perfect Fool, The (m), 11/7/21, George M. Cohan Theatre, 275
Perfect Lady, A (p), 10/28/14, Hudson Theatre, 21
Perfect Marriage, The (p), 11/16/32, Bijou Theatre, 14
Perfect Marriage, The (p), 10/26/44, Ethel Barrymore Theatre, 92
Perfect Match, The / Slow Memories (p), 11/16/70, Theatre de Lys, 2, (ANTA Matinee)
Perfect Party, The (p), 3/20/69, Tambellini's Gate Theatre, 22
Perfect Setup, The (p), 10/24/62, Cort Theatre, 5
Perfectly Scandalous (p), 5/13/31, Hudson Theatre, 5
Perfumed Lady, The (p), 3/12/34, Ambassador Theatre, 40
Pericas, La. See Difunta, La
Pericas, Las. See Program of 3 One-Acters
Perichole, La (m), 12/14/25, Jolson Theatre, 12
Perichole, La (m), 12/27/26, Jolson Theatre, 8
Pericles, Prince of Tyre (p), 5/13/71, CSC Repertory Theatre, 22
Period of Adjustment (p), 11/10/60, Helen Hayes Theatre, 132
Peripherie (p), 1/2/28, Cosmopolitan Theatre, 8
Perkins (p), 10/22/18, Henry Miller's Theatre, 23
Perplexed Husband, The (p), 9/2/12, Empire Theatre, 80
Perry's Mission / Rosalee Pritchett (p), 1/12/71, St. Marks Playhouse, 48
Persecution and Assassination of Marat as Performed by the Inmates of the Asylum of Charenton under the Direction of the Marquis de Sade (p), 12/27/65, Martin Beck Theatre, 145
Persecution and Assassination of Marat as Performed by the Inmates of the Asylum of Charenton Under the Direction of the Marquis de Sade, The (p), 1/3/67, Majestic Theatre, 55
Persia, a Desert Cheapie (m), 4/9/72, La Mama Experimental Theatre, 21
Persians, The (p), 4/15/70, St. George's Church, 21, (Phoenix Theatre)
Persians, The (p), 5/19/74, Circle Repertory Theatre, 19
Personal (p), 9/3/07, Bijou Theatre, 38
Personal Appearance (p), 10/17/34, Henry Miller's Theatre, 501
Personality (p), 8/27/21, Playhouse, 9
Persons Unknown (p), 10/25/22, Punch and Judy Theatre, 6
Peter and the Wolf (m), 12/18/71, Bil Baird Theatre, 131
Peter Flies High (p), 11/9/31, Gaiety Theatre, 8
Peter Ibbetson (p), 4/17/17, Republic Theatre, 71
Peter Ibbetson (p), 4/8/31, Shubert Theatre, 21
Peter Pan (p), 11/6/05, Empire Theatre, 223
Peter Pan (p) (Maude Adams), 12/24/06, Empire Theatre, 40
Peter Pan (p) (Maude Adams), 12/23/12, Empire Theatre, 24
Peter Pan (p) (Maude Adams), 12/21/15, Empire Theatre, 23
Peter Pan (p), 11/6/24, Knickerbocker Theatre, 120
Peter Pan (p), 11/26/28, Civic Repertory Theatre, 48
Peter Pan (p), 11/2/29, Civic Repertory Theatre, 30
Peter Pan (p), 11/15/30, Civic Repertory Theatre, 29
Peter Pan (p), 11/5/32, Civic Repertory Theatre, 10
Peter Pan (p), 4/24/50, Imperial Theatre, 321
Peter Pan (m), 10/20/54, Winter Garden Theatre, 152
Peter's Mother (p), 10/29/18, Playhouse, 15
Peter Weston (p), 9/18/23, Sam H. Harris Theatre, 23
Peterpat (p), 1/6/65, Longacre Theatre, 21
Petrified Forest, The (p), 1/7/35, Broadhurst Theatre, 194
Petrified Forest, The (p), 11/1/43, New Amsterdam Roof, 8
Petrified Forest, The (p), 1/21/74, St. Clement's Theatre, 16
Pets (Baby with a Knife / Silver Grey Toy Poodle / Pets) (p), 5/14/69, Provincetown Playhouse, 15
Petticoat Fever (p), 3/4/45, Ritz Theatre, 137
Petticoat Influence (p), 12/15/30, Empire Theatre, 98
Phantasmagoria Historia of D. Johann Fausten Magister, PhD, MD, DD, DL, Etc., A, 4/24/73, Truck and Warehouse Theatre, 1
Phantom Lady, The (p), 3/20/65, IASTA Institute, 12
Phantom Legion, The (p), 12/10/19, Playhouse, 5
Phantom Lover, The, 9/4/28, 49th St. Theatre, 15
Phantom Rival, The. See A Tale of the Wolf—same play, 10/6/14, Belasco Theatre, 127
Phantoms (p), 1/13/30, Wallack Theatre, 48
Phedre (p), 10/31/65, I.A.S.T.A. Theatre, 12
Phedre (p), 2/10/66, Greenwich Mews Theatre, 100
Phedre (p) (Marie Bell and Her Company), 10/20/63, Brooks Atkinson Theatre, 16
Phedre (p), 2/27/69, Hunter College Playhouse, 4
Phidelah Rice (p), 1/6/32, Belmont Theatre, 7
Philadelphia (p), 9/16/29, Mansfield Theatre, 32
Philadelphia, Here I Come! (p), 2/16/66, Helen Hayes Theatre, 326
Philadelphia Story, The (p), 3/28/39, Shubert Theatre, 417
Philanderer, The (p), 12/30/13, Little Theatre, 103
Philanderer, The / You Never Can Tell. See George Bernard Shaw Series, 5/12/58, Downtown Theatre, 32
Philanthropist, The (p), 3/15/71, Ethel Barrymore Theatre, 72
Philip Goes Forth (p), 1/12/31, Biltmore Theatre, 98
Philipp Hotz / The Firebugs (p), 11/26/69, Barbizon-Plaza Theatre, 6, (Schauspieltruppe Zurich)
Philoktetes (p), 1/13/59, Theatre de Lys, 1
Philoktetes / The Women at the Tomb (p), 4/24/61, One Sheridan Square, 6
Philosopher in the Apple Orchard, The (p), 1/20/11, Lyceum Theatre, 35
Philosophy in the Boudoir (p), 5/21/69, Gramercy Arts Theatre, 37
Phoebe of Quality Street (p), 5/9/21, Shubert Theatre, 16
Phoenix Too Frequent, A / Freight (p), 4/26/50, Fulton Theatre, 5
Phoenix '55 (r), 4/23/55, Phoenix Theatre, 97
Photo Finish (p), 2/12/63, Brooks Atkinson Theatre, 160
Physicists, The (p), 10/13/64, Martin Beck Theatre, 55
Piéton de l'Air, Le / Salut à Molière, 3/3/64, New York City Center, 8, (Théâtre de France, Renaud-Barrault Company)
Piccolo Teatro di Milano (The Servant of Two Masters), 2/23/60, New York City Center, 16
Pick a Number XV (r), 10/14/65, Plaza 9, 400
Pick-Up Girl (p), 5/3/44, 48th St. Theatre, 197
Pickwick (p), 9/5/27, Empire Theatre, 72
Pickwick (m), 10/4/65, 46th Street Theatre, 56
Picnic (p), 5/2/34, National Theatre, 2
Picnic (p), 2/19/53, Music Box Theatre, 477
Picnic on the Battlefield / Ionescopade (p), 1/12/73, Gotham Art Theatre
Picture of Dorian Gray, The (p), 8/28/63, Showboat Theatre, 23
Pictures in the Hallway, 9/16/56, Playhouse, 19
Pictures in the Hallway, 12/26/59, Phoenix Theatre, 11
Pictures in the Hallway (p), 12/16/64, Theatre de Lys, 71
Pictures in the Hallway, 4/29/71, Forum Theatre, 20
Pie in the Sky (p), 12/22/41, Playhouse, 6
Piece of Fog, A. See American Gothics
Pied Piper, The (m), 12/3/08, Majestic Theatre, 52
Pierre of the Plains (p), 10/12/08, Hudson Theatre, 32
Pierrot's Journey, 9/3/64, Philharmonic Hall, Lincoln Center, 8, (Prague Pantomime Theatre)
Pierrot the Prodigal, 9/6/16, Booth Theatre, 165
Pierrot the Prodigal (p), 3/6/25, 48th St. Theatre, 14
Pietro (p), 1/19/20, Criterion Theatre, 41
Piff! Paff!! Pouf!! (m), 4/2/04, Casino Theatre, 264
Piff! Paff!! Pouf! ! (m), 12/26/04, Majestic Theatre, 8
Pig Pen, The (p), 4/29/70, St. Clement's Church, 40, (American Place Theatre)
Pigeon, The (p), 3/12/12, Little Theatre, 64
Pigeon, The (p), 2/2/22, Greenwich Village Theatre, 92
Pigeons and People (p), 1/16/33, Sam H. Harris Theatre, 66
Pigeons / Conerico Was Here to Stay (p) (New Playwrights Series, Evening II), 3/3/65, Cherry Lane Theatre, 21
Piggy (m), 1/11/27, Royale Theatre, 79
Pigs (p), 9/1/24, Little Theatre, 347
Piker, The (p), 1/15/25, Eltinge Theatre, 43
Pilate's Daughter (p), 11/21/14, Century Theatre, 8
Pilgrim's Progress, The (m), 3/20/62, Gate Theatre, 8
Pilgrim's Progress, The, 4/24/73, Riverside Church, 13
Pilgrimage, The / The Last Night of Don Juan (p), 11/9/25, Greenwich Village Theatre, 16
Pillar to Post (p), 12/10/43, Playhouse, 27
Pillars of Society (p), 4/15/04, Lyric Theatre, 1
Pillars of Society (p), 3/28/10, Lyceum Theatre, 16
Pillars of Society, The (p), 10/14/31, 48th St. Theatre, 2
Pimpernel! (m), 1/6/64, Gramercy Arts Theatre, 3
Pin to See the Peepshow, A (p), 9/17/53, Playhouse, 1
Pin Up. See Command Performance
Pin Wheel. See Raymond Hitchcock's Pinwheel
Pinch Hitter, A (p), 6/1/22, Henry Miller's Theatre, 28
Pink Elephant, The (p), 4/22/53, Playhouse, 5
Pink Lady, The (m), 3/13/11, New Amsterdam Theatre, 312
Pink String and Sealing Wax (p), 9/5/57, Royal Playhouse, 4
Pinkville (p), 2/22/71, St. Clement's Church, 42, (American Place Theatre)
Pinocchio (m), 11/2/39, Ritz Theatre, 197
Pinocchio (m), 3/30/72, Felt Forum, 23
Pinocchio (m), 12/15/73, Bil Baird Theatre, 134
Pins and Needles (m), 2/1/22, Shubert Theatre, 46
Pins and Needles (r), 11/27/37, Labor Stage Theatre, 264
Pins and Needles 1939 (r), 4/20/39, Labor Stage Theatre, 680
Pinter Plays, The (p) (The Collection / The Dumbwaiter), 11/26/62, Cherry Lane Theatre, 578
Pinwheel (p), 2/3/27, Neighborhood Playhouse, 50
Pioneer Days / Circus Events / Neptune's Daughter (r), 11/28/06, New York Hippodrome, 288

Pipe Dream (m), 11/30/55, Shubert Theatre, 246
Piper Paid (p), 12/25/34, Ritz Theatre, 15
Piper, The (p), 1/30/11, New Theatre
Piper, The (p), 3/19/20, Fulton Theatre, 8
Pipes of Pan, The (p), 11/6/17, Hudson Theatre, 87
Pippa Passes (p), 11/12/06, Majestic Theatre, 9
Pippin (m), 10/23/72, Imperial Theatre, 669
Pique-Nique en Campagne / Guernica (p), 4/30/69, Barbizon-Plaza Theatre, 16, (Le Treteau de Paris)
Piraikon Theatron (Iphigenia in Aulis; Hippolytus) (p), 11/12/68, Felt Forum, 16
Piraikon Theatron of Athens (Medea; Electra) (p), 8/31/64, New York City Center, 16
Pirate, The (p), 11/25/42, Martin Beck Theatre, 176
Pirates of Penzance, The (m), 6/3/12, Casino Theatre, 28
Pirates of Penzance, The (m), 12/6/26, Plymouth Theatre, 128
Pirates of Penzance, The (m), 11/24/27, Royale Theatre, 9
Pirates of Penzance, The (m), 10/19/31, Erlanger Theatre, 8
Pirates of Penzance, The (m), 8/7/33, Majestic Theatre, 8
Pirates of Penzance, The (m), 4/9/34, Majestic Theatre, 8
Pirates of Penzance, The (m), 5/7/34, Majestic Theatre, 8
Pirates of Penzance, The (m), 7/22/35, Adelphi Theatre, 8
Pirates of Penzance, The (m), 8/22/35, Adelphi Theatre, 4
Pirates of Penzance, The (m), 4/20/36, Majestic Theatre, 8
Pirates of Penzance, The (m), 5/12/46, New York City Center, 4
Pirates of Penzance, The, 10/4/49, Mark Hellinger Theatre, 24, (Gilbert and Sullivan Rep.)
Pirates of Penzance, The (m) (S. M. Chartock's Gilbert & Sullivan Co.), 10/27/52, Mark Hellinger Theatre, 8
Pirates of Penzance, The (p), 10/6/55, Shubert Theatre, 8, (D'Oyly Carte Opera Co.)
Pirates of Penzance, The, 5/7/57, Shakespearewrights Theatre, 8, (American Savoyards)
Pirates of Penzance, The (m), 2/25/60, Jan Hus House
Pirates of Penzance, The (m), 9/6/61, Phoenix Theatre, 55
Pirates of Penzance, The (m), 3/28/64, New York City Center, 4
Pirates of Penzance, The (m), 11/24/64, New York City Center, 8, (D'Oyly Carte Company)
Pirates of Penzance, The (m), 5/23/66, Jan Hus Playhouse, 29, (American Savoyards)
Pirates of Penzance, The (m), 11/15/66, New York City Center, 7, (D'Oyly Carte Opera Co.)
Pirates of Penzance, The (m), 4/25/68, New York City Center, 7
Pirates of Penzance, The (m), 11/6/68, New York City Center, 3, (D'Oyly Carte Opera Co.)
Pirates of Penzance, The (m), 12/4/70, Fashion Institute Theatre, 6
Pirates of Penzance, The / Cox and Box (m), 9/6/34, Martin Beck Theatre, 14
Pirates of Penzance, The / Cox and Box (m), 2/17/44, Ambassador Theatre, 8
Pirates of Penzance, The / The Prodigal Son (m), 2/17/42, St. James Theatre, 11
Pirates of Penzance, The / Trial by Jury (m), 8/31/36, Martin Beck Theatre, 20
Pirates of Penzance, The / Trial by Jury (m), 10/7/40, 44th St. Theatre, 6
Pirates of Penzance, The / Trial by Jury (m), 1/5/48, Century Theatre, 16, (D'Oyly Carte Opera Co.)
Pit, The (p), 2/10/04, Lyric Theatre, 77
Pitter Patter (m), 9/28/20, Longacre Theatre, 111
Place for Chance, The, 5/14/64, Stage 73, 13
Place for Polly, A (p), 4/18/70, Ethel Barrymore Theatre, 1
Place in the Sun, A (p), 11/28/18, Comedy Theatre, 44
Place of Our Own, A (p), 4/2/45, Royale Theatre, 8
Place Without Doors, A (p), 12/22/70, Stairway Theatre, 30
Place Without Mornings, A (p), 1/10/72, Theatre de Lys, 2, (ANTA Matinee)
Places, Please (p), 11/12/37, John Golden Theatre, 3
Plain and Fancy (m), 1/27/55, Mark Hellinger Theatre, 461
Plain Jane (m), 5/12/24, New Amsterdam Theatre, 16
Plan M (p), 2/20/42, Belasco Theatre, 6
Plantation Revue, The (r), 7/17/22, 48th St. Theatre, 33
Plantation. See Contributions
Play / Dutchman / Two Executioners (p), 3/24/64, Cherry Lane Theatre, 32
Play, Genius, Play! (p), 10/30/35, St. James Theatre, 6
Play It Again, Sam (p), 2/12/69, Broadhurst, 453
Play's the Thing, The (p), 11/3/26, Henry Miller's Theatre, 313
Play's the Thing, The (p), 4/9/28, Empire Theatre, 24
Play's the Thing, The (p), 4/28/48, Booth Theatre, 244
Play's the Thing, The (p), 1/31/73, Roundabout Theatre, 64
Play's the Thing, The (p), 5/7/73, Bijou Theatre, 23
Play Strindberg (p), 6/3/71, Forum Theatre, 36
Play Strindberg (p), 9/29/71, Forum Theatre, 29
Play That on Your Old Piano (p), 10/14/65, Renata Theatre, 2
Play / The Lover (p), 1/4/64, Cherry Lane Theatre, 89
Play with a Tiger (p), 12/30/64, Renata Theatre, 23
Play without a Name, A (p), 11/26/28, Booth Theatre, 48
Playboy of the Western World, The (p), 11/11, Maxine Elliott's Theatre, (Irish Players)
Playboy of the Western World, The (p), 2/13, Wallack Theatre, (Irish Players)
Playboy of the Western World, The (p) (Thomas Mitchell), 4/16/21, Bramhall Playhouse, 36
Playboy of the Western World, The (p) (Sean Dillon), 1/2/30, Irish Theatre, 27
Playboy of the Western World, The (p), 10/20/32, Martin Beck Theatre, 2
Playboy of the Western World, The (p), 11/17/34, John Golden Theatre, 7
Playboy of the Western World, The (p), 10/26/46, Booth Theatre, 81
Playboy of the Western World, The (p), 5/8/58, Tara Theatre, 305
Playboy of the Western World, The (p), 1/7/71, Vivian Beaumont Theatre, 52
Playboy of the Western World, The / In the Train (p), 11/20/37, Ambassador Theatre, 9
Player Maid, The (p), 10/13/05, Liberty Theatre, 1
Player Queen, The / Shewing-Up of Blanco Posnet, The (p), 10/16/23, Neighborhood Playhouse, 49
Players from Japan, The, 3/4/30, Booth Theatre, 13
Players Inn. See Black Visions
Playing the Game (p), 12/19/27, Ritz Theatre, 8
Playing with Love (p), 2/26/29, Cherry Lane Theatre, 15
Playroom, The (p), 12/5/65, Brooks Atkinson Theatre, 33
Plays for Bleecker Street (Infancy / Childhood / Someone from Assisi) (p), 1/11/62, Circle in the Square, 349
Playwrights Cooperative Festival (Honor / Go Children Slowly) (p), 5/25/73, Cubiculo Theatre, 12
Playwrights Cooperative Festival (Mrs. Minter / Five Visits) (p), 6/15/73, Jean Cocteau Theatre
Playwrights Cooperative Festival (San Fernando Valley / Mother's Day / Hippy as a Lark) (p), 6/7/73, Stagelights II Theatre, 12
Playwrights Cooperative Festival (The Conquest of Everest / The Hero / Adora / L'Hopital Splendide) (p), 5/18/73, New York Theatre Ensemble, 10
Playwrights Cooperative Festival (Tonto / Magic Time / Roarshock) (p), 5/17/73, Cubiculo Theatre, 12
Plaza Suite (Visitor from Mamaroneck / Visitor from Hollywood / Visitor from Forest Hills) (p), 2/14/68, Plymouth Theatre, 1,097
Please Don't Cry and Say No (The Brown Overcoat / The Botany Lesson / Please Don't Cry and Say No) (p), 12/6/72, Circle in the Square, 15
Please Get Married (p), 2/10/19, Little Theatre, 160
Please Help Emily (p), 8/14/16, Lyceum Theatre, 40
Please, Mrs. Garibaldi (p), 3/16/39, Belmont Theatre, 4
Pleasure and Repentance, 4/21/74, Brooklyn Academy of Music, 5, (Royal Shakespeare Co.)
Pleasure Bound (r), 2/18/29, Majestic Theatre, 136
Pleasure Man (p), 10/1/28, Biltmore Theatre, 3
Pleasure of His Company, The (p), 10/22/58, Longacre Theatre, 474
Pleasure Seekers, The (m), 11/3/13, Winter Garden Theatre, 72
Plot Against the Chase Manhattan Bank, The (r), 11/26/63, Theatre East, 15
Plot Thickens, The (p), 9/5/22, Booth Theatre, 15
Plough and the Stars, The (p), 11/28/27, Hudson Theatre, 48
Plough and the Stars, The (p), 11/12/34, John Golden Theatre, 12
Plough and the Stars, The (p), 10/7/37, Ambassador Theatre, 4
Plough and the Stars, The (p), 12/6/60, Phoenix Theatre, 32
Plough and the Stars, The (p), 1/4/73, Vivian Beaumont Theatre, 44
Plume de Ma Tante, La (r), 11/11/58, Royale Theatre, 835
Plume de Ma Tante, La (r), 11/11/58, Royale Theatre, 835
Plumes in the Dust (p), 11/6/36, 46th St. Theatre, 11
Plutocrat, The (p), 2/20/30, Vanderbilt Theatre, 100
Plutus (p), 8/20/63, East River Park Amphitheatre
Pocket Watch, The (p), 1/5/66, Actors Playhouse, 725
Poetasters of Ispahan, The / Beauty and the Jacobin (p), 11/29/12, Comedy Theatre, 1
Point of Honor, A (p), 2/11/37, Fulton Theatre, 4
Point of No Return (p), 12/13/51, Alvin Theatre, 364
Point of View, The (p), 10/25/12, 48th St. Theatre, 1
Point of View, The (p), 11/4/12, Daly's Theatre, 8
Point Valaine (p), 1/16/35, Ethel Barrymore Theatre, 56
Poisoned by Pictures. See Potash and Perlmutter, Detectives, 8/31/26, Ritz Theatre, 48
Poker Session, The (p), 9/19/67, Martinique Theatre, 16
Poldekin (p), 9/9/20, Park Theatre, 42
Policeman, The / Androcles and the Lion (p), 11/21/61, Phoenix Theatre, 49
Polish Laboratory Theatre (The Constant Prince; Acropolis; Apocalypsis cum Figuris) (p), 10/16/69, Washington Square Methodist Church, 51
Polish Mime Theatre, The (r), 1/5/65, New York City Center, 16
Political Party, A (r), 9/26/63, 41st St. Theatre, 14
Polly (m), 10/10/25, Cherry Lane Theatre, 43
Polly (m), 1/8/29, Lyric Theatre, 15

Polly of Hollywood (m), 2/21/27, George M. Cohan Theatre, 24
Polly of the Circus (p), 12/23/07, Liberty Theatre, 160
Polly Preferred (p), 1/11/23, Little Theatre, 202
Polly Preferred (p), 8/20/23, Little Theatre
Polly with a Past (p), 9/6/17, Belasco Theatre, 315
Pollyanna (p), 9/18/16, Hudson Theatre, 112
Polonaise (m), 10/6/45, Alvin Theatre, 113
Polygamy (p), 12/1/14, Playhouse, 159
Polygamy / The Dickey Bird (p), 2/22/15, Park Theatre, 64
Pomander Walk (p), 12/20/10, Wallack Theatre, 143
Pomeroy's Past (p), 4/19/26, Longacre Theatre, 88
Pom-pom (m), 2/28/16, Cohan Theatre, 128
Ponder Heart, The (p), 2/16/56, Music Box Theatre, 149
Pony Cart, The (p), 9/14/54, Theatre de Lys, 16
Poor Bitos (p), 11/14/64, Cort Theatre, 17
Poor Little Rich Girl, The (p), 1/21/13, Hudson Theatre, 160
Poor Little Ritz Girl (p), 7/27/20, Central Theatre, 93
Poor Little Thing (p), 12/22/14, Bandbox Theatre, 31
Poor Nut, The (p), 4/27/25, Henry Miller's Theatre, 300
Poor Richard (p), 12/2/64, Helen Hayes Theatre, 118
Pop (m), 4/3/74, Players Theatre, 1
Poppa (p), 12/24/28, Biltmore Theatre, 98
Poppa Joe. See Mister Malatesta
Poppy (m), 9/3/23, Apollo Theatre, 346
Poppy God, The (p), 8/29/21, Hudson Theatre, 16
Popsy (p), 2/10/41, Playhouse, 4
Popularity (p), 10/1/06, Wallack Theatre, 24
Porgy (p), 10/10/27, Guild Theatre, 367
Porgy (p), 9/13/29, Martin Beck Theatre, 35
Porgy and Bess (m), 10/10/35, Alvin Theatre, 124
Porgy and Bess (m), 1/22/42, Majestic Theatre, 286
Porgy and Bess (m), 9/13/43, 44th St. Theatre, 24
Porgy and Bess (m), 2/7/44, New York City Center, 16
Porgy and Bess (m), 2/28/44, New York City Center, 48
Porgy and Bess (m), 3/10/53, Ziegfeld Theatre, 305
Porgy and Bess (m), 5/17/61, New York City Center, 16
Porgy and Bess (m), 5/6/64, New York City Center, 15
Pork (p), 5/5/71, La Mama Experimental Theatre Club, 10
Port o' London (p), 2/9/26, Daly's Theatre, 24
Port Royale (p), 5/24/60, Grace Church
Portmanteau Theatre Repertory. See Stuart Walker
Portofino (m), 2/21/58, Adelphi Theatre, 3
Portrait in Black (p), 5/14/47, Booth Theatre, 62
Portrait of a Lady (p), 12/21/54, ANTA Theatre, 7
Portrait of a Queen (p), 2/28/68, Henry Miller's Theatre, 60
Portrait of Gilbert, 12/28/34, Longacre Theatre, 3
Portrait of the Artist as a Young Man / The Barroom Monks (p), 5/28/62, Martinique Theatre, 300
Possessed, The (p), 10/24/39, Lyceum Theatre, 14
Possession (p), 10/2/28, Booth Theatre, 37
Possibilities (p), 12/4/68, Players Theatre, 1
Post Office, The (p), 12/10/20, Garrick Theatre, 5
Post Road (p), 12/4/34, Masque Theatre, 210
Postcards / Grin and Bare It! (p), 3/16/70, Belasco Theatre, 16
Postcards / The Club Bedroom (p), 12/4/67, Theatre de Lys, 2
Posterity for Sale (p), 5/11/67, American Place Theatre, 25
Postman Always Rings Twice, The (p), 2/25/36, Lyceum Theatre, 71
Postmark Zero (p), 11/1/65, Brooks Atkinson Theatre, 8
Pot Boiler, The / Autumn Fires / The Eternal Judith (p), 11/7/21, Princess Theatre, 8
Pot Luck (p), 9/29/21, Comedy Theatre, 28
Pot of Broth, A / The Land of Heart's Desire / Kathleen ni Houlihan (p), 6/3/03, Carnegie Lyceum Theatre, 2
Pot of Broth, A / Twenty Days in the Shade (p), 2/18/08, Savoy Theatre, 7
Potash and Perlmutter (p), 8/16/13, George M. Cohan Theatre, 441
Potash and Perlmutter (p), 4/5/35, Park Theatre, 18
Potash and Perlmutter, Detectives (Poisoned by Pictures) (p), 8/31/26, Ritz Theatre, 48
Potash and Perlmutter in Society. See Mark of the Beast, The
Potiphar's Wife (p), 12/24/28, Craig Theatre, 17
Potluck! (r), 7/7/66, Delacorte Theatre, 52
Potters, The (p), 12/8/23, Plymouth Theatre, 245
Potting Shed, The (p), 1/29/57, Bijou Theatre, 143
Potting Shed, The (p), 11/2/58, Broadway Congregational Church, 10
Pound on Demand / Androcles and the Lion (p), 12/19/46, International Theatre, 40
Poupees de Paris, Les (The Dolls of Paris) (r), 12/11/62, York Playhouse, 252
Pousse-Café (m), 3/18/66, 46th St. Theatre, 3
Poverty Is No Crime (p), 2/20/35, Majestic Theatre, 7
Power, 2/23/37, Ritz Theatre, 142
Power and the Glory, The (p), 12/10/58, Phoenix Theatre, 71
Power of Darkness, The (p), 1/15/20, Garrick Theatre, 40
Power of Darkness, The (p), 9/29/59, York Playhouse, 39
Power Without Glory (p), 1/13/48, Booth Theatre, 31
Prague Pantomime Theatre (Pierrot's Journey; Twenty-four Inventions), 9/3/64, Philharmonic Hall, Lincoln Center, 16
Prayer Meeting or the First Militant Minister. See A Black Quartet
Praying Curve (retitled The Love Thief) (p), 1/24/27, Eltinge Theatre, 32
Precedent (p), 4/14/31, Provincetown Playhouse, 184
Precious (p), 1/14/29, Royale Theatre, 24
Pre-Honeymoon (p), 4/30/36, Lyceum Theatre, 253
Prelude / Bury the Dead (p), 4/18/36, Ethel Barrymore Theatre, 97
Prelude to Exile (p), 11/30/36, Guild Theatre, 48
Premise, The (r), 11/22/60, Premise Theatre, 1,249
Prescott Proposals, The (p), 12/16/53, Broadhurst Theatre, 125
Present Arms (m), 4/26/28, Mansfield Theatre, 147
Present Laughter (p), 10/29/46, Plymouth Theatre, 158
Present Laughter (p), 1/31/58, Belasco Theatre, 6
Present Laughter (p), 1/14/71, Master Theatre, 14, (Equity Library Theatre)
Present Tense (Come Next Tuesday / Twas Brillig / So Please Be Kind / Present Tense) (p), 7/18/72, Sheridan Square Playhouse, 8
Preserving Mr. Panmure (p), 2/27/12, Lyceum Theatre, 31
President's Daughter, The (m), 11/3/70, Billy Rose Theatre, 72
Press Agent, The (m), 11/27/05, Lew Fields Theatre, 40
Pressing Business (p), 11/17/30, Republic Theatre, 16
Pretenders, The (p), 5/24/60, Cherry Lane Theatre, 16
Pretty Little Parlor (p), 4/17/44, National Theatre, 8
Pretty Mrs. Smith (m), 9/21/14, Casino Theatre, 48
Pretty Peggy (p), 3/23/03, Herald Sq. Theatre, 48
Pretty Peggy (p), 10/5/03, Madison Sq. Theatre, 32
Pretty Sister of Jose, The (p), 11/10/03, Empire Theatre, 58
Pretty Soft (p), 5/15/19, Morosco Theatre, 28
Pretzels (r), 5/17/74, Playhouse 2, 5, (New Phoenix Repertory Co.)
Price of Money, The (p), 8/29/06, Garrick Theatre, 42
Price of Peace, The (p), 3/21/01, Broadway Theatre, 60
Price, The (p), 11/1/11, Hudson Theatre, 77
Price, The (p), 2/7/68, Morosco Theatre, 425
Pride (p), 5/2/23, Morosco Theatre, 13
Pride and Prejudice (p), 11/5/35, Music Box Theatre, 219
Pride of Jennico, The (p), 3/6/00, Criterion Theatre, 111
Pride of Jennico, The (p), 9/3/00, Criterion Theatre, 32
Pride of Race, The (p), 1/11/16, Maxine Elliott's Theatre, 79
Pride's Crossing (p), 11/20/50, Biltmore Theatre, 8
Priest in the Cellar, The (p), 2/18/69, Blackfriars' Guild, 42
Prima Donna, The (p), 4/17/01, Herald Sq. Theatre, 36
Prima Donna, The (m), 11/30/08, Knickerbocker Theatre, 72
Prime of Miss Jean Brodie, The (p), 1/16/68, Helen Hayes Theatre, 379
Primer for Lovers, A (p), 11/18/29, Longacre Theatre, 24
Primitives (p), 10/29/69, La Mama Experimental Theatre Club, 12
Primrose Path, The (p), 5/6/07, Majestic Theatre, 16
Primrose Path, The (p), 1/4/39, Biltmore Theatre, 166
Prince and the Pauper, The (p), 11/1/20, Booth Theatre, 158
Prince Chap, The (p), 9/4/05, Madison Sq. Theatre, 106
Prince Chap, The (p), 4/15/07, Majestic Theatre, 24
Prince Consort, The (p), 3/6/05, New Amsterdam Theatre, 32
Prince of Bohemia, The (m), 1/13/10, Hackett Theatre, 20
Prince of India, The (p), 9/24/06, Broadway Theatre, 73
Prince of Pilsen, The (m), 3/17/03, Broadway Theatre, 143
Prince of Pilsen, The (m), 4/4/04, Daly's Theatre, 32
Prince of Pilsen, The (m), 4/3/05, New York Theatre, 40
Prince of Pilsen, The (m), 4/2/06, New York Theatre, 16
Prince of Pilsen, The (m), 5/6/07, Academy of Music, 32
Prince of Pilsen, The (m), 1/13/30, Jolson Theatre, 16
Prince Otto (p), 9/3/00, Wallack Theatre, 40
Prince Reuvaini (p), 11/17/67, Folksbiene Playhouse, 59
Prince There Was, A (p), 12/24/18, Cohan Theatre, 159
Princess April (m), 12/1/24, Ambassador Theatre, 24
Princess Beggar (m), 1/7/07, Casino Theatre, 40
Princess Charming (m), 10/13/30, Imperial Theatre, 56
Princess Chic, The (m), 2/17/00, Casino Theatre, 22
Princess Flavia (m), 11/2/25, Century Theatre, 152
Princess Ida (m), 4/13/25, Shubert Theatre, 40
Princess Ida (m), 9/27/34, Martin Beck Theatre, 10
Princess Ida (m), 10/12/36, Martin Beck Theatre, 12
Princess Ida (m), 10/13/55, Shubert Theatre, 8, (D'Oyly Carte Opera Co.)
Princess Ida (m), 5/18/61, Greenwich Mews Theatre, 12
Princess Ida (m), 5/26/66, Jan Hus Playhouse, 28, (American Savoyards)
Princess of Kensington, A (m), 8/31/03, Broadway Theatre, 41
Princess Pat, The (m), 9/29/15, Cort Theatre, 158
Princess Players, The, 3/14/13, Princess Theatre, 115
Princess Players, The, 9/27/13, Princess Theatre
Princess Players, The, 10/17/14, Princess Theatre
Princess Rebecca Birnbaum. See Monopoly
Princess Turandot (p), 11/12/26, Provincetown Playhouse, 34
Princess Turandot (p), 12/20/26, Greenwich Village Theatre, 16
Princess Turandot (p), 1/25/29, Mansfield Theatre, 5
Princess Virtue (m), 5/4/21, Central Theatre, 16
Priorities of 1942 (r), 3/12/42, 46th St. Theatre, 353

Prisoner of Second Avenue, The (p), 11/11/71, Eugene O'Neill Theatre, 788
Prisoner of Zenda, The (p), 9/21/08, Hackett Theatre
Prisoner, The (p), 12/28/27, Provincetown Playhouse, 40
Prisoners of War (p), 1/28/35, Ritz Theatre, 8
Private Affair, A (p), 5/14/36, Masque Theatre, 28
Private Ear, The / The Public Eye (p), 10/9/63, Morosco Theatre, 163
Private Life of the Master Race, The (p), 6/11/45, City College Auditorium, 6
Private Lives (p), 1/27/31, Times Sq. Theatre, 248
Private Lives (p), 10/4/48, Plymouth Theatre, 248
Private Lives (p), 5/19/68, Theatre de Lys, 9
Private Lives (p), 12/4/69, Billy Rose Theatre, 204
Privilege Car (p), 3/3/31, 48th St. Theatre, 48
Procès, Le (p), 11/17/52, Ziegfeld Theatre, 4
Processional (p), 1/12/25, Garrick Theatre, 105
Processional (p), 10/13/37, Maxine Elliott's Theatre, 81
Prodigal (p), 12/16/73, Circle Repertory Theatre, 19
Prodigal Husband, The (p), 9/7/14, Empire Theatre, 42
Prodigal Son, The (m), 9/4/05, New Amsterdam Theatre, 42
Prodigal Son, The / The Exception and the Rule (m,p) (Twin Bill), 5/20/65, Greenwich Mews Theatre, 141
Prodigal Son, The / The Pirates of Penzance (m), 2/17/42, St. James Theatre, 11
Prodigal, The (p), 2/11/60, Downtown Theatre, 164
Professor Bernhardi (p), 3/19/68, New York City Center, 6, (Vienna Burgtheater)
Professor Mamlock (p), 4/13/37, Daly's Theatre, 76
Professor's Love Story, The (p), 2/26/17, Knickerbocker Theatre, 48
Profligate, The (p), 3/17/00, Wallack Theatre, 4
Program of 3 One-Acters (La Difunta / Cruce de Vias / Las Pericas) (p), 10/31/69, Theatre East, 26, (Greenwich Mews Spanish Theatre)
Progress of Bora, the Tailor, The (p), 6/26/68, Forum Theatre, 6, (Atelje 212)
Projection Room, The / Neighbors (p), 1/13/69, Theatre de Lys, 2, (ANTA Matinee)
Prologue to Glory (p), 3/17/38, Maxine Elliott's Theatre, 169
Promenade (m), 6/4/69, Promenade Theatre, 259
Promenade, All! (p), 4/16/72, Alvin Theatre, 48
Promise (p), 12/30/36, Little Theatre, 29
Promise, The (p), 11/14/67, Henry Miller's Theatre, 23
Promises, Promises (m), 12/1/68, Shubert Theatre, 1281
Proof Through the Night (p), 12/25/42, Morosco Theatre, 11
Proposition, The (r), 3/24/71, Gramercy Arts Theatre, 1,109
Proposition, The (2nd Edition) (r), 9/16/71, Mercer Shaw Arena, 414
Proposition, The (3rd Edition) (r), 9/13/72, Mercer / Oscar Wilde Room, 656
Protective Custody (p), 12/28/56, Ambassador Theatre, 3
Proud Laird, The (p), 4/24/05, Manhattan Theatre, 7
Proud Prince, The (p), 10/12/03, Herald Square Theatre, 35
Proud Woman, A (p), 11/15/26, Maxine Elliott's Theatre, 8
Provincetown Follies (r), 11/3/35, Provincetown Playhouse, 63
Prozess, Der (p), 11/9/71, Barbizon-Plaza Theatre, 7, (Szene 71)
Prunella (p), 10/27/13, Little Theatre, 104
Prunella (p), 6/15/26, Garrick Theatre, 6
Prussian Suite (p), 1/31/74, Theatre Genesis
P.S. I Love You (p), 11/19/64, Henry Miller's Theatre, 12
Psychiatrists, The (p), 5/24/71, Lincoln Center Library Auditorium, 3, (Equity Library Theatre)
Psychic Pretenders, The (p), 12/24/71, New Lafayette Theatre
Public Eye, The / The Private Ear (p), 10/9/63, Morosco Theatre, 163
Public Relations (p), 4/6/44, Mansfield Theatre, 28
Pullman Car Hiawatha / Under Milk Wood (p), 12/3/64, Circle in the Square, 33
Punch, Judy & Co. (r), 6/1/03, Hammerstein's Paradise Roof Garden, 72
Puppet Show, 10/28/30, Belmont Theatre, 7
Puppet Theatre of Don Cristobal, The. See Retabilillo de Don Cristobal, El
Puppets, 3/9/25, Selwyn Theatre, 57
Puppets of Passion (p), 2/24/27, Masque Theatre, 12
Puppy Love (p), 1/27/26, 48th St. Theatre, 112
Pure in Heart, The (p), 3/20/34, Longacre Theatre, 7
Puritan, The (p), 1/23/36, Belmont Theatre, 4
Purity (p), 12/25/30, Ritz Theatre, 12
Purlie (m), 3/15/70, Broadway Theatre, 690
Purlie (m), 12/27/72, Billy Rose Theatre, 14
Purlie Victorious (p), 9/28/61, Cort Theatre, 261
Purlie Victorious (p), 3/7/69, Master Theatre, 9, (Equity Library Theatre)
Purple Canary, The (p), 4/22/63, Midway Theatre, 6
Purple Dust (p), 12/27/56, Cherry Lane Theater, 430
Purple Mask, The (p), 1/5/20, Booth Theatre, 139
Purple Road, The (m), 4/7/13, Liberty Theatre, 136
Pursuit of Happiness, The (p), 10/9/33, Avon Theatre, 248
Put It in Writing (r), 5/13/63, Theatre de Lys, 24
Put & Take (r), 8/23/21, Town Hall, 32
Puzzles of 1925 (r), 2/2/25, Fulton Theatre, 104
Pygmalion (p), 10/12/14, Park Theatre, 72
Pygmalion (p), 11/15/26, Guild Theatre, 143
Pygmalion (p), 5/11/27, Forrest Theatre, 2
Pygmalion (p), 1/25/38, Maxine Elliott's Theatre, 2
Pygmalion (p), 12/26/45, Ethel Barrymore Theatre, 179
Pygmalion (p), 10/25/72, Queens Playhouse, 29
Pyramids (p), 7/19/26, George M. Cohan Theatre, 32

Q

Quadrille (p), 11/3/54, Coronet Theatre, 150
Quaker Girl, The (m), 10/23/11, Park Theatre, 240
Quality Street (p), 11/11/01, Knickerbocker Theatre, 64
Quality Street (p), 1/6/08, Empire Theatre, 7
Quarantine (p), 12/16/24, Henry Miller's Theatre, 163
Quare Fellow, The (p), 10/20/58, Circle in the Square, 126
Quarter for the Ladies Room, A (r), 11/12/72, Village Gate, 1
Queen and the Rebels, The (p), 2/25/65, Theatre Four, 22
Queen at Home (p), 12/29/30, Times Square Theatre, 16
Queen Bee (p), 11/12/29, Belmont Theatre, 22
Queen Hatasu of Egypt (p), 5/7/23, Longacre Theatre, 1
Queen High (m), 9/8/26, Ambassador Theatre, 367
Queen o' Hearts (m), 10/10/22, Cohan Theatre, 40
Queen of Greece, The/Homo (p), 4/11/69, La Mama Experimental Theatre Club
Queen of the Moulin Rouge, The (m), 12/7/08, Circle Theatre, 160
Queen of the Movies, The (m), 1/12/14, Globe Theatre, 104
Queen's Husband, The (p), 1/25/28, Playhouse, 125
Queen Victoria (p), 11/15/23, 48th St. Theatre, 44
Queens of France. See Thornton Wilder's Triple Bill
Queer People (p), 2/15/34, National Theatre, 13
Question Mark Exclamation Point (?!) (r), 5/24/73, Little Church Around the Corner, 9
Question, The (p), 12/19/12, Daly's Theatre, 4
Quicksand (p), 2/13/28, Theatre Masque, 24
Quiet Please (p), 11/8/40, Guild Theatre, 16
Quincy Adams Sawyer (p), 8/7/02, Academy of Music, 36
Quinneys' (p), 10/18/15, Maxine Elliott's Theatre, 48
Quo Vadis (p) (Jeannette L. Gilder), 4/9/00, Herald Square Theatre, 32
Quo Vadis (p) (Stanislaus Stange), 4/9/00, New York Theatre, 96
Quo Vadis (p) (Stanislaus Stange), 12/31/00, Academy of Music, 32
Quoat-Quoat (p), 4/13/69, Barbizon-Plaza Theatre, 11, (Le Treteau de Paris)
Quotations from Chairman Mao Tse-Tung (p), 9/30/68, Billy Rose Theatre, 12, (Theatre 1969 Playwrights Repertory)

R

R. U. R. (p), 10/9/22, Garrick Theatre, 182
R. U. R. (p), 2/17/30, Martin Beck Theatre, 16
R. U. R. (p), 12/3/42, Ethel Barrymore Theatre, 4
Rabelais (m), 5/19/70, New York City Center, 16
Race of Hairy Men!, A (p), 4/29/65, Henry Miller's Theatre, 4
Race with the Shadow, The (p), 1/20/24, Garrick Theatre, 5
Rachel (p), 12/1/13, Knickerbocker Theatre, 16
Rack, The (p), 9/15/11, Playhouse, 11
Racket, The (p), 11/22/27, Ambassador Theatre, 120
Racketty-Packetty House (p), 12/23/12, Children's Theatre, 81
Radio City Music Hall Inaugural Program, 12/27/32, Radio City Music Hall, 1
Raffles (p), 11/1/10, Gaiety Theatre, 24
Raffles, the Amateur Cracksman (p), 10/27/03, Princess Theatre, 168
Ragged Army (p), 2/26/34, Selwyn Theatre, 2
Ragged Edge, The (p), 11/25/35, Fulton Theatre, 8
Raiders, The (p), 8/30/05, New York Hippodrome, 176
Raiders, The / A Yankee Circus on Mars (p), 4/12/05, New York Hippodrome, 120
Rain (p), 11/7/22, Maxine Elliott's Theatre, 648
Rain (p), 9/1/24, Gaiety Theatre, 104
Rain (p), 10/11/26, Century Theatre, 16
Rain (p), 2/12/35, Music Box Theatre, 47
Rain (p), 3/23/72, Astor Place Theatre, 7
Rain from Heaven (p), 12/24/34, John Golden Theatre, 99
Rain or Shine (m), 2/9/28, George M. Cohan Theatre, 360
Rainbow (m), 11/21/28, Gallo Theatre, 30
Rainbow (m), 12/18/72, Orpheum Theatre, 48
Rainbow Girl, The (m), 4/1/18, New Amsterdam Theatre, 160
Rainbow Jones (m), 2/13/74, Music Box Theatre, 1
Rainbow Rose (m), 3/16/26, Forrest Theatre, 55

Rainbow, The (p), 3/11/12, Liberty Theatre, 104
Rainmaker, The (p), 10/28/54, Cort Theatre, 124
Rainy Day in Newark, A (p), 10/22/63, Belasco Theatre, 6
Raisin (m), 10/18/73, 46th St. Theatre, 258
Raisin' Hell in the Son (p), 7/2/62, Provincetown Playhouse, 6
Raisin in the Sun, A (p), 3/11/59, Ethel Barrymore Theatre, 530
Rambler Rose (m), 9/10/17, Empire Theatre, 72
Ramblers, The (m), 9/20/26, Lyric Theatre, 291
Ramshackle Inn (p), 1/5/44, Royale Theatre, 216
Rang Tang (p), 7/12/17, Royale Theatre, 119
Ranger, The (p), 9/2/07, Wallack Theatre, 24
Ransom's Folly (p), 1/18/04, Hudson Theatre, 61
Rap, The (p), 4/6/31, Avon Theatre, 60
Rape of Lucretia, The (p), 12/29/48, Ziegfeld Theatre, 23
Rape of the Belt (p), 11/5/60, Martin Beck Theatre, 9
Rapid Transit (p), 4/7/27, Provincetown Playhouse, 18
Rapists, The (p), 6/28/66, Gate Theatre, 35
Raquel Meller, Senorita, 4/14/26, Empire Theatre, 38
Raquel Meller, Senorita, 10/25/26, Henry Miller's Theatre, 16
Rashomon (p), 1/27/59, Music Box Theatre, 159
Rashomon (p), 3/16/64, West Side YMCA, 8
Rashomon (p), 12/6/73, Master Theatre, 12, (Equity Library Theatre)
Rashomon (p), 4/14/73, CSC Repertory Theatre, 11
Rat Race, The (p), 12/22/49, Ethel Barrymore Theatre, 84
Rat's Mass, A (p), 9/17/69, La Mama Experimental Theatre Club
Rat, The (p), 2/10/25, Colonial Theatre, 137
Rate of Exchange (p), 4/1/68, Players Theatre, 1
Rats of Norway, The (p), 4/15/48, Booth Theatre, 4
Rats. See Collision Course
Ratten, Die (p), 4/12/66, New York City Center, 8, (The Bavarian State Theatre)
Rattle of a Simple Man (p), 4/17/63, Booth Theatre, 94
Ravenswood. See Bad Habits
Raw Meat (p), 3/22/33, Provincetown Playhouse, 12
Raymond Hitchcock's Pinwheel (r), 6/15/22, Earl Carroll Theatre, 35
Razzle Dazzle (r), 2/19/51, Arena, Hotel Edison, 8
Ready Money (p), 8/19/12, Maxine Elliott's Theatre, 128
Ready When You Are, C.B.! (p), 12/7/64, Brooks Atkinson Theatre, 80
Real Inspector Hound, The / After Magritte (p), 4/23/72, Theatre Four, 465
Real Reel (p), 4/14/71, La Mama Experimental Theatre Club, 5
Real Thing, The (p), 8/10/11, Maxine Elliott's Theatre, 60
Rebbitzen from Israel, The (m), 10/10/72, Mayfair Theatre, 166
Rebecca (p), 1/18/45, Ethel Barrymore Theatre, 20
Rebecca of Sunnybrook Farm (p), 10/3/10, Republic Theatre, 216
Rebel, The (p), 8/20/00, Academy of Music, 73
Rebellion (p), 10/3/11, Maxine Elliott's Theatre, 15
Rebound (p), 2/3/30, Plymouth Theatre, 124
Recapture (p), 1/29/30, Eltinge Theatre, 23
Recent Killing, A (p), 1/26/73, New Federal Theatre, 9
Reckoning, The (p), 2/12/07, Berkeley Lyceum Theatre, 73
Reckoning, The (p), 9/4/69, St. Marks Playhouse, 94
Reckoning, The / The Literary Sense (p), 1/13/08, Madison Square Theatre, 24
Reclining Figure (p), 10/7/54, Lyceum Theatre, 116
Recluse, The See Six from La Mama (1st Program)
Recorder, The. See The Memory Bank
Rector's Garden, The (p), 3/3/08, Bijou Theatre, 7
Red Blinds (p), 9/30/26, Maxine Elliott's Theatre, 20
Red Canary, The (m), 4/13/14, Lyric Theatre, 16
Red Cat, The (p), 9/19/34, Broadhurst Theatre, 14
Red Cross / Muzeeka (p), 4/28/68, Provincetown Playhouse, 65
Red Dawn, The (p), 8/6/19, 39th St. Theatre, 5
Red Dust (p), 1/2/28, Daly's Theatre, 8
Red Eye of Love (p), 6/12/61, Living Theatre, 161
Red Falcon, The (p), 10/7/24, Broadhurst Theatre, 15
Red Feather (m), 11/9/03, Lyric Theatre, 60
Red Geranium, The (p), 5/8/22, Princess Theatre, 16
Red Gloves (p), 12/4/48, Mansfield Theatre, 113
Red Harvest (p), 3/30/37, National Theatre, 15
Red Hat, The (p), 2/23/72, Blackfriars' Guild Theatre, 38
Red Horse Animation, The, 11/18/70, Guggenheim Museum
Red, Hot and Blue! (m), 10/29/36, Alvin Theatre, 181
Red Kloof, The (p), 9/21/01, Savoy Theatre, 41
Red Light Annie (p), 8/21/23, Morosco Theatre, 89
Red Lily, The. See The Scarlet Lily
Red Mill, The (m), 10/16/45, Ziegfeld Theatre, 531
Red Mill, The (m), 9/24/06, Knickerbocker Theatre, 274
Red Moon, The (m), 5/3/09, Majestic Theatre, 32
Red Pepper (m), 5/29/22, Shubert Theatre, 24
Red Petticoat, The (m), 11/13/12, Daly's Theatre, 61
Red Planet (p), 12/17/32, Cort Theatre, 7
Red Poppy, The (p), 12/20/22, Greenwich Village Theatre, 14
Red Rainbow, A (p), 9/14/53, Royale Theatre, 16
Red Riding Hood / The Heroes (p), 5/18/52, Comedy Club
Red Robe, The (m), 12/25/28, Shubert Theatre, 167
Red Rose, The (m), 6/22/11, Globe Theatre, 76
Red Roses for Me (p), 12/28/55, Booth Theatre, 29
Red Roses for Me (p), 11/27/61, Greenwich Mews Theatre, 176
Red Rust (p), 12/17/29, Martin Beck Theatre, 65
Red Velvet Coat, The / The Coggerers / Mr. Banks of Birmingham (p), 1/20/39, Hudson Theatre, 3
Red White and Black, The (r), 2/24/71, La Mama Experimental Theatre Club, 5
Red White and Black, The (r), 3/30/71, Players Theatre, 8
Red, White and Maddox (m), 1/26/69, Cort Theatre, 41
Red Widow, The (m), 11/6/11, Astor Theatre, 128
Redemption (p), 11/19/28, Ambassador Theatre, 20
Redemption of David Corson, The (p), 1/8/06, Majestic Theatre, 16
Redemption (The Living Corpse) (p), 10/3/18, Plymouth Theatre, 204
Redhead (m), 2/5/59, 46th St. Theatre, 452
Redhead (m), 1/12/68, Master Theatre, 15, (Equity Library Theatre)
Redskin, The (p), 3/1/06, Liberty Theatre, 26
Re-Echo (p), 1/10/34, Forrest Theatre, 5
Reflected Glory (p), 9/21/36, Morosco Theatre, 127
Refrigerators, The (p), 1/27/71, La Mama Experimental Theatre Club, 10
Regeneration, The (p), 9/1/08, Wallack Theatre, 39
Regina (m), 10/31/49, 46th St. Theatre, 56
Regular Feller, A, 9/15/19, Cort Theatre, 31
Regular Guy, A (p), 6/4/31, Hudson Theatre, 36
Rehan, Ada. See Ada Rehan
Rehearsal, The (p), 9/23/63, Royale Theatre, 110
Reinar Después de Morir (Rule After Death) (p) (Spanish Th. Repertory Co.), 11/19/53, Broadhurst Theatre, 31
Reine Morte, La (p), 2/15/66, New York City Center, 4, (Comédie Française)
Rejane, Gabrielle. See Gabrielle Rejane
Rejuvenation of Aunt Mary, The (p), 11/12/07, Garden Theatre, 56
Relapse, or Virtue in Danger, The (p), 11/22/50, Morosco Theatre, 30
Relations (p), 8/20/28, Masque Theatre, 105
Relations. See Friends and Relations
Reliquary of Mr. and Mrs. Potterfield, The. See Four Americans
Reluctant Debutante, The (p), 10/10/56, Henry Miller's Theatre, 134
Remains To Be Seen (p), 10/3/51, Morosco Theatre, 198
Remarkable Mr. Pennypacker, The (p), 12/30/53, Coronet Theatre, 221
Remember the Day (p), 9/25/35, National Theatre, 120
Remnant (p), 11/19/18, Morosco Theatre, 63
Remolienda, La, 2/2/68, Barbizon-Plaza Theatre, 6, (ITUCH Repertory Theatre of Chile)
Remote Control (p), 9/10/29, 48th St. Theatre, 79
Removalists, The (p), 1/20/74, Playhouse 2, 5, (New Phoenix Repertory Co.)
Renard / The Only Jealousy of Emer (m), 1/23/74, La Mama Experimental Theatre Club, 11
Renaud—Barrault Repertory Company. See Madeleine Renaud—Jean-Louis Barrault Repertory Co.
Rendezvous (p), 10/12/32, Broadhurst Theatre, 21
Rendezvous at Senlis (p), 2/27/61, Gramercy Arts Theatre, 10
Rented Earl, The (p), 2/8/15, Maxine Elliott's Theatre, 16
Report, The. See Fireworks
Reprise (p), 5/1/35, Vanderbilt Theatre, 1
Republic, The (m), 4/27/70, Free Store Theatre
Requiem for a Nun (p), 1/30/59, John Golden Theatre, 43
Rescuing Angel, The (p), 10/8/17, Hudson Theatre, 32
Resistible Rise Of Arturo VI, The (p), 12/22/68, Billy Rose Theatre, 15, (Minnesota Theatre Co.)
Respect for Riches (p), 5/11/20, Harris Theatre, 15
Respectful Prostitute, The / Church Street (p) (An Evening of Two Plays), 2/9/48, New Stages Theatre, 40
Respectful Prostitute, The / The Happy Journey to Trenton and Camden (p), 3/16/48, Cort Theatre, 318
Respectfully Yours (p), 5/13/47, Blackfriars' Theatre, 16
Restless Women (p), 12/26/27, Morosco Theatre, 24
Resurrection (p), 2/17/03, Hammerstein's Victoria Theatre, 88
Resurrection, The / Church Street (p), 11/19/34, John Golden Theatre, 2
Retabilillo de Don Cristobal, El / Zapatera Prodigiosa, La (The Puppet Theatre of Don Cristobal / The Shoemaker's Prodigious Wife) (p), 9/1/64, Delacorte Mobile Theatre, 6
Retreat to Pleasure (p), 12/17/40, Belasco Theatre, 23
Return Engagement (p), 11/1/40, John Golden Theatre, 8
Return from Jerusalem, The (p), 1/10/12, Hudson Theatre, 53
Return of Eve, The (p), 3/17/08, Herald Square Theatre, 29
Return of Peter Grimm, The (p), 10/17/11, Belasco Theatre, 231
Return of Peter Grimm, The (p), 9/21/21, Belasco Theatre, 78
Return of the Second City in "20,000 Frozen Grenadiers," The (r), 4/21/66, Square East Theatre, 29
Return of the Vagabond, The (p), 5/17/40, National Theatre, 3
Reunion (p), 4/11/38, Nora Bayes Theatre, 1
Reunion in New York (r), 2/21/40, Little Theatre, 89
Reunion in Vienna (p), 11/16/31, Martin Beck Theatre, 280

Reunion of Sorts (p), 10/14/69, Blackfriars' Theatre, 41
Revellers, The (p), 9/7/09, Maxine Elliott's Theatre, 15
Revelry (p), 9/12/27, Masque Theatre, 49
Revenge of the Law. See A Coney Island Cycle
Revenge, or the Pride of Lillian Le Mar / Mary's Manoeuvres (p), 2/25/13, Lyceum Theatre, 1
Revenge with Music (m), 11/28/34, New Amsterdam Theatre, 158
Revenger's Tragedy, The (p), 2/9/74, Abbey Theatre, 17, (CSC Repertory)
Revisor (The Inspector General) (p), 2/18/35, Majestic Theatre, 11
Revolt (p), 10/31/28, Vanderbilt Theatre, 29
Revolt, The (p), 4/1/15, Maxine Elliott's Theatre, 36
Revue of Revues, The (r), 9/27/11, Winter Garden Theatre, 55
Revue of the Classics / Hubbies in Distress (p), 4/12/21, Greenwich Village Theatre, 8
Revue Russe, 10/5/22, Booth Theatre, 20
Rhapsody (r), 11/22/44, Century Theatre, 13
Rhapsody in Black (r), 5/4/31, Sam H. Harris Theatre, 80
Rhapsody, The (p), 9/15/30, Cort Theatre, 16
Rhinoceros (p), 1/9/61, Longacre Theatre, 240
Rhinoceros (p), 9/18/61, Longacre Theatre, 16
Rich Full Life, The (p), 11/9/45, John Golden Theatre, 27
Rich Man, Poor Man (p), 10/5/16, 48th St. Theatre, 44
Rich Man's Son, A (p), 11/4/12, Harris Theatre, 32
Rich Mr. Hoggenheimer, The (m), 10/22/06, Wallack Theatre, 187
Rich Mrs. Repton, The (p), 11/16/04, Criterion Theatre, 5
Richard Carvel (p), 9/11/00, Empire Theatre, 128
Richard Farina: Long Time Coming and a Long Time Gone (m), 11/17/71, Fortune Theatre, 7
Richard II (p) (Maurice Evans), 2/5/37, St. James Theatre, 132
Richard II (p), 9/15/37, St. James Theatre, 38
Richard II (p) (Maurice Evans), 4/1/40, St. James Theatre, 32
Richard II (p) (Maurice Evans), 1/24/51, N.Y. City Center, 15
Richard II (p) (John Neville-Old Vic Co.), 10/23/56, Winter Garden Theatre, 27
Richard II (p) (Ben Hayes), 8/28/61, Wollman Memorial Skating Rink, 12
Richard III (p), 3/6/20, Plymouth Theatre, 27
Richard III (p), 1/1/21, Lexington Theatre, 2
Richard III (p), 12/26/21, Lexington Theatre, 2
Richard III (p), 3/29/30, Shubert Theatre, 2
Richard III (p) (Fritz Leiber), 1/3/31, Ambassador Theatre, 3
Richard III (p) (Walter Hampden), 12/27/34, 44th St. Theatre, 7
Richard III (p), 3/24/43, Forrest Theatre, 11
Richard III (p) (Richard Whorf), 2/8/49, Booth Theatre, 23
Richard III (p) (José Ferrer), 12/9/53, New York City Center, 15
Richard III (p) (George C. Scott), 11/25/57, Heckscher Theatre, 40
Richard Lovelace (p), 9/9/01, Garden Theatre, 40
Richard Morse Mime Theatre, The, 11/10/73, Theresa L. Kaufman Concert Hall, 5
Richard of Bordeaux (p), 2/14/34, Empire Theatre, 39
Richard Savage (p), 2/4/01, Lyceum Theatre, 26
Richelieu (p), 12/26/29, Hampden Theatre, 88
Richelieu (p), 12/26/34, 44th St. Theatre, 10
Richest Girl, The (p), 3/1/09, Criterion Theatre, 24
Richter's Wife (p), 2/27/05, Manhattan Theatre, 5
Riddle Me This (p), 2/25/32, John Golden Theatre, 100
Riddle Me This (p), 3/14/33, Hudson Theatre, 71
Riddle Woman, The (p), 10/23/18, Harris Theatre, 165
Ride a Black Horse (p), 5/25/71, St. Marks Playhouse, 24
Ride Across Lake Constance, The (p), 1/13/72, Forum Theatre, 20
Ride the Winds (m), 5/16/74, Bijou Theatre, 3
Rider of Dreams, The / Granny Maumee / Simon the Cyrenian (p), 4/5/17, Garden Theatre
Riders to the Sea (p), 11/4/32, Martin Beck Theatre, 2
Riders to the Sea (p), 12/7/34, John Golden Theatre, 2
Riders to the Sea / In the Shadow of the Glen / The Tinkers Wedding. See Three Plays by Synge, 3/6/57, Theatre East
Riders to the Sea / The Workhouse Ward (p), 8/4/20, Bramhall Theatre, 34
Right Age to Marry, The (p), 2/15/26, 49th St. Theatre, 33
Right Girl, The (m), 3/15/21, Times Square Theatre, 98
Right Honorable Gentleman, The (p), 10/19/65, Billy Rose Theatre, 118
Right Next to Broadway (p), 2/21/44, Bijou Theatre, 15
Right of Happiness (p), 4/2/31, Vanderbilt Theatre, 9
Right of Way, The (p), 11/4/07, Wallack Theatre, 34
Right This Way (m), 1/5/38, 46th St. Theatre, 14
Right To Be Happy, The (p), 3/26/12, Hudson Theatre, 31
Right To Dream, The (p), 5/26/24, Punch and Judy Theatre, 16
Right to Happiness, The (p), 1/11/12, Bijou Theatre, 12
Right To Kill, The (p), 2/15/26, Garrick Theatre, 16
Right To Love, The (p), 6/8/25, Wallack Theatre, 16
Right to Strike, The (p), 10/24/21, Comedy Theatre, 8
Right You Are If You Think You Are (p), 2/23/27, Guild Theatre, 58
Right You Are If You Think You Are (p), 3/5/64, Phoenix Theatre, 42
Right You Are (If You Think You Are) (p), 11/22/66, Lyceum Theatre, 42, (APA-Phoenix)
Right You Are If You Think You Are (p), 10/11/72, Roundabout Theatre, 31
Righteous Are Bold, The (p), 12/22/55, Holiday Theatre, 68
Rimers of Eldritch, The (p), 2/20/67, Cherry Lane Theatre, 32
Ring Around Elizabeth (p), 11/17/41, Playhouse, 10
Ring Round the Bathtub (p), 4/29/72, Martin Beck Theatre, 1
Ring 'Round the Moon (p), 11/23/50, Martin Beck Theatre, 68
Ring Two (p), 11/22/39, Henry Miller's Theatre, 5
Ringmaster, The (p), 8/9/09, Maxine Elliott's Theatre, 32
Ringside (p), 8/29/28, Broadhurst Theatre, 37
Ringside Seat (p), 11/22/38, Guild Theatre, 7
Rio Grande (p), 4/4/16, Empire Theatre, 55
Rio Rita (m), 2/2/27, Ziegfeld Theatre, 504
Riot (p), 12/19/68, Broadway United Church, 31, (OM Theatre Workshop)
Riot Act, The (p), 3/7/63, Cort Theatre, 44
Rip Van Winkle (p), 10/9/05, Wallack Theatre, 16
Rip Van Winkle (p), 7/15/47, New York City Center, 15
Ripples (m), 2/11/30, New Amsterdam Theatre, 55
Rise of Rosie O'Reilly, The (m), 12/25/23, Liberty Theatre, 97
Rise of Silas Lapham, The (p), 11/25/19, Garrick Theatre, 47
Rising of the Moon, The (p), 10/20/32, Martin Beck Theatre, 2
Rising of the Moon, The / Twenty Days in the Shade (p), 2/24/08, Savoy Theatre, 24
Rising Son, The (p), 10/27/24, Klaw Theatre, 16
Rita Coventry (p), 2/19/23, Bijou Theatre, 24
Ritzy (p), 2/10/30, Longacre Theatre, 32
Rivalry, The (p), 2/7/59, Bijou Theatre, 81
Rivals, The (p), 12/16/12, 39th St. Theatre
Rivals, The (p), 6/5/22, Empire Theatre, 8
Rivals, The (p), 5/7/23, 48th St. Theatre, 24
Rivals, The (p), 3/13/30, Erlanger Theatre, 20
Rivals, The (p), 1/14/42, Shubert Theatre, 54
River Line, The (p), 1/2/57, Carnegie Hall Playhouse, 15
River Niger, The (p), 12/5/72, St. Marks Playhouse, 120
River Niger, The (p), 3/27/73, Brooks Atkinson Theatre, 280
River, The. See Friday Night
Riverside Drive (p), 2/4/64, Theatre de Lys, 15
Riverwind (m), 12/11/62, Actors Playhouse, 443
Riverwind (m), 5/3/73, Master Theatre, 19, (Equity Library Theatre)
Riviera Girl, The (m), 9/24/17, New Amsterdam Theatre, 78
Road to Arcady, The (p), 11/25/12, Berkeley Theatre, 11
Road to Happiness, The (p), 8/30/15, Shubert Theatre, 48
Road to Happiness, The (p), 5/2/27, Forrest Theatre, 2
Road to Mandalay, The (m), 3/1/16, Park Theatre, 21
Road to Rome, The (p), 1/31/27, Playhouse, 392
Road to Rome, The (p), 5/21/28, Playhouse, 48
Road to Yesterday, The (p), 12/31/06, Herald Square Theatre, 216
Road Together, The (p), 1/17/24, Frazee Theatre, 1
Roads of Destiny (p), 11/27/18, Republic Theatre, 101
Roadside (p), 9/29/30, Longacre Theatre, 11
Roar China (p), 10/27/30, Martin Beck Theatre, 72
Roar Like a Dove (p), 5/21/64, Booth Theatre, 20
Roar of the Greasepaint—The Smell of the Crowd, The (m), 5/16/65, Shubert Theatre, 232
Roarshock. See Playwrights Cooperative Festival
Rob Roy (m), 9/15/13, Liberty Theatre, 24
Robbery, The (p) / Chinese Love (m) / Bridges (p) / The Choir Rehearsal (m), 2/28/13, Punch and Judy Theatre, 12
Robert Burns (p), 1/28/05, Carnegie Lyceum Theatre, 1
Robert E. Lee (p), 11/20/23, Ritz Theatre, 15
Robert Emmet (p), 8/18/02, 14th St. Theatre, 80
Robert Emmet (p), 12/28/04, 14th St. Theatre, 24
Roberta (m), 11/18/33, New Ambassador Theatre, 294
Robin Hood (m), 9/8/02, Academy of Music, 32
Robin Hood (m), 5/6/12, New Amsterdam Theatre, 64
Robin Hood (m), 11/18/29, Jolson Theatre, 16
Robin Hood (m), 1/27/32, Erlanger Theatre, 29
Robin Hood (m), 11/7/44, Adelphi Theatre, 15
Robin Landing (p), 11/18/37, 46th St. Theatre, 12
Robinson Crusoe, Jr. (m), 2/17/16, Winter Garden Theatre, 139
Rock Me, Julie (p), 2/3/31, Royale Theatre, 7
Rock-a-Bye Baby (m), 5/22/18, Astor Theatre, 85
Rockbound (p), 4/19/29, Cort Theatre, 19
Rockefeller and The Red Indians (p), 10/24/68, Ethel Barrymore Theatre, 4
Rocket to the Moon (p), 11/24/38, Belasco Theatre, 131
Roger Bloomer (p), 3/1/23, 48th St. Theatre, 50
Rogers Brothers in Central Park, The (m), 9/17/00, Hammerstein's Victoria Theatre, 72
Rogers Brothers in Harvard, The (m), 9/1/02, Knickerbocker Theatre, 63
Rogers Brothers in Ireland, The (m), 9/4/05, Liberty Theatre, 106
Rogers Brothers in Ireland, The (m), 9/3/06, New York Theatre, 16
Rogers Brothers in London, The (m), 9/7/03, Knickerbocker Theatre, 64
Rogers Brothers in Panama, The (m), 9/2/07, Broadway Theatre, 71
Rogers Brothers in Paris, The (m), 9/5/04, New Amsterdam Theatre, 72

Rogers Brothers in Washington, The (m), 9/2/01, Knickerbocker Theatre, 49
Roi se Meurt, Le (p), 4/15/74, American Place Theatre, 9, (Le Treteau de Paris)
Roll, Sweet Chariot (p), 10/2/34, Cort Theatre, 7
Rollicking Girl, The (m), 5/1/05, Herald Square Theatre, 192
Rollicking Girl, The (m), 4/16/06, New York Theatre, 32
Rolling Stones (p), 8/17/15, Harris Theatre, 115
Rolo's Wild Oat (p), 11/23/20, Punch and Judy Theatre, 34
Roly Poly / Without the Law, 11/21/12, Broadway Theatre, 60
Roly-Boly Eyes (m), 9/25/19, Knickerbocker Theatre, 100
Roman Candle (p), 2/3/60, Cort Theatre, 5
Roman Servant, A (p), 12/1/34, Longacre Theatre, 9
Romance (p), 2/10/13, Maxine Elliott's Theatre, 160
Romance (p), 2/28/21, Playhouse, 96
Romance and Arabella (p), 10/17/17, Harris Theatre, 29
Romance of Athlone, A (p), 3/18/01, 14th St. Theatre, 16
Romancin' Round (p), 10/3/27, Little Theatre, 24
Romanesques, The / Sweet and Twenty (p), 1/13/02, Madison Square Theatre, 32
Romanoff and Juliet (p), 10/10/57, Plymouth Theatre, 389
Romantic Age, The (p), 11/14/22, Comedy Theatre, 31
Romantic Mr. Dickens (p), 12/2/40, Playhouse, 8
Romantic Young Lady, The (p), 5/4/26, Neighborhood Playhouse, 25
Romantic Young Lady, The (p), 5/4/27, Forrest Theatre, 1
Romeo and Jeanette (p), 12/11/69, Master Theatre, 12, (Equity Library Theatre)
Romeo and Juliet (p), 2/16/03, Mrs. Osborn's Playhouse, 9
Romeo and Juliet (p) (Edmund Breese-Fernanda Eliscu), 5/25/03, Knickerbocker Theatre, 8
Romeo and Juliet (p) (George Ralph-Khyva St. Albans), 11/22/15, 44th St. Theatre, 24
Romeo and Juliet (p), 1/1/21, Lexington Theatre, 2
Romeo and Juliet (p), 12/26/21, Lexington Theatre, 2
Romeo and Juliet (p) (Fritz Leiber), 1/19/22, 48th St. Theatre, 2
Romeo and Juliet (p), 12/27/22, Longacre Theatre, 29
Romeo and Juliet (p), 1/24/23, Henry Miller's Theatre, 161
Romeo and Juliet (p), 11/12/23, Jolson Theatre, 7
Romeo and Juliet (p), 12/15/23, Times Square Theatre, 9
Romeo and Juliet (p) (Eva Le Gallienne-Donald Cameron), 4/21/30, Civic Repertory Theatre, 16
Romeo and Juliet (p), 10/6/30, Civic Repertory Theatre, 41
Romeo and Juliet (p), 2/1/33, Shakespeare Theatre, 13
Romeo and Juliet (p) (Basil Rathbone-Katharine Cornell), 12/20/34, Martin Beck Theatre, 78
Romeo and Juliet (p) (Maurice Evans-Katharine Cornell), 12/23/35, Martin Beck Theatre, 16
Romeo and Juliet (p), 5/9/40, 51st St. Theatre, 36
Romeo and Juliet (p) (Douglas Watson-Olivia de Havilland), 3/10/51, Broadhurst Theatre, 49
Romeo and Juliet (p), 2/23/56, Jan Hus House, 78
Romeo and Juliet (p) (John Neville-Claire Bloom), 10/24/56, Winter Garden Theatre, 29, (Old Vic Co.)
Romeo and Juliet (p) (Old Vic Co.), 2/13/62, New York City Center, 16
Romeo and Juliet (p) (Richard Novello-Sandra Mac Donald), 4/2/62, Midway Theatre, 3
Romeo and Juliet (p), 8/25/65, Delacorte Mobile Theatre, 12
Romeo and Juliet (p), 2/21/67, N.Y. City Center, 8, (Bristol Old Vic)
Romeo and Juliet (p), 8/14/68, Delacorte Theatre, 21
Romulus (p), 1/10/62, Music Box Theatre, 69
Ronde, La (p), 6/27/55, Circle in the Square, 132
Ronde, La (p), 5/9/60, Theatre Marquee, 272
Rondelay (m), 11/5/69, Hudson West Theatre, 11
Roof, The (p), 10/30/31, Charles Hopkins Theatre, 27
Room in Red and White, A (p), 1/18/36, 46th St. Theatre, 25
Room of Dreams, 11/3/30, Empire Theatre, 13
Room Service (p), 5/19/37, Cort Theatre, 496
Room Service (p), 4/6/53, Playhouse, 16
Room Service (p), 5/12/70, Edison Theatre, 71
Room, The / A Slight Ache (p), 12/9/64, Writers Stage Theatre, 343
Room 349 (p), 4/21/30, National Theatre, 15
Roomful of Roses, A (p), 10/17/55, Playhouse, 88
Rooming House, The. See Transfers
Rooms (Better Luck Next Time / A Walk in Dark Places) (p), 1/27/66, Cherry Lane Theatre, 54
Roosty (p), 2/14/38, Lyceum Theatre, 8
Roots (p), 3/6/61, Mayfair Theatre, 72
Roots (p), 1/8/64, Master Theatre, 9, (Equity Library Theatre)
Rope (p), 2/22/28, Biltmore Theatre, 32
Rope (p), 7/17/62, Actors Playhouse, 8
Rope Dancers, The (p), 11/20/57, Cort Theatre, 189
Rope's End (p), 9/19/29, Theatre Masque, 100
Rope, The / A Week from Today (p), 11/23/65, Theatre de Lys, 1, (ANTA Matinee)
Rosa Machree (p), 1/9/22, Lexington Theatre, 8
Rosalee Pritchett / Perry's Mission (p), 1/12/71, St. Marks Playhouse, 48
Rosalie (m), 1/10/28, New Amsterdam Theatre, 327
Rosalind / The Duke of Killicrankie (p), 9/6/15, Lyceum Theatre, 48
Rosalinda (m), 10/28/42, 44th St. Theatre, 520
Rosary, The (p), 10/24/10, Garden Theatre, 24
Rose (p), 10/28/69, Provincetown Playhouse, 8
Rose Bernd (p), 9/26/22, Longacre Theatre, 87
Rose Briar (p), 12/25/22, Empire Theatre, 89
Rose Girl, The (m), 2/11/20, Ambassador Theatre, 99
Rose in the Wilderness (p), 1/4/49, Master Institute Theatre, 2
Rose Maid, The (m), 4/22/12, Globe Theatre, 176
Rose o' Plymouth-town, A (p), 9/29/02, Manhattan Theatre, 21
Rose of Algeria, The (m), 9/20/09, Herald Square Theatre, 40
Rose of Alhambra, The (m), 2/4/07, Majestic Theatre, 26
Rose of China, The (m), 11/25/19, Lyric Theatre, 47
Rose of Panama, The (m), 1/22/12, Daly's Theatre, 24
Rose of Persia, The (m), 9/6/00, Daly's Theatre, 25
Rose of Stamboul, The (m), 3/7/22, Century Theatre, 111
Rose of the Rancho, The (p), 11/27/06, Belasco Theatre, 240
Rose of the Rancho, The (p), 8/31/07, Belasco Theatre, 87
Rose of the Rancho, The (p), 12/30/07, Academy of Music, 32
Rose Tattoo, The (p), 2/3/51, Martin Beck Theatre, 300
Rose Tattoo, The (p), 10/20/66, New York City Center, 78
Rose, The / A Light from St. Agnes / The Eyes of the Heart (p), 3/27/05, Manhattan Theatre, 3
Roseanne (p), 12/29/23, Greenwich Village Theatre, 41
Rosebloom (p), 1/5/72, Eastside Playhouse, 23
Rosedale (p), 4/18/13, Lyric Theatre, 23
Rose-Marie (m), 9/2/24, Imperial Theatre, 581
Rose-Marie (m), 1/24/27, Century Theatre, 49
Rosemary (p), 1/12/15, Empire Theatre, 15
Rosemary / The Alligators (p), 11/15/60, York Playhouse, 40
Rosencrantz and Guildenstern Are Dead (p), 10/16/67, Alvin Theatre, 421
Rosencrantz and Guildenstern Are Dead (p), 9/17/70, CSC Repertory Theatre, 45
Rosencrantz and Guildenstern Are Dead (p), 9/14/72, CSC Repertory Theatre
Rosencrantz and Guildenstern Are Dead (p), 1/5/74, Abbey Theatre, 35, (CSC Repertory)
Rosmersholm (p), 3/28/04, Princess Theatre, 8
Rosmersholm (p), 12/30/07, Lyric Theatre, 30
Rosmersholm (p), 2/7/24, Vanderbilt Theatre, 1
Rosmersholm (p), 5/5/25, 52nd St. Theatre, 47
Rosmersholm (p), 12/2/35, Sam S. Shubert Theatre, 8
Rosmersholm (p), 4/11/62, Fourth St. Theatre, 119
Ross (p), 12/26/61, Eugene O'Neill Theatre, 159
Rothschilds, The (m), 10/19/70, Lunt-Fontanne Theatre, 505
Rotters, The (p), 5/23/22, 39th St. Theatre, 16
Rouget de l'Isle / A Cigarette Maker's Romance (p), 11/12/02, Herald Square Theatre, 14
Round Table, The (p), 2/26/30, Gansevoort Theatre, 10
Round the Town (r), 5/21/24, Century Roof Theatre, 13
Round Trip (p), 5/29/45, Biltmore Theatre, 7
Round Up, The (p), 8/26/07, New Amsterdam Theatre, 155
Round Up, The (p), 8/31/08, Academy of Music, 35
Round with Ring, A (r), 10/27/69, Theatre de Lys, 2, (ANTA Matinee)
Rounders, The (m), 6/25/00, Casino Theatre, 35
Round-Up, The (p), 3/7/32, Majestic Theatre, 9
Route 1 (p), 11/17/64, One Sheridan Square, 1
Royal Box, The (p), 11/20/28, Belmont Theatre, 39
Royal Chef, The (m), 9/1/04, Lyric Theatre, 17
Royal Dramatic Theatre of Sweden, The (The Father, Long Day's Journey into Night, Miss Julie), 5/14/62, Cort Theatre, 8
Royal Family, A (p), 9/5/00, Lyceum Theatre, 175
Royal Family, The (p), 12/28/27, Selwyn Theatre, 343
Royal Family, The (p), 1/10/51, New York City Center, 16
Royal Fandango, A (p), 11/12/23, Plymouth Theatre, 24
Royal Fandango, The, 1/31/21, Neighborhood Playhouse, 14
Royal Fandango, The (Spanish ballet), 5/7/21, Neighborhood Playhouse, 12
Royal Gambit (p), 3/4/59, Sullivan St. Playhouse, 87
Royal Hunt of the Sun, The (p), 10/26/65, ANTA Theatre, 261
Royal Mounted, The (p), 4/6/08, Garrick Theatre, 32
Royal Rival, A (p), 8/26/01, Criterion Theatre, 112
Royal Rogue, A, 12/24/00, Broadway Theatre, 30
Royal Vagabond, The (m), 2/17/19, Cohan and Harris Theatre, 208
Royal Virgin, The (p), 3/17/30, Booth Theatre, 8
Rubicon, The (p), 2/21/22, Hudson Theatre, 135
Ruddigore (m), 5/20/27, Cosmopolitan Theatre, 19
Ruddigore (m), 8/10/31, Erlanger Theatre, 16
Ruddigore (m), 9/24/34, Martin Beck Theatre, 6
Ruddigore (m), 10/22/36, Martin Beck Theatre, 8
Ruddigore (m), 3/2/44, Ambassador Theatre, 3
Ruddigore (m), 10/20/55, Shubert Theatre, 8, (D'Oyly Carte Opera Co.)
Ruddigore (m), 4/14/60, Jan Hus House

Ruddigore (m), 12/23/64, New York City Center, 5, (D'Oyly Carte Opera Co.)
Ruddigore (m), 8/26/65, Jan Hus Playhouse, 28, (American Savoyards)
Ruddigore (m), 11/22/66, New York City Center, 4, (D'Oyly Carte Opera Co.)
Ruddigore (m), 3/4/71, Master Theatre, 22, (Equity Library Theatre)
Ruffian on the Stair, The. See Crimes of Passion
Rufus LeMaire's Affairs (r), 3/28/27, Majestic Theatre, 56
Rugantino (m), 2/6/64, Mark Hellinger Theatre, 28
Rugged Path, The (p), 11/10/45, Plymouth Theatre, 81
Ruggles of Red Gap (p), 12/25/15, Fulton Theatre, 33
"Ruined" Lady, The (p), 1/19/20, Playhouse, 33
Ruint (p), 4/7/25, Provincetown Playhouse, 30
Rule of Three, The (p), 2/16/14, Harris Theatre, 80
Rules of the Game, The (p), 12/19/60, Gramercy Arts Theatre, 46
Ruling Power, The, 3/14/04, Garrick Theatre, 23
Rumple (m), 11/6/57, Alvin Theatre, 45
Run, Little Chillun! (p), 3/1/33, Lyric Theatre, 130
Run, Little Chillun! (p), 8/11/43, Hudson Theatre, 16
Run Sheep Run (p), 11/3/38, Windsor Theatre, 12
Runaway, The (p), 10/9/11, Lyceum Theatre, 64
Runaways, The (m), 5/11/03, Casino Theatre, 167
Runnin' Wild (m), 10/29/23, Colonial Theatre, 224
Running for Office (m), 4/27/03, 14th St. Theatre, 48
Russell Patterson's Sketchbook (r), 2/6/60, Maidman Playhouse, 3
Russet Mantle (p), 1/16/36, Masque Theatre, 116
Russian Bank (p), 5/24/40, St. James Theatre, 11
Russian People, The (p), 12/29/42, Guild Theatre, 39
Rust (p), 1/31/24, Greenwich Village Theatre, 85
Ruth Draper, 11/14/32, Ritz Theatre, 9
Ruth Draper, 12/12/32, Ritz Theatre, 16
Ruth Draper, 12/26/34, Ethel Barrymore Theatre, 25
Ruth Draper, 1/19/36, Booth Theatre, 9
Ruth Draper, 1/12/47, Empire Theatre, 42
Ruth Draper, 12/28/47, Empire Theatre, 26
Ruth Draper, 1/25/54, Vanderbilt Theatre, 58
Ruth Draper, 12/25/56, Playhouse, 7
Ruth Draper and Paul Draper, 12/26/54, Bijou Theatre, 24
Rutherford and Son (p), 12/24/12, Little Theatre, 63
Rutherford and Son (p), 4/12/27, Grove St. Theatre, 23
Ryan Girl, The (p), 9/24/45, Plymouth Theatre, 48

S

S. S. Glencairn (p), 11/3/24, Provincetown Playhouse, 99
S. S. Glencairn (p), 1/9/29, Provincetown Playhouse, 96
S. S. Glencairn (p), 5/20/48, New York City Center, 14
S. S. Glencairn. See The Moon of the Caribbees / In the Zone / Bound East for Cardiff / The Long Voyage Home
S. S. Tenacity, The (p), 1/2/22, Belmont Theatre, 67
Sabrina Fair (p), 11/11/53, National Theatre, 318
Sacco-Vanzetti (m), 2/7/69, Master Theatre, 15, (Equity Library Theatre)
Sacrament of Judas, The / Raffles, the Amateur Cracksman (p), 12/21/03, Princess Theatre, 16
Sacred and Profane Love (p), 2/23/20, Morosco Theatre, 88
Sacred Flame, The (p), 11/19/28, Henry Miller's Theatre, 24
Sacred Flame, The (p), 10/7/52, President Theatre, 23
Sacrifice (p), 12/10/20, Garrick Theatre, 5
Sacrifice, The (p), 5/2/21, Greenwich Village Theatre, 2
Sadie Love (p), 11/29/15, Gaiety Theatre, 80
Sadie Thompson (m), 11/16/44, Alvin Theatre, 60
Safari 300 (r), 7/12/72, Mayfair Theatre, 17
Sag Harbor (p), 9/27/00, Republic Theatre, 76
Sail Away (m), 10/3/61, Broadhurst Theatre, 167
Sailor, Beware! (p), 9/28/33, Lyceum Theatre, 500
Sailor, Beware! (p), 5/3/35, Lafayette Theatre, 16
Sailors of Cattaro (p), 12/10/34, Civic Repertory Theatre, 96
Saint Joan (p), 12/28/23, Garrick Theatre, 214
Saint Joan (p) (Katharine Cornell), 3/9/36, Martin Beck Theatre, 89
Saint Joan (p) (Uta Hagen), 10/4/51, Cort Theatre, 140
Saint Joan (p) (Siobhan McKenna), 9/11/56, Phoenix Theatre, 77
Saint Joan (p), 2/20/62, New York City Center, 11, (Old Vic Co.)
Saint Joan (p), 1/4/68, Vivian Beaumont Theatre, 44
Saint of Bleecker Street, The (m), 12/27/54, Broadway Theatre, 92
Saint, The (p), 10/11/24, Greenwich Village Theatre, 17
Saint Wench (p), 1/2/33, Lyceum Theatre, 12
Saintliness of Margery Kempe, The (p), 2/2/59, York Playhouse, 17
Sakura (p), 12/25/28, Belmont Theatre, 7
Salad Days (m), 11/10/58, Barbizon-Plaza Theatre, 80
Salad of the Mad Cafe (r), 3/31/64, Masque Theatre, 16
Salamander, The (p), 10/23/14, Harris Theatre, 14
Sally (m), 12/21/20, New Amsterdam Theatre, 561
Sally (m), 9/17/23, New Amsterdam Theatre, 24
Sally (m), 5/6/48, Martin Beck Theatre, 36
Sally, George and Martha (p), 12/20/71, Theatre de Lys, 2, (ANTA Matinee)
Sally in Our Alley (m), 8/29/02, Broadway Theatre, 67
Sally, Irene and Mary (m), 9/4/22, Casino Theatre, 318
Sally, Irene and Mary (m), 3/23/25, 44th St. Theatre, 16
Salome (p), 5/22/22, Klaw Theatre, 8
Salome / The Chip Woman's Fortune (p), 5/7/23, Frazee Theatre, 8
Salome / The Marriage Game (p), 12/20/13, Comedy Theatre, 8
Salomy Jane (p), 1/19/07, Liberty Theatre, 122
Salomy Jane (p), 9/2/07, Academy of Music, 33
Salt Water (p), 11/26/29, John Golden Theatre, 87
Salut au Monde, 4/22/22, Neighborhood Playhouse, 8
Salut à Molière / Piéton de l'Air (p), 3/3/64, New York City Center, 8, (Théâtre de France, Renaud-Barrault Co.)
Saluta (m), 8/28/34, Imperial Theatre, 40
Salvation (p), 1/31/28, Empire Theatre, 31
Salvation, 3/11/69, Village Gate
Salvation (m), 9/24/69, Jan Hus Playhouse, 239
Salvation Nell (p), 11/17/08, Hackett Theatre, 71
Salvation on a String (Chair Endowed / The No 'Count Boy / Supper for the Dead) (p), 7/6/54, Theatre de Lys, 8
Salzburg Marionette Theatre (The Magic Flute; The Abduction from the Seraglio; Fledermaus; Snow White; Rumpelstiltskin) (m), 12/17/64, Town Hall, 39
Sam Abramvitch (p), 1/18/27, National Theatre, 14
Sam Houston (p), 10/16/06, Garden Theatre, 22
Sambo (m), 12/21/69, Public/Anspacher Theatre, 25
Sambo (m), 7/14/70, Delacorte Mobile Theatre, 22
Sammy on Broadway, 4/23/74, Uris Theatre, 14
Samson (p), 10/19/08, Criterion Theatre, 152
Samson and Delilah (p), 11/17/20, Greenwich Village Theatre, 139
San Fernando Valley. See Playwrights Cooperative Festival
San Toy (m), 10/1/00, Daly's Theatre, 65
San Toy (m), 3/4/01, Daly's Theatre, 103
San Toy (m), 4/7/02, Daly's Theatre, 32
San Toy (m), 4/17/05, Daly's Theatre, 24
Sancho Panza (m), 11/26/23, Hudson Theatre, 40
Sandalwood (p), 9/22/26, Gaiety Theatre, 39
Sandhog (m), 11/23/54, Phoenix Theatre, 48
Sandro Botticelli (p), 3/26/23, Provincetown Playhouse, 24
Sands of the Negev (p), 10/19/54, President Theatre, 64
Santa Claus / Calvary / Escurial (p), 7/21/60, Gate Theatre, 14
Sap of Life, The (m), 10/2/61, One Sheridan Square, 49
Sap Runs High, The (p), 2/4/36, Bijou Theatre, 24
Sap, The (p), 12/15/24, Apollo Theatre, 35
Sapho (p), 2/5/00, Wallack Theatre, 84
Sapho (p), 11/12/00, Wallack Theatre, 28
Sapho (p), 12/11/05, Herald Square Theatre, 8
Sapphire Ring, The (p), 4/15/25, Selwyn Theatre, 13
Sappho (p), 1/11/60, Renata Theatre, 9
Sappho and Phaon (p), 10/21/07, Lyric Theatre, 7
Sarah and the Sax / The Dirty Old Man (p), 5/14/64, Theatre de Lys, 16
Sarah Bernhardt Repertory, 12/5/10, Globe Theatre, 32
Sarah Bernhardt Repertory, 6/19/11, Globe Theatre, 4
Sarah Bernhardt Repertory, 12/4/16, Empire Theatre, 24
Sarah Bernhardt Repertory, 9/1/17, Knickerbocker Theatre, 16
Saratoga (m), 12/7/59, Winter Garden Theatre, 80
Sari (m), 1/13/14, Liberty Theatre, 151
Sari (m), 1/29/30, Liberty Theatre, 15
Satellite (p), 11/20/35, Bijou Theatre, 1
Satisfaction Guaranteed / Open 24 Hours (p), 2/11/69, Actors Playhouse, 22
Saturday It Rained / The White Dress / The Way Out / The March Heir / Family Exit / Counsel's Opinion (p), 12/13/32, Chanin Auditorium, 5
Saturday Night (p), 2/9/24, Cherry Lane Theatre, 8
Saturday Night (p), 10/25/26, Civic Repertory Theatre, 14
Saturday Night (p), 2/25/68, Sheridan Square Playhouse, 66
Saturday Night, A (p), 2/28/33, Playhouse, 39
Saturday Night Kid, The (p), 5/15/58, Provincetown Playhouse, 14
Saturday's Children (p), 1/26/27, Booth Theatre, 310
Saturday's Children (p), 4/9/28, Forrest Theatre, 16
Saturday to Monday (p), 10/1/17, Bijou Theatre, 16
Sauce for the Goose (p), 4/15/11, Playhouse, 2
Saucy Sally (p), 4/4/04, Lyceum Theatre, 28
Savage Rhythm (p), 12/31/31, John Golden Theatre, 12
Savages Under the Skin (p), 3/24/27, Greenwich Village Theatre, 28
Save It for Your Death Bed. See Triple Play
Save Me a Place at Forest Lawn / The Last Minstrel (p), 5/8/63, Pocket Theatre, 38
Save Me the Waltz (p), 2/28/38, Martin Beck Theatre, 8
Saved (p), 10/28/70, Brooklyn Academy of Music, 42, (Chelsea Theatre Center)
Saving Grace, The (p), 9/30/18, Empire Theatre, 96

Saving Grace, The (p), 4/18/63, Writers' Stage Theatre, 29
Say, Darling (p), 4/3/58, ANTA Theatre, 332
Say, Darling (p), 2/25/59, New York City Center, 16
Say, Darling (m), 11/12/65, Master Theatre, 17, (Equity Library Theatre)
Say It With Flowers (p), 12/3/26, Garrick Theatre, 2
Say Nothing (p), 1/27/65, Jan Hus House, 47
Say When (m), 6/26/28, Morosco Theatre, 15
Say When (m), 11/8/34, Imperial Theatre, 76
Say When (m), 12/4/72, Plaza 9 Theatre, 7
Scalawag (p), 3/29/27, 49th St. Theatre, 7
Scandal, The (p), 10/17/10, Garrick Theatre, 16
Scandal, The (p), 9/12/19, 39th St. Theatre, 318
Scandals (see George White's Scandals)
Scapin (m), 12/28/73, Billy Rose Theatre, 1, (City Center Acting Co.)
Scapin / Impromptu at Versailles (p), 3/9/64, Phoenix Theatre, 18
Scapino (p), 3/13/74, Brooklyn Academy of Music, 10, (Young Vic Co.)
Scapino (p), 5/18/74, Circle in the Square / Joseph E. Levine Theatre, 15, (Young Vic Co.)
Scaramouche (p), 10/24/23, Morosco Theatre, 61
Scarecrow, The (p), 1/17/11, Garrick Theatre, 23
Scarecrow, The (p), 6/16/53, Theatre de Lys
Scarlet Fox, The (p), 3/27/28, Masque Theatre, 79
Scarlet Lily, The (p), 1/29/27, Comedy Theatre, 57
Scarlet Lullaby (p), 3/10/68, Masque Theatre, 7
Scarlet Man, The (p), 8/22/21, Henry Miller's Theatre, 16
Scarlet Pages (p), 9/9/29, Morosco Theatre, 78
Scarlet Pimpernel, The (p), 10/24/10, Knickerbocker Theatre, 40
Scarlet Sister Mary (p), 11/25/30, Ethel Barrymore Theatre, 23
Scene of the Crime, The (p), 3/28/40, Fulton Theatre, 12
Scenes from American Life (p), 3/25/71, Forum Theatre, 30
Scent of Flowers, A (p), 10/20/69, Martinique Theatre, 72
Schauspieltruppe Zurich (The Marriage of Mr. Mississippi; Philipp Hotz / The Firebugs; Iphigenia in Tauris) (p), 11/19/69, Barbizon-Plaza Theatre, 13
Schemers (p), 9/15/24, Nora Bayes Theatre, 24
Schiller Theatre (Don Carlos; The Captain of Koepenick) (p), 11/24/64, New York State Theatre, 16
Schloss, Das (p), 11/19/68, Barbizon-Plaza Theatre, 6, (Die Brücke)
School (p), 12/16/13, Playhouse, 1
School Days (m), 9/14/08, Circle Theatre, 32
School for Brides (p), 8/1/44, Royale Theatre, 375
School for Husbands, The (p), 4/3/05, Wallack Theatre, 48
School for Husbands, The (p), 10/16/33, Empire Theatre, 111
School for Scandal, The (p) (Kyrle Bellew), 1/31/02, Wallack Theatre, 1
School for Scandal, The (p) (Ada Rehan), 2/13/05, Liberty Theatre, 8
School for Scandal, The (p), 12/27/09, New Theatre
School for Scandal, The (p), 3/12/23, National Theatre, 4
School for Scandal, The (p), 6/4/23, Lyceum Theatre, 8
School for Scandal, The (p), 10/22/25, Little Theatre, 85
School for Scandal, The (p), 12/6/25, Knickerbocker Theatre, 1
School for Scandal, The (p), 11/10/31, Ethel Barrymore Theatre, 23
School for Scandal, The (p), 6/23/53, Theatre de Lys
School for Scandal, The (p), 3/17/62, Folksbiene Playhouse, 21, (APA Repertory Co.)
School for Scandal, The (p), 1/24/63, Majestic Theatre, 60
School for Scandal, The (p), 11/21/66, Lyceum Theatre, 48, (APA-Phoenix)
School for Scandal, The (p), 9/28/72, Good Shepherd-Faith Church, 10, (City Center Acting Co.)
School for Virtue (p), 4/21/31, Longacre Theatre, 7
School for Wives, The (p), 2/16/71, Lyceum Theatre, 120, (Phoenix Theatre)
School Girl, The (p), 9/1/04, Daly's Theatre, 120
Schoolgirl (p), 11/20/30, Ritz Theatre, 21
Schoolhouse on the Lot (p), 3/22/38, Ritz Theatre, 55
Schoolmaster, The (p), 3/20/28, Provincetown Playhouse, 6
Schwieger (p), 3/23/26, Mansfield Theatre, 31
Score (p), 10/28/70, Martinique Theatre, 23
Scorpion, The (p), 11/27/33, Biltmore Theatre, 8
Scotch Mist (p), 9/20/26, Klaw Theatre, 16
Scotland Yard (p), 9/27/29, Sam H. Harris Theatre, 27
Scott and Zelda (p), 1/7/74, Theatre de Lys, 2, (Matinee Theatre)
Scrambled Wives (p), 8/5/20, Fulton Theatre, 68
Scrap of Paper, A (p), 5/11/14, Empire Theatre, 32
Scrap of Paper, The (p), 9/17/17, Criterion Theatre, 40
Scrape o' the Pen, The (p), 9/26/12, Weber Theatre, 76
Scratch (p), 5/6/71, St. James Theatre, 4
Screens, The (p), 12/2/71, Brooklyn Academy of Music, 27, (Chelsea Theatre Center)
Scuba Duba (p), 10/10/67, New Theatre, 704
Sea Dogs (p), 11/6/39, Maxine Elliott's Theatre, 16
Sea Horse, The (p), 3/3/74, Circle Repertory Theatre, 84
Sea Legs (m), 5/18/37, Mansfield Theatre, 15
Sea Woman, The (p), 8/24/25, Little Theatre, 32
Seacoast of Bohemia (r), 1/10/62, Second City at Square East, 258
Seagull, The (p), 5/20/16, Bandbox Theatre
Seagull, The (p), 4/9/29, Comedy Theatre, 33
Seagull, The (p), 9/16/29, Civic Repertory Theatre, 63
Seagull, The (p), 2/25/30, Waldorf Theatre, 8
Seagull, The (p), 3/28/38, Shubert Theatre, 40
Seagull, The (p), 5/11/54, Phoenix Theatre, 40
Seagull, The (p), 10/22/56, Fourth St. Theatre, 25
Seagull, The (p), 3/20/62, Folksbiene Playhouse, 10, (APA Repertory Co.)
Seagull, The (p), 4/5/64, Belasco Theatre, 32
Seagull, The (p), 10/25/73, Philip Nolan Theatre
Seagull, The (p), 1/23/74, Roundabout Theatre, 105
Seagulls Over Sorrento (p), 9/11/52, John Golden Theatre, 12
Search Me (p), 8/11/15, Gaiety Theatre, 13
Searching for the Sun (p), 2/19/36, 58th St. Theatre, 5
Searching Wind, The (p), 4/12/44, Fulton Theatre, 326
Season Changes, The (p), 12/23/35, Booth Theatre, 8
Season in the Sun (p), 9/28/50, Cort Theatre, 367
Season of Choice (p), 4/13/59, Barbizon-Plaza Theatre, 7
Second Best Bed (p), 6/3/46, Ethel Barrymore Theatre, 8
Second Comin', The (p), 12/8/31, Provincetown Playhouse, 9
Second Fiddle, The (p), 11/21/04, Criterion Theatre, 32
Second Hottest Show in Town, The (r), 6/28/71, Actors Playhouse
Second in Command, The (p), 9/2/01, Empire Theatre, 128
Second in Command, The (p), 11/3/13, Wallack Theatre, 11
Second Little Show, The (r), 9/2/30, Royale Theatre, 63
Second Man, The (p), 4/11/27, Guild Theatre, 178
Second Mrs. Aarons, The. See The World of Mrs. Solomon
Second Mrs. Tanqueray, The (p), 3/6/00, Wallack Theatre, 16
Second Mrs. Tanqueray, The (p), 10/8/02, Garden Theatre, 15
Second Mrs. Tanqueray, The (p), 2/3/13, 39th St. Theatre, 16
Second Mrs. Tanqueray, The (p), 10/27/24, Cort Theatre, 73
Second String, A (p), 4/13/60, Eugene O'Neill Theatre, 29
Second Threshold (p), 1/2/51, Morosco Theatre, 126
Secret Affairs of Mildred Wilde, The (p), 11/14/72, Ambassador Theatre, 23
Secret Concubine, The (p), 3/21/60, Carnegie Hall Playhouse, 6
Secret Life of Walter Mitty, The (m), 10/26/64, Players Theatre, 96
Secret Life of Walter Mitty, The (m), 1/11/73, Master Theatre, 19, (Equity Library Theatre)
Secret of Polichinelle, The (p), 1/19/04, Madison Square Theatre, 124
Secret of Suzanne, The / The Maid as Mistress (m), 5/14/44, Alvin Theatre, 2
Secret Orchard, The (p), 12/16/07, Lyric Theatre, 32
Secret Room, The (p), 11/7/45, Royale Theatre, 21
Secret Service (p), 11/8/15, Empire Theatre, 14
Secret Strings (p), 12/28/14, Longacre Theatre, 24
Secret, The (p), 12/23/13, Belasco Theatre, 143
Secrets (p), 12/25/22, Fulton Theatre, 172
Secrets of the Citizens Correction Committee (p), 10/17/73, Theatre at St. Clement's, 12
Security (p), 3/28/29, Maxine Elliott's Theatre, 24
Seducers, The. See Festival of New Italian Plays
See America First (m), 3/28/16, Maxine Elliott's Theatre, 15
See My Lawyer (p), 9/2/15, Eltinge Theatre, 12
See My Lawyer (p), 9/27/39, Biltmore Theatre, 224
See Naples and Die (p), 9/24/29, Vanderbilt Theatre, 62
See the Jaguar (p), 12/3/52, Cort Theatre, 5
Seed of the Brute (p), 11/1/26, Little Theatre, 72
Seeds in the Wind (p), 4/24/48, Lenox Hill Playhouse, 3
Seeds in the Wind (p), 5/25/48, Empire Theatre, 7
Seeing New York (m), 6/5/06, New York Roof, 75
Seeing Things (p), 6/17/20, Playhouse, 108
Seen But Not Heard (p), 9/17/36, Henry Miller's Theatre, 60
Seeniaya Ptitza (m), 12/28/24, Frolic Theatre, 80
See-Saw (p), 9/23/19, Cohan Theatre, 89
Seesaw (m), 3/18/73, Uris Theatre, 296
Seidman and Son (p), 10/15/62, Belasco Theatre, 216
Self and Lady (p), 10/8/00, Madison Sq. Theatre, 14
Self-Accusation / My Foot My Tutor (p), 4/27/71, Brooklyn Academy of Music, 7, (Chelsea Theatre Center)
Selling of the President, The (m), 3/22/72, Shubert Theatre, 5
Sellout, The (p), 9/6/33, Cort Theatre, 5
Semi-Detached (p), 3/10/60, Martin Beck Theatre, 4
Semi-Detached (p), 10/7/63, Music Box Theatre, 16
Senator Keeps House, The (p), 11/27/11, Garrick Theatre, 80
Send Me No Flowers (p), 12/5/60, Brooks Atkinson Theatre, 40
Sensations (m), 10/25/70, Theatre Four, 16
Sentinels (p), 12/25/31, Biltmore Theatre, 11
Separate Rooms (p), 3/23/40, Maxine Elliott's Theatre, 613
Separate Tables (p), 10/25/56, Music Box Theatre, 332
Septimus (p), 11/22/09, Hackett Theatre, 32
Seremonda (p), 1/1/17, Criterion Theatre, 48
Serena Blandish (p), 1/23/29, Morosco Theatre, 94
Serenade, The (m), 3/4/30, Jolson Theatre, 15
Sergeant Brue (m), 4/24/05, Knickerbocker Theatre, 152
Sergeant Kitty (m), 1/18/04, Daly's Theatre, 55

Serio-Comic Governess, The (p), 9/13/04, New Lyceum Theatre, 41
Serjeant Musgrave's Dance (p), 3/8/66, Theatre de Lys, 135
Serpent—A Ceremony, The, 5/16/69, Public Theatre, 4, (Open Theatre)
Serpent: A Ceremony, The (p), 5/29/70, Washington Square Methodist Church, 3, (Open Theatre)
Serpent's Tooth, A (p), 8/24/22, Little Theatre, 36
Serpent, The: A Ceremony (p), 5/29/70, Washington Square Methodist Church, 3, (Open Theatre)
Servant in the House, The (p), 3/23/08, Savoy Theatre, 80
Servant in the House, The (p), 10/19/08, Savoy Theatre, 48
Servant in the House, The (p), 4/24/18, Vieux Colombier Theatre, 21
Servant in the House, The (p), 5/2/21, Broadhurst Theatre, 3
Servant in the House, The (p), 4/7/25, 48th St. Theatre, 8
Servant in the House, The (p), 5/3/26, Broadhurst Theatre, 8
Servant of Two Masters, A / Beauty and the Beast (p), 1/23/65, Master Theatre, 6, (Equity Library Theatre)
Servant of Two Masters / He Is to Blame (p), 1/9/28, Cosmopolitan Theatre, 16
Servant of Two Masters, The (p) (Piccolo Teatro di Milano), 2/23/60, New York City Center, 16
Servant of Two Masters, The (p), 4/6/72, Master Theatre, 12, (Equity Library Theatre)
Service / A Night at an Inn (p), 4/15/18, Cohan Theatre, 16
Service for Two (p), 8/30/26, Gaiety Theatre, 24
Sesostra / Whirl of Society (m), 3/5/12, Winter Garden Theatre, 136
Set a Thief (p), 2/21/27, Empire Theatre, 80
Set My People Free (p), 11/3/48, Hudson Theatre, 29
Set to Music (r), 1/18/39, Music Box Theatre, 129
Seven (p), 12/27/29, Republic Theatre, 34
Seven Ages of Bernard Shaw, 11/21/66, Theatre de Lys, 2, (ANTA Matinee)
Seven at Dawn, The (p), 4/17/61, Actors Playhouse, 16
Seven Chances (p), 8/8/16, Cohan Theatre, 151
Seven Days (p), 11/10/09, Astor Theatre, 397
Seven Days' Leave (p), 1/17/18, Park Theatre, 156
Seven Days of Mourning (p), 12/16/69, Circle in the Square, 55
Seven Descents of Myrtle, The (p), 3/27/68, Ethel Barrymore Theatre, 29
Seven Keys to Baldpate (p), 9/22/13, Astor Theatre, 320
Seven Keys to Baldpate (p), 5/3/27, Garrick Theatre, 3
Seven Keys to Baldpate (p), 5/27/35, National Theatre, 8
Seven Lively Arts (r), 12/7/44, Ziegfeld Theatre, 182
Seven Meditations on Political Sado-Masochism, 11/9/73, Washington Square Methodist Church, 6, (Living Theatre)
Seven Sisters (p), 2/20/11, Lyceum Theatre, 32
Seven Year Itch, The (p), 11/20/52, Fulton Theatre, 1,141
Seventeen (p), 1/22/18, Booth Theatre, 225
Seventeen (m), 6/21/51, Broadhurst Theatre, 180
Seventeen Seventy Six (1776) (m), 3/16/69, 46th St. Theatre, 1217
Seventh Heart, The (m), 5/2/27, Mayfair Theatre, 16
Seventh Heaven (p), 10/30/22, Booth Theatre, 683
Seventh Heaven (m), 5/26/55, ANTA Theatre, 44
Seventh Trumpet, The (p), 11/21/41, Mansfield Theatre, 11
Seventy, Girls, Seventy (m), 4/15/71, Broadhurst Theatre, 36
Severed Head, A (p), 10/28/64, Royale Theatre, 29
Sex (p), 4/26/26, Daly's Theatre, 375
Sex Fable, The (p), 10/20/31, Henry Miller's Theatre, 33
Sextet (m), 3/3/74, Bijou Theatre, 9
Sextet (Six Aspects of Love) (p), 11/26/58, Royal Playhouse, 31
Sganarelle / Le Mariage Forcé / La Jalousie du Barbouille (p) (An Evening of 3 Farces), 5/6/58, Phoenix Theatre, 8
Sganarelle. See National Theatre of the Deaf
Sh! The Octopus (p), 2/21/28, Royale Theatre, 47
Shades of Night, The / On and Off (p), 4/1/01, Lyceum Theatre, 16
Shades of Night, The / The Lash of a Whip (p), 2/25/01, Lyceum Theatre, 40
Shadow and Substance (p), 1/26/38, John Golden Theatre, 206
Shadow and Substance (p), 11/3/59, Tara Theatre, 137
Shadow of a Gunman, The (p), 10/29/32, Martin Beck Theatre, 1
Shadow of a Gunman, The (p), 11/20/58, Bijou Theatre, 52
Shadow of a Gunman, The (p), 2/29/72, Sheridan Square Playhouse, 72
Shadow of Heroes (p), 12/5/61, York Playhouse, 20
Shadow of My Enemy, A (p), 12/11/57, ANTA Theatre, 5
Shadow of the Glen, The (p), 11/17/34, John Golden Theatre, 1
Shadow of the Glen, The / Birthright / Crabbed Youth and Age (p), 11/3/32, Martin Beck Theatre, 1
Shadow of the Hills (p), 1/28/29, Belmont Theatre, 9
Shadow, The (p), 1/25/15, Empire Theatre, 72
Shadow, The (p), 4/24/22, Klaw Theatre, 16
Shadow, The (p), 12/18/23, Eltinge Theatre, 24
Shadowed (p), 9/24/13, Fulton Theatre, 6
Shady Lady (m), 7/5/33, Shubert Theatre, 30
Shakespeare in Harlem / God's Trombones (p), 2/9/60, 41st St. Theatre, 32
Shakespeare Theatre Company, 11/17/32, Shakespeare Theatre, 249
Shakuntala (p), 4/28/19, Greenwich Village Theatre, 35
Shakuntala (p), 9/9/59, St. Marks Playhouse, 21
Shall We Join the Ladies? / Isabel (p), 1/13/25, Empire Theatre, 31
Sham (p), 3/27/09, Wallack Theatre, 65
Shame Woman, The (p), 10/16/23, Greenwich Village Theatre, 295
Shameen Dhu (p), 2/2/14, Grand Opera House, 32
Shanghai Gesture, The (p), 2/1/26, Martin Beck Theatre, 210
Shanghai Gesture, The (p), 9/6/26, Chanin's 48th St. Theatre, 121
Shanghai Gesture, The (p), 2/13/28, Century Theatre, 16
Shangri-La (m), 6/13/56, Winter Garden Theatre, 21
Shannons of Broadway, The (p), 9/26/27, Martin Beck Theatre, 288
Sharlee (m), 11/22/23, Daly's Theatre, 36
Sharon's Grave (p), 11/8/61, Maidman Playhouse, 6
Shatter'd Lamp, The (p), 3/21/34, Maxine Elliott's Theatre, 38
Shavings (p), 2/16/20, Knickerbocker Theatre, 122
Shaw Festival, A (Overruled / Buoyant Billions / Getting Married) (p), 5/26/59, Provincetown Playhouse, 155
Shay Duffin as Brendan Behan, 1/2/73, Abbey Theatre, 89
She Couldn't Say No (p), 8/31/26, Booth Theatre, 72
She Got What She Wanted (p), 3/4/29, Wallack Theatre, 118
She Had To Know (p), 2/2/25, Times Square Theatre, 81
She Lived Next to the Firehouse (p), 2/10/31, Longacre Theatre, 24
She Loves Me (m), 4/23/63, Eugene O'Neill Theatre, 302
She Loves Me (m), 4/18/69, Master Theatre, 15, (Equity Library Theatre)
She Loves Me Not (p), 11/20/33, 46th St. Theatre, 367
She Means Business (p), 1/26/31, Ritz Theatre, 8
She's a Good Fellow (m), 5/5/19, Globe Theatre, 120
She's in Again (p), 5/17/15, Gaiety Theatre, 48
She's My Baby (m), 1/3/28, Globe Theatre, 71
She Shall Have Music (m), 1/22/59, Martinique Theatre, 54
She Stoops To Conquer (p) (Eleanor Robson), 4/17/05, New Amsterdam Theatre, 24
She Stoops To Conquer (p), 11/11/12, 39th St. Theatre
She Stoops To Conquer (p), 6/9/24, Empire Theatre, 8
She Stoops To Conquer (p), 5/14/28, Erlanger Theatre, 16
She Stoops To Conquer (p), 12/28/49, New York City Center, 16
She Stoops To Conquer (p), 11/1/60, Phoenix Theatre, 31
She Stoops To Conquer (p), 1/3/61, Phoenix Theatre, 16
She Stoops To Conquer (p), 3/18/71, Cubiculo Theatre, 12
She Stoops To Conquer (p), 4/25/71, Roundabout Theatre, 46
She Walked in Her Sleep (p), 8/12/18, Playhouse, 80
She Would and She Did (p), 9/11/19, Vanderbilt Theatre, 36
Shearwater. See A Festival of Short Plays
Sheep on the Runway (p), 1/31/70, Helen Hayes Theatre, 105
Shelf, The (p), 9/27/26, Morosco Theatre, 32
Shelter (p), 1/25/26, Cherry Lane Theatre, 16
Shelter (m), 2/6/73, John Golden Theatre, 31
Shenyang Acrobatic Troupe of the People's Republic of China, 1/2/73, N.Y. City Center, 5
Shepherd King, The (p), 4/5/04, Knickerbocker Theatre, 27
Shepherd King, The (p), 2/20/05, New York Theatre, 48
Shepherd King, The (p), 12/3/06, Academy of Music, 28
Shepherd of Avenue B, The / Steal the Old Man's Bundle (p), 5/15/70, Fortune Theatre, 5
Sheppey (p), 4/18/44, Playhouse, 23
Sherlock Holmes (p), 11/3/02, Knickerbocker Theatre, 28
Sherlock Holmes (p), 3/6/05, Empire Theatre, 56
Sherlock Holmes, 10/11/15, Empire Theatre
Sherlock Holmes (p), 2/20/28, Cosmopolitan Theatre, 16
Sherlock Holmes (p), 11/25/29, New Amsterdam Theatre, 45
Sherlock Holmes (p), 10/30/53, New Century Theatre, 3
Sherman Was Right (p), 10/26/15, Fulton Theatre, 7
Sherry! (m), 3/28/67, Alvin Theatre, 72
Shewing-Up of Blanco Posnet, The / The Player Queen (p), 10/16/23, Neighborhood Playhouse, 49
Shidohogaku. See National Theatres of Japan
Shinbone Alley (m), 4/13/57, Broadway Theatre, 49
Shining Hour, The (p), 2/13/34, Booth Theatre, 120
Ship Comes In, A (p), 9/19/34, Morosco Theatre, 37
Ship, The (p), 11/20/29, Gansevoort Theatre, 17
Shipwrecked (p), 11/12/24, Wallack Theatre, 28
Shirley Kaye (p), 12/25/16, Hudson Theatre, 88
Shock of Recognition, The. See You Know I Can't Hear You When the Water's Running
Shoe Store (p), 3/1/71, Lincoln Center Library Auditorium, 3, (Equity Library Theatre)
Shoemaker and the Peddler, The (m), 10/14/60, East 74th St. Theatre, 43
Shoemaker's Holiday (m), 3/2/67, Orpheum Theatre, 6
Shoemaker's Holiday, The (p), 1/1/38, Mercury Theatre, 69
Shoemaker's Prodigious Wife, The. See Zapatera Prodigiosa, La
Shoes. See Contributions
Shoestring Revue (r), 2/28/55, President Theatre, 96
Shoestring '57 (r), 11/5/56, Barbizon-Plaza Theatre, 110
Sho-gun, The (m), 10/10/04, Wallack Theatre, 125
Shoo-Fly Regiment, The (m), 8/6/07, Bijou Theatre, 15
Shoot Anything with Hair That Moves (p), 2/2/69, Provincetown Playhouse, 17

Shoot the Works (r), 7/21/31, George M. Cohan Theatre, 87
Shooting Shadows (p), 6/26/24, Ritz Theatre, 12
Shooting Star (p), 6/12/33, Selwyn Theatre, 16
Shop at Sly Corner, The (p), 1/18/49, Booth Theatre, 7
Shore Leave (p), 8/8/22, Lyceum Theatre, 152
Short Bullins (How Do You Do? / A Minor Scene / Dialect Determinism / It Has No Choice) (p), 2/25/72, La Mama Experimental Theatre Club, 9
Short Eyes (p), 1/3/74, Theatre of the Riverside Church, 22
Short Eyes (p), 2/28/74, Public / Anspacher Theatre, 60
Shot in the Dark, A (p), 10/18/61, Booth Theatre, 389
Shout from the Rooftops (p), 10/28/64, Renata Theatre, 15
Show Boat (m), 12/27/27, Ziegfeld Theatre, 575
Show Boat (m), 5/19/32, Casino Theatre, 181
Show Boat (m), 1/5/46, Ziegfeld Theatre, 418
Show Boat (m), 9/7/48, New York City Center, 15
Show Boat (m), 5/5/54, New York City Center, 15
Show Boat (m), 4/12/61, New York City Center, 14
Show Boat (m), 7/19/66, New York State Theatre, 64
Show Booth, The / The Song of Songs (p), 4/3/23, Booth Theatre, 10
Show Girl (m), 7/2/29, Ziegfeld Theatre, 111
Show Girl (r), 1/12/61, Eugene O'Neill Theatre, 100
Show Girl, The (m), 5/5/02, Wallack Theatre, 64
Show Is On, The (r), 12/25/36, Winter Garden Theatre, 236
Show Is On, The (r), 9/18/37, Winter Garden Theatre, 17
Show Me Where the Good Times Are (m), 3/5/70, Edison Theatre, 29
Show of Wonders, The (r), 10/26/16, Winter Garden Theatre, 209
Show Shop, The (p), 12/31/14, Hudson Theatre, 156
Show Time (r), 9/16/42, Broadhurst Theatre, 342
Show-Off, The (p), 2/5/24, Playhouse, 571
Show-Off, The (p), 12/12/32, Hudson Theatre, 103
Show-Off, The (p), 5/31/50, Arena, Hotel Edison, 6
Show-Off, The (p), 12/5/67, Lyceum Theatre, 81, (APA-Phoenix)
Show-Off, The (p), 9/13/68, Lyceum Theatre, 19, (APA-Phoenix)
Shrike, The (p), 1/15/52, Cort Theatre, 161
Shrike, The (p), 11/25/53, New York City Center, 15
Shrike, The (p), 1/31/64, Master Institute–Equity Library Theatre, 10
Shrinking Bride, The (p), 1/17/71, Mercury Theatre, 1
Shubert Gaieties 1919 (r), 7/17/19, 44th St. Theatre, 87
Shuffle Along (m), 5/23/21, 63rd St. Music Hall, 484
Shuffle Along (m), 5/8/52, Broadway Theatre, 4
Shuffle Along of 1933, 12/26/32, Mansfield Theatre, 17
Shulamite, The (p), 10/29/06, Lyric Theatre, 25
Shunned (p), 12/20/60, Dickens Theatre
Siamese Connections (p), 6/8/72, Actors Studio Theatre, 6
Siamese Connections (p), 1/9/73, Public Theatre Annex, 64
Siberia (p), 1/16/05, Academy of Music, 32
Sick-a-Bed (p), 2/25/18, Gaiety Theatre, 80
Sidewalks of New York (m), 10/3/27, Knickerbocker Theatre, 112
Siege (p), 12/8/37, Longacre Theatre, 6
Siegfried (p), 10/20/30, Civic Repertory Theatre, 23
Siegfried at Stalingrad. See Festival of New Italian Plays
Sigh of Winter (p), 5/7/58, Theatre 74, 32
Sign in Sidney Brustein's Window, The (p), 10/15/64, Longacre Theatre, 101
Sign in Sidney Brustein's Window, The (p), 1/26/72, Longacre Theatre, 5
Sign of Jonah, The (p), 9/8/60, Players Theatre, 53
Sign of the Leopard (p), 12/11/28, National Theatre, 39
Sign of the Rose, The (p), 10/11/11, Garrick Theatre, 13
Sign on the Door, The (p), 12/19/19, Republic Theatre, 187
Signature (p), 2/14/45, Forrest Theatre, 2
Signs Along the Cynic Route (r), 12/14/61, Actors Playhouse, 93
Silence (p), 11/12/24, National Theatre, 199
Silence / Landscape (p), 4/2/70, Forum Theatre, 53
Silence / Landscape (p), 2/19/71, Forum Theatre, 6
Silent Assertion, The (p), 12/8/17, Bramhall Playhouse, 41
Silent Assertion, The (p), 3/21/23, Bramhall Playhouse, 70
Silent Call, The (p), 1/2/11, Broadway Theatre, 8
Silent House, The (p), 2/7/28, Morosco Theatre, 277
Silent House, The (p), 11/8/32, Ambassador Theatre, 15
Silent Night, Lonely Night (p), 12/3/59, Morosco Theatre, 124
Silent Partner, The (p), 5/11/72, Actors Studio, 12
Silent Voice, The (p), 12/29/14, Liberty Theatre, 71
Silent Witness, The (p), 8/10/16, Longacre Theatre, 52
Silent Witness, The (p), 3/23/31, Morosco Theatre, 80
Silhouettes (p), 9/8/69, Actors Playhouse, 8
Silk Stockings (m), 2/24/55, Imperial Theatre, 478
Silks and Satins (m), 7/15/20, George M. Cohan Theatre, 60
Silver Box, The (p), 3/18/07, Empire Theatre, 20
Silver Box, The (p), 1/17/28, Morosco Theatre, 23
Silver Cord, The (p), 12/20/26, John Golden Theatre, 130
Silver Fox, The (p), 9/5/21, Maxine Elliott's Theatre, 112
Silver Girl, The (p), 10/14/07, Wallack Theatre, 24
Silver Grey Toy Poodle. See Pets
Silver Queen (m), 4/11/73, La Mama Experimental Theatre Club, 10
Silver Slipper, The (m), 10/27/02, Broadway Theatre, 160
Silver Star, The (m), 11/1/09, New Amsterdam Theatre, 80
Silver Swan, The (m), 11/27/29, Martin Beck Theatre, 21
Silver Tassie, The (p), 10/23/29, Irish Theatre, 53
Silver Wedding, The (p), 8/11/13, Longacre Theatre, 16
Silver Whistle, The (p), 11/24/48, Biltmore Theatre, 219
Sim Sala Bim, 9/9/40, Morosco Theatre, 54
Simon Called Peter (p), 11/20/24, Klaw Theatre, 93
Simon the Cyrenian / The Rider of Dreams / Granny Maumee (p), 4/5/17, Garden Theatre
Simone, Mme. See Mme. Simone
Simple Simon (m), 2/18/30, Ziegfeld Theatre, 135
Simple Simon (m), 3/9/31, Majestic Theatre, 16
Simpleton of the Unexpected Isles, The (p), 2/18/35, Guild Theatre, 40
Simply Heavenly (m), 5/21/57, 85th St. Playhouse
Simply Heavenly (m), 8/20/57, Playhouse, 62
Sin of Pat Muldoon, The (p), 3/13/57, Cort Theatre, 5
Sinbad (m), 2/14/18, Winter Garden Theatre, 164
Sing and Whistle (p), 2/10/34, Fulton Theatre, 75
Sing for Your Supper (r), 4/24/39, Adelphi Theatre, 60
Sing High, Sing Low (p), 11/12/31, Sam H. Harris Theatre, 70
Sing, Israel, Sing (m), 5/11/67, Brooks Atkinson Theatre, 22
Sing Me No Lullaby (p), 10/14/54, Phoenix Theatre, 30
Sing Muse! (m), 12/6/61, Van Dam Theatre, 39
Sing Out Sweet Land (r), 12/27/44, International Theatre, 102
Sing Out the News (r), 9/24/38, Music Box Theatre, 105
Sing Till Tomorrow (p), 12/28/53, Royale Theatre, 8
Sing to Me Through Open Windows / The Day the Whores Came Out to Play Tennis (m), 3/15/65, Players Theatre, 24
Singapore (p), 11/14/32, 48th St. Theatre, 24
Singin' the Blues (m), 9/16/31, Liberty Theatre, 46
Singing Jailbirds (p), 12/6/28, Provincetown Playhouse, 79
Singing Rabbi, The (m), 9/10/31, Selwyn Theatre, 3
Single Man, A (p), 9/4/11, Empire Theatre, 104
Single Man at a Party (p), 4/21/59, Theatre Marquee, 22
Sinner (p), 2/7/27, Klaw Theatre, 129
Sinners (p), 1/7/15, Playhouse, 220
Sins of Society, The (p), 8/31/09, New York Theatre, 31
Sir Anthony (p), 11/19/06, Savoy Theatre, 16
Sir Harry Lauder, 4/21/30, Jolson Theatre, 9
Sire (p), 1/24/11, Criterion Theatre, 31
Siren, The (m), 8/28/11, Knickerbocker Theatre, 136
Sirena (p), 9/21/31, Waldorf Theatre, 8
Sirens, The (p), 5/15/74, Manhattan Theatre Club
Sister Beatrice / Brand (Act IV) (p), 4/14/10, New Theatre
Sister Oakes (p), 4/23/49, Lenox Hill Playhouse, 4
Sister Sadie (p), 3/17/72, La Mama Experimental Theatre Club
Sister Son/Ji. See Black Visions
Sisters (p), 12/24/27, Klaw Theatre, 10
Sisters of Mercy (r), 9/25/73, Theatre de Lys, 15
Sisters of the Chorus (p), 10/20/30, Ritz Theatre, 32
Sita (p), 1/12/31, Vanderbilt Theatre, 8
Sitting Pretty (m), 4/8/24, Fulton Theatre, 95
Six (r), 4/12/71, Cricket Playhouse, 8
Six Aspects of Love. See Sextet
Six Characters in Search of an Author (p), 10/30/22, Princess Theatre, 137
Six Characters in Search of an Author (p), 2/6/24, 44th St. Theatre, 14
Six Characters in Search of an Author (p), 4/15/31, Bijou Theatre, 13
Six Characters in Search of an Author (p), 12/11/55, Phoenix Theatre, 65
Six Characters in Search of an Author (p), 3/7/63, Martinique Theatre, 529
Six from La Mama, 1st Program (Thank You, Miss Victoria / This Is the Rill Speaking / Birdbath) (p), 4/11/66, Martinique Theatre, 1
Six from La Mama, 2nd Program (War / The Recluse / Chicago) (p), 4/12/66, Martinique Theatre, 2
Six Months' Option (p), 11/29/17, Princess Theatre, 28
Six O'Clock Theatre (p) (Hope Is the Thing with Feathers / Celebration / Afternoon Storm), 4/11/48, Maxine Elliott's Theatre, 8
Six Rms Riv Vu (p), 10/17/72, Helen Hayes Theatre, 247
Six-Cylinder Love (p), 8/25/21, Sam H. Harris Theatre, 430
Six-Fifty, The (p), 10/24/21, Hudson Theatre, 24
Sixth Finger in a Five Finger Glove (p), 10/8/56, Longacre Theatre, 2
Skidding (p), 5/21/28, Bijou Theatre, 469
Ski-Hi (m), 6/20/08, Madison Square Garden Roof Theatre, 25
Skin Deep (p), 10/17/27, Liberty Theatre, 8
Skin Game, The (p), 10/20/20, Bijou Theatre, 175
Skin of Our Teeth, The (p), 11/18/42, Plymouth Theatre, 355
Skin of Our Teeth, The (p), 8/17/55, ANTA Theatre, 22
Skipper & Co., Wall Street (p), 5/4/03, Garrick Theatre, 16
Skipper Next to God (p), 1/4/48, Maxine Elliott's Theatre, 93
Skirt, The (p), 11/7/21, Bijou Theatre, 8
Skits-Oh-Frantics! (r), 4/2/67, Bert Wheeler Theatre, 17
Skull, The (p), 4/3/28, Forrest Theatre, 96
Sky Farm (p), 3/17/02, Garrick Theatre, 48
Sky High (m), 3/2/25, Shubert Theatre, 217
Sky's the Limit, The (p), 12/17/34, Fulton Theatre, 24
Skydrift (p), 11/13/45, Belasco Theatre, 7

Skye (m), 2/1/71, Lincoln Center Library Auditorium, 3, (Equity Library Theatre)
Skylark (p), 10/11/39, Morosco Theatre, 256
Skylark, A (m), 4/4/10, New York Theatre, 24
Skylark, The (p), 7/25/21, Belmont Theatre, 24
Skyrocket (p), 1/11/29, Lyceum Theatre, 11
Skyscraper (m), 11/13/65, Lunt-Fontanne Theatre, 241
Skywriting. See Collision Course
Slag (p), 2/21/71, Public/Other Stage, 32
Slapstick Tragedy (The Mutilated / The Gnadiges Fraulein) (p), 2/22/66, Longacre Theatre, 7
Slave Ship (p), 11/18/69, Brooklyn Academy of Music, 45, (Chelsea Theatre Center)
Slave, The / The Toilet (p), 12/16/64, St. Marks Playhouse, 151
Slaves All (p), 12/6/26, Bijou Theatre, 8
Sleep (p), 2/10/72, American Place Theatre, 32
Sleep, My Pretty One (p), 11/2/44, Playhouse, 4
Sleep No More (p), 8/31/44, Cort Theatre, 7
Sleep of Prisoners, A (p), 10/16/51, St. James' Church, 31
Sleeping Beauty and the Beast, The (r), 11/4/01, Broadway Theatre, 241
Sleeping Clergyman, A (p), 10/8/34, Guild Theatre, 40
Sleeping Partners (p), 10/5/18, Bijou Theatre, 161
Sleeping Prince, The (p), 11/1/56, Coronet Theatre, 60
Sleepless Night, A (p), 2/18/19, Bijou Theatre, 71
Sleepy Hollow (m), 6/3/48, St. James Theatre, 12
Sleuth (p), 11/12/70, Music Box, 1,222
Slice of Life, A / Cousin Kate (p), 1/29/12, Empire Theatre, 48
Slight Ache, A / The Room (p), 12/9/64, Writers Stage Theatre, 343
Slight Case of Murder, A (p), 9/11/35, 48th St. Theatre, 70
Slightly Delirious (p), 12/31/34, Little Theatre, 8
Slightly Married (p), 10/25/43, Cort Theatre, 8
Slightly Scandalous (p), 6/13/44, National Theatre, 7
Slim Princess, The (m), 1/2/11, Globe Theatre, 104
Slow Dance on the Killing Ground (p), 11/30/64, Plymouth Theatre, 88
Slow Dance on the Killing Ground (p), 5/13/70, Sheridan Square Playhouse, 36
Slow Memories / The Perfect Match (p), 11/16/70, Theatre de Lys, 2, (ANTA Matinee)
Small Craft Warnings (p), 4/2/72, Truck and Warehouse Theatre, 194
Small Hours, The (p), 2/15/51, National Theatre, 20
Small Miracle (p), 9/26/34, John Golden Theatre, 118
Small Timers, The (p), 1/27/25, Punch and Judy Theatre, 47
Small War on Murray Hill (p), 1/3/57, Ethel Barrymore Theatre, 12
Small Wonder (r), 9/15/48, Coronet Theatre, 134
Smaller Than Life, 12/7/70, Lincoln Center Library Auditorium, 3, (Equity Library Theatre)
Smile at Me (r), 8/23/35, Fulton Theatre, 27
Smile of the World, The (p), 1/12/49, Lyceum Theatre, 5
Smile, Smile, Smile (m), 4/4/73, Eastside Playhouse, 7
Smiles (m), 11/18/30, Ziegfeld Theatre, 63
Smilin' Through (p), 12/30/19, Broadhurst Theatre, 175
Smiling Faces (m), 8/30/32, Shubert Theatre, 31
Smiling the Boy Fell Dead (m), 4/19/61, Cherry Lane Theatre, 22
Smith (p), 9/5/10, Empire Theatre, 112
Smith (m), 5/19/73, Eden Theatre, 17
Smokeweaver's Daughter, The (m), 4/14/59, Fourth St. Theatre, 16
Smoldering Flame / The Flame (p), 9/23/13, 48th St. Theatre, 7
Smooth as Silk (p), 2/22/21, Lexington Theatre, 16
Smooth as Silk (p), 4/21/21, Frazee Theatre, 30
Snafu (p), 10/25/44, Hudson Theatre, 156
Snapshots of 1921 (r), 6/2/21, Selwyn Theatre, 44
Snapshots of 1921 (r), 7/25/21, Selwyn Theatre, 16
Snark Was a Boojum, The (p), 9/1/43, 48th St. Theatre, 5
Snickering Horses / The Great Catherine / The Miser (p), 5/13/36, Experimental Theatre, 3
Snobs (p), 9/4/11, Hudson Theatre, 64
Snookie (p), 6/3/41, Golden Theatre, 15
Snow Maiden, The (p), 4/4/60, Madison Ave. Playhouse, 1
Snow White and the Seven Dwarfs (p), 11/7/12, Little Theatre, 72
So Am I (p), 1/27/28, Comedy Theatre, 28
So Long, Letty (m), 10/23/16, Shubert Theatre, 96
So Many Paths (p), 12/6/34, Ritz Theatre, 12
So Many Paths (p), 12/24/34, Ambassador Theatre, 16
So Much for So Much, 12/2/14, Longacre Theatre, 30
So Please Be Kind. See Present Tense
So Proudly We Hail (p), 9/22/36, 46th St. Theatre, 14
So This Is London! (p), 8/30/22, Hudson Theatre, 357
So This Is Politics (p), 6/16/24, Henry Miller's Theatre, 144
So Was Napoleon (Sap from Syracuse) (p), 1/8/30, Sam H. Harris Theatre, 25
Social Register, The (p), 11/9/31, Fulton Theatre, 97
Social Whirl, The (m), 4/9/06, Casino Theatre, 195
Social Whirl, The (m), 4/1/07, Majestic Theatre, 16
Society and the Bulldog (p), 1/18/08, Daly's Theatre, 17
Society Circus, A (m), 12/13/05, New York Hippodrome, 596
Society Girl (p), 12/30/31, Booth Theatre, 22
Society of American Singers Repertory, The, 9/30/18, Park Theatre
Soft Core Pornographer, The (p), 4/11/72, Stage 73 Theatre, 1
Sojourner Truth (p), 4/21/48, Kaufmann Auditorium YMHA, 22
Sold and Paid For (p), 12/7/00, Herald Square Theatre, 1
Sold to the Movies (Life Size / Type 424 Meet Type Oh— Oh, No! / Crossing the Gap) (p), 4/10/70, Gotham Art Theatre
Soldier's Wife (p), 10/4/44, John Golden Theatre, 255
Soldier, The (p), 4/10/73, Provincetown Playhouse, 8
Soldiers (p), 5/1/68, Billy Rose Theatre, 21
Soldiers and Women (p), 9/2/29, Ritz Theatre, 64
Soldiers of Fortune, 3/17/02, Savoy Theatre, 129
Solid Gold Cadillac, The (p), 11/5/53, Belasco Theatre, 526
Solid Ivory (p), 11/16/25, Central Theatre, 32
Solid South (p), 10/14/30, Lyceum Theatre, 23
Soliloquy (p), 11/28/38, Empire Theatre, 2
Solitaire (p), 3/12/29, Waldorf Theatre, 4
Solitaire (p), 1/27/42, Plymouth Theatre, 23
Solitaire / Double Solitaire (p), 9/30/71, John Golden Theatre, 36
Some Baby! (p), 8/12/15, Fulton Theatre, 72
Some Night (p), 9/23/18, Harris Theatre, 24
Some One in the House (p), 9/9/18, Knickerbocker Theatre, 32
Some Party (r), 4/15/22, Jolson 59th St. Theatre, 17
Somebody's Luggage (p), 8/28/16, 48th St. Theatre, 40
Somebody's Sweetheart (m), 12/23/18, Central Theatre, 224
Someone from Assisi / Infancy / Childhood. See Plays for Bleecker Street, 1/11/62, Circle in the Square, 349
Someone's Comin' Hungry (p), 3/31/69, Pocket Theatre, 16
Someone Waiting (p), 2/14/56, Golden Theatre, 15
Something About a Soldier (p), 1/4/62, Ambassador Theatre, 12
Something Different (p), 11/28/67, Cort Theatre, 103
Something for Nothing (p), 12/9/37, Windsor Theatre, 2
Something for the Boys (m), 1/7/43, Alvin Theatre, 422
Something Gay (p), 4/29/53, Morosco Theatre, 72
Something More! (p), 11/10/64, Eugene O'Neill Theatre, 15
Something More Important / The Old Woman / E & O E (p), 7/11/35, Chanin Auditorium, 12
Something To Brag About (p), 8/13/25, Booth Theatre, 4
Something Unspoken / Suddenly Last Summer. See Garden District
Sometime (m), 10/4/18, Shubert Theatre, 283
Sometime Jam Today (p), 2/12/67, Bouwerie Lane Theatre
Sometimes a Hard Head Makes a Soft Behind (p), 7/28/72, New Lafayette Theatre
Somewhere Else (m), 1/20/13, Broadway Theatre, 9
Son, Come Home, A. See The Electronic Nigger and Others
Son of Cock-Strong (m), 2/20/70, La Mama Experimental Theatre Club
Son of the People, A (p), 2/28/10, New Theatre
Son of the People, A (p), 3/28/10, Hackett Theatre, 7
Son Who Hunted Tigers in Jakarta, The. See Passing Through from Exotic Places
Son-Daughter, The (p), 11/19/19, Belasco Theatre, 223
Sondra. See Harold / Sondra
Song and Dance Man, The (p), 12/31/23, Hudson Theatre, 96
Song and Dance Man, The (p), 6/16/30, Fulton Theatre, 16
Song at Twilight, A. See Noel Coward in Two Keys
Song for a Certain Midnight (p), 9/16/59, Jan Hus House, 8
Song for the First of May, A (p), 10/22/71, Actors Playhouse, 5
Song of Bernadette, The (p), 3/26/46, Belasco Theatre, 3
Song of Israel (r), 3/21/72, Mayfair Theatre
Song of Norway (m), 8/21/44, Imperial Theatre, 860
Song of Songs / Maidens and Mistresses at Home at the Zoo. See Mistresses and Maidens, 1/21/59, Orpheum Theatre, 23
Song of Songs, The (p), 12/22/14, Eltinge Theatre, 191
Song of Songs, The / The Show Booth (p), 4/3/23, Booth Theatre, 10
Song of the Flame (m), 12/30/25, 44th St. Theatre, 224
Song of the Grasshopper (p), 9/28/67, ANTA Theatre, 4
Song of the Lusitanian Bogey (p), 1/2/68, St. Marks Playhouse, 40
Song of the Lusitanian Bogey (p), 7/23/68, St. Marks Playhouse, 24, (Negro Ensemble Co.)
Song Writer, The (p), 8/13/28, 48th St. Theatre, 54
Songs from Milkwood. See National Theatre of the Deaf
Sonny Boy (m), 8/16/21, Cort Theatre, 31
Sons and Soldiers (p), 5/4/43, Morosco Theatre, 22
Sons O' Fun (r), 12/1/41, Winter Garden Theatre, 742
Sons O' Guns (m), 11/26/29, Imperial Theatre, 297
Sonya (p), 8/15/21, 48th St. Theatre, 101
Soon (m), 1/12/71, Ritz Theatre, 3
Soon Jack November (p), 1/18/66, La Mama Experimental Theatre Club, 6
Soon Jack November (p), 6/2/72, Manhattan Theatre Club, 6
Sooner and Later / The Legend of the Dance, 3/31/25, Neighborhood Playhouse, 28
Sophie (p), 3/2/20, Greenwich Village Theatre, 79
Sophie (p), 12/25/44, Playhouse, 9
Sophie (m), 4/15/63, Winter Garden Theatre, 8
Sophisticrats, The (p), 2/13/33, Bijou Theatre, 2

Sorceress, The (p), 10/10/04, New Amsterdam Theatre, 36
Sothern, E. H. See Sothern-Marlowe
Sothern-Marlowe Repertory, 10/17/04, Knickerbocker Theatre, 48
Sothern-Marlowe Repertory, 10/16/05, Knickerbocker Theatre, 48
Sothern-Marlowe Repertory, 1/21/07, Lyric Theatre, 64
Sothern-Marlowe Repertory, 6/10/07, Academy of Music, 16
Sothern-Marlowe Repertory, 2/7/10, Academy of Music, 32
Sothern-Marlowe Repertory, 12/5/10, Broadway Theatre
Sothern-Marlowe Repertory, 7/3/11, Broadway Theatre
Sothern-Marlowe Repertory, 11/20/11, Manhattan Opera House
Sothern-Marlowe Repertory, 9/30/12, Manhattan Opera House, 40
Sothern-Marlowe Repertory, 9/22/13, Manhattan Opera House, 40
Sothern-Marlowe Repertory, 10/6/19, Shubert Theatre, 16
Sothern-Marlowe Shakespeare Repertory, 10/31/21, Century Theatre, 48
Sotoba Komachi / Han's Crime / The Damask Drum (p) (Three Modern Japanese Plays), 2/3/61, Players' Theatre, 45
Soul Kiss, The (m), 1/28/08, New York Theatre, 122
Sound of Hunting, A (p), 11/20/45, Lyceum Theatre, 23
Sound of Music, The (m), 11/16/59, Lunt-Fontanne Theatre, 1,443
Sound of Music, The (m), 4/26/67, New York City Center, 23
Sound of Silence, A (p), 3/8/65, Maidman Playhouse, 88
Sour Grapes (p), 9/6/26, Longacre Theatre, 40
Sourball (p), 8/5/69, Provincetown Playhouse, 1
South Pacific (p), 12/29/43, Cort Theatre, 5
South Pacific (m), 4/7/49, Majestic Theatre, 1,925
South Pacific (m), 5/4/55, New York City Center, 15
South Pacific (m), 4/24/57, New York City Center, 23
South Pacific (m), 4/26/61, New York City Center, 23
South Pacific (m), 6/2/65, New York City Center, 15
South Pacific (m), 6/12/67, New York State Theatre, 104
Southern Exposure (p), 9/26/50, Biltmore Theatre, 23
Southerners, The (m), 5/23/04, New York Theatre, 36
Southwest Corner, The (p), 2/3/55, Holiday Theatre, 36
Spanish Armada, The / Man out Loud, Girl Quiet (p), 4/3/62, Cricket Theatre, 16
Spanish Love (p), 8/17/20, Maxine Elliott's Theatre, 307
Spanish Theatre Repertory Company, 11/19/53, Broadhurst Theatre, 27
Speak Easy (p), 9/26/27, Mansfield Theatre, 57
Speaking of Murder (p), 12/19/56, Royale Theatre, 37
Speckled Band, The (p), 11/21/10, Garrick Theatre, 32
Speed (p), 9/9/11, Comedy Theatre, 33
Speed Gets the Poppys (m), 7/25/72, Mercer / Brecht Theatre, 7
Spell, The (p), 9/16/07, Majestic Theatre, 16
Spell, The (p), 5/11/08, Thalia Theatre, 7
Spellbinder, The (p), 9/5/04, Herald Square Theatre, 16
Spellbound (p), 2/15/27, Klaw Theatre, 2
Spellbound (p), 11/14/27, Earl Carroll Theatre, 24
Spenders, The (p), 10/5/03, Savoy Theatre, 41
Spendthrift, The (p), 4/11/10, Hudson Theatre, 88
Spice of 1922 (r), 7/6/22, Winter Garden Theatre, 85
Spider, The (p), 3/22/27, Chanin's 46th St. Theatre, 100
Spider, The (p), 2/27/28, Century Theatre, 16
Spiritualist, The (p), 3/24/13, 48th St. Theatre, 8
Spiro Who? (p), 5/18/69, Tamellini's Gate Theatre, 41
Spite Corner, 9/25/22, Little Theatre, 124
Spitfire, The (p), 4/25/10, Lyceum Theatre, 40
Spitting Image (p), 3/2/69, Theatre de Lys, 49
Spofford (p), 12/14/67, ANTA Theatre, 202
Spoilers, The (p), 3/11/07, New York Theatre, 16
Sponge Room, The / Squatt Betty (p), 2/24/64, East End Theatre, 49
Spook House (p), 6/3/30, Vanderbilt Theatre, 15
Spook Scandals (r), 12/8/44, President Theatre, 2
Spook Sonata, The (p), 1/24, Provincetown Playhouse, 22
Spook Sonata, The (p), 6/3/54, Living Theatre Studio
Spooks (p), 6/1/25, 48th St. Theatre
Spoon River Anthology, 9/29/63, Booth Theatre, 111
Spoon River Anthology, 4/30/73, Stage 73, 32
Sport of Kings, The (p), 5/4/26, Lyceum Theatre, 23
Sporting Days, 9/5/08, New York Hippodrome, 448
Sporting Thing to Do, The, 2/19/23, Ritz Theatre, 41
Spots of the Leopard, The (p), 9/24/63, Washington Sq. Theatre, 8
Spread Eagle (p), 4/4/27, Martin Beck Theatre, 80
Spreading the News (p), 10/31/32, Martin Beck Theatre, 2
Sprightly Romance of Marsac, The (p), 12/3/00, Republic Theatre, 32
Spring (p), 11/28/34, John Golden Theatre, 2
Spring Again (p), 11/10/41, Henry Miller's Theatre, 241
Spring Chicken, The (m), 10/8/06, Daly's Theatre, 66
Spring Chicken, The (m), 12/10/06, New Amsterdam Theatre, 25
Spring Chicken, The (m), 4/1/07, Daly's Theatre, 24
Spring Cleaning (p), 11/9/23, Eltinge Theatre, 292
Spring Dance (p), 8/25/36, Empire Theatre, 23
Spring Fever (p), 8/3/25, Maxine Elliott's Theatre, 56
Spring Freshet (p), 10/4/34, Plymouth Theatre, 12
Spring in Autumn (p), 10/24/33, Henry Miller's Theatre, 41
Spring Is Here (m), 3/11/29, Alvin Theatre, 104
Spring Maid, The (m), 12/26/10, Liberty Theatre, 192
Spring Meeting (p), 12/8/38, Morosco Theatre, 98
Spring's Awakening (p), 10/9/55, Provincetown Playhouse, 16
Spring Song (p), 12/21/27, Nora Bayes Theatre, 18
Spring Song (p), 10/1/34, Morosco Theatre, 40
Spring Thaw (p), 3/21/38, Martin Beck Theatre, 8
Spring, The, 1/31/21, Provincetown Playhouse, 2
Spring, The (p), 1/31/21, Princess Theatre, 21
Spring 3100 (p), 2/15/28, Little Theatre, 29
Springboard, The (p), 10/12/27, Mansfield Theatre, 37
Springtime (p), 10/19/09, Liberty Theatre, 79
Springtime Folly (p), 2/26/51, John Golden Theatre, 2
Springtime for Henry (p), 12/9/31, Bijou Theatre, 198
Springtime for Henry (p), 5/1/33, Ambassador Theatre, 16
Springtime for Henry (p), 3/14/51, John Golden Theatre, 53
Springtime of Youth (m), 10/26/22, Broadhurst Theatre, 68
Spy, The (p), 1/13/13, Empire Theatre, 64
Squab Farm, The (p), 3/13/18, Bijou Theatre, 45
Squall, The (p), 11/11/26, 48th St. Theatre, 262
Square Crooks (p), 3/1/26, Daly's Theatre, 144
Square in the Eye (p), 5/19/65, Theatre de Lys, 31
Square Peg, A (p), 1/27/23, Punch and Judy Theatre, 41
Square Root of Wonderful, The (p), 10/30/57, National Theatre, 45
Squaring the Circle (p), 10/3/35, Lyceum Theatre, 104
Squaring the Triangle / Divertissement / The Nightcap / Gutta Iconoclast / Pearls / The Good Women (p), 6/13/21, Apollo Theatre, 8
Squat Betty / The Sponge Room (p), 2/24/64, East End Theatre, 49
Squaw Man, The (p), 10/23/05, Wallack Theatre, 222
Squaw Man, The (p), 1/9/11, Broadway Theatre, 8
Squaw Man, The (p), 1/26/21, Astor Theatre, 50
Squealer, The (p), 11/12/28, Forrest Theatre, 66
St. Helena (p), 10/6/36, Lyceum Theatre, 63
St. Louis Woman (m), 3/30/46, Martin Beck Theatre, 113
Stag Movie (m), 1/3/71, Gate Theatre, 89
Stage Affair, A (p), 1/16/62, Cherry Lane Theatre, 8
Stage Door (p), 10/22/36, Music Box Theatre, 169
Staircase (p), 1/10/68, Biltmore Theatre, 61
Stairs, The (p), 11/7/27, Bijou Theatre, 8
Stalag 17 (p), 5/8/51, 48th St. Theatre, 472
Star and Garter (r), 11/26/00, Victoria Theatre, 29
Star and Garter (r), 6/24/42, Music Box Theatre, 605
Star Gazer, The (m), 11/26/17, Plymouth Theatre, 8
Star Spangled (p), 3/10/36, John Golden Theatre, 23
Star Spangled Family (p), 4/10/45, Biltmore Theatre, 5
Star Time (r), 9/12/44, Majestic Theatre, 120
Starbucks, The (p), 4/13/03, Daly's Theatre, 24
Starcross Story, The (p), 1/13/54, Royale Theatre, 1
Starlight (p), 3/3/25, Broadhurst Theatre, 71
Stars and Stripes. See Collision Course
Stars in Your Eyes (m), 2/9/39, Majestic Theatre, 127
Stars on Ice (r), 7/2/42, Center Theatre, 827
Star-Spangled Girl, The (p), 12/21/66, Plymouth Theatre, 262
Star-Wagon, The (p), 9/29/37, Empire Theatre, 221
State of the Union (p), 11/14/45, Hudson Theatre, 765
Stations of the Cross, The (p), 5/23/72, St. Clement's Church, 9, (Bread and Puppet Theatre)
Status Quo Vadis (p), 2/18/73, Brooks Atkinson Theatre, 1
Steadfast (p), 10/29/23, Ambassador Theatre, 8
Steal the Old Man's Bundle / The Shepherd of Avenue B (p), 5/15/70, Fortune Theatre, 5
Steam Roller, The (p), 11/10/24, Princess Theatre, 24
Steambath (p), 6/30/70, Truck and Warehouse Theatre, 127
Steel (p), 11/18/31, Times Sq. Theatre, 14
Steel (p), 12/19/39, Provincetown Playhouse, 9
Stempenyu (m), 11/14/73, Central Synagogue Auditorium, 66
Step Lively Boy (m), 1/31/73, Urban Arts Corps Theatre
Step Lively Boy / Croesus and the Witch (m), 3/15/73, Urban Arts Corps Theatre
Step on a Crack (p), 10/17/62, Ethel Barrymore Theatre, 1
Step This Way (m), 5/29/16, Shubert Theatre, 88
Stepdaughters of War (p), 10/6/30, Empire Theatre, 24
Stephen D. (p), 9/24/67, East 74th St. Theatre, 56
Stepping Out (p), 5/20/29, Fulton Theatre, 24
Stepping Sisters (p), 4/22/30, Waldorf Theatre, 327
Stepping Stones (p), 11/6/23, Globe Theatre, 241
Stepping Stones (p), 9/1/24, Globe Theatre, 40
Step-sister, The (p), 10/14/07, Garrick Theatre, 14
Steve (p), 9/28/12, Harris Theatre, 9
Stevedore (p), 4/18/34, Civic Repertory Theatre, 110
Stevedore (p), 10/1/34, Civic Repertory Theatre, 64
Stewed Prunes (r), 11/14/60, Circle in the Square
Stick-in-the-Mud (p), 11/30/35, 48th St. Theatre, 9
Sticks and Bones (p), 11/7/71, Public/Anspacher Theatre, 121
Sticks and Bones (p), 8/1/72, John Golden Theatre, 245

Stickup, The / Footsteps / A Little Act of Justice (p), 1/9/22, Provincetown Playhouse, 21
Stigma (p), 2/10/27, Cherry Lane Theatre, 11
Still Life. See Tonight at 8:30
Still Waters (p), 3/1/26, Henry Miller's Theatre, 16
Stitch in Time, A (p), 10/15/18, Fulton Theatre, 71
Stockade, 2/4/54, President Theatre, 6
Stolen Fruit (p), 10/7/25, Eltinge Theatre, 96
Stolen Orders (p), 9/24/15, Manhattan Opera House, 19
Stolen Story, The (p), 10/2/06, Garden Theatre, 15
Stomp (m), 11/16/69, Public/Martinson Theatre, 161
Stone for Danny Fisher, A (p), 10/21/54, Downtown National Theatre, 100
Stones of Jehoshaphat, The, 12/18/63, Rodale Theatre, 6
Stop! Look! Listen! (m), 12/25/15, Globe Theatre, 105
Stop Press (p), 3/19/39, Vanderbilt Theatre, 1
Stop the World—I Want to Get Off (m), 10/3/62, Sam S. Shubert Theatre, 556
Stop Thief (p), 12/25/12, Gaiety Theatre, 149
Stop, You're Killing Me (Laughs, Etc. / Terrible Jim Fitch / Bad Bad Jo-Jo) (p), 3/19/69, Stage 73, 39
Stop-Over (p), 1/11/38, Lyceum Theatre, 23
Stork Is Dead, The (p), 9/23/32, 48th St. Theatre, 28
Stork Mad (p), 9/30/36, Ambassador Theatre, 5
Stork, The (p), 1/26/25, Cort Theatre, 8
Storm Center (p), 11/30/27, Klaw Theatre, 29
Storm Operation (p), 1/11/44, Belasco Theatre, 23
Storm Over Patsy (p), 3/8/37, Guild Theatre, 48
Storm, The (p), 3/2/00, Carnegie Lyceum Theatre, 1
Storm, The (p), 10/2/19, 48th St. Theatre, 282
Storm, The (p), 3/30/62, Masque Theatre, 10
Story for a Sunday Evening, A (p), 11/17/50, Playhouse, 11
Story for Strangers, A (p), 9/21/48, Royale Theatre, 7
Story of Mary Surratt, The (p), 2/8/47, Henry Miller's Theatre, 11
Story of the Rosary, The (p), 9/7/14, Manhattan Opera House, 48
Story Theatre (r), 12/26/70, Ambassador Theatre, 243
Strada, La (m), 12/14/69, Lunt-Fontanne Theatre, 1
Straight Road, The (p), 1/7/07, Astor Theatre, 40
Straight Thru the Door (p), 10/4/28, 49th St. Theatre, 44
Strange Bedfellows (p), 1/14/48, Morosco Theatre, 229
Strange Case of Dr. Jekyll and Mr. Hyde, The (p), 2/26/23, Belmont Theatre, 4
Strange Child (p), 2/25/35, Majestic Theatre, 10
Strange Fruit (p), 11/29/45, Royale Theatre, 60
Strange Gods (p), 4/15/33, Ritz Theatre, 9
Strange Interlude (p), 1/30/28, John Golden Theatre, 426
Strange Interlude (p), 3/11/63, Hudson Theatre, 104
Strange Orchestra (p), 11/28/33, Playhouse, 1
Strange Play, A / According to Law (p), 6/1/44, Mansfield Theatre, 4
Strange Prince, The (p), 12/7/26, Booth Theatre, 1
Strange Prince, The (p), 12/28/26, 52nd St. Playhouse, 7
Strange Woman, The (p), 11/17/13, Lyceum Theatre, 88
Stranger Than Fiction (p), 3/5/17, Garrick Theatre, 16
Stranger, The (p), 12/21/11, Bijou Theatre, 28
Stranger, The (p), 2/12/45, Playhouse, 16
Strangers at Home (p), 9/14/34, Longacre Theatre, 11
Strangler Fig, The (p), 5/6/40, Lyceum Theatre, 8
Strangulation. See American Gothics
Straw Hat (p), 12/30/37, Nora Bayes Theatre, 4
Straw Hat Revue, The (r), 9/29/39, Ambassador Theatre, 75
Straw Hat, The (p), 10/14/26, American Laboratory Theatre, 57
Straw, The (p), 11/10/21, Greenwich Village Theatre, 20
Strawberry Blonde, The (p), 2/7/27, Bijou Theatre, 25
Stray Leaves, 6/28/33, Chanin Auditorium, 2
Street Scene (p), 1/10/29, Playhouse, 601
Street Scene (m), 1/9/47, Adelphi Theatre, 148
Street Singer (m), 9/17/29, Shubert Theatre, 189
Street Sounds (p), 10/14/70, La Mama Experimental Theatre Club
Street Wolf, The (p), 12/31/28, Garrick Theatre, 8
Streetcar Named Desire, A (p), 12/3/47, Barrymore Theatre, 855
Streetcar Named Desire, A (p), 5/23/50, New York City Center, 24
Streetcar Named Desire, A (p), 2/15/56, New York City Center, 15
Streetcar Named Desire, A (p), 4/26/73, Vivian Beaumont Theatre, 110
Streetcar Named Desire, A (p), 10/4/73, St. James Theatre, 53
Streets Are Guarded, The (p), 11/20/44, Henry Miller's Theatre, 24
Streets of New York, The (p), 10/6/31, 48th St. Theatre, 85
Streets of New York, The (m), 10/29/63, Maidman Playhouse, 318
Streets of Paris (r), 6/19/39, Broadhurst Theatre, 274
Strength of the Weak, The (p), 4/17/06, Liberty Theatre, 27
Strictly Dishonorable (p), 9/18/29, Avon Theatre, 563
Strictly for Kicks (r), 12/8/68, Hunter College Auditorium, 13, (Oxford & Cambridge Shakespeare Co.)
Strife (p), 11/17/09, New Theatre
Strike Heaven on the Face! (p), 1/15/73, Bijou Theatre, 2, (New Phoenix Repertory Sideshow)
Strike Me Pink (r), 3/4/33, Majestic Theatre, 122
Strike Up the Band (m), 1/14/30, Times Square Theatre, 191
String. See An Evening of One Acts
Strings, My Lord, Are False, The (p), 5/19/42, Royale Theatre, 15
Strip for Action (p), 9/30/42, National Theatre, 109
Strip Girl (p), 10/19/35, Longacre Theatre, 33
Stripped (p), 10/21/29, Ambassador Theatre, 24
Strollers, The (m), 6/24/01, Knickerbocker Theatre, 70
Strong Are Lonely, The (p), 9/29/53, Broadhurst Theatre, 7
Strong Breed, The / The Trials of Brother Jero (p), 11/9/67, Greenwich Mews Theatre, 115
Strong Man's House, A (p), 9/16/29, Ambassador Theatre, 24
Strong, The (p), 2/26/24, 49th St. Theatre, 2
Stronger Sex, The (p), 11/23/08, Weber Theatre, 48
Stronger than Love (p), 12/28/25, Belasco Theatre, 49
Stronger, The / Miss Julie (p), 2/21/56, Phoenix Theatre, 32
Stronger, The / Miss Julie (p), 11/10/65, Provincetown Playhouse, 11
Stronger, The / Pariah (p), 3/18/13, 48th St. Theatre, 1
Strongheart (p), 1/30/05, Hudson Theatre, 66
Strongheart (p), 8/28/05, Savoy Theatre, 32
Struggle Everlasting, The (p), 9/26/07, Hackett Theatre, 20
Strugglers, The (p), 11/6/11, Bijou Theatre, 8
Strut, Miss Lizzie (r), 6/3/22, Earl Carroll Theatre, 96
Stuart Walker Portmanteau Theatre Repertory, 11/27/16, 39th St. Theatre
Stuart Walker Portmanteau Theatre Repertory, 1/15/19, Punch and Judy Theatre
Stubborn Cinderella, A (m), 1/25/09, Broadway Theatre, 88
Stubborness of Geraldine, The (p), 11/3/02, Garrick Theatre, 64
Student Gypsy, or The Prince of Liederkrantz (m), 9/30/63, 54th St. Theatre, 16
Student King, The (m), 12/25/06, Garden Theatre, 40
Student Prince, The (m), 12/2/24, Jolson Theatre, 608
Student Prince, The (m), 1/29/31, Majestic Theatre, 45
Student Prince, The (m), 6/8/43, Broadway Theatre, 153
Student Prince, The (m), 7/13/61, Jan Hus House, 22
Studs Edsel (p), 3/7/74, Ensemble Studio Theatre, 10
Sty of the Blind Pig, The (p), 11/23/71, St. Marks Playhouse, 64
Styles in Acting (Dorothy Sands), 4/3/32, Booth Theatre, 2
Subject of Scandal and Concern, A / Captain Fantastic Meets the Ectomorph (p), 3/7/66, New Theatre Workshop, 3
Subject to Fits (p), 2/14/71, Public/Other Stage, 127
Subject Was Roses, The (p), 5/25/64, Royale Theatre, 832
Subscriber, The. See The Grab Bag
Substitute for Murder (p), 10/22/35, Ethel Barrymore Theatre, 15
Suburban Tragedy. See Monopoly
Subway Express (p), 9/24/29, Liberty Theatre, 270
Subway, The (p), 2/5/29, Masque Theatre, 23
Subway, The (p), 1/25/29, Cherry Lane Theatre, 35
Subways Are for Sleeping (m), 12/27/61, St. James Theatre, 205
Success (p), 1/28/18, Harris Theatre, 64
Success Story (p), 9/26/32, Maxine Elliott's Theatre, 120
Successful Calamity, A (p), 2/5/17, Booth Theatre, 144
Successful Calamity, A (p), 2/12/34, Cherry Lane Theatre
Such a Little Queen (p), 8/31/09, Hackett Theatre, 103
Such Is Life (p), 11/25/16, Princess Theatre, 9
Such Is Life (p), 8/31/27, Morosco Theatre, 22
Sudden and Accidental Reeducation of Horse Johnson, The (p), 12/18/68, Belasco Theatre, 5
Sudden End of Anne Cinquefoil, The (p), 1/10/61, East End Theatre, 2
Suddenly Last Summer / A Memory of Two Mondays (p), 10/30/64, Master Theatre, 9, (Equity Library Theatre)
Suddenly Last Summer / Something Unspoken. See Garden District
Suds in Your Eye (p), 1/12/44, Cort Theatre, 37
Sue, Dear (m), 7/10/22, Times Sq. Theatre, 97
Sugar (m), 4/9/72, Majestic Theatre, 505
Sugar Hill (m), 12/25/31, Forrest Theatre, 11
Suggs (p), 5/4/72, Forum Theatre, 20
Sultan of Sulu, The (m), 12/29/02, Wallack Theatre, 192
Sumidagawa. See National Theatres of Japan
Summer and Smoke (p), 10/6/48, Music Box Theatre, 102
Summer and Smoke (p), 4/24/52, Circle in the Square Theatre, 356
Summer Brave (p), 4/5/73, Master Theatre, 12, (Equity Library Theatre)
Summer Festival of Gilbert & Sullivan, A, 7/18/62, Jan Hus House, 14
Summer Night (p), 12/2/39, St. James Theatre, 4
Summer of Daisy Miller, The (p), 5/27/63, Phoenix Theatre, 17
Summer of the 17th Doll (p), 1/22/58, Coronet Theatre, 29
Summer of the 17th Doll (p), 10/13/59, Players Theatre, 137
Summer of the 17th Doll (p), 2/20/68, St. Marks Playhouse, 40
Summer Pygmies, The (p), 12/12/60, Jan Hus House, 16
Summer Widowers, The (m), 6/4/10, Broadway Theatre, 140
Summer Wives (p), 4/13/36, Mansfield Theatre, 8
Summertree (p), 3/3/68, Forum Theatre, 127
Summertree (p), 12/9/69, Players Theatre, 184
Sumurun (p), 1/16/12, Casino Theatre, 62
Sun and I, The (p), 3/20/49, New Stages Theatre, 23
Sun Dodgers, The (m), 11/30/12, Broadway Theatre, 29

Sun Field, The (p), 12/9/42, Biltmore Theatre, 5
Sun Kissed (p), 3/10/37, Little Theatre, 53
Sun Showers (m), 2/5/23, Astor Theatre, 48
Sun Up (p), 5/24/23, Provincetown Playhouse, 361
Sun Up (p), 10/22/28, Lucille La Verne Theatre, 137
Sunday (p), 11/15/04, Hudson Theatre, 79
Sunday Breakfast (p), 5/28/52, Coronet Theatre, 16
Sunday Dinner (p), 10/16/70, St. Clement's Church, 41, (American Place Theatre)
Sunday in New York (p), 11/29/61, Cort Theatre, 188
Sunday Man (p), 5/13/64, Morosco Theatre, 1
Sundown Beach (p), 9/7/48, Belasco Theatre, 7
Sunken Bell, The (p), 3/26/00, Knickerbocker Theatre, 40
Sunkist (r), 5/23/21, Globe Theatre
Sunny (m), 9/22/25, New Amsterdam Theatre, 517
Sunny Days (m), 2/8/28, Imperial Theatre, 101
Sunny Days (m), 10/1/28, Century Theatre, 32
Sunny Morning, A (p), 5/7/21, Neighborhood Playhouse, 12
Sunny Morning, A (p), 4/13/29, Civic Repertory Theatre, 2
Sunny Morning, A (p), 11/18/30, Civic Repertory Theatre
Sunny Morning, A / The Women Have Their Way (p), 12/7/35, Sam S. Shubert Theatre, 1
Sunny River (m), 12/4/41, St. James Theatre, 36
Sunrise at Campobello (p), 1/30/58, Cort Theatre, 556
Sunset (p), 5/12/66, 81st Street Theatre, 14
Sunset (p), 12/5/72, Brooklyn Academy of Music, 24, (Chelsea Theatre Center)
Sunshine (p), 8/17/26, Lyric Theatre, 15
Sunshine Boys, The (p), 12/20/72, Broadhurst Theatre, 538
Sunshine Girl, The (m), 2/3/13, Knickerbocker Theatre, 160
Sunshine Train, The, 6/15/72, Abbey Theatre, 214
Sunstroke. See Passing Through from Exotic Places
Sunup to Sundown (p), 2/1/38, Hudson Theatre, 7
Superstition of Sue, The (p), 4/4/04, Savoy Theatre, 8
Supper Club, The (m), 12/23/01, Winter Garden Theatre, 40
Supper for the Dead / Chair Endowed / The No 'Count Boy. See Salvation on a String, 7/6/54, Theatre de Lys, 8
Sure Fire (p), 10/20/26, Waldorf Theatre, 37
Surgeon, The (p), 10/27/32, Belmont Theatre, 6
Surprises of Love, The (p), 1/22/00, Lyceum Theatre, 41
Survival of St. Joan, The (m), 2/28/71, Anderson Theatre, 17
Survival of the Fittest, The (p), 3/14/21, Greenwich Village Theatre, 40
Survivors, The (p), 1/19/48, Playhouse, 8
Susan and God (p), 10/7/37, Plymouth Theatre, 287
Susan and God (p), 12/13/43, New York City Center, 8
Susan in Search of a Husband / A Tenement Tragedy (p), 11/20/06, Liberty Theatre, 14
Susan Slept Here (p), 7/11/61, 41st St. Theatre, 16
Susannah and the Elders (p), 10/18/59, Broadway Congregational Church, 10
Susie Is a Good Girl. See The Grab Bag
Suspect (p), 4/9/40, Playhouse, 31
Suspense (p), 8/12/30, Fulton Theatre, 7
Suzanna and the Elders (p), 10/29/40, Morosco Theatre, 30
Suzanne (p), 12/26/10, Lyceum Theatre, 64
Suzette (m), 11/24/21, Princess Theatre, 4
Suzi (m), 11/3/14, Casino Theatre, 55
Swan Song (p), 5/15/46, Booth Theatre, 158
Swan, The (p), 10/23/23, Cort Theatre, 253
Sweeney Todd (p), 7/16/24, Frazee Theatre, 67
Sweet Adeline (m), 9/3/29, Hamerstein Theatre, 233
Sweet Aloes (p), 3/2/36, Booth Theatre, 24
Sweet and Low (m), 11/17/30, 46th St. Theatre, 184
Sweet and Twenty (p), 12/30/01, Madison Sq. Theatre, 16
Sweet and Twenty / The Romanesques (p), 1/13/02, Madison Square Theatre, 32
Sweet Anne Page (m), 12/3/00, Manhattan Theatre, 29
Sweet Bird of Youth (p), 3/10/59, Martin Beck Theatre, 375
Sweet Chariot (p), 10/23/30, Ambassador Theatre, 3
Sweet Charity (p), 12/28/42, Mansfield Theatre, 8
Sweet Charity (m), 1/29/66, Palace Theatre, 608
Sweet Confusion / I Rise in Flame, Cried the Phoenix (p), 4/14/59, Theatre de Lys, 1
Sweet Enemy, The (p), 2/15/65, Actors Playhouse, 8
Sweet Eros / Witness (p), 11/21/68, Gramercy Arts Theatre, 78
Sweet Feet (m), 5/25/72, New Theatre, 6
Sweet Genevieve (p), 3/20/45, President Theatre, 1
Sweet Kitty Bellairs (p), 12/9/03, Belasco Theatre, 206
Sweet Kitty Bellairs (p), 9/3/04, Belasco Theatre, 25
Sweet Land of Liberty (p), 9/23/29, Knickerbocker Theatre, 8
Sweet Little Devil (m), 1/21/24, Astor Theatre, 120
Sweet Marie (m), 10/10/01, Hammerstein's Victoria Theatre, 28
Sweet Miani (m), 9/25/62, Players Theatre, 22
Sweet Mystery of Life (p), 10/11/35, Shubert Theatre, 11
Sweet Nell of Old Drury (p), 12/31/00, Knickerbocker Theatre, 18
Sweet Nell of Old Drury (p), 5/16/23, 48th St. Theatre, 51
Sweet River (p), 10/28/36, 51st St. Theatre, 5
Sweet Seventeen (p), 3/17/24, Lyceum Theatre, 72
Sweet Stranger (p), 10/21/30, Cort Theatre, 32
Sweetheart Shop, The (m), 8/31/20, Knickerbocker Theatre, 55
Sweetheart Time (m), 1/19/26, Imperial Theatre, 145
Sweethearts (m), 9/8/13, New Amsterdam Theatre, 136
Sweethearts (m), 9/21/29, Jolson Theatre, 17
Sweethearts (m), 1/21/47, Shubert Theatre, 288
Swifty (p), 10/16/22, Playhouse, 24
Swim Low Little Goldfish (p), 9/28/65, 41st Street Theatre, 1
Swing It (m), 7/22/37, Adelphi Theatre, 60
Swing Mikado, The (m), 3/1/39, New Yorker Theatre, 86
Swing Your Lady! (p), 10/18/36, Booth Theatre, 101
Swingers, The. See Four on a Garden
Swingin' the Dream (m), 11/29/39, Center Theatre, 13
Sword of the King, The (p), 10/6/02, Wallack Theatre, 48
Swords (p), 9/1/21, National Theatre, 36
Sybil (m), 1/10/16, Liberty Theatre, 168
Sylvelin (p), 11/16/20, Times Square Theatre, 2
Sylvia (p), 4/25/23, Provincetown Playhouse, 13
Sylvia Plath, 1/15/74, Brooklyn Academy of Music, 14, (Royal Shakespeare Co.)
Sylvia Runs Away (p), 8/20/14, Playhouse, 12
Symphony (p), 4/26/35, Cort Theatre, 3
Symphony in Two Flats (p), 9/16/30, Shubert Theatre, 47
Synthetic Sin (p), 10/10/27, 49th St. Theatre, 24

T

Ta Bouche, 3/14/29, Jolson Theatre, 12
Taboo (p), 4/4/22, Sam H. Harris Theatre, 3
Tailor-Made Man, A (p), 8/27/17, Cohan and Harris Theatre, 398
Tailor-Made Man, A (p), 10/21/29, Gallo Theatre, 8
Tainted Philanthropy (p), 11/26/12, Belasco Theatre, 1
Take a Bow (r), 6/15/44, Broadhurst Theatre, 12
Take a Chance (m), 11/26/32, Apollo Theatre, 246
Take a Giant Step (p), 9/24/53, Lyceum Theatre, 76
Take a Giant Step (p), 9/25/56, Jan Hus House, 264
Take Her, She's Mine (p), 12/21/61, Biltmore Theatre, 404
Take It As It Comes (p), 2/10/44, 48th St. Theatre, 16
Take It from Me (m), 3/31/19, 44th St. Theatre, 96
Take It from the Top, 11/22/67, Gramercy Arts Theatre, 15
Take Me Along (m), 10/22/59, Shubert Theatre, 448
Take Me to Bed / Time for Bed (p), 6/13/69, Provincetown Playhouse, 12
Take My Advice (p), 11/27/11, Fulton Theatre, 80
Take My Advice (p), 11/1/27, Belmont Theatre, 47
Take My Tip (p), 4/11/32, 48th St. Theatre, 24
Take One Step (m), 7/3/69, N.Y. Shakespeare Festival Mobile Theatre
Take the Air (m), 11/22/27, Waldorf Theatre, 208
Taking Chances (p), 3/17/15, 39th St. Theatre, 85
Tale of Kasane, The. See The National Theatre of the Deaf
Tale of the Wolf, The. See The Phantom Rival—same play, 10/7/25, Empire Theatre, 14
Tales of Rigo (m), 5/30/27, Lyric Theatre, 8
Talk About Girls (m), 6/14/27, Waldorf Theatre, 15
Talk of New York, The (m), 12/3/07, Knickerbocker Theatre, 157
Talker, The (p), 1/8/12, Harris Theatre, 144
Talking Parrot, The (p), 12/3/23, Frazee Theatre, 8
Talking to You / Across the Board on Tomorrow Morning (p), 8/17/42, Belasco Theatre, 8
Talking to You / Across the Board on Tomorrow Morning. See Two by Saroyan, 10/22/61, East End Theatre, 96
Tall and Rex. See Four Americans
Tall Story (p), 1/29/59, Belasco Theatre, 108
Talley Method, The (p), 2/24/41, Henry Miller's Theatre, 56
Tallulah, A Memory, 1/14/71, Lincoln Center Library Auditorium, 4
Tambourines to Glory (m), 11/2/63, Little Theatre, 24
Tamburlaine the Great (p), 1/19/56, Winter Garden Theatre, 20
Taming of Helen, The (p), 3/30/03, Savoy Theatre, 40
Taming of the Shrew, The (p) (Ada Rehan), 2/6/05, Liberty Theatre, 8
Taming of the Shrew, The (p), 5/11/21, Broadhurst Theatre, 4
Taming of the Shrew, The (p), 11/14/21, Century Theatre, 8, (Sothern-Marlowe Shakespeare Repertory)
Taming of the Shrew, The (p), 12/26/21, Lexington Theatre, 2
Taming of the Shrew, The (p), 10/15/23, Jolson Theatre, 7
Taming of the Shrew, The (p), 12/18/25, Klaw Theatre, 9
Taming of the Shrew, The (p) (Basil Sydney), 10/25/27, Garrick Theatre, 175
Taming of the Shrew, The (p), 3/27/30, Shubert Theatre, 1
Taming of the Shrew, The (p), 1/27/33, Shakespeare Theatre, 15

Taming of the Shrew, The (p) (Lunt-Fontanne), 9/30/35, Guild Theatre, 128
Taming of the Shrew, The (p) (Lunt-Fontanne), 2/5/40, Alvin Theatre, 8
Taming of the Shrew, The (p) (Margaret Webster), 4/25/51, New York City Center, 15
Taming of the Shrew, The (p), 2/20/57, Phoenix Theatre, 23, (ASFTA)
Taming of the Shrew, The (p), 3/6/63, Anderson Theatre, 39
Taming of the Shrew, The (p), 6/27/65, Delacorte Mobile Theatre, 26
Taming of the Shrew, The (p), 1/30/72, Roundabout Theatre, 45
Taming of the Shrew, The (p), 9/11/73, Performance Garage, 21
Taming of the Shrew, The (p), 3/7/74, Brooklyn Academy of Music, 12, (Young Vic Co.)
Tangerine (m), 8/9/21, Casino Theatre, 337
Tangerine (m), 8/7/22, Casino Theatre, 24
Tangled Lives (p), 1/22/26, Bramhall Playhouse, 31
Tangletoes (p), 2/17/25, 39th St. Theatre, 23
Tango (p), 1/18/69, Pocket Theatre, 67
Tantalizing Tommy (m), 10/1/12, Criterion Theatre, 31
Tante (p), 10/28/13, Empire Theatre, 79
Tantrum, The (p), 9/4/24, Cort Theatre, 28
Tanyard Street (p), 2/4/41, Little Theatre, 23
Tapestry in Gray (p), 12/27/35, Sam S. Shubert Theatre, 24
Taps (p), 9/17/04, Lyric Theatre, 25
Taps, 4/14/25, Broadhurst Theatre, 31
Tarnish (p), 10/1/23, Belmont Theatre, 255
Tarot (m), 12/11/70, Brooklyn Academy of Music, 13, (Chelsea Theatre Center)
Tarot (m), 3/4/71, Circle in the Square Theatre, 38
Tartuffe (p), 1/14/65, ANTA— Washington Square Theatre, 74
Tartuffe (p), 4/16/68, Barbizon-Plaza Theatre, 28, (Le Treteau de Paris)
Tartuffe (p), 7/2/68, Vivian Beaumont Theatre, 7, (Compagnie du Théâtre de la Cité de Villeurbanne)
Tarzan of the Apes (p), 9/7/21, Broadhurst Theatre, 13
Taste of Honey, A (p), 10/4/60, Lyceum Theatre, 376
Tattle Tales (r), 6/1/33, Broadhurst Theatre, 28
Tattooed Countess, The (m), 4/3/61, Barbizon-Plaza Theatre, 4
Tattooed Man, The (m), 2/18/07, Criterion Theatre, 59
Tavern, The (p), 9/27/20, George M. Cohan Theatre, 252
Tavern, The (p), 5/23/21, Hudson Theatre, 4
Tavern, The (p), 5/19/30, Fulton Theatre, 32
Tavern, The (p), 4/4/62, Folksbiene Playhouse, 14, (APA Repertory)
Tavern, The (p), 3/5/64, Phoenix Theatre, 15, (APA Repertory)
Taylor, Laurette Scenes from Shakespeare. See Laurette Taylor
Tchin-Tchin (p), 10/25/62, Plymouth Theatre, 222
Tea and Sympathy (p), 9/30/53, Ethel Barrymore Theatre, 712
Tea for Three (p), 9/19/18, Maxine Elliot's Theatre, 300
Tea Party / The Basement (p), 10/15/68, Eastside Playhouse, 176
Teach Me How To Cry (p), 4/5/55, Theatre de Lys, 48
Teahouse of the August Moon, The (p), 10/15/53, Martin Beck Theatre, 1,027
Teahouse of the August Moon, The (p), 11/8/56, New York City Center, 14
Teaser, The (p), 7/27/21, Playhouse, 29
Teaspoon Every Four Hours, A (p), 6/14/69, ANTA Theatre, 1 and 97 previews
Teatro Campesino, El (La Carpa de Los Rasquachis) (p), 4/19/73, Brooklyn Academy of Music, 10, (Chelsea Theatre Center)
Teatro dei Piccoli, 12/22/32, Lyric Theatre, 141
Teatro dei Piccoli of Rome. See Marionette Players, The
Teatro dei Piccoli, Vittorio Podrecca's, 1/8/34, Hudson Theatre, 45
Tel Aviv Drama Company (Dreyfus on Devil's Island; Monsieur Artaud), 9/20/73, Hunter College Playhouse, 4
Telemachus Clay (p), 11/15/63, The Writers' Stage, 125
Telephone Pole (p), 11/29/65, New Theatre Workshop, 3
Telephone, The / The Medium (m), 5/1/47, Ethel Barrymore Theatre, 212
Telephone, The / The Medium (m), 12/7/48, New York City Center, 40
Telephone, The / The Medium (m), 7/19/50, Arena, Edison Hotel, 110
Tell Her the Truth (m), 10/28/32, Cort Theatre, 11
Tell Me More (m), 4/13/25, Gaiety Theatre, 100
Tell Me, Pretty Maiden (p), 12/16/37, Mansfield Theatre, 28
Tell My Story (p), 3/15/39, Mercury Theatre, 1
Temper the Wind (p), 12/27/46, Playhouse, 35
Temperamental Journey, The (p), 9/4/13, Belasco Theatre, 124
Tempest, The (p) (Louis Calvert), 4/24/16, Century Theatre, 32
Tempest, The (p), 2/25/33, Shakespeare Theatre, 9
Tempest, The (p), 1/25/45, Alvin Theatre, 100
Tempest, The (p), 11/12/45, New York City Center, 24
Tempest, The (p), 12/28/59, East 74th St. Theatre, 18
Tempest, The (p), 7/6/62, Delacorte Theatre, Central Park, 22
Tempest, The (p), 1/26/74, Mitzi E. Newhouse Theatre, 81
Temporary Island, The (p), 3/14/48, Maxine Elliott's Theatre, 6
Temptation / Gaby / Hell, 4/27/11, Follies Bergère Theatre, 92
Ten Little Indians (p), 6/27/44, Broadhurst Theatre, 425
Ten Million Ghosts (p), 10/23/36, St. James Theatre, 11
Ten Minute Alibi (p), 10/17/33, Ethel Barrymore Theatre, 87
Ten Nights in a Barroom (p), 3/27/28, Wallack Theatre, 111
Ten Nights in a Barroom (p), 1/20/32, John Golden Theatre, 33
Ten Nights in a Barroom (m), 10/1/62, Greenwich Mews Theatre, 32
Ten Per Cent (p), 9/13/27, George M. Cohan Theatre, 23
Tender Trap, The (p), 10/13/54, Longacre Theatre, 101
Tender Trap, The (p), 8/22/61, 41st St. Theatre, 16
Tenderfoot, The (m), 2/22/04, New York Theatre, 81
Tenderloin (m), 10/17/60, 46th St. Theatre, 216
Tendresse, La (p), 9/25/22, Empire Theatre, 65
Tenement Tragedy, A / Susan in Search of a Husband (p), 11/20/06, Liberty Theatre, 14
Tenth Avenue (p), 8/15/27, Eltinge Theatre, 88
Tenth Man, The (p), 11/5/59, Booth Theatre, 623
Tenth Man, The (p), 11/8/67, New York City Center, 23
Tenth of an Inch Makes the Difference, A (p), 11/12/62, East End Theatre, 80
Tenting Tonight (p), 4/2/47, Booth Theatre, 46
Terence (p), 1/5/04, New York Theatre, 56
Terminal (p), 4/13/70, St. Clement's Church, 2, (Open Theatre)
Terminal, 5/26/70, Washington Square Methodist Church, 9, (Open Theatre)
Terminal, 9/15/73, St. Clement's Church Theatre, 5, (Open Theatre)
Terraces (p), 4/2/74, St. Marks Playhouse, 8
Terrible Angels, The (p), 11/1/71, Stage 73 Theatre
Terrible Jim Fitch. See Stop, You're Killing Me
Terrible Meek, The / The Flower of the Palace of Han (p), 3/19/12, Little Theatre, 39
Terrible Swift Sword, The (p), 11/15/55, Phoenix Theatre, 8
Terry, Ellen. See Ellen Terry
Tess of the D'Urbervilles (p), 5/6/02, Manhattan Theatre, 20
Tethered Sheep / The Maker of Dreams (p), 3/3/15, Neighborhood Playhouse
Tevya and His Daughters (p), 9/16/57, Carnegie Hall Playhouse, 80
Texas Nightingale, The (p), 11/20/22, Empire Theatre, 32
Thérèse (p), 10/9/45, Biltmore Theatre, 96
Théâtre de France (Renaud-Barrault Co.), 2/25/64, New York City Center, 24
Théâtre du Nouveau Monde, Le, 4/29/58, Phoenix Theatre, 16
Théâtre National Populaire, 10/14/58, Broadway Theatre, 23
Thais (p), 3/14/11, Criterion Theatre, 31
Thais (p), 6/18/31, President Theatre, 5
Thank You (p), 10/3/21, Longacre Theatre, 257
Thank You, Miss Victoria. See Six from La Mama (1st Program)
Thank You Svoboda (p), 3/1/44, Mansfield Theatre, 6
Thanks to You. See The Ghost Between
That Awful Mrs. Eaton (p), 9/29/24, Morosco Theatre, 16
That Championship Season (p), 5/2/72, Public/Newman Theatre, 144
That Championship Season (p), 9/14/72, Booth Theatre, 844
That Day (p), 10/3/22, Bijou Theatre, 15
That Ferguson Family (p), 12/22/28, Little Theatre, 129
That Five A.M. Jazz (The First / Five A.M. Jazz) (m), 10/19/64, Astor Place Playhouse, 94
That French Lady (p), 3/15/27, Ritz Theatre, 47
That Girl at the Bijou (r), 11/9/56, Bijou Theatre, 11
That Hat! (m), 9/23/64, Theatre Four, 1
That Lady (p), 11/22/49, Martin Beck Theatre, 79
That Man and I (p), 1/25/04, Savoy Theatre, 23
That Old Devil (p), 6/5/44, Playhouse, 16
That's Entertainment (r), 4/14/72, Edison Theatre, 4
That's Gratitude (p), 9/11/30, John Golden Theatre, 197
That's Gratitude (p), 6/16/32, Waldorf Theatre, 204
That's the Woman (p), 9/3/30, Fulton Theatre, 29
That Smith Boy (p), 2/20/26, Mayfair Theatre, 20
That Sort (p), 11/6/14, Harris Theatre, 25
That Summer—That Fall (p), 3/16/67, Helen Hayes Theatre, 12
That Thing at the Cherry Lane (r), 5/18/65, Cherry Lane Theatre, 7
Theatre (p), 11/12/41, Hudson Theatre, 69
Theatre: Fair of Opinion (r), 3/23/72, St. Clement's Church, 15
Theatre of Peretz, The (p), 11/5/63, Gate Theatre, 102
Theatre of the Absurd (9 Plays), 2/11/62, Cherry Lane Theatre, 55
Theatre on the Balustrade of Prague. See Button, Button
Theatre 1969 Playwrights Repertory (Box/Quotations from Chairman Mao Tse-Tung; The Death of Bessie Smith/The American Dream; Krapp's Last Tape/The Zoo Story; Happy Days (p), 9/30/68, Billy Rose Theatre, 32
Them's the Reporters (p), 5/29/35, Ethel Barrymore Theatre, 6
Theodora, the Queen (p), 1/31/34, Forrest Theatre, 6
There and Back / The Man Who Stole the Castle (p), 4/20/03, Princess Theatre, 48
There Is a Play Tonight (p), 2/15/61, Theatre Marquee, 15
There's a Girl in My Soup (p), 10/18/67, Music Box Theatre, 322
There's Always a Breeze (p), 3/2/38, Windsor Theatre, 5
There's Always Juliet (p), 2/15/32, Empire Theatre, 109
There's Always Juliet (p), 10/27/32, Ethel Barrymore Theatre, 20
There's Many a Slip (p), 9/15/02, Garrick Theatre, 20

There's Many a Slip / At the Telephone (p), 10/2/02, Garrick Theatre, 20
There's One in Every Marriage (p), 1/3/72, Royale Theatre, 16
There's Wisdom in Women (p), 10/30/35, Cort Theatre, 46
There Shall Be No Night (p), 4/29/40, Alvin Theatre, 115
There Shall Be No Night (p), 9/9/40, Alvin Theatre, 66
There Was a Little Girl (p), 2/29/60, Cort Theatre, 16
There You Are (m), 5/16/32, George M. Cohan Theatre, 8
These Are My Loves (Claire Luce), 4/18/60, Maidman Playhouse, 8
These Charming People (p), 10/6/25, Gaiety Theatre, 97
These Days (p), 11/12/28, Cort Theatre, 8
These Few Ashes (p), 10/30/28, Booth Theatre, 39
These Modern Women (p), 2/13/28, Eltinge Theatre, 24
These Two (p), 5/7/34, Henry Miller's Theatre, 8
Thesmophoriazusae (p), 12/13/55, Rooftop Theatre, 8
They All Come to Moscow (p), 5/11/33, Lyceum Theatre, 19
They All Want Something (p), 10/12/26, Wallack Theatre, 63
They Don't Make 'Em Like That Anymore (r), 6/8/72, Plaza 9 Music Hall, 32
They Don't Mean Any Harm (p), 2/23/32, Charles Hopkins Theatre, 15
They Got Jack (p), 1/17/66, New Theatre Workshop, 3
They Knew What They Wanted (p), 11/24/24, Garrick Theatre, 192
They Knew What They Wanted (p), 10/2/39, Empire Theatre, 24
They Knew What They Wanted (p), 2/16/49, Music Box Theatre, 61
They Never Grow Up (p), 4/7/30, Theatre Masque, 24
They Shall Not Die (p), 2/21/34, Royale Theatre, 62
They Should Have Stood in Bed (p), 2/13/42, Mansfield Theatre, 11
They Walk Alone (p), 3/12/41, Shubert Theatre, 21
Thief, The (p), 9/9/07, Lyceum Theatre, 281
Thief, The (p), 9/3/08, Empire Theatre, 16
Thief, The (p), 10/16/11, Daly's Theatre, 16
Thief, The (p), 4/22/27, Ritz Theatre, 86
Thieves (p), 4/7/74, Broadhurst Theatre, 62
Thieves' Carnival (p), 2/1/55, Cherry Lane Theatre, 152
Thieves' Carnival (p), 12/13/74, Gotham Art Theatre
Thin Ice (p), 9/30/22, Comedy Theatre, 105
Things. See Four Americans
Things That Almost Happen (Morton: The Patient / The Courtship of Kevin and Roxanne / Dominic's Lover) (p), 2/18/71, Provincetown Playhouse, 6
Things That Are Caesar's (p), 10/17/32, Martin Beck Theatre, 4
Things That Count, The (p), 12/8/13, Maxine Elliott's Theatre, 224
Third Best Sport (p), 12/30/58, Ambassador Theatre, 79
Third Degree, The (p), 2/1/09, Hudson Theatre, 168
Third Ear, The (r), 5/28/64, Premise Theatre, 150
Third Little Show, The (r), 6/1/31, Music Box Theatre, 136
Third Party, The (p), 8/3/14, 39th St. Theatre, 104
Third Person (p), 12/29/55, President Theatre, 76
Thirsty Soil (p), 2/3/37, 48th St. Theatre, 13
Thirteen Daughters (m), 3/2/61, 54th St. Theatre, 28
Thirteenth Chair, The (p), 11/20/16, 48th St. Theatre, 328
Thirty Days Hath September (p), 9/30/38, Hudson Theatre, 16
Thirty-nine East (p), 3/31/19, Broadhurst Theatre, 160
This Bird of Dawning Singeth All Night Long. See American Night Cry
This Bird of Dawning Singeth All Night Long. See Trainer, Dean, Liepolt and Company
This Fine-Pretty World (p), 12/26/23, Neighborhood Playhouse, 32
This Here Nice Place (p), 11/1/66, Theatre 80 St. Marks, 6
This Is New York, 11/28/30, Plymouth Theatre, 59
This Is the Army (r), 7/4/42, Broadway Theatre, 113
This Is the Rill Speaking. See Six from La Mama (1st Program)
This Man's Town (p), 3/10/30, Ritz Theatre, 9
This One Man, 10/21/30, Morosco Theatre, 39
This Our House (p), 12/11/35, 58th St. Theatre, 2
This Proud Pilgrimage (p), 6/8/40, Heckscher Theatre
This Rock (p), 2/18/43, Longacre Theatre, 36
This Side of Paradise (p), 2/21/62, Sheridan Square Playhouse, 87
This Thing Called Love (p), 9/17/28, Maxine Elliott's Theatre, 138
This Time Tomorrow (p), 11/3/47, Ethel Barrymore Theatre, 32
This, Too, Shall Pass (p), 4/30/46, Belasco Theatre, 63
This Was a Man (p), 11/23/26, Klaw Theatre, 31
This Was Burlesque (r), 3/6/62, Casino-East Theatre, 1,634
This Was Burlesque (r), 2/11/70, Hudson West Theatre, 106
This Way Out (p), 8/30/17, Cohan Theatre, 28
This Woman and This Man (p), 2/22/09, Maxine Elliott's Theatre, 24
This Woman Business, 12/7/26, Ritz Theatre, 63
This Year of Grace (r), 11/7/28, Selwyn Theatre, 158
Thistle in My Bed (p), 11/19/63, Gramercy Arts Theatre, 3
Thor, With Angels (p), 10/14/56, Broadway Congregational Church, 10
Thornton Wilder's Triple Bill (The Long Christmas Dinner / Queens of France / The Happy Journey to Trenton and Camden) (p), 9/6/66, Cherry Lane Theatre, 55
Thoroughbred (p), 11/6/33, Vanderbilt Theatre, 24
Thoroughbreds (p), 9/8/24, Vanderbilt Theatre, 16
Those Endearing Young Charms (p), 6/16/43, Booth Theatre, 60
Those That Play the Clowns (p), 11/24/66, ANTA Theatre, 4
Those We Love (p), 2/19/30, John Golden Theatre, 77
Those Who Walk in Darkness (p), 8/14/19, 48th St. Theatre, 28
Thou Desperate Pilot (p), 3/7/27, Morosco Theatre, 8
Thoughts (m), 3/19/73, Theatre de Lys, 24
Thoughts on the Instant of Greeting a Friend on the Street. See Collision Course
Thousand Clowns, A (p), 4/5/62, Eugene O'Neill Theatre, 428
Thousand Summers, A (p), 5/24/32, Selwyn Theatre, 47
Thousand Years Ago, A (p), 1/6/14, Shubert Theatre, 87
Thracian Horses, The (p), 9/27/61, Orpheum Theatre, 7
Three (p), 12/3/28, Edyth Totten Theatre, 8
Three and One (p), 10/25/33, Longacre Theatre, 77
Three at Judson (Harmony / Nice Place You Got Here / Three Sisters Who Are Not Sisters) (p), 6/5/65, Judson Memorial Church, 12
Three at the Cherry Lane. See Two Executioners / Dutchman / Play
Three Bags Full (p), 3/6/66, Henry Miller's Theatre, 33
Three Bears, The (p), 11/13/17, Empire Theatre, 39
Three by Ferlinghetti (Three Thousand Red Ants / The Alligation / The Victims of Amnesia) (p), 9/22/70, Jan Hus Theatre, 8
Three by Thurber (p), 3/7/55, Theatre de Lys, 2
Three Cheers (m), 10/15/28, Globe Theatre, 209
Three Daughters of Monsieur Dupont, The (p), 4/13/10, Comedy Theatre, 21
Three Doors (p), 4/23/25, Lenox Little Theatre, 27
Three Dramatic Monologues (Lorca), 3/24/58, Circle in the Square
Three Faces East (p), 8/13/18, Cohan and Harris Theatre, 335
Three for Diana (p), 4/21/19, Bijou Theatre, 32
Three for Tonight (r), 4/6/55, Plymouth Theatre, 85
Three from La Mama (This Is the Rill Speaking / Chicago / Birdbath) (p), 4/15/66, Martinique Theatre, 13
Three Hand Reel (Eternal Triangle / The Frying Pan / The Bridal Night) (p), 11/7/66, Renata Theatre, 72
Three Lights, The (p), 10/31/11, Bijou Theatre, 7
Three Little Business Men, The (p), 9/3/23, Thomashefsky's Broadway Theatre, 44
Three Little Girls (m), 4/14/30, Shubert Theatre, 104
Three Little Maids (m), 9/1/03, Daly's Theatre, 130
Three Live Ghosts (p), 9/29/20, Greenwich Village Theatre, 250
Three Men and a Woman (p), 1/11/32, Lyceum Theatre, 8
Three Men on a Horse (p), 1/30/35, Playhouse, 812
Three Men on a Horse (p), 10/9/42, Forrest Theatre, 28
Three Men on a Horse (p), 10/16/69, Lyceum Theatre, 100
Three Modern Japanese Plays (Sotoba Kamachi / Han's Crime / The Damask Drum), 2/3/61, Players Theatre, 45
Three Monkeys in a Glass. See Festival of New Italian Plays
Three Musketeers, The (m), 5/19/21, Manhattan Opera House, 5
Three Musketeers, The (m), 3/13/28, Lyric Theatre, 319
Three Musketeers, The (p), 6/25/68, Vivian Beaumont Theatre, 12, (Compagnie du Théâtre de la Cité de Villeurbanne)
Three of Hearts (p), 6/3/15, 39th St. Theatre, 20
Three of Us, The (p), 10/17/06, Madison Square Theatre, 227
Three on Broadway (r), 11/12/73, Theatre de Lys, 2, (Matinee Theatre)
Three One Acts (Monument to the Last Black Eunuch) (Home Cookin / Andrew / Oursides) (p), 4/19/72, New Federal Theatre, 6
Three Plays by Synge (In the Shadow of the Glen / The Tinker's Wedding / Riders to the Sea) (p), 3/6/57, Theatre East
Three Romeos, The (m), 11/13/11, Globe Theatre, 56
Three's a Crowd (p), 12/4/19, Cort Theatre, 12
Three's a Crowd (r), 10/15/30, Selwyn Theatre, 272
Three's a Family (p), 5/5/43, Longacre Theatre, 497
Three Showers (m), 4/5/20, Harris Theatre, 48
Three Sisters, The (p) (Moscow Art Theatre Repertory), 2/23, 59th St. Theatre
Three Sisters, The (p), 10/26/26, Civic Repertory Theatre, 36
Three Sisters, The (p), 10/27/27, Civic Repertory Theatre
Three Sisters, The (p), 10/13/30, Civic Repertory Theatre, 8
Three Sisters, The (p), 11/1/32, Civic Repertory Theatre, 4
Three Sisters, The (p), 10/14/39, Longacre Theatre, 9
Three Sisters, The (p), 12/21/42, Ethel Barrymore Theatre, 123
Three Sisters, The (p), 2/25/55, Fourth St. Theatre, 102
Three Sisters, The (p), 9/21/59, Fourth St. Theatre, 257
Three Sisters, The (p), 6/22/64, Morosco Theatre, 119, (Actor's Studio)
Three Sisters, The (p), 2/11/65, New York City Center, 8, (Moscow Art Theatre)
Three Sisters, The (p), 10/9/69, ANTA Theatre, 11, (American Conservatory Theatre)
Three Sisters, The (p), 6/11/70, Circle Theatre, 10
Three Sisters, The (p), 6/12/70, Circle Theatre, 10, (Experimental Prod.)
Three Sisters, The (p), 12/19/73, Billy Rose Theatre, 7, (City Center Acting Co.)
Three Sisters Who Are Not Sisters. See Three at Judson
Three Sisters Who Are Not Sisters / The Maids / In a Garden (p), 5/6/55, Tempo Playhouse, 63
Three Street Koans. See Kool Aid
Three Thousand Red Ants. See Three by Ferlinghetti

Three × Three (The Twenty-five Cent White Cap / George Washington Crossing the Delaware / Not Enough Rope) (p), 3/1/61, Maidman Theatre, 5
Three Times the Hour (p), 8/25/31, Avon Theatre, 16
Three To Make Ready (r), 3/7/46, Adelphi Theatre, 327
Three Twins (m), 6/15/08, Herald Square Theatre, 288
Three Waltzes (m), 12/25/37, Majestic Theatre, 122
Three Wise Fools (p), 10/31/18, Criterion Theatre, 316
Three Wise Fools (p), 3/1/36, John Golden Theatre, 9
Three Wishes for Jamie (m), 3/21/52, Mark Hellinger Theatre, 91
Three. . .With Women in Mind (Jeff Chandler / How a Nice Girl Named Janet Contracted Syphilis / I Hear It Kissing Me Ladies) (p), 11/14/70, Unit Theatre
Three-Cornered Moon (p), 3/16/33, Cort Theatre, 76
Threepenny Opera, The (m), 4/13/33, Empire Theatre, 12
Threepenny Opera, The (m), 3/10/54, Theatre de Lys, 96
Threepenny Opera, The (m), 9/20/55, Theatre de Lys, 2,611
Threepenny Opera, The (m), 10/27/66, Billy Rose Theatre, 16
Threepenny Opera, The (m), 10/13/72, WPA Theatre
Thrills (p), 4/16/25, Comedy Theatre, 12
Through the Night (p), 8/18/30, Masque Theatre, 16
Through the Years (m), 1/28/32, Manhattan Theatre, 20
Thru the Looking Glass / Alice in Wonderland (p), 12/12/32, Civic Repertory Theatre, 119
Thumbs Down (p), 8/6/23, 49th St. Theatre, 31
Thumbs Up (r), 12/27/34, St. James Theatre, 156
Thunder, 9/22/19, Criterion
Thunder in the Air (p), 11/11/29, 49th St. Theatre, 16
Thunder in the Index. See American Night Cry
Thunder on the Left (p), 10/31/33, Maxine Elliott's Theatre, 31
Thunder Rock (p), 11/14/39, Mansfield Theatre, 23
Thunder Rock (p), 2/26/56, Broadway Congregational Church, 10
Thunder Rock (p), 2/8/73, Master Theatre, 12, (Equity Library Theatre)
Thunderbolt, The (p), 11/12/10, New Theatre
Thunderbolt, The (p), 11/16/11, Lyric Theatre
Thurber Carnival, A (r), 2/26/60, ANTA Theatre, 127
Thurber Carnival, A (r), 9/5/60, ANTA Theatre, 96
Thurber Carnival, A (r), 10/1/65, Master Theatre, 9, (Equity Library Theatre)
Thursday Evening / Cornelius' Jewels / Nerves (p), 12/6/21, 15th St. Theatre, 2
Thy Name Is Woman (p), 11/15/20, Playhouse, 127
Thy Neighbor's Wife (p), 9/5/11, Lyceum Theatre, 15
Thy Will Be Done, 11/13/23, Century Theatre, 2
Tia Juana (p), 11/15/27, Bijou Theatre, 7
Tiao Ch'an, or the Beautiful Bait (p), 11/12/62, Longacre Theatre, 8, (Foo Hsing Theatre)
Tiao Ch'an, or The Beautiful Bait (p), 12/24/62, Morosco Theatre, 8, (Foo Hsing Theatre)
Ticket-of-Leave Man, the (p), 12/22/61, Midway Theatre, 31
Tickets, Please! (r), 4/27/50, Coronet Theatre, 245
Tickle Me (m), 8/17/20, Selwyn Theatre, 207
Ticklish Acrobat, 3/8/54, Amato Opera Theatre
Tick-Tack-Toe (r), 2/23/20, Princess Theatre, 32
Ti-Coq (p), 2/9/51, Broadhurst Theatre, 3
Tidbits of 1946 (p), 7/8/46, Plymouth Theatre, 8
Tide Rising (p), 1/25/37, Lyceum Theatre, 32
Tidings Brought to Mary, The (p), 12/25/22, Garrick Theatre, 32
Tie That Liberated, The (p), 3/7/21, Bramhall Playhouse, 21
Tiger at the Gates (p), 10/3/55, Plymouth Theatre, 217
Tiger at the Gates (p), 2/29/68, Vivian Beaumont Theatre, 44
Tiger Cats (p), 10/21/24, Belasco Theatre, 48
Tiger Rag, The (m), 2/16/61, Cherry Lane Theatre, 14
Tiger Rose (p), 10/3/17, Lyceum Theatre, 384
Tiger, The / The Typists (p), 2/4/63, Orpheum Theatre, 200
Tiger! Tiger! (p), 11/12/18, Belasco Theatre, 183
Tiger Tiger Burning Bright (p), 12/22/62, Booth Theatre, 33
Tight Britches (p), 9/11/34, Avon Theatre, 23
Tightwad, The (p), 4/16/27, 49th St. Theatre, 9
Ti-Jean and His Brothers (p), 7/20/72, Delacorte Theatre, 15
Till the Day I Die / Waiting for Lefty (p), 3/26/35, Longacre Theatre, 135
Tillie (p), 1/6/19, Henry Miller's Theatre, 32
Tillie's Nightmare (m), 5/5/10, Herald Square Theatre, 77
Timber House (p), 9/19/36, Longacre Theatre, 1
Time (p), 11/26/23, 39th St. Theatre, 51
Time and the Conways (p), 1/3/38, Ritz Theatre, 32
Time for Bed / Take Me to Bed (p), 6/13/69, Provincetown Playhouse, 12
Time for Elizabeth (p), 9/27/48, Fulton Theatre, 8
Time for Singing, A (m), 5/21/66, Broadway Theatre, 41
Time for the Gentle People, A (p), 5/25/67, Theatre East, 12
Time, Gentleman, Please! (r), 1/16/62, Strollers Theatre, 160
Time, Gentlemen, Please! (r), 11/4/61, Strollers Theatre, 80
Time Is a Dream (p), 4/22/24, Neighborhood Playhouse, 9
Time Limit! (p), 1/24/56, Booth Theatre, 127
Time of Storm, The (p), 2/26/54, Greenwich Mews Theatre
Time of the Cuckoo, The (p), 10/15/52, Empire Theatre, 263
Time of the Cuckoo, The (p), 10/27/58, Sheridan Square Playhouse, 105
Time of the Key, A (p), 9/11/63, Sheridan Square Playhouse, 7
Time of Vengeance (p), 12/10/59, York Playhouse, 69
Time of Your Life, The (p), 10/25/39, Booth Theatre, 185
Time of Your Life, The (p), 9/23/40, Guild Theatre, 32
Time of Your Life, The (p), 1/19/55, New York City Center, 15
Time of Your Life, The (p), 11/6/69, Vivian Beaumont Theatre, 52
Time Out for Ginger (p), 11/26/52, Lyceum Theatre, 248
Time Remembered (p), 11/12/57, Morosco Theatre, 248
Time Shadows (p), 6/21/71, Circle Theatre, 3
Time, the Place and the Girl, The (m), 8/5/07, Wallack Theatre, 32
Time, the Place and the Girl, The (m), 10/21/42, Mansfield Theatre, 13
Times Have Changed (p), 2/25/35, National Theatre, 32
Timon of Athens (p), 6/30/71, Delacorte Theatre, 19
Tin Pan Alley (p), 11/1/28, Biltmore Theatre, 77
Tin Top Valley (p), 2/27/47, ANT Playhouse, 45
Tinkers Wedding / Riders to the Sea / In the Shadow of the Glen. See Three Plays by Synge, 3/6/57, Theatre East
Tinsel Tarts in a Hot Coma (m), 11/7/71, Anderson Theatre
Tiny Alice (p), 12/29/64, Billy Rose Theatre, 167
Tiny Alice (p), 9/29/69, ANTA Theatre, 10, (American Conservatory Theatre)
Tip Top (m), 10/5/20, Globe Theatre, 241
Tipping the Winner (p), 9/23/14, Longacre Theatre, 13
Tip-Toes (m), 12/28/25, Liberty Theatre, 194
Tired Business Man, The (p), 6/4/29, Waldorf Theatre, 31
'Tis of Thee (r), 10/26/40, Maxine Elliott's Theatre, 1
'Tis Pity She's a Whore (p), 12/5/58, Orpheum Theatre, 204
Tit for Tat (p), 4/25/04, Savoy Theatre, 32
Title Mart, The, 2/20/06, Madison Square Theatre, 24
Title, The (p), 11/14/21, Belmont Theatre, 16
Titus Andronicus (p), 8/2/67, Delacorte Theatre, 17
Titus Andronicus (p), 1/29/72, CSC Repertory Theatre
To Be Continued (p), 4/23/52, Booth Theatre, 13
To Be or Not To Be . . . What Kind of a Question Is That? (r), 10/19/70, Barbizon-Plaza Theatre, 40
To Be Young, Gifted and Black (p), 1/2/69, Cherry Lane Theatre, 380
To Bury a Cousin (p), 5/16/67, Bouwerie Lane Theatre, 5
To Clothe the Naked (p), 4/27/67, Sheridan Square Playhouse, 30
To Damascus (p), 2/14/61, Theatre East, 16
To Dorothy, a Son (p), 11/19/51, John Golden Theatre, 8
To Have and to Hold (p), 3/4/01, Knickerbocker Theatre, 40
To Live Another Summer, To Pass Another Winter (r), 10/21/71, Helen Hayes Theatre, 173
To Love (p), 10/17/22, Bijou Theatre, 37
To My Husband, 6/1/36, Belmont Theatre, 24
To Quito and Back (p), 10/6/37, Guild Theatre, 46
To See Ourselves (p), 4/30/35, Ethel Barrymore Theatre, 23
To Tell You the Truth (p), 4/18/48, New Stages Theatre, 15
To the Chicago Abyss. See World of Ray Bradbury, The
To the Ladies (p), 2/20/22, Liberty Theatre, 128
To the Rescue. See The Paper Bag Players
To the Water Tower (r), 4/3/63, Second City at Square East, 312
Toast of the Town, The (p), 11/27/05, Daly's Theatre, 38
Tobacco Road (p), 12/4/33, Masque Theatre, 3,182
Tobacco Road (p), 9/5/42, Forrest Theatre, 34
Tobacco Road (p), 9/4/43, Ritz Theatre, 66
Tobacco Road (p), 3/6/50, 48th St. Theatre, 7
Tobacco Road (p), 5/10/60, Cricket Theatre
Tobias and the Angel (p), 4/28/37, Provincetown Playhouse, 22
Tobias and the Angel (p), 10/20/57, Broadway Congregational Church, 9
Toby's Bow (p), 2/10/19, Comedy Theatre, 144
Toby's Bow / Augustus Does His Bit (p), 3/12/19, Comedy Theatre, 5
Today (p), 10/6/13, 48th St. Theatre, 280
Toddles (p), 3/16/08, Garrick Theatre, 16
Toilet, The / The Slave (p), 12/16/64, St. Marks Playhouse, 151
'Toinette (m), 11/20/61, Theatre Marquee, 31
Tom Jones (m), 11/11/07, Astor Theatre, 65
Tom Moore (p), 8/31/01, Herald Square Theatre, 41
Tom Paine (p), 3/25/68, Stage 73, 295
Tom Sawyer (p), 12/25/31, Alvin Theatre, 4
Tommy (p), 1/10/27, Gaiety Theatre, 232
Tommy (p), 8/7/33, Forrest Theatre, 24
Tommy Rot (m), 10/20/02, Mrs. Osborn's Playhouse, 39
Tomorrow (p), 12/28/28, Lyceum Theatre, 10
Tomorrow and Tomorrow (p), 1/13/31, Henry Miller's Theatre, 206
Tomorrow's a Holiday (p), 12/30/35, John Golden Theatre, 8
Tomorrow's Harvest (p), 12/5/34, 49th St. Theatre, 4
Tomorrow the World (p), 4/14/43, Ethel Barrymore Theatre, 499
Tongues of Men, The (p), 11/10/13, Harris Theatre, 24
Tonight at 12 (p), 11/15/28, Hudson Theatre, 56
Tonight at 8:30 (p), 11/24/36, National Theatre, 113
Tonight at 8:30 (p), 2/20/48, National Theatre, 26
Tonight at 8:30 (p), 5/3/67, ANTA Theatre, 5

Tonight at 8:30 (p), 8/15/73, Lolly's Theatre Club
Tonight in Living Color (The Golden Fleece / The David Show) (p), 6/10/69, Actors Playhouse, 24
Tonight in Samarkand (p), 2/16/55, Morosco Theatre, 29
Tonight or Never (p), 11/18/30, Belasco Theatre, 231
Tonight's the Night (m), 12/24/14, Shubert Theatre, 108
Tonight We Improvise (p), 11/6/59, Living Theatre, 109
Tonto. See Playwrights Cooperative Festival
Too Hot for Maneuvers (p), 5/2/45, Broadhurst Theatre, 5
Too Late the Phalarope (p), 10/11/56, Belasco Theatre, 36
Too Many Boats (p), 9/11/34, Playhouse, 7
Too Many Cooks (p), 2/24/14, 39th St. Theatre, 223
Too Many Girls (m), 10/18/39, Imperial Theatre, 249
Too Many Heroes (p), 11/15/37, Hudson Theatre, 16
Too Many Husbands (p), 10/8/19, Booth Theatre, 102
Too Much Johnson (p), 1/15/64, Phoenix Theatre, 23
Too Much Party (p), 3/5/34, Masque Theatre, 8
Too True To Be Good (p), 4/4/32, Guild Theatre, 56
Too True To Be Good (p), 3/12/63, 54th St. Theatre, 94
Toot Sweet (r), 5/7/19, Princess Theatre, 45
Tooth of Crime, The (p), 3/7/73, Performing Garage, 123
Tooth of Crime, The (p), 2/2/74, Performing Garage
Toot-Toot! (m), 3/11/18, Cohan Theatre, 40
Top Banana (m), 11/1/51, Winter Garden Theatre, 350
Top o' th' World, The (m), 10/19/07, Majestic Theatre, 156
Top o' the Hill (p), 11/26/29, Eltinge Theatre, 15
Top Speed (m), 12/25/29, 46th St. Theatre, 104
Topaze (p), 2/12/30, Music Box Theatre, 159
Topaze (p), 8/18/30, Ethel Barrymore Theatre, 56
Topaze (p), 2/16/31, 49th St. Theatre, 8
Topaze (p), 12/27/47, Morosco Theatre, 1
Top-Hole (m), 9/1/24, Fulton Theatre, 104
Topics of 1923 (r), 11/20/23, Broadhurst Theatre, 143
Toplitzky of Notre Dame (m), 12/26/46, Century Theatre, 60
Top-Notchers (r), 5/29/42, 44th St. Theatre, 48
Topsy and Eva (m), 12/23/24, Sam H. Harris Theatre, 165
Torch Song (p), 8/27/30, Plymouth Theatre, 87
Torchbearers, The (p), 8/29/22, 48th St. Theatre, 128
Torches, The (p), 10/24/17, Bijou Theatre, 29
Toreador. See Four on a Garden
Toreador, The (m), 1/6/02, Knickerbocker Theatre, 146
Toreador, The (m), 2/22/04, Academy of Music, 16
Tortilla Flat (p), 1/12/38, Henry Miller's Theatre, 5
Total Eclipse (p), 2/23/74, Brooklyn Academy of Music, 32, (Chelsea Theatre Center)
Toto (p), 3/21/21, Bijou Theatre, 84
Touch (m), 11/8/70, Village Arena Theatre, 422
Touch and Go (r), 10/13/49, Broadhurst Theatre, 176
Touch of Brimstone, A (p), 9/22/35, John Golden Theatre, 96
Touch of the Poet, A (p), 10/2/58, Helen Hayes Theatre, 284
Touch of the Poet, A (p), 5/2/67, ANTA Theatre, 5
Touchstone (p), 2/3/53, Music Box Theatre, 7
Tough To Get Help (p), 5/4/72, Royale Theatre, 1
Tour de Four (r), 6/18/63, Writers Stage Theatre, 16
Tour. See Collision Course
Tourists, The (m), 8/25/06, Majestic Theatre, 132
Tovarich (p), 10/15/36, Plymouth Theatre, 356
Tovarich (p), 5/14/52, New York City Center, 15
Tovarich (m), 3/18/63, Broadway Theatre, 264
Tower Beyond Tragedy, The (p), 11/26/50, ANTA Playhouse, 32
Town Boy (p), 10/4/29, Belmont Theatre, 3
Town House (p), 9/23/48, National Theatre, 12
Town's Woman, The (p), 3/11/29, Craig Theatre, 16
Toy for Clowns, A / Wretched the Lionhearted (p), 9/12/62, East End Theatre, 2
Toymaker of Nurenberg, The (p), 11/25/07, Garrick Theatre, 24
Toys in the Attic (p), 2/25/60, Hudson Theatre, 556
Traffic, The (p), 11/16/14, New York Theatre, 8
Tragedian in Spite of Himself, A / The Bear / On the Harmfulness of Tobacco / The Wedding (p), 2/5/48, New York City Center, 14
Tragedy of Nan (p), 2/17/20, 39th St. Theatre, 4
Tragedy of Thomas Andros, The (m), 5/24/73, Circle Theatre, 20
Tragedy Rehearsed, A (p), 5/8/25, Neighborhood Playhouse, 38
Tragic 18 (p), 10/9/26, Charles Hopkins Theatre, 9
Tragical Historie of Doctor Faustus, The (p), 10/5/64, Phoenix Theatre, 64
Trail of the Lonesome Pine, The (p), 1/29/12, New Amsterdam Theatre, 32
Trainer, Dean, Liepolt and Company (The Acquisition / This Bird of Dawning Singeth All Night Long / The Young Master Dante) (p), 12/12/68, St. Clement's Church, 44, (American Place Theatre)
Traitor, The (p), 5/2/30, Little Theatre, 17
Traitor, The (p), 3/31/49, 48th St. Theatre, 67
Traitor, The (p), 9/4/59, 16th St. Theatre
Transfers (Transfers / The Rooming House / Dr. Galley) (p), 1/22/70, Village South Theatre, 36
Transfiguration (p), 10/13/70, Blackfriars' Guild, 41
Transgressor Rides Again, The (p), 5/20/69, Martinique Theatre, 1
Transplanting Jean (p), 1/3/21, Cort Theatre, 48
Transposed Heads, The (m), 2/10/58, Phoenix Theatre, 2
Trap, The (p), 2/19/15, Booth Theatre, 27
Trapped (p), 9/11/28, National Theatre, 15
Traveling Lady, The (p), 10/27/54, Playhouse, 30
Traveling Man, The / Merry Christmas, Daddy! / Editha's Burglar (p), 12/26/16, Cohan and Harris Theatre, 6
Traveling Salesman, The (p), 8/10/08, Liberty Theatre, 280
Traveller without Luggage (p), 9/17/64, ANTA Theatre, 44
Treasure (p), 10/4/20, Garrick Theatre, 34
Treasure Girl (m), 11/8/28, Alvin Theatre, 69
Treasure Island (p), 12/1/15, Punch and Judy Theatre, 205
Treasure Island (p), 12/25/31, Alvin Theatre, 4
Treat 'Em Rough (p), 10/4/26, Klaw Theatre, 24
Tree Grows in Brooklyn, A (m), 4/19/51, Alvin Theatre, 267
Tree Grows in Brooklyn, A (m), 4/15/66, Master Theatre, 14, (Equity Library Theatre)
Tree, The (p), 4/12/32, Park Lane Theatre, 7
Trees Die Standing, The (p), 10/12/69, Roosevelt Theatre, 53
Trelawney of the Wells (p), 6/1/25, Knickerbocker Theatre, 8
Trelawney of the Wells (p), 1/31/27, New Amsterdam Theatre, 56
Trelawny of the Wells (p), 1/1/11, Empire Theatre, 48
Trelawny of the Wells (p), 2/26/70, Public/Other Stage Theatre
Trelawny of the "Wells" (p), 10/11/70, Public/Anspacher Theatre, 67
Trench Fantasy, A / The Gypsy Trail (p), 1/24/18, Plymouth Theatre, 19
Treteau de Paris, Le (Le Grand Vizir / Le Cosmonaute Agricole; Lettre Morte / Architruc; Oh! Les Beaux Jours; La Jeune Fille a Marier / La Lacune / Les Chaises) (p), 4/7/70, Barbizon-Plaza Theatre, 37
Treteau de Paris, Le (Le Tartuffe; En Attendant Godot) (p), 4/16/68, Barbizon-Plaza Theatre, 40
Treteau de Paris, Le (Quoat-Quoat; Pique-Nique en Campagne / Guernica) (p), 4/13/69, Barbizon-Plaza Theatre, 27
Trevor. See Little Boxes
Trial by Jury (m), 2/28/42, St. James Theatre, 7
Trial by Jury / H.M.S. Pinafore (m), 5/8/33, St. James Theatre, 16
Trial by Jury / H.M.S. Pinafore (m), 4/16/34, Majestic Theatre, 16
Trial by Jury / H.M.S. Pinafore (m), 9/13/34, Martin Beck Theatre, 15
Trial by Jury / H.M.S. Pinafore (m), 8/12/35, Adelphi Theatre, 12
Trial by Jury / H.M.S. Pinafore (m), 4/27/36, Majestic Theatre, 16
Trial by Jury / H.M.S. Pinafore (m), 2/14/44, Ambassador Theatre, 7
Trial by Jury / H.M.S. Pinafore (m), 2/5/51, St. James Theatre, 8
Trial by Jury / H.M.S. Pinafore, 10/17/55, Shubert Theatre, 13, (D'Oyly Carte Opera Co.)
Trial by Jury / H.M.S. Pinafore (m), 11/19/64, New York City Center, 10, (D'Oyly Carte Opera Co.)
Trial by Jury / H.M.S. Pinafore (m), 6/7/66, Jan Hus Playhouse, 28, (American Savoyards)
Trial by Jury / The Pirates of Penzance (m), 8/31/36, Martin Beck Theatre, 20
Trial by Jury / The Pirates of Penzance (m), 10/7/40, 44th St. Theatre, 6
Trial by Jury / The Pirates of Penzance (m), 1/5/48, Century Theatre, 16
Trial Honeymoon (p), 11/3/47, Royale Theatre, 8
Trial Marriage (p), 1/31/27, Wallack Theatre, 26
Trial Marriage, The (p), 10/29/12, Hudson Theatre, 23
Trial of Dmitri Karamazov, The (p), 1/27/58, Jan Hus House, 32
Trial of Dr. Beck, The (p), 8/9/37, Maxine Elliott's Theatre, 24
Trial of Joan of Arc, The (p), 4/3/21, Century Theatre, 1
Trial of Joan of Arc, The (p), 4/12/21, Shubert Theatre, 31
Trial of Lee Harvey Oswald, The (p), 11/5/67, ANTA Theatre, 9
Trial of Mary Dugan, The (p), 9/19/27, National Theatre, 437
Trial of the Catonsville Nine, The (p), 2/7/71, Good Shepherd-Faith Church, 159
Trial of the Catonsville Nine, The (p), 6/2/71, Lyceum Theatre, 29
Trial, The (p), 6/14/55, Provincetown Playhouse, 131
Trial, The (p), 5/21/65, Master Theatre, 9, (Equity Library Theatre)
Trials of Brother Jero, The / The Strong Breed (p), 11/9/67, Greenwich Mews Theatre, 115
Trials of Oz, The (p), 12/19/72, Anderson Theatre, 15
Triangle, The, 2/20/06, Manhattan Theatre, 14
Trick for Trick (p), 2/18/32, Sam H. Harris Theatre, 70
Tricks (m), 1/8/73, Alvin Theatre, 8
Trifler, The (p), 3/16/05, Princess Theatre, 4
Trifles / Grotesques / The Moon of the Caribbees (p), 4/25/21, Provincetown Playhouse, 21
Trigger (p), 12/6/27, Little Theatre, 50
Trigon, The (p), 10/12/65, Stage 73, 70
Trilby (p), 5/8/05, New Amsterdam Theatre, 24
Trilby (p), 4/3/15, Shubert Theatre, 73
Trilby (p), 12/23/21, National Theatre, 12
Trimmed in Scarlet (p), 2/2/20, Maxine Elliott's Theatre, 14
Trio (p), 12/29/44, Belasco Theatre, 69
Trip to Bountiful, The (p), 11/3/53, Henry Miller's Theatre, 39
Trip to Bountiful, The (p), 2/26/59, Theatre East, 27
Trip to Japan, A (m), 9/4/09, New York Hippodrome, 447

Trip to Scarborough, A (p), 3/18/29, Cherry Lane Theatre, 30
Triple Crossed (p), 5/5/27, Morosco Theatre, 52
Triple Play (p), 4/14/59, Playhouse, 37
Triple Play (p), 11/3/68, Cherry Lane Theatre, 17
Triple-A Plowed Under (The Living Newspaper) (p), 3/14/36, Biltmore Theatre, 85
Triplets (p), 9/21/32, Masque Theatre, 3
Triumph (p), 10/14/35, Fulton Theatre, 8
Triumph of an Empress, The (p), 3/20/11, Garden Theatre, 32
Triumph of Love, The (p), 2/8/04, Criterion Theatre, 1
Triumph of Robert Emmet, The (p), 5/7/69, Frances Adler Theatre, 15
Triumph of the Egg, The (p), 2/10/25, Provincetown Playhouse, 23
Triumph of X, The (p), 8/24/21, Comedy Theatre, 29
Triumphant Bachelor, The (p), 9/15/27, Biltmore Theatre, 12
Troilus and Cressida (p), 6/6/32, Broadway Theatre, 8
Troilus and Cressida (p), 12/26/56, Winter Garden Theatre, 14, (Old Vic Co.)
Troilus and Cressida (p), 8/10/65, Delacorte Theatre, 15
Troilus and Cressida (p), 11/10/73, Mitzi E. Newhouse Theatre, 57
Trois Jeunes Filles Nues (Three Young Maids from the Folies Bergère) (m), 3/4/29, Jolson Theatre, 8
Trojan Incident, 4/21/38, St. James Theatre, 26
Trojan Women, The (p), 12/23/63, Circle in the Square, 600
Trojan Women, The (p), 9/3/65, Circle in the Square, 640
Troubadour, A / The Heather Field (p), 4/19/00, Carnegie Lyceum Theatre, 1
Trouble in Tahiti / Down in the Valley (m), 4/23/65, Master Theatre, 14, (Equity Library Theatre)
Trouble in Tahiti / Paul Draper / 27 Wagons Full of Cotton. See All in One
Troubled Waters (p), 6/3/65, Gate Theatre, 6
Troublemakers, The (p), 12/30/54, President Theatre, 55
Troupe du Roi, La / Amphitryon (p), 2/3/70, New York City Center, 6, (Comédie Française)
Trouper, The (p), 3/8/26, 52nd St. Theatre, 24
Troyka (p), 4/1/30, Hudson Theatre, 15
Truckline Cafe (p), 2/27/46, Belasco Theatre, 13
True to Form (p), 9/12/21, Bramhall Playhouse, 15
Truly Valiant (p), 1/9/36, 49th St. Theatre, 1
Trumpet Shall Sound, The, 12/10/26, American Laboratory Theatre, 30
Trumpets and Drums (p), 10/12/69, Roundabout Theatre, 40
Trumpets of the Lord (m), 12/31/63, Astor Place Playhouse, 161
Trumpets of the Lord (m), 4/29/69, Brooks Atkinson Theatre, 7
Truth (p), 1/7/07, Criterion Theatre, 34
Truth About Blayds, The (p), 3/14/22, Booth Theatre, 111
Truth About Blayds, The (p), 4/11/32, Belasco Theatre, 24
Truth Game, The, 12/29/30, Ethel Barrymore Theatre, 105
Truth, The (p), 4/14/14, Little Theatre, 55
Truth Wagon, The (p), 2/26/12, Daly's Theatre, 40
Try and Get It (p), 8/2/43, Cort Theatre, 8
Try It with Alice (p), 6/23/24, 52nd St. Theatre, 8
Try It, You'll Like It (m), 3/14/73, Mayfair Theatre, 87
Tubstrip (p), 5/17/73, Mercer / Brecht Theatre, 140 prevs.
Tug of War (p), 12/23/70, Roundabout Theatre, 21
Tumble In (m), 3/24/19, Selwyn Theatre, 128
Tumbler, The (p), 2/24/60, Helen Hayes Theatre, 5
Tunnel of Love, The (p), 2/13/57, Royale Theatre, 417
Turista, La (p), 3/4/67, American Place Theatre, 29
Turn to the Right! (p), 8/18/16, Gaiety Theatre, 435
Turning Point, The (p), 2/28/10, Hackett Theatre, 40
TV. See America Hurrah
Twanger (m), 11/15/72, Vandam Theatre, 23
Twas Brillig. See Present Tense
Tweedles (p), 8/13/23, Frazee Theatre, 96
Twelfth Night (p) (Viola Allen-John Blair), 2/8/04, Knickerbocker Theatre, 16
Twelfth Night (p), 2/22/04, Knickerbocker Theatre, 16
Twelfth Night (p), 1/11/05, Knickerbocker Theatre, 2
Twelfth Night (p), 1/26/10, New Theatre
Twelfth Night (p), 11/23/14, Liberty Theatre, 8
Twelfth Night (p), 2/14/21, Garrick Theatre, 1
Twelfth Night (p), 10/21/21, Century Theatre, 10, (Sothern-Marlowe Shakespeare Repertory)
Twelfth Night (p), 12/20/26, Civic Repertory Theatre, 25
Twelfth Night (p), 12/17/27, Civic Repertory Theatre, 9
Twelfth Night (p), 4/6/29, Civic Repertory Theatre, 2
Twelfth Night (p) (Fritz Leiber), 3/26/30, Shubert Theatre, 2
Twelfth Night (p), 10/15/30, Maxine Elliott's Theatre, 64
Twelfth Night (p), 1/14/31, Ambassador Theatre, 1
Twelfth Night (p), 11/18/32, Shakespeare Theatre, 17
Twelfth Night (p) (Helen Hayes-Maurice Evans), 11/19/40, St. James Theatre, 129
Twelfth Night (p), 12/2/41, Little Theatre, 15
Twelfth Night (p), 10/3/49, Empire Theatre, 48
Twelfth Night (p), 2/9/54, Jan Hus House, 98
Twelfth Night (p), 2/22/55, Jan Hus House, 14
Twelfth Night (p), 1/7/57, Shakespearewrights Theatre, 53
Twelfth Night (p), 12/9/58, Broadway Theatre, 14, (Old Vic Co.)
Twelfth Night (p), 8/6/69, Delacorte Theatre, 20
Twelfth Night (p), 12/29/69, Hunter College Playhouse, 7, (Oxford and Cambridge Shakespeare Co.)
Twelfth Night (p), 2/18/71, CSC Repertory Theatre, 16
Twelfth Night (p), 3/2/72, Vivian Beaumont Theatre
Twelfth Night (p), 9/26/73, Abbey Theatre, 21, (CSC Repertory)
Twelve Angry Men (p), 11/26/72, Queens Playhouse, 32
Twelve Angry Men (p), 12/3/72, Queens Playhouse, 17
Twelve Miles Out (p), 11/16/25, Playhouse, 188
Twelve Months Later (p), 3/26/00, Madison Square Theatre, 8
Twelve Pound Look, The / Alice-Sit-by-the-Fire (p), 2/13/11, Empire Theatre, 32
Twelve Thousand (p), 3/12/28, Garrick Theatre, 55
Twentieth Century (p), 12/29/32, Broadhurst Theatre, 154
Twentieth Century (p), 12/24/50, ANTA Playhouse, 218
Twenty Days in the Shade (p), 1/20/08, Savoy Theatre, 64
Twenty-five Cent White Cap / George Washington Crossing the Delaware / Not Enough Rope (3 × 3) (p), 3/1/62, Maidman
Twenty-five Dollars an Hour (p), 5/10/33, Masque Theatre 21 Playhouse, 5
Twenty-Four Inventions (Prague Pantomine Theatre), 9/10/64, Philharmonic Hall, Lincoln Center, 8
Twenty-Seven Wagons Full of Cotton / Trouble in Tahiti / Paul Draper. See All in One
Twenty-two Years (p), 1/4/72, Stage 73, 16
Twiddle-Twaddle (r), 1/1/06, Weber's Music Hall, 137
Twiddle-Twaddle (r), 11/12/06, Weber's Music Hall, 32
Twigs (p), 11/14/71, Broadhurst Theatre, 289
Twilight Walk (p), 9/24/51, Fulton Theatre, 8
Twin Beds (p), 8/14/14, Fulton Theatre, 411
Twin Bill (p,m) (The Exception and the Rule / The Prodigal Son), 5/20/65, Greenwich Mews Theatre, 141
Twin Sister, The (p), 3/3/02, Empire Theatre, 48
Twinkle, Twinkle (m), 11/16/26, Liberty Theatre, 167
Twirly Whirly (m), 9/11/02, Weber & Fields Music Hall, 244
Two Blind Mice (p), 3/2/49, Cort Theatre, 157
Two Blocks Away (p), 8/30/21, George M. Cohan Theatre, 47
Two Bouquets, The (m), 5/31/38, Windsor Theatre, 55
Two by Ionesco. See New Tenant, The / Victims of Duty
Two by Sainer (p) (The Bitch of Waverly Place / The Blind Angel), 4/1/65, Bridge Theatre, 50
Two by Saroyan (Talking to You / Across the Board on Tomorrow Morning) (p), 10/22/61, East End Theatre, 96
Two by Two (p), 2/23/25, Selwyn Theatre, 16
Two by Two (m), 11/10/70, Imperial Theatre, 352
Two Camps by Koutoukas (The Last Triangle / Only a Countess May Dance When She's Crazy) (p), 3/18/68, Actors Playhouse, 17
Two Executioners / Dutchman / Play (Three at the Cherry Lane) (p), 3/24/64, Cherry Lane Theatre, 32
Two Fellows and a Girl (p), 7/19/23, Vanderbilt Theatre, 132
Two for Fun (r), 2/13/61, Madison Ave. Playhouse, 34
Two for the Seesaw (p), 1/16/58, Booth Theatre, 750
Two for the Show (r), 2/8/40, Booth Theatre, 124
Two Gentlemen of Verona (p), 3/18/58, Phoenix Theatre, 28
Two Gentlemen of Verona (m), 7/22/71, Delacorte Theatre, 20
Two Gentlemen of Verona (m), 12/1/71, St. James Theatre, 613
Two Gentlemen of Verona (m), 7/31/73, Delacorte Mobile Theatre, 24
Two Girls Wanted (p), 9/9/26, Little Theatre, 324
Two Hundred Were Chosen (p), 11/20/36, 48th St. Theatre, 35
Two If by Sea (m), 2/6/72, Circle in the Square, 1
Two Is Company (m), 9/22/15, Lyric Theatre, 29
Two Little Brides (m), 4/23/12, Casino Theatre, 63
Two Little Girls in Blue (m), 5/3/21, Cohan Theatre, 135
Two Little Sailor Boys (p), 5/2/04, Academy of Music, 32
Two Married Men, 1/13/25, Longacre Theatre, 16
Two Mr. Wetherbys, The (p), 8/23/06, Madison Square Theatre, 21
Two Mrs. Carrolls, The (p), 8/14/44, Booth Theatre, 585
Two on an Island (p), 1/22/40, Broadhurst Theatre, 96
Two on the Aisle (r), 7/19/51, Mark Hellinger Theatre, 279
Two Orphans, The (p), 3/28/04, New Amsterdam Theatre, 56
Two Orphans, The (p), 4/5/26, Cosmopolitan Theatre, 32
Two Plays by Richard Wesley (The Past Is the Past / Going Through Changes) (p), 12/29/73, Billie Holiday Theatre
Two Roses, The (p), 11/21/04, Broadway Theatre, 29
Two's Company (r), 12/15/52, Alvin Theatre, 91
Two Schools, The (p), 9/30/02, Madison Square Theatre, 56
Two Seconds (p), 10/9/31, Ritz Theatre, 68
Two Strange Women (p), 1/10/33, Little Theatre, 15
Two Strangers from Nowhere (p), 4/7/24, Punch and Judy Theatre, 72
Two Thousand Eight and a Half (2008 1/2) (A Spaced Oddity) (m), 2/10/74, Truck and Warehouse Theatre
Two Thousand Nine Hundred Five or To-morrow Land. See Man from Now, The

Two Times One (The Last Straw / Duet for Solo Voice) (p), 3/9/70, St. Clement's Church Theatre, 35, (American Place Theatre)
Two × Two — Five (p), 11/28/27, Civic Repertory Theatre, 16
Two Virtues, The (p), 10/4/15, Booth Theatre, 64
Two Women (p), 11/29/10, Lyric Theatre, 47
Two Women and That Man (p), 10/18/09, Majestic Theatre, 16
Tyger! Tyger! And Other Burnings. See The National Theatre of the Deaf
Type 424 Meet Type Oh—Oh, No!. See Sold to the Movies
Typhoon, The (p), 3/11/12, Fulton Theatre, 96
Typists, The / The Tiger (p), 2/4/63, Orpheum Theatre, 200
Tyranny of Love, The (p), 2/28/21, Bijou Theatre, 27
Tyranny of Love, The (p), 5/2/21, Cort Theatre, 48
Tyranny of Tears, The / The Will (p), 9/29/13, Empire Theatre, 32
Tyrant, The (p), 11/12/30, Longacre Theatre, 13
Tyrants (p), 3/4/24, Cherry Lane Theatre, 14

U

UBU / Arden of Faversham (p), 2/70, La Mama Experimental Theatre Club
Ubu Roi (p), 6/28/68, Forum Theatre, 6, (Atelje 212)
Ubu Roi / The Heroes (p), 8/5/52, Cherry Lane Theatre
Uday Shankar Hindu Dancers and Musicians, The, 9/25/62, New York City Center, 8
Uhuruh (r), 3/20/72, City Center Downstairs Theatre, 8
Ulysses (p), 9/14/03, Garden Theatre, 65
Ulysses in Nighttown (p), 6/10/58, Rooftop Theatre, 206
Ulysses in Nighttown (p), 3/10/74, Winter Garden Theatre, 69
Umbrella, The (p), 5/26/65, Bouwerie Lane Theatre, 3
Un Bon Garçon (m), 3/18/29, Jolson Theatre, 4
Un Caprice / La Parisienne (p), 11/24/24, Henry Miller's Theatre, 8
Un Caprice / Le Jeu de l'Amour et du Hassard (Comédie Française), 11/15/55, Broadway Theatre, 8
Unborn, The (p), 11/29/15, Princess Theatre, 16
Unchastened Woman, The (p), 10/9/15, 39th St. Theatre, 193
Unchastened Woman, The (p), 2/16/26, Princess Theatre, 31
Uncle Harry (p), 5/20/42, Broadhurst Theatre, 430
Uncle Sam (p), 10/30/11, Liberty Theatre, 48
Uncle Sam's Money / The Worth of a Man / Lonesome Like / The Last Toast (p), 4/27/14, 48th St. Theatre, 1
Uncle Tom's Cabin (p) (Wilton Lackaye), 3/4/01, Academy of Music, 88
Uncle Tom's Cabin (p) (John Southerland), 5/20/07, Majestic Theatre, 24
Uncle Tom's Cabin (p), 12/26/21, Manhattan Opera House, 6
Uncle Tom's Cabin (p), 5/29/33, Alvin Theatre, 25
Uncle Vanya (p), 5/24/29, Morosco Theatre, 2
Uncle Vanya (p), 4/15/30, Cort Theatre, 80
Uncle Vanya (p), 9/22/30, Booth Theatre, 32
Uncle Vanya (p) (Old Vic Co.), 5/1/46, Century Theatre, 5
Uncle Vanya (p), 1/31/56, Fourth Century Theatre, 284
Uncle Vanya (p) (Novy Russby Teatr in orig. Russ.), 2/12/60, Master Institute Theatre, 6
Uncle Vanya (p), 1/24/71, Roundabout Theatre, 44
Uncle Vanya (p), 3/18/71, CSC Repertory Theatre, 15
Uncle Vanya (p), 6/4/73, Circle in the Square / Joseph E. Levine Theatre, 64
Uncle Vanya (p), 3/21/74, T. Schreiber Studio, 19
Uncle Willie (p), 12/20/56, Golden Theatre, 141
Uncommon Denominator, The (r), 5/7/63, Mermaid Theatre, 8
Unconquered, The (p), 2/13/40, Biltmore Theatre, 6
Under Cover (p), 9/14/03, Murray Hill Theatre, 90
Under Cover (p), 8/26/14, Cort Theatre, 349
Under Fire (p), 8/11/15, Hudson Theatre, 129
Under Glass (p), 10/30/33, Ambassador Theatre, 8
Under Many Flags (m), 8/31/12, New York Hippodrome, 445
Under Milk Wood (p), 10/15/57, Henry Miller's Theatre, 39
Under Milk Wood (p), 3/28/61, Circle in the Square, 202
Under Milk Wood / Pullman Car Hiawatha (p), 11/16/62, Circle in the Square, 54
Under Orders (p), 8/20/18, Eltinge Theatre, 167
Under Pressure (p), 2/21/18, Norworth Theatre, 28
Under Sentence (p), 10/3/16, Harris Theatre, 55
Under Southern Skies (p), 11/12/01, Republic Theatre, 71
Under the Counter (p), 10/3/47, Shubert Theatre, 27
Under the Gaslight (p), 4/2/29, Fay's Bowery Theatre, 21
Under the Gaslight (p), 12/8/67, Master Theatre, 9, (Equity Library Theatre)
Under the Greenwood Tree (p), 12/25/07, Garrick Theatre, 44
Under the Sycamore Tree (p), 3/7/60, Cricket Theatre, 41
Under the Weather (The Wen / Orange Souffle / Out from Under) (p), 10/27/66, Cort Theatre, 12
Under the Yum-Yum Tree (p), 11/16/60, Henry Miller's Theatre, 173
Under the Yum-Yum Tree (p), 5/28/64, Mayfair Theatre, 6
Under This Roof (p), 2/22/42, Windsor Theatre, 17
Under Two Flags (p), 2/5/01, Garden Theatre, 135
Undercover Cop / The Open and Shut Magic Company (p), 8/4/73, various street locations
Undercover Man (p), 6/2/66, Actors Playhouse, 22
Undercurrent, The (p), 2/3/25, Cort Theatre, 24
Underground (The Life and Times of J. Walter Smintheus / Jazznite) (p), 4/18/71, Public/Other Stage, 38
Undesirable Lady (p), 10/9/33, National Theatre, 24
Unexpected Husband (p), 6/2/31, 48th St. Theatre, 120
Unexpurgated Memoirs of Bernard Mergendeiler, The. See Collision Course
Unfair to Goliath (r), 1/25/70, Cherry Lane Theatre, 75
Unforeseen, The (p), 1/13/03, Empire Theatre, 111
Unicorn from the Stars (p), 2/20/70, Brooklyn Academy of Music, 4, (Chelsea Theatre Center)
Uniform of Flesh (p), 1/29/49, Lenox Hill Playhouse, 7
Uninvited Guest, The (p), 9/27/27, Belmont Theatre, 7
Union Pacific, 4/25/34, St. James Theatre, 4
Universal Nigger, The (p), 3/20/70, Brooklyn Academy of Music, 6, (Chelsea Theatre Center)
Unknown Purple, The (p), 9/14/18, Lyric Theatre, 273
Unknown Soldier and His Wife, The (p), 7/6/67, Vivian Beaumont Theatre, 149
Unknown Warrior, The (p), 10/29/28, Charles Hopkins Theatre, 8
Unknown Warrior, The (p), 10/22/31, Morosco Theatre, 4
Unknown Woman, The (p), 11/10/19, Maxine Elliott's Theatre, 64
Unleavened Bread (p), 1/26/01, Savoy Theatre, 12
Unlikely Heroes (Defender of the Faith / Epstein / Eli, the Fanatic) (p), 10/26/71, Plymouth Theatre, 23
Unseen Hand, The / Forensic and the Navigators (p), 4/1/70, Astor Place Theatre, 21
Unsinkable Molly Brown, The (m), 11/3/60, Winter Garden Theatre, 532
Unsophisticates, The (p), 12/30/29, Longacre Theatre, 8
Until the Monkey Comes (p), 6/20/66, Martinique Theatre, 56
Unto the Third (p), 4/20/33, Bijou Theatre, 4
Unto Thee a Garden, 10/14/68, Brooklyn Museum, 18
Unwelcome Mrs. Hatch, The (p), 11/25/01, Manhattan Theatre, 63
Unwritten Chapter, The (p), 10/11/20, Astor Theatre, 32
Unwritten Law, The (p), 2/7/13, Fulton Theatre, 19
Up and Down Broadway (m), 7/18/10, Casino Theatre, 72
Up and Up, The, 9/8/30, Biltmore Theatre, 81
Up Eden (m), 11/26/68, Jan Hus Playhouse, 8
Up from Nowhere (p), 9/8/19, Comedy Theatre, 40
Up in Central Park (m), 1/27/45, Century Theatre, 504
Up in Central Park (m), 5/19/47, New York City Center, 16
Up in Mabel's Room (p), 1/15/19, Eltinge Theatre, 229
Up in the Clouds (m), 1/2/22, Lyric Theatre, 89
Up Pops the Devil (p), 9/1/30, Masque Theatre, 146
Up She Goes (m), 11/6/22, Playhouse, 252
Up the Ladder (p), 3/6/22, Playhouse, 120
Up the Line (p), 11/22/26, Morosco Theatre, 25
Up to Thursday / Home Free! / Balls (p) (New Playwrights Series, Evening I), 2/10/65, Cherry Lane Theatre, 23
Up York State (p), 12/16/01, 14th St. Theatre, 56
Up York State (p), 9/16/01, 14th St. Theatre, 16
Ups-a-Daisy (m), 10/8/28, Shubert Theatre, 320
Upstart, The (p), 9/1/10, Maxine Elliott's Theatre, 4
Uptown West (p), 4/3/23, Earl Carroll Theatre, 89
U.S.A. (p), 10/28/59, Martinique Theatre, 256
U.S.A. (r), 10/1/72, Good Shepherd-Faith Church, 4, (City Center Acting Co.)
Usurper, The (p), 11/28/04, Knickerbocker Theatre, 28
UTBU (p), 1/4/66, Helen Hayes Theatre, 7
Utopia! (m), 5/6/63, Folksbiene Playhouse, 11
Utopia Limited (m), 4/7/60, Jan Hus House
Utopia Limited (m), 11/9/61, Jan Hus House, 12
Utopia Limited. See American Savoyards, 2/26/57, Shakespearewrights Theatre, 8

V

Vagabond King, The (m), 9/21/25, Casino Theatre, 511
Vagabond King, The (m), 6/29/43, Shubert Theatre, 55
Vagabond King, The (m), 11/23/61, Jan Hus House, 12
Vagabond, The (p), 12/27/23, Apollo Theatre, 4
Vagrant, The / The Witch / The Music Shop (p) (A Chekhov Sketchbook), 2/15/62, Gramercy Arts Theatre, 94
Vain Victory (r), 8/11/71, WPA Theatre, 25
Valley Forge (p), 12/10/34, Guild Theatre, 58
Valley of Content, The (p), 1/13/25, Apollo Theatre, 40
Valmouth (m), 10/6/60, York Playhouse, 14
Vamp, The (m), 11/10/55, Winter Garden Theatre, 60
Vampire, The (p), 1/18/09, Hackett Theatre, 24

Van Dych, The / The Children's Tragedy (p), 10/10/21, Greenwich Village Theatre, 8
Vanderbilt Cup, The (m), 1/16/06, Broadway Theatre, 143
Vanderbilt Cup, The (m), 1/7/07, New York Theatre, 40
Vanderbilt Revue, The (r), 11/5/30, Vanderbilt Theatre, 13
Vanity Fair (p), 1/7/11, New Theatre
Vanity of Nothing (p), 2/15/63, Rodale Theatre, 29
Variety Obit / Welcome to Andromeda (p), 2/12/73, Cherry Lane Theatre, 24
Varying Shore, The (p), 12/5/21, Hudson Theatre, 66
Vegetable, The (p), 4/10/29, Cherry Lane Theatre, 13
Vegetable, The (p), 10/26/63, Master's Institute—Equity Library Theatre, 10
Veils (p), 3/13/28, Forrest Theatre, 4
Veldt, The. See World of Ray Bradbury, The
Velvet Glove, The (p), 12/26/49, Booth Theatre, 152
Velvet Lady, The (m), 2/3/19, New Amsterdam Theatre, 136
Veneer (p), 11/12/29, Sam H. Harris Theatre, 31
Venetian Glass Nephew, The (p), 2/23/31, Vanderbilt Theatre, 8
Venetian Mirror, The (p), 3/18/27, Princess Theatre, 5
Venetian Romance, A (m), 5/2/04, Knickerbocker Theatre, 31
Venetian, The (p), 10/31/31, Masque Theatre, 9
Venetian Twins, The (p), 5/28/68, Henry Miller's Theatre, 32
Venturi: A Squeeze Play, The, 2/5/70, Thresholds Theatre, 24
Venus (p), 12/26/27, Masque Theatre, 8
Venus at Large (p), 4/12/62, Morosco Theatre, 4
Venus Observed (p), 2/13/52, Century Theatre, 86
Venus-Shot. See Command Performance
Vera Violetta (m), 11/20/11, Winter Garden Theatre, 112
Verge, The (p), 11/14/21, Provincetown Playhouse, 38
Vermont (p), 1/8/29, Erlanger Theatre, 16
Veronica / Bugs (p), 11/17/65, Pocket Theatre, 82
Veronica's Room (p), 10/25/73, Music Box, 75
Veronique (m), 10/30/05, Broadway Theatre, 81
Vertical Mobility: Sophia= (Wisdom) Part IV (p), 3/30/74, Ontological-Hysteric Theatre
Very Good, Eddie (m), 12/23/15, Princess Theatre, 341
Very Good Young Man, A (p), 8/19/18, Plymouth Theatre, 16
Very Idea, The (p), 8/9/17, Astor Theatre, 15
Very Minute, The (p), 4/9/17, Belasco Theatre, 32
Very Rich Woman, A (p), 9/30/65, Belasco Theatre, 28
Very Special Baby, A (p), 11/14/56, Playhouse, 5
Very Warm for May (m), 11/17/39, Alvin Theatre, 59
Very Wise Virgin, A (p), 6/2/27, Bijou Theatre, 20
Via Crucis (p), 11/12/23, Century Theatre, 4
Via Galactica (m), 11/28/72, Uris Theatre, 7
Via Wireless (p), 11/2/08, Liberty Theatre, 88
Vickie (p), 9/22/42, Plymouth Theatre, 48
Victim, The (p), 5/2/52, President Theatre, 3
Victims of Amnesia, The. See Three by Ferlinghetti
Victims of Duty (p), 1/19/60, Theatre de Lys
Victims of Duty (see The Victims)
Victims of Duty / The New Tenant. See Two by Ionesco, 5/24/64, Writers' Stage, 25
Victims, The (On the Hazards of Smoking Tobacco / Victims of Duty / Escurial) (p), 3/5/68, East 74th St. Theatre, 6
Victor Borge. See Comedy in Music
Victor, or the Children Take Over (p), 7/7/68, Forum Theatre, 5, (Atelje 212)
Victoria Regina (p), 12/26/35, Broadhurst Theatre, 204
Victoria Regina (p), 8/31/36, Broadhurst Theatre, 311
Victoria Regina (p), 10/3/38, Martin Beck Theatre, 87
Victors, The (p), 12/26/48, New Stages Theatre, 31
Victory Belles (p), 10/26/43, Mansfield Theatre, 85
Vida Es Sueno, La (Life Is a Dream) (p), 11/19/53, Broadhurst Theatre, 27
Video Free America, 4/24/73, Brooklyn Academy of Music, 14, (Chelsea Theatre Center)
Vie Parisienne, La (m) (Théâtre de France, Renaud-Barrault Company), 3/10/64, New York City Center, 8
Vienna Burgtheater (Professor Bernhardi; Das Konzert; Maria Stuart; Einen Jux Will Er Sich Machen) (p), 3/19/68, New York City Center, 24
Vienna Life (m), 1/23/01, Broadway Theatre, 35
Vienna Life. See Wiener Blut
Vierge Folle, La / La Coutouriere de Luneville / La Passe (p), 3/21/24, Gaiety Theatre, 6
Viet Rock (p), 11/10/66, Martinique Theatre, 62
View from the Bridge, A (p) (A View from the Bridge / A Memory of Two Mondays), 9/29/55, Coronet Theatre, 149
View from the Bridge, A (p), 1/28/65, Sheridan Square Playhouse, 780
View from under the Bridge, A (r), 8/5/64, Square East, 94
Viewing, The / Conditioned Reflex (p), 1/9/67, Theatre de Lys, 2, (ANTA Matinee)
Vigil, The (p), 5/21/48, Royale Theatre, 11
Vik (p), 4/29/14, Wallack Theatre, 5
Vikings, The (p), 5/12/30, New Yorker Theatre, 8
Villa of Madame Vidac, The (p), 9/30/59, Carnegie Hall Playhouse, 13
Village Green (p), 9/3/41, Henry Miller's Theatre, 30
Village Lawyer, The (p), 3/2/08, Garden Theatre, 17
Village Postmaster, The (p), 12/24/00, 14th St. Theatre, 16
Village Wooing (p), 8/11/55, Greenwich Mews Theatre, 103
Village Wooing / Darts (p), 1/10/74, AMDA Theatre, 13
Vincent (p), 9/30/59, Cricket Theatre, 55
Vinegar Buyer, The (p), 5/4/03, Savoy Theatre, 24
Vinegar Tree, The (p), 11/19/30, Playhouse, 233
Vintage '60 (r), 9/12/60, Brooks Atkinson Theatre, 8
Violet (p), 10/24/44, Belasco Theatre, 23
Violet, The / One, Two, Three (p), 9/29/30, Henry Miller's Theatre, 40
Virgin Man, The (p), 1/18/27, Princess Theatre, 64
Virgin of Bethulia, The (p), 2/23/25, Ambassador Theatre, 17
Virgin, The (p), 2/22/26, Maxine Elliott's Theatre, 57
Virginia (m), 9/2/37, Center Theatre, 60
Virginia Reel (p), 4/3/47, Princess Theatre, 5
Virginia Runs Away (p), 10/1/23, Klaw Theatre, 4
Virginian, The (p), 1/5/04, Manhattan Theatre, 138
Virginian, The (p), 10/16/05, Academy of Music, 16
Virginius (p), 9/16/07, Lyric Theatre, 22
Virility (p), 1/11/73, Actors Studio Theatre
Virtue (p), 11/16/22, Nora Bayes Theatre, 12
Virtue's Bed (p), 4/15/30, Hudson Theatre, 71
Virtuous Island, The / The Apollo of Bellac. See Double Bill of Jean Giraudoux's Plays, A), 4/9/57, Carnegie Hall Playhouse, 22
Visit, The (p), 5/5/58, Lunt-Fontanne Theatre, 189
Visit, The (p), 3/8/60, New York City Center, 16
Visit, The (p), 4/19/68, Master Theatre, 9, (Equity Library Theatre)
Visit, The (p), 11/25/73, Ethel Barrymore Theatre, 32, (New Phoenix Repertory Theatre)
Visit to a Small Planet (p), 2/7/57, Booth Theatre, 388
Visitor, The (p), 10/17/44, Henry Miller's Theatre, 23
Viva Madison Avenue! (p), 4/6/60, Longacre Theatre, 2
Viva O'Brien (m), 10/9/41, Majestic Theatre, 20
Vivat! Vivat Regina! (p), 1/20/72, Broadhurst Theatre, 116
Vivian's Papas (p), 8/17/03, Garrick Theatre, 49
Vogues (r), 3/27/24, Shubert Theatre, 114
Voice from the Minaret, The (p), 1/30/22, Hudson Theatre, 13
Voice in the Dark, A (p), 7/28/19, Republic Theatre, 134
Voice of McConnell, The (m), 12/25/18, Manhattan Opera House, 30
Voice of the Turtle, The (p), 12/8/43, Morosco Theatre, 1,557
Voice of the Turtle, The (p), 6/27/61, 41st St. Theatre, 150
Voices (p), 4/3/72, Ethel Barrymore Theatre, 8
Voices for a Mirror / The Curious Fern (p), 6/5/57, Master Institute
Volpone (p), 4/9/28, Guild Theatre, 160
Volpone (p), 3/10/30, Liberty Theatre, 8
Volpone (p) (Donald Wolfit), 2/24/47, Century Theatre, 3
Volpone (p) (Jose Ferrer), 1/8/48, New York City Center, 14
Volpone (p), 1/7/57, Rooftop Theatre, 130
Volpone (p) (Renaud-Berrault Repertory Co.), 2/4/57, Winter Garden Theatre, 4
Volpone (p), 6/22/67, New York Shakespeare Festival Mobile Theatre, 45
Voltaire (p), 3/20/22, Plymouth Theatre, 16
Vortex, The (p), 9/16/25, Henry Miller's Theatre, 157
Votes for Women (p), 3/15/09, Wallack Theatre, 16

W

Wait a Minim! (r), 3/7/66, John Golden Theatre, 457
Wait Till We're Married (p), 9/26/21, Playhouse, 56
Wait Until Dark (p), 2/2/66, Ethel Barrymore Theatre, 374
Waiting for Godot (p), 4/19/56, Golden Theatre, 59
Waiting for Godot (p), 1/21/57, Ethel Barrymore Theatre, 6
Waiting for Godot (p), 2/3/71, Sheridan Square Playhouse, 277
Waiting for Godot (p), 9/14/73, Jean Cocteau Theatre
Waiting for Godot. See also En Attendant Godot
Waiting for Lefty (p), 8/9/73, Manhattan Theatre Club, 10
Waiting for Lefty / Awake and Sing (p), 7/22/35, Belasco Theatre, 8
Waiting for Lefty / Awake and Sing (p), 9/9/35, Belasco Theatre, 24
Waiting for Lefty / The Bond (p), 12/13/67, Masque Theatre, 41
Waiting for Lefty / Till the Day I Die (p), 3/26/35, Longacre Theatre, 135
Wake Up and Dream (r), 12/30/29, Selwyn Theatre, 127
Wake Up, Darling (p), 5/2/56, Ethel Barrymore Theatre, 5
Wake Up, Jonathan (p), 1/17/21, Henry Miller's Theatre, 105
Walk a Little Faster (r), 12/7/32, St. James Theatre, 121
Walk Down Mah Street! (r), 6/12/68, Players Theatre, 135
Walk Hard (p), 11/30/44, Liberty Theatre, Harlem
Walk Hard (p), 3/27/46, Chanin Auditorium, 7
Walk in Dark Places, A. See Rooms
Walk in Darkness (p), 10/28/63, Greenwich Mews Theatre, 24
Walk into My Parlor (p), 11/19/41, Forrest Theatre, 29

Walk Together Children, 11/11/68, Greenwich Mews Theatre, 24
Walk Together Children, 3/16/72, Mercer/Brecht Theatre, 89
Walk Together Chillun (p), 2/2/36, Lafayette Theatre, 29
Walk with Music (m), 6/4/40, Ethel Barrymore Theatre, 55
Walker, Stuart. See Stuart Walker
Walking Gentleman, The (p), 5/7/42, Belasco Theatre, 6
Walking Happy (m), 11/26/66, Lunt-Fontanne Theatre, 161
Walking to Waldheim / Happiness (p), 11/10/67, Forum Theatre, 43
Walk-offs, The (p), 9/17/18, Morosco Theatre, 31
Walk-Up (p), 2/23/61, Provincetown Playhouse, 30
Wall Street (p), 4/20/27, Hudson Theatre, 21
Wall Street Girl, The (m), 4/15/12, Cohan Theatre, 56
Wall Street Scene (p), 10/18/37, Comedy Theatre, 3
Wall, The (p), 10/11/60, Billy Rose Theatre, 167
Wallflower (p), 1/26/44, Cort Theatre, 192
Walls of Jericho, The (p), 9/25/05, Savoy Theatre, 157
Walls of Jericho, The (p), 10/1/06, Hackett Theatre, 8
Walrus and the Carpenter, The (p), 11/8/41, Cort Theatre, 9
Waltz Dream, A (m), 1/27/08, Broadway Theatre, 111
Waltz in Goose Step (p), 11/1/38, Hudson Theatre, 7
Waltz of the Dogs, The (p), 4/25/28, 48th St. Theatre, 36
Waltz of the Toreadors, The (p), 1/17/57, Coronet Theatre, 132
Waltz of the Toreadors, The (p), 3/4/58, Coronet Theatre, 31
Waltz of the Toreadors, The (p), 4/6/59, Jan Hus House
Waltz of the Toreadors, The (p), 9/13/73, Circle in the Square / Joseph E. Levine Theatre, 85
Wanderer, The (p), 2/1/17, Manhattan Opera House, 108
Wanderers, The (r), 5/17/71, Orpheum Theatre, 3
Wandering Jew, The (p), 10/26/21, Knickerbocker Theatre, 69
Wandering Jew, The (p), 2/1/27, Cosmopolitan Theatre, 15
Wandering. See Collision Course
Wandering Stars (m), 11/11/66, Folksbiene Theatre
Wang (m), 4/18/04, Lyric Theatre, 57
Wanhope Building, The (p), 2/9/47, Princess Theatre, 5
Wanted (p), 7/2/28, Wallack Theatre, 16
Wanted (m), 1/19/72, Cherry Lane Theatre, 79
War and Peace (p), 1/11/65, Phoenix Theatre, 102
War and Peace (p), 3/21/67, Lyceum Theatre, 56, (APA-Phoenix)
War Games (p), 4/17/69, Fortune Theatre, 22
War President (p), 4/24/44, Shubert Theatre, 2
War. See Six from La Mama (1st Program)
War Song, The (p), 9/24/28, National Theatre, 80
Ware Case, The (p), 11/30/15, Maxine Elliott's Theatre, 47
Warm Body, A (p), 4/15/67, Cort Theatre, 1
Warm Peninsula, The (p), 10/20/59, Helen Hayes Theatre, 86
Warning—A Theme for Linda, The. See A Black Quartet
Warp (p), 2/14/72, Ambassador Theatre, 7
Warrens of Virginia, The (p), 12/3/07, Belasco Theatre, 190
Warrior's Husband, The (p), 3/11/32, Morosco Theatre, 83
Wars of the Roses, The (The Chronicles of King Henry VI, Part 1; The Chronicles of King Henry VI, Part 2; King Richard III) (p), 6/23/70, Delacorte Theatre, 55
Wars of the World (m), 9/5/14, New York Hippodrome, 229
Washington Heights (p), 9/29/31, Maxine Elliott's Theatre, 7
Washington Jitters (p), 5/2/38, Guild Theatre, 24
Washington Square Players, The, 2/19/15, Bandbox Theatre
Washington Square Players, The, 10/4/15, Bandbox Theatre
Washington Square Players, The, 8/30/16, Comedy Theatre
Washington Square Players, The, 10/31/17, Comedy Theatre
Washington Square Players, The (One-act plays) Children; The Age of Reason; The Magical City; Fire and Water; A Night of Snow; Helena's Husband; The Antick; Inferior; Literature; Overtones; The Honorable Lover; Whim; The Roadhouse in Arden, 1616-1916; The Clod; The Tenor; The Red Cloak
Washington Square Players, The (One-act Plays) Licensed; Interior; My Lady's Honor; The Shepherd in the Distance; Two Blind Beggars and One Less Blind; Love of One's Neighbor; In April; Forbidden Fruit; Saviors; A Miracle of St. Anthony; Eugenically Speaking; Another Interior; Moondown; A Bear
Washington Years, The (p), 3/11/48, ANT Playhouse, 7
Wasp's Nest, The (p), 10/25/27, Wallack Theatre, 31
Wasp, The (p), 3/27/23, Morosco Theatre, 86
Watch on the Rhine (p), 4/1/41, Martin Beck Theatre, 378
Watch Your Neighbor (p), 9/2/18, Booth Theatre, 48
Watch Your Step (m), 12/8/14, New Amsterdam Theatre, 175
Watched Pot, The (p), 10/28/47, Cherry Lane Theatre, 27
Watcher, The (p), 1/27/10, Comedy Theatre, 12
Watch-Pit (p), 1/30/69, Brooklyn Academy of Music, 3, (Chelsea Theatre Center)
Water Hen, The (p), 5/9/72, Brooklyn Academy of Music, 21, (Chelsea Theatre Center)
Watercolor / Criss-Crossing (p), 1/21/70, ANTA Theatre, 5
Watergate Scandals of '73, The (r), 6/28/73, Peach Pitts
Watering Place, The (p), 3/12/69, Music Box Theatre, 1
Waterloo Bridge (p), 1/6/30, Fulton Theatre, 64
Waters of Babylon, The (p), 11/8/65, New Theatre Workshop, 3
Wax Museum, The / The Innocent Party (p), 4/4/69, Brooklyn Academy of Music, 3, (Chelsea Theatre Center)
Way Down East (p), 12/14/03, Academy of Music, 48
Way Down East (p), 8/21/05, Academy of Music, 64
Way It Is, The (r), 12/2/69, New Lincoln Theatre, 60 previews
Way of the World, The (p), 11/4/01, Hammerstein's Victoria Theatre, 35
Way of the World, The (p), 11/17/24, Cherry Lane Theatre, 119
Way of the World, The (p), 6/1/31, Guild Theatre, 8
Way of the World, The (p), 10/2/54, Cherry Lane Theatre, 122
Way of the World, The (p), 2/13/74, Brooklyn Academy of Music, 5, (Actors Company)
Way Out, The / The March Heir / The Family Exit / Counsel's Opinion / Saturday It Rained / The White Dress (p), 12/13/32, Chanin Auditorium, 5
Way Things Happen, The (p), 1/28/24, Lyceum Theatre, 24
Ways and Means. See Tonight at 8:30
Wayward Saint, The (p), 2/17/55, Cort Theatre, 21
Wayward Stork, The (p), 1/19/66, 46th Street Theatre, 5
We All Do (p), 2/28/27, Bijou Theatre, 8
We Americans (p), 10/12/26, Sam H. Harris Theatre, 120
We Are No Longer Children (p), 3/31/32, Booth Theatre, 12
We Are Seven (p), 12/24/13, Maxine Elliott's Theatre, 21
We Bombed in New Haven (p), 10/16/68, Ambassador Theatre, 86
We Bombed in New Haven (p), 9/24/72, Circle in the Square, 1
We Can't Be as Bad as All That (p), 12/30/10, Nazimova's 39th St. Theatre, 19
We, Comrades Three (p), 12/20/66, Lyceum Theatre, 11, (APA-Phoenix)
We'd Rather Switch (r), 5/2/69, Mermaid Theatre
We Girls (p), 11/9/21, 48th St. Theatre, 30
We Have Always Lived in the Castle (p), 10/19/66, Ethel Barrymore Theatre, 9
We Moderns (p), 3/11/24, Gaiety Theatre, 23
We Never Learn (p), 1/23/28, Eltinge Theatre, 24
We're Civilized (m), 11/8/62, Jan Hus House, 22
We, the People (p), 1/20/33, Empire Theatre, 50
We've Got to Have Money (p), 8/20/23, Playhouse, 56
Weak Link, The (p), 3/4/40, Golden Theatre, 32
Weak Sisters (p), 10/13/25, Booth Theatre, 31
Weak Woman, A (p), 1/26/26, Ritz Theatre, 49
Weather Clear—Track Fast (p), 10/18/27, Hudson Theatre, 63
Weather Hen, The (p), 4/13/00, Manhattan Theatre, 1
Weather Permitting (p), 5/23/35, Masque Theatre, 4
Weavers, The (p), 12/14/15, Garden Theatre, 87
Web and the Rock, The (p), 3/19/72, Theatre de Lys, 9
Web, The (p), 6/27/32, Morosco Theatre, 24
Wedding Band (p), 9/26/72, Public / Newman Theatre, 175
Wedding Bells (p), 11/10/19, Harris Theatre, 168
Wedding Breakfast (p), 11/20/54, 48th St. Theatre, 113
Wedding Day, The (p), 12/10/09, Hackett Theatre, 1
Wedding of Iphigenia, The / Iphigenia in Concert (m), 12/16/71, Public/Martinson Hall, 139
Wedding, The / A Tragedian in Spite of Himself / The Bear / On the Harmfulness of Tobacco (p), 2/5/48, New York City Center, 14
Wedding, The / The Anniversary / On the High Road. See Evening with Chekhov, 4/20/61, Key Theatre, 61
Wedding Trip, The (m), 12/25/11, Broadway Theatre, 48
Wednesday's Child (p), 1/16/34, Longacre Theatre, 56
Week from Today, A / The Rope (p), 11/23/65, Theatre de Lys, 1, (ANTA Matinee)
Week-End (p), 10/22/29, John Golden Theatre, 12
Weekend (p), 3/13/68, Broadhurst Theatre, 21
Weep for the Virgins (p), 11/30/35, 46th St. Theatre, 9
Welcome Stranger (p), 9/13/20, Cohan and Harris Theatre, 307
Welcome to Andromeda / Variety Obit (p), 2/12/73, Cherry Lane Theatre, 24
Welcome to Our City (p), 9/12/10, Bijou Theatre, 16
Welded (p), 3/17/24, 39th St. Theatre, 24
Well of Romance, The (m), 11/7/30, Craig Theatre, 8
Well of the Saints, The (p), 9/10/21, Provincetown Playhouse, 8
Well of the Saints, The (p), 1/21/31, Barbizon Theatre, 5
Well of the Saints, The (p), 11/21/34, John Golden Theatre, 1
Wen, The. See Under the Weather
Werewolf, The (p), 8/25/24, 49th St. Theatre, 112
West of the Moon / The Blood Bugle (p), 6/28/61, New Playwrights Theatre, 6
West Point Cadet, The, 9/30/04, Princess Theatre, 4
West Side Story (m), 9/26/57, Winter Garden Theatre, 732
West Side Story (m), 4/27/60, Winter Garden Theatre, 249
West Side Story (m), 4/8/64, New York City Center, 31
West Side Story (m), 6/24/68, New York State Theatre, 89
Western Waters (p), 12/28/37, Hudson Theatre, 7
Wet Paint (r), 4/12/65, Renata Theatre, 16
What a Life (p), 4/13/38, Biltmore Theatre, 538
What a Rilling (m), 3/27/61, Folksbiene Theatre, 1

What Ails You? (p), 11/18/12, Criterion Theatre, 24
What! and Leave Bloomingdales? (Love in a Pub / Ellis Takes His Life Again / What! and Leave Bloomingdales? / Do You Know the Koran?) (p), 7/12/73, Little Church Around the Corner, 11
What Ann Brought Home (p), 2/21/27, Wallack Theatre, 106
What Big Ears (p), 4/20/42, Windsor Theatre, 8
What D'You Call It / According to Law / Devil Is a Good Man (p), 3/19/40, Provincetown Playhouse, 38
What D'You Want (p), 12/27/20, Provincetown Playhouse, 14
What Did We Do Wrong? (p), 10/22/67, Helen Hayes Theatre, 48
What Do We Know? (p), 12/23/27, Wallack Theatre, 35
What Every Woman Knows (p), 12/23/08, Empire Theatre, 198
What Every Woman Knows (p), 4/13/26, Bijou Theatre, 268
What Every Woman Knows (p), 11/8/46, International Theatre, 21
What Every Woman Knows (p), 12/22/54, New York City Center, 15
What Happened at 22 (p), 8/21/14, Harris Theatre, 19
What Happened to Jones (p), 8/30/17, 48th St. Theatre, 12
What Happened to Mary (p), 3/24/13, Fulton Theatre, 56
What If It Had Turned Up Heads (p), 10/13/72, New Lafayette Theatre, 29
What Is Love? (p), 9/19/14, Maxine Elliott's Theatre, 25
What It Means to a Woman (p), 11/19/14, Longacre Theatre, 12
What Makes Sammy Run? (m), 2/27/64, 54th St. Theatre, 540
What Money Can't Buy (p), 10/11/15, 48th St. Theatre, 8
What Never Dies (p), 12/28/26, Lyceum Theatre, 39
What Price Glory? (p), 9/5/24, Plymouth Theatre, 435
What's a Nice Country Like You Doing in a State Like This? (r), 4/19/73, Upstage at Jimmy's, 543
What's in a Name (m), 3/19/20, Maxine Elliott's Theatre, 87
What's In It for Me? (m), 7/30/73, Greenwich Mews Theatre, 12
What's It to You (r), 3/17/32, Provincetown Playhouse, 1
What's the Big Idea? (p), 3/23/26, Bijou Theatre, 23
What's the Matter with Susan? (p), 12/1/03, Bijou Theatre, 15
What's the Use (p), 9/6/26, Princess Theatre, 9
What's Up (m), 11/11/43, National Theatre, 63
What's Your Husband Doing (p), 11/12/17, 39th St. Theatre, 40
What's Your Wife Doing? (p), 10/1/23, 49th St. Theatre, 72
What Shall We Tell Caroline? / The Dock Brief (p), 11/21/61, Midway Theatre, 6
What the Butler Saw (p), 4/16/06, Garrick Theatre, 16
What the Butler Saw (p), 5/4/70, McAlpin Rooftop Theatre, 224
What the Doctor Ordered (p), 9/20/11, Astor Theatre, 21
What the Doctor Ordered (p), 8/18/27, Ritz Theatre, 20
What the Public Wants (p), 5/1/22, Garrick Theatre, 24
What the Wine Sellers Buy (p), 5/17/73, New Federal Theatre, 9
What the Wine Sellers Buy (p), 2/14/74, Vivian Beaumont Theatre, 37
. . . What Time of Night It Is (r), 5/3/73, Women's Interart Center, 9
What Women Do? (p), 7/20/25, Bijou Theatre, 16
What Would You Do? (p), 3/2/14, Hudson Theatre, 16
Whatever Goes Up (p), 11/25/35, Biltmore Theatre, 24
Whatever Possessed Her (p), 1/25/34, Mansfield Theatre, 4
Wheel, The (p), 8/29/21, Gaiety Theatre, 49
When Claudia Smiles (p), 2/2/14, 39th St. Theatre, 56
When Crummles Played / George Barnell / The Harlequinade (p), 10/1/28, Garrick Theatre, 40
When Did You Last See My Mother? (p), 1/4/67, Sheridan Square Playhouse, 11
When Dreams Come True (m), 8/18/13, Lyric Theatre, 64
When I Was a Child, 12/8/60, 41st St. Theatre, 38
When in Rome (p), 2/27/34, 49th St. Theatre, 7
When Johnny Comes Marching Home (m), 12/16/02, New York Theatre, 71
When Johnny Comes Marching Home (m), 5/7/17, New Amsterdam Theatre, 48
When Knighthood Was in Flower (p), 1/14/01, Criterion Theatre, 176
When Knighthood Was in Flower (p), 5/2/04, Empire Theatre, 16
When Knights Were Bold, 8/20/07, Garrick Theatre, 100
When Ladies Meet (p), 10/6/32, Royale Theatre, 187
When Ladies Meet (p), 5/15/33, Royale Theatre, 16
When Sweet Sixteen (m), 9/14/11, Daly's Theatre, 12
"When the Bough Breaks" (p), 2/16/32, 48th St. Theatre, 16
When the Owl Screams (r), 9/12/63, Second City at Square East, 204
When the Young Vine Blooms (p), 11/16/15, Garden Theatre, 23
When We Are Married (p), 12/25/39, Lyceum Theatre, 156
When We Are Young (p), 11/22/20, Broadhurst Theatre, 40
When We Dead Awake (p), 3/7/05, Knickerbocker Theatre, 3
When We Dead Awake (p), 3/27/05, Princess Theatre, 24
When We Dead Awaken (p), 5/17/26, Central Park Theatre, 7
When We Dead Awaken (p), 4/18/66, Masque Theatre, 6
When We Were Forty-one (r), 6/12/05, New York Roof Theatre, 66
When We Were Twenty-one (p), 2/5/00, Knickerbocker Theatre, 41
When We Were Twenty-one (p), 1/21/01, Knickerbocker Theatre, 42
When We Were Twenty-one (p), 10/18/06, Bijou Theatre, 3
When You Comin Back, Red Ryder? (p), 11/4/73, Circle Repertory Theatre, 19
When You Comin Back, Red Ryder? (p), 12/6/73, Eastside Playhouse, 228
When You Smile (m), 10/5/25, National Theatre, 49
Where Do We Go from Here? (p), 11/15/38, Vanderbilt Theatre, 15
Where Has Tommy Flowers Gone? (p), 10/7/71, Eastside Playhouse, 78
Where Ignorance Is Bliss (p), 9/3/13, Lyceum Theatre, 8
Where People Gather (p), 10/25/67, Gramercy Arts Theatre, 7
Where Poppies Bloom (p), 8/26/18, Republic Theatre, 104
Where's Charley? (m), 10/11/48, St. James Theatre, 792
Where's Charley? (m), 1/29/51, Broadway Theatre, 48
Where's Charley? (m), 5/25/66, N.Y. City Center, 15
Where's Daddy? (p), 3/2/66, Billy Rose, 21
Where's Your Husband? (p), 1/14/27, Greenwich Village Theatre, 19
Where's Your Wife (p), 10/4/19, Punch and Judy Theatre, 65
Where Stars Walk (p), 2/24/48, Mansfield Theatre, 14
Where There's a Will (p), 2/7/10, Weber Theatre, 64
Where There's a Will (p), 1/17/39, John Golden Theatre, 7
While Parents Sleep (p), 6/4/34, Playhouse, 16
While the Sun Shines (p), 9/19/44, Lyceum Theatre, 39
Whip, The (p), 11/22/12, Manhattan Opera House, 163
Whirl of New York, The (m), 6/13/21, Winter Garden Theatre, 124
Whirl of Society / Sesostra (m), 3/5/12, Winter Garden Theatre, 136
Whirl of the World, The (r), 1/10/14, Winter Garden Theatre, 161
Whirlpool (p), 12/3/29, Biltmore Theatre, 3
Whirlwind, The (p), 3/23/10, Daly's Theatre, 37
Whirlwind, The (p), 11/3/11, Daly's Theatre, 19
Whirlwind, The (p), 12/23/19, Standard Theatre, 31
Whiskey (p), 4/29/73, Theatre at St. Clement's Church
Whisper in God's Ear, A (p), 10/11/62, Cricket Theatre, 22
Whisper into My Good Ear / Mrs. Dally Has a Lover (p), 10/1/62, Cherry Lane Theatre, 48
Whisper to Me (p), 10/21/60, Players Theatre, 8
Whispering Friends (p), 2/20/28, Hudson Theatre, 112
Whispering Gallery, The (p), 2/11/29, Forrest Theatre, 81
Whispering Well, The (p), 12/4/20, Neighborhood Playhouse, 14
Whispering Wires (p), 8/7/22, 49th St. Theatre, 356
Whispers on the Wind (m), 6/3/70, Theatre de Lys, 15
Whistle in the Dark, A (p), 10/8/69, Mercury Theatre, 100
Whistler's Grandmother (p), 12/11/52, President Theatre, 24
Whistling in the Dark (p), 1/19/32, Ethel Barrymore Theatre, 144
Whistling in the Dark (p), 11/3/32, Waldorf Theatre, 123
Whistling Wizard and the Sultan of Tuffet, The (m), 12/20/69, Bil Baird Theatre, 179
Whistling Wizard and the Sultan of Tuffet, The (m), 10/17/70, Bil Baird Theatre, 33
Whistling Wizard and the Sultan of Tuffet, The (m), 10/17/73, Bil Baird Theatre, 36
White Cargo (p), 11/5/23, Greenwich Village Theatre, 864
White Cargo (p), 4/12/26, Daly's Theatre, 16
White Cargo (p), 12/29/60, Players Theatre, 10
White Cat, The, 11/2/05, New Amsterdam Theatre, 46
White Collars (p), 2/23/25, Cort Theatre, 104
White Desert (p), 10/18/23, Princess Theatre, 12
White Devil, The (p), 3/14/55, Phoenix Theatre
White Devil, The (p), 12/6/65, Circle in the Square, 152
White Dress, The / The Way Out / The March Heir / The Family Exit / Counsel's Opinion / Saturday It Rained (p), 12/13/32, Chanin Auditorium, 5
White Eagle, The (m), 12/26/27, Casino Theatre, 48
White Feather, The (p), 2/4/15, Comedy Theatre, 140
White Flame (p), 11/4/29, Vanderbilt Theatre, 8
White Gold (p), 11/2/25, Lenox Little Theatre, 16
White Guard, The (Days of the Turbins) (p), 3/4/35, Majestic Theatre, 10
White Hen, The (m), 2/16/07, Casino Theatre, 94
White Horse Inn (m), 10/1/36, Center Theatre, 211
White House Murder Case, The (p), 2/18/70, Circle in the Square, 119
White House, The, 5/19/64, Henry Miller's Theatre, 23
White Lies. See Black Comedy
White Lights (m), 10/11/27, Ritz Theatre, 31
White Lilacs (m), 9/10/28, Shubert Theatre, 138
White Magic (p), 1/24/12, Criterion Theatre, 21
White Man (p), 10/19/36, National Theatre, 6
White Mask (p), 3/19/22, Little Theatre, 1
White Nights / The Loves of Alonzo Fitz Clarence and Rosannah Ethelton (m), 2/6/74, Theatre of Riverside Church, 23
White Peacock, The (p), 12/26/21, Comedy Theatre, 102
White Rose and the Red, The (p), 3/16/64, Stage 73, 31
White Sister, The (m), 9/27/09, Daly's Theatre, 48
White Sister, The (m), 5/17/27, Wallack Theatre, 7
White Steed, The (p), 1/10/39, Cort Theatre, 136
White Villa, The (p), 2/14/21, Eltinge Theatre, 14
White Whore and the Bit Player, The (p), 2/5/73, St. Clement's Church Theatre, 18
White Wings (p), 10/15/26, Booth Theatre, 27
White-headed Boy, The (p), 9/15/21, Henry Miller's Theatre, 62
White-headed Boy, The (p), 10/20/32, Martin Beck Theatre, 2
White-Headed Boy, The (p), 12/1/34, John Golden Theatre, 3

Whiteoaks (p), 3/23/38, Hudson Theatre, 112
Whitewashed (p), 4/23/24, 52nd St. Theatre, 13
Whitewashing of Julia, The (p), 12/2/03, Garrick Theatre, 39
Whitman Portrait, A (p), 10/11/66, Gramercy Arts Theatre, 71
Whitsuntide (p), 3/26/72, Martinique Theatre, 1
Who Am I? (m), 12/4/71, Stage 73
Who Cares (r), 7/8/30, 46th St. Theatre, 30
Who Did It? (p), 6/9/19, Harris Theatre, 8
Who Goes There? (p), 2/20/05, Princess Theatre, 24
Who'll Save the Plowboy? (p), 1/9/62, Phoenix Theatre, 46
Who's Afraid of Virginia Woolf? (p), 10/13/62, Billy Rose Theatre, 644
Who's Afraid of Virginia Woolf? (p), 7/3/68, Forum Theatre, 7, (Atelje 212)
Who's Afraid of Virginia Woolf? in Spanish (p), 10/12/72, Gramercy Arts Theatre, 37, (Spanish Theatre Repertory Co.)
Who's Got His Own (p), 10/12/66, American Place Theatre, 19
Who's Happy Now? (p), 11/17/69, Village South Theatre, 32
Who's Who? (p), 9/11/13, Criterion Theatre, 52
Who's Who? (r), 3/1/38, Hudson Theatre, 23
Who's Who, Baby? (m), 1/29/68, Players Theatre, 16
Who Was That Lady I Saw You With? (p), 3/3/58, Martin Beck Theatre, 208
Whole Town's Talking, The (p), 8/29/23, Bijou Theatre, 174
Whole World Over, The (p), 3/27/47, Biltmore Theatre, 100
Whoop-Dee-Doo (m), 9/24/03, Weber & Fields Music Hall, 151
Whoop-Dee-Doo (m), 5/16/04, New Amsterdam Theatre, 14
Whoopee (m), 12/4/28, New Amsterdam Theatre, 255
Whoop-Up (m), 12/22/58, Shubert Theatre, 56
Whores, Wars and Tin Pan Alley (r), 6/16/69, Bitter End, 72
Why Do I Deserve This? (r), 1/18/66, Barbizon-Plaza Theatre, 12
Why Marry? (p), 12/25/17, Astor Theatre, 120
Why Men Leave Home (p), 9/12/22, Morosco Theatre, 138
Why Not? (p), 12/25/22, 48th St. Theatre, 123
Why Smith Left Home (p), 4/9/00, Madison Sq. Theatre, 24
Why Worry? (p), 8/23/18, Harris Theatre, 27
Wicked Age, The (p), 11/4/27, Daly's Theatre, 19
Wicked Cooks, The (p), 1/23/67, Orpheum Theatre, 16
Wide Open Cage, The (p), 12/10/62, Washington Sq. Theatre, 136
Widow by Proxy (p), 2/24/13, Cohan Theatre, 88
Widow by Proxy / Mrs. Peckham's Carouse (p), 4/21/13, Cohan Theatre, 24
Widow in Green, A (p), 11/20/31, Cort Theatre, 24
Widow Jones, The (p), 12/23/01, Bijou Theatre, 40
Widow's Might, The (p), 9/13/09, Liberty Theatre, 40
Widowers' Houses (p), 3/7/07, Herald Sq. Theatre, 16
Widowers' Houses (p), 3/2/59, Downtown Theatre, 107
Wiener Blut (m) (Vienna Life), 9/11/64, Lunt-Fontanne Theatre, 27
Wife Decides, The (p), 11/14/11, Weber Theatre, 31
Wife Hunters, The (m), 11/2/11, Herald Sq. Theatre, 36
Wife Insurance (p), 4/12/34, Ethel Barrymore Theatre, 4
Wife with a Smile, The / Boubouroche (p), 11/28/21, Garrick Theatre, 41
Wife without a Smile, A (p), 12/19/04, Criterion Theatre, 16
Wild and Wonderful (m), 12/7/71, Lyceum Theatre, 1
Wild Birds (p), 4/9/25, Cherry Lane Playhouse, 44
Wild Duck, The (p) (Nazimova), 3/11/18, Plymouth Theatre, 32
Wild Duck, The (p), 2/24/25, 48th St. Theatre, 110
Wild Duck, The (p), 11/19/28, 49th St. Theatre, 81
Wild Duck, The (p), 4/16/38, 49th St. Theatre, 3
Wild Duck, The (p), 12/26/51, New York City Center, 15
Wild Duck, The (p), 11/11/67, Lyceum Theatre, 45, (APA-Phoenix)
Wild Man of Borneo, The (p), 9/13/27, Bijou Theatre, 15
Wild Oats Lane (p), 9/6/22, Broadhurst Theatre, 14
Wild Rose, The (m), 5/5/02, Knickerbocker Theatre, 136
Wild Rose, The (m), 10/20/26, Martin Beck Theatre, 62
Wild Stunt Show, The (r), 4/9/74, Brooklyn Academy of Music, 21, (Chelsea Theatre Center)
Wild Waves (p), 2/19/32, Times Sq. Theatre, 25
Wild Wescotts, The (p), 12/24/23, Frazee Theatre, 25
Wildcat (m), 12/16/60, Alvin Theatre, 171
Wildcat, The (p), 11/26/21, Park Theatre, 74
Wilde! (p), 12/4/72, Theatre de Lys, 2, (ANTA Matinee)
Wilde Evening with Shaw, A, 3/5/63, 41st St. Theatre, 15
Wilderness, The (p), 1/23/01, Empire Theatre, 80
Wildfire (p), 9/7/08, Liberty Theatre, 64
Wildflowers (m), 2/7/23, Casino Theatre, 477
Will and the Way, The (p), 12/2/57, Theatre East, 9
Will Geer's Americana, 1/18/66, Theatre de Lys, 1, (ANTA Matinee)
Will Rogers' U.S.A., 5/6/74, Helen Hayes Theatre, 8
Will Shakespeare, 1/1/23, National Theatre, 64
Will Success Spoil Rock Hunter? (p), 10/13/55, Belasco Theatre, 444
Will the Mail Train Run Tonight? (m), 1/9/64, New Bowery Theatre, 8
Will, The / Tyranny of Tears (p), 9/29/13, Empire Theatre, 32
Willard, E. S. See E. S. Willard
William Gillette Repertory, 12/5/10, Empire Theatre
Willie Doesn't Live Here Anymore (p), 2/6/67, Theatre de Lys, 2, (ANTA Matinee)
Willow and I, The (p), 12/10/42, Windsor Theatre, 28
Willow Tree, The (p), 3/6/17, Cohan and Harris Theatre, 103
Wilson in the Promise Land (p), 5/26/70, ANTA Theatre, 7
Wind and the Rain, The (p), 2/1/34, Ritz Theatre, 119
Wind Is Ninety, The (p), 6/21/45, Booth Theatre, 108
Window Panes (p), 2/21/27, Mansfield Theatre, 32
Window Shopping (p), 12/23/38, Longacre Theatre, 11
Window Veil, The / Autumn Fires / Aria Da Capo (p), 6/10/21, Provincetown Playhouse, 11
Windows (p), 10/8/23, Garrick Theatre, 48
Wine of Choice (p), 2/21/38, Guild Theatre, 43
Wine, Women and Song (r), 9/28/42, Ambassador Theatre, 150
Winesburg, Ohio (p), 2/5/58, National Theatre, 13
Winged Victory (p), 11/20/43, 44th St. Theatre, 212
Wingless Victory, The (p), 12/23/26, Empire Theatre, 108
Wings Over Europe (p), 12/10/28, Martin Beck Theatre, 33
Winkelberg (p), 1/14/58, Renata Theatre, 48
Winner, The (p), 2/17/54, Playhouse, 30
Winners and Losers (p), 2/26/47, Henry St. Playhouse, 6
Winners. See Lovers
Winnie the Pooh (m), 11/23/67, Bil Baird Theatre, 156
Winnie the Pooh (m), 3/7/69, Bil Baird Playhouse, 58
Winnie the Pooh (m), 3/27/71, Bil Baird Theatre, 48
Winnie the Pooh (m), 10/29/72, Bil Baird Theatre, 44
Winslow Boy, The (p), 10/29/47, Empire Theatre, 218
Winsome Widow, A (m), 4/11/12, Moulin Rouge Theatre, 172
Winsome Winnie (m), 12/1/03, Casino Theatre, 56
Winter Bound (p), 11/12/29, Garrick Theatre, 39
Winter Garden, 3/20/11, Winter Garden Theatre, 32
Winter Journey (p), 3/12/68, Greenwich Mews Theatre, 15
Winter's Tale, The (p), 3/28/10, New Theatre
Winter's Tale, The (p), 2/4/21, Little Theatre, 1
Winter's Tale, The (p), 1/15/46, Cort Theatre, 39
Winter's Tale, The (p), 8/8/63, Delacorte Theatre, 21
Winter Soldiers (p), 11/29/42, Studio Theatre (New School or Social Research), 30
Winter'Tale, The (p) (Viola Allen-James Young), 12/26/04, Knickerbocker Theatre, 32
Winterfeast, The (p), 11/30/08, Savoy Theatre, 16
Winterset (p), 9/25/35, Martin Beck Theatre, 178
Winterset (p), 6/1/36, Martin Beck Theatre, 16
Winterset (p), 2/9/66, Jan Hus Playhouse, 30
Wisdom Tooth, The (p), 2/15/26, Little Theatre, 160
Wise Child (p), 1/27/72, Helen Hayes Theatre, 4
Wise Have Not Spoken, The (p), 2/10/54, Cherry Lane Theatre
Wise Tomorrow (p), 10/15/37, Biltmore Theatre, 3
Wisecrackers, The (p), 12/16/25, 5th Ave. Theatre, 13
Wiser They Are, The (p), 4/6/31, Plymouth Theatre, 40
Wish You Were Here (m), 6/25/52, Imperial Theatre, 598
Wisteria Trees, The (p), 3/29/50, Martin Beck Theatre, 165
Wisteria Trees, The (p), 2/2/55, New York City Center, 15
Witch, The (p), 2/14/10, New Theatre
Witch, The (p), 11/18/26, Greenwich Village Theatre, 28
Witch, The / The Music Shop / The Vagrant (p) (A Chekhov Sketchbook), 2/15/62, Gramercy Arts Theatre, 94
Witch Woman, The. See Kyhundor
Witches' Sabbath (p), 4/19/62, Madison Ave. Playhouse, 14
Witching Hour, The (p), 11/18/07, Hackett Theatre, 212
With a Silk Thread (p), 4/12/50, Lyceum Theatre, 15
With Privileges (p), 9/15/30, Vanderbilt Theatre, 48
Within Four Walls (p), 4/17/23, Selwyn Theatre, 15
Within the Gates (p), 10/22/34, National Theatre, 100
Within the Gates (p), 1/22/35, National Theatre, 40
Within the Law (p), 9/11/12, Eltinge Theatre, 541
Within the Law (p), 3/5/28, Cosmopolitan Theatre, 18
Without Love (p), 11/10/42, St. James Theatre, 110
Without Warning (p), 5/1/37, National Theatre, 17
Witness for the Defense, The (p), 12/4/11, Empire Theatre, 64
Witness for the Prosecution (p), 12/16/54, Henry Miller's Theatre, 645
Witness for the Prosecution (p), 3/4/66, Master Theatre, 9, (Equity Theatre)
Witness / Sweet Eros (p), 11/21/68, Gramercy Arts Theatre, 78
Wives of Henry VIII, The, 11/15/31, Avon Theatre, 63
Wives, The (p), 5/18/65, Stage 73, 33
Wizard of Oz, The (m), 1/21/03, Majestic Theatre, 293
Wizard of Oz, The (m), 3/21/04, Majestic Theatre, 48
Wizard of Oz, The (m), 11/27/68, Bil Baird Playhouse, 118
Wizard of Oz, The (m), 10/30/71, Bil Baird Theatre, 65
Wolf, The (p), 4/18/08, Bijou Theatre, 81
Wolves (p), 1/6/32, 49th St. Theatre, 28
Woman, 10/20/65, Gramercy Arts Theatre, 7
Woman Bites Dog (p), 4/17/46, Belasco Theatre, 5
Woman Brown, The (p), 12/8/39, Biltmore Theatre, 11

Woman Denied, A (p), 2/25/31, Ritz Theatre, 37
Woman Disputed, The (p), 9/28/26, Forrest Theatre, 87
Woman Haters, The (m), 10/7/12, Astor Theatre, 32
Woman in Room 13, The (p), 1/14/19, Booth Theatre, 175
Woman in the Case, The (p), 1/31/05, Herald Square Theatre, 89
Woman in the Case, The (p), 8/21/05, Madison Square Theatre, 8
Woman Is My Idea (p), 9/25/68, Belasco Theatre, 5
Woman Killed with Kindness, A / Granny Maumee (p), 3/30/14, Lyceum Theatre, 1
Woman of Bronze, The (p), 9/7/20, Frazee Theatre, 249
Woman of Bronze, The (p), 6/15/27, Lyric Theatre, 30
Woman of Destiny, A (p), 3/2/36, Willis Theatre, 35
Woman of Impulse, A (p), 3/1/09, Herald Square Theatre, 16
Woman of It, The (p), 1/14/13, 39th St. Theatre, 15
Woman of No Importance, A (p), 4/24/16, Fulton Theatre, 56
Woman of the Index, The (p), 8/29/18, 48th St. Theatre, 52
Woman of the Soil, A (p), 3/25/35, 49th St. Theatre, 24
Woman on the Jury, The (p), 8/15/23, Eltinge Theatre, 78
Woman's a Fool To Be Clever, A (p), 10/18/38, National Theatre, 7
Woman's Honor, A / 'Ile / The Maid of France (p), 5/20/18, Greenwich Village Theatre
Woman's Way, A (p), 2/22/09, Hackett Theatre, 112
Woman, The (p), 9/19/11, Republic Theatre, 247
Woman Who Laughed, The (p), 8/16/22, Longacre Theatre, 13
Women and Wine (p), 4/11/00, Manhattan Theatre, 69
Women at the Tomb, The / Fugue for Three Marys (p), 3/22/59, Broadway Congregational Church, 8
Women at the Tomb, The / Philoktetes (p), 4/24/61, One Sheridan Square, 6
Women Beware Women (p), 10/17/72, Good Shepherd-Faith Church, 7, (City Center Acting Co.)
Women Go On Forever (p), 9/7/27, Forrest Theatre, 118
Women Have Their Way, The (p), 11/18/30, Civic Repertory Theatre
Women Have Their Way, The / A Sunny Morning (p), 12/7/35, Sam S. Shubert Theatre, 1
Women Have Their Way, The / The Open Door (p), 1/27/30, Civic Repertory Theatre, 25
Women of Trachis / The Marrying Maiden (p), 6/22/60, Living Theatre, 50
Women of Twilight (p), 3/3/52, Plymouth Theatre, 8
Women, The (p), 12/26/36, Ethel Barrymore Theatre, 657
Women, The (p), 4/25/73, 46th Street Theatre, 63
Wonder Bar, The (m), 3/17/31, Nora Bayes Theatre, 86
Wonder Boy (p), 10/23/31, Alvin Theatre, 44
Wonderful Journey (p), 12/25/46, Coronet Theatre, 9
Wonderful Night, A (m), 10/31/29, Majestic Theatre, 125
Wonderful Thing, The (p), 2/17/20, Playhouse, 120
Wonderful Town (m), 2/25/53, Winter Garden Theatre, 559
Wonderful Town (m), 3/5/58, New York City Center, 16
Wonderful Town (m), 2/13/63, New York City Center, 16
Wonderful Town (m), 5/17/67, New York City Center, 23
Wonderful Visit, The (p), 2/12/24, Lenox Hill Theatre, 49
Wonderful Visit, The (p), 5/14/24, Princess Theatre, 92
Wonderful World of Burlesque, The (r), 4/28/65, Mayfair Theatre, 211
Wonderland (m), 10/24/05, Majestic Theatre, 73
Wood Demon, The (p), 3/3/67, Master Theatre, 9
Wood Demon, The (p), 1/29/74, Brooklyn Academy of Music, 10, (Actors Company)
Wooden Dish, The (p), 10/6/55, Booth Theatre, 12
Wooden Kimono (p), 12/27/26, Martin Beck Theatre, 201
Wooden Slipper, The (p), 1/3/34, Ritz Theatre, 5
Wooden Soldier, The (p), 6/22/31, Biltmore Theatre, 8
Woodland (m), 11/21/04, New York Theatre, 83
Woof, Woof (m), 12/25/29, Royale Theatre, 46
Wooing of Eve, The (p), 11/9/17, Liberty Theatre, 51
Wookey, The (p), 9/10/41, Plymouth Theatre, 134
Words and Music (r), 12/24/17, Fulton Theatre, 24
Words and Music (r), 4/16/74, John Golden Theatre, 53
Words Upon the Window Pane, The (p), 10/28/32, Martin Beck Theatre, 1
Work Is for Horses (p), 11/20/37, Windsor Theatre, 9
Workhouse Ward, The (p), 11/5/32, Martin Beck Theatre, 1
Workhouse Ward, The / Riders to the Sea (p), 8/4/20, Bramhall Theatre, 34
Workshop of the Players Art Second Annual International New Plays Festival (Far from the Summer, Far from the Sea / Forgotten Dreams / All Over Again / Apollo's Fate / Cleaning House / The Considered Opinion of Alexander Woollcott / Death / Fear / (p) The Flame Play / Frank Buck Can't Make It / The Goalie / Hara Kiri / Merle / The Refugees / Robert Benchley's Locomotive / Side Show), 6/19/73, WPA Theatre, 24
World and His Wife, The (p), 11/2/08, Daly's Theatre, 88
World of Carl Sandburg, The, 9/14/60, Henry Miller's Theatre, 29
World of Charles Aznavour, The (r), 10/14/65, Ambassador Theatre, 28
World of Gunter Grass, The (r), 4/26/66, Pocket Theatre, 80
World of Illusion (r), 6/24/64, Actors Playhouse
World of Kurt Weill in Song, The, 6/6/63, Key Theatre, 228
World of Kurt Weill in Song, The, 5/12/64, Jan Hus House, 80
World of Mrs. Solomon, The (Another Chance / The Second Mrs. Aarons) (p), 6/3/69, Fortune Theatre, 8
World of My America, The, 10/3/66, Greenwich Mews Theatre, 11
World of Pleasure, A (r), 10/14/15, Winter Garden Theatre, 116
World of Ray Bradbury, The (The Pedestrian / To The Chicago Abyss / the Veldt) (p), 10/8/65, Orpheum Theatre, 5
World of Sholom Aleichem, The, 5/1/53, Barbizon-Plaza Theatre
World of Suzie Wong, The (p), 10/14/58, Broadhurst Theatre, 508
World's a Stage, The, 5/12/69, Lyceum Theatre, 6
World's Full of Girls, The (p), 12/6/43, Royale Theatre, 9
World's My Oster, The (m), 7/31/56, Actors Playhouse, 40
World Waits, The (p), 10/25/33, Little Theatre, 29
World War 2½ (p), 3/24/69, Martinique Theatre, 1
World We Live In, The (p), 10/31/22, Jolson Theatre, 112
World We Make, The (p), 11/20/39, Guild Theatre, 80
Worlds of Oscar Brown, Jr., The, 2/18/65, Gramercy Arts Theatre, 53
Worlds of Shakespeare, The (p), 12/4/63, Carnegie Hall Theatre, 24
Worm in the Horseradish, A (p), 3/13/61, Maidman Playhouse, 89
Worth of a Man, The / Lonesome Like / The Last Toast / Uncle Sam's Money (p), 4/27/14, 48th St. Theatre, 1
Worth of a Woman, The (p), 2/12/08, Madison Sq. Theatre, 21
Would-Be Gentleman, The (p), 10/1/28, Civic Repertory Theatre, 34
Would-Be Gentleman, The (p), 9/21/29, Civic Repertory Theatre, 16
Would-Be Gentleman, The (p), 3/12/31, Civic Repertory Theatre, 3
Would-Be Gentleman, The (p), 1/9/46, Booth Theatre, 77
Woyzeck (p), 5/25/71, Fortune Theatre, 5
Woyzeck (p), 12/5/72, Barbizon-Plaza Theatre, 7, (Die Brücke)
Woyzeck / Die Mitschuldigen (p), 4/5/66, New York City Center, 8, (The Bavarian State Theatre)
Wrecker, The (p), 2/27/28, Cort Theatre, 40
Wrecking Ball, The (r), 4/15/64, Second City at Square East, 126
Wren, The (p), 10/10/21, Gaiety Theatre, 24
Wretched the Lionhearted / A Toy for Clowns (p), 9/12/62, East End Theatre, 2
Write Me a Murder (p), 10/26/61, Belasco Theatre, 196
Writing on the Wall, The (p), 4/26/09, Savoy Theatre, 32
Wrong Number (p), 3/13/34, Provincetown Playhouse, 17
Wrong Way Light Bulb, The (p), 3/4/69, John Golden Theatre, 7
Wuthering Heights (p), 4/27/39, Longacre Theatre, 12
Wuzit! (p), 9/28/70, Old Reliable Tavern

X

X Has No Value (p), 1/23/70, Public/Other Stage Theatre
Xmas in Las Vegas (p), 11/4/65, Ethel Barrymore Theatre, 4

Y

Y Avait un Prisonnier (p) (French Language), 1/24/38, Barbizon-Plaza Theatre
Yankee Circus on Mars, A / The Raiders (p), 4/12/05, New York Hippodrome, 120
Yankee Consul, The (m), 2/22/04, Broadway Theatre, 115
Yankee Consul, The (m), 1/24/05, Wallack Theatre, 47
Yankee Girl, The (m), 2/10/17, Herald Square Theatre, 92
Yankee Point (p), 11/23/42, Longacre Theatre, 24
Yankee Prince, The (m), 4/20/08, Knickerbocker Theatre, 28
Yankee Princess, The (m), 10/2/22, Knickerbocker Theatre, 80
Yankee Tourist, A, 8/12/07, Astor Theatre, 103
Yeah Man (r), 5/26/32, Park Lane Theatre, 2
Year Boston Won the Pennant, The (p), 5/22/69, Forum Theatre, 36
Year of the Dragon, The (p), 5/22/74, American Place Theatre, 26
Yearling, The (m), 12/10/65, Alvin Theatre, 3
Years Ago (p), 12/3/46, Mansfield Theatre, 206
Years of Discretion (p), 12/25/12, Belasco Theatre, 190
Yellow (p), 9/21/26, National Theatre, 132
Yellow Jack (p), 3/6/34, Martin Beck Theatre, 79
Yellow Jack (p), 2/27/47, International Theatre, 21
Yellow Jack (p), 12/11/64, Master Theatre, 9, (Equity Library Theatre)
Yellow Jacket, The (p), 11/4/12, Fulton Theatre, 80
Yellow Jacket, The (p), 11/9/16, Cort Theatre, 172
Yellow Jacket, The (p), 1/4/21, Cort Theatre, 10
Yellow Jacket, The (p), 11/7/28, Coburn Theatre, 129
Yellow Sands (p), 9/10/27, Fulton Theatre, 25
Yellow Sound, The (p), 5/11/72, Solomon R. Guggenheim Museum Auditorium
Yellow Ticket, The (p), 1/20/14, Eltinge Theatre, 183
Yeomen of the Guard, The (m), 5/1/33, St. James Theatre, 8

Yeomen of the Guard, The (m), 8/14/33, Majestic Theatre, 8
Yeomen of the Guard, The (m), 9/20/34, Martin Beck Theatre, 11
Yeomen of the Guard, The (m), 7/29/35, Adelphi Theatre, 12
Yeomen of the Guard, The (m), 8/26/35, Adelphi Theatre, 4
Yeomen of the Guard, The (m), 9/14/36, Martin Beck Theatre, 20
Yeomen of the Guard, The (m), 3/3/44, Ambassador Theatre, 1
Yeomen of the Guard, The (m), 2/2/48, Century Theatre, 16
Yeomen of the Guard, The (m), 10/3/55, Shubert Theatre, 8, (D'Oyly Carte Opera Co.)
Yeomen of the Guard, The (m), 2/18/60, Jan Hus House
Yeomen of the Guard, The (m), 4/27/61, Greenwich Mews Theatre, 6
Yeomen of the Guard, The (m), 3/18/64, New York City Center, 3
Yeomen of the Guard, The (m), 7/7/65, Jan Hus Playhouse, 35, (American Savoyards)
Yeomen of the Guard, The (m), 7/7/65, Jan Hus Playhouse, 22, (American Savoyards)
Yeomen of the Guard, The (m), 5/8/68, New York City Center, 3
Yeomen of the Guard, The. See American Savoyards, Shakespearewrights Theatre, 8
Yerma (p), 12/8/66, Vivian Beaumont Theatre, 56
Yerma (p), 2/25/71, Greenwich Mews Theatre, 60
Yerma (p), 10/18/72, Brooklyn Academy of Music, 16, (Nuria Espert Company of Spain)
Yes Is for a Very Young Man (p), 6/6/49, Cherry Lane Theatre
Yes Is for a Very Young Man (p), 3/4/63, Players Theatre, 1
Yes, M' Lord (p), 10/4/49, Booth Theatre, 87
Yes, My Darling Daughter (p), 2/9/37, Playhouse, 404
Yes, My Darling Daughter (p), 5/10/68, Master Theatre, 9, (Equity Library Theatre)
Yes or No (p), 12/21/17, 48th St. Theatre, 147
Yes Yes, No No (p), 12/31/68, Astor Place Theatre, 1
Yes, Yes, Yvette (m), 10/3/27, Sam H. Harris Theatre, 40
Yesterday's Magic (p), 4/14/42, Guild Theatre, 55
Yesterday's Orchids (p), 10/5/34, Fulton Theatre, 3
Yin Yang (p), 8/21/73, Space for Innovative Development, 36
Yin Yang (p), 8/21/73, St. Marks Playhouse
Yip Yip Yaphank (p), 8/19/18, Century Theatre, 32
Yokel Boy (m), 7/6/39, Majestic Theatre, 208
York State Folks (p), 8/19/05, Majestic Theatre, 31
Yosemite (p), 11/23/14, Daly's Theatre, 24
Yoshe Kalb (p), 12/28/33, National Theatre, 4
Yoshe Kalb (m), 10/22/72, Eden Theatre, 88
Yoshke Musikant (p), 11/4/72, Folksbiene Playhouse
You and I (p), 2/19/23, Belmont Theatre, 174
You Can't Sleep Here (p), 4/26/40, Barbizon-Plaza Theatre
You Can't Take It with You (p), 12/14/36, Booth Theatre, 837
You Can't Take It with You (p), 3/26/45, New York City Center, 17
You Can't Take It with You (p), 11/23/65, Lyceum Theatre, 240
You Can't Take It with You (p), 2/10/67, Lyceum Theater, 16, (APA-Phoenix)
You Can't Win (p), 2/16/26, Klaw Theatre, 2
You Know I Can't Hear You When the Water's Running (The Shock of Recognition / The Footsteps of Doves / I'll Be Home for Christmas / I'm Herbert) (p), 3/13/67, Ambassador Theatre, 756
You'll See Stars (p), 12/29/42, Maxine Elliott's Theatre, 4
You Never Can Tell (p), 1/9/05, Garrick Theatre, 129
You Never Can Tell (p), 4/5/15, Garrick Theatre
You Never Can Tell (p), 3/16/48, Martin Beck Theatre, 39
You Never Can Tell (p), 10/21/66, Master Theatre, 9, (Equity Library Theatre)
You Never Can Tell / The Philanderer. See George Bernard Shaw Series, 5/12/58, Downtown Theatre, 32
You Never Know (m), 9/21/38, Winter Garden Theatre, 78
You Never Know (m), 3/12/73, Eastside Playhouse, 8
You're a Good Man, Charlie Brown (m), 3/7/67, Theatre 80 St. Marks, 1,597
You're a Good Man, Charlie Brown (m), 6/1/71, John Golden Theatre, 32
You're in Love (m), 2/6/17, Casino Theatre, 167
You Said It (m), 1/19/31, 46th St. Theatre, 190
You Touched Me! (p), 9/25/45, Booth Theatre, 109
Young Abe Lincoln (m), 4/25/61, Eugene O'Neill Theatre, 27
Young Abe Lincoln (m), 2/13/71, Town Hall, 1
Young Alexander (p), 3/12/29, Biltmore Theatre, 7
Young America (p), 8/28/15, Astor Theatre, 105
Young American, A (p), 1/17/46, Blackfriars' Guild, 26
Young Among Themselves, The / The Pastry Shop (p), 6/10/70, The Extension, 10
Young and Beautiful, The (p), 10/1/55, Longacre Theatre, 65
Young and Fair, The (p), 11/22/48, Fulton Theatre, 24
Young and Fair, The (p), 12/27/48, International Theatre, 16
Young Blood (p), 11/24/25, Ritz Theatre, 72
Young Couple Wanted (p), 1/24/40, Maxine Elliott's Theatre, 13
Young Go First, The (p), 5/28/35, Park Theatre, 39
Young Idea, The (p), 3/18/32, Heckscher Theatre, 3
Young Love (p), 10/30/28, Masque Theatre, 87
Young Madam Conti (p), 3/31/37, Music Box Theatre, 22
Young Man's Fancy, A (p), 10/15/19, Playhouse, 13
Young Man's Fancy, A (p), 4/29/47, Plymouth Theatre, 335
Young Marrieds Play Monopoly. See Monopoly
Young Master Dante, The. See Trainer, Dean, Liepolt and Company
Young Mr. Disraeli (p), 11/10/37, Fulton Theatre, 6
Young Provincials, The (p), 9/18/58, Cricket Theatre, 13
Young Sinners (p), 11/28/29, Morosco Theatre, 229
Young Sinners (p), 4/20/31, New Yorker Theatre, 16
Young Sinners (p), 3/6/33, Ambassador Theatre, 68
Young Turk, The (m), 1/31/10, New York Theatre, 32
Young Visitors, The (p), 11/29/20, 39th St. Theatre, 16
Young Wisdom (p), 1/5/14, Criterion Theatre, 56
Young Woodley (p), 11/2/25, Belmont Theatre, 267
Younger Generation, The / Half an Hour (p), 9/25/13, Lyceum Theatre, 60
Younger Mrs. Parling, The (p), 1/26/04, Garrick Theatre, 36
Youngest, The (p), 12/22/24, Gaiety Theatre, 100
Your Humble Servant (p), 1/3/10, Garrick Theatre, 72
Your Loving Son (p), 4/4/41, Little Theatre, 3
Your Own Thing (m), 1/13/68, Orpheum Theatre, 933
Your Uncle Dudley (p), 11/18/29, Cort Theatre, 96
Your Woman and Mine (p), 2/27/22, Klaw Theatre, 48
Yours, A. Lincoln (p), 7/9/42, Shubert Theatre, 2
Yours Is My Heart (m), 9/5/46, Shubert Theatre, 36
Yours Truly (m), 1/25/27, Shubert Theatre, 127
Yours Truly (m), 3/12/28, Century Theatre, 24
Youth (p), 6/8/11, Bijou Theatre, 7
Youth (p) (Miles Mallison), 2/20/18, Comedy Theatre, 21
Youth (p), 10/26/20, Greenwich Village Theatre, 6
Yr. Obedient Husband (p), 1/10/38, Broadhurst Theatre, 8
Yvette (p), 5/13/04, Knickerbocker Theatre, 1
Yvette (m), 8/10/16, 39th St. Theatre, 4

Z

Zander the Great (p), 4/9/23, Empire Theatre, 162
Zapatera Prodigiosa, La (p), 2/2/74, INTAR Center
Zapatera Prodigiosa, La / Retabilillo de Don Cristobal, El (The Shoemaker's Prodigious Wife / The Puppet Theatre of Don Cristobal) (p), 9/1/64, Delacorte Mobile Theatre, 6
Zaza (p), 10/1/00, Criterion Theatre, 42
Zebra, The (p), 2/13/11, Garrick Theatre, 24
Zelda (p), 3/5/69, Ethel Barrymore Theatre, 5
Zeno (p), 8/25/23, 48th St. Theatre, 89
Zeppelin (p), 1/14/29, National Theatre, 72
Ziegfeld Follies (r), 7/8/07, Jardin de Paris, 70
Ziegfeld Follies (r), 6/15/08, Jardin de Paris, 120
Ziegfeld Follies (r), 6/14/09, Jardin de Paris, 64
Ziegfeld Follies (r), 6/20/10, Jardin de Paris, 88
Ziegfeld Follies (r), 6/26/11, Jardin de Paris, 80
Ziegfeld Follies (r), 10/21/12, Moulin Rouge, 88
Ziegfeld Follies (r), 6/16/13, New Amsterdam Theatre, 96
Ziegfeld Follies (r), 6/1/14, New Amsterdam Theatre, 112
Ziegfeld Follies (r), 6/21/15, New Amsterdam Theatre, 104
Ziegfeld Follies (r), 6/12/16, New Amsterdam Theatre, 112
Ziegfeld Follies (r), 6/12/17, New Amsterdam Theatre, 111
Ziegfeld Follies (r), 6/18/18, New Amsterdam Theatre, 151
Ziegfeld Follies (r), 6/16/19, New Amsterdam Theatre, 171
Ziegfeld Follies (r), 6/22/20, New Amsterdam Theatre, 123
Ziegfeld Follies (r), 6/21/21, Globe Theatre, 119
Ziegfeld Follies (r), 6/5/22, New Amsterdam Theatre, 541
Ziegfeld Follies (r), 10/20/23, New Amsterdam Theatre, 233
Ziegfeld Follies (r), 6/24/24, New Amsterdam Theatre, 520
Ziegfeld Follies (r), 8/16/27, New Amsterdam Theatre, 168
Ziegfeld Follies (r), 7/1/31, Ziegfeld Theatre, 164
Ziegfeld Follies (r), 1/4/34, Winter Garden Theatre, 182
Ziegfeld Follies (r), 1/30/36, Winter Garden Theatre, 115
Ziegfeld Follies (r), 9/14/36, Winter Garden Theatre, 112
Ziegfeld Follies (r), 4/1/43, Winter Garden Theatre, 553
Ziegfeld Follies (r), 3/1/57, Winter Garden Theatre, 123
Ziegfeld Girls of 1920 (r), 3/8/20, New Amsterdam Roof Theatre, 78
Ziegfeld Midnight Frolic (r), 10/2/19, New Amsterdam Roof Theatre, 171
Ziegfeld Midnight Frolic (r), 3/15/20, Ziegfeld Danse de Follies, 148
Ziegfeld Midnight Frolic (r), 9/2/20, New Amsterdam Roof Theatre, 135
Ziegfeld Midnight Frolic (r), 11/17/21, New Amsterdam Roof Theatre, 123
Ziegfeld Revue of 1926. See No Foolin'
Ziegfeld 9 O'Clock Frolic (r), 2/8/21, Ziegfeld Danse de Follies, 29
Zira (p), 9/21/05, Princess Theatre, 128
Zira (p), 4/16/06, Majestic Theatre, 24
Zizi (r), 11/21/64, Broadway Theatre, 49
Zombie (p), 2/10/32, Biltmore Theatre, 20
Zoo Story, The / Dutchman (p), 11/10/64, Village South Theatre, 134

Zoo Story, The / Krapp's Last Tape (p), 1/14/60, Provincetown Playhouse, 582
Zoo Story, The / Krapp's Last Tape (p), 6/8/65, Cherry Lane Theatre, 168
Zoo Story, The / Krapp's Last Tape (p), 10/9/68, Billy Rose Theatre, 6, (Theatre 1969 Playwrights Repertory)
Zoo Story, The / The American Dream (p), 5/28/63, Cherry Lane Theatre, 143
Zorba (m), 11/17/68, Imperial Theatre, 306
Zulu and the Zayda, The (p), 11/10/65, Cort Theatre, 179

Premieres in America

A

A
Stanley Nelson
May, 1973
Sloane House YMCA
356 W. 34th, N.Y.C.

A. Gorky, A Portrait (one-man show)
Michael A. Del Medico
8-24-73
St. Clement's Church
423 W. 46th, N.Y.C.

"A"-24: The L. Z. Masque
Louis Zukofsky
6-14-73
Cubiculo
414 W. 51st, N.Y.C.

A^3
James Bridges
5-15-69
Mark Taper Forum
Los Angeles, CA

Abdala — Jose Marti
4-13-72
New Federal Theatre at Henry Street Settlement Playhouse
466 Grand, N.Y.C.

Abelard and Heloise
Ronald Millar
1-19-71
Ahmanson Theatre Music Center
Mark Taper Forum
Los Angeles, CA

Abide in Darkness
12-14-73
Westbeth Playwrights Feminist Collective
155 Bank, N.Y.C.

Abortion: Women Tell It Like It Is
3-21-69
Washington Square Church
133 W. 4th, N.Y.C.

About Face (four one-acts)
Clayelle Dalfares & T. Frank Gutswa
7-19-71
Playbox
94 St. Mark's Pl., N.Y.C.

About Time
Theodore Barnes (book & lyrics); Al Carmines (music)
4-12-70
Judson Poet's Theatre
55 Wash. Sq. So., N.Y.C.

Above the Fire
Charles Deemer
5-13-71
University of Missouri
Columbia, MO

Abraham (A "New Theatre" piece)
5-14-69
E 52 University Theatre
University of Delaware
Newark, DE

Absence of Heroes, An
Alex Gotfryd & Robert C. Herron
11-21-72
WPA
333 Bowery, N.Y.C.

Absence of Light, An
David Toll
12-10-73
Equity Library Theatre
Library & Museum of the Performing Arts
111 Amsterdam, N.Y.C.

Absolute Power Over Movie Stars
Robert Patrick
5-11-68
Old Reliable Theatre Tavern
231 E. 3rd, N.Y.C.

Absolute Zero, The (with Every Buzzard's Son)
James Ty Hargrove
6-3-68
13th Street Theatre
50 W. 13th, N.Y.C.

Absurd Musical Revue for Children, The
1971
Contemporary Theatre
709 First Ave. W., Seattle, WA

Academy (with Waiting and Doorbell)
Mario Fratti
10-22-70
Cubiculo
414 W. 51st, N.Y.C.

Academy Workshop Production
5-25-72
Academy Theatre
Atlanta, GA

Acadie
Al Raymond
Spring, 1970
Fairfield University Playhouse
Fairfield, CT

Acamemnon
William Alfred
10-27-72
McCarter Theatre
Princeton, NJ

Acceptance
Dan Owens
11-8-73
Elma Lewis School of Fine Arts
Roxbury, MA

Accidental Angel
8-8-72
Little Lake Theatre
Canonsburg, PA

AC/DC
Heathcote Williams
2-23-71
Chelsea Theatre Center
30 Lafayette Ave., Brooklyn, NY

Acquaintance of Angels, An
Arranged by Patricia Cameron Peardon
4-25-72
Library & Museum of the Performing Arts
111 Amsterdam, N.Y.C.

Acquisition, The
David Trainer
12-12-68
American Place Theatre
N.Y.C.

Acrobats
Israel Horovitz
2-15-71
Theatre de Lys
N.Y.C.

Acropolis
Wyspianski
11-4-69
Polish Laboratory Theatre
Washington Square Church
133 W. 4th, N.Y.C.

Act of Violence
Stan Ross
Summer, 1970
Factory Theatre Lab
Toronto, CAN

Acting Up
William Ball
1-5-68
American Conservatory Theatre
San Francisco, CA

Actor, The
John Dooley
10-28-71
Triangle Theatre
316 E. 88th, N.Y.C.

Actorines and Actorettes
P. J. Barry
5-29-73
Fulton Theatre Company
Library & Museum of the Performing Arts
111 Amsterdam, N.Y.C.

Actors
Conrad Bromberg
7-19-73
Johnson State College
Johnson, VT

Actors on Acting
5-3-72
Ron Dener's Workshop
Good Shepherd Church
240 E. 31st, N.Y.C.

Acts of Love
Susan Yankowitz
1-18-73
Academy Theatre
Atlanta, GA

Ad Majorem Dei Gloriam
Josef Bush
9-9-68
Old Reliable Theatre Tavern
231 E. 3rd, N.Y.C.

Adam Had 'Em (with Southern Gothic)
Rock Kenyon
4-5-72
Playwright's Workshop Club
14 Waverly Pl., N.Y.C.

Adam's Rib (interpretations of the creation)
11-30-72
Hunter College
N.Y.C.

Adaptation
Elaine May
8-7-68
Berkshire Theatre Festival
Stockbridge, MA

Adolf Hitler or The Summoning
Kenneth Kelman
5-19-71
New Dramatists Workshop
424 W. 44th, N.Y.C.

Adora (with L'Habitat Splendid)
Jean Reavey
5-18-73
New York Theatre Ensemble
2 E. 2nd, N.Y.C.

Adultery
Sylvia Berry
6-1-73
Jacksonville Univ.
Jacksonville, FL

Adventures of Charlie and Belle, The
Erwin Protter
4-27-71
WPA
333 Bowery, N.Y.C.

Adventures of Huckleberry Finn, The
Adapted by Philip Hanson
4-17-72
Donnell Library
N.Y.C.

Adventures of Peter Pan, The
4-29-72
Mercer Arts Center
240 Mercer, N.Y.C.

Adventures of the Black Girl in Her Search for God, The
Christopher Isherwood
3-20-69
Mark Taper Forum
Los Angeles, CA

Adventures on Patch Street
Jane Shepard (book, lyrics, music)
5-15-70
Saverna Park Community Theatre
Saverna Park, MD

Aegina
James Costin
7-18-68
Missouri Repertory Theatre
Kansas City, MO

Aesop's Fables
Jon Swan (text); William Russo (music)
June, 1972
Chicago Free Theatre
Chicago, IL

Affair, The
Helen Duberstein
May, 1970
Westbeth
Bank St., N.Y.C.

Affairs of 8F
Harvey Zuckerman
12-11-73
Theatre 77 Repertory
23 E. 20th, N.Y.C.

Affirmations: Prose and Poetry in the American Vein
Day Tuttle
12-27-71
Library & Museum of the Performing Arts
111 Amsterdam, N.Y.C.

Afloat
5-10-72
Section 10
8 Waverly Pl., N.Y.C.

African Folk Tale, An
Roland Hayes
4-16-72
International Institute
Boston, MA

African People Theatre Experience
5-3-71
DeKalb Library
Bushwick & DeKalb Aves., Brooklyn, NY

African Star
John Jiler
7-23-24-71
Eugene O'Neill Memorial Theatre
Waterford, CT

After Liverpool
See: Games/After Liverpool

After Margritte
Tom Stoppard
4-23-72
Theatre Four
424 W. 55th, N.Y.C.

After the Ball (musical satire)
Shirley Broughton; John Herbert McDowell (music)
7-19-73
Cubiculo
414 W. 51st, N.Y.C.

After the Fashion Show (with Day to Day and The Classroom)
Maryat Lee
7-1-68
Soul and Latin Theatre
N.Y.C.

After the Wash
Ursule Molinaro
12-5-68
Playbox
94 St. Mark's Pl., N.Y.C.

After We Eat the Apple, We What?
Henry Fanelli
8-10-72
Cubiculo
414 W. 51st, N.Y.C.

After You, Mr. Hyde
Lee Thuna, Mel Mandel, Norman Sachs
6-24-68
Goodspeed Opera House
East Haddam, CT

Afternoon for a Baptism
Linda Dethman
5-14-70
University of Missouri
Columbia, MO

Afternoon for a Gay Death
Gene Lang
12-3-71
Omni Theatre Club
145 W. 18th, N.Y.C.

Afternoon Tea
Harvey Perr
9-25-73
New Theatre for Now
Los Angeles, CA

Age of the Stringless Bean, The
Ellsworth Whimby
10-16-70
Studio 808
154 W. 57th, N.Y.C.

Agreement on Damhaix, An (staged reading)
James Arden
3-16-72
Theatre Arts Experimental Workshop
117th St. & Amsterdam, N.Y.C.

Agreement, The
Douglas Taylor
2-13-70
American Repertory Theatre
37 W. 57th, N.Y.C.

Ah, Willy
Morris Carnovsky
5-24-73
YM-YWHA
92nd & Lexington, N.Y.C.

Ahead to the Stars
Mary Jean Parson
6-30-69
State Fair Grounds
Birmingham, AL

Aimee
William Goyen (book & lyrics); Worth Gardner (music)
12-2-73
Trinity Square Repertory Company
Providence, RI

Ain't Supposed To Die a Natural Death
Melvin Van Peebles
10-20-71
Ethel Barrymore Theatre
N.Y.C.

Air Force (with Hannibal)
7-23-72
Theatre of Gibberish
344 W. 36th, N.Y.C.

Ajax Fun Company, The (review)
June, 1970
Stage Lights Theatrical Club
218 W. 48th, N.Y.C.

Akokawe
Afolabi Ajayi
6-4-70
Negro Ensemble Company
St. Mark's Playhouse
133 Second, N.Y.C.

Alan, Carlos, Theresa
4-29-68
Studio 534 Theatre
534 W. 42nd, N.Y.C.

Albert's Bridge
Tom Stoppard
6-24-69
St. Albans Repertory Theatre
Washington, DC

Alberta Radiance (staged reading)
Robert Auletta
1-28-73
Yale Repertory Theatre
New Haven, CT

Alchemist, The
Fred Wagstaff
9-24-71
Pilgrims Theatre Company
Old South Church
Boston, MA

Alfred the Great
Israel Horovitz
3-16-73
Pittsburgh Playhouse
Pittsburgh, PA

Alice
Ryan Edwards
Spring, 1970
C. W. Post College
Greenvale, NY

Alice
Hot Peaches
1-18-73
Peach Pitts
200 W. 24th, N.Y.C.

Alice Is
Sally Lutyens (music)
11-5-71
Cambridge School
Weston, MA

Alice the Magnificent
Robert Higgins & Byron Tinsley
December, 1970
Charles Playhouse
Boston, MA

Alice, Through the Glass Lightly
Tom Eyen
4-14-68
Electric Circus
23 St. Mark's Pl., N.Y.C.

Alicia
Jeff Hochhauser
8-21-69
New York Theatre Ensemble
2 E. 2nd, N.Y.C.

Alimony
Jay Broad
8-2-71
Tappan Zee Playhouse
Nyack, NY

Alive and So Bold
Richard Joel Davis
2-11-71
Alice Theatre
137A W. 14th, N.Y.C.

Alive and Well in Argentina
Barry Pritchard
4-17-70
Syracuse Repertory Theatre
Syracuse, NY

Alive Today!
1-31-70
Total Theatre for Youth
West Side YWCA
51st & 8th, N.Y.C.

Alive (with Wet and Dry)
Leonard Melfi
10-3-68
Loft Workshop
152 Bleecker, N.Y.C.

All About Love and Other Fantasies
6-20-72
White Barn Theatre
Irwin, PA

All Dressed in White
Joan Durant
6-11-71
Playbox
94 St. Mark's Pl., N.Y.C.

All Is Bright
Marian Winters
3-4-70
University of Alabama Theatre
Southeastern Theatre Conference
Memphis, TN

All Junkies
Miguel Pinero
July, 1972
Street Theatre, Inc.
Ossining, NY

All of My Friends
Robert Upton (book & lyrics); Neal Tate (music)
9-9-71
Actor's Place
487 Hudson, N.Y.C.

All Over
Edward Albee
3-27-71
Martin Beck Theatre
302 W. 45th, N.Y.C.

All Over Again
William Kushner
6-19-73
WPA
333 Bowery, N.Y.C.

All the Girls Came Out to Play
Daniel Hollywood & Richard Thornblade
8-10-70
Falmouth Playhouse
Falmouth, MA

All the King's Horses
John McDonnell
12-7-73
Thomas Davis Irish Players
St. Barnabas School
241st St. & McLean, N.Y.C.

All the Old Familiar Places
Marjorie Taubenhaus
2-5-71
American Theatre Company
106 E. 14th, N.Y.C.

All Things Flow
Jack Shoemaker
5-5-72
Mercer Arts Center
240 Mercer, N.Y.C.

All Through the House
Anthony Scully
5-25-72
Manhattan Theatre Club
321 E. 73rd, N.Y.C.

All Together Now. . .
Nagle Jackson, Jeffrey Tambor & company members (book); G. Wood (lyrics & music)
6-8-73
Milwaukee Repertory Theatre
Milwaukee, WI

All We Are Saying. . .
6-12-70
James W. Johnson Theatre Arts Center
120 E. 110th, N.Y.C.

Allegation
Lawrence Ferlinghetti
4-6-68
Theatre Genesis
10th & 2nd, N.Y.C.

Allegro (revised version)
Richard Rodgers & Oscar Hammerstein
7-22-68
Goodspeed Opera House
East Haddam, CT

Allegros
Donald Harrington & Mark Brimitoin
7-15-70
La Mama ETC
74 E. 4th, N.Y.C.

Alley-Oop
Don Bevan, Donald R. Flynn
8-21-68
Gateway Playhouse
Bellport, L.I., NY

Alligator Man
Jack Kaplan
7-13-72
Cubiculo
414 W. 51st, N.Y.C.

Alligators Are Coming, The
Thaddeus Vane
Spring, 1970
Inner City Theatre
Los Angeles, CA

Almost on a Runway
Donna DeMatteo
6-17-71
H B Playwrights Foundation
124 Bank, N.Y.C.

Alpha Beta
E. A. Whitehead
5-3-73
Eastside Playhouse
334 E. 74th, N.Y.C.

Alpha Kappa
Marjorie Paradis
March, 1972
Broom Street Theatre
Madison, WI

Altogether Now?
Summer, 1973
Milwaukee Repertory Theater Co.
Milwaukee, WI

Aluminium Pigey, The (with The Daughter of Earl Siphon and The Story—Aunt Rollie)
Larry O'Connel
Spring, 1970
Second Group Theatre
McBurney YMCA
215 W. 23, N.Y.C.

Ambassador
Don Ettlinger & Anna Marie Barlow (book); Hal Hackaday (lyrics); Don Gohman (music)
6-28-72
LaSalle Music Theatre
Philadelphia, PA

Amelia and Jess
Ron Mele
2-11-68
Little Theatre
181 Bleecker, N.Y.C.

Amen
Guy Gauthier
5-21-72
Manhattan Theatre Club
321 E. 73rd, N.Y.C.

America the Beautiful (with Git)
9-10-70
Academy Theatre
Atlanta, GA

Americaliente
Jorge Diaz
11-9-71
Theatre of Latin America & Teatro del Nuevo Mundo
St. Clement's Church
423 W. 46th, N.Y.C.

American Asparagus Growers Annual Alligator Wrestling Contest, Barbecue and Jubilee, The
Jim Hardy
4-30-71
Loft Improvisational Players
Dowling College
Oakdale, NY

American Family versus American Art, The
Eli Siegel
9-13-69
Terrain Gallery
39 Grove, N.Y.C.

American Fantasies
James Schevill
4-12-72
Brown University
Providence, RI

American Glands
Conn Fleming
11-14-73
New Dramatists
424 W. 44th, N.Y.C.

American Gothic (with Thirty)
Walter Hadler
12-5-68
Theatre Genesis
10th & 2nd, N.Y.C.

American Modern
See: Canadian Gothic, American Modern

American Revolution, The: Part I
Paul Sills & Arnold Weinstein
9-26-73
Ford's Theatre
Washington, DC

American Revolutionary Road Company (revue)
1-6-73
Brandeis University
Waltham, MA

American Roulette
Tom McCormack
1-8-69
Greenfield Theatre
American Academy of Dramatic Arts
120 Madison, N.Y.C.

American Roulette
Sal Lombard
3-27-69
Nucleus Repertory Theatre
261 W. 34th, N.Y.C.

American Sunrise, The
The F.L.O.G. Theatre Company
6-6-69
New York Shakespeare Festival Public Theatre
425 Lafayette, N.Y.C.

American Triptych
Werner Liepolt
7-14-71
Eugene O'Neill Memorial Theatre
Waterford, CT

Americana Pastoral
Yabo Yablonsky
12-10-68
Greenwich Mews Theatre
141 W. 13th, N.Y.C.

Americans, The
8-27-69
La Mama ETC
74 E. 4th, N.Y.C.

Americka Cleopatra
Jackie Curtis
7-13-72
WPA
333 Bowery, N.Y.C.

Americomedia
Michael Procaccino
3-18-73
People's Bicentennial Commission
Washington Square Methodist Church
133 W. 4th, N.Y.C.

Amor de la Estanciera. . ., El
Adapted by Juan Carlos Uviedo
10-6-71
Grupo Bilingue at La Mama ETC
74 E. 4th, N.Y.C.

Amphitryon
Peter Hacks
5-28-70
Forum Theatre
Lincoln Center
N.Y.C.

Amphitryon
Heinrich von Kleist
12-14-70
La Mama ETC
Loeb Drama Center
Cambridge, MA

Amyntas
Torquato Tasso
4-10-70
Vickie Hayes Theatre Workshop
1741 Broadway, N.Y.C.

Ananias Twee
Stanley Kaplan
9-24-70
Columbia University
N.Y.C.

Ananse and the Dwarf Brigade
Efua T. Sutherland
2-5-71
Karamu House Theatre
Cleveland, OH

Anatol
Tom Jones (lyrics); Nancy Ford (music)
8-1-72
Provincetown Playhouse
Provincetown, MA

And Baby Makes Three
R. Deaudeux
January, 1973
Mafundi Institute
Los Angeles, Ca

. . . And Chocolate on Her Chin
Louis Florimonte
4-22-71
Theatre Crossroads
23 E. 20th, N.Y.C.

And Dorothy Parker Said
William Van Gieson
11-21-72
WPA
333 Bowery, N.Y.C.

. . . And His Light Green Hair (with The Light Blue Peignoir)
Jack Shoemaker
2-5-71
Gene Frankel Theater Workshop
115 MacDougal, N.Y.C.

. . .And I Am Black
Marvin Ullman
3-22-69
Henry Street Settlement Playhouse
466 Grand, N.Y.C.

And I Bet You Wish You Was Me Now
Susan Kosoff (book); Phillip Killian (lyrics); Jane Staab (music)
5-4-70
Library & Museum of the Performing Arts
111 Amsterdam, N.Y.C.

And I Met a Man
Lawrence Weinberg
4-10-70
Lincoln Square Theatre
Hotel Empire
Broadway & 63rd, N.Y.C.

And Last Week It Was a Mountain
6-20-71
Kaymar Gallery
548 LaGuardia Pl., N.Y.C.

And Never Been Kissed
7-24-73
Orleans Arena Theatre
Orleans, MA

And No Ceremony
Tevia Abrams
11-21-72
WPA
333 Bowery, N.Y.C.

And Other Caged Birds
Richard O'Donnell
3-25-69
Washington Theatre Club
Washington, DC

And People All Around
George Sklar
1-19-68
Meadowbrook Theatre
Oakland University
Rochester, MI

And Puppy Dog Tails
David Gaard
10-19-69
Bouwerie Lane Theatre
330 Bowery, N.Y.C.

And Santa Claus Says: Ho Ho Ho
Stanley Seidman
9-10-73
Theatre for the New City
113 Jane, N.Y.C.

And That's How the Rent Gets Paid, Part II
Jeff Weiss
4-20-73
La Mama ETC
74 E. 4th, N.Y.C.

And the Band Played On
Jon Buckaloo
1-26-68
Extension Theatre
128 E. 7th, N.Y.C.

And the Devil Makes Five
Walter Cool
2-26-71
Blackfriars' Guild
316 W. 57th, N.Y.C.

And the Old Man Had Two Sons
Elizabeth Levin
7-15-72
Eugene O'Neill Memorial Theatre
Waterford, CT

. . . And the Street Taketh Away
Frederick Dennis Greene
4-17-70
Minor Latham Playhouse
Barnard College
N.Y.C.

And They Put Handcuffs on the Flowers
Fernando Arrabal
10-14-71
Extension Theatre
277 Park Ave., N.Y.C.

And To Think Jesus Waited
Megan Reed Thomas
8-11-71
Kaymar Gallery
548 LaGuardia Pl., N.Y.C.

And Who's Little Boy Are You?
Rod Parker
5-3-71
McAlpin Rooftop Theatre
34th & 6th, N.Y.C.

And Who's Over There?
Maurice Siegel
7-28-72
New York Theatre Ensemble
2 E. 2nd, N.Y.C.

And Whose Little Girl Are You?
Andrew Colmar
5-8-70
Anthony Mannino Drama Tree
182 Fifth, N.Y.C.

Andrew
Rafic Taylor
1-28-72
Negro Ensemble Company
St. Mark's Playhouse
133 Second, N.Y.C.

Androgyny in Ostendorf
8-17-72
Washington Square Church
133 W. 4th, N.Y.C.

Android Project, The
Betzie Parker
5-11-73
Omni Theatre Club
145 W. 18th, N.Y.C.

Andromache
Jean Racine; Lionel Abel (translation)
4-27-73
WPA
333 Bowery, N.Y.C.

Anele
Peter Gorman
12-17-72
Direct Theatre
123 W. 71st, N.Y.C.

Angel Baby Honey Darling Dear (with The Golden Animal)
Robert Patrick
7-20-70
Old Reliable Theatre Tavern
231 E. 3rd, N.Y.C.

Angel Band/A Vision
Depot Company & James Hurt
2-18-72
Depot Theatre
University of Illinois
Urbana, IL

Angel Express
Joseph Caruso
11-12-71
Clark Center for the Performing Arts
West Side YWCA
8th Ave. & 51st, N.Y.C.

Angel Raziel, The
S. Ansky, adapted by Richard Vos
2-17-71
Nave Theatre
Columbia University
N.Y.C.

Angela
Sumner Arthur Long
8-27-68
Barn Theatre
Augusta, MI

Angelo
James Monos
5-1-69
Universalist Theatre
4 W. 76th, N.Y.C.

Angels Are Exhausted, The (Los Angeles Se Han Fatigado) (with La Hiel Nuestra de Cada Dia)
2-23-73
New Federal Theatre
N.Y.C.

Angels in Agony (with The Overseers)
Robert Patrick
7-1-68
Old Reliable Theatre Tavern
231 E. 3rd, N.Y.C.

Animal
Oliver Hailey
3-22-73
Academy Theatre
Atlanta, GA

Animals, The
Betzie Parker
6-23-72
Omni Theatre Club
145 W. 18th, N.Y.C.

Anna K
Eugenie Leontovich
5-7-72
Actor's Playhouse
100 Seventh Ave. So., N.Y.C.

Anna Luce
Irwin Mowat
8-11-68
Spingold Theatre
Brandeis University
Waltham, MA

Anna-Luse
David Mowat
11-30-72
CSC Repertory Theatre
89 W. 3rd, N.Y.C.

Annie
Michael Gibbens
6-5-72
New Old Reliable Theatre
231 E. 3rd, N.Y.C.

Anniversary Ball
Fred White
4-4-69
New York Theatre Ensemble
2 E. 2nd, N.Y.C.

Anniversary, The
Bill McIlwraith
8-1-73
U.R.G.E.N.T.
151 W. 46th, N.Y.C.

Another City, Another Land
Guy Hoffman
10-8-68
Gramercy Arts Theatre
N.Y.C.

Another Cross to Bridge
Bradford Riley
10-15-70
Playbox
94 St. Mark's Pl., N.Y.C.

Another Episode in the Life of Harry Ringel
Stanley Zawatsky
5-23-73
New York Theatre Ensemble
2 E. 2nd, N.Y.C.

Another Part of Us
Atlantic Avenue Theatre Group
8-26-71
Cuyler Warren Street Community Church
450 Warren, Brooklyn, NY

Another Time, Another Eden
A. R. Bell
5-14-70
Dramatis Personae
114 W. 14th, N.Y.C.

Answers
Tom Topor
6-7-8-72
WPA
333 Bowery, N.Y.C.

Anthony Burns
Pat Freni
3-22-72
Alliance Theatre
Atlanta, GA

Anthropologists, The
Benjamin Bradford
8-1-69
Stage Lights Theatrical Club
218 W. 48th, N.Y.C.

Anticlassical Presentation
Adapted by Gustavo Ames
10-20-71
La Mama ETC
74 E. 4th, N.Y.C.

Antigone
Mary Williams
3-28-69
First Unitarian Church
Brooklyn, NY

Antigone, Baby
Richard Allen Shur, adapted by Albert Evans
1-16-70
Riverdale Showcase
252nd St. & Riverdale Ave., Bronx, NY

Antigone Frankenstein Mysteries & Smaller Pieces Paradise Now
9-16-68
Living Theatre
Yale University
New Haven, CT

Antigone's Wedding
Michael Mathias
11-10-69
Old Reliable Theatre
231 E. 3rd, N.Y.C.

Antique Soft Tooth, The
Stephen Flaxman
10-17-68
Playbox
94 St. Mark's Pl., N.Y.C.

Antiques (revue)
Alan Greene & Laura Manning (lyrics & music); Dore Schary (special material)
6-19-73
Mercer Arts Center
240 Mercer, N.Y.C.

Anton Chekhov's Garden Party
Anton Chekhov; adapted by Elihu Winer
11-29-72
Roundabout Theatre
307 W. 26th, N.Y.C.

Antonio or The Message
Loula Anagnostaki
6-24-72
Westbeth Cabaret Theatre
155 Bank, N.Y.C.

Antony and Cleopatra (with Day Work)
Floyd Barbour
9-9-71
MIT Community Players
Cambridge, MA

Any Cow Will Do
2-5-69
Caravan Theatre
Cambridge, MA

Any Eve for Adam
6-27-72
Apple Hill Playhouse
Delmont, PA

Any Evening in October
Roma Greth
11-28-69
Theatre 13
201 W. 13th, N.Y.C.

Any Number Must Play
Edward Greenberg
9-25-70
New York Theatre Ensemble
2 E. 2nd, N.Y.C.

Any Resemblance To Persons Living or Dead. . .
Elliott Caplin
5-24-71
Gate Theatre
10th & 2nd Ave., N.Y.C.

Anyone for Men's Lib?
June Plager
2-29-73
One-Act Repertory Company at Lolly's Theatre Club
808 Lexington, N.Y.C.

Anything You Say Will Be Twisted
Ken Campbell
5-6-71
Agassiz Theatre
Radcliffe College
Cambridge, MA

Anyuta (with The Black Monk and Polinka)
Anton Chekhov, adapted by James Monos
2-5-71
Senior Dramatic Workshop Repertory Theatre
Studio 808, Carnegie Hall
881 Seventh, N.Y.C.

Apartment To Let
Glover Buck
5-12-71
Stagelights II Theatrical Club
125 W. 22nd, N.Y.C.

Apartment with the Big Monkey Is Still Available, The
Jeffrey Selby
6-8-72
WPA
333 Bowery, N.Y.C.

Apocalypse
Joel Schwartz
10-15-70
Mark Taper Forum
Los Angeles, CA

Apocalypsis Cum Figuris
T. S. Eliot, Dostoyefsky, Simone Weil & The Bible
11-18-69
Polish Laboratory Theatre
Washington Square Church
133 W. 4th, N.Y.C.

Apollo in New Hampshire
7-23-73
Dartmouth Players Repertory Company
Hanover, NH

Apollo's Fate
Stanley Seidman
6-19-73
WPA
333 Bowery, N.Y.C.

Appetites
Max G. Weine
1-21-70
Courtyard Playhouse
424 W. 45th, N.Y.C.

Applaud Yourself, Applaud (with The Great American Two Step)
Carl Ahlm
1-31-69
Wittenberg University Theatre
Springfield, OH

Applause
Betty Comden & Adolph Green (book); Charles Strouse & Lee Adams (music & lyrics)
1-26-70
Mechanic Theatre
Baltimore, MD

Apple Tree and I, The
Anthony Asnato (book & lyrics); Deborah Peek (music)
10-28-72
Theatre in the Church by the Bridge
328 E. 62nd, N.Y.C.

Applejuice
Francine Trevens
8-2-73
Joseph Jefferson Theatre Company
Little Church Around the Corner
11 E. 29th, N.Y.C.

Approaching Simone
Megan Terry
3-4-70
La Mama ETC
74 E. 4th, N.Y.C.

April
John Wolfson
9-24-71
Omni Theatre Club
145 W. 18th, N.Y.C.

Aquatic Chinee, The (and Seven Trumpets)
Tom LaBar
4-17-68
Playbox
94 St. Mark's Pl., N.Y.C.

Arabic Two
Ruth Rehrer Wolff
11-15-69
New Theatre Workshop
154 E. 54th, N.Y.C.

Architect and the Emperor of Assyria, The
Fernando Arrabal
3-26-69
American Conservatory Theatre
San Francisco, CA

Architruc (with Lettre Morte)
Robert Pinget
4-15-70
Barbizon-Plaza Theatre
N.Y.C.

Archy and Mehitabel
Don Marquis; Richard Gottlieb (adaptor)
6-1-73
Public Trust Theatre Company
Coconut Grove, FL

Are You a Virgin? (with Old Maid)
James Harter
11-19-73
Theatre for the New City
113 Jane, N.Y.C.

Are You Lookin' ?
Murray Mednick
3-15-73
Theatre Genesis
10th & 2nd Ave., N.Y.C.

Are You Now or Have You Ever Been?
Eric Bentley
11-10-72
Yale Repertory Theatre
New Haven, CT

Are You Now or Have You Ever Been Blue?
Leslie Weiner
7-28-71
Berkshire Theatre Festival
Stockbridge, MA

Are You Prepared To Be a United States Marine? (with I'm Glad I'm Not the Janitor Here)
Sandra Scoppettone
2-20-69
Cubiculo
414 W. 51st, N.Y.C.

Arena Conta Bolivar
Presented by The Arena Theatre of Sao Paulo
4-3-70
New York Shakspeare Festival Public Theatre
427 Lafayette, N.Y.C.

Arena Conta Zumbi
Presented by The Arena Theatre of Sao Paulo, Brasil
8-18-69
Theatre of Latin America
423 W. 46th, N.Y.C.

Arena (part of Blueberry Muffin Twice Removed)
Nancy Heiken
11-18-70
La Mama ETC
74 E. 4th, N.Y.C.

Arenas of Lutetia
Ronald Tavel
11-22-68
Judson Poets' Theatre
55 Wash. Sq. So., N.Y.C.

Aretha in the Ice Palace
Tom Eyen
1-16-70
Extension Theatre
277 Park Ave. So., N.Y.C.

Areyto (with Preciose Por Ser Un Encanto. . .)
Alfredo Matilla
11-18-71
Teatro de Orilla
Riverside Church
122nd & Riverside Dr., N.Y.C.

Ari
Leon Uris (book & lyrics); Walt Smith (music)
11-30-70
Shubert Theatre
Philadelphia, PA

Ariel
John Broek (book & lyrics)
2-14-72
Pace College
N.Y.C.

Armory, The (with The Big Black Box, Owl, and The Shiny Red Ball)
Cleve Hawbold
1-9-72
Park Avenue Community Theatre
Central Church
593 Park, N.Y.C.

Arnold Bliss Show, The
Robert Patrick
3-21-69
New York Theatre Ensemble
2 E. 2nd, N.Y.C.

Around the World with Annie M
3-4-73
Malachy Repertory Company
455 W. 51st, N.Y.C.

Arrangement for Children
Robert C. Herron
July, 1968
Eugene O'Neill Memorial Theatre
Waterford, CT

Arrangers, The
5-17-72
Boston Center for the Arts
Boston, MA

Art and Bart
Eduardo Garcia
1-8-71
New York Theatre Ensemble
2 E. 2nd, N.Y.C.

Art Lovers, The
H. N. Levitt
7-26-72
Hunter College
N.Y.C.

Art of Silence, The
Pocket Mime Circus of Boston
7-20-73
Fisherman' s Players
North Eastham, MA

Art of the Puppeteer, The
7-25-73
Theatre Group, Ltd.
Vergennes, VT

Arthur Isn't Here
Marj Mahle
6-17-70
Stage Lights Theatrical Club
218 W. 48th, N.Y.C.

Artichoke Man
Stanley Kaplan
5-4-73
Stage 73
321 E. 73rd, N.Y.C.

Artisan, The
John Rawd
8-27-72
Traveling Players Festival, Lewiston, Maine
Lincoln Center Plaza
N.Y.C.

Artist, The (multi-media piece)
Kenneth Koch (libretto); Paul Reif (music); Larry Rivers (visuals)
4-17-72
Whitney Museum
945 Madison, N.Y.C.

Artists for the Revolution
Eric Thompson
7-22-72
Eugene O'Neill Memorial Theatre
Waterford, CT

As Fate Would Have It
Brandon Blackman
9-11-70
Studio 808
154 W. 57th, N.Y.C.

As Happy As Kings
Jack Richardson
3-16-68
New Theatre Workshop
154 E. 54th, N.Y.C.

As the King (with The Boarders)
Peter Gorman
3-6-71
New York Theatre of the Americas
427 W. 59th, N.Y.C.

As You Can See
Steve Carter
6-17-68
Old Reliable Theatre Tavern
231 E. 3rd, N.Y.C.

As You Wait
Arthur Williams and Lois Dengrove (book & lyrics); Jade Woody (music)
11-30-73
New York Theatre Ensemble
Fortune Theatre
62 E. 4th, N.Y.C.

Asalto
Jose Vicente
5-18-70
La Mama ETC
74 E. 4th, N.Y.C.

Ashes of Mrs. Reasoner, The
Enid Rudd
9-17-68
Mineola Summer Theatre
Mineola, NY

Ashes (with A Minor Miscalculation)
Edwin Byrd
1-30-70
Free Music Store
359 E. 62nd, N.Y.C.

Asia and the Far East
Isaac Chochron
Spring, 1968
University of New Mexico
Albuquerque, NM

Ask Your Mamma (a jazz-mood piece)
Langston Hughes
10-18-69
Greenwich Mews Theatre
141 W. 13th, N.Y.C.

Aspasquanza (poetry recital)
11-26-71
Spencer Memorial Church
99 Clinton, Brooklyn, NY

Aspiration Flies, Curiosity Cries
Sri Chinmoy
11-19-71
Universalist Theatre
4 W. 76th, N.Y.C.

Assassin Guiteau, The
James Neyland
July, 1972
Heights Players
Brooklyn Heights, NY

Assassin, The
Alexander Panas
6-11-72
WBAI
359 E. 62nd, N.Y.C.

Assassination of Martin Luther King, The (with A Face Worth Saving and You May Well Be the Man . . .)
Frank Hogan
5-24-68
Knowhere East Theatre
736 Broadway, N.Y.C.

Assassination of Nigger Nate, The (with The Forgotten American)
Tony Barsha
1-8-70
Theatre Genesis
10th St. & 2nd, N.Y.C.

Assassination of the Pope, The
Jonathan Gillman
6-19-72
Manhattan Players
Atlantic City Playhouse
Atlantic City, NJ

Assassination, 1865
Stuart Vaughan
10-26-71
Goodman Theatre
Chicago, IL

Asses
Wilson Lehr
2-11-71
St. Peter's Church
346 W. 20th, N.Y.C.

Assumption Parish
Josef Bush
6-7-73
74 Below
74 Trinity Pl., N.Y.C.

Asylum
James P. White
4-15-73
Brown University
Providence, RI

A-Sylum
Williams Theatre Ensemble
January, 1973
Williams College
Williamstown, MA

At Least They Can't Say We Never Tried (with Games)
Pat Rioux
3-20-69
Loft Workshop
152 Bleecker, N.Y.C.

At the Tavern of the Raven
Alexander Panas
9-24-72
First Annual Edgar Allen Poe Festival
N.Y.C.

At War with the Mongols
Robert Heide
7-30-70
Brecht-West
New Brunswick, NJ

Atem
Mauricio Kagel
1-3-72
Cubiculo
414 W. 51st, N.Y.C.

Atlantic Crossing
Charles Mingus III (book & lyrics); Gunter Hampel (music)
7-15-72
Theater for the New City
113 Jane, N.Y.C.

Atlantis
Muriel Stursberg
5-22-70
New York Theatre Ensemble
2 E. 2nd, N.Y.C.

Atlantis and More (Part 3 of The Howard Klein Trilogy)
H. M. Koutoukas
5-19-69
Elgin Theatre
8th Ave. at 19th, N.Y.C.

Atsuhara
Kiyoko Yamaguchi; translated by Tamotsu Inukai; adapted by Michael Stoddard
8-18-72
St. Clement's Church
423 W. 46th, N.Y.C.

Attendant, The
Stratis Karras, translated by Evangelos Voutsinas
5-11-71
Dallas Theatre Center
Dallas, TX

Attic, The
Thomas P. Cullinan
5-7-70
Dobama Theatre
Cleveland, OH

Attica
Peter Schumann
7-1-72
Bread & Puppet Theatre
Brooklyn, NY

Au Pair Man, The
Hugh Leonard
11-23-73
Zellerbach Theatre
Philadelphia, PA

Audible Sigh
Lee Kalcheim
July, 1968
Eugene O'Neill Memorial Theatre
Waterford, CT

Audience Workshop
EVT Repertory Company
2-7-72
Dons Studio
202 E. 29th, N.Y.C.

Audition!
Stephen Holt (book & lyrics); John Braden (lyrics & music)
11-10-72
La Mama ETC
74 E. 4th, N.Y.C.

Audition, The
Dan Daniels
1-15-69
Free Store Theatre
14 Cooper Sq., N.Y.C.

Augustus
Jean Anouilh & Jean Aurenche
4-28-70
University of Minnesota
Morris, MN

Auntie Hamlet
Dan Isaac
1-28-70
Lincoln University Players
Lincoln University, PA

Aurora
Maria Irene Fornes
3-17-72
Theatre of the Riverside Church
490 Riverside Dr., N.Y.C.

Austringer, The
R. Wolf
3-18-73
Theatre Arts Corporation
Santa Fe, NM

Authors
Gordon Porterfield
8-20-68
Spingold Theatre
Brandeis University
Waltham, MA

Auto-Destruct
Jeff Wanshel
12-1-72
Magic Theatre
Steppenwolf
Berkeley, CA

Autograph Hound, The
James Prideaux
5-9-68
Playwrights' Unit
15 Vandam, N.Y.C.

Autumn Leaf
Paul Clarke
3-5-71
Imago Theater
Sloane House YMCA
356 W. 34th, N.Y.C.

Avanti!
Samuel Taylor
1-10-68
Shubert Theatre
New Haven, CT

Avenue 'A' Anthology
John Chodes
12-17-68
WPA Theatre
34 E. 4th, N.Y.C.

Away She Goes
3-15-68
Downstage Studio Theatre
321 W. 14th, N.Y.C.

Axe to Grind
Thomas Terefenko
4-22-68
Old Reliable Theatre Tavern
231 E. 3rd, N.Y.C.

B

Baba Goya
Steven Tesich
5-21-73
American Place Theatre
N.Y.C.

Babel (with The Man with Seven Toes)
Michael Ondaatje
7-6-72
St. Francis Xavier University Performing Group
Halifax, N.S., CAN

Babel-Babble
Joel Stone
11-8-73
St. Clement's Church
423 W. 46th, N.Y.C.

Babes Don't Cry Anymore
Michael Kallesser
2-20-68
Blackfriars' Guild
316 W. 57th, N.Y.C.

Babies
John Vincent Stoltenberg
4-23-70
Basement Coffee House
155 E. 22nd, N.Y.C.

Baboon!!!
Word Baker, Maria Irene Fornes, & Milburn Smith
10-5-72
Playhouse in the Park
Cincinnati, OH

Baboons Should Be Afraid
Owen Campbell
5-8-70
Stage Lights Theatrical Club
218 W. 48th, N.Y.C.

Babs and Judy Show, The
Stephen Holt (book & lyrics); John Braden (music)
2-15-72
WPA
333 Bowery, N.Y.C.

Baby Blue
Richard Blanning
2-3-72
University of Iowa
Iowa City, IA

Baby Mine (with Billy, Bobby, and Bunny)
John Vincent Stoltenberg
9-25-70
Columbia University
N.Y.C.

Babylon
Eric Thompson
10-4-73
New Dramatists
424 W. 44th, N.Y.C.

Babylon Captivity, The
Arthur Morey & Bobby Paul
2-4-71
Columbia University
N.Y.C.

Babysitter, The
W. Randolph Galvin
7-18-73
Black Curtain Dinner Theatre
Indianapolis, IN

Bacchae, The
Euripides; adapted by Kenneth Cavander
3-6-69
Yale University
New Haven, CT

Bach Is Always on Sundays
See: Facades

Bachelor Furnished
James Bridges
1-3-69
University of Calif.
Los Angeles, CA

Back Bog Beast Bait (with The Cowboy Mouth)
Sam Shepard
4-29-71
American Place Theatre
N.Y.C.

Back East (with Out West)
Andrew Mack
6-22-70
Second Group Theatre
McBurney YMCA
215 W. 23rd, N.Y.C.

Back to School
Barry Litvack
10-20-71
Clark Center for the Performing Arts
West Side YWCA
8th Ave. & 51st, N.Y.C.

Backdoor to Broadway (revue)
Fran Ziffer
5-12-73
Innercourt Theatre
504 Grand, N.Y.C.

Bad Day at Hot Rock's
Hal Craven
1-22-70
New York Theatre Ensemble
2 E. 2nd., N.Y.C.

Bad Guy
Stewart H. Benedict
12-17-70
Playbox
94 St. Mark's Pl., N.Y.C.

Bad Habits
Terrence McNally
8-10-71
John Drew Repertory Theatre
East Hampton, NY

Bad Habits of '71 (revue)
Frank Lee Wilde
4-29-71
New York Theatre Ensemble
2 E. 2nd, N.Y.C.

Bad Men in the West
William Saroyan
5-19-71
Stanford University
Stanford, CA

Bad News (with Failed Purposes)
Donald Kvares
6-21-71
Old Reliable Theatre Tavern
231 E. 3rd, N.Y.C.

Bad Place To Get Your Head, A (with Bead Tangle)
Robert Patrick
7-14-70
St. Peter's Church
346 W. 20th, N.Y.C.

Bad Play for an Old Lady
Elizabeth Johnson
5-9-69
Cubiculo
414 W. 51st, N.Y.C.

Bad Scene at Kent State
2-19-71
Liberty Revue
Washington Square Church
133 W. 4th, N.Y.C.

Bad Times in Bummersville
Joel Oppenheimer
5-31-68
Theatre Genesis
10th & 2nd, N.Y.C.

Badges
Robert Chicoine
February, 1970
Knox College
Galesburg, IL

Bag
Barry Knower
5-13-71
University of Missouri
Columbia, MO

Bag of Flies
Venable Herndon
8-1-68
Wagner College Auditorium
Staten Island, NY

Bag Woman, The
Joseph Caldwell
3-14-70
Hunter College Playhouse
N.Y.C.

Bah! Humburg (musical)
12-27-73
Robert F. Kennedy Theatre for Children
219 W. 48th, N.Y.C.

Bakke's Night of Fame
John McGrath
January, 1969
Stage Society Theatre
Los Angeles, CA

Balance
Gary Martin
7-10-69
Eugene O'Neill Memorial Theatre
Waterford, CT

Balancing Act
2-10-72
Tufts University
Medford, MA

Ball Game, The
Tom Thomas
11-7-73
Playwrights' Horizons
Clark Center for the Performing Arts
West Side YWCA, 8th Ave. & 51st, N.Y.C.

Ballad for a Firing Squad
Jerome Coopersmith; Martin Charnin; Edward Thomas
12-11-68
Theatre de Lys
N.Y.C.

Ballad of a Separated Couple
Meir Yannai, translated by Isaac Armony
12-6-68
New York Theatre Ensemble
2 E. 2nd, N.Y.C.

Ballad of Joe Smith, The
Thomas Donlon
1-19-68
Cooper Square Arts Theatre
35 Cooper Sq., N.Y.C.

Ballad of John Ogilvie
Ernest Ferlita, S. J.
10-8-68
Blackfriars' Guild
316 W. 57th, N.Y.C.

Ballad of Johnny Pot, The
Carolyn Richter (book & lyrics); Clinton Ballard (music)
4-26-71
Theatre Four
424 W. 55th, N.Y.C.

Ballad of Romeo and Juliet, The
Wally Harper and Paul Zakrzewski
5-3-73
Theatre of the Riverside Church
490 Riverside Dr., N.Y.C.

Ballad of Sanki Merser, The
Omar Paxon
March 1971?
Occidental College
Los Angeles, CA

Ballad of T and Lizard, The
P. Spoons Collier
6-4-70
WPA
34 E. 4th, N.Y.C.

Ballade
Arthur Samuels (book & lyrics) & Michel Conte
6-26-72
Fathers of the Confederation Memorial Centre
Charlottetown, Prince Edward Island, CAN

Ballads of the Bowery
Burgess Howard
2-28-73
Playwrights' Workshop Club
Bastiano's Studio
14 Cooper Sq., N.Y.C.

Ballerina Plays Ball, The
Lawrence Backstedt (book & lyrics); Lois Dengrove (music)
11-23-73
New York Theatre Ensemble
Fortune Theatre
62 E. 4th, N.Y.C.

Ballet Behind the Bridge
Lennox Brown
3-14-72
Negro Ensemble Company
St. Mark's Playhouse
133 Second Ave., N.Y.C.

Ballgame
Eric Gardner
3-1-71
Old Reliable Theatre Tavern
231 E. 3rd, N.Y.C.

Bananas
John White
12-4-68
Forum Theatre
Lincoln Center
N.Y.C.

Bandwagon (variety review for marionettes)
3-17-73
Bil Baird Theatre
59 Barrow, N.Y.C.

Bang?
Ken Eulo
3-19-69
Courtyard Playhouse
424 W. 45th, N.Y.C.

Bang! Bang!
David Newburge
6-30-69
Old Reliable Theatre Tavern
231 E. 3rd, N.Y.C.

Bang! Bang! You're Dead!
Mack Owen
1-29-69
University of Michigan Players
Ann Arbor, MI

Banker, The
Imre Goldstein
7-30-69
Old Reliable Theatre Tavern
231 E. 3rd, N.Y.C.

Baptizin', The
M. Carl Holman
Summer, 1971
Little Theatre
Tulsa, OK

Bar That Never Closes, The
Louisa Rose (book); Marco Vassi (fables); Louisa Rose & John Braswell (lyrics); Tom Mandel (music)
12-3-72
Astor Place Theatre
434 Lafayette, N.Y.C.

Barbarous Event No. 1: The Odyssey of Captain Brown
8-11-68
Spingold Theatre
Brandeis University
Waltham, MA

Barbary Shore
Jack Gelber
11-4-73
New York Shakespeare Festival
Public Theatre
425 Lafayette, N.Y.C.

Barbecue Pit, The
Donna DeMatteo
5-28-69
Theatre East
211 E. 60th, N.Y.C.

Barbeque, The
Theodore Fox
3-22-68
Courtyard Playhouse
424 W. 45th, N.Y.C.

Barber of Seville, The
Beaumarchais; new adaptation by James Ringo
10-20-72
St. Peter's Gate
132 E. 54th, N.Y.C.

Barnabas Among the Animals
Robert Karmon
10-25-68
Extension Theatre
128 E. 7th, N.Y.C.

Barracuda
Burt Marnik
1-29-70
Universalist Theatre
4 W. 76th, N.Y.C.

Barrel Full of Pennies, A
John Patrick
5-14-70
Playhouse on the Mall
Paramus, NJ

Bars of Dawn
John Boylan
1-12-68
Downstage Studio Theatre
321 W. 14th, N.Y.C.

Basement, The (with Tea Party)
Harold Pinter
10-15-68
Eastside Playhouse
334 E. 74th, N.Y.C.

Basic Training of Pavlo Hummel, The
David Rabe
5-20-71
New York Shakespeare Festival Public Theatre
425 Lafayette, N.Y.C.

Bathtub
Nick Boretz
11-13-69
Mannhardt Theatre Foundation
N.Y.C.

Bathtub Bandicott, The
David Lloyd
5-15-70
Gallery Theatre
Los Angeles, CA

Battering Ram
David Freeman
February, 1973
Tarragon Theatre
Toronto, Ontario, CAN

Battle for Heaven
Randolph Carter & Michael O'Shaughnessy
10-3-69
Elizabeth Seton College
Yonkers, NY

Battle of the Sexes, The
Philip Burton
1-22-69
Parish House Auditorium
Church of the Heavenly Rest
2 E. 90th, N.Y.C.

Battle of Valor, The
Norman Beim
2-27-70
Actors' Mobile Theatre
73rd & Broadway, N.Y.C.

Bead Tangle (with A Bad Place To Get Your Head)
Robert Patrick
7-14-70
St. Peter's Church
346 W. 20th, N.Y.C.

Bear Mountain
Bruce Kirle
4-12-71
Old Reliable Theatre Tavern
231 E. 3rd, N.Y.C.

Beast—A Nightmare Comedy
Robert Ost
2-3-72
West Side YWCA
8th Ave. & 51st, N.Y.C.

Beasts and Birds
Dynamite Theatre Ensemble
Brooklyn, NY

Beat the Wind
Winthrop Palmer
8-1-70
Southampton College
Southampton, L.I., NY

Beau Brummel and the Lady
William Devane
4-12-73
Ensemble Studio Theatre
549 W. 52nd, N.Y.C.

Beaudelaire
Arranged by Antoine Bouseiller, translated by Joachim Neugroschel
4-9-70
La Mama ETC
74 E. 4th, N.Y.C.

Beautification of Saint Dymphna, The
John Quinn
10-16-73
WPA
333 Bowery, N.Y.C.

Beautiful Dreamer: A Tribute to Martin Luther King
11-1-68
Poor People's Theatre
500 Riverside Dr., N.Y.C.

Beauty and the Beast
Oswald Rodriguez (adaptor)
1-4-73
La Mama ETC
74 E. 4th, N.Y.C.

Beauty and the Beast, The
Sandy Underwood
11-28-69
Stage Lights Theatrical Club
218 W. 48th, N.Y.C.

Beauty of Blackness, The
Voices, Inc.
6-28-69
Columbia University
N.Y.C.

Beauty of 1000 Stars, The
Gary Eldridge
3-24-68
Dramarena Repertory Theatre
158 W. 55th, N.Y.C.

Becoming (with The Many Lives of Wispy and Willo)
Betty Jean Lifton
5-5-73
Cathedral of St. John the Divine
Amsterdam & 112th, N.Y.C.

Bed, The
Robert Heide
12-7-70
Old Reliable Theatre Tavern
231 E. 3rd, N.Y.C.

Bed Was Full, The
Rosalyn Drexler
10-6-72
Moving Company
46 Great Jones, N.Y.C.

Bedlam
James Broughton
7-22-69
Eugene O'Neill Memorial Theatre
Waterford, CT

Bedroom, The
James Inman
12-2-71
Triangle Theatre
316 E. 88th, N.Y.C.

Bedtime Story, A
Frank McEnany
11-19-70
Factory Theatre Lab
Toronto, Ontario, CAN

Bee and the Butterfly, The (with Ruby Keller Is a Mother and Sunday Morning)
Charles Kerbs
1-31-69
Theatre of Our Discontent
127 W. 79th, N.Y.C.

Before I Wake
Trevor Reese
10-13-68
Greenwich Mews Theatre
141 W. 13th, N.Y.C.

Before Our Very Eyes
Michael Shurtleff & Charles Kerbs
11-8-68
Friday Workshop
229 Seventh, N.Y.C.

Before the War with the Eskimos
Adapted from J. D. Salinger by Niger Akoni
6-14-68
U.N. Theatre Voices of the N.Y. Theatre Ensemble
Covenant Theatre
310 E. 42nd, N.Y.C.

Before You Go
Laurence Holofcener
1-11-68
Laurence
N.Y.C.

Beggar's Opera
Tom Sankey
3-8-68
Theatre Genesis
10th & 2nd, N.Y.C.

Beginnings
The Beginnings Company & Mark J. Roth
2-17-71
Westbeth
Bank St., N.Y.C.

Behan (reading)
Ulick O'Connor
6-18-71
Chelsea Hotel
23rd St. & 8th Ave., N.Y.C.

Behavior Tableaux (sculpture-theatre work)
Scott Burton
4-19-72
Whitney Museum
N.Y.C.

Beheading, The
Thomas Muschamp
12-2-72
West End Presbyterian Church
105th & Amsterdam, N.Y.C.

Behind Every Man
Julie Berns
8-1-72
Apple Hill Playhouse
Delmont, PA

Behold! Cometh the Vanderkellans
William Wellington Mackey
3-31-71
Theatre de Lys
N.Y.C.

Being Black
Fred Rohan
9-1-72
Brothers and Sisters United, Staten Island
Lincoln Center Plaza
N.Y.C.

Belches
Anne Roby
3-2-72
Manhattan Theatre Club
321 E. 73rd, N.Y.C.

Believers, The
Josephine Jackson & Joseph A. Walker
5-9-68
Garrick Theatre
152 Bleecker, N.Y.C.

Bells, The
Leopold Lewis
12-7-72
Stagelights II Theatrical Club
125 W. 22nd, N.Y.C.

Bellymass
Jon Swan
11-14-68
Seattle Repertory Theatre
Seattle, WA

Benbow and Divorski
Michael Elliott King
12-6-68
Cubiculo
414 W. 51st, N.Y.C.

Bench, The
Nathan R. Teitel
Gramercy Arts Theatre
N.Y.C.

Bench, The (with The Shepherd)
Lawrence Holofcener
4-23-69
Playbox
94 St. Mark's Pl., N.Y.C.

Benjamin's Digs
Richard Heirich
1969
Yale University
New Haven, CT

Berlin Music Hall, 1920
1-26-68
Gruene Kakadu
544 E. 12th, N.Y.C.

Berlin to Broadway with Kurt Weill
Kurt Weill (music); Gene Lerner (text & format)
10-1-72
Theatre de Lys
N.Y.C.

Bernice and Lenore (reading)
Ann Meltzer
10-8-72
Theater for the New City
113 Jane, N.Y.C.

Bernie
Edward Gallardo
11-6-69
New York Theatre Ensemble
2 E. 2nd, N.Y.C.

Bessie Smith (with Harunobu and The Blue Centaur)
Piero Heliczer
2-18-71
Cinematheque
80 Wooster, N.Y.C.

Best Is Yet To Be, The
Margie Appleman
7-20-72
Manhattan Theatre Club
321 E. 73rd, N.Y.C.

Best Lookin' Man I Ever Saw, The (with The Eye Ball Tomb)
Raymond Schanze
2-19-69
La Mama ETC
9 St. Mark's Pl., N.Y.C.

Best of Friends
James Elward
7-6-70
Westport Country Playhouse
Westport, CT

Best We Can, The
Leslie E. Ornstein
7-12-72
Brooklyn College
Brooklyn, NY

Beste, Le
John Boylan
1-23-70
Downstage Studio Theatre
321 W. 14th, N.Y.C.

Bethlehem Steel
Bill Peters & John McAndrew
Fall, 1972
Yale University
New Haven, CT

Betrayal, The
Steve Press
2-23-73
Omni Theatre Club
145 W. 18th, N.Y.C.

Better Place, A
Robert Hogan
4-9-72
American Theatre Company
106 E. 14th, N.Y.C.

Better To Leave It Undercover?
Wesley J. Jensby
11-1-72
La Mama ETC
74 E. 4th, N.Y.C.

Between Two Worlds
Tony Vozzo
10-29-70
Hanson Place Central Methodist Church
Brooklyn, NY

Beyond Words (mime)
Created by Kenyon Martin
2-10-71
Brandeis University
Waltham, MA

Bicicletas, Las
Antonio Martinez-Ballesteros
9-4-72
08 Lab Theatre
115th & Broadway, N.Y.C.

Bicycle of the Lord
Robert A. Blackwell
10-27-70
MacLoren Playhouse
West Hollywood, CA

Big Alabama Wonder, The
Franklyn MacGregor
1-29-69
Courtyard Playhouse
424 W. 45th, N.Y.C.

Big Black Box, The (with Owl, The Shiny Red Ball, and The Armory)
Cleve Hawbold
1-9-72
Park Avenue Community Theatre
Central Church
593 Park, N.Y.C.

Big Broadcast on East 53rd, The
Dick Brukenfeld
3-1-73
Manhattan Theatre Club
321 E. 73rd, N.Y.C.

Big Charlotte
John Wallowitch (book & lyrics)
11-28-69
La Mama ETC
74 E. 4th, N.Y.C.

Big City Breakdown
Henry Zieger
1-23-69
Chelsea Theatre Center
30 Lafayette Ave., Brooklyn, NY

Big Coca-Cola Swamp in the Sky, The
Jay Broad
8-23-71
Westport Country Playhouse
Westport, CT

Big Gate, The
Albert Evans
6-19-69
Bronx Experimental Theatre
Bronx, NY

Big House, The
Lonnie Carter
10-31-71
Yale University
New Haven, CT

Big Klaus and Little Klaus
Hans Christian Andersen; D. Wenstrom (adaptor)
Apr., 1973
Florida State Theatre
Asolo, FL

Big Maude Saves the Day
Ellsworth Whimby
11-9-72
New York City League of Playwrights
162 W. 21st, N.Y.C.

Big Mother
Charles Dizenzo
2-9-73
Moving Company
46 Great Jones, N.Y.C.

Big Nose Mary Is Dead
Barry Pritchard
2-13-69
Off Center Theatre
Seattle Repertory Theatre
Seattle, WA

Big Show of 1928, The
1-24-72
O'Keefe Centre
Toronto, CAN

Big Show of 1936, The
5-30-72 (Had been touring previously)
Felt Forum
Madison Square Garden
N.Y.C.

Big Time Buck White
Joseph Dolan Tuotti
Spring, 1968
Frederick Douglas Theatre
Watts, CA

Big Time Buck White (musical version)
Joseph Dolan Tuotti (book); Oscar Brown, Jr. (music & lyrics)
2-12-69
Committee Theatre
San Francisco, CA

Big Top (with Ice)
Geraldine Krug
6-11-69
Unitarian Church of All Souls
80th St. & Lexington, N.Y.C.

Big Wheel A' Spinning and A' Spinning
Alonzo and the Players Eight
11-7-69
St. Luke's Church Parish House
Brooklyn, NY

Big Wolf
Harald Mueller
10-7-73
Whitman College
Walla Walla, WA

Bigfoot
Ronald Tavel
11-3-72
Theatre Genesis
2nd Ave. & 10th, N.Y.C.

Bill and William
James Addison
5-20-71
Playbox
94 St. Mark's Pl., N.Y.C.

Bill'Birthday (with Kolo and Mono)
Charles Kerbs
March, 1968
New Group Theatre
13th Street Theatre
50 W. 13th, N.Y.C.

Billiard Ball and Pi Lead Different Kinds of Lives, The
Don Katzman
7-27-72
Changing Scene
Denver, CO

Billy
Stephen Glassman (book); Ron Dante & Gene Allen (book & lyrics)
3-22-69
Billy Rose Theatre
208 W. 41st, N.Y.C.

Billy
Frederick Kirwin
4-18-73
Playwrights' Horizons
Clark Center for the Performing Arts
West Side YWCA, 8th Ave. & 51st, N.Y.C.

Billy Bailey and the Great American Refrigerator Come True
Fred Gordon
2-25-72
American Place Theatre
N.Y.C.

Billy, Bobby, and Bunny (with Baby Mine)
John Vincent Stoltenberg
9-25-70
Columbia University
N.Y.C.

Billy Hill
Gerome Ragni & Galt McDermott
11-27-73
Coconut Grove Playhouse
Miami, FL

Billy Noname
William Wellington Mackey (book); Johnny Brandon (lyrics & music)
3-2-70
Truck & Warehouse Theatre
79 E. 4th, N.Y.C.

Billy's Bass
Marlene Harding
10-31-73
Focus Two Coffee House
136 W. 74th, N.Y.C.

Bird Food
Nathan Barrett
9-14-73
New York Arts Theatre
25 E. 4th, N.Y.C.

Birdcatcher in Hell, The
Peter Schumann
6-30-71
Bread & Puppet Theatre
Central Park, N.Y.C.

Birds on the Wing
Peter Yeldham
4-8-69
O'Keefe Centre
Toronto, CAN

Birds, The
Aristophanes, adapted by Walter Kerr; music by "Woodsmoke"
Nov., 1971
Cleveland State University
Cleveland, OH

Birds, The (musical)
Seamus Murphy & Fred Lederman
8-19-69
Teenage Performing Arts Workshop
117th St. & Riverside Dr., N.Y.C.

Birth in a Tiny Container, A
Steven Braunstein
11-10-72
New York Theatre Ensemble
2 E. 2nd, N.Y.C.

Birth of a Nation
Edwin Treitler
3-14-69
Inner Theatre
356 Bowery, N.Y.C.

Birth of Venus, The (with Come Up and See My Casserole)
Frank Moffett Mosier
11-18-68
Library & Museum of the Performing Arts
111 Amsterdam, N.Y.C.

Birth to Death (dramatic reading)
James Joyce
11-10-71
St. Paul's Chapel
Columbia University
N.Y.C.

Bishop's Head, The
Marshall Yaeger
10-21-75
Assembly Theatre
113 Jane, N.Y.C.

Bitch
Andy Mulligan
9-6-72
Playwrights' Workshop Club
14 Waverly, N.Y.C.

Bitches
Eduardo Corbe
9-8-72
New York Theatre of the Americas
427 W. 59th, N.Y.C.

Biting Through
John Grimaldi
12-13-68
Cooper Square Arts Theatre
35 Cooper Sq., N.Y.C.

Bits and Pieces
Eli Wallach & Anne Jackson
7-20-70
Berkshire Theatre Festival
Stockbridge, MA

Bits and Pieces
George Hatch, Jr.
8-5-71
Gramercy Arts Theatre
N.Y.C.

Bitter Dialogue
Federico Garcia Lorca, John Olon-Scrymgeour (translator)
5-19-71
Stanford University
Stanford, CA

Bivouac
Lawrence Wunderlich
12-5-68
Playbox
94 St. Mark's Pl., N.Y.C.

Black and the White, The
Harold Pinter
3-1-68
West Side Actors' Theatre
252 W. 81st, N.Y.C.

Black and White (with Vanozza)
Lyon Phelps
11-9-70
Old Reliable Theatre Tavern
231 E. 3rd, N.Y.C.

Black Angels
Thom Shepard
12-2-71
Elma Lewis School of Fine Arts
Roxbury, MA

Black Back
LeRoi Jones (Imamu Amiri Baraka)
9-17-70
Playbox
94 St. Mark's Pl., N.Y.C.

Black Bards
Harvey Tavel, director
10-20-69
Old Reliable Theatre Tavern
231 E. 3rd, N.Y.C.

Black Caravans
12-7-73
Wellesley College
Wellesley, MA

Black Circles
J. H. Bryant
7-26-71
Halsey Street Block Association
Brooklyn, NY

Black Circles 'Round Angela (with Sheba)
Hazel Bryant
Feb., 1973
Afro-American Studio Total Theatre
415 W. 127th, N.Y.C..

Black, Cultured and Beautiful
9-1-72
La Rocque Bey African Dancers & Drummers
Lincoln Center Plaza
N.Y.C.

Black Cycle
Martie Charles
Afro-American Studio Total Theatre
415 W. 127th, N.Y.C.

Black Dada Nihilism (with Madheart)
Imamu Amiri Baraka (LeRoi Jones)
6-11-71
Afro-American Studio
15 W. 126th, N.Y.C.

Black Dragon Residence (Wu-Lung Yuan)
English version by Daniel S. P. Yang
4-2-70
University of Colorado
Boulder, CO

Black Evolution
Delano Stewart
10-24-71
Bed-Stuy Theatre
Belrose Ballroom
Bedford & St. Mark's Brooklyn, NY

Black Folk Tales
Julius Lester
8-27-71
Central Park, N.Y.C.

Black Genesis
Mel Winkler
3-5-72
New York University
N.Y.C.

Black Girl
J. E. Franklin
5-14-71
New Federal Theater
St. Augustine's Chapel
292 Henry, N.Y.C.

Black History from the Jewish Point of View
Morton Rothberger
11-28-69
New York Theatre Ensemble
2 E. 2nd, N.Y.C.

Black Is
June, 1970
Hall of Fame N.Y.U.

Black Is. . .We Are
Ron Mack
May, 1969
Negro Ensemble Company
St. Mark's Playhouse
133 Second, N.Y.C.

Black Is (with Dark Lady)
11-10-72
Featherbed Lane Community Freedom Theatre
Bronx, NY

Black Jesus
Ken Eulo
12-17-73
Stage Directors & Choreographers Workshop Foundation
Library & Museum of the Performing Arts
111 Amsterdam, N.Y.C.

Black Light Theater of Prague, The
9-27-71
New York City Center
131 W. 55th, N.Y.C.

Black Love
Sheryl Littles, Jenny Kellam, Carl Clay, Romaine Martin, Gil Fitts, & Don I. Lee
9-2-72
Lincoln Center Plaza
N.Y.C.

Black Macbeth
10-11-73
Caribbean-American Theatre Guild Theatre
Ansonia Hotel
74th St. & Broadway, N.Y.C.

Black Magic Anyone?
Leatrice El
1-19-72
Negro Ensemble Company
St. Mark's Playhouse
133 Second Ave., N.Y.C.

Black Manhood (with She's Dead Now and Two in the Back Room)
Earle Chisholm
5-21-70
Spencer Memorial Church
99 Clinton, Brooklynn Heights, NY

Black Mass (with Great Goodness of Life)
10-18-68
East Wind
23 E. 125th, N.Y.C.

Black Messiah, The
Richard D. Waters
8-16-68
Fisherman's Players
Wellfleet, MA

Black Mirror
Jackie Skarvellis
7-26-72
Bastiano's Studio
14 Cooper Sq., N.Y.C.

Black Monk, The (with Polinka and Anyuta)
Anton Chekhov, adapted by James Monos
2-5-71
Senior Dramatic Workshop Repertory Theatre
Carnegie Hall
881 Seventh, N.Y.C.

Black Quartet, A (see below)
4-25-69
Chelsea Theatre Center
30 Lafayette Ave., Brooklyn, NY
- **Gentleman Caller, The** by Ed Bullins
- **Prayer Meeting** by Ben Caldwell
- **Great Goodness of Life** by LeRoi Jones (not a premiere)
- **Warning, The — A Theme for Linda** by Ronald Milner

Black Shadow Black Prince
Walter Beaver (book & lyrics) & Ted Nichols (music)
2-12-71
California State College
Los Angeles, CA

Black Sun/Artaud
Robert Cordier
12-16-70
La Mama ETC
74 E. 4th, N.Y.C.

Black Terror, The
Richard Wesley
Feb., 1971
Howard University
Washington, DC

Black Titan
Based upon Aeschylus' Prometheus Bound
4-21-70
Group of Ancient Drama Society for Ethical Culture
2 W. 64th, N.Y.C.

Black Visions
4-4-72
New York Shakespeare Festival Public Theatre
425 Lafayette, N.Y.C.
- **Cop and Blow** by Neil Harris
- **Players Inn** by Neil Harris
- **Sister Son/Ji** by Sonia Sanchez
- **Gettin' It Together** by Richard Wesley

Black Voices
Cecil Alonzo
3-5-71
Courtyard Playhouse
424 W. 45th, N.Y.C.

Black Winter
Len Petersen
7-16-68
Academy Theatre
Lindsay, Ontario, CAN

Black Zion
Dick Goldberg
11-1-71
American Jewish Theatre
Boston University
Boston, MA

Blancs, Les
Lorraine Hansberry
11-15-70
Longacre Theatre
N.Y.C.

Blank Page Entitled Climax
Jeannie Lee
8-18-72
Theatre Wagon
Staunton, VA

Blank Playground
Gilles Larrain
9-16-69
Judson Poets' Theatre
55 Wash. Sq. So., N.Y.C.

Blanket, The (multi-media piece)
1-8-72
Film & Dance Theatre
42 E. 12th, N.Y.C.

Blasphemy of Arthur Rimbaud's Sister, The
Robert C. Herron
5-26-72
New York Theatre Ensemble
2 E. 2nd, N.Y.C.

Bleecker Street Alogical
Michael Kirby
4-16-70
Loft Workshop
152 Bleecker, N.Y.C.

Bless the Child
Irma Jurist, Bernice Blohm and Adelaide Bean
4-11-68
Proscenium Theatre, Karamu House
Cleveland, OH

Blimp, The
Garry Flemming
12-6-73
Playwrights' Workshop Club
Electric Circus
23 St. Mark's Pl., N.Y.C.

Blind Guy
Michael Mathias
11-1-68
New York Theatre Ensemble
2 E. 2nd, N.Y.C.

Blind Junkie, The
Peter Copani (book & lyrics); Robert Tuthill and Peter Copani (music)
8-28-71
Everyman Company
Lincoln Center Plaza
N.Y.C.

Blind Man's Bluff
Paul Takis
1-21-72
New York Theatre Ensemble
2 E. 2nd, N.Y.C.

Blind Spot, The
Roy Bradford
3-22-69
92nd St. YMHA Repertory Theatre
92nd & Lexington, N.Y.C.

Blindness
Ed Kelleher
11-13-70
Playbox
94 St. Mark'S Pl., N.Y.C.

Blip, Dip, Slug and Fantasia
Summer, 1972
Academy Theatre
Atlanta, GA

Bliss
Peter Copani
4-10-68
Extension Theatre
128 E. 7th, N.Y.C.

Blob That Ate Vermont, The
7-15-71
Bradford Repertory Theatre
Bradford, VT

Block, The
4-16-71
Soul & Latin Theatre
N.Y.C.

Block Twelve
Ric Besmanoff
9-11-70
Studio 808
154 W. 57th, N.Y.C.

Blood
John Eskow
2-27-69
Blood Theatre
Boston, MA

Blood
Doug Dyer
3-7-71
New York Shakespeare Festival Public Theatre
425 Lafayette, N.Y.C.

Blood and Mayonnaise
Ed Kelleher
11-5-71
Stage Lights Theatrical Club
218 W. 48th, N.Y.C.

Blood of the Pig and the Bite of the Dog, The
Elizabeth Johnson
12-19-68
Chelsea Theatre Center
30 Lafayette, Brooklyn, NY

Blood Red Roses
John Lewin (book & lyrics); Michael Valenti (music)
3-22-70
Golden Theatre
252 W. 45th, N.Y.C.

Blood Rites (with Junkies Are Full of Sh. . . and Fun Boot Dancers)
LeRoi Jones
11-21-70
Henry Street Playhouse
466 Grand, N.Y.C.

Blood, Sweat and Tears
8-24-68
Cafe Au Go-Go
152 Bleecker, N.Y.C.

Bloodsport
Milburn Smith
3-7-73
Playwrights' Horizons
Clark Center for the Performing Arts
West Side YWCA, 8th Ave. & 51st, N.Y.C.

Blu Doctor
11-20-70
St. Clement's Church
423 W. 46th, N.Y.C.

Blue Bitch
Sam Shepard
1-18-73
Theatre Genesis
2nd Ave. & 10th, N.Y.C.

Blue Boys
Allan Knee
11-29-72
Martinique Theatre
N.Y.C.

Blue Centaur, The (with Bessie Smith and Harunobu)
Piero Heliczer
2-18-71
Cinematheque
80 Wooster, N.Y.C.

Blue Horse
Dennis Must
10-13-72
Circus Family
4 Riverton, N.Y.C.

Blue Magi, The
Sally Dixon Wiener
12-11-72
St. Peter's Gate
132 E. 54th, N.Y.C.

Blue Man, The
Al Green
10-15-71
Playwright's Showcase
Houston, TX

Blue Raven Beauty
1969
Bread & Puppet Theatre
N.Y.C.

Blue Soap
Lennox Raphael
9-24-70
Free Store Theater
14 Cooper Sq., N.Y.C.

Blue Widow
James Monos
5-28-71
Senior Dramatic Workshop Repertory Theatre
Carnegie Hall
881 Seventh, N.Y.C.

Bluebeard
Charles Ludlam
3-24-70
La Mama ETC
74 E. 4th, N.Y.C.

Blueberry Muffin Twice Removed
See: Arena and Chamber Piece. . .

Bluebird of Happiness, The
Jerome Rosenberg
1973
District Attorney's Crime Prevention Education Drama Program
Queens, NY

Bluebird (with Star Bright)
Ted Menten
9-6-72
Mercer Arts Center
240 Mercer, N.Y.C.

Blues for Billy
Robert Somerfeld
1-3-69
Anthony Mannino Drama Tree
182 Fifth, N.Y.C.

Blues To Be Called Crazy When Crazy's All There Is, A
Claire Burch
5-26-73
St Clement's Church
423 W. 46th, N.Y.C.

Blunderer, The
Moliere, adapted by Sala Staw
11-4-71
La Mama ETC
74 E. 4th, N.Y.C.

Blunderer, The (and It Shouldn't Happen to a Dog)
7-15-68
Theatre in the Street
340 W. 28th, N.Y.C.

Boarders, The (with As the King)
Peter Gorman
3-6-71
New York Theatre of the Americas
427 W. 59th, N.Y.C.

Boarding House, The
Louis Florimonte
10-28-71
Changing Scene
Denver, CO

Boats
Adrienne Kennedy
10-7-69
Mark Taper Forum
Los Angeles, CA

Bob and Ray—The Two and Only
Bob Elliot & Ray Goulding
9-24-70
Golden Theatre
252 W. 45th, N.Y.C.

Bobby Goes to the Movies—1944
Larry O'Connel
3-23-70
Second Group Theatre
McBurney YMCA
215 W. 23rd, N.Y.C.

Boccaccio, From the Decameron
Kenneth Cavander
10-26-72
Manhattan Theatre Club
312 E. 73rd, N.Y.C.

Bodies (workshop reading)
Westbeth Playwrights Feminist Collective
Great Building Crack-up Gallery
251 W. 13th, N.Y.C.

Body and Soul
Helen Rathje
7-16-17-71
Eugene O'Neill Memorial Theatre
Waterford, CT

Body Indian
Hanay Geiogamah
10-25-72
American Indian Theatre Ensemble
La Mama ETC
74 E. 4th, N.Y.C.

Body of an American, The
Ross Alexander
5-6-69
La Mama ETC
74 E. 4th, N.Y.C.

Bodybuilders
Michael Weller
12-14-73
York College
Jamaica, NY

Boesman and Lena
Athol Fugard
6-22-70
Circle in the Square
159 Bleecker, N.Y.C.

Boiled Lobster Easter Pageant
Jack Smith
3-14-70
Plaster Foundation
36 Greene St., N.Y.C.

Bojo
William Dunas
11-2-70
Playwright's Unit
83 E. 4th, N.Y.C.

Bolshevik Empress, The
George Bernard Shaw
12-14-73
New York Arts Theatre
25 E. 4th, N.Y.C.

Bonus March
Wallace Hamilton
2-14-69
Center Stage
Baltimore, MD

Bonus, The
Maxwell Glanville
1-21-72
West Side YWCA
51st & 8th Ave., N.Y.C.

Boo Hoo (with Idyllic and On the Brink)
Philip Magdalany
6-17-72
West Side YWCA
51st & 8th Ave., N.Y.C.

Booji
Carlton & Barbara Molette
12-4-72
Spelman College
Atlanta, GA

Boom Boom Boom
David Rabe
11-8-73
New York Shakespeare Festival
Lincoln Center
N.Y.C.

Boor, The
Anton Chekhov; Gary Barker (translator)
Fall, 1973
Actors Theatre
Louisville, KY

Booth
Skip Largent
8-12-69
Jewel Box Theatre
Oklahoma City, OK

Borrowed Time
Robert Glaudini
2-3-72
Theatre Genesis
2nd Ave. & 10th, N.Y.C.

Borstal Boy
Brendan Behan, adapted by Frank McMahon
3-31-70
Lyceum Theatre
149 W. 45th, N.Y.C.

Boruk Giving Head (a mixed-media poetry show)
12-5-73
Cubiculo
414 W. 51st, N.Y.C.

Boston Party at Anniemae's House, The
Walter Jones
12-3-71
Ellen Stewart Theatre
240 E. 3rd, N.Y.C.

Botany Lesson, The
Joaquim Maria Machado de Assis; translated by Townsend Brewster
12-6-72
Circle in the Square
N.Y.C.

Botticelli
Terrence McNally
10-7-69
Mark Taper Forum
Los Angeles, CA

Bottled Room, The
Michael Mathias
10-18-68
New York Theatre Ensemble
2 E. 2nd, N.Y.C.

Bourgeois Gentleman, The
Moliere; translation by Michael Feingold
10-6-72
Yale Repertory Theatre
New Haven, CT

Box and Quotations from Chairman Mao Tse-Tung
Edward Albee
3-6-68
Studio Arena Theatre
Buffalo, NY

Box, The
H. N. Levitt
7-3-68
Hunter College Theatre Workshop
N.Y.C.

Box, The
Bronson Dudley
4-25-69
St. Peter's Gate
132 E. 54th, N.Y.C.

Box (with Joined)
Dan Owens
2-19-71
University of Massachusetts
Boston, MA

Boxcar, The
Matt Ellison
4-26-73
University of Montana
Missoula, MT

Boxer Garden, The
Peter Maeck
7-25-72
Stowe Summer Theatre
Stowe, VT

Boxes
Ralph Doty
4-28-73
Theatre Studio
Milbank Hall Barnard College
N.Y.C.

Boxing Match
Holly Solomon
3-17-72
98 Greene Street Loft
Clancy's Telstar Gym
146 W. 28th, N.Y.C.

Boy Blue
Stuart Levin
12-26-70
Cleveland Playhouse
Cleveland, OH

Boy Name Dog, A
Joseph Renard
1-12-73
WPA
333 Bowery, N.Y.C.

Boy on the Straightback Chair, The
Ronald Tavel
2-14-69
American Place Theatre
N.Y.C.

Boy on the Straightback Chair, The (new musical version)
Ronald Tavel
10-28-71
Theatre of the Lost Continent
113 Jane, N.Y.C.

Boy Who Came To Leave, A
Lee Kalcheim
5-29-73
Astor Place Theatre
434 Lafayette, N.Y.C.

Boys! Boys! Boys! (revue)
5-11-73
Dramatis Personae
114 W. 14th, N.Y.C.

Boys from U.S.A., The
Roger Kelly
4-26-69
Thomas Davis Irish Players
St. Jean's Auditorium
167 E. 75th, N.Y.C.

Boys in the Band, The
Mart Crowley
1-23-68
Playwright' Unit
15 Vandam, N.Y.C.

Bradleyville Trilogy, The
See: The Last Meeting of the Knights of the White Magnolia
The Oldest Living Graduate Lu
Ann Hampton Laverty Oberlander

Brainstorms Over Osaka
Ishamu Kawai
7-31-70
97 Crosby St., N.Y.C.

Brainwave
Benjamin Bradford
11-29-73
University of the Pacific
Stockton, CA

Brambles on the Sheepskin
Ramon Delgado
11-18-70
Kentucky Wesleyan College
Owensboro, KY

Brass Butterfly, The
William Golding
1-30-70
Chelsea Theatre Center
30 Lafayette, NY

Brave
Joseph Golden
3-30-70
ANTA Theatre
245 W. 52nd, N.Y.C.

Bread and Butter
Cecil P. Taylor
4-24-69
Washington Theatre Club
Washington, DC

Bread & Cinnamon
George Dal Lago
8-22-70
Henry Street Settlement Playhouse
466 Grand, N.Y.C.

Bread Tree, The
Kit Jones
11-15-71
St. Peter's Gate
132 E. 54th, N.Y.C.

Breadbasket
Jeannine O'Reilly
11-10-69
Old Reliable Theatre Tavern
231 E. 3rd, N.Y.C.

Breadbasket and Jade
Jeannine O'Reilly
2-9-73
American Women Playwrights Association
Columbia University School of the Arts Theatre
410 W. 117th, N.Y.C.

Break in the Skin, A
Ronald Ribman
10-13-72
Yale Repertory Theatre
New Haven, CT

Break in the Surface
Will Creed
3-3-71
Pretenders
106 E. 14th, N.Y.C.

Break It to Her Gently
Georges Feydeau
11-27-73
Stage Lights Theatrical Club
218 W. 48th, N.Y.C.

Break the Chains
Soul & Latin Theatre
2-6-72
New York University
N.Y.C.

Break Through
Bella Shafran
5-12-72
Playbox
94 St. Mark's Pl., N.Y.C.

Breakfast Past Noon
Ursule Molinaro
10-19-69
Dancers Studio Foundation
34 E. 10th, N.Y.C.

Breakout, The
Oyamo
7-27-72
Eugene O'Neill Memorial Theater
Waterford, CT

Breathing Space
Richard Browner
2-22-68
Triangle Theatre
316 E. 88th, N.Y.C.

Brecht on War
7-26-68
Theatre for Peace
423 W. 46th, N.Y.C.

Breech Baby, The
Leonard Melfi
3-28-68
Loft Workshop
152 Bleecker, N.Y.C.

Breeding Ground
Edward M. Cohen
4-14-71
Playwrights' Unit
83 E. 4th, N.Y.C.

Breeze from the Glue, A
Mart Crowley
1-31-73
Bucks County Playhouse
New Hope, PA

Brewstopher
David Wolf
10-19-73
St. Stephen's Church
120 W. 69th, N.Y.C.

Briar, Briar
Susan Kosoff & Jane Staab
8-21-73
Harwich Junior Theatre
West Harwich, MA

Bride Comes to Yellow Sky, The
Stephen Crane, adapted by Frank Crocitto
2-19-71
Assembly Theatre
113 Jane, N.Y.C.

Bride Wore Rice in Her Hair, The
Jerry Felix
3-10-71
Louisiana State University
New Orleans, LA

Bridegroom for Marcella, A (with Klara)
Ivan Klima, translated by Ruth Willard
5-24-69
La Mama ETC
74 E. 4th, N.Y.C.

Bridegroom of Death
Rock Kenyon
2-2-73
Cubiculo
414 W. 51st, N.Y.C.

Bridge
Oscar Brand (book, lyrics, music)
11-28-72
Greenwich Mews Theatre
141 W. 13th, N.Y.C.

Bridge, The
Mark Berman
2-14-69
New York Theatre Ensemble
2 E. 2nd, N.Y.C.

Bridge, The
Mario Fratti
2-11-72
Playwrights' Workshop Club
14 Waverly Pl., N.Y.C.

Brief Theatre
David Dozer
3-28-68
Loft Workshop
152 Bleecker, N.Y.C.

Brightower
Dore Schary
1-28-70
Golden Theatre
252 W. 45th, N.Y.C.

Bringing in the Sheep
William Andrews
5-6-71
Second Group Theatre
McBurney YMCA
215 W. 23rd, N.Y.C.

Bringing It All Back Home
Terrence McNally
11-19-70
C. W. Post College
Greenvale, NY

Britannicus
Jean Racine, translated by Samuel Solomon
12-3-69
Tufts University Theatre
Medford, MA

British Tournament and Tattoo, The
9-17-69
Madison Square Garden
N.Y.C.

Broken Cowboy, A
William Aue
7-20-71
WPA
333 Bowery, N.Y.C.

Broken Mirrors in a Junkyard
Blanche Mednick Oliak
10-13-72
New York Theatre Ensemble
2 E. 2nd, N.Y.C.

Broken Swing, The
Nomi Rubel
4-6-72
American Theatre Company
106 E. 14th, N.Y.C.

Bronx Is Next, The
Sonia Sanchez
10-1-70
Theatre Black
130 E. 7th, N.Y.C.

Brooklyn Bridge Is Falling Down (Sullivan's Wake and I Didn't Hear Nothing, I Live in the Back)
Joseph Hart
1-7-71
Cubiculo
414 W. 51st, N.Y.C.

Brooklyn Palace, The
5-20-71
St. Paul's Commuity Theatre
Brooklyn, NY

Brothel, The
Mario Fratti
2-3-72
West Side YWCA
8th Ave. & 51st, N.Y.C.

Brother Gorski
Emanuel Fried
3-15-73
Astor Place Theatre
434 Lafayette, N.Y.C.

Brother of Dragons
Ramon Delgado
10-23-73
Hardin-Simmons University
Abilene, TX

Brother to Dragons
Robert Penn Warren
11-21-68
Trinity Square Repertory
Providence, RI

Brother You're Next
Steve Waugh & Chris Roman
1-19-68
Cooper Square Arts Theatre
35 Cooper Sq., N.Y.C.

Brotherhood
Douglas Turner Ward
3-17-70
Negro Ensemble Company
St. Mark's Playhouse
133 Second, N.Y.C.

Brothers
Stephen White
2-13-72
Theatre Four
434 W. 55th, N.Y.C.

Brothers Ashkenazi, The
Adapted by Luba Kadison from I. J. Singer
10-31-70
Folksbiene Playhouse
875 E. Broadway, N.Y.C.

Brothers Karamazov, The
Chris Durang & Albert Innaurato (book & lyrics); Walter Jones (music)
Fall, 1973
Yale University
New Haven, CT

Brower Power
Albert G. Nalven
Summer, 1972
Brower Park Public Library
Brooklyn, NY

Brown Overcoat, The
Victor Sejour; translated by Townsend Brewster
12-6-72
Circle in the Square
159 Bleecker, N.Y.C.

Brown Pelican
George Sklar
2-9-71
Alliance Theatre Company
Atlanta, GA

Brownstone
Thomas P. Cullinan
10-15-70
Dobama Theatre
Cleveland, OH

Brownstone Urge, The
Gladys S. Foster & Allan Rieser
12-17-69
Actors' Playhouse
100 Seventh Ave. So., N.Y.C.

Brownsville Raid, 1916, The
P. J. Barry
6-6-69
Hudson Guild Theatre
441 W. 26th, N.Y.C.

Bruce
Gerry Carroll
7-30-31-71
Eugene O'Neill Memorial Theatre
Waterford, CT

Brunch, The
Gene Lang
5-7-71
Omni Theatre Club
145 W. 18th, N.Y.C.

Bubbles
James Lavin
8-9-72
Cubiculo
414 W. 51st, N.Y.C.

Buddha of Achiab, The
Paul W. Clark
9-12-69
Orient Expresso Coffee House
205 E. 81st, N.Y.C.

Buenos Aires, Hoy
2-18-72
Grupo Once al Sur
Extension Theatre
277 Park Ave. So., N.Y.C.

Buffalo Meat
Chico Garvin
2-11-70
La Mama ETC
74 E. 4th, N.Y.C.

Bums Rush, The
8-26-73
Yorktown Players
Sugar Loaf, NY

Bunny Boy (with A Rite for Bedtime)
Wallace Hamilton
8-20-71
Omni Theatre Club
145 W. 18th, N.Y.C.

Burberry Overcoat, The (with The Nun)
Irving Glusack
3-19-70
New York Theatre Ensemble
2 E. 2nd, N.Y.C.

Burden, The
Harry Sloan
4-16-71
Gene Frankel Theatre Workshop
115 MacDougal, N.Y.C.

Burghers of Calais, The
Edgar White
3-24-71
Theatre Company of Boston
Boston, MA

Burgomaster, The
Gert Hoffman
12-27-68
Brooks Theatre (Cleveland Playhouse)
Cleveland, OH

Burning City
Guerrilla Street Theatre Repertory
12-19-69
Alternate U
530 Sixth, N.Y.C.

Business Day: Frolic with the Family Bippus
2-21-73
Cubiculo
414 W. 51st, N.Y.C.

Business of Good Government, The
John Arden
12-24-69
Spencer Memorial Church
Brooklyn, NY

Business of Show, The (with Obscenity's End. . .)
John P. Connell
11-6-69
Triangle Theatre
316 E. 88th, N.Y.C.

Busy Dyin'
Sheila Hofstetter
7-4-73
Purdue University
West Lafayette, IN

But Can You Sing?
Richard Schafer & Terry Sandholzer
8-7-68
Playbox
94 St. Mark's Pl., N.Y.C.

But It Is Nothing
Maria Chorafa
12-6-68
Extension Theatre
277 Park Ave. So., N.Y.C.

But Most of Us Cry in Movies
Bruce Kirle
1-28-70
La Mama ETC
74 E. 4th, N.Y.C.

But Never Jam Today
Vinnette Carroll; music by Gershon Kingsley
4-23-69
New York City Center
N.Y.C.

But, Seriously. . .
Julius J. Epstein
2-27-69
Henry Miller's Theatre
N.Y.C.

Butcher's Scandal, The
Ned Bobkoff
11-17-71
La Mama ETC
74 E. 4th, N.Y.C.

Butler Carries the Sun Away, The
Stanley Nelson
2-11-71
Playbox
94 St. Mark's Pl., N.Y.C.

Butley
Simon Gray
10-31-72
Morosco Theatre
N.Y.C.

Buttered Side, The
5-5-70
Paper Mill Playhouse
Milburn, NJ

Butterflies Are Free
Leonard Gershe
8-11-69
Falmouth Playhouse
Falmouth, MA

Butterscotch Canyon
Guy Gauthier
11-28-69
New York Theatre Ensemble
2 E. 2nd, N.Y.C.

Button, Button
Theatre on the Balustrade
10-19-70
Hunter College Playhouse
N.Y.C.

Button, The
Ben Starr
2-9-70
Community Playhouse
Atlanta, GA

Button, The (with The Pussy and Chekhov's Grandmother)
Michael McClure
12-20-73
Theatre Genesis
2nd Ave. & 10th, N.Y.C.

Buy a Little Tenderness
Buriel Clay II
2-15-73
Negro Ensemble Company
133 Second, N.Y.C.

Buy Bonds, Buster!
Bob Miller & Bill Conklin (concept); Jack Holmes (book) & M. B. Miller (lyrics)
6-4-72
Theatre de Lys
N.Y.C.

Buying Out
Lawrence Roman
11-4-71
Studio Arena Theatre
Buffalo, NY

By Damn
Jim Mills
6-14-73
Ocala Civic Theatre
Ocala, FL

By Mutual Consent
Jeff Kindley
11-7-73
Manhattan Theatre Club
321 E. 73rd, N.Y.C.

C

Cabeza Del Bautista, La
9-30-70
Esta Noche Teatro (Madrid & Barcelona) La Mama ETC
Loeb Drama Center
Cambridge, MA

Cada Quien Su Vida (To Each His Own)
Luis G. Basurto
3-16-73
Teatro Caras Nuevas
114 W. 14th, N.Y.C.

Cadaver, The
Raymond Banachi
6-11-71
Playbox
94 St. Mark's Pl., N.Y.C.

Caddy and Clara
William D. Roberts
3-7-69
H B Playwrights Foundation
124 Bank, N.Y.C.

Cadence in the Land of Marvels. . .
Pedro Santaliz
April, 1973
Nuevo Teatro Pobre
124 W. 18th, N.Y.C.

Cadillac Dreams
Norman Jordan
10-11-68
Harlem Dramatic Arts Theatre
Judson Hall, N.Y.C.

Caesar
David Hardt & Company
9-2-72
Lincoln Center Plaza
N.Y.C.

Caesar at the Rubicon
Theodore H. White
2-12-71
McCarter Theatre
Princeton, NJ

Cafe Da Fé
Eugene Lion
4-4-70
New Theatre Workshop
154 E. 54th, N.Y.C.

Cafeteria Style
Morton Lichter
5-26-72
Academy Theatre
Atlanta, GA

Cage, The
Mario Fratti
1-7-71
Regent Theatre
Syracuse, NY

Cain
B. A. Boytin
2-1-70
Spencer Memorial Church
99 Clinton, Brooklyn Heights, NY

Cain's Mangoes
Abelardo Estorino
7-17-69
Duo Theatre Workshop
522 E. 12th, N.Y.C.

Calais and the Last Poets
1-4-72
Black Ghetto Theatre Company
Elma Lewis School of Fine Arts
Roxbury, MA

Calamity on the Campus, or, The Pot at the End of the Rainbow
Edward Cope
6-16-72
Theatre Suburbia
Houston, TX

Caliban
Michael Monroe
12-10-71
Company Theatre
Los Angeles, CA

California Wine
Laird Koenig
2-3-71
Playwrights' Unit
83 E. 4th, N.Y.C.

Caligula
Charles Stanley
2-2-73
Theatre for the New City
113 Jane, N.Y.C.

Call a Spade a Shovel
12-4-69
Princeton University
Princeton, NJ

Call Me Jacky
Enid Bagnold
8-17-71
Boothbay Playhouse
Boothbay, ME

Call of the Angry Owl, The
Emil Belasco
6-28-72
Playwrights' Workshop Club
14 Waverly Pl., N.Y.C.

Call of the Loom, The
Guy Gauthier
3-30-70
Old Reliable Theatre Tavern
231 E. 3rd, N.Y.C.

Callers
David Kranes
3-11-69
University of Utah
Salt Lake City, UT

Calling for Help
Peter Handke
11-1-73
Cambridge Ensemble
Old Cambridge Baptist Church
Cambridge, MA

Calling in Crazy
Henry Bloomstein
10-6-69
Fortune Theatre
62 E. 4th, N.Y.C.

Calm Down, Mother
Megan Terry
6-4-69
Atma Theatre
Boston, MA

Camembert Kumquats (with Weeds)
Ron Mele
4-13-69
Salvation Discotheque
1 Sheridan Sq., N.Y.C.

Camille
Alexandre Dumas; Charles Ludlam (adaptor)
5-2-73
Ridiculous Theatrical Company
13th Street Theatre
50 W. 13th, N.Y.C.

Camp, The
Griselda Gambara, translated by William I. Oliver
11-29-70
Cornell University
Ithaca, NY

Campion
William Griffin
7-20-71
Eugene O'Neill Memorial Theatre
Waterford, CT

Can't Kill Nothing, Won't Nothing Die
May, 1972
Margaret Fuller House
Cambridge, MA

Can the Frog Princess Find Happiness?
Joseph B. Baldwin
6-10-71
Jacksonville University
Jacksonville, FL

Canadian Gothic, American Modern
Joanna Glass
11-17-72
Manhattan Theatre Club
321 E. 73rd, N.Y.C.

Cancion de Cuna
Gregorio Martinez Sierra
11-30-73
Grupo Malditos
Teatro Caras Nuevas
114 W. 14th, N.Y.C.

Candaules Commissioner
Daniel C. Gerould
2-6-70
Chelsea Theatre Center
30 Lafayette Ave., Brooklyn, NY

Candide
Leonard Bernstein (music); new book by Sheldon Patinkin
7-6-71
Curran Theatre
San Francisco, CA

Candide
Organic Theatre
March, 1971
Body Politic
Chicago, IL

Candide (new version)
Hugh Wheeler (book); Richard Wilbur, Stephen Sondheim, John Latouche (lyrics); Leonard Bernstein (music)
12-18-73
Chelsea Theatre Center
Brooklyn Academy of Music
30 Lafayette, Brooklyn, NY

Candyapple, The
John Grissmer
11-23-70
Edison Theatre
240 W. 47th, N.Y.C.

Cannibals, The
George Tabori
10-17-68
American Place Theatre
N.Y.C.

Canterbury Tales
Martin Starkie; Nevill Coghill; Richard Hill & John Hawkins
12-9-68
American Theatre
St. Louis, MO

Canterbury Tales
Marya Bedernil & Janet Craft (adaptors)
Spring, 1973
University of Massachusetts
Amherst, MA

Canticle for Leibowitz, A
Walter Miller, Jr.
12-23-72
Yeshiva University
N.Y.C.

Canticle of a Nightingale
Ronald Tavel
6-13-73
New York Theatre Strategy Festival
Manhattan Theatre Club
321 E. 73rd, N.Y.C.

Canvas
David Roszkowski
1-4-73
Circle Theatre Company
2307 Broadway, N.Y.C.

Captain Jack's Revenge
Michael Smith
4-3-70
La Mama ETC
74 E. 4th, N.Y.C.

Captain of Kopenick, The
Carl Zuckmayer; John Mortimer (adaptor)
11-30-73
Hartke Theatre
Catholic University
Washington, DC

Captain Smight in His Glory
David Freeman
Fall, 1969
Theatre Company of Boston
Boston, MA

Captives of the Faceless Drummer
George Ryga
Summer, 1972
Lennoxville Festival
Lennoxville, Quebec, CAN

Car
McCrea Imbrie & Neil Seldon
5-6-72
CSC Repertory Theatre
89 W. 3rd, N.Y.C.

Car, The (with Control)
Jack Temchin
8-31-70
Old Reliable Theatre Tavern
231 E. 3rd, N.Y.C.

Car Used: Jazz, Blues Gospel
6-7-73
Afro-American Total Theatre
415 W. 127th, N.Y.C.

Caravaggio
Michael Straight
August, 1968
Vineyard Players
Vineyard Haven, MA

Caravan
The Theatre of All Possibilities
10-5-72
The Caravan from Dramaturgia
La Mama ETC
74 E. 4th, N.Y.C.

Card Game
Dick Higgins; compiled by Jerry Benjamin
11-8-72
Playwrights' Workshop Club
14 Waverly Pl., N.Y.C.

Card, The
Richard Reichman
8-5-69
Krannert Center for the Performing Arts
Urbana, IL

Care of the Body
Daniela Gioseffi
5-5-71
Cubiculo
414 W. 51st, N.Y.C.

Caricatura
Eli Alvarado
5-15-71
Spanish Players
Community Center Theatre
270 W. 89th, N.Y.C.

Carmilla
Wilford Leach (text); Ben Johnston (music)
11-25-70
La Mama ETC
74 E. 4th, N.Y.C.

Carnival
Albert Maurits
9-23-70
La Mama ETC
74 E. 4th, N.Y.C.

Carnival & Resurrection of the Blind God Orpheus
Monty Pike
9-9-68
Straight Theatre
San Francisco, CA

Carnival Song
Jimmy Justice
Nov., 1973
Afro-American Total Theatre
Martinique Theatre
N.Y.C.

Carol Channing with Ten Stout Hearted Men
3-16-70
O'Keefe Centre
Toronto, CAN

Carpa de los Rasquachis, La
4-19-73
El Teatro Campesino
Chelsea Theater Center
30 Lafayette, Brooklyn, NY

Carpenters, The
Steven Tesich
12-21-70
American Place Theatre
N.Y.C.

Carry Me Back to Morningside Heights
Robert Alan Arthur
2-12-68
Locust Theatre
Philadelphia, PA

Carry Me Back to Old Virginity
Jasper Oddo
11-8-73
Electric Circus
23 St. Mark's Pl. N.Y.C.

Carta à Franco 1972
Fernando Arrabal
3-10-72
Extension Theatre
277 Park Ave. So., N.Y.C.

Carta, La
Jose L. Gonzalez
5-26-73
Teatro Jurutungo
Gershwin Theatre Brooklyn College
Brooklyn, NY

Cartas Boca Abajo, Las
Anthony Buero Vallejo
6-15-73
Nuestro Teatro
Greenwich News Theatre
277 Park Ave. So., N.Y.C.

Cartoon
Murray Mednick
10-14-71
Theatre Genesis
10th & 2nd Ave., N.Y.C.

Cartouche
Anonymous
11-20-70
CAMI Theatre
165 W. 57th, N.Y.C.

Carving a Statue
Graham Greene
4-30-68
Gramercy Arts Theatre
N.Y.C.

Casa, La
Ermano Carsana
5-2-73
Teatro Italiano
Hunter College
N.Y.C.

Casa Vieja, La
Abelardo Estorino
11-12-71
New York Theatre of the Americas
427 W. 59th, N.Y.C.

Casanova and His Mother
Danny Lipman
7-20-72
Eugene O'Neill Memorial Theatre
Waterford, CT

Cascando
Samuel Beckett
4-28-70
University of Minnesota
Morris, MN

Case Against Roberta Guardino. . ., The
John Wolfson
12-19-73
Playwrights' Horizons
Clark Center for the Performing Arts
West Side YWCA, 8th Ave. & 51st, N.Y.C.

Case Book, The
Wesley St. Clair
3-7-70
Black Mask Players
34 W. 134th, N.Y.C.

Case Is Investigated, The
A. Arrufat
1-29-71
Potbelly Theatre Workshop
40 W. 18th, N.Y.C.

Cashmere Love (staged reading)
F. V. Hunt
5-20-73
American Women Playwright's Association
McBurney YMCA
215 W. 23rd, N.Y.C.

Casina
Plautus; translated by Lionel Casson
12-28-72
Shade Company
230 Canal, N.Y.C.

Cassandra and Aaron
Abigail Quart
2-9-73
Cubiculo
414 W. 51st, N.Y.C.

Cast Her as a Princess
Alfred Dumais
5-3-73
Schimmel Center for the Arts
Pace College
N.Y.C.

Casting
Joseph Ponzi
3-29-68
Judson Poets' Theatre
55 Wash. Sq. So., N.Y.C.

Castle on the Dee
David Levitt
5-9-70
Forest Hills High School
Forest Hills, NY

Castle, The
Ivan Klima, translated by Ruth Willard
12-3-68
Univ. of Michigan
Ann Arbor, MI

Castro Complex, The
Mel Arrighi
11-18-70
Stairway Theatre
225 W. 46th, N.Y.C.

Cat Among the Pigeons
Georges Feydeau; John Mortimer (translator)
10-8-71
Milwaukee Repertory Theatre
Milwaukee, WI

Cataclysmic Loves of Cooper and Looper and Their Friend Who Was Squashed by a Moving Van, The
Thomas A. Erhard
3-6-68
Highland High School
Albuquerque, NM

Catbox, The
David Libman
3-18-72
Hunter College Playwrights' Project
West Side YMCA
5 W. 63rd, N.Y.C.

Catch As Catch Can (with The Jesus Man)
Antony Bassae
12-21-70
Old Reliable Theatre Tavern
231 E. 3rd, N.Y.C.

Catch My Soul
Jack Good
3-5-68
Ahmanson Theatre
Los Angeles, CA

Catch-22
Joseph Heller
7-13-71
John Drew Repertory Theatre
East Hampton, NY

Catfood (with Soap)
H. N. Levitt
2-14-70
West Side YMCA
5 W. 63rd, N.Y.C.

Caught in the Act
Nagle Jackson
5-22-68
American Conservatory Theatre
San Francisco, CA

Cause City Jim Loves the Countess
Ronald Miglionico
5-31-68
Off Center Theatre
152 W. 66th, N.Y.C.

Caution: A Love Story
Tom Eyen (book & lyrics); Bruce Kerle (music)
4-2-69
La Mama ETC
74 E. 4th, N.Y.C.

Cave of the Wombats
Gerald Ashford
6-1-72
San Antonio Little Theatre
San Antonio, TX

Celebrate Me
Gloria Gonzalez & Edna Schappert
4-22-71
Playbox
94 St. Mark's Pl., N.Y.C.

Celebration
Tom Jones (book & lyrics); Harvey Schmidt (music)
1-22-69
Ambassador
215 W. 49th, N.Y.C.

Celebration: Jooz/Guns/Movies/The Abyss, The
Arthur Sainer
2-11-72
Theatre for the New City
151 Bank, N.Y.C.

Celebration, The
Ross Alexander
3-29-69
Little Theatre
West Side YMCA
5 W. 63rd, N.Y.C.

Celestina or The Spanish Bawd, La
Fernando de Rojas; adapted by Steve Abrams
9-22-71
La Mama ETC
74 E. 4th, N.Y.C.

Celia White Dove
Louis M. Ponderoso
11-24-69
Universalist Theatre
4 W. 76th, N.Y.C.

Cellar, The (with The Dishroom and The Motel)
Paul DeJohn
7-17-72
Manhattan Theatre Club
321 E. 73rd, N.Y.C.

Cemi en el Palacio de Jarlem
11-14-69
El Nuevo Teatro Pobre de America
Henry Street Settlement Playhouse
466 Grand, N.Y.C.

Cenci, The
Antonin Artaud
12-30-70
La Mama ETC
74 E. 4th, N.Y.C.

Cepillo de Dientes, El
Jorge Diaz
5-22-70
ADAL Performing Arts
682 Ave. of the Americas, N.Y.C.

Cerebrius Mentalus (with Interlude on a Train and To Beginningness)
Craig Wood
5-23-69
Wittenberg University Theatre
Springfield, OH

Ceremonies in Dark Old Men
Lonne Elder III
2-5-69
Negro Ensemble Company
St. Mark's Playhouse
133 Second, N.Y.C.

Ceremony for an Assassinated Black Man
Fernando Arrabal
4-1-72
Puerto Rican Traveling Theatre
124 W. 18th, N.Y.C.

Ceremony of the Birds, The
Spring, 1973
El Teatro Capesino
CA

Certain Kind of Woman, A (Part 1 of Grub)
Raymond Banachi
2-4-72
Playbox
94 St. Mark's Pl., N.Y.C.

Cervantes
Norman Corwin
9-5-73
American Theatre
Washington, DC

Chaconne in G Minor (with Wyatt and The Pecan Tree)
Piero Heliczer
2-11-71
Cinematheque
80 Wooster, N.Y.C.

Chamber Piece For Bearded Percussionist and Strouil (part of Blueberry Muffin Twice Removed)
James Cuomo
11-18-70
La Mama ETC
74 E. 4th, N.Y.C.

Chameleons, The (songs & dialogues on marriage)
2-4-72
Sheraton Commander Hotel
Cambridge, MA

Champagne's for Jake, Angel, The
Andrew Bro
2-13-69
Denison University
Granville, OH

Chandalika
Rabindranath Tagore
12-26-71
Boston Center for the Arts
Boston, MA

Change/Love Together/Organize: A Revival
Charlie L. Russell
7-28-72
National Black Theatre
9 E. 125th, N.Y.C.

Changes
Megan Terry
1-4-68
La Mama ETC
122 Second, N.Y.C.

Changes
Powell Shepherd
9-10-69
La Mama ETC
74 E. 4th, N.Y.C.

Changes (a circus of the mind tragi-comedy)
9-23-71
Theatre Two
Cambridge, MA

Changing Room, The
David Storey
11-17-72
Long Wharf Theatre
New Haven, CT

Charade
Michael Stewart
8-31-71
Cherry County Playhouse
Traverse City, MS

Chariot of the Sun, The
Lewis Gardner; (music) Oscar Brand
1-30-70
Portable Phoenix
Bronx, NY

Charlatans
Miguel de Cervantes; Paul Meacham (adaptation & lyrics); Joseph Smith (music)
5-16-72
WPA
333 Bowery, N.Y.C.

Charles Abbott and Son
Lewis S. Salzburg
3-10-71
Roundabout Theatre
307 W. 26th, N.Y.C.

Charles MacDeath
Lars Forssell
10-26-70
Old Reliable Theatre Tavern
231 E. 3rd, N.Y.C.

Charles Manson A.K.A. Jesus Christ
11-19-71
Theatre Passe Muraille
Toronto, Ontario, CAN

Charley and the Man with the Upside Down Eyes
Richard D. Waters
6-30-70
Fisherman's Players
North Eastham, MA

Charlie and Belle (with Sleeping Dogs)
David Libman
12-7-70
Assembly Theatre
113 Jane, N.Y.C.

Charlie Is My Darling Cried the Darling Little Girl
Dick Bakkerud
5-7-70
Tufts University
Medford, MA

Charlie Still Can't Win No Wars on the Ground (with The (Mis)Judgment)
Earl Anthony
1-8-71
New Federal Theatre
292 Henry, N.Y.C.

Charlie the Chicken
Jonathan Levy
8-11-72
American Shakespeare Festival
Stratford, CT

Charlie Was Here and Now He's Gone
Dennis G. Turner
6-6-71
Eastside Playhouse
334 E. 74th, N.Y.C.

Charlotte of the City (in Wash Rag) (with Readings from Vietnam)
Eric Goldman
6-4-71
Assembly Theatre
113 Jane, N.Y.C.

Chase Me, Comrade!
Ray Cooney
6-26-73
High Tor Summer Theatre
Fitchburg, MA

Che!
Lennox Raphael
3-22-69
Free Store Theatre
14 Cooper Sq., N.Y.C.

Che Guevara
Mario Fratti
Jan., 1969
Toronto Workshop Theatre
Toronto, CAN

Cheap Theatrics
Robert Patrick
6-27-69
Playbox
94 St. Mark's Pl., N.Y.C.

Cheap Trick, A
Charles Mingus
12-9-70
La Mama ETC
74 E. 4th, N.Y.C

Chekhov List, The
Joseph B. Baldwin
8-9-73
Changing Scene
Denver, CO

Chekhov's Grandmother (with The Button and The Pussy)
Michael McClure
12-20-73
Theatre Genesis
2nd Ave. & 10th, N.Y.C.

Chelem — Undzer Shtetl
6-7-70
YM-YWHA
92nd & Lexington, N.Y.C.

Chemin de Fer
Ed Kelleher
4-2-71
Stage Lights Theatrical Club
218 W. 48th, N.Y.C.

Chemmy Circle, The
Georges Feydeau, translated by Suzanne Grossmann
8-8-68
Niagara-on-the-Lake Theatre
Ontario, CAN

Cherry Soda Water (with The Gulf of Crimson)
Stephen Levi
5-11-30
H B Playwrights Foundation
124 Bank, N.Y.C.

Cheval Noir, Le
John Copley Quinn
1-7-72
Playbox
94 St. Mark's Pl., N.Y.C.

Chic Life, The
Arthur Marx and Robert Fisher
6-30-69
Westport Country Playhouse
Westport, CT

Chicago 70
5-25-70
Martinique Theatre,
N.Y.C.

Chicken Little's Ass Is Falling
Gloria Gonzalez
12-9-70
Playbox
94 St. Mark's Pl., N.Y.C.

Chicken Livers (or) The Butcher's Scandal
Ned Bobkoff
4-30-71
Dowling College
Oakdale, NY

Chickencoop Chinaman's Pregnant Pause, The (rehearsed reading)
Frank Chin
3-4-72
American Place Theatre
111 W. 46th, N.Y.C.

Child's Play
Robert Marasco
2-17-70
Royale Theatre
N.Y.C.

Child Went Forth, A
David Sawn
11-1-68
Dramarena Repertory Theatre
158 W. 55th, N.Y.C.

Children
Robert Elston & Harvey Keith
11-17-72
New Federal Theatre
Henry Street Settlement Playhouse
466 Grand, N.Y.C.

Children Are for Loving
Glory Van Scott
5-18-72
Library & Museum of the Performing Arts
111 Amsterdam, N.Y.C.

Children! Children!
Jack Horrigan
3-7-72
Ritz Theatre
219 W. 48th, N.Y.C.

Children Crossing (reading)
Andrea Karchmer
9-24-72
Theatre for the New City
113 Jane, N.Y.C.

Children in the Rain
Dennis McIntyre
2-6-70
New York Blood Center Auditorium
310 E. 67th, N.Y.C.

Children of Sanchez
Oscar Lewis; adapted by Vicente Lenero
June, 1972
Negreto Theatre
Mexico City, Mexico

Children's Crusade, The
William H. Hoffman (scenario); John H. Smead (music)
10-31-72
West Side YWCA
8th Ave. & 51st, N.Y.C.

Children's Games
Charles Hightower
5-22-69
Afro-American Theatre Workshop
Brooklyn College
NY

Children's Mass, The
Frederick Combs
5-16-73
Theatre de Lys
N.Y.C.

Children's Video Theatre, The
9-2-72
New Faith Children's Theatre Company
Lincoln Center Plaza
N.Y.C.

Children, The
Michael McGuire
12-17-72
New York Shakespeare Festival Public Theatre
425 Lafayette, N.Y.C.

Chinese and Dr. Fish, The
Murray Schisgal
2-14-70
Shubert Theatre
Philadelphia, PA

Chinese Dancer (with A Rehearsal)
Roberts Blossom
6-20-69
Judson Poets' Theatre
55 Wash. Sq. So., N.Y.C.

Chinese Friend, The (with The Family)
Mario Fratti
4-19-72
Playwrights' Workshop Club
14 Waverly Pl., N.Y.C.

Chinese Skin Shadow Plays
11-28-72
Asia Society
92nd St. YM-YWCA
92nd & Lexington, N.Y.C.

Chinese Wisecrackers
April, 1971 (?)
Chicago Project
Chicago, IL

Chip Woman's Fortune, The
Willis Richardson
November, 1973
Afro-American Studio
415 W. 127th, N.Y.C.

Chock Full
Nan Jesse
12-3-71
St. Peter's Church
346 W. 20th, N.Y.C.

Chocolate: A Black Musical
Chris Brown, Jr.
10-22-71
Henry Street Settlement Playhouse
466 Grand, N.Y.C.

Chocolate Covered Marshmallow
Stella Goren
6-24-71
Fiesta Hall
Los Angeles, CA

Choices
Peter Copani (book & lyrics); Robert Tuthill & Peter Copani (music)
8-23-72
People's Performing Company
Lincoln Center Plaza
N.Y.C.

Choking Up
Joseph Renard
11-16-73
WPA
333 Bowery, N.Y.C.

Christabel and the Rubicon
H. L. Moorman
8-26-69
Olney Theatre
Olney, MD

Christmas Carol, A (an adaptation of Dickens)
12-19-69
Dallas Theater Center
Dallas, TX

Christmas Dinner, The
William Devane
11-30-69
New Dramatists Workshop
424 W. 44th, N.Y.C.

Christmas in July
Michael Lewis
7-14-73
Street 70 Ensemble
Rockville Civic Center
Rockville, MD

Christmas Rappings (oratorio)
Al Carmines
12-14-69
Judson Poets' Theatre
55 Wash. Sq. So., N.Y.C.

Christmas Show, The
12-20-72
Contemporary Theatre
Seattle, WA

Christophe
John Gay
12-12-68
Chelsea Theatre Center
30 Lafayette, Brooklyn, NY

Christopher at Sheridan Squared
H. M. Koutoukas
11-11-71
Performing Garage
33 Wooster, N.Y.C.

Chronicle
Florence Stevenson
3-21-69
Chelsea Theatre Center
30 Lafayette, Brooklyn, NY

Chronicle of Nine
Florence Stevenson
11-9-70
Library & Museum of the Performing Arts
111 Amsterdam, N.Y.C.

Chronicles of Hell, The
Michel de Ghelderode
9-30-69
University of Michigan
Ann Arbor, MI

Chrysanthemum Forum
Ching-Yeh & Jing-Jyi Wu
7-29-70
La Mama ETC
Transfiguration Church
29 Mott St., N.Y.C.

Chumpanzee (with Willie Bignigga)
Charles Gordone
7-3-70
New Federal Theatre
292 Henry, N.Y.C.

Cinderella and the Hippie Prince
Alicia Carmona
3-7-71
New York Theater of the Americas
427 W. 59th, N.Y.C.

Cinderella Brown
J. Centola
5-11-73
Peach Pitts Hot Peaches Company
200 W. 24th, N.Y.C.

Cinderellagame
Paul Eerik Rummo, Andres Mannik & Mardi Valgemae (translator)
4-7-71
La Mama ETC
74 E. 4th, N.Y.C.

Cinders
Michael Carton
10-19-72
West Side YWCA
8th Ave. & 51st, N.Y.C.

Cinema of the Year Zero (staged reading)
Ira Hauptman
October, 1972
Manhattan Theatre Club
321 E. 73rd, N.Y.C.

Cinque
Leonard Melfi
5-29-71
Unit Theatre
157 W. 22nd, N.Y.C.

Circle in the Water, A
Gerry Raad
6-27-69
Hollywood Center Theatre
Hollywood, CA

Circle of Sound, The (an evening of song composed and sung by women)
8-10-73
Manhattan Theatre Club
321 E. 73rd, N.Y.C.

Circle, The
Tony Giordano
4-4-69
New York Theatre Ensemble
2 E. 2nd, N.Y.C.

Circles
Alexis Deveaux
3-4-73
Frederick Douglas Creative Arts Center
Salem United Methodist Church
2190 Seventh, N.Y.C.

Circo Dell'Arte
3-8-70
261 Bowery, N.Y.C.

Circus
Ilsa Gilbert
5-26-69
Old Reliable Theatre Tavern
231 E. 3rd, N.Y.C.

Circus, The
Gerry Young
1969
Ottowa University
Ottowa, CAN

Circus, The
Gerald Schoenewolf
8-6-71
New York Theater Ensemble
2 E. 2nd, N.Y.C.

Cities in Bezique
Adrienne Kennedy
1-4-69
New York Shakespeare Festival Public Theatre
425 Lafayette, N.Y.C.

City of Light
John Dodd
1-5-73
La Mama ETC
74 E. 4th, N.Y.C.

City of Light, The
James M. Auer
3-5-69
Theatre Americana
William D. Davies Building
Altadena, CA

City Scene (Paradise Gardens East and Conerico Was Here to Stay)
Frank Gagliano
3-10-69
Fortune Theatre
62 E. 4th, N.Y.C.

City Stops (The Final Experiment by Julie Bovasso; Manhattan Murder Mystery by Adrienne Kennedy; Port Authority by Leonard Melfi; Next Time by Ed Bullins; Boxes by Susan Yankowitz; Let It Bleed by Terrance McNally)
5-8-72
Bronx Community College
Bronx, NY

Clap Hands, Clap Hands, 'Till Daddy Comes Home
March, 1969
Spring Hill College
Mobile, AL

Claptailism of Palmola Christmas Spectacle
Jack Smith
12-19-70
Plaster Foundation
36 Greene, N.Y.C.

Clark and Myrna
Elliott Baker
8-1-72
Berkshire Theatre Festival
Stockbridge, MA

Clark Street, Duck Variations
6-27-72
St. Nicholas Theatre
Boston Center for the Arts
Boston, MA

Class, The
Gregory Rozakis
1-3-68
Playwrights' Workshop Club
14 Waverly Pl., N.Y.C.

Classroom, The (with After the Fashion Show and Day to Day)
Maryat Lee
7-1-68
Soul and Latin Theatre
N.Y.C.

Claudine
Donald Kvares, adapted by Robert Schroeder
11-15-68
Mannhardt Theatre Foundation
N.Y.C.

Clawing Hand, The
Joseph Di Stefano
6-4-71
Regina Theatre Center
Brooklyn, NY

Clean Sheets
John Boylan
11-19-71
Downstage Studio Theatre
321 W. 14th, N.Y.C.

Cleaning House
Robert Patrick
6-19-73
New Plays Festival
WPA
333 Bowery, N.Y.C.

Cleaning Solution, The
Deloss Brown
4-6-71
WPA
333 Bowery, N.Y.C.

Clearing House
Donald Kvares
4-29-71
Cubiculo
414 W. 51st, N.Y.C.

Cleobis & Bito
Ronald Tavel
3-27-68
Extension Theatre
128 E. 7th, N.Y.C.

Cleopatra Complex, The
1-8-71
Project Four
Park Ave. & 69th, N.Y.C.

Cleverest Son, The
Hardrick & Vernon Blackman
Fall, 1973
National Center of Afro-American Artists
Roxbury, MA

Cliche U.S.A.
Shirley Broughton (book); Robert Wolinsky (musical direction)
5-7-71
Theatre for Ideas Studio Theatre
112 W. 21st, N.Y.C.

Click!
Stan Hart
10-28-68
Mark Taper Forum
Los Angeles, CA

Clinic, The
Robert Goldman
10-26-73
Gene Frankel Workshop
Space for Innovative Development
344 W. 36th, N.Y.C.

Close Call (with Dialetic Dialogue in Double Time; Robbers' Nest; and Hogwash)
Barry Litvack
10-28-70
Playwrights' Unit
83 E. 4th, N.Y.C.

Closer Since the Shooting
Francine Winant
2-8-69
Judson Poets' Theatre
55 Wash. Sq. So., N.Y.C.

Closets
Regis Caddic
7-22-69
New Workshop Theatre
Brooklyn College
NY

Clouds, The
Aristophanes; William Arrowsmith (adaptor)
1971?
University of Massachusetts
Amherst, MA

Clown Alley
3-1-72
Astrodome
Houston, TX

Clown of Chocolate
Richard Minichiello
8-12-71
Calliope Theatre
Boston University
Boston, MA

Clowns, The
R. Boussom
May, 1973
South Coast Repertory Theatre
Costa Mesa, CA

Clowns (with On the Runway of Life Something's Always Taking Off)
Antonio Calabrese
6-18-72
Universalist Theatre
4 W. 76th, N.Y.C.

Clues and Cues
David De Rosier
Playbox
94 St. Mark's Pl., N.Y.C.

Clutch
David Epstein
4-2-70
Yale University
New Haven, CT

Coast to Coast
See: Back East and Out West

Cock Crows, The (with A Man Talking)
Allen Davis
2-22-72
Theatre of the Riverside Church
490 Riverside Dr., N.Y.C.

Cockade
Charles Wood
6-20-69
Assembly Theatre
113 Jane, N.Y.C.

Cockortwo
John Boylan
3-7-69
Downstage Studio Theatre
321 W. 14th, N.Y.C.

Cock-Strong
Tom Murrin
6-20-69
La Mama ETC
74 E. 4th, N.Y.C.

Cocktails with Mimi
Mary Chase
7-3-73
Barter Theatre
Abingdon, VA

Coco
Alan Jay Lerner (book & lyrics); André Previn (music)
12-18-69
Mark Hellinger Theatre
51st & Broadway, N.Y.C.

Cocteau
Andy Milligan
7-12-72
Playwrights' Workshop
14 Waverly Pl., N.Y.C.

Cocteau
Jewel Theatre
N.Y.C.
July, 1971
Players' Theatre
115 MacDougal, N.Y.C.

Coda
Evan Walker
Dec., 1972
D.C. Black Theatre Repertory Company
Washington, DC

Coffee Stand
Sharon Thei
4-27-72
St. Peter's Church
346 W. 20th, N.Y.C.

Coffins for Butterflies
Conceived by Aart
3-31-71
La Mama ETC
74 E. 4th, N.Y.C.

Coiled Spring, The
Stanley Taikeff
5-7-69
13th Street Theatre
50 W. 13th, N.Y.C.

Cold Day in Hell
Otis Bigelow
7-21-70
Brooklyn College
Brooklyn, NY

Cold Draft, A
Charles Pulaski
8-9-72
Playwrights' Workshop
14 Waverly Pl., N.Y.C.

Cold Feet
Marvin Pletzke
4-24-72
Players Theatre
115 MacDougal, N.Y.C.

Coldest War of All, The
Leo Brady and John Franceschina
7-17-68
Olney Theatre
Olney, MD

Colette
Elinor Jones
5-6-70
Ellen Stewart Theatre
240 E. 3rd, N.Y.C.

Collage
Richard Ronan
4-18-70
Riverside Theatre Workshop
224 Waverly Pl., N.Y.C.

Collection, The (with The Intruder)
Mell Lazarus
5-8-70
Anthony Mannino Drama Tree
182 Fifth, N.Y.C.

Collective Title
See: Her(r) Professor and Subtitles

Collective Works of Billy the Kid, The
Michael Ondaatje
7-10-73
Stratford Festival
Stratford, Ontario, CAN

Collision Course (a series, see titles below)
5-8-68
Cafe Au Go-Go
152 Bleecker, N.Y.C.
- **Stars and Stripes**
  by Leonard Melfi
- **Skywriting**
  by Rosalyn Drexler
- **Thoughts on the Instant of Greeting a Friend on the Street**
  by Jean-Claude Van Itallie and Sharon Thie
- **Thoughts**
  by Jean-Claude Van Itallie and Sharon Thie
- **Camera Obscura**
  by Robert Patrick
- **Metaphors**
  by Martin Duberman
- **Rats**
  by Israel Horovitz

Colonial Dudes, The
Martin Duberman
7-29-70
Caravan Theater
Dorset, VT

Colonial Fairy Tales, The or Zartan, Son of Tarzan
Jerome Savary
9-16-70
La Mama ETC
74 E. 4th., N.Y.C.

Color de Nuestra Piel, El
Celestina Gorostiza
4-15-72
Fordham University
113 W. 60th, N.Y.C.

Color for Cassandra's Dream, A
Dene Hammond
4-26-73
University of Missouri Theatre
Columbia, MO

Color Me Human
Richard D. Waters
7-14-72
Fisherman's Players
North Eastham, MA

Colors of Experience (reading)
Roni Dengel
1-20-71
Library & Museum of the Performing Arts
111 Amsterdam, N.Y.C.

Columbia, the Gem of the Ocean
Imamu Amiri Baraka (LeRoi Jones)
12-1-72
House of Kuumba
108 W. 112th, N.Y.C.

Come as You Are!
John Mortimer
7-11-72
Boothbay Playhouse
Boothbay, ME

Come Closer, You're Smothering Me
5-26-72
Caravan Theatre
Cambridge, MA

Come into My World
Paul Pierog
11-9-73
Anthony Mannino Drama Tree
182 Fifth, N.Y.C.

Come into the Garden Maude (with Shadows of the Evening)
Noel Coward
8-19-69
Boothbay Playhouse
Boothbay, ME

Come Summer
Will Holt (book & lyrics); David Baker (music)
1-25-69
O'Keefe Centre
Toronto, CAN

Come to the Station
Claude McNeal
7-28-71
St. Clement's Church
423 W. 46th, N.Y.C.

Come True (staged reading)
Fred Gordon
1-23-73
Manhattan Theatre Club
321 E. 73rd, N.Y.C.

Come Up and See My Casserole (with The Birth of Venus)
Frank Moffett Mosier
11-18-68
Library & Museum of the Performing Arts
111 Amsterdam, N.Y.C.

Comeback, The
Jack Gilhooley
6-25-73
Theatre for the New City
113 Jane, N.Y.C.

Comedia (ensemble creation)
5-18-73
Black Arts West
Seattle, WA

Comedy
Lawrence Carra (book); Hugo Peretti, Luigi Creatore, & George David Weiss (music & lyrics)
11-4-72
Colonial Theatre
Boston, MA

Comedy for Three Players, A
Clyde Ellsworth
10-10-69
Mainstream Theatre-Loft
20 E. 14th, N.Y.C.

Comedying
12-14-73
Theatre X
Milwaukee, WI

Coming Forth by Day of Osiris Jones
Conrad Aiken; adapted by Tom Shachtman
12-13-72
Actors' Experimental Unit
682 Sixth, N.Y.C.

Coming Forth by Lunch of Sgt. Stagg, The
Martin Shea
2-27-69
Cooper Square Arts Theatre
35 Cooper Sq., N.Y.C.

Coming Out!
Jonathan Katz
6-16-72
Gay Activists Alliance Firehouse
99 Wooster, N.Y.C.

Coming Together
Wally Harper & Paul Zakrzewski
12-19-71
Theatre of the Riverside Church
490 Riverside Dr., N.Y.C.

Comings and Goings
Megan Terry
2-9-68
St. Felix Street Playhouse
126 St. Felix, Brooklyn, NY

Commotion of Zebras, A (with Daddy)
Susan Miller
1-17-71
Alice Theatre
137A W. 14th, N.Y.C.

Commune
12-20-70
Performing Garage
33 Wooster, N.Y.C.

Community Kitchen
Alex Foster
March, 1969
Little Theatre
180 W. 135th, N.Y.C.

Community of Two, A
Jerome Chodorov
12-31-73
Playhouse
Wilmington, DE

Companion Plays, The
C. David Barrett
4-18-69
First Unitarian Church
Brooklyn, NY

Company
George Furth (book); Stephen Sondheim (music & lyrics)
3-26-70
Shubert Theatre
Boston, MA

Company of Wayward Saints, A
James Coakley
Summer, 1972
Northwestern University
Evanston, IL

Compensation
Pamela Lengyel
11-5-71
New York Theatre Ensemble
2 E. 2nd, N.Y.C.

Complaint Department Closes at Five, The
Edward M. Cohen
7-28-29-71
Eugene O'Neill Memorial Theatre
Waterford, CT

Complaint Department Closes at Five, The (reading)
Edward M. Cohen
4-8-73
New York Cultural Center
2 Columbus Circle, N.Y.C.

Complete Works of Studs Edsel, The
Percy Granger
8-29-72
Provincetown Playhouse
Provincetown, MA

Complexions Inside Out
Jan Quackenbush
3-6-68
La Mama ETC
122 Second, N.Y.C.

Compost
10-1-72
Princeton University
Princeton, NJ

Compressions
George Ryga
Spring, 1970
Playhouse Theatre Company
Vancouver, B.C., CAN

Concentric Circles
Benjamin Bradford
1-19-70
Old Reliable Theatre Tavern
231 E. 3rd, N.Y.C.

Concept II
3-26-69
La Mama ETC
74 E. 4th, N.Y.C.

Concept, The
Vernon Hinkle
7-9-69
Eugene O'Neill Memorial Theatre
Waterford, CT

Concept, The
Daytop Village
8-21-69
Gramercy Arts
N.Y.C.

Concept-Easy Poetry
Black Poetry Theatre
7-4-69
Paperback Theatre
80 Second, N.Y.C.

Concerning the Effects of Trimethyl-Chloride
John Ford Noonan
3-29-71
Old Reliable Theatre Tavern
231 E. 3rd, N.Y.C.

Concert at St. Ovide, The
Antonio Buero-Vallejo
11-25-73
Nuestro Teatro
Theatre 277
277 Park Ave. So., N.Y.C.

Concert for TPG
The Performance Group
12-12-71
Performing Garage
33 Wooster, N.Y.C.

Condition of Shadow: A Characterization of Poe
Jerry Rockwood (adaptor)
3-8-73
Cubiculo
414 W. 51st, N.Y.C.

Conditioning of Charlie One, The (staged reading)
Robert Karmon
2-21-73
Playwrights' Horizons
Clark Center for the Performing Arts
West Side YWCA, 8th Ave. & 51st, N.Y.C.

Conditions of Agreement
John Whiting
5-28-72
Roundabout Theatre
307 W. 26th, N.Y.C.

Conduct Unbecoming
Barry England
10-12-70
Ethel Barrymore Theatre
243 W. 47th, N.Y.C.

Coney Island
Yutaka Higashi; music by Itsuro Shimoda
10-28-70
La Mama ETC
74 E. 4th, N.Y.C.

Conference of the Birds, The
Peter Brook
6-1-73
International Centre for Theatre Research
Boston Center for the Arts
Boston, MA

Confession, The
Sarah Bernhardt
3-23-71
WPA
333 Bowery, N.Y.C.

Confessional for Street People
Paul Pierog
12-24-71
New York Theatre Ensemble
2 E. 2nd, N.Y.C.

Confessional (with I Can't Imagine Tomorrow)
Tennessee Williams
8-19-71
Maine Theatre Arts Festival
Bar Harbor, ME

Confessions of a Female Disorder
Susan Miller
7-19-73
Eugene O'Neill Memorial Theatre
Waterford, CT

Confessions of a Spent Youth
Vance Bourjaily
1-15-72
Cubiculo
414 W. 51st, N.Y.C.

Confessions of an Ignorant
Paul John Austin
2-19-68
New Theatre Workshop
154 E. 54th, N.Y.C.

Confidence Man, The
James Bowditch
12-2-70
Ripon College Theatre
Ripon, WI

Confines, The
George Carroll
2-27-70
Whitman College
Walla Walla, WA

Conflict of Interest, A
Jay Broad
2-9-72
Arena Stage
Washington, DC

Confused Smiths, The
Rafael Bunuel
3-14-69
Inner Theatre
356 Bowery, N.Y.C.

Confusion
Niall Toiban
1-22-73
Irish Arts Theatre
Toronto, CAN

Congratulations, You Have a New Disease
John Dooley
4-2-71
New York Theatre Ensemble
2 E. 2nd, N.Y.C.

Conjuror, The
Evan Hunter
11-5-69
University of Michigan
Ann Arbor, MI

Conquering Thursday
Elmer Kline
6-3-68
Old Reliable Theatre Tavern
231 E. 3rd, N.Y.C.

Conquest of Everest, The
Arthur Kopit
11-20-70
Assembly Theatre
113 Jane, N.Y.C.

Conquest of Mexico, The
Antonin Artaud
12-5-69
Blue Dome
33 Cornelia, N.Y.C.

Conrad: A Memory Play
Barbara Barrett
4-3-70
Royal Playhouse
219 Second Ave., N.Y.C.

Consensus (revue)
12-7-68
Cooperative Theatre
106 E. 14th, N.Y.C.

Considered Opinion of Alexander Woollcott, The
William Van Gieson
6-19-73
New Plays Festival
WPA
333 Bowery, N.Y.C.

Conspiracy
Aida Morales, James V. Hatch & Larry Garvin
2-27-70
Washington Square Church
133 W. 4th, N.Y.C.

Constant Prince, The
Pedro Calderon de la Barca; adapted by J. Slowacki
10-16-69
Polish Laboratory Theatre
Washington Square Church
N.Y.C.

Constantinople Smith
Charles L. Mee, Jr.
7-3-68
Playbox
94 St. Mark's Pl., N.Y.C.

Constructions
7-14-72
Boston Center for the Arts
Boston, MA

Contaminated Mysteries
Robert Reinhold
9-24-71
Playbox
94 St. Mark's Pl., N.Y.C.

Contest, The
Bernard Diamond
4-2-71
Omni Theatre Club
145 W. 18th, N.Y.C.

Contigo, Pan y Cebolla (with You, Bread and Onion)
Don Manuel Goristaza; adapted by Luis Reyes de la Maza; Jose Antonio Zavala (music & lyrics)
Spring, 1972
Teatro Del Bosque
Chapultepec Park
Mexico City, Mexico

Continental Divide
Oliver Hailey
5-6-70
Washington Theater Club
Washington, DC

Continued Departure (with The Door Is Open)
Arthur Gregor
1-29-70
Cubiculo
414 W. 51st, N.Y.C.

Contract, The
Joseph Golden
5-1-68
Fulton Theatre Company
119 Ninth, N.Y.C.

Contract, The
Joseph Lizardi
3-12-71
Senior Dramatic Workshop
Carnegie Hall
881 Seventh, N.Y.C.

Contractor, The
David Storey
11-19-71
Long Wharf Theatre
New Haven, CT

Contrast, The (musical version)
Royall Tyler; Don Pippin (music); adaptation by Anthony Stimac; Stephen Brown (lyrics)
8-3-72
Greenwich Mews Theatre
141 W. 13th, N.Y.C.

Contribution
Ted Shine
4-1-69
Negro Ensemble Company
St. Mark's Playhouse
133 Second, N.Y.C.

Contributions (Shoes, Plantation, and Contribution)
Ted Shine
3-9-70
Tambellini's Gate Theatre
162 Second, N.Y.C.

Control (with The Car)
Jack Temchin
8-31-70
Old Reliable Theatre Tavern
231 E. 3rd, N.Y.C.

Conversations in Comedy (participation show)
10-26-71
McHale Gaiety Cafe
750 Eighth, N.Y.C.

Conversion of the Jews (with Defender of the Faith and Epstein)
Philip Roth; adapted by Larry Arrick
7-30-70
Yale Repertory Theatre
East Hampton, NY

Convert, The (part of Petit Cabaret Solennel)
Arthur Williams
9-28-72
Theatre for the New City
113 Jane, N.Y.C.

Coocooshay
Robert Auletta
12-16-70
New York Shakespeare Festival
Public Theatre
425 Lafayette, N.Y.C.

Cookie Jar, The
John Clark Donahue
Mar., 1972
Children's Theatre Company of the Minneapol Institute of Arts
Minneapolis, MN

Cool Niggers
Green Lantern House Players
5-10-69
Eisner Lubin Auditorium
566 LaGuardia Pl., N.Y.C.

Cooler Near the Lake (revue)
The Second City
2-7-71
Plaza 9
Plaza Hotel
N.Y.C.

Cooler, The
Bruce Lehan
7-9-70
University of Minnesota
Minneapolis, MN

Co-Op, The
Barbara Garson & Fred Gardner
6-1-72
Theatre for the New City
151 Bank, N.Y.C.

Cop and Blow
See: Black Visions

Cop Out
John Guare
July, 1968
Eugene O'Neill Memorial Theatre
Waterford, CT

Coping
Pamela Lengyel
3-24-72
New York Theatre Ensemble
2 E. 2nd, N.Y.C.

Copout (with The Play Within)
Helen Duberstein
4-27-73
New York Theatre Ensemble
2 E. 2nd, N.Y.C.

Cops
Dashiell Hammett, adapted by Kenneth Cavander
8-5-70
Yale Repertory Theatre
East Hampton, NY

Cops and Robbers
Leslie Lee
Dec., 1970
La Mama ETC
74 E. 4th, N.Y.C.

Corn
Charles Ludlam (book); Virgil Young (music & lyrics)
11-20-72
13th Street Theatre
N.Y.C.

Corner of the Bed, A
Allen Jack Lewis
2-26-69
Gramercy Arts
N.Y.C.

Corner, The
Ed Bullins
Spring, 1969
Theatre Company of Boston
Boston, MA

Cornered
Robert Patrick
1-26-68
Gallery Theatre
99 E. 2nd, N.Y.C.

Cornflakes? and Dreams
2-17-68
Pageant Players
71 E. Broadway, N.Y.C.

Corporate Structure
Alam Mount
1-17-70
Pretenders Cooperative Theatre
106 E. 14th, N.Y.C.

'Corraspondence' School Meeting for Anna May Wong (a mystere)
6-3-72
New York Cultural Center
N.Y.C.

Corrupters, The
Gertrude Samuels
3-23-71
WPA
333 Bowery, N.Y.C.

Cosmic Forces
John Quinn
5-9-71
98 Greene St. Loft
98 Greene St., N.Y.C.

Cosmonaute Agricole, Le
Rene De Obaldia
4-7-70
Barbizon-Plaza Theatre
N.Y.C.

Couch (with The Crystal Pigs)
Gary Britton
9-19-69
Dramarena Repertory Theatre
158 W. 55th, N.Y.C.

Coucou Bazar (Le Bal de L'Hourloupe)
Jean Dubuffet
5-18-73
Guggenheim Museum
N.Y.C.

Could I Have My Wife Back, Please?
8-18-72
Abbey Playhouse
Philadelphia, PA

Count That Day Lost (with Judgment Day)
Stewart H. Benedict
3-4-71
Playbox
94 St. Mark's Pl., N.Y.C.

Counterpoint
Chad Mitchell
11-25-68
Bitter End
147 Bleecker, N.Y.C.

Country Doctor and Other Dreams, The
Dream Theater
November, 1971
Body Politic
Chicago, IL

Country Music
Michael Smith
12-16-71
Theatre Genesis
10th & 2nd, N.Y.C.

Country People
Maxim Gorki, translated by Alexander Bakshy in collaboration with Paul S. Nathan
1-9-70
Long Wharf Theatre
New Haven, CT

Country Woman, The
Turgenev; adaptation by Morris Carnovsky
3-17-72
Long Wharf Theatre
New Haven, CT

Couple
Sam McLanahan
8-30-73
13th Street Theatre
50 W. 13th, N.Y.C.

Couple O' Charleys, A
Michael Robert David
July, 1970
Eugene O'Neill Memorial Theatre
Waterford, CT

Cowboy Mouth, The (with Back Bog Beast Bait)
Sam Shepard & Patti Smith
4-29-71
American Place Theatre
N.Y.C.

Cowgirl and the Tiger, The
Summer, 1972
13th Street Theatre
50 W. 13th, N.Y.C.

Coyote Tracks (A Comic Enactment of a Nez Perce Tribal Legend)
Nancy Heiken
12-5-73
Native American Theatre Ensemble Company
La Mama ETC
74 E. 4th, N.Y.C.

Crabdance
Beverley Simon
9-16-69
Contemporary Theatre
Seattle, WA

Crane, Crane, Montrose and Crane
Jascha Kessler
1-2-68
American Place Theatre
N.Y.C.

Cranes and Peonies (Wonton Soup)
Jing-Jyi Wu & Ching-Yeh
12-30-70
La Mama ETC
74 E. 4th, N.Y.C.

Crawling Arnold
Jules Feiffer
4-22-68
New School
66 W. 12th, N.Y.C.

Crazy Niggers
Oyamo
7-18-73
Eugene O'Neill Memorial Theatre
Waterford, CT

Crazy Now
Richard Smithies & Maura Cavanagh (book & lyrics); Norman Sachs (music)
9-10-72
Eden Theatre
2nd Ave. & 12th, N.Y.C.

Cream of the Crop
Ben Karen
12-7-72
Triangle Theatre
316 E. 88th, N.Y.C.

Creating a Creche
Norman Taffel
12-9-73
Common Ground
70 Grand, N.Y.C.

Creation
1-24-70
Theatre Workshop Inc.
Boston, MA

Creation of the World and Other Business, The
Arthur Miller
10-2-72
Colonial Theatre
Boston, MA

Creative Collective
1969
Hollins College
Hollins, VA

Creditors
August Strindberg; translated by Frank Southerington
8-19-72
Theatre Wagon
Staunton, VA

Creeps
David Freeman
11-10-71
Tarragon Theatre
Toronto, CAN

Cremation, The
Paul Zindel
5-20-70
Playwrights' Unit
83 E. 4th, N.Y.C.

Cretan Bull, The
Kenneth Brown
4-24-69
Gotham Art
455 W. 43rd, N.Y.C.

Crickets, A Country Thing
Ralph Scholl
7-30-71
East Village Theatre
433 E. 6th, N.Y.C.

Crimes and Crimes
August Strindberg; new translation by Evert Sprinchorn
1-8-70
Yale Repertory Theatre
New Haven, CT

Crimes of Passion (The Ruffian on the Stairs and The Erpingham Camp)
Joe Orton
10-26-69
Astor Place Theatre
434 Lafayette, N.Y.C.

Criminals, The
Jose Triana
3-5-69
La Mama ETC
9 St. Mark's Pl., N.Y.C.

Crisis in Chucklewood
Charles Kading
3-27-72
California State College
Fullerton, CA

Criss-Crossing
Philip Magdalany
10-31-69
Playwrights' Unit
83 E. 4th, N.Y.C.

Crocodile and the Cockeyed Moose, The
Marvin Sandberg
7-16-68
Mill Run Playhouse
Niles, IL

Crocodile Smile, The
Jerome Lawrence & Robert E. Lee
8-18-70
Flat Rock Playhouse
Flat Rock, NC

Crocodiles (with The Riddle of the Palm Leaf)
Femi Euba
2-6-73
Negro Ensemble Company
St. Mark's Playhouse
133 Second, N.Y.C.

Croesus and the Witch
Vinnette Carroll (book); Micki Grant (music & lyrics)
8-10-71
Fort Greene Park, N.Y.C.

Cross Has Two Sides, A
Richard D. Waters
6-26-70
Fisherman's Players
North Eastham, MA

Crosslots (reading)
Lyon Phelps
1-16-72
Theatre for the New City
151 Bank, N.Y.C.

Crossroads
Manuel Mendez Ballester
8-5-69
Puerto Rican Traveling Theater
Riverside Park, N.Y.C.

Crown Matrimonial
Royce Ryton
10-2-73
Helen Hayes Theatre
N.Y.C.

Cruce De Vias (The Railroad Crossing)
Carlos Solorzano
10-31-69
Greenwich Mews Spanish Theater
Theatre East
211 E. 60th, N.Y.C.

Crucificado
Edgar White
1-19-73
New York University
N.Y.C.

Crucificado
6-13-72
Urban Art Corps
26 W. 20th, N.Y.C.

Cruising Speed 600 M.P.H.
Anna Marie Barlow
1-5-70
Theatre de Lys
N.Y.C.

Crumbs
Nancy Heiken
3-29-73
La Mama ETC
74 E. 4th, N.Y.C.

Crunch
John Buskin
2-1-73
Manhattan Theatre Club
321 E. 73rd, N.Y.C.

Cry for Us All
William Alfred (book); William Alfred & Phyllis Robinson (lyrics); Mitch Leigh (music)
1-30-70
Shubert Theatre
New Haven, CT

Cry in the Night from a Nice Jewish Boy in Trouble
Robert Lerner
12-3-71
St. Peter's Church
346 W. 20th, N.Y.C.

Cry in the Street
Rolf Lauckner
3-9-69
Harlem School of the Arts
141st & St. Nicholas, N.Y.C.

Cry of the Organ
Robert S. Ross
July, 1970
Eugene O'Neill Memorial Theatre
Waterford, CT

Cry of the People for Meat, The
Peter Schumann
3-27-69
Bread & Puppet Theatre
Columbia University
N.Y.C.

Cry Three
Clear Light Productions
11-28-71
First Baptist Church
Cambridge, MA

Cry Three (a multi-vision Jesus rock show)
12-15-71
Paulist Center
Boston, MA

Crystal and Fox
Brian Friel
4-9-70
Mark Taper Forum
Los Angeles, CA

Crystal Bird, The
12-18-69
Teachers College Drama Workshop
Columbia University
N.Y.C.

Crystal, Crystal Chandelier
7-31-73
Berkshire Playhouse
Stockbridge, MA

Crystal Pigs, The (with Couch)
Gary Britton
9-19-69
Dramarena Repertory Theatre
158 W. 55th, N.Y.C.

Crystallozoa
Herb Liebman
11-27-71
Supernova
451 W. Broadway, N.Y.C.

Cuban Thing, The
Jack Gelber
8-21-68
Berkshire Theatre Festival
Stockbridge, MA

Cuba-Si
Terrence McNally
12-5-68
Loft Workshop
152 Bleecker, N.Y.C.

Cuervos Estan de Luto, Los
Hugo Arguelles
5-22-71
Malditos
Community Center Theatre
270 W. 89th, N.Y.C.

Cultural Exchange — Nyet?
Richard Cave
1-19-68
Riverdale Showcase
252nd St. & Riverdale Ave., Bronx, NY

Cummings and Bowings
e. e. cummings
8-22-73
U.R.G.E.N.T.
151 W. 46th, N.Y.C.

Cummings and Stein Playing with Words
5-18-73
Sunday Brunch Company
Loeb Student Center New York Univ.
N.Y.C.

Cup, The
Nancy Wynn & Jane Dunlap
4-21-72
New York Theatre Ensemble
2 E. 2nd, N.Y.C.

Cure, The
Neal Weaver
6-15-73
CSC Repertory Theatre
89 W. 3rd, N.Y.C.

Curious Fauna
Kenneth McLean
6-24-71
University of Texas
Austin, TX

Current Rage, The
Carol Roper
6-7-73
Ensemble Studio Theatre
549 W. 52nd, N.Y.C.

Curse You, Spread Eagle (revue)
12-8-71
Washington Theatre Club
Washington, DC

Curve, The
Tankred Dorst
4-16-69
Venture Theatre Club
145 Eighth, N.Y.C.

Customs — Inspector in Baggy Pants, The
8-1-68
Rochester University Summer Theatre
Rochester, NY

Cuttaloosa (musical)
8-8-69
Washington Crossing State Park
Titusville, NJ

Cybele
Mario Fratti (book); Paul Dick (lyrics & music)
10-26-71
WPA
333 Bowery, N.Y.C.

Cycle of Spring
Rabindranath Tagore
4-16-71
Unity Center
143 W. 51st, N.Y.C.

Cycles
9-29-73
Womanspace Theatre
Washington Square Church
133 W. 4th, N.Y.C.

Cyclotron
Ching Yeh & Company
6-2-71
La Mama ETC
74 E. 4th, N.Y.C.

Cylinder, The
Copi
3-6-68
La Mama ETC
122 Second, N.Y.C.

Cymbals II
8-26-69
Lincoln Opera House
Lincoln, NH

Cyrano
Anthony Burgess (book & lyrics); Michael Lewis (music)
1-23-73
Tyrone Guthrie Theatre
Minneapolis, MN

Cyrano de Bergerac Edmond
Edmond Rostand; Anthony Burgess (translator)
12-10-71
Tyrone Guthrie Theatre
Minneapolis, MN

D

DA
Hugh Leonard
8-7-73
Olney Theatre
Olney, MD

Dada
Jacob Zilber
3-19-70
Cubiculo
414 W. 51st, N.Y.C.

Daddy
Earl McCarroll
11-3-69
Newtown Players
106 E. 86th, N.Y.C.

Daddy, Dear Daddy
6-20-72
Little Lake Theatre
Canonsburg, PA

Daddy Goodness
Louis Sapin, Richard Wright
6-4-68
Negro Ensemble Company
St. Mark's Playhouse
133 Second, N.Y.C.

Daddy's Little Girl
Harry Haugan
12-22-72
New York Theatre Ensemble
2 E. 2nd, N.Y.C.

Daddy (with A Commotion of Zebras)
Susan Miller
1-17-71
Alice Theatre
137A W. 14th, N.Y.C.

Dairies
V. Robert Coleman
6-17-68
Old Reliable Theatre Tavern
231 E. 3rd, N.Y.C.

Daisy Aldan on Great Jones Street
Daisy Aldan
1-5-73
Moving Company
46 Great Jones, N.Y.C.

Daisy Does It
Judith Gilhousen
11-5-71
New York Theatre Ensemble
2 E. 2nd, N.Y.C.

Dama Del Alba, La
Alejandro Casona
10-18-73
Nuestro Teatro
277 Park Ave. So., N.Y.C.

Damage Done, The
Cleve Thomas
5-24-73
Italics Mime Company
Trinity Methodist Church
Albany, NY

Damnation of Socrates Jones, The
Richard D. Waters
3-28-71
Players Communications Center
North Eastham, MA

Dance Next Door, The
David Trainer
7-29-69
Mark Taper Forum
Los Angeles, CA

Dance of Death at the Bronx Opera House, The
Robert Reinhold
5-17-72
Playwrights' Workshop
14 Waverly Pl., N.Y.C.

Dance to a Nosepicker's Drum
Maxwell Glanville & Alfred Rudolph Gray
3-28-70
773 Concourse Village East Bronx, NY

Dance Wi' Me
Greg Antonacci
2-12-71
La Mama ETC
74 E. 4th, N.Y.C.

Dancing Days
David Wesner
12-5-73
University of South Carolina
Columbia, SC

Dancing Mice, The
John Patrick
7-5-72
Berea Summer Theatre
Berea, OH

Dancing Picture Show, A
John Montgomery
10-19-72
Greenwich Mews Theatre
141 W. 13th, N.Y.C.

Dandelion Daydreams
Ed Graczyk
8-3-72
Midland Community Theatre
Midland, TX

Dandelion Wine
Ray Bradbury (book & lyrics); Larry Alexander (lyrics); Billy Goldenberg (music)
3-10-72
California State College
Fullerton, CA

Dangers of Great Literature, The
Gabriele Roepke
3-30-73
WPA
333 Bowery, N.Y.C.

Danish Modern
Tom LaBar; music by R. Stewart Powell
5-15-69
La Mama ETC
74 E. 4th, N.Y.C.

Danny 405
Conchata Ferrell
6-26-72
Circle Theatre Company
2307 Broadway, N.Y.C.

Dante's Divine Comedy (theatrical collage)
12-5-72
Fordham University
113 W. 60th, N.Y.C.

Daphnis and Chloe
Bruce Feld
12-8-68
Playwrights' Theatre Project
Dancers' Studio Workshop
34 E. 10th, N.Y.C.

Dark Lady (with Black Is)
11-10-72
Featherbed Lane Community Freedom Theatre
Bronx, NY

Dark Maiden from the Ninth Heaven, The
See: Late for Oblivion

Dark Symphony
Mical Whitaker
2-26-72
East River Players
Town Hall
113 W. 43rd, N.Y.C.

Darkroom
David Epstein
10-19-73
Yale Repertory Theatre
New Haven, CT

Darline's Mystery
Unknown
2-17-71
Brandeis University
Waltham, MA

Darning Needle, The
Donald Kvares
9-3-69
Old Reliable Theatre Tavern
231 E. 3rd, N.Y.C.

Darryl and Carol and Jenny and Kenny
Chris Durang
8-21-73
Manhattan Theatre Club
321 E. 73rd, N.Y.C.

Daughter of Earl Siphon, The (with The Aluminium Pigey and The Story—Aunt Rollie)
Larry O'Connel
Spring, 1970
Second Group Theatre
McBurney YMCA
215 W. 23rd, N.Y.C.

Daughter, The
7-6-73
Chicago Project/New York
Space for Innovative Development
344 W. 36th, N.Y.C.

David and Jonathan
Norman Beim
1-5-71
Assembly Theatre
113 Jane, N.Y.C.

David Show, The
A. R. Gurney, Jr.
10-31-68
Players Theatre
115 MacDougal, N.Y.C.

David Zlochower, Prominent Young American Playwright
David Zlochower
9-11-70
New York Theatre Ensemble
2 E. 2nd, N.Y.C.

Dawn (with The Successors)
Walter Turney
1-12-73
Playwright Horizons
Clark Center for the Performing Arts
West Side YWCA, 8th Ave. & 51st N.Y.C.

Day After the Fair, The
Frank Harvey
9-5-73
Auditorium Theatre
Denver, CO

Day Cornish Prince Came Home, The
Genan P. Tardu
9-7-72
W.B.I.
19 Union Sq. W., N.Y.C.

Day in the Life Of, A
Michael Shurtleff
1-10-69
Playbox
94 St. Mark's Pl., N.Y.C.

Day in the Life of an Actor, A (with Hamlet as in Hamburger)
John Dooley
5-13-70
Triangle Theatre
316 E. 88th, N.Y.C.

Day in the Life of Just About Everyone, A
Earl Wilson, Jr.
3-9-71
Bijou Theatre
357 W. 48th, N.Y.C.

Day in the Life of the Great Scholar Wu, A, from the Berliner Ensemble
3-6-69
Cubiculo
414 W. 51st, N.Y.C.

Day in the Port Authority, A
Gloria Gonzalez
Nov., 1973
St. Peter's Gate
16 E. 56th,
N.Y.C.

Day of the Golden Calf, The
Richard Hilger
4-2-70
Ripon College Theatre
Ripon, WI

Day of the Lion, The
Joel Wyman
10-28-68
Euclid Theatre (Cleveland Playhouse)
Cleveland, OH

Day of the Painter, The
Tom Topor
9-14-72
West Side YWCA
8th Ave. & 51st, N.Y.C.

Day of the Serpent
12-18-71
Four Winds Theatre
American Museum of Natural History
N.Y.C.

Day of the Serpent
12-8-71
Four Winds Theatre at American Museum of Natural History
N.Y.C.

Day They Gave the Babies Away, The
David Gaard
12-12-71
New Old Reliable Theatre
231 E. 3rd, N.Y.C.

Day They Took Grandfather Away, The
Ralph Scholl
9-29-72
New Village Theatre
433 E. 6th, N.Y.C.

Day to Day (with After the Fashion Show and The Classroom)
Maryat Lee
8-19-68
Soul and Latin Theatre,
N.Y.C.

Day Tours (Burger Deluxe; Play Ball or The Last Voyage of the Stadium People; Cackle)
Bruce Serlen
1-6-73
Hunter College Playwrights Project
West Side YMCA
5 W. 63rd, N.Y.C.

Day Work (with Antony and Cleopatra)
Floyd Barbour
9-9-71
MIT Community Players
Cambridge, MA

Days of the Commune, The
Bertolt Brecht; Leonard Lehrman translator)
3-17-71
Harvard University
Cambridge, MA

De Sade Illustrated
See: Philosophy in the Bedroom. . .

Dead Dentist, The
Ilsa Gilbert
2-5-68
Old Reliable Theatre Tavern
231 E. 3rd, N.Y.C.

Dead Letters
Howard Koch
5-3-71
Library & Museum of the Performing Arts
111 Amsterdam, N.Y.C.

Dead Wind in Aulis
William M. Meyers
8-13-71
University of Rhode Island Art Center
Kingston, RI

Deadline!!
Jerome Bayer
10-22-68
Educational Alliance
197 E. Broadway, N.Y.C.

Deaf, The
Jim Yeiser
Feb., 1970
University of Missouri
Columbia, MO

Deafman Glance
Robert Wilson
Dec. 1970
University Theatre
University of Iowa
Iowa City,IA

Dealers' Choice
Marsha Sheiness
6-20-73
Playwrights' Horizons
Clark Center for the Performing Arts
West Side YWCA, 8th Ave. & 51st, N.Y.C.

Dear Antoine
Jean Anouilh
7-20-73
Harvard Summer School Repertory Theatre
Loeb Drama Center
Cambridge, MA

Dear Janet Rosenberg, Dear Mr. Kooning (with Jakey Fat Boy)
Stanley Eveling
4-5-70
Gramercy Arts Theatre
N.Y.C.

Dear Love
Jerome Kilty
Nov., 1969
Wellesley College
Wellesley, MA

Dear Miss Peabody
Warren Murray
6-30-71
Dorset Playhouse
Dorset, VT

Dear Nobody
Terry Belanger and Jane Marla Robbins
6-24-68
Actors' Playhouse
100 Seventh Ave. So., N.Y.C.

Dear Oscar
Caryl Gabrielle Yound (book & lyrics); Addy O. Fieger (music)
10-9-71
Madison Avenue Methodist Church
N.Y.C.

Dear World
Jerome Lawrence, Robert E. Lee (book); Jerry Herman (music & lyrics)
2-6-69
Mark Hellinger Theatre
N.Y.C.

Death
Larry Fineberg
6-19-73
New Plays Festival
WPA
333 Bowery, N.Y.C.

Death and Life of Sneaky Fitch, The
James Rosenberg
10-16-68
Wisconsin State Univ.
Platteville, WI

Death and Re-Erection of Dr. Franklin, The
Eduardo Garcia
8-21-69
New York Theatre Ensemble
2 E. 2nd, N.Y.C.

Death Be Not Proud
4-15-73
Key '73 Players
Queensborough Community College
Queens, NY

Death by Desire (with Last Night I Dreamt I Was Julie Bravado)
H. M. Koutoukas
11-26-70
Elgin Theatre
171 Eighth Ave., N.Y.C.

Death Knocks
Woody Allen
8-7-68
Berkshire Theatre Festival
Stockbridge, MA

Death Lists
Ed Bullins
10-1-70
Theatre Black
130 E. 7th, N.Y.C.

Death of a Playwright
Burton Snyder
9-17-70
Playbox
94 St. Mark's Pl., N.Y.C.

Death of Adolph Hitler?, The
12-4-73
Triangle Theatre
316 E. 88th, N.Y.C.

Death of Black Jesus, The
Alfred Brenner
6-8-72
Karamu House Theatre
Cleveland, OH

Death of Eagles, The
Harding Lemay
August, 1969
University of Minnesota
Minneapolis, MN

Death of J. K., The
W. Nicholas Knight
12-8-71
Cubiculo
414 W. 51st, N.Y.C.

Death of Little Marcus, The
Herman Johnson
1-27-73
Negro Ensemble Company
St. Mark's Playhouse
133 Second, N.Y.C.

Death of Lord Chatterly, The
Christopher Frank
7-31-73
Roundabout Theatre
307 W. 26th, N.Y.C.

Death of Solly's Warren, The
Stuart Oderman
4-2-71
Omni Theatre Club
145 W. 18th, N.Y.C.

Death of the Siamese Twins, The
Louis Phillips
10-16-73
WPA
333 Bowery, N.Y.C.

Death Star, The
James Salter
11-12-73
St. Clement's Church
423 W. 46th, N.Y.C.

Death to the Brother
Kenneth Harrow
9-8-72
Omni Theatre Club
145 W. 18th, N.Y.C.

Death Wish
T. Frank Gutswa
11-15-72
Cubiculo
414 W. 51st, N.Y.C.

Death Wish, The
Philip Ashley Green
9-12-68
Playwrights' Workshop Club
14 Waverly Pl., N.Y.C.

Decadent White Bitch, The
Stuart Koch
5-25-73
New York Theatre Ensemble
2 E. 2nd, N.Y.C.

Decades
8-1-72
Thomas Playhouse
South Casco, ME

Decline and Fall of Fagus, The Roman Camp, The
David Sawn
6-13-69
Dramarena Repertory Theatre
158 W. 55th, N.Y.C.

Decline and Fall of Newark, New Jersey, The
Robert E. Young
4-25-69
New York Theatre Ensemble
2 E. 2nd, N.Y.C.

Deedle, Deedle Dumpling, My Son God
Brian McKinney
Apr., 1968
Carleton College
Northfield, MN

Deer Kill, The
Murray Mednick
4-30-70
Theatre Genesis
10th St. & 2nd, N.Y.C.

Defender of the Faith (with Conversion of the Jews and Epstein)
Philip Roth; adapted by Larry Arrick
Aug., 1970
Yale Repertory Theatre
East Hampton, NY

Definitely Militant
Polack Projectionists
5-10-69
Eisner Lubin Auditorium
566 LaGuardia Pl., N.Y.C.

Delicate Champions
Stephen Varble
12-29-71
Forum Theatre
Lincoln Center
N.Y.C.

Democracy and Esther (staged reading)
Romulus Linney
12-7-68
H B Playwrights Foundation
124 Bank, N.Y.C.

Demon
Wilford Leach; John Braswell (music)
1-9-72
La Mama ETC
74 E. 4th, N.Y.C.

Demon Mirror, The
Donna Carlson
2-23-68
Thresholds
23 E. 20th, N.Y.C.

Demons, The
Joseph Gifford & Stan Thomas
4-12-71
Boston University
Boston, MA

Depot
Herbert D. Greggs
11-16-72
St. Peter's Church
346 W. 20th, N.Y.C.

Destination Ashes
6-11-70
Theatre Black
130 E. 7th, N.Y.C.

Destiny Rag
Marvin Slateroff
5-25-68
Anthony Mannino Drama Tree
182 Fifth, N.Y.C.

Destroyers, The
Richard Davidson
1-15-68
Old Reliable Theatre Tavern
231 E. 3rd, N.Y.C.

Destroying Angels
Eugene Moore
2-27-71
Alliance Theatre
Atlanta, GA

Deus Ex Machinist
Norman Dietz
7-31-68
Barn Playhouse
Stony Point, NY

Devil His Due, The
Paul G. Enger, Richard Foltz, John Strauss, Adam Zeichner
5-10-68
St. Peter's Gate
132 E. 54th, N.Y.C.

Devil's Instrument, The
W. O. Mitchell
8-20-72
National Arts Centre
Ottawa, CAN

Dialectic Dialogue in Double Time (with Close Call; Robbers' Nest; and Hogwash)
Barry Litvack
10-28-70
Playwrights' Unit
83 E. 4th, N.Y.C.

Dialogue Between Didey Warbucks and Mama Vaseline, A
Ilsa Gilbert
12-8-69
Old Reliable Theatre Tavern
231 E. 3rd, N.Y.C.

Diamond
Ilse Perl
1-7-69
University of Utah
Salt Lake City, UT

Diaries of Adam and Eve, The
Mark Twain; adapted by Josephine Nichols
10-27-72
Milwaukee Repertory Theatre
Milwaukee, WI

Did Ya See the Lone Ranger?
Sean Michael
10-13-72
New York Theatre Ensemble
2 E. 2nd, N.Y.C.

Didn't We Go to Different Schools Together?
Joyce E. Widoff, Gene Casey, and others
Spring, 1970
Teen Theatre Workshop
Los Angeles, CA

Die Kleinburgerhochzeit (The Wedding Feast)
Bertolt Brecht
11-24-70
Barbizon-Plaza Theatre
N.Y.C.

Die Kurve
Tankred Dorst
11-24-70
Barbizon-Plaza Theatre
N.Y.C.

Diferencias I-IV (with The Tomb of Henry James)
Piero Heliczer
2-4-71
Cinematheque
80 Wooster, N.Y.C.

Different Times
Michael Brown (book, music, lyrics)
5-1-72
ANTA Playhouse
245 W. 52nd, N.Y.C.

Difficult Borning, A
Sylvia Plath
10-16-72
Cubiculo
414 W. 51st, N.Y.C.

Difficult Life of Uncle Fatso, The
Peter Schumann
2-13-70
Bread & Puppet Theatre
Brooklyn, NY

Dilemma of a Ghost, The
Christina Ama Ata Aidoo
7-27-73
Harlem School of the Arts Community Theatre
651 St. Nicholas, N.Y.C.

Dinner at the Ambassador's
Michael O'Reilly
3-12-73
Library & Museum of the Performing Arts
111 Amsterdam, N.Y.C.

Dinner for One
Joseph Renard
2-10-71
WPA
333 Bowery, N.Y.C.

Dinner for Three
Herbert Kramer
5-22-73
Lambs Theatre
130 W. 44th, N.Y.C.

Dionysia (after The Frogs by Aristophanes)
Al Gordon and Ray Pentzell
2-21-69
University of Toledo
Toledo, OH

Dionysus in '69
6-6-68
Performing Garage
33 Wooster, N.Y.C.

Dionysus Wants You!
9-16-71
New York Shakespeare Festival
425 Lafayette, N.Y.C.

Dioseros
Roberto Rodriguez Suarez
11-12-71
New York Theatre of the Americas
321 E. 73rd, N.Y.C.

Director, The
Art Hyde
2-16-68
West Side Theatre
585 Columbus Ave., N.Y.C.

Dirtiest Show in Town, The
Tom Eyen
4-4-70
La Mama ETC
74 E. 4th, N.Y.C.

Dirty Evening, A
Various authors
12-5-69
Inner Theatre
356 Bowery, N.Y.C.

Dirty Ferdie Comes Clean
Michael Groob (book & lyrics); Martin Siegel (music)
8-8-70
Henry Street Settlement Playhouse
466 Grand, N.Y.C.

Dirty Low Voice of Sex on TV, The
Newton Berry
7-17-69
New York Theatre Ensemble
2 E. 2nd, N.Y.C.

Disappointment in Sahara
Joseph Renard
10-5-71
WPA
333 Bowery, N.Y.C.

Disaster Strikes the Home
Charles Dizenzo
July, 1968
Eugene O'Neill Memorial Theatre
Waterford, CT

Discover America
Jeannine O'Reilly
8-12-69
Old Reliable Theatre Tavern
231 E. 3rd, N.Y.C.

Discovery of America, The
Diane de Prima
9-28-72
Theatre for the New City
113 Jane, N.Y.C.

Discreet Indiscretion, The
See: A Place for Polly

Dishroom, The (with The Motel and The Cellar)
Paul DeJohn
7-17-72
Manhattan Theatre Club
321 E. 73rd, N.Y.C.

Disintegration
Julian Miller
1-7-70
Hunter College
N.Y.C.

Disintegration of James Cherry, The
Jeff Wanshel
7-8-69
Eugene O'Neill Memorial Theatre
Waterford, CT

Disney on Parade
8-3-71
Madison Square Garden
N.Y.C.

Distance Ahead, A
Richard Garrick
5-16-73
Courtyard Playhouse
137 W. 14th, N.Y.C.

Disturbance of Mirrors, A
Pat Staten
7-25-72
Eugene O'Neill Memorial Theatre
Waterford, CT

Divine Words
12-9-71
University of Massachusetts
Boston, MA

Division Street
Adapted by Charles Kakatsakis
4-7-72
Theatre of the Riverside Church
490 Riverside Dr., N.Y.C.

Division Street
Studs Terkel; Ed Hayman & Ronald Kieft (adaptor)
12-2-11-71
University of Michigan
Flint, MI

Divorce of Judy and Jane, The
Arthur Whitney
4-26-72
Bijou Theatre
359 W. 48th, N.Y.C.

Do Not Go Gentle
Robert Upton
5-3-68
Judson Poets' Theatre
55 Wash. Sq. So., N.Y.C.

Do You Dig Shit?
Jeff Hochhauser
9-25-70
New York Theatre Ensemble
2 E. 2nd, N.Y.C.

Do You Know the Muffin Man
Milton Ward
3-11-70
Mercer-Hansberry
240 Mercer St., N.Y.C.

Do You Like Me? Say You Like Me
See: Triune

Doctor B. S. Black
Carlton Molette II
11-10-69
Spelman College
Atlanta, GA

Doctor, Doctor (very loosely adapted from Moliere's "Le Medecin Malgre Lui")
Hank Diers (book); Gene Wright (music & lyrics)
4-14-71
University of Miami
Coral Gables, FL

Doctor Quackenbush's Traveling Medicine Show Presents the Rope-Dancer
John Grimaldi
4-27-71
New York Theatre of the Americas
427 W. 59th, N.Y.C.

Dog Days
Walter Corwin
2-15-72
WPA
333 Bowery, N.Y.C.

Dog Ran Away, The
Brother Jonathan Ringhamp
4-9-72
New Theatre
154 E. 54th, N.Y.C.

Dog School, The
John White
4-25-69
American Theatre Club
310 E. 42nd, N.Y.C.

Dogs
Serge Gerstein
7-9-70
Washington Sqaure Church
133 W. 4th, N.Y.C.

Doin' It (revue)
5-21-72
West Side YWCA
8th Ave. & 51st, N.Y.C.

Doll's House, A
Henrik Ibsen; Christopher Hampton (adaptor)
Playhouse Theatre
359 W. 48th, N.Y.C.

Dolores
Juan Torrent
5-8-71
Muestra Teatral de Nueva York
Community Center Theatre
270 W. 89th, N.Y.C.

Dolphin Dreamer, The
Betty Jean Lifton
5-5-73
Drifting Traffic
Chichicastenango
189 Second, N.Y.C.

Dom Juan (sic)
Moliere; adapted by Kenneth Cavander
5-14-70
Yale Repertory Theatre
New Haven, CT

Dominus Marlowe — A Play on Dr. Faustus
Michael Monroe
Fall, 1973
Odyssey Theatre
Los Angeles, CA

Don Juan
Moliere; adaptation by Stephen Porter
10-19-72
Annenberg Center
Philadelphia, PA

Don Juan or The Viper of Seville
James Duckett
2-14-69
Tufts University
Medford, MA

Don Quixote in the City
1-13-70
Caravan Theater
Cambridge, MA

Don't Bother Me, I Can't Cope
Vinnette Carroll (conception); Micki Grant (lyrics & music)
10-8-70
Library & Museum of the Performing Arts
111 Amsterdam, N.Y.C.

Don't End My Song Before I Sing
Neil Yarema
July, 1968
Eugene O'Neill Memorial Theatre
Waterford, CT

Don't Fail Your Lovin' Daddy, Lily Plum
Anastazia Little (book & lyrics); Peter Schlosser (music)
9-22-71
New York Shakespeare Festival Public Theatre
425 Lafayette, N.Y.C.

Don't Frighten the Horses
Harold J. Kennedy
7-16-73
Pocono Playhouse
Mountainhome, PA

Don't Get Married, We Need You!
Albert D'Annibale
2-26-73
Mercer Arts Center
240 Mercer, N.Y.C.

Don't Leave Me Alone
Wallace Johnson
5-13-71
Theatre Crossroads
23 E. 20th, N.Y.C.

Don't Let Death Get You Down
Frank Miazga
9-29-72
New York Theatre Ensemble
2 E. 2nd, N.Y.C.

Don't Let It Go To Your Head
J. E. Gaines
1-20-72
New Federal Theatre
Henry Street Settlement Playhouse
466 Grand, N.Y.C.

Don't Move the Victory Column
Julian Barry
8-25-72
American Shakespeare Festival
Stratford, CT

Don't Play Us Cheap!
Melvin Van Peebles
5-16-72
Ethel Barrymore Theatre
243 W. 47th, N.Y.C.

Don't Shoot, Mable, It's Your Husband
Jerome Kilty
2-2-68
American Conservatory Theatre
San Francisco, CA

Don't Tell Lily (with Funn)
Robert Somerfeld
1-5-70
Fortune Theatre
62 E. 4th, N.Y.C.

Don't Touch That Dial
8-15-72
White Barn Theatre
Irwin, PA

Don't Walk on the Clouds
Marvin Gordon (book); John Aman (music)
11-5-71
St. Clement's Church
423 W. 46th, N.Y.C.

Don't You Know It's Raining?
Richard France
7-19-70
Dallas Theater Center
Dallas, TX

Done to Death
Fred Carmichael
8-5-70
Caravan Theater
Dorset, VT

Donner
Robert Murray
2-28-70
Professional Theatre
University of California at Davis

Donner Party, The
George Keithley & Charles Goff
1-12-73
Eaglet Theatre
15th & H St., Sacramento, CA

Donovan
Shirley Guy
11-19-69
Stage Lights Theatrical Club
218 W. 48th, NY.C.

Donut Lady, The
Ed Kelleher
4-25-69
Melting Pot Repertory Theatre
18 Bleecker, N.Y.C.

Door Is Open, The (with Continued Departure)
Arthur Gregor
1-29-70
Cubiculo
414 W. 51st, N.Y.C.

Doorbell (with Waiting and Academy)
Mario Fratti
10-22-70
Cubiculo
414 W. 51st, N.Y.C.

Doors, Limes and Other Hazards of City Life
Benjamin Barber
11-9-72
Riverside Theatre Workshop
224 Waverly Pl., N.Y.C.

Dopo Una Giornata di Lavoro Chiunque Puo Essere Brutale
Franco Zardo
12-11-73
Teatro Italiano
Hunter College, N.Y.C.

Doppelganger, The
Friedrich Duerrenmatt
4-10-70
Free Stage
236 E. 47th, N.Y.C.

Dos Historias
Oswaldo Dragum
5-8-71
Muestra Teatral de Nueva York
Community Center Theatre
270 W. 89th, N.Y.C.

Dos Viejos Panicos (Two Panicked Old Folks)
Virgilio Pinera
11-6-69
Duo Theatre Workshop
522 E. 12th, N.Y.C.

Double Axe, The
Robinson Jeffers, adapted by Richard Kuss
2-8-69
American Theatre Club
49 W. 20th, N.Y.C.

Double Bed, The (staged reading)
Eve Merriam
2-7-69
Universalitst Theatre
4 W. 76th, N.Y.C.

Double Five Flower Grotto
Ching-Yeh
6-21-72
La Mama ETC
74 E. 4th, N.Y.C.

Double Fraktur "L", A
Benjamin Bradford
1-24-72
New Old Reliable Theatre Tavern
231 E. 3rd, N.Y.C.

Double Solitaire
Michael Smith
9-27-73
Changing Scene
Denver, CO

Doubledecker for Dublin
See: Non-Stop Daily and Invincible

Doublers, The
Betzie Parker
11-1-70
Dancers Studio Foundation,
34 E. 10th, N.Y.C.

Dough
Steve Pomerantz
4-19-68
Troupe Theatre
167 W. 21st, N.Y.C.

Dough (with Waiting for Clarence)
F. V. Hunt
6-20-68
Dramarena Repertory Theatre
158 W. 55th, N.Y.C.

Doves, The
Michael Hanks
4-18-69
Knowhere East Theatre
736 Broadway, N.Y.C

Dowager's Hump, The
Daniel Haben Clark
11-17-71
La Mama ETC
74 E. 4th, N.Y.C.

Down by the River Where Waterlilies Are Disfigured Every Day
Julie Bovasso
12-20-71
Trinity Square Repertory Company
Providence, RI

Down East Stories
Mike Dodge
7-16-72
Eugene O'Neill Memorial Theatre
Waterford, CT

Down on the Farm
John von Hartz
Apr., 1971
New Dramatists
424 W. 44th, N.Y.C.

Down the Morning Line
Ramon G. Estevez
2-7-69
New York Shakespeare Festival Public Theatre
425 Lafayette, N.Y.C.

Downtown Holy Lady, The (rewrite of The Bag Woman, 1970)
Joseph Caldwell
9-28-72
Greenwich Mews Theatre
141 W. 13th, N.Y.C.

Dozens, The
Laird Koenig
3-13-69
Booth Theatre
N.Y.C.

Dr. Denton's Secret
Joseph Gath
4-5-73
Lolly's Theatre Club
808 Lexington, N.Y.C.

Dr. Faustus
Christopher Marlowe; Bill Tchakirides (adaptor)
5-10-73
Tensive Theatre
Flushing, NY

Dr. Faustus Lights the Lights
Gertrude Stein
4-24-72
La Mama ETC
74 E. 4th, N.Y.C.

Dr. Hero
Israel Horovitz
3-19-73
Shade Company
230 Canal, N.Y.C.

Dr. Kheal
Maria Irene Fornes
5-3-68
Judson Poets' Theatre
55 Wash. Sq. So., N.Y.C.

Dr. Quackenbush's Traveling Medicine Show and Magic Circus
2-20-73
74 Below
74 Trinity Pl., N.Y.C.

Dr. Selavy's Magic Theatre (The Mental Cure)
Richard Foreman (conception); Stanley Silverman (music); Tom Hendry (lyrics)
8-2-72
Lenox Arts Center
Lenox, MA

Dr. Xerox (with To Express My Life. . .)
Isaac Goldemburg
10-3-68
Cafe Four
522 E. 12th, N.Y.C.

Dracula
Bram Stoker; Crane Johnson (adaptor)
9-10-73
Royal Playhouse
219 Second, N.Y.C.

Dracula
Frederick Gaines
3-31-72
Asolo Theatre
Sarasota, FL

Dracula: Sabbat
Leon Katz
Jan. (?), 1970
Purdue University
Lafayette, IN

Dragon Bag, The
Brian Lo Verde
9-25-68
Playwrights' Workshop Club
14 Waverly Pl., N.Y.C.

Dragon Lady's Revenge, The
8-14-71
San Francisco Mime Troupe
San Francisco, CA

Dragons in the Wall (with The Thrilling Life of a Circus Performer Will One Day Be Yours)
Teresa Marffie
6-7-72
West Side YWCA
8th Ave. & 51st, N.Y.C.

Dramatic Montage
Maureen Bereskin
5-12-72
Columbia University
N.Y.C.

Dream Arena, The
6-4-71
Common Ground Theatre
70 Grand, N.Y.C.

Dream Etude (with Pat)
Michael Roy Denbo
4-25-70
New Theatre Workshop
154 E. 54th, N.Y.C.

Dream Event, A
5-20-72
Manhattan Theatre Club
321 E. 73rd, N.Y.C.

Dream Killers, The
Greg Reardon
3-3-72
Playbox
94 St. Mark's Pl., N.Y.C.

Dream Menace No. 67 and The Pit (a sermon)
Gylan Kain
11-27-72
New Federal Theatre
240 E. 3rd, N.Y.C.

Dream of a Blacklisted Actor
Conrad Bromberg
12-15-69
Theatre de Lys
N.Y.C.

Dream on Monkey Mountain, The
Derek Walcott
8-1-69
Eugene O'Neill Memorial Theatre
Waterford, CT

Dream Out of Time, A
Irv Bauer
11-8-70
Promenade Theatre
Broadway at 76th, N.Y.C.

Dream Play, A
August Strindberg; Evert Sprinchorn (translator)
11-3-71
La Mama ETC
74 E. 4th, N.Y.C.

Dream Song, The (with Frio's Progress)
John Forster (book, lyrics, & music)
12-3-72
Mercer Arts Center
240 Mercer, N.Y.C.

Dream Tantras for Western Massachusetts
Richard Foreman (text); Stanley Silverman (music)
8-12-71
Lenox Arts Center
Lenox, MA

Dreams (an improvisational play for children)
9-2-72
Riverdale Theatre Company
Lincoln Center Plaza
N.Y.C.

Dreams for Sale (with The Winner)
Arthur Williams
5-2-70
Open Space
37 St. Mark's Pl., N.Y.C.

Dreams (or An Adaptation: Dream)
Bill Duke
1-30-72
Negro Ensemble Company
St. Mark's Playhouse
133 Second Ave., N.Y.C.

Dress, The
Tim Randall
March, 1971
Kansas City University
Manhattan, KS

Dreyfus on Devil's Island
Michael Almaz
9-20-73
Tel Aviv Drama Company
Hunter College Playhouse
695 Park, N.Y.C.

Drifting Traffic
7-5-72
Space
344 W. 36th, N.Y.C.

Drill
Derrick Woodham
Dec., 1971
Center for the New Performing Art
Iowa City, IA

Drinking at the Falls (with F. . .!)
Guy Gauthier
3-23-70
Old Reliable Theatre Tavern
231 E. 3rd, N.Y.C.

Drinking Party, The
Adapted by Paul Shyre from Plato's "Symposium"
3-19-69
Library & Museum of the Performing Arts
111 Amsterdam, N.Y.C.

Drive-In Movie
Dallas Mayr
10-13-72
New York Theatre Ensemble
2 E. 2nd, N.Y.C.

Drivel
James Oneal
3-23-72
Changing Scene
Denver, CO

Drumbeats in Georgia
Paul Green
6-30-73
Jekyll Island, GA

Drummer Boy, The
Jean Basile
1-17-68
Royal Alexandra Theatre
Toronto, CAN

Drunkard, The (musical)
W.H.S. Smith, adapted by Bro Herod; music & lyrics by Barry Manilow
4-13-70
13th Street Theatre
150 W. 13th, N.Y.C.

Drunken Sister, The
Thornton Wilder
6-28-70
Spencer Memorial Church
99 Clinton, Brooklyn Heights, NY

Dry Run
Victor Lipton
9-29-72
New York Theatre Ensemble
2 E. 2nd, N.Y.C.

Duck Variations, The (with Clark Street: or, Perversity in Chicago)
David Mamet
6-27-72
St. Nicholas Theatre
Boston Center for the Arts
Boston, MA

Dudder Love
Walter Jones
10-12-72
New Federal Theatre
Henry Street Settlement Playhouse
466 Grand, N.Y.C.

Dude
Gerome Ragni (book & lyrics); Galt MacDermot (music)
10-9-72
Broadway Theatre
1681 Broadway, N.Y.C.

Dudes
Martin Duberman
8-23-72
John Drew Playhouse
East Hampton, L.I., NY

Duet
Joanne Joseph
10-20-71
Cubiculo
414 W. 51st, N.Y.C.

Duet for Solo Voice
David Scott Milton
3-9-70
American Place Theatre
N.Y.C.

Duet in Black
Michael Carras
6-4-70
WPA
34 E. 4th, N.Y.C.

Duplex, The: A Black Love Story in Four Movements
Ed Bullins
5-22-70
New Lafayette Theatre,
137th St. & 7th, N.Y.C.

During the War
Alice Nicholai
Nov. 1971
Friday Theatre
N.Y.C.

During the War (with I Want To Be with you)
Michael Shurtleff
6-6-73
Friday Theatre
N.Y.C.

Dustman, The
Tom Hennen
4-28-70
University of Minnesota
Morris, MN

Duty Bound
Allan Sloane
8-6-73
Loeb Student Center
New York Univ., N.Y.C.

Dwight Night (one-man revue)
Dwight Marfield
5-22-69
Melting Pot Theatre
18 Bleecker, N.Y.C.

Dybbuk, The
S. Ansky; John Hirsch (adaptor)
11-23-73
Manitoba Theatre Centre
Winnipeg, Manitoba, CAN

Dynel
Robert Patrick
12-16-68
Old Reliable Theatre Tavern
231 E. 3rd, N.Y.C.

Dyskolos
Menander; Guy M. Davenport (translator)
12-14-71
Jackson State College
Jackson, MS

E

E. L. Gruber
10-2-69
Stage Lights Theatrical Club
218 W. 48th, N.Y.C.

E. S. Peep
Leon Wittack
2-7-68
Playbox
94 St. Mark's Pl., N.Y.C.

Each His Own Tailcoat
Dario Fo
12-4-69
Cubiculo
414 W. 51st, N.Y.C.

Eagle
Jeffrey Selby
11-17-69
Old Reliable Theatre Tavern
231 E. 3rd, N.Y.C.

Eagle and the Serpent, The (with The Swallow)
Ernesto Fuentes
3-26-70
Duo Theatre Workshop
522 E. 12th, N.Y.C.

Earl of Ruston
C. C. & Ragan Courtney (book & lyrics); Peter Link (music)
5-5-71
Billy Rose Theatre
208 W. 41st, N.Y.C.

Early Morning
Edward Bond
11-18-70
La Mama ETC
74 E. 4th, N.Y.C.

Earth and Stars
Randolph Edmonds
Winter, 1971
Tennessee State University
Nashville, TN

Earth Must Be a Nice Planet the People Who Live Here Look So Happy, The
Robert Patrick
8-25-69
Old Reliable Theatre Tavern
231 E. 3rd, N.Y.C.

Earth Song
3-26-71
Boston College
Chestnut Hill, MA

Earthlight
Earthlight Theater
10-27-70
Gracie Square Theatre
334 E. 79th, N.Y.C.

Easiest Way, The (reading)
Eugene Walter
7-13-70
Opposites Company
39 Grove, N.Y.C.

East Side Story
5-18-72
United Palace Auditorium
175th & Broadway, N.Y.C.

East Side Story, The
David Kin
2-4-68
Educational Alliance
197 E. Broadway, N.Y.C.

Easter Egg, The
James Reaney
4-23-70
National Arts Centre
Ottawa, CAN

Easter Song for Jeanne Dixon, An
Christopher Mathewson
1-12-73
New York Theatre Ensemble
2 E. 2nd, N.Y.C.

Eastside-Westside
Treva Silverman
10-6-72
Playbox
94 St. Mark's Pl., N.Y.C.

Eat Cake
Jean–Claude van Itallie
8-19-71
Changing Scene
Denver, CO

Echoes
Lonny Chapman
10-12-73
Other Theatre at the Children's Mansion
351 Riverside Dr., N.Y.C.

Echoes
N. Richard Nash
7-6-72
University of Minnesota
Minneapolis, MN

Echoes from Kahlil Gibran (one-woman show)
Adapted by Kathryn Loder
3-8-72
Cubiculo
414 W. 51st, N.Y.C.

Eclectic Bunch, The
Cyril Simon
11-1-70
Grand Central YMCA
236 E. 47th, N.Y.C.

Eclipse
Harvey Flaxman
3-7-73
Dreyfuss College Theatre
Fairleigh Dickinson University
Madison, NJ

Eddie and Susanna in Love
Leonard Melfi
5-16-73
New York Theatre Strategy
Manhattan Theatre Club
321 E. 73rd., N.Y.C.

Edgar Allan Poe, His Stories and Poems
Philip Hanson (adaptor)
4-7-71
Library & Museum of the Performing Arts
111 Amsterdam, N.Y.C.

Edge of the Jungle
Philip Freund
4-2-73
New York Shakespeare Festival Public Theatre
425 Lafayette, N.Y.C.

Edith Stein
Arthur Giron
10-23-69
Arena Stage
Washington, DC

Education of Hyman Kaplan, The
Benjamin Zarin, Paul Nassau and Oscar Brand
3-1-68
Erlanger Theatre
Philadelphia, PA

Edward G., Like the Film Star
John Harvey Flint
December, 1973
Folger Theatre
Washington, DC

Edward the Second
Bertolt Brecht
4-22-71
Westbeth Cabaret
155 Bank, N.Y.C.

Eenie Meenie Minie Moe
Robert Schroeder
1-29-70
East River Players
132 E. 54th, N.Y.C.

El Asno
Jose Ruibal
9-22-72
Minor Latham Playhouse
Barnard College
N.Y.C.

El Auto de las Grandes Lluvias
Juan del Encina
12-15-69
Minor Latham Playhouse
Barnard College
N.Y.C.

Elagaralus
Martin Duberman
10-31-73
New Dramatists
424 W. 44th, N.Y.C.

Election Night
The Actors Company
3-11-72
Greenwich Mews Theatre
141 W. 13th, N.Y.C.

Electra
Euripides; new translation by Richard Gottlieb
3-19-71
Players Theatre of Greater Miami
Miami, FL

Electra Garrigo
Virgilio Pinera
9-22-73
New York Latin American Theatre Festival Spanish Theatre Repertory
Gramercy Arts Theatre
N.Y.C.

Electric Ice
Tom Sydorick
9-26-69
Playwrights' Unit
83 E. 4th, N.Y.C.

Electronic Nigger and Others, The (later retitled Three Plays By Ed Bullins)
Ed Bullins
2-29-68
American Place Theatre
N.Y.C.

Eleganterooneymismusissimus
Michael Goldman
4-29-70
Cubiculo
414 W. 51st, N.Y.C.

Elegy to a Down Queen
Leslie Lee
3-11-70
La Mama ETC
74 E. 4th, N.Y.C.

Elementary Logic
Robert Tieman
10-1-68
Nucleus Repertory Theatre
261 W. 54th, N.Y.C.

Elements, The
Hal Ackerman
2-5-70
Cubiculo
414 W. 51st, N.Y.C.

Elephant in the House, The
Berrilla Kerr
2-20-72
Circle Theatre Company
2307 Broadway, N.Y.C.

Elephants and People
Carla Joseph
11-5-71
New York Theatre Ensemble
2 E. 2nd, N.Y.C.

Elevator, The
Nelly Vivas
11-9-68
Cafe Four
522 E. 12th, N.Y.C.

Eleven Thousand Pieces of Jade
Bruce Harrison
9-20-68
Dramarena Repertory Theatre
158 W. 55th, N.Y.C.

Eleventh Dynasty, The
Wendell Metzger
6-20-69
Judson Poets' Theatre
55 Wash. Sq. So., N.Y.C.

Eli and Emily
Myron Levoy
5-16-69
New York Theatre Ensemble
2 E. 2nd, N.Y.C.

Eli Siegel's "Somewhere This" and Other Poems
Eli Siegel
8-30-69
Terrain Gallery
39 Grove, N.Y.C.

Eli, The Fanatic (part of Unlikely Heroes)
Philip Roth, adapted by Larry Arrick
10-26-71
Plymouth Theatre
N.Y.C.

Elinor Glyn Liquid Memorial Love Regatta, The
June Havoc (book & lyrics); Mel Malvin (music)
Feb., 1971
Repertory Theatre of New Orleans
New Orleans, LA

Elizabeth
Philip Lam
8-31-73
13th Street Theatre
50 W. 13th, N.Y.C.

Elizabeth I
Paul Foster
4-5-72
Lyceum Theatre
N.Y.C.

Elizabethan Talking Blues, The
7-1-72
Loft Theatre
Dowling College
Oakdale, NY

Elm Seed Theatre (puppet/people vaudeville)
Feb., 1973
Old Cambridge Baptist Church
Cambridge, MA

Elma Lewis School of the Arts
See also: National Center of Afro-American Artists

Elton
Lou Ferguson
3-23-73
Players' Workshop Club
83 E. 4th, N.Y.C.

Emanons
Stanley Nelson
4-17-68
Playwrights' Workshop Club
14 Waverly Pl., NY

Emerald Slippers, The
Jose Alcarez
9-1-70
Gramercy Arts Theatre
N.Y.C.

Emergency Brake, The
Nomi Rubel
4-20-69
Orient Expresso Coffee House
205 E. 81st, N.Y.C.

Emil's Leap
Thomas Terefenko
9-3-69
Old Reliable Theatre Tavern
231 E. 3rd, N.Y.C.

Emilia
Peter Schumann
3-2-71
Bread & Puppet Theatre
New York Shakespeare Public Theatre
425 Lafayette, N.Y.C.

Emily
Shirley Guy
Feb., 1970
Playbox
94 St. Mark's Pl., N.Y.C.

Emperor Henry IV
Luigi Pirandello; Stephen Rich (adaptor)
1-8-73
Royal Alexandra Theatre
Toronto, Ontario, CAN

Empire Builders, The
Boris Vian, translated by Simon Watson Taylor
10-1-68
Astor Place Theatre
434 Lafayette, N.Y.C.

Empire State
Tom LaBar
1-23-68
Caffee Cino
31 Cornelia, N.Y.C.

Empress Reflections, The
J. B. Rise
9-22-72
Playbox
94 St. Mark's Pl., N.Y.C.

Empty Bandwagon, The
Robert Nichols
6-30-69
Candlewood Theatre
New Fairfield, CT

En Pieces Detachees
Michel Trembay; Allan Van Meer (translator)
1-17-73
Manitoba Theatre Centre
Winnipeg, Manitoba, CAN

Enact
Linda Mussman
1-13-72
Manhattan Theatre Club
321 E. 73rd, N.Y.C.

Enchanted Miracle, A
12-7-73
Theatre for the New City
113 Jane, N.Y.C.

Enchanted (with Charley and The Party)
Slawomir Mrozek
8-6-68
Boothbay Playhouse
ME

Enclave, The
Arthur Laurents
2-21-73
Washington Theatre Club
Washington, DC

Encounter in a Beach Cottage
John Shinn
2-11-72
Playbox
94 St. Mark's Pl., N.Y.C.

Encounters
Paul Zakrzewski
8-13-69
Berkshire Theatre Festival
Stockbridge, MA

End Is Here, Baby, The ("hip" adaptation of Everyman)
Geraldine Fitzgerald & Brother Jonathan Ringhamp
8-10-68
Coney Island Houses
Boardwalk & W. 30th, Coney Island, NY

End of All Things Natural, The
Gerald Zoffer
9-11-69
Village South Theatre
15 Vandam, N.Y.C.

End of the Beginning, The
Paul Carter Harrison
4-19-68
St. Peter's Church
346 W. 20th, N.Y.C.

End of the Road
Daniel Morris
4-21-71
Dobama Theatre
Cleveland, OH

End of the World. . ., The
Keith Neilson
12-11-69
WPA
34 E. 4th, N.Y.C.

End (with The Pedestal)
Joseph Maher
7-28-72
American Shakespeare Festival
Stratford, CT

Endecott and the Red Cross
Robert Lowell
4-18-68
American Place Theatre
N.Y.C.

Enemies
Maxim Gorki
2-24-72
Yale University
New Haven, CT

Enemies
Maxim Gorky; translation by J. Kitty
11-9-72
Vivian Beaumont Theatre
Lincoln Center
N.Y.C.

Enemy Is Dead, The
Don Peterson
8-13-70
Berkshire Theatre Festival
Stockbridge, MA

Enemy of the People, An
Henrik Ibsen; translation by David Scanlan
2-28-69
Repertory Theatre of New Orleans
New Orleans, LA

Enemy of the People, An
Henrik Ibsen, New version by Betty Jane Wylie
11-20-70
St. Lawrence Centre
Toronto, Ontario, CAN

Engagement Baby, The
Stanley Shapiro
5-11-70
Colonial Theatre
Boston, MA

Enigma
John Patrick
6-12-73
Baldwin-Wallace College
Berea, OH

Enjoyables, The (musical variety show)
8-4-72
Playwrights' Workshop Club
14 Waverly Pl., N.Y.C.

Entanglements
12-27-73
Bard Theatre of Drama & Dance Group
Cubiculo
414 W. 51st, N.Y.C.

Enter a Free Man
Tom Stoppard
8-4-70
Olney Theatre
Olney, MD

Enter the Queen
Richard Ouzounian
1969
Fordham University
N.Y.C.

Entertainment, The
Raymond Platt
12-1-72
Stagelights II
125 W. 22nd, N.Y.C.

Entre-Nous
Michael Robert David
3-27-69
Playbox
94 St. Mark's Pl., N.Y.C.

Entrepreneurs of Avenue B, The (with The Last Act)
Jack Gilhooley
4-22-71
13th Street Theatre
50 W. 13th, N.Y.C.

Epic of Buster Friend, The
Richard Lenz
Summer, 1973
New Playwrights Series
American Shakespeare Festival
Stratford, CT

Epilogue
Kit Jones
2-9-68
Cooper Square Arts Theatre
35 Cooper Sq., N.Y.C.

Episode in the Life of an Author (with The Orchestra)
Jean Anouilh
9-16-69
Studio Arena Theatre
Buffalo, NY

Episodios de la Vida Intima
Ramon del Valle-Inclan; H. Dume (adaptor)
4-20-73
Dume Spanish Theatre
437 W. 46th, N.Y.C.

Epistle, An
Peter Grossman
4-12-71
Old Reliable Theatre Tavern
231 E. 3rd, N.Y.C.

Epstein (with Conversion of the Jews and Defender of the Faith)
Philip Roth, adapted by Larry Arrick
Aug., 1970
Yale Repertory Theatre
East Hampton, NY

Equinox
W. Lynn Ostergaard
5-16-72
Charles Camsell Hall
Ottawa, CAN

Equinox: A Fable of Leaves
Stephen Varble; Geoff Hendricks
5-6-72
Supernova
451 W. Broadway, N.Y.C.

Ergo
Jacob Lind
2-20-68
New York Shakespeare Festival Public Theatre
425 Lafayette, N.Y.C.

Eris
Lee Falk
11-7-70
American Theatre Company
106 E. 14th, N.Y.C.

Eros and Psyche (dance drama)
John Argue
4-25-72
Chelsea Theatre Center
30 Lafayette, Brooklyn, NY

Eros' Error
Fred Isler
10-15-70
Second Group Theatre
McBurney YMCA
215 W. 23, N.Y.C.

Erotic Tale of a Tall Girl, The
Frank Spierling
10-14-71
St. Clement's Church
423 W. 46th, N.Y.C.

Erpingham Camp, The
See: Crimes of Passion

Esa Cancion de Mierda
A. Adellach
5-14-71
Potbelly Theatre Workshop
40 W. 18th, N.Y.C.

Escape from Babylon
J. Ashton Brathwaite
7-6-73
P.S. 305
Brooklyn, NY

Escuadra Hacia La Muerte (The Condemned Squad)
Alfonso Sastre
2-3-73
Nuestro Teatro
Greenwich Mews Theatre
141 W. 13th, N.Y.C.

Esta Noche, Juntos, Amadonos Tanto
Maruxa Vilalta
11-10-73
New York Latin American Theater Festival
Spanish Theatre Repertory
Gramercy Arts Theatre
137 E. 27th, N.Y.C.

Estaban (rock musical based on Macbeth)
Brother Jonathan Ringhamp & Geraldine Fitzgerald
8-16-69
Wollman Rink
Prospect Park
Brooklyn, NY

Estaeban
8-23-71
Careers in the Arts Company
Lincoln Center Plaza
N.Y.C.

Et Cetera '68
4-26-68
Center Stage
Baltimore, MD

Eté (Summer)
Romain Weingarten; Sheppard Strudwick III & Margaret Baker (translators)
4-9-73
Cherry Lane Theatre
38 Commerce, N.Y.C.

Etched in Granite
Ivan Lawrence Becker
2-16-70
Riverside Plaza Hotel Theatre
253 W. 73rd, N.Y.C.

Ethiopia
Arthur Arent
11-20-68
Lincoln University
PA

Etimero III
Mateo P. Picornell
11-2-73
Intar Theatre
508 W. 53rd, N.Y.C.

Eunuchs of the Forbidden City
Charles Ludlam
4-5-72
Theatre for the New City
151 Bank, N.Y.C.

Eurynomous
Christopher Matthewson
5-25-70
Old Reliable Theatre Tavern
231 E. 3rd, N.Y.C.

Eux, ou La Prise de Pouvoir
Eduardo Manet
10-5-73
Theatre du Nouveau Monde
Montreal, Quebec, CAN

Evanescent Revue, An
Joel Miller
1-7-71
National Arts Centre
Ottawa, CAN

Eve and Adam
Joan Durant
12-10-71
Playbox
94 St. Mark's Pl., N.Y.C.

Even Steven
David Rogers
10-6-70
Playhouse on the Mall
Paramus, NJ

Evening, An
Jasper Oddo
10-22-68
Courtyard Playhouse
424 W. 45th, N.Y.C.

Evening and the Morning, The
Norman Dietz
3-10-69
St. Peter's Gate
132 E. 54th, N.Y.C.

Evening for Merlin Finch, An
Charles Dizenzo
6-3-68
New Dramatists Workshop
83 E. 4th, N.Y.C.

Evening of Broadway Hits, An
10-29-70
Theatre Royal
Las Vegas, NV

Evening of Bull with Peter Bull, An
11-19-73
Playhouse on the Mall
Paramus, NJ

Evening of Dostoyevsky, An
Adapted by Owen Hollander
9-3-69
Universalist Theatre
4 W. 76th, N.Y.C.

Evening of Emily Dickinson, An
Mildred Dunnock
9-28-72
Loeb Drama Center
Cambridge, MA

Evening of Identity, An (Gettin' It Together; It's Colored. It's Negro; Black Cycle)
5-13-71
Elma Lewis School of Fine Arts
Roxbury, MA

Evening of One Acts, An
John V. McKenna
July, 1971
Purdue University Theatre
Lafayette, IN

Evening of Originals, An
6-23-72
Heights Players
Brooklyn Heights, NY

Evening of Shaw, An
Bramwell Fletcher
8-26-73
John Drew Theatre
East Hampton, Long Island, NY

Evening of Thurber, An
Peter Turgeon
8-19-73
John Drew Theatre
East Hampton, Long Island, NY

Evening Raga (with Noctambule)
Josef Bush
6-14-71
Old Reliable Theatre Tavern
231 E. 3rd, N.Y.C.

Evening with Anne Bancroft, An
7-12-70
Berkshire Theatre Festival
Stockbridge, MA

Evening with Claire Bloom, An
8-3-70
Berkshire Theatre Festival
Stockbridge, MA

Evening with Dead Essex, An
Adrienne Kennedy
11-28-73
American Place Theatre
N.Y.C.

Evening with Eric Porter, An
5-26-73
Concord, MA

Evening with Glory Van Scott, An
11-4-71
Library & Museum of the Performing Arts
111 Amsterdam, N.Y.C.

Evening with James Agee, An
David McDowell
2-10-69
Theatre de Lys
N.Y.C.

Evening with Marvin Cohen, An
4-6-72
Cubiculo
414 W. 51st, N.Y.C.

Evening with Max Morath at the Turn of the Century, An
Max Morath
2-17-69
Jan Hus Auditorium
351 E. 74th, N.Y.C.

Evening with Max Roach, An
1-21-72
Negro Ensemble Company
St. Mark's Playhouse
133 Second, N.Y.C.

Evening with Richard Nixon and . . ., An
Gore Vidal
4-30-72
Shubert Theatre
N.Y.C.

Evening with Richard Ward, An
4-9-72
Center Stage
Baltimore, MD

Evening with Sweeney, An
T. S. Eliot, adapted by Eva Vizy
Summer, 1969
New Haven Free Theatre
New Haven, CT

Evening with the Poet-Senator, An
Leslie Weiner
3-21-73
Playhouse II
357 W. 48th, N.Y.C.

Events While Guarding the Bofors Gun
John McGrath
1-16-70
Playhouse Theatre Company
Vancouver, B.C., CAN

Ever After (with The Ploy)
Wendy Levine
4-9-70
St. Peter's Church
346 W. 20th, N.Y.C.

Everlasting Sorrow, The
Richard Helfer
7-6-71
Brooklyn College
Brooklyn, NY

Every Bridge Has a Splash
Alexander Panas
8-20-70
New York Theatre Ensemble
2 E. 2nd, N.Y.C.

Every Buzzard's Son (with The Absolute Zero)
James Ty Hargrove
6-3-68
13th Street Theatre
50 W. 13th, N.Y.C.

Everybody Knows My Business
Edward & Yolanda Gallardo
2-22-73
Manhattan Theatre Club
321 E. 73rd, N.Y.C.

Everybody's Looking for Something
Christophe Pierre & Lyle Thomas
7-19-72
Manhattan Theatre Club
321 E. 73rd, N.Y.C.

Everyman
Frederick Franck
1-11-73
Root Theatre Collective
Trinity Church
74 Trinity Pl., N.Y.C.

Everyman and the Cannon
Marvin Norinsky
9-5-68
Knowhere East Theatre Club
736 Broadway, N.Y.C.

Everyman II
8-18-68
Agassiz Theatre
Radcliff College
Cambridge, MA

Everyman (musical)
Thomas Babe, Timothy Mayer, Peter Ivers
8-15-68
Agassiz Theatre
Radcliff College
Cambridge, MA

Everything for Anybody (an amatorio in 12 parts)
Conceived by Louisa Rose & John Braswell
9-9-72
La Mama ETC
74 E. 4th, N.Y.C.

Everything's Fine
Stephen Mitchell (book & lyrics); Allen Matlick (music)
5-11-73
Little Recital Hall
Gershwin Theatre
Brooklyn College, Brooklyn, NY

Everything You Always Wanted To Know About Cole Porter (revue)
7-3-72
Falmouth Playhouse
Falmouth, MA

Evidence
Richard Foreman
4-21-72
Theatre for the New City
151 Bank, N.Y.C.

Evil That Men Do, The
Ed Jacobs
9-29-70
Bouwerie Lane Theatre
330 Bowery, N.Y.C.

Evolution
11-27-70
Bed-Stuy Theatre
1407 Bedford Ave., Brooklyn, NY

Evolution
American Mime Theatre; Tod Dockstader & James Reichert (music)
2-1-73
Town Hall
123 W. 43rd, N.Y.C.

Except for Susie Finkel
Joe Manchester & Gary Belkin
8-6-68
Playhouse on the Mall
Paramus, NJ

Exchanges
Walter Tyszka
2-16-73
New York Theatre Ensemble
2 E. 2nd, N.Y.C.

Executioners, The
Charles Kespert
7-19-72
Eugene O'Neill Memorial Theatre
Waterford, CT

Exejente, El
Stanley Nelson
8-13-71
Playbox
94 St. Mark's Pl., N.Y.C.

Exercise in Justice, An, or The Urge to Kill
Tristan Hewlitt
2-5-70
Inner Theatre
356 Bowery, N.Y.C.

Exercise, The
Lewis John Carlino
4-24-68
Golden Theatre
N.Y.C.

Exercises on Shakespeare
Warsaw Theatre Academy
April, 1972
American College Theatre Festival
Washington, DC

Ex-Expatriate, The
Donna deMatteo
July, 1972
H B Playwrights Foundation
124 Bank, N.Y.C.

Exhibition
Frank Spierling
6-15-68
Loft Workshop
152 Bleecker, N.Y.C.

Exile
Richard Sharp
3-19-71
Changing Scene
Denver, CO

Exit the Body
Fred Carmichael
8-8-71
Dorset Playhouse
Dorset, VT

Exit The King
Eugene Ionesco
1-9-68
Lyceum Theatre
N.Y.C.

Experience
Communicatus
7-10-70
Circle Theatre Company
2307 Broadway, N.Y.C.

Experience in Reality, An
8-23-72
Bed-Stuy Street Academy
Lincoln Center Plaza
N.Y.C.

Experiment Number One
Fourth Wall Demolition Company
3-19-71
Theatre Crossroads
23 E. 20th, N.Y.C.

Experimental Death Unit ■ (with Junkies Are Full of Sh . . .)
Imamu Amiri Baraka (LeRoi Jones)
9-18-72
Afro-American Studio
415 W. 12th, N.Y.C.

Experimental Drama
July, 1972
Good Shepherd Church
240 E. 31st, N.Y.C.

Experimental Leader, The
Paul Carter Harrison
Spring, 1968
St. Peter's Church
346 W. 20th, N.Y.C.

Experiments in Lyric Theatre
Masterworks Laboratory Theatre
4-6-70
Theatre-in-the-Courthouse
49 E. 2nd, N.Y.C.

Explorations
Donald Swann & Sydney Carter
11-4-70
Theatre of the Riverside Church
490 Riverside Dr., N.Y.C.

Exploratory Operation, An
Jonathan Levy
3-9-68
Elias A. Cohen Theatre
100th St. & West End Ave., N.Y.C.

Expressway, The
Robert Nichols
10-26-68
New York Shakespeare Festival Public Theatre
425 Lafayette, N.Y.C.

Extravaganza for Two Kings (musical fantasy)
Thomas Darien & Edward Six
12-7-72
Airline Theatre Wing
30 E. 31st, N.Y.C.

Eye Ball Tomb, The (with The Best Lookin' Man. . .)
Raymond Schanze
2-19-69
La Mama ETC
9 St. Mark's Pl., N.Y.C.

Eye in New York
Tom Eyen
11-9-69
La Mama ETC
74 E. 4th, N.Y.C.

Eyes of Chalk
Tone Brulin; adapted by David Villaire
6-7-72
St. Clement's Church
423 W. 46th, N.Y.C.

F

F. Jasmine Addams
Carson McCullers, G. Wood, Theodore Mann (book); G. Wood (lyrics & music)
10-27-71
Circle in the Square
159 Bleecker, N.Y.C.

F. . .! (with Drinking at the Falls)
Guy Gauthier
3-23-70
Old Reliable Theatre Tavern
231 E. 3rd, N.Y.C.

Fables Here and There
October, 1971
Tyrone Guthrie Theatre
Minneapolis, MN

Fabulous Miss Marie, The
Ed Bullins
3-3-71
New Lafayette Theatre
137th & 7th, N.Y.C.

Facades (The Price of Onions; Bach Is Always on Sundays; and Hotel de Dream)
Joe Caruso, Jr.
6-11-70
Cubiculo
414 W. 51st, N.Y.C.

Face Lift, The (improvisation company)
8-9-72
Manhattan Theatre Club
321 E. 73rd, N.Y.C.

Face Worth Saving, A (with The Assassination of M.L.K. and You May Well Be the Man. . .)
Frank Hogan
5-24-68
Knowhere East Theatre
736 Broadway, N.Y.C.

Faces
Norman Kline
5-28-68
Toronto Workshop Productions
Toronto, CAN

Fag!!!
William Kushner
6-18-71
New York Theatre Ensemble
2 E. 2nd, N.Y.C.

Faggot, The (an oratorio)
Al Carmines
4-13-73
Judson Poets' Theatre
55 Wash. Sq. So., N.Y.C.

Failed Purpose (with Bad News)
Donald Kvares
6-21-71
Old Reliable Theatre Tavern
231 E. 3rd, N.Y.C.

Fair and Warmer (musical)
8-13-73
Hampton Playhouse
Hampton, NH

Fair Exchange (with Pursuit)
Edmond Reynolds
11-11-69
Loyola University
Los Angeles, CA

Fairy Godmother
Maree Short (Madolin Cervantes)
2-8-71
Library & Museum of the Performing Arts
111 Amsterdam, N.Y.C.

Faldum
Herman Hesse
5-12-73
Chichicastenango
189 Second, N.Y.C.

Fall and Redemption of Man, The
John Brown
7-12-72
Tufts Summer Theatre
Medford, MA

Fall and Rise of Parity, The (shadow play)
Ed Baynard
4-2-71
98 Greene St. Loft
98 Greene St., N.Y.C.

Fall of Atlantis, The
Ed Wode
8-16-68
Cooper Square Arts Theatre
35 Cooper Sq., N.Y.C.

Fall River Ruins (with The Happiness Train and Pay Attention to the Ravel)
Donald Kvares
11-5-70
Theatre Crossroads
23 E. 20th, N.Y.C.

False Alarm
Virgilio Pinera
9-18-69
Duo Theatre Workshop
522 E. 12th, N.Y.C.

False Confessions
Pierre de Marivaux; W. S. Merwin (translator)
4-1-71
Master Theatre
103rd St. & Riverside Dr., N.Y.C.

Fame and the Reason Why
Arthur Miller
12-13-69
New Theatre Workshop
154 E. 54th, N.Y.C.

Familia de Justo Malgenio, La
Isabel Cuchi Coll
12-16-70
New York Theater of the Americas
427 W. 59th, N.Y.C.

Family Continues, The (with Ikke, Ikke, Nye, Nye, Nye, and The Great Nebula in Orion)
Lanford Wilson
5-21-72
Circle Theatre Company
2307 Broadway, N.Y.C.

Family, Family
12-14-73
Westbeth Playwrights Feminist Collective
155 Bank, N.Y.C.

Family Joke, The
David Starkweather
5-16-73
New York Theatre Strategy
Manhattan Theatre Club
321 E. 73rd, N.Y.C.

Family Meeting
William Wellington Mackey
1-28-72
La Mama ETC
74 E. 4th, N.Y.C.

Family, The (improvisational comedy group)
3-20-72
St. Peter's Gate
132 E. 54th, N.Y.C.

Family, The (with The Chinese Friend)
Mario Fratti
4-19-72
Playwrights' Workshop Club
14 Waverly Pl., N.Y.C.

Famous River Bottom Strategy of Etoe County, The (with The Transcontinental Redemption . . .)
John Snyder
4-10-70
Hudson Guild Theatre
441 W. 26th, N.Y.C.

Fan Club, The
Robert Hogan
11-30-72
American Theatre Company
106 E. 14th, N.Y.C.

Fanfare for a Revolution
Archie Shepp
2-3-72
Brooklyn College
Brooklyn, NY

Fanny Hill
4-14-71
Fortune Theatre
62 E. 4th, N.Y.C.

Fantasm
Maurice Peterson
11-8-72
Columbia University
N.Y.C.

Fantasy
Tobi Lewis
1-7-71
Playbox
94 St. Mark's Pl., N.Y.C.

Fantasy at the Kitchen
6-18-73
Mercer Arts Center
240 Mercer, N.Y.C.

Far from the Sea — Far from the Summer
Israel Eliraz
3-22-69
Basement Coffee House
155 E. 22nd, N.Y.C.

Farewell Party
Steve Fischer & Curtis Roberts
6-23-70
Playhouse on the Mall
Paramus, NJ

Farfarini's Dying
Stan Cornyn
2-5-73
St. Peter's Gate
132 E. 54th, N.Y.C.

Farm
Franklin Miller & Wayne Rindels
Dec., 1971
Center for the New Performing Art
Iowa City, IA

Farm Bill, The (with Galile)
Susan Dworkin
5-7-70
Triangle Theatre
316 E. 88th, N.Y.C.

Farmalla
10-22-71
Dume Grupo Estudio
437 W. 46th, N.Y.C.

Fashion
Anna Cora Mowatt (book); Richard Bimonte (book); James N. Wise (music)
5-2-73
Little Theatre
College of Wooster
Wooster, OH

Fashion (musical)
Anna Cora Mowatt (book); Anthony Stimac (book); Stephen Brown (lyrics); Don Pippin (music)
12-6-73
Greenwich Mews Theatre
141 W. 13th, N.Y.C.

Fatal Beauty
John Gruen
5-7-68
Loft Workshop
152 Bleecker, N.Y.C.

Father (Hagar and Ishmael section)
Paul Goodman
5-10-71
Theatre for Ideas Studio Theatre
112 W. 21st, N.Y.C.

Father's Day
Oliver Hailey
3-16-71
Golden Theatre
N.Y.C.

Father, The
August Strindberg; Samy Schmuel (adaptor)
10-19-73
Primitive Theatre
33 Howard, N.Y.C.

Fat-Lover, The
Charles Kerbs
8-27-72
New York Trust Company
The Goose and Gherkin
251 E. 50th, N.Y.C.

Fatty at the Boilers
R. Cary Bynum
6-13-69
First Unitarian Church
Brooklyn, NY

Fault, The
Kenneth Pressman
5-20-70
Playwright's Unit
83 E. 4th, N.Y.C.

Faust (mime)
Created by Kenyon Martin
2-10-71
Brandeis University
Waltham, MA

Fear
Jacob Lind
6-19-73
New Plays Festival
WPA
333 Bowery, N.Y.C.

Fear of Falling Apples (with The Sound of Eggs Breaking)
Dene Hammond
5-14-70
University of Missouri
Columbia, MO

Fear to Bring Children
Robin Culver
5-16-69
University of Missouri
Columbia, MO

Feast of the Chameleon, The
Peter Stambler
May, 1968
Martinique Theatre
N.Y.C.

Feasting with Panthers
Adrian Hall & Richard Cumming
4-18-73
Trinity Square Repertory Company
Providence, RI

Feathers
Kerry Newcomb
4-13-29-72
Dallas Theatre Company
Dallas, TX

Feiffer's People
Fall, 1969
Western State College
Gunnison, CO

Felicidad (a play for dolls, mannequins, masks, puppets, and people)
Ralque Halfi
6-20-73
La Mama ETC
74 E. 4th, N.Y.C.

Felix
Claude McNeal
2-23-72
Actors' Studio
432 W. 44th, N.Y.C.

?! (feminist revue)
Westbeth Playwrights' Feminist Collective
5-17-73
Joseph Jefferson Theatre Company
Little Church Around the Corner
11 E. 29th, N.Y.C.

Femme Fatale: The Three Faces of Gloria
Jackie Curtis
5-6-70
La Mama ETC
74 E. 4th, N.Y.C.

Ferril, Etc.
Thomas Hornsby Ferril; adapted by June Favre
11-1-72
Third Eye Theatre
Denver, CO

Ferryboat
Leonard Melfi
6-23-72
Moving Company
146 Great Jones, N.Y.C.

Festival of Carol's, A
John Hearn
3-20-68
Royal Alexandra Theatre
Toronto, CAN

Festival of Mimes, A
Rebecca, Richard Clairmont, Robert Molnar, Mimika and The New York Mime Duet
10-4-73
Cubiculo
414 W. 51st, N.Y.C.

F-F-F-Frozen
Elaine Denholtz
4-26-69
West Side YWCA
51st & 8th, N.Y.C.

Ffinest Ffamily in the Land
Henry Livings
4-14-72
PAF Playhouse
Long Island, NY

Fiaca, La
Richardo Talesnik
7-30-70
Henry Street Settlement Playhouse
466 Grand, N.Y.C.

Fiance, The
Philip Lam
3-1-71
Old Reliable Theatre Tavern
231 E. 3rd, N.Y.C.

Fiasco or The Unaccommodated Man
Bernard Saltzman
9-3-72
Jean Cocteau Theatre
43 Bond, N.Y.C.

Field, The
Michael Parriott
3-2-72
Manhattan Theatre Club
321 E. 73rd, N.Y.C.

Field, The
John B. Keane
5-21-71
Thomas Davis Irish Players
St. Jean Baptiste Auditorium
167 E. 75th, N.Y.C.

Fiesta in Madrid (based on the zarzuela "La Verbena de la Poloma")
Adapted by Tito Capobiance; music by Tomas Breton
5-28-69
New York City Center
N.Y.C.

Fifth Murder, The
Benjamin Bernard Zavin
8-20-72
Mercer Arts Center
240 Mercer, N.Y.C.

Fifth of Spread Eagle, A
12-16-70
Washington Theatre Club
Washington, DC

Fifth Season, The
Sylvia Regan
4-5-68
Baruch School
CCNY
23rd St. & Lexington, N.Y.C.

Fifth, The
Bradford Thomas Riley
4-27-70
Old Reliable Theatre Tavern
231 E. 3rd, N.Y.C.

Fifty Year Game of Gin Rummy, The
David Feldman
5-5-71
Brandeis University
Waltham, MA

Fig Leaves Are Falling, The
Allan Sherman (book & lyrics); Albert Hague (music)
11-25-68
Shubert Theatre
Philadelphia, PA

Figures
James Robiscoe
2-1-70
Spencer Memorial Church
99 Clinton Brooklyn Heights, NY

Figures at Chartres, The
Edgar White
1-24-69
New York Shakespeare Festival Public Theatre
425 Lafayette, N.Y.C.

Filling the Hole
Donald Kvares
5-22-70
New York Theatre Ensemble
2 E. 2nd, N.Y.C.

Film
Jane Culp
4-4-69
New York Theatre Ensemble
2 E. 2nd, N.Y.C.

Film Club, The
Merritt Abrash
July, 1970
Eugene O'Neill Memorial Theatre
Waterford, CT

Filthy Piranesi, The
William D. Roberts
3-13-69
Playhouse Theatre Company
Vancouver, B.C., CAN

Fin Mukool, The Grand Distraction
Frank Hogan
7-12-69
Eugene O'Neill Memorial Theatre
Waterford, CT

Final Commitment
Rose Sher
10-15-71
New York Theatre Ensemble
2 E. 2nd, N.Y.C.

Final Resting Place, The
William Finnegan
12-17-70
Columbia School of the Arts
440 W. 110th, N.Y.C.

Final Session
Michael Miller
5-22-70
St. Clement's Church
423 W. 46th, N.Y.C.

Final Solution to the Black Problem in the United States of America, The
Loften Mitchell
11-18-70
St. David's Episcopal Church
Bronx, NY

Final Solutions (pageant)
Jan Hartman
3-11-68
Felt Forum
Madison Square Garden, N.Y.C.

Fingernails Blue as Flowers
Ronald Ribman
12-22-71
American Place Theatre
N.Y.C.

Finishing Touches
Jean Kerr
1-9-73
Shubert Theatre
New Haven, CT

Finnegan's Wake
James Joyce; adaptation by David Kerry Heefner
4-24-69
Thresholds
23 E. 20th, N.Y.C.

Fire
John Roc
5-1-68
Spingold Theatre
Brandeis University
Waltham, MA

Fire Eater's Enemy, The
Tone Brulin
5-30-73
CSC Repertory
89 W. 3rd, N.Y.C.

Fire in the Mindhouse
Lance Mulcahy (music); Arnold Borget (lyrics)
4-2-71
Center Stage
Baltimore, MD

Firebugs, The
Max Frisch (new adaptation by Mordecai Gorelik)
6-23-68
Martinique Theatre
N.Y.C.

Fireworks for a Hot Fourth
Jon Swan
July, 1968
Eugene O'Neill Memorial Theatre
Waterford, CT

First Day of Us, The
Peter Copani (book); Elliot Siegel (lyrics); David McHugh (music)
7-14-70
Twin Rivers Theater
Binghamton, NY

First Death
Walter Leyden Brown
1-14-72
Extension Theatre
277 Park Ave. So., N.Y.C.

First Ladies Are in the Caboose, The
James Curtin
11-30-72
Jacksonville University
Jacksonville, FL

First Sin, The
Aharon Megged
3-16-73
New Federal Theatre
240 E. 3rd, N.Y.C.

First to See the Lights Go On
James B. Campbell
11-6-69
WPA
34 E. 4th, N.Y.C.

Fischer
Yoram Porat (Hillel Halkim, translator)
1-10-68
La Mama ETC
122 Second, N.Y.C.

Fishook of Orchid Lagoon Water Pageant
Jack Smith
5-9-70
Plaster Foundation
36 Greene, N.Y.C.

Five at the End
Patricia Livingston
4-23-71
Assembly Theatre
113 Jane, N.Y.C.

Five Characters in Three Parts
James Shields
5-8-69
Sloane House YMCA
356 W. 34th, N.Y.C.

Five Fits
Robert Reinhold
10-26-70
Old Reliable Theatre Tavern
231 E. 3rd, N.Y.C.

Five on the Black Hand Side
Charlie L. Russell
12-10-69
American Place Theatre
N.Y.C.

Five Pieces
James Shearwood
12-5-71
Dancers Studio Foundation
34 E. 10th, N.Y.C.

Five Star Saint
Edward A. Molloy
2-10-70
Blackfriars' Guild
316 W. 57th, N.Y.C.

Five Stars
William H. Hoffman
8-4-69
Old Reliable Theatre Tavern
231 E. 3rd, N.Y.C.

Five Thousand Feet High
Helen Duberstein
10-31-70
Westbeth
463 West Street, N.Y.C.

Five Visits
Donald Kvares
6-15-73
Jean Cocteau Theatre
43 Bond, N.Y.C.

Fix!
Mark Eisman
8-3-73
Eugene O'Neill Memorial Theatre
Waterford, CT

Flame Play, The
Christopher Mathewson
6-19-73
New Plays Festival
WPA
333 Bowery, N.Y.C.

Flame (with Vermin)
Shaunee Laurence
11-12-70
Playbox
94 St. Mark's Pl., N.Y.C.

Flaw, The
Ed Harkness
4-26-73
University of Montana
Missoula, MT

Flight
Richard Davidson
5-23-68
Charisma Cafe
33 Carmine, N.Y.C.

Flight from Hong Kong
Kazuko
12-11-70
La Mama ETC Chinatown Production
Henry Street Settlement Playhouse
N.Y.C.

Flight of Lindbergh, The (with A Lesson in Consent)
Bertolt Brecht; music by Kurt Weill; original material by Gordon Duffey and Richard Peaslee
5-25-69
New York City Theatre Workshop
Metropolitan Museum of Art
N.Y.C.

Flight 901
John Wolfson
4-17-70
Omni Theatre Club
145 W. 18th, N.Y.C.

Flip Side, The
Hugh & Margaret Williams
9-2-68
Shubert Theatre
New Haven, CT

Flite Cage (with Mission Beach)
Walter Hadler
5-3-69
Theatre Genesis
10th & 2nd, N.Y.C.

Flo's Boathouse
Charles Stewart
3-24-72
Down Stage Studio Theatre
321 W. 14th, N.Y.C.

Flo Under the Flag
Arthur Williams
2-8-69
Mannhardt Theatre Foundation
N.Y.C.

Florabel
Paul Kane
5-28-69
Playbox
94 St. Mark's Pl., N.Y.C.

Flounder Complex, The
Anthony Damat
7-20-68
Old Reliable Theatre Tavern
231 E. 3rd, N.Y.C.

Flower and Other Pieces, The
January, 1973
Theatre X
Milwaukee, WI

Flowered Path to the Big Time
John Ford Noonan
4-12-73
Ensemble Studio Theatre
549 W. 52nd, N.Y.C.

Flowers for the Trashman
Marvin X
5-8-70
Afro-American Studio
15 W. 126th, N.Y.C.

Flukes (The Whale Show)
Spring, 1973
Boston Conservatory Theatre
Boston, MA

Flush the Aquarium
Peter Gianino
5-19-69
University of North Carolina
Greensboro, NC

Fluted Fables
4-1-72
Street 70 Ensemble
Rockville Civic Center
Montgomery County, MD

Flying
The Surprise Troupe
5-2-70
Dramarena Repertory Theatre
158 W. 55th, N.Y.C.

Flying Fish, The
Glenn Graves
5-8-69
Playbox
94 St. Mark's Pl., N.Y.C.

Flying Sunflower, The
Robert Stewart and Gordon Duffey; Richard Peaslee
8-17-68
New York City Workshop
N.Y.C.

F.O.B.
Jeff Weiss
11-24-72
Mercer Arts Center
240 Mercer, N.Y.C.

Foghorn
Hanay Gelogamah
12-5-73
Native American Theatre Ensemble Company
La Mama ETC
74 E. 4th, N.Y.C.

Fold, Spindle, and Mutilate
Dan Callabreeze (book & lyrics); Richard DeRosa (music)
Feb., 1970
University of Hartford
Hartford, CT

Folks, Fun, and Fantasy
3-5-69
Waverly Players Gallery
327 Sixth, N.Y.C.

Follies
James Goldman (book); Stephen Sondheim (music & lyrics)
2-24-71
Colonial Theatre
Boston, MA

Fool Attached to His Bells, A
Lars Forssell
5-10-72
Queens College
N.Y.C.

Football (with The Report and Bellymass)
Jon Swan
11-14-68
Seattle Repertory Theatre
Seattle, WA

Footlocker
Charles Langdon
2-25-71
Changing Scene
Denver, CO

Footnote to Thucydides
Robert C. Herron
4-11-69
Actor's Place
487 Hudson St., N.Y.C.

Footnotes to Macbeth
Holly Solomon
2-19-71
98 Greene St. Loft
98 Greene St., N.Y.C.

Footsteps
Myron Levoy
5-22-70
New York Theatre Ensemble
2 E. 2nd, N.Y.C.

For Breakfast, Mr. Sachs
Kenneth Pressman
10-24-68
Playwrights' Unit
15 Vandam, N.Y.C.

For Her Enchanting Son
Richard Longchamps
3-12-71
American Theatre Company
106 E. 14th, N.Y.C.

For My People
9-9-68
Sheridan Square Playhouse
99 Seventh Ave. So., N.Y.C.

For the Use of the Hall
Oliver Hailey
4-26-73
Washington Theatre Club
Washington, DC

Foreigners, The
Michael McGrinder
3-2-73
Bastiano's Studio
14 Cooper Sq., N.Y.C.

Foreplay
Robert M. Lane
12-10-70
Bijou Theatre
N.Y.C.

Forget-Me-Not-Lane
Peter Nichols
4-6-73
Long Wharf Theatre
New Haven, CT

Forgotten American, The (with The Assassination of Nigger Nate)
Tony Barsha
1-8-70
Theatre Genesis
10th & 2nd, N.Y.C.

Forgotten Dreams
Patrick Broughton
6-19-73
New Plays Festival
WPA
333 Bowery, N.Y.C.

Fortune and Men's Eyes
John Herbert, with re-written text by Sal Mineo
1-9-69
Coronet Theatre
Los Angeles, CA

Forty Carats
Jay Allen
11-20-68
Shubert Theatre
New Haven, CT

Forty Years On (40 Years On)
Alan Bennett
8-3-70
Shaw Festival
Niagara-on-the-Lake, Ontario, CAN

Forty-Two Seconds from Broadway (42 Seconds from Broadway)
Louis Del Grande
3-11-73
Playhouse II
357 W. 48th, N.Y.C.

Found Objects
Marjorie Taubenhaus
10-11-71
American Theatre Company
106 E. 14th, N.Y.C.

Four Actors and a Restaurant (with Three Words in No Time and It's Got To Be Black or White)
Lyon Phelps
2-18-71
Judson Poet's Theatre
55 Wash. Sq. So., N.Y.C.

Four by Four
Lawrence Alson, Patricia Cooper, Oliver Hailey, William Hanley
1-30-69
Loft Workshop
152 Bleecker, N.Y.C.

Four Hundred Eleven Lines (411 Lines) (with Scene for Piano and Tape)
Tom Johnson
5-9-71
Dancers Studio Foundation
34 E. 10th, N.Y.C.

Four Hundred Years Overdue
The Alonzo Players
8-5-72
Twilight Theatre
Brooklyn, NY

Four Men and a Monster
Maryat Lee
12-11-68
Playhouse in the Park
Cincinnati, OH

Four No Plays (See below)
Tom Eyen
2-5-69
La Mama ETC
9 St. Mark's Place, N.Y.C.
Paradise Later
Fantasies and Smaller Pieces
Frankenstein's Wife
Antigone Meets Dionysus for Lunch

Four Note Opera, The
Tom Johnson
5-11-72
Cubiculo
414 W. 51st, N.Y.C.

Four of Them, The
Michael Shurtleff
2-18-72
Friday Theatre
N.Y.C.

Four on a Couch
Larry O'Connel & Andrew Mack
7-6-71
Second Group Theatre
McBurney YMCA
215 W. 23rd, N.Y.C.

Four on a Garden
Barillet and Gredy, adapted by Abe Burrows
10-21-70
Shubert Theatre
New Haven, CT

Four's Company
Davi Napoleon
11-8-73
Stage 7 Matrix
Greenwich Mews Theatre
141 W. 13th, N.Y.C.

Four Seasons, The
Arnold Wesker
3-14-68
Theatre Four
424 W. 55th, N.Y.C.

Four States of Mind
Frank Moffett Mosier
4-3-70
Actor's Place
487 Hudson, N.Y.C.

Four Stories Below the Ground (Alice in Wonderland; Angel of the Odd; Jeff Peters as a Personal Magnet; Sons of Liberty)
8-9-72
13th Street Theatre
50 W. 13th, N.Y.C.

Four Women
7-31-71
Manna House Drama Workshop
338 E. 106th, N.Y.C.

Four-in-Hand (reading)
Malvine Cole
3-19-72
Theatre for the New City
151 Bank, N.Y.C.

Foursome, The
E. A. Whitehead
11-8-72
Arena Stage
Washington, DC

Fourteen Ninety-One (1491)
Meredith Willson, Richard Morris, Ira Barnak
9-2-69
Los Angeles Music Center
Los Angeles, CA

Fourth Generation, The
Erwin Pally
5-21-71
Winslow Hall, YWCA
Cambridge, MA

Fourth Monkey, The
Eric Nicol
10-10-68
Playhouse Theatre Company
Vancouver, B.C., CAN

Fourth Ring, The
Leslie Holzer
12-17-70
13th Street Theatre
50 W. 13th, N.Y.C.

Fourth Wall, The (improvisational group)
9-4-68
Theatre East
211 East 60th, N.Y.C.

Fra Lorenzo or The Cardinal Sins
David R. Slavitt
8-17-70
Playwrights' Unit
83 E. 4th, N.Y.C.

Fragile Freight (with The Noisy Passenger and Un Passage)
Shelley Winters
12-30-70
Actor's Playhouse
100 Seventh Ave. So., N.Y.C.

Francesco: The Life and Times of the Cencis
Manuel Martin
6-1-73
Duo Theatre
La Mama ETC
74 E. 4th, N.Y.C.

Francis — Day, The
Brother Jonathan Ringhamp; Seymour Barab (music)
7-6-73
Everyman Company
La Mama ETC
74 E. 4th, N.Y.C.

Frank Buck Can't Make it
David Freeman
6-19-73
New Plays Festival
WPA
333 Bowery, N.Y.C.

Frank & Ella & Clara & Morris & the Telegram
Fran Lohman
4-27-71
WPA
333 Bowery, N.Y.C.

Frank Lee Wilde Show, The
8-25-69
Old Reliable Theatre Tavern
231 E. 3rd, N.Y.C.

Frank Merriwell
Skip Redwine, Larry Frank, Heywood Gould (book); Skip Redwine, Larry Frank (music & lyrics)
4-28-71
Longacre Theatre
N.Y.C.

Fraternal Order of Police (with Theory, Proof, Application; Slow Memories; and Inside My Head)
Barry Litvack
10-21-70
Playwright's Unit
83 E. 4th, N.Y.C.

Freak In (revue)
Robert Patrick
2-10-71
WPA
333 Bowery, N.Y.C.

Fred's Frisco Follies
8-21-73
Bay Bridge Holiday Inn
Emeryville, CA

Frederick
Terrill L. Gibson
5-26-71
Old West Church
Boston, MA

Frederick Douglas, An Evening in Memorium. . .
9-16-71
Triangle Theatre
316 E. 88th, N.Y.C.

Free! Free! Free!
Sally Ordway
4-19-69
West Side YMCA
5 W. 63rd, N.Y.C.

Free License — In the Late Afternoon
Sande Shurin
1-1-73
Drifting Traffic
Theatre for the New City
113 Jane, N.Y.C.

Free Ride
9-30-71
Theatre Passe Muraille
Toronto, CAN

Free Ride to Aunt Mercie's Soul, A
Jack Romano
3-15-68
Stage 9
96 W. Houston, N.Y.C.

Freedom of the City, The
Brian Friel
10-9-73
Goodman Theatre
Chicago, IL

Freedom Suite
Larry Jacobson and Macalester students (book); John Katsantonis (music)
2-14-70
Macalester College
St. Paul, MN

Freeman
Phillip Hayes Dean
1-23-73
American Place Theatre
N.Y.C.

French Comic Sketches
Allais, Courteline, etc.
11-18-72
French Art Theatre
111 W. 57th, N.Y.C.

French Gray
Josef Bush
9-23-68
Old Reliable Theatre Tavern
231 E. 3rd, N.Y.C.

French Revolution of May 1968, The
Serge Gavronsky
3-21-69
McMillan Theatre
Columbia University
N.Y.C.

Frenzy (with Solitude and The Revolution) (reading)
Tobi Louis
4-22-73
New York Cultural Center
2 Columbus Circle, N.Y.C.

Frere Jacques
Gerard Singer
6-6-68
Theatre 802
64th & 8th Ave., Brooklyn, NY

Freudian Memoirs of Viola Pickens (with Pay Attention to the Ravel)
Donald Kvares
7-7-72
Playbox
94 St. Mark's Pl., N.Y.C.

Friday Bench, The
Mario Fratti
1-20-71
Cubiculo
414 W. 51st, N.Y.C.

Friends and Relations
Eugene Yanni
10-14-71
Provincetown Playhouse
133 MacDougal, N.Y.C.

Friends Revisited
Stanley Zawatski
5-19-72
New York Theatre Ensemble
2 E. 2nd, N.Y.C.

Friends, The
Arnold Wesker
Summer, 1970
Stratford Festival
Stratford, CAN

Friends (1st part of trilogy Three Pieces Left)
Ransom Jeffrey
8-23-68
Dramarena Repertory Theatre
158 W. 55th, N.Y.C.

Frio's Progress (with The Dream Song)
John Forster
12-3-72
Mercer Arts Center
240 Mercer, N.Y.C.

Frog Frog
Mary Feldhaus-Weber
4-29-70
Cubiculo
414 W. 51st, N.Y.C.

Frog He Would A-Wooing Go, A
Jerry Devine
5-2-72
Masquers Theatre
Hollywood, CA

Frogs (work-in-progress)
6-2-73
Medicine Show Theatre Ensemble
Space for Innovative Development
344 W. 56th, N.Y.C.

From Fool to Hanged Man
William H. Hoffman
4-1-72
West Side YWCA
8th Ave. & 51st, N.Y.C.

From Israel with Laughter (revue)
10-16-69
Barbizon-Plaza, N.Y.C.

From Israel with Love
9-2-72
Auditorium
Santa Monica, CA

From Our Dissensions
8-5-71
Lenox Arts Center
Lenox, MA

From Shakespeare to Gordone
6-8-70
Sheridan Square Playhouse
99 Seventh Ave. So., N.Y.C.

From the Classifieds
Asher Coward
5-15-70
Extension Theatre
277 Park Ave. So., N.Y.C.

From the Graphis Series
Dick Higgins
12-24-71
New York Theatre Ensemble
2 E. 2nd, N.Y.C.

From the Second City (second edition)
10-14-69
Eastside Playhouse
334 E. 74th, N.Y.C.

From the Sublime to the Ridiculous: A Program of Pantomime
Bernard Kramer
6-21-73
Donnell Library
N.Y.C.

Frosted Glass Coffin, The (with A Perfect Analysis Given by a Parrot)
Tennessee Williams
5-1-70
Waterfront Playhouse
Key West, FL

Fuck Mother
Robert Peters
3-19-70
Cubiculo
414 W. 51st, N.Y.C.

Fuente Ovejuna
Lope de Vega, translated by Jill Booty
2-5-70
Columbia University
N.Y.C.

Fuente Ovejuna
Lope de Vega; Mario Pena (adaptor)
9-28-73
Intar Theatre
508 W. 53rd, N.Y.C.

Fuente Ovejuna
Lope de Vega; translated by William Colford
10-11-72
La Mama ETC
74 E. 4th, N.Y.C.

Fuera del Juego
Mario Pena
7-6-73
Teatro Caras Nuevas
114 W. 14th, N.Y.C.

Fuga
Jose L. Varona
11-25-70
New York Shakespeare Festival
Public Theatre
425 Lafayette, N.Y.C.

Full Circle
Erich Maria Remarque; Peter Stone (adaptor)
10-6-73
Eisenhower Theatre
Washington, DC

Full Eight Hours, A
David Hardy
6-7-72
La Mama ETC
74 E. 4th, N.Y.C.

Full Moon
Joan Durant
12-22-72
New York Theatre Ensemble
2 E. 2nd, N.Y.C.

Fun Boot Dancers (with Junkies Are Full of Sh. . . and Blood Rites)
Imamu Amiri Baraka (LeRoi Jones)
11-21-70
Henry Street Settlement Playhouse
466 Grand, N.Y.C.

Fun City
Lynne Carter
3-6-68
Jan Hus Auditorium
351 E. 74th, N.Y.C.

Fun City
Joan Rivers, Edgar Rosenberg, & Lester Colodny
11-29-71
National Theatre
Washington, DC

Fun House: A Victorian Carnival
Jenny Egan (compiler); Arnold Black (music)
4-22-72
Four Winds Theatre
Manhattan Theatre Club
321 E. 73rd, N.Y.C.

Funeral Games
Joe Orton
1-16-73
WPA
333 Bowery, N.Y.C.

Funeral Jazz (with Twenty Years from Now)
J. I. Rodale
3-3-69
Homer L. Ferguson High School
Newport News, VA

Funeral, The
William Packard
9-15-71
St. Peter's Church
346 W. 20th, N.Y.C.

Funk
Ricardo
3-5-70
Inner Theatre
356 Bowery, N.Y.C.

Funky Guacomole Bush, This
Stanley Seidman
9-27-68
Off Center Theatre
152 W. 66th, N.Y.C.

Funn (with Don't Tell Lily)
Robert Somerfeld
1-5-70
Fortune Theatre
62 E. 4th, N.Y.C.

Funny Face (musical)
Winter, 1973
Studio Arena
Buffalo, NY

Funny Men Are in Trouble, The (with Quietus)
Paul John Austin
11-20-72
St. Clement's Church
423 W. 46th, N.Y.C.

Funny Old Man, The
7-26-72
State University of New York
Stony Brook, L.I., NY

Funnytime
Seret Scott
2-15-73
Negro Ensemble Company
St. Mark's Playhouse
133 Second, N.Y.C.

Fur
Anna Belle Johnson
4-6-68
Theatre Genesis
10th & 2nd, N.Y.C.

Furniture, The
John Eckenrod
10-8-71
Senior Dramatic Repertory Theatre
Carnegie Hall
881 Seventh, N.Y.C.

Future Past, Future Present
Danielle Brantley
3-23-68
Dramarena Repertory Theatre
158 W. 55th, N.Y.C.

Futurities
Irvin Rinard
3-7-68
H B Playwrights Foundation
124 Bank, N.Y.C.

G

Gabriella
Ted Harris
3-26-68
Little Theatre
181 Bleecker, N.Y.C.

Gala Affair at the Hotel Plunge, A
Tom LaBar
2-16-70
Old Reliable Theatre Tavern
231 E. 3rd, N.Y.C.

Galavantin' Husband
Milburn Davis
1-27-73
Negro Ensemble Company
St. Mark's Playhouse
133 Second, N.Y.C.

Galile (with The Farm Bill)
Susan Dworkin
5-7-70
Triangle Theatre
316 E. 88th, N.Y.C.

Gallery of Characters
Sidney Morris
10-7-71
Bleecker Street Repertory Co.
AMDA Theatre
150 Bleecker, N.Y.C.

Gallery, The
Stephen Rausch
11-17-68
Wittenberg University Theatre
Springfield, OH

Game
John Ashby and Dorothy Ashby
3-21-68
Detroit Public Library
Detroit, MI

Game Is Stud, The
Edward Shanley
12-26-69
Hargrove Hotel
112 W. 72nd, N.Y.C.

Game of Adam & Eve, The
Ed Bullins
Spring, 1970
Theatre Company of Boston
Boston, MA

Game of Chance
Anton Chekhov; adapted by James Monos
3-25-73
One-Act Repertory Company
251 E. 50th, N.Y.C.

Game, The
Rafael Bunuel
3-5-70
Inner Theatre
356 Bowery, N.Y.C.

Game . . .?, The
Joseph Curran
July, 1970
Emmanuel Church
Boston, MA

Game, The
Dennis E. Noble
6-10-71
Jacksonville University
Jacksonville, FL

Games
Raymond Banachi
12-26-69
New York Theatre Ensemble
2 E. 2nd, N.Y.C.

Games
Charles Abbot & Fredric Dehn (sketches & lyrics); Howard Marren (music)
11-22-72
Mercer Arts Center
240 Mercer, N.Y.C.

Games (with At Least They Can't Say We Never Tried)
Pat Rioux
3-20-69
Loft Workshop
152 Bleecker, N.Y.C.

Games/After Liverpool
James Saunders
1-22-73
New Phoenix Theatre
Lyceum Theatre
149 W. 45th, N.Y.C.

Gandhi
Gurney Campbell
10-20-70
Playhouse
N.Y.C.

Gandhiji
Rose Leiman Goldemberg
July, 1970
Eugene O'Neill Memorial Theatre
Waterford, CT

Gannon
P. J. Barry
10-26-68
Fulton Theatre Company
119 Ninth, N.Y.C.

Gantry
Peter Bellwood (book); Fred Tobias (lyrics); Stanley Lebowsky (music)
1-17-70
George Abbott Theatre
152 W. 54th, N.Y.C.

Garbage Can Man
2-16-70
Actor's Playhouse
100 Seventh Ave. So., N.Y.C.

Garbage Collectors
Frank Steinkellner
1-18-73
Cubiculo
414 W. 51st, N.Y.C.

Garbage Hustler, The
George Savage & George Savage, Jr.
July 1969
Bowling Green University
Bowling Green, OH

Garbage Wine
Michael Hardstack
6-30-72
New York Theatre Ensemble
2 E. 2nd, N.Y.C.

Garden of Delights, A (with The Stylites)
Andrew Bauer
6-5-72
Manhattan Theatre Club
321 E. 73rd, N.Y.C.

Garden of Forking Paths, The
Alexander Panas
7-15-69
New Workshop Theatre
Brooklyn College
NY

Gas Stations of the Cross Religious Spectacle
Jack Smith
1-16-71
Plaster Foundation
36 Greene, N.Y.C.

Gaspard
Peter Handke
1-9-73
Studio Theatre
National Arts Centre
Ottawa, Ontario, CAN

Gay Desperado, The (with Magic Time and When Schwartz Meets Goldstein)
William Kushner
3-20-70
Play Lab
130 E. 7th, N.Y.C.

Geese
Gus Weill
1-12-69
Players' Theatre
115 MacDougal, N.Y.C.

Gemu (one-man show)
10-2-70
Alice Tully Hall
65th & Broadway, N.Y.C.

General Brutus, The
Jeff Wanshel
7-11-72
Eugene O'Neill Memorial Theatre
Waterford, CT

General Bullett (reading)
George Stiles
10-28-73
Aardvark Productions' Playreading Theatre
Electric Circus
23 St. Mark's Place, N.Y.C.

Generation Gap
Total Theatre for Youth
7-19-72
Donnell Library
N.Y.C.

Genesis!
Philip Bosakowsky
10-20-71
Villanova Theatre Company
La Mama ETC
74 E. 4th, N.Y.C.

Genesis Fue Manana, El (with El Girasol)
Jorge Diaz
12-12-71
New York Theatre of the Americas
427 W. 59th, N.Y.C.

Genesius
4-17-70
St. Genesius Theatre
Hollywood, CA

Gente, La
Edgar White
7-18-73
New York Shakespeare Festival
Astoria Park, Queens, NY

Geometric Progression
Benjamin Bradford
2-6-69
Theatre 13
201 W. 13th, N.Y.C.

George Dandin
Moliere; adapted by Joseph Renard
1-25-72
La Mama ETC
74 E. 4th, N.Y.C.

George M!
Michael Stewart and John & Fran Pascal (book), George M. Cohan & Mary Cohan
2-12-68
Fisher Theatre
Detroit, MI

George Porgie
George Birimisa
11-20-68
Cooper Square Arts Theatre
35 Cooper Sq., N.Y.C.

Georgia Man & Jamaican Woman
David Lewis
7-29-69
New Workshop Theatre
Brooklyn College
NY

Georgy
Tom Mankiewicz (book); Carole Bayer (lyrics); George Fischoff (music)
1-10-70
Shubert Theatre
New Haven, CT

Gershwin! A Cabaret Show
11-20-73
Manhattan Theatre Club
321 E. 73rd, N.Y.C.

Gershwin Years, The (revue)
6-29-73
Berkshire Playhouse
Stockbridge, MA

Gertrude
9-9-70
La Mama ETC
74 E. 4th, N.Y.C.

Gertrude Stein's First Reader
Gertrude Stein, adapted by Herbert Machiz; music by Ann Sternberg
8-27-69
Artists Theater Festival
Southampton, L.I., NY

Get Thee to Canterbury
Jan Steen & David Secter (book); lyrics by Mr. Secter; music by Paul Hoffert
1-25-69
Sheridan Square Playhouse
99 Seventh Ave. So., N.Y.C.

Get Yourself a Gun, Brother
Thomas Terefenko
7-20-68
Old Reliable Theatre Tavern
231 E. 3rd, N.Y.C.

Gettin' It Together
See: An Evening of Identity

Getting Ready
Grace Cavalieri
1-16-73
WPA
333 Bowery, N.Y.C.

Ghost Dance
Stuart Vaughan
Fall, 1973
Trinity Square Repertory Company
Providence, RI

Ghost Town
Albert Evans
1-19-68
Riverdale Showcase
252nd St. & Riverdale Ave. Bronx, NY

Giacomo de Trieste
Harry J. Pollock
January, 1971
Tulsa, OK

Gifts (mime)
Marge Helenchild
12-13-73
Women's Interart Center
549 W. 52nd, N.Y.C.

Gigi
Alan Jay Lerner (book & lyrics); Frederick Loewe (music)
5-15-73
Curran Theatre
San Francisco, CA

Gilbert
David S. Maranze & Marc Alan Zagoren
11-12-73
Library & Museum of the Performing Arts
111 Amsterdam, N.Y.C.

Gilgamesh
10-5-72
National Theatre of the Deaf
Rochester Institute of Technology
Rochester, NY

Gimmick, The (with To Kill a Devil)
Roger Furman
3-27-70
New Heritage Repertory
440 W. 110th, N.Y.C.

Gimpel the Fool
Isaac Bashevis Singer, adapted by Larry Arrick
8-19-70
Yale Repertory Theatre
East Hampton, NY

Ginger and the Painted Turtle
Nancy Somerfeld
1-28-71
Triangle Theatre
316 E. 88th, N.Y.C.

Gingerbread Lady, The
Neil Simon
11-4-70
Shubert Theatre
New Haven, CT

Gingham Dog, The
Lanford Wilson
9-26-68
Washington Theatre Club
Washington, DC

Girasol, El (with El Genesis Fue Manana)
Jorge Diaz
12-12-71
New York Theatre of the Americas
427 W. 59th, N.Y.C.

Girl and the Soldier, The
Jean-Claude van Itallie
10-7-69
Mark Taper Forum
Los Angeles, CA

Girl in the Dancing Box, The
Charles Kerbs
Novermber, 1972
Tulane University
New Orleans, LA

Girl in the House of Culture, The
Mats Odeen, David Mel Paul & Margareta Paul (translator)
1-4-71
Library & Museum of the Performing Arts
111 Amsterdam, N.Y.C.

Girl Who Has Everything, The
Henry Denker
4-10-73
Bucks County Playhouse
New Hope, PA

Girl with the Ring on Her Nose, The (with The Other One and Too Much) (One of four one-act plays presented under title About Women)
Mario Fratti
4-1-71
Loft Theatre
21 Bond, N.Y.C.

Girls Most Likely To Succeed, The
Dennis Andersen
5-9-73
Playwrights' Horizons
Clark Center for the Performing Arts West Side YWCA
8th Ave. & 51st, N.Y.C.

Git (with America the Beautiful)
9-10-70
Academy Theatre
Atlanta, GA

Give My Regards to Off Off Broadway
Tom Eyen
3-8-72
Playwrights' Workshop Club
14 Cooper Sq., N.Y.C.

Given: No Bread, An Encounter, and Dinner for 15
Morton Lichter
10-17-73
La Mama ETC
74 E. 4th, N.Y.C.

Giving Head
Boruk
11-24-73
Cubiculo
414 W. 51st, N.Y.C.

GKC — The Wit and Wisdom of Gilbert Keith Chesterton
Tony van Bridge (adaptor)
November, 1971
Neptune Theatre
Halifax, N.S., CAN

Gleaners, The
David Danielson
9-25-73
New Theatre for Now
Los Angeles, CA

Glickl Hameln Demands Justice
Max Bauman
2-13-72
Queens College
N.Y.C.

Global Village Video Rock Environment
12-4-69
Video Gallery
454 Broome, N.Y.C.

Glomming Through Life
Tom Hilt
1-23-68
Little Theatre
181 Bleecker, N.Y.C.

Gloria and Esperanza
Julie Bovasso
4-3-69
La Mama ETC
74 E. 4th, N.Y.C.

Gloriana
Dennis G. Turner
6-28-72
Atlantic City Playhouse
Atlantic City, NJ

Glorious Ruler, The
Michael Ackerman
6-30-69
Jan Hus Auditorium
351 E. 74th, N.Y.C.

Glory! Halleluhah!
Anna Marie Barlow
5-30-69
American Conservatory Theatre
San Francisco, CA

Glory Hole
John Boylan
10-25-68
Downstage Studio Theatre
321 W. 14th, N.Y.C.

Gnome Who Brought Happiness to All, The
Rose Sher
3-23-73
New York Theatre Ensemble
2 E. 2nd, N.Y.C.

Go Children Slowly
Arthur Sainer
5-25-73
Cubiculo
414 W. 51st, N.Y.C.

Go Directly To Jail, Do Not Pass Go
12-7-72
Blue Dome Rehearsal Hall
261 Bowery, N.Y.C.

Go on Downstairs (with Like Shoes)
Jordan A. Deutsch
1-17-69
Theatre of Our Discontent
Clifton Hotel
127 W. 79th, N.Y.C.

Go Out and See
John Ahern
4-20-72
Manhattan Theatre Club
321 E. 73rd, N.Y.C.

GOA
Asif Currimbhoy
2-19-68
Martinique Theatre
N.Y.C.

Goalie, The
Louis Phillips
6-19-73
New Plays Festival
WPA
333 Bowery, N.Y.C.

Go-Carts Coming Down the Road
Lyla Hay Owens
9-17-71
Pilgrims Theatre Company
Old South Church
Copley Square, Boston, MA

God Almighty
Tony Webster
Spring, 1970
Theatre West
Hollywood, CA

God and a Machine Are Hell, A
Stuart Milstein
6-25-71
Mercer Street Playhouse
240 Mercer, N.Y.C.

God Bless
Jules Feiffer
10-10-68
Yale University
New Haven, CT

God Bless Coney
John Glines (book, lyrics, & music)
5-3-72
Orpheum Theatre
126 Second, N.Y.C.

God Bless God; She Needs It!
Patricia Horan (book & lyrics); Victoria Vidal (lyrics & music)
10-5-72
Washington Square Church
133 W. 4th, N.Y.C.

God Bless You, Harold Fineberg
Maxine Fleischman
3-30-69
Actors' Playhouse
100 Seventh Ave. So., N.Y.C.

God Comes to Spoon River (reading)
7-17-71
Unity Center
143 W. 51st, N.Y.C.

God Is A (Guess What?)
Ray McIver
12-17-68
Negro Ensemble Company
St. Mark's Playhouse
133 Second, N.Y.C.

God Is Back, Black and Singing Gospel at the Fortune Theatre
Created by Al Miller
11-18-69
Fortune Theatre
62 E. 4th, N.Y.C.

God Is in the Streets Today
Mike Malone
8-26-72
Workshops for Careers in the Arts
Lincoln Center Plaza
N.Y.C.

God Knows
Elly Carr & Ruth Pleva
5-21-71
Playbox
94 St. Mark's Pl., N.Y.C.

God's Country
West End Acting Company
3-7-73
Courtyard Playhouse
137 W. 14th, N.Y.C.

God Says There Is No Peter Ott
Bill Hare
4-17-72
McAlpin Rooftop Theatre
34th St. & 6th, N.Y.C.

Godno
Joseph Ponzi
6-23-71
La Mama ETC
74 E. 4th, N.Y.C.

Gods Strike Back, The
Halstead Welles
July, 1971
University of California
Los Angeles, CA

Gods Want Sugar Smacks, The
Joseph Mountel
4-10-71
University of Missouri
Columbia, MO

Godspell
John-Michael Tebelak; Stephen Schwartz (music & lyrics)
2-24-71
La Mama ETC
74 E. 4th, N.Y.C.

Going Apes
Nick Hall
11-15-72
Theatre USA
University of South Alabama
Mobile, AL

Going For A Thrombo
Albert Bermel
7-31-68
Summer Repertory Theatre
Columbia University, N.Y.C.

Going Home
Edward Morris
12-10-71
Potbelly Theatre Workshop
40 W. 18th, N.Y.C.

Going Up!
Stewart H. Benedict
8-13-71
Playbox
94 St. Mark's Pl., N.Y.C.

Gold Watch
Momoko Iko
3-15-72
Inner City Theatre
Los Angeles, CA

Golden Animal, The (with Angel Baby Honey Darling Dear)
Robert Patrick
7-20-70
Old Reliable Theatre Tavern
231 E. 3rd, N.Y.C.

Golden Bat, The
Yutaka Higashi (director); Itsuro Shimoda (music)
6-17-70
La Mama ETC
74 E. 4th, N.Y.C.

Golden Circle, The
Robert Patrick
October, 1972
Spring Street Company
119 Spring, N.Y.C.

Golden Daffodil Dwarf, The, and Other Works
Daniela Gioseffi
1-4-73
St. Clement's Church
423 W. 46th, N.Y.C.

Golden Fleece, The
A. R. Gurney, Jr.
2-22-68
Playwrights' Unit
15 Vandam, N.Y.C.

Golden Hill
1-29-69
Western Illinois University
Macomb, Il

Golden Oldies
William Derringer
4-14-72
Playbox
94 St. Mark's Pl., N.Y.C.

Golden Rainbow
Ernest Kinoy & Walter Marks
2-4-68
Shubert Theatre
N.Y.C.

Golden Streets, The
Piri Thomas
8-12-70
Puerto Rican Traveling Theatre
Riverside Park, N.Y.C.

Gone Out
Tadeusz Rozewicz
1969
McMaster University
Hamilton, Ontario, CAN

Gone with the Wind
Horton Foote (book); Harold Rome (lyrics & music)
8-28-73
Chandler Pavilion
Los Angeles, CA

Good and Bad Times of Cady Francis McCullum and Friends, The
Portia Bohn (book); Richard Cumming (music & lyrics)
2-17-71
Trinity Square Repertory Company
Providence, RI

Good Catholic, The (reading)
Eric Bentley
9-20-68
H B Playwrights Foundation
124 Bank, N.Y.C.

Good Day for Pigs, A
Jon Surgal
Summer, 1970
Eugene O'Neill Memorial Theatre
Waterford, CT

Good Doctor, The
Neil Simon
11-5-73
Shubert Theatre
New Haven, CT

Good Evening (revue)
Peter Cook & Dudley Moore
10-15-73
Shubert Theatre
Boston, MA

Good Morning Blues
Jon Surgal
July, 1970
Eugene O'Neill Memorial Theatre
Waterford, CT

Good News, The
Paul G. Enger
1-4-73
Stage West
West Springfield, MA

Good People, The
Anne Layton
7-7-72
Omni Theatre Club
145 W. 18th, N.Y.C.

Good Seed, The (with Pupe Puppets)
Ralph Accardo
12-13-68
Stage 9
96 W. Houston, N.Y.C.

Good Soldier Schweik, The
New adaptation by Milan Kepel
1972
Cornell University
Ithaca, NY

Good Woman of Setzuan, The
Bertolt Brecht; new translation by Ralph Manheim
11-5-70
Vivian Beaumont Theatre
Lincoln Center
N.Y.C.

Goodby and Keep Cold
John Ford Noonan
7-16-70
Loft Theatre
21 Bond, N.Y.C.

Good-Bye
See: Fall River Ruins; The Happiness Train; and Pay Attention to the Ravel

Goodbye, Dan Bailey (reading)
Kenneth Bernard
12-12-69
Chelsea Theatre Center
30 Lafayette, Brooklyn, NY

Goodbye People, The
Herb Gardner
10-30-68
Locust Theatre
Philadelphia, PA

Goodbye People, The (revised)
Herb Gardner
8-10-72
Mark Taper Forum
Los Angeles, CA

Goodbye Profit Motive
Tom Shields & Martha Baird
4-29-72
Terrain Gallery
39 Grove, N.Y.C.

Goodbye Tomorrow
Sue Brock (book & lyrics); Carl Friberg (music)
3-23-73
Central Arts Cabaret
108 E. 64th, N.Y.C.

Goodnight, I Love You (with Thank You, Miss Victoria)
William H. Hoffman
8-26-68
Old Reliable Theatre Tavern
231 E. 3rd, N.Y.C.

Goodnight Jonathan/Night, Suzie
William Schlottmann
1-28-72
Stage Lights Theatrical Club
214 W. 48th, N.Y.C.

Gorf and the Blind Dyke
Michael McClure
Fall, 1973
Magic Theatre
San Francisco, CA

Gorilla, Gorilla
David Ball
3-17-71
Tufts University
Medford, MA

Gorillas
John Averill
Spring, 1973
Florida State University
Tallahassee, FL

Gosh, It's So Beautiful It Almost Looks Plastic
Louis Florimonte
11-12-70
Changing Scene
Denver, CO

Gossamer Wings
The Angels of Light
10-20-72
Theatre for the New City
113 Jane, N.Y.C.

Gown for His Mistress, A
Georges Feydeau; translated by Barnett Shaw
5-13-69
Dallas Theater Center
Dallas, TX

Grab Bag, The
Robert J. Thompson
11-4-68
Astor Place Theatre
434 Lafayette, N.Y.C.

Graduation (rock musical)
Jeff Hochhauser
2-12-71
New York Theatre Ensemble
2 E. 2nd, N.Y.C.

Graffiti (revue)
11-15-68
Charlie's
235 W. 52nd, N.Y.C.

Grail Green
See: Kool Aid

Gran Teatro del Mundo, El
Pedro Calderon de la Barca, with musical score by Manuel de Falla
12-8-68
St. Paul's Chapel
Columbia University, NY

Grand Mal Crick
Walter Hadler
1-7-71
Theatre Genesis
10th & 2nd, N.Y.C.

Grand Tarot
Charles Ludlam
Oct., 1969
Trocadero-Gloxinia Magic Mind Theatre
46 Great Jones, N.Y.C.

Grande de Coco-Cola, El
Ron House & Diz White
2-13-73
Mercer Arts Center
240 Mercer, N.Y.C.

Grandma's in the Cellar
Esquire Jauchem
7-16-72
Boston Center for the Arts
Boston, MA

Grandmother Is in the Strawberry Patch
H. M. Koutoukas
7-19-73
La Mama ETC
74 E. 4th, N.Y.C.

Grape Soda
Hal Craven
8-13-71
New York Theatre Ensemble
2 E. 2nd, N.Y.C.

Grass and Wild Strawberries
George Ryga
4-10-69
Playhouse Theatre Company
Vancouver, B.C., CAN

Grave Diggers of 1971
Reigh Hagen & Barbara Kahn
12-2-70
La Mama ETC
74 E. 4th, N.Y.C.

Grease (musical)
Jim Jacobs & Warren Casey
1-29-71
Kingston Mines Theatre
Chicago, IL

Great Airplane Snatch, The
Dan Greenburg
5-26-69
Stage 73
321 E. 73rd, N.Y.C.

Great American Desert, The
Jon Buckaloo
6-1-69
Loft Workshop
152 Bleecker, N.Y.C.

Great American Light War, The
D. Melmoth
6-23-71
St. Clement's Church
623 W. 46th, N.Y.C.

Great American Musical Comedy, The (nostalgic revue)
7-23-73
John Drew Theatre
East Hampton, L.I., NY

Great American Musical, The (revue)
Stan Keen (music)
9-18-73
Contemporary Theatre
Seattle, WA

Great American Pinball Machine, The
Charles Stanley
3-17-73
Clark Center for the Performing Arts
West Side YWCA
8th Ave. & 51st, N.Y.C.

Great American Refrigerator Come True, The
Fred Gordon
3-29-73
Ensemble Studio Theatre
549 W. 52nd, N.Y.C.

Great American Two Step, The (with Applaud Yourself, Applaud)
Carl Ahlm
1-31-69
Wittenberg University Theatre
Springfield, OH

Great Balls
Ellsworth Whimby
2-11-71
New York City League of Playwrights
Theatre Crossroads
23 E. 20th, N.Y.C.

Great Career, The (with An Evening for Merlin Finch)
Charles Dizenzo
12-26-68
Forum Theatre
Lincoln Center, N.Y.C.

Great Caribou Run, The
Bret Lyon
7-28-71
Tufts University
Medford, MA

Great Chinese Revolution, The
Anthony Scully
12-6-68
Yale University
New Haven, CT

Great Cross Country Race, The
6-30-68
Bristol Valley Playhouse
Naples, N.Y.C.

Great Fugue, The
F. M. Kimball
Apr., 1968
Theatre Company of Boston
Boston, MA

Great Goodness of Life (with Black Mass)
LeRoi Jones (Imamu Amiri Baraka)
10-18-68
East Wind
23 E. 125th, N.Y.C.

Great Hoss Pistol, A
Section Ten
5-16-73
New York University Theatre
111 Second, N.Y.C.

Great Jones Street (with Icarus Nine)
Bruce Serlen
2-12-73
Circle Theatre Company
2307 Broadway, N.Y.C.

Great MacDaddy, The
Paul Carter Harrison
1-12-73
Black Arts/West
Seattle, WA

Great Nebula in Orion, The (with Ikke, Ikke, Nye, Nye, Nye and The Family Continues)
Lanford Wilson
5-21-72
Circle Theatre Company
2307 Broadway, N.Y.C.

Great Rage of Philip Holtz, The (and Humulus the Mute)
8-6-68
Arena Theatre
Albany, NY

Great Scenes . . . An Introduction to Theatre
4-2-73
North Shore Music Circus
Beverly, MA

Great Tocks Island Dam, The
Jack Shoemaker
6-18-71
New York Theatre Ensemble
2 E. 2nd, N.Y.C.

Great White Computer, The
Peter Desbarrats
Spring, 1970
Centaur Theatre
Montreal, CAN

Great World and Timothy Colt, The
Louis Auchincloss
3-29-68
H B Playwrights Foundation
124 Bank, N.Y.C.

Great '57 Bank Robbery, The
Harry Haugan
12-22-72
New York Theatre Ensemble
2 E. 2nd, N.Y.C.

Greater Love
Carole Winner
8-9-73
Changing Scene
Denver, CO

Greatest Fairy Story Ever Told, The
Donald Howarth
11-24-73
St. Clement's Church
423 W. 46th, N.Y.C.

Greatshot
Arnold Weinstein & William Bolcom
5-8-69
Yale University
New Haven, CT

Green Julia
Paul Ableman
5-9-68
Washington Theatre Club
Washington, DC

Green Man and the Red Lady in the Red and Green Ladies Room, The
Guy Gauthier
6-26-70
New York Theatre Ensemble
2 E. 2nd, N.Y.C.

Green Thumb
Constance Conrad
10-28-72
Omni Theatre Club
145 W. 18th, N.Y.C.

Grey Lady Cantata, The
Peter Schumann
2-24-71
Bread & Puppet Theatre
New York Shakespeare Festival Public Theatre
425 Lafayette, N.Y.C.

Grin and Bear It! (with Postcards)
Tom Cushing; adapted by Ken McGuire
3-16-70
Belasco Theatre
N.Y.C.

Griot, The
C. Yarborough
3-29-73
La Mama ETC
74 E. 4th, N.Y.C.

Gris-Gris
Frank Gagliano
8-10-73
Eugene O'Neill Memorial Theatre
Waterford, CT

Grito
Ivan Acosta
6-12-70
Theatre of the Americas
124 W. 60th, N.Y.C.

Groove Tube
Kenneth Shapiro & Lane Sarasohn
10-10-69
Channel One Theatre
62 E. 4th, N.Y.C.

Grotesquerie
Harriet Ketchum
1-15-71
Anthony Mannino Drama Tree
182 Fifth, N.Y.C.

Grubby Devils, A Youth Rebellion, The
Total Theatre for Youth
4-18-72
Donnell Library
N.Y.C.

Guarapos
Pedro Santaliz
8-7-71
St. Clement's Church
423 W. 46th, N.Y.C.

Guernica (with Pique-Nique en Campagne)
Fernando Arrabal
4-30-69
Barbizon-Plaza Theatre
N.Y.C.

Guerra
G. Tito Shaw
June, 1970
Paperback Theatre
80 Second, N.Y.C

Guerre, Yes Sir!, La
Roch Carrier; translated by Suzanne Grossmann
8-4-72
Stratford Festival
Stratford, Ontario, CAN

Guess Who's Not Coming to Dinner
Norman Beim
3-11-71
P.S. 191
210 W. 61st, N.Y.C.

Guess Who the Noise Makers Are?
Jaheen Ishmaeli
9-20-73
Theatre Genesis
2nd Ave. & 10th, N.Y.C.

Guide, The
Harvey Breit & Patricia Rinehart
3-6-68
Hudson Theatre
N.Y.C.

Gulf of Crimson, The (with Cherry Soda Water)
Stephen Levi
5-11-68
H B Playwrights Foundation
124 Bank, N.Y.C.

Gum
Walter Corwin
4-6-71
WPA
333 Bowery, N.Y.C.

Gun
Charles Kespert, Frank Wittow, & company members
5-10-73
Academy Theatre
Atlanta, GA

Gun Play, A
Yale M. Udoff
1-8-71
Hartford Stage Company
Hartford, CT

Gunhill Road Express Is a Local, The
Randall Norcross
10-10-71
Theatre 23
23 E. 20th, N.Y.C.

Gunk
Robert Lowery (book); Dennis Burleson, Lauren Carner, Buckets Lowery (music)
2-10-71
University of Miami
Coral Gables, FL

Gunsight and Other Poems
Theodore Weiss; staged by Nancy Z. Rubin
4-19-72
Cubiculo
414 W. 51st, N.Y.C.

Guthrie
Glover Buck
8-20-68
Nucleus Repertory Theatre
261 W. 54th N.Y.C.

H

H Isolation
Lee Kissmann
1-31-69
Theatre Genesis
10th & 2nd, N.Y.C.

H. R. Pufnstuf Show
2-12-73
Felt Forum
Madison Square Garden
N.Y.C.

Ha Ha Play, The (with The Lamb)
Susan Yankowitz
11-27-70
Cubiculo
414 W. 51st, N.Y.C

Habit of Robins, A
Kenneth Bonnaffons
3-10-71
Louisiana State University
New Orleans, LA

Habital Splendid, L' (with Adora)
Jean Reavey
5-18-73
New York Theatre Ensemble
2 E. 2nd, N.Y.C.

Habitues
T. J. Camp III
11-19-73
Mama Hare's Tree
13th Street Theatre
50 W. 13th, N.Y.C.

Hadleyburg
Lewis Gardner (book & lyrics); Daniel Paget (music)
2-17-72
Minor Latham Playhouse
Barnard College
N.Y.C.

Hadrian VII
Peter Luke
1-8-69
Helen Hayes Theatre
N.Y.C.

Haftan (advertisement for an unfinished film)
Environmental Theatre of Saito Kikuo
12-1-73
Byrd Hoffman Foundation
147 Spring, N.Y.C.

Hajj Malik El: The Life and Death of Malcolm X
N. R. Davidson, Jr.
Spring, 1970
Theatre Company of Boston
Boston, MA

Halfway to Cephellenia
Jan., 1970
Massachusetts Institute of Technology
Cambridge, MA

Hallelujah
James Elward
8-22-72
Barnstormers
Tamworth, NH

Hallelujah or St. George and the Dragon
Peter Schumann
Summer, 1972
Bread & Puppet Theatre
Brooklyn, NY

Halloween
Sidney Michaels (book & lyrics); Mitch Leigh (music)
5-17-72
Florida State University
Tallahassee, FL

Hamburgers Are Impersonal (with Idabel's Fortune)
Ted Shine
7-9-71
Harlem School of the Arts Community Theatre
651 St. Nicholas, N.Y.C.

Hamhocks (with The Whiteshop)
Garrett Robinson
8-23-68
New Heritage Repertory Theatre
Madison at 127th, N.Y.C.

Hamlet
Shakespeare; adapted by Caca Aleksie
9-15-71
La Mama Belgrade
La Mama ETC
74 E. 4th, N.Y.C.

Hamlet and the 1001 Psychological Jingoleanisms of Prehistoric Landlordism of Rima-Puu
Jack Smith
August, 1971
Soho Theatre
131 Prince, N.Y.C.

Hamlet as in Hamburger (with A Day in the Life of an Actor)
John Dooley
5-13-70
Triangle Theatre
316 E. 88th, N.Y.C.

Hamlet of Gertrude Stein, The
10-25-71
Audio-Visual Group
98 Greene St. Loft, N.Y.C.

Hand That Cradles the Rock, The
8-29-73
Huron Country Playhouse
Grand Bend, Ontario, CAN

Hands of God, The
Carlos Solorzano
6-27-71
New York Theatre of the Americas
Studio 1
427 W. 59th, N.Y.C.

Handyrag
Carl Schiffman
9-29-72
New York Theatre Ensemble
2 E. 2nd, N.Y.C.

Hanging of William O'Donnell, The
David Helwig
June, 1970
Theatre Passe Muraille
Toronto, CAN

Hang-Ups and Cameos
George Koch
7-5-68
Tentarena
East Monticello, NY

Hannalore
Jere Admire
10-29-69
Spingold Theatre
Brandeis University
Waltham, MA

Hannibal (with Air Force)
7-23-72
Theatre of Gibberish
344 W. 36th, N.Y.C.

Happening with Butterfly McQueen and Her Friends, A
8-4-69
Bert Wheeler Theatre
250 W. 43rd, N.Y.C.

Happiness Bench, The
Thomas Bellin
Feb., 1968
Theatre East
Hollywood, CA

Happiness Cage, The
Dennis J. Reardon
2-11-70
New York Shakespeare Festival
Public Theatre
425 Lafayette, N.Y.C.

Happiness Is Just a Little Thing Called a Rolls-Royce
Arthur Alsberg & Robert Fisher
4-22-68
Locust Theatre
Philadelphia, PA

Happiness Train, The (with Fall River Ruins and Pay Attention to the Ravel)
Donald Kvares
11-5-70
Theatre Crossroads
23 E. 20th, N.Y.C.

Happy
William Kushner
2-11-71
Playbox
94 St. Mark's Pl., N.Y.C.

Happy Anniversary—Goodbye
7-26-71
Mountain Playhouse
Jennerstown, PA

Happy Apple, The
Terrence Feely
8-8-72
Flat Rock Playhouse
Flat Rock, NC

Happy Birthday, Wanda June
Kurt Vonnegut, Jr.
10-7-70
Theatre de Lys
N.Y.C.

Happy Days Are Here Again
Cecil P. Taylor
10-26-72
Manhattan Theatre Club
321 E. 73rd, N.Y.C.

Happy Days of Summer
Romain Weingarten
6-22-71
Shaw Festival
Niagara-on-the-Lake
Ontario, CAN

Happy End
Bertolt Brecht; adapted by Michael Feingold (book); Kurt Weill (music)
4-6-72
Yale Repertory Theatre
New Haven, CT

Happy Hunter, The
Georges Feydeau; translated by Barnett Shaw
10-24-72
Dallas Theatre Center
Dallas, TX

Happy Hypocrite, The
James Bredt, Edward Eager
9-5-68
Bouwerie Lane Theatre
330 Bowery, N.Y.C.

Happy New Year, Love
Erwin H. Lerner
3-22-68
Cooper Square Arts Theatre
35 Cooper Sq., N.Y.C.

Happy We (musical)
The Capers
2-21-71
Pine Manor Junior College
Chestnut Hill, MA

Happy-Go-Lucky (with Onward and Upward)
Andrew Witwer
12-4-69
Loft Workshop
152 Bleecker, N.Y.C.

Hara Kiri
Philip Zweig
6-19-73
New Plays Festival
WPA
333 Bowery, N.Y.C.

Harangues, The
Joseph A. Walker
1-13-70
Negro Ensemble Company
St. Mark's Playhouse
133 Second, N.Y.C.

Hard But Fair (revue)
Presented by the ex-inmates of the Women's House of Detention
3-9-72
Columbia University
N.Y.C.

Hard Core Soft Shoe (with Toyland)
Anna Belle Johnson
4-15-72
St. Peter's Church
346 W. 20th, N.Y.C.

Hard Job Being Old
Tom Martel (lyrics & music)
5-15-72
Edison Theatre
240 W. 47th, N.Y.C.

Hard Times
D. B. Gilles
11-6-73
Playwrights' Horizons
Clark Center for the Performing Arts
West Side YWCA, 8th Ave. & 51st, N.Y.C.

Hard To Be a Jew (new musical version)
Sholom Aleichem (book); Itzak Perlow (lyrics); Sholom Secunda (music)
10-28-73
Eden Theatre
2nd Ave. & 12th, N.Y.C.

Hardesty Park
William McCleery
9-5-72
Little Lake Theatre
Canonsburg, PA

Hark!
Robert Lorick (lyrics); Dan Goggin & Marvin Solley (music)
5-22-72
Mercer Arts Center
240 Mercer, N.Y.C.

Harlequin for Children
Remy Charlip & Burton Supree (book); Michael Corbett & Lynne Taylor (lyrics & music)
11-11-73
Clark Center for the Performing Arts
West Side YWCA
8th Ave. & 51st, N.Y.C.

Harlequin Play
William Kemp, Robert Jackson, Leslie Hurley & Martin Donovan
8-18-68
Provincetown Playhouse
Provincetown, MA

Harlequinade for Mourners
Shirley Guy
5-12-70
New York Theatre Workshop
154 E. 54th, N.Y.C.

Harlot and the Hunted, The
Arnold Meyers
11-6-73
Playwrights' Horizons
Clark Center for the Performing Arts
West Side YWCA, 8th Ave. & 51st, N.Y.C.

Harold and Perpetua
Michael Shurtleff
Nov., 1971
Friday Theatre
N.Y.C.

Harrison Progressive School, The (with Ruth and The Rabbi)
Stanley Nelson
10-23-68
Playwrights' Workshop Club
14 Waverly Pl., N.Y.C.

Harry
Augustus Edwards
4-9-71
New York Theatre Ensemble
2 E. 2nd, N.Y.C.

Harry and Edna Horowitz
James Edward Shannon
2-25-72
New York Theatre Ensemble
2 E. 2nd, N.Y.C.

Harry and the Angel
Norman Dietz
Feb., 1969
St. Peter's Gate
132 E. 54th, N.Y.C.

Harry's Night Out
John Crennan
12-13-68
Good Shepherd-Faith Church
152 W. 66th, N.Y.C.

Harunobu (with Bessie Smith and The Blue Centaur)
Piero Heliczer
2-18-71
Cinematheque
80 Wooster, N.Y.C.

Harvest
James Maloon
3-23-68
Dramarena Repertory Theatre
158 W. 55th, N.Y.C.

Harvey McLeod
Peter Schumann
Summer, 1972
Bread & Puppet Theatre
Brooklyn, NY

Hashish Club
L. Larsen & Company
Spring, 1973
Company Theatre
Los Angeles, CA

Hatfields and McCoys
Billy Edd Wheeler
6-20-70
Grandview State Park
Beckley, WV

Hatrack Named Georgie, A
Susan Scherman
1-27-72
St. Clement's Church
423 W. 46th, N.Y.C.

Haunted Host, The
Robert Patrick
7-29-68
Old Reliable Theatre Tavern
231 E. 3rd, N.Y.C.

Haunted Place, A
Philip Lo Giudice
12-3-71
Senior Dramatic Workshop Repertory Theatre
Studio 808, Carnegie Hall
881 Seventh, N.Y.C.

Haunting of Hill House, The
F. Andrew Leslie
5-24-68
Stage 9
96 W. Houston, N.Y.C.

Having Fun in the Bathroom
Leonard Melfi
4-11-68
La Mama ETC
122 Second, N.Y.C.

Hawk, The (new version)
Murray Mednick
2-5-73
Mercer Arts Center
240 Mercer, N.Y.C.

He' s a A Jones
G. Tito Shaw
1-11-73
New Group Theatre Company
Greenwich Mews Theatre
141 W. 13th, N.Y.C.

He Who Laughs Last
Antonio Calabrese
9-7-73
Playwrights' Workshop Club
Electric Circus
23 St. Mark's Place, N.Y.C.

Head 'Em Off at the Pass
1-5-72
Warehouse
Manitoba Theatre Center
Winnipeg, Manitoba, CAN

Head of Hair, The
Allen Davis
1-29-70
New Theatre Workshop
154 E. 54th, N.Y.C.

Head of His Time, A (with The Spayed Cat)
Michael McGrinder
5-17-72
Bastiano's Studio
14 Cooper Sq., N.Y.C.

Head of State
John Ahart & cast
Spring, 1973
University of Illinois
Urbana, IL

Headplay
Richard Reichman
January, 1971
Theater Workshop Boston
Boston Center for the Arts
Boston, MA

Hear Ye Hear Ye
8-24-71
Boston Repertory Theatre
Hyannis, MA

Hearing, The
Tony Barsha
3-26-71
Playbox
94 St. Mark's Pl., N.Y.C.

Heart's a Wonder, The
J. M. Synge, Nuala O'Farrell & Maureen Charlton (adaptors)
2-12-71
MacMillan Theatre
Toronto, CAN

Heat: Group Emanations with Music
New Theatre Ensemble
5-8-69
Hunter College Playhouse
N.Y.C.

Heathen Piper
Michael McGrinder
5-11-70
Old Reliable Theatre Tavern
231 E. 3rd, N.Y.C.

Heaven Grand in Amber Orbit
Jackie Curtis
10-9-69
Gotham Art
455 W. 43rd, N.Y.C.

Heaven Must Be Like This
Raymond Carlson
Nov., 1971
Friday Theatre
N.Y.C.

Heavenly Drugstore, The
Ricardo Castillo
11-6-69
New York Theatre Ensemble
2 E. 2nd, N.Y.C.

Heavy Duty Radio Theatre
David Dozer
Feb., 1971
Loft Workshop
21 Bond, N.Y.C.

Hedda Gabler
Henrik Ibsen; adapted by Christopher Hampton
2-17-71
Playhouse Theatre
359 W. 48th, N.Y.C.

Hedge of Serpents
Ramon Delgado
11-19-69
Kentucky Wesleyan College
Owensboro, KY

!Heimskringla! or The Stoned Angels
Paul Foster
3-28-70
La Mama ETC
74 E. 4th, N.Y.C.

Heirloom, The (Chinese drama)
10-16-71
Four Seas Amateur Players of Chinatown Transfiguration Church
Pace College
N.Y.C.

Heist, The
Robert Reinhold
1-15-71
Omni Theatre Club
145 W. 18th, N.Y.C.

Helen Haft Story, The
Tom Eyen
11-30-69
La Mama ETC
74 E. 4th, N.Y.C.

Helen's Hand
Raymond Platt
4-21-72
New York Theatre Ensemble
2 E. 2nd, N.Y.C.

Hello
Frank Orefice (book & lyrics); Frank Stuart (music)
5-4-72
Schimmel Center for the Arts
Pace College
N.Y.C.

Hello and Goodbye
Athol Fugard
11-11-68
Theatre de Lys
N.Y.C.

Hello, I Love You
Barry Berg
11-8-73
New Dramatists
424 W. 44th, N.Y.C.

Hello, Sucker
Robert Ennis Turoff & Larry Marks (book); Artie Harris (music & lyrics)
5-17-69
Casa Manana Dinner Theatre
Fort Worth, TX

Help, I Am
Robert Patrick
3-11-68
Old Reliable Theatre Tavern
231 E. 3rd, N.Y.C.

Help, I'm Single Again
Robert T. Littell
8-13-69
Frances Adler Theatre
211 W. 71st, N.Y.C.

Help Stamp Out Puritans
Walter Beaver (book & lyrics); Ted Nichols (music)
5-9-69
California State College
Los Angeles, CA

Helping Out
Patricia Cooper
8-13-68
Cafe Act IV
Provincetown, MA

Hemingway Meets Fitzgerald
6-22-68
Spencer Memorial Church
Brooklyn, NY

Hemingway Play, The
Frederic Hunter
7-21-73
Eugene O'Neill Memorial Theatre
Waterford, CT

Henry and Henrietta
Barbara Davenport
7-18-69
Eugene O'Neill Memorial Theatre
Waterford, CT

Henry's Daughter
Cavada Humphrey
2-20-73
Artists Theatre
Stage 73
321 E. 73rd, N.Y.C.

Her First Roman
Ervin Drake
7-29-68
Colonial Theatre
Boston, MA

Her Infinite Variety (scenes & music from Shakespeare)
8-30-71
Library & Museum of the Performing Arts
111 Amsterdam, N.Y.C.

Herbie's Door
Ron Taylor
6-24-71
American Shakespeare Festival
Stratford, CT

Here Are Ladies (one-woman show with Siobhan McKenna)
2-22-71
New York Shakespeare Festival Public Theatre
425 Lafayette, N.Y.C.

Here Be Dragons (with A Knack with Horses)
David Ward
12-5-70
St. Clement's Church
423 W. 46th, N.Y.C.

Here Comes the Groom
Samuel H. Cohen
10-8-73
Mayfair Theatre
235 W. 46th, N.Y.C.

Here's Where I Belong
Terrence McNally, Robert Waldman, Alfred Uhry
1-15-68
Shubert Theatre
Philadelphia, PA

Here You Are
Paul Pierog
12-2-71
Playbox Studio
94 St. Mark's Pl., N.Y.C.

Hermit's Cock, The
Allen Boretz
9-29-69
New Theatre Workshop
154 E. 54th, N.Y.C.

Hermosa Beach
Bruce Serlen
3-18-72
Hunter College Playwrights Project
West Side YMCA
5 W. 63rd, N.Y.C.

Hero (in-process production)
Israel Horovitz
5-7-71
New York Shakespeare Festival Public Theatre
425 Lafayette, N.Y.C.

Hero, The
Robert Noreault
6-12-69
New York Theatre Ensemble
2 E. 2nd, N.Y.C.

Hero, The
Arthur Kopit
10-3-70
Playbox
94 St. Mark's Pl., N.Y.C.

Herod and the Prophet Samuel (dramatic reading)
David Libman
12-8-73
Little Theatre
West Side YMCA
5 W. 63rd, N.Y.C.

Herodes (liturgical drama)
12-17-71
Church of the Ascension
5th Ave. at 10th, N.Y.C.

Herodiade
Stephane Mellarme
Mar., 1970
Mt. St. Agnes College
Baltimore, MD

Heroes and Failures
Warren Kliewer
11-2-73
St. Peter's Church
346 W. 20th, N.Y.C.

Her(r) Professor (with Subtitles)
Michael McGrinder
11-23-70
Old Reliable Theatre Tavern
213 E. 3rd, N.Y.C.

Heuristic (puppet play)
Jeannie Schindler
Apr., 1973
Portland State University
Portland, OR

Hexenkuechen
Anselm Hollo
Dec., 1971
Center for the New Performing Art
Iowa City, IA

Hey Dad Who Is This Guy Gershwin Anyway?
Jan., 1971
Paul's Mall Cabaret Theatre
Boston, MA

Hey Fellas
Matt Silverman
Apr., 1969
Martinique Theatre
N.Y.C.

Hey Look!
Rudas & Phillips Wylly; music by Lon Norman
Jan., 1969
Civic Center
San Francisco, CA

Hey Out There, Is There Anyone Out There?
Elaine Denholtz
2-16-73
New York Theatre Ensemble
2 E. 2nd, N.Y.C.

Hey, Porter (revue)
Cole Porter
6-18-73
Upstairs at the Buttery
Niagara-on-the-Lake, Ontario, CAN

Heyday
Herbert Appleman
9-28-72
New Dramatists
424 W. 44th, N.Y.C.

Hiel Nuestra de Cada Dia, La (Our Daily Bitterness) (with The Angels Are Exhausted)
Luis Rafael Sanchez
2-23-73
New Federal Theatre
240 E. 3rd, N.Y.C.

High John de Conquer
Afro-American Folkloric Troupe
4-22-69
New York City Center
N.Y.C.

High Rise
Charles Schmidt
12-10-71
Theatre Suburbia
Houston, TX

High Structure Falls Further, A
Benjamin Bradford
10-12-70
Old Reliable Theatre Tavern
231 E. 3rd, N.Y.C.

Hills Like White Elephants (with The Sea Change)
Ernest Hemingway
11-6-69
Universalist Theatre
4 W. 76th, N.Y.C.

Hip, Black and Angry
New Heritage Repertory Theatre
4-13-68
Loeb Student Center
Washington Square South & LaGuardia Pl., N.Y.C.

Hippie As a Lark
Robert Patrick
6-7-73
Stagelights II Theatrical Club
125 W. 22nd, N.Y.C.

His First Step
Oyamo
1-28-72
Negro Ensemble Company
St. Mark's Playhouse
133 Second, N.Y.C.

His Majesty, The Devil
6-10-71
Cabaret Theatre
St. Peter's Gate
132 E. 54th, N.Y.C.

Historia del Hombre que Dijo que No, La
Lydia M. Gonzalez
5-26-73
Teatro Jurutungo
Gershwin Theatre
Brooklyn College, Brooklyn, NY

History of the United States by Local 49 of the Brotherhood of Hot Dog Vendors of America, The
Walter A. Fairservis, Jr.
7-7-70
Brooklyn College
Brooklyn, NY

Hitch Hiker, The
Paul Harriman
4-21-72
University of Montana
Missoula, MT

Hitler
J. Ford
Fall, 1973
Actors Theatre of Louisville
Louisville, KY

Hmmm to the Creator
Edward Greenberg
6-3-68
Circle in the Square
N.Y.C.

Hocus Pocus
Jim Doyle
11-21-73
Manhattan Theatre Club
321 E. 73rd, N.Y.C.

Hogwash (with Dialectic Dialogue in Double Time; Close Call; and Robbers' Nest)
Barry Litvack
10-28-70
Playwrights's Unit
83 E 4th, N.Y.C.

Hold Up, The
Jean Nuchtern
6-6-69
Stage Lights Theatrical Club
218 W. 48th, N.Y.C.

Hole in the Sky, The
Douglas Nichols
11-12-70
Changing Scene
Denver, CO

Holey Trinity
Jeannine O'Reilly
6-8-71
WPA
333 Bowery, N.Y.C.

Holiday for Santa
Blanche Thebom (book & lyrics); Carleton Palmer (music)
Dec., 1970
Colony Square Theater
Atlanta, GA

Holiday, The
James Hashim
5-13-71
Clarion State College
Clarion, PA

Holland Tunnel of Love, The
F. V. Hunt
6-29-71
Roundabout Theatre
307 W. 26th, N.Y.C.

Holmes and Moriarty
Allen Sternfield
8-6-73
Eugene O'Neill Memorial Theatre
Waterford, CT

Holy Communion
Joe Pintauro
11-6-69
Loft Workshop
152 Bleecker, N.Y.C.

Holy Ghostly, The
Sam Shepard
11-29-72
New Village Theatre
433 E. 6th, N.Y.C.

Holy Moses (a "rock testament")
Hal Grego (book, lyrics & music)
2-8-73
Greenwich Mews Theatre
141 W. 13th, N.Y.C.

Homage at Night
Lars Gustafsson; translation by Yvonne Sandstroem
1-10-72
Library & Museum of the Performing Arts
111 Amsterdam, N.Y.C.

Hombre Sincero, Un: Jose Marti
Rene Buch
1-25-73
Spanish Theatre Repertory Company
Library & Museum of the Performing Arts
111 Amsterdam, N.Y.C.

Hombres y No
Manuel de Pedrolo
9-21-73
City University Graduate Center
33 W. 42nd, N.Y.C.

Home
David Storey
11-17-70
Morosco Theatre
N.Y.C.

Home Address
James Hurt
Apr., 1969
University of Illinois
Urbana, IL

Home Again — Home Again
Powell Shepherd
10-6-69
Old Reliable Theatre Tavern
231 E. 3rd, N.Y.C.

Home Away From, A
Glenn Allen Smith
4-28-69
Village South Theatre
15 Vandam, N.Y.C.

Home Fires
John Guare
4-7-69
Cort Theatre
N.Y.C.

Home Is Harlem
Summer, 1972
Experimental Theatre Group
Dept. of Psychiatry
Harlem Hospital, N.Y.C.

Home Life of the Buffalo
Richard Harrity
Summer, 1972
Hopkins Center
Dartmouth College
Hanover, NH

Home Monster
Stan Thomas
5-2-69
Spingold Theatre
Brandeis University
Waltham, MA

Home on the Range
LeRoi Jones (Imamu Amiri Baraka)
5-20-68
Fillmore East
Second Ave. & 6th, N.Y.C.

Home, The (reading)
Kent Anderson & Bengt Bratt; Robert Settles (translator)
1-11-71
Library & Museum of the Performing Arts
111 Amsterdam, N.Y.C.

Homecoming
David Martin
Mar. 22, 1968
Yale University
New Haven, CT

Homecookin'
Clay Goss
1-12-72
Negro Ensemble Company
St. Mark's Playhouse
133 Second Ave., N.Y.C.

Homefront
Martin Walser
12-14-72
Cubiculo
414 W. 51st, N.Y.C.

Homefront Blues
Jack Gilhooley
7-23-73
Stage 73
321 E. 73rd, N.Y.C.

Homer
Frank Fetters
7-30-68
Springfield Community Theatre
Springfield, MO

Hommel
James Shearwood
2-23-69
Dancers Studio Foundation
34 E. 10th, N.Y.C.

Homo (with The Queen of Greece)
Rochelle Owens
4-11-69
La Mama ETC
74 E. 4th, N.Y.C.

Honest Answer, An
Irving Glusack
11-26-71
New York Theatre Ensemble
2 E. 2nd, N.Y.C.

Honest-To-God Schnozzola, The
Israel Horovitz
July, 1968
Cafe Act IV
Provincetown, MA

Honesty
Jon Winer (book); Dave Meoli (music)
June, 1972
Wayland High School
Wayland, MA

Honesty Is the Best Policy
Barry Litvack
4-15-70
Cincinnati Playhouse in the Park
Cincinnati, OH

Honky-Tonk Trash
Hal Borske
6-15-72
La Mama ETC
74 E. 4th, N.Y.C.

Honor
Richard Foreman
5-25-73
Cubiculo
414 W. 51st, N.Y.C.

Honor America
Robert Lerner
5-24-70
Mainstream Theatre
20 E. 14th, N.Y.C.

Honor and Offer
Henry Livings
11-21-68
Playhouse in the Park
Cincinnati, OH

Hooded Gnome, The (Part 3 of Grub)
Frederick Bailey
2-4-72
Playbox
94 St. Mark's Pl., N.Y.C.

Hoofers, The (formerly entitled Tap Happening)
7-29-69
Mercury Theatre
136 E. 13th, N.Y.C.

Hoo-Hah!
Stanley Kaplan
4-3-72
New Old Reliable Theatre
231 E. 3rd, N.Y.C.

Hope for Life
Stanley Seidman
Summer, 1973
South Street Seaport, N.Y.C.

Hora de los Hombres Tristes, La
Arnaldo Rodriguez
9-20-73
Gama Company
Teatro LATA
114 W. 14th, N.Y.C.

Horatio
Ron Whyte
7-29-71
American Shakespeare Festival
Stratford, CT

Horay
David Kranes
3-11-73
New Phoenix Theatre
Lyceum Theatre
N.Y.C.

Horn in the West (revised version)
Kermit Hunter
6-23-72
Daniel Boone Amphitheatre
Boone, NC

Horrors
Bram Stoker's "Dracula," adapted by Kenneth Cavander
8-5-70
Yale Repertory Theatre
East Hampton, NY

Horrors of Dr. Moreau, The
H. G. Wells; adapted by Joel Stone
11-16-72
Jean Cocteau Theatre
43 Bond, N.Y.C.

Horseman, Pass By
Rocco Bufano & John Duffy
1-15-69
Fortune Theatre
62 E. 4th, N.Y.C.

Horseshoes
Paul Dexter
7-28-71
Cubiculo
414 W. 51st, N.Y.C.

Hosanna
Michel Tremblay; translated by William Glassco & John Van Burek
5-10-73
Théâtre de Quath'Sous
Montreal, Quebec, CAN

Hosea
John Larrson and John Gowans
June, 1971
Salvation Army Temple
120 W. 14th, N.Y.C.

Hostility at the Hacienda
Edward Cope
5-18-73
Theatre Suburbia
Houston, TX

Hot and Cold Heros
Joe Jakubowitz
5-9-73
13th Street Theatre
50 W. 13th, N.Y.C.

Hot Evening Rain
See: Thirty Years Past

Hot Feet
Paper Bag Players
7-16-69
Washington Square Park
N.Y.C.

Hot L Baltimore
Lanford Wilson
2-4-73
Circle Theatre Company
2307 Broadway, N.Y.C.

Hot Line
Andrew Witwer
3-27-69
Loft Workshop
152 Bleecker, N.Y.C.

Hot Summer Night
Ted Willis
12-15-68
New Day Repertory Theatre
New York University
566 LaGuardia Pl., N.Y.C.

Hot Tickets
Jeff Hochhauser
4-4-69
New York Theatre Ensemble
2 E. 2nd, N.Y.C.

Hot Voodoo
The Angels of Light
6-23-72
Theatre for the New City
151 Bank, N.Y.C.

Hotel China or Hcohtienla
Richard Foreman
12-8-71
Ontological-Hysteric Theatre
Cinematheque
80 Wooster, N.Y.C.

Hotel De Dream
See: FACADES

Hotel Happiness (with I Want to Fly)
Margaret Ford Taylor
3-16-72
Karamu House Theatre
Cleveland, OH

Hotel Paranoia
Max E. Verga
12-7-73
West Side Gay Theatre
W.S.D.G. Center
37 Ninth, N.Y.C.

Houdini
Muriel Rukeyser
7-3-73
Lenox Arts Center
Lenox, MA

Hough in Blazes
Jerome Max
11-5-71
University of Pennsylvania
Philadelphia, PA

House of Atreus Stone, The
Francis X. Kelly
1-20-70
Catholic University
Washington, DC

House of Breath
William Goyen
11-4-69
Trinity Square Repertory Company
Providence, RI

House of Fools, The
Joseph de Valdivielso
3-19-72
Greenwich Mews Theatre
141 W. 13th, N.Y.C.

House of Fun and Games, The
Shirley Guy
Sept., 1971
Kaymar Gallery
N.Y.C.

House of Leather, The
Frederick Gaines (book); Dale Menten (music & lyrics)
3-26-69
Cricket Theatre
Minneapolis, MN

House of Mourning
George Bass
8-28-68
Long Wharf Theatre
New Haven, CT

House of Yahweh, The
Jane Odin
11-1-72
Actors' Experimental Unit
682 Sixth, N.Y.C.

House on Chestnut Street, The
James Nichol
3-9-72
Theatre Calgary
Calgary, Alberta, CAN

House on Prince Street, The
Wallace Dace
Feb., 1971
Kansas State University
Manhatten, KS

House on the Cliff
George Batson
4-20-72
Church of Jesus Christ of Latter Day Saints
142 W. 81st, N.Y.C.

House Party
Ed Bullins
10-16-73
American Place Theatre
N.Y.C.

House Party — A Musical Memory
Rosetta LeNoire; Manny Cavaco & John Lenahan (music)
4-15-73
Amas Repertory Theatre
4 W. 76th, N.Y.C.

House Within the House Within, The
Joseph B. Baldwin
1968
University of Alabama
University, AL

Housewives' Cantata, The (revue)
11-5-73
St. Peter's Gate
16 E. 56th, N.Y.C.

How a Nice Girl Named Janet Contracted Syphilis (with Jeff Chandler)
David Shumaker
11-28-70
Unit Theatre
157 W. 22nd, N.Y.C.

How Do You Do
Ed Bullins
Fall, 1968
Theatre Company of Boston
Boston, MA

How Long Until the End of Morning
Cleve Thomas
1-21-72
Rubin Residence Hall
10th St. & 5th, N.Y.C.

How Mr. Mockinpott Was Cured of His Sufferings
Peter Weiss; Christopher Holme (translator)
5-26-73
Greenwich Mews Theatre
141 W. 13th, N.Y.C.

How Much, How Much?
Peter Keveson
4-20-70
Provincetown Playhouse
133 MacDougal, N.Y.C.

How Perfectly Nice
Gordon Tretick
10-17-68
Playbox
94 St. Mark's Pl., N.Y.C.

How Peter the Prick Found Love
William Kushner & Dennis Giesel
11-13-70
Playbox
94 St. Mark's Pl., N.Y.C.

How Prometheus Got Bound
8-10-68
Springold Theatre
Brandeis University
Waltham, MA

How St. Augustine Made It Saint
Stuart Koch
3-2-70
Old Reliable Theatre Tavern
231 E. 3rd, N.Y.C.

How Sweet and Fitting It Is
Joseph Renard
7-1-68
Old Reliable Theatre Tavern
231 E. 3rd, N.Y.C.

How the Company Went to an Island What Happened and Who Came Back
Centre Studio Company
11-26-70
National Arts Centre
Ottawa, CAN

How the Other Half Loves
Alan Ayckbourn
2-15-71
Royal Poinciana Playhouse
Palm Beach, FL

How the Puppets Formed a Government (improvisational)
4-1-69
Manitoba Theatre Centre
Winnipeg, Manitoba, CAN

How the Wind Comes
John Vincent Stoltenberg
1-30-69
Basement Coffee House
155 E. 22nd, N.Y.C.

How They Made It
Nancy Fales
4-30-70
La Mama ETC
74 E. 4th, N.Y.C.

How Thunder and Lightning Began
See: Late for Oblivion

How To Be a Successful Educator Without Really. . .
Lynn E. Haldeman (book, lyrics, music)
5-2-73
Catawba College
Salisbury, NC

How To Make a Woman
Summer, 1969
Caravan Theatre
Cambridge, MA

How To Select a Victim
Martin Kearns
9-3-70
Plaster Foundation
36 Greene, N.Y.C.

How To Steal an Election
William F. Brown, Joseph Michael (book); Oscar Brand (music & lyrics)
10-13-68
Pocket Theatre
NY

Howard Klein Trilogy, The
H. M. Koutoukas
12-25-68
71 Charles, N.Y.C.

Howie's
Richard A. Steel
Fall, 1972
Mermaid Theatre
Los Angeles, CA

Hub, The
Margaret Collins
8-20-72
Theater Wagon
Staunton, VA

Hubba, Hubba
June, 1970
Teen Theatre Workshop
Los Angeles, CA

Hubba Hubba
Jan & Gene Casey
8-16-71
Goodspeed Opera House
East Haddam, CT

Huck: An Adventure Musical
Maurice Tei Dunn, Peter Howard, Ford Hovis
3-10-73
Driftwood Company
Bouwerie Lane Theatre
330 Bowery, N.Y.C.

Huckleberry Finn (story theatre version)
4-21-71
Loeb Drama Center
Cambridge, MA

Huff and the Puff, The (with Whatever Happened to Hugging and Kissing)
Norman Wexler
4-17-70
Cleveland Playhouse
Cleveland, OH

Huh, Stan?
Hector Troy
11-8-69
Unit Theatre
157 W. 22nd, N.Y.C.

Human Condition: Commedia, The
Salvadore J. Coppola
6-9-72
Playwrights' Workshop Club
Bastiano's Studio
14 Cooper Sq., N.Y.C.

Humulus the Mute (and The Great Rage of Philip Holtz)
8-6-68
Arena Theatre
Albany, NY

Hung (with Roommates)
Tom Murrin
2-16-68
La Mama ETC
122 Second, N.Y.C.

Hunger and Thirst
Eugene Ionesco
7-16-69
Berkshire Theatre Festival
Stockbridge, MA

Hunger Artist, A
John Murrell
Summer, 1972
Okanagan Summer School of the Arts
Penticton, Alberta, CAN

Hungry Ones, The (with Sailors at an Exhibition and A Song for Helen)
Paul Rawlings
5-4-71
13th Street Theatre
50 W. 13th, N.Y.C.

Hunter, The
Murray Mednick
October, 1968
Theatre Genesis
10th & 2nd, N.Y.C.

Hunting of the Snark, The
Lewis Carroll; adapted by Donna Carlson
6-28-68
Thresholds
23 E. 20th, N.Y.C.

Hurricane of the Eye
Emanuel Peluso
6-20-69
La Mama ETC
74 E. 4th, N.Y.C.

Hurricane Season, The
John O'Neal
Feb., 1973
Free Southern Theatre
New Orleans, LA

Hurry, Harry
Jeremiah Morris, Lee Kalcheim, Susan Perkis (book); David Finkle (lyrics); Bill Weeden (music)
10-12-72
Ritz Theatre
219 W. 48th, N.Y.C.

Hush! Hush! (with Please 7:52 We Love You and The We Do It Agency)
Peter DiLeo
5-8-71
PAWorkshop
353 Ave. of the Americas, N.Y.C.

Hut A Yid A Landele
10-18-68
Barbizon-Plaza Theatre
N.Y.C.

Huui, Huui
Anne Olson Burr
11-16-68
New York Shakespeare Festival Public Theatre
425 Lafayette, N.Y.C.

Huzzy, The
Mars Hill
4-7-73
Black Arts Inc. of Albany
Afro-American Studio
415 W. 127th, N.Y.C.

Hyman' s Downfall
Sonia Goldberg (music & lyrics)
3-2-69
Straus Auditorium
Educational Alliance
197 E. Broadway, N.Y.C.

Hymie Finkelstein Used Lumber Company, The (musical)
Ernie Fahn
June, 1973
Karamu House Theatre
Cleveland, OH

Hymn to the Creator
See also: Rosensweig, F. C. (revision of above)

Hypatia 3
Michael McGrinder
10-17-72
WPA
333 Bowery, N.Y.C.

Hypothalamus
George Christodoulakis
7-17-73
Greek Arts Festival
Loeb Student Center
New York Univ., N.Y.C.

I

I Am a Woman
Viveca Lindfors
7-30-73
John Drew Theatre
East Hampton, Long Island, NY

I Am Not the Eiffel Tower
Ecaterina Oproiu
4-22-69
La Mama ETC
74 E. 4th, N.Y.C.

I Am the Chosen One
Benito Gutmacher
7-28-72
Mercer Arts Center
240 Mercer, N.Y.C.

I Bring You Flowers
William Lang
2-3-72
University of Missouri
Columbia, MO

I Came for a Job (with 'Til 2 in The Morning)
12-15-72
Long Island University
Flatbush Ave. Extension & DeKalb Ave., N.Y.C.

I Came to New York to Write
Robert Patrick
Mar., 1969
Old Reliable Theatre Tavern
231 E. 3rd, N.Y.C.

I Can't Go On Without You, Minna Mandelbaum!
Alex Byron
4-28-73
Hunter College Playwrights Project
West Side YMCA
5 W. 63rd, N.Y.C.

I Can't Imagine Tomorrow (with Confessional)
Tennessee Williams
8-19-71
Maine Theatre Arts Festival
Bar Harbor, ME

I'd Go to Heaven If I Was Good
Carole Leslie Thompson
9-17-73
Manhattan Theatre Club
321 E. 73rd, N.Y.C.

I'd Rather Be Dead Than Alone
Florence Aquino Kaufman & Ann Curry
8-4-72
Knickerbocker Creative Theatre Foundation
Hudson Guild Theatre
441 W. 26th, N.Y.C.

I'd Rather Sit Alone on a Pumpkin
Barry Berg
5-15-72
Neighborhood Playhouse School of the Theatre
340 E. 54th, N.Y.C.

I Didn't Hear Nothing, I Live in the Back
See: Brooklyn Bridge Is Falling Down

I Don't Care Who You Give It To, As Long As You Give Some To Me
Hal Craven
2-16-73
New York Theatre Ensemble
2 E. 2nd, N.Y.C.

I Don't Generally Like Poetry But Have You Read Trees? (revue)
Albert Innaurato & Chris Durang
Fall, 1972
Yale University
New Haven, CT

I Dreamt I Dwelt in Bloomingdale's
Jack Ramer & Ernest McCarty (lyrics); Ernest McCarty (music)
2-12-70
Provincetown Playhouse
133 MacDougal, N.Y.C.

I Flew to Fiji; You Went South (a mixed-media narrative)
Ping Chong
10-19-73
Silver Whale Gallery
21 Bleecker, N.Y.C.

I Got on Point Late in Life
Jeannine O'Reilly
5-25-70
Old Reliable Theatre Tavern
231 E. 3rd, N.Y.C.

I Have Always Believed in Ghosts
Michael Gibbens
9-4-72
New Old Reliable Theatre
231 E. 3rd, N.Y.C.

I Hear It Kissing Me Ladies
Arthur Sainer
11-14-70
Unit Theatre
157 W. 22nd, N.Y.C.

I'll Grind My Bones
Joan Durant
1-15-70
St. Peter's Church
346 W. 20th, N.Y.C.

I Love Thee Freely
Benjamin Bernard Zavin
9-17-73
Astor Place Theatre
434 Lafayette, N.Y.C.

I Love You
Ralph Scholl
2-19-70
New York Theatre Ensemble
2 E. 2nd, N.Y.C.

I Love You, Willie-Cat
Patrick O'Hearne
8-25-69
Hampton Playhouse
Hampton, NH

I'm Glad I'm Not the Janitor Here (with Are You prepared To Be a United States Marine?)
2-20-69
Cubiculo
414 W. 51st, N.Y.C.

I'm Glad You Asked That Question
Joanne Joseph
7-25-72
Washington Square Church
133 W. 4th, N.Y.C.

I'm Nobody
David Kranes
2-14-68
Extension Theatre
128 E. 7th, N.Y.C.

I'm Not Jewish and I Don't Know Why I'm Screaming
Stan Lachow
5-5-73
Cubiculo
414 W. 51st, N.Y.C.

I'm Read, You're Black
Lewis Cleckler
4-13-29-72
Dallas Theatre Center
Dallas, TX

I'm Really Here
Jean-Claude van Itallie
3-22-73
Academy Theatre
Atlanta, GA

I'm Solomon
Erich Segal, Anne Croswell, Ernest Gold
4-23-68
Shubert Theatre
New Haven, CT

I Married You for the Fun of It
Natalia Ginzburg; translated by John Hersey
2-17-72
Yale Repertory Company
New Haven, CT

I Never Sang for My Father
Robert Anderson
1-25-68
Longacre Theatre
N.Y.C.

I Only Just Got Here Myself
Michael Lewis
10-13-72
Street 70 Ensemble
Rockville Civic Center
Montgomery County, MD

I Only Want an Answer
Fred Denger; translated by Basil Ashmore
2-5-68
Stage 73
373 E. 73rd, N.Y.C.

I Remember Foxtrot
Tom Sydorick
3-28-68
Anthony Mannino Drama Tree
182 Fifth, N.Y.C.

I Said So
Terry Kester
9-17-69
Courtyard Playhouse
424 W. 45th, N.Y.C.

I, Said the Fly
June Havoc
9-20-73
Tyrone Guthrie Theatre
Minneapolis, MN

I Scream, You Scream, We All Scream
Rock Anthony
8-17-73
Provincetown Playhouse
133 MacDougal, N.Y.C.

I T'ought I Saw an Oedipus
Joseph Lazarus
6-5-70
Omni Theatre Club
145 W. 18th, N.Y.C.

I Tell the World Off Every Morning
Lou Michaels
10-26-73
Hells in Bells Bar
105 W. 13th, N.Y.C.

I Used to See My Sister
Norman Dietz
12-17-69
American Theatre Company Workshop
Alice's Studio
106 E. 14th, N.Y.C.

I Want To Be with You (with During the War)
Michael Shurtleff
6-6-73
Friday Theatre
N.Y.C.

I Want to Fly (with Hotel Happiness)
Margaret Ford Taylor
3-16-72
Karamu House Theatre
Cleveland, OH

I Went with Him and She Came with Me (theatre-dance piece)
1-18-73
Ambrose Arts Foundation
57 Laight, N.Y.C.

I Wish I Had a Name Like Isabel
Richard A. Schuster
3-23-73
New York Theatre Ensemble
2 E. 2nd, N.Y.C.

Icarus Nine (with Great Jones Street)
Bruce Serlen
2-12-73
Circle Theatre Company
2307 Broadway, N.Y.C.

Ice (with Big Top)
Geraldine Krug
6-11-69
Unitarian Church of All Souls
80th St. & Lexington, N.Y.C.

Ice Wolf
Joanna Kraus
10-18-73
Brooklyn College
Brooklyn, NY

Ice-Breaker
William Kushner
1-10-68
Playwright's Workshop Club
14 Waverly Pl., N.Y.C.

Idabel's Fortune
Ted Shine
1969
Howard University
Washington, DC

Idea, An
Richard Bernard
2-9-73
New Old Reliable Theatre
231 E. 3rd, N.Y.C.

Ideal State, The
Benjamin Bradford
10-24-69
Inner Theatre
356 Bowery, N.Y.C.

Ides of March, The
Jerome Kilty; adapted from the novel by Thornton Wilder
10-16-69
Loretto-Hilton Center
St. Louis, MO

Idlyyic (with Boo Hoo and On the Brink)
Philip Magdalany
6-17-72
West Side YWCA
8th Ave. & 51st, N.Y.C.

If Adventure's Your Dish
Seth Weeks
5-22-68
Playwrights' Workshop Club
14 Waverly Pl., N.Y.C.

If I Ruled the World
David A. Seiffer
4-23-71
Playbox
94 St. Mark's Pl., N.Y.C.

If You Please
Andre Breton & Phillipe Soupault
3-22-73
Academy Theatre
Atlanta, GA

If You're Gonna Stay
James Robiscoe
11-14-69
Cafe Déjà Vu
339 E. 10th, N.Y.C.

Ikke, Ikke, Nye, Nye, Nye (with The Great Nebula in Orion and The Family Continues)
Lanford Wilson
5-21-72
Circle Theatre Company
2307 Broadway, N.Y.C.

Ill Fated Voyage of Apollo 57, The
3-2-70
Old Reliable Theatre Tavern
231 E. 3rd, N.Y.C.

Illusion
Gerard D. Hottleman
12-11-69
Playbox
94 St. Mark's Pl., N.Y.C.

Illusionist Rex
Matthew Davison
11-12-71
Queens College
N.Y.C.

Illustrated Elephant, The
The Electric Circus Children's Theatre
2-4-68
Electric Circus
23 St. Mark's Pl., N.Y.C.

Illustration
Sean Michael
12-22-72
New York Theatre Ensemble
2 E. 2nd, N.Y.C.

Ilona and the Evil Eye People
Florence Miller
1-7-72
New York Theatre Ensemble
2 E. 2nd, N.Y.C.

Image of Elmo Doyle, The
Richard France
5-8-73
Lolly's Theatre Club
808 Lexington, N.Y.C.

Images
Carlo Grasso
9-17-71
New York Theatre Ensemble
2 E. 2nd, N.Y.C.

Images of the Coming Dead
Arthur Sainer
4-1-71
Open Space
37 St. Mark's Pl., N.Y.C.

Imaginary Invalid, The
Moliere; Allen Lorensen (adaptor)
Fall, 1973
Wayside Theatre
Washington, DC

Imitatin' Us, Imitatin' Us, Imitatin' Death
9-30-71
New African Company
Boston Center for the Arts
Boston, MA

Immaculate Misconception, The
W. Randolph Galvin
10-27-70
Cherry Lane Theatre
38 Commerce, N.Y.C.

Immigrant, The
John Quinn
10-15-70
Playbox
94 St. Mark's Pl., N.Y.C.

Immortal One, The
Ivan Goll
3-22-68
Gruene Kakadu
544 E. 12th, N.Y.C.

Imperial Hero Explains, The
Charles Langdon
7-13-72
Changing Scene
Denver, CO

Impersonator, The
James Magnuson
3-20-69
Lincoln University
Lincoln University, PA

Impossible Loves
Fernando Arrabal
7-17-69
Duo Theatre Workshop
522 E. 12th, N.Y.C.

Impossible Politician, The
Gregory Kenyon
5-31-72
Jacksonville University
Jacksonville, FL

Impression of Loving
Louise Thompson
3-12-73
Mercer Arts Center
240 Mercer, N.Y.C.

Impressions on Love
Grace and Ken Kimmins
10-21-69
Library & Museum of the Performing Arts
111 Amsterdam, N.Y.C.

Imprisoned
2-17-71
Brandeis University
Waltham, MA

Impromptu
Walter Tyszka
3-14-71
Brandeis University
Waltham, MA

Impulse (revue)
6-3-71
Stagelights II Theatrical Club
125 W. 22nd, N.Y.C.

In a Fine Castle
Derek Walcott
8-26-71
Mark Taper Forum
Los Angeles, CA

In Absence
Doric Wilson
12-12-68
Ensemble Project
Gotham Art
455 W. 43rd, N.Y.C.

In Another Part of the City
Edward Gallardo
7-24-70
New York Theatre Ensemble
2 E. 2nd, N.Y.C.

In Black and White (multi-media piece)
1-8-72
Film & Dance Theatre
42 E. 12th, N.Y.C.

In Case of Accident
Peter Simon
3-27-72
Eastside Playhouse
334 E. 74th, N.Y.C.

In Darkest Africa: A Ladies Guide to the Nile
Doris Baisley
11-17-72
WPA
333 Bowery, N.Y.C.

In Deepest Darkest Africa
Ron Hugar
11-18-71
New York City League of Playwrights
162 W. 21st, N.Y.C.

In Fashion
Jon Jory (book); Lonnie Burstein (lyrics); Jerry Blatt (music)
2-22-73
Actors Theatre
Louisville, KY

In His Own Write
Adrienne Kennedy & John Lennon & Victor Spinetti
8-20-68
Summer Theatre Festival
Kingston, RI

In My Father's Court
Adapted from Isaac Bashevis Singer
11-10-71
Folksbiene Playhouse
175 E. Broadway, N.Y.C.

In My Many Names and Days
Charles Fuller
6-16-72
New Federal Theatre
Henry Street Playhouse
466 Grand, N.Y.C.

In Need of Care
David E. Rowley
3-13-72
Library & Museum of the Performing Arts
111 Amsterdam, N.Y.C.

In Our Green Youth
George Savage & George Savage, Jr.
Jan., 1969
Santa Monica Playhouse
Santa Monica, CA

In Praise of Folly
Donald H. Julian
9-24-69
La Mama ETC
74 E. 4th, N.Y.C.

In Revue
7-17-73
Thomas Playhouse
South Casco, ME

In Search of the Cobra Jewels
Harvey Feinstein
10-4-72
Playwrights' Workshop Club
Bastiano's Studio
14 Cooper Sq., N.Y.C.

In Sheep's Clothing
Jean Marquis
1-8-71
Atlantic Avenue Theatre Group
Colony House
Brooklyn, NY

In the Absence of Fish
Gary Martin
7-31-70
New York Theatre Ensemble
2 E. 2nd, N.Y.C.

In the Bar of a Tokyo Hotel
Tennessee Williams
5-11-69
Eastside Playhouse
334 E. 74th, N.Y.C.

In the Beginning
Kenneth Cavander & Barbara Damashek (music)
6-29-71
John Drew Repertory Company
East Hampton, NY

In the Cage
William Van O'Connor
6-7-73
American Theatre Company
106 E. 14th, N.Y.C.

In the Can
Ken Gaburo
Apr., 1970
University of Oregon
Eugene, OR

In the Clap Shack
William Styron
12-15-72
Yale Repertory Theatre
New Haven, CT

In the Country's Night (with Late on a Sunday Afternoon)
Michael Shurtleff
11-9-69
Extension Theatre
277 Park Ave. So., N.Y.C.

In the Forests of the Night
John Crennan
5-3-68
Good Shepherd-Faith Church
152 W. 66th, N.Y.C.

In the Garden
Dallas Mayr
11-24-72
New York Theatre Ensemble
2 E. 2nd, N.Y.C.

In the Jungle of the Cities
Bertolt Brecht; new translation by Anselm Hollo
1971
New Repertory Theatre
236 E. 47th, N.Y.C.

In the Last Days
Norman Jordam
5-6-71
Karamu House Theatre
Cleveland, OH

In the Matter of J. Robert Oppenheimer
Heinar Kipphardt, translated by Ruth Speirs
5-24-68
Center Theatre Group
Los Angeles, CA

In the Midst of Life
Thronson, Shearer, McKernan
May, 1973
South Coast Repertory Theatre
Costa Mesa, CA

In the Mourning Time (black song & statement)
James Wigfall & Bill Cunningham
10-28-73
St. Clement's Church
423 W. 46th, N.Y.C.

In the Park
Ronald Young
July, 1972
Street Theatre, Inc.
Ossining, NY

In the Settling of the Wind
Mark J. Kurlansky
12-18-72
CSC Repertory Theatre
89 W. 3rd, N.Y.C.

In the Time of Harry Harass
Carolyn Rossi
10-25-71
Players Theatre
115 MacDougal, N.Y.C.

In the Wine Time
Ed Bullins
12-3-68
New Lafayette Theatre
137 St. & 7th Ave., N.Y.C.

In Three Zones
Wilford Leach
10-20-70
Charles Playhouse
Boston, MA

Incession (satirical review)
March, 1969
University of Illinois
Urbana, IL

Incest
Randolph Carter
4-2-71
Stage Lights Theatrical Club
218 W. 48th, N.Y.C.

Incident at Twilight (with The Stranger)
4-15-69
Basement Coffee House
155 E. 22nd, N.Y.C.

Incidents
John Cooper
3-23-72
Changing Scene
Denver, CO

Incinerator and Other Loves, The
Jean Maljean
11-15-68
New Hudson Guild
441 W. 26th, N.Y.C.

Incomparable Max, "An Evening of Beerbohm", The
Jerome Lawrence & Robert E. Lee
6-24-69
Barter Theatre
Abingdon, VA

Increased Difficulty of Concentration, The
Vaclav Havel
12-4-69
Forum Theatre
Lincoln Center
N.Y.C.

Incredible Christmas of Ebenezer Scrooge, The (musical)
11-23-72
13th Street Theatre
50 W. 13th, N.Y.C.

Incredible Outbreak of Semi-Nudity, The
Joseph B. Baldwin
6-9-71
Jacksonville University
Jacksonville, FL

Independence Night
Venable Herndon
9-23-70
Loft Theatre
21 Bond, N.Y.C.

Indian Experience, The
John Kauffman & Wayne Johnson
5-19-72
Contemporary Theatre
Seattle, WA

Indian Wants the Bronx, The
Israel Horovitz
1-17-68
Astor Place Theatre
434 Lafayette, N.Y.C.

Indiana Avenue
Debbie Wood
1-23-73
Negro Ensemble Company
St. Mark's Playhouse
133 Second, N.Y.C.

Indians
Arthur Kopit
5-6-69
Arena Stage
Washington, DC

In-Different Times
4-7-73
Total Theatre for Youth at Theatre of the Riverside Church
490 Riverside Dr., N.Y.C.

Indra-Nila: A Family Portrait of the God of Death
7-20-73
Cubiculo at Byrdcliffe
Woodstock, NY

Infection, The
Edward L. Gold
3-18-72
Hunter College Playwrights Project
West Side YMCA
5 W. 63rd, N.Y.C.

Infidelity Italian Style
See: Waiting; Doorbell; and Academy

Infinite Christmas
Cyril Griffin
12-23-70
Library & Museum of the Performing Arts
111 Amsterdam, N.Y.C.

Ingredients, or How To Get Laid in a Bakery Without Letting the Dough Fall
Christopher Mathewson
9-15-72
New York Theatre Ensemble
2 E. 2nd, N.Y.C.

Inheritors, The
Ronald Ribman
1-23-69
Yale University
New Haven, CT

Initiation, The
Nathan R. Teitel
2-24-70
Seattle Repertory Company
Seattle, WA

Injun
Guy Gauthier
4-23-71
Playbox
94 St. Mark's Pl., N.Y.C.

Inn People, The (musical based on Carlo Goldoni's La Locandiera)
Donald Walker & Arnold Goland
10-27-73
Bucks County Playhouse
New Hope, PA

Inner Circles (with Window Dressing and Scenes from Domestic Life)
9-25-69
Access Stage Media Workshop
Theatre East
211 E. 60th, N.Y.C.

Inner City (a street cantata)
Helen Miller (music); Eve Merriam (lyrics), Eve Merriam & Tom O'Horgan (book)
12-19-71
Ethel Barrymore Theatre
243 W. 47th, N.Y.C.

Inner City II
Eve Merriam (lyrics); Helen Miller (music)
10-11-73
Central Arts Cabaret
108 E. 64th, N.Y.C.

Inner Journey
James Hanley
3-20-69
Forum Theatre
Lincoln Center
N.Y.C.

Innocence
Ursule Molinaro
12-8-71
East Village Theatre
433 E. 6th, N.Y.C.

Innovations
John Grimaldi
10-4-68
Cooper Square Arts Theatre
35 Cooper Sq., N.Y.C.

Inook and the Sun
Henry Beissel
8-1-73
Stratford Festival
Stratford, Ontario, CAN

Inquiry, The
Ugo Betti
9-12-69
ADAL Performing Arts
682 Ave. of the Americas, N.Y.C.

Inside Broadway
Glory Van Scott
11-8-72
Library & Museum of the Performing Arts
111 Amsterdam, N.Y.C.

Inside My Head (with Theory, Proof, Application; Slow Memories; and Fraternal Order of Police)
Barry Litvack
10-21-70
Playwright's Unit
83 E. 4th, N.Y.C.

Inside Out
Betsy Bilton
4-17-70
Minor Latham Theatre
Barnard College
N.Y.C.

Inside Out (3 one-acts)
Berrilla Kerr
5-17-72
La Mama ETC
74 E. 4th, N.Y.C.

Insides of Orchid Price, The
Tobi Louis
3-14-69
West Side YMCA
5 W. 63rd, N.Y.C.

Insisting Invitations
Michael Holloway
Dec., 1971
Center for the New Performing Art
Iowa City, IA

Inspector of Stairs, The
Sandra Scoppettone
10-21-70
Assembly Theatre
113 Jane, N.Y.C.

Installment Plan
Insan Sauti (Robert S. Preston)
Nov., 1972
Massachusetts Correctional Institution
Norfolk, MA

Instant Replay
8-6-68
Downstairs at the Upstairs
N.Y.C.

Intelligent Young Ladies (World-Wise Women), The
Moliere; adapted by Josef Bush
11-26-71
WPA
333 Bowery, N.Y.C.

Interior Castle
John Braswell; Barbara Benary (music)
7-19-73
Lenox Arts Center
Lenox, MA

Interlude on a Train (with Cerebrius Mentalus and To Beginningness)
Craig Wood
5-23-69
Wittenberg University Theatre
Springfield, OH

Interludes
Cervantes
4-11-71
WPA
333 Bowery, N.Y.C.

International Wrestling Match, The
Jeff Weiss
1-8-69
La Mama ETC
9 St. Mark's Pl., N.Y.C.

Interplay
Tony Giordano
8-11-71
Kaymar Gallery
548 LaGuardia Pl., N.Y.C.

Interrogation
Louis E. Catron
4-18-69
Dramarena Repertory Theatre
158 W. 55th, N.Y.C.

Interrogation of Havana, The
Hans Magnus Enzenberger; Peter Mayer (translator)
12-27-71
Chelsea Theatre Center
30 Lafayette Ave., Brooklyn, NY

Interrogations
Patricia Cooper
3-5-70
Loft Workshop
152 Bleecker, N.Y.C.

Intersection (with The Newstand)
Bill Svanoe
3-13-69
Loft Workshop
152 Bleecker, N.Y.C.

Interview
Richard Hoag
3-28-68
Anthony Mannino Drama Tree
182 Fifth, N.Y.C.

Interview
12-14-73
Westbeth Playwrights Feminist Collective
155 Bank, N.Y.C.

Interview, The
E. E. Spitzer
11-10-68
Gene Frankel Theater Workshop
115 MacDougal, N.Y.C.

Interview, The
Peter Swet
6-4-73
Gene Frankel Theater Workshop
Mercer Arts Center
240 Mercer, N.Y.C.

Interview with F. Scott Fitzgerald, An
Paul Hunter
2-11-72
Playbox
94 St. Mark's Pl., N.Y.C.

Interview with God
L. A. Lambert (Miguel de Cervantes)
2-8-71
Library & Museum of the Performing Arts
111 Amsterdam, N.Y.C.

Into a Thousand Pieces
Emilie Green
4-17-70
Minor Latham Theatre
Barnard College
N.Y.C.

Into the Fire
6-29-71
John Drew Repertory Company
East Hampton, NY

Introduction
Melvin Frankel
July, 1970
Emmanuel Church
Boston, MA

Intruder, The (with The Collection)
Mell Lazarus
5-8-70
Anthony Mannino Drama Tree
182 Fifth, N.Y.C.

Intrusions
Mark Lutwak
Summer, 1971
Youth Workshop
Palo Alto, CA

Invaders, The
See: Los Invasores

Investigation into the Persecution of All Mankind, The
9-10-69
New York Theatre Ensemble
2 E. 2nd, N.Y.C.

Investigator, The
Reuben Ship
2-19-71
Liberty Revue
Washington Square Church
133 W. 4th, N.Y.C.

Invincible
Daniel Curley
Spring, 1970
Depot
Urbana, IL

Invitation to a Beheading
Vladimir Nabokov; adapted by Russell McGrath
3-8-69
New York Shakespeare Festival Public Theatre
425 Lafayette, N.Y.C.

Ionescapade
Eugene Ionesco; Robert Ackerman (adaptor)
1-12-73
New Repertory Company
455 W. 43rd, N.Y.C.

Iphegenia Again
Pat Staten
2-16-73
American Women Playwrights Association
Columbia University School of the Arts Theater
410 W. 117th, N.Y.C.

Irene
Hugh Wheeler, Harry Rigby, James Montgomery (book); Joseph McCarthy (lyrics); Charles Gaynor & Otis Clements (lyrics & music); Harry Tierney (music)
11-27-72
Royal Alexandra Theatre
Toronto, Ontario, CAN

Irish Rebel Theatre
8-9-72
Claidheamh Soluis
Abbey Theatre
136 E. 13th, N.Y.C.

Irish Tapes, The
John Reilly & Stefan Moore
10-13-73
Global Village
454 Broome, N.Y.C.

Is Anybody Listening (or Uptight)
Joseph Hayes
2-3-71
Florida State University
Tallahassee, FL

Is the Real You Really You?
John Tobias
3-4-68
Playhouse
Palm Beach, FL

Iscariot (dramatic sermon)
Frank Moffett Mosier
4-8-73
St. Luke's Chapel
487 Hudson, N.Y.C.

Ishtar
Robert S. Ross
7-17-71 (reading)
8-5&7-71 (performances)
Eugene O'Neill Memorial Theatre
Waterford, CT

Isla Sin Nombre
Pedro Santaliz
11-3-72
Nuevo Teatro Pobre de Americo
124 W. 18th, N.Y.C.

Island
Byrd Hoffman School for Byrds
7-27-73
Kuku Ryku Theatre Laboratory
147 Spring, N.Y.C.

Island
Anthony J. Ingrassia
3-16-72
New York Theatre Ensemble
2 E. 2nd, N.Y.C.

Island Surrounded by Sketches, An
Larry O'Connel
7-7-70
Second Group Theatre
McBurney YMCA
215 W. 23rd, N.Y.C.

Isle of Spice (reading)
Bella Shafran
4-6-70
New York Theatre Ensemble
2 E. 2nd, N.Y.C.

Israel Berkowitz Superstar
Richard D. Waters
8-25-72
Fisherman's Players
N. Eastham, MA

Israeli Mosiac
The Hebrew Stage of New York
12-13-69
Unit Theatre
157 W. 22nd, N.Y.C.

It Happened Here
Joseph Leonardo & Leslie Reidel
Summer, 1973
Carpenter Court
Philadelphia, PA

It Happens When They Take Away the Moon
7-4-68
Playwrights' Workshop Club
14 Waverly Pl., N.Y.C.

It Only Hurts When You Laugh
R. Finley Mullen
10-12-73
Cellar Theatre
Los Angeles, CA

It's a Wise Father Who Knows His Own Country
Carl Ahlm
10-20-68
Wittenberg University Theatre
Springfield, OH

It's All in Your Mime
Jack (Hill) and Graciela (Binaghi)
11-15-71
Library & Museum of the Performing Arts
111 Amsterdam, N.Y.C.

It's All Right To Be a Woman
3-24-71
Washington Square Church
133 W. 4th, N.Y.C.

It's All Right To Be a Woman Theatre (improvisational program)
2-16-73
Long Island University
Brooklyn, NY

It's Bad To Be Back!
Milton Polsky
2-26-68
13th Street Theatre
50 W. 13th, N.Y.C.

It's Colored, It's Negro
See: An Evening of Identity

It's Got To Be Black or White (with Three Words in No Time and Four Actors and A Restaurant)
Lyon Phelps
2-18-71
Judson Poet's Theatre
55 Wash. Sq. So., N.Y.C.

It's Never Too Late for Happiness
Kalman Lipson, Joseph Jacobs, Samuel Fershko
10-18-68
Anderson Theatre
66 Second, N.Y.C.

It's Nice Out, Isn't It?
Jack Heller
2-5-68
Old Reliable Theatre Tavern
231 E. 3rd, N.Y.C.

It's Up To You!
Florence Aquino, George Koch, & Wayne Sheridan
8-2-68
Tentarena
East Monticello, NY

It's 10 P.M., Do You Know Where Your Children Are?
George Wall
5-7-70
Changing Scene
Denver, CO

It Should Happen to a Dog
Wolf Mankowitz
1-27-72
St. Clement's Church
423 W. 46th, N.Y.C.

It Shouldn't Happen to a Dog (and The Blunderer)
7-15-68
Theatre in the Street
340 W. 28th, N.Y.C.

Iz She Izzy or Iz He Aintzy or Is They Both
Lonnie Carter
4-2-70
Yale Repertory Theatre
New Haven, CT

J

Jabberwock
Jerome Lawrence & Robert E. Lee
10-18-72
Ohio State University
Columbus, OH

Jabongo
Robert Unger
12-21-68
Unit Theatre
157 W. 22nd, N.Y.C.

Jack, Jack
Megan Terry
July, 1968
Firehouse Theatre
Minneapolis, MN

Jack Macgowran in the Works of Samuel Beckett
11-19-70
New York Shakespeare Festival
Public Theatre
425 Lafayette, N.Y.C.

Jack N's Awful Demands
Jonathan Levy
7-3-68
Playbox
94 St. Mark's Pl., N.Y.C.

Jack's Mother Is Missing Her Melons
Paul Corrigan
5-5-72
La Mama ETC
74 E. 4th, N.Y.C.

Jacques Brel Is Alive and Well and Living in Paris
Eric Blau and Mort Shuman
1-22-68
Village Gate
160 Bleecker, N.Y.C.

Jade
Jeannine O'Reilly
2-24-69
Old Reliable Theatre Tavern
231 E. 3rd, N.Y.C.

Jail Game
Barbara Barrett
1-13-68
Royal Playhouse
219 Second Ave., N.Y.C.

Jakey Fat Boy (with Dear Janet Rosenberg. . .)
Stanley Eveling
4-5-70
Gramercy Arts Theatre
N.Y.C.

James Bond Play, The
3-23-68
Pageant Players
71 E. Broadway, N.Y.C.

James Joyce Memorial Liquid Theatre
1969
Company Theatre
Los Angeles, CA

Jamimma
Martie Evans-Charles
3-16-72
New Federal Theatre
Henry Street Playhouse
466 Grand, N.Y.C.

Jane Eyre
Hal Shaper & Roy Harley Lewis (book); Hal Shaper (lyrics); Monty Stevens (music)
7-6-70
Fathers of Confederation Memorial Centre
Charlottetown, Prince Edward Island, CAN

Jar, The (with The License)
Luigi Pirandello
4-22-69
Sheridan Square Playhouse
99 Seventh Ave. So., N.Y.C.

Jardins Publique, Les
Mark Lamos (book); Philip Killian & Mark Lamos (music & lyrics)
5-4-70
Library & Museum of the Performing Arts
111 Amsterdam, N.Y.C.

Jason-Medea
3-19-71
Caravan Theatre
Cambridge, MA

Jaw Jacking Bout a Mission
6-25-70
Theatre Black
130 E. 7th, N.Y.C.

Jaws That Bite, The (staged reading)
Tony Giordano
6-6-73
Playwrights' Horizons
Clark Center for the Performing Arts
West Side YWCA, 8th Ave. & 51st, N.Y.C.

Jazz Circle
James Stevenson
6-20-69
Nucleus Repertory Theatre
261 W. 54th, N.Y.C.

Jazznite (with The Life and Times of J. Walter Smintheus under title Underground)
Walter Jones
4-13-71
New York Shakespeare Festival Public Theatre
425 Lafayette, N.Y.C.

Jeff Chandler (with How a Nice Girl Named Janet. . .)
David Shumaker
11-14-70
Unit Theatre
157 W. 22nd, N.Y.C.

Jelly F
John O'Keefe
Dec., 1971
Center for the New Performing Art
Iowa City, IA

Jenny Wiley
8-5-71
Jenny Wiley Summer Music Theatre
Prestonburg, KY

Jenusia
Rene de Obaldia
1-9-69
Cubiculo
414 W. 51st, N.Y.C.

Jesus Christ Superstar (Concert version presented at the Madison Ave., Baptist Church, N.Y.C., in spring of 1971)
Tim Rice (lyrics); Andrew Lloyd Webber (music)
10-12-71
Mark Hellinger Theatre
237 W. 51st, N.Y.C.

Jesus Is Seen by His Friends
Amos Kenan
3-22-73
Manhattan Theatre Club
321 E. 73rd, N.Y.C.

Jesus Man, The (with Catch As Catch Can)
Antony Bassae
12-21-70
Old Reliable Theatre Tavern
231 E. 3rd, N.Y.C.

Jesus Play
William H. Hoffman
9-16-71
Changing Scene
Denver, CO

Jewelry of the Dead (with Quiet Sunday)
Glover Buck
July, 1968
Nucleus Repertory Theatre
261 W. 54th, N.Y.C.

Jewish Prostitute, The
Irving Glusack
2-14-69
New York Theatre Ensemble
2 E. 2nd, N.Y.C.

J.F.K. (Seen earlier in the year at National Press Club, Washington)
Jeremiah Collins & Mark Williams
11-21-71
Circle in the Square
159 Bleecker, N.Y.C.

Jim Pavone and the Buzz Bomb
6-29-73
MUSE
1530 Bedford Ave., Brooklyn, NY

Jimmy
Mel Shavelson (book); Bill & Patti Jacob (music & lyrics)
9-8-69
Forrest Theatre
Philadelphia, PA

Jimmy Beam
John O'Keefe
Nov., 1970
Studio Theatre
Toronto, CAN

Jimmy Paradise
John Wolfson
5-16-68
Playwrights' Workshop Club
14 Waverly Pl., N.Y.C.

Jimmy Shine
Murray Schisgal
10-14-68
Forrest Theatre
Philadelphia, PA

Jimtown
Kathleen Kimball
3-17-72
Theatre Genesis
2nd Ave. & 10th, N.Y.C.

Jitney Vehicle, The (with Little B.S.)
Charles Briggs
12-7-73
Amas Repertory Theatre
263 W. 86th, N.Y.C.

Joan
Al Carmines
11-19-71
Judson Poet's Theatre
55 Wash. Sq. So., N.Y.C.

Jockey Club Stakes, The
William Douglas Home
11-1-72
Playhouse
Wilmington, DE

Joe Egg
Peter Nichols
2-1-68
Brooks Atkinson Theatre
N.Y.C.

Jogging it, Baby!
Bert Katz
5-17-70
Spencer Memorial Church
99 Clinton, Brooklyn, NY

John and Abigail
William Gibson
7-1-69
Berkshire Theatre Festival
Stockbridge, MA

John Henry Was a Steeldriving Man
Bruce Bernstein
4-15-71
Tufts University
Medford, MA

John Wayne Doesn't Hit Women
Frederick Feirstein
1-21-72
New York Theatre Ensemble
2 E. 2nd, N.Y.C.

Johnnas
Bill Gunn
2-1-73
Negro Ensemble Company
St. Mark's Playhouse
133 Second, N.Y.C.

Johnny Belinda
Mavor Moore and John Fenwick
7-1-68
Fathers of Confederation Memorial Centre
Charlottetown, Prince Edward Island, CAN

Johnny Comes Marching Home
1968
Bread & Puppet Theatre
N.Y.C.

Joined
Dan Owens
July, 1970
St. Cyprian' s Church
Roxbury, MA

Jonathan Jones
Guy Gauthier
10-27-72
New York Theatre Ensemble
2 E. 2nd, N.Y.C.

Jonathan Wild
Deloss Brown
5-19-71
Columbia University
N.Y.C.

Jones Man, The
Leonard Melfi
7-1-72
Actor's Experimental Unit
682 Sixth, N.Y.C.

Jongleurs (a miracle-grotesquerie)
4-6-72
Queens College
L.I. Expressway & Kissenga Blvd., N.Y.C.

Joseph (with Name Day)
Charles Kerbs
Nov., 1968
Playbox
N.Y.C.

Josephine Baker and Her International Revue
6-5-73
Carnegie Hall
N.Y.C.

Joshua
Federico Inclan
12-24-71
New York Theatre of the Americas
427 W. 59th, N.Y.C.

Journey into Blackness
Voices, Inc.
1-28-72
Mount Morris Park Center
N.Y.C.

Journey of Simon McKeever
Albert Maltz
6-1-68
Actor's Mobile Theatre
73rd & Broadway, N.Y.C.

Journey of Snow White, The
Al Carmines
2-26-71
Judson Poet's Theatre
55 Wash. Sq. So., N.Y.C.

Journey, The
Bill Russell & Lawrence Sacharow
11-4-71
Theatre for the New City
151 Bank, N.Y.C.

Journey to Bahia
Alfredo Dias Gomes; translated by Stanley Richards
7-16-70
Henry Street Settlement Playhouse
466 Grand, N.Y.C.

Journey to the Underworld (with Machine)
Jim Lucason
3-17-71
Brandeis University
Waltham, MA

Joy and Barbara
David Shumaker
4-4-73
Actors' Experimental Unit
682 Sixth, N.Y.C.

Joy of Mime, The
Robert Molnar
11-28-73
St. Bartholomew's Theatre
109 E. 50th, N.Y.C.

Joyce Dynel (revised version of Dynel)
Robert Patrick
4-7-69
Old Reliable Theatre Tavern
231 E. 3rd, N.Y.C.

Jub-Lee (mime)
Doug Day & Babs Fisher
Spring, 1969
The Depot
223 N. Broadway, Urbana, IL

Judah the Maccabee and Me (with The Plant That Talked Back)
Gertrude Samuels
1-27-70
Lambs Theatre
130 W. 44th, N.Y.C.

Judas
John W. Kirk
12-6-73
Westhoff Theatre
Illinois State University
Normal, IL

Judas Applause, The
Gary Munn
5-9-69
Chelsea Theatre Center
30 Lafayette, Brooklyn, Ny

Judgement, The Guest, and The Zodiac, The
Michael Carton
3-3-71
Playwrights' Unit
83 E. 4th, N.Y.C.

Judgment Day (with Count That Day Lost)
Stewart H. Benedict
3-4-71
Playbox
94 St. Mark's Pl., N.Y.C.

Judgment, The (with Metamorphosis)
Charles Dizenzo
4-8-72
American Place Theatre
N.Y.C.

Juke Box, The
Ed Baierlein
6-10-69
Changing Scene
Denver, CO

"Jules and Jim" Is Playing in This Godforsaken Town
Marion Fredd Towbin
1-12-72
Theatre Arts Experimental Workshop
117th & Amsterdam, N.Y.C.

Julia Caesar
Alan Causey
5-13-70
La Mama ETC
74 E. 4th, N.Y.C.

Juliet in Mantua
Robert Nathen
3-31-73
International Center
745 Seventh, N.Y.C.

Jump Crow (a musical mystery)
Grover Dale & Ted Hughes
7-5-72
Lenox Arts Center
Lenox, MA

Jumping Fool, The
Shirl Hendryx
2-9-70
Fortune Theatre
62 E 4th, N.Y.C.

Juncture of Billie Mapes, The
Susan Jack
7-26-73
Manhattan Theatre Club
321 E. 73rd, N.Y.C.

June/Moon
Jack Larson
10-7-69
Mark Taper Forum
Los Angeles, CA

Juniper Tree, The
Richard Lortz
3-30-72
Splinters Company
150 Bleecker, N.Y.C.

Junkies Are Full of Sh. . .
Imamu Amiri Baraka (LeRoi Jones)
July, 1972
Street Theatre, Inc.
Ossining, NY

Junkies Are Full of Sh. . . (with Blood Rites and Fun Boot Dancers)
Imamu Amiri Baraka (LeRoi Jones)
11-21-70
Henry Street Settlement Playhouse
466 Grand, N.Y.C.

Just Add Water
Summer, 1969
New Haven Free Theatre
New Haven, CT

Just Assassins, The
Albert Camus
7-27-73
West Side Community Repertory Theatre
252 W. 81st, N.Y.C.

Just Before Morning
Tom Oliver
Fall, 1968
Wesleyan University
Middletown, CT

Just Between Us
Peggy Cowles
2-20-73
Exchange Theatre
151 Bank, N.Y.C.

Just for Love
Henry Comer, Jill Showell, Michael Valenti
5-21-68
Central Library Theatre
Toronto, CAN

Just Keep Listening
John Kendrick
5-15-70
Unit Theatre
157 W. 22nd, N.Y.C.

Just Keep Listening (with When the Wine Is Cold)
John Kendrick
4-24-71
98 Greene St. Loft
98 Greene St., N.Y.C.

Just Passing Through
Andrew Mack
7-27-72
Second Group Theatre
McBurney YMCA
215 W. 23rd, N.Y.C.

Justice Box, The
Michael Robert David
6-2-71
Theatre de Lys
N.Y.C.

Justice Sterling
Rocky Roads
10-12-73
13th Street Theatre
50 W. 13th, N.Y.C.

Justifiable Homicide
Sheldron Feldner
12-3-70
Triangle Theatre
316 E. 88th, N.Y.C.

Justine
Robert Swerdlow
June, 1970
Global Village
Toronto, CAN

Jymi Cry
N. Davidson
Fall, 1973
Dashiki Project Theatre
New Orleans, LA

K

Kaaka-Makaakoo
Tone Brulin & Company
April, 1971
Otrabanda Company from CuraÜao
La Mama ETC
74 E. 4th, N.Y.C.

Kaddish
Allen Ginsberg
2-11-72
Chelsea Theatre Center
30 Lafayette, Brooklyn, NY

Kadensho, The
Ze-ami
1-20-72
Cubiculo
414 W. 51st, N.Y.C.

Kagekiyo
Seami; Arthur Waley (translator)
10-11-73
American Noh Theatre
Jefferson Market Library
425 Sixth, N.Y.C.

Kaleidoscope
Total Theatre for Youth
7-26-72
Donnell Library
N.Y.C.

Kaleidoscope: A Celebration from Minstrels to Mods
Mary Jean Parson
July, 1971
Alabama State Theatre
Birmingham, AL

Kali Mother
Milton Ward
10-23-73
Actors' Playhouse
100 Seventh Ave. So., N.Y.C.

Kalulu and His Money Farm
T. Mason
10-7-72
Children's Theatre Company
Minneapolis Institute of Arts
Minneapolis, MN

Kama Sutra, The (Part 1)
Tom Eyen
2-1-68
Playwrights' Workshop Club
14 Waverly Pl., N.Y.C.

Kangaroo Courtship
Julio Delatorre
5-6-71
Brooklyn College
Brooklyn, NY

Karl Marx Play, The
Rochelle Owens
3-16-73
American Place Theatre
N.Y.C.

Kaspar
Peter Handke
2-6-73
Chelsea Theatre Center
30 Lafayette, Brooklyn, NY

Keep Off the Grass
Ronald Alexander
4-3-72
Mechanic Theatre
Baltimore, MD

Keep, The
Michael Firth
3-22-71
Des Moines Community Playhouse
Des Moines, IA

Keep Your Shirt On, Buster
Francis Heilbut & Bob French
10-26-71
Gotham Art
455 W. 43rd, N.Y.C.

Keepers of the Hippo Horn
Peri Miller
5-28-71
Theatre for the New City
151 Bank, N.Y.C.

Kees By Boy
Gerbin Hellinga
1-25-73
Syracuse University
Syracuse, NY

Kennedy's Children
Robert Patrick
5-30-73
Playwrights' Horizons
Clark Center for the Performing Arts
West Side YWCA, 8th Ave. & 51st, N.Y.C.

Kenneth and Clarence
William DeVane
8-4-68
Playhouse on the Wharf
Provincetown, MA

Kentucky!
D. Stein
1-18-73
Actors Theatre
Louisville, KY

Kentucky Marriage Proposal, The
Anton Chekhov; adapted by Alice H. Houstle
10/72
College of Notre Dame of Maryland
Baltimore, MD

Kewperts and the Galoonghagleis, The (with Sure, This Is It!)
Sarah Delley
9-23-73
Community Loft
250 W. 106th, N.Y.C.

Keyhole, The
Jean Tardieu
Summer, 1970
Old Post Office Theatre
East Hampton, NY

Keyholes (Blank Pages: The Window; Christmas Carol)
Frank Marcus
11-20-73
WPA
333 Bowery, N.Y.C.

Kibbutz 52
Edward J. Sliva
1-16-70
Riverdale Showcase
252nd St. & Riverdale Ave., Bronx, NY

Kibosh, The
Steven M. Jacobson
9-9-69
Playbox
94 St. Mark's Pl., N.Y.C.

Kid, The
Robert Coover (book & lyrics); Stanley Walden (music)
11-17-72
American Place Theatre
N.Y.C.

Kidsnappers
Victor Noel
8-28-72
Club 22, Twenty-Two Players
Lincoln Center Plaza
N.Y.C.

Kill and Other Celebrations of Life
J. Robert Wills
1-21-69
Wittenberg University Theatre
Springfield, OH

Kill! Kill!
Herb Greer
6-3-71
Triangle Theatre
316 E. 88th, N.Y.C.

King and the Cup, The
Mark O. Lynch
3-23-73
University of Missouri Theatre
Columbia, MO

King Arthur
John Dryden
10-29-68
Municipal Theater
Atlanta, GA

King Cojo, El
Pablo Figueroa
2-10-73
Intar Theatre
508 W. 53rd, N.Y.C.

King David and David King
Martin Kalmanoff
10-12-69
Temple Ansche Chesed Theatre Auditorium
251 W. 100th, N.Y.C.

King Heroin
Al Fann
1970
Al Fann Theatrical Ensemble
N.Y.C.

King Is Dead, The
William Dunas
2-10-72
American Theatre Laboratory
219 W. 19th, N.Y.C.

King Is Dead, The (The Ballad for Dr. Martin Luther King)
5-20-71
Brooklyn College
Brooklyn, NY

King Midas and the Golden Touch
Ruth Eby (book); Jane D. White (music)
3-17-73
Lolly's Theatre Club
808 Lexington, N.Y.C.

King of Schnorrers, The
Paul Avila Mayer (book); Shimon Wincelberg & Diane Lampert (lyrics); Bernard Herrmann (music)
8-17-70
Goodspeed Opera House
East Haddam, CT

King of Spain, The
Bob Wilson
1-30-69
Anderson Theatre
66 Second, N.Y.C.

King of the United States, The
Jean-Claude van Itallie
5-15-72
Theatre for the New City
151 Bank, N.Y.C.

King's Crown and I, The
Alan Braunstein & John Braden
5-25-72
St. Clement's Church
423 W. 46th, N.Y.C.

King's Leave, The
Tom McLennon
4-20-72
University of Montana
Missoula, MT

King Solomon Is Dead
Frederick Gaines
7-7-69
Eugene O'Neill Memorial Theatre
Waterford, CT

Kingdom by the Sea
Helen Duberstein
10-20-71
Cubiculo
414 W. 51st, N.Y.C.

Kiss Now
Maxine Klein (book & lyrics); William S. Fischer (music)
4-19-71
Martinique Theatre
N.Y.C.

Kiss of Life, The
P. J. Barry
5-1-68
Fulton Theatre Company
119 Ninth, N.Y.C.

Kiss Rock
Maxine Klein, Jacqueline Bertrand, Carolyn Fellman
University of Minnesota
Minneapolis, MN

Kitchen Interlude (with Up and Down)
Charles Pulaski
10-2-69
Stage Lights Theatrical Club
218 W. 48th, N.Y.C.

Kitty Hawk
Leonard Jenkin
4-28-73
Theatre Studio
Barnard College
N.Y.C.

Klara (with A Bridegroom for Marcella)
Ivan Klima; translated by Ruth Willard
5-24-69
La Mama ETC
74 E. 4th, N.Y.C.

Kleinheit Demonstrates Tonight
Andrew Glaze
Dec., 1973
Cricket Theatre
Minneapolis, MN

Kleinhoff Demonstrates Tonight
Andrew Glaze
7-1-71
University of Texas
Austin, TX

Knack with Horses, A (with Here Be Dragons)
David Ward
12-5-70
St. Clement's Church
423 W. 46th, N.Y.C.

Knacker's ABC, The
Boris Vian
11-19-69
Columbia Players
Columbia University
N.Y.C.

Knight of the Lost Half-Hour
Summer, 1972
Milwaukee Repertory Theatre
Milwaukee, WI

Knight of the Twelfth Saucer, The
Marc Alan Zagoren
11-12-73
Library & Museum of the Performing Arts
111 Amsterdam, N.Y.C.

Knight-Mare's Nest, The
Ramon Delgado
5-13-71
University of Missouri
Columbia, MO

Knights of the Round Table
W. H. Auden (after Jean Cocteau)
7-5-68
Arts Theatre Festival
Southampton College, NY

Knock Knock Who Dat?
Richard Wesley
10-1-70
Theatre Black
130 E. 7th, N.Y.C.

Knots
R. D. Laing
6-22-72
Cubiculo
414 W. 51st, N.Y.C.

Ko-Ko-Ro
Linda Mussman
4-6-73
Zarattini Theatre
47 Bond, N.Y.C.

Kolo and Mono (with Bill's Birthday)
Charles Kerbs
Mar., 1968
New Group Theatre
13th Street Theatre
50 W. 13th, N.Y.C.

Kongi's Harvest
Wole Soyinka
4-9-68
Negro Ensemble Company
St. Mark's Playhouse
133 Second, N.Y.C.

Kooky Concert (revue)
Carolyn Rossi
10-8-72
Second Group Theatre
McBurney YMCA
215 W. 23rd, N.Y.C.

Kool Aid (Three Street Koans and Grail Green)
Merle Molofsky
11-3-71
Forum Theatre
Lincoln Center
N.Y.C.

Kouros
Nikos Kazantzakis
1-9-71
Spencer Memorial Church
99 Clinton Brooklyn, NY

Kramer, The
Mark Medoff
10-9-73
New Theatre for Now
Los Angeles, CA

Kryptonites and the Schismites, The: A Tale of Two Nations
6-1-73
WBAI Studio C
359 E. 62nd, N.Y.C.

Kumaliza
C. L. Burton
11-28-69
New York Shakespeare Festival Public Theatre
425 Lafayette, N.Y.C.

Kumquats (puppet show)
Cosmo Richard Falcon (book & lyrics); Gustavo Motta (music)
11-15-71
Village Gate
160 Bleecker, N.Y.C.

L

L'Adorabile Zitella
Giovanni Mina
5-2-73
Teatro Italiano at Hunter College
695 Park, N.Y.C.

L'Arlesienne
Daudet; new English text by Judith Searle & Basil Langton
11-19-71
Manhattan School of Music
120 Claremont, N.Y.C.

La Diestra de Dios Padre, En
Enrique Puenaventura
11-26-71
New York Theatre of the Americas
321 E. 73rd, N.Y.C.

La Difunta (The Dead Wife)
Miguel De Unamuno
10-31-69
Greenwich Mews Spanish Theatre
Theatre East
211 E. 60th, N.Y.C.

La La!
Jerry Fine
7-12-73
Changing Scene
Denver, CO

La Lacune
Eugene Ionesco
5-6-70
Barbizon-Plaza Theatre
N.Y.C.

La Mama Christmas Oratorio
12-24-69
La Mama ETC
74 E. 4th, N.Y.C.

L.A. Under Siege
Mayo Simon
8-2-70
Mark Taper Forum
Los Angeles, Ca

Labido Fury (a live cartoon nitemare)
12-7-73
Theater of Madness
Electric Circus
23 St. Mark's Pl., N.Y.C.

Labor Party
Robert T. Littell
4-28-70
Madison Center Theater
30 E. 31st, N.Y.C.

Labyrinthe
Fernando Arrabal
8-7-68
Spingold Theatre
Brandeis University
Waltham, MA

Ladies' Day at the Zoo
Clifford Fournier
4-24-70
New York Theatre Ensemble
2 E. 2nd, N.Y.C.

Ladies in Waiting
Peter DeAnda
6-17-68
Negro Ensemble Company
St. Mark's Playhouse
133 Second Ave., N.Y.C.

Ladies Kill Gentlemen
Michael Tonecki
6-18-70
Assembly Theatre
113 Jane, N.Y.C.

Lady and the Bandit, The
Lance Belville
11-8-73
Electric Circus
23 St. Mark's Pl., N.Y.C.

Lady and the Servant Girl, The
Myrna Lamb
April, 1969
Martinique Theatre
N.Y.C.

Lady and the Unicorn, The
1970
Theatre Wagon
Staunton, VA

Lady Audley's Secret (musical)
Douglas Seale (book); John Kuntz (lyrics); George Gochring (music)
7-24-69
Playhouse in the Park
Cincinnati, OH

Lady Chatterly's Lover
Edward Dork
5-31-68
Courtyard Playhouse
424 W. 45th, N.Y.C.

Lady Day: A Musical Tragedy
Aishah Rahman; Archie Shepp (music)
10-25-72
Chelsea Theatre Center
30 Lafayette, Brooklyn, NY

Lady Laura Pritchett, American
John White
7-23-69
Artists Theater Festival
Southampton, L.I., NY

Lady Macbeth in the Park
Susan Slade
5-13-71
Triangle Theatre
316 E. 88th, N.Y.C.

Lady Named Jo, A
Ben Finn
12-6-71
St. Peter's Gate
132 E. 54th, N.Y.C.

Ladybug (musical)
Dakota Don Peterson (book, lyrics, music)
11-16-72
Greenwich Mews Theatre
141 W. 13th, N.Y.C.

Lake of the Woods
Steven Tesich
12-22-71
American Place Theatre
N.Y.C.

Lamb, The (with The Ha Ha Play)
Susan Yankowitz
11-27-70
Cubiculo
414 W. 51st, N.Y.C.

Lament
Richard Longchamps
9-25-70
New York Theatre Ensemble
2 E. 2nd, N.Y.C.

Land I Love, The
Peter Copani
7-22-69
Playbox
94 St. Mark's Pl., N.Y.C

Land O' My Own
William B. Russell (book & lyrics); David Livingston (music)
6-13-70
Kentucky Theatre Under the Stars
Cave City, KY

Land of the Egyptians
G. Holmes Jones
8-28-72
Harlem Children's Theatre Co.
Lincoln Center Plaza
N.Y.C.

Landmarks
George Hammer
Fall, 1972
H B Playwrights Foundation
124 Bank, N.Y.C.

Landscape (with Silence)
Harold Pinter
4-2-70
Forum Theatre
Lincoln Center, N.Y.C.

Last Act, The (with The Entrepreneurs of Avenue B)
Jack Gilhooley
4-22-71
13th Street Theatre
50 W. 13th, N.Y.C.

Last Bangings
George Malko
2-14-70
New Theatre Workshop
154 E. 54th, N.Y.C.

Last Birthday, The
Michael Mathias
6-14-68
U.N. Theatre Voices of the N.Y. Theatre Ensemble
Covenant Theatre
310 E. 42nd, N.Y.C.

Last Catholic, The
Larry Gerst
11-12-71
College of Steubenville
Steubenville, OH

Last Chance Saloon, The
Andy Robinson
5-2-69
La Mama ETC
74 E. 4th, N.Y.C.

Last Known Positions at the Battle of Poitiers, The
Robert Jordan
6-11-68
Gotham Art
455 W. 43rd, N.Y.C.

Last Letters from Stalingrad
4-25-69
St. Peter's Gate
132 E. 54th, N.Y.C.

Last Night I Dreamt I Was Julie Bravado (with Death by Desire)
H. M. Koutoukas
11-26-70
Elgin Theatre
171 Eighth Ave., N.Y.C.

Last of Mrs. Lincoln, The
James Prideaux
11-10-72
Eisenhower Theatre
Kennedy Center for the Performing Arts
Washington, DC

Last of the Bummers, The
JoEllen Sheffield
6-11-70
Reese Palley Gallery
93 Prince St., N.Y.C.

Last of the Chorus Girls, The
William Narey
6-17-69
Assembly Theatre
113 Jane, N.Y.C.

Last of the Marx Brothers Writers, The
Louis Phillips
Spring, 1973
Brandeis University
Waltham, MA

Last of the Order, The
Richard V. Benner
5-6-70
Queens College
Flushing, NY

Last of the Red Hot Lovers
Neil Simon
11-26-69
Shubert Theatre
New Haven, CT

Last Pad, The
William Inge
12-6-70
13th Street Theatre
50 W. 13th, N.Y.C.

Last Poets
Kain David Nelson & Filipe Luciano
6-10-71
Cubiculo
414 W. 51st, N.Y.C.

Last Respects
Danny Lipman
2-21-72
University of Michigan
Ann Arbor, MI

Last Session, The
Dick Poston
5-9-73
Malachy Repertory Company
455 W. 51st, N.Y.C.

Last Straw, The (with Duet for Solo Voice by D. M. Milton)
Charles Dizenzo
3-9-70
American Place Theatre
N.Y.C.

Last Supper, The
Ed Wode
2-9-73
Gracie Theatre
423 E. 90th, N.Y.C.

Last Sweet Days of Isaac, The
Gretchen Cryer (book & lyrics); Nancy Ford (music)
1-26-70
Eastside Playhouse
334 E. 74th, N.Y.C.

Last Unicorn, The (Adapted from Peter Beagle's fantasy)
11-23-73
Arlington Street Church
Boston, MA

Late
Louis Florimonte
6-13-69
Cubiculo
414 W. 51st, N.Y.C.

Late for Oblivion (with Eurydice; The Dark Maiden from the Ninth Heaven; How Thunder and Lightning Began)
Holly Beye
7-22-71
Cubiculo
414 W. 51st, N.Y.C.

Late on a Sunday Afternoon (with In the Country's Night)
Michael Shurtleff
11-9-69
Extension Theatre
277 Park Ave. So., N.Y.C.

Late Show, The
Ken McGuire
6-17-71
Greenwich Mews Theatre
141 W. 13th, N.Y.C.

Latent Heterosexual, The
Paddy Chayevsky
3-15-68
Dallas Theatre Center
Dallas, TX

Latin American Theatre Fair (kaleidoscope of Latin American theatre & music)
3-23-72
St. Clement's Church
423 W. 46th, N.Y.C.

Latin American Trip (reading)
Arnaldo Calveyra
4-16-73
Theatre of Latin America
St. Clement's Church
423 W. 46th, N.Y.C.

Laugh Maker, The (musical)
G. Hertzog
10-19-71
Eden Theatre
2nd Ave. & 12th, N.Y.C.

Laundry
Gertrude Greenidge
1-23-73
Negro Ensemble Company
St. Mark's Playhouse
133 Second, N.Y.C.

Law and Order
Bill Hauptman
4-24-70
CR Acting Workshop
252 W. 81st, N.Y.C.

Lay of the Land, The (with We Agree; Cross-Country; and Australia Play)
Sally Ordway
11-12-71
New York Theatre Ensemble
2 E. 2nd, N.Y.C.

Leadbelly
Piero Heliczer
2-25-71
Cinematheque
80 Wooster, N.Y.C.

Leader, The
Paul Carter Harrison
4-19-68
St. Peter's Church
346 W. 20th, N.Y.C.

Leader, The
Joseph White
2-5-68
Old Reliable Theatre Tavern
231 E. 3rd, N.Y.C.

Lean and Hungry Priest, A
Warren Kliewer (book & lyrics); Dan Newmark (music)
Fall, 1973
Scorpio Rising
Los Angeles, Ca

Lean on the Wind (dramatic reading)
Frank Biancmano
10-23-72
Cubiculo
414 W. 51st, N.Y.C.

Lear
Edward Bond
4-13-73
Yale Repertory Theatre
New Haven, CT

Leaves of Grass
Stan Harts, Jr. (adapt. & music)
9-12-71
Theatre Four
424 W. 55th, N.Y.C.

Leaving Home
David French
May, 1972
Tarragon Theatre
Toronto, Ontario, CAN

Leb'n Auf Columbus, A (musical)
3-26-72
Educational Alliance
197 E. Broadway, N.Y.C.

Leda Had a Little Swan
Bamber Gascoigne
4-11-68
Cort Theatre
N.Y.C.

Ledger on the Lamp
Jonathan Marchant
7-16-71
Actors Theatre
49 E. 1st, N.Y.C.

Lee by Life – A Hodge Podge
Jerry Lee
3-1-68
Gallery Theatre
99 E. 2nd, N.Y.C.

Lee Harvey Oswald: A Far Mean Streak of Independence Brought on by Neglect
Michael Hastings
4-17-68
Theater Atlanta
Atlanta, GA

Left, Right, Left (with The Perfect Match)
William Derringer
2-14-69
Theatre of Our Discontent
Clifton Hotel
127 W. 79th, N.Y.C.

Left-Hand Mirror, The
William McQueen
1-9-70
Theatre West
1 W. 125th, N.Y.C.

Leftovers
Bronson Dudley
1-16-70
Riverdale Showcase
252nd St. & Riverdale Ave., Bronx, NY

Legacy
T. C. Gayle
Civic Theatre
Temple, TX

Legacy of Bessie Smith, The
Ruth Brisbane
3-6-72
St. Peter's Gate
132 E. 54th, N.Y.C.

Legacy, The
Kit Jones
1-3-69
Anthony Mannino Drama Tree
182 Fifth, N.Y.C.

Legend of Mr. Vee, The
Black Wheat Theatre
Dec., 1972
Emmanuel Church
Boston, MA

Legion
Peter Fusco
5-7-72
Supernova
451 W. Broadway, N.Y.C.

Lemon Sky
Lanford Wilson
July, 1968
Eugene O'Neill Memorial Theatre
Waterford, CT

Lemonade (with The Autograph Hound)
James Prideaux
12-13-68
Jan Hus Auditorium
351 E. 74th, N.Y.C.

Lenny
Tom Bissinger
3-17-70
Theatre of the Living Arts
Philadelphia, PA

Lenny
Julian Barry
5-26-71
Brooks Atkinson Theatre
N.Y.C.

Leonie Is Early (with Look, Don't Walk Around Naked)
Georges Feydeau; translated by James Clancy
7-4-69
Cornell University
Ithaca, NY

Leper, The
Gian-Carlo Menotti
4-22-70
Florida State University
Tallahasse, FL

Lesson in Consent, A (with The Flight of Lindbergh)
Bertolt Brecht; music by Paul Hindemith; original material by Gordon Duffey & Richard Peaslee
5-25-69
New York City Theatre Workshop
Metropolitan Museum of Art
N.Y.C.

Lesson in Dead Language
Adrienne Kennedy
4-22-71
Theatre Genesis
10th & 2nd, N.Y.C.

Let Me Hear You Smile
Leonora Thuna & Harry Cauley
12-26-72
Hannah Theatre
Cleveland, OH

Let Me Make One Thing Perfectly Clear
Michael Kortchmar
2-17-72
Manhattan Theatre Club
321 E. 73rd, N.Y.C.

Let's Hear It for Miss America
Gloria Gonzalez
5-25-70
Test Patterns Research Theatre
114 W. 14th, N.Y.C.

Let's You and Him Fight
John Welden
March 22, 1968
Yale University
New Haven, CT

Let Them Down, Gently
Gert Hoffman
1-29-68
Theatre de Lys
N.Y.C.

Let Your Fingers Do the Walking
H. N. Levitt
2-12-70
Hunter College
N.Y.C.

Lettre Morte (with Architruc)
Robert Pinget
4-15-70
Barbizon-Plaza Theatre
N.Y.C.

Leviticus
Edward Greenberg
Sept., 1970
Playwrights' Unit
83 E. 4th, N.Y.C.

Liars, Liars, Everywhere
Tom Farb
6-7-70
Master Institute Teenage Drama Workshop
103rd & Riverside Dr., N.Y.C.

Liars, The
Walter Beakel
12-27-68
Off Center Theatre
152 W. 66th, N.Y.C.

Lib Comes High
Joan Nourse
10-14-71
Blackfriars' Guild
316 W. 57th, N.Y.C.

Liberated Woman, A
Barry Reckford
3-17-71
La Mama ETC
74 E. 4th, N.Y.C.

Liberation (done with Oppression under the covering title Streets)
2-10-72
Emerson College
Boston, MA

Liberty Head Nickel, The
B. F. Dunn
9-10-68
Nucleus Repertory Theatre
261 W. 54th, N.Y.C.

Liberty Sometimes
Martin Ring
10-7-72
Omni Theatre Club
145 W. 18th, N.Y.C.

License, The (with The Jar)
Luigi Pirandello
4-22-69
Sheridan Square Playhouse
99 Seventh Ave. So., N.Y.C.

Lie, The
Ingmar Bergman
1-3-72
Swedish Drama Series
Library & Museum of the Performing Arts
111 Amsterdam, N.Y.C.

Life Among the Young People
Michael Shurtleff
4-10-68
Playbox
94 St. Mark's Pl., N.Y.C.

Life and Death in Detroit (with Strip Tease)
David MacLaren
12-8-72
New York Theatre Ensemble
2 E. 2nd, N.Y.C.

Life and Other Mistakes
Sandy Marshall
10-10-70
Playbox
94 St. Mark's Pl., N.Y.C.

Life and Times of J. Walter Smintheus, The
Edgar White
12-7-70
ANTA Matinee Series
Theatre de Lys
N.Y.C.

Life and Times of Joseph Stalin, The
Robert Wilson & Cynthia Lubar
12-14-73
Brooklyn Academy of Music
30 Lafayette, Brooklyn, NY

Life and Times of Sigmund Freud, The
Bob Wilson
12-18-69
Brooklyn Academy of Music
Brooklyn, NY

Life by Ferks – A Hodge Podge
Jerry Lee
3-8-68
Gallery Theatre
99 E. 2nd, N.Y.C.

Life Can Be Like Wow!
Marian Grudeff & Raymond Jessel
7-4-69
Fathers of Confederation Memorial Centre
Charlottetown, Prince Edward Island, CAN

Life in a Dream, A (rock contata)
Dave Bobrowitz & Gene Rempel
6-28-73
Cubiculo
414 W. 51st, N.Y.C.

Life in Bed
Joseph Renard
8-17-70
Old Reliable Theatre Tavern
231 E. 3rd, N.Y.C.

Life in Excellence
Anthony Calandra
5-9-73
Malachy Repertory Company
455 W. 51st, N.Y.C.

Life Is a Dream
Pedro Calderon de la Barca; translated by Kathleen Raine & R. M. Nadal
12-23-71
Greenwich Mews Spanish Theatre
141 W. 13th, N.Y.C.

Life Is a Dream
Pedro Calderon de la Barca; Edwin Honig (translator)
10-29-71
Brown University
Providence, RI

Life, Love, and Other Delusions Through the Eyes of James Thurber, Jules Feiffer
12-1-73
Showcase East
251 E. 50th, N.Y.C.

Life of a Man, The
Al Carmines
9-29-72
Judson Poets' Theatre
55 Wash. Sq. So., N.Y.C.

Life, The
Cary Pepper
9-29-72
New Village Theatre
433 E. 6th, N.Y.C.

Lifeguard, The
Robert Reinhold
10-29-71
Omni Theatre Club
145 W. 18th, N.Y.C.

Lifestring (with Rococo Joker)
James Eliason
Summer, 1972
Bronx Experimental Theatre
Vandam Theatre
15 Vandam, N.Y.C.

Ligeia
Edgar Allan Poe; adapted by Geddeth Smith
1-24-70
New York Historical Society
N.Y.C.

Light Blue Peignoir, The (with. . . And His Light Green Hair)
Jack Shoemaker
2-5-71
Gene Frankel Theater Workshop
115 MacDougal, N.Y.C.

Light Cell Death
Charles Kespert
1-4-73
Theatre Genesis
10th & 2nd Ave., N.Y.C.

Light, Lively and Yiddish
Ben Bonus (adaptor); A. Shulman & Wolf & Sylvia Youin (book & lyrics); Eli Rubenstein & A. Goldfaden (music)
10-27-70
Belasco Theatre
N.Y.C.

Lightnin' Bugs 'n' God 'n' Things
Bruce Peyton
2-16-73
Central Arts Cabaret
108 E. 64th, N.Y.C.

Lightning at a Funeral
David Pinner
3-3-71
Stanford University
Palo Alto, CA

Like a Tree, Like a Rock
3-14-69
Mainstream Theatre
20 E. 14th, N.Y.C.

Like Father, Like Fun
8-9-73
Huron Country Playhouse
Great Bend, Ontario, CAN

Like It Is!
Helen Kromer & Fredrick Silver
11-20-69
Riverside Church
122nd & Riverside Dr., N.Y.C.

Like It Is (revue)
8-14-69
Mount Union College
Alliance, OH

Like Nothing
Donald Kvares
5-1-70
New York Theatre Ensemble
2 E. 2nd, N.Y.C.

Like Ripe Red Apples
Elaine Berman
2-14-68
Extension Theatre
128 E. 7th, N.Y.C.

Like Shoes (with Go On Downstairs)
Jordan A. Deutsch
1-17-69
Theatre of Our Discontent
Clifton Hotel
127 W. 79th, N.Y.C.

Like Tender of Our Love We Make, The
John Arthur Anderson
4-12-72
New Village Theatre
433 E. 6th, N.Y.C.

Likely Saga of James T. Thayer, The
Rae Horan
4-26-73
University of Montana
Missoula, MT

Likely Story, A
Sally Raynor Higley
7-29-68
Playhouse
Kennebunkport, ME

Lily of the Valley of the Dolls
Robert Patrick
6-17-68
Old Reliable Theatre Tavern
231 E. 3rd, N.Y.C.

Lily, The Felon's Daughter
7-11-72
People's Theatre
YWCA
Cambridge, MA

Lime Green/Khaki Blue
Ben Piazza
3-26-69
Provincetown Playhouse
133 MacDougal, N.Y.C.

Limits
Michael Vittes
2-14-68
Theater 13
201 W. 13th, N.Y.C.

Lincoln Mask, The
V. J. Longhi
9-19-72
Kennedy Center for the Performing Arts
Washington, DC

Lion and the Jewel, The
Wole Soyinka
7-21-70
Playhouse in the Park
Philadelphia, PA

Lion Roams the Streets, A
Gordon Watkins
11-15-68
New Hudson Guild
441 W. 26th, N.Y.C.

Listen, Sean, to the Silhouette of Raindrops
John Hartnett
1-18-71
Old Reliable Theatre Tavern
231 E. 3rd, N.Y.C.

Listen to the Dutchess
Bruce Feld
4-2-71
Stage Lights Theatrical Club
218 W. 48th, N.Y.C.

Little Alice
Billy Dymond
8-29-72
Bridgton/Homestead Players, Bridgton, Me.
Lincoln Center Plaza
N.Y.C.

Little Baloney in Lieu of Luncheon, A
Norman & Sandra Dietz
1-8-68
St. Peter's Gate
132 E. 54th, N.Y.C.

Little Betty
Alexander Panas
9-30-70
Assembly Theatre
113 Jane, N.Y.C.

Little Black Book, The
Jean-Claude Carrier; adapted by Jerome Kilty
3-27-72
Eisenhower Theatre
Kennedy Center for the Performing Arts
Washington, DC

Little Boxes
John Bowen
12-3-69
New Theatre Workshop
154 E. 54th, N.Y.C.

Little B.S. (with The Jitney Vehicle)
Charles Briggs
12-7-73
Amas Repertory Theatre
263 W. 86th, N.Y.C.

Little Burgundy (with Manitoba)
Guy Gauthier
2-20-70
Judson Poet's Theatre
55 Wash. Sq. So., N.Y.C.

Little Gentleman, The
Yale M. Udoff
1-19-70
Fortune Theatre
62 E. 4th, N.Y.C.

Little History of a World
Juan Carlos Uviedo
2-10-71
La Mama ETC
74 E. 4th, N.Y.C.

Little Less Than Plato, A
Don Katzman
10-18-73
Changing Scene
Denver, CO

Little Mahagonny, The
Bertolt Brecht (book & lyrics); Kurt Weill (music)
5-13-71
Yale University
New Haven, CT

Little Match Girl Makes It Big, The ("revusical")
Paul Foster, Hal Craven, Peter Fusco, Stephen Holt, John Herbert McDowell, Lionel Hampton Mitchell, Jeannine O'Reilly, Robert Patrick, Joseph Renard
12-13-73
WPA
333 Bowery, N.Y.C.

Little Night Music, A
Hugh Wheeler (book); Stephen Sondheim (lyrics & music)
1-23-73
Colonial Theatre
Boston, MA

Little Old Lady
Barry Douglas
5-16-73
Courtyard Playhouse
137 W. 14th, N.Y.C.

Little Onion Annie
Ilsa Gilbert
7-16-71
Omni Theatre Club
145 W. 18th, N.Y.C.

Little Piece of Earth, A
Elayne Snyder
6-13-68
Theatre 13
201 W. 13th, N.Y.C.

Little Prince, The
Antoine de Saint-Exupery; adapted by David Zucker
4-12-72
Laurie Theatre
Brandeis University
Waltham, MA

Little Shepherd of Kingdom Come, The
Based on a story by John Fox, Jr.
6-30-72
Amphitheatre
Van, KY

Little Singing, a Little Dancing, A
Robert Kimmel Smith
7-14-15-71
Eugene O'Neill Memorial Theatre
Waterford, CT

Little Trips
Norman Taffel
Oct., 1970
Little Trips Theatre
70 Grand, N.Y.C.

Little Violet Picker, The
Jim Zack
4-13-70
Old Reliable Theatre Tavern
231 E. 3rd, N.Y.C.

Living End, The
Eleanor Hyde
2-16-68
West Side Theatre
585 Columbus, N.Y.C.

Living Room with Six Oppressions
Oscar Mandel
12-20-72
Playwright's Workshop Club
Bastiano's Studio
14 Cooper Sq., N.Y.C.

Local Stop
Marj Mahle
8-5-70
Assembly Theatre
113 Jane, N.Y.C.

Lockport (multi-media production)
March, 1971
New York Shakespeare Festival Public Theatre
425 Lafayette, N.Y.C.

Locomotive Munch
Jeff Weiss
3-4-72
La Mama ETC
74 E. 4th, N.Y.C.

Logical Room, The
John Crennan
11-26-71
New York Theatre Ensemble
2 E. 2nd, N.Y.C.

Lola-Lola and the Lucky Stars
J. R. Reynolds
3-30-73
Theatre for the New City
113 Jane, N.Y.C.

Lolita, My Love
Alan Jay Lerner (book & lyrics); John Barry (music)
2-15-71
Shubert Theatre
Philadelphia, PA

Lonely Hunting, The
Carson McCullers; adapted by George Gingell
1969
Springer Theatre Company
Columbus, GA

Lonely Ones, The
Bill Faulk
April, 1969
Central State College
Oklahoma City, OK

Long Black Block, The
Roger Furman
11-15-73
New Heritage Theatre
Brooklyn Academy of Music
30 Lafayette, Brooklyn, NY

Long Live Life
Jerome Kilty
4-28-68
American Conservatory Theatre
San Francisco, CA

Long Song
Charles Pulaski
6-12-69
New York Theatre Ensemble
2 E. 2nd, N.Y.C.

Long Time Coming and Long Time Gone, A (collage)
Based on the works of Richard Farina; Nancy Greenwald (adaptor)
7-1-71
Lenox Arts Center
Lenox, MA

Long War, The
Kevin O'Morrison
2-20-69
Triangle Theatre
316 E. 88th, N.Y.C.

Longest Afternoon of the Year, The
John Guare
4-11-69
Actor's Place
487 Hudson, N.Y.C.

Longest Day of My Life, The
Virgil Engeran
8-20-71
Pilgrims Theatre Company
Boston, MA

Longing for Worldly Pleasures
Asian American Troupe
4-21-72
La Mama ETC
74 E. 4th, N.Y.C.

Lonnie, James, Bernhardt and Zoowolski
John E. Sedlak
7-12-71 (reading)
8-6, 7-71 (performance)
Eugene O'Neill Memorial Theatre
Waterford, CT

Look at the Fifties, A
Al Carmines
4-14-72
Judson Poets' Theatre
55 Wash. Sq. So., N.Y.C.

Look Away
Jerome Kilty
1-7-73
Playhouse Theatre
359 W. 48th, N.Y.C.

Look, Don't Walk Around Naked (with Leonie Is Early)
Georges Feydeau, translated by James Clancy
7-4-69
Cornell University
Ithaca, NY

Look Me Up
Laurence Taylor (book)
10-6-71
Plaza 9
Plaza Hotel, N.Y.C.

Look Not Upon Me
Brenda Hicks
12-2-71
Elma Lewis School of Fine Arts
National Center of Afro-American Artists
Roxbury, MA

Look to the Lilies
Leonard Spigelgass (book); Sammy Cahn (lyrics); Jule Styne (music)
3-29-70
Lunt-Fontanne Theatre
205 W. 46th, N.Y.C.

Look To Your Rats
Paul Wienman
9-24-70
Columbia University
N.Y.C.

Look Where I'm At
James Leasor (book); Jordan Ramin (music); Frank Stanton, Murray Semos (lyrics)
3-3-71
Theater Four
424 W. 55th, N.Y.C.

Looking for Billy
T. Frank Gutswa
1-21-72
New York Theatre Ensemble
2 E. 2nd, N.Y.C.

Looking for Rosa
Jack Adler
10-18-68
New York Theatre Ensemble
2 E. 2nd, N.Y.C.

Loot
Joe Orton
3-18-68
Biltmore Theatre
N.Y.C.

Lord Jim
Daniel Stern
3-28-68
Artists' Repertory Theatre
20 E. 14th, N.Y.C.

Lord of the Flies
Andrew Bethell
June (?) 1970
St. Lawrence Centre
Toronto, CAN

Lords Adult Puppet Theatre
3-11-72
Staten Island Community College
Staten Island, NY

Lorelei
Kenny Solms & Gail Parent (book); Betty Comden & Adolph Green (lyrics); Jule Styne (music)
2-26-73
Civic Center Music Hall
Oklahoma City, OK

Lorenzaccio
Alfred de Musset; translation by John Lewin
6-6-72
Stratford Festival
Stratford, Ontario, CAN

Lorrie
Bernard M. Kahn
10-4-72
La Mama ETC
74 E. 4th, N.Y.C.

Los Angeles Se Han Fatigado
See: The Angels Are Exhausted

Los Invasores (The Invaders)
Egon Wolff
Dec., 1970
ADAL Theatre
682 Avenue of the Americas, N.Y.C.

Losers, The
Wesley St. John
7-13-71
New American Playwright Series
Brooklyn College
N.Y.C.

Losing Oneself (with Things as They Are)
Gina Collens
5-12-72
Theatre of the Americas
427 W. 59th, N.Y.C.

Losing Things (with Touch and Go)
Benjamin Bradford
12-6-72
Dept. of Theatre Arts
University of Kentucky
Lexington, KY

Lost Whaleboat, The
Clyde Ellsworth
4-6-72
Jean Cocteau Theatre
43 Bond, N.Y.C.

Lotta
Robert Montgomery
10-18-73
New York Shakespeare Festival
Public Theatre
425 Lafayette, N.Y.C.

Lou Gehrig Did Not Die of Cancer
Jason Miller
3-2-70
Library & Museum of the
Performing Arts
111 Amsterdam, N.Y.C.

Loud Silence, A (an evening of mime)
Siena Porter, Peter Ford, Billy Fink
12-1-72
Eclectic December Theatre
Central Arts Cabaret
108 E. 64th, N.Y.C.

Louis Gilbert's Genuine Mime Extravaganza
12-1-72
West Side YWCA
8th Ave. & 51st, N.Y.C.

Louis IX
Claude Brickell
3-19-71
Fortune Theatre
62 E. 4th, N.Y.C.

Louise
Milburn Mehlhop
6-7-72
WPA
333 Bowery, N.Y.C.

Louisville '59 (with So Dark Tonight)
Larry O'Connel
12-10-69
Second Group Theatre
McBurney YMCA
215 W. 23rd, N.Y.C.

Lovableness
Mordecai Newman
4-26-71
Minor Latham Playhouse
Barnard College
N.Y.C.

Love America or Live
Tosum Bayrak
11-7-70
Prince Street
N.Y.C.

Love and Let Love
John Lollos, Don Christopher,
Stanley Jay Gelber
1-2-68
Sheridan Square Playhouse
99 Seventh Ave. So., N.Y.C.

Love and Maple Syrup
Louis Negin
7-8-69
National Arts Centre
Ottawa, CAN

Love and Master Will
9-19-73
Opera House
Washington, DC

Love and War
Romulus Linney
11-21-68
H B Playwrights Foundation
124 Bank, N.Y.C.

Love Course, The
A. R. Gurney, Jr.
2-26-73
Library & Museum of the
Performing Arts
111 Amsterdam, N.Y.C.

Love Game
Tom Coble
6-2-72
Playbox
94 St. Mark's Pl., N.Y.C.

Love Game, The
George Gipe
Spring, 1972
Limestone Valley Dinner Theatre
Cockneyville, MD

Love Games of the Gods
7-3-71
Weathervane Theatre
Whitefield, NH

Love Gotta Come by Saturday Night
Ronnie Paris
1-8-73
Theatre de Lys
N.Y.C.

Love, Honor and Delay
See: Silverplate (same play)

Love in the Space Age
Mark Levine
10-22-70
Changing Scene
Denver, CO

Love in 1984
Stuart Koch
3-23-70
Old Reliable Theatre Tavern
231 E. 3rd, N.Y.C.

Love Is a Five Letter Word
Moliere; adapted by Wallace
Sterling & the Company
2-10-70
University of Akron
Akron, OH

Love Is a Time of Day
John Patrick
7-1-69
Playhouse on the Mall
Paramus, NJ

Love Is a Tuna Casserole
Gloria Gonzalez
8-6-71
New York Theatre Ensemble
2 E. 2nd, N.Y.C.

Love Man's Gone Away, The
P. J. Barry
10-30-70
Hudson Guild Theatre
441 W. 16th, N.Y.C.

Love Match
Christian Hamilton, Richard
Maltby, Jr.; David Shire
11-3-68
Palace West Theatre
Phoenix, AZ

Love Me, Love My Bread (a happening)
John Fischer
12-22-68
Loeb Student Center
Wash. Sq. So., N.Y.C.

Love Me or I'll Kill You
Daniel Haben Clark
10-7-68
Old Reliable Theatre Tavern
231 E. 3rd, N.Y.C.

Love of Art, The
Skip Rollet
5-28-69
St. Clement's Church
423 W. 46th, N.Y.C.

Love of Don Perlimplin, The
Federico Garcia Lorca; translation
by R. Brooke Lewis
8-19-72
Theatre Wagon
Staunton, VA

Love Suicide at Schofield Barracks, The
Romulus Linney
April, 1971
H B Playwrights Foundation
N.Y.C.

Love Two
George Nider (book & lyrics); Ed
Metz (music)
6-24-72
Theatre Unlimited
171 W. 85th, N.Y.C.

Love without Fear
Karl A. Tunberg
4-9-70
St. Peter's Church
346 W. 20th, N.Y.C.

Love Your Crooked Neighbor
Harold J. Chapler
12-29-69
Cherry Lane Theatre
38 Commerce, N.Y.C

Lovecraft's Follies
James Schevill
3-10-70
Trinity Square Repertory
Providence, RI

Love-Death of Madame Babinsky, The
John Wolfson
1-15-71
Omni Theatre Club
145 W. 18th, N.Y.C.

Loveliest Afternoon of the Year, The
John Guare
Nov., 1968
Loretto Hilton Center
St. Louis, MO

Lovely Ladies, Kind Gentlemen
John Patrick (book); Stan Freeman
& Franklin Underwood (lyrics &
music)
8-19-70
Shubert Theatre
Philadelphia, PA

Lovers
Brian Friel
7-25-68
Vivian Beaumont Theatre
Lincoln Center
N.Y.C.

Lovers and Other Strangers
Renee Taylor & Joseph Bologna
8-7-68
Berkshire Theatre Festival
Stockbridge, MA

Loves of William Shakespeare, The
Evangeline Machlin
Fall, 1969
Boston University
Boston, MA

Luba
Maryat Lee
Fall, 1969
Soul & Latin Theatre
N.Y.C.

Lucky Jim
Kingsley Amis
Summer, 1973
Northwestern University
Evanston, IL

Lucky Wonderful
Jackie Curtis, Ben Serrato
3-28-68
Playwrights' Workshop Club
14 Waverly Pl., N.Y.C.

Lucy Church Amiably
Gertrude Stein; adapted by Scott
Fields
6-4-72
Washington Square Church
133 W. 4th, N.Y.C.

Lulu Street
Ann Henry
Summer, 1972
Lennoxville Festival
Lennoxville, Quebec, CAN

Luminosity without Radiance: A Self-Portrait
Diane Kagan & Avra Petrides
4-3-73
Manhattan Theatre Club
321 E. 73rd, N.Y.C.

Lumpen
Simm Landres
6-17-71
University of Texas
Austin, TX

Luna Park
9-27-72
Theatre Laboratoire Vicinal of
Brussels
La Mama ETC
74 E. 4th, N.Y.C.

Luna (with A Quick Nut Bread To Make Your Mouth Water)
William H. Hoffman
7-6-70
Old Reliable Theatre Tavern
231 E. 3rd, N.Y.C.

Lunacies
5-11-73
Sixth Floor Theatre
150 Bleecker, N.Y.C.

Lunar Lunacy, Uncle Sam, and The Children of God
8-2-69
Alternate U
69 W. 14th, N.Y.C.

Lunatic, The Secret Sportsman and The Woman Next Door, The
Stanley Eveling
8-6-68
Spingold Theatre
Brandeis University
Waltham, MA

Lunch Hour
Craig Clinton
1-18-73
Manhattan Theatre Club
321 E. 73rd, N.Y.C.

Lunchbreak
Michael Wolfe
3-4-71
Playbox
94 St. Mark's Pl., N.Y.C.

Lydia's Rape
Lewis Michael Stern
7-23-68
New Workshop Theatre
Brooklyn College
NY

Lyle
Sidney Miller & Toby Garson (book); Toby Garson (lyrics); Janet Gari (music)
3-20-70
McAlpin Rooftop Theatre
34th St. & 6th, N.Y.C.

Lysistrata (Adaptation by Darrel deChaby)
Aristophanes
11-6-70
New York Theatre Ensemble
2 E. 2nd, N.Y.C.

Lysistrata (New adaptation by Michael Cacoyannis)
Aristophanes
11-13-72
Brooks Atkinson Theatre
N.Y.C.

Lysistrata (new rock musical version)
Aristophanes; music by Frank Vinciguerra & Danny Lieberstein
11-14-68
Hunter College Theatre Workshop
NY

M

Macbeth Did It
John Patrick
7-25-72
Flat Rock Playhouse
Flat Rock, NC

Macbett
Eugene Ionesco; Charles Marowitz (translator)
3-16-73
Yale Repertory Theatre
New Haven, Ct

MacDougal Street
Ed Setrakian
5-19-71
La Mama ETC
74 E. 4th, N.Y.C.

Macedonian Rag (with Prometheus and Pandora)
Gerry Giss
5-27-71
University of Montana
Missoula, MT

MacGowran in the Works of Beckett
See: Jack MacGowran in the Works of Samuel Beckett

Machiavelli
A. R. Bell
10-6-72
Dramatis Personae
114 W. 14th, N.Y.C.

Machiavelli and the Mandrake
7-3-70
Forestburgh Summer Theatre
Monticello, NY

Machine (with Journey to the Underworld)
Jim Lucason
3-17-71
Brandeis University
Waltham, MA

Macrune's Guevara
John Spurling
1-30-71
Whitman College
Walla Walla, WA

Mad Dog Blues
Sam Shepard
3-4-71
Theatre Genesis
10th & 2nd, N.Y.C.

Mad Ecologist, The
Thorn Crofter
1-12-73
Omni Theatre Club
145 W. 18th, N.Y.C.

Mad Spoofs
Albert Nulli
12-23-71
New York City League of Playwrights
162 W. 21st, N.Y.C.

Madam Mushroom (with The Rising Yeast)
Michael Mathias
4-22-70
Mainstream Theatre
20 E. 14th, N.Y.C.

Madam Odum
Louis Rivers
9-7-73
New Heritage Repertory Theatre
43 E. 125th, N.Y.C.

Madame de Sade
Yukio Mishima
10-30-72
Theatre de Lys
N.Y.C.

Made in the USA
Mary Chaffee & Art Bauman
4-10-69
Minor Latham Playhouse
Barnard College
N.Y.C.

Made in U.S.A.
8-6-73
Taconic Project
Spencertown, NY

Mademoiselle Colombe (musical version)
Jean Anouilh; Michael Valenti (music)
2-3-72
Stagelights II
125 W. 22nd, N.Y.C.

Madheart (with Black Dada Nihilism)
Imamu Amiri Baraka (LeRoi Jones)
6-11-71
Afro-American Studio
15 W. 126th, N.Y.C.

Madigan's Lock
Hugh Leonard
6-23-70
Olney Theatre
Olney, MD

Madman and Specialists
Wole Soyinka
8-1-70
Eugene O'Neill Memorial Theatre
Waterford, CT

Madman and the Nun, The
Stanislaw Witkiewicz
6-1-71
Inner City Theatre
Los Angeles, CA

Madness at Noon
Musical revue based on Works of Lewis Carroll
3-16-70
Cabaret Theatre
132 E. 54th, N.Y.C.

Madonna of the Trash Cans
Tony Preston
1-26-69
Theatre Market Place
Little Synagogue
27 E. 20th, N.Y.C.

Madrigal of Shakespeare, A
2-12-68
Theatre de Lys
121 Christopher, N.Y.C.

Maggie Flynn
Hugo Peretti, Luigi Creatore, George David Weiss
9-9-68
Fisher Theatre
Detroit, MI

Magic Cabbage
Janet Coleman
4-14-72
Teenage Theatre Games Workshop Project
St. Clement's Church
423 W. 46th, N.Y.C.

Magic Hype, The
J. Centola
10-12-73
Peach Pitts
200 W. 24th, N.Y.C.

Magic Isle, The
Adapted from original commedia dell'arte material of Russell Grave by Wesley van Tassel & Mark Ollington
7-1-68
Goodman Theatre
Chicago, IL

Magic Show of Dr. Ma-Gico, The
Kenneth Bernard
3-15-73
La Mama ETC
74 E. 4th, N.Y.C.

Magic Time (with The Gay Desperado and When Schwartz Meets Goldstein)
William Kushner
3-20-70
Play Lab
130 E. 7th, N.Y.C.

Magic Woofer-Tweeter, The
Tom Johnson
3-7-70
New York Shakespeare Festival Public Theatre
425 Lafayette, N.Y.C.

Magical Adventures of Skanderbeg & Skalawag, The
1-16-71
Terrain Gallery
39 Grove, N.Y.C.

Magic-Cine-Scene
Bohumil Svoboda
9-10-70
Dallas Theatre Center
Dallas, TX

Magnificent Thing to Be, A (musical)
Neal Love & Richard Wade
6-3-72
Little Theatre
Alexandria, VA

Magritte Skies
Yale M. Udoff
7-24-73
Eugene O'Neill Memorial Theatre
Waterford, CT

Mahagonny
Bertolt Brecht & Kurt Weill
4-28-70
Anderson Theatre
66 Second, N.Y.C.

Maid from Hue, The
Andres Monreal; Ricardo Castillo (translator)
4-30-71
New York Theatre of the Americas
427 W. 59th, N.Y.C.

Maids, The
12-29-71
La Mama ETC
74 E. 4th, N.Y.C.

Major Daley, Justice and the American Way
Michael Smith
10-20-68
Wittenberg University Theatre
Springfield, OH

Makbeth
11-20-69
Performance Garage
33 Wooster, N.Y.C.

Make Me Disappear
J. Marberger Stuart
5-13-69
Mercury Theatre
136 E. 13th, N.Y.C.

Makeshift
Donald Libman
1-29-72
Hunter College Playwrights Project
West Side YMCA
5 W. 63rd, N.Y.C.

Makin' It
Gertrude Greenidge, Walter Miles, Hazel Bryant (book); Jimmy Justice, Holly Hamilton (lyrics & music)
1-14-72
Afro-American Total Theatre
International House
500 Riverside Dr., N.Y.C.

Making It (with Pinky)
Jack Temchin
2-1-71
Old Reliable Theatre Tavern
231 E. 3rd, N.Y.C.

Making of Americans, The (opera)
Gertrude Stein; adapted by Leon Katz (lyrics); Al Carmines (music)
11-10-72
Judson Poets' Theatre
55 Wash. Sq. So., N.Y.C.

Making, The
Joseph Ponzi
5-3-68
Judson Poets' Theatre
55 Wash. Sq. So., N.Y.C.

Malcochon
Derek Walcott
4-1-69
Negro Ensemble Company
St. Mark's Playhouse
133 Second, N.Y.C.

Maleficio de la Mariposa, El
Federico Garcia Lorca
8-14-70
Tomkins Square Park
N.Y.C.

Malice in Wonderland
2-17-73
Black Experience Ensemble
Albany, NY

Mama
Neal DuBrock (book); John Clifton (music & lyrics)
1-6-72
Studio Arena Theatre
Buffalo, NY

Mama Went to the Movies
Irving Glusack
1-8-71
New York Theatre Ensemble
2 E. 2nd, N.Y.C.

Mamma, La
Andre Roussin
11-17-72
Teatro Caras Nuevas
114 W. 14th, N.Y.C.

Man Alive
John Dighton
8-25-70
Flat Rock Playhouse
Flat Rock, NC

Man and the Fly, The
Jose Ruibal
11-5-71
State University of New York
Binghamton, NY

Man and the Mosquito, The
Michael Mathias
9-20-68
Riverside Theatre Workshop
120th St. & Claremont Ave., N.Y.C.

Man and Woman
Joseph Ponzi
4-24-69
Gotham Art
455 W. 43rd, N.Y.C.

Man Behind the Legend, The
Yaacov Orland
10-24-71
YM-YWHA
92nd & Lexington, N.Y.C.

Man from Salem
7-18-68
Straight Wharf Theatre
Nantucket, MA

Man from the East, The
Stomu Yamash'ta
10-24-73
Red Buddha Theatre
Brooklyn Academy of Music
30 Lafayette, N.Y.C.

Man in a Bucket
Richard Brenner
2-11-71
Playbox
94 St. Mark's Pl., N.Y.C.

Man in a Bucket
Richard V. Benner
1-27-72
St. Clement's Church
423 W. 46th, N.Y.C.

Man in Space
Jon Swan
7-11-69
Eugene O'Neill Memorial Theatre
Waterford, CT

Man in the Glass Booth, The
Robert Shaw
9-26-68
Royale Theatre
N.Y.C.

Man in the Middle
Gordon Watkins
5-11-69
West Side YMCA
5 W. 63rd, N.Y.C.

Man Nobody Saw, The
10-17-69
Catholic Center
58 Wash. Sq. So., N.Y.C.

Man of the Voices, The
Aristides Meneghetti & Nelly Vivas
1-3-69
Cafe Four
522 E. 12th, N.Y.C.

Man Out of Darkness
William Gill
10-12-72
Playwrights' Horizons
West Side YWCA
8th Ave. & 51st, N.Y.C.

Man's a Man, A (rock musical)
Bertolt Brecht; Tim Hagerty (adaptor); P. Spoons Collier (music)
12-3-71
Bank Theatre
Brooklyn, NY

Man's Estate
Romulus Linney
1-18-68
H B Playwrights Foundation
124 Bank, N.Y.C.

Man Talking, A (with The Cock Crows)
Allen Davis
2-22-72
Theatre of the Riverside Church
490 Riverside Dr., N.Y.C.

Man Who Killed Tinkerbell, The
Robert Reiser
6-3-70
La Mama ETC
74 E. 4th, N.Y.C.

Man Who Lost the River, The
Bernard Sabath
2-7-68
Southern Illinois University
Carbondale, IL

Man with Expensive Tastes, The
7-27-71
Flat Rock Playhouse
Flat Rock, NC

Man with Seven Toes, The (with Babel)
Michael Ondaatje
7-6-72
St. Francis Xavier University Performing Group
Neptune Theatre
Halifax, Novia Scotia, CAN

Manchineel
Victor B. Miller
12-27-71
Cubiculo
414 W. 51st, N.Y.C.

Mandala
Seamus Murphy
11-5-72
Video Exchange
151 Bank, N.Y.C.

Mandragola
Niccolo Machiavelli; Cathy Roskam (translator)
2-15-73
Joseph Jefferson Theatre Company
Little Church-Around-the-Corner
11 E. 29th, N.Y.C.

Mandragola (musical)
Based on Niccolo Machiavelli
6-23-71
Brown University
Providence, RI

Mandrake the Magician
Lee Falk & Thayer Burch; George Quincy (music)
8-1-73
Lenox Arts Center
Lenox, MA

Manhattan on the Rocks (musical revue)
10-25-72
Bronx Community College
Bronx, NY

Manitoba (with Little Burgundy)
Guy Gauthier
2-20-70
Judson Poet's Theater
55 Wash. Sq. So., N.Y.C.

Mannomann
GRIPS Ensemble of Berlin
11-10-73
GRIPS Ensemble of Berlin at Theatre X
Milwaukee, WI

Many Happy Returns, A Review of Revues
Howard Dietz, Word Baker & Brooks Jones
6-13-70
Playhouse in the Park
Cincinnati, OH

Many Lives of Adam and Eve, The
Betty Jean Lifton
Fall, 1973
Proposition Workshop
Boston, MA

Many Lives of Wispy and Willo, The (with Becoming)
Betty Jean Lifton
5-5-73
Cathedral of St. John the Divine
112th & Amsterdam, N.Y.C.

Many Moods of the Black Experience, The
8-26-72
Artists Collective, Hartford, Connecticut
Lincoln Center Plaza
N.Y.C.

Marathon
2-5-71
Boston College
Boston, MA

Marco Polo Sings a Solo
John Guare
8-6-73
Nantucket Stage Company
Nantucket, MA

Marcolfa, La (with Not All Thieves Are Mischievous)
Dario Fo
7-24-69
Cubiculo
414 W. 51st, N.Y.C.

Margaret of Anjou
Shakespeare; adapted by Kenneth Janes
3-10-72
Barnard College
119th St. & Broadway, N.Y.C.

Margarie
Robert Tieman
9-3-68
Nucleus Repertory Theatre
261 W. 54th, N.Y.C.

Marie Vison, La
Shuji Terayama
7-8-70
La Mama ETC
74 E. 4th, N.Y.C.

Marjorie Daw
Sally Dixon Wiener
2-2-70
Library & Museum of the Performing Arts
111 Amsterdam, N.Y.C.

Mark
Betty Jane Wylie
7-19-72
Stratford Festival
Stratford, Ontario, CAN

Mark of Cain
Russell Freedman
8-13-71
Pilgrims Theatre Co.
Old South Church
Boston, MA

Marlene's Choice (with Rooftop)
Phillip Agree
2-11-72
13th Street Theatre
50 W. 13th, N.Y.C.

Marmalade Tree, The
Roma Greth
1-29-72
Riverdale Lab Theatre
252nd St. & Riverdale Ave. Bronx, NY

Marouf
Kenneth Cavander
12-11-73
Manhattan Theatre Club
321 E. 73rd, N.Y.C.

Marowitz Hamlet, The
Shakespeare; adapted by Charles Marowitz
8-9-72
Great Lakes Shakespearean Festival
Lakewood, OH

Marriage Museum, The
Elyse Nass
7-14-70
New Workshop Theatre
Brooklyn College
Brooklyn, NY

Marriage of the Telephone Company, The (with Out of Control)
Martin Craft
9-9-71
Actor's Playhouse
100 Seventh, N.Y.C.

Marriage on the New Made Moon Through No Fault of Our Own
Ed Harkness
4-21-72
University of Montana
Missoula, MT

Marriage, The
Bertolt Brecht
12-14-70
La Mama ETC
Loeb Drama Center
Cambridge, MA

Marriage, The
Witold Gombrowicz
4-12-72
Manhattan Theatre Club
321 E. 73rd, N.Y.C.

Married Couples Group, The
Florine Snider
1-26-73
New York Theatre Ensemble
2 E. 2nd, N.Y.C.

Marry Me! Marry Me!
Dennis Andersen
3-3-72
Playwrights' Horizons
Clark Center for the Performing Arts
West Side YWCA, 8th Ave. & 51st, N.Y.C.

Marty's Twice
Paul W. Clark
4-29-69
Phalanx Productions
Hotel Earle
103 Waverly Pl., N.Y.C.

Martyr, The
Now Theatre Ensemble
5-22-70
La Mama ETC
74 E. 4th, N.Y.C.

Martyrdom of Peter Ohey
Slawomir Mrozek
1969
Rutgers University
New Brunswick, NJ

Marvellous Misadventure of Sherlock Holmes, The
Thom Racina (book, lyrics, & music)
7-6-71
Goodman Theatre
Chicago, IL

Mary
Christopher Gore (book, lyrics); Howard Cable (music)
8-11-71
Fathers of Confederation Memorial Centre
Charlottetown, Prince Edward Island, CAN

Mary Dyer Hanged in Boston
Doris Baisley
2-9-71
Washington Square Church
133 W. 4th, N.Y.C.

Mary Jane
Kenneth Bernard
5-16-73
New York Theatre Strategy
Manhattan Theatre Club
321 E. 73rd, N.Y.C.

Mary Jean Maybee (with Wine Song)
Tony Mazzadra
9-11-70
The Assembly
113 Jane, N.Y.C.

Mary Stuart
Wolfgang Hildesheimer
3-3-73
Company Theatre
Los Angeles, CA

Masada (multi-action collage)
Hal Wicke & Anne Wilson
11-9-73
Packer Institute
Brooklyn, NY

Masha
Anton Chekhov; Tim Kelly (adaptor)
11-28-73
Manhattan Theatre Club
321 E. 73rd, N.Y.C.

Masks in Black '73 (revue)
Al Fann
8-16-73
St. Philips Center
207 W. 133rd, N.Y.C.

Masks in Brown, The
Al Fann
10-16-70
St. Philips Cultural Arts Center
207 W. 133rd, N.Y.C.

Masquenada
Richard Marc Rubin
3-25-71
Room 3H
40 E. 7th, N.Y.C.

Mass
Leonard Bernstein (music); Stephen Schwartz (text)
9-8-71
Opera House, Kennedy Center for the Performing Arts
Washington, DC

Mass for Actors and Audience. . .
Sydney Schubert Walter
4-25-69
La Mama ETC
74 E. 4th, N.Y.C.

Mass for Dionysis
James Maloon
11-19-69
Skidmore College Little Theatre
Saratoga Springs, NY

Massachusetts Trust
Megan Terry
8-21-68
Spingold Theatre
Brandeis University
Waltham, MA

Master Class
Jonathan Levy
2-22-73
Manhattan Theatre Club
321 E. 73rd, N.Y.C.

Master of the Blue Mineral Mines, The
Jonathan Levy
12-22-70
Playwrights' Unit
83 E. 4th, N.Y.C.

Master Psychoanalyst, The
Stanley Nelson
11-15-71
New Old Reliable Theatre
231 E. 3rd, N.Y.C.

Matador, El (a bullfight with songs)
Ricardo Castillo
12-25-70
New York Theater of the Americas
427 W. 59th, N.Y.C.

Matagorda
Henry Klussman
April, 1973
Theatre Suburbia
Houston, TX

Mates, The
Bernard Mendillo
10-16-73
Lolly's Theatre Club
808 Lexington, N.Y.C.

Matinee
Wallace Hamilton
12-10-71
Playbox
94 St. Mark's Pl., N.Y.C.

Matinee Ladies (with Volunteers for America)
Anne Commire
3-2-73
American Women Playwrights Association
Columbia University School of the Arts Theater
410 W. 117th, N.Y.C.

Matins (with Still Life)
Hal Ackerman
11-22-68
First Unitarian Church
Brooklyn, NY

Matter of Malnutrition, A
Ehud Manor
10-3-69
American Repertory Theatre
165 W. 57th, N.Y.C.

Matter of Pride, A
Frank D. Gilroy
1-7-71
Park Ave. Community Theatre
Central Church
Park & 64th, N.Y.C.

Matter Transformation No. 2 (interaction situation)
3-11-72
Apple
161 W. 23rd, N.Y.C.

Maude Marr
David K. Markay (book & lyrics); David Feinberg (music)
3-27-71
Stagelights II Theatrical Club
125 W. 22nd, N.Y.C.

Maxile
Rachel Erlanger
6-6-69
Riverdale Showcase
252nd & Riverdale Ave., Bronx, NY

Maybe That's Because I Love You
Raymond Banachi
1-7-71
Playbox
94 St. Mark's Pl., N.Y.C.

Me?
Martin Kinch
1973
Toronto Free Theatre
Toronto, Ontario, CAN

Me Nobody Knows, The
Will Holt (lyrics); Gary William Friedman (music)
5-18-70
Orpheum Theatre
126 Second, N.Y.C.

Me, You, Us and the Raincoat (multimedia presentation)
Fall, 1971
Theatre Passe Muraille
Toronto, Ontario, CAN

Meal, The
Mark O. Lynch
3-8-72
University of Missouri
Columbia, MO

Medal of Honor Winner
Albert Evans
6-6-69
Riverdale Showcase
252nd & Riverdale Ave., Bronx, NY

Medea
Richard Ronan
9-5-69
Riverside Theatre Workshop
224 Waverly Pl., N.Y.C.

Medea
Euripides; Samy Shmuel (adaptor)
12-16-73
Primitive Theatre
33 Howard, N.Y.C.

Medea
Euripides; Minos Volanakis (adaptor)
1-17-73
Circle in the Square
Joseph E. Levine Theatre
W. 50th St. & Broadway, N.Y.C.

Medea
Andrei Serban; Liz Swandos (music)
1-21-72
La Mama ETC
74 E. 4th, N.Y.C.

Medea en el Espejo
Jose Triana
12-9-71
New York Theatre of the Americas
321 E. 73rd, N.Y.C.

Medea in Africa
James Magnuson
5-21-68
Theatre Arts Center
120 E. 110th, N.Y.C.

Media Luz Los Tres, A
Miguel Mihura
10-7-70
Lucrezia Bori Theatre
684 Park, N.Y.C.

Medicine Show, The
4-27-72
St. Clement's Church
423 W. 46th, N.Y.C.

Medieval Tails (a story theatre production)
7-27-71
Theater Pennsylvania
Philadelphia, PA

Mee and Candy Coolidge
Bruce Feld
6-6-69
Riverdale Showcase
252nd & Riverdale Ave., Bronx, NY

Meek and a Feather in Her Hat, The
Jerome Kass
3-9-68
Elias A. Cohen Theatre
100th & West End Ave., N.Y.C.

Meeow!
Adaptation of Lewis Carroll
3-1-71
St. Peter's Gate
132 E. 54th, N.Y.C.

Meeting, A
Shaunee Laurence
9-17-70
Playbox
94 St. Mark's Pl., N.Y.C.

Meeting by the River, A
Christopher Isherwood & Don Bachardy
4-26-72
Mark Taper Forum
Los Angeles, CA

Meeting of Mimes, A
8-12-71
Cubiculo
414 W. 51st, N.Y.C.

Megilla of Itzik Manger, The
10-9-68
Golden Theatre
N.Y.C.

Melodrama in the Bronte Parsonage
Norma Crandall
5-9-69
Caravan House
132 E. 65th, N.Y.C.

Melodrama Play
Sam Shepard
1-27-68
La Mama ETC
122 Second, N.Y.C.

Melting Pot Park
Clarence Burton
3-15-68
Off Center Theatre
152 W. 66th, N.Y.C.

Memoirs of a Junkie
Paul Benjamin
3-20-71
Society for Ethical Culture
2 W. 64th, N.Y.C.

Memorandum, The
Vaclav Havel
4-23-68
New York Shakespeare Festival
Public Theatre
425 Lafayette, N.Y.C.

Memorial
Harvey Zuckerman
9-14-72
Playwrights' Horizons
West Side YWCA
8th Ave. & 51st, N.Y.C.

Memories of the Land: How Four Children Saved the World
Louis & John Biancato
9-16-72
St. Clement's Church
423 W. 46th, N.Y.C.

Memory Bank, The
Martin Duberman
1-11-70
Tambellini's Gate Theatre
162 Second, N.Y.C.

Memory Is a Spongecake
Raymond Platt
5-11-71
Stagelights II
125 W. 22nd, N.Y.C.

Memory of a Large Christmas (reading)
Lillian Smith, adapted by Eugenia Rawls
12-18-69
Library & Museum of the Performing Arts
111 Amsterdam, N.Y.C.

Memory of Childhood, A
Brooke C. Breslow
5-16-73
Courtyard Playhouse
137 W. 14th, N.Y.C.

Memphis Store Bought Teeth
E. Don Alldredge (book); William Fisher (music); D. Brian Wallach (lyrics)
12-29-71
Orpheum Theatre
126 Second, N.Y.C.

Men, Women, and God
Stan Lachow
11-7-73
Cubiculo
414 W. 51st, N.Y.C.

Menials, The
See: Testimonies

Mercy Drop
Robert Patrick
2-23-73
WPA
333 Bowery, N.Y.C.

Mercy Street
Anne Sexton
10-11-69
American Place Theatre
N.Y.C.

Merle
Josef Bush
6-19-73
New Plays Festival
WPA
333 Bowery, N.Y.C.

Merlin's Magic
Helen Avery
8-1-72
West Harwich Junior Theatre
West Harwich, MA

Merriam-Webster Pocket Mime Circus
4-22-72
Charles St. Meeting House
Boston, MA

Merry Death, A
Nikolai Evreinov; translated by Christopher Collins
8-19-72
Theatre Wagon
Staunton, VA

Merry Midnight Mass, A
Hot Peaches
12-21-73
Peach Pitts
200 W. 24th, N.Y.C.

Merry Wives
George Buza (book, lyrics, & music)
8-17-72
Berea Summer Theatre
Berea, OH

Merry Wives of Hotmatiki, The
Jack L. Bellamy
5-15-70
Community Playhouse
Long Beach, CA

Message from the Grassroots
Robert Riche
Oct., 1968
James Weldon Johnson Theatre Arts Center
120 E. 110th, N.Y.C.

Messiah, The
Martin Halpern
4-29-70
Brandeis University
Waltham, MA

Metamorphosis
Franz Kafka, John White (adaptor)
8-11-71
Loeb Drama Center
Cambridge, MA

Metamorphosis (with The Judgment)
Charles Dizenzo
4-8-72
American Place Theatre
N.Y.C.

Metaphysical Cop, The
David Scott Milton
5-31-68
Off Center Theatre
152 W. 66th, N.Y.C.

Metaphysical Rainstorm Blues, The
Pat Rule
7-26-73
Changing Scene
Denver, CO

Meteor, The
Friedrich Duerrenmatt
2-26-70
Arena Stage
Washington, DC

Mexican Bird Act
Dennis Must
3-7-71
Rutgers Community Center
200 Madison, N.Y.C.

Michael Bakunin
Gary Wurtzel
3-20-70
State University of New York at Binghamton
NY

Michael McClure on Toast
Michael McClure
1-27-73
Company Theatre
Los Angeles, CA

Michael, Michael
Lanny Turner
11-27-70
New York Theatre Ensemble
2 E. 2nd, N.Y.C.

Michigan South
Curt Dempster
12-18-73
Ensemble Studio Theatre
549 W. 52nd, N.Y.C.

Mickey
Mary Chase
12-12-68
Changing Scene
Denver, CO

Middle Class Black
Herbert Campbell
May, 1970
Bed-Stuy Theatre
1407 Bedford Ave., Brooklyn, NY

Middle Is the Deepest Part, The
Alan Harper
4-24-70
CR Acting Workshop
252 W. 81st, N.Y.C.

Middle, The
Richard A. Schuster
6-6-69
Stage Lights Theatrical Club
218 W. 48th, N.Y.C.

Mid-Kingdom of Lions
Roderic Mason Faber
5-16-69
Judson Poet's Theatre
55 Wash. Sq. So., N.Y.C.

Midsummer Gloxinia Madness
7-31-69
Theatre Genesis
10th & 2nd Ave., N.Y.C.

Midsummer Night's Trip
John Wolfson
11-24-69
New Dramatists
424 W. 44th, N.Y.C.

Midway
Peter Dee
1968
St. Clement's Church
423 W. 46th N.Y.C.

Mike, Downstairs
George Panetta
4-18-68
Hudson Theatre
N.Y.C.

Mikhal (dramatic reading)
David Pinski
5-4-73
Village Temple
33 E. 12th, N.Y.C.

Mildred
Robert Martin
12-3-71
St. Peter's Church
346 W. 20th, N.Y.C.

Mildred
Joseph Ponzi
2-25-72
Circle in the Square
159 Bleecker, N.Y.C.

Military Island
Peter Dee
7-26-68
Theatre for Peace
423 W. 46th, N.Y.C.

Mime Fantasia
9-27-72
Playwrights' Workshop Club
Bastiano's Studio
14 Cooper Sq., N.Y.C.

Mimosa Pudica
Curt Dempster
7-19-73
Johnson State College
Johnson, VT

Mind with the Dirty Man, The
Jules E. Tasca
7-12-72
Mark Taper Forum
Los Angeles, CA

Minding the Store
Robert Nichols
9-26-71
Theatre for the New City
151 Bank, N.Y.C.

Minerva V
Theatre Workshop of Boston
1-6-72
Boston Center for the Arts
Boston, MA

Minnie's Boys
Arthur Marx & Robert Fisher (book); Larry Grossman (music); Hal Hackaday (lyrics)
3-26-70
Imperial Theatre
N.Y.C.

Minor Miscalculation, A (with Ashes)
Edwin Byrd
1-30-70
Free Music Store
359 E. 62nd, N.Y.C.

Minstrel Boy, The
Herbert Moulton
2-28-70
Pretenders Cooperative Theatre
106 E. 14th, N.Y.C.

Minstrel Show
Bud Pitman
2-15-72
WPA
333 Bowery, N.Y.C.

Mira
Gucharian Das
5-20-70
La Mama ETC
74 E. 4th, N.Y.C.

Miracle Play
Joyce Carol Oates
12-30-73
Phoenix Theatre
Playhouse II
359 W. 48th, N.Y.C.

Mirage
John White
7-7-69
Dartmouth College
Hanover, NH

Mirage, Sheltered, Cornered
Robert Patrick
11-19-71
Playbox
94 St. Mark's Pl., N.Y.C.

Mirror for Women, A
Joyce Worsley
10-21-70
York Players
2 E. 90th, N.Y.C.

Mirror, The
Isaac Bashevis Singer
1-19-73
Yale Repertory Theatre
New Haven, CT

Mirrored Man
Richard Reich
4-7-72
New York City League of Playwrights
162 W. 21st, N.Y.C.

Mirrored Reflections
Robert Mull
8-30-73
Changing Scene
Denver, CO

Misanthrope, The
Moliere; Robert Hall & Lorraine Ross (adaptors)
11-3-73
CSC Repertory Company
Abbey Theatre
136 E. 13th, N.Y.C.

Misanthrope, The
Moliere; Tony Harrison (translator)
Summer, 1973
Williamstown Theatre
Williamstown, MA

Misbegotten Angels
Stanley Taikeff
12-12-70
West Side YMCA
5 W. 63rd, N.Y.C.

(Mis)Judgment, The (with Charlie Still Can't Win No Wars on the Ground)
Earl Anthony
1-8-71
New Federal Theatre
St. Augustine's Chapel
292 Henry, N.Y.C.

Miss Collins, The English Teacher
Arthur Kirson
Fall, 1973
American Theatre Company
106 E. 14th, N.Y.C.

Miss George Alliance
Edward Gallardo
5-5-72
Playbox
94 St. Mark's Pl., N.Y.C.

Miss Lizzie
Luigia M. Miller
1-12-71
Madison Ave. Presbyterian Church
921 Madison, N.Y.C.

Miss Pell Is Missing
Leonard Gershe
7-7-70
Flat Rock Playhouse
Flat Rock, NC

Miss Pete
Andrew Glaze
3-11-72
Trinity Presbyterian Church
422 W. 57th, N.Y.C.

Miss Thing or Never as Great
Jay Fletcher
6-8-72
Players Workshop
83 E. 4th, N.Y.C.

Miss Truth (a poetic suite on Sojourner Truth)
Glory Van Scott
1-23-72
Negro Ensemble Company
St. Mark's Playhouse
133 Second Ave., N.Y.C.

Miss Zatakri and Mister Jones
Rae Walker
4-5-72
Playwrights' Workshop Club
Bastiano's Studio
14 Cooper Sq., N.Y.C.

Missing Link, The
Arturo Parrilla
9-12-68
Cafe Four
522 E. 12th, N.Y.C.

Missing Note, The
Jane Staab
8-20-68
Junior Theatre
West Harwich, MA

Mission Beach (with Flite Cage)
Walter Hadler
5-3-69
Theatre Genesis
10th & 2nd Ave., N.Y.C.

Mister Gynt, Inc.
Henrik Ibsen; freely adapted by Mavis Taylor & Jerry Heymann
3-24-72
Asian American & Bilingual Troupes
La Mama ETC
74 E. 4th, N.Y.C.

Mister Jello
George Birimisa
3-20-68
Playbox
94 St. Mark's Pl., N.Y.C.

Mister Me
Jean Tardieu
7-1-70
Old Post Office Theatre
East Hampton, NY

Mister Price, or Tropical Madness
Stanislaw Witkiewicz; Daniel C. and Eleanor Gerould (translator)
7-15-71
Towson State College
Towson, MD

Mixed Doubles
Max G. Weine
6-6-73
Guild Studio 1
Ansonia Hotel
73rd & Broadway, N.Y.C.

Mixed Doubles
Fred Carmichael
8-24-72
Dorset Playhouse
Dorset, VT

Mixed Review
Larry O'Connel
2-23-73
Second Group Theatre
McBurney YMCA
215 W. 23rd, N.Y.C.

MMMMM!
Don Robar
5-23-72
Boston Center for the Arts
Boston, MA

Moby Dick
Herman Melville; adapted by Christopher Martin
4-23-70
CSC Repertory
89 W. 3rd, N.Y.C.

Mocking Bird, The
William Parchman
7-18-69
Eugene O'Neill Memorial Theatre
Waterford, CT

Mod Donna
Myrna Lamb (book & lyrics); Susan Bingham (music)
4-26-70
New York Shakespeare Festival Public Theatre
425 Lafayette, N.Y.C.

Modern Hamlet, A
John Guenther
4-3-73
Workshop of the Players' Art
333 Bowery, N.U.C.

Modern Hamlet, A (reading)
John Guenther
11-21-71
Jean Cocteau Theatre
43 Bond, N.Y.C.

Modern Statuary
Donald Kvares
5-15-68
Anthony Mannino Drama Tree
182 Fifth, N.Y.C.

Modern Times
Richard L. Hoffman
July, 1970
Eugene O'Neill Memorial Theatre
Waterford, CT

Moglie E' Necessaria, La
Pietro Aretino
5-2-73
Teatro Italiano
Hunter College
N.Y.C.

Moke-Eater, The
Kenneth Bernard
9-19-68
Playhouse of the Ridiculous
Park Ave. at 17th, N.Y.C.

Moliere or A Cabal of Hypocrites
Mikhail Bulgakov
8-1-73
Port Jefferson Summer Playhouse
Port Jefferson, NY

Molly
Louis Garfinkle & Leonard Adelson (book); Leonard Adelson & Mack David (lyrics); Jerry Livingston (music)
9-3-73
Shubert Theatre
Boston, MA

Molly's Dream
Maria Irene Fonnes
7-23-68
Boston University Workshop
Tanglewood, MA

Molly's O
Christopher Mathewson
5-5-72
Bastiano's Studio
14 Cooper Sq., N.Y.C.

Moment of Truth
David Litt
6-6-69
Riverdale Showcase
252nd & Riverdale Ave., Bronx, NY

Moments
Norman Charles
10-26-73
Theatre of Renewal
Stage Lights Theatrical Club
218 W. 48th, N.Y.C.

Moments and the Bramble
Ed Baierlein
2-5-70
Changing Scene
Denver, CO

Momma's Boy
Robert Johnson, Jr.
4-30-70
Tufts University
Medford, MA

Mon Reve Buckshot Blue
Jacquelin Megna
7-23-68
Summer Theatre Festival
Kingston, RI

Monday Night Varieties
John Ford Noonan
12-11-72
Theatre for the New City
113 Jane, N.Y.C.

Monday on the Way to Mercury Island (with Schubert's Last Serenade)
Julie Bovasso
6-30-71
La Mama ETC
74 E. 4th, N.Y.C.

Money-Back Guarantee, A (with The Petition)
Donald Flynn
3-18-72
Trinity Presbyterian Church
422 W. 57th, N.Y.C.

Monica (with Trysting Place and New Listings)
3-29-73
Shelter West Company
St. Stephen's Church
120 W. 69th, N.Y.C.

Monkey King, The
11-25-72
Four Seas Players
Schimmel Center for the Arts
Pace College, N.Y.C.

Monkey Man's Pick-Up (with No-Luggage People)
William Schlottmann
6-10-71
Cubiculo
414 W. 51st, N.Y.C.

Monkey of the Inkpot, The
Helen Duberstein
5-19-73
Actor's Experimental Unit
682 Sixth, N.Y.C.

Monkey Palace, The (part of triple bill entitled 3 by 3)
R. Cary Bynum
5-1-71
Hunter College Theatre Program
West Side YMCA
5 W. 63rd, N.Y.C.

Monkey Play
Jonathan Levy
9-14-72
Playwrights' Horizons
West Side YWCA
8th Ave. & 51st, N.Y.C.

Monkeys of the Organ Grinder, The
Kenneth Bernard
9-28-70
La Mama ETC
74 E. 4th, N.Y.C.

M.O.N.O.
Dalt Wonk
1-17-69
Cooper Square Arts Theatre
35 Cooper Sq., N.Y.C.

Monochrome (with Medusa of 47th Street)
Nancy Henderson
2-26-68
Old Reliable Theatre Tavern
231 E. 3rd, N.Y.C.

Monsieur Artaud
Michael Almaz
9-21-73
Tel Aviv Drama Company
Hunter College Playhouse
695 Park, N.Y.C.

Monsieur de Moliere
Mikhail Bulgakov; translated by Carl and Ellendea Proffer
11-19-72
Yale Repertory Theatre
New Haven, CT

Monster, The
John Francis Quinn
10-2-69
St. Peter's Church
346 W. 20th, N.Y.C.

Month of Fridays, A
Wallace Hamilton
8-17-73
West Side Gay Theatre
W.S.D.G. Center
37 Ninth Ave., N.Y.C.

Month of Sundays
Romeo Muller, Maury Laws, Jules Bass
9-16-68
Theatre de Lys
N.Y.C.

Montipasse
Michael Hardstack
10-31-73
Stagelights II
125 W. 22nd, N.Y.C.

Monument, The
Franklyn MacGregor
8-14-68
Courtyard Playhouse
424 W. 45th, N.Y.C.

Monuments
Diane DiPrima
3-5-68
Caffe Cino
31 Cornelia, N.Y.C.

Mood Indigo
Boris Vian; adapted by Andre Ernotte
1-26-72
Columbia University
N.Y.C.

Moon
Robert Heide
2-6-68
Caffe Cino
31 Cornelia, N.Y.C.

Moon Balloon, The (masque)
Kenneth Koch
12-31-69
Bethesda Fountain
Central Park, N.Y.C.

Moon Dreamers, The
Julie Bovasso
2-2-68
La Mama ETC
122 Second, N.Y.C.

Moon Walk
Betty Jean Lifton
12-13-69
Electric Circus
23 St. Mark's Pl., N.Y.C.

Moonchildren
Michael Weller
11-3-71
Arena Stage
Washington, DC

Moonlight File, The
Mick Daugherty
2-28-70
New York Theatre Workshop
154 E. 54th, N.Y.C.

Moonshot
Stephen H. Foreman
6-7-72
New Dramatists
424 W. 44th, N.Y.C.

Moral Facts
Terry Miller
7-8-69
New Workshop Theatre
Brooklyn College
NY

Morality
Charles Peters & Melvyn Morrow (book & lyrics); Wilfred Usher & John Mallord (music)
3-12-73
Mercer Arts Center
240 Mercer, N.Y.C.

More Power to You
Michael Shurtleff
12-7-69
Extension Theatre
277 Park Ave. So., N.Y.C.

More War in Store
Lonnie Carter
9-14-70
Old Reliable Theatre Tavern
231 E. 3rd, N.Y.C.

Morey and Paul at Midnight
Arthur Morey & Bobby Paul
12-10-71
Mercer Street Playhouse
240 Mercer, N.Y.C.

Morning, Noon and Night (3 one-act plays)
Israel Horovitz, Terrence McNally, and Leonard Melfi
11-28-68
Henry Miller's Theatre
N.Y.C.

Morning to Midnite
Georg Kaiser; Jonteta & Irma Bartenieff (adaptors)
5-24-73
Theatre for the New City
113 Jane, N.Y.C.

Moscow Circus on Ice
12-8-70
Madison Square Garden
N.Y.C.

Moses Plan, The
Francis Chesleigh
5-19-72
Hunter College Playwrights
West Side YMCA
5 W. 63rd, N.Y.C.

Moss Hart Celebration
4-12-70
University of Southern California
Los Angeles, CA

Mostly on the Morning Ceiling (with Return of Colorado Girl)
Robert Clapsadle
2-19-71
Assembly Theatre
113 Jane, N.Y.C.

Motel
Benjamin Bradford
6-22-70
Old Reliable Theatre Tavern
231 E. 3rd, N.Y.C.

Motel, The (with The Dishroom and The Cellar)
Paul DeJohn
7-17-72
Manhattan Theatre Club
321 E. 73rd, N.Y.C.

Mother
John Prince
3-14-69
Inner Theatre
356 Bowery, N.Y.C.

Mother Courage
Bertolt Brecht; George Tabori (adaptor)
11-17-71
University of California
Irvine, CA

Mother Courage and Her Children
Bertolt Brecht; translation by Chris Brandt & Edward C. Berkeley
10-19-72
Shade Company
230 Canal, N.Y.C.

Mother Earth (rock musical)
6-22-71
Marine's Theatre
San Francisco, CA

Mother Goose Go-Go
Jim Eiler (book & lyrics); Jim Eiler & Jeanne Bargy (music)
12-25-69
Ambassador Theatre
215 W. 49th, N.Y.C.

Mother Loved Us But She Died
New plays by Michael Shurtleff & Andrew Colmar
12-7-68
Playbox
94 St. Mark's Pl., N.Y.C.

Mother Lover, The
Jerome Weidman
2-1-69
Booth Theatre
N.Y.C.

Mother Mary's Honor Student
James Edward Shannon
9-17-71
New York Theatre Ensemble
2 E. 2nd, N.Y.C.

Mother of Pearl
Elaine Edelman
Oct., 1971
New Dramatists
424 W. 44th, N.Y.C.

Mother's Kisses, A
Bruce Jay Friedman, Richard Adler
9-21-68
Shubert Theatre
New Haven, CT

Mother's Womb with Window
Edward Leland
6-13-68
Changing Scene
Denver, CO

Mother Was Sober and It Was Was So Much Fun
Ed Setrakian
4-22-72
Kavookjian Auditorium
630 Second, N.Y.C.

Motherlove (with The Pelican)
August Strindberg; translated by Arvid Paulson
2-16-72
Cubiculo
414 W. 51st, N.Y.C.

Moths, The
Raffi Arzoomanian
6-17-68
Mark Taper Forum
Los Angeles, CA

Mourning in a Funny Hat
Dody Goodman
7-3-72
Gilford Playhouse
Gilford, NH

Movements and Moments from the Prophets
May, 1972
Boston Center for the Arts
Boston, MA

Movers, The
Clifford Browder
3-7-69
Anthony Mannino Drama Tree
182 Fifth, N.Y.C.

Movie, Movie on the Wall
Sally Ordway
10-28-68
Mark Taper Forum
Los Angeles, CA

Mozart as Dramatist
Walt Witover
5-18-73
Spencer Memorial Church
99 Clinton, Brooklyn, NY

Mr. and Ms. (scenes depicting struggle between the sexes)
9-14-72
Jean Cocteau Theatre
43 Bond, N.Y.C.

Mr. Baggy Pants
Jerry Lester
10-28-69
City Island Theatre
Bronx, NY

Mr. Dickens Reads Tonight!
Philip Von Kroopf
2-14-68
Heritage Repertory Productions
215 W. 23rd, N.Y.C.

Mr. Esteban
Geraldine Fitzgerald & Brother Jonathan Ringhamp (book & lyrics); Bryan Williams (music)
8-1-73
79th St. Theatre
Brooklyn, NY

Mr. Ollie's Here
Steve Saikin
11-20-68
Courtyard Playhouse
424 W. 45th, N.Y.C.

Mr. Optometrist
Stanley Nelson
4-17-68
Playwrights' Workshop Club
14 Waverly Pl., N.Y.C.

Mr. President
Nona Dearth
8-11-71
New Moon Magic Theatre
Provincetown, MA

Mr. Shandy
McCrea Imbrie & Neil Seldon
7-18-72
Roundabout Theatre
307 W. 26th, N.Y.C.

Mr. Tambo, Mr. Bones
Alexander Panas
Feb., 1969
Washington Theatre Club
Washington, DC

Mrs. Babb
Kelly & Bill Patton
8-1-70
Southampton College
Southampton, NY

Mrs. Erlynne's Daughter (early version of Lady Windermere's Fan)
Oscar Wilde; adapted by Randolph O'Donnell
7-14-72
Stagelights II
125 W. 22nd, N.Y.C.

Mrs. Lincoln
Thomas P. Cullinan
11-1-68
Cleveland Play House
Cleveland, OH

Mrs. Minter
Donald Kvares
2-14-72
Library & Museum of the Performing Arts
111 Amsterdam, N.Y.C.

Mrs. Peacock
Stanley Nelson
8-12-69
Old Reliable Theatre Tavern
231 E. 3rd, N.Y.C.

Mrs. President
M. David Samples
4-27-72
Johnston Center for Performing Arts
Lincoln College
Lincoln, IL

Mrs. Reynolds
Philip Hanson; adapted from Gertrude Stein
4-21-69
New York Public Library
N.Y.C.

Mrs. Snow
Kenneth S. Pressman
1-5-70
ANTA Matinee Series
Theatre de Lys
N.Y.C.

Mrs. Tidings' Mason-Dixon Medicine Man
John Heuer
6-4-73
Circle Theatre Company
2307 Broadway, N.Y.C.

Much Ado About Shakespeare
8-13-73
Taconic Project
Spencertown, NY

Mugnog
R. Hachfeld
12-1-73
Theatre X
Milwaukee, WI

Mulberry Bush, The
Phoebe Wray
9-15-69
Old Reliable Theatre Tavern
231 E. 3rd, N.Y.C.

Multicolored Maze, The
John Gilbert
10-10-69
Texas Tech University
Lubbock, TX

Multi-Media '71
8-16-71
Vineyard Players
Oak Bluffs, MA

Mummen Schanz (Swiss Mime Theatre)
10-27-73
Alice Tully Hall
65th & Broadway, N.Y.C.

Mundy Scheme, The
Brian Friel
12-11-69
Royale Theatre
N.Y.C.

Municipal Water System Is Not Trustworthy, The
Tom Anderson
9-16-68
Sullivan Street Playhouse
181 Sullivan, N.Y.C.

Munro
Jules Feiffer; Brooklyn Company (adaptor)
8-15-71
Prospect Park
Brooklyn, NY

Murder of Abel, The (passion play)
7-21-73
Twilight Theatre
Prospect Park Music Grove
Brooklyn, NY

Murderous Angels
Conor Cruise O'Brien
2-4-70
Mark Taper Forum
Los Angeles, CA

Museum Piece
Alan Mount
3-31-68
Cooperative Theatre
106 E. 14th, N.Y.C.

Museum Piece
Randolph Carter
4-25-69
Melting Pot Repertory Theatre
18 Bleecker, N.Y.C.

Music Box Players: Revue '72
Sue Semegran
4-7-72
California State College
Fullerton, CA

Music Box, The
Sheila Farmer
5-16-69
University of Missouri
Columbia, MO

Musical, A
10-26-72
Brooklyn College
Brooklyn, NY

Musical Cavalcade
8-15-72
Theatre of the Stars
Civic Center
Atlanta, GA

Musing
John E. Sedlak
5-15-73
Courtyard Playhouse
137 W. 14th, N.Y.C.

Mutations (later called The Mutation Show)
The Open Theatre
5-25-71
Loeb Drama Center
Cambridge, MA

Mutilation
Walter Hadler
5-18-72
Theatre Genesis
2nd Ave. & 10th, N.Y.C.

Mutual Decision, A
Lynne Honickman
5-18-71
Cubiculo
414 W. 51st, N.Y.C.

My Brother the Bride
Dean McIlnay & Richard Erickson
11-14-68
Theatre 13
201 W. 13th, N.Y.C.

My Country
Clyde Ellsworth
12-17-70
Mainstream Theatre
125 Fifth, N.Y.C.

My Daughter's Rated "X"
Arthur Marx & Robert Fisher
6-26-73
Kenley Players
Warren, OH

My Daughter, Your Son
Phoebe & Henry Ephron
5-13-69
Booth Theatre
N.Y.C.

My Flower (reading)
Manuel Maccarini
1-22-73
Theatre of Latin America
St. Clement's Church
423 W. 46th, N.Y.C.

My Foot My Tutor
Peter Handke
4-15-71
Bank Theatre
Brooklyn, NY

My House Is Your House
Lee Loeb & Sam Ross
10-15-70
Players Theatre
115 MacDougal, N.Y.C.

My Mama's Lemonade (with The Outhouse)
Dennis Spedaliere
3-22-71
Assembly Theatre
113 Jane, N.Y.C.

My Mama the General
Eli Shagia; Moshe Sachar (book); Nurit Hirsh & Lillian Lux (lyrics & music)
10-9-73
Burstein Theatre
250 W. 43rd, N.Y.C.

My Name Is Aram
William Saroyan; Philip Hanson (adaptor)
3-24-71
Library & Museum of the Performing Arts
111 Amsterdam, N.Y.C.

My Sister, My Sister
Ray Aranha
9-28-73
Hartford Stage Company
Hartford, CT

My Sister, My Spouse
Donald Sutherland
10-26-72
Changing Scene
Denver, CO

My Thank Is Full
Street 70 Ensemble with Lewis Black
9-16-73
Street 70 Ensemble
International Children's Festival
Vienna, VA

My Third Eye
1-26-72
National Theatre of the Deaf
Loeb Drama Center
Cambridge, MA

Mystery Cycle, The
Adapted by Nagle Jackson
Winter, 1972
American Conservatory Theatre
San Francisco, CA

Mystery Play
Jean-Claude Van Itallie
1-3-73
Cherry Lane Theatre
38 Commerce, N.Y.C.

Myth of Icarus, The
Miriam Iron
7-16-71
Actor's Theatre
49 E. 1st, N.Y.C.

Myth or Maybe Meth
Tom Murrin
10-2-69
Loft Workshop
152 Bleecker, N.Y.C.

Myth-Meat
Gerard Williams
11-28-69
Players Workshop
229 Seventh, N.Y.C.

Myth-Oedipus
1-19-72
St. Clement's Church
423 W. 46th, N.Y.C.

Myths of America Smith, The
Greg Antonacci
5-4-73
La Mama ETC
74 E. 4th, N.Y.C.

N

Na Haaz Z'an
Robert Shorty
10-25-72
American Indian Theatre Ensemble
La Mama ETC
74 E. 4th, N.Y.C.

Nada Que Ver (Out of It)
Griselda Gambaro
April, 1973
Spanish Theatre Repertory Company
Gramercy Arts Theatre
N.Y.C.

Naga Uta
Frank Parman
7-31-69
University of Illinois
Urbana, IL

Naked Don't Run, The
John Boylan
7-31-70
Down Stage Studio Theatre
321 W. 14th, N.Y.C.

Name Day (with Joseph)
Charles Kerbs
November, 1968
Playbox
N.Y.C.

Nameplate, The (with The Pickle and Souffle of Bot)
Raymond Platt
6-3-70
Stage Lights Theatrical Club
218 W. 48th, N.Y.C.

Nannies, The
Yiorgos Skourtis
7-8-72
Westbeth Cabaret Theatre
155 Bank, N.Y.C.

Naomi Court
Michael Sawyer
12-5-69
Actors Mobile Theatre
73rd & Broadway, N.Y.C.

Narrow Road to the Deep North
Edward Bond
10-30-69
Charles Playhouse
Boston, MA

Nash at Nine
Ogden Nash (verses & lyrics); Milton Rosenstock (music); Martin Charnin (conception)
5-17-73
Helen Hayes Theatre
N.Y.C.

Nation Is Born, A
Mary Wilton
7-3-70
Independence Hall
Philadelphia, PA

National Center of Afro-American Artists
See also: Elma Lewis School of Fine Arts

National Chinese Opera Theatre, The
Fall, 1973
Masonic Auditorium
Los Angeles, CA

National Health, The
Peter Nichols
8-26-71
Mark Taper Forum
Los Angeles, CA

National Lampoon's Lemmings (revue)
David Axelrod & others (dialogue & lyrics); Paul Jacobs & Christopher Guest (music)
1-25-73
Village Gate
160 Bleecker, N.Y.C.

Nativitie Playe, A
Frank Ball
12-14-69
Riverside Church
122nd & Riverside Dr., N.Y.C.

Natural Culmination
Richard de Blasi
8-11-72
Playbox
94 St. Mark's Pl., N.Y.C.

Naturally (staged Yoga entertainment)
4-14-73
Levy Shea Studio
100 E. 16th, N.Y.C.

Nature of the Crime
Larry Cohen
3-23-70
Bouwerie Lane Theatre
3rd Ave. & 2nd, N.Y.C.

Naughty, Naughty
Peter Copani
10-7-68
Old Reliable Theatre Tavern
231 E. 3rd, N.Y.C.

Naxos Bound
Josef Bush
6-9-69
Old Reliable Theatre Tavern
231 E. 3rd, N.Y.C.

Neighbors
James Saunders
3-28-68
Mannhardt Theatre Foundation
N.Y.C.

Neighbors — An East River Anthology
10-24-69
12 Steps Cafe-Theatre
44 W. 54th, N.Y.C.

Neighbors, The
Thomas Terefenko
2-24-69
Old Reliable Theatre Tavern
231 E. 3rd, N.Y.C.

Nellie Toole & Co.
Peter Keveson
9-24-73
Theatre Four
424 W. 55th, N.Y.C.

Nest, The
Tina Howe
4-9-70
Mercury Theatre
136 E. 13th, N.Y.C.

Netting of the Troupial, The
John Clark Donahue
3-2-73
Children's Theatre Company
Minneapolis Society of Fine Arts
Minneapolis, MN

Never Love a Poet (performed anthology of new poetry)
10-31-71
East Village Theatre
433 E. 6th, N.Y.C.

Never Tell Isobel
John Gruen
1-22-69
La Mama ETC
9 St. Mark's Pl., N.Y.C.

Neverfollow
Joseph Ponzi
1-9-69
Gotham Art
455 W. 43rd, N.Y.C.

New Crucifixion, A
Peter Schumann
3-4-70
Bread & Puppet Theatre
Spencer Memorial Church
99 Clinton, Brooklyn Heights, NY

New Deliverance, The
Stanislaw Witkiewicz; Daniel C. Gerould & Jadwiga Kosicka (translators)
2-8-73
CSC Repertory
89 W. 3rd, N.Y.C.

New Faces of '68
Leonard Sillman
5-2-68
Booth Theatre
N.Y.C.

New Haven Game, The
7-13-68
Long Wharf Theatre
New Haven, CT

New Listings (with Monica and Trysting Place)
3-29-73
Shelter West Company
St. Stephen's Church
120 W. 69th, N.Y.C.

New Mount Olive Motel, The
Steven Gethers
6-25-73
Ivoryton Playhouse
Ivoryton, CT

New Music Hall of Israel
10-2-69
Lunt-Fontanne Theatre
205 W. 46th, N.Y.C.

New Myth One (puppets)
Ann Jones; David Campbell (music)
August, 1971
New Myth Puppet Co.
N.Y.C.

New Orleans Orchid
Walter Hadler
3-15-73
Changing Scene
Denver, CO

New Play, A
Tom Eyen
1-16-70
Extension Theatre
277 Park Ave. So., N.Y.C.

New Shoes for Uncle Tom
Richard D. Waters
8-12-68
Fisherman's Players
Wellfleet, MA

New Theater Sketchbook
Multiple authors
7-16-69
Theatre in the Garden
Greenvale, NY

New York and Who To Blame It On
Joseph Hurley, Donald Moffat
7-9-68
Conference House Park
Staten Island, NY

New York City Mime Duet, The
9-6-72
Manhattan Theatre Club
321 73rd, N.Y.C.

New York Monster Show
4-27-72
New York University
8 Waverly Pl., N.Y.C.

New York Transit Authority, The
Joseph Lazarus
3-22-72
Bastiano's Studio
14 Cooper Sq., N.Y.C.

New/Play: (City) Closet Drama (with Naga Uta)
Frank Parman
2-12-70
Artichoke Theatre
Pittsburgh, PA

Newspaper Stories
1-4-69
Sixth Street Theatre
543 E. 6th, N.Y.C.

Newstand, The (with Intersection)
Bill Svanoe
3-13-69
Loft Workshop
152 Bleecker, N.Y.C.

Next
Terrence McNally
8-7-68
Berkshire Theatre Festival
Stockbridge, MA

Next Thing, The
Michael Smith
4-2-70
Changing Scene
Denver, CO

Next to the Last American Play, The
8-13-68
Blue Dome
Woodstock, NY

Next Year in Jerusalem
Martin Sherman
6-8-68
H B Playwrights Foundation
124 Bank, N.Y.C.

Nice Pizza, A
Warren Giarraputo
March 22, 1968
Yale University
New Haven, CT

Nice Place to Visit, A
David DeRosier & Allen Hirschberg
2-7-69
Grace Church
Brooklyn, NY

Nice Place to Visit–But, A
8-25-72
Mort Siegel Theatre
Sheridan Square Playhouse
99 Seventh Ave. So., N.Y.C.

Nice Place You Have Here
Margie Appleman
12-17-70
Omni Theatre Club
145 W. 18th, N.Y.C.

Nickel's Worth of New York, A (revue)
10-27-71
Stagelights II
125 W. 22nd, N.Y.C.

Nicol Williamson's Late Show
6-26-73
Eastside Playhouse
334 E. 74th, N.Y.C.

Nigger Heaven
Black Fire Company
12-3-72
JCCEO Community Theatre of Birmingham
Alabama Academy Theatre
Atlanta, GA

Nigger Killer, The
Milt McGriff
July, 1972
Street Theatre, Inc.
Ossining, NY

Nigger Nightmare
Walter Jones
6-24-71
New York Shakespeare Festival Public Theatre
425 Lafayette, N.Y.C.

Nigger-Game
8-26-72
Bed-Stuy Street Academy
Twilight Theatre
Brooklyn, NY

Night
William Jamieson
4-27-73
New York Theatre Ensemble
2 E. 2nd, N.Y.C.

Night at the Black Pig, A
Charles Nolte
2-27-70
University of Minnesota
Minneapolis, MN

Night Callers
Stephen Finn
4-13-71
University of Massachusetts
Boston, MA

Night Club or Bubi's Hideaway
Kenneth Bernard
9-17-70
Theater of the Ridiculous
La Mama ETC
74 E. 4th, N.Y.C.

Night for Ghosts, A
William Kushner
9-26-68
Playbox
94 St. Mark's Pl., N.Y.C.

Night Night
Tom Murrin
1-24-72
New Old Reliable Theatre
231 E. 3rd, N.Y.C.

Night of the Beautiful People, The
Gerry Raad
March, 1971
Will-o-Way Theatre
Bloomfield Hills, MI

Night of the Rooster, The
5-29-73
Boston Center for the Arts
Boston, MA

Night of the Witch
Donald Capezzona
4-13-69
Cooperative Theatre
106 E. 14th, N.Y.C.

Night Out, A
Harold Pinter
11-11-71
Park Avenue Community Theatre
593 Park, N.Y.C.

Night Pieces
4-25-73
St. John's Episcopal Church
Staten Island, NY

Night Thoreau Spent in Jail, The
Jerome Lawrence & Robert E. Lee
4-1-70
Ohio State University
Columbus, OH

Night Thoughts
Corinne Jacker
9-13-73
St. Clement's Church
423 W. 46th, N.Y.C.

Night Travelers
Gloria Gonzalez
9-29-72
Playbox
94 St. Mark's Pl. N.Y.C.

Night Watch
Lucille Fletcher
2-28-72
Morosco Theatre
217 W. 45th, N.Y.C.

Night Watchmen, The
Stratis Karras; translated by Van Voutsinas
Dallas Theater Center
Dallas, TX

Nightbirds
Andy Milligan
1-12-73
Cubiculo
414 W. 51st, N.Y.C.

Nightlight
Kenneth Brown
1-12-73
Hartford Stage Company
Hartford, CT

Nightpiece
Wolfgang Hildesheimer
4-29-71
Loft Theatre
21 Bond, N.Y.C.

Nightride
Lee Barton
12-9-71
Playwright's Unit
Vandam Theatre
15 Vandam, N.Y.C.

Nightstone
Elizabeth Brown
4-26-73
University of Montana
Missoula, MT

Nightwalk
Open Theater, with writing by Jean-Claude van Itallie, Sam Shepard, Megan Terry
9-8-73
Open Theater
St. Clement's Church
423 W. 46th, N.Y.C.

Nine Sentiments, The
Alfred Brooks
11-16-71
United Methodist Church
University Park, CO

Nine to Five to Zero (9 to 5 to 0)
Lawrence Wunderlich
5-3-69
Dancers Studio Foundation
34 E. 10th, N.Y.C.

Nite by Gorky
Daffi
11-13-70
La Mama ETC
74 E. 4th, N.Y.C.

Nitrogen
Rene De Obaldia
5-3-68
American Laboratory Theatre
219 W. 19th, N.Y.C.

Nitty Gritty of Mr. Charlie, The (The Just Society)
Philip Spensley
11-17-69
National Arts Centre
Ottawa, CAN

No Answer
William Hanley
3-23-69
Unit Theatre
157 W. 22nd, N.Y.C.

No Bed of Roses
Don Michaels
8-6-69
Showplace Summer Theatre
Oak Ridge, NJ

No Coward Soul
Margaret Webster
4-28-69
American Conservatory Theatre
San Francisco, CA

No Fit Place For a Child to Play
Edna St. Vincent Millay; arranged by Jere Jacob
9-25-70
Mainstream Theatre
20 E. 14th, N.Y.C.

No Fit Place for a Child to Play
9-16-73
Jean Cocteau Theatre
43 Bond, N.Y.C.

No Hard Feelings
Sam Bobrick & Ron Clark
2-16-73
Shubert Theatre
New Haven, CT

No Lark
Jeannine Bails
7-29-68
Old Reliable Theatre Tavern
231 E. 3rd, N.Y.C.

No More Rabbits
Albert Zuckerman & Richard Burwell
March 3, 1968
Queens College, Little Theatre
Flushing, NY

No, No Pinocchio
2-15-73
B. Gay Puppets
St. Patrick's School
420 95th St., Brooklyn, NY

No, No, Priscilla (musical)
6-28-71
Priscilla Beach Theatre
Manomet, MA

No One Writes Drawing Room Comedies Anymore
Stanley Nelson
11-13-69
Access
Theatre East
211 E. 60th, N.Y.C.

No Place To Be Somebody
Charles Gordone
5-4-69
New York Shakespeare Festival Public Theatre
425 Lafayette, N.Y.C.

No Sale
Michael McGrinder
5-26-69
Old Reliable Theatre Tavern
231 E. 3rd, N.Y.C.

No Sex Please, We're British
Anthony Marriott & Alistair Foot
10-2-72
Playhouse Theatre
Wilmington, DE

No Silver Saints
Robert Waldron
2-14-68
Florida State University Theatre
Tallahassee, FL

No Snakes in This Grass
James Magnuson
5-12-69
St. Peter's Gate
132 E. 54th, N.Y.C.

Noah and Sons
Edward J. Sliva
10-25-72
Riverdale Showcase
252nd St. & Riverdale Ave. Bronx, NY

Noah from A to Z
George Latshaw
8-10-73
Schoenbrunn Amphitheatre
New Philadelphia, OH

Nobody Cried When They Tore Down Broadway
John Braden (book, lyrics, & music)
9-24-71
Merce Cunningham Studio
55 Bethune, N.Y.C.

Nobody Ever Says Goodbye
Edward Gallardo
1-29-71
New York Theatre Ensemble
2 E. 2nd, N.Y.C.

Nobody Hears a Broken Drum
Jason Miller
12-12-68
Church of the Holy Trinity
316 E. 88th, N.Y.C.

Nobody Hears a Broken Drum (revised)
Jason Miller
2-16-73
Catholic University
Washington, DC

Nobody's Earnest
Arnold Sungaard (book); Ethan Ayer (lyrics); Alec Wilder
7-31-73
Williamstown Summer Theatre
Williamstown, MA

Noctambule (with Evening Raga)
Josef Bush
6-14-71
Old Reliable Theatre Tavern
231 E. 3rd, N.Y.C.

Nocturnes
Richard Reichman
5-5-71
Brandeis University
Waltham, MA

Noel Coward's Sweet Potato
7-22-68
Queen Elizabeth Theatre
Vancouver, B.C., CAN

Noh-Kyogen (Japan)
3-24-71
Carnegie Hall
881 Seventh, N.Y.C.

Noise of Strangers
Kenneth Janes
4-10-69
Minor Latham Playhouse
Barnard College
N.Y.C.

Noisy City Sam
Barbara Fisher Perry
8-4-70
45th Street Playground
Between 9th & 10th Aves., N.Y.C.

Noisy Passenger, The (with Un Passage and Fragile Freight)
Shelley Winters
12-30-70
Actor's Playhouse
100 Seventh Ave. So., N.Y.C.

No-Luggage People (with Monkey Man's Pick-Up)
William Schlottmann
6-10-71
Cubiculo
414 W. 51st, N.Y.C.

None of Us Are Ever Born Brave
Norman Harris
4-10-68
Afro Arts Theatre
222 W. 134th, N.Y.C.

None Whatever or The Master Critic
Ellen Gerrarlee
3-1-68
West Side Actors' Theatre
252 W. 81st, N.Y.C.

Non-Stop Daily (with Invincible)
Daniel Curley
Spring, 1970
Depot Theatre
Urbana, IL

Noo Jall
Jaime Carrero
8-27-73
Puerto Rican Traveling Theatre
Riverside Park, N.Y.C.

Nookie's Joint
D. Nathanson
6-24-71
Bank Theatre
Brooklyn, NY

Norman, Is That You?
Ron Clark & Sam Bobrick
2-19-70
Lyceum Theatre
N.Y.C.

Nosotros Somos Dios (We Are God)
Wilberto Canton
12-2-72
Greenwich Mews Theatre
141 W. 13th, N.Y.C.

Not All Thieves Are Mischievous (with La Marcolfa)
Dario Fo
7-24-69
Cubiculo
414 W. 51st, N.Y.C.

Not by Bed Alone
7-25-72
High Tor Summer Theatre
Fitchburg, MA

Not Entirely Nondescript but Persephone in the Sun
Bruce Kessler
11-5-69
La Mama ETC
74 E. 4th, N.Y.C.

Not Even a Sun Tan
Helen Yalof
11-29-73
Inner Tube Studios
148 Greene, N.Y.C.

Not I
Samuel Beckett
11-22-72
Forum Theatre
Lincoln Center
N.Y.C.

Not I, Said the Little Red Hen
Stephanie S. Tolan
2-1-71
Parish House Auditorium
2 E. 90th, N.Y.C.

Not Now, Darling
Ray Cooney & John Chapman
9-16-70
Fisher Theatre
Detroit, MI

Not Time's Fool; An Evening of Romantic Theatre
10-12-71
Theatre 23
23 E. 20th, N.Y.C.

Not Without Laughter
Joanna Featherstone
10-2-70
Library & Museum of the Performing Arts
111 Amsterdam, N.Y.C.

Note, The
Robert Somerfeld
12-19-72
Mercer Arts Center
240 Mercer, N.Y.C.

Nothin' But the Blues
Don Evans
Fall, 1972
H B Playwrights Foundation
124 Bank, N.Y.C.

Nothing for Thanks for Nothing
Jerome C. Small
11-21-69
Spencer Memorial Church
99 Clinton, Brooklyn, NY

Nothing Is Sacred
Guy Guden
4-13-73
Santa Barbara City College
Santa Barbara, CA

Nourish the Beast
See: Baba Goya

Novela de Las Nueve, La
Herminio Vargas
5-26-73
Teatro Jurutungo
Gershwin Theater
Brooklyn College, Brooklyn, NY

November People
Roma Greth
1-20-72
Actor's Place
487 Hudson, N.Y.C.

Now
George Haimsohn & John Aman
6-5-68
Cherry Lane Theatre
38 Commerce, N.Y.C.

Now
Walter Corwin
6-7-72
WPA
333 Bowery, N.Y.C.

Now It Makes Sense
Donald Flynn
8-26-69
Gateway Playhouse
Bellport, L.I., NY

Now She Dances
Doric Wilson
2-27-69
Playbox
94 St. Mark's Pl., N.Y.C.

Now There's Just the Three of Us
Michael Weller
10-19-71
Chelsea Theater Center
30 Lafayette Ave., Brooklyn, NY

Now We Are Free
James Lineberger
2-14-70
Spencer Memorial Church
99 Clinton Brooklyn Heights, NY

Nowhere To Run
Peter Copani
12-7-72
Playbox
94 St. Mark's Pl., N.Y.C.

Nuclear Hecuba
Robert Reinhold
10-23-70
Omni Theatre Club
145 W. 18th, N.Y.C.

Nude Gymnastics (with The Ugly)
Tom Miller
10-17-69
Playbox
94 St. Mark's Pl., N.Y.C.

Number Scene, The
Delia Anderson
3-14-69
Inner Theatre
356 Bowery, N.Y.C.

Nun, The (with The Burberry Overcoat)
Irving Glusack
3-19-70
New York Theatre Ensemble
2 E. 2nd, N.Y.C.

Nuns, The
Eduardo Manet; adapted by Don Parker & Paul Verdier
6-1-70
Cherry Lane Theatre
38 Commerce, N.Y.C.

O

O. F. Visigoths
Paul Stein & Charles Watts
Jan., 1969
Santa Monica Playhouse
Santa Monica, CA

O Happy Day (musical)
Susan Kosoff & Jane Staab
12-27-73
Bijou Theatre
359 W. 48th, N.Y.C.

Oba Waja (The King Is Dead)
Duro Lapido
5-20-71
Brooklyn College
Brooklyn, NY

Obituary of Dreams
Letitia Eldredge
7-20-73
La Mama ETC
74 E. 4th, N.Y.C.

Oblast Court Trial, The
Frank Daley
Nov., 1972
St. Patrick's College
Ottawa, CAN

Obnoxious in the First Degree
Anthony Calandra
9-7-73
Malachy Repertory Company
Our Lady of Peace Auditorium
237 E. 62nd, N.Y.C.

Obscene Verse of Magdalene Randallman, The
James Pendleton
7-13-72
Clarion State College
Clarion, PA

Obscenity's End or The Only Way Out Is In (with The Business of Show)
John P. Connell
11-6-69
Triangle Theatre
316 E. 88th, N.Y.C.

Obsidian
Bambi Hartgens
4-10-68
Old Reliable Theatre Tavern
231 E. 3rd, N.Y.C.

Obsidian
Frances Alenikoff
5-18-72
Washington Square Church
133 W. 4th, N.Y.C.

Oda-Oak Oracle
Tsegaye Gabre-Medhin
11-14-72
University of Minnesota
Minneapolis, MN

Odds and Ends
Milton Wisoff
3-25-69
Washington Theatre Club
Washington, DC

Ode to Black Women
6-14-71
Negro Ensemble Company
St. Mark's Playhouse
133 Second, N.Y.C.

Ode to Charley Parker
Edgar White
9-28-73
Studio Rivbea
24 Bond, N.Y.C.

Ododo
Joseph A. Walker & Dorothy Dindroe
9-13-68
Afro-American Studio
15 W. 126th, N.Y.C.

Oedipus
Seneca, adapted by Ted Hughes
7-9-70
Agassiz Theatre
Cambridge, MA

Oedipus
Sophocles, adapted by Anthony Sloan
2-15-70
Roundabout Theatre
307 W. 26th, N.Y.C.

Oedipus Mah-Jongg Scandal, The
Howard Moss
4-30-68
Cooperative Theatre
106 E. 14th, N.Y.C.

Oedipus Rex in Black Minor
5-13-71
Afro-American Theater Workshop
Brooklyn College
Brooklyn, NY

Oedipus the King
Sophocles; adaptation by Anthony Burgess
November, 1972
Tyrone Guthrie Theatre
Minneapolis, MN

Oedipus Tyrannos
Sophocles; adaptation by Benjamin Epperson
12-5-68
Theatre of All Possibilities
353 W. 57th, N.Y.C.

Oedipus Wrecks
Tony Kessick
3-1-68
Gallery Theatre
99 E. 2nd, N.Y.C.

Of Being Hit (with Our Sides)
Clay Goss
11-14-73
Billie Holiday Theatre
1368 Fulton, Brooklyn NY

Of the Fields Lately
David French
1973
Tarragon Theatre
Toronto, CAN

Ofay Watcher, The
Frank Cucci
9-15-69
Stage 73
373 E. 73rd, N.Y.C.

Off Among the Trees Somewhere
Richard Longchamps
6-14-73
H B Playwrights Foundation
124 Bank, N.Y.C.

Off the Wall (revue)
12-7-72
Manhattan Theatre Club
321 E. 73rd, N.Y.C.

Offending the Audience: A Speak-In
Peter Handke; translated by Michael Roloff
2-6-69
Gallery Players
1014 Fifth, N.Y.C.

Offerings (staged reading)
Tom McCormack
6-8-73
Playwrights' Horizons
Clark Center for the Performing Arts
West Side YWCA 8th Ave. & 51st, N.Y.C.

Office Murders, The
Martin Fox
11-14-73
Manhattan Theatre Club
321 E. 73rd, N.Y.C.

Office, The
David Beckman
11-1-70
Dancers Studio Theatre Foundation, Inc.
34 E. 10th, N.Y.C.

Off-Off Broadway
(One-woman show with Kay Carney)
3-21-73
Hunter College Playhouse
695 Park, N.Y.C.

Off-Season, The (2nd part of trilogy Three Pieces Left)
Ransom Jeffrey
7-19-68
Dramarena Repertory Theatre
158 W. 55th, N.Y.C.

Ogoo, I Was Called
Bernard Saltzman
3-12-70
Mainstream Theatre
20 E. 14th, N.Y.C.

Oh
Sandro Key-Aberg
7-3-68
Playbox
94 St. Mark's Pl, N.Y.C.

Oh, Baby!
Walter Boyd
4-21-72
Theatre Suburbia
Houston, TX

Oh, Calcutta
Kenneth Tynan and others
6-17-69
Eden Theatre
2nd Ave. & 12th, N.Y.C.

Oh Coward!
Noel Coward
10-4-72
New Theatre
154 E. 54th, N.Y.C.

Oh, Pioneers
Douglas Taylor
2-20-68
Milwaukee Repertory Theatre
Milwaukee, WI

Oh, Say Can You See L.A.
John Allen
2-8-68
Actors' Playhouse
100 Seventh Ave. So., N.Y.C.

Olathe Response, The
Jack E. Marshall & Rene Enriquez
4-5-71
Actor's Playhouse
100 Seventh Ave. So., N.Y.C.

Old Folks Duet
Harvey Zuckerman
6-16-73
Theatre 77 Repertory
23 E. 20th, N.Y.C.

Old Judge Mose is Dead
Joseph White
8-27-69
Hudson Guild Theatre
441 W. 26th, N.Y.C.

Old Lady With the Old Paper Bags, The
Anthony Howarth
11-24-72
New York Theatre Ensemble
2 E. 2nd, N.Y.C.

Old Maid (with Are You a Virgin?)
James Harter
11-19-73
Theatre for the New City
113 Jane, N.Y.C.

Old One Two, The
A. R. Gurney, Jr.
1-21-73
Brandeis University
Waltham, MA

Old Rat's Heart, The
Michael Smith
12-16-71
Theatre Genesis
2nd Ave. & 10th, N.Y.C.

Old Times
Harold Pinter
11-16-71
Billy Rose Theatre
208 W. 41st, N.Y.C.

Old Woman Broods, The
Tadeusz Rozewicz
6-2-72
La Mama ETC
74 E. 4th, N.Y.C.

Oldenberg
Barry Bermange
4-2-70
Playhouse in the Park
Cincinnati, OH

Older People
John Ford Noonan
5-14-72
New York Shakespeare Festival Public Theatre
425 Lafayette, N.Y.C.

Oli's Icecream Suit
Richard Ploetz
3-16-72
South Coast Repertory
Costa Mesa, CA

Ollojees of 1970 (revue)
11-20-70
Riverdale Showcase
Bronx, NY

Olu Clemente — The Philosopher of Baseball
Miguel Algarin & Jesus Abraham Laviera
8-30-73
Delacorte Theatre
Central Park
N.Y.C.

Olympian Games
Ovid ("Metamorphoses"); adapted by Kenneth Cavander & Barbara Damashek
10-8-70
Yale Repertory Theatre
New Haven, CT

On a Cambodian Highway
Brent Filson
4-27-73
Players' Workshop
83 E. 4th, N.Y.C.

On Account of Sid Shrycock
Marilyn Miller & Dale Gonyea
11-19-71
Kingston Mines
Chicago, IL

On Heaven and Heel (dramatic event evolved from the prose and poetry of William Blake)
1-22-72
Boston University
Boston, MA

On Stage
Walter Tyszka
10-13-72
New York Theatre Ensemble
2 E. 2nd, N.Y.C.

On the Boy Girl Thing
Richard Hoag
3-28-68
Anthony Mannino Drama Tree
182 Fifth, N.Y.C.

On the Brink (with Boo Hoo and Idyllic)
Philip Magdalany
6-17-72
West Side YWCA
8th Ave. & 51st St., N.Y.C.

On the Mantlepiece
Larry O'Connel
9-25-69
Second Group Theatre
McBurney YMCA
215 W. 23rd, N.Y.C.

On the Road
Tony Preston
1-15-68
Old Reliable Theatre Tavern
231 E. 3rd, N.Y.C.

On the Road (with Rags and Old Iron)
Tony Preston
2-22-72
Theatre of the Riverside Church
490 Riverside Dr., N.Y.C.

On the Runway of Life Something's Always Taking Off (with Clowns)
Antonio Calabrese
6-18-72
Rosebud Repertory Theatre
4 W. 76th, N.Y.C.

On Time
Felix Leon, Alfred Drake, Howard Da Silva
8-19-68
Goodspeed Opera House
East Haddam, CT

On Wall Street
Irwin Horowitz
8-20-69
Karma Theatre
Broadway & Rector, N.Y.C.

Once Upon a Playground
Jack Frakes
2-1-70
Spencer Memorial Church
99 Clinton Brooklyn Heights, NY

One!
Dick Williams
10-16-70
New Federal Theatre
292 Henry, N.Y.C.

One Family, Some Friends
John Jakes (book & lyrics); Gilbert M. Martin (music & lyrics)
7-9-71
Dayton Theatre Guild Playhouse
Dayton, OH

One Free Smile
Robert & Elizabeth Swerdlow & Malcolm Mills (book); Robert Swerdlow (music & lyrics)
11-15-73
Top-of-the-Gate
Bleecker & Thompson, N.Y.C.

One Hundred and First
Kenneth Cameron
1-26-68
Riverside Theatre Workshop
120th St. & Claremont Ave., N.Y.C.

One Hundred Miles from Nowhere (100 Miles from Nowhere)
Bill Solly (book, lyrics & music); Donald Ward (book)
12-4-73
Mama Hare's Tree
13th Street Theatre
50 W. 13th, N.Y.C.

One Is a Crowd
Beah Richards
5-24-71
Inner City Theatre
Los Angeles, CA

One Is One (one-man show with Julian Chagrin)
4-1-71
Catholic University
Washington, DC

One Lie and Half a Dream
Sydney Ladenheim
4-26-71
Minor Latham Playhouse
Barnard College
N.Y.C.

One More Fool
Peter Muller
11-18-71
New York Theatre of the Americas
321 E. 73rd, N.Y.C.

One More Spring
Robert E. Allen (book, lyrics, music)
12-24-73
Donnell Library
N.Y.C.

One Night Stands of a Noisy Passenger
See: The Noisy Passenger; Un Passage; Fragile Freight

One Out of Many
5-26-73
Puerto Rican Theatre Workshop
Gershwin Theatre
Brooklyn College, Brooklyn, NY

One Run, One Hit, No Eros
Fred Isler
3-24-71
Second Group Theatre
McBurney YMCA
215 W. 23rd, N.Y.C.

One, The
Oliver Pitcher
1-14-72
Negro Ensemble Company
St. Mark's Playhouse
133 Second Ave., N.Y.C.

One Thursday Last May
Art Wright
7-18-68
Cooper Square Arts Theatre
35 Cooper Sq., N.Y.C.

One Way Non-Stop (staged reading)
Thomas C. Rosica
December, 1972
Playwrights' Horizons
West Side YWCA
8th Ave. & 51st, N.Y.C.

One Wish to Broadway (musical)
Alaina Warren
3-27-71
Charles Playhouse
Boston, MA

One Wore Blue and One Wore Gray
Irene Lewis
Fall, 1973
Hartford Stage Company
Hartford, CT

One World at a Time
Richard F. Stockton
10-9-72
Lambs Theatre
130 W. 44th, N.Y.C.

One World Is Worth a Thousand Hair Dryers
Rick Kellogg
Feb., 1970
University of Missouri
Columbia, MO

One-Two-Three-Four, One-Two-Three-Four, One-Two. . .(1-2-3-4, 1-2-3-4, 1-2. . .)
Joseph Lazarus
7-10-70
Omni Theatre Club
145 W. 18th, N.Y.C.

Only a King (Part I): A Tragedy Suggested by the Death of James Forrestal
Chester Leo Smith
5-17-68
Kingston's Studio Theatre
Los Angeles, CA

Only a King (Part II—Rashamon Revisited): The Incredible Relationship of Haakon Chevalier and J. Robert Oppenheimer
Chester Leo Smith
5-24-68
Kingston's Studio Theatre
Los Angeles, CA

Only Bathtub in Cassis, The
Robert Fisher & Arthur Alsberg
3-26-69
Gallery Theatre
Los Angeles, CA

Only Fools Are Sad
Dan Almagor
11-22-71
Edison Theatre
240 W. 47th, N.Y.C.

Only Game in Town, The
Frank D. Gilroy
1-16-68
Mechanic Theatre
Baltimore, MD

Only One Angel Has a Knife
Muriel Stursberg
11-27-70
New York Theatre Ensemble
2 E. 2nd, N.Y.C.

Only the Shadow Knows
Danny Simon
8-31-71
Bucks County Playhouse
New Hope, PA

Ontological Proof of My Existence
Joyce Carol Oates
2-10-72
Cubiculo
414 W. 51st, N.Y.C.

Onward and Upward (with Happy-Go-Lucky)
Andrew Witwer
12-4-69
Loft Workshop
152 Bleecker, N.Y.C.

Oob Love Story, An
Hal Craven
5-16-69
New York Theatre Ensemble
2 E. 2nd, N.Y.C.

Oooooops!
Robert Patrick
5-12-69
Old Reliable Theatre Tavern
231 E. 3rd, N.Y.C.

Op
Frank Moffett Mosier
2-24-72
Actor's Place
487 Hudson, N.Y.C.

Open and Shut Magic Company, The
Robert Nichols
8-4-73
Theater for the New City
113 Jane, N.Y.C.

Opening, The
Charles Grodin
5-15-72
Tappan Zee Playhouse
Nyack, NY

Openings
Painted Women Ritual Theatre
6-9-72
Washington Square Church
133 W. 4th, N.Y.C.

Operation Sidewinder
Sam Shepard
3-12-70
Vivian Beaumont Theatre
Lincoln Center
N.Y.C.

Operation Thwack
Betzie Parker
3-24-72
Omni Theatre Club
145 W. 18th, N.Y.C.

Operetta
Kenyon Gordon
9-4-73
Mama Hare's Tree
13th Street Theatre
50 W. 13th, N.Y.C.

Ophelia
Kathleen St. John
3-29-73
La Mama ETC
74 E. 4th, N.Y.C.

Opium
Jean Cocteau; translated & adapted by Roc Brynner
10-5-70
Edison Theatre
240 W. 47th, N.Y.C.

Opposite Side of Sonny, The
Peter Copani (book & lyrics); John Ronan and Peter Copani (music)
5-3-73
People's Performing Company
Playbox
94 St. Mark's Pl., N.Y.C.

Oppression (done with Liberation under the covering title Streets)
2-7-72
Emerson College
Boston, MA

Opus Blue —Is Pink
Claude Kipnis Mime Theatre
2-26-72
Queensborough Community College
Bayside, NY

Opus Siniestrus
Leonora Carrington
2-19-73
Theatre of Latin America
St. Clement's Church
423 W. 46th, N.Y.C.

Oracles
Andy Wouk
9-19-73
Camera Obscura Theatre Company
La Mama ETC
74 E. 4th, N.Y.C.

Oracles — The Oedipus Story
Andy Wouk
9-12-73
La Mama ETC
74 E. 4th, N.Y.C.

Orchestra, The (with Episode in the Life of an Author)
Jean Anouilh
9-16-69
Studio Arena Theatre
Buffalo, NY

Ordinary Man, An
Mel Arrighi
9-9-68
Cherry Lane Theatre
38 Commerce, N.Y.C.

Oresteia in '71
Frank Huntington
Apr., 1971
Kent State University
Kent, OH

Orestes
Euripides
Feb., 1968
University of California Theatre
Berkeley, CA

Orestes
Gregory Rozakis
2-14-73
Playwrights' Workshop Club
Bastiano's Studio
14 Cooper Sq., N.Y.C.

Orestes (new rock version)
Euripides
7-2-70
Cubiculo
414 W. 51st, N.Y.C.

Orfeo for Me (staged reading)
Albert Fiorella
1-10-73
Manhattan Theatre Club
321 E. 73rd, N.Y.C.

Orgies Mysteries Theater
Hermen Nitsch
12-2-72
Mercer Arts Center
240 Mercer, N.Y.C.

Orgy on Saturday Night
Eugenia
4-17-69
Cooper Square Arts Theatre
35 Cooper Sq., N.Y.C.

Orientation, The (with Viva Lamour)
James Paul Dey
6-14-72
Cubiculo
414 W. 51st, N.Y.C.

Original Cast, The (improvisational troupe)
11-23-73
Broodje Restaurant
246 E. 51st, N.Y.C.

Original Child Bomb
Thomas Merton
3-12-71
St. Clement's Church
423 W. 46th, N.Y.C.

Orlando Furioso
Adapted by Eduardo Saguinetti
11-4-70
Bubble
Bryant Park, N.Y.C.

Orphan, The
David Rabe
4-18-73
New York Shakespeare Festival
Public Theatre
425 Lafayette, N.Y.C.

Orphans
11-10-73
Theatre of Encounter
247 W. 72nd, N.Y.C.

Orrin (with Sugar Mouth Sam Don't Dance No More)
Don Evans
10-12-72
H B Playwrights Foundation
124 Bank, N.Y.C.

Oscar
Adrian Hall & Richard Cumming
6-26-73
Trinity Square Repertory Company
Providence, RI

Oscar Wilde '73
Edward Shanley
12-9-72
Universalist Theatre
4 W. 76th, N.Y.C.

Ostrich, The
Hal Craven
11-28-69
New York Theatre Ensemble
2 E. 2nd, N.Y.C.

Ostriches
Roberto Rodriguez Suarez
2-8-71
Puerto Rican Players Group
Center for Puerto Rican Cultural Relations Auditorium
432 Third, N.Y.C.

Osvaldo Pradere y Su Teatro de Guinol
6-17-72
International Arts Relations
508 W. 53rd, N.Y.C.

Othello Seen Again: An Instance of Shakespearean Reality
1-30-72
Terrain Gallery
39 Grove, N.Y.C.

Other Cinderella, The
7-21-70
Lebanon Summer Playhouse
Lebanon, NH

Other One, The (with The Girl with a Ring on Her Nose and Too Much) (One of four one-act plays presented under title About Women)
Mario Fratti
4-1-71
Loft Theatre
21 Bond, N.Y.C.

Other People
Thomas Berger
7-1-70
Berkshire Theatre Festival
Stockbridge, MA

Other People's Junk (an adult puppet/mime show)
12-17-73
Exchange Theatre
151 Bank, N.Y.C.

Other Side of the Stars, The
Steve Press (book); Bonnie Arditi (lyrics); Joan Brown (music)
4-7-69
Triangle Theatre
316 E. 88th, N.Y.C.

Other Side of the Year, The
Roma Greth
2-6-69
Theatre 13
201 W. 13th, N.Y.C.

Other Side, The
Fred Vassi
3-12-68
Little Theatre
181 Bleecker, N.Y.C.

Other Voices, Other Rooms
Truman Capote; Anna Marie Barlow (adaptor)
10-4-73
Studio Arena Theatre
Buffalo, NY

Otho the Great
John Keats
6-18-70
Mainstream Theatre-Loft
20 E. 14th, N.Y.C.

Ottawa Man (adaptation of Gogol's Inspector General)
Mavor Moore
Summer, 1972
Lennoxville Festival
Lennoxville, Quebec, CAN

Our Darling Baby Boy
Howard Berland
8-26-72
Omni Theatre Club
145 W. 18th, N.Y.C.

Our Father's Failing
Israel Horovitz
7-21-73
Eugene O'Neill Memorial Theatre Foundation
Waterford, CT

Our Fourth Couple
Susan Cottrell
3-9-72
Whitman College
Walla Walla, WV

Our Lady of Late
William Dunas
4-28-72
Ambrose Arts Foundation
57 Laight, N.Y.C.

Our Play on the Future Has No Name
Howard Greenberger & Robert Reinhold
4-23-70
La Mama ETC
74 E. 4th, N.Y.C.

Our Thing
M. T. Teeners
8-27-71
Tentarena
Monticello, NY

Our Very Own Hole in the Ground
Bernard M. Kahn
10-6-72
La Mama ETC
74 E. 4th, N.Y.C.

Oursides (with Of Being Hit)
Clay Goss
11-14-73
Billie Holiday Theatre
1368 Fulton, Brooklyn, NY

Out Cry (revised version)
Tennessee Williams
1-18-73
Shubert Theatre
New Haven, CT

Out of Control
Joseph B. Baldwin
9-15-73
Actors' Experimental Unit
682 Sixth, N.Y.C.

Out of Control (with The Marriage of the Telephone Company)
Martin Craft
9-9-71
Actor's Playhouse
100 Seventh Ave. So., N.Y.C.

Out of the Deathcart
Charles Mingus
7-1-71
New York Shakespeare Festival Public Theatre
425 Lafayette, N.Y.C.

Out of the Grass and Into the Morning Glorious
Gerald W. Parowinchak
3-11-69
Theatre of the Arts
University of Waterloo
Waterloo, Ontario, CAN

Out There by Your Lonesome
Melvin Van Peebles
2-14-73
New York City Correctional Facility for Women
Riker's Island, NY

Out West (with Back East)
Andrew Mack
6-22-70
Second Group Theatre
McBurney YMCA
215 W. 23rd, N.Y.C.

Outcasts, The
Garrett Smith & Rolfie Lawson
8-21-69
Triangle Playhouse
Farmington, CT

Outfielders, The
Robert Lerner
11-6-69
WPA
34 E. 4th, N.Y.C.

Outhouse, The (with My Mama's Lemonade)
Dennis Spedaliere
3-22-71
Assembly Theatre
113 Jane, N.Y.C.

Outlaw Brothers
Barry Litvack (book); Christopher Allport, John Gerth, Richard Weissman (lyrics & music)
11-18-71
Bucks County Playhouse
New Hope, PA

Outsider, The
Wolfgang Borchert; translated by Elizabeth Isenstead
11-13-70
Anthony Mannino Drama Tree
182 Fifth, N.Y.C.

Over and Over
Wallace Johnson
6-2-69
Playwright's Opportunity Theatre
50 W. 13th, N.Y.C.

Overexposed
Elaine Berman
5-19-72
Hunter College Playwrights
West Side YMCA
5 W. 63rd, N.Y.C.

Overnight
William Inge
1-31-69
University of California
Los Angeles, CA

Overnight Bag, The
Stephan Taylor
3-23-70
Library & Museum of the Performing Arts
111 Amsterdam, N.Y.C.

Overseers, The (with Angels in Agony)
Robert Patrick
7-1-68
Old Reliable Theatre Tavern
231 E. 3rd, N.Y.C.

Overture for Ka Mountain and Gardenia Terrace
Bob Wilson
4-24-72
Studio Theatre
147 Spring, N.Y.C.

Owl Killer, The
Phillip Hayes Dean
11-4-73
New York Cultural Center
2 Columbus Circle, N.Y.C.

Owl (with The Big Black Box, The Shiny Red Ball, and The Armory)
Cleve Hawbold
1-9-72
Park Avenue Community Theatre
Central Church
593 Park, N.Y.C.

Owners
Caryl Churchill
5-14-73
Mercer Arts Center
240 Mercer, N.Y.C.

Ox-Roast
Dolores Walker & Andrew Piotrowski
10-21-68
Library and Museum of the Performing Arts
111 Amsterdam, N.Y.C.

Oy, What a Wedding
G. Israelev (book); Murray Rumshinsky (music); Jacobs (lyrics)
10-18-69
Anderson Theatre
66 Second Ave., N.Y.C.

O-Zoned
12-15-72
Theatre Genesis
10th & Second Ave., N.Y.C.

P

P from B
William Carlos Williams
6-1-73
Common Ground
70 Grand, N.Y.C.

Pacific Paradise (New Zealand Maori Co.)
10-16-72
Palace Theatre,
N.Y.C.

Pagador de Promesas, El
Alfredo Dias Gomes
4-30-71
ADAL Performing Arts
682 Ave. of the Americas, N.Y.C.

Painted Flowers (Morning of a Hero, I Am the Moon and Hide and Seek)
Glenn Graves
12-2-69
Provincetown Playhouse
133 MacDougal, N.Y.C.

Painted Women Ritual Theatre
3-22-73
Barnard College
N.Y.C.

Pair of Pelegics, A
Angelo Gnazzo
4-12-73
Ensemble Studio Theatre
549 W. 52nd, N.Y.C.

Pair of Steaks
Florence Miller
5-26-72
New York Theatre Ensemble
2 E. 2nd, N.Y.C.

Pair, The
Sholom Aleichem; adapted by Rina Elisha
10-8-69
La Mama ETC
74 E. 4th, N.Y.C.

Paisley Scar, The
William J. Norris
Summer, 1973
Actor's Workshop
Chicago, IL

Pal Joey '69
7-28-69
Ivoryton Playhouse
Ivoryton, CT

Palace at 4 A.M., The
Howard Moss
8-9-72
John Drew Playhouse
East Hampton, Long Island, NY

Palangana, La
Raul le Cardenas
6-30-71
ADAL Performing Arts
682 Ave. of the Americas, N.Y.C.

Palmer Way, The
Nicholas E. Baehr
11-17-72
West Side Gay Theatre
W.S.D.G. Center
37 Ninth, N.Y.C.

Palomares
Third World Puppets
6-11-70
St. Paul the Apostle Church
124 W. 60th, N.Y.C.

Panda and the Spy, The
Mary Virginia Heinlein
7-7-70
Goodman Theatre
Chicago, IL

Papers
Hans Ruesch
12-2-68
Provincetown Playhouse
133 MacDougal, N.Y.C.

Papers, The
Miles Smith
3-21-68
Detroit Public Library
Detroit, MI

Papp
Kenneth Cameron
4-17-69
American Place Theatre
N.Y.C.

Parabus Objective (with Pitfall for a Rational Man and Rehearsal)
Benjamin Bradford
3-17-72
Clarion State College
Clarion, PA

Parade, The
Gerald Miller
11-25-70
La Mama ETC
74 E. 4th, N.Y.C.

Paradise Kid, The
Donna DeMatteo
5-25-73
H B Playwrights Foundation
124 Bank, N.Y.C.

Paradise Slumming
Ronald Miglionico
10-30-71
Rutgers Community Center
200 Madison, N.Y.C.

Paraffin (with Rendezvous, Anyuta, and Polinka)
Anton Chekhov; adapted by James Monos
6-12-72
Circle Theatre
2307 Broadway, N.Y.C.

Paranoia Blues (revue)
Based on Jules Feiffer cartoons
Feb., 1970
State University of New York at Albany
NY

Paranoia Pretty (musical)
Levi and the Love Trust; Edwin Kapinos (music)
6-1-73
Theatre for the New City
113 Jane, N.Y.C.

Parapet, The
David Mueller
1-6-70
La Mama ETC
74 E. 4th, N.Y.C.

Parfumerie
Karen Johnson
10-5-71
Vandam Theatre
15 Vandam, N.Y.C.

Paris
Ping Chong & Meredith Monk
4-20-73
House
228 Broadway, N.Y.C.

Paris Is Out
Richard Seff
1-19-70
Brooks Atkinson Theatre
N.Y.C.
See: Will It Last? in 1969 list

Park
Paul Cherry (book & lyrics); Lance Mulcahy (music)
2-25-70
Center Stage
Baltimore, MD

Park, The
Ralph Scholl
1-27-72
Dons Studio
202 E. 29th, N.Y.C.

Park, The
Pat Rule
2-25-71
Changing Scene
Denver, CO

Part of a Darkness
James J. Fox
9-17-70
Mannhardt Theatre Foundation
N.Y.C.

Particle Theory
Richard Foreman
4-18-73
Theatre for the New City
113 Jane, N.Y.C.

Partnership, The
Aldo Giunta
10-24-73
New Dramatists
424 W. 44th, N.Y.C.

Party Clips
1-25-68
Theatre East
211 E. 60th, N.Y.C.

Party Day
Jack Winter
6-4-69
National Arts Centre
Ottawa, CAN

Party, The
William Parchman
7-11-69
Eugene O'Neill Memorial Theatre
Waterford, CT

Party, The (with Charley and Enchanted)
Slawomir Mrozek
8-6-68
Boothbay Playhouse
Boothbay, ME

Paschal Mystery of the Mass, The
4-7-73
Sacred Heart Church
455 W. 51st, N.Y.C.

Passacaglia
James Paul Dey
1-25-73
Cranium Theatre
277 Park Ave. So., N.Y.C.

Passage to E. M. Forster, A (reading)
Compiled by William Roerick & Thomas Coley
10-27-70
ANTA Matinee Series
Theatre de Lys
N.Y.C.

Passing Through from Exotic Places
Ronald Ribman
12-7-69
Sheridan Square Playhouse
99 Seventh Ave. So., N.Y.C.

Passing Through Liberia
Hal Ackerman
4-17-69
Cubiculo
414 W. 51st, N.Y.C.

Passion
Edward Bond
2-1-72
Yale Repertory Theatre
New Haven, CT

Passion and Other Plays
Stephen H. Foreman
6-9-72
New Dramatists
424 W. 44th, N.Y.C.

Passion of Antigona Perez, The
Luis Rafael Sanchez; translated by Charles Pilditch
5-17-72
Puerto Rican Traveling Theatre
Cathedral of St. John the Divine
Amsterdam Ave. & 112th St., N.Y.C.

Passion Play
Stephen H. Foreman
6-7-72
New Dramatists
424 W. 44th, N.Y.C.

Passover
Lloyd Gold
2-28-73
Spingold Theatre
Brandeis University
Waltham, MA

Past Is the Past, The
Richard Wesley
8-1-73
Eugene O'Neill Memorial Theatre
Waterford, CT

Pastime of Monsieur Robert, The
Howard Sackler
6-4-69
American Conservatory Theatre
San Francisco, CA

Pastry Shop, The (with The Young Among Themselves)
Ned Rorem
6-5-70
Extension Theatre
277 Park Ave. So., N.Y.C.

Pat (with Dream Etude)
Michael Roy Denbo
4-25-70
New Theatre Workshop
154 E. 54th, N.Y.C.

P.A.T.C.H. Theater Circus
8-12-73
Dramatic Society of Southampton
Southampton, L.I., NY

Paths of Destiny
Thomas Luce Summa
2-27-69
Casa Italiana
117th & Amsterdam, N.Y.C.

Pathways to Peace
6-11-72
Columbia University
N.Y.C.

Patient, The
Eileen Summers and Noel Warwick
10-17-68
Universalist Theatre
4 W. 76th, N.Y.C.

Patrick Pearse Motel, The
Hugh Leonard
8-22-72
Olney Theatre
Olney, MD

Patrick's Day
Bill Morrison
5-12-72
Long Wharf Theatre
New Haven, CT

Patrick's Dream
Thomas Terefenko
10-2-69
New York Theatre Ensemble
2 E. 2nd, N.Y.C.

Patriot for Me, A
John Osborne
9-15-69
National Theatre
Washington, DC

Patriots, The (1776)
Robert Munford
1-16-71
American Theatre Company
106 E. 14th, N.Y.C.

Paulina
Caleb Smith
11-10-68
Cans Underground Theatre
322 W. 55th, N.Y.C.

Pawn Takes King
T. Frank Gutswa
11-6-69
New York Theatre Ensemble
2 E. 2nd, N.Y.C.

Pay Attention to the Ravel (with Freudian Memoirs of Viola Pickins)
Donald Kvares
7-7-72
Playbox
94 St. Mark's Place, N.Y.C.

Pay Attention to the Ravel (with The Happiness Train and Fall River Ruins)
Donald Kvares
11-5-70
Theatre Crossroads
23 E. 20th, N.Y.C.

Pay the Piper
Lila Levant (book); Jack Labow (music & lyrics)
10-19-70
Cami Theatre
165 W. 57th, N.Y.C.

Peace
Aristophanes; adaptation by Timothy Reynolds, Al Carmines
11-1-68
Judson Poet's Theatre
55 Wash. Sq. So., N.Y.C.

Peace at Hand
Richard Wolf
2-12-73
Circle Theatre Company
2307 Broadway, N.Y.C.

Peace, Peace
Frank Crocitto
11-20-70
Assembly Theatre
113 Jane, N.Y.C.

Peacemaker, The
Carl Oglesby
4-9-70
Theatre Company of Boston
Boston University Theatre
Boston, MA

Peaches' Intimate Review, The
Hot Peaches
9-8-73
Judson Garden
239 Thompson, N.Y.C.

Peanut Butter & Jelly
Harris Freedman
5-9-70
Theatre of the University of the Streets
130 E. 7th, N.Y.C.

Pearl Necklace, The (musical)
Israel Bercovici
9-21-72
Jewish State Theatre of Bucharest
Brooklyn Academy of Music
30 Lafayette Ave., Brooklyn, NY

Pearls Stay On, The
Charlene Osgood Shuren
4-26-71
Assembly Theatre
113 Jane, N.Y.C.

Peas
Michael Smith
8-19-71
Changing Scene
Denver, CO

Peasant Life
Robert Nichols
4-5-68
Angry Arts
423 W. 46th, N.Y.C.

Pecan Tree, The (with Chaconne in G Minor and Wyatt)
Piero Heliczer
2-11-71
Cinematheque
80 Wooster, N.Y.C.

Peck's Bad Boy
Aurand Harris
7-24-73
Harwich Junior Theatre
West Harwich, MA

Pedestal, The (with End)
Joseph Mayer
7-28-72
American Shakespeare Festival
Stratford, CT

Pedro Gomez
Copley Davis
Fall, 1970
La Mise en Scene
New Orleans, LA

Peep Show, The (improvisational revue)
Tamara Horrocks
4-15-71
Bank Theatre
Brooklyn, NY

Pelican, The (with Motherlove)
August Strindberg; translated by Arvid Paulson
2-16-72
Cubiculo
414 W. 51st, N.Y.C.

Peloalambre No Se Rinde (original organic work)
June, 1973
Teatro de Orilla
214 E. 2nd, N.Y.C.

Penalty for Being Slow, The
Burton Snyder
1-25-68
Cooper Square Arts Theatre
35 Cooper Sq., N.Y.C.

Pendulum, The
Gerald Miller
10-1-69
La Mama ETC
74 E. 4th, N.Y.C.

Penelope G
10-19-73
Theatre X
Milwaukee, WI

Penitents
Roberto Rodriguez Suarez
5-29-69
Duo Theatre Workshop
522 E. 12th, N.Y.C.

Penny Wars, The
Elliott Baker
9-15-69
Colonial Theatre
Boston, MA

Penthouse Legend (original version of The Night of January 16th)
Ayn Rand
2-22-73
McAlpin Rooftop Theatre
34th & 6th, N.Y.C.

People Are Living There
Athol Fugard
11-18-71
Forum Theatre
Lincoln Center
N.Y.C.

People Are Trying To Put Opposites Together
Eli Seigal
8-11-68
Terrain Gallery
39 Grove, N.Y.C.

People's Heart, The
Benjamin Barber
11-25-69
Theatre 3
Forlini's Third Phase
111th & Broadway, N.Y.C.

People's Subways — No Sabireir
El Groupo Toane
4-29-72
New Federal Theatre
240 E. 3rd, N.Y.C.

People Show — '52, The
9-19-73
La Mama ETC
74 E. 4th, N.Y.C.

Peoria Impromptu, The
Deloss Brown
2-18-72
WPA
333 Bowery, N.Y.C.

Pequod
Roy S. Richardson
6-29-69
Mercury Theatre
136 E. 13th, N.Y.C.

Perfect Analysis Given by a Parrot, A (with The Frosted Glass Coffin)
Tennessee Williams
5-1-70
Waterfront Playhouse
Key West, FL

Perfect Gentleman, A
Herbert Appleman
July, 1970
Eugene O'Neill Memorial Theatre
Waterford, CT

Perfect Guest, The (staged reading)
Neil Vipond
5-13-70
Triangle Theatre
316 E. 88th, N.Y.C.

Perfect Match, The (with Left, Right, Left)
William Derringer
2-14-69
Theatre of Our Discontent
Clifton Hotel
127 W. 79th, N.Y.C.

Perfect Victory, The
Paul Rosefeldt
9-13-70
La Mise en Scene
New Orleans, LA

Perfection in Black
China Clark
1-16-72
Negro Ensemble Company
St. Mark's Playhouse
133 Second, N.Y.C.

Pericas, Las (The Parrots)
Nelson Dorr
10-31-69
Greenwich Mews Spanish Theatre
Theatre East
211 E. 60th, N.Y.C.

Pericles
H. M. Petrakis
8-27-68
Universalist Theatre
4 W. 76th, N.Y.C.

Perimeters
Poem by Charles Levendosky; dramatization by Frank Parman with Terry Moore
10-20-71
State University of New York
Buffalo, NY

Perry's Mission
Clarence Young III
1-21-71
Negro Ensemble Company
St. Mark's Playhouse
133 Second, N.Y.C.

Persia, A Desert Cheapie
Bernard Roth & John Vaccaro
4-9-72
Playhouse of the Ridiculous
La Mama ETC
74 E. 4th, N.Y.C.

Persians, The
Aeschylus; new adaptation by John Lewin
4-15-70
St. George's Church
Stuyvesant Square
N.Y.C.

Person to Person
Robert Gordon
Summer, 1970
Eugene O'Neill Memorial Theatre
Waterford, CT

Personally, I Like Peanut Butter and Jelly
8-8-73
Hyde Park Playhouse
Hyde Park, NY

Peter Pan Is a Dirty Old Man
Kirk Lovell
6-3-71
Village Arena
62 E. 4th, N.Y.C.

Peter Pan (new rock musical version)
King's Players
5-20-72
Library & Museum of the Performing Arts
111 Amsterdam Ave., N.Y.C.

Peter Sent Me
Kornel Petrovich Martinuk
12-6-69
Theatre
130 E. 7th, N.Y.C.

Petit Cabaret Solennel (revue)
9-28-72
Theatre for the New City
113 Jane, N.Y.C.

Petition, The
Donald Flynn
July, 1970
Eugene O'Neill Memorial Theatre
Waterford, CT

Petition, The (with A Moneyback Guarantee)
Donald Flynn
3-18-72
Trinity Presbyterian Church
422 W. 57th, N.Y.C.

Pets (Silver Gray Toy Poodle, Baby with a Knife, and Pets)
Richard Reich
5-14-69
Provincetown Playhouse
133 MacDougal, N.Y.C.

Petty-Bourgeois, The
Maxim Gorki; new adaptation by Jacques Chwat
3-17-72
WPA
333 Bowery, N.Y.C.

Petya, Prince of Pennsylvania
James Rosenfield
8-5-71
Changing Scene
Denver, CO

Pewter Pigeon, The
David Shumaker
10-23-71
Actors' Experimental Unit
682 Sixth, N.Y.C.

Phaethon
Thomas Terefenko
2-19-70
New York Theatre Ensemble
2 E. 2nd, N.Y.C.

Phantasmagoria Historia of D. Johann Fausten Magister, PhD, MD, DD, DL, Etc, A
Vasek Simek
4-24-73
Truck & Warehouse Theatre
79 E. 4th, N.Y.C.

Phase 3
Richard Cohen
10-11-68
Cooper Square Arts Theatre
35 Cooper Sq., N.Y.C.

Phigments
Ricardo Castillo
2-5-70
Inner Theatre
356 Bowery, N.Y.C.

Philanthropist, The
Christopher Hampton
3-15-71
Ethel Barrymore Theatre
N.Y.C.

Philosophy in the Bedroom by the Marquis de Sade
Arranged & compiled by William Haislip & Josef Bush
2-3-69
Old Reliable Theatre Tavern
231 E. 3rd, N.Y.C.

Philosophy in the Boudoir
Adapted by Eric Kahane; translated by Alex Szogyi
5-21-69
Gramercy Arts Theatre
N.Y.C.

Phoebus, You've Turned On!
Avra Petrides & Diane Kagan
10-21-70
La Mama ETC
74 E. 4th, N.Y.C.

Photographer
Otto Dijk
9-23-70
La Mama ETC
74 E. 4th, N.Y.C.

Photographs: Mary and Howard
Jean-Claude van Itallie
10-7-69
Mark Taper Forum
Los Angeles, CA

Photoplay
Cary Glaser
April, 1969
University of Illinois
Urbana, IL

Pickets at King's Rook Four, The
Marcia Pehr
4-28-73
Theatre Studio
Barnard College
N.Y.C.

Pickle, The (with The Nameplate and Souffle of Turbot)
Raymond Platt
6-3-70
Stage Lights Theatrical Club
218 W. 48th, N.Y.C.

Pickpocket, The
Ron Radice
Early 1972
Performing Arts Company
Woodstock, NY

Pickwickians at Manor Farm, The
Brian D. Barnes
7-22-70
Cubiculo
414 W. 51st, N.Y.C.

Picnic for Patricia, A
Belle Gitelman
2-17-68
Theatre East
211 E. 60th, N.Y.C.

Picture
Oliver Hailey
10-28-68
Mark Taper Forum
Los Angeles, CA

Picture Window or Day in the Life of Ellen Drew, Writer
1-16-73
Puppetry Guild of Greater New York
St. John's Episcopal Church
224 Waverly Pl., N.Y.C.

Picture Wire
Robert Patrick
8-13-70
St. Peter's Church
346 W. 20th, N.Y.C.

Pie Are Squared
Ira Weinstein
6-4-73
Gene Frankel Workshop
Mercer Arts Center
240 Mercer, N.Y.C.

Piece of Fog, A
Donald Kvares
3-2-70
Old Reliable Theatre Tavern
231 E. 3rd, N.Y.C.

Pieces
Stuart Kaplan (director); Jeremie Rachunow (music & lyrics)
12-12-69
Tube
177 MacDougal, N.Y.C.

Pieces
8-4-73
Teenage Theatre Workshop
Queens Playhouse
Flushing, NY

Pieces
Open Scene Troupe
1-21-72
Riverdale Neighborhood House
5521 Mosholu Ave., Bronx, NY

Pierre
Jacques Lanquirand
2-26-70
St. Lawrence Center for the Arts
Toronto, CAN

Pierrot Le Fou (Adaptation for the stage of Jean-Luc Goddard's film)
5-11-73
Ice & Fire Theatre Company
McBurney YMCA
215 W. 23rd, N.Y.C.

Pig!
Sydney Andreani & John Driver
4-22-70
La Mama ETC
74 E. 4th, N.Y.C.

Pig and the Spie, The
Jerry Ingram
2-11-72
Playbox
94 St. Mark's Pl., N.Y.C.

Pig in a Poke, A
Georges Feydeau; Richard Gottlieb (translator)
10-24-73
Public Trust Theatre Company
Coconut Grove, FL

Pig Pen, The
Ed Bullins
4-29-70
American Place Theatre
N.Y.C.

Pigeons
Edward Friedman
3-15-73
Cubiculo
414 W. 51st, N.Y.C.

Pigjazz (a pataphysical vaudeville)
The Decadent Poor
12-4-73
Nighthouse Theatre
249 W. 18th, N.Y.C.

Pilgrim's Process
January, 1973
Academy Theatre
Atlanta, GA

Pilgrimage
Louis Phillips
5-28-71
Production Workshop Club
80 Second, N.Y.C.

Pilgrims Progress
Orlin & Irene Corey
4-24-73
Theatre of the Riverside Church
490 Riverside Dr., N.Y.C.

Pillar of Sand
Eric Nicol
2-19-73
National Arts Centre
Ottawa, Ontario, CAN

Pimp
Martha Boesing
Academy Theatre
Atlanta, GA

Pine Tree and the Elm, The (staged reading)
Neal Bell
12-17-72
Manhattan Theatre Club
321 E. 73rd, N.Y.C.

Pineapple White
Jon Shirota
9-20-73
East-West Players
Los Angeles, CA

Ping Pong Match, The
Ann Meltzer
10-27-72
New York Theatre Ensemble
2 E. 2nd, N.Y.C.

Pining Wind (dance, film, music)
5-12-73
Centrifugal Theatre
Clark Center for the Performing Arts
West Side YWCA, 8th Ave. & 51st, N.Y.C.

Pinion
W. B. Yeats, adapted by Donna Carlson
12-4-69
Thresholds
23 E. 20th, N.Y.C.

Pink String and Sealing Wax
8-19-73
Huron Country Playhouse
Grand Bend, Ontario, CAN

Pinkville
George Tabori
8-13-70
Berkshire Theatre Festival
Stockbridge, MA

Pinky (with Making It)
Jack Temchin
2-1-71
Old Reliable Theatre Tavern
231 E. 3rd, N.Y.C.

Pinocchio
John Wood
1970
Manitoba Theatre Centre
Winnipeg, Manitoba, CAN

Pinocchio and The Fire Eater's Traveling Puppet Theatre
Tom Campbell (book); Richard Bone (lyrics & music)
4-28-73
New York Conservatory of Theatre Arts
Chapel Theatre
73rd & Broadway, N.Y.C.

Pippin
Roger O. Hirson (book); Stephen Schwartz (lyric & music)
9-20-72
Opera House
Kennedy Center for the Performing Arts
Washington, DC

Pique-Nique en Campagne (with Guernica)
Fernando Arrabal
4-30-69
Barbizon-Plaza Theatre
N.Y.C.

Pirate, The
Cole Porter; adapted by Lawrence Kasha & Hayden Griffin
8-12-68
Bucks County Playhouse
New Hope, PA

Pitfall for a Rational Man (with Rehearsal and Parabus Objective)
Benjamin Bradford
3-17-72
Clarion State College
Clarion, PA

Place without Doors, A
Marguerite Duras
11-20-70
Long Wharf Theatre
New Haven, CT

Place without Mornings, A
Robert Koesis
1-10-72
Theatre de Lys
N.Y.C.

Placebo
Jeannine O'Reilly
11-30-71
WPA
333 Bowery, N.Y.C.

Placeless, The
Lance Belville
6-19-73
New Plays Festival
WPA
333 Bowery, N.Y.C.

Plagueship — Nine Days Out of Barbados
Alexander Panas
5-22-72
Library & Museum of the Performing Arts
111 Amsterdam, N.Y.C.

Plan, The
Stanley Nelson
12-26-69
New York Theatre Ensemble
2 E. 2nd, N.Y.C.

Plant That Talked Back, The (with Judah the Macabee and Me)
Gertrude Samuels
1-27-70
Lambs Theatre
130 W. 44th, N.Y.C.

Plaster
Laurence Aulson
3-23-69
Unit Theatre
157 W. 22nd, N.Y.C.

Play
Kirk Lovell
3-22-71
Assembly Theatre
113 Jane, N.Y.C.

Play by Aleksander Solzhenitsyn, A
Aleksander Solzhenitsyn
10-13-70
Tyrone Guthrie Theatre
Minneapolis, MN

Play House
Joseph Gath
12-10-71
Mercer Street Playhouse
240 Mercer, N.Y.C.

Play It Again, Sam
Woody Allen
1-9-69
National Theatre
Washington, DC

Play Mary Play
Roy Kift
5-19-73
"Y" La Mama Workshop
YM-YWHA of Mid-Westchester
Scarsdale, NY

Play of the Weather, The
John Heywood
1972
Worcester Polytechnic Institute
Worcester, MA

Play on the Times
12-19-69
New York Shakespeare Festival Public Theatre
425 Lafayette, N.Y.C.

Play One
Stuart Koch
4-18-69
Dramarena Repertory Theatre
158 W. 55th, N.Y.C.

Play Strindberg
Friedrich Duerrenmatt
6-3-71
Forum Theatre
Lincoln Center
N.Y.C.

Play with a Message, A
Guy Gauthier
2-23-72
Bastiano's Studio
14 Cooper Sq., N.Y.C.

Play Within, The (with Copout)
Helen Duberstein
4-27-73
New York Theatre Ensemble
2 E. 2nd, N.Y.C.

Playboy?
Edward Cope
6-4-71
Southwest Theatre Guild
Houston, TX

Playboy of Seville, or, Supper with a Statue, The
Tirso de Molina
4-8-71
Cubiculo
414 W. 51st, N.Y.C.

Play-by-Play
Robert Patrick
12-20-72
La Mama ETC
74 E. 4th, N.Y.C.

Player Piano, The (with When I Dyed My Hair in Venice)
Helen Duberstein
6-11-73
Theatre for the New City
113 Jane, N.Y.C.

Playful Tyrant, The
Al Carmines
10-18-70
Judson Poet's Theatre
55 Wash. Sq. So., N.Y.C.

Playground
Tony Giordano
1-7-71
Playbox
94 St. Mark's Pl., N.Y.C.

Playing with Dolls
Julian Anderson
6-3-70
La Mama ETC
74 E. 4th, N.Y.C.

Playpen, The (with Up the Hill)
Tom Topor
6-9-69
Extension Theatre
277 Park Ave. So., N.Y.C.

Plays and Counterplays
3-3-73
Little Theatre
West Side YMCA
5 W. 63rd, N.Y.C.

Playstreet
Ted Harris
2-1-73
Negro Ensemble Company
St. Mark's Playhouse
133 Second, N.Y.C.

Playwrights Horizons
See also: West Side YWCA

Plaza Suite
Neil Simon
1-17-68
Shubert Theatre
New Haven, CT

Please Don't Cry and Say 'No'
Townsend Brewster
12-6-72
Circle-in-the-Square
159 Bleecker, N.Y.C.

Please 7:52 We Love You (with The We Do It Agency and Hush! Hush!)
Peter DiLeo
5-8-71
PAWorkshop
353 Ave. of the Americas, N.Y.C.

Pleasure Palace
Sharon Abramhoff
4-28-71
Brandeis University
Waltham, MA

Pleasure Seekers '69, The
George Koch
7-4-69
Tentarena
East Monticello, NY

Pleasure Seekers '70, The
George Koch
7-3-70
Tentarena
East Monticello, NY

Pleasure Seekers '71, The
George Koch
7-9-71
Tentarena
Monticello, NY

Pleasure Seekers ('73) (with The Starmakers)
George Koch
8-17-73
Tentarena
Monticello, NY

Plebians Rehearse the Uprising, The
Gunther Grass
Summer, 1968
Theatre Company of Boston
Boston, MA

Plot Counter Plot
Michael Procaccino
11-26-71
St. Clement's Church
423 W. 46th, N.Y.C.

Plotters
Benjamin Bradford
2-3-72
University of Missouri
Columbia, MO

Ploy, The (with Ever After)
Wendy Levine
4-9-70
St. Peter's Church
346 W. 20th, N.Y.C.

Pocahontas (musical)
Fall, 1973
Performing Arts Repertory Theatre
N.Y.C.

Pocketful of Posies
Sidney Morris
11-14-68
Airline Theatre Wing
353 W. 57th, N.Y.C.

Poe
7-14-71
Organic Theatre
Chicago, IL

Poe
Stanley Nelson
6-19-72
Little Firehouse Theatre
Oradell, NJ

Poe Show, The (reading)
Donald Rember
11-14-73
Hotel Diplomat
108 W. 43rd, N.Y.C.

Poemarena (program using original poetry from the community)
Conceived by Ron Dener
11-16-72
Church of the Good Shepherd
240 E. 31st, N.Y.C.

Poet and the Pill, The
George Jonas
4-6-70
National Arts Centre School Tour
Ottawa, CAN

Poet's Papers, The
David Starkweather
3-17-71
Tufts University
Medford, MA

Poetic Suite on Arabs and Israelis
Glory Van Scott
6-12-69
New York Ethical Culture Society
2 W. 64th, N.Y.C.

Poetry Reading, The
Stanley Nelson
10-25-72
Playwright's Workshop Club
Bastiano's Studio
14 Cooper Square, N.Y.C.

Poison Tree, The
Ronald Ribman
7-23-73
Playhouse in the Park
Philadelphia, PA

Poisoned Arts Traveling Radio
12-15-71
Manhattan Theatre Club
321 E. 73rd, N.Y.C.

Polinka (with The Black Monk and Anyuta)
Anton Chekhov, James Monos (adaptor)
2-5-71
Carnegie Hall
881 Seventh, N.Y.C.

Polish Laboratory Theatre (Acropolis, The Constant Prince & Apocalypsis Cum Figuris)
10-16-69
Brooklyn Academy of Music
Brooklyn, NY

Pomp.E-11
Ching-Yeh
11-1-72
Ling Chi Ma Theatre Company
La Mama ETC
74 E. 4th, N.Y.C.

Ponca City
Sam LeBlanc
9-13-70
Mise en Scene
New Orleans, LA

Poochie
Lou Rodgers
1-15-71
Anthony Mannino Drama Tree
182 Fifth, N.Y.C.

Poof!
Gerald Schoenewolf
1-7-72
New York Theatre Ensemble
2 E. 2nd, N.Y.C.

Pool Hall of the Heart, The
Joseph B. Baldwin
9-28-72
CSC Repertory Theatre
89 W. 3rd, N.Y.C.

Poor Little Match Girl, The
Arthur Williams
12-22-68
Judson Poets' Theatre
55 Wash. Sq. So., N.Y.C.

Poor Old Fool (musical)
Stuart Grossman
10-11-73
Provincetown Playhouse
133 MacDougal, N.Y.C.

Pope Alexander VI — The Bull of the Borgias
Lawrence J. Crockett
5-4-73
Renaissance Players
Cathedral of St. John the Divine
112th & Amsterdam, N..Y.C.

Porcelain Time, The
Ron Cowen
7-14-72
Eugene O'Neill Memorial Theatre
Waterford, CT

Pork
Andy Warhol
5-5-71
La Mama ETC
74 E. 4th, N.Y.C.

Port Authority
Leonard Melfi
1-7-72
Playbox
94 St. Mark's Pl., N.Y.C.

Portable Circus, The (satirical group)
9-25-73
Lolly's Theatre Club
808 Lexington, N.Y.C.

Portrait in Modern Obscurity, A
Victor Kossoy, Carl Larsen, Terry Miller, Walter Tyszka
7-23-68
New Workshop Theatre
Brooklyn College
Brooklyn, NY

Portrait of a Queen
William Francis
2-28-68
Henry Miller's Theatre
N.Y.C.

Portrait of Timmy, A
Off Boston Theatre Co.
2-6-71
Boston University
Boston, MA

Portraits in Glass
Richard Hoag
8-22-68
Playwrights' Workshop Club
14 Waverly Pl., N.Y.C.

Possessed, The
Dostoyefsky; new version by Robert Montgomery
1-7-71
Yale Repertory Theatre
New Haven, CT

Possibilities
Arthur Pittman
12-4-68
Players Theatre
115 MacDougal, N.Y.C.

Possible World of Jean Kerr, The
Teddy Handfield
10-15-71
Catholic University
Washington, DC

Post Mortem
Robert Karmon
6-10-71
Assembly Theatre
113 Jane, N.Y.C.

Postcards
James Prideaux
3-9-70
Belasco Theatre
N.Y.C.

Postman, The (part of triple bill titled 3 by 3)
Edward L. Gold
5-1-71
Hunter College Theatre Program
West Side YMCA
5 W. 63rd, N.Y.C.

Postmortem (with Where Are You Going Hollis Jay?)
Benjamin Bradford
1-7-71
Theatre Crossroads
23 E. 20th, N.Y.C.

Postscript
Merritt Abrash
7-30-70
Berkshire Theatre Festival
Stockbridge, MA

Pot Luck
Charles Langdon & Paul Folwell
5-6-71
Changing Scene
Denver, CO

Potpourri
Children's Theatre Company of the Minneapolis Institute of Arts
6-18-72
Fourth World Congress & General Assembly of the International Association of Theatre for Children and Youth
Albany, NY

Potsy
Lee Baxandall
6-22-72
St. Peter's Church
346 W. 20th, N.Y.C.

Pottstown Carnival, The
Roma Greth
6-23-72
Manhattan Players
Atlantic City Playhouse
Atlantic City, NJ

Potty, The
Robert Somerfeld
1-28-71
Triangle Theatre
316 E. 88th, N.Y.C.

Power
Peter Copani (book & lyrics); David McHugh (music)
5-31-73
Peoples Performing Company
Playbox
94 St. Mark's Pl., N.Y.C.

Power Machine, The
Jean Richards
1-12-73
New York Theatre Ensemble
2 E. 2nd, N.Y.C.

Power to the People
Janet Bruders
7-15-71
Second Group Theatre
McBurney YMCA
215 W. 23rd, N.Y.C.

Practical Ritual to Exorcise Frustration After Five Days of Rain, A
David Starkweather
3-27-70
Circle Theatre
2307 Broadway, N.Y.C.

Practice Makes Perfect
Robert M. Olds
Spring, 1973
Brigham City Community Theatre
Brigham City, UT

Praguero, El
8-9-72
Street Theatre
630 E. 6th, N.Y.C.

Praise the Law and Pass the Erudition
3-16-73
Harvard University
Cambridge, MA

Praxeis (Tormenta, While the Dew Is Still on the Roses, and Inferiorities)
Theodore Barnes
10-4-71
Theatre for the New City
151 Bank, N.Y.C.

Precieux, Les
Eugene Labiche
5-11-73
Cercle Francais
La Maison Francaise
New York Univ., N.Y.C.

Preciose Por Ser Un Encanto Por Ser Un Eden (with Areyto)
Alfredo Matilla
11-18-71
El Teatro de Orilla
Riverside Church
122nd & Riverside Dr., N.Y.C.

Precious Blood
Blake Leach
4-19-73
CSC Repertory Company
89 W. 3rd, N.Y.C.

Prelude to Hamlet
Samuel Sussman
11-10-72
Salt City Playhouse
Warehouse Theatre
Syracuse, NY

Present for Billy Sturgill, A
Howard Allen
10-16-70
Studio 808
154 W. 57th, N.Y.C.

Present Tense (with 'Twas Brillig; Come Next Tuesday; So Please Be Kind)
Frank D. Gilroy
7-18-72
Sheridan Square Playhouse
99 Seventh Ave. So., N.Y.C.

Present, The
Vicky Mealon
11-5-70
Studio 808
154 W. 57th, N.Y.C.

President Is Dead, The
Paul Shyre
11-12-71
Chabot College Theatre
San Francisco, CA

President's Daughter, The
Jacob Jacobs (lyrics); H. Kalmanov (book); Murray Rumshinsky (music)
11-3-70
Billy Rose Theatre
208 W. 41st, N.Y.C.

President's Gang, The
Jerome Lawrence & Robert E. Lee
8-10-73
Orpheum Theatre
San Francisco, CA

Prestidigitator, The
John Quinn
6-22-73
Discontiguous Theater of Transparent Manipulation
98 Greene Street Loft
98 Green, N.Y.C.

Prettybelle
Bob Merrill (book & lyrics); Jule Styne (music)
2-1-71
Shubert Theatre
Boston, MA

Prevalence of Mrs. Seal, The
Otis Bigelow
5-9-73
Spingold Theatre
Brandeis University
Waltham, MA

Priapus
William Kushner
6-13-68
Theatre 13
201 W. 13th, N.Y.C.

Price of Life, The
David Korr
12-2-71
American Theatre Company
106 E. 14th, N.Y.C.

Price of Onions, The
See: Facades

Price, The
Arthur Miller
1-17-68
Walnut St. Theatre
Philadelphia, PA

Priest in the Cellar, The
Rev. James S. Conlan
2-18-69
Blackfriars' Guild
316 W. 57th, N.Y.C.

Prime of Miss Jean Brodie, The
Jay Allen
1-16-68
Helen Hayes Theatre
N.Y.C.

Primitive Wonder, The
Dennis Jasudowicz
5-25-72
Academy Theatre
Atlanta, GA

Primitives
8-8-69
Theatre Company
Sloane House YMCA
356 W. 34th, N.Y.C.

Prince Hamlet
Philip Freund
3-25-72
Trinity Presbyterian Church
422 W. 57th, N.Y.C.

Prince of Peasantmania, The
Frank Gagliano
July, 1968
Eugene O'Neill Memorial Theatre
Waterford, CT

Princess Ivona
Witold Gombrowicz; translation by Krystyna Griffith Jones & Catherine Robins
4-17-70
Florida Presbyterian College
St. Petersburg, FL

Prism City
David Garvin
10-25-72
Bastiano's Studio
14 Cooper Square, N.Y.C.

Prison Sounds (collage)
Summer, 1972
Street Theatre, Inc.,
Ossining, NY
Lincoln Center Plaza,
N.Y.C.

Prisoner of Second Avenue, The
Neil Simon
10-12-71
Shubert Theatre
New Haven, CT

Private Passion of Seymour Porno, The
Stephen H. Foreman
6-7-72
New Dramatists
424 W. 44th, N.Y.C.

Private Private
Douglas Wedel
6-3-68
Mark Taper Forum
Los Angeles, CA

Private Turvey's War (revised version of Turvey)
Donald Harron (book); Elaine Campbell & John Fenwick (lyrics); Norman Campbell (music)
8-17-70
Fathers of Confederation Memorial Centre
Charlottetown, Prince Edward Island, CAN

Prize in the Cracker Jack Box, The
William Parchman
July, 1968
Eugene O'Neill Memorial Theatre
Waterford, CT

Process Is the Product, The (with White on White)
6-5-69
Dallas Theatre Center
Dallas, TX

Prodigal
10-13-70
Wagner College
Circle Theatre Company
2307 Broadway, N.Y.C.

Prodigal Daughter, The
David Turner
11-6-73
Eisenhower Theatre
Washington, DC

Prodigal Daughter, The
J. E. Franklin
8-21-71
Everyman Company
Lincoln Center Plaza
N.Y.C.

Prodigal in Black Stone
Lennox Brown
7-18-72
Eugene O'Neill Memorial Theatre
Waterford, CT

Professor Filarsky's Miraculous Invention
7-16-69
Arena Theatre
Albany, NY

Professor George
Marsha Sheiness
7-21-72
Eugene O'Neill Memorial Theatre
Waterford, CT

Progerian, The
Dallas Mayr
5-12-72
New York Theatre Ensemble
2 E. 2nd, N.Y.C.

Progress May Have Been All Right Once. . .
Ogden Nash
4-3-71
New Theatre Workshop
Stage 73
321 E. 73rd, N.Y.C.

Project III: Is Law in Order?
Paul Baker
11-25-69
Dallas Theatre Center
Dallas, TX

Project Omega: Lillian
Corinne Jacker
7-22, 23-71
Eugene O'Neill Memorial Theatre
Waterford, CT

Projection Room (with Respite and There Once Was a Hermit Named Dave)
Robert Somerfeld
10-17-68
Triangle Theatre
316 E. 88th, N.Y.C.

Promenade All
David V. Robison
6-30-71
Berkshire Theatre Festival
Stockbridge, MA

Prometheus and Pandora (with Macedonian Rag)
Gerry Giss
5-27-71
University of Montana
Missoula, MT

Prometheus Bound
Jerome Wheeler
1-9-71
University of Missouri
Columbia, MO

Prometheus (dramatic reading)
Clyde Ellsworth
4-8-70
Mainstream Theatre-Loft
20 E. 14th, N.Y.C.

Promises, Promises
Neil Simon, Burt Bacharach (music), Hal David (lyrics)
10-7-68
Colonial Theatre
Boston, MA

Promises To Keep
Robert Clapsadle
8-5-70
Assembly Theatre
113 Jane, N.Y.C.

Promoter, The
Ron Mele
12-17-70
Columbia School of the Arts
440 W. 110th, N.Y.C.

Prompter
Harvey Zuckerman
11-24-72
New York Theatre Ensemble
2 E. 2nd, N.Y.C.

Properly Introduced
Michael Koslow
11-9-69
Extension Theatre
277 Park Ave. So., N.Y.C.

Prophet, The
Bruce Thompson
10-22-70
Changing Scene
Denver, CO

Props, Interference
Bob Randall
11-7-70
New Theatre Workshop
154 E. 54th, N.Y.C.

Prosperall Rising!
Roderic Mason Faber
6-18-71
Theatre for the New City
151 Bank, N.Y.C.

Psalms of Two Davids
3-22-73
Loeb Drama Center
Cambridge, MA

Psych
Tony Vozzo
6-11-71
Spencer Memorial Church
99 Clinton, Brooklyn, NY

Psychiatrists, The
Ed Rombola
5-24-71
Library & Museum of the Performing Arts
111 Amsterdam, N.Y.C.

Psychic Pretenders, The
12-29-71
New Lafayette Theatre
137th & 7th, N.Y.C.

Psychlotron, The
Gene Borio
5-8-70
Stage 9
96 W. Houston, N.Y.C.

Public Prosecutor Is Sick of It All, A
Max Frisch
1-26-73
Arena Stage
Washington, DC

Pueblo
Stanley R. Greenburg
3-3-71
Arena Stage
Washington, DC

Puerto Rican Obituary
Pedro Pietri
11-18-71
El Teatro de Orilla
Riverside Church
122nd & Riverside Dr., N.Y.C.

Pumpkin
Richard Dotterer
6-1-72
Jacksonville University
Jacksonville, FL

Punch and Judas
Paul Lion
12-3-70
New York University
N.Y.C.

Punch and Judy in "A Revenge Play"
10-7-69
Mark Taper Forum
Los Angeles, CA

Pupe Puppets (with The Good Seed)
Ralph Accardo
12-13-68
Stage 9
96 W. Houston, N.Y.C.

Puppet Pusher, The
Patricia Horan
11-7-70
American Theatre Company
Alice's Studio
106 E. 14th, N.Y.C.

Puppets
James Shearwood
11-1-70
Dancers Studio Foundation
34 E. 10th, N.Y.C.

Puppy Love (with The Star Is Always Loved and Loved)
Peter Copani
5-15-68
Playbox
94 St. Mark's Pl., N.Y.C.

Pure Force Exhibit (electronic song and sound presentation)
8-2-72
State University of New York
Stony Brook, Long Island, NY

Pure Red
Grant Duay
1-3-69
New York Theatre Ensemble
2 E. 2nd, N.Y.C.

Purity
David Mowat
3-17-72
CSC Repertory Theatre
89 W. 3rd, N.Y.C.

Purlie
Davis-Roe-Udell (book); Peter Udell (lyrics); Gary Geld (music)
3-15-70
Broadway Theatre
N.Y.C.

Purple Heart
John Giorno
7-26-68
Fairleigh Dickinson University
Madison, NJ

Pursuit (with Fair Exchange)
Edmond Reynolds
11-11-69
Loyola University
Los Angeles, CA

Pushover
Jeff Weiss
11-7-73
La Mama ETC
74 E. 4th, N.Y.C.

Pussy, The (with The Button and Chekhov's Grandmother)
Michael McClure
12-20-73
Theatre Genesis
2nd Ave. & 10th, N.Y.C.

Put on Your Potato Jacket
Sam Smiley
Feb., 1970
University of Missouri
Columbia, MO

Pzazz '70 and All That Jazz, Baby
Donn Arden
July, 1969
Desert Inn
Las Vegas, NV

Q

Quad
Merrill Harris
2-18-70
La Mama ETC
74 E. 4th, N.Y.C.

Quarter for Sad Sackbut and Swallows
Roland Dubillard; J. Vincent Smith (adaptor)
4-14-73
Players Repertory Theatre
Miami, FL

Quarter for the Ladies Room, A
Ruth Batchelor (book & lyrics); John Clifton & Arthur Siegel (music)
11-12-72
Village Gate
160 Bleecker, N.Y.C.

Queen and Her Estates, The
Andrew Howard Jones
8-22-68
Spanish-English Theatre Arts School
219 E. 109th, N.Y.C.

Queen Can Lay Eggs, A
Robert S. Ross
July, 1970
Eugene O'Neill Memorial Theatre
Waterford, CT

Queen from Fire Island, The (later changed to The Count from Fire Island)
Spring, 1972
Greenwich Village Young Professionals
Boston Center for the Arts
Boston, MA

Queen of Cambia, The
Henry C. Timm (book); Barry Harwood (music)
5-13-71
Wheelock College Theatre
Boston, MA

Queen of Greece
Ronald Tavel
11-2-73
Theatre Genesis
2nd Ave. & 10th, N.Y.C.

Queen of Greece, The (with Homo)
Rochelle Owens
4-11-69
La Mama ETC
74 E. 4th, N.Y.C.

Queenside
C. Bishop & R. Skrentny
Summer, 1973
Milwaukee Repertory Theater Company
Milwaukee, WI

Questioning of Nick, The
Arthur Kopit
12-28-73
Stage 73
321 E. 73rd, N.Y.C.

Questions, The
John Hawkes
1-14-72
Players' Workshop
83 E. 4th, N.Y.C.

Quick Nut Bread To Make Your Mouth Water, A
William H. Hoffman
7-6-70
Old Reliable Theatre Tavern
231 E. 3rd, N.Y.C.

Quickie
Harvey Zuckerman
5-25-73
New York Theatre Ensemble
2 E. 2nd, N.Y.C.

Quiet in the Balcony (They Were Dependable; Jack Highstrung, All American; Taboo and the Princess from Popular Mechanics)
Larry O'Connel
4-1-71
Second Group Theatre
McBurney YMCA
215 W. 23rd, N.Y.C.

Quiet Sunday (with Jewelry of the Dead)
Glover Buck
July, 1968
Nucleus Repertory Theatre
261 W. 54th, N.Y.C.

Quietus (with The Funny Men Are in Trouble)
Paul John Austin
11-20-72
St. Clement's Church
423 W. 46th, N.Y.C.

Quoat, Quoat
Jacques Audiberti
4-13-69
Barbizon-Plaza Theatre
N.Y.C.

Quotations from Our Chairman, Mark Rudd
1969
Emerson College
Boston, MA

R

R. J. (A Musical Fable)
Jill Williams (book, lyrics, & music)
10-9-73
American Theatre
Washington, DC

Rabbits
Anna Belle Johnson
5-9-69
Anthony Mannino Drama Tree
182 Fifth, N.Y.C.

Rabbits Instead of Flowers
Jack Temchin
3-21-70
New Theatre Workshop
154 E. 54th, N.Y.C.

Rabelais
Jean-Louis Barrault, Compagnie Renaud-Barrault
5-11-70
Los Angeles Music Center
Los Angeles, CA

Rabinowitz Gambit, The
Rose Leiman Goldenberg
4-17-71
New Theatre Workshop
154 E. 54th, N.Y.C.

Race
Michal Kressy
2-21-69
New York Theatre Ensemble
2 E. 2nd, N.Y.C.

Rachael Lily Rosenbloom
Paul Jabara (book, lyrics & music)
11-26-73
Broadhurst Theatre
235 W. 44th, N.Y.C.

Rachel's Commitment
6-2-72
Harwich Winter Theatre
West Harwich, MA

Rafferty One by One
Rolf Fjelde
July, 1970
Eugene O'Neill Memorial Theatre
Waterford, CT

Rag Doll, The
Allen Davis
4-4-70
New Dramatists Workshop
424 W. 44th, N.Y.C.

Rage Over the Lost Beethoven (multi-media presentation)
Frank Parman (text); Lejaren Hiller (music)
2-19-72
State University of New York
Buffalo, NY

Rageous Comedy for Gruntled People, A
7-17-69
University of Rochester Summer Theatre
Rochester, NY

Rags
Wayne Sheridan (book & lyrics); George Koch (music)
4-26-69
Barbizon-Plaza Theatre
N.Y.C.

Rags
4-25-69
La Mama ETC
74 E. 4th, N.Y.C.

Rags
1-9-68
13th Street Theatre
50 W. 13th, N.Y.C.

Rags and Old Iron (with On the Road)
Tony Preston
2-22-72
Theatre of the Riverside Church
490 Riverside Drive, N.Y.C.

Ragtime Years, The
Max Morath
Winter, 1973
Denver, CO

Rain
Somerset Maugham; adapted and with music by Ron Link
4-24-70
Extension Theatre
277 Park Ave. So., N.Y.C.

Rainbow
James Rado (book, music, & lyrics); Ted Rado (book)
12-18-72
Orpheum Theatre
126 Second, N.Y.C.

Rainbow Jones
See: R. J.

Rainbow Sign, The
Louis E. Catron
4-28-71
College of William and Mary
Williamsburg, VA

Rainbows for Sale
John Ford Noonan
9-15-69
Old Reliable Theatre Tavern
231 E. 3rd, N.Y.C.

Raisin
Charlotte Zaltzberg & Robert Nemiroff (book); Robert Brittan (lyrics); Judd Woldin (music)
5-29-73
Arena Stage
Washington, DC

Rameses
6-12-70
Amphitheatre
Kentucky Lake State Park
Kentucky Lake, KY

Random Violence
Jane Chambers
5-17-73
Women's Interart Center
549 W. 52nd, N.Y.C.

Raoul Behind the Bush
Ron Mele
1968
New York Theatre Ensemble
2 E. 2nd, N.Y.C.

Rape, The
Newton Berry
1-17-69
New York Theatre Ensemble
2 E. 2nd, N.Y.C.

Rapes
Mario Fratti
12-20-72
Playwrights' Workshop Club
Bastiano's Studio
14 Cooper Square, N.Y.C.

Rapists, The
Dennis G. Turner
11-2-72
Washington Theatre Club
Washington, DC

Rare Find Towne
4-2-70
Dock Street Theatre
Charleston, SC

Raree Show, The
9-7-72
Four Winds Theatre
Federal Hall
Pine & Nassau Sts., N.Y.C.

Rashomon
Runosuke Akutagawa; Christopher Martin (adaptor)
4-14-73
CSC Repertory Company
89 W. 3rd, N.Y.C.

Raspberries
6-10-70
Cooperative Theatre
106 E. 14th, N.Y.C.

Rasputin
Lance Lee
7-19-69
Eugene O'Neill Memorial Theatre
Waterford, CT

Rat Wife, The (adapted from Little Eyolf)
Henrik Ibsen; adapted by Buzz Podewell
12-1-72
New York University
N.Y.C.

Rate of Exchange
Milo Thomas
4-1-68
Players Theatre
113 MacDougal, N.Y.C.

Rats — A Rondo for Rodents
Robert Swerdlow
Spring, 1972
St. Lawrence Arts Centre
Toronto, Ontario, CAN

Rats, The
Agatha Christie
12-22-73
Showcase East
251 E. 50th, N.Y.C.

Raven Rock, The
Leonard Melfi
3-28-69
Nassau Community College
Garden City, L.I., NY

Raw Guts and American Know-How
10-23-70
Old Reliable Theatre Tavern
231 E. 3rd, N.Y.C.

Raz Na Wesolo (Polish Actors' Ensemble)
11-9-73
John Hancock Hall
Boston, MA

Reach Out
12-19-69
Hudson Guild Theatre
441 W. 26th, N.Y.C.

Readings from Vietnam (with Charlotte of the City. . .)
Eric Goldman
6-4-71
Assembly Theatre
113 Jane, N.Y.C.

Ready on the Right (with That's the Ball Game)
Carlo Grasso
2-21-69
Nucleus Repertory Theatre
261 W. 54th, N.Y.C.

Real Inspector Hound, The
Tom Stoppard
1-16-70
Emerson College
Beacon St., Boston, MA

Real Reel
Frederic Baal
4-14-71
La Mama ETC
74 E. 4th, N.Y.C.

Reality: An Absurdist Entertainment
James Rosenfield
5-21-70
Changing Scene
Denver, CO

Rebbitzen from Israel, The
Pesach Burstein (book); Lili Amber (lyrics & music)
10-10-72
Mayfair Theatre
235 W. 46th, N.Y.C.

Recantation of Galileo Galilei, The
Eric Bentley
Fall, 1973
Wayne State University
Detroit, MI

Recent Killing, A
Imamu Amiri Baraka (LeRoi Jones)
1-26-73
New Federal Theatre
240 E. 3rd, N.Y.C.

Recess
Dolores Walker & Andrew Piotrowski
3-20-68
La Mama ETC
122 Second, N.Y.C.

Reckoning, The
Douglas Turner Ward
9-4-69
Negro Ensemble Company
St. Mark's Playhouse
133 Second, N.Y.C.

Recoil
5-17-72
Massachusetts Institute of Technology
Cambridge, MA

Recollections of a Civilized Man
Dennis E. Noble
6-1-72
Jacksonville University
Jacksonville, FL

Reconciliation
Ellen Nickolas
12-17-69
American Theatre Company
Alice's Studio
106 E. 14th, N.Y.C.

Reconstruction of Oliver Jones, The
Chris Assini
8-16-68
Cooper Square Arts Theatre
35 Cooper Sq., N.Y.C.

Recovery and Adjustment
Albert Baumel
5-24-71
Old Reliable Theatre Tavern
231 E. 3rd, N.Y.C.

Recuerdos De Tulipa
Manuel Reguera Saumell
8-27-70
Henry Street Settlement House
466 Grand, N.Y.C.

Red
Jules Renard; adapted by Stewart H. Benedict
5-12-72
Playbox
94 St. Mark's Pl., N.Y.C.

Red Burning Light of the American Way of Life, The (with A Vietnamese Wedding)
Maria Irene Fornes
4-12-69
La Mama ETC
74 E. 4th,
N.Y.C.

Red Convertible, The
Enrique Buenaventura, Antony Sampson (translator)
7-27-71
Stratford Festival
Stratford, Ontario, CAN

Red Hat, The
Maureen Martin
2-23-72
Blackfriars' Guild
316 W. 57th, N.Y.C.

Red Horse Animation, The
Lee Breuer
11-18-70
Guggenheim Museum
1071 Fifth, N.Y.C.

Red Lips (with Stalin)
Ed Wode
12-2-70
Free Store Theatre
14 Cooper Sq., N.Y.C.

Red Pumps, The
Jeannine O'Reilly
12-1-72
WPA
333 Bowery, N.Y.C.

Red Raspberry Revue, The
Cash Baxter, Herb Buchanan, George Schneider, Art Weller, Gene Raskin
6-15-71
Windmill Dinner Theatre
Houston, TX

Red's My Color, What's Yours?
Norman Wexler
3-18-70
Cleveland Playhouse
Cleveland, OH

Red, the White, and the Black, The
Eric Bentley
2-24-71
La Mama ETC
74 E. 4th, N.Y.C.

Red, White, and Maddox
Jay Broad and Don Tucker
10-3-68
Theater Atlanta
Atlanta, GA

Redemption Center
Ron Cowen
July, 1968
Eugene O'Neill Memorial Theatre
Waterford, CT

Redhead (part, along with Genet's Maids, of a double bill called Sweet Asylum)
4-17-72
Theatre Two
Cambridge, MA

Reety in Hell
Stephen Holt (book & lyrics); Donald Harrington (music)
5-8-73
WPA
333 Bowery, N.Y.C.

Reflection, Reflection
David Morgan
7-9-72
Hunter College Summer Repertory Theatre
695 Park Ave., N.Y.C.

Reflections
Patricia Cooper
4-13-69
Loft Workshop
152 Bleecker, N.Y.C.

Reflections
The Third World Revelationists
8-13-70
New Federal Theatre
292 Henry, N.Y.C.

Reflections/Void
Nov., 1971
Stage 1
Boston Center for the Arts
Boston, MA

Refractions
Caleb Smith
2-8-69
Cans Underground Theatre
322 W. 55th, N.Y.C.

Refrigerators, The
Mario Fratti
1-27-71
La Mama ETC
74 E. 4th, N.Y.C.

Refugees
Donald Kvares
2-11-72
New York Theatre Ensemble
2 E. 2nd, N.Y.C.

Reg'lar Miss America, A
Bernice Lee
5-25-73
Omni Theatre Club
145 W. 18th, N.Y.C.

Regeneration
Beverlee Galli
7-16-71
Omni Theatre Club
145 W. 18th, N.Y.C.

Rehearsal for Death
George Batson
2-9-73
West Side Gay Theatre
W.S.D.G. Center
37 Ninth, N.Y.C.

Rehearsal (with Pitfall for a Rational Man and Parabus Objective)
Benjamin Bradford
3-17-72
Clarion State College
Clarion, PA

Relations
Lynne Honickman
5-6-71
Cubiculo
414 W. 51st, N.Y.C.

Relationships and Other Mistakes
Paul Pierog
4-14-72
New York Theatre Ensemble
2 E. 2nd, N.Y.C.

Relationships of Man (dramatic reading)
1-13-72
Lyric Players
St. George Library Center
Staten Island, NY

Relatively Speaking
Alan Ayckbourn
6-29-70
Gilford Playhouse
Gilford, NH

Relentless Smile, The
Geraldine Wall
2-3-72
New York University
Bronx, NY

Religion
Al Carmines
10-26-73
Judson Poets' Theatre
55 Wash. Sq. So., N.Y.C.

Religion and Politics: Two Farces
Ricardo Castillo
12-9-71
New York Theatre of the Americas
321 E. 73rd, N.Y.C.

Religious Spectacle of Atlantis
Jack Smith
4-18-70
Reptilian Theatrical Company
Plaster Foundation
36 Greene, N.Y.C.

Reliquary of Mr. and Mrs. Potterfield, The
Stephen H. Foreman
10-19-71
Chelsea Theatre Center
30 Lafayette Ave., Brooklyn, NY

Relitivity's Track
Berman Venet
5-27-68
Judson Poet's Theatre
55 Wash. Sq. So., N.Y.C.

Remains of Carter Simpson, The
Randolph O'Donnell
12-11-69
Drawing Room Drama Workshop
155 Second, N.Y.C.

Remaking of Audience, The
Robert Karmon
4-24-68
Extension Theatre
128 E. 7th, N.Y.C.

Remember Me!
Ronald Alexander
7-24-72
Lakewood Playhouse
Skowhegan, ME

Remember the Alamo
Barry Litvack
1-19-70
American Place Theatre
N.Y.C.

Remolienda, La
1-10-68
University of California
Riverside, CA

Remote Asylum
Mart Crowley
12-1-70
Center Theatre Group
Ahmanson Th.
Los Angeles, CA

Removalists, The
David Williamson
10-26-73
Cleveland Playhouse
Cleveland, OH

Rendezvous
James Monos, adapted from Anton Chekhov
4-3-69
Universalist Theatre
4 W. 76th, N.Y.C.

Rendezvous
Keith Engar & Crawford Gates
4-25-68
University of Utah
Salt Lake City, UT

Rendezvous (La Chasse)
Georges Feydeau; Frederick Mullett (translator); Jon Jory (adaptor)
Nov., 1973
Actors Theatre
Louisville, KY

Rendezvous (with Anyuta, Paraffin, and Polinka)
Anton Chekhov; adapted by James Monos
6-12-72
Circle Theatre
2307 Broadway, N.Y.C.

Renegade in Retrospect
Frank Parman
Fall, 1971
Theatre Passe Muraille
Toronto, Ontario, CAN

Report Here
Jean Maljean
3-6-70
Hudson Guild Theatre
441 W. 26th, N.Y.C.

Report on the State of the Hudson, A
Lee Hays
5-9-70
Cafe Hey Brother
144 W. 90th, N.Y.C.

Report to an Academy, A
Franz Kafka
4-16-69
Venture Theatre Club
145 Eighth, N.Y.C.

Report (with Football and Bellymass), The
Jon Swan
11-14-68
Seattle Repertory Theatre
Seattle, WA

Republic, The
Ed Wode; music by Carman Moore
4-27-70
Free Store Theatre
14 Cooper Sq., N.Y.C.

Requiem for a Junkie
James Garfield Storey
5-31-72
York College Black Students Players
Jamaica Jewish Center
Jamaica, NY

Requiem for a Play (reading)
William Kranz
11-11-68
Playwrights' Workshop Club
14 Waverly Pl., N.Y.C.

Requiem for Brother X
William Wellington Mackey
1-5-73
Players' Workshop
83 E. 4th, N.Y.C.

Requiem Por Yarini
Carlos Felipe
9-25-72
Compania Repertorio Dume
Library & Museum of the Performing Arts
111 Amsterdam, N.Y.C.

Requiem/A Celebration
The Intense Family
6-9-71
Cubiculo
414 W. 51st, N.Y.C.

Re-Run (with Welcome Home, Joe)
Delano Stewart
10-12-73
Bed-Stuy Theatre
Brooklyn, NY

Respects
Jerry Spindel
7-22-71
Eugene O'Neill Memorial Theatre
Waterford, CT

Respite (with Projection Room and There Once Was a Hermit Named Dave)
Robert Somerfeld
10-17-68
Triangle Theatre
316 E. 88th, N.Y.C.

Responsive Scene
11-19-71
Manhattan Theatre Club
321 E. 73rd, N.Y.C.

Restaurant
Dan Greenburg
Oct., 1970
Yale University
New Haven, CT

Restaurant, The
Thomas Terefenko
4-14-69
Old Reliable Theatre Tavern
231 E. 3rd, N.Y.C.

Restoration of Arnold Middleton, The
David Storey
8-10-72
Circle Theatre
2307 Broadway, N.Y.C.

Return of Colorado Girl (with Mostly on the Morning Ceiling)
Robert Clapsadle
2-19-71
Assembly Theatre
113 Jane, N.Y.C.

Return of Peggy Atherton, The
Malcolm Stewart
8-22-72
Boothbay Playhouse
Boothbay, ME

Return of the Guru, The
Stuart Koch
2-2-70
Old Reliable Theatre Tavern
231 E. 3rd, N.Y.C.

Return of the Phoenix, The (Chinese musical fantasy)
Tisa Chang
7-5-73
La Mama ETC
74 E. 4th, N.Y.C.

Return, The
Guy Parker
5-15-72
Manhattan Theatre Club
321 E. 73rd, N.Y.C.

Reunion
11-30-73
Academy Theatre
Atlanta, GA

Reunion Among Ruins
David Kerry Heefner
5-12-72
New York Theatre Ensemble
2 E. 2nd, N.Y.C.

Reunion of Sorts
Mary Drahos
10-14-69
Blackfriars' Guild
316 W. 57th, N.Y.C.

Reunion: School of Byrds, Class of 1970
Michael Sckoloff
Dec., 1971
Center for the New Performing Art
Iowa City, IA

Reunion, The
John Hartnett
2-2-70
Old Reliable Theatre Tavern
231 E. 3rd, N.Y.C.

Reunion, The (part of Hits, Bits and Skits)
Lee Hunkins
1-21-72
West Side YWCA
8th & 51st, N.Y.C.

Rev. Brown's Daughter
Walter Jones
11-1-73
La Mama ETC
74 E. 4th, N.Y.C.

Revelation of John the Divine, The
Susanne Elyse
9-24-71
Zeta Theatre
30th & Lexington, N.Y.C.

Reverend Ferdinand and Bessie Mae
Nat White
3-15-71
Old Reliable Theatre Tavern
231 E. 3rd, N.Y.C.

Revolt in the Leper Colony (with Sylvia)
Sheldon Cholst
4-13-73
New York Theatre Ensemble
2 E. 2nd, N.Y.C.

Revolting Theatre, The
6-28-69
Washington Square Church
135 W. 4th, N.Y.C.

Revolucion, La
Isaac Chochron
October, 1971
New York Theatre of the Americas
427 W. 59th, N.Y.C.

Revolution
Jonn Sillings
11-3-69
C. W. Post College
Greenvale, NY

Revolution
Archie Shepp
5-19-68
Olatunji Center of African Culture
43 E. 125th, N.Y.C.

Revolution in a Teacup
Rosemary Ingham
4-20-72
University of Montana
Missoula, MT

Revolution Starts Inside, The
Martin Robbins
4-24-70
Northeastern University
Boston, MA

Revolution, The (with Solitude and Frenzy) (reading)
Tobi Louis
4-22-73
New York Cultural Center
2 Columbus Circle, N.Y.C.

Revolutionaires Don't Sit in the Orchestra
Gloria Gonzalez
2-2-73
Omni Theatre Club
145 W. 18th, N.Y.C.

Revue at Moon, The
Summer, 1972
East Hampton, Long Island, NY

Revue, The
Avery Corman, Edward Kleban, Bobby Paul, Dan Greenberg, Edward Pomerantz
10-19-72
Manhattan Theatre Club
321 E. 73rd, N.Y.C.

Reward, The
Jerry Fine
7-12-73
Changing Scene
Denver, CO

Rhesus Umbrella, The
Jeff Wanshel
4-2-70
Yale University
New Haven, CT

Rhubarb and Roses
Omar Paxon
1969
Occidental College
Los Angeles, CA

Rhythm of Violence
Lewis Nkosi
12-14-72
Brooklyn College
Brooklyn, NY

Rice Balls
Fragrant Shoes
10-16-71
New York University
N.Y.C.

Richard's Cork Leg
Brendan Behan
10-10-73
Krannert Center for the Performing Arts
University of Illinois Theatre
Urbana-Champaign, IL

Richard Third Time
Steven Bush & Rick McKenna
Fall, 1973
Toronto Workshop
Toronto, CAN

Richman's Follies Burlesque '72
8-16-72
Meadowbrook Theatre Restaurant
Cedar Grove, NJ

Riddle of the Palm Leaf, The (with Crocodiles)
Femi Euba
2-6-73
Negro Ensemble Company
St. Mark's Playhouse
133 Second, N.Y.C.

Ride a Black Horse
John Scott
July, 1970
Eugene O'Neill Memorial Theatre
Waterford, CT

Ride Across Lake Constance, The
Peter Handke; translation by Michael Roloff
1-13-72
Forum Theatre
Lincoln Center
N.Y.C.

Ride Over Them with Love
Pamela Hawthorn & Hutchison Shandro
1969-70
Playhouse Theatre Company
Vancouver, CAN

Ride, The
Raymond Gentry
4-24-70
Theatre in the Loft
8 Waverly Pl., N.Y.C.

Ridiculous Young Ladies, The (Preciosity Ridiculed)
Moliere; Josef Bush (adaptor)
11-26-71
WPA
333 Bowery, N.Y.C.

Rifiuto, Il
Mario Fratti
6-14-72
Cubiculo
414 W. 51st, N.Y.C.

Right On! Dope Is Death
Vance Amaker
9-19-70
Martin Luther King Jr. Memorial Theatre
Ninth Ave. at 27th St., N.Y.C.

Ring Around the Bathtub
Jane Trahey
12-3-70
Alley Theatre
709 Berry St., N.Y.C.

Ring Around the Rosy
Edward Greenberg
Dec., 1971
New Dramatists
424 W. 44th, N.Y.C.

Ring-A-Levio (musical)
Donald Ross (book); Jason Darrow (lyrics); Lance Mulcahy (music)
1-4-73
Studio Arena Theatre
Buffalo, NY

Riot
January, 1968
Arlington St. Church
Boston, MA

Rise and Decline of the Birdbrain Dinosaur, The
Rose Sher
3-12-71
New York Theatre Ensemble
2 E. 2nd, N.Y.C.

Rise and Fall of the Usurous Shylock, The
Leonard Pailet
4-5-70
Whitman College
Walla Walla, WA

Rising Yeast, The (with Madam Mushroom) (dramatic reading)
Michael Mathias
4-22-70
Mainstream Theatre
20 E. 14th, N.Y.C.

Rite for Bedtime, A (with Bunny Boy)
Wallace Hamilton
8-20-71
Omni Theatre Club
145 W. 18th, N.Y.C.

Rite On
Imogunla Alakoye
3-4-73
Frederick Douglass Creative Arts Center
Salem United Methodist Church
2190 Seventh Ave. at 129th, N.Y.C.

Rites II
Joseph Gifford
Fall, 1969
Boston University
Boston, MA

Rite(s) On! Rite of Spring
Stanley Nelson
5-20-71
WPA
333 Bowery, N.Y.C.

Ritomagiadanza
Alejandra Dondines
3-17-72
Extension Theatre
277 Park Ave. So., N.Y.C.

Rivals, The (musical)
Richard Brimsley Sheridan
11-8-68
1010 Players
Park Ave. at 85th, N.Y.C.

River Kids
Roberta Rosenthal & Randy Buck
11-13-70
Lexington High School Auditorium
Lexington, MA

River Niger, The
Joseph A. Walker
11-28-72
Negro Ensemble Company
St. Mark's Playhouse
133 Second, N.Y.C.

Road from Ithaca, The
Stephen Sweeney
4-13-71
University of Massachusetts
Boston, MA

Road Where the Wolves Run, A
Claris Nelson
11-26-72
Circle Theatre Company
2307 Broadway, N.Y.C.

Roar Shock
Christopher Matthewson
5-17-73
Cubiculo
414 W. 51st, N.Y.C.

Roaring Good Time, A
Johann Nestroy, translated by Corliss Phillabaum
3-13-69
University of Wisconsin-Milwaukee
Milwaukee, WI

Robbers' Nest (with Dialectic Dialogue in Double Time and Close Call)
Barry Litvack
10-28-70
Playwrights' Unit
83 E. 4th, N.Y.C.

Robert Benchley's Locomotive
William Van Gieson
6-19-73
New Plays Festival
WPA
333 Bowery, N.Y.C.

Robert Bliss Show, The
Robert Patrick
3-28-69
New York Theatre Ensemble
2 E. 2nd, N.Y.C.

Robert Frost, with Rhyme and Reason
11-28-73
Open Eye
78 Fifth, N.Y.C.

Roberta Flack Fan Club, The
Hal Craven
2-11-72
New York Theatre Ensemble
2 E. 2nd, N.Y.C.

Robespierre's Woman
Eric Thompson
2-4-71
Paperback Studio
80 Second, N.Y.C.

Robin Hood
Sharon O'Brien; Fred Palmisano (music)
January, 1973
Le Petit Theatre
New Orleans, LA

Rock (musical) (showcase production)
Ron Campbell & Stan Trogen
10-16-73
Black Renaissance Company
Playbox
94 St. Mark's Pl., N.Y.C.

Rock the World
Louise Heck Naughton
11-28-73
Theatre 77 Repertory
23 E. 20th, N.Y.C.

Rockefeller and the Red Indians
Ray Galton & Alan Simpson
9-16-68
Colonial Theatre
Boston, MA

Rocker, The
Richard Wilson Hayes
6-5-68
Playbox
94 St. Mark's Pl., N.Y.C.

Rococo Joker (with Lifestring)
James Eliason
Summer, 1972
Bronx Experimental Theatre
Vandam Theatre
15 Vandam, N.Y.C.

Roger and Arlene — A Premarital Farce
Bruce Berkow
6-30-72
New York Theatre Ensemble
2 E. 2nd, N.Y.C.

Rogues' Trial, The
Ariano Suassuna
11-8-73
Loeb Drama Center
Cambridge, MA

Roman Circus
Tom LaBar
3-27-70
St. Clement's Church
423 W. 46th, N.Y.C.

Roman Conquest
John Patrick
8-22-73
Baldwin-Wallace College
Berea, OH

Romania That's the Old Country
Allen Joseph
12-13-68
New York Shakespeare Festival
Public Theatre
425 Lafayette, N.Y.C.

Romantic Age of Elizabeth Barrett Browning, The
(One-woman show with Joan Fontaine)
8-9-73
John Drew Theatre
East Hampton, L.I., NY

Rome, Rome
Louis Guss
11-5-71
Cubiculo
414 W. 51st, N.Y.C.

Ronde, La (new version)
Arthur Schnitzler
10-4-68
Rising Sun Theatre
344 W. 36th, N.Y.C.

Rondelay
Hal Jordan (music); Jerry Douglas (book & lyrics)
11-5-69
Hudson West Theatre
353 W. 57th, N.Y.C.

Rooftop (with Marlene's Choice)
Phillip Agree
2-11-72
13th Street Theatre
50 W. 13th, N.Y.C.

Rook, The
Lawrence Osgood
Spring, 1970
University of Michigan
Ann Arbor, MI

Room A
Vernon Jordan
12-6-73
Playwrights' Workshop Club
Electric Circus
23 St. Mark's Pl., N.Y.C.

Room for One Woman
S. J. Bergman
2-22-73
Loeb Drama Center
Cambridge, MA

Room 47 (staged reading)
Arnold Meyers
10-22-72
Manhattan Theatre Club
321 E. 73rd, N.Y.C.

Roomers
Peter Gorman
5-7-73
Library & Museum of the Performing Arts
111 Amsterdam, N.Y.C.

Roommates, The
M. J. Bevans
3-20-72
Manhattan Theatre Club
321 E. 73rd, N.Y.C.

Roommates (with Hung)
Thomas Martin
2-16-68
La Mama ETC
122 Second, N.Y.C.

Rooted
Alexander Buzo
1-7-72
Hartford Stage Company
Hartford, CT

Roots
Gilbert Moses
10-3-69
Afro-American Studio
15 W. 126th, N.Y.C.

Roots
Emalyn Caliva
11-29-73
Library & Museum of the Performing Arts
111 Amsterdam, N.Y.C.

Roots (stories compiled by participants)
Root Theatre Collective
5-4-72
Trinity Church
74 Trinity Pl., N.Y.C.

Rope Dance Five, The
Louis Phillips
3-11-71
Production Workshop Club
80 Second, N.Y.C.

Rosa De Papel, La
9-30-70
Esta Noche Teatro (Madrid & Barcelona)
La Mama ETC
Loeb Drama Center, Cambridge, MA

Rosalee Pritchett
Carlton & Barbara Molette
3-23-70
Spelman College
Atlanta, GA

Rose
Emanuel Fried
10-28-69
Provincetown Playhouse
133 MacDougal, N.Y.C.

Rose Festival, The (with The Winner)
Arthur Williams
10-28-71
St. Peter's Church
346 W. 20th, N.Y.C.

Rose Man, The
Leon Gillen
7-28-69
Eugene O'Neill Memorial Theatre
Waterford, CT

Rosebloom
Harvey Perr
7-31-69
Mark Taper Forum
Los Angeles, CA

Rosensweig, F. C.
See: Hymn to the Creator (earlier version of same)

Rothschilds, The
Sherman Yellen (book); Sheldon Harnick (lyrics); Jerry Bock (music)
8-11-70
Fisher Theatre
Detroit, MI

Rotunda (musical satire)
12-27-73
American Theatre
Washington, DC

Rouge Atomique
N. Richard Nash
3-25-73
One-Act Repertory Company
251 E. 50th, N.Y.C.

Round and Round the Naked Round
A. R. Bell
Jan., 1974
Dramatis Personae
114 W. 14th N.Y.C.

Round Trip
Jean Nuchtern
4-15-71
American Theatre Company
106 E. 14th, N.Y.C.

Round with Ring, A
Nathan R. Teitel & Haila Stoddard
10-27-69
Theatre de Lys
N.Y.C.

Routes (To Black Mountain)
Huddled Masses Experimental Workshop
11-29-73
Library & Museum of the Performing Arts
111 Amsterdam, N.Y.C.

Routines for Roger, Ross, Rita, The Eskimo, and Doctor Jim
Frank Miazga
3-6-72
New Old Reliable Theatre
231 E. 3rd, N.Y.C.

Rowena
July, 1972
Manchester Art Center
Mancester, VT

Roy Vacio, El
Wilfredo Blanco
12-31-71
New York Theatre of the Americas
427 W. 59th, N.Y.C.

Royal Box, The
Eugene Dolgoff
5-21-70
Bronx Community College
184th & Walton Bronx, NY

Royal Flesh
Mary Feldhaus-Weber
6-7-71
Judson Poets' Theatre
55 Wash. Sq. N.Y.C.

Royal Pardon, or The Soldier Who Became an Actor, The
8-1-73
Rochester Univ. Summer Theatre
Rochester, NY

Royal Rape of Ruari Macasmunde, The
Richard F. Stockton & Richard T. Herd
3-2-73
Virginia Museum
Richmond, VA

Rubber Nickels
Michael Tennenbaum (book); Jason Shulman (music & lyrics)
5-11-72
Brooklyn College
Brooklyn, NY

Ruby Keeler Is a Mother (with The Bee and the Butterfly and Sunday Morning)
Charles Kerbs
1-31-69
Theatre of Our Discontent
Clifton Hotel
127 W. 79th, N.Y.C.

Ruff Dues Tag the Sweet Story
Ronald Miglionico
11-1-68
Old Center Theatre
152 W. 66th, N.Y.C.

Ruin, The
Jorge Luis Borges; Oswald Rodriguez (adaptor)
3-7-73
La Mama ETC
74 E. 4th, N.Y.C.

Rules for the Running of Trains, etc. on the Erie Railway, To Go into Effect January 1, 1862, Section Ten
11-7-69
Extension Theatre
277 Park Ave. So., N.Y.C.

Rules of the Game
Steven Shea
7-17-73
Manhattan Theatre Club
321 E. 73rd, N.Y.C.

Ruling Class, The
Peter Barnes
1-15-71
Arena Stage
Washington, DC

Rumor de Fuego y Agua
5-15-71
Spanish Players
Community Center Theatre
270 W. 89th, N.Y.C.

Runaway
Ron Felber
6-12-69
St. Benedict's Preparatory School
Newark, NJ

Runesglee
1969
Adelphi University
Garden City, NY

Runner Stumbles, The
Milan Stitt
Summer, 1972
Berkshire Festival
Stockbridge, MA

Rural Bone Show
Will Allen
6-5-72
New Old Reliable Theatre
231 E. 3rd, N.Y.C.

Ruth and the Rabbi (with The Harrison Progressive School)
Stanley Nelson
10-23-68
Playwrights' Workshop Club
14 Waverly Pl., N.Y.C.

S

Sabbot, The
Gerald Miller
11-25-70
Niagara Community College The Now Theatre Repertory Company
La Mama ETC
74 E. 4th, N.Y.C.

Saboo
Theatre Laboratoire Vicinal
12-8-70
Caravan Theatre
Cambridge, MA

Sacred Guard
Ken Rubenstein
4-11-73
La Mama ETC
74 E. 4th, N.Y.C.

Sacrifice, The
Herb Liebman
5-7-71
Supernova
451 W. Broadway, N.Y.C.

Safari 300
Tad Truesdale & Richie Havens
7-12-72
Mayfair Theatre
235 W. 46th, N.Y.C.

Safe and Sound
Laura Olsher
6-9-71
Jacksonville University
Jacksonville, FL

Safe at Last
James V. Hatch & Larry Garvin
2-9-73
New Village Theatre
433 E. 6th, N.Y.C.

Sailors at an Exhibition (with The Hungry Ones and A Song for Helen
Paul Rawlings
5-4-71
13th Street Theatre
50 W. 13th, N.Y.C.

Saints, Sinners, and Scriabin
7-26-70
Expression of the Two Arts Theatre
102 W. 29th, N.Y.C.

Salem Chronicles
2-10-72
Old Town Hall
Salem, MA

Salesman, The
Wendell Phillips, Jr.
5-10-70
Triangle Theatre
316 E. 88th, N.Y.C.

Sally, George and Martha
Sam Dann
12-20-71
Theatre de Lys
N.Y.C.

Salome
Oscar Wilde; adapted by Andy & Irene Robinson
6-10-70
La Mama ETC
74 E. 4th, N.Y.C.

Salome
Oscar Wilde; new adaptation by Joaquin La Habana
11-24-72
Playwrights' Workshop Club
Bastiano's Studio
14 Cooper Square, N.Y.C.

Saloon
Sally Netzel
4-13 - 29-72
Dallas Theatre Center
Dallas, TX

Salted Arrows
Tony Brazina
11-13-73
Playwrights' Horizons
Clark Center for the Performing Arts
West Side YWCA, 8th Ave. & 51st, N.Y.C.

Saltflowers
Tom Oliver
9-26-68
Playwrights' Unit
15 Vandam, N.Y.C.

Salvation
Peter Link & C. C. Courtney
3-11-69
Village Gate
160 Bleecker, N.Y.C.

Salvation Army Band
Lee Goldman
3-16-69
WPA
34 E. 4th, N.Y.C.

Salvation Army, The
Robert Patrick
9-23-68
Old Reliable Theatre Tavern
231 E. 3rd, N.Y.C.

Salzburg Great Theatre of the World, The
Hugo von Hofmannsthal, trans. by Lisel Mueller & John Reich
10-4-68
Goodman Theatre
Chicago, IL

Sam and Lil
Marj Mahle
May, 1970
Universalist Theatre
4 W. 76th, N.Y.C.

Sambo
Ron Steward (words); Neal Tate (music)
6-14-69
La Mama ETC
74 E. 4th, N.Y.C.

Samson and Delilah
Jean Flynn & Anthony Osnato
10-28-72
Theatre in the Church by the Bridge
328 E. 62nd, N.Y.C.

San Fran Scandals
San Francisco Mime Troupe
Summer 1973
San Francisco Mime Troupe
San Francisco, CA

Sand
F. V. Hunt
2-23-73
American Women Playwrights Association
Columbia University School of the Arts Theatre
410 W. 117th, N.Y.C.

Sand Castle, The
Warren Giarraputo
6-7-71
Judson Poets' Theatre
55 Wash. Sq. So., N.Y.C.

Sandbox, The
Kent Anderson
2-5-73
Donnell Library
N.Y.C.

Sandburg Odyssey, A
David Glazer
4-20-72
Manhattan Theatre Club
321 E. 73rd, N.Y.C.

Sandra and the Janitor
William Packard
10-11-68
H B Playwrights Foundation
124 Bank, N.Y.C.

Sans Everything
Lydia Simmons
5-14-71
Theatre Projects
161 W. 22nd, N.Y.C.

Santa Anita '42
Allan Knee
9-12-73
Playwrights' Horizons
Clark Center for the Performing Arts
West Side YWCA, 8th Ave. & 51st, N.Y.C.

Santa Juana de America
Andres Lizarraga
3-10-71
New York Theater of the Americas
427 W. 59th, N.Y.C.

Santacqua
Joanna Glass
12-12-69
H B Playwrights Foundation
124 Bank, N.Y.C.

Satan Goes to the Opera
Stanley Nelson
7-13-73
Theatre 77 Repertory
23 E. 20th, N.Y.C.

Satirical Earful, A
Portable Radio Circus
12-15-73
Community Loft
250 W. 106th, N.Y.C.

Satisfaction Guaranteed (with Open 24 Hours)
Roger N. Cornish
2-11-69
Actor's Playhouse
100 Seventh Ave. So., N.Y.C.

Saturday Night
Jerome Kass
2-25-68
Sheridan Square Playhouse
99 Seventh Ave. So., N.Y.C.

Satyr Play
See: The Searching Satyrs

Satyricon
Paul Foster
5-14-72
Playhouse of the Ridiculous
La Mama ETC
74 E. 4th, N.Y.C.

Satyricon, The
Based on material by Petronius, Juvenal, Tacitus and Minsky; Tom Hendry (book & lyrics) Stanley Silverman (music)
7-4-69
Avon Theatre
Stratford Festival
Stratford, Ontario, CAN

Savage
Conceived by Maxine Klein
2-22-71
Boston University
Boston, MA

Savage in the Sandwich Isles, A
Mark Twain
7-4-73
Manhattan Players
Atlantic City Playhouse
Atlantic City, NJ

Save the Children
August, 1971
Kawmba House
106 W. 112th, N.Y.C.

Saved
Edward Bond
12-5-68
Yale University
New Haven, CT

Saving Grace, The
John Tobias
2-20-70
Playwright's Unit
83 E. 4th, N.Y.C.

Saviour Queen, The
Jefferson Bayley
5-21-71
Players Theatre of Greater Miami
Miami, FL

Say It Loud (gospel show)
5-18-70
Library & Museum of the Performing Arts
111 Amsterdam, N.Y.C.

Say When
Keith Winter (book & lyrics); Arnold Goland (music)
12-4-72
Plaza 9
Plaza Hotel
59th St. & 5th, N.Y.C.

Saying Something
2-16-73
Space for Innovative Development
344 W. 36th, N.Y.C.

Sayings of Mao Tse-Tung, The
1-28-68
Jackson Poets' Theatre
55 Wash. Sq. So., N.Y.C.

Scaffold for Marionettes, A
C. Lester Franklin
1-31-68
Theatre of the Living Arts
Philadelphia, PA

Scandal Point
John Patrick
2-20-68
Playhouse on the Mall
Paramus, NJ

Scandalous Affair of Mrs. Kettle and Mrs. Moon, The
J. B. Priestley
8-13-68
Boothbay Playhouse
Boothbay, ME

Scapegoat, The
Henry Kendrick
6-1-73
Jacksonville University
Jacksonville, FL

Scarlet Lullabye
Elliott Taubenslag
3-10-68
Masque Theatre
440 W. 42nd, N.Y.C.

Scavengers
Hal Ackerman
2-28-69
Theatre of Our Discontent
Clifton Hotel
127 W. 79th, N.Y.C.

Scene
Margaret Barbour Gilbert
Fall, 1970
Mise en Scene
New Orleans, LA

Scene for Piano and Tape (with 411 Lines)
Tom Johnson
5-9-71
Dancers Studio Foundation
34 E. 10th, N.Y.C.

Scenes and Things
Jerrold Brody & Tony Forrest
4-15-71
Playbox
94 St. Mark's Pl., N.Y.C.

Scenes for Laughter and Tears
8-12-72
Festival Repertory Company
Twilight Theatre
Brooklyn, NY

Scenes from American Life
A. R. Gurney, Jr.
10-27-70
Studio Arena Theatre
Buffalo, NY

Scenes from Domestic Life (with Window Dressing and Inner Circles)
9-25-69
Theatre East
211 E. 60th, N.Y.C.

Scent of Flowers, A
James Saunders
10-20-69
Martinique Theatre
N.Y.C.

Schiediker Calls
Ed Gruber
8-1-69
Gene Frankel Theatre Workshop
115 MacDougal, N.Y.C.

Schizzo Hey Ride (satirical revue)
Salvatore J. Coppola
9-12-73
Manhattan Theatre Club
321 E. 73rd, N.Y.C.

Schloss, Das (The Castle)
Franz Kafka; dramatized by Max Brod
11-19-68
Barbizon-Plaza Theatre
N.Y.C.

School for Buffoons
Michel de Ghelderode
6-7-73
Space for Innovative Development
344 W. 36th, N.Y.C.

School for Wives, The
Moliere; Richard Wilbur (translator)
2-16-71
Lyceum Theatre
N.Y.C.

School Play: An Experiment in Ensemble Acting
5-17-69
La Mama ETC
74 E. 4th, N.Y.C.

Schubert's Last Serenade (with Monday on the Way to Mercury Island)
Julie Bovasso
6-30-71
La Mama ETC
74 E. 4th, N.Y.C.

Score
Jerry Douglas
10-28-70
Martinique Theatre
N.Y.C.

Score No. 1
5-12-69
Theatre Genesis
10th St. & 2nd Ave., N.Y.C.

Score, The (staged reading)
Ira Hayes Fuchs
6-27-73
Playwrights' Horizons
Clark Center for the Performing Arts
West Side YWCA, 8th Ave. & 51st, N.Y.C.

Scott and Zelda
Paul Hunter
Fall, 1973
Oxford Theatre
Los Angeles, CA

Scoutmaster's Revenge, The (with The Three)
Irwin Shapiro
4-16-71
Clark Center for the Performing Arts
West Side YWCA
8th Ave. & 51st, N.Y.C.

Scraping Bottom
David Scott Milton
1-3-69
New York Theatre Ensemble
2 E. 2nd, N.Y.C.

Scratch
Archibald MacLeish
4-7-71
Colonial Theatre
Boston, MA

Scream Revolution
Peter Copani
11-6-69
New York Theatre Ensemble
2 E. 2nd, N.Y.C.

Screen Play
3-2-73
Blue Dome Rehearsal Hall
261 Bowery, N.Y.C.

Screens, The
Jean Genet
12-7-71
Chelsea Theatre Center
30 Lafayette, Brooklyn, NY

Sculptors, The
Mike Toburen
March, 1971
Kansas State University
Manhattan, KS

Sea Change, The (with Hills Like White Elephants)
Ernest Hemingway
11-6-69
Universalist Theatre
4 W. 76th, N.Y.C.

Seagull, The
Anton Chekhov; Jean-Claude van Itallie (adaptor)
October, 1973
McCarter Theatre
Princeton, NJ

Seance
1-21-71
Atlanta Memorial Arts Center
Atlanta, GA

Search for the Bull, The
Eric Bass Puppets
12-5-73
Open Eye
78 Fifth, N.Y.C.

Searchers, The
See: The Searching Satyrs

Searching Satyrs, The (Ichneutae)
Sophocles; Sande Shurin (adaptor)
3-19-73
Theatre for the New City
113 Jane, N.Y.C.

Season in Hell: The Essence of Rimbaud, A
Rimbaud; adapted by David Kerry Heefner
4-16-70
Thresholds
23 E. 20th, N.Y.C.

Season in the Congo, A
Aime Cesaire; translated by Ralph Manheim
6-27-70
Paperback Theatre
80 Second, N.Y.C.

Season of the Carnival
Stuart Oderman
5-5-72
Omni Theatre Club
145 W. 18th, N.Y.C.

Second Chance
Bette Zeigler
7-28-72
New York Theatre Ensemble
2 E. 2nd, N.Y.C.

Second Coming of Bert, The
Ronald Chudley
1-4-69
Oakland University
Rochester, MI

Second Coming, The
Janet Giles
8-13-68
Universalist Theatre
4 W. 76th, N.Y.C.

Second Cummings: A Montage in Movement, Speech and Sound
e. e. cummings
12-14-70
Library & Museum of the Performing Arts
111 Amsterdam, N.Y.C.

Second Door Left
Alexander Popovic
4-1-70
La Mama ETC
74 E. 4th, N.Y.C.

Second Hottest Show in Town (improvisational show)
6-28-71
Actor's Playhouse
100 Seventh Ave. So., N.Y.C.

Second Shepherd's Play, The
William Packard (adaptor)
12-19-73
H B Playwrights Foundation
124 Bank, N.Y.C.

Second Story Girl
11-24-73
Pace College
N.Y.C.

Secret Affairs of Mildred Wild, The
Paul Zindel
10-9-72
Shubert Theatre
New Haven, CT

Secret Attendance
Matthew Davison
10-31-71
East Village Theatre
433 E. 6th, N.Y.C.

Secret Garden, The
New adaptation by Susan Kosoff
8-15-72
West Harwich Junior Theater
West Harwich, MA

Secret Place, The
Garrett Morris
12-16-72
Playwrights' Horizons
West Side YWCA
8th Ave. & 51st, N.Y.C.

Secret, The
Thomas Terefenko
8-7-68
Playbox
94 St. Mark's Pl., N.Y.C.

Secretary Bird, The
William Douglas Home
7-6-70
Cape Playhouse
Dennis, MA

Secretary, The
Bruce Feld
1-26-69
Theatre Market Place
The Little Synagogue
27 E. 20th, N.Y.C.

Secrets
Patricia Cooper
11-14-68
Loft Workshop
152 Bleecker, N.Y.C.

Secrets of the Citizens' Correction Committee
Ronald Tavel
10-15-73
St. Clement's Church
423 W. 46th, N.Y.C.

Section 8
Gerald Jackson
5-25-71
Jewel Theatre
N.Y.C.

See Johnny . . .
Jeff Hochhauser
4-24-70
New York Theatre Ensemble
2 E. 2nd, N.Y.C.

See Other Side (with Obsidian and Tinkle, Tinkle)
Robert Patrick
4-10-68
Old Reliable Theatre Tavern
231 E. 3rd, N.Y.C.

Seeing–Eye Dog with an Eye for Women, The
James Magnuson
4-13-72
Changing Scene
Denver, CO

Seek and You Shall Find
Directed by Oscar Brown, Jr.
5-19-72
Julia Richman H.S.
2nd Ave. & 67th, N.Y.C.

Seesaw
Michael Stewart (book); Dorothy Fields (lyrics); Cy Coleman (music)
1-12-73
Fisher Theatre
Detroit, MI

Selections from Lewis Carroll (multi-media event)
Barbara Schoenfeld & Russell Schwartz
5-15-69
Hunter Playhouse
63rd & Lexington, N.Y.C.

Self-Accusation
Peter Handke, translated by Michael Roloff
5-22-70
St. Clement's Church
423 W. 46th, N.Y.C.

Self-Destruct
Albert Evans
1-29-72
Riverdale Lab Theatre
252nd St. & Riverdale Ave. Bronx, NY

Selling of the President, The
Stuart Hample (book); Jack O'Brien (lyrics); Bob James (music)
3-30-71
American Conservatory Theatre
San Francisco, CA

Seneca Scampers
8-15-73
Geneva Summer Theatre
Geneva, NY

Sengakuji
Kenji Haguta
4-29-71
Radcliffe College
Cambridge, MA

Sensations
Paul Zakrzewski & Wally Harper
Summer, 1970
Berkshire Theatre Festival
Stockbridge, MA

Sense of Wild Flowers, A
Bruce Comer
4-3-68
La Mama ETC
122 Second, N.Y.C.

Senseless Play, A
Joseph Ponzi
5-15-68
Judson Poets' Theatre
55 Wash. Sq. So., N.Y.C.

Sensuous Woman, The
July, 1972
Priscilla Beach Theatre
Plymouth, MA

September Tea
John Pawley
Jan., 1970
ANTA Theatre
Arcata, CA

Sepulchrum (liturgical drama)
4-18-73
Stage 7 Matrix
New York University Chapel
58 Wash. Square So., N.Y.C.

Serenade
Nancy Heiken
7-19-73
La Mama ETC
74 E. 4th, N.Y.C.

Serenade at the Villa
11-17-72
All Saints Church
60th St. bet. 2nd & 3rd, N.Y.C.

Serenading Louie
Lanford Wilson
4-1-70
Washington Theater Club
Washington, DC

Serpent: A Work in Progress, The
Jean-Claude van Itallie
3-2-68
Colgate University
Hamilton, NY

Serpentine
J. E. Neyland
6-4-69
Playbox
94 St. Mark's Pl., N.Y.C.

Servant of Two Masters, The
Carlo Goldoni, Kenneth Cavander (adaptor); Barbara Damashek (music)
7-27-71
John Drew Repertory Company
East Hampton, NY

Serving of Verse, A
Walt Witcover
2-7-73
Masterworks Laboratory Theatre
Spencer Memorial Church
Remson & Clinton Sts., Brooklyn Heights, NY

Set It Down with Gold on Lasting Pillars
Frederick Bailey
8-13-71
Playbox
94 St. Mark's Pl., N.Y.C.

Seven Days of Mourning
L. S. Simckes
12-16-69
Circle in the Square
159 Bleecker, N.Y.C.

Seven Descents of Myrtle, The
Tennessee Williams
2-29-68
Walnut St. Theatre
Philadelphia

Seven in Search
11-8-68
Universalist Theatre
4 W. 76th, N.Y.C.

Seven Meditations on Political Sado-Masochism
The Living Theatre
6-30-73
Washington Square Methodist Church
133 Fourth, N.Y.C.

Seven Trumpets (and The Aquatic Chinee)
Tom LaBar
4-17-68
Playbox
94 St. Mark's Pl., N.Y.C.

Seventeen Seventy-Six (1776)
Peter Stone (book); Sherman Edwards (music & lyrics)
2-10-69
Shubert Theatre
New Haven, CT

Seventy—Girls—Seventy! (70—Girls—70!)
Fred Ebb & Norman Martin (book); Fred Ebb (lyrics); John Kander (music)
3-6-71
Forrest Theatre
Philadelphia, PA

Several Barrels of Trash
Vincent Terrell
7-16-71
Arlington Street Church
Boston, MA

Sextet (Yes)
Lanford Wilson
2-11-71
Circle Theatre Company
2307 Broadway, N.Y.C.

Sexual Practices in Heaven
Mar., 1971
Theatre Erotica
30 W. 48th, N.Y.C.

Sganarelle
Moliere; new translation by Albert Bermel
1-12-70
ANTA Theatre
245 W. 52nd, N.Y.C.

Shades of Black (revue)
Voices, Inc.
1-21-72
Mount Morris Park Center
N.Y.C.

Shadow Ripens, The
Murray Mednick
5-30-69
Theatre Genesis
10th & 2nd, N.Y.C.

Shadowplay
Gertrude Greenidge
1-19-68
Riverdale Showcase
252nd St. & Riverside Ave., Bronx, NY

Shadows, A Dream Opera
Martha Boesing (libretto); Paul Boesing (music)
3-2-73
Academy Theatre
Atlanta, GA

Shadows of the Evening (with Come into the Garden Maude)
Noel Coward
8-19-69
Boothbay Playhouse
Boothbay, ME

Shaggy Dog Story, A
Stanley Marcus
9-27-68
Off Center Theatre
152 W. 66th, N.Y.C.

Shakespeare Games
H. Wesley Balk
11-6-70
University of Minnesota
Minneapolis, MN

Shakespeare Heaven
SUNY at Buffalo Company and Gordon Rogoff
12-10-70
State University of New York at Buffalo
Buffalo, NY

Shakespeare: His Men and Women
1-31-73
Library & Museum of the Performing Arts
111 Amsterdam, N.Y.C.

Shakespeare/Dance and Drama
9-25-73
Opera House
Washington, DC

Shall We Gather at the River
Maurice Noel
5-3-72
Cubiculo
414 W. 51st, N.Y.C.

Shalom
Dean Brelis
3-21-69
Newport Players Guild
Newport Performing Arts Center
Newport, RI

Shanghai Loca
Alexis Del Lago
3-16-73
13th Street Theatre
50 W. 13th, N.Y.C.

Shango De Ima
Pepe Carril; adapted by Susan Sherman
1-1-70
La Mama ETC
74 E. 4th, N.Y.C.

Shapes and Shadows
Canadian Mime Theatre
Summer, 1971
Stratford Festival
Stratford, Ontario, CAN

Share a Secret
David Sawn
7-19-68
Dramarena Repertory Theatre
158 W. 55th, N.Y.C.

Share the Men
Emily Hellman
6-1-73
Jacksonville University
Jacksonville, FL

Shark and the Man Who Satisfied It, The
Allen Katzman
10-18-73
Changing Scene
Denver, CO

Shaved Splits
Sam Shepard
7-29-70
La Mama ETC
74 E. 4th, N.Y.C.

Shay
Anne Commire
7-28-73
Eugene O'Neill Memorial Theatre
Waterford, CT

Shay Duffin as Brendan Behan
Brendan Behan; Shay Duffin (adaptor)
1-2-73
Abbey Theatre
136 E. 13th, N.Y.C.

She Played Good Piano
P. J. Barry
1-23-70
Hudson Guild Theatre
441 W. 26th, N.Y.C.

She's Dead Now (with Two in the Back Room and Black Manhood)
Earle Chisholm
5-21-70
Spencer Memorial Church
99 Clinton St., Brooklyn Heights, NY

She Was a Lazy Witch (with The Travelling Sisters)
John Kirkpatrick
11-17-72
West Side Gay Theatre
W.S.D.G. Center
37 Ninth, N.Y.C.

Sheba (with Black Circles 'Round Angela)
Hazel Bryant & J. Justice
2-9-73
Afro-American Total Theatre
415 W. 127th, N.Y.C.

Sheep on the Runway
Art Buchwald
12-22-69
Shubert Theatre
New Haven, Ct

Sheila
Anthony J. Ingrassia
3-12-71
New York Theatre Ensemble
2 E. 2nd, N.Y.C.

Shekhina (The Bride)
Leon Katz
12-3-71
La Mama ETC
74 E. 4th, N.Y.C.

Shellgame
Douglas Bankson
7-17-68
Playbox
94 St. Mark's Pl., N.Y.C.

Shelter
Gretchen Cryer (book & lyrics); Nancy Ford (music)
2-6-73
Golden Theatre
252 W. 45th, N.Y.C.

Shemp Liebowitz
Hal Craven

Shenandoah
Delmore Schwartz
4-25-69
American Theatre Club
310 E. 42nd, N.Y.C.

Shenyang Acrobatic Troupe of the Peoples' Republic of China
11-22-72
National Arts Centre
Ottawa, Ontario, CAN

Shepherd of Avenue B, The
Lawrence Holofcener
5-15-70
Fortune Theatre
62 E. 4th, N.Y.C.

Shepherd, The (with The Bench)
Lawrence Holofcener
4-23-69
Playbox
94 St. Mark' s Pl., N.Y.C.

Sheriff Who Had No Horse, The
P. J. Barry
4-19-71
Library & Museum of the Performing Arts
111 Amsterdam, N.Y.C.

Sherlock Holmes
William Gillette; adapted by Dennis Rosa
12-22-72
Cleveland Playhouse
Cleveland, OH

Sherwood
R. Cary Bynum
1-29-72
Hunter College Playwrights Project
West Side YMCA
5 W. 63rd, N.Y.C.

Shiny Red Ball, The
Cleve Hawbold
1-9-72
Park Avenue Community Theatre
Central Church
593 Park, N.Y.C.

Shiny Red Ball, The (with Big Black Box, Owl, and The Armory)
Cleve Baubold
1-9-72
Park Avenue Community Theatre
Central Church
Park Ave. & 64th, N.Y.C.

Ship of the Righteous
Nikolai Evreinov
Summer, 1970
Theatre Wagon
Staunton, VA

Shiskebab!
F. V. Hunt
4-19-68
Troupe Theatre
167 W. 21st, N.Y.C.

Sho Is Hot in the Cotton Patch (or Miss Weaver)
Ted Shine
1968
Negro Ensemble Company
St. Mark's Playhouse
133 Second, N.Y.C.

Shoe Shine Tragedy
James Magnuson
5-27-68
Circle in the Square
N.Y.C.

Shoe Store
Shirley Rhodes
3-1-71
Library & Museum of the Performing Arts
111 Amsterdam, N.Y.C.

Shoe Story
Robert Cunningham
2-24-73
Ten-Ten Players
1010 Park, N.Y.C.

Shoot Anything with Hair that Moves
Donald Ross
2-2-69
Provincetown Playhouse
133 MacDougal, N.Y.C.

Shooting Gallery
Israel Horovitz
6-7-72
WPA
333 Bowery, N.Y.C.

Short Bullins
Ed Bullins
12-15-71
La Mama ETC
74 E. 4th, N.Y.C.

Short Magical Ministry of the Reverend Doctor John Faust, The
J. Ranelli
11-17-72
Cleveland Playhouse
Cleveland, OH

Short Season, The
Anne Paolucci
5-7-70
Cubiculo
414 W. 51st, N.Y.C.

Short Stories
Anton Chekhov
6-10-71
Fortune Theatre
62 E. 4th, N.Y.C.

Short Stuff
Ed Bullins
6-1-70
New Dramatists Workshop
424 W. 44th, N.Y.C.

Short Sweet Life, A
Edna Schappert
11-5-71
New York Theatre Ensemble
2 E. 2nd, N.Y.C.

Show Me Where the Good Times Are
Lee Thuna (book); Rhoda Roberts (lyrics); Kenneth Jacobson (music)
3-5-70
Edison Theatre
240 W. 47th, N.Y.C.

Show No. 39
10-25-72
People Show
La Mama ETC
74 E. 4th, N.Y.C.

Show No. 44
10-18-72
People Show
La Mama ETC
74 E. 4th, N.Y.C.

Show or Goat
Lars Forssell
2-26-73
Donnell Library
N.Y.C.

Shower
Ronald Tavel
3-27-68
Extension Theatre
128 E. 7th, N.Y.C.

Shrinking Bride, The
Jonathan Levy
1-11-71
Mercury Theatre
134 E. 13th, N.Y.C.

Shropshire Lad, A
7-31-73
Ibsen-Shaw Festival
Cabrini College
Radnor, PA

Shuffle-Off
Stanley Nelson
4-17-68
Playwright's Workshop Club
14 Waverly Pl., N.Y.C.

Shufflings
Kenneth Janes
2-27-69
Minor Latham Playhouse
Barnard College
N.Y.C.

Shuttle USA
1-16-72
Sanders Theatre
Cambridge, MA

Si de las Ninas, El
Moratin
8-26-71
Greenwich Mews Spanish Theatre
141 W. 13th, N.Y.C.

Siamese Connection
Dennis J. Reardon
3-16-71
University of Michigan
Ann Arbor, MI

Sick Fare
5-20-71
University of the Streets Repertory Company
130 E. 7th, N.Y.C.

Sid Arthur and His Psyche Dahlia-nce
Sheldon Cholst
8-11-72
New York Theatre Ensemble
2 E. 2nd, N.Y.C.

Siddhartha
Marin Kapell (adaptor)
4-30-71
University Heights Presbyterian Church
Bronx, NY

Side Show
Joseph Renard
6-19-73
New Plays Festival Workshop of the Players Art
333 Bowery, N.Y.C.

Siege, The
Jovan Hristic
1970
Santa Barbara, CA

Siena, Rebecca (mimes)
3-26-72
Jean Cocteau Theatre
43 Bond, N.Y.C.

Significance of Love, Etc., The
Bruce Feld
5-1-69
WPA
34 E. 4th, N.Y.C.

Signorina, La
Marc Alan Zagoren
12-20-69
New York Cultural Center
N.Y.C.

Signpost to Murder
Monte Doyle
7-6-70
Candlewood Theatre
New Fairfield, CT

Silence (with Landscape)
Harold Pinter
4-2-70
Forum Theatre
Lincoln Center
N.Y.C.

Silent Men, The
Robert Somerfeld
10-25-68
Anthony Mannino Drama Tree
182 Fifth, N.Y.C.

Silent Partner, The
Clifford Odets
5-11-72
Actors' Studio
432 W. 44th, N.Y.C.

Silent Prayer
Stephen Varble
3-14-73
La Mama ETC
74 E. 4th, N.Y.C.

Silhouette of God, The (with The Virtues of Adultery)
Joseph Okpaku
1-15-69
Stanford University
Palo Alto, CA

Silhouettes
Ted Harris
5-30-68
Playwrights' Workshop Club
14 Waverly Pl., N.Y.C.

Silver Queen
Paul Foster (book & lyrics); John Braden (lyrics & music)
4-11-73
La Mama ETC
74 E. 4th, N.Y.C.

Silver Skies (with The Youth Rebellion, Tarquin Truth Beauty, and Camera Obscura)
Robert Patrick
4-28-69
Old Reliable Theatre Tavern
231 E. 3rd, N.Y.C.

Silverplate
Lee Thuna
7-12-71
Candlewood Theatre
New Fairfield, CT

Simba, Simba, Umgawa
Rock Kenyon
7-31-70
New York Theatre Ensemble
2 E. 2nd, N.Y.C.

Simone
Antonio Calabrese (book, lyrics, & music); Rosalie Calabrese (lyrics & music)
10-11-73
Playwrights' Workshop Club
Electric Circus
23 St. Mark's Pl., N.Y.C.

Simone
Megan Terry
3-4-70
La Mama ETC
74 E. 4th, N.Y.C.

Sin Bandera
Jaime Carrero
1-11-73
Puerto Rican Traveling Theatre Company
Experimental Lab
124 W. 18th, N.Y.C.

Sinfonia En No Sostenido
Hermilo Salazar
6-27-73
Teatro Caras Nuevas
114 W. 14th, N.Y.C.

Sing a Rainbow
Betty Keller
Spring, 1970
Playhouse Theatre Company
Vancouver, CAN

Sing All a Green Willow
Paul Green
3-28-69
University of North Carolina
Chapel Hill, NC

Singer with a Big Band
Tom Eyen
5-5-72
Bastiano's Studio
14 Cooper Square, N.Y.C.

Singin' Hare Krishna (with Snows of Spring)
Guy Gauthier
2-19-71
New York Theatre Ensemble
2 E. 2nd, N.Y.C.

Singing in a Lonely Cage, The
Roger Kenvin
8-2-73
Joseph Jefferson Theatre Company
Little Church Around the Corner
11 E. 29th, N.Y.C.

Singing Newspaper, The
7-25-72
Washington Square Church
133 W. 4th, N.Y.C.

Single Double Kingsize
John Vincent Stoltenberg
4-12-71
Columbia University Theatre Troupe
Nave Theatre
440 W. 110th, N.Y.C.

Singles and Doubles
Michael McGrinder
12-8-69
Old Reliable Theatre Tavern
231 E. 3rd, N.Y.C.

Sinister Cambodian Forebodings
Ishamu Kawai
6-13-70
30 E. 14th, N.Y.C.

Sir Slob and the Princess
George Garrett
2-26-72
Ten-ten Players
1010 Park Ave., N.Y.C.

Sissies' Scrapbook
Larry Kamer
11-14-73
Playwrights' Horizon
Clark Center for the Performing Arts
West Side YWCA, 8th Ave. & 51st, N.Y.C.

Sissy
Seth Allen
11-9-72
The Playhouse of the Ridiculous
La Mama ETC
74 E. 4th, N.Y.C.

Sister
Glenn Allen Smith
5-17-68
Venture Theatre Club
145 Eighth, N.Y.C.

Sister Florence, Sister Joan
Henry C. Timm
10-15-70
Wheelock College
Boston, MA

Sister Sadie and the Son of Sam
6-29-68
New Dramatists Workshop
83 E. 4th, N.Y.C.

Sister Son/Ji
Sonia Sanchez
1-16-72
Negro Ensemble Company
St. Mark's Playhouse
133 Second, N.Y.C.

Sisters
Jonathan Halpern
11-13-70
Stage Lights Theatrical Club
218 W. 48th, N.Y.C.

Sisters of Mercy
Leonard Cohen; Gene Lesser (adaptor)
7-5-73
Shaw Festival
Niagara-on-the-Lake
Ontario, CAN

Sisyphus and the Blue-Eyed Cyclops
Garland Thompson
1-14-72
Negro Ensemble Company
St. Mark's Playhouse
133 Second, N.Y.C.

Sisyphus (mime program)
Frank Josef Bogner
5-16-73
New York University Theatre
111 Second, N.Y.C.

Sitting (with Saving Grace)
John Tobias
7-21-72
American Shakespeare Festival
Stratford, CT

Six
Charles Strouse (book, lyrics, & music)
4-12-71
Cricket Theatre
162 Second, N.Y.C.

Six Foot Tricycle, The
Craig Carnelia (book, music, & lyrics)
4-30-71
Theatre of the Riverside Church
490 Riverside Dr., N.Y.C.

Six Hundred Dollars and a Mule (musical)
Lester Wilson (conception); Lester Wilson & Arthur Smalls, Jr. (music)
8-28-73
Huntington Hartford Theatre
Los Angeles, CA

Six Rms Riv Vu (6 Rms Riv Vu)
Bob Randall
9-11-72
Colonial Theatre
Boston, MA

Six, Seven, and Eight
Roger N. Cornish
6-1-72
Jacksonville University
Jacksonville, FL

Six Studies for Three Voices
e. e. cummings, arranged by Barrie Landauer
2-23-69
Dancers Studio Foundation
34 E. 10th, N.Y.C.

Sixteenth Century Ur Hamlet (16th Century Ur Hamlet)
Anonymous
1-30-70
Spencer Memorial Church
99 Clinton, Brooklyn Heights, NY

Skin Tight
Frank Cucci
4-1-68
New Theatre Workshop
154 E. 54th, N.Y.C.

Sky High
The Angels of Light
4-28-72
Theatre for the New City
151 Bank, N.Y.C.

Sky Is Falling, The (play reading)
Raymond Banachi
12-21-70
New York Theatre Ensemble
2 E. 2nd, N.Y.C.

Sky of Faces, A
Joseph B. Baldwin
5-17-73
Changing Scene
Denver, CO

Sky's the Limit
8-9-72
Surflight Summer Theatre
Beach Haven, NJ

Sky Salesman, The
Robert Nichols
9-9-72
Theatre for the New City
Abington Square, N.Y.C.

Sky Theatre Jubilee
Afro-American Total Theatre
7-30-73
Theatre of the Riverside Church
490 Riverside Dr., N.Y.C.

Skye
Avery Corman & Dan Rustin (book & lyrics); Ben Finn (music)
2-1-71
Library & Museum of the Performing Arts
111 Amsterdam, N.Y.C.

Slag
David Hare
2-21-71
New York Shakespeare Festival Public Theatre
425 Lafayette, N.Y.C.

Slaughterhouse Play
Susan Yankowitz
10-20-71
New York Shakespeare Festival Public Theatre
425 Lafayette, N.Y.C.

Slave of Love
Paul Morse (book & music); Michael Holmes & Paul Morse (lyrics)
3-15-71
New York Theatre of the Americas
427 W. 59th, N.Y.C.

Slave Ship
LeRoi Jones (Imamu Amiri Baraka)
11-18-69
Chelsea Theatre Center
30 Lafayette, Brooklyn, NY

Sleep
Jack Gelber
2-10-72
American Place Theatre
N.Y.C.

Sleep of Demons, A
Herbert D. Greggs
1-28-68
Cooperative Theatre
106 E. 14th, N.Y.C.

Sleeping Bag, The
Robert Patrick
5-6-68
13th Street Theatre
50 W. 13th, N.Y.C.

Sleeping Dogs (with Charlie and Belle)
David Libman
12-7-70
Assembly Theatre
113 Jane, N.Y.C.

Sleepless
John Hartnett
1-19-70
Old Reliable Theatre Tavern
231 E. 3rd, N.Y.C.

Sleuth
Anthony Shaffer
10-22-70
National Theatre
Washington, DC

Slightly Higher on the West Coast
Arranged and adapted by Frances Bardacke & John Sinor
8-7-69
Old Globe Theatre
Balboa Park, CA

Slip into the Street
Carla Joseph
2-18-72
New York Theatre Ensemble
2 E. 2nd, N.Y.C.

Slivovitz
Joel Schwartz
5-15-69
Mark Taper Forum
Los Angeles, CA

Slow Memories (with Theory, Proof, Application; Inside My Head; and Fraternal Order of Police)
Barry Litvack
10-21-70
Playwrights' Unit
83 E. 4th, N.Y.C.

Sludge
Paul J. Curtis
7-20-73
American Mime Theatre
Emelin Theatre
Mamaroneck, NY

Slum Song
Stephen H. Foreman
1-18-71
New Theatre Workshop
154 E. 54th, N.Y.C.

Smaller Than Life
Dorothy Vann & Jim Evering
12-7-70
Library & Museum of the Performing Arts
111 Amsterdam, N.Y.C.

Smart Assets
Edward Cope
3-13-70
Theatre Suburbia
Houston, TX

Smash!
Tony Barsha
11-26-71
New York Theatre Ensemble
2 E. 2nd, N.Y.C.

Smile Orange
Trevor Rhone
8-6-72
Eugene O'Neill Memorial Theatre
Waterford, CT

Smile, Smile, Smile (revision of Comedy)
Robert Russell (book); Luigi Creatore, Hugo Peretti & George David Weiss (lyrics & music)
2-20-73
Bucks County Playhouse
New Hope, PA

Smile Your Little Smile on Me
Michael Shurtleff
Nov., 1971
Friday Theatre
N.Y.C.

Smith
Dean Fuller, Tony Hendra, Matt Dubey (book); Dean Fuller & Matt Dubey (lyrics & music)
5-19-73
Eden Theatre
12th & 2nd Ave., N.Y.C.

Smith, Here!
Edward Greenberg
3-23-70
Old Reliable Theatre Tavern
231 E. 3rd, N.Y.C.

Smorgasbord (concert drawn from repertoire of solo shows)
Philip Hanson
6-19-73
Library & Museum of the Performing Arts
111 Amsterdam, N.Y.C.

Smudge
Myron Levoy
6-10-71
New York Theatre Ensemble
2 E. 2nd, N.Y.C.

Snapshots
William Derringer
1-17-72
Manhattan Theatre Club
321 E. 73rd, N.Y.C.

Snob, The (with The Strong Sex)
Carl Sternheim
2-16-68
Players' Workshop of the English Speaking Theatre
229 Seventh, N.Y.C.

Snow White
Walter J. Wallace (adaptor)
5-16-73
Seamen's Church Institute
15 State, N.Y.C.

Snow White Goes West
7-4-72
Dartmouth College
Hanover, NH

Snowbound King, The
Raymond Platt
12-24-70
New York Theatre Ensemble
2 E. 2nd, N.Y.C.

Snows of Spring (with Singin' Hare Krishna)
Guy Gauthier
2-19-71
New York Theatre Ensemble
2 E. 2nd, N.Y.C.

So Dark Tonight (with Louisville '59)
Larry O'Connel
12-10-69
Second Group Theatre
McBurney YMCA
215 W. 23rd, N.Y.C.

So Early in the Morning
Noel Hamilton
4-15-73
McBurney YMCA
215 W. 23rd, N.Y.C.

So Long My Tottie
Jenny Egan
8-3-71
South St.
Seaport, N.Y.C.

So Who's Goldberg?
Louis Del Grande
4-9-73
Stage Directors & Choreographers Foundation
Library & Museum of the Performing Arts
111 Amsterdam, N.Y.C.

Soap Opera
John Gruen
May, 1968
Loft Workshop
152 Bleecker, N.Y.C.

Soap (with Catfood)
H. N. Levitt
2-14-70
West Side YMCA
5 W. 63rd, N.Y.C.

Sociability
Charles Dizenzo
7-26-71
Old Post Office Theatre
East Hampton, NY

Socrates Is
Charles Langdon
2-25-71
Changing Scene
Denver, CO

Socrates Is Mortal
Robert Gordon
July, 1970
Eugene O'Neill Memorial Theatre
Waterford, CT

Sodom and Gomorrah
A. R. Bell
10-1-71
Dramatis Personae
114 W. 14th, N.Y.C.

Soft Core Pornographer, The
Martin Stone & John Heller
4-11-72
Stage 73
321 E. 73rd, N.Y.C.

Softly and Consider the Nearness
Rosalyn Drexler
8-6-68
Playhouse on the Wharf
Provincetown, MA

Softness of Damon's Underwear, The
Robert C. Herron
9-17-71
New York Theatre Ensemble
2 E. 2nd, N.Y.C.

Sol Enterrado, El
Juan Penalver
6-30-71
ADAL Performing Arts
682 Ave. of the Americas, N.Y.C.

Solar Invention; Morning Star
Conceived & directed by Robert Schwartz
6-16-69
La Mama ETC
74 E. 4th, N.Y.C.

Solarium
Walter Hadler
6-14-68
Theatre Genesis
2nd Ave. & 10th, N.Y.C.

Sold to the Movies
Gerard Marchette
4-10-70
Gotham Art
455 W. 43rd, N.Y.C.

Soldier, The
N. D. Bellitto
3-14-73
Provincetown Playhouse
133 MacDougal, N.Y.C.

Soldiers
Robert Georgalas
5-1-70
Bronx Community College
Bronx, NY

Soldiers, The
Rolf Hochhuth
2-28-68
Royal Alexandra Theatre
Toronto, CAN

Solid Walls
Patricia Horan
4-25-69
American Theatre Club
310 E. 42nd, N.Y.C.

Solitaire, Double Solitaire
Robert Anderson
2-12-71
Long Wharf Theatre
New Haven, CT

Solitude (with Frenzy and the Revolution) (reading)
Tobi Louis
4-23-73
New York Cultural Center
2 Columbus Circle, N.Y.C.

Solness (The Master Builder)
Henrik Ibsen; Albert Weiner (adaptor)
1-25-73
Lolly's Theatre Club
808 Lexington, N.Y.C.

Solos
5-7-73
Byrd Hoffman School of Byrds
147 Spring, N.Y.C.

Solver's Secret Revolutionary Pig Sings, The
Peter Copani
10-14-71
Greenwich House
27 Barrow, N.Y.C.

Some Men Are Good at That
Elaine Denholtz
11-20-70
Assembly Theatre
113 Jane, N.Y.C.

Some of My Best Friends Are Women (revue)
2-1-72
Finch College Auditorium
N.Y.C.

Someone's Comin' Hungry
McCrea Imbrie & Neil Seldon
3-31-69
Pocket Theatre
N.Y.C.

Something About Anne
Anita Loos (book); Ralph Blane (lyrics); James Gregory (music)
10-14-73
Clark Theatre
Birmingham, AL

Something About Yesterday
Susan H. Schulman
6-7-72
WPA
333 Bowery, N.Y.C.

Something Afoot
James McDonald, David Voss, Robert Gerlach
3-8-72
Alliance Theatre
Atlanta, GA

Something Else
Robert Patrick
1-12-73
New York Theatre Ensemble
2 E. 2nd, N.Y.C.

Something for Kitty Genovese
Sandra Scoppettone
11-1-70
Dancers Studio Foundation
34 E. 10th, N.Y.C.

Something in the Wind
Arlene Fanale
11-16-73
Irondequoit Community Theatre
Eastridge High School
Brockport, NY

Something Special
M. T. Trouper
8-21-70
Tentarena
Monticello, NY

Sometimes a Hard Head Makes a Soft Behind
J. E. Gaines
7-26-72
New Lafayette Theatre
7th Ave. & 137th, N.Y.C.

Sometimes in New Jersey
Larry O'Connel
2-17-72
Second Group Theatre
McBurney YMCA
215 W. 23rd, N.Y.C.

Somewhere in Between
Katherine Rao
3-8-72
Cubiculo
414 W. 51st, N.Y.C.

Son, Come Home, A
Ed Bullins
3-14-69
Hudson Guild Theatre
441 W. 26th, N.Y.C.

Son Come Home (with Soul Gone Home)
8-10-71
New African Company
Boston Center for the Arts
Boston, MA

Son for Helen, A (with Sailors at an Exhibition and The Hungry Ones)
Paul Rawlings
5-4-71
13th Street Theatre
50 W. 13th, N.Y.C.

Son of Cock-Strong
Tom Murrin
2-20-70
La Mama ETC
74 E. 4th, N.Y.C.

Son of Jesse James, The
Arthur Givens
3-28-68
Fulton Theatre Company
119 Ninth, N.Y.C.

Son of Man and the Family
Timothy Taylor & Adrian Hall
11-18-70
Trinity Square Repertory Company
Providence, RI

Son of Man, The
Richard D. Waters
7-1-70
Fisherman's Players
North Eastham, MA

Sonata for Mott Street
Joseph Hart
2-23-70
Cubiculo
414 W. 51st, N.Y.C.

Sondheim—A Musical Tribute
3-11-73
Shubert Theatre,
N.Y.C.

Song at Twilight, A
Noel Coward
8-19-69
Boothbay Playhouse
Boothbay, ME

Song for Cyrano, A
Jose Ferrer (book & lyrics); Robert Wright & George Forrest (music)
3-1-73
Hope College
Holland, MI

Song for Rent
4-22-71
Brassiere Foundation Theatre
141 Prince, N.Y.C.

Song for the First of May, A
Ted Pezzulo
10-22-71
Actor's Playhouse
100 Seventh Ave. So., N.Y.C.

Song of Hiawatha, The
Edwin Roberts (music); Bill Tehakirides (adaptation)
7-20-72
Whitney Museum
N.Y.C.

Song of Israel (revue)
3-21-72
Mayfair Theatre
235 W. 46th, N.Y.C.

Song of Sara (poetry of Sara Teasdale)
Daniel Jahn (music)
5-3-73
Cubiculo
414 W. 51st, N.Y.C.

Song of the Lusitanian Bogey
Peter Weiss
1-2-68
Negro Ensemble Company
St. Mark's Playhouse
133 Second, N.Y.C.

Song of the Morning Star
Barney Kremer
5-14-69
South Dakota Playwrights Theatre
Sioux Falls Community Playhouse
Sioux Falls, SD

Song of Walt Whitman
Richard Davidson
6-5-69
Nucleus Repertory Theatre
261 W. 54th, N.Y.C.

Songs: An Evening of Mime
Richard Clairmont
10-3-73
Cubiculo
414 W. 51st, N.Y.C.

Songs for a Saturday Night
Summer, 1973
Scarborough Summer Playhouse
Briarcliff Manor, NY

Songs from Milk Wood
Dylan Thomas, special adaptation by Bernard Bragg & Dorothy Miles
1-12-70
ANTA Theatre
245 W. 52nd, N.Y.C.

Songs of Innocence and Experience: An Evening with Richard Clairmont
5-4-73
Sixth Floor Theatre
150 Bleecker, N.Y.C.

Sonny and Lazlo
Irving Glusack
7-31-70
New York Theatre Ensemble
2 E. 2nd, N.Y.C.

Soon
Scott Fagan, Joseph Martinez Kookoolis, Robert Greenwald
1-12-71
Ritz Theatre
219 W. 48th, N.Y.C.

Sophia - (Wisdom) Part III
Richard Foreman
12-8-72
Cinematheque
80 Wooster, N.Y.C.

Sophistication of America, The
Jack Adler
8-23-68
New York Theatre Ensemble Workshop
2 Wash. Sq., N.Y.C.

Sotoba Komachi
Kwanami
2-21-73
American Noh Theatre
Jefferson Market Library
426 Sixth, N.Y.C.

Souffle of Turbot (with The Pickle and the Nameplate)
Raymond Platt
6-3-70
Stage Lights Theatrical Club
218 W. 48th, N.Y.C.

Soul Gone Home (with Son Come Home)
8-10-71
New African Company
Boston Center for the Arts
Boston, MA

Soul of a Stripper, The
Ilsa Gilbert
1-27-71
Assembly Theatre
113 Jane, N.Y.C.

Soul Pieces
Freddie Roach
12-1-69
Bert Wheeler Theatre
250 W. 43rd, N.Y.C.

Soul Theatre: A Celebration of Shouts
1-28-72
International Student Center
Cambridge, MA

Soul Yesterday and Today
Langston Hughes & Bob Teague, arranged by Rosetta LeNoire
8-28-69
Amas Repertory Theatre
Central Park Mall
N.Y.C.

Sound
2-4-72
Emerson College
Boston, MA

Sound and Light at Ford's Theatre
Charles Guggenheim & Harry Muheim
7-21-70
Ford's Theatre
Washington, DC

Sound of a Different Drum, The
A. R. Bell
8-23-68
Dramatis Personae
114 W. 14th, N.Y.C.

Sound of a Woman, The
Frank Spierling
3-16-72
St. Clement's Church
423 W. 46th, N.Y.C.

Sound of Bread Breaking, The
Feb., 1970
Lea College
Albert Lea, MN

Sound of Eggs Breaking, The (with Fear of Falling Apples)
Dene Hammond
5-14-70
University of Missouri
Columbia, MO

Sound of Murder, The
William Fairchild
7-14-69
Ogunquit Playhouse
Ogunquit, ME

Soundings
Patricia Cooper
3-23-69
Unit Theatre
157 W. 22nd, N.Y.C.

Soundings
Richard Longchamps
1-23-70
American Theatre Company
Alice's Studio
106 E. 14th, N.Y.C.

Soundings
Donald Swann & Sydney Carter
11-6-70
Madison Avenue Presbyterian Church
921 Madison Ave., N.Y.C.

Sounds of a Silent Man
Basil Wallace
3-28-73
La Mama ETC
74 E. 4th, N.Y.C.

Soup
Tony Giordano
2-6-69
Theatre 13
201 W. 13th, N.Y.C.

Sourball
Robert Shure
8-5-69
Provincetown Playhouse
133 MacDougal, N.Y.C.

Southern Gothic (with Adam Had 'Em)
Rock Kenyon
4-5-72
Playwrights' Workshop Club
Bastiano's Studio
14 Cooper Square, N.Y.C.

Space Mass
Connie Demby
4-9-70
Mannhardt Theatre Foundation, N.Y.C.

Space Play Phase 2
Stan Thomas
1969
Ark
15 Lansdowne St., Boston, MA

Space Play/Midnight Mass
Stan Thomas
8-14-68
Spingold Theatre
Brandeis University
Waltham, MA

Spayed Cat, The (with A Head of His Time)
Michael McGrinder
5-17-72
Bastiano's Studio
14 Cooper Sq., N.Y.C.

Spears That Roar for Blood
Pat Hyland
9-20-72
Playwrights' Workshop Club
Bastiano's Studio
14 Cooper Square, N.Y.C.

Special Assignment in Enemy Territory, A
Norman Kennedy
2-14-68
Extension Theatre
128 E. 7th, N.Y.C.

Specimen, A
Judith Gilhousen
9-15-72
New York Theatre Ensemble
2 E. 2nd, N.Y.C.

Speed
Grant Duay
12-27-68
New York Theatre Ensemble
2 E. 2nd, N.Y.C.

Speed Gets the Poppys
Lila Levant (book & lyrics); Lorenzo Fuller (lyrics & music)
7-25-72
Mercer Arts Center
240 Mercer, N.Y.C.

Spider People, The
Harvard Law School Drama Society
4-11-69
New York University
N.Y.C.

Spider Rabbit
Michael McClure
Fall, 1973
Magic Theatre
San Francisco, CA

Spiders, The
Werner Aspenstrom
1-8-73
Library & Museum of the Performing Arts
111 Amsterdam, N.Y.C.

Spiritual History, The
6-1-68
Pageant Players
71 E. Broadway, N.Y.C.

Spiritual Oasis of Lucky Landlord Paradise Slideshow
Jack Smith
6-5-71
Plaster Foundation
36 Greene, N.Y.C.

Spiro Who?
William M. Meyers; music by Phil Ochs
5-18-69
Gate Theatre
10th & 2nd, N.Y.C.

Spitting Image
Colin Spencer
3-2-69
Theatre de Lys
N.Y.C.

Splash
Robert Reinhold
3-2-73
Playwrights Workshop Club
Bastiano's Studio
14 Cooper Sq., N.Y.C.

Splinters
Keith Carsey & Larry Hamilton
3-25-71
Stagelights II
125 W. 22nd, N.Y.C.

Split Level
Robert Heide
5-5-72
Bastiano's Studio
14 Cooper Square, N.Y.C.

S.P.O. (reading)
Louis M. Ponderoso
6-4-71
Extension Theatre
277 Park Ave So., N.Y.C.

Spoilers, The
Drama Workshop of the East Harlem Youth Center
2-25-70
New York Public Library
125th Street Branch, N.Y.C.

Spotlights
Guy Gauthier
1-22-70
New York Theatre Ensemble
2 E. 2nd, N.Y.C.

Spread Eagle IV (revue)
Multiple authors
6-4-69
Washington Theatre Club
Washington, DC

Spread Eagle Papers
9-21-72
Washington Theatre Club
Washington, DC

Spread Eagle Strikes Back (revue)
6-27-68
Washington Theatre Club
Washington, DC

Spread Eagle (V)
See: A Fifth of Spread Eagle

Spring at Merino
Constance Cox
8-20-69
Forestburgh Summer Theater
Monticello, NY

Spring Bouquet
Silvia Bandyke
10-28-72
Omni Theatre Club
145 W. 18th, N.Y.C.

Spring Offensive, The
Arthur Sainer
6-6-73
Bridge Collective
Supernova
451 W. Broadway, N.Y.C.

Spring Thaw '69 (revue)
4-21-69
Royal Alexandra Theatre
Toronto, CAN

Spring Thaw '71
Robert & Elizabeth Swerdlow (book); Robert Swerdlow (music & lyrics)
3-17-71
Global Village
Toronto, CAN

Spring – Voices
Andy Robinson
12-4-69
La Mama ETC
74 E. 4th, N.Y.C.

Sprintorgasmuss
Wilhelm Penny
12-11-69
La Mama ETC
74 E. 4th, N.Y.C.

Squanto
James Magnuson
Spring, 1973
Princeton University
Princeton, NJ

Square Peg, The
Lee Hunkins
3-17-72
American Community Theatre
Bed-Stuy Civic Center
Brooklyn, NY

Square Root of Hip
Burt French
8-22-72
Playhouse 101
Milford, NH

Squirrel Island
Nomi Rubel
11-28-69
Stage Lights Theatrical Club
218 W. 48th, N.Y.C.

S.R.O.
Ken Eulo
Summer, 1971
Eugene O'Neill Memorial Theatre
Waterford, CT

St. Dynamite's Ragtime Dance
Robert Capece
3-18-72
Actors' Experimental Unit
682 Sixth, N.Y.C.

St. Hydro Clemency
Megan Terry & Tom O'Horgan
12-9-73
St. Clement's Church
423 W. 46th, N.Y.C.

St. Jermyn
Andrew Glaze
5-16-69
First Unitarian Church
Brooklyn, NY

St. Joan of the Stockyards
Bertolt Brecht; Frank Jones (translator)
4-27-71
University of Pennsylvania
Philadelphia, PA

St. Julian the Hospitaler
Gustave Flaubert; adapted by Kenneth Cavander
8-19-70
Yale Repertory Theatre
East Hampton, NY

Stab at Getting Laid in New York. . ., A
Hal Craven
7-17-69
New York Theatre Ensemble
2 E. 2nd, N.Y.C.

Stag at Bay, The (staged reading)
Charles MacArthur & Nunnally Johnson
2-22-72
Florida State University
Tallahassee, FL

Stag Movie
David Newburge (book & lyrics); Jacques Urbont (music)
1-3-71
Gate Theatre
2nd & 10th, N.Y.C.

Stag Party
Leonard Webb
1-17-71
Baldwin-Wallace College
Berea, OK

Stage Leers and Love Songs
Mary Silverman (book & lyrics); Stanley Silverman (music)
8-15-73
Lenox Arts Center
Lenox, MA

Staircase
Charles Dyer
1-10-68
Biltmore Theatre
N.Y.C.

Stalin (with Red Lips)
Ed Wode
12-2-70
Free Store Theatre
14 Cooper Sq., N.Y.C.

Stand in the Mountains, A
Peter Taylor
Nov., 1968
Dramatic Club
Kenyon College
Gambier, OH

Stanley
Dean Kaner (book & lyrics); Dean Kaner & Myron Goodman (music)
10-11-73
Bloomington Civic Theatre
Bloomington, MN

Star Bright (with Bluebird)
Ted Menten
9-6-72
Mercer Arts Center
240 Mercer, N.Y.C.

Star Is Always Loved and Loved, The (with Puppy Love)
Peter Copani
5-15-68
Playbox
94 St. Mark's Pl., N.Y.C.

Starmakers, The (with The Pleasure Seekers)
8-17-73
Tentarena
Monticello, NY

Starry Night ("puppets, people & music")
12-27-71
Universalist Theatre
4 W. 76th, N.Y.C.

Starry Night Theatre (improvisational)
11-14-71
Jean Cocteau Theatre
43 Bond, N.Y.C.

State
Richard deBlasi
11-27-70
New York Theatre Ensemble
2 E. 2nd, N.Y.C.

Station, The
Wesly St. Clair
11-14-69
Black Mask Players
34 W. 134th, N.Y.C.

Stations of the Cross
Peter Schumann
5-23-72
Bread & Puppet Theatre
St. Clement's Church
423 W. 46th, N.Y.C.

Status Quo Vadis
Donald Driver
8-26-71
Ivanhoe Theatre
Chicago, IL

Steal the Old Man's Bundle
Kenneth Pressman
5-15-70
Fortune Theatre
62 E. 4th, N.Y.C.

Steambath
Bruce Jay Friedman
6-30-70
Truck & Warehouse Theatre
79 E. 4th, N.Y.C.

Step Lively, Boy (musical)
Vinnette Carroll & Micki Grant
1-31-73
Urban Arts Corps
26 W. 20th, N.Y.C.

Stephanie
5-16-73
Boston Center for the Arts
Boston, MA

Stephen Foster
Earl Hobson Smith
7-12-73
Minnesota Centennial Showboat
Minneapolis, MN

Steps
Jerzy Kosinski
9-25-70
Columbia University
N.Y.C.

Sticks and Bones
David Rabe
1969
Villanova University
Villanova, PA

Sticks and Stones
James Reaney
1973
Tarragon Theatre
Toronto, Ontario, CAN

Sticks and Stones (revue)
Kelly Fitzpatrick & Ed Geldart
10-22-68
Charlie's
235 W. 52nd, N.Y.C.

Still Falling
Nancy Walter; John Franzen (music)
7-10-71
Firehouse Theatre
San Francisco, CA

Still Life
McCrea Imbrie & Timothy Imbrie
3-1-73
CSC Repertory Theatre
89 W. 3rd, N.Y.C.

Still Life with Apples
Ruth Rehrer Wolff
July, 1968
Eugene O'Neill Memorial Theatre
Waterford, CT

Still Life (with Matins)
Hal Ackerman
11-22-68
First Unitarian church
Brooklyn, N.Y.C.

Stinkin' from Drinkin' (musical)
12-3-71
Bank Theatre
Brooklyn, NY

Stinking from Drinking
July, 1971
Old Reliable Theatre
231 E. 3rd, N.Y.C.

Stolen Words
Joao Perry
10-6-71
La Mama ETC
74 E. 4th, N.Y.C.

Stomp
11-16-69
New York Shakespeare Festival Public Theatre
425 Lafayette, N.Y.C.

Stone Cycle
Powell Shepherd & Art O'Reilly
1-19-70
Old Reliable Theatre Tavern
231 E. 3rd, N.Y.C.

Stoned
James Rosenfield
1-29-70
Changing Scene
Denver, CO

Stooping To Pick up a Tame Bird, I Discovered a Wild Goose
10-3-69
Dramarena Repertory Theatre
158 W. 55th, N.Y.C.

Stop the Parade
Marsha Sheiness
11-13-73
Playwrights' Horizons
Clark Center for the Performing Arts
West Side YWCA, 8th Ave. & 51st, N.Y.C.

Stop the Presses (musical)
9-12-72
White Barn Theatre
Irwin, PA

Stop, You're Killing Me!
James Leo Herlihy
3-19-69
Stage 73
321 E. 73rd, N.Y.C.

Stops
Robert Auletta
2-1-72
Yale Repertory Theatre
New Haven, CT

Storkwood
Mark Dunster
6-4-73
Playwrights' Horizons
Clark Center for the Performing Arts
West Side YWCA, 8th Ave. & 51st, N.Y.C.

Story—Aunt Rollie or Before and After, The (with The Aluminium Pigey and The Daughter of Earl Siphon)
Larry O'Connel
Spring, 1970
Second Group Theatre
McBurney YMCA
215 W. 23, N.Y.C.

Story Structure (improvisational musical scenes)
4-7-72
Theatre of the Riverside Church
490 Riverside Dr., N.Y.C.

Story Teller, A (with The Summer's Breeze)
Irving Glusack
8-25-72
New York Theatre Ensemble
2 E. 2nd, N.Y.C.

Story Theatre (Grimms' Fairytales and Aesop)
Paul Sills
1-23-69
Yale University
New Haven, CT

Story Theatre (2) ("Metamorphoses" by Ovid)
Paul Sills
11-27-69
Yale University
New Haven, CT

Story Theatre (3) Repertory
See: Gimpel the Fool; St. Julian the Hospitaler; and Olympian Games

Strada, La
Lionel Bart (music & lyrics); Charles K. Peck, Jr. (book)
10-25-69
Fisher Theatre
Detroit, MI

Straight from the Ghetto
Neil Harris & Miguel Pinero
11-4-73
Theatre of the Riverside Church
490 Riverside Dr., N.Y.C.

Straight Up
Syd Cheatle
6-28-73
Missouri Repertory Theatre
University of Missouri
Kansas City, MO

Straights of Messina, The
David Starkweather
11-28-73
Circle Theatre Company
2307 Broadway, N.Y.C.

Strains
Jeannine O'Reilly
6-8-70
Old Reliable Theatre Tavern
231 E. 3rd, N.Y.C.

Strange Festival, The
Robert Goldstein
Dec., 1972
181 Christopher St., N.Y.C.

Stranger, The (with Incident at Twilight)
4-15-69
Basement Coffee House
Baruch College
N.Y.C.

Strangulation
Donald Kvares
12-17-70
St. Peter's Church
346 W. 20th, N.Y.C.

Straphangers, The
Robert Somerfeld
1-5-73
Amas Repertory Theatre
4 W. 76th, N.Y.C.

Strays (with Third Ride on a Merry Go Round)
Blanche Mednick Oliak
3-23-73
New York Theatre Ensemble
2 E. 2nd, N.Y.C.

Stream Has Shown Me My Semblance True, The
7-10-72
Elgin Theatre
N.Y.C.

Street Corner
Richard Wesley
Summer, 1972
Street Theatre, Inc., Ossining, NY
Lincoln Center Plaza
N.Y.C.

Street Jesus
Peter Copani
8-25-73
Peoples Performing Company
Lincoln Center Plaza
N.Y.C.

Street King
Bruce Peyton
2-26-73
Theatre for the Forgotten
26 W. 84th, N.Y.C.

Street Life
Joseph Washington
8-22-72
Brownsville Theater Project
Lincoln Center Plaza, N.Y.C.

Street Plays and Other Events
Pageant Players
1-10-70
Pageant Players
450 Broome St., N.Y.C.

Street Sounds
Ed Bullins
10-14-70
La Mama ETC
74 E. 4th, N.Y.C.

Strictly for Kicks (revue)
12-9-68
Oxford and Cambridge Shakespeare Company
Hunter College
N.Y.C.

Strike Heaven on the Face
Richard Wesley
1-15-73
New Phoenix Theatre
Lyceum Theatre
N.Y.C.

Strindberg Brothers, The
Oyvind Fahlstrom
6-11-68
Gotham Art
455 W. 43rd, N.Y.C.

String
Alice Childress
4-1-69
Negro Ensemble Company
St. Mark's Playhouse
133 Second, N.Y.C.

Strings Snapping
Andy Wolf
11-14-72
Manhattan Theatre Club
321 E. 73rd, N.Y.C.

Strip Tease (with Life and Death in Detroit)
David MacLaren
12-8-72
New York Theatre Ensemble
2 E. 2nd, N.Y.C.

Strolling
Black Vibrations
10-29-70
Bedford-Lincoln Neighborhood Museum
Bedford Ave. & Lincoln Pl., Brooklyn, NY

Strong Men, The
Stratis Karras
7-15-72
Westbeth Cabaret Theatre
155 Bank, N.Y.C.

Strongbox, The (with The Snob)
Carl Sternheim
2-23-68
Cooper Union
N.Y.C.

Struck
Sandra Scoppettone
7-31-72
Eugene O'Neill Memorial Theatre
Waterford, CT

Struggle for a Soul
2-4-72
Emerson College
Boston, MA

Strumpfbandoperette, Die
6-2-72
New School
66 W. 12th, N.Y.C.

Student Life
1-4-69
6th Street Theatre
543 E. 6th, N.Y.C.

Stuffings
James Prideaux
5-3-71
Library & Museum of the Performing Arts
111 Amsterdam, N.Y.C.

Stump Removal
Tone Brulin
Spring, 1972
Otrabanda Company
Ohio University
Athens, OH

Sty of the Blind Pig, The
Phillip Hayes Dean
11-23-71
Negro Ensemble Company
St. Mark's Playhouse
133 Second, N.Y.C.

Stylites, The (with A Garden of Delights)
Andrew Bauer
6-5-72
Manhattan Theatre Club
321 E. 73rd, N.Y.C.

Sub-Lease
Larry Meyers
10-28-72
Omni Theatre Club
145 W. 18th, N.Y.C.

Subtitles (with Her(r) Professor)
Michael McGrinder
11-23-70
Old Reliable Theatre Tavern
231 E. 3rd, N.Y.C.

Subway, A Piece in Motion
6-11-70
Reese Palley Gallery
93 Prince St., N.Y.C.

Successors, The (with Dawn)
Walter Turney
1-12-73
Playwrights' Horizons
Clark Center for the Performing Arts
West Side YWCA, 8th Ave. & 51st, N.Y.C.

Suddenly at Home
Francis Durbridge
7-9-73
Westport Country Playhouse
Westport, CT

Sue Barton Student Nurse Loves Frankenstein
Carl Larsen (book & lyrics); Patricia Lehrmann (music)
1-23-70
Hudson Guild Theatre
441 W. 26th, N.Y.C.

Sue Barton Student Nurse's Dilemma
Carl Larsen; music by Patricia Lehrmann
2-21-68
Fulton Theatre Company
119 Ninth, N.Y.C.

Suffragette
John McNamara & James Dudley
3-8-73
Agassiz Theatre
Radcliff College
Cambridge, MA

Sugar
Peter Stone (book); Bob Merrill (lyrics); Jule Styne (music)
1-17-72
Opera House
Washington, DC

Sugar Mouth Sam Don't Dance No More (with Orrin)
Don Evans
10-12-72
H B Playwrights Foundation
124 Bank, N.Y.C.

Suggs
David Wiltse
5-4-72
Forum Theatre
Lincoln Center
N.Y.C.

Suicide Exhibition
Dale Blair
5-8-71
Theatre KIVA
150 Bleecker, N.Y.C.

Suicide in Alexandria
Nelly Vivas
12-16-70
La Mama ETC
74 E. 4th, N.Y.C.

Sultan of Tuffet, The (with The Whistling Wizard)
Bil Baird & Alan Stern
12-20-69
Bil Baird Theatre
59 Barrow, N.Y.C.

Summer Days
Romain Weingarten, Suzanne Grossmann (translator)
5-31-71
National Arts Centre
Ottawa, CAN

Summer Ghost, A
Claude Fredericks
3-7-69
Players Workshop
229 Seventh, N.Y.C.

Summer's Breeze, The (with A Story Teller)
Irving Glusack
8-25-72
New York Theatre Ensemble
2 E. 2nd, N.Y.C.

Summertime
Ugo Betti
4-2-70
WPA
34 E. 4th, N.Y.C.

Summertree
Ron Cowen
3-3-68
Forum Theatre
Lincoln Center
N.Y.C.

Sun Deck
Lee Franklin Merriweather
12-12-70
Inner Court Theatre
504 Grand, N.Y.C.

Sun Is a Red Dwarf, The
Myron Levoy
4-25-69
New York Theatre Ensemble
2 E. 2nd, N.Y.C.

Sun's Morning
Franklin Engel & Miranda McDermott
7-7-71
Provincetown Playhouse
133 MacDougal, N.Y.C.

Sunday
Joseph Scott Kierland
4-15-73
Eugene O' Neill Theatre Center
New York Cultural Center
2 Columbus Circle, N.Y.C.

Sunday Circus (varied theatrical programs)
7-2-72
Cornell University
Ithaca, NY

Sunday Comics (revue)
5-26-72
Elgin Theatre
N.Y.C.

Sunday Dinner
Joyce Carol Oates
10-16-70
American Place Theatre
N.Y.C.

Sunday Drive
Michael Morris
1-31-69
Catholic University
Washington, DC

Sunday Morning (with The Bee and the Butterfly and Ruby Keeler Is a Mother)
Charles Kerbs
1-31-69
Theatre of Our Discontent
Clifton Hotel
127 W. 79th, N.Y.C.

Sunday Promenade, The
Lars Forssell
10-31-68
Thresholds
23 E. 20th, N.Y.C.

Sundeck
Leon Wittack
12-5-70
Cubiculo
414 W. 51st, N.Y.C.

Sundial, The
Ursule Molinaro
2-18-72
New Village Theatre
433 E. 6th, N.Y.C.

Sunshine Boys, The
Neil Simon
11-20-72
Shubert Theatre
New Haven, CT

Sunshine Town
Mavor Moore (book, lyrics, music)
7-29-68
Fathers of Confederation Memorial Centre
Charlottetown, Prince Edward Island, CAN

Sunshine Train, The (gospel musical)
Conceived by William E. Hunt
6-15-72
Abbey Theatre
136 E. 13th, N.Y.C.

Sun/The Gentle (The Penetrating Wind)
Chris Parker & David Sundance
Dec., 1971
Center for the New Performing Art
Iowa City, IA

Superfreak!
Donald L. Brooks
8-8-69
Playbox
94 St. Mark's Pl., N.Y.C.

Suppose I Fall?
Stan Edelson
Spring, 1973
Caravan Theatre
Cambridge, MA

Supreme Commander, The
Murray Moltner
4-21-72
New York Theatre Ensemble
2 E. 2nd, N.Y.C.

Supreme Equal, The
Charles Langdon
7-13-72
Changing Scene
Denver, CO

Sure, This Is It! (with The Kewperts and the Galoonghaleis)
9-23-73
Community Loft
250 W. 106th, N.Y.C.

Surprise
Fred Carmichael
8-27-69
Dorset Playhouse
Dorset, VT

Surprise Package!
M. T. Teeners
8-16-68
Tentarena
East Monticello, NY

Surprise Party, The
Lee Kalcheim
5-18-70
New Dramatists Workshop
424 W. 44th, N.Y.C.

Surrealm (rock cartoon)
6-17-73
Theatre of Madness
Bank Theatre
Brooklyn, NY

Survival of Saint Joan, The (a rock concert)
James Lineberger (book & lyrics); Ruffin (music)
4-15-70
Playwrights' Unit
83 E. 4th, N.Y.C.

Survival (with Up, Up, and Away)
Michael Kortchmar
11-20-73
BRC (Black Renaissance Co.)
Playbox
94 St. Mark's Pl., N.Y.C.

Surviving Death in Three Acts
Nancy Fales
5-2-73
Active Trading Company
N.Y.C.

Susan Peretz at the Manhattan Theatre Club
Megan Terry
5-24-73
New York Theatre Strategy Festival
Manhattan Theatre Club
321 E. 73rd, N.Y.C.

Swallow, The (with The Eagle and the Serpent)
Ernesto Fuentes
3-26-70
Duo Theatre Workshop
522 E. 12th, N.Y.C.

Swallowed
12-6-73
Theatre Two
Cambridge, MA

Swan Song (part of a bill entitled Troika)
Anton Chekhov; new adaptation by Morris Carnovsky
3-17-72
Long Wharf Theatre
New Haven, CT

Sweet Enemy, The
Joyce Carol Oates
3-9-73
Cubiculo
414 W. 51st, N.Y.C.

Sweet Eros
Terrence McNally
8-4-68
Cafe Act IV
Provincetown, MA

Sweet Feet
Dan Graham (book); Don Brockett (music & lyrics)
5-25-72
New Theatre
154 E. 54th, N.Y.C.

Sweet Shoppe Myriam, The
Ivan Klima, Ruth Willard (translator)
2-4-71
Cubiculo
414 W. 51st, N.Y.C.

Sweet Tom
Myron Levoy
7-3-69
Playbox
94 St. Mark's Pl., N.Y.C.

Sweetness
Jeffrey Moss
5-15-72
La Mama ETC
74 E. 4th, N.Y.C.

Sweetpea and Honey
James Edward Shannon
4-5-72
Playwrights' Workshop Club
Bastiano's Studio
14 Cooper Square, N.Y.C.

Swinger, The
Alan Rubenstein
8-27-70
Black River Playhouse
Chester, NJ

Switchblade-Machete
Davy Paul
4-12-71
Sweetness & Light Satirical Theatre
Omaha, NB

Swung
Richard Lenz
12-5-69
Extension Theatre
277 Park Ave. So., N.Y.C.

Syllables
B. S. Bull
1-22-71
Assembly Theatre
113 Jane, N.Y.C.

Sylvia (with Revolt in the Leper Colony)
Sheldon Cholst
4-13-73
New York Theatre Ensemble
2 E. 2nd, N.Y.C.

Symbiosis Golden
Glover Buck
2-25-70
Stage Lights Theatrical Club
218 W. 48th, N.Y.C.

System, The
Clarence Young III
8-26-72
Theatre West, Dayton Ohio
Lincoln Center Plaza
N.Y.C.

T

T. R. Tuffe
Moliere (improvised adaptation)
10-18-72
Theater One Twenty
120th & Broadway, N.Y.C.

Tabernacle
Paul Carter Harrison
9-4-70
Antioch College
Yellow Springs, OH

Tabula-Rasa
Multi-media program featuring short plays by Megan Terry, Sally Ordway, Susan Yankowitz, Sharon Thei Bill Russell, Ed Bullins, Jean-Claude van Itallie
2-25-72
Brooklyn Academy of Music
30 Lafayette, Brooklyn, NY

Tackle That Snowman
R. Gordon
January, 1973
Mafundi Institute
Los Angeles, CA

Tadpole
Jules E. Tasca
9-18-73
New Theatre for Now
Los Angeles, CA

Tag
Ted Jordan
Dec., 1971
Center for the New Performing Art
Iowa City, IA

Take My Wife
Marvin Sandberg
8-5-69
Boothbay Playhouse
Boothbay, ME

Take One Step
Gerald Freedman & John Morris
6-25-68
New York Shakespeare Festival Public Theatre
425 Lafayette, N.Y.C.

Take Very Good Care of Yourself
Michael Shurtleff
12-1-72
Friday Theatre
N.Y.C.

Take Your Chair with You
Mark Decker
12-22-73
Community Loft
250 W. 106th, N.Y.C.

Take Your Pic (musical)
4-11-72
New England Life Hall
Boston, MA

Taking Care of Business
Marvin X
10-3-69
Afro-American Studio
15 W. 126th, N.Y.C.

Tale for Christmas Eve, A, or, The Comic Why of Suffering,
Susan Jack
7-18-73
Manhattan Theatre Club
321 E. 73rd, N.Y.C.

Tales of Hoffmann
E. T. A. Hoffman; Josef Bush (adaptor)
2-16-73
WPA
333 Bowery, N.Y.C.

Tales of the Revolution and Other American Fables
Jane Chambers
8-3-72
Eugene O'Neill Memorial Theatre
Waterford, CT

Tales of Women
Max G. Weine
11-3-72
Guild Studio One
Broadway at 73rd, N.Y.C.

Talking Love
11-13-73
Theatre for the New City
113 Jane, N.Y.C.

Tall and Rex
David Wiltse
10-26-71
Chelsea Theatre Center
30 Lafayette, Brooklyn, NY

Tallulah, A Memory
Eugenia Rawls
1-14-71
Library & Museum of the Performing Arts
111 Amsterdam, N.Y.C.

Talus (Hadrian's Wall)
Ronald W. Lackman
5-20-70
Madison Center Theatre
30 E. 31st, N.Y.C.

Tamarand
10-4-72
Caravan from Dramaturgia
La Mama ETC
74 E. 4th, N.Y.C.

Taming of the Beast
Robert Weingarten
4-9-70
St. Peter's Church
346 W. 20th, N.Y.C.

Tanuki, The Mischievous Racoon
Clive Rickabaugh (adaptor)
9-21-68
Goodman Theatre
Chicago, IL

Tapdance Your Traumas Away (a comic-tragic revue)
7-12-73
74 Below
74 Trinity Pl., N.Y.C.

Tarquin Truth Beauty (with The Youth Rebellion, Silver Skies, and Camera Obscura)
Robert Patrick
4-28-69
Old Reliable Theatre Tavern
231 E. 3rd, N.Y.C.

Tattletale Teapot, The
Ronnie Schleuter
4-6-68
Hudson Guild Theatre
119 Ninth, N.Y.C.

Tavern of the Raven
Alexander Panas
2-25-72
Southern Methodist University
Dallas, TX

Tavern, The
George M. Cohan, John McCabe (book & lyrics); Mary Cohan (music)
2-18-70
Interlochen Center for the Arts
Interlochen, MI

Taxi Dance Hall, The
Norman Taffel
12-3-71
Common Ground Theatre
70 Grand, N.Y.C.

Tea Party (with The Basement)
Harold Pinter
10-15-68
Eastside Playhouse
334 E. 74th, N.Y.C.

Teacups
Henry Morrison
1-16-73
WPA
333 Bowery, N.Y.C.

Team, The
Stuart Oderman
9-24-71
Omni Theatre Club
145 W. 18th, N.Y.C.

Teams
Drew Kalter
11-24-71
Cubiculo
414 W. 51st, N.Y.C.

Teaspoon Every Four Hours, A
Jackie Mason & Mike Morton
6-14-69
ANTA Theatre
245 W. 52nd, N.Y.C.

Tecumseh
Allen Eckhert
6-30-73
Chillicothe, OH

Teddy Bears Never Mate in Captivity
Dene Hammond
2-3-72
University of Missouri
Columbia, MO

Teeth of Mons Herbert, The
Philip LaZebnik (book, lyrics, music)
8-2-73
Unitarian Church
Columbia, MO

Telemachus Friend
Sally Dixon Wiener
4-17-72
St. Peter's Gate
130 E. 54th, N.Y.C.

Tell It Like It Is (folk musical)
Mar., 1971
Less-McRae College
Banner Elk, NC

Tell It to Angela
James M. Auer
7-17-71
Lawrence University
Appleton, WI

Tell Me, Worthy Editor
Jerome Bayer
3-5-72
Educational Alliance
197 E. Broadway, N.Y.C.

Tell Me You Don't Love Me, Charlie Moon
Michael Shurtleff
2-15-70
Extension Theatre
277 Park Ave. So., N.Y.C.

Tell Pharoah
Loften Mitchell
Feb., 1970
South Carolina State College
Orangeburg, SC

Temptation of Father Joe, The
K. P. Whittaker
8-25-73
Carpenter's Hall
Brooklyn, NY

Ten Best Martyrs of the Year, The
Seymour Simckes
10-18-73
Theatre for the New City
113 Jane, N.Y.C.

Ten Million B.C. Economic Spectacle of Jungola (10 Million B.C. Economic Spectacle of Jungola)
Jack Smith
3-6-71
Plaster Foundation
36 Greene, N.Y.C.

Ten O'Clock Scholar
Lewis Bianci & Milburn Smith
2-13-69
Royal Poinciana Playhouse
Palm Beach, FL

Ten Plus One (various authors; see below)
11-22-68
New York Theatre Ensemble
2 E. 2nd, N.Y.C.
Walk Me Home
by William Kushner
Three Month Seduction, The
by Hal Craven
Hiatus
by Cesar Torres
Emil's Leap
by Thomas Terefenko
Tuesday
by Joan Durant
Requiem for a Dead Duck
by Richard Hoag
Toyland
by Anna Belle Johnson
Barrage
by Grant Duay
Halloween Years, The
by Tony Giordano

Tennis, Anyone (1st installment of The Park)
F. V. Hunt
2-22-68
Troupe Theatre
167 W. 21st, N.Y.C.

Terminal
Open Theatre Company
4-13-70
St. Clement's Church
423 W. 46th, N.Y.C.

Termites, The
Jacques Burdick
Mar., 1968
Pillory Theatre
Adelphi University
Garden City, L.I., NY

Terraced Apartment, The
Steve Carter
2-26-68
Old Reliable Theatre Tavern
231 E. 3rd, N.Y.C.

Terrible Angels, The (Los Angeles Terribles)
Roman Chalbaud; translated by Alick Gay Kaplan and Paul Miranda
8-13-70
Henry Street Settlement Playhouse
466 Grand, N.Y.C.

Testimonies (Al & Big Mama, Mr. Zion, The Menials)
James Edward Shannon
5-26-71
La Mama ETC
74 E. 4th, N.Y.C.

Testing Bit, The
Raymond Platt
5-22-70
New York Theatre Ensemble
2 E. 2nd, N.Y.C.

Thank You, Miss Victoria (with Goodnight I Love You)
William H. Hoffman
8-26-68
Old Reliable Theatre Tavern
231 E. 3rd, N.Y.C.

Thanks, Courteous Wall
R. David Cox
7-3-72
Manhattan Players
Atlantic City Playhouse
Atlantic City, NJ

That Championship Season
Jason Miller
5-2-72
New York Shakespeare Festival Public Theatre
425 Lafayette, N.Y.C.

That Great Big Touchdown in the Sky!
Stanford Kopit
6-26-69
Spencer Memorial Church
99 Clinton, Brooklyn, NY

That Man from Moscow!
Nickolai Gogol; adapted by Marge Adelberg
4-20-70
McPherson Playhouse
Victoria, CAN

That Means You
Tom Williams
10-4-73
University of Missouri
Columbia, MO

That Old Rockabye
Susan Yankowitz
3-8-68
Cooper Square Arts Theatre
35 Cooper Sq., N.Y.C.

That One and the Other
Eric Concklin
1-6-69
Old Reliable Theatre Tavern
231 E. 3rd, N.Y.C.

That's Entertainment
Howard Dietz & Arthur Schwartz (music & lyrics)
4-14-72
Edison Theatre
240 W. 47th, N.Y.C.

That's the Ball Game (with Ready on the Right)
Carlo Grasso
2-21-69
Nucleus Repertory Theatre
261 W. 54th, N.Y.C.

That's the Game, Jack
Douglas Taylor
4-11-69
Milwaukee Repertory Theatre
Milwaukee, WI

That Simple Light May Rise Out of Complicated Darkness
Peter Schumann
12-12-72
Bread & Puppet Theatre
St. Clement's Church
423 W. 46th, N.Y.C.

Theatre Carnival (Très Chic by Michael Vittes; Ye Fish and Little Gods by Roma Greth; Tomorrow's Horrorscope by Richard Erickson & Dean McIlnay)
5-2-69
Theatre 13
201 W. 13th, N.Y.C.

Theatre of Light
2-28-69
Cassen-Stern Studio
727 Sixth, N.Y.C.

Theatre Romantique (mime dramas)
Gabriel Oshen
3-30-73
Fly-By-Night Presentations
Brooklyn, NY

Theatre Whose Stage Is the Street, The
Bertolt Brecht
2-27-69
Minor Latham Playhouse
Barnard College
N.Y.C.

Theatre-Go-Round
July, 1972
Theatre-Go-Round
Coolfont, WV

Theatregraphs
Jim Hardy
11-17-71
La Mama ETC
74 E. 4th, N.Y.C.

Theatro
Eugene Yanni
4-27-68
Theatre of Encounter
247 W. 72nd, N.Y.C.

Theory, Proof, Application (with Slow Memories; Inside My Head; and Fraternal Order of Police)
Barry Litvack
10-21-70
Playwrights' Unit
83 E. 4th, N.Y.C.

Therapy, The
Richard Morris
4-26-73
University of Missouri Theatre
Columbia, MO

There Are Men Too Gentle to Live Among Wolves
James Kavanaugh; adapted by Paul Werth
11-6-72
Mark Taper Forum
Los Angeles, CA

There Aren't Any
Harris Freedman
9-12-69
Cafe Déjà vu
339 E. 10th, N.Y.C.

There Is a Place for a Nice Girl in the Big City
David E. Rowley & Michael Shurtleff
2-4-72
Friday Theatre
N.Y.C.

There Once Was a Hermit Named Dave (with Respite and Projection Room)
Robert Somerfeld
10-17-68
Triangle Theatre
316 E. 88th, N.Y.C.

There's a Shadow Over This Land
The Black Night Ensemble
2-21-70
Danny's Restaurant
345 W. 46th, N.Y.C.

There's Egypt in Your Dreamy Eyes
Helen Bed and the Broken Springs
1-5-73
Playwrights' Workshop Club
Bastiano's Studio
14 Cooper Sq., N.Y.C.

There's Nothing More Obscene Than Plastic Lillies
Pat Rule
6-29-72
Changing Scene
Denver, CO

There's One in Every Marriage
Georges Feydeau (Le Dindon), Suzanne Grossmann & Paxton Whitehead (adaptors)
8-6-71
Stratford Festival
Stratford, Ontario, CAN

There Was a Little Girl
Susan Yankowitz
3-1-68
Cooper Square Arts Theatre
35 Cooper Sq., N.Y.C.

There Was a Tribe of Indians (with When Princes Could Be Waiters)
George Hammer
12-9-72
H B Playwrights Foundation
124 Bank, N.Y.C.

These Black Ghettos
Richard Toussaint
5-2-69
Black Mask Players
Kennedy Community Center
34 W. 134th, N.Y.C.

They Came
Bonnie Beardsley
1-20-71
Cubiculo
414 W. 51st, N.Y.C.

They Came from Spain
Margaret Harper
9-2-71
Palo Duro Canyon
Canyon, TX

They Don't Make 'em Like That Any More (revue)
6-6-72
Plaza Hotel
N.Y.C.

They Got Jack
Ed Kelleher
5-9-71
Dancers Studio Foundation
34 E. 10th, N.Y.C.

They Saw the Marching Band Go Round the Grandstand
2-22-73
Trust
American Theatre Laboratory
219 W. 19th, N.Y.C.

They Saw the Whole Zoo
Robert Andrew Bonnard
3-6-68
Extension Theatre
128 E. 7th, N.Y.C.

They Told Me That You Came This Way
David Epstein
12-6-68
Yale University
New Haven, CT

Thief
David Trainer
Summer, 1968
Eugene O'Neill Memorial Theatre
Waterford, CT

Thief of Bagdad, The
Christopher Cable (book & lyrics); Lew Kesler (music)
3-27-72
Pixie Judy Troupe
Plaza 9
Plaza Hotel, N.Y.C.

Thief, The
Steve Whitson
3-11-71
Production Workshop Club
80 Second, N.Y.C.

Thing Called Love, A
Matthew Ahern
5-27-68
11 Trinity Square Ontario, CAN

Thing Itself, The
Arthur Sainer
11-30-72
Theatre for the New City
113 Jane, N.Y.C.

Thing of Beauty, A
Charles M. Kray
6-10-71
Jacksonville University
Jacksonville, FL

Things
Thomas Terefenko
3-27-69
Playbox
94 St. Mark's Pl., N.Y.C.

Things
David Kranes
10-26-71
Chelsea Theatre Center
30 Lafayette, Brooklyn, NY

Things as They Are (with Losing Oneself)
Gina Collens
5-12-72
Theatre of the Americas
427 W. 59th, N.Y.C.

Things That Almost Happen
Claude McNeal
6-6-70
Unit Theatre
157 W. 22nd, N.Y.C.

Things To Hear, Things To See (An Evening with Huckleberry Finn)
Stephen Brown & Clay Boland
12-19-69
Chelsea Theatre Center
30 Lafayette, Brooklyn, NY

Things Went Badly in Westphalia
Martin Sherman
6-30-73
Southampton College Dramtic Society
Southampton, Long Island, NY

Third Commune, The
The Performance Group
12-8-71
Performing Garage
33 Wooster, N.Y.C.

Third Corner
Nina Robbins
6-1-71
Assembly Theatre
113 Jane, N.Y.C.

Third Generation
Jean Maljean
3-1-68
Lyric Players
Elmhurst, NY

Third Ride on a Merry Go Round (with Strays)
Blanche Mednick Oliak
3-23-73
New York Theatre Ensemble
2 E. 2nd, N.Y.C.

Thirty (with American Gothic)
Walter Hadler
12-5-68
Theatre Genesis
2nd Ave. & 10th, N.Y.C.

Thirty Years Past (Not Me, Boy and Hot Evening Rain)
Frederick Bailey
10-22-71
Playbox
94 St. Mark's Pl., N.Y.C.

This Agony, This Triumph
Reginald Rose
1-7-72
Stage West
West Springfield, MA

This God Business
Doral Chenoweth
3-17-71
13th Street Theatre
50 W. 13th, N.Y.C.

This House Has Quiet Rooms
Larry Jon Maness
5-28-71
Harwich Winter Theatre
West Harwich, MA

This Is a Recording
Susan Zeder
5-6-72
Southern Methodist University
Dallas, TX

This Is no Movie
1-18-73
Laughing Alley
Boston, MA

This Is Our Living Room
R. P. Dicky
3-19-71
Changing Scene
Denver, CO

This One's for the Fat Lady
12-2-73
Academy Theatre
Atlanta, GA

This Side of Paradise
8-2-71
Ring-A-Round Playhouse
Sturbridge, MA

This Way Out
Esteman de Leon
3-16-73
Omni Theatre Club
145 W. 18th, N.Y.C.

This Way to the Rose Garden
Don Tucker (music & lyrics); Roger N. Cornish (book & lyrics)
1-12-72
Alliance Theatre
Atlanta, GA

Thorp
Robert Myers
2-18-72
Academy Theatre
Atlanta, GA

Those Who Play the Clowns
Antonio Calabrese
7-13-73
Provincetown Repertory Company
Provincetown Playhouse
133 MacDougal, N.Y.C.

Thou Shalt Not Lie!
Franz Grillparzer
Fall, 1973
H B Playwrights Foundation
124 Bank, N.Y.C.

Thoughts
Lamar Alford
12-6-72
La Mama ETC
74 E. 4th, N.Y.C.

Thoughts on My Back
Megan Reed Thomas
5-21-70
Stage Lights Theatrical Club
218 W. 48th, N.Y.C.

Three
Raymond Gasper
3-18-70
Queens College Little Theatre
Flushing, NY

Three Ball Blues
Mark Berman
2-26-68
13th Street Theatre
50 W. 13th,
N.Y.C.

Three Big Sillies, The
Poor People's Puppets
10-13-72
Balloon Face Maggie's
111 St. Mark's Place, N.Y.C.

Three Black Households
James Edward Shannon
6-16-72
Adam Clayton Powell Auditorium
144 W. 138th, N.Y.C.

Three by Eliscue
Edward Eliscue
June, 1973
Courtyard Playhouse
137 W. 14th, N.Y.C.

Three by Shearwood (On Ship, Painting Day, and Jack B. Nimble)
6-14-69
Dancers Studio Foundation
34 E. 10th, N.Y.C.

Three by Two (Across the Bed; Playhouse; Matinee)
2-11-72
Gene Frankel Theatre Workshop
Mercer Arts Center
240 Mercer, N.Y.C.

Three Cuckolds, The (adapted from a 16th century scenario)
Leon Katz
2-27-69
Library & Museum of the Performing Arts
111 Amsterdam, N.Y.C.

Three Daughters, The (with The Wise and Foolish Maidens)
Transcribed by Fletcher Collins
1969
Mary Baldwin College
Staunton, VA
at Folger Shakespeare Library
Washington, DC

Three Drag Queens from Daytona (3 Drag Queens from Daytona)
Tom Eyen
6-10-73
La Mama ETC
74 E. 4th, N.Y.C.

Three Goats and a Blanket
Robert J. Hilliard & Woodie Kling
5-4-71
Coconut Grove Playhouse
Miami, FL

Three Grotescas
Rafael Bunuel
2-27-71
New York Theatre of the Americas
Studio 1
427 W. 59th, N.Y.C.

Three Hundred Sixty-Five Days (365 Days)
Adapted & directed by H. Wesley Balk from the novel by R. G. Glasser
11-16-71
Shevlin Arena Theatre
University of Minnesota
Minneapolis, MN

Three Lives
Joan Durant
12-22-72
New York Theatre Ensemble
2 E. 2nd, N.Y.C.

Three Maries, The (Cornish medieval play)
Kenneth Janes, adaptor
12-2-70
Barnard College Theatre Company
117th St. & Amsterdam Ave., N.Y.C.

Three Nocturnes
Richard Reichman
3-22-71
University of Texas
Austin, TX

Three Non-Shakespearian One Acts
Gabriele Roepke
4-22-71
WPA
333 Bowery, N.Y.C.

Three on a Bench
Doris Estrada
11-17-72
West Side Gay Theatre
W.S.D.G. Center
37 Ninth, N.Y.C.

Three on Broadway (anthology of American musical theatre)
11-12-73
Theatre de Lys
N.Y.C.

Three One Acts (Homecookin'; Andrew; Oursides)
Clay Goss
4-19-72
New Federal Theatre
240 E. 3rd, N.Y.C.

Three Original One-Act Plays
3-21-68
West Side YMCA
5 W. 63rd, N.Y.C.

Three Piece Set
Marty Davis
3-16-73
Anthony Mannino Drama Tree
182 Fifth, N.Y.C.

Three Plays
Michael Mathias
5-3-68
Riverside Theatre Workshop
Claremont Ave., N.Y.C.

Three Plays (If I Were the Only Boy; It's To Laugh; Double D)
Stan Lachow
2-22-73
Cranium Theatre
277 Park Ave. So., N.Y.C.

Three's a Crowd
Donald Kvares
1-22-70
New York Theatre Ensemble
2 E. 2nd, N.Y.C.

Three Scenic Views Through the Marvelous Eyes of a Soozie
Jack Kreuger
10-21-73
Brooklyn Museum
Brooklyn, NY

Three Sisters, The (new experimental version)
Anton Chekhov
6-12-70
Circle Theatre
2307 Broadway, N.Y.C.

Three Sons
Richard Lortz
Oct., 1970
Wagner College Auditorium
Staten Island, NY

Three Stops to Purgatory
Lucy Lee Flippen
8-21-69
New York Theatre Ensemble
2 E. 2nd, N.Y.C.

Three Stories High (showcase)
Winifred Wolfe
2-2-73
Mercer Arts Center
240 Mercer, N.Y.C.

Three Street Koans
See: Kool Aid

Three Temptations, The
Charles Williams
3-5-70
General Theological Seminary
175 Ninth Ave. at 20th, N.Y.C.

Three, The (with The Scoutmaster's Revenge)
Irwin Shapiro
4-16-71
Clark Center for the Performing Arts
West Side YWCA
8th Ave. & 51st, N.Y.C.

Three Thousand Five Hundred Indians, Sisters (3500 Indians, Sisters)
Stanley Seidman
7-10-72
Manhattan Theatre Club
321 E. 73rd, N.Y.C.

Three Thousand Five Hundred Indians (3500 Indians)
Stanley Seidman
5-31-68
Off Center Theatre
152 W. 66th, N.Y.C.

Three Times Toby
S. M. Schneble
4-24-69
Loft Workshop
152 Bleecker, N.Y.C.

Three Triangles (Mother's Day, Birds, and A Suitable Name)
William Kushner
9-10-71
New York Theatre Ensemble
2 E. 2nd, N.Y.C.

Three, Two, One (Not Much Limping, Monuments, May & December)
Gertrude Stein, Diane de Prima, James Waring
1-26-69
Mannhardt Theatre Foundation
N.Y.C.

Three Words in No Time (with It's Got To Be Black or White and Four Actors and a Restaurant)
Lyon Phelps
2-18-71
Judson Poets' Theatre
55 Wash. Sq. So., N.Y.C.

Three X Garcia (3 X Garcia)
Eduardo Garcia
2-18-71
Stagelights II
125 W. 22nd, N.Y.C.

Threshold of Pain
Hal Ackerman
12-27-68
New York Theatre Ensemble
2 E. 2nd, N.Y.C.

Thrilling Life of a Circus Performer Will One Day Be Yours, The (with Dragons in the Wall)
Teresa Marffie
6-7-72
West Side YWCA
8th Ave. & 51st St., N.Y.C.

Through a Glass Brightly
Fred Wagstaff
8-27-71
Pilgrims Theatre Company
Boston, MA

Throw-Away Kids, The
8-25-72
Freedom House Players, Madison, Wisconsin
Lincoln Center Plaza, N.Y.C.

Thunder in the Index
Phillip Hayes Dean
1-23-69
Chelsea Theatre Center
30 Lafayette Ave., Brooklyn, NY

Thunderstorms, New York Style
Hal Craven
7-7-72
New York Theatre Ensemble
2 E. 2nd, N.Y.C.

Thursday Night Self-Improvement Class, The
Jerry Fine
7-12-73
Changing Scene
Denver, CO

Tick, Tick . . .
Gary Engler
8-1-73
Drama Workshop
Theatre Calgary
Calgary, Alberta, CAN

Ticket
Richard Longchamps
11-7-70
American Theatre Company
Alice's Studio
106 E. 14th, N.Y.C.

Ticklish Acrobat, The
Robert Hivner
January, 1969
University of California
Irvine, CA

Tidings, Comfort, and Joy
Joseph Gath, Edna Schappert, Gloria Gonzalez
11-15-71
Playbox
94 St. Mark's Pl., N.Y.C.

Ti-Jean and His Brothers
Derek Walcott
7-26-72
New York Shakespeare Festival
Delacorte Theatre
Central Park, N.Y.C.

'Til 2 in the Morning (with I Came for a Job)
12-15-72
Long Island University
Brooklyn, NY

Tilt
Joel Schwartz
5-13-69
Mark Taper Forum
Los Angeles, CA

Tim Plus Two
Andrew Colmar
2-13-68
Little Theatre
181 Bleecker, N.Y.C.

Timberlines
Jeannine O'Reilly
2-16-70
Old Reliable Theatre Tavern
231 E. 3rd, N.Y.C.

Time Changes (a dramatic multimedia rock trip)
Harry Palmer
1-21-70
Ford Theatre
New England Mutual Hall
Boston, MA

Time for Bed — Take Me to Bed
Charles Love
6-13-69
Provincetown Playhouse
133 MacDougal, N.Y.C.

Time Is the Stream
John David Pollack
6-27-70
Hutchinson Theatre
Raymond, NH

Time Passage (mixed media play)
Franklin Engel & Miranda McDermott
6-28-73
Studio 10
321 E. 73rd, N.Y.C.

Time Shadows
Helen Duberstein
6-21-71
Circle Theatre Company
2307 Broadway, N.Y.C.

Time to Heal, A
Martin Bard & Leroy Lassane
10-3-69
Riverside Church
122nd & Riverside Dr., N.Y.C.

Times Square
Leonard Melfi
1-25-68
La Mama ETC
122 Second, N.Y.C.

Time-Space-Light Environment
June Blum
11-23-70
Flatsfixed Gallery
453 W. Broadway, N.Y.C.

Time-Time Tattoo
10-6-72
Paula Cooper Gallery
100 Prince, N.Y.C.

Timon's Beach
Gordon Rogoff
7-30-69
Berkshire Theatre Festival
Stockbridge, MA

Tingalary Bird, The
Mary Melwood
10-31-70
New York University
N.Y.C.

Tinkle, Tinkle
Thomas Terefenko
4-10-68
Old Reliable Theatre Tavern
231 E. 3rd, N.Y.C.

Tippicanoe and Deja Vu
Jan., 1973
Second City
Chicago, IL

Tissue Paper Lies
Maurice Noel; Jeremiah Murray (music)
11-30-72
West Side YWCA
8th Ave. & 51st, N.Y.C.

Tistou
Rafael V. Blanco
12-4-73
Lolly's Theatre Club
808 Lexington, N.Y.C.

To All Things Black and Beautiful
5-8-71
Africana Studies and Research Center
Cornell University
Ithaca, NY

To Be or Not To Be! (musical)
Edward Cashman & Joseph Lewis
4-6-73
Catholic University
Washington, DC

To Be or Not To Be—What Kind of Question Is That?
J. Ritterman & Zvi Reisel (sketches); Max Meszel (lyrics); Eli Rubenstein (music)
10-19-70
Barbizon-Plaza Theatre
N.Y.C.

To Be Young, Gifted and Black
Lorraine Hansberry, ed. by Robert Nemiroff
1-2-69
Cherry Lane Theatre
38 Commerce, N.Y.C.

To Beginningness (with Cerebrius Mentalus and Interlude on a Train)
Craig Wood
5-23-69
Wittenberg University Theatre
Springfield, OH

To Catch a Crooked Crown
Nat White
1-22-68
13th Street Theatre
50 W. 13th, N.Y.C.

To Children, With Love
Michael Lewis
8-5-72
Street 70 Ensemble
Rockville Civic Center
Montgomery County, MD

To Dream a Dinosaur
George Latshaw
7-2-71
University of Oklahoma
Norman, OK

To Everything There Is a Season
Betty Keller
Spring, 1970
Playhouse Theatre Company
N.Y.C.

To Express My Life I Have My Death (with Dr. Xerox)
Cesar Vallejo; adapted by Isaac Goldenburg
10-3-68
Cafe Four
522 E. 12th, N.Y.C.

To Kill a Devil (with The Gimmick)
Roger Furman
3-27-70
New Heritage Repertory
440 W. 110th, N.Y.C.

To Langston Hughes with Love
6-12-70
Afro-American Studio for Acting and Speech
15 W. 126th, N.Y.C.

To Live Another Summer. . .
Hayim Hefer and others
10-21-71
Helen Hayes Theatre
N.Y.C.

To Love Us Is to Pay Us
William Dunas
9-21-72
Tears Reality Corporation
330 Broome, N.Y.C.

To the Rescue
Paper Bag Players
3-17-73
Hunter College
N.Y.C.

Toby the Talking Turtle
John & Jan Hepler
1-26-73
College of Wooster
Wooster, OH

Toccata
Ted Pezullo
7-18-72
Jean Cocteau Theatre
43 Bond, N.Y.C.

Today We Killed Molly Bloom (workshop staging)
Eric Thompson
11-30-72
New Dramatists
424 W. 44th, N.Y.C.

Today We Saw a Turtle
David Kerry Heefner
9-12-69
Thresholds
23 E. 20th, N.Y.C.

Together Again for the Very First Time
4-25-69
West End Collegiate Church
245 W. 77th, N.Y.C.

Together Tonight Loving Each Other So Much
Maruxa Vilalta
11-4-71
New York Theatre of the Americas
321 E. 73rd, N.Y.C.

Tokalitta (historical drama)
Summer, 1973
State Parks, GA

Tokyo Diary
Marci Sutin (book & lyrics); Itsuro Shimoda (music)
11-5-71
La Mama ETC
74 E. 4th, N.Y.C.

Tom
Alexander Buzo
12-19-73
Arena Stage
Washington, DC

Tom Jones
Austin Pendleton (book); Joseph Mathewson & Peter Bergman (lyrics); Robert Archer (music)
3-30-69
Extension Theatre
277 Park Ave. So., N.Y.C.

Tom Jones
New adaptation with music by Sally Nusbaum & Alexander Maissel
7-26-72
Forestburgh Summer Theatre
Monticello, NY

Tom Piper
Ed Lakso
7-14-69
Goodspeed Opera House
East Haddam, CT

Tom Swift and His . . . (revue)
Dinglefest Theatre Company
5-16-73
Body Politic
Chicago, IL

Tomb of Henry James, The (with Diferencias I-IV)
Piero Heliczer
2-4-71
Cinematheque
80 Wooster, N.Y.C.

Tomorrow
Horton Foote
4-15-68
H B Playwrights Foundation
124 Bank, N.Y.C.

Tomorrow's Horrorscope
Richard Erickson & Dean McIlnay
5-2-69
Theatre 13
201 W. 13th, N.Y.C.

Tongue Tied Tales (silent movie mime)
Nancy Z. Rubin
3-30-73
WPA
333 Bowery, N.Y.C.

Tonight's the Night
Michael Shurtleff
4-11-69
Actor's Place
487 Hudson, N.Y.C.

Tonight We Improvise
The Mort Siegel Players
7-5-73
Cubiculo
414 W. 51st, N.Y.C.

Tonight We Improvise (without Pirandello) or Tonight We Torture the Audience
Tom Eyen
2-1-68
Playwrights' Workshop Club
14 Waverly Pl., N.Y.C.

Tonto
Guy Gauthier
3-26-71
Playbox
94 St. Mark's Pl., N.Y.C.

Tony and the Call Girl
Ciro Baldinucci
3-20-70
Play Lab
130 E. 7th, N.Y.C.

Too Bad About Sparrow
J. J. Coyle
4-9-73
Library & Museum of the Performing Arts
111 Amsterdam, N.Y.C.

Too Much (with The Girl with the Ring on Her Nose and The Other One) (One of four one-act plays presented under title About Women)
Mario Fratti
4-1-71
Loft Theatre
21 Bond, N.Y.C.

Too Young for Spring
Jerry Oddo
8-1-71
Barter Theatre
Abingdon, VA

Toohey in Transit
Collective Movement Theatre
12-7-73
Huntington Ave. YMCA
Boston, MA

Tooth of Crime, The
Sam Shepard
11-9-72
McCarter Theatre
Princeton, NJ

Top Hat
Paul C. Harrison
1-12-72
Negro Ensemble Company
St. Mark's Playhouse
133 Second, N.Y.C.

Top Hat
Paul Carter Harrison
1-5-73
Players' Workshop
83 E. 4th, N.Y.C.

Tosca
Victorien Sardou; Joseph Renard (translator)
2-24-73
WPA
333 Bowery, N.Y.C.

Toscanini and Picasso
Calder Willingham
6-24-68
Playhouse
Kennebunkport, ME

Total Eclipse
Christopher Hampton
Oct., 1972
Folger Theatre Group
Washington, DC

Total Eclipse of Stephanie Schreck, The
Vincent Ventola
10-30-69
Emerson College
Boston, MA

Total Recall
Richard Foreman
12-30-70
Ontological-Hysteric Theatre
Cinematheque
80 Wooster, N.Y.C.

Total Theatre for Youth
1-27-71
Clark Center for the Performing Arts
West Side YWCA
8th Ave. & 51st, N.Y.C.

Touch
Gareth Mann Sitz
2-19-70
Dramarena Repertory Theatre
158 W. 55th, N.Y.C.

Touch, A Communal Musical
Kenn Long & Amy Saltz (book); Kenn Long (lyrics); Kenn Long & Jim Cozier (music)
11-8-70
Village Arena Theatre
62 E. 4th, N.Y.C.

Touch and Go (with Losing Things)
Benjamin Bradford
12-6-72
Dept. of Theatre Arts
University of Kentucky
Lexington, KY

Touch of Brightness, A
Partap Sharma
7-19-72
Brooklyn College
Brooklyn, NY

Touch of Orpheus, A
Wallace Hamilton
1-7-72
Omni Theatre Club
145 W. 18th, N.Y.C.

Tough To Get Help!
Steve Gordon
5-4-72
Royale Theatre
N.Y.C.

Tower of Babel, The
Arthur Morey & Bobby Paul
2-4-71
Columbia University
N.Y.C.

Toy Show
Leon Katz
11-5-70
La Mama ETC
74 E. 4th, N.Y.C.

Toyland (with Hard Core Soft Shoe)
Anna Belle Johnson
4-15-72
St. Peter's Church
346 W. 20th, N.Y.C.

Très Chic
Michael Vittes
5-2-69
Theatre 13
201 W. 13th, N.Y.C.

Tragedy, A
Vladimir Mayakovsky
Fall, 1973
Cambridge Ensemble
Old Cambridge Baptist Church
Cambridge, MA

Tragedy in Pantomime, A
Clyde Ellsworth
3-12-70
Mainstream Theatre-Loft
20 E. 14th, N.Y.C.

Tragedy of Homer Sills, The
Tony Barsha
12-2-70
La Mama ETC
74 E. 4th, N.Y.C.

Tragedy of Thomas Andros, The
Ronald Wilcox
5-24-73
Circle Theatre Repertory
2307 Broadway, N.Y.C.

Tragedy's Prevention, A
Jean Richards
Spring, 1973
District Attorney's Crime Prevention Education Drama Program
Queens, NY

Tragic Side of Joe Fonebone, The
4-5-72
Boston Center for the Arts
Boston, MA

Tra-La-La, Ha-Ha!
Ellen Pahl
4-15-72
Malachy Players
457 W. 51st, N.Y.C.

Tramp
Arthur Spilliaert
9-20-72
Theatre Laboratoire Vicinal of Brussels
La Mama ETC
74 E. 4th, N.Y.C.

Trampa, La
Myrna Casas
11-26-71
New York Theatre of the Americas
427 W. 59th, N.Y.C.

Transcontinental Redemption of Buster C. Dunn, The (with The Famous River Bottom Strategy . . .)
John Snyder
4-10-70
Hudson Guild Theatre
441 W. 26th, N.Y.C.

Transfers
Conrad Bromberg
1-22-70
Village South Theatre
15 Vandam, N.Y.C.

Transfiguration
Brendan Larnen
10-13-70
Blackfriars' Guild
316 W. 57th, N.Y.C.

Transfiguration of Benno Blimpie, The
Albert Innaurato
8-6-73
Eugene O'Neill Memorial Theatre
Waterford, CT

Transformations
7-19-72
University of Rochester
Rochester, NY

Transformations, A Church Ritual
Edgar White
4-23-72
New York Shakespeare Festival Public Theatre
425 Lafayette, N.Y.C.

Transformations (staged reading)
Anne Sexton
4-12-73
Cubiculo
414 W. 51st, N.Y.C.

Transgressions
Jeffrey Selby
7-9-71
CSC Repertory Theatre
89 W. 3rd, N.Y.C.

Transgressor Rides Again, The
Aldo Giunta
5-20-69
Martinique Theatre
N.Y.C.

Trap, The
Henry Salerno
12-20-72
Playwrights' Workshop Club
Bastiano's Studio
14 Cooper Square, N.Y.C.

Trapshod
A.E.O. Goldman
May, 1971
Actor's Voyage East
N.Y.C.

Travellers, The
Ewan MacColl
5-1-68
Toronto Workshop Productions
12 Alexander St., Toronto, CAN

Travelling Sisters, The (with She Was a Lazy Witch)
John Kirkpatrick
11-17-72
West Side Gay Theatre
W.S.D.G. Center
37 Ninth Ave., N.Y.C.

Travels of Benjamin the Third
Adapted from S. Y. Abramovitch by Ben Bonus, T. Yonasovitch, Charles Tauber
10-28-69
Gindi Theatre of Judaism
Hollywood, CA

Treatment, The
Raymond Gentry
11-25-69
Forlin's Third Phase
Theatre 3
111th & Broadway, N.Y.C.

Treatment, The (with Soap Opera)
John Gruen
May, 1968
Loft Workshop
152 Bleecker, N.Y.C.

Trec
Arlie Stewart
11-23-69
Theatre Black
Eisner-Lubin Auditorium
New York University, N.Y.C.

Tree
Tom Oliver
7-25-69
Eugene O'Neill Memorial Theatre
Waterford, CT

Tree Choppers
Ron Mele
12-27-68
New York Theatre Ensemble
2 E. 2nd, N.Y.C.

Tree Climber, The (Ya Talli' Ash-Shagara)
Tewfik al-Hakim; translated by Denys Johnson-Davies
3-20-70
Alfred University Theatre
Alfred, NY

Trees Die Standing, The
Alejandro Casona; Yiddish adaptation by Ida Kaminska
10-12-69
Roosevelt Theatre
145 & 7th, N.Y.C.

Trial and Death of Socrates, The
Aliki Nord
1-8-68
Library & Museum of the Performing Arts
111 Amsterdam, N.Y.C.

Trial of A. Lincoln, The
James Damico
4-3-70
Hartford Stage Company
Hartford, CT

Trial of Anne Opie Wehrer. . ., The
Robert Ashley
5-26-69
Electric Circus
23 St. Mark's Pl., N.Y.C.

Trial of Hutton Daniels, The
Russell Rammingjay
4-2-71
Assembly Theatre
113 Jane, N.Y.C.

Trial of James McNeil Whistler, The
Don Phillip Palmer
12-27-73
On Broadway Theatre
San Francisco, CA

Trial of Lenny Bruce, The
4-23-71
Boston University
Boston, MA

Trial of Secundus Generation Blackman versus Hannah and William A. Blackman, The
Robert Kya-Hill
6-28-68
Theatre West
2301 W. 3rd, Dayton, OH

Trial of the Catonsville Nine, The
Daniel Berrigan
8-6-70
Mark Taper Forum
Los Angeles, CA

Trial of William Tell, The
Richard D. Waters
8-23-71
Fisherman's Players
North Eastham, MA

Trials and Tribs of Henry Gibbs, The
Robert Houston
8-1-73
International House
500 Riverside Dr., N.Y.C.

Trials of Oz, The
Geoff Robertson; Buzzy Linhart, Mick Jagger, John Lennon, Yoko Ono (music)
12-19-72
Anderson Theatre
66 Second, N.Y.C.

Tribal Music Pool
Angus MacLise & Jonathan Chernoble
12-5-69
Alternate U
530 Sixth, N.Y.C.

Tribute to Mother
Jeannine O'Reilly
5-12-69
Old Reliable Theatre Tavern
231 E. 3rd, N.Y.C.

Trick of the Eye
Chad Henderson
12-10-71
Playbox
94 St. Mark's Pl., N.Y.C.

Tricks
Jon Jory (book); Lonnie Burstein (lyrics); Jerry Blatt (music)
10-14-71
Actor's Theatre
Louisville, KY

Tricycle, The
Fernando Arrabal
1-9-70
Inner Theatre
356 Bowery, N.Y.C.

Trip . . .
Christopher Newton (book & lyrics); Allan Rae (music)
1-7-71
Theatre Calgary
Calgary, Alberta, CAN

Trip into Blackness, A
Youth Development Agency Drama Workshop
2-25-70
New York Public Library
115th Street Branch, N.Y.C.

Trip, The
Eric Krebs
11-28-69
Focus Coffeehouse
163 W. 74th, N.Y.C.

Trip, The
Michael Ondaatje
3-2-70
National Arts Centre School Tour
Ottawa, CAN

Trip, The
Arranged by Margaret Wilkins
2-8-70
Wesley Players
Naperville, IL

Trip to Another Dream
Mickey Maroni
5-6-70
Thwaites Night Watch Theatre
536 City Island Ave., N.Y.C.

Triple Image (Lunchtime Concert, The Inhabitants, and Coda)
Owen Wymark
4-26-68
Thresholds
23 E. 20th, N.Y.C.

Triple Play
Randolph Carter
11-3-68
Cherry Lane Theatre
38 Commerce, N.Y.C.

Triple Play (three one-acts)
Celia Karston, Denise Chavez, James Crump
May, 1973
Dallas Theatre Center
Dallas, TX

Tripping
Donald Kvares
12-24-71
New York Theatre Ensemble
2 E. 2nd, N.Y.C.

Trips
Mark Berman
Feb., 1971
Purdue University Theatre
Lafayette, IN

Tristan
Peter Schumann
6-26-70
Bread & Puppet Theatre
Brooklyn, NY

Triumph of Robert Emmet, The
Bache McEvers Whitlock
5-7-69
Frances Adler Theatre
211 W. 71st, N.Y.C.

Triune (Communication Gap; Do You Like Me? Say You Like Me; Willyum)
David Sawn, Frank Rizzo, Phil Balestrino
2-3-71
13th Street Theatre
50 W. 13th, N.Y.C.

Trotter
2-8-72
TSOCC Players
Roxbury, MA

Trouble Begins at Eight, The
Mark Twain; adapted by Randy Kim
3-25-72
Park Slope Cultural Center
186 St. John's Place Brooklyn, NY

Trouble in Territoon City, The
Arthur Givens
2-14-68
Fulton Theatre Company
119 Ninth, N.Y.C.

Trouble with Portnoy, The
Martha Baird
8-30-69
Terrain Gallery
39 Grove, N.Y.C.

True History of Squire Jonathan and His Unfortunate Treasure, The
John Arden
2-18-72
New Village Theatre
433 E. 6th, N.Y.C.

True Story
Eric Krebs
3-27-70
Focus Coffeehouse
163 W. 74th, N.Y.C.

Trumpet in the Land
Paul Green
7-3-70
Tuscaranus Valley Amphitheatre
New Philadelphia, OH

Trumpet of the New Moon (musical)
8-20-72
Manhattan Players
Atlantic City Playhouse
Atlantic City, NJ

Trust, The
William Dunas
12-4-71
Clark Center for the Performing Arts
West Side YWCA
8th Ave. & 51st, N.Y.C.

Truth About Chance, The
Robert M. Cory
March, 1971
Kansas State University
Manhattan, KS

Truth About It The: A Play
Otis Maclay
5-8-69
Loft Workshop
152 Bleecker, N.Y.C.

Try It! You'll Like It!
Jacob Jacobs & Max Zalatoff (book); Jacob Jacobs (lyrics); Alexander Olshenetsky (music)
3-14-73
Mayfair Theatre
235 W. 46th, N.Y.C.

Trysting Place (with Monica and New Listings)
3-29-73
Shelter West Company
St. Stephen's Church
120 W. 69th, N.Y.C.

Tsk, Mary, Tsk
Stanley Nelson
3-20-70
Stage Lights Theatrical Club
218 W. 48th, N.Y.C.

Tub
James Nichol
Summer, 1972
Provincial Summer School in Drama
Drumheller, Alberta, CAN

Tubs, The
Terrence McNally
12-21-73
Yale Repertory Theatre
New Haven, CT

Tubstrip
A. J. Kronengold
5-17-73
Mercer Arts Center
240 Mercer, N.Y.C.

Tucholsky (musical)
10-20-71
Brandeis University
Waltham, MA

Tug of War
Alan Rossett
12-11-70
Roundabout Theatre
307 W. 26th, N.Y.C.

Tunnel under Baymiller Street
Henry S. Humphrey
2-17-73
Lab Theatre
Mt. St. Joesph's College
Cincinnati, OH

Turds in Hell
Charles Ludlam
11-8-68
Gate Theatre
2nd Ave. & 10th, N.Y.C.

Turn Off the Dark
7-17-69
Queens College
Flushing, NY

Turnabouts, The (participation program)
4-29-72
St. Peter's Church
346 W. 20th, N.Y.C.

Turtlenecks
Bruce Jay Friedman & Jacques Levy
8-6-73
Fisher Theatre
Detroit, MI

TV Room, The
Ann Meltzer
2-9-73
Moving Company
46 Great Jones, N.Y.C.

Twanger
Ronnie Britton (book, lyrics, music)
11-15-72
Vandam Theatre
15 Vandam, N.Y.C.

Twee's Play
Stanley Kaplan
1-7-72
New York Theatre Ensemble
2 E. 2nd, N.Y.C.

Twelve Noon (12 Noon)
Victor Palmer Eschbach
11-13-70
La Mama ETC
74 E. 4th, N.Y.C.

Twentieth-Century Tar (20th-Century Tar)
Tom Sydorick
7-7-71
Cubiculo
414 W. 51st, N.Y.C.

Twenty–Three Years Later
Michael Weller
Fall, 1973
New Theatre for Now
Los Angeles, CA

Twenty Years from Now (with Funeral Jazz)
J. I. Rodale
3-3-69
Homer L. Ferguson High School
Newport News, VA

Twenty-Three Thousand Pieces of String (23,000 Pieces of String)
Christopher Jones
10-25-68
Anthony Mannino Drama Tree
182 Fifth, N.Y.C.

Twenty-Two Years (22 Years)
Bob Sickinger
5-20-71
New York Theatre Ensemble
2 E. 2nd, N.Y.C.

Twice Upon a Time (improvised tales)
7-25-73
Manhattan Theatre Club
321 E. 73rd, N.Y.C.

Twigs
George Furth
10-18-71
Playhouse
Wilmington, DE

Twin Brothers, The
George C. Fosgate (book & lyrics); George C. Fosgate & Dorothy Simpson (music)
8-3-72
Edson Hall
University of Minnesota
Morris, MN

Twist
John White
11-7-69
Cubiculo
414 W. 51st, N.Y.C.

Two at the Bar
11-18-69
Forlini's Third Phase
Theatre 3
111th & Broadway, N.Y.C.

Two by Two
Peter Stone (book); Martin Charnin (lyrics); Richard Rodgers (music)
9-14-70
Shubert Theatre
New Haven, CT

Two Camps by Koutoukas
H. M. Koutoukas
3-18-68
Actors Playhouse
100 Seventh Ave. So., N.Y.C.

Two Character Play, The
Tennessee Williams
7-8-71
Ivanhoe Theatre
Chicago, IL

Two Friends
Mark Sheinbaum
10-1-68
Nucleus Repertory Theatre
261 W. 54th, N.Y.C.

Two from Lost and Found
John Ford Noonan
4-22-71
Loft Theatre
21 Bond, N.Y.C.

Two from Soho
See: The Last of the Bummers and Subway

Two Gentlemen of Verona
Shakespeare; John Guare & Mel Shapiro (book); John Guare (lyrics); Galt MacDermot (music)
7-27-71
New York Shakespeare Festival
Delacorte Theatre
N.Y.C.

Two Girls and a Sailor
Edward M. Cohen
9-13-73
St. Clement's Church
423 W. 46th, N.Y.C.

Two If By Sea
Priscilla B. Dewey & Constantine Hutchins, Jr.
1-27-70
Theatre Company of Boston
Boston, MA

Two in All
Mike & Julie Wilson
4-26-72
Henry Street Settlement Playhouse
466 Grand, N.Y.C.

Two in the Back Room (with Black Manhood and She's Dead Now)
Earle Chisholm
5-21-70
Spencer Memorial Church
99 Clinton St., Brooklyn Heights, NY

Two New One Act Plays
Rafael Bunuel
4-25-68
La Mama ETC
122 Second, N.Y.C.

Two Nights in the Country
Martin Craft
2-23-72
Courtyard Playhouse
137 W. 14th, N.Y.C.

Two Nocturnes (Duet and Octet)
Richard Reichman
11-20-69
Artichoke Theatre
UACM
Pittsburgh, PA

Two Plays
F. V. Hunt
11-9-70
Assembly Theatre
113 Jane, N.Y.C.

Two Plus One Equals Two
Stuart Oderman
5-4-73
Omni Theatre Club
145 W. 18th, N.Y.C.

Two Saints
See: Gimpel the Fool and St. Julian the Hospitaler

Two Sisters, The
Frank Moffett Mosier
12-16-73
Actor's Place
487 Hudson, N.Y.C.

Two Times One
See: Duet for Solo Voice and The Last Straw

Two Virgins (multi-media work)
Fusion II and Joe West
3-24-71
Cubiculo
414 W. 51st, N.Y.C.

Tyrant Apostle, The
Richard D. Waters
7-15-70
Fisherman's Players
North Eastham, MA

U

U Turn
Michael Graham
5-28-69
St. Clement's Church
423 W. 46th, N.Y.C.

Ubu Bound
Alfred Jarry
10-25-73
Nighthouse Theatre
249 W. 18th, N.Y.C.

Ubu Cocu
Alfred Jarry
3-7-69
Open Theatre
N.Y.C.

Ugly, The (with Nude Gymnastics)
Tom Miller
10-17-69
Playbox
94 St. Mark's Pl., N.Y.C.

Umpapah!
M. dePury
7-17-73
Theatre Arts Corp.
Santa Fe, NM

Un Belle Di
Robert Patrick
1-26-68
Gallery Theatre
99 E. 2nd, N.Y.C.

Un' Ora Mia Moglie
Midi Mannocci
12-11-73
Teatro Italiano
Hunter College, N.Y.C.

Un Passage (with The Noisy Passenger and Fragile Freight)
Shelley Winters
12-30-70
Actor's Playhouse
100 Seventh Ave. So., N.Y.C.

Uncle Albert Auditions the Word
Albert G. Nalven
5-14-71
Cubiculo
414 W. 51st, N.Y.C.

Uncle Scrooge MacDuck and the Pill (reading)
Augusto Boal
3-19-73
Theatre of Latin America
St. Clement'Church
423 W. 46th, N.Y.C.

Uncle, The
Philip Lam
10-6-72
13th Street Theatre
50 W. 13th, N.Y.C.

Uncle Tom?
Delano Stuart
10-5-73
Bed-Stuy Theatre
Brooklyn, NY

Uncle Vanya
Anton Chekhov; Albert Todd & Mike Nichols (translators)
6-4-73
Circle in the Square/Joseph E. Levine Theatre
50th St. West of Broadway, N.Y.C.

Under MacDougal Street
James Prideaux
3-9-72
Cubiculo
414 W. 51st, N.Y.C.

Under Papa's Picture
George Tibbles & Joe Connelly
5-1-73
Off Broadway Theatre
San Diego, CA

Under the Cross Eyed Eagle
Elmer Kline
4-22-68
Old Reliable Theatre Tavern
231 E. 3rd, N.Y.C.

Undercover Cop
Robert Nichols
8-27-72
Theatre for the New City
Lincoln Center Plaza
N.Y.C.

Underground Bird, The
2-20-70
New York University
N.Y.C.

Undertaking, The
David Trainer
4-3-68
Playwrights' Unit
15 Vandam, N.Y.C.

Underwriter, The
John Robinson
10-6-69
Old Reliable Theatre Tavern
231 E. 3rd, N.Y.C.

Unfair to Goliath
Ephraim Kishon, adapted & with lyrics by Herbert Appleman; music by Menachem Zur
1-25-70
Cherry Lane Theatre
38 Commerce, N.Y.C.

Unfinished Song, The
Feb., 1970
Howard University
Washington, DC

Unforseen Death of a Butterfly on a Feather, The
Robert J. Landy
5-22-69
Adams School Great Hall
248 E. 31st, N.Y.C.

Unidentified Flying Angel
Charles Langdon
5-11-72
Changing Scene
Denver, CO

Unified Sensibility: An Ecological Review of U.S.
Tom Eagan
11-14-70
Playbox
94 St. Mark's Pl., N.Y.C.

Union, The
Ransom Jeffrey
2-27-70
Professional Theater Program
University of Michigan
Ann Arbor, MI

United States vs. Julius and Ethel Rosenberg, The
Donald Freed
3-14-69
Cleveland Playhouse
Cleveland, OH

Universal Nigger, The
Gordon Porterfield
3-20-70
Chelsea Theatre Center
30 Lafayette, Brooklyn, NY

Unjust Do Not Prosper
Herb Martin (lyrics); Kenneth Mills (music)
6-21-73
Afro-American Cultural Theatre
P.S. 103
Madison Ave. 127th, N.Y.C.

Unknown Chinaman, The
Kenneth Bernard (book, lyrics, and music)
7-8-71
Magic Theatre
Omaha, NB

Unknown Soldier, The
Warren Frost
Spring, 1973
Theatre-in-the-Round
Minneapolis, MN

Unnatural Act
Paul Fleisher & Friends
6-25-73
Mercer Arts Center
240 Mercer, N.Y.C.

Unpleasant Evening with H. L. Mencken, An
Paul Shyre
7-13-71
Central City Festival
Central City, CO

Unscheduled Appearance
Rick Bailey
10-27-72
New York Theatre Ensemble
2 E. 2nd, N.Y.C.

Unseen Hand, The
Sam Shepard
12-26-69
La Mama ETC
74 E. 4th, N.Y.C.

Untamed Land, The (folk musical)
6-26-73
Westbury Music Fair
Westbury, L.I., NY

Unta-The
Dale Worsley
6-7-72
La Mama ETC
74 E. 4th, N.Y.C.

Untitled
Michael Graham
11-28-68
New York Shakespeare Festival Public Theatre
425 Lafayette, N.Y.C.

Untitled
11-29-72
Academy Community Theatre
Central Presbyterian Church
Atlanta, GA

Untitled Play
Lanford Wilson
1-26-68
Judson Poets' Theatre
55 Wash. Sq. So., N.Y.C.

Untitled Play
Paul John Austin
11-29-71
Manhattan Theatre Club
321 E. 73rd, N.Y.C.

Unto Thee a Garden
Jenny Egan
10-14-68
Four Winds Theatre, Inc.
Brooklyn Museum
N.Y.C.

Up and Down (with Kitchen Interlude)
Charles Pulaski
10-2-69
Stage Lights Theatrical Club
218 W. 48th, N.Y.C.

Up Eden
Robert Rosenblum & Howard Shuman
11-26-68
Jan Hus Auditorium
351 E. 74th, N.Y.C.

Up! (revue)
Gwendolyn Gunn, Patricia Horan, Chryse Maile, Sally Ordway, Andrew Piotrowski, Dolores Walker, & Susan Yankowitz
2-17-72
Westbeth Cabaret
155 Bank, N.Y.C.

Up the Creek
Donald Flynn
8-17-71
Corning Summer Theatre
Corning, NY

Up the Hill (with The Playpen)
Tom Topor
6-9-69
Extension Theatre
277 Park Ave. So., N.Y.C.

Up, Up, and Away (with Survival)
Michael Kortchmar
11-20-73
Black Renaissance Company
Playbox
94 St. Mark's Pl., N.Y.C.

Upon This Rock
Bernice Reagon
January, 1973
D.C. Black Theater Repertory Company
Washington, DC

Uproar in the House
Anthony Marriott & Alistair Foot
9-1-70
Allenberry Playhouse
Boiling Springs, PA

Upside Down Cake, The
Jeffrey Selby
3-30-70
Old Reliable Theatre Tavern
231 E. 3rd, N.Y.C.

Upstairs Sleeping
Harvey Perr
3-22-69
Henry Street Settlement Playhouse
466 Grand, N.Y.C.

Upsy Downsy Lane
Alan Miller & Milan Kymlicks
10-31-70
St. Lawrence Centre
Toronto, CAN

Uptaught
Helen Duberstein, Brian Jayne, Chryse Maile, Robert Patrick, Robert Reiser, Matthew & William Sanders, Stanley Nelson, Sally Ordway
3-1-73
Kranny's Nook
Brooklyn, NY

Uptight
William H. Hoffman
10-28-68
Old Reliable Theatre Tavern
231 E. 3rd, N.Y.C.

Uptight
Gunther Grass
3-17-72
Arena Stage
Washington, DC

Uptown Express
John Eckenrod
5-28-71
Carnegie Hall
881 Seventh, N.Y.C.

Upturned Face, The
Stephen Crane, adapted by Frank Crocitto
12-18-70
Assembly Theatre
113 Jane, N.Y.C.

Urban Blight
Conceived and staged by Isaiah Sheffer
1-2-70
Cubiculo
414 W. 51st, N.Y.C.

Urban Crisis, The
Al Carmines
10-19-69
Judson Poets' Theatre
55 Wash. Sq. So., N.Y.C.

Urination of Gylan Kain, The
Gylan Kain
2-23-73
Players' Workshop
83 E. 4th, N.Y.C.

Us vs. Nobody
Hal DeWindt
2-5-72
Negro Ensemble Company
St. Mark's Playhouse
133 Second, N.Y.C.

Ushers, The
James Schevill
11-18-71
Brown University
Providence, RI

V

V . . .
Therese Gibbons
3-15-72
Provincetown Playhouse
133 MacDougal, N.Y.C.

Vain Victory
Jackie Curtis
5-26-71
La Mama ETC
74 E. 4th, N.Y.C.

Val, Christie and the Others
Elizabeth Auer (book & lyrics); Joe Bousard (music)
10-15-73
Equity Library Theatre
Library & Museum of the Performing Arts
111 Amsterdam, N.Y.C.

Valentine Rainbow (revue)
Robert Patrick
1-25-72
La Mama ETC
74 E. 4th, N.Y.C.

Valentine's Day
Ron Cowen (book & lyrics); Saul Naishtat (music)
12-27-69
American Conservatory Theatre
San Francisco, CA

Valija, La
Julio Mauricio
11-20-70
Potbelly Theater Workshop
40 W. 18th, N.Y.C.

Valley of Unrest, The
Edgar Allen Poe
12-11-69
Dramatic Society of Stevens Institute
Hoboken, NJ

Vampire Show, The
Charles Pulaski
8-1-69
Stage Lights Theatrical Club
218 W. 48th, N.Y.C.

Vampyre Freako
12-18-70
Ellen Klein Mime Troupe & Medicine Show
83 Leonard St. N.Y.C.

Van Gogh
Arthur Sainer
2-25-70
La Mama ETC
74 E. 4th, N.Y.C.

Vanity Fair
Maura Cavanagh Smithies (book & lyrics); Mildred Kayden (music)
8-12-69
Orleans Arena Theatre
Orleans, MA

Vanity Wake
Powell Shepherd & Ken Hill
1-14-70
Old Reliable Theatre Tavern
231 E. 3rd, N.Y.C.

Vanozza (with Black and White)
Lyon Phelps
11-9-70
Old Reliable Theatre Tavern
231 E. 3rd, N.Y.C.

Vapors
Jamil Zakkai
7-15-69
Eugene O'Neill Memorial Theatre
Waterford, CT

Variation on a Theme
Terence Rattigan
8-20-68
Boothbay Playhouse
Boothbay, ME

Variations of Freedom (Part III)
Drama Workshop of the Lab
8-30-72
Brownsville Lab Theater Arts, Inc.
Lincoln Center Plaza, N.Y.C.

Variety Obit (with Welcome to Andromeda)
Ron Whyte & Robert Satuloff (book & lyrics); Mel Marvin (music)
2-12-73
Cherry Lane Theatre
38 Commerce, N.Y.C.

Vasco
Georges Schehade
2-17-68
Dallas Theatre Center
Dallas, TX

Vatzlav
Slawomir Mrozek, translated by Ralph Manheim
Summer, 1970
Stratford Festival
Stratford, CAN

V.D. Vietnam
Peter Grossman
12-10-71
Clark Center for the Performing Arts
West Side YWCA
8th Ave. & 51st, N.Y.C.

Vegetable Night or Prototype IV
Luther Burbank Dingleberry Festival
10-29-70
Northern Illinois University
DeKalb, IL

Venetian Twins, The
Carlo Goldoni
5-28-68
Henry Miller's Theatre
N.Y.C.

Venetian Twins, The
Carlo Goldoni, adapted by Robert David Macdonald
6-18-70
Tyrone Guthrie Theatre
Minneapolis, MN

Venice—The Agony of a City
Franco Zardo
4-24-72
Cubiculo
414 W. 51st, N.Y.C.

Venture, The: A Squeeze Play
John Parkinson
2-5-70
Thresholds
23 E. 20th, N.Y.C.

Verbatim
Luther Burbank Dinglefest
9-27-72
Body Politic
Chicago, IL

Vermilion, A Farce
Ron Mele
1-17-69
New York Theatre Ensemble
2 E. 2nd, N.Y.C.

Vermin (with Flame)
Shaunee Laurence
11-12-70
Playbox
94 St. Mark's Pl., N.Y.C.

Veronica' s Room
Ira Levin
9-22-73
Shubert Theatre
New Haven, CT

Vespers
Jeannine O'Reilly
9-3-69
Old Reliable Theatre Tavern
231 E. 3rd, N.Y.C.

Vessel (an opera epic)
Meredith Monk and The House
10-18-71
9 Great Jones St. (Parts I & II), Wooster St. (Part III)
N.Y.C.

Via Galactica
Christopher Gore & Judith Ross (book); Christopher Gore (lyrics); Galt MacDermot (music)
11-28-72
Uris Theatre
51st St. W. of Broadway, N.Y.C.

Vicious Circle, The
Shelly Valfer
8-13-73
Theatre for the New City
113 Jane, N.Y.C.

Victims of Amnesia (with The Alligation)
Lawrence Ferlinghetti
4-9-70
Cubiculo
414 W. 51st, N.Y.C.

Victor
Roger Vitrac; Stephen Mitchell (translator)
7-9-69
Artists Theatre Festival
Southampton, L.I., NY

Victoria's House
Fred Carmichael
8-21-68
Playhouse
Dorset, VT

Video-Rock Environment: Aquarian Festival
John Reilly, Ira Schneider, Rudi Stern, Jud Yalku
11-21-69
Global Village
454 Broome, N.Y.C.

Vienna Burgtheater
3-19-68
City Center
131 W. 55th, N.Y.C.

Vienna Eisrevue
10-22-69
Felt Forum
Madison Square Garden, N.Y.C.

Vigil, The
Walter Evans
5-16-69
University of Missouri
Columbia, MO

Vigil (theatre event)
Norman Taffel
4-2-72
70 Grand, N.Y.C.

Village, The: A Party
Charles Fuller
10-18-68
McCarter Theatre
Princeton, NJ

Village Variety
3-8-68
Little Theatre
181 Bleecker, N.Y.C.

Vimazoluleka
Levy Rossell
4-5-69
Mannhardt Theatre Foundation
N.Y.C.

Vinyl Visits an FM Station
Ronald Tavel
5-20-70
Playwrights' Unit
83 E. 4th, N.Y.C.

Vinyl Vists an F.M. Station
Ronald Tavel
4-27-72
Theatre of the Lost Continent
113 Jane, N.Y.C.

V.I.P., The
Stanley Seidman
3-19-71
Dramatis Personae
114 W. 14th, N.Y.C.

Virgin (a rock opera)
Father John O'Reilly
11-17-72
Village East Theatre
104 Second, N.Y.C.

Virility
Ed Satrakian
1-11-73
Actors Studio
432 W. 44th, N.Y.C.

Virtues of Adultery, The (with The Silhouette of God)
Joseph Okpaku
1-15-69
Stanford University
Palo Alto, CA

Visit to the Queen of England, A
Rosett Di Chiara
9-6-68
Fulton Theatre Company
119 Ninth, N.Y.C.

Visitatio Sepulchri, Peregrinus, Planctus Mariae
Prepared by W. L. Smolden
May, 1968
St. George's Church
Stuyvesant Sq., N.Y.C.

Visitor, The
Rudy Gray
Hunter College Playwrights Project
West Side YMCA
5 W. 63rd, N.Y.C.

Visitors vs. The Hometeam, The
Bruce Feld
6-18-71
WPA
333 Bowery, N.Y.C.

Vita Che Mi Devi, La
Franca Petracci
12-11-73
Teatro Italiano
Hunter College
N.Y.C.

Viva Lamour (with The Orientation)
James Paul Dey
6-14-72
Cubiculo
414 W. 51st, N.Y.C.

Vivat! Vivat Regina!
Robert Bolt
12-27-71
Shubert
Boston, MA

Voice from Another Season, The
Meladin Zarubica (book & lyrics); Nelson Riddle (music)
9-9-69
Royce Hall
University of California
Los Angeles, CA

Voice Is Coming, The or A Voice to Be Heard
Guy Gauthier
1-7-72
Playbox
94 St. Mark's Place, N.Y.C.

Voice of Charlie Pont, The
Douglas Fairbairs
12-31-71
Players Theatre of Greater Miami
Miami, FL

Voice of the Gene
Elwoodson Williams
8-15-69
Bed-Stuy Theatre
1407 Bedford Ave., Brooklyn, NY

Voice of the Ghetto
Rodney K. Douglas
11-14-69
Black Mask Players
34 W. 134th, N.Y.C.

Voice To Call Your Own, A
Clayelle Dalfares
4-23-71
Playbox
94 St. Mark's Pl., N.Y.C.

Voices
Richard Lortz
2-26-72
Shubert Theatre
New Haven, CT

Void in Wisconsin
Guy Guden
1972
Santa Barbara City College
Santa Barbara, CA

Volunteers for America (with Matinee Ladies)
Anne Commire
3-2-73
American Women Playwrights Association
Columbia University School of the Arts Theatre
410 W. 117th, N.Y.C

Voyage to Arcturus, A
3-4-70
Theatre Genesis
10th & 2nd, N.Y.C.

W

Wait, The
Barry Anbinder
12-18-73
Brooklyn College
Brooklyn, NY

Waiting for Clarence (with Dough)
F. V. Hunt
6-20-68
Dramarena Repertory Theatre
158 W. 55th, N.Y.C.

Waiting Room
Laurence Cantor
12-13-68
New York University
Bronx, NY

Waiting (with Doorbell and Academy)
Mario Fratti
10-22-70
Cubiculo
414 W. 51st, N.Y.C.

Wake
David Shelton
4-26-73
University of Missouri Theatre
Columbia, MO

Wake for the Late Captain Hasan Tursun Efendi . . ., The
Tosum Bayrak
2-26-71
Sonraed Galleries
141 Prince, N.Y.C.

Wake Me Up When It's Over
Diane English
7-20-70
New London Barn Playhouse
New London, NH

Wake, The
Steve Allen
9-28-71
Masquers Theatre
Hollywood, CA

Walden Pond
Joseph Renard
3-21-72
WPA
333 Bowery, N.Y.C.

Walk Down Mah Street
Norman & Patricia Curtis
6-12-68
Players Theatre
115 MacDougal, N.Y.C.

Walk Me Home
William Kushner
1-7-72
Playbox
94 St. Mark's Place, N.Y.C.

Walk Together Children (new edition)
Vinnie Burrows
Mercer Arts Center
240 Mercer, N.Y.C.

Walk Together Children: The Black Scene in Prose, Poetry, and Song
11-11-68
Greenwich Mews Theatre
141 W. 13th, N.Y.C.

Walking, The
Michael Mathias
3-12-70
Mainstream Theatre
20 E. 14th, N.Y.C.

Wall Between, The
Richard Usem
4-25-69
New York Theatre Ensemble
2 E. 2nd, N.Y.C.

Walls
Improvisational play by Soul and Latin Theatre
3-19-71
Soul & Latin Theatre
Theatre Arts Center
120 E. 110th, N.Y.C.

Walls of the Ghetto
Tony Vozzo
5-22-70
Brooklyn College
Brooklyn, NY

Walrus Said, The
Cary Pepper
11-28-73
Theatre 77 Repertory
23 E. 20th, N.Y.C.

Walsh
Sharon Pollock
11-7-73
Theatre Calgary
Calgary, Alberta, CAN

Waltz Invention, The
Vladimir Nabokov
11-21-68
Eastside Theatre
St. Paul, MN

Waltz Me Around Again
Norman Barasch & Carroll Moore
7-9-68
Playhouse on the Mall
Paramus, NJ

Wanderer in the Earth
Mark J. Kurlansky
11-1-73
Gershwin Theatre
Brooklyn College
Brooklyn, NY

Wanderers, The
From the stories of Eudora Welty
5-17-71
Orpheum Theatre
126 Second, N.Y.C.

Wanted
David Epstein (book); Al Carmines (music & lyrics)
9-17-71
Judson Poets' Theater
55 Wash. Sq. So., N.Y.C.

Wanted
Clay Goss
6-6-73
D.C. Black Repertory Company
Washington, DC

Wanted: One Princess
Seth A. Schweitzer
3-14-71
Brandeis University
Waltham, MA

Wanton Soup
Ching-Yeh
10-8-69
La Mama ETC
74 E. 4th, N.Y.C.

War
Stephen McCorkle
10-24-69
Inner Theatre
356 Bowery, N.Y.C.

War
Rose Leiman Goldemberg
5-21-71
East Village Theatre
433 E. 6th, N.Y.C.

War Babies (improvisational group)
8-26-72
Focus Two Coffee House
163 W. 74th, N.Y.C.

War Games
Neal Weaver
4-17-69
Fortune Theatre
62 E. 4th, N.Y.C.

War, Women and Other Trivia
George Bernard Shaw, Max Beerbohm
7-26-71
Shaw Festival
Niagara-on-the-Lake
Ontario, CAN

Warehouse, The
Jean Forest
3-11-68
Old Reliable Theatre Tavern
231 E. 3rd, N.Y.C.

Warm Bodies
Anthony West
5-16-70
New Theatre Workshop
154 E. 54th, N.Y.C.

Warm-Blooded Dame, A: An Evening With Miss Sally-Jane Heit
Doris Adler (sketches); Shirly Grossman (music & lyrics)
10-18-71
Library & Museum of the Performing Arts
111 Amsterdam, N.Y.C.

Warmth of Winter, The
Anthony Grabowski
6-23-68
Wedgewood Dinner Theatre
Williamsburg, VA

Warp
Stuart Gordon & Lenny Kleinfeldt
12-8-71
Body Politic
Chicago, IL

Warp I: My Battlefield, My Body
Bury St. Edmund & Stuart Gordon
2-14-73
Ambassador Theatre
215 W. 49th, N.Y.C.

Warplay
Based on war poems by Vietnam Veterans
5-20-72
Brooklyn Company
Brooklyn YMCA
9th St. & 6th, Brooklyn, NY

Warren Harding
Steven Shea
7-28-72
Eugene O'Neill Memorial Theatre
Waterford, CT

Was There Ever a Harry Potts?
9-21-72
Changing Scene
Denver, CO

Washington Irving, the Gentleman from Sleepy Hollow
Laurens Moore
10-20-70
Limestoné College
Gaffney, SC

Washington Square
Kenneth Jerome (book & lyrics); Jerome Walman (book & music)
3-22-72
Washington Theatre Club
Washington, DC

Watch the Fords Go By
Bob Arnebeck
Oct., 1970
Agassiz Elementary School
Cambridge, MA

Watch-Pit, The
Kit Jones
1-30-69
Chelsea Theatre Center
30 Lafayette Ave., Brooklyn, NY

Water Hen, The
Stanislaw Witkiewicz, translated by Daniel C. Gerould & C. S. Durek
3-2-71
Towson State College
Towson, MD

Water Strike!
Edna Schappert
7-16-71
New York Theatre Ensemble
2 E. 2nd, N.Y.C.

Water Works at Lincoln, The
Walter Hadler
11-7-69
Theatre Genesis
10th & 2nd, N.Y.C.

Watercolor
Philip Magdalany
1-21-70
ANTA Theatre
245 W. 52nd, N.Y.C.

Watergate Classics
Isaiah Sheffer
11-16-73
Yale Repertory Theatre
New Haven, CT

Watergate Scandals of '73
Hot Peaches
6-28-73
Peach Pitts
200 W. 24th, N.Y.C.

Watering Place, The
Lyle Kessler
3-12-69
Music Box Theatre
N.Y.C.

Waves, The
Virginia Wolff, adapted by Joyce Whitcomb and Gail Bell
2-26-68
Library & Museum of the Performing Arts
111 Amsterdam, N.Y.C.

Way It Is, The
12-2-69 (previews)
New Lincoln Theatre
63rd & Broadway, N.Y.C.

Way of Life, A
Murray Schisgal
2-4-69
ANTA Theatre
245 W. 52nd, N.Y.C.

W.C.
Milton Sperling & Sam Locke (book); Al Carmines (music & lyrics)
6-15-71
Painter's Mill Music Fair
Owings Mills, MD

We Agree
See: The Lay of the Land

We'd Rather Switch
Larry Crane
5-2-69
Mermaid Theatre
420 W. 42nd, N.Y.C.

We Do Feel for You, Daniel (with You Can't Tell a Cover by Its Color)
Stanley Zawatsky
12-8-72
New York Theatre Ensemble
2 E. 2nd, N.Y.C.

We Do It Agency, The (with Please 7:52 We Love You and Hush! Hush!)
Peter DiLeo
5-8-71
PAWorkshop
353 Ave. of the Americas, N.Y.C.

We Got a Lot of Lovin' To Do
5-3-70
Emanu-El Midtown YM-YMHA
344 E. 14th, N.Y.C.

We Hate To See You Go
Michael McGrinder
8-31-70
Old Reliable Theatre Tavern
231 E. 3rd, N.Y.C.

We'll Start a New Day
Menagerie
Feb., 1970
Mod Scene
157 Bleecker, N.Y.C.

We're Off To See the Wizard
Edna Schappert
9-29-72
Playbox
94 St. Mark's Pl., N.Y.C.

We Righteous Bombers
Kingsley B. Bass, Jr.
7-30-70
Wayne State University
Detroit, MI

We . . . The President
Louis McKinley
Jan., 1973
Theatre Suburbia
Houston, TX

We Three You and I
William Greenland
July, 1970
Factory Theatre Lab
Toronto, CAN

Weaving and Other Things
Muriel Mand
6-28-73
Primitive Theatre
33 Howard, N.Y.C.

Web, A (with The Workout)
Albert Bermel
11-24-70
Assembly Theatre
113 Jane, N.Y.C.

Web and the Rock, The
Thomas Wolfe; Dolores Sutton (adaptor)
2-24-71
Washington Theatre Club
Washington, DC

Web, The
Trevor Rhone
7-25-72
Eugene O'Neill Memorial Theatre
Waterford, CT

Wedding Dress, The
Nelson Rodrigues
12-11-70
New York Theater of the Americas
427 W. 59th, N.Y.C.

Wedding Feast, The
See: Die Kleinburgerhochzeit

Wedding Night
Carl Schiffman
12-22-72
New York Theatre Ensemble
2 E. 2nd, N.Y.C.

Wedding of Iphigenia Plus Iphigenia in Concert, The
Doug Dyer (adaptor); Peter Link (music)
12-16-71
New York Shakespeare Festival Public Theatre
425 Lafayette, N.Y.C.

Wedding Rehearsal, A
Madge Ritter
11-13-69
Spencer Memorial Church
Remsen & Clinton Sts., Brooklyn Heights, NY

Wedding, The
Anton Chekhov; new adaptation by Morris Carnovsky
3-17-72
Long Wharf Theatre
New Haven, CT

Wee Diamond Ring, A
Irma R. Jones
3-7-69
Stage Lights Theatrical Club
218 W. 48th, N.Y.C.

Weed Garden, A
Janice Rice
8-9-73
Changing Scene
Denver, CO

Weeds (with Camembert Kumquats)
Ron Mele
4-13-69
Salvation Discotheque
1 Sheridan Sq., N.Y.C.

Weekend
Gore Vidal
2-14-68
Shubert Theatre
New Haven, CN

Welcome Back Billy Baby
James Edward Shannon
May, 1973
Black Experience Dramatic Workshop
Adam Clayton Powell Auditorium
N.Y.C.

Welcome Home
Edmund Hartman
12-7-72
Ivanhoe Theatre
Chicago, IL

Welcome Home, Gabriel
Tom Lanter
6-9-71
Jacksonville University
Jacksonville, FL

Welcome Home, Joe (with Re-Run)
Delano Stewart
10-12-73
Bed-Stuy Theatre
Brooklyn, NY

Welcome to Andromeda (with Variety Obit)
Ron Whyte
2-12-73
Cherry Lane Theatre
38 Commerce, N.Y.C.

Welcome to Serenity Farms
Garry White
11-11-68
Mark Taper Forum
Los Angeles, CA

Welfare Lady, The
Tony Villani
2-14-71
Dancers Studio Foundation
34 E. 10th, N.Y.C.

Well . . . Fair
Anne Roby (book & lyrics); Sandy Alpert (music)
10-5-72
Manhattan Theatre Club
321 E. 73rd, N.Y.C.

Well Stillwell
Sam Bernstein
1-14-71
Lesley-Ellis School
34 Concord Ave. Cambridge, MA

Well-Mannered Corpse, The
Manuel Trujillo
12-19-69
Duo Theatre Workshop
522 E. 12th, N.Y.C.

Wells of Fancy
Pocket Mime Theatre
11-1-73
Church of the Covenant
Boston, MA

Wet and Dry (with Alive)
Leonard Melfi
10-3-68
Loft Workshop
152 Bleecker, N.Y.C.

Whale
Kent Jarratt
11-30-71
WPA
333 Bowery, N.Y.C.

What a Day
Michael A. del Medico
8-5-71
Cloisters
N.Y.C.

What a Day for a Miracle!
Henry Myers & E. Y. Harburg (book); E. Y. Harburg (lyrics); Larry Ornstein & Jeff Chandler (music)
4-29-71
University of Vermont
Burlington, VT

What About Tomorrow?
Norman Parker
7-28-71
St. Clement's Church
423 W. 46th, N.Y.C.

What! And Leave Bloomingdale's? (with Love in a Pub; Ellis Takes His Life Again; and Do You Know the Koran?)
Marion Towbin & David Finkle
7-12-73
Joseph Jefferson Theatre Company
Little Church Around the Corner
11 E. 29th, N.Y.C.

What Can You Buy for a Token?
Eddy Allen
9-14-73
West Side Gay Theatre
W.S.D.G. Center
37 Ninth, N.Y.C.

What Color Is Love?
Darlene Young
12-6-72
Bastiano's Studio
14 Cooper Sq., N.Y.C.

What Do They Know About Love Uptown?
Jerold C. Dukor
11-7-68
WPA Theatre
34 E. 4th, N.Y.C.

What Else Have You Got in the Closet?
Laslo Vadnay & Hans Wilhelm
7-15-68
Bucks County Playhouse
New Hope, PA

What Ever Happened to Kimchee Fook?
P. J. Barry
4-10-72
Library & Museum of the Performing Arts
111 Amsterdam, N.Y.C.

What Happened to the Thorne's Place
Arthur Kopit
8-29-72
Peru and Landover, VT

What If It Had Turned Up Heads?
J. E. Gaines
3-10-72
American Place Theatre
N.Y.C.

What in the World Is Wrong? (revue)
Frank Lee Wilde
1-16-70
Spencer Memorial Church
99 Clinton, Brooklyn Heights, NY

What Is a Man?
1-22-73
Theatre at Noon
St. Peter's Gate
132 E. 54th, N.Y.C.

What Is Going On?
Ben Caldwell
11-23-73
New Federal Theatre
240 E. 3rd, N.Y.C.

What Is Making Gilda so Grey?
Tom Eyen
3-28-70
La Mama ETC
74 E. 4th, N.Y.C.

What is Woman?
Women of Burning City Street Theatre
10-25-70
St. Peter's Church
346 W. 20th, N.Y.C.

What Makes Daddy Run?
Mass Transit Street Theatre
December, 1973
Mass Transit Street Theatre
N.Y.C.

What Reason Could I Give
Dan Owens
7-26-73
Eugene O'Neill Memorial Theatre
Waterford, CT

What's a Nice Country Like You Doing in a State Like This?
Ira Gasman (lyrics); Cary Hoffman (music); Bernie Travis
10-16-72
St. Peter's Gate
132 E. 54th, N.Y.C.

What's Expected?
Mitchell Weiss (book, lyrics, & music)
Winter, 1972
Oberlin College
Oberlin, OH

What's Going on Outside Anyhow?
Hamotak
1-12-73
Playbox
94 St. Mark' s Pl., N.Y.C.

What's in It for Me?
Michael Groob (book); Paul Morse (music)
7-30-73
Greenwich Mews Theatre
141 W. 13th, N.Y.C.

What's the Game Now?
Peter Copani
3-13-69
Playbox
94 St. Mark's Pl., N.Y.C.

What the Butler Saw
Joe Orton
5-4-70
McAlpin Rooftop Theatre
34th & 6th Ave., N.Y.C.

What the Wine Sellers Buy
Ronald Milner
5-17-73
New Federal Theatre
240 E. 3rd, N.Y.C.

What Time of Night It Is (musical history)
Patricia Horan & Marjorie DeFazio
6-17-73
Women's Interart Center
549 W. 52nd, N.Y.C.

What You Didn't Know, Papa
Robert Shulman
11-16-68
Frances Adler Theatre
23 W. 73rd, N.Y.C.

Whatever Happened to Hugging and Kissing? (with The Huff and the Puff)
Norman Wexler
4-17-70
Cleveland Playhouse
Cleveland, OH

Whatever Happened to the Sons?
Rose Sher
3-23-73
New York Theatre Ensemble
2 E. 2nd, N.Y.C.

Wheelbarrow, The
Jere Berger
May, 1968
Martinique Theatre
N.Y.C.

Wheeling Reds
Walter Hadler
5-24-73
Theatre Genesis
10th & 2nd Ave., N.Y.C.

When Do the Words Come True?
John Meyer (book, lyrics, & music)
4-13-71
Bucks County Playhouse
New Hope, PA

When I Dyed My Hair in Venice (with The Player Piano)
Helen Duberstein
6-11-73
Theatre for the New City
113 Jane, N.Y.C.

When Johnny Comes Dancing Home Again
Tom Eyen
2-1-68
Playwrights' Workshop Club
14 Waverly Pl., N.Y.C.

When Johnny Comes Marching Home
Richard Davidson
7-24-68
Studio 58
150 W. 58th, N.Y.C.

When Mother Was Sober It Was So Much Fun
Ed Setrakian
7-8-72
Cherry Lane Theatre
38 Commerce, N.Y.C.

When Princes Could Be Waiters (with There Was a Tribe of Indians)
George Hammer
12-9-72
H B Playwrights Foundation
124 Bank, N.Y.C.

When Schwartz Meets Goldstein (with The Gay Desperado and Magic Time)
William Kushner
3-20-70
Play Lab
130 E. 7th, N.Y.C.

When the Bough Breaks
Peter Copani
12-26-69
New York Theatre Ensemble
2 E. 2nd, N.Y.C.

When the Wine Is Cold (with Just Keep Listening)
John Kendrick
4-24-71
98 Greene St. Loft
98 Greene, N.Y.C.

When They Let You Out of the Looney Bin, Make Sure You Have a Plan
Richard Hoag
1-17-69
Anthony Mannino Drama Tree
182 Fifth, N.Y.C.

When To Water the Milk
Lynn Root & Harry Clork
6-1-71
Shady Lane Farm Playhouse
Marengo, IL

When We Dead Awaken
Henrik Ibsen; Michael Feingold (translator)
10-14-71
Yale Repertory Theatre
New Haven, CT

When We Last Saw Our Hero
7-13-71
Millbrook Playhouse
Mill Hall, PA

When We Were Married
7-16-69
Theatre by the Grove
Indiana, PA

When You Comin' Back, Red Ryder?
Mark Medoff
6-25-73
Circle Theatre Company
2307 Broadway, N.Y.C.

Where Are You Going Hollis Jay? (with Postmortem)
Benjamin Bradford
1-7-71
Theatre Crossroads
23 E. 20th, N.Y.C.

Where Did Mr. Foster Go?
Ted Pezzulo
5-10-70
Triangle Theatre
316 E. 88th, N.Y.C.

Where Did You Put It When You Had It?
Doris Schwerin
7-30-69
Eugene O'Neill Memorial Theatre
Waterford, CT

Where Do We Go from Here?
Carla Joseph
6-2-72
New York Theatre Ensemble
2 E. 2nd, N.Y.C.

Where Do We Go from Here?
John Ford Noonan
8-2-73
Johnson State College
Johnson, VT

Where Else Would a Bull Live?
William Derringer
6-16-72
Manhattan Theatre Club
321 E. 73rd, N.Y.C.

Where Has Tommy Flowers Gone?
Terrence McNally
1-7-71
Yale Repertory Theatre
New Haven, CT

Where Is Everyone?
The Genesis Theatre Company
9-26-70
St. Brigid's Church
Ave. B & 9th St., N.Y.C.

Where Is Sicily?
1969
University of Calif.
Santa Barbara, CA

Where It's At!
Maura Cavanagh & Richard Smithies (book & lyrics); Norman Sachs (music)
8-4-70
Arena Theatre
Orleans, MA

Where the Green Bananas Grow
Allen Davis
3-16-72
H B Playwrights Foundation
124 Bank, N.Y.C.

Where the Music Is
Anna Marie Barlow
Oct., 1968
Louisiana State University
Baton Rouge, LA

Where Two or Three Are
2-8-69
London Missioners
The Little Synagogue
27 E. 20th, N.Y.C.

Where We At
Martie Charles
1-16-72
Negro Ensemble Company
St. Mark's Playhouse
133 Second, N.Y.C.

Which Way to the E-Ring?
Don Miller
6-3-68
Circle in the Square
N.Y.C.

While Shakespeare Slept
Tim Kelly
4-15-72
Sneaker Players
Library & Museum of the Performing Arts
111 Amsterdam, N.Y.C.

Whip Lady, The
David Zlochower
2-6-71
Clark Center for Performing Arts
West Side YMCA
5 W. 63rd, N.Y.C.

Whiskey
Terrence McNally
4-29-73
St. Clement's Church
423 W. 46th, N.Y.C.

Whispers on the Wind
John B. Kuntz (book & lyrics); Lor Crane (music)
6-3-70
Theatre de Lys
N.Y.C.

Whistle in the Dark, A
Thomas Murphy
2-9-68
Long Wharf Theatre
New Haven, CT

Whistling Wizard, The (with The Sultan of Tuffet)
Bil Baird & Alan Stern
12-20-69
Bil Baird Theatre
59 Barrow, N.Y.C.

White Clouds, Black Dreams
6-21-73
Hedgerow Theatre
Moylan, PA

White House Murder Case, The
Jules Feiffer
2-18-70
Circle in the Square
159 Bleecker, N.Y.C.

White on White (with The Process Is the Product)
6-5-69
Dallas Theatre Center
Dallas, TX

Whiteshop, The (with Hamhocks)
Garrett Robinson
8-23-68
New Heritage Repertory Theatre
Madison at 127th, N.Y.C.

Whitsuntide
Tom LaBar
5-6-71
St. Clement's Church
423 W. 46th, N.Y.C.

Who Am I?
Seymour Barab (book, music & lyrics)
12-4-71
Stage 73
321 E. 73rd, N.Y.C.

Who Builds This Lofty Structure
David J. Kennedy
7-9-68
New Workshop Theatre
Brooklyn College
Nostrand Ave. & Ave. H, N.Y.C.

Who Can Tell?
Hank Warner
2-25-71
Changing Scene
Denver, CO

Who Is Seamus Murphy and Why Does He Do These Awful Things . . . (dance & film event)
3-3-73
Playwrights' Horizons
Clark Center for the Performing Arts, West Side YWCA
8th Ave. & 51st, N.Y.C.

Who Killed My Bald Sister Sophie or The Saga of Sophie
Tom Eyen
2-20-68
Caffe Cino
31 Cornelia, N.Y.C.

Who Killed Santa Claus?
Terrence Feely
2-14-72
Royal Poinciana Playhouse
Palm Beach, FL

Who Needs a Waltz?
Fred Carmichael
8-9-73
Dorset Playhouse
Dorset, VT

Who's a Lady?
Annette Miller
5-31-71
Brandeis University
Waltham, MA

Who's Crazy?
Jane Roberts
8-7-72
New Old Reliable Theatre
231 E. 3rd, N.Y.C.

Who's Hungry?
Edward Belling
4-26-71
Old Reliable Theatre Tavern
231 E. 3rd, N.Y.C.

Who's Over There?
Maurice Siegel
7-28-72
New York Theatre Ensemble
2 E. 2nd, N.Y.C.

Who's Weaker?
Shaw, Shakespeare, Moliere, etc., arranged and directed by Luz Castanos
3-7-72
Barnard College Theatre Company
Barnard College
N.Y.C.

Who's Who, Baby?
Guy Bolton and Johnny Brandon
1-29-68
Players Theatre
115 MacDougal, N.Y.C.

Who Said Freddy Was Dead?
Houston Owens
10-23-73
Alcorn A&M College
Lorman, MS

Who Shot Hedda?
10-13-73
Takala Society
Universalist Theatre
4 W. 76th, N.Y.C.

Who Stole the American Crown Jewels? (opera)
Jean Reavey (libretto); Norman Siegel (music)
4-26-71
Cubiculo
414 W. 51st, N.Y.C.

Who Wants To Be the Lone Ranger?
Lee Kalcheim
5-26-71
Mark Taper Forum
Los Angeles, CA

Whodunit
Richard Ellington
2-12-68
Provincetown Playhouse
133 MacDougal, N.Y.C.

Whole Truth and the Honest Man, The
Cleve Hawbold
2-18-73
One-Act Repertory Company
251 E. 50th,
N.Y.C.

Whores of Babylon
Bill Vehr
3-22-68
Ridiculous Repertory
Gate Theatre
2nd Ave. at 10th, N.Y.C.

Whores of Broadway, The
Gregory Rozakis
10-21-71
Cubiculo
414 W. 51st, N.Y.C.

Whores, Wars and Tin Pan Alley
An evening of Kurt Weill
6-16-69
Bitter End
147 Bleecker, N.Y.C.

Why Are We in Vietnam?
Norman Mailer
8-11-71
New Moon Magic Theatre
Provincetown, MA

Why Hannah's Skirt Won't Stay Down
Tom Eyen
6-6-69
La Mama ETC
74 E. 4th, N.Y.C.

Why I Went Crazy
Charles Dizenzo
7-14-69
Westport Country Playhouse
Westport, CT

Why You Shouldn't Go Rabbit Hunting on Your Honeymoon
Paul Pierog
8-13-70
St. Peter's Church
346 W. 20th, N.Y.C.

Wicked John and the Devil (American Folk Opera)
Jeff Sweet (lyrics and music)
7-19-73
Cubiculo
414 W. 51st, N.Y.C.

Wicked Women Revue
Westbeth Feminist Collective
1-13-73
Theatre for the New City
113 Jane, N.Y.C.

Widow's Mite, The
Kenneth Cooney
7-31-69
Machine Shop Playhouse
Redding, CA

Widowing of Mrs. Holroyd, The
D. H. Lawrence
11-16-73
Long Wharf Theatre
New Haven, CT

Wiglaf: A Myth for Actors
12-20-73
Rutgers Theatre Workshop
Cubiculo
414 W. 51st, N.Y.C.

Wild and Wonderful
Bob Brotherton, Phil Phillips & Bob Miller (book); Bob Goodman (lyrics & music)
12-7-71
Lyceum Theatre
149 W. 45th, N.Y.C.

Wild Embrace (scenes, songs, & sonnets)
7-22-73
Central Church
593 Park, N.Y.C.

Wild Flower
Robbie McCauley
1-23-73
Negro Ensemble Company
St. Mark's Playhouse
133 Second, N.Y.C.

Wild Hunch, The, An Evening of Violence, or Three Theatrical Events
Julian Miller
6-11-71
Hunter College
N.Y.C.

Wild Ride to a Special Moon, A
Chad Henderson
3-24-72
Omni Theatre Club
145 W. 18th, N.Y.C.

Wilde
Frederick Gaines
7-26-68
Asolo Theatre
Sarasota, FL

Wiley and the Hairy Man
Susan Zeder
3-14-72
Southern Methodist University
Dallas, TX

Will I See You in the City?
Peggy Simon
9-9-68
Old Reliable Theatre Tavern
231 E. 3rd, N.Y.C.

Will It Last?
Richard Seff
10-14-69
Playhouse on the Mall
Paramus, NJ

Will Rogers' U.S.A.
Paul Shyre
1-5-70
Loretto Hilton Center
St. Louis, MO

Will the Real Danny Boy Please Stand Up?
Aaron Weingarten
7-3-68
Hunter College Theatre Workshop
N.Y.C.

Will the Real Mae West. . .?
David Sawn
2-19-70
Dramarena Repertory Theatre
158 W. 55th, N.Y.C.

Will the "Real" Rich Cristy Please Stand Up
Allen Schrader, Alan Sandy, Jimmie Haskell
Fall, 1970
San Fernando Valley State College
CA

Willie
Joseph Ponzi
10-22-70
New York Shakespeare Festival Public Theatre
425 Lafayette, N.Y.C.

Willie Bignigga (with Chimpanzee)
Charles Gordone
7-3-70
New Federal Theatre
292 Henry St., N.Y.C.

Willie Heavyshoes
Robert Nichols
8-4-73
Theatre for the New City
113 Jane, N.Y.C.

Willie the Germ
Murray Mednick
5-10-68
Theatre Genesis
10th & 2nd, N.Y.C.

Willyum
See: Triune

Window Dressing (with Scenes from Domestic Life and Inner Circles)
9-25-69
Theatre East
211 E. 60th, N.Y.C.

Window, The
Ellen Gerrarlee
4-11-69
West Side Actors Theatre
252 W. 81st, N.Y.C.

Windy City, The
John T. Kelley
5-18-72
Theatre East
Los Angeles, CA

Wine in the Wilderness
Alice Childress
2-19-71
New Heritage Repertory Theatre
43 E. 125th, N.Y.C.

Wine Song (with Mary Jean Maybee)
Tony Mazzadra
9-11-70
Assembly Theatre
113 Jane, N.Y.C.

Winging It (musical)
Jeff Sweet (book, lyrics, music)
5-30-73
Musical Theatre Lab
St. Clement's Church
423 W. 46th, N.Y.C.

Winner
Clement Fowler
12-12-73
U.R.G.E.N.T.
151 W. 46th, N.Y.C.

Winner, The
Mimi Lams
8-20-71
The Everyman Company
Lincoln Center Plaza
N.Y.C.

Winner, The (with Dreams for Sale)
Arthur Williams
5-2-70
Open Space
37 St. Mark's Pl., N.Y.C.

Winnie the Pooh (rock musical)
7-5-72
Harvard University
Cambridge, MA

Winning Hearts and Minds
Adapted by Paula Kay Pierce
8-1-72
New York Shakespeare Festival Public Theatre
425 Lafayette, N.Y.C.

Winter Journey
Clifford Odets
3-12-68
Greenwich Mews Theatre
141 W. 13th, N.Y.C.

Winter Night
Shirley Guy
3-30-71
Theatre Packaging Group
13th Street Theatre
50 W. 13th, N.Y.C.

Winter's Tale in Georgia, A
Thomas Babe
6-30-68
Radcliffe College
Cambridge, MA

Winter Soldiers
Dorothy Kobak
1-30-71
Little Broadway Theatre
27 E. 20th, N.Y.C.

Wipe-Out Games (Jeux de Massacre)
Eugene Ionesco
4-14-71
Arena Stage
Washington, DC

Wise and Foolish Maidens, The (with The Three Daughters)
Transcribed by Fletcher Collins
1969
Mary Baldwin College
Staunton, VA
at Folger Shakespeare Library
Washington, DC

Wise Child
Simon Gray
1-27-72
Helen Hayes Theatre
N.Y.C.

Wishes and Saturdays
5-30-72
Theatre of the Riverside Church
490 Riverside Dr., N.Y.C.

Wisp in the Wind
Jack Cunningham
4-1-73
One-Act Repertory Company
251 E. 50th, N.Y.C.

Wisping the Wind
Stephen Weld
4-5-73
Changing Scene
Denver, CO

Witch and Willy, The
1-4-69
6th Street Theatre
543 E. 6th, N.Y.C.

Witch That Was Good, The
Maria Clara Macado
6-20-70
St. Paul the Apostle Church
124 W. 60th, N.Y.C.

With Music by the Bird. . .
Gracie Carroll and G. Hobson Waller
1-15-68
Old Reliable Theatre Tavern
231 E. 3rd, N.Y.C.

With This Rose I Thee Wake
Kenneth Patchen
Fall, 1973
Ensemble Theatre Company
Nashville, TN

Witness
Terrence McNally
11-21-68
Gramercy Arts Theatre
N.Y.C.

Witnesses
William Murray
7-1-68
Mark Taper Forum
Los Angeles, CA

Wizard of Oz, The
11-27-68
Bil Baird Theatre
59 Barrow, N.Y.C.

Wizard of Oz, The (puppet version)
Arthur Cantor & Bil Baird (book); E. Y. Harburg (lyrics); Harold Arlen (music)
10-30-71
Bil Baird Theatre
59 Barrow, N.Y.C.

Wizard of Us, The
Hot Peaches
11-9-72
Mercer Arts Center
240 Mercer, N.Y.C.

Wodehouse & Shakespeare (one-man show)
Alfred Hyslop
1-6-72
Barnard College
N.Y.C.

Wolves, The
Robert Koesis
1-14-70
Washington Theater Club
Washington, DC

Woman is my Idea
Don Liljenquist
9-25-68
Belasco Theatre
N.Y.C.

Woman of the Dunes
Kobo Abe; Peter Coe (translator)
11-19-71
Cleveland Playhouse
Cleveland, OH

Woman Play, The
8-25-72
Streetcorner Society
East Lansing, MI

Woman Potion
3-23-73
Earth Onion Women's Theatre
Washington Square Church
133 W. 4th, N.Y.C.

Woman's Kingdom, A
Anton Chekhov; James Monos (adaptor)
4-9-73
Theatre Insight
Mercer Arts Center
240 Mercer, N.Y.C.

Woman Who Pleased Everybody, The
Rose Sher
10-13-72
New York Theatre Ensemble
2 E. 2nd, N.Y.C.

Women Beware Women
Thomas Middleton
Fall, 1968
Harvard Dramatic Club
Loeb Drama Center
Cambridge, MA

Women in Red/Black
Based on work by five Feminist playwrights
5-24-73
330 Broome, N.Y.C.

Women of Ancient Greece
Dolores Brandon
1-22-73
Donnell Library
N.Y.C.

Women's Representative, The
Sun Yu; David Gaard (adaptor)
6-1-73
Night House Theatre
249 W. 18th, N.Y.C.

Women's Rites (Thesmophoriazusae)
Aristophanes; Hardy Hansen (translator)
3-9-73
New York Theatre Ensemble
2 E. 2nd, N.Y.C.

Women, Two Men and a Moose, The
Mia Anderson
Summer, 1972
Lennoxville Festival
Lennoxville, Quebec, CAN

Wonder, Try (Sketchy Version)
Charles Atlas
12-28-73
Exchange Theatre
151 Bank, N.Y.C.

Wonderful Ice Cream Suit, The
Ray Bradbury
10-10-73
Organic Theatre
Chicago, IL

Wonderful Tang, The
Beaumont Bruestle (book & lyrics); Charles Swier
7-30-70
Tufts University
Medford, MA

Wonderfull Yeare, The
Edgar White
10-24-69
New York Shakespeare Festival Public Theatre
425 Lafayette, N.Y.C.

Wooden Nickels
Susan Yankowitz
2-22-73
Theatre for the New City
113 Jane, N.Y.C.

Woodrow Wilson in the Promised Land
Roland van Zandt
12-9-69
Trinity Square Repertory Company
Providence, RI

Work of Art, A
Anton Chekhov
4-26-73
New York University
35 Fifth, N.Y.C.

Work Out, The (with The Web)
Albert Bermel
11-12-71
Clark Center for the Performing Arts
West Side YWCA
8th Ave. & 51st, N.Y.C.

Working Bee, The
Neal Graham
5-11-72
Changing Scene
Denver, CO

Worl's Champeen Lip Dansuh an' Wahtah Mellon Jooglah
Charles Gordone
5-26-69
New York Shakespeare Festival Public Theatre
425 Lafayette, N.Y.C.

World, Birth of a Nation
Wayne County
12-18-70
New York Theatre Ensemble
2 E. 2nd, N.Y.C.

World Festival of Magic and Occult, The
12-14-71
Felt Forum
8th Ave., N.Y.C.

World of Mrs. Solomon, The
Fannie Fertik
6-3-69
Fortune Theatre
62 E. 4th, N.Y.C.

World of William Blake, The (multi-media piece)
1-8-72
Film & Dance Theatre
42 E. 12th, N.Y.C.

World Split Open, The (a journey thru women's poetry 1650-1950)
3-14-73
Manhattan Theatre Club
321 E. 73rd, N.Y.C.

World Tipped Over and Laying on Its Side, The
Mary Feldhaus Weber
4-26-69
West Side YWCA
51st & 8th, N.Y.C.

World Turned Upside Down, The
Marceine Sweetser
2-20-69
Cornell University
Ithaca, NY

World War 2 1/2
Roger O. Hirson
3-24-69
Martinique Theatre
N.Y.C.

World, World, Go Away
Betty Lambert
Spring, 1970
Playhouse Theatre Company
Vancouver, B.C., CAN

Worms
Roma Greth
3-7-69
Anthony Mannino Drama Tree
182 Fifth, N.Y.C.

Worms, The
Eduardo Corbe
6-9-72
Repertory VII
New York Theatre of the Americas
427 W. 59th, N.Y.C.

Wounds of Love, The
John T. Dugan
4-10-69
University of Utah
Salt Lake City, UT

Wranglings in a Soul Box
The Youth of the Third World
3-27-71
Clark Center for the Performing Arts
West Side YWCA
8th Ave. & 51st, N.Y.C.

Wrapped in Cellophane
Eugene A. Sylvester III
11-5-70
Studio 808
154 W. 57th, N.Y.C.

Wrath of Achilles, The
Sheldon Cholst
October, 1971
Theatre of Joy
131 Prince, N.Y.C.

Wrath of God, The
Joseph Renard
11-16-73
WPA
333 Bowery, N.Y.C.

Wrecking Corporation of America, The
Hal Craven
10-9-70
New York Theatre Ensemble
2 E. 2nd, N.Y.C.

Wrong Gone Dreamer
Walter Leyden Brown; music by Calvin Hampton
5-9-69
Extension Theatre
277 Park Ave. So., N.Y.C.

Wrong Side of the Moon, The
Ron McLarty
10-16-72
Library & Museum of the Performing Arts
111 Amsterdam, N.Y.C.

Wrong Way Light Bulb, The
Leonard Spigelgass
3-4-69
Golden Theatre
252 W. 45th, N.Y.C.

Wrong Way to Paradise
John O'Neal
3-30-73
Free Southern Theatre
New Orleans, LA

Wuziz
Donald Kvares; music by Elise Bretton
9-28-70
Old Reliable Theatre Tavern
231 E. 3rd, N.Y.C.

Wyatt (with Chaconne in G Minor and The Pecan Tree)
Piero Heliczer
2-11-71
Cinematheque
80 Wooster, N.Y.C.

X

X and Y — Revolt on Campus
Trudi Sachs
11-10-72
Cubiculo
414 W. 51st, N.Y.C.

X Communication
January, 1973
Theatre X
Milwaukee, WI

X Has No Value
Cherrilyn Miles
1-16-70
New York Shakespeare Festival Public Theatre
425 Lafayette, N.Y.C.

Xircus
Donald L. Brooks
5-12-71
St. Peter's Church
346 W. 20th, N.Y.C.

Xmas Cards
Antony Bassae
12-30-70
Old Reliable Theatre Tavern
231 E. 3rd, N.Y.C.

Y

Yard of Sun, A
Christopher Fry
11-10-70
St. Lawrence Arts Centre
Toronto, CAN

Ye Fish and Little Gods
Roma Greth
5-2-69
Theatre 13
201 W. 13th, N.Y.C.

Year Boston Won the Pennant, The
John Ford Noonan
5-22-69
Forum Theatre
Lincoln Center
N.Y.C.

Year of the Hikers, The
John B. Keane
1-13-73
St. Jean Baptiste Auditorium
167 E. 75th, N.Y.C.

Years of the Locust
Norman Holland
2-8-68
Trinity Square Repertory
Providence, RI

Yegor Bulichov
Maxim Gorki; adapted by Joan Isserman
12-18-70
Long Wharf Theatre
New Haven, CT

Yellow Bird, The
(Adaptation of Tennessee Williams' short story)
11-9-69
Assembly Theatre
113 Jane, N.Y.C.

Yellow Peril
Mark Zalk
4-22-71
Theatre Crossroads
23 E. 20th, N.Y.C.

Yellow Peril, The
John Perkins
2-10-73
Negro Ensemble Company
St. Mark's Playhouse
133 Second, N.Y.C.

Yellow Sound, The (multi-media event)
Based on a script by Vasily Kandinsky
5-11-72
Guggenheim Museum
N.Y.C.

Yes, Yes, No, No
Ronnie Paris
12-31-68
Astor Place Theatre
434 Lafayette, N.Y.C.

Yesterday Ended Last Night
Pearl Fein
3-17-73
Stage Lights Theatrical Club
218 W. 48th, N.Y.C.

Yesterday's Good Girl
7-28-70
Towers Cabaret Theatre
Cedar Grove, NJ

Yin Yang (poetry, dance, music)
Joseph A. & Dorothy A. Dinroe Walker
6-30-72
Afro-American Studio
415 W. 127th, N.Y.C.

Yoshe Kalb (new musical production)
I. J. Singer; David Licht (adaptation); Maurice Rauch (music)
10-22-72
Eden Theatre
Second Ave. & 12th St., N.Y.C.

Yoshke Muzikant
Ossip Dimow (music); Z. Mlotek
11-4-72
Folksbiene Playhouse
175 E. Broadway, N.Y.C.

You Can't Tell a Cover by Its Color (with We Do Feel for You, Daniel)
Stanley Zawatsky
12-8-72
New York Theatre Ensemble
2 E. 2nd, N.Y.C.

You Don't Stand a Chinaman's Chance in This World Baby 'Cause They're Gonna Get You in the End Anyhow
David Libman
6-6-72
Manhattan Theatre Club
321 E. 33rd, N.Y.C.

You Find Out Young
Jeff Hochhauser
8-17-72
Playbox
94 St. Mark's Pl., N.Y.C.

You Gotta Deal with It
Neal Tate (book, lyrics, & music)
8-8-73
Theatre for the New City
113 Jane, N.Y.C.

You May Well Be the Man Who Lives Forever But Just in Case You Don't (with The Assassination of Martin Luther King and A Face Worth Saving)
Frank Hogan
5-24-68
Knowhere East Theatre Club
736 Broadway, N.Y.C.

You're Immoral, Nelly Lockridge
Nick Cosentino
9-22-72
New York City League of Playwrights
162 W. 21st, N.Y.C.

You Two Stay Here, the Rest Come with Me
Allan Rae (music); Christopher Newton (book); Wally Grieve & Christopher Newton (lyrics)
1-8-70
Theatre Calgary
Calgary, CAN

You Wanna Hear Luck?
Ruth Pleva; Elly Carr (book & lyrics); Herb Sweet (music)
3-31-72
Stagelights II Theatrical Club
125 W. 22nd, N.Y.C.

Young Among Themselves, The (with The Pastry Shop)
Ned Rorem
6-5-70
Extension Theatre
277 Park Ave. So., N.Y.C.

Young Joseph
Walter Corwin
10-5-71
WPA
333 Bowery, N.Y.C.

Young Marrieds at Play
Jerome Kass
3-7-69
Players Workshop
229 Seventh, N.Y.C.

Young Martin Luther King Jr.
Alice Childress
5-6-69
Symphony Hall
Newark, NJ

Young Master Dante, The
Werner Liepolt
12-12-68
American Place Theatre
N.Y.C.

Your Move Next
L. Charles Gray
6-2-72
Presbyterian Players of St. Albans
190th St. & 119th Ave., N.Y.C.

Your Own Thing
Donald Driver, Hal Hester, Danny Apolina
1-13-68
Orpheum
126 Second, N.Y.C.

Your Unhappiness with Me Is of No Concern to Readers
Helen Duberstein
5-7-71
Omni Theatre Club
145 W. 18th, N.Y.C.

Youth Rebellion, The (with Silver Skies, Tarquin Truth Beauty, and Camera Obscura)
Robert Patrick
4-28-69
Old Reliable Theatre Tavern
231 E. 3rd, N.Y.C.

Yucca Flats
Adam Lefevre (book & lyrics); Michael Arkin & Jay Allison (music)
9-21-73
Manhattan Theatre Club
321 E. 73rd, N.Y.C.

Yukisag
Dalt Wonk
7-10-69
WPA
34 E. 4th, N.Y.C.

Z

Zarf, I Love You
11-28-69
Courtyard Playhouse
424 W. 45th, N.Y.C.

Zelda
Sylvia Regan
3-5-69
Ethel Barrymore Theatre
243 W. 47th, N.Y.C.

Zing
George Haimsohn (book & lyrics); John Aman (music)
9-30-71
Bucks County Playhouse
New Hope, PA

Zombies of the Twentieth Century
Antonio Saldana
5-5-72
Chapel of the Intercession
Broadway & 155th St., N.Y.C.

Zoo
Vercors, translated by James Clancy
3-14-68
Cornell University
Ithaca, NY

Zorba
Joseph Stein, John Kander, Fred Ebb
10-7-68
Shubert Theatre
New Haven, CT

Zorra y Las Uvas, La (The Fox and the Grapes)
Guilhermo Figueiredo
5-26-72
Teatro Caras Nuevas
114 W. 14th, N.Y.C.

Zou (revue)
12-4-73
Blue Angel,
N.Y.C.

Zuber
Eric Krebs
5-5-72
CSC Repertory Theatre
89 W. 3rd, N.Y.C.

Zykove, The
Maxim Gorki; translated by Alexander Bakshy and Paul S. Nathan
12-1-72
St. Peter's Gate
132 E. 54th, N.Y.C.

A

Abbot, Charles
Games

Abe, Kobo
Woman of the Dunes

Abel, Lionel
Andromache

Ableman, Paul
Green Julia

Abramhoff, Sharon
Pleasure Palace

Abramovich, S. Y.
Travels of Benjamin the Third

Abrams, Steve
Celestina or The Spanish Bawd, La

Abrams, Tevia
And No Ceremony

Abrash, Merritt
Film Club, The
Postscript

Accardo, Ralph
Good Seed, The (with Pupe Puppets)
Pupe Puppets (with The Good Seed)

Ackerman, Hal
Elements, The
Matins (with Still Life)
Passing Through Liberia
Scavengers
Still Life (with Matins)
Threshold of Pain

Ackerman, Michael
Glorious Ruler, The

Ackerman, Robert
Ionescapade

Acosta, Ivan
Grito

Adams, Lee
Applause

Addison, James
Bill and William

Adelberg, Marge
That Man from Moscow!

Adellach, A.
Esa Cancion de Mierda

Adelson, Leonard
Molly

Adler, Doris
Warm-Blooded Dame, A: An Evening With Miss Sally-Jane Heit

Adler, Jack
Looking for Rosa
Sophistication of America, The

Adler, Richard
Mother's Kisses, A

Admire, Jere
Hannalore

Aeschylus
Persians, The

Agree, Phillip
Marlene's Choice (with Rooftop)
Rooftop (with Marlene's Choice)

Ahern, John
Go Out and See

Ahern, Matthew
Thing Called Love, A

Ahlm, Carl
Applaud Yourself, Applaud (with The Great American Two Step)
Great American Two Step, The (with Applaud Yourself, Applaud)
It's a Wise Father Who Knows His Own Country

Aidoo, Christina Ama Ata
Dilemma of a Ghost, The

Aiken, Conrad
Coming Forth by Day of Osiris Jones

Ajayi, Afolabi
Akokawe

Akoni, Niger
Before the War with the Eskimos

Akutagawa, Runosuke
Rashomon

Alakoye, Imogunla
Rite On

Albee, Edward
All Over
Box and Quotations from Chairman Mao Tse-Tung

Alcarez, Jose
Emerald Slippers, The

Aldan, Daisy
Daisy Aldan on Great Jones Street

Aleichem, Sholom
Hard To Be a Jew (new musical version)
Pair, The

Aleksie, Caca
Hamlet

Alenikoff, Frances
Obsidian

Alexander, Larry
Dandelion Wine

Alexander, Ronald
Keep Off the Grass
Remember Me!

Alexander, Ross
Body of an American, The
Celebration, The

Alford, Lamar
Thoughts

Alfred, William
Acamemnon
Cry for Us All

Algarin, Miguel
Olu Clemente — The Philosopher of Baseball

Al-Hakim, Tewfik
Tree Climber, The (Ya Talli' Ash-Shagara)

Alldredge, E. Don
Memphis Store Bought Teeth

Allen, Eddy
What Can You Buy for a Token?

Allen, Gene
Billy

Allen, Howard
Present for Billy Sturgill, A

Allen, Jay
Forty Carats
Prime of Miss Jean Brodie, The

Allen, John
Oh, Say Can You See L.A.

Allen, Robert E.
One More Spring

Allen, Seth
Sissy

Allen, Steve
Wake, The

Allen, Will
Rural Bone Show

Allen, Woody
Death Knocks
Play It Again, Sam

Allison, Jay
Yucca Flats

Allport, Christopher
Outlaw Brothers

Almagor, Dan
Only Fools Are Sad

Almaz, Michael
Dreyfus on Devil's Island
Monsieur Artaud

Alonzo, Cecil
Black Voices

Alpert, Sandy
Well . . . Fair

Alsberg, Arthur
Happiness Is Just a Little Thing Called a Rolls-Royce
Only Bathtub in Cassis, The

Alson, Lawrence
Four by Four

Alvarado, Eli
Caricatura

Amaker, Vance
Right On! Dope Is Death

Aman, John
Don't Walk on the Clouds
Now
Zing

Amber, Lili
Rebbitzen from Israel, The

Ames, Gustavo
Anticlassical Presentation

Amis, Kingsley
Lucky Jim

Anagnostaki, Loula
Antonio or The Message

Anbinder, Barry
Wait, The

Andersen, Dennis
Girls Most Likely To Succeed, The
Marry Me! Marry Me!

Andersen, Hans Christian
Big Klaus and Little Klaus

Anderson, Delia
Number Scene, The

Anderson, John Arthur
Like Tender of Our Love We Make, The

Anderson, Julian
Playing with Dolls

Anderson, Kent
Home, The (reading)
Sandbox, The

Anderson, Mia
Women, Two Men and a Moose, The

Anderson, Robert
I Never Sang for My Father
Solitaire, Double Solitaire

Anderson, Tom
Municipal Water System Is Not Trustworthy, The

Andreani, Sydney
Pig!

Andrews, William
Bringing in the Sheep

Anouilh, Jean
Augustus
Dear Antoine
Episode in the Life of an Author (with The Orchestra)
Mademoiselle Colombe (musical version)
Orchestra, The (with Episode in the Life of an Author)

Ansky, S.
Angel Raziel, The
Dybbuk, The

Anthony, Earl
Charlie Still Can't Win No Wars on the Ground (with The (Mis)Judgment)
(Mis)Judgment, The (with Charlie Still Can't Win No Wars on the Ground)

Anthony, Rock
I Scream, You Scream, We All Scream

Antonacci, Greg
Dance Wi' Me
Myths of America Smith, The

Apolina, Danny
Your Own Thing

Appleman, Herbert
Heyday
Perfect Gentleman, A
Unfair to Goliath

Appleman, Margie
Best Is Yet To Be, The
Nice Place You Have Here

Aquino, Florence
It's Up To You!

Aranha, Ray
My Sister, My Sister

Archer, Robert
Tom Jones

Arden, Donn
Pzazz '70 and All That Jazz, Baby

Arden, James
Agreement on Damhaix, An (staged reading)

Arden, John
Business of Good Government, The
True History of Squire Jonathan and His Unfortunate Treasure, The

Arditi, Bonnie
Other Side of the Stars, The

Arent, Arthur
Ethiopia

Aretino, Pietro
Moglie E' Necessaria, La

Argue, John
Eros and Psyche (dance drama)

Arguelles, Hugo
Cuervos Estan de Luto, Los

Aristophanes
Birds, The
Clouds, The
Lysistrata (Adaptation by Darrel deChaby)
Lysistrata (New adaptation by Michael Cacoyannis)
Lysistrata (new rock musical version)
Peace
Women's Rites (Thesmophoriazusae)

Arkin, Michael
Yucca Flats

Arlen, Harold
Wizard of Oz, The (puppet version)

Armony, Isaac
Ballad of a Separated Couple

Arnebeck, Bob
Watch the Fords Go By

Arrabal, Fernando
And They Put Handcuffs on the Flowers
Architect and the Emperor of Assyria, The
Carta à Franco 1972
Ceremony for an Assassinated Black Man
Guernica (with Pique-Nique en Campagne)
Impossible Loves
Labyrinthe
Pique-Nique en Campagne (with Guernica)
Tricycle, The

Arrick, Larry
Conversion of the Jews (with Defender of the Faith and Epstein)
Defender of the Faith (with Conversion of the Jews and Epstein)
Eli, The Fanatic (part of Unlikely Heroes)
Epstein (with Conversion of the Jews and Defender of the Faith)
Gimpel the Fool

Arrighi, Mel
Castro Complex, The
Ordinary Man, An

Arrowsmith, William
Clouds, The

Arrufat, A.
Case Is Investigated, The

Artaud, Antonin
Cenci, The
Conquest of Mexico, The

Arzoomanian, Raffi
Moths, The

Ashby, Dorothy
Game

Ashby, John
Game

Ashford, Gerald
Cave of the Wombats

Ashley, Robert
Trial of Anne Opie Wehrer. . ., The

Ashmore, Basil
I Only Want an Answer

Asnato, Anthony
Apple Tree and I, The

Aspenstrom, Werner
Spiders, The

Assini, Chris
Reconstruction of Oliver Jones, The

Atlas, Charles
Wonder, Try (Sketchy Version)

Auchincloss, Louis
Great World and Timothy Colt, The

Auden, W. H.
Knights of the Round Table

Audiberti, Jacques
Quoat, Quoat

Aue, William
Broken Cowboy, A

Auer, Elizabeth
Val, Christie and the Others

Auer, James M.
City of Light, The
Tell It to Angela

Auletta, Robert
Alberta Radiance (staged reading)
Coocooshay
Stops

Aulson, Laurence
Plaster

Aurenche, Jean
Augustus

Aurthur, Robert Alan
Carry Me Back to Morningside Heights

Austin, Paul John
Confessions of an Ignorant
Funny Men Are in Trouble, The (with Quietus)
Quietus (with The Funny Men Are in Trouble)
Untitled Play

Averill, John
Gorillas

Avery, Helen
Merlin's Magic

Axelrod, David
National Lampoon's Lemmings (revue)

Ayckbourn, Alan
How the Other Half Loves
Relatively Speaking

Ayer, Ethan
Nobody's Earnest

B

Baal, Frederic
Real Reel

Babe, Thomas
Everyman (musical)
Winter's Tale in Georgia, A

Bacharach, Burt
Promises, Promises

Bachardy, Don
Meeting by the River, A

Backstedt, Lawrence
Ballerina Plays Ball, The

Baehr, Nicholas E.
Palmer Way, The

Bagnold, Enid
Call Me Jacky

Baierlein, Ed
Juke Box, The
Moments and the Bramble

Bailey, Frederick
Hooded Gnome, The (Part 3 of Grub)
Set It Down with Gold on Lasting Pillars
Thirty Years Past (Not Me, Boy and Hot Evening Rain)

Bailey, Rick
Unscheduled Appearance

Bails, Jeannine
No Lark

Baird, Bil
Sultan of Tuffet, The (with The Whistling Wizard)
Whistling Wizard, The (with The Sultan of Tuffet)
Wizard of Oz, The (puppet version)

Baird, Martha
Goodbye Profit Motive
Trouble with Portnoy, The

Baisley, Doris
In Darkest Africa: A Ladies Guide to the Nile
Mary Dyer Hanged in Boston

Baker, David
Come Summer

Baker, Elliott
Clark and Myrna
Penny Wars, The

Baker, Margaret
Eté (Summer)

Baker, Paul
Project III: Is Law in Order?

Baker, Word
Baboon!!!
Many Happy Returns, A Review of Revues

Bakkerud, Dick
Charlie Is My Darling Cried the Darling Little Girl

Bakshy, Alexander
Country People
Zykove, The

Baldinucci, Ciro
Tony and the Call Girl

Baldwin, Joseph B.
Can the Frog Princess Find Happiness?
Chekhov List, The
House Within the House Within, The
Incredible Outbreak of Semi-Nudity, The
Out of Control
Pool Hall of the Heart, The
Sky of Faces, A

Balestrino, Phil
Triune (Communication Gap; Do You Like Me? Say You Like Me; Willyum)

Balk, H. Wesley
Shakespeare Games
Three Hundred Sixty-Five Days (365 Days)

Ball, David
Gorilla, Gorilla

Ball, Frank
Nativitie Playe, A

Ball, William
Acting Up

Ballard, Clinton
Ballad of Johnny Pot, The

Ballester, Manuel Mendez
Crossroads

Banachi, Raymond
Cadaver, The
Certain Kind of Woman, A (Part 1 of Grub)
Games
Maybe That's Because I Love You
Sky Is Falling, The (play reading)

Bandyke, Silvia
Spring Bouquet

Bankson, Douglas
Shellgame

Barab, Seymour
Francis — Day, The
Who Am I?

Baraka, Imamu Amiri (LeRoi Jones)
Black Dada Nihilism (with Madheart)
Columbia, the Gem of the Ocean
Experimental Death Unit #1 (with Junkies Are Full of Sh . . .)
Fun Boot Dancers (with Junkies Are Full of Sh. . . and Blood Rites)
Junkies Are Full of Sh. . . (with Blood Rites and Fun Boot Dancers)
Junkies Are Full of Sh. . .
Madheart (with Black Dada Nihilism)
Recent Killing, A

Barasch, Norman
Waltz Me Around Again

Barber, Benjamin
Doors, Limes and Other Hazards of City Life
People's Heart, The

Barbour, Floyd
Antony and Cleopatra (with Day Work)
Day Work (with Antony and Cleopatra)

Bard, Martin
Time to Heal, A

Bardacke, Frances
Slightly Higher on the West Coast

Bargy, Jeanne
Mother Goose Go-Go

Barker, Gary
Boor, The

Barlow, Anna Marie
Ambassador
Cruising Speed 600 M.P.H.
Glory! Halleluhah!
Other Voices, Other Rooms
Where the Music Is

Barnak, Ira
Fourteen Ninety-One (1491)

Barnes, Brian D.
Pickwickians at Manor Farm, The

Barnes, Peter
Ruling Class, The

Barnes, Theodore
About Time
Praxeis (Tormenta, While the Dew Is Still on the Roses, and Inferiorities)

Barrault, Jean-Louis
Rabelais

Barrett, Barbara
Conrad: A Memory Play
Jail Game

Barrett, C. David
Companion Plays, The

Barrett, Nathan
Bird Food

Barry, John
Lolita, My Love

Barry, Julian
Don't Move the Victory Column
Lenny

Barry, P. J.
Actorines and Actorettes
Brownsville Raid, 1916, The
Gannon
Kiss of Life, The
Love Man's Gone Away, The
She Played Good Piano
Sheriff Who Had No Horse, The
What Ever Happened to Kimchee Fook?

Barsha, Tony
Assassination of Nigger Nate, The (with The Forgotten American)
Forgotten American, The (with The Assassination of Nigger Nate)
Hearing, The
Smash!
Tragedy of Homer Sills, The

Bart, Lionel
Strada, La

Bartenieff, Irma
Morning to Midnite

Bartenieff, Jonteta
Morning to Midnite

Barton, Lee
Nightride

Basile, Jean
Drummer Boy, The

Bass, George
House of Mourning

Bass, Jules
Month of Sundays

Bass, Kingsley B., Jr.
We Righteous Bombers

Bassae, Antony
Catch As Catch Can (with The Jesus Man)
Jesus Man, The (with Catch As Catch Can)
Xmas Cards

Basurto, Luis G.
Cada Quien Su Vida (To Each His Own)

Batchelor, Ruth
Quarter for the Ladies Room, A

Batson, George
House on the Cliff
Rehearsal for Death

Baubold, Cleve
Shiny Red Ball, The (with Big Black Box, Owl, and The Armory)

Bauer, Andrew
Garden of Delights, A (with The Stylites)
Stylites, The (with A Garden of Delights)

Bauer, Irv
Dream Out of Time, A

Bauman, Art
Made in the USA

Bauman, Max
Glickl Hameln Demands Justice

Baumel, Albert
Recovery and Adjustment

Baxandall, Lee
Potsy

Baxter, Cash
Red Raspberry Revue, The

Bayer, Carole
Georgy

Bayer, Jerome
Deadline!!
Tell Me, Worthy Editor

Bayley, Jefferson
Saviour Queen, The

Baynard, Ed
Fall and Rise of Parity, The (shadow play)

Bayrak, Tosum
Love America or Live
Wake for the Late Captain Hasan Tursun Efendi . . ., The

Beakel, Walter
Liars, The

Bean, Adelaide
Bless the Child

Beardsley, Bonnie
They Came

Beaumarchais
Barber of Seville, The

Beaver, Walter
Black Shadow Black Prince
Help Stamp Out Puritans

Boytin, B. A.
Cain

Bradbury, Ray
Dandelion Wine
Wonderful Ice Cream Suit, The

Braden, John
Audition!
Babs and Judy Show, The
King's Crown and I, The
Nobody Cried When They Tore Down Broadway
Silver Queen

Bradford, Benjamin
Anthropologists, The
Brainwave
Concentric Circles
Double Fraktur "L", A
Geometric Progression
High Structure Falls Further, A
Ideal State, The
Losing Things (with Touch and Go)
Motel
Parabus Objective (with Pitfall for a Rational Man and Rehearsal)
Pitfall for a Rational Man (with Rehearsal and Parabus Objective)
Plotters
Postmortem (with Where Are You Going Hollis Jay?)
Rehearsal (with Pitfall for a Rational Man and Parabus Objective)
Touch and Go (with Losing Things)
Where Are You Going Hollis Jay? (with Postmortem)

Bradford, Roy
Blind Spot, The

Brady, Leo
Coldest War of All, The

Bragg, Bernard
Songs from Milk Wood

Brand, Oscar
Bridge
Chariot of the Sun, The
Education of Hyman Kaplan, The
How To Steal an Election

Brandon, Dolores
Women of Ancient Greece

Brandon, Johnny
Billy Noname
Who's Who, Baby?

Brandt, Chris
Mother Courage and Her Children

Brantley, Danielle
Future Past, Future Present

Braswell, John
Bar That Never Closes, The
Demon
Everything for Anybody (an amatorio in 12 parts)
Interior Castle

Brathwaite, J. Ashton
Escape from Babylon

Bratt, Bengt
Home, The (reading)

Braunstein, Alan
King's Crown and I, The

Braunstein, Steven
Birth in a Tiny Container, A

Brazina, Tony
Salted Arrows

Brecht, Bertolt
Days of the Commune, The
Die Kleinburgerhochzeit (The Wedding Feast)
Edward the Second
Flight of Lindbergh, The (with A Lesson in Consent)
Good Woman of Setzuan, The
Happy End
In the Jungle of the Cities
Lesson in Consent, A (with The Flight of Lindbergh)
Little Mahagonny, The
Mahagonny
Man's a Man, A (rock musical)
Marriage, The
Mother Courage
Mother Courage and Her Children
St. Joan of the Stockyards
Theatre Whose Stage Is the Street, The

Bredt, James
Happy Hypocrite, The

Breit, Harvey
Guide, The

Brelis, Dean
Shalom

Brenner, Alfred
Death of Black Jesus, The

Brenner, Richard
Man in a Bucket

Breslow, Brooke C.
Memory of Childhood, A

Breton, Andre
If You Please

Breton, Tomas
Fiesta in Madrid (based on the zarzuela "La Verbena de la Poloma")

Bretton, Elise
Wuziz

Breuer, Lee
Red Horse Animation, The

Brewster, Townsend
Botany Lesson, The
Brown Overcoat, The
Please Don't Cry and Say 'No'

Brickell, Claude
Louis IX

Bridges, James
A^3
Bachelor Furnished

Briggs, Charles
Jitney Vehicle, The (with Little B.S.)
Little B.S. (with The Jitney Vehicle)

Brimitoin, Mark
Allegros

Brisbane, Ruth
Legacy of Bessie Smith, The

Brittan, Robert
Raisin

Britton, Gary
Couch (with The Crystal Pigs)
Crystal Pigs, The (with Couch)

Britton, Ronnie
Twanger

Bro, Andrew
Champagne's for Jake, Angel, The

Broad, Jay
Alimony
Big Coca-Cola Swamp in the Sky, The
Conflict of Interest, A
Red, White, and Maddox

Brock, Sue
Goodbye Tomorrow

Brockett, Don
Sweet Feet

Brod, Max
Schloss, Das (The Castle)

Brody, Jerrold
Scenes and Things

Broek, John
Ariel

Bromberg, Conrad
Actors
Dream of a Blacklisted Actor
Transfers

Brook, Peter
Conference of the Birds, The

Brooks, Alfred
Nine Sentiments, The

Brooks, Donald L.
Superfreak!
Xircus

Brotherton, Bob
Wild and Wonderful

Broughton, James
Bedlam

Broughton, Patrick
Forgotten Dreams

Broughton, Shirley
After the Ball (musical satire)
Cliche U.S.A.

Browder, Clifford
Movers, The

Brown, Chris Jr.
Chocolate: A Black Musical

Brown, Deloss
Cleaning Solution, The
Jonathan Wild
Peoria Impromptu, The

Brown, Elizabeth
Nightstone

Brown, Joan
Other Side of the Stars, The

Brown, John
Fall and Redemption of Man, The

Brown, Kenneth
Cretan Bull, The
Nightlight

Brown, Lennox
Ballet Behind the Bridge
Prodigal in Black Stone

Brown, Michael
Different Times

Brown, Oscar Jr.
Big Time Buck White (musical version)

Brown, Stephen
Contrast, The (musical version)
Fashion (musical)
Things To Hear, Things To See (An Evening with Huckleberry Finn)

Brown, Walter Leyden
First Death
Wrong Gone Dreamer

Brown, William F.
How To Steal an Election

Browner, Richard
Breathing Space

Bruders, Janet
Power to the People

Bruestle, Beaumont
Wonderful Tang, The

Brukenfeld, Dick
Big Broadcast on East 53rd, The

Brulin, Tone
Eyes of Chalk
Fire Eater's Enemy, The
Stump Removal

Bryant, Hazel
Black Circles 'Round Angela (with Sheba)
Makin' It
Sheba (with Black Circles 'Round Angela)

Bryant, J. H.
Black Circles

Brynner, Roc
Opium

Buch, Rene
Hombre Sincero, Un: Jose Marti

Buchanan, Herb
Red Raspberry Revue, The

Buchwald, Art
Sheep on the Runway

Buck, Glover
Apartment To Let
Guthrie
Jewelry of the Dead (with Quiet Sunday)
Quiet Sunday (with Jewelry of the Dead)
Symbiosis Golden

Buck, Randy
River Kids

Buckaloo, Jon
And the Band Played On
Great American Desert, The

Buenaventura, Enrique
Red Convertible, The

Buero-Vallejo, Antonio
Concert at St. Ovide, The

Bufano, Rocco
Horseman, Pass By

Bulgakov, Mikhail
Moliere or A Cabal of Hypocrites
Monsieur de Moliere

Bull, B. S.
Syllables

Bullins, Ed
Corner, The
Death Lists
Duplex, The: A Black Love Story in Four Movements
Electronic Nigger and Others, The (later retitled Three Plays By Ed Bullins)
Fabulous Miss Marie, The
Game of Adam & Eve, The
Gentleman Caller, The
House Party
How Do You Do
In the Wine Time
Pig Pen, The
Short Bullins
Short Stuff
Son, Come Home, A
Street Sounds
Tabula-Rasa

Bunuel, Rafael
Confused Smiths, The
Game, The
Three Grotescas
Two New One Act Plays

Burch, Claire
Blues To Be Called Crazy When Crazy's All There Is, A

Burch, Thayer
Mandrake the Magician

Burdick, Jacques
Termites, The

Burgess, Anthony
Cyrano
Cyrano de Bergerac Edmond
Oedipus the King

Burleson, Dennis
Gunk

Burr, Anne Olson
Huui, Huui

Burrows, Abe
Four on a Garden

Burrows, Vinnie
Walk Together Children (new edition)

Burstein, Lonnie
In Fashion
Tricks

Burstein, Pesach
Rebbitzen from Israel, The

Burton, C. L.
Kumaliza

Burton, Clarence
Melting Pot Park

Burton, Philip
Battle of the Sexes, The

Burton, Scott
Behavior Tableaux (sculpture-theatre work)

Burwell, Richard
No More Rabbits

D

Fried, Emanuel
Brother Gorski
Rose

Friedman, Bruce Jay
Mother's Kisses, A
Steambath
Turtlenecks

Friedman, Edward
Pigeons

Friedman, Gary William
Me Nobody Knows, The

Friel, Brian
Crystal and Fox
Freedom of the City, The
Lovers
Mundy Scheme, The

Frisch, Max
Firebugs, The
Public Prosecutor Is Sick of It All, A

Frost, Warren
Unknown Soldier, The

Fry, Christopher
Yard of Sun, A

Fuchs, Ira Hayes
Score, The (staged reading)

Fuentes, Ernesto
Eagle and the Serpent, The (with The Swallow)
Swallow, The (with The Eagle and the Serpent)

Fugard, Athol
Boesman and Lena
Hello and Goodbye
People Are Living There

Fuller, Charles
In My Many Names and Days
Village, The: A Party

Fuller, Dean
Smith

Fuller, Lorenzo
Speed Gets the Poppys

Furman, Roger
Gimmick, The (with To Kill a Devil)
Long Black Block, The
To Kill a Devil (with The Gimmick)

Furth, George
Company
Twigs

Fusco, Peter
Legion
Little Match Girl Makes It Big, The ("revusical")

G

Gaard, David
And Puppy Dog Tails
Day They Gave the Babies Away, The
Women's Representative, The

Gabre-Medhin, Tsegaye
Oda-Oak Oracle

Gaburo, Ken
In the Can

Gagliano, Frank
City Scene (Paradise Gardens East and Conerico Was Here to Stay)
Gris-Gris
Prince of Peasantmania, The

Gaines, Frederick
Dracula
House of Leather, The
King Solomon Is Dead
Wilde

Gaines, J. E.
Don't Let It Go To Your Head
Sometimes a Hard Head Makes a Soft Behind
What If It Had Turned Up Heads?

Gallardo, Edward
Bernie
Everybody Knows My Business
In Another Part of the City
Miss George Alliance
Nobody Ever Says Goodbye

Gallardo, Yolanda
Everybody Knows My Business

Galli, Beverlee
Regeneration

Galton, Ray
Rockefeller and the Red Indians

Galvin, W. Randolph
Babysitter, The
Immaculate Misconception, The

Gambara, Griselda
Camp, The
Nada Que Ver (Out of It)

Garcia, Eduardo
Art and Bart
Death and Re-Erection of Dr. Franklin, The
Three X Garcia (3 X Garcia)

Gardner, Eric
Ballgame

Gardner, Fred
Co-Op, The

Gardner, Herb
Goodbye People, The
Goodbye People, The (revised)

Gardner, Lewis
Chariot of the Sun, The
Hadleyburg

Gardner, Worth
Aimee

Garfinkle, Louis
Molly

Gari, Janet
Lyle

Garrett, George
Sir Slob and the Princess

Garrick, Richard
Distance Ahead, A

Garson, Barbara
Co-Op, The

Garson, Toby
Lyle

Garvin, Chico
Buffalo Meat

Garvin, David
Prism City

Garvin, Larry
Conspiracy
Safe at Last

Gascoigne, Bamber
Leda Had a Little Swan

Gasman, Ira
What's a Nice Country Like You Doing in a State Like This?

Gasper, Raymond
Three

Gates, Crawford
Rendezvous

Gath, Joseph
Dr. Denton's Secret
Play House
Tidings, Comfort, and Joy

Gauthier, Guy
Amen
Butterscotch Canyon
Call of the Loom, The
Drinking at the Falls (with F. . .!)
F. . .! (with Drinking at the Falls)
Green Man and the Red Lady in the Red and Green Ladies Room, The
Injun
Jonathan Jones
Little Burgundy (with Manitoba)
Manitoba (with Little Burgundy)
Play with a Message, A
Singin' Hare Krishna (with Snows of Spring)
Snows of Spring (with Singin' Hare Krishna)
Spotlights
Tonto
Voice Is Coming, The or A Voice to Be Heard

Gavronsky, Serge
French Revolution of May 1968, The

Gay, John
Christophe

Gayle, T. C.
Legacy

Gaynor, Charles
Irene

Geiogamah, Hanay
Body Indian

Gelber, Jack
Barbary Shore
Cuban Thing, The
Sleep

Gelber, Stanley Jay
Love and Let Love

Geld, Gary
Purlie

Geldart, Ed
Sticks and Stones (revue)

Gelogamah, Hanay
Foghorn

Genet, Jean
Screens, The

Gentry, Raymond
Ride, The
Treatment, The

Georgalas, Robert
Soldiers

Gerlach, Robert
Something Afoot

Gerould, Daniel C.
Candaules Commissioner
Mister Price, or Tropical Madness
New Deliverance, The
Water Hen, The

Gerould, Eleanor
Mister Price, or Tropical Madness

Gerrarlee, Ellen
None Whatever or The Master Critic
Window, The

Gershe, Leonard
Butterflies Are Free
Miss Pell Is Missing

Gerst, Larry
Last Catholic, The

Gerstein, Serge
Dogs

Gerth, John
Outlaw Brothers

Gethers, Steven
New Mount Olive Motel, The

Gianino, Peter
Flush the Aquarium

Giarraputo, Warren
Nice Pizza, A
Sand Castle, The

Gibbens, Michael
Annie
I Have Always Believed in Ghosts

Gibbons, Therese
V . . .

Gibson, Terrill L.
Frederick

Gibson, William
John and Abigail

Giesel, Dennis
How Peter the Prick Found Love

Gifford, Joseph
Demons, The
Rites II

Gilbert, Ilsa
Circus
Dead Dentist, The
Dialogue Between Didey Warbucks and Mama Vaseline, A
Little Onion Annie
Soul of a Stripper, The

Gilbert, John
Multicolored Maze, The

Gilbert, Margaret Barbour
Scene

Giles, Janet
Second Coming, The

Gilhooley, Jack
Comeback, The
Entrepreneurs of Avenue B, The (with The Last Act)
Homefront Blues
Last Act, The (with The Entrepreneurs of Avenue B)

Gilhousen, Judith
Daisy Does It
Specimen, A

Gill, William
Man Out of Darkness

Gillen, Leon
Rose Man, The

Gilles, D. B.
Hard Times

Gillette, William
Sherlock Holmes

Gillman, Jonathan
Assassination of the Pope, The

Gilroy, Frank D.
Matter of Pride, A
Only Game in Town, The
Present Tense (with 'Twas Brillig; Come Next Tuesday; So Please Be Kind)

Gingell, George
Lonely Hunting, The

Ginsberg, Allen
Kaddish

Ginzburg, Natalia
I Married You for the Fun of It

Giordano, Tony
Circle, The
Halloween Years, The
Interplay
Jaws That Bite, The (staged reading)
Playground
Soup

Giorno, John
Purple Heart

Gioseffi, Daniela
Care of the Body
Golden Daffodil Dwarf, The, and Other Works

Gipe, George
Love Game, The

Giron, Arthur
Edith Stein

Giss, Gerry
Macedonian Rag (with Prometheus and Pandora)
Prometheus and Pandora (with Macedonian Rag)

Gitelman, Belle
Picnic for Patricia, A

Giunta, Aldo
Partnership, The
Transgressor Rides Again, The

Givens, Arthur
Son of Jesse James, The
Trouble in Territoon City, The

Griffin, Hayden
Pirate, The

Griffin, William
Campion

Grillparzer, Franz
Thou Shalt Not Lie!

Grimaldi, John
Biting Through
Doctor Quackenbush's Traveling Medicine Show Presents the Rope-Dancer
Innovations

Grissmer, John
Candyapple, The

Grodin, Charles
Opening, The

Groob, Michael
Dirty Ferdie Comes Clean
What's in It for Me?

Grossman, Larry
Minnie's Boys

Grossman, Peter
Epistle, An
V.D. Vietnam

Grossman, Shirly
Warm-Blooded Dame, A: An Evening With Miss Sally-Jane Heit

Grossman, Stuart
Poor Old Fool (musical)

Grossmann, Suzanne
Chemmy Circle, The
Guerre, Yes Sir!, La
Summer Days
There's One in Every Marriage

Gruber, Ed
Schiediker Calls

Grudeff, Marian
Life Can Be Like Wow!

Gruen, John
Fatal Beauty
Never Tell Isobel
Soap Opera
Treatment, The (with Soap Opera)

Guare, John
Cop Out
Home Fires
Longest Afternoon of the Year, The
Loveliest Afternoon of the Year, The
Marco Polo Sings a Solo
Two Gentlemen of Verona

Guden, Guy
Nothing Is Sacred
Void in Wisconsin

Guenther, John
Modern Hamlet, A
Modern Hamlet, A (reading)

Guest, Christopher
National Lampoon's Lemmings (revue)

Guggenheim, Charles
Sound and Light at Ford's Theatre

Gunn, Bill
Johnnas

Gunn, Gwendolyn
Up! (revue)

Gurney, A. R., Jr.
David Show, The
Golden Fleece, The
Love Course, The
Old One Two, The
Scenes from American Life

Guss, Louis
Rome, Rome

Gustafsson, Lars
Homage at Night

Gutmacher, Benito
I Am the Chosen One

Gutswa, T. Frank
About Face (four one-acts)
Death Wish
Looking for Billy
Pawn Takes King

Guy, Shirley
Donovan
Emily
Harlequinade for Mourners
House of Fun and Games, The
Winter Night

H

Hachfeld, R.
Mugnog

Hackaday, Hal
Ambassador
Minnie's Boys

Hacks, Peter
Amphitryon

Hadler, Walter
American Gothic (with Thirty)
Flite Cage (with Mission Beach)
Grand Mal Crick
Mission Beach (with Flite Cage)
Mutilation
New Orleans Orchid
Solarium
Thirty (with American Gothic)
Water Works at Lincoln, The
Wheeling Reds

Hagen, Reigh
Grave Diggers of 1971

Hagerty, Tim
Man's a Man, A (rock musical)

Hague, Albert
Fig Leaves Are Falling, The

Haguta, Kenji
Sengakuji

Hailey, Oliver
Animal
Continental Divide
Father's Day
For the Use of the Hall
Four by Four
Picture

Haimsohn, George
Now
Zing

Haislip, William
Philosophy in the Bedroom by the Marquis de Sade

Haldeman, Lynn E.
How To Be a Successful Educator Without Really. . .

Halfi, Ralque
Felicidad (a play for dolls, mannequins, masks, puppets, and people)

Halkim, Hillel
Fischer

Hall, Adrian
Feasting with Panthers
Oscar
Son of Man and the Family

Hall, Nick
Going Apes

Hall, Robert
Misanthrope, The

Halpern, Jonathan
Sisters

Halpern, Martin
Messiah, The

Hamilton, Christian
Love Match

Hamilton, Holly
Makin' It

Hamilton, Larry
Splinters

Hamilton, Noel
So Early in the Morning

Hamilton, Wallace
Bonus March
Bunny Boy (with A Rite for Bedtime)
Matinee
Month of Fridays, A
Rite for Bedtime, A (with Bunny Boy)
Touch of Orpheus, A

Hammer, George
Landmarks
There Was a Tribe of Indians (with When Princes Could Be Waiters)
When Princes Could Be Waiters (with There Was a Tribe of Indians)

Hammerstein, Oscar
Allegro (revised version)

Hammett, Dashiell
Cops

Hammond, Dene
Color for Cassandra's Dream, A
Fear of Falling Apples (with The Sound of Eggs Breaking)
Sound of Eggs Breaking, The (with Fear of Falling Apples)
Teddy Bears Never Mate in Captivity

Hamotak
What's Going on Outside Anyhow?

Hampel, Gunter
Atlantic Crossing

Hample, Stuart
Selling of the President, The

Hampton, Calvin
Wrong Gone Dreamer

Hampton, Christopher
Doll's House, A
Hedda Gabler
Philanthropist, The
Total Eclipse

Handfield, Teddy
Possible World of Jean Kerr, The

Handke, Peter
Calling for Help
Gaspard
Kaspar
My Foot My Tutor
Offending the Audience: A Speak-In
Ride Across Lake Constance, The
Self-Accusation

Hanks, Michael
Doves, The

Hanley, James
Inner Journey

Hanley, William
Four by Four
No Answer

Hansberry, Lorraine
Blancs, Les
To Be Young, Gifted and Black

Hansen, Hardy
Women's Rites (Thesmophoriazusae)

Hanson, Philip
Adventures of Huckleberry Finn, The
Edgar Allan Poe, His Stories and Poems
Mrs. Reynolds
My Name Is Aram
Smorgasbord (concert drawn from repertoire of solo shows)

Harburg, E. Y.
What a Day for a Miracle!
Wizard of Oz, The (puppet version)

Harding, Marlene
Billy's Bass

Hardstack, Michael
Garbage Wine
Montipasse

Hardy, David
Full Eight Hours, A

Hardy, Jim
American Asparagus Growers Annual Alligator Wrestling Contest, Barbecue and Jubilee, The
Theatregraphs

Hare, Bill
God Says There Is No Peter Ott

Hare, David
Slag

Hargrove, James Ty
Absolute Zero, The (with Every Buzzard's Son)
Every Buzzard's Son (with The Absolute Zero)

Harkness, Ed
Flaw, The
Marriage on the New Made Moon Through No Fault of Our Own

Harnick, Sheldon
Rothschilds, The

Harper, Alan
Middle Is the Deepest Part, The

Harper, Margaret
They Came from Spain

Harper, Wally
Ballad of Romeo and Juliet, The
Coming Together
Sensations

Harriman, Paul
Hitch Hiker, The

Harrington, Donald
Allegros
Reety in Hell

Harris, Artie
Hello, Sucker

Harris, Aurand
Peck's Bad Boy

Harris, Merrill
Quad

Harris, Neil
Cop and Blow
Players Inn
Straight from the Ghetto

Harris, Norman
None of Us Are Ever Born Brave

Harris, Ted
Gabriella
Playstreet
Silhouettes

Harrison, Bruce
Eleven Thousand Pieces of Jade

Harrison, Paul Carter
End of the Beginning, The
Experimental Leader, The
Great MacDaddy, The
Leader, The
Tabernacle
Top Hat

Harrity, Richard
Home Life of the Buffalo

Harron, Donald
Private Turvey's War (revised version of Turvey)

Harrow, Kenneth
Death to the Brother

Hart, Joseph
Brooklyn Bridge Is Falling Down (Sullivan's Wake and I Didn't Hear Nothing, I Live in the Back)
Sonata for Mott Street

Hart, Stan
Click!

Harter, James
Are You a Virgin? (with Old Maid)
Old Maid (with Are You a Virgin?)

Hartgens, Bambi
Obsidian

Hartman, Edmund
Welcome Home

Hartman, Jan
Final Solutions (pageant)

I

J

L

M

O

Oates, Joyce Carol
Miracle Play
Ontological Proof of My Existence
Sunday Dinner
Sweet Enemy, The

O'Brien, Conor Cruise
Murderous Angels

O'Brien, Jack
Selling of the President, The

O'Brien, Sharon
Robin Hood

Ochs, Phil
Spiro Who?

O'Connel, Larry
Aluminium Pigey, The (with The Daughter of Earl Siphon and The Story—Aunt Rollie)
Bobby Goes to the Movies—1944
Daughter of Earl Siphon, The (with The Aluminium Pigey and The Story—Aunt Rollie)
Four on a Couch
Island Surrounded by Sketches, An
Louisville '59 (with So Dark Tonight)
Mixed Review
On the Mantlepiece
Quiet in the Balcony (They Were Dependable; Jack Highstrung, All American; Taboo and the Princess from Popular Mechanics)
So Dark Tonight (with Louisville '59)
Sometimes in New Jersey
Story—Aunt Rollie or Before and After, The (with The Aluminium Pigey and The Daughter of Earl Siphon)

O'Connor, Ulick
Behan (reading)

O'Connor, William Van
In the Cage

Oddo, Jasper
Carry Me Back to Old Virginity
Evening, An

Oddo, Jerry
Too Young for Spring

Odeen, Mats
Girl in the House of Culture, The

Oderman, Stuart
Death of Solly's Warren, The
Season of the Carnival
Team, The
Two Plus One Equals Two

Odets, Clifford
Silent Partner, The
Winter Journey

Odin, Jane
House of Yahweh, The

O'Donnell, Randolph
Mrs. Erlynne's Daughter (early version of Lady Windermere's Fan)
Remains of Carter Simpson, The

O'Donnell, Richard
And Other Caged Birds

O'Farrell, Nuala
Heart's a Wonder, The

Oglesby, Carl
Peacemaker, The

O'Hearne, Patrick
I Love You, Willie-Cat

O'Horgan, Tom
Inner City (a street cantata)
St. Hydro Clemency

O'Keefe, John
Jelly F
Jimmy Beam

Okpaku, Joseph
Silhouette of God, The (with The Virtues of Adultery)
Virtues of Adultery, The (with The Silhouette of God)

Olds, Robert M.
Practice Makes Perfect

Oliak, Blanche Mednick
Broken Mirrors in a Junkyard
Strays (with Third Ride on a Merry Go Round)
Third Ride on a Merry Go Round (with Strays)

Oliver, Tom
Just Before Morning
Saltflowers
Tree

Oliver, William I.
Camp, The

Ollington, Mark
Magic Isle, The

Olon-Scrymgeour, John
Bitter Dialogue

Olshenetsky, Alexander
Try It! You'll Like It!

Olsher, Laura
Safe and Sound

O'Morrison, Kevin
Long War, The

Ondaatje, Michael
Babel (with The Man with Seven Toes)
Collective Works of Billy the Kid, The
Man with Seven Toes, The (with Babel)
Trip, The

Oneal, James
Drivel

O'Neal, John
Hurricane Season, The
Wrong Way to Paradise

Ono, Yoko
Trials of Oz, The

Oppenheimer, Joel
Bad Times in Bummersville

Oproiu, Ecaterina
I Am Not the Eiffel Tower

Ordway, Sally
Free! Free! Free!
Lay of the Land, The (with We Agree; Cross-Country; and Australia Play)
Movie, Movie on the Wall
Tabula-Rasa
Up! (revue)
Uptaught

Orefice, Frank
Hello

O'Reilly, Art
Stone Cycle

O'Reilly, Father John
Virgin (a rock opera)

O'Reilly, Jeannine
Breadbasket
Breadbasket and Jade
Discover America
Holey Trinity
I Got on Point Late in Life
Jade
Little Match Girl Makes It Big, The ("revusical")
Placebo
Red Pumps, The
Strains
Timberlines
Tribute to Mother
Vespers

O'Reilly, Michael
Dinner at the Ambassador's

Orland, Yaacov
Man Behind the Legend, The

Ornstein, Larry
What a Day for a Miracle!

Ornstein, Leslie E.
Best We Can, The

Orton, Joe
Crimes of Passion (The Ruffian on the Stairs and The Erpingham Camp)
Funeral Games
Loot
What the Butler Saw

Osborne, John
Patriot for Me, A

Osgood, Lawrence
Rook, The

O'Shaughnessy, Michael
Battle for Heaven

Oshen, Gabriel
Theatre Romantique (mime dramas)

Osnato, Anthony
Samson and Delilah

Ost, Robert
Beast—A Nightmare Comedy

Ostergaard, W. Lynn
Equinox

Ouzounian, Richard
Enter the Queen

Ovid
Olympian Games

Owen, Mack
Bang! Bang! You're Dead!

Owens, Dan
Acceptance
Box (with Joined)
Joined
What Reason Could I Give

Owens, Houston
Who Said Freddy Was Dead?

Owens, Lyla Hay
Go-Carts Coming Down the Road

Owens, Rochelle
Homo (with The Queen of Greece)
Karl Marx Play, The
Queen of Greece, The (with Homo)

Oyamo
Breakout, The
Crazy Niggers
His First Step

P

Packard, William
Funeral, The
Sandra and the Janitor
Second Shepherd's Play, The

Paget, Daniel
Hadleyburg

Pahl, Ellen
Tra-La-La, Ha-Ha!

Pailet, Leonard
Rise and Fall of the Usurous Shylock, The

Pally, Erwin
Fourth Generation, The

Palmer, Carleton
Holiday for Santa

Palmer, Don Phillip
Trial of James McNeil Whistler, The

Palmer, Harry
Time Changes (a dramatic multimedia rock trip)

Palmer, Winthrop
Beat the Wind

Palmisano, Fred
Robin Hood

Panas, Alexander
Assassin, The
At the Tavern of the Raven
Every Bridge Has a Splash
Garden of Forking Paths, The
Little Betty
Mr. Tambo, Mr. Bones
Plagueship — Nine Days Out of Barbados
Tavern of the Raven

Panetta, George
Mike, Downstairs

Paolucci, Anne
Short Season, The

Paradis, Marjorie
Alpha Kappa

Parchman, William
Mocking Bird, The
Party, The
Prize in the Cracker Jack Box, The

Parent, Gail
Lorelei

Paris, Ronnie
Love Gotta Come by Saturday Night
Yes, Yes, No, No

Parker, Betzie
Android Project, The
Animals, The
Doublers, The
Operation Thwack

Parker, Chris
Sun/The Gentle (The Penetrating Wind)

Parker, Don
Nuns, The

Parker, Guy
Return, The

Parker, Norman
What About Tomorrow?

Parker, Rod
And Who's Little Boy Are You?

Parkinson, John
Venture, The: A Squeeze Play

Parman, Frank
Naga Uta
New/Play: (City) Closet Drama (with Naga Uta)
Perimeters
Rage Over the Lost Beethoven (multi-media presentation)
Renegade in Retrospect

Parowinchak, Gerald W.
Out of the Grass and Into the Morning Glorious

Parrilla, Arturo
Missing Link, The

Parriott, Michael
Field, The

Parson, Mary Jean
Ahead to the Stars
Kaleidoscope: A Celebration from Minstrels to Mods

Pascal, Fran
George M!

Pascal, John
George M!

Patchen, Kenneth
With This Rose I Thee Wake

Patinkin, Sheldon
Candide

Patrick, John
Barrel Full of Pennies, A
Dancing Mice, The
Enigma
Love Is a Time of Day
Lovely Ladies, Kind Gentlemen
Macbeth Did It
Roman Conquest
Scandal Point

Smith, Chester Leo
Only a King (Part I): A Tragedy Suggested by the Death of James Forrestal
Only a King (Part II— Rashamon Revisited): The Incredible Relationship of Haakon Chevalier and J. Robert Oppenheimer

Smith, Earl Hobson
Stephen Foster

Smith, Garrett
Outcasts, The

Smith, Geddeth
Ligeia

Smith, Glenn Allen
Home Away From, A
Sister

Smith, J. Vincent
Quarter for Sad Sackbut and Swallows

Smith, Jack
Boiled Lobster Easter Pageant
Claptailism of Palmola Christmas Spectacle
Fishook of Orchid Lagoon Water Pageant
Gas Stations of the Cross Religious Spectacle
Hamlet and the 1001 Psychological Jingoleanisms of Prehistoric Landlordism of Rima-Puu
Religious Spectacle of Atlantis
Spiritual Oasis of Lucky Landlord Paradise Slideshow
Ten Million B.C. Economic Spectacle of Jungola (10 Million B.C. Economic Spectacle of Jungola)

Smith, Joseph
Charlatans

Smith, Lillian
Memory of a Large Christmas (reading)

Smith, Michael
Captain Jack's Revenge
Country Music
Double Solitaire
Major Daley, Justice and the American Way
Next Thing, The
Old Rat's Heart, The
Peas

Smith, Milburn
Baboon!!!
Bloodsport
Ten O'Clock Scholar

Smith, Miles
Papers, The

Smith, Patti
Cowboy Mouth, The (with Back Bog Beast Bait)

Smith, Robert Kimmel
Little Singing, a Little Dancing, A

Smith, Walt
Ari

Smith, W.H.S.
Drunkard, The (musical)

Smithies, Maura Cavanagh
Vanity Fair

Smithies, Richard
Crazy Now
Where It's At!

Smolden, W. L.
Visitatio Sepulchri, Peregrinus, Planctus Mariae

Snider, Florine
Married Couples Group, The

Snyder, Burton
Death of a Playwright
Penalty for Being Slow, The

Snyder, Elayne
Little Piece of Earth, A

Snyder, John
Famous River Bottom Strategy of Etoe County, The (with The Transcontinental Redemption . . .)
Transcontinental Redemption of Buster C. Dunn, The (with The Famous River Bottom Strategy . . .)

Solley, Marvin
Hark!

Solly, Bill
One Hundred Miles from Nowhere (100 Miles from Nowhere)

Solms, Kenny
Lorelei

Solomon, Holly
Boxing Match
Footnotes to Macbeth

Solomon, Samuel
Britannicus

Solorzano, Carlos
Cruce De Vias (The Railroad Crossing)
Hands of God, The

Solzhenitsyn, Aleksander
Play by Aleksander Solzhenitsyn, A

Somerfeld, Nancy
Ginger and the Painted Turtle

Somerfeld, Robert
Blues for Billy
Don't Tell Lily (with Funn)
Funn (with Don't Tell Lily)
Note, The
Potty, The
Projection Room (with Respite and There Once Was a Hermit Named Dave)
Respite (with Projection Room and There Once Was a Hermit Named Dave)
Silent Men, The
Straphangers, The
There Once Was a Hermit Named Dave (with Respite and Projection Room)

Sondheim, Stephen
Candide (new version)
Company
Follies
Little Night Music, A

Sophocles
Oedipus
Oedipus the King
Oedipus Tyrannos
Searching Satyrs, The (Ichneutae)

Soupault, Phillipe
If You Please

Southerington, Frank
Creditors

Soyinka, Wole
Kongi's Harvest
Lion and the Jewel, The
Madman and Specialists

Spedaliere, Dennis
My Mama's Lemonade (with The Outhouse)
Outhouse, The (with My Mama's Lemonade)

Speirs, Ruth
In the Matter of J. Robert Oppenheimer

Spencer, Colin
Spitting Image

Spensley, Philip
Nitty Gritty of Mr. Charlie, The (The Just Society)

Sperling, Milton
W.C.

Spierling, Frank
Erotic Tale of a Tall Girl, The
Exhibition
Sound of a Woman, The

Spigelgass, Leonard
Look to the Lilies
Wrong Way Light Bulb, The

Spilliaert, Arthur
Tramp

Spindel, Jerry
Respects

Spinetti, Victor
In His Own Write

Spitzer, E. E.
Interview, The

Sprinchorn, Evert
Crimes and Crimes
Dream Play, A

Spurling, John
Macrune's Guevara

St. Clair, Wesley
Case Book, The
Station, The

St. Edmund, Bury
Warp I: My Battlefield, My Body

St. John, Kathleen
Ophelia

St. John, Wesley
Losers, The

Staab, Jane
And I Bet You Wish You Was Me Now
Briar, Briar
Missing Note, The
O Happy Day (musical)

Stambler, Peter
Feast of the Chameleon, The

Stanley, Charles
Caligula
Great American Pinball Machine, The

Stanton, Frank
Look Where I'm At

Starkie, Martin
Canterbury Tales

Starkweather, David
Family Joke, The
Poet's Papers, The
Practical Ritual to Exorcise Frustration After Five Days of Rain, A
Straights of Messina, The

Starr, Ben
Button, The

Staten, Pat
Disturbance of Mirrors, A
Iphegenia Again

Staw, Sala
Blunderer, The

Steel, Rchard A.
Howie's

Steen, Jan
Get Thee to Canterbury

Stein, D.
Kentucky!

Stein, Gertrude
Dr. Faustus Lights the Lights
Gertrude Stein's First Reader
Lucy Church Amiably
Making of Americans, The (opera)
Mrs. Reynolds
Three, Two, One (Not Much Limping, Monuments, May & December)

Stein, Joseph
Zorba

Stein, Paul
O. F. Visigoths

Steinkellner, Frank
Garbage Collectors

Stern, Alan
Sultan of Tuffet, The (with The Whistling Wizard)
Whistling Wizard, The (with The Sultan of Tuffet)

Stern, Daniel
Lord Jim

Stern, Lewis Michael
Lydia's Rape

Stern, Rudi
Video-Rock Environment: Aquarian Festival

Sternberg, Ann
Gertrude Stein's First Reader

Sternfield, Allen
Holmes and Moriarty

Sternheim, Carl
Snob, The (with The Strong Sex)
Strongbox, The (with The Snob)

Stevens, Monty
Jane Eyre

Stevenson, Florence
Chronicle
Chronicle of Nine

Stevenson, James
Jazz Circle

Steward, Ron
Sambo

Stewart, Arlie
Trec

Stewart, Charles
Flo's Boathouse

Stewart, Delano
Black Evolution
Re-Run (with Welcome Home, Joe)
Welcome Home, Joe (with Re-Run)

Stewart, Malcolm
Return of Peggy Atherton, The

Stewart, Michael
Charade
George M!
Seesaw

Stewart, Robert
Flying Sunflower, The

Stiles, George
General Bullett (reading)

Stimac, Anthony
Contrast, The (musical version)
Fashion (musical)

Stitt, Milan
Runner Stumbles, The

Stockton, Richard F.
One World at a Time
Royal Rape of Ruari Macasmunde, The

Stoddard, Haila
Round with Ring, A

Stoddard, Michael
Atsuhara

Stoker, Bram
Dracula
Horrors

Stoltenberg, John Vincent
Babies
Baby Mine (with Billy, Bobby, and Bunny)
Billy, Bobby, and Bunny (with Baby Mine)
How the Wind Comes
Single Double Kingsize

Stone, Joel
Babel-Babble
Horrors of Dr. Moreau, The

Stone, Martin
Soft Core Pornographer, The

Stone, Peter
Full Circle
Seventeen Seventy-Six (1776)
Sugar
Two by Two

Stoppard, Tom
After Margritte
Albert's Bridge
Enter a Free Man
Real Inspector Hound, The

Storey, David
Changing Room, The
Contractor, The
Home
Restoration of Arnold Middleton, The

Storey, James Garfield
Requiem for a Junkie

Straight, Michael
Caravaggio

U

V

W

Wagstaff, Fred
Alchemist, The
Through a Glass Brightly

Walcott, Derek
Dream on Monkey Mountain, The
In a Fine Castle
Malcochon
Ti-Jean and His Brothers

Walden, Stanley
Kid, The

Waldman, Robert
Here's Where I Belong

Waldron, Robert
No Silver Saints

Waley, Arthur
Kagekiyo

Walker, Dolores
Ox-Roast
Recess
Up! (revue)

Walker, Donald
Inn People, The (musical based on Carlo Goldoni's La Locandiera)

Walker, Dorothy A. Dinroe
Yin Yang (poetry, dance, music)

Walker, Evan
Coda

Walker, Joseph A.
Believers, The
Harangues, The
Ododo
River Niger, The
Yin Yang (poetry, dance, music)

Walker, Rae
Miss Zatakri and Mister Jones

Wall, George
It's 10 P.M., Do You Know Where Your Children Are?

Wall, Geraldine
Relentless Smile, The

Wallace, Basil
Sounds of a Silent Man

Wallace, Walter J.
Snow White

Wallach, D. Brian
Memphis Store Bought Teeth

Wallach, Eli
Bits and Pieces

Waller, G. Hobson
With Music by the Bird. . .

Wallowitch, John
Big Charlotte

Walman, Jerome
Washington Square

Walser, Martin
Homefront

Walter, Eugene
Easiest Way, The (reading)

Walter, Nancy
Still Falling

Walter, Sydney Schubert
Mass for Actors and Audience. . .

Wanshel, Jeff
Auto-Destruct
Disintegration of James Cherry, The
General Brutus, The
Rhesus Umbrella, The

Ward, David
Here Be Dragons (with A Knack with Horses)
Knack with Horses, A (with Here Be Dragons)

Ward, Donald
One Hundred Miles from Nowhere (100 Miles from Nowhere)

Ward, Douglas Turner
Brotherhood
Reckoning, The

Ward, Milton
Do You Know the Muffin Man
Kali Mother

Warhol, Andy
Pork

Waring, James
Three, Two, One (Not Much Limping, Monuments, May & December)

Warner, Hank
Who Can Tell?

Warren, Alaina
One Wish to Broadway (musical)

Warren, Robert Penn
Brother to Dragons

Warwick, Noel
Patient, The

Washington, Joseph
Street Life

Waters, Richard D.
Black Messiah, The
Charley and the Man with the Upside Down Eyes
Color Me Human
Cross Has Two Sides, A
Damnation of Socrates Jones, The
Israel Berkowitz Superstar
New Shoes for Uncle Tom
Son of Man, The
Trial of William Tell, The
Tyrant Apostle, The

Watkins, Gordon
Lion Roams the Streets, A
Man in the Middle

Watts, Charles
O. F. Visigoths

Waugh, Steve
Brother You're Next

Weaver, Neal
Cure, The
War Games

Webb, Leonard
Stag Party

Webber, Andrew Lloyd
Jesus Christ Superstar (Concert version presented at the Madison Ave., Baptist Church, N.Y.C., in spring of 1971)

Weber, Mary Feldhaus
World Tipped Over and Laying on Its Side, The

Webster, Margaret
No Coward Soul

Webster, Tony
God Almighty

Wedel, Douglas
Private Private

Weeden, Bill
Hurry, Harry

Weeks, Seth
If Adventure's Your Dish

Weidman, Jerome
Mother Lover, The

Weil, Simone
Apocalypsis Cum Figuris

Weill, Gus
Geese

Weill, Kurt
Berlin to Broadway with Kurt Weill
Flight of Lindbergh, The (with A Lesson in Consent)
Happy End
Little Mahagonny, The
Mahagonny
Whores, Wars and Tin Pan Alley

Weinberg, Lawrence
And I Met a Man

Weine, Max G.
Appetites
Mixed Doubles
Tales of Women

Weiner, Albert
Solness (The Master Builder)

Weiner, Leslie
Are You Now or Have You Ever Been Blue?
Evening with the Poet-Senator, An

Weingarten, Aaron
Will the Real Danny Boy Please Stand Up?

Weingarten, Robert
Taming of the Beast

Weingarten, Romain
Eté (Summer)
Happy Days of Summer
Summer Days

Weinstein, Arnold
American Revolution, The: Part I
Greatshot

Weinstein, Ira
Pie Are Squared

Weiss, George David
Comedy
Maggie Flynn
Smile, Smile, Smile (revision of Comedy)

Weiss, Jeff
And That's How the Rent Gets Paid, Part II
F.O.B.
International Wrestling Match, The
Locomotive Munch
Pushover

Weiss, Mitchell
What's Expected?

Weiss, Peter
How Mr. Mockinpott Was Cured of His Sufferings
Song of the Lusitanian Bogey

Weiss, Theodore
Gunsight and Other Poems

Weissman, Richard
Outlaw Brothers

Weld, Stephen
Wisping the Wind

Welden, John
Let's You and Him Fight

Weller, Art
Red Raspberry Revue, The

Weller, Michael
Bodybuilders
Moonchildren
Now There's Just the Three of Us
Twenty-Three Years Later

Welles, Halstead
Gods Strike Back, The

Wells, H. G.
Horrors of Dr. Moreau, The

Welty, Eudora
Wanderers, The

Wenstrom, D.
Big Klaus and Little Klaus

Werth, Paul
There Are Men Too Gentle to Live Among Wolves

Wesker, Arnold
Four Seasons, The
Friends, The

Wesley, Richard
Black Terror, The
Gettin' It Together
Knock Knock Who Dat?
Past Is the Past, The
Street Corner
Strike Heaven on the Face

Wesner, David
Dancing Days

West, Anthony
Warm Bodies

Wexler, Norman
Huff and the Puff, The (with Whatever Happened to Hugging and Kissing)
Red's My Color, What's Yours?
Whatever Happened to Hugging and Kissing? (with The Huff and the Puff)

Wheeler, Billy Edd
Hatfields and McCoys

Wheeler, Hugh
Candide (new version)
Irene
Little Night Music, A

Wheeler, Jerome
Prometheus Bound

Whimby, Ellsworth
Age of the Stringless Bean, The
Big Maude Saves the Day
Great Balls

Whitaker, Mical
Dark Symphony

Whitcomb, Joyce
Waves, The

White, Diz
Grande de Coco-Cola, El

White, Edgar
Burghers of Calais, The
Crucificado
Figures at Chartres, The
Gente, La
Life and Times of J. Walter Smintheus, The
Ode to Charley Parker
Transformations, A Church Ritual
Wonderfull Yeare, The

White, Fred
Anniversary Ball

White, Garry
Welcome to Serenity Farms

White, James P.
Asylum

White, Jane D.
King Midas and the Golden Touch

White, John
Bananas
Dog School, The
Lady Laura Pritchett, American
Metamorphosis
Mirage
Twist

White, Joseph
Leader, The
Old Judge Mose is Dead

White, Nat
Reverend Ferdinand and Bessie Mae
To Catch a Crooked Crown

White, Stephen
Brothers

White, Theodore H.
Caesar at the Rubicon

Whitehead, E. A.
Alpha Beta
Foursome, The

Whitehead, Paxton
There's One in Every Marriage

Whiting, John
Conditions of Agreement

Whitlock, Bache McEvers
Triumph of Robert Emmet, The

Whitney, Arthur
Divorce of Judy and Jane, The

Whitson, Steve
Thief, The

Whittaker, K. P.
Temptation of Father Joe, The

Whyte, Ron
Horatio
Variety Obit (with Welcome to Andromeda)
Welcome to Andromeda (with Variety Obit)

Wicke, Hal
Masada (multi-action collage)

Widoff, Joyce E.
Didn't We Go to Different Schools Together?

Wiener, Sally Dixon
Blue Magi, The
Marjorie Daw
Telemachus Friend

Wienman, Paul
Look To Your Rats

Wigfall, James
In the Mourning Time (black song & statement)

Wilbur, Richard
Candide (new version)
School for Wives, The

Wilcox, Ronald
Tragedy of Thomas Andros, The

X

Y

Z

Premieres of American Plays Abroad

Dec. 9, 1948, *A Giant's Strength,* by Upton Sinclair. Torch Theatre, London, England. Directed by Richard Lake; produced by Forty-eight Theatre.

Mar. 22, 1949, *The Rising Wind,* by Lee Gilbert. Library Theatre, Manchester, England. Directed by Peter Cotes; produced by Peter Cotes Prod., Ltd., with the Arts Council.

Aug. 22, 1949, *The Cocktail Party,* by T. S. Eliot. Lyceum Theatre, Edinburgh, Scotland. Directed by E. Martin Browne; produced by Sherek Players, Ltd.

Sept. 21, 1949, *The Golden Door,* by Sylvia Regan. Embassy, Swiss Cottage, London, England. Directed by Robert Mitchell.

Mar. 30, 1950, *The Platinum Set,* by Reginald Denham and Mary Orr. Saville Theatre, London, England. Directed by Roy Rich; produced by Stanley French and Dan O'Neil.

May 15, 1950, *Sorry, Wrong Number,* by Lucille Fletcher. Water Gate, London, England. Directed by Robert Henderson.

June 19, 1950, *The Blessed and the Damned* (an Orson Welles program); comprised of *The Unthinking Lobster,* a fable by Orson Welles, music by Tony Aubin; and *Time Runs,* a tragedy by Orson Welles, music by Duke Ellington. Theatre Edouard VII, Paris, France. Directed by Orson Welles; produced by Pleiades Company.

Oct. 30, 1951, *Third Person,* by Andrew Rosenthal. Arts, London, England. Directed by Roy Rich; produced by Alec Clunes.

Dec. 10, 1951, *The Importance of Wearing Clothes,* by Lawrence Langner. New Boltons, London, England. Directed by Peter Cotes.

Feb. 21, 1952, *Red Letter Day,* by Andrew Rosenthal. Garrick, London, England. Directed by Murray Macdonald; produced by Jack de Leon with Mark Marvin.

Apr. 23, 1952, *Under the Sycamore Tree,* by Sam Spewack. Aldwych, London, England. Directed by Peter Glenville; produced by Tennent Prods., Ltd.

Sept. 23, 1952, *The Hanging Judge,* by Raymond Massey, based on a novel by Bruce Hamilton. New, London, England. Directed by Michael Powell; produced by Bronson Albery, Michael Powell and Walter P. Chrysler, Jr.

Dec. 3, 1952, *Sweet Peril,* by Mary Orr and Reginald Denham. St. James's, London, England. Direcled by Norman Marshall; produced by Daniel Mayer.

Mar. 6, 1953, *Sud (Southland),* by Julien Green. Théâtre de l'Athénée, Paris, France. Directed by Jean Mercure.

Aug. 28, 1953, *The Confidential Clerk,* by T. S. Eliot. Lyceum, Edinburgh, Scotland. Directed by E. Martin Browne; produced by Henry Sherek.

Feb. 23, 1954, *Gigi,* a comedy by Colette, adapted for the theatre by Colette and Anita Loos. Théâtre des Arts, Paris, France. Directed by Jean Meyer; produced by Alexandra Roubé-Jansky.

Mar. 1, 1954, *L'Ennemi,* by Julien Green. Théâtre des Bouffes Parisiens, Paris, France. Directed by Fernand Ledoux; produced by Jacques Truchot.

Apr. 3, 1954, *Wedding in Paris,* a musical comedy by Vera Caspary, music by Hans May. Hippodrome, London, England. Directed by Charles Hickman; produced by George and Alfred Black.

July 27, 1954, *The Wooden Dish,* by Edmund Morris. Phoenix, London, England. Directed by Joseph Losey; produced by E. P. Clift.

Aug. 23, 1954, *The Matchmaker,* by Thornton Wilder. Lyceum, Edinburgh, Scotland. Directed by Tyrone Guthrie; produced by Tennent Prods., Ltd.

June 16, 1955, *Moby Dick,* adapted by Orson Welles from Herman Melville's novel. Duke of York's Theatre, London, England. Directed by Orson Welles; produced by Oscar Lewenstein and Wolf Mankowitz with Martin Gabel and Henry Margolis.

July 11, 1955, *The One and Only,* by Andrew Rosenthal. Royal, Windsor, England. Directed by John Counsell; produced by Windsor Repertory Company.

Aug. 9, 1955, *Requiem for a Nun,* by William Faulkner. Schauspielhaus, Zurich, Switzerland. Directed by Leopold Lindtberg; produced by Dr. Oskur Walterlin.

Aug. 22, 1955, *A Life in the Sun,* by Thornton Wilder. Assembly Hall, Edinburgh, Scotland. Directed by Tyrone Guthrie; produced by The Edinburgh Festival Society with Tennent Prods., Ltd.

Feb. 10, 1956, *Long Day's Journey into Night,* by Eugene O'Neill. Royal Dramatic Theatre, Stockholm, Sweden. Directed by Bengt Ekerots; produced by Dr. Karl Gierow.

Apr. 30, 1956, *The Clockwork House,* by Rosemary Casey. Leatherhead Theatre, Leatherhead, England. Directed by Jordan Lawrence; produced by Leatherhead Repertory Company.

Sept. 20, 1956, *L'Ombre,* by Julien Green. Théâtre Antoine, Paris, France. Directed by Jean Meyer; produced by Simone Berriau.

Jan. 29, 1957, *The Crystal Heart,* by William Archibald, music by Baldwin Bergerson. Lyceum, Edinburgh, Scotland. Directed by

Bill Butler; produced by Toby Rowland, Ltd. (by special arrangement with Lyn Austin, Thomas Noyes, and Roger L. Stevens, in association with Charles Pratt, Jr.).

Feb. 11, 1957, *Olive Ogilvie,* by Henry Denker. Lyceum, Edinburgh, Scotland. Directed by Henry Denker.

Feb. 16, 1957, *Moord Op De Onschuldigen (A Slaughter of Innocents),* by William Saroyan. Koninklijke Schouwberg, The Hague, Netherlands. Directed by Albert van Dalsum; produced by Haagshe Comedie Company.

Mar. 29, 1957, *A Touch of the Poet,* by Eugene O'Neill. Royal Dramatic Theatre, Stockholm, Sweden.

Sept. 19, 1957, *All Kinds of Men,* by Alex Samuels. Arts, London, England. Directed by Robert Mitchell; produced by London Arts Theatre Committee, Ltd.

Sept. 20, 1957, *Bernice,* a one-act play by Thornton Wilder; *The Wreck on the 5:25,* a one-act play by Thornton Wilder. Congress Hall, Berlin, Germany. Produced by ANTA.

July 31, 1958, *Brouhaha,* by George Tabori. Theatre Royal, Brighton, England. Directed by Peter Hall; produced by International Playwrights' Theatre and Robert L. Joseph and Lester Osterman.

Aug. 25, 1958, *The Elder Statesman,* by T. S. Eliot. Lyceum, Edinburgh, Scotland. Directed by E. Martin Browne; produced by Henry Sherek.

Sept. 18, 1958, *Hughie,* a one-act play by Eugene O'Neill. Royal Dramatic Theatre, Stockholm, Sweden. Directed by Bengt Ekerots.

Oct. 7, 1958, *Shadow of Heroes,* by Robert Ardrey. Piccadilly, London, England. Directed by Peter Hall; produced by Ruby Rowland, Ltd.

Apr. 13, 1959, *The Hidden River,* by Ruth and Augustus Goetz, based on a novel by Storm Jameson. Cambridge Theatre, London, England. Directed by John Dexter (original director, Dennis Arundel); produced by Pelham and Arthur Prods., Ltd.

July 2, 1959, *The Tiny Closet,* a one-act play by William Inge; *The Night of the Iguana,* a one-act play by Tennessee Williams; *Too Close for Comfort,* a one-act play by Jack Dunphy. Teatro Caio Melisso, Spoleto, Italy. Directed by Frank Corsaro; produced by Festival of Two Worlds.

Sept. 15, 1959, *The Ginger Man,* by J. P. Donleavy. Fortune, London, England. Directed by Philip Wiseman; produced by Spur Prods., Ltd. (P. Wiseman and T. Walton).

Sept. 28, 1959, *Die Zoo-Geschicte (The Zoo Story),* by Edward Albee, adapted by Pinkas Braun. Werkstatt des Schiller-Theater, Berlin, Germany. Directed by Walter Henn.

Nov. 16, 1959, *Bachelor Flat,* by Budd Grossman. Richmond, Richmond, England. Directed by Jack Williams; produced by David Pelham Prods., Ltd. with Richmond Theatre Prods., Ltd.

Apr. 6, 1960, *Sam, The Highest Jumper of Them All,* by William Saroyan. Theatre Royal, Stratford, London, England. Directed by William Saroyan; produced by Theatre Workshop Company.

Apr. 21, 1960, *Der Tod Der Bessie Smith (The Death of Bessie Smith),* by Edward Albee. Schlosspark, Berlin, Germany. Directed by Walter Henn.

June 30, 1960, *Innocent as Hell,* by Andrew Rosenthal. Lyric, Hammersmith, London, England. Directed by Vida Hope; produced by Thane Parker.

Oct. 1, 1960, *Camelot,* by Alan Jay Lerner (based on *The Once and Future King,* by T. H. White), music by Frederick Loewe. O'Keefe Center for the Performing Arts, Toronto, Canada. Directed by Moss Hart; produced by Lerner, Loewe & Hart.

Dec. 6, 1960, *Fairy Tales of New York,* by J. P. Donleavy. Pembroke, Croydon, London, England. Directed by Philip Wiseman; produced by Pembroke Theatre, Ltd. and Spur Prods., Ltd.

Dec. 11, 1960, *The Typists, The Postman,* and *A Simple Kind of Love Story,* three one-act plays by Murray Schisgal. British Drama League, London, England.

June 1, 1961, *Mrs. Schonnenschein (Mrs. Sunshine),* by Eugene Lovett. Tribune Theater, Berlin, Germany. Directed by Illo von Janko.

Sept. 4, 1961, *Kwamina,* by Robert Alan Aurthur, music and lyrics by Richard Adler. O'Keefe Center for the Performing Arts, Toronto, Canada. Directed by Robert Lewis; produced by Alfred de Liagre, Jr.

Oct. 19, 1961, *Ducks and Lovers,* by Murray Schisgal. Arts Theatre Club, London, England. Directed by Philip Saville; produced by Michael Codron, Ltd. & David Hall, Ltd.

Nov. 22, 1961, *Echo from Afar,* by Jack Pullman. Twentse Schouwburg, Enschede, Netherlands. Directed by Theo Kling; produced by Toneelgroep Centrum (Amsterdam Company).

Dec. 17, 1961, *Das Lange Weihnachtsmahl (The Long Christmas Dinner),* an opera, libretto by Thornton Wilder, music by Paul Hindemith. National, Mannheim, Germany. Directed by Hans Schüler; conducted by Paul Hindemith.

Jan. 10, 1962, *Ebbe (Ebb),* by Fenn Guernsey, German translation by Erwin Barth. Hessisches Staatstheater, Kleines Haus, Wiesbaden, Germany. Directed by Detlof Krüger.

Mar. 1, 1962, *Die Alkestiade (The Alcestiad),* an opera, libretto by Thornton Wilder, music by Louise Talma. Stadische Buhnen, Frankfort-am-Main, Germany. Directed by Harry Buckwitz; conducted by Wolfgang Bennert.

July 2, 1962, *Foxy,* a musical, book by Ring Lardner, Jr., and Ian Hunter, lyrics by Johnny Mercer, music by Robert Emmett Dolan. Palace Grand, Dawson City, Yukon Territory, Canada. Directed by Robert Lewis; produced by Stanley Gilkey and Robert Whitehead.

July 10, 1962, *The Milk Train Doesn't Stop Here Anymore,* by Tennessee Williams. Teatro Nuovo, Spoleto, Italy. Directed by Herbert Machiz; produced by Festival of Two Worlds.

Nov. 9, 1962, *Bygg Dig Allt Hogre Boningar (More Stately Mansions),* by Eugene O'Neill, Swedish adaptation by Karl Gierow and Sven Barthel. Royal Dramatic Theatre, Stockholm, Sweden. Directed by Stig Torsslow.

Nov. 16, 1962, *Die Iden Des Marz (The Ides of March),* by Jerome Kilty, adapted from Thornton Wilder's novel, translated into German by Ludwig Berger. Renaissance, Berlin, Germany. Directed by Jerome Kilty.

Mar. 27, 1963, *Parlor Magic,* by John Howard Lawson. Mecklenburgisches Staatstheater, Schwerin, East Germany. Directed by Erhard Kunkel.

Apr. 18, 1963, *Luv,* by Murray Schisgal. Arts, London, England.

July 3, 1963, *Just Wild About Harry,* by Henry Miller. Teatro Caio Melisso, Spoleto, Italy. Directed by Herbert Machiz; produced by Festival of Two Worlds.

Nov. 14, 1963, *Pocahontas,* a musical, with book, music and lyrics by Kermit Goell. Lyric, London, England. Directed by Michael Manuel; produced by Stephen Mitchell with Michael Manuel.

Dec. 29, 1963, *Heute ist Unabhangigkeitstag (Independence Day),* by William Hanley. Werkstatt des Schiller-Theater, Berlin, Germany. Directed by Gert Omar Leutner.

June 2, 1964, *The Easter Man,* by Evan Hunter. Birmingham Repertory Theatre, Birmingham, England. Directed by John Harrison; produced by Jack Minster, H.M. Tennent Ltd. and John Gale (retitled *A Race of Hairy Men* in New York).

Sept. 29, 1964, *Games,* by Fred Sadoff. New Arts Theatre Club, London, England. Directed and produced by Fred Sadoff.

Oct. 5, 1964, *A Singular Man,* by J. P. Donleavy. Cambridge Arts Theatre, Cambridge, England. Directed by Philip Wiseman; produced by Spur Productions Ltd. and Richard Rhys.

Feb. 16, 1965, *Forests of the Night,* by Arnold Sundgaard. Gate Theatre, Dublin, Ireland. Directed by Louis Lentin; produced by Mitch Miller and M. O'Malley O'Donohue Productions.

Mar. 1965, *Mysteries,* by Julian Beck and Judith Malina. 140 Theatre, Brussels, Belgium. Directed by Julian Beck and Judith Malina; produced by Living Theatre of New York.

Oct. 1965, *Frankenstein,* by Judith Malina and Julian Beck. XXIV Festival Internazionale Biennale, Venice, Italy. Directed by Julian Beck and Judith Malina; produced by Living Theatre of New York.

Apr. 5, 1966, *The Prime of Miss Jean Brodie,*

by Jay Presson Allen. Princess Theatre, Torquay, England. Directed by Peter Woods; produced by Donald Albery (for Calabash Productions) by arrangement with Whitehead-Stevens Productions, Inc.

May 26, 1966, *The Bellow Plays* (*Out from Under/Orange Souffle/The Wen*) by Saul Bellow. Jeannetta Cochrane Theatre, Holborn, London, England. Directed by Charles Marowitz; produced by the London Traverse Theatre Company.

Sept. 27, 1966, *The Others,* by Richard Lortz. Leatherhead Theatre Club, Leatherhead, England. Directed by Robert Cartland; produced by Brian Jackson.

Dec. 10, 1966, *Eris,* by Lee Falk. Theatre La Bruyère, Paris, France. Directed by Georges Vitaly; produced by Ludmila Vlasto.

Dec. 20, 1966, *Warte bis Jeff Kommt (Wait Until Jeff Comes*), by Robert Storey. Schauspielhaus Hansa, West Berlin, Germany. Directed by Paul Esser; produced by Schauspielhaus Hansa.

Apr. 13, 1967, *World War 2 1/2,* by Roger O. Hirson, New Theatre, London, England. Directed by Peter Coe; produced by Geoffrey Russell.

July 3, 1967, *Minor Murder,* by Reginald Denham and Mary Orr. Royal Theatre, Brighton, England. Directed by Reginald Denham; produced by John Gale Productions and Eagle Productions.

Mar. 13, 1968, *Staring at the Sun,* by Alfred Aiken. Vaudeville Theatre, London, England. Directed and produced by Peter Cotes.

July 4, 1968, *Indians,* by Arthur Kopit. Aldwych Theatre, London, England. Directed by Jack Gelber; produced by the Royal Shakespeare Company.

July 8, 1968, *Janie Jackson,* by Robert P. Hillier. Manchester Opera House, Manchester, England. Directed and produced by Peter Cotes (for Cotes Logan Productions).

Sept. 16, 1968, *Out of the Question,* by Ira Wallach. Manchester Opera House, Manchester, England. Directed by Nigel Patrick; produced by John Roberts and Doris Cole Abrahams, in association with Commonwealth United Entertainment.

Fall, 1968, *Fucknam,* by Tuli Kupferberg. Lilla Teatern, Lund, Sweden. Presented by the Lilla Teatern Theatre Workshop.

May 13, 1969, *And These Is Not All...!,* by James Paul Dey. Mercury Theatre, London, England. Directed by Jean-Pierre Voos; produced by International Theatre Club Ensemble.

Aug. 19, 1969, *Kein Problem (No Problem)* by Norman Krasna translated by Karl Wittlinger, originally titled *Blue Hour*. Komoedie am Kurfuerstendamm Theater, West Berlin, Germany. Directed by Wolfgang Spier; produced by Hans and Juergen Woelffer.

Sept. 2, 1969, *The Spoils of Poynton,* adapted by Robert Manson Myers, with additions by Basil Ashmore. May Fair Theatre, London, England. Directed by Basil Ashmore; presented by Vincent Shaw Associates and Jimmy Wollheim.

Oct. 21, 1969, *A Man and His Wife,* by Guy Bolton. Alexandra Theatre, Birmingham, England. Directed by Geoffrey Edwards; produced by the Alexandra Repertory Company.

Oct. 29, 1969, *My Little Boy... My Big Girl,* by Naomi and David Robison. Fortune Theatre, London, England. Directed by Eric Porter; produced by James Varner and Lou Levy for Loner Productions and in association with R. J. Kahn.

Jan. 2, 1970, *Gone with the Wind,* book by Kazuo Kikuta, music and lyrics by Harold Rome. Imperial Theatre, Tokyo. Directed by Joe Layton; produced by Kazuo Kikuta & Toho Co., Ltd., in association with Joe Layton.

Spring, 1970, *Isabel's a Jezebel,* book and lyrics by William Dumaresq, music by Galt MacDermot. Mercury Theatre, London, England. Directed by Diane Despins; produced by the Gate Theatre Co., Ltd.

June 1, 1970, *The Heretics,* by Morris West. Ashcroft Theatre, Croydon, London, England. Directed by Morris West and Joseph O'Conor; presented by Douglas Pollard.

Sept. 14, 1970, *Cancer,* by Michael Weller. Royal Court Theatre, London, England. Directed by Roger Hendricks Simon; produced by Royal Court in association with Martin Rosen and Nepenthe Productions (retitled *Moonchildren* in New York).

Feb. 16, 1971, *Flash Gordon and the Angels,* by David Zane Mairowitz. Open Space Theatre, London, England. Directed by Walter Donohue; produced by Open Space Theatre.

Aug. 2, 1971, *Pork,* by Andy Warhol. Round House, London, England. Directed by Anthony J. Ingrassia; produced by Ira D. Gale in association with Lynsey and Haydn Productions, Ltd.

Aug. 31, 1971, *Jump!,* by Larry Gelbart. Queen's Theatre, London, England. Directed by Charles Marowitz; produced by James Verner (for Bloomsbury Plays Ltd.) in association with Open Space Theatre.

Sept. 14, 1971, *Ambassador,* book by Don Ettlinger, lyrics by Hal Hackady, music by Don Gohman. Palace Theatre, Manchester, England. Directed by Stone Widney; produced by Genesius Productions and Julie C. Daugherty Productions, Ltd.

Apr. 1972, *High Time,* by Alan Rossett. Hampstead Theatre Club, Hampstead, London.

May 3, 1972, *Gone with the Wind,* book by Horton Foote, lyrics and music by Harold Rome. Drury Lane Theatre, London, England. Directed by Joe Layton; produced by Harold Fielding.

May 31, 1972, *Nobody Loves Wednesday,* by Allan Weiss. Arts Theatre Club, London, England. Directed by Malcolm Taylor; produced by Howard Kent.

July 1972, *The Tooth of Crime,* by Sam Shepard. Open Space Theatre, London, England. Directed by Charles Marowitz.

July 13, 1972, *Rock Carmen,* adapted by Buck Spurr and Herb Hendler. Roundhouse Theatre, London, England. Directed by Irving Davies; produced by Buck Spurr and Herb Hendler, in association with the London Rock Carmen Co. and Videocassette Enterprises.

Sept. 26, 1972, *Bunny,* by Norman Krasna. Belgrade Theatre, Coventry, England. Directed by Alexander Dore; produced by Paul Elliott and Duncan C. Weldon.

Nov. 6, 1972, *I and Albert,* book by Jay Allen, music by Charles Strouse, lyrics by Lee Adams. Piccadilly Theatre, London, England. Directed by John Schlesinger; produced by Lewis M. Allen and Si Litvinoff, in association with Theatre Projects and Richard Lukins.

Dec. 1972, *The Old Man's Comforts,* by Perry Pontac. Open Space Theatre, London, England. Directed by Charles Marowitz.

Jan. 29, 1973, *Small Craft Warnings,* by Tennessee Williams. Hampstead Theatre Club, London, England. Directed by Vivian Matalon; produced by Eddie Kulukundis and Eric Kilner.

Mar. 1973, *Geography of a Horse Dreamer,* by Sam Shepard. Theatre Upstairs, Royal Court Theatre, London, England. Produced by the English Stage Company.

Oct. 8, 1973, *Harold and Maude,* by Colin Higgins; French adaptation by Jean-Claude Carrière. Théâtre Récamier, Paris, France. Directed by Jean-Louis Barrault.

Oct. 11, 1973, *Section Nine,* by Philip Magdalany. The Place Theatre, London, England. Directed by Charles Marowitz; produced by the Royal Shakespeare Company.

Nov. 20, 1973, *Gomes,* by David Swift and Sidney Sheldon. Queen's Theatre, London, England. Directed by Peter Coe; produced by Bernard Delfont and Richard M. Mills.

Apr. 8, 1974, *Children,* by A. J. Gurney, Jr., Mermaid Theatre, London, England. Directed by Alan Strachan; produced by Mermaid Theatre Trust.

Theatre Group Biographies

The Acting Company, A National Repertory Theater, (formerly the City Center Acting Company), 130 W. 56th St., New York, NY 10019, tel. (212) 489-8548.
Artistic Director: John Houseman; *Producing Director:* Margot Harley; *Executive Director:* Porter Van Zandt; *Associate Artistic Director:* Jack O'Brien; *Founders:* John Houseman, Margot Harley.

In the winter of 1971-72, members of the first graduating class of the Drama Division of the Juilliard School began a series of public appearances in a repertory of plays staged by such outstanding American directors as Gerald Freedman, Michael Kahn, John Houseman, Boris Tumarin, and Eugene Lesser. Public acceptance and critical acclaim led to a crucial decision—to hold together this ensemble of young, highly trained actors in a permanent, independent theatrical group.

On July 3, 1972, The Acting Company opened its first professional season at the Saratoga Performing Arts Festival in the distinguished company of the NY City Ballet and the Philadelphia Orchestra. The five plays performed that summer formed the basis for the City Center Acting Company's first New York season, presented in September 1972 at the Good Shepherd Church in Lincoln Center.

Since July 1972, members of The Acting Company have been employed at full Equity salaries. And they have had the opportunity which few young American actors of their generation are able to enjoy—that of mastering their profession while performing the great literature of the theatre in productions directed and designed by artistically acclaimed professionals.

As the country's only permanent touring repertory company, The Acting Company has performed nineteen plays in ninety-two cities in thirty states at universities and art centers across the nation, as well as filled engagements in such cities as Boston, Philadelphia, Denver, New York, St. Louis, Washington, D.C., San Francisco, and Los Angeles.

Between 1972 and 1975, the repertory included *The School for Scandal, The Three Sisters, Love's Labour's Lost, The Beggar's Opera, Time of Your Life, She Stoops to Conquer, Measure for Measure, Edward II, Women, Beware Women!, The Hostage, The Lower Depths, Next Time I'll Sing to You,* and *Arms and the Man.*

In the course of its national tours, the company also offers classical and contemporary plays especially adapted for young audiences, as well as master classes, seminars, workshops, and demonstrations—all carefully designed and developed in collaboration with the faculties of the institutions visited. Thus, the members of The Acting Company perform an invaluable national, educational, and artistic function, carrying as they do a unique repertory of classical and contemporary plays and passing on the exceptional resources of their special training.

Actors' Equity Association, 1500 Broadway, New York, NY 10036, tel. (212) 869-8530. Branch offices: John Van Eyck, 360 North Michigan Ave., Room 1401, Chicago IL 60601, tel. (312) 641-0393; Edward Weston, 6430 Sunset Blvd., Hollywood, CA 90028, tel. (213) 462-2334; Harry Polland, c/o Brundage, Neyhart, Grodin and Beeson, 100 Bush St., San Francisco, CA 94104, tel. (415) YU 6-4060.
President: Theodore Bikel; *1st Vice-President:* Carl Harms; *2nd Vice-President:* Nancy Lynch; *3rd Vice-President:* Jeanna Belkin; *4th Vice-President:* Iggie Wolfington; *Recording Secretary:* Barbara Colton; *Treasurer:* Randy Phillips; *Midwest Regional Vice-President:* George Womack; *Western Regional Vice-President:* Bern Hoffman; *Presidents Emeritus:* Ralph Bellamy, Frederick O'Neal. *Executive Secretary:* Donald Grody; *Assistant Executive Secretaries:* Willard Swire, Vincent Donahue, Edward Weston, John Van Eyck; *Administrative Aide to the Executive Secretary:* Dan Hogan; *Executive Assistant to the Executive Secretary:* Judith Weston; *Director, Governmental Relations:* Jack Golodner, 815 16th St., N.W., Washington, D.C. 20006; *Counsel:* Cohn, Glickstein, Lurie, Ostrin & Lubell; *Chorus Executive Secretaries Emeritus:* Dorothy Bryant, Ruth Richmond; *Chorus Counsel Emeritus:* Rebecca Brownstein.

Actors' Equity Association is the labor union that negotiates minimum conditions and enforces members' contracts for all professional performers in the legitimate theatre in the US. Founded May 26, 1913, by 112 actors meeting in New York City following months of preparatory work in 1912 and 1913 on a constitution and bylaws, Equity's unique contribution to the labor movement was the principle of arbitration of disputes.

The founding of Equity rose out of recognition of the need for a bargaining agency to represent the performer. Since the mid-1880s, actors had been increasingly exploited by managers who set policies against which few actors could prevail. There was no minimum wage; there was no pay for unlimited rehearsal time, which could be of indefinite duration; road companies were frequently stranded in remote areas because of managers who defaulted; actors could be dismissed without notice; actors had to supply their own costumes; casts were often laid off without salary or prior notice when a bad week at the box office necessitated temporary closing.

Six years after its establishment, Equity went on strike in order to secure acceptance as the actors' bargaining agent by the Producing Managers' Association. The strike lasted for a month, involved eight cities, closed thirty-seven plays and prevented sixteen others from opening, and the cost to all parties was some $3 million. The International Alliance of Theatrical and Stage Employees and the American Federation of Musicians supported Equity, whose membership increased from 2,700 to about 14,000 during the course of the strike, and whose treasury grew during the same period from $13,500 to $120,000, although the strike cost over $5,000 a day.

Settlement was reached when the managers signed a five-year contract agreeing to practically all of Equity's demands. Five years later, in 1924, a contract was signed that established the Equity shop and bonding agreements requiring that managers put up funds to guarantee salaries and transportation for actors. Later important gains were: in 1928, protection against the importation of alien actors; in 1929, protection from exorbitant commissions by franchising theatrical representatives; in 1933, the minimum wage; in 1935, the first payment of rehearsal expense money—$15 weekly; in 1960, establishment of a welfare fund and pension plan; in 1964, equalization of rehearsal pay and minimum salary (effective 1967) and acceptance of the "Principal Interview" clause to be included in nearly all Equity contracts, stating that on specific days producers will see any Equity member without appointment.

In addition to the legitimate stage, Equity has organized the industrial shows field and resident, children's, and dinner theatres; established rules governing relationships between talent agents and actors; organized the agency's jurisdiction in Canada (Canadian Equity became a separate organization in 1976); and constantly worked for better working conditions, particularly backstage safety and sanitary standards.

Equity has been a leader in civil rights since 1947 when it barred members from appearing at the National Theatre, Washington, D.C., because of discrimination, and in 1961 Equity and the League of NY Theatres agreed that no Equity member should be required to perform in any place where discrimination against actors or audience because of race, religion, or color is practiced.

In addition to its main concern with negotiation of minimum conditions and enforcement of member contracts, Equity has supported Equity Library Theatre, and had representatives in Washington urging Congressional passage of laws favoring the arts and the theatrical professional. It publishes a monthly newspaper, *Equity*, for all members, which is edited by Helaine Feldman, and issues notices of chorus auditions.

The organization is governed by an elected and non-salaried 65-member council and 10 officers. Since its founding, the organization has had nine presidents: Francis Wilson (1913-20); John Emerson (1920-28); Frank Gilmore (1928-37); Arthur Byron (1938-40); Bert Lytell (1940-46); Clarence Derwent (1946-52); Ralph Bellamy (1952-64); Frederick O'Neal (1964-73); and Theodore Bikel (1973-to date).

The Council appoints the Executive Secretary, who is responsible for executing Equity policy and administering the Equity contract. Among the more than thirty committees are the Advisory Committee on Chorus Affairs, the Stock Committee, the Dinner Theatre Committee, the Off-Broadway Committee, and the Pay TV Committee.

Performers become members of Actors' Equity by joining after the signing of an Equity contract with a manager or under reciprocal agreement with either or both the Screen Actors Guild (SAG) and the American Federation of Television and Radio Artists (AFTRA). Actors' Equity Association is a branch of the Associated Actors and Artistes of America, the organization from which performer unions receive their jurisdictional charters. Equity is a AFL-CIO affiliate, belongs to the Federation Internationale des Acteurs, and is a member of AFL-CIO Central Trades and Labor Council in New York City and of New York State, Illinois, California, Chicago, San Francisco, and Los Angeles labor federations.

The Actors Studio, Inc., 432 W. 44th St., New York, NY 10036, tel. (212) PL 7-0870. *Corporate Board:* Lee Strasberg, Cheryl Crawford, Carl Schaeffer, Arthur Penn, Shelley Winters, Eli Wallach, Burgess Meredith, Liska March, Lee Grant, Mark Rydell, Milton Sperling.

The Actors Studio is a theatre workshop for professional actors that was founded in 1947 by Elia Kazan, Cheryl Crawford, and Robert Lewis, who sought to establish a place where actors could work together during long runs or between engagements in order to continue their development. The present membership, which is for life, is approximately 400. Performers are invited to membership as a result of auditions. More than 1,000 auditions are held annually, from which five or six performers are invited to join.

In 1955, the Actors Studio purchased its present building, where the Actors Unit holds regular classes twice a week, under the direction of Lee Strasberg. Observing privileges are granted to visiting theatre professionals from all over the world. The studio established a Playwrights Unit in 1956, a Directors Unit in 1960, and a Production Unit in 1962.

The Actors Studio's first Broadway production was a revival of Eugene O'Neill's *Strange Interlude* (Hudson Th., Mar. 11, 1963), with a cast that included Betty Field, Jane Fonda, Ben Gazzara, Pat Hingle, Geoffrey Horne, Geraldine Page, William Prince, and Franchot Tone. Subsequent productions included June Havoc's *Marathon '33* (ANTA, Dec. 22, 1963); Arnold Weinstein's *Dynamite Tonight* (York Playhouse, Mar. 15, 1964); James Costigan's *Baby Want a Kiss* (Little, Apr. 19, 1964); James Baldwin's *Blues for Mister Charlie* (ANTA, Apr. 23, 1964); and a revival of Anton Chekhov's *The Three Sisters* (Morosco, June 22, 1964).

The Actor's Workshop, San Francisco, CA

Following their graduation from New York University, Jules Irving and Herbert Blau acted professionally in New York and elsewhere. It was while working for their degrees at Stanford University that they began thinking of establishing the organization which became the Actor's Workshop.

With Irving as managing director and Blau as consulting director, the group was officially launched in 1952, with a one-performance production of Philip Barry's *Hotel Universe,* financed from personal savings and presented to an invited audience of 50. By 1960, the Actor's Workshop had presented 40 plays, including the American premiere of Bertolt Brecht's *Mother Courage* and West Coast premieres of several other important works. In 1958, the company played a six-week engagement in New York in Samuel Beckett's *Waiting for Godot,* later appearing in the same work at the Brussels World's Fair.

In 1959, the Actor's Workshop received a Ford Foundation grant to produce an original play by Sidney Michaels entitled *The Plaster Bambino,* the cast of which included Viveca Lindfors and Burgess Meredith. In 1960, the Ford Foundation offered the workshop a challenge grant of $156,000 to augment its company and add to its program. The following year an apprentice program was set which functioned within the professional repertory company.

In 1965 Irving and Blau resigned to become directors of the Theatre Company of Lincoln Center and were succeeded by Kenneth Kitch, managing director, and John Hancock, artistic director. The final performance of the Actor's Workshop took place Aug. 6, 1966.

Actor's Workshop productions, presented in two centrally located San Francisco theatres, the Marines' Theatre and the Encore, have included Philip Barry's *Hotel Universe* (Feb. 28, 1952); John Van Druten's *I Am a Camera* (May 16, 1952); Henrik Ibsen's *Hedda Gabbler* (Oct. 10, 1952); Federico Garcia Lorca's *Blood Wedding* (Dec. 4, 1952); John Millington Synge's *Playboy of the Western World* (Feb. 26, 1953); Tennessee Williams' *Summer and Smoke* (Apr. 3, 1953); Molière's *The Miser* (June 1, 1953); Aristophanes' *Lysistrata* (Oct. 23, 1953); Christopher Fry's *Venus Observed* (Dec. 25, 1953); Arthur Miller's *Death of a Salesman* (Feb. 26, 1954); Anton Chekhov's *The Cherry Orchard* (June 25, 1954); Noel Coward's *Tonight at 8:30* (Aug. 20, 1954); Sophocles' *Oedipus Rex* and *Pierre Patelin* (anon.) (Oct. 8, 1954); Arthur Miller's *The Crucible* (Dec. 3, 1954); Tennessee Williams' *Camino Real* (July 10, 1955); Alfred Hayes' *The Girl on the Via Flaminia* (Aug. 19, 1955); and the world premiere of David Mark's *Captive at Large* (Aug. 25, 1955).

Also, Oscar Wilde's *The Importance of Being Earnest* (Oct. 14, 1955); John Millington Synge's *Deirdre of the Sorrows* (Nov. 25, 1955); the American premiere of Bertolt Brecht's *Mother Courage* (Jan. 13, 1956); August Strindberg's *Miss Julie* and *The Stronger* (Sept. 4, 1956); Sean O'Casey's *Plough and the Stars* (Oct. 12, 1956); Clifford Odets' *The Flowering Peach* (Dec. 7, 1956); Samuel Beckett's *Waiting for Godot* (Feb. 28, 1957); William Wycherly's *The Country Wife* (Mar. 22, 1957); Robert Hivnor's *The Ticklish Acrobat* (June 22, 1957); Graham Greene's *The Potting Shed* (Sept. 27, 1957); Jean Giraudoux' *Tiger at the Gates* (Dec. 13, 1957); the world premiere of Herbert Blau's *A Gift of Fury* (Mar. 14, 1958); Eugene O'Neill's *The Iceman Cometh* (July 11, 1958); the world premiere of George Hitchcock's *Prometheus Found* (Aug. 21, 1958); Jean Anouilh's *Waltz of the Toreadors* (Sept. 26, 1958); Tennessee Williams' *Garden District* (Nov. 28, 1958); John Osborne's *The Entertainer* (Feb. 6, 1959); Jean Cocteau's *The Infernal Machine* (Apr. 30, 1959); Samuel Beckett's *Endgame* (May 10, 1959); the American premiere of Yuko Mishima's *3 Japanese Noh Plays* (June, 4, 1959); Sean O'Casey's *Cock-a-Doodle Dandy* (June 19, 1959); the world premiere of George Hitchcock's *The Busy Martyr* (Sept. 10, 1959); the world premiere of Sidney Michaels' *The Plaster Bambino* (Sept. 16, 1959); John Osborne's *Epitaph for George Dillon* (Oct. 31, 1959); Eugene Ionesco's *Jack* and *The Chairs* (Dec. 18, 1959); George Bernard Shaw's *The Devil's Disciple* (Jan. 15, 1960); Friedrich Duerrenmatt's *The Marriage of Mr. Mississippi* (May 13, 1960); the American premiere of Harold Pinter's *The Birthday Party* (July 15, 1960); and the American premiere of John Whiting's *Saint's Day* (July 1, 1960).

Also, the world premiere of Miriam Stovall's *The Rocks Cried Out* (Nov. 10, 1960); Ben Jonson's *The Alchemist* (Nov. 23, 1960); Eugene O'Neill's *A Touch of the Poet* (Dec. 7, 1960); the world premiere of Hamilton Wright and Guy Andros' *Twinkling of an Eye* (Jan. 11, 1961); Samuel Beckett's *Krapp's Last Tape* and Edward Albee's *The Zoo Story* (Feb. 7, 1961); William Shakespeare's *King Lear* (Mar. 29, 1961); George Bernard Shaw's *Misalliance* (May 10, 1961); a revival of Samuel Beckett's *Waiting for Godot*; the American premiere of John Arden's *Serjeant Musgrave's Dance* (Oct. 13, 1961); Anton Chekhov's *The Three Sisters* (Nov. 17, 1961); Jean Anouilh's *Becket* (Dec. 23, 1961); the world premiere of Mark Harris' *Friedman & Son* (Jan. 6, 1962); August Strindberg's *Dance of Death* (Mar. 16, 1962); William Shakespeare's *Henry IV, Part 1* (Apr. 21, 1962); Samuel Beckett's *Happy Days* (Sept. 14, 1962); William Shakespeare's *Twelfth Night* (Oct. 5, 1962); Tennessee Williams' *The Glass Menagerie* (Nov. 9, 1962); Bertolt Brecht's *Galileo* (Dec. 14, 1962); Harold Pinter's *The Dumbwaiter* and the American premiere of Robert Symonds' *A Slight Ache* (Dec. 28, 1962); the world premiere of Herbert Blau's *Telegraph Hill* (Jan. 18, 1963); Ben Jonson's *Volpone* (Feb. 22, 1963); Jean Genet's *The Balcony* (Mar. 29, 1963); George Bernard Shaw's *Major Barbara* (May 3, 1963); the American premiere of Carl Sternheim's *The Underpants* (Apr. 12, 1963); Federico Garcia Lorca's *The House of Bernarda Alba* (Sept. 13, 1963); William Shakespeare's *The Taming of the Shrew* (Oct. 4, 1963); Harold Pinter's *The Caretaker* (Nov. 15, 1963); James Schevill's *The Master* and Maria Irene Fornes' *There! You Died* (Nov. 29, 1963); Bertolt Brecht's *The Caucasian Chalk Circle* (Dec. 13, 1963); Conrad Bromberg's *The Defense of Taipei* (Jan. 31, 1964); J. P. Donleavy's *The Ginger Man* (Feb. 21, 1964); Max Frisch's *The Firebugs* (Feb. 28, 1964); Tennessee Williams' *The Night of the Iguana* (Apr. 3, 1964); Enid Bagnold's *The Chalk Garden* (Apr. 24, 1964); and Aristophanes' *The Birds* (May 15, 1964).

Also, Ben Jonson's *Volpone* (Aug. 5, 1964); Millard Lampell's *The Wall* (Oct. 16, 1964); William Wycherly's *The Country Wife* (Nov. 27, 1964); Anton Chekhov's *Uncle Vanya* (Jan. 1, 1965); Graham Greene's *The Living Room* and Harold Pinter's *The Collection* (Feb. 11, 1965); Tennessee Williams' *The Milk Train Doesn't Stop Here Anymore* (July 23, 1965); Bertolt Brecht's *The History of the Lamentable Reign of Edward II* (Oct. 22, 1965); Saul Bellow's *The Last Analysis* (Nov. 26, 1965); Rick Cluchey's *The Cage* (Dec. 11, 1965); (Dec. 12, 1965); Molière's *Don Juan* (Dec. 31, 1965); August Strindberg's *The Father* (Feb. 4, 1966); William Shakespeare's *A Midsummer Night's Dream* (Mar. 11, 1966); and Bertolt Brecht's *A Man's a Man* (July 23, 1966).

Alley Theatre, 615 Texas Ave., Houston, TX 77002, tel. (713) 228-9341, 228-8421.
President: McClelland Wallace; *Vice-President:* J. W. Link; *Vice-President:* Mrs Dudley C. Sharp; *Secretary:* R. D. Richards: *Treasurer:* Richard B. Counts, *Producing Director:* Nina Vance; *Managing Director:* Iris Siff; *Business Manager:* Bill Halbert.

Activity toward the establishment of Alley Theatre began when Nina Vance mailed 214 postcards to individuals who would be interested in starting a new theatre in Houston. The first production was Harry Brown's *A Sound of Hunting* (Nov. 1947), which was presented in a small dance studio at the end of an alley at 3617 Main St., Houston, seating 87 people.

In 1949, Alley Theatre moved to a converted attic-fan factory at 709 Berry Ave. Initially, none of the participants received a salary, the first paid employee being a custodian. With the production of Jean Giraudoux's *The Enchanted* (Aug. 1951), Alley Theatre attained semi-professional status, and following a production of Arthur Miller's *Death of a Salesman* (Feb. 1954) the Alley received a charter from Actors' Equity Association and attained full professional status.

In 1958, Alley Theatre was invited to represent American theatre at the Brussels World's Fair.

Alley Theatre moved to its present location at 615 Texas Ave. in 1968. The first production in this new building was Bertolt Brecht's *Galileo* (Nov. 1968). A multi-million dollar structure situated in the center of downtown Houston's business, professional, and cultural complex, the building was funded partially by a $2.5 million grant from the Ford Foundation. Additional funds were derived from Houston Endowment Corporation and donations from private individuals and corporations in Houston. The building includes two stages: one large theatre with a thrust stage and an auditorium seating 798; and an arena theatre seating 296.

The Alley Academy, the theatre's first acting school, was established in 1951; classes were offered to students from pre-school age to adult. In 1964, the school was reorganized as Alley Theatre Merry-Go-Round School with a six-semester program covering all phases of theatre for students in the fourth through twelfth grades. In addition, two adult workshops are held throughout the year: one emphasizes beginning techniques, and the second concentrates on various acting styles. The theatre has a forty-week apprentice program, offering college graduates the opportunity to gain professional experience.

In December 1974, the theatre's producing director, Nina Vance, was awarded a special $200,000 "artistic director's discretionary fund" prize by the Andrew W. Mellon Foundation. It is to be used over a period of three or more years in ways Miss Vance thinks most beneficial, and is a one-time award given in recognition of Alley Theatre's importance as an American theatre.

Alley Theatre's productions include: Harry Brown's *A Sound of Hunting* (Nov. 18, 1947); Jeffrey Dell's *Payment Deferred* (Feb. 3, 1948); Lillian Hellman's *Another Part of the Forest* (Apr. 6, 1948); *Caroline* (May 9, 1948); Clifford Odets' *Clash by Night* (Oct. 5, 1948); Norman Krasna's *John Loves Mary* (Nov. 30, 1948); Lillian Hellman's *The Children's Hour* (Feb. 8, 1949); Rose Franken's *Another Language* (Apr. 5, 1949); Julian Thompson's *The Warrior's Husband* (May 17, 1949); Eugene O'Neill's *Desire Under the Elms* (July 12, 1949); Irwin Shaw's *The Gentle People* (Oct. 25, 1949); Jean-Paul Sartre's *No Exit* (Dec. 7, 1949); Ronald Alexander's *Season with Ginger* (Feb. 7, 1950); George Bernard Shaw's *Dark Lady of the Sonnets* and *Man of Destiny* (Mar. 21, 1950); Moss Hart's *Light Up the Sky* (Apr. 25, 1960); Maxwell Anderson's *Wingless Victory* (June 20, 1950); Tennessee Williams' *Summer and Smoke* (Aug. 8, 1950); Clifton Sage and Hal Lewis' *Joshua Beene and God* (Nov. 1, 1950); Walter O. Jensen and David Westheimer's *The Magic Fallacy* (Dec. 31, 1950); *The Sleeping Beauty* (Jan. 27, 1950); Stephen Vincent Benét's *On Time and Nightmares* (Feb. 13, 1951); Clifford Odets' *Golden Boy* (Fet. 13, 1951); Ronald Alexander's *Angelica* (June 5, 1951); John Patrick's *The Hasty Heart* (July 12, 1951); Maurice Valency's adaptation of Jean Giraudoux' *The Enchanted* (Aug. 23, 1951); Fay Kanin's *Goodbye, My Fancy* (Sept. 27, 1951); Robert Ardrey's *Thunder Rock* (Nov. 15, 1951); and Mel Dinelli's *The Man* (Dec. 31, 1951).

Also, August Strindberg's *Miss Julia* (sic) (Feb. 12, 1952); Howard Lindsay and Russel Crouse's *Life with Mother* (Apr. 24, 1952); *Cinderella* (Mar. 8, 1952); *Rumpelstiltskin* (May 24, 1952); Arthur Laurents' *Home of the Brave* (June 26, 1952); Rudolf Beisier's *The Barretts of Wimpole Street* (July 21, 1952); *Aladdin* (Oct. 3, 1952); Thornton Wilder's *The Skin of Our Teeth* (Nov. 6, 1952); George Manker Watters and Arthur Hopkins' *Burlesque* (Dec. 25, 1952); Donald Bevan and Edmund Trzcinski's *Stalag 17;* Tennessee Williams' *The Rose Tattoo* (Feb. 5, 1953); William Glickman and Joseph Stein's *My Dear Delinquents* (Apr. 21, 1953); Maxwell Anderson's *Elizabeth the Queen* (June 23, 1953); John Van Druten's *I Am a Camera* (Aug. 6, 1953); Peter Blackmore's *Miranda* (Oct. 1, 1953); Ferenc Molnar's *The Play's the Thing;* Arthur Miller's *Death of a Salesman* (Feb. 23, 1954); Mary Chase's *Mrs. McThing* (Apr. 22, 1954); Joseph Kramm's *The Shrike* (May 27, 1954); Louis Verneuil's *Affairs of State* (July 1, 1954); Victor Clement and Francis Swann's *Open House* (Sept. 14, 1954); William Inge's *Picnic* (Oct. 19, 1954); Sam and Bella Spewack's *My 3 Angels* (Dec. 16, 1955); Arthur Miller's *All My Sons* (Dec. 25, 1955); Frederick Knott's *Dial 'M' for Murder* (Mar. 1, 1955); Christopher Fry's *The Lady's Not for Burning* (Apr. 15, 1955); Moss Hart's *Light Up the Sky* (May 17, 1955); Liam O'Brien's *The Remarkable Mr. Pennypacker* (July 12, 1955); N. Richard Nash's *The Rainmaker* (Sept. 13, 1955); Tennessee Williams' *The Glass Menagerie* (Oct. 25, 1955); Max Shulman and Robert Paul Smith's *The Tender Trap* (Dec. 25, 1956); Henrik Ibsen's *Hedda Gabler* (Feb. 25, 1956); Sylvia Regan's *The Fifth Season* (Mar. 20, 1956); Edith Sommer's *Roomful of Roses* (May 29, 1956); Sidney Kingsley's *Detective Story* (July 17, 1956); James Lee's *Career* (Aug. 28, 1956); Samuel Taylor's *Sabrina Fair* (Sept. 25, 1956); Guy Bolton's adaptation of Marcelle Maurette's *Anastasia* (Nov. 8, 1956); Jerome Chodorov and Joseph Fields' *Anniversary Waltz* (Dec. 25, 1956); Arthur Miller's *A View from the Bridge* (Feb. 13, 1957); Lillian Hellman's adaptation of Jean Anouilh's *The Lark* (Apr. 4, 1957); Theodore Reeves' *Wedding Breakfast* (May 23, 1957); Henry Denker and Ralph Berkey's *Time Limit!*

(June 27, 1957); Ronald Alexander's *Time Out for Ginger* (Aug. 8, 1957); Enid Bagnold's *The Chalk Garden* (Oct. 3, 1957); George Axelrod's *Will Success Spoil Rock Hunter?* (Nov. 7, 1957); and Thornton Wilder's *The Matchmaker* (Dec. 26, 1957).

Also, William Douglas Home's *The Reluctant Debutante* (Feb. 6, 1958); *Three Love Affairs* (one-act plays by Fry, O'Casey, and Coward) (Mar. 6, 1958); William Shakespeare's *Julius Caesar* (Apr. 17, 1958); Paddy Chayefsky's *Middle of the Night* (May 15, 1958); Leslie Stevens' *Champagne Complex* (June 19, 1958); Liam O'Brien's *The Remarkable Mr. Pennypacker* (July 24, 1958); Anita Loos' adaptation of Colette's *Gigi* (Sept. 4, 1958); Maurice Valency's adaptation of Jean Giraudoux' *The Madwoman of Chaillot* (Oct. 9, 1958); Agatha Christie's *Spider's Web* (Nov. 12, 1958); Collins Bell's *The Wonderful Cure* (Nov. 27, 1958); Joseph Fields and Peter DeVries' *Tunnel of Love* (Dec. 23, 1958); Arthur Miller's *The Crucible* (Feb. 5, 1959); Richard Bissell, Abe Burrows and Marian Bissell's *Say, Darling* (Mar. 25, 1959); Tennessee Williams' *Orpheus Descending* (May 7, 1959); Ronald Alexander's *Holiday for Lovers* (June 4, 1959); Eugene O'Neill's *The Iceman Cometh* (July 6, 1959); Harry Kurnitz's *Once More, with Feeling* (Aug. 6, 1959); Samuel Beckett's *Waiting for Godot* (Sept. 9, 1959); Norman Krasna's *Who Was That Lady I Saw You With?* (Oct. 6, 1959); Fay and Michael Kanin's *Rashomon* (Nov. 11, 1959); Lucienne Hill's adaptation of Jean Anouilh's *Waltz of the Toreadors* (Dec. 10, 1959); Herman Wouk's *The Caine Mutiny Court-Martial* (Jan. 13, 1960); William Saroyan's *The Cave Dwellers* (Feb. 17, 1960); Noel Coward's *Nude with Violin* (Mar. 16, 1960); Eugene O'Neill's *Moon for the Misbegotten* (Apr. 13, 1960); Dore Schary's *Sunrise at Campobello* (May 12, 1960); Norman Barasch and Carroll Moore's *Make a Million* (June 14, 1960); Joshua Logan and Thomas Heggen's *Mr. Roberts* (July 20, 1960); Frank Gagliano's *Library Raid* (Oct. 12, 1960); S. N. Behrman's *Jane*, based on a story by Somerset Maugham (Nov. 9, 1960); Maurice Valency's adaptation of Jean Giraudoux' *Ondine* (Dec. 14, 1960); Lillian Hellman's *The Little Foxes* (Jan. 17, 1961); Arthur Miller's adaptation of Henrik Ibsen's *An Enemy of the People* (Feb. 22, 1961); Samuel Taylor's *The Happy Time* (Mar. 16, 1961); Luigi Pirandello's *Six Characters in Search of an Author* (Apr. 19, 1961); *Friends and Lovers* (four one-act plays by Chekhov, O'Neill, and O'Casey) (May 10, 1961); Terrence Rattigan's *The Winslow Boy* (June 6, 1961); Tennessee Williams' *Period of Adjustment* (July 12, 1961); *John Brown's Body* (Aug. 15, 1961); George Bernard Shaw's *Misalliance* (Oct. 17, 1961); William Inge's *Come Back, Little Sheba* (Nov. 15, 1961); and Ben Jonson's *Volpone* (Dec. 12, 1961).

Also, Leonard Spigelgass' *A Majority of One* (Jan. 2, 1962); William Shakespeare's *Hamlet* (Mar. 7, 1962); *Volpone* (return engagement, Apr. 6, 1962); George Garrett's *Garden Spot*, U.S.A. (Apr. 25, 1962); *One Woman Show* (May 10, 1962); William Gibson's *The Miracle Worker* (May 16, 1962); S. N. Behrman's *Amphitryon 38*, adapted from Jean Giraudoux (June 27, 1962); Lillian Hellman's *Toys in the Attic* (July 19, 1962); Joseph Fields and Jerome Chodorov's *The Ponder Heart* (Aug. 16, 1962); Lucienne Hill's translation of Jean Anouilh's *Becket* (Oct. 24, 1962); Brendan Behan's *The Hostage* (Nov. 28, 1962); Howard Lindsay and Russel Crouse's *Life with Father* (Jan. 9, 1963); William Shakespeare's *The Taming of the Shrew* (Feb. 27, 1963); J. B. Priestley's *An Inspector Calls* (Apr. 24, 1963); Eugene O'Neill's *Long Day's Journey into Night* (May 22, 1963); Mary Chase's *Bernardine* (July 3, 1963); Ugo Betti's *The Queen and the Rebels* (Oct. 23, 1963); Miles Malleson's adaptation of Molière's *The Imaginary Invalid* (Dec. 4, 1963); Mary Chase's *Harvey* (Jan. 15, 1964); Anton Chekhov's *The Three Sisters* (Feb. 26, 1964); Gore Vidal's *The Best Man* (Apr. 8, 1964); Michael Redgrave's adaptation of Henry James' *The Aspern Papers* (May 20, 1964); Arthur Kopit's *Oh Dad, Poor Dad, Mamma's Hung You in the Closet and I'm Feelin' So Sad* (June 24, 1964).

In addition, Euripides' *The Trojan Women* (Nov. 25, 1964); Paddy Chayefsky's *The Tenth Man* (Jan. 6, 1965); Harry Brown's *A Sound of Hunting* (Feb. 17, 1965); Ann Jellico's *The Knack* (Mar. 31, 1965); Paul Zindel's *The Effect of Gamma Rays on Man-in-the-Moon Marigolds* (world premiere, May 12, 1965); George Bernard Shaw's *The Devil's Disciple* (Oct. 13, 1965); Eugene O'Neill's *Ah, Wilderness!* (Nov. 23, 1965); Luigi Pirandello's *Right You Are (If You Think You Are)* (Jan. 5, 1966); George S. Kaufman and Moss Hart's *You Can't Take It with You* (Feb. 16, 1966); Jean Giraudoux' *Duel of Angels* (Mar. 30, 1966); Arnold Perl's *The World of Sholom Aleichem* (Oct. 19, 1966); Alexander Ostrovsky's *Dairy of a Scoundrel* (Nov. 30, 1966); Friedrich Duerrenmatt's *The Physicists* (Jan. 11, 1967); Anton Chekhov's *The Seagull* (Feb. 22, 1967); Howard Lindsay and Russel Crouse's *The Great Sebastians* (May 5, 1967); Harold Pinter's *The Caretaker* (July 18, 1967); Edward Albee's *A Delicate Balance* (Oct. 5, 1967); and Molière's *The Miser* (Nov. 30, 1967).

Furthermore, George Bernard Shaw's *Candida* (Jan. 25, 1968); Bertolt Brecht's *Galileo* (Nov. 26, 1968); George Bernard Shaw's *Saint Joan* (Jan. 9, 1969); Keith Waterhouse and Willis Hall's *Billy Liar* (Feb. 13, 1969); Shaw's *Don Juan in Hell* (Feb. 28, 1969); Robert David MacDonald's adaptation of Erwin Piscator's *War* and *Peace*, based on Leo Tolstoi's novel (Apr. 3, 1969); Slawomir Mrozek's *Charlie* and *Out at Sea* (Apr. 17, 1969); Moss Hart's *Light Up the Sky* (May 8, 1969); Tad Mosel's *All the Way Home* (June 12, 1969); Tennessee Williams' *The Rose Tattoo* (Oct. 16, 1969); Edward Albee's *Everything in the Garden* (Nov. 27, 1969); and Molière's *Tartuffe* (Dec. 4, 1969).

Also, Saul Levitt's *The Andersonville Trial* (Jan. 22, 1970); Jerome Kilty's *Dear Liar* (Feb. 5, 1970); Brandon Thomas' *Charley's Aunt* (Mar. 12, 1970); Norman Corwin's *The World of Carl Sandburg*, adapted from Sandburg's writings (Apr. 16, 1970); Noel Coward's *Blithe Spirit* (Apr. 30, 1970); Jerome Kilty's *Dear Love* (Sept. 17, 1970); Eugene O'Neill's *Mourning Becomes Electra* (Oct. 22, 1970); Jane Trahey's *Ring Round the Bathtub* (world premiere, Dec. 3, 1970); Jerome Lawrence and Robert E. Lee's *The Night Thoreau Spent in Jail* (Jan. 14, 1971); Thornton Wilder's *Our Town* (Feb. 25, 1971); Jay Allen's *The Prime of Miss Jean Brodie* (Apr. 8, 1971); Frederick Knott's *Dial 'M' for Murder* (May 20, 1971); Slawomir Mrozek's *Tango* (May 21, 1971); Tennessee Williams' *Camino Real* (Oct. 21, 1971); John Dos Passos and Paul Shyre's *U.S.A.* (Nov. 15, 1971); Georges Feydeau's *A Flea in Her Ear* (Dec. 2, 1971); and Joe Orton's *What the Butler Saw* (Dec. 23, 1971);

Additionally, Charles Aidman's *Spoon River*, adapted from Edgar Lee Masters' poems (Jan. 20, 1972); David Westheimer's *My Sweet Charlie* (Jan 10, 1972); Peter Luke's *Hadrian VII* (Mar. 2, 1972); William Shakespeare's *The Taming of the Shrew* (Apr. 13, 1972); John Morasco's *Child's Play* (May 25, 1972); Michel de Ghelderode's *Pantagleize* (Oct. 19, 1972); Kurt Vonnegut, Jr.'s *Happy Birthday, Wanda June* (Nov. 24, 1972); Howard Lindsay and Russel Crouse's *Life with Father* (Nov. 30, 1972); Brendan Behan's *The Hostage* (Jan. 18, 1973); Edward Albee's *All Over* (Jan. 23, 1973); Elinor Jones' *Colette* (Mar. 1, 1973); Molière's *School for Wives* (Apr. 12, 1973); *Jacques Brel Is Alive and Well and Living in Paris* (May 24, 1973); Jerome Lawrence and Robert E. Lee's *Inherit the Wind* (Oct. 18, 1973); Eugene O'Neill's *Ah, Wilderness!* (Nov. 29, 1973); Tennessee Williams' *The Purification* (Nov. 23, 1973); Denise Le Brun's *Encore!* (Dec. 26, 1973); William Shakespeare's *A Midsummer Night's Dream* (Jan. 17, 1974); Friedrich Duerrenmatt's *Comedy of Marriage (Play Strindberg)* (Feb. 28, 1974); Ted Tiller's *Count Dracula* (Apr. 11, 1974); *The Decline and Fall of the Entire World as Seen through the Eyes of Cole Porter* (May 23, 1974); George Greanias' *Wilson* (Oct. 17, 1974); George S. Kaufman and Moss Hart's *The Man Who Came to Dinner* (Nov. 28, 1974); Charles Dickens' *A Christmas Carol* (Dec. 13, 1974); William Shakespeare's *Twelfth Night* (Jan. 16, 1975), Tennessee Williams' *A Streetcar Named Desire* (Feb. 27, 1975); Jack Kirkland's *Tobacco Road* (Apr. 10, 1975); and Shirley Mezvensky Lauro's *The Contest* (world premiere, May 22, 1975).

American Academy of Dramatic Arts, 120 Madison Ave., New York, NY 10016, tel. (212) MU 6-9244; 300 E. Green St., Pasadena, CA 91101, tel. (213) 795-7556.

Board of Directors: President: Louis Hager; *Vice-Presidents:* Leonel Kahn and Gordon A. Rust; *Secretary:* Warren Caro. *Members of the Board:* Worthington Miner and Frances Fuller, co-chairmen; Mrs. William C. Breed, Jr., Lillian Gish, Donald R. Seawell, Dr. Edward Mortola, Mrs. David Granger, Armina Marshall, Mrs. Arnold Schwartz. *Director of the American Academy:* Charles W. Raison.

The American Academy of Dramatic Arts stems from the first dramatic training school in the English-speaking theatre. On October 3, 1884, Franklin Haven Sargent founded the Lyceum Theatre School of Acting in New York City. The institution was later known as the New York School of Acting, and then by its present name. In 1899, the school received a charter from the Regents of the University of the State of New York, and a new charter was issued in 1952, citing the Academy as "a non-stock, non-profit educational institution."

In 1973, the American Academy was

authorized to award an Associate of Occupational Studies degree to those students who successfully complete the two-year program curriculum. In 1974, the American Academy opened a branch of the school in Pasadena, Calif. Graduates of this branch receive an Associate in Arts degree.

The American Academy of Dramatic Arts offers a course comprised of theatre history, fencing, make-up, acting styles, singing, voice and speech, movement, mime and acting in the first year. The second year, which is by invitation only, focuses primarily on rehearsal and performance. Evening and Saturday classes are offered also.

Among the alumni are Edward G. Robinson, Cecil B. DeMille, Garson Kanin, Kirk Douglas, Rosalind Russell, Hume Cronyn, Spencer Tracy, Jason Robards, Robert Redford, and Cleavon Little.

American Conservatory Theatre, 450 Geary St., San Francisco, CA 94102, tel. (415) 771-3880.

General Director: William Ball; *Executive Producer:* James B. McKenzie; *Executive Director and Resident Stage Director:* Edward Hastings; *Resident Stage Director and Conservatory Director:* Allen Fletcher; *Development Director:* Edith Markson; *Artists and Repertory Director:* Robert Bonaventura.

The American Conservatory Theatre (A.C.T.), San Francisco's resident professional theatre, was founded by William Ball in 1965 with financial support from the Rockefeller Foundation, Carnegie-Mellon University, Pittsburgh, Pa., and the Pittsburgh Playhouse. After playing its premiere season in Pittsburgh, the company moved in 1967 to San Francisco, where, in the next nine seasons it presented over a hundred productions to an audience of nearly 3 million at the Geary and Marines' Memorial theatres. The company also has played engagements in New York City, Chicago, Los Angeles, Phoenix, Denver, and Honolulu and has been seen on PBS television in *Under Milk Wood* (1966), *Misalliance* (1967), *Glory! Hallelujah!* and *Act Now* (both 1969), and *Cyrano de Bergerac* (1974).

The California Association for A.C.T. was established in 1966 to raise money at the time the company moved to San Francisco. Ford, Rockefeller, and Mellon Foundation matching grants have helped the company, as have sums from the National Endowment for the Arts. Local support has come from the San Francisco Foundation, the city of San Francisco, the California Arts Commission, and such corporations as the Crocker National Bank and Standard Oil of California. A Ford Foundation grant of $2 million helped A.C.T. purchase a long-term lease on the Geary Theatre, thereby assuring the company's continuity in San Francisco.

A.C.T. operates a full-time theatre training program, seeking to provide performers with a creative environment for continuing training, so that they may broaden and deepen their skills. The repertory of the theatre provides an opportunity for actors and actresses to practice the methods and techniques learned in A.C.T. training sessions, classes, workshops, and seminars. In addition to this program, which is for company members, A.C.T. offers instruction to selected young people from all over the country through its Advanced Training Program. There is also a ten-week Summer Training Congress for school and university students who come from institutions throughout the US to learn A.C.T. training techniques, and similar training is available through an evening extension program to interested residents of the local community. Finally, the Young Conservatory offers young people from eight to eighteen an opportunity to learn A.C.T. techniques. Scholarships and fellowships are provided by A.C.T. for talented students who need such financial aid. The success of an Asian-American scholarship program instituted in 1973 led to the establishment of the Asian-American Workshop, and A.C.T. hopes to involve other ethnic minorities in similar conservatory programs and as members of the performing company.

During its first season (1965-66), played in Pittsburgh, A.C.T. produced Molière's *Tartuffe,* Luigi Pirandello's *Six Characters in Search of an Author,* Edward Albee's *Tiny Alice,* Tennessee Williams' *The Rose Tattoo,* William Shakespeare's *King Lear,* Arthur Miller's *Death of a Salesman,* Jean Giraudoux' *The Apollo of Bellac,* Jean Anouilh's *Antigone,* André Obey's *Noah,* Carlo Goldoni's *The Servant of Two Masters,* George Bernard Shaw's *The Devil's Disciple,* Martin Duberman's *In White America,* Dylan Thomas's *Under Milk Wood,* and the revue *Beyond the Fringe.* The first San Francisco season (1967) repeated the Molière, Pirandello, Albee, Miller, and Thomas plays and *Beyond the Fringe* and added Samuel Beckett's *Endgame* and *Krapp's Last Tape,* Brandon Thomas' *Charley's Aunt,* George Bernard Shaw's *Man and Superman,* Joseph Kesselring's *Arsenic and Old Lace,* Thornton Wilder's *Our Town,* Jerome Kilty's *Dear Liar,* George Kelly's *The Torch-Bearers,* Eugene O'Neill's *Long Day's Journey into Night,* Anton Chekhov's *The Seagull,* and Edward Albee's *The Zoo Story.*

Subsequent San Francisco seasons included: (1967-68) William Gibson's *Two for the Seesaw,* Arthur Miller's *The Crucible,* Jean Anouilh's *Thieves' Carnival,* Donald Hall's *An Evening's Frost,* Tennessee Williams' *A Streetcar Named Desire,* Dylan Thomas's *Under Milk Wood,* Jerome Kilty's *Dear Liar,* Martin Duberman's *In White America,* Molière's *The Misanthrope* and *Tartuffe,* William Shakespeare's *Twelfth Night* and *Hamlet,* Edward Albee's *The American Dream, A Delicate Balance, The Zoo Story,* and *Tiny Alice,* Thornton Wilder's *Our Town,* Eugene O'Neill's *Long Day's Journey into Night,* Brandon Thomas's *Charley's Aunt,* Samuel Beckett's *Endgame,* Hall Hester, Danny Apolinar, and Donald Driver's *Your Own Thing,* and world premieres of Jerome Kilty's *Don't Shoot, Mable, It's Your Husband* and *Long Live Life,* Nagle Jackson's *Caught in the Act,* and Brian McKinney's *Deedle, Deedle Dumpling, My Son God;* (1968-69) Georges Feydeau's *A Flea in Her Ear,* George Bernard Shaw's *The Devil's Disciple,* Jules Feiffer's *Little Murders,* Charles Dyer's *Staircase,* Anton Chekhov's *Three Sisters,* Arbuzov's *The Promise,* Tom Stoppard's *Rosencrantz and Guildenstern Are Dead,* the American premiere of Arrabal's *The Architect and the Emperor of Assyria,* John Murray and Allen Boretz's *Room Service,* Anna Marie Barlow's *Glory! Hallelujah!,* Brendan Behan's *The Hostage,* Arthur Kopit's *Oh Dad, Poor Dad, Mamma's Hung You in the Closet and I'm Feeling so Sad,* Edward Albee's *A Delicate Balance,* Martin Duberman's *In White America,* and the musical *Hair;* (1969-70) Oscar Wilde's *The Importance of Being Earnest,* Sophocles' *Oedipus Rex,* George Bernard Shaw's *Saint Joan,* Athol Fugard's *The Blood Knot,* David Halliwell's *Little Malcolm and His Struggle Against the Eunuchs,* Peter Luke's *Hadrian VII,* Tennessee Williams' *The Rose Tattoo,* William Shakespeare's *The Tempest* and *Hamlet,* George M. Cohan's *The Tavern,* Tom Stoppard's *Rosencrantz and Guildenstern Are Dead,* Luigi Pirandello's *Six Characters in Search of an Author,* and Elaine May and Terrence McNally's *Adaptation/Next.*

Also, (1970-71) William Shakespeare's *The Merchant of Venice* and *The Tempest,* John Vanbrugh's *The Relapse,* Paddy Chayefsky's *The Latent Heterosexual,* William Saroyan's *The Time of Your Life,* Henrik Ibsen's *An Enemy of the People,* the world premiere of the musical *The Selling of the President,* Peter Luke's *Hadrian VII,* Paul Shyre's *Will Rogers' U.S.A.,* Gretchen Cryer and Nancy Ford's *The Last Sweet Days of Isaac,* the musical *Hair, Max Morath at the Turn of the Century,* Ron Thronson and Toni Shearer's *Mother Earth,* Mary Chase's *Harvey,* Molière's *School for Wives,* and Paul Zindel's *The Effect of Gamma Rays on Man-in-the-Moon Marigolds;* (1971-72) George Bernard Shaw's *Caesar and Cleopatra,* William Shakespeare's *Antony and Cleopatra,* Arthur Wing Pinero's *Dandy Dick,* Clifford Odets's *Paradise Lost,* Noel Coward's *Private Lives,* David Storey's *The Contractor,* Anthony Shaffer's *Sleuth,* Tom Stoppard's *Rosencrantz and Guildenstern Are Dead,* George M. Cohan's *The Tavern,* and Stephen Schwartz and John Michael Tebelak's *Godspell;* (1972-73) Edmond Rostand's *Cyrano de Bergerac,* John Guare's *The House of Blue Leaves,* Nagel Jackson's *Mystery Cycle,* Henrik Ibsen's *A Doll's House,* George S. Kaufman and Moss Hart's *You Can't Take It with You,* Jason Miller's *That Championship Season,* William Shakespeare's *The Merchant of Venice,* Arthur Miller's *The Crucible,* and Vinnette Carroll and Micki Grant's *Don't Bother Me, I Can't Cope.*

Also (1973-74) William Shakespeare's *The Taming of the Shrew,* Lanford Wilson's *The Hot l Baltimore,* Molière's *The Miser,* Federico Garcia Lorca's *The House of Bernarda Alba,* Noel Coward's *Tonight at 8:30,* Anton Chekhov's *The Cherry Orchard,* George Abbott and Philip Dunning's *Broadway,* Edmond Rostand's *Cyrano de Bergerac,* George S. Kaufman and Moss Hart's *You Can't Take It with You,* the review *Oh Coward!,* and Paul Shyre's *Will Rogers' U.S.A.;* (1974-75) William Shakespeare's *Richard III* and *The Taming of the Shrew,* Edmond Rostand's *Cyrano de Bergerac,* Allen Fletcher's translation of Henrik Ibsen's *The Pillars of the Community,* Ron Whyte and Mel Marvin's *Horatio,* Tom Stoppard's *Jumpers,* Elmer Rice's *Street Scene,* Peter Barnes's *The Ruling Class,* Marc Blitzstein's adaptation of Bertolt Brecht and Kurt Weill's *The Threepenny Opera,* James McDonald, David Vos, and Robert Gerlach's *Some-*

thing's Afoot, Oliver Hailey's *Father's Day,* Neil Simon's *The Sunshine Boys,* and the musical *Grease.*

American Mime Theatre, 192 Third Ave., New York, NY 10003, tel. (212) 777-1710.
Director: Paul J. Curtis.

The American Mime Theatre was founded by Paul J. Curtis in 1952. Mr. Curtis is also president of American Mime, Inc., incorporated as a nonprofit tax-exempt foundation in 1970 for the purpose of promoting American mime internationally. It has received funding from the NY State Council on the Arts, the Capezio Foundation, the Rockefeller Foundation, and private individuals.

Mr. Curtis calls the American Mime Theatre a "complete theatre medium with a body of aesthetic laws that govern every aspect of its activities from teaching syllabus to script material." Members of the company "are silent actors who play symbolic activities in characterization and express their characters honestly through a form of movement that is both telling and beautiful. They perform a repertory of American mime plays which are created for this medium by the company."

The American Mime Theatre has performed at theatres, universities, and other institutions throughout the US, including ANTA West Coast Drama Festival, Bard College, Cooper Union, Briarcliff (N.Y.) College, Brooklyn Academy of Music, Gallaudet College, Pratt Institute, the Baltimore Museum of Art, and Equity Library Theatre. The company also offers classes at its studio space and at outside institutions, such as Cornell University; the New School, where over 6,000 performers have received training; Jacob's Pillow, Lee, Mass.; and Sarah Lawrence College, Bronxville, N.Y.

American National Theatre and Academy, 245 W. 52nd St., New York, NY 10019, (212) PL 7-4133.
Chairman of the Board: Donald Seawell; *Secretary:* Alfred de Liagre, Jr.; *Treasurer:* Jean Dalrymple; *Board of Directors:* Walter Abel, Warren Caro, Jack Morrison, Roger L. Stevens, Robert Whitehead, Audrey Wood.

The American National Theatre and Academy (ANTA) was created on July 5, 1935, when President Franklin D. Roosevelt signed its charter. The charter had been secured by a group of citizens and came into being through an enactment by Congress. A section of the preamble of this charter stated, "A national theatre should bring to the people throughout the country their heritage of the great drama of the past and the best of the present, which has been too frequently unavailable to them under existing conditions."

Though created by national legislation, it was understood that there was to be no federal funding available to the organization. It was not until 1945 that the board of directors was reorganized to include people from the working theatre and from affiliated groups. A membership structure was set up and various activities began to take place under the auspices of the American National Theatre and Academy.

Among ANTA's activities have been: a nationwide theatre information and advisory service, an artist and speaker program, a photographic loan service, a job counseling service, a publications program, an annual theatre assembly. It serves as the United States Centre of the International Theatre Institute.

In its efforts to be a national organization and to work toward the decentralization of the American theatre, ANTA has set up regional chapters. In addition to the Greater New York Chapter, there are regional directors for the following areas: Atlanta, Ga.; Des Moines, Iowa; Boston, Mass.; Los Angeles, Calif.; San Francisco, Calif.; and University Park, Fla.

On March 31, 1950, ANTA acquired the former Guild Theatre on New York's 52nd Street, which is now known as the ANTA Playhouse, and where many of the ANTA sponsored productions have taken place.

Under ANTA sponsorship, foreign theatre companies and artists have appeared in the United States and American players have taken American plays abroad. Future plans envisage an ANTA television program and an ANTA Star Revival Theatre.

American Negro Theatre.

The American Negro Theatre was organized in 1940, and its first productions were presented in a theatre in the basement of the New York Public Library branch on West 135th St. A few years later the organization defined itself as "a permanent cooperative acting company coordinating and perfecting the related arts of the theatre; eventually deriving its own theatre craft and acting style by combining all standard form and putting to artful use the fluency and rhythm that lies in the Negro's special gifts."

Certainly the outstanding success of the American Negro Theatre was its production of Philip Yordan's *Anna Lucasta,* which opened at an uptown theatre, June 16, 1944. The following August, under the auspices of John Wildberg, the production opened on Broadway at the Mansfield Theatre (now the Brooks Atkinson), where it ran for 957 performances. The original company took the production to London in October 1947, where it was also well received.

The group was under the direction of Abram Hill, and such performers as Hilda Simms, Earle Hyman, Frederick O'Neal, Alvin Childress, and Alice Childress came to the fore in its productions.

In 1953, the group undertook a year's tour of Europe in a repertory program, opening in Southsea, England, Apr. 20, 1953, with *Anna Lucasta* and *Square Ring;* but there has been little subsequent activity from the American Negro Theatre.

American Negro Theatre productions include Theodore Browne's *Natural Man* (Library Th., 135th St., May 7, 1941); Curtis Cooksey's *Starlight* (Library Th., 135th St., June 3, 1942); Phoebe and Henry Ephron's *Three's a Family* (Library Th., 135th St., Nov. 18, 1943); Philip Yordan's *Anna Lucasta* (Library Th., 135th St., June 16, 1944); Abram Hill's *Walk Hard* (Library Th., 135th St., Nov. 30, 1944); Owen Dodson's *Garden of Time* (Library Th., 135th St., Mar. 7, 1945); a revival of Abram Hill's *Walk Hard* (Chanin Aud., Mar. 27, 1946); Dan Hammerman's *Henri Christophe* (Library Th., 135th St., June 6, 1945); Samuel M. Kootz' *Home Is the Hunter* (ANT Playhouse, Dec. 20, 1945); Abram Hill's *On Strivers' Row* (ANT Playhouse, Feb. 28, 1946); Kurt Unkelbach's *The Peacemaker* (ANT Playhouse, Nov. 25, 1946); Walter Caroll's *Tin Top Valley* (ANT Playhouse, Feb. 27, 1947); John Colton and Clemence Randolph's *Rain* (ANT Playhouse, Dec. 26, 1947); Nat Sherman's *The Washington Years* (ANT Playhouse, Mar. 11, 1948); Katharine Garrison Chapin's *Sojourner Truth* (ANT Playhouse, Apr. 23, 1948); Harry Wagstaff Gribble's *Almost Faithful* (ANT Playhouse, June 2, 1948); Nicholas Bela's *Skeletons* and Jonathan Tree's *The Fisherman* (Master Institute Th., Nov. 19, 1948); and Kenneth White's *Freight* and John Millington Synge's *Riders to the Sea* (Harlem Children's Center, Feb. 3, 1949).

The American Place Theatre, 111 W. 46th St., New York, NY 10036, tel. (212) 246-3730.
Board of Trustees: Chairman: Alan U. Schwartz; *Treasurer:* Russell Banks; *Director:* Wynn Handman; *Associate Director:* Julia Miles; *Director of Development:* Constance Kelly.

Wynn Handman and Sidney Lanier founded the American Place Theatre in 1964 for the purpose of finding, developing, and staging new American plays. It is not a repertory company, but hires actors to fit the requirements of each new play produced. Playwrights are aided in the creation of their work by critical and financial support. Exploration of new forms and styles is also encouraged. Often while the play is still being written, there are collaboration and consultation between the writer and the director, followed by a preliminary production and then a full-scale professional production with a five-week run for American Place subscribers. A distinctive aspect of American Place policy is that the audience is frequently invited to participate in discussions of the plays following performances.

Initially, the American Place was housed at St. Clement's Church in New York City. In 1971, it moved to what was then the first new legitimate theatre in the Broadway-Times Square area since 1928. The first commercial theatre built under a new theatre-district zoning code in New York City, American Place Theatre is located on the lower levels of the 43-story J. P. Stevens Building. The 299-seat auditorium with a thrust stage is designed for adaptability to the needs of various productions. In addition, there are rehearsal areas, a cabaret theatre, and spaces for workshops and experimental productions.

American Place is a nonprofit group. It has been aided by grants from the Ford and Rockefeller foundations, the National Endowment for the Arts, and New York State. Membership is limited to 16,000, but American Place works to broaden the theatre audience by distribution of specially priced tickets to faculty and student groups and senior citizens and to such special groups as Phoenix House and hospital organizations.

Numerous awards have been won by playwrights, performers, directors, and designers connected with American Place productions, and American Place Theatre received the Margo Jones Award in 1966 for bringing the works of "poets, novelists, and scholars to the living theater"; it has also received the New England Theatre Conference Special Award.

During its initial (1964-65) season, American Place Theatre produced Robert Lowell's *The Old Glory* (Nov. 1, 1964) and Ronald Ribman's *Harry, Noon and Night* (May 9, 1965). Subsequent productions (many of which moved on to regular Broadway or off-Broadway runs) include: William Alfred's *Hogan's Goat* (Nov. 11, 1965); Paul Goodman's *Jonah* (Feb. 15, 1966); Ronald Ribman's *The Journey of the Fifth Horse* (Apr. 21, 1966); a double-bill of two one-act plays, May Swenson's *The Floor* and Bruce Jay Friedman's *23 Pat O'Brien Movies* (May 11, 1966); Ronald Milner's *Who's Got His Own* (Oct. 12, 1966); Cecil Dawkins's *The Displaced Person* (Dec. 29, 1966); Sam Shepard's *La Turista* (Mar. 4, 1967); Niccolo Tucci's *Posterity for Sale* (May 11, 1967); Frank Gagliano's *Father Uxbridge Wants To Marry* (Oct. 28, 1967); Ronald Ribman's *The Ceremony of Innocence* (Jan. 1, 1968); Ed Bullins' *The Electronic Nigger and Others* (Mar. 6, 1968); Robert Lowell's *Endecott and the Red Cross* (May 7, 1968); George Tabori's *The Cannibals*, a program of three one-act plays consisting of David Trainer's *The Acquisition*, Phillip Hayes Dean's *This Bird of Dawning*, and Werner Liepolt's *The Young Master Dante* (Dec. 12, 1968); Ronald Tavel's *Boy on the Straight-Back Chair*, and Kenneth Cameron's *Papp* (Apr. 17, 1969).

Also, Anne Sexton's *Mercy Street* (Oct. 11, 1969); Charlie L. Russell's *Five on the Black Hand Side* (Dec. 10, 1969), a double-bill of the two one-act plays, Charles Dizenzo's *The Last Straw* and David Scott Milton's *Duet for Solo Voice* (Mar. 9, 1970); Ed Bullins' *The Pig Pen* (Apr. 29, 1970); Joyce Carol Oates's *Sunday Dinner* (Oct. 16, 1970); Steve Tesich's *The Carpenters* (Dec. 10, 1970); George Tabori's *Pinkville* (Feb. 22, 1971); Sam Shepard's *Back Bog Beast Bait* (Apr. 29, 1971); two one-act plays, Ronald Ribman's *Fingernails Blue as Flowers* and Steve Tesich's *Lake of the Woods* (Dec. 6, 1971); Jack Gelber's *Sleep* (Feb. 10, 1972); Charles Dizenzo's *Metamorphosis* (Apr. 8, 1972); Frank Chin's *The Chickencoop Chinaman* (May 27, 1972); Robert Coover's *The Kid* (Nov. 2, 1972); Phillip Hayes Dean's *Freeman* (Jan. 25, 1973); Rochelle Owens' *The Karl Marx Play* (Mar. 16, 1973); Steve Tesich's *Baba Goya* (May 9, 1973); and Ed Bullins' *House Party* (Oct. 16, 1973); David Scott Milton's *Bread* (Jan. 12, 1974); a program of four one-act plays consisting of William Hauptman's *Shearwater*, Lonnie Carter's *Cream Cheese*, Maria Irene Fornes's *Dr. Kheal*, Robert Coover's *Love Scene* (Mar. 6, 1974); and Frank Chin's *The Year of the Dragon* (May 22, 1974).

American Repertory Theatre.
Managing Directors: Cheryl Crawford, Eva Le Gallienne, Margaret Webster.

The formation of the American Repertory Theatre occurred in 1946. It was announced as an organization "whose reason for being is its faith in the public's desire to see in the living theatre the finest dramatic creations of the present and the past."

The "Plan for the American Repertory Theatre" further stated: "We need a theatre that would be for the drama what a library is for literature or a symphony orchestra for music . . ." It then went on to develop the plan for bringing such a theatre into being.

According to plan, the first production, William Shakespeare's *King Henry VIII*, opened at the International Theatre, N.Y.C., Nov. 6, 1946, followed by James M. Barrie's *What Every Woman Knows*, Nov. 8, and Henrik Ibsen's *John Gabriel Borkman*, Nov. 19. The casts included Eva Le Gallienne, Margaret Webster, Walter Hampden, Victor Jory, June Duprez, Richard Waring, Ernest Truex, and Philip Bourneuf. The three plays were performed in repertory, with others later added to the schedule.

American Repertory Theatre productions included William Shakespeare's *King Henry VIII* (Internatl., Nov. 6, 1946); James M. Barrie's *What Every Woman Knows* (Internatl., Nov. 8, 1946); Henrik Ibsen's *John Gabriel Borkman* (Internatl., Nov. 19, 1946); George Bernard Shaw's *Androcles and the Lion* and Sean O'Casey's *Pound on Demand* (Internatl., Dec. 19, 1946); Sidney Howard and Paul de Kruif's *Yellow Jack* (Internatl., Feb. 27, 1947); and Eva Le Gallienne and Florida Friebus' adaptation of *Alice in Wonderland* (Internatl., Apr. 5, 1947).

American Shakespeare Theatre, Stratford, CT 06497, tel. (203) 378-7321.
Chairman: Harold Shaw; *President:* Konrad Matthaei; *Vice-Presidents:* William W. Goodman, Robert M. Keefe, Robert Whitehead; *Treasurer:* Harvey L. Koizim; *Secretary:* Armina Marhsall. *Artistic Director:* Michael Kahn; *Managing Director:* William Stewart; *Director of Educational Planning and Development:* Mary Hunter Wolf.

In 1950, the late Lawrence Langner, a founder and director of the Theatre Guild, announced his concept of a theatre to be built on the banks of the Housatonic River in Stratford, Conn.: "The Theatre that will be built to house Shakespeare's plays will be patterned after the old Globe Theatre in London and will have approximately 1,600 seats. It will, however, include every appropriate improvement that has been developed since, making it possible to adapt it to any kind of production—Elizabethan or modern."

Plans embodying Mr. Langner's ideas were drawn up by the architect Edwin Howard; the Connecticut legislature enacted a law chartering the American Shakespeare Festival Theatre and Academy—American Shakespeare Theatre (AST) since 1972—as a nonprofit institution; funds came from individual contributors and from donations made by corporations, foundations, and organizations. At the groundbreaking ceremonies in October 1954, Katharine Cornell turned the first shovelful of earth; construction commenced in January 1955 and in July the American Shakespeare Theatre began its first season.

The production for opening night (July 12) was William Shakespeare's *Julius Caesar*, directed by Denis Carey and with a cast that included Jack Palance as Cassius, Christopher Plummer as Marc Antony, Hurd Hatfield as Caesar, and Leora Dana as Portia. The other production of the first season was *The Tempest* (Aug. 1, 1955). Since then, AST's presentations have included: (1956) *King John*, *Measure for Measure*, and *The Taming of the Shrew;* (1957) *Othello*, *The Merchant of Venice*, and *Much Ado About Nothing;* (1958) *Hamlet*, *A Midsummer Night's Dream*, and *The Winter's Tale;* (1959) *Romeo and Juliet*, *The Merry Wives of Windsor*, and *All's Well That Ends Well;* (1960) *Twelfth Night*, *The Tempest*, and *Antony and Cleopatra;* (1961) *Macbeth*, *As You Like It*, and *Troilus and Cressida;* (1962) *Henry IV, Part I; Richard II*; and a special presentation, *Shakespeare Revisited;* (1963) *King Lear*, *The Comedy of Errors*, *Henry V*, and George Bernard Shaw's *Caesar and Cleopatra;* and (1964) *Hamlet*, *Much Ado About Nothing*, and *Richard III*.

Also, (1965) *Romeo and Juliet*, *Coriolanus*, *The Taming of the Shrew*, and *King Lear;* (1966) *Julius Caesar*, *Twelfth Night*, *Falstaff* (*Henry IV, Part 2*), and T. S. Eliot's *Murder in the Cathedral;* (1967) *Macbeth*, *The Merchant of Venice*, *A Midsummer Night's Dream*, and Jean Anouilh's *Antigone;* (1968) *As You Like It*, *Love's Labour's Lost*, *Richard II*, and George Bernard Shaw's *Androcles and the Lion;* (1969) *Henry V*, *Much Ado About Nothing*, *Hamlet*, and Anton Chekhov's *The Three Sisters;* (1970) *Othello*, *All's Well That Ends Well*, and George Bernard Shaw's *The Devil's Disciple;* (1971) *The Tempest*, *The Merry Wives of Windsor*, and Eugene O'Neill's *Mourning Becomes Electra;* (1972) *Julius Caesar*, *Antony and Cleopatra*, and George Bernard Shaw's *Major Barbara;* (1973) *Measure for Measure*, *Macbeth*, and William Wycherley's *The Country Wife;* (1974) *Twelfth Night*, *Romeo and Juliet*, and Tennessee Williams' *Cat on a Hot Tin Roof;* and (1975) *King Lear*, *The Winter's Tale*, and Thornton Wilder's *Our Town*.

AST's inaugural season was eight weeks long. This was later extended, and by the end of the 1975 season nearly 6 million people had seen plays at the theatre in Strattord, Conn. Beginning in 1959, the schedule included spring performances for junior and senior high school students, about 100,000 of whom came each year from twelve states; a total of approximately 2 million students had seen AST productions by 1975.

Formerly, beginning in 1954 and on the birthday of William Shakespeare, AST made annual awards "in recognition of works which stimulate appreciation of Shakespeare and the classical theatre." As examples, Yale University received the award for its 1954 Shakespeare Festival, Hallmark Cards for its telecast of *King Richard II*, and Joseph Papp for his Shakespeare productions in New York City's Central Park. The William Benton Awards were established in 1970 by the former US senator, publisher, and AST trustee and presented to members of the AST company for creative achievement. Awards winners include: (1970) John Ventantonio and Mary Wright; (1971) Robert Blumenfeld and Garland Wright; (1972) Charles T. Harper and Stephen Schnetzer.

American Theatre Association, 1317 "F" St., NW, Washington, DC 20004, tel. (202) 737-5606.
President: Ann S. Hill; *President-elect:* O. G. Brockett; *Executive Director:* Anthony Reid.

The American Theatre Association (formerly American Educational Theatre Association) was formed in 1936 as an organization of persons and institutions interested in noncommercial theatre. Currently it is composed of the American Community Theatre Association, Army Theatre Arts Association, National Association of Schools of Theatre, National Children's Theatre Association, Secondary School Theatre Association, University and College Theatre Association, the University Resident Theatre Association, and the American Theatre Student League. Its membership is over 6,500.

The association's publication program includes *Educational Theatre Journal, Children's Theatre Review, Secondary School Journal* (quarterly), *Theatre News* (monthly), various annual directories and bibliographies, and the "Books of the Theatre" series. The association produces the annual American College Theatre Festival and the biennial Festival of American Community Theatre, and holds an annual convention as well as numbers of regional and state conferences. Research and program activities are carried on within each constituent association as well as by ATA as a whole. Liaison is maintained with other national organizations and agencies as well as with international groups, and the association is represented on the US Commission of UNESCO.

The purposes of the American Theatre Association include: "affirming the contribution of theatre to the improvement of the quality of life, stimulating and conducting research in the nature and history of theatre education, advising and consulting appropriate public and private agencies about the status and condition of theatre, providing a forum for the exchange of ideas and experiences concerning theatre."

Arena Stage (including the **Kreeger Theater),** 6th and Maine Ave., SW, Washington, DC 20024, tel.: executive offices (202) 347-0931; box office (202) 638-6700.
Producing Director: Zelda Fichandler; *Executive Director:* Thomas C. Fichandler; *Associate Producer:* George Touliatos; *Associate Executive Director:* Alton Miller.

Arena Stage, one of America's first regional theatres, began operations in 1950 in a converted movie theatre ("The Hippodrome"). In 1956 the theatre moved to a reconditioned brewery ("The Old Vat"), and in 1961 to a permanent home in the architectural award-winning Arena, located in Washington's modern "Southwest Waterfront" district. In 1971 it opened also the adjacent Kreeger Theater. The growth of Arena through these moves has parallelled—and, to some extent, propelled—the emergence of a newly invigorated American theatre.

By building a theatre-conscious local audience and weaning them away from the hit-or-miss Broadway syndrome; by encouraging new playwrights, actors, designers, and directors; and by insisting on the highest artistic standards, Arena has earned respect across the country and around the world. In 1973, Arena was selected by the US State Department and the Soviet Ministry of Culture as the first such troupe to take American drama on tour to Moscow and Leningrad, where performances of *Our Town* and *Inherit the Wind* won acclaim.

The following year, Arena presented the English-language premiere of Elie Wiesel's *Zalmen, or the Madness of God* (May 3, 1974) for stage audiences and for network television. World premieres at Arena include Howard Sackler's *The Great White Hope* (Dec. 12, 1967); *Raisin* (May 23, 1973), the musical version of Lorraine Hansberry's *Raisin in the Sun*; and the first professional performance of Jerome Lawrence and Robert E. Lee's *The Night Thoreau Spent in Jail* (Oct. 23, 1970). US premieres include John Whiting's *The Devils* (Oct. 30, 1963); Arthur Kopit's *Indians* (May 6, 1969); Peter Barnes's *The Ruling Class* (Jan. 15, 1971); Eugene Ionesco's *Wipe-Out Games* (Apr. 9, 1971); Michael Weller's *Moonchildren* (Oct. 29, 1971); Gunter Grass's *Uptight* (Mar. 17, 1972); and Max Frisch's *A Public Prosecutor Is Sick of It All* (Jan. 31, 1973).

Arena is supported by a broad-based community of small contributors (about 5,000 individuals and families) and by the National Endowment for the Arts and several foundations. The Living Stage, a free improvisational touring company of professional actors who bring theatre for children to inner city neighborhoods, constitutes one of several continuing programs.

Associated Actors and Artistes of America, 165 W. 46th St., New York, NY 10036, tel. (212) 245-8295.
President: Frederick O'Neal; *Vice-Presidents:* Chester Migden, *1st;* DeLloyd Tibbs, *2nd;* H. O'Neil Shanks, *3rd;* Penny Singleton, *4th;* Donald Grody, *5th; Treasurer:* Harold M. Hoffman; *Executive Secretary:* Sanford I. Wolff.

The Associated Actors and Artistes of America, known as the "Four A's," is the parent organization of all the performing arts trade unions. It was organized on July 18, 1919, and now has a membership of 73,000.

The following organizations are affiliated with the Four A's: Actors' Equity Association, American Federation of Television and Radio Artists, American Guild of Musical Artists, American Guild of Variety Artists, Association Puertorriquena de Artistas y Tecnicos del Espectaculo, Hebrew Actors Union, Italian Actors Union, Screen Actors Guild, and Screen Extras Guild.

Association of Producing Artists (APA).
The Association of Producing Artists (APA) was founded in January 1960 by Ellis Rabb as a workshop for professional actors, directors, and designers. The company made its debut under the sponsorship of the Bermuda Theatre Guild, Hamilton, Bermuda, in May 1960. This engagement was followed by a tour (Summer 1960) of the Bucks County Playhouse, New Hope, Pa.; Theatre-by-the-Sea, Matunuck, R.I.; and John Drew Memorial Theatre, East Hampton, N.Y.; and a season at the McCarter Theatre, Princeton, N.J.

The repertory for the first year included Arthur Schnitzler's *Anatol*, Anton Chekhov's *The Seagull*, William Shakespeare's *The Taming of the Shrew*, Luigi Pirandello's *Right You Are (If You Think You Are)*, George Bernard Shaw's *Man and Superman*, Molière's *Scapin*, William Butler Yeats's *The Cat and the Moon*, Gilbert and Sullivan's *Cox and Box*, Christopher Fry's *The Lady's Not for Burning*, George M. Cohan's *The Tavern*, and Oscar Wilde's *The Importance of Being Earnest*. The McCarter season also included William Shakespeare's *King Lear, A Midsummer Night's Dream, Twelfth Night, As You Like It*, and *Hamlet*. APA presented some of these plays at the Fred Miller Theatre, Milwaukee, Wisc. (Oct.-Dec. 1961). The company first appeared in New York City with a presentation of Robert Sheridan's *The School for Scandal* (Folksbiene Playhouse, Mar. 17, 1962).

APA began making annual visits to Ann Arbor, Mich., under the sponsorship of the Professional Theatre Program of the University of Michigan in October 1962. The second New York City season began in February 1964 under the aegis of the Phoenix Theatre (q.v.), a project of Theatre Incorporated, as APA at the Phoenix. Repertory seasons were put on by the group each year in New York, California, Michigan, Toronto, and other localities. In 1966 the Lyceum Theatre became the New York City base.

There were many interesting and successful productions during the APA-Phoenix partnership, which ended in April 1969 with a revival of Noel Coward's *Private Lives* during the eighth season at the University of Michigan. Mounting financial problems that seem to be inherent in the operation of a nonprofit repertory company and lack of governmental support were the primary reasons for the dissolution.

In addition to the productions already listed, APA's repertory included Molière's *Impromptu at Versailles*, Maxim Gorki's *The Lower Depths*, Erwin Piscator's adaptation of Leo Tolstoi's *War and Peace*, Jean Giraudoux's *Judith*, George S. Kaufman and Moss Hart's *You Can't Take It with You*, Henrik Ibsen's *The Wild Duck*, Archibald MacLeish's *Herakles*, Richard Baldridge's arrangement of writings by Walt Whitman, *We Comrades Three*, Page Johnson's *Sweet of You To Say So*, Michel de Ghelderode's *Escurial, Pantagleize*, and *The Chronicles of Hell*, Jean-Paul Sartre's *The Flies*, Eugene Ionesco's *Exit the King*, George Kelly's *The Show-Off*, Anton Chekhov's *The Cherry Orchard*, Molière's *The Misanthrope*, Sean O'Casey's *Cock-a-Doodle Dandy*, T. S. Eliot's *The Cocktail Party*, William Shakespeare's *Macbeth*, Brendan Behan's *The Hostage*, and Samuel Beckett's *Play*.

Association of Theatrical Press Agents and Managers, 268 W. 47th St., New York, NY 10036, tel. (212) JU 2-3750.
President: B. Merle Debuskey; *Vice-President:* Arthur Rubin; *Secretary-Treasurer:* Richard B. Weaver; *Business Agent:* Milton M. Pollack.

The Association of Theatrical Press Agents and Managers (ATPAM) is composed of two groups of theatre workers: company managers and house managers; and press agents and advance (touring) press agents. The organization came about through the amalgamation of several earlier groups concerned with the welfare of those working in these business phases of the theatre. When the press agents joined with the association in 1938, ATPAM, as we know it today, came into being.

The association operates much as the other trade union groups of the theatre: to secure maximum benefits for its members and to represent them in dealing with other theatre groups.

It is a national organization, and an affiliate of the AFL-CIO.

Barter Theatre, Abingdon, VA 24210, tel. (703) 628-2281.

President: Fillmore McPherson; *Vice-Presidents:* Charles J. Harkrader and William A. Stuart; *Secretary/Treasurer:* James P. Jones; *Assistant Secretary/Treasurer and Business Manager:* Pearl Hayter.

Producing Director: Rex Partington.

America's longest running professional repertory theatre, the Barter Theatre, was founded at Abingdon, Va., in 1933 by Robert Porterfield, with the plan of exchanging food for drama. After their first season of theatre—in an abandoned schoolhouse in the fertile farmland of southwest Virginia—the troupe of twenty-two New York actors and actresses who had gone to Abingdon instead of languishing on depression-starved Broadway counted $4.30 in the till from the 35¢ admission fee, plus an aggregate weight gain of over three hundred pounds! The performers literally ate the "box-office receipts," with patrons bringing chicken, ham, and other farm produce to barter at the theatre in exchange for seats at performances of plays.

Since 1933, Barter Theatre, operated by the Barter Foundation, Inc., has continued to provide professional theatre in the Appalachian region and numbers among its "alumni" Patricia Neal, Gregory Peck, Ernest Borgnine, and a host of other well-known stage, film, and television actors. In 1939, Mr. Porterfield instituted the Barter Theatre of Virginia Award for an outstanding performer of the New York season, entitling the winner to choose two actors for Barter's intern program and also giving him or her an acre of land in Abingdon, a ham, and a platter off which to eat it. Among winners of the Award have been Tallulah Bankhead, Ralph Bellamy, Shirley Booth, Hume Cronyn, and Helen Hayes. The Barter has toured nationally and internationally; their most famous tour took them to Denmark, where, at the invitation of the National Theatre of Denmark, they presented *Hamlet* at Kronberg Castle, Shakespeare's setting for the play.

In 1946, Barter Theatre was designated as the State Theatre of Virginia, the first state theatre in America. In 1953, Mr. Porterfield acquired for Barter Theatre the seats, stage curtain, lamps, and other interior fittings of the Empire Theatre in New York City, which was scheduled to be demolished. Dozens of theatre people worked as volunteers to move all the desired furnishings out of the Empire during one weekend and into the vans of a Virginia moving company that had agreed to help Mr. Porterfield in this project that brought the shining splendor of an old Broadway theatre to the mountains of Virginia. Following Robert Porterfield's death, Rex Partington was selected in 1972 by the board as artistic director/manager.

In addition to its Equity company, selected by auditions in New York City and other theatre centers, Barter operates a two-year internship program in professional theatre and a summer apprentice program. Barter is a member of the League of Resident Theatres.

Black Theatre Alliance, 162 W. 56th St., Suite 303, New York, NY 10019, tel. (212) 247-5840.

President: Hazel J. Bryant, Director of the Afro American Total Theatre; *Vice-President:* Jesse DeVore, Managing Director of Voices, Inc.; *Secretary:* Mical Whitaker, Artistic Director of The East River Players; *Treasurer:* Yusef Iman, Director of the Weusi Kuumba Troupe.

Board Members: all the preceding, plus Ernie McClintock, who preceded Hazel Bryant as president and who is Executive Director of the Afro American Studio Theatre; Lubaba Lateef, Director of Brownsville Laboratory Theatre; and Aduke Aremu, Director of Harlem Children's Theatre.

Board Members-at-Large: Joseph Walker, Director of the Demi Gods; Emory Taylor, Director of the Harlem Opera Society; and Fred Hudson, Director of the Frederick Douglass Creative Arts Center.

The Black Theatre Alliance is a nonprofit organization comprised of twenty-one New York City companies, three New York State units, and six out-of-state organizations. The Alliance was incorporated in 1971 with a budget of $15,000; four years later its budget was $150,000. Funding has been made available by the Rockefeller Brothers' Fund, the New York Foundation, Edward John Noble Foundation, the Shubert Foundation, the NY State Council on the Arts, the National Endowment for the Arts, and other sources.

The Alliance was founded to solve common problems, share information and resources, and to create an instrument to validate black theatre and dance companies as community institutions. Primary goals are to organize audience development programs; to give technical and administrative assistance to theatres; to act as an information clearinghouse on theatre and theatre-related activities; and to develop special projects of the black theatre community.

The Alliance conducts an annual theatre festival and workshops on theatre management, directs audience development services through AUDELCO, and conducts a theatre technical training program in lighting and scene design. The Alliance also sponsored formation of the Frank Silvera Writers' Workshop, founded and directed by Garland Lee Thompson. The Alliance established a central scene shop, maintains a manuscript collection of plays at the Schomburg Center in New York City, and runs an emergency loan program for members. Publications of the Alliance are *The Black Theatre Resource Directory,* which lists black playwrights, directors, technicians, etc., and a quarterly newsletter. The Alliance also issues a weekly calendar, *Theatre Notes,* which is published in the *Amsterdam News.*

The Boston Repertory Theatre, Inc., 1 Boylston Place, Boston MA 02116, tel. (616) 423-6580 and 423-7586.

General Manager: Esquire Jauchem.

The Boston Repertory Theatre was founded by Esquire Jauchem in 1970 as a cooperative in which the actors hold administrative and technical positions and serve as trustees of the corporation in addition to performing in the works produced by the company. The first productions were mounted at a Hyannis, Mass., junior high school in the summer of 1971, but from the outset a main goal of the company was to become established in its own building in Boston, where, from 1972 to 1974, plays were staged in the First and Second Church auditorium. In 1975, the Boston Repertory purchased a structure in one of Boston's oldest sections. After renovations and alterations, this building housed all aspects of the Boston Repertory's operations, containing scenery and costume shops, administrative offices, and a 230-seat theatre.

At the time of this acquisition, the original staff was expanded with administrative and technical specialists to help in management and maintenance; these individuals also became trustees and members of the cooperative. In addition, it was decided to hire performers and directors from outside the organization in order to stimulate the artistic development of Boston Repertory.

The company has staged nearly thirty productions to date since its first season, which included William Saroyan's *The Beautiful People,* Jean Cocteau's *The Knights of the Round Table,* and Edmond Rostand's *The Romantics.* In the second season (1972-73)—its first in Boston—the company gave the world premiere of Antoine de Saint Exupery's *The Little Prince,* as adapted and directed by David Zucker, an actor-member of the cooperative; this production ran for three years and then went on national tour. Other plays presented by the company include: (1972-73) James Thurber's *The Thirteen Clocks,* adapted and directed by Greg Meeh, a member of the company; *Mime Magic* by David Zucker; the Boston premiere of Jerome Lawrence and Robert E. Lee's *The Night Thoreau Spent in Jail; Grandma's in the Cellar,* created by Mr. Jauchem and the entire company; (1973-74) David Zucker's adaptation of George Orwell's *Animal Farm,* which he also directed; and (1974-75) the Boston premiere of Mark Medoff's *When You Comin Back, Red Ryder?* and world premiere of company member Robin Brecker's *The Cheer of Our Christmas.*

In addition to its rotating repertory, running for 40-50 weeks a year, the company presents, with the aid of the Massachusetts Council on the Arts and Humanities, "Theatre for a Dollar" shows, providing opportunity to produce experimental works and enabling theatregoers to attend by paying a token admission.

Brooklyn Academy of Music. *See* Chelsea Theater Center of Brooklyn

CSC Repertory, Abbey Theatre, 136 W. 13th Street, New York, NY 10003, tel. (212) 677-4210, 477-5770.

President: Christopher Martin; *Vice-President:* Harris Laskawy; *Secretary-Treasurer:* Kathryn Wyman; *Board of Directors:* William Snow, Paul Doniger; *Artistic Director:* Christopher Martin; *Managing Director:* William Glass.

Christopher Martin, Harris Laskawy, and Kathryn Wyman founded CSC as the Classic Stage Company in 1967 for the purpose of producing theatre classics in a manner that would make them as exciting and meaningful to a contemporary audience as they had been for their original audiences. The first performances were given in January 1967 at Riverside Church in New York City; in the fall of the same year CSC moved to Rutgers Church, West 73rd Street, New York City, remaining there for a year. There followed approximately a year in a loft theatre on Greenwich Village's Bleecker Street, followed by another move in the fall of 1969 to 89 W. 3rd Street, a converted shoe factory, which was the group's home until the spring of 1973. During those four years, the company was incorporated as CSC Repertory and received its first grants from the National Endowment for the Arts and the NY State Council on the Arts. Box-office and critical success led to bigger audiences and the need for a larger theatre with professional equipment, and in mid-1973 CSC moved to the Abbey Theatre. In 1974, CSC received a *Village Voice* Off-Broadway (Obie) award special citation for theatrical excellence.

Besides an annual subscription season, CSC tours regularly, visiting college and university campuses in New York and New Jersey, and also presents a new play series, using performers other than members of the regular CSC company. Productions for each CSC season include: (1968-69) Christopher Fry's *The Lady's Not for Burning*, William Shakespeare's *Hamlet*, George Bernard Shaw's *Man and Superman*, Jean Anouilh's *Poor Bitos* and *The Cavern*, Anton Chekhov's *Uncle Vanya*, and Molière's *Tartuffe;* (1969-70) Cyril Tourneur's *The Revenger's Tragedy*, Jean Anouilh's *Poor Bitos*, Anton Chekhov's *Uncle Vanya*, George Bernard Shaw's *Man and Superman*, Ugo Betti's *Goat Island* and Christopher Martin's adaptation of *Moby Dick;* (1970-71) William Shakespeare's *Hamlet, Pericles*, and *Twelfth Night*, Tom Stoppard's *Rosencrantz and Guildenstern Are Dead*, Herman Melville's *Moby Dick*, and George Bernard Shaw's *Man and Superman*.

Also, (1971-72) Peter Weiss's *Marat/Sade*, William Shakespeare's *Julius Caesar* and *Titus Andronicus*, and Gogol's *The Inspector General;* (1972-73) Tom Stoppard's *Rosencrantz and Guildenstern Are Dead*, Harold Pinter's *The Homecoming*, William Shakespeare's *The Tempest, Macbeth*, and *Measure for Measure*, John Whiting's *The Devils*, Joe Orton's *Look* and Ronosuke Akutagawa's *Rashomon;* (1973-74) Herman Melville's *Moby Dick*, William Shakespeare's *Twelfth Night*, August Strindberg's *Miss Julie*, Harold Pinter's *The Homecoming*, Molière's *The Misanthrope*, Tom Stoppard's *Rosencrantz and Guildenstern Are Dead*, Cyril Tourneur's *The Revenger's Tragedy*, Harold Pinter's *The Dwarfs* and *The Dumb Waiter*, Dylan Thomas's *Under Milk Wood*, and Henrik Ibsen's *Hedda Gabler;* and (1974-75) Christopher Marlowe's *Edward II*, Henrik Ibsen's *Hedda Gabler*, William Shakespeare's *The Tempest*, Christopher Fry's *The Lady's Not for Burning*, Jean Anouilh's *Antigone*, and Georg Buchner's *Woyzeck*.

Chelsea Theater Center of Brooklyn, Brooklyn Academy of Music, 30 Lafayette Ave., Brooklyn, NY 11217, tel. (212) 783-5110.

Artistic Director: Robert Kalfin; *Executive Director:* Michael David; *Production Director:* Burl Hash.

Chelsea Theater Center of Brooklyn is a nonprofit theatre organization founded in the Chelsea section of Manhattan in 1965 by Robert Kalfin. In 1969, it moved to the Brooklyn Academy of Music, becoming established there as the resident theatre of Brooklyn. A board of directors governs the business affairs of the corporation, and all artistic and policy decisions are left to the artistic, executive, and production directors. There is no resident company; actors, directors, and designers are hired to fill the requirements of each production. Similarly, the physical aspect of the theatre may be adapted to fit the needs of each play. Somewhat more than half of Chelsea's tickets are sold on a subscription basis.

Funds from the Ford, Rockefeller, Noble, Shubert, and Mellon foundations, the Kaplan Fund, the National Endowment for the Arts, and the New York City Office of Cultural Affairs supplement the loyal support Chelsea draws from the immediate community as well as from the greater metropolitan area.

In addition to being in residence in Brooklyn, Chelsea began operating in October 1973 the Westside in Manhattan, a theatre in a renovated church on West 43rd Street. There are two performing spaces: upstairs is the 299-seat performing space used to house Chelsea's successful productions after they have completed their Brooklyn engagements and to present special projects that do not fit into the regular Brooklyn season; downstairs is the Brooklyn Navy Yard, a cabaret featuring varied entertainment as well as serving food and drink. Its profits help support the Chelsea in Brooklyn.

Chelsea Theater Center performers, directors, and designers have received numerous awards for work done at the center. Chelsea itself was cited by the *Village Voice* Off-Broadway (Obie) award committee (1969-70) for outstanding achievement; the center also received a Vernon Rice Drama Desk Award (1971-72) and a special award of the New England Theater Conference.

From its first (1965-66) through its tenth (1974-75) season, the Chelsea produced nearly a hundred plays, including (1968-69) John Gay's *Christophe*, John Hawkes's *The Innocent Party* and *The Wax Museum*, and *A Black Quartet;* (1969-70) Imamu Baraka's (Leroi Jones) *Slave Ship*, Daniel C. Gerold's *Candaules, Commissioner*, William Golding's *The Brass Butterfly*, and William Butler Yeats's *The Unicorn from the Stars;* (1970-71) Edward Bond's *Saved*, Joe McCord's *Tarot*, Heathcote Williams's *AC/DC*, and Peter Handke's *My Foot My Tutor* and *Self-Accusation;* (1971-72) Jean Genet's *The Screens*, Hans Magnus Enzensberger's *The Interrogation of Havana*, Allen Ginsberg's *Kaddish*, John Gay's *The Beggar's Opera*, and Stanislaw Ignacy Witkiewicz's *The Water Hen;* (1972-73) Aishah Rahman's *Lady Day: A Musical Tragedy*, Isaac Babel's *Sunset*, Peter Handke's *Kaspar*, and a series of guest productions presented by The New Theater of Palo Alto, Calif., the Iowa Theater Lab, El Teatro Campesino, and Video Free America; (1973-74) David Storey's *The Contractor*, Hugh Wheeler's adaptation of *Candide* with music by Leonard Bernstein, Christopher Hampton's *Total Eclipse*, and *The Madhouse Company;* (1974-75) Megan Terry's *Hothouse*, Isaac Bashevis Singer's *Yentle the Yeshiva Boy*, Allan Knee's *Santa Anita '42*, John Gay's *Polly: An Opera*, Jim Wann and Bland Simpson's *Diamond Studs*, and guest appearances by El Teatro Campesino and the San Francisco Mime Troupe.

Circle in the Square, 1633 Broadway on 50th St., New York, NY 10019, (201) 581-3270.

Artistic Director: Theodore Mann; *Managing Director:* Paul Libin.

The Circle in the Square developed from the Loft Players, a workshop group which started in a midtown loft in October 1949. Their first production was a revival of Edna St. Vincent Millay's *Aria da Capo* and Federico Garcia Lorca's *The Love of Don Perlimplin and Belisa in the Garden* (Master Institute Th., Mar. 24, 1950).

After a successful summer at the Maverick Theatre, Woodstock, N.Y., the group returned to New York City with a profit of $300. The founding members: Jose Quintero, Emilie Stevens, Jason Wingreen, and Theodore Mann raised $7,000 to lease a defunct Greenwich Village nightclub at 5 Sheridan Square. They converted the space into a three-sided arena theatre named Circle in the Square and opened with *Dark of the Moon* (Feb. 2, 1951).

Its first great success came in the second season with the revival of *Summer and Smoke* (Apr. 24, 1952). Subsequent hits were *The Grass Harp* and *The Girl on the Via Flaminia*. The latter was transferred to Broadway when the theatre was closed in March 1954 due to building code violations. *The King and the Duke* reopened the theatre in June 1955.

Leigh Connell served as co-producer with Theodore Mann and Jose Quintero from 1955 to 1961. In January 1960 the company was forced to move because the building was scheduled for demolition. The remodeled Amato Theatre at 159 Bleecker St. became the new Circle in the Square and *Our Town*, which had opened on Mar. 23, 1959, moved in on Jan. 8, 1960, to continue a successful run. A theatre school was opened in 1961. Mr. Quintero severed his connections with Circle in the Square in 1964.

A new theatre, Circle in the Square/Joseph E. Levine Theatre, with a seating capacity of 650, was designed and built for the organization into the basement of the Uris Office Building at Broadway and 50th St. The formal opening occurred on Nov. 15, 1972, with a revival of Eugene O'Neill's *Mourning Becomes Electra*.

Circle in the Square productions or co-productions include (1951) *Dark of the Moon, Amata, Antigone* (Anouilh) and *The Enchanted;* (1952) *Bonds of Interest, Yerma, Burning Bright* and *Summer and Smoke;* (1953) *The Grass Harp* and *American Gothic;* (1954) *The Girl on the Via Flaminia;* (1955) *The King and the Duke, La Ronde*, and *Cradle Song;* (1956) *The Iceman Cometh;* (1958) *Children of Darkness* and *The Quare Fellow;* (1959) Our Town; and (1960) *The Balcony* and *Camino Real*.

Also, (1961) *Under Milk Wood* and *Smiling the Boy Fell Dead;* (1962) *Plays for Bleecker Street, Under Milk Wood* and *Pullman Car Hiawatha;* (1963) *Desire Under the Elms, The Trojan Women, Six Characters in Search of an Author* and *Trumpets of the Lord;* (1964) *Othello;* (1965) *The White Devil, Baal*, and *Live Like Pigs;* (1966) *Eh?* and *Six from La Mama;* (1967) *Drums in the Night, Iphigenia in Aulis*, and *A Midsummer Night's Dream;* (1968) *A Moon for the Misbegotten;* (1969) *Little Murders* and *Seven Days of Mourning;* (1970) *The White House Murder Case, Chicago 70*, and *Boesman and Lena;* (1971) *The Last Analysis* and *F. Jasmine Addams;* and (1972) *Joan*.

On Broadway, Circle in the Square has produced (1954) *The Girl on the Via Flaminia;* (1956) *The Innkeepers* and *Long Day's Journey into Night;* (1962) *General Seeger* and *Great Day in the Morning;* (1963) *Strange Interlude;* (1964) *Hughie;* (1965); *And Things That Go Bump in the Night, The Royal Hunt of the Sun* and *The Zulu and the Zayda* (1969) *Trumpets of the Lord;* (1972) *Mourning Becomes Electra;* (1973) *Medea, Here Are Ladies, Uncle Vanya, The Waltz of the Toreadors* and *The Iceman Cometh;* and (1974) *An American Millionaire* and *Scapino.*

At Ford's Theatre, Washington, D.C., Circle in the Square presented (1969) *A Moon for the Misbegotten, Trumpets of the Lord* and *Iphigenia in Aulis* and (1970) *Autumn Garden, Will Rogers' U.S.A.* and *Max Morath at the Turn of the Century.*

Circle Repertory Company. Theatre address: 99 Seventh Ave. South, New York, NY 10014, tel. (212) 924-7100; office address: 186 W. 4th St., New York, NY 10014, tel. (212) 691-3210.
Artistic Director: Marshall W. Mason; *Executive Director:* Jerry Arrow.

Chairman: Dr. Paul F. Cranefield; *President:* Robert L. Thirkield; *Vice-President:* Lanford Wilson; *Treasurer:* Marilyn A. Sutter; *Secretary:* Eugene Aleinikoff, Esq.; *Directors:* Tanya Berezin, Dr. William L. Bradley, Jacques Chabrier, Harold Clurman, Edith Gordon, Norman Lloyd, Marshall W. Mason.

Circle Repertory Company was founded in 1969 by Marshall W. Mason, Rob Thirkield, Tanya Berezin, and Lanford Wilson. Having worked together off-off Broadway since 1965, they evolved an informal alliance with actors who shared their artistic goals. As "The American Theater Project," they scored a major success in London in 1968 with Mr. Wilson's *Home Free!* and *The Madness of Lady Bright.*

Back in America, they located a home on upper Broadway in New York City and began a series of workshops, which met thirty hours a week for six months; Circle Repertory began to emerge. Rob Thirkield directed the first production, David Starkweather's *A Practical Ritual To Exorcise Frustration After Five Days of Rain.* Mason then created a controversial event, two alternating productions of Anton Chekhov's *The Three Sisters*—one "traditional," the other "experimental." After a season of only thirty performances, Circle received grants from the NY State Council on the Arts and the Peg Santvoord Foundation.

In the second season (1970-71), the workshop production program (a central source of creativity) was developed. *Princess Ivona, The Ghost Sonata, The Doctor in Spite of Himself,* and Lanford Wilson's *Sextet (Yes)* were the major productions. Then the company went to Woodstock, N.Y., for a summer of workshops during which they reworked *The Three Sisters* and *The Ghost Sonata.* The summer strengthened the group's methods and spirit.

On the schedule of the third season (1971-72), the new versions of Chekhov and Strindberg were presented to enthusiastic receptions, as were the new American plays on the schedule—Berrilla Kerr's *Elephant in the House,* Helen Duberstein's *Time Shadows,* and three new one-act plays by Lanford Wilson.

The fourth season (1972-73) started with a repeat of Wilson's three one-acts and was followed by Claris Nelson's *A Road Where the Wolves Run.* Next came Wilson's *The Hot l Baltimore,* written especially for the company; it opened in January 1973 and was still running at the end of 1975. The fourth season was completed with a revival of Henrik Ibsen's *When We Dead Awaken* and Ronald Wilcox's *The Tragedy of Thomas Andros.*

The Circle's recognition grew during its fifth year (1973-74). Mark Medoff's *When You Comin' Back, Red Ryder?,* which had originated in the workshop program, opened the season and subsequently moved to off-Broadway. Richard Lortz's *Prodigal* and Roy London's *The Amazing Activity of Charlie Contrare* experimented with different forms, and then Edward J. Moore's *The Sea Horse* scored another success and followed *The Hot l Baltimore* and *When You Comin' Back, Red Ryder?* to off-Broadway. Three Circle productions were running concurrently with e. e. cummings's *him* and Aeschylus' *The Persians* at Circle. The workshop program included the premiere of Megan Terry's *Hot House,* later presented at Chelsea Theatre.

As the sixth season (1974-75) began, Tennessee Williams's *Battle of Angels* had its premiere at Circle's new home, the former Sheridan Square Playhouse. Lanford Wilson's *The Mound Builders* and Corinne Jacker's *Harry Outside* together won a total of six Obies. *Down by the River Where Waterlilies Are Disfigured Every Day* displayed the talent of Julie Bovasso, and Lanford Wilson demonstrated his abilities as a director with the production of a new play and playwright—*Not to Worry* by A. E. Santaniello.

Circle will continue to devote itself to productions of the works of the finest new American writers and strive to make the action of the play become the experience of the audience.

City Center Acting Company. *See* The Acting Company.

Civic Repertory Theatre, 105 W. 14th St., New York, NY
President: Eva Le Gallienne.

William Lyon Phelps wrote in 1932: "One of the great events in the history of the American stage took place on Oct. 25, 1926, when Eva Le Gallienne opened the Civic Repertory Theatre."

Miss Le Gallienne had taken over the old 14th Street Theatre, renamed it the Civic Repertory Theatre, gathered a company, and began a season of repertory. The opening production was Jacinto Benavente's *Saturday Night.* The second night, Anton Chekhov's *The Three Sisters* was added.

By 1932, the Civic Repertory had presented 1,024 performances of 31 plays. Among the most popular of its productions were Gregorio and Maria Martinez Sierra's *The Cradle Song,* James M. Barrie's *Peter Pan,* Anton Chekhov's *The Cherry Orchard,* William Shakespeare's *Romeo and Juliet,* and Susan Glaspell's *Alison's House.*

In addition to the working repertory company, an apprentice group was established, which consisted of from 30 to 50 students between the ages of 15 and 30 who received training at no tuition charge.

In 1933, the financial crisis and other economic problems brought about the demise of the venture, and in the spring of that year Miss Le Gallienne closed the theatre.

Productions of the Civic Repertory Theatre (not including revivals put back in repertory) included Jacinto Benavente's *Saturday Night* (Oct. 25, 1926); Anton Chekhov's *The Three Sisters* (Oct. 26, 1926); Henrik Ibsen's *The Master Builder* (Nov. 1, 1926); Henrik Ibsen's *John Gabriel Borkman* (Nov. 9, 1926); Carlo Goldoni's *The Mistress of the Inn* (Nov. 22, 1926); William Shakespeare's *Twelfth Night* (Dec. 20, 1926); Gregorio and Maria Martinez Sierra's *The Cradle Song* (Jan. 24, 1927); Susan Glaspell's *Inheritors* (Mar. 7, 1927); Hermann Heijermans' *The Good Hope* (Oct. 18, 1927); Gustav Weid's *2 x 2 = 5* (Nov. 28, 1927); Walter Ferris' *The First Stone* (Jan. 13, 1928); Max Mohr's *Improvisations in June* (Feb. 23, 1928); Henrik Ibsen's *Hedda Gabler* (Mar. 26, 1928); Molière's *L'Invitation au voyage* (Oct. 4, 1928); Anton Chekhov's *The Cherry Orchard* (Oct. 15, 1928); James M. Barrie's *Peter Pan* (Nov. 26, 1928); Serafin and Joaquin Alvarez Quintero's *Lady from Alfaqueque* (Jan. 14, 1929); Anton Chekhov's *On the High Road* (Jan. 14, 1929); Leonid Andreyev's *Katerina* (Feb. 25, 1929); Serafin and Joaquin Alvarez Quintero's *A Sunny Morning* (Apr. 13, 1929); Anton Chekhov's *The Seagull* (Sept. 16, 1929); Claude Anet's *Mademoiselle Bourrat* (Oct. 7, 1929); Leo Tolstoy's *The Living Corpse* (Dec. 6, 1929); Alfred Sutro's *The Open Door* and Serafin and Joaquin Alvarez Quintero's *The Women Have Their Way* (Jan. 27, 1930); William Shakespeare's *Romeo and Juliet* (Apr. 21, 1930); Arthur Schnitzler's *The Green Cockatoo* (Oct. 9, 1930); Jean Giraudoux' *Siegfried* (Oct. 20, 1930); Susan Glaspell's *Alison's House* (Dec. 1, 1930); Alexandre Dumas fils' *Camille* (Jan. 26, 1931); Ferenc Molnar's *Liliom* (Oct. 26, 1932); Eleanor Holmes Hinkley's *Dear Jane* (Nov. 14, 1932); and Eva Le Gallienne and Florida Friebus' adaptation of *Alice in Wonderland* and *Thru the Looking Glass* (Dec. 12, 1932).

The Cleveland Play House, 2040 E. 86th St., Cleveland, OH 44106, tel. (216) 795-7000.
Director: Richard Oberlin; *Associate Director:* Larry Tarrant; *Business Manager:* James Sweeney. *Officers and Trustees: President:* Harold Fallon; *Vice-Presidents:* G. Robert Klein, Mrs. Frederick A. Oldenburg, Joseph E. Adams; *Treasurer:* George D. Kirkham; *Secretary:* Mrs. Frederick A. Oldenburg; *Trustees:* Lewis J. Affelder, Richard T. Baker, Ralph A. Colbert, Mrs. Robert P. Dalton, George Dobrea, Mrs. Robert F. Doolittle, Arthur E. Earley, Chester R. Edwards, C. W. Elliott, Mrs. Alvin B. Fisher, Alvin B. Fisher, Reverend John Frazier, Miss Lillian Gish, Joel Grey, Robert D. Gries, Mrs. Shattuck W. Hartwell, Jr., Miss Helen Hayes, Edward A. Hinkle, William M. Jones, Mrs. Jack W. Kelly, Jack W. Lampl, Jr., David F. Leahy, Leonard B. Lebby, Mrs. Gordon Long, Harvey O. Mierkee, Jr., Max Muller, Mrs. David W. Murray, Jr., George Oliva, Jr., William A. Polster, H. Chapman Rose, Frederic H. Roth, Mrs. Thomas H. Roulston, Mrs. Victor J. Scaravilli, Leland Schubert, David L. Stashower, Mrs. Marc A. Wyse.

Charles S. Brooks, the first president of the Cleveland Play House, recalled in a history of the organization that the idea of establishing the Play House was first discussed in the early fall of 1914. Shortly thereafter, informal Sunday evening programs were being presented.

In 1917, title was taken to a church building. A stage was constructed in the altar area, and seating was available for approximately 200. Through this period, Raymond O'Neil was the theatre's director. In 1921, Mr. O'Neil resigned and Frederic McConnell became the director, bringing with him K. Elmo Lowe and Max Eisenstat. Under this directorship the Play House was transformed from a little theatre to the institution it has become. The theatre was enlarged, the repertory and the number of performances were increased, and the entire scope of the Cleveland Play House broadened.

In 1926, the 86th Street Theatre was built. Francis E. Drury and his wife purchased the property for the Play House, and money was raised to erect the theatre. The new building was formally dedicated April 9, 1927, but it had been used for rehearsal, meetings, and informal programs since early that year. The Play House Summer Theatre, Chautauqua, N.Y., was inaugurated in 1929.

Mr. McConnell retired in 1958 and was succeeded by K. Elmo Lowe, who held the reins of the theatre until 1969. He was succeeded by the late William Greene. Rex Partington was named managing director in 1970 and was followed by Richard Oberlin in 1971. Mr. Oberlin was named director in the following year.

In 1972, the Ford Foundation gave the Play House a $225,000 cash reserve grant, a challenge grant, contingent on the Play House's balancing its budget over a four-year period. The Play House has successfully met this challenge grant to date. The theatre also receives funding from the National Endowment for the Arts, Ohio Arts Council, Cleveland Foundation, the Martha Holden Jennings Foundation, many local foundations, and individual contributors.

Today, the Cleveland Play House maintains three stages: the Francis E. Drury Theatre, and the Charles S. Brooks Theatre at the East 86th St. address, both proscenium stages, and the Euclid-77th St. Theatre, which also houses a private dining room and bar, the Play House Club. The Play House has a salaried company and staff of 85, enjoys appearances by distinguished artists and the services of guest directors, and maintains a student festival and matinee program, a youth theatre, taught by professionals, an artist-in-the-classroom program—The Play House Comes to School—and a nontuition apprentice training program.

By the end of its 1974-75 season of thirteen productions, the Cleveland Play House had presented 1,253 productions during the fifty-nine consecutive seasons of its lifetime. Sixty-six of the plays were world or American premieres. Among them are Sacha Guitry's *The Illusionist* (1928) and *The Fall of Bergop-Zoom* (1929), Elmer Rice's *Not for Children* (1936), Tennessee Williams and William Windham's *You Touched Me* (1943), Maxwell Anderson's *Eve of St. Mark* (1943), Maurice Valency's *The Thracian Horses* (1944), Thomas Hill and Alan Alda's *Job* (1958), Jon Jory's *Tipsy Rebellion* (1959), William Paterson's *A Profile of Benjamin Franklin* and his *A Profile of Holmes* (both 1966), Thomas Cullinan's *Mrs. Lincoln* (1968), Donald Freed's *The United States vs. Julius & Ethel Rosenberg* (1968), Peter Coe's *Woman in the Dunes* (1971), Christopher Fry's *A Yard of Sun* (1972), David Williamson's *The Removalists* (1973), and Kevin O'Morrison's *The Morgan Yard* (1973).

Dallas Theater Center, 3436 Turtle Creek Blvd., Dallas, TX 75216, tel. (214) 526-0107.
Chairman Emeritus: Paul M. Raigorodsky; *Chairman of the Board:* Waldo E. Stewart; *President:* Charles J. Wyly, Jr.; *Chairman, Executive Committee:* Richard C. Marcus; *Vice-Chairman, Executive Committee:* Alan M. May; *Vice-Presidents:* Mrs. Morris Harrell, Dr. Charles Hunter, Erle Rawlins, III, Jack Wahlquist; *Secretary:* Donald J. Malouf; *Assistant Secretary:* V. Bryan Medlock, Jr.; *Treasurer:* Dan W. Cook, III; *Managing Director:* Paul Baker.

The Dallas Theater Center was built in 1959 by Dallas citizens under the leadership of Robert D. Stecker, Sr., and Beatrice Handel to house a resident professional theatre group. It is sustained by its patrons and a committed board of directors led through the years by such people as Paul M. Raigorodsky and Waldo E. Stewart.

The center, which in 1973 was presented as a gift by its board of directors to the City of Dallas, is the only public theatre designed by American architect Frank Lloyd Wright, and houses the 416-seat Kalita Humphreys Theater and the 56-seat Down Center Stage.

Paul Baker, the Center's founding director, has staged such productions as *Hamlet, Hamlet, ESP, Macbeth, Of Time and the River, Journey to Jefferson* and *Jack Ruby, All-American Boy.* The production of *Journey to Jefferson* won the Jury Prize at the Theatre of Nations Festival in Paris in 1964, and the Margo Jones Award was presented to Mr. Baker in 1968 in recognition of the Center's "daring and continuous new play production" (over sixty-five world or American premieres have been staged). The center's full-time resident company is augmented by an experienced group of professional journeymen and apprentices who are working toward M.F.A. degrees through Trinity University, San Antonio, Texas.

The theatre center also operates a large and active teen-children's theatre program, produces a series of plays for children, and is active in numerous community affairs projects.

Drama Desk, c/o Tom McMorrow, New York *Daily News,* 220 E. 42d St., New York, NY 10017, MU 2-1234.
President: Tom McMorrow; *Vice-President:* Debbi Wasserman; *Treasurer:* Tony Clark; *Secretary:* Lillian Africano.

The Drama Desk, founded in 1949 as an association of writers on the legitimate theatre, is a chartered nonprofit corporation operating under by-laws ratified Nov. 4, 1974. Membership includes critics, reporters, editors, writers, and commentators in all media on the New York theatre.

Monthly luncheon meetings are held at Rosoff's 1899 Theatre Restaurant on West 43rd Street, and actors, directors, producers, playwrights, designers and others working in the theater are invited to talk to and with the members.

The Dramatists Guild, Inc., 234 W. 44th St., NY 10036, tel. (212) 563-2233.
President: Stephen Sondheim; *Vice-President:* Richard Lewine; *Secretary:* Sheldon Harnick; *Treasurer:* Dore Schary; *Executive Director:* David E. LeVine, Esq.

The following data is based on a Dramatists Guild booklet *The Dramatists Guild,* by George Middleton and also on Mr. Middleton's personal records.

The Dramatists Guild was born out of earlier organizations and attempts to secure just dealings for the playwright. In 1878, Steele MacKay and Clay M. Greene organized the American Dramatic Authors' Society "to secure protection of their work." In 1891, 33 dramatists came together under the leadership of Bronson Howard in the Society of American Dramatists and Composers. The latter was primarily a social group, but it endeavored to represent the dramatist in business dealings.

The Authors League of America, Inc., which held its initial organizational meeting December 27, 1911, included playwrights among its members. The constitution and by-laws of the Authors League was adopted December 13, 1912. On April 8, 1913, Winston Churchill, the American novelist, was elected first president and Theodore Roosevelt, vice-president. There were only three playwrights on ALA's Council, and none were members of the Executive Committee. A dramatic subcommittee was appointed in 1914 to work "towards the standardization of a dramatic contract" between playwrights and producers. Members of this committee included Bayard Veiller, Harvey O'Higgins, Edwin Milton Royle, Edgar Selwyn, and George Middleton.

"In 1915, a proposed contract was the first feeble effort to stake out the ill-defined rights of the League's dramatist members. In 1917, another 'Standard Contract' was drawn up, but likewise died a-borning. This was reworked in 1920, yet its use was not mandatory and its terms were not enforceable to abolish the many trade abuses which had accumulated."

As a result of the Actors' Equity strike for recognition in 1919, the Executive Committee of the Authors League granted Channing Pollock's suggestion that Dramatists form "an autonomous committee." Thirty-two "working dramatists" joined and a "Dramatists Committee" of 112 was created. Out of this, the Dramatists Guild, as now known, was born. The League became "a sort of holding company or federation of Guilds." Owen Davis became the first Dramatists Guild President.

"The pocket nerve of every dramatist was touched when a secret deal was discovered, in 1925, whereby Fox Films was contracting with seven Broadway theatrical managers to back plays, take half the profits and obtain all film rights without competitive bidding.

"The Dramatists Guild officers then were Arthur Richman, President; Otto Harbach, Vice-President; Percival Wilde, Secretary; Harry E. Smith, Treasurer; and George Middleton, Chairman of Board. They decided aggressive action was necessary. Thirty leading playwrights met secretly on Dec. 7, 1925, formed a committee to report what drastic moves should be deemed advisable to protect their rights. Channing Pollock became Chairman, with Cosmo Hamilton, George Kelly, Roi Cooper Magrue, A. E. Thomas, Rita Weiman, and George Middleton. Each of the 30 agreed to be bound by the report, to be prepared for submission to managers, and to forfeit to the group $1,000 as 'liquidated damages' in event of breach.

"On Jan. 7, 1926, at the Hotel Roosevelt, N.Y., George Kelly read to 121 members, who by then had been signed up, what was the most important manifesto any organized group of playwrights ever made. This was approved without protest. The Committee, appointed to draw up the demands considered imperative, was Rachel Crothers, Eugene O'Neill, John Emerson, Gene Buck, Otto Harbach, George Kelly, George S. Kaufman, Le Roi Clemens, Channing Pollock, Roi Cooper Magrue, J. Hartley Manners, and George Middleton (Chairman).

"On Feb. 2, 1926, at a closed meeting of members, the proposed terms for a Minimum Basic Agreement (M.B.A.) were submitted and unanimously adopted by the original 30, plus many new recruits. Each author pledged to withhold plays, submit no new scripts or undertake any contracts until the producers would sign the proposed enforceable Agreement. These demanded and were granted a conference. A joint-meeting was held on Mar. 11, 1926, at which every manager listed agreed to be bound to any result finally worked out. The two groups named their confreres (which were augmented from time to time): For Guild: Arthur Richman, Chairman; J. Hartley Manners, Roi Cooper Magrue, Owen Davis, James Forbes, Otto Harbach, Gene Buck, John Emerson, Channing Pollock, Marc Connelly, and George Middleton (Secretary); for managers: Wm. A. Brady, Chairman; Lee Shubert, Sam Harris, Arthur Hammerstein, Joseph P. Bickerton, Edgar Selwyn, Brock Pemberton, Warren Munsell, and Laurence Weber.

"They met daily for weeks. With few exceptions, most managers saw justice in many of the authors' claims. The Guild would not yield its control of the copyright, nor permit unauthorized changes in any script. It insisted on 'open competitive bidding' for the film rights in plays by removing the sale from existing managerial control. It demanded a floor on royalties, below which a manager could never go; which thus protected every first play author. It imposed no ceiling, however, on those who could demand higher terms.

"Most vital, to make the Agreement enforceable: no Guild member could enter into any contract with any manager who had *not* signed the Basic Agreement; no manager, who had signed, could enter into any contract with any playwright *not* a Guild member. It was thus open to all managers and all dramatists who accepted and observed the agreed-upon terms and conditions. But no restrictions were placed on any production where neither manager nor author was signatory to the Agreement, nor was any effort made to control the theatres where any such plays might be produced. After five months of intense activity, during which all scripts were withheld from the market, the Five-Year M.B.A. was signed on Apr. 27, 1926, and business was efficiently resumed—more or less happily.

"As one outstanding firm of managers did not sign the M.B.A., though it had been pledged to do so, the question of its possible tie-up (through long options and lower terms) with British Authors and their scripts became vital. The Chairman of Board, then George Middleton, went secretly to London, with President Richman as confidant, and arranged to address the British Authors' Society at an open meeting on June 16, 1927. The objects of the Guild and Basic Agreement were explained. Cooperation was asked—and given.

"Among those contacted who signed up were: Major Ian Hay Beith, Sir Arthur Pinero, Sir James Barrie, Arnold Bennett, St. John Ervine, John Drinkwater, Frederick Lonsdale, Harley Granville-Barker, W. J. Locke, A. A. Milne, Henry Arthur Jones, Clemence Dane, John Masefield, and George Bernard Shaw. Noel Coward, Somerset Maugham, Michael Arlen, Ashley Dukes, and John Galsworthy had previously signed."

George Middleton became Guild President in October 1927. He did much to establish and strengthen relations with authors' societies throughout Europe.

As of October 1964, The Dramatists Guild, Inc., began to function as a separate corporation. Formerly the Dramatists Guild and the Authors Guild were divisions of the Authors League of America, Inc., and all members paid dues to the League. Now, both Authors and Dramatists guilds are incorporated (and the League continues to be). The guilds will continue to operate as blood brothers within the League, but they will control their own finances.

The minimum basic agreement was revised in 1931, 1936, 1941, 1946, 1955, and 1961. Because of the economic conditions in the theatre, related complications due to the rising costs of stage production, and certain legal questions which had arisen since the expiration of the 1941 agreement, a new basic agreement was negotiated and became effective on June 14, 1955.

Since July 23, 1928, the Guild has had an agreement with the Society of Authors Representatives, Inc. This agreement defines the author-agent relationship and obligations.

The Guild serves the playwright as advisor, watchdog, bill collector, and bonding agent. With the Authors League, the Guild attempts to promote legislation designed to strengthen the copyright protection of literary and artistic works, both nationally and internationally. They are also engaged in a campaign for revision of the income tax laws to meet the problems peculiar to authors.

In 1936, at the suggestion of the late Sidney Howard, then President of the Dramatists Guild, the Dramatists Play Service was formed to correct abuses and protect the author's rights in the amateur market. The Play Service has an autonomous board of directors composed of playwrights and participating agents. It is an agency to which dramatists entrust the handling of the non-professional (amateur) acting rights of their plays and the publication of acting versions of them.

Equity Library Theatre, 165 W. 46th St., New York, NY 10036, tel. (212) PL 7-1710 *Directors:* Robin Craven, ***President:*** Paul Austin, Edmund Gaynes, Earle Hyman, David Leary, Alan Manson, Natalie Priest, Dorothy Sands.

Equity Library Theatre (ELT), sponsored by Actors' Equity Association, is a professional showcase providing free theatre to the entire New York City metropolitan area. It was founded in 1943 by actor Sam Jaffe, representing Equity, and George Freedley, then curator of the NY Public Library Theatre Collection, for the twofold purpose of giving actors a chance to practice their art, thereby maintaining their professional skills, and to create new theatre audiences by developing a love of the theatre among people who cannot afford to attend commercial offerings.

Early productions were put on in New York public libraries for professional and neighborhood audiences. ELT was incorporated as a nonprofit organization in 1949 and moved into its own theatre, the Lenox Hill Playhouse, East 70th Street. In 1961, ELT moved to the Master Theater, Riverside Drive, where during each October-to-May season it presents eight revivals—four plays and four musicals. In addition, six experimental workshop productions—so-called ELT Informals—original works, dramatizations of published materials not originally intended for the stage, and new theatrical forms—are presented at the Library and Museum of the Performing Arts, Lincoln Center. Each production has a different cast, director, and crew, all of whom are volunteers.

ELT gives all performers, whether with or without previous experience, a chance to display their talents to proven audiences of producers, agents, directors, and others in casting positions, and nearly two-thirds of the artists appearing in ELT productions have obtained employment as a direct result of this participation. Artists who have been aided in their careers through appearing in ELT shows include Charlton Heston, James Earl Jones, Richard Kiley, Jason Robards, Jr., Kim Stanley, Rod Steiger, and Jo Van Fleet. ELT is also valuable as a training ground for potential theatrical professionals, and it has been helpful in placing many of its volunteer technicians through an informal placement service.

There is no admission charge to ELT shows, but some contributions are made at performances. In addition, approximately 550 patrons make donations. These include individuals and the Charlepeg, JJC, Rodgers and Hammerstein, Scherman, and Shubert Foundations, and the John Golden Fund. Equity supplies 12 percent of ELT financing, and the NY State Council on the Arts and the National Endowment for the Arts both provide generous support.

ELT reaches out to a wide community through distribution of free tickets to many organizations serving minority groups, youth, the aged, the hospitalized and handicapped. It also cooperates with various schools and colleges in New York and nearby states in theatre education programs.

Eugene O'Neill Memorial Theater Center, Inc., 305 Great Neck Rd., Waterford, CT 06385, tel. (203) 443-5378; 1860 Broadway, New York, NY 10023, tel. (212) 264-1485.

President: George C. White; *Vice-President:* David Hays; *Executive Vice-President:* George Thorn; *Treasurer:* Peter Van Slyck; *Corporate Secretary:* Francis J. Pavetti.

The O'Neill Theater was established by George C. White in 1964. It is located on an eight-acre site at Waterford, Conn., near New London, overlooking Long Island Sound, and the museum and library of the theatre center are in Monte Cristo Cottage, the former home of James O'Neill, actor and father of Eugene O'Neill.

Projects conducted by the theatre center include the National Playwrights Conference, established in 1965. Under the artistic direction of Lloyd Richards since 1968, the conference runs four weeks each summer, during which between twelve and twenty new plays are given staged readings by professional actors. Emphasis is on talented new playwrights and the development of new approaches and new techniques by established playwrights. Readings and stagings are supplemented by evaluation and discussion among the playwrights and theatre professionals.

The National Critics Institute, running concurrently with the conference, was established in 1968 and is directed by Ernest Schier. Its purpose is to help professional critics explore the performing arts and to expand their skills in theatre, film, and dance criticism.

The National Theatre of the Deaf, founded in 1966 by designer and director David Hays, uses deaf actors trained to communicate with facial expression and the use of the body as well as with sign language and vocal expression, in which all members of the company have varying degrees of capability. The company has made several coast-to-coast tours, appeared twice on Broadway, and toured in western Europe, Yugoslavia, and Israel.

The National Theatre Institute, directed by Larry Arrick, is an experimental laboratory in theatre arts training, comprising ten weeks of intensive workshop sessions, three weeks of rehearsal, and a two-week bus and truck tour to college, university, high school, and community theatres throughout northeastern United States.

The Center's Creative Arts in Education program brings professional performing, visual, and literary artists into school systems for direct involvement with students and teachers, and the American Theatre Treasury is the Center's video-tape archive of theatre history.

Folger Theatre Group, 201 East Capitol St., SE, Washington, DC 20003, tel. (202) 546-4000.
Producer: Louis W. Scheeder; *General Manager:* Larry Verbit; *Company Manager:* Mary Ann DeBarbieri; *Public Relations Director:* Pat Bailey; *Technical Director:* Thom Shovestull; *Production Stage Manager:* David M. Levine.

The Folger Theatre Group is a division of the Folger Shakespeare Library, O.B. Hardison, Jr., director. The Library was founded in May 1930 and named after Henry Clay Folger, former president of the Standard Oil Company in New York. Mr. Folger spent nearly 50 years assembling a collection of rare books and manuscripts relating to Shakespeare, including 79 first folios. The Library now houses the largest collection of Shakespearean materials in the United States, and no other library in the world has a collection of Shakespeare's works larger than in the Folger.

The Theatre Group was founded in 1970 by Dr. Hardison and Richmond Crinkley. It is dedicated to the presentation of new plays and innovative productions of the work of Shakespeare. Housed in a replica Elizabethan theatre inside the Folger Library, the group now presents a five-play season October through June. In addition to Shakespeare's plays, the Folger Theatre Group has presented five premiere productions and seven American premieres over the past six years.

Among the American premieres, *Creeps* by David Freeman and *Medal of Honor Rag* by Tom Cole were transferred to New York. *Creeps* was selected as one of the ten best plays of the 1973-74 season, and *Medal of Honor Rag* is still playing as of this writing (Apr. 6, 1976.)

Other American premieres include Christopher Hampton's *Total Eclipse* (1972); John Harvey Flint's *Edward G., Like the Film Star* (1973); David Storey's *The Farm* (1974); Michael Ondaatje's *The Collected Works of Billy the Kid;* and a play by Ben Jonson never before done in the United States, *Bartholomew Fair* (1973).

Premiere productions include Percy Granger's *The Complete Works of Studs Edsel* (1972); a musical adaptation of Shakespeare's *Love's Labour's Lost* (1974); G. Tito Shaw's *He's Got a Jones* (1975); Michael Menaugh's *Natural and Unnatural Acts;* and *Dionysus Wants You* by Richmond Crinkley.

The group has done eight Shakespearean productions in addition to the adaptation of *Love's Labour's Lost,* including: *Romeo and Juliet* (1972); *Henry IV, Part 1* (1974); *The Tempest* (1975); *All's Well That Ends Well; Henry V; The Comedy of Errors; The Winter's Tale;* and *Twelfth Night.* Other productions include *Landscape* and *Silence* (1971); *The Revenger's Tragedy* (1971); *Subject to Fits* (1972); *The Inspector General* (1974); *The Promise;* and *Happy Days.*

Free Southern Theater, 1328 Dryades St., New Orleans, LA 70113, tel. (office) (504) 581-5091; (theatre) (504) 581-5114.
Producing Director: John O'Neal; *Associate Producer:* Bill Rouselle; *Artistic Director:* Earl Billings; *Technical Director:* Ben Spillman; *Administrative Assistant:* Charlene Mays; *Community Relations Director:* Jesse Morrell; *Production Stage Manager:* Chakula Cha Jua. *Board of Directors:* Robert Aulston, John Britton, Juggy Butler, Maxine Copelin, Dave Dennis, Carol Feinman, Al Gourrier, Ernest Jones, Gilbert Moses, Alden McDonald, John O'Neal, Robert Perkins, Isaac Reynolds, Milton Upton, Roxy Wright, Wallace Young.

Gilbert Moses and John O'Neal founded the Free Southern Theater (FST) at Tougaloo College, near Jackson, Miss., in 1963; two years later FST moved to New Orleans. The purpose of the organization was, and is, to support the struggle for human rights among black people, to promote black consciousness, and to educate black people in rural areas and in city ghettos. It does this by presenting plays aimed primarily at working-class audiences, who attend performances of either the small resident company in New Orleans or its touring companies throughout the Southern states. FST is a nonprofit tax-exempt organization operating with an annual budget of approximately $230,000. It has received grants from the Rockefeller and Ford foundations, the National Endowment for the Arts, and the City of New Orleans.

Among works produced by FST are Ron Milner's *The Warning—A Theme for Linda;* Roger Furman's *To Kill a Devil,* Sharon Stockard Martin's *Edifying Further Elaborations on the Mentality of a Chore,* Lorraine Hansberry's *A Raisin in the Sun,* FST Writers Workshop's *We Are the Suns,* Chakula Cha Jua and Leppaine Chiphe's *A Black Experience,* John O'Neal's *The Hurricane Season,* Kenneth Odom's *The Curing Melon,* and John O'Neal's *When the Opportunity Scratches, Itch It.*

Goodman Theatre Center of the Art Institute of Chicago, 200 S. Columbus Drive, Chicago, IL 60603, tel. (312) 443-3811.
Artistic Director: William Woodman; *Managing Director:* John Economos. For the Art Institute of Chicago—*Chairman:* James W. Alsdorf; *President:* E. Laurence Chalmers, Jr.; Committee on Goodman Theatre, *Chairman:* Stanley M. Freehling.

Goodman Theatre Center was founded in 1925 as a memorial gift to The Art Institute of Chicago from the family of a promising poet-playwright, Kenneth Sawyer Goodman. Fifty years old in 1975, Goodman Theatre Center is the second oldest continuing regional theatre in the nation. Designed by Howard Van Doren Shaw, it was literally the nation's first "underground" theatre—a city ordinance prohibited buildings of more than one story along what was then Chicago's lake shore, so with the exception of the box office and business office, the physical plant is all below ground level.

A totally self-contained producing unit, the theatre maintains its own shops for costume and set design and construction, as well as electronic shops and property storage. The main proscenium auditorium, seating 683 in a continental arrangement, has handsome wood-paneled walls and an Izenour electronic pre-set lighting system.

Always conceived as a resident professional theatre, the Goodman ran from 1925 to 1930 with a company of actors. In 1930, the depression caught up with the arts, and in the absence of an endowment the Art Institute converted the theatre into a drama school. In 1969 Goodman was re-established as a professional theatre. Each play in the six-play subscription season is individually cast and designed, drawing from the nationwide talent pool.

In 1973, William Woodman became Goodman's first new artistic director in seventeen years. Under his guidance in 1974, Goodman launched its Stage 2 series devoted to professional productions of experimental works and works-in-progress.

The Group Theatre.

The Group Theatre began as a studio group of the Theatre Guild. Its first production was Paul Green's *The House of Connelly,* which opened Sept. 23, 1931, in New York City. An announcement of the organization had defined the Group Theatre as "an organization of actors and directors formed with the ultimate aim of creating a permanent acting company to maintain regular New York seasons."

The final production under Group Theatre auspices was Irwin Shaw's *Retreat to Pleasure,* which opened Dec. 17, 1940. In that decade, however, the Group Theatre had produced plays by Clifford Odets, Irwin Shaw, Paul Green, John Howard Lawson, Marc Blitzstein, Sidney Kingsley, Maxwell Anderson and Robert Ardrey. The casts of these productions had included Luther Adler, Stella Adler, Sanford Meisner, Clifford Odets, Art Smith, J. Edward Bromberg, Morris Carnovsky, John Garfield, Phoebe Brand, Frances Farmer, Sylvia Sidney, and Franchot Tone. Such directors and/or producers as Harold Clurman, Cheryl Crawford, Lee Strasberg, and Erwin Piscator had worked with the group.

An account of the excitement that the Group Theatre provided the American theatre during its history appears in Harold Clurman's book *The Fervent Years.*

Group Theatre productions included Paul Green's *The House of Connelly* (Martin Beck Th., Sept. 28, 1931); Claire and Paul Sifton's *1931* (Mansfield, Dec. 10, 1931); Maxwell Anderson's *Night Over Taos* (48th St. Th., Mar. 9, 1932); John Howard Lawson's *Success Story* (Maxine Elliott's Th., Sept. 26, 1932); Dawn Powell's *Big Night* (Maxine Elliott's Th., Jan. 17, 1933); Sidney Kingsley's *Men in White* (Broadhurst, Sept. 26, 1933); John Howard Lawson's *Gentlewomen* (Cort, Mar. 22, 1934); Melvin Levy's *Gold Eagle Guy* (Morosco, Nov. 28, 1934); Clifford Odets' *Awake and Sing!* (Belasco, Feb. 19, 1935); Clifford Odets' *Till the Day I Die* and *Waiting for Lefty* (Longacre, Mar. 26, 1935); a revival of Clifford Odets' *Awake and Sing!* and *Waiting for Lefty* (Belasco, Sept. 9, 1935); Nellise Child's *Weep for the Virgins* (46th St. Th., Nov. 30, 1935); Clifford Odets' *Paradise Lost* (Longacre, Dec. 9, 1935); Erwin Piscator and Lena Goldschmidt's *The Case of Clyde Griffiths* (Ethel Barrymore Th., Mar. 13, 1936); Paul Green's *Johnny Johnson* (44th St. Th., Nov. 19, 1936); Clifford Odets' *Golden Boy* (Belasco, Nov. 4, 1937); Robert Ardrey's *Casey Jones* (Fulton, Feb. 19, 1938); Clifford Odets' *Rocket to the Moon* (Belasco, Nov. 24, 1938); Irwin Shaw's *The Gentle People* (Belasco, Jan. 5, 1939); a revival of Clifford Odets' *Awake and Sing!* (Windsor, Mar. 7, 1939); William Saroyan's *My Heart's in the Highlands* (Guild, Apr. 13, 1939); Irwin Shaw's *Quiet City* (Belasco, Apr. 16, 1939; Robert Ardrey's *Thunder Rock* (Mansfield, Nov. 14, 1939); Clifford Odets' *Night Music* (Broadhurst, Feb. 22, 1940); and Irwin Shaw's *Retreat to Pleasure* (Belasco, Dec. 17, 1940).

The Guthrie Theater Foundation, The Guthrie Theater, Vineland Place, Minneapolis, MN 55403, tel. (612) 377-2824.

Chairman of the Board: Mrs. Edward C. Brown, Jr.; *President:* James H. Binger; *Vice-President:* Robert J. Dayton; *Executive Vice-President for Artistic Affairs:* Michael Langham; *Executive Vice-President for Operations:* Donald Schoenbaum; *Vice-President:* Wesley O. Brustad; *Treasurer:* Bruce K. MacLaury; *Secretary:* Mrs. Thomas J. Morison; *Artistic Director:* Michael Langham; *Managing Director:* Donald Schoenbaum; *Resources Development and Extension Director:* Wesley O. Brustad; *Associate Directors:* Len Cariou, David Feldshuh, Eugene Lion; *Literary Manager:* Barbara Field Nosanow.

As early as 1959, while working together on the musical *Juno,* Oliver Rea and Peter Zeisler began talking about establishing a permanent repertory company outside of New York City. They discussed the idea with Tyrone Guthrie, who had recently set up the Shakespeare Festival in Stratford, Ontario, Canada. These three then canvassed the United States for the proper site and eventually settled upon Minneapolis and St. Paul, Minnesota's Twin Cities.

The Walker Art Center of Minneapolis welcomed the proposal with a $400,000 grant and a tract of land upon which the theatre could be erected. The Minnesota Theatre Company was established "to develop a permanent resident repertory theatre company presenting four or more plays in repertory each summer season from May through September at the highest possible level of artistic excellence."

Under this organization, the Tyrone Guthrie Theater Foundation was set up "to provide an attractive, efficient new theatre suitable for use by the theatre company during the summer season and by the Walker Art Center and other performing arts groups during the winter season."

The Guthrie building initially had an open framework surround (removed in 1974) enclosing a glass front, making interior lobby areas visible from the outside. The auditorium seats 1,437 in a 200-degree arc around an asymmetrical thrust stage designed by Guthrie and his principal designer, Tanya Moiseiwitsch. No seat is more than 52 feet from stage center. The stage, about 32 by 35 feet and three steps above floor level, is surrounded by a floor-level strip of additional acting area and can be plugged to transform its steps to stage level space when necessary. The stage can be trapped in any location and is served by full upstage entrance areas as well as two ramps at downstage corners leading beneath the audience.

Mr. Guthrie died in 1971 and was succeeded as artistic director by Michael Langham who had directed at Stratford-upon-Avon, England; Stratford, Ontario, Canada; and other leading theatres in North America and in Europe. Donald Schoenbaum had become managing director in 1970. Under the leadership of Mr. Langham and Mr. Schoenbaum, the Guthrie began expanding activities to include an enlarged season of plays on the main stage of the theatre, a more extensive touring program to bring plays and theatre activities and speakers to all parts of the Upper Midwest, and the establishment of a second theatre to be known as the Guthrie 2 for the presentation of new theatre works and methods and alternative theatre forms that are out of place on the main stage of the Guthrie Theater. In addition, the Guthrie will continue its twice-weekly series of prose and dramatic readings presented free before matinee performances. The Guthrie is also beginning to explore further possibilities of working in such important areas as prisons and old-age homes.

Several extensive midwest tours have taken the Guthrie acting company before audiences that rarely see live performances. People in these outlying areas are joining local arts councils dedicated to making future tours of the Guthrie and other organizations possible. Not only has the Guthrie fulfilled its founders' aim of establishing a first-class professional theatre far removed from Broadway, but it has introduced professional theatre into the life experience of people in the most rural areas.

The Guthrie's main stage operates on a rotating repertory system, presenting at least two, most often three, and sometimes as many as four or five plays on as many nights. The season has traditionally run from early summer to the following winter, although this is being lengthened.

The theatre opened May 7, 1963, with William Shakespeare's *Hamlet.* A listing by year of productions that followed includes: (1963-64) Molière's *The Miser,* Anton Chekhov's *The Three Sisters,* and Arthur Miller's *Death of a Salesman;* (1964-65) William Shakespeare's *Henry V,* George Bernard Shaw's *Saint Joan,* Tennessee Williams' *The Glass Menagerie,* and Ben Jonson's *Volpone;* (1965-66) William Shakespeare's *Richard III,* William Congreve's *The Way of the World,* Anton Chekhov's *The Cherry Orchard,* Bertolt Brecht's *The Caucasian Chalk Circle,* and Molière's *The Miser;* (1966-67) Thornton Wilder's *The Skin of Our Teeth,* August Strindberg's *The Dance of Death,* William Shakespeare's *As You Like It,* George Bernard Shaw's *The Doctor's Dilemma,* and Eugene O'Neill's *S. S. Glencairn;* (1967-68) Thomas Dekker's *The Shoemaker's Holiday,* Jean Anouilh's *Thieves' Carnival,* Barrie Stavis's *Harpers Ferry,* John Lewin's *The House of Atreus,* and Friedrich Duerrenmatt's *The Visit;* (1968-69) William Shakespeare's *Twelfth Night,* John Arden's *Serjeant Musgrave's Dance,* Henrik Ibsen's *The Master Builder,* Bertolt Brecht's *The Resistible Rise of Arturo Vi,* George F. Kaufman and Marc Connelly's *Merton of the Movies,* and *The House of Atreus;* (1969-70) William Shakespeare's *Julius Caesar,* S. J. Perelman's *The Beauty Part,* Harold Pinter's *The Homecoming,* Eugene O'Neill's *Mourning Becomes Electra,* and Anton Chekhov's *Uncle Vanya;* (1970-71) Carlo Goldoni's *The Venetian Twins,* Lonne Elder's *Ceremonies in Dark Old Men,* William Shakespeare's *The Tempest,* Bertolt Brecht's *A Man's a Man,* and Paul Avila Mayer's adaptation, *A Play by Aleksandr Solzhenitsyn;* (1971-72) Edmond Rostand's *Cyrano de Bergerac,* William Shakespeare's *The Taming of the Shrew,* George Bernard Shaw's *Misalliance,* Eugene O'Neill's *A Touch of the Poet,* Alexander Ostrovsky's *The Diary of a Scoundrel,* and *Fables Here and Then;* (1972-73) William Shakespeare's *A Midsummer Night's Dream,* John Steinbeck's *Of Mice and Men,* John Vanbrugh's *The Relapse,* Eugene Labiche and Marc-Michel's *An Italian Straw Hat,* Sophocles' *Oedipus the King,* translated by Anthony Burgess, and Anthony Burgess and Michael Lewis's musical *Cyrano;* (1973-74) Jean Anouilh's *Becket,* Sophocles' *Oedipus the King,* Nikolai Gogol's *The Government Inspector,* Sean O'Casey's *Juno and the Paycock,* June Havoc's *I, Said the Fly,* Samuel Beckett's *Waiting for Godot,* and

William Shakespeare's *The Merchant of Venice;* (1974-75) William Shakespeare's *King Lear* and *Love's Labour's Lost,* Arthur Miller's *The Crucible,* Molière's *Tartuffe,* Richard Brinsley Sheridan's *The School for Scandal,* and *Everyman;* (1975-76) Joseph Kesselring's *Arsenic and Old Lace,* Harold Pinter's *The Caretaker,* Tennessee Williams' *A Streetcar Named Desire,* Joe Orton's *Loot,* Dylan Thomas' *Under Milk Wood,* Noel Coward's *Private Lives,* Bertolt Brecht's *Mother Courage and Her Children,* Charles Dickens' *A Christmas Carol* (adapted by Barbara Nosanow), and William Shakespeare's *Measure for Measure.*

Herbert Berghof Studio, 120 Bank St., New York, NY 10014, tel. (212) OR 5-2370.

The Herbert Berghof (HB) Studio came into being in 1945, and its career has been directed, in the main, by Herbert Berghof and Uta Hagen.

A pamphlet published by the studio announces, "Conceived as an artistic and working home, it offers an outlet for practice and growth for the professional theatre artists, and an opportunity for the young to establish roots in their intended craft."

The Herbert Berghof Studio offers courses in acting techniques, speech and voice, directing, movement, costume and make-up, and playwriting. There is also a series of young people's classes.

Institute for Advanced Studies in the Theatre Arts, 310 W. 56th St., New York, NY 10019, tel. (212) 581-3133.
President and Treasurer: John D. Mitchell; *Vice-President and Secretary:* Miriam P. Mitchell; *Administrative Vice-President:* Mary W. John. *Chairman, Board of Trustees:* John F. Wharton; *Board of Trustees:* Robert Epstein, Rosamond Gilder, John D. Mitchell, Reta Shacknove Schwartz; *Music Director:* Raymond Hargrave; *Executive Secretary:* Gilbert Lee Forman; *Business Manager:* C. George Willard.

In 1958, the Institute for Advanced Studies in the Theatre Arts (IASTA) was chartered by the Board of Regents of the University of the State of New York. It was founded by Dr. and Mrs. John D. Mitchell in the belief that American actors and directors could benefit their own stage art by practical study of the theatre of other countries. To this end a program was launched whereby theatre specialists from different countries are brought over to work with American professional actors for a period of four to ten weeks at a time. The actors are selected by audition and each director takes his cast through a translated version of a play, which is explained and analyzed, while the actors learn, rehearse, and finally perform before an invited audience. Among those who have been enrolled in IASTA are over seventy actors who have worked with two or more of the visiting directors; some have worked with as many as nine.

In the course of its work, IASTA has commissioned eleven translations of international classics. Several of these have already been published, and *White Snake* is now available from David R. Godine, Boston, in *The Red Pear Garden* collection.

Leading directors from foreign countries are invited for six-week terms to direct a play in their theatrical tradition. These productions have included such plays as Friedrich Schiller's *Love and Intrigue,* directed by Willi Schmidt; Molière's *The Misanthrope,* directed by Jacques Charon; Anton Chekhov's *The Cherry Orchard,* direcled by Yuri Zavadski; Hanjuro's *Narukami,* directed by Onoe Baiko; William Congreve's *The Way of the World,* directed by George Devine; Sophocles' *Electra,* directed by Dimitrios Rondiris; in association with A. C. Scott, *The Butterfly Dream,* directed by Hu Hung-Yen and Hu Yung-Fang; Gozzi's *The Green Bird,* directed by Giovanni Poli; Stanislaw Wyspianski's *The Wedding,* directed by Erwin Axer; Lope de Vega's *The Knight from Olmedo,* directed by Jose Tamayo; Bertolt Brecht's *The Good Woman of Setzuan,* directed by Gert Weymann; Pierre Marivaux' *The False Confessions,* directed by Robert Manuel; Bhasa's *The Vision of Vasavadatta,* directed by Mrinalini Sarabhai; Shakespeare's *Macbeth,* directed by John Blatchley; Komparu's *Ikkaku Sennin,* directed by Sadayo Kita; Pédro Calderon's *The Phantom Lady,* directed by Jose Luis Alonso; the medieval drama *Mary of Nijmeghen,* directed by Johan de Meester; Jean-Baptiste Racine's *Phedre,* directed by Paul-Emile Deiber; John Webster's *The Duchess of Malfi,* directed by Desmond O'Donovan; Namiki's *Kanjincho,* directed by Matsumoto Koshiro VII and Nakamura Matagoro II; Eugéne Labiche's *Gladiator's 30 Millions,* directed by Paul-Emile Deiber; Valdivielso's *The House of Fools,* directed by Miguel Narros. Additional IASTA productions include *The Heiress, Juno and the Paycock, Enrico IV, Tartuffe, Antigone,* and *White Snake.* IASTA produced for the Fourth International Arts Festival, Monaco, at the invitation of her SHS Princess Grace, *Do Your Own Thing.* Seven of IASTA's productions have been presented in Washington, D.C., upon the invitation of the Library of Congress. IASTA was awarded a grant from the Rockefeller Foundation in support of its program in world theatre.

International Alliance of Theatrical Stage Employes and Moving Picture Machine Operators of the United States and Canada, 1270 Ave. of the Americas, New York, NY 10020, tel. (212) CI 5-4369.
President: Walter F. Diehl; *General Secretary-Treasurer:* Harold F. Chadwick; *1st Vice-President:* George J. Flaherty; *2nd Vice-President:* A. L. "Pat" Travers; *3rd Vice-President:* Paul G. Robertson; *4th Vice-President:* Edward C. Powell; *5th Vice-President:* Adrian Short, Jr.; *6th Vice-President:* John J. Nolan; *7th Vice-President:* J. E. Johnson; *8th Vice-President:* John J. Ryan; *International Trustees:* James F. Sullivan, James J. Riley, William L. Daniel.

IATSE was organized nationally on July 17, 1893, and internationally on October 1, 1902. It is composed of approximately 950 local unions covering the United States and Canada.

Among the craftsmen in the legitimate theatre belonging to this union are sound technicians, make-up artists and hair stylists, publicists, scenic artists, stage employees, and theatrical wardrobe attendants.

The International Theatre Institute of the United States, Inc. 1860 Broadway, New York, NY 10023, tel. (212) 245-3950.
President: Rosamond Gilder; *Director:* Martha W. Coigney; *Associate Director:* Maurice McClelland; *Assistant Director:* Peggy C. Hansen; *Library Director:* Elizabeth Burdick; *Library Assistant:* Crawford K. Wright; *Board of Directors:* Martha W. Coigney, Eldon Elder, Rosamond Gilder, David E. LeVine, Porter McCray, Harold Prince, Ellen Stewart, George C. White.

The International Theatre Institute was chartered by UNESCO in 1948 "to promote the exchange of knowledge and practice in the theatre arts" throughout the world. Centers are established in sixty countries; there is a central office in UNESCO's Paris headquarters, with Jean Darcante as Secretary General, at 1, rue Miollis, Paris 15, France.

The American Center, the International Theatre Institute of the United States, Inc. (ITI/US), is an independent, tax-exempt service organization. It exists to serve the needs of theatre professionals and to further communication among theatre people around the world. In practice its aims are reflected in special projects and in ongoing programs, such as foreign visitor services, publications, information exchange, library and research, and representation at theatre meetings.

Every year ITI/US receives and plans programs for several hundred foreign theatre people during their visits to the United States and assists American theatre professionals in their plans for foreign travel and study, putting them in touch with their "opposite numbers" throughout the world. Ten times a year, ITI/US publishes *Theatre Notes,* providing current information about nonprofit professional theatre groups traveling abroad or about equivalent groups from other countries coming to the United States. ITI/US has published five issues of *Theatre,* annual surveys of American theatre, and a volume on *Contemporary Stage Design—U.S.A.* It also distributes *International Theatre Information,* published by the Paris office. The U.S. center promotes the attendance of leading theatre experts at international meetings, especially those organized by the ITI: the international congresses, meetings of such ITI special committees as those on music, youth, and the Third World, and so on. The U.S. center is the source of a constant exchange of information among ITI centers and theatre people and it now has an outstanding international theatre library where the latest information on world theatre can be found in the 250 publications received monthly and in a large book collection.

In addition to an ever-increasing "exchange of knowledge and practice," ITI/US has carried forward various special projects, the most recent (1974-75) being the organization of the first American exhibition of scene and costume design, shown at Lincoln Center for the Performing Arts in New York in December 1974, due to be shown at the Third Prague Quadrennial in 1976, and then to tour the United States.

Judson Poets' Theater, 55 Washington Square South, New York, NY 10012, tel. (212) SP 7-0033.
Administrative Director: Rev. Al Carmines.

The Judson Poets' Theater was founded in September 1961 as a program of the Judson Memorial Church. The first organizers were

Al Carmines and Robert Nichols; the first resident director was Lawrence Kornfeld.

The theatre was founded to produce the work of new playwrights in an experimental and communal atmosphere. Its major contributions have been musicals, of which nine have been commercially produced. Works produced by the theatre have received numerous awards including 11 Obies, the Drama Desk Award, and the Vernon Rice Award.

Productions first presented at Judson include George Denison's *Vaudeville Skit* (Aug. 24, 1962); Gertrude Stein's *What Happened* (Sept. 19, 1963); Rosalyn Drexler's *Home Movies* (May 19, 1964); Maria Irene Fornes' *Promenade* (Apr. 8, 1965); Timothy Reynolds' translation of Aristophanes' *Peace* (Nov. 7, 1968); David Epstein's *Wanted* (Sept. 17, 1971); and Gertrude Stein's *Listen to Me*—all of these in collaboration with Mr. Carmines as musicals. Other productions were Sam Shepard's *Red Cross* (Jan. 20, 1966) and Mr. Carmines' *The Journey of Snow White* (Feb. 26, 1971); *Joan* (Nov. 19, 1971); *A Look at the Fifties* (Apr. 14, 1972); and *The Faggot* (Apr. 13, 1973).

The Judson Poets' Theater has presented over 200 works with such directors as Lawrence Kornfeld, Jacques Levy, Remy Charlip, and choreographers Dan Waggoner, Katherine Litz, and Gus Solomons, Jr. The theatre also produces large dramatic and musical oratorios which are open to all participants and often involve casts of 80 to 100 performers.

Kreeger Theater. *See* Arena Stage

La Mama E.T.C. (Experimental Theatre Club), 74A E. 4th St., New York, NY 10003, tel. (212) 254-6468
Executive Director: Ellen Stewart; *Artistic Director:* Wilford Leach.

Miss Stewart organized her first coffeehouse theatre as a showcase for the works of promising new playwrights and opened it in a basement at 312 E. 9th Street on July 27, 1962.

Because of alleged building and zoning violations, she was forced to move to a loft at 82 Second Ave. and subsequently to another hall at 122 Second Ave. During these moves her organization became known as Cafe La Mama—the "Mama" being Miss Stewart. To avoid the harassment of inspectors from numerous city agencies, Cafe La Mama was reorganized as La Mama E.T.C., a private club which sold weekly memberships rather than charging admissions.

At its inception and for a number of years thereafter, the group was supported almost entirely by Miss Stewart from her earnings as a clothing designer. As the company expanded its activities, influence, and reputation around the world, foundations have become generous with their financial support.

An acting company under the direction of Tom O'Horgan was organized in 1964, and it made the first of many European tours the following year. The impact of the La Mama presentations and techniques has been so strong that over twenty La Mama groups have been established in Europe, South America, Australia, and Japan. La Mama opened at its present headquarters at 74A E. 4th Street on Apr. 2, 1969, and the Annex Theatre at 66 E. 4th Street opened on Oct. 18, 1974. There is also a workshop facility nearby on Great Jones Street. The three locations include six performance spaces.

Although the company still presents new plays by aspiring playwrights, since 1970 the emphasis has shifted to the presentation of works by experimental performing groups. Several of these troupes are permanent residents of the La Mama complex.

Since its inception, La Mama E.T.C. has presented well over 300 productions by some 200 playwrights. Among the many playwrights and directors who have been given a public hearing and a push by Miss Stewart are: Paul Foster, Sam Shepard, Jean-Claude van Itallie, Tom Eyen, Lanford Wilson, Leonard Melfi, Israel Horovitz, Rochelle Owens, Adrienne Kennedy, Charles Ludlam, Megan Terry, Julie Bovasso, Tom O'Horgan, John Vaccaro, Ed Setrakian, and Andrei Serban.

The Lambs, c/o Lotos Club, 5 E. 66th St., New York, NY 10021, tel. (212) RE 7-7100
Shepherd: Tom Dillon

The Lambs club was organized in 1874, primarily as a supper club. The charter members were George H. McLean, Henry T. Montague, Edward Arbott, Henry Beckett, and Arthur Wallack.

The club moved into a home on 44th Street, which had a theatre designed by Stanford White, in 1904. The membership of the club is limited to men, with some members chosen from outside the theatre.

Over a period of many years, The Lambs staged an annual show, called the Lambs Gambol, in which members appeared without remuneration. The productions were staged in New York and toured key cities throughout the United States.

In late 1974, due to mounting financial problems, the hundred-year-old club was forced into bankruptcy and the building was sold. At the present time the club is using the facilities of the Lotos Club.

The League of New York Theatres and Producers, 226 W. 47th St., New York, NY 10036, tel. (212) 582-4455
President: Richard D. Barr; *1st Vice-President:* Robert Whitehead; *2nd Vice-President:* Samuel Schwartz; *3rd Vice-President:* Alexander H. Cohen; *4th Vice-President:* Bernard Jacobs; *Secretary:* Morton Gottlieb; *Treasurer:* Joseph P. Harris; *Executive Director:* Irving W. Cheskin; *Asst. Executive Director:* Ruth Green; *Board of Governors:* Spofford Beadle, Arthur Cantor, William Court Cohen, Maxine Fox, Lee Guber, T. Edward Hambleton, Norman Kean, Marvin A. Krauss, Edgar Lansbury, Konrad Matthaei, Jerome Minskoff, James Nederlander, Lester Osterman, Stuart Ostrow, Joel Schenker, Gerald Schoenfeld, Albert W. Selden, Diana Shumlin, Eugene Wolsk, Kermit Bloomgarden, Herman Levin, Louis A. Lotito, and Harold Prince.

The League of New York Theatres was founded in 1930, "to protect the general public, patrons of the theatre, owners of theatrical entertainments, operators of theatres and reputable theatre ticket brokers against the evils of speculation in theatre tickets."

These aims were amended and enlarged in 1931, in 1933 (under the impetus of the enactment of the National Recovery Act), and again in 1938. The statement of aims at that date were:

1. To effectuate and bring about amicable adjustment of labor disputes in the theatrical industry in the City of New York;
2. To make on behalf of its members all agreements with other organizations, to carry out one or more purposes of the league;
3. To procure and effect uniformity and certainty in the customs and usages of the theatrical industry; and those having an interest therein;
4. To effect economy in the conduct of the business of its members;
5. To eliminate unfair and unjust practices.

Most of the league's energies today are expended in the labor field. It has basic agreements with the Dramatists Guild and ten trade unions. In 1938, in conjunction with Actors' Equity Association, the league promulgated a Theatre Ticket Code of Fair Practice. In 1940, this code was strengthened by enactment of state law limiting the premium on ticket speculation.

The league's present name was adopted in 1973.

League of Off-Broadway Theatres and Producers, c/o Paul Libin, Circle in the Square Theatre, 1633 Broadway, New York, NY 10019.
President: Paul Libin; *Secretary:* Dorothy Olim.

Several groups with similar titles and objectives had been organized in New York City before the League of Off-Broadway Theatres and Producers became established as the official representative for off-Broadway producers and theatre owners. The league evolved from the Off-Broadway Theatre Association, Inc., which was formed on Oct. 18, 1955. The league is the spokesman for producers and theatre owners engaged in off-Broadway theatre production activities. Its principal function is negotiating wage and working-condition contracts with the unions and guilds whose members work in off-Broadway productions. As of January 1974, the league claimed 57 off-Broadway theatres as members. The number of producers was not reported.

Lincoln Center Repertory Company. See Repertory Theatre of Lincoln Center

Long Wharf Theatre, 222 Sargent Drive, New Haven, CT 06511, tel. (203) 787-4284.
Chairman of the Board of Directors: C. Newton Schenck; *Artistic Director:* Arvin Brown; *Executive Director:* M. Edgar Rosenblum.

Long Wharf Theatre was founded in 1965 by Harlan Kleiman and Jon Jory. A New Haven warehouse near the harbor was renovated, a three-quarter round thrust stage was added, and seating for 441 persons was installed. Remodeling in 1974 increased seating capacity by 43 seats. Arvin Brown directed Long Wharf's production of *Long Day's Journey into Night* during the theatre's first season and, as artistic director of the organization since 1967, has presented a wide range of plays from premiere productions to dramatic classics to revivals. The theatre's seven-play season runs from mid-October through mid-June each year.

Long Wharf Theatre's major auxiliary activity is its Young People's Theatre, which appears at the theatre on weekends and tours through the week, performing and conducting educational workshops in a three-state area. Young People's Theatre has been involved in projects with autistic children at Connecticut Valley Hospital and with psychiatric outpatients at a community center in New Haven.

Arthur Miller's *The Crucible* was Long Wharf's opening production on July 4, 1965. Other presentations of the first season, which ran through May 1966, were: Brendan Behan's *The Hostage*, Rick Besoyan's *Little Mary Sunshine*, Peter Shaffer's *The Private Ear* and *The Public Eye*, Sean O'Casey's *The Plough and the Stars*, Ben Jonson's *Volpone*, Gilbert and Sullivan's *The Pirates of Penzance*, Euripides' *The Trojan Women*, Noel Coward's *Hay Fever*, Anton Chekhov's *Uncle Vanya*, Richard Brinsley Sheridan's *The Rivals*, and Eugene O'Neill's *Long Day's Journey*.

Later productions, by season, were: (1966-67) the American premieres of David Kranes's *The Loon Hunt* and *I'm Nobody*, of Jerry Blatt's *Thumby*, and of John Arden's *The Happy Haven*, as well as presentations of Joan Littlewood and Ted Allan's *Oh! What a Lovely War*, Anton Chekhov's *Three Sisters*, Kaufman and Hart's *The Man Who Came to Dinner*, George Bernard Shaw's *Misalliance*, Bertolt Brecht's *Mother Courage and Her Children*, George M. Cohan's *The Tavern*, and Tennessee Williams' *Night of the Iguana;* (1967-68) Tennessee Williams' *The Glass Menagerie*, Jean Anouilh's *The Rehearsal*, J. M. Synge's *The Playboy of the Western World*, John Murray and Allen Boretz's *Room Service*, the American premiere of Thomas Murphy's *A Whistle in the Dark*, Molière's *A Doctor in Spite of Himself* and Eugene Ionesco's *The Bald Soprano*, Edward Albee's *Tiny Alice*, and George Bernard Shaw's *Don Juan in Hell;* (1968-69) James Goldman's *The Lion in Winter*, Ferenc Molnar's *The Play's the Thing*, John Osborne and Anthony Creighton's *Epitaph for George Dillon*, Jean-Claude van Itallie's *America Hurrah*, Israel Horovitz's *The Indian Wants the Bronx* and *It's Called the Sugar Plum*, Dylan Thomas' *Under Milk Wood*, and Henrik Ibsen's *Ghosts;* (1969-70) Molière's *Tartuffe*, Slawomir Mrozek's *Tango*, Cole Porter, Lawrence Kasha and Hayden Griffin's *The Pirate*, the American premiere of Maxim Gorki's *Country People*, Peter Shaffer's *Black Comedy* and *The White Liars*, Peter Nichols's *A Day in the Death of Joe Egg*, Charles Aidman's adaptation of Edgar Lee Masters' *Spoon River Anthology*, and Herb Gardner's *A Thousand Clowns;* (1970-71) Thornton Wilder's *The Skin of Our Teeth*, the American premieres of Marguerite Duras's *A Place without Doors* and Joan Isserman's adaptation of Maxim Gorki's *Yegor Bulichov*, Oliver Goldsmith's *She Stoops To Conquer*, the world premiere of Robert Anderson's *Solitaire/Double Solitaire*, Athol Fugard's *The Blood Knot*, George Bernard Shaw's *Heartbreak House*, and Arthur Miller's *The Price*.

Also (1971-72) Kaufman and Hart's *You Can't Take It with You*, the American premiere of David Storey's *The Contractor*, Tennessee Williams' *A Streetcar Named Desire*, William Shakespeare's *Hamlet*, William Congreve's *The Way of the World*, Morris Carnovsky's *Troika: An Evening of Russian Comedy*, Eugene O'Neill's *The Iceman Cometh*, and the world premiere of Bill Morrison's *Patrick's Day;* (1972-73) Christopher Fry's *The Lady's Not for Burning*, the American premiere of David Storey's *The Changing Room*, Laurence Stallings and Maxwell Anderson's *What Price Glory?*, Arthur Wing Pinero's *Trelawny of the "Wells,"* Sean O'Casey's *Juno and the Paycock*, the American premiere of Peter Nichols' *Forget-Me-Not Lane*, and August Strindberg's *Dance of Death* and *Miss Julie;* (1973-74) Henrik Ibsen's *The Master Builder*, the American premiere of D. H. Lawrence's *The Widowing of Mrs. Holroyd*, Paul Osborn's *Morning's at Seven*, the American premiere of Edna O'Brien's *A Pagan Place*, Anton Chekhov's *The Seagull*, Peter Nichols' *The National Health*, and Bertolt Brecht's *The Resistible Rise of Arturo Ui;* (1974-75) the American premieres of David Rudkin's *Afore Night Come*, Richard Venture's *You're Too Tall, But Come Back in Two Weeks*, and Athol Fugard, John Kani, and Winston Ntshona's *Sizwe Banzi Is Dead* and *The Island*, George Bernard Shaw's *Pygmalion*, Shakespeare's *Richard III*, Beaumont and Fletcher's *Knight of the Burning Pestle* and Igor Stravinsky's *The Soldier's Tale*, and Eugene O'Neill's *Ah, Wilderness!*

Long Wharf Theatre productions seen on television include *The Contractor* (Jan., 1974), *The Widowing of Mrs. Holroyd* (May, 1974), and *Forget-Me-Not Lane* (Mar., 1975), all on the PBS series Theatre in America, and in 1971 the company appeared by invitation at the Edinburgh (Scotland) International Festival, where it presented *Solitaire/Double Solitaire* and *You Can't Take It with You*. In addition, several Long Wharf productions have been shown in New York City. These, with dates of New York openings, are *A Whistle in the Dark* (Apr. 1968), *A Place without Doors* (Stairway Th., Dec. 22, 1970), *Solitaire/Double Solitaire* (John Golden Th., Sept. 30, 1971), *The Changing Room* (Morosco, Mar. 6, 1973), *The Contractor* (Chelsea Theater Center of Brooklyn, Brooklyn Academy of Music, Oct. 17, 1973), and *The National Health* (Circle in the Square/Joseph E. Levine Th., Oct. 10, 1974). *The Changing Room* was selected by the NY Drama Critics as best play of the 1972-73 season, and it brought an Antoinette Perry (Tony) award to John Lithgow as best supporting actor in a play and Drama Desk awards to Michael Rudman as outstanding director and David Jenkins as outstanding scene designer.

Manhattan Theatre Club, Inc., 321 E. 73rd St., New York, NY 10021, tel. (212) BU 8-2500.

Artistic/Executive Director: Lynne Meadow; *Associate Director:* Tomm Bullard; *Managing Director:* Kathleen Norris; *Casting and Literary Director:* Stephen Pascal; *Technical Director:* William D. Anderson; *Public Relations Director:* Joel Wald; *Assistant to the Managing Director:* Trudy Brown. *Board of Directors: Chairman:* A. E. Jeffcoat; *President:* Richard M. Ticktin; *Treasurer:* Martin Abrahams; *Secretary:* Peregrine Whittlesey; *Members of the Board:* Gerald Freund, Alfred S. Goldfield, Sinclair Jacobs, Margaret Kennedy, Honor Moore, Lynne Meadow, Jacques C. Nordeman, Muriel Rafalsky, Stephen Sondheim, Edwin R. Stern III, Stanley Stillman, Beatrice Straight, George White.

The Manhattan Theatre Club (MTC), founded in 1970 by a group of private citizens, is a multi-theatre, nonprofit institution primarily dedicated to the development and presentation of new work in the theatre, but featuring as well an opera season, revivals of the classics, a poetry series, a classroom program, and musical evenings.

MTC is located in the century-old Bohemian National Hall on New York City's East 73rd Street, where it uses four performance spaces on three floors: a 170-seat proscenium theatre (the off-Broadway house Stage 73); a 100-seat thrust-stage theatre; a 65-seat studio amphitheatre; and a cabaret for late-night entertainment. Several rehearsal studios, which are also rented to other groups, are located in the building.

Through the efforts of Miss Meadow and a full-time staff of seven, the MTC has given first productions to a number of plays that were later produced commercially, including Terrence McNally's *Bad Habits*, Mark Medoff's *The Wager*, and Michael Sawyer's *Naomi Court*, which had a four-month run at Stage 73. The MTC has been proud of these presentations, but its major commitment is to provide a forum for a variety of work, some of which, while not destined for commercial life, is still worthy of display in MTC's unique context.

Among highlights of MTC's first three seasons are the following: (1972-73) New York premieres of Kenneth Cavander's *Boccaccio;* Joanna Glass's *Canadian Gothic/American Modern;* Jonathan Levy's *Charlie the Chicken* and *Master Class*, Bertolt Brecht and Kurt Weill's opera *Little Mahagonny;* and the New York Theatre Strategy Festival of twenty playwrights, including Terrence McNally's *Bad Habits;* (1973-74) revivals of Clifford Odets's *Waiting for Lefty*, Henrik Ibsen's *Little Eyolf*, and the Guillaume Apollinaire–Francois Poulenc opera *The Breasts of Tiresias;* the world premiere of Aleksandr Solzhenitsyn's *Candle in the Wind;* the American premiere of Thomas Murphy's *The Morning after Optimism;* and the New York premieres of Mark Medoff's *The Wager;* Richard Wesley's *The Sirens; A Circle of Sound;* Michael Sawyer's *Naomi Court;* and Carlisle Floyd's opera *Markheim;* and (1974-75) revivals of Anton Chekhov's *The Seagull* in a new English version by Jean-Claude van Itallie, and S. N. Behrman's *End of Summer;* and New York premieres of Corinne Jaker's *Bits and Pieces;* Joseph Landon's *Blessing;* Milan Stitt's *The Runner Stumbles;* Edward Bond's *The Sea;* and Thomas Pasatieri's opera *Signor Deluso* on a double-bill with Gustav Holst's opera *Savitri*.

Margo Jones Theatre, 1411 Commerce St., Dallas, TX 75201.

President: Arthur L. Kramer, Jr.; *Vice-President and Treasurer:* De Witt Ray; *Vice-Presidents:* Waldo Stewart, Keith Baker, John Carver; *Secretary:* Mrs. Jake Hamon; *Administrator:* Edmund G. Peterson; *Founding President:* Eugene McDermott.

When Margo Jones (1913-1955) founded Theatre '47 in Dallas in 1947, she gave new impetus to the American theatre. It sparked the current growth in theatres in the major cities of the United States, created a new interest in theatre-in-the round, and brought to the fore new talent among playwrights and actors.

The organization, which would update its name each year (Theatre '48, Theatre '49, etc.), was located in the Gulf Oil Building in Dallas' State Fair Park until 1959, when it acquired the Maple Theatre and changed its mode of production to proscenium staging. Nine productions were offered over a 27-week season.

Different directors attempted to carry on Miss Jones's work following her death in 1955, but the venture came to an end on Dec. 25, 1959. The final production was William Shakespeare's *Othello*.

Productions for the Margo Jones Theatre included William Inge's *Farther Off from Heaven* (June 3, 1947); Martyn Coleman's *How Now, Hecate* (June 10, 1947); Vera Matthews' *Third Cousin* (June 22, 1947); Henrik Ibsen's *Hedda Gabler* (June 24, 1947); Tennessee Williams' *Summer and Smoke* (July 8, 1947); Henrik Ibsen's *The Master Builder* (Nov. 3, 1947); Tennessee Williams' *The Last of My Solid Gold Watches, Portrait of a Madonna,* and *This Property Is Condemned* (Nov. 17, 1947); Vivian Connell's *Throng O' Scarlet* (Dec. 1, 1947); William Shakespeare's *The Taming of the Shrew* (Dec. 15, 1947); Manning Gurian's *Lemple's Old Man* (Dec. 29, 1947); Oscar Wilde's *The Importance of Being Earnest* (Jan. 12, 1948); Joseph Hayes's *Leaf and Bough* (Jan. 27, 1948); Barton MacLane's *Black John* (Feb. 9, 1948); Molière's *The Learned Ladies* (Nov. 8, 1948); Shirland Quinn's *Here's to Us* (Nov. 29, 1948); William Shakespeare's *Twelfth Night* (Dec. 20, 1948); Vivian Johannes' *Skaal* (Jan. 10, 1949); Tom Purefoy's *Sting in the Tail* (Jan. 31, 1949); Anton Chekhov's *The Seagull* (Feb. 21, 1949); Oliver Goldsmith's *She Stoops to Conquer* (Mar. 14, 1949); Dorothy Parker and Ross Evans' *The Coast of Ilyria* (Apr. 4, 1949); and a revival of Oscar Wilde's *The Importance of Being Earnest* (May 9, 1949).

Also, George Bernard Shaw's *Heartbreak House* (Nov. 7, 1949); Sari Scott's *An Old Beat-Up Woman* (Nov. 28, 1949); William Shakespeare's *Romeo and Juliet* (Dec. 19, 1949); George Sessions and Perry and Loren Disney's *My Granny Van* (Jan. 9, 1950); Sean O'Casey's *Cock-a-Doodle Dandy* (Jan. 30, 1950); Henrik Ibsen's *Ghosts* (Feb. 20, 1950); Muriel Roy Botton's *The Golden Porcupine* (Mar. 13, 1950); Owen Crump's *Southern Exposure* (Apr. 3, 1950); Oscar Wilde's *Lady Windermere's Fan* (Nov. 6, 1950); William McCleery's *A Play for Mary* (Nov. 27, 1950); William Shakespeare's *Merchant of Venice* (Dec. 18, 1950); A. B. Shiffrin's *The Willow Tree* (Jan. 8, 1951); Edward Caulfield's *An Innocent in Time* (Jan. 29, 1951); Sigmund Miller's *One Bright Day* (Feb. 19, 1951); George Bernard Shaw's *Candida* (Mar. 12, 1951); Frank Duane's *Walls Rise Up* (Apr. 2, 1951); Alden Nash's *The Sainted Sisters* (Nov. 7, 1951); Irving Phillips' *One Foot in Heaven* (Dec. 3, 1951); William Shakespeare's *A Midsummer Night's Dream* (Dec. 23, 1951); Ronald Alexander's *A Gift for Cathy* (Jan. 21, 1952); Edward Caulfield's *The Blind Spot* (Feb. 11, 1952); August Strindberg's *The Father* (Mar. 10, 1952); Edwin Justus Mayer's *I Am Laughing* (Mar. 31, 1952); Vera Marshall's *So in Love* (Apr. 28, 1952); Vivian Connell's *Goodbye Your Majesty* (Nov. 3, 1952); William Shakespeare's *Hamlet* (Nov. 24, 1952); *The Rising Heifer* (Dec. 22, 1952); Eugene Raskin's *The Last Legend* (Jan. 12, 1953); John Briard Harding's *Uncle Marston* (Feb. 9, 1953); Rosemary Casey's *Late Love* (Mar. 2, 1953); Lesley Storm's *The Day's Mischief* (Mar. 30, 1953); and Richard Sheridan's *The Rivals* (Apr. 20, 1953).

Also, Burgess Drake's *The Footpath Way* (Nov. 2, 1953); Harry Garnick's *The Guilty* (Nov. 23, 1953); Alejandro Casona's *Happy We'll Be* (Dec. 14, 1953); Sari Scott's *Oracle Junction* (Jan. 4, 1954); Samson Raphaelson's *The Heel* (Jan. 25, 1954); Milton Robertson's *A Rainbow at Home* (Feb. 15, 1954); William Alexander Guthrie's *The Embarcation for the Happy Isles* (Mar. 8, 1954); the musical *Horatio*, with book by Ira Wallach, music by David Baker, and lyrics by Sheldon Harnick (Mar. 9, 1954); Tennessee Williams' *The Purification* and Jean Giraudoux' *The Apollo of Bellac* (Mar. 29, 1954); Ronald Alexander's *The Inevitable Circle* (June 8, 1954); John Rodell's *The Brothers* (June 29, 1954); Reginald Denham and Conrad Smith's *A Dash of Bitters* (July 20, 1954); William Case's *Sea-Change* (Aug. 10, 1954); Ben Jonson's *Volpone* (Aug. 31, 1954); Albert Dickason's *Marry-Go-Round* (Nov. 8, 1954); William Shakespeare's *As You Like It* (Nov. 29, 1954); Edward Hunt's *The Hemlock Cup* (Dec. 20, 1954); Jerome Lawrence and Robert E. Lee's *Inherit the Wind* (Jan. 10, 1955); Jean Dalrymple and Charles Robinson's *The Feathered Fauna* (Jan. 31, 1955); Bernard C. Schoenfeld's *The Summer of the Fancy Dress* (Feb. 21, 1955); George Bernard Shaw's *Misalliance* (Mar. 14, 1955); Stephen Grey's *Ghost of a Chance* (Apr. 4, 1955); and the musical *La Belle Lulu,* with book by Frederick Jackson and Irving Phillips, music by Offenbach and Charles Previn, and lyrics by Irving Phillips (Apr. 25, 1955).

Also, George Bernard Shaw's *Pygmalion* (June 13, 1955); Greer Johnson's *Whisper to Me* (June 27, 1955); Joseph Hayes' *The Girl from Boston,* Anna Marie Barlow and S. Brooke White's *Cold Christmas* (July 25, 1955); John Vari's *Farewell, Farewell Eugene* (Aug. 7, 1955); Ferenc Molnar's *Somebody* (Nov. 7, 1955); Gene Radano's *The World Is Yours* (Nov. 28, 1955); George Bernard Shaw's *The Dark Lady of the Sonnets* and *Man of Destiny* (Dec. 19, 1955); Neal Roper's *Love in a Tutu* (Jan. 9, 1956); Maura Laverty's *Tolka Row* (Jan. 30, 1956); Molière's *The School for Wives* (Feb. 20, 1956); James Bridie's *Mr. Gillie* (Mar. 12, 1956); Patricia Toudry's *The Sand Castle* (Apr. 2, 1956); Violet Welles' *The Spring Affair* (Apr. 23, 1956); Eleanor and Leo Bayer's *The Third Best Sport* (May 14, 1956); Jacinto Benavente's *Love Goes to School* (Jan. 18, 1956); Albert Mannheimer and Frederick Kohner's *Stalin Allee* (Nov. 5, 1956); Milton Kramer's *Lawyer* (Nov. 27, 1956); S. I. Abelow and Robert Cenedella's *The Small Servant* (Dec. 18, 1956); Don Liljenquist's *Women Is My Idea* (Jan. 8, 1957); Richard Reich's *The Tin Cup* (Jan. 29, 1957); Somerset Maugham's *The Circle* (Feb. 9, 1957); Elinor Lenz' *The Second Wind* (Mar. 12, 1957); and Norbert Faulkner and Samuel R. Golding's *The Most Fashionable Crime* (Apr. 2, 1957).

Also, Anton Chekhov's *Uncle Vanya* (Apr. 23, 1957); Tennessee Williams' *The Glass Menagerie* (May 13, 1957); Paul Vincent Carroll's *The Devil Came from Dublin* (Oct. 29, 1957); Lynn Riggs' *Roadside* (Nov. 19, 1957); George Bernard Shaw's *Androcks and the Lion* (Dec. 10, 1957; Kate Furness' *Heat of Noontide* (Dec. 31, 1957); Katherine Morrill's *And So, Farewell* (Jan. 21, 1958); Molière's *The Doctor in Spite of Himself* (Feb. 11, 1958); Harry Granick's *The Hooper Law* (Mar. 4, 1958); Carl Oglesby's *Season of the Beast* (Mar. 4, 1958); Sheridan Gibney's *Penelope's Web* (Nov. 3, 1958); Robert Penn Warren's *Willie Stark: His Rise and Fall* (Nov. 25, 1958); *Legends and Fables,* a double-bill of Kurt Weill's *Down in the Valley* and James Thurber's *Fables for Our Times* (Dec. 16, 1958); Charles Robinson's *October Gal* (Jan. 6, 1959); Ruth and Augustus Goetz' *The Heiress* (Jan. 27, 1959); Royall Tyler's *The Contrast* (Feb. 17, 1959); Eugene O'Neill's *A Moon for the Misbegotten* (Mar. 31, 1959); William Shakespeare's *Much Ado About Nothing* (Mar. 31, 1959); *Une Nuit Chez Vous Madame* (Apr. 21, 1959); Kenneth Cameron's *Physician for Fools* (Oct. 6, 1959); the musical *Leave It to Me,* with book by Bella and Samuel Spewack, music and lyrics by Cole Porter (Oct. 27, 1959); Warren Tute's *A Few Days in Greece* (Nov. 17, 1959); and William Shakespeare's *Othello* (Dec. 8, 1959).

McCarter Theatre Company, West College Road and University Place, Princeton, NJ 08540, tel. (609) 452-3617.
Producing Director, Michael Kahn.

The McCarter Theatre Company, formed in 1960, is a resident acting company and producing organization currently presenting a six-play season in addition to booked-in attractions which include programs of classical and popular music, dance, and film.

The company's season runs from October to December and February to April and consists of productions of the classics, infrequently performed plays by master playwrights, and, whenever possible, new plays. Michael Kahn, who became McCarter's producing director in 1974, provides artistic leadership at both the McCarter Theatre and the American Shakespeare Theatre in Stratford, Conn., a dual role that has established an association which is productive both financially, with occasionally shared production costs, and artistically, by giving artists the opportunity to work together during much of the year.

The McCarter Theatre, built in 1928, is owned and maintained by Princeton University and has a proscenium stage and seating capacity of 1,077. The Princeton University Program in Theatre brings together students and McCarter professionals; the subsequent exposure of students to live drama is not expected to prepare them for professional careers, but rather to sharpen their perceptions and to supplement the rest of their academic work.

In addition to the University's financial support, the company is aided by the National Endowment for the Arts, the New Jersey State Council on the Arts, corporate and private donors, and several foundations.

Plays produced during the 1974-75 and 1975-76 seasons include: *Beyond the Horizon* by Eugene O'Neill; *'Tis Pity She's a Whore* by John Ford; *Mother Courage and Her Chil-*

dren by Bertolt Brecht; *Kingdom of Earth* by Tennessee Williams; *Romeo and Juliet* by William Shakespeare; *A Grave Undertaking* by Lloyd Gold (world premiere); *The Royal Family* by George S. Kaufman and Edna Ferber; *Section Nine* by Philip Magdalany (American premiere); *The Heiress* by Ruth and Augustus Goetz, suggested by Henry James' novel *Washington Square; Awake and Sing* by Clifford Odets; and *The Winter's Tale* by William Shakespeare.

Minnesota Theatre Company Foundation. *See* Guthrie Theatre Foundation

National Repertory Theatre.
Producers: Michael Dewell, Frances Ann Dougherty; *Directors:* Eva Le Gallienne, Jack Sydow.

The National Repertory Theatre was organized in 1961 by New York's Phoenix Theatre to carry the work of the theatre outside New York. In autumn 1961 the company toured with Maxwell Anderson's *Elizabeth the Queen* and Friedrich Schiller's *Mary Stuart* in an adaptation by Jean Stock Goldstone and John Reich. The acting troupe was headed by Eva Le Gallienne, Faye Emerson, Scott Forbes, and Frederic Worlock. The American National Theatre and Academy shared in the sponsorship, and the company traveled 50,000 miles, using plane, bus, train, and station wagon as means of transportation. During the 1963-64 season, the company again toured, this time with Arthur Miller's *The Crucible,* Eva Le Gallienne's adaptation of Anton Chekhov's *The Seagull,* and Christopher Fry's *Ring 'Round the Moon,* ending the tour in New York City, playing the first two mentioned plays in repertory.

Elizabeth the Queen and *Mary Stuart* opened at the Academy of Music, Northampton, Mass., Oct. 19, 1961, and closed at the Auditorium, Rochester, N.Y., Apr. 14, 1962; *The Crucible, The Seagull,* and *Ring'Round the Moon* opened in Greensboro, N.C., Oct. 5, 1963, and closed at the Auditorium, Dallas, Tex., Mar. 29, 1964. *The Seagull* opened in New York City at the Belasco Theatre, Apr. 5, 1964, and *The Crucible* opened the following night at the same theatre.

In following seasons, the company presented, in New York and on tour, *Liliom, She Stoops To Conquer* and *Hedda Gabler; The Madwoman of Chaillot, The Rivals* and *The Trojan Women; The Tempest, Lil' Abner* and *Hotel Universe; Tonight at 8:30, A Touch of the Poet* and *The Imaginary Invalid;* and *She Stoops to Conquer, John Brown's Body* and *The Comedy of Errors.*

The National Theatre of the Deaf, 305 Great Neck Rd., Waterford, CT 06385, tel. (203) 443-5378; New York office: 1860 Bway, Suite 1012, New York, NY 10023, tel. (212) 246-2277.
Producing Director: David Hays; *Tour Director and Press Representative:* Mack Scism.

The concept of a professional company of deaf performers was formed in the 1950s by government officials, notably Mary Switzer and Boyce Williams, and by Dr. Edna Simon Levine, a psychologist working with the deaf. The purpose of such a company would be to serve as a public relations device, raising the visibility and image of the deaf population, a much misunderstood minority. These plans were not realized until 1966, when David Hays brought the project to the newly formed Eugene O'Neill Memorial Theater Center.

As a professional theatre person working within a professional theatre organization, David Hays always had a goal that was largely artistic: to found a first-class permanent theatre company that would create a new theatre form. However, in achieving the artistic goal, the social benefits envisioned by officials at the Dept. of Health, Education and Welfare have followed as natural fallout.

The National Theatre of the Deaf (NTD) is a professional touring theatre company of deaf actors who perform in a highly theatricalized visual language—sign-mime—based on the deafs' unique form of communication, sign language. The company includes two to four hearing actors, or "speakers," who are worked into the action of the play to create an extraordinary blend of visual and spoken language.

The NTD, which is largely funded by the US Office of Education, Dept. of Health, Education and Welfare, holds workshops and performances for many deaf schools and community groups; but the majority of the audiences are hearing. The company has made seventeen national tours and two Broadway appearances; has toured extensively abroad playing most of the major European festivals; made nationally broadcast television specials for NBC and CBS; and appears every year on the acclaimed NET children's program, Sesame Street. Major NTD productions include *Sganarelle, Songs from Milkwood, Woyzeck,* and *The Dybbuk.* On three occasions, the company has created its own material through improvisation: *My Third Eye, Gilgamesh,* and most recently, *Parade.*

The Negro Ensemble Company, St. Marks Playhouse, 133 Second Ave., New York, NY 10003, tel. (212) 667-3939.
Artistic Director: Douglas Turner Ward; *Executive Director:* Robert Hooks; *Administrative Director:* Frederick Garrett; *Administrative Consultant and Company Manager:* Gerald S. Krone.

On May 15, 1967, the Ford Foundation announced a grant of $434,000 to the newly organized Negro Ensemble Company for the establishment of a professional theatre company and workshop to develop black actors, playwrights, directors, technicians, and managers.

The group was founded by Douglas Turner Ward, Robert Hooks, and Gerald S. Krone with the aim of providing a new off-Broadway platform for a repertoire to include works on racial themes and problems, to expand opportunities for experienced Negro theatre artists, and to offer professional training to potential new talent with materials which emphasize the Negro identity. The training program was the outgrowth of a workshop that Mr. Hooks had begun in 1964.

The Ford Foundation has continued to be an important financial support to the company throughout the years.

The company leased the St. Marks Playhouse at 133 Second Ave. and opened on Jan. 2, 1968, with the American premiere of Peter Weiss' *The Song of the Lusitanian Bogey.*

In May 1969 the company performed at the World Theatre Season at the Aldwych Theatre in London and at the Rome Theatre Festival. They have also made national tours of the United States.

One of the group's great successes, Joseph A. Walker's *The River Niger* (Dec. 5, 1972), moved to Broadway (Brooks Atkinson Th., Mar. 25, 1973). The company's productions include: *Song of the Lusitanian Bogey* (Jan. 2, 1968), *Summer of the 17th Doll* (Feb. 20, 1968), *Kongi's Harvest* (Apr. 14, 1968), *Daddy Goodness* (June 4, 1968), *"God Is a (Guess What?)"* (Dec. 17, 1968), *Ceremonies in Dark Old Men* (Feb. 4, 1969), *An Evening of One Acts: String, Contribution; Malcochon* (Mar. 25, 1969), *Man Better Man* (July 2, 1969), *The Reckoning* (Sept. 4, 1969), *The Harangries* (Dec. 30, 1969), *Brotherhood* and *Day of Absence* (Mar. 10, 1970), *Akokawe* (*Initiation*) (May 19, 1970), *Ododo* (*Truth*) (Nov. 17, 1970), *Perry's Mission* and *Rosalee Pritchett* (Jan. 12, 1971), *The Dream on Monkey Mountain* (Mar. 9, 1971), *Ride a Black Horse* (May 25, 1971), *The Sty of the Blind Pig* (Nov. 16, 1971), *A Ballet Behind the Bridge* (Mar. 7, 1972), *Frederick Douglass . . . Through His Own Words* (May 9, 1972), *The River Niger* (Dec. 5, 1972), *The Great Macdaddy* (Feb. 12, 1974), *A Season-within-a-Season: Black Sunlight* (Mar. 19, 1974); *Nowhere to Run, Nowhere to Hide* (Mar. 26, 1974); *Terraces* (Apr. 2, 1974); and *Heaven and Hell's Agreement* (Apr. 9, 1974).

In addition to the plays listed above, the company has presented many workshop productions as well as music and dance programs.

New Drama Forum Association, Inc., 164 W. 79th St., Apt. 6B, New York, NY 10024, tel. (212) 799-3853.
President: Marilyn Stasio; *First Vice-President:* Hugh Southern; *Second Vice-President:* Margaret Croyden; *Secretary:* John Beaufort; *Treasurer:* Stuart W. Little.

The New Drama Forum began as a group of eleven individuals sharing an interest in the theatre who met informally and unofficially in the fall of 1974; during the spring of 1975 the original members invited several other people to participate, bringing the total involved to about forty, and the following summer the group was incorporated.

Regular meetings, which officially began in October 1975, are held at Sardi's Restaurant, N.Y.C., on the second Monday of each month as luncheon seminars on theatre topics. There are, in addition, occasional afternoon parties or receptions open to guests. The Forum has membership, nominating, and programs committees.

The purpose of the New Drama Forum, as stated in its charter, is to provide a forum for the exchange of ideas among people interested and actively involved in the theatre: critics, writers, editors, scholars, and officers of nonprofit organizations. Guests are usually creative theatre people: writers, producers, directors, actors, and others.

In 1967, the NTD started its annual summer program, The Professional School for Deaf Theatre Personnel. The school attracts deaf students interested in theatre from all over the country for an intensive five-week course in NTD's theatre techniques. In 1968, the first Little Theatre of the Deaf was created to perform children's programs. Since

1970, the large company has divided itself into two Little Theatre of the Deaf companies to tour schools and communities here and abroad. The Little Theatre of the Deaf has played Australia, Scandinavia, the Vienna Festival, and in 1972 was selected to represent the US at the ASSITEJ international theatre conference where it won the Jennie Heiden Award for excellence in professional children's theatre.

Neighborhood Playhouse School of the Theatre, 340 E. 54th St., New York NY 10022, tel. (212) MU 8-3770.
Director: Paul Morrison; *Administrative Director:* Oleta Carns D'Ambry; *Head of Acting Dept.:* Sanford Meisner; *Librarian:* Alice Owen. *President:* Robert Whitehead; *Vice-President:* Tony Randall; *Treasurer:* Frederick H. Rohlfs; *Secretary:* Oleta Carns D'Ambry; *Directors:* Martha Graham, Eli Wallach.

Out of the drama activities on behalf of the neighborhood children on New York's lower East Side came the Neighborhood Playhouse. The Henry Street Settlement had been serving the area for more than twenty years when Irene Lewisohn and Alice Lewisohn Crowley began a professional theatre venture there. Out of the street festivals and the holiday theatricals developed the memorable productions of *The Little Clay Cart, The Dybbuk, The Madras House,* and the various *Grand Street Follies.*

From 1915 until 1927, the Neighborhood Playhouse maintained a permanent repertory company, classes in theatre and the allied arts, and costume and scene workshops. In 1928, the Neighborhood School of the Theatre was founded upon this tradition. The history of the Neighborhood Playhouse can be traced in Alice Lewisohn Crowley's work bearing that title (1959).

A catalogue of the school informs the young theatre aspirant that, "We offer you a stern apprenticeship of two years under teachers each of whom is an artist in his field and therefore an exacting taskmaster. Come here only if you are willing to work with the intensity necessary to meet the standards which these teachers will hold for you."

Courses are offered in acting, dance, voice, and speech. Guest instructors offer special courses. Public performances are given by the students in the school's well-equipped playhouse. The school maintains an excellent library for its students. Graduates of the Neighborhood Playhouse School of the Theatre include many distinguished actors and actresses and many important figures in the teaching of theatre.

The New Dramatists, Inc.; 424 W. 44th Street, New York, NY 10036, tel. (212) PL 7-6960.
Chairman of the Board of Directors: L. Arnold Weissberger, *President:* Mary K. Frank; *Vice-President:* Zilla Lippmann; *Treasurer:* Francis Neuwirth; *Secretary:* Joan C. Daly; *Program Director:* Jeff Peters; *Coordinator:* Stephen Harty.

The New Dramatists, Inc., was founded in 1949 by Howard Lindsay, Russel Crouse, John Golden, Moss Hart, Oscar Hammerstein II, Michaela O'Harra, Richard Rodgers, and John Wharton. The group was organized, first informally and later as a nonprofit corporation, to encourage and develop the new playwriting talent of America. This objective has been met through the years with a five-point "Plan for Playwrights" involving workshop productions, panel discussions, production observerships, craft discussion seminars, and theatre admissions.

Since its inception in 1949, the New Dramatists has provided a comprehensive program of development for more than 400 playwrights. Among the many New Dramatists members who have received Broadway and off-Broadway productions are Robert Anderson, Joe Masteroff, Paddy Chayefsky, William Inge, Rosalyn Drexler, Sidney Michaels, James Goldman, Horton Foote, and James Baldwin. Membership in the organization customarily numbers around forty, but the sole restriction on membership is the interest of talented writers. In an average year, the workshop program sponsors fifteen full stagings, twenty rehearsed readings, and thirty panel discussions of new plays by members, while actors, directors, and technicians contribute their services toward the refinement of these new plays. Since the New Dramatists is a purely service organization, requiring neither fees of its members nor admission charges of its audiences, funding for its programs is traditionally based on the generosity of the theatre profession and philanthropic foundations.

New York Drama Critics' Circle, 29 W. 46th St., New York, NY 10036.
President: Douglas Watt; *Vice-President:* Emory Lewis; *Treasurer:* John Beaufort; *Secretary:* Joseph T. Shipley.

The initial meetings of the New York Drama Critics' Circle were held in 1927, at the instigation of Kelcey Allen. The organization was patterned after that of the London Drama Critics Circle. It was not, however, until October 22, 1935, that the Circle was officially formed. The purpose, as stated in the organization's constitution, is "the fostering and rewarding of merit in the American theatre, and the awarding of a prize to be known as the Drama Critics Prize, for the best new play by an American playwright produced in New York during the theatrical season."

The award for that first season, 1935-36, was given to Maxwell Anderson's *Winterset.* In recent years, the Circle has made awards, additionally, to the best play by a foreign dramatist and to the best musical of the season. In 1962, the rules of balloting were altered. The new resolution states, "There shall be one ballot cast for the Best Play—drama or musical, regardless of the country of its origin. If there is no majority on the first ballot, each voting member will list three plays in order of his preference. First choice will count 3 points; second choice, 2 points; third choice, 1 point. The play amassing most points receives the award. If a foreign work should win the award, the Circle may, if it chooses, name a Best American Play. If an American play wins, the Circle may choose a Best Foreign Play. Whether to choose a musical is, as heretofore, left to the discretion of the Circle."

The Circle also holds meetings to discuss problems of the theatre, etc., and often receives visits from fellow critics visiting from abroad.

New York Shakespeare Festival, 425 Lafayette St., New York, NY 10003, (212) 677-1750
Producer: Joseph Papp
The New York Shakespeare Festival was chartered by the State of New York Education Department, November 19, 1954, to "encourage and cultivate interest in poetic drama with emphasis on the works of William Shakespeare and his Elizabethan contemporaries, and to establish an annual summer Shakespeare Festival."

Early productions were presented in the auditorium of the Emanuel Presbyterian Church at 729 East 6th Street, on Manhattan's lower East Side. No admission was charged and most of the company worked without recompense.

During the summer of 1956, the company presented its productions at an outdoor amphitheatre on the East River near Grant Street. During the 1957 season, with the aid of the N.Y.C. Parks Dept., performances were presented in several of the city's parks. All of these were presented without an admission charge. The plays were presented on a 35′ x 30′ Renaissance-style stage, which opened up from a trailer truck. During the winter months, the productions were played at the Heckscher Auditorium and in New York City high schools.

With the exception of the summer of 1961, performances have been given at Belvedere Lake in Central Park. During 1961, these were held at the Wollman Rink in Central Park, while the Delacorte Theatre was being constructed.

In 1962 the New York Shakespeare Festival acquired a permanent home at the Delacorte Theatre in Central Park. For the first time, in 1963, the Festival offered contributors a choice of reserved seats for any performance during the run of each play. With this exception, the productions are presented without admission charge.

On January 5, 1966, Mr. Papp announced that the New York Shakespeare Festival had purchased the Astor Library landmark building at 425 Lafayette Street as headquarters for year-round activities. The building, renamed the New York Shakespeare Festival Public Theater, would be converted into a performing arts center with at least two theatres, rehearsal rooms, exhibition halls and a film theatre.

The first theatre to be completed, the Florence Sutro Anspacher Theatre, opened on Oct. 29, 1967, with *Hair.* Martinson Hall opened November 16, 1969, with *Stomp.* The Estelle R. Newman Theatre opened Oct. 4, 1970, with *The Happiness Cage.* The Public Theatre Annex, across the street from the main building, opened Feb. 29, 1972, with *Black Visions.* Workshop productions are presented in a space called The Other Stage.

In March 1971 the New York City Council approved the purchase of the Astor Library building by the city and leased it back to the New York Shakespeare Festival for $1.00 a year. This helped reduce the debt the company had incurred to purchase and remodel the property.

On March 6, 1973, Lincoln Center, Inc., announced that Joseph Papp and his New York Shakespeare Festival group would replace the Repertory Theatre of Lincoln Center. Mr. Papp's board of directors would also replace the Repertory Theatre board. The New York Shakespeare Festival planned to continue its activities at the Public Theater complex on Lafayette Street, as well as the summer season at the Delacorte Theatre in Central Park. In May 1973, Mrs. Samuel I. Newhouse made a gift of $1,000,000 to the company to help defray production expenses at Lincoln Center. The Forum Theatre was renamed the Mitzi E. Newhouse Theatre.

The first program of the New York Shakespeare Festival, entitled *An Evening with Shakespeare and Marlowe*, was given in November 1954; and, in January 1955, a program called *Shakespeare's Women Characters* was presented.

Subsequent productions of Shakespeare's plays, except where indicated, have included *Much Ado About Nothing*, *Cymbeline*, *As You Like It*, *Two Gentlemen of Verona*, and *Romeo and Juliet* (1955); *Much Ado About Nothing*, Thomas Middleton and William Rowley's *The Changeling*, *Julius Caesar*, *The Taming of the Shrew*, and *Titus Andronicus* (1956); *Romeo and Juliet* (touring) (1960); *Much Ado About Nothing*, *A Midsummer Night's Dream*, and *King Richard II* (1961); *Julius Caesar* (touring), *The Merchant of Venice*, *The Tempest*, and *King Lear* (1962); *Macbeth* (touring), *Antony and Cleopatra*, *As You Like It*, *The Winter's Tale* and *Twelfth Night* (touring) (1963); *A Midsummer Night's Dream* (touring), *Hamlet*, *Othello*, and Sophocles' *Electra* (1964). *Love's Labour's Lost*, *Coriolanus*, *Troilus and Cressida*, *King Henry V* (touring), *The Taming of the Shrew* (touring) and *Romeo and Juliet* in Spanish (touring) (1965); *All's Well That Ends Well*, *Measure for Measure*, *King Richard III*, *Macbeth* in English and Spanish (touring) and a revue for children, *Potluck!* (touring) (1966), also poetry, music and dance programs; *The Comedy of Errors*, *King John*, *Titus Andronicus*, *Volpone* (touring), and poetry music and dance programs (1967).

On October 29, 1967, the New York Shakespeare Festival Public Theatre inaugurated its first season with *Hair*, book and lyrics by Gerome Ragni and James Redo, music by Galt MacDermot (Florence Sutro Anspacher Theatre). It was followed by Shakespeare's *Hamlet* (Anspacher Th., Dec. 26, 1967); Jakov Lind's *Ergo* (Anspacher Th., Mar. 3, 1968); Vaclav Havel's *The Memorandum* (Anspacher Th., May 5, 1968) translated by Vera Blackwell; and several workshop productions.

The 1968 summer season included *King Henry IV, Part I*, *King Henry IV, Part 2*, *Romeo and Juliet*, *Hamlet* (touring), *Take One Step* (touring) and poetry, music and dance programs. Anne Burr's *Huui Huui* (Anspacher Th., Nov. 16, 1968); Adrienne Kennedy's *Cities in Beique*, two one-act plays: *The Owl Answers* and *A Beast's Story* (Anspacher Th., Jan. 4, 1969); Russell McGrath's *Invitation to a Beheading* (Anspacher Th., Mar. 8, 1969); Charles Gordone's *No Place To Be Somebody* (Anspacher Th., May 4, 1969); and six workshop productions.

The 1969 summer season included Henrik Ibsen's *Peer Gynt* translated by Michael Meyer, Shakespeare's *Twelfth Night*, Sophocles' *Electra* (touring) and dance programs. Later the company presented *Stomp* (Martinson Hall, Nov. 16, 1969) created by The Combine; Ron Steward and Neal Tate's *Sambo* (Anspacher Th., Dec. 12, 1969); Myrna Lamb & Susan H. Bingham's *Mod Donna* (Anspacher Th., Apr. 24, 1970); and several workshop productions.

The summer of 1970 Shakespeare presentation, entitled *The Wars of the Roses*, included *The Chronicles of King Henry VI, Part 1* adapted from *King Henry VI, Part 1* and *King Henry VI, Part 2; The Chronicles of King Henry, Part 2* adapted from *King Henry VI, Part 2* and *King Henry VI, Part 3;* and *King Richard III*. A special performance of all three productions was given beginning at 7 p.m. on June 27, 1970, and ending eleven hours later at dawn on Sunday. *Sambo* (touring) and dance programs completed the summer season. The season at The Public Theatre included Dennis J. Reardon's *The Happiness Cage* (Estelle R. Newman Th., Oct. 4, 1970); Arthur Wing Pinero's *Trelawny of the Wells* (Anspacher Th., Oct. 11, 1970); *Jack MacGowran in the Works of Samuel Beckett* (Newman Th., Nov. 19, 1970); Robert Montgomery's *Subject to Fits* (Anspacher Th., Feb. 14, 1971); David Hare's *Slag* (Other Stage, Feb. 21, 1971); *Here Are Ladies* (Newman Th., Feb. 22, 1971), a one-woman show with Siobhan McKenna; The Blood Company's *Blood* (Martinson Hall, Mar. 7, 1971), conceived by Doug Dyer; *Underground* (Other Stage, Apr. 18, 1971), two one-act plays: *Jazznite* by Walter Jones and *The Life and Times of J. Walter Sminthers* by Edgar White; the Organic Theatre Company's adaptation of Voltaire's *Candide* (South Hall, Apr. 14, 1971); David Rabe's *The Basic Training of Pavlo Hummel* (Newman Th., May 20, 1971); and several workshop productions.

Summer 1971 brought *Timon of Athens*, *Cymbeline*, and *Two Gentlemen of Verona*, adapted by John Guare and Mel Shapiro, music by Galt MacDermot, lyrics by John Guare (at the Delacorte Th. and touring), and the New York Dance Festival. The Public Theatre season opened with Greg Antonacci's *Dance Wi' Me* (Anspacher Th., June 10, 1971); Walter Jones' *Nigger Nightmare* (Other Stage, June 24, 1971); David Rabe's *Sticks and Bones* (Anspacher Th., Nov. 7, 1971, transferred to John Golden Th., Mar. 1, 1972); Richard Wesley's *The Black Terror* (Other Stage, Nov. 10, 1971); *Two Gentlemen of Verona* (St. James Th., reopened for Broadway run Dec. 1, 1971); Doug Dyer, Peter Link, and Gretchen Cryer's adaptation of Euripides: *The Wedding of Iphigenia* and *Iphigenia in Concert* (Martinson Hall, Dec. 16, 1971); *Black Visions*, four one-act plays: *SisterSon/ji* by Sonia Sanchez, *Players Inn* by Neil Harris, *Cop and Blow* by Neil Harris, *Gettin' It Together* by Richard Wesley (Public Theatre Annex, Feb. 29, 1972); Jason Miller's *That Championship Season* (Newman Th., May 2, 1972); John Ford Noonan's *Older People* (Anspacher Th., May 14, 1972); Murray Mednick's *The Hunter* (Public Theatre Annex, May 23, 1972); and workshop productions.

The 1972 summer productions were *Hamlet*, Derek Walcott's *Ti-Jean and His Brothers*, music by Andre Tanker, lyrics by Walcott and Tanker (at the Delacorte Th., and touring); *Much Ado About Nothing*, and the New York Dance Festival. At the Public Theatre were *The Corner* by Ed Bullins (Other Stage, June 22, 1972); the Bread and Puppet Theatre production of *Coney Island Cycle*, three plays by Peter Schuman: *Revenge of the Law*, *Harvey McLeod* and *Hallelujah* (Martinson Th., Sept. 7, 1972); Jason Miller's *That Championship Season* (Booth Th., transferred for Broadway run Sept. 14, 1972); Alice Childress's *Wedding Band* (Newman Th., Sept. 26, 1972); the summer production of *Much Ado About Nothing* (Winter Garden, reopened for Broadway run Nov. 11, 1972); Michael McGuire's *The Children* (Newman Th., Nov. 28, 1972); Anton Chekhov's *The Cherry Orchard* (Anspacher Th., Dec. 7, 1972); Dennis J. Reardon's *Siamese Connections* (Public Theatre Annex, Jan. 9, 1973); David Rabe's *The Orphan* (Anspacher Th., Mar. 30, 1973); and workshop productions.

In the summer of 1973 were presented *As You Like It*, *King Lear*, *Two Gentlemen of Verona* (touring). The Public Theatre presented Robert Montgomery's *Lotta* (Anspacher Th., Oct. 18, 1973); *More Than You Deserve*, book by Michael Weller, music by Jim Steinman, lyrics by Weller and Steinman (Newman Th., Nov. 21, 1973); Jack Gelber's *Barbary Shore* (Anspacher Th., Dec. 18, 1973); Edgar White's *Les Femmes Noires* (Other Stage, Feb. 21, 1974); Miguel Piñero's *Short Eyes* (Anspacher Th., Feb. 28, 1974); Jay Broad's *The Killdeer* (Newman Th., Mar. 12, 1974); and workshop productions. *Much Ado About Nothing* was telecast (CBS, Feb. 2, 1973; PBS, Apr. 8 and 13, 1974). *Wedding Band* was telecast (ABC, Apr. 24, 1974).

During its first season, the New York Shakespeare Festival at Lincoln Center presented David Rabe's *Boom Boom Room* (Vivian Beaumont Th., Nov. 8, 1973); Shakespeare's *Troilus and Cressida* (Mitzi E. Newhouse Th., Nov. 10, 1973); Hugh Leonard's *The Au Pair Man* (Beaumont Th., Dec. 27, 1973); Shakespeare's *The Tempest* (Newhouse Th., Jan. 26, 1974); Ron Milner's *What the Wine-Sellers Buy* (Beaumont Th., Feb. 14, 1974); August Strindberg's *The Dance of Death*, adapted by A. J. Antoon from Elizabeth Sprigge's translation (Beaumont Th., Apr. 4, 1974); William Shakespeare's *Macbeth* (Newhouse Th., Apr. 13, 1974); and Miguel Piñero's *Short Eyes* (Beaumont Th., May 23, 1974, transferred from the Anspacher Th.).

Off Off Broadway Alliance (OOBA), 162 W. 56th St., New York, NY 10019, tel. (212) 757-4473.

President: Christopher Martin, CSC Repertory; *Vice-President:* Robert Moss, Playwrights Horizons; *Secretary:* Cathy Roskam, Joseph Jefferson Theatre Co.; *Treasurer:* Eve Adamson, Jean Cocteau Repertory; *Executive Director, OOBA Service Office:* Virginia R. Kahn.

The Off Off Broadway Alliance is a cooperative organization established to promote recognition for off-off Broadway as a significant cultural force in New York City and the nation. The Alliance was formed in response to the Black-Baumol *Study of New York Theatre*, published in January 1972, which suggested solutions for a number of the problems of its subject but neglected other important elements, such as the importance of a flourishing off-off Broadway arena to the development of the American theatre.

An OOBA service office was established in September 1972 to provide supportive administrative and public relations services to off-off Broadway theatre companies. As of June 1975, sixty-five nonprofit theatre companies were OOBA members, all based in Manhattan.

Oregon Shakespearean Festival Association, 15 S. Pioneer St., P.O. Box 605, Ashland, OR 97520, tel. (503) 482-2111. *Founder and Development Consultant:* Angus L. Bowmer; *Producing Director:* Jerry Turner; *General Manager:* William W. Patton; *President of the Board of Directors:* Ray Jackson.

The Oregon Shakespearean Festival was founded in 1935 by Angus Bowmer, who was producing director until his retirement in 1971, when he was succeeded by Jerry Turner. The Festival is a repertory theatre dedicated to producing the complete Shakespeare canon, as well as a variety of classical European and American works. A nonprofit corporation, the Festival provides both a training ground for preprofessional actors and technicians and a unique educational opportunity for its audience. Both the company and its audience come from all over the country.

Dr. Turner has stated the following as goals for the Festival: "To present the plays of Shakespeare and other major writers in such good faith that the audience can experience most completely the vitality of the chief literary figures common to English, European, and American cultural heritage. To amend and expand the fund of theatrical scholarship, especially with regard to the Elizabethan drama, through experience and experiment. And to provide theatre artists with a stimulating and substantial classical theatre."

The summer season consists of six productions—four Shakespearean and two non-Shakespearean. They are presented in the Festival's two theatres, an outdoor Elizabethan stagehouse modeled after London's Fortune Theatre and the modern, indoor Angus Bowmer Theatre built in 1970. The season lasts for approximately twelve weeks with two performances daily.

The Festival also offers an eight-week spring season entitled Festival/STAGE II consisting of four plays, only one of which is Shakespearean. The spring season was inaugurated in 1970 in answer to a need for expansion in repertory as well as audience capacity. The four plays rotate Tuesday through Sunday in the Angus Bowmer Theatre.

In conjunction with its two seasons, the Festival's Institute of Renaissance Studies sponsors courses for teachers and students emphasizing study of the current plays in relation to a variety of subjects, from stage techniques to classroom teaching methods. The faculty includes members of the Festival staff along with distinguished guests from all over the world.

Other education programs include the School Theatre Project in which teams of actors visit schools throughout the Northwest with presentations for English and drama classes, a summer lecture series, and special student matinee performances followed by post-play discussions with actors and directors.

The Oregon Shakespearean Festival had produced the entire canon by 1958; many of Shakespeare's works have been presented many different times. The Festival is now midway through its third presentation of all the chronicle history plays. Non-Shakespearean performances include such works as *The Duchess of Malfi, The Alchemist, Volpone, Antigone, Oedipus the King, The Imaginary Invalid, Hedda Gabler, The Glass Menagerie, Under Milk Wood, A Man for All Seasons, Charley's Aunt, The Crucible, Dance of Death, Waiting for Godot,* and *Our Town,* among others.

The Paper Bag Players, 50 Riverside Dr., New York, NY 10024, tel. (212) EN 2-0431. *Director:* Judith Martin; *Administrator:* Ludith Liss; *Composer:* Donald Ashwander; *Featured Actor:* Irving Burton.

Judith Martin and friends founded The Paper Bag Players in 1958 as a contemporary theatre for children. The ten original productions created by the company since its beginning are fast-moving one-hour revues—musical and dramatic sketches—developed for children, but appealing as well to adults.

Miss Martin develops the story, directs, and designs props and scenery, using household articles and discards; Mr. Ashwander composes original music for the skits; and a younger actor, actress and a stagehand are hired each season, bringing the size of the performing company to five. The children in the audience are invited to participate in the shows, joining the songs and offering critical suggestions.

The Paper Bag Players have appeared in New York City at Hunter College Playhouse, the Forum and Alice Tully Hall (both at Lincoln Center), the Brooklyn Academy of Music, The Living Theatre, Henry Street Settlement House, and Kaufmann Auditorium at the 92nd Street YM-YWHA. They have toured in nineteen states and Washington, D.C.; performed in London, England, at the Royal Court Th. (1968, 1970, 1972), and at the Young Vic (1973); conducted workshops for the Egyptian Ministry of Culture, Cairo, Egypt (1975); for the Institute for the Intellectual Development of Children and Young Adults, Teheran, Iran (1975); appeared in Tel Aviv, Haifa, and Jerusalem during the 1975 Festival of Israel; and at the 1976 Holland Festival.

On television, they have presented two specials on NET, *My Horse Is Waiting* (1969) and *Dandelion* (1973); Thames Television, London, showed thirteen half-hour specials throughout the United Kingdom, Sweden, and Australia (1972); and in 1975 they appeared on the Today Show (NBC); Eyewitness News (ABC); and other programs.

Awards received by the Paper Bag Players include a Village Voice Off-Bway (Obie) special citation in 1965 and an Obie award in 1972; a citation from the American Theatre Association in 1971; a NY State Award (1974); and a N.Y.C. Bicentennial Certificate (1975).

Phoenix Theatre, 149 W. 45th St., New York, NY 10036, tel. (212) 765-1620. *Managing Director:* T. Edward Hambleton

The Phoenix Theatre was organized in 1953 by T. Edward Hambleton and Norris Houghton to provide theatre of high quality that would attract both artist and theatregoer and would be available at reasonable prices. The company leased the Yiddish Art Theatre, 189 Second Ave., New York City, refurbished and renamed it the Phoenix Theatre. The first production, *Madam, Will You Walk,* by Sidney Howard, opened on Dec. 1, 1953, during a citywide newspaper strike. The company remained at the Second Avenue location for eight years.

In 1957, Theatre Incorporated, a nonprofit corporation, assumed sponsorship of Phoenix Theatre. A permanent acting company was instituted in 1958 under the direction of Stuart Vaughn. After three years, financial strains forced the dissolution of the acting company, and the organization moved to the off-Broadway East 74th St. Theatre, 334 E. 74th St., in September 1961.

In February 1964, Phoenix Theatre assumed the sponsorship of the Association of Producing Artists (APA). This marriage lasted until April 1969. For three more seasons (1969-72) after that the Phoenix Theatre continued to produce plays both on and off Broadway. Then for the twentieth season of continuous production another reorganization was effected. The New Phoenix Repertory Theatre, with Harold Prince, Stephen Porter, and Michael Montel as artistic directors, opened at the Zellerbach Theatre of the Annenberg Center at the University of Pennsylvania in Philadelphia. The company performed at several other university centers as well as presenting short seasons in Manhattan and Brooklyn. In 1975 the company settled in the Playhouse, 357 W. 48th St., New York City.

Phoenix Theatre has sponsored a wide variety of experimental presentations as well as the major productions. In twenty-three seasons the company has staged more than 150 productions—new plays, revivals, musicals, ballets, modern dance, operas, mimes, and marionette shows. The list includes: (1953-54) *Madam, Will You Walk;* William Shakespeare's *Coriolanus;* John Latouche and Jerome Moross' *The Golden Apple;* and Anton Chekhov's *The Seagull;* (1954-55) Robert Ardrey's *Sing Me No Lullaby;* Earl Robinson and Waldo Salt's *Sandhog;* George Bernard Shaw's *The Doctor's Dilemma;* Henrik Ibsen's *The Master Builder;* and *Phoenix '55* by Ira Wallach, David Craig, and David Baker; (1955-56) Aldyth Morris' *The Carefree Tree;* Luigi Pirandello's *Six Characters in Search of an Author;* August Strindberg's *Miss Julie* and *The Stronger;* Ivan Turgenev's *A Month in the Country;* and Ogden Nash and Vernon Duke's *The Littlest Revue;* and (1956-57) George Bernard Shaw's *Saint Joan;* Aleksandr Ostrovski's *Diary of a Scoundrel;* Bertolt Brecht's *The Good Woman of Setzuan;* William Shakespeare's *Measure for Measure* and *The Taming of the Shrew;* John Webster's *The Duchess of Malfi;* and *Livin' the Life* by Dale Wasserman, Bruce Geller, and Jack Urbont.

Also (1957-58) Friedrich Schiller's *Mâry Stuart;* Karl Capek's *The Makropoulos Secret;* Eugene Ionesco's *The Chairs* and *The Lesson;* Jean Cocteau's *The Infernal Machine;* the Stratford (Canada) Festival productions of William Shakespeare's *Two*

Gentlemen of Verona and Heinrich Von Kleist's *The Broken Jug;* and Le Théâtre du Nouveau Monde productions of Molière's *Le Malade Imaginaire, Le Mariage Forcé, Sganarelle,* and *La Jalousie du Barbouille;* (1958-59) T. S. Eliot's *The Family Reunion;* Graham Greene's *The Power and the Glory,* as adapted by Denis Cannan and Pierre Bost; George Farquhar's *The Beaux' Stratagem;* and *Once Upon a Mattress* by Mary Rodgers, Jay Thompson, Marshall Barer, and Dean Fuller; (1959-60) Eugene O'Neill's *The Great God Brown;* Aristophanes' *Lysistrata;* Sean O'Casey's *Pictures in the Hallway;* Henrik Ibsen's *Peer Gynt;* and William Shakespeare's *Henry IV, Parts 1* and *2;* (1960-61) the Stratford (Canada) Festival production of Gilbert and Sullivan's *H.M.S. Pinafore;* Oliver Goldsmith's *She Stoops To Conquer;* Sean O'Casey's *The Plough and the Stars;* Dion Boucicault's *The Octoroon;* and William Shakespeare's *Hamlet;* and (1961-62) the Stratford (Canada) Festival production of Gilbert and Sullivan's *The Pirates of Penzance;* Slawomir Mrozek's *The Policemen;* George Bernard Shaw's *The Dark Lady of the Sonnets;* Frank D. Gilroy's *Who'll Save the Plowboy?;* and Arthur Kopit's *Oh Dad, Poor Dad, Mamma's Hung You in the Closet and I'm Feelin' So Sad.*

Also (1962-63) Robert E. Sherwood's *Abe Lincoln in Illinois;* William Shakespeare's *The Taming of the Shrew;* Eugene Schwarz's *The Dragon;* and Thornton Wilder's *The Matchmaker;* (1963-64) Paul Klein and Fred Ebb's *Morning Sun;* James Saunders' *Next Time I'll Sing to You;* William Gillette's *Too Much Johnson;* Margaret Webster's *The Brontes;* and (with APA) Luigi Pirandello's *Right You Are;* George M. Cohan's *The Tavern;* Molière's *Scapin* and *Impromptu at Versailles;* and Maxim Gorki's *The Lower Depths;* and (1964-65) Christopher Marlowe's *Doctor Faustus;* and (with APA) George Bernard Shaw's *Man and Superman;* Leo Tolstoi's *War and Peace* as adapted by Alfred Neumann, Erwin Piscator, and Guntram Prufer; and Jean Giraudoux's *Judith.*

All productions for the seasons 1965-66 through 1968-69 were with APA and included: (1965-66) Henrik Ibsen's *The Wild Duck;* Archibald MacLeish's *Herakles;* Samuel Beckett's *Krapp's Last Tape;* and George S. Kaufman and Moss Hart's *You Can't Take It with You;* (1966-67) Brendan Behan's *The Hostage;* Richard Brinsley Sheridan's *The School for Scandal;* Luigi Pirandello's *Right You Are;* Richard Baldridge's *We, Comrades Three,* adapted from writings of Walt Whitman; Henrik Ibsen's *The Wild Duck;*Leo Tolstoi's *War and Peace;* and George S. Kaufman and Moss Hart's *You Can't Take It with You;* (1967-68) Michel de Ghelderode's *Pantagleize;* George Kelly's *The Show-Off;* Eugene Ionesco's *Exit the King;* and Anton Chekhov's *The Cherry Orchard;* and (1968-69) George Kelly's *The Show-Off* (on tour); Michel de Ghelderode's *Pantagleize* (on tour); Molière's *The Misanthrope;* Sean O'Casey's *Cock-a-Doodle Dandy;* T. S. Eliot's *The Cocktail Party;* and William Shakespeare's *Hamlet.*

Also (1969-70) Mary Chase's *Harvey;* José Triana's *The Criminals;* and Aeschylus' *The Persians;* (1970-71) Daniel Berrigan's *The Trial of the Catonsville Nine* and Molière's *The School for Wives;* (1971-72) Mary Chase's *Harvey* (on tour); Molière's *The School for Wives* (on tour); and Conor Cruise O'Brien's *Murderous Angels;* (1972-73) Eugene O'Neill's *The Great God Brown* and Molière's *Don Juan;* (1973-74) Friedrich Duerrenmatt's *The Visit;* Georges Feydeau's *Chemin de Fer;* and Philip Barry's *Holiday;* (1974-75) William Congreve's *Love for Love;* Luigi Pirandello's *The Rules of the Game;* and Carson McCullers' *The Member of the Wedding;* and (1975-76) Tennessee Williams' *27 Wagons Full of Cotton* and Arthur Miller's *A Memory of Two Mondays;* Sidney Howard's *They Knew What They Wanted;* William Gillette's *Secret Service;* and Bella and Sam Spewack's *Boy Meets Girl.*

The Players, 16 Gramercy Park, New York, NY 10003, tel. (212) GR 5-6116.
President: Alfred Drake; *First Vice-President:* Roland Winters; *Second Vice-President:* Peter Turgeon; *Secretary:* Ralph Camargo; *Treasurer:* Wilfred J. Halpern.

The Players is situated in a brownstone mansion built originally in 1845 for banker Elihu Townsend. In the 1880s the house was owned by the Hon. Clarkson N. Potter, U.S. Congressman. Potter's widow sold it in 1887 to Edwin Booth, who commissioned architect Stanford White to remove the brownstone stoop, substitute Greek columns and a street-level entrance with projecting wrought-iron lanterns. The gas jets still flicker in the twin lamps, and The Players has become a registered national historic landmark.

For years Edwin Booth had had a consuming desire to serve the theatre in a way other than with his recognized ability to "suit the action to the word, the word to the action"—a manner in which he could encourage the "social advantages so necessary for what is termed 'the elevation of the stage.'" In the late 1870s, Booth enjoyed the hospitality of the famed Garrick Club of London and conceived the idea of a similar club in New York. His dream began to take definite shape in July 1887 aboard a yacht at anchor in Boothbay Harbor, Me., where the prominent financier Elias C. Benedict hosted a company of friends on the *Oneida:* Mr. Booth, Lawrence Barrett, Thomas Bailey Aldrich, Laurence Hutton, William Bispham, and Parke Godwin. There The Players was conceived.

Before going on tour that September, Booth, after consulting with playwright and theatre manager Augustin Daly and Union Square Theatre manager Albert M. Palmer, made the final decision to assume the cost of housing The Players. On Jan. 6, 1888, Daly invited fifteen friends of the actor to breakfast at Delmonico's—the fifteen who were to become the incorporators of The Players: actors Joseph Jefferson, John Drew, Lawrence Barrett, James Lewis, Henry Edwards, and John A. Lane, banker turned actor; Albert M. Palmer and Augustin Daly; lawyers Joseph F. Daly and Stephen H. Olin; businessman William Bispham; Professor Brander Matthews; authors Laurence Hutton and Samuel L. Clemens; and Gen. William Tecumseh Sherman.

Today, membership in The Players, resident and nonresident, is approaching the 1,000 mark. In over three quarters of a century the club has had seven presidents: Booth, Jefferson, Drew, Walter Hampden, Howard Lindsay, Dennis King, and currently Alfred Drake. It was Booth's conception that The Players was not to be solely an actors' haunt or even a sacred theatrical sanctum. It was to be a gentlemen's social club where actors and dramatists of repute would mingle in good fellowship with craftsmen of the fine arts as well as those of the performing arts, and the membership was to include bankers, lawyers, and businessmen who would be categorized as Patrons of the Arts. In addition, the club was formally charged with the primary duty of building up "a library relating especially to the history of the American stage, and the preservation of pictures, bills of the play, photographs and curiosities," forming a repository where the great and colorful personalities who molded the American theatre, and who continue to direct its destinies, should come alive for future generations. Booth's nucleus of 1,000 volumes was augmented by hundreds of additions and became The Players Library. Because it was and is such a vital and vibrant organism, it was destined, in the interest of the arts, to open its doors to the world of theatre research. This it did officially in 1957 as The Walter Hampden Memorial Library at The Players, named in honor of the club's fourth president, one of this century's most renowned actors. Now permanently chartered under the Education Law of the State of New York, the library's statement of purpose includes the clause: "to establish and maintain for the use of the public a library devoted to the advancement of the arts in general and the drama in particular."

Between 1922 and 1940 The Players presented all-star revivals for one week only, of famous plays known as "The Players Revivals." All business details, staging, and publicity of these productions were undertaken exclusively by club members.

Playwrights' Company.
The Playwrights' Company was organized in 1938 by five American dramatists; Maxwell Anderson, S. N. Behrman, Sidney Howard, Elmer Rice and Robert E. Sherwood banded together to share in the responsibilities and rights of their own productions. Later, Kurt Weill and Robert Anderson became partner dramatists, and John Wharton and Roger L. Stevens also became partners in the organization.

The first production was Robert E. Sherwood's *Abe Lincoln in Illinois,* which opened Oct. 15, 1938. Over the years, the Playwrights' Company took part in the production of plays by other than the partners of the company.

With the production of Gore Vidal's *The Best Man* in 1960, the Playwrights' Company announced its dissolution. Of the founding members, Maxwell Anderson, Sidney Howard, and Robert E. Sherwood had died, as had Kurt Weill.

Works produced or co-produced by the Playwrights' Company included Robert E. Sherwood's *Abe Lincoln in Illinois* (Plymouth Th., Oct. 15, 1938); Maxwell Anderson's *Knickerbocker Holiday* (Ethel Barrymore Th., Oct. 19, 1938); Elmer Rice's *American Landscape* (Cort, Dec. 3, 1938); S. N. Behrman's *No Time for Comedy* (Ethel Barrymore Th., Apr. 17, 1939); Maxwell Anderson's *Key Largo* (Ethel Barrymore Th., Nov. 27, 1939); Elmer Rice's *Two on an Island* (Broadhurst, Jan. 22, 1940); Robert E.

Sherwood's *There Shall Be No Night* (Alvin, Apr. 29, 1940); Maxwell Anderson's *Journey to Jerusalem* (Natl., Oct. 5, 1940); Elmer Rice's *Flight to the West* (Guild, Dec. 30, 1940); S. N. Behrman's *The Talley Method* (Henry Miller's Th., Feb. 24, 1941); Maxwell Anderson's *Candle in the Wind* (Shubert, Oct. 22, 1941); Maxwell Anderson's *The Eve of St. Mark* (Cort, Oct. 7, 1942); S. N. Behrman's *The Pirate* (Martin Beck Th., Nov. 25, 1942); Sidney Kingsley's *The Patriots* (Natl., Jan. 29, 1943); Elmer Rice's *A New Life* (Royale, Sept. 15, 1943); Maxwell Anderson's *Storm Operation* (Belasco, Jan. 11, 1944); Robert E. Sherwood's *The Rugged Path* (Plymouth, Nov. 10, 1945); Elmer Rice's *Dream Girl* (Coronet, Dec. 14, 1945); Maxwell Anderson's *Truckline Café* (Belasco, Feb. 27, 1946); Maxwell Anderson's *Joan of Lorraine* (Alvin, Nov. 18, 1946); the musical *Street Scene,* book by Elmer Rice, lyrics by Langston Hughes, music by Kurt Weill (Adelphi, Jan. 9, 1947); Maxwell Anderson's *Anne of the Thousand Days* (Shubert, Dec. 8, 1948); Garson Kanin's *The Smile of the World* (Lyceum, Jan. 12, 1949); Maxwell Anderson and Kurt Weill's *Lost in the Stars* (Music Box, Oct. 20, 1949); Sidney Kingsley's *Darkness at Noon* (Alvin, Jan. 13, 1951); Elmer Rice's *Not for Children* (Coronet, Feb. 13, 1951); Jan de Hartog's *The Fourposter* (Ethel Barrymore Th., Oct. 24, 1951); Maxwell Anderson's *Barefoot in Athens* (Martin Beck Th., Oct. 31, 1951); Elmer Rice's *The Grand Tour* (Martin Beck Th., Dec. 10, 1951); Stanley Young's *Mr. Pickwick* (Plymouth, Sept. 17, 1952); George Tabori's *The Emperor's Clothes* (Ethel Barrymore Th., Feb. 9, 1953); Robert Anderson's *Tea and Sympathy* (Ethel Barrymore Th., Sept. 30, 1953); Samuel Taylor's *Sabrina Fair* (Natl., Nov. 11, 1953); and Jane Bowles' *In the Summer House* (Playhouse, Dec. 29, 1953).

Also, Elmer Rice's *The Winner* (Playhouse, Feb. 17, 1954); Jean Giraudoux' *Ondine* (46th St. Th., Feb. 18, 1954); Robert Anderson's *All Summer Long* (Coronet, Sept. 23, 1954); Horton Foote's *The Traveling Lady* (Playhouse, Oct. 27, 1954); Maxwell Anderson's *The Bad Seed* (46th St. Th., Dec. 8, 1954); Tennessee Williams' *Cat on a Hot Tin Roof* (Morosco, Mar. 24, 1955); Baruch Lumet's *Once Upon a Tailor* (Cort, May 23, 1955); Jean Giraudoux' *Tiger at the Gates* (Plymouth, Oct. 3, 1955); Joseph Fields and Jerome Chodorov's *The Ponder Heart* (Music Box, Feb. 16, 1956); Leslie Stevens' *The Lovers* (Martin Beck Th., May 10, 1956); Robert E. Sherwood's *Small War on Murray Hill* (Ethel Barrymore Th., Jan. 3, 1957); Jean Anouilh's *Time Remembered* (Morosco, Nov. 12, 1957); Noel Coward's *Nude with Violin* (Belasco, Nov. 14, 1957); Morton Wishengrad's *The Rope Dancers* (Cort, Nov. 20, 1957); William Wycherley's *The Country Wife* (Adelphi, Nov. 27, 1957); Ray Lawler's *Summer of the Seventeenth Doll* (Coronet, Jan. 22, 1958); Phoebe Ephron's *Howie* (46th St. Th., Sept. 17, 1958); Samuel Taylor and Cornelia Otis Skinner's *The Pleasure of His Company* (Longacre, Oct. 22, 1958); Milton Geiger's *Edwin Booth* (46th St. Th., Nov. 24, 1958); Elmer Rice's *Cue for Passion* (Henry Miller's Th., Nov. 25, 1958); Alec Coppel's *The Gazebo* (Lyceum, Dec. 12, 1958); Noel Coward's *Look After Lulu* (Henry Miller's Th., Mar. 3, 1959); Joseph Stein and Marc Blitzstein's *Juno* (Winter Garden, Mar. 3, 1959); and Gore Vidal's *The Best Man* (Morosco, Mar. 31, 1960).

Producers' Theatre. 1545 Broadway, New York, NY 10036, tel. (212) PL 7-6900.
Roger L. Stevens, Robert Whitehead, Robert W. Dowling.

The Producers' Theatre was formed in 1953 by Messrs. Stevens, Whitehead, and Dowling. At the time of its formation, the company had assets of $1,000,000 and three leased Broadway theatres.

Producers' Theatre has produced or co-produced T. S. Eliot's *The Confidential Clerk* (Morosco, Feb. 11, 1954); William Archibald's *Portrait of a Lady* (ANTA, Dec. 21, 1954); Clifford Odets' *The Flowering Peach* (Belasco, Dec. 28, 1954); Joyce Grenfell's *Joyce Grenfell Requests the Pleasure. . . .* (Bijou, Oct. 10, 1955); Christopher Marlowe's *Tamburlaine the Great* (Winter Garden, Jan. 19, 1956); Terrence Rattigan's *Separate Tables* (Music Box, Oct. 25, 1956); George Bernard Shaw's *Major Barbara* (Martin Beck Th., Oct. 30, 1956); Terrence Rattigan's *The Sleeping Prince* (Coronet, Nov. 1, 1956); Jean Anouilh's *The Waltz of the Toreadors* (Coronet, Jan. 17, 1957); Arnold Schulman's *A Hole in the Head* (Plymouth, Feb. 28, 1957); Maxwell Anderson and Brendan Gill's *The Day the Money Stopped* (Belasco, Feb. 20, 1958); Friedrich Duerrenmatt's *The Visit* (Lunt-Fontanne, May 5, 1958); Eugene O'Neill's *A Touch of the Poet* (Helen Hayes Th., Oct. 2, 1958); Walter and Jean Kerr, Leroy Anderson, and Joan Ford's musical *Goldilocks* (Lunt-Fontanne, Oct. 11, 1958); Albert Beich and William H. Wright's *The Man in the Dog Suit* (Coronet, Oct. 30, 1958); S. N. Behrman's *The Cold Wind and the Warm* (Morosco, Dec. 8, 1958); and William Shakespeare's *Much Ado About Nothing* (Lunt-Fontanne, Sept. 17, 1959).

The Repertory Company of the Virginia Museum Theatre, Boulevard and Grove, Richmond, VA 23221, tel. (804) 770-6333.
Producing Director: Keith Fowler; *General Manager:* Loraine Slade.

The Virginia Museum Theatre (VMT) was established in 1955 as a division of the Virginia Museum of Fine Arts. Housed in an intimate 500-seat proscenium theatre, the VMT was initially organized as a community theatre, with a staff of professional directors and designers and amateur actors. In 1972, Keith Fowler founded the professional Equity repertory company, which now offers a 6-month season each year and a repertory consisting of classics and new artistic works. The theatre also sponsors a conservatory, which offers tuition-free classes to members of the community, and a resident apprenticeship program for advanced theatre students. The resident apprenticeship program is accredited by Virginia Polytechnic Institute and State University.

VMT repertory productions since 1972 have included Edmond Rostand's *Cyrano de Bergerac,* Keith Fowler's adaptation of Charles Dicken's *A Christmas Carol,* Joe Orton's *Loot,* William Shakespeare's *Macbeth,* Jerome Lawrence and Robert E. Lee's *The Night Thoreau Spent in Jail,* the American premiere of Richard F. Stockton's *The Royal Rape of Ruari Macasmunde (Prisoner of the Crown), Jacques Brel Is Alive and Well. . .,* Arthur Kopit's *Indians, A Victorian Christmas Panto,* Athol Fugard's *The Blood Knot,* William Shakespeare's *The Taming of the Shrew,* the world premiere of *Democracy,* John Clifton and Ben Tarver's *The Man with a Load of Mischief,* the musical *Purlie,* based on Ossie Davis' *Purlie Victorious,* Thornton Wilder's *Our Town,* Peter Handke's *Kaspar,* Molière's *The Miser,* the American premiere of *Our Father,* William Shakespeare's *Much Ado About Nothing,* and Jack Kirkland's *Tobacco Road,* adapted from Erskine Caldwell's novel.

The Repertory Theatre of Lincoln Center, Inc.

On February 15, 1960, the Repertory Theatre of Lincoln Center was founded under the auspices of the Lincoln Center for the Performing Arts. It was constituted as a non-profit, professional, institutional theatre with Robert Whitehead and Elia Kazan as co-directors. The training program for the company of 26 actors began on October 1, 1962. The first production, the world premiere of Arthur Miller's *After the Fall,* was presented at the ANTA-Washington Square Theatre on January 23, 1964.

The ANTA-Washington Square Theatre was erected as a temporary home for the Repertory Theatre until its permanent home, the Vivian Beaumont Theatre at Lincoln Center, was completed.

During its first season, the company presented, in addition to *After the Fall,* Eugene O'Neill's *Marco Millions* (ANTA-Washington Sq. Th., Feb. 20, 1964); and the world premiere of S. N. Behrman's *But for Whom Charlie* (ANTA-Washington Sq. Th., Mar. 12, 1964).

During the second season at the ANTA-Washington Square Theatre, the company presented Middleton and Rowley's *The Changeling* (Oct. 29, 1964), Arthur Miller's *Incident at Vichy* (Dec. 3, 1964) and Molière's *Tartuffe* (Jan. 14, 1965).

In October 1964 Elia Kazan relinquished his position as co-director of the company and in December 1964 Robert Whitehead also resigned his post as administrator of the company due to difficulties with the board of directors. On January 25, 1965, the board of directors announced the appointment of Herbert Blau and Jules Irving, founders and co-producing directors of the San Francisco Actors Workshop, as co-producing directors of the Repertory Theatre of Lincoln Center. They began their duties on March 1, 1965.

The third season began with the opening of the Vivian Beaumont Theatre at Lincoln Center on October 21, 1965, with Georg Buechner's *Danton's Death*; and continued with William Wycherley's *The Country Wife* (Dec. 9, 1965); Jean-Paul Sartre's *The Condemned of Altona* (Feb. 3, 1966), adapted by Justin O'Brien; Bertolt Brecht's *The Caucasian Chalk Circle* (Mar. 24, 1966), English version by Eric Bentley.

During the fourth season, the company presented Ben Jonson's *The Alchemist* (Oct. 13, 1966); Federico Garcia Lorca's *Yerma* (Dec. 8, 1966), translation by W. S. Merwin; Leo Lehman's *The East Wind* (Feb. 9, 1967); Bertolt Brecht's *Galileo* (Apr. 13, 1967), adapted by Charles Laughton. Mr. Blau resigned as co-director in January 1967. Mr.

Irving continued as director of the company.

During the fifth season, the company presented George Bernard Shaw's *Saint Joan* (Jan 4, 1968); Jean Giraudoux' *Tiger at the Gates* (Feb. 29, 1968), adapted by Christopher Fry; Edmond Rostand's *Cyrano de Bergerac* (Apr. 25, 1968), English version by James Forsyth. The company also presented its first season in the Forum Theatre with two one-act plays by Mayo Simon, *Walking to Waldheim* and *Happiness* (Nov. 10, 1967); and Ron Cowen's *Summertree* (Mar. 3, 1968).

During the sixth season, the productions were Shakespeare's *King Lear* (Vivian Beaumont Th., Nov. 7, 1968); William Gibson's *A Cry of Players* (Vivian Beaumont Th., Nov. 14, 1968); Charles Dizenzo's two one-act plays *An Evening for Merlin Finch* and *A Great Career* (Forum Th., Dec. 5, 1968); Heinar Kipphardt's *In the Matter of J. Robert Oppenheimer* (Vivian Beaumont Th., Mar. 6, 1969), translated by Ruth Spiers; James Hanley's *The Inner Journey* (Forum Th., Mar. 20, 1969); Molière's *The Miser* (Vivian Beaumont Th., May 8, 1969), based on a translation by H. Baker and J. Miller; John Ford Noonan's *The Year Boston Won the Pennant* (Forum Th., May 22, 1969); and *In the Matter of J. Robert Oppenheimer* played a return engagement (Vivian Beaumont Th., June 26, 1969).

In the seventh season, the company presented William Saroyan's *The Time of Your Life* (Vivian Beaumont Th., Nov. 6, 1969); Vaclav Havel's *The Increased Difficulty of Concentration* (Forum Th., Dec. 4, 1969), translated by Vera Blockwell; Tennessee Williams' *Camino Real* (Vivian Beaumont Th., Jan. 8, 1970); Jeff Wanshel's *The Disintegration of James Cherry* (Forum Th., Jan. 29, 1970); Sam Shepard's *Operation Sidewinder* (Vivian Beaumont Th., Mar. 12, 1970); Harold Pinter's one-act plays *Landscape* and *Silence* (Forum Th., Apr. 2, 1970); George S. Kaufman and Marc Connelly's *Beggar on Horseback* (Vivian Beaumont Th., May 14, 1970); Peter Hack's *Amphitryon* (Forum Th., May 28, 1970), translated by Ralph Manheim.

During the eighth season, the company presented Bertolt Brecht's *The Good Woman of Setzuan* (Vivian Beaumont Th., Nov. 5, 1970), translated by Ralph Manheim; John Millington Synge's *The Playboy of the Western World* (Vivian Beaumont Th., Jan. 7, 1971); Harold Pinter's *The Birthday Party* (Forum Th., Feb. 5, 1971); Mr. Pinter's one-act plays *Landscape* and *Silence* (Forum Th., Feb. 9, 1971); Henrik Ibsen's *An Enemy of the People* (Vivian Beaumont Th., Mar. 11, 1971), adapted by Arthur Miller; A. R. Gurney, Jr.'s *Scenes from American Life* (Forum Th., Mar. 25, 1971), adapted by Paul Shyre; Sophocles' *Antigone* (Vivian Beaumont Th., May 13, 1971), English version by Dudley Fitts and Robert Fitzgerald; Friedrich Duerrenmatt's *Play Strindberg* (Forum Th., June 3, 1971), based on August Strindberg's *The Dance of Death*, translated by James Kirkup.

In the fall of 1970 a plan was formulated for the City Center of Music and Drama, which operates the New York State Theatre at Lincoln Center, to take over the operation of the building and theatres used by the Repertory Company. The Repertory Company was to become a tenant and thus be relieved of the responsibility and expense for the year-round upkeep of the property.

The City Center announced a $5,200,000 remodeling plan for the building. A cinematheque with theatres to show the films was to be built in the basement area of the Forum Theatre. That auditorium, universally praised as the best theatre space in the Lincoln Center complex, was to be reconstructed in a smaller backstage area. The ensuing public opposition and controversy caused the entire plan to be abandoned in December 1971.

During the ninth season, the company presented Friedrich Schiller's *Mary Stuart* (Vivian Beaumont Th., Nov. 11, 1971), freely translated and adapted by Stephen Spender; Athol Fugard's *People Are Living Here* (Forum Th., Nov. 18, 1971); Edward Bond's *Narrow Road to the Deep North* (Vivian Beaumont Th., Jan. 6, 1972); Peter Handke's *The Ride across Lake Constance* (Forum Th., Jan. 13, 1972), translated by Michael Roloff; Shakespeare's *Twelfth Night* (Vivian Beaumont Th., Mar. 2, 1972); Ed Bullins' *The Duplex* (Forum Th., Mar. 9, 1972); Arthur Miller's *The Crucible* (Vivian Beaumont Th., Apr. 27, 1972); David Wiltse's *Suggs* (Forum Th., May 4, 1972).

At the beginning of the tenth season in October 1972, Jules Irving announced his resignation to take effect at the end of the season because the board of directors was unable to fund the season in the Forum Theatre. The company presented Maxim Gorki's *Enemies* (Vivian Beaumont Th., Nov. 9, 1972), English version by Jeremy Brooks and Kitty Hunter-Blair; two programs of one-act plays by Samuel Beckett, *Happy Days* and *Act Without Words I* (Forum Th., Nov. 20, 1972) and *Krapp's Last Tape* and *Not I* (Forum Th., Nov. 22, 1972); Sean O'Casey's *The Plough and the Stars* (Vivian Beaumont Th., Jan. 4, 1973); Shakespeare's *The Merchant of Venice* (Vivian Beaumont Th., Mar. 1, 1973); Tennessee Williams' *A Streetcar Named Desire* (Vivian Beaumont Th., Apr. 26, 1973).

On March 6, 1973, Lincoln Center, Inc., announced that Joseph Papp and his New York Shakespeare Festival Company would replace the Repertory Theatre of Lincoln Center. Mr. Papp's board of directors also replaced the Repertory Theatre board. The Repertory Company played its final performance of *A Streetcar Named Desire* on July 29, 1973. For further information on the continuing activities at the Vivian Beaumont Theatre and the Forum Theatre see the article on the New York Shakespeare Festival.

Roundabout Theatre Company, 333 W. 23rd St., New York, NY 10011, tel. (212) 924-7161.

Producing Director: Gene Feist; *Executive Director:* Michael Fried.

The Roundabout Theatre Company was founded by Gene Feist in the spring of 1965 as a state-chartered, nonprofit educational institution. From the beginning, the intention was to present the great plays of the past and also revivals of worthy plays of more recent vintage at very modest admission prices.

In November 1966, the company began its first season with a production of August Strindberg's *The Father* in a 144-seat basement theatre beneath a supermarket at 307 W. 26th St. The Roundabout functioned as an off-Broadway group with casts of both professional and nonprofessional actors. As the company grew and developed, it became a professional off-Broadway organization with a year-round schedule of activities. Many of its productions tour New York City schools and other school systems in the metropolitan area. An in-house program for directors, playwrights, and performers is also maintained.

Starting with 100 subscribers during its first season, by the 1973-74 season the Roundabout subscribers had grown to 14,000. In August 1974, the RKO 23rd Street Cinema was leased and remodeled to provide expanded production facilities and seating capacity of 300. The new theatre is called Stage One. The theatre on 26th Street, now called Stage Two, will be used for experimental productions, workshop activities, and the educational program.

Roundabout Theatre productions have included (1966-67) *The Father, The Miser, Peleas and Melisande, and Pins and Needles;* (1967-68) *Waiting for Lefty, The Bond, King Lear, The Importance of Being Earnest;* (1968-69) *Journey's End, King Lear, Candida,* and *Dance of Death;* (1969-70) *Trumpets and Drums, Macbeth, Oedipus,* and *Lady from Maxim's;* (1970-71) *Hamlet, Tug of War, Uncle Vanya, Chas. Abbott & Son,* and *She Stoops To Conquer;* (1972 summer season) *The Fan, The Lover, The Creditors, The Wax Museum, Mr. Shandy, Box and Cox, How He Lied to Her Husband,* and *The Bacchae;* (1971-72) *The Master Builder, The Taming of the Shrew, Misalliance,* and *Conditions of Agreement;* (1973 summer season) *The Caretaker, Miss Julie, The Death of Lord Chatterly,* and *Hamlet;* (1972-73) *Right You Are, Chekhov's Garden Party, American Gothics, The Play's the Thing,* and *Ghosts;* (1973-74) *The Father, The Seagull, The Circle,* and *The Burnt Flowerbed.*

Society of Stage Directors and Choreographers, 1619 Broadway, New York, NY 10019, tel. (212) CI 6-5118.

President: Lloyd Richards; *Executive Vice-President:* Mary Hunter; *Vice-President:* James Hammerstein; *Secretary:* Charles Olsen; *Treasurer:* Billy Matthews; *Executive Secretary:* Mildred Traube.

The Society of Stage Directors and Choreographers is the newest of the theatre trade union groups. Though formed in 1959, it was not until August 1962 that the group was recognized by the League of New York Theatres & Producers, and its minimum basic agreement signed. It now has collective agreements with the League of Off Broadway Theatres & Producers and the League of Resident Theatres.

At present, the Society has approximately 500 members and speaks for most of the legitimate theatre's directors and choreographers.

Stage Periodicals

One of the earliest American publications to carry news of the theatre was the *Spirit of the Times*, published weekly in New York from 1831 to 1861. (A similar periodical, *Wilkes' Spirit of the Times*, ran from 1859 to 1902.) Describing itself as "a chronicle of the turf, agriculture, field sports, literature and the stage," the newspaper carried articles, interviews, obituaries, and reviews of theatrical and musical presentations both in the United States and abroad, particularly London and Paris. Under the heading "Movements of Actors," it carried news of touring actors and productions in the US and Canada.

In 1853, the New York *Clipper* joined the scene and appeared weekly until 1924. Like the *Spirit of the Times,* the *Clipper* carried news of the theatre and sporting world. This paper was read by professionals for casting news and news of business arrangements. Actors "at liberty" advertised in its columns for positions.

From 1879 until 1922, the *New York Dramatic Mirror* ranked as the leading theatre newspaper. At one point in its career, it announced "the *Mirror* is the American Dramatic authority and the ablest journal devoted to the stage in the world. It is read in every city of the Union, and its circulation is double that of any theatrical paper." The publication probably gained its widest audience under the editorship of Harrison Grey Fiske, who assumed the post in 1880 when he was only twenty. Fiske was in command until 1911 and it was through the pages of the New York *Dramatic Mirror* that he waged his battle against the Syndicate.

Today's leading theatre newspaper is *Variety,* which was founded in 1905 by Sime Silverman, who served as its editor-publisher until his death in 1933. Abel Green then became editor, and he continued in this position until his death in 1973, when *Variety's* publisher, Syd Silverman (grandson of the founder), took over as Executive Editor. *Variety* has been called "The Bible of Show Business." The publication details developments in all phases of show business: stage, cinema, radio, television, night club, concert, opera, recordings, etc. It is written in a language which has been developed by *Variety* writers over the years . . . an amalgam of slang, abbreviation, Broadwayese and show business parlance.

Billboard reports not only the legitimate theatre but also circus, carnival, pop music, coin and vending machines. It was founded in 1894 by W. H. Donaldson.

Casting information for the stage, cinema, radio, television, modeling, etc., is reported in *Show Business* (founded as *Actor Cues* in 1941). It is one of the several publications of Leo Shull reporting the day-to-day happenings in show business. More recently (1959) *Back Stage* has chronicled news of the legitimate theatre, film, and television.

For many years, the leading popular stage periodical was *Theatre Magazine.* From 1901 until April 1931, it carried reviews of the new plays on Broadway, interviews with the stars and chatty articles, several features each month and all liberally illustrated with scenes from the plays and portraits of stage favorites. The editor and chief drama critic for *Theatre Magazine* from 1901 until 1926 was Arthur Hornblow. His reviews, "Mr. Hornblow Goes to the Play," were widely read by audience and professionals alike.

Theatre Arts Magazine began as "an illustrated quarterly" in Detroit, Michigan, in November 1916. Sheldon Cheney was the first editor, assisted by a panel of distinguished contributing editors. The magazine carried illustrated articles on the art of the theatre, on little theatre, stage publications, etc. In January 1924, the periodical became a monthly. It continued until February 1948, to campaign for a better theatre, to bring to the attention of its readers important new theatre talents, to encourage the community and educational theatres. In spring 1948, a new *Theatre Arts* (combined with *Stage Magazine)* made its debut. The new publication was more of a popular magazine, with reviews, articles, profuse illustrations, and a full-length play in each issue. The new *Theatre Arts* was edited by Charles MacArthur, and continued, under various editors until spring 1964, when it ceased publication. *Stage Magazine* had its genesis in 1925, when the Theatre Guild inaugurated publication of a quarterly, mainly designed to inform readers of Theatre Guild activities. This periodical became a monthly and eventually branched out on its own as *Stage Magazine.* Under various editors and publishers, *Stage Magazine* continued until 1941, taking, on the whole, a rather light view of theatre, cinema, night clubs and other entertainment media.

The theatre of social and political protest in the 1930s was ably documented by *New Theatre,* edited by Herbert Kline and then Ben Blake. This monthly magazine of drama, film, and dance, was published in New York by the Workers Theatres of America and the Workers Dance League. *New Theatre* began publication in January 1934 (superseding *Workers Theatre* [1931-33] which had been published by the Workers Laboratory Theatre), and continued publishing until November 1936. It was revived briefly for two issues in March and April 1937, under the title *New Theatre and Film.* The magazine contained articles, reviews, interviews on productions and personalities in the United States and abroad, as well as texts of short plays or scenes. Contributors included Clifford Odets, Harold Clurman, Langston Hughes, Lincoln Kirstein, V. I. Pudovkin.

The Drama Review (TDR) is a scholarly quarterly now published under the auspices of the School of Arts of New York University. Founded in 1955 as the *Carleton Drama Review* in Northfield, Minnesota, it moved to New Orleans in 1957 and changed its title to the *Tulane Drama Review.* In 1967, the magazine moved to its present home with the editorial and business staffs intact. The current editor is Michael Kirby; Richard Schechner, who was the editor for many years, remains on the masthead as a contributing editor. The magazine features well-researched articles on a wide variety of theatrical subjects, with each number devoted to a different topic.

Huntington Hartford, producer, writer, museum founder and patron of the arts, established in 1960 *Show, the Magazine of the Arts,* an illustrated monthly periodical with feature articles, reviews, etc., and was its publisher until 1965.

There are several stage periodicals aimed primarily at the student and/or amateur. *Players Magazine,* published bi-monthly by the National Collegiate Players in De Kalb, Illinois, has been serving college and community theatres since 1924. It devotes considerable space to activities among college theatre groups but also concerns itself with professional theatre. In recent years, it has printed an annual list of premiere productions throughout the country. *Dramatics,* which started as the *High School Thespian* in 1929, is now published bi-monthly in Cincinnati by the International Thespian Society, "an organization of teachers and students devoted to the advancement of theatre arts in the secondary schools." Primarily, it describes production activities of high school theatre clubs, but it also has articles on personalities and professional productions which would be of interest to secondary school students.

Attempts have been made from time to time to publish specialized periodicals. In 1937, *The One Act Play Magazine,* edited by William Kozlenko, aimed to publish worthwhile endeavors in the area of one-act plays. Many interesting plays and promising playwrights were given an audience during the publication's approximately five years of life.

Various theatrical unions, subscription clubs, and similar organizations publish house organs to keep their members abreast of pertinent developments on the theatrical scene. Many associations such as the American Society for Theatre Research, the American Theatre Association (formerly the American Educational Theatre Association), and the Theatre Library Association, publish both a newsletter of current events and a journal of research articles. Most of these publications are described in the accounts of the organizations.

Theatre Arts Magazine. *See* Stage Periodicals

The Theatre Collection of the New York Public Library, Library and Museum of the Performing Arts, 111 Amsterdam Ave., New York, NY 10023, tel. (212) 799-2200. *Curator:* Paul Myers.

The Theatre Collection of the New York Public Library was established in 1931 due, in large part, to the gift to the library of the collections of David Belasco and Robinson Locke. George Freedley was engaged to organize the Collection and in June 1933 a section in the Main Reading Room of the Library's Central Building at Fifth Avenue and 42nd Street was opened to the public. In 1965, the Theatre Collection opened in new quarters at the Lincoln Center for the Performing Arts as part of the Library-Museum of the Performing Arts.

The Collection contains material of historic interest as well as contemporary material. Current clipping folders are maintained on persons active in theatre, cinema, radio, television, vaudeville, night clubs, carnival and circus, as well as on productions and organizations in all these media. In addition, programmes, reviews, press books and photographs of such productions are preserved and catalogued for reference use.

Among the large collections, in addition to the Belasco and Locke collections mentioned above, are:

The George Becks Collection of prompt books, principally of eighteenth and nineteenth century productions;

The Hiram Stead Collection of programmes, prints and letters about the British Theatre from, roughly, 1672-1932;

The Henin Collection on the French theatre of the eighteenth and nineteenth centuries;

Photographic collections of Carl Van Vechten, the Vandamm Studio, G. Maillard Kesslere, the White Studio, Alfredo Valente, and Bruguiere.

The Theatre Collection also includes collections of scrapbooks and other memorabilia of specific artists such as Townsend Walsh, Sophie Tucker, Lee Simonson, Gilbert Gabriel, Aline Bernstein, John Golden, R. H. Burnside, and Gertrude Lawrence. In 1964, Hallie Flanagan turned over a large amount of material about her administration of the Federal Theatre Project and her teaching career in drama at Vassar College. Additional collections include the working papers of Jerome Lawrence and Robert E. Lee, Leland Hayward, Burl Ives, Katharine Cornell and Guthrie McClintic, the Actor's Workshop (San Francisco), and the Vivian Beaumont Theatre (N.Y.C.).

Records of producing firms are also preserved, including Klaw and Erlanger, Jones and Green, the Playwrights' Company, Chamberlain and Lyman Brown, and the Provincetown Playhouse.

The Theatre Collection is adding a collection of films and videotapes of plays in performance and interviews with artists concerning their professional careers and productions with which they have been associated.

Theatre Communications Group, 355 Lexington Ave., New York, NY 10017, tel. (212) 697-5230.
Director: Peter Zeisler; *Associate Directors:* Jean Guest, Lindy Zesch; *Board of Directors:* Arthur Ballet, Arvin Brown, Gordon Davidson, Karl Eigsti, Alvin Epstein, Michael Feingold, Thomas Fichandler, Geraldine Fitzgerald, Earle Gister, Michael Kahn, Robert Kalfin, Woodie King, Edith Markson, Robert Moss, Sara O'Connor, Harold Prince, Lloyd Richards, W. Duncan Ross, Joan Sandler, Richard Schechner, Peter Zeisler.

Theatre Communications Group (TCG) is the national service organization for the nonprofit professional theatre in the US. With a grant from the Ford Foundation, it was founded in 1961 "to help raise standards and aid in the development of the nonprofit professional theatre." Its programs were originally directed toward supporting resident professional theatres, but were completely revised in 1972 to reflect the growth and diversity of the American noncommercial theatre. TCG has been under the direction of Peter Zeisler since that year and now offers more than twenty programs and services to resident, experimental, ethnic, and other theatre institutions, to independent theatre artists, and to professional theatre training programs. Activities include a casting service; national student auditions; subscription consultation; management services; a referral service for theatre artists, administrators, and technicians; a series of workshops and conferences; an annual fiscal survey of theatres; and a variety of publications, including *Theatre Profiles,* a reference series on theatre companies throughout the country.

Theatre Development Fund, 1564 Broadway, New York, NY 10036, tel. (212) 757-4883.
President: Mrs. Russel Crouse; *Vice-President:* John E. Booth; *Secretary:* Lloyd Richards; *Treasurer:* Stuart W. Little; *Directors:* Stephen Benedict, Dick Brukenfeld, Irving Cheskin, Harold Clurman, Mrs. Beatrice Straight Cookson, Mrs. Kitty Carlisle Hart, August Heckscher, Edward F. Kook, Erika Munk, Alan Pryce-Jones, Lawrence Rogers II, Joan Sandler, Moses Shapiro, Richard Weinstein.
Executive Director: Hugh Southern; *Administrator:* Mary Hays; *Special Projects Director:* Janet E. Gracey; *Development Services Director:* Vincent Marron; *Costume Collection Administrator:* Whitney Blausen; *TKTS General Manager:* William Orton.

Theatre Development Fund (TDF) is a nonprofit corporation founded in 1967 to aid productions of worthwhile plays in the commercial theatre. With the support of endowment funds from both public and private sources, TDF purchases blocks of tickets for performances of particular presentations during the early weeks of their runs. The tickets are then sold at lower prices to students and others who might not be able to afford the full rate. A twofold purpose is thereby served: a good production receives financial aid and begins to build an audience and the audience for all theatre is expanded.

By the 1970s, the Fund had broadened its scope of activities to provide support for almost every area of theatre and dance, offering low-cost admissions to a wide variety of plays and dance events for the benefit of students, teachers, union members, clergymen, retired persons, and others who might otherwise be unable to attend.

Ticket subsidy programs have been developed for Broadway and off Broadway, voucher programs for off-off Broadway theatre and for dance companies in New York. The Times Square Theatre Centre (TKTS) markets otherwise unsold theatre tickets at half price on the day of performance. It is the only TDF program available to the general public.

TDF also administers The Costume Collection for the NY State Council on the Arts. The Collection provides professional costumes to nonprofit performing arts organizations operating on low budgets.

The Theatre Guild, 27 W. 53rd St., New York, NY 10019, tel. (212) CI 5-8257.
Administrative Director: Armina Marshall.

The Theatre Guild was formally organized early in 1919 under a board of managers including Rollo Peters, Philip Moeller, Helen Freeman, Helen Westley, Justus Sheffield, Lawrence Langner, Lee Simonson. The organization was an outgrowth of the Washington Square Players (see elsewhere).

Its initial production was Jacinto Benavente's *Bonds of Interest,* which opened Apr. 19, 1919. The play was a translation by John Garrett Underhill and the cast included Rollo Peters, Helen Freeman, Helen Westley, Dudley Digges (later a director of the Theatre Guild), Augustin Duncan, Edna St. Vincent Millay, and Mary Blair.

Its first success, however, was St. John Ervine's *John Ferguson,* which opened May 12, 1919. On Nov. 10, 1920, the Theatre Guild produced their first George Bernard Shaw play, *Heartbreak House,* a noteworthy fact in that the organization was to become the prime producer of Shaw's plays in New York for many years. In 1925, the Theatre Guild opened its own theatre in New York City, The Guild Theatre (now called the ANTA Playhouse); it was often referred to as "the house that Shaw built."

During the 1920s, the Theatre Guild endeavored to produce the plays of outstanding young American dramatists, as well as those of important playwrights of the European theatre. Of the latter, the roster included works by Tolstoy, Molnar, Lenormand, Andreyev, Claudel, and Strindberg. Of the playwrights, the Theatre Guild presented new plays by Eugene O'Neill, Sidney Howard, Elmer Rice, John Howard Lawson, and S. N. Behrman.

By the late 1920s, the Theatre Guild was a flourishing organization with a large subscription audience. Through the American Theatre Society, it also had a guaranteed subscription audience in many of the key cities of the United States. During this period, the Theatre Guild was managed by Lawrence Langner, Theresa Helburn, Lee Simonson, Helen Westley, Philip Moeller, and Maurice Wertheim.

Outstanding actors and directors were most eager to appear in Theatre Guild productions, and for a time there was almost a regular acting company, which included such personalities as Lynn Fontanne, Alfred Lunt, Earle Larrimore, and Henry Travers.

The Theatre Guild suffered seriously during the lean years of the 1930s and into the early 1940s. The subscription audiences dwindled, production costs mounted, and many of their productions were not box-office successes. However, the organization's fortunes turned with the opening of *Oklahoma!* (St. James Th., N.Y.C., Mar. 31, 1943). Richard Rodgers had written music for the Theatre Guild's *Garrick Gaieties* in the 1920s, and now, teamed with Oscar Hammerstein II, made musical theatre history with *Oklahoma!* and rescued the Theatre Guild from its financial doldrums.

In 1948, the Theatre Guild branched out into the medium of radio with the Theatre Guild on the Air, sponsored by United States Steel. For eight years the program continued on radio, and, in 1955, a similar series was presented on television.

Today, the Theatre Guild continues as a producing organization under the leadership of Philip Langner, president, and Armina Marshall, vice-president. The Guild continues its Five Play Subscription Series in New York, and the Theatre Guild-American Theatre Society Subscription on the road. The Theatre Guild also operates a theatre-oriented travel agency—Theatre Guild Abroad. In addition, the Guild has a film department headed by Philip Langner, who has produced for the Guild *Judgment at Nuremberg, The Pawnbroker, Born to Win, Slaves,* and *A Child Is Waiting.*

Works which have been produced and coproduced by the Theatre Guild include Jacinto Benavente's *The Bonds of Interest* (Garrick Th., Apr. 19, 1919); St. John Ervine's *John Ferguson* (Garrick, May 12, 1919); John Masefield's *The Faithful* (Garrick, Oct. 13, 1919); Lillian Sabine's *The Rise of Silas Lapham* (Garrick, Nov. 25, 1919); Leo Tolstoy's *The Power of Darkness* (Garrick, Jan. 19, 1920); St. John Ervine's *Jane Clegg* (Garrick, Feb. 23, 1920); August Strindberg's *The Dance of Death* (Garrick, May 9, 1920); David Pinski's *The Treasure* (Garrick, Oct. 4, 1920); George Bernard Shaw's *Heartbreak House* (Garrick, Nov. 10, 1920); David Liebovitz' *John Hawthorne*

(Garrick, Jan. 23, 1921); A. A. Milne's *Mr. Pim Passes By* (Garrick, Feb. 28, 1921); Ferenc Molnar's *Liliom* (Garrick, Apr. 20, 1921); Emile Verhaeren's *The Cloister* (Garrick, June 6, 1921); Arthur Richman's *Ambush* (Garrick, Oct. 10, 1921); Deneys Amiel and Andre Obey's *The Wife with a Smile* and Georges Courteline's *Bourbouroche* (Garrick, Nov. 28, 1921); Leonid Andreyev's *He Who Gets Slapped* (Garrick, Jan. 9, 1922); George Bernard Shaw's *Back to Methuselah* (Garrick, Feb. 27, 1922); Arnold Bennett's *What the Public Wants* (Garrick, May 1, 1922); Georg Kaiser's *From Morn to Midnight* (Garrick, May 21, 1922); Karl Capek's *R. U. R.* (Garrick, Oct. 9, 1922); A. A. Milne's *The Lucky One* (Garrick, Nov. 20, 1922); Paul Claudel's *The Tidings Brought to Mary* (Garrick, Dec. 25, 1922); Henrik Ibsen's *Peer Gynt* (Garrick, Feb. 5, 1923); Elmer Rice's *The Adding Machine* (Garrick, Mar. 19, 1923); and George Bernard Shaw's *The Devil's Disciple* (Garrick, Apr. 23, 1923).

Also, John Galsworthy's *Windows* (Garrick, Oct. 8, 1923); H. R. Lenormand's *The Failures* (Garrick, Nov. 19, 1923); *Aucassin and Nicolete* (anon., 12th century, French) (Garrick, Dec. 23, 1923); George Bernard Shaw's *Saint Joan* (Garrick, Dec. 28, 1923); *Nala and Damayanti* (anon., Hindu) (Garrick, Jan. 4, 1924); Wilhelm von Scholz' *The Race with the Shadow* (Garrick, Jan. 20, 1924); Earnest Vajda's *Fata Morgana* (Garrick, Mar. 3, 1924); Ferenc Molnar's *The Guardsman* (Garrick, Oct. 13, 1924); Sidney Howard's *They Knew What They Wanted* (Garrick, Nov. 24, 1924); John Howard Lawson's *Processional* (Garrick, Jan. 12, 1925); A. A. Milne's *Ariadne* (Garrick, Feb. 23, 1925); George Bernard Shaw's *Caesar and Cleopatra* (Garrick, Apr. 13, 1925); the revue *Garrick Gaieties* (1st edition) (Garrick, June 8, 1925); George Bernard Shaw's *Arms and the Man* (Guild, Sept. 14, 1925); Ferenc Molnar's *The Glass Slipper* (Guild, Oct. 19, 1925); George Bernard Shaw's *The Man of Destiny* and *Androcles and the Lion* (Klaw, Nov. 23, 1925); Marcel Pagnol and Paul Nivoix' *Merchants of Glory* (Guild, Dec. 14, 1925); Franz Werfel's *Goat Song* (Guild, Jan. 25, 1926); Nicholas Evreinov's *The Chief Thing* (Guild, Jan. 25, 1926); C. K. Monro's *At Mrs. Beam's* (Guild, Apr. 26, 1926); the revue *Garrick Gaieties* (2nd edition) (Garrick, May 10, 1926); Franz Werfel's *Juarez and Maximilian* (Guild, Oct. 11, 1926); George Bernard Shaw's *Pygmalion* (Guild, Nov. 15, 1926); Sidney Howard's *Ned McCobb's Daughter* (John Golden, Nov. 29, 1926); Sidney Howard's *The Silver Cord* (John Golden, Dec. 20, 1926); Jacques Copeau and Jean Croue's *The Brothers Karamazov* (Guild, Jan. 3, 1927); Luigi Pirandello's *Right You Are If You Think You Are* (Guild, Feb. 23, 1927); S. N. Behrman's *The Second Man* (Guild, Apr. 11, 1927); Dorothy and DuBose Heyward's *Porgy* (Guild, Oct. 10, 1927); George Bernard Shaw's *The Doctor's Dilemma* (Guild, Nov. 21, 1927); Eugene O'Neill's *Marco Millions* (Guild, Jan. 9, 1928); Eugene O'Neill's *Strange Interlude* (John Golden, Jan. 30, 1928); and Ben Jonson's *Volpone* (Guild, Apr. 9, 1928).

Also, George Bernard Shaw's *Major Barbara* (Guild, Nov. 19, 1928); Robert Nichols and Maurice Browne's *Wings Over Europe* (Martin Beck Th., Dec. 10, 1928); Sil-Vara's *Caprice* (Guild, Dec. 31, 1928); Eugene O'Neill's *Dynamo* (Martin Beck Th., Feb. 11, 1929); Beatrice Blackmar and Bruce Gould's *Man's Estate* (Biltmore, Apr. 1, 1929); Frantisek Langer's *The Camel Through the Needle's Eye* (Martin Beck Th., Apr. 15, 1929); Leonhard Frank's *Karl and Anna* (Guild, Oct. 7, 1929); Romain Rolland's *The Game of Love and Death* (Guild, Nov. 25, 1929); V. Kirchon and A. Oupensky's *Red Rust* (Martin Beck Th., Dec. 17, 1929); S. N. Behrman's *Meteor* (Guild, Dec. 23, 1929); a revival of Karl Capek's *R. U. R.* (Guild, Feb. 17, 1930); George Bernard Shaw's *The Apple Cart* (Martin Beck Th., Feb. 24, 1930); a revival of Eugene O'Neill's *Marco Millions* (Liberty, Mar. 3, 1930); a revival of Ben Jonson's *Volpone* (Liberty, Mar. 10, 1930); Ivan Turgenev's *A Month in the Country* (Guild, Mar. 17, 1930); Philip Barry's *Hotel Universe* (Martin Beck Th., Apr. 14, 1930); the revue *Garrick Gaieties* (3rd edition) (Guild, June 4, 1930; reopened Oct. 16, 1930); S. Tretyakov's *Roar China!* (Martin Beck Th., Oct. 27, 1930); Maxwell Anderson's *Elizabeth the Queen* (Guild, Nov. 3, 1930); Claire and Paul Sifton's *Midnight* (Guild, Dec. 29, 1930); Lynn Riggs' *Green Grow the Lilacs* (Guild, Jan. 26, 1931); Hans Chlumberg's *Miracle at Verdun* (Martin Beck, Mar. 19, 1931); George Bernard Shaw's *Getting Married* (Guild, Mar. 30, 1931); Eugene O'Neill's *Mourning Becomes Electra* (Guild, Oct. 26, 1931); Robert E. Sherwood's *Reunion in Vienna* (Martin Beck Th., Nov. 16, 1931); Sophocles' *Oedipus Rex* (Martin Beck Th., Jan. 15, 1932);Denis Johnston's *The Moon in the Yellow River* (Guild, Feb. 29, 1932); George Bernard Shaw's *Too True To Be Good* (Guild, Apr. 4, 1932); Owen and Donald Davis' *The Good Earth* (Guild, Oct. 17, 1932); S. N. Behrman's *Biography* (Guild, Dec. 12, 1932); George O'Neil's *American Dream* (Guild, Feb. 21, 1933); Maxwell Anderson's *Both Your Houses* (Royale, Mar. 6, 1933); Luigi Chiarelli's *The Mask and the Face* (Guild, May 8, 1933); Eugene O'Neill's *Ah, Wilderness!* (Guild, Oct. 2, 1933); Molière's *The School for Husbands* (Empire, Oct. 16, 1933); Maxwell Anderson's *Mary of Scotland* (Alvin, Nov. 27, 1933); Eugene O'Neill's *Days without End* (Henry Miller's Th., Jan. 8, 1934); John Wexley's *They Shall Not Die* (Royale, Feb. 21, 1934); and Dawn Powell's *Jig Saw* (Ethel Barrymore Th., Apr. 30, 1934).

Also, James Bridie's *A Sleeping Clergyman* (Guild, Oct. 8, 1934); Maxwell Anderson's *Valley Forge* (Guild, Dec. 10, 1934); S. N. Behrman's *Rain from Heaven* (John Golden, Dec. 24, 1934); Margaret Kennedy's *Escape Me Never* (Shubert, Jan. 21, 1935); George Bernard Shaw's *The Simpleton of the Unexpected Isles* (Guild, Feb. 18, 1935); the revue *Parade* (Guild, May 20, 1935); John Haynes Holmes and Reginald Lawrence's *If This Be Treason* (Music Box, Sept. 23, 1935); William Shakespeare's *The Taming of the Shrew* (Guild, Sept. 30, 1935); DuBose Heyward, Ira Gershwin, and George Gershwin's musical *Porgy and Bess* (Alvin, Oct. 10, 1935); Dodie Smith's *Call It a Day* (Morosco, Jan. 28, 1936); S. N. Behrman's *End of Summer* (Guild, Feb. 17, 1936); Robert E. Sherwood's *Idiot's Delight* (Shubert, Mar. 24, 1936); Julius and Philip Epstein's *And Stars Remain* (Guild, Oct. 12, 1936); William McNally's *Prelude to Exile* (Guild, Nov. 30, 1936); Leopold L. Atlas' *But for the Grace of God* (Guild, Jan. 12, 1937); Maxwell Anderson's *The Masque of Kings* (Shubert, Feb. 8, 1937); Bruno Frank's *Storm Over Patsy* (Guild, Mar. 8, 1937); Ben Hecht's *To Quito and Back* (Guild, Oct. 6, 1937); Jean Giraudoux' *Amphitryon '38* (Shubert, Nov. 1, 1937); Gaston Baty's *Madame Bovary* (Broadhurst, Nov. 16, 1937); Sidney Howard's *The Ghost of Yankee Doodle* (Guild, Nov. 22, 1937); S. N. Behrman's *Wine of Choice* (Guild, Feb. 21, 1938); Anton Chekhov's *The Seagull* (Shubert, Mar. 28, 1938); John Boruff and Walter Hart's *Washington Jitters* (Guild, May 2, 1938); Andre Birabeau's *Dame Nature* (Booth, Sept. 26, 1938); Philip Barry's *The Philadelphia Story* (Shubert, Mar. 28, 1939); William Saroyan's *The Time of Your Life* (Booth, Oct. 25, 1939); a revival of William Shakespeare's *The Taming of the Shrew* (Alvin, Feb. 5, 1940); Benjamin Glazer's adaptation of Ernest Hemingway's *The Fifth Column* (Alvin, Mar. 6, 1940); Robert E. Sherwood's *There Shall Be No Night* (Alvin, Apr. 29, 1940); William Saroyan's *Love's Old Sweet Song* (Plymouth, May 2, 1940); a revival of Robert E. Sherwood's *There Shall Be No Night* (Alvin, Sept. 9, 1940); a revival of William Saroyan's *The Time of Your Life* (Guild, Sept. 23, 1940); a revival of William Shakespeare's *Twelfth Night* (St. James, Nov. 19, 1940); the pre-Bway tryout of Tennessee Williams' *The Battle of Angels* (opened Wilbur, Boston, Mass., Dec. 20, 1940), which closed out of town; Philip Barry's *Liberty Jones* (Shubert, Feb. 5, 1941); and the pre-Bway tryout of Carl Zuckmayer and Fritz Kortner's *Somewhere in France* (opened Natl., Washington, D.C., Apr. 28, 1941), which closed out of town.

Also, a revival of Eugene O'Neill's *Ah, Wilderness!* (Guild, Oct. 2, 1941); Maxwell Anderson's *Candle in the Wind* (Shubert, Oct. 22, 1941); Sophie Treadwell's *Hope for a Harvest* (Guild, Nov. 26, 1941); Patterson Greene's *Papa Is All* (Guild, Jan. 6, 1942); Richard Brinsley Sheridan's *The Rivals* (Shubert, Jan. 14, 1942); Emlyn Williams' *Yesterday's Magic* (Guild, Apr. 14, 1942); Philip Barry's *Without Love* (St. James, Nov. 10, 1942); Ketti Frings' *Mr. Sycamore* (Guild, Nov. 13, 1942); S. N. Behrman's *The Pirate* (Martin Beck Th., Nov. 25, 1942); Konstantin Simonov's *The Russian People* (Guild, Dec. 29, 1942); Richard Rodgers and Oscar Hammerstein II's musical *Oklahoma!* (St. James, Mar. 31, 1943); William Shakespeare's *Othello* (Shubert, Oct. 19, 1943); Paul Osborne's *The Innocent Voyage* (Belasco, Nov. 15, 1943); S. N. Behrman's *Jacobowsky and the Colonel* (Martin Beck Th., Mar. 14, 1944); L. Bush-Fekete and Mary Helen Fay's *Embezzled Heaven* (Natl., Oct. 31, 1944); Walter Kerr's *Sing Out, Sweet Land!* (Internatl., Dec. 27, 1944); Philip Barry's *Foolish Notion* (Martin Beck Th., Mar. 13, 1945); Richard Rodgers and Oscar Hammerstein II's *Carousel* (Majestic, Apr. 19, 1945); a revival of William Shakespeare's *Othello* (NY City Ctr., May 22, 1945); S. N. Behrman's *Dunnigan's Daughter* (John Golden Th., Dec. 26, 1945); William Shakespeare's *The Winter's Tale* (Cort, Jan. 15, 1946); the pre-Bway tryout of William Shakespeare's *The Merry Wives of Windsor* (opened Playhouse, Wilmington, Del., Mar. 15, 1946), which closed out of town; a revival of Leonid Andreyev's

He Who Gets Slapped (Booth, Mar. 20, 1946); Eugene O'Neill's *The Iceman Cometh* (Martin Beck Th., Oct. 9, 1946); George Kelly's *The Fatal Weakness* (Royale, Nov. 19, 1946); Glendon Swarthout and John Savacool's *O'Daniel* (Princess, Feb. 23, 1947); Oscar Wilde's *The Importance of Being Earnest* (Royale, Mar. 3, 1947); William Congreve's *Love for Love* (Royale, May 26, 1947); Richard Rodgers and Oscar Hammerstein II's musical *Allegro* (Majestic, Oct. 10, 1947); Terrence Rattigan's *The Winslow Boy* (Empire, Oct. 29, 1947); Jan de Hartog's *This Time Tomorrow* (Ethel Barrymore Th., Nov. 3, 1947); and George Bernard Shaw's *You Never Can Tell* (Martin Beck Th., Mar. 16, 1948).

Also, Dorothy Heyward's *Set My People Free* (Hudson, Nov. 3, 1948); Robert McEnroe's *The Silver Whistle* (Biltmore, Nov. 24, 1948); John Van Druten's *Make Way for Lucia* (Cort, Dec. 22, 1948); a revival of Richard Rodgers and Oscar Hammerstein II's musical *Carousel* (NY City Ctr., Jan. 25, 1949); Jean Pierre Aumont's *My Name Is Aquilon* (Lyceum, Feb. 9, 1949); S. N. Behrman's *I Know My Love* (Shubert, Nov. 2, 1949); William Shakespeare's *As You Like It* (Cort, Jan. 26, 1950); the musical *Arms and the Girl,* with book by Herbert and Dorothy Fields and Rouben Mamoulian, music by Morton Gould, and lyrics by Dorothy Fields (46th St. Th., Feb. 2, 1950); William Inge's *Come Back, Little Sheba* (Booth, Feb. 15, 1950); John Patrick's *The Curious Savage* (Martin Beck Th., Oct. 24, 1950); Christopher Fry's *The Lady's Not for Burning* (Royale, Nov. 8, 1950); Sir John Vanbrugh's *The Relapse* (Morosco, Nov. 22, 1950); a revival of Richard Rodgers and Oscar Hammerstein II's *Oklahoma!* (Bway, May 29, 1951); a revival of George Bernard Shaw's *Saint Joan* (Cort, Oct. 4, 1951); John Patrick's *Lo and Behold* (Booth, Dec. 12, 1951); Jean Anouilh's *Legend of Lovers* (Plymouth, Dec. 26, 1951); S. N. Behrman's *Jane* (Coronet, Feb. 1, 1952); Christopher Fry's *Venus Observed* (Century, Feb. 13, 1952); George Bernard Shaw's *The Millionairess* (Shubert, Oct. 17, 1952); Peter Ustinov's *The Love of Four Colonels* (Shubert, Jan. 15, 1953); William Inge's *Picnic* (Music Box, Feb. 19, 1953); Horton Foote's *The Trip to Bountiful* (Henry Miller's, Nov. 3, 1953); Charles Morgan's *Home Is the Hero* (Booth, Sept. 22, 1954); Albert Husson's *The Heavenly Twins* (Booth, Nov. 4, 1955); Thornton Wilder's *The Matchmaker* (Royale, Dec. 5, 1955); Henry Denker and Ralph Berkey's *Time Limit!* (Booth, Jan. 24, 1956); and Bill Hoffman's *Affair of Honor* (Ethel Barrymore Th., Apr. 6, 1956).

Also, the musical *Bells Are Ringing,* with book and lyrics by Betty Comden and Adolph Green, music by Jule Styne (Shubert, Nov. 29, 1956); Joseph Fields and Peter DeVries' *The Tunnel of Love* (Royale, Feb. 13, 1957); Ray Lawler's *The Summer of the Seventeenth Doll* (Coronet, Jan. 22, 1958); Dore Schary's *Sunrise at Campobello* (Cort, Jan. 30, 1958); *A Party with Betty Comden and Adolph Green* (John Golden Th., Dec. 23, 1958); Eleanor and Leo Bayer's *Third Best Sport* (Ambassador, Dec. 30, 1958); Ruth Ford and William Faulkner's *Requiem for a Nun* (John Golden Th., Jan. 30, 1959); Leonard Spigelgass' *A Majority of One* (Shubert, Feb. 16, 1959); *Triple Play* (Playhouse, Apr. 15, 1959); Florence Lowe and Caroline Francke's *The 49th Cousin* (Ambassador, Oct. 27, 1960); Arthur Laurents' *Invitation to a March* (Music Box, Oct. 29, 1960); the musical *The Unsinkable Molly Brown,* with music and lyrics by Meredith Willson, book by Richard Morris (Winter Garden, Nov. 3, 1960); Robertson Davies' *Love and Libel,* or, *The Ogre of the Provincial World* (Martin Beck Th., Dec. 7, 1960); Leo Lieberman's *The Captains and the Kings* (Playhouse, Jan. 2, 1962); Ernest Kinoy's *Something About a Soldier* (Ambassador, Jan. 4, 1962); Santha Rama Rau's *A Passage to India* (Ambassador, Jan. 31, 1962); Elick Moll's *Seidman and Son* (Belasco, Oct. 15, 1962); and Leonard Spigelgass' *Dear Me, the Sky Is Falling* (Music Box, Mar. 2, 1963).

Also, Paul Shyre's *The Child Buyer,* adapted from John Hersey's novel (Garrick, Dec. 21, 1964); Ben Kerner's *All Women Are One* (Gate, Jan. 7, 1965); Peter Shaffer's *The Royal Hunt of the Sun* (ANTA, Oct. 26, 1965); Keith Waterhouse and Willis Hall's *Help Stamp Out Marriage* (Booth, Sept. 29, 1966); Harold Pinter's *The Homecoming* (Music Box, Jan. 5, 1967); the musical *Darling of the Day* with book by Nunnally Johnson, music by Jule Styne, and lyrics by E. Y. Harburg (George Abbott, Jan. 27, 1968); Alan Ayckbourn's *Absurd Person Singular* (Music Box, Oct. 8, 1974); and *Musical Jubilee* (St. James, Nov. 13, 1975).

Theatre Library Association, 111 Amsterdam Ave., New York, NY 10023.
President: Dr. Robert M. Henderson, Chief, General Library and Museum of the Performing Arts, New York Public Library at Lincoln Center, 111 Amsterdam Ave., New York, NY 10023; *Vice-President:* Hobart Berolzheimer, Mark Wilson Collection of Literature Dept., Free Library of Philadelphia, Logan Sq., Philadelphia, PA 19403; *Secretary-Treasurer:* Richard M. Buck, Assistant to the Chief, Performing Arts Research Center, New York Public Library at Lincoln Center, 111 Amsterdam Ave., New York, NY 10023; *Recording Secretary:* Paul R. Palmer, 560 Riverside Dr., Apt. 21B, New York, NY 10027. (Send all general correspondence to Richard M. Buck, Secretary-Treasurer: Theatre Library Assn., 111 Amsterdam Ave., New York, NY 10023.)

Executive Board: The officers are, for 1975-1978, Mrs. Robin Craven, 360 E. 55th St., New York, NY 10022; William Green, Dept. of English, Queens College, Flushing, NY 11367; Paul Myers, Curator, Theatre Collection, Performing Arts Research Center, New York Public Library at Lincoln Center, 111 Amsterdam Ave., New York, NY 10023; Miss Jeanne T. Newlin, Curator, Theatre Collection, Harvard College Library, Cambridge, MA 02138.

For 1972-1976, Dr. Francis R. Hodge, Dept. of Drama, Univ. of Texas, Austin, TX 78712; Brooks McNamara, Dept. of Drama and Cinema, New York Univ., Washington Sq., New York, NY 10003; Mrs. Sally T. Pavetti, Eugene O'Neill Theatre Foundation, Inc., Box 206, Waterford, CT 06385; Mrs. John F. Wharton, 141 E. 72nd St., New York, NY 10021.

Honorary, Miss Rosamond Gilder, 24 Gramercy Park, New York, NY 10003; Mrs. Marguerite McAneny, 67 Grover Ave., Princeton, NJ 08540; Louis A. Rachow, Librarian, Walter Hampden Memorial Library, The Players, 16 Gramercy Park, New York, NY 10003; Miss Helen Willard, 8 Chauncy St., Cambridge, MA 02138. *Committee Chairmen: Program & Special Events:* Hobart Berolzheimer; *Publications:* Brooks McNamara.

The Theatre Library Association was founded in 1937 as an affiliate of the American Library Association. Its stated purpose is "to further the interests of gathering, preserving, and making available through libraries, museums, and private collections and records (books, photographs, playbills, etc.) of theatre in all its forms."

The membership of the association is made up of curators, librarians, collectors, both individual and institutional. Periodic meetings are held. Over the years, the Theatre Library Association has sponsored and aided in the publication of works regarding theatre research and collections. It also publishes the quarterly *Broadside,* distributed to members of the association, and the annual *Performing Arts Resources.*

The Theatre Union.
Secretary: Margaret Larkin; *Treasurer:* Charles R. Walker; *Audience Manager:* Sylvia Regan; *Counsel:* H. William Fitelson; *Executive Board:* Michael Blankfort, Sylvia Fenningston, Joseph Freeman, Samuel H. Friedman, Mary Fox, Manuel Gomez, John Henry Hammond, Jr., Albert Maltz, Liston M. Oak, Paul Peters, George Sklar, Tom Tippett, Victor Wolfson.

The Theatre Union was one of the most active enterprises of the depression years. The organization took over the Civic Repertory Theatre, pledging itself to low admission prices—ranging from 30 cents to $1.50. It maintained a studio training group and, in addition to its regular season, presented special Sunday performances of experimental works.

The first production was George Sklar and Albert Maltz' *Peace on Earth* (Nov. 29, 1933), which ran for 18 weeks, its audience including more than 12,000 unemployed who were provided with free admission through the contributions of those who saw the play.

Subsequent productions included Paul Peters and George Sklar's *Stevedore* (Apr. 18, 1934; revived Oct. 1, 1934); Friedrich Wolf's *Sailors of Cattaro* (Dec. 10, 1934); Albert Maltz' *Black Pit* (Mar. 20, 1935); Bertolt Brecht's *Mother* (Nov. 19, 1935); Albert Bein's *Let Freedom Ring* (Dec. 17, 1935); Victor Wolfson's *Bitter Stream* (Mar. 30, 1936); and John Howard Lawson's *Marching Song* (Feb. 17, 1937).

Trinity Square Repertory Company, 201 Washington St., Providence, RI 02903, tel. (401) 521-1100.
Director: Adrian Hall; *Assistant to the Director:* Marion Simon; *Composer-in-Residence and Director of Educational Services:* Richard Cumming; *Set Designers:* Eugene Lee, Robert D. Soule; *Lighting Designers:* Roger Morgan, John McLain; *Costume Designers:* James Berton Harris, Betsey Potter; *Properties Designer:* Sandra Nathanson; *Stage Managers:* William Radka, Beverly Andreozzi; *Technical Director:* Shaun Curran; *Guest Directors:* Word Baker,

Larry Arrick, Brooks Jones.

In 1964, Trinity Square Repertory Company began presenting plays in a theatre that had been created by the remodeling of the auditorium of Providence's Trinity United Methodist Church at a cost of $3,000, which had been pledged by the trustees of the new organization. Adrian Hall, with a background of ten years in professional and regional theatre, was engaged as the company's director and has led it since the beginning, presenting each season programs of both old and new plays, but always giving attention to the work of new American playwrights.

In the summer of 1965, a new production was presented each week at the University of Rhode Island and during the 1965–66 season, aided by Rockefeller Foundation and US Office of Education grants, Trinity Square staged twenty performances of *Twelfth Night* for high-school audiences throughout the state. Then a three-year federal grant under Project Discovery helped the company launch a regular program of plays in Rhode Island high schools and relieved some of the financial uncertainty of the early years. State and local sources continued the funding after the expiration of the federal grant and by the season 1972–73 a student audience of over 15,000 attended fifty-four performances of four different plays. The company also runs theatre workshops in the schools as part of the arts program.

Outside the state, Trinity Square has toured throughout New England and played in such cities as Cincinnati, Phoenix, and Philadelphia. In 1968, the company appeared by invitation at the Edinburgh (Scotland) Festival, the first American regional theatre so honored, and in May 1970, it made its New York City debut, participating in the ANTA Showcase for Regional Theatre. Also in 1970, Mr. Hall and Trinity Square received the Margo Jones Award for outstanding work in encouragement of new American playwrights. In 1973, the company was selected as one of the regional theatres for the PBS television series Theatre in America, and the work presented, *Feasting with Panthers,* was seen by a national television audience in March 1974. For the 1973–74 season, the company moved into a new home—the Lederer Theatre Project—a renovated movie house containing two separate performing spaces.

Productions (by season) of Trinity Square Repertory Company since its beginning include: (1963-64) Federico Garcia Lorca's *The House of Bernarda Alba,* Brendan Behan's *The Hostage,* Tennessee Williams' *Orpheus Descending,* and Edward Albee's *The American Dream* and *The Death of Bessie Smith;* (1964-65) Howard Richardson and William Berney's *Dark of the Moon,* Jean Anouilh's *The Rehearsal,* Harold Pinter's *The Caretaker,* Anton Chekhov's *Uncle Vanya,* Eugene O'Neill's *Desire Under the Elms,* George Bernard Shaw's *Don Juan in Hell,* Trevanian's *All to Hell Laughing* (premiere, Apr. 7, 1965), and Edward Albee's *The Zoo Story;* (1965-66) Arthur Miller's *The Crucible,* Molière's *Tartuffe,* Jean Genet's *The Balcony,* William Shakespeare's *Twelfth Night,* Eugene O'Neill's *Long Day's Journey into Night,* Gabriel Gladstone's *The Eternal Husband* (premiere, Mar. 3, 1966), J. M. Synge's *The Playboy of the Western World,* and the Edward Albee double-bill *The American Dream* and *The Zoo Story;* (1966-67) George Bernard Shaw's *Saint Joan,* Tennessee Williams' *A Streetcar Named Desire,* Kenward Elmslie and Claibe Richardson's *The Grass Harp* (premiere, Dec. 27, 1966), Eugene O'Neill's *Ah, Wilderness!,* William Shakespeare's *A Midsummer Night's Dream,* John Hawkes's *The Questions* and LeRoi Jones's *Dutchman* on a double-bill, Harold Pinter's *The Birthday Party,* and Anton Chekhov's *The Three Sisters;* (1967-68) Bertolt Brecht and Kurt Weill's *The Threepenny Opera,* William Shakespeare's *Julius Caesar,* Oscar Wilde's *The Importance of Being Earnest,* Norman Holland's *Years of the Locust* (premiere, Feb. 8, 1968), Henrik Ibsen's *An Enemy of the People,* and Racine's *Phaedra;* (1968-69) Sean O'Casey's *Red Roses for Me,* Robert Penn Warren's *Brother to Dragons* (premiere, Nov. 21, 1968), William Shakespeare's *Macbeth,* Trinity Square's adaptation of Herman Melville's *Billy Budd* (premiere, Mar. 3, 1969), and James Joyce's *Exiles;* (1969-70) Robert Lowell's *The Old Glory,* William Goyen's *House of Breath, Black/White* (premiere, Nov. 4, 1969), Roland Van Zandt's *Wilson in the Promise Land* (premiere, Dec. 9, 1969), Thornton Wilder's *The Skin of Our Teeth,* and James Schevill's *Lovecraft's Follies* (premiere, Mar. 10, 1970); (1970-71) Moss Hart and George S. Kaufman's *You Can't Take It with You,* Jules Feiffer's *Little Murders,* Elaine May's *Adaptation* and Terrence McNally's *Next* on a double-bill, Portia Bohn's *The Good and Bad Times of Cady Francis McCullum and Friends* (premiere, Feb. 17, 1971), Timothy Taylor and Adrian Hall's *Son of Man and the Family* (premiere, Nov. 18, 1970), William Shakespeare's *The Taming of the Shrew,* William Congreve's *Love for Love,* Mary Chase's *Harvey,* and *The Threepenny Opera.*

Also (1971-72) Robert Marasco's *Child's Play,* William Shakespeare's *Troilus and Cressida,* Julie Bovasso's *Down by the River Where Waterlilies Are Disfigured Every Day* (premiere, Dec. 20, 1971), Molière's *The School for Wives,* and Arthur Miller's *The Price;* (1972-73) Harold Pinter's *Old Times,* Douglas Seale's *Lady Audley's Secret,* Peter Shaffer's *The Royal Hunt of the Sun,* Molière's *The School for Wives,* and Adrian Hall and Richard Cumming's *Feasting with Panthers* (premiere, Apr. 18, 1973); (1973-74) Robert Penn Warren's *Brother to Dragons,* Israel Horovitz's *Alfred the Great* (premiere, Nov. 28, 1973), Oliver Hailey's *For the Use of the Hall* (premiere, Jan. 2, 1974), Sam Shepard's *The Tooth of Crime,* William Gillette's *Sherlock Holmes,* Stuart Vaughan's *Ghost Dance* (premiere, Nov. 1, 1973), William Goyen and Worth Gardner's *Aimée* (premiere, Dec. 6, 1973), and Robert Bolt's *A Man for All Seasons.*

United Scenic Artists of America, Local 829, 1540 Broadway, New York, NY 10036, tel. (212) 575-5120.

President: Ben Edwards; *Vice-President:* Peggy Clark; *Treasurer:* Robert Rowe Paddock; *Recording Secretary:* Betty Coe Armstrong; *Financial Secretary:* Stanley Cappiello; *Business Representatives:* Andy Clores and Abe Kanter.

The United Scenic Artists of America is the trade union embracing all persons involved in the decor of production in the theatre, motion pictures, and television—scenic artists, scenic designers, and costume designers (for all areas), and lighting designers (for the theatre only). Affiliated, also are mural artists and makers of dioramas, models, and display.

University Players.

The University Players included among its members Henry Fonda, Joshua Logan, Myron McCormick, Mildred Natwick, Barbara O'Neill, Kent Smith, James Stewart, Margaret Sullivan, and Bretaigne Windust. Their first productions were presented at Falmouth, Mass., during the summer of 1928. The prime movers of the University Players were Bretaigne Windust and Charles Leatherbee. The company was recruited from among their theatre-minded friends, mainly at Harvard and Princeton, but also from other colleges.

The company spent five summers (until after the summer of 1932) at Falmouth, and played some touring engagements during the winter months. Norris Houghton's book entitled *But Not Forgotten* (1952) is a history of the University Players.

From 1928 through 1930, the group called itself the University Players Guild; in 1931, they changed their name to the University Players; and, for their last summer season, 1932, they became the Theatre Unit, Inc.

In summer 1928, the company presented at the Elizabeth Theatre, Falmouth, Mass., A. A. Milne's *The Dover Road;* Eugene O'Neill's *Beyond the Horizon;* George Kelly's *The Torch Bearers;* Sem Benelli's *The Jest;* Eleanor Robson and Harriet Ford's *In the Next Room;* Annie Nathan Meyer's *The New Way;* James Gleason and Richard Taber's *Is Zat So;* and Bayard Veiller's *The Thirteenth Chair.*

In summer 1929, they moved into a theatre they had built at Old Silver Beach, called the University Players Guild Theatre, where they presented Tom Cushing's *The Devil in the Cheese;* Owen Davis' *The Donovan Affair;* Frederick Lonsdale's *The Last of Mrs. Cheyney;* Sutton Vane's *Outward Bound;* Thomas Fallon's *The Last Warning;* George Kaufman and Marc Connelly's *Merton of the Movies;* Samuel Shipman and John B. Hymer's *Crime;* Porter Emerson Brown's *The Bad Man;* Melchior Lengyel and Lajos Biro's *The Czarina;* and Margaret Kennedy and Basil Dean's *The Constant Nymph.* Summer 1930 productions included Leslie Howard's *Murray Hill;* John Floyd's *The Wooden Kimono;* Saki's *The Watched Pot;* Jean Ferguson Black's *Thunder on the Left;* Karl Capek's *The Makropoulos Secret;* George Dunning Gribble's *The Masque of Venice;* Edwin Justus Mayer's *The Firebrand;* Hatcher Hughes' *Hell-Bent fer Heaven;* Noel Coward's *The Marquise;* and James M. Barrie's *A Kiss for Cinderella.* Summer 1931 productions included Philip Barry's *Paris Bound;* Roland Pertwee and Harold Dearden's *Interference;* A. A. Milne's *Mr. Pim Passes By;* George Abbott and Ann Preston Bridgers' *Coquette;* Jacques Duval's *Her Cardboard Lover;* Bayard Veiller's *The Trial of Mary Dugan;* Ferenc Molnar's *The Guardsman;* Sean O'Casey's *Juno and the Paycock;* John G. Brandon and George Pickett's *The Silent House;* and Eugene Labiche and Marc-Michel's *The Italian Straw Hat.*

Beginning October 1931, the University

Players produced an 18-week season at the Maryland Theatre in Baltimore. The works presented included Tom Cushing's *The Devil in the Cheese;* A. A. Milne's *Mr. Pim Passes By;* Hatcher Hughes' *Hell-Bent fer Heaven;* Margaret Kennedy and Basil Dean's *The Constant Nymph;* Alberto Casella's *Death Takes a Holiday;* David Belasco's *It's a Wise Child;* Arnold Ridley's *The Ghost Train;* George Kaufman and Edna Ferber's *The Royal Family;* George Abbott and Ann Preston Bridgers' *Coquette;* Gilbert Seldes' adaptation of Aristophanes' *Lysistrata;* James M. Barrie's *Mary Rose;* S. N. Behrman's *The Second Man;* John Wexley's *The Last Mile;* Rachel Crothers' *Let Us Be Gay;* Philip Barry's *Paris Bound;* Bayard Veiller's *The Trial of Mary Dugan;* and Don Marquis' *The Dark Hours.*

In summer 1932, at their theatre at Old Silver Beach, they presented Booth Tarkington's *Magnolia;* Arnold Ridley's *The Ghost Train;* John Balderston's *Berkeley Square;* David Belasco's *It's a Wise Child;* Lawrence Gross and Edward Childs Carpenter's *Whistling in the Dark;* Gilbert Seldes' adaptation of Aristophanes' *Lysistrata;* Alberto Casella's *Death Takes a Holiday;* and Allan Scott and George Haight's *Goodbye Again.*

At the Maryland Theatre in Baltimore, October 1932, they presented John Van Druten's *There's Always Juliet* and Frank McGrath's *Carry Nation.*

Urban Arts Corps, 26 W. 20th St., New York, NY 10011, tel. (212) 924-7820. *Artistic Director:* Vinnette Carroll; *Managing Director:* Barbara Hauptman; *Chairman of the Board:* John B. Hightower; *Vice-President:* Evelyn Cunningham.

Vinnette Carroll, then director of the NY State Council on the Arts' Ghetto Arts Program, organized the Urban Arts Corps (UAC) in 1967 as a summer project to send black and Puerto Rican youths into New York City's ghetto communities to present programs of songs, plays, and poetry readings to minority-group audiences. All the material utilized was written by blacks and Puerto Ricans, many of them corps members, who also guided ghetto youths in creating their own theatre projects. In 1968, UAC became a year-round program and in May 1969 moved into its Chelsea district home in New York City.

UAC produced Shirley Jackson's *The Lottery* and Joseph White's *Old Judge Mose Is Dead* (Clark Ctr. for the Performing Arts, New York City, 1968); the black musical *But Never Jam Today,* Miss Carroll's adaptation of Lewis Carroll's *Alice in Wonderland* (Black Expo, NY City Ctr., Apr. 1969); toured the Virgin Islands with Errol John's *Moon on a Rainbow Shawl* (July 1969); toured New York City playgrounds, streets, and schools with a revival of *But Never Jam Today* (July 1970); performed in a television special, *Send for Me* (NBC, Sept. 1970); produced the musical *Don't Bother Me, I Can't Cope,* with music and lyrics by Micki Grant (Oct. 1970); staged revivals of *Moon on a Rainbow Shawl* (Dec. 17, 1970) and *Don't Bother Me, I Can't Cope* (Feb. 1971). The last was revived again (June 1971) in repertory with a musical version of Irwin Shaw's *Bury the Dead,* with music and lyrics by Micki Grant. UAC also produced the musical *Croesus and the Witch,* adapted by Vinnette Carroll from a black folk tale with music and lyrics by Micki Grant (Aug. 24, 1971); toured in *Don't Bother Me, I Can't Cope* (Ford's Th., Washington, D.C., Sept. 1971; New Locust Th., Philadelphia, Oct. 1971; Vest Pocket Th., Detroit, Mich., Nov. 1971); presented Langston Hughes's *Black Nativity* (Church of the Holy Communion, N.Y.C., Dec. 22, 1971); visited Philadelphia with *Don't Bother Me, I Can't Cope* (Jan. 1972); and opened an extended New York City run of the last (Playhouse Th., Apr. 19, 1972), which moved to Broadway (Edison Th., June 1972); produced *Step Lively, Boy,* a new version of *Bury the Dead* (Feb. 7, 1973); Jean-Paul Sartre's *The Flies* (Dec. 6, 1973); a dramatic version of Robert Penn Warren's *All the King's Men* (May 14, 1974); and a new musical by Vinnette Carroll and Micki Grant, *The Ups and Downs of Theophilus Maitland* (Jan. 1975).

Variety. *See* Stage Periodicals

Virginia Museum Theatre. *See* Repertory Company of the Virginia Museum Theatre

Washington Square Players.

The Washington Square Players began its career in 1915. Early that year the members rented the Bandbox Theatre on New York's East 57th Street and drew up a manifesto. This document said, in part, "The Washington Square Players, Inc.—an organization which takes its name from the district where it originated—is composed of individuals who believe in the future of the theatre in America, and includes playwrights, actors and producers, working with a common end in view."

The Washington Square Players' career lasted four years, during which it produced 62 one-act plays and pantomimes and six long plays. It was out of the Washington Square Players that the Theatre Guild evolved (see elsewhere). A complete history of the venture can be found in Walter Prichard Eaton's *The Theatre Guild: The First Ten Years* (1929).

The first production, a bill of three one-act plays and a pantomime, took place Feb. 19, 1915. The plays were: *Licensed* by Basil Lawrence (pseudonym, for Lawrence Langner); *Eugenically Speaking* by Edward Goodman, who also directed the production; and Maurice Maeterlinck's *Interior.* The pantomime was the anonymously written *Another Interior.* Subsequently that season (Feb. 19, 1915-May 30, 1915), the following were presented: John Reed's *Moondown;* Murdock Pemberton's *My Lady's Honor;* Philip Moeller's *Two Blind Beggars and One Less Blind;* Leonid Andreyev's *Love of One's Neighbor;* Maurice Maeterlinck's *A Miracle of St. Anthony;* Holland Hudson's *The Shepard in the Distance;* Rose Pastor Stokes' *In April;* Edward Goodman's *Saviors;* Anton Chekhov's *A Bear;* and George Jay Smith's *Forbidden Fruit.* During the next season (Oct. 4, 1915-May 31, 1916), the following were presented: Harvey White's *Fire and Water;* Roberto Bracco's *A Night of Snow;* Philip Moeller's *Helena's Husband;* Percy MacKaye's *The Antick;* Arthur Schnitzler's *Literature;* Alice Gerstenberg's *Overtones;* Roberto Bracco's *The Honorable Lover;* Alfred de Musset's *Whims;* Lewis Beach's *The Clod;* Philip Moeller's *The Roadhouse in Arden, 1616-1916;* Josephine A. Meyer and Lawrence Langner's *The Red Cloak;* Guy Bolton and Tom Carlton's *Children;* Cecil Dorrian's *The Age of Reason;* Zoe Akins' *The Magical City;* Maurice Relonde's *Pierre Patelin;* Maurice Maeterlinck's *Aglavaine and Selzette;* and Anton Chekhov's *The Seagull.*

During the third season (Aug. 30, 1916-May 26, 1917) at the Comedy Theatre, the following were presented: Nicholas Evreinov's *A Merry Death;* Alice Brown's *The Sugar House;* Georges de Porto-Riche's *Lover's Luck;* Philip Moeller's *Sisters of Susanne;* Susan Glaspell's *Trifles;* Lawrence Langner's *Another Way Out;* Takeda Izumo's *Bushido;* Karl Ettlinger's *Altruism;* Leonid Andreyev's *The Life of Man;* Georges Courteline's *A Private Account;* Maurice Maeterlinck's *The Death of Tintagiles;* Kenneth Sawyer Goodman and Ben Hecht's *The Hero of Santa Maria;* Edward Massey's *Plots and Playwrights;* Hermann Barr's *The Poor Fool;* Bosworth Cocker's *The Last Straw;* Molière's *Sganarelle;* Henrik Ibsen's *Ghosts,* and August Strindberg's *Pariah.* During the fourth season (Sept. 19, 1917-Apr. 27, 1918), again at the Comedy Theatre, the following were presented: Lawrence Langner's *The Family Exit,* which was produced with Edward L. George; Eugene O'Neill's *In the Zone;* Fenimore Merrill's *The Avenue;* Grace Latimer Wright's *Blind Alleys;* Jacinto Benavente's *His Widow's Husband;* Zona Gale's *Neighbors;* Samuel Kaplan's *The Critic's Comedy;* Theodore Dreiser's *The Girl in the Coffin;* J. Garcia Pimentel and Beatrice de Holthoir's *Yum Chapab;* Susan Glaspell and George Cram Cook's *Suppressed Desires;* George Cronyn's *The Sandbar Queen;* Frank Dare's *Habit;* Philip Moeller's *The Beautiful Legend of Pokey;* the Chinese play entitled *The Poisoned Flower;* Miles Malleson's *Youth;* George Bernard Shaw's *Mrs. Warren's Profession;* Elmer L. Reizenstein's *The Home of the Free;* Harold Brighouse's *Lonesome Like;* Oscar Wilde's *Salome;* Susan Glaspell's *Close the Book;* and Theresa Helburn's *Enter the Hero.*

Yale Repertory Theatre and Yale School of Drama, 222 York St., New Haven, CT 06520, tel. (203) 436-1600; (203) 436-1589. *Yale Repertory Theatre: Director:* Robert Brustein; *Associate Director:* Alvin Epstein; *Managing Director:* Robert J. Orchard.

Yale School of Drama: Dean: Robert Brustein; *Dean of Faculty and Students:* Howard Stein.

The Yale Repertory Theatre is a professional repertory company in residence at Yale University. The company was formed in 1966, growing out of the Yale School of Drama, the renowned conservatory for professional theatre training.

The YRT concentrates largely on the production of classics, with emphasis on new interpretations and modern insights; on premieres of new plays, generally by young American playwrights; as well as rediscovery of certain works of musical theatre (frequently produced in association with the Yale School of Music), such as the Bertolt Brecht-Kurt Weill *Rise and Fall of the City of Mahagonny* and *Happy End,* and combining for the first time scores by Henry Purcell with Shakespeare's *The Tempest* and *A Midsum-*

mer Night's Dream. Since its inception in 1966, the theatre has presented over seventy productions, including twenty-six world premieres by American playwrights, ten American premieres, and six new translations. The YRT offers a forty-week season of seven productions on a subscription basis, and the plays are performed in rotating repertory.

The close relationship between the professional company and the conservatory is demonstrated by the fact that most YRT members also teach in the School of Drama, while certain selected drama students are invited to join either the staff or the permanent company following graduation.

School of Drama: A Department of Drama was founded at Yale in 1924, through the generosity of Edward S. Harkness, and in 1955, the department was reorganized as a separate graduate professional school. Although the school is organized on a graduate basis and offers the majority of students a three-year course toward a Master of Fine Arts degree, the main objective of the program is to train the students for professional work in the theatre and its allied branches.

There are seven major courses of study offered: playwriting; acting/directing; scene, costume, and lighting design; theatre design and technology; theatre administration; and theatre criticism and dramatic literature. There are thirty-three permanent members of faculty and eight visiting lecturers.

Theatre Building Biographies

ABC Radio Theatre, 202 W. 58th St., between Broadway and 7th Ave.
(See John Golden Theatre)

ABC Television Studio, 238 W. 44th St., between Broadway and 8th Ave.
(See Little Theatre)

Abbey's Theatre, 1396 Broadway, northeast corner of 38th St. Owners, Abbey, Schoeffel and Grau. Architects, Carrère and Hastings. Opened November 8, 1893, with *Beckett.*
Re-opened as:
KNICKERBOCKER THEATRE, September 14, 1896, with *Half a King*
Demolished 1930

Acme Theatre, 247 W. 48th St., between Broadway and 8th Ave.
(See Edythe Totten Theatre)

Adelphi Theatre, 152 W. 54th St., between 7th Ave. and the Avenue of the Americas.
(See Craig Theatre)

Aerial Gardens, on the roof of the New Amsterdam Theatre, 214 W. 42nd St., between 7th and 8th Aves. Owners, Klaw and Erlanger. Opened June 6, 1904, with *A Little Bit of Everything.*
Re-opened as:
ZIEGFELD DANSE DE FOLLIES, March 29, 1915, with *Ziegfeld Midnight Frolic*
DRESDEN, April 3, 1923, with *Cinders*
FROLIC, September 10, 1923, with *Teatro dei Piccoli*
NBC TIMES SQUARE STUDIO, 1930
WOR-MUTUAL RADIO THEATRE, September 12, 1937
NEW AMSTERDAM ROOF, November 1, 1943, with *The Petrified Forest*
NBC TIMES SQUARE TELEVISION STUDIO, September 15, 1951

Alice Tully Hall, in Lincoln Center, 1941 Broadway between 65th & 66th Sts. Owner, Lincoln Center for the Performing Arts. Architects, Pietro Belluschi and Catalano & Westermann. Opened September 11, 1969, with a concert.

Alvin Theatre, 250 W. 52nd St., between Broadway and 8th Ave. Owner, Alvin Theatre Corporation. Architect, Herbert J. Krapp. Opened November 22, 1927, with *Funny Face.*

Amato Opera Theatre, 159 Bleecker St.
(See New Stages Theatre)

Ambassador Theatre, 215 W. 49th St., between Broadway and 8th Ave. Owners, Lee and J. J. Shubert. Architect, Herbert J. Krapp. Opened February 11, 1921, with *The Rose Girl.*

Amberg Theatre, southwest corner of Irving Place and 15th St.
(See Irving Hall)

American Academy of Dramatic Arts, 245 W. 52nd St., between Broadway and 8th Ave.
(See Guild Theatre)

American Music Hall, 260 W. 42nd St., through to 41st St. and onto 8th Ave.
(See American Theatre)

American Music Hall, 139-41 E. 55th St., between Lexington and 3rd Aves. Erected as a church in 1852. Converted into theatre, and opened March 14, 1934, with *The Drunkard.*

American Place Theatre, 111 W. 46th St., between Broadway and Avenue of the Americas. Owner, Fisher Brothers 47th Corp. Architect, Richard D. Kaplan. Designer, Frank Trotta. Opened December 6, 1971, with *Fingernails Blue as Flowers* and *Lake of the Woods.*

American Show Shop, 247 W. 48th St., between Broadway and 8th Ave.
(See Edythe Totten Theatre)

American Theatre, 260 W. 42nd St. through to 41st St. and onto 8th Ave. Owner, T. Henry French. Architect, Charles C. Haight. Opened May 22, 1893, with *The Prodigal Daughter.*
Re-opened as:
AMERICAN MUSIC HALL, November 16, 1908, with vaudeville
LOEW'S AMERICAN, 1911
AMERICAN MUSIC HALL, 1929, as a burlesque theatre
Demolished 1932

Anco Theatre, 254 W. 42nd St., between 7th and 8th Aves.
(See Lew Fields' Theatre)

Anderson Yiddish Theatre, 66 2nd Ave. at 4th St.
(See Public Theatre)

Anne Nichols' Little Theatre, 238 W. 44th St., between Broadway and 8th Ave.
(See Little Theatre)

Anta Playhouse, 245 W. 52nd St., between Broadway and 8th Ave.
(See Guild Theatre)

Anta Theatre, 245 W. 52nd St., between Broadway and 8th Ave.
(See Guild Theatre)

Apollo Theatre, 219 W. 42nd St., between 7th and 8th Aves.
(See Bryant Theatre)

Artef Theatre, 108 W. 41st St., between Broadway and the Avenue of the Americas.
(See Comedy Theatre)

Artef Theatre, 247 W. 48th St., between Broadway and 8th Ave.
(See Edythe Totten Theatre)

Artef Theatre, 22 W. 63rd St., between Central Park West and Broadway.
(See Davenport Theatre)

Assembly Theatre, 104 W. 39th St.
(See Princess Theatre)

Astor Theatre, 1537 Broadway, northwest corner of 45th St. Owners, Wagenhals and Kemper. Architect, George Keister. Opened September 21, 1906, with *A Midsummer Night's Dream.*

Avery Fisher Hall, Broadway and 64th St.
(See Philharmonic Hall)

Avon Theatre, 251 W. 45th St., between Broadway and 8th Ave.
(See Klaw Theatre)

B. S. Moss' Broadway, 1681 Broadway, southwest corner 53rd St.
(See B. S. Moss' Colony)

B. S. Moss' Colony, 1681 Broadway, southwest corner 53rd St. Owner, B. S. Moss. Architect, Eugene DeRosa. Opened December 25, 1924, with *The Thief of Bagdad* (cinema).
Re-opened as:
UNIVERSAL'S COLONY, February 7, 1926
B. S. MOSS' BROADWAY, December 8, 1930, with *The New Yorkers*
EARL CARROLL'S BROADWAY, September 27, 1932, with *Earl Carroll's Vanities*
BROADWAY, December 26, 1932, with a vaudeville policy
B.S. MOSS' BRÓADWAY, October 12, 1935, with a film policy
CINE ROMA, February 25, 1937, with *Lealta Di Donna* (cinema)
BROADWAY, November 13, 1940, with *Fantasia* (cinema)

Barbizon-Plaza Theatre, 106 Central Park South at Avenue of the Americas. Owner, Barbizon-Plaza Hotel. Opened in 1930 with a concert.

Banvard's Museum, 1221 Broadway, between 29th and 30th Sts. Owner, John Banvard. Opened June 17, 1867, with *Banvard's Panorama of the Mississippi, The Hymn of Four Nations, Jenny Lind at Last, A Husband for an Hour.*
Re-opened as:
WOOD'S MUSEUM AND METROPOLITAN THEATRE, August 31, 1868, with *Married by Lanterns, Sixty-Six*
WOOD'S MUSEUM AND MENAGERIE, August 30, 1869, with *The Water Nymphs* and *Masaniello*
BROADWAY THEATRE, December 26, 1876, with *Coerinia*
DALY'S THEATRE, September 17, 1879, with *Love's Young Dream*
Demolished 1920

Bayes Theatre, 216 W. 44th St., between Broadway and 8th Ave.
(See Lew Fields' 44th St. Roof Garden)

Belasco Theatre, 111 W. 44th St. between Broadway and the Avenue of the Americas.
(See Stuyvesant Theatre)

Belasco Theatre, 207 W. 42nd St., between 7th and 8th Aves.
(See Theatre Republic)

Belmont Theatre, 125 W. 48th St., between 7th Ave. and the Avenue of the Americas.
(See Norworth Theatre)

Bijou Theatre, 209 W. 45th St., between Broadway and 8th Ave. Owner, J. J. Shubert. Architect, Herbert J. Krapp. Opened April 12, 1917, with *The Knife.*
Re-opened as:
D. W. GRIFFITH THEATRE, October 3, 1962, with *The Connection* (cinema)
TOHO CINEMA, January 22, 1963, with *Yojimbo* (cinema)
BIJOU THEATRE, January 14, 1973, with *The Enemy Is Dead.*

Billy Rose Music Hall, 1697 Broadway, west side of Broadway between 53rd and 54th Sts.
(See Hammerstein's Theatre)

Billy Rose Theatre, 208 W. 41st St., between 7th and 8th Aves.
(See National Theatre)

Biltmore Theatre, 261 W. 47th St., between Broadway and 8th Ave. Owner, Chanin Theatre Corporation. Architect, Herbert J. Krapp. Opened December 7, 1925, with *Easy Come Easy Go.*

Bleecker Street Playhouse, 159 Bleecker St.
(See New Stages Theatre)

Booth Theatre, 222 W. 45th St., between Broadway and 8th Ave. Owners, Winthrop Ames and Shubert Theatre Corp. Architect, Henry B. Herts. Opened October 16, 1913, with *The Great Adventure.*

Bouwerie Lane Theatre, 330 Bowery at Bond St. Owners, Bruce & Honey Becker. Opened November 1, 1963, with *The Immoralist.*

Bramhall Theatre, 138 E. 27th St., between Lexington and 3rd Aves. Owner, Butler Davenport. Opened April 1, 1915, with *Importance of Coming and Going.*
Re-opened as:
DAVENPORT THEATRE, January 17, 1923
GRAMERCY ARTS THEATRE, May 1959, with *Oedipus*

Broadhurst Theatre, 235 W. 44th St., between Broadway and 8th Ave. Owners, Lee and J. J. Shubert and Affiliated Theatre Building Co., Inc. Architect, Herbert J. Krapp. Opened September 27, 1917, with *Misalliance.*

Broadway Theatre, 1221 Broadway, west side of Broadway between 29th and 30th Sts.
(See Banvard's Museum)

Broadway, 1681 Broadway, southwest corner 53rd St.
(See B. S. Moss' Colony)

Brooks Atkinson Theatre, 256 W. 47th St., between Broadway and 8th Ave.
(See Mansfield Theatre)

Bryant Theatre, 219 W. 42nd St., between 7th and 8th Aves. Opened 1910, as a film and vaudeville house.
Re-opened as:
APOLLO THEATRE, November 18, 1920, with *Jimmie*

CBS Radio Playhouse, 238 W. 44th St., between Broadway and 8th Ave.
(See Little Theatre)

CBS Radio Playhouse, 1697 Broadway, west side of Broadway between 53rd and 54th Sts.
(See Hammerstein's Theatre)

CBS Radio Playhouse (1), 139 W. 44th St., between Broadway and the Avenue of the Americas.
(See Hudson Theatre)

CBS Radio Playhouse (3), 242 W. 45th St., between Broadway and 8th Ave.
(See Royale Theatre)

CBS Radio Playhouse (4), 254 W. 54th St., between Broadway and 8th Ave.
(See Gallo Theatre)

CBS Radio Playhouse (4), 223 W. 48th St., between Broadway and 8th Ave.
(See Ritz Theatre)

CBS Radio Playhouse (5), 109 W. 39th St., between Broadway and the Avenue of the Americas.
(See Maxine Elliott's Theatre)

Candler Theatre, 226 W. 42nd St., between 7th and 8th Aves. Owners, George Kleine, Cohan and Harris, Sol Bloom. Opened May 7, 1914, with *Antony and Cleopatra* (cinema).
Re-opened as:
COHAN AND HARRIS THEATRE, October 25, 1916, with *Object—Matrimony*
SAM H. HARRIS THEATRE, February 21, 1921, with *Welcome Stranger*

Carnegie Hall, 154 W. 57th St., southeast corner of 7th Ave.
(See Music Hall)

Caruso Theatre, 247 W. 48th St., between Broadway and 8th Ave.
(See Edythe Totten Theatre)

Casa Manana, southeast corner 7th Ave. and 50th St.
(See Earl Carroll Theatre)

Casino, southeast corner 7th Ave. and 50th St.
(See Earl Carroll Theatre)

Casino De Paree, 254 W. 54th St., between Broadway and 8th Ave.
(See Gallo Theatre)

Casino East, 189 2nd Ave., southeast corner 12th St.
(See Yiddish Art Theatre)

Casino Theatre, southeast corner of Broadway and 39th St. Owner, Rudolph Aronson. Architects, Kimball and Wisedell. Opened October 21, 1882, with *The Queen's Lace Handkerchief.*
Demolished 1930

Castles-in-the-Air, 216 W. 44th St., between Broadway and 8th Ave.
(See Lew Fields' 44th St. Roof Garden)

Center Theatre, southeast corner Avenue of the Americas and 49th St.
(See RKO Roxy Theatre)

Central Theatre, 1567 Broadway at 47th St. Owner, the Shuberts. Architect, Herbert J. Krapp. Opened September 9, 1918, with *Forever After.*
Re-opened as:
SHUBERT CENTRAL THEATRE, 1922
CENTRAL THEATRE, 1923
COLUMBIA THEATRE, March 24, 1934, with a burlesque show
CENTRAL THEATRE, June 1934
GOTHAM THEATRE
HOLIDAY THEATRE, May 1951
ODEON THEATRE, December 26, 1957, with *Pursuit of the Graf Spee* (cinema)
FORUM THEATRE, June 17, 1959, with *Middle of the Night* (cinema)

Century Opera House, Central Park West, 62nd to 63rd Sts.
(See New Theatre)

Century Theatre, Central Park West, 62nd to 63rd Sts.
(See New Theatre)

Century Theatre, 932 7th Ave., west side of 7th Ave., between 58th and 59th Sts.
(See Jolson's 59th Street Theatre)

Century Theatre, 189 2nd Ave., southwest corner 12th St.
(See Yiddish Art Theatre)

Chanin's 46th St. Theatre, 226 W. 46th St., between Broadway and 8th Ave. Owner, Chanin Construction Co. Architect, Herbert J. Krapp. Opened December 24, 1924, with *The Greenwich Village Follies.*
Re-opened as:
46TH ST. THEATRE, October 10, 1932, with *Of Thee I Sing*

Charles Hopkins Theatre, 153 W. 49th St., between 7th Ave. and the Avenue of the Americas.
(See Punch and Judy Theatre)

Cherry Lane Theatre, 38 Commerce St. Owner, Bedford Mews Corp. Opened February 9, 1924, with *Saturday Night.*
Re-opened as:
NEW PLAYWRIGHTS THEATRE, 1927
CHERRY LANE THEATRE, 1928
PAUL GILMORE'S CHERRY LANE THEATRE, 1931
GILMORE MUSIC HALL, 1934
GILMORE CHERRY LANE MYSTERY THEATRE, 1935
GILMORE'S CHERRY LANE THEATRE, 1937
CHERRY LANE THEATRE, September 4, 1945, with *Murder without Crime*

Cine Roma, 1681 Broadway, southwest corner of 53rd St.
(See B. S. Moss' Colony)

Cinema, 153 W. 49th St., between 7th Ave. and the Avenue of the Americas.
(See Punch and Judy Theatre)

Cinema Dante, southwest corner of the Avenue of the Americas and 39th St.
(See Princess Theatre)

Cinema Verdi, southwest corner of the Avenue of the Americas and 39th St.
(See Princess Theatre)

Circle in the Square, 5 Sheridan Sq. Owners, The Loft Players. Opened February 2, 1951, with *Dark of the Moon.*
Demolished 1960

Circle in the Square, 159 Bleecker St.
(See New Stages Theatre)

Circle in the Square/Joseph E. Levine Theatre, 1633 Broadway on 50th St. west of Broadway. Owner, Uris Corporation, Architect, Allen Sayles. Opened October 26, 1972, with special all-star benefit. First production, *Mourning Becomes Electra,* opened November 15, 1972.

Circle Music Hall, 1825 Broadway, southwest corner of 60th St. Owners, Charles E. Evans and W. D. Mann. Announced a vaudeville policy, September 1900, but did not open.
Re-opened as:
CIRCLE THEATRE, November 26, 1902, with *Aristocracy*

Circle Theatre, 1825 Broadway, southwest corner of 60th St.
(See Circle Music Hall)

City Theatre, 116 E. 14th St., between 3rd and Park Aves. South. Owners, City Theatre Co. (Timothy D. Sullivan, George J. Kraus, William Fox, Timothy P. Sullivan). Opened April 18, 1910, with *Miss Innocence.*
Re-opened as:
FOX'S CITY THEATRE, November 1910, as a vaudeville house
YIDDISH ART THEATRE, December 10, 1928, with *Success*
CITY THEATRE, 1929, as a film theatre
Demolished 1952

Civic Repertory Theatre, 105 W. 14th St., between the Avenue of the Americas and 7th Ave.
(See Theatre Francais)

Coburn Theatre, 22 W. 63rd St., between Central Park West and Broadway.
(See Davenport Theatre)

Cohan and Harris Theatre, 226 W. 42nd St., between 7th and 8th Aves.
(See Candler Theatre)

Colonial Theatre, 1887 Broadway, west side of Broadway between 62nd and 63rd Sts. Owners, Thompson and Dundy with Tom W. Ryley. Opened February 12, 1905, with *A Duel in the Snow* and *The Athletic Girl.*
Re-opened as:
HAMPDEN'S THEATRE, October 11, 1925, with *Hamlet*
RKO COLONIAL, 1931
HARKNESS THEATRE, April 9, 1974, with the Harkness Ballet

Columbia Radio Playhouse, 251 W. 45th St., between Broadway and 8th Ave.
(See Klaw Theatre)

Columbia Theatre, 1567 Broadway at 47th St.
(See Central Theatre)

Columbus Circle Theatre, 5 Columbus Circle.
(See Majestic Theatre)

Comedy Theatre, 108 W. 41st St., between Broadway and the Avenue of the Americas. Owners, Sam S. and Lee Shubert. Architect, D. G. Malcolm. Opened September 6, 1909, with *The Melting Pot.*
Re-opened as:
WILLIAM COLLIER'S COMEDY THEATRE, November 28, 1910, with *I'll Be Hanged If I Do*
COMEDY THEATRE, September 1, 1913, with *Her Own Money*
MERCURY THEATRE, November 11, 1937, with *Julius Caesar*
ARTEF THEATRE, during the run of *Uriel Acosta,* which opened December 29, 1939
Demolished 1942

Concert Theatre, 202 W. 58th St., between Broadway and 7th Ave.
(See John Golden Theatre)

Coronet Theatre, 230 W. 49th St., between Broadway and 8th Ave.
(See Forrest Theatre)

Cort Theatre, 148 W. 48th St., between 7th Ave. and the Avenue of the Americas. Owner, John Cort. Architect, Edward B. Corey. Opened December 20, 1912, with *Peg o' My Heart.*

Cosmopolitan, 5 Columbus Circle.
(See Majestic Theatre)

Craig Theatre, 152 W. 54th St., between 7th Ave. and the Avenue of the Americas. Owner, Houston Properties Corp. Architects, R. E. Hall & Co. Opened December 24, 1928, with *Potiphar's Wife.*
Re-opened as:
ADELPHI THEATRE, November 27, 1934, with *The Lord Blesses the Bishop*
RADIANT CENTER, December 1940
YIDDISH ART THEATRE, October 18, 1943, with *The Family Carnovsky*
ADELPHI THEATRE, April 20, 1944, with *Allah Be Praised*
54TH STREET THEATRE, October 8, 1958, with *Drink to Me Only*
GEORGE ABBOTT THEATRE, November 14, 1965
Demolished

Cricket Theatre, 162 2nd Ave., east side of 2nd Ave. between 10th and 11th Sts. Opened November 26, 1957, with *A Palm Tree in a Rose Garden.*

Criterion Theatre, east side of Broadway between 44th and 45th Sts.
(See Olympia)

D. W. Griffith Theatre, 209 W. 45th St., between Broadway and 8th Ave.
(See Bijou Theatre)

Daly's Theatre, 1221 Broadway, between 29th and 30th Sts.
(See Banvard's Museum)

Daly's 63rd St. Theatre, 22 W. 63rd St., between Central Park West and Broadway.
(See Davenport Theatre)

Davenport Theatre, 138 E. 27th St., between Lexington and 3rd Aves.
(See Bramhall Theatre)

Davenport Theatre, 22 W. 63rd St., between Central Park West and Broadway. Owned by an estate represented by W. F. Clare. Started as a theatre in 1909, but never completed. Opened 1913 as a temple.
Re-opened as:
63RD ST. MUSIC HALL, December 25, 1919, with movies for children
DALY'S 63RD ST. THEATRE, October 3, 1922, with *Dolly Jordan*
COBURN THEATRE, November 7, 1928, with *The Yellow Jacket*
RECITAL THEATRE, January 26, 1932, with *Lady Windermere's Fan*
PARK LANE THEATRE, April 12, 1932, with *The Tree*
GILMORE'S 63RD ST. THEATRE, December 27, 1934, with *Jealousy*
EXPERIMENTAL THEATRE, March 4, 1936, with *Chalk Dust*
ARTEF THEATRE, October 4, 1937, with *The Outlaw*
DALY'S 63RD ST. THEATRE, March 1, 1938
Demolished

Delacorte Theatre, Central Park near 80th St. Owner, N.Y.C. Dept. of Parks. Architect, N.Y.C. Dept of Parks. Consultant & Stage Designer, Eldon Elder. Opened June 18, 1962, with *The Merchant of Venice.*

Downtown Theatre, 85 E. 4th St. west of 2nd Ave. Opened January 3, 1956, with *Don Juan.*
Re-opened as:
EAST END THEATRE, January 10, 1961, with *The Sudden End of Anne Cinquefoil.*

Dresden, atop the New Amsterdam Theatre, 214 W. 42nd St., between 7th and 8th Aves.
(See Aerial Gardens)

Earl Carroll Theatre, southeast corner 7th Ave. and 50th St. Owner, Earl Carroll. Architect, George Keister. Opened July 5, 1923, with *Earl Carroll's Vanities of 1923.*

Re-opened as:
CASINO, May 19, 1932, with *Show Boat*
FRENCH CASINO, December 25, 1934, as a theatre restaurant
CASA MANANA, January 19, 1938, as a theatre-restaurant
Demolished 1939

Earl Carroll's Broadway, 1681 Broadway, southwest corner 53rd St.
(See B. S. Moss' Colony)

East End Theatre, 85 E. 4th St., west of 2nd Ave.
(See Downtown Theatre)

East 74th Street Theatre, 334 E. 74th St. between 1st & 2nd Aves. Owner, Day Tuttle. Designer, Barrie Greenbie. Remodeled and re-opened May 19, 1959, with *Lysistrata.*
Re-opened as:
PHOENIX 74TH STREET THEATRE, September 18, 1961
PHOENIX THEATRE, November 21, 1961 with *Androcles and the Lion* and *The Policemen*
EAST 74TH STREET THEATRE, October 22, 1965 with *Hotel Passionato*
EASTSIDE PLAYHOUSE, October 15, 1968 with *Tea Party* and *The Basement*

Eastside Playhouse, 334 E. 74th St., between 1st & 2nd Aves.
(See East 74th Street Theatre)

Eden Theatre, 189 2nd Ave., southwest corner 12th St.
(See Yiddish Art Theatre)

Edison Theatre, 240 W. 47th St., between Broadway & 8th Ave. Owner, Edison Theatre Corp. Opened March 5, 1970, with *Show Me Where the Good Times Are.*

Edythe Totten Theatre, 247 W. 48th St., between Broadway and 8th Ave. Owner, Edythe Totten Theatre Corp. Opened October 6, 1926, with *Secret Sands.*
Re-opened as:
PRESIDENT THEATRE, January 7, 1929, with *The Guinea Pig*
HINDENBURG THEATRE, March 30, 1932, with *Mein Leopold* (cinema)
CARUSO THEATRE, February 1, 1933, with *My Cousin* (cinema)
MIDGET THEATRE, December 25, 1933
PRESIDENT THEATRE, February 15, 1934, with *Legal Murder*
ARTEF THEATRE, October 12, 1934, with *Recruits*
ACME THEATRE, September 7, 1937, with *Al Chet* (cinema)
AMERICAN SHOW SHOP, December 13, 1937, with *Murder Sails at Midnight*
SHOW SHOP, April 14, 1938, with *Emil* (cinema)
GILMORE'S 48TH ST. THEATRE, July 1938
48TH ST. THEATRE, December 1938
PRESIDENT THEATRE, September 1944
Converted into part of Mamma Leone's Restaurant, 1956

Eltinge Theatre, 236 W. 42nd St., between 7th and 8th Aves. Owner, A. H. Woods. Architect, Thomas A. Lamb. Opened September 11, 1912, with *Within the Law.*
Re-opened as:
LAFFMOVIE, 1943, as a cinema
EMPIRE, 1954, as a cinema

Elysée, 202 W. 58th St., between Broadway and 7th Ave.
(See John Golden Theatre)

Empire Theatre, 1430 Broadway at 40th St. Owners, Al Hayman and Frank Sanger. Architect, J.B. McElfatrick & Co. Opened January 25, 1893, with *The Girl I Left Behind Me.*
Demolished 1953

Empire Theatre, 236 W. 42nd St., between 7th and 8th Aves.
(See Eltinge Theatre)

Equity, 48th Street Theatre, 157 W. 48th St., between 7th Ave. and the Avenue of the Americas.
(See 48th St. Theatre)

Erlanger's Theatre, 246 W. 44th St., between Broadway and 8th Ave. Owner, Caesar Theatre Corporation. Architects, Warren and Wetmore. Opened September 26, 1927, with *The Merry Malones.*
Re-opened as:
ST. JAMES THEATRE, December 7, 1932, with *Walk a Little Faster.*

Estelle R. Newman Theatre, 425 Lafayette St., south of 8th St. Owner, New York Shakespeare Festival Public Theatre. Architect, Giorgio Cavaglieri. Opened October 4, 1970, with *The Happiness Cage.*

Ethel Barrymore Theatre, 243 W. 47th St., between Broadway and 8th Ave. Owners, Lee and J. J. Shubert. Architect, Herbert J. Krapp. Opened December 20, 1928, with *The Kingdom of God.*

Eugene O'Neill Theatre, 230 W. 49th St., between Broadway and 8th Ave.
(See Forrest Theatre)

Evergreen Theatre, 55 E. 11th St., between Broadway & University Pl.
(See Renata Theatre)

Experimental Theatre, 22 W. 63rd St., between Central Park West and Broadway.
(See Davenport Theatre)

Federal Music Theatre, 254 W. 54th St., between Broadway and 8th Ave.
(See Gallo Theatre)

51st St. Theatre, 237 W. 51st St., between Broadway and 8th Ave.
(See Hollywood Theatre)

54th St. Theatre, 152 W. 54th St., between 7th Ave. and the Avenue of the Americas.
(See Craig Theatre)

58th St. Theatre, 202 W. 58th St., between Broadway and 7th Ave.
(See John Golden Theatre)

Filmarte, 202 W. 58th St., between Broadway and 7th Ave.
(See John Golden Theatre)

Fine Arts Theatre, 202 W. 58th St., between Broadway and 7th Ave.
(See John Golden Theatre)

Florence Sutro Anspacher Theatre, 425 Lafayette St., south of 8th St. Owner, New York Shakespeare Festival Public Theatre Architect, Giorgio Cavaglieri. Opened October 17, 1967, with *Hair.*

Folies Bergere, 210 W. 46th St., between Broadway and 8th Ave. Owners, Henry B. Harris and Jesse L. Lasky. Architects, Herts and Tallant. Opened April 27, 1911, as a theatre-restaurant, with *Hell, Temptation* and *Gaby.*
Re-opened as:
FULTON THEATRE, October 20, 1911, with *The Cave Man*
HELEN HAYES THEATRE, November 21, 1955, with *Tiger at the Gates*

Folies Marigny, 216 W. 44th St., between Broadway and 8th Ave.
(See Lew Fields' 44th St. Roof Garden)

Folksbiene Yiddish Theatre, 175 East Broadway. Opened December 15, 1959, with *A Thousand and One Nights.*

Forrest Theatre, 230 W. 49th St., between Broadway and 8th Ave. Owners, Lee and J. J. Shubert. Architect, Herbert J. Krapp. Opened November 24, 1925, with *Mayflowers.*
Re-opened as:
CORONET, December 14, 1945, with *Dream Girl*
EUGENE O'NEILL THEATRE, November 19, 1959

41st St. Theatre, 125 W. 41st St., between Broadway and the Avenue of the Americas. Opened April 16, 1957, with *Oscar Wilde.*

44th St. Roof Theatre, 216 W. 44th St., between Broadway and 8th Ave.
(See Lew Fields' 44th St. Roof Garden)

44th St. Theatre, 216 W. 44th St., between Broadway and 8th Ave.
(See Weber and Fields' Music Hall)

46th St. Theatre, 226-36 W. 46th St., between Broadway and 8th Ave.
(See Chanin's 46th St. Theatre)

48th St. Theatre, 157 W. 48th St., between 7th Ave. and the Avenue of the Americas. Owner, William A. Brady. Architect, William A. Swasey. Opened August 12, 1912, with *Just Like John.*
Re-opened as:
EQUITY, 48TH ST. THEATRE, October 2, 1922, with *Malvaloca*
48TH ST. THEATRE, June 1, 1925, with *Spooks*
WINDSOR THEATRE, November 20, 1937, with *Work Is for Horses*
48TH ST. THEATRE, September 1, 1943
Demolished 1955

48th St. Theatre, 247 W. 48th St., between Broadway and 8th Ave.
(See Edythe Totten Theatre)

Forum Theatre, northwest corner of Lincoln Center, 65th St. east of Amsterdam Ave. Owner, Lincoln Center for the Performing Arts. Architect, Eero Saarinen & Associates and Jo Mielziner, collaborating designer. Opened April 3, 1966, with *Berlin's Mine.*
Re-opened as:
MITZI E. NEWHOUSE THEATRE, November 10, 1973, with *Troilus and Cressida*

Forum Theatre, 1567 Broadway at 47th St.
(See Central Theatre)

14th St. Theatre, 105 W. 14th St., between the Avenue of the Americas and 7th Ave.
(See Theatre Francais)

4th Street Theatre, 83 E. 4th St., west of 2nd Ave. Opened October 26, 1954, with *The Dybbuk.*
Re-opened as:
WRITERS' STAGE, October 30, 1962, with *P.S. 193*
NEW DRAMATISTS WORKSHOP, October 1965
PLAYWRIGHTS UNIT, June 1969
PLAYERS WORKSHOP, November 1971, with *The Slave* and *Open 24 Hours*

Fox's City Theatre, 116 E. 14th St., between 3rd Ave. and Park Ave. South.
(See City Theatre)

Frazee Theatre, 254 W. 42nd St., between 7th and 8th Aves.
(See Lew Fields' Theatre)

French Casino, southeast corner of 7th Ave. and 50th St.
(See Earl Carroll Theatre)

Frolic, atop the New Amsterdam Theatre, 214 W. 42nd St., between 7th and 8th Aves.
(See Aerial Gardens)

Fulton Theatre, 210 W. 46th St., between Broadway and 8th Ave.
(See Folies Bergere)

Gaiety Theatre, 1547 Broadway, west side of Broadway between 45th and 46th Sts. Owners, Klaw and Erlanger. Architects, Herts and Tallant. Opened September 4, 1909, with *The Fortune Hunter.*
Re-opened as:
VICTORIA THEATRE, September 4, 1943, with *The City That Stopped Hitler—Heroic Stalingrad* (cinema)

Gallo Theatre, 254 W. 54th St., between Broadway and 8th Ave. Owner, Fortune Gallo. Opened November 7, 1927, with *La Boheme* (opera)
Re-opened as:
NEW YORKER THEATRE, May 12, 1930, with *The Vikings*
CASINO DE PAREE, December 13, 1933
PALLADIUM, January 16, 1936
FEDERAL MUSIC THEATRE, 1937
NEW YORKER THEATRE, March 21, 1939, with *The Swing Mikado*
CBS RADIO PLAYHOUSE (4), 1943

Garrick Theatre, 65 W. 35th St., between 5th Ave. and the Avenue of the Americas.
(See Harrigan's Theatre)

Gate Theatre, 162 2nd Ave., east side of 2nd Ave. between 10th and 11th Sts. Opened December 6, 1957, with *The Brothers Karamazov.*

Gayety Theatre, 189 2nd Ave., southwest corner 12th St.
(See Yiddish Art Theatre)

George Abbott Theatre, 152 W. 54th St., between 7th Ave. and the Avenue of the Americas.
(See Craig Theatre)

George M. Cohan's Theatre, 1482 Broadway, southeast corner of 43rd St. Owners, Cohan and Harris. Architect, George Keister. Opened February 13, 1911, with *Get-Rich-Quick Wallingford.*
Demolished 1938

Giglio's Radio Theatre, 216 W. 44th St., between Broadway and 8th Ave.
(See Lew Fields' 44th St. Roof Garden)

Gilmore Cherry Lane Mystery Theatre, 38 Commerce St.
(See Cherry Lane Theatre)

Gilmore Music Hall, 38 Commerce St.
(See Cherry Lane Theatre)

Gilmore's Cherry Lane Theatre, 38 Commerce St.
(See Cherry Lane Theatre)

Gilmore's 48th St. Theatre, 247 W. 48th St., between Broadway and 8th Ave.
(See Edythe Totten Theatre)

Gilmore's 63rd St. Theatre, 22 W. 63rd St., between Central Park West and Broadway.
(See Davenport Theatre)

Globe Theatre, 1555 Broadway, between 46th and 47th Sts., and 205 W. 46th St., between Broadway and 8th Ave. Owner, Charles Dillingham. Architects, Carrère and Hastings. Opened January 10, 1910, with *The Old Town.*
Re-opened as:
LUNT-FONTANNE THEATRE, May 5, 1958, with *The Visit*

Golden Theatre, 242 W. 45th St., between Broadway and 8th Ave.
(See Royale Theatre)

Gotham Theatre, 1567 Broadway at 47th St.
(See Central Theatre)

Gramercy Arts Theatre, 138 E. 27th St., between Lexington and 3rd Aves.
(See Bramhall Theatre)

Grand Opera House, northwest corner of 8th Ave. and 23rd St.
(See Pike's Opera House)

Greenwich Village Theatre, 220 W. 4th St., at 7th Ave. Owner, Frank Conroy. Opened November 15, 1917, with *The Festival of Bacchus, Efficiency, Behind a Watteau Picture.*
Re-opened as:
IRISH THEATRE, December 26, 1929, with *The Playboy of the Western World*
Demolished 1930

Guild Theatre, 245 W. 52nd St., between Broadway and 8th Ave. Owner, Theatre Guild. Architects, C. Howard Crane, Kenneth Franzheim, Charles Hunter Bettis. Opened April 13, 1925, with *Caesar and Cleopatra.*
Re-opened as:
WOR MUTUAL THEATRE, March 19, 1943
ANTA PLAYHOUSE, March 31, 1950
AMERICAN ACADEMY OF DRAMATIC ARTS, 1953
ANTA THEATRE, December 20, 1954, with *Portrait of a Lady*

Hackett Theatre, 254 W. 42nd St., between 7th and 8th Aves.
(See Lew Fields' Theatre)

Hammerstein's Theatre, 1697 Broadway, west side of Broadway between 53rd and 54th Sts. Owner, Arthur Hammerstein. Architect, Herbert J. Krapp. Opened November 30, 1927, with *Golden Dawn.*
Re-opened as:
MANHATTAN THEATRE, September 8, 1931, with *Free For All*
BILLY ROSE MUSIC HALL, June 21, 1934, as a theatre-restaurant
MANHATTAN MUSIC HALL, November 27, 1934
MANHATTAN THEATRE, February 14, 1936, with *American Holiday*
CBS RADIO PLAYHOUSE, September 1936

Hampden's Theatre, 1887 Broadway, west side of Broadway between 62nd and 63rd Sts.
(See Colonial Theatre)

Harkness Theatre, 1887 Broadway, west side of Broadway between 62nd and 63rd Sts.
(See Colonial Theatre)

Harrigan's Theatre, 65 W. 35th St., between 5th Ave. and the Avenue of the Americas. Owner, Edward Harrigan. Architect, Francis H. Kimball. Opened December 29, 1890, with *Reilly and the Four Hundred.*
Re-opened as:
GARRICK THEATRE, April 23, 1895, with *Arms and the Man*
THEATRE DU VIEUX COLOMBIER, November 20, 1917, with *Les Fourberies de Scapin*
GARRICK THEATRE, April 19, 1919, with *Bonds of Interest*
Demolished 1932

Harris Theatre, 254 W. 42nd St., between 7th and 8th Aves.
(See Lew Fields' Theatre)

Haverly's Theatre, 105 W. 14th St., between the Avenue of the Americas and 7th Ave.
(See Theatre Francais)

Helen Hayes Theatre, 210 W. 46th St., between Broadway and 8th Ave.
(See Folies Bergere)

Henry Miller's Theatre, 124 W. 43rd St., between Broadway and the Avenue of the Americas. Owner, Henry Miller. Architects, H. C. Ingalls and Paul R. Allen. Opened April 1, 1918, with *The Fountain of Youth.*

Hindenburg Theatre, 247 W. 48th St., between Broadway and 8th Ave.
(See Edythe Totten Theatre)

Hippodrome, 6th Avenue, between 43rd and 44th Sts. Owners, Frederic W. Thompson and Elmer S. Dundy. Opened April 12, 1905, with *A Yankee Circus on Mars.*
Demolished 1939

Holiday Theatre, 1567 Broadway at 47th St.
(See Central Theatre)

Hollywood Theatre, 1655 Broadway and 237 W. 51st St., around northwest corner, Broadway and 51st St. Owner, Warner Brothers. Architect, Thomas W. Lamb. Opened April 22, 1930, with *Hold Everything* (cinema); opened, as legitimate house, December 13, 1934, with *Calling All Stars.*
Re-opened as:
51ST ST. THEATRE, October 28, 1936, with *Sweet River*
HOLLYWOOD THEATRE, August 11, 1937, with *The Life of Emile Zola* (cinema)
51ST ST. THEATRE, May 9, 1940, with *Romeo and Juliet*
WARNER BROTHERS THEATRE, August 15, 1947, with *Life with Father* (cinema)
MARK HELLINGER THEATRE, January 22, 1949, with *All for Love*

Hudson Playhouse, 121 Christopher St., between Bleecker and Greenwich Sts. Opened in the 1920s as a neighborhood cinema.
Re-opened as:
THEATRE DE LYS, October 27, 1952, with *Frankie and Johnny*

Hudson Theatre, 139 W. 44th St., between Broadway and the Avenue of the Americas. Owner, Henry B. Harris. Architects, McElfatrick & Co. Opened October 19, 1903, with *Cousin Kate.*
Re-opened as:
CBS RADIO PLAYHOUSE NO. 1, February 3, 1934
HUDSON THEATRE, February 15, 1937, with *An Enemy of the People*

Imperial Theatre, 249 W. 45th St., between Broadway and 8th Ave. Owners, 249 West

45th Street, Inc. Architect, Herbert J. Krapp. Opened December 25, 1923, with *Mary Jane McKane.*

International Theatre, 5 Columbus Circle. (See Majestic Theatre)

Irish Theatre, 220 W. 4th St., at 7th Ave. (See Greenwich Village Theatre)

Irving Hall, southwest corner of Irving Place and 15th St. Opened December 20, 1860, with a ball.
Re-opened as:
AMBERG THEATRE, December 1, 1888, with *Ein Erflog*
IRVING PLACE THEATRE, May 8, 1893, with *Ivanhoe*
Presently warehouse for S. Klein

Irving Place Theatre, southwest corner of Irving Place and 15th St. (See Irving Hall)

John Golden Theatre, 252 W. 45th St., between Broadway and 8th Ave. (See Theatre Masque)

John Golden Theatre, 202 W. 58th St., between Broadway and 7th Ave. Owner, John Golden. Architect, Harrison G. Wiseman. Opened November 1, 1926, with *Two Girls Wanted.*
Re-opened as:
58TH ST. THEATRE, September 17, 1935, with *Few Are Chosen*
FILMARTE, September 20, 1936, with *La Kermesse Héroique* (cinema)
FINE ARTS THEATRE, April 2, 1940, with *The Life of Giuseppe Verdi* (cinema)
CONCERT THEATRE, February 14, 1942, with *Of V We Sing*
ROCK CHURCH, 1943
58TH ST. THEATRE, January 15, 1946
ABC RADIO THEATRE, April 1946
ELYSÉE, January 28, 1948, with *Fanny* (cinema)
ABC TELEVISION THEATRE

Jolson's 59th Street Theatre, 932 7th Ave., west side of 7th Ave., between 58th and 59th Sts. Owner, the Shuberts. Architect, Herbert J. Krapp. Opened Oct. 6, 1921, with *Bombo.*
Re-opened as:
SHAKESPEARE THEATRE, November 17, 1932, with *A Midsummer Night's Dream*
VENICE THEATRE, November 26, 1934, with *Africana*
YIDDISH ART THEATRE, September 20, 1937, with *The Brothers Ashkenazi*
JOLSON THEATRE, May 26, 1942, with *Comes the Revelation*
MOLLY PICON THEATRE, October 12, 1942, with *Oy Is Dus A Leben*
CENTURY THEATRE, April 8, 1944, with *Follow the Girls*
NBC THEATRE, March 29, 1954
VIDEO TAPE CENTER, Fall, 1959
Demolished 1962

Jolson Theatre, 932 7th Ave., west side of 7th Ave., between 58th and 59th Sts. (See Jolson's 59th Street Theatre)

Klaw Theatre, 251 W. 45th St., between Broadway and 8th Ave. Owner, Marc Klaw, Inc. Architect, Eugene DeRosa. Opened March 2, 1921, with *Nice People.*
Re-opened as:
AVON THEATRE, September 18, 1929, with *Strictly Dishonorable*
COLUMBIA RADIO PLAYHOUSE, September 1934
Demolished January 1954

Knickerbocker Theatre, 1396 Broadway, northeast corner of 38th St. (See Abbey's Theatre)

Labor Stage, southwest corner of the Avenue of the Americas and 39th St. (See Princess Theatre)

Laffmovie, 236 W. 42nd St., between 7th and 8th Aves. (See Eltinge Theatre)

Laura Keene's 14th St. Theatre, 105 W. 14th St., between the Avenue of the Americas and 7th Ave. (See Theatre Francais)

Lew Fields' 44th St. Roof Garden, atop Weber and Fields' New Music Hall, 216 W. 44th St., between Broadway and 8th Ave. Owners, the Shuberts. Architect, William Albert Swasey. Opened June 5, 1913, with *All Aboard.*
Re-opened as:
FOLIES MARIGNY, January 1914
CASTLES-IN-THE-AIR, June 14, 1915, with *Look Who's Here*
44TH ST. ROOF THEATRE, December 1, 1917, with *Over the Top*
NORA BAYES THEATRE, December 30, 1918, with *Ladies First*
BAYES THEATRE, September 11, 1922, with *East Side—West Side*
THOMASHEFSKY'S BROADWAY THEATRE, September 3, 1923, with *The Three Little Business Men*
BAYES THEATRE, May 12, 1924, with *Two Strangers from Nowhere*
GIGLIO'S RADIO THEATRE, August 28, 1937, with *La Figlia Brutta*
NORA BAYES THEATRE, December 15, 1937, with *Fickle Women*
Demolished July 1945

Lew Fields' Mansfield Theatre, 256 W. 47th St., between Broadway and 8th Ave. (See Mansfield Theatre)

Lew Fields' Theatre, 254 W. 42nd St., between 7th and 8th Aves. Owner, Oscar Hammerstein. Opened December 5, 1904, with *It Happened in Nordland.*
Re-opened as:
HACKETT THEATRE, August 27, 1906, with *The Little Stranger*
HARRIS THEATRE, August 31, 1911, with *Maggie Pepper*
FRAZEE THEATRE, September 7, 1920, with *The Woman of Bronze*
WALLACK'S THEATRE, November 12, 1924, with *Shipwrecked*
ANCO THEATRE erected on the site, 1940

Liberty Theatre, 234 W. 42nd St., between 7th and 8th Aves. Owners, Klaw and Erlanger Amusement Co. Architects, Herts and Tallant. Opened October 10, 1904, with *The Rogers Brothers in Paris.*

Little Met, southwest corner of the Avenue of the Americas and 39th St. (See Princess Theatre)

Little Theatre, 238 W. 44th St., between Broadway and 8th Ave. Owner, Winthrop Ames. Architects, H. C. Ingalls and F. B. Hoffman, Jr. Opened March 12, 1912, with *The Pigeon.*
Re-opened as:
CBS RADIO PLAYHOUSE, February 1935
ANNE NICHOLS' LITTLE THEATRE, September 28, 1936, with *Pre-Honeymoon*
LITTLE THEATRE, December 7, 1937, with *Edna His Wife*
NEW YORK TIMES HALL, January 1942
ABC TELEVISION STUDIO, 1959
LITTLE THEATRE, October 26, 1963, with *Tambourines to Glory*
WINTHROP AMES THEATRE, September 7, 1964, with *The Subject Was Roses*
LITTLE THEATRE, March 1965.

Loew's American, 260 W. 42nd St., through to 41st St. and onto 8th Ave. (See American Theatre)

Loew's 42nd St. Theatre, 162 E. 42nd St., southeast corner of Lexington Ave. (See Murray Hill Theatre)

Loew's Ziegfeld, northwest corner of the Avenue of the Americas and 54th St. (See Ziegfeld Theatre)

Longacre Theatre, 220 W. 48th St., between Broadway and 8th Ave. Owner, Frazee Realty Co. Architect, Henry B. Herts. Opened May 1, 1913, with *Are You a Crook?*

Lunt-Fontanne Theatre, 205 W. 46th St., between Broadway and 8th Ave. (See Globe Theatre)

Lucille La Verne Theatre, southwest corner of the Avenue of the Americas and 39th St. (See Princess Theatre)

Lyceum, 105 W. 14th St., between the Avenue of the Americas and 7th Ave. (See Theatre Francais)

Lyceum Theatre, 149 W. 45th St., between Broadway and the Avenue of the Americas. Owner, Daniel Frohman. Architects, Herts and Tallant. Opened November 2, 1903, with *The Proud Prince.*

Lyric Theatre, 213 W. 42nd St. between 7th & 8th Aves. Owner, Reginald DeKoven. Architect, V. Hugo Koehler. Opened October 12, 1903, with *Old Heidelberg.*

McAlpin Rooftop Theatre, Broadway & 34th St. Owner, McAlpin Hotel. Designer, Jack Blackman. Opened March 20, 1970, with *Lyle.*

Maidman Playhouse, 416 W. 42nd St., between 9th and 10th Aves. Owner, Irving Maidman. Designed by Russell Patterson. Opened February 6, 1960, with *Russell Patterson's Sketchbook.*

Majestic Theatre, 245 W. 44th St., between Broadway and 8th Ave. Owner, Chanin Theatres Corp. Architect, Herbert J. Krapp. Opened March 28, 1927, with *Rufus LeMaire's Affairs.*

Majestic Theatre, 5 Columbus Circle. Owners, E. D. Stair and A. L. Wilbur. Architect, John H. Duncan. Opened January 21, 1903, with *The Wizard of Oz.*
Re-opened as:
PARK THEATRE, October 23, 1911, with *The Quaker Girl*
PARK MUSIC HALL, September 15, 1922, with burlesque
COSMOPOLITAN, August 2, 1923, with *Little Old New York* (cinema)
THE THEATRE OF YOUNG AMERICA, October 5, 1934, with *The Chinese Nightingale*

PARK THEATRE, 1935, with motion pictures
INTERNATIONAL THEATRE, October 30, 1944, with *Ballet International*
COLUMBUS CIRCLE THEATRE, December 13, 1945, with *G. I. Hamlet*
INTERNATIONAL THEATRE, August 13, 1946
NBC TELEVISION THEATRE, January 1949
Demolished June 1954

Manhattan Music Hall, 1697 Broadway, west side of Broadway between 53rd and 54th Sts.
(See Hammerstein's Theatre)

Manhattan Theatre, 1697 Broadway, west side of Broadway between 53rd and 54th Sts.
(See Hammerstein's Theatre)

Mansfield Theatre, 256 W. 47th St., between Broadway and 8th Ave. Owner, Chanin Construction Company. Architect, Herbert J. Krapp. Opened February 15, 1926, with *The Night Duel.*
Re-opened as:
LEW FIELDS' MANSFIELD THEATRE, April 26, 1928, with *Present Arms*
MANSFIELD THEATRE, March 4, 1929, with *Indiscretion*
BROOKS ATKINSON THEATRE, September 12, 1960, with *Vintage '60*

Mark Hellinger Theatre, 1655 Broadway and 237 W. 51st St., between Broadway and 8th Ave.
(See Hollywood Theatre)

Martin Beck Theatre, 302 W. 45th St., between 8th and 9th Aves. Owner, Martin Beck. Architect, G. Albert Lansburgh. Opened November 11, 1924, with *Madame Pompadour.*

Martinique Theatre, 49 W. 32nd St., east of Broadway. Owner, Martinique Hotel. Opened March 11, 1958, with *The Crucible.*

Martinson Hall, 425 Lafayette St., south of 8th St. Owner, New York Shakespeare Festival Public Theatre. Architect, Giorgio Cavaglieri. Opened November 16, 1969, with *Stomp.*

Maxine Elliott's Theatre, 109 W. 39th St., between Broadway and the Avenue of the Americas. Owners, Lee Shubert and Maxine Elliott. Architect, Marshall & Fox. Opened December 30, 1908, with *The Chaperon.*
Re-opened as:
MUTUAL RADIO THEATRE NO. 1, November 3, 1941
CBS RADIO PLAYHOUSE NO. 5, 1944
Demolished 1959

Mayfair Theatre, 235 W. 46th St. between Broadway & 8th Ave. Owners, Norman Twain & Irving Maidman. Designer, Russell Patterson. Opened March 6, 1961, with *Roots.*

Mecca Temple, 131 W. 55th St., between the Avenue of the Americas and 7th Ave. Opened 1924 as the headquarters of the Nobles of the Order of the Mystic Shrine.
Re-opened as:
NEW YORK CITY CENTER, December 13, 1943, with *Susan and God*

Mercer Arts Center, 240 Mercer St., between Bleecker & 3rd Sts.
(See Mercer Street Playhouse Center)

Mercer-Brecht Theatre, 240 Mercer St., between Bleecker & 3rd Sts. Opened March 16, 1972, with *Walk Together Children.*
(See Mercer Street Playhouse Center)

Mercer-Hansbury Theatre, 240 Mercer St., between Bleecker & 3rd Sts. Opened January 7, 1970, with *Love and Maple Syrup.*
(See Mercer Street Playhouse Center)

Mercer-O'Casey Theatre, 240 Mercer St., between Bleecker & 3rd Sts. Opened February 8, 1970, with *Exchange.*
(See Mercer Street Playhouse Center)

Mercer-Oscar Wilde Room, 240 Mercer St., between Bleecker & 3rd Sts. Opened January 1972 with *The Proposition.*
(See Mercer Arts Playhouse Center)

Mercer-Shaw Arena Theatre, 240 Mercer St., between Bleecker & 3rd Sts. Opened April 3, 1970, with *Dark of the Moon.*
(See Mercer Street Playhouse Center)

Mercer Street Playhouse Center, 240 Mercer St., between Bleecker & 3rd Sts. Lessors, Art D'Lugoff, Bert D'Lugoff & Seymour Kaback. (A complex of theatres, cabarets, bar, restaurant, boutique, school & workshops.)
Re-opened as:
MERCER ARTS CENTER, January 1972
Building collapsed August 3, 1973

Mercury Theatre, 108 W. 41st St., between Broadway and the Avenue of the Americas.
(See Comedy Theatre)

Metropolitan Opera House, Broadway to 7th Ave., 39th to 40th Sts. Owner, Metropolitan Opera Association. Architect, Cady, Berg and See. Opened October 22, 1883, with *Faust.*
Demolished 1967

Metropolitan Opera House, west side of Lincoln Center Plaza, Broadway at 64th St. Owner, Lincoln Center for the Performing Arts. Architect, Wallace K. Harrison. Opened September 16, 1966, with *Antony and Cleopatra.*

Midget Theatre, 247 W. 48th St., between Broadway and 8th Ave.
(See Edythe Totten Theatre)

Midway Theatre, 420 W. 42nd St., between 9th and 10th Aves. Owner, Maidman Playhouses, Inc. Opened April 2, 1962, with *Romeo and Juliet.*

Minskoff Theatre, 200 W. 45th St. on Broadway between 44th and 45th Sts. Owner, Sam Minskoff & Sons. Architect, Robert Allan Jacobs of Kahn & Jacobs. Opened March 13, 1973, with *Irene.*

Mitzi E. Newhouse Theatre, northwest corner of Lincoln Center, 65th St., east of Amsterdam Ave.
(See Forum Theatre)

Molly Picon Theatre, 932 7th Ave., west side of 7th Ave., between 58th and 59th Sts.
(See Jolson's 59th Street Theatre)

Morosco Theatre, 217 W. 45th St., between Broadway and 8th Ave. Owners, Lee and J. J. Shubert. Architect, Herbert J. Krapp. Opened February 5, 1917, with *Canary Cottage.*

Murray Hill Theatre, 162 E. 42nd St., southeast corner of Lexington Ave. Owner, Frank R. Murtha. Opened October 19, 1896, with *In Mexico—1848.*
Re-opened as:
LOEW'S 42ND ST. THEATRE, 1917
Demolished 1951

Music Box Theatre, 239 W. 45th St., between Broadway and 8th Ave. Owners, Sam H. Harris and Irving Berlin. Architect, C. Howard Crane. Opened September 22, 1921, with *Music Box Revue of 1921.*

Music Hall, 154 W. 57th St., southeast corner 7th Ave. Owner, Andrew Carnegie. Architect, William Burnett Tuthill. Opened May 5, 1891, with a concert.
Re-opened as:
CARNEGIE HALL, 1898

Mutual Radio Theatre No. 1, 109 W. 39th St., between Broadway and the Avenue of the Americas.
(See Maxine Elliott's Theatre)

NBC Television Theatre, northwest corner of the Avenue of the Americas and 54th St.
(See Ziegfeld Theatre)

NBC Television Theatre, 5 Columbus Circle.
(See Majestic Theatre)

NBC Theatre, 932 7th Ave., west side of 7th Ave., between 58th and 59th Sts.
(See Jolson's 59th Street Theatre)

NBC Times Square Studio, atop the New Amsterdam Theatre, 214 W. 42nd St., between 7th and 8th Aves.
(See Aerial Gardens)

NBC Times Square Television Studio, atop the New Amsterdam Theatre, 214 W. 42nd St., between 7th and 8th Aves.
(See Aerial Gardens)

National Theatre, 208 W. 41st St., between 7th and 8th Aves. Owners, Walter C. Jordan and the Shuberts. Architect, William N. Smith. Opened September 1, 1921, with *Swords.*
Re-opened as:
BILLY ROSE THEATRE, October 18, 1959, with *Heartbreak House.*

Nazimova's Theatre, 119 W. 39th St., between Broadway & 6th Ave. Owners, the Shuberts. Architect, William A. Swasey. Opened April 18, 1910, with *Little Eyolf.*
Re-opened as:
39TH STREET THEATRE, March 13, 1911, with *As a Man Thinks*
Demolished 1928

New Amsterdam Roof, 214 W. 42nd St., between 7th and 8th Aves.
(See Aerial Gardens)

New Amsterdam Theatre, 214 W. 42nd St., between 7th and 8th Aves. Owners, Klaw and Erlanger. Architects, Herts and Tallant. Opened November 2, 1903, with *A Midsummer Night's Dream.*

New Dramatists Workshop, 83 E. 4th St., west of 2nd Ave.
(See 4th Street Theatre)

New Playwrights Theatre, 38 Commerce St.
(See Cherry Lane Theatre)

New Stages Theatre, 159 Bleecker St. Owner, New Stages, Inc. Remodeled from a former cinema and opened, December 21, 1947, with *Lamp at Midnight.*
Re-opened as:
BLEECKER STREET PLAYHOUSE, January 23,

1950, with *The Creditors*
AMATO OPERA THEATRE, July 14, 1951, with *Il Barbiere di Siviglia*
CIRCLE IN THE SQUARE, January 8, 1960, with *Our Town*

New Theatre, Central Park West, 62nd to 63rd Sts. Owner, The New Theatre Company. Architects, Carrère and Hastings. Opened November 6, 1909, with *Antony and Cleopatra.*
Re-opened as:
CENTURY THEATRE, October 21, 1911, with *The Garden of Allah*
CENTURY OPERA HOUSE, September 15, 1913, with *Aida*
CENTURY THEATRE, September 23, 1915, with *Ned Wayburn's Town Topics*
Demolished 1930

The New Theatre, 154 E. 54th St. Owner, Daniel H. Larezzo, Jr. Architect, Alan Robert Sayles. Opened May 27, 1964, with *The Knack.*

New York City Center, 131 W. 55th St., between the Avenue of the Americas and 7th Ave.
(See Mecca Temple)

New York State Theatre, south side of Lincoln Center Plaza, Broadway at 64th St. Built by Lincoln Center for the Performing Arts for the State of New York. Architect, Philip Johnson. Opened April 23, 1964, with New York City Ballet Company and the Music Theatre of Lincoln Center participating in an inaugural program.

New York Theatre, east side of Broadway between 44th and 45th Sts.
(See Olympia)

New York Times Hall, 238 W. 44th St., between Broadway and 8th Ave.
(See Little Theatre)

New Yorker Theatre, 254 W. 54th St., between Broadway and 8th Ave.
(See Gallo Theatre)

Nora Bayes Theatre, 216 W. 44th St., between Broadway and 8th Ave.
(See Lew Fields' 44th St. Roof Garden)

Norworth Theatre, 125 W. 48th St., between 7th Ave. and the Avenue of the Americas. Owners, The Norworth Holding Company. Opened January 28, 1918, with *Odds and Ends of 1917.*
Re-opened as:
BELMONT THEATRE, April 1918
THEATRE PARISIEN, November 19, 1919, with *La Main Gauche*
BELMONT THEATRE, February 23, 1920, with *The Passion Flower*
Demolished 1951

Odeon Theatre, 1567 Broadway at 47th St.
(See Central Theatre)

Olympia, east side of Broadway between 44th and 45th Sts. Owner, Oscar Hammerstein. Architect, J. B. McElfatrick & Co. The complex consisted of a music hall, a concert hall, a theatre, a roof garden, etc. Opening of what was called the **Lyric Theatre,** November 25, 1895, with *Excelsior, Jr.* The **Music Hall** opened with Yvette Guilbert, December 17, 1895.
MUSIC HALL re-opened as:
NEW YORK THEATRE, April 24, 1899, with *The Man in the Moon*
LYRIC THEATRE, reopened as:
CRITERION THEATRE, August 29, 1899, with *The Girl from Maxim's*
VITAGRAPH THEATRE, February 7, 1914, as a cinema theatre
CRITERION THEATRE, September 11, 1916, with *Paganini*
Demolished 1935

Orpheum Theatre, 126 2nd Ave. at 8th St. Lessors, Julian Bercovici & Leo Garin. Designer, John McNamara. Opened September 23, 1958, with *The American Mime Theatre.*

Palladium, 254 W. 54th St., between Broadway and 8th Ave.
(See Gallo Theatre)

Palmer's Theatre, northeast corner of Broadway and 30th St.
(See Wallack's Theatre)

Park Lane Theatre, 22 W. 63rd St., between Central Park West and Broadway.
(See Davenport Theatre)

Park Music Hall, 5 Columbus Circle.
(See Majestic Theatre)

Park Theatre, 5 Columbus Circle.
(See Majestic Theatre)

Paul Gilmore's Cherry Lane Theatre, 38 Commerce St.
(See Cherry Lane Theatre)

Philharmonic Hall, Broadway and 64th St. Owner, Lincoln Center for the Performing Arts. Architect, Max Abramovitz. Opened Sept. 23, 1962, with a concert.
Re-opened as:
AVERY FISHER HALL, September 20, 1973

Phoenix 74th Street Theatre, 334 E. 74th St., between 1st and 2nd Aves.
(See East 74th Street Theatre)

Phoenix Theatre, 189 2nd Ave., southwest corner 12th St.
(See Yiddish Art Theatre)

Phoenix Theatre, 334 E. 74th St. between 1st & 2nd Aves.
(See East 74th Street Theatre)

Phyllis Anderson Theatre, 66 2nd Ave. at 4th St.
(See Public Theatre)

Pike's Opera House, northwest corner 8th Ave. and 23rd St. Owner, Samuel N. Pike. Opened January 9, 1868, with *Il Trovatore.*
Re-opened as:
GRAND OPERA HOUSE, February 1869, during an engagement of an opera bouffe company
RKO 23RD STREET, 1938, as a cinema
Demolished July 1960

Players Workshop, 83 E. 4th St., west of 2nd Ave.
(See 4th Street Theatre)

Playhouse Theatre, 137 W. 48th St., between 7th Ave. and the Avenue of the Americas, Owner, William A. Brady. Architect, Charles A. Rich. Opened April 15, 1911, with *Sauce for the Goose.*
Demolished 1968

Playhouse Theatre, 359 W. 48th St., between 8th & 9th Aves. Owners, Paramount Twin-Arts Corp. Opened May 17, 1970, with *Lemon Sky.*

Playwrights Unit, 83 E. 4th St., west of 2nd Ave.
(See 4th Street Theatre)

Plymouth Theatre, 236 W. 45th St., between Broadway and 8th Ave. Owners, Lee and J. J. Shubert. Architect, Herbert J. Krapp. Opened October 10, 1917, with *A Successful Calamity.*

President Theatre, 247 W. 48th St., between Broadway and 8th Ave.
(See Edythe Totten Theatre)

Princess Theatre, 104 W. 39th St. Owner, F. Ray Comstock. Architect, W. Albert Swasey. Opened March 14, 1913, with the Princess Players in a bill of five plays: *The Switchboard, Fear, Fancy Free, Any Night* and *A Tragedy of the Future.*
Re-opened as:
LUCILLE LA VERNE THEATRE, October 22, 1928, with *Sun-Up*
PRINCESS THEATRE, April 4, 1929, with *He Walked in Her Sleep*
ASSEMBLY THEATRE, October 16, 1929, with *Lolly*
REO, 1933, as a cinema
LABOR STAGE, November 27, 1937, with *Pins and Needles*
THEATRE WORKSHOP, 1944
CINEMA DANTE, October 31, 1947, with *Lucia de Lammermoor* (cinema)
LITTLE MET, April 22, 1948, with *Not Guilty* (cinema)
CINEMA VERDI, April 16, 1952, with *La Forza del Destino* (cinema)
Demolished June 1955

Provincetown Playhouse, 133 MacDougal St., between 3rd and 4th Sts. Owner, Mrs. Jennie Belardi. Opened November 22, 1918, with *The Princess Marries, The Page, Where the Cross is Made, Gee-Rusalem.*

Public Theatre, 66 2nd Ave. at 4th St. Owner, Schulman-Goldberg Public Theatre. Architects, H. Craig Severance & David M. Oltarsh. Opened January 29, 1927, with *Parisian Love*
Re-opened as:
PHYLLIS ANDERSON THEATRE, November 5, 1957 with *The Girl of the Golden West*
ANDERSON YIDDISH THEATRE, October 18, 1958 with *A Family Mishmash*

Public Theatre, 425 Lafayette St.
(See Estelle R. Newman Theatre, Florence Sutro Anspacher Theatre, Martinson Hall)

Punch and Judy Theatre, 153 W. 49th St., between 7th Ave. and the Avenue of the Americas. Owner, Charles Hopkins. Architects, Murray & Dana. Opened November 10, 1914, with *The Marriage of Colombine.*
Re-opened as:
CHARLES HOPKINS THEATRE, January 21, 1926, with *The Makropoulos Secret*
CINEMA, 1933
WESTMINSTER CINEMA, April 20, 1934, with *Just Smith* (cinema)
WORLD THEATRE, October 1, 1935

RKO Center Theatre, southeast corner Avenue of the Americas and 49th St.
(See RKO Roxy Theatre)

RKO Roxy Theatre, southeast corner Avenue of the Americas and 49th St. Owner, Rockefeller Center. Architects, Reinhart and Hofmeister, Corbett, Harrison, and MacMurray, Hood and Foulihoux. Opened December 29, 1932, with *The Animal Kingdom* (cinema) and stage show.
Re-opened as:
RKO CENTER THEATRE, December 14, 1933, with *Little Women* (cinema)
CENTER THEATRE, September 22, 1934, with *The Great Waltz*
Demolished 1954

RKO 23rd Street, northwest corner 8th Ave. and 23rd St.
(See Pike's Opera House)

Radiant Center, 152 W. 54th St., between 7th Ave. and the Avenue of the Americas.
(See Craig Theatre)

Recital Theatre, 22 W. 63rd St., between Central Park West and Broadway.
(See Davenport Theatre)

Renata Theatre, 55 E. 11th St., between Broadway & University Pl. Owner, Oscar Zurer. Opened October 28, 1964, with *Shout from the Rooftops.*
Re-opened as:
EVERGREEN THEATRE, October 24, 1967, with *The Beard*

Reo, southwest corner of the Avenue of the Americas and 39th St.
(See Princess Theatre)

Republic Theatre, 207 W. 42nd St., between 7th and 8th Aves.
(See Theatre Republic)

Ritz Theatre, 223 W. 48th St., between Broadway and 8th Ave. Owners, Lee and J. J. Shubert. Architect, Herbert J. Krapp. Opened March 21, 1921, with *Mary Stuart* (Drinkwater).
Re-opened as:
CBS RADIO PLAYHOUSE (4), October 9, 1939
RITZ, 1943

Rock Church, 202 W. 58th St., between Broadway and 7th Ave.
(See John Golden Theatre)

Royale Theatre, 242 W. 45th St., between Broadway and 8th Ave. Owners, Chanin Theatres Corporation. Architect, Herbert J. Krapp. Opened January 11, 1927, with *Piggy.*
Re-opened as:
GOLDEN THEATRE, September 26, 1934, with *Small Miracle*
CBS RADIO PLAYHOUSE (3), December 1936
ROYALE THEATRE, December 19, 1940, with *Cue for Passion*

St. James Theatre, 246 W. 44th St., between Broadway and 8th Ave.
(See Erlanger Theatre)

Sam H. Harris Theatre, 226 W. 42nd St., between 7th and 8th Aves.
(See Candler Theatre)

Sam S. Shubert Theatre, 225 W. 44th St., between Broadway and 8th Ave. Owners, Shubert Theatrical Co. Architect, Henry B. Herts. Opened September 29, 1913, with Forbes-Robertson Repertory

Selwyn Theatre, 229 W. 42nd St., between 7th and 8th Aves. Owner, Selwyn and Company. Architect, George Keister. Opened October 3, 1918, with *Information Please.*

Shakespeare Theatre, 932 7th Ave., west side of 7th Ave., between 58th and 59th Sts.
(See Jolson's 59th Street Theatre)

Show Shop, 247 W. 48th St., between Broadway and 8th Ave.
(See Edythe Totten Theatre)

Shubert Central Theatre, 1567 Broadway at 47th St.
(See Central Theatre)

63rd St. Music Hall, 22 W. 63rd St., between Central Park West and Broadway.
(See Davenport Theatre)

Stage 73, 321 E. 73rd St., between 1st & 2nd Aves. Designer, Jack Blackman. Opened May 10, 1962, with *If Five Years Pass.*

Stuyvesant Theatre, 111 W. 44th St., between Broadway and the Avenue of the Americas. Owner, David Belasco. Plans and specifications by David Belasco; General Contractor, M. R. Bimberg, Architect, George Keister. Opened October 16, 1907, with *A Grand Army Man.*
Re-opened as:
BELASCO THEATRE, September 3, 1910, with *The Lily*

Sullivan St. Playhouse, 181 Sullivan St., south of Bleecker St. Lessors, Lee Paton & David Long. Opened August 27, 1957, with *Sweeny Todd, the Demon Barber of Fleet Street.*

Theatre De Lys, 121 Christopher St., between Bleecker and Greenwich Sts.
(See Hudson Playhouse)

Theatre Du Vieux Colombier, 65 W. 35th St., between 5th Ave. and the Avenue of the Americas.
(See Harrigan's Theatre)

Theatre East, 211 E. 60th St., between 2nd & 3rd Aves. Owner, Bridge Estates, Inc. Designer, Abraham Grossman. Opened April 10, 1956, with *The Beautiful People.*

Theatre Four, 424 W. 55th St., between 9th & 10th Aves. Owner, David & Carmel Ross. Architect, Louis Gardner with Lee Schoen. Designer, Hugh Hardy. Opened November 14, 1962, with *The Cherry Orchard.*

Theatre Francais, 105 W. 14th St., between the Avenue of the Americas and 7th Ave. Owners, M. Guignet and M. C. Drivet. Opened May 26, 1866, with *Nos Allies* and *Les Rendezvous Bourgeois.*
Re-opened as:
LAURA KEENE'S 14TH ST. THEATRE, April 11, 1871, with *Nobody's Child*
LYCEUM, September 11, 1873, with *The Hunchback of Notre Dame*
HAVERLY'S THEATRE, March 31, 1879, with *Le Petit Duc*
14TH ST. THEATRE, August 21, 1886, with *Paquita*
CIVIC REPERTORY THEATRE, October 25, 1926, with *Saturday Night*
Demolished 1938

Theatre Marquee, 110 E. 59th St. east of Park Ave. Owner, Columbia Broadcasting System. Operators & Designers, Irwin Stahl, Paul E. Davis & Hans Wigert. Opened March 18, 1957, with *The Trojan Women.*
Demolished 1962

Theatre Masque, 252 W. 45th St., between Broadway and 8th Ave. Owners, Chanin Theatres Corp. Architect, Herbert J. Krapp. Opened February 24, 1927, with *Puppets of Passion.*
Re-opened as:
JOHN GOLDEN THEATRE, February 2, 1937, with *And Now Goodbye*

The Theatre of Young America, 5 Columbus Circle.
(See Majestic Theatre)

Theatre Parisien, 125 W. 48th St., between 7th Ave. and the Avenue of the Americas.
(See Norworth Theatre)

Theatre Republic, 207 W. 42nd St., between 7th and 8th Aves. Owner, Oscar Hammerstein. Architects, J. B. McElfatrick & Co. Opened September 27, 1900, with *Sag Harbor.*
Re-opened as:
BELASCO THEATRE, September 29, 1902, with *Du Barry*
REPUBLIC THEATRE, August 22, 1910, with *Bobby Burnit*
VICTORY THEATRE, May 9, 1942, as a cinema

Theatre 74, 334 E. 74th St., between 1st and 2nd Aves. Owners, Theatre 74. Opened March 25, 1958, with *Asmodee*
(See East 74th Street Theatre)

Theatre Workshop, southwest corner of the Avenue of the Americas and 39th St.
(See Princess Theatre)

39th Street Theatre, 119 W. 39th St., between Broadway & 6th Ave.
(See Nazimova's Theatre)

Thomashefsky's Broadway Theatre, 216 W. 44th St., between Broadway and 8th Ave.
(See Lew Fields' 44th St. Roof Garden)

Times Square Theatre, 219 W. 42nd St., between 7th & 8th Aves. Owner, the Selwyns. Architect, Eugene DeRosa. Opened September 30, 1920, with *The Mirage.*

Tobis Vanderbilt, 148 W. 48th St., between 7th Ave. and the Avenue of the Americas.
(See Vanderbilt Theatre)

Toho Cinema, 209 W. 45th St., between Broadway and 8th Ave.
(See Bijou Theatre)

Town Hall, 119 W. 43rd St., between 7th Ave. and the Avenue of the Americas. Owner, The League for Political Education. Architects, McKim, Mead and White. Opened January 21, 1921, with a meeting advocating the right to public school education without vaccination.

Truck and Warehouse Theatre, 79 E. 4th St. Owner, Bruce Mailman. Opened March 2, 1970, with *Billy Noname.*

Universal's Colony, 1681 Broadway, southwest corner 53rd St.
(See B. S. Moss' Colony)

Uris Theatre, 1633 Broadway, between 50th and 51st Sts. Owner, Uris Corporation. Architect, Theatre Planning Associates—

Ralph Alswang, designer. Opened November 19, 1972, with *Via Galactica.*

Vanderbilt Theatre, 148 W. 48th St., between 7th Ave. and the Avenue of the Americas. Owner, Lyle Andrews. Architects, DeRosa and Pereira. Opened March 7, 1918, with *Oh, Look!*
Re-opened as:
TOBIS VANDERBILT, September 1931
VANDERBILT, December 29, 1931, with *Mr. Papavert*
Demolished 1954

Venice Theatre, 932 7th Ave., west side of 7th Ave., between 58th and 59th Sts.
(See Jolson 59th Street Theatre)

Victoria Theatre, northwest corner 7th Ave. and 42nd St. Owner, Oscar Hammerstein. Architect, J. B. McElfatrick & Co. Opened March 2, 1899, with *The Reign of Error.* Demolished 1915, RIALTO THEATRE erected on site.

Victoria Theatre, 1547 Broadway, between 45th and 46th Sts.
(See Gaiety Theatre)

Victory Theatre, 207 W. 42nd St., between 7th and 8th Aves.
(See Theatre Republic)

Video Tape Center, 932 7th Ave., west side of 7th Ave., between 58th and 59th Sts.
(See Jolson 59th Street Theatre)

Vitagraph Theatre, east side of Broadway between 44th and 45th Sts.
(See Olympia)

Vivian Beaumont Theatre, northwest corner of Lincoln Center, 65th St. at Amsterdam Ave. Owner, Lincoln Center for the Performing Arts. Architect, Eero Saarinen & Associates and Jo Mielziner, collaborating designer. Opened October 12, 1965, with *Danton's Death.*

Waldorf Theatre, 116 W. 50th St., between 7th Ave. and the Avenue of the Americas. Owners, Mayson Realty Company. Architect, Herbert J. Krapp. Opened October 20, 1926, with *Sure Fire.*
Converted into stores, 1937.

Wallack's Theatre, northeast corner of Broadway and 30th St. Owner, Lester Wallack. Opened January 4, 1882, with *The School for Scandal.*
Re-opened as:
PALMER THEATRE, October 8, 1888, with *Les Precieuses Ridicules, La Joie Fait Peur* and two monologues by Constant Coquelin.
WALLACK'S THEATRE, December 7, 1896
Demolished 1915

Wallack's Theatre, 254 W. 42nd St., between 7th and 8th Aves.
(See Lew Fields' Theatre)

Warner Brothers Theatre, 1655 Broadway, between 51st and 52nd Sts.
(See Hollywood Theatre)

Weber and Fields' 44th St. Theatre, 216 W. 44th St., between Broadway and 8th Ave.
(See Weber and Fields' Music Hall)

Weber and Fields' Music Hall, 216 W. 44th St., between Broadway and 8th Ave. Owners, the Shuberts. Architect, William A. Swasey. Opened January 23, 1913, with *The Man with Three Wives.*
Re-opened as:
WEBER AND FIELDS' 44TH THEATRE, March 27, 1913, with *The Geisha*
44TH ST. THEATRE, December 29, 1913, with *The Girl on the Film*
Demolished July 1945

Westminster Cinema, 153 W. 49th St., between 7th Ave. and the Avenue of the Americas.
(See Punch and Judy Theatre)

William Collier's Comedy Theatre, 108 W. 41st St., between Broadway and the Avenue of the Americas.
(See Comedy Theatre)

Windsor Theatre, 157 W. 48th St., between 7th Ave. and the Avenue of the Americas.
(See 48th Street Theatre)

Winter Garden Theatre, 1634 Broadway, east side of Broadway between 50th and 51st Sts. Owners, Winter Garden Company. Architect. William A. Swasey. Opened March 20, 1911, with *"Bow Sing"* and *La Belle Paree.*

Winthrop Ames Theatre, 238 W. 44th St., between Broadway and 8th Ave.
(See Little Theatre)

Wood's Museum and Menagerie, 1221 Broadway, west side of Broadway between 29th and 30th Sts.
(See Banvard's Museum)

Wood's Museum and Metropolitan Theatre, 1221 Broadway, west side of Broadway, between 29th and 30th Sts.
(See Banvard's Museum)

World Theatre, 153 W. 49th St., between 7th Ave. and the Avenue of the Americas.
(See Punch and Judy Theatre)

Wor-Mutual Radio Theatre, atop the New Amsterdam Theatre, 214 W. 42nd St., between 7th and 8th Aves.
(See Aerial Gardens)

Wor-Mutual Theatre, 245 W. 52nd St., between Broadway and 8th Ave.
(See Guild Theatre)

Writers' Stage, 83 E. 4th St., west of 2nd Ave.
(See 4th Street Theatre)

Yiddish Art Theatre, 189 2nd Ave., southwest corner 12th St. Owner, Yiddish Art Theatre. Architect, Louis Jaffee. Opened November 17, 1926, with *The Tenth Commandment.*
Re-opened as:
YIDDISH FOLKS THEATRE, 1934
CENTURY THEATRE, September 9, 1937, as a cinema
PHOENIX THEATRE, December 1, 1953, with *Madam Will You Walk*
CASINO EAST, December 9, 1961, with *Gezunt and Meshuga*
GAYETY THEATRE, 1965 with Burlesque show
EDEN THEATRE, May 11, 1969, with *Oh, Calcutta*

Yiddish Art Theatre, 116 E. 14th St., between 3rd Ave. and Park Ave. South.
(See City Theatre)

Yiddish Art Theatre, 152 W. 54th St., between 7th Ave. and the Avenue of the Americas.
(See Craig Theatre)

Yiddish Art Theatre, 932 7th Ave., west side of 7th Ave., between 58th and 59th Sts.
(See Jolson 59th Street Theatre)

Yiddish Folks Theatre, 189 2nd Ave., southwest corner 12th St.
(See Yiddish Art Theatre)

Ziegfeld Danse De Follies, atop the New Amsterdam Theatre, 214 W. 42nd St., between 7th and 8th Aves.
(See Aerial Gardens)

Ziegfeld Theatre, northwest corner of the Avenue of the Americas and 54th St. Owner, Florenz Ziegfeld, Jr. Architects, Joseph Urban and Thomas A. Lamb. Opened February 2, 1927, with *Rio Rita.*
Re-opened as:
LOEW'S ZIEGFELD, a motion picture theatre, April 22, 1933, with *Rasputin and the Empress*
ZIEGFELD THEATRE, December 7, 1944, with *Seven Lively Arts*
NBC TELEVISION THEATRE, November 1, 1955
ZIEGFELD THEATRE, January 29, 1963, with *An Evening with Maurice Chevalier*
Demolished 1967

Awards

Academy of Motion Picture Arts and Sciences Awards. The Oscars.

Academy awards are given annually for outstanding work in all phases of the motion picture industry. Below are complete listings of winners by years in those categories in which theatre professionals might be honored for excellence in film making.

ACTOR

1927-28 Emil Jannings *(The Way of All Flesh)*
1928-29 Warner Baxter *(In Old Arizona)*
1929-30 George Arliss *(Disraeli)*
1930-31 Lionel Barrymore *(A Free Soul)*
1931-32 Wallace Berry *(The Champ)*; Fredric March *(Dr. Jekyll and Mr. Hyde)*
1932-33 Charles Laughton *(The Private Life of Henry VIII)*
1934 Clark Gable *(It Happened One Night)*
1935 Victor McLaglen *(The Informer)*
1936 Paul Muni *(The Story of Louis Pasteur)*
1937 Spencer Tracy *(Captains Courageous)*
1938 Spencer Tracy *(Boys Town)*
1939 Robert Donat *(Goodbye, Mr. Chips)*
1940 James Stewart *(The Philadelphia Story)*
1941 Gary Cooper *(Sergeant York)*
1942 James Cagney *(Yankee Doodle Dandy)*
1943 Paul Lukas *(Watch on the Rhine)*
1944 Bing Crosby *(Going My Way)*
1945 Ray Milland *(The Lost Weekend)*
1946 Fredric March *(The Best Years of Our Lives)*
1947 Ronald Coleman *(A Double Life)*
1948 Laurence Olivier *(Hamlet)*
1949 Broderick Crawford *(All the King's Men)*
1950 Jose Ferrer *(Cyrano de Bergerac)*
1951 Humphrey Bogart *(The African Queen)*
1952 Gary Cooper *(High Noon)*
1953 William Holden *(Stalag 17)*
1954 Marlon Brando *(On the Waterfront)*
1955 Ernest Borgnine *(Marty)*
1956 Yul Brynner *(The King and I)*
1957 Alec Guinness *(The Bridge on the River Kwai)*
1958 David Niven *(Separate Tables)*
1959 Charlton Heston *(Ben-Hur)*
1960 Burt Lancaster *(Elmer Gantry)*
1961 Maximilian Schell *(Judgment at Nuremberg)*
1962 Gregory Peck *(To Kill a Mockingbird)*
1963 Sidney Poitier *(Lilies of the Field)*
1964 Rex Harrison *(My Fair Lady)*
1965 Lee Marvin *(Cat Ballou)*
1966 Paul Scofield *(A Man for All Seasons)*
1967 Rod Steiger *(In the Heat of the Night)*
1968 Cliff Robertson *(Charley)*
1969 John Wayne *(True Grit)*
1970 George C. Scott *(Patton)*
1971 Gene Hackman *(The French Connection)*
1972 Marlon Brando *(The Godfather)*
1973 Jack Lemmon *(Save the Tiger)*
1974 Art Carney *(Harry and Tonto)*
1975 Jack Nicholson (*One Flew Over the Cuckoo's Nest*)

ACTRESS

1927-28 Janet Gaynor *(Seventh Heaven)*
1928-29 Mary Pickford *(Coquette)*
1929-30 Norma Shearer *(The Divorcee)*
1930-31 Marie Dressler *(Min and Bill)*
1931-32 Helen Hayes *(The Sin of Madelon Claudet)*
1932-33 Katharine Hepburn *(Morning Glory)*
1934 Claudette Colbert *(It Happened One Night)*
1935 Bette Davis *(Dangerous)*
1936 Luise Rainer *(The Great Ziegfeld)*
1937 Luise Rainer *(The Good Earth)*
1938 Bette Davis *(Jezebel)*
1939 Vivien Leigh *(Gone With the Wind)*
1940 Ginger Rogers *(Kitty Foyle)*
1941 Joan Fontaine *(Suspicion)*
1942 Greer Garson *(Mrs. Miniver)*
1943 Jennifer Jones *(The Song of Bernadette)*
1944 Ingrid Bergman *(Gaslight)*
1945 Joan Crawford *(Mildred Pierce)*
1946 Olivia de Havilland *(To Each His Own)*
1947 Loretta Young *(The Farmer's Daughter)*
1948 Jane Wyman *(Johnny Belinda)*
1949 Olivia de Havilland *(The Heiress)*
1950 Judy Holliday *(Born Yesterday)*
1951 Vivien Leigh *(A Streetcar Named Desire)*
1952 Shirley Booth *(Come Back, Little Sheba)*
1953 Audrey Hepburn *(Roman Holiday)*
1954 Grace Kelly *(The Country Girl)*
1955 Anna Magnani *(The Rose Tattoo)*
1956 Ingrid Bergman *(Anastasia)*
1957 Joanne Woodward *(The Three Faces of Eve)*
1958 Susan Hayward *(I Want to Live)*
1959 Simone Signoret *(Room at the Top)*
1960 Elizabeth Taylor *(Butterfield 8)*
1961 Sophia Loren *(Two Women)*
1962 Anne Bancroft *(The Miracle Worker)*
1963 Patricia Neal *(Hud)*
1964 Julie Andrews *(Mary Poppins)*
1965 Julie Christie *(Darling)*
1966 Elizabeth Taylor *(Who's Afraid of Virginia Woolf?)*
1967 Katharine Hepburn *(Guess Who's Coming to Dinner?)*
1968 Katharine Hepburn *(The Lion in Winter)*; Barbra Streisand *(Funny Girl)*
1969 Maggie Smith *(The Prime of Miss Jean Brodie)*
1970 Glenda Jackson *(Women in Love)*
1971 Jane Fonda *(Klute)*
1972 Liza Minnelli *(Cabaret)*
1973 Glenda Jackson *(A Touch of Class)*
1974 Ellen Burstyn *(Alice Doesn't Live Here Anymore)*
1975 Louise Fletcher *(One Flew Over the Cuckoo's Nest)*

SUPPORTING ACTOR

1936 Walter Brennan *(Come and Get It)*
1937 Joseph Schildkraut *(The Life of Emile Zola)*
1938 Walter Brennan *(Kentucky)*
1939 Thomas Mitchell *(Stage Coach)*
1940 Walter Brennan *(The Westerner)*
1941 Donald Crisp *(How Green Was My Valley)*
1942 Van Heflin *(Johnny Eager)*
1943 Charles Coburn *(The More the Merrier)*
1944 Barry Fitzgerald *(Going My Way)*
1945 James Dunn *(A Tree Grows in Brooklyn)*
1946 Harold Russell *(The Best Years of Our Lives)*
1947 Edmund Gwenn *(Miracle on 34th Street)*
1948 Walter Huston *(Treasure of Sierra Madre)*
1949 Dean Jagger *(Twelve O'Clock High)*
1950 George Sanders *(All About Eve)*
1951 Karl Malden *(A Streetcar Named Desire)*
1952 Anthony Quinn *(Viva Zapata!)*
1953 Frank Sinatra *(From Here to Eternity)*
1954 Edmond O'Brien *(The Barefoot Contessa)*
1955 Jack Lemmon *(Mister Roberts)*
1956 Anthony Quinn *(Lust for Life)*
1957 Red Buttons *(Sayonara)*
1958 Burl Ives *(The Big Country)*
1959 Hugh Griffith *(Ben-Hur)*
1960 Peter Ustinov *(Spartacus)*
1961 George Chakiris *(West Side Story)*
1962 Ed Begley *(Sweet Bird of Youth)*
1963 Melvyn Douglas *(Hud)*
1964 Peter Ustinov *(Topkapi)*
1965 Martin Balsam *(A Thousand Clowns)*
1966 Walter Matthau *(The Fortune Cookie)*
1967 George Kennedy *(Cool Hand Luke)*
1968 Jack Albertson *(The Subject Was Roses)*
1969 Gig Young *(They Shoot Horses, Don't They?)*
1970 John Mills *(Ryan's Daughter)*
1971 Ben Johnson *(The Last Picture Show)*
1972 Joel Grey *(Cabaret)*
1973 John Houseman *(The Paper Chase)*
1974 Robert De Niro *(The Godfather, Part II)*
1975 George Burns *(The Sunshine Boys)*

SUPPORTING ACTRESS

1936 Gale Sondergaard *(Anthony Adverse)*
1937 Alice Brady *(In Old Chicago)*
1938 Fay Bainter *(Jezebel)*
1939 Hattie MacDaniel *(Gone With the Wind)*
1940 Jane Darwell *(The Grapes of Wrath)*
1941 Mary Astor *(The Great Lie)*
1942 Teresa Wright *(Mrs. Miniver)*
1943 Katina Paxinou *(For Whom the Bell Tolls)*
1944 Ethel Barrymore *(None But the Lonely Heart)*
1945 Ann Revere *(National Velvet)*
1946 Anne Baxter *(The Razor's Edge)*
1947 Celeste Holm *(Gentleman's Agreement)*
1948 Claire Trevor *(Key Largo)*
1949 Mercedes McCambridge *(All the King's Men)*
1950 Josephine Hull *(Harvey)*
1951 Kim Hunter *(A Streetcar Named Desire)*
1952 Gloria Grahame *(The Bad and the Beautiful)*
1953 Donna Reed *(From Here to Eternity)*
1954 Eva Marie Saint *(On the Waterfront)*
1955 Jo Van Fleet *(East of Eden)*
1956 Dorothy Malone *(Written on the Wind)*
1957 Miyoshi Umeki *(Sayonara)*
1958 Wendy Hiller *(Separate Tables)*
1959 Shelley Winters *(The Diary of Anne Frank)*
1960 Shirley Jones *(Elmer Gantry)*
1961 Rita Moreno *(West Side Story)*
1962 Patty Duke *(The Miracle Worker)*
1963 Margaret Rutherford *(The V.I.P.'s)*
1964 Lila Kedrova *(Zorba the Greek)*
1965 Shelley Winters *(A Patch of Blue)*
1966 Sandy Dennis *(Who's Afraid of Virginia Woolf?)*
1967 Estelle Parsons *(Bonnie and Clyde)*
1968 Ruth Gordon *(Rosemary's Baby)*
1969 Goldie Hawn *(Cactus Flower)*
1970 Helen Hayes *(Airport)*
1971 Cloris Leachman *(The Last Picture Show)*
1972 Eileen Heckart *(Butterflies Are Free)*
1973 Tatum O'Neal *(Paper Moon)*
1974 Ingrid Bergman *(Murder on the Orient Express)*
1975 Lee Grant *(Shampoo)*

DIRECTION

1927-28 Frank Borzage *(Seventh Heaven)*; Lewis Milestone *(Two Arabian Knights)*
1928-29 Frank Lloyd *(The Devine Lady)*
1929-30 Lewis Milestone *(All Quiet on the Western Front)*
1930-31 Norman Taurog *(Skippy)*
1931-32 Frank Borzage *(Bad Girl)*
1932-33 Frank Lloyd *(Cavalcade)*
1934 Frank Capra *(It Happened One Night)*
1935 John Ford *(The Informer)*
1936 Frank Capra *(Mr. Deeds Goes to Town)*
1937 Leo McCarey *(The Awful Truth)*
1938 Frank Capra *(You Can't Take It with You)*
1939 Victor Fleming *(Gone With the Wind)*
1940 John Ford *(The Grapes of Wrath)*
1941 John Ford *(How Green Was My Valley)*
1942 William Wyler *(Mrs. Miniver)*
1943 Michael Curtiz *(Casablanca)*
1944 Leo McCarey *(Going My Way)*
1945 Billy Wilder *(The Lost Weekend)*
1946 William Wyler *(The Best Years of Our Lives)*
1947 Elia Kazan *(Gentleman's Agreement)*
1948 John Huston *(Treasure of Sierra Madre)*
1949 Joseph L. Mankiewicz *(A Letter to Three Wives)*
1950 Joseph L. Mankiewicz *(All About Eve)*
1951 George Stevens *(A Place in the Sun)*
1952 John Ford *(The Quiet Man)*
1953 Fred Zinnemann *(From Here to Eternity)*
1954 Elia Kazan *(On the Waterfront)*
1955 Delbert Mann *(Marty)*
1956 George Stevens *(Giant)*
1957 David Lean *(The Bridge on the River Kwai)*
1958 Vincente Minnelli *(Gigi)*
1959 William Wyler *(Ben-Hur)*
1960 Billy Wilder *(The Apartment)*
1961 Robert Wise and Jerome Robbins *(West Side Story)*
1962 David Lean *(Lawrence of Arabia)*
1963 Tony Richardson *(Tom Jones)*
1964 George Cukor *(My Fair Lady)*
1965 Robert Wise *(The Sound of Music)*
1966 Fred Zinnemann *(A Man for All Seasons)*
1967 Mike Nichols *(The Graduate)*
1968 Carol Reed *(Oliver!)*
1969 John Schlesinger *(Midnight Cowboy)*
1970 Franklin J. Shaffner *(Patton)*
1971 William Friedkin *(The French Connection)*
1972 Bob Fosse *(Cabaret)*
1973 George Roy Hill *(The Sting)*
1974 Francis Ford Coppola *(The Godfather, Part II)*
1975 Milos Forman *(One Flew Over the Cuckoo's Nest)*

WRITING

1927-28 Original Story: Ben Hecht *(Underworld)*
Adaptation: Benjamin Glazer *(Seventh Heaven)*
Title Writing: Joseph Farnham *(The Fair Co-ed; Laugh, Clown, Laugh; Telling the World)*
1928-29 Writing: Hans Kraly *(The Patriot)*
1929-30 Writing: Frances Marion *(The Big House)*
1930-31 Original Story: John Monk Saunders *(The Dawn Patrol)*
Adaptation: Howard Estabrook *(Cimarron)*
1931-32 Original Story: Francis Marion *(The Champ)*
Adaptation: Edwin Burke *(Bad Girl)*
1932-33 Original Story: Robert Lord *(One Way Passage)*
Adaptation: Victor Heerman, Sarah Y. Mason *(Little Women)*
1934 Original Story: Arthur Caesar *(Manhattan Melodrama)*
Screenplay: Robert Riskin *(It Happened One Night)*
1935 Original Story: Ben Hecht, Charles MacArthur *(The Scoundrel)*
Screenplay: Dudley Nichols *(The Informer)*
1936 Original Story: Sheridan Gibney, Pierre Collings *(The Story of Louis Pasteur)*
Screenplay: Sheridan Gibney, Pierre Collings *(The Story of Louis Pasteur)*
1937 Original Story: William A. Wellman, Robert Carson *(A Star Is Born)*
Screenplay: Norman Reilly Raine, Heinz Herald, Geza Herczeg *(The Life of Emile Zola)*
1938 Original Story: Dore Schary, Eleanore Griffin *(Boys Town)*
Screenplay: George Bernard Shaw *(Pygmalion)*
Adaptation: W. P. Lipscomb, Cecil Lewis, Ian Dalrymple *(Pygmalion)*
1939 Original Story: Lewis R. Foster *(Mr. Smith Goes to Washington)*
Screenplay: Sidney Howard *(Gone With the Wind)*
1940 Original Story: Benjamin Glazer, John S. Toldy *(Arise My Love)*
Screenplay: Donald Ogden Stewart *(The Philadelphia Story)*
Original Screenplay: Preston Sturges *(The Great McGinty)*

1941 Original Story: Harry Segall *(Here Comes Mr. Jordan)*
Screenplay: Sidney Buchman, Seton I. Miller *(Here Comes Mr. Jordan)*
Original Screenplay: Herman J. Mankiewicz, Orson Welles *(Citizen Kane)*

1942 Original Story: Emeric Pressburger *(The Invaders)*
Screenplay: Arthur Wimperis, George Froeschel, James Hilton, Claudine West *(Mrs. Miniver)*
Original Screenplay: Ring Lardner, Jr., Michael Kanin *(Woman of the Year)*

1943 Original Story: William Saroyan *(The Human Comedy)*
Screenplay: Jules J. Epstein, Philip G. Epstein, Howard Koch *(Casablanca)*
Original Screenplay: Norman Krasna *(Princess O'Rourke)*

1944 Original Story: Leo McCarey *(Going My Way)*
Screenplay: Frank Butler, Frank Cavett *(Going My Way)*
Original Screenplay: Lamar Trotti *(Wilson)*

1945 Original Story: Charles G. Booth *(The House on 92nd Street)*
Screenplay: Charles Brackett, Billy Wilder *(The Lost Weekend)*
Original Screenplay: Richard Schweizer *(Marie-Louise)*

1946 Original Story: Clemence Dane *(Vacation from Marriage)*
Screenplay: Robert E. Sherwood *(The Best Years of Our Lives)*
Original Screenplay: Muriel Box, Sydney Box *(The Seventh Veil)*

1947 Original Story: Valentine Davies *(Miracle on 34th Street)*
Screenplay: George Seaton *(Miracle on 34th Street)*
Original Screenplay: Sidney Sheldon *(The Bachelor and the Bobby Soxer)*

1948 Motion Picture Story: Richard Schweizer, David Wechsler *(The Search)*
Screenplay: John Huston *(Treasure of Sierra Madre)*

1949 Motion Picture Story: Douglas Morrow *(The Stratton Story)*
Screenplay: Joseph L. Mankiewicz *(A Letter to Three Wives)*
Story and Screenplay: Robert Pirosh *(Battleground)*

1950 Motion Picture Story: Edna Anhalt, Edward Anhalt *(Panic in the Streets)*
Screenplay: Joseph L. Mankiewicz *(All About Eve)*
Story and Screenplay: Charles Brackett, Billy Wilder, D. M. Marshamn, Jr. *(Sunset Boulevard)*

1951 Motion Picture Story: Paul Dehn, James Bernard *(Seven Days to Noon)*
Screenplay: Michael Wilson, Harry Brown *(A Place in the Sun)*
Story and Screenplay: Alan Jay Lerner *(An American in Paris)*

1952 Motion Picture Story: Fredric M. Frank, Theodore St. John, Frank Cavett *(The Greatest Show on Earth)*
Screenplay: Charles Schnee *(The Bad and the Beautiful)*
Story and Screenplay: T. E. B. Clarke *(The Lavender Hill Mob)*

1953 Motion Picture Story: Ian McLellan Hunter *(Roman Holiday)*
Screenplay: Daniel Taradash *(From Here to Eternity)*
Story and Screenplay: Charles Brackett, Walter Reisch, Richard Breen *(Titanic)*

1954 Motion Picture Story: Philip Yordan *(Broken Lance)*
Screenplay: George Seaton *(The Country Girl)*
Story and Screenplay: Budd Schulberg *(On the Waterfront)*

1955 Motion Picture Story: Daniel Fuchs *(Love Me or Leave Me)*
Screenplay: Paddy Chayefsky *(Marty)*
Story and Screenplay: William Ludwig, Sonya Levien *(Interrupted Melody)*

1956 Motion Picture Story: Robert Rich *(The Brave One)*
Screen Adaptation: James Poe, John Farrow, S. J. Perelman *(Around the World in 80 Days)*
Original Screenplay: Albert Lamorisse *(The Red Balloon)*

1957 Original Story and Screenplay: George Wells *(Designing Woman)*
Screenplay: Pierre Boulle *(The Bridge on the River Kwai)*

1958 Original Story and Screenplay: Nathan E. Douglas, Harold Jacob Smith *(The Defiant Ones)*
Screenplay: Alan Jay Lerner *(Gigi)*

1959 Original Story and Screenplay: Story by Russell Rouse, Clarence Greene; screenplay by Stanley Shapiro, Maurice Richlin *(Pillow Talk)*
Screenplay: Neil Paterson *(Room at the Top)*

1960 Original Story and Screenplay: Billy Wilder, I. A. L. Diamond *(The Apartment)*
Screenplay: Richard Brooks *(Elmer Gantry)*

1961 Original Story and Screenplay: William Inge *(Splendor in the Grass)*
Screenplay: Abby Mann *(Judgment at Nuremberg)*

1962 Original Story and Screenplay: Ennio De Concini, Alfredo Giannetti, Pietro Germi *(Divorce-Italian Style)*
Screenplay: Horton Foote *(To Kill a Mockingbird)*

1963 Original Story and Screenplay: James R. Webb *(How the West Was Won)*
Screenplay: John Osborne *(Tom Jones)*

1964 Adaptation: Edward Anhalt *(Beckett)*
Original Screenplay: S. H. Barnett, Peter Stone, Frank Tarloff *(Father Goose)*

1965 Adaptation: Robert Bolt *(Doctor Zhivago)*
Original Screenplay: Frederick Raphael *(Darling)*

1966 Adaptation: Robert Bolt *(A Man for All Seasons)*
Original Screenplay: Pierre Uytterhoeven, Claude Lelouch *(A Man and a Woman)*

1967 Adaptation: Stirling Silliphant *(In the Heat of the Night)*
Original Screenplay: William Rose *(Guess Who's Coming to Dinner)*

1968 Adaptation: James Goldman *(The Lion in Winter)*
Original Screenplay: Mel Brooks *(The Producers)*

1969 Adaptation: Walter Salt *(Midnight Cowboy)*
Original Screenplay: William Goldman *(Butch Cassidy and the Sundance Kid)*

1970 Adaptation: Ring Lardner, Jr. *(M*A*S*H)*
Original Screenplay: Francis Ford Coppola, Edmund North *(Patton)*

1971 Adaptation: Ernest Tidyman *(The French Connection)*
Original Screenplay: Paddy Chayefsky *(The Hospital)*

1972 Adaptation: Mario Puzo, Francis Ford Coppola *(The Godfather)*
Original Screenplay: Jeremy Larner *(The Candidate)*

1973 Adaptation: William Peter Blatty *(The Exorcist)*
Original Screenplay: David S. Ward *(The Sting)*

1974 Adaptation: Mario Puzo, Francis Ford Coppola *(The Godfather, Part II)*
Original Screenplay: Robert Towne *(Chinatown)*

1975 Adaptation: Lawrence Hauben, Bo Goldman *(One Flew Over the Cuckoo's Nest)*
Original Screenplay: Frank Pierson *(Dog Day Afternoon)*

MUSIC—SONG

1934 "The Continental" from *The Gay Divorcee;* music by Con Conrad, lyrics by Herb Magidson

1935 "Lullaby of Broadway" from *Gold Diggers of 1935;* music by Harry Warren, lyrics by Al Dubin

1936 "The Way You Look Tonight" from *Swing Time;* music by Jerome Kern, lyrics by Dorothy Fields

1937 "Sweet Leilani" from *Waikiki Wedding;* music and lyrics by Harry Owens

1938 "Thanks for the Memory" from *The Big Broadcast of 1938;* music by Ralph Ranger, lyrics by Leo Robin

1939 "Over the Rainbow" from *The Wizard of Oz;* music by Harold Arlen, lyrics by E. Y. Harburg

1940 "When You Wish Upon a Star" from *Pinocchio;* music by Ned Washington, lyrics by Leigh Harline

1941 "The Last Time I Saw Paris" from *Lady Be Good;* music by Jerome Kern, lyrics by Oscar Hammerstein II

1942 "White Christmas" from *Holiday Inn;* music and lyrics by Irving Berlin

1943 "You'll Never Know" from *Hello, Frisco, Hello;* music by Harry Warren, lyrics by Mack Gordon

1944 "Swinging on a Star" from *Going My Way;* music by James Van Heusen, lyrics by Johnny Burke

1945 "It Might As Well Be Spring" from *State Fair;* music by Richard Rodgers, lyrics by Oscar Hammerstein II

1946 "On the Atchison, Topeka and Sante Fe" from *The Harvey Girls;* music by Harry Warren, lyrics by Johnny Mercer

1947 "Zip-A-Dee-Doo-Dah" from *Song of the South;* music by Allie Wrubel, lyrics by Ray Gilbert

1948 "Buttons and Bows" from *The Paleface;* music and lyrics by Jay Livingston and Ray Evans

1949 "Baby, It's Cold Outside" from *Neptune's Daughter;* music and lyrics by Frank Loesser

1950 "Mona Lisa" from *Captain Carey,*

U.S.A.; music and lyrics by Ray Evans and Jay Livingston
1951 "In the Cool, Cool, Cool of the Evening" from *Here Comes the Groom;* music by Hoagy Carmichael, lyrics by Johnny Mercer
1952 "High Noon" ("Do Not Forsake Me, Oh My Darlin'") from *High Noon;* music by Dimitri Tiomkin, lyrics by Ned Washington
1953 "Secret Love" from *Calamity Jane;* music by Sammy Fain, lyrics by Paul Francis Webster
1954 "Three Coins in the Fountain" from *Three Coins in the Fountain;* music by Jule Styne, lyrics by Sammy Cahn
1955 "Love Is a Many-Splendored Thing" from *Love Is a Many-Splendored Thing;* music by Sammy Fain, lyrics by Paul Francis Webster
1956 "Whatever Will Be, Will Be" ("Que Sera, Sera") from *The Man Who Knew Too Much;* music and lyrics by Jay Livingston and Ray Evans
1957 "All the Way" from *The Joker Is Wild;* music by James Van Heusen, lyrics by Sammy Cahn
1958 "Gigi" from *Gigi;* music by Fredrick Loewe, lyrics by Alan Jay Lerner
1959 "High Hopes" from *A Hole in the Head;* music by James Van Heusen, lyrics by Sammy Cahn
1960 "Never on Sunday" from *Never on Sunday;* music and lyrics by Manos Hadjidakis
1961 "Moon River" from *Breakfast at Tiffany's;* music by Henry Mancini, lyrics by Johnny Mercer
1962 "Days of Wine and Roses" from *Days of Wine and Roses;* music by Henry Mancini, lyrics by Johnny Mercer
1963 "Call Me Irresponsible" from *Papa's Delicate Condition;* music by James Van Heusen, lyrics by Sammy Cahn
1964 "Chim Chim Cheree" from *Mary Poppins;* by Richard M. Sherman and Robert B. Sherman
1965 "The Shadow of Your Smile" from *The Sandpiper;* music by Johnny Mandel, lyrics by Paul Francis Webster
1966 "Born Free" from *Born Free;* music by John Barry, lyrics by Don Black
1967 "Talk to the Animals" from *Dr. Doolittle;* by Leslie Bricusse
1968 "The Windmills of Your Mind" from *The Thomas Crown Affair;* music by Michel Legrand, lyrics by Alan and Marilyn Bergman
1969 "Raindrops Keep Falling on My Head" from *Butch Cassidy and the Sundance Kid;* music by Burt Bacharach, lyrics by Hal David
1970 "For All We Know" from *Lovers and Other Strangers;* music by Fred Karlin, lyrics by Robb Wilson and Arthur James
1971 Theme from *Shaft;* by Isaac Hayes
1972 "The Morning After" from *The Poseidon Adventure;* music by Al Kasha, lyrics by Joel Hirschhorn
1973 "The Way We Were" from *The Way We Were;* music by Marvin Hamlisch, lyrics by Alan and Marilyn Bergman
1974 "We May Never Love Like This Again" from *The Towering Inferno;* music by Al Kasha, lyrics by Joel Hirschhorn
1975 "I'm Easy" from *Nashville;* by Keith Carradine

American Academy of Arts and Letters

MEDAL FOR GOOD SPEECH

Awarded from time to time by the board of directors of the American Academy of Arts and Letters to recognize correct utterance in the use of language on the stage and in radio and television.

1924 Walter Hampden
1927 Edith Wynne Matthison
1928 Otis Skinner
1929 Julia Marlowe
1930 George Arliss
1932 Alexandra Carlisle
1933 Lawrence Tibbett
1935 Lynn Fontanne
1936 Ina Claire
1944 Paul Robeson
1945 Eva Le Gallienne
1946 Ethel Barrymore
1947 Alfred Lunt
1948 Judith Anderson
1949 Jose Ferrer
1950 Grace George
1951 Claude Rains
1957 Edward R. Murrow
1959 Katharine Cornell
1961 Fredric March
1962 Julie Harris

The American Shakespeare Festival Theatre Shakespeare Awards

First presented in 1954, the Shakespeare Awards were given annually by the Board of Trustees of the American Shakespeare Festival Theatre "in recognition of works which stimulate appreciation of Shakespeare and the classical theatre."

1954 Yale University
Constance Collier
Joyce C. Hall of Hallmark
MGM—John Houseman
New York City Center
WNYC
1955 Antioch College
Dr. Frank Baxter
Shakespeare Association of America
Jack Landau and the Phoenix Theatre
Helge Kökeritz and Charles Tyler Prouty Judith Anderson
1956 Professor Alfred Harbage
Constance Welch
Maurice Evans
The Shakespearewrights
Noah Greenberg and the Pro Musica Antiqua
Sir Laurence Olivier
The Brattle Players
Lawrence Langner
1957 Joseph Papp
Louis B. Wright and Virginia L. Freund of the Folger Library
Penguin Books and Harry F. Paroissien
Professor Henry Wells
NBC-TV's Producers Showcase
1958 Sir Laurence Olivier
Katharine Hepburn
B. Iden Payne
Lyn Ely
William F. and Elisebeth S. Friedman
1959 No Awards
1960 No Awards
1961 Sir Tyrone Guthrie
The Oregon Shakespeare Festival
The Shakespeare Guilds of America
Bert Lahr
1962 Margaret Leighton
Dr. Bernard Beckerman
San Diego Shakespeare Festival
Shakespeare Recording Society
1963 M. J. Rathbone and Standard Oil Company (New Jersey)
Dr. George F. Reynolds
Oliver Rea
Helen Hayes
(Awards Discontinued)

ATA Award of Merit

ATA Citation for Distinguished Service to the Theatre

ATA—ITI World Theatre Award

(See American Theatre Association)

American Theatre Association

ATA AWARD OF MERIT

This award is presented annually for distinguished service to educational theatre by the American Theatre Association (formerly American Educational Theatre Association).

1956 Kenneth MacGowan
1957 Brooks Atkinson
1958 B. Iden Payne
1959 John Gassner
1960 Hubert C. Heffner
1961 Rosamond Gilder
1962 Samuel Selden
1963 Glenn Hughes
1964 Edward C. Cole
1965 William P. Halstead
1966 Jack Morrison
1967 Frank M. Whiting
1968 Loren Winship
1969 Arnold S. Gillette
1970 Theodore Fuchs
1971 Winifred Ward
1972 Lee Norvelle
1973 James Butler
1974 Barnard Hewitt
1975 Monroe Lippman

ATA CITATION FOR DISTINGUISHED SERVICE TO THE THEATRE

1963 Tyrone Guthrie
1964 Allardyce Nicoll
1965 George Freedley
1966 Roger Stevens
1967 Walter Kerr
1968 Thornton Wilder
1969 Helen Hayes
1970 Harold Clurman
1971 John Houseman
1972 Eva Le Gallienne
1973 Joseph Papp
1974 Peggy Wood
1975 Jo Mielziner

ATA—ITI WORLD THEATRE AWARD

1967 Dora Stratou, Greece

1968 Tyrone Guthrie, Ireland
1969 Michel Saint Denis, France
1970 Jean-Louis Barrault, France
1971 Laurence Olivier, Britain
1972 Peter Brook, Britain
1973 Paul Robeson, U.S.A.
1974 Michael Langham, U.S.A.
1975 Ellen Stewart, U.S.A.

The American Theatre Wing Antoinette Perry Awards. The Tony Awards.

Beginning in 1947, the Antoinette Perry (Tony) Awards have been given yearly for "Distinguished Achievement in Theatre." The awards are named after Antoinette Perry (1888-1946), one-time chairman of the board and head of the American Theatre Wing during World War War II.

ACTOR, DRAMATIC STAR

1947 Jose Ferrer *(Cyrano de Bergerac)*
Fredric March *(Years Ago)*
1948 Henry Fonda *(Mister Roberts)*
Paul Kelly *(Command Decision)*
Basil Rathbone *(The Heiress)*
1949 Rex Harrison *(Anne of the Thousand Days)*
1950 Sidney Blackmer *(Come Back, Little Sheba)*
1951 Claude Rains *(Darkness at Noon)*
1952 Jose Ferrer *(The Shrike)*
1953 Tom Ewell *(The Seven Year Itch)*
1954 David Wayne *(The Teahouse of the August Moon)*
1955 Alfred Lunt *(Quadrille)*
1956 Paul Muni *(Inherit the Wind)*
1957 Frederic March *(Long Day's Journey into Night)*
1958 Ralph Bellamy *(Sunrise at Campobello)*
1959 Jason Robards, Jr. *(The Disenchanted)*
1960 Melvyn Douglas *(The Best Man)*
1961 Zero Mostel *(Rhinoceros)*
1962 Paul Scofield *(A Man for All Seasons)*
1963 Arthur Hill *(Who's Afraid of Virginia Woolf?)*
1964 Alec Guinness *(Dylan)*
1965 Walter Matthau *(The Odd Couple)*
1966 Hal Holbrook *(Mark Twain Tonight)*
1967 Paul Rogers *(The Homecoming)*
1968 Martin Balsam *(You Know I Can't Hear You When the Water's Running)*
1969 James Earl Jones *(The Great White Hope)*
1970 Fritz Weaver *(Child's Play)*
1971 Brian Bedford *(The School for Wives)*
1972 Cliff Gorman *(Lenny)*
1973 Alan Bates *(Butley)*
1974 Michael Moriarty *(Find Your Way Home)*
1975 John Kani and Winston Ntshona *(Sizwe Banzi Is Dead* and *The Island)*
1976 John Wood *(Travesties)*

ACTRESS, DRAMATIC STAR

1947 Ingrid Bergman *(Joan of Lorraine)*
Helen Hayes *(Happy Birthday)*
1948 Judith Anderson *(Medea)*
Katharine Cornell *(Antony and Cleopatra)*
Jessica Tandy *(A Streetcar Named Desire)*
1949 Martita Hunt *(The Madwoman of Chaillot)*
1950 Shirley Booth *(Come Back, Little Sheba)*
1951 Uta Hagen *(The Country Girl)*
1952 Julie Harris *(I Am a Camera)*
1953 Shirley Booth *(Time of the Cuckoo)*
1954 Audrey Hepburn *(Ondine)*
1955 Nancy Kelly *(The Bad Seed)*
1956 Julie Harris *(The Lark)*
1957 Margaret Leighton *(Separate Tables)*
1958 Helen Hayes *(Time Remembered)*
1959 Gertrude Berg *(A Majority of One)*
1960 Anne Bancroft *(The Miracle Worker)*
1961 Joan Plowright *(A Taste of Honey)*
1962 Margaret Leighton *(The Night of the Iguana)*
1963 Uta Hagen *(Who's Afraid of Virginia Woolf?)*
1964 Sandy Dennis *(Any Wednesday)*
1965 Irene Worth *(Tiny Alice)*
1966 Rosemary Harris *(The Lion in Winter)*
1967 Beryl Reid *(The Killing of Sister George)*
1968 Zoe Caldwell *(The Prime of Miss Jean Brodie)*
1969 Julie Harris *(Forty Carats)*
1970 Tammy Grimes *(Private Lives)*
1971 Maureen Stapleton *(The Gingerbread Lady)*
1972 Sada Thompson *(Twigs)*
1973 Julie Harris *(The Last of Mrs. Lincoln)*
1974 Colleen Dewhurst *(A Moon for the Misbegotten)*
1975 Ellen Burstyn *(Same Time, Next Year)*
1976 Irene Worth *(Sweet Bird of Youth)*

ACTOR, DRAMATIC—FEATURED OR SUPPORTING

1949 Arthur Kennedy *(Death of a Salesman)*
1951 Eli Wallach *(The Rose Tattoo)*
1952 John Cromwell *(Point of No Return)*
1953 John Williams *(Dial 'M' for Murder)*
1954 John Kerr *(Tea and Sympathy)*
1955 Francis L. Sullivan *(Witness for the Prosecution)*
1956 Ed Begly *(Inherit the Wind)*
1957 Frank Conroy *(The Potting Shed)*
1958 Henry Jones *(Sunrise at Campobello)*
1959 Charles Ruggles *(The Pleasure of His Company)*
1960 Roddy McDowall *(The Fighting Cock)*
1961 Martin Gabel *(Big Fish, Little Fish)*
1962 Walter Matthau *(A Shot in the Dark)*
1963 Alan Arkin *(Enter Laughing)*
1964 Hume Cronyn *(Hamlet)*
1965 Jack Albertson *(The Subject Was Roses)*
1966 Patrick Magee *(Marat/Sade)*
1967 Ian Holm *(The Homecoming)*
1968 James Patterson *(The Birthday Party)*
1969 Al Pacino *(Does a Tiger Wear a Necktie?)*
1970 Ken Howard *(Child's Play)*
1971 Paul Sand *(Story Theatre)*
1972 Vincent Gardenia *(The Prisoner of Second Avenue)*
1973 John Lithgow *(The Changing Room)*
1974 Ed Flanders *(A Moon for the Misbegotten)*
1975 Frank Langella *(Seascape)*
1976 Edward Herrmann *(Mrs. Warren's Profession)*

ACTRESS, DRAMATIC—FEATURED OR SUPPORTING

1947 Patricia Neal *(Another Part of the Forest)*
1949 Shirley Booth *(Goodbye, My Fancy)*
1951 Maureen Stapleton *(The Rose Tattoo)*
1952 Marian Winter *(I Am a Camera)*
1953 Beatrice Straight *(The Crucible)*
1954 Jo Van Fleet *(The Trip to Bountiful)*
1955 Patricia Jessel *(Witness for the Prosecution)*
1956 Una Merkel *(The Ponder Heart)*
1957 Peggy Cass *(Auntie Mame)*
1958 Anne Bancroft *(Two for the Seesaw)*
1959 Julie Newmar *(Marriage-Go-Round)*
1960 Anne Revere *(Toys in the Attic)*
1961 Colleen Dewhurst *(All the Way Home)*
1962 Elizabeth Ashley *(Take Her, She's Mine)*
1963 Sandy Dennis *(A Thousand Clowns)*
1964 Barbara Loden *(After the Fall)*
1965 Alice Ghostly *(The Sign in Sidney Brustein's Window)*
1966 Zoe Caldwell *(Slapstick Tragedy)*
1967 Marian Seldes *(A Delicate Balance)*
1968 Zena Walker *(A Day in the Death of Joe Egg)*
1969 Jane Alexander *(The Great White Hope)*
1970 Blythe Danner *(Butterflies Are Free)*
1971 Rae Allen *(And Miss Reardon Drinks a Little)*
1972 Elizabeth Wilson *(Sticks and Bones)*
1973 Leora Dana *(The Last of Mrs. Lincoln)*
1974 Frances Sternhagen *(The Good Doctor)*
1975 Rita Moreno *(The Ritz)*
1976 Shirley Knight *(Kennedy's Children)*

PLAY

1948 *Mister Roberts*
1949 *Death of a Salesman*
1950 *The Cocktail Party*
1951 *The Rose Tattoo*
1952 *The Fourposter*
1953 *The Crucible*
1954 *The Teahouse of the August Moon*
1955 *The Desperate Hours*
1956 *The Diary of Anne Frank*
1957 *Long Day's Journey into Night*
1958 *Sunrise at Campobello*
1959 *J.B.*
1960 *The Miracle Worker*
1961 *Becket*
1962 *A Man for All Seasons*
1963 *Who's Afraid of Virginia Woolf?*
1964 *Luther*
1965 *The Subject Was Roses*
1966 *Marat/Sade*
1967 *The Homecoming*
1968 *Rosencrantz and Guildenstern Are Dead*
1969 *The Great White Hope*
1970 *Borstal Boy*
1971 *Sleuth*
1972 *Sticks and Bones*
1973 *That Championship Season*
1974 *The River Niger*
1975 *Equus*
1976 *Travesties*

AUTHOR, PLAY

1948 Thomas Heggen and Joshua Logan
1949 Arthur Miller
1950 T. S. Eliot
1951 Tennessee Williams
1952 Jan de Hartog
1953 Arthur Miller
1954 John Patrick
1955 Joseph Hayes
1956 Frances Goodrich and Albert Hackett
1957 Eugene O'Neill
1958 Dore Schary
1959 Archibald MacLeish

1960 William Gibson
1961 Jean Anouilh
1962 Robert Bolt
1963 Edward Albee
1964 John Osborne
1965 Neil Simon

DIRECTOR

1947 Elia Kazan *(All My Sons)*
1949 Elia Kazan *(Death of a Salesman)*
1950 Joshua Logan *(South Pacific)*
1951 George S. Kaufman *(Guys and Dolls)*
1952 Jose Ferrer *(The Shrike, Stalag 17,* and *The Fourposter)*
1953 Joshua Logan *(Picnic)*
1954 Alfred Lunt *(Ondine)*
1955 Robert Montgomery *(The Desperate Hours)*
1956 Tyrone Guthrie *(The Matchmaker)*
1957 Moss Hart *(My Fair Lady)*
1958 Vincent J. Donehue *(Sunrise at Campobello)*
1959 Elia Kazan *(J.B.)*
1960 Arthur Penn *(The Miracle Worker)*
1961 John Gielgud *(Big Fish, Little Fish)*
1962 Noel Willman *(A Man for All Seasons)*
1963 Alan Schneider *(Who's Afraid of Virginia Woolf?)*
1964 Mike Nichols *(Barefoot in the Park)*
1965 Mike Nichols *(Luv* and *The Odd Couple)*
1966 Peter Brook *(Marat/Sade)*
1967 Peter Hall *(The Homecoming)*
1968 Mike Nichols *(Plaza Suite)*
1969 Peter Dews *(Hadrian VII)*
1970 Joseph Hardy *(Child's Play)*
1971 Peter Brooke *(A Midsummer Night's Dream)*
1972 Mike Nichols *(The Prisoner of Second Avenue)*
1973 A. J. Antoon *(That Championship Season)*
1974 Jose Quintero *(A Moon for the Misbegotten)*
1975 John Dexter *(Equus)*
1976 Ellis Rabb *(The Royal Family)*

PRODUCER, PLAY

1948 Leland Heyward
1949 Kermit Bloomgarden and Walter Fried
1950 Gilbert Miller
1951 Cheryl Crawford
1952 Playwrights Company
1953 Kermit Bloomgarden
1954 Maurice Evans and George Schaefer
1955 Howard Erskine and Joseph Hayes
1956 Kermit Bloomgarden
1957 Leigh Connell, Theodore Mann and Jose Quintero
1958 Lawrence Langner, Theresa Helburn, Armina Marshall, and Dore Schary
1959 Alfred de Liagre, Jr.
1960 Fred Coe
1961 David Merrick
1962 Robert Whitehead and Roger L. Stevens
1963 Theatre '63 (Richard Barr and Clinton Wilder)
1964 Herman Shumlin
1965 Claire Nichtern
1968 David Merrick Arts Foundation
1971 Helena Bonfills, Morton Gottlieb, and Michael White

ACTOR, MUSICAL STAR

1948 Paul Hartman *(Angel in the Wings)*
1949 Ray Bolger *(Where's Charley?)*
1950 Ezio Pinza *(South Pacific)*
1951 Robert Alda *(Guys and Dolls)*
1952 Phil Silvers *(Top Banana)*
1953 Thomas Mitchell *(Hazel Flagg)*
1954 Alfred Drake *(Kismet)*
1955 Walter Slezak *(Fanny)*
1956 Ray Walston *(Damn Yankees)*
1957 Rex Harrison *(My Fair Lady)*
1958 Robert Preston *(The Music Man)*
1959 Richard Kiley *(Redhead)*
1960 Jackie Gleason *(Take Me Along)*
1961 Richard Burton *(Camelot)*
1962 Robert Morse *(How To Succeed in Business Without Really Trying)*
1963 Zero Mostel *(A Funny Thing Happened on the Way to the Forum)*
1964 Bert Lahr *(Foxy)*
1965 Zero Mostel *(Fiddler on the Roof)*
1966 Richard Kiley *(Man of La Mancha)*
1967 Robert Preston *(I Do! I Do!)*
1968 Robert Goulet *(The Happy Time)*
1969 Jerry Orbach *(Promises, Promises)*
1970 Cleavon Little *(Purlie)*
1971 Hal Linden *(The Rothschilds)*
1972 Phil Silvers *(A Funny Thing Happened on the Way to the Forum)*
1973 Ben Vereen *(Pippin)*
1974 Christopher Plummer *(Cyrano)*
1975 John Cullum *(Shenandoah)*
1976 George Rose *(My Fair Lady)*

ACTRESS, MUSICAL STAR

1948 Grace Hartman *(Angel in the Wings)*
1949 Nanette Fabray *(Love Life)*
1950 Mary Martin *(South Pacific)*
1951 Ethel Merman *(Call Me Madam)*
1952 Gertrude Lawrence *(The King and I)*
1953 Rosalind Russell *(Wonderful Town)*
1954 Dolores Gray *(Carnival in Flanders)*
1955 Mary Martin *(Peter Pan)*
1956 Gwen Verdon *(Damn Yankees)*
1957 Judy Holliday *(Bells Are Ringing)*
1958 Thelma Ritter *(New Girl in Town)*
Gwen Verdon *(New Girl in Town)*
1959 Gwen Verdon *(Redhead)*
1960 Mary Martin *(The Sound of Music)*
1961 Elizabeth Seal *(Irma La Douce)*
1962 Anna Maria Alberghetti *(Carnival!)*
Diahann Carroll *(No Strings)*
1963 Vivien Leigh *(Tovarich)*
1964 Carol Channing *(Hello Dolly!)*
1965 Liza Minnelli *(Flora, the Red Menace)*
1966 Angela Lansbury *(Mame)*
1967 Barbara Harris *(The Apple Tree)*
1968 Patricia Routledge *(Darling of the Day)*
Leslie Uggams *(Hallelujah, Baby!)*
1969 Angela Lansbury *(Dear World)*
1970 Lauren Bacall *(Applause)*
1971 Helen Gallagher *(No, No, Nanette)*
1972 Alexis Smith *(Follies)*
1973 Glynis Johns *(A Little Night Music)*
1974 Virginia Capers *(Raisin)*
1975 Angela Lansbury *(Gypsy)*
1976 Donna McKechnie *(A Chorus Line)*

SCENIC DESIGNER

1948 Horace Armistead *(The Medium)*
1949 Jo Mielziner for his "work throughout the '48-'49 season" *(Sleepy Hollow, Summer and Smoke, Anne of the Thousand Days, Death of a Salesman,* and *South Pacific)*
1950 Jo Mielziner *(The Innocents)*
1951 Boris Aronson *(The Rose Tattoo, The Country Girl* and *Season in the Sun)*
1952 Jo Mielziner *(The King and I)*
1953 Raoul Pene du Bois *(Wonderful Town)*
1954 Peter Larkin *(Ondine* and *The Teahouse of the August Moon)*
1955 Oliver Messel *(House of Flowers)*
1956 Peter Larkin *(No Time for Sergeants* and *Inherit the Wind)*
1957 Oliver Smith *(My Fair Lady)*
1958 Oliver Smith *(West Side Story)*
1959 Donald Oenslager *(A Majority of One)*
1960 Howard Bay *(Toys in the Attic)*
Oliver Smith *(The Sound of Music)*
1961 Oliver Smith *(Becket* and *Camelot)*
1962 Will Steven Armstrong *(Carnival!)*
1963 Sean Senny *(Oliver!)*
1964 Oliver Smith *(Hello, Dolly!)*
1965 Oliver Smith *(Baker Street, Luv* and *The Odd Couple)*
1966 Howard Bay *(Man of La Mancha)*
1967 Boris Aronson *(Cabaret)*
1968 Desmond Heeley *(Rosencrantz and Guildenstern Are Dead)*
1969 Boris Aronson *(Zorba)*
1970 Jo Mielziner *(Child's Play)*
1971 Boris Aronson *(Company)*
1972 Boris Aronson *(Follies)*
1973 Tony Walton *(Pippin)*
1974 Franne and Eugene Lee *(Candide)*
1975 Carl Toms *(Sherlock Holmes)*
1976 Boris Aronson *(Pacific Overtures)*

COSTUME DESIGNER

1947 Lucinda Ballard for her "several current plays" *(Happy Birthday, Another Part of the Forest, Street Scene, John Loves Mary,* and *The Chocolate Soldier)*
David Ffolkes *(Henry VIII)*
1948 Mary Percy Schenck *(The Heiress)*
1949 Lemuel Ayers *(Kiss Me, Kate)*
1950 Aline Bernstein *(Regina)*
1951 Miles White *(Bless You All)*
1952 Irene Sharaff *(The King and I)*
1953 Miles White *(Hazel Flagg)*
1954 Richard Whorf *(Ondine)*
1955 Cecil Beaton *(Quadrille)*
1956 Alvin Colt *(Pipe Dream)*
1957 Cecil Beaton *(My Fair Lady)*
1958 Motley *(The First Gentleman)*
1959 Rouben Ter-Arutunian *(Redhead)*
1960 Cecil Beaton *(Saratoga)*
1961 Motley *(Becket)*
Tony Duquette and Adrian *(Camelot)*
1962 Lucinda Ballard *(The Gay Life)*
1963 Anthony Powell *(The School for Scandal)*
1964 Freddy Wittop *(Hello, Dolly!)*
1965 Patricia Zipprodt *(Fiddler on the Roof)*
1966 Gunilla Palmstierna Weiss *(Marat/Sade)*
1967 Patricia Zipprodt *(Cabaret)*
1968 Desmond Heeley *(Rosencrantz and Guildenstern Are Dead)*
1969 Louden Sainthill *(Canterbury Tales)*
1970 Cecil Beaton *(Coco)*
1971 Raoul Pene de Bois *(No, No, Nanette)*
1972 Florence Klotz *(Follies)*
1973 Florence Klotz *(A Little Night Music)*
1974 Franne Lee *(Candide)*
1975 Geoffrey Holder *(The Wiz)*
1976 Florence Klotz *(Pacific Overtures)*

STAGE TECHNICIAN

1948 George Gebart
George Pierce ("for twenty-five years

of courteous service as the backstage doorman of the Embassy Theatre")
1950 Joe Lynn (master propertyman, *Miss Liberty)*
1951 Richard Raven *(The Autumn Garden)*
1952 Peter Feller *(Call Me Madam)*
1953 Abe Kurnit (master propertyman, *You Were Here)*
1954 John Davis ("for consistently good work as a theatre technician, currently with *Picnic")*
1955 Richard Rodda (stage technician, *Peter Pan)*
1956 Harry Green
1957 Howard McDonald *(Major Barbara)*
1958 Harry Romar (master electrician, *Time Remembered)*
1959 Sam Knapp (master electrician, *The Music Man)*
1960 John Walters (chief carpenter, *The Miracle Worker)*
1961 Teddy Van Bemmel (master electrician, *Becket)*
1962 Michael Burns (master electrician, *A Man for All Seasons)*
1963 Solly Pernick (production propertyman, *Mr. President)*

ACTOR, MUSICAL—FEATURED OR SUPPORTING

1947 David Wayne *(Finian's Rainbow)*
1950 Myron McCormick *(South Pacific)*
1951 Russell Nype *(Call Me Madam)*
1952 Yul Brynner *(The King and I)*
1953 Hiram Sherman *(Two's Company)*
1954 Harry Belafonte *(Almanac)*
1955 Cyril Ritchard *(Peter Pan)*
1956 Russ Brown *(Damn Yankees)*
1957 Sydney Chaplin *(Bells Are Ringing)*
1958 David Burns *(The Music Man)*
1959 Russell Nype *(Goldilocks)* tied with the Cast of *La Plume de Ma Tante*
1960 Tom Bosley *(Fiorello!)*
1961 Dick Van Dyke *(Bye Bye Birdie)*
1962 Charles Nelson Reilly *(How To Succeed in Business Without Really Trying)*
1963 David Burns *(A Funny Thing Happened on the Way to the Forum)*
1964 Jack Cassidy *(She Loves Me)*
1965 Victor Spinetti *(Oh, What a Lovely War)*
1966 Frankie Michaels *(Mame)*
1967 Joel Grey *(Cabaret)*
1968 Hiram Sherman *(How Now, Dow Jones)*
1969 Ronald Holgate *(1776)*
1970 Rene Auberjonois *(Coco)*
1971 Keene Curtis *(The Rothschilds)*
1972 Larry Blyden *(A Funny Thing Happened on the Way to the Forum)*
1973 George S. Irving *(Irene)*
1974 Tommy Tune *(Seesaw)*
1975 Ted Ross *(The Wiz)*
1976 Sammy Williams *(A Chorus Line)*

ACTRESS MUSICAL—FEATURED OR SUPPORTING

1950 Juanita Hall *(South Pacific)*
1951 Isabel Bigley *(Guys and Dolls)*
1952 Helen Gallagher *(Pal Joey)*
1953 Sheila Bond *(Wish You Were Here)*
1954 Gwen Verdon *(Can-Can)*
1955 Carol Haney *(The Pajama Game)*
1956 Lotte Lenya *(The Threepenny Opera)*
1957 Edie Adams *(Li'l Abner)*
1958 Barbara Cook *The Music Man)*
1959 Pat Stanley *(Goldilocks)* tied with the Cast of *La Plume de Ma Tante*
1960 Patricia Neway *(The Sound of Music)*
1961 Tammy Grimes *(The Unsinkable Molly Brown)*
1962 Phyllis Newman *(Subways Are for Sleeping)*
1963 Anna Quayle *(Stop the World—I Want to Get Off)*
1964 Tessie O'Shea *(The Girl Who Came to Supper)*
1965 Maria Karnilova *(Fiddler on the Roof)*
1966 Beatrice Arthur *(Mame)*
1967 Peg Murrey *(Cabaret)*
1968 Lillian Hayman *(Hallelujah, Baby!)*
1969 Marian Mercer *(Promises, Promises)*
1970 Melba Moore *(Purlie)*
1971 Patsy Kelly *(No, No, Nanette)*
1972 Linda Hopkins *(Inner City)*
1973 Patricia Elliott *(A Little Night Music)*
1974 Janie Sell *(Over Here!)*
1975 Dee Dee Bridgewater *(The Wiz)*
1976 Kelly Bishop *(A Chorus Line)*

MUSICAL PLAY

1949 *Kiss Me, Kate*
1950 *South Pacific*
1951 *Guys and Dolls*
1952 *The King and I*
1953 *Wonderful Town*
1954 *Kismet*
1955 *The Pajama Game*
1956 *Damn Yankees*
1957 *My Fair Lady*
1958 *The Music Man*
1959 *Redhead*
1960 *Fiorello!* tied with *The Sound of Music*
1961 *Bye Bye Birdie*
1962 *How To Succeed in Business Without Really Trying*
1963 *A Funny Thing Happened on the Way to the Forum*
1964 *Hello, Dolly!*
1965 *Fiddler on the Roof*
1966 *Man of La Mancha*
1967 *Cabaret*
1968 *Hallelujah, Baby!*
1969 *1776*
1970 *Applause*
1971 *Company*
1972 *Two Gentlemen of Verona*
1973 *A Little Night Music*
1974 *Raisin*
1975 *The Wiz*
1976 *A Chorus Line*

AUTHOR, MUSICAL PLAY

1949 Bella and Samuel Spewack
1950 Oscar Hammerstein II and Joshua Logan
1951 Jo Swerling and Abe Burrows
1952 Oscar Hammerstein II
1953 Joseph Fields and Jerome Chodorov
1954 Charles Lederer and Luther Davis
1955 George Abbott and Richard Bissell
1956 George Abbott and Douglass Wallop
1957 Alan Jay Lerner
1958 Meredith Willson and Frank Lacey
1959 Herbert and Dorothy Fields, Sidney Sheldon, and David Shaw
1960 Jerome Weidman and George Abbott tied with Howard Lindsay and Russel Crouse
1961 Michael Stewart
1962 Abe Burrows, Jack Weinstock, and Willie Gilbert
1963 Bert Shevelove and Larry Gelbart
1964 Michael Stewart
1965 Joseph Stein
1971 George Furth
1972 John Guare, Mel Shapiro
1973 Hugh Wheeler
1974 Hugh Wheeler
1975 James Lee Barrett, Peter Udell, Philip Rose
1976 James Kirkwood, Nicholas Dante

DIRECTOR, MUSICAL PLAY

1960 George Abbott *(Fiorello!)*
1961 Gower Champion *(Bye Bye Birdie)*
1962 Abe Burrows *(How To Succeed in Business Without Really Trying)*
1963 George Abbott *(A Funny Thing Happened on the Way to the Forum)*
1964 Gower Champion *(Hello, Dolly!)*
1965 Jerome Robbins *(Fiddler on the Roof)*
1966 Albert Marre *(Man of La Mancha)*
1967 Harold Prince *(Cabaret)*
1968 Gower Champion *(The Happy Time)*
1969 Peter Hunt *(1776)*
1970 Ron Field *(Applause)*
1971 Harold Prince *(Company)*
1972 Harold Prince, Michael Bennett *(Follies)*
1973 Bob Fosse *(Pippin)*
1974 Harold Prince *(Candide)*
1975 Geoffrey Holder *(The Wiz)*
1976 Michael Bennett *(A Chorus Line)*

COMPOSER, MUSICAL PLAY

1949 Cole Porter
1950 Richard Rodgers
1951 Frank Loesser
1952 Richard Rodgers
1953 Leonard Bernstein
1954 Aleksandr Borodin
1955 Richard Adler and Jerry Ross
1956 Richard Adler and Jerry Ross
1957 Frederick Loewe
1958 Meredith Willson
1959 Albert Hague
1960 Jerry Bock tied with Richard Rodgers
1961 No Award
1962 Richard Rodgers
1963 Lionel Bart
1964 Jerry Herman

COMPOSER AND LYRICIST

1965 Jerry Bock and Sheldon Harnick
1966 Mitch Leigh and Joe Darion
1967 Joe Kander and Fred Ebb
1968 Jule Styne, Betty Comden, Adolph Green

MUSICAL SCORE

1971 Stephen Sondheim
1972 Stephen Sondheim
1973 Stephen Sondheim
1974 Frederick Loewe and Alan Jay Lerner
1975 Charlie Smalls
1976 Marvin Hamlisch and Edward Kleban

CHOREOGRAPHER

1947 Agnes de Mille *(Brigadoon)*
Michael Kidd *(Finian's Rainbow)*
1948 Jerome Robbins *(High Button Shoes)*
1949 Gower Champion *(Lend An Ear)*
1950 Helen Tamiris *(Touch and Go)*
1951 Michael Kidd *(Guys and Dolls)*
1952 Robert Alton *(Pal Joey)*
1953 Donald Saddler *(Wonderful Town)*
1954 Michael Kidd *(Can-Can)*
1955 Bob Fosse *(The Pajama Game)*
1956 Bob Fosse *(Damn Yankees)*
1957 Michael Kidd *(My Fair Lady)*
1958 Jerome Robbins *(West Side Story)*

1959 Bob Fosse *(Redhead)*
1960 Michael Kidd *(Destry Rides Again)*
1961 Gower Champion *(Bye Bye Birdie)*
1962 Agnes de Mille *(Kwamina)*
Joe Layton *(No Strings)*
1963 Bob Fosse *(Little Me)*
1964 Gower Champion *(Hello, Dolly!)*
1965 Jerome Robbins *(Fiddler on the Roof)*
1966 Bob Fosse *(Sweet Charity)*
1967 Ron Field *(Cabaret)*
1968 Gower Champion *(The Happy Time)*
1969 Joe Layton *(George M!)*
1970 Ron Field *(Applause)*
1971 Donald Saddler *(No, No, Nanette)*
1972 Michael Bennett *(Follies)*
1973 Bob Fosse *(Pippin)*
1974 Michael Bennett *(Seesaw)*
1975 George Faison *(The Wiz)*
1976 Michael Bennett, Robert Avian *(A Chorus Line)*

MUSICAL DIRECTOR

1949 Max Meth *(As the Girls Go)*
1950 Maurice Abravanel *(Regina)*
1951 Lehman Engel *(The Consul)*
1952 Max Meth *(Pal Joey)*
1953 Lehman Engel *(Wonderful Town* and the Gilbert and Sullivan Season)
1954 Louis Adrian *(Kismet)*
1955 Thomas Schippers *(The Saint of Bleecker Street)*
1956 Hal Hastings *(Damn Yankees)*
1957 Franz Allers *(My Fair Lady)*
1958 Herbert Greene *(The Music Man)*
1959 Salvatore Dell'Isola *(Flower Drum Song)*
1960 Frederick Dvonch *(The Sound of Music)*
1961 Franz Allers *(Camelot)*
1962 Elliot Lawrence *(How To Succeed in Business Without Really Trying)*
1963 Donald Pippin *(Oliver!)*
1964 Shepard Coleman *(Hello, Dolly!)*

PRODUCER, MUSICAL PLAY

1949 Saint-Subber and Lemuel Ayers
1950 Oscar Hammerstein II, Richard Rodgers, Joshua Logan and Leland Hayward
1951 Cy Feuer and Ernest Martin
1952 Richard Rodgers and Oscar Hammerstein II
1953 Robert Fryer
1954 Charles Lederer
1955 Frederick Brisson, Robert Griffith and Harold S. Prince
1956 Frederick Brisson, Robert Griffith and Harold S. Prince in association with Albert B. Taylor
1957 Herman Levin
1958 Kermit Bloomgarden and Herbert Greene in association with Frank Productions
1959 Robert Fryer and Lawrence Carr
1960 Robert Griffith and Harold S. Prince tied with Leland Hayward and Richard Halliday
1961 Ed Padula
1962 Cy Feuer and Ernest Martin in association with Frank Productions
1963 Harold S. Prince
1964 David Merrick
1965 Harold Prince
1968 Albert Selden, Hal James, Jane C. Nussbaum, and Harry Rigby
1971 Harold Prince

LIGHTING DESIGNER

1970 Jo Mielziner *(Child's Play)*
1971 H. R. Poindexter *(Story Theatre)*
1972 Tharon Musser *(Follies)*
1973 Jules Fisher *(Pippin)*
1974 Jules Fisher *(Ulysses in Nighttown)*
1975 Neil Peter Jampolis *(Sherlock Holmes)*
1976 Tharon Musser *(A Chorus Line)*

SPECIAL AWARDS

1947 Dora Chamberlain
Mr. and Mrs. Ira Katzenberg
Jules Leventhal
Burns Mantle
P. A. MacDonald
Arthur Miller
Vincent Sardi, Sr.
Kurt Weill
1948 Vera Allen
Paul Beisman
Joe E. Brown
Robert Dowling
Experimental Theatre, Inc.
Rosamond Gilder
June Lockhart
Mary Martin
Robert Porterfield
James Whitmore
1950 Maurice Evans
1951 Ruth Green
1952 Charles Boyer
Judy Garland
Edward Kook
1953 Beatrice Lillie
Danny Kaye
Equity Community Theatre
1955 Proscenium Productions
1956 *The Threepenny Opera*
Theatre Collection of the New York Public Library
1957 American Shakespeare Festival and Academy
Jean-Louis Barrault—French Repertory
Robert Russell Bennett
William Hammerstein
Paul Shire
1958 New York Shakespeare Festival
Mrs. Martin Beck
1959 John Gielgud
Howard Lindsay and Russel Crouse
1960 John D. Rockefeller III
James Thurber and Burgess Meredith
1961 David Merrick
The Theatre Guild
1962 Brooks Atkinson
Franco Zeffirelli
Richard Rodgers
1963 Irving Berlin
W. McNeil Lowrey
The *Beyond the Fringe* Troupe
1964 Eva Le Gallienne
1965 Gilbert Miller
Oliver Smith
1966 Helen Menken (posthumous)
1968 Audrey Hepburn
Carol Channing
Pearl Bailey
David Merrick
Maurice Chevalier
APA–Phoenix Theatre
Marlene Dietrich
1969 National Theatre Company of Great Britain
Negro Ensemble Company
Rex Harrison
Leonard Bernstein
Carol Burnett
1970 Noel Coward
Alfred Lunt and Lyn Fontanne
New York Shakespeare Festival
Barbra Streisand
1971 Elliott Norton
Ingram Ash
Playbill
Roger L. Stevens
1972 The Theatre Guild—American Theatre Society
Richard Rodgers
Fiddler on the Roof
Ethel Merman
1973 John Lindsay
Actors' Fund of America
Shubert Organization
1974 Liza Minnelli
Bette Midler
Peter Cook and Dudley Moore, *Good Evening*
A Moon for the Misbegotten
Candide
Actors' Equity Association
Theatre Development Fund
John F. Wharton
Harold Friedlander
1975 Neil Simon
Al Hirschfeld
1976 Thomas H. Fitzgerald
George Abbott
Mathilde Pinkus
Arena Stage
Circle in the Square

Best Plays

Best Plays *has been published annually since 1926 with the intent "to cover, as completely and accurately as possible, the activities of the theatrical season in New York." The book contains excerpts and descriptive synopses of "the ten best plays of the year." The editor selects those ten plays which "represent the best judgment of the editor, variously confirmed by the public's endorsement."*

Burns Mantle was editor of Best Plays *until his death, February 9, 1948 (editions 1919-1920 through 1946-1947); John Chapman succeeded him as editor (editions 1947-1948 through 1951-1952). Louis Kronenberger was editor of volumes 1952-1953 through 1960-1961; Henry Hewes edited the 1961-1962 through 1963-1964 editions; and since then Otis L. Guernsey, Jr., has been editor.*

The following volumes of Best Plays *supplement the annual editions for the years 1899-1919:* The Best Plays of 1894-1899, *edited by John Chapman and Garrison P. Sherwood and published in 1955;* The Best Plays of 1899-1909, *edited by Burns Mantle and Garrison P. Sherwood and published in 1947; and* The Best Plays of 1909-1914, *edited by Burns Mantle and Garrison P. Sherwood and published in 1933.*

Plays chosen to represent the theatre seasons from 1894 to 1975 are as follows:

1894-1899
The Case of Rebellious Susan, by Henry Arthur Jones
The Heart of Maryland, by David Belasco
Secret Service, by William Gillette
The Little Minister, by James M. Barrie
Trelawny of the Wells, by Sir Arthur Wing Pinero
1899-1909
Barbara Frietchie, by Clyde Fitch

The Climbers, by Clyde Fitch
If I Were King, by Justin Huntley McCarthy
The Darling of the Gods, by David Belasco
The County Chairman, by George Ade
Leah Kleschna, by C. M. S. McLellan
The Squaw Man, by Edwin Milton Royle
The Great Divide, by William Vaughn Moody
The Witching Hour, by Augustus Thomas
The Man from Home, by Booth Tarkington and Harry Leon Wilson

1909-1919
The Easiest Way, by Eugene Walter
Mrs. Bumpstead-Leigh, by Harry James Smith
Disraeli, by Louis N. Parker
Romance, by Edward Sheldon
Seven Keys to Baldpate, by George M. Cohan
On Trial, by Elmer Reizenstein
The Unchastened Woman, by Louis Kaufman Anspacher
Good Gracious Annabelle, by Clare Kummer
Why Marry?, by Jesse Lynch Williams
John Ferguson, by St. John Ervine

1919-1920
Abraham Lincoln, by John Drinkwater
Clarence, by Booth Tarkington
Beyond the Horizon, by Eugene G. O'Neill
Declassee, by Zoe Akins
The Famous Mrs. Fair, by James Forbes
The Jest, by Sem Benelli
Jane Clegg, by St. John Ervine
Mamma's Affair, by Rachel Barton Butler
Wedding Bells, by Salisbury Field
Adam and Eva, by George Middleton and Guy Bolton

1920-1921
Deburau, adapted from the French of Sacha Guitry by H. Granville-Barker
The First Year, by Frank Craven
Enter Madame, by Gilda Varesi and Dolly Byrne
The Green Goddess, by William Archer
Liliom, by Ferenc Molnar
Mary Rose, by James M. Barrie
Nice People, by Rachel Crothers
The Bad Man, by Porter Emerson Browne
The Emperor Jones, by Eugene G. O'Neill
The Skin Game, by John Galsworthy

1921-1922
Anna Christie, by Eugene G. O'Neill
A Bill of Divorcement, by Clemence Dane
Dulcy, by George S. Kaufman and Marc Connelly
He Who Gets Slapped, adapted from the Russian of Leonid Andreyev by Gregory Zilboorg
Six Cylinder Love, by William Anthony McGuire
The Hero, by Gilbert Emery
The Dover Road, by Alan Alexander Milne
Ambush, by Arthur Richman
The Circle, by William Somerset Maugham
The Nest, by Paul Geraldy and Grace George

1922-1923
Rain, by John Colton and Clemence Randolph
Loyalties, by John Galsworthy
Icebound, by Owen Davis
You and I, by Philip Barry
The Fool, by Channing Pollock
Merton of the Movies, by George S. Kaufman and Marc Connelly, based on the novel of the same name by Harry Leon Wilson
Why Not?, by Jesse Lynch Williams
The Old Soak, by Don Marquis
R.U.R., by Karel Capek, translated by Paul Selver
Mary the 3rd, by Rachel Crothers

1923-1924
The Swan, translated from the Hungarian of Ferenc Molnar by Melville Baker
Outward Bound, by Sutton Vane
The Show-Off, by George Kelly
The Changelings, by Lee Wilson Dodd
Chicken Feed, by Guy Bolton
Sun-Up, by Lula Vollmer
Beggar on Horseback, by George S. Kaufman and Marc Connelly
Tarnish, by Gilbert Emery
The Goose Hangs High, by Lewis Beach
Hell-Bent Fer Heaven, by Hatcher Hughes

1924-1925
What Price Glory?, by Laurence Stallings and Maxwell Anderson
They Knew What They Wanted, by Sidney Howard
Desire Under the Elms, by Eugene G. O'Neill
The Firebrand, by Edwin Justus Mayer
Dancing Mothers, by Edgar Selwyn and Edmund Goulding
Mrs. Partridge Presents, by Mary Kennedy and Ruth Hawthorne
The Fall Guy, by James Gleason and George Abbott
The Youngest, by Philip Barry
Minick, by Edna Ferber and George S. Kaufman
Wild Birds, by Dan Totheroh

1925-1926
Craig's Wife, by George Kelly
The Great God Brown, by Eugene G. O'Neill
The Green Hat, by Michael Arlen
The Dybbuk, by S. Ansky, Henry G. Alsberg-Winifred Katzin translation
The Enemy, by Channing Pollock
The Last of Mrs. Cheney, by Frederick Lonsdale
Bride of the Lamb, by William Hurlbut
The Wisdom Tooth, by Marc Connelly
The Butter and Egg Man, by George S. Kaufman
Young Woodley, by John van Druten

1926-1927
Broadway, by Philip Dunning and George Abbott
Saturday's Children, by Maxwell Anderson
Chicago, by Maurine Watkins
The Constant Wife, by William Somerset Maugham
The Play's the Thing, by Ferenc Molnar
The Road to Rome, by Robert Emmet Sherwood
The Silver Cord, by Sidney Howard
The Cradle Song, translated from the Spanish of G. Martinez Sierra by John Garrett Underhill
Daisy Mayme, by George Kelly
In Abraham's Bosom, by Paul Green

1927-1928
Strange Interlude, by Eugene G. O'Neill
The Royal Family, by Edna Ferber and George S. Kaufman
Burlesque, by George Manker Watters and Arthur Hopkins
Coquette, by George Abbott and Ann Bridgers
Behold the Bridegroom, by George Kelly
Porgy, by DuBose and Dorothy Heyward
Paris Bound, by Philip Barry
Escape, by John Galsworthy
The Racket, by Bartlett Cormack
The Plough and the Stars, by Sean O'Casey

1928-1929
Street Scene, by Elmer Rice
Journey's End, by R.C. Sherriff
Wings Over Europe, by Robert Nichols and Maurice Browne
Holiday, by Philip Barry
The Front Page, by Ben Hecht and Charles MacArthur
Let Us Be Gay, by Rachel Crothers
Machinal, by Sophie Treadwell
Little Accident, by Floyd Dell and Thomas Mitchell
The Kingdom of God, by G. Martinez Sierra; English version by Helen and Harley Granville-Barker

1929-1930
The Green Pastures, by Marc Connelly (adapted from *Ol' Man Adam and His Chillun* by Roark Bradford)
The Criminal Code, by Martin Flavin
Berkeley Square, by John Balderston
Strictly Dishonorable, by Preston Sturges
The First Mrs. Fraser, by St. John Ervine
The Last Mile, by John Wexley
June Moon, by Ring W. Lardner and George S. Kaufman
Michael and Mary, by A. A. Milne
Death Takes a Holiday, by Walter Ferris (adapted from the Italian of Alberto Casella)
Rebound, by Donald Ogden Stewart

1930-1931
Elizabeth the Queen, by Maxwell Anderson
Tomorrow and Tomorrow, by Philip Barry
Once in a Lifetime, by George S. Kaufman and Moss Hart
Green Grow the Lilacs, by Lynn Riggs
As Husbands Go, by Rachel Crothers
Alison's House, by Susan Glaspell
Five-Star Final, by Louis Wietzenkorn
Overture, by William Bolitho
The Barretts of Wimpole Street, by Rudolf Besier
Grand Hotel, adapted from the German of Vicki Baum by W. A. Drake

1931-1932
Of Thee I Sing, by George S. Kaufman and Morrie Ryskind; music and lyrics

by George and Ira Gershwin
Mourning Becomes Electra, by Eugene G. O'Neill
Reunion in Vienna, by Robert Emmet Sherwood
The House of Connelly, by Paul Green
The Animal Kingdom, by Philip Barry
The Left Bank, by Elmer Rice
Another Language, by Rose Franken
Brief Moment, by S. N. Behrman
The Devil Passes, by Benn W. Levy
Cynara, by H. M. Harwood and R. F. Gore-Browne

1932-1933
Both Your Houses, by Maxwell Anderson
Dinner at Eight, by George S. Kaufman and Edna Ferber
When Ladies Meet, by Rachel Crothers
Design for Living, by Noel Coward
Biography, by S. N. Behrman
Alien Corn, by Sidney Howard
The Late Christopher Bean, adapted from the French of Rene Fauchois by Sidney Howard
Pigeons and People, by George M. Cohan
One Sunday Afternoon, by James Hagan

1933-1934
Mary of Scotland, by Maxwell Anderson
Men in White, by Sidney Kingsley
Dodsworth, by Sinclair Lewis and Sidney Howard
Ah, Wilderness!, by Eugene O'Neill
They Shall Not Die, by John Wexley
Her Master's Voice, by Clare Kummer
No More Ladies, by A. E. Thomas
Wednesday's Child, by Leopold Atlas
The Shining Hour, by Keith Winter
The Green Bay Tree, by Mordaunt Shairp

1934-1935
The Children's Hour, by Lillian Hellman
Valley Forge, by Maxwell Anderson
The Petrified Forest, by Robert Emmet Sherwood
The Old Main, by Zoe Akins
Accent on Youth, by Samson Raphaelson
Merrily We Roll Along, by George S. Kaufman and Moss Hart
Awake and Sing, by Clifford Odets
The Farmer Takes a Wife, by Frank B. Elser and Marc Connelly
Lost Horizons, by John Hayden
The Distaff Side, by John van Druten

1935-1936
Winterset, by Maxwell Anderson
Idiot's Delight, by Robert Emmet Sherwood
End of Summer, by S. N. Behrman
First Lady, by Katharine Dayton and George S. Kaufman
Victoria Regina, by Laurence Housman
Boy Meets Girl, by Bella and Samuel Spewack
Dead End, by Sidney Kingsley
Call It a Day, by Dodie Smith
Ethan Frome, by Owen Davis and Donald Davis
Pride and Prejudice, by Helen Jerome

1936-1937
High Tor, by Maxwell Anderson
You Can't Take It with You, by Moss Hart and George S. Kaufman
Johnny Johnson, by Paul Green; music by Kurt Weill
Daughters of Atreus, by Robert Turney
Stage Door, by Edna Ferber and George S. Kaufman
The Women, by Clare Boothe
St. Helena, by R. C. Sheriff and Jeanne de Casalis
Yes, My Darling Daughter, by Mark Reed
Excursion, by Victor Wolfson
Tovarich, by Jacques Deval and Robert Emmet Sherwood

1937-1938
Of Mice and Men, by John Steinbeck
Our Town, by Thornton Wilder
Shadow and Substance, by Paul Vincent Carroll
On Borrowed Time, by Paul Osborn
The Star-Wagon, by Maxwell Anderson
Susan and God, by Rachel Crothers
Prologue to Glory, by E. P. Conkle
Amphitryon 38, by S. N. Behrman
Golden Boy, by Clifford Odets
What a Life, by Clifford Goldsmith

1938-1939
Abe Lincoln in Illinois, by Robert Emmet Sherwood
The Little Foxes, by Lillian Hellman
Rocket to the Moon, by Clifford Odets
The American Way, by George S. Kaufman and Moss Hart
No Time for Comedy, by S. N. Behrman
The Philadelphia Story, by Philip Barry
The White Steed, by Paul Vincent Carroll
Here Come the Clowns, by Philip Barry
Family Portrait, by Lenore Coffee and William Joyce Cowen
Kiss the Boys Good-Bye, by Clare Boothe

1939-1940
There Shall Be No Night, by Robert Emmet Sherwood
The World We Make, by Sidney Kingsley
Life with Father, by Howard Lindsay and Russel Crouse
The Man Who Came to Dinner, by George S. Kaufman and Moss Hart
The Male Animal, by James Thurber and Elliott Nugent
The Time of Your Life, by William Saroyan
Skylark, by Samson Raphaelson
Margin for Error, by Clare Boothe
Morning's at Seven, by Paul Osborn

1940-1941
Native Son, by Paul Green and Richard Wright
Watch on the Rhine, by Lillian Hellman
The Corn Is Green, by Emlyn Williams
Lady in the Dark, by Moss Hart; lyrics by Ira Gershwin, music by Kurt Weill
Arsenic and Old Lace, by Joseph Kesselring
My Sister Eileen, by Joseph Fields and Jerome Chodorov
Flight to the West, by Elmer Rice
Claudia, by Rose Franken Meloney
Mr. and Mrs. North, by Owen Davis
George Washington Slept Here, by George S. Kaufman and Moss Hart

1941-1942
In Time to Come, by Howard Koch
The Moon Is Down, by John Steinbeck
Blithe Spirit, by Noel Coward
Junior Miss, by Jerome Chodorov and Joseph Fields
Candle in the Wind, by Maxwell Anderson
Letters to Lucerne, by Fritz Rotter and Allen Vincent
Jason, by Samson Raphaelson
Angel Street, by Patrick Hamilton
Uncle Harry, by Thomas Job
Hope for a Harvest, by Sophie Treadwell

1942-1943
The Patriots, by Sidney Kingsley
The Eve of St. Mark, by Maxwell Anderson
The Skin of Our Teeth, by Thornton Wilder
Winter Soldiers, by Dan James
Tomorrow the World, by James Gow and Arnaud d'Usseau
Harriet, by Florence Ryerson and Colin Clements
The Doughgirls, by Joseph Fields
The Damask Cheek, by John van Druten and Lloyd Morris
Kiss and Tell, by F. Hugh Herbert
Oklahoma! by Oscar Hammerstein II, music by Richard Rodgers

1943-1944
Winged Victory, by Moss Hart
The Searching Wind, by Lillian Hellman
The Voice of the Turtle, by John van Druten
Decision, by Edward Chodorov
Over 21, by Ruth Gordon
Outrageous Fortune, by Rose Franken
Jacobowsky and the Colonel, by S. N. Behrman
Storm Operation, by Maxwell Anderson
Pick-Up Girl, by Elsa Shelley
The Innocent Voyage, by Paul Osborn

1944-1945
A Bell for Adano, by Paul Osborn
I Remember Mama, by John van Druten
The Hasty Heart, by John Patrick
The Glass Menagerie, by Tennessee Williams
Harvey, by Mary Chase
The Late George Apley, by John P. Marquand and George S. Kaufman
Soldier's Wife, by Rose Franken
Anna Lucasta, by Philip Yordan
Foolish Notion, by Philip Barry
Dear Ruth, by Norman Krasna

1945-1946
State of the Union, by Howard Lindsay and Russel Crouse
Home of the Brave, by Arthur Laurents
Deep Are the Roots, by Arnaud d'Usseau and James Gow
The Magnificent Yankee, by Emmet Lavery
Antigone, by Jean Anouilh, adapted by Lewis Galantiere
O Mistress Mine, by Terence Rattigan
Born Yesterday, by Garson Kanin

Dream Girl, by Elmer Rice
The Rugged Path, by Robert Emmet Sherwood
Lute Song, by Will Irwin and Sidney Howard

1946-1947
All My Sons, by Arthur Miller
The Iceman Cometh, by Eugene G. O'Neill
Joan of Lorraine, by Maxwell Anderson
Another Part of the Forest, by Lillian Hellman
Years Ago, by Ruth Gordon
John Loves Mary, by Norman Krasna
The Fatal Weakness, by George Kelly
The Story of Mary Surratt, by John Patrick
Christopher Blake, by Moss Hart
Brigadoon, by Alan Jay Lerner; music by Frederick Loewe

1947-1948
A Streetcar Named Desire, by Tennessee Williams
Mister Roberts, by Thomas Heggen and Joshua Logan
Command Decision, by William Wister Haines
The Winslow Boy, by Terence Rattigan
The Heiress, by Ruth and Augustus Goetz
Allegro, by Oscar Hammerstein II; music by Richard Rodgers
Eastward in Eden, by Dorothy Gardner
Skipper Next to God, by Jan de Hartog
An Inspector Calls, by J. B. Priestley
Me and Molly, by Gertrude Berg

1948-1949
Death of a Salesman, by Arthur Miller
Anne of the Thousand Days, by Maxwell Anderson
The Madwoman of Chaillot, by Maurice Valency, adapted from the French of Jean Giraudoux
Detective Story, by Sidney Kingsley
Edward, My Son, by Robert Morley and Noel Langley
Life with Mother, by Howard Lindsay and Russell Crouse
Light Up the Sky, by Moss Hart
The Silver Whistle, by Robert Edward McEnroe
Two Blind Mice, by Samuel Spewack

1949-1950
The Cocktail Party, by T. S. Eliot
The Member of the Wedding, by Carson McCullers
The Innocents, by William Archibald
Lost in the Stars, by Maxwell Anderson; music by Kurt Weill
Come Back, Little Sheba, by William Inge
The Happy Time, by Samuel Taylor
The Wisteria Trees, by Joshua Logan
I Know My Love, by S. N. Behrman
The Enchanted, by Maurice Valency, adapted from a play by Jean Giraudoux
Clutterbuck, by Benn W. Levy

1950-1951
Guys and Dolls, by Jo Swerling and Abe Burrows; music and lyrics by Frank Loesser
Darkness at Noon, by Sidney Kingsley and Arthur Koestler
Billy Budd, by Louis O. Coxe and Robert Chapman
The Autumn Garden, by Lillian Hellman
Bell, Book and Candle, by John van Druten
The Country Girl, by Clifford Odets
The Rose Tattoo, by Tennessee Williams
Season in the Sun, by Walcott Gibbs
Affairs of State, by Louis Verneuil
Second Threshold, by Philip Barry

1951-1952
Mrs. McThing, by Mary Coyle Chase
The Shrike, by Joseph Kramm
I Am a Camera, by John van Druten
The Fourposter, by Jan de Hartog
Point of No Return, by Paul Osborn
Barefoot in Athens, by Maxwell Anderson
Venus Observed, by Christopher Fry
Jane, by S. N. Behrman and Somerset Maugham
Gigi, by Anita Loos and Colette
Remains To Be Seen, by Howard Lindsay and Russel Crouse

1952-1953
The Time of the Cuckoo, by Arthur Laurents
Bernardine, by Mary Coyle Chase
Dial 'M' for Murder, by Frederick Knott
The Climate of Eden, by Moss Hart
The Love of Four Colonels, by Peter Ustinov
The Crucible, by Arthur Miller
The Emperor's Clothes, by George Tabori
Picnic, by William Inge
Wonderful Town, by Joseph Fields and Jerome Chodorov; lyrics by Betty Comden and Adoph Green; music by Leonard Bernstein
My 3 Angels, by Sam and Bella Spewack; adapted from *La Cuisine des Anges* by Albert Husson

1953-1954
The Caine Mutiny Court-Martial, by Herman Wouk
In the Summer House, by Jane Bowles
The Confidential Clerk, by T. S. Eliot
Take a Giant Step, by Louis Peterson
The Teahouse of the August Moon, by John Patrick
The Immoralist, by Ruth and Augustus Goetz
Tea and Sympathy, by Robert Anderson
The Girl on the Via Flaminia, by Alfred Hayes
The Golden Apple, by John Latouche; music by Jerome Moross
The Magic and the Loss, by Julian Funt

1954-1955
The Boy Friend, by Sandy Wilson
The Living Room, by Graham Greene
Bad Seed, by Maxwell Anderson
Witness for the Prosecution, by Agatha Christie
The Flowering Peach, by Clifford Odets
The Desperate Hours, by Joseph Hayes
The Dark Is Light Enough, by Christopher Fry
Bus Stop, by William Inge
Cat on a Hot Tin Roof, by Tennessee Williams
Inherit the Wind, by Jerome Lawrence and Robert E. Lee

1955-1956
A View from the Bridge, by Arthur Miller
Tiger at the Gates, by Jean Giraudoux, translated by Christopher Fry
The Diary of Anne Frank, by Frances Goodrich and Albert Hackett
No Time for Sergeants, by Ira Levin
The Chalk Garden, by Enid Bagnold
The Lark, by Jean Anouilh, adapted by Lillian Hellman
The Matchmaker, by Thornton Wilder
The Ponder Heart, by Joseph Fields and Jerome Chodorov
My Fair Lady, by Alan Jay Lerner; music by Frederick Loewe
Waiting for Godot, by Samuel Beckett

1956-1957
Separate Tables, by Terence Rattigan
Long Day's Journey into Night, by Eugene O'Neill
A Very Special Baby, by Robert Alan Arthur
Candide, by Lillian Hellman; lyrics by Richard Wilbur, John Latouche, Dorothy Parker, music by Leonard Bernstein
A Clearing in the Woods, by Arthur Laurents
The Waltz of the Toreadors, by Jean Anouilh, translated by Lucienne Hill
The Potting Shed, by Graham Greene
Visit to a Small Planet, by Gore Vidal
Orpheus Descending, by Tennessee Williams
A Moon for the Misbegotten, by Eugene O'Neill

1957-1958
Look Back in Anger, by John Osborne
Under Milk Wood, by Dylan Thomas
Time Remembered, by Jean Anouilh, adapted by Patricia Moyes
The Rope Dancers, by Morton Wishengrad
Look Homeward, Angel, by Ketti Frings
The Dark at the Top of the Stairs, by William Inge
Summer of the 17th Doll, by Ray Lawler
Sunrise at Campobello, by Dore Schary
The Entertainer, by John Osborne
The Visit, by Friedrich Duerrenmatt, adapted by Maurice Valency

1958-1959
A Touch of the Poet, by Eugene O'Neill
The Pleasure of His Company, by Samuel Taylor with Cornelia Otis Skinner
Epitaph for George Dillon, by John Osborne and Anthony Creighton
The Disenchanted, by Budd Schulberg and Harvey Breit
The Cold Wind and the Warm, by S. N. Behrman
J.B., by Archibald MacLeish
Requiem for a Nun, by William Faulkner and Ruth Ford
Sweet Bird of Youth, by Tennessee Williams
A Raisin in the Sun, by Lorraine Hansberry
Kataki, by Shimon Wincelberg

1959-1960

The Tenth Man, by Paddy Chayefsky
Five Finger Exercise, by Peter Shaffer
The Andersonville Trial, by Saul Levitt
The Deadly Game, by Friedrich Duerrenmatt, adapted by James Yaffe
Caligula, by Albert Camus, translated and adapted by Justin O'Brien
Toys in the Attic, by Lillian Hellman
The Best Man, by Gore Vidal
Duel of Angels, by Jean Giraudoux, translated and adapted by Christopher Fry
A Thurber Carnival, by James Thurber; conceived and directed by Burgess Meredith
Fiorello!, by Jerome Weidman and George Abbott; lyrics by Sheldon Harnick, music by Jerry Bock

1960-1961
The Hostage, by Brendan Behan
A Taste of Honey, by Shelagh Delaney
Becket, by Jean Anouilh, translated by Lucienne Hill
Period of Adjustment, by Tennessee Williams
All the Way Home, by Tad Mosel
Rhinoceros, by Eugene Ionesco, translated by Derek Prouse
Mary, Mary, by Jean Kerr
The Devil's Advocate, by Dore Schary
Big Fish, Little Fish, by Hugh Wheeler
A Far Country, by Henry Denker

1961-1962
The Caretaker, by Harold Pinter
How To Succeed in Business Without Really Trying, by Jack Weinstock, Willie Gilbert and Abe Burrows; music and lyrics by Frank Loesser
The Complaisant Lover, by Graham Greene
Gideon, by Paddy Chayefsky
A Man for All Seasons, by Robert Bolt
Stone and Star (Shadow of Heroes), by Robert Ardrey
The Night of the Iguana, by Tennessee Williams
The Egg, by Felicien Marceau, translated by Robert Schlitt
Oh Dad, Poor Dad, Mama's Hung You in the Closet and I'm Feelin' So Sad, by Arthur L. Kopit
A Thousand Clowns, by Herb Gardner

1962-1963
Stop the World—I Want to Get Off, by Leslie Bricusse and Anthony Newley
Who's Afraid of Virginia Woolf?, by Edward Albee
Tchin-Tchin, by Sidney Michaels, based on the play by Francois Billetdoux
P.S. 193, by David Rayfiel
The Collection, by Harold Pinter
The Milk Train Doesn't Stop Here Anymore, by Tennessee Williams
Andorra, by Max Frisch, translated by Michael Bullock
Mother Courage and Her Children: A Chronicle of the Thirty Years' War, by Bertolt Brecht, English version by Eric Bentley
Rattle of a Simple Man, by Charles Dyer
She Loves Me, by Joe Masteroff; music by Jerry Bock, lyrics by Sheldon Harnick

1963-1964
After the Fall, by Arthur Miller
Barefoot in the Park, by Neil Simon
Chips with Everything, by Arnold Wesker
The Deputy, by Rolf Hochhuth
Dylan, by Sidney Michaels
Hello, Dolly!, by Michael Stewart, suggested by Thornton Wilder's *The Matchmaker;* music and lyrics by Jerry Herman
Luther, by John Osborne
Next Time I'll Sing to You, by James Saunders
The Passion of Josef D., by Paddy Chayefsky
The Rehearsal, by Jean Anouilh

1964-1965
The Subject Was Roses, by Frank D. Gilroy
Fiddler on the Roof, by Joseph Stein, Jerry Bock, Sheldon Harnick
The Physicists, by Friedrich Duerrenmatt
Luv, by Murray Schisgal
The Odd Couple, by Neil Simon
Poor Bitos, by Jean Anouilh
Slow Dance on the Killing Ground, by William Hanley
Incident at Vichy, by Arthur Miller
The Toilet, by LeRoi Jones
Tiny Alice, by Edward Albee

1965-1966
Generation, by William Goodhart
The Royal Hunt of the Sun, by Peter Shaffer
Hogan's Goat, by William Alfred
Man of La Mancha, by Dale Wasserman, Joe Darion, and Mitch Leigh
Inadmissable Evidence, by John Osborne
It's a Bird, It's a Plane, It's SUPERMAN, by David Newman, Robert Benton, Lee Adams, and Charles Strauss
Cactus Flower, by Abe Burrows, based on a play by Pierre Barillet and Jean-Pierre Gredy
Marat/Sade, by Peter Weiss
Philadelphia, Here I Come!, by Brian Friel
The Lion In Winter, by James Goldman

1966-1967
A Delicate Balance, by Edward Albee
The Killing of Sister George, by Frank Marcus
Hamp, by John Wilson
Cabaret, by Joe Masteroff, John Kander and Fred Ebb
The Apple Tree, by Jerry Bock and Sheldon Harnick
America Hurrah, by Jean-Claude van Itallie
The Homecoming, by Harold Pinter
Black Comedy, by Peter Shaffer
You're a Good Man, Charlie Brown, by John Gordon and Clark Gesner
You Know I Can't Hear You When the Water's Running, by Robert Anderson

1967-1968
After the Rain, by John Bowen
Scuba Duba, by Bruce Friedman
Rosencrantz and Guildenstern Are Dead, by Tom Stoppard
Staircase, by Charles Dyer
Your Own Thing, by Donald Driver
A Day in the Death of Joe Egg, by Peter Nichols
The Price, by Arthur Miller
Plaza Suite, by Neil Simon
I Never Sang for My Father, by Robert Anderson
The Boys in the Band, by Mart Crowley

1968-1969
Lovers, by Brian Friel
The Man in the Glass Booth, by Robert Shaw
The Great White Hope, by Howard Sackler
In the Matter of J. Robert Oppenheimer, by Heinar Kipphardt
Forty Carats, by Jay Allen
Hadrian VII, by Peter Luke
Celebration, by Tom Jones and Harvey Schmidt
1776, by Peter Stone and Sherman Edwards
No Place To Be Somebody, by Charles Gordone
Adaptation, by Elaine May and *Next,* by Terrence McNally

1969-1970
Indians, by Arthur Kopit
Butterflies Are Free, by Leonard Gershe
Last of the Red Hot Lovers, by Neil Simon
Child's Play, by Robert Marasco
The Effect of Gamma Rays on Man-in-the-Moon Marigolds, by Paul Zindel
Applause, by Betty Comden, Adolph Green, Lee Adams, and Charles Strouse
Company, by George Furth and Stephen Sondheim
The White House Murder Case, by Jules Feiffer
What the Butler Saw, by Joe Orton
The Serpent: A ceremony written by Jean-Claude van Itallie in collaboration with the Open Theatre under the direction of Joseph Chaikin

1970-1971
Boesman and Lena, by Athol Fugard
Steambath, by Bruce Jay Friedman
Conduct Unbecoming, by Barry England
Sleuth, by Anthony Shaffer
The Trial of the Catonsville Nine, by Father Daniel Berrigan
Home, by David Storey
The Gingerbread Lady, by Neil Simon
The House of Blue Leaves, by John Guare
The Philanthropist, by Christopher Hampton
Follies, by James Goldman and Stephen Sondheim

1971-1972
Where Has Tommy Flowers Gone?, by Terrence McNally
The Screens, by Jean Genet
That Championship Season, by Jason Miller
Ain't Supposed To Die a Natural Death, by Melvin Van Peeples
Sticks and Bones, by David Rabe
The Prisoner of Second Avenue, by Neil Simon
Old Times, by Harold Pinter
Vivat! Vivat Regina!, by Robert Bolt
Moonchildren, by Michael Weller
Small Craft Warnings, by Tennessee Williams

1972-1973
6 Rms Riv Vu, by Bob Randall
Butley, by Simon Gray
Green Julia, by Paul Ableman
The Creation of the World and Other Business, by Arthur Miller
The River Niger, by Joseph A. Walker
The Sunshine Boys, by Neil Simon
Finishing Touches, by Jean Kerr
The Changing Room, by David Storey
The Hot l Baltimore, by Lanford Wilson
A Little Night Music, by Hugh Wheeler and Stephen Sondheim

1973-1974
The Contractor, by David Storey
Bad Habits, by Terrence McNally
Find Your Way Home, by John Hopkins
Short Eyes, by Miguel Pinero
Creeps, by David E. Freeman
Noel Coward in Two Keys, by Noel Coward
Jumpers, by Tom Stoppard
The Good Doctor, by Neil Simon
When You Comin Back, Red Ryder?, by Mark Medoff
The Sea Horse, by Edward J. Moore

1974-1975
Equus, by Peter Shaffer
The Wager, by Mark Medoff
The Island, by Athol Fugard, John Kani and Winston Ntshoa
The Ritz, by Terrence McNally
All Over Town, by Murray Schisgal
The National Health, by Peter Nichols
Seascape, by Edward Albee
The Taking of Miss Janie, by Ed Bullins
A Chorus Line, by Michael Bennett, James Kirkwood and Nicholas Dante, Marvin Hamlisch, and Edward Kleban
Same Time, Next Year, by Bernard Slade

The Delia Austrian Medals

(See Drama League of New York)

The Barter Theatre of Virginia Awards

The Barter Theatre of Virginia Award honors an outstanding contribution to the theatre by an American during the current season. The recipient receives "an acre of land near Abingdon, Virginia, and a ham and a platter to eat it off of." With the Award goes the privilege of nominating two young performers at New York auditions for jobs at this theatre.

1939 Laurette Taylor *(Outward Bound)*
1940 Dorothy Stickney *(Life with Father)*
1941 Ethel Barrymore *(The Corn Is Green)*
1942 Mildred Natwick *(Blithe Spirit)*
1943 No Award
1944 No Award
1945 No Award
1946 Louis Calhern *(The Magnificent Yankee)*
1947 Helen Hayes *(Happy Birthday)*
1948 Tallulah Bankhead *(Private Lives)*
1949 Henry Fonda *(Mister Roberts)*
1950 Shirley Booth *(Come Back, Little Sheba)*
1951 Fredric March *(The Autumn Garden)*
1952 Cornelia Otis Skinner *(Paris 90)*
1953 Rosalind Russell *(Wonderful Town)*
1954 David Wayne *(The Teahouse of the August Moon)*
1955 Mary Martin *(Peter Pan)*
1956 Julie Harris *(The Lark)*
1957 Ethel Merman *(Happy Hunting)*
1958 Ralph Bellamy *(Sunrise at Campobello)*
1959 Robert Whitehead *(Lincoln Center)*
1960 George Abbott (author-director of *Fiorello!)*
1961 Hume Cronyn *(Big Fish, Little Fish)*
1962 Abe Burrows *(How To Succeed in Business Without Really Trying)*
1963 David Merrick (producer)
1964 Robert Preston *(Nobody Loves an Albatross)*
1965 Roger L. Stevens
1966 No Award
1967 No Award
1968 Tom Prideaux
1969 Pearl Bailey
No award since 1969

Marc Blitzstein Award for the Musical Theatre

(See National Institute of Arts and Letters)

Brandeis University Creative Arts Awards

Presented annually to recognize outstanding artistic contributions during a lifetime of distinguished achievement.

THEATRE ARTS
Award

1957 Hallie Flanagan Davis
1958 Stark Young
1959 George Kelly
1960 Thornton Wilder
1961 Lillian Hellman
1962 S. N. Behrman
1963 Jo Mielziner
1964 Cheryl Crawford
1965 Tennessee Williams
1966 Eva Le Gallienne
1967 Jerome Robbins
1968 Richard Rodgers
1969 Boris Aronson
1970 Arthur Miller
1972 Alfred Lunt and Lynn Fontanne
1974 Helen Hayes

Citation

1957 The Shakespearewrights
1958 Paul Shyre
1959 Richard Hayes
1960 William Alfred
1961 Julian Beck and Judith Malina
1962 James P. Donleavy
1963 Joseph Papp
1964 Jack Richardson
1965 Michael Smith
1966 Alvin Epstein
1967 Ellen Stewart
1968 Tom O'Horgan
1969 The Negro Ensemble Company
1970 The Open Theater
1972 The New Dramatists
1974 Arena Stage

Cue Entertainers of the Year

1961 Diahann Carroll
1962 Zero Mostel
1963 Barbra Streisand
1964 Sammy Davis, Jr.
1965 Mike Nichols
1966 Barbara Harris
1967 Pearl Bailey
1968 Burt Bacharach and Hal David
1969 Barbra Streisand
1970 Danny Kaye
1971 Neil Simon
1972 Diana Ross
1973 Debbie Reynolds
1974 Dustin Hoffman

The Clarence Derwent Awards

In 1945, the actor Clarence Derwent (1884-1959) established an award in his name to give annual recognition to the best actor and actress appearing in non-featured roles. Four awards are made each year, two in New York and two in London, although the British awards were not begun until 1948. The award consists of a $500 stipend to each of the American recipients and a £50 stipend to each of the British recipients.

1945 Judy Holliday *(Kiss Them for Me)*
Frederick O'Neal *(Anna Lucasta)*
1946 Barbara Bel Geddes *(Deep Are the Roots)*
Paul Douglas *(Born Yesterday)*
1947 Tom Ewell *(John Loves Mary)*
Margaret Phillips *(Another Part of the Forest)*
1948 Catherine Ayers *(A Long Way from Home)*
Lou Gilbert *(Hope Is the Thing with Feathers)*
British:
Jessica Spencer *(Royal Circle)*
Colin Gordon *(The Happiest Days of Your Life)*
1949 Leora Dana *(The Madwoman of Chaillot)*
Ray Walston *(Summer and Smoke)*
British:
Gwen Cherrell *(The Beaux' Stratagem)*
Robin Bailey *(The Rivals)*
1950 Gloria Lane *(The Consul)*
Douglas Watson *(That Lady* and *The Wisteria Trees)*
British:
Daphne Arthur *(The Holly and the Ivy)*
Denholm Elliott *(Venus Observed)*
1951 Phyliss Love *(The Rose Tattoo)*
Logan Ramsey *(The High Ground)* who tied with Frederick Warriner *(Getting Married)*
British:
Frances Rowe *(Who Goes There!)*
Hugh Griffith *(Point of Departure)*
1952 Anne Meacham *(The Long Watch)*
Iggie Wolfington *(Mrs. McThing)*
British:
Valerie Hanson *(Nightmare Abbey)*
Paul Rogers *(The Other Heart)*
1953 Jenny Egan *(The Crucible)*
David J. Stewart *(Camino Real)*
British:
Brenda de Banzie *(Murder Mistaken)*
Ernest Clark *(Escapade)*
1954 Vilma Kurer *(The Winner)*
David Lewis *(King of Hearts)*
British:
Patricia Jessel *(Witness for the Prosecution)*
Richard Wordsworth *(Venice Preserved)*

1955 Vivian Nathan *(Anastasia)*
Fritz Weaver *(The White Devil)*
British:
Beryl Measor *(Separate Tables)*
Noel Willman *(The Prisoner)*
1956 Frances Sternhagen *(The Admirable Bashville)*
Gerald Hiken *(Uncle Vanya)*
British:
Margaret Vines *(Morning's at Seven)*
Timothy Bateson *(Waiting for Godot)*
1957 Joan Croyden *(The Potting Shed)*
Ellis Rabb *(The Misanthrope)*
British:
Megs Jenkins *(A View from the Bridge)*
Derek Godfrey *(Cymbaline)*
1958 Collin Wilcox *(The Day the Money Stopped)*
George C. Scott *(As You Like It)*
British:
Lally Bowers *(Dinner with the Family)*
Paul Daneman *(Henry VI, Parts 1, 2, and 3)*
1959 David Hurst *(Look After Lulu)*
Lois Nettleton *(God and Kate Murphy)*
British:
Avice Landone *(Not in the Book)*
Alan Bates *(Long Day's Journey into Night)*
1960 Rochelle Oliver *(Toys in the Attic)*
William Daniels *(The Zoo Story)*
British:
Pauline Jameson *(The Aspern Papers)*
Alec McCowan *(As You Like It)*
1961 Rosemary Murphy *(Period of Adjustment)*
Eric Christmas *(Little Moon of Alban)*
British:
Rachel Roberts *(Platonov)*
Peter Woodthorpe *(The Caretaker)*
1962 Rebecca Darke *(Who'll Save the Plowboy?)*
Gene Wilder *(The Complaisant Lover)*
British:
Judi Dench *(The Cherry Orchard)*
John Moffatt *(Luther)*
1963 Jessica Walter *(Photo Finish)*
Gene Hackman *(Children from Their Games)*
British:
Jessie Evans *(The Keep)*
Frank Finlay *(Chips with Everything)*
1964 Joyce Ebert *(The Trojan Women)*
Richard McMurray *(A Case of Libel)*
British:
Eileen Atkins *(Exit the King)*

1965 Elizabeth Hubbard *(The Physicists)*
James Sanchez *(Conerico Was Here to Stay)*
British:
Jeanne Hepple *(The Crucible)*
Ian McKellen *(A Scent of Flowers)*
1966 Jeanne Hepple *(Serjeant Musgrave's Dance)*
Christopher Walken *(The Lion in Winter)*
British:
Gemma Jones *(The Cavern)*
Edward Hardwicke *(A Flea in Her Ear)*
Special award: Thomas Ahearne *(Hogan's Goat)*
1967 Reva Rose *(You're a Good Man, Charlie Brown)*
Austin Pendleton *(Hail Scrawdyke!)*
Special award: Philip Bosco *(The Alchemist)*
British:
Vickery Turner *(The Prime of Miss Jean Brodie)*
Paul Eddington *(Jarrocks)*
1968 Catherine Burns *(The Prime of Miss Jean Brodie)*
David Birney *(Summertree)*
British:
Ann Dyson *(The Daughter-in-Law)*
Timothy West *(The Italian Girl)*
1969 Marlene Warfield *(The Great White Hope)*
Ron O'Neal *(No Place To Be Somebody)*
British:
Elizabeth Spriggs *(A Delicate Balance)*
Gordon Jackson *(Hamlet)*
1970 Pamela Payton-Wright *(The Effect of Gamma Rays on Man-in-the-Moon Marigolds)*
Jeremiah Sullivan *(A Scent of Flowers)*
British:
Denise Coffey *(The Bandwagon)*
Robert Eddison *(Edward II)*
1971 Katherine Helmond *(House of Blue Leaves)*
James Wood *(Saved)*
British:
Rosemary McHale *(Slag)*
Michael Bates *(Forget-Me-Not Lane)*
1972 Pamela Bellwood *(Butterflies Are Free)*
Richard Backus *(Promenade, All)*
British:
Heather Canning *(Miss Julie)*
Richard O'Callaghan *(Butley)*
1973 Mary Gorman *(Hot l Baltimore)*
Christopher Murney *(Tricks)*
British:
Bridget Turner *(Time and Time Again)*
Alan McNaughton *(Misanthrope)*
1974 Ann Reinking *(Over Here)*
Thomas Christopher *(Noel Coward in Two Keys)*
British:
Anna Carteret *(Saturday, Sunday, Monday)*
John Tordoff *(Misalliance)*
1975 Marybeth Hurt *(Love for Love)*
Reyno *(The First Breeze of Summer)*
British:
Dorothy Reynolds *(What Every Woman Knows)*
Mike Gwilyn *(King John)*

The Donaldson Awards

Established in 1944 in memory of W. H. Donaldson (1864-1925), founder of The Billboard Magazine. *The award was discontinued after 1955.*

PLAY DIVISION

Play

1943-44 *The Voice of the Turtle*
1944-45 *The Glass Menagerie*
1945-46 *State of the Union*
1946-47 *All My Sons*
1947-48 *A Streetcar Named Desire*
1948-49 *Death of a Salesman*
1949-50 *The Member of the Wedding*
1950-51 *Darkness at Noon*
1951-52 *The Shrike*
1952-53 *Picnic*
1952-53 *The Crucible*
1953-54 *The Tea House of the August Moon*
1954-55 *Cat on a Hot Tin Roof*

First Play

1945-46 *Born Yesterday*
1946-47 *No Exit*
1947-48 *Mister Roberts*
1948-49 *Edward, My Son*
1949-50 *The Member of the Wedding*
1950-51 *Billy Budd*
1951-52 *The Shrike*
1952-53 *The Love of Four Colonels*
1953-54 *Tea and Sympathy*
1954-55 *Inherit the Wind*

Direction

1943-44 Moss Hart *(Winged Victory)*
1944-45 John van Druten *(I Remember Mama)*
1945-46 Garson Kanin *(Born Yesterday)*
1946-47 Elia Kazan *(All My Sons)*
1947-48 Elia Kazan *(A Streetcar Named Desire)*
1948-49 Elia Kazan *(Death of a Salesman)*
1949-50 Harold Clurman *(The Member of the Wedding)*
1950-51 Daniel Mann *(The Rose Tattoo)*
1951-52 Jose Ferrer *(The Shrike)*
1952-53 Joshua Logan *(Picnic)*
1953-54 Elia Kazan *(Tea and Sympathy)*
1954-55 Elia Kazan *(Cat on a Hot Tin Roof)*

Performance (Male)

1943-44 Paul Robeson *(Othello)*
1944-45 Frank Fay *(Harvey)*
1945-46 Louis Calhern *(The Magnificent Yankee)*
1946-47 Laurence Olivier *(Oedipus)*
1947-48 Paul Kelly *(Command Decision)*
1948-49 Lee J. Cobb *(Death of a Salesman)*
1949-50 Sidney Blackmer *(Come Back, Little Sheba)*
1950-51 Claude Rains *(Darkness at Noon)*
1951-52 Jose Ferrer *(The Shrike)*
1952-53 Tom Ewell *(The Seven-Year Itch)*
1953-54 Lloyd Nolan *(The Caine Mutiny Court-Martial)*
1954-55 Paul Muni *(Inherit the Wind)*

Performance (Female)

1943-44 Margaret Sullivan *(The Voice of the Turtle)*
1944-45 Laurette Taylor *(The Glass Menagerie)*
1945-46 Judy Holliday *(Born Yesterday)*
1946-47 Ingrid Bergman *(Joan of Lorraine)*
1947-48 Judith Anderson *(Medea)*
1948-49 Martita Hunt *(The Madwoman of Chaillot)*
1949-50 Shirley Booth *(Come Back, Little Sheba)*
1950-51 Uta Hagen *(The Country Girl)*
1951-52 Julie Harris *(I Am a Camera)*
1952-53 Shirley Booth *(Time of the Cuckoo)*
1953-54 Deborah Kerr *(Tea and Sympathy)*
1954-55 Kim Stanley *(Bus Stop)*

Supporting Performance (Male)

1943-44 Jose Ferrer *(Othello)*
1944-45 Anthony Ross *(The Glass Menagerie)*
1945-46 Marlon Brando *(Truckline Cafe)*
1946-47 Tom Ewell *(John Loves Mary)*
1947-48 Karl Malden *(A Streetcar Named Desire)*
1948-49 Arthur Kennedy *(Death of a Salesman)*
1949-50 Dennis King *(The Devil's Disciple)*

1950-51 Eli Wallach *(The Rose Tattoo)*
1951-52 John Cromwell *(Point of No Return)*
1952-53 John Williams *(Dial 'M' for Murder)*
1953-54 John Kerr *(Tea and Sympathy)*
1954-55 Ed Begley *(Inherit the Wind)*

Supporting Performance (Female)

1943-44 Audrey Christie *(The Voice of the Turtle)*
1944-45 Josephine Hull *(Harvey)*
1945-46 Barbara Bel Geddes *(Deep Are the Roots)*
1946-47 Margaret Phillips *(Another Part of the Forest)*
1947-48 Kim Hunter *(A Streetcar Named Desire)*
1948-49 Mildred Dunnock *(Death of a Salesman)*
1949-50 Julie Harris *(The Member of the Wedding)*
1950-51 Phyllis Love *(The Rose Tattoo)*
1951-52 Marian Winters *(I Am a Camera)*
1952-53 Kim Stanley *(Picnic)*
1953-54 Jo Van Fleet *(The Trip to Bountiful)*
1954-55 Eileen Heckart *(The Bad Seed)*

Debut Performance (Male)

1945-46 Paul Douglas *(Born Yesterday)*
1946-47 Claude Dauphin *(No Exit)*
1947-48 James Whitmore *(Command Decision)*
1948-49 Charles Boyer *(Red Gloves)*
1949-50 Brandon Dewilde *(The Member of the Wedding)*
1950-51 Denholm Elliott *(Ring 'Round the Moon)*
1951-52 John Hodiak *(The Chase)*
1952-53 Menasha Skulnick *(The Fifth Season)*
1953-54 Louis Jourdan *(The Immoralist)*
1954-55 Buddy Hackett *(Lunatics and Lovers)*

Debut Performance (Female)

1945-46 Susan Douglas *(He Who Gets Slapped)*
1946-47 Patricia Neal *(Another Part of the Forest)*
1947-48 June Lockhart *(For Love or Money)*
1948-49 Martita Hunt *(The Madwoman of Chaillot)*
1949-50 Joan Lorring *(Come Back, Little Sheba)*
1950-51 Dominique Blanchar *(L'Ecole des Femmes)*
1951-52 Audrey Hepburn *(Gigi)*
1952-53 Geraldine Page *(Mid-Summer)*
1953-54 Deborah Kerr *(Tea and Sympathy)*
1954-55 Loretta Leversee *(Home Is the Hero)*

Settings

1943-44 Stewart Chaney *(The Voice of the Turtle)*
1944-45 George Jenkins *(I Remember Mama)*
1945-56 Jo Mielziner *(Dream Girl)*
1946-47 Cecil Beaton *(Lady Windermere's Fan)*
1947-48 Jo Mielziner *(A Streetcar Named Desire)*
1948-49 Jo Mielziner *(Death of a Salesman)*
1949-50 Jo Mielziner *(The Innocents)*
1950-51 Frederick Fox *(Darkness at Noon)*
1951-52 Cecil Beaton *(The Grass Harp)*
1952-53 Lemuel Ayers *(Camino Real)*
1953-54 Peter Larkin *(The Teahouse of the August Moon)*
1954-55 Peter Larkin *(Inherit the Wind)*

Costumes

1943-44 Motley *(Lovers and Friends)*
1944-45 Lucinda Ballard *(I Remember Mama)*
1945-46 Motley *(Pygmalion)*
1946-47 Cecil Beaton *(Lady Windermere's Fan)*
1947-48 David Ffolkes *(Man and Superman)*
1948-49 Christian Berard *(The Madwoman of Chaillot)*
1949-50 James Bailey *(As You Like It)*
1950-51 Oliver Messel *(Romeo and Juliet)*
1950-51 Castillo *(Ring 'Round the Moon)*
1951-52 Audrey Gruddas *(Caesar and Cleopatra)*
1952-53 Lemuel Ayers *(Camino Real)*
1953-54 Richard Whorf *(Ondine)*
1954-55 Cecil Beaton *(Quadrille)*

MUSICAL DIVISION

Musicals

1943-44 *Carmen Jones*
1944-45 *Carousel*
1945-46 *Show Boat*
1946-47 *Finian's Rainbow*
1947-48 *High Button Shoes*
1948-49 *South Pacific*
1949-50 *The Consul*
1950-51 *Guys and Dolls*
1951-52 *Pal Joey*
1952-53 *Wonderful Town*
1953-54 *The Golden Apple*
1954-55 *The Pajama Game*

Direction

1943-44 Hassard Short *(Carmen Jones)*
1944-45 Rouben Mamoulian *(Carousel)*
1945-46 George Abbott *(Billion Dollar Baby)*
1946-47 Joshua Logan *(Annie Get Your Gun)*
1947-48 George Abbott *(High Button Shoes)*
1948-49 Joshua Logan *(South Pacific)*
1949-50 Gian-Carlo Menotti *(The Consul)*
1950-51 George S. Kaufman *(Guys and Dolls)*
1951-52 David Alexander *(Pal Joey)*
1952-53 George Abbott *(Wonderful Town)*
1953-54 Albert Marre *(Kismet)*
1954-55 George Abbott and Jerome Robbins *(The Pajama Game)*

Performance (Male)

1943-44 Bobby Clark *(Mexican Hayride)*
1944-45 John Raitt *(Carousel)*
1945-46 Ray Bolger *(Three to Make Ready)*
1946-47 David Wayne *(Finian's Rainbow)*
1947-48 Paul Hartman *(Angel in the Wings)*
1948-49 Alfred Drake *(Kiss Me, Kate)*
1949-50 Todd Duncan *(Lost in the Stars)*
1950-51 Yul Brynner *(The King and I)*
1951-52 Phil Silvers *(Top Banana)*
1952-53 Thomas Mitchell *(Hazel Flagg)*
1953-54 Alfred Drake *(Kismet)*
1954-55 Cyril Ritchard *(Peter Pan)*

Performance (Female)

1943-44 Mary Martin *(One Touch of Venus)*
1944-45 Beatrice Lillie *(Seven Lively Arts)*
1945-46 Betty Garrett *(Call Me Mister)*
1946-47 Ethel Merman *(Annie Get Your Gun)*
1947-48 Nanette Fabray *(High Button Shoes)*
1948-49 Mary Martin *(South Pacific)*
1949-50 Patricia Neway *(The Consul)*
1950-51 Shirley Booth *(A Tree Grows in Brooklyn)*
1951-52 Vivienne Segal *(Pal Joey)*
1952-53 Rosalind Russell *(Wonderful Town)*
1953-54 Shirley Booth *(By the Beautiful Sea)*
1954-55 Mary Martin *(Peter Pan)*

Supporting Performance (Male)

1943-44 Kenny Baker *(One Touch of Venus)*
1944-45 Burl Ives *(Sing Out, Sweet Land)*
1945-46 Tom Helmore *(The Day Before Spring)*
1946-47 David Wayne *(Finian's Rainbow)*
1947-48 Jack McCauley *(High Button Shoes)*
1948-49 Myron McCormick *(South Pacific)*
1949-50 Wally Cox *(Dance Me a Song)*
1950-51 Russell Nype *(Call Me Madam)*
1951-52 Tony Bavaar *(Paint Your Wagon)*
1952-53 Jack Whiting *(Hazel Flagg)*
1953-54 Harry Belafonte *(Almanac)*
1954-55 Cyril Ritchard *(Peter Pan)*

Supporting Performance (Female)

1943-44 June Havoc *(Mexican Hayride)*
1944-45 Joan McCracken *(Bloomer Girl)*
1945-46 Carol Bruce *(Show Boat)*
1946-47 Polyna Stoska *(Street Scene)*
1947-48 Nanette Fabray *(High Button Shoes)*
1948-49 Juanita Hall *(South Pacific)*
1949-50 Gloria Lane *(The Consul)*
1950-51 Doretta Morrow *(The King and I)*
1951-52 Helen Gallagher *(Pal Joey)*
1952-53 Edith Adams *(Wonderful Town)*
1953-54 Gwen Verdon *(Can-Can)*
1954-55 Carol Haney *(The Pajama Game)*

Debut Performance (Male)

1945-46 Jules Munshin *(Call Me Mister)*
1946-47 Albert Sharpe *(Finian's Rainbow)*
1947-48 Sid Caesar *(Make Mine Manhattan)*
1948-49 Ezio Pinza *(South Pacific)*
1949-50 Wally Cox *(Dance Me a Song)*
1950-51 Robert Alda *(Guys and Dolls)*
1951-52 Tony Bavaar *(Paint Your Wagon)*
1952-53 Ronny Graham *(New Faces of 1952)*
1953-54 Billy De Wolfe *(Almanac)*
1954-55 David Daniels *(Plain and Fancy)*

Debut Performance (Female)

1945-46 Pearl Bailey *(St. Louis Woman)*
1946-47 Marion Bell *(Brigadoon)*
1947-48 Valerie Bettis *(Inside U.S.A.)*
1948-49 Yvonne Adair *(Lend an Ear)*
1949-50 Gloria Lane *(The Consul)*
1950-51 Vivian Blaine *(Guys and Dolls)*
1951-52 Olga San Juan *(Paint Your Wagon)*
1952-53 Edith Adams *(Wonderful Town)*
1953-54 Hermione Gingold *(Almanac)*
1954-55 Julie Andrews *(The Boy Friend)*

Dancer (Male)

1943-44 Paul Haakon *(Mexican Hayride)*
1944-45 Peter Birch *(Carousel)*
1945-46 Ray Bolger *(Three to Make Ready)*
1946-47 James Mitchell *(Brigadoon)*
1947-48 Harold Lang *(Look Ma, I'm Dancin')*

1948-49 Ray Bolger *(Where's Charley?)*
1949-50 Jack Cole *(Alive and Kicking)*
1950-51 Harold Lang *(Make a Wish)*
1951-52 Harold Lang *(Pal Joey)*
1952-53 John Brascia *(Hazel Flagg)*
1953-54 Jonathan Lucas *(The Golden Apple)*
1954-55 Daniel Nagrin *(Plain and Fancy)*

Dancer (Female)

1943-44 Sono Osato *(One Touch of Venus)*
1944-45 Bambi Linn *(Carousel)*
1945-46 Joan McCracken *(Billion Dollar Baby)*
1946-47 Anita Alvarez *(Finian's Rainbow)*
1947-48 Valerie Bettis *(Inside U.S.A.)*
1948-49 Viola Essen *(Along Fifth Avenue)*
1949-50 Anita Alvarez *(Gentlemen Prefer Blondes)*
1950-51 Janet Collins *(Out of This World)*
1951-52 Gemze De Lappe *(Paint Your Wagon)*
1952-53 Nora Kaye *(Two's Company)*
1953-54 Gwen Verdon *(Can-Can)*
1954-55 Carol Haney *(The Pajama Game)*

Book

1943-44 Oscar Hammerstein II *(Carmen Jones)*
1944-45 Oscar Hammerstein II *(Carousel)*
1945-46 Oscar Hammerstein II *(Show Boat)*
1946-47 E. Y. Harburg and Freddy Saidy *(Finian's Rainbow)*
1947-48 Oscar Hammerstein II *(Allegro)*
1948-49 Oscar Hammerstein II and Joshua Logan *(South Pacific)*
1949-50 Gian-Carlo Menotti *(The Consul)*
1950-51 Jo Swerling and Abe Burrows *(Guys and Dolls)*
1951-52 John O'Hara *(Pal Joey)*
1952-53 Joseph Fields and Jerome Chodorov *(Wonderful Town)*
1953-54 John Latouche *(The Golden Apple)*
1954-55 George Abbott and Richard Bissell *(The Pajama Game)*

Score

1943-44 Georges Bizet *(Carmen Jones)*
1944-45 Richard Rodgers *(Carousel)*
1945-46 Jerome Kern *(Show Boat)*
1946-47 Irving Berlin *(Annie Get Your Gun)*
1947-48 Richard Rodgers *(Allegro)*
1948-49 Richard Rodgers *(South Pacific)*
1949-50 Gian Carlo Menotti *(The Consul)*
1950-51 Frank Loesser *(Guys and Dolls)*
1951-52 Richard Rodgers *(Pal Joey)*
1952-53 Leonard Bernstein *(Wonderful Town)*
1953-54 Alexander Borodin *(Kismet)*
1954-55 Richard Adler and Jerry Ross *(The Pajama Game)*

Lyrics

1943-44 Oscar Hammerstein II *(Carmen Jones)*
1944-45 Oscar Hammerstein II *(Carousel)*
1945-46 Oscar Hammerstein II *(Show Boat)*
1946-47 Irving Berlin *(Annie Get Your Gun)*
1947-48 Oscar Hammerstein II *(Allegro)*
1948-49 Oscar Hammerstein II *(South Pacific)*
1949-50 Gian-Carlo Menotti *(The Consul)*
1950-51 Frank Loesser *(Guys and Dolls)*
1951-52 Lorenz Hart *(Pal Joey)*
1952-53 Betty Comden and Adolph Green *(Wonderful Town)*
1953-54 John Latouche *(The Golden Apple)*
1954-55 Richard Adler and Jerry Ross *(The Pajama Game)*

Dance Direction)

1943-44 Agnes de Mille *(One Touch of Venus)*
1944-45 Agnes de Mille *(Carousel)*
1945-46 Jerome Robbins *(Billion Dollar Baby)*
1946-47 Agnes de Mille *(Brigadoon)*
1947-48 Jerome Robbins *(High Button Shoes)*
1948-49 Gower Champion *(Lend an Ear)*
1949-50 Jack Cole *(Alive and Kicking)*
1950-51 Jerome Robbins *(The King and I)*
1951-52 Robert Alton *(Pal Joey)*
1952-53 Jerome Robbins *(Two's Company)*
1953-54 Michael Kidd *(Can-Can)*
1954-55 Jerome Robbins *(Two's Company)*

Settings

1943-44 Howard Bay *(Carmen Jones)*
1944-45 Howard Bay *(Up in Central Park)*
1945-46 Robert Edmond Jones *(Lute Song)*
1946-47 Oliver Smith *(Brigadoon)*
1947-48 Oliver Smith *(High Button Shoes)*
1948-49 Lemuel Ayers *(Kiss Me, Kate)*
1949-50 Oliver Smith *(Gentlemen Prefer Blondes)*
1950-51 Jo Mielziner *(The King and I)*
1951-52 Oliver Smith *(Pal Joey)*
1952-53 Raoul Pene du Bois *(Wonderful Town)*
1953-54 William and Jean Eckart *(The Golden Apple)*
1954-55 Oliver Messel *(House of Flowers)*

Costumes

1943-44 Raoul Pene du Bois *(Carmen Jones)*
1944-45 Miles White *(Bloomer Girl)*
1945-46 Robert Edmond Jones *(Lute Song)*
1946-47 David Ffolkes *(Brigadoon)*
1947-48 Miles White *(High Button Shoes)*
1948-49 Lemuel Ayers *(Kiss Me, Kate)*
1949-50 Miles White *(Gentlemen Prefer Blondes)*
1950-51 Irene Sharaff *(The King and I)*
1951-52 Miles White *(Pal Joey)*
1952-53 Lemuel Ayers *(My Darlin' Aida)*
1953-54 Lemuel Ayers *(Kismet)*
1954-55 Oliver Messel *(House of Flowers)*

Drama League of New York

THE DELIA AUSTRIAN MEDALS

The Delia Austrian Medal is awarded annually by the Drama League of New York. The selection is made by the entire membership of the Drama League for "the most distinguished performance of the season."

1935 Katharine Cornell *(Romeo and Juliet)*
1936 Helen Hayes *(Victoria Regina)*
1937 Maurice Evans *(Richard III)*
1938 Cedric Hardwicke *(Shadow and Substance)*
1939 Raymond Massey *(Abe Lincoln in Illinois)*
1940 Paul Muni *(Key Largo)*
1941 Paul Lukas *(Watch on the Rhine)*
1942 Judith Evelyn *(Angel Street)*
1943 Alfred Lunt and Lynn Fontanne *(The Pirate)*
1944 Elisabeth Bergner *(The Two Mrs. Carrolls)*
1945 Mady Christians *(I Remember Mama)*
1946 Louis Calhern *(The Magnificent Yankee)*
1947 Ingrid Bergman *(Joan of Lorraine)*
1948 Judith Anderson *(Medea)*
1949 Robert Morley *(Edward My Son)*
1950 Grace George *(The Velvet Glove)*
1951 Claude Rains *(Darkness at Noon)*
1952 Julie Harris *(I Am a Camera)*
1953 Shirley Booth *(Time of the Cuckoo)*
1954 Josephine Hull *(The Solid Gold Cadillac)*
1955 Viveca Lindfors *(Anastasia)*
1956 David Wayne *(The Ponder Heart)*
1957 Eli Wallach *(Major Barbara)*
1958 Ralph Bellamy *(Sunrise at Campobello)*
1959 Cyril Ritchard *(The Pleasure of His Company)*
1960 Jessica Tandy *(Five Finger Exercise)*
1961 Hume Cronyn *(Big Fish, Little Fish)*
1962 Paul Scofield *(A Man for All Seasons)*
1963 Charles Boyer *(Lord Pengo)*
1964 Alec Guinness *(Dylan)*
1965 John Gielgud *(Tiny Alice)*
1966 Richard Kiley *(Man of La Mancha)*
1967 Rosemary Harris *(The Wild Duck)*
1968 Zoe Caldwell *(The Prime of Miss Jean Brodie)*
1969 Alec McCowan *(Hadrian VII)*
1970 James Stewart *(Harvey)*
1971 Anthony Quayle *(Sleuth)*
1972 Eileen Atkins and Claire Bloom *(Vivat! Vivat! Regina)*
1973 Alan Bates *(Butley)*
1974 Christopher Plummer *(The Good Doctor)*
1975 John Wood *(Sherlock Holmes)*

The Dramatists Guild

ELIZABETH HULL—KATE WARRINER AWARD

This award is presented by The Dramatists Guild to a playwright for an outstanding work dealing with a controversial subject involving political, religious, or social mores.

1970-1971 David Rabe *(The Basic Training of Pavlo Hummel)*
1971-1972 Phillip Hayes Dean *(The Sty of the Blind Pig)*
1972-1973 Joseph A. Walker *(The River Niger)*
1973-1974 Terrence McNally *(Bad Habits)* and Miguel Pinero *(Short Eyes)*
1974-1975 Edward Albee *(Seascape)*

The George Freedley Memorial Award

(See Theatre Library Association)

John Simon Guggenheim Memorial Foundation Fellowships

The following is a list of the recipients of Guggenheim Fellowships in drama. These awards are given to citizens of Canada, the Phillippines, the United States, the Latin American republics, and the British Caribbean area. The awards are made to men and women, age 30 to 40, who have already demonstrated unusual productive ability in their fields.

FELLOWS IN DRAMA

1928 Paul Green, Lynn Riggs
1930 Ellsworth Conkle
1931 Emjo Basshe, Katherine Clugston
1936 Leopold L. Atlas, Albert Bein, Robert Turney

1937 Robert Ardrey
1938 Arthur Arent
1942 Alexander Greendale
1946 Arthur Ranous Wilmut
1948 Theodore Ward
1949 John Latouche
1951 Arnold Olaf Sundgaard
1954 Denis W. Johnston
1956 Harry Miles Muheim
1958 Lionel Abel, Loften Mitchell
1959 William Blackwell Branch
1960 Joshua Greenfield
1961 Robert Goode Hogan
1963 Henry W. Butler, Jack Gelber
1964 Jan S. Hartman, Herbert H. Lieberman, Jack C. Richardson
1965 Albert Bermel, Kenneth H. Brown, LeRoi Jones, Arnold Weinstein
1966 Jack Gelber, Errol John, Terrence McNally, Gabriela Roepke
1967 Charles Dizenzo, Adrienne Kennedy, Arthur Kopit
1968 Leon Gillen, Sam Shepard
1969 Terrence McNally
1970 Benjamin Caldwell, Rosalyn Drexler, Tom Eyen, Ronald Ribman
1971 Julie Bovasso, Ed Bullins, Lonnie Carter, Charles Ludlam, Rochelle Owens, Sam Shepard
1972 Kenneth Bernard, Maria Irene Fornes, Wilford Leach, Jerome Max, Robert S. Montgomery, Jose Morales, Lanford Wilson
1973 Frederick Gaines, Charles F. Gordon, Myrna Lamb, Murray Mednick, Barry Reckord, Ronald Tavel, Jean-Claude van Itallie, Joseph A. Walker
1974 Paul Foster, Frank Gagliano, Juan Jose Gurrola, William Hoffman, Mark Medoff, Susan Yankowitz
1975 Richard Foreman, Albert F. Innaurato, Philip Magdalany, Jeff Weiss, Augusto Boal

FELLOWS IN STAGE DESIGN AND PRODUCTION

1926 Hallie Flanagan
1929 Remo Bufano, James Light
1934 Charles Norris Houghton
1935 Mordecai Gorelik, Cleon Throckmorton
1937 Stewart Chaney
1938 Samuel Selden
1939 William S. Clark II
1940 Howard Bay
1949 John Waldhorn Gassner
1950 Boris Aronson, Rosamond Gilder
1955 Monroe Lippman, Charles Ensign Rogers
1956 Alan Leo Schneider
1959 Basil Langton, Richard Moody, Louis Sheaffer
1960 Ann Hitchcock Holmes
1961 Benjamin Hunniger, Dorothy Jeakins
1962 Herbert Blau
1967 Hector Azar
1970 Joseph Chaikin, Henry May
1971 George Izenour
1973 Augusto Boal, Gordon Rogoff
1975 Joseph Chaikin, Richard Schechner

Elizabeth Hull—Kate Warriner Award

(See The Dramatists Guild)

The Kelcey Allen Awards

Established by Abraham Mandelstam in memory of Kelcey Allen (1875-1951), drama editor and drama critic of Women's Wear Daily *from 1915 until his death.*

1955 Vincent Sardi, Sr.
1956 George Freedley
1957 Mrs. Martin Beck
1958 Walter Vincent
1959 May Davenport Seymour
1960 Benjamin P. Kaye
1961 Lee Strasberg
1962 Edward F. Kook
1963 Rosamond Gilder
1964 Peggy Wood
1965 John Gassner
1966 John F. Wharton
1967 John V. Lindsay
1968 Brooks Atkinson
(Discontinued)

The Margo Jones Awards

The Margo Jones Award was established in 1961 by Jerome Lawrence and Robert E. Lee in memory of Margo Jones (1913-1955). The award, which consists of a commemorative medal and stipend, is given annually "to the producing manager of an American or Canadian theatre whose policy of presenting new dramatic works continues most faithfully in the tradition of Margo Jones."

1962 Lucille Lortel, White Barn Playhouse
1963 Michael Ellis, Bucks County Playhouse
1964 Judith Rutherford Marechal and Mrs. Roy MacGregor Watt
1965 Richard Barr, Edward Albee and Clinton Wilder, Theatre 64
1966 Sidney Lanier and Wynn Handman, American Place Theatre
1967 Harlan P. Kleiman and Jon Jory, Long Wharf Theatre
1968 Paul Baker, Dallas Theater Center
1969 Davey Marlin-Jones, Washington Theatre Club
Ellen Stewart, Cafe La Mama
1970 Adrian Hall, Trinity Square Repertory Company
Gordon Davidson and Edward Parone, Los Angeles Center Theatre
1971 Joseph Papp, New York Shakespeare Festival Public Theatre
1972 Zelda Fichandler, Arena Stage
1973 Jules Irving, Repertory Theatre of Lincoln Center
1974 Douglas Turner Ward, Negro Ensemble Company
1975 Paul Weidner, Hartford Stage Company

Maharam Theatrical Design Awards

The Maharam award was established in 1965 to honor outstanding scenic and costume design in Broadway and off-Broadway plays and musicals. It is awarded annually by the Joseph Maharam Foundation.

1964-65 Scenic: Boris Aronson for *Fiddler on the Roof*
Ming Cho Lee for *Electra*
Costume: Jane Greenwood for *Tartuffe*
1965-66 Scenic: Howard Bay for *Man of La Mancha*
Costume: Noel Taylor for *Slapstick Tragedy*
1966-67 Scenic: Boris Aronson for *Cabaret*
Costume: Jeanne Button for *Macbird!*
1967-68 Scenic: Peter Wexler for *The Happy Time*
Ming Cho Lee for *Ergo*
Costume: Nancy Potts for *Pantagleize*, also *Hair*
1968-69 Scenic: Jo Mielziner for *1776*, Julian Beck for *Frankenstein*
Costume: Patricia Zipprodt for *1776*
1969-70 Scenic: Boris Aronson for *Company*
Jo Mielziner for *Child's Play*
Costume: Theoni V. Aldredge for *Peer Gynt*
1970-71 Scenic: Peter Larkin for *Les Blancs*
Boris Aronson for *Follies*
Costume: Raoul Pene DuBois for *No! No! Nanette!*
Special Citation: Clarke Dunham for *The Me Nobody Knows*
1971-72 Scenic: Kurt Lundell for *Ain't Supposed To Die a Natural Death*
Robert U. Taylor for *The Beggar's Opera*
Costume: Willa Kim for *Screens*
1972-73 Scenic: Douglas W. Schmidt for *Enemies*
Robin Wagner for *Seesaw*
Costume: Theoni V. Aldredge for *Much Ado About Nothing*
1973-74 Scenic: Franne and Eugene Lee for *Candide*
Ed Wittstein for *Ulysses in Nightown*
Costume: Franne Lee for *Candide*
1974-75 Scenic: Robin Wagner for *A Chorus Line*
Robert Wilson for *Letter for Queen Victoria*
Costume: Carrie F. Robbins for *Polly*

Medal for Good Speech

(See American Academy of Arts and Letters)

The George Jean Nathan Awards

In accordance with provisions in the will of the late George Jean Nathan (1882-1958), the George Jean Nathan Award was established "to encourage and assist in developing the art of drama criticism and the stimulation of intelligent theatre going." A selection committee made up of the English department chairmen from Cornell, Princeton, and Yale meets annually to cite the author of the "best piece of drama criticism published during the previous year, whether an article, treatise or book." Accompanying the award is a stipend of $5,000.

1959 Harold Clurman *(Lies Like Truth)*
1960 C. L. Barber *(Shakespeare's Festive Comedy)*
1961 Jerry Tallmer *(The Village Voice* reviews)
1962 Robert Brustein *(The New Republic* reviews)
1963 Walter Kerr *(The Theatre in Spite of Itself)*
1964 Elliot Norton *(Reviews, Newspaper and Television)*

1965 Gerald Weales *(Drama Survey* reviews)
1966 Eric Russell Bentley (articles, two of which appeared in the *Tulane Drama Review)*
1967 Elizabeth Hardwick *(New York Review of Books,*reviews and discussions)
1968 Martin Gottfried *(A Theatre Divided: The Postwar American Stage)*
1969 John Lahr (essays)
1970 John Simon (reviews)
1971 Richard Gilman *(Common and Uncommon Masks: Writings on Theatre 1961-1970)*
1972 Jay Carr (reviews, . . . *Detroit News)*
1973 Stanley Kauffman *(New Republic* reviews)
1974 Albert Bermel (reviews)

National Institute of Arts and Letters

MARC BILTZSTEIN AWARD FOR THE MUSICAL THEATRE

An award administered by the National Institute of Arts and Letters and presented to a composer, lyricist, or librettist to encourage the creation of works of merit for the musical theatre.

1965 William Bolcom
1968 Jack Beeson

The New England Theatre Conference Awards

The New England Theatre Conference was established in order "to develop, expand, and assist theatre activity on the community, educational and professional levels in New England," and has presented awards and citations at its annual convention each October since 1957.

OUTSTANDING CREATIVE ACHIEVEMENT IN THE AMERICAN THEATRE AWARD

1957 Jo Mielziner
1958 Joshua Logan
1959 Richard Rodgers and Oscar Hammerstein II
1960 Moss Hart
1961 Howard Lindsay and Russel Crouse
1962 Lawrence Langner
1963 Joseph Papp
1964 Elia Kazan, Robert Whitehead and Harold Clurman (of the Repertory Theater of Lincoln Center)
1965 Morris Carnovsky
1966 William Gibson
1967 David Hays
1968 David Merrick
1969 Arthur Miller
1970 Harold Prince
1971 The Open Theatre
1972 John Houseman
1973 Lillian Hellman
1974 Elliot Norton
1975 Eva Le Gallienne

New England Theatre Conference Annual Awards and Citations

SPECIAL AWARDS

Presented since 1957 to individuals, groups, and organizations beyond the New England region to recognize and honor national achievement, contribution, or innovation in the interest, support, and advancement of theatre on a national level.

1957 *Hill and Wang* (publishers) of New York
1958 *Norris Houghton* of the Phoenix Theatre, New York
1959 *Playhouse 90* "in recognition of the consistent excellence of its production of television plays in a format permitting truly dramatic scope and impact."
1960 *David Susskind* "for courage and vision in planning and producing for TV outstanding works of dramatic literature."
1961 *National Thespian Society* "for active and consistent service to Secondary Schools as a guiding force in setting standards of excellence, and in developing appreciation of the art and craft of theatre."
Grove Press "for their vision and courage in publishing the great contemporary avant garde works of the theatre."
1962 *The Living Theatre* (of New York) "for creating and maintaining a successful repertory, and for performing consistently, against great odds, the newer and more experimental forms of drama."
1963 *Frederick O'Neal* "for over thirty-five years a distinguished leader in the American Theatre: actor in all dramatic media, stage director, theatre organizer, author and lecturer; administrator of Actors' Equity Association, The Negro Actors' Guild of America, and other key theatrical organizations; negotiator and defender of civil and artistic rights."
1964 *Richard Boone* "for conceiving, producing and starring in, 'The Richard Boone Show,' a dramatic weekly television series using a permanent repertory company and presented during the 1963-1964 season; for unequaled dedication to the highest standards of excellence in television writing, acting, directing and production."
Raymond Sovey "for your several distinguished professional careers as designer, teacher and friend of generations of theatre students; for your enthusiasm, imagination, artistry and shining talents; and most of all, for the magnificent example you have set and for what you continue to bring to the theatre of our time."
Jewish Theological Seminary of America "for producing 'The Eternal Light,' a pioneer religious dramatic series, which for over twenty years has dramatized for millions of listeners and viewers the universal values of Jewish tradition; for its unfailing high standards of production; for its faithfulness to its original concept of providing literate and dramatic nonsectarian programs; and for its place in the mainstream of contemporary religious ecumenicism."
1965 *Free Southern Theatre* "for its dedication, despite segregationist harassment and insufficient money and equipment, to the mission of introducing quality theatre to the underprivileged and culturally deprived communities of the Deep South; and for its success in developing an exciting degree of interaction between its actors and its audience."
Adrienne Kennedy "playwright; for illuminating a nightmare world in contemporary America with compassion, honesty and humility, giving force and scope by the public art of the theatre to a profoundly personal vision, and transmuting her sense of people's inner anguish into brilliantly imaginative plays for the theater of today."
Alvin Ailey "for having brought to audiences abroad and at home a vivid theatre dance that has drawn upon the heritage and culture of the American Negro with power and imagination."
John Gassner "author, educator, critic, wise and devoted friend of the American Theatre; he has discovered and helped to develop some of its worthiest artists, has bridged the gap between its commercial and academic ventures, and has upheld the highest standard of the art of drama in a productive lifetime dedicated to excellence."
1966 *American Place Theatre* "for its pioneering project in the aiding and encouragement of the craft of playwriting for writers in other literary fields. It has established a place where talented men of letters may, without fear of failure, apply their talents to a new field of endeavor, thus enriching their experiences and the body of American dramatic literature."
Viola Spolin "teacher and author; for her contribution to many successful professional, educational, community, and children's theatre artists, as well as to teachers seeking more stimulating and effective methods of instruction within a variety of fields, including elementary and secondary education, occupational therapy, speech therapy, and religion; for the development, organization, and presentation of her system of 'Theatre Games,' a practicable method for fostering the creative process by permitting the individual to heighten his own awareness and understanding of himself, of others, and of the world they share."
1967 *Horace Armistead* "artist, designer, teacher. As an artist-designer, your settings have created glorious worlds in which actors have lived. As a teacher, your inspiration has led gifted artists to grow."
Theodore Fuchs "a pioneer in the development of high standards in technical production for the educational theatre; author of the first comprehensive book on the art and science of modern stage lighting; advisor and consultant for outstanding educational theatre plants across the nation; and inspiring teacher of many of the leaders in the American Theatre today."
Earle Hyman "for more than two decades a distinguished actor whose portrayals on stage and television, here

and abroad, have brought lustre to both classical and modern roles. Having taught himself Norwegian, he became the first United States actor to perform before Scandinavians in their own tongue, and has since won repeated critical and popular acclaim for his powerful interpretations of Shakespeare and O'Neill."

1967 *Stanley McCandless* "teacher, whose work in the classroom and in the laboratory has helped to light up the stages of our theatres."

1968 *Orlin and Irene Corey* "theatre artists for enriching audiences in this country, as well as Canada, Europe and South Africa, with thoughtful theatre of significance, providing inspiration and leadership to fellow artists in the entire field of professional and non-professional theatre, particularly those in religious drama and children's theatre."

Lyn Ely "for bringing Shakespearian drama to secondary school students and teachers through your touring program,'Theater in Education,' since 1955; and for your pioneer work in this field in New England, the Northeast and the South, which has made it easier for those who have since imitated your idea."

Tom O'Horgan "for bringing back to the theatre the ingredients of spectacle; for 'celebrating' the theatrical experience as an exhiliarating and free art form; and for striving to make the dramatic art a true synthesis of all the arts."

1969 *Karl Malden* "actor, gentleman and teacher; internationally established as a professional of the highest artistry, he has actively manifested the realization that the future of the craft of acting lies in the training of the young...by giving of his time and energies through university activities, he has set an ever-growing example for his peers."

Julius L. Novick "for his pioneering descriptive and evaluative study, 'Beyond Broadway: The Quest for Permanent Theatres.' His achievement is welcome testimony that all the country's a stage."

The Playwrights' Unit "theatre workshop extraordinary, committed to an entire operation of new plays by untested playwrights in a completely professional environment, this production company has actively and energetically shaped the course of the contemporary theatre."

Budd Schulberg and The Watts Writers' Workshop "internationally acclaimed author, whose sensitivity and insight led to the establishment of an organization which has met the urban and cultural crises by providing a place for the encouragement and development of new writers seeking an avenue to set forth a distinct body of American literature."

Edwin Sherin "actor-director, whose vision and efforts have re-established the theatrical production as a collaborative creation of artists working as an ensemble."

1970 *Boris Aronson* "in recognition of close to fifty years of innovative set design for the American stage. His work has reflected both the stage craftsman's understanding of the practical theatre and the artist's sensitivity to the meaning of the drama. His sets have been more than display cases—they have been designs in which the drama can truly live."

Michael Butler "your appreciation of the message and new sounds of *Hair* convinced you to do something about its future. That artistic decision ushered in 'The Age of Aquarius'—and 'let the sun shine in' Opening night on April 29, 1968 changed Broadway—and the American musical theatre. What a piece of work is Michael Butler!"

Joe Layton "distinguished director-choreographer, who, for more than a decade, has enriched the American musical theatre with his imaginative choreography and artistic staging; and for his contributions to the development of the musical stage as a unique and vital part of the American theatre."

Peter Stone "distinguished writer for the musical theatre, motion pictures and television; in recognition of his contributions to the art of the American musical; and in particular, for his inspiring book for the award-winning musical play, *1776.*"

1971 *Merce Cunningham* "brilliant choreographer and unique dancer, one of the great innovators of our time, who has given new meanings to time, space and form, thus creating a new art for us all."

The Chelsea Theater Center at the Brooklyn Academy of Music, New York "for continuing to produce some of America's most exciting theatre through a commitment to relevant, brilliant works and to new and challenging theatrical forms."

1972 *American Playwrights Theatre* "for realizing its aim of serving a truly decentralized theater by offering new plays to non-commercial theatres, and by encouraging a working relationship between American dramatists and the play producers of university, community and resident theatres in a creative adventure."

Harold Scott "eminent black artist; for brilliance as an actor, and sensitivity and imagination as a director; and particularly for his unselfish and dedicated efforts as a teacher working with young people in educational institutions throughout the country."

1973 *Alexander H. Cohen* "in recognition of his achievement in promoting the cause of the American theater through the annual Tony Awards shows."

Patricia Zipprodt "for her creative excellence, imagination and integrity in the art of costume design, and for the innovative example she has set as an inspiration for other designers."

1974 *Zelda Fichandler* "one of the pioneers of the American regional theatre movement, founder of the Arena Stage of Washington, D.C., creator and artistic director of two great theaters, producer of nearly two hundred plays, and director of many. More than any individual, she is responsible for the extraordinary new interest in theater in the nation's capitol. More than all but a few, she has shown the way and held up the torch for those who would restore the theatre to the people of the United States."

Brooks Atkinson "a New Englander by birth, education and earliest cultural ties, he began his career as reporter, teacher, play reviewer and editor in this region. As chronicler and critic of Broadway's theatre spanning half a century, he brings us now, in his latest book, *The Lively Years, 1920-1973,* fresh reminders of the plays that, by mirroring the salient issues of their times, have expanded the scope of the American theatre."

Louis Sheaffer "despite different warnings and with laudable recklessness, his thirst for the fountain of truth and servitude to every desire under the elms enabled him to explore more stately mansions than any dreamy kid; after a strange interlude of 17 years of overcoming every fog and web in the zone of O'Neill scholarship, he completed the long journey home; his monumental study, written with a touch of the poet and welded with gold, will continue to be read days without end beyond the horizon, from Cardiff to the Caribbees."

1975 *Theatre Development Fund* of New York "for its commitment to the development of audiences, without which there is no future for the American theatre; and for its encouragement and support of the best that the professional theatre can offer, from experimental to Broadway showcase and regional theatre."

The Village Voice "to voice our gratitude for this newspaper's unflagging commitment to the theatre—not only off-Broadway, off-off-Broadway and on Broadway, but also elsewhere in America and abroad; and for its creation of the annual Obie Awards to signalize distinguished achievement. In the past two decades, no other periodical has matched its record of comprehensive and intelligent coverage of the stage. We wish it a prideful 20th birthday and many happy reviews of the day."

New England Theatre Conference Annual Awards and Citations

MOSS HART MEMORIAL AWARD

Presented annually since 1962. This award is given by the Boston Record-American *and* Sunday Advertiser *through the Conference to a New England theatre group—selected by a committee of judges—in recognition of an outstanding production of a play which stressed the virtues of freedom and human dignity and accents the positive virtues of courage, faith and hope. The purpose of this award is to stimulate the production in New*

England of plays which exemplify this spirit of the free world.

1962 Winner: Drama Club of State College at Fitchburg, Mass., for its production of *The Diary of Anne Frank.* Honorable Mentions: Wachusett Regional High School at Holden, Mass., for its production of *The Skin of Our Teeth.* Williamstown Summer Theatre, Williamstown, Mass., for its production of *The Miracle Worker.*

1963 Winner: Scitamard Players, Providence, R.I., for its production of *A Raisin in the Sun.* Honorable Mentions: Brandeis University Forum Theatre, Waltham, Mass., for its production of *The Skin of Our Teeth.* Weston Drama Workshop, Weston, Mass., for its production of *Home of the Brave.*

1964 Winner: Community Players, Concord, N.H., for its production of *Inherit the Wind.* Honorable Mention: Harlequin Players of State College at North Adams, Mass., for its production of *Antigone.*

1965 Winner: The People's Theater, Cambridge, Mass., for its production of *Noah.* Honorable Mentions: Powder & Wig, Colby College, Waterville, Me., for its production of *A Man for All Seasons.* Town Players, Pittsfield, Mass., for its production of *A Far Country.*

1966 Winner: Wheelock College Drama Club, Boston, Mass., for its production of *Jacobowsky and the Colonel.* Honorable Mentions: Arlington Friends of the Drama, Arlington, Mass., for its production of *A Man for All Seasons.* Theatre Company of Boston, Boston, Mass., for its production of *Yes Is for a Very Young Man.*

1967 Winner: Arlington Friends of the Drama, Arlington, Mass., for its production of *The Crucible.*

1968 Winner: Staples High School Players, Westport, Conn., for its production of *War and Pieces* (original). Honorable Mention: Arlington Friends of the Drama, Arlington, Mass., for its production of *The Madwoman of Chaillot.*

1969 No Award Given.

1970 Winner: Staples High School Players, Westport, Conn., for its production of *Soldier, Soldier* (adaptation of *Bury the Dead).* Honorable Mention: Notre Dame College, Manchester, N.H., for its production of *Amahl and the Night Visitors.*

1971 Winner: University of Hartford Players, West Hartford, Conn., for its production of *The Ceremony of Innocence.* Honorable Mention: Community Players, Concord, N.H., for its production of *A Hatful of Rain.*

1972 Winner: Arlington Friends of the Drama, Arlington, Mass., for its production of *Fiddler on the Roof.* Honorable Mention: Rhode Island College Theatre, Providence, R.I., for its production of *The Caucasian Chalk Circle.*

1973 Winner: Reagle Players, Waltham Summer Theatre, Waltham, Mass., for its production of *1776.* Honorable Mention: Peabody Veterans Memorial High School, Drama Guild, Peabody, Mass., for its production of *Becket.*

1974 Winner: Harwich Winter Theatre, West Harwich, Mass., for its production of *Uncle Vanya.* Honorable Mentions: Acadia Repertory Theatre, Somesville, Me., for its production of *The Electra (Sophocles).* Brattleboro Union High School, Drama Group, Brattleboro, Vt., for its production of *Our Town.* Reagle Players, Waltham Summer Theatre, Waltham, Mass., for its production of *A Man for All Seasons.*

1975 Winner: Concord Players, Concord, Mass., for its production of *A Flurry of Birds* (new bicentennial play). Honorable Mention: Arlington Friends of the Drama, Arlington, Mass., for its production of *Ah, Wilderness!*

The New York Drama Critics' Circle Awards

Established in 1936, the New York Drama Critics' Circle Awards are given annually by the New York Drama Critics' Circle. Although the award was originally given to the "Best American Play," over the years it has been enlarged to include four categories, "Best American Play," "Best Foreign Play," "Best Musical Production," and "Best Play." The recipients are chosen by the voting members of the Critics' Circle who in 1975-76 were Clive Barnes (New York Times), *Harold Clurman* (The Nation), *Brendan Gill* (The New Yorker), *William Glover* (Associated Press), *Martin Gottfried* (New York Post), *Henry Hewes* (Saturday Review/World), *Ted Kalem* (Time), *Walter Kerr* (New York Times), *Jack Kroll* (Newsweek), *Emory Lewis* (The Record), *Hobe Morrison* (Variety), *Norman Nadel* (Scripps-Howard), *Julius Novick* (The Village Voice), *Edith Oliver* (The New Yorker), *George Oppenheimer* (Newsday), *William Raidy* (Newhouse Chain), *Marilyn Stasio* (Cue), *John Simon* (New York Magazine), *Allan Wallach* (Newsday), *Douglas Watt* (The Daily News), *Richard Watts* (New York Post), *and Edwin Wilson* (The Wall Street Journal). *See* Theatre Group Biographies *for voting rules.*

1936 Best American Play: *Winterset*

1937 Best American Play: *High Tor*

1938 Best American Play: *Of Mice and Men*
Best Foreign Play: *Shadow and Substance*

1939 Best Foreign Play: *The White Steed*

1940 Best American Play: *The Time of Your Life*

1941 Best American Play: *Watch on the Rhine*
Best Foreign Play: *The Corn Is Green*

1942 Best Foreign Play: *Blithe Spirit*

1943 Best American Play: *The Patriots*

1944 Best Foreign Play: *Jacobowsky and the Colonel*

1945 Best American Play: *The Glass Menagerie*

1946 Best Musical Production: *Carousel*

1947 Best American Play: *All My Sons*
Best Foreign Play: *No Exit*
Best Musical Production: *Brigadoon*

1948 Best American Play: *A Streetcar Named Desire*
Best Foreign Play: *The Winslow Boy*

1949 Best American Play: *Death of a Salesman*
Best Foreign Play: *The Madwoman of Chaillot*
Best Musical Production: *South Pacific*

1950 Best American Play: *The Member of the Wedding*
Best Foreign Play: *The Cocktail Party*
Best Musical Production: *The Consul*

1951 Best American Play: *Darkness at Noon*
Best Foreign Play: *The Lady's Not for Burning*
Best Musical Production: *Guys and Dolls*

1952 Best American Play: *I Am a Camera*
Best Foreign Play: *Venus Observed*
Best Musical Production: *Pal Joey*
Special Citation: *Don Juan in Hell*

1953 Best American Play: *Picnic*
Best Foreign Play: *The Love of Four Colonels*
Best Musical Production: *Wonderful Town*

1954 Best American Play: *The Teahouse of the August Moon*
Best Foreign Play: *Ondine*
Best Musical Production: *The Golden Apple*

1955 Best American Play: *Cat on a Hot Tin Roof*
Best Foreign Play: *Witness for the Prosecution*
Best Musical Production: *The Saint of Bleecker Street*

1956 Best American Play: *The Diary of Anne Frank*
Best Foreign Play: *Tiger at the Gates*
Best Musical Production: *My Fair Lady*

1957 Best American Play: *Long Day's Journey into Night*
Best Foreign Play: *The Waltz of the Toreadors*
Best Musical Production: *The Most Happy Fella*

1958 Best American Play: *Look Homeward, Angel*
Best Foreign Play: *Look Back in Anger*
Best Musical Production: *The Music Man*

1959 Best American Play: *A Raisin in the Sun*
Best Foreign Play: *The Visit*
Best Musical Production: *La Plume de Ma Tante*

1960 Best American Play: *Toys in the Attic*
Best Foreign Play: *Five Finger Exercise*
Best Musical Production: *Fiorello!*

1961 Best American Play: *All the Way Home*
Best Foreign Play: *A Taste of Honey*
Best Musical Production: *Carnival!*

1962 Best American Play: *The Night of the Iguana*
Best Foreign Play: *A Man for All*

Seasons
Best Musical Production: *How To Succeed in Business Without Really Trying*
1963 Best Play: *Who's Afraid of Virginia Woolf?*
Special Citation: *Beyond the Fringe*
1964 Best Play: *Luther*
Best Musical Production: *Hello, Dolly!*
Special Citation: *The Trojan Women*
1965 Best Play: *The Subject Was Roses*
Best Musical: *Fiddler on the Roof*
1966 Best Play: *The Persecution and Assassination of Marat as Performed by the Inmates of the Asylum of Charenton under the Direction of the Marquis de Sade*
Best Musical: *Man of La Mancha*
1967 Best Play: *The Homecoming*
Best Musical: *Cabaret*
1968 Best Play: *Rosencrantz and Guildenstern Are Dead*
Best Musical: *Your Own Thing*
1969 Best Play: *The Great White Hope*
Best Musical: *1776*
1970 Best Play: *Borstal Boy*
Best American Play: *The Effect of Gamma Rays on Man-in-the-Moon Marigolds*
Best Musical: *Company*
1971 Best Play: *Home*
Best American Play: *The House of Blue Leaves*
Best Musical: *Follies*
1972 Best Play: *That Championship Season*
Best Foreign Play: *The Screens*
Best Musical: *Two Gentlemen of Verona*
Special Citations: *Sticks and Bones, Old Times*
1973 Best Play: *The Changing Room*
Best American Play: *The Hot l Baltimore*
Best Musical: *A Little Night Music*
1974 Best Play: *The Contractor*
Best American Play: *Short Eyes*
Best Musical: *Candide*
1975 Best Play: *Equus*
Best American Play: *The Taking of Miss Janie*
Best Musical: *A Chorus Line*

The Oscars

(See Academy of Motion Picture Arts and Sciences)

The Newspaper Guild of New York Awards in Theatre. Page One Awards.

First given in 1945, the Page One Award was awarded for theatrical achievement in the current season. Selections were made annually (with the exception of 1963, when no award was made because of the newspaper strike) by a board of judges composed of New York journalists. Page One Awards in the theatre were discontinued after 1965.

1945 Laurette Taylor
Deep Are the Roots
On the Town
1946 *Call Me Mister*
1947-48 Clarence Derwent, President of Actors' Equity Association
1949 *Death of a Salesman*
1950 Alec Guinness
Irene Worth
Maurice Evans (recipient of a citation)
1951 Shirley Booth
1952 Jose Ferrer
1953 Victor Moore
1954 John Latouche and Jerome Moross *(The Golden Apple)*
1955 Kim Stanley
Albert Salmi
1956 Paul Muni
1957 Jose Quintero
1958 New York Shakespeare Festival
1959 John Gielgud
Elia Kazan
Geraldine Page
Gwen Verdon
1960 The Living Theatre
1961 Circle in the Square
Joan Plowright
Tammy Grimes
1962 *The Caretaker*
Margaret Leighton
Paul Scofield
1963 No Award
1964 Alec Guinness (for his performance in *Dylan)*
1965 *Fiddler on the Roof*

The Nobel Prizes for Literature

American and foreign Nobel laureates who are playwrights, or authors who have written plays.

1903 Björnstjerne Björnson (Norway)
1904 Jose Echegaray (Spain)
1910 Paul Heyse (Germany)
1912 Gerhart Hauptmann (Germany)
1913 Rabindranath Tagore (India)
1915 Romain Rolland (France)
1922 Jacinto Benavente (Spain)
1923 William Butler Yeats (Ireland)
1925 George Bernard Shaw (England)
1930 Sinclair Lewis (U.S.)
1932 John Galsworthy (England)
1934 Luigi Pirandello (Italy)
1936 Eugene O'Neill (U.S.)
1947 André Gide (France)
1948 T. S. Eliot (England)
1951 Pär Lagerkvist (Sweden)
1957 Albert Camus (France)
1962 John Steinbeck (U.S.)
1969 Samuel Beckett (Ireland—France)

Outer Circle Awards

The Outer Circle Awards have been presented annually since 1950 by the Outer Circle, an organization of writers who cover the New York Theatre for out-of-town newspapers and national publications.

1950 Best play: *The Cocktail Party*
Best musical: *The Consul*
Outstanding performance in minor roles: Daniel Reed *(Come Back, Little Sheba),* Sheila Guyse *(Lost in the Stars)*
1951 Best play: *Billy Budd*
Best musical: *Guys and Dolls*
Best supporting performance: Nomi Mitty *(A Tree Grows in Brooklyn)*
1952 Best play: *Point of No Return*
1953 Best musical: *Wonderful Town.* No award for play.
1954 Best play: *The Caine Mutiny Court-Martial*
Best musical: *Kismet*
Best supporting performance, drama: Eva Marie Saint *(The Trip to Bountiful)*
Best supporting performance, musical: Bibi Osterwald *(The Golden Apple)*
1955 Best play: *Inherit the Wind*
Best musical: *Three for Tonight*
Outstanding performances in supporting roles: Crahan Denton *(Bus Stop),* Gretchen Wyler *(Silk Stockings)*
1956 Best play: *Diary of Anne Frank*
Best musical: *My Fair Lady*
Distinguished performance: Anthony Franciosa *(Hatful of Rain)*
Cited: Alice Pearce *(Fallen Angels);* Peter Larkin, designer *(No Time for Sergeants)*
1957 Best play: *Long Day's Journey into Night*
Best musical: *My Fair Lady*
Distinguished performance, drama: Inga Swenson *(The First Gentleman)*
Distinguished performance, musical: Stubby Kaye *(Li'l Abner)*
Cited: New York City Center Light Opera Co.; Osbert Lancaster, designer *(Hotel Paradiso)*
1958 Best play: *Look Homeward, Angel*
Best musical: *Music Man*
Distinguished performance, drama: Henry Jones *(Sunrise at Campobello)*
Distinguished performance, musical: Jacquelyn McKeever *(Oh Captain!)*
Best set designer: Rouben Ter-Arutunian *(Who Was That Lady I Saw You With)*
Special award: Joe Papp
1959 Best play: *The Visit*
Distinguished performance, drama: Diana Sands *(A Raisin in the Sun)*
Distinguished performance, musical: Tommy Rall *(Juno)*
Set design: Oliver Messel *(Rashomon)*
Special citation: Hal Holbrook *(Mark Twain Tonight)*
1960 Best play: *The Miracle Worker*
Best musical: *Bye Bye Birdie*
Distinguished performance, drama: Risa Schwartz *(The Tenth Man)*
Distinguished performance, musical: Cecil Kellaway *(Greenwillow)*
Special citation: National Phoenix Co. *(Mary Stuart* on tour)
1961 Most over-all creative contribution to the season: *Rhinoceros*
Most effective and imaginative individual contribution to a stage production: Gower Champion *(Carnival!)*
Best ensemble acting: *Big Fish, Little Fish*
Distinguished performance, musical: Don Tompkins *(Wildcat)*
Outstanding achievement in designing set: Oliver Smith *(Camelot)*
Special citation: American Shakespeare Festival Theatre and Academy
1962 Most over-all creative contribution to the season: *No Strings;* George Abbott *(A Funny Thing Happened on the Way to the Forum)*
Best revival: *Anything Goes*
For his contribution to *How To Succeed in Business. . . .*: Rudy Vallee
Most original play and production: *Oh Dad, Poor Dad, . . .*

"For being the first American to play Eliza in *My Fair Lady*": Margot Moser
Special citations: George Freedley; National Repertory Theatre

1963 Outstanding American playwright of the season: Edward Albee
Outstanding staging: Alan Schneider *(Who's Afraid of Virginia Woolf?)*
Outstanding ensemble acting: Cast of *Who's Afraid of Virginia Woolf?*
Outstanding new playwright: Murray Schisgal *(The Tiger* and *The Typists)*
Achievement in staging: William Ball *(Six Characters in Search of an Author)*
Special citations: Alexander H. Cohen; Helen Hayes; Maurice Evans; *Oliver!* "Outstanding creative production"

1964 For "the inspiration it is giving other communities": Lincoln Center for the Performing Arts
Outstanding revival (of a classic play): *The Trojan Women*
Outstanding revival (of a modern play): *The Lower Depths*
Outstanding new playwright: Frank D. Gilroy *(The Subject Was Roses)*
"For consistently fine achievement in the theatre": Beatrice Lillie *(High Spirits)*
"Honoring her first Broadway appearance in an original Broadway production": Carol Burnett *(Fade Out-Fade In)*
"For an outstanding performance in a musical": Inga Swenson *(110 in the Shade)*
"For an outstanding performance": Lee Allen *(Marathon '33)*
"Outstanding debut": Barbara Loden *(After the Fall)*
Posthumous award: Carol Haney, choreographer

1965 City Center Light Opera Company (for consistent excellence)
Tartuffe
Oh, What a Lovely War!
Zero Mostel *(Fiddler on the Roof)*
Mike Nichols (for directing four hits)
Tommy Steele *(Half a Sixpence)*
Sol Hurok (for importing distinguished foreign attractions)
William Hanley (outstanding new playwright)
Association of Producing Artists (for continued progress in repertory)

1966 *Man of La Mancha*
Wait a Minim!
Frank Loesser (for the revival of his work at City Center)
David Merrick (for his contribution to the season)
Institute for Advanced Studies in the Theatre Arts (for its revival of *Phedre*)
Gwen Verdon *(Sweet Charity)*
Angela Lansbury and Beatrice Arthur *(Mame)*
David Donnelly and Patrick Bedford *(Philadelphia, Here I Come)*
Peter Brook (direction, *Marat/Sade*)

1967 *Cabaret*
You're a Good Man, Charlie Brown
America Hurrah
You Know I Can't Hear You When the Water's Running
Martin Balsam *(You Know I Can't Hear You When the Water's Running)*
Alexander H. Cohen (for producing *The Homecoming* and *Black Comedy* and his work in revitalizing the Tony Awards)
Melina Mercouri *(Illya Darling)* and Leslie Uggams *(Hallelujah, Baby!)* (outstanding new personalities)
Joseph Hirsch (direction, *Galileo*)
Constance Towers *(The Sound of Music* revival)
Bil and Cora Baird (for establishing a permanent puppet theatre)

1968 *Rosenkrantz and Guildenstern Are Dead*
The Price
George M!
Your Own Thing
Pearl Bailey and Cab Calloway *(Hello, Dolly!)*
Zoe Caldwell
Harold Gary *(The Price)*
Herman Shumlin (for his career as a director and for his playwriting debut with *Spofford*)
Mike Nichols (direction, *Plaza Suite*)
The Forum and The Public theatres (as important new forces in the American theatre)
Joel Grey *(George M!)*
Helen Hayes *(The Show-Off)*
Zena Jasper *(Saturday Night)*

1969 Sherman Edwards (composer, lyricist, *1776*)
Edwin Sherin (direction, *The Great White Hope*)
Elaine May (direction and author of first part, *Adaptation/Next*)
Lonnie Elder III *(Ceremonies in Dark Old Men)*
Lorraine Serabian *(Zorba)*
Dames at Sea
The Front Page
Linda Lavin *(Little Murders* and *Cop-Out)*
Jules Feiffer *(Little Murders)*
Jean Rosenthal (for contributions to stage lighting)
David Hays (for work with the National Theatre of the Deaf)

1970 *Child's Play*
Company
The Last Sweet Days of Isaac
The White House Murder Case
Brian Bedford *(Private Lives)*
Sandy Duncan *(The Boy Friend)*
Bonnie Franklin *(Applause)*
Lewis J. Stadlen *(Minnie's Boys)*
Frank Grimes and Niall Toibin *(Borstal Boy)*

1971 *Follies*
A Midsummer Night's Dream (Peter Brook)
No, No, Nanette!
Joseph Papp (New York Shakespeare Festival)
Paul Sills *(Story Theatre)*
The Phoenix Theatre (for productions of *The School for Wives* and *The Trial of the Catonsville Nine*)
John Guare (playwright, *The House of Blue Leaves*)
Claire Bloom (*Hedda Gabler* and *A Doll's House*)
Anthony Quayle and Keith Baxter *(Sleuth)*
Susan Bloch (press agent)

1972 *Sticks and Bones*
That Championship Season
Don't Bother Me, I Can't Cope
Chelsea Theatre Center and Equity Library Theatre (for distinctive contributions to the theatre)
Robert Morse *(Sugar)*
Brock Peters *(Lost in the Stars)*
Sada Thompson *(Twigs)*
Marlyn Criss *(Kaddish)*
Rosemary Harris *(Old Times)*
John Houseman (for a long-standing contribution to the theatre as writer and director)

1973 Christopher Plummer *(Cyrano)*
Michele Lee *(Seesaw)*
Debbie Reynolds *(Irene)*
Ellis Rabb (direction, *A Streetcar Named Desire*)
Bob Fosse (direction, *Pippin*)
Julie Harris *(The Last of Mrs. Lincoln)*
The entire cast of *The Women* (for ensemble playing)

1974 *A Moon for the Misbegotten*
Candide
Noel Coward in Two Keys
Carol Channing *(Lorelei)*
George Rose *(My Fat Friend)*
Doris Roberts *(Bad Habits)*
Janie Sell and Ann Reinking *(Over Here)*
Sammy Cahn
Patrician Birch (choreography)
Mark Medoff (playwright, *When You Comin Back, Red Ryder?*)

1975 Arts Council of Great Britain
Equus
Peter Shaffer (playwright, *Equus*)
Anthony Hopkins and Peter Firth *(Equus)*
Ellen Burstyn and Charles Grodin (for outstanding ensemble playing, *Same Time, Next Year*)
Maggie Smith *(Private Lives)*
Geraldine Page *(Absurd Person Singular)*
John Cullum and Chip Ford *(Shenandoah)*
Tovah Feldshuh *(Rodgers and Hart, Yentl, Dreyfus in Rehearsal)*
Leslie Lee (playwright, *First Breeze of Summer*)
Tom Jones and Harvey Schmidt (contributions to the musical theatre through the Portfolio Studio)
Long Wharf Theatre

Page One Awards

(See Newspaper Guild of New York)

The Pulitzer Prizes for Drama

The Pulitzer Prize for drama is awarded yearly to "the original American play performed in New York which shall best represent the educational value and power of the stage in raising the standard of good morals and good manners."

1917-18 *Why Marry?*, by Jesse Lynch Williams
1918-19 No Award
1919-20 *Beyond the Horizon*, by Eugene O'Neill
1920-21 *Miss Lulu Bett*, by Zona Gale
1921-22 *Anna Christie*, by Eugene O'Neill
1922-23 *Icebound*, by Owen David
1923-24 *Hell-Bent fer Heaven*, by Hatcher Hughes

1924-25 *They Knew What They Wanted,* by Sidney Howard
1925-26 *Craig's Wife,* by George Kelly
1926-27 *In Abraham's Bosom,* by Paul Green
1927-28 *Strange Interlude,* by Eugene O'Neill
1928-29 *Street Scene,* by Elmer Rice
1929-30 *The Green Pastures,* by Marc Connelly
1930-31 *Alison's House,* by Susan Glaspell
1931-32 *Of Thee I Sing,* by George S. Kaufman, Morrie Ryskind, and Ira and George Gershwin
1932-33 *Both Your Houses,* by Maxwell Anderson
1933-34 *Men in White,* by Sidney Kingsley
1934-35 *The Old Maid,* by Zoe Akins
1935-36 *Idiot's Delight,* by Robert E. Sherwood
1936-37 *You Can't Take It with You,* by Moss Hart and George S. Kaufman
1937-38 *Our Town,* by Thornton Wilder
1938-39 *Abe Lincoln in Illinois,* by Robert E. Sherwood
1939-40 *The Time of Your Life,* by William Saroyan
1940-41 *There Shall Be No Night,* by Robert E. Sherwood
1941-42 No Award
1942-43 *The Skin of Our Teeth,* by Thornton Wilder
1943-44 No Award
1944-45 *Harvey,* by Mary Coyle Chase
1945-46 *State of the Union,* by Howard Lindsay and Russel Crouse
1946-47 No Award
1947-48 *A Streetcar Named Desire,* by Tennessee Williams
1948-49 *Death of a Salesman,* by Arthur Miller
1949-50 *South Pacific,* by Richard Rodgers, Oscar Hammerstein II and Joshua Logan
1950-51 No Award
1951-52 *The Shrike,* by Joseph Kramm
1952-53 *Picnic,* by William Inge
1953-54 *The Teahouse of the August Moon,* by John Patrick
1954-55 *Cat on a Hot Tin Roof,* by Tennessee Williams
1955-56 *The Diary of Anne Frank,* by Frances Goodrich and Albert Hackett
1956-57 *Long Day's Journey into Night,* by Eugene O'Neill
1957-58 *Look Homeward, Angel,* by Ketti Frings
1958-59 *J.B.,* by Archibald MacLeish
1959-60 *Fiorello!,* by Jerome Weidman, George Abbott, Sheldon Harnick, and Jerry Bock
1960-61 *All the Way Home,* by Tad Mosel
1961-62 *How To Succeed in Business Without Really Trying,* by Abe Burrows, Willie Gilbert, Jack Weinstock, and Frank Loesser
1962-63 No Award
1963-64 No Award
1964-65 *The Subject Was Roses,* by Frank D. Gilroy
1965-66 No Award
1966-67 *A Delicate Balance,* by Edward Albee
1967-68 No Award
1968-69 *The Great White Hope,* by Howard Sackler
1969-70 *No Place To Be Somebody,* by Charles Gordone
1970-71 *The Effect of Gamma Rays on Man-in-the-Moon Marigolds,* by Paul Zindel
1971-72 No Award
1972-73 *That Championship Season,* by Jason Miller
1973-74 No Award
1974-75 *Seascape,* by Edward Albee

The Shubert Foundation Awards

Established in 1954 in the memory of Sam S. Shubert (1875-1905), the Shubert Foundation Award is given annually "In recognition of the most outstanding individual contribution to the New York theatrical season."

1954 Victor Borge
1955 Joshua Logan
1956 Kermit Bloomgarden
1957 Roger L. Stevens
1958 David Merrick
1959 Sol Hurok
1960 George Abbott
1961 Oliver Smith
1962 No Award
1963 Alexander H. Cohen
1964 No Award
1965 Mike Nichols
1966 Richard Rodgers
1967 Vincent Sardi, Sr.
1968 Neil Simon
1969 Hal Prince
1970 No Award
1971 Danny Kaye
1972 No Award
1973 Robert Whitehead

Theatre Library Association

THE GEORGE FREEDLEY MEMORIAL AWARD

This award was established in 1968 by The Theatre Library Association in memory of George Freedley, the theatre historian, critic, author, and first curator of The New York Public Library Theatre Collection. It honors a published work in the field of theatre in the United States relating to live performance, including vaudeville, puppetry, pantomime, and circus—biography, history, and criticism. Awards are presented to authors on the basis of scholarship, readability, and general contribution to the broadening of knowledge.

1968 Louis Shaeffer, *O'Neill, Son and Playwright*
Honorable Mention:
Edward Craig, *Gordon Craig*
Walther R. Volbach, *Adolphe Appia, Prophet of the Modern Theatre*
1969 Charles H. Shattuck, *The Hamlet of Edwin Booth*
1970 Brooks Atkinson, *Broadway*
Honorable Mention:
Joseph Leach, *Bright Particular Star: The Life and Times of Charlotte Cushman*
1971 James M. Symons, *Meyerhold's Theatre of the Grotesque: The Post-Revolutionary Production*
1972 John Houseman, *Run-through*
Lael Wertenbaker and Jean Rosenthal, *The Magic of Light*
Honorable Mention:
Marvin Rosenberg, *The Masks of King Lear*
1973 Stephen Orgel and Roy Strong, *Inigo Jones: The Theatre of the Stuart Court*
Honorable Mention:
Richard Leacraft, *The Development of the English Playhouse*
Louis Shaeffer, *O'Neill, Son and Artist*
1974 Robert C. Toll, *Blacking Up: The Minstrel Show in Nineteenth-century America*
Honorable Mention:
John F. Wharton, *Life Among the Playwrights*

THE THEATRE LIBRARY ASSOCIATION AWARD

This award was established in 1973 for the purpose of honoring a book in the areas of recorded performance, including motion pictures and television, to complement the Association's George Freedley Memorial Award, which is presented to books related to live performance.

1973 Donald Bogle, *Toms, Coons, Mulattoes, Mammies, and Bucks*
Honorable Mention:
David G. Yellin, *Fred Freed and the Television Documentary*
1974 Gerald S. Lesser, *Children and Television: Lessons from Sesame Street*

The Daniel Blum THEATRE WORLD Awards

Given each year since 1945 by Daniel Blum, editor of Theatre World, *the Theatre World Award is made in recognition of "Promising Personalities" who have appeared throughout the season. (For the 1944-45 and 1945-46 seasons, the recipients of the Theatre World Awards were not cited for a particular performance, therefore we have listed all of their credits for those seasons.)*

1944-45 Bambi Linn *(Carousel)*
Judy Holliday *(Kiss Them for Me)*
Richard Davis *(Kiss Them for Me)*
John Lund *(The Hasty Heart)*
Betty Comden *(On the Town)*
John Raitt *(Carousel)*
Margaret Phillips *(The Late George Apley)*
Richard Hart *(Dark of the Moon)*
Charles Lang *(Down to Miami* and *The Overtons)*
Donald Murphy *(For Keeps, Signature,* and *Common Ground)*
Nancy Noland *(Common Ground)*
1945-46 Beatrice Pearson *(The Mermaids Singing)*
Marlon Brando *(Truckline Cafe)*
Barbara Bel Geddes *(Deep Are the Roots)*
Paul Douglas *(Born Yesterday)*
Burt Lancaster *(A Sound of Hunting)*
Patricia Marshall *(The Day Before Spring)*
Bill Callahan *(Call Me Mister)*
Wendell Corey *(The Wind Is Ninety* and *Dream Girl)*
Mary James *(Apple of His Eye)*
1946-47 David Wayne *(Finian's Rainbow)*
Marion Bell *(Brigadoon)*
Peter Cookson *(Message for Margaret)*
Patricia Neal *(Another Part of the Forest)*

James Mitchell *(Brigadoon)*
Ellen Hanley *(Barefoot Boy with Cheek)*
Keith Andes *(The Chocolate Soldier)*
John Jordan *(The Wanhope Building)*
Dorothea MacFarland *(Oklahoma!)*
Ann Crowley *(Carousel)*
George Keane *(Brigadoon)*

1947-48 Douglas Watson *(Antony and Cleopatra)*
Meg Mundy *(The Respectful Prostitute)*
James Whitemore *(Command Decision)*
Valerie Bettis *(Inside U.S.A.)*
Whitfield Conner *(Macbeth)*
Patricia Wymore *(Hold It)*
Ralph Meeker *(Mister Roberts)*
Peggy Maley *(Joy to the World)*
Edward Bryce *(The Cradle Will Rock)*
June Lockhart *(For Love or Money)*
Mark Dawson *(High Button Shoes)*
Estelle Loring *(Inside U.S.A.)*

1948-49 Carol Channing *(Lend an Ear)*
Tod Andrews *(Summer and Smoke)*
Mary McCarty *(Sleepy Hollow)*
Gene Nelson *(Lend an Ear)*
Allyn McLerie *(Where's Charley?)*
Byron Palmer *(Where's Charley?)*
Cameron Mitchell *(Death of a Salesman)*
Jean Carson *(Bravo)*
Julie Harris *(Sundown Beach)*
Bob Scheerer *(Lend an Ear)*
Doe Avedon *(The Young and Fair)*
Richard Derr *(The Traitor)*

1949-50 Charlton Heston *(Design for a Stained Glass Window)*
Priscilla Gillette *(Regina)*
Rick Jason *(Now I Lay Me Down to Sleep)*
Grace Kelly *(The Father)*
Don Hammer *(The Man)*
Marcia Henderson *(Peter Pan)*
Charles Nolte *(Design for a Stained Glass Window)*
Lydia Clarke *(Detective Story)*
Roger Price *(Tickets, Please!)*
Nancy Andrews *(Touch and Go)*
Phil Arthur *(With a Silk Thread)*
Barbara Brade *(The Velvet Glove)*

1950-51 Richard Burton *(The Lady's Not for Burning)*
Barbara Ashley *(Out of This World)*
Russell Nype *(Call Me Madam)*
Maureen Stapleton *(The Rose Tattoo)*
Eli Wallach *(The Rose Tattoo)*
Isabel Bigley *(Guys and Dolls)*
William Smithers *(Romeo and Juliet)*
Jack Palance *(Darkness at Noon)*
Marcia Van Dyke *(A Tree Grows in Brooklyn)*
Martin Brooks *(Burning Bright)*
Pat Crowley *(Southern Exposure)*
James Daly *(Major Barbara and Mary Rose)*
Cloris Leachman *(A Story for a Sunday Evening)*

1951-52 Audrey Hepburn *(Gigi)*
Patricia Benoit *(Glad Tidings)*
Tony Bavaar *(Paint Your Wagon)*
Charles Proctor *(Twilight Walk)*
Virginia de Luce *(New Faces of 1952)*
Kim Stanley *(The Chase)*
Ronny Graham *(New Faces of 1952)*
Helen Wood *(Seventeen)*
Conrad Janis *(The Brass Ring)*
Peter Conlow *(Courtin' Time)*
Diana Herbert *(The Number)*
Dick Kallman *(Seventeen)*
Marian Winters *(I Am a Camera)*
Eric Sinclair *(Much Ado About Nothing)*

1952-53 Geraldine Page *(Mid-Summer)*
Paul Newman *(Picnic)*
Eileen Heckart *(Picnic)*
Ray Stricklyn *(The Climate of Eden)*
Edith Adams *(Wonderful Town)*
Rosemary Harris *(The Climate of Eden)*
John Kerr *(Bernardine)*
Gwen Verdon *(Can-Can)*
Johnny Stewart *(Bernadine)*
Richard Kiley *(Misalliance)*
Penelope Munday *(The Climate of Eden)*
Peter Kelley *(Two's Company)*
Gloria Marlow *(In Any Language)*
Sheree North *(Hazel Flagg)*

1953-54 James Dean *(The Immoralist)*
Carol Haney *(The Pajama Game)*
Leo Penn *(The Girl on the Via Flaminia)*
Orson Bean *(Almanac)*
Eva Marie Saint *(The Trip to Bountiful)*
Harry Belafonte *(Almanac)*
Kay Medford *(Lullaby)*
Joan Diener *(Kismet)*
Ben Gazzara *(End As a Man)*
Elizabeth Montgomery *(Late Love)*
Jonathan Lucas *(The Golden Apple)*
Scott Merrill *(The Threepenny Opera)*

1954-55 Christopher Plummer *(The Dark Is Light Enough)*
Anthony Perkins *(Tea and Sympathy)*
Jacqueline Brookes *(The Cretan Woman)*
Loretta Leversee *(Home Is the Hero)*
Jack Lord *(The Traveling Lady)*
Dennis Patrick *(The Wayward Saint)*
Shirl Conway *(Plain and Fancy)*
Julie Andrews *(The Boy Friend)*
David Daniels *(Plain and Fancy)*
Page Johnson *(In April Once)*
Mary Fickett *(Tea and Sympathy)*
Barbara Cook *(Plain and Fancy)*

1955-56 Andy Griffith *(No Time for Sergeants)*
Anthony Franciosa *(A Hatful of Rain)*
Susan Strasberg *(The Diary of Anne Frank)*
Jayne Mansfield *(Will Success Spoil Rock Hunter?)*
Richard Davalos *(A View from the Bridge)*
Sarah Marshal *(The Ponder Heart)*
Laurence Harvey *(Island of Goats)*
Earle Hyman *(Mister Johnson)*
Gaby Rodgers *(Mister Johnson)*
Diane Cilento *(Tiger at the Gates)*
Al Hedison *(A Month in the Country)*
John Michael King *(My Fair Lady)*
Susan Johnson *(The Most Happy Fella)*
Fritz Weaver *(The Chalk Garden)*

1956-57 Sydney Chaplin *(Bells Are Ringing)*
Inga Swenson *(The First Gentleman)*
Peter Palmer *(Li'l Abner)*
Jason Robards *(Long Day's Journey into Night)*
Sylvia Daneel *(The Tunnel of Love)*
Carol Lynley *(The Potting Shed)*
Peter Donat *(The First Gentleman)*
Pippa Scott *(Child of Fortune)*
George Grizzard *(The Happiest Millionaire)*
Peggy Cass *(Auntie Mame)*
Cliff Robertson *(Orpheus Decending)*
Bradford Dillman *(Long Day's Journey into Night)*

1957-58 Joan Hovis *(Love Me Little)*
Robert Morse *(Say, Darling)*
Wynne Miller *(Li'l Abner)*
Colleen Dewhurst *(Children of Darkness)*
George C. Scott *(Richard III)*
Eddie Hodges *(The Music Man)*
Jacquelyn McKeever *(Oh Captain!)*
Richard Easton *(The Country Wife)*
Carol Lawrence *(West Side Story)*
Anne Bancroft *(Two for the Seesaw)*
Warren Berlinger *(Blue Denim)*
Timmy Everett *(The Dark at the Top of the Stairs)*

1958-59 Paul Roebling *(A Desert Incident)*
Ben Piazza *(Kataki)*
Tammy Grimes *(Look After Lulu)*
Larry Hagman *(God and Kate Murphy)*
Dolores Hart *(The Pleasure of His Company)*
William Shatner *(The World of Suzie Wong)*
Susan Oliver *(Patate)*
Lou Antonio *(The Buffalo Skinner)*
Ina Ballin *(A Majority of One)*
Rip Torn *(Sweet Bird of Youth)*
Pat Suzuki *(Flower Drum Song)*
Roger Mollien (of the French Theatre National Populaire)
Richard Cross *(Maria Golovin)*

1959-60 Carol Burnett *(Once Upon a Mattress)*
Jane Fonda *(There Was a Little Girl)*
Warren Beatty *(A Loss of Roses)*
Anita Gillette *(Russell Patterson's Sketchbook)*
George Maharis *(The Zoo Story)*
Donald Madden *(Julius Caesar)*
Patty Duke *(The Miracle Worker)*
John McMartin *(Little Mary Sunshine)*
Eileen Brennan *(Little Mary Sunshine)*
Elisa Loti *(Come Share My House)*
Dick Van Dyke *(The Boys Against the Girls)*
Lauri Peters *(The Sound of Music)*

1960-61 Robert Goulet *(Camelot)*
James MacArthur *(Invitation to a March)*
Joyce Bulifant *(Whisper to Me)*
June Harding *(Cry of the Raindrop)*
Dennis Cooney *(Every Other Evil)*
Joan Hackett *(Call Me by My Rightful Name)*
Bruce Yarnell *(The Happiest Girl in the World)*
Ron Husmann *(Tenderloin)*
Nancy Dussault *(Do Re Mi)*

1961-62 John Stride *(Romeo and Juliet)*
Barbara Harris *(Oh, Dad, Poor Dad, Mamma's Hung You in the Closet and I'm Feelin' So Sad)*
Don Galloway *(Bring Me a Warm Body)*
Brenda Vaccaro *(Everybody Loves Opal)*
Sean Garrison *(Half-Past Wednesday)*
Janet Margolin *(Daughter of Silence)*
Peter Fonda *(Blood, Sweat and Stanley Poole)*
Robert Redford *(Sunday in New York)*
Karen Morrow *(Sing, Muse!)*
James Earl Jones *(Moon on a Rainbow Shawl)*

Elizabeth Ashley *(Take Her, She's Mine)*
Keith Baxter *(A Man for All Seasons)*
1962-63 Dorothy Loudon *(Nowhere To Go But Up)*
Liza Minnelli *(Best Foot Forward)*
Swen Swenson *(Little Me)*
Robert Drivas *(Mrs. Dally Has a Lover)*
Bob Gentry *(Angels of Anadarko)*
Estelle Parsons *(Mrs. Dally Has a Lover)*
Melinda Dillon *(Who's Afraid of Virginia Woolf?)*
Brandon Maggart *(Put It in Writing)*
Julienne Marie *(The Boys from Syracuse)*
Diana Sands *(Tiger, Tiger Burning Bright)*
Alan Arkin *(Enter Laughing)*
1963-64 Jennifer West *(Dutchman)*
Kitty Lester *(Cabin in the Sky)*
Barbara Loden *(After the Fall)*
Imelda De Martin *(The Amorous Flea)*
Philip Proctor *(The Amorous Flea)*
Gloria Bleezarde *(Never Live Over a Pretzel Factory)*
Gilbert Price *(Jerico-Jim Crow)*
Alan Alda *(Fair Game for Lovers)*
Claude Giraud *(Phedre)*
John Tracy *(Telemachus Clay)*
1964-65 Michael O'Sullivan *(Tartuffe)*
Carolyn Coates *(The Trojan Women)*
Victor Spinetti *(Oh, What a Lovely War!)*
Bea Richards *(The Amen Corner)*
Joanna Pettit *(Poor Richard)*
Jaime Sanchez *(Conerico Was Here To Stay* and *The Toilet)*
Clarence Williams III *(Slow Dance on the Killing Ground)*
Linda Lavin *(Wet Paint)*
Robert Walker *(I Knock at the Door* and *Pictures in the Hallway)*
Joyce Jillson *(The Roar of the Greasepaint, The Smell of the Crowd)*
Luba Lisa *(I Had a Ball)*
1965-66 Faye Dunaway *(Hogan's Goat)*
David Carradine *(The Royal Hunt of the Sun)*
Gloria Foster *(Medea)*
John Davidson *(Oklahoma!)*
John Cullum *(On a Clear Day You Can See Forever)*
Zoe Caldwell *(Slapstick Tragedy)*
Lesley Ann Warren *(Drat! The Cat!)*
Jerry Lanning *(Mame)*
Robert Hooks *(Where's Daddy?* and *Day of Absence)*
April Shawhan *(3 Bags Full)*
Richard Mulligan *(Mating Dance* and *Hogan's Goat)*
Sandra Smith *(Any Wednesday)*
1966-67 Bonnie Bedelia *(My Sweet Charlie)*
Richard Benjamin *(The Star Spangled Girl)*
Dustin Hoffman *(Eh?)*
Reva Rose *(You're a Good Man, Charlie Brown)*
Sheila Smith *(Mame)*
Terry Kiser *(Fortune and Men's Eyes)*
Robert Salvio *(Hamp)*
Connie Stevens *(The Star Spangled Girl)*
Pamela Tiffin *(Dinner at Eight)*
Jon Voight *(That Summer—That Fall)*
Christopher Walken *(The Rose Tattoo)*
Leslie Uggams *(Hallelujah, Baby!)*
1967-68 David Birney *(Summertree)*
Pamela Burnell *(Arms and the Man)*
Sandy Duncan *(Ceremony of Innocence)*
Jordan Christopher *(Black Comedy)*
Julie Gregg *(The Happy Time)*
Jack Crawder *(Hello, Dolly!)*
Stephen Joyce *(Stephen D)*
Bernadette Peters *(George M!)*
Alice Playten *(Henry, Sweet Henry)*
Mike Reysent *(The Happy Time)*
Rusty Thacker *(Your Own Thing)*
Brenda Smiley *(Scuba Duba)*
1968-69 Jane Alexander *(The Great White Hope)*
David Cryer *(Come Summer)*
Ed Evanko *(Canterbury Tales)*
Blythe Danner *(The Miser)*
Lauren Jones *(Does a Tiger Wear a Necktie?)*
Ken Howard *(1776)*
Ron Liebman *(We Bombed in New Haven)*
Marian Mercer *(Promises, Promises)*
Jill O'Hara *(Promises, Promises)*
Ron O'Neal *(No Place To Be Somebody)*
Al Pacino *(Does a Tiger Wear a Necktie?)*
Marlene Warfield *(The Great White Hope)*
1969-70 Susan Brown *(Company)*
Donny Burks *(Billy Noname)*
Catherine Burns *(Dear Janet Rosenberg, Dear Mr. Kooning)*
Len Cariou *(Henry V* and *Applause)*
Bonnie Franklin *(Applause)*
David Holliday *(Coco)*
Katharine Houghton *(A Scent of Flowers)*
David Rounds *(Child's Play)*
Melba Moore *(Purlie)*
Lewis J. Stadlen *(Minnie's Boys)*
Kristoffer Tabori *(How Much, How Much?)*
Fredricka Weber *(The Last Sweet Days of Isaac)*
1970-71 Clifton Davis *(Do It Again)*
Julie Garfield *(Uncle Vanya)*
Martha Henry (Lincoln Center Repertory Company)
Michael Douglas *(Pinkville)*
James Naughton *(Long Day's Journey into Night)*
Tricia O'Neil *(Two by Two)*
Ayn Ruyman *(The Gingerbread Lady)*
Kipp Osborne *(Butterflies Are Free)*
Roger Rathborn *(No, No, Nanette)*
Jennifer Salt *(Father's Day)*
Joan Van Ark *(School for Wives)*
Walter Willison *(Two by Two)*
1971-72 Jonelle Allen *(Two Gentlemen of Verona)*
William Atherton *(Sugga)*
Richard Backus *(Promenade, All!)*
Mureen Anderman *(Moonchildren)*
Adrienne Barbeau *(Grease)*
Robert Foxworth *(The Crucible)*
Jess Richards *(On the Town)*
Cara Duff-McCormick *(Moon Children)*
Elaine Joyce *(Sugar)*
Ben Vereen *(Jesus Christ Superstar)*
Beatrice Winde *(Ain't Supposed To Die a Natural Death)*
James Woods *(Moonchildren)*
1972-73 Patricia Elliott *(A Little Night Music)*
James Farentino *(A Streetcar Named Desire)*
Brian Farrell *(The Last of Mrs. Lincoln)*
Kelly Garrett *(Mother Earth)*
Victor Garber *(Ghosts)*
Mori Gorman *(The Hot l Baltimore)*
Trish Hawkins *(The Hot l Baltimore)*
Laurence Gittard *(A Little Night Music)*
Monte Markham *(Irene)*
D. Jamin-Bartlett *(A Little Night Music)*
Jennifer Warren *(6 Rms Riv Vu)*
John Rubinstein *(Pippin)*
1973-74 Mark Baker *(Candide)*
Maureen Brennan *(Candide)*
Conchata Farrell *(The Sea Horse)*
Ralph Carter *(Raisin)*
Thom Christopher *(Noel Coward in Two Keys)*
Ernestine Jackson *(Raisin)*
Ann Reinking *(Over Here)*
John Driver *(Over Here)*
Michael Moriarty *(Find Your Way Home)*
Janie Sell *(Over Here)*
Mary Woronov *(Boom Boom Room)*
Joe Morton *(Raisin)*

The Tony Awards

(See American Theatre Wing Antoinette Perry Awards)

The Annual VARIETY New York Drama Critics Poll

In 1939, Variety *began to publish the results of an annual poll taken of drama critics selected from major New York daily newspapers and nationally circulated magazines. The following is a listing of the winners of each poll in their respective categories. The poll has been discontinued.*

BEST PERFORMANCE BY A MALE LEAD IN A STRAIGHT PLAY

1939 Maurice Evans *(Hamlet)*
1940 Alfred Lunt *(There Shall Be No Night)* tied with Barry Fitzgerald *(Juno and the Paycock)*
1941 Paul Lukas *(Watch on the Rhine)*
1942 Burgess Meredith *(Candida)*
1943 Alfred Lunt *(The Pirate)*
1944 Elliott Nugent *(The Voice of the Turtle)*
1945 Frank Fay *(Harvey)*
1946 Laurence Olivier *(Henry IV, Part 1* and *Oedipus)*
1947 Dudley Digges *(The Iceman Cometh)* tied with Fredric March *(Years Ago)*
1948 Paul Kelly *(Command Decision)*
1949 Lee J. Cobb *(Death of a Salesman)*
1950 Alec Guinness *(The Cocktail Party)*
1951 Claude Rains *(Darkness at Noon)*
1952 Jose Ferrer *(The Shrike)*
1953 Victor Moore *(On Borrowed Time)*
1954 Lloyd Nolan *(The Caine Mutiny Court-Martial)*
1955 Paul Muni *(Inherit the Wind)*
1956 Michael Redgrave *(Tiger at the Gates)*
1957 Fredric March *(Long Day's Journey into Night)*
1958 Ralph Bellamy *(Sunrise at Campobello)*
1959 Jason Robards *(The Disenchanted)*
1960 Jason Robards *(Toys in the Attic)*

1961 Laurence Olivier (as Henry II in *Becket)*
1962 Paul Scofield *(A Man for All Seasons)*
1963 Arthur Hill *(Who's Afraid of Virginia Woolf?)*
1964 Alec Guinness *(Dylan)*
1965 Walter Matthau *(The Odd Couple)*
1966 Nicol Williamson *(Inadmissable Evidence)*
1967 Paul Rogers *(The Homecoming)*
1968 Albert Finney *(A Day in the Death of Joe Egg)*
1969 James Earl Jones *(The Great White Hope)*
1970 Fritz Weaver *(Child's Play)*
1971 Ralph Richardson *(Home)*
1972 Jason Robards *(The Country Girl)*

BEST PERFORMANCE BY A FEMME LEAD IN A STRAIGHT PLAY

1939 Judith Anderson *(Family Portrait)* tied with Ethel Waters *(Mamba's Daughters)*
1940 Sara Allgood *(Juno and the Paycock)*
1941 Gertrude Lawrence *(Lady in the Dark)*
1942 Judith Anderson *(Macbeth)*
1943 Tallulah Bankhead *(The Skin of Our Teeth)*
1944 Margaret Sullavan *(The Voice of the Turtle)*
1945 Laurette Taylor *(The Glass Menagerie)*
1946 Betty Field *(Dream Girl)*
1947 Ingrid Bergman *(Joan of Lorraine)*
1948 Judith Anderson *(Medea)*
1949 Martita Hunt *(The Madwoman of Chaillot)*
1950 Shirley Booth *(Come Back, Little*
1951 Uta Hagen *(The Country Girl)* tied with Maureen Stapleton *(The Rose Tattoo)*
1952 Julie Harris *(I Am a Camera)*
1953 Shirley Booth *(Time of the Cuckoo)* tied with Geraldine Page *(Mid-Summer)*
1954 Audrey Hepburn *(Ondine)* tied with Deborah Kerr *(Tea and Sympathy)*
1955 Kim Stanley *(Bus Stop)*
1956 Julie Harris *(The Lark)*
1957 Florence Eldridge *(Long Day's Journey into Night)*
1958 Jo Van Fleet *(Look Homeward, Angel)*
1959 Geraldine Page *(Sweet Bird of Youth)*
1960 Anne Bancroft *(The Miracle Worker)*
1961 Joan Plowright *(A Taste of Honey)*
1962 Margaret Leighton *(The Night of the Iguana)*
1963 Uta Hagen *(Who's Afraid of Virginia Woolf?)*
1964 Sandy Dennis *(Any Wednesday)*
1965 Bea Richards *(The Amen Corner)* tied with Irene Worth *(Tiny Alice)*
1966 Rosemary Harris *(The Lion in Winter* and *You Can't Take It with You)*
1967 Beryl Reid *(The Killing of Sister George)*
1968 Zoe Caldwell *(The Prime of Miss Jean Brodie)*
1969 Jane Alexander *(The Great White Hope)*
1970 Tammy Grimes *(Private Lives)*
1971 Maureen Stapleton *(The Gingerbread Lady)*
1972 Sada Thompson *(Twigs)*

BEST PERFORMANCE BY A MALE LEAD IN A MUSICAL

1942 Danny Kaye *(Let's Face It)*
1943 Alfred Drake *(Oklahoma!)*
1944 Bobby Clark *(Mexican Hayride)*
1945 John Raitt *(Carousel)*
1946 Ray Bolger *(Three to Make Ready)*
1947 Bobby Clark *(Would-Be Gentleman)*
1948 Paul Hartman *(Angel in the Wings)* tied with Jack McCauley *(High Button Shoes)*
1949 Ezio Pinza *(South Pacific)*
1950 George Guetary *(Arms and the Girl)* tied with Todd Duncan *(Lost in the Stars)*
1951 Yul Brynner *(The King and I)*
1952 Phil Silvers *(Top Banana)*
1953 Jack Whiting *(Hazel Flagg)*
1954 Alfred Drake *(Kismet)*
1955 Walter Slezak *(Fanny)*
1956 Rex Harrison *(My Fair Lady)*
1957 Fernando Lamas *(Happy Hunting)*
1958 Robert Preston *(The Music Man)*
1959 Andy Griffith *(Destry Rides Again)*
1960 Tom Bosley *(Fiorello!)*
1961 Richard Burton *(Camelot)*
1962 Robert Morse *(How To Succeed in Business Without Really Trying)*
1963 Sid Caesar *(Little Me)*
1964 Steve Lawrence *(What Makes Sammy Run?)*
1965 Zero Mostel *(Fiddler on the Roof)*
1966 Richard Kiley *(Man of La Mancha)*
1967 Robert Preston *(I Do! I Do!)*
1968 No Selection
1969 Jerry Orbach *(Promises, Promises)*
1970 Cleavon Little *(Purlie)*
1971 Hal Linden *(The Rothschilds)*
1972 Phil Silvers *(A Funny Thing Happened on the Way to the Forum)*

BEST PERFORMANCE BY A FEMME LEAD IN A MUSICAL

1942 Eve Arden *(Let's Face It)*
1943 Ethel Merman *(Something for the Boys)*
1944 Mary Martin *(One Touch of Venus)*
1945 Beatrice Lillie *(Seven Lively Arts)*
1946 Ethel Merman *(Annie Get Your Gun)*
1947 Marion Bell *(Brigadoon)*
1948 Beatrice Lillie *(Inside U.S.A.)*
1949 Mary Martin *(South Pacific)*
1950 Patricia Neway *(The Consul)*
1951 Shirley Booth *(A Tree Grows in Brooklyn)*
1952 Vivienne Segal *(Pal Joey)*
1953 Rosalind Russell *(Wonderful Town)*
1954 Shirley Booth *(By the Beautiful Sea)* tied with Renee Jeanmaire *(The Girl in Pink Tights)*
1955 Gwen Verdon *(Damn Yankees)*
1956 Julie Andrews *(My Fair Lady)*
1957 Judy Holliday *(Bells Are Ringing)*
1958 Lena Horne *(Jamaica)*
1959 Ethel Merman *(Gypsy)*
1960 Mary Martin *(The Sound of Music)*
1961 Tammy Grimes *(The Unsinkable Molly Brown)*
1962 Diahann Carroll *(No Strings)*
1963 Barbara Cook *(She Loves Me)* tied with Vivien Leigh *(Tovarich)*
1964 Carol Channing *(Hello, Dolly!)*
1965 Elizabeth Allen *(Do I Hear A Waltz?)* tied with Liza Minnelli *(Flora, the Red Menace)*
1966 Gwen Verdon *(Sweet Charity)*
1967 Barbara Harris *(The Apple Tree)*
1968 Patricia Routledge *(Darling of the Day)*
1969 Maria Karnilova *(Zorba)* tied with Angela Lansbury *(Dear World)*
1970 Lauren Bacall *(Applause)*
1971 Alexis Smith *(Follies)*
1972 Jonelle Allen *(Two Gentlemen of Verona*

BEST PERFORMANCE BY AN ACTOR IN A SUPPORTING PART

1942 Joseph Buloff *(Spring Again)*
1943 Rhys Williams *(Harriet)*
1944 Jose Ferrer *(Othello)* tied with Montgomery Clift *(The Searching Wind)* and Arnold Korff *(The Searching Wind)*
1945 Frederick O'Neal *(Anna Lucasta)*
1946 Marlon Brando *(Truckline Cafe)*
1947 Tom Ewell *(John Loves Mary)* tied with David Wayne *(Finian's Rainbow)*
1948 Karl Malden *(A Streetcar Named Desire)*
1949 No Choice
1950 Robert Flemyng *(The Cocktail Party)* tied with Kent Smith *(The Wisteria Trees)*
1951 Eli Wallach *(The Rose Tattoo)*
1952 John Cromwell *(Point of No Return)*
1953 John Williams *(Dial 'M' for Murder)*
1954 John Kerr *(Tea and Sympathy)*
1955 Ed Begley *(Inherit the Wind)*
1956 Anthony Franciosa *(A Hatful of Rain)*
1957 Frank Conroy *(The Potting Shed)*
1958 Henry Jones *(Sunrise at Campobello)*
1959 Walter Matthau *(Once More, With Feeling)*
1960 Robert Morse *(Take Me Along)*
1961 Martin Gabel *(Big Fish, Little Fish)*
1962 Charles Nelson Reilly *(How To Succeed in Business Without Really Trying)*
1963 Alan Arkin *(Enter Laughing)*
1964 Hume Cronyn *(Hamlet)*
1965 John Heffernan *(Tiny Alice)* tied with Victor Spinetti *(Oh, What a Lovely War!)*
1966 Eamon Kelly *(Philadelphia, Here I Come!)* tied with Hirma Sherman *(Where's Daddy?)* and Robert Symonds *(The Caucasian Chalk Circle)*
1967 Joel Grey *(Cabaret)*
1968 Harold Gary *(The Price)*
1969 Al Pacino *(Does a Tiger Wear a Necktie?)*
1970 Ken Howard *(Child's Play)*
1971 Paul Sand *(Story Theatre* and *Metamorphoses)*
1972 Vincent Gardenia *(The Prisoner of Second Avenue)*

BEST PERFORMANCE BY AN ACTRESS IN A SUPPORTING PART

1942 Jessica Tandy *(Yesterday's Magic)*
1943 Aline MacMahon *(The Eve of St. Mark)*
1944 Terry Holmes *(Manhattan Nocturne)*
1945 Josephine Hull *(Harvey)*
1946 Barbara Bel Geddes *(Deep Are the Roots)*
1947 Margaret Phillips *(Another Part of the Forest)*
1948 Kim Hunter *(A Streetcar Named Desire)*

1949 Mildred Dunnock *(Death of a Salesman)*
1950 Julie Harris *(The Member of the Wedding)*
1951 Joan Loring *(The Autumn Garden)*
1952 Marian Winters *(I Am a Camera)*
1953 Kim Stanley *(Picnic)*
1954 Carol Haney *(The Pajama Game)*
1955 Patricia Jessel *(Witness for the Prosecution)* tied with Elaine Stritch *(Bus Stop)*
1956 Diane Cilento *(Tiger at the Gates)* tied with Sarah Marshall *(The Ponder Heart)*
1957 Mildred Natwick *(The Waltz of the Toreadors)*
1958 Eileen Heckart *(The Dark at the Top of the Stairs)*
1959 Sandra Church *(Gypsy)*
1960 Kay Medford *(Bye Bye Birdie)*
1961 Rosemary Murphy *(Period of Adjustment)*
1962 Sandy Dennis *(A Thousand Clowns)* tied with Barbra Streisand *(I Can Get It for You Wholesale)*
1963 Zorah Lampert *(Mother Courage and Her Children)*
1964 Barbara Loden *(After the Fall)*
1965 Alice Ghostley *(The Sign in Sidney Brustein's Window)*
1966 Zoe Caldwell *(Slapstick Tragedy)*
1967 Rosemary Murphy *(A Delicate Balance)*
1968 Pert Kelton *(Spofford)* tied with Zena Walker *(A Day in the Death of Joe Egg)*
1969 Marian Mercer *(Promises, Promises)*
1970 Melba Moore *(Purlie)*
1971 Mona Washbourne *(Home)*
1972 Frances Sternhagen *(The Sign in Sidney Brustein's Window)*

MOST PROMISING NEW ACTOR

1942 Nicholas Conte *(Jason)*
1943 Skippy Homeier *(Tommorrow the World)*
1944 Montgomery Clift *(The Searching Wind)*
1945 Richard Basehart *(The Hasty Heart)* tied with John Lund *(The Hasty Heart)*
1946 No Choice
1947 Arthur Kennedy *(All My Sons)*
1948 Marlon Brando *(A Streetcar Named Desire)*
1949 Ray Walston *(Summer and Smoke)*
1950 David Cole *(The Innocents)* tied with Douglas Watson *(The Wisteria Trees)*
1951 Eli Wallach *(The Rose Tattoo)*
1952 Brandon de Wilde *(Mrs. McThing)*
1953 John Kerr *(Bernadine)*
1954 Ben Gazzara *(End As a Man)*
1955 George Grizzard *(The Desperate Hours)* tied with Buddy Hackett *(Lunatics and Lovers)*
1956 Andy Griffith *(No Time for Sergeants)*
1957 Jason Robards *(Long Day's Journey into Night)*
1958-60 No Choice
1961 Philip Bosco *(The Rape of the Belt)*
1962 Peter Fonda *(Blood, Sweat and Stanley Poole)*
1963 Alan Arkin *(Enter Laughing)*
1964 Lee Allen *(Marathon '33)*
1965 No Choice
1966 Donal Donnelly *(Philadelphia, Here I Come!)*
1967 Michael Crawford *(Black Comedy)*
1968 No Choice
1969 Al Pacino *(Does a Tiger Wear a Necktie?)*
1970 Frank Grimes *(Borstal Boy)*
1971 No Choice
1972 Richard Backus *(Promenade, All!)*

MOST PROMISING NEW ACTRESS

1942 Mary Anderson *(Guest in the House)* tied with Judith Evelyn *(Angel Street)* and Beverly Roberts *(Uncle Harry)*
1943 Joan Caulfield *(Kiss and Tell)*
1944 Terry Holmes *(Manhattan Nocturne)*
1945 Joan Tetzel *(I Remember Mama)*
1946 No Choice
1947 Patricia Neal *(Another Part of the Forest)*
1948 Meg Mundy *(The Respectful Prostitute)*
1949 No Choice
1950 Marcia Henderson *(Peter Pan)*
1951 Maureen Stapleton *(The Rose Tattoo)*
1952 Julie Harris *(I Am a Camera)* tied with Audrey Hepburn *(Gigi)*
1953 Iris Mann *(The Children's Hour)* tied with Kim Stanley *(Picnic)*
1954 Eva Marie Saint *(The Trip to Bountiful)*
1955 No Choice
1956 Susan Strasberg *(The Diary of Anne Frank)*
1957 Inga Swenson *(The First Gentleman)*
1958 Anne Bancroft *(Two for the Seesaw)*
1959 No Choice
1960 Jane Fonda *(There Was a Little Girl)*
1961 No Choice
1962 Barbara Harris *(From the Second City)*
1963 Melinda Dillon *(Who's Afraid of Virginia Woolf?)*
1964 Barbara Loden *(After the Fall)*
1965 No Choice
1966 Glenda Jackson *(Marat/Sade)*
1967 Leslie Uggams *(Hallelujah, Baby!)*
1968 Zena Walker *(A Day in the Death of Joe Egg)*
1969 Lauren Jones *(Does a Tiger Wear a Necktie?)*
1970 Catherine Bacon *(The Penny Wars)* tied with Blythe Danner *(Butterflies Are Free)*
1971 No Choice
1972 No Choice

BEST DIRECTOR

1942 Shepard Traube *(Angel Street)*
1943 Elia Kazan *(The Skin of Our Teeth)*
1944 Moss Hart *(Winged Victory)*
1945 John van Druten *(I Remember Mama)*
1946 No Choice
1947 John Gielgud *(The Importance of Being Earnest)* tied with Elia Kazan *(All My Sons)*
1948 Joshua Logan *(Mister Roberts)*
1949 Elia Kazan *(Death of a Salesman)*
1950 Peter Glenville *(The Innocents)*
1951 George S. Kaufman *(Guys and Dolls)*
1952 Jose Ferrer *(The Shrike)*
1953 Joshua Logan *(Picnic)*
1954 Robert Lewis *(The Teahouse of the August Moon)*
1955 Herman Shumlin *(Inherit the Wind)*
1956 Moss Hart *(My Fair Lady)*
1957 Jose Quintero *(Long Day's Journey into Night)*
1958 George Roy Hill *(Look Homeward, Angel)*
1959 Elia Kazan *(Sweet Bird of Youth)*
1960 Gower Champion *(Bye Bye Birdie)*
1961 Gower Champion *(Carnival!)* tied with Franklin Schaffner *(Advise and Consent)*
1962 Donald McWhinnie *(The Caretaker)* tied with Noel Willman *(A Man for All Seasons)*
1963 Alan Schneider *(Who's Afraid of Virginia Woolf?)*
1964 Gower Champion *(Hello, Dolly!)*
1965 Mike Nichols *(The Odd Couple* and *Luv)*
1966 Peter Brook *(Marat/Sade)*
1967 Peter Hall *(The Homecoming)*
1968 Derek Goldby *(Rosencrantz and Guildenstern Are Dead* and *Loot)*
1969 Edwin Sherin *(The Great White Hope)*
1970 Harold Prince *(Company)*
1971 Peter Brook *(A Midsummer Night's Dream)*
1972 Jeff Bleckner *(Sticks and Bones)*

BEST SCENIC DESIGNER

1942 Howard Bay *(Brooklyn, U.S.A.)*
1943 Lemuel Ayers *(The Pirate)*
1944 Stewart Chaney *(The Voice of the Turtle)*
1945 George Jenkins *(Dark of the Moon)*
1946 Jo Mielziner *(Dream Girl)* tied with Robert Edmond Jones *(Lute Song)*
1947 Jo Mielziner *(Another Part of the Forest)*
1948 Jo Mielziner *(A Streetcar Named Desire)*
1949 Jo Mielziner *(Death of a Salesman)*
1950 Jo Mielziner *(The Innocents)*
1951 Jo Mielziner *(The King and I)*
1952 Cecil Beaton *(The Grass Harp)* tied with Jo Mielziner *(The Flight into Egypt)*
1953 Jo Mielziner *(Can-Can)*
1954 Peter Larkin *(The Teahouse of the August Moon)*
1955 Peter Larkin *(Inherit the Wind)*
1956 Jo Mielziner *(The Most Happy Fella)* tied with Oliver Smith *(My Fair Lady)*
1957 Oliver Smith *(Candide)* tied with Rouben Ter-Arutunian *(New Girl in Town)*
1958 No Choice
1959 Oliver Messel *(Rashamon)* tied with Oliver Smith *(Destry Rides Again)*
1960 Cecil Beaton *(Saratoga)* tied with Ben Edwards *(Heartbreak House)*
1961 Oliver Smith *(Camelot)*
1962 David Hays *(No Strings)*
1963 Sean Kenny *(Oliver!)*
1964 Oliver Smith *(Hello, Dolly!)*
1965 Boris Aronson *(Fiddler on the Roof)* tied with Oliver Smith *(Baker Street* and *Luv)*
1966 Howard Bay *(Man of La Mancha)*
1967 Boris Aronson *(Cabaret)*
1968 Desmond Heeley *(Rosencrantz and Guildenstern Are Dead)*
1969 Ming Cho Lee *(Billy)*
1970 Boris Aronson *(Company)*
1971 Boris Aronson *(Follies)*
1972 John Bury *(Old Times)*

BEST COSTUME DESIGNER

1956 Cecil Beaton *(My Fair Lady)*
1957 Motley *(The First Gentleman)*

1958-59 No Choice
1960 Cecil Beaton *(Saratoga)*
1961 Adrian and Tony Duquette *(Camelot)*
1962 Lucinda Ballard *(The Gay Life)* tied with Fred Voelpel and Donald Brooks *(No Strings)*
1963 Anthony Powell *(The School for Scandal)*
1964 Freddy Wittop *(Hello, Dolly!)*
1965 Motley *(Baker Street)*
1966 Robert Mackintosh *(Mame)*
1967 Patricia Zipprodt *(Cabaret)*
1968 Desmond Heeley *(Rosencrantz and Guildenstern Are Dead)*
1969 Patricia Zipprodt *(1776)*
1970 Cecil Beaton *(Coco)*
1971 Florence Klotz *(Follies)*
1972 Theoni V. Aldredge *(Two Gentlemen of Verona)*

BEST COMPOSER

1943 Richard Rodgers *(Oklahoma!)*
1944 Kurt Weill *(One Touch of Venus)*
1945 Richard Rodgers *(Carousel)*
1946 Irving Berlin *(Annie Get Your Gun)*
1947 Frederick Loewe *(Brigadoon)*
1948 Jerome Moross *(Ballet Ballads)*
1949 Richard Rodgers *(South Pacific)*
1950 Gian-Carlo Menotti *(The Consul)*
1951 Frank Loesser *(Guys and Dolls)*
1952 Frederick Loewe *(Paint Your Wagon)*
1953 Leonard Bernstein *(Wonderful Town)*
1954 Richard Adler and Jerry Ross *(The Pajama Game)*
1955 Harold Arlen *(House of Flowers)*
1956 Frederick Loewe *(My Fair Lady)*
1957 Leonard Bernstein *(Candide)*
1958 Meredith Willson *(The Music Man)*
1959 Harold Rome *(Destry Rides Again)* tied with Jule Styne *(Gypsy)*
1960 Richard Rodgers *(The Sound of Music)*
1961 Bob Merrill *(Carnival!)*
1962 No Choice
1963 Jerry Bock *(She Loves Me)*
1964 Jerry Herman *(Hello, Dolly!)*
1965 Jerry Bock *(Fiddler on the Roof)*
1966 Mitch Leigh *(Man of La Mancha)*
1967 John Kander *(Cabaret)*
1968 Galt MacDermot *(Hair)*
1969 Burt Bacharach *(Promises, Promises)*
1970 Stephen Sondheim *(Company)*
1971 Stephen Sondheim *(Follies)*
1972 Galt MacDermot *(Two Gentlemen of Verona)*

BEST CHOREOGRAPHER

1945 Agnes de Mille *(Carousel)*
1946 Helen Tamiris *(Annie Get Your Gun)*
1947 Agnes de Mille *(Brigadoon)* tied with Michael Kidd *(Finian's Rainbow)*
1948 Jerome Robbins *(High Button Shoes)*
1949 Hanya Holm *(Kiss Me, Kate)*

BEST LYRICIST

1945 Oscar Hammerstein II *(Carousel)*
1946 Harold Rome *(Call Me Mister)*
1947 E. Y. Harburg *(Finian's Rainbow)*
1948 John Latouche *(Ballet Ballads)*
1949 Oscar Hammerstein II *(South Pacific)*
1950 No Choice
1951 Frank Loesser *(Guys and Dolls)*
1952-53 No Choice
1954 Richard Adler and Jerry Ross *(The Pajama Game)*
1955 Richard Adler and Jerry Ross *(Damn Yankees)*
1956 Alan Jay Lerner *(My Fair Lady)*
1957 Richard Wilbur, John Latouche and Dorothy Parker *(Candide)*
1958 Meredith Willson *(The Music Man)*
1959 Stephen Sondheim *(Gypsy)*
1960 Sheldon Harnick *(Fiorello!)*
1961 Alan Jay Lerner *(Camelot)*
1962 Frank Loesser *(How To Succeed in Business Without Really Trying)*
1963 Sheldon Harnick *(She Loves Me)*
1964 Jerry Herman *(Hello, Dolly!)*
1965 Sheldon Harnick *(Fiddler on the Roof)*
1966 Jerry Herman *(Mame)*
1967 Fred Ebb *(Cabaret)*
1968 Gerome Ragni and James Rado *(Hair)*
1969 Hal David *(Promises, Promises)*
1970 Stephen Sondheim *(Company)*
1971 Stephen Sondheim *(Follies)*
1972 John Guare *(Two Gentlemen of Verona)*

BEST LIBRETTIST

1946 Herbert and Dorothy Fields *(Annie Get Your Gun)*
1947 Alan Jay Lerner *(Brigadoon)*
1948 John Latouche *(Ballet Ballads)*
1949 Oscar Hammerstein II and Joshua Logan *(South Pacific)*

OUTSTANDING BROADWAY PRODUCER

1970 Harold Prince

MOST PROMISING PLAYWRIGHT

1947 Arthur Miller *(All My Sons)*
1948 William W. Haines *(Command Decision)*
1949 Robert E. McEnroe *(The Silver Whistle)*
1950 William Inge *(Come Back, Little Sheba)*
1951 Louis O. Coxe and Robert Chapman *(Billy Budd)*
1952 Joseph Kramm *(The Shrike)*
1953 George Axelrod *(The Seven Year Itch)*
1954 Robert Anderson *(Tea and Sympathy)*
1955 Jerome Lawrence and Robert E. Lee *(Inherit the Wind)*
1956 Paddy Chayefsky *(Middle of the Night)* tied with Michael Gazzo *(A Hatful of Rain)*
1957 Gore Vidal *(Visit to a Small Planet)*
1958 No Choice
1959 Lorraine Hansberry *(A Raisin in the Sun)*
1960 Jack Gelber *(The Connection)*
1961 Shelagh Delany *(A Taste of Honey)*
1962 Herb Gardner *(A Thousand Clowns)*
1963 Edward Albee *(Who's Afraid of Virginia Woolf?)*
1964 Frank D. Gilroy *(The Subject Was Roses)*
1965 William Hanley *(Slow Dance on the Killing Ground)*
1966 Brian Friel *(Philadelphia, Here I Come!)*
1967 No Choice
1968 Tom Stoppard *(Rosencrantz and Guildenstern Are Dead)*
1969 John Guare *(Cop-Out)*
1970 Robert Marasco *(Child's Play)*
1971 Christopher Hampton *(The Philanthropist)*
1972 David Rabe *(Sticks and Bones)*

The Village Voice Off-Broadway Awards. The Obies.

At the end of the 1955-56 theatre season, The Village Voice *initiated its annual Off-Broadway (Obie) Awards in order to give recognition to theatrical achievement in the off-Broadway theatre. The awards are made by a panel of judges which is selected each season. Categories and the titles of categories have been changed from year to year, awards have not been made in each category every year, and in 1969 specific categories were eliminated entirely.*

BEST PRODUCTION

1956 *Uncle Vanya*
1957 *Exiles*
1958 No Award
1959 *Ivanov*
1960 *The Connection*
1961 *Hedda Gabler*
1962 No Award
1963 *Six Characters in Search of an Author* (play)
The Boys from Syracuse (musical)
1964 *The Brig* (play)
What Happened (musical)
1965 *The Cradle Will Rock* (musical)

BEST ACTRESS

1956 Julie Bovasso *(The Maids)*
1957 Colleen Dewhurst *(The Taming of the Shrew, The Eagle Has Two Heads,* and *Camille)*
1958 Anne Meacham *(Suddenly Last Summer)*
1959 Kathleen Maguire *(Time of the Cuckoo)*
1960 Eileen Brennan *(Little Mary Sunshine)*
1961 Anne Meacham *(Hedda Gabler)*
1962 Barbara Harris *(Oh Dad, Poor Dad, Mamma's Hung You in the Closet and I'm Feelin' So Sad)*
1963 Colleen Dewhurst *(Desire Under the Elms)*
1966 Jane White *(Coriolanus* and *Love's Labour's Lost)*
1968 Billie Dixon *(The Beard)*
1971 Ruby Dee *(Boesman and Lena)*

BEST ACTOR

1956 Jason Robards *(The Iceman Cometh)* tied with George Voskovec *(Uncle Vanya)*
1957 William Smithers *(The Seagull)*
1958 George C. Scott *(Richard III, As You Like It* and *Children of Darkness)*
1959 Alfred Ryder *(I Rise in Flame, Cried the Phoenix)*
1960 Warren Finnerty *(The Connection)*
1961 Khigh Dhiegh *(In the Jungle of Cities)*
1962 James Earl Jones (N.Y. Shakespeare Festival, *Clandestine on the Morning Line, The Apple,* and *Moon on a Rainbow Shawl)*
1963 George C. Scott *(Desire Under the Elms)*
1964 No Award
1965 No Award
1966 Dustin Hoffman *(The Journey of the Fifth Horse)*
1967 Seth Allen *(Futz)*
1968 Al Pacino *(The Indian Wants the Bronx)*
1971 Jack MacGowran *(Beckett)*

BEST DIRECTOR

1956 Jose Quintero *(The Iceman Cometh)*

1957 Gene Frankel *(Volpone)*
1958 No Award
1959 William Ball *(Ivanov)* tied with Jack Ragotzy *(Time of the Cuckoo* and *A Clearing in the Woods)*
1960 Gene Frankel *(Machinal)*
1961 Gerald A. Freedman *(The Taming of the Shrew)*
1962 John Wulp *(Red Eye of Love)*
1963 Alan Schneider *(The Pinter Plays)*
1964 Judith Malina *(The Brig)*
1965 Ulu Grosbard *(A View from the Bridge)*
1967 Tom O'Horgan *(Futz)*
1968 Michael A. Schultz *(Song of the Lusitanian Bogey)*

BEST NEW PLAY

1956 *Absalom,* by Lionel Abel
1957 *A House Remembered,* by Louis A. Lippa
1958 *Endgame,* by Samuel Beckett
1959 *The Quare Fellow,* by Brendan Behan
1960 *The Connection,* by Jack Gelber
1961 *The Blacks,* by Jean Genet
1962-63 No Award
1964 *Play,* by Samuel Beckett
1965 *The Old Glory,* by Robert Lowell
1966 *The Journey of the Fifth Horse,* by Ronald Ribman
1970 *The Effect of Gamma Rays on Man-in-the-Moon Marigolds,* by Paul Zindel, and *Approaching Simone,* by Megan Terry
1971 *House of Blue Leaves,* by John Guare
1973 *The Hot l Baltimore,* by Lanford Wilson, and *The River Niger,* by Joseph A. Walker
1974 *Short Eyes,* by Miguel Pinero
1975 *The First Breeze of Summer,* by Leslie Lee

MISCELLANEOUS PLAY AWARDS

Best Foreign Play:

1960 *The Balcony,* by Jean Genet
1962 *Happy Days,* by Samuel Beckett
1968 *The Memorandum,* by Vaclav Havel
1970 *What the Butler Saw,* by Joe Orton
1974 *The Contractor,* by David Storey

Best American Play:

1962 *Who'll Save the Plowboy?,* by Frank D. Gilroy
1964 *Dutchman,* by LeRoi Jones

Best Adaptation:

1958 *The Brothers Karamazov,* by Boris Tumarin and Jack Sydow

Best Revival:

1958 *The Crucible,* by Arthur Miller (directed in revival by Word Baker)

Best Comedy:

1958 *Comic Strip,* by George Panetta

Best One-Act Play:

1958 *Guests of the Nation,* by Neil McKenzie

Distinguished Plays:

1960 *Krapp's Last Tape,* by Samuel Beckett
The Prodigal, by Jack Richardson
The Zoo Story, by Edward Albee
1964 *Home Movies,* by Rosalyn Drexler
Funnyhouse of a Negro, by Adrienne Kennedy
1965 *Promenade* and *The Successful Life of Three,* by Maria Irene Fornes
1966 *Good Day,* by Emanuel Peluso
Chicago, Icarus's Mother, and *Red Cross,* by Sam Shepard
1967 *Futz,* by Rochelle Owens
La Turista, by Sam Shepard
1968 *Muzeeka,* by John Guare
The Indian Wants the Bronx, by Israel Horovitz
Forensic and the Navigators and *Melodrama Play,* by Sam Shepard
1970 *The Deer Kill,* by Murray Mednick
The Increased Difficulty of Concentration, by Vaclav Havel
1973 *The Tooth of Crime,* by Sam Shepard
Big Foot, by Ronald Tavel
What If I Had Turned Up Heads?, by J. E. Gaines
1974 *Bad Habits,* by Terrence McNally
When You Comin Back, Red Ryder?, by Mark Medoff
The Great MacDaddy, by Paul Carter Harrison

DISTINGUISHED PLAYWRITING

1971 Ed Bullins *(The Fabulous Miss Marie* and *In New England Winter)*
David Rabe *(The Basic Training of Pavlo Hummel)*
1975 Ed Bullins *(The Taking of Miss Janie)*
Lanford Wilson *(The Mound Builders)*
Wallace Shawn *(Our Late Night)*
Sam Shepard *(Action)*

DISTINGUISHED FOREIGN PLAYS

1971 *Boesman and Lena,* by Athol Fugard
AC/DC, by Heathcote Williams
Dream on Monkey Mountain, by Derek Walcott
1973 *Not I,* by Samuel Beckett
Kaspar, by Peter Handke

DISTINGUISHED PRODUCTION

1971 *The Trial of the Catonsville Nine*

BEST MUSICAL

1956 *The Threepenny Opera,* by Bertolt Brecht and Kurt Weill, in an adaptation by Marc Blitzstein
1959 *A Party with Betty Comden and Adolph Green*
1962 *Fly Blackbird,* by C. Jackson, James Hatch, and Jerome Eskow
1968 *In Circles,* by Gertrude Stein and Al Carmines
1970 *The Last Sweet Days of Isaac,* by Gretchen Cryer and Nancy Ford, and *The Me Nobody Knows,* by Robert Livingston, Gary William Friedman, and Will Holt

BEST REVUE

1959 *Diversions,* by Steven Vinaver

BEST OFF-BROADWAY PRODUCTION

1961 *The Premise,* produced and directed by Theodore Flicker

BEST THEATRE PIECE

1972 The Open Theatre *(The Mutation Show)*

BEST PERFORMANCES

1964 Gloria Foster *(In White America)*
1965 Roscoe Lee Browne, Frank Langella, Lester Rawlins *(The Old Glory)*
1970 Sada Thompson *(The Effect of Gamma Rays on Man-in-the-Moon Marigolds)*

DISTINGUISHED DIRECTION

1964 Lawrence Kornfeld
1966 Remy Charlip and Jacques Levy
1968 John Hancock and Rip Torn
1970 Alan Arkin, Melvin Bernhardt, Maxine Klein, and Gilbert Moses
1971 John Berry, Jeff Bleckner, Gordon Davidson, John Hirsch, and Lawrence Kornfeld
1972 Wilford Leach and John Braswell, Mel Shapiro, Michael Smith, and Tom Sydorick
1973 Jack Gelber, William E. Lathan, and Marshall W. Mason
1974 Marvin Felix Camillo, Robert Drivas, David Licht, John Pasquin, and Harold Prince
1975 Lawrence Kornfeld, Marshall W. Mason, and Gilbert Moses

DISTINGUISHED PERFORMANCES, ACTRESSES

1956 Peggy McCay, Shirlee Emmons, Frances Sternhagen, and Nancy Wickwire
1957 Marguerite Lenert, Betty Miller, and Jutta Wolf
1958 Tammy Grimes, Grania O'Malley, and Nydia Westman
1959 Rosina Fernhoff, Anne Fielding, and Nancy Wickwire
1960 Patricia Falkenhain, Elisa Loti, and Nancy Marchand
1961 Joan Hackett, Gerry Jedd, and Surya Kumari
1962 Sudie Bond, Vinnette Carroll, Rosemary Harris, and Ruth White
1963 Jacqueline Brookes, Olympia Dukakis, Anne Jackson, and Madeline Sherwood
1964 Joyce Ebert, Lee Grant, Estelle Parsons, Diana Sands, and Marian Seldes
1965 Margaret De Priest, Rosemary Harris, Francis Sternhagen, Sada Thompson
1966 Clarice Blackburn, Mari-claire Charbe, Gloria Foster, Sharon Gains, and Florence Tarlow
1967 Bette Henritze
1968 Jean David, Mari Gorman, and Peggy Pope
1970 Rue McClanahan, Roberta Maxwell, Frederika Weber, and Pamela Payton-Wright
1971 Susan Batson, Margaret Braidwood, and Joan MacIntosh
1972 Salome Bey, Marilyn Chris, Marilyn Sokol, Kathleen Widdoes, and Elizabeth Wilson
1973 Mari Gorman, Lola Pashalinski, Alice Playten, Roxie Roker, and Jessica Tandy
1974 Barbara Barrie, Conchata Ferrell, Loretta Greene, Barbara Montgomery, Zipora Speizman, and Elizabeth Sturges
1975 Cara Duff-MacCormick, Priscilla Smith, Tanya Berezin, and Tovah Feldshuh

DISTINGUISHED PERFORMANCES, ACTORS

1956 Gerald Hiken, Alan Ansara, Roberts Blossom, and Addison Powell
1957 Thayer David, Michael Kane, and Arthur Malet
1958 Leonardo Cimino, Jack Cannon, Robert Gerringer, and Michael Higgins

1959 Zero Mostel, Lester Rawlins, and Harold Scott
1960 William Daniels, Donald Davis, Vincent Gardenia, John Heffernan, and Jock Livingston
1961 Godfrey M. Cambridge, James Coco, and Lester Rawlins
1962 Clayton Corzatte, Geoff Garland, Gerald O'Laoughlin, and Paul Roebling
1963 Joseph Chaikin, Michael O'Sullivan, James Patterson, and Eli Wallach
1964 Philip Burns, David Hurst, Taylor Mead, Jack Warden, and Ronald Weyand
1965 Brian Bedford, Roberts Blossom, Robert Duvall, and James Earl Jones
1966 Frank Langella, Michael Lipton, Kevin O'Connor, Jess Osuna, and Douglas Turner
1967 Tom Aldredge, Robert Bonnard, Alvin Epstein, Neil Flanagan, Stacy Keach, Terry Kiser, Eddie McCarty, Robert Salvio, and Rip Torn
1968 John Cazale, James Coco, Cliff Gorman, Moses Gunn, and Roy R. Scheider
1970 Beeson Carroll, Vincent Gardenia, Harold Gould, Anthony Holland, Lee Kissman, Ron Leibman, and Austin Pendleton
1971 Hector Elizondo, Donald Ewer, Sonny Jimm, Stacy Keach, Harris Laskawy, William Schallert, and James Woods
1972 Maurice Blanc, Alex Bradford, Ron Faber, Danny Sewell, and Ed Zang
1973 Hume Cronyn, James Hilbrant, Stacy Keach, Christopher Lloyd, Charles Ludlam, Douglas Turner Ward, and Sam Waterston
1974 Joseph Buloff and Kevin Conway
1975 Reyno, Moses Gunn, Dick Latessa, Kevin McCarthy, Stephen D. Newman, Christopher Walken, and Ian Trigger

SETS, LIGHTING, OR COSTUMES

1956 Klaus Holm, Alvin Colt
1957 No Award
1958 No Award
1959 David Hays, Will Steven Armstrong and Nikola Cernovich
1960 David Hays
1961 No Award
1962 Norris Houghton
1963 No Award
1964 Julian Beck
1965 Willa Kim
1966 Lindsey Decker and Ed Wittstein
1967 John Dodd
1968 Robert La Vigna
1971 John Scheffler
1974 Theoni V. Aldredge, Holmes Easley, and Christopher Thomas
1975 Robert U. Taylor, John Lee Beatty

VISUAL EFFECTS

1972 *Video Free America*

MUSIC

1959 David Amram
1961 Teiji Ito
1964 Al Carmines
1972 Micki Grant and Liz Swados
1974 Bill Elliott

SPECIAL CITATIONS

1956 The Phoenix Theatre, the Shakespearean Workshop Theatre (later the New York Shakespeare Festival), and the Tempo Playhouse
1957 Paul Shyre
1958 The Phoenix Theatre, the Theatre Club, and Lucille Lortel
1959 Hal Holbrook
1960 Brooks Atkinson
1961 Bernard Frechtman
1962 Ellis Rabb and *The Hostage*
1963 Jean Erdman and *The Second City*
1964 The Judson Memorial Church
1965 The Paper Bag Players, Caffe Cino and Cafe La Mama
1966 Joseph H. Dunn, H. M. Koutoukas, Peter Schumann, Theatre for Ideas, and Theatre in the the Street
1967 La Mama Troupe, The Open Theatre, Tom Sankey, The Second Story Players, and Jeff Weiss
1968 The Fortune Society, The Negro Ensemble Company, San Francisco Mime Troupe, and El Teatro Campesino
1970 Chelsea Theatre Center, Gardner Compton and Emile Ardolino, *Elephant Steps,* Andre Gregory, The Ridiculous Theatrical Company, and Theatre of the Ridiculous
1971 *Orlando Furioso* and Kirk Kirksey
1972 Charles Stanley, Meredith Monk, Theatre of Latin America, and Free the Army
1973 Richard Foreman, San Francisco Mime Troupe, City Center Acting Company, Workshop of the Player's Art
1974 The Bread and Puppet Theatre, The Brooklyn Academy of Music, CSC Repertory Company, and Robert Wilson
1975 Andrei Serban, The Royal Shakespeare Company, Charles Ludlam, The Henry Street Settlement, Charles Pierce, and Mabou Mines

1969 AWARDS

The judges for this year altered the form of the awards, substituting for specific categories general citations for outstanding achievement.

The Living Theatre *(Frankenstein)*
Jeff Weiss *(The International Wrestling Match)*
Julie Bovasso *(Gloria and Esperanza)*
Judith Malina and Julian Beck *(Antigone)*
Israel Horovitz *(The Honest-to-God Schnozzola)*
Jules Feiffer *(Little Murders)*
Ronald Tavel *(The Boy on the Straight-Back Chair)*
Nathan George and Ron O'Neal *(No Place To Be Somebody)*
Arlene Rothlein *(The Poor Little Match Girl)*
Theatre Genesis
The Open Theatre *(The Serpent)*
OM Theatre *(Riol)*
The Performance Group *(Dionysus in '69)*

SPECIAL 20-YEAR OBIES 1975

Judith Malina and Julian Beck
Ted Mann and the Circle in the Square
Joseph Papp
Ellen Stewart
The Fantasticks

Biographical Bibliography

Abbott, George 1887-
Abbott, George. *Mister Abbott.* New York: Random House, 1963.

Abington, Frances 1731-1815
The Life of Mrs. Abington (formerly Miss Barton), Celebrated Comic Actress. London: Reader, 1888.

Ackland, Rodney 1908-
Ackland, Rodney. *The Celluloid Mistress; or, The Custard Pie of Dr. Caligari.* London: Wingate, 1954.

Adams, Joey 1911-
Adams, Joey. *Cindy and I.* New York: Crown, 1957.
—. *From Gags to Riches.* New York: Frederick Fell, 1946.
—. *On the Road for Uncle Sam.* New York: Bernard Geis, 1963.

Adams, Maude 1872-1953
Davies, Acton. *Maude Adams.* New York: Frederick A. Stokes, 1901.
Patterson, Ada. *Maude Adams.* New York: Meyer Brothers, 1907.
Robbins, Phyllis. *Maude Adams, An Intimate Portrait.* New York: Putnam, 1956.
The Young Maude Adams. Francestown, N.H.: Marshall Jones, 1959.

Ade, George 1866-1944
Ade, George (ed. by Terence Tobin). *Letters of George Ade.* West Lafayette, Ind.: Purdue Univ., 1973.
Kelly, Fred C. *George Ade, Warmhearted Satirist.* Indianapolis: Bobbs-Merrill, 1947.
Matson, Lowell. *Ade, Who Needed None.* Oklahoma City: 1962.

Agate, James Evershed 1877-1947
Agate, James. *Ego, the Autobiography of James Agate.* London: Hamilton, 1935.
—. *Ego 2; Being More of the Autobiography. . . .* London: Gollancz, 1936.
—. *Ego 3; Being Still More of the Autobiography. . . .* London: Harrap, 1938.
—. *Ego 4; Yet More of the Autobiography. . . .* London: Harrap, 1940.
—. *Ego 5; Again More of the Autobiography. . . .* London: Harrap, 1943.
—. *Ego 6; Once More the Autobiography. . . .* London: Harrap, 1944.
—. *Ego 7; Even More of the Autobiography. . . .* London: Harrap, 1945.
—. *Ego 8; Continuing the Autobiography. . . .* London: Harrap, 1946.
—. *Ego 9; Concluding the Autobiography of James Agate.* London: Harrap, 1948.
—. *A Shorter Ego; [an Abridged Version of] the Autobiography of James Agate.* London: Harrap, 1945-49; 3 vols.
—. *The Later Ego, Consisting of Ego 8 and Ego 9.* New York: Crown, 1951.

Aherne, Brian 1902-
Aherne, Brian. *A Proper Job.* Boston: Houghton Mifflin, 1969.

Albanesi, Margharita 1899-1923
Albanesi, Effie Adelaide Maria. *Meggie Albanesi.* London: Hodder, 1928.

Albee, Edward 1928-
Amacher, Richard E. *Edward Albee.* New York: Twayne, 1969.
Cohn, Ruby. *Edward Albee.* Minneapolis: Univ. of Minnesota, 1969.
Debusscher, Gilbert (trans. by Anne D. Williams). *Edward Albee: Tradition and Renewal.* Brussels: American Study Center, 1967.

Aldridge, Ira Frederick 1807-1867
Malone, Mary. *Actor in Exile; The Life of Ira Aldridge.* New York: Crowell-Collier, 1969.
Marshall, Herbert. *Further Research on Ira Aldridge, The Negro Tragedian.* Carbondale: Southern Illinois Univ., 197-.
— and Stock, Mildred. *Ira Aldridge, The Negro Tragedian.* London: Rockliff, 1958. Rockliff, 1958.
Trommer, Marie. *Ira Aldridge, American Negro Tragedian and Taras Shevchenko, Poet of the Ukraine; Story of a Friendship.* Brooklyn, N.Y.: Trommer, 1939.

Alexander, Sir George 1858-1918
Mason, Alfred E. W. *Sir George Alexander & the St. James Theatre.* London: Macmillan, 1935.

Allan, Maud 1883-1956
Allan, Maud. *My Life and Dancing.* London: Everett, 1908.

Allen, Fred 1894-1956
Allen, Fred. *Treadmill to Oblivion.* Boston: Little, Brown, 1954.
—. *Much Ado About Me.* Boston: Little, Brown, 1956.
—. (ed. by Joe McCarthy) *Fred Allen's Letters.* Garden City: Doubleday, 1965.

Allen, Gracie 1906-1964
See: Burns, George.

Allen, Woody 1935-
Lax, Eric. *On Being Funny: Woody Allen and Comedy.* New York: Charterhouse, 1975.

Alleyn, Edward 1566-1626
Collier, John P. *Memoirs of Edward Allen, Founder of Dulwich College; Including Some New Particulars Respecting Shakespeare, Ben Jonson, Massinger, Marston, Dekker, etc.* London: Shakespeare Society, 1843.
Hosking, G. L. *The Life and Times of Edward Alleyn, Actor, Master of the King's Bears, Founder of the College of God's Gift at Dulwich.* London: Cape, 1952.
The Alleyn Papers; A Collection of Original Documents Illustrative of the Life and Times of Edward Alleyn, and of the Early English Stage and Drama. London: Shakespeare Society, 1843.

Ambrosi, Marietta
Ambrosi, Marietta. *When I Was a Girl in Italy.* Boston: Lothrop, Lee & Shepart, 1906.

Anderson, John Henry 1814-1874
Findlay, James B. *Professor Anderson and His Theatre.* Shanklin (Isle of Wight): J. B. Findlay, 1967.

Anderson, John Murray 1886-1954
Anderson, Hugh Abercrombie. *Out without My Rubbers.* New York: Library Publishers, 1954.

Anderson, Mary 1859-1940
Anderson, Mary. *A Few Memories.* New York: Harper, 1896.
—. *A Few More Memories.* London: Hutchinson, 1936.
Farrar, J. Maurice. *Mary Anderson; The Story of Her Life and Professional Career.* London: Bogue, 1884.
Frey, Albert Romer. *Mary Anderson in Her Dramatic Roles.* New York: W. J. Kelly, 1892.
Williams, Henry Llewellyn. *The "Queen of the Drama."* New York: Williams, 1885.
Winter, William. *Stage Life of Mary Anderson.* New York: G. J. Coombes, 1896.

Anderson, Maxwell 1888-1959
Clark, Barrett H. *Maxwell Anderson, the Man and His Plays.* New York: Samuel French, 1933.

Andrews, Julie 1935-
Cottrell, John. *Julie Andrews; The Story of a Star.* London: Barker, 1969.
Windeler, Robert. *Julie Andrews.* New York: Putnam, 1970.

Angelou, Maya 1928-
Angelou, Maya. *Gather Together in My Name.* New York: Random House, 1974.
—. *I Know Why the Caged Bird Sings.* New York: Random House, 1970.

Annunzio, Gabriele d' (Rapagnetta) 1863-1938
Antongini, Tommaso. *D'Annunzio.* Boston: Little, Brown, 1938.
Griffin, Gerald. *Gabriele d'Annunzio; The Warrior Bard.* London: Long, 1935.
Gullace, Giovanni. *Gabriele d'Annunzio in France; A Study in Cultural Relations.* Syracuse, N.Y.: Syracuse Univ., 1966.
Jullian, Phillippe (trans. by Stephen Hardman). *D'Annunzio.* New York: Viking, 1973.
Nardelli, Frederico and Livingston, Albert Arthur. *Gabriel, the Archangel.* New York: Harcourt, Brace, 1931.
Rhodes, Anthony. *D'Annunzio, the Poet as Superman.* New York: McDowell, Obolensky, 1960.
Winwar, Frances. *Wingless Victory.* New York: Harper, 1956.
See also: Duse, Eleanora.

Anouilh, Jean 1910-
Archer, Marguerite. *Jean Anouilh.* New York: Columbia Univ., 1971.
Della Fazia, Alba. *Jean Anouilh.* New York: Twayne, 1969.

Antoine, Andre Leonard 1857-1943
Antoine, Andre (trans. by Marvin A. Carlson). *Memories of the Theatre-Libre.* Coral Gables, Fla.: Univ. of Miami, 1964.
Waxman, Samuel Montefiore. *Antoine and the Theatre-Libre.* Cambridge: Harvard, 1926.

Appia, Adolphe 1862-1928
Volbach, Walther R. *Adolphe Appia, Prophet of the Modern Theater; A Profile.* Middletown, Conn.: Wesleyan Univ., 1968.

Archer, William 1856-1924
Archer, Charles. *William Archer: His Life, Work and Friendships.* New Haven: Yale Univ., 1931.

Arliss, George 1868-1946
Arliss, George. *My Ten Years in the Studios.* Boston: Little, Brown, 1940.
—. *Up the Years from Bloomsbury.* Boston: Little, Brown, 1927.

Armitage, Merle 1893-
Armitage, Merle. *Accent on America.* New York: Weyhe, 1944.

Arnaud, Yvonne 1892-1958
Malet, Oriel (pseud). *Marraine; A Portrait of My Godmother.* London: Heinemann, 1961.

Arnold, Edward 1890-1956
Arnold, Edward. *Lorenzo Goes to Hollywood.* New York: Liveright, 1940.

Arnould, Sophie 1740-1802
Douglas, Robert B. *Sophie Arnould, Actress and Wit.* Paris: Carrington, 1898.

Aronson, Rudolph 1856-1919
Aronson, Rudolph. *Theatrical and Musical Memoirs.* New York: McBride, Nast, 1913.

Artaud, Antonin 1896-1948
Greene, Naomi. *Antonin Artaud: Poet without Words.* New York: Simon & Schuster, 1971.
Knapp, Bettina L. *Antonin Artaud; Man of Vision.* New York: Lewis, 1969.

Arvold, Alfred G. 1882-1957
Arvold, Alfred G. *Alfred . . . In Everyman's Life.* Fargo, N.D.: Arvold Library, 1957.

Asche, Oscar 1872-1936
Asche, Oscar. *Oscar Asche; His Life.* London: Hurst & Blackett, 1929.

Ashcroft, Peggy 1907-
Keown, Eric. *Peggy Ashcroft.* London: Rockliff, 1955.

Ashton, Frederick 1906-
Barnes, Clive. *Frederick Ashton and His Ballets.* New York: Dance Perspectives, 1961.
Dominic, Zoë and Gilbert, John S. *Frederick Ashton: A Choreographer and His Ballets.* London: Harrap, 1971.

Ashwell, Lena 1872-1957
Ashwell, Lena. *Myself a Player.* London: Joseph, 1936.

Astaire, Fred 1899-
Astaire, Fred. *Steps in Time.* New York: Harper, 1959.
Croce, Arlene. *The Fred Astaire & Ginger Rogers Book.* New York: Outerbridge & Lazard, 1972.
Green, Stanley and Goldblatt, Burt. *Starring Fred Astaire.* New York: Dodd, Mead, 1973.
Hackl, Alfons. *Fred Astaire and His Work.* Vienna: Ed. Austria International, 1970.
Thompson, Howard. *Fred Astaire.* New York: Falcoln Enterprises, 1970.

Aston, Tony fl. 1712-1731
Nicholson, Watson. *Anthony Aston, Stroller and Adventurer . . .* South Haven, Mich.: 1920.

Astor, Mary 1906-
Astor, Mary. *My Story: An Autobiography.* Garden City: Doubleday, 1959.
—. *A Life on Film.* New York: Delacorte, 1971.

Avril, Jane 1868-1942
Shercliff, Jose. *Jane Avril of the Moulin Rouge.* Philadelphia: Macrae Smith, 1954.

Baddeley, Sophia Snow 1745-1786
Steele, Elizabeth. *The Memoirs of Mrs. Sophia Baddeley, Late of Drury Lane Theatre.* London: 1787.

Bagnold, Enid 1889-
Bagnold, Enid. *Enid Bagnold's Autobiography.* Boston: Little, Brown, 1970.

Bailey, Mollie 1841-1918
Bailey, Olga. *Mollie Bailey, The Circus Queen of the Southwest.* Dallas: Harben-Spotts, 1943.

Bailey, Pearl 1918-
Bailey, Pearl. *The Raw Pearl.* New York: Harcourt, Brace & World, 1968.
—. *Talking to Myself.* New York: Harcourt, Brace, Jovanovich, 1971.

Bairnsfather, Bruce 1887-1959
Bairnsfather, Bruce. *The Bairnsfather Case, as Tried before Mr. Justice Busby.* London: Putnam, 1920.
—. *Old Bill Looks at Europe.* New York: Dodge, 1935.

Baker, George Pierce 1866-1935
Kinne, Wisner Payne. *George Pierce Baker and the American Theatre.* Cambridge: Harvard Univ., 1954.
George Pierce Baker, a Memorial. New York: Dramatists Play Service, 1939.

Bakst, Leon 1868-1924
Bakst, Leon. *Bakst; A Monograph.* New York: Coward-McCann, 1927.
Levinson, André. *Bakst, the Story of the Artist's Life.* London: Bayard, 1923.
Lister, Raymond. *The Muscovite Peacock; A Study of the Art of Leon Bakst.* Cambridge, England: Golden Head Press, 1954.
Spencer, Charles. *Leon Bakst.* New York: St. Martin's, 1973.

Balaban, A. J. 1889-1962
Balaban, A. J., as told to his wife, Carrie Balaban. *Continuous Performance.* New York: Putnam, 1942.

Balanchine, George 1904-
Taper, Bernard. *Balanchine.* New York: Macmillan, 1974.

Baldwin, James 1924-
Baldwin, James. *No Name in the Street.* New York: Dial, 1972.
Eckman, Fern M. *The Furious Passage of James Baldwin.* New York: Evans, 1966.

Bancroft, George Pleydell 1868-1956
Bancroft, George P. *Stage and Bar; Recollections of George Pleydell Bancroft. . .* London: Faber & Faber, 1939.

Bancroft, Marie 1839-1921
Bancroft, Squire 1841-1926
Bancroft, Squire. *Empty Chairs.* New York: Frederick A. Stokes, 1925.
— and Bancroft, Marie. *Mr. and Mrs. Bancroft On and Off the Stage.* London: R. Bentley, 1885; 2 vols.

— and Bancroft, Marie. *The Bancrofts; Recollections of Sixty Years.* London: Murray, 1909.

Bandmann, Daniel Edward 1840-1905
Bandmann, Daniel Edward. *An Actor's Tour; or, Seventy Thousand Miles with Shakespeare.* New York: Brentano, 1886.

Bankhead, Tallulah 1903-1968
Bankhead, Tallulah. *Tallulah; My Autobiography.* New York: Harper, 1952.
Brian, Denis. *Tallulah, Darling.* New York: Pyramid, 1972.
Campbell, Sandy. *A Streetcar Named Desire: B.* New York: Campbell, 1974.
Gill, Brendan. *Tallulah.* New York: Holt, Rinehart & Winston, 1972.
Israel, Lee. *Miss Tallulah Bankhead.* New York: Putnam, 1972.
Tunney, Kieran. *Tallulah: Darling of the Gods.* New York: Dutton, 1973.

Bankson, Budd 1916-
Bankson, Budd. *I Should Live So Long.* Philadelphia: Lippincott, 1952.

Bannister, John 1760-1836
Adolphus, John. *Memoirs of John Bannister, Comedian.* London: Bentley, 1838.

Barker, Harley Granville
See: Granville-Barker, Harley.

Barnabee, Henry Clay 1833-1917
Varney, George Leon (ed.). *Reminiscences of Henry Clay Barnabee.* Boston: Chapple, 1913.

Barnes, Al G. 1862-1931
Robeson, Dave. *Al G. Barnes, Master Showman.* Caldwell, Idaho: Caxton, 1935.

Barnes, J[ohn] H. 1850-1925
Barnes, John H. *Forty Years on the Stage.* London: Chapman & Hall, 1914.

Barnes, Kenneth R. 1878-1957
Hartnoll, Phyllis (ed.). *Welcome Good Friends.* London: Davies, 1958.

Barnum, Phineas Taylor 1810-1891
Barnum, Phineas T. *The Life of P. T. Barnum.* New York: Redfield, 1855.
—. *Struggles and Triumphs; or, Forty Years' Recollections of P. T. Barnum.* Hartford: J. B. Burr, 1869.
— (ed. by Waldo R. Browne). *Barnum's Own Story; The Autobiography of P. T. Barnum, Combined and Condensed from the Various Editions Published during His Lifetime.* New York: Viking, 1927.
Benton, Joel. . . .*Life of Hon. Phineas T. Barnum* . . . Philadelphia: Edgewood, 1891.
Fitzsimons, Raymund. *Barnum in London.* London: Bles, 1969.
Harris, Neil. *Humbug; The Art of P. T. Barnum.* Boston: Little, Brown, 1973.
Jefferson, Caleb. *Life and History of P. T. Barnum, the Greatest Living Showman.* London: Hansard, 1889.
Romer, Frank. *P. T. Barnum.* Washington: Judd and Detweiler, 1933.
Root, Harvey Woods. *The Unknown Barnum.* New York: Harper, 1927.
Sutton, Felix. *Master of Ballyhoo.* New York: Putnam, 1968.
Wallace, Irving. *The Fabulous Showman.* New York: Knopf, 1959.
Werner, Morris Robert. *Barnum.* New York: Harcourt, Brace, 1923.

Barrault, Jean-Louis 1910-
Barrault, Jean-Louis (trans. by Barbara Wall). *Reflections on the Theatre.* London: Rockliff, 1951.
—. (trans. by Joseph Chiari) *The Theatre of Jean-Louis Barrault.* London: Barrie and Rockliff, 1961.
—. (trans. by Jonathan Griffin) *Memories for Tomorrow.* London: Thames and Hudson, 1974.

Barrett, Lawrence 1838-1891
Barron, Elwyn A. *Lawrence Barrett, A Professional Sketch.* Chicago: Knight & Leonard, 1889.

Barrie, James Matthew 1860-1937
Asquith, Cynthia. *Portrait of Barrie.* London: Barrie, 1954.
Barrie, James Matthew. *The Greenwood Hat.* New York: Scribner, 1938.
Barton, Frederick. *J. M. Barrie.* New York: Holt, 1929.
Braybrooke, Patrick. *J. M. Barrie; A Study in Fairies and Mortals.* Philadelphia: Lippincott, 1925.
Chalmers, Patrick. *The Barrie Inspiration.* London: P. Davies, 1938.
Cockburn, J. M. *A Birthplace in Thrums; The Story of J. M. Barrie.* Edinburgh: National Trust for Scotland, 1964.
Darton, F. J. Harvey. *J. M. Barrie.* New York: Holt, 1929.
Dunbar, Janet. *J. M. Barrie; The Man behind the Image.* Boston: Houghton Mifflin, 1970.
Geduld, Harry M. *Sir James Barrie.* New York: Twayne, 1971.
Green, Roger L. *J. M. Barrie.* New York: H. Z. Walck, 1961.
Hammerton, John Alexander. *J. M. Barrie and His Books.* London: Marshall, 1900.
—. *Barrie; The Story of a Genius.* New York: Dodd, Mead, 1929.
Kennedy, John. *Thrums and the Barrie Country.* London: H. Cranton, 1930.
Mackail, Denis George. *Barrie; The Story of J. M. B.* New York: Scribner, 1941.
Moult, Thomas. *Barrie.* London: Cape, 1928.
Roy, James Alexander. *James Matthew Barrie; An Appreciation.* New York: Scribner, 1938.
Walbrook, Henry Mackinnon. *J. M. Barrie and the Theatre.* London: F. V. White, 1922.
Letters of J. M. Barrie. New York: Scribner, 1947.

Barrington, Rutland 1853-1922
Barrington, Rutland. *Rutland Barrington. A Record of Thirty-five Year's Experience on the English Stage.* London: Richards, 1908.
—. *More Rutland Barrington.* London: Richards, 1911.

Barry, Philip 1896-1949
Roppolo, Joseph P. *Philip Barry.* New York: Twayne, 1965.

Barrymore Family
Alpert, Hollis. *The Barrymores.* New York: Dial, 1964.

Barrymore, Diana 1921-1960
Barrymore, Diana and Frank, Gerold. *Too Much, Too Soon.* New York: Holt, 1957.

Barrymore, Elaine
Barrymore, Elaine and Dody, Sandford. *All My Sins Remembered.* New York: Appleton-Century-Crofts, 1964.

Barrymore, Ethel 1879-1959
Barrymore, Ethel. *Memories, an Autobiography.* New York: Harper, 1955.

Barrymore, John 1882-1942
Barrymore, John. *Confessions of an Actor.* Indianapolis: Bobbs-Merrill, 1926.
Fowler, Gene. *Good Night, Sweet Prince.* Philadelphia: Blackiston, 1945.
Power-Waters, Alma, *John Barrymore, the Legend and the Man.* New York: Messner, 1941.
See also: Strange, Michael.

Barrymore, Lionel 1878-1954
Barrymore, Lionel, as told to Cameron Shipp. *We Barrymores.* New York: Appleton-Century-Crofts, 1951.

Bateman, Isabel (Mother Isabel Mary) 1854-1934
From Theatre to Convent; Memories of Mother Isabel Mary, C.S.M.V. London: Society for Promoting Christian Knowledge, 1936.

Baum, Vicki 1888-1960
Baum, Vicki. *It Was All Quite Different; The Memoirs of Vicki Baum.* New York: Funk & Wagnalls, 1964.
[Published in England as: *I Know What I'm Worth.* London: M. Joseph, 1964.]

Baylis, Lilian 1874-1937
Findlater, Richard. *Lilian Baylis; The Lady of the Old Vic.* London: Allen Lane, 1975.
Thorndike, Sybil and Russell. *Lilian Baylis.* London: Chapman & Hall, 1938.
Williams, E. Harcourt, (ed.). *Vic-Wells; The Work of Lilian Baylis.* London: Cobden-Sanderson, 1938.

Beaton, Cecil 1904-
Beaton, Cecil. *Photobiography.* Garden City: Doubleday, 1951.
—. *It Gives Me Great Pleasure.* London: Weidenfeld & Nicolson, 1955.
—. *The Wandering Years; Diaries: 1922-39.* Boston: Little, Brown, 1961.
—. *The Years Between; Diaries: 1939-44.* New York: Holt, Rinehart & Winston, 1965.
—. *My Bolivian Aunt: A Memoir.* London: Weidenfeld & Nicolson, 1971.
—. *The Happy Years; Diaries: 1944-48.* London: Weidenfeld & Nicolson, 1972.

Beaumarchais, Pierre-Augustin 1732-1799
Cox, Cynthia. *The Real Figaro; The Extraordinary Career of Caron de Beaumarchais.* London: Longmans, 1962.
Dalsème, René (trans. by Hannaford Bennett). *Beaumarchais, 1732-1799.* New York: Putnam, 1929.
Frischauer, Paul (trans. by Margaret Goldsmith). *Beaumarchais, Adventurer in the Century of Women.* New York: Viking, 1935.
Hazard, Blanche E. *Beaumarchais and the American Revolution.* Boston: E. L. Slocomb, 1910.
Johnson, Margaret L. *Beaumarchais and His Opponents; New Documents on His Lawsuits.* Richmond, Va: Whittet & Shepperson, 1936.
Kite, Elizabeth S. *Beaumarchais and the War of American Independence.* Boston: R. G. Badger, 1918; 2 vols.

Lemaitre, Georges E. *Beaumarchais.* New York: Knopf, 1949.
Loménie, Louis L. (trans. by Henry S. Edwards). *Beaumarchais and His Times.* New York: Harper, 1857.
Rivers, John. *Figaro: The Life of Beaumarchais.* London: Hutchinson, 1922.

Beaumont, Francis c.1584-1616
Appleton, William W. *Beaumont and Fletcher; A Critical Study.* London: Allen & Unwin, 1956.
Gayley, Charles M. *Beaumont, the Dramatist.* New York: Century, 1914.
Wallis, Lawrence B. *Fletcher, Beaumont & Company, Entertainers to the Jacobean Gentry.* New York: King's Crown, 1947.
See also: Fletcher, John.

Beck, Julian 1925-
See: Malina, Judith.

Beckett, Samuel 1906-
Cohn, Ruby. *Back to Beckett.* Princeton: Princeton Univ., 1974.
Harvey, Lawrence E. *Samuel Beckett; Poet & Critic.* Princeton: Princeton Univ., 1970.
Scott, Nathan A. *Samuel Beckett.* London: Bowes & Bowes, 1969.
Sen, Supti. *Samuel Beckett: His Mind and Art.* Calcutta: Firma K. L. Mukhopadhyay, 1970.
Simpson, Alan. *Beckett and Behan and a Theatre in Dublin.* London: Routledge and Kegan Paul, 1962.
Tindall, William Y. *Samuel Beckett.* New York: Columbia Univ., 1964.
Beckett at 60: A Festschrift. London: Calder & Boyars, 1967.

Bedford, Paul John 1792-1871
Bedford, Paul John. *Recollections and Wanderings of Paul Bedford; Facts, Not Fancies.* London: Strand, 1867.

Beerbohm, Max 1872-1956
Beerbohm, Max. *Letters to Reggie Turner.* London: Hart-Davis, 1964.
Behrman, S. N. *Portrait of Max.* New York: Random House, 1960.
Cecil, David. *Max.* Boston: Houghton Mifflin, 1965.
Felstiner, John. *The Lies of Art; Max Beerbohm's Parody and Caricature.* New York: Knopf, 1972.
Lynch, Bohun. *Max Beerbohm in Perspective.* London: Heinemann, 1921.
McElderry, Bruce R, Jr. *Max Beerbohm.* New York: Twayne, 1972.
Mix, Katherine L. *Max and the Americans.* Brattleboro, Vt.: Greene, 1974.
Riewald, J. G. *Sir Max Beerbohm, Man and Writer.* The Hague: Nijhoff, 1953.

Behan, Brendan 1923-1964
Behan, Beatrice (with Des Hickey and Gus Smith). *My Life with Brendan.* Los Angeles: Nash, 1974.
Behan, Brendan. *Borstal Bay.* London: Hutchinson, 1958.
—. *Confessions of an Irish Rebel.* New York: Bernard Geis Associates, 1966.
Behan, Dominic. *My Brother Behan.* New York: Simon & Schuster, 1965.
Jeffs, Rae. *Brendan Behan: Man and Showman.* London: Hutchinson, 1966.
McCann, Sean, (ed.). *The World of Brendan Behan.* New York: Twayne, 1965.
O'Connor, Ulick. *Brendan Behan.* London: Hamilton, 1970.
Simpson, Alan. *Beckett and Behan and a Theatre in Dublin.* London: Routledge & Paul, 1962.

Behn, Aphra 1640-1689
Hahn, Emily. *Aphra Behn.* London: Cape, 1951.
West, Victoria Sackville. *Aphra Behn.* New York: Viking, 1928.

Behrman, S. N. 1893-1973
Asher, Don. *The Eminent Yachtsman and the Whorehouse Piano Player.* New York: Coward, McCann & Geoghegan, 1973.
Behrman, S. N. *The Worcester Account.* New York: Random House, 1954.
—. *People in a Diary.* Boston: Little, Brown, 1972.

Belasco, David 1859-1931
Belasco, David. *Plays Produced under the Stage Direction of David Belasco.* New York: 1925.
Marker, Lise-Lone. *David Belasco: Naturalism in the American Theatre.* Princeton: Princeton Univ., 1975.
Timberlake, Craig. *The Life and Work of David Belasco, the Bishop of Broadway.* New York: Library Publishers, 1954.
Winter, William. *The Life of David Belasco.* New York: Moffat, Yard, 1918; 2 vols.

Bell, Mary Hayley 1914-
Bell, Mary Hayley. *What Shall We Do Tomorrow? The Story of My Families.* Philadelphia: Lippincott, 1968.

Bellamy, George Anne c.1727-1788
Bellamy, George Anne. *An Apology for the Life of George Anne Bellamy, Late of Covent-Garden Theatre.* London: Bell, 1785.
Hartmann, Cyril Hughes. *Enchanting Bellamy.* London: Heinemann, 1956.

Belmont, Eleanor
See: Robson, Eleanor.

Benchley, Robert Charles 1889-1945
Benchley, Nathaniel. *Robert Benchley, a Biography.* New York: McGraw-Hill, 1955.
Redding, Robert. *Starring Robert Benchley.* Albuquerque: Univ. of New Mexico, 1973.
Rosmond, Babette. *Robert Benchley: His Life and Good Times.* Garden City: Doubleday, 1970.
Yates, Norris W. *Robert Benchley.* New York: Twayne, 1968.

Bennett, Constance 1905-1965
McBride, Mary Margaret. *The Life Story of Constance Bennett.* New York: Star Library Publications, 1932.

Bennett, Joan 1910-
Bennett, Joan and Kibbee, Lois. *The Bennett Playhill.* New York: Holt, Rinehart & Winston, 1970.

Benois, Alexander Nikolayevich 1870-1960
Benois, Aleksandr Nikolayevich (trans. by Moura Budberg). *Memoirs.* London: Chatto & Windus, 1960.
—. *Memoirs. Volume II.* London: Chatto & Windus, 1964.
— (trans. by Mary Britnieva). *Reminiscences of the Russian Ballet.* London: Putnam, 1947.

Benson, Frank R. 1858-1939
Benson, Constance, *Mainly Players: Bensonian Memories.* London: Butterworth, 1926.
Benson, Frank R. *My Memoirs.* London: Benn, 1930.
Trewin, John Courtenay. *Benson and the Bensonians.* London: Barrie & Rockliff, 1960.

Berg, Gertrude 1899-1966
Berg, Gertrude, with Berg, Cherney. *Molly and Me.* New York: McGraw-Hill, 1961.

Bergman, Ingrid 1916-
Brown, Curtis F. *Ingrid Bergman.* New York: Pyramid, 1973.
Steele, Joseph Henry. *Ingrid Bergman: An Intimate Portrait.* New York: McKay, 1959.

Berkeley, Busby 1895-1976
Pike, Bob and Martin, Dave. *The Genius of Busby Berkeley.* Los Angeles: Sherbourne Press, 1974.
Thomas, Tony and Terry, Jim. *The Busby Berkeley Book.* New York: Graphic Society, 1973.

Berle, Milton 1908-
Berle, Milton and Frankel, Haskel. *Milton Berle.* New York: Delacorte, 1974.

Berlin, Irving 1888-
Ewen, David. *The Story of Irving Berlin.* New York: Holt, 1950.
Freedland, Michael. *Irving Berlin.* New York: Stein & Day, 1974.
Woollcott, Alexander. *The Story of Irving Berlin.* New York: Putnam, 1925.

Bernardi, Berel 1872?-1932
Bernardi, Jack. *My Father, the Actor.* New York: Norton, 1971.

Bernhardt, Sarah 1844-1923
Agate, May. *Madame Sarah.* London: Home & Van Thal, 1946.
Arthur, George. *Sarah Bernhardt.* London: Heinemann, 1923.
Baring, Maurice. *Sarah Bernhardt.* London: Davies, 1933.
Bernhardt, Lysiane Sarah (trans. by Vyvyan Holland). *Sarah Bernhardt, My Grandmother.* New York: Hurst & Blackett, 1949.
Bernhardt, Sarah. *Memories of My Life.* New York: D. Appleton, 1923.
Berton, Thérèse. *Sarah Bernhardt as I Knew Her; The Memories of Madame Pierre Benton as Told to Basil Woon.* London: Hurst & Blackett, 1923.
Brereton, Austin. *Sarah Bernhardt; An Illustrated Memoir.* Sydney: Marcus & Andrew, 1891.
Gallus, A. *Sarah Bernhardt; Her Artistic Life.* New York: R. H. Russell, 1901.
Geller, G. J. (trans. by E. S. G. Potter). *Sarah Bernhardt.* London: Duckworth, 1933.
Hahn, Reynaldo (trans. by Ethel Thompson). *Sarah Bernhardt.* London: Mathews & Marrot, 1932.
Noble, Iris. *Great Lady of the Theatre, Sarah Bernhardt.* New York: Messner, 1960.
Richardson, Joanna. *Sarah Bernhardt.* London: Max Reinhardt, 1959.
Row, Arthur. *Sarah the Divine; The Biography of Sarah Bernhardt.* New York: Comet, 1957.
Rueff, Suze. *I Knew Sarah Bernhardt.* London: Muller, 1951.
Skinner, Cornelia Otis. *Madame Sarah.* Boston: Houghton Mifflin, 1967.

Taranow, Gerda. *Sarah Bernhardt: The Art within the Legend.* Princeton: Princeton Univ., 1972.
Verneuil, Louis (trans. by Ernest Boyd). *The Fabulous Life of Sarah Bernhardt.* New York: Harper, 1942.
The Amours of Sarah, the Eccentric. Boston: G. V. Barton, 188-.

Berry, William Henry 1872-1951
Berry, William Henry. *Forty Years in the Limelight.* London: Hutchinson, 1939.

Betterton, Thomas 1635-1710
Gildon, Charles. *The Life of Mr. Thomas Betterton, the Late Eminent Tragedian.* London: Gosling, 1710.
Lowe, Robert William. *Thomas Betterton.* London: Paul, Trench, Trübner, 1891.
An Account of the Life of That Celebrated Tragedian, Mr. Thomas Betterton. London: Robinson, 1749.
The Life and Times of That Excellent and Renowned Actor Thomas Betterton . . . London: Reader, 1888.

Betty, William Henry West 1791-1874
Democritus, Junior. *The Young Roscius Dissected; or, an Account of the Parentage, Birth, and Education of William Henry West Betty; Strictures on His Acting; Reasons for the Decline of His Popularity.* London: 1805.
Harley, George Davies. *An Authentic Biographical Sketch of the Life, Education, and Personal Character of William Henry West Betty, the Celebrated Young Roscius.* London: Phillips, 1804.
Jackson, John. *Strictures Upon the Merits of Young Roscius.* London: Longman, Hurst, Rees, & Orme, 1804.
Playfair, Giles. *The Prodigy; A Study of the Strange Life of Master Betty.* London: Secker & Warburg, 1967.
The Young Roscius. Biographical Memories of William Hen. West Betty . . . New York: McDermut, 1806.
The Wonderful Theatrical Progress of W. Hen. West Betty, the Infant Roscius . . . with an Accurate Sketch of His Life. London: Barnard & Sultzer, 1804.

Bibiena Family, 17th-18th centuries
Mayor, Alpheus Hyatt. *The Bibiena Family.* New York: Bittner, 1945.

Blow, Sydney 1878-1961
Blow, Sydney. *The Ghost Walks on Fridays, In and Out of the Stage Door.* London: Heath Cranton, 1935.
—. *Through Stage Doors; or, Memories of Two in the Theatre.* Edinburgh: W. & R. Chambers, 1958.

Blumenthal, George 1862-1943
Blumenthal, George. *My Sixty Years in Show Business.* New York: F. C. Osberg, 1936.

Boker, George Henry 1823-1890
Bradley, Edward S. *George Henry Boker, Poet and Patriot.* Philadelphia: Univ. of Pennsylvania, 1927.

Boleslawski, Richard 1889-1937
Boleslavski, Richard and Woodward, Helen. *Lances Down; Between the Fires in Moscow.* Indianapolis: Bobbs-Merrill, 1932.

Bolton, Guy 1886-
See: Wodehouse, Pelham G.

Booth, Barton 1681-1733
Victor, Benjamin. *Memoirs of the Life of Barton Booth.* London: Watts, 1733.

Booth Family
Kimmel, Stanley Preston. *The Mad Booths of Maryland.* Indianapolis: Bobbs-Merrill, 1940; 2d rev. New York: Dover, 1970.
Mahoney, Ella V. *Sketches of Tudor Hall and the Booth Family.* Belair, Md.: 1925.

Booth, Edwin 1833-1893
Booth, Edwin (ed. by Daniel J. Watermeier). *Between Actor and Critic; Selected Letters of Edwin Booth and William Winter.* Princeton: Princeton Univ., 1971.
Clarke, Asia Booth. *The Elder and the Younger Booth.* Boston: J. R. Osgood, 1882.
Copeland, Charles Townsend. *Edwin Booth.* Boston: Small, Maynard, 1901.
Goodale, Katherine. *Behind the Scenes with Edwin Booth.* Boston: Houghton Mifflin, 1931.
Grossman, Edwina Booth. *Edwin Booth; Recollections by His Daughter.* New York: Century, 1894.
Hutton, Laurance. *Edwin Booth.* New York: Harper, 1893.
Lockridge, Richard. *Darling of Misfortune: Edwin Booth: 1833-1893.* New York: Century, 1932.
Power-Waters, Alma. *The Story of Young Edwin Booth.* New York: Dutton, 1955.
Royle, Edwin Milton. *Edwin Booth as I Knew Him.* New York: The Players, 1933.
Ruggles, Eleanor. *Prince of Players.* New York: Norton, 1953.
Skinner, Otis. *The Last Tragedian.* New York: Dodd, Mead, 1939.
Winter, William. *Edwin Booth in Twelve Dramatic Characters.* Boston: J. R. Osgood, 1872.
—. *Life and Art of Edwin Booth.* New York and London: Macmillan, 1893.

Booth, John Wilkes 1839-1865
Baker, Ray Stannard. *The Capture, Death and Burial of J. Wilkes Booth.* Chicago: Poor Richard, 1940.
Bates, Finis L. *Escape and Suicide of John Wilkes Booth, Assassin of President Lincoln.* Memphis: Pilcher, 1907.
Clarke, Asia Booth. *The Unlocked Book: A Memoir of John Wilkes Booth.* London: Faber & Faber, 1938.
Ferguson, William J. *I Saw Booth Shoot Lincoln.* Boston: Houghton Mifflin, 1930.
Forrester, Izola Louise. *This One Mad Act; The Unknown Story of John Wilkes Booth and His Family.* Boston: Cushman & Flint, 1937.
Jones, Thomas A. *J. Wilkes Booth; An Account of His Sojourn in Southern Maryland after the Assassination of Abraham Lincoln, His Passage Across the Potomac, and His Death in Virginia.* Chicago: Laird & Lee, 1893.
Leonardi, Dell. *The Reincarnation of John Wilkes Booth: A Case Study in Hypnotic Regression.* Old Greenwich, Conn.: Devin-Adair, 1975.
Miller, Ernest C. *John Wilkes Booth—Oilman.* New York: Exposition Press, 1947.
Stern, Philip Van Doren. *The Man Who Killed Lincoln.* New York: Random House, 1939.
Townsend, George A. *The Life, Crime, and Capture of John Wilkes Booth.* New York: Dick & Fitzgerald, 1865.
Weichmann, Louis J. (ed. by Floyd Risvold). *A True History of the Assassination of Abraham Lincoln.* New York: Knopf, 1975.
Wilson, Francis. *John Wilkes Booth; Fact and Fiction of Lincoln's Assassination.* Boston: Houghton Mifflin, 1929.
Woods, Rufus. *The Weirdest Story in American History; The Escape of John Wilkes Booth.* Wenatchee, Wash.: 1944.

Booth, Junius Brutus 1796-1852
Booth, Junius Brutus. *Memoirs of Junius Brutus Booth.* London: Chapple, 1817.
Clarke, Asia Booth. *Booth Memorials. Passages, Incidents, and Anecdotes in the Life of Junius Brutus Booth (the Elder).* New York: Carleton, 1866.
—. *The Elder and the Younger Booth.* Boston: J. R. Osgood, 1882.
Gould, Thomas B. *The Tragedian; an Essay on the Histrionic Genius of Junius Brutus Booth.* New York: Hurd & Houghton, 1868.
The Actor; or, A Peep Behind the Curtain. Being Passages in the Lives of Booth and Some of His Contemporaries. New York: W. H. Graham, 1846.

Bostock, Edward H. 1858-1940
Bostock, E. H. *Menageries, Circuses and Theatres.* London: Chapman & Hall, 1927.

Boucicault, Dion 1822-1890
Hogan, Robert. *Dion Boucicault.* New York: Twayne, 1969.
Walsh, Townsend. *The Career of Dion Boucicault.* New York: Dunlap Society, 1915.

Bowman, Laura 1881-1957
Antoine, Le Roi. *Achievement: The Life of Laura Bowman.* New York: Pageant Press, 1961.

Brady, William A. 1863-1950
Brady, William A. *The Fighting Man.* Indianapolis: Bobbs-Merrill, 1916.
—. *Showman.* New York: Dutton, 1937.

Bragdon, Claude 1866-1946
Bragdon, Claude. *The Secret Springs.* London: A. Dakers, Ltd., 1938. [Published in U.S. as: *More Lives than One.* New York: Knopf, 1938.]

Bragg, Bernard 1928-
Powers, Helen. *Signs of Silence: Bernard Bragg and the National Theatre of the Deaf.* New York: Dodd, Mead, 1972.

Brahm, Otto 1856-1912
Newmark, Maxim. *Otto Brahm, the Man and the Critic.* New York: G. E. Stechert, 1938.

Brando, Marlon 1924-
Carey, Gary. *Brando!* New York: Pocket Books, 1973.
Fiore, Carlo. *Bud: The Brando I Knew.* New York: Delacorte, 1974.
Jordan, Rene. *Marlon Brando.* New York: Pyramid, 1973.
Morella, Joe and Epstein, Edward Z. *Brando; The Unauthorized Biography.* New York: Crown, 1973.
Offen, Ron. *Brando.* Chicago: Regnery, 1973.
Shipman, David. *Brando.* London: Macmillan, 1974.
Thomas, Bob. *Marlon: Portrait of the Rebel as an Artist.* New York: Random House, 1974.

Brecht, Bertolt 1898-1956
Demetz, Peter, (ed.). *Brecht; A Collection of Critical Essays.* Englewood Cliffs, N.J.: Prentice-Hall, 1962.
Esslin, Martin. *Brecht: A Choice of Evils; A Critical Study of the Man, His Work and His Opinions.* London: Eyre & Spottiswoode, 1959.
—. *Bertolt Brecht.* New York: Columbia Univ., 1969.
Ewen, Frederic. *Bertolt Brecht; His Life, His Art, and His Times.* New York: Citadel, 1967.
Haas, Willy (trans. by Max Knight and Joseph Fabry). *Bert Brecht.* New York: Ungar, 1970.
Hill, Claude. *Bertolt Brecht.* New York: Twayne, 1974.
Lyons, Charles R. *Bertolt Brecht; The Despair and the Polemic.* Carbondale: Southern Illinois Univ., 1968.
Witt, Hubert, comp. (trans. by John Peet). *Brecht—As They Knew Him.* New York: International Publishers, 1974.

Brice, Fanny 1891-1951
Katkov, Norman. *The Fabulous Fanny.* New York: Knopf, 1953.

Bridie, James 1888-1951
Bannister, Winifred. *James Bridie and His Theatre.* London: Rockliff, 1955.
Bridie, James. *One Way of Living.* London: Constable, 1939.
Luyben, Helen L. *James Bridie: Clown and Philosopher.* Philadelphia: Univ. of Pennsylvania, 1965.

Brook, Peter 1925-
Trewin, John C. *Peter Brook: A Biography.* London: Macdonald, 1971.

Brooke, Gustavus Vaughan 1818-1860
Lawrence, W. J. *The Life of Gustavus Vaughan Brooke.* Belfast: W. and G. Baird, 1892.

Brooks, Geraldine 1925-
See: Schulberg, Budd.

Broun, Heywood Hale 1918-
Broun, Heywood Hale. *A Studied Madness.* Garden City: Doubleday, 1965.

Brown, Gilmor ?-1960
Green, Harriet L. *Gilmor Brown, Portrait of a Man—and an Idea.* Pasadena, Calif.: Burns, 1933.

Brown, Joe E. 1892-1973
Brown, Joe E. *Your Kids and Mine.* Garden City: Doubleday, 1944.
—, as told to Ralph Hancock. *Laughter Is a Wonderful Thing.* New York: Barnes, 1956.

Brown, John Mason 1900-1969
Brown, John Mason. *Many a Watchful Night.* New York: Whittlesey House, 1944.
Stevens, George. *Speak for Yourself, John: The Life of John Mason Brown with Some of His Letters and Many of His Opinions.* New York: Viking, 1974.

Browne, Maurice 1881-1955
Browne, Maurice. *Too Late to Lament; An Autobiography.* London: Gollancz, 1955.

Bryant, Billy
Bryant, Billy. *Children of Ol' Man River.* New York: Furman, 1936.

Bull, Peter 1912-
Bull, Peter. *I Know the Face, But . . .* London: Davies, 1959.
—. *I Say, Look Here! The Rather Random Reminiscences of a Round Actor in the Square.* London: Davies, 1965.
—. *Life Is a Cucumber.* London: Peter Davies, 1973.

Bulwer-Lytton, Lord Edward George Earle Lytton 1803-1873
Bulwer-Lytton, Edward. *Letters of Bulwer-Lytton to Macready . . . 1836-1866.* Newark, N.J.: Carteret Book Club, 1911.
—. *The Life Letters and Library Remains of Edward Bulwer, Lord Lytton, by His Son.* London: Paul, Trench, 1883; 2 vols.
Escott, T. H. S. *Edward Bulwer, First Baron Lytton of Knebworth: A Social, Personal, and Political Monograph.* London: Routledge, 1910.
Frost, William A. *Bulwer Lytton; an Exposure of the Errors of His Biographers.* London: Lynwood, 1913.
Lytton (2nd Earl), Victor. *The Life of Edward Bulwer, First Lord Lytton, by His Grandson.* London: Macmillan, 1913; 2 vols.
—. *Bulwer-Lytton.* London: Home & Van Thal, 1948.
Sadleir, Michael. *Bulwer and His Wife; a Panorama, 1803-1836.* London: Constable, 1933.
Stewart, C. Nelson. *Bulwer Lytton as Occultist.* London: Theosophical Pub. House, 1927.

Burbage, Richard c.1567-1619
Stopes, Charlotte C. *Burbage and Shakespeare's Stage.* London: Maring, 1913.
Wallace, Charles. *The First London Theatre: Materials for a History.* Omaha: Univ. of Nebraska, 1913.

Burke, Billie 1885-1970
Burke, Billie with Shipp, Cameron. *With a Feather on My Nose.* New York: Appleton-Century-Crofts, 1949.
—. *With Powder on My Nose.* New York: Coward-McCann, 1959.
See also: Ziegfeld, Florenz.

Burns, George 1896-
Burns, George with Lindsay, Cynthia Hobart. *I Love Her, That's Why!* New York: Simon & Schuster, 1955.

Burt, Frank A. ?-1964
Young, Miriam Burt. *Mother Wore Tights.* New York: McGraw-Hill, 1944.

Burton, Percy 1878-1948
Burton, Percy as told to Lowell Thomas. *Adventures Among Immortals; Percy Burton—Impressario . . .* New York: Dodd, Mead, 1937.

Burton, Philip 1904-
Burton, Philip. *Early Doors; My Life and the Theatre.* New York: Dial, 1969.

Burton, Richard 1925-
Cottrell, John and Cashin, Fergus. *Richard Burton.* London: Barker, 1971.

Burton, William E. 1804-1860
Keese, William Linn. *William E. Burton, Actor, Author, and Manager.* New York: Putnam, 1885.

Cahn, Sammy 1913-
Cahn, Sammy. *I Should Care; The Sammy Cahn Story.* New York: Arbor House, 1974.

Calvert, Adelaide Helen 1837-1921
Calvert, Mrs. Charles. *Sixty-eight Years on the Stage.* London: Mills & Boon, 1911.

Campbell, Mrs. Patrick 1865-1940
Campbell, Mrs. Patrick. *My Life and Some Letters.* New York: Dodd, Mead, 1922.
Dent, Alan. *Mrs. Patrick Campbell.* London: Museum Press, 1961.
Shaw, George Bernard (ed. by Alan Dent). *Bernard Shaw and Mrs. Patrick Campbell, Their Correspondence.* New York: Knopf, 1952.

Camus, Albert 1913-1960
Breé, Germaine. *Camus.* New Brunswick, N.J.: Rutgers Univ., 1972.
King, Adele. *Albert Camus.* New York: Grove, 1964.
Lebesque, Morvan (trans. by T. C. Sharman). *Portrait of Camus.* New York: Herder & Herder, 1971.
Luppé, Robert De (trans. by John Cumming and J. Hargreaves). *Albert Camus.* London: Merlin, 1967.
Maquet, Albert (trans. by Herma Briffault). *Albert Camus: The Invincible Summer.* New York: Braziller, 1958.
O'Brien, Conor Cruise. *Albert Camus of Europe and Africa.* New York: Viking, 1970.
Parker, Emmett. *Albert Camus; The Artist in the Arena.* Madison: Univ. of Wisconsin, 1965.
Proix, Robert, ed. (trans. by Gregory H. Davis). *Albert Camus and the Men of the Stone.* San Francisco: Greenwood, 1971.
Quilliot, Roger (trans. by Emmett Parker). *The Sea and Prisons; A Commentary on the Life and Thought of Albert Camus.* University, Ala.: Univ. of Alabama, 1970.
Scott, Nathan A. *Albert Camus.* London: Bowes & Bowes, 1969.
Thody, Philip. *Albert Camus, 1913-1960.* London: Hamilton, 1961.

Cantor, Eddie 1893-1964
Cantor, Eddie, as told to David Freedman. *My Life Is in Your Hands.* New York: Harper, 1928.
—with Kesher, Jane. *Take My Life.* Garden City: Doubleday, 1957.
— (ed. by Phyllis Rosenteur). *The Way I See It.* Englewood Cliffs, N.J.: Prentice-Hall, 1959.

Case, Frank 1877-1946
Case, Frank. *Tales of a Wayward Inn.* New York: Frederick A. Stokes, 1938.
—. *Do Not Disturb.* New York: Frederick A. Stokes, 1940.
Harriman, Margaret Case. *The Vicious Circle; The Story of the Algonquin Round Table.* New York: Rinehart, 1951.
—. *Blessed Are the Debonair.* New York: Rinehart, 1956.

Casson, Lewis 1875-1969
See: Thorndike, Sybil.

Chapin, Harold 1886-1915
Chapin, Harold. *Soldier and Dramatist.* London: Lane, 1916.

Chase, Ilka 1905-
Chase, Ilka. *Free Admission.* Garden City: Doubleday, 1948.
—. *Past Imperfect.* Garden City: Doubleday, 1942.

Chekhov, Anton 1860-1904

Bruford, Walter H. *Anton Chekhov*. New Haven: Yale Univ., 1957.
Chekhov, Anton. (trans. by S. S. Koteliansky and Philip Tomlinson). *The Life and Letters of Anton Chekhov*. New York: George B. Doran, 1925.
— (trans. by Constance Garnett). *The Letters of Anton Pavlovitch Tchehov to Olga Leonardovna Knipper*. New York: G. H. Doran, 1925.
— (trans. by S. S. Koteliansky, Leonard Woolf, and Constance Burnett). *Personal Papers*. New York: Lear, 1948.
— (trans. by Sidonie Lederer). *The Selected Letters of Anton Chekhov*. New York: Farrar, Straus, 1955.
— (trans. by Michael Henry Heim and Simon Karlinsky). *Letters of Anton Chekhov*. New York: Harper & Row, 1973.
— (ed. by Avrahm Yarmolinsky). *Letters of Anton Chekhov*. New York: Viking, 1973.
Chukovsky, Kornei (trans. by Pauline Rose). *Chekhov the Man*. New York: Hutchinson, 1945.
Elton, Oliver. *Chekhov, the Taylorian Lecture, 1929*. London: Oxford, 1929.
Gerhardi, William A. *Anton Chekhov; A Critical Study*. New York: Duffield, 1923.
Gilles, Daniel (trans. by Charles Markmann). *Chekhov: Observer without Illusion*. New York: Funk & Wagnalls, 1968.
Gorky, Maxim, Kuprin, Alexander and Bunin, I. A. (trans. by S. S. Koteliansky and Leonard Woolf). *Reminiscences of Anton Chekhov*. New York: B. W. Huebsch, 1921.
Hingley, Ronald. *Chekhov; A Biographical and Critical Study*. New York: Barnes & Noble, 1966.
Katzer, Julius, (ed.). *A. P. Chekhov, 1860-1960*. Moscow: Foreign Languages Publishing House, 1961.
Koteliansky, S. S., (ed.). *Anton Tchekhov; Literary and Theatrical Reminiscences*. London: Routledge, 1927.
Lafitte, Sophie (trans. by Moura Budberg and Gordon Latta). *Chekhov*. New York: Scribner, 1975.
Llewellyn Smith, Virginia. *Anton Chekhov and the Lady with the Dog*. New York: Oxford, 1973.
Magarshack, David. *Chekhov, a Life*. London: Faber & Faber, 1952.
—. *Chekhov, the Dramatist*. New York: Hill & Wang, 1960.
Saunders, Beatrice. *Tchekhov, the Man*. London: Centaur, 1960.
Simmons, Ernest J. *Chekhov; A Biography*. Boston: Little, Brown, 1962.
Toumanova, Nina Andronikova. *Anton Chekhov; The Voice of Twilight Russia*. New York: Columbia Univ., 1937.
Yermilov, Vladimir (trans. by Ivy Litvinov). *Anton Pavlovich Chekhov, 1860-1904*. Moscow: Foreign Language Publishing House, 195-.

Chevalier, Albert 1861-1923
Chevalier, Albert. *Albert Chevalier. A Record by Himself*. London: Macqueen, 1895.
—. *Before I Forget—The Autobiography of a Chevalier d'Industrie*. London: T. F. Unwin, 1902.

Chevalier, Maurice 1889-1972
Boyer, William. *The Romantic Life of Maurice Chevalier*. London: Hutchinson, 1937.
Chevalier, Maurice, as told to Percy Cudlipp. *Maurice Chevalier's Own Story*. London: Nash & Grayson, 1930.
—. *The Man in the Straw Hat; My Story*. New York: Crowell, 1949.
—, as told to Eileen and Robert Mason Pollock. *With Love*. Boston: Little, Brown, 1960.
— (trans. by Cornelia Higginson). *I Remember It Well*. New York: Macmillan, 1970.
Ringfold, Gene and Bodeen, Dewitt. *Chevalier; The Films and Career of Maurice Chevalier*. Secaucus, N.J.: Citadel, 1973.

Cibber, Charlotte (Mrs. Richard Charke) ?-1760
Charke, Charlotte Cibber. *A Narrative of the Life of Mrs. Charlotte Charke*. London: Reeve, 1755.

Cibber, Colley 1671-1757
Ashley, Leonard R. N. *Colley Cibber*. New York: Twayne, 1955.
Barker, Richard Hindry. *Mr. Cibber of Drury Lane*. New York: Columbia Univ., 1939.
Cibber, Colley. *An Apology for the Life of Mr. Colley Cibber*. London: Watts, 1740.
Habbema, D.M.E. *An Appreciation of Colley Cibber, Actor and Dramatist . . .* Amsterdam: H. J. Paris, 1928.
Senior, F. Dorothy. *The Life and Times of Colley Cibber*. London: Constable, 1928.

Cibber, Susannah Maria Arne (Mrs. Theophilus Cibber) 1714-1766
An Account of the Life of that Celebrated Actress, Mrs. Susannah Maria Cibber. London: Reader, 1887.

Clairon, Hyppolite 1723-1803
Clairon, Claire Joseph Hyppolite (trans. from the French). *Memoirs of Hyppolite Clairon, the Celebrated French Actress*. London: O. G. & J. Robinson, 1800.

Clapp, Henry Austin 1841-1904
Clapp, Henry Austin. *Reminiscences of a Dramatic Critic*. Boston: Houghton Mifflin, 1902.

Clarence, O. B. 1870-1955
Clarence, O. B. *No Complaints*. London: Cape, 1943.

Clark, Bobby 1888-1960
Taylor, Robert Lewis. *The Running Pianist*. Garden City; Doubleday, 1950.

Clarke, J[oseph] I. C. 1846-1925
Clarke, Joseph I. C. *My Life and Memories*. New York: Dodd, Mead, 1925.

Claudel, Paul 1868-1955
Chaigne, Louis (trans. by Pierre De Fontnouvelle). *Paul Claudel, the Man and the Mystic*. New York: Appleton-Century-Crofts, 1961.
Claudel, Paul (trans. by Henry L. Stuart). *Letters to a Doubter [1907-1914]*. New York: A. & C. Boni, 1927.
— (trans. by John Russell). *The Correspondence, 1899-1926, between Paul Claudel and Andre Gide*. New York: Pantheon, 1952.
— (trans. by Christine Trollope). *Claudel on the Theatre*. Coral Gables, Fla.: Univ. of Miami, 1972.
Du Sarment, A. (trans. by William Howard). *Letters from Paul Claudel, My Godfather*. Westminster, Md.: Newman Press, 1964.
Waters, Harold A. *Paul Claudel*. New York: Twayne, 1970.

Clive, Kitty (Catherine Raftor) 1711-1785
Fitzgerald, Percy. *The Life of Mrs. Catherine Clive*. London: Reader, 1888.

Clunes, Alec 1912-1970
Trewin, J. C. *Alec Clunes*. London: Rockliff, 1958.

Clurman, Harold 1901-
Clurman, Harold. *The Fervent Years; The Story of the Group Theatre and the Thirties*. New York: Knopf, 1950.
—. *All People Are Famous*. New York: Harcourt, Brace, Jovanovich, 1974.

Cochran, C. B. 1872-1951
Cleugh, James. *Charles Blake Cochran, Lord Bountiful*. London: Pallas, 1946.
Cochran, Charles Blake. *The Secrets of a Showman*. London: Heinemann, 1925.
—. *I Had Almost Forgotten*. London: Hutchinson, 1932.
—. *Cock-a-Doodle-Do*. London: J. M. Dent, 1941.
—. *Showman Looks On*. London: J. M. Dent, 1945.
Graves, Charles. *The Cochran Story*. London: W. H. Allen, 1951.
Heppner, Samuel. *Cockie*. London: Frewin, 1969.

Cocteau, Jean 1891-1963
Brown, Frederick. *An Impersonation of Angels; A Biography of Jean Cocteau*. New York: Viking, 1968.
Cocteau, Jean (trans. by Mary C. Hoeck). *Maalesh; A Theatrical Tour in the Middle East*. London: Owen, 1956.
— (trans. by Margaret Crosland and Sinclair Road). *Opium; The Diary of a Cure*. New York: Grove, 1958.
— (trans. by Wallace Fowlie). *Journals*. Bloomington: Indiana Univ., 1964.
— (trans. by Richard Howard). *Professional Secrets*. New York: Farrar, Straus & Giroux, 1970.
Crosland, Margaret. *Jean Cocteau*. New York: Nevill, 1955.
Fowlie, Wallace. *Jean Cocteau; The History of a Poet's Age*. Bloomington: Indiana Univ., 1966.
Gilson, Rene (trans. by Ciba Vaughan). *Jean Cocteau*. New York: Crown, 1969.
Knapp, Bettina. *Jean Cocteau*. New York: Twayne, 1970.
Peters, Arthur K. *Jean Cocteau and Andre Gide: An Abrasive Friendship*. New Brunswick: Rutgers Univ., 1973.
Sprigge, Elizabeth and Kimm, Jean-Jacques. *Jean Cocteau; The Man and the Mirror*. New York: Coward-McCann, 1968.
Steegmuller, Francis. *Cocteau: A Biography*. Boston: Little, Brown, 1970.

Coffin, C[harles] Hayden 1862-1935
Coffin, Charles H. *Hayden Coffin's Book, Packed with Acts and Facts*. London: Alston Rivers, 1930.

Cohan, George M. 1878-1942
Cohan, George M. *Twenty Years on Broadway and the Years It Took to Get There*. New York: Harper, 1925.
McCabe, John. *George M. Cohan: The Man Who Owned Broadway*. Garden City: Doubleday, 1973.
Morehouse, Ward. *George M. Cohan, Prince of the American Theatre*. Philadelphia: J. B. Lippincott, 1943.

Cohn, Harry 1891-1958
Thomas, Bob. *King Cohn; The Life and Times of Harry Cohn.* New York: Putnam, 1967.

Coleman, John 1831-1904
Coleman, John. *Fifty Years of an Actor's Life.* London: Hutchinson, 1904.

Collier, Constance 1878-1955
Collier, Constance. *Harlequinade; The Story of My Life.* London: Lane, 1929.

Colman, George (the elder) 1732-1794
Page, Eugene R. *George Colman, the Elder.* New York: Columbia Univ. Press, 1935.
See also: Colman, George (the younger).

Colman, George (the younger) 1762-1836
Bagster-Collins, Jeremy. *George Colman, the Younger, 1762-1836.* New York: King's Crown, 1946.
Colman, George, the younger. *Random Records.* London: Colburn and Bentley, 1830; 2 vols.
Peake, Richard B. *Memoirs of the Colman Family, Including Their Correspondence with the Most Distinguished Personages of Their Time.* London: Bentley, 1841; 2 vols.

Colum, Padraic 1881-
Bowen, Zack R. *Padraic Colum; A Biographical-Critical Introduction.* Carbondale: Southern Illinois Univ., 1970.

Compton, Fay 1894-
Compton, Fay. *Rosemary, Some Remembraces.* London: Alston Rivers, 1926.

Compton, Henry 1805-1877
Compton, Charles and Edward (eds.). *Memoir of Henry Compton.* London: Tinsley, 1879.

Congreve, William 1670-1729
Congreve, William (ed. by John C. Hodges). *Letters & Documents.* London: Macmillan, 1964.
Gosse, Edmund. *Life of William Congreve.* New York: Scribner, 1924.
Hodges, John C. *William Congreve, the Man; A Biography from New Sources.* London: Oxford Univ., 1941.
Lynch, Kathleen Martha. *A Congreve Gallery.* Cambridge: Harvard Univ., 1951.
Novak, Maximillian E. *William Congreve.* New York: Twayne, 1971.
Taylor, Daniel Crane. *William Congreve.* London: Oxford Univ., 1931.

Connelly, Marc 1890-
Connelly, Marc. *Voices Offstage.* Chicago: Holt, Rinehart & Winston, 1968.
Nolan, Paul T. *Marc Connelly.* New York: Twayne, 1969.

Conried, Heinrich 1855-1909
Moses, Montrose J. *The Life of Heinrich Conried.* New York: Crowell, 1916.

Constanduros, Mabel -1957
Constanduros, Mabel. *Shreds and Patches.* London: Lawson & Dunn, 1946.

Conti, Italia 1874-1946
Selby-Lowndes, Joan. *The Conti Story.* London: Collins, 1954.

Cooke, George Frederick 1756-1812
Dunlap, William. *The Life of George Fred. Cooke.* London: Colburn, 1813; 2 vols.

Cooper, Diana (Lady Duff Cooper) 1892-
Cooper, Diana. *The Rainbow Comes and Goes.* Boston: Houghton Mifflin, 1958.
—. *The Light of Common Day.* Boston: Houghton Mifflin, 1959.
—. *Trumpets from the Steep.* Boston: Houghton, 1960.

Cooper, Gladys 1889-1971
Cooper, Gladys. *Gladys Cooper.* London: Hutchinson, 1931.
Stokes, Sewell. *Without Veils; The Intimate Biography of Gladys Cooper.* London: Davies, 1953.

Corneille, Pierre 1606-1684
Abraham, Claude K. *Pierre Corneille.* New York: Twayne, 1972.
Guizot, Francois Pierre Guillaume, *Corneille and His Times.* New York: Harper, 1852.

Cornell, Katharine 1898-1974
Cornell, Katharine (as told to Ruth Woodbury Sedgwick). *I Wanted to Be An Actress.* New York: Random House, 1939.
Malvern, Gladys. *Curtain Going Up.* New York: Messner, 1944.
See also: McClintic, Guthrie.

Cosgrave, Luke 1862-1949
Cosgrave, Luke. *Theatre Tonight.* Hollywood: House-Warven, 1952.

Courtneidge, Cicely 1893-
Courtneidge, Cicely. *Cicely.* London: Hutchinson, 1953.
Hulbert, Jack. *The Little Woman's Always Right.* London: W. H. Allen, 1975.

Courtneidge, Robert 1859-1939
Courtneidge, Robert. *"I Was an Actor Once."* London: Hutchinson, 1930.

Coward, Noel 1899-1973
Braybrooke, Patrick. *Amazing Mr. Noel Coward.* London: Archer, 1933.
Castle, Charles. *Noel.* London: W. H. Allen, 1972.
Coward, Noel. *Present Indicative.* Garden City: Doubleday, Doran, 1937.
—. *Future Indefinite.* Garden City: Doubleday, 1954.
— (ed. by John Hadfield). *A Last Encore.* Boston: Little, Brown, 1973.
Greacen, Robert. *The Art of Noel Coward.* Aldington: Hand and Flower Press, 1953.
Marchant, William. *The Privilege of His Company.* Indianapolis: Bobbs-Merrill, 1975.
Morley, Sheridan. *A Talent to Amuse.* Garden City: Doubleday, 1969.

Cowell, Joseph 1792-1863
Cowell, Joseph. *Thirty Years Passed Among the Players in England and America.* New York: Harper, 1844.

Cowell, Samuel 1820-1864
Disher, M. Willson (ed.). *The Cowells in America.* London: Oxford Univ., 1934.

Cox, Wally 1924-1973
Cox, Wally. *My Life as a Small Boy.* New York: Simon & Schuster, 1961.

Crabtree, Lotta 1847-1924
Bates, Helen Marie. *Lotta's Last Season.* Brattleboro, Vt.: E. L. Hildreth, 1940.
Dempsey, David. *The Triumphs and Trials of Lotta Crabtree.* New York: Morrow, 1968.
Jackson, Phyllis W. *Golden Footlights; The Merry-Making Career of Lotta Crabtree.* New York: Holiday House, 1949.
Rourke, Constance. *Troupers of the Gold Coast.* New York: Harcourt, Brace, 1928.

Craig, Edith (Edith Wardell) 1869-1947
Adlard, Eleanor (ed.). *Edy; Recollections of Edith Craig.* London: Muller, 1949.

Craig, Edward Gordon 1872-1966
Bablet, Denis. *Edward Gordon Craig* (trans. by Daphne Woodward). New York: Theatre Arts, 1966.
Craig, Edward Gordon. *Index to the Story of My Days.* London: Hulton, 1957.
Leeper, Janet. *Edward Gordon Craig: Designs for the Theatre.* Harmondsworth, Middlesex: Penguin, 1948.
Rood, Arnold. *Edward Gordon Craig, Artist of the Theatre, 1872-1966; a Memorial Exhibition in the Amsterdam Gallery* [*of The New York Public Library*]. *Catalogue.* New York: The New York Public Library, 1967.
Rose, Enid. *Gordon Craig and the Theatre.* London: Low, Marston, 1931.

Crane, William H. 1845-1928
Crane, William H. *Footprints and Echoes.* New York: Dutton, 1927.

Cressy, Will M. 1863-1930
Cressy, Will M. *Continuous Vaudeville.* Boston: Badger, 1914.

Cushman, Charlotte 1816-1876
Barrett, Lawrence. *Charlotte Cushman.* New York: Dunlap Society, 1889.
Price, W. T. *A Life of Charlotte Cushman.* New York: Brentano, 1894.
Leach, Joseph. *Bright Particular Star; The Life & Times of Charlotte Cushman.* New Haven: Yale Univ., 1970.
Stebbins, Emma, (ed.). *Charlotte Cushman: Her Letters and Memories of Her Life.* Boston: Houghton, Osgood, 1879.
Waters, Clara Erskine. *Charlotte Cushman.* Boston: J. R. Osgood, 1882.

Dalrymple, Jean 1910-
Dalrymple, Jean. *September Child.* New York: Dodd, Mead, 1963.
—. *From the Last Row.* Clifton, N.J.: James T. White, 1975.

Daly, Augustin 1838-1899
Daly, Joseph Francis. *The Life of Augustin Daly.* New York: Macmillan, 1917.
Dithmar, Edward A. *Memories of Daly's Theatre.* New York: 1897.
Felheim, Marvin. *The Theatre of Augustin Daly.* Cambridge: Harvard University, 1956.
See also: Ranous, Dora.

Daly, Arnold 1875-1927
Goldsmith, Berthold H. *Arnold Daly.* New York: James T. White, 1927.

Dandridge, Dorothy 1924-1965
Dandridge, Dorothy and Conrad, Earl. *Everything and Nothing; The Dorothy Dandridge Tragedy.* New York: Abelard-Schuman, 1970.

D'Avenant, Sir William 1606-1668
Harbage, Alfred. *Sir William D'Avenant, Poet, Venturer, 1606-1668.* Philadelphia: Univ. of Pennsylvania, 1935.
Marchant, Edgar C. *Sir William D'Avenant;*

An Informal Address. Oxford: Davenant Society, Lincoln College, 1936.
Nethercot, Arthur H. *Sir William D'Avenant, Poet Laureate and Playwright-Manager.* New York: Russell & Russell, 1967.

Davenport, E. L. 1815-1877
Edgett, Edwin Francis (ed.). *Edward Loomis Davenport.* New York: Dunlap Society, 1901.

Davis, Bette 1908-
Davis, Bette. *The Lonely Life.* New York Putnam, 1962.
Noble, Peter. *Bette Davis; A Biography.* London: Skelton Robinson, 1948.
Stine, Whitney with Davis, Bette. *Mother Goddam.* New York: Hawthorn, 1974.
Vermilye, Jerry. *Bette Davis.* New York: Pyramid, 1973.

Davis, Owen 1874-1956
Davis, Owen. *I'd Like to Do It Again.* New York: Farrar & Rinehart, 1931.
—. *My First Fifty Years in the Theatre.* Boston: Walter H. Baker, 1950.

Davis, Sammy, Jr. 1925-
Davis, Sammy, Jr. and Boyar, Jane and Burt. *Yes I Can; The Story of Sammy Davis, Jr.* New York: Farrar, Straus & Giroux, 1965.

De Angelis, Jefferson 1859-1933
De Angelis, Jefferson and Harlow, Alvin E., *A Vagabond Trouper.* New York. Harcourt, Brace, 1931.

Deburau, Jean-Baptiste Gaspard 1796-1846
Janin, Jules (trans. by Winifred Katzin). *Deburau.* New York: R. M. McBride, 1928.
Kozik, Francis (trans. by Dora Round). *Pierrot.* London: Harrap, 1942. [Published in U.S. as: *The Great Deburau.* New York: Farrar & Rinehart, 1942]

De Courville, Albert P. 1887-1960
De Courville, Albert. *I Tell You.* London: Chapman & Hall, 1928.

De Frece, Lady (Matilda Alice Powles) 1864-1952
See: Tilley, Vesta.

Dekker, Thomas 1570-c.1632
Hunt, Mary L. *Thomas Dekker; A Study.* New York: Columbia Univ., 1911.

Delsarte, François 1811-1871
Shawn, Ted. *Every Little Movement; A Book about Francois Delsarte.* Pittsfield, Mass.: Eagle Print and Binding, 1963.

De Mille, Agnes 1908-
de Mille, Agnes. *Dance to the Piper.* Boston: Little, Brown, 1952.
—. *And Promenade Home.* Boston: Little, Brown, 1958.
—. *Speak to Me, Dance with Me.* Boston: Little, Brown, 1973.

Derwent, Clarence 1884-1959
Derwent, Clarence. *The Derwent Story.* New York: Henry Schuman, 1953.

Desmond, Florence 1905-
Desmond, Florence. *Florence Desmond.* London: Harrap, 1953.

De Wolfe, Elsie 1865-1950
Bemelmans, Ludwig. *To the One I Love the Best.* New York: Viking, 1955.
De Wolfe, Elsie. *After All.* New York: Harper, 1935.

Dibdin, Charles 1745-1814
Dibdin, Charles. *The Public Undeceived . . . Containing a Statement of All the Material Facts Relative to His Pension.* London: Chapple, 1807.

Dibdin, Charles Isaac Mungo 1768-1833
Dibdin, Charles Isaac Mungo. (ed. by George Speaight). *Professional & Literary Memoirs of Charles Dibdin the Younger . . .* London: Society for Theatre Research, 1956.

Dibdin, Thomas 1771-1841
Dibdin, Thomas John. *The Reminiscences of Thomas Dibdin . . .* London: Colburn, 1834.

Dietz, Howard 1896-
Dietz, Howard. *Dancing in the Dark.* New York: Quadrangle, 1974.

Digges, (John) Dudley West 1720-1786
Digges, West. *Letters which Passed between Mr. West Digges, Comedian, and Mrs. Sarah Ward, 1752-1759 . . .* Edinburgh: Stevenson, 1833.

Doggett, Thomas c.1670-1721
Cook, Theodore Andrea. *Thomas Doggett Deceased: A Famous Comedian.* London: Constable, 1908.

Donahue, Jack ?-1930
Donahue, Jack. *Letters of a Hoofer to His Ma.* New York: Cosmopolitan Book, 1931.

Donaldson, Walter 1793?-1877
Donaldson, Walter. *Recollections of an Actor.* London: Maxwell, 1865.

Donisthorpe, G. Sheila 1898-1946
Donisthorpe, Gladys Sheila. *Show Business; A Book of the Theatre.* London: Fortune Press, 1943.

Draper, Ruth 1884-1956
Zabel, Morton Dauwen. *The Art of Ruth Draper.* Garden City: Doubleday, 1960.

Drew, John 1853-1927
Dithmar, Edward A. *John Drew.* New York: Frederick A. Stokes, 1900.
Drew, John. *My Years on the Stage.* New York: Dutton, 1922.
Wood, Peggy. *A Splendid Gypsy: John Drew.* New York: Dutton, 1928.

Drew, Louisa Lane 1820-1897
Drew, Louisa. *Autobiographical Sketch of Mrs. John Drew.* New York: Scribner, 1899.

Drinkwater, John 1882-1937
Drinkwater, John. *Inheritance; The First Book of an Autobiography.* New York: Holt, 1931.
—. *Discovery; Being the Second Book of an Autobiography, 1897-1913.* Boston: Houghton Mifflin, 1933.

Dryden, John 1631-1700
Dryden, John (ed. by Charles E. Ward). *The Letters of John Dryden, with Letters Addressed to Him.* Durham, N.C.: Duke Univ., 1942.
Eliot, T. S. *John Dryden, the Poet, the Dramatist, the Critic.* New York: Holliday, 1932.
Hollis, Christopher. *Dryden.* London: Duckworth, 1933.
Johnson, Samuel (ed. by Alfred Milnes). *Lives of Dryden and Pope.* Oxford: Clarendon, 1885.
Osborn, James M. *John Dryden.* Gainesville: Univ. of Florida, 1965.
Saintsbury, George E. *Dryden.* New York: Harper, 1887.
Scott, Sir Walter (ed. by Bernard Kreissman). *The Life of John Dryden.* Lincoln: Univ. of Nebraska, 1963.
Ward, Charles E. *The Life of John Dryden.* Chapel Hill: Univ. of North Carolina, 1961.
Young, Kenneth. *John Dryden: A Critical Biography.* London: Sylvan Press, 1954.

Duff, Mrs. Mary Ann (née Dyke) 1794-1857
Ireland, Joseph Norton . . . *Mrs. Duff . . .* Boston: J. R. Osgood, 1882.

Duke, Vernon 1903-1969
Duke, Vernon. *Passport to Paris.* Boston: Little, Brown, 1955.

Dukes, Ashley, 1885-1959
Dukes, Ashley. *The Scene Is Changed.* London: Macmillan, 1942.

Du Maurier, Gerald 1873-1934
Du Maurier, Daphne. *Gerald; a Portrait.* London: Gollancz, 1934.

Dumas, Alexandre (Père) 1802-1870
Davidson, Arthur F. *Alexandre Dumas, Père; His Life and Works.* Philadelphia: Lippincott, 1902.
Dumas, Alexandre (trans by A. Craig Bell). *My Memoirs.* London: Owen, 1961.
Fitzgerald, Percy. *The Life and Adventures of Alexander Dumas.* London: Tinsley, 1873; 2 vols.
Gorman, Herbert S. *The Incredible Marquis, Alexandre Dumas . . .* New York: Farrar & Rinehart, 1929.
See also: Dumas, Alexandre (fils).

Dumas, Alexandre (Fils) 1824-1895
Gribble, Francis H. *Dumas, Father and Son.* New York: Dutton, 1930.
Maurois, André (trans. by Gerard Hopkins). *The Titans, a Three-Generation Biography of the Dumas.* New York: Harper, 1957. [Published in England as: *Three Musketeers.*]
Saunders, Edith. *The Prodigal Father; Dumas Père et Fils and "The Lady of the Camellias."* London: Longmans, Green, 1951.
Taylor, Frank A. *The Theatre of Alexandre Dumas Fils.* Oxford: Clarendon, 1937.

Dunham, Katherine 1910-
Dunham, Katherine. *A Touch of Innocence.* New York: Harcourt, Brace, 1959.
Harnan, Terry. *African Rhythm—American Dance: A Biography of Katherine Dunham.* New York: Knopf, 1974.

Dunlap, William 1766-1839
Canary, Robert H. *William Dunlap.* New York: Twayne, 1970.
Coad, Oral Sumner. *William Dunlap; A Study of His Life and Works and of His Place in Contemporary Culture.* New York: Dunlap Society, 1917.
Dunlap, William. *Diary of William Dunlap (1766-1839).* New York: The Society, 1930; 3 vols.

Dunsany, Alfred, Lord (Edward John Moreton Drax Plunkett) 1878-1957
Dunsany, Edward J.M.D.P., 18th baron. *Patches of Sunlight.* New York: Heinemann, 1938.
Littlefield, Hazel. *Lord Dunsany: King of Dreams; a Personal Portrait.* New York: Exposition Press, 1959.
Bierstadt, Edward H. *Dunsany, the Dramatist.* Boston: Little, Brown, 1917.

Durang, John 1768-1822
Durang, John (ed. by Alan S. Downer). *The Memoir of John Durang, American Actor, 1785-1816.* Pittsburgh: Univ. of Pittsburgh, 1966.

Durante, Jimmy 1893-
Cahn, William. *Good Night, Mrs. Calabash; The Secret of Jimmy Durante.* New York: Duell, Sloan and Pearce, 1963.
Fowler, Gene. *Schnozzola; The Story of Jimmy Durante.* New York: Viking, 1951.

Duse, Eleanora 1858-1924
Anfuso, Bernice Sciorra. *The Passing Star; Eleanora Duse in America.* Los Angeles: 1956.
Bordeux, Jeanne. *Eleanora Duse: The Story of Her Life.* London: Hutchinson, 1924.
Harding, Bertita. *Age Cannot Wither; The Story of Duse and d'Annunzio.* Philadelphia: Lippincott, 1947.
Le Gallienne, Eva. *The Mystic in the Theatre: Eleanora Duse.* New York: Farrar, Straus & Giroux, 1966.
Mapes, Victor. *Duse and the French.* New York: Dunlap Society: 1898
Rheinhardt, Emil Alphons (trans. by Willa and Edwin Muir). *The Life of Eleanora Duse.* London: Secker, 1930.
Symons, Arthur. *Eleanora Duse.* London: Mathews, 1926.
See also: Annunzio, Gabriele D'.

Eagels, Jeanne 1894-1929
Doherty, Edward. *The Rain Girl.* Philadelphia: Macrae-Smith, 1930.

East, John M. 1866-1924
East, John M. *'Neath the Mask: The Story of the East Family.* London: Allen & Unwin, 1967.

Edwardes, George 1852-1915
Bloom, Ursula. *Curtain Call for the Guv'nor.* London: Hutchinson, 1954.

Egan, Pierce 1772-1849
Egan, Pierce. *The Life of an Actor . . .* New York: Appleton, 1904.
Reid, John C. *Bucks and Bruisers: Pierce Egan and Regency England.* London: Routledge & Paul, 1971.

Eliot, T. S. (Thomas Stearns Eliot) 1888-1965
Bergonzi, Bernard. *T. S. Eliot.* New York: Macmillan, 1972.
Howarth, Herbert. *Notes on Some Figures Behind T. S. Eliot.* Boston: Houghton Mifflin, 1964.
Kirk, Russell. *Eliot and His Age; T. S. Eliot's Moral Imagination in the Twentieth Century.* New York: Random House, 1972.
Kojecky, Roger. *T. S. Eliot's Social Criticism.* London: Faber & Faber, 1971.
Levy, William T. and Scherle, Victor. *Affectionately, T. S. Eliot; The Story of a Friendship, 1947-1965.* Philadelphia: Lippincott, 1968.
Margolis, John D. *T. S. Eliot's Intellectual Development, 1922-1939.* Chicago: Univ. of Chicago, 1972.
Matthews, Thomas S. *Great Tom; Notes Towards the Definition of T. S. Eliot.* New York: Harper & Row, 1974.
Sencourt, Robert. *T. S. Eliot, a Memoir.* New York: Dodd, Mead, 1971.
Tate, Allen, (ed.) *T. S. Eliot: The Man and His Work; A Critical Evaluation by Twenty-Six Distinguished Writers.* New York: Dell, 1966.

Elitch, Mary ?-1936
Dier, Caroline. *The Lady of the Gardens, Mary Elitch Long.* Hollywood: Hollycrofters, 1932.

Elkins, Hillard 1929-
Davis, Christopher. *The Producer.* New York: Harper & Row, 1972.

Ellington, Duke 1899-1974
Dance, Stanley. *The World of Duke Ellington,* New York: Scribner, 1970.
Ellington. Duke. *Music Is My Mistress.* Garden City: Doubleday, 1973.
Schaaf, Martha A. *Duke Ellington: Young Music Master.* Indianapolis: Bobbs-Merrill, 1975.

Elliott, Maxine 1868-1940
Forbes Robertson, Diana. *My Aunt Maxine.* New York: Viking, 1964.

Elliston, Robert William 1774-1831
Raymond, George. *The Life and Enterprises of R. W. Elliston, Comedian.* London: Routledge, 1857.

Ellsler, John Adam 1822-1900
Ellsler, John Adam (ed. by Weston, Effiie Ellsler). *The Stage Memories of John A. Ellsler.* Cleveland: Rowfant Club, 1950.

Endrey, Eugene
Endrey, Eugene. *Beg, Borrow and Squeal.* New York: Pageant Press, 1963.

Engel, Lehman 1910-
Engel, Lehman. *The Bright Day.* New York: Macmillan, 1974.

Enters, Angna 1907-
Enters, Angna. *Silly Girl, A Portrait of Personal Remembrance.* Cambridge, Mass.: Houghton Mifflin, 1944.
—. *First Person Plural.* New York: Stackpole, 1937.
—. Artist's Life. New York: Coward-McCann, 1955.

Espinosa, Edouard 1872-1950
Espinosa, Edouard. *And Then He Danced.* London: Low, Marston, 1948.

Etherege, Sir George 1635?-1691
Etherege, George. *Letters of Sir George Etherege.* Berkeley: Univ. of California, 1973.
McCamic, Frances S. *Sir George Etherege, a Study in Restoration Comedy (1660-1680).* Cedar Rapids, Iowa: Torch Press, 1931.

Euripides. c. 486-407 B.C.
Bates, William N. *Euripides; A Student of Human Nature.* Philadelphia: Univ. of Pennsylvania, 1930.
Grube, George. *The Drama of Euripides.* London: Methuen, 1941.
Lucas, Frank L. *Euripides and His Influence.* Boston: Marshall Jones, 1923.
Mahaffy, John P. *Euripides.* London: Macmillan, 1879.
Melchinger, Siegfried (trans. by Samuel R. Rosenbaum). *Euripides.* New York: Ungar, 1972.
Murray, Gilbert. *Euripides and His Age.* New York: Holt, 1913.

Evans, Edith 1888-
Trewin, John C. *Edith Evans.* London: Rockliff, 1954.

Eytinge, Rose 1835-1911
Eytinge, Rose. *The Memories of Rose Eytinge.* New York: Frederick A. Stokes, 1905.

Fairbrother, Sydney (Sydney Parselle Cowell) 1872-1941
Fairbrother, Sydney. *Through an Old Stage Door.* London: Muller, 1939.

Farmer, Frances 1914-1970
Farmer, Frances. *Will There Really Be a Morning?* New York: Putnam, 1972.

Farren, Elizabeth (Countess of Derby) 1759-1829
Broadbent, R. J. *Elizabeth Farren, Countess of Derby.* Edinburgh: Ballantyne, Hanson, 1910.

Faucit, Helen (Helen Saville, Lady Martin) 1817-1898
Martin, Sir Theodore. *Helena Faucit (Lady Martin).* Edinburgh: Blackwood, 1900.

Fay, Frank 1897-1961
Fay, Frank. *How to Be Poor.* New York: Prentice-Hall, 1945.

Fechter, Charles Albert 1824-1879
Field, Kate. *Charles Albert Fechter.* Boston: J. R. Osgood, 1882.

Fellows, Dexter William 1871-1937
Fellows, Dexter W. and Freeman, Andrew A. *This Way to the Big Show.* New York: Viking, 1936.

Fenton, Lavinia (Duchess of Bolton) 1708-1760
Pearce, Charles E. *"Polly Peachum"; Being the Story of Lavinia Fenton (Duchess of Bolton) and "The Beggar's Opera."* New York: Brentano, 1913.

Fennell, James 1766-1816
Fennell, James. *An Apology for the Life of James Fennell.* Philadelphia: Moses Thomas, 1814.

Ferber, Edna 1887-1968
Dickinson, Rogers. *Edna Ferber.* Garden City: Doubleday, Page, 1925.
Ferber, Edna. *A Kind of Magic.* Garden City: Doubleday, 1963.
—. *A Peculiar Treasure.* Garden City: Doubleday, 1939.

Feydeau, Georges 1862-1921
Pronko, Leonard C. *Georges Feydeau.* New York: Ungar, 1975.

Field, Al G. 1852-1921
Field, Al G. *Watch Yourself Go By.* Columbus, O.: Spohr & Glenn, 1912.

Field, Nathan 1587-1620
Brinkley, Roberta F. *Nathan Field, the*

Field, Sid 1904-1950
Fisher, John. *What a Performance: A Life of Sid Field.* London: Leo Cooper, 1975.

Fields, Gracie 1898-
Fields, Gracie. *Sing as We Go.* Garden City: Doubleday, 1961.

Fields, Lew 1867-1941
See: Weber, Joe.

Fields, W. C. 1879-1946
Fields, W. C. *W. C. Fields by Himself; His Intended Autobiography.* Englewood Cliffs, N.J.: Prentice-Hall, 1973.
Fowler, Gene. *Minutes of the Last Meeting.* New York: Viking, 1954.
Monti, Carlotta with Rice, Cy. *W. C. Fields & Me.* Englewood Cliffs, N.J.: Prentice-Hall, 1971.
Taylor, Robert Lewis. W. C. *Fields, His Follies and Fortunes.* Garden City: Doubleday, 1949.

Fisher, Clara (Mrs. James Maeder) 1811-1898
A Sketch of the Life of Miss Clara Fisher, the Lilliputian Actress. London: 1819.
Maeder, Clara (ed. by Douglas Taylor) *Autobiography of Clara Fisher Maeder.* New York: Dunlap Society, 1897.

Fiske, Minnie Maddern 1865-1932
Binns, Archie. *Mrs. Fiske and the American Theatre.* New York: Crown, 1955.
Griffith, Frank Carlos. *Mrs. Fiske.* New York: Neale, 1912.
Woollcott, Alexander (ed.). *Mrs. Fiske. Her Views on Actors, Acting, and the Problems of Production.* New York: Century, 1917.

Fitch, Clyde 1865-1909
Bell, Archie. *The Clyde Fitch I Knew.* New York: Broadway Pub. Co., 1909.
Moses, Montrose J. and Gerson, Virginia. *Clyde Fitch and His Letters.* Boston: Little, Brown, 1924.

Fletcher, John 1579-1625
See: Beaumont, Francis.

Fletcher, Tom 1873-1954
Fletcher, Tom. *One Hundred Years of the Negro in Show Business.* New York: Burdge, 1954.

Fleury (Abraham-Joseph Bénard) 1750-1822
Lafitte, Jean Baptiste Pierre (ed. by Theodore Hook). *Adventures of an Actor: Comprising a Picture of the French Stage During a Period of Fifty Years.* London: Colburn, 1842.

Fogerty, Elsie 1866-1945
Cole, Marion. *Fogie: The Life of Elsie Fogerty, C.B.E. . . .* London: Davies, 1967.

Fonda Family (Henry, Jane and Peter)
Brough, James. *The Fabulous Fondas.* New York: McKay, 1973.
Springer, John. *The Fondas; The Films and Careers of Henry, Jane, and Peter Fonda.* New York: Citadel, 1970.

Fonda, Jane 1937-
Kiernan, Thomas. *Jane.* New York: Putnam, 1973.

Fontanne, Lynn 1887-
See: Lunt, Alfred.

Foote, Samuel 1720-1777
Fitzgerald, Percy H. *Samuel Foote.* London: Chatto & Windus, 1910.
Trefman, Simon. *Sam Foote, Comedian, 1720-1777.* New York: New York Univ., 1971.

Forbes-Robertson, Johnston 1853-1937
Forbes-Robertson, Johnston. *A Player under Three Reigns.* Boston: Little, Brown, 1925.

Ford, John 1586-c.1639
Sargeaunt, M. Joan. *John Ford.* Oxford: Blackwell, 1935.

Forrest, Edwin 1806-1872
Alger, William Rounseville. *Life of Edwin Forrest, the American Tragedian.* Philadelphia: Lippincott, 1877.
Barrett, Lawrence. *Edwin Forrest.* Boston: J. R. Osgood, 1881.
Harrison, Gabriel. *Edwin Forrest: The Actor and the Man.* Brooklyn, N. Y.: 1889.
Moody, Richard. *Edwin Forrest, First Star of the American Stage.* New York: Knopf, 1960.
Moses, Montrose J. *The Fabulous Forrest; The Record of an American Actor.* Boston: Little, Brown, 1929.
Rees, James. *The Life of Edwin Forrest.* Philadelphia: T. B. Peterson, 1874.

Forrest, Sam 1870-1944
Forrest, Sam. *Variety of Miscellanea.* New York: 1939.

Foy, Eddie 1856-1928
Foy, Eddie and Harlow, Alvin F. *Clowning Through Life.* New York: Dutton, 1928.

Frederick, Pauline 1885-1938
Elwood, Muriel. *Pauline Frederick, On and Off the Stage.* Chicago: Kroch, 1940.

Frohman, Charles 1860-1915
Marcosson, Isaac F. and Frohman, Daniel. *Charles Frohman: Manager and Man.* New York: Harper, 1916.

Frohman, Daniel 1851-1940
Frohman, Daniel. *Daniel Frohman Presents.* New York: Citadel, 1935.
—. *Memories of a Manager.* Garden City: Doubleday, Page, 1911.
—. *Encore.* New York: Citadel, 1937.

Fry, Charles 1845-1928
Fry, F. Charlton. *Charles Fry; His Life and His Work.* London: J. M. Baxter, 1932.

Fry, Christopher 1907-
Stanford, Derek. *Christopher Fry Album.* London: Nevill, 1952.

Furse, Jill ?-1944
Whistler, Laurence. *The Initials in the Heart.* London: Hart-Davis, 1964.

Gaige, Crosby 1882-1949
Gaige, Crosby. *Footlights and Highlights.* New York: Dutton, 1948.

Gale, Zona (Mrs. William Llewellyn Breese) 1874-1938
Derleth, August W. *Still Small Voice; The Biography of Zona Gale.* New York: Appleton-Century, 1940.
Simonson, Harold P. *Zona Gale.* New York: Twayne, 1962.

Galsworthy, John 1867-1933
Barker, Dudley. *The Man of Principle; A Biography of John Galsworthy.* Briarcliff Manor, N.Y.: Stein & Day, 1969.
Galsworthy, Ada. *Over the Hills and Far Away.* [. . . memories of travel with her husband . . .] London: Hale, 1937.
Galsworthy, John (ed. by Edward Garnett). *Letters from John Galsworthy, 1900-1932.* London: Cape, 1934.
Holloway, David. *John Galsworthy.* London: Morgan-Grampian, 1968.
Marrot, Harold V. *The Life and Letters of John Galsworthy.* London: Heinemann, 1935.
Morris, Margaret. *My Galsworthy Story; Including 67 Hitherto Unpublished Letters.* London: Owen, 1967.
Mottram, Ralph. *For Some We Loved; An Intimate Portrait of Ada and John Galsworthy.* London: Hutchinson, 1956.
Ould, Hermon. *John Galsworthy.* London: Chapman & Hall, 1934.
Reynolds, Mabel E. *Memories of John Galsworthy, by His Sister.* London: Hale, 1936.
Sauter, Rudolf. *Galsworthy the Man: An Intimate Portrait.* London: Owen, 1967.
Wilson, Asher B. *John Galsworthy's Letters to Leon Lion.* The Hague: Mouton, 1968.

Ganthony, Robert ?-1931
Ganthony, Robert. *Random Recollections.* London: H. J. Drane, 1899.

Garcia Lorca, Federico 1899-1936
Gibson, Ian. *The Death of Lorca.* Chicago: J. P. O'Hara, 1973.
Cobb, Carl W. *Federico Garcia Lorca.* New York: Twayne, 1967.

Garfield, John 1913-1952
Swindell, Larry. *Body and Soul: The Story of John Garfield.* New York: Morrow, 1975.

Garland, Judy 1922-1969
Dahl, David and Kehoe, Barry. *Young Judy.* New York: Mason/Charter, 1975.
Deans, Mickey and Pinchot, Ann. *Weep No More, My Lady.* New York: Hawthorn, 1972.
Di Orio, Al. *Little Girl Lost: The Life and Hard Times of Judy Garland.* New Rochelle, N.Y.: Arlington House, 1974.
Edwards, Anne. *Judy Garland.* New York: Simon & Schuster, 1975.
Finch, Christopher. *Rainbow: The Stormy Life of Judy Garland.* New York: Grosset & Dunlap, 1975.
Frank, Gerold. *Judy.* New York: Harper & Row, 1975.
Juneau, James. *Judy Garland.* New York: Pyramid, 1974.
Steiger, Brad. *Judy Garland.* New York: Ace, 1969.
Torme, Mel. *The Other Side of the Rainbow with Judy Garland on the Dawn Patrol.* New York: Morrow, 1970.

Garrick, David 1717-1779
Barton, Margaret. *Garrick.* London: Faber & Faber, 1948.
Burnim, Kalman A. *David Garrick, Director.* Pittsburgh: Univ. of Pittsburgh, 1961.
Davies, Thomas. *Memoirs of the Life of David Garrick, Esq.* London: 1780.
Fitzgerald, Percy H. *The Life of David Garrick.* London: Tinsley Brothers, 1868.

Garrick, David (ed. by James Boaden). *The Private Correspondence of David Garrick* . . . London: Colburn & Bentley, 1831-32.
— (ed. by George Pierce Baker). *Some Unpublished Correspondence of David Garrick.* Boston: Houghton Mifflin, 1907.
— (ed. by Ryllis Clair Alexander). *The Diary of David Garrick* . . . New York: Oxford, 1928.
—. (ed. by David Mason Little). *Pineapples of Finest Flavor* . . . Cambridge: Harvard Univ., 1930.
— (ed. by George Winchester Stone, Jr.). *The Journal of David Garrick* . . . New York: Modern Language Association, 1939.
— (ed. by Earl Spencer and Christopher Dobson). *Letters of David Garrick and Georgiana, Countess Spencer, 1759-1779.* Cambridge: Roxburghe Club, 1960.
— (ed. by David M. Little and George M. Kahrl). *The Letters of David Garrick.* Cambridge: Belknap, 1963; 3 vols.
Hedgcock, Frank A. *A Cosmopolitan Actor, David Garrick and His Friends.* London: Stanley Paul, 1912.
Knight, Joseph. *David Garrick.* London: Paul, Trench, Trubner, 1894.
Lenanton, Carola (Oman). *David Garrick.* London: Hodder & Stoughton, 1958.
Murphy, Arthur. *The Life of David Garrick* . . . London: Wright, 1801.
Parsons, Florence. *Garrick and His Circle.* London: Methuen, 1906.

Gay, John 1685-1732
Gay, John (ed. by C. F. Burgess). *The Letters of John Gay.* Oxford: Clarendon, 1966.
Gaye, Phoebe. *John Gay, His Place in the Eighteenth Century.* London: Collins, 1938.
Irving, William Henry. *John Gay, Favorite of the Wits.* Durham, N.C.: Duke Univ., 1940.
Melville, Lewis. *Life and Letters of John Gay.* London: Daniel O'Connor, 1921.
Sherwin, Oscar. *Mr. Gay.* New York: John Day, 1929.
Warner, Oliver. *John Gay.* London: Longmans, Green, 1964.

Geddes, Norman Bel 1893-1958
Geddes, Norman Bel (ed. by William Kelley). *Miracle in the Evening.* Garden City: Doubleday, 1960.

Genet, Jean 1910-
Choukri, Mohamed (trans. by Paul Bowles). *Jean Genet in Tangier.* New York: Ecco, 1975.
Driver, Tom F. *Jean Genet.* New York: Columbia Univ., 1966.
Genet, Jean (trans. by Bernard Frechtman). *The Thieve's Journal.* New York: Grove, 1964.
Sartre, Jean-Paul (trans. by Bernard Frechtman). *Saint Genet, Actor and Martyr.* New York: Braziller, 1963.

Gershwin, George 1898-1937
Altman, Frances. *George Gershwin, Master Composer.* Minneapolis: T. S. Denison, 1968.
Armitage, Merle. *George Gershwin: Man and Legend.* New York: Duell, Sloan and Pearce, 1958.
—. (ed.). *George Gershwin.* London: Longmans, Green, 1938.
Ewen, David. *George Gershwin, His Journey to Greatness.* Englewood Cliffs, N.J.: Prentice-Hall, 1970.
—. *A Journey to Greatness; The Life and Music of George Gershwin.* New York: Holt, 1956.
—. *The Story of George Gershwin.* New York: Holt, 1943.
Goldberg, Isaac. *George Gershwin, a Study in American Music.* New York: Ungar, 1958.
Jablonski, Edward and Stewart, Lawrence D. *The Gershwin Years.* Garden City: Doubleday, 1958.
Kimball, Robert and Simon, Alfred. *The Gershwins.* New York: Atheneum, 1973.
Payne, Robert. *Gershwin.* London: R. Hale, 1962.
Rushmore, Robert. *The Life of George Gershwin.* New York: Crowell-Collier, 1966.
Schwartz, Charles. *Gershwin: His Life and Music.* London: Abelard-Schuman, 1974.
Stewart, Lawrence D. *The Gershwins; Words upon Music.* New York: Verve Records, 1959.

Gershwin, Ira. 1896-
Gershwin, Ira. *Lyrics on Several Occasions* . . . New York: Knopf, 1959.
See also: Gershwin, George.

Gibson, William 1914-
Gibson, William. *A Mass for the Dead.* New York: Atheneum, 1968.
—. *A Season in Heaven.* New York: Atheneum, 1974.
—. *The Seesaw Log; A Chronicle of the Stage Production.* . . . New York: Knopf, 1959.

Gielgud, John 1904-
Anthony, Gordon. *John Gielgud.* (Camera studies). London: Bles, 1938.
Fordham, Hallam (comp.). *John Gielgud; An Actor's Biography in Pictures.* London: Lehmann, 1952.
Gielgud, John. *Early Stages.* New York: Macmillan, 1939.
—. *Distinguished Company.* London: Heinemann Educational, 1972.
Gilder, Rosamond. *John Gielgud's Hamlet.* New York and Toronto: Oxford Univ., 1937.
Hayman, Ronald. *John Gielgud.* New York: Random House, 1971.

Gielgud, Val 1900-
Gielgud, Val. *Years in a Mirror.* London: Bodley Head, 1965.
—. *Years of the Locust.* London: Nicholson & Watson, 1947.

Gilbert, Anne 1821-1904
Gilbert, Anne. *The Stage Reminiscences of Mrs. Gilbert.* New York: Scribner, 1901.

Gilbert, William Schwenck 1836-1911
Baily, Leslie. *The Gilbert and Sullivan Book.* London: Cassell, 1952.
—. *Gilbert and Sullivan: Their Lives and Times.* New York: Viking, 1974.
Browne, Edith A. *W. S. Gilbert.* New York: Lane, 1907.
Cellier, François and Bridgeman, Cunningham. *Gilbert, Sullivan and D'Oyly Carte; Reminiscences of the Savoy and the Savoyards.* London: Pitman, 1914.
Dark, Sidney and Grey, Rowland. *W. S. Gilbert; His Life and Letters.* London: Methuen, 1923.
Darlington, William A. *The World of Gilbert and Sullivan.* New York: Crowell, 1950.
Fitzgerald, Percy. *The Savoy Opera and the Savoyards.* London: Chatto & Windus, 1894.
Goldberg, Isaac. *The Story of Gilbert and Sullivan; or, The "Compleat" Savoyard.* New York: Simon & Schuster, 1928.
—. *Sir Wm.* [sic] *S. Gilbert: A Study in Modern Satire.* Boston: Stratford, 1913.
Jacobs, Arthur. *Gilbert and Sullivan.* London: Parrish, 1951.
Jones, John Bush (comp.). *W. S. Gilbert: A Century of Scholarship and Commentary.* New York: New York Univ., 1970.
Mander, Raymond and Mitchenson, Joe. *A Picture History of Gilbert and Sullivan.* London: Vista, 1962.
Pearson, Hesketh. *Gilbert and Sullivan.* New York: Harper, 1935.
—. *Gilbert: His Life and Strife.* London: Methuen, 1957.
Purdy, Claire Lee. *Gilbert and Sullivan, Masters of Mirth and Melody.* New York: Messner, 1947.
Searle, Townley. *Sir William Schwenck Gilbert; a Topsy-Turvey Adventure.* London: Alexander-Ousley, 1931.
Sutton, Max K. *W. S. Gilbert.* New York: Twayne, 1975.
Williamson, Audrey. *Gilbert & Sullivan Opera; A New Assessment.* New York: Macmillan, 1953.
Wood, Roger. *A D'Oyly Carte Album; A Pictorial Record of the Gilbert and Sullivan Operas.* London: A. and C. Black, 1953.

Gill, Brendan 1914-
Gill, Brendan. *Here at The New Yorker.* New York: Random House, 1975.

Gillette, William ?-1937
Cook, Doris E. *Sherlock Holmes and Much More.* Hartford: Connecticut Historical Society, 1970.

Gillmore, Margalo 1897-
Gillmore, Margalo. *Four Flights Up.* Boston: Houghton Mifflin, 1964.
— and Collinge, Patricia. *The B.O.W.S.* New York: Harcourt, Brace, 1945.

Giraudoux, Jean 1882-1944
Inskip, Donald P. *Jean Giraudoux; The Making of a Dramatist.* London: Oxford Univ., 1958.
Lemaître, Georges. *Jean Giraudoux: The Writer and His Work.* New York: Ungar, 1971.
Le Sage, Laurence. *Jean Giraudoux; His Life and His Works.* University Park: Penn. State Univ., 1959.

Gish, Lillian 1896-
Gish, Lillian. *Dorothy and Lillian Gish.* New York: Scribner, 1973.
Gish, Lillian with Pinchot, Ann. *Lillian Gish; The Movies, Mr. Griffith, and Me.* Englewood Cliffs, N.J.: Prentice-Hall, 1969.
Paine, Albert Bigelow. *Life and Lillian Gish.* New York: Macmillan, 1932.
Wagenknecht, Edward C. *Lillian Gish; An Interpretation.* Seattle: Univ. of Washington, 1927.

Gish, Dorothy 1898-1968
See: Gish, Lillian.

Glagolin, Boris 1879-1948
Mazurova, Alexandra N. *Revelation of a Russian Actor.* Campbell, Calif.: 1944.

Gogol, Nikolai (Nicholas) Vassilievitch 1809-1852
Gogol, Nikolai (trans. by Carl R. Proffer and Vera Krivoshein). *Letters of Nikolai Gogol.*

Ann Arbor: Univ. of Michigan, 1967.
Lavrin, Janko. *Nikolai Gogol (1809-1852), a Centenary Survey.* London: Sylvan Press, 1951.
Magarshack, David. *Gogol: A Life.* London: Faber & Faber, 1957.
Nabokov, Vladimir. *Nikolai Gogol.* Norfolk, Conn.: New Directions, 1944.
Setchkarev, Vsevold (trans. by Robert Kramer). *Gogol; His Life and Works.* New York: New York Univ., 1965.
Troyat, Henri (trans. by Nancy Amphoux). *Divided Soul; The Life of Gogol.* Garden City: Doubleday, 1973.

Golden, John 1874-1955
Golden, John and Shore, Viola Brothers. *Stage-Struck John Golden.* New York: Samuel French, 1930.

Goldoni, Carlo 1707-1793
Chatfield-Taylor, H. C. *Goldoni: A Biography.* New York: Duffield, 1913.
Coppins, Edward. *Alfieri and Goldoni; Their Lives and Adventures.* London: Addey, 1857.
Goldoni, Carlo (trans. by John Black). *Memoirs of Carlo Goldoni.* New York: Knopf, 1926.
Kennard, Joseph. *Goldoni and the Venice of His Time.* New York: Macmillan, 1920.

Goldsmith, Oliver 1728-1774
Balderston, Katharine C. *The History and Sources of Percy's Memoir of Goldsmith.* Cambridge, England: Cambridge Univ., 1926.
Black, William. *Goldsmith.* New York: Harper, 1879.
Dobson, Austin. *Life of Oliver Goldsmith.* London: Walter Scott, 1888.
Forster, John. *The Life and Times of Oliver Goldsmith.* London: Chapman & Hall; 2 vols.
Freeman, William. *Oliver Goldsmith.* London: Jenkins, 1951.
Goldsmith, Oliver. *The Autobiography of Oliver Goldsmith.* Toronto: Ryerson Press, 1943.
Gwynn, Stephen. *Oliver Goldsmith.* London: Butterworth, 1935.
Irving, Washington. *Oliver Goldsmith.* New York: Putnam, 1849.
Kent, Elizabeth. *Goldsmith and His Booksellers.* Ithaca: Cornell Univ., 1933.
King, Richard A. *Oliver Goldsmith.* London: Methuen, 1910.
Moore, Frank F. *The Life of Oliver Goldsmith.* New York: Dutton, 1911.
Neal, Minnie M. *Oliver Goldsmith.* New York: Pageant, 1955.
Prior, James. *The Life of Oliver Goldsmith.* Philadelphia: E. L. Carey and A. Hart, 1837.
Scott, Temple. *Oliver Goldsmith Bibliographically and Biographically Considered, Based on the Collection of Material in the Library of W. M. Elkins, Esq.* New York: Bowling Green, 1928.
Sells, A. Lytton. *Oliver Goldsmith; His Life and Works.* London: Allen & Unwin, 1975.
Sherwin, Oscar. *Goldy; The Life and Times of Oliver Goldsmith.* New York: Twayne, 1961.
Wardle, Ralph M. *Oliver Goldsmith.* Hamden, Conn.: Archon Books, 1969.

Goodman, Cardell 1653-1713?
Wilson, John Harold. *Mr. Goodman, the Player.* Pittsburgh: Univ. of Pittsburgh, 1964.

Goodwin, Nat C. 1857-1919
Goodwin, Nat C. *Nat Goodwin's Book.* Boston: Richard G. Badger, 1914.

Gordon, Max 1892-
Gordon, Max with Funke, Lewis. *Max Gordon Presents.* New York: Bernard Geis, 1963.

Gordon, Ruth 1896-
Gordon, Ruth. *Myself Among Others.* New York: Atheneum, 1971.

Gorki, Maxim (Alexi Maximovitch Pyeshkov) 1868-1936
Borras, F. M. *Maxim Gorky the Writer; An Interpretation.* Oxford: Clarendon, 1967.
Gorki, Maxim (trans. by Gertrude M. Foakes). *In the World.* New York: Century, 1917.
— (trans. by Veronica Dewey). *Reminiscences of My Youth.* London: Heinemann, 1924.
— (trans. by Leonard Wolfe and others). *Reminiscences.* New York: Dover, 1946.
— (trans. by Isidor Schneider). *Autobiography of Maxim Gorky: My Childhood. In the World. My Universities.* New York: Citadel, 1949.
— (trans. by Helen Altschuler). *My Universities.* Moscow: Foreign Languages Publishing House, 1952.
— (trans. by Lydia Weston, ed. by Peter Yershov). *Letters of Gorky and Andreev.* New York: Columbia Univ., 1958.
— (trans. by Margaret Wettlin). *Childhood.* London: Oxford Univ., 1961.
— (trans. by Margaret Wettlin). *My Apprenticeship.* Moscow: Foreign Language Publishing House, 1962.
— (trans. by Moura Budberg). *Fragments from My Diary.* New York: Praeger, 1972.
— (trans. by Ronald Wilks). *My Apprenticeship.* Baltimore: Penguin, 1974.
Habermann, Gerhard E. (trans. by Ernestine Schlant). *Maksim Gorki.* New York: Ungar, 1971.
Hare, Richard. *Maxim Gorky: Romantic Realist and Conservative Revolutionary.* London: Oxford Univ., 1962.
Holtzman, Filia. *The Young Maxim Gorky, 1868-1902.* New York: Columbia Univ., 1948.
Kaun, Alexander S. *Maxim Gorki and His Russia.* London: Cape & Smith, 1931.
Levin, Dan. *Stormy Petrel; The Life and Work of Maxim Gorky.* New York: Appleton-Century, 1965.
Olgin, Moissaye J. *Maxim Gorky, Writer and Revolutionist.* New York: International Publishers, 1933.
Roskin, Alexander (trans. by D. L. Fromberg). *From the Banks of the Volga; The Life of Maxim Gorky.* New York: Philisophical Library, 1946.
Wolfe, Bertram D. *The Bridge and the Abyss; The Troubled Friendship of Maxim Gorky and V. I. Lenin.* New York: Praeger, 1967.

Gozzi, Count Carlo 1720-1806
Gozzi, Carlo (trans. by John Addington Symonds). *Useless Memoirs of Carlo Gozzi.* London: Oxford Univ., 1962.

Grady, Billy -1973
Grady, Billy. *The Irish Peacock; The Confessions of a Legendary Talent Agent.* New Rochelle, N.Y.: Arlington House, 1972.

Graham, Joe F. 1850-1933
Graham, Joe F. *An Old Stock-Actor's Memories.* London: Murray, 1930.

Graham, Martha 1894-
Armitage, Merle (ed.). *Martha Graham.* Los Angeles: Armitage, 1937.
Leatherman, Leroy. *Martha Graham; Portrait of the Lady as an Artist.* New York: Knopf, 1966.
McDonagh, Don. *Martha Graham.* New York: Praeger, 1973.
Morgan, Barbara. *Martha Graham; Sixteen Dances in Photographs.* New York: Duell, Sloan and Pearce, 1941.

Granach, Alexander 1879-1945
Granach, Alexander (trans. by Willard Trask). *There Goes an Actor.* Garden City: Doubleday, Doran, 1945.

Granlund, Nils Thor (N. T. G.) 1882-1957
Granlund, Nils Thor, Feder, Sid and Hancock, Ralph. *Blondes, Brunettes and Bullets.* New York: McKay, 1957.

Granville-Barker, Harley 1877-1946
Purdom, Charles Benjamin. *Harley Granville Barker, Man of the Theatre, Dramatist, and Scholar.* Cambridge: Harvard Univ., 1956.
Shaw, George Bernard (ed. by C. B. Purdom). *Letters to Granville Barker.* New York: Theatre Arts, 1957.
Whitworth, Geoffrey. *Harley Granville-Barker, 1877-1946; A Reprint of a Broadcast . . .* London: Sidgwick & Jackson, 1948.

Graves, George 1876-1949
Graves, George. *Gaieties & Gravities; The Autobiography of a Comedian.* London: Hutchinson, 1931.

Green, Martyn 1899-
Green, Martyn. *Here's a How-De-Do; My Life in Gilbert and Sullivan.* New York: Norton, 1952.

Green, Paul 1894-
Adams, Agatha B. (ed. by Richard Walser). *Paul Green of Chapel Hill.* Chapel Hill: Univ. of North Carolina Library, 1951.
Clark, Barrett H. *Paul Green.* New York: R. M. McBride, 1928.
Kenny, Vincent S. *Paul Green.* New York: Twayne, 1971.

Greene, Graham 1904-
Greene, Graham. *A Sort of a Life.* New York: Simon & Schuster, 1971.
Wyndham, Francis. *Graham Greene.* Harlow, Eng.: Longmans, Green, 1968.

Greet, Sir Philip (Ben) 1857-1936
Isaac, Winifred F.E.C. *Ben Greet and the Old Vic.* London: Greenbank Press, 1964.

Gregory, Lady Augusta 1852-1932
Coxhead, Elizabeth. *Lady Gregory; A Literary Portrait.* New York: Harcourt, Brace & World, 1961.
Gregory, Anne. *Me and Nu; Childhood at Coole.* Gerrards Cross, Eng.: Smythe, 1970.
Gregory, Isabella Augusta (ed. by Lennox Robinson). *Journals, 1916-1930.* New York: Macmillan, 1947.
—. *Our Irish Theatre: A Chapter of Autobiography.* New York: Putnam, 1913.

—. (ed. by Colin Smythe). *Seventy Years. Being the Autobiography of Lady Gregory.* Gerrards Cross, Eng.: Smythe, 1974.
See also: Synge, John Millington.

Gregory, Dick 1932-
Gregory, Dick with Lipsyte, Robert. *Nigger; An Autobiography.* New York: Dutton, 1964.

Grein, Jacob Thomas 1862-1935
Orme, Michael (pseud.). *J. T. Grein; The Story of a Pioneer, 1862-1935.* London: Murray, 1936.
Schoonderwoerd, Nicolaas. *J. T. Grein, Ambassador of the Theatre, 1862-1935; A Study in Anglo-Continental Theatrical Relations.* Assen: Van Gorcum, 1963.

Grimaldi, Joseph ("Joey") 1779-1837
Dickens, Charles. *Memoirs of Joseph Grimaldi.* London: Bentley, 1846.
—. (ed. by Richard Findlater). *Memoirs of Joseph Grimaldi.* New York: Stein & Day, 1968.
Findlater, Richard. *Grimaldi, King of Clowns.* London: MacGibbon & Kee, 1955.

Grock (Adrien Wettach) 1880-1959
Wettach, Adrien (trans. by Madge Pemberton). *Grock: Life's a Lark.*.London: Heinemann, 1931.

Grossmith, George (the Younger) 1874-1935
Grossmith, George. *"G. G."* London: Hutchinson, 1933.
—. *A Society Clown; Reminiscences . . .* Bristol, Eng.: J. W. Arrowsmith, 1888.

Grossmith, Walter Weedon 1852-1919
Grossmith, Weedon. *From Studio to Stage; Reminiscences of Weedon Grossmith.* London: Lane, 1913.

Grotowski, Jerzy 1933-
Temkine, Raymonde (trans. by Alex Szogyi). *Grotowski.* New York: Avon, 1972.

Guilbert, Yvette 1865-1944
Geffroy, Gustave (trans. by Barbara Sessions). *Yvette Guilbert.* New York: Walker, 1968.
Guilbert, Yvette (trans. by Beatrice De Holthoir). *The Song of My Life; My Memories.* London: Harrap, 1929.
— and Simpson, Harold. *Yvette Guilbert; Struggles and Victories.* London: Mills & Boon, 1910.
Knapp, Bettina and Chipman, Myra. *That Was Yvette; The Biography of Yvette Guilbert, the Great Diseuse.* New York: Holt, Rinehart & Winston, 1964.

Guinness, Alec 1914-
Tynan, Kenneth. *Alec Guinness.* London: Rockliff, 1953.

Hart, Tony 1855-1891
See: Harrigan, Edward.

Harvey, Laurence 1928-1973
Stone, Paulene. *One Tear Is Enough.* London: Michael Joseph, 1975.

Hauptmann, Gerhart 1862-1946
Behl, Carl F. W. (trans. by Helen Taubert). *Gerhart Hauptmann, His Life and Work.* Wurzburg: Holzner-Verlag, 1956.
Garten, Hugh F. *Gerhart Hauptmann.* New Haven: Yale Univ., 1954.
Holl, Karl. *Gerhart Hauptmann; His Life and Work, 1862-1912.* Chicago: A. C. McClurg, 1913.
Pohl, Gerhart (trans. by William I. Morgan). *Gerhart Hauptmann and Silesia; A Report on the German Dramatist's Last Days in His Occupied Homeland.* Grand Forks: Univ. of North Dakota, 1962.

Havoc, June 1916-
Havoc, June. *Early Havoc.* New York: Simon & Schuster, 1959.

Hawtrey, Sir Charles 1858-1923
Hawtrey, Charles H. (ed. by W. Somerset Maugham). *The Truth at Last from Charles Hawtrey.* London: Butterworth, 1924.

Hayes, Helen 1900-
Brown, Catherine Hayes. *Letters to Mary.* New York: Random House, 1940.
— with Funke, Lewis. *A Gift of Joy.* New York: Evans, 1965.
— with Dody, Sanford. *On Reflection; An Autobiography.* New York: Evans, 1968.
See also: Loos, Anita.

Hazlitt, William 1778-1830
Baker, Herschel. *William Hazlitt.* Cambridge: Harvard Univ., 1962.
Birrell, Augustine. *William Hazlitt.* New York: Macmillan, 1902.
Hazlitt, Sarah and William (ed. by Willard H. Bonner). *The Journals of Sarah and William Hazlitt, 1822-1831.* Buffalo: Univ. of Buffalo, 1959.
Hazlitt, William Carew. *The Hazlitts; An Account of Their Origin and Descent, with Autobiographical Particulars of William Hazlitt (1778-1830). . . .* Edinburgh: Ballantyne, Hanson, 1911.
—. (ed.) *Lamb and Hazlitt; Further Letters and Records. . . .* New York: Dodd, Mead, 1899.
—. *Memoirs of William Hazlitt, with Portions of His Correspondence.* London: Bentley, 1867; 2 vols.
Howe, Percival. *The Life of William Hazlitt.* New York: G. H. Doran, 1923.
Maclean, Catherine M. *Born under Saturn.* London: Collins, 1943.
Pearson, Hesketh. *The Fool of Love.* London: Hamilton, 1934.
Priestley, J. B. *William Hazlitt.* London: Longmans, Green, 1960.
Wardle, Ralph M. *Hazlitt.* Lincoln: Univ. of Nebraska, 1971.

Hebbel, Christian Friedrich 1813-1863
Purdie, Edna. *Friedrich Hebbel.* London: Oxford Univ., 1932.
Rees, George B. *Friedrich Hebbel as a Dramatic Artist; A Study of His Dramatic Theory and of Its Relationship to His Dramas.* London: G. Bell, 1930.

Hecht, Ben 1894-1964
Hecht, Ben. *A Child of the Century.* New York: Simon & Schuster, 1954.
—. *Gaily, Gaily.* Garden City: Doubleday, 1963.
Yessipova, Marie Armstrong. *My First Husband.* New York: Greenberg, 1932.

Guitry, Sacha 1885-1957
Guitry, Sacha (trans. by Lewis Galantiere). *If Memory Serves.* Garden City: Doubleday, Doran, 1935.
Harding, James. *Sacha Guitry: The Last Boulevardier.* New York: Scribner, 1968.

Guthrie, Tyrone 1900-1971
Guthrie, Tyrone. *A Life in the Theatre.* New York: McGraw-Hill, 1959.

Gwyn, Nell 1650-1687
Bax, Clifford. *Pretty, Witty Nell; An Account of Nell Gwyn and Her Environment.* London: Chapman & Hall, 1932.
Benjamin, Lewis S. *Nell Gwyn; The Story of Her Life . . .* New York: G. H. Doran, 1924.
Bevan, Bryan. *Nell Gwyn, Vivacious Mistress of Charles II.* New York: Roy, 1969.
Chesterton, Cecil E. *Nell Gwyn.* London: T. N. Foulis, 1912.
Cunningham, Peter. *The Story of Nell Gwyn . . .* London: Bradbury & Evans, 1852.
Dasent, Arthur I. *Nell Gwynne, 1650-1687 . . .* London: Macmillan, 1924.
Hazelton, George C., Jr. *Mistress Nell; a Merry Tale of a Merry Time (Twixt Fact and Fancy).* New York: Scribner, 1901.
Wilson, John H. *Nell Gwyn, Royal Mistress.* New York: Pellegrini & Cudahy, 1952.

Haggard, Stephen 1911-1943
Haggard, Stephen. *I'll Go to Bed at Noon; a Soldier's Letter to His Son.* London: Faber & Faber, 1944.
Hassall, Christopher Vernon. *The Timeless Quest.* London: Barker, 1948.

Hammerstein, Oscar 1847-1919
Cone, John F. *Oscar Hammerstein's Manhattan Opera Company.* Norman: Univ. of Oklahoma, 1966.
Sheean, Vincent. *Oscar Hammerstein I; The Life and Exploits of an Impresario.* New York: Simon & Schuster, 1956.

Hammerstein, Oscar, II 1895-1960
See: Rodgers, Richard.

Hammond, Percy 1873-1936
Adams, Franklin P. and others. *Percy Hammond, a Symposium in Tribute.* Garden City: Doubleday, Doran, 1936.

Hardwicke, Cedric 1893-1964
Hardwicke, Cedric. *Let's Pretend; Recollections and Reflections of a Lucky Actor.* London: Grayson & Grayson, 1932.
—, as told to James Brough. *A Victorian in Orbit.* Garden City: Doubleday, 1961.

Harker, Joseph C. 1855-1927
Harker, Joseph C. *Studio and Stage.* London: Nisbet, 1924.

Harrigan, Edward 1843-1911
Kahn, Jr., E. J., *The Merry Partners; The Age and Stage of Harrigan and Hart.* New York: Random House, 1955.

Harris, Jed 1900-
Harris, Jed. *Watchman, What of the Night? An Episode Out of a Fabulous Broadway Career.* Garden City: Doubleday, 1963.

Harrison, Rex 1908-
Harrison, Rex. *Rex.* New York: Morrow, 1974.

Harrity, Richard 1907-1973
Harrity, Richard. *The World Famous Harrity Family.* New York: Trident, 1968.

Hart, Moss 1904-1961
Hart, Moss. *Act One.* New York: Random House, 1959.

Helburn, Theresa 1887-1959
Helburn, Theresa. *A Wayward Quest.* Boston: Little, Brown, 1960.

Hellinger, Mark 1903-1947
Bishop, Jim. *The Mark Hellinger Story.* New York: Appleton-Century-Crofts, 1952.

Hellman, Lillian 1907-
Hellman, Lillian. *An Unfinished Woman; A Memoir.* Boston: Little, Brown, 1969.
—. *Pentimento; A Book of Portraits.* Boston: Little, Brown, 1973.
Moody, Richard. *Lillian Hellman, Playwright.* New York: Pegasus, 1972.

Helpmann, Robert 1909-
Anthony, Gordon. *Robert Helpmann.* London: Home & Van Thal, 1946.
Brahms, Caryl. *Robert Helpmann, Choreographer.* London: B. T. Batsford, 1943.
Gurlay, J. Logan (ed.). *Robert Helpmann Album.* Glasgow: Stage and Screen, 1948.
Walker, Kathrine S. *Robert Helpmann; An Illustrated Study of His Work, with a List of His Appearances on Stage and Screen.* London: Rockliff, 1957.

Henslowe, Philip ?-1616
Collier, John P. *Diary of Philip Henslowe from 1591 to 1609.* London: Shakespeare Society, 1845.
Henslowe, Philip (ed. by Walter W. Greg). *Henslowe's Diary.* London: A. H. Bullen, 1904-08; 2 vols.

Hepburn, Katharine 1909-
Higham, Charles. *Kate.* New York: Norton, 1975.
Marill, Alvin H. *Katharine Hepburn.* New York: Pyramid, 1973.
See also: Tracy, Spencer.

Heraud, John A. 1799-1887
Heraud, Edith. *Memoirs of John A. Heraud.* London: Redway, 1898.

Heyward, DuBose 1885-1940
Allen, Hervey. *DuBose Heyward; A Critical and Biographical Sketch.* New York: Doran, 192-.
Durham, Frank. *DuBose Heyward, the Man Who Wrote Porgy.* Columbia: Univ. of South Carolina, 1954.

Hicks, Sir Edward Seymour 1871-1949
Hicks, Edward Seymour. *Between Ourselves.* London: Cassell, 1930.
—. *Hail Fellow Well Met.* London: Staples, 1949.
—. *Me and My Missus; Fifty Years on the Stage.* London: Cassell, 1939.
—. *Night Lights: Two Men Talk of Life and Love and Ladies...* London: Cassell, 1938.
—. *Seymour Hicks: Twenty-four Years of an Actor's Life.* London: Alston Rivers, 1910.

Hill, Benson Earle ?-1845
Hill, Benson E. *Playing About; or, Theatrical Anecdotes and Adventures . . .* London: Sams, 1840.

Hill, George Handel ("Yankee Hill") 1809-1849
Hill, George H. *Scenes from the Life of an Actor.* New York: Garrett, 1853.
Northall, William K. (ed.). *Life and Recollections of Yankee Hill; Together with Anecdotes and Incidents of His Travels.* New York: Burgess, 1850.

Holland, George 1791-1870
Maclay, William B. *Holland Memorial; Sketch of the Life of George Holland, the Veteran Comedian, with Dramatic Reminiscences.* New York: Morrell, 1871.

Hollingshead, John 1827-1904
Hollingshead, John. *My Lifetime.* London: Law, Marston, 1895.

Holloway, Stanley 1890-
Holloway, Stanley, as told to Dick Richards. *Win a Little Bit O'Luck.* New York: Stein & Day, 1967.

Holm, Hanya 1893-
Sorell, Walter. *Hanya Holm; The Biography of an Artist.* Middletown, Conn.: Wesleyan Univ., 1969.

Hopkins, Arthur 1878-1950
Hopkins, Arthur. *To a Lonely Boy.* Garden City: Doubleday, Dorn, 1937.

Hopper, De Wolf 1858-1935
Hopper, De Wolf. *Once a Clown, Always a Clown.* Boston: Little, Brown, 1927.

Horniman, Annie Elizabeth Fredericka 1860-1937
Flannery, James W. *Miss Annie F. Horniman and the Abbey Theatre.* London: Oxford Univ., 1971.

Houseman, John 1902-
Houseman, John. *Run-Through; A Memoir.* New York: Simon & Schuster, 1972.

Housman, Laurence 1865-1959
Housman, Laurence. *The Unexpected Years.* Indianapolis: Bobbs-Merrill, 1936.

Howard, Bronson 1842-1908
American Dramatists and Composers Society. *In Memoriam: Bronson Howard, 1842-1908 . . .* New York: Marion Press, 1910.

Howard, J. Bannister 1867-1946
Howard, J. Bannister. *Fifty Years a Showman.* London: Hutchinson, 1938.

Howard, Leslie 1893-1943
Colvin, Ian. *Flight 777.* London: Evans Bros., 1957.
Howard, Leslie Ruth. *A Quite Remarkable Father.* New York: Harcourt, Brace, 1959.

Howe, J. B. -1908
Howe, J. B. *A Cosmopolitan Actor . . . His Adventures All Over the World.* London: Bedford, 1888.

Hoyt, Charles Hale 1860-1900
Hunt, Douglas L. *The Life and Work of Charles H. Hoyt.* Nashville, Tenn.: Joint University Libraries, 1945.

Hughes, Langston 1902-1967
Dickinson, Donald C. *A Bio-Bibliography of Langston Hughes, 1902-1967.* Hamden, Conn.: Archon Books, 1972.
Emanuel, James A. *Langston Hughes.* New York: Twayne, 1967.
Hughes, Langston. *The Big Sea.* New York: Knopf, 1945.
—. *I Wonder as I Wander; An Autobiographical Journey.* New York: Rinehart, 1956.
Meltzer, Milton. *Langston Hughes.* New York: Crowell, 1968.
Rollins, Charlamae H. *Black Troubadour: Langston Hughes.* Chicago: Rand McNally, 1970.

Hugo, Victor Marie, Viscount 1802-1885
Barbou, Alfred (trans. by Frances A. Shaw). *Victor Hugo: His Life and Works.* Chicago: S. C. Griggs, 1881.
— (trans. by Ellen E. Frewer). *Victor Hugo and His Time.* New York: Harper, 1882.
Blemont, Emile (ed.). *Memorial Life of Victor Hugo.* Boston: Estes & Lauriat.
Cappon, James. *Victor Hugo: A Memoir and a Study.* Edinburgh: W. Blackwood, 1885.
Drouet, Juliette (ed. by Louis Gimbaud and trans. by Theodora Davidson). *The Love Letters of Juliette Drouet to Victor Hugo.* New York: McBride, Nast, 1914.
Duclaux, Agnes Mary. *Victor Hugo.* London: Constable, 1921.
Edwards, Samuel. *Victor Hugo; A Tumultuous Life.* New York: McKay, 1971.
Escholier, Raymond (trans. by Lewis Galantiere). *Victor Hugo.* New York: Payson & Clarke, 1930.
Grant, Elliott M. *The Career of Victor Hugo.* Cambridge: Harvard Univ., 1945.
Giese, William F. *Victor Hugo, the Man and the Poet.* New York: Dial, 1926.
Guyer, Foster. *The Titan: Victor Hugo.* New York: S. F. Vanni, 1955.
Haggard, Andrew. *Victor Hugo; His Work and Love.* London: Hutchinson, 1923.
Houston, John P. *Victor Hugo.* New York: Twayne, 1974.
Hugo, Adele (trans. by C. E. Wilbour). *Victor Hugo.* New York: Carleton, 1863.
Hugo, Victor (ed. by P. Meurice). *The Letters of Victor Hugo, to His Family, to Sainte-Beuve and Others.* Boston: Houghton, Mifflin, 1896.
— (ed. by P. Meurice). *The Letters of Victor Hugo from Exile and After the Fall of the Empire.* Boston: Houghton, Mifflin, 1898.
— (trans. by John W. Harding). *The Memoirs of Victor Hugo.* New York: Dillingham, 1899.
— (trans. by Elizabeth W. Latimer). *The Love Letters of Victor Hugo, 1820-1822.* New York: Harper, 1901.
Josephson, Matthew. *Victor Hugo, a Realistic Biography of the Great Romantic.* Garden City: Doubleday, Doran, 1942.
Marzials, Frank T. *The Life of Victor Hugo.* London: Scott, 1888.
Maurois, André (trans. by Gerard Hopkins). *Olympio; The Life of Victor Hugo.* New York: Harper, 1956.
— (trans. by Oliver Bernard). *Victor Hugo and His World.* New York: Viking, 1966.
Swinburne, Algernon. *Victor Hugo.* New York: Worthington, 1886.
Wack, Henry W. *The Romance of Victor Hugo and Juliette Drouet.* New York: Putnam, 1905.

Hull, Josephine 1886-1957
Carson, William G. B. *Dear Josephine.* Norman: Univ. of Oklahoma, 1963.

Hunter, Ruth
Hunter, Ruth. *Come Back on Tuesday.* New York: Scribner, 1945.

Hurlbut, Gladys
Hurlbut, Gladys. *Next Week East Lynne!* New York: Dutton, 1950.

Ibsen, Henrik 1828-1906
Bradbrook, Muriel C. *Ibsen, the Norwegian; A Revaluation.* London: Chatto & Windus, 1946.
Gosse, Edmund William. *Henrik Ibsen.* New

Orgel, Stephen and Strong, Roy. *Inigo Jones, The Theatre of the Stuart Court.* Berkeley: Univ. of California, 1973; 2 vols.
Ramsey, Stanley C. *Inigo Jones.* London: Benn, 1924.
Summerson, John. *Inigo Jones.* Harmondsworth: Penquin, 1966.

Jones, Robert Edmond 1887-1954
Pendleton, Ralph (ed.). *The Theatre of Robert Edmond Jones.* Middletown, Conn.: Wesleyan Univ., 1958.

Jonson, Ben c.1573-1637
Bamborough, John B. *Ben Jonson.* London: Longmans, Green, 1959.
Chute, Marchette. *Ben Jonson of Westminster.* New York: Dutton, 1953.
Herford, C. H. and Simpson, Percy. *Ben Jonson: The Man and His Work.* Oxford: Clarendon, 1925; 2 vols.
Linklater, Eric. *Ben Jonson and King James.* London: Cape, 1931.
Palmer, John L. *Ben Jonson.* New York: Viking, 1934.
Smith, George Gregory. *Ben Jonson.* London: Macmillan, 1919.
Steel, Byron [Francis Steegmüller]. *O Rare Ben Jonson.* New York: Knopf, 1927.
Swinburne, Algernon. *A Study of Ben Jonson.* London: Chatto & Windus, 1889.
Symonds, John Addington. *Ben Jonson.* London: Longmans, Green, 1888.

Jordan, Dorothy (née Bland) 1761-1816
Boaden, James. *The Life of Mrs. Jordan.* London: Bull, 1831.
Fothergill, Brian. *Mrs. Jordan, Portrait of an Actress.* London: Faber & Faber, 1965.
Jerrold, Clare A. *The Story of Dorothy Jordan.* London: Nash, 1914.
Jordan, Dorothy (ed. by A. Aspinall). *Mrs. Jordan and Her Family; Being the Unpublished Correspondence of Mrs. Jordan and the Duke of Clarence, Later William IV.* London: A. Barker, 1951.
Sergeant, Philip W. *Mrs. Jordan: Child of Nature.* London: Hutchinson, 1913.
Public and Private Life of that Celebrated Actress, Miss Bland, otherwise Mrs. Ford, or, Mrs. Jordan. London: Duncombe, 1886.

Jouvet, Louis 1891-1951
Knapp, Bettina Liebowitz. *Louis Jouvet; Man of the Theatre.* New York: Columbia Univ., 1958.

Judith, Mme. 1827-1912
Judith [Julie Bernot] (trans. by Mrs. A. Bell). *My Autobiography.* London: Nash, 1912.

Kaminska, Ida 1899-
Kaminska, Ida (trans. by Curt Leviant). *My Life, My Theater.* New York: Macmillan, 1973.

Kane, Whitford 1882-1956
Kane, Whitford. *Are We All Met?* London: Mathews & Marrot, 1931.

Kanin, Garson 1912-
Kanin, Garson. *Hollywood.* New York: Viking, 1974.

Karloff, Boris 1887-1969
Gifford, Denis. *Karloff: The Man, the Monster, the Movies.* New York: Curtis Books, 1973.
Jensen, Paul M. *Boris Karloff and His Films.* New York: A. S. Barnes, 1975.
Underwood, Peter. *Horror Man: The Life of Boris Karloff.* London: Frewin, 1972.

Karno, Fred 1866-1941
Adeler, Edwin and West, Con. *Remember Fred Karno? The Life of a Great Showman.* London: Long, 1939.
Gallagher, J. P. *Fred Karno: Master of Mirth and Tears.* London: Hale, 1971.

Kaufman, George S. 1889-1961
Teichmann, Howard. *George S. Kaufman; An Intimate Portrait.* New York: Atheneum, 1972.
Meredith, Scott. *George S. Kaufman and His Friends; A Biography.* Garden City: Doubleday, 1974.
See also: Hart, Moss.

Kaye, Danny 1918-
Richards, Dick. *The Life Story of Danny Kaye.* London: Convoy, 1949.
Singer, Kurt. *The Danny Kaye Saga.* London: Hale, 1957.

Kazan, Elia 1909-
Ciment, Michel. *Kazan on Kazan.* New York: Viking, 1974.

Kean, Charles 1811?-1868
Cole, John W. *The Life and Theatrical Times of Charles Kean.* London: Bentley, 1859.
Kean, Charles (ed. by William G. B. Carson). *Letters of Mr. and Mrs. Charles Kean, Relating to Their American Tours.* St. Louis, Mo.: Washington Univ., 1945.
—. (ed. by J. M. D. Hardwick). *Emigrant in Motley; The Journey of Charles and Ellen Kean in Quest of a Theatrical Fortune in Australia and America.* London: Rockliff, 1954.

Kean, Edmund 1787-1833
Disher, Maurice Wilson. *Mad Genius.* London: Hutchinson, 1950.
Hawkins, F. W. *The Life of Edmund Kean.* London: Tinsley Bros., 1869; 2 vols.
Hillebrand, Harold Newcomb. *Edmund Kean.* New York: Columbia Univ., 1933.
Macqueen-Pope, W. J. *Edmund Kean; The Story of an Actor.* Edinburgh: Nelson, 1960.
Molloy, Joseph Fitzgerald. *The Life and Adventures of Edmund Kean.* London: Downey, 1897.
Playfair, Giles. *Kean.* New York: Dutton, 1939.
Procter, Bryan W. *The Life of Edmund Kean.* New York: Harper, 1835.

Keene, Laura 1820-1873
Greanan, John. *The Life of Laura Keene.* Philadelphia: Rodgers, 1897.

Kelly, Frances Maria 1790-1882
Francis, Basil. *Fanny Kelly of Drury Lane.* London: Rockliff, 1950.
Holman, L. E. *Lamb's "Barbara S__"; The Life of Frances Maria Kelly, Actress.* London: Methuen, 1935.

Kelly, Gene 1912-
Hirschhorn, Clive. *Gene Kelly.* London: W. H. Allen, 1974.

Kelly, Michael ?-1826
Kelly, Michael. *Reminiscences of Michael Kelly, of the King's Theatre, and Theatre Royal Drury Lane.* London: Colburn, 1826; 2 vols.

Kelly, Walter C. 1873-1939
Kelly, Walter C. *Of Me I Sing; An Informal Autobiography.* New York: Dial, 1953.

Kemble, Charles 1775-1854
Williamson, Jane. *Charles Kemble, Man of the Theatre.* Lincoln: Univ. of Nebraska, 1970.

Kemble, Fanny 1809-1893
Armstrong, Margaret Neilson. *Fanny Kemble, A Passionate Victorian.* New York: Macmillan, 1938.
Bobbé, Dorothie. *Fanny Kemble.* New York: Minton, Balch, 1931.
Driver, Leota Stultz. *Fanny Kemble.* Chapel Hill: Univ. of North Carolina, 1933.
Gibbs, Henry. *Affectionately Yours, Fanny; Fanny Kemble and the Theatre.* New York: Jarrolds, 1947.
Kemble, Frances Anne. *Journal.* Philadelphia: Carey, Lea & Blanchard, 1835.
—. *Record of a Girlhood.* London: Bentley, 1878.
—. *Records of Later Life.* New York: Holt, 1882.
—. *Further Records, 1848-1883.* New York, Holt, 1891.
— (ed. by Fanny Kemble Wister). *Fanny, the American Kemble: Her Journals and Unpublished Letters.* Tallahassee: South Pass Press, 1972.
Kerr, Laura. *Footlights to Fame.* New York: Funk & Wagnalls, 1962.
Rushmore, Robert. *Fanny Kemble.* New York: Crowell-Collier, 1970.
Wise, Winifred E. *Fanny Kemble; Actress, Author, Abolitionist.* New York: Putnam, 1967.
Wright, Constance. *Fanny Kemble and the Lovely Land.* New York: Dodd, Mead, 1972.

Kemble, John Philip 1757-1823
Baker, Herschel C. *John Philip Kemble; The Actor in His Theatre.* Cambridge: Harvard Univ., 1942.
Boaden, James. *Memoirs of the Life of John Philip Kemble, Esq.* Philadelphia: R. H. Small, 1825.
Child, Harold H. *Shakespearian Productions of John Philip Kemble.* London: Milford, 1935.
Fitzgerald, Percy H. *Kembles; an Account of the Kemble Family, Including the Lives of Mrs. Siddons and Her Brother John Philip Kemble.* London: Tinsley, 1871; 2 vols.
Williams, John A. *Memoirs of John Philip Kemble.* London: J. B. Wood, 1817.

Kendal, Madge 1848-1935
Kendal, William H. 1843-1917
Kendal, Margaret. *Dramatic Opinions.* Boston: Little, Brown, 1890.
—. *Dame Madge Kendal.* London: Murray, 1933.
Pemberton, T. Edgar. *The Kendals.* New York: Dodd, Mead, 1900.

Kendall, Henry 1897-1962
Kendall, Henry. *I Remember Romano's.* London: MacDonald, 1960.

Kern, Jerome 1885-1945
Ewen, David. *The Story of Jerome Kern.* New York: Holt, 1953.
—. *The World of Jerome Kern, a Biography.* New York: Holt, 1960.

Keys, Nelson 1886-1939
Carstairs, John P. *"Bunch," a Biography of Nelson Keys.* London: Hurst & Blackett, 1941.

Killigrew, Thomas (the elder) 1612-1683
Harbage, Alfred. *Thomas Killigrew, Cavalier Dramatist, 1612-83*. Philadelphia: Univ. of Pennsylvania, 1930.

Kleist, Heinrich von 1777-1811
Blankenagel, John Carl. *The Attitude of Heinrich von Kleist toward the Problems of Life*. Baltimore: Johns Hopkins, 1917.
March, Richard. *Heinrich von Kleist*. New Haven: Yale Univ. 1954.

Komisarjevsky, Theodore 1882-1954
Komisarjevsky, Theodore. *Myself and the Theatre*. New York: Dutton, 1930.

Kops, Bernard 1926-
Kops, Bernard. *The World Is a Wedding*. New York: Coward-McCann, 1963.

Kotzebue, August Friedrich Ferdinand von 1761-1819
Kotzebue, Augustus von (trans. by Anne Plumptre). *Sketch of the Life and Literary Career of Augustus von Kotzebue; with the Journal of His Tour to Paris, at the close of the year 1790*. London: H. D. Symonds, 1800.
— (trans. by Benjamin Beresford). *The Most Remarkable Year in the Life of Augustus von Kotzebue; Containing an Account of His Exile into Siberia, and of the Other Extraordinary Events which Happened to Him in Russia*. London: Phillips, 1802; 3 vols.
—. *Sketch of the Life and Literary Career of Augustus von Kotzebue; with the Journal of His Exile to Siberia*. London: Hunt and Clarke, 1827; 2 vols.

Kraft, Hy 1899-1975
Kraft, Hy. *On My Way to the Theatre*. New York: Macmillan, 1971.

Kreymborg, Alfred 1883-1966
Kreymborg, Alfred. *Troubadour; An Autobiography*. New York: Boni & Liveright, 1925.

Kyd, Thomas 1558-1594
Freeman, Arthur. *Thomas Kyd: Facts and Problems*. Oxford: Clarendon, 1967.

Lahr, Bert 1895-1967
Lahr, John. *Notes on a Cowardly Lion*. New York: Knopf, 1969.

Landis, Jessie Royce 1904-1972
Landis, Jessie Royce. *You Won't Be So Pretty (But You'll Know More)*. London: W. H. Allen, 1954.

Lane, Lupino 1892-1959
White, James D. *Born to Star: The Lupino Lane Story*. London: Heinemann, 1957.

Lang, (Alexander) Matheson 1879-1948
Lang, Matheson. *Mr. Wu Looks Back; Thoughts and Memories*. London: Paul, 1941.

Langner, Lawrence 1890-1962
Langner, Lawrence. *The Magic Curtain*. New York: Dutton, 1951.
—. *G. B. S. and the Lunatic; Reminiscences of the Long, Lively, and Affectionate Friendship between George Bernard Shaw and the Author*. New York: Atheneum, 1963.

Langtry, Lily 1852-1929
Brough, James. *The Prince and the Lily*. New York: Coward-McCann, 1975.
Dudley, Ernest. *The Gilded Lily*. London: Odhams, 1958.
Gerson, Noel B. *Because I Loved Him; The Life and Loves of Lillie Langtry*. New York: Morrow, 1971.
Langtry, Lillie. *The Days I Knew*. New York: Doran, 1925.
Sichel, Pierre. *The Jersey Lily*. Englewood Cliffs, N.J.: Prentice-Hall, Inc. 1958.

Lano, David 1874-
Lano, David. *A Wandering Showman, I*. East Lansing: Michigan State Univ., 1957.

Lauder, Sir Harry 1870-1950
Irving, Gordon. *Great Scot; The Life Story of Sir Harry Lauder, Legendary Laird of the Music Hall*. London: Frewin, 1968.
Lauder, Harry. *Harry Lauder at Home and on Tour*. London: Greening, 1907.
—. *A Minstrel in France*. New York: Hearst, 1918.
—. *Roamin' in the Gloamin'*. London: Hutchinson, 1928.
—. *Wee Drappies*. New York: R. M. McBride, 1932.
Malvern, Gladys. *Valiant Minstrel, the Story of Harry Lauder*. New York: J. Messner, 1943.

Laughton, Charles 1899-1962
Lanchester, Elsa. *Charles Laughton and I*. New York: Harcourt, Brace, 1938.
Singer, Kurt. *The Laughton Story; An Intimate Story of Charles Laughton*. Philadelphia: J. C. Winston, 1954.

Lavallière, Eve 1866-1929
McReavy, Lawrence L. *Eve Lavallière; A Modern Magdalen, (1866-1929)*. St. Louis, Mo.: Herder, 1935.
Murphy, Edward F. *Mademoiselle Lavallière*. Garden City: Doubleday, 1948.
Willette, Henriette (trans. by Mary B. M. Sands). *Lavallière: Actress & Saint*. London: Sands, 1934.

Laver, James 1899-
Laver, James. *Museum Piece; or, The Education of an Iconographer*. Boston: Houghton, 1964.

Lawrence, Gertrude 1898-1952
Aldrich, Richard Stoddard. *Gertrude Lawrence as Mrs. A*. New York: Greystone, 1954.
Lawrence, Gertrude. *A Star Danced*. Garden City: Doubleday, Doran, 1945.

Laye, Evelyn 1900-
Laye, Evelyn. *Boo, To My Friends*. London: Hurst & Blackett, 1959.

Leavitt, Michael Bennett 1843-1935
Leavitt, Michael Bennett. *Fifty Years in Theatrical Management*. New York: Broadway Publishing, 1912.

Leblanc, Georgette (Maeterlinck) 1876-1941
See: Maeterlinck, Maurice.

Lecouvreur, Adrienne 1692-1730
Richtman, Jack. *Adrienne Lecouvreur: The Actress and the Age*. Englewood Cliffs, N.J.: Prentice-Hall, 1971.

Lee, Gypsy Rose 1914-1970
Lee, Gypsy Rose. *Gypsy*. New York: Harper, 1957.

Lee, Henry 1765-1836
Lee, Henry. *Memoirs of a Manager*. Taunton, Eng.: Bragg, 1830.

Le Gallienne, Eva 1899-
Le Gallienne, Eva. *At 33*. New York: Longmans, Green, 1934.
—. *With a Quiet Heart*. New York: Viking, 1953.

Leigh, Vivien 1913-1967
Dent, Alan. *Vivien Leigh; A Bouquet*. London: Hamilton, 1969.
Robyns, Gwen. *Light of a Star*. London: Frewin, 1968.
See also: Olivier, Laurence.

LeMaître, Frederic 1800-1876
Baldick, Robert. *The Life and Times of Frederick Lemaître*. London: Hamilton, 1959.

Leman, Walter 1810-
Leman, Walter M. *Memories of an Old Actor*. San Francisco: Roman, 1886.

Leno, Dan (George Galvin) 1860-1904
Leno, Dan. *Dan Leno, Hys Booke*. London: Greening, 1905.
Wood, Jay. *Dan Leno*. London: Methuen, 1905.

Leonard, Eddie 1875-1941
Leonard, Eddie. *What a Life, I'm Telling You*. New York: Eddie Leonard, 1934.

Leslie, Fred 1855-1892
Vincent, William T. *Recollections of Fred Leslie*. London: Paul, Trench, Trubner, 1894.

Lessing, Gotthold Ephraim 1729-1781
Brown, F. Andrew. *Gotthold Ephraim Lessing*. New York: Twayne, 1971.
Garland, Henry B. *Lessing: The Founder of Modern German Literature*. Cambridge, Eng.: Bowes, 1937.
Rolleston, Thomas W. *Life and Writings of Gotthold Ephraim Lessing*. London: Walter Scott, 1889.
Sime, James. *Lessing*. Boston: J. R. Osgood, 1877.
Stahr, Adolf (trans. by E. P. Evans). *The Life and Works of Gotthold Ephraim Lessing*. Boston: W. V. Spencer, 1866; 2 vols.

Lewes, Charles Lee 1740-1803
Lewes, Charles Lee. *Memoirs of Charles Lee Lewes*. London: Phillips, 1805.

Lewis, Joe E.
Cohn, Art. *The Joker Is Wild*. New York: Random House, 1955.

Lillie, Beatrice 1898-
Lillie, Beatrice with Brough, James. *Every Other Inch a Lady*. Garden City: Doubleday, 1972.

Lion, Leon M. 1879-1947
Lion, Leon M. *The Surprise of My Life*. New York: Hutchinson, 1948.
See also: Galsworthy, John.

Lister, Moira 1923-
Lister, Moira. *The Very Merry [Widow] Moira*. London: Hodder & Stoughton, 1969.

Livingstone, Belle
Livingstone, Belle. *Belle of Bohemia*. London: John Hamilton, 1927.
—. *Belle Out of Order*. New York: Holt, 1959.

Lloyd, Marie 1870-1922

York: Scribner, 1907.
Heiberg, Hans (trans. by Joan Tate). *Ibsen: A Portrait of the Artist.* London: Allen & Unwin, 1969.
Ibsen, Bergliot (trans. by Gerik Schielderup). *The Three Ibsens; Memoirs of Henrik Ibsen, Suzannah Ibsen and Sigurd Ibsen.* New York: American-Scandinavian Foundation, 1952.
Ibsen, Henrik (trans. by J. N. Laurvik and M. Morison). *Letters of Henrik Ibsen.* New York: Fox, Duffield, 1905.
— (trans. by Arne Kildal). *Speeches and New Letters.* Boston: R. G. Badger, 1910.
— (ed. by Evert Sprinchorn). *Letters and Speeches.* New York: Hill & Wang.
Jaeger, Henrik (trans. by William Morton Payne). *Henrik Ibsen, 1828-1888; A Critical Biography.* Chicago: A. C. McClurg, 1890.
Jorgenson, Theodore. *Henrik Ibsen: Life and Drama.* Northfield, Minn.: St. Olaf Norwegian Institute, 1963.
Koht, Halvdan (trans. by Ruth McMahon and Hanna Larsen). *The Life of Ibsen.* New York: Norton, 1931; 2 vols.
MacFall, Haldane. *Ibsen, the Man, His Art and His Significance.* New York: Shepard, 190-.
Meyer, Michael L. *Henrik Ibsen.* London: Hart-Davis, 1967-71; 3 vols.
Moses, Montrose. *Henrik Ibsen; The Man and His Plays.* Boston: Little, Brown, 1908.
Roberts, R. Ellis. *Henrik Ibsen; A Critical Study.* London: Secker, 1912.
Rose, Henry. *Henrik Ibsen: Poet, Mystic and Moralist.* London: A. C. Fifield, 1913.
Shaw, George Bernard. *The Quintessence of Ibsenism, Now Completed to the Death of Ibsen.* London: Constable, 1913.
Zucker, Adolf E. *Ibsen, the Master Builder.* New York: Holt, 1929.

Inchbald, Mrs. Elizabeth (née Simpson) 1753-1821
Inchbald, Elizabeth (ed. by James Boaden). *Memoirs of Mrs. Inchbald . . .* London: Bentley, 1833.
Littlewood, S. R. *Elizabeth Inchbald and Her Circle: The Life Story of a Charming Woman (1753-1821).* London: O'Connor, 1921.

Inge, William 1913-1973
Shuman, Robert B. *William Inge.* New York: Twayne, 1965.

Ionesco, Eugene 1912-
Bonnefoy, Claude (trans. by Jan Dawson). *Conversations with Eugene Ionesco.* New York: Holt, Rinehart & Winston, 1971.
Ionesco, Eugene (trans. by Helen R. Lane). *Present Past, Past Present; A Personal Memoir.* New York: Grove, 1971.

Irving, Henry 1838-1905
Archer, William. *Henry Irving, Actor and Manager; A Critical Study.* London: Field & Tuer, 1883.
Austin, Louis Frederic. *Henry Irving in England and America, 1838-1884.* London: T. F. Unwin, 1884.
Brereton, Austin. *Henry Irving.* London: Bogue, 1883.
—. *The Lyceum and Henry Irving.* London: Lawrence & Bullen, 1903.
—. *The Life of Henry Irving.* London: Longmans, Green, 1908; 2 vols.
—. *"H. B." and Laurence Irving.* Boston: Small, Maynard, 1923.
Craig, Edward Gordon. *Henry Irving.* New York: Longmans, Green, 1930.
Fitzgerald, Percy H. *Sir Henry Irving, a Biography.* Philadelphia: G. W. Jacobs, 1906.
Hatton, Joseph. *Henry Irving's Impressions of America.* Boston: J. R. Osgood, 1884.
Hiatt, Charles. *Henry Irving; A Record and Review.* London: Bell, 1899.
Irving, Laurence. *Henry Irving, the Actor and His World.* London: Faber & Faber, 1951.
—. *The Precarious Crust.* London: Chatto & Windus, 1971.
Jones, Henry Arthur. *The Shadow of Henry Irving.* New York: Morrow, 1931.
Macfall, Haldane. *Sir Henry Irving.* Edinburgh: T. N. Foulis, 1906.
Marshall, Francis A. *Henry Irving, Actor and Manager; A Criticism of a Critic's Criticism, by an Irvingite.* London: Routledge, 1883.
Melville, E. J. *"Thorough"; A Short Sketch on the Life and Work of Mr. Henry Irving.* London: Darling, 1879.
Menpes, Mortimer. *Henry Irving.* London: A. and C. Black, 1906.
Pollock, Walter H. *Impressions of Henry Irving, Gathered in Public and Private during a Friendship of Many Years.* London: Longmans, Green, 1908.
Russell, Percy. *Sir Henry Irving.* London: S. Champness, 1896.
St. John, Christopher. *Henry Irving.* London: Green Sheaf, 1905.
Saintsbury, Harry A., (ed.). *We Saw Him Act; A Symposium on the Art of Sir Henry Irving.* London: Hurst & Blackett, 1939.
Scott, Clement W. *From "The Bells" to "King Arthur"; A Critical Record of the First-Night Productions at the Lyceum Theatre from 1871 to 1895.* London: Macqueen, 1896.
Stoker, Bram. *Personal Reminiscences of Henry Irving.* New York: Macmillan, 1906; 2 vols.
Winter, William. *Henry Irving.* New York: G. J. Coombes, 1885.

Jackson, Sir Barry 1879-1961
Bishop, George W. *Barry Jackson and the London Theatre.* London: Barker, 1933.

Jacob, Naomi 1889-1964
Jacob, Naomi. *Me; A Chronicle about Other People.* London: Hutchinson, 1933.
—. *Me Again.* London: Hutchinson, 1937.
—. *More About Me.* London: Hutchinson, 1939.
—. *Me in Wartime.* London: Hutchinson, 1940.
—. *Me—Looking Back.* London: Hutchinson, 1950.
—. *Me—Yesterday and To-day.* London: Hutchinson, 1957.

James, Julia -1964
James, Julia. *Mother Signed the Contract.* London: Davies, 1957.

Janis, Elsie 1889-1956
Janis, Elsie. *The Big Show; My Six Months with the American Expeditionary Forces.* New York: Cosmopolitan Book, 1919.
—. *So Far, So Good!* New York: E. P. Dutton, 1932.

Jeffers, Robinson 1887-1962
Adamic, Louis. *Robinson Jeffers; A Portrait.* Seattle: Univ. of Washington, 1929.
Bennett, Melba. *The Stone Mason of Far House; The Life and Work of Robinson Jeffers.* Los Angeles: Ritchie, 1966.
Coffin, Arthur B. *Robinson Jeffers; Poet of Inhumanism.* Madison: Univ. of Wisconsin, 1971.
Jeffers, Robinson (ed. by Ann N. Ridgeway). *The Selected Letters of Robinson Jeffers, 1897-1962.* Baltimore: Johns Hopkins, 1968.
Powell, Lawrence C. *Robinson Jeffers; The Man and the Artist.* New York: Boni & Liveright, 1926.

Jefferson, Joseph 1829-1905
Dole, Nathan H. *Joseph Jefferson at Home.* Boston: Estes, 1898.
Farjeon, Eleanor. *Portrait of a Family.* New York: Stokes, 1936.
Jefferson, Eugenie P. *Intimate Recollections of Joseph Jefferson.* New York: Dodd, Mead, 1909.
Jefferson, Joseph. *The Autobiography of Joseph Jefferson.* New York: Century, 1890.
—. *"Rip Van Winkle"; The Autobiography of Joseph Jefferson.* New York: Appleton-Century-Crofts, 1950.
—. (ed. by Alan S. Downer). *Autobiography.* Cambridge: Harvard Univ., 1964.
Malvern, Gladys. *Good Troupers All.* Philadelphia: Macrae-Smith, 1945.
Wilson, Francis. *Joseph Jefferson, Reminiscences of a Fellow Player.* New York: Scribner, 1906.
Winter, William. *The Jeffersons.* Boston: J. R. Osgood, 1881.
—. *Life and Art of Joseph Jefferson.* New York: Macmillan, 1894.

Jerome, Jerome Klapka 1859-1927
Faurot, Ruth Marie. *Jerome K. Jerome.* New York: Twayne, 1975.
Jerome, Jerome K. *On the Stage—and Off: The Brief Career of a Would-Be Actor.* New York: Holt, 1891.
—. *My Life and Times.* New York: Harper, 1926.
Moss, Alfred. *Jerome K. Jerome; His Life and Work (from Poverty to the Knighthood of the People).* London: Selwyn & Blount, 1928.

Jessel, George 1898-
Jessel, George. *So Help Me.* New York: Random House, 1943.
—. *This Way, Miss.* New York: Holt, 1955.

Jolson, Al 1886-1950
Freedland, Michael. *Jolson.* New York: Stein & Day, 1972.
Jolson, Harry, as told to Alban Emley. *Mistah Jolson.* Hollywood: House-Warven, 1952.
Sieben, Pearl. *The Immortal Jolson.* New York: Fell, 1962.

Jones, Henry Arthur 1851-1929
Cordell, Richard A. *Henry Arthur Jones and the Modern Drama.* New York: Long and Smith, 1932.
Jones, Doris A. *Taking the Curtain Call; The Life and Letters of Henry Arthur Jones.* New York: Macmillan, 1930.

Jones, Inigo 1573-1652
Cunningham, Peter. *Inigo Jones. A Life of the Architect.* London: Shakespeare Society, 1848.
Gotch, John Alfred. *Inigo Jones.* London: Methuen, 1928.

Farson, Daniel. *Marie Lloyd & Music Hall.* London: Tom Stacey, 1972.
Jacob, Naomi. *"Our Marie."* London: Hutchinson, 1936.

Loftus, Cissie 1876-1943
McCarthy, Justin Huntly. *Cissie Loftus; An Appreciation.* New York: R. H. Russell, 1899.

Logan, Olive 1839-1909
Logan, Olive. *The Mimic World.* Philadelphia: New-World, 1871.

Lonsdale, Frederick 1881-1954
Donaldson, Frances. *Freddy.* Philadelphia: Lippincott, 1957.

Loos, Anita 1893-
Hayes, Helen and Loos, Anita. *Twice Over Lightly.* New York: Harcourt, Brace, Jovanovich, 1972.
Loos, Anita. *A Girl Like I.* New York: Viking, 1966.
—. *Kiss Hollywood Goodbye.* New York: Viking, 1974.

Loraine, Robert 1876-1935
Loraine, Winifred. Head Wind; The Story of Robert Loraine. New York: Morrow, 1939.

Lover, Samuel -1868
Bernard, William. *The Life of Samuel Lover.* New York: Appleton, 1874.

Luce, Clare Boothe 1903-
Hatch, Alden. *Ambassador Extraordinary, Clare Boothe Luce.* New York: Holt, 1956.
Henle, Faye. *Au Clare de Luce; Portrait of a Luminous Lady.* New York: Daye, 1943.
Shadegg, Stephen C. *Clare Boothe Luce;* New York: Simon & Schuster, 1970.

Ludlow, Noah Miller 1795-1886
Ludlow, Noah Miller. *Dramatic Life as I Found It.* St. Louis, Mo.: G. I. Jones, 1880.

Lugne-Poe, Aurelien-Marie 1869-1940
Jasper, Gertrude R. *Adventure in the Theatre; Lugne-Poe and the Theatre de l'Oeuvre to 1899.* New Brunswick, N.J.: Rutgers Univ., 1947.

Lunt, Alfred 1893-
Freedley, George. *The Lunts.* London: Rockliff, 1957.
Zolotow, Maurice. *Stagestruck; The Romance of Alfred Lunt and Lynn Fontanne.* New York: Harcourt, Brace & World, 1965.

Lupino, Stanley 1894-1942
Lupino, Stanley. *From the Stocks to the Stars; An Unconventional Autobiography.* London: Hutchinson, 1934.

Lytton, Sir Henry Alfred 1867-1936
Lytton, Henry A. *The Secrets of a Savoyard.* London: Jarrolds, 1922.
—. *A Wandering Minstrel, Reminiscences.* London: Jarrolds, 1933.

MacArthur, Charles 1895-1956
Hecht, Ben. *Charlie; The Improbable Life and Times of Charles Mac Arthur.* New York: Harper, 1957.
See also: Hayes, Helen.

Mackaye, Steele 1842-1894
Mackaye, Percy. *Epoch.* New York: Boni and Liveright, 1927; 2 vols.

Macklin, Charles 1699-1797
Appleton, William. *Charles Macklin; An Actor's Life.* Cambridge: Harvard Univ., 1960.
Cook, William. *Memoirs of Charles Macklin, Comedian.* London: Asperne, 1804.
Kirkman, James T. *Memoirs of the Life of Charles Macklin; Esq.* London: Lackington, Allen, 1799.
Parry, Edward A. *Charles Macklin.* London: Paul, Trench, Trubner, 1891.

MacLiammoir, Micheal 1899-
MacLiammoir, Micheal. *All for Hecuba.* London: Methuen, 1947.
—. *Each Actor on His Ass.* London: Routledge & Paul, 1961.
—. *An Oscar of No Importance.* London: Heinemann, 1968.

Macready, William Charles 1793-1873
Archer, William. *William Charles Macready.* London: Paul, Trench, Trubner, 1890.
Downer, Alan S. *The Eminent Tragedian William Charles Macready.* Cambridge: Harvard Univ., 1966.
Macready, William Charles (ed. by William Toynbee). *The Diaries of William Charles Macready,* 1833-1851. New York: Putnam, 1912; 2 vols.
— (ed. by Sir Frederick Pollock). *Macready's Reminiscences, and Selections from His Diaries and Letters.* New York: Harper, 1875.
Pollock, Juliet. *Macready As I Knew Him.* London: Remington, 1884.
Trewin, J. C. *Mr. Macready, a Nineteenth-Century Tragedian and His Theatre.* London: Harrap, 1955.
Macready, William Charles (ed. by J. C. Trewin). *The Journal of William Charles Macready, 1832-1851.* London: Longmans, 1967.

Maeder, Clara Fisher 1811-1898
Maeder, Clara Fisher (ed. by Douglas Taylor). *Autobiography of Clara Fisher Maeder.* New York: Dunlap Society, 1897.

Maeterlinck, Maurice (Count) 1862-1949
Bailly, Auguste (trans. by Fred Rothwell). *Maeterlinck.* London: Rider, 1931.
Bithell, Jethro. *Life and Writings of Maurice Maeterlinck.* London: Walter Scott, 1913.
Clark, MacDonald. *Maurice Maeterlinck, Poet and Philosopher.* New York: Stokes, 1916.
Halls, W. D. *Maurice Maeterlinck; A Study of His Life and Thought.* Oxford: Clarendon, 1960.
Harry, Gerard (trans. by A. Allinson). *Maurice Maeterlinck: A Biographical Study; with Two Essays by M. Maeterlinck.* London: Allen, 1910.
Knapp, Bettina. *Maurice Maeterlinck.* New York: Twayne, 1975.
Leblanc, Georgette (trans. by Janet Flanner). *Souvenirs: My Life with Maeterlinck.* New York: Dutton, 1932.
Mahony, Patrick. *The Magic of Maeterlinck.* Hollywood: House-Warven, 1952.
Moses, Montrose J. *Maurice Maeterlinck; a Study.* New York: Duffield, 1911.

Malina, Judith 1926-
Malina, Judith. *The The Enormous Despair.* New York: Random House, 1972.

Maney, Richard 1892-1968
Maney, Richard. *Fanfare; The Confessions of a Press Agent.* New York: Harper, 1957.

Mansfield, Richard 1857-1907
Wilstach, Paul. *Richard Mansfield: The Man and the Actor.* New York: Scribner's, 1908.
Winter, William. *Life and Art of Richard Mansfield, with Selections from His Letters.* New York: Moffat, Yard, 1910; 2 vols.

Mantell, Robert Bruce 1854-1928
Bulliet, Clarence Joseph. *Robert Mantell's Romance.* Boston: J. W. Luce, 1918.

Marble, Danforth ?-1849
Falconbridge. *Dan Marble.* New York: Dewitt & Davenport, 1851.

Marbury, Elisabeth 1856-1933
Marbury, Elisabeth. *My Crystall Ball.* New York: Boni & Liveright, 1924.

Marlowe, Julia 1865-1950
Barry, John D. *Julia Marlowe.* Boston: E. H. Bacon, 1907.
russell, Charles Edward. 2Julia Marlowe, Her Life and Art. New York: Appleton, 1926.
Sothern, E. H. (ed. by Fairfax Downey) *Julia Marlowe's Story.* New York: Rinehart, 1954.
See also: Sothern, Edward Hugh.

Marlowe, Christopher 1564-1593
Bakeless, Hohn. *Christopher Marlowe; The Man in His Time.* New York: Morrow, 1937.
—. *The Tragicall History of Christopher Marlowe.* Hamden, Conn.: Archon, 1964.
Boas, Frederick S. *Marlowe and His Circle; A Biographical Survey.* London: Milford, 1931.
—. *Christopher Marlowe; A Biographical and Critical Study.* Oxford: Clarendon, 1940.
Brooke, C. F. Tucker. *The Life of Marlowe.* New York: Dial, 1930.
Eccles, Mark. *Christopher Marlowe in London.* Cambridge: Harvard Univ., 1925.
Henderson, Philip. *Christopher Marlowe.* London: Longmans, Green, 1952.
—. *And Morning in His Eyes.* New York: Haskell House, 1972.
Hoffman, Calvin. *The Murder of the Man Who Was "Shakespeare."* New York: Messner, 1955.
Hotson, J. Leslie. *The Death of Christopher Marlowe.* Cambridge: Harvard Univ., 1925.
Ingram, John H. *Christopher Marlowe and His Associates.* London: Richards, 1904.
Kocher, Paul H. *Christopher Marlowe; A Study of His Thought, Learning, and Character.* Chapel Hill: Univ. of North Carolina, 1946.
Lewis, J. G. *Christopher Marlowe: Outlines of His Life and Work.* London: W. W. Gibbings, 1891.
Norman, Charles. *The Muses' Darling.* New York: Rinehart, 1946.
Poirier, Michel. *Christopher Marlowe.* London: Chatto & Windus, 1951.
Ross Williamson, Hugh. *Kind Kit; An Informal Biography of Christopher Marlowe.* New York: St. Martin's, 1973.
Rowse, Alfred L. *Christopher Marlowe; His Life and Work.* New York: Harper, 1964.
Tannenbaum, Samuel A. *The Assassination of Christopher Marlowe (A New View).* New York: Tenny, 1928.
Wraight, Annie D. *In Search of Christopher Marlowe; A Pictorial Biography.* London: Macdonald, 1965.

Marquis, Don 1878-1937
Anthony, Edward. *O Rare Don Marquis; A Biography.* Garden City: Doubleday, 1962.

Martin-Harvey, Sir John 1863-1944
Disher, Maurice Willson. *The Last Romantic.* London: Hutchinson, 1948.
Martin-Harvey, John. *The Autobiography of Sir John Martin-Harvey.* London: Low, Marston, 1933.
The Book of Martin Harvey . . . comp. and ed. by R.N.G.-A. London: Walker, 1930.
Edgar, George. *Martin Harvey; Some Pages of His Life.* London: Richards, 1912.

Martyn, Edward 1859-1924
Courtney, Marie Therese. *Edward Martyn and the Irish Theatre.* New York: Vantage, 1956.
Gwynn, Denis. *Edward Martyn and the Irish Revival.* London: Cape, 1930.

The Marx Brothers
Adamson, Joseph. *Groucho, Harpo, Chico, and Sometimes Zeppo. A History of the Marx Brothers and a Satire on the Rest of the World.* New York: Simon & Schuster, 1973.
Crichton, Kyle. *The Marx Brothers.* Garden City: Doubleday, 1950.
Eyles, Allen. *The Marx Brothers; Their World of Comedy.* New York: A. S. Barnes, 1969.
Marx, Arthur. *Life with Groucho.* New York: Simon & Schuster, 1954.
—. *Son of Groucho.* New York: McKay, 1972.
Marx, Groucho. *Groucho and Me.* New York: Bernard Geis, 1959.
—. *The Groucho Letters.* New York: Simon & Schuster, 1967.
— and Anobile, Richard J. *The Marx Bros. Scrapbook* New York: Norton, 1973.
Marx, Harpo, with Barber, Rowland. *Harpo Speaks!* London: Gollancz, 1961.

Massinger, Philip 1583-1640
Dunn, Thomas A. *Philip Massinger, the Man and the Playwright.* London: Nelson, 1957.
Lawless, Donald S. *Philip Massinger and His Associates.* Muncie, Ind.: Ball State Univ., 1967.

Mathews, Charles 1776-1835
Arnold, Samuel J. *Forgotten Facts in the Memoirs of Charles Mathews, Comedian, Recalled in a Letter to Mrs. Mathews, His Biographer.* London: Ridgway, 1839.
Mathews, Anne. *Memoirs of Charles Mathews, Comedian.* London: Bentley, 1839; 4 vols.
—. *The Life and Correspondence of Charles Mathews, the Elder, Comedian.* London: Routledge, Warne & Routledge, 1860.

Mathews, Charles James 1803-1878
Mathews, Charles James (ed. by Charles Dickens). *The Life of Charles James Mathews.* London: Macmillan, 1879; 2 vols.

Matthews, A. E. 1869-1960
Matthews, Alfred Edward. *Matty.* London: Hutchinson, 1952.

Matthews, Brander 1852-1929
Matthews, Brander. *These Many Years; Recollections of a New Yorker.* New York: Scribner, 1917.

Maude, Cyril 1862-1951
Brereton, Austin. *Cyril Maude; a Memoir.* London: Eyre & Spottiswoode, 1914.
De Bordove, Rudolph. *A Photographic and Descriptive Biography of Mr. Cyril Maude.* Westminster: Abbey Press, 1909.
Maude, Cyril. *Behind the Scenes with Cyril Maude.* London: Murray, 1927.
—. *Lest I Forget.* New York: J. H. Sears, 1928.

Maugham, W. Somerset 1874-1965
Brophy, John. *Somerset Maugham.* London: Longmans, Green, 1952.
Brown, Ivor. *W. Somerset Maugham.* London: International Textbook, 1970.
Cordell, Richard A. *W. Somerset Maugham.* New York: Nelson, 1937.
—. *Somerset Maugham; A Biographical and Critical Study.* Bloomington: Indiana Univ., 1961.
Kanin, Garson. *Remembering Mr. Maugham.* New York: Atheneum, 1966.
Maugham, Robert C. R. *Somerset and All the Maughams.* New York: New American Library, 1966.
Maugham, W. Somerset. *Strictly Personal.* Garden City: Doubleday, Doran, 1941.
—. *The Summing Up.* Garden City: Doubleday, Doran, 1938.
—. *A Writer's Notebook.* Garden City: Doubleday, 1949.
Menard, Wilmon. *The Two Worlds of Somerset Maugham.* Los Angeles: Sherbourne, 1965.
Naik, M. K. *W. Somerset Maugham.* Norman: Univ. of Oklahoma, 1966.
Nichols, Beverly. *A Case of Human Bondage.* London: Secker & Warburg, 1966.
Pfeiffer, Karl G. *W. Somerset Maugham; A Candid Portrait.* New York: Norton, 1959.

Mayakovsky, Vladimir Vladimirovich 1894-1930
Shklovsky, Viktor (trans. by Lily Feiler). *Mayakovsky and His Circle.* New York: Dodd, Mead, 1972.
Woroszylski; Viktor (trans. by Boleslaw Taborski). *The Life of Mayakovsky.* New York: Orion Press, 1971.

McCarthy, Lillah 1875-1960
Mc Carthy, Lillah. *Myself and My Friends.* London: Butterworth, 1933.

McClintic, Guthrie -1961
McClintic, Guthrie. *Me and Kit.* Boston: Little, 1955.
See also: Cornell, Katharine.

McCullough, John 1832-1885
Clark, Susie Champney. *John McCullough as Man, Actor, and Spirit.* Boston: Murray and Emery, 1905.
In Memory of John McCullough. New York: De Vinne, 1889.

Mei Lan-Fang 1894-1943
Leung, George Kin. *Mei Lan-Fang, Foremost Actor in China.* Shanghai: Commercial Press, 1929.
Scott, A. C. *Mei Lan-Fang. Leader of the Pear Garden.* Hong Kong: Hong Kong Univ., 1959.

Melville, Alan 1910-
Melville, Alan. *Merely Melville.* London: Hodder & Stoughton, 1970.

Menken, Adah Isaacs 1835-1868
Falk, Bernard. *The Naked Lady; or, Storm Over Adah.* London: Hutchinson, 1934.
Fleischer, Nathaniel S. *Reckless Lady; The Life Story of Adah Isaacs Menken.* New York: Press of C. J. O'Brien, 1941.
Lesser, Allen. *Enchanting Rebel.* New York: Beechhurst Press, 1947.
Lewis, Paul. *Queen of the Plaza.* New York: Funk & Wagnalls, 1964.

Merivale, Herman Charles 1839-1906
Merivale, Herman Charles. *Bar, Stage & Platform; Autobiographic Memories.* London: Chatto & Windus, 1902.

Merman, Ethel 1909-
Merman, Ethel, as told to Pete Martin. *Who Could Ask for Anything More.* Garden City: Doubleday, 1955.

Merrill, John 1875-
Merrill, John. *Son of Salem.* New York: Vantage, 1953.

Merry, Anne Brunton 1768-1808
Doty, Gresdna Ann. *The Career of Mrs. Anne Brunton Merry in the American Theatre.* Baton Rouge, La.: Louisiana State Univ., 1971.

Meyerhold, Vsevolod Emilievich 1874-1942
Hoover, Marjorie L. *Meyerhold: The Art of Conscious Theater.* Amherst: Univ. of Mass., 1974.
Symons, James M. *Meyerhold's Theatre of the Grotesque; The Post-Revolutionary Productions, 1920-1932.* Coral Gables, Fla.: Univ. of Miami, 1971.

Michael, Edward 1853-1950
Michael, Edward and Booth, J. B. *Tramps of a Scamp.* London: T. W. Laurie, 1928.

Middleton, George 1880-1967
Middleton, George. *These Things Are Mine; The Autobiography of a Journeyman Playwright.* New York: Macmillan, 1947.

Middleton, Thomas ?-1627
Brittin, Norman A. *Thomas Middleton.* New York: Twayne, 1972.

Miller, Ann 1919-
Miller, Ann with Norma Lee Browning. *Miller's High Life.* Garden City: Doubleday, 1972.

Miller, Arthur 1915-
Hogan, Robert. *Arthur Miller.* Minneapolis: Univ. of Minnesota, 1964.
Moss, Leonard. *Arthur Miller.* New York: Twayne, 1967.
Nelson, Benjamin. *Arthur Miller; Portrait of a Playwright.* New York: McKay, 1970.

Miller, Henry 1860-1926
Morse, Frank Philip. *Backstage with Henry Miller.* New York: Dutton, 1938.

Mills, Bertram 1873-1938
Williamson, A. Stanley. *On the Road with Bertram Mills.* London: Chatto & Windus, 1938.

Mills, Hayley 1946-
Mills, John 1908-
Mills, Juliet 1941-
See: Bell, Mary Hayley.

Millward, Jessie 1861-1932
Millward, Jessie (with J. B. Booth). *Myself and Others.* London: Hutchinson, 1923.

Minnelli, Vincente
Minnelli, Vincente and Arce, Hector. *I*

Remember It Well. Garden City: Doubleday, 1974.

Mistinguett 1875-1956
Mistinguett (trans. by Hubert Griffith). *Mistinguett and Her Confessions.* London: Hurst & Blackett, 1938.
—. (trans. by Lucienne Hill). *Mistinguett, Queen of the Paris Night.* London: Elek Books, 1954.

Mitchell, Yvonne 1925-
Mitchell, Yvonne. *Actress.* London: Routledge & Paul, 1957.

Modjeska, Helena 1840-1909
Altemus, Jameson Torr. *Helena Modjeska.* New York: J. S. Ogilvie, 1883.
Coleman, Arthur and Marion. *Wanderers Twain; Modjeska and Sienkiewicz: A View from California.* Cheshire, Conn: Cherry Hill Books, 1964.
Coleman, Marion. *Fair Rosalind; The American Career of Helena Modjeska.* Cheshire, Conn: Cherry Hill Books, 1969.
Gronowicz, Antoni. *Modjeska Her Life and Loves.* New York: Thomas Yoseloff, 1956.
Modjeska, Helena. *Memories and Impressions of Helena Modjeska; An Autobiography.* New York: Macmillan, 1910.
— (trans. by Michael Kwapiszewski). *Letters to Emilia, Record of a Friendship; Seven Letters of Helena Modjeska to a Friend Back Home.* Cheshire, Conn.: Cherry Hill Books, 1967.

Moffat, Graham 1866-1951
Moffat, Graham. *Join Me in Remembering; The Life and Reminiscences of the Author of "Bunty Pulls the Strings."* Camps Bay, South Africa: W. L. Moffat, 1955.

Molière, Jean-Baptiste 1622-1673
Ashton, Harry. *Molière.* London: Routledge, 1930.
Bulgakov, Mikhail (trans. by Mirra Ginsburg). *The Life of Monsieur de Molière.* New York: Funk & Wagnalls, 1970.
Chapman, Percy Addison. *The Spirit of Molière.* London: H. Milford, Oxford Univ., 1940.
Chatfield-Taylor, Hobart Chatfield. *Molière; A Biography.* New York: Duffield, 1906.
Fernandez, Ramon (trans. by Wilson Follett). *Molière; The Man Seen through the Plays.* New York: Hill & Wang, 1958.
Lewis, Dominic B. *Molière: The Comic Mask.* New York: Coward-McCann, 1959.
Matthews, Brander. *Molière, His Life and His Works.* New York: Russell & Russell, 1910.
Palmer, John L. *Molière.* New York: Brewer and Warren, 1930.
Tilley, Arthur A. *Molière.* New York: Macmillan, 1921.
Trollope, Henry. *The Life of Molière.* London: Constable, 1905.
Vincent, Leon H. *Molière.* Boston: Houghton Mifflin, 1902.
Walker, Hallam. *Molière.* New York: Twayne, 1971.

Molnar, Ferenc 1878-1952
Molnar, Ferenc (trans. by Barrows Mussey). *Companion in Exile; Notes for an Autobiography.* New York: Gaer, 1950.

Montez, Lola 1818-1861
Darling, Amanda. *Lola Montez.* New York: Stein & Day, 1972.
D'Auvergne, Edmund. *Lola Montez, an Adventuress of the Forties.* New York: Brentano, 1924.
Foley, Doris. *The Divine Eccentric; Lola Montez and the Newspapers.* Los Angeles: Westernlore Press, 1969.
Goldberg, Isaac. *Queen of Hearts; The Passionate Pilgrimage of Lola Montez.* New York: John Day, 1936.
Holdredge, Helen. *The Woman in Black.* New York: Putnam, 1955.
Lewis, Oscar. *Lola Montez; The Mid-Victorian Bad Girl in California.* San Francisco: Colt Press, 1938.
Ross, Ishbel. *The Uncrowned Queen; Life of Lola Montez.* New York: Harper & Row, 1972.
Wyndham, Horace. *The Magnificent Montez; from Courtesan to Convert.* London: Hutchinson, 1935.

Montgomery, Robert 1904-
McBride, Mary Margaret. *The Life Story of Robert Montgomery.* New York: Screen Star Library, 1932.

Montherlant, Henry de 1896-1972
Becker, Lucille. *Henry de Montherlant; A Critical Biography.* Carbondale: Southern Illinois Univ., 1970.

Moody, William Vaughn 1869-1910
Brown, Maurice F. *Estranging Dawn: The Life and Works of William Vaughn Moody.* Carbondale: Southern Illinois Univ., 1973.
Halpern, Martin. *William Vaughn Moody.* New York: Twayne, 1964.
Henry, David D. *William Vaughn Moody; A Study.* Boston: Humphries, 1934.
Moody, William Vaughn (ed. by D. G. Mason). *Some Letters of William Vaughn Moody.* Boston: Houghton Mifflin, 1913.
— (ed. by Percy Mackaye). *Letters to Harriet.* Boston: Houghton Mifflin, 1935.

Moore, Eva 1870-1955
Moore, Eva. *Exits and Entrances.* London: Chapman & Hall, 1923.

Moore, Grace 1901-1947
Moore, Grace. *You're Only Human Once.* Garden City: Doubleday, Doran, 1944.

Morehouse, Ward 1898-1966
Morehouse, Ward. *Forty-five Minutes Past Eight.* New York: Dial, 1939.
—. *Just the Other Day; From Yellow Pines to Broadway.* New York: McGraw-Hill, 1953.

Morgan, Helen 1900-1941
Maxwell, Gilbert. *Helen Morgan: Her Life and Legend.* New York: Hawthorn, 1974.

Morley, Robert 1908-
Morley, Robert and Stokes, Sewell. *Robert Morley; A Reluctant Autobiography.* New York: Simon & Schuster, 1966.

Morosco, Oliver 1875-1945
Morosco, Helen M. and Dugger, Leonard Paul. *Life of Oliver Morosco; The Oracle of Broadway.* Caldwell, Idaho: Caxton Printers, 1944.

Morris, Clara 1844-1925
Harriott, Clara (Morris). *Life on the Stage; My Personal Experiences and Recollections.* New York: McClure, Phillips, 1901.
—. *Stage Confidences; Talks about Players and Play Acting.* Boston: Lothrop, 1902.
—. *The Life of a Star.* New York: McClure, Phillips, 1906.

Morris, Felix 1850-1900
Morris, Felix. *Reminiscences.* New York: International Telegram, 1892.

Mountfort, William 1664-1692
Borgman, Albert S. *The Life and Death of William Mountfort.* Cambridge: Harvard Univ., 1935.

Mowatt, Anna Cora 1819-1870
Barnes, Eric Wollencott. *The Lady of Fashion: The Life and the Theatre of Anna Cora Mowatt.* New York: Scribner, 1955.
Butler, Mildred A. *Actress in Spite of Herself; The Life of Anna Cora Mowatt.* New York: Funk & Wagnalls, 1966.
Ritchie, Anna Cora Mowatt. *Autobiography of an Actress; or, Eight Years on the Stage.* Boston: Ticknor, Reed & Fields, 1854.

Mozart, George 1864?-1947
Mozart, George. *Limelight.* London: Hurst & Blackett, 1938.

Munden, Joseph Shepherd 1758-1832
Munden, Thomas S. *Memoirs of Joseph Shepherd Munden, Comedian.* London: Bentley, 1844.

Muni, Paul 1895-1967
Druxman, Michael. *Paul Muni: His Life and His Films.* South Brunswick: A. S. Barnes, 1974.
Lawrence, Jerome. *Actor: The Life and Times of Paul Muni.* New York: Putnam, 1974.

Murray, Ken 1903-
Murray, Ken. *Life on a Pogo Stick.* Philadelphia: John C. Winston, 1960.

Nathan, George Jean 1882-1958
Frick, Constance. *The Dramatic Criticism of George Jean Nathan.* Ithaca, N.Y.: Cornell Univ., 1943.
Goldberg, Isaac. *The Theatre of George Jean Nathan; Chapters and Documents toward a History of the New American Drama.* New York: Simon & Schuster, 1926.
Hatteras, Owen (pseud.). *Pistols for Two.* New York: Knopf, 1917.
Nathan, George Jean. *The Bachelor Life.* New York: Reynal & Hitchcock, 1941.

Neagle, Anna 1904-
Neagle, Anna. *There's Always Tomorrow.* London: W. H. Allen, 1974.

Neal, Patricia 1926-
Farrell, Barry. *Pat and Roald.* New York: Random House, 1969.

Neilson, Adelaide 1848-1880
De Leine, M. A. *Lilian Adelaide Neilson: A Memorial Sketch, Personal and Critical.* London: Newman, 1881.
Langford, Laura Holloway. *Adelaide Neilson.* New York: Funk & Wagnalls, 1885.

Neilson, Julia 1869-1957
Neilson, Julia. *This for Remembrance.* London: Hurst & Blackett, 1940.

Nemirovich-Danchenko, V. I. 1858-1943
Nemirovich-Danchenko, Vladimir Ivanovich (trans. by John Cournos). *My Life in the Russian Theatre.* Boston: Little, Brown, 1936.

Nesbit, Evelyn ?-1967

Langford, Gerald. *The Murder of Stanford White.* Indianapolis: Bobbs-Merrill, 1962.
Nesbit, Evelyn. *Prodigal Days; The Untold Story.* New York: Messner, 1934.
Samuels, Charles. *The Girl in the Red Velvet Swing.* New York: Fawcett, 1953.
Thaw, Harry K. *The Traitor; Being the Untampered with, Unrevised Account of the Trial and All that Led Up to It.* Philadelphia: Dorrance, 1926.

Nesbitt, Cathleen 1888-
Nesbitt, Cathleen. *A Little Love and Good Company.* London: Faber & Faber, 1975.

Neville, John 1925-
Trewin, John C. *John Neville.* London: Barrie & Rockliff, 1961.

Newman, Paul 1925-
Hamblett, Charles. *Paul Newman.* London: W. H. Allen, 1975.

Nijinsky, Vaslav 1890-1950
Beaumont, Cyril W. *Vaslav Nijinsky.* London: Beaumont, 1932.
Bourman, Anatole and Lyman, Dorothy. *The Tragedy of Nijinsky.* New York: McGraw-Hill, 1936.
Buckle, Richard. *Nijinsky.* London: Weidenfeld & Nicolson, 1971.
Kirstein, Lincoln. *Nijinsky Dancing.* New York: Knopf, 1975.
Magriel, Paul. *Nijinsky.* New York: Holt, 1947.
Nijinsky, Romola. *Nijinsky.* New York: Simon & Schuster, 1934.
—. *The Last Years of Nijinsky.* New York: Simon & Schuster, 1952.
Nijinsky, Vaslav (ed. by Romola Nijinsky). *The Diary of Vaslav Nyjinsky.* New York: Simon & Schuster, 1936.
Reiss, Francoise (trans. by Helen and Stephen Haskell). *Nijinsky, A Biography.* New York: Pitman, 1960.
Whitworth, Geoffrey. *The Art of Nijinsky.* London: Chatto & Windus, 1913.

Novello, Ivor 1893-1951
MacQueen-Pope, W. J. *Ivor.* London: W. H. Allen, 1952.
Noble, Peter. *Ivor Novello; Man of the Theatre.* London: Falcon Press, 1951.

Noverre, Jean Georges 1727-1810
Lynham, Deryck. *The Chevalier Noverre, Father of Modern Ballet.* London: Sylvan Press, 1950.
Noverre, Charles Edwin (ed.). *The Life and Works of the Chevalier Noverre.* London: Jarrold, 1882.

Nugent, Elliott 1899-
Nugent, Elliott. *Events Leading up to the Comedy.* New York: Trident, 1965.

Nugent, J. C. 1878-1947
Nugent, John Charles. *It's a Great Life.* New York: Dial, 1940.

Oakley, Annie 1866-1926
Cooper, Courtney Ryley. *Annie Oakley, Woman at Arms.* New York: Duffield, 1927.
Havighurst, Walter. *Annie Oakley of the Wild West.* New York: Macmillan, 1954.
Swartwout, Annie Fern. *Missie, an Historical Biography of Annie Oakley.* Blanchester, Ohio: Brown, 1947.

O'Brady, Frederic
O'Brady, Frederic. *All Told.* New York: Simon & Schuster, 1964.

O'Brien, Pat 1899-
O'Brien, Pat. *The Wind at My Back.* Garden City: Doubleday, 1964.

O'Casey, Sean 1880-1964
Armstrong, William A. *Sean O'Casey.* London: Longmans, Green, 1967.
Benstock, Bernard. *Sean O'Casey.* Lewisburg: Bucknell Univ., 1971.
Cowasjee, Saros. *Sean O'Casey; The Man Behind the Plays.* London: St. Martin's, 1963.
Fallon, Gabriel. *Sean O'Casey; The Man I Knew.* Boston: Little Brown, 1965.
Koslow, Jules. *The Green and the Red; Sean O'Casey . . . the Man and His Plays.* New York: Arts, 1949.
Krause, David. *Sean O'Casey; The Man and His Work.* New York: Macmillan, 1960.
—. *A Self-Portrait of the Artist as a Man; Sean O'Casey's Letters.* Dublin: Dolmen, 1968.
O'Casey, Eileen. *Sean.* London: Macmillan, 1971.
O'Casey, Sean. *I Knock at the Door.* London: Macmillan, 1939.
—. *Pictures in the Hallway.* London: Macmillan, 1942.
—. *Drums under the Windows.* London: Macmillan, 1945.
—. *Inishfallen, Fare Thee Well.* New York: Macmillan, 1949.
—. *Rose and Crown.* London: Macmillan, 1952.
—. *Sunset and Evening Star.* New York: Macmillan, 1954.
— (ed. by David Krause). *The Letters of Sean O'Casey: Vol. 1, 1910-41.* New York: Macmillan, 1975.

Odets, Clifford 1906-1963
Shuman, Robert B. *Clifford Odets.* New York: Twayne, 1962.
Weales, Gerald. *Clifford Odets, Playwright.* New York: Pegasus, 1971.

O'Hara, John 1905-1970
Farr, Finis. *O'Hara.* Boston: Little, Brown, 1973.
Grebstein, Sheldon. *John O'Hara.* New York: Twayne, 1966.

O'Keeffe, John 1747-1833
O'Keeffe, John. *Recollections of the Life of John O'Keeffe.* Philadelphia: Carey & Lea, 1827.

Olcott, Chauncey 1860-1932
Olcott, Rita. *Song in His Heart.* New York: House of Field, 1939.

Oldfield, Anne ("Nance") 1683-1730
Egerton, William. *Faithful Memoirs of the Life, Amours, and Performances of that Justly Celebrated Actress, Mrs. Anne Oldfield.* London: Brotherton, 1731.
Gore-Browne, Robert F. *Gay Was the Pit; The Life and Times of Anne Oldfield, Actress (1683-1730).* London: Reinhardt, 1957.
Oldys, William. *Memoirs of Mrs. Anne Oldfield.* London: 1741.
Robins, Edward. *The Palmy Days of Nance Oldfield.* London: Heinemann, 1898.

Oliver, Vic 1898-1964
Oliver, Vic. *Mr. Showbusiness.* London: Harrap, 1954.

Olivier, Laurence 1907-
Barker, Felix. *The Oliviers; A Biography.* London: Hamilton, 1953.
Cottrell, John. *Laurence Olivier.* Englewood Cliffs, N.J.: Prentice-Hall, 1975.
Darlington, William A. *Laurence Olivier.* London: Morgan Grampian, 1968.
Fairweather, Virginia. *Olivier; An Informal Portrait.* New York: Coward-McCann, 1969.
Gourlay, Logan (ed.). *Olivier.* New York: Stein & Day, 1974.

O'Neill, Eugene 1888-1953
Alexander, Doris. *The Tempering of Eugene O'Neill.* New York: Harcourt, Brace & World, 1962.
Boulton, Agnes. *Part of a Long Story.* Garden City: Doubleday, 1958.
Bowen, Croswell, with Shane O'Neill. *The Curse of the Misbegotten.* New York: McGraw-Hill, 1959.
Clark, Barrett H. *Eugene O'Neill; The Man and His Plays.* New York: McBride, 1933.
Frenz, Horst (trans. by Helen Seba). *Eugene O'Neill.* New York: Ungar, 1971.
Gassner, John. *Eugene O'Neill.* Minneapolis: Univ. of Minnesota, 1965.
Gelb, Arthur and Barbara. *O'Neill.* New York: Harper & Row, 1974.
O'Neill, Eugene (ed. by Donald Gallup). *Inscriptions: Eugene O'Neill to Carlotta Monterey O'Neill.* New Haven: 1960.
Sheaffer, Louis. *O'Neill, Son and Playwright.* Boston: Little, Brown, 1968.
Skinner, Richard Dana. *Eugene O'Neill; A Poet's Quest.* New York: Longmans, 1935.

O'Neill, Maire 1887-1952
See: Synge, John Millington

Osborne, John 1929-
Carter, Alan. *John Osborne.* Edinburgh: Oliver & Boyd, 1969.

Owens, John E. 1823-1886
Owens, Mary, C. S. *Memories of the Professional and Social Life of John E. Owens.* Baltimore: John Murphy, 1892.

Pagnol, Marcel 1895-1974
Pagnol, Marcel (trans. by Rita Barisse). *The Days Were Too Short.* Garden City: Doubeday, 1960.
— (trans. by Rita Barisse). *The Time of Secrets.* Garden City: Doubleday, 1962.

Palmer, Lilli 1914-
Palmer, Lilli. *Fat Lilly—Good Child.* New York: Macmillan, 1975.

Papp, Joseph 1921-
Little, Stuart W. *Enter Joseph Papp.* New York: Coward, McCann & Geoghegan, 1974.

Parker, Dorothy 1893-1967
Keats, John. *You Might As Well Live; The Life and Times of Dorothy Parker.* New York: Simon & Schuster, 1970.

Parker, Henry Taylor 1867-1934
McCord, David. *H. T. P.; Portrait of a Critic.* New York: Coward-McCann, 1935.

Pascal, Gabriel 1894-1954
Pascal, Valerie. *The Disciple and His Devil: Gabriel Pascal, Bernard Shaw.* New York: McGraw-Hill, 1970.

Pastor, Tony 1837-1908
Zellers, Parker. *Tony Pastor: Dean of the Vaudeville Stage.* Ypsilanti: Eastern Michigan Univ., 1971.

Pavlova, Anna 1882-1931
Beaumont, Cyril. *Anna Pavlova.* London: C. W. Beaumont, 1932.
Dandre, Victor E. *Anna Pavlova.* London: Cassell, 1932.
Franks, Arthur Henry (ed.). *Pavlova.* London: Burke, 1956.
Hyden, Walford. *Pavlova.* Boston: Little, 1931.
Kerensky, Oleg. *Anna Pavlova.* New York: Dutton, 1973.
Magriel, Paul. *Pavlova, an Illustrated Monograph.* New York: Holt, 1947.
Malvern, Gladys. *Dancing Star.* New York: Messner, 1942.
May, Helen. *The Swan, the Story of Anna Pavlova.* Edinburgh: Nelson, 1958.
Oliveroff, Andre, as told to John Gill. *Flight of the Swan; A Memory of Anna Pavlova.* New York: Dutton, 1932.
Oukrainsky, Serge (trans. by I. M.). *My Two Years with Anna Pavlova.* Los Angeles: Suttonhouse Pub., 1940.
Stier, Theodore. *With Pavlova Round the World.* London: Hurst & Blackett, 1927.
Svetloff, Valerian (trans. by A. Grey). *Anna Pavlova.* Paris: M. de Brunoff, 1922.

Payne, John Howard 1791-1852
Brainard, Charles H. *John Howard Payne: A Biographical Sketch of the Author of "Home, Sweet Home"* . . . Washington, D. C.: G. A. Coolidge, 1885.
Chiles, Rosa P. *John Howard Payne; American Poet, Actor, Playwright, Consul and Author of "Home, Sweet Home."* Washington, D. C.: W. F. Roberts, 1930.
Hanson, Willis T., Jr. *The Early Life of John Howard Payne, with Contemporary Letters Hitherto Unpublished.* Boston: Bibliophile Society, 1913.
Harrison, Gabriel. *John Howard Payne, Dramatist, Poet, Actor and Author of Home, Sweet Home! His Life and Writings.* Philadelphia: Lippincott, 1885.
Overmyer, Grace. *America's First Hamlet.* New York: New York Univ., 1957.
Pennypacker, Morton. *The John Howard Payne Memorial "Home, Sweet Home," East Hampton, Long Island, New York.* East Hampton: Board of Trustees . . ., 1935.
Shelley, Mary W. *The Romance of Mary W. Shelley, John Howard Payne and Washington Irving.* Boston: Bibliophile Society, 1907.

Payton, Corse 1867-1934
Andrews, Gertrude. *The Romance of a Western Boy; The Story of Corse Payton.* Brooklyn, N.Y.: Andrews Press, 1901.

Peele, George c1558-c1598
Horne, David H. *The Life and Minor Works of George Peele.* New Haven: Yale Univ., 1952.

Peile, Frederick Kinsey 1862-1934
Peile, Kinsey. *Candied Peel; Tales without Prejudice.* London: A. & C. Black, 1931.

Perrella, Robert ("Father Bob")
Perrella, Robert. *They Call Me the Showbiz Priest.* New York: Trident, 1973.

Pertwee, Roland 1886-1963
Pertwee, Roland. *Master of None.* London: Davies, 1940.

Petrova, Olga 1886-
Petrova, Olga. *Butter with My Bread.* Indianapolis; New York: Bobbs-Merrill, 1942.

Phelps, Samuel 1804-1878
Allen, Shirley S. *Samuel Phelps and Sadler's Wells Theatre.* Middletown, Conn.: Wesleyan Univ., 1971.
Coleman, John. *Memoirs of Samuel Phelps.* London: Remington, 1886.
Phelps, W. May and Forbes-Robertson, J. *The Life and Life-Work of Samuel Phelps.* London: Sampson Low, Marston, Searle, & Rivington, 1886.

Philips, Francis Charles 1849-1921
Philips, F. C. *My Varied Life.* London: Nash, 1914.

Picon, Molly 1898-
Picon, Molly, as told to Eth Clifford Rosenberg. *So Laugh a Little.* New York: Messner, 1962.

Pinero, Arthur Wing 1855-1934
Dunkel, Wilbur D. *Sir Arthur Pinero; A Critical Biography with Letters.* Chicago: Univ. of Chicago, 1941.
Fyre, Henry Hamilton. *Arthur Wing Pinero, Playwright.* London: Greening, 1902.
—. *Sir Arthur Pinero's Plays and Players.* New York: Macmillan, 1930.
Lazenby, Walter. *Arthur Wing Pinero.* New York: Twayne, 1972.
Pinero, Arthur Wing (ed. by J. P. Wearing). *The Collected Letters of Sir Arthur Pinero.* Minneapolis: Univ. of Minnesota, 1974.

Pirandello, Luigi 1867-1936
Giudice, Gaspare (trans. by Alastair Hamilton). *Pirandello.* New York: Oxford Univ., 1975.
MacClintock, Lander. *The Age of Pirandello.* Bloomington: Indiana Univ., 1951.
Ragusa, Olga. *Luigi Pirandello.* New York: Columbia Univ., 1968.
Starkie, Walter F. *Luigi Pirandello, 1867-1936.* New York: Dutton, 1937.

Piscator, Erwin 1893-1966
Innes, C. D. *Erwin Piscator's Political Theatre.* Cambridge, Eng.: University Press, 1972.
Ley-Piscator, Maria. *The Piscator Experiment: The Political Theatre.* New York: J. H. Heineman, 1967.

Pitou, Augustus 1843-1915
Pitou, Augustus. *Masters of the Shaw as Seen in Retrospection by One Who Has Been Associated with the American Stage for Nearly Fifty Years.* New York: Neale, 1914.

Planché, James Robinson 1796-1880
Planché, James Robinson. *Recollections and Reflections.* London: Low, Marston, 1901.

Playfair, Sir Nigel Ross 1874-1934
Playfair, Giles. *My Father's Son.* London: Bles, 1937.
Playfair, Sir Nigel Ross. *Hammersmith Hoy.* London: Faber & Faber, 1930.

Poel, William 1852-1934
Speaight, Robert. *William Poel and the Elizabethan Revival.* Melbourne: Heinemann, 1954.

Pollock, Channing 1880-1946
Pollock, Channing. *Harvest of My Years.* Indianapolis: Bobbs-Merrill, 1943.
—. *Adventures of a Happy Man.* New York: Crowell, 1939.

Porter, Cole 1891-1964
Kimball, Robert (ed.). *Cole.* New York: Holt, Rinehart & Winston, 1971.
Eells, George. *The Life that Late He Led.* New York: Putnam, 1967.
Porter, Cole (as told to Richard G. Hubler). *The Cole Porter Story.* Cleveland: World Pub., 1965.

Power, Tyrone 1797-1841
Power, Tyrone. *Impressions of America, during the Years 1833, 1834, and 1835.* London: Bentley, 1836; 2 vols.

Power, Tyrone 1869-1931
Winter, William. *Tyrone Power.* New York: Moffat, Yard, 1913.

Powers, James T. 1862-1943
Powers, James T. *Twinkle Little Star; Sparkling Memories of Seventy Years.* New York: Putnam, 1939.

Preminger, Otto 1906-
Frischauer, Willi. *Behind the Scenes with Otto Preminger; An Unauthorized Biography.* New York: Morrow, 1973.

Priestley, John Boynton 1894-
Brown, Ivor. *J. B. Priestley.* London: Longmans, Green, 1957.
Cooper, Susan. *J. B. Priestley; Portrait of an Author.* London: Heinemann, 1970.
Evans, Gareth. *J. B. Priestley, the Dramatist.* London: Heinemann, 1964.
Pogson, Rex. *J. B. Priestley and the Theatre.* Clevedon, Eng.: Triangle, 1947.
Priestley, J. B. *Midnight on the Desert, Being an Excursion into Autobiography during a Winter in America, 1935-36.* New York: Harper, 1937.
—. *Rain upon Godshill; A Further Chapter of Autobiography.* London: Heinemann, 1939.
—. *Margin Released; A Writer's Reminiscences and Reflections.* New York: Harper, 1962.

Prince, Harold (Hal) 1928-
Prince, Hal. *Contradictions: Notes on Twenty-Six Years in the Theatre.* New York: Dodd, Mead, 1974.

Proctor, Frederick Freeman 1851-1929
Marston, William Moulton and Feller, John Henry. *F. F. Proctor Vaudeville Pioneer.* New York: Richard R. Smith, 1943.

Quin, James 1693-1766
The Life of Mr. James Quin, Comedian. London: Bladon, 1766.

Quinn, Anthony 1915-
Quinn, Anthony. *The Original Sin: A Self-Portrait.* Boston: Little, Brown, 1972.

Quintero, Jose 1924-
Quintero, Jose. *If You Don't Dance, They Beat You.* Boston: Little, Brown, 1974.

Rachel 1821(?)-1858
Agate, James. *Rachel.* New York: Viking, 1928.
Barrera, Mme. A. de. *Memoirs of Rachel.* New York: Harper, 1858.

Beauvallet, Leon. *Rachel and the New World.* New York: Dix, Edwards, 1856.
Falk, Barnard. *Rachel, the Immortal.* London: Hutchinson, 1935.
Gribble, Francis. *Rachel; Her Stage Life and Her Real Life.* New York: Scribner, 1911.
Kennard, Nina H. *Rachel.* London: W. H. Allen, 1885.
Morrison, Peggy. *Rachel; An Interpretation.* London: Collins, 1947.
Richardson, Joanna. *Rachel.* London: Reinhardt, 1956.

Racine, Jean Baptiste 1639-1699
Blaze de Bury, Marie. *Racine and the French Classical Drama.* London: Knight, 1845.
Brereton, Geoffrey. *Jean Racine; A Critical Biography.* London: Cassell, 1951.
Clark, Alexander. *Jean Racine.* Cambridge: Harvard Univ., 1939.
Duclaux, Mary. *The Life of Racine.* New York: Harper, 1925.
Giraudoux, Jean (trans. by P. Mansell Jones). *Racine.* Cambridge: Fraser, 1938.
Knapp, Bettina. *Jean Racine: Mythos and Renewal in Modern Theater.* University: Univ. of Alabama, 1971.

Rambert, Marie
Haskell, Arnold. *Marie Rambert Ballet.* London: British-Continental Press, 1930.
Rambert, Marie. *Quicksilver; The Autobiography of Marie Rambert.* London: Macmillan, 1972.

Randall, Harry 1860-1932
Randall, Harry. *Harry Randall, Old Time Comedian.* London: Low, Marston, 1931.

Ranous, Dora ?-1916
Ranous, Dora Knowlton Thompson. *Diary of a Daly Debutante; Being Passages from the Journal of Augustin Daly's Famous Company of Players.* New York: Duffield, 1910.

Rathbone, Basil 1892-1967
Rathbone, Basil. *In and Out of Character.* Garden City: Doubleday, 1962.
Druxman, Michael B. *Basil Rathbone: His Life and His Films.* New York: A. S. Barnes, 1975.

Reade, Charles 1814-1884
Burns, Wayne. *Charles Reade; A Study in Victorian Authorship.* New York: Bookman Associates, 1961.
Coleman, John. *Charles Reade as I Knew Him.* London: Treherne, 1904.
Elwin, Malcolm. *Charles Reade.* London: Cape, 1931.
Reade, Charles (comp. by Charles L. Reade and Compton Reade). *Charles Reade, Dramatist, Novelist, Journalist; A Memoir, Compiled Chiefly from His Literary Remains.* London: Chapman & Hall, 1887; 2 vols.

Reader, Ralph 1903-
Reader, Ralph. *It's Been Terrific.* London: Laurie, 1953.
—. *Ralph Reader Remembers.* Folkestone: Bailey & Swinfen, 1974.

Redfield, William 1927-
Redfield, William F. *Letters from an Actor.* New York: Viking, 1967.

Redgrave, Michael 1908-
Findlater, Richard. *Michael Redgrave, Actor.* London: Heinemann, 1956.
Redgrave, Michael. *Mask or Face, Reflections in an Actor's Mirror.* New York: Theatre Arts, 1958.

Reed, Joseph Verner 1902-1973
Reed, Joseph Verner. *The Curtain Falls.* New York: Harcourt, Brace, 1935.

Rehan, Ada 1860-1916
Winter, William. *Ada Rehan: A Study.* New York: 1891.

Reid, Wallace 1892-1923
Reid, Bertha Westbrook. *Wallace Reid.* New York: Sorg, 1923.

Reinhardt, Max 1873-1943
Carter, Huntly. *The Theatre of Max Reinhardt.* London: F. and C. Palmer, 1914.
Sayler, Oliver M. *Max Reinhardt and His Theatre.* New York: Brentano, 1924.

Resnik, Muriel
Resnik, Muriel. *Son of Any Wednesday.* New York: Stein & Day, 1965.

Reynolds, Frederick 1764-1841
Reynolds, Frederick. *The Life and Times of Frederick Reynolds.* London: Colburn, 1826; 2 vols.

Rice, Dan 1823-1900
Brown, Maria Ward. *The Life of Dan Rice.* Long Branch, N.J.: 1901.
Gillette, Don Carle. *He Made Lincoln Laugh.* New York: Exposition Press, 1967.
Kunzog, John C. *The One-Horse Show.* Jamestown, N.Y.: 1962.

Rice, Elmer 1892-1967
Durham, Frank. *Elmer Rice.* New York: Twayne, 1970.
Hogan, Robert G. *The Independence of Elmer Rice.* Carbondale: Southern Illinois Univ., 1965.
Rice, Elmer. *Minority Report.* New York: Simon & Schuster, 1963.

Richardson, Ralph 1902-
Hobson, Harold. *Ralph Richardson.* London: Rockliff, 1958.

Richman, Harry 1895-1972
Richman, Harry with Richard Gehman. *A Hell of a Life.* New York: Duell, 1966.

Ricketts, Charles 1866-1931
Ricketts, Charles S. (ed. by Cecil Lewis). *Self-Portrait: Taken from the Letters & Journals of Charles Ricketts.* London: Davies, 1939.

Ristori, Adelaide 1821-1906
Field, Kate. *Adelaide Ristori, a Biography.* New York: John A. Gray and Green, 1867.
Ristori, Adelaide (trans. by Mantellini, G.). *Memoirs and Artistic Studies of Adelaide Ristori.* New York: Doubleday, Page, 1907.

Roberts, Joan 1922-
Roberts, Joan. *Never Alone.* New York: McMullen, 1954.

Robertson, Thomas William 1829-1871
Pemberton, Thomas Edgar. *The Life and Writings of T. W. Robertson.* London: Bentley, 1893.

Robertson, W. Graham 1867-1948
Robertson, Walford Graham (ed. by Kerriston Preston). *Letters.* London: Hamilton, 1953.
Robertson, W. Graham. *Life Was Worth Living.* New York: Harper, 1931. [English title: *Time Was.*]
—. *Letters to Frances White Emerson from W. Graham Robertson.* Cambridge, Mass.: 1950.

Robeson, Paul 1898-1976
Graham, Shirley. *Paul Robeson, Citizen of the World.* New York: Messner, 1946.
Hoyt, Edwin P. *Paul Robeson, the American Othello.* Cleveland: World, 1967.
Robeson, Eslanda Goode. *Paul Robeson, Negro.* London: Gollancz, 1930.
Robeson, Paul. *Here I Stand.* Boston: Beacon, 1971.

Robey, Sir George (George Edward Wade) 1869-1954
Cotes, Peter. *George Robey, "The Darling of the Halls."* London: Cassell, 1972.
Robey, George. *Looking Back on Life.* London: Constable, 1933.
Wilson, Albert Edward. *Prime Minister of Mirth.* London: Odhams Press, 1956.

Robins, Elizabeth 1862-1952
Robins, Elizabeth. *Both Sides of the Curtain.* London: Heinemann, 1940.
James, Henry. *Theatre and Friendship; Some Henry James Letters.* New York: Putnam, 1932.

Robinson, Edward G. 1893-1973
Robinson, Edward G. with Leonard Spigelgass. *All My Yesterdays.* New York: Hawthorn, 1973.
Robinson, Edward G., Jr. *My Father—My Son.* New York: Frederick Fell, 1958.

Robinson, Lennox 1886-1958
O'Neill, Michael J. *Lennox Robinson.* New York: Twayne, 1964.
Robinson, Lennox. *Curtain Up.* London: M. Joseph, 1942.
—. *I Sometimes Think.* Dublin: Talbot, 1956.
— and Thomas, and Dorman, Nora (Robinson). *Three Homes.* London: Joseph, 1938.

Robinson, Mary Darby ("Perdita") 1758-1800
Makower, Stanley V. *Perdita, a Romance in Biography.* New York: Appleton, 1908.
Robinson, Mary Darby (ed. by Mary Elizabeth Robinson). *Memoirs of the Late Mrs. Robinson.* New York: Swords, Mesier, and Davis, 1802.
Steen, Marguerite. *Lost One; A Biography of Mary (Perdita) Robinson.* London: Methuen, 1937.

Robson, Eleanor 1879-
Belmont, Eleanor (Robson). *The Fabric of Memory.* New York: Farrar, Straus & Cudahy, 1957.

Robson, Flora 1902-
Dunbar, Janet. *Flora Robson.* London: Harrap, 1960.

Robson, Frederick (the elder) 1821-1864
Sala, George A. *Robson: A Sketch.* London: J. C. Hotten, 1864.

Rodgers, Richard 1902-
Hammerstein, Oscar, II 1895-1960
Ewen, David. *Richard Rodgers.* New York: Holt, 1957.
Richard Rodgers Fact Book. New York: Lynn Farnol Group, 1968.
Rodgers and Hammerstein Fact Book. New York: Lynn Farnol Group, 1955.

Taylor, Deems. *Some Enchanted Evenings; The Story of Rodgers and Hammerstein.* New York: Harper, 1953.
Green, Stanley. *The Rodgers and Hammerstein Story.* New York: Day, 1963.

Rodway, Philip 1876-1932
Rodway, Phyllis and Slingsby, Lois Rodway. *Philip Rodway and a Tale of Two Theatres.* Birmingham: Cornish, 1934.

Rogers, Paul 1917-
Williamson, Audrey. *Paul Rogers.* London: Rockliff, 1956.

Rogers, Will 1879-1935
Alworth, E. Paul. *Will Rogers.* New York: Twayne, 1974.
Brown, William R. *Imagemaker: Will Rogers and the American Dream.* Columbia: Univ. of Missouri, 1970.
Croy, Homer. *Our Will Rogers.* New York: Duell, Sloan and Pearce, 1953.
Day, Donald. *Will Rogers.* New York: McKay, 1962.
Ketchum, Richard M. *Will Rogers; His Life and Times.* New York: American Heritage, 1973.
Lait, Jack. *Our Will Rogers.* New York: Greenberg, 1935.
Milsten, David Randolph. *An Appreciation of Will Rogers.* San Antonio, Tex.: Naylor, 1935.
O'Brien, Patrick Joseph. *Will Rogers, Ambassador of Good Will, Prince of Wit and Wisdom.* Philadelphia: John C. Winston, 1935.
Payne, William Howard and Lyons, Jake G. (comps.). *Folks Say of Will Rogers; A Memorial Anecdotage.* New York: Putnam, 1936.
Rogers, Betty. *Will Rogers, His Wife's Story.* Indianapolis: Bobbs-Merrill, 1941.
Rogers, Will (ed. by Donald Day). *Autobiography.* Boston: Houghton Mifflin, 1949.
—. *Will Rogers: Wit and Wisdom.* New York: F. A. Stokes, 1936.
—. *The Illiterate Digest.* New York: A. & C. Boni, 1924.
Trent, Spi M. *My Cousin Will Rogers.* New York: G. P. Putnam, 1938.

Romberg, Sigmund 1887-1951
Arnold, Elliott. *Deep in My Heart.* New York: Duell, Sloan and Pearce, 1949.

Rose, Billy 1899-1966
Conrad, Earl. *Billy Rose, Manhattan Primitive.* Cleveland: World, 1968.
Gottlieb, Polly Rose. *The Nine Lives of Billy Rose.* New York: Crown, 1968.
Rose, Billy. *Wine, Women and Words.* New York: Simon & Schuster, 1948.

Roth, Lillian 1910-
Roth, Lillian. *Beyond My Worth.* New York: Frederick Fell, 1958.
— with Mike Connolly and Gerold Frank. *I'll Cry Tomorrow.* New York: Frederick Fell, 1954.

Runyon, Damon 1884-1946
Hoyt, Edwin P. *A Gentleman of Broadway.* Boston: Little, Brown, 1964.
Runyon, Damon (Jr.). *Father's Footsteps.* New York: Random House, 1954.
Weiner, Edward H. *The Damon Runyon Story.* New York: Longmans, Green, 1948.

Russell, Lillian 1861-1922
Burke, John. *Duet in Diamonds; The Flamboyant Saga of Lillian Russell and Diamond Jim Brady in America's Gilded Age.* New York: Putnam, 1972.
Morell, Parker. *Lillian Russell; The Era of Plush.* New York: Random House, 1940.

Rutherford, Margaret 1892-1972
Keown, Eric. *Margaret Rutherford.* London: Rockliff, 1956.
Rutherford, Margaret (as told to Gwen Robyns). *Margaret Rutherford.* London: W. H. Allen, 1972.

Ryley, Samuel William 1759-1837
Ryley, Samuel William. *The Itinerant, or, Memoirs of an Actor.* London: Taylor & Hessey, 1808; 3 vols.

Salvini, Tommaso 1829-1916
Salvini, Tommaso. *Leaves from the Autobiography of T. Salvini.* New York: Century, 1893.

Sanders, George 1906-1972
Sanders, George. *Memoirs of a Professional Cad.* New York: Putnam, 1960.

Sanger, George 1827-1911
Coleman, George Sanger. *The Sanger Story.* London: Hodder & Stoughton, 1956.
Sanger, George. *Seventy Years a Showman.* New York: Dutton, 1926.

Sarcey, Francisque 1827-1899
Sarcey, Francisque (trans. by Elisabeth Luther Cary). *Recollections of Middle Life.* New York: Scribner, 1893.

Sardou, Victorien 1831-1908
Hart, Jerome A. *Sardou and the Sardou Plays.* Philadelphia: Lippincott, 1913.
Roosevelt, Blanche. *Victorien Sardou, Poet, Author, and Member of the Academy of France; A Personal Study.* London: Paul, Trench, Trubner, 1892.

Saroyan, William 1908-
Floan, Howard R. *William Saroyan.* New York: Twayne, 1966.
Saroyan, William. *My Name Is Aram.* New York: Harcourt, 1940.
—. *The Bicycle Rider in Beverly Hills.* New York: Scribner, 1952.
—. *Here Comes, There Goes, You Know Who.* New York: Simon & Schuster, 1961.
—. *Not Dying.* New York: Harcourt, Brace & World, 1963.
—. *Days of Life and Death and Escape to the Moon.* New York: Dial, 1970.
—. *Places Where I've Done Time.* New York: Praeger, 1972.

Sartre, Jean-Paul 1905-
Carson, Ronald A. *Jean-Paul Sartre.* Valley Forge, Pa.: Judson, 1974.
Peyre, Henri. *Jean-Paul Sartre.* New York: Columbia Univ., 1968.
Sartre, Jean-Paul (trans. by Bernard Frechtman). *The Words.* New York: Braziller, 1964.
Thody, Philip. *Sartre; A Biographical Introduction.* New York: Scribner, 1971.

Savo, Jimmy (Sava) 1895-1960
Savo, Jimmy. *I Bow to the Stones; Memories of a New York Childhood.* New York: Frisch, 1963.
—. *Little World, Hello!* New York: Simon & Schuster, 1947.

Schildkraut, Joseph 1896-1964
Schildkraut, Joseph. *My Father and I.* New York: Viking, 1959.

Schiller, Johann Christoph Friedrich Von 1759-1805
Boyesen, Hjalmar H. *Goethe and Schiller; Their Lives and Works.* New York: Scribner, 1879.
Carlyle, Thomas. *The Life of Friedrich Schiller: Comprehending an Examination of His Works.* London: Chapman & Hall, 1888.
Carus, Paul. *Friedrich Schiller; A Sketch of His Life and an Appreciation of His Poetry.* Chicago: Open Court, 1905.
Duentzer, Heinrich (trans. by Percy E. Pinkerton). *The Life of Schiller.* London: Macmillan, 1883.
Garland, H. B. *Schiller.* London: Harrap, 1949.
Heiseler, Bernt Von (trans. by John Bednall). *Schiller.* London: Eyre & Spottiswoode, 1962.
Kuhnemann, Eugen (trans. by Katharine Royce). *Schiller.* Boston: Ginn, 1912; 2 vols.
Meakin, Annette M. B. *Goethe and Schiller, 1785-1805; The Story of a Friendship.* London: Griffiths, 1932; 3 vols.
Nevinson, Henry W. *Life of Friedrich Schiller.* New York: Whittaker, 1889.
Palleske, Emil (trans. by Lady Wallace). *Schiller's Life and Works.* London: 1860; 2 vols.
Parry, Ellwood C. *Friedrich Schiller in America. A Contribution to the Literature of the Poet's Centenary, 1905.* Philadelphia: Americana Germanica Press, 1905.
Schiller, J.C.F. von (trans. by J. L. Weisse). *Letters of Schiller, Selected from His Private Correspondence, Prior to His Marriage.* Boston: S. N. Dickinson, 1841.
— (trans. by George H. Calvert). *Correspondence between Schiller and Goethe, from 1794 to 1805.* New York: Wiley & Putnam, 1845.
— (trans. by Leonard Simpson). *Correspondence of Schiller with Korner, Comprising Sketches and Anecdotes of Goethe, the Schlegels, Wieland...* London: R. Bentley, 1849; 3 vols.
Thomas, Calvin. *The Life and Works of Friedrich Schiller.* New York: Holt, 1902.

Schnitzler, Arthur 1862-1931
Liptzin, Solomon. *Arthur Schnitzler.* New York: Prentice-Hall, 1932.
Schnitzler, Arthur (trans. by Catherine Hutter). *My Youth in Vienna.* New York: Holt, Rinehart & Winston, 1970.

Scofield, Paul 1922-
Trewin, J. C. *Paul Scofield.* London: Rockcliff, 1956.

Scribe, Eugene 1791-1861
Arvin, Neil Cole. *Eugene Scribe and the French Theatre, 1815-1860.* Cambridge: Harvard Univ., 1924.

Shakespeare, William 1564-1616
Acheson, Arthur. *Shakespeare's Lost Years in London, 1586-1592; Giving New Light on the Pre-sonnet Period.* London: B. Quaritch, 1920.
Adams, Joseph Quincy. *A Life of William Shakespeare.* Boston: Houghton Mifflin, 1923.
Alexander, Peter. *Shakespeare.* New York: Oxford Univ., 1964.
Bagehot, Walter. *Shakespeare, the Man.* New York: McClure Phillips, 1901.

Baynes, T. Spencer. *Shakepeare; His Life and Times.* New York: Hurst, 191-.
Bentley, Gerald E. *Shakespeare; A Biographical Handbook.* New Haven: Yale Univ., 1961.
Bohn, Henry G. *The Biography and Bibliography of Shakespeare.* London: 1863.
Brandes, Georg. *William Shakespeare.* New York: Macmillan, 1924.
Brinkworth, Edwin R. C. *Shakespeare and the Bawdy Court of Stratford.* Chichester: Phillimore, 1972.
Brooke, Charles F. Tucker. *Shakespeare of Stratford; A Handbook for Students.* New Haven: Yale Univ., 1926.
Brooks, Alden. *Will Shakespeare, Factotum and Agent.* New York: Round Table, 1937.
Brown, Ivor. *Shakespeare.* Garden City: Doubleday, 1949.
—. *How Shakespeare Spent the Day.* New York: Hill and Wang, 1964.
—. *The Women in Shakespeare's Life.* New York: Coward-McCann, 1969.
Burgess, Anthony. *Shakespeare.* New York: Knopf, 1970.
Butler, Pierce, (comp.). *Materials for the Life of Shakespeare.* Chapel Hill: Univ. of North Carolina, 1930.
Calmour, Alfred C. *Fact and Fiction about Shakespeare; with Some Account of the Playhouses, Players, and Playwrights of His Period.* London: H. Williams, 1894.
Chambers, Edmund K. *William Shakespeare; A Study of Facts and Problems.* Oxford: Clarendon, 1930; 3 vols.
Chambrun, Clara. *Shakespeare, Actor-Poet, as Seen by His Associates, Explained by Himself, and Remembered by the Succeeding Generation.* New York: Appleton, 1927.
—. *Shakespeare: A Portrait Restored.* London: Hollis & Carter, 1957.
Chute, Marchette. *Shakespeare of London.* New York: Dutton, 1949.
Collier, J. Payne. *New Facts Regarding the Life of Shakespeare, in a Letter to Thomas Amyot.* London: T. Rodd, 1835.
Cundall, Joseph. *Annals of the Life and Work of William Shakespeare, Collected from the Most Recent Authorities.* London: Low, Marston & Rivington, 1886.
Dall, Caroline Healey. *What We Really Know About Shakespeare.* Boston: Roberts, 1886.
Dawson, Giles E. *The Life of William Shakespeare.* Ithaca, N.Y.: Cornell Univ., 1958.
Drake, Nathan. *Shakespeare and His Times.* London: Cadell and Davies, 1817.
Drinkwater, John. *Shakespeare.* London: Duckworth, 1933.
Eccles, Mark. *Shakespeare in Warwickshire.* Madison: Univ. of Wisconsin, 1961.
Elton, Charles I. (ed. by A. Hamilton Thompson). *William Shakespeare, His Family and Friends.* London: Murray, 1904.
Field, Arthur. *Recent Discoveries Relating to the Life and Works of William Shakespeare.* London: Mitre, 1954.
Fleay, Frederick G. *A Chronicle History of the Life and Work of William Shakespeare, Player, Poet, and Playmaker.* London: J. C. Nimmo, 1886.
Fripp, Edgar I. *Shakespeare, Man and Artist.* London: Oxford Univ., 1938; 2 vols.
Fullom, Stephen W. *History of William Shakespeare, Player and Poet: with New Facts and Traditions.* London: Saunders, Otley, 1862.
Furnivall, Frederick J. *Shakespeare; Life and Work.* London: Cassell, 1910.
Gollancz, Israel. *Life of Shakespeare.* New York: Univ. Society, 1901.
Gray, Arthur. *A Chapter in the Early Life of Shakespeare. Polesworth in Arden.* Cambridge: Univ. Press, 1926.
Gray, Joseph W. *Shakespeare's Marriage, His Departure from Stratford and Other Incidents in His Life.* London: Chapman & Hall, 1905.
Halliday, Frank Ernest. *Shakespeare.* New York: Yoseloff, 1961.
—. *Shakespeare, a Pictorial Biography.* New York: Viking, 1964.
Halliwell-Phillips, James O. *The Life of William Shakespeare.* London: J. R. Smith, 1848.
—. *Outlines of the Life of Shakespeare.* London: Longmans, Green, 1882.
Harbage, Alfred. *Conceptions of Shakespeare.* Cambridge: Harvard Univ., 1966.
Harris, Frank. *The Man Shakespeare and His Tragic Life-story.* New York: Kennerley, 1909.
Harrison, George B. *Shakespeare under Elizabeth.* New York: Holt, 1933.
—. *Introducing Shakespeare.* Baltimore: Penguin, 1966.
Hazlitt, William C. *Shakespeare Himself and His Work: A Biographical Study.* London: Quaritch, 1908.
Hotson, Leslie. *Shakespeare versus Shallow.* Boston: Little, Brown, 1931.
Hunter, Joseph. *New Illustrations of the Life, Studies, and Writings of Shakespeare.* London: J. B. Nichols, 1845.
Keen, Alan and Lubbock, Roger. *The Annotator; The Pursuit of an Elizabethan Reader of Halle's Chronicle Involving Some Surmises about the Early Life of William Shakespeare.* New York: Macmillan, 1954.
Knight, Charles. *William Shakespeare.* London: Knight, 1843.
Lamborn, Edmund and Harrison, George. *Shakespeare, the Man and His Stage.* London: Oxford, 1923.
Lee, Sidney. *A Life of William Shakespeare.* New York: Macmillan, 1916.
Lewis, Benjamin Roland. *The Shakespeare Documents; Facsimiles, Transliterations, Translations & Commentary.* Westport, Conn.: Greenwood, 1969; 2 vols.
Mabie, Hamilton W. *William Shakespeare, Poet, Dramatist, and Man.* New York: Macmillan, 1907.
Macardle, Dorothy (ed. by George Bott). *Shakespeare, Man and Boy.* London: Faber & Faber, 1961.
Malone, E. *The Life of William Shakespeare.* London: 1821.
Masson, David (ed. by R. Masson). *Shakespeare Personally.* New York: Dutton, 1914.
May, Robin. *Who Was Shakespeare?: The Man, the Times, the Works.* New York: St. Martin's, 1974.
McCurdy, Harold G. *The Personality of Shakespeare; A Venture in Psychological Method.* New Haven: Yale Univ., 1953.
Montague, William K. *The Man of Stratford—the Real Shakespeare.* New York: Vantage, 1964.
Neil, Samuel. *Shakespere; A Critical Biography and an Estimate of the Facts, Fancies, and Fabrications, Regarding His Life and Works, Which Have Appeared in Remote and Recent Literature.* London: Houlston and Wright, 1861.
Norman, Charles. *So Worthy a Friend: William Shakespeare.* New York: Rinehart, 1947.
Parrott, Thomas. *William Shakespeare; A Handbook.* New York: Scribner, 1934.
Pearson, Hesketh. *A Life of Shakespeare.* London: Carroll & Nicholson, 1949.
Pohl, Frederick. *Like to the Lark; The Early Years of Shakespeare.* New York: C. N. Potter, 1972.
Quennell, Peter. *Shakespeare.* Cleveland: World, 1963.
Raleigh, Walter A. *Shakespeare.* London: Macmillan, 1907.
Reese, Max M. *Shakespeare; His World & His Work.* London: Buffalo: C. W. Moulton, 1890.
Rolfe, William J. *Shakespeare the Boy; with Sketches of the Home and School Life, the Games and Sports, the Manners, Customs and Folk-Lore of the Time.* New York: Harper, 1896.
Rosignoli, Maria Pia (trans. by Mary Kanani). *The Life and Times of Shakespeare.* London: Hamlyn, 1968.
Rowse, A. L. *William Shakespeare.* New York: Harper & Row, 1963.
—. *Shakespeare the Man.* New York: Harper & Row, 1973.
Schoenbaum, S. *William Shakespeare; A Documentary Life.* New York: Oxford Univ., 1975.
Shore, William T. *Shakespeare's Self.* London: Allan, 1920.
Skottowe, Augustine. *The Life of Shakespeare; Enquiries into the Originality of His Dramatic Plots and Characters; and Essays on the Ancient Theatres and Theatrical Usages.* London: Longmans, Green, 1824; 2 vols.
Smart, John S. *Shakespeare; Truth and Tradition.* New York: Longmans, Green, 1928.
Snider, Denton J. *A Biography of William Shakespeare, Set Forth as His Life Drama.* St. Louis: William Harvey Minor, 1922.
Spencer, Hazelton. *Art and Life of William Shakespeare.* New York: Harcourt, 1940.
Sprague, Homer B. *Studies in Shakespeare. (First Series).* Boston: Pilgrim Press, 1916.
Stopes, Charlotte C. *Shakespeare's Family; Being a Record of the Ancestors and Descendants of William Shakespeare, with Some Account of the Ardens.* London: Stock, 1901.
Thorpe, William G. *The Hidden Lives of Shakespeare and Bacon and Their Business Connection; with Some Revelations of Shakespeare's Early Struggles, 1587-1592.* London: Cheswick Press, 1897.
Turner, Robert Y. *Shakespeare's Apprenticeship.* Chicago: Univ. of Chicago, 1974.
Van Doren, Mark. *Shakespeare.* New York: Holt, 1939.
Wagenknecht, Edward. *The Personality of Shakespeare.* Norman: Univ. of Oklahoma, 1972.
Walter, James. *Shakespeare's True Life.* London: Walter, 1890.
Wendell, Barrett. *William Shakespeare, a Study in Elizabethan Literature.* New York: Scribner, 1894.
White, Richard G. *Memoirs of the Life of William Shakespeare.* Boston: Little, Brown, 1865.
Williams, Frayne. *Mr. Shakespeare of the Globe.* New York: Dutton, 1941.

Wilson, John Dover. *Essential Shakespeare; A Biographical Adventure.* New York: Macmillan, 1932.
Wright, Louis B. and Fowler, Elaine W. *A Visual Guide to Shakespeare's Life and Times.* New York: Pocket Books, 1975.
Yeatman, John P. *The Gentle Shakspere: A Vindication.* London: Roxburghe Press, 1896.

Shaw, George Bernard 1856-1950
Bentley, Eric. *Bernard Shaw, 1856-1950.* New York: New Directions, 1957.
Brown, Ivor. *Shaw in His Time.* London: Nelson, 1965.
Burton, Richard. *Bernard Shaw: The Man and the Mask.* New York: Holt, 1916.
Chappelow, Allan (ed.). *Shaw the Villager and Human Being.* New York: Macmillan, 1962.
— (ed.). *Shaw—"the Chucker-Out."* New York: AMS, 1971.
Chesterton, Gilbert Keith. *George Bernard Shaw.* New York: Lane, 1910.
Colbourne, Maurice. *The Real Bernard Shaw.* London: Dent, 1949.
Coolidge, Olivia. *George Bernard Shaw.* Boston: Houghton Mifflin, 1968.
Du Cann, Charles G. *The Loves of George Bernard Shaw.* New York: Funk & Wagnalls, 1963.
Dukore, Bernard F. *Bernard Shaw, Director.* London: Allen & Unwin, 1971.
Dunbar, Janet. *Mrs. G. B. S.* New York: Harper & Row, 1963.
Ervine, St. John. *Bernard Shaw, His Life, Work and Friends.* New York: Morrow, 1956.
Esdaile, Ernest. *Show Me Shaw; Mr. Bernard Shaw's Conversion to the Films.* London: Mitre, 1941.
Farmer, Henry G. *Bernard Shaw's Sister and Her Friends; A New Angle on G. B. S.* Leiden: E. J. Brill, 1959.
Hackett, J. P. *Shaw, George versus Bernard.* New York: Sheed & Ward, 1937.
Hamon, Augustin (trans. by Eden and Cedar Paul). *The Twentieth-Century Moliere: Bernard Shaw.* New York: F. H. Stokes, 1916.
Hardwick, Michael and Mollie. *The Bernard Shaw Companion.* New York: St. Martin's, 1974.
Harris, Frank. *Bernard Shaw; An Unauthorized Biography Based on First Hand Information.* New York: Simon & Schuster, 1931.
Henderson, Archibald. *Bernard Shaw, Playboy and Prophet.* New York: Appleton-Century, 1932.
—. *George Bernard Shaw: Man of the Century.* New York: Appleton-Century-Crofts, 1956.
Irvine, William. *The Universe of G. B. S.* New York: Whittlesey House, 1949.
Jackson, Holbrook. *Bernard Shaw.* London: E. G. Richards, 1907.
Joad, Cyrile. *Shaw.* London: Gollancz, 1949.
Kauffmann, Ralph J. (ed.). *G. B. Shaw; A Collection of Critical Essays.* Englewood Cliffs, N.J.: Prentice-Hall, 1965.
Laing, Allan M. (ed.). *In Praise of Bernard Shaw; An Anthology for Old and Young.* London: Muller, 1949.
Loewenstein, Fritze. *Bernard Shaw through the Camera; 238 Photos.* London: B. and H. White, 1948.
Matthews, John F. *George Bernard Shaw.* New York: Columbia Univ., 1969.
McCabe, Joseph. *George Bernard Shaw; A Critical Study.* New York: Kennerley, 1914.
Mencken, Henry Louis. *George Bernard Shaw, His Plays.* Boston: J. W. Luce, 1905.
Minney, Rubeigh J. *Recollections of George Bernard Shaw.* Englewood Cliffs, N.J.: Prentice-Hall, 1969.
O'Donovan, John. *Shaw and the Charlatan Genius; A Memoir.* Chester Springs, Pa.: Dufour Editions, 1966.
Palmer, John L. *George Bernard Shaw; Harlequin or Patriot?* New York: Century, 1915.
Pascal, Valerie. *The Disciple and His Devil: Gabriel Pascal, Bernard Shaw.* New York: McGraw-Hill, 1970.
Patch, Blanche E. *Thirty Years with G. B. S.* New York: Dodd, Mead, 1951.
Pearson, Hesketh. *G. B. S. A Full Length Portrait.* New York: Harper, 1942.
—. *G. B. S., a Postscript.* New York: Harper, 1950.
Rattray, Robert F. *Bernard Shaw: A Chronicle and an Introduction.* London: Duckworth, 1934.
Rider, Dan. *Adventures with Bernard Shaw.* London: M. and M. Kennerley, 1907.
Rosset, B. C. *Shaw of Dublin; The Formative Years.* University Park: Pennsylvania State Univ., 1964.
Shanks, Edward B. *Bernard Shaw.* London: Nisbet, 1924.
Shaw, Charles M. *Bernard's Brethren; with Comments by Bernard Shaw.* New York: Holt, 1939.
Shaw, George Bernard. *Shaw Gives Himself Away; An Autobiographical Miscellany.* Newtown, Montgomeryshire: Gregynog Press, 1939.
—. *Sixteen Self Sketches.* New York: Dodd, Mead, 1949.
—. *Advice to a Young Critic, and Other Letters.* New York: Crown, 1955.
—. *To a Young Actress. The Letters of Bernard Shaw to Molly Tompkins.* New York: C. N. Potter, 1960.
— (ed. by Dan H. Laurence). *Collected Letters, 1874-1910.* London: Reinhardt, 1965-72; 2 vols.
— (comp. by Stanley Weintraub). *Shaw; An Autobiography, Selected from His Writings.* New York: Weybright and Talley, 1969-70; 2 vols.
Skimpole, Herbert. *Bernard Shaw; the Man and His Work.* London: Allen & Unwin, 1918.
Smith, J. Percy. *The Unrepentant Pilgrim; A Study of the Development of Bernard Shaw.* Boston: Houghton Mifflin, 1965.
Titterton, William R. *So This Is Shaw.* London: D. Organ, 1945.
Tompkins, Peter. *Shaw and Molly Tompkins in Their Own Words.* London: Blond, 1961.
Wall, Vincent. *Bernard Shaw, Pygmalion to Many Players.* Ann Arbor: Univ. of Michigan, 1973.
Ward, Alfred C. *Bernard Shaw.* London: Longmans, Green, 1951.
Weintraub, Stanley. *Private Shaw and Public Shaw; A Dual Portrait of Lawrence of Arabia and GBS.* New York: Braziller, 1963.
—. *Journey to Heartbreak; The Crucible Years of Bernard Shaw, 1914-1918.* New York: Weybright & Talley, 1971.
Williamson, Audrey. *Bernard Shaw: Man and Writer.* New York: Crowell-Collier, 1963.
Wilson, Colin. *Bernard Shaw; A Reassessment.* London: Hutchinson, 1969.
Winston, Stephen (ed.). *G. B. S. 90; Aspects of Bernard Shaw's Life and Work.* London: Hutchinson, 1946.
—. *Days with Bernard Shaw.* New York: Vanguard, 1949.
—. *Shaw's Corner.* London: Hutchinson, 1952.
—. *Jesting Apostle; The Private Life of Bernard Shaw.* New York: Dutton, 1957.
Woodbridge, Homer E. *George Bernard Shaw, Creative Artist.* Carbondale: Southern Illinois Univ., 1963.
See also: Campbell, Mrs. Patrick; Granville-Barker, Harley; Langner, Lawrence; Pascal, Gabriel; Terry, Ellen.

Sheldon, Edward Brewster 1886-1946
Barnes, Eric W. *The Man Who Lived Twice.* New York: Scribner, 1956.

Shelton, George 1852-1932
Shelton, George. *It's Smee.* London: Benn, 1928.

Sheridan, Richard Brinsley 1751-1816
Bingham, Madeleine. *Sheridan; The Track of a Comet.* London: Allen & Unwin, 1972.
Butler, Eliza M. *Sheridan; A Ghost Story.* New York: R. R. Smith, 1931.
Darlington, William A. *Sheridan.* New York: Macmillan, 1933.
Fitzgerald, Percy. *Lives of the Sheridans.* London: Bentley, 1886; 2 vols.
Foss, Kenelm. *Here Lies Richard Brinsley Sheridan.* London: Secker, 1939.
Gibbs, Lewis. *Sheridan: His Life and His Theatre.* New York: Morrow, 1948.
Glasgow, Alive. *Sheridan of Drury Lane.* New York: Frederick A. Stokes, 1940.
Lefanu, Alicia. *Memoirs of the Life and Writings of Mrs. Frances (Chamberlaine) Sheridan; with Remarks upon a Late Life of the Right Hon. R. B. Sheridan.* London: G. and W. B. Whittaker, 1824.
Moore, Thomas. *Memoirs of the Life of the Right Honourable Richard Brinsley Sheridan.* Philadelphia: H. C. Carey & I. Lea, 1825.
Oliphant, Margaret O. *Sheridan.* New York: Harper, 1883.
Rae, William F. *Sheridan.* New York: Holt, 1896; 2 vols.
Rhodes, R. C. *Harlequin Sheridan.* Oxford: Blackwell, 1933.
Sadleir, Michael. *The Political Career of Richard Brinsley Sheridan . . . Followed by Some Hitherto Unpublished Letters of Mrs. Sheridan.* Oxford: Blackwell, 1919.
Sanders, L. C. *Life of Richard Brinsley Sheridan.* London: Scott, 1890.
Sheridan, Betsy (ed. by William Lefanu). *Betsy Sheridan's Journal; Letters from Sheridan's Sister, 1784-1786, and 1788-1790.* New Brunswick, N. J.: Rutgers Univ., 1960.
Sheridan, Richard Brinsley. *A Short Memoir of the Life of the Late Right Honourable Richard Brinsley Sheridan . . . To Which Is Added a Report of His Celebrated Speech . . . 1788.* London: Booth, 1816.
— (ed. by Cecil Price). *The Letters of Richard Brinsley Sheridan.* Oxford: Clarendon, 1966; 3 vols.
Sheridaniana; or, Anecdotes of the Life of Richard Brinsley Sheridan; His Tabletalk and Bon Mots. London: Colburn, 1826.
Sherwin, Oscar. *Uncorking Old Sherry; The*

Life and Times of Richard Brinsley Sheridan. New York: Twayne, 1960.
Sichel, Walter S. *Sheridan.* Boston: Houghton, 1909; 2 vols.
Watkins, John. *Memoirs of the Public and Private Life of the Right Hon. R. B. Sheridan; with a Particular Account of His Family and Connexions.* London: Colburn, 1817; 2 vols.

Sheridan, Thomas 1719-1788
Sheldon, Esther K. *Thomas Sheridan of Smock-Alley.* Princeton, N.J.: Princeton Univ., 1967.

Sherriff, Robert Cedric 1896-1975
Sherriff, Robert C. *No Leading Lady.* London: Gollancz, 1968.

Sherwood, Robert Emmett 1896-1955
Brown, John Mason. *The Worlds of Robert E. Sherwood; Mirror to His Times, 1896-1939.* New York: Harper, 1965.
—. *The Ordeal of a Playwright; Robert E. Sherwood and the Challenge of War.* New York: Harper, 1970.
Meserve, Walter J. *Robert E. Sherwood, Reluctant Moralist.* New York: Pegasus, 1970.
Shuman, Robert B. *Robert E. Sherwood.* New York: Twayne, 1964.

Shirley, James 1596-1666
Forsythe, Robert S. *Relations of Shirley's Plays to Elizabethan Drama.* New York: Columbia Univ., 1914.
Nason, Arthur H. *James Shirley, Dramatist.* New York: A. H. Nason, 1915.

Shubert, Jacob J. 1880?-1963
Shubert, Lee 1875-1953
Shubert, Sam S. 1875-1905
Stagg, Jerry. *The Brothers Shubert.* New York: Random House, 1968.

Siddons, Sarah (Kemble) 1755-1831
Boaden, James. *Memoirs of Mrs. Siddons.* London: Colburn, 1827; 2 vols.
Campbell, Thomas. *Life of Mrs. Siddons.* London: Wilson; 1834, 2 vols.
Ffrench, Yvonne. *Mrs. Siddons: Tragic Actress.* London: Cobden-Sanderson, 1936.
Fitzgerald, Percy H. *Kembles; An Account of the Kemble Family, Including the Lives of Mrs. Siddons, and Her Brother John Philip Kemble.* London: Tinsley, 1871; 2 vols.
Jonson, Marian. *A Troubled Grandeur; The Story of England's Great Actress, Sarah Siddons.* Boston: Little, Brown, 1972.
Kennard, Nina H. *Mrs. Siddons.* Boston: Roberts Brothers, 1887.
Knapp, Oswald G. (ed.). *Artist's Live Story, Told in Letters of Sir Thomas Lawrence, Mrs. Siddons and Her Daughters.* New York: Longmans, 1904.
MacKenzie, Kathleen. *The Great Sarah; The Life of Mrs. Siddons.* London: Evans, 1968.
Manvell, Roger. *Sarah Siddons.* London: Heinemann, 1970.
Parsons, Florence. *Incomparable Siddons.* London: Methuen, 1909.
Royde-Smith, Naomi. *Portrait of Mrs. Siddons; A Study in Four Parts.* New York: Viking, 1933.

Sienkiewicz, Henryk 1846-1916
Gardner, Monica M. *The Patriot Novelist of Poland, Henryk Sienkiewicz.* London: J. M. Dent, 1926.
Lednicki, Waclaw. *Henryk Sienkiewicz, 1846-1946.* New York: Polish Institute of Arts and Sciences in America, 1948.
Sienkiewicz, Henryk (ed. and trans. by Charles Morley). *Portrait of America; Letters of Henryk Sienkiewicz.* New York: Columbia Univ., 1959.
See also: Modjeska, Helena

Sillman, Leonard 1908-
Sillman, Leonard. *Here Lies Leonard Sillman, Straightened Out at Last.* New York: Citadel, 1959.

Silverman, Sime 1873-1933
Stoddart, Dayton. *Lord Broadway, Variety's Sime.* New York: Funk, 1941.

Silvers, Phil 1911-
Silvers, Phil with Saffron, Robert. *This Laugh Is on Me.* Englewood Cliffs, N. J.: Prentice-Hall, 1973.

Simonson, Lee 1888-1967
Simonson, Lee. *Part of a Lifetime; Drawings and Designs, 1919-1940.* New York: Duell, Sloan and Pearce, 1943.

Skinner, Cornelia Otis 1901-
Kimbrough, Emily. *We Followed Our Hearts to Hollywood.* New York: Dodd, Mead, 1943.
Skinner, Cornelia Otis and Kimbrough, Emily. *Our Hearts Were Young and Gay.* New York: Dodd, Mead, 1942.
See also: Skinner, Otis.

Skinner, Otis 1858-1942
Skinner, Cornelia Otis. *Family Circle.* Boston: Houghton Mifflin, 1948.
Skinner, Otis. *Footlights and Spotlights.* Indianapolis: Bobbs-Merrill, 1924.

Slezak, Walter 1902-
Slezak, Walter. *What Time's the Next Swan.* Garden City: Doubleday, 1962.

Smith, Albert 1816-1860
Fitzsimons, Raymund. *The Baron of Piccadilly; The Travels and Entertainments of Albert Smith, 1816-1860.* London: Bles, 1967.

Smith, Harry Bache 1860-1936
Smith, Harry Bache. *First Nights and First Editions.* Boston: Little, Brown, 1931.

Smith, Solomon Franklin 1801-1869
Smith, Sol. *Theatrical Apprenticeship.* Philadelphia: Carey & Hart, 1848.
—. *The Theatrical Journey-work and Anecdotical Recollections of Sol Smith.* Philadelphia: T. B. Peterson, 1854.
—. *Theatrical Management in the West and South for Thirty Years.* New York: Harper, 1868.

Soldene, Emily 1840-1912
Soldene, Emily. *My Theatrical and Musical Recollections.* London: Downey, 1897.

Sondheim, Stephen 1930-
Zadan, Craig. *Sondheim & Co.* New York: Macmillan, 1974.

Sophocles 496-406 B.C.
Bates, William N. *Sophocles, Poet and Dramatist.* Philadelphia: Univ. of Pennsylvania, 1940.
Letters, Francis J. H. *The Life and Work of Sophocles.* New York: Sheed & Ward, 1953.
Melchinger, Siegfried (trans. by David A. Scrase). *Sophocles.* New York: Ungar, 1974.
Sheppard, John T. *The Wisdom of Sophocles, an Essay.* London: Allen & Unwin, 1947.
Webster, Thomas B. *An Introduction to Sophocles.* London: Oxford, 1936.

Sorel, Cecile 1875-
Sorel, Cecile (trans. by Stead, Philip John). *Cecile Sorel, an Autobiography.* New York: Staples, 1953.

Sothern, Edward Askew 1826-1881
De Fontaine, Felix Gregory. *Birds of a Feather Flock Together; or, Talks with Sothern.* New York: G. W. Carleton, 1870.
Pemberton, Thomas Edgar. *A Memoir of Edward Askew Sothern.* London: Bentley, 1889.

Sothern, Edward Hugh 1859-1933
Sothern, Edward Hugh. *The Melancholy Tale of "Me."* New York: Scribner, 1916.
See also: Marlowe, Julia.

Stanislavsky, Constantin 1863-1938
Gorchakov, Nikolai M. (trans, by Miriam Goldina). *Stanislavsky Directs.* New York: Funk & Wagnalls, 1954.
Margarshack, David. *Stanislavsky; A Life.* London: MacGibbon and Kee, 1950.
Stanislavsky, Constantin (trans. by J. J. Robbins). *My Life in Art.* Boston: Little, Brown, 1924.
— (trans. by Elizabeth Reynolds Hapgood). *Stanislavski's Legacy.* New York: Theatre Arts Books, 1958.
—. (trans. by Vic Schneierson). *Man and Actor. Stanislavsky and the World Theatre. Stanislavsky's Letters.* Moscow: Progress Publishers, 1964.

Steele, Sir Richard 1672-1729
Aitken, George A. *The Life of Richard Steele.* London: Isbister, 1889; 2 vols.
Connely, Willard. *Sir Richard Steele.* New York: Scribner, 1934.
Dobson, Austin. *Richard Steele.* New York: Appleton, 1886.
Loftis, John. *Steele at Drury Lane.* Berkeley: Univ. of California, 1952.
Montgomery, Henry R. *Memoirs of the Life and Writings of Sir Richard Steele.* Edinburgh: W. P. Nimmo, 1865; 2 vols.
Steele, Richard. *Mr. Steele's Apology for Himself and His Writings; Occasioned by His Expulsion from the House of Commons.* London: Burleigh, 1714.
—. *The Epistolary Correspondence of Sir Richard Steele.* London: John Nichols, 1809.
— (ed. by R. Brimley Johnson). *The Letters of Richard Steele.* London: Lane, 1927.
— (ed. by Rae Blanchard). *The Correspondence of Richard Steele.* London: Oxford Univ., 1941.
Winton, Calhoun. *Captain Steele; The Early Career of Richard Steele.* Baltimore: Johns Hopkins, 1964.
—. *Sir Richard Steele, M. P.; The Later Career.* Baltimore: Johns Hopkins, 1970.

Stein, Gertrude 1874-1946
Anderson, Sherwood (ed. by Ray Lewis White). *Sherwood Anderson/Gertrude Stein: Correspondence and Personal Essays.* Chapel Hill: Univ. of North Carolina, 1972.
Brinnin, John M. *The Third Rose—Gertrude*

Stein and Her World. New York: Grove, 1961.
Greenfeld, Howard. *Gertrude Stein*. New York: Crown, 1973.
Hoffman, Frederick. *Gertrude Stein*. Minneapolis: Univ. of Minnesota, 1961.
Mellow, James R. *Charmed Circle: Gertrude Stein & Company*. New York: Praeger, 1974.
Rogers, William G. *When This You See Remember Me; Gertrude Stein in Person*. New York: Rinehart, 1948.
Sprigge, Elizabeth. *Gertrude Stein: Her Life and Work*. London: Hamilton, 1957.
Stein, Gertrude. *The Autobiography of Alice B. Toklas*. New York: Harcourt, Brace, 1933.
—. *Wars I Have Seen*. New York: Random House, 1945.
—. *Everybody's Autobiography*. New York: Random House, 1937.
Toklas, Alice B. *What Is Remembered*. New York: Holt, Rinehart & Winston, 1963.
— (ed. by Edward Burns). *Staying on Alone; Letters of Alice B. Toklas*. New York: Liveright, 1973.
Wilson, Ellen. *They Named Me Gertrude Stein*. New York: Farrar, Straus & Giroux, 1973.

Stern, Ernest 1876-1954
Stern, Ernest. *My Life, My Stage*. London: Gollancz, 1951.

Stirling, Fanny 1813-1895
Allen, Percy. *The Stage Life of Mrs. Stirling*. London: T. F. Unwin, 1922.

Stirling, W. Edward 1891-1948
Stirling, W. Edward. *Something to Declare; The Story of My English Theatre Abroad*. London: Muller, 1942.

Stoddart, James Henry 1827-1907
Stoddart, J. H. *Recollections of a Player*. New York: Century, 1902.

Stone, Fred 1873-1959
Stone, Fred. *Rolling Stone*. New York: Whittlesey House, 1945.

Strange, Michael 1890-1950
Strange, Michael. *Who Tells Me True*. New York: Scribner, 1940.

Stratton, Charles Sherwood 1838-1883
See: Thumb, Tom.

Streisand, Barbra 1942-
Jordan, Rene. *I'm the Greatest Star; The Barbra Streisand Story: An Unauthorized Biography*. New York: Putnam, 1975.
Spada, James. *Barbra, the First Decade: The Films and Career of Barbra Streisand*. Secaucus, N.J.: Citadel, 1974.

Strindberg, August 1849-1912
Campbell, George A. *Strindberg*. London: Duckworth, 1933.
Collis, John S. *Marriage and Genius; Strindberg and Tolstoy, Studies in Tragi-Comedy*. London: Cassell, 1963.
Klaf, Franklin S. *Strindberg; The Origin of Psychology in Modern Drama*. New York: Citadel, 1963.
Lamm, Martin (trans. by Harry G. Carlson). *August Strindberg*. New York: Blom, 1971.
Lind-af-Hageby, Lizzy. *August Strindberg; The Spirit of Revolt*. London: S. Paul, 1913.
—. *August Strindberg; A Study*. London: A. K. Press, 1928.
McGill, Vivian J. *August Strindberg; The Bedeviled Viking*. New York: Brentano, 1930.
Mortensen, Brita Maud and Downs, Brian W. *Strindberg; An Introduction to His Life and Work*. Cambridge: Univ. Press, 1949.
Sprigge, Elizabeth. *The Strange Life of August Strindberg*. New York: Macmillan, 1949.
Steene, Birgitta. *The Greatest Fire; A Study of August Strindberg*. Carbondale: Southern Illinois Univ., 1973.
Strindberg, Freda (trans. by Ethel T. Scheffauer). *Marriage with Genius*. London: Cape, 1937.
Strindberg, August. *Legends; Autobiographical Sketches*. London: Melrose, 1912.
— (trans. by Claud Field). *The Inferno*. New York: Putnam, 1913.
— (trans. by Arvid Paulson). *Letters of Strindberg to Harriet Bosse*. New York: Grosset & Dunlap, 1959.
— (trans. by Mary Sandbach). *Inferno*. London: Hutchinson, 1962.
— (ed. by Torsten Eklund; trans. by Mary Sandbach). *From an Occult Diary; Marriage with Harriet Bosse*. New York: Hill & Wang, 1965.
— (rev. and ed. by Evert Sprinchorn). *A Madman's Defense*. New York: Anchor, 1967.
— (trans. by Arvid Paulson). *Days of Loneliness*. New York: Phaedra, 1971.
Uddgren, Gustaf (trans. by Axel John Uppvall). *Strindberg, the Man*. New York: Haskell House, 1972.
Uppvall, Axel Johan. *August Strindberg; A Psychoanalytic Study with Special Reference to the Oedipus Complex*. New York: Haskell House, 1970.

Sullivan, Arthur 1842-1900
Allen, Reginald with D'Luhy, Gale R. *Sir Arthur Sullivan: Composer & Personage . . . Catalog of an Exhibition, 13 Feb. to 20 April 1975*. New York: Pierpont Morgan Library, 1975.
Findon, Benjamin W. *Sir Arthur Sullivan; His Life and Music*. London: Nisbet, 1904.
Lawrence, Arthur. *Sir Arthur Sullivan: Life Story, Letters and Reminiscences*. Chicago: H. S. Stone, 1900.
Sullivan, Herbert and Flower, Newman. *Sir Arthur Sullivan; His Life, Letters & Diaries*. London: Cassell, 1927.
Wells, Walter J. *Souvenir of Sir Arthur Sullivan*. London: Newnes, 1901.
Wyndham, Henry S. *Arthur Seymour Sullivan*. London: Paul, Trench, Trubner, 1926.
Young, Percy M. *Sir Arthur Sullivan*. London: Dent, 1971.
See also: Gilbert, William Schwenk.

Sullivan, Barry 1824-1891
Lawrence, William John. *Barry Sullivan; A Biographical Sketch*. London: W. and G. Baird, 1893.
Sillard, Robert M. *Barry Sullivan and His Contemporaries; A Histrionic Record*. London: T. F. Unwin, 1901.

Sutro, Alfred 1863-1933
Sutro, Alfred. *Celebrities and Simple Souls*. London: Duckworth, 1933.

Svoboda, Josef 1920-
Burian, Jarka. *The Scenography of Joseph Svoboda*. Middletown, Conn.: Wesleyan Univ., 1971.

Swaffer, Hannen 1879-1962
Driberg, Tom. *"Swaff": The Life and Times of Hannen Swaffer*. London: Macdonald, 1974.

Swears, Herbert ?-1946
Swears, Herbert. *When All's Said and Done*. London: Bles, 1937.

Synge, John Millington 1871-1909
Bourgeoise, Maurice. *John Millington Synge and the Irish Theatre*. London: Constable, 1913.
Corkery, Daniel. *Synge, and Anglo-Irish Literature; A Study*. London: Longmans, 1931.
Coxhead, Elizabeth. *J. M. Synge and Lady Gregory*. London: Longmans, Green, 1962.
Gerstenberger, Donna. *John Millington Synge*. New York: Twayne, 1965.
Greene, David H. and Stephens, Edward M. *J. M. Synge, 1871-1909*. New York: Macmillan, 1959.
Johnston, Denis. *John Millington Synge*. New York: Columbia Univ., 1965.
Masefield, John. *John M. Synge: A Few Personal Recollections, with Biographical Notes*. New York: Macmillan, 1915.
Skelton, Robin. *J. M. Synge and His World*. New York: Viking, 1971.
Stephens, Edward. *My Uncle John: Edward Stephens's Life of J. M. Synge*. New York: Oxford Univ., 1974.
Strong, Leonard A. G. *John Millington Synge*. London: Allen & Unwin, 1941.
Synge, John Millington. *The Autobiography of J. M. Synge*. Chester Springs, Pa.: Dufour Editions, 1965.
— (ed. by Alan Price). *The Autobiography of J. M. Synge*. London: Oxford Univ., 1965.
— (ed. by Ann Saddlemyer). *Letters to Molly; John Millington Synge to Maire O'Neill, 1906-1909*. Cambridge: Harvard Univ., 1971.
—. *My Wallet of Photographs: The Collected Photographs of J. M. Synge*. London: Oxford Univ., 1971.
— (comp. by Ann Saddlemyer). *Some Letters of John M. Synge to Lady Gregory and W. B. Yeats*. Dublin: Cuala Press, 1971.
Synge, Samuel. *Letters to My Daughter. Memories of John Millington Synge*. Dublin: Talbot, 1931.
Yeats, William B. *Synge and the Ireland of His Time*. Dublin: Cuala Press, 1911.

Talma, Francois Joseph 1763-1826
Collins, Herbert F. *Talma*. London: Faber & Faber, 1964.

Taylor, Charles A. ?-1942
Taylor, Dwight. *Blood-and-Thunder*. New York: Atheneum, 1962.

Taylor, Laurette 1884-1946
Courtney, Marguerite. *Laurette*. New York: Rinehart, 1955.
Taylor, Laurette. *"The Greatest of These—."* New York: Doran, 1918.

Taylor, Tom 1817-1880
Tolles, Winton. *Tom Taylor and the Victorian Drama*. New York: Columbia Univ., 1940.

Tellegen, Lou 1883-1934
Tellegen, Lou. *Women Have Been Kind*. New York: Vanguard, 1931.

Tempest, Marie 1866-1942
Bolitho, Hector. *Marie Tempest*. London: Cobden-Sanderson, 1936.

Terriss, William 1847-1897
Smythe, Arthur J. *The Life of William Terriss, Actor.* Westminster: Constable, 1898.

Terry, Ellen 1848-1928
Craig, Edward Gordon. *Ellen Terry and Her Secret Self.* New York: Dutton, 1932.
Hiatt, Charles. *Ellen Terry and Her Impersonations.* London: G. Bell, 1898.
Manvell, Roger. *Ellen Terry.* New York: Putnam, 1968.
Pemberton, T. Edgar. *Ellen Terry and Her Sisters.* New York: Dodd, Mead, 1902.
Scott, Clement. *Ellen Terry.* New York: F. A. Stokes, 1900.
St. John, Christopher. *Ellen Terry.* New York: Lane, 1907.
Terry, Ellen. *The Heart of Ellen Terry.* London: Mills & Boon, 1928.
— (ed. by Christopher St. John). *Ellen Terry and Bernard Shaw; A Correspondence.* London: Reinhardt & Evans, 1949.

Thomas, Augustus 1857-1934
Thomas, Augustus. *The Print of My Remembrance.* New York: Scribner, 1922.

Thomas, Brandon 1856-1914
Brandon-Thomas, Jevan. *Charley's Aunt's Father.* London: Douglas Saunders, with MacGibbon and Kee, 1955.

Thompson, Alexander M. 1861-1948
Thompson, Alex. M. *Here I Lie.* London: Routledge, 1937.

Thorndike, Sybil 1882-
Casson, John. *Lewis & Sybil; A Memoir.* London: Collins, 1972.
Sprigge, Elizabeth. *Sybil Thorndike Casson.* London: Gollancz, 1971.
Thorndike, Russell. *Sybil Thorndike.* London: Butterworth, 1929.
Trewin, J. C. *Sybil Thorndike.* London: Rockliff, 1955.

Thurber, James Grover 1894-1961
Bernstein, Burton. *Thurber.* New York: Dodd, Mead, 1975.
Holmes, Charles S. *The Clocks of Columbus; The Literary Career of James Thurber.* New York: Atheneum, 1972.
Morsberger, Robert E. *James Thurber.* New York: Twayne, 1964.
Thurber, James. *The Years with Ross.* Boston: Little, Brown, 1959.

Tilley, Vesta 1864-1952
De Frece, Lady Matilda. *Recollections of Vesta Tilley.* London: Hutchinson, 1934.

Todd, Michael 1907-1958
Cohn, Art. *The Nine Lives of Michael Todd.* New York: Random House, 1958.

Toole, John Lawrence 1830-1906
Toole, John Lawrence. *Reminiscences of J. L. Toole.* London: Hurst & Blackett, 1889.

Travers, Ben 1886-
Travers, Benjamin. *Vale of Laughter.* London: Bles, 1957.

Tree, Herbert Beerbohm 1853-1917
Beerbohm, Max. *Herbert Beerbohm Tree; Some Memories of Him and His Art.* New York: Dutton, 1920.
Cran, Marion. *Herbert Beerbohm Tree.* London: Lane, Bodley Head, 1907.
Pearson, Hesketh. *Beerbohm Tree, His Life and Laughter.* London: Methuen, 1956.

Tree, Viola 1884-1938
Tree, Viola. *Castles in the Air; The Story of My Singing Days.* London: L. & V. Woolf, 1926.

Tucker, Sophie 1884-1966
Tucker, Sophie. *Some of These Days.* Garden City: Doubleday, Doran, 1945.

Turgenev, Ivan Sergeyevich 1818-1883
Garnett, Edward W. *Turgenev.* London: Collins, 1917.
Lloyd, J. A. T. *Two Russian Reformers; Ivan Turgenev, Leo Tolstoy.* New York: Lane, 1911.
—. *Ivan Turgenev.* London: Hale, 1942.
Magarshack, David. *Turgenev; A Life.* London: Faber & Faber, 1954.
Turgenev, Ivan (ed. by E. Halperine-Kaminsky; trans, by Ethel M. Arnold). *Tourgueneff and His French Circle.* London: T. F. Unwin, 1898.
— (trans. by David Magarshack). *Literary Reminiscences and Autobiographical Fragments.* New York: Farrar, Straus & Cudahy, 1958.
— (trans. by Edgar H. Lehrman). *Letters, a Selection.* New York: Knopf, 1961.
— (trans. by Nora Gottlieb and Raymond Chapman). *Letters to an Actress; The Story of Ivan Turgenev and Marya Gavrilovna Savina.* Athens: Ohio Univ., 1973.
Yarmolinsky, Abraham. *Turgenev; The Man, His Art and His Age.* New York: Century, 1926.
Zhitova, Varvara N. (trans. by A. S. Mills). *The Turgenev Family.* London: Harvill, 1947.

Tyler, George C. 1867-1946
Tyler, George C. and Furnas, J. C. *Whatever Goes Up.* Indianapolis: Bobbs-Merrill, 1934.

Ustinov, Peter 1921-
Thomas, Tony. *Ustinov in Focus.* New York: A. S. Barnes, 1971.
Ustinov, Nadia Benois. *Klop and the Ustinov Family.* London: Sidgwick & Jackson, 1973.
Willans, Geoffrey. *Peter Ustinov.* London: Peter Owen, 1957.

Vakhtangov, Eugen V. 1883-1922
Gorchakov, Nikolai M. (trans. by G. Ivanov-Mumjiev). *The Vakhtangov School of Stage Art.* Moscow: Foreign Language Publishing House, 1961.
Simonov, Ruben N. (trans. by Miriam Goldina). *Stanislavsky's Protègé: Eugene Vakhtangov.* New York: DBS Publications, 1969.

Vanbrugh, Irene 1872-1949
Vanbrugh, Irene. *To Tell My Story.* New York: Hutchinson, 1949.

Vanbrugh, Sir John 1664-1726
Harris, Bernard A. *Sir John Vanbrugh.* London: Longmans, 1967.
Whistler, Laurence. *Sir John Vanbrugh, Architect & Dramatist, 1664-1726.* London: Cobden-Sanderson, 1938.

Vanbrugh, Violet 1867-1942
Vanbrugh, Violet. *Dare To Be Wise.* London: Hodder & Stoughton, 1925.

Vandenhoff, George 1820-1884
Vandenhoff, George. *Dramatic Reminiscences; or, Actors and Actresses in England and America.* London: T. W. Copper, 1860.

Van Druten, John 1901-1957
Van Druten, John. *The Way to the Present; A Personal Record.* London: Joseph, 1938.
—. *The Widening Circle; A Personal Search.* New York: Scribner, 1957.

Vega Carpio, Lope Felix de 1562-1635
Flores, Angel. *Lope de Vega; Monster of Nature.* New York: Brentano, 1930.
Hayes, Francis C. *Lope de Vega.* New York: Twayne, 1967.
Holland, H. R. *Some Account of the Life and Writings of Lope Felix de Vega Carpio.* London: Longmans, Hurst, 1806.
Rennert, Hugo Albert. *The Life of Lope de Vega, 1562-1635.* Philadelphia: Campion, 1904.

Veiller, Bayard 1869-1943
Veiller, Bayard. *The Fun I've Had.* New York: Reynal & Hitchcock, 1941.

Vestris, Madame 1797-1856
Appleton, William. *Madame Vestris and the London Stage.* New York: Columbia Univ., 1974.
Pearce, Charles. *Madame Vestris and Her Times.* London: S. Paul, 1923.
Waitzkin, Leo. *The Witch of Wych Street; A Study of the Theatrical Reforms of Madame Vestris.* Cambridge: Harvard Univ., 1933.
Williams, Clifford J. *Madame Vestris.* London: Sidgwick & Jackson, 1973.

Vidal, Gore 1925-
Dick, Bernard F. *The Apostate Angel.* New York: Random House, 1974.
White, Ray L. *Gore Vidal.* New York: Twayne, 1968.

Vincent, Mary Ann 1818-1887
Richardson, James B. *Mrs. James R. Vincent; A Memorial Address. . . .* Cambridge, Mass.: Riverside Press, 1911.
Fiftieth Anniversary of the First Appearance on the Stage of Mrs. J. R. Vincent, Boston's Favorite Actress. Fifty Years of an Actress' Life. Boston: Daly, 1885.

Wagner, Charles L. ?-1956
Wagner, Charles L. *Seeing Stars.* New York: Putnam, 1940.

Walker, Thomas ("Whimsical") 1851-1934
Walker, Whimsical. *From Sawdust to Windsor Castle.* London: S. Paul, 1922.

Wallace, Edgar 1875-1932
Curtis, Robert G. *Edgar Wallace—Each Way.* London: Long, 1932.
Lane, Margaret. *Edgar Wallace, the Biography of a Phenomenon.* New York: Doubleday, Doran, 1939.
Wallace, Ethel King. *Edgar Wallace.* London: Hutchinson, 1932.
Wallace, Edgar. *Edgar Wallace; A Short Autobiography.* London: Hodder & Stoughton, 1929.
—. *My Hollywood Diary; The Last Work of Edgar Wallace.* London: Hutchinson, 1932.

Wallack, James William 1791?-1864
A Sketch of the Life of James William Wallack (Senior), Late Actor and Manager. New York: Morrell, 1865.

Wallack, Lester 1820-1888
Wallack, Lester. *Memories of Fifty Years.* New York: Scribner, 1889.

Ward, Genevieve 1838-1922
Gustafson, Zadel Barnes. *Genevieve Ward.* Boston: James R. Osgood, 1882.
Ward, Genevieve and Whiteing, Richard. *Both Sides of the Curtain.* London: Cassell, 1918.

Warde, Frederick 1851-1935
Warde, Frederick. *Fifty Years of Make-Believe.* New York: International Press Syndicate, 1920.

Wareing, Alfred 1876-1942
Isaac, Winifred F.E.C. *Alfred Wareing.* London: Green Bank Press, 1946.

Warren, William 1812-1888
Life and Memoirs of William Warren. Boston: Daly, 1882.

Waters, Ethel 1900-
Waters, Ethel and Samuels, Charles. *His Eye Is on the Sparrow.* Garden City: Doubleday, 1951.
Waters, Ethel. *To Me It's Wonderful.* New York: Harper & Row, 1972.

Watkins, Harry ?-1894
Skinner, Maud and Otis. *One Man in His Time; The Adventures of H. Watkins, Strolling Player, 1845-1863, from His Journal.* Philadelphia: Univ. of Pennsylvania, 1938.

Weber, Joe 1867-1942
Isman, Felix. *Weber and Fields, Their Tribulations, Triumphs and Their Associates.* New York: Boni & Liveright, 1924.

Webster, Ben 1864-1947
See: Webster, Margaret.

Webster, John 1580?-1625?
Brooke, Rupert. *John Webster and the Elizabethan Drama.* New York: Lane, 1916.
Scott-Kilvert, Ian. *John Webster.* London: Longmans, Green, 1964.

Webster, Margaret 1905-1972
Webster, Margaret. *The Same Only Different: Five Generations of a Great Theatre Family.* New York: Knopf, 1969.
—. *Don't Put Your Daughter on the Stage.* New York: Knopf, 1972.

Wedekind, Frank 1864-1918
Gittleman, Sol. *Frank Wedekind.* New York: Twayne, 1969.

Weiss, Peter 1916-
Best, Otto (trans. by Ursule Molinaro). *Peter Weiss.* New York: Ungar, 1975.
Hilton, Ian. *Peter Weiss: A Search for Affinities.* London: Wolff, 1970.

Welles, Orson 1915-
Bessy, Maurice (trans. by Ciba Vaughan). *Orson Welles.* New York: Crown, 1971.
Cowie, Peter. *A Ribbon of Dreams; The Cinema of Orson Welles.* New York: A. S. Barnes, 1973.
Fowler, Roy Alexander. *Orson Welles.* London: Pendulum, 1946.
McBride, Joseph. *Orson Welles.* New York: Viking, 1972.
Noble, Peter. *The Fabulous Orson Welles.* London: Hutchinson, 1956.

Wemyss, Francis Courtney 1797-1859
Wemyss, Francis Courtney. *Twenty-Six Years of the Life of an Actor and Manager.* New York: Burgess, Stringer, 1847.

Wesker, Arnold 1932-
Hayman, Ronald. *Arnold Wesker.* London: Heinemann, 1970.
Ribalow, Harold U. *Arnold Wesker.* New York: Twayne, 1965.

West, Mae 1893-
West, Mae. *Goodness Had Nothing to Do with It.* Englewood Cliffs, N.J.: Prentice-Hall, 1959.
— (ed. by Joseph Weintraub). *The Wit and Wisdom of Mae West.* New York: Avon, 1970.
—. *On Sex, Health & ESP.* London: W. H. Allen, 1975.

Wharton, John F. 1894-
Wharton, John F. *Life Among the Playwrights; Being Mostly the Story of the Playwrights Producing Company, Inc.* New York: Quadrangle, 1974.

Whiffen, Mrs. Thomas 1845-1936
Whiffen, Mrs. Thomas. *Keeping Off the Shelf.* New York: Dutton, 1928.

Whitty, Dame May 1865-1948
See: Webster, Margaret.

Wilde, Oscar 1854-1900
Brasol, Boris L. *Oscar Wilde, the Man, the Artist, the Martyr.* New York: Scribner, 1938.
Bremont, Anna de. *Oscar Wilde and His Mother; A Memoir.* London: Everett, 1914.
Broad, Lewis. *The Friendships and Follies of Oscar Wilde.* London: Hutchinson, 1954.
Byrne, Patrick. *The Wildes of Merrion Square; The Family of Oscar Wilde.* New York: Staples, 1953.
Cooper, Pritchard, A. H. *Conversations with Oscar Wilde.* London: Allan, 1931.
Croft-Cooke, Rupert. *The Unrecorded Life of Oscar Wilde.* New York: McKay, 1972.
Douglas, Lord Alfred. *Oscar Wilde and Myself.* New York: Duffield, 1914.
—. *My Friendship with Oscar Wilde, Being the Autobiography of Lord Alfred Douglas.* New York: Coventry, 1932.
—. *Oscar Wilde; A Summing-Up.* London: Duckworth, 1940.
Ervine, St. John Greer. *Oscar Wilde; A Present Time Appraisal.* New York: Morrow, 1952.
Fido, Martin. *Oscar Wilde.* New York: Viking, 1973.
Gide, André (trans. by S. Mason). *Oscar Wilde, a Study.* Oxford: Holywell, 1905.
— (trans. by Bernard Frechtman). *Oscar Wilde: In Memoriam (Reminiscences) De Profundis.* New York: Philosophical Library, 1949.
Harris, Frank. *Oscar Wilde; His Life and Confessions, . . . Including the Hitherto Unpublished Full and Final Confession, by Lord Alfred Douglas and My Memories of Oscar Wilde, by Bernard Shaw.* New York: Covici, Friede, 1930.
Holland, Vyvyan. *Son of Oscar Wilde.* New York: Dutton, 1954.
—. *Oscar Wilde, a Pictorial Biography.* New York: Viking, 1960.
Hyde, Harford. *Oscar Wilde; The Aftermath.* London: Methuen, 1963.
Ingleby, Leonard. *Oscar Wilde.* London: T. W. Laurie, 1907.
Jullian, Philippe (trans. by Violet Wyndham). *Oscar Wilde.* New York: Viking, 1969.
Lewis, Lloyd and Smith, Henry J. *Oscar Wilde Discovers America (1882).* New York: Harcourt, 1936.
O'Sullivan, Vincent. *Aspects of Wilde.* New York: Holt, 1936.
Pollard, Percival (ed. and trans.). *In Memoriam, Oscar Wilde, by Ernest La Jeunesse, André Gide and Franz Blei.* Greenwich, Conn.: Literary Collector Press, 1905.
Ransome, Arthur. *Oscar Wilde; A Critical Study.* London: Methuen, 1913.
Renier, Gustaaf J. *Oscar Wilde.* New York: Appleton-Century, 1933.
Sherard, Robert H. *The Life of Oscar Wilde.* New York: Kennerley, 1907.
—. *The Real Oscar Wilde.* London: Laurie, 1915.
—. *Bernard Shaw, Frank Harris & Oscar Wilde.* New York: Greystone, 1937.
Wilde, Oscar (ed. by Robert Ross). *De profundis.* New York: Putnam, 1909.
—. *After Reading: Letters of Oscar Wilde to Robert Ross.* Westminster: Beaumont, 1921.
—. *After Berneval; Letters of Oscar Wilde to Robert Ross.* Westminster: Beaumont, 1922.
—. *Some Letters of Oscar Wilde to Alfred Douglas, 1892-1897 (Heretofore Unpublished).* San Francisco: J. H. Nash, 1924.
— (ed. by John Rothenstein). *Sixteen Letters from Oscar Wilde.* London: Faber & Faber, 1930.
—. *De Profundis, Being the First Complete and Accurate Version of "Epistola: In Carcere et Vinculis," the Last Prose Work in English of Oscar Wilde.* New York: Philosophical Library, 1950.
— (ed. by Rupert Hart-Davis). *Letters.* New York: Harcourt, Brace & World, 1962.
Winwar, Frances. *Oscar Wilde and the Yellow Nineties.* New York: Harper, 1958.
Woodcock, George. *The Paradox of Oscar Wilde.* New York: Boardman, 1950.

Wilder, Alec 1907-
Wilder, Alec. *Letters I Never Mailed; Clues to a Life.* Boston: Little, Brown, 1975.

Wilder, Thornton 1897-
Burbank, Rex. *Thornton Wilder.* New York: Twayne, 1961.
Goldstone, Richard H. *Thornton Wilder: An Intimate Portrait.* New York: Dutton, 1975.
Grebanier, Bernard. *Thornton Wilder.* Minneapolis: Univ. of Minnesota, 1964.

Wilkinson, Tate 1739-1803
Wilkinson, Tate. *Memoirs of His Own Life.* York: Wilson, Spence & Mawman, 1790.
—. *The Wandering Patentee.* York: Wilson, Spence & Mawman, 1795.

Wilks, Robert 1665-1732
Curll, Edmund. *The Life of that Eminent Comedian, Robert Wilks, Esq.* London: Curll, 1733.

Williams, Bert 1876-1922
Charters, Ann. *Nobody: The Story of Bert Williams.* New York: Macmillan, 1970.
Rowland, Mabel (ed.). *Bert Williams, Son of Laughter; A Symposium . . .* New York: English Crafters, 1923.

Williams, Bransby 1870-1961
Williams, Bransby. *An Actor's Story.* London: Chapman & Hall, 1909.
—. *Bransby Williams.* London: Hutchinson, 1954.

Williams, Emlyn 1905-

Findlater, Richard. *Emlyn Williams; An Illustrated Study of His Work.* London: Rockliff, 1956.
Williams, Emlyn. *George: An Early Autobiography.* New York: Random House, 1961.
—. *Emlyn: An Early Autobiography, 1927-1935.* New York: Viking, 1974.

Williams, Tennessee 1914-
Donahue, Francis. *The Dramatic World of Tennessee Williams.* New York: Ungar, 1964.
Falk, Signi L. *Tennessee Williams.* New York: Twayne, 1962.
Maxwell, Gilbert. *Tennessee Williams and Friends.* Cleveland: World, 1965.
Nelson, Benjamin. *Tennessee Williams: The Man and His Work.* New York: Obolensky, 1961.
Steen, Mike. *A Look at Tennessee Williams.* New York: Hawthorn, 1969.
Tischler, Nancy M. *Tennessee Williams: Rebellious Puritan.* New York: Citadel, 1961.
Weales, Gerald. *Tennessee Williams.* Minneapolis: Univ. of Minnesota, 1965.
Williams, Edwina Dakin, as told to Lucy Freeman. *Remember Me to Tom.* New York: Putnam, 1963.

Williamson, James Cassius 1845-1913
Dicker, Ian G. *J.C.W.—A Short Biography of James Cassius Williamson.* Sydney: Elizabeth Tudor Press, 1974.
Tait, Viola. *A Family of Brothers: The Taits and J. C. Williamson; A Theatre History.* Melbourne: Heinemann, 1971.

Wills, W. G. 1828-1891
Wills, Freeman. *W. G. Wills, Dramatist and Painter.* London: Longmans, Green, 1898.

Willson, Meredith 1902-
Willson, Meredith. *And There I Stood with My Piccolo.* Garden City: Doubleday, 1948.
—. *Eggs I Have Laid.* New York: Holt, 1955.
—. *"But He Doesn't Know the Territory."* New York: Putnam, 1959.

Wilson, Albert Edward 1885-1960
Wilson, Albert E. *Playgoer's Pilgrimage.* New York: S. Paul, 1948.

Wilson, Edmund 1895-1972
Wilson, Edmund. *A Piece of My Mind; Reflection at Sixty.* New York: Farrar, Straus & Cudahy, 1956.
—. *A Prelude; Landscapes, Characters and Conversations from the Earlier Years of My Life.* New York: Farrar, Straus & Giroux, 1967.
—. *Upstate; Records and Recollections of Northern New York.* New York: Farrar, Straus & Giroux, 1971.
— (ed. by Leon Edel). *The Twenties.* New York: Farrar, Straus & Giroux, 1975.

Wilson, Francis 1854-1935
Wilson, Francis. *Francis Wilson's Life of Himself.* Boston: Houghton Mifflin, 1924.

Wilson, Sandy 1924-
Wilson, Sandy. *I Could Be Happy.* London: Michael Joseph, 1975.

Winchell, Walter 1897-1972
McKelway, St. Clair. *Gossip; The Life and Times of Walter Winchell.* New York: Viking, 1940.
Stuart, Lyle. *The Secret Life of Walter Winchell.* New York: Boars' Head Books, 1953.
Thomas, Bob. *Winchell.* Garden City: Doubleday, 1971.
Weiner, Edward. *Let's Go to Press; A Biography of Walter Winchell.* New York: Putnam, 1955.

Winston, James 1773-1843
Winston, James (ed. by Alfred L. Nelson and Gilbert B. Cross). *Drury Lane Journal: Selections from James Winston's Diaries, 1819-1827.* London: Society for Theatre Research, 1974.

Wodehouse, Pelham G. 1881-1975
Cazalet-Keir, Thelma (ed.). *Homage to P. G. Wodehouse.* London: Barrie & Jenkins, 1973.
French, Robert B.D. *P. G. Wodehouse.* New York: Barnes & Noble, 1967.
Jasen, David A. *P. G. Wodehouse: A Portrait of a Master.* New York: Mason and Lipscomb, 1974.
Wodehouse, P. G. *Performing Flea; A Self-portrait in Letters.* London: Jenkins, 1953.
—. *America, I Like You.* New York: Simon & Schuster, 1956.
—. *Over Seventy: An Autobiography with Digressions.* London: Jenkins, 1957.
— and Bolton, Guy. *Bring on the Girls; The Improbable Story of Our Life in Musical Comedy, with Pictures to Prove It.* New York: Simon & Schuster, 1953.
Wind, Herbert W. *The World of P. G. Wodehouse.* New York: Praeger, 1972.

Woffington, Margaret ("Peg") 1720-1760
Daly, Augustin. *Woffington.* Philadelphia: Globe Printing House, 1888.
Dunbar, Janet. *Peg Woffington and Her World.* Boston: Houghton Mifflin, 1968.
Lucey, Janet C. *Lovely Peggy; The Life and Times of Margaret Woffington.* Watford, Herts: Hurst & Blackett, 1952.
Molloy, Joseph F. *The Life and Adventures of Peg Woffington.* London: Downey, 1897.

Wolfit, Donald 1902-1968
Harwood, Ronald. *Sir Donald Wolfit, C.B.E.: His Life and Work in the Unfashionable Theatre.* London: Secker & Warburg, 1971.
Wolfit, Donald. *First Interval.* London: Odhams, 1954.

Wood, Peggy 1894-
Wood, Peggy. *Actors—and People; Both Sides of the Footlights.* New York: Appleton, 1930.
—. *How Young You Look, Memoirs of a Middle-Sized Actress.* New York: Farrar & Rinehart, 1941.
—. *Arts and Flowers.* New York: Morrow, 1963.

Wood, William Burke 1779-1861
Wood, William B. *Personal Recollections of the Stage; Embracing Notices of Actors, Authors, and Auditors, During a Period of Forty Years.* Philadelphia: H. C. Baird, 1855.

Woollcott, Alexander 1887-1943
Adams, Samuel H. *A. Woollcott, His Life and His World.* New York: Reynal & Hitchcock, 1945.
Hoyt, Edwin Palmer. *Alexander Woollcott: The Man Who Came to Dinner.* New York: Abelard-Schuman, 1968.
Philistina. *Alec the Great, an Account of the Curious Life and Extraordinary Opinions of the Late Alexander Woollcott.* New York: Avalon, 1943.
Wollcott, Alexander (ed. by Beatrice Kaufman and Joseph Hennessey). *The Letters of Alexander Woollcott.* New York: Viking, 1944.

Worthing, Frank 1866-1910
Winter, William J. (ed.). *In Memory of Frank Worthing, Actor, . . .* New York: 1910.

Wright, Richard 1908-1960
Bakish, David. *Richard Wright.* New York: Ungar, 1973.
Bone, Robert A. *Richard Wright.* Minneapolis: Univ. of Minnesota, 1969.
Fabre, Michel (trans. by Isabel Barzun). *The Unfinished Quest of Richard Wright.* New York: Morrow, 1973.
Kinnamon, Keneth. *The Emergence of Richard Wright; A Study in Literature and Society.* Urbana: Univ. of Illinois, 1973.
McCall, Dan. *The Example of Richard Wright.* New York: Harcourt, Brace & World, 1969.
Senna, Carl. *Black Boy; Notes . . .* Lincoln, Neb.: Cliff's Notes, 1971.
Webb, Constance. *Richard Wright; A Biography.* New York: Putnam, 1968.
Williams, John A. *The Most Native of Sons; A Biography of Richard Wright.* Garden City: Doubleday, 1970.
Wright, Richard. *Black Boy, a Record of Childhood and Youth.* Cleveland: World, 1945.

Wycherley, William 1640-1716
Connely, Willard. *Brawny Wycherley; First Master in English Modern Comedy.* New York: Scribner, 1930.
Gildon, Charles. *Memoirs of the Life of William Wycherley, Esq; with a Character of His Writings.* London: Curll, 1718.
Vernon, Paul F. *William Wycherley.* London: Longmans, Green, 1965.

Wyndham, Charles 1837-1919
Pemberton, T. Edgar. *Sir Charles Wyndham, a Biography.* London: Hutchinson, 1904.
Shore, Florence T. *Sir Charles Wyndham.* London: Lane, 1908.

Wynn, Keenan 1916-
Wynn, Keenan, as told to James Brough. *Ed Wynn's Son.* Garden City: Doubleday, 1959.

Yeats, William Butler 1865-1939
Bushrui, Suheil B. and Munro, J. M. (ed.). *Images and Memories; A Pictorial Record of the Life and Work of W. B. Yeats.* Beirut: Dar El-Mashreq, 1970.
Cowell, Raymond. *W. B. Yeats.* London: Evans, 1969.
Ellmann, Richard. *Yeats, the Man and the Masks.* New York: Dutton, 1948.
Fraser, George S. *W. B. Yeats.* London: Longmans, Green, 1954.
Gibbon, Monk. *The Masterpiece and the Man; Yeats as I Knew Him.* London: Hart-Davis, 1959.
Gogarty, Oliver S. *William Butler Yeats: A Memoir.* Dublin: Dolmen, 1963.
Gwynn, Stephen L. (ed.). *Scattering Branches; Tributes to the Memory of W. B. Yeats.* New York: Macmillan, 1940.
Harper, George M. *Yeats's Golden Dawn.* New York: Barnes & Noble, 1974.

Hone, Joseph Maunsell. *W. B. Yeats, 1865-1939.* New York: Macmillan, 1943.
—. *William Butler Yeats; The Poet of Contemporary Ireland.* Dublin: Maunsel, 1915.
Jeffares, A. Norman and Cross, K. G. W. *In Excited Reverie; A Centenary Tribute to William Butler Yeats, 1865-1939.* London: Macmillan, 1965.
Jeffares, A. Norman. *W. B. Yeats, Man and Poet.* New Haven: Yale Univ., 1949.
Krans, Horatio. *William Butler Yeats, and the Irish Literary Revival.* New York: McClure, Phillips, 1904.
Marcus, Phillip L. *Yeats and the Beginning of the Irish Renaissance.* Ithaca: Cornell Univ., 1970.
Masefield, John. *Some Memories of W. B. Yeats.* New York: Macmillan, 1940.
Menon, V. K. Narayana. *The Development of William Butler Yeats.* Edinburgh: Oliver & Boyd, 1942.
Orel, Harold. *The Development of William Butler Yeats, 1885-1900.* Lawrence: Univ. of Kansas, 1968.
Pollock, John H. *William Butler Yeats.* London: Duckworth, 1935.
Rajan, Balachandra. *W. B. Yeats, a Critical Introduction.* London: Hutchinson Univ., 1965.
Ronsley, Joseph. *Yeats's Autobiography; Life as Symbolic Pattern.* Cambridge, Mass.: Harvard Univ., 1968.
Tindall, William Y. *W. B. Yeats.* New York: Columbia Univ., 1966.
Ure, Peter. *Yeats, the Playwright.* New York: Barnes & Noble, 1963.
Yeats, William Butler. *Reveries over Childhood and Youth.* New York: Macmillan, 1916.
—. *The Trembling of the Veil.* London: T. W. Laurie, 1922.
—. *Dramatis Personae, 1896-1902.* New York: Macmillan, 1936.
—. *The Autobiography of William Butler Yeats, Consisting of: Reveries over Childhood and Youth, The Trembling of the Veil, and Dramatis Personae.* New York: Macmillan, 1938.
—. *Pages from a Diary Written in Nineteen Hundred and Thirty.* Dublin: Cuala Press, 1944.
— (ed. by Roger McHugh). *Letters to Katherine Tynan.* New York: McMullen, 1953.
— (ed. by Ursula Bridge). *W. B. Yeats and T. Sturge Moore: Their Correspondence, 1901-1937.* London: Routledge & Paul, 1953.
— (ed. by Allan Wade). *Letters.* London: Hart-Davis, 1954.
— (ed. by Roger McHugh). *Ah, Sweet Dancer: W. B. Yeats, Margot Ruddock; a Correspondence.* New York: Macmillan, 1971.
— (ed. by Denis Donoghue). *Memoirs.* New York: Macmillan, 1973.

Young, Charles Mayne 1777-1856

Young, Julian C. *A Memoir of Charles Mayne Young, Tragedian.* New York: Macmillan, 1871.

Youngman, Henny 1906-

Youngman, Henny (as confessed to Carroll, Carroll). *Take My Wife . . . Please! My Life and Laughs.* New York: Putnam, 1973.

Yurka, Blanche 1893-1974

Yurka, Blanche. *Dear Audience.* Englewood Cliffs, N.J.: Prentice-Hall, 1959.
—. *Bohemian Girl: Blanche Yurka's Theatrical Life.* Athens: Ohio Univ., 1970.

Zangwill, Israel 1864-1926

Adams, Elsie. *Israel Zangwill.* New York: Twayne, 1971.
Leftwich, Joseph. *Israel Zangwill.* London: Clarke, 1956.
Wohlgelernter, Maurice. *Israel Zangwill; A Study.* New York: Columbia Univ., 1964.

Ziegfeld, Florenz 1869-1932

Cantor, Eddie and Freedman, David. *Ziegfeld, the Great Glorifier.* New York: A. H. King, 1934.
Carter, Randolph. *The World of Flo Ziegfeld.* New York: Praeger, 1974.
Higham, Charles. *Ziegfeld.* Chicago: Regnery, 1972.
Ziegfeld, Patricia. *The Ziegfelds' Girl: Confessions of an Abnormally Happy Childhood.* Boston: Little, Brown, 1964.

Zola, Emile 1840-1902

Bernard, Marc (trans. by Jean M. Leblon). *Zola.* New York: Grove, 1960.
Carter, Lawson A. *Zola and the Theatre.* New Haven: Yale, 1963.
Friedman, Lee M. *Zola & the Dreyfus Case; His Defense of Liberty and Its Enduring Significance.* Boston: Beacon, 1937.
Grant, Elliott M. *Emile Zola.* New York: Twayne, 1966.
Hemmings, F. W. *Emile Zola.* Oxford: Clarendon, 1966.
Josephson, Matthew. *Zola and His Time; The History of His Martial Career in Letters.* New York: Macaulay, 1928.
Sherard, Robert H. *Emile Zola; A Biographical & Critical Study.* London: Chatto & Windus, 1893.
The Trial of Emile Zola; Continuing M. Zola's Letter to President Faure Relating to the Dreyfus Case, and a Full Report of the Fifteen Days' Proceedings in the Assize Court of the Seine, Including Testimony of Witnesses and Speeches of Counsel. New York: B. R. Tucker, 1898.
Vizetelly, Ernest A. *With Zola in England. A Story of Exile.* London: Chatto & Windus, 1899.
—. *Emile Zola, Novelist and Reformer; An Account of His Life & Work.* London: Lane, 1904.
Wilson, Angus. *Emile Zola; An Introductory Study of His Novels.* London: Secker & Warburg, 1952.

Zuckmayer, Karl 1896-

Zuckmayer, Karl (trans. by E. R. Hapgood). *Second Wind.* London: Harrap, 1941.
— (trans. by Richard and Clara Winston). *A Part of Myself.* New York: Harcourt, Brace, Jovanovich, 1970.

Zweig, Stefan 1881-1942

Allday, Elizabeth. *Stefan Zweig; A Critical Biography.* Chicago: J. P. O'Hara, 1972.
Arens, Hanns (ed.). (trans. by Christobel Fowler). *Stefan Zweig; A Tribute to His Life and Work.* London: W. H. Allen, 1951.
Prater, D. A. *European of Yesterday; A Biography of Stefan Zweig.* Oxford: Clarendon, 1972.
Romains, Jules (trans. by James Whitall). *Stefan Zweig, Great European.* New York: Viking, 1941.
Zweig, Friderike. *Stefan Zweig.* New York: Crowell, 1946.
Zweig, Stefan. *The World of Yesterday, an Autobiography.* New York: Viking, 1943.

Necrology

A

AABEL, Hauk
Actor
b. Unknown
d. Oslo, Norway, Dec. 1961

AANRUD, Hans
Novelist, Playwright
b. Unknown, 1864
d. Oslo, Norway, Jan. 9, 1953, Age 89

AARONS, Alexander A.
Producer
b. Philadelphia, PA, 1891
d. Beverly Hills, CA, March 15, 1943, Age 52

AARONS, Alfred E.
Producer, Composer
b. Philadelphia, PA, Nov. 16, 1865
d. New York, NY, Nov. 16, 1936, Age 71

AARONSON, Irving
Bandleader, Composer
b. Unknown, 1895
d. Hollywood, CA, March 10, 1963, Age 68

AASEN, John
Performer
b. Unknown, 1887
d. Mendocino, CA, Aug. 1, 1938, Age 51

ABARBANELL, Lina
Performer, Producer
b. Berlin, Germany, Feb. 3, 1880
d. New York, NY, Jan. 6, 1963, Age 82

ABBE, Charles S.
Performer
b. Windham, CT, 1859
d. Norwalk, CT, June 6, 1932, Age 73

ABBEY, Henry Edwin
Manager
b. Akron, OH, June 27, 1846
d. New York, NY, Oct. 17, 1896, Age 50

ABBEY, May Evers (Mrs. George Lessey)
Performer
b. Hartford, CT, 1872
d. New York, NY, Aug. 20, 1952, Age 80

ABBOTT, Al
Performer
b. Unknown, 1884
d. Reseda, CA, Sept. 4, 1962, Age 78

ABBOTT, Bessie
Prima donna
b. Riverside, NY, 1877
d. New York, NY, Feb. 9, 1919, Age 42

ABBOTT, Bud (William A. Abbott)
Actor
b. Asbury Park, NJ, Oct. 2, 1898
d. Woodland Hills, CA, April 25, 1974, Age 75

ABBOTT, C.
Performer
b. Unknown, 1726
d. Knottingley (near Ferrybridge), Aug. 8, 1817, Age 89

ABBOTT, Clara Barnes
Musical director
b. Chicago, IL, 1874
d. Philadelphia, PA, Aug. 28, 1956, Age 82

ABBOTT, Dolly (Emily Horn) (Mrs. H. Harrington)
Performer
b. Cleveland, OH, 1887
d. Hartford, CT, May 31, 1955, Age 68

ABBOTT, Dorothy L.
Performer
b. Covington, KY, 1886
d. Covington, KY, Apr. 12, 1937, Age 51

ABBOTT, Edward B.
Performer
b. Unknown, 1882
d. Atlantic City, NJ, Nov. 24, 1932, Age 50

ABBOTT, Edward S. (Edward S. Sanders)
Performer
b. Anson, TX, 1914
d. New York, NY, Dec. 21, 1936, Age 22

ABBOTT, Emma
Performer
b. Chicago, IL, Dec. 9, 1850
d. Salt Lake City, UT, Jan. 12, 1891, Age 40

ABBOTT, Harry
Press Representative
b. Unknown, 1861
d. New York, NY, March 9, 1942, Age 81

ABBOTT, Marion
Performer
b. Danville, KY, 1866
d. Philadelphia, PA, Jan. 15, 1937, Age 71

ABBOTT, Nancy Ann
Actress, Doll designer and manufacturer
b. San Francisco, CA, 1901
d. San Mateo, CA, Aug. 10, 1964, Age 63

ABBOTT, Paul
Performer
b. Unknown
d. Unknown, July 1872

ABBOTT, William
Actor
b. England, 1789
d. U.S.A., 1843, Age 54

ABBOTT, Yarnell
Painter, Writer, Lecturer
b. Philadelphia, PA, 1871
d. Philadelphia, PA, June 24, 1938, Age 67

ABDUSHELLI, Zurab
Announcer
b. Georgia, Russia, 1913
d. Washington, DC, May 30, 1957, Age 44

ABEL, Alfred
Actor
b. Unknown, 1865
d. Berlin, Germany, Dec. 12, 1937, Age 72

ABEL, Neal
Performer
b. Unknown, 1882
d. Los Angeles, CA, Dec. 2, 1952, Age 70

ABELES, Edward S.
Actor
b. St. Louis, MO, Nov. 4, 1869
d. New York, NY, July 10, 1919, Age 49

ABINGDON, William L. (William Lepper)
Actor
b. Towchester, Northamptonshire, England, May 2, 1859
d. New York, NY, May 18, 1918, Age 59

ABINGTON, Frances (Frances Barton)
Actress
b. England, 1731
d. London, England, March 4, 1815, Age 83

ABORN, Milton
Producer
b. Marysville, CA, Unknown
d. New York, NY, Nov. 12, 1933, Age 69

ABORN, Sargent
Producer, Music publisher
b. Unknown
d. New Rochelle, NY, Feb. 6, 1956, Age 89

ABRANCHES, Aura (Mrs. Joaquin Grijo)
Actress, Playwright
b. Unknown
d. Lisbon, Portugal, March 23, 1962, Age 67

ACCIUS, Lucius
Playwright
b. Unknown, c170 B.C.
d. Unknown, 86 B.C.

ACHARD, Marcel
Playwright, Director
b. Ste.-Foy-les-Lyon, France, July 5, 1900
d. Unknown, Sept. 4, 1974, Age 74

ACHURCH, Janet
Actress, Producer
b. Unknown, Jan. 17, 1864
d. Unknown, Sept. 11, 1916, Age 52

ACKERMAN, Irene
Performer, Writer
b. New York, NY, Unknown
d. Mt. Vernon, NY, Nov. 5, 1916, Age 45

ACKERMAN, P. Dodd Sr.
Designer
b. Florida, Unknown
d. Ft. Myers, FL, Jan. 5, 1963, Age 87

ACKERMANN, Charlotte
Actress
b. Unknown, 1757
d. Unknown, 1774, Age 17

ACKERMANN, Dorothea
Actress
b. Unknown, 1752
d. Unknown, 1821

ACKERMANN, Konrad Ernst
Actor
b. Unknown, 1710
d. Unknown, 1771

ACTMAN, Irving
Musician, Composer, Conductor
b. New York, NY, June 2, 1907
d. New York, NY, Sept. 24, 1967, Age 60

ADAIR, Jean (Violet McNaughton)
Actress
b. Hamilton, Ontario, CAN, Unknown
d. New York, NY, May 11, 1953, Age 80

ADAMOV, Arthur
Playwright
b. Caucasus, Russia, 1908
d. Paris, France, March 16, 1970, Age 61

ADAMS, Abigail
Actress
b. Unknown
d. Beverly Hills, CA, Feb. 13, 1955, Age 37

ADAMS, Alice Baldwin (Mrs. Burton Adams)
Actress
b. Unknown
d. Englewood, NJ, Feb. 11, 1936, Age 83

ADAMS, Dr. Joseph Quincy
Shakespearean scholar, Educator
b. Greenville, SC, March 23, 1881
d. Washington, DC, Nov. 10, 1946, Age 65

ADAMS, Edwin
Actor
b. Medford, MA, Feb. 3, 1834
d. Philadelphia, PA, Oct. 25, 1877, Age 43

ADAMS, Frank R.
Librettist, Lyricist, Journalist
b. Unknown
d. White Lake, MI, Oct. 8, 1963, Age 80

ADAMS, Frank Steward
Theatre organist
b. Unknown
d. White Plains, NY, Feb. 22, 1964, Age 79

ADAMS, Franklin Pierce
Columnist, Performer
b. Chicago, IL, Nov. 15, 1881
d. New York, NY, March 23, 1960, Age 78

ADAMS, Ida
Performer
b. Unknown
d. Unknown, Nov. 1960, Age 72

ADAMS, Jill
Dancer
b. Unknown
d. California-Nevada border (auto crash), March 30, 1964, Age 41

ADAMS, Kathryn
Actress
b. St. Louis, MO, Unknown
d. Hollywood, CA, Feb. 17, 1959, Age 65

ADAMS, Leslie
Actor
b. Stark, FL, Unknown
d. New York, NY, March 26, 1936, Age 49

ADAMS, Lionel
Actor
b. New Orleans, LA, Unknown
d. New York, NY, Aug. 10, 1952, Age 86

ADAMS, Margie (Mrs. H. Wilmot Young)
Actress
b. London, Ontario, CAN, Aug. 4, 1881
d. Ogdensburg, NY, May 27, 1937, Age 55

ADAMS, Maude
Actress
b. Salt Lake City, UT, Nov. 11, 1872
d. Tannersville, NY, July 17, 1953, Age 80

ADAMS, Nicholas (Nathan Anspach)
Actor
b. New York, NY, Unknown
d. New York, NY, Oct. 23, 1935, Age 64

ADAMS, Nick (Nicholas Adamshock)
Actor
b. Nanticoke, PA, July 10, 1935
d. Beverly Hills, CA, Feb. 7, 1968, Age 36

ADAMS, Samuel Hopkins
Author
b. Dunkirk, NY, Jan. 26, 1871
d. Beaufort, SC, Nov. 16, 1958, Age 87

ADAMS, Suzanne
Prima donna
b. Cambridge, MA, Nov. 28, 1872
d. London, England, Feb. 5, 1953, Age 80

ADAMS, W. Davenport
Dramatic critic, Theatre historian
b. Unknown
d. Unknown, July 26, 1904, Age 52

ADDISON, Joseph
Playwright, Poet
b. Milston, Wiltshire, England, May 1, 1672
d. Unknown, June 17, 1719, Age 47

ADE, George
Playwright, Humorist, Journalist
b. Kentland, IN, Feb. 9, 1866
d. Kentland, IN, May 16, 1964, Age 78

ADLER, Adolph J.
Theatre owner-manager
b. Unknown
d. New York, NY, Dec. 24, 1961, Age 77

ADLER, Allen A.
Producer, Writer
b. New York, NY, Unknown
d. New York, NY, Jan. 30, 1964, Age 47

ADLER, Buddy (E. Maurice Adler)
Film executive, Film producer
b. New York, NY, Unknown
d. Hollywood, CA, July 12, 1960, Age 51

ADLER, Felix
Screen writer
b. Unknown
d. Woodland Hills, CA, March 25, 1963, Age 72

ADLER, Frances (Mrs. Joseph Shoengold)
Actress, Teacher
b. New York, NY, 1891
d. New York, NY, Dec. 13, 1964, Age 73

ADLER, Hyman
Actor, Producer
b. Unknown
d. New York, NY, June 27, 1945, Age 62

ADLER, Jacob P.
Actor
b. Odessa, Russia, 1855
d. New York, NY, April 1, 1926, Age 71

ADLER, Sarah (née Levitzka)
Actress
b. Odessa, Russia, Unknown
d. New York, NY, April 28, 1953, Age 95

ADOREE, Renee (Renée de la Fointe)
Actress
b. Lille, France, 1902
d. Sunland, CA, Oct. 5, 1933, Age 31

ADRIAN, Gilbert
Costume designer
b. Waterbury, CT, Unknown
d. Hollywood, CA, Sept. 13, 1959, Age 56

ADRIAN, Max
Actor
b. Ireland, Nov. 1, 1903
d. Surrey, England, Jan. 19, 1973, Age 69

AESCHYLUS
Playwright
b. Eleusis, Attica, 525 B.C.
d. Gela, Sicily, 456 B.C.

AFINOGENOV, Alexander Mikolaevich
Playwright
b. Odessa, Russia, 1904
d. Moscow, U.S.S.R., Nov. 4, 1941, Age 41

AFRIQUE, (Alexander Witkin)
Performer
b. Johannesburg, South Africa, Unknown
d. London, England, Dec. 17, 1961, Age 54

AGAR, Florence Leonide Charvin
Actress
b. Valence, France, Sept. 18, 1836
d. Algeria, Aug. 17, 1891, Age 54

AGAR, Grace Hale
Performer
b. Unknown
d. Los Angeles, CA, Nov. 20, 1963, Age 74

AGATE, James Evershed
Critic, Author
b. Manchester, England, Sept. 9, 1877
d. London, England, June 6, 1947, Age 69

AHLERS, Anny
Actress
b. Hamburg, Germany, 1906
d. London, England, March 14, 1933, Age 26

AHLERT, Fred E.
Composer
b. New York, NY, Sept. 19, 1892
d. New York, NY, Oct. 20, 1953, Age 61

AHLSCHLAGER, Walter W. Sr.
Architect
b. Chicago, IL, July 20, 1887
d. Dallas, TX, March 28, 1965, Age 77

AHRENDT, Carl Frederick William
Actor
b. Lauterborg, Germany, Nov. 7, 1842
d. Greenville, MS, June 11, 1909, Age 66

AIKEN, Frank Eugene
Actor, Manager
b. Boston, MA, Aug. 31, 1840
d. New York, NY, Oct. 17, 1910, Age 70

AIKEN, George L.
Playwright, Actor
b. Boston, MA, 1830
d. Unknown, April 27, 1876, Age 45

AINLEY, Henry
Actor, Producer, Director
b. Leeds, England, Aug. 21, 1879
d. London, England, Oct. 31, 1945, Age 66

AINLEY, Richard
Actor
b. Stanmore, Middlesex, England, Dec. 23, 1910
d. London, England, May 18, 1967, Age 66

AINSLEE, Adra
Actress
b. Unknown
d. Lima, OH, Jan. 13, 1963, Age 87

AINSWORTH, Helen Shumate
Performer, Talent representative
b. San Francisco, CA, Unknown
d. West Hollywood, CA, Aug. 18, 1961, Age 59

AINSWORTH, Sydney (Charles Sydney)
Actor
b. Manchester, England, Unknown
d. Madison, WI, May 21, 1922, Age 50

AISTON, Arthur C.
Producer
b. South Lee, MA, Aug. 30, 1868
d. Unknown, Feb. 26, 1924, Age 58

AKED, Muriel
Actress
b. Bingley, Yorkshire, England, Nov. 9, 1887
d. Settle, Yorkshire, England, March 21, 1955, Age 67

AKIMOU, Nikolai
Stage Director, Designer
b. Leningrad, Russia, 1901
d. Moscow, Russia, Sept. 5, 1968, Age 67

AKINS, Zoö
Playwright, Novelist
b. Unknown, Humansville, MO
d. Oct. 30, 1886, Los Angeles, CA, Age Oct. 29, 1958

AKST, Harry
Songwriter
b. Unknown, Aug. 15, 1894
d. Hollywood, CA, March 31, 1963, Age 68

ALARCON y MENDOZA, Juan Ruiz di
Playwright
b. Mexico, 1588
d. Unknown, 1639

ALBANI, Emma (Marie Louise Cecilia Emma Lajuenesse)
Prima donna
b. Chambly, CAN, Nov. 1, 1847
d. London, England, April 3, 1930, Age 82

ALBAUGH, John W. Sr.
Actor-Manager
b. Baltimore, MD, Sept. 30, 1837
d. Jersey City, NJ, Feb. 11, 1909, Age 71

ALBAUGH, John W. Jr.
Actor-Manager
b. New York, NY, 1867
d. Baltimore, MD, April 7, 1910, Age 43

ALBEE, Edward Franklin
Vaudeville producer, Theatre executive
b. Maine, 1857
d. Palm Beach, FL, March 11, 1930, Age 72

ALBERNI, Luis
Actor
b. Spain, Unknown
d. Woodland Hills, CA, Dec. 23, 1962, Age 75

ALBERS, Hans
Actor
b. Unknown
d. Munich, Germany, July 24, 1960, Age 67

ALBERTSON, Frank
Actor
b. Unknown
d. Santa Monica, CA, Feb. 29, 1964, Age 55

ALBERTSON, Lillian
Actress, Producer, Director
b. CA, Unknown
d. Los Angeles, CA, Aug. 24, 1962, Age 81

ALBERY, James
Playwright
b. London, England, May 4, 1838
d. London, England, Aug. 15, 1889, Age 51

ALDEN, John
Actor, Director
b. Unknown
d. Sydney, Australia, Nov. 10, 1962, Age 55

ALDEN, Mary Maguire
Actress
b. New Orleans, LA, Unknown
d. Woodland Hills, CA, July 2, 1946, Age 63

ALDERSON, Clifton
Performer, Producer
b. Stockton-on-Tees, England, Aug. 13, 1964
d. Unknown, May 31, 1930, Age 65

ALDRICH, Louis (Lyon)
Performer, Producer
b. Ohio, Oct. 1, 1843
d. Kennebunkport, ME, June 17, 1901, Age 57

ALDRICH, Richard
Drama critic
b. Providence, RI, July 31, 1863
d. Rome, Italy, June 2, 1937, Age 73

ALDRICH, Thomas Bailey
Playwright
b. Portsmouth, NH, 1836
d. Unknown, March 19, 1907, Age 70

ALDRIDGE, Ira Frederick
Actor, (The African Roscius)
b. New York, NY, 1807
d. Lodz, Poland, Aug. 10, 1867, Age 60

ALEICHEM, Sholom (Rabinovich)
Author, Playwright
b. Pereiaslov (Poltova), Ukraine, 1859
d. Brooklyn, NY, 1916

ALEXANDER, Ross (Ross Alexander Smith)
Actor
b. Brooklyn, NY, July 27, 1907
d. Hollywood, CA, Jan. 2, 1937, Age 29

ALEXANDER, Sir George (George Alexander Gibb Samson)
Actor-Manager
b. Reading, England, June 19, 1858
d. London, England, Mar. 16, 1918, Age 59

ALEXANDRE, René
Actor, Secretary of Comédie Française
b. Unknown
d. Paris, France, Aug. 19, 1946, Age 61

ALFIERI, Count Vittorio Amedeo
Playwright
b. Asti, Italy, Jan. 17, 1749
d. Unknown, Oct. 8, 1803, Age 54

ALISON, George
Performer
b. London, England, Unknown
d. Norwalk, CT, Jan. 14, 1936, Age 70

ALLAN, Louise Rosalie (née Despréaux)
Actress
b. Unknown, 1810
d. Unknown, 1856, Age 46

ALLAN, Maud
Performer
b. Toronto, CAN, 1883
d. Los Angeles, CA, Oct. 7, 1956, Age 73

ALLEGRO, Anita
Actress
b. Unknown
d. Hollywood, CA, April 28, 1964

ALLEN, Charles Leslie
Performer
b. Boston, MA, June 12, 1830
d. Stamford, CT, Feb. 23, 1917, Age 86

ALLEN, Fred (John Florence Sullivan)
Actor
b. Cambridge, MA, 1894
d. New York, NY, March 17, 1956, Age 61

ALLEN, Gracie (née Grace Ethel Rosalie Cecile Allen)
Comedienne
b. San Francisco, CA, July 26, 1906
d. Hollywood, CA, Aug. 27, 1964, Age 58

ALLEN, Inglis
Playwright
b. Unknown
d. Unknown, March 2, 1943, Age 63

ALLEN, Joseph
Actor
b. Bristol, England, Jan. 2, 1840
d. Unknown, 1917

ALLEN, Joseph (McGurn)
Actor
b. Boston, MA, Unknown
d. Newton, MA, Sept. 9, 1952, Age 80

ALLEN, Joseph Jr.
Actor
b. Boston, MA, Unknown
d. Patchogue, L.I., NY, Nov. 9, 1963, Age 44

ALLEN, Kelcey (Eugene Kuttner)
Drama critic
b. Brooklyn, NY, Nov. 11, 1875
d. New York, NY, July 23, 1951, Age 75

ALLEN, Lester
Actor
b. England, Unknown
d. North Hollywood, CA, Nov. 6, 1949, Age 58

ALLEN, Louise (Mrs. Willie Collier)
Actress
b. New York, NY, Unknown
d. Unknown, Nov. 9, 1909, Age 36

ALLEN, Mrs. Vivian Beaumont
Philanthropist
b. Unknown
d. New York, NY, Oct. 10, 1962

ALLEN, Percy
Drama critic
b. Unknown
d. London, England, Feb. 1959, Age 86

ALLEN, Rita (Mrs. Rita Allen Cassel)
Producer
b. Unknown
d. New York, NY, July 2, 1968, Age 56

ALLEN, Susan Westford
Performer
b. Unknown
d. Bayshore, L.I., NY, June 13, 1944, Age 79

ALLEN, Viola (Mrs. Peter B. Duryea)
Actress
b. Huntsville, AL, Oct. 27, 1867
d. New York, NY, May 9, 1948, Age 80

ALLEYN, Edward
Actor, (Founder of Dulwich College)
b. St. Botolph, Bishopgate, London, England, Sept. 1, 1566
d. England, Nov. 26, 1626, Age 60

ALLGOOD, Sarah
Actress
b. Dublin, Ireland, Oct. 31, 1883
d. Woodland Hills, CA, Sept. 13, 1950, Age 66

ALMA-TADEMA, Sir Lawrence
Designer
b. Dronrijp, Frisia, The Netherlands, Jan. 8, 1836
d. Unknown, June 25, 1912, Age 76

ALPERT, Mickey (né Milton I. Alpert)
Artists representative, Personal manager
b. Holliston, MA, April 9, 1904
d. New York, NY, Sept. 22, 1965, Age 61

ALPHONSINE, (Fleury)
Actress
b. Paris, France, 1829
d. Unknown, 1883, Age 54

ALTHOFF, Charles R.
Actor
b. Unknown
d. Irvington, NJ, Oct. 14, 1962, Age 72

ALTON, Robert (Robert Alton Hart)
Choreographer
b. Bennington, VT, Unknown
d. Hollywood, CA, June 12, 1957, Age 54

ALVAREZ, Albert Raymond (Albert Raymond Gouron)
Singer
b. Bordeaux, France, 1861
d. Nice, France, 1933, Age 72

AMAYA, Carmen
Dancer
b. Barcelona, Spain, Nov. 2, 1913
d. Bagur, Spain, Nov. 19, 1963, Age 50

AMBER, Mabel
Actress
b. Elmira, NY, Unknown
d. Englewood, NJ, Oct. 7, 1945, Age 79

AMBER, Maude
Actress
b. Brookfield, OH, Unknown
d. San Francisco, CA, Aug. 24, 1938, Age 66

AMBERG, Gustave
Manager
b. Prague, Czechoslovakia, 1844
d. New York, NY, May 22, 1921, Age 77

AMBIENT, Mark
Playwright, Actor
b. Rastrick, Yorkshire, England, June 20, 1860
d. Brighton, England, Aug. 11, 1937, Age 77

AMES, Adrienne (Adrienne Ruth McClure)
Performer
b. Fort Worth, TX, Unknown
d. New York, NY, May 31, 1947, Age 39

AMES, Gerald
Actor
b. Blackheath, England, Sept. 12, 1881
d. Unknown, July 2, 1933, Age 51

AMES, Percy
Actor
b. Brighton, England, Unknown
d. New York, NY, March 28, 1936, Age 62

AMES, Robert
Actor
b. Hartford, CT, March 23, 1889
d. New York, NY, Nov. 27, 1931, Age 42

AMES, Winthrop
Producer
b. North Easton, MA, Nov. 25, 1870
d. Boston, MA, Nov. 3, 1937, Age 66

AMHERST, J. H.
Playwright, Actor
b. London, England, 1776
d. Philadelphia, PA, Aug. 12, 1851, Age 75

AMIC, Henry
Playwright
b. Unknown
d. Unknown, Feb. 5, 1929, Age 75

AMSDEN, Minneola
Performer
b. Unknown
d. Detroit, MI, Aug. 8, 1962, Age 75

AMUNARRIZ, Raul Cancio
Actor
b. Unknown
d. Madrid, Spain, Oct. 23, 1961

ANCEY, Georges (Georges de Curnieu)
Playwright
b. Unknown, 1860
d. Unknown, 1926, Age 66

ANCLIFFE, Charles
Composer
b. Unknown
d. Unknown, Dec. 20, 1953, Age 72

ANDERSEN, Hans Christian
Poet, Playwright, Novelist
b. Odense, Denmark, 1805
d. Unknown, 1875

ANDERSON, Clair Mathes
Actress
b. Detroit, MI, Unknown
d. Venice, CA, March 23, 1964, Age 68

ANDERSON, Dallas
Performer
b. Scotland, Unknown
d. Richmond, VA, Nov. 16, 1934, Age 60

ANDERSON, Florence
Wardrobe mistress, Performer
b. Liverpool, England, Unknown
d. New York, NY, Nov. 25, 1962, Age 80

ANDERSON, Garland
Playwright, Lecturer
b. Wichita, KS, Unknown
d. New York, NY, May 31, 1939, Age 53

ANDERSON, John Hargis
Drama critic, Author
b. Pensacola, FL, Oct. 18, 1896
d. New York, NY, July 16, 1943, Age 46

ANDERSON, John Henry
Actor, (The Wizard of the North)
b. Unknown, 1814
d. Unknown, Feb. 2, 1874, Age 59

ANDERSON, John Murray
Producer, Director
b. St. John's, Newfoundland, CAN, Sept. 20, 1886
d. New York, NY, Jan. 30, 1954, Age 67

ANDERSON, Julia (Mrs. Frank Broaker née Lüth)
Actress, Playwright
b. Hjuring, Denmark, Mar. 3, 1864
d. New York, NY, July 3, 1950, Age 86

ANDERSON, Mary Antoinette (Mrs. Antonio de Navarro)
Actress
b. Sacramento, CA, July 28, 1859
d. Broadway, Worcestershire, England, May 29, 1940, Age 80

ANDERSON, Maxwell
Playwright
b. Atlantic, PA, Dec. 15, 1888
d. Stamford, CT, Feb. 28, 1959, Age 70

ANDERSON, Percy
Costume and scenic designer
b. Unknown
d. London, England, Oct. 30, 1928, Age 77

ANDERSON, Phyllis Stohl
Literary representative
b. Brigham City, UT, Unknown
d. New York, NY, Nov. 28, 1956, Age 49

ANDERSON, Sherwood
Playwright, Author
b. Camden, OH, Sept. 13, 1876
d. Colon, Panama, March 8, 1941, Age 64

ANDRE, Gwili
Actress
b. Copenhagen, Denmark, Unknown
d. Venice, CA, Feb. 5, 1959, Age 51

ANDRE, Major John
Pageant creator
b. Unknown, 1751
d. Unknown, 1780, Age 29

ANDREWS, Adora
Actress
b. Denver, CO, Unknown
d. Harrison, NY, Sept. 18, 1956, Age 84

ANDREWS, Albert Gracia
Actor
b. Buffalo, NY, Unknown
d. New York, NY, Nov. 26, 1950, Age 93

ANDREWS, Elizabeth
Actress
b. London, England, Jan. 21, 1821
d. Holmesburg, PA, March 30, 1910, Age 89

ANDREWS, Lois (Lorraine Gourley)
Actress
b. Huntington Park, CA, Unknown
d. Encino, CA, April 5, 1968, Age 44

ANDREWS, Louise (Mrs. Arthur (Bugs) Baer)
Performer
b. Unknown
d. New York, NY, Nov. 14, 1950

ANDREWS, Lyle D.
Theatre manager, Treasurer
b. New York, NY, Unknown
d. Hempstead, NY, Jan. 17, 1950, Age 79

ANDREWS, Tod
Actor
b. New York, NY, Nov. 10, 1920
d. Beverly Hills, CA, Nov. 7, 1972, Age 51

ANDREYEV, Leonid Nikolaievitch
Playwright
b. Orel, Russia, June 1871
d. Unknown, Sept. 12, 1919, Age 48

ANDRONICUS, Lucius Livius
Translator, Producer
b. Unknown, c284 B.C.
d. Unknown, 204 B.C.

ANGELY, Louis
Playwright, Actor
b. Leipzig, Germany, Feb. 1, 1787
d. Berlin, Germany, Nov. 16, 1835, Age 48

ANGLIN, Margaret
Actress
b. Ottawa, CAN, April 3, 1876
d. Toronto, CAN, Jan. 7, 1958, Age 81

ANNUNZIO, Gabriele d'
(Rapagnetta), Playwright, Poet
b. Unknown, Francavilla al Mare near Pescara, Italy
d. March 12, 1863, Gardone Riviera, Italy, Age March 1, 1938

ANSELL, John
Composer and musical director
b. London, England, March 26, 1874
d. Marlow, Buckinghamshire, England, Dec. 15, 1948, Age 74

ANSELL, Mary (Mrs. Gilbert Cannon, formerly Mrs. James M. Barrie)
Actress
b. Unknown
d. Biarritz, France, 1950

ANSKY, S. A. (Solomon Rappaport)
Playwright
b. Unknown, 1863
d. Vilna, Lithuania, 1920

ANSON, Albert Edward
Performer
b. England, Sept. 14, 1879
d. Monrovia, CA, June 25, 1936, Age 56

ANSON, George William
Actor
b. Montrose, Scotland, Nov. 25, 1847
d. Unknown, Aug. 2, 1920, Age 72

ANSPACH, Elizabeth (Margravine of)
Playwright
b. Unknown
d. Unknown, Jan. 13, 1828, Age 78

ANSPACHER, Louis Kaufman
Playwright, Lecturer
b. Cincinnati, OH, March 1, 1878
d. Nashville, TN, May 10, 1947, Age 69

ANSTEY, F. (Thomas Anstey Guthrie)
Novelist, Playwright
b. London, England, Aug. 8, 1856
d. Unknown, March 10, 1934, Age 77

ANTHEIL, George Johann Carl
Composer, Writer
b. Trenton, NJ, July 8, 1900
d. New York, NY, Feb. 12, 1959, Age 58

ANTHONY, Carl
Performer
b. Unknown
d. Spencertown, NY, July 27, 1930, Age 52

ANTHONY, Jack (John Anthony Herbertson)
Performer
b. Dennistown, Glasgow, Scotland, Unknown
d. Dunbar, Scotland, Feb. 28, 1962, Age 61

ANTOINE, André Leonard
Producer, Critic
b. founder of Théâtre Libre of Paris, Limoges, France
d. 1857, Pouliguen, Brittany, France, Age Oct. 1943

ANTONA-TRAVERSI, Camillo
Playwright
b. Unknown
d. Unknown, Aug. 30, 1926, Age 69

ANZENGRUBER, Ludwig
Actor, Playwright
b. Austria, 1839
d. Unknown, 1889

APOLLINAIRE, Guillaume
Poet, Playwright
b. Monaco, Aug. 26, 1880
d. Paris, France, Nov. 10, 1918, Age 37

APPEL, Anna (née Bercovici)
Actress
b. Bucharest, Rumania, Unknown
d. New York, NY, Nov. 19, 1963

APPIA, Adolphe
Designer, Inventor
b. Geneva, Switzerland, Sept. 1, 1862
d. Nyon, Switzerland, Feb. 29, 1928, Age 65

APPLETON, George J.
Manager
b. Unknown
d. New York, NY, Sept. 5, 1926, Age 82

APPLIN, George
Playwright, Novelist
b. Unknown
d. Unknown, Sept. 11, 1949, Age 76

ARBUCKLE, Maclyn
Actor
b. San Antonio, TX, 1863
d. Waddington, NY, March 31, 1931, Age 68

ARBUCKLE, Roscoe (Fatty)
Actor, Director
b. San Jose, CA, March 24, 1887
d. New York, NY, June 29, 1933, Age 46

ARCARO, Flavia
Performer
b. Mejico, TX, June 22, 1876
d. Bronx, NY, April 8, 1937, Age 61

ARCHER, Belle (née Mingle)
Actress
b. Easton, PA, Sept. 5, 1858
d. Warren, PA, Sept. 19, 1900, Age 42

ARCHER, Fred R.
Special Effects photographer
b. Unknown
d. Hollywood, CA, April 29, 1963, Age 75

ARCHER, Harry
Composer
b. Creston, IA, Feb. 21, 1888
d. New York, NY, April 23, 1960, Age 72

ARCHER, Thomas
Actor, Playwright
b. Unknown
d. Unknown, May 11, 1848, Age 59

ARCHER, William
Critic, Playwright
b. Perth, Scotland, Sept. 23, 1856
d. Unknown, Dec. 27, 1924, Age 68

ARCHIBALD, William
Playwright
b. Trinidad, West Indies, March 7, 1924
d. New York, NY, Dec. 27, 1970, Age 53

ARDEN, Edwin Hunter Pendleton
Performer, Playwright
b. St. Louis, MO, Feb. 13, 1864
d. New York, NY, Oct. 2, 1918, Age 54

ARDEN, Victor (Lewis J. Fulks)
Orchestra leader
b. Wenona, IL, Unknown
d. New York, NY, July 30, 1962, Age 69

ARENT, Arthur
Playwright
b. Jersey City, NJ, Sept. 29, 1904
d. New York, NY, May 18, 1972, Age 67

ARETINO, Pietro
Playwright
b. Unknown, 1492
d. Unknown, 1556

ARGENTINA, (Antonia Mercé)
Dancer
b. Buenos Aires, Argentina, Unknown
d. Unknown, July 18, 1936, Age 45

ARGENTINITA, (Encarnació n Lopez)
Dancer
b. Buenos Aires, Argentina, March 3, 1905
d. New York, NY, Sept. 24, 1945, Age 44

ARIOSTO, Ludovico
Poet, Playwright
b. Reggio, Italy, 1474
d. Venice, Italy, 1533

ARISTOPHANES
Playwright
b. Athens, Greece, c448 B.C.
d. Unknown, c388 B.C.

ARISTOTLE
Author, Philosopher, Scientist
b. Stagira, Chalcidice (Macedonia), 384 B.C.
d. Chalcis, Euboea, 322 B.C.

ARKELL, Reginald
Playwright, Lyricist
b. Lechlade, Gloucestershire, England, Oct. 14, 1882
d. Cricklade, England, May 1, 1959, Age 76

ARLEN, Michael (Dikran Kouyoumdjian)
Author, Playwright
b. Roustchouk, Bulgaria, Nov. 16, 1895
d. New York, NY, June 23, 1956, Age 60

ARLISS, Florence Montgomery
Actress
b. Unknown
d. London, England, March 11, 1950, Age 77

ARLISS, George (Augustus George Andrews)
Actor, Author
b. London, England, April 10, 1868
d. London, England, Feb. 5, 1946, Age 77

ARMAT, Thomas
Inventor of the Vitascope
b. Fredericksburg, VA, Oct. 26, 1866
d. Washington, DC, Sept. 30, 1948, Age 81

ARMENDARIZ, Pedro
Actor
b. Churubusco, Mexico City, Mexico, Unknown
d. Los Angeles, CA, June 18, 1963, Age 51

ARMETTA, Henry
Performer
b. Palermo, Italy, July 4, 1888
d. San Diego, CA, Oct. 21, 1945, Age 57

ARMIN, Robert
Actor
b. Unknown, c1568
d. Unknown, c1611

ARMITAGE, Walter W.
Actor, Author, Producer
b. Johannesburg, South Africa, Unknown
d. New York, NY, Feb. 22, 1953, Age 46

ARMSTRONG, Harry (Henry W.)
Songwriter
b. Sommerville, MA, July 22, 1879
d. Bronx, NY, Feb. 28, 1951, Age 71

ARMSTRONG, Maj. Edwin H.
Inventor, Engineer
b. New York, NY, Dec. 18, 1890
d. New York, NY, Feb. 1, 1954, Age 63

ARMSTRONG, Ned (Edwin)
Press representative
b. Unknown
d. Doylestown, PA, July 13, 1961, Age 55

ARMSTRONG, Paul
Playwright
b. near St. Joseph, MO, April 25, 1869
d. New York, NY, Aug. 30, 1915, Age 46

ARMSTRONG, Sir Harry Gloster K.C.M.G., K.B.E.
Actor, British Consul at New York
b. Unknown
d. Unknown, Feb. 6, 1938, Age 77

ARMSTRONG, Sir William C.B.E.
Actor, Director, Producer
b. Edinburgh, Scotland, Nov. 30, 1882
d. Bournville, Birmingham, England, Oct. 5, 1952, Age 69

ARMSTRONG, Will H.
Performer
b. Unknown
d. Hollywood, CA, July 28, 1943, Age 74

ARMSTRONG, Will Steven
Designer
b. New Orleans, LA, March 26, 1930
d. New Mexico, Aug. 12, 1969, Age 39

ARMSTRONG, William (Billy) (William M. Devine)
Performer
b. Philadelphia, PA, Unknown
d. Philadelphia, PA, April 30, 19(?), Age 87

ARNA, Lissy
Actress
b. Unknown
d. Berlin, Germany, Jan. 22, 1964, Age 64

ARNAUD, Yvonne
Actress
b. Bordeaux, France, Dec. 20, 1892
d. London, England, Sept. 20, 1958, Age 65

ARNDT, Felix
Composer
b. New York, NY, May 20, 1889
d. Harmon-on-Hudson, NY, Oct. 16, 1918, Age 29

ARNE, Thomas Augustine
Playwright, Composer
b. Unknown
d. London, England, March 5, 1778, Age 68

ARNO, Sig
actor, director
b. Unknown, Dec. 27, 1895
d. Hamburg, Germany, Aug. 17, 1975, Age 79

ARNOLD, Eddie (Arnold Wendorff)
Performer
b. Unknown
d. Sunderland, England, Aug. 30, 1962, Age 34

ARNOLD, Edward (Guenther Schneider)
Actor
b. New York, NY, Feb. 18, 1890
d. Encino, CA, April 26, 1956, Age 66

ARNOLD, Franz
Playwright
b. Berlin, Germany, April 28, 1878
d. London, England, Sept. 29, 1960, Age 82

ARNOLD, Jack (Arnold Jack Gluck)
Performer
b. Unknown
d. New York, NY, June 15, 1962, Age 59

ARNOLD, Laura
Actress, Talent representative
b. Indianapolis, IN, Unknown
d. Yonkers, NY, Aug. 17, 1962, Age c73

ARNOLD, Lilian
Talent representative
b. Boston, MA, Nov. 24
d. New York, NY, June 2, 1974

ARNOLD, Matthew
Poet, Critic
b. Laleham-on-Thames, England, Dec. 24, 1822
d. Liverpool, England, April 15, 1888, Age 65

ARNOLD, Reggie
Performer
b. Unknown
d. U.S. Army Base, Germany, Jan. 19, 1963, Age 43

ARNOLD, Samuel James
Producer, Playwright
b. Unknown
d. Unknown, Aug. 16, 1852

ARNOLD, Seth
Actor
b. London, England, Unknown
d. New York, NY, Jan. 3, 1955, Age 70

ARNOT, Louise (Mrs. Mary Louise Gunn)
Actress
b. Unknown
d. New York, NY, Aug. 16, 1919, Age 76

ARNOULD, Sophie (Magdeleine Sophie Arnould)
Actress
b. Paris, France, Feb. 14, 1740
d. Unknown, Oct. 22, 1802, Age 62

ARONSON, Rudolph
Composer, Producer
b. New York, NY, April 8, 1856
d. New York, NY, Feb. 4, 1919, Age 62

ARTAUD, Antonin
Director, Poet, Playwright, Actor, Producer
b. Marseilles, France, Sept. 4, 1896
d. Ivry-sur-Seine, France, March 4, 1948, Age 51

ARTHUR, Helen
Administrator, Lawyer, Press rep.
b. Lancaster, WI, Unknown
d. New York, NY, Dec. 10, 1939, Age 60

ARTHUR, Joseph (Joseph Arthur Smith)
Playwright
b. Centerville, IN, 1848
d. New York, NY, Feb. 20, 1906, Age 57

ARTHUR, Julia (Mrs. Benjamin P. Cheney, née Ida Lewis)
Actress
b. Hamilton, Ontario, CAN, May 3, 1869
d. Boston, MA, March 28, 1950, Age 80

ARTHUR, Paul
Performer
b. Albany, NY, July 19, 1859
d. Unknown, May 12, 1928, Age 68

ARTHURS, George
Playwright, Lyricist
b. Manchester, England, April 13, 1875
d. Harrow, England, March 14, 1944, Age 68

ARTOIS, Armand d'
Playwright
b. Unknown
d. Unknown

ARTZYBASHEV, Mikhail Petrovitch
Novelist, Playwright
b. Unknown, 1878
d. Unknown, 1927

ARVOLD, Alfred G.
Educator, Little Theatre initiator
b. Whitewater, WI, Jan. 15, 1882
d. Fargo, ND, April 16, 1957, Age 75

ASBAJE Y RAMIREZ DE CANTILLANA, Juana Inés de a/k/a Sor Juana Inés de la Cruz
Poet, Playwright
b. Mexico, 1651
d. Unknown, 1695

ASCH, Sholem
Novelist, Playwright
b. Kutno, Poland, Nov. 1, 1880
d. London, England, July 10, 1957, Age 76

ASCHE, Oscar (John Stanger Heiss Oscar Asche)
Actor, Producer, Playwright
b. Geelong, Australia, Jan. 26, 1872
d. Marlow, Bucks, England, March 23, 1936, Age 65

ASH, Arty
Performer
b. Unknown
d. Unknown, Feb. 6, 1954, Age 61

ASH, Gordon
Performer
b. Unknown
d. Unknown, April 19, 1929, Age 52

ASHE, Warren
Actor
b. New York, NY, Unknown
d. Madison, CT, Sept. 19, 1947, Age 44

ASHER, Max
Actor, Make-up man
b. Unknown
d. Hollywood, CA, April 15, 1957, Age 77

ASHFORD, Harry
Actor
b. London, England, Unknown
d. Whitestone, L.I., NY, April 10, 1926, Age 68

ASHLEY, Annie (Mrs. John Barton, née Drolet)
Actress
b. San Francisco, CA, Unknown
d. New York, NY, Nov. 15, 1947, Age 82

ASHLEY, Helen (Mrs. Clarence S. Spencer, née Hurt)
Actress, Writer
b. Unknown
d. New York, NY, April 3, 1954, Age 75

ASHLEY, Minnie (Mrs. William Astor Chanler, Mrs. Beatrice Winthrop Ashley Chanler)
Performer
b. Fall River, MA, 1875
d. Portland, ME, June 19, 1945, Age 62

ASHTON, Mrs. Sylvia
Actress
b. Denver, CO, Unknown
d. Hollywood, CA, Nov. 18, 1940, Age 60

ASHWELL, Lena (Lady Simson, née Lena Pocock)
Actress, Producer
b. Fall River, MA, Sept. 28, 1872
d. Unknown, March 13, 1957, Age 84

ASKAM, Perry
Actor, Singer
b. Seattle, WA, Unknown
d. San Francisco, CA, Oct. 22, 1961

ASKIN, Harry
Manager, Producer
b. Philadelphia, PA, Unknown
d. New York, NY, Sept. 30, 1934, Age 67

ASQUITH, Mary
Actress, Literary rep., Playwright
b. Unknown
d. Brooklyn, NY, Dec. 22, 1942, Age 69

ASTLEY, John
Actor, Circus performer and proprietor
b. Unknown
d. Unknown, Oct. 19, 1821, Age 53

ASTLEY, Philip
Performer, Producer, Equestrian
b. London, England, Jan. 8, 1742
d. Unknown, Oct. 20, 1814, Age 72

ASTON, Tony (Anthony) (a/k/a Matt Medley)
Performer, (first actor in America)
b. Unknown, (fl. 1712-1731)

ASTOR, Adelaide (Mrs. George Grossmith, Jr.)
Actress
b. Birmingham, England
d. London, England, May 25, 1951

ATCHLEY, Hooper
Actor
b. Unknown
d. Hollywood, CA, Nov. 16, 1943, Age 57

ATES, Roscoe
Actor
b. Hattiesburg, MS, Unknown
d. Encino, CA, March 1, 1962, Age 67

ATHERTON, Alice (Mrs. Willie Edouin, née Hogan)
Performer
b. Unknown, 1860
d. New York, NY, Feb. 4, 1899, Age 39

ATHERTON, Daisy
Actress
b. England, Unknown
d. New York, NY, Dec. 18, 1961, Age 80

ATKINS, Alfred
Actor
b. Unknown
d. London, England, May 10, 1941, Age 41

ATKINSON, Charles H.
Minstrel
b. Unknown
d. Boston, MA, Feb. 2, 1909, Age 72

ATKINSON, Frank
Performer, Script writer
b. Unknown
d. Pinner, Hatch End, England, Feb. 23, 1963, Age 72

ATKINSON, George H.
Press representative
b. Unknown
d. New York, NY, Oct. 10, 1955, Age 75

ATLAS, Leopold
Playwright
b. Brooklyn, NY, 1907
d. North Hollywood, CA, Sept. 30, 1954, Age 46

ATTERIDGE, Harold R.
Librettist
b. Lake Forrest, IL, July 9, 1886
d. Lynbrook, NY, Jan. 15, 1938, Age 51

ATWELL, Ben H.
Press representative
b. Syracuse, NY, Unknown
d. Los Angeles, CA, Feb. 21, 1951, Age 74

ATWELL, Roy (John Leroy Atwell)
Actor, Writer
b. Syracuse, NY, Unknown
d. New York, NY, Feb. 6, 1962, Age 83

ATWILL, Lionel
Actor, Producer
b. Croyden, England, March 1, 1885
d. Pacific Palisades, CA, April 22, 1946, Age 61

ATWOOD, Lorena E. (Mrs. Harry C. Bradley)
Performer
b. San Francisco, CA, Unknown
d. Hollywood, CA, June 3, 1947

AUBIGNAC, François Hèdeli, Abbé d'
Critic
b. Unknown, 1604
d. Unknown, 1676

AUDE, Joseph
Playwright
b. Unknown, 1755
d. Unknown, 1841

AUDRAN, Edmond
Composer
b. Lyons, France, April 12, 1840
d. Tierceville, France, Aug. 17, 1901, Age 61

AUER, Mischa (né Mischa Ounskowski)
Actor
b. St. Petersburg, Russia, Nov. 17, 1905
d. Rome, Italy, March 5, 1967, Age 61

AUERBACH, Artie (Arthur)
Performer, Photographer-reporter
b. New York, NY, Unknown
d. Van Nuys, CA, Oct. 3, 1957, Age 54

AUERBACH-LEVY, William
Caricaturist, Artist
b. Brest-Litovsk, Unknown
d. Ossining, NY, June 29, 1961, Age 75

AUG, Edna
Performer
b. Cincinnati, OH, 1878
d. Willow, NY, Nov. 30, 1938, Age 60

AUGARDE, Adrienne
Performer
b. Unknown
d. Unknown, March 17, 1913

AUGARDE, Amy
Actress
b. London, England, July 7, 1868
d. Reigate, England, April 1, 1959, Age 90

AUGARDE, Gertrude (Mrs. George Henry Trader)
Actress
b. Unknown
d. East Islip, L.I., NY, Sept. 10, 1959

AUGIER, Guillaume Victor Emile
Playwright
b. Valence, France, Sept. 17, 1820
d. Paris, France, Oct. 25, 1889, Age 69

AUGUST, Edwin
Actor, Director, Author
b. Unknown
d. Hollywood, CA, Mar. 4, 1964, Age 81

AULT, Marie (Mrs. J. A. Paterson)
Actress
b. Wigan, Lancashire, England, Sept. 2, 1870
d. London, England, May 9, 1951, Age 80

AURIOL, Jean Baptiste
Clown
b. Unknown
d. Passy, France, Sept. 1881, Age 76

AUSTIN, Charles
Performer
b. Unknown, 1878
d. Unknown, 1944

AUSTIN, Jennie (Mrs. Joseph Hurtig)
Performer
b. Unknown
d. New York, NY, Oct. 19, 1938, Age c48

AUSTIN, Joseph
Actor, Producer
b. Unknown
d. Unknown, March 31, 1821, Age 81

AUSTIN, Louis Frederick
Critic, Playwright
b. Unknown
d. Unknown, Sept. 13, 1905

AVRIL, Jane
Dancer
b. Unknown, 1868
d. Paris, France, Feb. 1943, Age 75

AXT, William L.
Composer, Conductor
b. Unknown
d. Ukiah, CA, Feb. 13, 1959, Age 71

AYALA, Adelardo López de
Playwright
b. Unknown, 1828
d. Unknown, 1879

AYER, Nat. D. (Nathaniel Davis Ayer)
Composer
b. Boston, MA, Unknown
d. Bath, England, Sept. 19, 1952, Age 65

AYERS, Agnes
Actress
b. Carbondale, IL, 1896
d. Unknown, Dec. 25, 1940, Age 42

AYERS, Lemuel
Scenic and costume designer, Producer
b. New York, NY, Jan. 22, 1915
d. New York, NY, Aug. 14, 1955, Age 40

AYERTON, Randle
Performer
b. Chester, England, Aug. 9, 1869
d. Stratford-on-Avon, England, May 28, 1940, Age 70

AYLIFF, Henry Kiell
Actor, Producer, Director
b. Grahamstown, South Africa, Unknown
d. Cambridge, England, May 28, 1949, Age 77

AYLMER, David
Actor
b. Unknown
d. London, England, July 20, 1964, Age 31

AYME, Marcel
Playwright, Novelist, Screen writer
b. Joigny, France, March 29, 1902
d. Paris, France, Oct. 14, 1967, Age 65

AYNESWORTH, Allan (E. Abbott-Anderson)
Actor
b. Royal Military College, Sandhurst, England, April 14, 1864
d. Camberley, Surrey, England, Aug. 22, 1959, Age 95

AYRTON, Robert
Actor
b. Unknown
d. Unknown, May 18, 1924

B

BACH, Fernand (Charles Joseph Pasquier)
Performer
b. Unknown
d. Nogent le Rotrou, France, Nov. 19, 1953, Age 72

BACH, Reginald
Actor, Director
b. Shepperton, London, England, Sept. 3, 1886
d. New York, NY, Jan. 6, 1941, Age 54

BACKUS, E. Y.
Actor, Stage Manager
b. Danielson, CT, Unknown
d. Westport, CT, Nov. 12, 1914, Age 62

BACKUS, George
Performer, Playwright
b. Columbus, OH, 1858
d. Merrick, NY, May 21, 1939, Age 81

BACON, David Gaspar G. Jr.
Actor
b. Jamaica Plains, MA, March 24, 1914
d. Venice, CA, Sept. 12, 1942, Age 29

BACON, Faith
Performer
b. Unknown
d. Chicago, IL, Sept. 26, 1956, Age 45

BACON, Francis Viscount St. Albans
Essayist, Playwright
b. London, England, Jan. 22, 1561
d. Unknown, 1626

BACON, Frank
Actor, Playwright
b. Marysville, CA, Jan. 16, 1864
d. Chicago, IL, Nov. 19, 1922, Age 58

BACON, Jane
Actress
b. Unknown
d. Hollywood, CA, Sept. 27, 1956, Age 89

BACON, Phannel
Playwright
b. Unknown
d. Unknown, Jan. 10, 1783, Age 82

BADDELEY, Robert
Actor
b. Unknown, 1733
d. London, England, Nov. 20, 1794, Age 61

BADDELEY, Sophia Snow
Actress
b. Unknown, 1745
d. Unknown, July 1, 1786, Age 41

BADGER, Clarence
Film director
b. Unknown
d. Sidney, Australia, June 17, 1964, Age 84

BAER, Max (Maximilian Adelbert Baer)
Pugilist, Performer
b. Omaha, NB, Feb. 11, 1909
d. Hollywood, CA, Nov. 21, 1959, Age 50

BAGGOT, King
Actor, Director
b. St. Louis, MO, 1880
d. Hollywood, CA, July 11, 1948, Age 68

BAHN, Chester B.
Journalist, Editor
b. Liverpool, NY, Unknown
d. Burbank, CA, Jan. 8, 1962, Age 68

BAHR, Hermann
Playwright, Critic, Novelist
b. Linz, Austria, July 19, 1863
d. Munich, Germany, Jan. 15, 1934, Age 70

BAILEY, Bryan
First director of Belgrade Theatre
b. Unknown
d. Coventry, England, March 25, 1960, Age 38

BAILEY, Frankie (Frankie Walters Robinson)
Actress
b. New Orleans, LA, May 29, 1859
d. Los Angeles, CA, July 8, 1953, Age 94

BAILEY, James A.
Circus proprietor
b. Detroit, MI, July 4, 1847
d. Mount Vernon, NY, April 11, 1906, Age 59

BAILEY, Margery
Shakespearean authority, Educator
b. Salt Lake City, UT, 1891
d. Palo Alto, CA, June 19, 1963, Age 72

BAILEY, Mildred (Mildred Rinker)
Singer
b. . . .on an Indian reservation, WA, Unknown
d. Poughkeepsie, NY, Dec. 12, 1951, Age 48

BAILEY, William N.
Director, Actor
b. Milwaukee, WI, Unknown
d. Hollywood, CA, Nov. 8, 1962, Age 76

BAILLIE, Joanna
Playwright
b. Bothwell Manse, Lanarkshire, Scotland, Sept. 11, 1762
d. Hampstead, England, Feb. 23, 1851, Age 88

BAINES, Florence
Actress, Producer
b. Unknown
d. Unknown, Dec. 30, 1918, Age 41

BAINTER, Fay
Actress
b. Los Angeles, CA, Dec. 7, 1892
d. Beverly Hills, CA, April 16, 1968, Age 76

BAIRD, Cora (née Cora Burlar Eisenberg)
Puppeteer, Actress
b. New York, NY, Jan. 26, 1912
d. New York, NY, Dec. 6, 1967, Age 55

BAIRD, Dorothea (Mrs. Henry B. Irving)
Actress
b. Teddington, England, May 20, 1875
d. Broadstairs, Kent, England, Sept. 24, 1933, Age 58

BAIRD, Stuart
Performer
b. Boston, MA, Unknown
d. New York, NY, Oct. 28, 1947, Age 66

BAIRNSFATHER, Bruce
Playwright, Cartoonist
b. Muree, India, July 1887
d. Norton, Worcestershire, England, Sept. 29, 1959, Age 71

BAJOR, Gisi
Actress
b. Unknown
d. Budapest, Hungary, Feb. 12, 1951, Age 55

BAKALEINIKOFF, Mischa
Conductor
b. Russia, Unknown
d. Los Angeles, CA, Aug. 1, 1960, Age 70

BAKER, Belle (Becker)
Performer
b. New York, NY, Unknown
d. Los Angeles, CA, April 28, 1957, Age 62

BAKER, Benjamin A.
Actor, Producer, Playwright
b. New York, NY, 1818
d. New York, NY, Sept. 1890

BAKER, Daniel E.
Performer
b. New York, NY, Unknown
d. Englewood, NJ, Dec. 6, 1939, Age 78

BAKER, David Erskine
Author
b. Unknown
d. Unknown, Feb. 16, 1767, Age 37

BAKER, Dorothy
Author, Playwright
b. Missoula, MT, April 21, 1907
d. Unknown, 1968, Age 61

BAKER, George Pierce
Author, Educator
b. Providence, RI, April 4, 1866
d. New York, NY, Jan 6, 1935, Age 68

BAKER, Lee
Actor
b. Ovid, MI, Unknown
d. Los Angeles, CA, Feb. 24, 1948, Age 72

BAKER, Lewis J.
Performer
b. Russia, Unknown
d. Rochester, NY, June 7, 1962, Age 79

BAKER, Phil
Performer
b. Philadelphia, PA, Aug. 24, 1896
d. Copenhagen, Denmark, Dec. 1, 1963, Age 67

BAKER, Tarkington
Press representative
b. Unknown
d. New York, NY, Jan. 1, 1924, Age 45

BAKST, Leon
Designer, Painter
b. Petrograd, Russia, 1868
d. Paris, France, Dec. 27, 1924, Age 57

BALABAN, A. J.
Theatre executive
b. Chicago, IL, 1889
d. New York, NY, Nov. 1, 1962, Age 73

BALDERSTON, John Lloyd
Playwright
b. Philadelphia, PA, Oct. 22, 1889
d. Beverly Hills, CA, March 8, 1954, Age 64

BALE, John Bishop of Ossary
Playwright
b. Unknown, 1495
d. Unknown, Nov. 11, 1563, Age 68

BALFE, Michael William
Composer
b. Dublin, Ireland, May 15, 1808
d. Rowney Abbey, Hertfordshire, England, Oct. 20, 1870, Age 62

BALFOUR, William
Actor
b. Unknown
d. New York, NY, April 13, 1964, Age 89

BALIEFF, Nikita
Performer, Impresario
b. Rostow-on-Don, Russia, 1877
d. New York, NY, Sept. 3, 1936, Age 59

BALL, Ernest R.
Song Writer
b. Cleveland, OH, July 21, 1878
d. Santa Ana, CA, May 3, 1927, Age 49

BALL, J. Meredith
Conductor, Composer
b. Unknown
d. Unknown, Feb. 22, 1915, Age 77

BALL, Lewis
Actor
b. Unknown
d. Teignmouth, England, Feb. 14, 1905, Age 84

BALL, Suzan
Actress
b. Buffalo, NY, Feb. 3, 1933
d. North Hollywood, CA, Aug. 5, 1955, Age 22

BALLARD, Frederick
Playwright
b. Lincoln, NB, 1884
d. Lincoln, NB, Sept. 24, 1957, Age 72

BALLIN, Hugo
Producer, Director, Painter
b. New York, NY, Unknown
d. Santa Monica, CA, Nov. 27, 1956, Age 76

BALLIN, Mabel (Mrs. Hugo Ballin)
Actress
b. Philadelphia, PA, Unknown
d. Santa Monica, CA, July 24, 1958, Age 73

BALMAIN, Rollo
Actor, Producer
b. Unknown
d. Unknown, Dec. 5, 1920, Age 63

BALZAC, Honoré de
Playwright, Novelist
b. Tours, France, May 20, 1799
d. Paris, France, Aug. 18, 1850, Age 51

BAMBERGER, Theron
Producer, Press representative
b. Philadelphia, PA, Unknown
d. New York, NY, Sept. 14, 1953, Age 59

BANCROFT, George
Actor
b. Philadelphia, PA, Unknown
d. Santa Monica, CA, Oct. 2, 1956, Age 74

BANCROFT, George Pleydell
Playwright, Novelist, Actor
b. London, England, Nov. 1, 1868
d. Taplow, England, March 1, 1956, Age 87

BANCROFT, Lady (Marie Effie Wilton)
Actress-Manager
b. Doncaster, England, Jan 12, 1839
d. Folkstone, England, May 22, 1921, Age 82

BANCROFT, Sir Squire
Actor-Manager
b. Unknown, May 14, 1841
d. Unknown, April 19, 1926, Age 84

BANDMANN, Daniel E.
Actor-Manager
b. Cassel, Germany, 1840
d. Missoula, MT, Nov. 23, 1905, Age 65

BANDMANN-PALMER, Mrs. (Millicent Palmer)
Actress-Manager
b. Lancaster, England, Unknown
d. Kew, England, Jan 6, 1926, Age 81

BANG, Herman Joachim
Playwright
b. Unknown, April 20, 1857
d. Unknown, Jan. 29, 1912, Age 54

BANGS, Frank C.
Performer
b. Alexandria, VA, Oct. 12, 1833
d. Atlantic City, NJ, June 12, 1908, Age 74

BANGS, John Kendrick
Author, Playwright
b. Yonkers, NY, May 27, 1862
d. Atlantic City, NJ, Jan. 21, 1922, Age 59

BANIM, John
Playwright, Novelist, Poet
b. Unknown
d. Unknown, Aug. 13, 1842, Age 44

BANKHEAD, Tallulah
Actress
b. Huntsville, AL, Jan. 31, 1903
d. New York, NY, Dec. 12, 1968, Age 65

BANKS, John
Playwright
b. Unknown, c1650
d. Unknown, 1706

BANKS, Leslie J.
Actor
b. West Derby, England, June 9, 1890
d. London, England, April 21, 1952, Age 61

BANKS, Monty (Mario Bianchi)
Actor, Director
b. Nice, France, 1897
d. Arona, Italy, Jan. 7, 1950, Age 52

BANNERMAN, Margaret
Actress
b. Toronto, Canada, Dec. 15, 1896
d. Englewood, NJ, Apr. 25, 1976, Age 79

BANNISTER, Charles
Actor
b. Unknown, 1738
d. London, England, Oct. 26, 1804

BANNISTER, Harry
Performer
b. Holland, MI, Sept. 29, 1893
d. New York, NY, Feb. 26, 1961, Age 72

BANNISTER, John
Actor
b. Deptford, England, May 12, 1760
d. Unknown, Nov. 6, 1836, Age 76

BANNISTER, Nathaniel Harrington
Playwright, Actor
b. Unknown, Jan. 3, 1813
d. New York, NY, 1847

BANTOCK, Leedham
Actor, Playwright
b. Unknown
d. Unknown, Oct. 15, 1928, Age 58

BANVILLE, Théodore Faullain de
Playwright, Poet
b. Unknown, 1823
d. Unknown, March 13, 1891, Age 68

BARA, Theda (Theodosia Goodman) (Mrs. Charles Brabin)
Actress
b. Cincinnati, OH, 1890
d. Los Angeles, CA, April 7, 1955, Age c65

BARAGREY, John
Actor
b. Haleyville, AL, April 15, 1918
d. New York, NY, Aug. 4, 1975, Age 57

BARBIER, George
Actor
b. Philadelphia, PA, Unknown
d. Hollywood, CA, July 19, 1945, Age 80

BARBIER, Jules
Playwright
b. Unknown
d. Unknown, Jan. 17, 1901, Age 75

BARBOR, H. R.
Playwright, Business Manager
b. Lowestoft, England, Jan. 1, 1893
d. Unknown, Jan. 13, 1933, Age 40

BARD, Wilkie
Actor
b. London, England, 1870
d. Hugden, England, May 5, 1944, Age 70

BARING, Hon. Maurice
Playwright, Essayist
b. Unknown, April 27, 1874
d. Beauly, Scotland, Dec. 14, 1945, Age 71

BARKER, Jack
Actor
b. Unknown
d. Cleveland, OH, July 18, 1950, Age 55

BARKER, James Nelson
Playwright
b. Philadelphia, PA, June 17, 1784
d. Unknown, March 9, 1858, Age 73

BARKER, Reginald
Director, Actor
b. Bothwell, Scotland, Unknown
d. Los Angeles, CA, Feb. 23, 1945, Age 59

BARKER, Richard
Actor, Stage manager
b. Unknown
d. Unknown, Aug. 1, 1903, Age 69

BARLACH, Ernst
Artist, Playwright
b. Wedel, Holstein, Germany, Jan. 2, 1870
d. Güstrow, Mecklemburg, Germany, Oct. 25, 1938, Age 68

BARLOW, Billie (Minnie)
Performer
b. London, England, July 18, 1862
d. Unknown, Feb. 11, 1937, Age 74

BARLOW, Reginald
Actor
b. Springfield, MA, Unknown
d. Hollywood, CA, July 6, 1943, Age 76

BARNABEE, Henry Clay
Actor
b. Portsmouth, NH, Nov. 14, 1833
d. Jamaica Plains, MA, Dec. 16, 1917, Age 84

BARNARD, Annie (Lady Carlton)
Actress
b. Unknown
d. Unknown, Sept. 26, 1941

BARNARD, Charles
Playwright
b. Unknown
d. Unknown, April 11, 1920, Age 82

BARNARD, Ivor
Actor
b. London, England, June 13, 1887
d. Unknown, June 30, 1953, Age 66

BARNES, Barnabee
Playwright
b. Unknown
d. Unknown, Dec. 1609, Age 40

BARNES, Charlotte Mary Sanford
Actress, Playwright
b. Unknown, 1818
d. Unknown, April 14, 1863, Age 45

BARNES, Howard
Critic, Television Writer
b. London, England, Nov. 26, 1904
d. New York, NY, March 12, 1968, Age 64

BARNES, J. H.
Performer
b. England, Feb. 26, 1850
d. Unknown, Nov. 10, 1925, Age 75

BARNES, Joe ("Uncle Joe")
Performer
b. Unknown
d. Southend, England, March 28, 1964, Age 59

BARNES, John
Performer
b. Unknown, 1761
d. Unknown, 1841

BARNES, Mabel Thomas (Mrs. Bernard R. Baranoski)
Performer
b. Unknown
d. Kansas City, MO, Nov. 14, 1962

BARNES, Sir Kenneth (Ralph)
Educator
b. Heavitree, Exeter, England, Sept. 11, 1878
d. Kingston Gorse, Sussex, England, Oct. 16, 1957, Age 79

BARNES, T. Roy
Actor
b. Lincolnshire, England, Unknown
d. Hollywood, CA, March 30, 1937, Age 56

BARNET, Robert Ayers
Librettist, Playwright
b. New York, NY, Sept. 3, 1853
d. New York, NY, June 1933, Age 79

BARNETT, C. Z.
Performer
b. Unknown
d. Unknown, 1890, Age 88

BARNETT, Chester A.
Actor
b. Piedmont, MO, Unknown
d. Jefferson City, MO, Sept. 22, 1947, Age 62

BARNETT, Morris
Playwright, Actor
b. Unknown
d. Unknown, March 18, 1856, Age 56

BARNUM, George William
Actor
b. Unknown
d. Philadelphia, PA, March 30, 1937, Age 84

BARNUM, Phineas Taylor
Manager, Circus proprietor
b. Danbury, CT, July 5, 1810
d. Bridgeport, CT, April 7, 1891, Age 80

BARON, Lewis
Actor
b. Unknown
d. Unknown, March 2, 1920, Age 82

BARON, Maurice
Composer, Conductor
b. Lille, France, Jan. 1, 1889
d. Oyster Bay, NY, Sept. 5, 1964, Age 75

BARON, Michael
Actor, Playwright
b. Paris, France, c1653
d. Unknown, Dec. 22, 1729, Age 76

BARRACLOUGH, Sydney
Performer
b. Unknown
d. Unknown, March 1930, Age 61

BARRAS, Charles M.
Actor, Playwright
b. Philadelphia, PA, March 17, 1826
d. Cos Cob, CT, March 31, 1873, Age 47

BARRATT, Walter Augustus
Composer, Producer, Conductor
b. Scotland, Unknown
d. New York, NY, April 12, 1947, Age 73

BARRATT, Watson
Scenic designer
b. Salt Lake City, UT, June 27, 1884
d. New York, NY, July 6, 1962, Age 78

BARRE, Albert
Playwright
b. Unknown
d. Unknown, May 31, 1910, Age 54

BARRETT, George (Charles Frederick Barrett)
Actor
b. Leeds, England, 1869
d. Unknown, June 13, 1935, Age 66

BARRETT, George Edward
Actor
b. Unknown, 1849
d. Unknown, 1894

BARRETT, George Horton
Actor
b. Exeter, England, 1794
d. New York, NY, Sept. 5, 1860, Age 66

BARRETT, Henry Michael
Actor
b. Liverpool, England, Unknown
d. London, England, June 15, 1872, Age 68

BARRETT, Ivy Rice
Performer
b. Unknown
d. Hollywood, CA, Nov. 8, 1962, Age 64

BARRETT, Jimmie
Actress
b. Unknown
d. Queens, NY, June 20, 1964, Age 80

BARRETT, Lawrence
Actor-Manager
b. Detroit, MI, 1838
d. New York, NY, March 20, 1891, Age 52

BARRETT, Mrs. George H. ("Mrs. Henry")
Actress
b. Unknown
d. Unknown, April 20, 1857, Age 55

BARRETT, Oscar Sr.
Composer, Conductor, Producer
b. Unknown
d. St. Margaret's Bay, Kent, England, July 1, 1941, Age 95

BARRETT, Oscar Jr.
Manager
b. London, England, March 19, 1875
d. Unknown, July 11, 1943, Age 68

BARRETT, Wilson
Actor-Manager, Playwright
b. Essex, England, Feb. 18, 1846
d. Unknown, July 22, 1904, Age 57

BARRI, Odoardo
Composer
b. Unknown
d. Unknown, Jan. 23, 1920, Age 85

BARRIE, Sir James Matthew
Playwright, Novelist
b. Kirriemuir, Scotland, May 9, 1860
d. London, England, June 19, 1937, Age 77

BARRIERE, Théodore
Playwright
b. Unknown, 1823
d. Unknown, 1877

BARRINGTON, Rutland (George Rutland Barrington-Fleet)
Actor, Author
b. Penge, Jan. 15, 1853
d. Unknown, June 1, 1922, Age 69

BARRIS, Harry
Composer, Performer
b. New York, NY, Unknown
d. Burbank, CA, Dec. 13, 1962, Age 57

BARRON, Marcus
Actor
b. Unknown
d. Unknown, March 15, 1944, Age 75

BARRON, Mark
Journalist, Critic, Playwright
b. Waco, TX, Unknown
d. New York, NY, Aug. 15, 1960, Age 55

BARROSO, Ary
Composer
b. Unknown
d. Rio de Janeiro, Brazil, Feb. 9, 1964, Age 60

BARROWS, James C.
Performer
b. Unknown
d. Hollywood, CA, Dec. 7, 1925, Age 72

BARRY, Ann Spranger (Crawford)
Actress
b. Unknown
d. Unknown, Nov. 29, 1801, Age 67

BARRY, Bobby
Performer, Actor
b. Unknown
d. Englewood, NJ, March 23, 1964, Age 78

BARRY, Elaine
Performer
b. Unknown
d. . . .near Etowah, TN, Jan. 30, 1948

BARRY, Elizabeth
Actress
b. England, 1658
d. England, Nov. 7, 1713, Age 55

BARRY, Fred
Actor
b. Unknown
d. Montreal, CAN, Aug. 17, 1964

BARRY, Helen
Actress
b. Unknown
d. Unknown, Sept. 1904, Age 51

BARRY, Lydia (Mrs. George Felix)
Actress
b. Brooklyn, NY, Unknown
d. Rumson, NJ, July 3, 1932, Age 56

BARRY, Philip
Playwright
b. Rochester, NY, June 18, 1896
d. New York, NY, Dec. 3, 1949, Age 53

BARRY, Sheil
Actor
b. Unknown
d. Middleton, Lancashire, England, March 13, 1897, Age 55

BARRY, Spranger
Actor
b. Dublin, Ireland, Nov. 20, 1719
d. Unknown, January 7, 1777, Age 58

BARRY, Thomas
Actor, Producer
b. England, July 27, 1798
d. Boston, MA, Feb. 11, 1876, Age 77

BARRY, Tom (Hal Donahue)
Screen writer, Playwright
b. Kansas City, MO, Unknown
d. Hollywood, CA, Nov. 7, 1931, Age 47

BARRY, Viola
Actress
b. Unknown
d. Hollywood, CA, April 2, 1964, Age 70

BARRYMORE, Diana
Actress
b. New York, NY, March 3, 1921
d. New York, NY, Jan. 25, 1960, Age 38

BARRYMORE, Ethel
Actress
b. Philadelphia, PA, Aug. 15, 1879
d. Beverly Hills, CA, June 18, 1959, Age 79

BARRYMORE, Georgie Drew (Georgiana)
Actress
b. Unknown, 1856
d. Santa Barbara, CA, July 2, 1893, Age 37

BARRYMORE, John
Actor
b. Philadelphia, PA, Feb. 15, 1882
d. Hollywood, CA, June 29, 1942, Age 60

BARRYMORE, Lionel
Actor
b. Philadelphia, PA, April 28, 1878
d. Chatsworth, CA, Nov. 15, 1954, Age 76

BARRYMORE, Maurice (Herbert Blythe)
Actor
b. India, 1847
d. Amityville, L.I., NY, March 26, 1905, Age 57

BARRYMORE, Mrs. William
Actress
b. Unknown
d. Unknown, Dec. 30, 1862

BARRYMORE, William
Actor
b. Unknown
d. Edinburgh, Scotland, July 1830, Age 72

BARRYMORE, William Henry (R. N. Blewitt)
Actor
b. Unknown
d. Unknown, Feb. 16, 1845

BARTELS, Louis John
Actor
b. Chicago, IL, Unknown
d. Hollywood, CA, March 4, 1932, Age 36

BARTET, Julia
Actress
b. Paris, France, Unknown
d. Paris, France, Nov. 1941, Age 87

BARTH, Cecil
Producer
b. Unknown
d. Unknown, Dec. 10, 1949, Age 84

BARTHELMESS, Richard Semler
Actor
b. New York, NY, 1895
d. Southampton, L.I., NY, Aug. 17, 1963, Age 68

BARTHOLDI, Fred
Theatre manager
b. Unknown
d. Miami Beach, FL, Nov. 22, 1961, Age 58

BARTHOLOMAE, Philip H.
Playwright, Producer
b. Chicago, IL, Unknown
d. Winnetka, IL, Jan. 5, 1947, Age 67

BARTHOLOMEW, Ann
Playwright
b. Unknown
d. Unknown, Aug. 18, 1862

BARTLETT, Clifford
Actor
b. Cardiff, Wales, June 14, 1903
d. London, England, Dec. 25, 1936, Age 33

BARTLETT, Josephine (Mrs. Harold Perry)
Performer
b. Morris, IL, Unknown
d. Chicago, IL, Oct. 14, 1910, Age 48

BARTLEY, George
Actor
b. Bath, England, 1782
d. Unknown, July 22, 1858, Age 76

BARTLEY, Mrs. George
Actress
b. Unknown
d. Unknown, Jan. 14, 1850, Age 66

BARTOLOZZI, Josephine (Mrs. James R. Anderson)
Performer
b. Unknown
d. Unknown, May 1, 1848, Age 41

BARTON, James
Actor
b. Gloucester, NJ, Nov. 1, 1890
d. Mineola, L.I., NY, Feb. 19, 1962, Age 71

BARTON, John
Performer
b. Germantown, PA, May 1, 1872
d. New York, NY, Dec. 23, 1946, Age 74

BARTON, Sam
Performer
b. Unknown
d. New York, NY, Oct. 8, 1941, Age 46

BARTON, Ward J.
Performer
b. Unknown
d. New York, NY, April 12, 1963, Age 87

BARTSCH, Hans
Producer, Literary representative
b. Germany, Unknown
d. Bullville, NY, July 10, 1952, Age 68

BARTY, Jack (John Bartholomew)
Actor
b. London, England, Dec. 31, 1888
d. Streatham, London, England, Nov. 25, 1942, Age 54

BARWICK, Edwin
Actor
b. Unknown
d. Unknown, May 5, 1928, Age 70

BASCOMB, A. W.
Performer
b. London, England, July 5, 1880
d. Unknown, Dec. 10, 1939, Age 59

BASHOR, Wilma
Exec. dir. of Motion Picture Relief Fund
b. Unknown
d. Hollywood, CA, April 26, 1964, Age 75

BASSERMAN, Albert
Actor
b. Mannheim, Germany, Sept. 7, 1867
d. Zurich, Switzerland, May 15, 1952, Age 85

BASSERMAN, Else (née Schiff)
Actress, Author
b. Leipzig, Germany, Unknown
d. Baden-Baden, Germany, May 30, 1961, Age 83

BASSERMANN, August
Actor, Director
b. Unknown, 1848
d. Unknown, 1931

BASSET, Serge
Playwright, Critic, Journalist
b. Unknown
d. Unknown, June 29, 1917

BASSETT, Russell
Actor
b. Milwaukee, WI, Unknown
d. New York, NY, May 8, 1918, Age 72

BASSHE, Emjo
Playwright, Director
b. Vilna, Russia, Unknown
d. New York, NY, Oct. 28, 1939, Age 40

BATAILLE, Henry
Playwright
b. Nimes, France, 1872
d. Paris, France, March 2, 1922, Age 49

BATEMAN, Ellen Douglas (Mrs. Claude Greppo)
Actress
b. Unknown, 1844
d. Unknown, 1936

BATEMAN, Hezekiah Linthicum
Producer
b. Maryland, 1812
d. London, England, March 22, 1875, Age 62

BATEMAN, Isabel Emilie
Actress-Manager
b. U.S.A., 1854
d. Wantage, England, June 10, 1934, Age 79

BATEMAN, Jessie
Actress
b. U.S.A., Aug. 2, 1877
d. Windsor, England, Nov. 14, 1940, Age 63

BATEMAN, Kate (Mrs. George Crowe)
Actress, Educator
b. Baltimore, MD, Oct. 7, 1842
d. London, England, April 8, 1917, Age 74

BATEMAN, Mrs. H. L. (Sidney Frances Cowell)
Actress, Author, Producer
b. New York, NY, 1823
d. London, England, Jan. 13, 1881, Age 57

BATEMAN, Virginia Frances (Mrs. Edward Compton)
Actress
b. Maryland, Jan. 1, 1853
d. London, England, May 4, 1940, Age 87

BATES, Blanche (Mrs. George Creel)
Actress
b. Portland, OR, Aug. 25, 1873
d. San Francisco, CA, Dec. 25, 1941, Age 68

BATES, Florence (née Rabe)
Actress
b. Texas, 1888
d. Burbank, CA, Jan. 31, 1954, Age 65

BATES, Marie
Performer
b. Boston, MA, Unknown
d. Glenbrook, CT, March 12, 1923, Age 70

BATES, Thorpe
Performer
b. London, England, Feb. 11, 1883
d. Unknown, May 23, 1958, Age 75

BATES, William
Performer, (played first low comedian American Negro character May 22, 1795)

BATH, Albert J. "Pop"
Performer
b. Unknown
d. Unknown, Columbus, OH, Age Feb. 14, 1964

BATIE, Frank
Actor
b. Norwich, NY, Unknown
d. Norwich, NY, Dec. 31, 1949, Age 69

BATTY, Archibald
Actor
b. North Mymms Vicarage, Hertshire, England, Nov. 6, 1887
d. Budleigh Salterton, England, Nov. 24, 1961, Age 74

BATY, Gaston
Producer, Director, Author, Actor
b. Unknown, 1885
d. Unknown, Oct. 1952

BAUGHAN, Edward Algernon
Drama, Music and Film Critic
b. London, England, Dec. 2, 1865
d. Unknown, Nov. 26, 1938, Age 72

BAUM, Lyman Frank
Playwright, Novelist
b. Chittenango, NY, May 15, 1856
d. Unknown, May 6, 1919, Age 62

BAUM, Morton
Co-Founder N.Y. City Center
b. New York, NY, 1905
d. New York, NY, Feb. 7, 1968, Age 62

BAUM, Vicki
Novelist, Playwright, Screenwriter
b. Vienna, Austria, Jan. 24, 1888
d. Hollywood, CA, Aug. 29, 1960, Age 72

BAUR, Franklyn
Singer
b. Unknown
d. Brooklyn, NY, Feb. 24, 1950, Age 46

BAUR, Harry
Actor
b. Unknown
d. Unknown, April 1943

BAX, Clifford
Playwright, Journalist
b. London, England, July 13, 1886
d. London, England, Nov. 18, 1962, Age 76

BAXTER, Alan
actor
b. East Cleveland, OH, Nov. 19, 1908
d. Woodland Hills, CA, May 8, 1976, Age 67

BAXTER, Barry
Performer
b. Newton, North Wales, Aug. 5, 1894
d. New York, NY, May 27, 1922, Age 27

BAXTER, Beverley (Sir)
Critic, Editor, Writer
b. Toronto, CAN, Unknown
d. Haslemere, England, April 26, 1964, Age 73

BAXTER, Lora
Performer
b. Unknown
d. New York, NY, June 16, 1955, Age 47

BAXTER, Warner
Actor
b. Unknown
d. Beverly Hills, CA, May 7, 1951, Age 59

BAYES, Nora
Performer
b. Milwaukee, WI, 1880
d. New York, NY, March 19, 1928, Age 48

BAYLIS, Lillian
Producer, (Old Vic Co. & Sadler's Wells)
b. London, England, May 9, 1874
d. Unknown, Nov. 25, 1937, Age 63

BAYLY, Thomas Haynes
Playwright
b. Unknown
d. Unknown, April 22, 1839, Age 41

BAYNTON, Henry
Actor
b. Warwick, England, Sept. 23, 1892
d. Unknown, Jan. 2, 1951, Age 58

BEACH, William
Actor
b. Unknown
d. Philadelphia, PA, Dec. 1, 1926, Age 52

BEAL, Royal
Actor
b. Brookline, MA, June 2, 1899
d. Keene, NH, May 20, 1969, Age 69

BEALBY, George
Actor
b. Unknown
d. Unknown, June 18, 1931, Age 54

BEARD, John
Performer
b. Unknown, c1716
d. Unknown, Feb. 5, 1791, Age 75

BEASLEY, Byron
Actor
b. Unknown
d. Detroit, MI, Jan. 28, 1927, Age 55

BEATTY, May
Actress
b. Christchurch, New Zealand, Unknown
d. Unknown, April 1, 1945, Age 64

BEAUCHAMP, John
Actor
b. Unknown
d. Unknown, May 25, 1921, Age 70

BEAUDET, Louise
Performer
b. St. Emilie, Quebec, CAN, Unknown
d. New York, NY, Dec. 31, 1947, Age 87

BEAUMARCHAIS, Pierre-Augustin Caron de
Playwright
b. Paris, France, Jan. 24, 1732
d. Paris, France, May 18, 1799, Age 67

BEAUMONT, Diana
Actress
b. Unknown
d. London, England, June 21, 1964, Age 55

BEAUMONT, Francis
Playwright
b. Unknown, c1584
d. Unknown, March 6, 1616, Age 32

BEAUMONT, Muriel (Lady du Maurier)
Actress
b. Unknown, April 14, 1881
d. Unknown, Nov. 27, 1957, Age 78

BEAUMONT, Nellie
Actress
b. Unknown
d. Concord, NH, Oct. 26, 1938, Age 68

BEAUMONT, Rose
Actress
b. Unknown
d. Miami, FL, May 1938

BEAVERS, Louise
Actress
b. Unknown
d. Hollywood, CA, Oct. 26, 1962, Age 60

BEAZLEY, Samuel
Playwright, Architect, Designer
b. Unknown, 1786
d. Unknown, Oct. 12, 1851, Age 65

BEBAN, George
Actor
b. San Francisco, CA, 1873
d. Los Angeles, CA, Oct. 5, 1928, Age 55

BECK, Martin
Producer, Theatre manager
b. Czechoslovakia, c1869
d. New York, NY, Nov. 16, 1940, Age 71

BECKER, John C.
Scene designer and builder
b. Unknown
d. Sarasota, FL, May 3, 1963, Age 81

BECKETT, Gilbert A.
Playwright
b. Unknown
d. Unknown, Aug. 30, 1856, Age 45

BECKETT, Scotty
Actor
b. Oakland, CA, Oct. 4, 1920
d. Hollywood, CA, May 10, 1968, Age 38

BECKINGHAM, Charles
Playwright, Poet
b. Unknown
d. Unknown, Feb. 19, 1731, Age 31

BECQUE, Henri
Playwright
b. Paris, France, 1837
d. Unknown, May 12, 1899, Age 62

BEDDOES, Thomas Lovell
Playwright, Poet
b. Clifton, England, 1803
d. Unknown, 1849

BEDFORD, Harry
Comedian
b. Unknown
d. Unknown, Dec. 18, 1939, Age 66

BEDFORD, Henry
Actor, Playwright
b. Unknown
d. Unknown, Feb. 2, 1923, Age 77

BEDFORD, Paul
Actor
b. Unknown, 1792
d. Unknown, Jan. 11, 1871, Age 78

BEDINI, Jean
Producer
b. Unknown
d. New York, NY, Nov. 8, 1956, Age 85

BEECHAM, Sir Joseph
Producer
b. Unknown
d. Unknown, Oct. 23, 1916, Age 68

BEECHAM, Sir Thomas
Conductor
b. Unknown
d. London, England, March 8, 1961, Age 81

BEECHER, Janet
Actress
b. Jefferson City, MO, Oct. 21, 1884
d. Washington, CT, Aug. 6, 1955, Age 71

BEERBOHM, Sir Max
Drama critic, Caricaturist, Writer
b. London, England, Aug. 24, 1872
d. Rapallo, Italy, May 20, 1956, Age 83

BEERY, Noah Sr.
Actor
b. Kansas City, MO, Jan. 1, 1883
d. Hollywood, CA, April 1, 1946, Age 63

BEERY, Wallace
Actor
b. Kansas City, MO, April 1, 1881
d. Beverly Hills, CA, April 15, 1949, Age 68

BEESTON, Christopher
Actor, Producer
b. Unknown, c1570
d. Unknown, 1638

BEESTON, William
Actor, Producer
b. Unknown, c1606
d. Unknown, 1682

BEET, Alice
Actress
b. Hull, England, Unknown
d. Unknown, Dec. 26, 1931

BEGLEY, Ed
Actor
b. Hartford, CT, March 25, 1901
d. Los Angeles, CA, April 29, 1970, Age 69

BEHAN, Brendan
Playwright, Journalist, Poet
b. Dublin, Ireland, Feb. 9, 1923
d. Dublin, Ireland, March 20, 1964, Age 41

BEHN, Mrs. Aphra
Playwright, Novelist, Poet
b. Wye, Kent, England, 1640
d. Unknown, April 16, 1689, Age 48

BEHRMAN, S. N.
Playwright
b. Worcester, MA, June 9, 1893
d. New York, NY, Sept. 9, 1973, Age 80

BEHYMER, L. E. (Lynden Ellsworth)
Impresario
b. Shelbyville, IL, Unknown
d. Los Angeles, CA, Dec. 16, 1947, Age 85

BEHYMER, Minetta S. (Mrs. L. E. Behymer)
Impresario
b. Unknown
d. Los Angeles, CA, Oct. 2, 1958, Age 93

BEITH, Sir John Hay (Ian Hay)
Playwright, Novelist
b. Unknown, April 17, 1876
d. Hampshire, England, Sept. 22, 1952, Age 76

BEJART, Armande Grésinde Claire Elizabeth (Mme. Molière)
Actress
b. Unknown, 1642
d. Unknown, Nov. 3, 1700, Age 58

BEJART, Madeleine
Actress
b. Unknown, 1618
d. Unknown, 1672

BELA, Nicholas
Actor, Playwright
b. Hungary, Unknown
d. New York,NY, Nov. 18, 1963, Age 63

BELASCO, David
Producer, Playwright
b. San Francisco, CA, July 25, 1859
d. New York, NY, May 14, 1931, Age 71

BELASCO, Edward
Producer
b. San Francisco, CA, Unknown
d. San Francisco, CA, Oct. 9, 1937, Age 63

BELASCO, Frederick
Manager, Producer
b. Unknown
d. San Francisco, CA, Dec. 21, 1920, Age 59

BELASCO, Genevieve
Actress
b. London, England, Unknown
d. New York, NY, Nov. 17, 1956, Age 84

BELCHAM, Henry
Theatrical journalist
b. Unknown
d. Unknown, Feb. 9, 1917, Age 67

BELL, Archie
Critic, Playwright
b. Unknown
d. Unknown, Jan. 28, 1943, Age 65

BELL, Clarence F.
Press representative
b. Unknown
d. New York, NY, Feb. 20, 1963, Age 66

BELL, Digby Valentine
Actor
b. Milwaukee, WI, 1851
d. Unknown, June 20, 1917, Age 66

BELL, Dr. Campton
Educator
b. Unknown
d. Denver, CO, Dec. 7, 1963, Age 58

BELL, Gaston
Actor
b. Boston, MA, Sept. 27, 1877
d. Woodstock, NY, Dec. 11, 1963, Age 86

BELL, John
Publisher
b. Unknown, 1745
d. Unknown, 1831, Age 86

BELL, John Jay
Playwright
b. Unknown, 1871
d. Unknown, 1938

BELL, Lady (Hugh) (Dame Florence Evelyn Eleanor Bell)
Playwright, Novelist
b. Paris, France, 1851
d. Unknown, May 16, 1930, Age 78

BELL, Laura Joyce
Performer
b. London, England, Unknown
d. New York, NY, May 29, 1904, Age 46

BELL, Leslie R.
Conductor, Composer, Arranger, Educator
b. Unknown
d. Toronto, CAN, Jan. 19, 1962, Age 55

BELL, Rex (George Belden)
Actor, Politician
b. Chicago, IL, Unknown
d. Las Vegas, NV, July 4, 1962, Age 58

BELL, Richard
Actor
b. Unknown
d. Unknown, Jan. 25, 1672

BELL, Robert
Playwright
b. Unknown
d. Unknown, April 12, 1867, Age 67

BELL, Stanley (C.B.E.)
Producer, Director
b. Nottingham, England, Oct. 8, 1881
d. Unknown, Jan. 4, 1952, Age 70

BELLAMY, Daniel (the younger)
Playwright
b. Unknown
d. Unknown, Feb. 15, 1788

BELLAMY, George
Actor
b. Unknown
d. Unknown, Dec. 26, 1944, Age 78

BELLAMY, George Anne
Actress
b. Unknown, c1727
d. Unknown, Feb. 16, 1788

BELLAMY, Henry Ernest
Producer
b. Oxford, England, Unknown
d. Cheltenham, England, Feb. 7, 1932, Age 70

BELLAMY, Thomas
Playwright
b. Unknown
d. Unknown, Aug. 29, 1800, Age 55

BELLAMY, Thomas Ludford
Performer, Director
b. Unknown
d. Unknown, Jan. 3, 1843, Age 73

BELLEROSE, (Pierre Le Messier)
Actor, Producer
b. Unknown, c1600
d. Unknown, c1670

BELLEW, Cosmo Kyrle
Actor
b. Unknown
d. Hollywood, CA, Jan. 25, 1948, Age 62

BELLEW, H. Kyrle (Harold)
Performer
b. Prescot, England, March 28, 1855
d. Unknown, Nov. 2, 1911, Age 56

BELLWOOD, Bessie
Performer
b. Unknown, 1847
d. Unknown, Sept. 24, 1896, Age 49

BELMORE, Alice (Cliffe)
Actress
b. London, England, Unknown
d. New York, NY, July 31, 1943, Age 73

BELMORE, Bertha
Actress
b. Manchester, England, Dec. 20, 1882
d. Barcelona, Spain, Dec. 14, 1953, Age 70

BELMORE, Daisy
Actress
b. England, Unknown
d. New York, NY, Dec. 12, 1954, Age 80

BELMORE, George
Actor
b. Unknown
d. Unknown, Sept. 27, 1956

BELMORE, Herbert
Actor
b. Unknown
d. Unknown, March 15, 1952, Age 77

BELMORE, Lionel
Actor
b. England, Unknown
d. Hollywood, CA, Jan. 30, 1953, Age 86

BELOT, Adolphe
Playwright
b. Unknown
d. Unknown, Dec. 17, 1890, Age 61

BELWIN, Alma
Performer
b. Unknown
d. Boston, MA, May 3, 1924

BENADERET, Bea
Actress
b. New York, NY, April 4, 1906
d. Los Angeles, CA, Oct. 13, 1968, Age 62

BENATZKY, Ralph
Composer
b. Moravske-Budejovice, June 5, 1884
d. Zurich, Switzerland, Oct. 17, 1957, Age 73

BENAVENTE y MARTINEZ, Jacinto
Playwright
b. Madrid, Spain, Aug. 12, 1866
d. Madrid, Spain, July 14, 1954, Age 87

BENCHLEY, Robert Charles
Humorist, Drama critic, Author, Actor
b. Worcester, MA, Sept. 15, 1889
d. New York, NY, Nov. 21, 1945, Age 56

BENDA, Wladyslaw Theodor
Artist
b. Poland, Unknown
d. New York, NY, Dec. 2, 1948, Age 75

BENDER, Dr. Milton
Actor's business manager, Dentist
b. Unknown
d. New York, NY, March 1, 1964, Age 69

BENDIX, Doreen
Actress
b. Unknown
d. Unknown, Aug. 7, 1931, Age 25

BENDIX, William
Actor
b. New York, NY, Jan. 14, 1906
d. Los Angeles, CA, Dec. 14, 1964, Age 58

BENDON, Bert
Performer, Sketch writer
b. Glasgow, Scotland, Unknown
d. Glasgow, Scotland, April 20, 1964

BENEDICT, Lew
Minstrel
b. Buffalo, NY, Unknown
d. New York, NY, Feb. 13, 1920, Age 80

BENELLI, Sem
Playwright
b. Prato, Toscana, Unknown
d. Zoagli, Italy, Dec. 18, 1949, Age 72

BENET, Harry
Producer, Director
b. Unknown
d. Unknown, Sept. 15, 1948, Age 71

BENET, Stephen Vincent
Playwright, Poet
b. Pennsylvania, July 22, 1898
d. New York, NY, March 13, 1943, Age 44

BENHAM, Arthur
Playwright
b. Unknown
d. Unknown, Sept. 7, 1895, Age 23

BENINI, Ferruccio
Playwright, Actor
b. Unknown, 1854
d. Unknown, 1925

BENJAMIN, C. B.
Theatre Manager
b. Unknown
d. Unknown, Aug. 22, 1951, Age 65

BENNETT, Barbara
Actress
b. Palisades, NJ, Unknown
d. Montreal, CAN, Aug. 8, 1958, Age 52

BENNETT, Belle
Actress
b. Unknown
d. Hollywood, CA, Nov. 4, 1932, Age 42

BENNETT, Constance Campbell
Actress
b. New York, NY, Oct. 22, 1904
d. Fort Dix, NJ, July 24, 1965, Age 59

BENNETT, (Enoch) Arnold
Playwright, Critic, Novelist
b. Shelton, Staffordshire, England, May 27, 1867
d. London, England, May 27, 1931, Age 63

BENNETT, George John
Actor
b. Unknown
d. Unknown, Sept. 21, 1879, Age 79

BENNETT, Johnstone
Actress
b. Unknown, 1870
d. Unknown, April 14, 1906, Age 36

BENNETT, Julia
Actress
b. Unknown
d. Unknown, Sept. 30, 1903, Age 79

BENNETT, Mrs. Joseph
Actress
b. Unknown
d. Unknown, Jan. 10, 1943, Age 84

BENNETT, Richard
Actor
b. Indiana, May 21, 1873
d. Los Angeles, CA, Oct. 22, 1944, Age 71

BENNISON, Louis
Actor
b. San Francisco, CA, Unknown
d. New York, NY, June 9, 1929, Age 46

BENOIS, Alexander Nikolayevich
Designer, Painter
b. St. Petersburg, Russia, 1870
d. Paris, France, Feb. 9, 1960, Age 90

BENRIMO, Joseph Harry
Performer, Playwright, Director
b. San Francisco, CA, June 21, 1874
d. New York, NY, March 26, 1942, Age 67

BENSON, Lady (née Gertrude Constance Samwell)
Actress
b. Unknown
d. Unknown, Jan. 19, 1946, Age 86

BENSON, Ruth
Actress
b. Fort Logan, MT, June 26, 1873
d. Unknown, Oct. 30, 1948, Age 75

BENSON, Sally
Playwright, Writer
b. St. Louis, MO, Sept. 3, 1897
d. Woodland Hills, CA, July 19, 1972, Age 75

BENSON, Sir Frank Robert
Actor-Manager
b. Alresford, England, Nov. 4, 1858
d. London, England, Dec. 31, 1939, Age 81

BENT, Buena
Actress
b. London, England, Unknown
d. Unknown, Dec. 17, 1957

BENT, Marion (Mrs. Pat Rooney)
Performer
b. Bronx, NY, Dec. 23, 1879
d. Bronx, NY, July 28, 1940, Age 60

BENTHALL, Michael
Director
b. London, England, Feb. 8, 1919
d. London, England, Sept. 6, 1974, Age 55

BENTLEY, Doris
Actress
b. Unknown
d. Unknown, Feb. 25, 1944

BENTLEY, Grendon
Actor
b. Bromyard, England, April 8, 1877
d. Unknown, April 27, 1956, Age 79

BENTLEY, Irene
Performer
b. Baltimore, Md., Unknown
d. Allenhurst, NJ, June 3, 1940, Age 70

Bentley, Richard
Playwright
b. Unknown
d. Unknown, Oct. 26, 1782, Age 74

BENTLEY, Spencer
Actor, Announcer
b. Unknown
d. Cuernevaca, Mexico, Nov. 28, 1963, Age 53

BENTLEY, Walter
Actor
b. Unknown
d. Unknown, Sept. 18, 1927, Age 79

BENZON, Otto
Playwright
b. Unknown, 1856
d. Unknown, 1927

BERAIN, Jean (the elder)
Designer
b. Unknown, 1637
d. Unknown, 1711

BERANGER, Clara (Mrs. William C. De Mille)
Screen writer, Educator
b. Baltimore, Md., Unknown
d. Hollywood, CA, Sept. 10, 1956, Age 70

BERARD, Christian
Designer, Artist
b. France, Unknown
d. Paris, France, Feb. 12, 1949, Age 46

BERENDT, Rachel (Monique Arkell)
Actress
b. Paris, France, Unknown
d. Paris, France, Jan. 19, 1957

BERESFORD, Harry
Actor
b. London, England, Nov. 4, 1867
d. Los Angeles, CA, Oct. 4, 1944, Age 77

BERG, Ellen (Mrs. Robert Edeson)
Actress
b. Unknown
d. Unknown, May 30, 1906, Age 32

BERG, Gertrude (née Gertrude Edelstein)
Actress, Playwright
b. New York, NY, Oct. 3, 1899
d. New York, NY, Sept. 14, 1966, Age 66

BERG, Michael C.
Performer
b. New York, NY, Unknown
d. Miami, FL, July 10, 1964, Age 78

BERGEL, John Graham
Critic, Journalist
b. London, England, March 1, 1902
d. Unknown, Nov. 15, 1941, Age 39

BERGEN, Nella
Performer
b. Brooklyn, NY, Dec. 2, 1873
d. Unknown, April 24, 1919, Age 46

BERGERAC, Savinien de Cyrano de
Author, Poet, Playwright
b. Unknown, 1619
d. Paris, France, 1655

BERGERE, Valerie
Performer
b. Metz, Alsace-Lorraine, 1867
d. Hollywood, CA, Sept. 16, 1938, Age 71

BERGMAN, Henry
Performer
b. Unknown
d. San Antonio, TX, Nov. 6, 1962, Age 75

BERGMAN, Hjalmar
Playwright, Novelist
b. Orebro, Sweden, 1883
d. Berlin, Germany, Jan. 1, 1931, Age 47

BERGSTROM, Hjalmar
Playwright
b. Copenhagen, Denmark, 1868
d. Unknown, 1914

BERI, Ben (Hogan)
Performer
b. Unknown
d. Vancouver, WA, Jan. 18, 1963, Age 51

BERINGER, Mrs. Oscar (Aimée Daniell)
Playwright, Authoress
b. Philadelphia, PA, 1856
d. Bournemouth, England, Feb. 17, 1936, Age 79

BERINGER, Vera
Actress, Playwright, Teacher
b. London, Mar. 2, 1879
d. London, England, Jan. 29, 1964, Age 84

BERKELEY, Arthur
Actor
b. Unknown
d. Hollywood, CA, July 29, 1962, Age 66

BERKELEY, Gertrude (Mrs. Gertrude Berkeley Enos)
Performer
b. Plattsburg, NY, Unknown
d. Hollywood, CA, June 14, 1946, Age 81

BERKELEY, Reginald Cheyne
Playwright, Novelist, Screenwriter
b. London, England, Aug. 18, 1890
d. Los Angeles, CA, March 30, 1935, Age 44

BERLEIN, Annie Mack
Actress
b. Dublin, Ireland, Unknown
d. New York, NY, June 22, 1935, Age 85

BERLYN, Alfred
Journalist, Drama critic, Playwright
b. London, England, 1860
d. Unknown, July 14, 1936, Age 76

BERLYN, Ivan
Actor
b. Unknown
d. Unknown, Dec. 11, 1934, Age 67

BERNARD, Barney
Actor
b. Rochester, NY, Aug. 17, 1877
d. New York, NY, Mar. 21, 1924, Age 46

BERNARD, Dick
Actor
b. Unknown
d. Unknown, Dec. 25, 1925, Age 60

BERNARD, Dorothy (Mrs. A. H. Van Beuren)
Actress
b. Unknown, July 25, 1890
d. Hollywood, CA, Dec. 15, 1955, Age 65

BERNARD, Kitty
Performer
b. Unknown
d. Rentoul, IL, Sept. 6, 1962

BERNARD, Leon
Actor
b. Unknown
d. Unknown, Nov. 19, 1935, Age 58

BERNARD, Sam
Actor
b. Birmingham, England, June 3, 1863
d. Shipboard, May 18, 1927, Age 63

BERNARD, Sam
Actor
b. Unknown
d. Los Angeles, CA, July 5, 1950, Age 61

BERNARD, Tristan
Playwright
b. Besancon, Doubs, France, Sept. 7, 1866
d. Paris, France, Dec. 7, 1947, Age 81

BERNARD, W. Bayle
Playwright
b. Unknown
d. Unknown, Aug. 5, 1875, Age 67

BERNAUER, Rudolph
Playwright, Librettist, Producer
b. Hungary, Unknown
d. London, England, Nov. 27, 1953, Age 73

BERNEY, William
Playwright
b. Unknown
d. Los Angeles, CA, Nov. 23, 1961, Age 40

BERNHARDT, Maurice
Producer
b. Unknown
d. Unknown, Dec. 21, 1928, Age 65

BERNHARDT, Sarah Henriette Rosine (Bernard)
Actress
b. Paris, France, Oct. 23, 1844
d. Paris, France, March 26, 1923, Age 78

BERNIE, Ben (Anzelevitz)
Performer, Musician
b. New York, NY, Unknown
d. Beverly Hills, CA, Oct. 20, 1943, Age 52

BERNSTEIN, Aline (née Frankau)
Designer, Writer
b. New York, NY, Dec. 22, 1881
d. New York, NY, Sept. 7, 1955, Age 74

BERNSTEIN, Henry Leon Gustave Charles
Playwright
b. Paris, France, June 20, 1876
d. Paris, France, Nov. 27, 1953, Age 77

BERNSTEIN, Herman
Theatre, executive, Production manager
b. New York, NY, Unknown
d. New York, NY, Nov. 2, 1963, Age 58

BERR, Georges
Actor, Playwright
b. Unknown
d. Unknown, July 25, 1942, Age 74

BERR DU TURIQUE, Julien
Playwright
b. Unknown
d. Unknown, July 5, 1923, Age 60

BERRY, William Henry
Actor
b. London, England, March 23, 1872
d. Unknown, May 2, 1951, Age 81

BERTE, Charles
Playwright, Journalist
b. Unknown
d. Unknown, May 26, 1908, Age 33

BERTE, Heinrich
Composer
b. Galgócz, May 8, 1858
d. Vienna, Austria, Aug. 25, 1924, Age 66

BERTON, Pierre
Actor, Playwright
b. Unknown
d. Unknown, Oct. 24, 1912, Age 70

BERTRAM, Arthur
Business manager
b. Blackheath, England, March 24, 1860
d. Unknown, Dec. 30, 1955, Age 95

BERTRAM, Eugene
Actor
b. Greenwich, England, Dec. 16, 1872
d. Unknown, Nov. 21, 1941, Age 69

BERTRAM, Frank
Actor
b. Unknown
d. Unknown, March 23, 1941, Age 70

BESIER, Rudolf
Playwright, Journalist
b. Java, July 2, 1878
d. London, England, June 15, 1942, Age 63

BESOYAN, Rick
Playwright, Composer, Lyricist, Actor
b. Reedley, CA, July 2, 1924
d. Sayville, NY, March 13, 1970, Age 45

BEST, Edna
Actress
b. Hove, England, March 3, 1900
d. Geneva, Switzerland, Sept. 19, 1974, Age 74

BEST, Willie
Actor
b. Unknown
d. Hollywood, CA, Feb. 27, 1962, Age 46

BETTAMY, F. G.
Critic, Journalist
b. Unknown
d. Unknown, Feb. 27, 1942, Age 73

BETTELHEIM, Edwin Sumner
Publisher, Editor, (N.Y. Dramatic News)
b. Albany, NY, Sept. 28, 1865
d. Unknown, Jan. 15, 1938, Age 75

BETTERTON, Mrs. Thomas (Mary Sanderson)
Actress
b. Unknown, c1647
d. Unknown, April 11, 1712

BETTERTON, Thomas
Actor, Playwright
b. Unknown, 1635
d. Unknown, April 28, 1710, Age 75

BETTI, Ugo
Playwright, Jurist
b. Camerino, Italy, 1892
d. Unknown, June 10, 1953, Age 61

BETTY, William Henry West
Actor, (The Young Roscius)
b. Shrewsbury, England, Sept. 13, 1791
d. London, England, Aug. 24, 1874, Age 82

BEVAN, Billy
Actor
b. Australia, Unknown
d. Escondido, CA, Nov. 26, 1957, Age 70

BEVANS, Phillippa
Actress
b. London, England, Unknown
d. New York, NY, May 10, 1968, Age 55

BEVERIDGE, J. D.
Performer
b. Dublin, Ireland, Oct. 28, 1844
d. Unknown, April 8, 1926, Age 81

BEVERLEY, Henry Roxby
Actor
b. Unknown
d. Unknown, Feb. 1, 1863, Age 67

BEVERLEY, Hilda
Actress
b. Unknown
d. Unknown, Jan. 24, 1942

BEVERLEY, Mrs. W. R.
Actress-Manager
b. Unknown
d. Unknown, May 1, 1851, Age 75

BEVERLEY, William Roxby
Actor, Producer
b. Unknown
d. Unknown, July 25, 1842, Age 69

BEVERLEY, William Roxby (the younger)
Scenic designer
b. Unknown, c1814
d. Unknown, May 17, 1889, Age 75

BIBIENA, Alessandro
Designer, Architect
b. Unknown, 1687
d. Unknown, 1769

BIBIENA, Antonio
Designer, Architect
b. Unknown, 1700
d. Unknown, 1774

BIBIENA, Carlo
Designer, Architect
b. Unknown, 1728
d. Unknown, 1787

BIBIENA, Ferdinando
Designer, Architect
b. Unknown, 1657
d. Unknown, 1743

BIBIENA, Francesco
Designer, Architect
b. Unknown, 1659
d. Unknown, 1739

BIBIENA, Giovanni Maria
Designer, Architect
b. Unknown, 1704
d. Unknown, 1769

BIBIENA, Giuseppe
Designer, Architect
b. Unknown, 1696
d. Unknown, 1757

BIBO, Irving
Composer
b. Unknown
d. Hollywood, CA, May 2, 1962, Age 72

BICKEL, George L.
Actor
b. Saginaw, MI, Unknown
d. Los Angeles, CA, June 5, 1941, Age 78

BICKERSTAFFE, Isaac
Playwright
b. Unknown, 1735
d. Unknown, 1812

BICKFORD, Charles
Actor
b. Cambridge, MA, Jan. 1, 1891 or 1889
d. Los Angeles, CA, Nov. 9, 1967, Age 78

BIDOU, Henri
Critic
b. Unknown
d. Unknown, Feb. 1943, Age 70

BIGELOW, Charles A.
Performer
b. Cleveland, OH, Dec. 12, 1862
d. Unknown, March 12, 1912, Age 49

BIGGERS, Earl Derr
Playwright, Author
b. Warren, OH, Aug. 26, 1884
d. Pasadena, CA, April 5, 1933, Age 48

BIGWOOD, G. B.
Actor
b. Unknown
d. Unknown, Feb. 11, 1913, Age 84

BILHAUD, Paul
Playwright
b. Unknown
d. Unknown, Jan. 9, 1933, Age 78

BILLINGS, William
Composer
b. Boston, MA, Oct. 7, 1746
d. Boston, MA, Sept. 26, 1800, Age 54

BILLINGTON, Elizabeth
Actress
b. Unknown
d. Unknown, Aug. 25, 1818, Age 49

BILLINGTON, Fred
Actor
b. Unknown
d. Unknown, Nov. 2, 1917, Age 63

BILLINGTON, John
Actor
b. Unknown
d. Unknown, Sept. 5, 1904, Age 75

BILLINGTON, Mrs. John (Adeline Mortimer)
Actress
b. Unknown
d. Unknown, Jan. 20, 1917, Age 93

BILLSBURY, John H.
Producer, Theatre operator, Agent, Singer
b. Unknown
d. Hollywood, CA, June 30, 1964, Age 78

BILTON, Belle (Countess of Clancarty)
Actress
b. Unknown
d. Unknown, Dec. 31, 1908, Age 38

BINDER, Fred (Falls)
Performer
b. Brooklyn, NY, Unknown
d. Cincinnati, OH, Jan. 27, 1963

BINDER, Sybille
Actress
b. Vienna, Austria, Unknown
d. Dusseldorf, Germany, June 30, 1962, Age 62

BING, Herman
Actor
b. Frankfort am Maine, Germany, Unknown
d. Hollywood, CA, Jan. 9, 1947, Age 57

BINGHAM, Amelia
Actress
b. Hicksville, OH, March 20, 1869
d. New York, NY, Sept. 1, 1927, Age 58

BINGHAM, J. Clarke
Actor
b. England, Unknown
d. New York, NY, Dec. 4, 1962, Age 65

BINGHAM, Leslie (Mrs. Joseph Byron Totten)
Performer
b. Boston, MA, Unknown
d. Adamson, NJ, Feb. 8, 1945, Age 61

BINYON, Robert Laurence
Playwright, Poet
b. Lancaster, England, Aug. 10, 1869
d. Reading, England, March 10, 1943, Age 73

BIRCH, Frank (O.B.E.)
Producer, Actor
b. London, England, Dec. 5, 1889
d. Unknown, Feb. 14, 1956, Age 66

BIRCH, Samuel
Playwright
b. Unknown
d. Unknown, Dec. 10, 1841, Age 84

BIRD, Charles A.
Manager
b. Lockport, NY, Unknown
d. Hornell, NY, Nov. 11, 1925, Age 70

BIRD, Robert Montgomery
Playwright
b. New Castle, DE, Feb. 5, 1806
d. Unknown, Jan. 23, 1854, Age 47

BIRD, Theophilus
Actor, Producer
b. Unknown, 1608
d. Unknown, 1664

BIRD (BOURNE), William
Actor
b. Unknown
d. Unknown, 1624

BIRKETT, Viva
Performer
b. Exeter, England, Feb. 14, 1887
d. Unknown, June 26, 1934, Age 47

BIRMINGHAM, George A. (James Owen Hannay)
Playwright, Novelist
b. Belfast, Ireland, July 16, 1865
d. London, England, Feb. 2, 1950, Age 84

BIRO, Lajos
Playwright
b. Hungary, Unknown
d. London, England, Sept. 9, 1948, Age 68

BIRRELL, Francis
Critic, Playwright
b. Unknown
d. Unknown, Jan. 2, 1935, Age 44

BISHOP, Alfred
Performer
b. Liverpool, England, Feb. 7, 1848
d. Unknown, May 22, 1928, Age 80

BISHOP, Kate
Actress
b. Unknown, Oct. 1, 1847
d. Unknown, June 12, 1923, Age 75

BISHOP, Richard
Actor
b. Unknown
d. Sharon, CT, May 28, 1956, Age 58

BISHOP, Will
Dancer
b. Unknown
d. Unknown, Nov. 24, 1944, Age 76

BISHOP, William
Actor
b. Oak Park, IL, July 16, 1918
d. Malibu, CA, Oct. 3, 1959, Age 41

BISPHAM, David
Singer
b. Philadelphia, PA, Jan. 5, 1857
d. New York, NY, Oct. 2, 1921, Age 64

BISSON, Alexandre
Playwright
b. Unknown
d. Unknown, Jan. 28, 1912, Age 64

BIZET, Georges
Composer
b. Paris, France, Oct. 25, 1838
d. Bougival, France, June 3, 1875, Age 36

BJORKMAN, Edwin August
Novelist, Poet, Critic, Translator
b. Unknown, Oct. 19, 1866
d. Asheville, NC, Nov. 16, 1951, Age 85

BJORNSON, Björn
Actor, Playwright
b. Unknown
d. Oslo, Norway, April 14, 1942, Age 82

BJORNSON, Björnstjerne
Playwright, Poet, Novelist
b. Kvikne, Osterdalen, Norway, Dec. 8, 1832
d. Paris, France, April 26, 1910, Age 77

BLACK, George
Producer, Director
b. Birmingham, England, April 20, 1890
d. Unknown, March 4, 1945, Age 54

BLACKMAN, Fred. J.
Director, Producer
b. Unknown
d. Unknown, July 1951, Age 74

BLACKMER, Sidney
Actor
b. Salisbury, NC, July 13, 1895
d. New York, NY, Oct. 5, 1973, Age 78

BLACKWELL, Carlyle
Actor
b. Troy, PA, Unknown
d. Miami, FL, June 17, 1955, Age 71

BLAIR, Eugenie
Actress
b. Columbia, SC, Unknown
d. Chicago, IL, May 13, 1922, Age 54

BLAIR, Mary (Mary Blair Eakin)
Actress
b. Pittsburgh, PA, Unknown
d. Pittsburgh, PA, Sept. 17, 1947, Age 52

BLAKELEY, James
Performer
b. Hull, England, 1873
d. Unknown, Oct. 19, 1915, Age 42

BLAKISTON, Clarence
Actor
b. Giggleswick, England, April 23, 1864
d. Unknown, March 23, 1943, Age 78

BLANCHAR, Pierre
Actor
b. Philippeville, Algeria, Unknown
d. Paris, France, Nov. 21, 1963, Age 67

BLANCHARD, Edward Leman
Playwright, Critic, Journalist
b. Unknown, 1820
d. Unknown, Sept. 4, 1889, Age 68

BLANCHARD, William
Actor
b. Unknown, 1769
d. Unknown, 1835

BLANCHE, Ada
Actress
b. London, England, July 16, 1862
d. Unknown, Jan. 1, 1953, Age 90

BLANCHE, Belle (Blanche Minzesheimer)
Performer
b. New York, NY, June 2, 1891
d. New York, NY, March 27, 1963, Age 72

BLAND, George
Actor
b. Unknown
d. Unknown, 1807

BLAND, Harcourt
Actor
b. Unknown
d. Unknown, Nov. 18, 1875, Age 64

BLAND, James
Performer
b. Unknown, 1798
d. London, England, July 17, 1861, Age 63

BLAND, James A.
Songwriter, Performer
b. Flushing, NY, Oct. 22, 1854
d. Philadelphia, PA, May 5, 1911, Age 56

BLAND, John
Playwright
b. Unknown
d. Unknown, Nov. 1788

BLAND, R. Henderson
Actor, Playwright, Poet
b. Unknown
d. Unknown, Aug. 20, 1941

BLANDE, Edith
Actress
b. Unknown
d. Unknown, May 10, 1923, Age 64

BLANDICK, Clara
Actress
b. Hong Kong, China, Unknown
d. Hollywood, CA, April 15, 1962, Age 81

BLANEY, Charles Edward
Producer, Author
b. Columbus, OH, Unknown
d. New Canaan, CT, Oct. 21, 1944, Age 78

BLANEY, Henry Clay
Producer, Actor, Playwright
b. Center Moriches, NY, Sept. 11, 1908
d. New York, NY, Jan. 22, 1964, Age 57

BLAU, Bela
Producer
b. Hungary, Unknown
d. New York, NY, Oct. 21, 1940, Age 44

BLAYNEY, May (Mrs. A. E. Matthews)
Actress
b. England, Unknown
d. Wepener, Orange, Free State, South Africa, Feb. 10, 1953, Age 79

BLEDSOE, Earl
Performer
b. Unknown
d. . . .near Joplin, MO, Feb. 10, 1962

BLEDSOE, Jules
Actor, Composer
b. Waco, TX, Dec. 29, 1898
d. Hollywood, CA, July 14, 1943, Age 44

BLINN, Holbrook
Actor
b. San Francisco, CA, Jan. 23, 1872
d. Croton, NY, June 24, 1928, Age 56

BLINN, Nellie Holbrook
Actress
b. Unknown
d. Unknown, July 5, 1909

BLISS, Hebe
Actress
b. Unknown
d. Unknown, Oct. 2, 1956, Age 79

BLISSETT, Francis
Performer
b. Unknown
d. Unknown, Dec. 13, 1824, Age 82

BLITZSTEIN, Marc
Composer
b. Philadelphia, PA, March 2, 1905
d. Fort de France, Martinique, West Indies, Jan. 22, 1964, Age 58

BLOCK, Anita Cahn
Journalist, Play reader, Lecturer
b. New York, NY, Aug. 22, 1882
d. New York, NY, Dec. 11, 1967, Age 85

BLOCK, William J.
Manager
b. Springfield, IL, Unknown
d. Kansas City, MO, April 12, 1932, Age 63

BLODGET, Alden S.
Producer-Manager for wife, C. O. Skinner
b. Flushing, NY, Unknown
d. Bay Shore, NY, June 11, 1964, Age 80

BLOMFIELD, Derek
Actor
b. London, Aug. 31, 1920
d. Britanny, France, July 23, 1964, Age 44

BLOOD, Adele
Actress
b. Unknown
d. Unknown, Sept. 13, 1936, Age 50

BLOODGOOD, Clara (Mrs. Clara S. Laimbeer, née Stephens)
Actress
b. New York, NY, 1870
d. Baltimore, MD, Dec. 5, 1907, Age 37

BLOOMGARDEN, Kermit
Producer
b. Brooklyn, NY, Dec. 15, 1904
d. New York, NY, Sept. 20, 1976, Age 71

BLORE, Eric
Actor
b. London, England, Dec. 23, 1887
d. Woodland Hills, CA, March 1, 1959, Age 71

BLOSSOM, Henry Martyn Jr.
Playwright
b. St. Louis, MO, May 10, 1866
d. New York, NY, March 23, 1919, Age 52

BLOW, Mark
Actor, Producer
b. Unknown
d. Unknown, June 10, 1921, Age 49

BLOW, Sydney (Jellings-Blow)
Playwright, Actor
b. London, England, March 6, 1878
d. Lugano, Switzerland, June 1, 1961, Age 83

BLOWITZ, William F.
Press representative
b. Pittsburgh, PA, Unknown
d. New York, NY, March 14, 1964, Age 48

BLUE, Monte
Actor, Press representative
b. Indianapolis, IN, Unknown
d. Milwaukee, WI, Feb. 18, 1963, Age 73

BLUM, Daniel
Editor, Author
b. Chicago, IL, Oct. 1, 1899
d. New York, NY, Feb. 24, 1965, Age 65

BLUM, Ernest
Playwright
b. Unknown
d. Unknown, Sept. 18, 1907, Age 71

BLUMENTHAL, Oscar
Playwright, Critic
b. Unknown, 1852
d. Unknown, 1917, Age 65

BLUMENTHAL, Richard M.
Producer
b. Paris, France, Unknown
d. Hollywood, CA, Jan. 14, 1962, Age 55

BLUMENTHAL-TAMARINA, Maria
Actress
b. Unknown
d. Unknown, Nov. 4, 1938, Age 79

BLYDEN, Larry
Actor, Director
b. Houston, TX, June 23, 1925
d. Agadir, Morocco, June 6, 1975, Age 49

BLYTHE, Coralie
Performer
b. Unknown, 1880
d. Unknown, July 24, 1928, Age 48

BOADEN, James
Playwright, Biographer
b. Unknown, 1762
d. Unknown, Feb. 16, 1839, Age 76

BOAG, William
Performer, Manager
b. Charleston, SC, Unknown
d. Dongan Hills, S.I., NY, June 1, 1939, Age 72

BOARDMAN, Lillian (Mrs. Lillian Boardman Smith)
Actress
b. Bay City, MI, Unknown
d. New York, NY, Sept. 19, 1953, Age 60

BOCAGE, (Pierre-François Tousey)
Actor, Producer
b. Unknown, 1797
d. Unknown, Aug. 30, 1863, Age 65

BODE, Milton
Actor, Producer
b. Birmingham, England, Jan. 7, 1860
d. Unknown, Jan. 10, 1938, Age 78

BODENHEIM, Maxwell (Bodenheimer)
Poet, Author, Performer
b. Hermansville, MS, May 26, 1893
d. New York, NY, Feb. 7, 1954, Age 60

BOGART, David
Singer, Actor
b. Unknown
d. New York, NY, April 7, 1964, Age 81

BOGART, Humphrey
Actor
b. New York, NY, Dec. 25, 1900
d. Holmby Hills, CA, Jan 14, 1957, Age 56

BOGDANOFF, Rose
Designer
b. Philadelphia, PA, Unknown
d. New York, NY, Jan. 19, 1957, Age 53

BOGUSLAWSKI, Wojciech
Producer, Director, Playwright
b. Unknown, 1757
d. Unknown, 1829

BOHNEN, Roman
Actor
b. St. Paul, MN, Unknown
d. Hollywood, CA, Feb. 24, 1949, Age about 50

BOILEAU, Nicolas (Boileau-Despréaux)
Poet, Critic
b. Paris, France, c1633
d. Unknown, 1711

BOISROBERT, François le Nutel de Abbé
Playwright, Cleric
b. Unknown, 1592
d. Unknown, 1662

BOITO, Arrigo
Poet, Composer
b. Unknown, 1842
d. Unknown, 1918, Age 76

BOKER, George Henry
Playwright, Poet, Diplomat
b. Philadelphia, PA, Oct. 6, 1823
d. Unknown, Jan. 2, 1890, Age 66

BOLAND, Mary
Actress
b. Philadelphia, PA, Jan. 28, 1885
d. New York, NY, June 23, 1965, Age 80

BOLES, John
Actor, Singer
b. Greenville, TX, Oct. 28, 1896
d. San Angelo, TX, Feb. 27, 1969, Age 73

BOLESLAWSKI, Richard
Actor, Director, Author, Educator
b. Warsaw, Poland, Feb. 4, 1889
d. Hollywood, CA, Jan. 17, 1937, Age 47

BOLEY, May
Performer
b. Washington, DC, Unknown
d. Hollywood, CA, Jan. 7, 1963, Age 81

BOLLER, Robert O. Sr.
Architect
b. Unknown
d. Dallas, TX, Nov. 24, 1962, Age 75

BOLLINGER, Anne (Mrs. Jack T. Nielson)
Singer
b. Lewiston, IA, Unknown
d. Zurich, Switzerland, July 11, 1962, Age 39

BOLM, Adolph
Dancer, Choreographer
b. St. Petersburg, Russia, 1887
d. Hollywood, CA, April 16, 1951, Age 67

BOLTON, Jack
Talent representative
b. Unknown
d. Hollywood, CA, Oct. 17, 1962, Age 60

BOLTON, Whitney
Drama critic
b. Washington, DC, July 23, 1900
d. New York, NY, Nov. 4, 1969, Age 69

BOND, Acton
Actor
b. Unknown
d. Unknown, Nov. 29, 1941, Age 80

BOND, Bert (Herbert Rowley)
Performer
b. Unknown
d. Leeds, England, July 1964, Age 81

BOND, Carrie Jacobs
Composer, Publisher
b. Janesville, WI, Aug. 11, 1862
d. Hollywood, CA, Dec. 28, 1946, Age 84

BOND, Frederick Drew
Actor
b. New York, NY, Sept. 12, 1861
d. Whitestone, L.I., NY, Feb. 9, 1914, Age 52

BOND, Jessie
Actress
b. London, England, Jan. 11, 1853
d. Worthing, Sussex, England, June 17, 1942, Age 89

BOND, Ward
Actor
b. Bendelmen, NB, Unknown
d. Dallas, TX, Nov. 5, 1960, Age about 56

BONFILS, Helen
Producer, Newspaper publisher
b. Peekskill, NY, Nov. 26, 1889
d. Denver, CO, June 6, 1972, Age 82

BONIFACE, George C. Jr.
Performer
b. Unknown
d. Unknown, Jan. 3, 1912, Age 78

BONIFACE, Mrs. George C.
Actress
b. Unknown
d. Unknown, Oct. 13, 1883

BONNER, Isabel
Actress
b. Pittsburgh, PA, Unknown
d. Los Angeles, CA, July 1, 1955, Age 47

BONSALL, Bessie
Performer
b. Unknown
d. Paris, Ontario, CAN, Dec. 15, 1963, Age 92

BONSTELLE, Jessie (Laura Justine Bonesteele)
Actress
b. . . .near Greece, NY, Unknown
d. Detroit, MI, Oct. 14, 1932, Age about 66

BOOR, Frank
Manager
b. Rio de Janeiro, Brazil, Unknown
d. Unknown, April 10, 1938, Age 73

BOOSEY, William
Producer, Music publisher
b. Unknown
d. Unknown, April 17, 1933, Age 69

BOOTH, Agnes
Performer
b. Unknown, 1847
d. Unknown, Jan. 2, 1910, Age 63

BOOTH, Barton
Playwright, Actor
b. Unknown, 1681
d. Unknown, May 10, 1733, Age 52

BOOTH, Blanche De Bar
Actress
b. Unknown
d. Unknown, April 14, 1930, Age 86

BOOTH, Edwin Thomas
Actor-Manager
b. Belair, MD, Nov. 13, 1833
d. New York, NY, June 7, 1893, Age 60

BOOTH, Hope
Actress
b. Toronto, CAN, 1872
d. New York, NY, Dec. 18, 1933, Age 60

BOOTH, John Wilkes
Actor
b. Hartford County, MD, 1839
d. Bowling Green, VA, April 26, 1865, Age 26

BOOTH, Junius Brutus
Actor
b. London, England, May 1, 1796
d. on board the Mississippi steamboat "J. N. Sheneworth", Nov. 30, 1852, Age 56

BOOTH, Junius Brutus (the younger)
Actor
b. Charleston, SC, 1821
d. Manchester, MA, Sept. 16, 1883, Age 61

BOOTH, Junius Brutus III
Actor
b. Boston, MA, Unknown
d. Brightlingsea, England, Dec. 6, 1912, Age about 45

BOOTH, Nesdon
Actor
b. Unknown
d. Hollywood, CA, March 25, 1964, Age 45

BOOTH, Sallie
Actress
b. Unknown
d. Unknown, Feb. 28, 1902, Age 65

BOOTH, Sarah
Actress
b. Birmingham, England, 1794
d. Unknown, Dec. 30, 1867, Age 75

BOOTH, Sydney Barton
Actor
b. Boston, MA, Jan. 29, 1873
d. Stamford, CT, Feb. 5, 1937, Age 64

BORDEN, Olive
Actress
b. Baltimore, MD, 1907
d. Los Angeles, CA, Oct. 1, 1947, Age 40

BORDONI, Irene
Performer
b. France, Jan. 16, 1895
d. New York, NY, March 19, 1953, Age 58

BOREO, Emile
Performer
b. Poland, Unknown
d. New York, NY, July 27, 1951, Age 66

BORODIN, Aleksandr
Composer
b. St. Petersburg, Russia, Oct. 30, 1833
d. St. Petersburg, Russia, Feb. 15, 1887, Age 53

BOROWSKY, Marvin S.
Educator, Writer
b. Hammonton, NJ, Sept. 28, 1907
d. Los Angeles, CA, July 5, 1969, Age 60

BORTHWICK, A. T.
Critic, Journalist
b. Unknown
d. Unknown, May 22, 1943, Age 65

BOSILLO, Nick
Performer
b. Unknown
d. Hollywood, CA, May 19, 1964, Age 80

BOSTON, Nelroy Buck
Actress
b. Unknown
d. Van Nuys, CA, Feb. 28, 1962, Age 51

BOSWORTH, Hobart Van Zandt
Actor, Director, Writer
b. Marietta, OH, 1867
d. Glendale, CA, Dec. 20, 1943, Age 76

BOTTOMLY, Gordon
Playwright, Poet
b. Keighley, Yorkshire, England, Feb. 20, 1874
d. Oare, England, Aug. 25, 1948, Age 74

BOTTOMLY, Roland
Actor
b. Liverpool, England, Unknown
d. New York, NY, Jan. 5, 1947, Age 67

BOUCHER, François
Designer
b. Unknown, 1703
d. Unknown, 1770, Age 67

BOUCHER, Victor
Actor
b. Rouen, France, Unknown
d. Ville d'Avray, France, Feb. 22, 1942, Age 62

BOUCICAULT, Aubrey
Actor, Playwright
b. London, England, June 23, 1869
d. Unknown, July 10, 1913, Age 44

BOUCICAULT, Dion (Dionysius Lardner Bourcicault)
Actor, Playwright
b. Dublin, Ireland, Dec. 1822
d. New York, NY, Sept. 18, 1890, Age 68

BOUCICAULT, Dion George (Darley George Boucicault)
Director, Actor, Producer
b. New York, NY, May 23, 1859
d. Hurley, Buckinghamshire, England, June 25, 1929, Age 70

BOUCICAULT, Mrs. Dion (Agnes Kelly Robertson)
Actress
b. Edinburgh, Scotland, Dec. 25, 1833
d. London, England, Nov. 6, 1916, Age 82

BOUCICAULT, Nina
Performer
b. Marylebone, London, England, Feb. 27, 1967
d. Ealing, London, England, Aug. 1950, Age 83

BOUGHTON, Rutland
Composer
b. Aylesbury, England, 1878
d. Unknown, Jan. 25, 1960, Age 82

BOURCHIER, Arthur
Actor-Manager
b. Speen, Berkshire, England, June 22, 1863
d. Unknown, Sept. 14, 1927, Age 64

BOURDET, Edouard
Playwright, Director
b. Saint-Germain en Laye, France, 1887
d. Paris, France, Jan. 17, 1945, Age 57

BOURGET, Paul
Playwright, Poet, Critic, Novelist
b. Unknown, 1852
d. Unknown, Dec. 25, 1935, Age 83

BOURVIL, (né Andre Raimbourg)
Actor
b. Normandy, France, Unknown
d. Paris, France, Sept. 23, 1976, Age 57

BOWDLER, Thomas
Editor
b. Unknown, 1754
d. Unknown, Feb. 24, 1825, Age 70

BOWER, Marian
Playwright
b. Unknown
d. Unknown, Oct. 5, 1945

BOWERS, D. P.
Actor
b. Unknown
d. Unknown, June 6, 1857, Age 35

BOWERS, Mrs. D. P.
Actress
b. Unknown
d. Unknown, Nov. 6, 1895, Age 65

BOWERS, Robert Hood
Composer, Condustor
b. Chambersburg, PA, May 24, 1877
d. New York, NY, Dec. 29, 1941, Age 64

BOWERS, Viola (Mrs. Viola Bowers Simmons)
Performer
b. Worcester, MA, Unknown
d. New York, NY, June 27, 1962, Age 79

BOWES, Major Edward E.
Manager, Promoter
b. San Francisco, CA, Unknown
d. Rumson, NJ, June 13, 1946, Age about 72

BOWKETT, Sidney
Playwright
b. Unknown
d. Unknown, Oct. 10, 1937, Age 69

BOWMAN, Laura
Actress
b. Unknown, 1881
d. Los Angeles, CA, March 29, 1957, Age 76

BOWNE, Owen O.
Dancer
b. Unknown
d. St. Petersburg, FL, Jan. 1963, Age 84

BOWYER, Frederick
Playwright, Songwriter
b. Unknown
d. Unknown, Dec. 25, 1936, Age 87

BOYAR, Benjamin A.
Production general manager, Producer
b. Hartford, CT, Unknown
d. New York, NY, Feb. 21, 1964, Age 69

BOYD, William Henry
Actor
b. New York, NY, Unknown
d. Hollywood, CA, March 20, 1935, Age 45

BOYER, Rachel
Actress
b. Unknown
d. Unknown, Aug. 11, 1935, Age 70

BOYLE, Roger (Earl of Orrery)
Playwright
b. Unknown
d. Unknown, Oct. 16, 1679, Age 58

BOYLE, William
Playwright
b. County Louth, Ireland, April 4, 1853
d. Unknown, March 6, 1923, Age 69

BOYNE, Leonard
Actor, Producer
b. Westmeath, Ireland, April 11, 1853
d. Unknown, April 17, 1920, Age 67

BRACCO, Roberto
Playwright
b. Unknown
d. Unknown, April 21, 1943, Age 82

BRACEGIRDLE, Mrs. Anne
Actress
b. Unknown, c1663
d. Unknown, Sept. 14, 1748, Age 85

BRACKENRIDGE, Hugh Henry
Playwright
b. Scotland, 1748
d. Unknown, 1816, Age 68

BRACKETT, Charles
Critic, Writer, Producer
b. Saratoga Springs, NY, Nov. 26, 1892
d. Bel-Air, CA, March 9, 1969, Age 76

BRACKMAN, Marie L.
Singer
b. Unknown
d. Holyoke, MA, March 8, 1963, Age 90

BRADBURY, James H.
Performer
b. Old Town, ME, Oct. 12, 1857
d. Clifton, S.I., NY, Oct. 12, 1940, Age 83

BRADEL, John F.
Stage manager, Union executive
b. Unknown
d. Louisville, KY, Jan. 16, 1962, Age 79

BRADEN, Frank
Press representative
b. Unknown
d. Providence, RI, May 3, 1962, Age 76

BRADFORD, James M.
Performer
b. Cincinnati, OH, Unknown
d. Akron, OH, June 8, 1933, Age 89

BRADLEY, H. Dennis
Playwright
b. Unknown
d. Unknown, Nov. 20, 1934, Age 56

BRADLEY, Leonora
Actress
b. New York, NY, Unknown
d. Boston, MA, May 31, 1935, Age 80

BRADLEY, Oscar
Musical conductor
b. London, England, Unknown
d. Norwalk, CT, Aug. 31, 1948, Age 55

BRADSHAW, Fanny
Actrees - Teacher
b. Pittsburgh, PA, Dec. 27, 1897
d. New York, NY, June 26, 1973, Age 75

BRADT, Clifton E. (Clif)
Critic
b. Schenectady, NY, Unknown
d. Albany, NY, Nov. 2, 1961, Age 62

BRADY, Alice
Actress
b. New York, NY, Nov. 2, 1892
d. New York, NY, Oct. 28, 1939, Age 47

BRADY, Hugh
Actor
b. Unknown
d. Greenwich, CT, March 4, 1921, Age 40

BRADY, Veronica
Actress
b. Dublin, Ireland, 1890
d. Twickenham, England, Jan. 19, 1964, Age 75

BRADY, William A. Jr.
Producer
b. New York, NY, 1900
d. Colt's Neck, NJ, Sept. 26, 1935, Age 35

BRADY, William Aloysius
Producer
b. San Francisco, CA, June 19, 1863
d. New York, NY, Jan. 6, 1950, Age 86

BRAGA, Eurico
Actor, Producer, Journalist
b. Rio de Janeiro, Brazil, Unknown
d. Lisbon, Portugal, Nov. 19, 1962, Age 68

BRAGDON, Claude Fayette
Author, Designer, Architect
b. Oberlin, OH, Unknown
d. New York, NY, Sept. 17, 1946, Age 80

BRAHAM, David
Composer
b. London, England, 1838
d. New York, NY, April 11, 1905, Age 67

BRAHAM, Harry
Performer
b. London, England, Unknown
d. Staten Island, NY, Sept. 21, 1923, Age 73

BRAHAM, Horace
Actor
b. London, England, July 29, 1893
d. New York, NY, Sept. 7, 1955, Age 62

BRAHAM, Lionel
Actor
b. Yorkshire, England, Unknown
d. Hollywood, CA, Oct. 6, 1947, Age 68

BRAHAM, Philip
Composer, Conductor
b. London, England, June 18, 1881
d. Unknown, May 2, 1934, Age 52

BRAHM, Otto (Otto Abrahamsohn)
Performer, Manager
b. Unknown, 1856
d. Unknown, Dec. 1912, Age 56

BRAITHWAITE, Dame Lillian
Actress
b. Ramsgate, England, 1873
d. London, England, Sept. 17, 1948, Age 75

BRAMSON, Karen
Playwright
b. Unknown
d. Unknown, Jan. 27, 1936

BRAMSON, Sam
Talent representative
b. Kansas City, MO, Unknown
d. New York, NY, April 4, 1962, Age 60

BRAND, Barbarina (Lady Dacre)
Playwright
b. Unknown
d. Unknown, May 17, 1854, Age 86

BRAND, Hannah
Actress, Playwright, Poet
b. Unknown
d. Unknown, March 11, 1821

BRAND, Oswald
Actor, Playwright
b. Unknown
d. Unknown, Aug. 19, 1909, Age 52

BRANDES, Georg Morris Cohen
Critic
b. Copenhagen, Denmark, Feb. 4, 1842
d. Copenhagen, Denmark, Feb. 19, 1927, Age 85

BRANDES, Marthe
Actress
b. Unknown
d. Unknown, April 28, 1930, Age 68

BRANDON, Jocelyn
Playwright
b. Unknown
d. Unknown, May 24, 1948, Age 82

BRANDT, George
Producer
b. Brooklyn, NY, Oct. 1, 1916
d. New York, NY, Nov. 12, 1963, Age 47

BRANSCOMBE, Arthur
Playwright
b. Unknown
d. Unknown, Feb. 20, 1924

BRASSEUR, Albert
Actor
b. Unknown
d. Unknown, May 13, 1932, Age 70

BRASSEUR, Jules
Actor, Producer
b. Unknown
d. Unknown, Oct. 6, 1890, Age 61

BRATTON, John Walter
Composer
b. Wilmington, DE, Jan. 21, 1867
d. Brooklyn, NY, Feb. 7, 1947, Age 80

BRAYTON, Lily (Mrs. Oscar Asche)
Actress
b. Hindley, England, June 23, 1876
d. Dawlish, Devon, England, April 30, 1953, Age 76

BRECHER, Egon
Actor, Director
b. Czechoslovakia, Feb. 16, 1885
d. Los Angeles, CA, Aug. 12, 1946, Age 61

BRECHT, Bertolt (Eugen Berthold Friedrich Brecht)
Playwright
b. Ausburg, Bavaria, Germany, Feb. 10, 1898
d. East Germany, Aug. 14, 1956, Age 58

BREESE, Edmund
Actor
b. Brooklyn, NY, June 18, 1871
d. New York, NY, April 6, 1936, Age 64

BREIT, Harvey
Playwright, Novelist, Poet, Editor
b. New York, NY, Nov. 27, 1909
d. New York, NY, April 9, 1968, Age 58

BRENDEL, El
Actor
b. Philadelphia, PA, Unknown
d. Hollywood, CA, April 9, 1964, Age about 73

BRENNAN, Frederick Hazlitt
Novelist, Screenwriter
b. St. Louis, MO, Unknown
d. Hidden Valley, CA, June 30, 1962, Age 60

BRENNAN, J. Keirn (Jack)
Composer
b. Unknown
d. Hollywood, CA, Feb. 4, 1948, Age 74

BRENNAN, Jay
Performer, Screenwriter
b. Baltimore, MD, Unknown
d. Brooklyn, NY, Jan. 14, 1961, Age 78

BRENTANO, Felix
Producer
b. Vienna, Austria, Unknown
d. Bronx, NY, June 23, 1961, Age 52

BRENTANO, Lowell
Playwright, Novelist, Editor
b. New York, NY, Unknown
d. New York, NY, July 8, 1950, Age 55

BRERETON, Austin
Critic, Producer, Biographer
b. Liverpool, England, July 13, 1862
d. Unknown, Nov. 20, 1922, Age 60

BRERETON, Thomas
Playwright
b. Unknown
d. Unknown, Feb. 12, 1722, Age 31

BRETON DE LOS HERREROS, Manuel
Playwright
b. Unknown, 1796
d. Unknown, 1873

BRETT, Arabella
Actress
b. Unknown
d. Unknown, 1803

BRETT, Stanley
Performer
b. St. Heliers, Jersey, England, Nov. 18, 1879
d. Unknown, Nov. 9, 1923, Age 43

BREWER, George E. Jr.
Playwright
b. Unknown
d. Unknown, Feb. 20, 1968

BRIAN, Donald
Actor, Singer
b. St. John's, Newfoundland, Feb. 17, 1877
d. Great Neck, L.I., NY, Dec. 22, 1948, Age 71

BRICE, Fanny (née Borach)
Performer
b. New York, NY, Oct. 29, 1891
d. Hollywood, CA, May 29, 1951, Age 59

BRICE, Monte (Marvelle Brice)
Writer, Producer, Director
b. U.S.A., Unknown
d. London, England, Nov. 8, 1962, Age 71

BRIDIE, James (Dr. Osborne Henry Mavor)
Playwright
b. Glasgow, Scotland, Jan. 3, 1888
d. Edinburgh, Scotland, Jan. 29, 1951, Age 63

BRIEUX, Eugène
Playwright
b. Paris, France, Jan. 19, 1858
d. Nice, France, Dec. 6, 1932, Age 74

BRIGGS, Harlan
Actor
b. Blissfield, MI, Unknown
d. Hollywood, CA, Jan. 26, 1952, Age 72

BRIGGS, Matt
Performer
b. Unknown
d. Seattle, WA, June 10, 1962, Age 79

BRIGHOUSE, Harold
Playwright, Novelist
b. Eccles, Lancashire, England, July 26, 1882
d. London, England, July 25, 1958, Age 76

BRIQUET, Jean (Adolf Philipp)
Composer, Playwright, Actor
b. Hamburg, Germany, Jan. 29, 1864
d. New York, NY, July 30, 1936, Age 72

BRISCOE, Lottie (Mrs. Harry Mountford)
Actress
b. St. Louis, MO, Unknown
d. New York, NY, March 19, 1950, Age 79

BRISSON, Carl (né Pederson)
Singer, Actor
b. Copenhagen, Denmark, Dec. 24, 1895
d. Copenhagen, Denmark, Sept. 26, 1958, Age 62

BRITTON, Clifton
Director
b. Unknown
d. Goldsboro, NC, Feb. 10, 1963, Age 52

BROADHURST, George Howells
Playwright
b. Walsall, England, June 3, 1866
d. Santa Barbara, CA, Jan. 31, 1952, Age 85

BROADHURST, Thomas W.
Playwright
b. Old Wedensfield, South Staffordshire, England, Unknown
d. New York, NY, May 1, 1936, Age 78

BROCKBAND, Harrison
Performer
b. Liverpool, England, Unknown
d. New York, NY, Nov. 30, 1947, Age 80

BRODERICK, Helen (Mrs. Lester Crawford)
Actress
b. Philadelphia, PA, 1891
d. Beverly Hills, CA, Sept. 25, 1959, Age 68

BROKE, Charles Frederick Tucker
Critic, Scholar
b. Morgantown, WV, June 4, 1883
d. New Haven, CT, June 22, 1946, Age 63

BROMBERG, J. Edward (Joseph)
Actor
b. Temesvar, Hungary, Dec. 25, 1903
d. London, England, Dec. 6, 1951, Age 47

BROME, Alexander
Playwright
b. Unknown
d. Unknown, June 30, 1666, Age 46

BROME, Richard
Playwright
b. Unknown, c1590
d. Unknown, 1653

BROMFIELD, Louis
Novelist, Playwright
b. Mansfield, OH, Dec. 27, 1896
d. Columbus, OH, March 18, 1956, Age 59

BROMLEY, Nellie
Actress
b. Unknown
d. Unknown, Oct. 27, 1939, Age 89

BROMLEY-DAVENPORT, Arthur
Actor, Baginton, Warwickshire, England
b. Oct. 29, 1867, Unknown
d. Dec. 15, 1946, 79

BRONTE, Charlotte
Novelist
b. Thornton, England, April 21, 1816
d. Haworth, England, March 31, 1955, Age 38

BROOKE, Cynthia
Actress
b. Australia, Dec. 15, 1875
d. New York, NY, Sept. 11, 1949, Age 74

BROOKE, Emily
Actress
b. Unknown
d. Unknown, Aug. 9, 1953

BROOKE, Gustavus Vaughan
Actor
b. Unknown, 1818
d. Bay of Biscay, 1860

BROOKE, H. Sullivan
Composer, Conductor
b. Unknown
d. Unknown, July 7, 1923

BROOKE, Henry
Playwright
b. Rantavan, County Covan, Ireland, 1703
d. Ireland, Oct. 10, 1783, Age 80

BROOKE, Mrs. Frances
Playwright, Librettist
b. Unknown
d. Unknown, Jan. 1789, Age 65

BROOKFIELD, Charles Hallam Elton
Actor, Author, Censor
b. Unknown, May 19, 1857
d. Unknown, Oct. 20, 1913, Age 56

BROOKFIELD, Sydney F.
Critic
b. Unknown
d. France, Sept. 3, 1916

BROOK-JONES, Elwyn
Actor
b. Unknown
d. Reading, England, Sept. 4, 1962, Age 51

BROOKS, May K. (Mrs. Marty Brooks)
Performer
b. Unknown
d. Hollywood, CA, April 4, 1963, Age 68

BROOKS, Shirley
Playwright
b. Unknown
d. Unknown, Feb. 23, 1874, Age 57

BROPHY, Edward
Actor
b. New York, NY, Unknown
d. Pacific Palisades, CA, May 27, 1960, Age 65

BROUGH, Fanny Whiteside
Actress
b. Unknown, 1854
d. Unknown, 1914, Age 60

BROUGH, Lionel
Actor
b. Unknown, 1836
d. Unknown, 1900, Age 64

BROUGH, Mary
Actress
b. London, England, April 16, 1863
d. Unknown, Sept. 30, 1934, Age 71

BROUGH, Mrs. Robert (Florence Trevelyan)
Actress
b. Unknown
d. Unknown, Jan. 7, 1932, Age 73

BROUGH, Robert
Actor, Producer
b. Unknown
d. Unknown, April 14, 1906, Age 49

BROUGH, Robert Barnabas
Playwright
b. Unknown, 1828
d. Unknown, 1860, Age 32

BROUGH, Sydney
Actor
b. Unknown, 1868
d. Unknown, 1911, Age 43

BROUGH, William
Playwright
b. Unknown, 1826
d. Unknown, March 13, 1870, Age 44

BROUGHAM, John
Playwright, Producer
b. Dublin, Ireland, 1810
d. New York, NY, June 7, 1880, Age 70

BROUGHTON, Simon J.
Performer
b. Unknown
d. Youngstown, OH, Jan. 7, 1964, Age 80

BROUN, Heywood Campbell
Playwright, Critic
b. Brooklyn, NY, Dec. 7, 1888
d. New York, NY, Dec. 18, 1939, Age 51

BROWN, Albert O.
Producer
b. New York, NY, Unknown
d. New York, NY, March 6, 1945, Age 73

BROWN, Bertrand
Song writer, Press representative
b. Norborne, MO, Unknown
d. Bronx, NY, June 3, 1964, Age 75

Brown, Carrie Clarke Ward
Performer
b. Virginia City, NV, Unknown
d. Hollywood, CA, Feb. 6, 1926, Age 64

BROWN, Chamberlain
Talent representative
b. Unknown
d. New York, NY, Nov. 11, 1955, Age 67

BROWN, Charles D.
Actor
b. Council Bluffs, IA, Unknown
d. Hollywood, CA, Nov. 25, 1948, Age 60

BROWN, Clark
Manager
b. Mankato, MN, Unknown
d. Ashtabula, OH, May 5, 1943, Age 67

BROWN, Colonel T. Allston
Historian
b. Unknown
d. Philadelphia, PA, April 2, 1918, Age 83

BROWN, David Paul
Playwright
b. Philadelphia, PA, 1795
d. Unknown, 1875

BROWN, George Anderson
Actor
b. Unknown
d. Providence, RI, June 18, 1920, Age 81

BROWN, Gilmorn
Producer, Director, Educator
b. New Salem, ND, Unknown
d. Palm Springs, CA, Jan 10, 1960, Age 73

BROWN, John Mason
Critic
b. Louisville, KY, July 3, 1900
d. New York, NY, March 16, 1969, Age 68

BROWN, Lew
Song writer, Producer
b. Odessa, Russia, Dec. 10, 1893
d. New York, NY, Feb. 5, 1958, Age 64

BROWN, Lionel
Playwright, TV writer
b. Unknown
d. Bicton, England, June 16, 1964, Age 78

BROWN, Lyman C.
Talent representative
b. Hartford, CT, Unknown
d. New York, NY, March 31, 1961, Age 60

BROWN, Martin
Performer, Playwright
b. Montreal, CAN, June 22, 1885
d. New York, NY, Feb. 13, 1936, Age 50

BROWN, Nacio Herb (Ignacio)
Composer
b. Deming, NM, Feb. 22, 1896
d. San Francisco, CA, Sept. 28, 1964, Age 68

BROWN, Pamela
Actress
b. London, England, July 8, 1917
d. London, England, Sept. 18, 1975, Age 58

BROWN, Reed Jr.
Actor
b. Texas, Unknown
d. Mount Vernon, NY, July 26, 1962, Age 63

BROWN, Sedley
Actor, Director
b. Unknown
d. Los Angeles, CA, Sept. 29, 1928, Age 72

BROWN, Wally
Actor
b. Unknown
d. Unknown, Nov. 13, 1961, Age 87

BROWNE, Maurice
Actor, Producer
b. Reading, England, Feb. 12, 1881
d. Torquay, Devon, England, Jan. 21, 1955, Age 74

BROWNE, Porter Emerson
Playwright
b. Beverly, MA, June 22, 1879
d. Norwalk, CT, Sept. 20, 1934, Age 55

BROWNE, W. Graham
Performer, Director
b. Ireland, Jan. 1, 1870
d. Hampstead, England, March 11, 1937, Age 67

BROWNE, Walter
Performer, Playwright
b. Hull, Yorkshire, England, May 7, 1856
d. Unknown, Feb. 9, 1911, Age 56

BROWNE, Wynyard Barry
Playwright, Author
b. Unknown
d. Norwich, Norfolk, England, Feb. 19, 1964, Age 52

BROWNING, Edith
Performer
b. Unknown
d. Baltimore, MD, Jan. 26, 1926, Age 51

BROWN-POTTER, Mrs. James (née Cora Urquhart)
Actress
b. New Orleans, LA, May 15, 1859
d. Beaulieu-sur-Mer, France, Feb. 12, 1936, Age 76

BRUCE, Betty
Dancer, Singer
b. New York, NY, May 2, 1925
d. New York, NY, July 18, 1974, Age 49

BRUCE, Geraldine
Actress
b. Unknown
d. Congers, NY, Aug. 24, 1953, Age 72

BRUCE, Nigel
Actor
b. Ensenada, Mexico, Feb. 4, 1895
d. Santa Monica, CA, Oct. 8, 1953, Age 58

BRUCE, Tony
Actor
b. Unknown
d. Unknown, March 3, 1937, Age 27

BRUCKNER, Ferdinand
Adaptor
b. Unknown
d. Unknown, Dec. 5, 1958, Age 67

BRUNING, Albert
Actor
b. Berlin, Germany, Unknown
d. New York, NY, April 9, 1929, Age 70

BRUNS, Edna
Performer
b. Unknown
d. New York, NY, July 23, 1960, Age 80

BRUNS, Julia
Performer
b. St. Louis, MO, 1895
d. Unknown, Dec. 24, 1927, Age 32

BRUNTON, Ann (Mrs. Merry)
Actress
b. England, 1768
d. U.S.A., 1808, Age 40

BRUNTON, John
Actor
b. Unknown, 1741
d. Unknown, 1822, Age 81

BRUNTON, John (the younger)
Actor, Theatre manager
b. Unknown, 1775
d. Unknown, 1849, Age 74

BRUNTON, Louisa
Actress
b. Unknown, 1779
d. Unknown, 1860, Age 81

BRYAN, Hal (Johnson Clark)
Actor
b. Tansley, Derbyshire, England, Sept. 23, 1891
d. Unknown, Aug. 14, 1948, Age 57

BRYAN, Herbert George
Producer
b. Torquay, Devon, England, Unknown
d. Unknown, May 28, 1948

BRYANT, Charles E.
Actor
b. England, 1879
d. Mt. Kisco, NY, Aug. 7, 1948, Age 68

BRYANT, Dan (Daniel Webster O'Brien)
Minstrel, Producer
b. Troy, NY, May 9, 1833
d. New York, NY, April 10, 1875, Age 41

BRYANT, J. V.
Performer
b. Ayr, Scotland, May 26, 1889
d. Unknown, March 2, 1924, Age 34

BRYANT, Nana
Actress
b. Cincinnati, OH, Unknown
d. Hollywood, CA, Dec. 24, 1955, Age 67

BRYANT, Willie
Actor, Writer, Disk jockey
b. Unknown
d. Los Angeles, CA, Feb. 9, 1964, Age 56

BUCALOSSI, Brigata
Composer, Musical director
b. Unknown
d. Unknown, Dec. 21, 1924

BUCALOSSI, Ernest
Composer, Musical director
b. Unknown
d. Unknown, April 15, 1933, Age 69

BUCALOSSI, Procida
Composer, Musical director
b. Unknown
d. Unknown, May 10, 1918, Age 86

BUCHAN, Annabelle Whitford
Performer
b. Unknown
d. Chicago, IL, Nov. 30, 1961, Age 83

BUCHANAN, Charles L.
Critic
b. Unknown
d. New York, NY, March 10, 1962, Age 77

BUCHANAN, Jack
Performer
b. Helensburgh, Scotland, April 2, 1891
d. London, England, Oct. 20, 1957, Age 66

BUCHANAN, Robert
Playwright
b. Unknown
d. Unknown, June 10, 1901, Age 59

BUCHANAN, Thompson
Playwright
b. New York, NY, June 21, 1877
d. Louisville, KY, Oct. 15, 1937, Age 60

BUCHANAN, Virginia
Actress
b. Unknown
d. Unknown, Dec. 22, 1931, Age 88

BUCHNER, Georg
Playwright
b. Goddelan-bei-Darmst, Prussia, Oct. 17, 1813
d. Zurich, Switzerland, Feb. 19, 1837, Age 23

BUCK, Gene (Eugene Edward)
Producer, Songwriter
b. Detroit, MI, Aug. 8, 1885
d. Manhasset, NY, Feb. 24, 1957, Age 71

BUCK, Inez
Performer
b. Unknown
d. Oakland, CA, Sept. 6, 1957, Age 67

BUCKHAM, Bernard
Critic, Journalist
b. Unknown
d. Sussex, England, Dec. 28, 1963, Age 82

BUCKLER, Hugh C.
Actor
b. Southampton, England, Unknown
d. Lake Malibu, CA, Oct. 31, 1936, Age 66

BUCKLER, John
Actor
b. London, England, Unknown
d. Lake Malibu, CA, Oct. 31, 1936, Age 40

BUCKLEY, Annie (or Anna)
Performer
b. New York, NY, Unknown
d. New York, NY, Nov. 26, 1916, Age 44

BUCKLEY, Charles T.
Manager
b. Unknown
d. New York, NY, Aug. 25, 1920

BUCKLEY, F. Rauson
Actor
b. Unknown
d. Unknown, Sept. 15, 1943, Age 77

BUCKLEY, Floyd
Actor
b. Chatham, NY, Unknown
d. Flushing, NY, Nov. 14, 1956, Age 82

BUCKSTONE, J. C.
Actor
b. Sydenham, England, Dec. 9, 1858
d. Unknown, Sept. 24, 1924, Age 65

BUCKSTONE, John Baldwin
Actor, Playwright, Producer
b. Unknown, 1802
d. Unknown, Oct. 31, 1879, Age 77

BUCKSTONE, Rowland
Actor
b. Sydenham, Kent, England, March 29, 1860
d. London, England, Sept. 13, 1922, Age 62

BUEHLER, Arthur
Actor
b. Unknown
d. Hollywood, CA, Dec. 1, 1962, Age 68

BUFANO, Remo
Designer, Puppeteer
b. Italy, Unknown
d. . . .in airplane crash in Pennsylvania, June 17, 1948, Age 54

BUHLER, Richard
Performer
b. Washington, DC, Unknown
d. Washington, DC, March 27, 1925, Age 48

BULFINCH, Charles
Architect
b. Unknown, 1763
d. Unknown, 1844, Age 81

BULGAKOV, Leo
Actor, Producer
b. Tula, Russia, March 22, 1889
d. Binghamton, NY, July 20, 1948, Age 59

BULGAKOV, Mikhail Afanasyev
Playwright, Novelist
b. Russia, 1891
d. Moscow, U.S.S.R., March 10, 1940, Age 49

BULGER, Harry
Comedian
b. Unknown
d. Freeport, L.I., NY, April 15, 1926, Age 54

BULLOCK, Christopher
Actor, Playwright
b. Unknown
d. Unknown, April 5, 1724, Age 34

BULLOCK, Dr. John Malcolm
Critic, Playwright, Genealogist
b. Aberdeen, Scotland, Aug. 26, 1867
d. Unknown, March 6, 1938, Age 70

BULWER-LYTTON, Lord Edward George Earle Lytton
Playwright, Novelist, Poet
b. London, England, May 1803
d. Unknown, Jan. 18, 1873, Age 69

BUNCE, Oliver Bell
Playwright
b. Unknown, 1828
d. Unknown, 1890, Age 62

BUNN, Alfred
Librettist, Manager
b. Unknown, 1798
d. Unknown, Dec. 20, 1860

BUNNY, John
Actor
b. New York, NY, Sept. 1, 1863
d. Unknown, April 26, 1915, Age 51

BURANI, Michelette (Mme. Georges Barrare)
Actress
b. Asnieres, Paris, France, Unknown
d. Eastchester, NY, Oct. 27, 1957, Age 75

BURBADGE, Cuthbert
Actor, Producer
b. Unknown, c1566
d. Unknown, buried Sept. 16, 1636

BURBADGE, James
Actor, Producer
b. Hertfordshire, England, c1530
d. Unknown, buried Feb. 2, 1597

BURBAGE, Richard
Actor
b. Unknown, c1567
d. Unknown, March 13, 1619, Age 51

BURBECK, Frank
Performer
b. Unknown
d. New York, NY, Feb. 20, 1930, Age 74

BURGESS, Neil
Actor, Playwright
b. Boston, MA, June 29, 1846
d. New York, NY, Feb. 19, 1910, Age 63

BURGOYNE, General John
Playwright
b. Unknown, 1722
d. Unknown, June 4, 1792, Age 70

BURK, John Daly
Playwright
b. Ireland, Unknown
d. Unknown, April 11, 1808

BURKE, Billie
Actress
b. Washington, DC, Aug. 6, 1886
d. Los Angeles, CA, May 14, 1970, Age 84

BURKE, Charles
Performer
b. Unknown, 1822
d. Unknown, Nov. 10, 1854, Age 32

BURKE, Johnny
Lyricist
b. Antioch, CA, Oct. 3, 1908
d. New York, NY, Feb. 25, 1964, Age 55

BURKE, Myra
Actress
b. Unknown
d. Unknown, Feb. 9, 1944, Age 79

BURNABY, G. Davy
Performer, Author
b. Buckland, Hertfordshire, England, April 7, 1881
d. Unknown, April 17, 1949, Age 68

BURNACINI, Lodovico Ottavio
Designer
b. Unknown, 1636
d. Unknown, 1707

BURNAND, Sir Francis Cowley
Playwright, Editor, (of Punch Magazine)
b. Unknown, Nov. 29, 1836
d. Unknown, April 21, 1917, Age 80

BURNELL, Buster
Dancer, Choreographer
b. Unknown
d. New York, NY, Jan. 2, 1964, Age 41

BURNET, Dana
Playwright, Author
b. Unknown
d. Stonington, CT, Oct. 22, 1962, Age 74

BURNETT, Frances Hodgson
Playwright
b. Manchester, England, Nov. 24, 1849
d. Plandone, L.I., NY, Oct. 30, 1924, Age 74

BURNHAM, Charles C.
Producer, Theatre manager
b. New York, NY, Unknown
d. Winter Park, FL, Jan. 19, 1938, Age 85

BURNS, Anne K.
Playwright, Lyricist
b. Jerome, ID, Unknown
d. New York, NY, Sept. 20, 1968, Age 82

BURNS, David
Actor
b. New York, NY, June 22, 1902
d. Philadelphia, PA, March 12, 1971, Age 68

BURNS, Jerry "Pop"
Performer
b. Unknown
d. Unknown, New York, NY, Age Jan. 4, 1962

BURNS, Nat (Nat Burden Haines)
Actor
b. Philadelphia, PA, Unknown
d. New York, NY, Nov. 8, 1962, Age 75

BURNSIDE, R. H. (Richard)
Producer, Director
b. Glasgow, Scotland, 1870
d. Metuchen, NJ, Sept. 14, 1952, Age 82

BURNUP, Peter
Film critic, Journalist
b. Unknown
d. Morecambe, England, July 14, 1964, Age 73

BURR, Courtney
Producer
b. Kansas, Unknown
d. New York, NY, Oct. 17, 1961, Age 70

BURROWES, James
Actor
b. Unknown
d. Lynn, MA, May 20, 1926, Age 84

BURRY, Solen
Actor
b. Unknown
d. Long Island City, NY, June 8, 1953, Age 50

BURT, Frank A. (Augustus Berek)
Performer
b. Unknown
d. Brooklyn, NY, April 3, 1964, Age 82

BURT, Frederick
Actor
b. Lincoln, NB, Unknown
d. Twenty-nine Palms, CA, Oct. 2, 1943, Age 67

BURT, Harriet
Actress
b. Troy, NY, Oct. 5, 1885
d. Kansas City, MO, May 22, 1935, Age 47

BURT, Laura (Mrs. Henry W. Stanford)
Actress
b. Ramsey, Isle of Man, Unknown
d. Bronx, NY, Oct. 16, 1952, Age 80

BURT, William P.
Actor, Director
b. Unknown
d. Denver, CO, Feb. 23, 1955, Age 88

BURTON, Langhorne
Performer
b. Somersby, Lincolnshire, England, Dec. 25, 1872
d. Unknown, Dec. 6, 1949, Age 77

BURTON, Percy
Business manager
b. Tamworth, England, March 7, 1878
d. Unknown, Nov. 19, 1948, Age 70

BURTON, Robert
Actor
b. Boston, MA, Unknown
d. New York, NY, June 17, 1955, Age 46

BURTON, William E.
Manager, Performer
b. England, 1804
d. New York, NY, Feb. 10, 1860, Age 56

BURTON, William H.
Actor
b. Unknown
d. New York, NY, March 15, 1926, Age 81

BURTWELL, Frederick
Actor
b. Unknown
d. Unknown, Nov. 16, 1948

BUSBY, Amy
Actress
b. Rochester, NY, Unknown
d. East Stroudsburg, PA, July 13, 1957, Age 85

BUSCH, Mae (Mrs. Thomas C. Tate)
Actress
b. Melbourne, Australia, 1902
d. San Fernando Valley, CA, April 19, 1946

BUSH, Anita
Theatre Founder - Actress
b. Washington, DC, Unknown
d. New York, NY, Feb. 16, 1974

BUSH, Frank
Monologist
b. Unknown
d. Mount Vernon, NY, Nov. 14, 1927, Age 71

BUSLEY, Jessie
Actress
b. Albany, NY, March 10, 1869
d. New York, NY, April 20, 1950, Age 80

BUSNACH, William
Playwright
b. Unknown
d. Unknown, Jan, 1907, Age 75

BUTI, Carlo
Singer
b. Unknown
d. Florence, Italy, Nov. 16, 1963, Age 61

BUTLER, Alice Augarde
Performer
b. London, England, Nov. 4, 1868
d. Philadelphia, PA, Nov. 11, 1919, Age 51

BUTLER, Charles
Actor
b. Unknown
d. New York, NY, Aug. 27, 1920, Age 64

BUTLER, Rachel Barton
Playwright
b. Unknown
d. Greenwich, CT, Nov. 24, 1920

BUTLER, Richard William
Journalist, Critic, Playwright
b. London, England, May 21, 1844
d. Unknown, Dec. 1928, Age 84

BUTLER, Samuel
Actor
b. Unknown
d. Unknown, July 17, 1945, Age 48

BUTTERFIELD, Everett
Actor
b. Portland, ME, Unknown
d. New York, NY, March 6, 1925, Age 40

BUTTERWORTH, Charles Edward
Actor
b. South Bend, IN, July 26, 1896
d. Hollywood, CA, June 13, 1946, Age 49

BUTTERWORTH, Walter T.
Actor
b. Unknown
d. Hollywood, CA, March 10, 1962, Age 69

BYFORD, Roy
Performer
b. London, England, Jan. 12, 1873
d. Unknown, Jan. 31, 1939, Age 66

BYNNER, Witter
Poet, Playwright, Author
b. Brooklyn, NY, Aug. 1881
d. Sante Fe, NM, June 1, 1968, Age 86

BYRD, Sam
Actor
b. Mount Olive, NC, Jan. 18, 1908
d. Durham, NC, Nov. 14, 1955, Age 47

BYRNE, Francis M.
Actor
b. Newport, RI, Aug. 3, 1875
d. Unknown, Feb. 6, 1923, Age 47

BYRNE, James A.
Performer
b. Norwich, CT, Unknown
d. Camden, NJ, March 19, 1927, Age 59

BYRON, Arthur William
Actor
b. Brooklyn, NY, April 3, 1872
d. Unknown, July 17, 1943, Age 71

BYRON, Henrietta (Mrs. Barney Fagan)
Performer
b. Unknown
d. Philadelphia, PA, June 1, 1924

BYRON, Henry James
Playwright, Actor
b. Manchester, England, 1834
d. Unknown, 1884

BYRON, Kate (Mrs. Oliver Doud Byron née Mary Kate Rehan)
Actress
b. Unknown
d. Montclair, NJ, Dec. 21, 1920, Age 75

BYRON, Lord George Gordon
Poet, Playwright
b. London, England, Jan. 22, 1788
d. Missolonghi, Greece, April 19, 1824, Age 36

BYRON, Oliver Doud
Actor
b. Frederick City, MD, Nov. 14, 1842
d. Long Branch, NJ, Oct. 22, 1920, Age 77

C

CABOT, Eliot
Performer
b. Boston, MA, June 22, 1899
d. New York, NY, June 17, 1938, Age 39

CAHILL, Lily
Performer
b. Texas, Unknown
d. San Antonio, TX, July 20, 1955, Age 69

CAHILL, Marie (Mrs. Daniel V. Arthur)
Performer
b. Brooklyn, NY, 1870
d. New York, NY, Aug. 23, 1933, Age 63

CAHN, Julius
Manager
b. Unknown
d. Fort Lee, NJ, May 13, 1921

CAIL, Harold L.
Critic
b. Unknown
d. Portland, ME, Aug. 30, 1968, Age 66

CAILLAVET, Gaston Arman de
Playwright
b. Unknown
d. Unknown, Jan. 13, 1915, Age 44

CAIN, Patrick J.
Scenery warehouse operator
b. New York, NY, Unknown
d. New York, NY, May 13, 1949, Age 70

CAIN, Robert
Actor
b. Unknown
d. New York, NY, April 27, 1954, Age 67

CAINE, Georgia
Actress
b. Unknown
d. Hollywood, CA, April 4, 1964, Age 88

CAINE, Sir Hall (Thomas Henry Hall Caine)
Playwright
b. Douglas, Isle of Man, May 14, 1853
d. Isle of Man, Aug. 31, 1931, Age 78

CALDARA, Orme
Actor
b. Unknown
d. Saranac Lake, NY, Oct. 21, 1925, Age 50

CALDER, King
Actor
b. Unknown
d. Hollywood, CA, June 28, 1964, Age 65

CALDERON DE LA BARCA, Pedro
Playwright
b. Madrid, Spain, 1600
d. Unknown, May 25, 1681, Age 81

CALDWELL, Anne
Playwright, Lyricist
b. Boston, MA, Unknown
d. Beverly Hills, CA, Oct. 22, 1936, Age 60

CALDWELL, Henry
Producer, Actor
b. Unknown
d. London, England, Nov. 28, 1961, Age 42

CALHERN, Louis (Carl Henry Vogt)
Actor, Director
b. Brooklyn, NY, Feb. 19, 1895
d. Nara, Japan, May 12, 1956, Age 61

CALHOUN, Eleanor (Princess Lazarovich-Hrebelianovich)
Actress
b. Visalia, CA, Unknown
d. New York, NY, Jan. 9, 1957, Age 92

CALLAHAN, Billy (Mrs. Rosalee Valenzio)
Performer
b. Unknown
d. Whitestone, Queens, NY, Feb. 21, 1964, Age 53

CALLIGAN, Edward O.
Talent representative
b. Unknown
d. Santa Monica, CA, Sept. 21, 1962, Age 64

CALLOT, Jacques
Engraver, Designer
b. Nancy, France, 1592
d. Unknown, 1635

CALTHROP, Dion Clayton
Author, Artist, Designer, Litterateur
b. Unknown, London, England
d. May 2, 1878

CALTHROP, Donald
Actor-Manager
b. London, England, April 11, 1888
d. Unknown, July 15, 1940, Age 52

CALVERT, Adelaide Helen (née Biddles or Bedells)
Actress, Playwright
b. Unknown, 1837
d. Unknown, 1921, Age 84

CALVERT, Charles
Actor-Manager
b. Unknown, 1828
d. Unknown, 1879, Age 51

CALVERT, Louis
Actor, Producer
b. Manchester, England, Nov. 25, 1859
d. Unknown, July 9, 1923, Age 63

CAMARGO, Mlle. Marie Anne de Cupis de
Dancer
b. Unknown, 1710
d. Unknown, April 28, 1770, Age 60

CAMERON, Beatrice (Mrs. Richard Mansfield)
Actress
b. Troy, NY, 1868
d. New London, CT, July 12, 1940, Age 72

CAMERON, Donald
Actor
b. Canada, Unknown
d. West Cornwall, CT, July 11, 1955, Age 66

CAMERON, Hugh
Actor
b. Duluth, MN, Unknown
d. New York, NY, Nov. 9, 1941, Age 62

CAMERON, Kathryn
Actress
b. Unknown
d. New York, NY, Jan. 1, 1954, Age 71

CAMPANINI, Cleofonte
Impresario
b. Parma, Italy, Unknown
d. Chicago, IL, Dec. 19, 1919, Age 60

CAMPBELL, Bartley
Playwright
b. Pittsburgh, PA, Aug. 12, 1843
d. Unknown, July 30, 1888, Age 44

CAMPBELL, Charles
Actor
b. Scotland, Unknown
d. New York, NY, July 25, 1964, Age 59

CAMPBELL, Frances
Actress
b. Unknown
d. Unknown, July 9, 1948

CAMPBELL, Herbert
Performer
b. Unknown, 1844
d. Unknown, 1904, Age 60

CAMPBELL, Mrs. Patrick (Beatrice Stella Tanner)
Actress
b. Kensington, London, England, Feb. 9, 1865
d. Pau, France, April 9, 1940, Age 75

CAMPEAU, Frank
Actor
b. Detroit, MI, Unknown
d. Hollywood, CA, Nov. 5, 1943, Age 79

CAMUS, Albert
Playwright, Novelist, Essayist
b. Mondovi, Algeria, Nov. 7, 1913
d. Sens, France, Jan. 4, 1960, Age 46

CANFIELD, William F.
Performer
b. Unknown
d. New York, NY, Feb. 16, 1925, Age 64

CANNAN, Gilbert
Playwright
b. Manchester, England, June 25, 1884
d. Unknown, June 30, 1955, Age 71

CANSINO, Gabriel
Dancer, Dance teacher
b. Unknown
d. San Francisco, CA, March 2, 1963, Age 50

CANTOR, Eddie (né Edward Israel Iskowitz)
Comedian, Actor
b. New York, NY, Jan. 31, 1892
d. Beverly Hills, CA, Oct. 10, 1964, Age 72

CANTOR, Nat
Actor
b. Unknown
d. Queens, NY, May 16, 1956, Age 59

CAPEK, Josef
Playwright, Painter
b. Czechoslovakia, 1887
d. Unknown, 1927

CAPEK, Karel
Playwright, Producer
b. Malé, Syatonovice, Bohemia, Czechoslovakia, Jan. 9, 1890
d. Prague, Czechoslovakia, Dec. 25, 1938, Age 48

CAPON, William
Scene designer, Architect
b. Unknown, 1757
d. Unknown, 1827

CAPRICE, June (Mrs. Harry Millarde) (June Elizabeth Millarde)
Actress
b. Boston, MA, 1899
d. Hollywood, CA, Nov. 9, 1936, Age 37

CAPUS, Alfred
Journalist, Novelist, Playwright
b. Aix-en-Provence, France, 1858
d. Unknown, 1922

CARBREY, John
Performer
b. Unknown
d. Covina, CA, Dec. 12, 1962, Age 77

CARD, Kathryn (or Cathryn)
Actress
b. Unknown
d. Costa Mesa, CA, March 1, 1964, Age 71

CARDER, Emmeline
Actress
b. Unknown
d. London, England, Nov. 17, 1961

CAREW, James
Actor
b. Goshen, IN, Feb. 5, 1876
d. London, England, April 4, 1938, Age 62

CAREW, Ora
Actress
b. Unknown
d. Hollywood, CA, Oct. 26, 1955, Age 62

CAREY, George Saville
Actor, Playwright
b. Unknown
d. Unknown, July 10, 1807, Age 65

CAREY, Harry
Actor
b. New York, NY, 1878
d. Brentwood, CA, Sept. 21, 1947, Age 69

CAREY, Henry
Playwright, Musician
b. Unknown, 1690
d. Unknown, 1743, Age 174

CAREY, Joseph A.
Actor
b. Unknown
d. Brooklyn, NY, Jan. 9, 1964, Age 81

CAREY, Rev. Thomas
Co-founder and director of Blackfriars' Guild
b. Chicago, IL, June 19, 1904
d. New York, NY, May 8, 1972, Age 67

CARHART, James L.
Performer
b. West Bloomfield, MI, Dec. 24, 1843
d. Port Washington, L.I., NY, May 4, 1937, Age 93

CARLE, Richard
Actor, Playwright
b. Somerville, MA, July 7, 1871
d. Hollywood, CA, June 28, 1941, Age 69

CARLETON, Henry Guy
Playwright, Inventor
b. Fort Union, NM, June 21, 1856
d. Unknown, Dec. 10, 1910, Age 54

CARLETON, Marjorie
Playwright, Novelist
b. Unknown
d. Newton, MA, June 4, 1964

CARLILE, James
Actor, Playwright
b. Unknown
d. July 12, 1691

CARLISLE, Alexandra (Alexandra Swift)
Actress
b. London, England, Jan. 15, 1886
d. New York, NY, April 21, 1936, Age 50

CARLTON, Kathleen
Actress
b. Unknown
d. Iver, England, Jan. 2, 1964, Age 65

CARNEY, Kate (Mrs. George Barclay)
Performer
b. Unknown, Aug. 15, 1869
d. London, England, Jan. 1, 1950, Age 80

CARPENTER, Edward Childs
Playwright, Novelist
b. Philadelphia, PA, Dec. 13, 1872
d. Torrington, CT, Oct. 7, 1950, Age 77

CARPENTER, Paul
Actor
b. Montreal, CAN, Unknown
d. London, England, June 12, 1964, Age 43

CARR, Alexander
Performer, Playwright
b. Rumni, Russia, March 7, 1878
d. Hollywood, CA, Sept. 19, 1946, Age 68

CARR, Jane (née Rita Brunström)
Actress
b. Whitley Bay, Northumberland, England, Aug. 1, 1909
d. Unknown, Sept. 29, 1957, Age 48

CARR, Joseph William Comyns
Critic, Editor, Playwright
b. London, England, 1849
d. Unknown, 1916

CARR, Philip (Philip Alfred Vansittart Comyns Carr)
Critic, Journalist
b. Unknown
d. London, England, Aug. 6, 1957, Age 82

CARR-COOK, Madge
Actress
b. Yorks, England, June 28, 1856
d. Unknown, Sept. 20, 1933, Age 77

CARRE, Albert
Director, Playwright
b. Strasbourg, France, 1852
d. Paris, France, Dec. 12, 1938, Age 86

CARRE, Michel
Playwright
b. Unknown
d. Unknown, June 27, 1872, Age 53

CARRICK, Hartley
Playwright
b. Unknown, Nov. 15, 1881
d. Unknown, Nov. 24, 1929, Age 48

CARRIGAN, Thomas J.
Actor
b. Lapeer, MI, Unknown
d. Lapeer, MI, Oct. 2, 1941, Age 55

CARRILLO, Leo
Actor
b. Los Angeles, CA, Aug. 6, 1881
d. Santa Monica, CA, Sept. 10, 1961, Age 80

CARRINGTON, Evelyn
Actress
b. Unknown
d. Hollywood, CA, Nov. 21, 1942, Age 66

CARRINGTON, Frank
Producer, Director
b. Angel Island, CA, Sept. 13, 1901
d. Millburn, NJ, July 3, 1975, Age 73

CARRINGTON, Katherine
Actress
b. East Orange, NJ, Unknown
d. New York, NY, May 2, 1953, Age 43

CARRINGTON, Murray
Actor
b. Upper Norwood, England, March 13, 1885
d. Unknown, Dec. 2, 1941, Age 56

CARROLL, Albert
Actor
b. Oak Park, IL, Unknown
d. Chicago, IL, Dec. 1, 1956, Age 61

CARROLL, Earl
Producer, Playwright, Songwriter
b. Pittsburgh, PA, Jan. 23, 1892
d. Airplane Crash near Mt. Carmel, PA, June 17, 1948, Age 56

CARROLL, Garnet H.
Producer, Theatre owner, Actor
b. Unknown
d. Melbourne, Australia, Aug. 23, 1964, Age 61

CARROLL, Harry
Composer
b. Unknown
d. Santa Barbara, CA, Dec. 26, 1962, Age 70

CARROLL, Lawrence W.
Theatre Manager
b. Unknown
d. North Hollywood, CA, Feb. 7, 1963, Age 65

CARROLL, Leo G.
Actor
b. Weedon, England, 1892
d. Hollywood, CA, Oct. 16, 1972, Age 80

CARROLL, Nancy (née Ann Veronica LaHiff)
Actress
b. New York, NY, Nov. 19, 1909
d. New York, NY, Aug. 6, 1965, Age 60

CARROLL, Patrick Francis
Theatre librarian
b. Fall River, MA, Nov. 22, 1902
d. Hicksville, NY, March 16, 1965, Age 62

CARROLL, Paul Vincent
Playwright
b. Dundalk, Ireland, July 10, 1900
d. London, England, Oct. 20, 1968, Age 68

CARROLL, Richard Field
Performer
b. Boston, MA, Oct. 27, 1865
d. New York, NY, June 26, 1925, Age 59

CARROLL, Sydney W.
Critic, Author, Journalist
b. Melbourne, Australia, Feb. 16, 1877
d. Unknown, Aug. 24, 1958, Age 81

CARSON, Charles L.
Publisher
b. Unknown
d. Unknown, Jan. 2, 1901

CARSON, Jack
Actor
b. Carman, Manitoba, CAN, Unknown
d. Encino, CA, Jan. 2, 1963, Age 52

CARSON, Lionel
Editor
b. Unknown, May 30, 1875
d. London, England, Jan. 24, 1937, Age 63

CARSON, S. Murray
Performer, Playwright
b. London, England, March 17, 1865
d. Unknown, April 20, 1917, Age 52

CARTER, Desmond
Playwright, Lyricist
b. Bristol, England, Unknown
d. London, England, Feb. 3, 1939

CARTER, Leslie
Actor
b. Unknown
d. Unknown, Oct. 4, 1921, Age 48

CARTER, Lincoln J.
Playwright
b. Unknown
d. near Goshen, IN, July 13, 1926, Age 61

CARTER, Mrs. Leslie (née Caroline Louise Dudley)
Actress
b. Lexington, KY, June 10, 1862
d. Brentwood Heights, Santa Monica, CA, Nov. 13, 1937, Age 75

CARTON, Richard Claude (R. C. Critchett)
Playwright
b. London, England, May 10, 1853
d. London, England, March 31, 1928, Age 74

CARTWRIGHT, Charles (Morley)
Actor
b. England, March 7, 1855
d. Unknown, Nov. 5, 1916, Age 61

CARUS, Emma
Performer
b. Berlin, Germany, March 18, 1879
d. Unknown, Nov. 18, 1927, Age 48

CARVER, Kathryn
Actress
b. Unknown
d. Elmhurst, L.I., NY, July 18, 1947, Age 41

CARVER, Louise
Performer
b. Unknown
d. Los Angeles, CA, Jan. 19, 1956, Age 87

CARVER, Lynne
Actress
b. Unknown
d. New York, NY, Aug. 12, 1955, Age 38

CARVILL, Henry J.
Actor
b. Unknown
d. Unknown, March 11, 1941, Age 74

CARYLL, Ivan (Felix Tilken)
Composer, Conductor
b. Liege, Belgium, 1861
d. New York, NY, Nov. 29, 1921, Age 60

CASEY, Pat
Talent representative, Film executive
b. Springfield, MA, Unknown
d. Hollywood, CA, Feb. 7, 1962, Age 87

CASH, William F. ("Ardo the Frog")
Performer
b. Unknown
d. New York, NY, April 15, 1963, Age over 80

CASHEL, Oliver
Actor
b. Unknown
d. Unknown, Aug. 26, 1747

CASSIDY, J. Rice
Actor
b. Unknown
d. Unknown, May 11, 1927, Age 66

CASSON, Lewis Sir
Actor, Producer
b. Birkenhead, England, Oct. 26, 1875
d. London, England, May 16, 1969, Age 93

CASSON, Louis
Actor, Producer
b. Unknown
d. Unknown, Jan. 23, 1950

CASTLE, Betty (Mrs. Ray Parker)
Performer
b. Unknown
d. Glendale, CA, April 30, 1962, Age 47

CASTLE, Egerton
Playwright
b. Unknown, March 12, 1858
d. London, England, Sept. 17, 1920, Age 62

CASTLE, Irene
Performer, Dancer, Actress
b. New Rochelle, NY, 1892
d. Eureka Springs, AR, Jan. 25, 1969, Age 77

CASTLE, Vernon (Vernon Castle Blythe)
Performer, Dancer
b. England, 1887
d. Forth Worth, TX, Feb. 15, 1918, Age 31

CASTRO Y BELLVIS, Guillénde
Playwright
b. Valencia, Spain, 1569
d. Unknown, 1631

CATLETT, Walter
Actor
b. San Francisco, CA, Feb. 4, 1889
d. Woodland Hills, CA, Nov. 14, 1960, Age 71

CAVANAUGH, Hobart
Actor
b. Virginia City, NV, Unknown
d. Woodland Hills, CA, April 26, 1950, Age 63

CAVANNA, Elise (Mrs. James Welton)
Actress
b. Unknown
d. Hollywood, CA, May 12, 1963, Age 61

CAVENDER, Glenn W.
Performer
b. Unknown
d. Hollywood, CA, Feb. 9, 1962, Age 78

CAVENDISH, Ada (Mrs. Frank Marshall)
Actress
b. Unknown, 1847
d. London, England, Oct. 5, 1895, Age 48

CAWTHORN, Joseph
Actor
b. New York, NY, March 29, 1867
d. Beverly Hills, CA, Jan. 21, 1949, Age 81

CAYVAN, Georgia
Performer
b. Bath, ME, 1858
d. Unknown, Nov. 19, 1906, Age 48

CECCHETTI, Enrico
Dancer, Teacher
b. Italy, 1850
d. Unknown, Nov. 16, 1928, Age 78

CELESTE, Céline
Actress, Dancer
b. Unknown, 1814
d. Unknown, 1882, Age 68

CELLI, Faith
Actress
b. Kensington, London, England, Nov. 27, 1888
d. Unknown, Dec. 16, 1942, Age 54

CELLIER, Alfred
Composer
b. London, England, Dec. 1, 1844
d. London, England, Dec. 28, 1891, Age 47

CELLIER, Frank
Actor, Producer
b. Surbiton, England, Feb. 23, 1884
d. London, England, Sept. 27, 1948, Age 64

CENTLIVRE, Mrs. Susannah (Freeman)
Actress, Playwright
b. Lincolnshire, England, c1667
d. Unknown, Dec. 1, 1723, Age 56

CERRITO, Fanny
Dancer, Choreographer
b. Unknown, 1821
d. Unknown, 1899, Age 78

CERVANTES SAAVEDRA, Miguel de
Novelist, Playwright
b. Alcalá de Henares, Spain, Oct. 9, 1547
d. Unknown, April 23, 1616, Age 68

CHALMERS, Thomas Hardie
Opera singer, Actor, Film director, Editor, Writer
b. New York, NY, Oct. 20, 1884
d. Greenwich, CT, June 12, 1966, Age 81

CHALZEL, Leo
Actor
b. Dayton, OH, Unknown
d. Westport, CT, July 16, 1953, Age 52

CHAMBERS, Charles Haddon
Playwright
b. Stanmore, Australia, April 22, 1860
d. London, England, March 28, 1921, Age 60

CHAMBERS, Henry Kellett
Playwright
b. Sydney, Australia, Nov. 28, 1867
d. Great Neck, L.I., NY, Sept. 5, 1935, Age 67

CHAMBERS, Lyster
Actor
b. Michigan, Unknown
d. New York, NY, Jan. 27, 1947, Age 71

CHAMBERS, Norma
Actress
b. Dinwiddie County, VA, Unknown
d. New York, NY, May 2, 1953

CHAMBERS, Ralph
Actor
b. Uniontown, PA, Unknown
d. New York, NY, March 16, 1968, Age 76

CHAMPION, Harry
Performer
b. Unknown, 1866
d. London, England, Jan. 14, 1942, Age 76

CHAMPMESLE, Charles Chevillet
Actor, Playwright
b. Unknown, 1642
d. Paris, France, 1701, Age 59

CHAMPMESLE, Marie Desmares
Actress
b. Unknown, 1642
d. Unknown, May 15, 1698, Age 56

CHANDLER, Helen (Mrs. Walter Piascik)
Actress
b. New York, NY, Feb. 1, 1909
d. Hollywood, CA, April 30, 1965, Age 56

CHANDLER, Jeff (Ira Grossel)
Actor
b. Brooklyn, NY, Unknown
d. Culver City, CA, June 17, 1961, Age 42

CHANEY, Lon
Actor
b. Colorado Springs, CO, April 1, 1883
d. Los Angeles, CA, Aug. 26, 1930, Age 47

CHANEY, Stewart
Stage designer
b. Kansas City, MO, June 23, 1910
d. East Hampton, NY, Nov. 9, 1969, Age 59

CHANFRAU, Francis S.
Actor
b. New York, NY, Feb. 22, 1824
d. Jersey City, NJ, Oct. 2, 1884, Age 60

CHANFRAU, Mrs. F. S. (Henrietta Baker a/k/a Jeannette Davis)
b. Philadelphia, PA, 1837
d. Burlington, NJ, Sept. 21, 1909, Age 72

CHANSLOR, Roy
Screenwriter, Novelist
b. Clay County, MO, Unknown
d. Encino, CA, April 16, 1964, Age 64

CHAPEL, Eugenia (Mrs. Henri Dardier)
Actress, Theatre executive
b. Unknown
d. New York, NY, April 21, 1964, Age 52

CHAPIN, Alice
Actress
b. Unknown
d. Keene, NH, July 6, 1934, Age 76

CHAPIN, Harold
Playwright
b. Brooklyn, NY, 1886
d. Loos, Sept. 26, 1915

CHAPMAN, Blanche (Mrs. H. C. Ford)
Performer
b. Convington, KY, Unknown
d. Rutherford, NJ, June 7, 1941, Age 90

CHAPMAN, Edythe
Actress
b. Unknown
d. Glendale, CA, Oct. 15, 1948, Age 85

CHAPMAN, George
Playwright
b. Unknown, c1559
d. Unknown, May 12, 1634, Age 77

CHAPMAN, Henry
Actor
b. Unknown, 1822
d. Unknown, 1865, Age 43

CHAPMAN, John
Drama critic
b. Denver, CO, June 25, 1900
d. Westport, CT, Jan. 19, 1972, Age 71

CHAPMAN, William
Performer, Showboat Proprietor
b. England, 1764
d. Unknown, 1839, Age 75

CHARIG, Phil
Composer
b. Unknown
d. New York, NY, July 21, 1960, Age 58

CHARLES, Fred
Actor
b. Unknown
d. London, England, July 26, 1904, Age 75

CHARLESON, Mary
Actress
b. Unknown
d. Woodland Hills, CA, Dec. 3, 1961, Age 76

CHARLOT, André
Producer
b. Paris, France July 26, 1882
d. Woodland Hills, CA, May 20, 1956, Age 73

CHARLTON, Harold C.
Actor
b. Unknown
d. Unknown, April 26, 1954

CHARPENTIER, Gustave
Composer
b. Dieuze, Lorraine, France, June 25, 1860
d. Paris, France, Feb. 18, 1956, Age 95

CHARTERS, Spencer
Actor
b. Duncannon, PA, Unknown
d. Hollywood, CA, Jan. 25, 1943, Age 68

CHASE, Pauline
Performer
b. Washington, DC, May 20, 1885
d. Tunbridge Wells, England, March 3, 1962, Age 76

CHASE, William B.
Music critic, Drama critic
b. Syracuse, NY, Unknown
d. Whitefield, NH, Aug. 25, 1948, Age 76

CHATHAM, Pitt
Performer
b. Unknown
d. Unknown, July 6, 1923, Age 37

CHATRIAN, Louis Gratien Charles Alexandre
Playwright
b. Soldatenthal, Alsace, France, 1826
d. Unknown, Sept. 3, 1890, Age 63

CHATTERTON, Ruth
Actress
b. New York, NY, Dec. 24, 1893
d. Norwalk, CT, Nov. 24, 1961, Age 67

CHAUMONT, Céline
Actress
b. Unknown
d. Unknown, Feb. 4, 1926, Age 78

CHAUVENET, Virginia
Performer
b. Harrisburg, PA, Unknown
d. New York, NY, March 6, 1949, Age 65

CHEATHAM, Kitty (Catherine Smiley Bugge Cheatham)
Actress
b. Nashville, TN, Unknown
d. Greenwich, CT, Jan. 5, 1946, Age 81

CHEKHOV, Anton Pavlovich
Playwright, Writer
b. Taganrog, Russia, Jan. 17, 1860
d. Baden-Weiler, South Germany, July 2, 1904, Age 44

CHEKHOV, Michael Alexandrovich
Actor, Director, Educator
b. St. Petersburg, Russia, Aug. 29, 1891
d. Beverly Hills, CA, Sept. 30, 1955, Age 64

CHENIER, Marie Joseph
Playwright
b. Unknown, 1764
d. Unknown, 1811

CHERRY, Addie (Cherry Sisters) (Addie Rose Alma Cherry)
Performer
b. Wheaton, IL, Unknown
d. Cedar Rapids, IA, Oct. 25, 1942, Age 83

CHERRY, Andrew
Actor, Playwright
b. Limerick, Ireland, Jan. 11, 1762
d. Monmouth, England, Feb. 12, 1812, Age 50

CHERRY, Charles
Actor
b. Greenwich, Kent, England, Nov. 19, 1872
d. Unknown, Sept. 2, 1931, Age 59

CHERRY, Effie (Cherry Sisters)
Performer
b. Indian Creek, IA, Unknown
d. Cedar Rapids, IA, Aug. 5, 1944, Age c65

CHERRY, Ellen (Cherry Sisters)
Performer
b. Indian Creek, IA, Unknown
d. Cedar Rapids, IA, 1934, Age 71

CHERRY, Jessie (Cherry Sisters)
Performer
b. Indian Creek, IA, Unknown
d. Unknown, 1903, Age 67

CHERRY, Lizzie (Cherry Sisters) (Elizabeth Cherry)
Performer
b. Indian Creek, IA, Unknown
d. Cedar Rapids, IA, May 12, 1936, Age 67

CHERRY, Malcolm
Actor, Playwright
b. Liverpool, England, May 17, 1878
d. Unknown, April 13, 1925, Age 46

CHERRYMAN, Rex
Actor
b. California, Unknown
d. Le Havre, France, Aug. 10, 1928, Age 30

CHESNEY, Arthur
Actor
b. London, England, Unknown
d. London, England, Aug. 29, 1949, Age 67

CHESTER, Samuel K.
Performer
b. Unknown
d. New York, NY, March 19, 1921, Age 87

CHESTERTON, Gilbert Keith
Playwright, Critic, Novelist, Poet
b. London, England, May 29, 1874
d. Beaconsfield, Buckinghamshire, England, June 14, 1936, Age 62

CHETTLE, Henry
Playwright
b. Unknown, c1560
d. Unknown, 1607

CHETWOOD, William Rufus
Playwright
b. Unknown
d. Unknown, March 3, 1766

CHEVALIER, Albert
Actor
b. London, England, March 21, 1861
d. London, England, July 10, 1923, Age 62

CHEVALIER, Gus
Performer
b. Unknown
d. Unknown, Nov. 20, 1947, Age 56

CHEVALIER, Maurice
Actor - singer
b. Paris, France, Sept. 12, 1888
d. Paris, France, Jan. 1, 1972, Age 83

CHEVALIER, May
Actress
b. Unknown
d. Unknown, Jan. 16, 1940

CHIKAMATSU, Monzayemon
Playwright
b. Hagi, Japan, c1653
d. Unknown, 1724, Age 72

CHILD, Harold Hannyngton
Critic, Journalist, Actor
b. Gloucester, England, June 20, 1869
d. Unknown, Nov. 8, 1945, Age 76

CHILDERS, Naomi
Actress
b. Unknown
d. Hollywood, CA, May 9, 1964, Age 71

CHILDS, Gilbert
Actor
b. Unknown
d. London, England, Sept. 24, 1931

CHISHOLM, Robert
Actor
b. Milbourne, Australia, April 18, 1898
d. Unknown, Nov. 1960, Age 62

CHIVOT, Henri
Playwright
b. Unknown
d. Unknown, Sept. 18, 1897, Age 67

CHOATE, Edward
Theatre manager, Producer
b. New York, NY, Nov. 23 1908
d. New York, NY, July 23, 1975, Age 66

CHOPIN, Frederic
Composer
b. Zelazowa Wola, Poland, Feb. 22, 1810
d. Paris, France, Oct. 17, 1849, Age 39

CHOTZINOFF, Samuel
Music director of NBC, Critic, Playwright
b. Vitebsk, Russia, Unknown
d. New York, NY, Feb. 9, 1964, Age 74

CHRISTIANS, Mady (née Marguerita Maria Christians)
Actress
b. Vienna, Austria, Jan. 19, 1900
d. Norwalk, CT, Oct. 28, 1951, Age 51

CHRISTIE, Al
Producer, Director
b. London, Ontario, CAN, Unknown
d. Beverly Hills, CA, April 14, 1951, Age about 64

CHRISTIE, Charles H.
Producer
b. Unknown
d. Hollywood, CA, Oct. 1, 1955, Age 75

CHRISTIE, George
Actor
b. Philadelphia, PA, Feb. 27, 1873
d. Toms River, NJ, May 20, 1949, Age 76

CHRISTIE, John
Impresario
b. Unknown
d. Glydebourne, England, July 4, 1962, Age 80

CHRISTY, Edwin P.
Actor, (founder of the Christy Minstrels)
b. Unknown
d. New York, NY, May 21, 1862, Age 47

CHRISTY, Floyd
Performer
b. Unknown
d. Hollywood, CA, May 21, 1962, Age 55

CHRISTY, Ken
Actor
b. Unknown
d. Hollywood, CA, July 23, 1962, Age 67

CHURCHILL, Berton
Actor
b. Toronto, CAN, Dec. 9, 1876
d. New York, NY, Oct. 10, 1940, Age 63

CHURCHILL, Charles
Playwright
b. Unknown
d. Unknown, Nov. 24, 1764, Age 33

CHURCHILL, Winston
Playwright, Novelist
b. St. Louis, MO, Nov. 10, 1871
d. Winter Park, FL, March 12, 1947, Age 75

CIBBER, Charlotte (Mrs. Richard Charke)
Performer
b. Unknown
d. Unknown, c1760

CIBBER, Colley
Playwright, Actor, Poet, Producer
b. London, England, 1671
d. London, England, Dec. 11, 1757, Age 86

CIBBER, Susanna Maria Arne (Mrs. Theophilus Cibber)
Actress, Singer
b. Unknown, 1714
d. Unknown, Jan. 30, 1766, Age 51

CIBBER, Theophilus
Actor
b. Unknown, 1703
d. Irish Sea, Oct. 16, 1758, Age 54

CINO, Joe
Coffee house owner, Off-off Broadway producer
b. Buffalo, NY, Nov. 12, 1931
d. New York, NY, April 2, 1967, Age 36

CINQUEVALLI, Paul
Performer
b. Poland, 1859
d. England, 1918

CIRKER, Mitchell
Set designer
b. New York, NY, Unknown
d. Forest Hills, NY, Feb. 4, 1953, Age 70

CLAIRE, Helen
Actress
b. Union Springs, AL, Oct. 18, 1911
d. Birmingham, AL, Jan. 12, 1974, Age 68

CLAIRON, Hypolyte (Claire Josèphe Hippolyte Léris de la Tude Clairon)
Actress
b. Unknown, 1723
d. Unknown, Jan. 31, 1803, Age 80

CLAPHAM, Charlie
Performer
b. Unknown
d. Unknown, July 1959, Age 65

CLAPP, Charles (Sunny)
Songwriter
b. Battle Creek, MI, Unknown
d. Van Nuys, CA, Dec. 9, 1962, Age 63

CLAPP, Charles Edwin Jr.
Producer, Writer
b. Pittsburgh, PA, Unknown
d. Charlottesville, VA, Jan. 2, 1957, Age 57

CLARE, Phyllis
Actress
b. London, England, Unknown
d. Unknown, Nov. 1, 1947, Age 42

CLARENCE, O. B.
Actor
b. London, England, March 25, 1870
d. Unknown, Oct. 2, 1955, Age 85

CLARETIE, Jules
Playwright, Critic, Producer
b. Unknown, 1840
d. Unknown, Dec. 23, 1913, Age 73

CLARK, Barrett Harper
Author, Editor
b. Toronto, CAN, Aug. 26, 1890
d. Briarcliff Manor, NY, Aug. 5, 1953, Age 62

CLARK, Bobby
Performer, Actor
b. Springfield, OH, June 16, 1888
d. New York, NY, Feb. 12, 1960, Age 71

CLARK, Buddy (Samuel Goldberg)
Singer
b. Boston, MA, July 26, 1911
d. Hollywood, CA, Oct. 1, 1949, Age 38

CLARK, Charles Dow
Actor
b. St. Albans, VT, Unknown
d. New York, NY, March 26, 1959, Age 89

CLARK, Cuthbert
Musical director, Composer
b. London, England, Jan. 25, 1869
d. Unknown, Aug. 1953, Age 84

CLARK, E. Holman
Actor
b. East Hothley, Sussex, England, April 22, 1864
d. London, England, Sept. 7, 1925, Age 61

CLARK, Ethel Schneider
Actress
b. Unknown
d. Hollywood, CA, Feb. 18, 1964, Age 48

CLARK, Fred
Actor
b. Lincoln, CA, March 9, 1914
d. Santa Monica, CA, Dec. 5, 1968, Age 54

CLARK, Harry
Actor
b. Unknown
d. New York, NY, Feb. 28, 1956, Age 45

CLARK, Marguerite
Actress
b. Cincinnati, OH, Feb. 22, 1887
d. New York, NY, Sept. 25, 1940, Age 53

CLARK, Rose Francis Langdon
Performer
b. Unknown
d. Hollywood, CA, Jan. 27, 1962, Age 80

CLARK, T. Sealey
Publisher, (The Green Room Book)
b. Unknown
d. Unknown, April 1, 1909, Age 59

CLARK, Wallis H.
Actor
b. Essex, England, March 2, 1888
d. North Hollywood, CA, Feb. 14, 1961, Age 72

CLARK, William T.
Actor
b. Unknown
d. Brooklyn, NY, Sept. 14, 1925, Age 62

CLARKE, Creston
Performer
b. Philadelphia, PA, Aug. 30, 1865
d. Unknown, March 21, 1910, Age 44

CLARKE, George
Performer
b. Brooklyn, NY, June 28, 1840
d. Unknown, Oct. 3, 1900, Age 60

CLARKE, George
Actor
b. Bromley, Middlesex, England, April 11, 1886
d. Unknown, Dec. 21, 1946, Age 60

CLARKE, H. Saville
Playwright
b. Unknown
d. London, England, Oct. 5, 1893, Age 52

CLARKE, Harry Corson
Performer
b. New York, NY, Unknown
d. Los Angeles, CA, March 3, 1923, Age 62

CLARKE, J. I. C.
Playwright
b. Unknown, 1846
d. New York, NY, Feb. 27, 1925, Age 78

CLARKE, John Sleeper
Actor-Manager
b. Baltimore, MD, Sept. 3, 1833
d. London, England, Sept. 24, 1899, Age 66

CLARKE, Wilfred
Actor, Author, Producer
b. Philadelphia, PA, Unknown
d. New York, NY, April 27, 1945, Age 77

CLAUDEL, Paul
Playwright
b. Villeneuve-sur-Fere, France, Aug. 6, 1868
d. Paris, France, Feb. 23, 1955, Age 86

CLAXTON, Kate
Actress
b. Somerville, NJ, 1850
d. New York, NY, May 5, 1924, Age 74

CLAY, Cecil
Playwright
b. Unknown
d. Unknown, May 25, 1920, Age 73

CLAYTON, Bessie
Performer
b. Philadelphia, PA, Unknown
d. Long Branch, NJ, July 16, 1948, Age 63

CLAYTON, Hazel (Mrs. Mack Hilliard)
Actress
b. Unknown
d. Forest Hills, NY, March 8, 1963, Age 77

CLAYTON, Herbert
Producer, Playwright, Actor
b. London, England, Dec. 1, 1876
d. Unknown, Feb. 16, 1931, Age 54

CLAYTON, Lou
Singer, Manager
b. New York, NY, Unknown
d. Santa Monica, CA, Sept. 12, 1950, Age 63

CLEMENT, Clay
Actor
b. Unknown
d. Watertown, NY, Oct. 20, 1956, Age 68

CLEMENT, Frank
Critic, Novelist
b. Unknown
d. Unknown, June 3, 1937

CLEMENTS, Colin
Playwright, Author
b. Omaha, NB, Unknown
d. Philadelphia, PA, Jan. 29, 1948, Age 53

CLEMENTS, Dudley
Actor
b. New York, NY, Unknown
d. New York, NY, Nov. 3, 1947, Age 58

CLEVELAND, George
Actor
b. Unknown
d. Burbank, CA, July 15, 1957, Age 71

CLEWLOW, F. D.
Director Scottish National Theatre
b. Unknown
d. Unknown, June 13, 1957, Age 72

CLIFF, Laddie
Performer
b. Bristol, England, Sept. 3, 1891
d. Montana, Vermala, Switzerland, Dec. 8, 1937, Age 46

CLIFFE, H. Cooper (H. Clifford Cooper)
Actor
b. Oxford, England, July 19, 1862
d. New York, NY, May 2, 1939, Age 76

CLIFFORD, Charles
Actor
b. Unknown
d. Unknown, Jan. 22, 1943

CLIFFORD, Gordon
Lyricist
b. Providence, RI, March 28, 1902
d. Las Vegas, NV, June 11, 1968, Age 65

CLIFFORD, Jack (Virgil Montani)
Actor, Dancer
b. Unknown
d. New York, NY, Nov. 10, 1956, Age 76

CLIFFORD, Kathleen (Mrs. Meo Illitch)
Actress
b. Unknown
d. Hollywood, CA, Jan. 11, 1963, Age 75

CLIFFORD, Mrs. W. K.
Author, Playwright
b. Unknown
d. Unknown, April 21, 1929

CLIFT, Montgomery
Actor
b. Omaha, NB, Oct. 17, 1920
d. New York, NY, July 23, 1966, Age 45

CLIFTON, Elmer
Actor, Director
b. Unknown
d. Hollywood, CA, Oct. 15, 1949, Age 59

CLIFTON, Josephine
Performer
b. Philadelphia, PA, Unknown
d. Unknown, Nov. 21, 1847, Age 34

CLINE, Maggie
Actress
b. Haverhill, MA, 1857
d. Fair Haven, NJ, June 11, 1934, Age 77

CLINTON, Kate
Actress
b. Unknown
d. Unknown, June 6, 1935

CLIUTMAS, Harry F.
Performer
b. Unknown
d. Newington, NH, May 8, 1964, Age 83

CLIVE, Colin (Clive-Greig)
Actor
b. St. Malo, France, Jan. 20, 1900
d. Hollywood, CA, June 25, 1937, Age 37

CLIVE, Edward E.
Actor, Producer, Director
b. Monmouthshire, England, Unknown
d. North Hollywood, CA, June 6, 1940, Age about 60

CLIVE, Kitty (Catherine Raftor)
Actress
b. Unknown, 1711
d. Unknown, 1785

CLUBLEY, John Sherwood
Actor, Director
b. Unknown
d. New York, NY, April 29, 1964

CLUNES, Alec
Actor, Manager, Producer
b. London, England, May 17, 1912
d. London, England, March 13, 1970, Age 57

CLYDE, Jean
Actress
b. Unknown
d. Helensburgh, Scotland, 1962, Age 73

COBB, Irvin S.
Author, Humorist, Actor
b. Paducah, KY, June 23, 1876
d. New York, NY, March 11, 1944, Age 67

COBB, Lee J.
Actor
b. New York City, NY, Dec. 9, 1911
d. Woodland Hills, CA, Feb. 11, 1976, Age 65

COBORN, Charlie (Colin Whitton McCallum)
Performer, Songwriter
b. Unknown, 1852
d. London, England, Nov. 23, 1945, Age 93

COBURN, Charles Douville
Actor, Producer
b. Macon, GA, June 19, 1877
d. New York, NY, Aug. 30, 1961, Age 84

COBURN, Ivah Wills (Mrs. Charles)
Actress
b. Appleton, MO, c1882
d. New York, NY, April 27, 1937, Age 57

COCHRAN, Sir Charles Blake
Producer, Actor
b. Lindfield, Sussex, England, Sept. 25, 1872
d. London, England, Jan. 31, 1951, Age 78

COCHRANE, Frank
Actor
b. England, Unknown
d. London, England, 1962, Age 89

COCKBURN, Catherine
Playwright
b. Unknown
d. Unknown, May 11, 1749, Age 69

COCKBURN, John M.
Drama critic, Author
b. Unknown
d. Dundee, Scotland, July 6, 1964, Age 66

COCTEAU, Jean
Poet, Author, Director, Playwright
b. Maisons-Laffitte, France, July 5, 1889
d. Milly-La-Foret, France, Oct. 11, 1963, Age 74

CODY, Bill
Actor
b. Unknown, Santa Monica, CA
d. Jan. 24, 1948, 57

CODY, Ethel (née Sack)
Actress
b. Philadelphia, PA, Unknown
d. Rockledge, PA, Nov. 21, 1957, Age 62

CODY, Lew (Louis J. Cote, Jr.)
Actor
b. Waterville, ME, Feb. 22, 1887
d. Beverly Hills, CA, May 31, 1934, Age 47

CODY, William Frederick (Buffalo Bill)
Producer, Performer
b. . . .near Le Clair, Scott County, IA, Feb. 26, 1846
d. Denver, CO, Jan. 10, 1917, Age 70

COFFIN, C. Hayden
Actor
b. Manchester, England, April 22, 1862
d. Unknown, Dec. 8, 1935, Age 73

COGERT, Jed
Actor
b. Unknown
d. Brooklyn, NY, Dec. 25, 1961, Age 80

COGHLAN, Charles Francis
Actor, Playwright
b. Paris, France, 1841
d. Galveston, TX, Nov. 27, 1899, Age 58

COGHLAN, Gertrude Evelyn (Mrs. Augustus Pitou)
Actress
b. Hertfordshire, England, Feb. 1, 1876
d. Bayside, NY, Sept. 11, 1952, Age 76

COGHLAN, Rosalind (Mrs. Richard Pitman)
Actress
b. Unknown
d. Forest Hills, NY, Sept. 27, 1937, Age 51

COGHLAN, Rose
Actress
b. Peterborough, England, March 18, 1851
d. Harrison, NY, April 2, 1932, Age 81

COHAN, George Michael
Actor, Playwright, Composer, Producer
b. Providence, RI, July 3, 1878
d. New York, NY, Nov. 5, 1942, Age 64

COHAN, Helen Frances Costigan (Mrs. Jere Cohan)
Actress
b. Unknown, 1854
d. Monroe, NY, Aug. 26, 1928, Age 74

COHAN, Jere J. (Jeremiah John Cohan)
Performer
b. Providence, RI, 1848
d. Monroe, NY, Aug. 1, 1917, Age 69

COHAN, Josephine (Mrs. Fred Niblo)
Performer
b. Providence, RI, 1876
d. New York, NY, July 12, 1916, Age 40

COHEN, Frederick
Director, Composer, Producer, Educator
b. Bonn, Germany, June 23, 1904
d. New York, NY, March 10, 1967, Age 62

COHEN, Katie
Actress
b. Unknown
d. Unknown, Jan. 24, 1946, Age 82

COHEN, Octavus Roy
Playwright, Author
b. Charleston, SC, June 26, 1891
d. Los Angeles, CA, Jan. 6, 1959, Age 67

COHEN, Sara B.
Performer
b. Unknown
d. Des Moines, IA, March 15, 1963, Age 82

COHN, Harry
Performer, Producer, Film executive
b. New York, NY, July 23, 1891
d. Phoenix, AZ, Feb. 27, 1958, Age 66

COKAYNE, Sir Aston
Playwright
b. Unknown
d. Unknown, Feb. 10, 1684, Age 75

COKE, Richard
Actor
b. Unknown
d. Unknown, Oct. 13, 1955, Age 63

COLBRON, Grace Isabel
Playwright
b. New York, NY, Unknown
d. Wilmington, DE, Sept. 8, 1943

COLE, Bob
Librettist, Lyricist
b. Unknown, 1869
d. Unknown, 1912

COLE, Jack
Choreograher, Director, Dancer
b. New Brunswick, NJ, April 27, 1914
d. Los Angeles, CA, Feb. 17, 1974, Age 59

COLEMAN, Carole (née Betty Huneycutt)
Performer
b. Charlotte, NC, Unknown
d. York, SC, Aug. 21, 1964, Age 42

COLEMAN, John
Playwright, Producer
b. Unknown
d. Unknown, April 22, 1904, Age 72

COLEMAN, Warren R.
Actor, Singer, Director
b. Newark, NJ, Unknown
d. Martha's Vineyard, MA, Jan. 13, 1968, Age 67

COLERIDGE, Amy
Actress
b. Unknown
d. Unknown, Aug. 4, 1951, Age 85

COLERIDGE, Samuel Taylor
Playwright, Poet
b. Devon, England, 1772
d. Unknown, July 25, 1834, Age 61

COLETTE, (Sidonie Gabrielle Claudine Colette Gauthier-Villas de Jouvenel Goudeket)
Writer
b. Sait-Sauveur-en-Puisaye, France, Jan. 28, 1873
d. Paris, France, Aug. 3, 1954, Age 81

COLLEANO, Bonar Jr.
Actor
b. New York, NY, March 14, 1923
d. Birkenhead, England, Aug. 17, 1958, Age 35

COLLEANO, Bonar Sr. (Edgar James Sullivan)
Performer
b. Unknown
d. London, England, March 7, 1957, Age over 60

COLLIER, Constance
Actress, Teacher
b. Windsor, England, Jan. 22, 1878
d. New York, NY, April 25, 1955, Age 77

COLLIER, J. Walter
Manager
b. Unknown
d. Long Branch, NJ, Aug. 20, 1920, Age 60

COLLIER, Jeremy
Author, Cleric
b. Unknown, 1650
d. Unknown, April 26, 1726, Age 75

COLLIER, John Payne
Historian, Critic
b. Unknown, 1789
d. Unknown, Sept. 18, 1883, Age 94

COLLIER, Lizzie Hudson
Actress
b. Unknown
d. Staten Island, NY, Oct. 26, 1924, Age 60

COLLIER, William
Actor, Playwright
b. New York, NY, Nov. 12, 1866
d. Beverly Hills, CA, Jan. 13, 1944, Age 77

COLLINGE, Patricia
Actress
b. Dublin, Ireland, Sept. 20, 1894
d. New York, NY, April 10, 1974, Age 81

COLLINGHAM, G. G. (Mary Helen White)
Playwright
b. Unknown
d. Unknown, June 20, 1923

COLLINS, Bert
Performer
b. Unknown
d. Fresno, CA, Oct. 4, 1962, Age 63

COLLINS, Charles
Drama critic, Editor, Writer
b. Unknown
d. Chicago, IL, March 3, 1964, Age 83

COLLINS, Daniel
Performer
b. Unknown
d. Rochester, NY, March 16, 1964, Age 76

COLLINS, Frank
Actor, Producer
b. London, England, Sept, 18, 1878
d. Unknown, May 31, 1957, Age 78

COLLINS, John
Actor, Poet
b. Unknown
d. Unknown, May 2, 1808, Age 65

COLLINS, José
Actress
b. London, England May 23, 1887,
d. London, England, Dec. 6, 1958, Age 71

COLLINS, Lottie
Performer
b. Unknown, 1866
d. Unknown, May 2, 1910, Age 44

COLLINS, May
Actress
b. Unknown
d. Fairfield, CT, May 6, 1955, Age 49

COLLINS, Ray
Actor
b. Sacramento, CA, Dec. 10, 1889
d. Santa Monica, CA, July 11, 1965, Age 75

COLLINS, Russell Henry
Actor
b. Indianapolis, IN, Oct. 6, 1897
d. Hollywood, CA, Nov. 14, 1965, Age 68

COLLINS, Sam (Samuel Vagg)
Performer
b. Unknown, 1826
d. Unknown, 1865

COLLINS, Sewell
Playwright, Producer, Critic
b. Denver, CO, 1876
d. London, England, Feb. 15, 1934, Age 57

COLLINS, Ted
Radio and TV producer, Director
b. New York, NY, Unknown
d. Lake Placid, NY, May 27, 1964, Age 64

COLLINS, Una
Actress
b. Unknown
d. Dublin, Ireland, June 1, 1964, Age 45

COLLINS, Wilkie
Playwright, Novelist
b. London, England, Jan. 1824
d. Unknown, Sept. 23, 1889, Age 65

COLLISON, Wilson
Playwright, Screenwriter
b. Gloucester, OH, Nov. 5, 1893
d. Beverly Hills, CA, May 24, 1941, Age 47

COLLUM, John
Actor
b. Unknown
d. Hollywood, CA, Aug. 28, 1962, Age 36

COLLYER, Dan
Performer
b. Unknown
d. Chicago, IL, March 30, 1918

COLLYER, June (Dorothea Heermance)
Actress
b. New York, NY, Unknown
d. Los Angeles, CA, March 16, 1968, Age 61

COLMAN, George (the elder)
Playwright, Producer
b. Florence, Italy, 1732
d. Unknown, Aug. 14, 1794, Age 62

COLMAN, George (the younger)
Playwright, Censor, Producer
b. Unknown, Oct. 21, 1762
d. Unknown, Oct. 17, 1836, Age 74

COLMAN, Ronald
Actor
b. Richmond, Surrey, England, Feb. 9, 1891
d. Santa Barbara, CA, May 19, 1958, Age 67

COLOMBIER, Marie
Actress, Novelist
b. Unknown, c1842
d. Unknown, 1910

COLONY, Alfred T.
Actor
b. Unknown
d. Keene, NH, May 27, 1964

COLTON, John B.
Playwright
b. near Minneapolis, MN, Unknown
d. Gainesville, TX, Dec. 28, 1946, Age 60

COLTRANE, John
Musician
b. Hamlet, NC, Sept. 23, 1926
d. Huntington, NY, July 17, 1967, Age 40

COMELLI, Attilio
Scene and costume designer
b. Unknown
d. Unknown, Sept. 3, 1925, Age 67

COMERFORD, Maurice
Publisher, (The Stage)
b. Unknown
d. Unknown, Nov. 9, 1903, Age 49

COMPTON, Betty (Mrs. Theodore T. Knappen) (née Violet Halling Compton)
Performer
b. Isle of Wight, Unknown
d. New York, NY, July 12, 1944, Age 37

COMPTON, Edward (Mackenzie)
Actor, Producer
b. London, England, Jan. 14, 1854
d. Unknown, July 15, 1918, Age 64

COMPTON, Francis (né Francis Sidney Mackenzie)
Actor
b. Malvern, Worcestershire, England, May 4, 1885
d. Stamford, CT, Sept. 17, 1964, Age 79

COMPTON, Henry (Charles Mackenzie)
Actor
b. Scotland, 1805
d. Unknown, 1877

COMPTON, Katherine Mackenzie (Mrs. R.C. Carton)
Actress
b. Unknown, 1853
d. Unknown, 1928, Age 75

COMPTON, Mrs. Edward (Virginia Frances Bateman)
Actress, Producer
b. Maryland, Jan. 1, 1853
d. London, England, May 4, 1940, Age 87

COMPTON, Sydney
Actor
b. Unknown
d. Unknown, July 7, 1938

COMSTOCK, Anthony B.
Reformer, Censor
b. New Caanan, CT, 1844
d. Unknown, 1915

COMSTOCK, F. Ray
Producer
b. Buffalo, NY, 1880
d. Boston, MA, Oct. 15, 1949, Age 69

COMSTOCK, Nanette
Performer
b. Albany, NY, July 17, 1873
d. Unknown, June 17, 1942, Age 69

CONCHITA, (Mrs. J. Leo Shaw née Maria de la Concepcion Conchita Serafina Bacigalupi
Actress
b. Unknown
d. South Colby, WA, June 13, 1940, Age 79

CONDELL, Henry
Actor, Editor
b. Unknown
d. Unknown, Dec. 1627

CONGREVE, William
Playwright
b. Bardsley, England, 1670
d. England, Jan. 19, 1729, Age 58

CONKEY, Thomas
Singer
b. Unknown
d. New York, NY, April 3, 1927, Age 45

CONKLING, Charles A. (Charles Ames)
Dancer
b. Unknown
d. New York, NY, May 1964, Age 57

CONLAN, Frank
Actor
b. Unknown
d. East Islip, NY, Aug. 24, 1955, Age 81

CONLIN, Jimmy
Actor
b. Unknown
d. Encino, CA, May 7, 1962, Age 77

CONLIN, Ray Sr. (né William O'Connor)
Performer
b. Unknown
d. Chicago, IL, Feb. 22, 1964, Age 73

CONNELL, F. Norreys (Conal O'Riordan)
Playwright, Novelist, Actor
b. Ireland, 1874
d. Unknown, June 18, 1948, Age 74

CONNELLY, Edward
Performer
b. Unknown
d. Hollywood, CA, Nov. 21, 1928, Age 73

CONNER, E. S. (Edmon Sheppard)
Actor
b. Philadelphia, PA, Sept. 9, 1809
d. Rutherford, NJ, Dec. 15, 1891, Age 82

CONNERS, Barry
Playwright, Actor
b. Oil City, PA, May 31, 1883
d. Hollywood, CA, Jan. 5, 1933, Age 49

CONNESS, Robert
Actor
b. La Salle County, IL, Unknown
d. Portland, ME, Jan. 15, 1941, Age 73

CONNOLLY, Bobby
Dance director, Film producer
b. Unknown
d. Encino, CA, Feb. 29, 1944, Age 49

CONNOLLY, Michael
Composer
b. Unknown
d. Unknown, Aug. 11, 1911, Age 80

CONNOLLY, Walter
Actor
b. Cincinnati, OH, Apr. 8, 1887
d. Beverly Hills, CA, May 28, 1940, Age 53

CONOR, Harry
Performer
b. Unknown
d. Roxbury, MA, April 1931, Age 75

CONQUEST, Arthur
Actor
b. London, England, 1875
d. London, England, Dec. 6, 1945, Age 70

CONQUEST, Benjamin Oliver
Actor, Producer
b. Cornhill, London, England, 1805
d. Unknown, 1872

CONQUEST, Fred
Actor
b. London, England, 1870
d. Bembridge, Isle of Wight, England, March 19, 1941, Age 70

CONQUEST, George
Actor
b. Unknown, 1858
d. Unknown, 1926

CONQUEST, George Augustus
Actor, Playwright, Producer
b. Unknown, 1837
d. Unknown, May 14, 1901, Age 64

CONQUEST, Ida (Mrs. Riccardo Bertelli)
Actress
b. Boston, MA, 1876
d. New York, NY, June 12, 1937, Age 61

CONRAD, Con (Conrad K. Dober)
Composer
b. New York, NY, June 18, 1891
d. Van Nuys, CA, Sept. 28, 1938, Age 49

CONRAD, Eugene J.
Playwright, Screenwriter
b. New York, NY, Unknown
d. Hollywood, CA, Jan. 28, 1964, Age 69

CONRAD, Robert Taylor
Playwright, Actor
b. Philadelphia, PA, 1810
d. Unknown, June 27, 1858, Age 48

CONROY, Frank
Actor
b. Derby, England, Unknown
d. Paramus, NJ, Feb. 24, 1964, Age 73

CONSTANDUROS, Mabel (née Tilling)
Actress, Playwright
b. London, England, Unknown
d. Unknown, Feb. 8, 1957, Age 77

CONTI, Italia
Actress, Teacher
b. London, England, 1874
d. Unknown, Feb. 8, 1946, Age 72

CONWAY, Curt
Actor
b. Boston, MA, May 4, 1915
d. Los Angeles, CA, April 10, 1974, Age 59

CONWAY, Frederick Bartlett
Actor, Producer
b. Clifton, Bristol, England, Feb. 10, 1819
d. Manchester, MA, Sept. 7, 1874, Age 55

CONWAY, Hugh (Fargus)
Playwright
b. Unknown
d. Unknown, May 15, 1885, Age 37

CONWAY, Jack
Actor, Film director
b. Graceville, MN, Unknown
d. Pacific Palisades, CA, Oct. 11, 1952, Age 65

CONWAY, Minnie (Mrs. Osmond Tearle a/k/a Marianne Levy)
Actress
b. New York, NY, 1854
d. England, Oct. 9, 1896, Age 42

CONWAY, (Rugg) William Augustus
Actor
b. Unknown, 1789
d. . . . drowned, Atlantic Ocean, 1828

CONWAY, Sarah Crocker (Mrs. F. B. Conway)
Actress, Producer
b. Litchfield, CT, 1834
d. Brooklyn, NY, April 1875, Age 40

CONYERS, Joseph
Actor
b. Unknown
d. New York, NY, July 5, 1920, Age 60

COOK, Charles Emerson
Agent, Author, Producer, Director
b. Parsonville, ME, Unknown
d. New York, NY, June 8, 1941, Age 71

COOK, Donald
Actor
b. Portland, OR, Sept. 26, 1901
d. New Haven, CT, Oct. 1, 1961, Age 60

COOK, Edward Dutton
Critic, Journalist
b. Unknown, 1829
d. Unknown, Sept. 11, 1883, Age 54

COOK, George Cram
Producer, Writer, Educator, Director
b. Iowa, 1873
d. Delphi, Greece, 1924

COOK, Joe (Joseph Lopez)
Performer
b. Evansville, IN, 1890
d. Clinton Hollow, NY, May 16, 1959, Age 69

COOK, John Russell
Theatre librarian
b. Plymouth, MA, April 9, 1911
d. New York, NY, April 3, 1964, Age 53

COOK, Ken
Actor
b. Unknown
d. Hollywood, CA, Dec. 28, 1963, Age 49

COOK, Madge Carr
Actress
b. Yorkshire, England, 1856
d. Syosset, L.I., NY, Sept. 20, 1933, Age 77

COOK, Will Marion
Composer
b. Washington, DC, Unknown
d. New York, NY, July 18, 1944, Age 75

COOKE, Alexander (a/k/a Sander Cooke)
Actor
b. Unknown
d. Unknown, . . . buried Feb. 25, 1614

COOKE, Eddie
Manager, Press representative
b. New York, NY, Unknown
d. New York, NY, Jan. 15, 1942, Age 73

COOKE, George Frederick
Actor
b. England, 1756
d. New York, NY, Sept. 26, 1812, Age 55

COOKE, Harry
Performer
b. Manchester, NH, Unknown
d. Forest Hills, NY, March 21, 1958, Age 56

COOKE, Marjorie Benton
Writer, Monologist
b. Unknown
d. Manila, Philipine Islands, April 26, 1920, Age 44

COOKE, Thomas
Playwright
b. Unknown
d. Unknown, Dec. 20, 1756, Age 53

COOKE, Thomas Coffin
Actor
b. Montgomery, AL, Unknown
d. Bayside, NY, June 10, 1939, Age 65

COOKE, Thomas Potter
Actor
b. Marylebone, London, England, April 23, 1786
d. London, England, April 4, 1864, Age 78

COOKMAN, Anthony V. (Albert Victor Cookman)
Drama Critic
b. Unknown, 1894
d. London, England, April 29, 1962, Age 67

COOKSEY, Curtis
Performer
b. Kentucky, Dec. 9, 1892
d. Hollywood, CA, April 19, 1962, Age 69

COOKSON, S. A.
Actor
b. Unknown
d. Unknown, Feb. 27, 1947, Age 78

COOLIDGE, Philip
Actor
b. Concord, MA, Aug. 25, 1908
d. Los Angeles, CA, May 23, 1967, Age 58

COOP, Colin
Actor
b. Unknown
d. Unknown, Aug. 7, 1937

COOPER, Ashley
Actor
b. Sydney, Australia, Unknown
d. New York, NY, Jan. 3, 1952, Age 70

COOPER, Charles Kemble
Actor
b. Unknown
d. Unknown, Sept. 13, 1923, Age 69

COOPER, Clifford
Actor
b. Unknown
d. Fulham, London, England, April 1, 1895, Age 76

COOPER, Edward
Actor
b. Unknown
d. Surrey, England, July 1956

COOPER, Frances (Mrs. T. H. Lacy)
Actress
b. Unknown
d. Unknown, April 21, 1872, Age 53

COOPER, Frank Kemble
Performer
b. Worcester, England, May 22, 1857
d. Unknown, Dec. 27, 1918, Age 61

COOPER, Frederick
Actor
b. London, England, 1890
d. Unknown, Jan. 1945, Age 55

COOPER, Gary (Frank James Cooper)
Actor
b. Helena, Mt, May 7, 1901
d. Holmby Hills, CA, May 13, 1961, Age 60

COOPER, Giles
Playwright, Television writer, Actor
b. Carrick Mines, County Dublin, Ireland, Aug. 9, 1918
d. near London, England, Dec. 2, 1966, Age 48

COOPER, Gladys
Actress
b. Lewisham, England, Dec. 18, 1889
d. Henley-on-Thames, England, Nov. 17, 1971, Age 82

COOPER, Margaret
Performer
b. Unknown
d. Unknown, Dec. 27, 1922

COOPER, Melville
Actor
b. Birmingham, England, Oct. 15, 1896
d. Hollywood, CA, March 29, 1973, Age 76

COOPER, Mrs. Clifford (Agnes Kemble)
Actress
b. Unknown, 1823
d. Unknown, April 3, 1895, Age 72

COOPER, Richard
Actor
b. Harrow-on-the-Hill, Middlesex, England, July 16, 1893
d. Unknown, June 1947, Age 53

COOPER, Thomas Abthorpe
Performer
b. England, 1776
d. U.S.A., April 21, 1849, Age 72

COOPER, Violet Kemble (Mrs. Walter Ferris)
Actress
b. London, England, 1889
d. Los Angeles, CA, Aug. 17, 1961, Age 72

COOTE, Bert
Actor, Playwright
b. London, England, 1867
d. Cricklewood, London, England, Sept. 2, 1938, Age 70

COPEAU, Jacques
Playwright
b. Paris, France, 1878
d. Beaune, France, Oct. 20, 1949, Age 70

COPELAND, Isabella (Mrs. J. B. Buckstone)
Actress
b. Unknown
d. Unknown, Dec. 15, 1912, Age 73

COPELAND, Mary Dowell
Performer
b. Fort Worth, TX, Unknown
d. New York, NY, April 9, 1963, Age 48

COPPEE, François Edouard Joachim
Playwright, Poet, Novelist
b. Paris, France, 1842
d. Unknown, May 23, 1908, Age 66

COQUELIN, Benoît Constant
Actor, Writer
b. Boulogne-sur-Mer, France, Jan. 23, 1841
d. Pont-aux-Dames, France, Jan. 27, 1909, Age 68

COQUELIN, Ernest Alexandre Honoré
Actor, Author
b. Unknown 1848
d. Unknown, Feb. 8, 1909, Age 60

COQUELIN, Jean
Actor, Producer
b. Unknown, 1865
d. Unknown, Oct. 3, 1944, Age 79

CORBETT, James J.
Actor
b. San Francisco, CA, 1866
d. Bayside, NY, Feb. 18, 1933, Age 66

CORBETT, Leonora
Actress
b. London, England, June 28, 1908
d. Vleuten, the Netherlands, July 29, 1960, Age 52

CORBIN, John
Critic, Novelist
b. Chicago, IL, May 2, 1870
d. Unknown, Aug. 30, 1959, Age 89

CORCORAN, Katherine (Mrs, James A. Herne)
Actress
b. Abbeyleix, Ireland, 1857
d. Astoria, NY, Feb. 8, 1943, Age 86

COREY, Wendell
Actor, President Academy of Motion Picture Arts & Sciences
b. Dracut, MA, March 20, 1914
d. Woodland Hills, CA, Nov. 8, 1968, Age 54

CORINNE, (Corinne Belle De Briou)
Performer
b. New Orleans, LA, Dec. 25, 1873
d. Unknown, 1937, Age 63

CORNEILLE, Pierre
Playwright
b. Rouen, France, June 6, 1606
d. Paris, France, Oct. 1, 1684, Age 78

CORNEILLE, Thomas
Playwright
b. Rouen, France, 1625
d. Les Andelys, France, 1709

CORNELL, Katharine
Actress
b. Berlin, Germany, Feb. 16, 1898
d. Vineyard Haven, MA, June 9, 1974, Age 81

CORREL, Gladis
Performer
b. Unknown
d. Hollywood, CA, May 19, 1962, Age 70

CORRIGAN, Emmett (Antoine Zilles)
Actor
b. Amsterdam, Holland, June 5, 1868
d. Hollywood, CA, Oct. 29, 1932, Age 64

CORT, Harry Linsley
Producer, Author
b. Seattle, WA, Unknown
d. New York, NY, May 6, 1937, Age 44

CORT, John
Manager
b. Newark, NJ, Unknown
d. Stamford, CT, Nov. 17, 1929, Age 70

CORTHELL, Herbert
Performer
b. Boston, MA, Unknown
d. Hollywood, CA, Jan 23, 1947, Age 69

COSSA, Pietro
Playwright
b. Unknown, 1830
d. Unknown, 1881

COSSART, Ernest
Actor
b. Chelthenham, England, Sept. 24, 1876
d. New York, NY, Jan. 21, 1951, Age 74

COSTELLO, Helene
Actress
b. New York, NY, Unknown
d. California, Jan. 26, 1957, Age 53

COSTELLO, Lou (Louis Francis Costello)
Actor
b. Paterson, NJ, March 6, 1906
d. Beverly Hills, CA, March 3, 1959, Age 53

COSTELLO, Maurice (Maurice George Washington Costello)
Actor
b. Pittsburgh, PA, Feb. 22, 1877
d. Hollywood, CA, Oct. 29, 1950, Age 73

COSTELLO, Tom
Comedian
b. Unknown, 1863
d. Unknown, Nov. 8, 1943, Age 80

COTOPOULI, Marika
Actress
b. Greece, Unknown
d. Athens, Greece, Sept. 11, 1954, Age 68

COTTON, Charles
Playwright
b. Unknown
d. Unknown, Feb. 16, 1687, Age 57

COTTON, Fred Ayers
Actor, Union executive
b. Hastings, NB, Unknown
d. New York, NY, Jan. 28, 1964, Age 57

COTTON, Lucy
Performer
b. Unknown
d. Miami Beach, FL, Dec. 12, 1948, Age 57

COTTON, Robert F.
Actor
b. England, Unknown
d. London, England, Sept. 27, 19--

COTTRELLY, Mathilde (née Meyer) (Mrs. Mathilde Wilson)
Performer
b. Hamburg, Germany, Feb. 7, 1851
d. Tuckerton, NJ, June 16, 1933, Age 82

COTTS, Campbell (Sir William Campbell Mitchell-Cotts)
Actor
b. Unknown
d. London, England, Feb. 19, 1964, Age 61

COULDOCK, Charles Walter
Actor
b. London, England, 1815
d. Unknown, 1898

COULTER, Frazer
Actor
b. Smith Falls, Ontario, CAN, Aug. 20, 1848
d. East Islip, NY, Jan. 26, 1937, Age 88

COURTELINE, Georges
Author, Playwright
b. Unknown, 1861
d. Unknown, June 25, 1929

COURTENAY, William Leonard
Actor
b. Worcester, MA, June 19, 1875
d. Rye, NY, April 20, 1933, Age 57

COURTENEY, Fay
Actress
b. San Francisco, CA, Unknown
d. New York, NY, July 18, 1943, Age 65

COURTLEIGH, Edna (Mrs. William Courtleigh)
Actress
b. Unknown
d. Hollywood, CA, July 25, 1962, Age 77

COURTLEIGH, William
Actor
b. Guelph, Ontario, CAN, June 28, 1867
d. Rye, NY, Dec. 27, 1930, Age 63

COURTNEIDGE, Charles
Actor
b. Unknown
d. Unknown, June 13, 1935

COURTNEIDGE, Mrs. Robert (Rosie Nott)
Actress
b. Unknown
d. Unknown, Aug. 27, 1914, Age 46

COURTNEIDGE, Robert
Producer, Playwright, Actor
b. Glasgow, Scotland, June 29, 1859
d. Unknown, April 6, 1939, Age 79

COURTNEIDGE, Rosaline
Actress
b. London, England, Aug. 19, 1903
d. Unknown, Dec. 8, 1926, Age 23

COURTNEY, Fay
Singer, Comedienne
b. Clay County, TX, Unknown
d. New York, NY, Feb. 14, 1941, Age 45

COURTNEY, John
Actor, Playwright
b. Unknown
d. Unknown, Feb. 17, 1865, Age 61

COURTNEY, Oscar W.
Performer
b. Unknown
d. Chicago, IL, June 18, 1963, Age 85

COURTNEY, William Leonard
Critic, Author, Journalist
b. Poona, India, Jan. 5, 1850
d. Unknown, Nov. 1, 1928, Age 78

COWAN, Jerome
Actor
b. New York, NY, Oct. 6, 1897
d. Hollywood, CA, Jan. 24, 1972, Age 74

COWARD, Noel
Playwright - Composer - Actor
b. Teddington, England, Dec. 16, 1899
d. Blue Harbor, Jamaica, British West Indies, March 26, 1973, Age 73

COWDEN, Irene
Actress
b. Unknown
d. England, Nov. 15, 1961

COWELL, Joseph Leathley
Actor
b. England, 1792
d. England, 1863

COWELL, Samuel Houghton
Actor
b. London, England, 1820
d. Unknown, 1864

COWELL, Sydney
Actress
b. London, England, 1846
d. Unknown, Nov. 5, 1925, Age 79

COWEN, Laurence
Playwright, Theatre proprietor
b. Hull, England, 1865
d. Hampstead, London, England, Oct. 7, 1942, Age 77

COWEN, Louis
Critic, Playwright
b. Unknown
d. Unknown, Dec. 16, 1925, Age 69

COWEN, William Joyce
Playwright
b. Unknown
d. London, England, Jan. 1964, Age 76

COWL, Jane
Actress
b. Boston, MA, Dec. 14, 1884
d. Santa Monica, CA, June 22, 1950, Age 65

COWLES, Eugene
Actor
b. Stanstead, Quebec, CAN, Unknown
d. Boston, MA, Sept. 22, 1948, Age 88

COWLEY, Abraham
Playwright, Poet
b. Unknown, 1618
d. Unknown, July 28, 1667, Age 49

COWLEY, Eric
Actor
b. Southsea, Hants, England, June 11, 1886
d. Unknown, Sept. 8, 1948, Age 62

COWLEY, Mrs. Hannah (née Parkhouse)
Playwright
b. Tiverton, England, 1743
d. Unknown, March 11, 1809, Age 66

COWLEY, Richard
Actor
b. Unknown
d. Unknown, . . . buried March 12, 1619

COWPER, Clara (Mrs. William Calvert)
Actress
b. Unknown
d. Unknown, March 13, 1917

COX, Wally
Actor
b. Detroit, MI, Dec. 6, 1924
d. Bel Air, CA, Feb. 15, 1973, Age 48

COYLE, John E.
Actor
b. Unknown
d. London, England, July 15, 1964, Age 70

COYNE, Joseph
Actor
b. New York, NY, March 27, 1867
d. Virginia Water, Surrey, England, Feb. 17, 1941, Age 73

COYNE, Joseph Stirling
Playwright
b. Unknown
d. Unknown, July 18, 1868, Age 64

CRABTREE, Charlotte ("Lotta")
Performer
b. New York, NY, Nov. 7, 1847
d. Boston, MA, Sept. 25, 1924, Age 76

CRAIG, Edith (Edith Wardell)
Actress
b. England, Dec. 9, 1869
d. Small Hythe, Kent, England, March 27, 1947, Age 77

CRAIG, Edward Gordon
Designer, Director, Actor, Writer
b. Stevenage, Herts, England, Jan. 16, 1872
d. Vence, France, July 29, 1966, Age 94

CRAIG, Hardin
Shakespeare Scholar, Editor
b. Owensboro, KY, June 29, 1875
d. Houston, TX, Oct. 13, 1968, Age 93

CRAIG, John
Actor-manager
b. Columbia County, TN, Unknown
d. Woodmere, L.I., NY, Aug. 23, 1932, Age 64

CRAMER, Edd
Actor
b. Unknown
d. New York, NY, Dec. 21, 1963, Age 39

CRANE, Edith (Mrs. Tyrone Power)
Actress
b. New York, NY, 1865
d. Unknown, Jan 3, 1912, Age 46

CRANE, William Henry
Actor
b. Leicester, Ma, April 30, 1845
d. Hollywood, CA, March 7, 1928, Age 82

CRATER, Allene
Actress
b. Unknown
d. Burbank, CA, Aug. 13, 1957, Age 77

CRAVEN, Arthur Scott (Capt. A. K. Harvey-James)
Actor, Playwright
b. Unknown
d. Unknown, April 15, 1917

CRAVEN, Frank
Actor, Author, Director
b. Boston, Ma, 1875
d. Beverly Hills, CA, Sept. 1, 1945, Age 70

CRAVEN, Hawes (Henry Hawes Craven Green)
Scene Painter
b. Unknown, 1837
d. Unknown, 1910

CRAVEN, Henry Thornton
Actor, Playwright
b. London, England, Feb. 26, 1818
d. Brixton, London, England, April 14, 1905, Age 87

CRAVEN, Ruby
Actress
b. Australia, Unknown
d. Milford, CT, March 10, 1964, Age 76

CRAVEN, Tom
Actor, Author, Producer
b. London, England, July 26, 1868
d. Unknown, Aug. 5, 1919, Age 51

CRAWFORD, Anne (Imelda Crawford, Mrs. Wallace Douglas)
Actress
b. Haifa, Palestine, Nov. 22, 1920
d. London, England, Oct. 17, 1956, Age 35

CRAWFORD, Clifton
Comedian
b. Edinburgh, Scotland, Unknown
d. London, England, June 3, 1920, Age 45

CRAWFORD, Francis Marion
Playwright, Novelist
b. Unknown, Aug. 2, 1854
d. Unknown, April 9, 1909, Age 54

CRAWFORD, Jack R.
Educator
b. Washington, DC, April 1, 1878
d. West Haven, CT, Aug. 8, 1968, Age 90

CRAWFORD, Jesse
Organist, Teacher
b. Woodland, CA, Unknown
d. Los Angeles, CA, May 27, 1962, Age 67

CRAWLEY, J. Sayre
Actor
b. Heyford, England, Unknown
d. New York, NY, Mar. 7, 1948, Age c70

CREBILLON, Prosper Jolyot de
Playwright
b. Unknown, 1674
d. Unknown, 1762

CREEL, Frances
Actress
b. Unknown
d. San Francisco, CA, Feb. 18, 1957, Age 43

CREGAR, (Samuel) Laird
Actor
b. Philadelphia, PA, 1916
d. Hollywood, CA, Dec. 9, 1944, Age 28

CRESSY, William
Actor
b. Unknown, 1863
d. St. Petersburg, FL, May 7, 1930, Age 65

CRESWELL, Helen
Actress
b. Unknown
d. London, England, Feb. 7, 1949, Age 103

CREWE, Bertie
Theatrical architect
b. Unknown
d. Unknown, Jan. 10, 1937, Age 74

CREWS, Laura Hope
Actress
b. San Francisco, CA, Unknown
d. New York, NY, Nov. 13, 1942, Age 62

CRICHTON, Kyle S.
Playwright
b. Peale, PA, Nov. 6, 1896
d. New York, NY, Nov. 24, 1960, Age 64

CRISP, Samuel
Playwright
b. Unknown
d. Unknown, April 24, 1783

CROCKER, Henry
Producer
b. Unknown
d. Unknown, Oct. 12, 1937, Age 62

CROFT, Anne
Actress
b. Skirlaugh, Hull, England, Aug. 17, 1896
d. Unknown, March 23, 1959, Age 62

CROKER, T. F. Dillon
Historian
b. Barnes, England, Aug. 26, 1831
d. Unknown, Feb. 6, 1912, Age 80

CROKER-KING, Charles H.
Actor
b. Rook Holme, Yorkshire, England, April 30, 1873
d. Unknown, Oct. 25, 1951, Age 77

CROLY, George
Novelist, Playwright, Critic
b. Dublin, Ireland, 1780
d. Unknown, 1860

CROMPTON, William H.
Actor
b. Manchester, England, 1843
d. Unknown, Oct. 23, 1909, Age 66

CROMWELL, Richard (Roy Radabaugh)
Actor
b. Los Angeles, CA, Unknown
d. Hollywood, CA, Oct. 11, 1960, Age 50

CRONE, Adeline (Dutton) Leipnik
Performer
b. Unknown
d. Cincinnati, OH, July 29, 1962, Age 70

CROOK, John Composer
Conductor
b. London, England, Unknown
d. Unknown, Nov. 10, 1922

CROPPER, Roy
Actor
b. Jamaica Plain, Boston, MA, 1898 (?)
d. Miami, FL, May 14, 1954, Age 58

CROSBY, Edward Harold
Playwright, Critic
b. Boston, MA, Unknown
d. Boston, MA, Dec. 2, 1934, Age 75

CROSBY, Hazel (Hazel Crosby Brown)
Performer
b. Unknown
d. Petaluma, CA, June 19, 1964, Age 74

CROSMAN, Henrietta Foster
Actress
b. Wheeling, WV, Sept. 2, 1861
d. Pelham Manor, NY, Oct. 31, 1944, Age 83

CROSSLEY-TAYLOR, E. W.
Theatre manager
b. Unknown
d. London, England, 1963, Age 68

CROTHERS, Rachel
Playwright
b. Bloomington, IL, 1878
d. Danbury, CT, July 5, 1958, Age 79

CROUSE, Russel
Playwright, Producer, Writer
b. Findlay, OH, Feb. 20, 1893
d. New York, NY, April 3, 1966, Age 73

CROWNE, John
Playwright
b. Unknown, c1640
d. Unknown, c1710

CRUMIT, Frank
Performer, Song writer
b. Jackson, OH, 1888
d. New York, NY, Sept. 7, 1943, Age 54

CRUZE, James (Bosen)
Actor, Film director
b. Ogden, UT, 1884
d. Hollywood, CA, Aug. 4, 1942, Age 58

CUENCA, Pedro Fernandez
Actor
b. Unknown
d. Unknown, Dec. 9, 1940

CUEVA, Juan de la
Poet, Playwright
b. Seville, Spain, c1550
d. Unknown, c1615

CULLEN, Edward L.
Actor, Radio announcer
b. Buffalo, NY, Unknown
d. New York, NY, July 27, 1964, Age 69

CULLEY, Frederick
Actor
b. Plymouth, England, March 9, 1879
d. Unknown, Nov. 3, 1942, Age 63

CULLINAN, Ralph
Actor
b. Unknown
d. New York, NY, April 4, 1950, Age 68

CULLMAN, Howard S.
Theatrical investor
b. New York City, NY, Sept. 23, 1891
d. New York City, June 29, 1972, Age 81

CULVER, David Jay
Critic, Editor
b. Harrison, NY, Oct. 21, 1902
d. New York, NY, March 22, 1968, Age 65

CUMBERLAND, Gerald
Playwright, Critic, Novelist
b. Manchester, England, May 7, 1879
d. Unknown, Jan. 2, 1926, Age 47

CUMBERLAND, John
Publisher
b. Unknown
d. Unknown, June 13, 1866, Age 79

CUMBERLAND, Richard
Playwright
b. Cambridge, England, 1732
d. Unknown, May 7, 1811, Age 79

CUMMINGS, Edward Estlin
Poet, Playwright, Essayist
b. Cambridge, MA, Oct. 14, 1894
d. North Conway, NH, Sept. 3, 1962, Age 67

CUMMINGS, Vicki
Actress, Singer
b. Northhampton, MA, 1913
d. New York, NY, Nov. 30, 1969, Age 56

CUNNINGHAM, Arthur
Actor
b. San Francisco, CA, Unknown
d. San Francisco, CA, Nov. 29, 1955, Age 67

CUNNINGHAM, George
Actor, Choreographer, Director
b. Unknown
d. Los Angeles, CA, May 1, 1962, Age 58

CUNNINGHAM, John
Actor, Playwright
b. Unknown
d. Unknown, Sept. 18, 1773, Age 44

CUREL, François de Vicomte
Playwright
b. Lorraine, France, 1854
d. Unknown, c1928

CURLL, Edmund
Publisher
b. Unknown
d. Unknown, Dec. 11, 1747, Age 72

CURRAN, Homer F.
Producer
b. Springfield, MO, Unknown
d. Beverly Hills, CA, July 18, 1952, Age 67

CURRIE, Clive
Actor
b. Birmingham, England, March 26, 1877
d. Unknown, May 25, 1935, Age 58

CURRIE, Finlay
Actor
b. Edinburgh, Scotland, Jan. 20, 1878
d. Gerrards Cross, England, May 9, 1968, Age 90

CURRIER, Frank
Actor
b. Unknown
d. Hollywood, CA, April 22, 1928, Age 71

CURTIS, Alan (Harry Ueberroth)
Actor
b. Chicago, IL, Unknown
d. New York, NY, Feb. 1, 1953, Age 43

CURTIS, Allen
Actor, Film director
b. Unknown
d. Hollywood, CA, Nov. 24, 1961, Age 84

CURTIZ, David
Actor, Film director, Film editor
b. Budapest, Hungary, Unknown
d. Hollywood, CA, May 23, 1962, Age 68

CURTO, Ramada
Playwright
b. Unknown
d. Lisbon, Portugal, Oct. 27, 1961, Age 75

CURWEN, Patric
Actor
b. London, England, Dec. 14, 1884
d. Unknown, May 31, 1949, Age 64

CURZON, Frank (Francis Arthur Deeley)
Producer, Actor
b. Wavertree, Liverpool, England, Sept. 17, 1868,
d. Unknown, July 2, 1927, Age 58

CUSHING, Catherine Chisholm
Playwright, Songwriter, Librettist
b. Ohio, Unknown
d. New York, NY, Oct. 19, 1952

CUSHING, Tom (Charles C. Strong Cushing)
Playwright
b. New Haven, CT, Oct. 27, 1879
d. Boston, MA, March 6, 1941, Age 61

CUSHMAN, Charlotte Saunders
Actress
b. Boston, MA, July 23, 1816
d. Boston, MA, Feb. 18, 1876, Age 59

CUSHMAN, Susan
Actress
b. Unknown, 1822
d. Unknown, 1859, Age 37

CUSTIS, George Washington Parke
Playwright, Author
b. Unknown, 1781
d. Unknown, 1857, Age 70

CUTLER, Kate
Actress
b. London, England, Aug. 14, 1870
d. Unknown, May 14, 1955, Age 84

CUTLER, Peggy (Mrs. Douglas Furber)
Actress
b. Unknown
d. Unknown, July 31, 1945

CUTTS, Patricia
Actress
b. London, England, July 20, 1931
d. London, England, Sept. 6, 1974, Age 48

CZETTEL, Ladislas Philip
Designer
b. Budapest, Hungary, Unknown
d. New York, NY, March 5, 1949, Age 55

D

DABBS, Dr. H. R.
Playwright
b. Unknown
d. Unknown, June 10, 1913

DABORNE, Robert
Playwright
b. Unknown
d. Unknown, March 23, 1628

DADSWELL, Pearl
Performer
b. Unknown
d. London, England, June 1, 1963, Age 47

DAGMAR, Marie
Actress
b. Unknown
d. Unknown, June 15, 1925

DAI, Lin
Actress
b. Unknown
d. Hong Kong, British Crown Colony, July 17, 1964, Age 33

DAILEY, Peter F.
Performer
b. New York, NY, 1868
d. Unknown, May 23, 1908, Age 40

DAINTON, Marie (Née Sharlach)
Performer
b. Russia, June 30, 1881
d. Unknown, Feb. 1, 1938, Age 56

DALBERG, Baron Wolfgang Heribert von
Producer
b. Unknown, 1750
d. Unknown, 1806

D'ALBERT, George
Performer
b. Unknown
d. Unknown, Aug. 17, 1949, Age 71

DALE, Alan (Alfred J. Cohen)
Critic, Playwright
b. Birmingham, England, May 14, 1861
d. Unknown, May 21, 1928, Age 67

DALE, Esther
Actress
b. Beaufort, SC, Unknown
d. Los Angeles, CA, July 23, 1961, Age 75

DALE, Margie (Mrs. Nicholas Rinaldo)
Performer
b. Unknown
d. Buffalo, NY, Aug. 1962, Age 54

DALIN, Olaf
Playwright
b. Unknown, 1708
d. Unknown, 1763, Age 55

DALMORES, Charles
Actor
b. Nancy, France, Jan. 1, 1871
d. Hollywood, CA, Dec. 6, 1939, Age 68

DALTON, Charles
Actor
b. England, Aug. 29, 1864
d. Stamford, CT, June 11, 1942, Age 77

DALY, Arnold (Peter Christopher Arnold Daly)
Actor
b. Brooklyn, NY, Oct. 4, 1875
d. New York, NY, Jan. 12, 1927, Age 51

DALY, Dan
Performer
b. Unknown, 1858
d. Unknown, March 26, 1904, Age 46

DALY, Dixie (Rosie Francis) (Mrs. Tony King)
Performer
b. Unknown
d. Leicester, England, 1963, Age 66

DALY, (John) Augustin
Producer, Author
b. Plymouth, NC, July 20, 1838
d. Paris, France, June 7, 1899, Age 60

DALY, Lawrence
Actor, Producer
b. Unknown
d. Unknown, Nov. 13, 1900, Age 38

DALY, Mae (Mrs. Margaret DeLeo)
Performer
b. Unknown
d. Miami Beach, FL, March 7, 1962, Age 70

DALY, Mark
Actor
b. Edinburgh, Scotland, Aug. 23, 1887
d. Unknown, Sept. 27, 1957, Age 70

DAM, H. J. W.
Playwright
b. Unknown
d. Unknown, April 26, 1906, Age 47

DAMALA, Jacques
Actor
b. Unknown
d. Unknown, Aug. 18, 1889, Age 40

DAMERAL, George
Singer
b. Hastings, MN, Unknown
d. Glendale, CA, July 10, 1936, Age 57

DAMON, Les
Actor
b. Unknown
d. Hollywood, CA, July 20, 1962, Age 53

DAMROSCH, Walter Johannes
Conductor, Composer
b. Breslau, Silesia (Prussia), Jan. 30, 1862
d. New York, NY, Dec. 22, 1950, Age 88

DANA, Henry
Producer
b. London, England, Jan. 1, 1855
d. Unknown, Sept. 4, 1921, Age 66

DANA, Mary Louise
Actress
b. Unknown
d. New York, NY, Dec. 10, 1946, Age 70

DANBY, Charles
Actor
b. Unknown
d. Unknown, Sept. 7, 1906, Age 48

DANCE, George Sir
Playwright, Librettist, Manager
b. Nottingham, England, 1858
d. Unknown, Oct. 22, 1932, Age 74

DANCHENKO, Vladimir Ivanovich Nemirovich
Director, Educator, Author
b. Unknown, 1859
d. Unknown, 1943

DANCOURT, Florent Carton Playwright
Lawyer, Poet
b. Fontainebleu, France, 1661
d. Unknown, 1725

DANDO, W. P.
Inventor, ("Flying Ballet")
b. Unknown
d. Unknown, Nov. 11, 1944, Age 92

DANDY, Jess
Performer
b. Rochester, NY, Unknown
d. Brookline, MA, April 15, 1923, Age 53

DANE, Clemence
Playwright, Novelist, Screenwriter
b. Blackheath, England, Unknown
d. London, England, March 28, 1965, Age 77

DANE, Essex
Actor, Playwright
b. London, England, Unknown
d. New London, Ct, July 18, 1962, Age 96

DANE, Karl (Rasmus Karl Thekelsen Gottlieb)
Actor
b. Copenhagen, Denmark, 1887
d. Unknown, April 14, 1934, Age 47

DANFORTH, William
Actor, Singer
b. Syracuse, NY, May 13, 1867
d. Skaneateles, NY, April 16, 1941, Age 73

DANGEVILLE, Marie Anne Botot
Actress
b. Unknown, 1714
d. Unknown, 1796

DANIEL, Billy
Choreographer
b. Unknown
d. Hollywood, CA, May 15, 1962, Age 50

DANIEL, George ("D. G.")
Critic
b. Unknown
d. Unknown, March 30, 1864, Age 74

DANIEL, Rita
Actress
b. Unknown
d. Unknown, July 14, 1951

DANIEL, Samuel
Playwright, Poet
b. Somersetshire, England, 1562
d. Unknown, Oct. 14, 1619, Age 57

DANIELL, Henry
Actor
b. London, England, May 5, 1894
d. Santa Monica, CA, Oct. 13, 1963, Age 69

DANIELS, Bebe
Actress
b. Dallas, TX, Jan. 14, 1901
d. London, England, March 16, 1971, Age 71

DANIELS, Frank Albert
Actor
b. Dayton, OH, 1860
d. West Palm Beach, FL, Jan. 12, 1935, Age 74

DANJURO, Ichikawa
Actor, Producer
b. Unknown
d. Unknown, Oct. 1903

DANKS, Hart Pease
Composer
b. New Haven, CT, April 6, 1834
d. Philadelphia, PA, Nov. 20, 1903, Age 69

D'ANNUNZIO, Lola
Actress
b. Unknown
d. Meade, KS, June 5, 1956, Age 26

DANTE, Ethel (Mrs. Alice O'Neil)
Actress
b. Unknown
d. Unknown, March 30, 1954, Age 92

DANVERS, Billy
Actor
b. Liverpool, England, Unknown
d. Manchester, England, March 20, 1964, Age 75

DANVERS, Johnny (or Johnnie)
Actor, Minstrel
b. Yorkshire, England, Nov. 19, 1870
d. Brixton, England, April 1, 1939, Age 68

D'ARCY, Belle
Performer
b. New York, NY, Unknown
d. Portland, ME, Nov. 2, 1936, Age 64

D'ARCY, Hugh Antoine
Actor, Manager
b. France, Unknown
d. New York, NY, Nov. 11, 1925, Age 82

DARE, Eva
b. Unknown
d. Unknown, Oct. 15, 1931

DARE, Richard
Actor
b. Unknown
d. Chalfont St. Giles, England, Feb. 3, 1964, Age 41

DARE, Virginia
Actress
b. Unknown
d. Hollywood, Ca, July 8, 1962

DAREWSKI, Herman
Composer, Musical director
b. Minsk, Russia, April 17, 1883
d. Unknown, June 2, 1947, Age 64

DAREWSKI, Max
Composer, Conductor
b. Manchester, England, Nov. 3, 1894
d. Unknown, Sept. 25, 1929, Age 34

DARGAN, Olive Tilford
Poet, Playwright, Novelist
b. Grayson County, KY, Unknown
d. Asheville, NC, Jan. 22, 1968, Age 99

DARK, Sidney
Critic, Journalist
b. Unknown, Jan. 14, 1874
d. Unknown, Oct. 11, 1947, Age 73

DARMONT, Albert
Actor, Playwright
b. Unknown
d. Unknown, Jan. 1909, Age 45

DARNLEY, Herbert
Actor, Playwright, Songwriter
b. Unknown
d. Unknown, Feb. 7, 1947, Age 75

DARNLEY, J. H.
Playwright, Actor
b. Unknown
d. Unknown, April 29, 1938, Age 81

DARNTON, Charles
Drama critic
b. Adrian, MI, Unknown
d. Hollywood, CA, May 18, 1950, Age 80

DARRAGH, Miss (Letitia Marion Dallas)
Actress
b. Unknown
d. Unknown, Dec. 15, 1917

DARRELL, Charles
Playwright
b. Unknown
d. Unknown, March 25, 1932

D'ARVILLE, Camille
Performer
b. Overrysel, Holland, June 21, 1863
d. San Francisco, CA, Sept. 10, 1932, Age 69

DASHINGTON, James J.
Performer
b. Unknown
d. Philadelphia, PA, Feb. 11, 1962, Age 84

D'AUBAN, Ernest
Director
b. Unknown
d. Unknown, Feb. 3, 1941, Age 67

DAUDET, Alphonse
Playwright, Novelist
b. Nimes, France, May 13, 1840
d. Paris, France, Dec. 16, 1897, Age 57

DAUDET, Ernest
Playwright
b. Unknown, 1837
d. Unknown, Aug. 20, 1921, Age 84

DAUNCEY, Sylvanus
Playwright, Producer
b. Unknown
d. Unknown, Nov. 24, 1912, Age 48

DAUNT, William
Actor
b. Dublin, Ireland, Aug. 21, 1893
d. Unknown, Oct. 1, 1938, Age 44

D'AVENANT, Sir William
Playwright, Producer, Poet Laureate
b. Oxford, England, Feb. 1606
d. London, England, April 17, 1668, Age 63

DAVENPORT, Butler
Actor, Producer, Playwright
b. New York, NY, 1871
d. New York, NY, April 7, 1958, Age 87

DAVENPORT, Edgar Longfellow
Actor
b. Unknown, 1862
d. Unknown, 1918, Age 56

DAVENPORT, Edward Loomis
Actor
b. Unknown, 1815
d. Unknown, Sept. 1, 1877, Age 61

DAVENPORT, Eva (Mrs. Neil O'Brien)
Actress
b. London, England, Unknown
d. White Plains, NY, Sept. 26, 1932, Age 74

DAVENPORT, Fanny Elizabeth Vining
Actress
b. Unknown, 1829
d. Canton, PA, July 20, 1891

DAVENPORT, Fanny Lily Gypsy
Actress
b. London, England, April 10, 1850
d. South Duxbury, MA, Sept. 26, 1898, Age 48

DAVENPORT, George Gosling
Actor
b. Unknown
d. Unknown, March 13, 1814, Age 56

DAVENPORT, Harry George Bryant
Actor
b. New York, NY, Jan. 19, 1866
d. Hollywood, CA, Aug. 9, 1949, Age 83

DAVENPORT, Jean Margaret (Mrs. Lander)
Actress
b. Unknown, 1829
d. Unknown, Aug. 3, 1903, Age 74

DAVENPORT, Mary
Actress
b. Unknown
d. Unknown, June 26, 1916, Age 65

DAVENPORT, May (Mrs. William Seymour)
Actress
b. Boston, MA, July 21, 1856
d. New York, NY, Feb. 10, 1927, Age 70

DAVEY, Peter
Theatre manager
b. London, England, Nov. 11, 1857
d. Unknown, May 26, 1946, Age 88

DAVID, Worton
Composer
b. Unknown
d. Unknown, Nov. 15, 1940

DAVIDSON, Dore
Actor, Playwright
b. Unknown
d. New York, NY, March 7, 1930, Age 80

DAVIDSON, Maitland
Critic
b. Unknown
d. Unknown, Jan. 1, 1936, Age 62

DAVIES, Acton
Critic
b. St. John's, Quebec, CAN, 1870
d. Unknown, June 12, 1916, Age 46

DAVIES, Ben
Actor
b. Swansea Valley, Wales, Jan. 6, 1858
d. Unknown, March 28, 1943, Age 85

DAVIES, Betty-Ann
Actress
b. London, England, Dec. 24, 1910
d. Manchester, England, May 14, 1955, Age 44

DAVIES, Harry Parr
Composer
b. Briton Ferry, Glamorganshire, Scotland, May 24, 1914
d. Unknown, Oct. 14, 1955, Age 41

DAVIES, Hubert Henry
Playwright
b. Woodley, Cheshire, England, March 30, 1869
d. Unknown, Aug. 17, 1917, Age 48

DAVIES, Lilian
Actress
b. Lynmouth, North Devon, England, Jan 18, 1895
d. Unknown, March 3, 1932, Age 37

DAVIES, Marion (Marion Cecilia Douras)
Actress
b. Brooklyn, NY, Jan. 3, 1897
d. Los Angeles, CA, Sept. 22, 1961, Age 64

DAVIES, Thomas
Biographer, Writer
b. Unknown
d. Unknown, May 5, 1785, Age 73

DAVIOT, Gordon (Elizabeth Mackintosh)
Playwright, Novelist
b. Inverness, Scotland, Unknown
d. Unknown, Feb. 13, 1952, Age 55

DAVIS, Ann
Actress
b. Unknown
d. Unknown, Sept. 3, 1961, Age 68

DAVIS, Blevins
Producer, Playwright
b. Osceola, MO, May 26, 1903
d. London, England, July 16, 1971, Age 68

DAVIS, Boyd
Performer
b. Santa Rosa, CA, June 19, 1885
d. Hollywood, CA, Jan 25, 1963, Age 77

DAVIS, Charles Belmont
Critic
b. Philadelphia, PA, Unknown
d. Asheville, NC, Dec. 10, 1926, Age 60

DAVIS, Eddie
Writer
b. New York, NY, Unknown
d. New York, NY, July 30, 1958, Age 58

DAVIS, Fay
Actress
b. Boston, MA, Dec. 15, 1872
d. Unknown, Feb. 26, 1945, Age 72

DAVIS, H. O.
Journalist, Film executive, Producer
b. Unknown
d. Palm Springs, CA, Aug. 28, 1964, Age 87

DAVIS, Harry E.
Producer, Educator
b. Little Mountain, SC, Aug. 25, 1905
d. Chapel Hill, NC, Sept. 15, 1968, Age 63

DAVIS, Jessie Bartlett
Actress
b. near Moris, IL, 1861
d. Chicago, IL, May 14, 1905, Age 44

DAVIS, Joan (Madonna Josephine Davis)
Actress
b. St. Paul, MN, June 29, 1913(?)
d. Palm Springs, CA, May 23, 1961, Age 53

DAVIS, Owen
Playwright
b. Portland, ME, Jan 29, 1874
d. New York, NY, Oct. 14, 1956, Age 82

DAVIS, Owen Jr.
Performer, Playwright, Producer
b. New York, NY, Oct. 6, 1907
d. New York, NY (Drowned in Long Island Sound), May 22, 1949, Age 42

DAVIS, Richard Harding
Playwright, Author
b. Philadelphia, PA, April 18, 1864
d. Mt. Kisco, NY, April 11, 1916, Age 52

DAVIS, Tom Buffen
Producer
b. London, England, 1867
d. Unknown, Dec. 14, 1931, Age 64

DAVIS, Willis J.
Theatre Manager
b. Newman, GA, Unknown
d. Naples, FL, Nov. 24, 1963, Age 76

DAVISON, Maria
Actress
b. Unknown
d. Unknown, May 30, 1858, Age 78

DAWE, Carlton
Playwright, Novelist
b. Unknown
d. Unknown, May 30, 1935, Age 69

DAWSON, Ivo
Actor
b. Unknown
d. Unknown, March 7, 1934, Age 54

DAWSON, Jenny
Actress
b. Unknown
d. Unknown, Dec. 21, 1936

DAWSON, Ralph
Film editor
b. Unknown
d. Hollywood, CA, Nov. 15, 1962, Age 65

DAY, Cyrus L.
Drama Teacher, Writer
b. New York, NY, Dec. 2, 1900
d. Hamilton, Bermuda, July 5, 1968, Age 67

DAY, Edith
Actress
b. Minneapolis, MN, April 10, 1896
d. London, England, May 1, 1971, Age 75

DAY, John
Playwright
b. Unknown
d. Unknown, July 23, 1584

DAY, John
Playwright
b. Cawston, Norfolk, England, c1574
d. Unknown, c1640

DAY, Juliette (Mrs. Paul Le Brocque Whitney)
Actress
b. Unknown
d. Huntington, NY, Sept. 18, 1957, Age 63

DAY, Roy
Actor, Librarian
b. Unknown
d. Stamford, CT, April 14, 1963, Age 75

DAYMAN, Bain Sr.
Voice teacher
b. Unknown
d. Hollywood, CA, June 9, 1964, Age 68

DAYNE, Blanche (Mrs. Will Cressy)
Actress
b. Troy, NY, Unknown
d. Hackensack, NJ, June 27, 1944, Age 73

DAZEY, Charles Turner
Playwright
b. Lima, IL, Aug. 12, 1853
d. Quincy, IL, Feb. 9, 1938, Age 84

DAZIE, Mlle. (née Daisy Peterkin) (Mrs. Cornelius Fellowes)
Performer
b. St. Louis, MO, Sept. 16, 1884
d. Miami Beach, FL, Aug. 12, 1952, Age 67

DEAGON, Arthur
Comedian
b. Kilmarnock, Scotland, Unknown
d. Boston, MA, Sept. 4, 1927, Age 56

DEAN, Alexander
Director, Educator
b. Newburyport, MA, Unknown
d. Cohasset, MA, July 29, 1939, Age 46

DEAN, James
Actor
b. Marion, IN, Unknown
d. Paso Robles, CA, Sept. 20, 1955, Age 24

DEAN, John W. (Jack)
Actor
b. Bridgeport, CT, Unknown
d. New York, NY, June 23, 1950, Age 75

DEAN, Julia
Actress
b. St. Paul, MN, May 13, 1880
d. Hollywood, CA, Oct. 18, 1952, Age 72

DEAN, Julia (Hayne-Cooper)
Actress
b. Dutchess County, NY, 1830
d. Boston, MA, March 6, 1868, Age 37

DE ANGELIS, Jefferson
Actor
b. San Francisco, CA, Nov. 30, 1859
d. Orange, NJ, March 20, 1933, Age 73

DE ANGELO, Carlo
Actor, Director
b. Unknown
d. Cornwall, NY, Jan 2, 1962, Age 66

DEANS, F. Harris
Critic,, Playwright, Novelist
b. Woolwich, England, April 10, 1886
d. Unknown, Feb. 12, 1961, Age 74

DEARLY, Max
Actor
b. Unknown
d. Unknown, June 2, 1943, Age 69

DEARNER, Mrs. Percy
Playwright
b. Unknown
d. Unknown, July 11, 1915, Age 43

DEARTH, Harry
Actor
b. London, England, 1876
d. Unknown, April 18, 1933, Age 56

DEAVES, Ada
Performer
b. Unknown
d. New York, NY, Sept. 18, 1920, Age 64

DE BELLEVILLE, Frederic
Actor
b. Liège, Belgium, Feb. 17, 1857
d. New York, NY, Feb. 25, 1923, Age 66

DEBENHAM, Cicely
Actress
b. Aylesbury, England, April 17, 1891
d. Unknown, Nov. 7, 1955, Age 64

DE BOER VAN RIJK, Esther
Actress
b. Unknown
d. Unknown, Sept. 7, 1937, Age 84

DE BORNIER, Henri
Playwright
b. Unknown
d. Unknown, Jan. 28, 1901, Age 75

DEBURAU, Charles
Actor, Pantomimist
b. Paris, France, 1829
d. Bordeaux, France, Dec. 7, 1873, Age 44

DEBURAU, Jean-Baptiste Gaspard
Actor, Pantomimist
b. Constanza, Romania, July 31, 1796
d. Paris, France, June 7, 1846, Age 49

DE BURGH, Aimee
Actress
b. Aberdeen, Scotland, Unknown
d. Unknown, April 2, 1946

DE CARMO, Pussy (Passidonio De Cardo)
Performer
b. Portugal, Unknown
d. Pittsburgh, PA, Jan. 19, 1964, Age 63

DE CISNEROS, Eleonora
Actress
b. New York, NY, Nov. 1, 1878
d. New York, NY, Feb. 3, 1934, Age 55

DE CORDOBA, Pedro
Actor
b. New York, NY, Sept. 28, 1881
d. Hollywood, CA, Sept. 17, 1950, Age 68

DE CORDOVA, Rudolph
Actor, Playwright
b. Kingston, Jamaica, 1860
d. Unknown, Jan. 11, 1941, Age 81

DECOURCELLE, Adrien
Playwright
b. Unknown
d. Unknown, Aug. 6, 1892, Age 69

DECOURCELLE, Pierre
Playwright
b. Unknown
d. Unknown, Oct. 10, 1926, Age 71

DECOURSEY, Nettie (Mrs. Edward C. Jameson)
Singer, Performer
b. Unknown
d. Merrimack, NH, March 12, 1964, Age 95

DE COURVILLE, Albert P.
Producer, Director
b. London, England, March 26, 1887
d. Unknown, March 1960, Age 72

DE CROISSET, Francis
Playwright
b. Unknown
d. Unknown, Nov. 8, 1937, Age 52

DE CUREL, François Viscomte
Playwright
b. Unknown
d. Unknown, April 26, 1928, Age 64

DEETER, Jasper
Producer, Director, Actor, Teacher
b. Mechanicsburg, PA, July 31, 1893
d. Media, PA, May 31, 1972, Age 78

DEEVY, Teresa
Playwright
b. Unknown
d. Waterford, Ireland, Jan. 19, 1963, Age 60

DE FERAUDY, Maurice
Actor
b. Unknown
d. Unknown, May 12, 1873, Age 73

DE FLERS, Robert
Playwright
b. Unknown
d. Unknown, Aug. 1, 1927, Age 56

DE FOE, Louis Vincent
Drama Critic
b. Adrian, MI, July 18, 1869
d. New York, NY, March 13, 1922, Age 52

DE FOREST, Marian
Playwright, Drama Critic
b. Buffalo, NY, Unknown
d. Buffalo, NY, Feb. 17, 1935, Age 70

DE GRASSE, Sam
Actor
b. Unknown
d. Hollywood, CA, Nov. 29, 1953, Age 78

DE GRESAC, Fred
Playwright, Librettist
b. Unknown
d. Unknown, Feb. 20, 1943, Age 75

DEJAZET, Pauline Virginie
Actress
b. Paris, France, 1798
d. Paris, France, Dec. 1, 1875, Age 77

DEKKER, Albert (Albert Van Dekker)
Actor
b. Brooklyn, NY, Dec. 20, 1905
d. Hollywood, CA, May 5, 1968, Age 62

DEKKER, Thomas
Playwright
b. London, England, c1570
d. Unknown, c1641, Age 61

DE KOVEN, Henry Louis Reginald
Composer, Conductor, Critic
b. Middletown, CT, April 3, 1859
d. Chicago, IL, Jan. 16, 1920, Age 60

DELAFIELD, E. M. (Edmée 3 Elizabeth Monica de la Pasture)
Playwright, Novelist
b. Hove, Sussex, England, 1890
d. Unknown, Dec. 2, 1943, Age 53

DELAIR, Paul
Playwright
b. Unknown
d. Unknown, Jan. 18, 1894, Age 52

DE LA MOTTE, Marguerite
Actress
b. Unknown, 1902
d. San Francisco, CA, March 10, 1950, Age 47

DELANEY, Charles
Actor
b. Unknown
d. Hollywood, CA, Aug. 31, 1959, Age 67

DELANEY, Maureen
Actress
b. Ireland, Unknown
d. London, England, March 27, 1961, Age 73

DE LANGE, Herman
Actor
b. Amsterdam, Holland, Dec. 6, 1851
d. Unknown, Aug. 4, 1929, Age 77

DELANOY, Edmond
Actor
b. Unknown
d. Unknown, Dec. 30, 1888, Age 71

DE LA PASTURE, Mrs. Henry (Lady Hugh Clifford)
Playwright, Novelist
b. Naples, Italy, 1866
d. Unknown, Oct. 30, 1945, Age 78

DE LA ROCHE, Mazo
Playwright, Novelist
b. Newmarket, Ontario, CAN, Jan. 15, 1879
d. Toronto, CAN, July 12, 1961, Age 81

DE LAROUX, Hugues
Playwright
b. Unknown
d. Unknown, Nov. 1925

DELAUNEY, Louis Arsène
Actor
b. Unknown, 1826
d. Unknown, Sept. 22, 1903, Age 77

DELAVIGNE, Germain
Playwright
b. Unknown
d. Unknown, Nov. 30, 1868, Age 78

DELAVIGNE, Jean François Casimir
Playwright
b. Le Havre, France, 1793
d. Unknown, Dec. 11, 1843, Age 50

DĒL CAMPO, Santiago
Playwright, Author, Lecturer
b. Chile, Unknown
d. Madrid, Spain, Nov. 19, 1963, Age 45

DE LEON, Jack
Producer
b. Panama, Aug. 12, 1897
d. Unknown, Sept. 21, 1956, Age 59

DE LEON, Millie
Performer
b. Unknown
d. New York, NY, Aug. 6, 1922, Age 52

DE LETRAZ, Jean
Playwright
b. Unknown
d. Unknown, June 4, 1954, Age 57

DELF, Harry
Performer, Songwriter, Playwright
b. Unknown
d. New York, NY, Feb. 7, 1964, Age 72

DELL, Floyd
Playwright, Novelist
b. Barry, IL, June 28, 1887
d. Bethesda, MD, July 23, 1969, Age 82

DELMORE, Ralph
Actor
b. New York, NY, Unknown
d. Unknown, Nov. 21, 1923, Age 70

DE LOUTHERBOURG, Philippe Jacques
Scenic designer
b. Strasbourg, Alsace, France, Oct. 31, 1740
d. Unknown, March 12, 1812, Age 71

DELPINI, Carlo
Pantomimist
b. Unknown
d. Unknown, Feb. 13, 1828, Age 88

DE LUSSAN, Zelie
Performer
b. New York, NY, Unknown
d. Unknown, Dec. 18, 1949, Age 85

DE MAR, Carrie (Mrs. Joseph Hart Boudrow)
Performer
b. Unknown
d. Cold Spring, NY, Feb. 23, 1963, Age 87

DEMAREST, Rubin
Actor
b. Unknown
d. Hollywood, CA, Sept. 20, 1962, Age 76

DE MARTHOLD, Jules
Playwright
b. Unknown
d. Unknown, May 5, 1927, Age 85

DE MAX, Edouard
Actor
b. Unknown
d. Unknown, Oct. 28, 1924, Age 55

DE MENDOZA, Don Fernando Diaz
Actor, Producer
b. Unknown
d. Unknown, Oct. 20, 1930

DE MILLE, Cecil Blount
Actor, Film producer, Director
b. Ashfield, MA, Aug. 12, 1881
d. Hollywood, CA, Jan. 21, 1959, Age 77

DE MILLE, Henry C.
Playwright, Manager
b. North Carolina, 1850
d. Pompton, NJ, Feb. 10, 1893, Age 42

DeMILLE, Mrs. Beatrice M.
Talent representative
b. Unknown
d. Hollywood, CA, Oct. 8, 1923

DE MILLE, Mrs. Cecil (Constance Adams)
Actress
b. East Orange, NJ, Unknown
d. Hollywood, CA, July 17, 1960, Age 87

DE MILLE, William C.
Playwright, Producer, Director, Educator
b. Washington, NC, July 25, 1878
d. Playa del Rey, CA, March 5, 1955, Age 76

DEMING, Will
Actor
b. Unknown
d. Unknown, Sept. 13, 1926, Age 55

DE MINIL, Renée
Actress
b. Unknown
d. Unknown, May 1941

DEMPSEY, Clifford
Actor
b. Winsted, CT, Unknown
d. Atlantic Highlands, NJ, Sept. 4, 1938, Age 73

DENIM, Kate
Actress
b. Unknown
d. Unknown, Feb. 5, 1907, Age 70

D'ENNERY, Adolphe Eugène Philippe
Playwright, Novelist
b. Paris, France, 1811
d. Unknown, 1899, Age 88

DENNING, Will H.
Actor
b. Unknown
d. London, England, Sept. 13, 1926, Age 55

DENNIS, Dr. Russell (M.D.)
Doctor, Actor
b. Unknown
d. New York, NY, May 29, 1964, Age 48

DENNIS, John
Critic, Playwright
b. Unknown, 1657
d. Unknown, Jan. 6, 1734, Age 76

DENNIS, Will (Stephen Townshend)
Actor, Playwright
b. Unknown
d. Unknown, May 20, 1914, Age 54

DENNISON, Frank
Actor, Orchestra conductor
b. England, Unknown
d. Ottawa, CAN, July 6, 1964, Age 63

DENNISTON, Reynolds
Actor
b. Dunedin, New Zealand, Unknown
d. New York, NY, Jan. 29, 1943, Age 62

DENNY, Ernest
Playwright
b. Unknown, July 20, 1869
d. Unknown, Sept. 20, 1943, Age 74

DENNY, Reginald Leigh Dugmore
Actor
b. Richmond, England, Nov. 20, 1891
d. Richmond, England, June 16, 1967, Age 75

DENNY, William Henry Leigh (Dugmore)
Actor
b. Balsall Heath, Birmingham, England, Oct. 22, 1853
d. Unknown, Aug. 31, 1915, Age 61

DENTON, Frank (Bellamy)
Actor
b. Louth, Lincolnshire, England, 1878(?)
d. Unknown, Feb. 23, 1945, Age 71

DENVILLE, Alfred
Actor, Producer
b. Nottingham, England, 1876
d. Unknown, March 23, 1955, Age 79

DE PALOWSKI, Gaston
Editor, (Comoedia)
b. Unknown
d. Unknown

de PASQUALI, Bernice
Singer
b. near Boston, MA
d. Omaha, NB, April 3, 1925

DE REYES, Consuelo
Director, Playwright
b. Leamington Spa, Warwickshire, England, Dec. 5, 1893
d. Unknown, May 27, 1948, Age 54

DE ROSE, Peter
Songwriter
b. New York, NY, March 10, 1896
d. New York, NY, April 23, 1953, Age 57

DERRICK, Samuel
Playwright
b. Unknown
d. Unknown, March 28, 1769, Age 45

DERWENT, Clarence
Actor
b. London, England, March 23, 1884
d. New York, NY, Aug. 6, 1959, Age 75

DERWENT, Elfrida
Actress
b. England, Unknown
d. Islip, NY, July 5, 1958, Age over 80

DESCLEE, Aimée Olympe
Actress
b. Unknown, 1836
d. Unknown, March 9, 1874, Age 37

DESEINE, Mlle. (Catherine Marie Jeanne Dupré, Mme. Dufresne)
Actress
b. Unknown
d. Unknown, 1759

DE SELINCOURT, Hugh
Critic, Playwright
b. London, England, June 15, 1878
d. Unknown, Jan 20, 1951, Age 72

DESHAYES, Paul
Actor
b. Unknown
d. Unknown, April 14, 1891, Age 57

DE SILVA, Frank
Actor
b. India, Unknown
d. New York, NY, March 20, 1968, Age 78

DE SILVA, Nina (Lady John Martin-Harvey née Angelita Helena de Silva)
Actress
b. Unknown, Aug. 28, 1868
d. Surrey, England, May 29, 1949, Age 80

DESJARDINS, Marie Catherine Hortense
Playwright, Poet, Novelist
b. Unknown, 1632
d. Unknown, 1683

DESLYS, Gaby (Gabrielle)
Performer
b. Marseilles, France, 1884
d. Paris, France, Feb. 11, 1920, Age 36

DESMOND, William
Actor
b. California, 1878
d. Hollywood, CA, Nov. 2, 1949, Age 71

DE SOLLA, Rachel
Actress
b. Unknown
d. Unknown, Nov. 24, 1920

DeSOUSA, May
Actress
b. Chicago, IL, 1882
d. Chicago, IL, Aug. 10, 1948, Age 66

DESPRES, Suzanne
Actress
b. Unknown
d. Unknown, July 1951, Age 76

DESPREZ, Frank
Playwright, Journalist
b. Bristol, England, Feb. 10, 1853
d. Unknown, Nov. 22, 1916, Age 63

DESTOUCHES, Philippe Néricault
Playwright, Diplomat
b. Unknown, 1680
d. Unknown, 1754

DESVALLIERES, Maurice
Playwright
b. Paris, France, Oct. 3, 1857
d. Unknown, March 23, 1926, Age 68

DE SYLVA, B. G. (Buddy) (George Gard De Sylva)
Author, Producer, Librettist
b. New York, NY, Jan. 27, 1896
d. Hollywood, CA, July 11, 1950, Age 54

DEVAL, Jacques
Playwright, Novelist
b. Paris, France, June 27, 1890
d. Paris, France, Dec. 19, 1972, Age 81

DEVERE, Francesca
Actress
b. Washington State, Unknown
d. Port Townsend, WA, Sept. 11, 1952, Age 61

DE VERE, George F.
Actor
b. Unknown
d. Unknown, Dec. 24, 1910, Age 75

DEVEREAUX, Jack
Actor
b. Unknown
d. New York, NY, Jan. 19, 1958, Age 76

DEVEREAUX, Louise Drew (Mrs. Jack Devereaux)
Actress
b. New York, NY, Unknown
d. New York, NY, April 23, 1954, Age 72

DEVEREUX, William
Actor, Playwright
b. Unknown
d. Unknown, June 18, 1945, Age 75

DEVINE, George
Director, Actor
b. London, England, Nov. 20, 1910
d. London, England, Jan. 20, 1966, Age 55

DEVRIENT, Eduard
Actor, Producer
b. Unknown, 1801
d. Unknown, Oct. 1877, Age 76

DEVRIENT, Emil
Actor
b. Unknown, 1803
d. Unknown, Aug. 1872, Age 68

DEVRIENT, Karl
Actor
b. Unknown, 1797
d. Unknown, 1872

DEVRIENT, Ludwig
Actor, Producer
b. Holland, 1784
d. Berlin, Germany, Dec. 30, 1832, Age 48

DEVRIENT, Max
Actor
b. Unknown, 1857
d. Unknown, June 25, 1929, Age 71

DEVRIENT, Otto
Actor, Director
b. Unknown, 1838
d. Oldenburg, Germany, 1894

DEWHURST, Jonathan
Actor
b. Unknown
d. Unknown, Aug. 1, 1913

DeWILDE, Brandon
Actor
b. Brooklyn, NY, April 9, 1942
d. Lakewood, CA, July 6, 1972, Age 30

DeWOLFE, Billy
Actor
b. Wollaston, MA, Feb. 18, 1907
d. Los Angeles, CA, March 5, 1974, Age 67

DE WOLFE, Elsie (Lady Mendl)
Performer, Author, Interior decorator
b. New York, NY, Dec. 20, 1865
d. Versailles, France, July 12, 1950, Age 84

DEXTER, Aubrey (Douglas Peter Jonas)
Actor
b. London, England, March 29, 1898
d. Unknown, May 1958, Age 60

DEXTER, Elliot
Actor
b. Unknown, 1870
d. Unknown, June 23, 1941, Age 71

DIAMOND, Lillian (Lilian Patrick)
Performer, Wardrobe mistress
b. Unknown
d. Sunderland, England, 1962, Age 73

DIAMOND, William
Actor, Playwright
b. Unknown
d. Unknown, Jan. 2, 1812, Age 62

DIBDIN, Charles
Playwright, Songwriter, Composer
b. Unknown, 1745
d. Unknown, July 25, 1814, Age 69

DIBDIN, Charles Isaac Mungo
Producer, Playwright
b. Unknown, 1768
d. Unknown, June 14, 1833, Age 65

DIBDIN, Thomas John
Actor, Playwright, Songwriter
b. Unknown, 1771
d. Unknown, Sept. 16, 1841, Age 70

DICK, C. S. Cotsford
Playwright
b. Unknown
d. Unknown, Aug. 28, 1911, Age 64

DICKENS, Charles John Huffman
Playwright, Novelist
b. Landport, Portsea, England, Feb. 7, 1812
d. Unknown, June 9, 1870, Age 58

DICKEY, Paul
Actor, Playwright, Director
b. Chicago, IL, May 12, 1885
d. New York, NY, Jan. 8, 1933, Age 47

DICKINSON, Maggie
Actress
b. Unknown
d. Unknown, June 16, 1949

DICKSON, Gloria
Actress
b. Unknown
d. Hollywood, CA, April 10, 1945, Age 28

DICKSON, Lamont
Actor
b. Unknown
d. Unknown, May 7, 1944

DICKSON, Lydia
Comedienne
b. Unknown
d. Los Angeles, CA, April 2, 1928, Age 40

DIDEROT, Denis
Critic, Playwright, Encyclopedist
b. Langres, Champagne, France, 1713
d. Unknown, 1784

DIDRING, Ernst
Playwright
b. Unknown, 1868
d. Unknown, 1931

DIETZ, Linda
Actress
b. Unknown
d. Poughkeepsie, NY, Sept. 6, 1920

DIEUDONNE, M.
Actor
b. Unknown
d. Unknown, Dec. 31, 1922, Age 91

DIGGES, Dudley
Actor, Producer
b. Dublin, Ireland, 1879
d. New York, NY, Oct. 24, 1947, Age 68

DIGGES, (John) Dudley West
Actor
b. Unknown, 1720
d. Unknown, 1786, Age 66

DILLINGHAM, Charles Bancroft
Producer
b. Hartford, CT, May 30, 1868
d. New York, NY, Aug. 30, 1934, Age 66

DILLON, Charles
Actor, Producer
b. Unknown
d. Unknown, Jan. 24, 1881, Age 62

DILLON, Charles E.
Actor
b. Unknown
d. New Orleans, LA, Jan 29, 1964, Age 76

DILLON, Clara
Actress
b. Unknown
d. Unknown, Feb. 27, 1898, Age 53

DILLON, Frances
Actress
b. Unknown
d. Unknown, Sept. 2, 1947, Age 75

DILLON, Thomas Patrick
Performer
b. Unknown
d. Hollywood, CA, Sept. 15, 1962, Age 66

DI LORENZO, Tina
Actress
b. Unknown
d. Unknown, April 1, 1930, Age 57

DINEHART, Alan
Actor, Director, Playwright
b. St. Paul, MN, Oct. 3, 1889
d. Hollywood, CA, July 17, 1944, Age 54

DINGLE, Charles
Actor
b. Wabash, IN, Unknown
d. Worcester, MA, Jan. 19, 1956, Age 68

DINGLE, TOM
Dancer
b. Unknown
d. New York, NY, Sept. 6, 1925, Age 38

DINGWALL, Alexander W.
Producer
b. Unknown
d. Unknown, July 27, 1918, Age 60

DIOR, Christian
Costume designer, Couturier
b. Granville, France, Jan. 21, 1905
d. Montecatini, Italy, Oct. 24, 1957, Age 52

DIPPEL, Johann Andreas
Singer, Manager
b. Kassel, Germany, Nov. 30, 1866
d. Hollywood, CA, May 19, 1932, Age 65

DITHMAR, Edward A.
Critic, Historian
b. New York, NY, May 22, 1854
d. New York, NY, Oct. 16, 1917, Age 63

DITRICHSTEIN, Leo James
Actor, Playwright
b. Tomesbar, Hungary, Jan. 6, 1865
d. Vienna, Austria, June 28, 1928, Age 63

DIX, Lillian
Actress
b. Unknown
d. New York, NY, Oct. 10, 1922, Age 58

DIX, Richard (Ernest Carlton Brimmer)
Actor
b. St. Paul, MN, July 18, 1894
d. Hollywood, CA, Sept. 20, 1949, Age 55

DIXEY, Henry E.
Actor-Manager
b. Boston, MA, Jan. 6, 1859
d. Atlantic City, NJ, Feb. 25, 1943, Age 84

DIXEY, Phyllis
Performer
b. Unknown
d. Epsom, England, June 2, 1964, Age 50

DIXON, Alfred
Speech teacher
b. Unknown
d. New York, NY, April 1964, Age 53

DIXON, Campbell
Playwright, Critic
b. Ouse, Tasmania, Australia, Dec. 10, 1895
d. Unknown, May 25, 1960, Age 64

DIXON, Conway
Actor
b. Unknown
d. Unknown, Jan. 18, 1943, Age 69

DIXON, Lee
Actor
b. Brooklyn, NY, 1911
d. New York, NY, Jan. 8, 1953, Age 42

DIXON, Lillian B.
Performer
b. Unknown
d. Van Nuys, CA, March 23, 1962, Age 69

DIXON, Thomas Jr.
Playwright, Novelist
b. Shelby, NC, Jan. 11, 1864
d. Raleigh, NC, April 3, 1946, Age 82

DMITREVSKY, Ivan Afanasyevich
Actor, Head of Russian State Theatre
b. Unknown, 1733
d. Unknown, 1821, Age 88

DODD, Emily
Actress
b. Unknown
d. Brooklyn, NY, Sept. 21, 1944

DODD, James William
Actor
b. Unknown, 1734
d. Unknown, 1796, Age 62

DODD, Lee Wilson
Playwright, Novelist, Poet
b. Franklin, PA, July 11, 1879
d. New York, NY, May 16, 1933, Age 53

DODDS, Jack
Dancer
b. Unknown
d. Hollywood, CA, June 2, 1962, Age 35

DODDS, (William) Jamieson
Actor
b. Newcastle-on-Tyne, England, Sept. 17, 1884
d. Unknown, Dec. 1942, Age 58

DODSLEY, James
Publisher
b. Unknown
d. Unknown, Feb. 19, 1797, Age 73

DODSLEY, Robert
Playwright, Publisher
b. Mansfield, England, 1703
d. Unknown, Dec. 25, 1764, Age 61

DODSON, John E.
Actor
b. London, England, Sept. 25, 1857
d. New York, NY, Dec. 9, 1931, Age 74

DODSWORTH, Charles
Actor
b. Unknown
d. Unknown, May 1920

DOGGETT, Thomas
Actor
b. Unknown, c1670
d. Unknown, Sept. 22, 1721

D'OISELY, Maurice
Actor
b. Unknown
d. Unknown, July 12, 1949, Age 66

DOLAN, Michael J.
Actor
b. Unknown
d. Unknown, Oct. 21, 1954, Age 70

DOLAN, Robert Emmett
Composer, Conductor
b. Hartford, CT, Aug. 3, 1908
d. Westwood, CA, Sept. 24, 1972, Age 64

DOLARO, Hattie
Actress
b. Unknown
d. Unknown, April 18, 1941, Age 80

DOLENZ, George
Actor
b. Trieste, Italy, Unknown
d. Hollywood, CA, Feb. 8, 1963, Age 55

DOLLY, Jenny (Yansci Deutsch)
Actress, Dancer
b. Hungary, Oct. 25, 1892
d. Hollywood, CA, June 1, 1941, Age 48

DONAGHEY, Frederick
Critic, Manager, Playwright
b. Philadelphia, PA, 1870
d. Chicago, IL, Nov. 8, 1937, Age 67

DONAHUE, Jack
Dancer, Comedian
b. Charlestown, MA, Unknown
d. New York, NY, Oct. 1, 1930, Age 38

DONALDSON, Arthur
Performer, Dramist, Director, Producer
b. Norsholm, Sweden, April 5, 1869
d. Long Island, NY, Sept. 28, 1955, Age 86

DONALDSON, Walter
Actor, Author
b. Unknown, 1793
d. Unknown, Dec. 19, 1877, Age 84

DONALDSON, Walter
Songwriter
b. Brooklyn, NY, Feb. 15, 1893
d. Santa Monica, CA, July 15, 1947, Age 54

DONAT, Robert
Actor
b. Withington, Manchester, England, March 18, 1905
d. London, England, June 9, 1958, Age 53

DONATH, Ludwig
Actor, Teacher
b. Vienna, Austria, March 6, 1907
d. New York, NY, Sept. 29, 1967, Age 60

DONEHUE, Vincent Julian
Director
b. Whitehall, NY, Sept. 22, 1915
d. New York, NY, Jan. 17, 1966, Age 50

DONELLY, Henry V.
Actor, Producer
b. Unknown
d. Unknown, Feb. 15, 1910, Age 49

DONISTHORPE, G. Sheila
Playwright, Novelist
b. London, England, Dec. 17, 1898
d. Unknown, Sept. 1, 1946, Age 47

DONLEVY, Brian
Actor
b. Portadown, County Armagh, Ireland, Feb. 9, 1903
d. Woodland Hills, CA, April 6, 1972, Age 69

DONNAY, Charles Maurice
Playwright
b. Paris, France, 1859
d. Unknown, March 31, 1945, Age 85

DONNELLY, Dorothy Agnes
Librettist, Actress, Playwright
b. New York, NY, Jan. 28, 1880
d. New York, NY, Jan. 3, 1928, Age 48

DONOVAN, Walter
Performer, Composer
b. East Cambridge, MA, Unknown
d. North Hollywood, CA, Jan. 10, 1964, Age 75

DOOLEY, James
Performer
b. Unknown
d. Freeport, L.I., NY, Feb. 24, 1949, Age 69

DORAN, Charles
Actor
b. Unknown
d. Folkestone, England, April 5, 1964, Age 87

DORAN, Dr. John
Historian
b. London, England, March 11, 1807
d. London, England, Jan. 25, 1878, Age 70

DORIVAL, Georges
Actor
b. Unknown
d. Unknown, July 16, 1939, Age 78

D'ORME, Aileen
Actress
b. London, England, Feb. 14, 1877
d. Unknown, Aug. 1939, Age 62

DORNEY, Richard
Manager
b. Unknown
d. New York, NY, Jan. 16, 1921, Age 79

DORNTON, Charles
Actor, Producer
b. Unknown
d. Unknown, May 11, 1900

DORO, Marie (Marie Kathryn Stewart)
Actress
b. Duncannon, PA, May 25, 1882
d. New York, NY, Oct. 9, 1956, Age 74

d'ORSAY, Lawrence (Dorset William Lawrence)
Actor
b. Peterborough, Northhamptonshire, England, Aug. 19, 1853
d. London, England, Sept. 13, 1931, Age 78

DORSEY, Jimmy (James Francis Dorsey)
Bandleader, Musician
b. Shenandoah, PA, Unknown
d. New York, NY, June 12, 1957, Age 53

DORSEY, Tommy
Bandleader, Musician
b. Mahanoy Plane, PA, Nov. 19, 1905
d. Greenwich, CT, Nov. 26, 1956, Age 51

DORVAL, (Marie Thomase Amélie Delaunay)
Actress
b. Unknown, 1798
d. Unknown, 1849, Age 51

DORVIGNY, (Louis François Archambault)
Actor, Playwright
b. Unknown, 1742
d. Unknown, 1812, Age 70

DOSTOIEVSKY, Feodor Mikhailovich
Playwright, Novelist
b. Moscow, Russia, Oct. 30, 1821
d. Unknown, Feb. 1, 1881, Age 59

DOUCET, Catharine
Actress
b. Richmond, VA, Unknown
d. New York, NY, June 24, 1958, Age 83

DOUGLAS, Byron
Actor
b. Unknown
d. New York, NY, April 21, 1935, Age 70

DOUGLAS, Dorothea
Performer
b. Unknown
d. Des Plaines, IL, Oct. 2, 1962, Age 79

DOUGLAS, Marie Booth
Actress
b. Unknown
d. Unknown, March 9, 1932, Age 75

DOUGLAS, Paul
Actor
b. Philadelphia, PA, April 11, 1907
d. Hollywood, CA, Sept. 11, 1959, Age 52

DOUGLAS, R. H.
Actor
b. Unknown
d. Unknown, April 1, 1935

DOUGLAS, Richard
Scenic artist
b. Unknown
d. Unknown, July 22, 1911, Age 67

DOUGLASS, David
Actor-Manager
b. Unknown
d. Jamaica, British West Indies, 1786

DOUGLASS, John
Producer, Playwright
b. Unknown
d. Unknown, Jan. 31, 1874, Age 59

DOUGLASS, John
Producer, Playwright
b. Unknown
d. Unknown, Jan. 13, 1917

DOUGLASS, Margaret
Actress
b. Dallas, TX, Unknown
d. New York, NY, Oct. 24, 1949, Age 53

DOUGLASS, Vincent
Playwright
b. London, England, Sept. 25, 1900
d. Unknown, Sept. 26, 1926, Age 26

DOW, Ada
Actress
b. Unknown
d. New York, NY, May 19, 1926, Age 79

DOW, Alexander
Playwright
b. Unknown
d. Unknown, July 31, 1779

DOWD, Harrison
Actor
b. Madison, CT, Aug. 15, 1897
d. New York, NY, Dec. 19, 1964, Age 67

DOWLING, Eddie
Actor, Director, Playwright
b. Woonsocket, RI, Dec. 9, 1894
d. Smithfield, RI, Feb. 18, 1976, Age 81

DOWLING, Joan
Actress
b. Laindon, Essex, England, Jan. 6, 1928
d. Unknown, May 31, 1954, Age 26

DOWLING, Robert W.
Producer
b. New York, NY, Sept. 9, 1895
d. New York, NY, Aug. 28, 1973, Age 77

DOWNING, Robert
Actor, Director, Playwright, Historian
b. Sioux City, IA, April 26, 1914
d. Denver, CO, June 14, 1975, Age 61

DOWNING, Robert L.
Actor
b. Washington, DC, Oct. 28, 1857
d. Middletown, MD, Oct. 1, 1944, Age 86

DOWTON, Emily
Actress
b. Unknown
d. Unknown, Jan. 1924, Age 84

DOWTON, William
Actor
b. Unknown, 1764
d. Unknown, 1851, Age 87

DOYLE, James
Dancer
b. Lowell, MA, Unknown
d. New York, NY, June 13, 1927, Age 38

DOYLE, John T.
Actor
b. St. Louis, MO, Unknown
d. New York, NY, Oct. 16, 1935, Age 62

DOYLE, Len
Performer
b. Unknown
d. Port Jarvis, NY, Dec. 6, 1959, Age 66

DOYLE, Mariam
Actress, Producer
b. Unknown
d. Wilton, CT, Sept. 18, 1962

DOYLE, Sir Arthur Conan
Playwright, Novelist
b. Edinburgh, Scotland, May 22, 1859
d. Unknown, July 7, 1930, Age 71

D'OYLY CARTE, Richard
Manager
b. London, England, May 3, 1844
d. London, England, April 3, 1901, Age 56

D'OYLY CARTE, Rupert
Producer
b. Hampstead, England, Nov. 3, 1876
d. London, England, Sept. 12, 1948, Age 71

DRACHMANN, Holger Henrik Herholdt
Poet, Playwright
b. Copenhagen, Denmark, 1846
d. Copenhagen, Denmark, 1908, Age 62

DRAGO, Cathleen
Actress
b. Unknown
d. Unknown, Dec. 24, 1938

DRAKE, Frances Ann Denny
Actress, Producer
b. Unknown
d. Unknown, Sept. 1, 1875, Age 77

DRANGE, Emily (Mrs. Lynn Overman)
Performer
b. Unknown
d. Torrance, CA, Dec. 30, 1961, Age 63

DRAPER, Joseph
Performer
b. Unknown
d. New York, NY, June 30, 1962, Age 55

DRAPER, Ruth
Monologist
b. New York, NY, Dec. 2, 1884
d. New York, NY, Dec. 30, 1956, Age 72

DRAYSON, Edith
Actress
b. Unknown
d. Unknown, May 30, 1926, Age 37

DRAYTON, Alfred
Actor
b. Brighton, England, Nov. 1, 1881
d. Unknown, April 26, 1949, Age 67

DREHER, Walter Arthur
Actor
b. Argentina, Unknown
d. New York, NY, Feb. 5, 1962, Age 61

DREISER, Edward M.
Actor
b. Unknown
d. Springfield Gardens, NY, Jan. 29, 1958, Age 84

DREISER, Theodore
Playwright, Novelist
b. Terre Haute, IN, Aug. 27, 1871
d. California, Dec. 28, 1945, Age 74

DRESSER, Paul (Dreiser)
Performer, Songwriter
b. Terre Haute, IN, April 21, 1857
d. Brooklyn, NY, Jan. 30, 1906, Age 48

DRESSLER, Marie (Leila Koerber)
Actress
b. Cobourg, CAN, Nov. 9, 1869
d. Santa Barbara, CA, July 28, 1934, Age 64

DREVER, Constance
Actress
b. Coonoor, Neilgherry Hills, Madras, India, Unknown
d. Unknown, Sept. 21, 1948, Age 68

DREW, John Sr.
Actor, Producer
b. Dublin, Ireland, 1827
d. Unknown, May 21, 1862, Age 34

DREW, John
Actor
b. Philadelphia, PA, Nov. 13, 1853
d. San Francisco, CA, July 9, 1927, Age 73

DREW, Louisa (Mrs. Jack Devereaux)
Actress
b. New York, NY, Unknown
d. New York, NY, April 23, 1954, Age 72

DREW, Louisa Lane (Mrs. John Drew)
Actress-Manager
b. Lambeth, London, England, Jan. 10, 1820
d. Larchmont, NY, Aug. 31, 1897, Age 77

DREW, Lucille McVey
Actress
b. Unknown
d. Hollywood, CA, Nov. 3, 1925, Age 35

DREYFUSS, Michael
Actor, Director
b. Unknown
d. New York, NY, March 30, 1960, Age 32

DRINKWATER, Albert Edwin
Playwright, Producer, Actor
b. Warwick, England, Unknown
d. Unknown, Jan. 27, 1923, Age 71

DRINKWATER, John
Actor, Playwright, Poet
b. Leytonstone, Essex, England, June 1, 1882
d. London, England, March 25, 1937, Age 54

DROUET, Robert
Actor, Playwright
b. Clinton, IA, March 27, 1870
d. Unknown, Aug. 17, 1914, Age 44

DRUCE, Herbert
Actor, Producer
b. Twickenham, England, May 20, 1870
d. New York, NY, April 6, 1931, Age 60

DRUMMOND, Alexander M.
Educator
b. Auburn, NY, July 15, 1884
d. Ithaca, NY, Nov. 29, 1956, Age 72

DRUMMOND, Dolores (née Green)
Actress
b. London, England, Feb. 3, 1834
d. Unknown, July 14, 1926, Age 92

DRURY, Lt.-Col. William Price
Playwright
b. Unknown, 1861
d. Unknown, Jan. 21, 1949, Age 87

DRYDEN, John
Playwright, Poet, Critic
b. Aldwinkle, Northamptonshire, England, Aug. 9, 1631
d. London, England, May 1, 1700, Age 68

DUBIN, Al
Lyricist
b. Zurich, Switzerland, Unknown
d. New York, NY, Feb. 11, 1945, Age 54

DUBOIS, Gene (Mrs. Milton H. Bayne)
Actress
b. Unknown
d. New York, NY, Jan. 21, 1962, Age 61

DUBOSC, Gaston
Actor
b. Unknown
d. Unknown, Aug. 1941, Age 81

DUBOURG, A. W.
Playwright
b. Unknown
d. Unknown, July 8, 1910, Age 80

DUCIS, Jean François
Playwright, Adaptor
b. Unknown, 1733
d. Versailles, France, 1816

DUCLOS, (Marie Anne de Châteauneuf)
Actress
b. Unknown, 1688 (?)
d. Unknown, June 18, 1748, Age 78

DU CROISY, Philibert Gassot
Actor
b. Unknown, 1626
d. Unknown, 1695, Age 69

DUDLAY, Adeline
Actress
b. Unknown
d. Unknown, Nov. 15, 1934, Age 76

DUDLEY, Walter Bronson (Bide)
Drama critic, Author
b. Minneapolis, MN, Sept. 8, 1877
d. New York, NY, Jan. 4, 1944, Age 66

DUFF, John
Actor
b. Ireland, 1787
d. U.S.A., 1831, Age 44

DUFF, Mrs. Mary Ann (née Dyke)
Actress
b. London, England, 1794
d. Unknown, Sept. 5, 1857, Age 63

DUFFY, Henry (Terry)
Producer, Actor
b. Chicago, IL, Unknown
d. Woodland Hills, CA, Nov. 18, 1961, Age 71

DUFFY, Herbert
Actor
b. Unknown
d. Rochester, MN, Nov. 23, 1952

DUFLOS, Raphael
Actor
b. Unknown
d. Unknown, Jan. 21, 1946, Age 88

DUFRESNE, (Abraham Alexis Quinault)
Actor
b. Unknown, 1693
d. Unknown, 1767, Age 74

DUFRESNE, Charles
Actor, Producer
b. Unknown, c1611
d. Unknown, c1684

DUFRESNY, Charles Rivière
Playwright
b. Unknown, 1654
d. Unknown, 1724, Age 70

DUGAZON, Jean Baptiste Henri Gourgaud
Actor
b. Unknown, 1746
d. Unknown, Oct. 11, 1809, Age 63

DUGAZON, Louise Rosalie
Actress
b. Unknown
d. Unknown, Sept. 21, 1821, Age 66

DUGAZON, Marie Marguerite Gourbaud
Actress
b. Unknown, 1742
d. Unknown, 1799, Age 59

DUGGAN, Edmund
Producer, Actor
b. Unknown
d. Unknown, Aug. 2, 1938, Age 72

DUGGAN, Maggie
Actress
b. Unknown
d. Unknown, Oct. 5, 1919, Age 59

DUKE, Vernon (né Vladimir Dukelsky)
Composer
b. Parafianovo, Russia, Oct. 10, 1903
d. Santa Monica, CA, Jan. 17, 1969, Age 65

DUKES, Ashley
Writer, Drama critic, Producer
b. Bridgwater, England, May 29, 1885
d. London, England, May 4, 1959, Age 73

DULAC, Arthur (De Ravenne)
Actor
b. France, Unknown
d. Hollywood, CA, Sept. 18, 1962, Age 52

DULLIN, Charles
Actor, Producer
b. Yenne, Savoie, France, 1885
d. Unknown, Dec. 11, 1949, Age 64

DULLZELL, Paul
Performer, Former Sec'y., Treasurer AEA
b. Boston, MA, June 15, 1879
d. Flushing, NY, Dec. 21, 1961, Age 82

DUMAS, Alexandre (père) (Alexandre Davy de la Pailleterie)
Playwright, Novelist
b. Villers-Cotterets, France, July 24, 1802
d. Puys, France, Dec. 5, 1870, Age 68

DUMAS, Alexandre (fils)
Playwright, Novelist
b. Paris, France, July 27, 1824
d. Marly-le-Roi, France, Nov. 27, 1895, Age 71

DU MAURIER, George Louis Palmella Busson
Playwright, Painter, Novelist
b. Paris, France, March 6, 1834
d. Unknown, Oct. 8, 1896, Age 62

DU MAURIER, Lt.-Col. Guy
Playwright
b. Unknown, 1865
d. France, 1916

DU MAURIER, Sir Gerald Hubert Edward
Actor, Playwright, Producer
b. Hampstead, England, March 26, 1873
d. London, England, April 11, 1934, Age 61

DUMENY, Camille
Actor
b. Unknown
d. Unknown, July 28, 1920, Age 62

DUMESNIL, Marie Françoise
Actress
b. Unknown, 1713
d. Unknown, 1803, Age 91

DUMKE, Ralph
Actor
b. South Bend, IN, Unknown
d. Sherman Oaks, CA, Jan. 4, 1964, Age 64

DUMONT, Louise
Actress
b. Unknown
d. Unknown, May 18, 1932

DUNCAN, Augustin
Actor, Producer, Director
b. San Francisco, CA, April 12, 1873
d. Astoria, NY, Feb. 20, 1954, Age 80

DUNCAN, Isadora
Dancer
b. San Francisco, CA, 1878
d. Nice, France, Sept. 14, 1927, Age 49

DUNCAN, Malcolm
Actor
b. Brooklyn, NY, Sept. 19, 1878
d. Bayshore, NY, May 2, 1942, Age 63

DUNCAN, Rosetta
Actress, Performer
b. Los Angeles, CA, 1902
d. Berwyn, IL, Dec. 4, 1959, Age 57

DUNCAN, William
Actor
b. Unknown
d. Hollywood, CA, Feb. 8, 1961, Age 81

DUNCAN, WIlliam Cary
Playwright
b. North Brookfield, MA, Feb. 6, 1874
d. Unknown, Nov. 21, 1945, Age 71

DUNLAP, William
Playwright, Manager, Historian, Painter
b. Perth Amboy, NJ, Feb. 19, 1766
d. New York, NY, Sept. 28, 1839, Age 73

DUNN, Arthur
Actor
b. New York, NY, Unknown
d. New York, NY, Dec. 6, 1932, Age 66

DUNN, Edwin Wallace
Press representative
b. La Crosse, WI, Unknown
d. New York, NY, June 29, 1931, Age 73

DUNN, Gregg
Actor
b. Unknown
d. Hollywood, CA, May 14, 1964, Age 48

DUNN, J. Malcolm
Actor
b. London, England, Unknown
d. Beechurst, Queens, L.I., NY, Oct. 10, 1946, Age 70

DUNN, James Howard
Actor
b. New York, NY, Nov. 2, 1906
d. Santa Monica, CA, Sept. 3, 1967, Age 61

DUNN, Joseph Barrington
Actor
b. Grand Rapids, MI, Unknown
d. Brooklyn, NY, Sept. 12, 1920, Age 58

DUNN, Michael (né Gary Neil Miller)
Actor
b. Shattuck, OK, Oct. 20, 1934
d. London, England, Aug. 29, 1973, Age 39

DUNNING, Philip
Playwright
b. Meriden, CT, Dec. 11, 1891
d. Westport, CT, July 20, 1968, Age 76

DUNPHIE, Charles J.
Critic
b. Unknown
d. Unknown, July 7, 1908, Age 87

DUNSANY, Alfred Lord (Edward John Moreton Drax Plunkett)
Playwright, Poet
b. London, England, July 24, 1878
d. Dublin, Ireland, Oct. 25, 1957, Age 79

DUNVILLE, (Wallon), T. E.
Performer
b. Unknown, c1870
d. Unknown, 1924

DU PARC, Marquise-Thérèse de Gorla
Actress
b. Unknown, 1633
d. Unknown, 1668, Age 35

DU PARC, René Berthelot
("Gros-René"), Actor
b. Unknown
d. 1630, Unknown, Age 1664

du PONT, Paul
Costume designer
b. Bradford, PA, Unknown
d. New York, NY, April 20, 1957, Age 51

DUPREE, Minnie
Actress
b. La Crosse, WI, Jan. 19, 1873
d. New York, NY, May 23, 1947, Age 74

DUPREZ, Fred
Actor
b. Detroit, MI, Sept. 6, 1884
d. Unknown, Oct. 29, 1938, Age 54

DUPREZ, May Moore
Performer
b. Unknown
d. Unknown, Jan. 2, 1946, Age 57

DUPUIS, Adolphe
Actor
b. Unknown
d. Unknown, Oct. 24, 1891, Age 67

DURAND, Edouard
Actor
b. France, Unknown
d. Port Chester, NY, July 31, 1926, Age 55

DURANG, Charles
Author, Historian
b. Unknown, 1796
d. Unknown, Feb. 15, 1870, Age 74

DURBIN, Maud (Mrs. Otis Skinner)
Actress, Author
b. Hannibal, MO, Unknown
d. New York, NY, Dec. 25, 1936, Age 66

DURET, Marie
Actress
b. Unknown
d. Unknown, April 1881

D'URFEY, Thomas
Playwright, Songwriter
b. Exeter, England, 1653
d. Unknown, Feb. 26, 1723, Age 70

DURGIN, Cyrus W.
Critic, Editor
b. Lowell, MA, Oct. 18, 1907
d. Boston, MA, Dec. 14, 1962, Age 55

DURKIN, James
Actor
b. Unknown
d. Unknown, March 12, 1934, Age 55

DURU, Alfred
Playwright
b. Unknown
d. Unknown, Dec. 29, 1889, Age 60

DURYEA, Dan
Actor
b. White Plains, NY, Jan. 23, 1907
d. Hollywood, CA, June 7, 1968, Age 61

DURYEA, Mary
Actress
b. Unknown
d. Oradell, NJ, July 20, 1949, Age 80

DUSE, Eleanora
Actress
b. . . . on a train between Venice and Vigevano, Italy, Oct. 3, 1858
d. Pittsburgh, PA, April 21, 1924, Age 65

DuSOUCHET, Henry A.
Playwright, Author
b. Mount Vernon, IN, Aug. 24, 1852
d. Kingston, NY, Oct. 27, 1922, Age 70

DU TERREAUX, Louis Henry
Playwright
b. Unknown
d. Unknown, March 31, 1878, Age 37

DUVAL, Georges
Playwright
b. Unknown
d. Unknown, Sept. 28, 1919, Age 72

DUVERNOIS, Henri
Playwright
b. Unknown
d. Paris, France, Jan. 29, 1937, Age 61

DWYER, Ada
Actress
b. Salt Lake City, UT, Unknown
d. Washington, DC, July 4, 1952, Age 89

DYALL, Franklin
Actor, Director
b. Liverpool, England, Feb. 3, 1874
d. Unknown, May 8, 1950, Age 76

DYE, Carol Finch
Actress
b. Guttenberg, IA, Unknown
d. New York, NY, June 10, 1962, Age 31

DYSON, LAURA
Actress
b. Unknown
d. Unknown, Sept. 1, 1950, Age 80

E

EADIE, Dennis
Actor, Producer
b. Glasgow, Scotland, Jan. 14, 1875
d. Unknown, June 10, 1928, Age 53

EAGELS, Jeanne
Actress
b. Kansas City, MO, 1894
d. New York, NY, Oct. 3, 1929, Age 35

EAMES, Clare
Actress
b. Hartford, CT, 1896
d. London, England, Nov. 8, 1930, Age 34

EARLE, Lilias
Actress
b. Unknown
d. Unknown, March 25, 1935, Age 62

EARLE, Virginia
Actress, Singer
b. Cincinnati, OH, Aug. 6, 1875
d. New Jersey, Sept. 21, 1937, Age 62

EASTLAKE, Mary
Actress
b. Unknown
d. Unknown, Aug. 5, 1911, Age 55

EASTMAN, Frederick
Actor
b. London, England, Dec. 30, 1859
d. Unknown, Dec. 8, 1920, Age 60

EATON, Mary
Actress
b. Norfolk, VA, Unknown
d. Hollywood, CA, Oct. 10, 1948, Age 46

EATON, Walter Prichard
Critic, Educator, Author, Historian
b. Malden, MA, Aug. 24, 1878
d. Chapel Hill, NC, Feb. 26, 1957, Age 78

EBERLE, Eugene A.
Actor
b. Bangor, ME, April 7, 1840
d. Chatham, NY, Oct. 23, 1917, Age 77

EBSWORTH, Joseph
Playwright
b. Unknown
d. Unknown, June 17, 1868, Age 79

EBSWORTH, Mary Emma
Playwright
b. Unknown
d. Unknown, Oct. 13, 1881, Age 87

EBURNE, Maude
Actress
b. Unknown
d. Hollywood, CA, Oct. 15, 1960, Age 85

ECHEGARAY, José
Playwright
b. Unknown, Madrid, Spain
d. 1832

EDDINGER, Wallace
Actor
b. Albany, NY, July 14, 1881
d. Pittsburgh, PA, Jan. 8, 1929, Age 47

EDDY, Edward
Actor
b. Unknown, 1822
d. Unknown, 1875

EDDY, Nelson
Singer, Actor
b. Providence, RI, June 29, 1901
d. Miami Beach, FL, March 6, 1967, Age 65

EDESON, Robert
Actor
b. New Orleans, LA, Jan. 3, 1868
d. Hollywood, CA, March 24, 1931, Age 62

EDGAR, Marriott
Actor, Playwright
b. Colvend, Kircudbright, Oct. 5, 1880
d. Unknown, May 4, 1951, Age 70

EDGAR, Mrs. Richard (Jennie Taylor)
Actress
b. Unknown
d. Unknown, May 22, 1937, Age 81

EDGAR, Tripp
Actor
b. Unknown
d. Unknown, Feb. 21, 1927

EDGETT, Edwin F.
Historian, Critic
b. Unknown
d. Unknown, March 13, 1946, Age 79

EDINGTON, May
Author
b. Unknown
d. Rondebosch, South Africa, June 17, 1957

EDISON, Thomas Alva
Inventor, Lighting designer
b. Milan, OH, Feb. 11, 1847
d. West Orange, NJ, Oct. 18, 1931, Age 84

EDISS, Connie
Actress
b. Brighton, England, Aug. 11, 1871
d. London, England, April 18, 1934, Age 62

EDNEY, Florence
Actress
b. London, England, June 2, 1879
d. New York, NY, Nov. 24, 1950, Age 71

EDOUIN, May
Actress
b. Unknown
d. Unknown, Sept. 1944

EDOUIN, Rose
Actress
b. Brighton, England, Jan. 29, 1844
d. Unknown, Aug. 24, 1925, Age 81

EDOUIN, Willie (William Frederick Boyer)
Performer
b. Unknown, 1846
d. Unknown, April 14, 1908, Age 62

EDWARDES, Conway
Playwright
b. Unknown
d. Unknown, May 5, 1880

EDWARDES, Felix
Producer
b. London, England, Unknown
d. London, England, Feb. 6, 1954, Age 83

EDWARDES, George
Manager
b. Dublin, Ireland, Oct. 8, 1852
d. London, England, Oct. 4, 1915, Age 63

EDWARDS, Alan
Actor
b. New York, NY, Unknown
d. Los Angeles, CA, May 8, 1954, Age 61

EDWARDS, Bruce
Manager
b. Scotland, Unknown
d. Fort Wayne, IN, Jan. 16, 1927, Age 54

EDWARDS, Gus (Simon)
Songwriter, Actor, Film director
b. Hohensalza, Germany, Aug. 18, 1879
d. Los Angeles, CA, Nov. 7, 1945, Age 66

EDWARDS, Henry
Actor, Songwriter, Actor, Film director, Prod.
b. Unknown, Sept. 18, 1883
d. Crobham, England, Nov. 2, 1952, Age 69

EDWARDS, Julian
Composer
b. Manchester, England, Dec. 11, 1855
d. Yonkers, NY, Sept. 29, 1910, Age 54

EDWARDS, Osman
Playwright, Critic
b. Liverpool, England, Feb. 18, 1864
d. Unknown, May 1, 1936, Age 72

EDWARDS, Richard
Poet, Playwright
b. Unknown
d. Unknown, Oct. 31, 1566, Age 43

EDWARDS, Richard
Playwright
b. Unknown
d. Unknown, Nov. 19, 1604, Age 81

EDWARDS, Susie
Performer
b. Unknown
d. Chicago, IL, Dec. 5, 1963, Age 65

EDWARDS, Virginia (Mrs. William Hunter)
Actress, Teacher, Playwright
b. Unknown
d. Hollywood, CA, March 7, 1964

EDWIN, T. Emery
Actor
b. Unknown
d. New York, NY, June 24, 1951, Age 79

EFFRAT, John
Director, Actor, Producer, Union executive
b. New York, NY, March 8, 1908
d. New York, NY, May 14, 1965, Age 57

EGAN, Frank C.
Producer
b. Chicago, IL, Unknown
d. Los Angeles, CA, March 5, 1927, Age 55

EGAN, Michael
Playwright, Press representative, Prod.
b. Kilkenny, Ireland, June 26, 1895
d. Unknown, July 27, 1956, Age 61

EGAN, Mishska
Actor
b. Unknown
d. Hollywood, CA, Feb. 15, 1964, Age 73

EGAN, Pierce
Playwright, Novelist, Journalist
b. Unknown, 1772
d. Unknown, Aug. 3, 1849, Age 77

EGERTON, George (Mrs. R. Golding Bright)
Playwright, Writer
b. Melbourne, Australia, Unknown
d. Unknown, Aug. 12, 1945, Age 86

EGRI, Lajos
Creative writing teacher, Story analyst
b. Hungary, Jan. 4, 1888
d. Hollywood, CA, Feb. 7, 1967, Age 79

EHRENSPERGER, Harold A.
Educator, Writer
b. Indianapolis, IN, Aug. 12, 1897
d. Lower Gilmanton, NH, Nov. 5, 1973, Age 75

EINSTEIN, Harry (Parkyakarkus)
Performer
b. Unknown
d. Hollywood, CA, Nov. 24, 1958, Age 54

EKHOF, Konrad
Actor, Director
b. Unknown, 1720
d. Gotha, Germany, 1778

ELDRED, Arthur
Actor
b. London, England, Unknown
d. Unknown, Dec. 10, 1942, Age 66

ELDRIDGE, Louisa
Actress
b. Unknown
d. Unknown, Nov. 9, 1905, Age 76

ELEN, Gus (Ernest Augustus)
Performer
b. London, England, July 22, 1862
d. Unknown, Feb. 17, 1940, Age 77

ELINORE, Kate
Performer
b. Unknown
d. Indianapolis, IN, Dec. 30, 1924, Age 49

ELIOT, Arthur
Playwright, Producer
b. Unknown
d. Unknown, Oct. 8, 1936, Age 62

ELIOT, Max (Mrs. Granville Ellis)
Critic, Author
b. Unknown
d. Unknown, Feb. 21, 1911

ELIOT, Thomas Stearns
Poet, Critic, Playwright
b. St. Louis, MO, Sept. 26, 1888
d. London, England, Jan. 4, 1965, Age 76

ELKINS, Marie Louise
Producer
b. Unknown
d. Hollwyood, CA, Dec. 12, 1961, Age 71

ELLINGER, Desiree
Actress
b. Manchester, England, Unknown
d. London, England, April 30, 1951, Age 57

ELLINGTON, Duke (né Edward Kennedy Ellington)
Conductor, Composer, Pianist
b. Washington, DC, April 29, 1899
d. New York, NY, May 24, 1974, Age 75

ELLIOT, Arthur
Actor
b. India, Unknown
d. Bennington, VT, April 17, 1936, Age 78

ELLIOT, William
Actor, Manager
b. Boston, MA, Unknown
d. New York, NY, Dec. 5, 1931, Age 52

ELLIOTT, Alonzo (ZO)
Composer, Lyricist
b. Manchester, NH, Unknown
d. Wallingford, CT, June 24, 1964, Age 73

ELLIOTT, Dick
Actor
b. Unknown
d. Hollywood, CA, Dec. 22, 1961, Age 75

ELLIOTT, G. H.
Performer
b. Lancashire, England, Unknown
d. Brighton, England, Nov. 19, 1962, Age 78

ELLIOTT, Gertrude (Lady Forbes-Robertson)
Actress
b. Rockland, ME, Dec. 14, 1874
d. Kent, England, Dec. 24, 1950, Age 74

ELLIOTT, John Tiffany
Literary representative
b. Unknown
d. Westhampton Beach, NY, Oct. 1963, Age 48

ELLIOTT, Madge
Actress
b. Kensington, London, England, May 12, 1898
d. New York, NY, Aug. 8, 1955, Age 57

ELLIOTT, Maxine (Jessie McDermot)
Actress, Producer
b. Rockland, ME, Feb. 5, 1868
d. Juan Les Pins, France, Mar. 5, 1940, Age 72

ELLIOTT, William
Actor, Director, Producer
b. Boston, MA, Dec. 4, 1885
d. New York, NY, Feb. 5, 1932, Age 46

ELLIS, Anthony L.
Critic, Producer
b. Unknown
d. Unknown, Sept. 23, 1944

ELLIS, Brandon
Playwright
b. Unknown
d. Unknown, Jan. 6, 1916, Age 87

ELLIS, Edith
Playwright
b. Coldwater, MI, Unknown
d. New York, NY, Dec. 27, 1960, Age 86

ELLIS, Edward
Actor
b. Coldwater, MI, Nov. 12, 1872
d. Beverly Hills, CA, July 26, 1952, Age 79

ELLIS, Evelyn
Performer
b. Unknown
d. Saranac Lake, NY, June 5, 1958, Age 64

ELLIS, Max
Production executive
b. Unknown
d. Cleveland, OH, June 25, 1964, Age 50

ELLIS, Walter W.
Playwright
b. London, England, 1874
d. Unknown, Jan. 21, 1956, Age 81

ELLIS-FERMOR, Una Mary
Critic, Educator
b. Unknown, 1894
d. Unknown, 1958

ELLISON, Sydney
Director
b. Unknown
d. Unknown, Dec. 21, 1930, Age 61

ELLISTON, Grace (née Grace Rutter)
Actress
b. Memphis, TN, Unknown
d. Lenox, MA, Dec. 14, 1950, Age 72

ELLISTON, Robert William
Actor, Producer
b. Unknown, 1774
d. Unknown, 1831

ELLSLER, Effie (Mrs. John A. Ellsler née Euphemia Murray)
Actress
b. Philadelphia, PA, Nov. 21, 1823
d. Nutley, NJ, Dec. 12, 1918, Age 95

ELLSLER, Effie
Actress
b. Cleveland, OH, Unknown
d. Los Angeles, CA, Oct. 8, 1942, Age 87

ELLSTEIN, Abraham
Composer, Conductor
b. Unknown
d. New York, NY, March 22, 1963, Age 56

ELPHISTONE, Emma (Mrs. J. Sheridan Knowles)
Actress
b. Unknown
d. Unknown, May 10, 1888, Age 81

ELSER, Frank B.
Novelist, Playwright
b. Fort Worth, TX, Unknown
d. St. George's, Grenada, British West Indies, Jan. 31, 1935, Age 50

ELSIE, Lily
Performer
b. Wortley, England, April 8, 1886
d. Palehouse Common, Sussex, England, Dec. 16, 1962, Age 76

ELSSLER, Fanny
Dancer
b. Vienna, Austria, June 23, 1810
d. Unknown, Nov. 27, 1884, Age 73

ELTINGE, Julian (William Dalton)
Actor
b. Newtonville, MA, May 14, 1883
d. New York, NY, March 7, 1941, Age 57

ELTON, Frank
Actor
b. Unknown
d. Unknown, Jan. 13, 1954, Age 73

ELTON, George
Actor
b. Sheffield, England, March 22, 1875
d. Unknown, Dec. 14, 1942, Age 67

ELTON (ELT), Edward William
Actor
b. Unknown, 1794
d. Unknown, 1843, Age 49

ELVIN, (Keegan), Joe
Performer
b. Unknown, 1862
d. Unknown, 1935, Age 73

EMDEN, Henry
Scenic artist
b. Unknown
d. Unknown, Jan. 8, 1930, Age 78

EMDEN, Margaret
Actress
b. Unknown
d. Unknown, Feb. 13, 1946

EMERALD, Connie (Mrs. Stanley Lupino)
Actress
b. Unknown
d. Barstow, CA, Dec. 26, 1959, Age 68

EMERSON, Hope
Actress
b. Hawarden, IA, Unknown
d. Hollywood, CA, April 24, 1960, Age 62

EMERSON, John
Playwright, Actor, Director
b. Sandusky, OH, May 28, 1874
d. Pasadena, CA, March 8, 1956, Age 81

EMERSON, Mary
Actress
b. Unknown
d. Utica, NY, Feb. 11, 1921

EMERTON, Roy (né Hugh Fitzray Emerton)
Actor
b. Burford, Oxfordshire, England, Oct. 9, 1892
d. Unknown, Nov. 30, 1944, Age 52

EMERY, Edward
Actor
b. London, England, May 13, 1861
d. New York, NY, May 7, 1938, Age 77

EMERY, Edwin T.
Performer, Director
b. Philadelphia, Pa, Unknown
d. New York, NY, June 24, 1951, Age 78

EMERY, Frederick
Actor
b. Unknown
d. Unknown, Sept. 21, 1930, Age 65

EMERY, Gilbert (Gilbert Emery Bensley Pottle)
Playwright, Actor
b. Naples, NY, Unknown
d. Unknown, Oct. 27, 1945, Age 70

EMERY, John
Actor
b. New York City, NY, 1822
d. New York City, NY, Nov. 16, 1965, Age 59

EMERY, Louise
Actress
b. Unknown
d. Unknown, April 1943

EMERY, Pollie
Actress
b. Bolton, Lancastershire, England, May 10, 1875
d. Unknown, Oct. 31, 1958, Age 83

EMERY, Rose
Actress
b. Unknown
d. Unknown, March 12, 1934, Age 89

EMERY, Samuel Anderson
Actor
b. Unknown, 1817
d. Unknown, 1881, Age 64

EMERY, Winifred
Actress
b. Manchester, England, Aug. 1, 1862
d. Unknown, July 15, 1924, Age 61

EMIL-BEHNKE, Kate
Drama instructor
b. Unknown
d. Unknown, April 1957, Age 86

EMMET, Katherine
Actress
b. San Francisco, CA, Unknown
d. New York, NY, June 6, 1960, Age 78

EMMETT, Dan (Daniel Decatur Emmett)
Minstrel, Songwriter
b. Mount Vernon, OH, Oct. 29, 1815
d. Mount Vernon, OH, June 28, 1904, Age 88

EMMETT, J. K.
Actor
b. Unknown
d. Unknown, Jan. 15, 1891, Age 50

EMNY, Fred
Performer
b. Unknown, 1865
d. Unknown, 1917

EMPY, Guy
Songwriter, Actor, Director, Author
b. Unknown
d. Wadsworth, KS, Feb. 22, 1963, Age 79

ENCINA, Juan del
Playwright
b. Unknown, c1468
d. Unknown, c1537

ENDORE, Guy
Playwright - Film writer
b. New York, NY, July 4, 1901
d. Hollywood, CA, Feb. 12, 1970, Age 69

ENGELS, Georg
Playwright, Actor
b. Unknown
d. Unknown, Oct. 31, 1907, Age 61

ENGLAND, Daisy
Actress
b. Unknown
d. Unknown, March 7, 1943, Age 81

ENGLANDER, Ludwig
Composer
b. Vienna, Austria, 1859
d. Far Rockaway, NY, Sept. 13,1914, Age 55

ENGLEFIELD, Violet
Actress
b. Unknown, 1886
d. Unknown, March 22, 1946, Age 60

ENGLUND, Maude Beatrice Galbraith (Mrs. Arthur Englund)
Singer
b. Unknown, 1891
d. Hollywood, CA, Dec. 7, 1962, Age 71

ENNERY, Adolphe D'
Playwright
b. Unknown
d. 1812, Unknown, Age Jan. 26, 1899

ENNIUS, Quintus
Poet, Playwright
b. Rudia, Italy, 239 B.C.
d. Unknown, 169 B.C.

ENRIGHT, Sara
Actress, Talent representative
b. Unknown, 1888
d. New York, NY, Feb. 23, 1963, Age 75

ENTHOVEN, Gabrielle
Theatre archivist
b. London, England, Jan. 12, 1868
d. Unknown, Aug. 18, 1950, Age 82

ENTWISTLE, Lillian Millicent (Peg)
Actress
b. Unknown
d. San Francisco, CA, Sept. 10, 1932

EPHRIAM, Lee
Producer
b. Hopkinsonville, KY, July 7, 1877
d. London, England, Sept. 26, 1953, Age 76

EPHRON, Phoebe
Playwright
b. New York, NY, Jan. 26, 1916
d. New York, NY, Oct. 13, 1971, Age 57

EPICHARMUS
Playwright
b. Cos, Greece, c550 B.C.
d. Syracuse, Sicily, c460 B.C.

EPSTEIN, Philip G.
Playwright, Screenwriter
b. New York, NY, Unknown
d. Hollywood, CA, Feb. 7, 1952, Age 42

ERCKMANN, Emile
Playwright, Novelist
b. Phalsbourg, Lorraine, France, May 20, 1822
d. Lunéville, France, March 14, 1899, Age 76

ERIC, Fred
Actor
b. Peru, IN, 1874
d. New York, NY, April 17, 1935, Age 61

ERLANGER, Abraham L.
Producer
b. Buffalo, NY, May 4, 1860
d. New York, NY, March 7, 1930, Age 69

ERMOLIEFF, Joseph N.
Producer
b. Russia, 1890
d. Hollywood, CA, Feb. 20, 1962, Age 72

ERNST, Paul Carl Friedrich
Playwright
b. Elbingerode, Harz, Germany, 1866
d. Unknown, 1933

ERROL, Leon
Actor
b. Sydney, Australia, July 3, 1881
d. Hollywood, CA, Oct. 12, 1951, Age 70

ERSKINE, John
Educator, Author, Musician
b. New York, NY, Oct. 5, 1879
d. New York, NY, June 2, 1951, Age 71

ERSKINE, Sir David
Playwright
b. Unknown
d. Unknown, Oct. 22, 1837, Age 65

ERSKINE, Wallace
Actor
b. England, Unknown
d. Massapequa, NY, Jan. 6, 1943, Age 81

ERVINE, St. John
Playwright - Critic
b. Belfast, Ireland, Dec. 28, 1883
d. London, England, Jan. 24, 1971, Age 87

ERWIN, Stu (né Stuart Philip Erwin)
Actor
b. Squaw Valley, CA, Feb. 14, 1903
d. Beverly Hills, CA, Dec. 21, 1967, Age 64

ESLER, Lemist
Playwright, Educator, Actor
b. Unknown, 1888
d. New York, NY, Nov. 7, 1960, Age 72

ESMOND, Annie
Actress
b. Unknown, Sept. 27, 1873
d. Unknown, Jan. 4, 1945, Age 71

ESMOND, Henry Vernon (Henry Vernon Jack)
Performer, Playwright
b. Hampton Court, England, Nov. 30, 1869
d. Unknown, April 17, 1922, Age 52

ESTCOURT, Richard
Actor, Playwright
b. Unknown, 1668
d. Unknown, Aug. 1712, Age 44

ESTEN, Mrs. (Harriet Pye)
Actress
b. Unknown, 1763
d. Unknown, April 29, 1865, Age 102

ETHEL, Agnes
Performer
b. Unknown, 1853
d. Unknown, May 26, 1903, Age 50

ETHEREGE, Sir George
Playwright
b. Unknown, c16355
d. Unknown, 1691

ETHERINGTON, James
Actor
b. Wheatley Hill, Durham, England, April 16, 1902
d. Unknown, June 16, 1948, Age 46

EULENBERG, Herbert
Playwright, Poet
b. Muhlheim, Germany, Jan. 25, 1876
d. Düsseldorf, Germany, Sept. 4, 1949, Age 73

EURIPIDES
Playwright
b. Phyla, Attica, Greece, c486 B.C.
d. Unknown, 407 B.C.

EUSTACE, Jennie
Actress
b. Troy, NY, Oct. 23, 1865
d. Dobbs Ferry, NY, July 10, 1936, Age 70

EVANS, Caradoc
Playwright, Novelist
b. Landyssul, Wales, Unknown
d. Unknown, Jan. 11, 1945, Age 70

EVANS, Charles Evan
Actor, Producer, Impressario
b. Rochester, NY, Sept. 6, 1856
d. Santa Monica, CA, April 16, 1945, Age 88

EVANS, Edwin
Music critic
b. Unknown
d. Unknown, March 3, 1945, Age 70

EVANS, Evan E.
Performer
b. Unknown, 1875
d. Homestead, PA, July 22, 1962, Age 73

EVANS, Norman
Performer
b. Unknown
d. Blackpool, England, Nov. 25, 1962, Age 61

EVANS, Rothbury
Actor
b. Unknown
d. Unknown, Nov. 11, 1944, Age 81

EVANS, Will
Actor, Playwright
b. London, England, May 29, 1873
d. London, England, April 11, 1931, Age 58

EVARTS, William H. (William Hentz)
Actor
b. Roxbury, MA, Unknown
d. South Portland, ME, June 6, 1940, Age 73

EVELYN, Judith (née Judith Evelyn Allen)
Actress
b. Seneca, SD, March 20, 1913
d. New York, NY, May 7, 1967, Age 54

EVERARD, Walter
Actor
b. Unknown
d. Unknown, April 11, 1924, Age 74

EVEREST, Barbara
Actress
b. England, June 9, 1890
d. London, England, Feb. 9, 1968, Age 77

EVERETT, Sophie
Performer
b. Unknown
d. Sarasota, FL, March 18, 1963, Age 88

EVERLEIGH, Kate
Actress
b. Unknown
d. Unknown, Feb. 8, 1926, Age 62

EVERTON, Paul
Actor
b. New York, NY, Sept. 19, 1868
d. Hollywood, CA, Feb. 26, 1948, Age 79

EVESSON, Isabelle
Actress
b. St. Louis, MO, Unknown
d. Stamford, CT, Aug. 9, 1914, Age 51

EVETT, Robert
Actor, Producer
b. Warwickshire, England, Oct. 16, 1874
d. Unknown, Jan. 15, 1949, Age 74

EWALD, Johannes
Poet, Playwright
b. Unknown, 1743
d. Unknown, 1781

EWELL, Caroline
Actress
b. Unknown
d. Unknown, June 8, 1909, Age 69

EYRE, Gerald
Actor
b. Unknown
d. Unknown, Aug. 7, 1885

EYRE, John Edmund
Playwright
b. Unknown
d. Unknown, April 11, 1816, Age 48

EYRE, Laurence
Playwright
b. Chester, PA, 1881
d. Bronx, NY, June 6, 1959, Age 78

EYTHE, William
Actor, Producer
b. Mars, PA, April 7, 1918
d. Hollywood, CA, Jan. 26, 1957, Age 38

EYTINGE, Rose
Actress
b. Philadelphia, PA, Nov. 21, 1835
d. Unknown, Dec. 20, 1911, Age 76

F

FABER, Leslie
Actor
b. Newcastle-on-Tyne, England, Aug. 30, 1879
d. London, England, Aug. 5, 1929, Age 50

FABRE, Emile
Playwright
b. France, 1869
d. Paris, France, Sept. 25, 1955, Age 86

FABRIZI, Mario
Performer
b. Unknown, 1925
d. London, England, April 5, 1963, Age 38

FAGAN, Barney
Actor, Author
b. Boston, MA, 1850
d. Bay Shore, NY, Jan. 12, 1937, Age 87

FAGAN, James Bernard
Actor, Playwright, Producer
b. Glasgow, Scotland, May 10, 1873
d. Hollywood, CA, Feb. 17, 1933, Age 59

FAIRBANKS, Douglas (né Ulman)
Actor
b. Denver, CO, May 23, 1883
d. Santa Monica, CA, Dec. 12, 1939, Age 56

FAIRBROTHER, Sydney (Sydney Parselle Cowell)
Actress
b. Unknown, July 31, 1872
d. Unknown, Jan. 10, 1941, Age 68

FAIRFAX, Lettice
Actress
b. Unknown, March 26, 1876
d. Unknown, Dec. 25, 1948, Age 72

FAIRMAN, Austin
Actor, Playwright
b. London, England, 1892
d. Dedham, MA, March 26, 1964, Age 72

FALCONER, Edmund
Actor, Producer, Playwright, 1815
b. Unknown
d. Unknown, Sept. 29, 1879, Age 64

FALCONI, Arturo
Actor
b. Unknown
d. Unknown, Nov. 12, 1934

FALK, Sawyer
Educator
b. Key West, FL, Dec. 9, 1898
d. Paris, France, Aug. 31, 1961, Age 62

FALL, Leo
Composer
b. Olmütz, Feb. 2, 1873
d. Vienna, Austria, Sept. 15, 1925, Age 52

FANCOURT, Darrell
Actor
b. London, England, March 8, 1888
d. London, England, Aug. 29, 1953, Age 65

FARADAY, Philip Michael
b. London, England, Jan. 1, 1875
d. Unknown, Feb. 6, 1944 , Age 69

FARJEON, Benjamin Leopold
Playwright, Novelist
b. Unknown
d. Unknown, July 23, 1903, Age 65

FARJEON, Herbert
Sketch writer, Critic, Producer
b. South Hampstead, England, March 5, 1887
d. London, England, May 3, 1945, Age 58

FARJEON, Joseph Jefferson
Playwright, Novelist
b. London, England, June 4, 1883
d. Hove, Sussex, England, June 6, 1955, Age 72

FARLEY, Charles
Actor, Playwright
b. Unknown
d. Unknown, Jan. 28, 1859, Age 87

FARNIE, H. B.
Playwright
b. Unknown
d. Unknown, Sept. 22, 1889

FARNOL, Lynn
Press representative
b. Marion, PA, Unknown
d. New York, NY, March 30, 1963, Age 63

FARNUM, Dustin
Actor
b. Hampton Beach, NH, May 27, 1874
d. New York, NY, July 5, 1929, Age 55

FARNUM, Franklyn
Actor
b. Boston, MA, Unknown
d. Woodland Hills, CA, July 4, 1961, Age 83

FARNUM, G. Dustin
Actor
b. Unknown
d. Unknown, Feb. 19, 1912, Age 65

FARNUM, William
Actor
b. Boston, MA, July 4, 1876
d. Hollywood, CA, June 5, 1953, Age 76

FARQUHAR, George
Playwright
b. Londonderry, Ireland, c1678
d. London, England, April 28, 1707, Age about 28

FARR, Florence
Actress
b. Unknown
d. Unknown, April 29, 1917, Age 57

FARRELL, Catherine F.
Performer
b. Unknown
d. Woonsocket, RI, Aug. 27, 1964, Age 73

FARRELL, Glenda
Actress
b. Enid, OK, June 30, 1904
d. New York, NY, May 1, 1971, Age 66

FARRELL, Marguerite
Actress
b. Unknown
d. Buffalo, NY, Jan. 26, 1951, Age 62

FARREN, Elizabeth (Countess of Derby)
Actress
b. Unknown, 1759
d. Unknown, April 21, 1829, Age 70

FARREN, Fred
Actor, Dancer
b. London, England, Unknown
d. London, England, May 7, 1956, Age 82

FARREN, George Francis
Actor
b. Boston, MA, Unknown
d. New York, NY, April 21, 1935, Age 74

FARREN, George Percy
Actor
b. Unknown
d. Unknown, Aug. 18, 1861

FARREN, Henry
Actor
b. Unknown, 1826
d. St. Louis, MO, 1860

FARREN, Nellie (Mrs. Robert Soutar)
Actress
b. Lancashire, England, April 10, 1848
d. London, England, April 28, 1904, Age 56

FARREN, Percival
Actor, Producer
b. Unknown, 1784
d. Unknown, 1843, Age 59

FARREN, William
Actor
b. Unknown, 1725
d. Unknown, 1795, Age 70

FARREN, William
Actor
b. Unknown, 1786
d. Unknown, 1861, Age 75

FARREN, William
Actor
b. Unknown, 1825
d. Siena, Italy, Sept. 26, 1908, Age 83

FARREN, William (Percival)
Actor
b. Unknown, Aug. 2, 1853
d. Unknown, Sept. 7, 1937, Age 84

FARROW, John Villiers
Film director, Film producer
b. Sydney, Australia, Unknown
d. Beverly Hills, CA, Jan. 27, 1963, Age 56

FAUCIT, Harriet (née Diddear)
Actress
b. Penzance, Cornwell, England, July 31, 1789
d. Unknown, 1857

FAUCIT, Helen (Helen Saville, Lady Martin)
Actress
b. London, England, Oct. 11, 1817
d. Bryntysilio, Vale of Llangollen, Wales, Oct. 1898, Age 81

FAULKNER, William
Novelist, Playwright
b. New Albany, MS, Sept. 25, 1897
d. Oxford, MS, July 6, 1962, Age 64

FAUST, Lotta
Performer
b. Unknown, 1881
d. New York, NY, Jan. 25, 1910, Age 29

FAVART, Charles Simon
Playwright, Producer
b. Paris, France, 1710
d. Unknown, 1792, Age 82

FAVART, Edmée
Actress
b. Unknown
d. Unknown, Oct. 29, 1941

FAVART, Madame (Marie Justine Benoiste Duronceray)
Actress
b. Unknown, 1727
d. Unknown, April 21, 1772, Age 44

FAVART, Mme. Maria
Actress
b. Unknown, 1833
d. Unknown, Nov. 11, 1908, Age 75

FAVERSHAM, Edith Campbell
Actress
b. Unknown
d. New York, NY, May 21, 1945, Age 61

FAVERSHAM, Julie Opp
Actress
b. New York, NY, 1871
d. New York, NY, April 8, 1921, Age 50

FAVERSHAM, William
Actor
b. London, England, Feb. 12, 1868
d. Bay Shore, L.I., NY, April 7, 1940, Age 72

FAWCETT, Charles S.
Actor, Playwright
b. Unknown, 1855
d. Unknown, Nov. 23, 1922, Age 67

FAWCETT, George D.
Actor
b. Fairfax County, VA, Aug. 25, 1860
d. Nantucket, MA, June 6, 1939, Age 78

FAWCETT, Marion (née Katherine Roger Campbell)
Actress, Director
b. Aberdeen, Scotland, Nov. 25, 1886
d. Unknown, July 1957, Age 70

FAWCETT, Owen
Performer
b. Unknown, 1839
d. Unknown, Feb. 21, 1904, Age 65

FAY, Edward M.
Theatre owner, Performer
b. Unknown
d. Providence, RI, Feb. 13, 1964, Age 88

FAY, Frank
Actor
b. San Francisco, CA, Nov. 17, 1897
d. Santa Monica, CA, Sept. 25, 1961, Age 63

FAY, Frank G. (or J.)
Actor
b. Dublin, Ireland, 1870
d. Dublin, Ireland, Jan 2, 1931, Age 60

FAY, William George
Actor, Producer, Director
b. Dublin, Ireland, Nov. 12, 1872
d. London, England, Oct. 27 1947, Age 74

FAYOLLE, Berthe
Actress
b. Unknown
d. Unknown, May 17, 1934, Age 68

FAZENDA, Louis (Mrs. Hal Wallis)
Actress
b. Lafayette, IN, Unknown
d. Holmby Hills, CA, April 17, 1962, Age 67

FEATHERSTON, Vane (Featherstonhaugh)
Actress
b. London, England, Dec. 16, 1864
d. Unknown, Nov. 6, 1948, Age 83

FECHTER, Charles Albert
Actor-Manager
b. London, England, Oct. 23, 1824
d. . . . near Philadelphia, PA, Aug. 5, 1879, Age 54

FEINBERG, Abe I.
Talent representative
b. Unknown
d. New York, NY, Jan. 20, 1962, Age 71

FEINMAN, Sigmund
Actor
b. Unknown
d. Unknown, July 1, 1909, Age 52

FELDMAN, Charles K.
Producer, Talent Agent
b. New York, NY, April 26, 1905
d. Beverly Hills, CA, May 25, 1968, Age 63

FELIX, Hugo
Composer
b. Unknown, 1866
d. Unknown, Aug. 25, 1934, Age 62

FELIX, Mlle. Sarah
Actress
b. Unknown
d. Unknown, Jan. 13, 1877, Age 59

FELLOWES, Rockcliffe
Actor
b. Ottawa, CAN, Unknown
d. Los Angeles, CA, Jan. 28, 1950, Age 65

FELLOWES-ROBINSON, Dora
Producer
b. Unknown
d. Unknown, May 26, 1946

FELLOWS, Dexter William
Press representative
b. Boston, MA, 1871
d. Hattiesburg, MS, Nov. 28, 1937, Age 66

FELYNE, Renée
Actress
b. Unknown, 1884
d. April 27, 1910, 26

FENDALL, Percy
Playwright, Novelist
b. Unknown
d. Unknown, Nov. 29, 1917

FENN, Frederick George
Playwright, Critic
b. Bishop Stortford, England, Nov. 6, 1868
d. Unknown, Jan. 2, 1924, Age 55

FENN, George Manville
Playwright
b. Unknown, 1831
d. Unknown, Aug. 27, 1909, Age 78

FENNELL, James
Actor, Playwright
b. Unknown, 1766
d. Unknown, June 13, 1816, Age 49

FENOUX, Jacques
Actor
b. Unknown
d. Unknown, July 19, 1930

FENTON, Frank
Actor
b. Hartford, CT, 1906
d. Hollywood, CA, July 24, 1957, Age 51

FENTON, Lavinia (Duchess of Bolton)
Actress
b. Unknown, 1708
d. Unknown, Jan. 24, 1760, Age 52

FENTON, Mabel (Mrs. Charles J. Rose, née Ada Towne)
Actress
b. Van Buren County, MI, Unknown
d. Los Angeles, CA, April 19, 1931, Age 63

FENWICK, Irene (Frizzel)
Actress
b. Chicago, IL, 1887
d. Beverly Hills, CA, Dec. 24, 1936, Age 49

FEODOROVNA, Vera
Actress
b. Unknown
d. Unknown, Feb. 24, 1910

FERBER, Edna
Playwright, Author
b. Kalamazoo, MI, Aug. 15, 1887
d. New York, NY, April 16, 1968, Age 82

FERGUSON, Barney
Performer
b. Unknown
d. Bernardsville, NJ, Aug. 28, 1924, Age 71

FERGUSON, Elsie
Actress
b. New York, NY, Aug. 19, 1883
d. New London, CT, Nov. 15, 1961, Age 78

FERGUSON, Frank
Actor, Playwright
b. Boston, MA, Unknown
d. New York, NY, Sept. 8, 1937, Age 74

FERGUSON, William
Performer
b. Unknown
d. Hutchison, KS, Sept. 19, 1961, Age 41

FERGUSON, William J.
Actor
b. Unknown
d. Pikesville, MD, May 4, 1930, Age 85

FERNALD, Chester Bailey
Playwright
b. Boston, MA, March 18, 1869
d. Unknown, April 10, 1938, Age 69

FERNANDEZ, Bijou
Actress
b. New York, NY, Unknown
d. New York, NY, Nov. 7, 1961, Age 84

FERRAR, Ada
Actress
b. Unknown
d. Unknown, Jan. 8, 1951, Age 84

FERRAR, Beatrice
Actress
b. London, England, Unknown
d. Unknown, Feb. 12, 1958, Age 82

FERRAR, Gwen
Actress
b. London, England, July 14, 1899
d. Unknown, Dec. 25, 1944, Age 45

FERRARI, Paolo
Playwright
b. Unknown, 1822
d. Unknown, 1889, Age 67

FERRARI, William
Art director
b. Unknown
d. Hollywood, CA, Sept. 10, 1962, Age 61

FERRAVILLA, Edoardo
Actor, Playwright
b. Unknown, 1846
d. Unknown, Oct. 31, 1915, Age 69

FERRERS, George
Playwright
b. Unknown
d. Unknown, Jan. 11, 1579, Age 79

FERRERS, Helen
Actress
b. Cockham, Berks, England, Unknown
d. Unknown, Feb. 1, 1943, Age 77

FERRIER, Paul
Playwright
b. Montpellier, France, 1843
d. Unknown, Sept. 11, 1920, Age 77

FERRY, Felix (Féfé)
Producer
b. Bucharest, Romania, Unknown
d. Bad Homburg, Germany, Nov. 12, 1953, Age 56

FEUCHTWANGER, Lion
Novelist, Playwright
b. Munich, Germany, 1884
d. Los Angeles, CA, Dec. 21, 1959, Age 74

FEUILLET, Octave
Playwright, Novelist
b. St. Lò, France, 1821
d. Unknown, Dec. 29, 1890, Age 69

FEVAL, Paolo
Playwright
b. Unknown
d. Unknown, March 8, 1887, Age 69

FEYDEAU, Georges
Playwright
b. Paris, France, 1862
d. Unknown, June 5, 1921, Age 58

FFOLLIOTT, Gladys
Actress
b. Ireland, Unknown
d. Unknown, Feb. 1, 1928, Age 69

FIDDES, Josephine (Mrs. Dominic Murray)
Actress
b. Unknown
d. Unknown, March 1923, Age 85

FIELD, Al G. (Alfred Griffen Field)
Minstrel
b. Leesburg, VA, 1852
d. Columbus, OH, April 3, 1921, Age 72

FIELD, Ben
Actor
b. Unknown
d. Unknown, Oct. 21, 1939, Age 61

FIELD, Betty
Actress
b. Boston, MA, Feb. 8, 1918
d. Hyannis, MA, Sept. 13, 1973, Age 54

FIELD, Edward Salisbury
Playwright, Artist
b. Indianapolis, IN, Unknown
d. Zaca Lake, CA, Sept. 20, 1936, Age 56

FIELD, Joseph M.
Actor, Playwright
b. Unknown
d. Unknown, Jan. 28, 1856, Age 46

FIELD, Kate
Actress, Author
b. Unknown
d. Unknown, May 19, 1896, Age 57

FIELD, Lila (Lillia Scholefield)
Playwright
b. Unknown
d. Unknown, Feb. 9, 1954

FIELD, Nathan
Actor, Playwright
b. Unknown, 1587
d. Unknown, 1620, Age 33

FIELD, Nathaniel
Actor, Playwright
b. Unknown
d. Unknown, Feb. 20, 1633, Age 46

FIELD, Rachel
Playwright, Novelist
b. New York, NY, Sept. 19, 1894
d. Los Angeles, CA, March 14, 1942, Age 47

FIELD, Sid (né Sidney Arthur Field)
Comedian
b. Edgbaston, Birmingham, England, April 1, 1904
d. Surrey, England, Feb. 3, 1950, Age 45

FIELDING, Edward (Edward B. Elkins)
Actor
b. Brooklyn, NY, Unknown
d. Beverly Hills, CA, Jan. 10, 1945, Age 65

FIELDING, Henry
Playwright, Novelist
b. Sharpham Park, Somerset, England, April 22, 1707
d. Unknown, Oct. 8, 1754, Age 47

FIELDING, Marjorie
Actress
b. Gloucester, England, 1892
d. Unknown, Dec. 28, 1956, Age 64

FIELDS, Arthur
Performer, Songwriter
b. Philadelphia, PA, Aug. 6, 1888
d. Largo, FL, March 29, 1953, Age 64

FIELDS, Arthur B. "Buddy"
Songwriter, Musician
b. Vienna, Austria, Sept. 24, 1889
d. Detroit, MI, Oct. 4, 1965, Age 76

FIELDS, Benny
Singer
b. Milwaukee, WI, June 14, 1894
d. New York, NY, Aug. 16, 1959, Age 65

FIELDS, Dorothy
Lyricist, Librettist
b. Allenhurst, NJ, July 15, 1905
d. New York, NY, March 28, 1974, Age 68

FIELDS, Harry D.
Performer, Writer
b. Unknown
d. Hollywood, CA, Nov. 12, 1961, Age 65

FIELDS, Herbert
Librettist, Performer
b. New York, NY, July 26, 1897
d. New York, NY, March 24, 1958, Age 60

FIELDS, Joseph Albert
Playwright, Producer, Director, Screenwriter
b. New York, NY, Feb. 21, 1895
d. Beverly Hills, CA, March 3, 1966, Age 71

FIELDS, Lew (Lewis Maurice Schanfields)
Actor, Producer
b. New York, NY, Jan. 1, 1867
d. Beverly Hills, CA, July 20, 1941, Age 74

FIELDS, W. C. (William Claude Dukinfield)
Actor, Juggler
b. Philadelphia, PA, April 9, 1879
d. Pasadena, CA, Dec. 25, 1946, Age 67

FIELDS, William
Press representative
b. Unknown
d. New York, NY, April 24, 1961, Age 62

FIGMAN, Max
Actor, Director
b. Vienna, Austria, Unknown
d. Bayside, Queens, NY, Feb. 13, 1952, Age 85

FIGMAN, Oscar
Actor
b. Unknown
d. Neponsit, L.I., NY, July 18, 1930, Age 48

FILIPPI, Rosina
Actress
b. Venice, Italy, Oct. 31, 1866
d. Unknown, Feb. 27, 1930, Age 63

FILKINS, Grace (Grace Sweetman)
Actress
b. Philadelphia, PA, Unknown
d. New York, NY, Sept. 16, 1962, Age 97

FINCH, Flora
Actress
b. England, 1869
d. Hollywood, CA, Jan. 4, 1940, Age 71

FINDLAY, Ruth
Actress
b. Unknown
d. Unknown, July 13, 1949, Age 45

FINDLAY, Thomas B.
Actor
b. Guelph, Ontario, CAN, Unknown
d. Aylmer, Quebec, CAN, May 29, 1941, Age 67

FINDON, B. W.
Critic, Editor
b. Unknown, Feb. 6, 1859
d. Unknown, July 20, 1943, Age 84

FINE, Aaron
Playwright, Author, Illustrator
b. Unknown
d. New York, NY, Oct. 21, 1963, Age 46

FINN, Henry James
Actor, Playwright
b. Unknown, c1790
d. Long Island Sound, 1840

FINNELL, Carrie (Carrie Finnell Morris)
Performer
b. Convington, KY, Unknown
d. Fayetteville, OH, Nov. 14, 1963, Age 70

FINNEY, Mary
Actress
b. Spokane, WA, Sept. 30, 1906
d. New York, NY, Feb. 26, 1973, Age 66

FIORILLI, Tiberio
Actor
b. Unknown, 1608
d. Unknown, Dec. 7, 1694, Age 86

FISCHER, Alice (Harcourt)
Actress
b. Terre Haute, IN, Unknown
d. New York, NY, June 23, 1947, Age 78

FISCHER, Clifford C.
Producer
b. Belgium, Unknown
d. Westwood, NJ, Oct. 11, 1951, Age 69

FISHER, Clara (Mrs. James Maeder)
Actress
b. London, England, July 14, 1811
d. Metuchen, NJ, Nove. 12, 1898, Age 87

FISHER, Fred
Composer, Publisher
b. Cologne, Germany, Sept. 30, 1875
d. New York, NY, Jan. 14, 1942, Age 66

FISHER, Harry E.
Performer
b. England, Unknown
d. Brooklyn, NY, May 28, 1923, Age 55

FISHER, Irving
Actor
b. Unknown
d. Flushing, L.I., NY, Feb. 4, 1959, Age 73

FISHER, Jane (Mrs. George Vernon)
Actress
b. Unknown
d. Unknown, 1869

FISHER, John C.
Manager, Producer
b. Louisville, KY, Unknown
d. Chicago, IL, Dec. 17, 1921, Age 67

FISHER, Lola
Actress
b. Chicago, IL, 1892
d. Yonkers, NY, Oct. 15, 1926, Age 34

FISHER, Sallie
Actress
b. Unknown
d. Twenty-Nine Palms, CA, June 8, 1950, Age 69

FISHMAN, Henry
Actor
b. Russia, Unknown
d. Cincinnati, OH, Feb. 3, 1964, Age 76

FISKE, Harrison Grey
Producer, Playwright, Drama critic
b. Harrison, NY, July 30, 1861
d. New York, NY, Sept. 3, 1942, Age 81

FISKE, Minnie Maddern (Mary Augusta Davey)
Actress, Director, Producer
b. New Oreleans, LA, Dec. 19, 1865
d. Hollis, L.I., NY, Feb. 15, 1932, Age 66

FISKE, Stephen
Critic, Journalist, Producer
b. New Brunswick, NJ, Nov. 22, 1840
d. Unknown, April 27, 1916, Age 75

FITCH, (William) Clyde
Playwright
b. Elmira, NY, May 2, 1865
d. Chalons-sur-Marne, France, Sept. 4,1909, Age 44

FITTS, Dudley
Critic, Translator, Educator
b. Boston, MA, April 28, 1903
d. Lawrence, MA, July 10, 1968, Age 65

FITZ, Charles E.
Actor
b. Unknown
d. Philadelphia, PA, July 10, 1920

FITZBALL, Edward
Librettist, Lyricist
b. Unknown, 1792
d. Unknown, Oct. 27, 1873, Age 81

FITZGERALD, Barry
Performer
b. Dublin, Ireland, March 10, 1888
d. Dublin, Ireland, Jan. 4, 1961, Age 72

FITZGERALD, Cissy (Mrs. Cissy Tucker)
Actress
b. England, Unknown
d. Ovingdean, England, May 5, 1941, Age 67

FITZGERALD, F. Scott (Francis Scott Key Fitzgerald)
Novelist, Playwright
b. St. Paul, MN, Sept. 24, 1896
d. Hollywood, CA, Dec. 21, 1940, Age 44

FITZGERALD, Lilian
Performer
b. Unknown
d. New York, NY, July 9, 1947

FITZGERALD, Mrs. Florence Irene Dimrock
Actress
b. Unknown
d. Hartford, CT, Jan. 31, 1962, Age 72

FITZGERALD, Percy Hetherington
Playwright, Critic, Historian
b. Fane Valley, County Louth, Ireland, 1834
d. Unknown, Nov. 24, 1925, Age 91

FITZGERALD, S. J. Adair
Playwright, Historian
b. Unknown, Nov. 9, 1859
d. Unknown, Oct. 23, 1925, Age 65

FITZGIBBON, Louis A.
Performer
b. Unknown
d. Salem, MA, Nov. 30, 1961, Age 81

FLANAGAN, Bud (Robert Winthrop)
Comedian, Song writer
b. England, 1896
d. Kingston, England, Oct. 20, 1968, Age 72

FLANAGAN, Hallie
Director, Author, Teacher
b. Redfield, SD, Aug. 27, 1890
d. Old Tappan, NJ, July 23, 1969, Age 78

FLANAGAN, Richard
Producer
b. Unknown
d. Unknown, May 17, 1917, Age 68

FLANDERS, Michael
Lyricist, Actor
b. London, England, March 1, 1922
d. Wales, April 14, 1975, Age 53

FLATEAU, Georges
Actor
b. Unknown
d. Unknown, Feb. 13, 1953, Age 71

FLAVIN, Martin
Playwright, Author
b. San Francisco, CA, Nov. 2, 1883
d. Carmel, CA, Dec. 27, 1967, Age 84

FLEAY, Frederick Gard
Shakespearean authority
b. Unknown
d. Unknown, March 10, 1909, Age 78

FLECK, Johann Friedrich Ferdinand
Actor, Director
b. Unknown, 1757
d. Berlin, Germany, 1801, Age 44

FLECKER, (Herman) James Elroy
Poet, Playwright
b. Unknown, 1884
d. Unknown, 1915, Age 31

FLEETWOOD, Charles
Producer
b. Unknown
d. Unknown, c1745

FLEISCHMAN, Maurice L.
Theatre owner
b. Unknown
d. Miami Beach, FL, Nov. 17, 1963, Age 79

FLEISCHMANN, Julius
Philanthropist, Producer
b. Cincinnati, OH, April 29, 1900
d. Cincinnati, OH, Oct. 22, 1968, Age 68

FLEMING, Alice
Actress
b. Brooklyn, NY, Unknown
d. New York, NY, Dec. 6, 1952, Age 70

FLEMING, George (Constance Fletcher)
Playwright
b. Unknown, 1858
d. Unknown, June 6, 1938, Age 80

FLEMING, Noel
Actor
b. Unknown
d. Unknown, Nov. 17, 1950, Age 67

FLEMING, William
Actor
b. Unknown
d. New York, NY, Jan. 7, 1921, Age 83

FLEMMING, Claude
Actor
b. Sydney, New South Wales, Australia, Feb. 22, 1884
d. Unknown, March 24, 1952, Age 68

FLERS, P. L.
Playwright
b. Unknown
d. Unknown, Sept. 10, 1932, Age 65

FLERS, Robert de la Moote-Ango Marquis de
Playwright
b. Unknown, 1872
d. Unknown, 1927, Age 55

FLETCHER, John
Playwright, Poet
b. Sussex, England, 1579
d. Southwark, London, England, Aug. 29, 1625, Age 45

FLETCHER, Percy
Composer, Conductor
b. Derby, England, Dec. 12, 1879
d. Unknown, Sept. 10, 1932, Age 52

FLEURY, (Abraham-Joseph Benard)
Actor
b. Unknown, 1750
d. Unknown, 1822

FLEXNER, Anne Crawford
Playwright
b. Georgetown, KY, June 27, 1874
d. Providence, RI, Jan. 11, 1955, Age 80

FLOOD, John
Actor
b. Unknown
d. Ulster, NY, Oct. 6, 1924

FLORENCE, Mrs. William Jermyn (Malvina Pray Littell)
Actress
b. Unknown, 1831
d. Unknown, Feb. 18, 1906, Age 75

FLORENCE, William Jermyn (Bernard Conlin)
Actor, Writer
b. Albany, NY, July 26, 1831
d. Philadelphia, PA, Nov. 19, 1891, Age 60

FLORY, Regine
Actress, Dancer
b. Unknown, July 24, 1894
d. Unknown, June 17, 1926, Age 31

FLOWER, Sir Archibald
Executive, Shakespeare Memorial Theatre
b. Stratford-on-Avon, England, Unknown
d. Stratford-on-Avon, England, Nov. 22, 1950, Age 85

FLOWLER, Gene (Eugene Devlan)
Playwright, Novelist, Journalist
b. Denver, CO, 1890
d. West Hollywood, CA, July 2, 1960, Age 70

FLOYD, Gwendolen
Actress
b. Unknown
d. Unknown, Nov. 23, 1950, Age 80

FLYNN, Errol
Actor
b. Hobart, Tasmania, Australia, June 20, 1909
d. Vancouver, British Columbia, CAN, Oct. 14, 1959, Age 50

FLYNN, Hazel
Journalist, Press representative
b. Unknown
d. Santa Monica, CA, May 15, 1964, Age 65

FOGARTY, Frank
Performer
b. Unknown
d. Brooklyn, NY, April 6, 1925, Age 50

FOGERTY, Elsie
Actress, (Founder of Central School of Speech Training and Dramatic Art)
b. Sydenham, Kent, England, 1866
d. Unknown, July 4, 1945, Age 79

FOKINE, Michel
Choreographer, Dancer
b. Leningrad, Russia, April 26, 1880
d. New York, NY, Aug. 22, 1942, Age 62

FOLGER, Henry Clay
Shakespearean authority, (Founder of Folger Collection and Library)
b. Unknown, 1857
d. Unknown, June 11, 1930

FOLKINA, Vera
Dancer
b. Russia, Unknown
d. Jackson Heights, NY, July 29, 1958, Age 69

FOLLIS, Dorothy
Actress
b. Newark, NJ, 1802
d. New York, NY, Aug. 15, 1923, Age 31

FONVIZIN, Denis Ivanovich
Playwright
b. Unknown, 1744
d. Unknown, 1792

FOOTE, John Taintor
Playwright
b. Leadville, CO, Unknown
d. Los Angeles, CA, Jan. 28, 1950, Age 69

FOOTE, Lydia (Lydia Alice Legge)
Actress
b. Unknown, 1844
d. Unknown, 1892, Age 48

FOOTE, Samuel
Actor, Playwright, Producer
b. Unknown, 1720
d. Unknown, Oct. 21, 1777, Age 56

FORBES, Athol (Rev. Forbes Phillips)
Playwright
b. Unknown
d. Unknown, May 29, 1917, Age 50

FORBES, James
Playwright
b. Salem, Ontario, Sept. 2, 1871
d. Frankfort a/M, Germany, May 26, 1938, Age 66

FORBES, Ralph
Actor
b. London, England, Sept. 30, 1905
d. New York, NY, March 31, 1951, Age 45

FORBES-ROBERTSON, Eric
Actor
b. Unknown, 1865
d. Unknown, 1935, Age 70

FORBES-ROBERTSON, Frank
Actor
b. Unknown, Aug. 1, 1885
d. Unknown, March 15, 1947, Age 61

FORBES-ROBERTSON, Jean
Actress
b. London, England, March 16, 1905
d. London, England, Dec. 24, 1962, Age 57

FORBES-ROBERTSON, Norman
Actor, Manager, Playwright
b. London, England, Sept. 24, 1858
d. London, England, Sept. 29, 1932, Age 74

FORBES-ROBERTSON, Sir Johnston
Actor, Producer
b. London, England, Jan. 16, 1853
d. St. Margaret's Bay, Dover, England, Nov. 6, 1937, Age 84

FORD, Francis
Actor
b. Unknown
d. Hollywood, CA, Sept. 5, 1953, Age 71

FORD, Harriet
Playwright
b. Seymour, CT, Unknown
d. New York, NY, Dec. 12, 1949, Age 86

FORD, Harrison
Performer
b. Unknown
d. Woodland Hills, CA, Dec. 2, 1957, Age 73

FORD, John
Playwright
b. Ilsington, Devon, England, 1586
d. Devon, England, c1640, Age 53

FORD, John
Performer
b. Unknown
d. Hot Springs, AR, March 12, 1963, Age 81

FORD, John Thomson
Theatre manager
b. Unknown, 1829
d. Unknown, 1894

FORD, Paul
Actor
b. Baltimore, MD, Nov. 2, 1901
d. Mineola, NY, April 12, 1976, Age 74

FORD, Wallace (né Samuel Jones)
Actor
b. Balton, Lancashire, England, Feb. 12, 1898
d. Woodland Hills, CA, June 11, 1966, Age 68

FORDE, Florrie
Performer
b. Australia, 1876
d. Unknown, April 18, 1940, Age 64

FORDE, Hal
Actor
b. Ireland, Unknown
d. Philadelphia, PA, Dec. 4, 1955, Age 78

FOREPAUGH, Adam
Producer
b. Philadelphia, PA, Feb. 28, 1830
d. Unknown, Jan. 22, 1890, Age 59

FOREPAUGH, John A.
Producer
b. Unknown
d. Unknown, June 8, 1895

FORMAN, Justice Miles
Playwright, Novelist
b. Unknown
d. Unknown, May 7, 1915, Age 39

FORNIA, Mme. Rita
Singer
b. California, Unknown
d. Paris, France, Oct. 27, 1922, Age 44

FORREST, Arthur
Actor
b. Bayreuth, Germany, Unknown
d. New York, NY, May 16, 1933, Age 74

FORREST, Edwin
Actor, Producer
b. Philadelphia, PA, March 9, 1806
d. Philadelphia, PA, Dec. 12, 1872, Age 66

FORREST, Mrs. Edwin (Catherine Norton Sincliar)
Actress
b. Unknown, 1817
d. Unknown, June 16, 1891, Age 74

FORREST, Sam
Director, Actor, Author
b. Richmond, VA, Nov. 30, 1870
d. New York, NY, April 30, 1944, Age 73

FORRESTER, Frederick C.
Actor
b. Unknown
d. Bronx, NY, Oct. 14, 1952, Age 80

FORRESTER, Jack
Performer
b. Unknown
d. Unknown, Jan. 10, 1963, Age 59

FORSTER, John
Biographer, Critic
b. Unknown, 1812
d. Unknown, Feb. 2, 1876, Age 63

FORSTER, Rudolf
Actor
b. Groebming, Austria, 1884
d. Bad Aussee, Austria, Oct. 25, 1968, Age 84

FORSTER, Wilfred
Actor
b. Ryle, Isle of Wight, England, Nov. 8, 1872
d. Unknown, April 3, 1924, Age 51

FORSYTH, Bertram
Actor, Playwright
b. Unknown
d. Unknown, Sept. 15, 1927, Age 40

FORSYTH, Matthew
Actor, Director
b. Croydon, England, Aug. 8, 1896
d. Unknown, Aug. 25, 1954, Age 58

FORTESCUE, Julia (Lady Gardner)
Actress
b. Unknown
d. Unknown, Nov. 3, 1899

FORTESCUE, May (née Finney)
Actress
b. Unknown, Feb. 9, 1862
d. Unknown, Sept. 2, 1950, Age 88

FORTESCUE, Viola
Actress
b. Columbus, GA, Unknown
d. New York, NY, Sept. 16, 1953, Age 78

FOSS, George R.
Actor, Director
b. Dover, England, Nov. 25, 1859
d. Unknown, March 12, 1938, Age 78

FOSTER, Basil S.
Actor
b. Malvern, England, Feb. 12, 1882
d. Unknown, Sept. 30, 1959, Age 77

FOSTER, Lillian
Actress
b. Centralia, IL, Unknown
d. New York, NY, May 15, 1949, Age 63

FOSTER, Stephen Collins
Composer, Songwriter
b. Lawrenceville, PA, July 4, 1826
d. New York, NY, Jan. 13, 1864, Age 37

FOWLER, Gertrude
Actress
b. Unknown
d. New York, NY, June 5, 1935, Age 42

FOX, Della
Performer
b. St. Louis, MO, Oct. 13, 1871
d. Unknown, June 16, 1913, Age 41

FOX, George Washington Lafayette
Performer, Producer
b. Unknown, 1825
d. Unknown, Oct. 24, 1877, Age 52

FOX, Harry
Performer
b. Unknown
d. Woodland Hills, CA, July 20, 1959, Age about 77

FOX, Sidney
Actress
b. New York, NY, Dec. 10, 1910
d. Unknown, Nov. 14, 1942, Age 31

FOX, Stuart
Performer
b. Cleveland, OH, Unknown
d. New York, NY, June 17, 1951, Age 57

FOY, Eddie (Edwin Fitzgerald)
Comedian
b. New York, NY, March 9, 1856
d. Kansas City, MO, Feb. 16, 1928, Age 71

FOY, Richard
Performer, Theatre manager
b. Unknown
d. Dallas, TX, April 4, 1947, Age 42

FRANCE, Charles Vernon
Actor
b. Bradford, England, June 30, 1868
d. Unknown, April 13, 1949, Age 80

FRANCIS, J. O.
Playwright
b. Unknown
d. Unknown, Oct. 1, 1956, Age 74

FRANCIS, M. E.
Playwright, Novelist
b. Killiney Park, Dublin, Ireland, Unknown
d. Unknown, May 9, 1930, Age 72

FRANCIS, Robert
Actor
b. Unknown
d. Burbank, CA, July 3, 1955, Age 25

FRANCK, Hans
Novelist, Playwright
b. Unknown
d. Frankenhorst, West Germany, April 18, 1964, Age 85

FRANK, Bruno
Playwright
b. Stuttgart, Germany, June 13, 1887
d. Unknown, June 20, 1945, Age 58

FRANKAU, Ronald
Performer
b. London, England, Feb. 22, 1894
d. Eastbourne, Sussex, England, Sept. 11, 1951, Age 57

FRANKLIN, Harold B.
Producer, Director
b. New York, NY, April 4, 1890
d. Mexico City, Mexico, April 21, 1941, Age 51

FRANKLIN, Irene
Actress, Songwriter
b. New York, NY, June 13, 1876
d. Englewood, NJ, June 16, 1941, Age 65

FRANKLYN, Beth
Actress
b. Unknown
d. Baltimore, MD, March 5, 1956, Age 83

FRASER, Claud Lovat
Designer
b. Unknown, 1890
d. Unknown, June 18, 1921, Age 31

FRASER-SIMPSON, Harold
Composer
b. London, England, Aug. 15, 1878
d. Inverness, Scotland, Jan. 19, 1944, Age 65

FRAWLEY, T. Daniel
Actor, Producer
b. Washington, DC, Unknown
d. Tottenville, NY, April 26, 1936, Age 72

FRAZEE, Harry Herbert
Manager
b. Peoria, IL, June 29, 1880
d. New York, NY, June 4, 1929, Age 48

FREDERICI, Blanche
Actress
b. Unknown
d. Unknown, Dec. 23, 1933, Age 55

FREDERICK, Pauline (née Libbey)
Actress
b. Boston, MA, Aug. 12, 1885
d. Beverly Hills, CA, Sept. 19, 1938, Age 53

FREDERICKS, Albert
Producer
b. Unknown
d. Unknown, June 26, 1901, Age 61

FREDERICKS, Fred
Producer
b. Unknown
d. Unknown, Feb. 22, 1939, Age 75

FREDERICKS, Sam
Producer
b. Unknown
d. Unknown, Dec. 1922, Age 46

FREDMAN, Alice
Co-founder of Phoenix and Renaissance Theatre Societies
b. Unknown
d. Unknown, Aug. 9, 1950, Age 71

FREEAR, Louie
Actress
b. London, England, Nov. 26, 1871
d. Unknown, March 20, 1939, Age 67

FREEBORN, Cassius
Composer, Musical director
b. Unknown
d. New York, NY, May 8, 1954, Age 76

FREEDLEY, George Reynolds
Theatre historian, Library curator, Author
b. Richmond, VA, Sept. 5, 1904
d. Bay Shore, NY, Sept. 11, 1967, Age 63

FREEDLEY, Vinton
Manager, Producer
b. Philadelphia, PA, Nov. 5, 1891
d. New York, NY, June 5, 1969, Age 77

FREEDMAN, Lenore
Actress
b. Unknown
d. Houston, TX, May 6, 1964

FREEL, Aleta
Actress
b. Jersey City, NJ, Unknown
d. Hollywood, CA, Dec. 7, 1935, Age 28

FREEMAN, Charles J.
Vaudeville booker, Journalist
b. Unknown
d. Dallas, TX, Aug. 25, 1964, Age 82

FREEMAN, H. A.
Producer
b. Unknown
d. Unknown, Feb. 15, 1929

FREEMAN, Max
Actor
b. Unknown
d. Unknown, March 28, 1912

FREEMAN, Stella
Actress
b. South Norwood, England, April 26, 1910
d. Unknown, May 13, 1936, Age 26

FREEZER, Herbert J.
Investor
b. Unknown
d. New York, NY, June 30, 1963, Age 61

FREGOLI, Leopold
Protean Artist
b. Unknown
d. Unknown, Nov. 28, 1936, Age 69

FRENCH, Herbert C.
Dancer, Stage director
b. Unknown
d. New London, CT, Jan. 27, 1924, Age 33

FRENCH, Samuel
Publisher
b. Unknown
d. Unknown, April 9, 1898, Age 76

FRENCH, Stanley
Producer, BBC Executive
b. London, England, Jan. 27, 1908
d. London, England, May 14, 1964, Age 56

FRENCH, T. Henry
Producer, Publisher
b. Unknown
d. Unknown, Dec. 1, 1902

FREY, Nathaniel (né Fichtenbaum)
Actor
b. New York, NY, Aug. 3, 1923
d. New York, NY, Nov. 7, 1970, Age 47

FRIED, Walter
Producer, Manager
b. New York, NY, April 23, 1910
d. New York, NY, May 28, 1975, Age 65

FRIEDLAND, Anatole
Composer, Performer
b. St. Petersburg, Russia, March 21, 1888
d. Atlantic City, NJ, July 24, 1938, Age 50

FRIEDMAN, Max
Songwriter, performer
b. Unknown
d. Pittsburgh, PA, Aug. 20, 1964, Age 76

FRIML, Rudolf
Composer
b. Prague, Czechoslovakia, Dec. 7, 1879
d. Los Angeles, CA, Nov. 12, 1972, Age 92

FRISCO, Joe (Louis Wilson Joseph)
Performer
b. Milan, IL, Unknown
d. Woodland Hills, CA, Feb. 16, 1958, Age 68

FRITH, John Leslie
Actor, Playwright
b. London, England, Sept. 28, 1889
d. London, England, Feb. 2, 1961, Age 71

FRITH, Walter
Playwright, Novelist
b. Unknown
d. Unknown, July 25, 1941

FROELICH, William J.
Performer
b. Chicago, IL, Unknown
d. Butte, MT, 1963, Age 60

FROHMAN, Charles
Producer
b. Sandusky, OH, June 17, 1860
d. . . . on board Lusitania, May 7, 1915, Age 54

FROHMAN, Daniel
Producer, Author
b. Sandusky, OH, August 22, 1851
d. New York, NY, Dec. 26, 1940, Age 89

FROHMAN, Gustave
Producer
b. Sandusky, OH, 1855
d. New York, NY, Aub. 16, 1930, Age 75

FRY, Charles
Performer, Director
b. Unknown, 1845
d. Unknown, Dec. 12, 1928, Age 83

FULDA, Ludwig
Playwright
b. Frankfort a/M, Germany, July 15, 1862
d. Berlin, Germany, March 30, 1939, Age 76

FULLER, Leland F.
Art director
b. Unknown, 1899
d. Hollywood, CA, Oct. 9, 1962, Age 63

FULLER, Loie
Actress, Dancer
b. Fullersburg, IL, 1863
d. Paris, France, Jan. 1, 1928, Age 65

FULLER, Mollie
Actress
b. Boston, MA, 1865
d. Hollywood, CA, Jan. 5, 1933, Age 68

FULTON, Charles J. (Foss)
Actor
b. Unknown, July 23, 1857
d. Unknown, July 18, 1938, Age 80

FULTON, Maude
Actress, Playwright
b. Eldorado, KS, May 14, 1881
d. Los Angeles, CA, Nov. 9, 1950, Age 69

FURBER, Douglas
Playwright
b. London, England, May 13, 1885
d. Unknown, Feb. 19, 1961, Age 75

FURLEY, Shelagh
Actress
b. Unknown
d. Unknown, Nov. 30, 1951

FURNISS, Grace Livingston
Playwright
b. New York, NY, Unknown
d. New York, NY, April 20, 1938, Age 74

FURNIVAL, Dr. F. J.
Shakespearean scholar
b. Unknown, 1825
d. Unknown, July 2, 1910, Age 85

FURSE, Roger
Costume designer
b. Ightham, England, Sept. 11, 1903
d. Corfu, Greece, Aug. 19, 1972, Age 68

FURST, William Wallace
Composer
b. Unknown, 1852
d. Freeport, L.I., NY, June 11, 1917, Age 65

FURTADO, Teresa (Mrs. J. S. Clarke)
Actress
b. Unknown, 1845
d. Unknown, Aug. 9, 1877, Age 32

FYFE, H. Hamilton
Critic, Playwright, Journalist
b. London, England, Sept. 28, 1869
d. Unknown, June 15, 1951, Age 81

FYFFE, Will
Actor
b. Dundee, Scotland, 1885
d. St. Andrews, Scotland, Dec. 14, 1947, Age 62

FYLES, Franklin
Playwright, Critic
b. Unknown
d. Unknown, July 4, 1911, Age 64

G

GABLE, (William) Clark
Actor
b. Cadiz, OH, Feb. 1, 1901
d. Hollywood, CA, Nov. 16, 1960, Age 59

GABRIEL, Gilbert Wolf
Drama critic
b. Brooklyn, NY, Jan. 18, 1890
d. Mt. Kisco, NY, Sept. 3, 1952, Age 62

GACHET, Alice (Alice Mary Gachet de la Fourniere)
Actress, Director, Teacher
b. Unknown
d. London, England, Oct. 27, 1960

GADE, Jacob
Composer, Musician
b. Unknown
d. Assens, Denmark, Feb. 20, 1963, Age 83

GAIGE, Crosby
Producer, Director
b. Nelson, NY, 1882
d. Peekskill, NY, March 8, 1949, Age 66

GAITES, Joseph M.
Producer, Director
b. . . . near Pittsburgh, PA, Unknown
d. Boston, MA, Dec. 4, 1940, Age 67

GALDOS, Benito Pérez
Novelist, Playwright
b. Las Palmas, Canary Islands, 1845
d. Madrid, Spain, 1920

GALE, Zona (Mrs. William Llewllyn Breese)
Playwright, Novelist
b. Portage, WI, Aug. 26, 1874
d. Chicago, IL, Dec. 27, 1938, Age 64

GALIPAUX, Felix
Actor, Playwright
b. Unknown
d. Unknown, Dec. 7, 1931, Age 71

GALLAGHER, Richard S. (Skeets)
Actor
b. Terre Haute, IN, July 28, 1896
d. Santa Monica, CA, May 22, 1955, Age 58

GALLAND, Bertha
Actress
b. . . . near Wilkes-Barre, PA, Nov. 15, 1876
d. Unknown, Nov. 20, 1932, Age 56

GALLATIN, Alberta
Actress
b. Unknown
d. New York, NY, Aug. 25, 1948, Age 87

GALLI, Rosina
Dancer
b. Unknown
d. Unknown, April 30, 1940, Age 45

GALLIARI, Bernardino
Designer
b. Adorno, Italy, Nov. 3, 1707
d. Aunorno, Italy, March 31, 1794, Age 86

GALLIARI, Fabrizio
Designer
b. Andorno, Italy, Sept. 28, 1709
d. Treviglio, Italy, June 1790, Age 80

GALLIARI, Gaspare
Designer
b. Italy, 1761
d. Milan, Italy, 1823

GALLIARI, Giovanni Designer
b. Italy, 1746
d. Treviglio, Italy, 1818

GALLIARI, Giuseppino
Designer
b. Andorno, Italy, 1752
d. Milan, Italy, 1817

GALLIMORE, Catherine (Anderson)
Performer
b. Unknown
d. Lake Carey, PA, Sept. 3, 1962, Age 57

GALLO, Alberto
Choreographer, Dance teacher
b. Unknown
d. New York, NY, April 18, 1964, Age 75

GALLO, Fortune
Showman - Producer
b. Torremaggiore, Italy, May 9, 1878
d. New York, NY, March 28, 1970, Age 91

GALLON, Nellie Tom
Actress
b. Unknown
d. Unknown, Feb. 1, 1938

GALLON, Tom
Playwright, Novelist
b. Unknown
d. Unknown, Nov. 2, 1914, Age 48

GALLOWAY, Louise
Actress
b. Michigan, Unknown
d. Brookfield, MA, Oct. 10, 1949, Age 70

GALM, Tina
Performer
b. Unknown
d. Frankfort-am-Main, Germany, Oct. 10, 1962, Age 81

GALSWORTHY, John
Playwright, Novelist
b. Coombe, Surrey, England, Aug. 14, 1867
d. Hampstead, England, Jan. 31, 1933, Age 65

GALT, John
Theatrical writer, Biographer
b. Unknown
d. Unknown, April 11, 1839, Age 59

GALVANI, Dino
Actor
b. Milan, Italy, Oct. 27, 1890
d. Unknown, Sept. 14, 1960, Age 69

GAMBLE, Theodore Roosevelt (Ted)
Theatre and Broadcasting executive
b. Unknown
d. San Francisco, CA, May 18, 1960, Age 54

GAMBLE, Warburton
Actor
b. Unknown
d. Unknown, Aug. 27, 1945, Age 62

GANDILLOT, Leon
Playwright
b. Unknown
d. Unknown, Sept. 22, 1912, Age 50

GANTHONY, Richard
Playwright, Actor
b. Unknown
d. Unknown, April 29, 1924, Age 67

GANTHONY, Robert
Playwright, Performer
b. Unknown
d. Unknown, March 12, 1931, Age 82

GARAT, Henri
Actor
b. Unknown
d. Toulon, France, Aug. 13, 1959, Age 57

GARCIA GUTIERREZ, Antonio
Playwright
b. Chiclana, Cádiz, Spain, c1813
d. Unknown, 1884

GARCIA LORCA, Federico
Playwright, Poet
b. Fuente Vaqueros, Andalusia, Spain, April 15, 1899
d. Granada, Spain, Aug. 19, 1936, Age 37

GARD, Alex
Artist
b. Russia, Unknown
d. New York, NY, June 1, 1948, Age 48

GARDELLA, Tess
Actress
b. Wilkes-Barre, PA, Unknown
d. Brooklyn, NY, Jan. 3, 1950, Age 52

GARDEN, E. W.
Actor
b. London, England, April 27, 1845
d. Unknown, Oct. 17, 1939, Age 94

GARDNER, Charles A.
Actor, Composer
b. Unknown
d. Unknown, Feb. 15, 1924, Age 76

GARDNER, Ed (Edward Francis Gardner né Poggenburg)
Performer
b. Astoria, Queens, NY, Unknown
d. Hollywood, CA, Aug. 17, 1963, Age 62

GARDNER, Jack
Actor
b. Unknown
d. Encino, CA, Sept. 30, 1950, Age 77

GARDNER, Shayle
Actor
b. Auckland, New Zealand, Aug. 22, 1890
d. Unknown, May 17, 1945, Age 55

GARFIELD, John (Jules Garfinkel)
Performer
b. New York, NY, March 4, 1913
d. New York, NY, May 21, 1952, Age 39

GARGAN, Edward F.
Actor
b. Unknown
d. New York, NY, Feb. 19, 1964, Age 62

GARLAND, Hamlin
Novelist, Playwright
b. West Salem, WI, Sept. 14, 1860
d. Hollywood, CA, March 4, 1940, Age 79

GARLAND, Robert
Drama critic
b. Baltimore, MD, April 29, 1895
d. New York, NY, Dec. 27, 1955, Age 60

GARNETT, Edward
Playwright, Critic
b. Unknown, 1868
d. Unknown, Feb. 19, 1937, Age 69

GARRETT, Oliver H. P.
Playwright, Scenarist
b. New Bedford, MA, Unknown
d. New York, NY, Feb. 23, 1952, Age 54

GARRICK, David
Actor, Playwright, Producer
b. Hereford, England, Feb. 19, 1717
d. Hampton, England, Jan. 20, 1779, Age 62

GARRICK, Helen Collier
Actress
b. Unknown
d. Goshen, NY, Dec. 9, 1954, Age 87

GARRICK, Mrs. David (Eva Marie Veigel or Violetti)
Actress, Dancer
b. Vienna, Austria, 1724
d. London, England, Oct. 16, 1822, Age 98

GARRICK, Richard T.
Actor
b. Unknown
d. Hollywood, CA, Aug. 21, 1962, Age 83

GARRY, Charles
Actor
b. Unknown
d. Unknown, June 6, 1939, Age 68

GARRY, Claude
Actor
b. Unknown
d. Unknown, Aug. 1918, Age 41

GARSIDE, John
Actor, Designer
b. Salford, Manchester, England, April 21, 1887
d. Unknown, April 18, 1958, Age 71

GARUTSO, Stephen E.
Optical engineer
b. Russia, Unknown
d. Hollywood, CA, Jan. 17, 1964

GARVIE, Edward
Actor
b. Meriden, CT, Unknown
d. New York, NY, Feb. 17, 1939, Age 73

GASNIER, Louis
Actor, Director
b. France, Unknown
d. Hollywood, CA, Feb. 15, 1963, Age 87

GASSMAN, Josephine (Mrs. Josephine Sullivan)
Performer
b. Unknown
d. Youngstown, OH, Jan. 24, 1962, Age 82

GASSNER, John Waldhorn
Theatre historian, Critic, Anthologist, Producer, Educator, Playwright
b. Maramaros-Sziget, Hungary, Jan. 30, 1903
d. New Haven, CT, April 2, 1967, Age 64

GASTELLE, Stella
Actress
b. Unknown
d. Unknown, Nov. 1936

GASTON, George
Actor
b. Lockport, NY, Jan. 27, 1843
d. Englewood, NJ, Jan. 14, 1937, Age 93

GATES, Eleanor
Playwright, Novelist
b. Shakopee, MN, Sept. 26, 1875
d. Los Angeles, CA, March 7, 1951, Age 75

GATES, Ruth
Actress
b. Denton, TX, Oct. 28, 1888
d. New York, NY, May 23, 1966, Age 77

GATTI-CASAZZA, Guilio
Opera impresario, Manager
b. Udine, Italy, Unknown
d. Ferrara, Italy, Sept. 2, 1940, Age About 74

GATTIE, A. W.
Playwright
b. Unknown
d. Unknown, Sept. 21, 1925, Age 69

GAUGE, Alexander
Actor
b. Unknown
d. Unknown, Aug. 29, 1960, Age 46

GAUL, George
Actor
b. Philadelphia, PA, Sept. 22, 1885
d. Unknown, Oct. 6, 1939, Age 54

GAULTIER-GARGUILLE, (Huges Guéru)
Actor, Farceur
b. Unknown, c1573
d. Unknown, 1633

GAUNT, Percy
Songwriter
b. Philadelphia, PA, 1852
d. Palenville, NY, Sept. 5, 1896, Age 44

GAUTIER, Théophile
Critic, Poet
b. Tarbes, France, Aug. 31, 1811
d. Nueilly, France, Oct. 22, 1872, Age 61

GAWTHORNE, Peter A.
Actor
b. Queen's County, Ireland, Sept. 1, 1884
d. London, England, March 17, 1962, Age 77

GAXTON, William (Arturo Gaxiola)
Performer
b. San Francisco, CA, Dec. 2, 1893
d. New York, NY, Feb. 2, 1963, Age 69

GAY, John
Playwright, Poet
b. Barnstaple, Devon, England, Sept. 1685
d. Unknown, Dec. 4, 1732, Age 47

GAY, Maisie (née Munro-Noble)
Actress
b. London, England, Jan. 7, 1883
d. London, England, Sept. 13, 1945, Age 62

GAY, Maria
Singer
b. Barcelona, Spain, Unknown
d. New York, NY, July 29, 1943, Age 64

GAY, Noel (Reginald Moxon Armitage)
Composer
b. Wakefield, Yorkshire, England, July 15, 1898
d. Unknown, March 4, 1954, Age 55

GAY, Walter
Actor
b. Unknown
d. Unknown, Jan. 8, 1936, Age 73

GAYER, Echlin
Actor
b. Unknown
d. New York, NY, Feb. 14, 1926, Age 48

GAYLER, Charles
Playwright
b. New York, NY, April 1, 1820
d. Brooklyn, NY, May 28, 1892, Age 72

GAYNOR, Charles
Lyricist, Composer
b. Winthrop Highlands, MA, April 3, 1909
d. Washington, DC, Dec. 18, 1975, Age 66

GEBERT, Ernst
Conductor, Teacher
b. Berlin, Germany, Unknown
d. Hollywood, CA, Nov. 22, 1961, Age 59

GEDDES, Norman Bel
Designer, Producer
b. Adrian, MI, April 27, 1893
d. New York, NY, May 8, 1958, Age 65

GEE, George
Actor
b. Unknown
d. Coventry, England, Oct. 17, 1959, Age 64

GEIRINGER, Jean (Hans)
Librettist, Lyricist
b. Vienna, Austria, Unknown
d. New York, NY, Feb. 20, 1962, Age 62

GEMIER, Firmin
Actor, Producer
b. Aubervilliers, France, Feb. 13, 1865
d. Paris, France, Nov. 26, 1933, Age 68

GENDRON, Pierre
Actor
b. Unknown
d. Hollywood, CA, Nov. 27, 1956, Age 60

GENEE, Alexander
Dancer, Director
b. Unknown
d. Unknown, June 29, 1938, Age 88

GENEST, Rev. John
Historian
b. Unknown
d. Unknown, Dec. 15, 1839, Age 75

GENIAT, Marcelle (Eugenie Martin)
Actress
b. Petrograd, Russia, Unknown
d. Paris, France, Sept. 28, 1959, Age 80

GENN, Edward P.
Producer
b. Unknown
d. Unknown, Nov. 4, 1947, Age 50

GENTLEMAN, Francis
Actor, Playwright
b. Dublin, Ireland, 1728
d. Dublin, Ireland, Dec. 21, 1784, Age 56

GENTRY, Amelia
Performer
b. Unknown
d. Hollywood, CA, June 15, 1963, Age 40

GENTRY, Bob
Performer
b. Unknown
d. Georgia, Nov. 28, 1962, Age 44

GEORGE, A. E.
Actor
b. Lincoln, England, July 22, 1869
d. Unknown, Nov. 10, 1920, Age 51

GEORGE, Gladys
Actress
b. Patton, ME, Sept. 13, 1904
d. Hollywood, CA, Dec. 8, 1954, Age 50

GEORGE, Grace
Actress
b. New York, NY, Dec. 25, 1879
d. New York, NY, May 19, 1961, Age 81

GEORGE, Marie
Performer
b. New York, NY, June 25, 1879
d. Unknown, July 14, 1955, Age 76

GEORGE, Mlle. (Marguerite Joséphine Weimer)
Actress, Teacher
b. Unknown, 1787
d. Unknown, 1867, Age 80

GERALD, Ara (Mrs. Ara Gerald Clarke née Fitzgerald)
Actress, Opera singer
b. Sydney, Australia, Unknown
d. Fort Lauderdale, FL, April 2, 1957, Age 63

GERALD, Florence
Actress
b. Canton, MS, Unknown
d. New York, NY, Sept. 6, 1942, Age 84

GERALD, Frank (Francis Gates Pearson)
Actor
b. Liverpool, England, 1855
d. Kennington, Oxford, England, July 16, 1942, Age 86

GERHARD, Karl (Karl Gerhard Johnson)
Actor, Songwriter
b. Unknown
d. Stockholm, Sweden, April 22, 1964, Age 73

GERMAINE, Auguste
Playwright, Critic
b. Unknown
d. Unknown, Dec. 1915, Age 53

GERMON, Effie
Actress
b. Unknown
d. Unknown, March 5, 1914, Age 66

GEROULE, Henri
Playwright
b. Unknown
d. Unknown, Nov. 28, 1934

GERRARD, Teddie (Thérése Théodora Gérard Cabrié)
Actress
b. Argentina, May 2, 1892
d. Unknown, Aug. 31, 1942, Age 50

GERSHWIN, George (Jacob Gershwin)
Composer
b. Brooklyn, NY, Sept. 26, 1898
d. Hollywood, CA, July 11, 1937, Age 38

GERSTMAN, Felix G.
Impresario, Producer
b. Vienna, Austria, Unknown
d. New York, NY, Jan. 11, 1967, Age 68

GEST, Morris
Producer
b. Vilna, Russia, Jan. 17, 1881
d. New York, NY, May 16, 1942, Age 61

GETCHELL, Dr. Charles Munro
Educator
b. Gardiner, ME, Aug. 22, 1909
d. University, MS, April 22, 1963, Age 54

GETZ, Johnnie G.
Performer
b. Cincinnati, OH, Unknown
d. Cincinnati, OH, Jan. 7, 1964, Age 84

GHELDERODE, Michel de
Playwright
b. Ixelles, Brussels, Belgium, 1898
d. Brussels, Belgium, April 1, 1962, Age 63

GHERARDI, Evaristo
Actor, Playwright
b. Unknown, c1663
d. Unknown, 1700

GHIONE, Franco
Conductor, Composer
b. Acqui, Italy, Aug. 26, 1886
d. Rome, Italy, Jan. 1964, Age 77

GHOSAL, Mrs. (Srimati Svarnakumari Devi)
Novelist, Playwright, Poet, Editor
b. Unknown, 1857
d. Unknown, 1932

GIACOMETTI, Paolo
Playwright
b. Unknown, 1816
d. Unknown, 1882, Age 66

GIACOSA, Giuseppe
Playwright, Librettist
b. Unknown, 1847
d. Unknown, 1906, Age 59

GIBBONS, Arthur
Producer
b. Addlestone, Surrey, England, Jan. 21, 1871
d. Unknown, Aug. 17, 1935, Age 64

GIBBONS, Cedric
Art director
b. New York, NY, Unknown
d. Westwood, CA, July 26, 1960, Age 65

GIBBONS, Irene (Mrs. Elliot Gibbons née Irene Lentz)
Costume designer
b. . . . near Baker, MT, Dec. 8, 1907
d. Hollywood, CA, Nov. 15, 1962, Age 61

GIBBONS, Rose
Actress
b. Unknown
d. Oakland, CA, Aug. 13, 1964, Age 78

GIBBS, Mrs. (Mrs. George Colman née Mary Logan)
Actress
b. Unknown, 1770
d. Brighton, England, 1844

GIBBS, Nancy (Mrs. W. Arthur J. Govan)
Actress
b. Wales, Unknown
d. Liverpool, England, Oct. 13, 1956, Age 63

GIBBS, Robert Paton
Actor
b. Scranton, PA, Unknown
d. Clifton, S.I., NY, Feb. 22, 1940, Age 81

GIBBS, Wolcott
Author, Drama critic, Playwright
b. New York, NY, 1902
d. Ocean Beach, Fire Island, NY, Aug. 16, 1958, Age 56

GIBSON, Hoot (Edmund Richard Gibson)
Actor
b. Tekamah, NB, Aug. 6, 1892
d. Woodland Hills, CA, Aug. 23, 1962, Age 70

GIBSON, Preston
Playwright
b. Washington, DC, Unknown
d. New York, NY, Feb. 15, 1937, Age 57

GIDDENS, George
b. Bedfont, Middlesex, England, June 17, 1845
d. New York, NY, Nov. 21, 1920, Age 75

GIDE, Andre Paul Guillaume
Shakespearean translator, Novelist
b. Paris, France, Nov. 22, 1869
d. Paris, France, Feb. 19, 1951, Age 81

GIDEON, Johnny
Historian
b. Unknown
d. Unknown, Nov. 29, 1901, Age 78

GIDEON, Melville J.
Composer, Singer
b. New York, NY, May 21, 1884
d. Unknown, Nov. 11, 1933, Age 49

GIESLER, Jerry (Harold Lee Giesler)
Theatrical lawyer
b. Wilton Junction, IA, Unknown
d. Beverly Hills, CA, Jan. 1, 1962, Age 75

GIFFARD, Henry
Actor, Producer
b. Unknown, 1694
d. Unknown, Oct. 29, 1772, Age 78

GIFFEN, Robert Lawrence
Producer, Director, Author's rep.
b. Tecumseh, NB, Unknown
d. Brooklyn, NY, March 16, 1946, Age 73

GIFFORD, Gordon
Performer
b. Unknown
d. Chicago, IL, Jan. 25, 1962, Age 48

GILBERT, Billy
Actor
b. Louisville, KY, Sept. 12, 1894
d. Hollywood, CA, Sept. 23, 1971, Age 77

GILBERT, George Henry
Dancer
b. Unknown
d. Unknown, 1866

GILBERT, Jean (Herr Winterfeld)
Composer
b. Germany, 1879
d. Unknown, Jan. 4, 1943, Age 63

GILBERT, John (Pringle)
Actor
b. Logan, UT, 1897
d. Beverly Hills, CA, Jan. 9, 1936, Age 38

GILBERT, John Gibbs
Actor
b. Boston, MA, Feb. 27, 1810
d. Boston, MA, June 17, 1889, Age 79

GILBERT, Mercedes
Performer
b. Unknown
d. New York, NY, March 1, 1952, Age 58

GILBERT, Mrs. George Henry (née Ann Hartley)
Actress, Dancer
b. Unknown, Oct. 21, 1821
d. Chicago, IL, Dec. 2, 1904, Age 83

GILBERT, Sir William Schwenck
Lyricist, Playwright, Poet
b. London, England, Nov. 18, 1836
d. Harrow, Middlesex, England, May 29, 1911, Age 74

GILBERT, Walter
Actor
b. Brooklyn, NY, Unknown
d. Brooklyn, NY, Jan. 13, 1947, Age 60

GILCHRIST, Connie (Countess of Orkney)
Actress, Dancer
b. Unknown, 1865
d. Unknown, May 9, 1946, Age 81

GILCHRIST, Rubina
Actress
b. Unknown
d. Unknown, Feb. 28, 1956

GILDEA, Agnes
Actress
b. Unknown
d. East Islip, L.I., NY, Feb. 2, 1964, Age 90

GILDEA, Mary
Actress
b. Unknown
d. Rockland County, NY, Feb. 19, 1957, Age about 72

GILDER, Jeanette
Critic, Playwright
b. Unknown
d. Unknown, Jan. 17, 1916, Age 66

GILDON, Charles
Playwright
b. Unknown
d. Unknown, Jan. 12, 1724, Age 59

GILL, Basil
Actor
b. Birkenhead, Cheshire, England, March 10, 1877
d. Hove, England, April 23, 1955, Age 78

GILL, Henry
Singer
b. Unknown
d. Unknown, Sept. 2, 1954, Age 55

GILL, Paul (Gilbert Wilson Snow)
Actor
b. Unknown
d. Portland, ME, Dec. 7, 1953, Age 38

GILLESPIE, Richard Henry
Producer
b. Morpeth, Northumberland, England, Sept. 10, 1878
d. Unknown, May 20, 1952, Age 73

GILLETTE, William
Playwright, Actor
b. Hartford, CT, July 24, 1855
d. Unknown, April 29, 1937, Age 81

GILLIE, Jean
Actress
b. London, England, Oct. 14, 1915
d. Unknown, Feb. 19, 1949, Age 33

GILLILAND, Helen
Actress
b. Belfast, Ireland, Jan. 31, 1897
d. Unknown, Nov. 24, 1942, Age 45

GILLILAND, Thomas
Theatrical chronicler, Author
b. Unknown
d. Unknown, c1816

GILLMORE, Frank
Actor, Union official
b. New York, NY, May 14, 1867
d. New York, NY, March 29, 1943, Age 75

GILMAN, Ada
Actress
b. Unknown
d. Philadelphia, PA, Dec. 18, 1921, Age 67

GILMORE, Douglas
Actor
b. Unknown
d. New York, NY, July 26, 1950, Age 47

GILMOUR, Brian
Actor
b. Unknown, Nov. 10, 1894
d. Unknown, May 18, 1954, Age 59

GILMOUR, Gordon
Actor, Playwright
b. Unknown
d. Aberdour, Fife, Scotland, March 8, 1962, Age 48

GILMOUR, John H.
Actor, Producer
b. Unknown
d. Yonkers, NY, Nov. 1922, Age 65

GILPIN, Charles Sidney
Actor
b. Richmond, VA, Nov. 20, 1878
d. Eldridge Park, NJ, May 6, 1930, Age 51

GILSON, Lottie (Lyda Deagon)
Performer
b. New York, NY, Unknown
d. New York, NY, July 10, 1912, Age 43

GINGOLD, Baroness Hélêne
Playwright, Novelist, Poet
b. Unknown
d. Unknown, Dec. 10, 1926

GINISTY, Paul
Playwright, Critic
b. Unknown
d. Unknown, March 5, 1932, Age 66

GINTY, Elizabeth Beall
Playwright
b. Wisconsin, Unknown
d. New York, NY, Nov. 15, 1949, Age 86

GIRALDI, Giovanni Battista ("Il Cinthio")
Novelist, Playwright
b. Ferrara, Italy, 1504
d. Unknown, 1573

GIRARD, Kate
Actress
b. Unknown
d. Unknown, March 22, 1885

GIRARDOT, Etienne
Actor
b. London, England, Unknown
d. Hollywood, CA, Nov. 10, 1939, Age 83

GIRAUD, Giovanni
Playwright
b. Unknown
d. Unknown, Oct. 1, 1834, Age 57

GIRAUDOUX, Jean
Playwright, Diplomat
b. Bellac, France, Oct. 29, 1882
d. Paris, France, Jan. 31, 1944, Age 61

GISH, Dorothy
Actress
b. Massillon, OH, March 11, 1898
d. Rapallo, Italy, June 4, 1968, Age 70

GITANA, Gertie (Mrs. Gertrude Mary Ross, née Astbury)
Performer
b. Longport, Staffordshire, England, 1887
d. Haverstock Hill, London, England, Jan. 5, 1957, Age 70

GIVENS, Jimmie (James Amos Givens)
Performer
b. Unknown
d. Newark, NJ, Feb. 19, 1964, Age 47

GIVLER, Mary Louise (Mrs. Oscar Shaw)
Performer
b. Carlisle, PA, Unknown
d. Manhasset, L.I., NY, March 30, 1964, Age 77

GLADMAN, FLORENCE (Mrs. Andreé Charlot)
Performer, Producer
b. Unknown
d. Unknown, Aug. 19, 1956, Age 66

GLASER, Lulu
Actress
b. Allegheny, PA, June 2, 1874
d. Norwalk, CT, Sept. 5, 1958, Age 84

GLASPELL, Susan
Playwright, Novelist
b. Davenport, IA, July 1, 1882
d. Provincetown, MA, July 27, 1948, Age 66

GLASS, Montague Marsden
Playwright
b. Manchester, England, July 23, 1877
d. Westport, CT, Feb. 3, 1934, Age 56

GLASSFORD, David
Actor
b. Sydney, Australia, April 17, 1866
d. New York, NY, Oct. 17, 1935, Age 69

GLEASON, James
Actor, Playwright, Producer
b. New York, NY, May 23, 1886
d. Woodland Hills, CA, April 12, 1959, Age 72

GLEASON, Lucile Webster
Actress
b. Pasadena, CA, Unknown
d. Brentwood, CA, May 18, 1947, Age 59

GLEASON, Russell
Performer
b. Unknown
d. New York, NY, Dec. 25, 1945, Age 36

GLENDINNING, Ernest
Actor
b. Ulverston, England, Feb. 19, 1884
d. South Coventry, CT, May 17, 1936, Age 52

GLENDINNING, John
Actor, Producer
b. Whitehaven, England, Nov. 30, 1857
d. Unknown, July 16, 1916, Age 58

GLENNY, Charles H.
Actor
b. Glasgow, Scotland, June 20, 1857
d. Unknown, Oct. 1, 1922, Age 65

GLENVILLE, Shaun
Actor
b. Ireland, May 16, 1884
d. London, England, Dec. 28, 1968, Age 84

GLOSSOP, Joseph
Actor, Producer
b. Unknown
d. Unknown, Jan. 1835

GLOSSOP, Mrs. Joseph (Elizabeth Feron)
Actress
b. Unknown
d. Unknown, May 9, 1853, Age 58

GLOSSOP-HARRIS, Florence
Actress, Producer
b. London, England, Oct. 8, 1883
d. Unknown, Oct. 26, 1931, Age 48

GLOVER, Charles William
Composer
b. Unknown
d. Unknown, March 23, 1863, Age 57

GLOVER, Edmund
Producer
b. Unknown, 1813
d. Unknown, 1860

GLOVER, Halcott
Playwright
b. Cambridge, England, May 31, 1877
d. Unknown, May 5, 1949, Age 71

GLOVER, Julia (née Betterton)
Actress
b. Unknown, 1781
d. Unknown, 1850, Age 69

GLYNNE, Mary
Actress
b. Penarth, South Wales, Jan. 25, 1898
d. Unknown, Sept. 19, 1954, Age 56

GOBERMAN, Max
Conductor
b. Philadelphia, PA, Unknown
d. Vienna, Austria, Dec. 31, 1962, Age 51

GODD, Barbara
Actress
b. Unknown
d. Unknown, Nov. 18, 1944

GODDARD, Charles W.
Playwright
b. Portland, ME, Nov. 26, 1879
d. Unknown, Jan. 11, 1951, Age 71

GODDEN, Jimmy
Actor
b. Maidstone, England, Aug. 11, 1879
d. Unknown, March 5, 1955, Age 75

GODFREY, G. W.
Playwright
b. Unknown
d. Unknown, April 10, 1897, Age 53

GODFREY, Renee Haal
Performer
b. Unknown
d. Unknown, May 2, 1964, Age 44

GODFREY, Thomas Jr.
Playwright
b. Unknown, 1736
d. Unknown, Aug. 3, 1763, Age about 27

GODWIN, Edward William
Designer, Architect
b. Unknown, 1833
d. Unknown, Oct. 6, 1886, Age 53

GOETHE, Johann Wolfgang von
Playwright, Poet, Novelist
b. Frankfort-am-Main, Germany, Aug. 28, 1749
d. Weimar, Germany, March 22, 1832, Age 82

GOETZ, Augustus
Playwright
b. Buffalo, NY, Unknown
d. New York, NY, Sept. 30, 1957, Age 56

GOETZ, E. Ray
Producer, Songwriter
b. Buffalo, England, June 12, 1886
d. Greenwich, CT, June 12, 1954, Age 68

GOETZL, Dr. Anselm
Composer
b. Bohemia, Unknown
d. Barcelona, Spain, Jan. 9, 1923, Age 44

GOFTON, E. Story
Actor
b. Unknown
d. Unknown, May 1, 1939, Age 92

GOGOL, Nikolai (Nicholas) Vassilievitch
Playwright, Novelist
b. Sorochintsky, Poltav, Russia, March 31, 1809
d. Unknown, Feb. 21, 1852, Age 42

GOLDBERG, Nathan
Actor, Producer
b. Austria, Unknown
d. Brooklyn, NY, Dec. 5, 1961, Age 74

GOLDEN, John
Producer, Playwright, Songwriter, Actor
b. New York, NY, June 27, 1874
d. Bayside, NY, June 17, 1955, Age 80

GOLDER, Jennie
Actress
b. Unknown
d. Unknown, July 11, 1928, Age 34

GOLDER, Lew
Producer
b. Unknown
d. Philadelphia, PA, Dec. 7, 1962, Age 78

GOLDFADEN, Abraham
Playwright, Producer, Teacher
b. Old Constantine (Volhynia), Russia, 1840
d. New York, NY, 1908

GOLDIE, F. Wyndham
Actor
b. Rochester, Kent, England, July 5, 1897
d. Unknown, Sept. 26, 1957, Age 60

GOLDMAN, Edwin Franko
Conductor, Composer
b. Louisville, KY, Jan. 1, 1878
d. New York, NY, Feb. 21, 1956, Age 78

GOLDNER, Charles
Actor, Producer
b. Vienna, Austria, Dec. 7, 1900
d. Unknown, April 15, 1955, Age 54

GOLDONI, Carlo
Playwright
b. Venice, Italy, 1707
d. Paris, France, Feb. 6, 1793, Age 86

GOLDSMITH, Oliver
Playwright, Poet
b. Pallas, Forney, Longford County, Ireland, Nov. 10, 1728
d. London, England, April 4, 1774, Age 45

GOLDSTEIN, Jennie
Actress
b. New York, NY, 1897
d. New York, NY, Feb. 9, 1960, Age 63

GOMEZ, Thomas
Actor
b. New York, NY, July 10, 1905
d. Santa Monica, CA, June 19, 1971, Age 65

GONCOURT, Edmond Louis Antoine Huot de
Novelist, Essayist, Playwright
b. Nancy, France, May 26, 1822
d. Champrosay, France, July 16, 1896, Age 74

GONCOURT, Jules Alfred Huot de
Novelist, Essayist, Playwright
b. Paris, France, Dec. 17, 1830
d. Paris, France, June 20, 1870, Age 39

GOOD, Kip
Actor, Production assistant
b. Unknown
d. Gadsden, AL, May 1, 1964

GOODALE, George P.
Drama critic
b. Unknown
d. Detroit, MI, May 7, 1920, Age 77

GOODALL, Charlotte
Actress
b. Unknown
d. Unknown, July 19, 1830

GOODALL, Edyth
Actress
b. Dundee, Scotland, Feb. 20, 1886
d. Unknown, July 22, 1929, Age 47

GOODMAN, Edward
Playwright, Producer, Director
b. New York, NY, Unknown
d. New York, NY, Oct. 2, 1962, Age 74

GOODMAN, Jules Eckert
Playwright, Journalist
b. Gervals, OR, Nov. 2, 1876
d. Peekskill, NY, July 10, 1962, Age 85

GOODMAN, Philip
Producer, Playwright
b. Philadelphia, PA, Unknown
d. New York, NY, July 20, 1940, Age 55

GOODRICH, Arthur F.
Playwright
b. New Britain, CT, Feb. 18, 1878
d. New York, NY, June 26, 1941, Age 63

GOODRICH, Louis (né Abbot-Anderson)
Actor
b. Sandhurst, England, Unknown
d. Unknown, Jan. 27, 1945, Age 72

GOODWIN, Nat C.
Actor
b. Boston, MA, July 25, 1857
d. New York, NY, Jan. 31, 1919, Age 61

GOOSSENS, Sir Eugene
Composer, Conductor
b. Unknown
d. Hillingdon, England, June 13, 1962, Age 69

GORCEY, Bernard
Actor
b. Unknown
d. Hollywood, CA, Sept. 12, 1955, Age 67

GORDIN, Jacob
Playwright
b. Ukraine, Russia, 1853
d. Unknown, June 11, 1909, Age 56

GORDON, Douglas
Actor, Producer
b. London, England, March 12, 1871
d. Unknown, Oct. 26, 1935, Age 64

GORDON, G. Swayne
Actor
b. Baltimore, MD, Unknown
d. New York, NY, June 23, 1949, Age 69

GORDON, Gavin
Actor, Singer, Composer
b. Ayr, Scotland, Nov. 24, 1901
d. London, England, Nov. 18, 1970, Age 68

GORDON, George Lash
Actor, Playwright
b. Unknown
d. Unknown, March 18, 1895

GORDON, Gloria
Actress
b. Unknown
d. Hollywood, CA, Nov. 23, 1962

GORDON, Huntley
Actor
b. Unknown
d. Hollywood, CA, Dec. 7, 1956, Age 69

GORDON, James M.
Actor, Director
b. Unknown
d. Unknown, Feb. 22, 1944, Age 86

GORDON, Leon
Writer, Actor, Film producer
b. Brighton, Sussex, England, Jan. 12, 1895
d. Hollywood, CA, Jan. 4, 1960, Age 64

GORDON, Mack (Morris Gittler)
Lyricist, Performer
b. Warsaw, Poland, Unknown
d. New York, NY, Feb. 28, 1959, Age 54

GORDON, Paul
Actor
b. Brooklyn, NY, Unknown
d. Florence, Italy, May 3, 1929, Age 43

GORDON, Vera
Actress
b. Russia, 1886
d. Beverly Hills, CA, May 8, 1948, Age 61

GORDON, Walter
Playwright, Actor
b. Unknown
d. Unknown, Jan. 20, 1892

GORDON-LENNOX, Cosmo
Playwright
b. Unknown, Aug. 17, 1869
d. Unknown, July 31, 1921, Age 51

GORE, Mrs. Catherine
Playwright
b. Unknown
d. Unknown, Jan. 29, 1861, Age 62

GORKI, Maxim (Alexi Maximovitch Pyeshkov)
Playwright, Novelist
b. Nizhni-Novgorod, Russia, March 28, 1868
d. Gorki, U.S.S.R., June 18, 1936, Age 68

GOSSE, Sir Edmund William
Biographer, Translator
b. London, England, Sept. 21, 1849
d. London, England, May 16, 1928, Age 79

GOSSMAN, Irving
Actor, Producer
b. Boston, MA, Unknown
d. West Palm Beach, FL, March 24, 1964, Age 63

GOSSON, Stephen
Playwright, Poet
b. Canterbury, England, 1554
d. Unknown, Feb. 13, 1642, Age 85

GOT, Edmond François Jules
Actor, Librettist
b. Unknown, 1822
d. Unknown, 1901, Age 79

GOTTESFELD, Chone
Playwright, Author
b. Russia, Unknown
d. New York, NY, Jan. 27, 1964, Age 73

GOTTLIEB, Arthur
Producer
b. Brooklyn, NY, Unknown
d. New York, NY, Dec. 24, 1962, Age 63

GOTTLIEB, David
Costumer
b. Unknown
d. New York, NY, May 21, 1962, Age 81

GOTTLOBER, Sigmund
Program publisher
b. Beltz, Rumania, Sept. 10, 1888
d. New York, NY, Aug. 14, 1967, Age 78

GOTTSCHALK, Ferdinand
Actor, Playwright
b. London, England, Feb. 28, 1858
d. London, England, Nov. 10, 1944, Age 86

GOTTSCHALL, Rudolf von
Playwright
b. Unknown
d. Unknown, March 28, 1909, Age 85

GOTTSCHED, Johann Christoph
Producer, Critic
b. . . . near Koenigsburg, Germany, 1700
d. Unknown, 1766

GOULD, Bernard (Sir Bernard Partridge)
Actor, Cartoonist, Painter
b. Unknown
d. Unknown, Aug. 9, 1945, Age 84

GOULD, Billy
Actor
b. Unknown
d. New York, NY, Feb. 1, 1950, Age 81

GOULD, Edith Kingdon
Actress
b. Unknown
d. New York, NY, Nov. 13, 1921, Age 60

GOULD, Fred
Playwright, Producer
b. Unknown
d. Unknown, Dec. 30, 1917, Age 76

GOULD, Harold
Performer
b. New York, NY, Unknown
d. New York, NY, July 17, 1952, Age 78

GOULD, Howard
Actor
b. St. Anthony, MN, Unknown
d. Wintrhop, MA, Feb. 3, 1938, Age 74

GOULDING, Edmund
Actor, Author, Composer
b. London, England, March 20, 1891
d. Los Angeles, CA, Dec. 24, 1959, Age 68

GOUNOD, Charles François
Composer
b. Paris, France, June 17, 1818
d. St. Cloud, France, Oct. 18, 1893, Age 75

GOW, James
Playwright
b. Creston, IA, Aug. 23, 1907
d. New York, NY, Feb. 11, 1952, Age 44

GOWARD, Annie (Mrs. Charles Fawcett)
Actress
b. Unknown
d. Unknown, March 21, 1907, Age 48

GOWARD, Mary Ann (Mrs. Robert Keeley)
Actress, Producer
b. Unknown, 1806
d. Unknown, 1899

GOZZI, Count Carlo
Playwright
b. Venice, Italy, 1720
d. Unknown, 1806

GRABBE, Christian Dietrich
Actor, Poet, Playwright
b. Unknown, 1801
d. Unknown, Sept. 12, 1836, Age 35

GRACE, Amy
Actress
b. Unknown
d. Unknown, Aug. 11, 1945, Age 73

GRAFFENRIED-VILLARS, Baron Emmanuel de
Playwright
b. Unknown
d. Bern, Switzerland, June 14, 1964, Age 69

GRAHAM, Ernest
Actor
b. Unknown
d. Unknown, Feb. 7, 1945, Age 67

GRAHAM, George
Actor
b. Dorchester, England, Unknown
d. Chicago, IL, Nov. 16, 1939, Age 64

GRAHAM, Harry Joscelyn Clive
Playwright, Lyricist
b. London, England, Dec. 23, 1874
d. Unknown, Oct. 30, 1936, Age 61

GRAHAM, J. F.
Actor, Producer
b. Unknown, 1850
d. Unknown, Nov. 27, 1932, Age 82

GRAHAM, Morland
Actor
b. Partick, Glasgow, Scotland, Aug. 8, 1891
d. Unknown, April 8, 1949, Age 57

GRAHAM, Ronald
Actor
b. Scotland, Unknown
d. New York, NY, July 4, 1950, Age 38

GRAHAM, Virginia (Mrs. Beatrice Graham Van Breems)
Actress
b. Unknown
d. New York, NY, July 24, 1964, Age 45

GRAINGER, Percy
Composer, Musician
b. Australia, Unknown
d. White Plains, NY, Feb. 20, 1961, Age 78

GRANACH, Alexander
Actor
b. Ukraine, 1879
d. New York, NY, March 1945, Age 65

GRANBY, Cornelius W.
Actor, Producer
b. Unknown
d. Unknown, Sept. 4, 1886, Age 82

GRAND, Georges
Actor
b. Unknown
d. Unknown, March 31, 1921, Age 60

GRANDIN, Elmer
Actor
b. Unknown
d. Patchogue, NY, May 19, 1933, Age 72

GRANDJEAN, Louise
Actress
b. Unknown
d. Unknown, May 21, 1934, Age 64

GRANDVAL, Charles François Racot de
Actor
b. Unknown, 1711
d. Unknown, 1784, Age 73

GRANIER, Jeanne
Actress
b. Unknown
d. Unknown, Dec. 19, 1939, Age 88

GRANLUND, Nils Thor "N. T. G."
Producer
b. Unknown, Lapland, Sweden
d. 1882, Las Vagas, NV, Age April 21, 1957

GRANOVSKY, Alexander (Abraham Azarch)
Actor, Producer, Director
b. Moscow, Russia, 1890
d. Paris, France, March 11, 1937, Age 47

GRANT, Barney (John Leo Younger)
Performer
b. Unknown
d. Sydney, Australia, Jan. 24, 1962, Age 50

GRANT, Maxwell
Sketch writer
b. Unknown
d. New York, NY, Aug. 5, 1961, Age 39

GRANT, Sydney
Actor
b. Unknown
d. Santa Monica, CA, July 12, 1953, Age 80

GRANT, W. F.
Actor
b. Unknown
d. Unknown, Jan. 5, 1923

GRANVILLE, Bernard
Actor
b. Chicago, IL, July 4, 1886
d. Hollywood, CA, Oct. 5, 1936, Age 50

GRANVILLE, George (Viscount Lansdowne)
Playwright
b. Unknown
d. Unknown, Jan. 30, 1735, Age 68

GRANVILLE, Sydney
Performer
b. Bolton, Lancashire, England, Unknown
d. Stockport, England, Dec. 27, 1959, Age 79

GRANVILLE-BARKER, Harley
Actor-Manager, Playwright
b. London, England, Nov. 25, 1877
d. Paris, France, Aug. 31, 1946, Age 68

GRANVILLE-BARKER, Helen (née Gates)
Playwright, Novelist, Poet
b. Unknown
d. Paris, France, Feb. 16, 1950

GRAPEWIN, Charles
Actor
b. Xenia, OH, Dec. 20, 1869
d. Corona, CA, Feb. 2, 1956, Age 86

GRASSO, Giovanni
Actor
b. Sicily, 1875
d. Unknown, 1930

GRATTAN, H. Plunkett
Playwright, Actor
b. Unknown
d. Unknown, Dec. 25, 1889, Age 81

GRATTAN, Lawrence
Actor, Playwright
b. Concord, NH, Unknown
d. New York, NY, Dec. 9, 1941, Age 71

GRATTON, Harry
Actor, Playwright
b. London, England, April 25, 1867
d. Unknown, Sept. 25, 1951, Age 84

GRAU, Maurice
Producer
b. Unknown, 1851
d. Unknown, March 13, 1907, Age 58

GRAU, Maurice
Talent representative
b. Natick, MA, Oct. 21, 1857
d. Bronx, NY, March 10, 1934, Age 76

GRAU, Robert
Theatrical writer, Author, Producer
b. Unknown
d. Unknown, Aug. 9, 1916

GRAUMAN, Sid (Sidney Patrick Grauman)
Theatre executive
b. Indianapolis, IN, March 17, 1879
d. Hollywood, CA, March 5, 1950, Age 71

GRAVES, Clo (Richard Dehan)
Playwright, Novelist
b. Unknown
d. Unknown, Dec. 3, 1932, Age 70

GRAVES, George
Actor
b. London, England, Jan. 1, 1876
d. London, England, April 2, 1949, Age 73

GRAVES, Laura
Actress
b. Unknown
d. Unknown, March 20, 1925, Age 55

GRAY, Gilda (Mary or Marianna Michalski)
Singer, Dancer
b. Poland, Unknown
d. Hollywood, CA, Dec. 22, 1959, Age about 60

GRAY, Ida M.
Actress
b. Unknown
d. Unknown, Nov. 16, 1942, Age 84

GRAY, Leonard
Performer
b. Unknown
d. Newport Beach, CA, March 28, 1964, Age 50

GRAY, Thomas
Song writer
b. New York, NY, Unknown
d. New York, NY, Nov. 30, 1924, Age 36

GRAY, William (John W. Kolb)
Actor, Playwright
b. Unknown
d. New York, NY, Feb. 16, 1943, Age 83

GRAYSON, Bette (Mrs. Clifford Odets née Lipper)
Actress
b. Unknown
d. New York, NY, Feb. 22, 1954, Age 32

GREATHEED, Bertie
Playwright
b. Unknown
d. Unknown, Jan. 16, 1826, Age 66

GREAZA, Walter
Actor
b. St. Paul, MN, Jan. 1, 1897
d. New York, NY, June 1, 1973, Age 76

GREEN, Abel
Editor, Writer
b. New York, NY, June 3, 1900
d. New York, NY, May 10, 1973, Age 72

GREEN, Dennis
Actor, Playwright
b. Unknown
d. Unknown, Nov. 10, 1954, Age 50

GREEN, Dorothy (Mrs. Alfred A. Harris)
Actress
b. Herts, England, June 30, 1886
d. London, England, Jan. 14, 1961, Age 74

GREEN, Dorothy (Mrs. Norman November)
Actress
b. Unknown
d. New York, NY, Nov. 16, 1963, Age 71

GREEN, Dr. Carelton
Educator, Teacher
b. Unknown
d. Stratford-on-Avon, England, Aug. 3, 1962, Age 52

GREEN, Isadore
Journalist
b. Unknown
d. London, England, Jan. 25, 1963, Age 59

GREEN, James Burton
Songwriter, Pianist
b. Unknown
d. Mt. Vernon, NY, Nov. 17, 1922, Age 48

GREEN, Marion
Actor
b. Janesville, IA, March 8, 1890
d. Rye, NY, March 17, 1956, Age 66

GREEN, Martyn
Actor, Singer
b. London, England, Apr. 22, 1899
d. New York, NY, Feb. 8, 1975, Age 75

GREEN, Mitzi
Actress
b. Bronx, NY, Oct. 22, 1920
d. Huntington Beach, CA, May 24, 1969, Age 48

GREEN, Morris
Producer
b. Unknown
d. Washington, DC, May 22, 1963, Age 73

GREEN, Richard
Actor
b. Unknown
d. Unknown, Jan. 16, 1914, Age 49

GREENBANK, Henry H. (Harry)
Playwright, Librettist, Lyricist
b. Unknown
d. Unknown, Feb. 26, 1899, Age 33

GREENBANK, Percy
Librettist, Lyricist
b. London, England, Jan. 24, 1878
d. Rickmansworth, England, Dec. 8, 1968, Age 90

GREENE, Clay M.
Actor, Playwright
b. San Francisco, CA, Unknown
d. San Francisco, CA, Sept. 5, 1933, Age 83

GREENE, Eric (Edith Elizabeth Greene)
Actress
b. Portsmouth, England, Jan. 14, 1876
d. Unknown, Sept. 11, 1917, Age 41

GREENE, Norman
Actor
b. Unknown
d. Unknown, July 1945, Age 66

GREENE, Patterson
Critic, Playwright
b. Unknown, Sept. 20, 1899
d. Los Angeles, CA, Jan. 27, 1968, Age 69

GREENE, Robert
Playwright
b. Norwich, England, 1558
d. Unknown, Sept. 3, 1592, Age 33

GREENE, Walter
Journalist
b. Unknown
d. Hollywood, CA, March 24, 1963, Age 69

GREENER, Dorothy
Actress
b. Gateshead, England, Oct. 16, 1917
d. New York, NY, Dec. 6, 1971, Age 54

GREENLEAF, (Roger) Raymond
Actor
b. Gloucester, MA, Nov. 27, 1892
d. Woodland Hills, CA, Oct. 29, 1963, Age 70

GREENSTREET, Sydney Hughes
Actor
b. Sandwich, Kent, England, Dec. 27, 1879
d. Hollywood, CA, Jan. 18, 1954, Age 74

GREENWALD, Joseph
Actor
b. New York, NY, Unknown
d. Santa Barbara, CA, April 1, 1938, Age 60

GREET, Clare
Actress
b. Unknown, June 14, 1871
d. Unknown, Feb. 14, 1939, Age 67

GREET, Maurice
Actor
b. England, Unknown
d. Washington, DC, May 29, 1951, Age 70

GREET, Mildred C.
Actress, Teacher
b. Unknown
d. Washington, DC, June 25, 1964, Age 64

GREET, Sir Philip (Ben)
Actor-Manager
b. London, England, Sept. 24, 1857
d. London , England, May 17, 1936, Age 78

GREGG, Everley
Actress
b. Bishop Stoke, Hantshire, England, Oct. 26, 1903
d. Unknown, June 8, 1959, Age 55

GREGOR, Nora
Actress
b. Unknown
d. Unknown, Jan. 20, 1949

GREGORY, Dora
Actress
b. Dulwich, England, Sept. 2, 1872
d. Unknown, March 5, 1954, Age 81

GREGORY, Lady Augusta (née Persse)
Playwright, Director
b. Roxborough, Galway, Ireland, March 1852
d. Galway, Ireland, May 23, 1932, Age 80

GREIN, Jacob Thomas
Critic, Producer, etc.
b. Amsterdam, Holland, Oct. 11, 1862
d. London, England, June 23, 1935, Age 72

GREIVE, Thomas
Scenic artist
b. Unknown, 1799
d. Unknown, April 16, 1882, Age 82

GREIVE, William
Scenic artist
b. Unknown, 1800
d. Unknown, Nov. 12, 1844, Age 44

GRENEKER, Claude P.
Press representative
b. Newberry, SC, Unknown
d. New York, NY, April 7, 1949, Age 68

GRENET-DANCOURT, E.
Playwright
b. Unknown
d. Unknown, Feb. 1913, Age 54

GRESHAM, Herbert
Actor, Director
b. London, England, Unknown
d. Mount Vernon, Feb. 23, 1921, Age 68

GREW, Mary
Actress
b. London, England, Aug. 21, 1902
d. England, March 20, 1971, Age 68

GREY, Clifford (née Davis)
Librettist, Lyricist
b. Birmingham, England, Jan. 5, 1887
d. Unknown, Sept. 26, 1941, Age 54

GREY, Frank Herbert
Composer, Conductor
b. Unknown
d. Unknown, Oct. 3, 1951, Age 67

GREY, Jane (Mary E. Tyrrell)
Actress
b. Middlebury, VT, May 22, 1883
d. New York, NY, Nov. 9, 1944, Age 61

GREY, Katherine
Actress
b. San Francisco, CA, Dec. 27, 1873
d. Orleans, MA, March 21, 1950, Age 76

GREY, Lytton
Actor
b. Unknown
d. Unknown, Jan. 9, 1931, Age 80

GREY, Marie de
Actress, Producer
b. Unknown
d. Unknown, Oct. 21, 1897

GREY, Marion
Actress
b. Unknown
d. Unknown, May 26, 1949, Age 74

GREY, Sylvia
Performer
b. Unknown
d. Unknown, May 6, 1958, Age 92

GRIBBON, Harry
Actor
b. New York, NY, Unknown
d. Woodland Hills, CA, July 28, 1961, Age 75

GRIBOYEDOV, Alexander Sergeivich
Playwright, Diplomat
b. Russia, 1795
d. Unknown, 1829

GRIEG, Edvard Hagerup
Composer
b. Bergen, Norway, June 15, 1843
d. Bergen, Norway, Sept. 4, 1907, Age 64

GRIEG, Nordahl
Playwright
b. Unknown, 1902
d. Unknown, 1943, Age 41

GRIEVE, John Henderson
Scenic artist
b. Unknown, 1770
d. Unknown, 1845, Age 75

GRIFFEN, Benjamin
Actor, Playwright
b. Unknown
d. Unknown, Feb. 18, 1740, Age 60

GRIFFIN, Arthur
Actor
b. Boston, MA, Unknown
d. Fall River, MA, Feb. 6, 1953, Age 75

GRIFFIN, Gerald
Playwright
b. Unknown
d. Unknown, June 12, 1840, Age 36

GRIFFIN, Gerald
Actor, Singer, Songwriter
b. Chicago, IL, Unknown
d. Rhinebeck, NY, Jan. 11, 1962, Age 70

GRIFFITH, Hubert
Critic, Writer
b. London, England, Oct. 4, 1896
d. Unknown, March 2, 1953, Age 56

GRIFFITH, Linda
Actress
b. Unknown
d. New York, NY, July 26, 1949, Age 65

GRIFFITH, Lydia Eliza (Mrs. James Seymour)
Actress
b. Unknown, 1832
d. Unknown, 1897

GRIFFITH, Raymond
Actor, Producer
b. Unknown
d. Hollywood, CA, Nov. 25, 1957, Age 70

GRIFFITH, Robert E.
Producer, Stage manager, Actor
b. Metheun, MA, Unknown
d. Port Chester, NY, June 7, 1961, Age 54

GRILLPARZER, Franz
Playwright
b. Vienna, Austria, 1791
d. Unknown, Jan. 10, 1872, Age 80

GRIMALDI, George H.
Playwright
b. Unknown
d. Unknown, April 12, 1951, Age 58

GRIMANI, Julia (Mrs. Charles Wayne Young)
Actress
b. Unknown
d. Unknown, July 17, 1806, Age 21

GRIMWOOD, Herbert
Actor
b. Walthamstow, England, March 7, 1875
d. Unknown, Dec. 1, 1929, Age 54

GRINGORE, Pierre (Gringoire)
Playwright, Poet
b. Unknown, 1480
d. Unknown, 1539

GRISI, Carlotta
Dancer
b. Unknown, 1819
d. Unknown, June 5, 1899, Age 79

GRISIER, Georges
Playwright
b. Unknown
d. Unknown, June 5, 1909, Age 56

GRISMER, Joseph Rhode
Actor, Playwright, Producer
b. Albany, NY, Nov. 4, 1849
d. New York, NY, March 5, 1922, Age 72

GRISWOLD, Grace (née Hall)
Actress, Playwright
b. Ashtabula, OH, Unknown
d. Unknown, June 13, 1927, Age 55

GROENVELD, Ben
Actor
b. Unknown
d. Amsterdam, Netherlands, Feb. 14, 1962, Age 63

GROODY, Louise
Actress
b. Waco, TX, March 26, 1897
d. Unknown, Sept. 16, 1961, Age 64

GROPPER, Milton Herbert
Playwright
b. New York, NY, Dec. 26, 1896
d. New York, NY, Oct. 27, 1955, Age 58

GROS-GUILLAUME, (Robert Guérin)
Actor, Farceur
b. Unknown, 1600
d. Unknown, 1634

GROSSMITH, Ena
Actress
b. London, England, Aug. 14, 1896
d. Unknown, March 20, 1944, Age 47

GROSSMITH, George
Actor, Composer, Author, Entertainer
b. Unknown, Dec. 9, 1847
d. Unknown, March 1, 1912, Age 64

GROSSMITH, George (the Younger)
Comedian, Author, Producer
b. London, England, May 11, 1874
d. London, England, June 6, 1935, Age 61

GROSSMITH, Lawrence
Actor
b. London, England, March 29, 1877
d. Hollywood, CA, Feb. 21, 1944, Age 66

GROSSMITH, Walter Weedon
Actor, Playwright, Painter
b. London, England, 1852
d. Unknown, June 14, 1919, Age 67

GROVE, F. C.
Playwright
b. Unknown
d. Unknown, Aug. 16, 1902

GROVE, Fred (née Palmer)
Actor
b. London, England, Nov. 25, 1851
d. Unknown, Jan. 31, 1927, Age 75

GROVER, Leonard
Playwright
b. Unknown
d. Brooklyn, NY, March 7, 1926, Age 92

GROVES, Charles
Actor
b. Unknown
d. Unknown, July 8, 1909, Age 65

GROVES, Charles
Actor
b. Manchester, England, Nov. 22, 1875
d. Unknown, May 23, 1955, Age 79

GROVES, Fred
Actor
b. London, England, Aug. 8, 1880
d. Unknown, June 4, 1955, Age 74

GRUBE, Max
Actor, Playwright
b. Unknown
d. Unknown, Dec. 27, 1934, Age 80

GRUENBERG, Louis
Composer
b. Brest-Litovsk, Poland, Aug. 3, 1884
d. Los Angeles, CA, June 9, 1964, Age 79

GRUNDGENS, Gustaf
Actor, Director
b. Düsseldorf, Germany, Unknown
d. Manila, Philippines, Oct. 7, 1963, Age 63

GRUNDY, Sydney
Playwright
b. Manchester, England, March 23, 1848
d. Unknown, July 4, 1914, Age 66

GRUNWALD, Alfred
Librettist
b. Vienna, Austria, Unknown
d. New York, NY, Feb. 24, 1951, Age 67

GRUVER, Elbert A.
Stage Manager
b. Unknown
d. New York, NY, Nov. 11, 1962, Age 57

GUARD, Kit
Actor
b. Unknown
d. Woodland Hills, CA, July 18, 1961, Age 67

GUARD, William J.
Press representative
b. Limerick, Ireland, Unknown
d. New York, NY, March 3, 1932, Age 70

GUERRERO, Maria
Actress
b. Unknown, 1868
d. Unknown, Jan. 23, 1928, Age 59

GUILBERT, Yvette
Singer, Actress, Teacher
b. Paris, France, 1865
d. Aix-en-Provence, France, Feb. 2, 1944, Age 79

GUILFOYLE, Paul
Actor, Director
b. Jersey City, NJ, Unknown
d. Hollywood, CA, June 27, 1961, Age 58

GUIMARD, La (Madeleine)
Dancer
b. Unknown, 1743
d. Unknown, May 4, 1816, Age 73

GUIMERA, Angel
Playwright
b. Santa Cruz de Tenerife, Canary Islands, Spain, May 6, 1845
d. Barcelona, Spain, July 18, 1924, Age 79

GUINAN, Texas (Mary Louise Cecelia)
Actress, Entertainer
b. Waco, TX, Unknown
d. Vancouver, B.C., CAN, Nov. 5, 1933

GUIOL, Fred
Screenwriter, Director
b. Unknown
d. Bishop, CA, May 23, 1964, Age 66

GUITRY, Jean
Actor
b. Unknown
d. Unknown, Sept. 12, 1920, Age 38

GUITRY, Lucien
Actor, Playwright, Producer
b. Paris, France, 1860
d. Paris, France, June 1, 1925, Age 65

GUITRY, Sacha
Actor, Playwright
b. St. Petersburg, Russia, Feb. 21, 1885
d. Paris, France, July 24, 1957, Age 72

GULLAN, Campbell
Actor, Director
b. Glasgow, Scotland, Unknown
d. Unknown, Dec. 1, 1939

GUMM, Suzanne (Mrs. Jack Cathcart née Mary Jane Gumm)
Performer
b. Unknown
d. Las Vegas, NV, May 26, 1964, Age 48

GUNNING, Louise
Actress
b. Unknown
d. Sierra Madre, CA, July 24, 1960, Age 82

GUNTER, A. C.
Playwright, Novelist
b. Unknown
d. Unknown, Feb. 24, 1907, Age 59

GURNEY, Claud
Director
b. Westmoors, Dorset, England, April 26, 1897
d. Unknown, May 21, 1946, Age 49

GURNEY, Edmund
Actor
b. Unknown
d. New York, NY, Jan. 14, 1925, Age 73

GUSYEV, Victor Mikhailovich
Playwright
b. Unknown, 1908
d. Unknown, 1944

GUTERSON, Vladimar (Wally)
Orchestra conductor
b. Unknown
d. Hollywood, CA, March 28, 1964

GUTHRIE, Tyrone Sir
Director, Actor
b. Tunbridge Wells, England, July 2, 1900
d. Dublin, Ireland, May 15, 1971, Age 70

GUTZKOW, Karl Ferdinand
Playwright, Author
b. Unknown, 1811
d. Unknown, 1878

GWENN, Edmund
Actor
b. London, England, Sept. 26, 1875
d. Woodland Hills, CA, Sept. 6, 1959, Age 83

GWINNETT, Richard
Playwright
b. Unknown
d. Unknown, April 16, 1717

GWYN, Nell (Eleanor)
Actress
b. England, 1650
d. London, England, Nov. 13, 1687, Age 37

GWYNNE, Julia (Mrs. George Edwards)
Actress
b. Unknown
d. Unknown, July 10, 1934, Age 78

GWYTHER, Geoffrey Matheson
Actor, Composer
b. Unknown, 1890
d. Bryn Mawr, PA, July 27, 1944, Age 54

H

HAAS, Hugo
Actor, Director, Producer
b. Czechoslovakia, Feb. 19, 1902
d. Vienna, Austria, Unknown, Age 67

HAAS, Robert M.
Art director
b. Unknown
d. Costa Mesa, Ca, Dec. 17, 1962, Age 73

HAASE, Friedrich
Actor
b. Unknown
d. Unknown, March 17, 1911, Age 83

HABINGTON, William
Playwright
b. Unknown
d. Unknown, Nov. 30, 1654, Age 49

HACKER, Maria (Mrs. Lauritz Melchoir)
Actress
b. Unknown
d. Sherman Oaks, CA, Feb. 20, 1963

HACKETT, Charles
Singer
b. Worcester, MA, Unknown
d. Jamaica, NY, Jan. 1, 1942, Age 52

HACKETT, Florence
Actress
b. Unknown
d. New York, NY, Aug. 21, 1954, Age 72

HACKETT, James Henry
Actor
b. Unknown, 1800
d. Unknown, Dec. 28, 1871, Age 71

HACKETT, James Keteltas
Actor, Producer
b. Wolf Island, Ontario, CAN, Sept. 8, 1869
d. Paris, France, Nov. 8, 1926, Age 57

HACKETT, Mrs. J. H.
Actress
b. Unknown
d. Unknown, Oct. 27, 1909, Age 74

HACKETT, Mrs. J. H. (Catherine Lee Sugg)
Actress
b. Unknown, 1797
d. Unknown, Dec. 9, 1845, Age 48

HACKETT, Raymond
Actor
b. New York, NY, July 15, 1902
d. Los Angeles, CA, July 7, 1958, Age 55

HACKETT, Walter
Playwright, Producer, Director
b. Oakland, CA, Nov. 10, 1876
d. New York, NY, Jan. 20, 1944, Age 67

HACKNEY, Mabel (Mrs. Laurence Irving)
Actress
b. Unknown
d. Unknown, May 29, 1914

HADDON, Archibald
Press representative, Critic, Playwright
b. Ironbridge, England, Dec. 2, 1871
d. Unknown, Oct. 15, 1942, Age 70

HADDON, Peter (Peter Tildsley)
Actor, Author, Theatre manager
b. Rawtenstall, Lancashire, England, Mar. 31, 1898
d. London, England, Sept. 7, 1962, Age 64

HADING, Jane (Jeanette Hadingue)
Actress
b. France, March 25, 1859
d. Nice, France, Dec. 31, 1933, Age 74

HADING, Jane (Jeanne Alfredine Trefouret)
Actress
b. Unknown
d. Neuilly, France, Feb. 18, 1941, Age 81

HAGAN, James B.
Actor, Playwright, Manager
b. Dan Diego, CA, Unknown
d. Cincinnati, OH, Sept. 1, 1947, Age 65

HAGGARD, Stephen
Actor
b. Guatemala City, Guatemala, March 21, 1911
d. Unknown, Feb. 1943, Age 31

HAGGIN, James Ben Ali
Designer
b. New York, NY, 1882
d. New York, NY, Sept. 2, 1951, Age 69

HAGGOTT, John Cecil
Producer, Director
b. Denver, CO, Unknown
d. Saugatuck, CT, Aug. 20, 1964, Age 50

HAIG, Emma
Actress
b. Unknown
d. Unknown, June 9, 1939, Age 41

HAINES, Herbert E.
Composer, Conductor
b. Manchester, England, 1880
d. Unknown, April 21, 1923, Age 43

HAINES, J. Talbot
Playwright
b. Unknown
d. Unknown, May 18, 1843, Age 45

HAINES, Rhea (Mrs. Rhea Haines Case)
Actress
b. Unknown
d. Hollywood, CA, March 12, 1964, Age 69

HAINES, Robert Terrel
Actor, Playwright, Director
b. Muncie, IN, Feb. 3, 1870
d. New York, NY, May 6, 1943, Age 73

HALBE, Max
Playwright
b. Güttland, Danzig, East Prussia, Oct. 4, 1865
d. near Neuotting, Upper Bavaria, Germany, Nov. 30, 1944, Age 79

HALE, Alan
Actor
b. Washington, DC, 1892
d. Hollywood, CA, Jan. 22, 1950, Age 57

HALE, Dorothy
Actress
b. Pittsburgh, PA, Unknown
d. New York, NY, Oct. 21, 1938, Age 33

HALE, Edward Everett III
Actor
b. Hewlitt, NY, Unknown
d. New York, NY, March 19, 1953, Age 46

HALE, George
Dance director
b. New York, NY, Unknown
d. New York, NY, Aug. 15, 1956, Age 54

HALE, J. Robert (né Hale-Munro)
Actor
b. Newton Abbott, Devon, England, March 25, 1874
d. Maidenhead, Berkshire, England, April 18, 1940, Age 66

HALE, John
Performer, Theatrical manager
b. Unknown
d. Englewood, NJ, May 4, 1947, Age 88

HALE, Louise Closser
Actress, Playwright
b. Chicago, IL, Oct. 13, 1872
d. Los Angeles, CA, July 26, 1933, Age 60

HALE, Philip
Author, Playwright
b. Norwich, VT, Unknown
d. Boston, MA, Nov. 30, 1934, Age 80

HALE, Ruth
Critic, Press representative
b. Rogersville, TN, Unknown
d. New York, NY, Sept. 18, 1934, Age 48

HALE, Sonnie (John Robert Hale-Munro)
Actor, Playwright, Director
b. London, England, May 1, 1902
d. London, England, June 9, 1959, Age 57

HALES, Thomas
Playwright
b. Gloucestershire, England, c1740
d. Unknown, Dec. 27, 1780, Age 40

HALEVY, Léon
Playwright
b. Unknown
d. Unknown, Sept. 10, 1883, Age 80

HALEVY, Ludovic
Playwright
b. Paris, France, 1834
d. Paris, France, May 8, 1908, Age 74

HALL, Alexander
Director
b. Boston, MA, 1894
d. San Francisco, CA, July 30, 1968, Age 74

HALL, Anmer (Alderson Burrell Horne)
Director, Producer, Actor
b. London, England, Nov. 22, 1863
d. Unknown, Dec. 22, 1953, Age 90

HALL, Dorothy
Actress
b. Bradford, PA, Unknown
d. New York, NY, Feb. 3, 1953, Age 47

HALL, James
Actor
b. Dallas, TX, Oct. 22, 1900
d. Jersey City, NJ, June 7, 1940, Age 39

HALL, Josephine
Actress
b. East Greenwich, RI, Unknown
d. Apponaug, RI, Dec. 1920

HALL, Juanita
Actress, Singer
b. Keyport, NY, Nov. 6, 1901
d. Bayshore, NY, Feb. 28, 1968, Age 66

HALL, Mrs. S. C.
Playwright
b. Unknown
d. Unknown, Jan. 30, 1881, Age 81

HALL, Owen (James Davis)
Librettist, Lyricist, Playwright
b. Dublin, Ireland, 1853
d. Harrowgate, England, April 10, 1907, Age 53

HALL, Pauline
Performer
b. Cincinnati, OH, Feb. 26, 1860
d. Yonkers, NY, Dec. 29, 1919, Age 59

HALL, Porter
Actor
b. Unknown
d. Los Angeles, CA, Oct. 6, 1953, Age 65

HALL, Thurston
Performer
b. Boston, MA, May 1882
d. Beverly Hills, CA, Feb. 20, 1958, Age 75

HALLAM, Adam
Actor
b. Unknown
d. Unknown, 1738

HALLAM, Ann
Actress
b. Unknown
d. Unknown, June 5, 1740

HALLAM, Basil
Actor
b. London, England, April 3, 1889
d. Unknown, Aug. 20, 1916, Age 27

HALLAM, Lewis
Manager
b. Unknown, 1714
d. Jamaica, British West Indies, 1756, Age 42

HALLAM, Lewis Jr.
Actor-Manager
b. Unknown, 1740
d. Unknown, Nov. 1, 1808, Age 68

HALLAM, Mrs. Lewis
Actress
b. Unknown
d. Unknown, 1773

HALLAM, Nancy
Actress
b. Unknown, 1759
d. Unknown, 1761

HALLAM, Sarah
Actress, fl. 1770-1775

HALLAM, Thomas
Actor
b. Unknown
d. Unknown, May 11, 1735

HALLAM, William
Actor-Manager
b. Unknown
d. Unknown, 1758, Age 46

HALLARD, Charles Maitland
Actor
b. Edinburgh, Scotland, Oct. 26, 1865
d. Unknown, March 21, 1942, Age 76

HALLATT, Henry
Actor
b. Whitehaven, England, Feb. 1, 1888
d. Unknown, July 24, 1952, Age 64

HALLATT, W. H.
Actor, Producer
b. Unknown
d. Unknown, Nov. 9, 1927, Age 80

HALL-CAINE, Lily
Actress
b. Unknown
d. Unknown, June 1, 1914

HALLIDAY, Andrew
Playwright
b. Unknown
d. Unknown, April 10, 1877, Age 46

HALLIDAY, John
Actor
b. Brooklyn, NY, Sept. 14, 1880
d. Honolulu, HI, Oct. 17, 1947, Age 67

HALLIDAY, Lena
Actress
b. Unknown
d. Unknown, Dec. 19, 1937

HALLIDAY, Richard
Producer
b. Denver, CO, April 3, 1905
d. Brasilia, Brazil, March 3, 1973, Age 67

HALLIWELL-PHILLIPS, James Orchard
Historian, Author
b. Unknown
d. Unknown, Dec. 3, 1888, Age 68

HALPERIN, Nan
Performer
b. Unknown
d. Long Island, NY, May 30, 1963, Age 65

HAMBLETON, Anne B. C.
Education Dept. Phoenix Theatre
b. Unknown
d. Unknown, March 18, 1962, Age 24

HAMBLIN, Mrs. T. S.
Actress
b. Unknown
d. Unknown, May 8, 1849

HAMBLIN, Mrs. T. S. (Mary Shaw)
Actress
b. Unknown
d. Unknown, July 4, 1873, Age 56

HAMBLIN, Thomas Sowerby
Actor, Manager
b. London, England, 1800
d. Unknown, Jan. 8, 1853, Age 52

HAMELIN, Clement
Actor
b. Unknown
d. Unknown, July 4, 1957

HAMER, Robert
Director
b. Unknown
d. London, England, Dec. 4, 1963, Age 52

HAMILTON, Cicely (née Cicely Mary Hammill)
Playwright, Actress, Writer
b. Unknown, 1872
d. Unknown, Dec. 6, 1952, Age 80

HAMILTON, Clayton
Playwright, Critic
b. Brooklyn, NY, Nov. 14, 1881
d. New York, NY, Sept. 17, 1946, Age 64

HAMILTON, Cosmo (né Gibbs)
Playwright, Novelist
b. Unknown, 1879
d. Shanley Green, Surrey, England, Oct. 14, 1942, Age 63

HAMILTON, Diana
Actress, Playwright
b. London, England, July 15, 1898
d. Unknown, Oct. 3, 1951, Age 53

HAMILTON, Hale (Hale Rice Hamilton)
Actor
b. Topeka, KS, Feb. 28, 1880
d. Hollywood, CA, May 19, 1942, Age 62

HAMILTON, Henry
Playwright, Actor
b. Nunhead, Surrey, England, Unknown
d. Unknown, Sept. 4, 1918, Age 65

HAMILTON, John F.
Actor
b. New York, NY, Nov. 7, 1893
d. Paramus, NJ, July 11, 1967, Age 73

HAMILTON, Mahlon
Actor
b. Unknown
d. Woodland Hills, CA, June 20, 1960, Age 77

HAMILTON, Patrick
Playwright
b. London, England, 1904
d. Sheringham, England, Sept. 24, 1962, Age 58

HAMLEY-CLIFFORD, Molly
Actress
b. Unknown
d. Unknown, June 7, 1956

HAMLIN, George
Director, Producer, Educator
b. Chicago, IL, July 25, 1920
d. Canandaigua, NY, June 17, 1964, Age 43

HAMMER, Will
Impresario
b. Unknown
d. Guildford, England, June 1, 1957, Age 69

HAMMERSTEIN, Arthur
Producer
b. New York, NY, 1873
d. Palm Beach, FL, Oct. 12, 1955, Age 82

HAMMERSTEIN, Elaine Allison (Mrs. James Walter Kays)
Performer
b. Unknown, 1898
d. Tiajuana, Mexico, Aug. 13, 1948, Age 50

HAMMERSTEIN, Oscar
Impresario
b. Berlin, Germany, May 8, 1847
d. New York, NY, Aug. 1, 1919, Age 72

HAMMERSTEIN, Oscar II
Lyricist, Librettist, Producer
b. New York, NY, July 12, 1895
d. Doylestown, PA, Aug. 23, 1960, Age 65

HAMMOND, Aubrey
Costume and Scenic designer
b. Folkestone, England, Sept. 18, 1893
d. Unknown, March 19, 1940, Age 46

HAMMOND, Dorothy (Lady Standing)
Actress
b. London, England, Unknown
d. Unknown, Nov. 23, 1950, Age 76

HAMMOND, Percy
Drama critic
b. Cadiz, OH, March 7, 1873
d. New York, NY, April 25, 1936, Age 63

HAMMOND, Virginia
Actress
b. Scranton, PA, Unknown
d. Washington, DC, April 6, 1972, Age 78

HAMPDEN, Walter (Walter Hampden Dougherty)
Actor-Manager
b. Brooklyn, NY, June 30, 1879
d. Hollywood, CA, June 11, 1955, Age 75

HAMPTON, Louise
Actress
b. Stockport, England, Unknown
d. Unknown, Feb. 10, 1954, Age 73

HAMPTON, Mary
Actress
b. Kentucky, Unknown
d. New York, NY, Feb. 1, 1931, Age 63

HAMPTON, Myra
Actress
b. Unknown
d. Unknown, July 19, 1945, Age 44

HAMSUN, Knut
Poet, Playwright
b. Lom, Grudrandsdal, Norway, Aug. 4, 1859
d. near Grimstad, Norway, Feb. 19, 1952, Age 92

HAMUND, St. John
Actor
b. Unknown
d. Unknown, April 25, 1929, Age 58

HANBURY, Lily
Actress
b. Unknown
d. Unknown, March 5, 1908, Age 33

HANCOCK, Tony
Comedian
b. Hall Green, Birmingham, England, May 12, 1924
d. Sydney, Australia, June 22, 1968, Age 44

HANDY, William Christopher
Composer
b. Florence, AL, Nov. 16, 1873
d. New York, NY, March 28, 1958, Age 84

HANDYSIDE, Clarence
Actor
b. Montreal, CAN, Unknown
d. Philadelphia, PA, Dec. 20, 1931, Age 77

HANEY, Carol
Choreographer, Performer
b. New Bedford, MA, Dec. 24, 1924
d. New York, NY, May 10, 1964, Age 39

HANEY, J. Francis (Will J. Haney)
Performer
b. Unknown
d. Milan, IN, April 11, 1964

HANFORD, Charles B.
Actor
b. Unknown
d. Washington, DC, Oct. 16, 1926, Age 67

HANKIN, Edward Charles St. John
Playwright
b. Unknown, 1869
d. Unknown, June 16, 1909, Age 39

HANN, Walter
Scenic artist
b. London, England, Jan. 11, 1838
d. Unknown, July 1922, Age 84

HANRAY, Lawrence
Actor
b. London, England, May 16, 1874
d. Unknown, Nov. 28, 1947, Age 73

HANSBERRY, Lorraine Vivian
Playwright
b. Chicago, IL, May 19, 1930
d. New York, NY, Jan. 12, 1965, Age 34

HANSEN, Hans
Performer
b. Germany, Unknown
d. Bronx, NY, June 18, 1962, Age 76

HANSEN, Juanita
Actress
b. Unknown
d. West Hollywood, CA, Sept. 26, 1961, Age 66

HANSEN, Laura
Actress
b. Unknown
d. Unknown, Nov. 26, 1914

HANSON, Kitty (Mrs. W. H. Berry)
Actress
b. Unknown
d. Unknown, Jan. 16, 1947, Age 76

HAPGOOD, Norman
Critic, Playwright
b. Chicago, IL, 1868
d. Unknown, April 29, 1937, Age 69

HARBACH, Otto
Librettist, Lyricist
b. Salt Lake City, UT, Aug. 18, 1873
d. New York, NY, Jan. 24, 1963, Age 89

HARBEN, Hubert
Actor
b. London, England, July 12, 1878
d. Unknown, Aug. 24, 1941, Age 63

HARBEN, Joan
Actress
b. London, England, Feb. 22, 1909
d. Unknown, Oct. 19, 1953, Age 44

HARBURY, Charles
Actor
b. Unknown
d. Staten Island, NY, Jan. 6, 1928, Age 85

HARBY, Isaac
Playwright, Critic, Editor
b. Unknown, 1788
d. Unknown, 1828, Age 40

HARCOURT, Cyril
Playwright, Actor
b. Unknown
d. Unknown, March 4, 1924, Age 52

HARCOURT, James
Actor
b. Headingly, Leeds, Yorkshire, England, April 20, 1873
d. Unknown, Feb. 18, 1951, Age 77

HARDACRE, John Pitt
Producer, Actor
b. Bradford, England, Nov. 2, 1855
d. Unknown, June 5, 1933, Age 77

HARDIE, A. C.
Actor
b. Unknown
d. Unknown, Jan. 31, 1939

HARDIE, Russell
Actor
b. Buffalo, NY, May 20, 1904
d. Clarence, NY, July 21, 1973, Age 69

HARDING, Alfred
Actor
b. Unknown
d. Unknown, Feb. 10, 1945

HARDING, J. Rudge
Actor
b. Unknown
d. Unknown, April 24, 1932, Age 70

HARDING, Lyn (David Llewellyn Harding)
Actor
b. Newport, England, Oct. 12, 1867
d. Southend, Sussex, England, Dec. 26, 1952, Age 85

HARDMUTH, Paul
Actor
b. Germany, Unknown
d. London, England, Feb. 5, 1962, Age 73

HARDS, Ira
Actor, Director
b. Geneva, IL, June 24, 1872
d. West Norwalk, Ct, May 2, 1938, Age 65

HARDWICKE, Cedric Webster Sir
Actor, Director
b. Lye, Stourbridge, Worcestershire, England, Feb. 19, 1893
d. New York, NY, Aug. 6, 1964, Age 71

HARDY, Alexandre
Playwright, Actor
b. Paris, France, c1572
d. Unknown, 1631

HARDY, Cherry
Actress
b. London, England, Unknown
d. New York, NY, Dec. 23, 1963, Age 74

HARDY, Oliver
Actor
b. Unknown, 1892
d. North Hollywood, CA, Aug. 7, 1957, Age 65

HARDY, Sam B.
Actor
b. New Haven, CT, March 21, 1883
d. Hollywood, CA, Oct. 16, 1935, Age 52

HARE, (John) Gilbert
Actor
b. Ireland, March 23, 1869
d. Unknown, May 21, 1951, Age 82

HARE, Lumsden
Actor, Director
b. Tipperary, Ireland, Unknown
d. Beverly Hills, CA, Aug. 28, 1964, Age 90

HARE, Mrs. Kate
Actress
b. Unknown
d. Unknown, Aug. 24, 1957, Age 83

HARE, Sir John (Fairs)
Actor, Producer
b. Giggleswick, Yorkshire, England, May 16, 1844
d. London, England, Dec. 28, 1921, Age 77

HARKER, Frederick
Actor
b. Unknown
d. Unknown, Oct. 4, 1941, Age 79

HARKER, Joseph C.
Scenic artist
b. Levenshulme, Manchester, England, Oct. 17, 1855
d. Unknown, April 15, 1927, Age 71

HARKINS, Marion
Performer
b. Unknown
d. New York, NY, Feb. 1, 1962, Age 68

HARKINS, William S. Actor
b. Unknown
d. Unknown, July 1, 1945, Age 89

HARLAN, Otis
Actor
b. Zanesville, OH, Dec. 29, 1865
d. Martinsville, IN, Jan. 20, 1940, Age 74

HARLOW, Gertrude
Actress
b. Unknown
d. Unknown, Aug. 22, 1947, Age 73

HARLOW, Jean (Harlean Carpenter)
Actress
b. Kansas City, MO, 1911
d. Hollywood, CA, June 7, 1937, Age 26

HARNED, Virginia (Hickes) (Mrs. E. H. Sothern)
Actress
b. Boston, MA, May 29, 1868
d. New York,NY, April 29, 1946, Age 77

HARNER, Dolly
Performer
b. Unknown
d. Unknown, March 15, 1956, Age 89

HARNEY, Benjamin Robertson
Composer, Performer
b. Unknown, c1872
d. Philadelphia, PA, Feb. 28, 1938

HARPER, Fred
Performer
b. Unknown
d. New York, NY, Feb. 24, 1963, Age 60

HARRIGAN, Edward (Ned)
Actor, Producer, Playwright
b. New York, NY, Oct. 26, 1845
d. New York, NY, June 6, 1911, Age 67

HARRIGAN, William
Actor
b. New York, NY, March 27, 1886
d. New York, NY, Feb. 1, 1966, Age 79

HARRINGTON, Alice
Actress
b. Marlboro, MA, Unknown
d. Greenwich, CT, June 6, 1954, Age 81

HARRINGTON, Florence
Actress
b. Unknown
d. Unknown, Jan. 24, 1942, Age 80

HARRINGTON, Pat Sr., (né Daniel Patrick Harrington)
Actor, Performer
b. Montreal, Canada, 1900
d. Islip, NY, Sept. 2, 1965, Age 64

HARRIS, Asa
Singer, Arranger, Pianist, (original Ink Spots)
b. Unknown
d. Chicago, IL, June 11, 1964, Age 54

HARRIS, Audrey Sophia (Mrs. George Devine)
Scenery & costume designer (Motley)
b. Hayes, Kent, England, July 2, 1901
d. London, England, March 1966, Age 65

HARRIS, Augustus Glossop
Actor, Producer
b. Unknown, 1825
d. Unknown, April 19, 1873, Age 47

HARRIS, Charles A. "Honey"
Performer
b. Unknown
d. Unknown, San Ysidro, CA, Age Jan. 10, 1962

HARRIS, Charles Kassell
Composer, Publisher
b. Poughkeepsie, NY, May 1, 1867
d. New York, NY, Dec. 22, 1930, Age 63

HARRIS, Clare
Actress
b. Unknown
d. Unknown, July 5, 1949, Age 59

HARRIS, Elmer Blaney
Playwright, Screenwriter
b. Chicago, IL, Jan. 11, 1878
d. Washington, DC, Sept. 6, 1966, Age 88

HARRIS, Frank
Journalist, Author, Playwright
b. Galway, Ireland, Feb. 14, 1856
d. Nice, France, Aug. 26, 1931, Age 75

HARRIS, George W.
Scenic designer and artist
b. Unknown
d. Unknown, Feb. 14, 1929, Age 49

HARRIS, Henry B.
Producer
b. St. Louis, MO, Dec. 1, 1866
d. Unknown, April 15, 1912, Age 45

HARRIS, Herbert H.
Producer
b. New York, NY, c1896
d. New York, NY, March 21, 1949, Age 52

HARRIS, Joseph
Actor, Playwright
b. Unknown, 1661
d. Unknown, 1699

HARRIS, Leonore
Actress
b. Unknown
d. New York, NY, Sept. 27, 1953, Age 74

HARRIS, Mildred
Actress
b. Cheyenne, WY, 1901
d. Hollywood, CA, July 20, 1944, Age 42

HARRIS, Mitchell
Performer
b. Unknown
d. New York, NY, Nov. 17, 1948, Age 65

HARRIS, Sam H.
Producer
b. New York, NY, Feb. 3, 1872
d. New York, NY, July 3, 1941, Age 69

HARRIS, Sir Augustus Henry Glossop
Actor, Producer, Playwright
b. Paris, France, 1852
d. Folkestone, England, June 22, 1896, Age 44

HARRIS, Sylvia
Producer
b. New York, NY, May 15, 1906
d. New York, NY, Nov. 11, 1966, Age 60

HARRIS, Will J.
Producer, Director, Songwriter
b. New York, NY, March 14, 1900
d. Chicago, IL, Dec. 14, 1967, Age 73

HARRIS, William
Producer
b. Unknown
d. Unknown, Nov. 25, 1916, Age 83

HARRIS, William Jr.
Producer, Director
b. Boston, MA, July 22, 1884
d. New York, NY, Sept. 2, 1946, Age 62

HARRISON, Austin
Critic, Playwright
b. Unknown, 1873
d. Unknown, July 14, 1928, Age 55

HARRISON, Duncan
Playwright, Manager
b. Toronto, CAN, Unknown
d. New Rochelle, NY, March 13, 1934, Age 72

HARRISON, Fanny (Mrs. Isaac Cohen)
Actress
b. Unknown
d. Unknown, Feb. 15, 1909, Age 70

HARRISON, Frederick
Producer, Actor
b. London, England, Unknown
d. Unknown, June 13, 1926, Age 72

HARRISON, Gabriel
Actor, Author, Producer
b. Unknown
d. Unknown, Dec. 15, 1902, Age 84

HARRISON, Lee
Performer
b. Unknown
d. Greenwich, CT, Oct. 29, 1916, Age 50

HARRISON, Louis
Playwright, Comedian
b. Philadelphia, PA, Unknown
d. New York, NY, Oct. 23, 1936, Age 70

HARRISON, Mona
Actress
b. Edinburgh, Scotland, Unknown
d. Unknown, Jan. 2, 1957

HARRISON, Richard Berry
Actor
b. London, Ontario, CAN, 1864
d. New York, NY, March 14, 1935, Age 70

HARRISON, Robert
Actor
b. Denver, CO, Unknown
d. New York, NY, April 3, 1953, Age 68

HARRITY, Richard
Playwright, Actor
b. Newport News, VA, May 22, 1907
d. Franklin, NH, Jan. 19, 1973, Age 65

HARROLD, Orville
Singer
b. Muncie, IN, Unknown
d. Norwalk, CT, Oct. 23, 1933, Age 55

HARRON, Robert
Actor
b. Unknown, 1894
d. New York, NY, Sept. 5, 1920, Age 26

HART, Annie
Performer
b. Unknown
d. Fair Haven, NJ, June 13, 1947, Age 87

HART, Bernard
Producer, Stage manager
b. New York, NY, April 21, 1911
d. New York, NY, Aug. 18, 1964, Age 53

HART, Bernard Solomon
Producer, Stage manager
b. New York, NY, April 21, 1911
d. New York, NY, Aug. 18, 1964, Age 53

HART, John
Producer, Theatre executive
b. Unknown
d. Canford Cliffs, Dorset, England, March 28, 1937

HART, Joseph
Performer, Producer
b. Unknown
d. New York, NY, Oct. 3, 1921, Age 59

HART, Lorenz
Lyricist
b. New York, NY, May 2, 1895
d. New York, NY, Nov. 22, 1943, Age 48

HART, Moss
Playwright, Producer, Director
b. New York, NY, Oct. 24, 1904
d. Palm Springs, CA, Dec. 20, 1961, Age 57

HART, Richard
Actor
b. Providence, RI, April 14, 1915
d. New York, NY, Jan. 2, 1951, Age 35

HART, Teddy
Actor
b. New York, NY, Sept. 25, 1897
d. Los Angeles, CA, Feb. 17, 1971, Age 73

HART, Tony (Anthony J. Cannon)
Actor
b. Worcester, MA, July 25, 1855
d. Worcester, MA, Nov. 4, 1891, Age 36

HART, William S.
Actor, Producer
b. Newburgh, NY, Dec. 6, 1870
d. Los Angeles, CA, June 23, 1946, Age 75

HARTE, Francis Bret
Playwright, Novelist
b. Albany, NY, Aug. 25, 1836
d. . . .near London, England, May 5, 1902, Age 65

HARTLEBEN, Otto Erich
Playwright
b. Unknown
d. Unknown, Feb. 11, 1905, Age 50

HARTLEY, Elizabeth (née White)
Actress
b. North of England, 1751
d. Woolwich, England, Feb. 1, 1824, Age 73

HARTMAN, Don
Screenwriter, Producer, Director
b. Brooklyn, NY, Unknown
d. Palm Springs, CA, March 23, 1958, Age 57

HARTMAN, Grace (Grace Barrett Hartman Abbott)
Dancer
b. San Francisco, CA, Unknown
d. Van Nuys, CA, Aug. 8, 1955, Age 48

HARTMAN, Paul
Dancer, Actor
b. San Francisco, CA, Unknown
d. Los Angeles, CA, Oct. 2, 1973, Age 69

HARTWIG, Walter
Producer
b. Milwaukee, WI, Unknown
d. New York, NY, Jan. 17, 1941, Age 61

HARTZENBUSCH, Juan Eugenio
Playwright, Translator, Editor
b. Spain, 1806
d. Unknown, 1880

HARVEY, Don C.
Performer
b. Unknown
d. Hollywood, CA, April 24, 1963, Age 51

HARVEY, Forrester
Actor
b. Unknown
d. Unknown, Dec. 14, 1945, Age 55

HARVEY, Frank
Playwright, Actor, Producer
b. Unknown
d. Unknown, March 29, 1903, Age 62

HARVEY, Georgette
Actress
b. St. Louis, MO, Unknown
d. New York, NY, Feb. 17, 1952, Age 69

HARVEY, Georgia
Actress
b. Nova Scotia, Unknown
d. New York, NY, May 17, 1960, Age 85

HARVEY, Laurence (né Larushka Misha Skikne)
Actor
b. Yonishkis, Lithuania, Oct. 1, 1928
d. London, England, Nov. 26, 1973, Age 45

HARVEY, Lilian
Actress, Singer, Dancer
b. London, England, Jan. 1907
d. Antibes, France, July 27, 1968, Age 61

HARVEY, May
Actress
b. Unknown
d. Unknown, June 17, 1930

HARVEY, Morris
Actor, Author
b. London, England, Sept. 25, 1877
d. Unknown, Aug. 24, 1944, Age 66

HARVEY, Paul
Actor
b. Sandwich, IL, Unknown
d. Hollywood, CA, Dec. 14, 1955, Age 71

HARVEY, Rupert
Actor
b. Iron Bridge, Shropshire, England, Jan. 1, 1887
d. Unknown, July 7, 1954, Age 67

HARVEY, Sir John Martin
Actor, Producer
b. Wyvenhoe, Essex, England, June 22, 1863
d. Unknown, May 14, 1944, Age 80

HARWOOD, H. M.
Playwright
b. Eccles, Lancashire, England, March 29, 1874
d. Unknown, April 19, 1959, Age 85

HARWOOD, Harry
Actor
b. New York, NY, Unknown
d. Portland, ME, Aug. 1, 1926, Age 78

HARWOOD, John
Actor, Director
b. London, England, Feb. 29, 1876
d. Unknown, Dec. 26, 1944, Age 68

HARWOOD, John E.
Actor
b. Unknown, 1771
d. New York, NY, 1809

HASCALL, Lon (Laurence)
Actor
b. Grand Rapids, MI, Unknown
d. New York, NY, Dec. 13, 1932, Age 60

HASSALL, Christopher
Performer, Poet, Lyricist
b. London, England, March 24, 1912
d. Chatham, England, April 25, 1963, Age 51

HASSELL, George
Actor
b. Birmingham, England, Unknown
d. Chatsworth, CA, Feb. 17, 1937, Age 56

HASTINGS, B. Macdonald
Playwright, Critic
b. Unknown
d. Unknown, Feb. 21, 1928, Age 46

HASTINGS, Sir Patrick
Playwright
b. Unknown, March 17, 1880
d. Unknown, Feb. 26, 1952, Age 71

HASWELL, Percy (Mrs. George Fawcett)
Actress
b. Austin, TX, Unknown
d. Nantucket, MA, June 13, 1945, Age 74

HATCH, Frank
Actor, Playwright, Director
b. Marysville, CA, Unknown
d. Richmond Hill, NY, Oct. 25, 1938, Age 74

HATCH, Ike (Isaac Flower Hatch)
Performer
b. U.S.A., Unknown
d. London, England, Dec. 26, 1961, Age 69

HATHERTON, Arthur
Actor
b. Unknown
d. Unknown, June 11, 1924

HATTON, Adele Bradford
Actress
b. Unknown
d. Unknown, April 10, 1957, Age 76

HATTON, Fanny Locke
Playwright
b. Chicago, IL, Unknown
d. New York, NY, Nov. 27, 1939, Age 69

HATTON, Frederick H.
Drama critic, Playwright
b. Peru, IL, July 30, 1879
d. Rutland, IL, April 13, 1946, Age 66

HATTON, Joseph
Playwright, Journalist
b. Unknown
d. Unknown, July 31, 1907, Age 68

HAUCH, Johannes Carsten
Playwright, Teacher
b. Unknown, 1790
d. Unknown, 1872

HAUPTMANN, Carl
Playwright
b. Unknown
d. Unknown, Feb. 4, 1921

HAUPTMANN, Gerhart
Playwright
b. Obersalzbrunn, Silesia, Germany, Nov. 15, 1862
d. Unknown, June 8, 1946, Age 83

HAVARD, William
Actor, Playwright
b. Unknown
d. Unknown, Feb. 20, 1778, Age 68

HAVER, Phyllis
Actress
b. Douglas, KS, Unknown
d. Sharon, CT, Nov. 19, 1960, Age 60

HAVILAND, Augusta
Actress
b. Unknown
d. Unknown, Oct. 25, 1925

HAVILAND, William
Actor, Producer
b. Bristol, England, 1860
d. Unknown, Sept. 19, 1917, Age 57

HAVLIN, John H.
Manager
b. Unknown
d. Miami, FL, Dec. 17, 1924, Age 77

HAWKESWORTH, Walter
Playwright
b. Unknown
d. Unknown, Oct. 1606

HAWKINS, Anthony Hope
Playwright
b. London, England, Unknown
d. Walton, Surrey, England, July 8, 1933, Age 70

HAWKINS, Etta
Actress
b. Unknown
d. Unknown, July 13, 1945, Age 80

HAWKINS, Jack
Actor
b. London, England, Sept. 14, 1910
d. London, England, July 18, 1973, Age 62

HAWKINS, Stockwell
Actor
b. Monmouth, England, Oct. 20, 1874
d. Unknown, March 25, 1927, Age 52

HAWKS, Wells
Press representative
b. Unknown
d. Unknown, Dec. 4, 1941, Age 71

HAWLEY, Dudley
Actor
b. England, Unknown
d. New York, NY, March 29, 1941, Age 62

HAWLEY, Esther
Writer
b. Chicago, IL, Nov. 2, 1906
d. New York, NY, Nov. 4, 1968, Age 62

HAWORTH, Joseph
Actor
b. Unknown, 1855
d. Unknown, Aug. 28, 1903, Age 48

HAWTHORNE, David
Actor
b. Unknown
d. Unknown, June 18, 1942

HAWTHORNE, Grace
Actress, Producer
b. Unknown
d. Unknown, May 1922, Age 62

HAWTREY, George P.
Actor, Playwright
b. Unknown
d. Unknown, Aug. 17, 1910, Age 64

HAWTREY, Sir Charles
Actor, Producer, Playwright
b. Eton, England, Sept. 21, 1858
d. London, England, July 30, 1923, Age 64

HAWTREY, William P.
Actor
b. Unknown
d. Unknown, Jan. 6, 1914, Age 57

HAWTRY, Anthony
Actor, Producer
b. Claygate, Surrey, England, Jan. 22, 1909
d. Unknown, Oct. 18, 1954, Age 45

HAY, Ian (Maj. Gen. John Hay Beith)
Playwright
b. Scotland, April 17, 1876
d. Petersfield, Hampshire, England, Sept. 22, 1952, Age 76

HAY, Mary (née Caldwell)
Actress
b. Fort Bliss, TX, Aug. 22, 1901
d. Inverness, CA, June 4, 1957, Age 55

HAYDON, Florence
Actress
b. Holborn, London, England, Unknown
d. Unknown, July 21, 1918, Age 80

HAYDON, John S.
Actor
b. Unknown
d. Unknown, Nov. 19,1907, Age 70

HAYE, Helen
Actress
b. Assam, India, Aug. 28, 1874
d. London, England, Sept. 1, 1957, Age 83

HAYES, Ada
Performer
b. Unknown
d. Brooklyn, NY, June 8, 1962, Age 87

HAYES, F. W.
Playwright, Painter
b. Unknown
d. Unknown, Sept. 7, 1918, Age 70

HAYES, Hubert
Playwright
b. Unknown
d. Asheville, NC, July 30, 1964

HAYES, Milton
Performer
b. Unknown
d. Unknown, Dec. 18, 1940, Age 56

HAYES, Reginald
Actor
b. Unknown
d. Unknown, June 27, 1953

HAYMAN, Al
Producer
b. San Francisco, CA, Unknown
d. Unknown, Feb. 9, 1917, Age 67

HAYMAN, Alf
Producer
b. Wheeling, WV, 1865
d. New York, NY, May 14, 1921, Age 56

HAYMAN, Leonard
Performer
b. Plymouth, England, Unknown
d. Vancouver, British Columbia, CAN, Jan. 17, 1962, Age 61

HAYNES, Alfred W.
Performer
b. Lynn, MA, Unknown
d. Lynn, MA, Nov. 10, 1924, Age 63

HAYNES, T. P.
Actor
b. Unknown
d. Unknown, Feb. 16, 1915, Age 65

HAYS, William Shakespeare
Songwriter, Journalist
b. Louisville, KY, July 1837
d. Louisville, KY, July 1907, Age 70

HAYWARD, Leland Agent - Producer
Nebraska City, NE
b. Sept. 13, 1902, Yorktown Heights, NY
d. March 18, 1971, 68

HAYWELL, Frederick (Hawley)
Actor, Playwright
b. Unknown
d. Unknown, March 13, 1889, Age 62

HAYWOOD, Mrs. Eliza
Actress, Playwright
b. Unknown
d. Unknown, Feb. 25, 1756, Age 63

HAZLETON, George C.
Playwright
b. Boscobel, WI, Unknown
d. New York, NY, June 24, 1921, Age 53

HAZLEWOOD, C. H.
Playwright
b. Unknown
d. Unknown, May 31, 1875, Age 52

HAZLITT, William
Critic
b. Maidstone, Kent, England, 1778
d. Unknown, Sept. 18, 1830, Age 52

HAZZARD, John E. (Jack)
Actor, Playwright
b. New York, NY, Unknown
d. Great Neck, LI, NY, Dec. 2, 1935, Age 54

HEALY, Gerald
Performer, Playwright, Producer
b. Unknown
d. London, England, March 9, 1963, Age 45

HEARN, James
Actor
b. Unknown
d. Unknown, Nov. 10, 1913, Age 40

HEATH, Caroline (Mrs. Wilson Barrett)
Actress
b. Unknown
d. Unknown, July 26, 1887, Age 52

HEATH, Ida
Performer
b. Unknown
d. Unknown, March 20, 1950, Age 77

HEATHCOTE, A. M.
Playwright
b. Unknown
d. Unknown, Aug. 5, 1934, Age 87

HEATHERLY, Clifford
Actor
b. Unknown
d. Unknown, Sept. 16, 1937, Age 48

HEBBEL, Christian Friedrich
Playwright, Poet
b. Wesselburen, Holstein, Germany, 1813
d. Vienna, Austria, Dec. 13, 1863, Age 50

HEBERT, Fred
Producer, Director
b. St. Paul, MN, July 4, 1911
d. Newark, NJ, March 7, 1972, Age 60

HECHT, Ben
Playwright, Screenwriter, Novelist
b. New York, NY, Feb. 28, 1894
d. New York, NY, April 18, 1964, Age 70

HEDBURG, Franz
Playwright
b. Unknown, 1828
d. Stockholm, Sweden, 1908

HEDBURG, Tor
Playwright, Novelist, Critic
b. Unknown, 1862
d. Unknown, 1931

HEDLEY, H. B.
Lyricist, Composer
b. Unknown
d. Unknown, June 2, 1931, Age 41

HEFLIN, Van
Dancer, Actor
b. Walters, OK, Dec. 13, 1910
d. Unknown, July 23, 1971, Age 70

HEGGEN, Thomas O.
Playwright, Novelist
b. Fort Dodge, IA, Dec. 23, 1919
d. New York, NY, May 19, 1949, Age 29

HEGGIE, O. P.
Actor
b. South Australia, Sept. 17, 1879
d. Hollywood, CA, Feb. 7, 1936, Age 56

HEIBERG, Gunnar
Playwright, Critic
b. Oslo, Norway, 1857
d. Unknown, Feb. 21, 1929, Age 72

HEIBERG, Johan Ludvig
Poet, Playwright, Critic
b. Unknown, 1791
d. Unknown, 1860

HEIDT, Joseph
Press representative
b. Liberty, NY, Unknown
d. Detroit, MI, Aug. 16, 1962, Age 52

HEIJERMANS, Hermann (a/k/a Samuel Falkland)
Playwright
b. Rotterdam, Netherlands, 1864
d. Unknown, Nov. 22, 1924, Age 59

HEIN, Albert
Actor
b. Unknown
d. Unknown, April 13, 1949, Age 81

HEIN, Silvio
Composer
b. New York, NY, March 15, 1879
d. Saranac Lake, NY, Dec. 19, 1928, Age 49

HEINLEIN, Mary Virginia
Educator, Theatre expert
b. Bridgeport, OH, Unknown
d. Poughkeepsie, NY, Dec. 25, 1961, Age 58

HELBURN, Theresa
Producer, Playwright
b. New York, NY, Jan. 12, 1887
d. Norwalk, CT, Aug. 18, 1959, Age 72

HELD, Anna
Actress
b. Paris, France, March 18, 1873
d. Unknown, Aug. 13, 1918, Age 45

HELLER, Jeanne
Actress
b. Unknown
d. Unknown, Nov. 29, 1908

HELLINGER, Mark
Columnist, Author
b. New York, NY, March 21, 1903
d. Hollywood, CA, Dec. 21, 1947, Age 44

HELMORE, Arthur
Performer
b. Unknown
d. Unknown, June 14, 1941, Age 83

HELMSLEY, Charles Thomas Hunt
Actor, Business manager
b. London, England, Dec. 1, 1865
d. Unknown, Nov. 27, 1940, Age 74

HELTON, Alf
Actor
b. England, Unknown
d. Forest Hills, NY, March 6, 1937, Age 78

HEMINGE, John
Actor, Editor
b. Unknown, 1556
d. Unknown, Oct. 10, 1630, Age 74

HEMINGWAY, Ernest
Novelist, Writer, Playwright
b. Oak Park, IL, July 21, 1899
d. Ketcham, ID, July 2, 1961, Age 62

HEMINGWAY, Marie
Actress
b. Yorkshire, England, 1893
d. Unknown, June 11, 1939, Age 46

HEMMERDE, Edward George
Playwright
b. Peckham, England, Nov. 13, 1871
d. Unknown, May 24, 1948, Age 76

HEMMING, Alfred
Actor
b. Unknown
d. Unknown, Dec. 17, 1942, Age 91

HEMSLEY, Estelle
Actress
b. Boston, MA, 1892
d. New York, NY, Nov.4, 1968, Age 76

HEMSLEY, Harry May
Performer
b. Unknown
d. Unknown, April 8, 1951, Age 73

HEMSLEY, W. T.
Scenic artist
b. Newcastle-on-Tyne, England, June 2, 1850
d. Unknown, Feb. 8, 1918, Age 67

HENDERSON, Alex F.
Producer
b. London, England, May 4, 1866
d. Unknown, June 13, 1933, Age 67

HENDERSON, David
Producer, Performer
b. Unknown
d. Unknown, May 26, 1908, Age 54

HENDERSON, Del
Actor, Director
b. Unknown
d. Woodland Hills, CA, Dec. 2, 1956, Age 79

HENDERSON, Grace
Actress
b. Ann Arbor, MI, Unknown
d. Bronx, NY, Oct. 30, 1944, Age 84

HENDERSON, Jack
Actor
b. Unknown
d. New York, NY, Jan. 1, 1957, Age 79

HENDERSON, John Raymond
Press representative
b. Colorado Springs, CO, Unknown
d. Athens, Greece (airplane accident), Oct. 1, 1937, Age 48

HENDERSON, Lucius
Performer, Producer, Film director
b. Unknown
d. New York, NY, Feb. 19, 1947, Age 86

HENDERSON, Marie (Mrs. George Ringold)
Actress
b. Unknown
d. Unknown, Feb. 26, 1902, Age 58

HENDERSON, Mrs. Laura
Producer
b. Unknown
d. Unknown, Nov. 29, 1944, Age 80

HENDERSON, Ray
Composer
b. Buffalo, NY, Dec. 1, 1896
d. Greenwich, CT, Dec. 31, 1970, Age 74

HENDRICKS, Ben
Actor
b. Buffalo, NY, Unknown
d. Hollywood, CA, April 30, 1930, Age 65

HENDRIE, Ernest
Actor, Playwright
b. Unknown, June 10, 1859
d. Unknown, March 11, 1929, Age 69

HENLEY, E. J.
Actor
b. Unknown
d. Unknown, Oct. 16, 1898, Age 36

HENLEY, Herbert James
Critic
b. Sevenoaks, Kent, England, April 1, 1882
d. Unknown, Dec. 22, 1937, Age 55

HENLEY, William Ernest
Playwright, Poet, Journalist
b. Gloucester, England, 1849
d. Unknown, July 11, 1903, Age 53

HENNEQUIN, Alfred
Playwright
b. Unknown
d. Unknown, Aug. 7, 1887

HENNEQUIN, Maurice
Playwright
b. Unknown
d. Unknown, Sept. 3, 1926

HENNESSY, Roland Burke
Critic
b. Unknown
d. Unknown, Feb. 1, 1939, Age 69

HENNINGS, Betty
Actress
b. Unknown
d. Unknown, Oct. 30, 1939, Age 89

HENRI, Louie (Lady Lytton)
Actress
b. Unknown
d. Unknown, May 2, 1947, Age 84

HENRIQUES, Madeline
Actress
b. Unknown
d. Unknown, May 11, 1929, Age 85

HENRY, Charles
Author, Director
b. Putney, England, April 13, 1890
d. Little Chalfont, England, Feb. 28, 1968, Age 77

HENRY, Creagh
Actor
b. Unknown
d. Unknown, Feb. 26, 1946

HENRY, John
Performer, Producer
b. Ireland, 1738
d. Unknown, Oct. 16 or 23, 1794

HENRY, Martin
Producer
b. Brighton, England, Jan. 1, 1872
d. Unknown, Sept. 4, 1942, Age 70

HENSEL, Sophie Friederike (née Sparmann)
Actress
b. Unknown, 1738
d. Unknown, 1789

HENSLOWE, Philip
Producer
b. Unknown
d. Unknown, Jan. 6, 1616

HENSON, Leslie
Actor, Producer, Director
b. London, England, Aug. 3, 1891
d. Harrow Weald, Middlesex, England, Dec. 2, 1957, Age 66

HENTSCHEL, Carl
Founder of the Playgoers & "O. P." Clubs
b. Unknown
d. Unknown, Jan. 9, 1930, Age 65

HERALD, Heinz
Playwright, Screenwriter
b. Unknown
d. Kreuth, Germany, July 22, 1964, Age about 75

HERAUD, John A.
Playwright, Critic
b. Unknown, 1799
d. Unknown, April 20, 1887, Age 86

HERBERT, F. Hugh
Playwright
b. Vienna, Austria, Unknown
d. Hollywood, CA, May 17, 1958, Age 60

HERBERT, Henry
Actor, Producer
b. London, England, Unknown
d. Flushing, Ny, Feb. 20, 1947, Age 68

HERBERT, Holmes
Actor
b. Unknown
d. Hollywood, CA, Dec. 26, 1956, Age 78

HERBERT, Hugh
Actor, Playwright
b. Binghamton, NY, Unknown
d. North Hollywood, CA, March 12, 1952, Age 66

HERBERT, Joseph
Comedian, Librettist
b. Liverpool, England, Unknown
d. New York, NY, Feb. 18, 1923, Age 56

HERBERT, Louisa
Actress, Producer
b. Unknown
d. Unknown, April 10, 1921, Age 89

HERBERT, Sir Henry
Master of the Revels
b. Unknown, 1596
d. Unknown, April 27, 1673, Age 77

HERBERT, Victor
Composer, Conductor
b. Dublin, Ireland, Feb. 1, 1859
d. New York, NY, May 26, 1924, Age 65

HERCZEG, Ferenc
Playwright
b. Versecz, Hungary, Sept. 22, 1863
d. Budapest, Hungary, 1950, Age 87

HERCZEG, Geza
Playwright
b. Hungary, Unknown
d. Rome, Italy, Feb. 28, 1954, Age 65

HERENDEEN, Fred
Playwright, Author
b. Unknown
d. Charlotte, NC, June 4, 1962, Age 68

HERFORD, Beatrice (Mrs. Beatrice Herford Hayward)
Actress, Monologist, Author
b. Manchester, England, Unknown
d. Seaconnet Point, RI, July 18, 1952, Age 84

HERMAN, Henry
Playwright, Director
b. Unknown
d. Unknown, Sept. 25, 1894, Age 62

HERMANN, David
Actor, Director, Producer
b. Unknown, 1876
d. Unknown, 1930, Age 54

HERMANT, Abel
Playwright, Critic
b. Unknown
d. Unknown, Oct. 7, 1950, Age 86

HERNDON, Agnes
Actress
b. White Sulphur Springs, VA, Unknown
d. Whitestone, L.I., NY, Dec. 31, 1920

HERNDON, Richard Gilbert
Producer
b. Paris, France, Unknown
d. Philadelphia, PA, July 11, 1958, Age 85

HERNE, James A. (Ahearn)
Actor, Playwright, Producer
b. Cohoes, NY, Feb. 1, 1839
d. Unknown, June 2, 1901, Age 62

HERNE, Julie A.
Actress, Playwright
b. Unknown
d. New York, NY, Feb. 24, 1955, Age 74

HERNE, (Katherine) Chrystal (Mrs. Harold S. Pollard)
Actress
b. Dorchester, MA, June 16, 1883
d. Boston, MA, Sept. 19, 1950, Age 67

HERNE, Katherine Corcoran
Actress
b. Abbeyleix, Ireland, 1857
d. Astoria, NY, Feb. 8, 1943, Age 86

HERON, Bijou (Mrs. Henry Miller née Hélène Stoepel)
Actress
b. New York, NY, Unknown
d. New York, NY, March 18, 1937, Age 75

HERON, Dalziel
Actor
b. Unknown
d. Unknown, Aug. 8, 1911

HERON, Matilda Agnes
Actress, Playwright
b. Unknown, 1830
d. Unknown, 1877, Age 47

HERRAUD, Marcel
Actor, Director
b. Unknown
d. Unknown, June 11, 1953, Age 55

HERRING, Fanny
Actress
b. Unknown
d. Unknown, May 18, 1906, Age 85

HERSHEY, Burnet
Playwright
b. Rumania, Dec. 13, 1896
d. Miami Beach, FL, Dec. 13, 1971, Age 75

HERSHOLT, Jean
Actor
b. Copenhagen, Denmark, July 12, 1886
d. Beverly Hills, CA, June 2, 1956, Age 69

HERTZ, Henrik
Playwright
b. Unknown, c1798
d. Unknown, 1870

HERVIEU, Paul
Playwright
b. Neuilly-sur-Seine, France, Sept. 2, 1857
d. Unknown, Oct. 25, 1915, Age 58

HERZ, Ralph C.
Actor
b. Paris, France, March 25, 1878
d. Atlantic City, NJ, July 12, 1921, Age 43

HERZBRUN, Bernard
Art director
b. Unknown
d. Hollywood, CA, Jan. 7, 1964, Age 72

HESLEWOOD, Tom
Actor, Designer
b. Hessle, Yorkshire, England, April 8, 1868
d. Unknown, April 28, 1959, Age 91

HESTOR, George
Actor
b. Tresco, Isles of Scilly, England, Oct. 6, 1877
d. Unknown, Dec. 3, 1925, Age 48

HEWITT, Agnes
Actress
b. India, Unknown
d. Unknown, Feb. 24, 1924, Age 61

HEWITT, Henry
Actor
b. London, England, Dec. 28, 1885
d. Newbury, England, Aug. 23, 1968, Age 82

HEWITT, John Hill
Songwriter, Journalist
b. New York, NY, July 11, 1801
d. Baltimore, MD, Oct. 7, 1890, Age 89

HEWLETT, Maurice
Playwright
b. Unknown, Jan. 22, 1861
d. Unknown, June 15, 1923, Age 62

HEWSON, J. James
Playwright, Journalist
b. Unknown
d. Unknown, June 3, 1923, Age 71

HEYBURN, Weldon
Actor
b. Unknown
d. Hollywood, CA, May 18, 1951, Age 46

HEYDT, Louis Jean Jr.
Actor
b. Montclair, NJ, April 17, 1905
d. Boston, MA, Jan. 29, 1960, Age 54

HEYES, Herbert
Actor
b. Unknown
d. Hollywood, CA, May 31, 1958, Age 68

HEYSE, Paul
Playwright
b. Unknown
d. Unknown, April 2, 1914, Age 84

HEYWARD, Dorothy
Playwright
b. Wooster, OH, June 6, 1890
d. Unknown, Nov. 19, 1961, Age 71

HEYWARD, DuBose
Playwright, Novelist, Poet
b. Charleston, SC, Aug. 31, 1885
d. Tryon, NC, June 16, 1940, Age 54

HEYWOOD, John
Playwright
b. Unknown, c1497
d. Malines, France, 1580

HEYWOOD, Thomas
Actor, Playwright
b. Unknown, c1570
d. Unknown, 1641

HIBBARD, Edna
Actress
b. California, Unknown
d. New York, NY, Dec. 26, 1942, Age 47

HIBBERT, Henry George
Critic, Journalist, Editor
b. Nottingham, England, April 4, 1862
d. Unknown, March 7, 1924, Age 61

HICHENS, Robert Smythe
Playwright, Novelist
b. Speldhurst, Kent, England, Nov. 14, 1864
d. Unknown, July 20, 1950, Age 85

HICKMAN, Alfred
Actor
b. Unknown
d. Unknown, April 9, 1931, Age 57

HICKMAN, Howard
Actor
b. Unknown
d. Hollywood, CA, Dec. 31, 1949, Age 69

HICKS, Newton Treen ("Bravo" Hicks)
Actor
b. Unknown
d. Unknown, Feb. 21, 1873, Age 62

HICKS, Russell
Actor
b. Baltimore, MD, Unknown
d. West Los Angeles, CA, June 1, 1957, Age 62

HICKS, Sir Edward Seymour
Actor, Playwright, Producer
b. St. Helier, Isle of Jersey, England, Jan. 30, 1871
d. Hampshire, England, April 6, 1949, Age 78

HIGGIE, T. H.
Actor, Playwright
b. Unknown
d. Unknown, March 24, 1893, Age 85

HIGGINS, David
Actor, Playwright
b. Chicago, IL, Unknown
d. Brooklyn, NY, June 30, 1936, Age 78

HIGHLAND, George A.
Producer, Director
b. Unknown
d. Unknown, April 16, 1954

HIGNETT, H. R.
Actor
b. Ringway, Cheshire, England, Jan. 29, 1870
d. Unknown, Dec. 17, 1959, Age 89

HIKEN, Nat
Playwright
b. Chicago, IL, June 23, 1914
d. Brentwood, CA, Dec. 7, 1968, Age 54

HILL, Aaron
Playwright
b. Unknown, 1685
d. Unknown, Feb. 8, 1750, Age 64

HILL, Annie (Mrs. H. De Lange)
Actress
b. Unknown
d. Unknown, March 6, 1943

HILL, Benson
Actor, Playwright
b. Unknown
d. Unknown, Sept. 17, 1845, Age 49

HILL, Billy (William Joseph Hill)
Songwriter
b. Boston, MA, July 14, 1899
d. New York, NY, Dec. 24, 1940, Age 41

HILL, Frederic Stanhope
Actor, Playwright
b. Unknown
d. Unknown, April 7, 1851, Age 46

HILL, George Handel ("Yankee Hill")
Performer
b. Unknown, Oct. 9, 1809
d. Unknown, Sept. 27, 1849, Age 39

HILL, Jennie
Actress
b. Unknown, 1851
d. Streatham, England, June 28, 1896, Age 45

HILL, John J.
Press representative
b. Unknown
d. Hollywood, CA, July 1, 1962, Age 70

HILL, Sinclair (Gerard Arthur Lewin Sinclair-Hill)
Director
b. Kingston-on-Thames, England, June 10, 1896
d. Unknown, March 1945, Age 48

HILL, Walter Osborn
Actor
b. Unknown
d. Albany, NY, Aug. 24, 1963, Age 87

HILL, Wesley
Actor
b. Baltimore, MD, Unknown
d. New York, NY, Dec. 1930, Age 55

HILLIARD, Bob
Lyricist
b. New York, NY, Jan. 28, 1918
d. Hollywood, NY, Feb. 1, 1971, Age 53

HILLIARD, Kathlyn
Actress
b. Glasgow, Scotland, April 17, 1896
d. Unknown, Oct. 7, 1933, Age 37

HILLIARD, Robert C.
Actor
b. New York, NY, May 28, 1857
d. New York, NY, June 6, 1927, Age 70

HILLMAN, Michael
Actor, Producer
b. Capetown, South Africa, Dec. 7, 1902
d. Unknown, March 23, 1941, Age 38

HILTON, James
Writer
b. Lancashire, England, Unknown
d. Long Beach, CA, Dec. 20, 1954, Age 54

HILYARD, Maud
Actress
b. Unknown
d. Unknown, June 4, 1926

HINDEMITH, Paul
Composer, Conductor, Teacher
b. Hanau, Germany, Nov. 16, 1895
d. Frankfort a/M, Germany, Dec. 28, 1963, Age 68

HINE, Hubert
Actor, Director
b. Unknown
d. Unknown, Oct. 13, 1950, Age 59

HINES, Dixie
Press respresentative
b. Unknown
d. New York, NY, Oct. 1, 1928, Age 56

HINSHAW, William W.
Actor, Singer, Producer
b. Union, IA, Unknown
d. Washington, DC, Nov. 27, 1947, Age 80

HIPPISLEY, John
Actor, Playwright
b. Unknown
d. Unknown, Feb. 12, 1748

HIPPISLEY, John (the younger)
Actor, Playwright
b. Unknown
d. Unknown, Jan. 1, 1767

HIRSCH, Louis Achille
Composer
b. New York, NY, Nov. 28, 1887
d. New York, NY, May 13, 1924, Age 36

HIRSCH, Max
Theatrical executive
b. Unknown
d. Blue Point, L.I., NY, July 23, 1925, Age 61

HIRSCHBEIN, Peretz
Playwright, Actor, Producer
b. Grodno, Lithuania, 1880
d. Unknown, 1949

HITCHCOCK, Raymond
Actor
b. Auburn, NY, Oct. 22, 1865
d. Beverly Hills, CA, Nov. 24, 1929, Age 64

HITCHCOCK, Robert
Historian, Actor
b. Unknown
d. Unknown, 1809

HITE, Mabel
Actress
b. Kentucky, Unknown
d. Unknown, Oct. 22, 1912, Age 26

HOADLEY, Dr. Benjamin
Playwright
b. Unknown
d. Unknown, Aug. 10, 1757, Age 51

HOADLEY, John
Playwright, Poet
b. Unknown
d. Unknown, March 16, 1776, Age 64

HOARE, Prince
Playwright
b. Unknown
d. Unknown, Dec. 22, 1834, Age 80

HOBAN, Agnes E.
Performer
b. Unknown
d. Kansas City, MO, Nov. 6, 1962, Age 73

HOBART, Doty
Playwright
b. Unknown
d. New York, NY, Nov. 16, 1958, Age 72

HOBART, George V.
Playwright
b. Cape Breton, N.S., Jan. 16, 1867
d. Cumberland, MD, Jan. 31, 1926, Age 59

HOBBES, (Herbert) Halliwell
Actor
b. Stratford-upon-Avon, England, Nov. 16, 1877
d. Santa Monica, CA, Feb. 20, 1962, Age 84

HOBBES, John Oliver (Mrs. Craigie)
Playwright, Novelist
b. Unknown
d. Unknown, Aug. 13, 1906, Age 38

HOBBS, Frederick
Theatre manager, Actor
b. Christchurch, New Zealand, July 29, 1880
d. Unknown, April 11, 1942,, Age 61

HOBBS, Jack
Actor
b. London, England, Sept. 28, 1893
d. Brighton, England, June 4, 1968, Age 74

HOBSON, Maud
Actress
b. Unknown
d. Unknown, Jan. 6, 1913

HOCHULI, Paul
Journalist
b. Unknown
d. Houston, TX, March 24, 1964, Age 60

HODGDON, Samuel K.
Vaudeville manager
b. Saco, ME, Unknown
d. New York, NY, April 6, 1922, Age 69

HODGE, Dr. Merton (Horace Emerton Hodge)
Playwright
b. Gisborne, New Zealand, March 13, 1904
d. Unknown, Oct. 10, 1958, Age 54

HODGE, William T.
Actor, Playwright
b. Albion, NY, Nov. 1, 1874
d. Greenwich, CT, Jan. 30, 1932, Age 57

HODGES, Horace
Actor, Playwright
b. Unknown, Dec. 19, 1865
d. Unknown, July 6, 1951, Age 86

HODGINS, Earle
Actor
b. Unknown
d. Hollywood, CA, April 14, 1964, Age 65

HODGKINSON, John (Meadowcroft)
Actor, Producer
b. Manchester, England, c1765
d. New York, NY, Sept. 12, 1805

HODGKINSON, Mrs. John
Actress
b. Unknown
d. Unknown, 1803

HODIAK, John
Actor
b. Pittsburgh, PA, April 16, 1914
d. Tarzana, CA, Oct. 19, 1955, Age 41

HODSON, Henrietta (Mrs. Henry Labouchère)
Actress, Producer
b. Unknown, 1841
d. Unknown, Oct. 30, 1910, Age 69

HODSON, James Landsdale
Playwright, Novelist, Journalist
b. Hazlehurst, Lancashire, England, Unknown
d. London, England, Aug. 28, 1956, Age 65

HODSON, Kate
Actress
b. Unknown
d. Unknown, April 17, 1917

HODSON, Nellie (Mrs. Charles Macdona)
Actress
b. Unknown
d. Unknown, March 16, 1940

HODSON, Sylvia (Mrs. John S. Blythe)
Actress
b. Unknown
d. Unknown, July 20, 1893

HOEY, Dennis (Samuel David Hyams)
Actor
b. London, England, March 30, 1893
d. Unknown, July 25, 1960, Age 67

HOEY, William
Actor, Producer
b. Unknown
d. Unknown, June 29, 1897

HOFER, Chris (Martin Christopher Hofer)
Press representative, Actor
b. New York, NY, Unknown
d. Rome, Italy, Feb. 11, 1964, Age 44

HOFFE, Monckton (Reaney Monckton Hoffe-Miles)
Playwright, Actor
b. Connemara, Ireland, Dec. 26, 1880
d. London, England, Nov. 4, 1951, Age 70

HOFFMAN, Aaron
Playwright
b. St. Louis, MO, Oct. 31, 1880
d. New York, NY, May 27, 1924, Age 43

HOFFMAN, Bill (Elwood C.)
Playwright, Writer
b. Detroit, MI, Unknown
d. New York, NY, Jan. 22, 1962, Age 44

HOFFMAN, Gertrude
Dancer
b. Montreal, CAN, Unknown
d. Washington, DC, June 3, 1955, Age 57

HOFFMAN, Max
Musical director, Conductor
b. Germany, Unknown
d. Hollywood, CA, May 21, 1963, Age 88

HOFFMAN, Max Jr.
Performer
b. Norfolk, VA, Unknown
d. New York, NY, March 31, 1945, Age 43

HOFLICH, Lucie
Actress
b. Unknown
d. Unknown, Oct. 1956, Age 73

HOFMANNSTHAL, Hugo von
Playwright, Poet
b. Vienna, Austria, 1874
d. Vienna, Austria, July 15, 1929, Age 55

HOGARTH, Lionel
Performer
b. Quincy, MA, April 16, 1874
d. Amityville, L.I., NY, April 15, 1946, Age 72

HOIER, Thomas P.
Performer
b. Denmark, Unknown
d. New York, NY, Dec. 20, 1951, Age 74

HOLBERG, Ludwig Baron
Playwright, Author, Producer
b. Bergen, Norway, 1684
d. Denmark, Jan. 28, 1754, Age 70

HOLBROOK, Ann Catherine
Actress, Author
b. Unknown
d. Unknown, Jan. 1837, Age 56

HOLCROFT, Thomas
Actor, Playwright
b. Unknown, c1744
d. Unknown, March 23, 1809, Age 64

HOLIDAY, Billie (Eleanora Fagan Holiday)
Singer
b. Baltimore, MD, Unknown
d. New York, NY, July 17, 1959, Age 44

HOLINSHED, Raphael
Historian
b. Chesshire, England, Unknown
d. Unknown, c1580

HOLLAND, Charles
Actor
b. Unknown
d. Unknown, Dec. 7, 1796, Age 33

HOLLAND, Charles
Actor
b. Unknown
d. Unknown, 1849, Age 71

HOLLAND, E. M. (Edmund Milton)
Performer
b. Unknown, Sept. 7, 1848
d. New York, NY, Nov. 24, 1913, Age 65

HOLLAND, Fanny
Actress
b. Unknown
d. Unknown, June 18, 1931, Age 83

HOLLAND, George
Actor
b. England, 1791
d. New York, NY, Dec. 20, 1870, Age 79

HOLLAND, George
Actor
b. Unknown
d. Unknown, Feb. 17, 1910, Age 63

HOLLAND, Joseph Jefferson
Actor
b. Unknown, 1860
d. New York, NY, Sept. 25, 1926, Age 65

HOLLAND, Mildred
Actress
b. Chicago, IL, April 9, 1869
d. New York, NY, Jan. 27, 1944, Age 74

HOLLES, Antony
Actor
b. London, England, Jan. 17, 1901
d. Unknown, Nov. 5, 1950, Age 49

HOLLIDAY, Judy (née Judith Tuvim)
Actress
b. New York, NY, June 21, 1922
d. New York, NY, June 7, 1965, Age 42

HOLLINGSHEAD, John
Producer,, Playwright,, Journalist
b. Unknown, 1827
d. Unknown, Oct. 10, 1904, Age 77

HOLLINGSWORTH, Alfred
Actor
b. Unknown
d. Glendale, CA, June 20, 1926, Age 52

HOLLIS, William
Actor, Producer
b. Liverpool, England, July 15, 1867
d. Unknown, Sept. 10, 1947, Age 80

HOLLOWAY, W. J.
Actor, Producer
b. Unknown
d. Unknown, April 6, 1913

HOLLOWAY, William Edwyn
Actor, Director
b. Adelaide, Australia, Sept. 18, 1885
d. Unknown, June 30, 1952, Age 66

HOLMAN, Joseph G.
Actor, Playwright
b. Unknown
d. Unknown, Aug. 24, 1817, Age 53

HOLMAN, Libby
Actress - Singer
b. Cincinnati, OH, May 23, 1906
d. Stanford, CT, June 19, 1971, Age 65

HOLME, Myra (Lady Pinero)
Actress
b. Unknown
d. Unknown, June 30, 1919

HOLMES, Helen (Mrs. Helen Holmes Saunders)
Actress
b. Unknown, 1892
d. Hollywood, CA, July 9, 1950, Age 58

HOLMES, Phillips
Actor
b. Grand Rapids, MI, 1907
d. Ontario, CAN, Aug. 12, 1942, Age 34

HOLMES, Ralph
Actor
b. New York, NY, Unknown
d. New York, NY, Nov. 15, 1945, Age 30

HOLMES, Robert
Actor
b. Isle of Wight, England, Jan. 7, 1899
d. Unknown, July 10, 1945, Age 46

HOLMES, Taylor
Actor
b. Newark, NJ, May 16, 1878
d. Hollywood, CA, Sept. 30, 1959, Age 81

HOLMES, Wendell
Actor
b. Unknown
d. Paris, France, April 26, 1962, Age 47

HOLT, Clarence
Actor, Producer
b. Unknown
d. Unknown, Sept. 27, 1903, Age 77

HOLT, Clarence
Actor
b. Unknown
d. New York, NY, July 5, 1920

HOLT, Harold
Impresario
b. Unknown
d. Unknown, Sept. 3, 1953, Age 67

HOLT, Jack
Actor
b. Winchester, VA, May 31, 1888
d. Sawtelle, CA, Jan. 18, 1951, Age 62

HOLTZMAN, David M.
Producer, Lawyer
b. Brooklyn, NY, Feb. 21, 1908
d. New York, NY, March 2, 1965, Age 57

HOLZMAN, Benjamin F.
Talent representative, Press representative
b. Unknown
d. Hollywood, CA, May 8, 1963, Age 72

HOMAN, Gertrude
Actress
b. Unknown
d. Glen Cove, L.I., NY, May 29, 1951, Age 71

HOME, Rev. John
Playwright
b. Unknown, 1722
d. Unknown, Sept. 5, 1808, Age 85

HOMFREY, Gladys
Actress
b. Unknown
d. Unknown, March 10, 1932, Age 83

HONEGGER, Arthur
Composer
b. Le Havre, France, 1892
d. Paris, France, Nov. 27, 1955, Age 63

HONEY, George Alfred
Actor
b. Unknown, May 1823
d. London, England, May 28, 1880, Age 57

HONNER, Robert
Actor, Producer
b. Unknown
d. Unknown, Dec. 31, 1852, Age 43

HONRI, Percy (Percy Harry Thompson)
Performer
b. Unknown
d. Sussex, England, Sept. 24, 1953, Age 78

HOOD, Captain Basil
Librettist, Lyricist
b. Unknown, April 5, 1864
d. London, England, Aug. 7, 1917, Age 53

HOOK, Theodore
Playwright
b. Unknown
d. Unknown, Aug. 24, 1842, Age 53

HOOKER, Brian
Playwright, Composer
b. New London, CT, Unknown
d. New London, CT, Dec. 28, 1946, Age 66

HOOLE, John
Playwright
b. Unknown
d. Unknown, Aug. 2, 1803, Age 75

HOOPER, Edward
Actor, Producer
b. Unknown
d. Unknown, Jan. 27, 1865, Age 70

HOPE, Adele Blood
Actress, Promoter
b. Unknown
d. Yonkers, NY, Sept. 13, 1936, Age 50

HOPE, Anthony (Sir Anthony Hope-Hawkins)
Playwright, Novelist
b. London, England, Feb. 9, 1863
d. Unknown, July 8, 1933, Age 70

HOPE, Mabel Ellams
Playwright
b. Unknown
d. Unknown, July 24, 1937

HOPE, Maidie
Actress
b. London, England, Feb. 15, 1881
d. Unknown, April 18, 1937, Age 56

HOPE, Vida
Actress, Director
b. Unknown
d. Chelmsford, England, Dec. 23, 1963, Age 45

HOPKINS, Arthur
Producer, Director
b. Cleveland, OH, Oct. 4, 1878
d. New York, NY, March 22, 1950, Age 71

HOPKINS, Bob
Actor
b. Unknown
d. Hollywood, CA, Oct. 5, 1962, Age 44

HOPKINS, Charles
Producer, Director, Actor
b. Philadelphia, PA, Jan. 1, 1884
d. New York, NY, Jan. 1, 1953, Age 69

HOPKINS, Miriam
Actress
b. Bainbridge, GA, Oct. 18, 1902
d. New York, NY, Oct. 9, 1972, Age 69

HOPPER, Charles H.
Actor
b. Unknown
d. Unknown, June 17, 1916, Age 53

HOPPER, De Wolf (William De Wolf Hopper)
Actor
b. New York, NY, March 30, 1858
d. Kansas City, MO, Sept. 23, 1935, Age 77

HOPPER, Edna Wallace (Mrs. Albert O. Brown)
Actress
b. San Francisco, CA, Jan. 17, 1864 or 74
d. New York, NY, Dec. 14, 1959, Age 95 or 85

HOPPER, Hedda (née Elda Furry)
Columnist, Actress
b. Hollidaysburg, PA, June 2, 1890
d. Hollywood, CA, Feb. 1, 1966, Age 75

HOPPER, Rika
Actress
b. Unknown
d. Amsterdam, Holland, Dec. 1963, Age 86

HOPWOOD, Avery
Playwright
b. Cleveland, OH, May 28, 1882
d. Juan-les-Pines, France, July 1, 1928, Age 46

HORITZ, Joseph F.
Performer
b. Unknown
d. Philadelphia, PA, Dec. 4, 1961, Age 87

HORKHEIMER, Herbert M.
Producer
b. Unknown
d. Hollywood, CA, April 27, 1962, Age 80

HORNBLOW, Arthur
Author, Historian, Editor
b. Manchester, England, Unknown
d. Asbury Park, NJ, May 6, 1942, Age 77

HORNER, Lottie
Talent representative
b. Unknown
d. Hollywood, CA, July 7, 1964

HORNIMAN, Annie Elizabeth Fredericka
Producer
b. Forest Hill, London, England, Oct. 3, 1860
d. London, England, Aug. 6, 1937, Age 76

HORNIMAN, Roy
Playwright, Novelist, Actor, Producer
b. Unknown
d. Unknown, Oct. 11, 1930, Age 62

HORNSBY, Nancy
Actress
b. London, England, May 11, 1910
d. Unknown, Sept. 1958, Age 48

HORSMAN, Charles
Actor, Playwright
b. Unknown
d. Unknown, Aug. 4, 1886, Age 61

HORSNELL, Horace
Critic, Playwright, Novelist
b. St. Leonards, Sussex, England, 1883
d. Unknown, Feb. 10, 1949, Age 66

HORWIN, C. Jerome
Playwright
b. New York, NY, Unknown
d. Hollywood, CA, April 24, 1954, Age 49

HOSCHNA, Karl
Composer
b. Kuschwarda, Bohemia, Aug. 16, 1877
d. Unknown, Dec. 23, 1911, Age 34

HOTVEDT, Phyllis Shaw
Actress
b. Unknown
d. Norwalk, CT, May 12, 1964, Age 53

HOUGH, Will M.
Librettist, Lyricist
b. Unknown
d. Carmel, CA, Nov. 20, 1962, Age 80

HOUGHTON, Belle
Performer
b. Unknown
d. London, England, July 14, 1964, Age 95

HOUGHTON, (William) Stanley
Playwright
b. Unknown, 1881
d. Unknown, Dec. 11, 1913, Age 32

HOUSE, Billy
Actor
b. Unknown
d. Woodland Hills, CA, Sept. 23, 1961, Age 71

HOUSMAN, Laurence
Author, Playwright
b. England, July 18, 1865
d. Shepton Mallet, Somerset, England, Feb. 20, 1959, Age 93

HOUSTON, George Fleming
Performer
b. Hampton, NJ, Unknown
d. Hollywood, CA, Nov. 12, 1944, Age 47

HOWARD, Andree
Dancer, Choreographer
b. Unknown, Oct. 3, 1910
d. London, England, April 18, 1968, Age 57

HOWARD, Art
Performer
b. Unknown
d. Hollywood, CA, May 28, 1963, Age 71

HOWARD, Bronson
Playwright, Journalist
b. Detroit, MI, Oct. 7, 1842
d. Avon-by-the-Sea, NJ, Aug. 4, 1908, Age 65

HOWARD, Cecil
Critic, Historian
b. Unknown
d. Unknown, Sept. 20, 1895, Age 59

HOWARD, Cordelia (Mrs. Edmund J. MacDonald)
Actress
b. Providence, RI, Feb. 1, 1848
d. Belmont, MA, Aug. 10, 1941, Age 93

HOWARD, Eugene (né Isidore Levkowitz)
Performer, Actor
b. Neustadt, Germany, July 7, 1881
d. New York, NY, Aug. 1, 1965, Age 84

HOWARD, George
Manager
b. Unknown
d. Vancouver, WA, March 17, 1921, Age 55

HOWARD, George Bronson
Playwright, Author
b. Unknown
d. Los Angeles, CA, Nov. 20, 1922, Age 38

HOWARD, J. B.
Producer, Actor
b. Unknown
d. Unknown, May 14, 1895, Age 54

HOWARD, J. Bannister
Producer
b. London, England, Feb. 27, 1867
d. Unknown, Jan. 27, 1946, Age 78

HOWARD, John Tasker
Composer, Author, Editor, Educator
b. Brooklyn, NY, Nov. 30, 1890
d. West Orange, NJ, Nov. 19, 1964, Age 73

HOWARD, Joseph E.
Performer, Composer
b. New York, NY, Feb. 12, 1867
d. Chicago, IL, May 19, 1961, Age 94

HOWARD, Keble (John Keble Bell)
Playwright, Novelist
b. Basingstoke, England, June 8, 1875
d. Unknown, March 29, 1928, Age 52

HOWARD, Leslie (né Stainer)
Actor, Playwright, Director
b. London, England, April 3, 1893
d. in airplane between Lisbon and London, June 1, 1943, Age 50

HOWARD, Norah
Actress
b. London, England, Dec. 12, 1901
d. Unknown, April 1968, Age 66

HOWARD, Sam
Talent representative, Performer
b. Unknown
d. Hollywood, CA, April 20, 1964, Age 61

HOWARD, Sidney Coe
Playwright
b. Oakland, CA, June 26, 1891
d. Tyringham, MA, Aug. 23, 1939, Age 48

HOWARD, Sir Robert
Playwright
b. Unknown
d. Unknown, Sept. 3, 1698, Age 72

HOWARD, Sydney
Actor
b. Yeadon, near Leeds, England, Aug. 7, 1885
d. London, England, June 12, 1946, Age 60

HOWARD, Walter
Actor, Playwright, Producer
b. Leamington, England, March 7, 1866
d. Unknown, Oct. 6, 1922, Age 56

HOWARD, William W.
Theatre executive
b. Chicago, IL, Unknown
d. New York, NY, Oct. 30, 1963, Age 65

Howard, Willie (William Levkowitz)
Comedian
b. Neustadt, Germany, April 13, 1886
d. New York, NY, Jan. 12, 1949, Age 62

HOWE, Henry (Hutchinson)
Actor
b. Unknown, 1812
d. Unknown, March 10, 1896, Age 83

HOWE, J. B.
Actor
b. Unknown
d. Unknown, March 9, 1908, Age 79

HOWE, Julia Ward
Playwright, Poet
b. New York, NY, May 27, 1819
d. Oak Glen, RI, Oct. 17, 1910, Age 91

HOWELL, John
Actor
b. Penmaenmawr, Carnarvonshire, Wales, Aug. 13, 1888
d. Unknown, Aug. 4, 1928, Age 39

HOWELLS, William Dean
Playwright, Editor, Critic
b. Martins Ferry, OH, March 1, 1837
d. New York, NY, May 11, 1920, Age 83

HOWLAND, Alan
Actor
b. Unknown
d. Unknown, Nov. 1, 1946, Age 47

HOWLAND, Jobyna
Actress
b. Indianapolis, IN, March 31, 1880
d. Los Angeles, CA, June 7, 1936, Age 56

HOWLAND, Olin
Actor
b. Unknown
d. Hollywood, CA, Sept. 20, 1959, Age 63

HOWSON, Frank A.
Actor
b. Unknown
d. Unknown, July 9, 1945, Age 66

HOWSON, John
Performer
b. Unknown
d. Unknown, Dec. 16, 1887

HOYT, Caroline Miskel
Actress
b. Unknown
d. Unknown, Oct. 2, 1898, Age 25

HOYT, Charles Hale
Playwright
b. Concord, NH, July 26, 1860
d. Unknown, Nov. 20, 1900, Age 40

HOYT, Julia
Actress
b. New York, NY, Unknown
d. New York, NY, Oct. 31, 1955, Age 58

HOYT, Mrs. Charles H. (Flora Walsh)
Actress
b. Unknown
d. Unknown, Jan. 22, 1893

HROTSVITHA OF GANDERSHEIM, (a/k/a Hrotsuitha; Hrotswitha; or Roswitha)
Playwright
b. Germany, c935
d. Unknown, c973, Age 38

HUBAN, Eileen
Actress
b. Loughrea, Galway, Ireland, 1895
d. New York, NY, Oct. 22, 1935, Age 39

HUBBEL, Raymond
Composer
b. Urbana, OH, June 1, 1879
d. Miami, FL, Dec. 13, 1954, Age 75

HUBER, Harold
Actor
b. New York, NY, Unknown
d. New York, NY, Sept. 29, 1959, Age 49

HUBERT, George
Performer
b. Unknown
d. Hollywood, CA, May 8, 1963, Age 82

HUDD, Walter
Actor, Playwright, Teacher
b. London, England, Feb. 20, 1898
d. London, England, Jan. 20, 1963, Age 64

HUDMAN, Wesley
Actor
b. Unknown
d. Williams, AZ, Feb. 29, 1964, Age 48

HUDSON, Charles
Actor, Playwright
b. Unknown
d. Unknown, July 10, 1897

HUFFMAN, Jessie C.
Director, Producer
b. Unknown
d. Unknown, June 22, 1935, Age 66

HUGHES, Langston
Playwright, Poet
b. Joplin, MO, Feb. 1, 1902
d. New York, NY, May 22, 1967, Age 65

HUGHES, Adelaide
Performer
b. Glendora, CA, Unknown
d. New York, NY, Aug. 20, 1937, Age 20

HUGHES, Adelaide
Dancer
b. Unknown
d. Jamaica, NY, Jan. 21, 1960, Age 70

HUGHES, Annie
Actress
b. Southampton, England, Oct. 10, 1869
d. Unknown, Jan. 7, 1954, Age 84

HUGHES, Archie
Actor
b. Unknown
d. Unknown, 1860

HUGHES, Ernest
Performer, Historian
b. Unknown
d. Cleveland, OH, Feb. 11, 1962, Age 82

HUGHES, Fanny (Mrs. Edward Swanborough)
Actress
b. Unknown
d. Unknown, Jan. 12, 1888, Age 45

HUGHES, Glenn A.
Teacher, Director, Playwright
b. Cozad, NB, Dec. 7, 1894
d. Seattle, WA, March 21, 1964, Age 69

HUGHES, Hatcher
Playwright
b. Polkville, NC, 1883
d. New York, NY, Oct. 18, 1945, Age 62

HUGHES, Henry
Actor
b. Unknown
d. Unknown, Oct. 11, 1872, Age 62

HUGHES, John
Playwright
b. Unknown
d. Unknown, Feb. 17, 1720, Age 41

HUGHES, Lloyd
Actor
b. Unknown
d. San Gabriel, CA, June 6, 1958, Age 61

HUGHES, Margaret
Actress
b. Unknown, c1643
d. Unknown, 1719

HUGHES, Rupert
Author, Playwright, Critic
b. Lancaster, MO, Jan. 31, 1872
d. Los Angeles, CA, Sept. 9, 1956, Age 84

HUGO, Victor Marie, Viscount
Playwright, Poet, Novelist
b. Besançon, France, Feb. 26, 1802
d. Paris, France, May 22, 1885, Age 83

HUGUENET, Felix
Actor
b. Lyons, France, 1858
d. Unknown, Nov. 19, 1926, Age 68

HULBERT, Claude
Performer
b. Unknown
d. Sydney, Australia, Jan. 22, 1964, Age 63

HULL, Josephine (née Sherwood)
Actress
b. Newtonville, MA, Jan. 3, 1886
d. Bronx, NY, March 12, 1957, Age 71

HULL, Shelly
Actor
b. Louisville, KY, Unknown
d. New York, NY, Jan. 14, 1919, Age 35

HULL, Thomas
Actor, Playwright
b. Unknown
d. Unknown, April 22, 1808, Age 80

HUME, Benita
Actress
b. London, England, 1906
d. Egerton, England, Nov. 1, 1967, Age 61

HUME, Fergus
Playwright, Novelist
b. Unknown
d. Unknown, July 12, 1932, Age 73

HUMIERES, Robert d'
Playwright
b. Unknown
d. Unknown

HUMPERDINCK, Prof. Engelbert
Composer
b. Unknown
d. Berlin, Germany, Sept. 28, 1921, Age 67

HUMPHREY, Doris (Mrs. Charles Francis Woodford)
Choreographer, Dancer
b. Oak Park, IL, Unknown
d. New York, NY, Dec. 29, 1958, Age 63

HUMPHREYS, Cecil
Actor
b. Cheltenham, England, July 21, 1883
d. New York, NY, Nov. 6, 1947, Age 64

HUMPHRIES, John
Actor
b. Unknown
d. Unknown, Sept. 28, 1927, Age 63

HUNEKER, James Gibbons
Critic
b. Philadelphia, PA, Jan. 31, 1859
d. Brooklyn, NY, Feb. 9, 1921, Age 64

HUNT, Al
Press representative
b. Unknown
d. Sutton, England, Aug. 15, 1964, Age 45

HUNT, (James Henry) Leigh
Critic, Poet
b. Southgate, Middlesex, England, 1784
d. Putney, England, Aug. 28, 1859, Age 75

HUNT, Martita
Actress
b. Argentina, Jan. 30, 1900
d. London, England, June 13, 1969, Age 69

HUNTER, Glenn
Actor
b. Highland Mills, NY, 1893
d. Bronx, NY, Dec. 30, 1945, Age 52

HUNTER, Harrison
Actor
b. England, Unknown
d. Boston, MA, Jan. 2, 1923

HUNTER, Jackie
Actor
b. Canada, Unknown
d. London, England, Nov. 21, 1951, Age 50

HUNTER, Richard
Actor
b. Unknown
d. Santa Monica, CA, Dec. 22, 1962, Age 87

HUNTLEY, George Patrick
Actor
b. Fermoy, County Cork, Ireland, July 13, 1868
d. London, England, Sept. 21, 1927, Age 59

HUNTLEY, Grace
Actress
b. Unknown
d. Unknown, Oct. 11, 1896

HUPFELD, Herman
Songwriter
b. Montclair, NJ, Unknown
d. Montclair, NJ, June 8, 1951, Age 57

HURGON, Austen A.
Playwright, Director
b. Unknown
d. Unknown, June 24, 1942, Age 74

HUROK, Sol
Impresario
b. Pogar, Russia, April 9, 1888
d. New York, NY, March 5, 1974, Age 86

HURST, Brandon
Actor
b. London, England, Unknown
d. Hollywood, CA, July 15, 1947, Age 81

HURST, Fannie
Author
b. Hamilton, OH, Oct. 18, 1889
d. New York, NY, Feb. 23, 1968, Age 78

HURTIG, Louis
Producer
b. Unknown
d. New York, NY, July 22, 1924, Age 53

HURWITCH, Moses
Playwright
b. Unknown, 1844
d. Unknown, 1910

HUSCH, Richard J. (pseudonym, Richard Gerard)
Lyricist
b. New York, NY, Unknown
d. New York, NY, July 2, 1948, Age 72

HUSSEY, Jimmy
Actor
b. Chicago, IL, Jan. 19, 1891
d. Unknown, Nov. 20, 1930, Age 39

HUSTON, Walter
Actor
b. Toronto, CAN, April 6, 1884
d. Beverly Hills, CA, April 7, 1950, Age 66

HUTCHINSON, Dorothy (Mrs. Frank Della Lana)
Singer, Teacher
b. Washington, DC, Unknown
d. Washington, DC, Oct. 16, 1962, Age 80

HUTCHINSON, Emma
Actress, Producer
b. Unknown
d. Unknown, Oct. 29, 1817, Age 72

HUTCHISON, Percy
Actor, Producer
b. Stratford-upon-Avon, England, 1875
d. Unknown, April 18, 1945, Age 69

HUTTON, Joseph
Actor, Playwright
b. Philadelphia, PA, 1787
d. Newbern, NC, 1828

HUTTON, Laurence
Critic, Author
b. Unknown
d. Unknown, June 10, 1904, Age 60

HUXLEY, Aldous Leonard
Novelist, Essayist, Playwright
b. Godalming, Surrey, England, July 26, 1894
d. Hollywood, CA, Nov. 22, 1963, Age 69

HYEM, Constance Ethel
Actress
b. London, England, Unknown
d. Unknown, April 13, 1928, Age 54

HYLAND, Augustin Allen
Performer
b. Unknown
d. Hollywood, CA, Feb. 8, 1963, Age 58

HYLTON, Jack
Producer, Musician, Performer
b. Bolten, Lancashire, England, July 2, 1892
d. Unknown, Jan. 29, 1965, Age 72

HYLTON, Millie
Actress
b. Birmingham, England, Feb. 8, 1868
d. Unknown, Sept. 1, 1920, Age 52

HYLTON, Richard
Performer
b. Unknown
d. San Francisco, CA, May 12, 1962, Age 41

HYMER, John B.
Playwright
b. Nashville, TN, Unknown
d. Los Angeles, CA, June 16, 1953, Age 77

HYMER, Warren
Actor
b. Unknown
d. Los Angeles, CA, March 25, 1948, Age 42

I

IBERT, Jacques
Composer, Lyricist
b. Paris, France, Aug. 15, 1890
d. Paris, France, Feb. 5, 1962, Age 71

IBSEN, Henrik
Playwright
b. Skien, Norway, March 20, 1828
d. Oslo, Norway, May 23, 1906, Age 78

ICHIKAWA, Sadanje
Actor
b. Unknown
d. Unknown, Feb. 23, 1940, Age 59

IFFLAND, August Wilhelm
Actor, Playwright, Producer
b. Hanover, Germany, April 19, 1759
d. Berlin, Germany, Sept. 22, 1814, Age 55

ILLINGTON, Margaret (Mrs. Edward J. Bowes née Maud Light)
Actress
b. Bloomington, IL, July 23, 1881
d. Miami Beach, FL, March 11, 1934, Age 52

ILLINGTON, Marie
Actress
b. Unknown
d. Unknown, Feb. 3, 1927, Age 71

IMHOF, Roger
Performer
b. Rock Island, IL, Unknown
d. Beverly Hills, CA, April 15, 1958, Age 83

INCE, Ralph W.
Actor, Director
b. Boston, MA, Unknown
d. Kensington, England, April 11, 1935, Age 50

INCHBALD, Joseph
Actor
b. Unknown
d. Unknown, June 6, 1779

INCHBALD, Mrs. Elizabeth (née Simpson)
Playwright, Actress
b. Unknown, 1753
d. Unknown, Aug. 1, 1821, Age 68

INCLEDON, Charles ("The Wandering Melodist")
Performer
b. Unknown
d. Unknown, Feb. 11, 1826, Age 63

INESCOURT, Elaine
Actress
b. Unknown
d. Brighton, England, July 7, 1964, Age 87

INGE, William
Playwright
b. Independence, KS, May 3, 1913
d. Hollywood Hills, CA, June 10, 1973, Age 60

INGERSOLL, William
Actor
b. Lafayette, IN, Unknown
d. Hollywood, CA, May 7, 1936, Age 76

INGLE, Charles (August Chevalier)
Composer
b. Unknown
d. Unknown, Feb. 26, 1940, Age 77

INGRAM, Rex
Actor
b. Aboard the "Robert E. Lee" on the Mississippi River, Oct. 20, 1895
d. Hollywood, CA, Sept. 19, 1969, Age 73

INTROPODI, Ethel
Actress
b. New York, NY, Unknown
d. New York, NY, Dec. 18, 1946, Age 50

INTROPODI, Josie
Actress
b. New York, NY, Unknown
d. New York, NY, Sept. 19, 1941, Age 75

IRELAND, Anthony
Actor
b. Peru, Feb. 5, 1902
d. London, England, Dec. 4, 1957, Age 55

IRELAND, Joseph Norton
Historian
b. Unknown
d. Unknown, Dec. 29, 1898, Age 81

IRELAND, William Henry
Author of Shakespeare Forgeries
b. Unknown, 1775
d. Unknown, April 17, 1835, Age 59

IRISH, Annie (Lady Fladgate)
Actress
b. Warloys, Hunts, England, April 21, 1865
d. Unknown, May 20, 1947, Age 82

IRVINE, Harry
Actor
b. British India, Unknown
d. Nyack, NY, Aug. 7, 1951, Age 77

IRVINE, Robin
Actor
b. London, England, Dec. 21, 1901
d. Unknown, April 28, 1933, Age 31

IRVING, Ben
Executive, Actors Equity
b. Brooklyn, NY, March 15, 1919
d. New York, NY, Feb. 7, 1968, Age 48

IRVING, Daisy
Actress
b. Ireland, Unknown
d. Unknown, April 10,1938

IRVING, Ethel
Actress
b. Unknown, Sept. 5, 1869
d. Bexhill, England, May 3, 1963, Age 93

IRVING, Henry Brodribb
Actor, Producer, Author
b. London, England, Aug. 5, 1870
d. Unknown, Oct. 17, 1919, Age 49

IRVING, Isabel
Actress
b. Bridgeport, CT, Feb. 28, 1871
d. Nantucket, MA, Sept. 1, 1944, Age 73

IRVING, Joseph Henry
Actor
b. Unknown
d. Unknown, Sept. 6, 1870, Age 31

IRVING, K. Ernest
Composer, Conductor
b. Godalming, Surrey, England, Nov. 6, 1878
d. Unknown, Oct. 24, 1953, Age 74

IRVING, Lawrence Sidney Brodribb
Actor, Producer, Playwright
b. London, England, Dec. 21, 1871
d. Drowned in St. Lawrence River, CAN, May 29, 1914, Age 42

IRVING, Mrs. Joseph
Actress
b. Unknown
d. Unknown, Dec. 7, 1925, Age 80

IRVING, Sir Henry (John Henry Brodribb)
Actor, Producer
b. Keinton Mandeville, Somerset, England, Feb. 6, 1838
d. Bradford, England, Oct. 13, 1905, Age 67

IRVING, Washington
Playwright, Author, Diplomat
b. New York, NY, April 3, 1783
d. Tarrytown, NY, Nov. 28, 1859, Age 76

IRWIN, Edward
Actor, Playwright
b. Leeds, England, March 7, 1867
d. Unknown, Feb. 25, 1937, Age 69

IRWIN, Felix
Actor
b. Unknown
d. Unknown, Nov. 30, 1950, Age 57

IRWIN, Flo (Campbell)
Performer
b. Whitby, Ontario, CAN, Unknown
d. Los Angeles, CA, Dec. 21, 1930, Age 71

IRWIN, May
Actress
b. Whitby, Ontario, CAN, June 27, 1862
d. New York, NY, Oct. 22, 1938, Age 76

ISAACS, Edith J. R. (Rich)
Stage expert, Editor, Author
b. Milwaukee, WI, March 27, 1878
d. White Plains, NY, Jan. 10, 1956, Age 77

ISHAM, Frederic S.
Playwright, Novelist
b. Unknown
d. New York, NY, Sept. 6, 1922, Age 57

ISOLA, Emile
Theatre manager
b. Unknown
d. Unknown, May 17, 1945, Age 85

ISOLA, Vincent
Producer
b. Algeria, Unknown
d. Paris, France, Sept. 1947, Age 85

IVAN, Rosalind
Actress, Playwright
b. London, England, Unknown
d. New York, NY, April 6, 1959, Age 77

IVERS, James D.
Editor of the Motion Picture Herald
b. Unknown
d. Hackensack, NJ, June 12, 1964, Age 54

J

JACKLEY, George
Comedian
b. Unknown
d. Unknown, Jan. 26, 1950, Age 65

JACKMAN, Isaac
Playwright
b. Unknown, fl. 1795

JACKSON, Charles
Playwright, Author
b. Summit, NJ, April 6, 1903
d. New York, NY, Sept. 21, 1968, Age 65

JACKSON, Ethel
Actress
b. New York, NY, Nov. 1, 1877
d. East Islip, NY, Nov. 23, 1957, Age 80

JACKSON, Joe (Joseph Francis Jiranek)
Comedian
b. Vienna, Austria, Unknown
d. New York, NY, May 14, 1942, Age 62

JACKSON, John
Actor, Playwright
b. Unknown
d. Unknown, Dec. 4, 1806, Age 76

JACKSON, Sir Barry Vincent
Stage impresario, Playwright
b. Birmingham, England, Sept. 6, 1879
d. Birmingham, England, April 3, 1961, Age 81

JACOB, Naomi
Novelist, Actress, Politician
b. Ripon, Yorkshire, England, Unknown
d. Sirmione, Lake Garda, Italy, Aug. 27, 1964, Age 80

JACOBI, Maurice
Musical director
b. Unknown
d. Unknown, Feb. 11, 1939

JACOBI, Victor
Composer
b. Budapest, Hungary, Oct. 22, 1883
d. New York, NY, Dec. 11, 1921, Age 38

JACOBS, William Wymark
Playwright, Novelist
b. London, England, Sept. 8, 1863
d. Unknown, Sept. 1, 1943, Age 79

JACOBSEN, L. H.
Critic
b. Unknown
d. Unknown, Jan. 4, 1941, Age 81

JACOBSON, Sam
Performer
b. Unknown
d. Toledo, OH, May 12, 1964, Age 89

JAGGARD, William
Printer, Publisher
b. Unknown, 1568
d. Unknown, 1623

JAHR, Adolf
Actor
b. Unknown
d. Stockholm, Sweden, April 19, 1964, Age 70

JALLAND, Henry
Producer
b. Horncastle, Lincolnshire, England, Aug. 7, 1861
d. Unknown, June 17, 1928, Age 67

JAMES, Cairns
Actor
b. Unknown
d. Unknown, Oct. 7, 1946, Age 81

JAMES, Charles James
Scenic artist, Producer
b. Unknown
d. Unknown, Oct. 2, 1888, Age 84

JAMES, Clifton (Meyrich Edward Clifton James)
Actor
b. Unknown
d. Worthing, England, May 8, 1963, Age 65

JAMES, David
Actor, Producer
b. Unknown, 1839
d. Unknown, Oct. 2, 1893, Age 54

JAMES, David Jr.
Actor, Director
b. Unknown
d. Unknown, April 25, 1917

JAMES, Gerald
Actor, Theatre manager
b. Unknown
d. Southend, England, Jan. 5, 1964, Age 77

JAMES, Henry
Playwright, Novelist
b. New York, NY, April 15, 1843
d. London, England, Feb. 28, 1916, Age 72

JAMES, Horace D.
Actor
b. Unknown
d. Orange, NJ, Oct. 16, 1925, Age 72

JAMES, Julia
Actress
b. Unknown
d. England, July 1964, Age 74

JAMES, Kate
Actress
b. Unknown
d. Unknown, Nov. 2, 1913, Age 59

JAMES, Louis
Actor, Producer
b. Tremont, IL, Oct. 3, 1842
d. Helena, MT, March 5, 1910, Age 67

JAMES, Rian
Novelist, Screenwriter, Playwright
b. Unknown
d. Newport Beach, CA, April 26, 1953, Age 53

JAMESON, House
Actor
b. Austin, TX, Dec. 17, 1902
d. Danbury, CT, April 23, 1971, Age 68

JANAUSCHEK, Madame Francesca Romana Magdalena
Actress
b. Prague, Czechoslovakia, 1830
d. New York State, Nov. 28, 1904, Age 74

JANIN, Jules Gabriel
Journalist, Critic
b. Unknown, 1804
d. Unknown, 1874

JANIS, Elsie (Bierbower)
Actress, Author
b. Columbus, OH, March 16, 1889
d. Beverly Hills, CA, Feb. 26, 1956, Age 66

JANNINGS, Emil
Actor
b. Brooklyn, NY, 1886
d. Lake Wolfgang, Zinkenbach, Austria, Jan. 2, 1950, Age 63

JANS, Harry
Performer
b. Unknown
d. Hollywood, CA, Feb. 4, 1962, Age 62

JANSEN, Marie
Actress
b. Unknown, 1857
d. Unknown, March 20, 1914

JANVIER, Emma
Comedienne
b. Unknown
d. New York, NY, Aug. 31, 1924

JARBEAU, Vernona
Actress
b. Unknown
d. Unknown, Oct. 16, 1914, Age 53

JARDINE, Betty (Elizabeth McKittrick Jardine)
Actress
b. Heaton Moor, Manchester, England, Unknown
d. Unknown, Feb. 28, 1945

JARMAN, Herbert
Actor, Director
b. Unknown
d. Unknown, Nov. 14, 1919, Age 48

JARRETT, Henry C. (the elder)
Manager
b. Unknown
d. Unknown, Aug. 2, 1886

JARRETT, Henry C.
Producer
b. Baltimore, MD, Unknown
d. Unknown, Oct. 14, 1903, Age 76

JARRY, Alfred
Poet, Critic, Playwright, Artist
b. Laval, Mayenne, France, Sept. 8, 1873
d. Paris, France, Nov. 1, 1907, Age 34

JAY, Ernest
Actor
b. London, England, Sept. 18, 1893
d. Unknown, Feb. 8, 1957, Age 63

JAY, Harriet (a/k/a Charles Marlowe)
Playwright, Actress, Novelist
b. London, England, 1863
d. Eilford, Essex, England, Dec. 21, 1932, Age 69

JAY, Isabel
Actress
b. London, England, Oct. 17, 1879
d. Unknown, Feb. 26, 1927, Age 47

JAY, John Herbert
Theatre manager, Producer
b. London, England, Oct. 19, 1871
d. Unknown, Jan. 19, 1942, Age 70

JEANS, Ursula
Actress
b. Simla, India, May 5, 1906
d. London, England, April 21, 1973, Age 66

JEAYES, Allan
Actor, Playwright
b. Hampstead, London, England, Unknown
d. London, England, Sept. 20, 1963, Age 78

JECKS, Clara
Actress
b. Unknown
d. Unknown, Jan. 5, 1951, Age 94

JEDD, Gerry
Performer
b. Cleveland, OH, Dec. 21, 1924
d. New York, NY, Nov. 28, 1962, Age 37

JEFFERIES, Douglas
Actor
b. Hampstead, London, England, April 21, 1884
d. Unknown, Dec. 1959, Age 75

JEFFERS, Robinson
Playwright, Poet
b. Pittsburgh, PA, Jan. 10, 1887
d. Carmel, CA, Jan. 20, 1962, Age 75

JEFFERSON, Charles Burke
Actor, Manager
b. Unknown, 1851
d. Unknown, 1908

JEFFERSON, Cornelia Frances (née Thomas)
Actress, Singer
b. Unknown, 1796
d. Unknown, 1849

JEFFERSON, Joseph
Actor
b. Unknown, 1774
d. Unknown, Aug. 4, 1832, Age 58

JEFFERSON, Joseph
Actor, Scenic Painter
b. Unknown, 1804
d. Unknown, 1842

JEFFERSON, Joseph
Actor, Producer
b. Philadelphia, PA, Feb. 20, 1829
d. Palm Beach, FL, April 23, 1905, Age 76

JEFFERSON, Joseph Warren
Actor
b. Unknown
d. New York, NY, April 30, 1919, Age 49

JEFFERSON, Thomas
Actor, Producer
b. Unknown, 1732
d. Unknown, 1797

JEFFERSON, Thomas
Actor
b. Unknown
d. Hollywood, CA, April 2, 1932, Age 76

JEFFERSON, William Winter
Actor
b. London, England, Unknown
d. Honolulu, HI, Feb. 1946, Age 70

JEFFREYS, Ellis (Minnie Gertrude Ellis Jeffreys)
Actress
b. Colombo, Ceylon, May 17, 1872
d. Surrey, England, Jan. 21, 1943, Age 70

JEFFREYS-GOODFRIEND, Ida
Actress
b. Unknown
d. New York, NY, Feb. 16, 1926, Age 70

JEFFRIES, Maud
Actress
b. Mississippi, Dec. 14, 1869
d. Unknown, Sept. 27, 1946, Age 76

JEFFRYS, George
Playwright, Poet
b. Unknown
d. Unknown, Aug. 17, 1755, Age 77

JEHLINGER, Charles
Educator, Actor
b. Macomb, IL, March 7, 1866
d. New York, NY, July 29, 1952, Age 86

JENKS, Frank
Actor
b. Des Moines, IA, Unknown
d. Los Angeles, CA, May 13, 1962, Age 59

JENNINGS, Dewitt C.
Actor
b. Cameron, MO, Unknown
d. Hollywood, CA, March 1, 1937, Age 65

JENNINGS, Gertrude E.
Playwright, Actress
b. Unknown
d. Fittleworth, Sussex, England, Sept. 28, 1958, Age 81

JEPHSON, Robert
Playwright, Poet
b. Unknown
d. Unknown, May 31, 1803, Age 67

JERMINGHAM, Edward
Playwright, Poet
b. Unknown
d. Unknown, Nov. 17, 1812, Age 85

JEROME, Ben M.
Composer
b. New York, NY, Unknown
d. Huntington, L.I., NY, Nov. 27, 1938, Age 55

JEROME, Edwin
Actor
b. Unknown
d. Pasadena, CA, Sept. 10, 1959, Age 73

JEROME, Jerome Klapka
Playwright, Novelist
b. Walsall, England, May 2, 1859
d. Unknown, June 14, 1927, Age 68

JEROME, Sadie (née Witkowski)
Actress
b. New York, NY, 1876
d. Unknown, April 30, 1950, Age 74

JEROME, William
Lyricist
b. Cornwall-on-Hudson, NY, Unknown
d. New York, NY, June 25, 1932, Age 67

JERROLD, Douglas William
Playwright
b. Unknown, 1803
d. Unknown, June 8, 1857, Age 54

JERROLD, Mary
Actress
b. London, England, Dec. 4, 1877
d. London, England, March 3, 1955, Age 77

JERROLD, William Blanchard
Playwright
b. Unknown, 1826
d. Unknown, March 10, 1884, Age 57

JESSE, Fryniwyd Tennyson (Mrs. H. M. Harwood)
Playwright, Novelist
b. Unknown
d. London, England, Aug. 6, 1958, Age 69

JESSEL, Patricia
Actress
b. Hong Kong, Oct. 15, 1920
d. London, England, June 8, 1968, Age 47

JESSNER, Leopold
Director, Producer
b. Koenigsberg, Germany, 1878
d. Los Angeles, CA, DEC. 13, 1945, Age 67

JESSOP, George H.
Playwright
b. Unknown
d. Unknown, March 21, 1915

JESSUP, Stanley
Actor
b. Chester, NY, Unknown
d. New York, NY, Oct. 26, 1945, Age 67

JEVON, Thomas
Actor, Playwright
b. Unknown
d. Unknown, Dec. 20, 1688

JEWETT, Henry
Actor, Producer
b. Australia, Unknown
d. West Newton, MA, June 24, 1930, Age 68

JOB, Thomas
Author, Playwright, Educator
b. Conwill Elvet, Carmarthen, So. Wales, Aug. 10, 1900
d. Santa Monica, CA, July 31, 1947, Age 46

JODDRELL, Richard Paul
Playwright
b. Unknown
d. Unknown, Jan. 26, 1831, Age 85

JOHN, Alice
Actress
b. Llanelly, Wales, Unknown
d. Binghamton, NY, Aug. 9, 1956, Age 75

JOHN, Evan (né Simpson)
Actor, Playwright, Director
b. London, England, April 9, 1901
d. Unknown, 1953, Age 52

JOHNSON, Albert Richard
Scene designer, Director, Producer, Architect
b. La Crosse, WI, Feb. 1, 1910
d. New York, NY, Dec. 21, 1967, Age 57

JOHNSON, Charles
Playwright
b. Unknown
d. Unknown, March 11, 1748, Age 69

JOHNSON, Dr. Samuel
Playwright, Critic, Poet, etc.
b. Lichfield, England, Sept. 18, 1709
d. London, England, Dec. 13, 1784, Age 75

JOHNSON, Dr. W. Gerald
Playwright, Director, Actor
b. Unknown
d. Hartford, CT, Feb. 7, 1963, Age 51

JOHNSON, Elizabeth
Actress
b. Unknown, 1790
d. Unknown, 1810

JOHNSON, Emory
Actor, Director
b. Unknown
d. San Mateo, CA, April 18, 1960, Age 66

JOHNSON, Ethel May
Performer, Composer
b. Unknown
d. Santa Monica, CA, May 23, 1964, Age 76

JOHNSON, Greer
Playwright
b. London, KY, Jan. 20, 1920
d. New York, NY, Oct. 30, 1974, Age 54

JOHNSON, Hall
Musician - Playwright
b. Athens, GA, 1888
d. New York, NY, April 30, 1970, Age 82

JOHNSON, Harold (Chic) Ogden
Performer
b. Chicago, IL, March 5, 1891
d. Las Vegas, NV, Feb. 25, 1962, Age 70

JOHNSON, Isa
Actress
b. Unknown
d. Unknown, April 1, 1941

JOHNSON, J. Rosamond
Composer, Actor
b. Jacksonville, FL, 1873
d. New York, NY, Nov. 11, 1954, Age 81

JOHNSON, Katie
Actress
b. Unknown
d. Elham, England, May 4, 1957, Age 78

JOHNSON, William ("Bill")
Actor, Singer
b. Baltimore, MD, Unknown
d. Flemington, NJ, March 6, 1957, Age 41

JOHNSRUD, Harold
Actor
b. Spokane, WA, Unknown
d. New York, NY, Dec. 24, 1939, Age 35

JOHNSTON, Arthur James
Composer
b. Unknown
d. Unknown, May 1, 1954, Age 56

JOHNSTON, Moffat
Actor
b. Edinburgh, Scotland, Aug. 18, 1886
d. Norwalk, CT, Nov. 3, 1935, Age 49

JOHNSTONE, Clarence (Layton and Johnstone)
Performer
b. Unknown
d. Unknown, 1953

JOHNSTONE, J. B.
Actor, Playwright
b. Unknown
d. Unknown, April 25, 1891, Age 88

JOHNSTONE, Madge
Actress
b. Unknown
d. Unknown, May 27, 1913

JOHNSTONE-SMITH, George
Actor, Producer
b. Unknown
d. Worcester, England, 1963, Age 81

JOINER, Barbara (Mrs. George Kingdon Parsons)
Performer
b. Unknown
d. New York, NY, Dec. 29, 1961, Age 61

JOLLY, George
Actor, Teacher
b. Unknown, 1640
d. Unknown, 1673

JOLSON, Al (Asa Yoelson)
Actor, Singer
b. St. Petersburg, Russia, May 26, 1886
d. San Francisco, CA, Oct. 23, 1950, Age 64

JOLSON, Harry
Performer
b. Srednik, Poland, Unknown
d. Hollywood, CA, April 26, 1953, Age 71

JONES, (Charles) Buck
Actor
b. Vincennes, IN, Unknown
d. Boston, MA, Nov. 30, 1942, Age 53

JONES, Douglas P. Jr.
Actor, Director
b. Unknown
d. Paris, France, June 15, 1964, Age 38

JONES, Dr. Joseph Steven
Playwright, Manager, Actor
b. Boston, MA, Sept. 28, 1809
d. Unknown, Dec. 29, 1877, Age 68

JONES, Edward
Composer, Conductor
b. Unknown
d. Unknown, Aug. 10, 1917

JONES, Henry Arthur
Playwright, Author
b. Grandborough, Buckinghamshire, England, Sept. 20, 1851
d. Unknown, Jan. 7, 1929, Age 77

JONES, Inigo
Architect, Scenic Designer
b. London, England, July 15,1573
d. London, England, July 21, 1652, Age 79

JONES, Isham
Composer, Band Leader
b. Coalton, OH, Jan. 31, 1894
d. Hollywood, CA, Oct. 19, 1956, Age 62

JONES, J. Matheson
Clown, Director, Author
b. Unknown
d. Unknown, Aug. 12, 1931, Age 83

JONES, J. Wilton
Playwright
b. Unknown
d. Unknown, March 1, 1897, Age 43

JONES, John Price
Actor
b. Unknown
d. Nashville, TN, April 7, 1961, Age 70

JONES, Margo
Producer
b. Livingston, TX, Dec. 12, 1913
d. Dallas, TX, July 25, 1955, Age 41

JONES, Maria B. (Mrs. Francis Phillips)
Actress, Playwright
b. Unknown
d. Unknown, Feb. 11, 1873, Age 27

JONES, Phyllis Ann
Performer
b. Unknown
d. Rose Valley, PA, Found strangled, June 11, 1962, Age 24

JONES, Richard ("Gentleman Jones")
Actor
b. Unknown
d. Unknown, Aug. 30, 1851, Age 73

JONES, Robert Edmond
Scenic designer
b. Milton, NH, Dec. 12, 1887
d. Milton, NH, Nov. 26, 1954, Age 66

JONES, Rozene Kemper
Actress
b. Unknown
d. Hollywood, CA, July 8, 1964, Age 74

JONES, Rupel Johnson
Educator
b. Athens, OH, April 4, 1895
d. Norman, OK, Nov. 17, 1964, Age 69

JONES, Samuel Major
Actor
b. Birkenhead, England, Unknown
d. Unknown, Aug. 25, 1952, Age 89

JONES, Sidney
Composer
b. Leeds, England, 1869
d. London, England, Jan. 29, 1946, Age 77

JONES, Stanley D.
Songwriter, Actor
b. Unknown
d. Los Angeles, CA, Dec. 13, 1963, Age 49

JONES, Stephen
Biographer
b. Unknown
d. Unknown, Dec. 20, 1827, Age 64

JONES, T. C. (né Thomas Craig Jones)
Actor
b. Scranton, PA, Oct. 26, 1920
d. Duarte, CA, Sept. 25, 1971, Age 50

JONSON, Ben
Playwright, Poet
b. Westminster, London, England, c1573
d. Westminster, London, England, Aug. 6, 1637, Age 63

JOPE-SLADE, Christine
Playwright, Novelist
b. Unknown
d. Unknown, May 2, 1942, Age 49

JOPLIN, Scott
Composer, Musician
b. Texarkana, TX, Nov. 24, 1868
d. New York, NY, April 4, 1919, Age 50

JORDAN, Bernard
Performer
b. Halifax, Yorkshire, England, Unknown
d. Los Angeles, CA, 1962, Age 77

JORDAN, Dorothy (née Bland)
Actress
b. Near Waterford, Ireland, c1762
d. St. Cloud, France, July 3, 1816

JORDAN, Marian ("Fibber McGee and Molly") (née Marian Driscoll)
Performer
b. Peoria, IL, April 16, 1898
d. Encino, CA, April 7, 1961, Age 62

JORDAN, Walter C.
Literary representative, Producer
b. New York, NY, Unknown
d. New York, NY, Nov. 13, 1951, Age 74

JOSEPH, Harry
Theatre owner
b. London, England, Unknown
d. Leeds, England, 1962, Age 64

JOUVET, Louis
Actor, Director
b. Crozon, Finisterre, Brittany, France, 1887
d. Paris, France, Aug. 16, 1951, Age 63

JOY, Leonard W.
Producer
b. Unknown
d. New York, NY, Nov. 21, 1961, Age 65

JOY, Nicholas
Actor
b. Paris, France, Unknown
d. Philadelphia, PA, March 16, 1964, Age 81

JOY, Nicholas
Actor
b. Paris, France, Jan. 31, 1883
d. Philadelphia, PA, March 6, 1964, Age 81

JOYCE, Alice
Actress
b. Missouri, 1890
d. Hollywood, CA, Oct. 9, 1955, Age 65

JOYCE, Archibald
Composer
b. Unknown
d. Sutton, England, March 22, 1963, Age 89

JOYCE, James
Playwright, Novelist
b. Dublin, Ireland, Feb. 2, 1882
d. Zurich, Switzerland, Jan. 13, 1941, Age 58

JOYCE, Peggy Hopkins (née Margaret Upton)
Performer
b. Norfolk, VA, Unknown
d. New York, NY, June 12, 1957, Age 63

JOYCE, Walter
Actor
b. Unknown
d. Unknown, June 2, 1916, Age 81

JUCH, Emma
Actress
b. Unknown
d. Unknown, March 6, 1939, Age 78

JUDITH, Mme. (Julie Bernot)
Actress
b. Unknown
d. Unknown, Oct. 27, 1912, Age 85

JULIET, Miss (Juliet Delf)
Performer
b. Unknown
d. New York, NY, March 24, 1962, Age 74

JULLIEN, Jean
Playwright
b. Lyons, France, Dec. 4. 1854
d. Unknown, Sept. 1919, Age 64

JUVARRA, Filippo
Architect, Designer
b. Unknown, 1676
d. Unknown, 1736

K

KAART, Hans
Singer
b. Unknown
d. Amsterdam, Holland, 1963, Age 39

KACHALOV, Vasili Ivanovich (Shverubovich)
Actor
b. Unknown, 1875
d. Unknown, Oct. 1948, Age 73

KAGEN, Sergius
Composer
b. St. Petersburg, Russia, Unknown
d. New York, NY, March 1, 1964, Age 55

KAHN, Florence (Lady Beerbohm)
Actress
b. Memphis, TN, March 3,1878
d. Rapallo, Italy, Jan. 13, 1951, Age 72

KAHN, Gus
Lyricist
b. Germany, Unknown
d. Beverly Hills, CA, Oct. 8, 1941, Age 54

KAHN, L. Stanley
Producer, Stockbroker
b. New York, NY, Unknown
d. New York, NY, Aug. 10, 1964, Age 66

KAHN, Otto Hermann
Theatre and arts patron
b. Mannheim, Germany, Feb. 21, 1867
d. New York, NY, March 29, 1934, Age 68

KAINZ, Josef
Actor
b. Unknown, 1858
d. Unknown, 1910

KAISER, Georg
Playwright
b. Magdeburg, Germany, Nov. 25, 1878
d. Unknown, June 5, 1945, Age 66

KALB, Marie
Actress
b. Unknown
d. Unknown, March 22, 1930, Age 76

KALICH, Bertha
Actress
b. Lemberg, Poland, May 17, 1874
d. New York, NY, April 18, 1939, Age 64

KALIZ, Armand
Actor, Songwriter
b. Unknown
d. Unknown, Feb. 1, 1941, Age 49

KALMAN, Emmerich
Composer
b. Siotok, Hungary, Oct. 24, 1882
d. Paris, France, Oct. 30, 1953, Age 71

KALMAR, Bert
Composer, Author, Performer
b. New York, NY, Unknown
d. Hollywood, CA, Sept. 17, 1947, Age 63

KAMBISIS, Joannes
Playwright
b. Unknown, 1872
d. Unknown, 1902

KAMMER, Klaus
Actor
b. Hanover, Germany, Unknown
d. Berlin, Germany, May 9, 1964, Age 35

KANE, Whitford
Actor
b. Larne, Ireland, Jan. 30, 1881
d. New York, NY, Dec. 17, 1956, Age 75

KANER, Ruth
Producer, Theatre operator, Actress
b. Brooklyn, NY, Unknown
d. Queens, NY, April 12, 1964

KAPLAN, Eddie "Nuts"
Talent representative, Performer
b. Unknown
d. New York, NY, July 20, 1964, Age 57

KAPPELER, Alfred
Actor
b. Zurich, Switzerland, Unknown
d. New York, NY, Oct. 30, 1945, Age 69

KARLOFF, Boris (né William Henry Pratt)
Actor
b. Dulwich, England, Nov. 23, 1887
d. Midhurst, Sussex, England, Feb. 2, 1969, Age 81

KARLWEIS, Oscar Leopold
Actor
b. Vienna, Austria, Unknown
d. New York, NY, Jan. 24, 1956, Age 61

KARSON, Kit (Alexander R. G. Miller)
Performer
b. Unknown
d. Worcester, MA, Jan. 2, 1940, Age 65

KARSON, Nat
Scenic designer, Producer
b. Zurich, Switzerland, Unknown
d. New York, NY, Sept. 27, 1954, Age 46

KARTOUSCH, Louise
Performer
b. Unknown
d. Vienna, Austria, Feb. 13, 1964, Age 78

KATZENELSON, Isaac
Producer
b. Unknown, 1886
d. Unknown, c1941

KAUFMAN, George S.
Director, Playwright, Critic
b. Pittsburgh, PA, Nov. 16, 1889
d. New York, NY, June 2, 1961, Age 71

KAUFMAN, Harry A.
Director
b. Unknown
d. Unknown, Nov. 18, 1944, Age 57

KAUFMAN, S. Jay
Playwright, Press representative
b. Unknown, Feb. 15, 1886
d. Bronx, NY, June 20, 1957, Age 71

KAUSER, Alice
Play broker, Author's representative
b. Budapest, Hungary, Unknown
d. New York, NY, Sept. 10, 1945, Age 73

KAVANAGH, Patrick
Poet, Playwright, Journalist
b. County Monaghan, Ireland, Unknown
d. Dublin, Ireland, Nov. 30, 1967, Age 62

KAYE, Albert Patrick (A. P.)
Actor
b. Ringwood, Hunts, England, 1878
d. Washingtonville, NY, Sept. 7, 1946, Age 68

KAYE, Carmen
Performer
b. Unknown
d. London, England, April 23, 1962

KAZAN, Molly Day Thacher
Playwright, Poet
b. South Orange, NJ, Unknown
d. New York, NY, Dec. 13, 1963, Age about 55

KAZANTZAKIS, Nikos
Novelist, Poet, Playwright
b. Crete, 1883
d. Freiburg, Germany, Oct. 26, 1957, Age 74

KEALY, Tom (Thomas J. Kealy)
Press representative
b. County Limerick, Ireland, May 8, 1874
d. Unknown, Feb. 12, 1949, Age 75

KEAN, Charles John
Actor, Producer
b. Waterford, Ireland, 1811
d. Unknown, Jan. 22, 1868, Age 57

KEAN, Edmund
Actor
b. London, England, Nov. 4, 1787
d. Richmond, England, May 15, 1833, Age 45

KEAN, Mrs. Charles (Ellen Tree)
Actress
b. Unknown, 1806
d. Unknown, Aug. 20, 1880, Age 74

KEANE, Doris
Actress
b. Michigan, Dec. 12, 1881
d. New York, NY, Nov. 25, 1945, Age 63

KEARNEY, Kate
Actress
b. Unknown
d. Unknown, May 20, 1926, Age 85

KEARNEY, Patrick
Playwright
b. Columbus, OH, Unknown
d. New York, NY, March 28, 1933, Age 36

KEARNS, Allen
Actor
b. Canada, 1893
d. Albany, NY, April 20, 1956, Age 62

KEARNS, Joseph
Actor
b. Salt Lake City, UT, Unknown
d. Los Angeles, CA, Feb. 17, 1962, Age 55

KEATING, Fred (Frederick Serrano Keating)
Performer
b. New York, NY, Unknown
d. New York, NY, June 29, 1961, Age 64

KEATING, John G.
Critic, Editor
b. New York, NY, June 8, 1919
d. New York, NY, Jan. 29, 1968, Age 50

KEATING, Larry
Performer
b. St. Paul, MN, Unknown
d. Hollywood, CA, Aug. 26, 1963, Age 67

KEELEY, Robert
Actor, Producer
b. Unknown, 1793
d. Unknown, 1869

KEEN, Malcolm
Actor
b. Bristol, England, Aug. 8, 1887
d. England, Jan. 30, 1970, Age 82

KEENAN, Frank
Actor
b. Dubuque, IA, April 8, 1858
d. New York, NY, Feb. 24, 1929, Age 70

KEENE, Laura (Mary Moss)
Actress-Manager
b. London, England, 1820
d. Montclair, NJ, Nov. 4, 1873, Age 53

KEENE, Thomas Wallace (Eagelson)
Actor
b. Unknown, 1840
d. Unknown, 1898

KEENE, Tom (George Duryea)
Performer
b. New York, NY, Unknown
d. Glendale, CA, Aug. 4, 1963, Age 65

KEGLEY, Kermit
Actor, Director
b. Pulaski, VA, Nov. 12, 1918
d. Fenton, MO, Feb. 19, 1974, Age 55

KEIGHTLEY, Cyril
Actor
b. Wellington, N. S. W., Australia, Nov. 10, 1875
d. New York, NY, Aug. 14, 1929, Age 53

KEITH, Benjamin Franklin
Vaudeville producer, Theatre proprietor
b. Hillsboro Bridge, NH, 1846
d. Unknown, 1914

KEITH, Ian
Actor
b. Boston, MA, Feb. 27, 1899
d. New York, NY, March 26, 1960, Age 61

KELCEY, Herbert (Lamb)
Actor
b. London, England, Oct. 10, 1855
d. Unknown, July 10, 1917, Age 61

KELLARD, Ralph (Thomas J. J. Kelly)
Actor
b. New York, NY, June 16, 1884
d. New York, NY, Feb. 5, 1955, Age 70

KELLERD, John E.
Actor
b. Kensington, London, England, May 14, 1863
d. New York, NY, June 8, 1929, Age 66

KELLY, Ann
Actress
b. Unknown
d. Unknown, April 5, 1852, Age 103

KELLY, Anthony Paul
Playwright
b. Chicago, IL, Unknown
d. New York, NY, Sept. 26, 1932, Age 37

KELLY, Eva (Mrs. G. P. Huntley)
Actress
b. Lockhaven, PA, Sept. 18, 1880
d. Unknown, Nov. 16, 1948, Age 68

KELLY, Fanny
Actress, Producer
b. Unknown
d. Unknown, Dec. 6, 1882, Age 92

KELLY, Frances Maria
Actress, Teacher
b. Unknown, 1790
d. Unknown, 1882

KELLY, Gregory
Actor
b. New York, NY, Unknown
d. New York, NY, July 9, 1927, Age 36

KELLY, Hugh
Playwright
b. Unknown, 1739
d. Unknown, Feb. 3, 1777, Age 38

KELLY, James
Performer, Union official
b. Unknown
d. Hollywood, CA, May 5, 1964, Age 49

KELLY, John
Playwright
b. Unknown
d. Unknown, July 16, 1751, Age 71

KELLY, Lew
Performer
b. St. Louis, MO, Unknown
d. Los Angeles, CA, June 10, 1944, Age 65

KELLY, Michael
Actor, Composer
b. Unknown
d. Unknown, Oct. 9, 1826, Age 62

KELLY, Paul
Actor
b. Brooklyn, NY, Aug. 9, 1899
d. Beverly Hills, CA, Nov. 6, 1956, Age 57

KELLY, Robert
Actor
b. Chicago, IL, Unknown
d. Lewiston, ME, June 19, 1949, Age 74

KELLY, W. W.
Producer
b. USA, Dec. 16, 1853
d. Unknown, Sept. 19, 1933, Age 79

KELLY, Walter C.
Actor
b. Mineville, NY, Oct. 29, 1873
d. Philadelphia, PA, Jan. 6, 1939, Age 65

KELLY, William J.
Performer
b. Newburyport, MA, June 16, 1875
d. New York, NY, May 17, 1949, Age 73

KELT, John (Eric Forbes-Robertson)
Actor
b. Unknown
d. Unknown, March 9, 1935, Age 70

KELTON, Pert
Actress
b. Great Falls, MT, 1909
d. Ridgewood, NJ, Oct. 30, 1968, Age 61

KEMBLE, Adelaide (a/k/a Adelaide Sartoris)
Playwright, Singer
b. Unknown, 1814
d. Unknown, Aug. 4, 1879, Age 65

KEMBLE, Charles
Actor
b. Brecknock, South Wales, 1775
d. Unknown, Nov. 12, 1854, Age 79

KEMBLE, Elizabeth (Mrs. Whitlock)
Actress
b. Unknown
d. Unknown, Feb. 27, 1836, Age 64

KEMBLE, Fanny (Frances Anne)
Actress
b. London, England, 1809
d. London, England, Jan. 15, 1893, Age 83

KEMBLE, Frances (Mrs. Twiss)
Actress
b. Unknown
d. Unknown, Oct. 1, 1822, Age 62

KEMBLE, Harry
Actor
b. Unknown
d. Unknown, June 22, 1836, Age 45

KEMBLE, Henry
Actor
b. Unknown, 1848
d. Unknown, 1907

KEMBLE, John Mitchell
Examiner of plays
b. Unknown
d. Unknown, March 26, 1857, Age 49

KEMBLE, John Philip
Actor, Producer
b. Prescot, Lancashire, England, 1757
d. Lausanne Switzerland, Feb. 26, 1823, Age 66

KEMBLE, Mrs. Charles (Maria Theresa de Camp)
Actress
b. Unknown, c1773
d. Unknown, Sept. 3, 1838, Age 65

KEMBLE, Mrs. J P. (Priscilla Hopkins)
Actress
b. Unknown, 1755
d. Unknown, May 14, 1845, Age 89

KEMBLE, Mrs. Roger (Sarah Ward)
Actress
b. Unknown
d. Unknown, April 25,1807

KEMBLE, Mrs. Stephen (Elizabeth Satchell)
Actress
b. Unknown
d. Unknown, Jan. 20, 1841, Age 78

KEMBLE, Roger
Actor
b. Unknown, 1721
d. Unknown, Dec. 6, 1802, Age 81

KEMBLE, Stephen
Actor
b. Unknown, 1758
d. Unknown, June 5, 1822, Age 64

KEMP, Robert (Robertson)
Critic
b. Paris, France, Unknown
d. Paris, France, July 3, 1959, Age 73

KEMP, Thomas Charles
Critic
b. Birmingham, England, April 30, 1891
d. Unknown, Jan. 3, 1955, Age 64

KEMP, William
Actor
b. Unknown, 1580
d. Unknown, 1603

KEMPER, Collin
Producer
b. Cincinnati, Ohio, Feb. 17, 1870
d. Bronxville, NY, Nov. 27, 1955, Age 85

KENDAL, Dame Madge (Margaret Robertson) (Mrs. W. H. Grimston)
Actress
b. 58 Cleethorpes Road, Grimsby, Lincolnshire, England, March 15, 1849
d. Chorley Wood Common, Hertfordshire, England, Sept. 14, 1935, Age 86

KENDAL, William Hunter (Grimston)
Actor, Producer
b. London, England, Dec. 16, 1843
d. Unknown, Nov. 6, 1917, Age 73

KENDALL, Henry
Producer, Actor
b. London, England, May 28, 1897
d. France, June 9, 1962, Age 65

KENDALL, Kay (Justine Kay Kendall McCarthy)
Actress
b. Withensea, Yorkshire, England, May 21, 1926
d. London, England, Sept. 6, 1959, Age 33

KENDALL, Marie
Performer
b. Unknown
d. London, England, May 5, 1964, Age 90

KENNARD, Jane (Lothian)
Actress
b. Cincinnati, OH, Unknown
d. New York, NY, Feb. 11, 1938, Age 75

KENNAWAY, James
Playwright, Screenwriter
b. Scotland, 1928
d. London, England, Dec. 21, 1968, Age 40

KENNEDY, Beulah (Beulah K. Rafael)
Performer
b. St. Louis, MO, Unknown
d. Stockton, CA, May 11, 1964, Age 71

KENNEDY, Charles Lamb
Critic, Playwright
b. Unknown
d. Unknown, Aug. 25, 1881, Age 58

KENNEDY, Charles Rann
Playwright, Actor
b. Derby, England, Feb. 14, 1871
d. Westwood, Los Angeles, CA, Feb. 16, 1950, Age 79

KENNEDY, Edgar
Actor
b. Monterey, CA, Unknown
d. Woodland Hills, CA, Nov. 9, 1948, Age 58

KENNEDY, H. A.
Playwright, Critic
b. Unknown
d. Unknown, June 21, 1905, Age 50

KENNEDY, Joyce
Actress
b. London, England, July 1, 1898
d. Unknown, March 12, 1943, Age 44

KENNEDY, Maurice
Theatre Manager
b. Unknown
d. England, 1962, Age 51

KENNEDY, Merna
b. Unknown
d. Los Angeles, CA, Dec. 20, 1944, Age 35

KENNEY, Jack
Actor
b. Unknown
d. Hollywood, CA, May 26, 1964, Age 76

KENNEY, James
Playwright
b. Unknown
d. Unknown, July 25, 1849, Age 69

KENNINGHAM, Charles
Actor
b. Unknown
d. Unknown, Oct. 24, 1925

KENT, Charles
Actor
b. England, Unknown
d. Brooklyn, NY, May 21, 1923, Age 69

KENT, Crawford
Actor
b. Unknown
d. Hollywood, CA, May 14, 1953, Age 72

KENT, S. Miller
Actor
b. Unknown
d. Unknown, Nov. 12, 1948, Age 86

KENT, William
Performer
b. St. Paul, MN, Unknown
d. New York, NY, Oct. 4, 1945, Age 59

KENYON, Charles
Playwright
b. Unknown
d. Hollywood, CA, June 27, 1961, Age 79

KEOGH, J. A.
Actor, Director
b. Unknown
d. Unknown, Nov. 30, 1942

KEOGH, William T.
Producer
b. Unknown
d. Unknown, Oct. 28, 1947, Age 87

KEOWN, Eric
Critic
b. Unknown
d. Worplesdon, England, Feb. 15, 1963, Age 58

KERBY, Marion
Actress, Singer
b. (in the south) USA, Unknown
d. Hollywood, CA, Dec. 18, 1956, Age 79

KERKER, Gustave Adolph
Composer
b. Herford, Westphalia, Germany, Feb. 28, 1857
d. New York, NY, June 29, 1923, Age 66

KERN, Jerome David
Composer
b. New York, NY, Jan. 27, 1885
d. New York, NY, Nov. 11, 1945, Age 60

KERNAN, Joseph Lewis
Theatre manager, Talent representative
b. Unknown
d. Phoenix, AZ, July 1964, Age 83

KEROUL, Henri (Queyroul)
Playwright
b. Corte, Corsica, Feb. 8, 1857
d. Unknown, April 14, 1921, Age 64

KERR, Dr. Alfred
Critic, Journalist
b. Unknown
d. Unknown, Oct. 12, 1948, Age 80

KERR, Frederick (Frederick Grinham Keen)
Actor, Director
b. London, England, Oct. 11, 1858
d. London, England, May 2, 1933, Age 74

KERR, Sophie
Novelist, Author, Playwright
b. Denton, MD, Aug. 23, 1880
d. New York, NY, Feb. 6, 1965, Age 84

KERRIGAN, J. Warren
Actor
b. Unknown, 1880
d. Balboa Island, CA, June 9, 1947, Age 67

KERRIGAN, Joseph M.
Actor
b. Dublin, Ireland, Unknown
d. Hollywood, CA, April 29, 1964, Age 76

KERRY, Norman
Actor
b. Unknown
d. Hollywood, CA, Jan. 12, 1956, Age 66

KERSHAW, Willette (née Mansfield)
Actress, Producer
b. Clifton Heights, St. Louis, MO, June 17, 1890
d. Honolulu, HI, May 4, 1960, Age 69

KESSELRING, Joseph Otto
Playwright, Author, Actor
b. New York, NY, June 21, 1902
d. Kingston, NY, Nov. 5, 1967, Age 65

KESSLER, David
Actor
b. Russia, Unknown
d. New York, NY, May 14, 1920, Age 61

KESSLER, Joseph
Actor
b. Unknown
d. Unknown, Feb. 22, 1933, Age 51

KESTER, Paul
Playwright
b. Delaware, OH, Nov. 2, 1870
d. Lake Mohegan, NY, June 20, 1933, Age 62

KEY, Kathleen
Actress
b. Unknown
d. Woodland Hills, CA, Dec. 21, 1954, Age 57

KEY, Pat Ann
Performer
b. Unknown
d. Shoreham, Sussex, England, Oct. 22, 1962

KEYS, Nelson
Actor
b. London, England, Aug. 7, 1886
d. London, England, April 26, 1939, Age 52

KHMELYOV, Nikolai Pavlovich
Actor, Director
b. Unknown, 1901
d. Unknown, Nov. 1945, Age 44

KIBBEE, Guy
Actor
b. El Paso, TX, March 6, 1882
d. East Islip, L.I., NY, May 24, 1956, Age 74

KIDD, Kathleen
Actress
b. CAN, Unknown
d. Toronto, CAN, Feb. 23, 1961

KIDDER, Kathryn (Mrs. Louis Kaufman Anspacher)
Actress
b. Newark, NJ, Dec. 23, 1867
d. New York, NY, Sept. 7, 1939, Age 71

KIEPURA, Jan
Singer, Actor
b. Sosnowiecz, Poland, May 16, 1902
d. Rye, NY, Aug. 15, 1966, Age 64

KIESLER, Frederick John
Architect, Scene designer, Artist
b. Vienna, Austria, Sept. 22, 1890
d. New York, NY, Dec. 27, 1965, Age 75

KILBRIDE, Percy
Actor
b. San Francisco, CA, July 16, 1888
d. Los Angeles, CA, Dec. 11, 1964, Age 76

KILGALLEN, Dorothy
Columnist, Journalist
b. Chicago, IL, July 3, 1913
d. New York, NY, Nov. 8, 1965, Age 52

KILGOUR, Joseph Turnbull
Actor
b. Ayr, Ontario, CAN, July 11, 1863
d. Bay Shore, L.I., NY, April 20, 1933, Age 69

KILLIGREW, Charles
Producer
b. Unknown, 1665
d. Unknown, Jan. 1725, Age 60

KILLIGREW, Sir William
Playwright
b. Unknown, 1606
d. Unknown, Oct. 1695, Age 89

KILLIGREW, Thomas (the elder)
Actor, Producer, Playwright
b. Unknown, 1612
d. Unknown, Nov. 19, 1683, Age 71

KILLIGREW, Thomas (the younger)
Playwright
b. Unknown, 1657
d. Unknown, July 1719, Age 62

KILMOREY, Earl of (Lord Newry)
Producer, Playwright
b. Unknown
d. Unknown, July 28, 1915, Age 73

KILPACK, Bennett
Actor
b. England, Unknown
d. Santa Monica, CA, Aug. 17, 1962, Age 79

KIMBALL, Louis (né Conaughy)
Actor
b. Marshalltown, IA, May 19, 1889
d. Unknown, Jan. 29, 1936, Age 46

KIMBERLEY, Mrs. F. G.
Playwright, Producer
b. Unknown
d. Unknown, Dec. 27, 1939, Age 62

KIMMINS, Anthony
Playwright, Film producer
b. Unknown
d. Hurstpierpoint, Sussex, England, May 19, 1964, Age 62

KING, Ada
Actress
b. Unknown
d. Unknown, June 8, 1940, Age 78

KING, Cecil
Actor
b. Fermoy, County Cork, Ireland, Unknown
d. Unknown, Sept. 21, 1958, Age 83

KING, Charles
Actor, Singer
b. New York, NY, Oct. 31, 1889
d. London, England, Jan. 11, 1944, Age 54

KING, Claude
Actor
b. Northampton, England, Jan. 15, 1876
d. Unknown, Sept. 18, 1941, Age 65

KING, Dennis
Actor - Singer
b. Coventry, England, Nov. 2, 1897
d. New York, NY, May 21, 1971, Age 73

KING, Edith (Mrs. Dennis King, née Wright)
Actress
b. White Haven, PA, 1897
d. Denver, CO, Sept. 26, 1963, Age 65

KING, Emmett C.
Actor
b. Griffin, GA, Unknown
d. Hollywood, CA, April 21, 1953, Age 87

KING, Nosmo (Vernon Watson)
Performer
b. Unknown
d. Unknown, Jan. 13, 1949, Age 63

KING, Robert A. ("Bobo") (Robert Keiser)
Composer
b. New York, NY, Sept. 20, 1862
d. New York, NY, April 13, 1932, Age 69

KING, Tom
Actor
b. Unknown, 1730
d. Unknown, 1804

KING, Victor
Performer
b. Unknown
d. London, England, June 22, 1964, Age 72

KINGDON, Frank
Actor
b. Providence, RI, Unknown
d. Englewood, NJ, April 9,1937, Age 72

KINGDON, John M.
Playwright
b. Unknown
d. Unknown, July 24, 1876

KINGDON-GOULD, Edith Maughan (Mrs. George Jay Gould)
Actress
b. Brooklyn, NY, Unknown
d. Lakewood, NJ, Nov. 13, 1921, Age 60

KINGSFORD, Walter
Actor
b. Red Hill, England, Unknown
d. North Hollywood, CA, Feb. 7, 1958, Age 73

KINGSLEY, Grace
Journalist, Columnist
b. Unknown
d. Hollywood, CA, Oct. 8, 1962, Age 89

KINGSLEY, Mary
Actress
b. Unknown
d. Unknown, Sept. 15, 1936, Age 74

KINGSLEY, Walter
Press representative
b. Unknown
d. New York, NY, Feb. 14, 1929, Age 52

KINGSTON, Gertrude (Silver née Konstam)
Actress, Producer
b. London, England, 1866
d. London, England, Nov. 8, 1937, Age 71

KINGSTON, Sam F.
Manager
b. Dublin, Ireland, Unknown
d. New York, NY, June 17, 1929, Age 63

KINNELL, Murray
Actor
b. England, Unknown
d. Santa Barbara, CA, Aug. 14, 1954, Age 65

KINSELLA, Kathleen
Actress
b. England, Unknown
d. Washington, DC, March 25, 1961, Age 83

KIRALFY, Bolossy
Producer, Dancer
b. Hungary, Unknown
d. London, England, March 6, 1932, Age 84

KIRALFY, Imré
Producer
b. Unknown
d. Brighton, England, April 27, 1919, Age about 74

KIRBY, Hudson
Actor
b. Unknown
d. Unknown, March 8, 1848, Age 29

KIRBY, John
Actor
b. Unknown
d. Unknown, March 18, 1930, Age 36

KIRK, John
Actor, Producer, Director
b. Wilmington, DE, Unknown
d. New York, NY, May 23, 1948, Age 86

KIRKE, John
Playwright
b. Unknown, 1638
d. Unknown, 1643

KIRKLAND, Jack
Playwright, Producer
b. St. Louis, MO, July 25, 1902
d. New York, NY, Feb. 22, 1969, Age 66

KIRKLAND, Muriel
Actress
b. Yonkers, NY, Aug. 19, 1903
d. New York, NY, Sept. 25, 1971, Age 68

KIRKMAN, Francis
Playwright, Publisher
b. Unknown
d. 1674

KIRKWOOD, Gertrude Robinson
Actress
b. Unknown
d. Hollywood, CA, March 19, 1962, Age 71

KIRKWOOD, Jack
Performer
b. Scotland, Aug. 6, 1894
d. Las Vegas, NV, Aug. 2, 1964, Age 69

KIRWAN, Patrick
Actor, Producer, Director
b. Ireland, Unknown
d. Unknown, Feb. 13, 1929, Age 67

KISFALUDY, Károly
Playwright, Author
b. Unknown, 1788
d. Unknown, 1830

KISTEMAECHERS, Henry
Playwright
b. Floreffe, Oct. 13, 1872
d. Unknown, Jan. 21, 1938, Age 65

KITCHEN, Fred
Performer
b. Unknown
d. Unknown, April 1, 1951, Age 77

KITTREDGE, George Lyman
Educator, Shakespearean scholar
b. Boston, MA, Feb. 28,1860
d. Barnstable, MA, July 23, 1941, Age 81

KLAUBER, Adolph
Actor, Producer, Critic
b. Louisville, KY, April 29, 1879
d. Louisville, KY, Dec. 7, 1933, Age 54

KLAW, Marc
Producer
b. Paducah, KY, May 29, 1858
d. Hassocks, Sussex, England, June 14, 1936, Age 78

KLEIN, Charles
Librettist, Playwright
b. London, England, Jan. 7, 1867
d. on the Lusitania, May 7, 1915, Age 48

KLEIN, Manuel
Composer, Conductor
b. London, England, Dec. 6, 1876
d. London, England, June 1, 1919, Age 42

KLEIN, Paul
Press representative, Advertising exec.
b. Unknown
d. Flushing, NY, May 10, 1964, Age 61

KLEIST, Heinrich von
Playwright
b. Frankfort-on-Oder, Germany, Oct. 18, 1777
d. Potsdam, Germany, Nov. 21, 1811, Age 34

KNAPP, Fred L.
Performer
b. Unknown
d. Monterey Park, CA, Oct. 5, 1962, Age 67

KNEPP, Mary
Actress
b. Unknown
d. Unknown, 1677

KNIGHT, John (née Houser)
Actor
b. Payne, OH, Unknown
d. New York, NY, June 11, 1964, Age 64

KNIGHT, Joseph
Critic, Historian
b. Unknown, 1829
d. Unknown, June 23, 1907, Age 78

KNIGHT, Julius
Actor
b. Dumfries, Scotland, 1863
d. Unknown, Feb. 21, 1941, Age 78

KNIGHT, Percival
Comedian, Playwright
b. Unknown
d. Switzerland, Nov. 27, 1923, Age 50

KNIGHT, Thomas
Actor, Playwright
b. Unknown
d. Unknown, Feb. 4, 1820

KNIPPER-CHEKHOVA, Olga Leonardovna (Mrs. Anton Chekhov)
Actress
b. Unknown, 1870
d. Moscow, Russia, March 22, 1959, Age 88

KNOBLOCK, Edward (Knoblauch)
Actor, Author
b. New York, NY, April 7, 1874
d. London, England, July 19, 1945, Age 71

KNOTT, Roselle (Agnes Roselle)
Actress
b. Hamilton, Ontario, CAN, 1870
d. Unknown, Jan. 28, 1948, Age 77

KNOWLES, Alec ("Sir Affable")
Journalist
b. Aberdeenshire, Scotland, Oct. 23, 1850
d. Unknown, October 15, 1917, Age 66

KNOWLES, James Sheridan
Actor, Playwright
b. Unknown, 1784
d. Unknown, Nov. 30, 1862, Age 78

KNOWLES, Richard George
Comedian
b. Canada, 1858
d. London, England, Jan. 1, 1919, Age 60

KOBER, Arthur
Playwright, Writer
b. Brody, Austria-Hungary, Aug. 25, 1900
d. New York, NY, June 12, 1975, Age 74

KOCH, Frederick Henry
Educator
b. Covington, KY, Sept. 12, 1877
d. Miami, FL, Aug. 16, 1944, Age 66

KOCH, Heinrich Gottfried
Actor, Producer
b. Unknown, 1703
d. Unknown, 1775

KOENIG, John
Designer
b. Berlin, Germany, 1910
d. Richmond, VA, Feb. 1, 1963, Age 52

KOHLMAR, Lee
Performer
b. Unknown
d. North Hollywood, CA, May 15, 1946, Age 74

KOKERITZ, Helge
Shakespearean authority, Educator
b. Gotland, Sweden, Unknown
d. Falköping, Sweden, March 1964, Age 61

KOLB, Thérèse
Actress
b. Altkrich, France, Jan. 19, 1856
d. Unknown, Aug. 19, 1935, Age 79

KOLBENHAYER, Guido
Playwright
b. Unknown
d. Wolfsratshausen, Germany, April 12, 1962, Age 83

KOLKER, Henry
Actor
b. Berlin, Germany, Nov. 13, 1874
d. Los Angeles, CA, July 15, 1947, Age 72

KOLLMAR, Richard
Producer, Actor
b. Ridgewood, NJ, Dec. 31, 1910
d. New York, NY, Jan. 7, 1971, Age 60

KOMISARJEVSKAYA, Vera Fedorovna
Actress, Producer
b. Russia, 1864
d. Russia, 1910

KOMISARJEVSKY, Theodore
Director, Producer, Writer
b. Venice, Italy, May 23, 1882
d. Darien, CT, April 17, 1954, Age 71

KOOY, Pete
Actor
b. Unknown
d. Hollywood, CA, April 20, 1963

KORDA, Sir Alexander Producer
Director
b. Turkeve, Hungary, Unknown
d. London, England, Jan. 23, 1956, Age 62

KORDA, Zoltan
Producer, Director
b. Turkeve, Hungary, May 3, 1895
d. Beverly Hills, CA, Oct. 13, 1961, Age 66

KORFF, Arnold
Actor
b. Vienna, Austria, Aug. 2, 1870
d. New York, NY, June 2,1944, Age 73

KOSLOFF, Theodore
Dancer, Actor, Teacher
b. Russia, Unknown
d. Los Angeles, CA, Nov. 22, 1956, Age 74

KOTZEBUE, August Friedrich Ferdinand von
Playwright
b. Weimar, Germany, 1761
d. Mannheim, Germany, March 23, 1819, Age 57

KOVACS, Ernie
Actor
b. Trenton, NJ, Jan. 23, 1919
d. Beverly Hills, CA, Jan. 13, 1962, Age 43

KOVAL, Rene
Actor
b. Unknown
d. Unknown, Aug. 17, 1936, Age 50

KRAFT, Hy
Playwright
b. New York, NY, April 30, 1899
d. New York, NY, July 29, 1975, Age 74

KRAMER, Wright
Actor
b. Chicago, IL, Unknown
d. Hollywood, CA, Nov. 14, 1941, Age 71

KRAUS, Werner
Actor
b. Gestungshausen, Coburg, Germany, June 23, 1884
d. Vienna, Austria, Oct. 20, 1959, Age 75

KREISLER, Fritz
Composer, Musician
b. Vienna, Austria, Unknown
d. New York, NY, Jan. 29, 1962, Age 86

KREYMBORG, Alfred
Poet, Playwright
b. New York, NY, Dec. 10, 1883
d. Milford, CT, Aug. 14, 1966, Age 82

KRUGER, Alma
Actress
b. Pittsburgh, PA, Unknown
d. Seattle, WA, April 5, 1960, Age 88

KRUGER, Fred H.
Actor
b. Unknown
d. Hollywood, CA, Dec. 5, 1961, Age 48

KRUGER, Otto
Actor
b. Toledo, OH, Sept. 6, 1885
d. Los Angeles, CA, Sept. 6, 1974, Age 89

KRUTCH, Joseph Wood
Author, Naturalist, Critic
b. Knoxville, TN, Nov. 23, 1893
d. Tucson, AZ, May 22, 1970, Age 76

KUMMER, Clare (née Clare Rodman Bacher)
Playwright
b. Unknown
d. Carmel, CA, April 22, 1958, Age 85

KUMMER, Frederic Arnold
Playwright
b. Catonsville, MD, Aug. 5, 1873
d. Baltimore, MD, Nov. 22, 1943, Age 70

KUN, Magda
Actress
b. Szaszregen, Hungary, Feb. 7, 1912
d. Unknown, Nov. 7, 1945, Age 33

KURNITZ, Harry
Playwright, Novelist, Screenwriter
b. New York, NY, Jan. 5, 1908
d. Los Angeles, CA, March 18, 1968, Age 60

KURTY, Hella
Actress
b. Vienna, Austria, Unknown
d. Unknown, Nov. 7, 1954, Age 48

KURZ, Joseph Felix von
Playwright, Actor, Director
b. Unknown, 1715
d. Unknown, 1784

KYD, Thomas
Playwright
b. Unknown, 1558
d. St. Mary Colchurch, London, England, Dec. 1594, Age 36

KYLE, Howard
Actor
b. Unknown
d. New York, NY, Dec. 1, 1950, Age 89

KYNASTON, Edward (Ned)
Actor
b. Unknown, c1640
d. Unknown, 1706

KYRLE, Judith
Actress
b. Unknown
d. Unknown, March 21, 1922

L

LA BADIE, Florence
Actress
b. Unknown, 1893
d. Unknown, 1917

LABICHE, Eugène
Playwright
b. Paris, France, 1815
d. Unknown, Jan. 23, 1888, Age 72

LABOUCHERE, Henry
Producer
b. Unknown
d. Unknown, Jan. 15, 1912, Age 81

LACEY, Marion
Actress
b. Unknown
d. Unknown, Sept. 1915, Age 95

LACKAYE, Wilton
Actor
b. Loudon County, VA, Sept. 30, 1862
d. New York, NY, Aug. 22, 1932, Age 69

LACKEY, Kenneth
Performer
b. Indiana, Unknown
d. Columbus, NC, April 16, 1976, Age 74

LACY, Frank
Actor
b. Penge, England, July 9, 1867
d. Unknown, Aug. 10, 1937, Age 70

LACY, James
Patentee of Drury Lane
b. Unknown
d. Unknown, Jan. 21, 1774

LACY, John
Actor, Playwright
b. Unknown
d. Unknown, Sept. 17, 1681

LACY, Rophino
Composer, Playwright
b. Unknown
d. Unknown, Sept. 20, 1867, Age 70

LACY, Thomas Hailes
Playwright, Bookseller
b. Unknown
d. Unknown, Aug. 1, 1873, Age 63

LACY, Walter
Actor
b. Unknown
d. Unknown, Dec. 13, 1898, Age 89

LADD, Alan (Alan Walbridge Ladd)
Actor
b. Hot Springs, AR, Sept. 3, 1913
d. Palm Springs, CA, Jan. 29, 1964, Age 50

LAFERRIERE, Adolphe
Actor
b. Unknown
d. Unknown, July 15, 1877, Age 77

LAFFERTY, Wilson (Gene Wilson)
Performer
b. Unknown
d. Clarksburg, VA, Aug. 24, 1962

LaFOLLETTE, Fola
Actress
b. Madison, WI, Sept. 10, 1882
d. Arlington, VA, Feb. 17, 1970, Age 97

LAFONT, Pierre
Actor
b. Unknown
d. Unknown, April 18, 1873, Age 77

LA GRANGE, Charles Varlet
Actor
b. Unknown
d. Unknown, March 1, 1692, Age 52

LAGRANGE, Felix
Actor
b. Unknown
d. Unknown, Oct. 15, 1901, Age 75

LA GRANGE, Marie Ragueneau
Actress
b. Unknown, 1639
d. Unknown, 1737

LA GRANGE-CHANCEL, Joseph de
Playwright
b. Unknown, 1677
d. Unknown, 1758

LAHR, Bert (né Irving Lahrheim)
Actor, Comedian
b. New York, NY, Aug. 13, 1895
d. New York, NY, Dec. 4, 1967, Age 72

LAIDLER, Francis
Producer
b. Yorkshire, England, Jan. 7, 1870
d. Unknown, Jan. 6, 1955, Age 85

LAIT, Jack (Jacquin)
Author, Critic, Editor
b. New York, NY, March 13, 1883
d. Beverly Hills, CA, April 1, 1954, Age 71

LAKE, Lew
Performer, Producer
b. Unknown
d. London, England, Nov. 5, 1939, Age 65

LALOR, Frank
Performer
b. Washington, DC, Aug. 20, 1869
d. New York, NY, Oct. 15, 1932, Age 63

LA MARR, Barbara (Reatha Watson)
Actress
b. Unknown
d. Altadena, CA, Jan. 31, 1926, Age 30

LAMB, Charles
Essayist, Author, Critic
b. London, England, 1775
d. Edmonton, England, Dec, 27, 1834, Age 59

LAMBART, Ernest
Actor
b. Ireland, Unknown
d. New York, NY, June 27, 1945, Age 71

LAMBART, Richard (Eric Leighton)
Actor
b. Unknown
d. Unknown, Jan. 6, 1924

LAMBDIN, John O.
Critic
b. Unknown
d. Baltimore, MD, April 25, 1923, Age 50

LAMBELET, Napoleon
Composer, Musical director
b. Corfu, Greece, Feb. 27, 1864
d. Unknown, Sept. 25, 1932, Age 68

LAMBERT, Lawson
Theatre manager
b. Bombay, India, Aug. 29, 1870
d. Unknown, March 8, 1944, Age 73

LAMBERTI, Professor
Performer
b. Unknown
d. Hollywood, CA, March 13, 1950, Age 58

LAMI, Eugène Louis
Designer
b. Unknown, 1800
d. Unknown, 1890

LAMMERS, Paul
Director
b. Sacramento, CA, Aug. 28, 1921
d. Rochester, NY, June 12, 1968, Age 46

LANCASTER-WALLIS, Ellen
Actress, Producer
b. Unknown
d. Unknown, March 7, 1940, Age 86

LANDAU, David
Actor
b. Philadelphia, PA, Unknown
d. Los Angeles, CA, Sept. 20, 1935, Age 57

LANDAU, Jack
Director
b. Braddock, PA, Jan. 5, 1925
d. Boston, MA, March 16, 1967, Age 42

LANDECK, Ben
Playwright
b. London, England, Oct. 24, 1864
d. Unknown, Jan. 6, 1928, Age 63

LANDER, Charles Oram
Actor
b. Unknown
d. Unknown, Sept. 8, 1934, Age 71

LANDER, Jean Margaret Davenport (née Donald)
Actress
b. Wolverhampton, England, 1829
d. Lynn, MA, Aug. 2, 1903, Age 74

LANDI, Elissa (Elizabeth Marie Christine Kuehnelt)
Actress, Playwright, Novelist
b. Venice, Italy, Dec. 6, 1904
d. Kingston, NY, Oct. 21, 1948, Age 43

LANDIS, Carole (Frances Lillian Mary Ridste)
Actress
b. Fairchild, WI, Jan. 1, 1919
d. Brentwood, CA, July 5, 1948, Age 29

LANDIS, Jessie Royce
Actress
b. Chicago, IL, Nov. 25, 1906
d. Danbury, CT, Feb. 2, 1972, Age 67

LANE, Grace
Actress
b. England, Jan. 13, 1876
d. Hove, England, Jan. 14, 1956, Age 80

LANE, Lupino
Performer, Producer
b. London, England, June 16, 1892
d. London, England, Nov. 10, 1959, Age 67

LAN-FANG, Mei
Actor
b. Peiping, China, 1894
d. Unknown, Aug. 10, 1943, Age 49

LANG, (Alexander) Matheson
Actor, Producer, Playwright
b. Montreal, CAN, May 15, 1879
d. Bridgetown, Barbados, April 11, 1948, Age 68

LANG, Eva Clara
Actress
b. Columbus, OH, Unknown
d. Los Angeles, CA, April 6, 1933, Age 48

LANG, Gertrude
Performer
b. Unknown
d. New York, NY, Oct. 2, 1941, Age 42

LANG, Gertrude
Actress
b. Unknown
d. Unknown, Nov. 15, 1942

LANG, Harold
Dancer, Actor
b. San Francisco, CA, Dec. 21, 1931
d. Cairo, Egypt, Nov. 16, 1975, Age 43

LANG, Harry
Actor
b. Unknown
d. Hollywood, CA, Aug. 3, 1953, Age 58

LANG, Howard (Frederick Lange)
Actor
b. Unknown
d. Hollywood, CA, Jan. 26, 1941, Age 65

LANG, Ludwig
Organizer of Oberammergau Passion Play
b. Unknown
d. Unknown, Oct. 18, 1932, Age 88

LANG, Peter
Actor, Singer
b. Unknown
d. New York, NY, Aug. 20, 1932, Age 73

LANGBAINE, Gerard
Historian
b. Unknown
d. Unknown, June 23, 1692, Age 35

LANGDON, Harry
Actor
b. Council Bluffs, IA, June 15, 1885
d. Hollywood, CA, Dec. 22, 1944, Age 60

LANGE, Sven
Playwright
b. Unknown
d. Unknown, Jan. 6, 1930, Age 62

LANGFORD, Abraham
Playwright
b. Unknown
d. Unknown, Sept. 17, 1774, Age 63

LANGFORD, William
Actor
b. Montreal, CAN, Unknown
d. New York, NY, July 27, 1955, Age 35

LANGNER, Lawrence
Producer, Lawyer
b. Swansea, Wales, May 30, 1890
d. New York, NY, Dec. 26, 1962, Age 72

LANGTRY, Mrs. Lily (Emilie Charlotte Le Breton)
Actress, Producer
b. Isle of Jersey, England, Oct. 13, 1852
d. Monaco, Feb. 12, 1929, Age 76

LANIA, Leon (Lasser Herman)
Journalist, Screenwriter
b. Unknown
d. Munich, Germany, Nov. 10, 1961

LANNER, Mme. Katti
Dancer, Ballet mistress
b. Unknown
d. Unknown, Nov. 15, 1908, Age 80

LANTELME, Mlle.
Actress
b. Unknown
d. Unknown, July 26, 1911

LANZA, Mario (Alfred Arnold Cocozza)
Singer, Actor
b. South Philadelphia, PA, Unknown
d. Rome, Italy, Oct. 7, 1959, Age 38

LAPORTE, Pierre François
Producer
b. Unknown
d. Unknown, Sept. 26, 1841, Age 58

LA RAE, Grace
Actress
b. Unknown
d. Unknown, March 1956

LARDNER, Ring W.
Author, Humorist
b. Niles, MI, March 6, 1885
d. East Hampton, L.I., NY, Sept. 25, 1933, Age 48

LARIMORE, Earle
Actor
b. Portland, OR, Unknown
d. New York, NY, Oct. 23, 1947, Age 48

LARNED, Mel
Singer
b. Unknown
d. New York, NY, July 2, 1955, Age 30

LARQUEY, Pierre
Actor
b. Unknown
d. Paris, France, April 17, 1962, Age 78

LARRA, Mariano José de
Novelist, Playwright
b. Madrid, Spain, 1809
d. Unknown, 1837

LARRIMORE, Francine
Actress
b. Verdun, France, Aug. 22, 1898
d. New York, NY, March 7, 1975, Age 76

LA RUE, Grace
Actress
b. Kansas City, MO, 1882
d. Burlingame, CA, March 12, 1956, Age 74

LASCOE, Henry
Actor
b. Unknown
d. Hollywood, CA, Sept. 1, 1964, Age 52

LA SHELLE, Kirke
Librettist, Lyricist, Manager
b. Unknown, 1863
d. Unknown, May 16, 1905, Age 42

LASHWOOD, George
Performer
b. Unknown
d. Unknown, Jan. 20, 1942, Age 79

LASKY, Jesse Louis
Producer, Film executive
b. San Jose, CA, Unknown
d. Beverly Hills, CA, Jan. 13, 1958, Age 77

LATEINER, Joseph
Playwright
b. Unknown, 1853
d. Unknown, 1935

LATHAM, Fred G.
Director, Manager
b. England, Unknown
d. New York, NY, Jan. 31, 1943, Age 90

LATHAM, Hope (Mrs. Louise Brega Kemper)
Actress
b. Canada, Unknown
d. Bronxville, NY, April 10, 1951, Age 79

LATIMER, Henry
Performer
b. Unknown
d. London, England, Jan. 25, 1963, Age 86

LATOUCHE, John Treville
Composer, Lyricist
b. Richmond, VA, Nov. 13, 1917
d. Calais, VT, Aug. 7, 1956, Age 38

LAUDER, Sir Harry
Performer
b. Portobello, Scotland, Aug. 14, 1870
d. Strathaven, Lenarkshire, Scotland, Feb. 26, 1950, Age 79

LAUGHLIN, Anna (Mrs. Dwight V. Monroe)
Singer
b. Sacramento, CA, Unknown
d. New York, NY, March 6, 1937, Age 52

LAUGHTON, Charles
Actor, Director
b. Scarborough, England, July 1, 1899
d. Hollywood, CA, Dec. 15, 1962, Age 63

LAURI, Edward
Actor, Stage Manager
b. Unknown
d. Unknown, Jan. 9, 1919

LAURIE, Joe Jr.
Actor, Writer
b. New York, NY, 1892
d. New York, NY, April 29, 1954, Age 62

LAVALLIERE, Eve
Actress
b. Naples, Italy, 1866
d. Unknown, July 10, 1929, Age 61

LAVEDAN, Henri
Playwright
b. Orléans, France, April 9, 1859
d. Unknown, Aug. 1940, Age 81

LA VERE, Earl
Performer
b. Unknown
d. New York, NY, Jan. 25, 1962, Age 71

LA VERNE, Lucille
Actress
b. Memphis, TN, Nov. 8, 1872
d. Culver City, CA, March 4, 1945, Age 72

LAVERNE, Pattie
Actress
b. Unknown
d. Unknown, April 24, 1916

LAW, Arthur
Playwright
b. Unknown, March 22, 1844
d. Unknown, April 2, 1913, Age 69

LAW, Jenny Lou
Actress
b. Athens, OH, Unknown
d. Pittsburgh, PA, Jan. 1, 1961, Age 39

LAWFORD, Betty
Actress
b. London, England, Unknown
d. New York, NY, Nov. 20, 1960, Age 50

LAWFORD, Ernest
Actor
b. England, Unknown
d. New York, NY, Dec. 27, 1940, Age 70

LAWLOR, Charles B.
Performer
b. Dublin, Ireland, Unknown
d. New York, NY, May 31, 1925, Age 73

LAWRENCE, Adrian
Actor, Producer
b. Unknown
d. Unknown, Sept. 2, 1953, Age 79

LAWRENCE, Boyle
Playwright, Lyricist
b. London, England, 1869
d. Unknown, Dec. 30, 1951, Age 82

LAWRENCE, C. E.
Playwright, Novelist
b. Unknown
d. Unknown, March 14, 1940, Age 69

LAWRENCE, D. H.
Playwright, Novelist, Poet, Painter
b. Eastwood, Nottinghamshire, England, Sept. 11, 1885
d. Unknown, March 3, 1940, Age 54

LAWRENCE, Florence
Actress
b. Unknown, 1888
d. Unknown, 1938

LAWRENCE, Georgia
Actress
b. Unknown
d. Palatka, FL, Jan. 12, 1923, Age 46

LAWRENCE, Gerald
Actor
b. London, England, March 23, 1873
d. Unknown, May 16, 1957, Age 84

LAWRENCE, Gertrude (née Klasen)
Actress
b. London, England, July 4, 1898
d. New York, NY, Sept. 6, 1952, Age 54

LAWRENCE, Lawrence Shubert Sr.
Theatre executive, Producer
b. Syracuse, NY, Oct. 1, 1894
d. Philadelphia, PA, Apr. 15, 1965, Age 70

LAWRENCE, Margaret
Actress
b. Trenton, NJ, Aug. 2, 1889
d. New York, NY, June 9, 1929, Age 39

LAWRENCE, Reginald
Playwright, Educator
b. Rahway, NJ, March 4, 1900
d. New York, NY, Nov. 20, 1967, Age 67

LAWRENCE, Vincent S.
Playwright
b. Roxbury, MA, 1890
d. Corpus Christi, TX, Nov. 25, 1946, Age 56

LAWRENCE, Walter N.
Manager
b. Unknown
d. Bronxville, NY, Feb. 28, 1920, Age 62

LAWRENCE, William
Actor
b. Unknown
d. Boston, MA, March 17, 1921

LAWRENCE, William John
Historian, Playwright
b. Belfast, Ireland, Oct. 29, 1862
d. Unknown, Aug. 8, 1940, Age 77

LAWSON, John
Actor
b. Unknown
d. Unknown, Nov. 25, 1920, Age 55

LAWSON, Mary
Actress
b. Darlington, England, Aug. 30, 1910
d. Unknown, May 4, 1941, Age 30

LAWSON, Robb
Critic
b. Unknown
d. Unknown, March 30, 1947, Age 74

LAWSON, Wilfrid
Actor
b. Bradford, Yorkshire, England, Jan. 14, 1900
d. London, England, Oct. 10, 1966, Age 66

LAWSON, Winifred
Singer, Actress
b. London, England, Nov. 15, 1894
d. England, Nov. 30, 1961, Age 67

LAWTON, Frank
Performer
b. Unknown
d. Unknown, April 16, 1914

LAWTON, Thais
Actress
b. Louisville, KY, June 18, 1881
d. New York, NY, Dec. 18, 1956, Age 75

LEA, Marion (Mrs. Langdon Mitchell)
Actress
b. Philadelphia, PA, Unknown
d. New York, NY, June 7, 1944, Age 83

LEAKE, James
Patentee of Covent Garden Theatre
b. Unknown
d. Unknown, Aug. 15, 1791, Age 76

LEAMAR, Alice
Performer
b. Unknown
d. Unknown, Nov. 30, 1950, Age 81

LEAMORE, Tom
Comedian, Dancer
b. Unknown
d. Unknown, Sept. 6, 1939, Age 73

LEARY, Gilda
Actress
b. England, Unknown
d. New York, NY, April 17, 1927, Age 31

LEAVITT, Michael Bennett
Manager
b. Posen, Poland, 1843
d. Miami Beach, FL, June 27, 1935, Age 92

LE BARGY, Charles Gustave Auguste
Actor, Playwright
b. La Chapelle, Seine, France, 1858
d. Unknown, Feb. 5, 1936, Age 77

LE BARON, William
Playwright, Film producer
b. Elgin, IL, Feb. 16, 1883
d. Los Angeles, CA, Feb. 9, 1958, Age 75

LEBEDEFF, Ivan
Actor
b. Russia or Lithuania, Unknown
d. Los Angeles, CA, March 31, 1953, Age 58

LEBLANC, Georgette (Maeterlinck)
Actress
b. Rouen, France, 1876
d. Unknown, Oct. 26, 1941, Age 65

LECLERCQ, Pierre
Playwright, Novelist
b. Unknown
d. Langley, Bucks, England, Jan. 24, 1932

LE CLERQ, Florence
Actress
b. Unknown
d. Unknown, April 15, 1960, Age 89

LECOCQ, Alexandre Charles
Composer
b. Paris, France, June 3, 1832
d. Paris, France, Oct. 24, 1918, Age 86

LECOUVREUR, Adrienne
Actress
b. Damery, France, April 5, 1692
d. Paris, France, March 20, 1730, Age 38

LECUONA, Ernesto
Composer
b. Guanbacoa, Cuba, Unknown
d. Santa Cruz de Tenerife, Canary Islands, Spain, Nov. 29, 1963, Age 68

LEDERER, George W.
Producer, Director
b. Wilkes-Barre, PA, 1861
d. Jackson Heights, NY, Oct. 8, 1938, Age 77

LEDERER, George W. Jr.
Talent representative
b. Unknown
d. New York, NY, Dec. 17, 1924, Age 33

LEDERER, Gretchen
Actress
b. Unknown
d. Anaheim, CA, Dec. 20, 1955, Age 64

LEDGER, Edward
Editor, Publisher
b. Unknown
d. Unknown, Sept. 24, 1921

LEDGER, Frederick
Editor, Publisher
b. Unknown
d. Unknown, June 14, 1874

LEE, Auriol
Actress, Director
b. London, England, Sept. 13, 1880
d. near Hutchinson, July 2, 1941, Age 60

LEE, Belinda
Actress
b. Devon, England, Unknown
d. near Baker, CA, March 13, 1961, Age 26

LEE, Bert
Librettist, Songwriter
b. Rosensthorpe, Yorkshire, England, June 11, 1880
d. Unknown, Jan. 23, 1946, Age 65

LEE, Canada (Leonard Lionel Cornelius Canegata)
Actor, Producer
b. New York, NY, March 3, 1907
d. New York, NY, May 8, 1952, Age 45

LEE, Charles
Performer
b. Unknown
d. Unknown, March 25, 1947, Age 71

LEE, Florence (Mrs. Del Henderson)
Actress
b. Unknown
d. Hollywood, CA, Sept. 1, 1962, Age 74

LEE, Gypsy Rose (née Rose Louise Hovick)
Entertainer, Writer
b. Seattle, WA, Jan. 9, 1914
d. Los Angeles, CA, April 26, 1970, Age 56

LEE, Harry A.
Manager
b. San Francisco, CA, Unknown
d. Atlantic City, NJ, Aug. 2, 1919, Age 76

LEE, Henry
Actor, Playwright
b. Unknown
d. Unknown, March 30, 1836, Age 70

LEE, Henry
Performer
b. Unknown
d. Unknown, Nov. 9, 1910, Age 53

LEE, Jane
Actress
b. Unknown
d. New York, NY, March 17, 1957, Age 45

LEE, Jean (Mrs. Jess Mack)
Performer
b. Unknown
d. Boston, MA, March 8, 1963

LEE, Jennie (Mrs. W. Cartright)
Actress
b. Unknown
d. Hollywood, CA, Aug. 4, 1925, Age 75

LEE, Jennie ("Jo")
Actress
b. London, England, Unknown
d. Unknown, May 3, 1930, Age 84

LEE, Jennie (Mrs. J. P. Burnett)
Actress
b. Unknown
d. London, England, May 3, 1930, Age 72

LEE, Lillie (Mrs. Hugh Jay Didcott)
Actress, Dancer
b. Unknown
d. Unknown, Aug. 5, 1941, Age 81

LEE, Nathaniel
Playwright, Poet
b. Unknown, c1653
d. Unknown, buried May 6, 1692, Age 39

LEE, Nelson
Playwright, Producer
b. Unknown
d. Unknown, Jan. 2, 1872, Age 65

LEE, Sammy
Dance Director
b. Unknown
d. Woodland Hills, CA, March 30, 1968, Age 78

LEE, Sophia
Playwright
b. Unknown
d. Unknown, March 13, 1824, Age 74

LEFAUR, André
Actor
b. Unknown
d. Unknown

LE FEUVRE, Guy
Singer, Composer
b. Ottawa, CAN, Oct. 17, 1883
d. Unknown, Feb. 15, 1950, Age 66

LEFFLER, George
Producer, Booking manager
b. New York, NY, Unknown
d. New York, NY, Aug. 5, 1951, Age 77

LEFTWICH, Alexander
Director, Producer
b. Unknown
d. Hollywood, CA, Jan. 13, 1947, Age 63

LEGAT, Nicholas
Dancer, Ballet Master
b. Unknown
d. Unknown, Jan. 24, 1937, Age 67

LEGOUVE, Ernest Gabriel Jean Baptiste
Playwright, Poet, Novelist
b. Unknown, 1807
d. Unknown, March 14, 1903, Age 96

LEGRAND, Marc-Antoine
Actor
b. Unknown, 1673
d. Unknown, Jan. 7, 1728, Age 54

LE GUERE, George
Actor
b. Memphis, TN, Unknown
d. New York, NY, Nov. 21, 1947, Age 76

LEHAR, Franz
Composer
b. Komaron, Hungary, April 30, 1870
d. Bad Ischl, Austria, Oct. 24, 1948, Age 78

LE HAY, John (Healy)
Performer
b. Ireland, March 25, 1854
d. Unknown, Nov. 2, 1926, Age 72

LEIBER, Fritz
Actor
b. Chicago, IL, Jan. 31, 1883
d. Pacific Palisades, CA, Oct. 14, 1949, Age 66

LEICESTER, Ernest
Actor
b. Unknown, June 11, 1866
d. Unknown, Oct. 5, 1939, Age 73

LEICESTER, George F.
Actor
b. Unknown
d. Unknown, June 23, 1916, Age 72

LEIGH, Andrew George
Actor, Director
b. Brighton, England, Nov. 30, 1887
d. Brighton, England, April 21, 1957, Age 69

LEIGH, Gracie (née Ellis)
Actress
b. Unknown
d. Unknown, June 24, 1950, Age 75

LEIGH, Henry S.
Playwright
b. Unknown
d. Unknown, June 16, 1883, Age 46

LEIGH, J. H.
Producer, Actor, Shakespearean scholar
b. Unknown
d. Unknown, March 1, 1934, Age 75

LEIGH, Mary (née Eveleigh)
Actress
b. London, England, Feb. 11, 1904
d. Unknown, March 19, 1943, Age 38

LEIGH, Philip
Actor
b. Unknown
d. Unknown, June 19, 1935, Age 55

LEIGH, Vivien (née Vivian Mary Hartley)
Actress
b. Darjeeling, India, Nov. 5, 1913
d. London, England, July 8, 1967, Age 53

LEIGHTON, Alexes
Actress
b. Unknown
d. Unknown, Sept. 1926

LEIGHTON, Bert (James Albert Leighton)
Performer, Songwriter
b. Beacher, IL, Unknown
d. San Francisco, CA, Feb. 10, 1964, Age 87

LEIGHTON, Harry
Actor
b. Unknown
d. Bayshore, L.I., NY, May 30, 1926, Age 60

LEIGHTON, Queenie
Actress
b. Unknown, July 18, 1872
d. Unknown, Nov. 19, 1943, Age 71

LEKAIN (CAIN), Henri Louis
Actor
b. Unknown, 1729
d. Paris, France, Feb. 8, 1778, Age 49

LELY, Durward
Actor
b. Unknown
d. Unknown, Feb. 29, 1944, Age 91

LEMAITRE, (Antoine Louis Prosper) Frédéric
Actor
b. Le Havre, France, 1800
d. Unknown, Jan. 26, 1876, Age 75

LEMAITRE, Jules François Elie
Playwright, Critic, Poet, Novelist
b. Vennecy, Loiret, France, Aug. 27, 1853
d. Paris, France, Aug. 7, 1914, Age 60

LE MAY, Alan
Novelist, Screenwriter, Producer, Director
b. Unknown
d. Hollywood, CA, April 27, 1964, Age 64

LEMERCIER, (Louis Jean) Népomucène
Playwright
b. Unknown, 1771
d. Unknown, 1840

LEMON, Mark
Playwright, Editor
b. Unknown, 1809
d. Unknown, May 23, 1870, Age 60

LeMOYNE, Sarah Cowell
Actress
b. New York, NY, July 22, 1859
d. Unknown, July 17, 1915, Age 56

LE MOYNE, W. J. (William)
Actor
b. Unknown, 1831
d. Unknown, Nov. 6, 1905, Age 74

LENDER, Marcelle
Actress
b. Unknown
d. Unknown, Sept. 26, 1926, Age 64

LENGEL, William Charles
Editor, Writer, Playwright, Lawyer
b. Durango, CO, June 27, 1888
d. New York, NY, Oct. 11, 1965, Age 77

LENIHAN, Winifred
Actress
b. Brooklyn, NY, Unknown
d. Sea Cliff, L.I., NY, July 27, 1964, Age 66

LENNARD, Arthur
Performer
b. Unknown
d. Unknown, Jan. 14, 1954, Age 86

LENNARD, Horace
Playwright, Lyricist
b. Unknown
d. Unknown, Sept. 2, 1920

LENNOX, Lottie
Performer
b. Unknown
d. Unknown, March 9, 1947, Age 61

LENO, Dan Jr. (Sydney Paul Galvin)
Performer, Writer
b. Unknown
d. London, England, Jan. 2, 1962, Age 70

LENORMAND, Henri-René
Playwright
b. Unknown, Paris, France
d. May 3, 1882, Paris, France, Age Feb. 17, 1951

LENSKY, Alexander Pavlovich
Actor, Producer, Director
b. Unknown, 1847
d. Unknown, 1908

LEON, Victor
Librettist
b. Unknown
d. Vienna, Austria, April 1940, Age 82

LEON, W. D. (W. D. Glassock)
Performer, Theatre operator
b. Unknown
d. San Antonio, TX, July 1964, Age 78

LEONARD, Eddie (Lemuel Gordon Toney)
Comedian, Songwriter
b. Richmond, VA, Unknown
d. New York, NY, July 29, 1941, Age 70

LEONARD, Jack E.
Comedian, Actor
b. Chicago, IL, April 24, 1911
d. New York, NY, May 11, 1973, Age 62

LEONARD, Marion
Actress
b. Unknown
d. Woodland Hills, CA, Jan. 9, 1956, Age 75

LEONARD, Robert
Performer
b. Unknown
d. Brooklyn, NY, Jan. 5, 1948, Age 59

LEONARD, Robert Z.
Actor, Director, Singer
b. Chicago, IL, Oct. 7, 1889
d. Beverly Hills, CA, Aug. 27, 1968, Age 78

LEONARD-BOYNE, Eva (née Boyne)
Actress
b. London, England, 1885
d. New York, NY, April 12, 1960, Age 74

LEONCAVALLO, Ruggero
Composer
b. Naples, Italy, March 8, 1858
d. Montecatini, Italy, Aug. 9, 1919, Age 61

LEONE, Henry
Actor, Singer
b. Unknown
d. Mount Vernon, NY, June 9, 1922, Age 64

LEONE, Maude
Actress
b. Unknown
d. Unknown, March 13, 1930, Age 45

LEONI, Franco
Composer
b. Unknown
d. Unknown, Feb. 8, 1949, Age 84

LEONIDOV, Leonid Mironovich
Actor, Director
b. Unknown, 1873
d. Moscow, Russia, 1941

LERAND, M.
Actor
b. Unknown
d. Unknown, March 16, 1920, Age 56

LERMONTOV, Mikhail Yurevich
Poet, Playwright
b. Unknown, 1814
d. Pyatagorsk, Russia, July 15 or 27, 1841

LERNER, Joseph Yehuda
Playwright, Translator
b. Unknown, 1849
d. Unknown, 1907

LE SAGE, Alain René
Novelist, Playwright
b. Unknown
d. 1668, Unknown, Age 1747

LESLIE, Amy (a/k/a Lillie West)
Actress, Drama critic
b. West Burlington, IA, Oct. 11, 1860
d. Chicago, IL, July 3, 1939, Age 78

LESLIE, Fanny
Actress
b. Unknown
d. Unknown, Feb. 8, 1935, Age 78

LESLIE, Fred (Frederick Hobson)
Actor, Playwright
b. Woolwich, England, 1855
d. Unknown, Dec. 7, 1892, Age 37

LESLIE, Henry
Playwright
b. Unknown
d. Unknown, March 4, 1881, Age 51

LESLIE, Lew (Lew Lessinsky)
Manager, Producer, Composer, Author
b. Unknown, 1886 (?)
d. Orangeburg, NY, March 10, 1963, Age about 75

LESLIE, Tom (né Thomas Veale)
Performer
b. Unknown
d. Birmingham, England, March 26, 1964, Age 68

LESSING, Gotthold Ephraim
Playwright, Poet, Critic
b. Kametz, Saxony, Germany, Jan. 22, 1729
d. Braunschweig, Germany, Feb. 15, 19781, Age 52

LESTER, Alfred (Leslie)
Actor
b. Nottingham, England, Oct. 25, 1874
d. Unknown, May 6, 1925, Age 50

LESTOCQ, George
Actor, Director
b. Unknown
d. Unknown, Dec. 6, 1924

LESTOCQ, William (Lestocq Boileau Wooldridge)
Actor, Manager, Playwright
b. Unknown
d. London, England, Oct. 16, 1920, Age 69

L'ESTRANGE, Julian
Actor
b. Unknown, Aug. 6, 1878
d. Unknown, Oct. 22, 1918, Age 40

LeSUEUR, Hal
Actor
b. Unknown
d. Los Angeles, CA, May 3, 1963, Age 59

LE THIERE, Roma Guillon
Actress
b. Unknown
d. Unknown, Jan. 8, 1903

LEVAN, Harry
Performer
b. Unknown
d. Knoxville, TN, Jan. 10, 1963, Age 61

LEVENTHAL, Joseph Jules
Producer
b. near Minsk, Russia, March 3, 1889
d. New York, NY, April 13, 1949, Age 60

LEVEY, Ethel (Grace Ethelia)
Actress
b. San Francisco, CA, Nov. 22, 1880
d. New York, NY, Feb. 27, 1955, Age 74

LEVICK, Gus
Actor
b. Unknown
d. Unknown, July 8, 1909, Age 55

LEVIN, Charles
Film production manager
b. Unknown
d. Hollywood, CA, Nov. 11, 1962, Age 63

LEVINE, Joseph
Lawyer
b. Unknown
d. New York, NY, June 8, 1964, Age 68

LEVITT, Paul
Actor, Producer, Director
b. Unknown
d. Los Angeles, CA, Sept. 15, 1968, Age 41

LEVY, Benn W.
Playwright, Director
b. London, England, March 7, 1900
d. Oxford, England, Dec. 7, 1973, Age 73

LEVY, Helen Marsh (Mrs. Arthur Jay Levy)
Journalist
b. Hartford, CT, Unknown
d. Norwalk, CT, Feb. 3, 1962

LEVY, J. Langley
Critic, Journalist
b. Unknown
d. Unknown, May 11, 1945, Age 74

LEVY, José G.
Theatre manager, Playwright
b. Unknown, Portsmouth, England
d. June 29, 1884

LEVY, Sylvan
Performer
b. Unknown
d. New York, NY, Oct. 30, 1962, Age 56

LEWES, Charles Lee
Actor
b. Unknown, 1740
d. Unknown, 1803

LEWES, George Henry
Playwright, Critic
b. Unknown, 1817
d. Unknown, Nov. 28, 1878, Age 61

LEWINSKY, Josef
Actor
b. Unknown
d. Unknown, Feb. 27, 1907, Age 72

LEWIS, Ada
Actress
b. New York, NY, Unknown
d. Hollis, L.I., NY, Sept. 24, 1925, Age 50

LEWIS, Arthur
Actor, Producer
b. Hampstead, England, Aug. 19, 1846
d. New York, NY, June 13, 1930, Age 83

LEWIS, Bertha
Actress
b. London, England, May 12, 1887
d. Unknown, May 8, 1931, Age 44

LEWIS, Catherine
Actress
b. Unknown
d. Unknown, Feb. 15, 1942, Age 88

LEWIS, Edward
Actor
b. Unknown
d. Unknown, April 23, 1922

LEWIS, Eric (Fred Eric Lewis Tuffley)
Actor
b. Northampton, England, Oct. 23, 1855
d. Unknown, April 1, 1935, Age 79

LEWIS, Frank A.
Director of American Civic Opera Co.
b. Unknown
d. Poughkeepsie, NY, April 20, 1963, Age 71

LEWIS, Fred (né Till)
Actor
b. Kingston-on-Thames, England, Dec. 23, 1860
d. Unknown, Dec. 25, 1927, Age 67

LEWIS, Frederick G.
Actor
b. Oswego, NY, Feb. 14, 1873
d. Amityville, NY, March 19, 1946, Age 73

LEWIS, Ida
Actress
b. Unknown
d. Unknown, April 21, 1935, Age 86

LEWIS, James
Actor
b. Unknown
d. Unknown, Sept. 10, 1896, Age 59

LEWIS, Jeffreys
Actress
b. London, England, Unknown
d. New York, NY, April 29, 1926, Age 69

LEWIS, Leopold
Playwright
b. Unknown
d. Unknown, Feb. 23, 1890, Age 62

LEWIS, Lloyd Downs
Critic, Historian, Playwright
b. Spring Valley, IN, 1891
d. Libertyville, IL, April 21, 1949, Age 57

LEWIS, Matthew Gregory ("Monk")
Playwright
b. Unknown, 1775
d. Unknown, May 14, 1818, Age 42

LEWIS, Mitchell
Actor
b. Unknown
d. Hollywood, CA, Aug. 24, 1956, Age 76

LEWIS, Philip
Musical director
b. Unknown
d. Unknown, Oct. 20, 1931

LEWIS, Sam
Performer
b. Unknown
d. New York, NY, Jan. 11, 1964

LEWIS, Sheldon
Performer
b. Unknown
d. San Gabriel, CA, May 7, 1958, Age 89

LEWIS, Sinclair
Novelist, Playwright, Actor
b. Sauk Center, MN, Feb. 7, 1885
d. Rome, Italy, Jan. 10, 1951, Age 65

LEWIS, Ted (né Theodore Leopold Friedman)
Performer
b. Circleville, OH, June 6, 1891
d. New York, NY, Aug. 25, 1971, Age 80

LEWIS, William Thomas ("Gentleman Lewis")
Actor, Producer
b. Unknown, 1749
d. Unknown, Jan. 13, 1811, Age 62

LEWIS, Windsor
Director
b. New York, NY, Nov. 21, 1918
d. New York, NY, May 15, 1972, Age 53

LEWISOHN, Alice
Director, Writer, Philanthropist
b. New York, NY, Unknown
d. Zurich, Switzerland, Jan. 6, 1972, Age 88

LEWISOHN, Irene
Founder of Neighborhood Playhouse
b. New York, NY, Unknown
d. New York, NY, April 4, 1944, Age about 50

LEWISOHN, Victor Max
Actor
b. London, England, April 21, 1897
d. Unknown, Nov. 13, 1934, Age 37

LEYBOURNE, George (Joe Saunders) (a/k/a "Champagne Charlie")
Performer
b. England, 1842
d. Unknown, 1884, Age 42

LEYEL, Carl F. (Leijel)
Producer
b. County Durham, England, Dec. 30, 1875
d. Unknown, Oct. 1, 1925, Age 49

LEYSSAC, Paul
Performer, Author
b. France, Unknown
d. Copenhagen, Denmark, Aug. 20, 1946

LEYTON, George
Performer
b. Unknown
d. Unknown, June 5, 1948, Age 84

LIBBEY, James Aldrich
Singer
b. Unknown
d. San Francisco, CA, April 29, 1925, Age 53

LIDGETT, Dr. Scott
Administrator, (Old Vic)
b. Unknown
d. Unknown, 1953, Age 98

LIEBLER, Theodore A.
Producer
b. New York, NY, Unknown
d. Old Greenwich, CT, April 23, 1941, Age 89

LIEBLING, Leonard
Librettist, Critic, Editor
b. New York, NY, Feb. 7, 1874
d. New York, NY, Oct. 28, 1945, Age 70

LIEBURG, Max
Playwright
b. Unknown
d. Corfu, Greece, June 12, 1962, Age 63

LIGHT, James
Director
b. Pittsburgh, PA, Unknown
d. New York, NY, Feb. 11, 1964, Age 69

LILINA, Maria Petrovna (Mme. Konstantin Stanislavsky née Perevozchikova)
Actress
b. Unknown, 1866
d. Moscow, Russia, Aug. 24, 1954, Age 77

LILLIES, Leonard
Producer
b. Chudleigh, Devonshire, England, Sept. 18, 1860
d. Unknown, Aug. 2, 1923, Age 62

LILLO, George
Playwright
b. Moorfields, London, England, Feb. 4, 1693
d. London, England, Sept. 3, 1739, Age 46

LIMBERT, Roy
Theatre, manager, Producer, Co-founder of the Malvern Festival
b. Surbiton, Surrey, England, Dec. 26, 1893
d. Unknown, Nov. 29, 1954, Age 60

LINCKE, Paul
Composer
b. Berlin, Germany, Nov. 7, 1866
d. Klausthal-Zellerfeld, Germany, Sept. 4, 1946, Age 79

LINCOLN, Elmo (Otto E. Linkenhelt)
Actor
b. Unknown, 1889
d. Hollywood, CA, June 27, 1952, Age 63

LIND, Letty
Actress, Dancer
b. Unknown, Dec. 21, 1862
d. Unknown, Aug. 27, 1923, Age 60

LINDER, Max
Actor
b. Unknown
d. Unknown, Nov. 1, 1925, Age 41

LINDO, Frank
Actor, Producer, Playwright
b. Unknown
d. Unknown, April 9, 1933, Age 68

LINDSAY, Howard
Playwright, Director, Producer, Actor
b. Waterford, NY, March 29, 1889
d. New York, NY, Feb. 11, 1968, Age 78

LINDSAY, James
Actor
b. Devonshire, England, Feb. 26, 1869
d. Unknown, June 9, 1928, Age 59

LINDSLEY, Guy
Actor
b. St. Louis, MO, Unknown
d. New York, NY, May 26, 1923

LING, Richie
Actor, Singer
b. London, England, Unknown
d. New York, NY, March 5, 1937, Age 70

LINGARD, Horace
Producer, Actor
b. Unknown
d. Unknown, Jan. 12, 1927, Age 89

LINK, Adolf
Actor
b. Budapest, Hungary, Unknown
d. New York, NY, Sept. 24, 1933, Age 81

LINLEY, Betty
Actress
b. Malmesbury, England, Unknown
d. New York, NY, May 9, 1951, Age 61

LINLEY, George
Playwright, Composer
b. Unknown
d. Unknown, Sept. 10, 1865, Age 67

LINLEY, William
Playwright, Composer
b. Unknown
d. Unknown, May 6, 1835, Age 64

LINNIT, Sidney E.
Producer
b. Unknown
d. London, England, Aug. 12, 1956, Age 58

LION, Leon M.
Actor, Director, Producer, Playwright
b. London, England, March 12, 1879
d. Unknown, March 28, 1947, Age 68

LIPMAN, Clara
Actress
b. Chicago, IL, Dec. 6, 1869
d. New York, NY, June 22, 1952, Age 82

LIPSCOMB, William Percy
Playwright
b. Merton, Surrey, England, 1887
d. Unknown, July 24, 1958, Age 70

LIPTON, George
Singer, Actor
b. Unknown
d. Sparta, NJ, March 9, 1962, Age 45

LISITZKY, Professor Ephram E.
Educator, Poet, Shakespearean scholar
b. Russia, Unknown
d. New Orleans, LA, June 25, 1962, Age 77

LISTER, Francis
Actor
b. London, England, Apr. 2, 1899
d. London, England, Oct. 28, 1951, Age 52

LISTON, John
Actor
b. Unknown, 1776
d. Unknown, 1846

LISTON, Victor
Performer, Theatre manager
b. Unknown, 1838
d. Unknown, 1913

LITT, Jacob
Producer
b. Unknown
d. Unknown, Sept. 27, 1905

LITTELL, Robert
Critic, Editor
b. Milwaukee, WI, May 25, 1896
d. New York, NY, Dec. 5, 1963, Age 67

LITTLE, C. P.
Actor, Journalist
b. Unknown
d. Unknown, Jan. 18, 1914

LITTLEDALE, Richard
Actor
b. Unknown
d. Unknown, Jan. 31, 1951, Age 47

LITTLEFIELD, Catherine
Dancer, Choreographer
b. Philadelphia, PA, Sept. 16, 1904
d. Unknown, Nov. 19, 1951, Age 47

LITTLEFIELD, Emma
Actress
b. Unknown
d. Unknown, June 23, 1934, Age 53

LITTLEFIELD, Lucien
Actor
b. San Antonio, TX, Unknown
d. Hollywood, CA, June 4, 1960, Age 64

LITTLER, F. R.
Theatre manager
b. Unknown
d. Unknown, March 13, 1940, Age 60

"LITTLE TICH"
(Harry Relph), Performer
b. England, Unknown
d. Hendon, London, England, Feb. 10, 1928, Age 59

LIVERIGHT, Horace Brisbin
Producer, Director, Publisher
b. Osceola Mills, PA, Dec. 10, 1886
d. New York, NY, Sept. 24, 1933, Age 46

LIVESEY, Jack
Actor
b. Barry, South Wales, June 11, 1901
d. Unknown, Oct. 12, 1961, Age 60

LIVESEY, Sam
Actor
b. Flintshire, Scotland, Oct. 14, 1873
d. Unknown, Nov. 7, 1936, Age 63

LIVINGSTON, Deacon (Murray)
Performer
b. Unknown
d. Pittsburgh, PA, Feb. 1, 1963, Age about 75

LLEWELLYN, Fewlass
Actor, Director, Playwright
b. Hull, England, March 5, 1866
d. Unknown, June 16, 1941, Age 75

LLEWELYN, Alfred H.
Actor
b. Unknown
d. Albequerque, NM, Apr. 6, 1964, Age 71

LLOYD, Al
Performer
b. Unknown
d. Hollywood, CA, July 10, 1964, Age 80

LLOYD, Alice (née Wood)
Performer
b. Unknown
d. Bandstead, England, Nov. 16, 1949, Age 76

LLOYD, Frederick William
Actor
b. London, England, Jan. 15, 1880
d. Unknown, Nov. 25, 1949, Age 69

LLOYD, Grace (Grace Lloyd Hyman)
Performer
b. Unknown
d. Banstead, Surrey, England, 1961, Age 86

LLOYD, John
Actor
b. Unknown
d. Unknown, Feb. 28, 1944, Age 74

LLOYD, Marie (Matilda Alice Victoria Wood)
Performer
b. London, England, Feb. 12, 1870
d. London, England, Oct. 7, 1922, Age 52

LLOYD, Rosie
Performer
b. Unknown
d. Unknown, Jan. 19, 1944, Age 64

LOCKE, Edward
Playwright, Actor
b. Stourbridge, Worcestershire, England, Oct. 18, 1869
d. East Islip, NY, April 1, 1945, Age 75

LOCKE, Robinson
Critic, Editor
b. Toledo, OH, March 15, 1856
d. Toledo, OH, April 20, 1920, Age 64

LOCKE, Will H.
Playwright
b. Unknown
d. Unknown, Oct. 7, 1950, Age 82

LOCKE, William John
Playwright, Novelist
b. Barbados, B. W. I., March 20, 1863
d. Unknown, May 15, 1930, Age 67

LOCKETT, Louis
Performer, Dancer
b. New York, NY, Unknown
d. Los Angeles, CA, July 29, 1964, Age 71

LOCKHART, Gene (Eugene)
Actor, Playwright
b. London, Ontario, CAN, July 18, 1891
d. Santa Monica, CA, March 31, 1957, Age 65

LOCKWOOD, Harold
Actor
b. Unknown, 1887
d. Unknown, 1918

LODER, George
Composer
b. Unknown
d. Unknown, July 15, 1868, Age 52

LOEB, Philip
Actor
b. Philadelphia, PA, 1894
d. New York, NY, Sept. 1, 1955, Age 61

LOEHNER-BEDA, Dr.
Librettist
b. Unknown
d. Unknown, Nov. 1939

LOESSER, Frank
Composer, Lyricist
b. New York, NY, June 29, 1910
d. New York, NY, July 28, 1969, Age 59

LOEW, Marcus
Theatre and Film executive
b. New York, NY, May 7, 1870
d. Glen Cove, NY, Sept. 7, 1927, Age 57

LOFTUS, Kitty
Actress
b. Kenilworth, Scotland, June 16, 1867
d. Unknown, March 17, 1927, Age 59

LOFTUS, Marie
Actress
b. Unknown
d. Unknown, Dec. 7, 1940, Age 83

LOFTUS, Marie Cecilia (Cissie)
Actress
b. Glasgow, Scotland, Oct. 22, 1876
d. New York, NY, July 12, 1943, Age 66

LOGAN, Cornelius A.
Playwright, Actor
b. Baltimore, MD, May 4, 1806
d. near Wheeling, WV, Feb. 22, 1853, Age 46

LOGAN, Ella
Actress, Singer
b. Glasgow, Scotland, March 6, 1913
d. Burlingame, CA, May 1, 1969, Age 56

LOGAN, Olive
Playwright, Actress
b. Unknown, 1839
d. Unknown, April 27, 1909, Age 70

LOGAN, Stanley
Actor, Producer, Director
b. Earlsfield, England, Unknown
d. New York, NY, Jan. 30, 1953, Age 67

LOMBARD, Carole (Carol Jane Peters)
Actress
b. Fort Wayne, IN, Oct. 6, 1909
d. air crash near Las Vegas, NV, Jan. 16, 1942, Age 32

LOMBARD, Harry
Performer
b. Unknown
d. Beloit, WI, Feb. 4, 1963, Age 74

LONDON, Ernest A.
Performer
b. Unknown
d. Staten Island, NY, June 21, 1964, Age 85

LONDON, Jack (John Griffith London)
Playwright, Novelist
b. San Francisco, CA, Jan. 12, 1876
d. Glen Ellen, CA, Nov. 22, 1916, Age 40

LONDON, Tom (Leonard Clapham)
Actor
b. Unknown
d. Hollywood, CA, Dec. 5, 1963, Age 81

LONERGAN, Lester
Actor, Director
b. Ireland, Unknown
d. Lynn, MA, Aug. 13, 1931, Age 62

LONERGAN, Lester
Actor
b. Unknown
d. New York, NY, Dec. 23, 1959, Age 65

LONG, John Luther
Playwright
b. Philadelphia, PA, 1861
d. Unknown, Oct. 31, 1927, Age 66

LONG, Mary Elitch
Theater owner and manager
b. Philadelphia, PA, Unknown
d. Denver, CO, July 16, 1936, Age 86

LONG, Nick Jr.
Dancer
b. Unknown
d. New York, NY, Aug. 31, 1949, Age 43

LONGFORD, Sixth Earl of (Edward Arthur Henry Pakenham)
Playwright, Producer
b. Unknown, Dec. 29, 1902
d. Unknown, Feb. 4, 1961, Age 58

LONSDALE, H. G.
Actor
b. Unknown
d. Unknown, July 12, 1923

LONSDALE, (Leonard) Frederick
Playwright
b. Island of Jersey, Channel Islands, England, Feb. 5, 1881
d. London, England, April 4, 1954, Age 73

LONSDALE, Thomas J.
Lyricist
b. Unknown
d. Unknown, June 13, 1928

LOOFBOURROW, John G.
Actor, Journalist
b. Oberlin, OH, Unknown
d. Venice, FL, Feb. 24, 1964, Age 61

LOPEZ, Sabatino
Playwright
b. Unknown
d. Unknown, Oct. 27, 1951, Age 84

LORAINE, Henry
Actor
b. Unknown
d. Unknown, July 10, 1899, Age 80

LORAINE, Robert
Actor, Producer
b. New Brighton, Liskard, Cheshire, England, Jan. 14, 1876
d. London, England, Dec. 23, 1935, Age 59

LORD, Pauline
Actress
b. Hanford, CA, Aug. 8, 1890
d. Alamogordo, NM, Oct. 10, 1950, Age 60

LORIMER, Wright
Actor, Producer, Playwright
b. Unknown, 1874
d. Unknown, Dec. 22, 1911, Age 37

LORNE, Marion (Mrs. Walter Hackett)
Actress
b. Pennsylvania, 1888
d. New York, NY, May 9, 1968, Age 82

LORRAINE, Emily
Actress
b. England, Unknown
d. New York, NY, July 6, 1944, Age 66

LORRAINE, Lillian (Mary Ann Brennan)
Actress
b. San Francisco, CA, Jan. 1, 1892
d. New York, NY, April 17, 1955, Age 63

LORRE, Peter
Actor
b. Rosenburg, Hungary, June 26, 1904
d. Hollywood, CA, March 23, 1964, Age 59

LOSCH, Tilly
Dancer
b. Vienna, Austria, Nov. 15, 1907
d. New York, NY, Dec. 24, 1975, Age 68

LOSEE, Frank
Actor
b. Brooklyn, NY, Unknown
d. Yonkers, NY, Nov. 14, 1937, Age 81

LOTINGA, Ernie
Performer, Director
b. Sunderland, England, Unknown
d. Unknown, Oct. 28, 1951, Age 75

LOTTA, Charlotte (or Carlotta Crabtree)
Actress
b. New York, NY, Nov. 7, 1847
d. Unknown, Sept. 25, 1924, Age 76

LOVAT, Nancie (Mrs. Walter E. Masters)
Actress
b. England, July 7, 1900
d. Worcester, MA, Aug. 16, 1946, Age 46

LOVE, Mabel (née Watson)
Actress
b. England, Unknown
d. Weybridge, England, May 15, 1953, Age 78

LOVE, Montagu
Actor
b. Portsmouth, Hants, England, 1877
d. Beverly Hills, CA, May 17, 1943, Age 66

LOVEJOY, Frank
Actor
b. Bronx, NY, March 28, 1914
d. New York, NY, Oct. 2, 1962, Age 48

LOVELL, George William
Playwright
b. Unknown
d. Unknown, May 13, 1878, Age 74

LOVELL, Mrs
Playwright
b. Unknown
d. Unknown, April 2, 1877, Age 73

LOVELL, Raymond
Actor
b. Montreal, CAN, April 13, 1900
d. London, England, Oct. 1, 1953, Age 53

LOVER, Samuel
Playwright, Novelist, Poet
b. Unknown
d. Unknown, July 6, 1868, Age 70

LOWE, Joshua
Journalist
b. Unknown
d. Unknown, March 21, 1945, Age 72

LOWE, K. Elmo
Actor - Director
b. San Antonio, TX, Aug. 27, 1899
d. Cleveland, OH, Jan. 26, 1971, Age 71

LOWE, Robert
Actor
b. Washington, DC, Unknown
d. New Dorp, S.I., NY, Sept. 21, 1939, Age 64

LOWELL, Helen (Robb)
Actress
b. New York, NY, June 2, 1866
d. Hollywood, CA, June 28, 1937, Age 71

LOWENFIELD, Henry
Producer
b. Unknown
d. Unknown, Nov. 20, 1931, Age 72

LOWIN, John
Actor
b. Unknown, 1576
d. Unknown, 1653

LOWNE, Charles Macready
Actor
b. Unknown
d. Unknown, July 30, 1941, Age 78

LOWRY, John
Business executive
b. Unknown
d. Mount Vernon, NY, Nov. 3, 1962, Age 79

LUBITSCH, Ernst
Director, Actor
b. Berlin, Germany, Jan. 28, 1892
d. Bel Air, CA, Nov. 30, 1947, Age 55

LUCAN, Arthur
Performer
b. Unknown
d. Unknown, May 17, 1954, Age 67

LUCAS, Rupert
Actor
b. Unknown
d. Unknown, Jan 13, 1953, Age 57

LUCK, Booth P.
Actor
b. Unknown
d. Richfield, IL, Jan. 13, 1962, Age 52

LUCY, Arnold
Actor
b. Unknown
d. Unknown, Dec. 15, 1945

LUDERS, Gustav
Composer
b. Bremen, Germany, Dec. 13, 1865
d. Unknown, Jan. 24, 1913, Age 47

LUDLOW, Noah Miller
Actor, Producer, Author
b. New York, NY, July 3, 1795
d. St. Louis, MO, Jan. 9, 1886, Age 90

LUDWIG, Emil (Emil Cohn)
Novelist, Playwright
b. Breslau, Germany, Jan. 28, 1881
d. Ascona, Switzerland, Sept. 17, 1948, Age 67

LUDWIG, Otto
Novelist, Playwright
b. Unknown, 1813
d. Unknown, 1865

LUGNE-POE, Aurélien-Marie
Actor, Producer
b. San Francisco, CA, Dec. 27, 1869
d. Avignon, France, June 19, 1940, Age 70

LUGOSI, Bela
Actor
b. Lugos, Hungary, Oct. 20, 1884
d. Los Angeles, CA, Aug. 16, 1956, Age 71

LUKAS, Paul (né Paul Lukacs)
Actor
b. Budapest, Hungary, May 26, 1894
d. Tangier, Morocco, Aug. 15, 1971, Age 76

LUMIERE, Auguste
Inventor, Scientist
b. Besançon, France, 1862
d. Lyons, France, April 10, 1954, Age 92

LUMIERE, Louis
Inventor, Film producer
b. France, 1864
d. Bandol, France, June 6, 1948, Age 83

LUMLEY, Ralph R.
Playwright
b. Unknown
d. Unknown, May 27, 1900, Age 35

LUNACHARSKY, Anatoli Vasilevich
First Commissar of Education in Soviet Russia, Critic, Playwright
b. Unknown, 1875
d. Unknown, 1933

LUNN, Joseph
Playwright
b. Unknown
d. Unknown, Dec. 12, 1863, Age 79

LUPINO, Barry
Performer
b. London, England, Jan. 7, 1884
d. Brighton, England, Sept. 26, 1962, Age 78

LUPINO, George
Actor, pantomimist
b. Birmingham, England, 1853
d. London, England, March 10, 1932, Age 79

LUPINO, Mark
Actor
b. Unknown
d. Unknown, April 4, 1930, Age 36

LUPINO, Stanley
Actor, Playwright, Producer
b. London, England, May 15, 1894
d. London, England, June 10, 1942, Age 48

LUTHER, Anna
Actress
b. Unknown
d. Hollywood, CA, Dec. 16, 1960, Age 67

LUTHER, Lester
Actor, Teacher
b. Unknown
d. Hollywood, CA, Jan. 19, 1962, Age 74

LYLE, Lyston (Edward Gibson)
Actor
b. Unknown
d. Unknown, Feb. 19, 1920, Age 64

LYLY, John
Playwright, Poet
b. Unknown, 1554
d. Unknown, Nov. 30, 1606, Age 52

LYMAN, Abe (né Simon)
Bandleader, Songwriter
b. Chicago, IL, Unknown
d. Beverly Hills, CA, Oct. 23, 1957, Age 60

LYMAN, Tommy
Singer
b. Unknown
d. Chicago, IL, March 12, 1964, Age 73

LYND, Rosa (Lady Chetwynd)
Actress
b. New York, NY, July 23, 1884
d. Unknown, Oct. 8, 1922, Age 38

LYNN, Diana
Actress
b. Los Angeles, CA, Unknown
d. Los Angeles, CA, Dec. 18, 1971, Age 45

LYNN, William H.
Actor
b. Providence, RI, Unknown
d. New York, NY, Jan. 5, 1952, Age 63

LYON, John Henry Hobart
Shakespeare scholar, Educator
b. Unknown
d. New York, NY, Dec. 18, 1961, Age 83

LYON, T. E.
Actor, Playwright
b. Unknown
d. Unknown, June 23, 1869, Age 57

LYONNET, Henry
Biographer, Historian
b. Unknown
d. Unknown, Feb. 4, 1933, Age 80

LYONS, Edmund D.
Actor
b. Unknown
d. Unknown, June 16, 1906, Age 55

LYRIC, Dora
Performer
b. Unknown
d. London, England, Dec. 7, 1962, Age 83

LYTELL, Bert
Actor
b. New York, NY, Feb. 24, 1885
d. New York, NY, Sept. 28, 1954, Age 69

LYTELL, Wilfred
Actor
b. Unknown
d. Salem, NY, Sept. 10, 1954, Age 62

LYTTELTON, Dame Edith (née Balfour)
Playwright, Administrator
b. Unknown
d. London, England, Sept. 2, 1948, Age 83

LYTTON, Doris (née Partington)
Actress
b. Manchester, England, Jan. 23, 1893
d. Unknown, Dec. 3, 1953, Age 60

LYTTON, Lord (Edward George Earle Lytton Bulwer-Lytton)
Playwright, Novelist
b. London, England, May 25, 1803
d. Unknown, Jan. 18, 1873, Age 69

LYTTON, Sir Henry Alfred
Actor
b. London, England, Jan. 3, 1867
d. London, England, Aug. 15, 1936, Age 69

LYVEDEN, Lord (Percy Vernon)
Actor
b. Unknown
d. Unknown, Dec. 28, 1926, Age 69

M

MacARTHUR, Charles
Playwright
b. Scranton, PA, Nov. 5, 1895
d. New York, NY, April 21, 1956, Age 60

MacARTHUR, Mary
Actress
b. New York, NY, Feb. 15, 1930
d. New York, NY, Sept. 22, 1949, Age 19

MacBRIDE, Donald
Actor
b. Unknown
d. Los Angeles, CA, June 21, 1957, Age 63

MacCAFFREY, George
Critic
b. Galway, Ireland, Sept. 15, 1870
d. Unknown, March 12, 1939, Age 68

MacCARTHY, Sir Desmond
Author, Critic
b. Plymouth, England, 1877
d. Unknown, June 7, 1952, Age 75

MacCOLL, James
Actor
b. Unknown
d. New York, NY, April 18, 1956, Age 44

MacDERMOTT, G. H. (Gilbert Hastings Farrell)
Actor, Playwright
b. Unknown, 1845
d. Unknown, May 8, 1901, Age 56

MACDONA, Charles
Actor, Producer
b. Dublin, Ireland, Unknown
d. Brighton, England, Nov. 15, 1946, Age 86

MacDONAGH, Donagh
Playwright, Poet, Judge
b. Ireland, Unknown
d. Dublin, Ireland, Jan. 1, 1968, Age 55

MACDONALD, Andrew
Playwright, Poet
b. Unknown
d. Unknown, Aug. 22, 1790, Age 35

MacDONALD, Ballard
Songwriter
b. Portland, OR, Unknown
d. Forest Hills, L.I., NY, Nov. 17, 1935, Age 52

MacDONALD, Christie
Actress
b. Picton, Nova Scotia, Feb. 28, 1875
d. Fairfield, CT, July 25, 1962, Age 87

MacDONALD, Donald
Actor
b. Denison, TX, March 13, 1898
d. New York, NY, Dec. 9, 1959, Age 61

MacDONALD, James Weatherby
Actor
b. Unknown
d. Santa Cruz, CA, Aug. 31, 1962, Age 63

MacDONALD, Jeanette Anna
Actress, Singer
b. Philadelphia, PA, June 18
d. Houston, TX, Jan. 14, 1965, Age 57

MacDONALD, Katherine
Actress
b. Unknown
d. Santa Barbara, CA, June 4, 1956, Age about 64

MacDONOUGH, Glen
Librettist
b. Unknown
d. Stamford, CT, March 30, 1924, Age 57

MacDOWELL, William Melbourne
Actor
b. South River, NJ, Unknown
d. Decoto, CA, Feb. 18, 1941, Age 84

MacFARREN, George
Playwright, Producer
b. Unknown
d. Unknown, April 24, 1843, Age 54

MacGEACHEY, Charles
Manager
b. Unknown
d. New York, NY, Dec. 24, 1921, Age 62

MacGOWAN, Kenneth
Author, Historian, Film prod., Educator
b. Winthrop, MA, 1888
d. West Los Angeles, CA, April 27, 1963, Age 74

MacGREGOR, Robert M.
Editor, Publisher
b. Pittsfield, MA, Aug. 5, 1911
d. New York, NY, Nov. 22, 1974, Age 63

MACHIAVELLI, Niccolo di Bernardo dei
Playwright, Author, Philosopher
b. Florence, Italy, May 3, 1469
d. Florence, Italy, June 22, 1527, Age 58

MACK, Andrew (William Andrew McAloon)
Actor, Singer
b. Boston, MA, Unknown
d. Bayside, L.I., NY, May 21, 1931, Age 67

MACK, Annie
Actress
b. Unknown
d. Unknown, June 28, 1935, Age 85

MACK, George E.
Performer
b. Unknown
d. Cheyenne, WY, May 20, 1948, Age 82

MACK, Nila (MacLoughlin)
Actress, Writer, Producer, Director
b. Arkansas City, KS, Unknown
d. New York, NY, Jan. 20, 1953, Age 62

MACK, Wilbur
Performer
b. Unknown
d. Hollywood, CA, March 13, 1964, Age 91

MACK, Willard (Charles W. McLaughlin)
Actor, Playwright, Director
b. Morrisburg, Ontario, CAN, Sept. 18, 1878
d. Brentwood Heights, CA, Nov. 18, 1934, Age 56

MACKAY, Fenton
Playwright
b. Unknown
d. Unknown, March 1929

MACKAY, Frank Finley
Actor
b. Unknown
d. Coytesville, NJ, May 5, 1923, Age 92

MACKAY, Leonard
Actor
b. Unknown
d. Unknown, Jan. 3, 1929, Age 53

MACKAY, W. Gayer
Actor, Playwright
b. Unknown
d. Unknown, March 1920

MacKAYE, Percy
Playwright, Poet
b. New York, NY, March 16, 1875
d. Cornish, NH, Aug. 31, 1956, Age 81

MacKAYE, Steele (James Morrison Steele Mackaye)
Actor-manager, Playwright, etc.
b. Buffalo, NY, June 6, 1842
d. Timpas, CO, Feb. 25, 1894, Age 51

MACKEN, Walter
Playwright, Novelist, Actor, Director
b. Galway, Ireland, May 3, 1915
d. Galway, Ireland, April 22, 1967, Age 51

MacKENNA, Kenneth (Leo Mielziner, Jr.)
Actor, Director, Editor
b. Canterbury, NH, Aug. 19, 1899
d. Santa Monica, CA, Jan. 15, 1962, Age 62

MacKENZIE, Ronald
Playwright
b. Unknown
d. Unknown, Aug. 12, 1932, Age 29

MacKINLAY, Jean Stirling (Mrs. Harcourt Williams)
Actress
b. London, England, 1882
d. Unknown, Dec. 15, 1958, Age 76

MacKINTOSH, William
Actor
b. Unknown
d. Unknown, Jan. 5, 1929, Age 73

MACKLIN, F. H.
Actor
b. Unknown
d. Unknown, May 3, 1903, Age 54

MACKLIN, (McLaughlan or Melaghlin) Charles
Actor, Playwright
b. Gortinaven, Donegal, Ireland, 1699
d. London, England, July 11, 1797, Age 97

MACKLIN, Mrs. F. H. (Blanche Henri)
Actress
b. Unknown
d. Unknown, April 9, 1904, Age 55

MacLAREN, Archibald
Playwright
b. Unknown
d. Unknown, 1826, Age 71

MacLAREN, Ivor
Performer, Producer
b. Wimbledon, England, Unknown
d. London, England, Oct. 30, 1962, Age 58

MacLARNIE, Thomas
Actor
b. North Adams, MA, Unknown
d. Brighton, MA, Dec. 1, 1931, Age 60

MacLEAN, R. D. (Shepherd)
Actor
b. New Orleans, LA, March 7, 1859
d. Unknown, June 27, 1948, Age 89

MacLEOD, Angus
Producer, Manager
b. Unknown
d. London, England, Feb. 4, 1962, Age 82

MacMANUS, Clive
Critic, Journalist
b. Highgate, London, England, Unknown
d. Unknown, May 3, 1953

MacMILLAN, Violet
Actress
b. Unknown
d. Grand Rapids, MI, Dec. 28, 1953, Age 66

MacNALLY, Leonard
Playwright
b. Unknown
d. Unknown, Feb. 13, 1820, Age 68

MacNAMARA, Brinsley (John Weldon)
Actor, Playwright, Novelist
b. Unknown
d. Dublin, Ireland, Feb. 4, 1963, Age 72

MacNEICE, Louis
Poet, Playwright, Radio producer
b. Belfast, Northern Ireland, Sept. 12, 1907
d. London, England, Sept. 3, 1963, Age 55

MACOWAN, Norman
Playwright, Actor
b. St. Andrews, Scotland, Jan. 2, 1877
d. Hastings, England, Dec. 31, 1961, Age 84

MacPHERSON, Quinton ("Mr. Hymack")
Actor
b. Unknown
d. Unknown, Jan. 2, 1940, Age 69

MacQUEEN, W. J.
Press representative, Historian
b. Devonshire, England, April 11, 1888
d. Unknown, June 27, 1960, Age 72

MacQUOID, Percy
Costume and scenic designer
b. Unknown, 1852
d. Unknown, March 20, 1925, Age 73

MacRAE, Arthur
Playwright, Actor
b. London, England, March 17, 1908
d. Brighton, England, Feb. 25, 1962, Age 53

MacREADY, William
Actor, Producer
b. Unknown
d. Unknown, April 11, 1829, Age 74

MacREADY, William Charles
Actor, Producer
b. London, England, March 3, 1793
d. Weston-Super-Mare, England, April 29, 1873, Age 80

MACY, Carleton
Actor
b. Unknown
d. East Islip, L.I., NY, Oct. 17, 1946, Age 85

MADDEN, Richard
Literary representative
b. Poughkeepsie, NY, Unknown
d. New York, NY, May 8, 1951, Age 71

MADISON, Cleo
Actress
b. Unknown
d. Burbank, CA, March 11, 1964, Age 81

MAEDER, Frederick George
Actor, Playwright
b. Unknown
d. Unknown, April 8, 1891, Age 50

MAETERLINCK, Maurice (Count)
Playwright, Poet
b. Ghent, Belgium, Aug. 29, 1862
d. French Riviera near Nice, May 6, 1949, Age 86

MAGINN, Dr. William
Critic
b. Unknown
d. Unknown, Aug. 21, 1942, Age 49

MAGRANE, Thais
Actress
b. St. Louis, MO, Unknown
d. Suffern, NY, Jan. 28, 1957, Age 79

MAHELOT, Laurent
Scenic artist, Designer, Mechanic
b. Unknown, 1634

MAHR, Herman Carl (Curly)
Composer-Arranger
b. Unknown
d. Duarte, CA, Feb. 27, 1964, Age 62

MAINE, Bruno (Bruno Jalmar Manninen)
Designer
b. Tampere, Finland, Oct. 6, 1896
d. New York, NY, July 30, 1962, Age 65

MAINWARING, Ernest
Actor
b. East Grinstead, England, May 22, 1876
d. Unknown, Oct. 22, 1941, Age 65

MAIR, George Herbert
Critic, Journalist
b. Unknown, May 8, 1887
d. Unknown, Jan. 2, 1926, Age 39

MAIRET, Jean
Playwright, Diplomat
b. Unknown, 1604
d. Unknown, 1686

MAITLAND, Lauderdale
Actor
b. London, England, Unknown
d. Unknown, Feb. 28, 1929, Age 52

MAJERONI, Mario
Actor
b. Unknown
d. New York, NY, Nov. 18, 1931, Age 61

MAJILTON, Charles
Actor, Producer
b. Unknown
d. Unknown, Nov. 27, 1931, Age 85

MAJOR, Charles
Playwright
b. Unknown
d. Unknown, Feb. 13, 1913, Age 55

MAJOR, Clare Tree
Producer
b. England, Unknown
d. New York, NY, Oct. 9, 1954, Age 74

MAKEHAM, Eliot
Actor
b. London, England, Dec. 22, 1882
d. London, England, Feb. 8, 1956, Age 73

MALCOLM, Marion P.
Performer
b. Unknown
d. Chicago, IL, Feb. 24, 1964, Age 50

MALINOFSKY, Max
Performer, Theatre manager
b. Unknown
d. New York, NY, May 10, 1963, Age 70

MALLALIEU, Aubrey
Actor
b. Liverpool, England, June 8, 1873
d. Unknown, May 28, 1948, Age 74

MALLALIEU, William
Actor
b. Unknown
d. Unknown, Feb. 27, 1927, Age 81

MALLESON, Miles
Actor, Dramatist
b. Croydon, England, May 25, 1888
d. London, England, March 15, 1969, Age 80

MALLORY, Boots (Patricia)
Actress
b. New Orleans, LA, Unknown
d. Santa Monica, CA, Dec. 1, 1958, Age 45

MALLORY, Burton
Performer
b. Unknown
d. New York, NY, Dec. 29, 1962, Age 79

MALLORY, Rene
Actress
b. Unknown
d. Unknown, Nov. 24, 1931, Age 24

MALONE, Andrew E.
Critic, Author, Journalist
b. Unknown
d. Unknown, April 13, 1939

MALONE, Edmund
Shakespearean authority
b. Ireland, 1741
d. Unknown, April 25, 1812, Age 70

MALONE, Elizabeth
Actress
b. Unknown
d. Unknown, April 21, 1955, Age 75

MALONE, J. A. E.
Producer, Director
b. Mhow, India, Unknown
d. Unknown, Feb. 3, 1929, Age 69

MALONE, Pick (Andrew Pickens Maloney) "Pick and Pat"
Performer
b. Unknown
d. New York, NY, Jan. 22, 1962, Age 69

MALTBY, Alfred
Actor, Playwright
b. Unknown
d. Unknown, Feb. 12, 1901

MANDEL, Frank
Author, Producer
b. Unknown
d. Hollywood, CA, April 20, 1958, Age 74

MANDEL, Mike
Stage manager
b. Unknown
d. Chicago, IL, Feb. 8, 1963, Age 69

MANDELL, Israel
Performer
b. Unknown
d. New York, NY, Sept. 16, 1962, Age 60

MANEY, Richard
Press agent
b. Chinook, MT, June 11, 1891
d. Norwalk, CT, June 30, 1968, Age 77

MANKIEWICZ, Herman J.
Playwright, Critic
b. New York, NY, Unknown
d. Hollywood, CA, March 5, 1953, Age 56

MANLEY, Mary
Playwright
b. Unknown
d. Unknown, July 11, 1724, Age 61

MANN, Charlton
Producer, Playwright
b. London, England, July 2, 1876
d. Unknown, March 27, 1958, Age 81

MANN, Louis
Actor, Playwright, Producer
b. New York, NY, April 20, 1865
d. New York, NY, Feb. 15, 1931, Age 65

MANNERING, Doré Lewin
Actor
b. Unknown, Poland
d. Jan. 19, 1879

MANNERING, Mary (Florence Friend)
Actress
b. London, England, April 29, 1876
d. Los Angeles, CA, Jan. 21, 1953, Age 76

MANNERS, J. (John) Hartley
Playwright, Actor
b. London, England, Aug. 10, 1870
d. New York, NY, Dec. 19, 1928, Age 58

MANNES, Leopold Damrosch
Musician, Educator, Co-inventor of Kodachrome film
b. Unknown
d. Menemsha, Martha's Vineyard, MA, Aug. 11, 1964, Age 64

MANNING, Ambrose
Actor
b. Unknown
d. Unknown, March 22, 1940, Age 79

MANNING, Otis
Performer
b. near Toledo, OH, Unknown
d. Atlanta, GA, Feb. 9, 1963, Age 50

MANNION, Moira
Actress
b. Unknown
d. London, England, Aug. 15, 1964, Age 46

MANNY, Charles
Performer
b. Unknown
d. New York, NY, Feb. 15, 1962, Age 71

MANOLA, Marion
Performer
b. Unknown
d. Unknown, Oct. 7, 1914, Age 48

MANSFIELD, Alfred F.
Actor, Director
b. Unknown
d. Unknown, April 19, 1938, Age 60

MANSFIELD, Alice
Actress
b. Unknown
d. Unknown, Feb. 17, 1938, Age 80

MANSFIELD, Richard
Actor, Producer
b. Berlin, Germany, May 24, 1854
d. New London, CT, Aug. 30, 1907, Age 53

MANTELL, Bruce
Actor
b. Atlantic Highlands, NJ, Unknown
d. Hollywood, CA, Oct. 24, 1933, Age 24

MANTELL, Robert Bruce
Actor, Producer
b. Irvine, Ayrshire, Scotland, Feb. 7, 1854
d. Atlantic Highlands, NJ, June 27, 1928, Age 74

MANTLE, Robert Burns
Drama critic, Author, Historian
b. Watertown, NY, Dec. 23, 1873
d. Forest Hills, L.I., NY, Feb. 9, 1948, Age 74

MANTZIUS, Karl
Actor, Author
b. Unknown
d. Unknown, May 17, 1921, Age 61

MANZONI, Alessandro
Author, Playwright
b. Milan, Italy, 1785
d. Unknown, 1873

MANZOTTI, Luigi
Choreographer
b. Unknown
d. Unknown, March 16, 1905, Age 70

MAPES, Victor
Playwright, Producer
b. New York, NY, March 10, 1870
d. Cannes, France, Sept. 27, 1943, Age 73

MARANO, Charles
Talent representative
b. Unknown
d. Philadelphia, PA, July 1, 1964, Age 61

MARAVAN, Lila (née Muschamp)
Actress
b. Unknown
d. Unknown, Aug. 29, 1950, Age 54

MARBERG, Lili
Actress
b. Unknown
d. Vienna, Austria, April 7, 1962, Age 84

MARBLE, Danforth
Actor
b. Unknown, 1810
d. St. Louis, MO, May 13, 1849, Age 39

MARBLE, Emma
Actress
b. Buffalo, NY, Unknown
d. New York, NY, July 26, 1930, Age 88

MARBURY, Elisabeth
Author, Authors' representative
b. New York, NY, 1856
d. New York, NY, Jan. 22, 1933, Age 76

MARCELLA, Marco ("Fatso Marco")
Performer
b. Unknown
d. South Amboy, NJ, Oct. 27, 1962, Age 53

MARCELLUS, George W.
Actor
b. Unknown
d. Philadelphia, PA, March 8, 1921, Age 80

MARCH, Fredric
Actor
b. Racine, WI, Aug. 31, 1897
d. Los Angeles, CA, April 14, 1975, Age 77

MARCH, Hal
Actor
b. San Francisco, CA, April 22, 1920
d. Los Angeles, CA, Jan. 19, 1970, Age 49

MARCH, Nadine
Actress
b. London, England, July 30, 1898
d. Unknown, Oct. 10, 1944, Age 46

MARCHAND, Leopold
Playwright
b. Unknown
d. Paris, France, Nov. 25, 1952, Age 61

MARCHANT, Frank
Playwright
b. Unknown
d. Unknown, Dec. 17, 1878, Age 41

MARCIN, Max
Playwright
b. Posen, Germany, May 6, 1879
d. Tucson, AZ, March 30, 1948, Age 68

MARC-MICHEL, (Marc Antoine Amedée Michel)
Playwright
b. Marseilles, France, 1812
d. Paris, France, 1868, Age 56

MARGETSON, Arthur
Actor
b. London, England, April 27, 1897
d. London, England, Aug. 12, 1951, Age 54

MARGUERITTE, Victor
Playwright, Novelist
b. Blidah, Algeria, Dec. 1, 1866
d. Unknown, March 23, 1942, Age 75

MARINELLI, H. B.
Vaudeville agent
b. Thuringia, Germany, 1864
d. Paterson, NJ, Jan. 7, 1924, Age 59

MARINOFF, Fania
Actress
b. Odessa, Russia, March 20, 1890
d. Englewood, NJ, Nov. 17, 1971, Age 81

MARION, Dave (David Marion Graves)
Playwright, Manager, Actor
b. Toledo, OH, Unknown
d. New York, NY, Sept. 15, 1934, Age 73

MARION, George F.
Performer, Producer
b. San Francisco, CA, July 16, 1860
d. Carmel, CA, Nov. 30, 1945, Age 85

MARION, George F. Jr.
Librettist, Actor, Lyricist, Screenwriter
b. Boston, MA, Aug. 30, 1899
d. New York, NY, Feb. 25, 1968, Age 68

MARIVAUX, Pierre Carlet de Chamberlain de
Playwright
b. Paris, France, Feb. 4, 1688
d. Unknown, Feb. 12, 1763, Age 75

MARKBY, Robert Brenner
Actor
b. Unknown
d. Unknown, Jan. 1908, Age 66

MARKHAM, Pauline
Actress
b. Unknown
d. Unknown, March 20, 1919, Age 72

MARKS, Mrs. Josephine Preston Peabody
Playwright, Poetess
b. Unknown
d. Cambridge, MA, Dec. 4, 1922

MARLBOROUGH, Leah
Actress
b. Unknown
d. Unknown, Dec. 21, 1954, Age 85

MARLOW, George
Actor
b. Unknown
d. Unknown, May 20, 1939, Age 62

MARLOW, Harry
Performer
b. London, England, Unknown
d. London, England, Jan. 19, 1957, Age 75

MARLOWE, Christopher
Playwright, Poet
b. Canterbury, England, 1564
d. Deptford, London, England, June 1, 1593, Age 29

MARLOWE, Frank
Actor
b. Unknown
d. Hollywood, CA, March 30, 1964, Age 60

MARLOWE, Julia (Sarah Frances Frost)
Actress
b. Caldbeck, Cumberlandshire, Scotland, Aug. 17, 1866
d. New York, NY, Nov. 12, 1950, Age 84

MARMION, Shackerley
Playwright
b. Unknown
d. Unknown, Jan. 1639, Age 36

MAROT, Gaston
Playwright
b. Unknown
d. Unknown, 1916

MARQUIS, Donald Robert Perry
Playwright, Novelist
b. Walnut, IL, July 29, 1878
d. Forest Hills, NY, Dec. 29, 1937, Age 59

MARQUIS, Marjorie Vonnegut
Actress
b. Indianapolis, IN, Unknown
d. New York, NY, Oct. 25, 1936, Age 44

MARRIOTT, Alice
Actress, Producer
b. Unknown
d. London, England, Dec. 25, 1900, Age 76

MARRIOTT, G. M.
Actor
b. Unknown
d. Unknown, Sept. 3, 1940, Age 81

MARRIOTT, Moore
Actor
b. Unknown
d. Unknown, Dec. 11, 1949, Age 64

MARRYAT, Florence (Mrs. Francis Lean)
Actress, Novelist
b. Unknown, 1837
d. London, England, Oct. 27, 1899

MARS, Antony
Playwright
b. Vence, France, Oct. 22, 1861
d. Unknown, Feb. 17, 1915, Age 53

MARS, Mlle. (Anne Françoise Hippolyte Bontet)
Actress
b. Paris, France, 1779
d. Unknown, March 20, 1847, Age 68

MARS, Severin
Actor, Mime
b. Unknown
d. Unknown, July 17, 1921, Age 43

MARSH, Alexander
Actor, Producer
b. Unknown
d. Unknown, Nov. 5, 1947

MARSH, Leo A.
Journalist
b. Unknown
d. Unknown, Nov. 5, 1936, Age 42

MARSHAK, Samuel
Playwright, Poet
b. Unknown
d. Moscow, U.S.S.R., July 4, 1964, Age 77

MARSHALL, Alan
Actor
b. Sydney, Australia, Unknown
d. Chicago, IL, July 9, 1961, Age 52

MARSHALL, Captain Robert
Playwright
b. Unknown
d. Unknown, July 1, 1910, Age 47

MARSHALL, Edward
Actor
b. Unknown
d. Unknown, Feb. 26, 1904, Age 78

MARSHALL, Frank
Playwright
b. Unknown
d. Unknown, Dec. 28, 1889, Age 49

MARSHALL, Frank
Critic, Journalist
b. Unknown
d. Unknown, Oct. 19, 1939, Age 81

MARSHALL, Herbert
Actor
b. London, England, May 23, 1890
d. Beverly Hills, CA, Jan. 21, 1966, Age 75

MARSHALL, Percy F.
Actor
b. Unknown
d. Unknown, Dec. 28, 1927, Age 68

MARSHALL, Tully (née Phillips)
Actor
b. Nevada City, CA, April 13, 1864
d. Encino, CA, March 9, 1943, Age 78

MARSON, Aileen
Actress
b. Unknown
d. Unknown, May 4, 1939, Age 26

MARSTON, Henry
Actor
b. Unknown
d. Unknown, March 23, 1883, Age 79

MARSTON, John
Playwright
b. Unknown, 1575
d. Unknown, June 25, 1634, Age 59

MARSTON, John
Actor
b. Unknown
d. New York, NY, Sept. 2, 1962, Age 72

MARSTON, John Westland
Playwright
b. Unknown, 1819
d. Unknown, Jan. 5, 1890, Age 70

MARSTON, Mrs. Henry
Actress
b. Unknown
d. Unknown, March 5, 1887, Age 78

MARTHOLD, Jules de
Playwright
b. Paris, France, 1842
d. Unknown, May 1927, Age 85

MARTIN, Boyd
Critic, Director, Educator
b. Unknown
d. Louisville, KY, April 16, 1963, Age 76

MARTIN, Edie
Actress
b. Unknown
d. London, England, Feb. 23, 1964, Age 84

MARTIN, John E.
Actor
b. Unknown, 1770
d. Unknown, 1807

MARTIN, Mildred Palmer
Critic
b. Unknown
d. Sussex, England, March 14, 1962, Age 59

MARTIN, Mrs. Jacques (Lillian Gerome)
Actress
b. Michigan, 1863
d. New York, NY, July 11, 1936, Age 73

MARTIN, Owen
Actor
b. Unknown
d. Saranac Lake, NY, May 4, 1960, Age 71

MARTIN, Tom
Artists' representative
b. Unknown
d. New York, NY, Dec. 17, 1962, Age 58

MARTIN, Townsend
Writer
b. New York, NY, Unknown
d. New York, NY, Nov. 22, 1951, Age 55

MARTINDEL, Edward
Actor
b. Unknown
d. Woodland Hills, CA, May 4, 1955, Age 80

MARTINE, Stella (Mrs. Stella Martine Sweet)
Actress
b. Unknown
d. New York, NY, Nov. 20, 1961, Age 81

MARTINEZ DE LA ROSA, Francisco de
Playwright, Poet, Novelist, Statesman
b. Granada, Spain, 1787
d. Unknown, 1862

MARTINEZ SIERRA, Gregorio
Playwright, Author, Producer
b. Madrid, Spain, 1881
d. Madrid, Spain, Oct. 1, 1947, Age 66

MARTIN-HARVEY, Sir John
Actor, Producer
b. Wyvenhoe, Essex, England, 1863
d. London, England, May 14, 1944, Age 81

MARTINOT, Sadie (Sarah)
Actress
b. Jamaica, NY, Dec. 19, 1861
d. Ogdensburg, NY, May 7, 1923, Age 61

MARTYN, Eliza (Miss Inverarity)
Actress
b. Unknown
d. Unknown, Dec. 27, 1846, Age 33

MARTYN, May (Lady Playfair)
Actress
b. Unknown
d. Unknown, June 7, 1948, Age 72

MARX, Chico (Leonard Marx)
Performer
b. New York, NY, 1891
d. Hollywood, CA, Oct. 11, 1961, Age 70

MARX, Harpo (né Adolph Marx)
Comedian, Musician
b. New York, NY, Nov. 23, 1893
d. Hollywood, CA, Sept. 28, 1964, Age 70

MARY, Jules
Playwright
b. Launois-sur-Vence, Ardennes, France, March 20, 1851
d. Unknown, July 1922, Age 71

MASEFIELD, John
Poet laureate, Playwright
b. Ledbury, Herefordshire, England, June 1, 1878
d. Berkshire, England, May 12, 1967, Age 88

MASKELL, Fanny
Actress
b. Unknown
d. Unknown, Feb. 1919, Age 90

MASON, Alfred Edward Woodley
Playwright, Novelist
b. London, England, May 7, 1865
d. London, England, Nov. 22, 1948, Age 83

MASON, Ann
Actress
b. Virginia, Unknown
d. New York, NY, Feb. 6, 1948, Age 50

MASON, Elliot C.
Actress
b. Glasgow, Scotland, Unknown
d. Unknown, June 20, 1949, Age 52

MASON, Homer B.
Performer
b. Unknown
d. Van Nuys, CA, Sept. 27, 1959, Age 80

MASON, John
Actor
b. Orange, NJ, Oct. 28, 1857
d. Unknown, Jan. 12, 1919, Age 61

MASON, Lawrence
Critic, Educator
b. Chicago, IL, Unknown
d. Toronto, CAN, Dec. 9, 1939, Age 57

MASON, LeRoy
Actor
b. Unknown
d. Hollywood, CA, Oct. 13, 1947, Age 44

MASON, Lesley
Press representative, Journalist
b. Roselle, NJ, Unknown
d. Laguna, CA, March 24, 1964, Age 76

MASON, Reginald
Actor
b. San Francisco, CA, June 27, 1882
d. Hermosa Beach, CA, July 10, 1962, Age 80

MASSEN, Louis F.
Actor, Director
b. Paris, France, Unknown
d. Moresemere, NJ, March 25, 1925, Age 67

MASSEY, Blanche
Actress
b. Unknown
d. Unknown, Sept. 27, 1929, Age 51

MASSINGER, Philip
Playwright
b. Salisbury, England, 1583
d. Unknown, buried March 18, 1640, Age 56

MASSINGHAM, Dorothy
Actress, Playwright
b. Highgate, London, England, Dec. 12, 1889
d. Unknown, March 30, 1933, Age 43

MATHER, Aubrey
Actor
b. Minchinhampton, England, Dec. 17, 1885
d. Stanmore, England, Jan. 15, 1958, Age 72

MATHER, Sydney
Actor
b. England, Unknown
d. New York, NY, April 18, 1925, Age 49

MATHEWS, Charles Sr.
Actor
b. London, England, June 28, 1776
d. Plymouth, England, June 28, 1835, Age 59

MATHEWS, Charles James
Actor, Playwright
b. Liverpool, England, Dec. 26, 1803
d. Manchester, England, June 24, 1878, Age 74

MATHEWS, Mrs. Charles Sr. (Anne Jackson)
Actress
b. Unknown
d. Unknown, Oct. 12, 1869, Age 87

MATHEWS, Mrs. Charles J. (Lizzie Davenport)
Actress
b. Unknown
d. Unknown, Jan. 4, 1899

MATHIS, June
Actress, Screenwriter
b. Unknown
d. New York, NY, July 26, 1927, Age 35

MATKOWSKY, Aldabert
Actor
b. Unknown
d. Unknown, March 16, 1909, Age 52

MATTESON, Ruth
Actress
b. San Jose, CA, Dec. 8, 1909
d. Westport, CT, Feb. 5, 1975, Age 65

MATTHEWS, A. E. (Alfred Edward)
Actor
b. Bridlington, Yorkshire, England, Nov. 22, 1869
d. Bushey Heath, London, England, July 25, 1960, Age 90

MATTHEWS, Bache
Literary advisor to Birmingham Repertory Theatre
b. Birmingham, England, March 23, 1876
d. Unknown, Oct. 12, 1948, Age 72

MATTHEWS, (James) Brander
Playwright, Historian, Critic, Educator
b. New Orleans, LA, 1852
d. Unknown, March 31, 1929, Age 77

MATTHISON, Arthur
Playwright
b. Unknown
d. Unknown, May 21, 1883, Age 57

MATTHISON, Edith Wynne (Mrs. Charles Rann Kennedy)
Actress
b. Birmingham, England, Nov. 23, 1875
d. West Los Angeles, CA, Sept. 23, 1955, Age 79

MATTOCKS, Isabella Hallam
Actress
b. Unknown, 1746
d. Unknown, June 25, 1826, Age 80

MATURIN, Eric
Actor
b. India, May 30, 1883
d. Unknown, Oct. 17, 1957, Age 74

MATURIN, Reverend Charles
Playwright
b. Unknown
d. Unknown, Oct. 30, 1824, Age 42

MATZENAUER, Margarette
Singer, Actress
b. Unknown
d. Van Nuys, CA, May 19, 1963, Age 81

MAUDE, Charles Raymond
Actor
b. Unknown
d. Unknown, Nov. 14, 1943, Age 61

MAUDE, Cyril
Actor, Producer
b. London, England, April 24, 1862
d. Torquay, England, Feb. 20, 1951, Age 88

MAUGHAM, William Somerset
Playwright, Novelist, Writer
b. Paris, France, Jan. 25, 1874
d. St. Jean Cap-Ferrat, France, Dec. 16, 1965, Age 91

MAULE, Robin
Actor
b. London, England, Nov. 23, 1924
d. Unknown, March 2, 1942, Age 17

MAUREY, Max
Producer
b. Paris, France, Unknown
d. Unknown, Feb. 27, 1947, Age 76

MAURICE, (Maurice Mouvet)
Dancer
b. Unknown
d. Unknown, May 18, 1927, Age 41

MAURICE, Edmund (Edmund Fitz-Maurice Lenon)
Actor
b. Unknown
d. Unknown, April 6, 1928, Age 65

MAURICE, Mary
Actress
b. Ohio, 1844
d. Unknown, 1918

MAURICE, Newman
Actor, Producer, Author
b. Unknown
d. Unknown, Sept. 11, 1920

MAWDESLEY, Robert
Actor
b. Unknown
d. Unknown, Sept. 30, 1953, Age 53

MAWSON, Edward R.
Actor
b. Unknown
d. Unknown, May 20, 1917, Age 55

MAX, (Alexandre) Edouard de
Actor
b. Jassy, Romania, Feb. 14, 1869
d. Paris, France, 1925, Age 56

MAXEY, Paul
Actor
b. Wheaton, IL, Unknown
d. Pasadena, CA, June 3, 1963, Age 55

MAXWELL, Edwin
Actor
b. Dublin, Ireland, Unknown
d. Falmouth, MA, Aug. 13, 1948, Age 58

MAXWELL, Elsa
Performer, Author, Hostess
b. Keokuk, IA, May 24, 1883
d. New York, NY, Nov. 1, 1963, Age 80

MAXWELL, Gerald
Critic, Actor
b. London, England, March 19, 1862
d. Unknown, Jan. 14, 1930, Age 67

MAXWELL, Meg
Actress
b. Unknown
d. Unknown, 1955

MAXWELL, Vera K.
Actress
b. Unknown
d. New York, NY, May 1, 1950, Age 58

MAY, Akerman
Talent representative
b. London, England, Nov. 12, 1869
d. Unknown, March 21, 1933, Age 63

MAY, Edna (Mrs. Oscar Lewisohn née Edna May Petty)
Actress, Singer
b. Syracuse, NY, Sept. 2, 1875
d. Lausanne, Switzerland, Jan. 2, 1948, Age 72

MAY, Hans
Composer
b. Vienna, Austria, 1891
d. Unknown, Jan. 1, 1959, Age 67

MAY, Olive (Countess of Drogheda)
Actress
b. Unknown
d. Unknown, Nov. 24, 1947

MAY, Olive (Mrs. John W. Albaugh)
Actress
b. Chicago, IL, Unknown
d. Beverly Hills, CA, July 26, 1938, Age 65

MAYAKOVSKY, Vladimir Vladimirovich
Poet, Playwright
b. Georgia, 1894
d. Unknown, 1930

MAYBRICK, Michael (Stephen Adams)
Singer, Composer
b. Unknown
d. Unknown, Aug. 26, 1913, Age 69

MAYE, Bernyce (Bernyce Atz Moore)
Performer
b. Sioux City, IA, Unknown
d. San Francisco, CA, March 30, 1962, Age 52

MAYER, Daniel
Producer, Impresario
b. Unknown, 1856
d. Unknown, Aug. 20, 1928, Age 72

MAYER, Dot
Performer
b. Unknown
d. Long Beach, NY, Aug. 23, 1964, Age about 68

MAYER, Edwin Justus
Playwright
b. New York, NY, 1897
d. New York, NY, Sept. 11, 1960, Age 63

MAYER, Gaston
Producer
b. London, England, 1869
d. Unknown, Jan. 18, 1923, Age 53

MAYER, Henri
Actor
b. Paris, France, Unknown
d. Unknown, Oct. 1941, Age 80

MAYER, Louis B.
Producer, Film executive
b. Minsk, Russia, July 4, 1885
d. Los Angeles, CA, Oct. 29, 1957, Age 72

MAYER, Marcus
Producer
b. Unknown
d. Unknown, May 8, 1918, Age 77

MAYER, Sylvain
Playwright
b. Unknown
d. Unknown, Sept. 13, 1948, Age 85

MAYERL, Billy (Joseph W. Mayerl)
Composer, Conductor
b. London, England, May 31, 1902
d. Unknown, March 27, 1959, Age 56

MAYERS, Wilmette K.
Singer
b. Unknown
d. New York, NY, May 19, 1964

MAYFIELD, Cleo (Mrs. Cecil Lean, née Empy)
Actress
b. Unknown
d. New York, NY, Nov. 8, 1954, Age 57

MAYHALL, Jerome "Jerry"
Musical director, Arranger
b. Unknown
d. Pittsburgh, PA, Aug. 12, 1964, Age 70

MAYHEW, Henry
Playwright
b. Unknown
d. Unknown, July 25, 1887, Age 74

MAYHEW, Horace
Playwright
b. Unknown
d. Unknown, April 30, 1872, Age 53

MAYHEW, Kate
Actress
b. Indianapolis, IN, Sept. 2, 1853
d. New York, NY, June 16, 1944, Age 90

MAYHEW, Stella (Izetta Estelle Sadler)
Actress
b. Pittsburgh, PA, Unknown
d. New York, NY, May 2, 1934, Age 59

MAYNARD, Gertrude
Actress
b. Montreal, CAN, Unknown
d. New York, NY, March 22, 1953, Age 48

MAYNE, Eric
Actor
b. Dublin, Ireland, Unknown
d. Hollywood, CA, Feb. 10, 1947, Age 81

MAYO, Frank
Performer, Producer
b. Boston, MA, 1839
d. on a train near Omaha, NB, June 8, 1896, Age 57

MAYO, Frank
Actor
b. Unknown
d. Laguna Beach, CA, July 9, 1963, Age 74

MAYO, Harry
Actor
b. Unknown
d. Woodland Hills, CA, Jan. 6, 1964, Age 65

MAYO, Margaret (Lilian Clatten)
Playwright, Actress
b. Brownsville, IL, Nov. 19, 1882
d. Ossining, NY, Feb. 25, 1951, Age 68

MAYO, Mrs. Frank
Actress
b. Unknown
d. Unknown, Oct. 30, 1896

MAYO, Sam
Comedian, Songwriter
b. Unknown
d. London, England, March 31, 1938, Age 63

McATEE, Ben
Actor
b. Unknown
d. Hollywood, CA, Dec. 3, 1961, Age 58

McBRIDE, John S.
Ticket agent
b. Unknown
d. Amityville, L.I., NY, Nov. 28, 1961, Age 84

McCABE, May North
Actress
b. Unknown
d. New York, NY, June 2, 1949, Age 76

McCALL, Lizzie
Actress
b. Unknown
d. Unknown, April 18, 1942, Age 84

McCAMMON, Bessie J.
Actress, Teacher
b. Cincinnati, OH, Unknown
d. New York, NY, March 2, 1964, Age 80

McCANDLESS, Stanley Russell
Educator, Lighting designer, Author
b. Chicago, IL, May 9, 1897
d. West Haven, CT, Aug. 4, 1967, Age 70

McCARTEN, John
Drama critic
b. Philadelpia, PA, Sept. 10, 1916
d. New York, NY, Sept. 25, 1974, Age 63

McCARTHY, Justin Huntly
Playwright, Author
b. London, England, Sept. 30, 1860
d. Putney, England, March 21, 1936, Age 75

McCARTHY, Lillah
Actress
b. Cheltenham, England, Sept. 22, 1875
d. London, England, April 15, 1960, Age 84

McCLAIN, John Wilcox
Drama critic, Journalist
b. Marion, OH, Aug. 7, 1904
d. London, England, May 3, 1967, Age 62

McCLEERY, Albert
Producer
b. Fort Worth, TX, Unknown
d. New York, NY, May 13, 1972, Age 60

McCLELLAND, Donald
Actor
b. Unknown
d. New York, NY, Nov. 15, 1955, Age 52

McCLENDON, Rose
Actress
b. New York, NY, 1885
d. New York, NY, July 12, 1936, Age 51

McCLINTIC, Guthrie
Director
b. Seattle, WA, Aug. 6, 1893
d. Sneedens Landing, NY, Oct. 29, 1961, Age 68

McCOMAS, Carroll
Performer
b. Albuquerque, NM, Unknown
d. New York, NY, Nov. 9, 1962, Age 76

McCOMB, Kate
Actress
b. Unknown
d. New York, NY, April 15, 1959, Age 87

McCONNELL, Forrest W. (Peewee)
Performer
b. Independence, KS, Unknown
d. Independence, KS, Jan. 11, 1962, Age 51

McCONNELL, Lulu
Performer
b. Kansas City, MO, Unknown
d. Hollywood, CA, Oct. 9, 1961, Age 80

McCORMACK, Frank
Actor
b. Washington, DC, Unknown
d. Connecticut, May 22, 1941, Age 65

McCORMACK, John
Performer, Singer
b. Athlone, Ireland, June 14, 1884
d. Booterstown, Ireland, Sept. 16, 1945, Age 61

McCormick, Arthur L.
Playwright
b. Port Huron, MI, Unknown
d. New York, NY, June 25, 1954, Age 81

McCORMICK, F. J. (Peter Judge)
Actor
b. Skerries, Ireland, Unknown
d. Dublin, Ireland, April 24, 1947, Age about 50

McCORMICK, Myron
Actor
b. Albany, IN, Feb. 8, 1908
d. New York, NY, July 30, 1962, Age 54

McCOY, Frank
Producer
b. Unknown
d. New York, NY, Jan. 16, 1947, Age 58

McCRACKEN, Joan
Actress, Dancer
b. Philadelphia, PA, Dec. 31, 1922
d. New York, NY, Nov. 1, 1961, Age 38

McCULLERS, Carson
Novelist, Playwright
b. Columbus, GA, Feb. 19, 1917
d. Nyack, NY, Sept. 29, 1967, Age 50

McCULLOUGH, John Edward
Performer, Producer
b. . . .near Londonderry, Ireland, Nov. 15, 1837
d. Philadelphia, PA, Nov. 8, 1885, Age 48

McCUTCHEON, Wallace
Actor
b. Unknown
d. Los Angeles, CA, Jan. 27, 1928, Age 47

McDANIEL, Hattie
Actress
b. Wichita, KS, Unknown
d. Hollywood, CA, Oct. 26, 1952, Age 57

McDERMOTT, Aline
Actress
b. Unknown
d. New York, NY, Feb. 16, 1951, Age 70

McDERMOTT, William F.
Critic, Journalist
b. Unknown
d. Bratenahl, OH, Nov. 16, 1958, Age 67

McDONALD, Ray
Actor, Dancer
b. Boston, MA, Unknown
d. New York, NY, Feb. 20, 1959, Age 35

McEARCHAN, Malcolm ("Jetsam")
Performer
b. Unknown
d. Unknown, Jan. 17, 1945, Age 61

McEVOY, Charles
Playwright
b. London, England, June 30, 1879
d. Unknown, Feb. 17, 1929, Age 49

McEVOY, J. P. (Joseph Patrick)
Librettist, Playwright
b. New York, NY, Jan. 10, 1894
d. New City, NY, Aug. 8, 1958, Age 64

McFARLANE, George
Singer
b. Kingston, Ontario, CAN, Unknown
d. Hollywood, CA, Feb. 22, 1932, Age 55

McGEE, Harold J.
Actor
b. Schenectady, NY, Unknown
d. New York, NY, Feb. 23, 1955, Age 55

McGHEE, Paul A.
Educator
b. Unknown
d. New York, NY, Aug. 6, 1964, Age 64

McGIVER, John
Actor, Writer
b. New York, NY, Nov. 5, 1913
d. West Fulton, NY, Sept. 1975, Age 61

McGLYNN, Frank
Actor
b. San Francisco, CA, Oct. 26, 1866
d. Newburgh, NY, May 17, 1951, Age 84

McGOWAN, John P.
Actor, Director
b. Unknown
d. Unknown, March 26, 1952, Age 72

McGOWAN, Oliver
Actor, Director
b. Kipling, AL, Aug. 22, 1907
d. Hollywood, CA, Aug. 23, 1971, Age 64

McGREGOR, Malcolm
Actor
b. Unknown, 1892
d. Hollywood, CA, April 29, 1945, Age 53

McGREGOR, Parke (Cushnie)
Actor
b. Unknown
d. Hollywood, CA, Dec. 5, 1962, Age 55

McGUIRE, William Anthony
Playwright, Film producer
b. Chicago, IL, July 9, 1885
d. Beverly Hills, CA, Sept. 16, 1940, Age 55

McHENRY, Nellie
Actress
b. Unknown
d. Unknown, May 4, 1935, Age 82

McHUGH, James Francis (Jimmy)
Composer
b. Boston, MA, July 10, 1896
d. Beverly Hills, CA, May 23, 1969, Age 74

McHUGH, Jimmy
Composer, Music publisher
b. Boston, MA, July 10, 1896
d. Beverly Hills, CA, May 23, 1969, Age 72

McINTOSH, Burr
Actor, Author
b. Wellsville, OH, Aug. 11, 1862
d. Hollywood, CA, April 28, 1942, Age 79

McINTOSH, Madge
Actress, Director
b. Calcutta, India, April 8, 1875
d. Unknown, Feb. 19, 1950, Age 74

McINTYRE, Frank
Actor
b. Ann Arbor, MI, Feb. 25, 1879
d. Ann Arbor, MI, June 8, 1949, Age 70

McINTYRE, James T.
Performer
b. Kenosha, WI, Aug. 8, 1857
d. Noyack, L.I., NY, Aug. 18, 1937, Age 80

McINTYRE, John T.
Playwright, Novelist
b. Philadelphia, PA, Unknown
d. Philadelphia, PA, May 21, 1951, Age 79

McINTYRE, Leila
Performer
b. Unknown
d. Los Angeles, CA, Jan. 9, 1953, Age 71

McINTYRE, Molly
Performer
b. Unknown
d. New York, NY, Jan. 29, 1952, Age 65

McKAY, Frederick E.
Critic, Producer
b. Unknown
d. Unknown, Feb. 29, 1944, Age 72

McKECHNIE, James
Actor
b. Glasgow, Scotland, Unknown
d. London, England, May 7, 1964, Age 53

McKEE, John
Actor, Director
b. Belfast, Ireland, Unknown
d. New York, NY, Dec. 28, 1953, Age Eighties

McKENNA, William J.
Songwriter
b. Jersey City, NJ, Unknown
d. Jersey City, NJ, March 4, 1950, Age 69

McKENNEY, Ruth
Author - Screenwriter
b. Mishawaka, IN, Nov. 18, 1911
d. New York, NY, July 25, 1972, Age 60

McKINNEL, Norman
b. Maxwelltown, Kirkcudbrightshire, N. B., Feb. 10, 1870
d. Unknown, March 29, 1932, Age 62

McKNIGHT, Tom
Author, Producer
b. Unknown
d. Oxnard, CA, April 22, 1963, Age 62

McLAGLEN, Victor
Actor
b. Tunbridge Wells, England, Dec. 11, 1886
d. Newport Beach, CA, Nov. 7, 1959, Age 72

McLAUGHLIN, John
Composer, Pianist, Conductor
b. Lynn, MA, Feb. 17, 1897
d. Queens, NY, June 15, 1968, Age 71

McLELLAN, C. M. S. (Hugh Morton)
Playwright, Librettist, Lyricist
b. Maine, 1865
d. Unknown, Sept. 22, 1916, Age 51

McLELLAN, G. B.
Producer
b. Unknown
d. Unknown, Feb. 1, 1932, Age 65

McLEOD, Helen
Actress
b. Unknown
d. Bakersfield, CA, April 20, 1964, Age 40

McMAHON, Horace
Actor
b. South Norwalk, CT, May 17, 1907
d. Norwalk, CT, Aug. 17, 1971, Age 64

McMANUS, John L.
Musical director
b. Unknown
d. New York, NY, April 20, 1963, Age 71

McMASTER, Anew
Actor
b. Ireland, Unknown
d. Dublin, Ireland, Aug. 24, 1962, Age 72

McMILLAN, Lida (Snow)
Actress
b. Cincinnati, OH, Unknown
d. New York, NY, March 29, 1940, Age 71

McNALLY, John J.
Dramatic critic, Playwright
b. Charlestown, MA, Unknown
d. Brooklyn, NY, March 25, 1931, Age 76

McNAMARA, Daniel I. (Dan)
Press representative, Editor
b. Unknown
d. New York, NY, Feb. 20, 1962, Age 76

McNAMARA, Edward J.
Actor
b. Paterson, NJ, Unknown
d. Boston, MA (on train), Nov. 10, 1944, Age 57

McNAY, Evelyn (Mrs. William Mollison)
Actress
b. Unknown
d. Unknown, Jan. 21, 1944, Age 73

McNUTT, Patterson
Playwright, Producer
b. Urbana, IL, Unknown
d. New York, NY, Oct. 23, 1948, Age 52

McPETERS, Taylor
Actor
b. Unknown
d. Hollywood, CA, April 16, 1962, Age 62

McQUOID, Rose Lee
Actress
b. Unknown
d. Hollywood, CA, May 4, 1962, Age 75

McRAE, Bruce
Actor
b. India, Jan. 15, 1867
d. New York, NY, May 7, 1927, Age 60

McRAE, Duncan
Director, Actor
b. Unknown
d. Unknown, Feb. 4, 1931

McSHANE, Kitty
Actress
b. Unknown
d. London, England, March 24, 1964, Age 66

McVICKER, Horace
Manager
b. Chicago, IL, Unknown
d. Sea Bright, NJ, July 30, 1931, Age 75

McVICKER, J. H.
Actor, Producer
b. Unknown
d. Unknown, March 7, 1896, Age 74

McWADE, Robert
Actor, Producer
b. Unknown
d. Unknown, March 5, 1913, Age 78

McWADE, Robert
Actor
b. Buffalo, NY, Unknown
d. Culver City, CA, Jan. 20, 1938, Age 56

MEACHUM, James H. ("Dad")
Performer
b. Shelbyville, IN, Unknown
d. Los Angeles, CA, Feb. 24, 1963, Age 70

MEAKINS, Charles
Actor
b. Unknown
d. Elora, Ontario, CAN, May 5, 1951, Age 70

MEARS, J. H.
Director, Lyricist
b. Unknown
d. Unknown, July 26, 1956, Age 78

MEASOR, Adela
Actress
b. Ireland, Sept. 2, 1860
d. Unknown, June 9, 1933, Age 72

MEDCRAFT, Russell Graham
Playwright
b. Unknown
d. New York, NY, Sept. 29, 1962, Age 65

MEDFORD, Mark
Actor, Producer, Playwright
b. Unknown
d. London, England, Jan. 4, 1914

MEEHAN, John
Art Director
b. Unknown
d. Hollywood, CA, May 15, 1963, Age 61

MEEK, Donald
Actor
b. Glasgow, Scotland, 1880
d. Hollywood, CA, Nov. 18, 1946, Age 66

MEEK, Kate
Actress
b. Unknown
d. New York, NY, Aug. 3, 1925, Age 87

MEGRUE, Roi Cooper
Playwright
b. New York, NY, June 12, 1883
d. New York, NY, Feb. 27, 1927, Age 43

MEHAFFEY, Harry S.
Actor
b. Unknown
d. New York, NY, Dec. 23, 1963, Age 56

MEIGHAN, Thomas
Actor
b. Pittsburgh, PA, April 9, 1879
d. Great Neck, NY, July 8, 1936, Age 57

MEI LAN-FANG, (see Lan-fang, Mei)
Performer
b. Unknown
d. Shanghai, China, Aug. 8, 1943

MEILHAC, Henri
Playwright
b. Paris, France, 1831
d. Paris, France, July 6, 1897, Age 66

MELLER, Harro
Playwright, Actor
b. Germany, Unknown
d. New York, NY, Dec. 26, 1963, Age 56

MELLER, Raquel (Francisca Marquez Lopez)
Actress
b. Madrid, Spain, Unknown
d. Barcelona, Spain, July 26, 1962, Age 74

MELLISH, Fuller (Leclerq)
Actor
b. England, Jan. 3, 1865
d. New York, NY, Dec. 7, 1936, Age 71

MELLISH, Fuller Jr.
Actor
b. Unknown
d. Forest L.I., LI, NY, Feb. 8, 1930, Age 35

MELLON, Ada
Actress
b. Unknown
d. Unknown, Aug. 19, 1914

MELLON, Mrs. Alfred (Sarah Jane Woolgar)
b. Unknown, 1824
d. Unknown, Sept. 8, 1909, Age 85

MELMOTH, Courtney (Samuel Jackson Pratt)
Actor, Playwright
b. Unknown, 1749
d. Unknown, Oct. 4, 1814, Age 64

MELMOTH, Mrs. Charlotte
Actress
b. Unknown, 1749
d. Unknown, 1823

MELNOTTE, Violet (Mrs. Frank Wyatt)
Producer, Actress
b. Birmingham, England, 1856
d. Unknown, Sept. 17, 1935, Age 79

MELTZER, Charles Henry
Music and drama critic, Playwright
b. London, England, Unknown
d. New York, NY, Jan. 14, 1936, Age 83

MELVILLE, Andrew (Emm)
Producer, Director, Actor, Playwright
b. Unknown
d. Portslade, Brighton, England, March 4, 1938, Age 52

MELVILLE, Emilie
Actress
b. Unknown
d. Unknown, May 20, 1932, Age 82

MELVILLE, Frederick
Producer, Playwright, Actor
b. Swansea, Wales, 1876
d. Unknown, April 5, 1938, Age 62

MELVILLE, Rose
Actress
b. Terre Haute, IN, Jan. 30, 1873
d. Lake George, NY, Oct. 8, 1946, Age 73

MELVILLE, Walter
Producer, Playwright
b. London, England, 1875
d. Unknown, Feb. 28, 1937, Age 62

MELVILLE, Winifred (Wright)
Actress
b. Unknown
d. Unknown, June 12, 1950, Age 40

MELVILLE, Winnie
Actress
b. Unknown
d. Unknown, Sept. 19, 1937, Age 42

MENANDER
Playwright
b. Athens, Greece, 342 B.C.
d. Unknown, 291 B.C.

MENCKEN, Henry Louis
Critic, Author
b. Baltimore, MD, Sept. 12, 1880
d. Baltimore, MD, Jan. 29, 1956, Age 75

MENDELSSOHN, Eleanora
Actress
b. Berlin, Germany, Unknown
d. New York, NY, Jan. 24, 1951, Age 51

MENDELSSOHN, Felix
(Mendelssohn-Bartholdy, Jakob Ludwig Felix)
Composer
b. Hamburg, Germany, Feb. 3, 1809
d. Leipzig, Germany, Nov. 4, 1847, Age 38

MENDES, Catulle Abraham
Critic, Playwright
b. Bordeaux, France, May 22, 1841
d. St. Germain-en-Laye, France, Feb. 8, 1909, Age 67

MENDES, Moses
Playwright
b. Unknown
d. Unknown, Feb. 4, 1758

MENDUM, Georgie Drew
Actress
b. Unknown
d. New York, NY, July 30, 1957, Age 82

MENJOU, Adolphe
Actor
b. Pittsburgh, PA, Feb. 18, 1890
d. Beverly Hills, CA, Oct. 29, 1963, Age 73

MENKEN, Adah Isaacs (Dolores Adios Fuertos)
Actress
b. New Orleans, LA, 1835
d. Paris, France, Aug. 10, 1868, Age 33

MENKEN, Helen
Actress, Teacher, Philanthropist
b. New York, NY, Dec. 12, 1901
d. New York, NY, March 27, 1966, Age 64

MENZIES, William Cameron
Art director
b. New Haven, CT, Unknown
d. Beverly Hills, CA, March 5, 1957, Age 60

MERANDE, Doro
Actress
b. Columbia, KS, Unknown
d. Miami, FL, Nov. 1, 1975, Age 70s

MERANTE, Louis
Dancer, Choreographer
b. Unknown
d. Unknown, Jan. 6, 1887, Age 58

MERCER, Beryl
Actress
b. Seville, Spain, Aug. 13, 1882
d. Santa Monica, CA, July 28, 1939, Age 56

MERCER, Johnny
Lyricist, Composer
b. Savannah, GA, Nov. 18, 1910
d. Los Angeles, CA, June 25, 1976, Age 66

MERCIER, Louis Sébastien
Playwright
b. Unknown, 1740
d. Unknown, 1814

MERIMEE, Prosper
Playwright, Novelist
b. Paris, France, Sept. 28, 1803
d. Cannes, France, Sept. 23, 1870, Age 67

MERIVALE, Bernard
Playwright
b. Newcastle-on-Tyne, England, July 15, 1882
d. Unknown, May 10, 1939, Age 56

MERIVALE, Herman Charles
Playwright
b. Unknown, 1839
d. Unknown, Jan. 14, 1906, Age 67

MERIVALE, Mrs. Herman (Elizabeth)
Playwright
b. Unknown
d. Unknown, Nov. 20, 1932, Age 85

MERIVALE, Philip
Actor
b. Rehutia, India, Nov. 2, 1886
d. Los Angeles, CA, March 13, 1946, Age 59

MERLIN, Frank
Actor, Author, Playwright, Director, Producer
b. County Cork, Ireland, 1892
d. Bay Shore, NY, March 1, 1968, Age 76

MERRICK, Leonard
Playwright, Novelist
b. Belsize Park, England, Feb. 21, 1864
d. Unknown, Aug. 7, 1939, Age 75

MERRILL, Louis
Performer
b. Unknown
d. Hollywood, CA, April 7, 1963, Age 52

MERRITT, Paul
Playwright
b. Unknown
d. Unknown, July 7, 1895

MERRY, Mrs. Robert (Ann Brunton)
Actress
b. Unknown, 1763
d. Unknown, June 28, 1808, Age 45

MERRY, Robert
Playwright, Poet
b. Unknown
d. Unknown, Dec. 14, 1798, Age 43

MERVYN (HIMMEL), Lee
Performer
b. Unknown
d. Cleveland, OH, Jan. 16, 1962, Age 34

MESSITER, Eric
Actor
b. Unknown
d. London, England, Sept. 13, 1960, Age 68

MESTAYER, Anna Maria (Mrs. C. R. Thorne, Sr.)
Actress
b. Unknown
d. Unknown, 1881

MESTEL, Jacob
Actor, Director
b. Poland, Unknown
d. New York, NY, Aug. 6, 1958, Age 74

METASTASIO, (Pietro Armando Domenico Trapassi)
Playwright, Librettist
b. Unknown, 1698
d. Unknown, 1782

METAXA, Georges
Actor
b. Bucharest, Romania, Sept. 11, 1899
d. Monroe, LA, Dec. 8, 1950, Age 51

METCALFE, James Stetson
Drama critic
b. Buffalo, NY, June 27, 1858
d. New York, NY, May 26, 1927, Age 68

METENIER, Oscar
Playwright, Director
b. Sancoins, Cher, France, Jan. 17, 1859
d. Unknown, Feb. 1913, Age 54

METHOT, Mayo
Actress
b. Portland, OR, Unknown
d. Portland, OR, June 9, 1951, Age 47

METZ, Theodore
Songwriter
b. Hanover, Germany, March 14, 1848
d. New York, NY, Jan. 12, 1936, Age 87

MEURICE, Paul
Playwright
b. Unknown
d. Unknown, Dec. 10, 1905, Age 85

MEYER, Ernest
Literary representative
b. Unknown
d. Unknown, Nov. 5, 1927, Age 50

MEYER, George W.
Composer
b. Boston, MA, Jan. 1, 1884
d. New York, NY, Aug. 28, 1959, Age 75

MEYER, Louis
Producer, Journalist
b. Birmingham, England, Oct. 20, 1871
d. Unknown, Feb. 1, 1915, Age 43

MEYER-FORSTER, Wilhelm
Playwright
b. Unknown
d. Unknown, March 17, 1934, Age 72

MEYERHOLD, Vsevolod Emilievich
Producer, Director, Actor
b. Paris, France, Jan. 1, 1874
d. Unknown, March 17, 1942, Age 68

MEYNELL, Clyde
Actor, Producer
b. Dover, England, April 7, 1867
d. Unknown, June 18, 1934, Age 67

MICHAEL, Edward
Producer
b. Unknown
d. Unknown, Feb. 4, 1950, Age 97

MICHALESCO, Michael
Actor
b. Russia, Unknown
d. New York, NY, April 28, 1957, Age 72

MIDDLETON, Edgar
Playwright
b. London, England, Nov. 26, 1894
d. Unknown, April 10, 1939, Age 44

MIDDLETON, George
Manager
b. Boston, MA, Unknown
d. South Pasadena, CA, Feb. 14, 1926, Age 81

MIDDLETON, George
Playwright, Author
b. Paterson, NJ, Oct. 27, 1880
d. Washington, DC, Dec. 23, 1967, Age 87

MIDDLETON, Guy
Actor
b. Hove, Sussex, England, Dec. 14, 1907
d. London, England, July 30, 1973, Age 65

MIDDLETON, Thomas
Playwright
b. London, England, 1570
d. Unknown, July 4, 1627, Age 57

MIELZINER, Jo
Scenic designer
b. Paris, France, March 19, 1901
d. New York, NY, March 15, 1976, Age 74

MIKHOELS, Salomon (Salomon Mikhailovich Vovsky)
Actor, Producer
b. Dvinsk, Russia, 1890
d. Moscow, Russia, 1948

MILANO, Frank
Performer
b. Wilmington, DE, Unknown
d. Hudson, NY, Dec. 15, 1962

MILES, Carlton
Playwright, Talent rep., Drama critic
b. Fergus Falls, MN, Unknown
d. New York, NY, Sept. 18, 1954, Age over 70

MILES, George Henry
Playwright, Poet, Novelist
b. Unknown
d. Unknown, July 24, 1871, Age 46

MILES, Jackie
Performer
b. Kiev, Russia, 1913
d. Los Angeles, CA, April 24, 1968, Age 54

MILJAN, John
Actor
b. Lead, SD, Unknown
d. Hollywood, CA, Jan. 24, 1960, Age 67

MILLAR, Douglas
Producer
b. Unknown
d. Unknown, May 1943, Age 67

MILLAR, Gertie (Countess of Dudley)
Actress
b. Bradford, Yorkshire, England, Feb. 21, 1879
d. Chiddingford, England, April 25, 1952, Age 73

MILLAR, Mack
Press representative
b. Unknown
d. Hollywood, CA, Nov. 8, 1962, Age 57

MILLAR, Robins
Critic, Author, Journalist
b. British Columbia, CAN, Unknown
d. Glasgow, Scotland, Aug. 12, 1968, Age 79

MILLARD, Edward R. "Rocky"
Performer
b. Unknown
d. Glendale, CA, Dec. 13, 1963

MILLARD, Evelyn
Actress, Producer
b. Kensington, London, England, Sept. 18, 1869
d. Unknown, Nov. 9, 1941, Age 71

MILLAUD, Albert
Playwright
b. Unknown
d. Unknown, Oct. 22, 1892, Age 47

MILLAY, Edna St. Vincent (Mrs. Eugen Jan Boissevan)
Playwright, Performer, Poet
b. Rockland, ME, Feb. 22, 1892
d. Austerlitz, NY, Oct. 19, 1950, Age 58

MILLER, Alice Duer
Playwright, Novelist
b. New York, NY, July 28, 1874
d. New York, NY, Aug. 22, 1942, Age 68

MILLER, Arthur
Playwright
b. Unknown
d. Unknown, July 17, 1935

MILLER, Bob
Song plugger, Music publisher
b. Unknown
d. Yuland, NY, July 7, 1964, Age 73

MILLER, Clarence
Stagehand
b. Unknown
d. Nutley, NJ, Feb. 23, 1963, Age 67

MILLER, David
Actor, Director
b. Glasgow, Scotland, March 31, 1871
d. Unknown, Jan. 1, 1933, Age 61

MILLER, David Prince
Producer
b. Unknown
d. Unknown, May 24, 1873, Age 65

MILLER, Gilbert Heron
Producer
b. New York, NY, July 3, 1884
d. New York, NY, Jan. 2, 1969, Age 84

MILLER, Henry
Actor-manager
b. London, England, Feb. 1, 1860
d. New York, NY, April 9, 1926, Age 66

MILLER, Irene Bliss
Publicity representative
b. Unknown
d. Naples, FL, Oct. 6, 1962, Age 86

MILLER, James
Playwright
b. Unknown
d. Unknown, April 26, 1744, Age 38

MILLER, Joaquin (Cincinnatus Hiner (Heine) Miller)
Playwright
b. near Liberty, IN, Sept. 8, 1837
d. Oakland, CA, Feb. 17, 1913, Age 75

MILLER, Joseph or Josias ("Joe Miller")
Actor
b. Unknown, 1684
d. Unknown, Aug. 16, 1738, Age 54

MILLER, Malcolm E.
Critic
b. Unknown
d. Maryville, TN, May 21, 1963

MILLER, Marilyn (Mary Ellen Reynolds)
Actress, Dancer
b. Findley, OH, Sept. 1, 1898
d. New York, NY, April 7, 1936, Age 37

MILLER, Max (Thomas Henry Sargent)
Performer
b. Unknown
d. Brighton, England, May 7, 1963, Age 68

MILLER, Truman "Gene"
Stage manager, Actor
b. Unknown
d. Unknown, Pittsburgh, PA, Age April 24, 1963

MILLER, Walter
b. Unknown, 1892
d. Unknown, 1940

MILLER, Wesley C.
Sound engineer
b. Unknown
d. Hollywood, CA, April 19, 1962, Age 65

MILLER, Wyn
Producer, Playwright
b. Unknown
d. Unknown, May 30, 1932, Age 85

MILLETT, Maude
Actress
b. Rajumpûr, India, Nov. 8, 1867
d. Unknown, Feb. 16, 1920, Age 52

MILLOCKER, Karl
Composer
b. Unknown, 1842
d. Baden, Germany, Dec. 31, 1899, Age 57

MILLS, Annette
Performer
b. Unknown
d. Unknown, Jan. 10, 1955, Age 60

MILLS, Carley
Composer, Author
b. Unknown
d. New York, NY, Oct. 20, 1962, Age 65

Mills, Florence
Comedienne, Singer
b. Washington, DC, Jan. 25, 1895
d. New York, NY, Nov. 1, 1927, Age 32

MILLS, Frank (Frank Ransom)
Actor
b. Kendal, MI, 1870
d. Michigan Sanitarium, June 11, 1921, Age 51

MILLS, Guy
Performer
b. Unknown
d. Chichester, England, Oct. 15, 1962, Age 64

MILLS, Horace
Actor, Playwright
b. Portsmouth, England, Sept. 1, 1864
d. Unknown, Aug. 14, 1941, Age 76

MILLS, Kerry (Frederick Allen Mills)
Composer, Song Publisher
b. Philadelphia, PA, Feb. 1, 1869
d. Hawthorne, CA, Dec. 5, 1948, Age 79

MILLS, Mrs. Clifford
Playwright
b. Unknown
d. Unknown, July 2, 1933, Age 70

MILLWARD, Charles
Playwright
b. Unknown
d. Unknown, June 7, 1892, Age 62

MILLWARD, Jessie
Actress
b. Liverpool, England, July 14, 1861
d. London, England, July 13, 1932, Age 71

MILMAN, Dean
Playwright
b. Unknown
d. Unknown, Sept. 24, 1868, Age 77

MILNE, Alan Alexander
Playwright, Author, Poet
b. London, England, Jan. 18, 1882
d. Sussex, England, Jan. 31, 1956, Age 74

MILTERN, John E.
Actor
b. New Britain, CT, Unknown
d. Los Angeles, CA, Jan. 15, 1937, Age 67

MILTON, John
Playwright, Poet
b. Cheapside, London, England, Dec. 9, 1608
d. Bunhill, London, England, Nov. 6, 1674, Age 65

MILTON, Maud
Actress
b. Gravesend, England, March 24, 1859
d. Unknown, Nov. 19, 1945, Age 86

MILTON, Mrs. Arthur (Milton-Rays)
Actress
b. Unknown
d. Unknown, April 24, 1936

MILWARD, Dawson
Actor
b. Woolwich, England, July 13, 1870
d. Unknown, May 15, 1926, Age 56

MINCIOTTI, Esther
Actress
b. Italy, Unknown
d. Jackson Heights, Queens, NY, April 15, 1962, Age 74

MINER, Henry Clay
Theatre manager, Producer
b. Brooklyn, NY, Unknown
d. Greenwich, CT, Aug. 10, 1950, Age 84

MINEVITCH, Borrah
Musician
b. Kiev, Russia, Unknown
d. Paris, France, June 26, 1955, Age 52

MINSHULL, George T.
Actor, Producer
b. Unknown
d. Unknown, April 16, 1943, Age 87

MINSKY, Abraham Bennet
Producer
b. New York, NY, March 1, 1881
d. New York, NY, Sept. 5, 1949, Age 68

MINSKY, Mollie (Mrs. Abraham B. Minsky)
Theatre executive
b. New York, NY, Unknown
d. New York, NY, May 14, 1964, Age 69

MINTURN, Harry L.
Producer, Actor
b. Unknown
d. Chicago, IL, March 7, 1963, Age 79

MINZEY, Frank
Actor
b. Massachusetts, Unknown
d. Lake George, NY, Nov. 12, 1949, Age 70

MIRANDA, Carmen (Marie de Carno da Canbra)
Dancer, Actress
b. Portugal, Unknown
d. Beverly Hills, CA, Aug. 5, 1955, Age 41

MIRBEAU, Octave
Playwright
b. Travières, Calvados, France, Feb. 16, 1848
d. Unknown, Feb. 16, 1917, Age 69

MISSA, Edmond
Composer
b. Unknown
d. Unknown, Jan. 29, 1910

MISTINGUETT, (Jeanne Marie Bourgeois)
Performer
b. La Pointe de Raquet, Engien-Les-Bains, France, c1875
d. Bougival, Paris, France, Jan. 5, 1956, Age 82

MITCHELL, Abbie
Actress
b. Unknown
d. New York, NY, March 16, 1960, Age 76

MITCHELL, Dodson Lomax
Actor, Playwright
b. Memphis, TN, Jan. 23, 1868
d. New York, NY, June 2, 1939, Age 71

MITCHELL, Earle
Actor
b. La Plata, MO, Unknown
d. New York, NY, Feb. 17, 1946, Age 64

MITCHELL, Esther
Actress
b. Newcastle, New So. Wales, Australia, Unknown
d. New York, NY, Nov. 26, 1953, Age 56

MITCHELL, George
Actor
b. Larchmont, NY, Feb. 21, 1905
d. Washington, DC, Jan. 18, 1972, Age 66

MITCHELL, Grant
Actor
b. Columbus, OH, June 17, 1874
d. Los Angeles, CA, May 1, 1957, Age 82

MITCHELL, Joseph
Playwright
b. Unknown
d. Unknown, Feb. 6, 1738, Age 63

MITCHELL, Julian
Director, Producer
b. Unknown
d. Long Branch, NJ, June 24, 1926, Age 72

MITCHELL, Julien
Actor
b. Glossop, Derbyshire, England, Nov. 13, 1888
d. Unknown, Nov. 4, 1954, Age 66

MITCHELL, Langdon Elwyn
Playwright, Poet
b. Philadelphia, PA, Feb. 17, 1862
d. Philadelphia, PA, Oct. 21, 1935, Age 73

MITCHELL, Mae
Performer
b. Unknown
d. New Jersey, bet. Feb. 19—April 20, 1963, Age 52

MITCHELL, Maggie (Margaret Julia)
Actress
b. New York, NY, 1832
d. New York, NY, March 22, 1918, Age 86

MITCHELL, Millard
Actor
b. Havana, Cuba, Aug. 14, 1903
d. Santa Monica, CA, Oct. 13, 1953, Age 50

MITCHELL, Mrs. Langdon
Performer
b. Philadelphia, PA, Unknown
d. New York, NY, June 7, 1944

MITCHELL, Rhea
Actress
b. Unknown
d. Hollywood, CA, Sept. 16, 1957, Age 63

MITCHELL, Theodore
Press representative, Critic
b. Lexington, KY, Unknown
d. Beechurst, NY, Feb. 23, 1938, Age 63

MITCHELL, Thomas
Actor, Director, Playwright
b. Elizabeth, NJ, July 11, 1895
d. Beverly Hills, CA, Dec. 17, 1962, Age 70

MITCHELL, William
Producer, Actor
b. England, 1798
d. Unknown, 1856

MITFORD, Mary Russell
Playwright
b. Unknown
d. Unknown, Jan. 10, 1855, Age 67

MIX, Tom
Actor
b. Mix Run near Dubois, Clearfield County, PA, 1880 (?)
d. Florence, AZ (auto accident), Oct. 12, 1940

MIZNER, Wilson
Playwright
b. Benicia, CA, 1876
d. Los Angeles, CA, April 3, 1933, Age 56

MODENA, Giacomo
Actor
b. 1766, Unknown
d. 1841

MODENA, Gustavo
Actor, Producer
b. Unknown, 1803
d. Unknown, 1861

MODJESKA (MODRZEJEWSKA), Helena (née Opido)
Actress
b. Cracow, Poland, Oct. 12, 1844
d. Bay City, CA, April 8, 1909, Age 65

MOELLER, Philip
Author, Producer, Director
b. New York, NY, Aug. 26, 1880
d. New York, NY, April 26, 1958, Age 77

MOFFAT, Graham
Actor, Playwright
b. Glasgow, Scotland, Feb. 21, 1866
d. Unknown, Dec. 12, 1951, Age 85

MOFFAT, Margaret
Actress
b. Edinburgh, Scotland, Oct. 11, 1882
d. Unknown, Feb. 19, 1942, Age 59

MOFFAT, Mrs. Graham
Actress
b. Spital, England, Jan. 7, 1873
d. Unknown, Feb. 19, 1943, Age 70

MOFFATT, Sanderson
Actor
b. Unknown
d. Unknown, Jan. 1, 1918

MOFFETT, Cleveland
Playwright, Journalist
b. Unknown
d. Unknown, Oct. 14, 1926, Age 63

MOFFETT, Harold
Actor
b. Chicago, IL, Aug. 9, 1892
d. Unknown, Nov. 7, 1938, Age 46

MOHR, Gerald
Actor
b. New York, NY, June 11, 1914
d. Stockholm, Sweden, Nov. 10, 1968, Age 54

MOISSI, Alexander
Actor
b. Trieste, Austria, 1880
d. Vienna, Austria, March 22, 1935, Age 54

MOK, Michel
Press representative
b. Amsterdam, Holland, Unknown
d. New York, NY, Feb. 2, 1961, Age 72

MOLESWORTH, Ida
Actress, Producer
b. near Calcutta, India, Unknown
d. Unknown, Oct. 14, 1951

MOLIERE, Jean-Baptiste Poquelin de
Playwright, Poet, Actor, Director
b. Paris, France, baptized Jan. 15, 1622
d. Paris, France, Feb. 17, 1673, Age 51

MOLINA, Tirso de (Gabriel Téllez)
Playwright, Cleric
b. Madrid, Spain, c1571
d. Unknown, March 12, 1648

MOLLISON, William
Actor, Director
b. London, England, Dec. 24, 1893
d. Unknown, Oct. 19, 1955, Age 61

MOLLOY, Charles
Playwright
b. Unknown
d. Unknown, July 16, 1767

MOLLOY, J. L.
Composer
b. Unknown
d. Unknown, Feb. 8, 1909, Age 71

MOLNAR, Ferenc
Playwright
b. Budapest, Hungary, Jan 12, 1878
d. New York, NY, April 1, 1952, Age 74

MOLNAR, Lily
Actress
b. Unknown
d. Unknown, Oct. 20, 1950

MONACO, Jimmy (James V.)
Composer
b. Genoa, Italy, Jan. 13, 1885
d. Beverly Hills, CA, Dec. 17, 1945, Age 60

MONAKHOV, Nickolai Fedorovich
Actor
b. Unknown, 1875
d. Unknown, 1936

MONCK, Nugent
Actor, Director
b. Welshampton, Salop, England, Feb. 4, 1877
d. Unknown, Oct. 1958, Age 81

MONCKTON, Lionel
Composer, Music critic
b. Unknown
d. Unknown, Feb. 15, 1924, Age 62

MONCRIEFF, Murri
Actor
b. Unknown
d. Unknown, May 21, 1949

MONCRIEFF, William (George) Thomas
Playwright, Producer
b. Unknown, 1794
d. Unknown, Dec. 3, 1857

MONKHOUSE, Allan
Playwright, Critic, etc.
b. Barnard Castle, Durham, England, May 7, 1858
d. Unknown, Jan. 10, 1936, Age 77

MONKHOUSE, Harry
Actor
b. Unknown
d. Unknown, Feb. 18, 1901, Age 47

MONNA-DELZA, Mlle.
Actress
b. Unknown
d. Unknown, May 5, 1921

MONNOT, Marguerite
Composer, Pianist
b. Unknown
d. Paris, France, Oct. 12, 1961, Age 58

MONROE, Frank
Actor
b. Jersey City, NJ, Unknown
d. Bay Shore, NY, June 19, 1937, Age 73

MONROE, George W.
Actor
b. Philadelphia, PA, Unknown
d. Atlantic City, NJ, Jan. 29, 1932, Age 75

MONROE, Marilyn (Norman Jean Mortenson or Baker)
Actress
b. Los Angeles, CA, June 1, 1926
d. Brentwood, CA, Aug. 5, 1962, Age 36

MONTA, Rudolph
Lawyer
b. Unknown
d. Hollywood, CA, April 15, 1963, Age 62

MONTAGUE, Charles Edward
Critic, Author
b. Ealing, England, Jan. 1, 1867
d. Unknown, May 28, 1928, Age 61

MONTAGUE, Emmeline (Mrs. Henry Compton)
Actress
b. Unknown
d. Unknown, Dec. 31, 1910

MONTAGUE, Harry
Actor, Songwriter
b. Unknown
d. Amityville, L.I., NY, March 20, 1927, Age 83

MONTAGUE, Louise
Performer
b. Unknown, 1871
d. Unknown, 1906

MONTAGUE, Rita
Actress, Playwright
b. Unknown
d. Hollywood, CA, May 5, 1962, Age 78

MONTAGUE (MANN), Henry James
Actor
b. Unknown, 1844
d. Unknown, 1878

MONTANSIER, Marguerite (née Brunet)
Actress, Producer
b. Unknown, 1730
d. Unknown, 1820

MONTDORY, (Guillaume Desgilberts)
Actor, Producer
b. Unknown, 1594
d. Unknown, 1651

MONTEFIORE, Eade
Producer, Director, Author
b. Charmouth, England, Feb. 6, 1866
d. Unknown, Sept. 26, 1944, Age 78

MONTEREY, Carlotta
Actress
b. San Francisco, CA, Unknown
d. Westwood, NJ, Nov. 18, 1970, Age 82

MONTESOLE, Max
Playwright, Director
b. Unknown
d. Unknown, Sept. 19, 1942, Age 52

MONTEUX, Pierre
Conductor
b. Paris, France, April 4, 1875
d. Hancock, ME, July 1, 1964, Age 89

MONTEZ, Lola (Marie Dolores Eliza Rosanna Gilbert)
Actress, Dancer
b. Limerick, Ireland, 1818
d. Astoria, L.I., NY, Jan. 17, 1861, Age 42

MONTEZ, Maria (Marie Africa Gracis Vidal de Santos Silas)
Actress
b. Barahona, Dominican Republic, June 6, 1920
d. Suresnes, France, Sept. 7, 1951, Age 31

MONTGOMERY, David Craig
Actor, Producer
b. St. Joseph, MO, April 21, 1870
d. Unknown, April 20, 1917, Age 47

MONTGOMERY, Douglass (né Robert Douglas Montgomery)
Actor
b. Los Angeles, CA, Oct. 29, 1908
d. Norwalk, CT, July 23, 1966, Age 57

MONTGOMERY, Florence (Mrs. George Arliss)
Actress
b. Unknown
d. London, England, March 12, 1950, Age 77

MONTGOMERY, Marshall
Ventriloquist
b. Brooklyn, NY, Unknown
d. Brooklyn, NY, Sept. 30, 1942, Age 55

MONTGOMERY & STONE, See David Craig Montgomery See Fred A. Stone
Performers

MONTMENIL, (René-André Le Sage)
Actor
b. Unknown, 1695
d. Unknown, 1743, Age 48

MOODIE, Louise M. R.
Actress
b. Unknown
d. Unknown, Aug. 9, 1934, Age 88

MOODY, William Vaughan
Playwright
b. Spencer, IN, July 8, 1869
d. California, Oct. 17, 1910, Age 41

MOORE, Carrie
Actress
b. Albury, New South Wales, Australia, July 20, 1883
d. Unknown, Sept. 5, 1956, Age 73

MOORE, Charles J.
Performer
b. Washington, DC, Unknown
d. Sarasota, FL, Sept. 14, 1962, Age 84

MOORE, Decima
Actress
b. Unknown
d. England, Feb. 18, 1964, Age 93

MOORE, Edward
Playwright
b. Unknown, 1712
d. Unknown, Feb. 28, 1757, Age 44

MOORE, Eulabelle
Actress
b. Garrison, TX, Unknown
d. New York, NY, Nov. 30, 1964, Age 61

MOORE, Eva
Actress
b. Brighton, England, Feb. 9, 1870
d. Unknown, April 27, 1955, Age 85

MOORE, F. Frankfort
Playwright, Poet, Novelist
b. Unknown
d. Unknown, May 11, 1931, Age 75

MOORE, Florence (Mrs. John Ogden Kerner)
Actress, Singer
b. Philadelphia, PA, Unknown
d. Darby, PA, March 23, 1935, Age 49

MOORE, George
Playwright, Poet, Novelist
b. Moore Hall, County Mayo, Ireland, Feb. 24, 1852
d. Unknown, Jan. 21, 1933, Age 80

MOORE, Grace
Opera singer, Actress
b. Del Rio, TN, Dec. 5, 1901
d. . . .near Copenhagen, Denmark, Jan. 25, 1947, Age 45

MOORE, Hilda
Actress
b. Unknown
d. Unknown, May 18, 1929, Age 42

MOORE, Jessie (Mrs. Cairns James)
Actress
b. Brighton, England, Unknown
d. London, England, Nov. 28, 1910

MOORE, Maggie
Actress
b. San Francisco, CA, 1847
d. Unknown, March 15, 1926, Age 79

MOORE, Mary (Lady Wyndham)
Actress, Producer
b. London, England, July 3, 1861
d. Unknown, April 6, 1931, Age 69

MOORE, Matt
Actor
b. Ireland, Jan. 8, 1890
d. Hollywood, CA, Jan. 21, 1960, Age 70

MOORE, Monette
Performer
b. Unknown
d. Anaheim, CA, Oct. 21, 1961, Age 50

MOORE, Owen
Actor, Producer
b. Ireland, 1886
d. Beverly Hills, CA, June 9, 1939, Age 52

MOORE, Percy
Actor
b. Montreal, CAN, Unknown
d. New York, NY, April 8, 1945, Age 67

MOORE, Raymond
Producer
b. Baltimore, MD, Unknown
d. New York, NY, March 8, 1940, Age 42

MOORE, Robert Francis
Drama editor for Billboard, Critic
b. Brooklyn, NY, Unknown
d. Brooklyn, NY, Feb. 25, 1964, Age 69

MOORE, Tom
Actor
b. County Meath, Ireland, Unknown
d. Santa Monica, CA, Feb. 12, 1955, Age 71

MOORE, Victor Frederick
Performer
b. Hammonton, NJ, Feb. 24, 1876
d. East Islip, L.I., NY, July 24, 1962, Age 86

MOOREHEAD, Agnes
Actress
b. Clinton, MA, Dec. 6, 1906
d. Rochester, MN, April 30, 1974, Age 67

MOORHEAD, Jean
Actress
b. Ellisville, MS, Unknown
d. Lindwood, NJ, Nov. 1, 1953, Age 39

MORALES, Noro
Musician, Composer
b. Puerto Rico, Jan. 2, 1913
d. Santurce, Puerto Rico, Jan. 14, 1964, Age 51

MORAN, George (Moran & Mack)
Performer
b. Elwood, KS, 1881
d. Oakland, CA, Aug. 1, 1949, Age 67

MORAN, Lee
Actor
b. Unknown
d. Woodland Hills, CA, April 24, 1961, Age 73

MORAN, Patsy
Actress
b. Unknown
d. Hollywood, CA, Dec. 10, 1968, Age 63

MORAN, Polly (Mrs. Martin T. Malone née Pauline Therese Moran)
Actress
b. Chicago, IL, June 28, 1885
d. Hollywood, CA, June 25, 1952, Age 66

MORAND, Eugéne
Playwright
b. Petrograd, Russia, March 17, 1855
d. Unknown, Jan. 1930, Age 74

MORAND, Marcellus Raymond
Actor
b. Bury, Lancashire, England, Dec. 17, 1860
d. Unknown, March 5, 1922, Age 61

MORDANT, Edwin
Actor
b. Baltimore, MD, Unknown
d. Hollywood, CA, Feb. 15, 1942, Age 74

MORDKIN, Mikhail M.
Dancer, Ballet Master
b. Moscow, Russia, Unknown
d. Millbrook, NJ, July 15, 1944, Age 63

MORE, Hannah
Playwright
b. Unknown
d. Unknown, Sept. 7, 1833, Age 78

MOREAU, Angéle
Actress
b. Unknown
d. Unknown, March 4, 1897, Age 40

MOREHOUSE, Ward
Drama critic, Journalist, Playwright
b. Savannah, GA, Nov. 24, 1899
d. New York, NY, Dec. 7, 1966, Age 67

MORENO, Marguerite (Lucie Monceau)
Actress
b. Paris, France, Unknown
d. Touzac, Lot, France, July 14, 1948, Age 77

MORGAN, Charles Langbridge
Playwright, Critic
b. Kent, England, Jan. 22, 1894
d. London, England, Feb. 6, 1958, Age 64

MORGAN, Charles S. Jr.
Producer, Director
b. Pennsylvania, Unknown
d. Philadelphia, PA, Nov. 28, 1950, Age 75

MORGAN, Claudia
Actress
b. Brooklyn, NY, June 12, 1912
d. Unknown, Sept. 17, 1974, Age 62

MORGAN, Frank (Francis Philip Wuppermann)
Actor
b. New York, NY, June 1, 1890
d. Beverly Hills, CA, Sept. 18, 1949, Age 59

MORGAN, Helen
Singer, Actress
b. Danville, IL, 1900
d. Chicago, IL, Oct. 8, 1941, Age 41

MORGAN, Joan (Mrs. Scott McKay)
Actress
b. Memphis, TN, Unknown
d. New York, NY, Oct. 11, 1962, Age 43

MORGAN, Merlin
Conductor, Composer
b. Unknown
d. Unknown, April 25, 1924, Age 47

MORGAN, Ralph (né Wuppermann)
Actor
b. New York, NY, July 6, 1883
d. New York, NY, June 11, 1956, Age 72

MORGAN, Sydney
Actor
b. Dublin, Ireland, Oct. 21, 1885
d. Unknown, Dec. 5, 1931, Age 46

MORGAN, William
Actor
b. Unknown
d. Unknown, Jan. 2, 1944, Age 92

MORGENTHAU, Rita Wallach
Direc. of Neighborhood Playhouse School
b. Unknown
d. New York, NY, April 8, 1964, Age 84

MORLAY, Gaby (Blanche Fumoleau)
Actress
b. Bakra, Algeria, 1890
d. Nice, France, July 4, 1964, Age 71

MORLEY, Christopher
Playwright, Novelist, Poet
b. Haverford, PA, Unknown
d. Roslyn Heights, L. I., NY, March 28, 1957, Age 66

MORLEY, Harry William
Actor
b. Unknown
d. Unknown, June 29, 1953, Age 82

MORLEY, Prof. Henry
Critic, Playwright
b. Unknown, 1822
d. Unknown, May 14, 1894, Age 71

MORLEY, Victor
Actor
b. Greenwich, England, Unknown
d. New York, NY, June 29, 1953, Age 82

MORNINGSTAR, Carter
Scenic Designer
b. Lanstowne, PA, Unknown
d. Mexico City, Mexico, Feb. 18, 1964, Age 53

MOROSCO, Oliver (Mitchell)
Producer, Author, Director
b. Logan, UT, 1876
d. Hollywood, CA, Aug. 25, 1945, Age 69

MORRELL, H. H. (Mackenzie)
Producer, Actor
b. Unknown
d. Unknown, Jan. 8, 1916

MORRIS, Chester
Actor
b. New York, NY, Feb. 16, 1901
d. New Hope, PA, Sept. 11, 1970, Age 69

MORRIS, Clara (Morrison)
Actress, Writer
b. Toronto, CAN, March 17, 1846
d. New Canaan, CT, Nov. 20, 1925, Age 79

MORRIS, Felix
Actor
b. Berkenhead, England, April 5, 1850
d. New York, NY, Jan. 13, 1900, Age 49

MORRIS, Lily
Performer
b. Unknown
d. Unknown, Oct. 3, 1952, Age 68

MORRIS, Mary
Actress
b. Swampscott, MA, June 24, 1895
d. New York, NY, Jan. 16, 1970, Age 74

MORRIS, Maynard
Talent representative
b. Unknown
d. New York, NY, Jan. 25, 1964, Age 65

MORRIS, McKay
Actor
b. Fort Sam Houston, TX, Dec. 22, 1891
d. Forest Hills, L. I., NY, Oct. 3, 1955, Age 63

MORRIS, Mowbray
Critic, Journalist
b. Unknown
d. Unknown, June 20, 1911, Age 63

MORRIS, Mrs. Cleze Gill
Performer
b. Unknown
d. Greensboro, NC, Dec. 1, 1963, Age 78

MORRIS, Mrs. Felix
Actor
b. Hannibal, MO, Unknown
d. Princeton, NJ, April 17, 1954

MORRIS, Mrs. Owen
Actress
b. Unknown, 1753
d. Unknown, 1826

MORRIS, Owen
Actor
b. Unknown, 1759
d. Unknown, 1790

MORRIS, Wayne
Actor
b. Los Angeles, CA, 1914
d. Oakland, CA, Sept. 14, 1959, Age 45

MORRIS, William
Theatre booking agent
b. Schwartzenau, Germany, Unknown
d. New York, NY, Nov. 1, 1932, Age 59

MORRIS, William
Actor
b. Boston, MA, Jan. 1, 1861
d. Unknown, Jan. 11, 1936, Age 75

MORRISON, Adrienne
Actress
b. New York, NY, Unknown
d. New York, NY, Nov. 20, 1940, Age 57

MORRISON, George E.
Critic, Playwright
b. Cheshunt, Hertshire, England, Jan. 8, 1860
d. Unknown, Nov. 19, 1930, Age 70

MORRISON, Henrietta Lee
Actress
b. Unknown
d. Unknown, Dec. 29, 1948, Age 79

MORRISON, Howard Priestly
Actor, Director, Producer
b. Baltimore, MD, Unknown
d. Kew Gardens, L. I., NY, Jan. 26, 1938, Age 66

MORRISON, Jack
Actor
b. Newcastle-on-Tyne, England, April 6, 1887
d. Unknown, May 4, 1948, Age 61

MORRISON, Lewis
Actor, Producer
b. Unknown, 1845
d. Unknown, Aug. 18, 1906, Age 61

MORRISSEY, John F.
Actor
b. Unknown
d. Unknown, Oct. 6, 1941, Age 58

MORRISSEY, John J.
Actor
b. Detroit, MI, Unknown
d. New York, NY, July 24, 1925, Age 70

MORRISSEY, Will
Actor, Songwriter, Author, Producer
b. Unknown
d. Santa Barbara, CA, Dec. 16, 1957, Age 72

MORROS, Boris
Musical director, Producer
b. Russia, Unknown
d. New York, NY, Jan. 9, 1963, Age about 70

MORROW, Doretta
Actress, Singer
b. Brooklyn, NY, Jan. 22, 1926
d. London, England, Feb. 28, 1968, Age 42

MORSE, Theodore F.
Composer, Song publisher
b. Washington, DC, 1873
d. New York, NY, May 25, 1924, Age 51

MORSE, Woolson
Composer
b. Charlestown, MA, Feb. 24, 1858
d. New York, NY, May 3, 1897, Age 39

MORTIMER, Charles
Actor
b. Unknown
d. Unknown, Sept. 27, 1913, Age 82

MORTIMER, Charles
Actor
b. Unknown
d. London, England, April 1864, Age 79

MORTIMER, Dorothy
Actress
b. Unknown
d. New York, NY, Feb. 15, 1950, Age 52

MORTIMER, James
Playwright
b. Unknown
d. Unknown, Feb. 24, 1911, Age 77

MORTIMER, Lee (Mortimer Lieberman)
Columnist
b. Chicago, IL, Unknown
d. New York, NY, March 1, 1963, Age 58

MORTON, Clara
Performer
b. Unknown
d. Detroit, MI, May 2, 1948, Age 66

MORTON, Edward A.
Playwright, Critic
b. Unknown
d. Unknown, July 6, 1922

MORTON, Harry K.
Actor
b. Unknown
d. New York, NY, May 9, 1956, Age 67

MORTON, Hugh (see McLellan, C. M. S.)

MORTON, James J.
Performer
b. Boston, MA, Unknown
d. Islip, NY, April 10, 1938, Age 76

MORTON, John Maddison
Playwright
b. Unknown, 1811
d. Unknown, Dec. 19, 1891, Age 80

MORTON, Kitty
Actress
b. Detroit, MI, Unknown
d. New York, NY, April 25, 1927, Age 65

MORTON, Maggie
Actress, Producer
b. Unknown
d. Unknown, Dec. 31, 1939, Age 82

MORTON, Martha
Playwright
b. New York, NY, Oct. 10, 1870 (?)
d. New York, NY, Feb. 18, 1925, Age about 60

MORTON, Michael
Playwright
b. Unknown
d. Unknown, Jan. 11, 1931, Age 76

MORTON, Sam
Actor
b. Detroit, MI, Unknown
d. Detroit, MI, Oct. 28, 1941, Age 79

MORTON, Thomas
Playwright
b. Unknown, c1764
d. Unknown, March 28, 1838, Age 74

MORTON, Thomas
Playwright
b. Unknown
d. Unknown, Jan. 18, 1879, Age 76

MORTON, William
Producer
b. Unknown, Jan. 1838
d. Unknown, July 5, 1938, Age 100

MOSCOVITCH, Maurice (né Masskoff)
Actor
b. Odessa, Russia, Nov. 23, 1871
d. Hollywood, CA, June 18, 1940, Age 68

MOSCOWITZ, Jennie (née Silverstein)
Actress
b. Jassy, Romania, Unknown
d. New York, NY, July 26, 1953, Age 85

MOSENTHAL, Solomon Hermann
Playwright
b. Unknown
d. Unknown, Feb. 17, 1877, Age 56

MOSER, Gustav von
Playwright
b. Unknown
d. Unknown, Oct. 23, 1903, Age 78

MOSER, Hans (né Jean Juliet)
Actor
b. Unknown
d. Vienna, Austria, June 19, 1964, Age 84

MOSES, Harry
Producer
b. Chicago, IL, Unknown
d. New York, NY, Aug. 31, 1937, Age 64

MOSES, Montrose Jonas
Critic, Editor, Author, Historian
b. New York, NY, Sept. 2, 1878
d. New York, NY, March 29, 1934, Age 55

MOSKOWITZ, Dr. Henry
Lawyer
b. Unknown
d. Unknown, Dec. 18, 1936, Age 57

MOSKOWITZ, Maurice (see Maurice Moscovitch)

MOSKVIN, Ivan Mikhailovich
Performer
b. Moscow, Russia, 1874
d. Moscow, U.S.S.R., Feb. 16, 1946, Age 72

MOSS, Hugh
Playwright, Director
b. Unknown
d. Unknown, June 23, 1926, Age 70

MOSS, Paul
Producer
b. New York, NY, Unknown
d. New York, NY, Feb. 25, 1950, Age 70

MOSS, Sir Edward
Theatre executive
b. Unknown, 1852
d. Unknown, 1912

MOSS, W. Keith
Founder of The Spotlight , Actor, Director
b. Unknown, Manchester, England
d. March 29, 1892

MOSSOP, Henry
Actor
b. Ireland, 1729
d. London, England, 1774

MOTTEUX, Peter
Playwright
b. Unknown
d. Unknown, Feb. 18, 1718, Age 58

MOTTLEY, John
Playwright
b. Unknown
d. Unknown, 1750, Age 58

MOUILLOT, Frederick
Producer, Playwright
b. Unknown
d. Unknown, Aug. 4, 1911, Age 47

MOUILLOT, Gertrude (née Davison)
Actress, Producer
b. Unknown
d. Colchester, England, Nov. 24, 1961, Age 91

MOULAN, Frank
Singer, Actor
b. New York, NY, July 24, 1875
d. New York, NY, May 13, 1939, Age 63

MOUNET, Jean Paul Sully
Actor
b. Bergerac, Dordogne, France, Oct. 5, 1847
d. Unknown, Feb. 10, 1922, Age 74

MOUNET-SULLY, Jean (Jean Sully Mounet)
Actor
b. Bergerac, France, Feb. 27, 1841
d. Unknown, March 1, 1916, Age 75

MOUNTAIN, Earl B.
Performer
b. Unknown
d. Kew Gardens, L. I., NY, March 1, 1962, Age 74

MOUNTFORD, Harry
Actor, Playwright, Editor
b. Dublin, Ireland, Unknown
d. New York, NY, June 4, 1950, Age 79

MOUNTFORT, Susanna Percival
Actress
b. Unknown, 1667
d. Unknown, 1703

MOUNTFORT, William
Actor, Playwright
b. Unknown, 1664
d. Unknown, Dec. 9, 1692, Age 28

MOUVET, Maurice
Dancer
b. Switzerland, Unknown
d. Lausanne, Switzerland, May 18, 1927, Age 40

MOWAT, Anna Cora (Mrs. A. C. Mowatt Ritchie née Ogden)
Playwright, Actress
b. Bordeaux, France, 1819
d. London, England, July 21, 1870, Age 51

MOWBRAY, Alan
Actor, Writer, Director
b. London, England, Aug. 18, 1897
d. Hollywood, CA, March 25, 1969, Age 72

MOWBRAY, Thomas
Actor, Playwright
b. Unknown
d. Unknown, Aug. 1900, Age 77

MOZART, George
Performer
b. Great Yarmouth, England, Unknown
d. London, England, Dec. 10, 1947, Age 83

MOZEEN, Thomas
Actor, Playwright
b. Unknown
d. Unknown, March 28, 1768

MUDIE, George
Actor
b. Unknown
d. Unknown, Dec. 28, 1918, Age 59

MULCASTER, G. H.
Actor
b. London, England, June 27, 1891
d. England, Jan. 19, 1964, Age 73

MULDENER, Louise
Actress
b. Brooklyn, NY, Unknown
d. New York, NY, May 10, 1938, Age 84

MULHOLLAND, J. B.
Producer, Actor
b. Unknown, Nov. 11, 1858
d. Unknown, June 2, 1925, Age 66

MULLALLY, Don
Actor, Playwright, Director
b. St. Louis, MO, Unknown
d. Duarte, CA, April 1, 1933, Age 48

MULLE, Ida
Actress, Singer
b. Boston, MA, Unknown
d. New York, NY, Aug. 5, 1934, Age 75

MUNDAY, Anthony
Playwright
b. Unknown, 1553
d. Unknown, buried Aug. 10, 1633, Age 80

MUNDEN, Joseph Shepherd
Actor
b. London, England, 1758
d. Unknown, 1832

MUNDIN, Herbert
Actor
b. St. Helen's, Lancashire, England, Aug. 21, 1898
d. Unknown, March 5, 1939, Age 40

MUNI, Paul (né Frederich Weisenfreund)
Actor
b. Lemberg, Austria, Sept. 22, 1895
d. Santa Barbara, CA, Aug. 25, 1967, Age 71

MUNK, Kaj (Kaj Harald Leininger Petersen)
Playwright, Clergyman
b. Maribo, Denmark, Jan. 13, 1898
d. near Silkeborg, Denmark, Jan. 4, 1944, Age 46

MUNRO, George
Playwright, Journalist
b. Unknown
d. Ballochmyle, Scotland, April 15, 1968, Age 66

MUNSELL, Warren P. Jr.
Playwright, Theatre manager
b. New York, NY, Unknown
d. Olney, MD, July 28, 1952, Age 37

MUNSHIN, Jules
Actor
b. New York, NY, Feb. 22, 1915
d. New York, NY, Feb. 19, 1970, Age 54

MUNSON, Ona
Actress
b. Portland, OR, June 16, 1906
d. New York, NY, Feb. 11, 1955, Age 48

MURDOCH, Frank Hitchcock
Playwright, Performer
b. Unknown
d. Unknown, Nov. 13, 1872, Age 29

MURDOCH, James Edward
Performer
b. Unknown, 1811
d. Cincinnati, OH, May 19, 1893, Age 82

MURDOCK, Henry
Drama critic
b. Philadelphia, PA, Unknown
d. Philadelphia, PA, April 20, 1971, Age 69

MURFIN, Jane
Playwright, Screenwriter
b. Ypsilanti, MI, Unknown
d. Brentwood, CA, Aug. 10, 1955, Age 62

MURPHY, Arthur
Actor, Playwright
b. Unknown, 1727
d. Unknown, June 18, 1805, Age 77

MURPHY, James
Playwright
b. Unknown
d. Unknown, Jan. 5, 1759, Age 33

MURPHY, John Daly (John Daly Conlon)
Actor
b. County Kildare, Ireland, Unknown
d. New York, NY, Nov. 20, 1934, Age 61

MURPHY, John T. ("Guffer")
Performer
b. Unknown
d. Lynn, MA, Aug. 22, 1964, Age 64

MURPHY, Tim
Actor
b. Rupert, VT, Unknown
d. New York, NY, Jan. 11, 1928, Age 67

MURRAY, Alma
Actress
b. London, England, Nov. 21, 1854
d. Unknown, July 3, 1945, Age 90

MURRAY, Charles
Actor, Playwright
b. Unknown
d. Unknown, Nov. 8, 1821, Age 67

MURRAY, David Christie
Playwright, Actor, etc.
b. Unknown
d. Unknown, Aug. 1, 1907, Age 60

MURRAY, Douglas
Playwright
b. Unknown
d. Unknown, Aug. 6, 1936, Age 73

MURRAY, Elizabeth M.
Performer
b. Unknown
d. Philadelphia, PA, March 27, 1946, Age 75

MURRAY, Gaston
Actor
b. Unknown
d. Unknown, Aug. 8, 1889, Age 63

MURRAY, Henry Valentine
Performer
b. Unknown
d. Chicago, IL, May 31, 1963, Age 71

MURRAY, J. Harold
Actor, Singer
b. South Berwich, ME, Feb. 17, 1891
d. Killingsworth, CT, Dec. 11, 1940, Age 49

MURRAY, John J.
Performer
b. Unknown
d. St. Petersburg, FL, Feb. 18, 1924

MURRAY, Mae (née Marie Adrienne Koenig)
Actress, Performer
b. Portsmouth, VA, May 10, 1889
d. Woodland Hills, CA, March 23, 1965, Age 75

MURRAY, Mrs. Gaston (Fanny Hughes)
Actress
b. Unknown
d. Unknown, Jan. 15, 1891, Age 61

MURRAY, Paul
Director, Producer
b. Cork, Ireland, July 15, 1885
d. Unknown, Oct. 17, 1949, Age 64

MURRAY, Prof. Gilbert (George Gilbert Aimé Murray)
Playwright, Translator, Educator
b. Sydney, Australia, Jan. 2, 1866
d. Oxford, England, May 20, 1957, Age 91

MURRAY, Thomas Cornelius
Playwright
b. County Cork, Ireland, 1873
d. Dublin, Ireland, March 7, 1959, Age 86

MURRAY, Will
Actor, Director
b. Unknown
d. Unknown, March 17, 1955, Age 77

MURRAY, William H.
Playwright, Producer
b. Unknown
d. Unknown, May 6, 1852, Age 62

MURRAY, Wynn (Mrs. William A. Rau)
Singer, Actress
b. Carbondale, PA, Unknown
d. Fort Meade, MD, Feb. 6, 1957, Age 35

MUSKERRY, William
Playwright
b. Unknown
d. Unknown, July 1918

MUSSET, Alfred de (Louis Charles Alfred de Musset)
Playwright, Poet, Novelist
b. Paris, France, Dec. 11, 1810
d. Unknown, May 2, 1857, Age 46

MYERBERG, Michael
Producer
b. Baltimore, MD, Aug. 5, 1906
d. Baltimore, MD, Jan. 6, 1974, Age 67

MYERS, Bessie Allen
Performer
b. San Francisco, CA, Unknown
d. San Francisco, CA, June 15, 1964

MYERS, Harry C.
Actor
b. New Haven, CT, 1882
d. Hollywood, CA, Dec. 25, 1938, Age 56

N

NADIR, Moishe (Isaac Reiss)
Playwright
b. Galicia, Austria-Hungary, 1885
d. Woodstock, NY, June 8, 1943, Age 58

NAEVIUS, Gnaeus
Playwright
b. Unknown, c270 B.C.
d. Africa, c199 B.C.

NAGEL, Claire (Mrs. Arthur Hammerstein)
Actress
b. Buffalo, NY, Unknown
d. Reno, NV, Nov. 11, 1921, Age 25

NAGEL, Conrad
Actor
b. Keokuk, IA, March 16, 1897
d. New York, NY, Feb. 24, 1970, Age 72

NAGLE, Urban
Founder of Blackfriars' Guild, Playwright, Educator
b. Providence, RI, Sept. 10, 1905
d. Cincinnati, OH, March 11, 1965, Age 59

NAINBY, Robert
Actor
b. Dublin, Ireland, June 14, 1869
d. Unknown, Feb. 17, 1948, Age 78

NAISH, J. Carrol
Actor
b. New York, NY, Jan. 21, 1901
d. La Jolla, CA, Jan. 24, 1973, Age 72

NALDI, Nita
Actress
b. New York, NY, 1897
d. New York, NY, Feb. 17, 1961, Age 63

NANSEN, Betty
Actress
b. Unknown
d. Unknown, March 15, 1943, Age 67

NAPIER, Frank
Actor, Director
b. Unknown
d. Unknown, Jan. 7, 1949, Age 45

NARES, Geoffrey
Actor, Designer
b. London, England, June 10, 1917
d. Unknown, Aug. 20, 1942, Age 25

NARES, Owen
Actor, Producer
b. Maiden Erleigh, England, Aug. 11, 1888
d. Unknown, July 31, 1943, Age 54

NASH, Florence
Actress
b. Troy, NY, Oct. 2, 1888
d. Hollywood, CA, April 2, 1950, Age 61

NASH, George Frederick
Actor
b. Philadelphia, PA, Unknown
d. Amityville, NY, Dec. 31, 1944, Age 71

NASH, Mary
Actress
b. Troy, NY, Aug. 15, 1885
d. Paramus, NJ, June 28, 1965, Age 76

NASH, Ogden
Poet, Author, Lyricist
b. Rye, NY, Aug. 19, 1902
d. Baltimore, MD, May 19, 1971, Age 68

NASHE, Thomas
Poet, Playwright
b. Unknown, 1567
d. Unknown, 1601

NASSOUR, Edward
Producer, Inventor
b. Colorado Springs, CO, Unknown
d. Sherman Oaks, CA, Dec. 15, 1962, Age 45

NATAN, Emile
Producer
b. Romania, Unknown
d. Paris, France, Dec. 1962, Age 62

NATHAN, Ben
Actor, Producer, Talent representative
b. Unknown
d. Unknown, May 9, 1919, Age 61

NATHAN, George Jean
Drama critic, Author
b. Fort Wayne, IN, Feb. 14, 1882
d. New York, NY, April 8, 1958, Age 76

NATION, W. H. C.
Producer, Playwright, Composer
b. Exeter, England, 1843
d. Unknown, March 17, 1914, Age 71

NAUDAIN, May
Actress
b. Burlington, IA, Oct. 12, 1880
d. Jacksonville, FL, Feb. 8, 1923, Age 42

NAZIMOVA, Alla
Actress
b. Yalta, Crimea, Russia, May 22, 1879
d. Los Angeles, CA, July 13, 1945, Age 66

NEALE, Frederick
Producer, Playwright
b. Unknown
d. Unknown, Dec. 11, 1856

NEDERLANDER, David T.
Theatre operator
b. Detroit, MI, May 24, 1886
d. Grosse Point, MI, Oct. 14, 1967, Age 81

NEELY, Henry M.
Actor, Writer, Director, Lecturer
b. Unknown
d. Elmhurst, L. I., NY, May 1, 1963, Age 84

NEIL, Ross (Isabella Harwood)
Playwright
b. Unknown
d. Unknown, June 1888, Age 48

NEILAN, Marshall
Director, Actor
b. California, 1891
d. Woodland Hills, CA, Oct. 26, 1958, Age 67

NEILL, James
Actor
b. Unknown
d. Glendale, CA, March 15, 1931, Age 70

NEILL, James
Actor
b. Missoula, MT, Unknown
d. New York, NY, May 22, 1962, Age 65

NEILSON, Ada
Actress
b. Unknown, 1846
d. Unknown, Jan. 25, 1905, Age 58

NEILSON, Francis
Author, Critic
b. Birkenhead, Cheshire, England, Unknown
d. Port Washington, NY, April 13, 1961, Age 94

NEILSON, Harold V.
Actor, Producer
b. Manchester, England, Jan. 8, 1874
d. Unknown, Feb. 17, 1956, Age 82

NEILSON, Lilian Adelaide (Elizabeth Ann Brown)
Actress
b. Leeds, England, March 3, 1848
d. Paris, France, Aug. 15, 1880, Age 32

NEILSON-TERRY, Dennis
Actor, Manager, Director
b. London, England, Oct. 21, 1895
d. Bulawayo, South Africa, July 14, 1932, Age 36

NEILSON-TERRY, Julia
Actress
b. London, England, June 12, 1868
d. London, England, May 27, 1957, Age 88

NELSON, Alice Brainerd
Director, Teacher
b. Unknown
d. Middlebury, VT, March 7, 1963, Age 79

NELSON, Carrie
Actress
b. Unknown
d. Unknown, Dec. 9, 1916, Age 80

NELSON, Eliza (Mrs. H. T. Craven)
Actress
b. Unknown
d. Unknown, March 21, 1908, Age 81

NELSON, Gordon
Actor
b. Unknown
d. New York, NY, Feb. 19, 1956, Age 58

NEMIROVICH-DANCHENKO, Vladimir Ivanovich
Actor, Producer
b. Tiflis, Russia, 1858
d. Moscow, U.S.S.R., April 25, 1943, Age 85

NERULOS, Jacob Rizos
Playwright
b. Unknown, 1778
d. Unknown, 1850

NESBIT, Evelyn (Mrs. Harry K. Thaw)
Showgirl, Dancer, Model
b. Tarentum, PA, 1885
d. Santa Monica, CA, Jan. 17, 1967, Age 82

NESBITT, Tom
Actor
b. England, 1890
d. South Africa, March 31, 1927, Age 36

NESTROY, Johann Nepomuk
Actor, Playwright
b. Unknown, 1801
d. Unknown, 1862

NETHERSOLE, Louis
Producer, Press Representative
b. Unknown
d. Unknown, March 14, 1936, Age 71

NETHERSOLE, Olga Isabel
Actress, Producer
b. Kensington, England, Jan. 18, 1866
d. Bournemouth, England, Jan. 9, 1951, Age 81

NETTLEFOLD, Archibald
Producer
b. London, England, 1870
d. Unknown, Nov. 29, 1944, Age 74

NETTLEFOLD, Frederick John
Actor, Producer
b. Hastings, England, 1867
d. Unknown, Nov. 25, 1949, Age 82

NEUBER, Frederika Carolina (née Weissenborn)
Actress, Producer
b. Reichenberg, Germany, March 9, 1697
d. Dresden, Germany, Nov. 30, 1760, Age 63

NEVADA, Mme. Emma
Singer
b. Nevada City, CA, Unknown
d. Liverpool, England, June 20, 1940, Age 81

NEVILLE, Harry
Performer
b. Unknown
d. Hempstead, L.I., NY, Jan. 26, 1945, Age 77

NEVILLE, John Gartside
Actor, Producer
b. Unknown
d. Unknown, March 16, 1874, Age 87

NEVILLE, (Thomas) Henry (Gartside)
Actor, Producer
b. Unknown, 1837
d. Unknown, June 19, 1910, Age 73

NEWALL, Guy
Actor
b. Isle of Wight, England, May 25, 1885
d. Unknown, Feb. 28, 1937, Age 51

NEWCOMBE, Caroline
Actress
b. Unknown
d. Unknown, Dec. 18, 1941, Age 69

NEWELL, Tom D.
Actor
b. Unknown
d. Unknown, July 24, 1935, Age 45

NEWNHAM-DAVIS, Lt. Col. Nathaniel
Playwright, Critic
b. London, England, Nov. 6, 1854
d. Unknown, May 28, 1917, Age 62

NEWTE, Horace Wykeham Can
Playwright
b. Unknown
d. Unknown, Dec. 25, 1949, Age 80

NEWTON, Henry Chance ("Carados")
Critic, Playwright
b. London, England, March 13, 1854
d. Unknown, Jan. 2, 1931, Age 76

NEWTON, Kate
Actress
b. Unknown
d. Unknown, May 13, 1940, Age 94

NEWTON, Robert
Actor
b. Shaftsbury, Dorsetshire, England, June 1, 1905
d. Beverly Hills, CA, March 25, 1956, Age 50

NEWTON, Theodore
Actor
b. Lawrenceville, NJ, Unknown
d. Hollywood, CA, Feb. 23, 1963, Age 58

NIBLO, Fred Sr.
Actor, Film director
b. York, NB, Unknown
d. New Orleans, LA, Nov. 11, 1948, Age 74

NIBLO, William
Actor, Producer
b. Unknown
d. Unknown, Aug. 21, 1878, Age 89

NICANDER, Edwin (Nicander Edwin Rau)
b. New York, NY, Unknown
d. College Point, Queens, NY, Jan. 1, 1951, Age 74

NICHOLLS, Harry
Actor, Playwright
b. London, England, March 1, 1852
d. Unknown, Nov. 29, 1926, Age 74

NICHOLS, Anne
Playwright, Director, Producer, Actress
b. Dales Mills, GA, Nov. 26, 1891
d. Englewood Cliffs, NJ, Sept. 15, 1966, Age 74

NICHOLS, Guy
Actor
b. Unknown
d. Hempstead, L. I., NY, Jan. 23, 1928, Age 65

NICHOLS, Robert Malise Bowyer
Playwright, Poet
b. England, Unknown
d. Cambridge, England, Dec. 17, 1944, Age 51

NICHOLSON, John
Actor
b. Charleston, IL, Unknown
d. New York, NY, June 24, 1934, Age 61

NICHOLSON, Sir William
Designer, Artist
b. Unknown
d. Unknown, May 16, 1949, Age 77

NICKINSON, Isabella (Mrs. Charles M. Walcot)
Actress
b. Unknown, 1847
d. Unknown, 1906

NICODEMI, Dario
Playwright, Actor
b. Italy, Unknown
d. Unknown, Sept. 24, 1934, Age 60

NICOL, Emma
Actress
b. Unknown
d. Unknown, Nov. 1877, Age 76

NICOL, Harry N.
Vaudeville agent
b. Unknown
d. London, England, Oct. 5, 1962, Age 73

NIELSEN, Alice
Singer, Actress
b. Nashville, TN, 1876
d. New York, NY, March 8, 1943, Age 66

NIGHTINGALE, Alfred
General Manager of D'Oyly Carte Co.
b. Unknown
d. London, England, Jan. 18, 1957, Age 67

NIJINSKY, Vaslav
Dancer, Choreographer
b. Kiev, Russia, Feb. 28, 1890
d. London, England, April 8, 1950, Age 60

NILLSON, Carlotta
Actress
b. Sweden, c1878
d. New York, NY, Dec. 31, 1951, Age 73

NILSON, Einar
Composer, Conductor
b. Unknown
d. Hollywood, CA, April 20, 1964, Age 83

NILSSON, Christine
Singer
b. Unknown
d. Copenhagen, Denmark, Nov. 22, 1921

NIRDLINGER, Charles Frederic
Playwright, Critic
b. Unknown
d. Atlantic City, NJ, May 13, 1940, Age 77

NISBET, J. F.
Critic, Playwright
b. Unknown
d. Unknown, March 31, 1899, Age 47

NISITA, Giovanni
Singer, Teacher
b. Unknown
d. Queens Village, NY, Nov. 24, 1962, Age 66

NIXON, Hugh
Actor
b. Unknown
d. New York, NY, Jan. 27, 1921, Age 62

NIXON-NIRDLINGER, Fred G.
Theatre owner
b. Unknown
d. Nice, France, March 11, 1931, Age 54

NOAH, Mordecai Manuel
Playwright
b. Philadelphia, PA, July 14, 1785
d. New York, NY, May 22, 1851, Age 65

NOBLES, Dolly
Actress
b. Cincinnati, OH, Unknown
d. Brooklyn, NY, Oct. 6, 1930, Age 67

NOBLES, Milton (Tamey)
Actor
b. Cincinnati, OH, Dec. 1847
d. Brooklyn, NY, June 14, 1924, Age 76

NOBLES, Milton Jr.
Actor
b. Brooklyn, NY, Unknown
d. Chester, PA, Feb. 22, 1925, Age 32

NOLAN, Mary (a/k/a Imogene (Bubbles) Wilson, née Mary Imogene Robertson)
Actress
b. Louisville, KY, 1906
d. Hollywood, CA, Oct. 31, 1948, Age 42

NOONAN, Tommy
Actor, Producer
b. Bellingham, WA, April 29, 1922
d. Woodland Hills, CA, April 24, 1968, Age 46

NORCROSS, Frank
Actor
b. Unknown
d. Glendale, CA, Sept. 13, 1926, Age 70

NORCROSS, Hale
Actor
b. San Francisco, CA, Unknown
d. New York, NY, Oct. 15, 1947, Age 70

NORCROSS, Joseph M.
Performer
b. Unknown
d. Springfield, MA, Feb. 28, 1925, Age 84

NORDSTROM, Clarence
Actor
b. Chicago, IL, March 13, 1893
d. East Orange, NJ, Dec. 13, 1968, Age 75

NORMAN, E. B.
Actor, Director, Producer
b. Unknown
d. Unknown, Oct. 26, 1930, Age 77

NORMAN, Karyl George
Performer
b. Unknown
d. Hollywood, FL, July 23, 1947, Age 51

NORMAN, Norman J.
Producer
b. Pennsylvania, Nov. 12, 1870
d. London, England, Oct. 10, 1941, Age 70

NORMAN, Norman V.
Actor, Producer
b. Somerset, England, Oct. 24, 1864
d. Unknown, Feb. 26, 1943, Age 78

NORMAND, Mabel
Actress
b. Boston, MA, Nov. 10, 1894
d. Monrovia, CA, Feb. 23, 1930, Age 35

NORREYS, Rose
Actress
b. Unknown
d. Unknown, Dec. 2, 1946, Age 84

NORRIE, Anna
Actress
b. Unknown
d. Unknown, July 1957, Age 97

NORRIS, Ernest E.
Actor
b. Unknown
d. London, England, Dec. 28, 1935, Age 70

NORRIS, Lee
Actress, Author
b. Unknown
d. Baldwin, L.I., NY, Feb. 28, 1964, Age 59

NORRIS, William (William Norris Block)
Actor
b. New York, NY, June 15, 1870
d. New York, NY, March 20, 1929, Age 58

NORTHCOTT, John
Critic
b. Unknown
d. Unknown, June 30, 1905, Age 62

NORTHCOTT, Richard
Music critic, Archivist
b. London, England, Aug. 1, 1871
d. Unknown, Jan. 22, 1931, Age 59

NORTON, Barry (Alfredo deBiraben)
Actor
b. Argentina, Unknown
d. Hollywood, CA, Aug. 24, 1956, Age 51

NORTON, Frederic
Composer
b. Manchester, England, Dec. 15, 1946

NORTON, Jack (Mortimer J. Naughton)
Actor
b. Brooklyn, NY, Unknown
d. Saranac Lake, NY, Oct. 15, 1958, Age 69

NORTON, Thomas
Playwright
b. Unknown, 1532
d. Unknown, 1584

NORWOOD, Eille
Actor
b. York, England, Oct. 11, 1861
d. Unknown, Dec. 24, 1948, Age 87

NORWORTH, Jack
Actor, Composer
b. Philadelphia, PA, Jan. 5, 1879
d. Laguna Beach, CA, Sept. 1, 1959, Age 80

NOTT, Cicely (Mrs. Sam Adams)
Actress
b. Unknown
d. Unknown, Jan. 3, 1900, Age 67

NOVELLI, Ermete
Actor, Producer
b. Lucca, Italy, May 5, 1851
d. Rome, Italy, Jan. 30, 1919, Age 67

NOVELLO, Ivor
Actor, Composer, Producer, Playwright
b. Cardiff, Wales, Jan. 15, 1893
d. London, England, March 6, 1951, Age 58

NOZIERE, Fernand (Weyl)
Playwright, Critic
b. Unknown
d. Passy, France, March 25, 1931, Age 57

NUGENT, John Charles
Actor, Playwright
b. Niles, OH, April 6, 1878
d. New York, NY, April 21, 1947, Age 79

NUGENT, Moya
Actress
b. Unknown, 1901
d. London, England, Jan. 26, 1954, Age 52

NUMES, Armand
Actor, Playwright
b. Unknown
d. Unknown, May 2, 1933, Age 75

NUNES, Léon
Playwright
b. Unknown
d. Unknown, July 29, 1911

NYE, Tom F.
Actor
b. Unknown
d. Unknown, Jan. 13, 1925, Age 78

NYITRAY, Emil
Playwright
b. Unknown
d. Milford, CT, May 20, 1922

OAKLAND, Will (Herman Hinrichs)
Performer
b. Jersey City, NJ, 1883
d. Bloomfield, NJ, May 15, 1956, Age 73

OAKMAN, Wheeler
Actor
b. Washington, DC, Unknown
d. Van Nuys, CA, March 19, 1949, Age 59

OATES, Cicely
Actress
b. Unknown
d. Unknown, Dec. 23, 1934, Age 45

OBER, Harold
Literary representative
b. Unknown
d. New York, NY, Oct. 31, 1959, Age 78

OBER, Robert (Robert Howard Ober)
Actor
b. Bunker Hill, IL, Sept. 3, 1881
d. New York, NY, Dec. 7, 1950, Age 69

OBERLE, Thomas
Actor
b. Unknown
d. Unknown, Nov. 7, 1906

O'BRIEN, Barry
Actor, Producer, Talent Representative
b. London, England, Dec. 23, 1893
d. London, England, Dec. 25, 1961, Age 69

O'BRIEN, Justin
Playwright, Educator
b. Chicago, IL, Nov. 26, 1906
d. New York, NY, Dec. 7, 1968, Age 62

O'BRIEN, Kate
Playwright, Novelist
b. Limerick, Ireland, Dec. 3, 1897
d. Faversham, England, Aug. 13, 1974, Age 76

O'BRIEN, Neil
Actor
b. Unknown
d. Unknown, Oct. 18, 1909, Age 55

O'BRIEN, William
Actor, Playwright
b. Unknown
d. Unknown, Sept. 2, 1815, Age 79

O'CASEY, Sean (né Shaun O'Cathasaigh)
Playwright, Author
b. Dublin, Ireland, March 30, 1880
d. Torquay, England, Sept. 18, 1964, Age 84

OCHS, Al
Talent representative
b. Unknown
d. Hollywood, CA, July 16, 1964, Age 70

OCHS, Lillian
Talent Representative
b. Unknown
d. Hollywood, CA, June 15, 1964

O'CONNELL, Hugh
Actor
b. New York, NY, Aug. 4, 1898
d. Hollywood, CA, Jan. 19, 1943, Age 44

O'CONNOR, Charles William
Press representative, Journalist
b. Roscommon, Ireland, Feb. 15, 1878
d. Unknown, Nov. 28, 1955, Age 77

O'CONNOR, Edwin
Playwright
b. Providence, RI, July 29, 1918
d. Boston, MA, March 23, 1968, Age 49

O'CONNOR, Frank né Michael O'Donovan)
Author, Novelist, Educator, Playwright
b. Cork, Ireland, 1903
d. Dublin, Ireland, March 10, 1966, Age 63

O'CONNOR, (Jim) James F. (a/k/a "Gene Knight")
Journalist
b. Troy, NY, Unknown
d. New York, NY, March 18, 1963, Age 70

O' CONNOR, Robert
Actor
b. Unknown
d. Chicago, IL, March 4, 1947

O'CONNOR, Robert Emmett
Actor
b. Milwaukee, WI, Unknown
d. Hollywood, CA, Sept. 4, 1962, Age 77

O'CONNOR, Rod
Actor, Announcer
b. Unknown
d. Hollywood, CA, June 5, 1964, Age 51

O'CONNOR, Una
Actress
b. Belfast, Ireland, Oct. 23, 1880
d. New York, NY, Feb. 4, 1959, Age 78

O'DALY, Cormac (Dick Forbes)
Playwright
b. Unknown
d. Unknown, Aug. 29, 1949, Age 55

O'DAY, Alice
Actress
b. Unknown
d. Unknown, Dec. 7, 1937

ODELL, E. J.
Actor
b. Unknown
d. Unknown, May 26, 1928, Age 93

ODELL, George Clinton Densmore
Historian
b. Newburgh, NY, March 16, 1866
d. New York, NY, Oct. 17, 1949, Age 82

ODELL, Maude
Actress
b. Beaufort, SC, Unknown
d. New York, NY, Feb. 27, 1937, Age 65

ODELL, Thomas
Producer, Playwright
b. Unknown
d. Unknown, May 24, 1749, Age 58

O'DEMPSEY, Brigit (Mrs. W. S. Fay)
Actress
b. Unknown
d. London, England, Dec. 1, 1952, Age 65

ODETS, Clifford
Playwright, Director, Actor
b. Philadelphia, PA, July 18, 1906
d. Los Angeles, CA, Aug. 14, 1963, Age 57

ODILON, Helene
Actress
b. Unknown
d. Unknown, Feb. 9, 1939, Age 75

ODINGSELLS, Gabriel
Playwright
b. Unknown
d. Unknown, Feb. 10, 1734, Age 44

O'DONNELL, Charles H.
Performer
b. Unknown
d. Pompano Beach, FL, Sept. 10, 1962, Age 76

O'DONOVAN, Fred
Actor, Director
b. Dublin, Ireland, Oct. 14, 1889
d. Unknown, July 19, 1952, Age 62

OEHLENSCHLAEGER, Adam Gottlob
Poet, Playwright
b. Vesterbro, Denmark, 1779
d. Unknown, 1850

OELRICHS, Blanche (Michael Strange)
Actress, Author
b. Unknown
d. Unknown, Nov. 5, 1950, Age 60

OENSLAGER, Donald
Designer
b. Harrisburg, PA, March 7, 1902
d. Waccabuc, NY, June 21, 1975, Age 73

O'FARRELL, Talbot
Performer
b. Unknown
d. Unknown, Sept. 2, 1952, Age 72

OFFENBACH, Jacques
Composer
b. Cologne, Germany, June 20, 1819
d. Paris, France, Oct. 4, 1880, Age 61

OFFERMAN, George Sr.
Actor
b. Unknown
d. Hollywood, CA, March 5, 1938, Age 58

OFFERMAN, George Jr.
Actor
b. Chicago, IL, Unknown
d. New York, NY, Jan. 14, 1963, Age 45

OGILVIE, Glencairn Stuart
Playwright
b. Haslemere, Surrey, England, March 27, 1858
d. Unknown, March 7, 1932, Age 73

O'HANLON, Redmond L.
Policeman, Shakespearean authority
b. Unknown
d. West New Brighton, NY, July 3, 1964, Age 48

O'HARA, Fiske
Singer, Actor
b. Ireland, Unknown
d. Hollywood, CA, Aug. 2, 1945, Age 67

O'HARA, John
Actor
b. Unknown
d. St. Kilda, Australia, July 15, 1929, Age 70

O'HARA, John
Writer
b. Pottsville, PA, Jan. 31, 1905
d. Princeton, NJ, April 11, 1970, Age 65

O'HARA, Kane
Playwright
b. Unknown
d. Unknown, June 17, 1782, Age 69

O'HIGGINS, Harvey J.
Playwright
b. London, Ontario, CAN, Nov. 14, 1876
d. Unknown, Feb. 28, 1929, Age 52

OHNET, Georges
Playwright
b. Paris, France, April 3, 1848
d. Unknown, May 5, 1918, Age 70

O'KEEFFE, John
Playwright
b. Ireland, 1747
d. Unknown, Feb. 4, 1833, Age 85

OKEY, Jack
Art director
b. Unknown
d. Hollywood, CA, Jan. 8, 1963, Age 75

OLAND, Warner
Actor
b. Umea, Vesterbotten, Sweden, Oct. 3, 1880
d. Stockholm, Sweden, Aug. 6, 1938, Age 57

OLCOTT, Chauncey (Chancellor John Olcott)
Actor, Singer, Songwriter
b. Buffalo, NY, July 21, 1858
d. Monte Carlo, Monaco, March 18, 1932, Age 73

OLCOTT, Sidney (John S. Alcott)
Director, Actor
b. Unknown
d. Hollywood, CA, Dec. 16, 1949, Age 76

OLDFIELD, Anne ("Nance")
Actress
b. London, England, 1683
d. London, England, Oct. 23, 1730, Age 47

OLDHAM, Derek
Actor, Singer
b. Accrington, England, March 29, 1892
d. England, March 20, 1968, Age 75

OLDMIXON, John
Playwright
b. Unknown
d. Unknown, July 9, 1742, Age 69

OLDMIXON, Mrs. (née Georgina Sidus)
Actress, Teacher
b. Unknown
d. Unknown, 1835/6

OLESEN, Otto K.
Lighting equipment expert
b. Denmark, Unknown
d. Hollywood, CA, Jan. 5, 1964, Age 72

OLIVE, Edyth
Actress
b. Newton Abbot, Devonshire, England, Unknown
d. London, England, Nov. 7, 1956, Age 84

OLIVER, Edna May (née Nutter)
Actress
b. Malden, MA, Sept. 1885
d. Hollywood, CA, Nov. 9, 1942, Age 57

OLIVER, Olive
Actress
b. California, Unknown
d. San Francisco, CA, Nov. 7, 1961, Age 90

OLIVER, Vic (Viktor Olivier Samek)
Performer, Musician
b. Vienna, Austria, 1898
d. Johannesburg, South Africa, Aug. 15, 1964, Age 66

OLLENDORF, Paul
Publisher
b. Unknown
d. Unknown, Dec. 18, 1920

OLSEN, Moroni
Actor, Director
b. Ogden, UT, Unknown
d. Los Angeles, CA, Nov. 22, 1954, Age 65

OLSEN, Ole (John Siguard Olsen)
Performer
b. Peru, IN, Nov. 6, 1892
d. Albuquerque, NM, Jan. 26, 1963, Age 70

OLVER, Hal
Press representative
b. Unknown
d. New York, NY, Jan. 21, 1963, Age 70

O'MALLEY, Rex
Actor, Director
b. London, Jan. 2, 1901
d. New York City, NY, May 1, 1976, Age 75

O'NEIL, Peggy
Actress
b. Gneeveguilla, Co. Kerry, Ireland, June 16, 1898
d. London, England, Jan. 7, 1960, Age 61

O'NEILL, Eugene Gladstone
Playwright
b. New York, NY, Oct. 16, 1888
d. Boston, MA, Nov. 27, 1953, Age 65

O'NEILL, Frank B.
Business manager
b. Cranbrook, Kent, England, Oct. 31, 1869
d. Unknown, Dec. 28, 1959, Age 90

O'NEILL, Henry Joseph
Actor
b. Orange, NJ, Unknown
d. Hollywood, CA, May 18, 1961, Age 69

O'NEILL, James
Actor
b. Kilkenny, Ireland, Nov. 15, 1847
d. New London, CT, Aug. 10, 1920, Age 72

O'NEILL, James Jr.
Actor
b. Unknown
d. Trenton, NJ, Nov. 8, 1923, Age 43

O'NEILL, Joseph J.
Performer
b. Unknown
d. Bridgeport, CT, Aug. 26, 1962, Age 66

O'NEILL, Maire (née Allgood)
Actress
b. Dublin, Ireland, 1887
d. London, England, Nov. 2, 1952, Age 65

O'NEILL, Norman
Composer, Conductor
b. London, England, March 14, 1875
d. Unknown, March 3, 1934, Age 58

O'NEILL, Sally
Actress
b. Bayonne, NJ, Oct. 23, 1912
d. Galesburg, IL, June 18, 1968, Age 55

ONOE, Kikugoro
Actor, Teacher
b. Tokyo, Japan, 1885
d. Unknown, 1949

OPERTI, LeRoi
Singer - Actor
b. Boston, MA, Dec. 9, 1895
d. New York, NY, June 22, 1971, Age 75

OPP, Julie (Mrs. William Faversham)
Actress
b. New York, NY, Jan. 28, 1871
d. New York, NY, April 8, 1921, Age 50

ORBASANY, Irma (Mrs. Ernest Garrett)
Performer
b. Unknown
d. Ashurst, England, 1961, Age 95

ORCZY, Baroness Emmuska (Mrs. Montague Barstow)
Playwright, Novelist
b. Tarnäors, Hungary, Unknown
d. London, England, Nov. 12, 1947, Age 80

ORD, Simon
Producer
b. Muirhouselaw, Scotland, Feb. 15, 1874
d. Unknown, May 11, 1944, Age 70

ORDONNEAU, Maurice
Playwright
b. Saintes, France, June 18, 1854
d. Unknown, Dec. 1916, Age 62

ORME, Denise (Duchess of Leinster Née Jessie Smither)
Actress
b. Unknown, Aug. 26, 1884
d. London, England, Oct. 20, 1960, Age 76

ORME, Michael Mrs. J. T. Grein Née Alice Augusta Greeven)
Actress, Playwright, Critic
b. Unknown, 1894
d. London, England, July 16, 1944, Age 50

O'RORKE, Brefni
Actor
b. Unknown
d. Unknown, Nov. 11, 1946, Age 57

O'ROURKE, J. A.
Actor
b. Unknown
d. Unknown, June 17, 1937, Age 55

O'ROURKE, Tex
Performer, Promotor
b. Ysleta, TX, Unknown
d. New York, NY, May 14, 1963, Age 77

ORR, Christine (Mrs. Robin Stark)
Playwright, Novelist
b. Unknown
d. Edinburgh, Scotland, May 1963, Age 63

ORR, Forrest H.
Performer
b. Dallas, TX, Unknown
d. Paterson, NJ, April 20, 1963, Age 63

ORRY-KELLY
Costume designer
b. Kaima, Australia, Unknown
d. Hollywood, CA, Feb. 26, 1964, Age 67

ORSKA, Marie
Actress
b. Unknown
d. Unknown, May 16, 1930

ORTH, Frank
Actor
b. Unknown
d. Hollywood, CA, March 17, 1962, Age 82

ORTON, Joe
Playwright
b. Leicester, England, Unknown
d. London, England, Aug. 9, 1967, Age 34

OSBORN, E. W.
Critic
b. Winthrop, ME, Oct. 24, 1860
d. Unknown, May 4, 1930, Age 69

OSBORNE, Lennie (Bud)
Actor
b. Unknown
d. Hollywood, CA, Feb. 2, 1964, Age 79

OSBOURNE, Lloyd
Playwright, Novelist
b. San Francisco, CA, Unknown
d. Glendale, CA, May 23, 1947, Age 79

OSGOOD, Charles
Manager
b. Unknown
d. New York, NY, May 26, 1922, Age 63

OSHINS, Julie
Actor
b. Brooklyn, NY, Unknown
d. New York, NY, May 9, 1956, Age 50

OSTERMAN, Kathryn (Mrs. Jacob Rosenthal)
Actress
b. Unknown
d. New York, NY, Aug. 25, 1956, Age 73

OSTERWA, Juliusz
Actor, Director, Producer
b. Poland, 1885
d. Poland, 1947

OSTLER, William
Actor
b. Unknown, 1601-20

OSTROVSKY, Alexander Nicholayevitch
Playwright
b. Moscow, Russia, April 12, 1823
d. Moscow, Russia, June 14, 1886, Age 63

OTIS, Elita Proctor
Actress
b. Cleveland, OH, Unknown
d. Pelham, NY, Aug. 13, 1927, Age 76

OTWAY, Grace
Actress
b. Unknown
d. Unknown, May 6, 1935

OTWAY, Thomas
Playwright
b. Sussex, England, 1651
d. Unknown, April 14, 1685, Age 34

OULD, Hermon
Playwright, Author
b. London, England, Dec. 14, 1885
d. London, England, Sept. 21, 1951, Age 64

OULTON, W. C.
Historian
b. Unknown
d. Unknown, 1820, Age 50

OURSLER, Fulton
Playwright, Novelist, Editor
b. Baltimore, MD, Jan. 22, 1893
d. New York, NY, May 24, 1952, Age 59

OUSPENSKAYA, Maria
Actress, Teacher
b. Tula, Russia, July 29, 1876
d. Hollywood, CA, Dec. 3, 1949, Age 73

OVERMAN, Lynne
Actor
b. Maryville, MO, Sept. 19, 1887
d. Hollywood, CA, Feb. 19, 1943, Age 55

OVERTON, Frank
Actor
b. Babylon, NY, March 12, 1918
d. Pacific Palisades, CA, April 24, 1967, Age 49

OWEN, Harold
Playwright
b. Burslem, Staffordshire, England, May 3, 1872
d. Unknown, May 10, 1930, Age 58

OWEN, Reginald
Actor
b. Hertfordshire, England, Aug. 5, 1887
d. Boise, ID, Nov. 5, 1972, Age 85

OWENS, John Edmond
Actor
b. London, England, 1823
d. Unknown, 1886

OWENS, William
Actor
b. Unknown
d. Chicago, IL, Aug. 20, 1926, Age 63

OXBERRY, William
Actor, Biographer, Publisher
b. Unknown, Dec. 18, 1784
d. London, England, June 9, 1824, Age 39

OXBERRY, William Henry
Actor, Playwright
b. London, England, April 21, 1808
d. London, England, 1852

OXENFORD, Edward
Playwright, Librettist
b. Unknown
d. Unknown, March 21, 1929, Age 82

OXENFORD, John
Playwright, Critic
b. Camberwell, Surrey, England, 1812
d. Unknown, Feb. 21, 1877, Age 64

OYSHER, Moishe
Actor, Cantor
b. Lipkon, Bessarabia, Unknown
d. New Rochelle, NY, Nov. 27, 1958, Age 51

OZELL, John
Playwright
b. Unknown
d. Unknown, Oct. 15, 1743

P

PACKER, Netta
Performer
b. Unknown
d. Hollywood, CA, Nov. 7, 1962, Age 65

PAGDEN, Leonard
Actor
b. Unknown
d. Unknown, March 24, 1928, Age 66

PAGE, Ashley
Actor
b. Unknown
d. Unknown, Oct. 18, 1934, Age 67

PAGE, Norman
Actor, Director
b. Nottingham, England, Unknown
d. Unknown, July 4, 1935, Age 59

PAGE, Philip
Critic, Writer
b. St. Alban's, England, July 17, 1889
d. England, Dec. 1968, Age 80

PAGE, Rita
Actress
b. London, England, Aug. 16, 1906
d. Unknown, Dec. 19, 1954, Age 48

PAGE, Will A.
Press representative
b. Unknown
d. New York, NY, July 20, 1928, Age 55

PAGET, Cecil
Theatre manager
b. Unknown
d. Unknown, March 26, 1955

PAGNOL, Marcel
Playwright - Director
b. Marseilles, France, Feb. 28, 1895
d. Paris, France, April 18, 1974, Age 79

PAIGE, Mabel (née Roberts)
Actress
b. New York, NY, Unknown
d. Van Nuys, CA, Feb. 8, 1954, Age 74

PAILLERON, Edouard
Playwright
b. Unknown, 1834
d. Unknown, April 20, 1899, Age 65

PAINTER, Eleanor (Mrs. Charles H. Strong)
Singer, Actress
b. Walkerville, IA, 1890
d. Cleveland, OH, Nov. 4, 1947, Age 57

PALETTE, Billy (William Robinson)
Performer
b. Bradford, England, Unknown
d. Leicester, England, 1963

PALFREY, May Lever (Mrs. Weedon Grossmith)
Actress
b. England, May 1, 1867
d. England, Oct. 31, 1929, Age 62

PALLADIO, Andrea
Architect
b. Unknown, 1518
d. Unknown, 1580

PALLANT, Walter
Playwright
b. Unknown
d. Unknown, Aug. 2, 1904, Age 45

PALLENBERG, Max
Actor
b. Unknown, 1877
d. Unknown, June 26, 1934, Age 57

PALLETTE, Eugene
Actor
b. Winfield, KS, Unknown
d. Los Angeles, CA, Sept. 3, 1954, Age 65

PALMER, Albert Marshman
Producer
b. North Stonington, CT, July 27, 1838
d. New York, NY, March 7, 1905, Age 66

PALMER, Charles
Critic, Journalist
b. Unknown, Sept. 9, 1869
d. Unknown, Oct. 25, 1920, Age 51

PALMER, John Leslie
Critic, Author
b. Oxford, England, Sept. 4, 1885
d. Hampstead, England, Aug. 5, 1944, Age 58

PALMER, Minnie
Actress
b. Philadelphia, PA, March 31, 1860
d. Bay Shore, L.I., NY, May 21, 1936, Age 76

PANETTA, George
Playwright
b. New York, NY, Aug. 6, 1915
d. Brooklyn, NY, Oct. 16, 1969, Age 54

PANGBORN, Franklin
Actor
b. Newark, NJ, Unknown
d. Santa Monica, CA, July 20, 1958, Age about 65

PANZER, Paul W.
Actor
b. Unknown
d. Hollywood, CA, Aug. 15, 1958, Age 86

PARAGA, Marco
Playwright
b. Milan, Italy, 1862
d. Unknown, Jan. 31, 1929, Age 66

PARKE, Walter
Playwright
b. Unknown
d. Unknown, Dec. 6, 1922

PARKER, Cecil
Actor
b. Hastings, England, Sept. 3, 1897
d. Brighton, England, April 21, 1971, Age 73

PARKER, Dorothy (née Dorothy Rothschild)
Author, Lyricist, Playwright, Poet
b. West End, NJ, Aug. 22, 1893
d. New York, NY, June 7, 1967, Age 73

PARKER, Flora
Actress
b. Unknown
d. Hollywood, CA, Sept. 9, 1950, Age 67

PARKER, Frank
Stage manager, Director
b. Unknown, Feb. 17, 1862
d. Unknown, Dec. 20, 1926, Age 64

PARKER, George D.
Producer, Director
b. Unknown
d. Unknown, May 29, 1937, Age 64

PARKER, Henry Taylor (H.T.P.)
Critic
b. Boston, MA, April 29, 1867
d. Boston, MA, March 29, 1934, Age 66

PARKER, John
Theatrical Journalist, Historian, Editor
b. New York, NY, July 28, 1875
d. London, England, Nov. 18, 1952, Age 77

PARKER, Lew
Actor
b. Brooklyn, NY, Oct. 29, 1907
d. New York, NY, Oct. 27, 1972, Age 64

PARKER, Lottie Blair
Actress, Playwright
b. Oswego, NY, Unknown
d. Great Neck, NY, Jan. 5, 1937, Age 78

PARKER, Louis Napoleon
Playwright, Composer
b. Calvados, France, Oct. 21, 1852
d. Devonshire, England, Sept. 21, 1944, Age 91

PARKER, Sir Gilbert
Novelist, Playwright
b. Camden East, Ontario, CAN, Unknown
d. London, England, Sept. 6, 1932, Age 69

PARKHIRST, Douglass
Actor, Author
b. Unknown
d. New York, NY, May 20, 1964, Age 50

PARNELL, James
Actor
b. Unknown
d. Hollywood, CA, Dec. 27, 1961, Age 38

PARRISH, Helen
Actress
b. Columbus, GA, Unknown
d. Hollywood, CA, Feb. 22, 1959, Age 35

PARRY, Sefton Henry
Producer
b. Unknown
d. Unknown, Dec. 18, 1887, Age 65

PARRY, Sir Edward Abbott (Judge Parry)
Playwright
b. Unknown
d. Unknown, Dec. 1, 1943, Age 80

PARRY, Tom
Actor, Playwright
b. Unknown
d. Unknown, Dec. 5, 1862, Age 56

PARSLOE, Charles T.
Actor
b. Unknown
d. Unknown, Jan. 22, 1898, Age 61

PARSONS, Allan
Critic
b. London, England, March 6, 1888
d. Unknown, Jan. 15, 1933, Age 44

PARSONS, Percy
Actor
b. Louisville, KY, June 12, 1878
d. Unknown, Oct. 3, 1944, Age 66

PASCAL, André
(Baron Henri de Rothschild), Playwright, Producer
b. Unknown
d. Unknown

PASCAL, Ernest
Screen writer, Playwright, Author, Union exec.
b. London, England, Jan. 11, 1896
d. Los Angeles, CA, Nov. 4, 1966, Age 70

PASCAL, Gabriel (Gabor Pascal)
Director
b. Hungary, 1894
d. New York, NY, July 6, 1954, Age 60

PASCOE, Charles Eyre
Editor
b. Unknown
d. Unknown, Nov. 9, 1912, Age 70

PASSMORE, Walter
Actor
b. London, England, May 10, 1867
d. Unknown, Aug. 29, 1946, Age 79

PASTON, George (Emily Morse Symonds)
Playwright, Novelist
b. Unknown
d. London, England, Sept. 11, 1936

PASTOR, Tony (Antonio)
Producer, Performer, etc.
b. New York, NY, May 1837
d. Unknown, Aug. 26, 1908, Age 71

PATEMAN, Robert
Actor
b. Unknown, Oct. 17, 1840
d. Unknown, June 8, 1924, Age 83

PATHE, Charles
Producer, Film executive
b. Paris, France, Unknown
d. Monte Carlo, Monaco, Dec. 25 , 1957, Age 94

PATRICK, Jerome
Actor
b. New Zealand, Unknown
d. New York, NY, Sept. 26, 1923, Age 40

PATRICOLA, Tom
Actor, Director
b. New Orleans, LA, Jan. 22, 1891
d. Pasadena, CA, Jan. 1, 1950, Age 58

PATSTON, Doris (Mrs. Doris Sheeyan or Sheehan)
Actress
b. Islington, England, Unknown
d. New York, NY, June 12, 1957, Age 53

PATTERSON, Ada
Critic
b. Unknown
d. Unknown, June 26, 1939

PATTERSON, Elizabeth
Actress
b. Savannah, TN, Nov. 22, 1874
d. Los Angeles, CA, Jan. 31, 1966, Age 91

PATTERSON, James
Actor
b. Derry, PA, June 29, 1932
d. New York, NY, Aug. 19, 1972, Age 40

PATTERSON, Joseph Medill
Publisher, Novelist, Playwright
b. Chicago, IL, Jan. 6, 1879
d. New York, NY, May 26, 1946, Age 67

PATTERSON, Marjorie
Actress
b. Unknown
d. Unknown, March 12, 1948, Age 61

PAUKER, Dr. Edmond
Literary representative
b. Budapest, Hungary, Unknown
d. New York, NY, May 6, 1962, Age 74

PAUL, Howard
Playwright, Performer
b. Unknown
d. Unknown, Dec. 9, 1905, Age 75

PAUL, Mrs. Howard (Isabella Featherstone)
Actress
b. Unknown
d. Unknown, June 6, 1879, Age 46

PAULDING, Frederick (Dodge)
Actor, Author
b. West Point, NY, Jan. 22, 1859
d. Rutherford, NJ, Sept. 6, 1937, Age 78

PAULL, Harry Major
Playwright
b. Monmouth, England, Jan. 6, 1854
d. Unknown, Nov. 29, 1934, Age 80

PAULO, Signor
Clown
b. Unknown
d. Unknown, July 27, 1835, Age 48

PAULTON, Edward Antonio
Playwright, Lyricist
b. Glasgow, Scotland, Unknown
d. Hollywood, CA, March 20, 1939, Age 73

PAULTON, Harry
Actor, Playwright
b. Wolverhampton, England, March 16, 1842
d. Unknown, April 17, 1917, Age 75

PAULTON, Tom
Actor, Playwright
b. Unknown
d. Unknown, March 25, 1914, Age 76

PAUMIER, Alfred
Actor, Playwright
b. Liverpool, England, Nov. 14, 1870
d. Unknown, Jan. 25, 1951, Age 80

PAUNCEFORT, Claire
Actress
b. Unknown
d. Unknown, Nov. 23, 1924

PAUNCEFORT, George
Actor
b. Unknown
d. Los Angeles, CA, March 25, 1942, Age 72

PAUNCEFORT, Georgina
Actress
b. Unknown
d. Unknown, Dec. 19, 1895, Age 70

PAWLE, J. Lennox
Actor
b. London, England, April 27, 1872
d. Hollywood, CA, Feb. 22, 1936, Age 63

PAWLEY, William
Actor
b. Kansas City, MO, Unknown
d. New York, NY, June 15, 1952, Age 47

PAWSON, Hargrave
Actor
b. England, Dec. 6, 1902
d. Unknown, Jan. 26, 1945, Age 42

PAXINOV, Katina
Actress
b. Piraeus, Greece, 1900
d. Athens, Greece, Feb. 22, 1973, Age 72

PAXTON, Sydney (Sydney Paxton Hood)
Actor, Producer
b. London, England, June 25, 1860
d. Unknown, Oct. 13, 1930, Age 70

PAYNE, B. Iden
Director, Producer, Educator
b. Newcastle-on-Tyne, England, Sept. 5, 1881
d. Austin, TX, April 6, 1976, Age 94

PAYNE, Edmund
Actor
b. Unknown, 1865
d. Unknown, July 1, 1914, Age 49

PAYNE, George Adney
Producer
b. Unknown
d. Unknown, May 15, 1907, Age 60

PAYNE, John Howard
Performer, Playwright
b. New York, NY, 1791
d. Tunis, North Africa, April 9, 1852, Age 60

PAYNE, Walter
Producer, Theatre executive
b. London, England, Unknown
d. Unknown, Oct. 30, 1949, Age 76

PAYNE, William Louis
Actor
b. Elmira, NY, Unknown
d. Hollywood, CA, Aug. 14, 1953, Age 80

PAYNE-JENNINGS, Victor
Producer
b. Ashstead, Surrey, England, May 2, 1900
d. New York, NY, June 17, 1962, Age 62

PAYNTON, Harry
Performer
b. Unknown
d. Brooklyn, NY, July 26, 1964, Age 74

PAYSON, Blanche
Actress
b. Unknown
d. Hollywood, CA, July 3, 1964, Age 83

PAYTON, Barbara (née Redfield)
Actress
b. Cloquet, MN, Nov. 16, 1927
d. San Diego, CA, May 8, 1967, Age 39

PAYTON, Corse
Actor, Producer
b. Centreville, IA, Dec. 18, 1867
d. Brooklyn, NY, Feb. 23, 1934, Age 66

PEACOCK, Bertram
Performer
b. Philadelphia, PA, Unknown
d. New York, NY, April 28, 1963, Age 79

PEAKE, R. B.
Playwright
b. Unknown
d. Unknown, Oct. 24, 1847, Age 55

PEAL, Gilbert
Performer
b. Lithuania, Unknown
d. Oakland City, IN, Jan. 7, 1964, Age 76

PEARCE, Alice
Actress
b. New York, NY, Oct. 16, 1917
d. Los Angeles, CA, March 3, 1966, Age 48

PEARCE, Sam
Theatre curator
b. Los Angeles, CA, Sept. 12, 1909
d. Lobachsville, PA, Sept. 12, 1971, Age 62

PEARSON, Hesketh
Biographer, Author, Actor
b. Hawford, Worcestershire, England, Feb. 20, 1887
d. London, England, April 9, 1964, Age 77

PEARSON, Leon Morris
Critic, Newscaster
b. Evanston, IL, Oct. 15, 1899
d. New York, NY, April 29, 1963, Age 63

PEARSON, Molly
Actress
b. Edinburgh, Scotland, Unknown
d. Newton, CN, Jan. 26, 1959, Age 83

PEARSON, Virginia
Performer
b. Kentucky, Unknown
d. Los Angeles, CA, June 6, 1958, Age 72

PEELE, George
Playwright, Actor
b. London, England, c1558
d. Unknown, c1598

PEFFER, Crawford A.
Booking Agent
b. Unknown
d. Portland, ME, Dec. 12, 1961, Age 94

PEIL, Charles Edward ("Johnny Jones" a/k/a "Edward Peil, Jr.")
Actor
b. Unknown
d. San Andreas, CA, Nov. 7, 1962, Age 54

PEIL, Edward J.
Actor
b. Unknown
d. Hollywood, CA, Dec. 29, 1958, Age 70

PEILE, Frederick Kinsey
Actor, Playwright
b. Allahabad, India, Dec. 20, 1862
d. Unknown, April 13, 1934, Age 71

PELHAM, Meta
Actress
b. Unknown
d. Unknown, Nov. 29, 1948, Age 98

PELISSIER, Harry Gabriel
Actor, Producer, Composer
b. Finchley, England, 1874
d. Unknown, Sept. 25, 1913, Age 39

PELLY, Farrell
Performer
b. County Galway, Ireland, Unknown
d. New York, NY, April 23, 1963, Age 72

PEMBERTON, Brock
Producer, Director
b. Leavenworth, KS, Dec. 14, 1885
d. New York, NY, March 11, 1950, Age 64

PEMBERTON, Henry W.
Actor
b. Unknown
d. Orlando, FL, July 26, 1952, Age 77

PEMBERTON, John Wyndham
Producer
b. Gwalior, India, Oct. 31, 1883
d. Unknown, Aug. 6, 1947, Age 63

PEMBERTON, Sir Max
Playwright, Journalist, Novelist
b. Birmingham, England, June 19, 1863
d. Unknown, Feb. 22, 1950, Age 86

PEMBERTON, Thomas Edgar
Playwright, Biographer
b. Unknown
d. Unknown, Sept. 28, 1905, Age 56

PENDENNIS, Rose
Actress
b. Unknown
d. Unknown, April 10, 1943

PENLEY, Belville S.
Producer, Author
b. Unknown
d. Unknown, July 26, 1940

PENLEY, Sampson
Actor, Playwright
b. Unknown
d. Unknown, May 28, 1838

PENLEY, William Sydney
Actor, Producer
b. St. Peter's Margate, England, Nov. 19, 1851
d. Unknown, Nov. 11, 1912, Age 61

PENMAN, Lea
Actress
b. Red Cloud, NB, Unknown
d. Hollywood, CA, Oct. 12, 1962, Age 67

PENNICK, Ronald "Jack"
Actor
b. Unknown, Portland,OR
d. Manhattan Beach, CA, Aug. 16, 1964, Age 69

PENNINGTON, Ann
Dancer, Actress
b. Wilmington, DE, Dec. 23, 1893
d. Unknown, Nov. 4, 1971, Age 77

PENNINGTON, W. H.
Actor
b. Unknown
d. Unknown, May 1, 1923, Age 91

PEPUSCH, Dr. John Christopher
Composer
b. Berlin, Germany, 1667
d. England, July 20, 1752, Age 85

PEPYS, Samuel
Diarist
b. London, England, Feb. 23, 1633
d. Clapham, England, May 26, 1703, Age 70

PERCEVAL-CLARK, Perceval
Actor
b. London, England, Nov. 25, 1881
d. Unknown, June 6, 1938, Age 57

PERCIVAL, Horace
Actor
b. Unknown
d. Middlesex, England, Nov. 9, 1961, Age 75

PERCIVAL, Walter C.
Actor, Playwright
b. Chicago, IL, Unknown
d. Hollywood, CA, Jan. 28, 1934, Age 46

PERCY, Edward (Edward Percy Smith)
Playwright
b. London, England, Jan. 5, 1891
d. England, May 28, 1968, Age 77

PERCY, George (George Percy Groves-Raines)
Performer
b. Unknown
d. Guernsey, Channel Islands, England, Dec. 1962, Age 90

PERCY, S. Esmé
Actor, Director
b. London, England, Aug. 8, 1887
d. Brighton, England, June 16, 1957, Age 69

PERCY, William Stratford
Actor
b. Melbourne, Australia, Dec. 23, 1872
d. Unknown, June 19, 1946, Age 73

PERETZ, Isaac Leob
Poet, Writer, Playwright
b. Zamoscz, Poland, 1851
d. Warsaw, Poland, 1915

PEREZ-GALDOS, Benito
Playwright
b. Las Palmas, Canary Islands, Spain, 1845
d. Unknown, Jan. 5, 1920, Age 75

PERICAUD, Louis
Playwright
b. Unknown
d. Unknown, Nov. 12, 1909

PERKINS, David Fessenden
Actor, Author, Playwright
b. Unknown
d. New York, NY, Dec. 31, 1962, Age 77

PERKINS, Osgood
Actor
b. West Newton, MA, May 16, 1892
d. Washington, DC, Sept. 21, 1937, Age 45

PERKINS, Walter E.
Actor
b. Biddeford, ME, Unknown
d. Brooklyn, NY, June 3, 1925, Age 55

PERL, Arnold
Playwright - Producer
b. New York, NY, April 14, 1914
d. New York, NY, Dec. 11, 1971, Age 57

PERLMAN, William J.
Playwright, Director, Producer
b. Unknown
d. New York, NY, Nov. 18, 1954, Age 72

PERMAIN, Fred W.
Actor, Producer
b. Unknown
d. Unknown, Dec. 29, 1933

PERRINS, Leslie
Actor
b. Mosley, Birmingham, England, Unknown
d. Esher, Surrey, England, Dec. 13, 1962, Age 60

PERRY, Albert H.
Actor
b. Detroit, MI, Unknown
d. St. George, S.I., NY, May 6, 1933, Age 63

PERRY, Antoinette (Mrs. Frank W. Frueauff)
Actress, Producer, Director
b. Denver, CO, June 27, 1888
d. New York, NY, June 28, 1946, Age 58

PERRY, Florence
Actress
b. Unknown
d. Unknown, Dec. 19, 1949, Age 80

PERRY, Irma (Irma Hinton Le Gallienne)
Actress
b. Unknown
d. Menton, France, March 15, 1955, Age 79

PERRY, Mary
Actress
b. Gainesville, GA, Unknown
d. New York, NY, March 6, 1971, Age 63

PERRY, Robert E.
Actor, Director
b. Unknown
d. Hollywood, CA, Jan. 8, 1962, Age 83

PERRY, Ronald
Performer
b. Unknown
d. Dublin, Ireland, April 26, 1963, Age 53

PERTWEE, Roland
Playwright, Novelist
b. Brighton, England, 1886(?)
d. London, England, April 26, 1963, Age 78

PERUGINI, Signor (John Chatterton)
Actor
b. England, Unknown
d. Philadelphia, PA, Dec. 4, 1914, Age 59

PETERS, Brandon
Actor
b. Troy, NY, Unknown
d. New York, NY, Feb. 27, 1956, Age 63

PETERS, Charles Rollo
Scene designer, Actor, Director, Producer, Artist
b. Paris, France, Sept. 25, 1892
d. Monterey, CA, Jan. 21, 1967, Age 74

PETERS, Fred (Frederick P. Tuite)
Actor
b. Unknown
d. Hollywood, CA, April 23, 1963, Age 78

PETERS, Rollo
Scenic designer, Actor
b. Paris, France, Sept. 25, 1892
d. Unknown, Jan. 21, 1967, Age 74

PETERS, Susan (Suzanne Carnahan)
Actress
b. Spokane, WA, Unknown
d. Visalia, CA, Oct. 23, 1952, Age 31

PETERSEN, Karen
Actress
b. Unknown
d. Unknown, Feb. 16, 1940, Age 37

PETIPA, Marius
Dancer, Choreographer
b. Unknown, 1822
d. Unknown, July 14, 1910, Age 88

PETLEY, E. S.
Actor
b. Unknown
d. Unknown, June 30, 1945, Age 69

PETLEY, Frank E.
Actor
b. Old Charlton, Kent, England, March 28, 1872
d. Unknown, Jan. 12, 1945, Age 72

PETRASS, Sari
Actress
b. Budapest, Hungary, Nov. 5, 1890
d. Unknown, Sept. 7, 1930, Age 39

PETRIE, David Hay
Actor
b. Dundee, Scotland, July 16, 1895
d. Unknown, July 30, 1948, Age 53

PETTITT, Henry
Playwright
b. Unknown
d. Unknown, Dec. 24, 1893, Age 45

PHARAR, Renée
Actress, Sculptress
b. Unknown
d. New London, CT, Aug. 17, 1962, Age 83

PHELPS, Dodie (Mrs. Irving Newhoff)
Performer
b. Unknown
d. Hollywood, CA, April 6, 1963, Age 65

PHELPS, Leonard P.
Manager
b. Baltimore, MD, Unknown
d. New York, NY, March 15, 1924, Age 73

PHELPS, Samuel
Actor, Producer
b. Unknown, 1804
d. Unknown, Nov. 6, 1878, Age 74

PHILIP, James E.
Actor, Composer
b. Unknown
d. Unknown, June 21, 1910, Age 42

PHILIPE, Gérard
Actor
b. Cannes, France, Dec. 4, 1922
d. Paris, France, Nov. 25, 1959, Age 36

PHILIPP, Adolph (a/k/a Jean Briquet)
Playwright, Composer, Actor
b. Hamburg, Germany, Jan. 29, 1864
d. New York, NY, July 30, 1936, Age 72

PHILIPPI, Herbert M.
Author, Teacher of Stagecraft and Design
b. Columbia, MO, July 12, 1906
d. Bellingham, WA, Dec. 9, 1958, Age 52

PHILIPS, F. C.
Playwright, Novelist, Producer
b. Brighton, England, Feb. 3, 1849
d. Unknown, April 21, 1921, Age 72

PHILIPS, William
Playwright
b. Unknown
d. Unknown, Dec. 12, 1734

PHILLIPS, Acton
Producer
b. Unknown
d. Unknown, July 29, 1940, Age 86

PHILLIPS, Albert
Actor
b. Edwardsville, IN, Unknown
d. New York, NY, Feb 24, 1940, Age 65

PHILLIPS, Jack
Stage Manager, Director
b. Unknown
d. London, England, Feb. 14, 1956, Age 55

PHILLIPS, Kate (née Goldney)
Actress
b. Essex, England, July 28, 1856
d. England, Sept. 9, 1931, Age 75

PHILLIPS, Minna
Performer
b. Sydney, New South Wales, Australia, Unknown
d. New Orleans, LA, Jan. 17, 1963, Age 91

PHILLIPS, Mrs. Alfred
Playwright, Actress
b. Unknown
d. Unknown, Aug. 12, 1876, Age 54

PHILLIPS, Norma
Actress
b. Baltimore, MD, 1893
d. New York, NY, Nov. 11, 1931, Age 38

PHILLIPS, Stephen
Playwright, Poet, Actor
b. Somertown, England, July 28, 1864
d. Unknown, Dec. 9, 1915, Age 51

PHILLIPS, Watts
Playwright
b. Unknown
d. Unknown, Dec. 2, 1874, Age 45

PHILLPOTTS, Eden
Playwright, Novelist
b. Mount Aboo, India, Nov. 4, 1862
d. Unknown, Dec. 29,1960, Age 98

PHYSIOC, Joseph Allen
Scenic artist
b. Richmond, VA, Unknown
d. Columbia, SC, Aug. 3, 1951, Age 86

PIAF, Edith (Edith Giovanna Gassion)
Singer
b. Paris, France, Dec. 19, 1915
d. Paris, France, Oct. 11, 1963, Age 47

PICARD, André
Playwright
b. Unknown, Paris, France
d. 1874

PICARD, Louis Baptiste
Playwright, Actor, Founder Odéon Th.
b. Unknown, 1769
d. Unknown, 1828

PICHEL, Irving
Actor, Film director
b. Pittsburgh, PA, Unknown
d. La Canada, CA, July 13, 1954, Age 63

PICKARD, Helena (Mrs. Cedric Hardwicke)
Actress
b. Handsworth, Sheffield, Yorkshire, England, Oct. 13, 1900
d. Reading, England, Sept. 27, 1959, Age 58

PICKARD, Mae (Former Countess Cowley)
Actress
b. Unknown
d. Unknown, June 3, 1946

PICKERING, J. Russell
Producer
b. Unknown
d. Unknown, April 16, 1947, Age 67

PICKETT, Ingram B.
Actor, Politician
b. Unknown
d. Santa Fe, NM, Feb. 14, 1963, Age 64

PICKFORD, Jack (Jack Smith)
Actor, Producer
b. Toronto, CAN, Unknown
d. Paris, France, Jan. 3, 1933, Age 36

PICKFORD, Lottie (Smith)
Actress
b. Toronto, CAN, 1895
d. Beverly Hills, CA, Dec. 9, 1936, Age 41

PIDDOCK, J. C.
Actor
b. Unknown
d. Unknown, Dec. 3, 1919, Age 56

PIDGEON, Edward Everett
Drama editor
b. Charlottestown, Nova Scotia, Unknown
d. New York, NY, Aug. 30, 1941, Age 75

PIERAT, Marie-Thérèse (né e Pelletier)
Actress
b. Paris, France, Unknown
d. Unknown, May 30, 1934, Age 48

PIERLOT, Francis
Actor
b. Unknown
d. Hollywood, CA, May 11, 1955, Age 79

PIGOTT, Tempe
Performer
b. Unknown
d. Hollywood, CA, Oct. 13, 1962, Age 78

PILCER, Harry
Dancer, Performer
b. New York, NY, Unknown
d. Cannes, France, Jan. 14, 1961, Age 75

PILGRIM, James
Playwright, Actor, Stage manager
b. Bromley, Kent, England, Dec. 7, 1825
d. Philadelphia, PA, March 14, 1877, Age 51

PINCHOT, Rosamond
Actress
b. New York, NY, Oct. 26, 1904
d. Old Brookville, NY, Jan. 24, 1938, Age 33

PINDER, Powis
Actor
b. Unknown
d. Unknown, July 25, 1941, Age 68

PINERO, Sir Arthur Wing
Playwright, Actor
b. Islington, London, England, May 24, 1855
d. London, England, Nov. 23, 1934, Age 79

PINK, Wal (Walter Augustus Pink)
Playwright, Actor
b. London, England, Unknown
d. Unknown, Oct. 27, 1922, Age 60

PINKARD, Maceo
Composer
b. Unknown
d. New York, NY, July 19, 1962, Age 65

PINO, Rosario
Actress
b. Unknown
d. Unknown, July 15, 1933

PINZA, Ezio
Singer
b. Rome, Italy, May 18, 1892
d. Stamford, CT, May 9, 1957, Age 64

PIRANDELLO, Luigi
Author, Producer, Novelist, Poet
b. Girgenti, Sicily, June 28, 1867
d. Rome, Italy, Dec. 10, 1936, Age 69

PIRANESI, Giovanni Battista
Designer
b. Unknown, 1720
d. Unknown, 1778

PISCATOR, Erwin Friedrich Max
Producer, Director, Playwright
b. Ulm, Kreis Werzlar, Germany, Dec. 17, 1893
d. Starnberg, Bavaria, Germany, March 30, 1966, Age 72

PISEMSKY, Alexei Feofilaktovich
Novelist, Actor, Playwright
b. near Moscow, Russia, 1820
d. Unknown, 1881

PITMAN, Richard
Actor, Talent representative
b. Boston, MA, Unknown
d. Jamaica, NY, Nov. 13, 1941, Age 67

PITOEFF, Georges
Actor, Producer, Director
b. Tiflis, Russia, 1885
d. Geneva, Switzerland, Sept. 18, 1939, Age 54

PITOEFF, Ludmilla
Performer
b. Tiflis, Russia, 1896
d. Rueil near Paris, France, Sept. 15, 1951, Age 55

PITOU, Augustus
Producer, Playwright
b. New York, NY, Feb. 23, 1843
d. Unknown, Dec. 4, 1915, Age 72

PITT, Archie (née Selinger)
Actor, Director
b. Unknown, 1885
d. Unknown, Nov. 12, 1940, Age 55

PITT, Fanny Addison
Actress
b. England, Unknown
d. Philadelphia, PA, Jan. 7, 1937, Age 93

PITT, Felix
Actor
b. Unknown
d. Unknown, June 1922

PITTS, Zasu (Eliza Susan Pitts) Mrs. John E. Woodall)
Actress
b. Parsons, KS, Jan. 3, 1898
d. Hollywood, CA, June 7, 1963, Age 65

PIXERECOURT, René Charles Guilbert
Playwright
b. Unknown
d. 1773, Unknown, Age 1844

PIXLEY, Frank
Composer, Playwright
b. Richfield, OH, Nov. 21, 1867
d. San Diego, CA, Dec. 31, 1919, Age 52

PLACIDE, Caroline (Mrs. William Rufus Blake)
Actress
b. Unknown
d. Unknown, May 21, 1881

PLACIDE, Henry
Actor
b. Unknown, 1799
d. New York, NY, Jan. 23, 1870, Age 70

PLANCHE, James Robinson
Playwright, Scholar
b. London, England, Feb. 27, 1796
d. London, England, May 30, 1880, Age 84

PLANK, Thomas C.
Performer
b. Unknown
d. New York, NY, Oct. 19, 1962, Age 34

PLATO
Author, Philosopher, Critic
b. Athens, Greece, 428/427 B.C.
d. Unknown, 348/347 B.C., Age 80

PLATT, Joseph B.
Designer, Art director
b. Plainfield, NJ, March 26, 1895
d. Wayne, PA, Feb. 6, 1968, Age 72

PLAUTUS, (Titus Maccuis)
Playwright, Poet, Actor
b. Sarsina, Umbria, c254 B.C.
d. Unknown, 184 B.C., Age 70

PLAYFAIR, Arthur
Actor
b. Elichpoor, India, Oct 20, 1869
d. Unknown, Aug. 28, 1918, Age 48

PLAYFAIR, Sir Nigel
Actor, Playwright, Producer, Director
b. London, England, July 1, 1874
d. London, England, Aug. 19, 1934, Age 60

PLEASANT, Richard
Press representative
b. Denver, CO, Unknown
d. New York, NY, July 4, 1961, Age 52

PLYMPTON, Eben
Actor
b. Boston, MA, Feb. 7, 1853
d. Unknown, April 12, 1915, Age 62

POCOCK, Isaac
Playwright, Painter
b. Unknown, 1782
d. Unknown, Aug. 24, 1835

PODESTA, Italo
Conductor
b. Unknown
d. Parma, Italy, Aug. 15, 1964, Age 79

POE, Edgar Allen
Critic, Poet, Author
b. Boston, MA, Jan. 19, 1809
d. Baltimore, MD, Oct. 7, 1849, Age 40

POEL, William (Pole)
Shakespearean Director, Actor, Producer
b. London, England, July 22, 1852
d. Unknown, Dec. 13, 1934, Age 82

POGANY, Willy
Designer
b. Szeged, Hungary, Unknown
d. New York, NY, July 30, 1955, Age 72

POGODIN, Nikolai F.
Playwright
b. Unknown
d. Moscow, USSR, Sept. 19, 1962, Age 61

POINTER, Sidney
Actor
b. Unknown
d. Unknown, May 16, 1955

POISSON, Paul
Actor
b. Unknown, 1658
d. Unknown, 1735

POISSON, Raymond ("Belleroche")
Actor, Playwright
b. Unknown, c1630
d. Unknown, 1690

POLACEK, Louis Vask
Performer
b. New York, NY, Oct. 30, 1920
d. Baltimore, MD, March 11, 1963, Age 42

POLAIRE, Mlle. (Emilie Marie Bouchard)
Actress, Singer
b. Agha, Algeria, May 13, 1879
d. Champigny-sur-Marne, France, Oct. 14, 1939, Age 60

POLAN, Lou
Actor
b. Ukraine, Russia, June 15, 1904
d. Freeport, ME, March 3, 1976, Age 71

POLGAR, Alfred
Playwright
b. Vienna, Austria, Unknown
d. Zurich, Switzerland, April 24, 1955, Age 81

POLINI, Emily
Actress
b. Unknown
d. Unknown, July 31, 1927

POLINI, G. M.
Producer
b. Unknown
d. Unknown, Sept. 22, 1914, Age 63

POLINI, Marie (Mrs. Owen Nares)
Actress
b. Shoreham, Sussex, England, Unknown
d. Unknown, May 1960

POLLACK, Lew
Songwriter
b. New York, NY, Unknown
d. Los Angeles, CA, Jan. 18, 1946, Age 50

POLLARD, Harry
Director, Actor
b. Republic City, KS, Unknown
d. Pasadena, CA, July 6, 1934, Age 55

POLLARD, Harry (Snub)
Performer
b. Melbourne, Australia, Unknown
d. Burbank, CA, Jan. 19, 1962, Age 72

POLLOCK, Allan
Actor
b. London, England, Unknown
d. England, Jan. 18, 1942, Age 64

POLLOCK, Anna (Marble)
Press representative, Author
b. Chicago, IL, Unknown
d. New York, NY, March 31, 1946, Age 65

POLLOCK, Channing
Playwright
b. Washington, DC, March 4, 1880
d. Shoreham, L.I., NY, Aug. 17, 1946, Age 66

POLLOCK, Gordon W.
Producer
b. Unknown
d. Lake Erie, April 15, 1956, Age 28

POLLOCK, Horace
Actor
b. Unknown
d. London, England, Jan. 11, 1964, Age 92

POLLOCK, John
Theatrical representative and manager
b. Salt Lake City, UT, Unknown
d. New York, NY, July 29, 1945, Age 64

POLLOCK, Louis
Screenwriter, Press representative
b. Unknown
d. Hollywood, CA, Aug. 23, 1964, Age 60

POLLOCK, William
Critic
b. Eastbourne, England, Nov. 21, 1881
d. Unknown, Oct. 27, 1944, Age 62

POLO, Eddie
Actor, Acrobat
b. Unknown
d. Hollywood, CA, June 14, 1961, Age 86

POMEROY, Jay (Joseph Pomeranz)
Director
b. Theodosia, Crimea, Russia, April 13, 1895
d. Unknown, June 1, 1955, Age 60

PONCIN, Marcel
Actor
b. Unknown
d. Unknown, June 8, 1953

POND, Anson Phelps
Playwright
b. Unknown
d. New York, NY, Jan. 22, 1920, Age 71

PONISI, Madame (né e Elizabeth Hanson)
Actress
b. Huddersfield, Yorkshire, England, Dec. 15, 1818
d. Washington, DC, Feb. 19, 1899, Age 80

PONSARD, François
Playwright
b. Vienna, Austria, 1814
d. Unknown, 1867

PONSONBY, Eustace
Composer, Actor
b. Unknown
d. Unknown, April 15, 1924

POOL, F. C.
Business Mgr. of D'Oyly Carte Opera Co.
b. Unknown
d. Unknown, Sept. 12, 1944, Age 69

POOLE, John
Playwright
b. Unknown
d. Unknown, Feb. 5, 1872, Age 87

POPE, Alexander
Actor
b. Unknown
d. Unknown, March 22, 1835, Age 72

POPE, Elizabeth
Actress
b. Unknown
d. Unknown, March 15, 1797, Age 53

POPE, Jane
Actress
b. Unknown, 1742
d. Unknown, July 30, 1818, Age 76

POPE, Maria Ann
Actress
b. Unknown
d. Unknown, June 18, 1803, Age 28

POPE, Mrs. W. Coleman
Actress
b. Yorkshire, England, 1809
d. Indianapolis, IN, March 16, 1880, Age 71

POPE, T. Michael
Critic, Journalist
b. Unknown
d. Unknown, Oct. 17, 1930, Age 55

POPE, Thomas
Actor
b. Unknown
d. Unknown, Feb. 1604

POPE, William Coleman
Actor
b. Unknown
d. Indianapolis, IN, June 1, 1868

POREL, Paul (Paul Désiré Parfouru)
Producer, Actor
b. Lessay, France, Oct. 25,1843
d. Paris, France, Aug. 4, 1917, Age 73

PORTEN, Henny
Actress
b. Unknown
d. Berlin, Germany, Oct. 15, 1960, Age 70

PORTEOUS, Gilbert
Actor
b. London, England, May 19, 1868
d. Unknown, Sept. 6, 1928, Age 60

PORTER, Caleb
Actor
b. London, England, Sept 1, 1867
d. Unknown, March 13, 1940, Age 72

PORTER, Cole
Composer, Lyricist
b. Peru, IN, June 9, 1891
d. Santa Monica, CA, Oct. 16, 1964, Age 73

PORTER, Harry A.
Actor
b. Unknown
d. Indianapolis, IN, Sept. 24, 1920, Age 52

PORTER, Neil
Actor, Director
b. London, England, Jan. 10, 1895
d. Unknown, April 21, 1944, Age 49

PORTER, Quincy
Composer, Educator
b. New Haven, CT, Feb. 7, 1897
d. Bethany, CT, Nov. 12, 1966, Age 69

PORTERFIELD, Robert H.
Director - Actor
b. Austinville, VA, Dec. 21, 1905
d. Abingdon, VA, Oct. 28, 1971, Age 65

PORTMAN, Eric
Actor
b. Halifax, England, July 13, 1903
d. Cornwall, England, Dec. 7, 1970, Age 67

PORTO-RICHE, George de
Playwright, Poet
b. Bordeaux, France, May 20, 1849
d. Paris, France, Sept. 5, 1930, Age 81

POSSART, Ernst Ritter von
Actor, Producer
b. Berlin, Germany, May 11, 1841
d. Unknown, April 8, 1921, Age 79

POST, Guy Bates
Actor
b. Seattle, WA, 1875
d. Los Angeles, CA, Jan. 16, 1968, Age 92

POST, Guy Bates
Actor
b. Seattle, WA, Sept. 22, 1875
d. Unknown, 1946, Age 71

POTEL, Victor
Actor
b. Unknown
d. Hollywood, CA, March 8, 1947, Age 57

POTTER, Paul M.
Playwright
b. Brighton, England, June 3, 1853
d. New York, NY, March 7, 1921, Age 67

POUGIN, Arthur
Historian, Critic
b. Unknown
d. Unknown, Aug. 8, 1921, Age 78

POULENC, Francis
Composer
b. Unknown
d. Paris, France, Jan. 30, 1963, Age 64

POULSEN, Johannes
Actor, Director
b. Unknown
d. Unknown, Oct. 14, 1938, Age 57

POUNDS, Charles Courtice
Actor
b. London, England, May 30, 1862
d. Unknown, Dec. 21, 1927, Age 65

POWELL, Charles Stuart
Actor-Manager
b. Unknown
d. Unknown, April 26, 1811, Age 62

POWELL, Dick (Richard Ewing Powell)
Actor, Producer, Director
b. Mountain View, AK, Nov. 14, 1904
d. Hollywood, CA, Jan. 2, 1963, Age 58

POWELL, Ellis
Actress
b. Unknown
d. London, England, May 1, 1963, Age 57

POWELL, George
Actor, Playwright, Director
b. Unknown, 1668
d. Unknown, Dec. 14, 1714, Age 46

POWELL, Walter Templer
Actor, Producer
b. Unknown
d. Unknown, June 29, 1949

POWELL, William
Actor, Patentee
b. Unknown, 1735
d. Bristol, England, July 3, 1769, Age 34

POWER, Clavering
Actor
b. Unknown
d. Unknown, Nov. 26, 1931, Age 89

POWER, Nelly
Actress
b. Unknown
d. Unknown, Jan. 20, 1887, Age 32

POWER, Rosine (Mrs. George Parker)
Actress
b. England, 1840
d. England, March 1932, Age 92

POWER, Sir George
Actor
b. Unknown
d. Unknown, Oct. 17, 1928, Age 81

POWER, Tyrone
Actor, Playwright
b. Kilmacthomas, Ireland, Nov. 2, 1797
d. Atlantic Ocean, sinking of S. S. President, March 24, 1841, Age 43

POWER, Tyrone
Actor
b. London, England, May 2, 1869
d. Hollywood, CA, Dec. 30, 1931, Age 62

POWER, Tyrone
Actor
b. Cincinnati, OH, May 5, 1913
d. Madrid, Spain, Nov. 15, 1958, Age 45

POWERS, Arba Eugene
Actor
b. Houlton, ME, Unknown
d. Saranac Lake, NY, Jan. 7, 1935, Age 62

POWERS, Harry J.
Producer, Theatre owner
b. Nenagh, Tipperary, Ireland, Unknown
d. Morristown, NJ, Feb. 21, 1941, Age 81

POWERS, James T.
Actor
b. New York, NY, April 26, 1862
d. New York, NY, Feb. 10, 1943, Age 80

POWERS, Leona
Actress
b. Salida, CO, Mar. 13, 1896
d. Unknown, Jan. 7, 1970, Age 73

POWERS, Marie
Singer, Actress
b. Mount Carmel, PA, Unknown
d. New York, NY, Dec. 29, 1973, Age 60s

POWERS, Tom
Actor
b. Owensboro, KY, July 7, 1890
d. Hollywood, CA, Nov. 9, 1955, Age 65

PRAGER, Stanley
Director - Actor
b. New York, NY, Jan. 8, 1917
d. Hollywood, CA, Jan. 16, 1972, Age 55

PRATT, Muriel
Actress, Director
b. Nottingham, England, Unknown
d. Unknown, Jan. 15, 1945, Age 54

PRATT, Samuel Jackson ("Courtney Melmoth")
Playwright, Actor
b. Unknown
d. Unknown, Oct. 4, 1814, Age 64

PRATT, Theodore
Novelist, Playwright
b. Minneapolis, MN, April 26, 1901
d. Delray Beach, FL, Dec. 15, 1969, Age 68

PRAY, Isaac Clark
Playwright, Actor, Producer
b. Unknown
d. Unknown, Nov. 28, 1869, Age 56

PREEDY, George R. (Gabrielle Margaret Vere Campbell Long)(Marjorie Bowen a/k/a Joseph Shearing)
Playwright, Novelist
b. Hayling Island, Hants, England, 1888
d. London, England, Dec. 23, 1952, Age 64

PREHAUSER, Gottfried
Actor
b. Unknown, 1699
d. Unknown, 1769

PREISSER, Cherry (Mrs. David J. Hopkins)
Dancer
b. Unknown
d. Sydney, Australia, July 12, 1964, Age 46

PRESANO, Rita
Actress
b. Unknown
d. Unknown, Sept. 18, 1935, Age 70

PRESBREY, Eugene Wyley
Actor, Playwright
b. Williamsburg, MA, March 13, 1853
d. Hollywood, CA, Sept. 9, 1931, Age 78

PRESTON, Jessie
Actress
b. Unknown
d. Unknown, Feb. 6, 1928, Age 51

PRESTON, William
Playwright, Poet
b. Unknown
d. Unknown, Feb. 2, 1807, Age 53

PREVILLE, (Pierre Louis Dubus)
Actor
b. Unknown, 1721
d. Unknown, 1799

PREVOST, Marcel
Playwright, Novelist
b. Paris, France, May 1, 1862
d. Unknown, April 8, 1941, Age 78

PREVOST, Marie
Actress
b. Sarnia, Ont., CAN, Nov. 2, 1898 (?)
d. Hollywood, CA, Jan. 21, 1937, Age 44

PREWETT, Eda Valerga
Singer, Dancer
b. Unknown
d. Oakland, CA, Aug. 1964, Age 81

PRICE, Dennis
Actor
b. Twyford, Berkshire, England, June 23, 1915
d. Guernsey, Channel Islands, Oct. 7, 1973, Age 58

PRICE, Eleazer D.
Manager, Press representative
b. Tecumseh, MI, Unknown
d. New York, NY, May 24, 1935, Age 86

PRICE, George E.
Performer, Stockbroker
b. New York, NY, 1900
d. New York, NY, May 10, 1964, Age 64

PRICE, George N.
Performer
b. Unknown
d. Salisbury, New Brunswick, CAN, April 28, 1962, Age 86

PRICE, Kate
Actress
b. County Cork, Ireland, 1873
d. Hollywood, CA, Jan. 4, 1943, Age 69

PRICE, Lorain M.
Performer
b. Unknown
d. Mexico City, Mexico, June 26, 1963, Age 53

PRICE, Stanley L.
Actor
b. Unknown
d. Hollywood, CA, July 13, 1955, Age 55

PRICE, Stephen
Producer, Theatre manager
b. Unknown, 1783
d. Unknown, 1840

PRICE, Will
Director, Dialogue Coach
b. Unknown
d. Magnolia, MS, July 4, 1962, Age 49

PRICE, William Thompson
Critic, Playwright, Reader
b. Unknown
d. Unknown, May 3, 1920, Age 73

PRICE-DRURY, Lt. Col. W.
Playwright
b. Unknown
d. Unknown, Jan. 21, 1949, Age 87

PRINCE, Adelaide (né e Rubenstein)
Actress
b. London, England, Unknown
d. Shawnee-on-Delaware, PA, Apr. 4, 1941, Age 84

PRINCE, Lillian (Mrs. William Mead)
Actress
b. Unknown
d. New York, NY, Feb. 25, 1962, Age 68

PRINSEP, Val
Playwright, Artist
b. Unknown
d. Unknown, Nov. 11, 1904, Age 66

PRITCHARD, Dick
Theatre manager
b. Unknown
d. Hollywood, CA, June 25, 1963, Age 58

PROBY, David
Actor
b. Unknown
d. Vancouver, B.C., CAN, May 7, 1964, Age 21

PROCTOR, Bryan Waller ("Barry Cornwall")
Playwright
b. Unknown
d. Unknown, Oct. 5, 1874, Age 87

PROCTOR, Frederick Francis
Theatre manager, Vaudeville producer
b. Dexter, ME, 1851
d. Larchmont, NY, Sept. 4, 1929, Age 78

PROCTOR, Joseph
Actor, Producer
b. Unknown
d. Unknown, Oct. 2, 1897, Age 81

PROUTY, Jed
Actor
b. Boston, MA, Unknown
d. New York, NY, May 10, 1956, Age 77

PRUD'HOMME, Cameron Worsley
Actor, Director, Writer
b. Auburn, CA, Dec. 16, 1892
d. Pompton Plains, NJ, Nov. 27, 1967, Age 74

PRYCE, Richard
Playwright, Novelist
b. Boulogne, France, Unknown
d. Unknown, May 30, 1942, Age 79

PRYDE, Ted
Performer
b. Unknown
d. London, England, Dec. 2, 1963

PRYNNE, William
Author
b. Unknown
d. Unknown, Oct. 24, 1669, Age 69

PRYOR, Arthur
Composer, Bandmaster
b. St. Joseph, MO, Unknown
d. West Long Branch, NJ, June 18, 1942, Age 71

PRYSE, Hugh (John Hwfa Pryse)
Actor
b. London, England, Nov. 11, 1910
d. Unknown, Aug. 11, 1955, Age 44

PUCK, Harry
Performer, Songwriter
b. Unknown
d. Metuchen, NJ, Jan. 29, 1964, Age 71

PULASKI, Jack (Isme Beringer Pulaski)
Theatrical reporter, Editor, Critic
b. Cuthbert, GA, Unknown
d. New York, NY, July 16, 1948

PURCELL, Gertrude
Performer, Playwright
b. Unknown
d. Hollywood, CA, May 1, 1963, Age 67

PURDELL, Reginald
Actor
b. Clapham, London, England, Nov. 4, 1896
d. London, England, April 22, 1953, Age 56

PURVIANCE, Edna
Actress
b. Paradise Valley, NV, 1895
d. Woodland Hills, CA, Jan. 13, 1958, Age 62

PUSHKIN, Alexander Sergeyevitch
Poet, Playwright
b. Moscow, Russia, May 26, 1799
d. St. Petersburg, Russia, Jan. 29, 1837, Age 37

PYE, Henry James
Playwright, Poet Laureate
b. Unknown
d. Unknown, Aug. 11, 1813, Age 58

Q

QUARTERMAINE, Charles
Actor
b. Richmond, Surrey, England, Dec. 30, 1877
d. Unknown, Aug. 1958, Age 80

QUARTERMAINE, Leon
Actor
b. Richmond, England, Sept. 24, 1876
d. Salisbury, England, June 25, 1967, Age 90

QUIGLEY, Martin
Publisher of Movie Trade Periodicals
b. Unknown, May 6, 1890
d. New York, NY, May 4, 1964, Age 74

QUILTER, Roger
Composer
b. Brighton, England, Unknown
d. London, England, Sept. 21, 1953, Age 75

QUIN, James
Actor
b. Unknown, 1693
d. Unknown, 1766

QUINAULT, Philippe
Playwright, Librettist
b. Unknown, 1635
d. Unknown, 1688

QUINLAN, Gertrude
Performer
b. Vermont, Unknown
d. New York, NY, Nov. 29, 1963

QUINLAN, John C.
Actor
b. New Zealand, Unknown
d. White Plains, NY, Dec. 1, 1954, Age 62

QUINN, Arthur Hobson
Author, Educator
b. Philadelphia, PA, Feb. 9, 1875
d. Philadelphia, PA, Oct. 16, 1960, Age 85

QUINN, Mary (Mrs. Dudley Digges, Maire Roden Quinn)
Actress
b. County Fermanagh, Ireland, Unknown
d. Bay Shore, L.I., NY, Aug. 21, 1947

QUINTERO, Joaquín Alvarez
Playwright
b. Utrera, Spain, Jan. 21, 1873
d. Madrid, Spain, June 14, 1944, Age 71

QUINTERO, Serafin Alvarez
Playwright
b. Utrera, Spain, March 26, 1871
d. Madrid, Spain, April 12, 1938, Age 67

QUINTON, Mark
Playwright, Actor
b. Unknown
d. Unknown, Oct. 8, 1891, Age 32

R

RACHEL, Lydia
Actress
b. Unknown
d. Unknown, June 1915

RACHEL, Madame (Elizabeth Félix)
Actress
b. Mumpf, Switzerland, Feb. 28, 1820
d. Cannet, France, Jan. 3, 1858, Age 37

RACINE, Jean Baptiste
Playwright, Poet
b. La Ferti-Milan, France, baptized Dec. 22, 1639
d. Unknown, April 21, 1699, Age 59

RADFORD, Basil
Actor
b. Chester, England, June 25,1897
d. Unknown, Oct. 20, 1952, Age 55

RAFFERTY, Pat
Singer
b. Unknown
d. Unknown, Dec. 11, 1952, Age 91

RAGLAN, James (Thomas James Raglan Cornewall-Walker)
Actor
b. Redhill, Surrey, England, Jan. 6, 1901
d. London, England, Nov. 15, 1961, Age 60

RAGLAND, "Rags"
(John Morgan Ragland), Performer
b. Unknown, Louisville, KY
d. Unknown, Hollywood, CA, Age Aug. 20, 1946

RAIMU, Jules
Actor
b. Toulon-sur-mer, France, Dec. 17, 1883
d. Paris, France, Sept. 20, 1946, Age 62

RAIMUND, Ferdinand
Playwright, Actor
b. Unknown, 1790
d. Unknown, 1836

RAINGER, Ralph
Composer
b. New York, NY, Oct. 7, 1901
d. Unknown, Oct. 23, 1942, Age 41

RAINS, Claude
Actor
b. London, England, Nov. 10, 1889
d. Laconia, NH, May 30, 1967, Age 77

RAISIN, Jean-Baptiste
Actor
b. Unknown, 1655
d. Unknown, 1693

RAJAH, Raboid (Ray Boyd)
Performer
b. Unknown
d. Miami Beach, FL, Jan. 11, 1962

RALEIGH, Cecil (Rowlands)
Playwright
b. Unknown, Jan. 27, 1856
d. Unknown, Nov. 10, 1914, Age 58

RALEIGH, Mrs. Cecil (Saba)
Actress
b. Unknown
d. Unknown, Aug. 22, 1923, Age 57

RALPH, Jessie (Mrs. William Patton née Jessie Ralph Chambers)
Actress
b. Gloucester, MA, Unknown
d. Gloucester, MA, May 30, 1944, Age 79

RAMSAYE, Terry
Editor, Cinema historian
b. Tonganoxie, KS, Unknown
d. Norwalk, CT, Aug. 19, 1954, Age 68

RAMSEY, Alicia
Playwright
b. London, England, Unknown
d. Unknown, May 7, 1933

RAMSEY, Nelson
Actor
b. Unknown
d. Unknown, April 5, 1929, Age 66

RANALOW, Frederick Baring
Actor
b. Dublin, Ireland, Nov. 7, 1873
d. Unknown, Dec. 8, 1953, Age 80

RAND, Bill (William George Engler)
Performer
b. Unknown
d. Boston, MA, Nov. 5, 1961

RANDOLPH, Eva
Actress
b. Unknown
d. New York, NY, Nov. 22, 1927, Age 64

RANDOLPH, Louise
Actress
b. Leavenworth, KS, Unknown
d. Port Chester, NY, Nov. 2, 1953, Age 83

RANDOLPH, Thomas
Playwright, Poet
b. Unknown
d. Unknown, March 1635, Age 29

RANKEN, Frederick W.
Librettist, Lyricist
b. Troy, NY, Unknown
d. New York, NY, Oct. 17, 1905, Age 36

RANKIN, Arthur McKee
Performer, Manager
b. Sandwich, Ontario, CAN, Feb. 6, 1841
d. San Francisco, CA, April 17, 1914, Age 73

RANKIN, Doris (Mrs. Lionel Barrymore)
Actress
b. Unknown, c1880
d. Washington, DC, c1946

RANKIN, Gladys (Mrs. Sidney Drew)
Actress
b. Unknown
d. Unknown, Jan. 9, 1914, Age 40

RANKIN, Mrs. McKee (Kitty Blanchard)
Actress
b. Unknown, 1847
d. Unknown, Dec. 14, 1911, Age 64

RANKIN, Phyllis (Mrs. Harry Davenport)
Actress
b. New York, NY, Aug. 31, 1874
d. Canton, PA, Nov. 17, 1934, Age 60

RANKIN (DAVENPORT), Arthur
Performer, Writer
b. New York, NY, Unknown
d. Hollywood, CA, March 22, 1947, Age 50

RANOE, Cecilia (Mrs. F. C. Burnand)
Actress
b. Unknown
d. Unknown, April 10, 1870, Age 27

RANSOME, John W.
Actor
b. Unknown
d. New York, NY, Aug. 12, 1929, Age 69

RAPHAEL, Enid
Actress, Performer
b. Unknown
d. New York, NY, March 5, 1964

RAPHAEL, John N. ("Percival")
Playwright, Critic, Journalist
b. Unknown, May 16, 1868
d. Unknown, Feb. 23, 1917, Age 48

RASCH, Albertina (Mrs. Dimitri Tiomkin)
Choreographer, Ballerina
b. Vienna, Austria, 1896
d. Woodland Hills, CA, Oct. 2, 1967, Age 76

RASCOE, Burton
Critic, Playwright
b. Fulton, KY, Oct. 22, 1892
d. Unknown, March 19, 1957, Age 64

RASUMNY, Mikhail
Actor
b. Odessa, Russia, Unknown
d. Los Angeles, CA, Mar. 12, 1938, Age 28

RATHBONE, Basil
Actor
b. Johannesburg, Transvaal, South Africa, June 13, 1892
d. New York, NY, July 21, 1967, Age 75

RATHBONE, Guy B.
Actor
b. Liverpool, England, May 28, 1884
d. Unknown, April 21, 1916, Age 31

RATHBONE, Ouida
Playwright, Designer, Actress
b. Madrid, Spain, Dec. 14, 1887
d. New York, NY, Nov. 29, 1974, Age 86

RATOFF, Gregory
Actor, Director, Producer
b. Samara, Russia, April 20, 1893
d. Solothurn, Switzerland, Dec. 14, 1960, Age 67

RAVENSCROFT, Edward
Playwright, fl. 1671-97

RAWLING, Sylvester
Critic
b. Saltash, England, Unknown
d. New York, NY, Feb. 16, 1921, Age 63

RAWLINS, W. H.
Actor
b. Unknown
d. Unknown, Dec. 29, 1927

RAWLINSON, Herbert
Actor
b. Brighton, England, Unknown
d. Los Angeles, CA, July 12, 1953, Age 67

RAWLSTON, Zelma
Actress
b. Unknown
d. Unknown, Oct. 30, 1915

RAWSON, Graham
Playwright
b. London, England, Oct. 22, 1890
d. Unknown, 1955, Age 65

RAY, Charles
Actor, Film producer
b. Jacksonville, IL, 1891
d. Hollywood, CA, Nov. 23, 1943, Age 52

RAY, John William
Actor, Playwright
b. Unknown
d. Unknown, Sept. 1871, Age 64

RAYMOND, Charles
Playwright
b. Unknown
d. Unknown, May 11, 1911

RAYMOND, John T. (John O'Brien)
Performer
b. Unknown, 1836
d. Unknown, April 10, 1887, Age 51

RAYMOND, Maud (Mrs. Gus Rogers)
Performer
b. New York, NY, Unknown
d. Rockville Centre, L. I., NY, May 10, 1961, Age 89

RAYNE, Leonard
Actor, Producer
b. Unknown, March 6, 1869
d. Unknown, June 19, 1925, Age 56

RAYNER, Alfred
Actor
b. Unknown
d. Unknown, Jan. 20, 1898, Age 75

RAYNER, Lionel Benjamin
Actor, Producer
b. Unknown
d. Unknown, Sept. 24, 1855, Age 69

RAYNER, Minnie
Actress
b. London, England, May 2, 1869
d. Unknown, Dec. 13, 1941, Age 72

REA, Alec L.
Producer
b. Liverpool, England, Jan. 30, 1878
d. Unknown, Feb. 11, 1953, Age 75

REA, William J.
Actor
b. Belfast, Ireland, April 11, 1884
d. Unknown, Nov. 27, 1932, Age 48

REACH, Angus B.
Playwright
b. Unknown
d. Unknown, Nov. 25, 1856, Age 35

READE, Charles
Playwright, Novelist
b. Ipseden, Oxfordshire, England, June 8, 1814
d. Shepherd's Bush, London, England, April 11, 1884, Age 69

REDE, Thomas Leman
Actor, Playwright
b. Unknown, 1799
d. Unknown, Dec. 12, 1932, Age 33

REDE, William Leman
Actor, Playwright
b. Unknown, 1802
d. Unknown, April 3, 1847, Age 45

REDFERN, W. B.
Producer
b. Unknown
d. Unknown, Aug. 21, 1923, Age 83

REDFIELD, William
Actor
b. New York, NY, Jan. 26, 1927
d. New York, NY, Aug. 17, 1976, Age 49

REDFORD, George Alexander
Film censor, Examiner of plays
b. Unknown
d. Unknown, Nov. 10, 1916

REDMAN, Ben Ray
Literary critic, Author
b. Brooklyn, NY, Feb. 21, 1896
d. Hollywood, CA, Aug. 2, 1962, Age 66

REDMOND, T. C.
Actor
b. Unknown
d. Unknown, Aug. 9, 1937, Age 80

REDMOND, William
Actor
b. Unknown
d. Unknown, Oct. 9, 1915

REDSTONE, Willy
Composer, Musical director
b. Unknown
d. Unknown, Sept. 30, 1949, Age 66

REECE, Brian
Actor
b. Unknown
d. London, England, April 12, 1962, Age 48

REECE, Robert
Playwright
b. Unknown
d. Unknown, July 8, 1891, Age 53

REED, Alfred German
Composer, Performer
b. Unknown
d. Unknown, March 10, 1895, Age 48

REED, Carl D.
Producer
b. Unknown
d. Cortland, NY, July 11, 1962, Age 79

REED, Florence
Actress
b. Philadelphia, PA, Jan. 10, 1883
d. East Islip, NY, Nov. 21, 1967, Age 84

REED, Isaac
Critic, Historian
b. Unknown
d. Unknown, Jan. 5, 1807, Age 65

REED, Jared
Performer
b. Columbia, SC, Unknown
d. New York, NY, Sept. 11, 1962, Age 38

REED, Joseph
Playwright
b. Unknown
d. Unknown, Aug. 15, 1787, Age 64

REED, Joseph Verner Sr.
Producer
b. Nice, France, Jan. 18, 1902
d. New York, NY, Nov. 25, 1973, Age 71

REED, Mrs. German (Priscilla Horton)
Actress
b. Unknown
d. Unknown, March 18, 1895, Age 77

REED, Roland
Performer, Manager
b. Unknown, 1852
d. Unknown, March 30, 1901, Age 48

REED, Thomas German
Performer
b. Unknown
d. Unknown, March 21, 1888, Age 70

REESE, James W.
Actor
b. Buena Vista, GA, Unknown
d. New York, NY, Feb. 17, 1960, Age 62

REEVE, Wybert
Actor, Producer
b. Unknown
d. Unknown, Nov. 15, 1906, Age 77

REEVES, George
Actor
b. Woodstock, IA, Unknown
d. Hollywood, CA, June 16, 1959, Age 45

REEVES, Jim ("Gentleman Jim")
Singer, Actor
b. Unknown
d. Plane Crash near Nashville, TN, July 31, 1964, Age 39

REEVES, Theodore
Playwright
b. Unknown, Oct. 10, 1910
d. Hollywood, CA, March 18, 1973, Age 62

REEVES-SMITH, Harry
Actor
b. Scarborough, England, 1862
d. Unknown, Jan. 29, 1938, Age 75

REEVES-SMITH, Olive
Actress
b. Ewell, England, Nov. 23, 1894
d. New York, NY, July 20, 1972, Age 57

REGNARD, Jean-François
Playwright
b. Unknown, 1655
d. Unknown, Sept. 4, 1709, Age 54

REGNAULT, Mme.
Actress
b. Unknown
d. Unknown, Aug. 1887

REGNIER, (François Joseph Pierre Tousez)
Actor, Teacher
b. Unknown, 1807
d. Unknown, April 28, 1885, Age 78

REHAN, Ada (Crehan)
Actress
b. Limerick, Ireland, April 22, 1860
d. New York, NY, Jan. 8, 1916, Age 55

REHAN, Mary
Actress, Lawyer
b. Chippewa Falls, WI, Unknown
d. Rochester, MN, Aug. 28, 1963, Age 76

REICHER, Emmanuel
Actor, Director
b. Unknown, 1849
d. Unknown, 1924

REID, Francis Ellison
Press representative
b. Lancaster, PA, Unknown
d. New York, NY, Oct. 3, 1933, Age 67

REID, Hal (James Hallock Reid)
Playwright
b. Unknown
d. Unknown, May 22, 1920, Age 60

REID, Wallace
Actor
b. St. Louis, MO, April 15, 1892
d. Hollywood, CA, Jan. 18, 1923, Age 30

REILLY, Anastasia (Mrs. Theodore Buhl)
Performer
b. Unknown
d. Grosse Pointe, MI, Dec. 28, 1961, Age 58

REIMERS, Georg
Actor
b. Unknown
d. Unknown, April 15, 1936, Age 76

REINER, Ethel Linder
Producer
b. Brooklyn, NY, Unknown
d. Barbados, Feb. 8, 1971, Age 65

REINER, Fritz
Conductor
b. Hungary, 1888
d. New York, NY, Nov. 15, 1963, Age 74

REINGOLDS, Kate
Actress
b. Unknown
d. Unknown, July 11, 1911, Age 75

REINHARDT, Max (Goldmann)
Actor, Author, Producer, Director
b. Baden, Austria, Sept. 9, 1873
d. New York, NY, Oct. 31, 1943, Age 70

REIS, Irving
Director
b. New York, NY, Unknown
d. Woodland Hills, CA, July 3, 1953, Age 47

REJANE, Mme. (Gabrielle Charlotte Réju)
Actress-Manager
b. Paris, France, June 6, 1857
d. Paris, France, June 14, 1920, Age 63

RELPH, George
Actor
b. Cullercoats, England, Jan. 27, 1888
d. London, England, April 24, 1960, Age 72

REMARQUE, Erich Maria
Author, Playwright
b. Osnabruck, Germany, June 22, 1898
d. Locarno, Switzerland, Sept. 25, 1970, Age 72

RENAD, Frederick (Cooper)
Actor
b. Unknown
d. Unknown, May 30, 1939, Age 73

RENARD, Jules
Playwright
b. Unknown
d. Unknown, May 23, 1910, Age 46

RENAULT, Francis
Performer
b. Unknown
d. New York, NY, May 20, 1955, Age 62

RENDLE, Thomas McDonald
Critic, Journalist, Historian
b. Plymouth, England, April 14, 1856
d. Unknown, Feb. 7, 1926, Age 69

RENNIE, Hugh
Actor, Director
b. England, Unknown
d. New York, NY, Sept. 27, 1953, Age 50

RENNIE, James
Actor, Writer
b. Toronto, Canada, April 18, 1890
d. New York, NY, July 31, 1965, Age 75

RENNIE, John
Actor
b. Unknown
d. Unknown, Aug. 20, 1952, Age 77

RENNIE, Michael
Actor
b. Yorkshire, England,, Aug. 25, 1909
d. Harrogate, England, June 10, 1971, Age 61

RENOIR, Pierre
Actor
b. Unknown
d. Paris, France, March 11, 1952, Age 66

RENOUF, Henry
Actor
b. Unknown
d. Unknown, July 24, 1913, Age 53

RESOR, Stanley Burnet
Business executive
b. Cincinnati, OH, Unknown
d. New York, NY, Oct. 20, 1962, Age 83

RESSLER, Benton Crews
Performer
b. Unknown
d. Saranac Lake, NY, May 29, 1963

RESZKE, Jean de
Opera singer
b. Warsaw, Poland, Jan. 14, 1850
d. Nice, France, April 3, 1925, Age 75

RETFORD, Ella
Performer
b. Ireland, Unknown
d. London, England, June 29, 1962, Age 76

REVEL, Harry
Composer
b. London, England, Dec. 21, 1905
d. New York, NY, Nov. 3, 1958, Age 53

REVELLE, Arthur Hamilton (Engström)
Actor
b. Gibralter, Spain, Unknown
d. Nice, France, April 11, 1958, Age 85

REVILLE, Robert (Barrett)
Actor
b. Unknown
d. Unknown, Oct. 26, 1893

REYNOLDS, Adeline De Walt
Actress
b. . . .near Vinton, IA, Sept. 19, 1862
d. Hollywood, CA, Aug. 13, 1961, Age 98

REYNOLDS, Craig (Harold Hugh Enfield)
Actor
b. Anaheim, CA, 1907
d. Hollywood, CA, Oct. 22, 1949, Age 42

REYNOLDS, E. Vivian
Actor, Stage manager
b. London, England, June 24, 1866
d. Unknown, May 13, 1952, Age 85

REYNOLDS, Frank E.
Director, Producer, Actor
b. Unknown
d. Belfast, Ireland, Oct. 8, 1962, Age 57

REYNOLDS, Frederick
Playwright
b. Unknown, 1764
d. Unknown, April 16, 1841, Age 77

REYNOLDS, James
Designer, Author, Artist
b. Warrenton, VA, Unknown
d. Bellagio, Italy, July 1957, Age 65

REYNOLDS, Jane Louisa (Lady Brampton)
Actress
b. Unknown
d. Unknown, Nov. 17, 1907, Age 83

REYNOLDS, Thomas
Producer, Director
b. Unknown
d. Unknown, Jan. 25, 1947, Age 67

REYNOLDS, Tom
Actor
b. Paddington, London, England, Aug. 9, 1866
d. Unknown, July 25, 1942, Age 75

REYNOLDS, Vera
Actress
b. Unknown
d. Woodland Hills, CA, April 22, 1962, Age 61

REYNOLDS, Walter
Playwright, Producer
b. Unknown
d. Unknown, March 26, 1941, Age 89

REYNOLDSON, T. H.
Actor, Playwright
b. Unknown
d. Unknown, July 1888, Age 80

RHODES, Harrison
Playwright
b. Cleveland, OH, June 2, 1871
d. Unknown, Sept. 1929, Age 58

RHODES, Percy William
Actor
b. Unknown
d. Unknown, Nov. 1956, Age 85

RHODES, Raymond Compton
Critic, Playwright
b. Birmingham, England, Sept. 27, 1887
d. Unknown, Oct. 3, 1935, Age 48

RIAL, Louise
Actress
b. Unknown
d. New York, NY, Aug. 9, 1940, Age 90

RIBNER, Irving
Educator
b. Brooklyn, NY, Aug. 29, 1921
d. Long Island, NY, July 2, 1972, Age 50

RICARDEL, Molly (Boehnel)
Playwright, Actress
b. Unknown
d. East Meadow, L. I., NY, March 30, 1963, Age 56

RICCOBONI, Luigi ("Lelio")
Actor, Producer, Author
b. Unknown, c1675
d. Unknown, 1753

RICE, Andy
Performer, Writer
b. Austria, Unknown
d. Dallas, TX, Feb. 17, 1963, Age 82

RICE, Charles
Actor, Producer
b. Unknown
d. Unknown, April 12, 1880, Age 60

RICE, Edward Everett
Composer, Producer, Playwright
b. Brighton, MA, Dec. 21, 1848
d. New York, NY, Nov. 16, 1924, Age 75

RICE, Elmer (né Elmer Leopold Reizenstein)
Playwright, Director, Educator
b. New York, NY, Sept. 28, 1892
d. Southampton, England, May 8, 1967, Age 74

RICE, Fanny
Actress
b. Lowell, MA, Unknown
d. New York, NY, July 10, 1936, Age 77

RICE, Gitz
Songwriter
b. Unknown
d. New York, NY, Oct. 16, 1947, Age 56

RICE, Thomas Dartmouth ("Jim Crow")
Performer
b. New York, NY, 1808
d. New York, NY, Sept. 18, 1860, Age 52

RICE, Vernon
Drama editor
b. St. Louis, MO, Unknown
d. New York, NY, May 6, 1954, Age 46

RICH, Charles J.
Manager
b. Boston, MA, 1855
d. Boston, MA, week of May 13, 1921, Age 66

RICH, Christopher
Producer
b. Unknown
d. Unknown, Nov. 4, 1714

RICH, Helen
Performer, Business executive
b. Unknown
d. New York, NY, Aug. 28, 1963, Age 66

RICH, John
Actor, Producer
b. England, c1682
d. England, Nov. 26, 1761, Age 79

RICH, Lillian
Actress
b. Unknown
d. Woodland Hills, CA, Jan. 5, 1954

RICHARD, Al
Talent representative, Performer
b. Unknown
d. East Greenwich, RI, June 6, 1962, Age 69

RICHARD, Georges
Actor, Producer, Playwright
b. Unknown
d. Unknown, Nov. 16, 1891, Age 60

RICHARDS, Addison
Actor
b. Unknown
d. Hollywood, CA, March 22, 1964, Age 61

RICHARDS, Cicely
Actress
b. London, England, Unknown
d. Unknown, April 8, 1933, Age 83

RICHARDS, Col. A. Bate
Playwright, Producer
b. Unknown
d. Unknown, June 12, 1876, Age 56

RICHARDS, Donald
Actor
b. New York, NY, Unknown
d. Ridgewood, NJ, Sept. 26, 1953, Age 34

RICHARDS, Gordon
Actor
b. England, Unknown
d. Hollywood, CA, Jan. 13, 1964, Age 70

RICHARDS, Richard R.
Press representative
b. Unknown
d. New York, NY, Jan. 1925, Age 52

RICHARDSON, Foster
Singer
b. Unknown
d. Unknown, Jan. 30, 1942, Age 52

RICHARDSON, Frank
Playwright, Novelist, Critic
b. London, England, 1871
d. Unknown, Aug. 1, 1917, Age 46

RICHARDSON, Frankie
Performer
b. Unknown
d. Philadelphia, PA, Jan. 30, 1962, Age 63

RICHARDSON, Leander
Playwright, Journalist
b. Cincinnati, OH, Feb. 28, 1856
d. Unknown, Feb. 2, 1918, Age 61

RICHEPIN, Jacques
Playwright, Poet
b. Paris, France, March 20, 1880
d. Unknown, Sept. 2, 1946, Age 66

RICHEPIN, Jean
Playwright, Poet, Novelist
b. Medéah, Algeria, Feb. 4, 1849
d. Unknown, Dec. 12, 1926, Age 77

RICHMAN, Arthur
Playwright
b. New York, NY, April 16, 1886
d. New York, NY, Sept. 10, 1944, Age 58

RICHMAN, Charles J.
Actor
b. Chicago, IL, Jan. 12, 1870
d. Bronx, NY, Dec. 1, 1940, Age 70

RICHMAN, Harry
Singer - Performer
b. Cincinnati, OH, Aug. 10, 1895
d. Hollywood, CA, Nov. 3, 1972, Age 77

RICHMOND, Susan
Actress
b. London, England, Dec. 5, 1894
d. Unknown, Jan, 1959, Age 64

RICHTER, Paul
Actor
b. Germany, Unknown
d. Vienna, Austria, Dec. 30, 1961, Age 65

RICKETTS, Charles
Designer, Painter, Sculptor, Author
b. Geneva, Switzerland, Oct. 2, 1866
d. Unknown, Oct. 7, 1931, Age 65

RIDDELL, George
Actor
b. Unknown
d. Unknown, March 20, 1944, Age 80

RIDGELY, Cleo (Mrs. James Horne)
Actress
b. Unknown
d. Glendale, CA, Aug. 18, 1962, Age 68

RIDGES, Stanley
Actor
b. Southampton, England, Unknown
d. Westbrook, CT, April 22, 1951, Age 59

RIDGEWAY, Peter
Actor, Producer
b. Unknown
d. Unknown, Nov. 23, 1938, Age 44

RIDGEWAY, Philip Sr.
Actor, Director
b. London, England, Nov. 3, 1891
d. Unknown, Oct. 27, 1954, Age 62

RIETTI, Victor
Actor, Producer, Translator
b. Ferrara, Italy, Feb. 28, 1888
d. London, England, Dec. 4, 1963, Age 75

RIGBY, Arthur (William Turner)
Comedian, Playwright
b. London, England, July 25, 1870
d. London, England, April 17, 1944, Age 73

RIGBY, Edward
Actor
b. Ashford, Kent, England, Feb. 5, 1879
d. Unknown, April 5, 1951, Age 72

RIGBY, Frank J.
Musician, Teacher
b. Unknown
d. Portland, ME, Feb. 13, 1963, Age 100

RIGGS, Lynn
Playwright
b. Claremore, OK, Aug. 31, 1899
d. New York, NY, June 30, 1954, Age 54

RIGGS, Ralph
Actor
b. St. Paul, MN, Unknown
d. New York, NY, Sept. 16, 1951, Age 66

RIGHTON, Edward C.
Actor, Playwright
b. Unknown
d. Unknown, Jan. 1, 1899

RIGNOLD, George
Actor, Producer
b. Leicester, England, Unknown
d. Unknown, Dec. 16, 1912, Age 74

RIGNOLD, Henry
Actor
b. Unknown
d. Unknown, Sept. 17, 1873, Age 62

RIGNOLD, Lionel (Rignall)
Actor, Producer
b. London, England, Unknown
d. Unknown, Nov. 13, 1919, Age 69

RIGNOLD, Marie (née D'Altra)
Actress
b. Unknown
d. Unknown, Sept. 7, 1932, Age 84

RIGNOLD, Susan
Actress
b. Unknown
d. Unknown, July 16, 1895

RIGNOLD, William
Actor
b. Unknown
d. Unknown, Dec. 22, 1904, Age 68

RIGNOLD, William Henry
Actor
b. Unknown
d. Unknown, Nov. 24, 1910

RILEY, Edna Goldsmith
Playwright
b. Unknown
d. New York, NY, May 3, 1962, Age 82

RILEY, Lawrence
Playwright
b. Bradford, PA, 1891
d. Stamford, CT, Nov. 29, 1975, Age 78

RINEHART, Mary Roberts
Writer
b. Pittsburgh, PA, Aug. 12, 1876
d. New York, NY, Sept. 22, 1958, Age 82

RING, Blanche
Actress
b. Boston, MA, April 24, 1876
d. Santa Monica, CA, Jan. 13, 1961, Age 84

RING, Frances (Mrs. Thomas Meighan)
Actress
b. Unknown, July 4, 1882
d. Hollywood, CA, Jan. 15, 1951, Age 68

"RIP"
(Georges Thénon), Author
b. Unknown
d. Paris, France, May 1941

RISCOE, Arthur
Actor
b. Sherburn-in-Elmet, Yorkshire, England, Nov. 19, 1896
d. Unknown, Aug. 6, 1954, Age 57

RISDON, Elizabeth
Actress
b. Wandsworth, London, England, 1887
d. Santa Monica, CA, Dec. 20, 1958, Age 71

RISQUE, W. H.
Librettist, Author
b. Unknown
d. Unknown, Aug. 17, 1916

RISTORI, Adelaide (Marchesa Capranica del Grillo)
Actress
b. Cividale del Frinli, Italy, Jan. 29, 1822
d. Rome, Italy, Oct. 9, 1906, Age 84

RITCHIE, Adele
Actress
b. Philadelphia, PA, Dec. 21, 1874
d. Laguna Beach, CA, April 24, 1930, Age 55

RITTENHOUSE, Florence
Actress
b. Philadelphia, PA, Unknown
d. New York, NY, March 28, 1929, Age 35

RITTER, John P.
Playwright
b. Unknown
d. Newark, NJ, Aug. 3, 1920, Age 62

RITTER, Thelma
Actress
b. Brooklyn, NY, Feb. 14, 1905
d. New York, NY, Feb. 5, 1969, Age 63

RIVERS, Alfred
Actor
b. Unknown
d. Unknown, March 27, 1955, Age 88

RIVES, Amelie (Princess Troubetzkoy)
Dramatist, Novelist
b. Richmond, VA, Unknown
d. Charlottesville, VA, June 15, 1945, Age 81

RIVOIRE, André
Playwright, Critic, Poet
b. Unknown
d. Unknown

ROACH, Thomas A.
Performer
b. Unknown
d. Waltham, MA, 1962, Age 51

ROACHE, Viola
Actress
b. Norfolk, England, Oct. 3, 1885
d. Hollywood, CA, May 17, 1961, Age 75

ROBARDS, Jason Sr.
Actor
b. Hillsdale, MI, Unknown
d. Sherman Oaks, CA, April 4, 1963, Age 70

ROBBINS, Sir Alfred
Critic, Playwright, Journalist
b. Launceston, England, Aug. 1, 1856
d. Unknown, March 10, 1931, Age 74

ROBE, Annie
Actress
b. Unknown
d. Unknown, July 1922

ROBER, Richard
Performer
b. Unknown
d. Santa Monica, CA, May 26, 1952, Age 46

ROBERDEAU, John Peter
Playwright
b. Unknown
d. Unknown, Jan. 7, 1815, Age 60

ROBERTI, Lyda
Actress
b. Warsaw, Poland, May 20, 1909
d. Los Angeles, CA, Mar. 12, 1938, Age 28

ROBERTS, Arthur
Performer
b. London, England, Sept. 21, 1852
d. Unknown, Feb. 27, 1933, Age 80

ROBERTS, C. Luckeyth (Luckey)
Composer-Singer-Actor
b. Philadelphia, PA, Aug. 7, 1893
d. New York, NY, Feb. 5, 1968, Age 74

ROBERTS, Cledge
Actor, Director
b. Unknown
d. New York, NY, June 14, 1957, Age 52

ROBERTS, Florence (Mrs. Frederick Vogeling)
Actress
b. Los Angeles, CA, Unknown
d. Los Angeles, CA, July 17, 1927, Age 56

ROBERTS, Florence (Mrs. Walter Gale)
Actress
b. Frederick, MD, March 16, 1861
d. Hollywood, CA, July 6, 1940, Age 79

ROBERTS, Florence Smythe (Mrs. Theodore)
Actress
b. Unknown
d. Hollywood, CA, Aug. 29, 1925, Age 47

ROBERTS, Hans
Actor
b. Unknown
d. Jamaica, L. I., NY, May 2, 1954, Age 80

ROBERTS, J. H.
Actor
b. London, England, July 11, 1884
d. Unknown, Feb. 1, 1961, Age 76

ROBERTS, Jimmy (Robert Thomas Edmeades)
Performer
b. Indiana, Unknown
d. San Francisco, CA, Feb. 19, 1962, Age 60

ROBERTS, Nancy (Annette Finley)
Actress
b. Unknown
d. London, England, June 25, 1962, Age 70

ROBERTS, Ralph
Actor
b. Shikapur, India, Unknown
d. Unknown, Oct. 31, 1944, Age 75

ROBERTS, Sir Randal
Actor, Producer, Playwright
b. Unknown
d. Unknown, Oct. 10, 1899, Age 62

ROBERTS, Theodore
Actor
b. San Francisco, CA, Oct. 8, 1861
d. Hollywood, CA, Dec. 14, 1928, Age 67

ROBERTSHAW, Jerrold
Actor
b. Allerton, Yorkshire, England, March 28, 1866
d. Unknown, Feb. 14, 1941, Age 74

ROBERTSON, Agnes
Actress
b. Edinburgh, Scotland, Dec. 25, 1833
d. London, England, Nov. 6, 1916, Age 82

ROBERTSON, Alex
Playwright, Author, Broadcaster
b. Dundee, Scotland, Unknown
d. Edinburgh, Scotland, Aug. 21, 1964, Age 64

ROBERTSON, Donald
Actor
b. Edinburgh, Scotland, Unknown
d. Chicago, IL, May 20, 1926, Age 66

ROBERTSON, East
Actress
b. Unknown
d. Unknown, Nov. 19, 1916

ROBERTSON, Hermine
Actress
b. Unknown
d. Hollywood, CA, Jan. 10, 1962, Age 61

ROBERTSON, Ian (Forbes-)
Actor, Stage manager
b. London, England, Oct. 13, 1858
d. Unknown, Jan. 11, 1936, Age 77

ROBERTSON, Jerome
Performer
b. Unknown
d. Memphis, TN, Oct. 17, 1962, Age 62

ROBERTSON, John
Scene designer
b. Unknown
d. New Brunswick, NJ, March 18, 1962, Age 35

ROBERTSON, Maud
Actress
b. Unknown
d. Unknown, Nov. 22, 1930

ROBERTSON, Mrs. Thomas
Actress, Producer
b. Unknown
d. Unknown, Dec. 19, 1855, Age 87

ROBERTSON, Orie O.
Actor, Stuntman
b. Unknown
d. Hollywood, CA, April 14, 1964, Age 83

ROBERTSON, Pax
Actress, Director
b. Unknown
d. Unknown, Sept. 20, 1948

ROBERTSON, Thomas William
Playwright
b. Newark, England, Jan. 9, 1829
d. London, England, Feb. 3, 1871, Age 42

ROBERTSON, Thomas William Shafto
Actor, Producer
b. Unknown
d. London, England, May 24, 1895, Age 37

ROBERTSON, W. Graham
Playwright
b. Unknown, July 8, 1867
d. Surrey, England, Sept. 4, 1948, Age 81

ROBESON, Paul
Singer, Actor
b. Princeton, NJ, Apr. 9, 1898
d. Philadelphia, PA, Jan. 23, 1976, Age 77

ROBINA, Fanny
Actress
b. Unknown
d. Unknown, Feb. 13, 1927, Age 65

ROBINA, Florrie
Actress
b. Unknown
d. Unknown, June 9, 1953, Age 86

ROBINS, Edward H.
Actor
b. Shamokin, PA, Oct. 15, 1880
d. Paramus, NJ, July 27, 1955, Age 74

ROBINS, Elizabeth
Actress, Author
b. Louisville, KY, Aug. 6, 1862
d. Brighton, May 18, 1952, Age 89

ROBINS, Gertrude L.
Actress, Playwright
b. Unknown
d. Unknown, Dec. 25, 1917, Age 31

ROBINS, William A.
Musical director, Composer
b. Unknown
d. Unknown, Aug. 23, 1948, Age 81

ROBINSON, Anna (former Countess Rosslyn)
Actress
b. Wisconsin, Unknown
d. New York, NY, Oct. 5, 1917, Age 47

ROBINSON, Bertrand
Actor, Playwright
b. Creston, IA, Unknown
d. Bronx, NY, Feb. 4, 1959, Age 70

ROBINSON, Bill
Dancer, Actor
b. Richmond, VA, May 25, 1878
d. New York, NY, Nov. 25, 1949, Age 71

ROBINSON, E. M.
Actor
b. London, England, Jan. 12, 1855
d. Unknown, June 14, 1932, Age 77

ROBINSON, (Esmé Stuart) Lennox
Playwright, Director
b. Douglas, Cork, Ireland, Oct. 4, 1886
d. Dublin, Ireland, Oct. 14, 1958, Age 72

ROBINSON, Ethan M.
Vaudeville Manager
b. Unknown
d. New York, NY, Dec. 3, 1919, Age 47

ROBINSON, Forrest
Actor
b. Unknown
d. Los Angeles, CA, Jan. 1924, Age 65

ROBINSON, Frederic Charles Patey
Actor
b. London, England, July 22, 1832
d. Brighton, England, Oct. 18, 1912, Age 80

ROBINSON, J. Russel
Composer, Lyricist, Performer
b. Indianapolis, IN, Unknown
d. Palmdale, CA, Sept. 30, 1963, Age 71

ROBINSON, "Perdita"
(Mary Darby Robinson), Actress, Poet
b. College Green, Bristol, England, Nov. 27, 1758
d. Englefield Cottage, Surrey, England, Dec. 26, 1800, Age 42

ROBINSON-DUFF, Frances
Actress, Teacher
b. Blue Hill, ME, Unknown
d. New York, NY, Oct. 30, 1951, Age 74

ROBSON, Frederick (the elder) (Thomas Robson Brownbill)
Actor
b. Margate, England, 1821
d. London, England, Aug. 11, 1864, Age 43

ROBSON, Frederick (the younger)
Actor
b. Unknown
d. Unknown, March 16, 1919, Age 72

ROBSON, Mat
Actor
b. Unknown
d. Unknown, Dec. 22, 1899, Age 69

ROBSON, May (née Robison)
Actress
b. Melbourne, Australia, April 19, 1865
d. Beverly Hills, CA, Oct. 20, 1942, Age 77

ROBSON, Mrs. Stuart (May Waldron)
Actress
b. Unknown
d. Louisville, LA, Dec. 22, 1924, Age 56

ROBSON, Stuart (Henry Robson Stuart)
Actor, Producer
b. Annapolis, MD, March 4, 1836
d. New York, NY, April 29, 1903, Age 67

ROBSON, Stuart Jr.
Actor
b. Unknown
d. New York, NY, Aug. 21, 1946

ROBSON, William ("The Old Playgoer")
Author

ROBYN, Dr. Alfred G.
Organist, Composer
b. St. Louis, MO, Unknown
d. New York, NY, Oct. 18, 1935, Age 75

ROCH, Madeleine
Actress
b. France, Unknown
d. France, Dec. 9, 1930, Age 46

ROCHELLE, Edward
Actor
b. Unknown
d. Unknown, April 16, 1908, Age 56

ROCHIN, Paul
Actor
b. Unknown
d. Hollywood, CA, May 5, 1964, Age 75

ROCK, Charles (Arthur Charles Rock de Fabeck)
Actor
b. Vellore, India, May 30, 1866
d. Unknown, July 12, 1919, Age 53

ROCK, William
Comedian, Dancer
b. Unknown
d. Philadelphia, PA, June 27, 1922, Age 53

ROCKWELL, Florence
Actress
b. St. Louis, MO, Unknown
d. Stamford, CT, March 24, 1964, Age 76

RODE, Helge
Playwright
b. Unknown, 1870
d. Unknown, 1937

RODENBACH, Georges
Poet, Playwright, Novelist
b. Tournai, Belgium, July 16, 1855
d. Unknown, 1898

RODGERS, Carrie Cecil (Mrs. Jimmy Rodgers)
Talent representative
b. Unknown
d. San Antonio, TX, Nov. 28, 1961, Age 59

RODGERS, James
Producer
b. Unknown
d. Unknown, Jan. 6, 1890, Age 74

RODGERS, Jimmy
Performer
b. Meridian, MS, 1897
d. Unknown, 1933, Age 35

RODNEY, Frank
Actor
b. Unknown
d. Unknown, Aug. 14, 1902, Age 43

RODNEY, Stratton
Actor
b. Unknown
d. Unknown, March 13, 1932, Age 67

RODWAY, Philip
Producer
b. Unknown
d. Unknown, Feb. 2, 1932, Age 55

RODWELL, G. H.
Composer, Playwright
b. Unknown
d. Unknown, Jan. 22, 1852, Age 50

RODZINSKI, Artur
Conductor
b. Spalato, Dalmatia, Unknown
d. Boston, MA, Nov. 27, 1958, Age 64

ROE, Bassett
Actor
b. Folkestone, England, Sept. 10, 1860
d. Unknown, Nov. 2, 1934, Age 74

ROEBUCK, Captain Disney
Actor, Producer
b. Unknown
d. Sea Point, Cape Town, South Africa, March 22, 1885, Age 66

ROEDER, Benjamin F.
Producer
b. New York, NY, Unknown
d. New York, NY, May 4, 1943, Age 77

ROGERS, Charles R.
Producer, Film executive
b. Unknown
d. Hollywood, CA, March 29, 1957, Age 64

ROGERS, Emmett (né Emmett Martine Sweet)
Producer, Director, Actor
b. Trenton, NJ, Nov. 30, 1915
d. New York, NY, Oct. 31, 1965, Age 49

ROGERS, Gus (né Solomon)
Actor
b. Unknown, 1869
d. Unknown, Oct. 19, 1908, Age 39

ROGERS, John R. ("Yours Merrily")
Press representative, Producer
b. Cincinnati, OH, Unknown
d. New York, NY, Oct. 7, 1932, Age 92

ROGERS, Lora
Performer
b. Unknown
d. Providence, RI, Dec. 23, 1948, Age 74

ROGERS, Louise Mackintosh
Actress
b. Unknown
d. Beverly Hills, CA, Nov. 1, 1933, Age 68

ROGERS, Max (né Solomon)
Actor
b. New York, NY, Unknown
d. Far Rockaway, NY, Dec. 26, 1932, Age 59

ROGERS, Stanwood
Art director
b. Unknown
d. Hollywood, CA, Jan. 2, 1963, Age 65

ROGERS, Will (William Penn Adair Rogers)
Philosopher, Comedian, Actor
b. Oolagah, Indian Territory, Nov. 4, 1879
d. Point Barrow, AK, Aug. 15, 1935, Age 55

ROHMER, Sax (Arthur Sarsfield Ward)
Playwright, Novelist, Composer
b. Birmingham, England, Feb. 15, 1886
d. Unknown, June 2, 1959, Age 73

ROJAS ZORILLA, Francisco de
Playwright
b. Toledo, Spain, 1607
d. Unknown, 1648

ROLAND, Ida
Actress
b. Vienna, Austria, Feb. 18, 1881
d. Unknown, March 28, 1951, Age 70

ROLAND, Ruth
Actress
b. San Francisco, CA, Aug. 26, 1893
d. Los Angeles, CA, Sept. 22, 1937, Age 44

ROLLAND, Romain
Playwright, Novelist, Critic, Historian
b. Clamecy, Nièvre, France, Jan. 2, 1866
d. Vezelay, Yonne, France, Dec. 30, 1944, Age 78

ROLLE, Georges
Playwright, Producer
b. Unknown
d. Unknown, Oct. 3, 1916

ROLLO, Billy
Actor, Stage manager
b. Unknown
d. Manhasset, L. I., NY, May 7, 1964, Age 40

ROLLY, Jeanne
Actress
b. Unknown
d. Unknown, Dec. 14, 1929, Age 70

ROLSTON, William
Actor, Director, Stage manager
b. Unknown
d. London, England, April 17, 1964

ROLT, Richard
Playwright
b. Unknown
d. Unknown, March 2, 1770, Age 45

ROLYAT, Dan (Herbert Taylor)
Actor
b. Birmingham, England, Nov. 11, 1872
d. Unknown, Dec. 10, 1927, Age 55

ROMAINS, Jules
Playwright, Novelist
b. St. Julien-Chapteuil, France, Aug. 26, 1885
d. Unknown, Nov. 20, 1942, Age 57

ROMANI, Felice
Poet, Librettist
b. Unknown, 1788
d. Unknown, 1865

ROMANO, Charles
Actor
b. London, England, Unknown
d. New York, NY, Aug. 9, 1937, Age 38

ROMANO, Jane
Actress
b. New York, NY, Unknown
d. New York, NY, Aug. 2, 1962, Age 33

ROMBERG, Sigmund
Composer
b. Szeged, Hungary, July 29, 1887
d. New York, NY, Nov. 9, 1951, Age 64

ROMER, Anne (Mrs. William Brough)
Actress
b. Unknown
d. Unknown, Feb. 1, 1852, Age 23

ROMER, Robert
Actor
b. Unknown
d. Unknown, April 5, 1874, Age 66

ROMEYN, Jane (Mrs. Fred Desch)
Actress
b. Unknown
d. Hollywood, CA, May 5, 1963, Age 62

ROOKE, Irene
Actress
b. Bridport, England, Unknown
d. Unknown, June 14, 1958, Age 80

ROONEY, Pat
Performer
b. New York, NY, July 4, 1880
d. New York, NY, Sept. 9, 1962, Age 82

ROOT, George Frederick
Songwriter
b. Sheffield, MA, Aug. 30, 1820
d. Bailey Island, ME, Aug. 6, 1895, Age 74

RORIE, Yvonne
Actress
b. Dundee, Scotland, Nov. 28, 1907
d. Unknown, Feb. 1, 1959, Age 51

RORKE, John
Actor
b. Unknown
d. Unknown, July 21, 1957, Age 65

RORKE, Kate (Mrs. Douglas Cree)
Actress, Teacher
b. London, England, Feb. 22, 1866 (?)
d. Hertfordshire, England, July 31, 1945, Age 81

RORKE, Mary
Actress
b. London, England, Feb. 14, 1858
d. Unknown, Oct. 12, 1938, Age 80

ROSA, Carl (Rose)
Producer
b. Unknown
d. London, England, April 30, 1889, Age 46

ROSA, Nera
Actress
b. Unknown
d. New York, NY, July 19, 1920, Age 80

ROSAR, Annie
Performer
b. Unknown
d. Hollywood, CA, Aug. 1, 1963, Age 75

ROSBAUD, Hans
Conductor
b. Graz, Austria, Unknown
d. Lugano, Switzerland, Dec. 29, 1962, Age 68

ROSCIUS GALLUS, Quintus
Actor
b. Solonium near Lanuvium, c126 B.C.
d. Unknown, 62 B.C.

ROSE, Adrian (Arthur Reed Ropes)
Lyricist, Librettist
b. Lewisham, England, Dec. 28, 1859
d. Unknown, Sept. 10, 1933, Age 73

ROSE, Betty Clarke
Actress
b. Unknown
d. Hollywood, CA, Feb. 2, 1947

ROSE, Billy (né William Samuel Rosenberg)
Producer, Theatre owner, Composer, Lyricist
b. New York, NY, Sept. 6, 1899
d. Montego Bay, Jamaica, Feb. 10, 1966, Age 66

ROSE, Clarkson
Actor, Songwriter
b. Dudley, England, Dec. 8, 1890
d. Eastbourne, England, Apr. 23, 1968, Age 77

ROSE, Edward
Actor, Playwright
b. Unknown
d. Unknown, Dec. 31, 1904, Age 55

ROSE, Edward Everett
Playwright
b. Stanstead, Quebec, CAN, Feb. 11, 1862
d. Fremond, WI, April 2, 1939, Age 77

ROSE, Harry
Performer
b. Unknown
d. Hollywood, CA, Dec. 10, 1962, Age 70

ROSEBERY, Arthur
Producer, Playwright
b. Unknown
d. Unknown, Feb. 11, 1928

ROSELLE, Amy (Mrs. Arthur Dacre, née Hawkins)
b. London, England, 1854
d. Sydney, Australia, Nov. 17, 1895, Age 41

ROSELLE, William
Actor
b. New York, NY, Unknown
d. New York, NY, June 1, 1945, Age 67

ROSENBAUM, Edward Sr.
Manager
b. Unknown
d. New York, NY, Dec. 1927, Age 72

ROSENBERG, Sarah
Actress
b. Unknown
d. Hollywood, CA, June 16, 1964, Age 90

ROSENFELD, Sydney
Playwright
b. Richmond, VA, Oct. 26, 1855
d. New York, NY, June 14, 1931, Age 75

ROSENTHAL, Harry
Composer, Pianist, Actor
b. Belfast, Ireland, Unknown
d. Beverly Hills, CA, May 10, 1953, Age 60

ROSENTHAL, J. J. ("Jake")
Theatrical manager, Talent representative
b. Cincinnati, OH, Unknown
d. Los Angeles, CA, July 1923, Age 60

ROSENTHAL, Jean
Lighting designer
b. New York, NY, March 16, 1912
d. New York, NY, May 1, 1969, Age 57

ROSHANARA, (Olive Craddock)
Dancer
b. India, Unknown
d. Asheville, NC, July 14, 1926

ROSS, Anthony
Actor
b. New York, NY, 1906
d. New York, NY, Oct. 26, 1955, Age 49

ROSS, Charles J. (née Kelly)
Actor
b. Montreal, CAN, Feb. 18, 1859
d. North Asbury Park, NJ, June 15, 1918, Age 59

ROSS, David
Director, Producer
b. St. Paul, MN, June 17, 1922
d. St. Paul, MN, April 13, 1966, Age 43

ROSS, Herbert (Tait)
Actor
b. Calcutta, India, Oct. 3, 1865
d. London, England, July 18, 1934, Age 68

ROSS, Jerry (Jerold Rosenberg)
Composer, Lyricist
b. Bronx, NY, March 9, 1926
d. New York, NY, Nov. 11, 1955, Age 29

ROSS, Mabel Fenton
Actress
b. Van Buren County, MI, Unknown
d. Hollywood, CA, April 19, 1931, Age 63

ROSS, Martin
Playwright, Teacher
b. Unknown
d. Los Angeles, CA

ROSS, Robert
Actor, Director
b. Port Colborne, Ontario, CAN, Unknown
d. New York, NY, Feb. 23, 1954, Age 52

ROSS, Thomas W.
Actor
b. Boston, MA, Jan. 22, 1875
d. Torrington, CT, Nov. 14, 1959, Age 84

ROSS, William
Performer
b. Unknown
d. Pittsburgh, PA, Feb. 25, 1963, Age 38

ROSSE, Frederick
Composer
b. Unknown
d. Unknown, June 20, 1940, Age 73

ROSSE, Russell
Actor, Producer
b. Unknown
d. Unknown, May 15, 1910

ROSSI, Ernesto Fortunato Giovanni
Actor
b. Unknown, 1827
d. Unknown, 1897

ROSSLYN, Elaine
Performer
b. Unknown
d. Blackpool, England, March 1964

ROSTAND, Edmond
Playwright, Poet
b. Marseilles, France, April 1, 1868
d. Paris, France, Dec. 2, 1918, Age 50

ROTHE, Anita
Actress
b. Alexandria, VA, Unknown
d. Bronx, NY, Jan. 9, 1944, Age 77

ROTRON, Jean
Playwright
b. Dreux, France, 1609
d. Dreux, France, 1650

ROUGHWOOD, Owen
Actor
b. London, England, June 9, 1876
d. Unknown, May 30, 1947, Age 70

ROUNSEVILLE, Robert
Singer, Actor
b. Attleboro, MA, March 25, 1914
d. New York, NY, Aug. 6, 1974, Age 60

ROUS, Helen (Shaw)
Actress
b. Carlow, Ireland, Unknown
d. Unknown, March 23, 1934, Age 71

ROUSBY, William Wybert
Actor, Producer
b. Unknown
d. Unknown, Sept. 10, 1907, Age 72

ROUTLEDGE, Calvert
Producer, Actor
b. Unknown
d. Unknown, May 22, 1916

ROUVEROL, Mrs. Aurania
Playwright
b. Palo Alto, CA, Unknown
d. Palo Alto, CA, June 23, 1955, Age 69

ROWE, George Fawcett
Playwright, Actor
b. Unknown, 1834
d. Unknown, Sept. 4, 1889

ROWE, Nicholas
Playwright, Poet
b. Unknown, 1674
d. Unknown, Dec. 6, 1718, Age 44

ROWE, Sir Reginald
Managing Governor of the Old Vic and Sadler's Wells
b. Unknown
d. Unknown, Jan. 21, 1945, Age 75

ROWLAND, H. W.
Producer
b. Unknown
d. Unknown, June 21, 1937, Age 70

ROWLAND, Mabel
Actress
b. Philadelphia, PA, Unknown
d. Hollywood, CA, Feb. 21, 1943, Age 61

ROWLAND, Margery
Critic
b. Pinner, Middlesex, England, Sept. 9, 1910
d. Unknown, Oct. 13, 1945, Age 35

ROWLANDS, Gaynor
Actress, Dancer
b. Unknown
d. Unknown, July 18, 1906

ROWLEY, J. W.
Performer
b. Unknown
d. Unknown, March 23, 1925, Age 78

ROWLEY, Samuel
Playwright, Actor
b. Unknown
d. Unknown, 1624

ROWLEY, William
Actor, Playwright
b. Unknown, c1585
d. Unknown, c1638

ROWSON, Susanna Haswell
Playwright, Actress
b. Unknown
d. Unknown, March 2, 1824, Age 62

ROX, John Jefferson
Lyricist, Composer
b. Unknown
d. Davis Park, Great South Bay, L. I., NY, Aug. 5, 1957, Age 50

ROXBOROUGH, Picton
Actor
b. Unknown
d. Unknown, July 9, 1932, Age 61

ROYAARDS, William (Wilhelm)
Actor, Director
b. Unknown
d. Unknown, Jan. 25, 1929, Age 62

ROYALE, Harry M.
Performer
b. Unknown
d. Libertyville, IL, April 7, 1963, Age 88

ROYCE, Brigham
Actor
b. Memphis, TN, Unknown
d. Baltimore, MD, March 2, 1933, Age 69

ROYCE, Edward
Producer
b. Unknown
d. London, England, June 15, 1964, Age 93

ROYCE, Edward William
Actor
b. Eversholt, Bedfordshire, England, Aug. 11, 1841
d. Unknown, Jan. 24, 1926, Age 84

ROYCE, Julian (Gardner)
Actor
b. Bristol, England, March 26, 1870
d. Unknown, May 10, 1946, Age 76

ROYCE, Virginia
Actress
b. Unknown
d. Hollywood, CA, July 8, 1962, Age 30

ROYDE-SMITH, Naomi
Playwright
b. Lanwrst, Wales, Unknown
d. London, England, July 28, 1964, Age 89

ROYLE, Edwin Milton
Actor, Playwright
b. Lexington, MO, March 2, 1862
d. New York, NY, Feb. 16, 1942, Age 79

ROYLE, Selena Fetter
Actress
b. Kentucky, Unknown
d. Van Nuys, CA, May 10, 1955, Age 95

ROZE, Raymond
Composer, Conductor
b. London, England, 1875
d. Unknown, March 31, 1920, Age 45

RUBEN, Jose
Actor, Director
b. Paris, France, Dec. 8, 1888
d. New York, NY, April 28, 1969, Age 80

RUBENS, Alma
Actress
b. San Francisco, CA, 1898
d. Los Angeles, CA, Jan. 22, 1931, Age 32

RUBENS, Maurie or Maury (Maurice)
Composer
b. New York, NY, Unknown
d. Hollywood, CA, July 24, 1948, Age 55

RUBENS, Paul Alfred
Composer, Playwright
b. Unknown, 1875
d. Falmouth, England, Feb. 4, 1917, Age 42

RUBIN, Menachem
Actor, Director
b. Poland, Unknown
d. New York, NY, June 18, 1962, Age 67

RUBY, Harry
Songwriter
b. New York, NY, Jan. 27, 1895
d. Woodland Hills, CA, Feb. 23, 1974, Age 79

RUEDA, Lope de
Actor, Producer, Playwright
b. Unknown, 1510
d. Unknown, 1565

RUGGERI, Ruggero
Actor
b. Unknown
d. Unknown, July 20, 1953, Age 81

RUHL, Arthur Brown
Drama critic, Journalist
b. Rockford, IL, Unknown
d. Jackson Heights, NY, June 7, 1935, Age 58

RUIZ, Federico
Composer
b. Galicia, Spain, Unknown
d. Mexico City, Mexico, Nov. 1961, Age 72

RUMAN, Sig (né Siegfried Albon Rumann)
Actor
b. Hamburg, Germany, Unknown
d. Julian, CA, Feb. 14, 1967, Age 82

RUMSHINSKY, Joseph M.
Composer
b. Vilna, Russia, Unknown
d. Kew Gardens, NY, Feb. 6, 1956, Age 74

RUNYON, Damon
Playwright, Journalist, Author
b. Manhattan, KS, Oct. 4, 1884
d. New York, NY, Dec. 10, 1946, Age 62

RUSINYOL, Santiago (Rusiol y Prats)
Playwright, Painter
b. Catalan, Spain, 1861
d. Unknown, June 13, 1931

RUSKIN, Sybil
Actress
b. Unknown
d. Unknown, Feb. 10, 1940

RUSSELL, Agnes (Mrs. C. W. Somerset)
Actress
b. Unknown
d. Unknown, July 10, 1947, Age 73

RUSSELL, Annie
Actress
b. Liverpool, England, Jan. 12, 1864
d. Winter Park, FL, Jan. 16, 1936, Age 72

RUSSELL, Byron (Patrick Joseph Russell)
Actor
b. Clonmel, Tipperary, Ireland, Unknown
d. New York, NY, Sept. 4, 1963, Age 79

RUSSELL, Gail
Actress
b. Chicago, IL, Unknown
d. West Los Angeles, CA, April 26, 1961, Age 36

RUSSELL, H. Scott
Actor
b. Malvern, England, Sept. 25, 1868
d. Unknown, Aug. 28, 1949, Age 80

RUSSELL, Henry
Conductor
b. Moorhead, MN, Sept. 4, 1913
d. Sherman Oaks, CA, April 14, 1968, Age 54

RUSSELL, Henry
Composer, Performer
b. Sheerness, England, Dec. 24, 1812
d. London, England, Dec. 8, 1900, Age 87

RUSSELL, Howard
Actor
b. Unknown
d. Unknown, Nov. 15, 1914, Age 81

RUSSELL, Lewis
Actor
b. Unknown
d. Los Angeles, CA, Nov. 12, 1961, Age 76

RUSSELL, Lillian (Helen Louise Leonard)
Singer, Actress
b. Clinton, IA, Dec. 4, 1861
d. Pittsburgh, PA, June 6, 1922, Age 60

RUSSELL, Mabel (Mabel Scott former Countess Russell)
Actress
b. Unknown
d. Maidenhead, England, Sept. 22, 1908, Age 36

RUSSELL, Mabel (Mrs. Hilton Philipson)
Actress, M.P.
b. Unknown, Jan. 1, 1887
d. Brighton, England, Jan. 8, 1951, Age 64

RUSSELL, Marie Booth (Mrs. R. B. Mantell)
Actress
b. Unknown
d. Unknown, Oct. 31, 1911

RUSSELL, Samuel Thomas ("Jerry Sneak" Russell)
Actor
b. Unknown
d. Unknown, Feb. 25, 1845, Age 79

RUSSELL, Sol Smith
Actor
b. Brunswick, MO, June 15, 1848
d. Washington, DC, April 28, 1902, Age 53

RUSSELL, William
Actor, Director
b. Unknown, 1884
d. Unknown, 1929

RUSSELL, William Clark
Biographer
b. Unknown
d. Unknown, Nov. 8, 1911, Age 67

RUSSELL OF LIVERPOOL, Lord (Sir Edward Richard Russell)
Critic, Editor
b. London, England, Aug. 9, 1834
d. Unknown, Feb. 20, 1920, Age 85

RUTHERFORD, Margaret
Actress
b. London, England, May 11, 1892
d. Buckinghamshire, England, May 22, 1972, Age 80

RUTHERSTON, Albert Daniel
Artist, Designer
b. Bradford, England, Dec. 5, 1883
d. Unknown, July 14, 1953, Age 69

RYAN, Conny
Performer
b. Unknown
d. West Haven, CT, May 12, 1963, Age 62

RYAN, Kate
Actress
b. Boston, MA, Unknown
d. Brookline, MA, Nov. 27, 1922, Age 65

RYAN, Lacy
Actor
b. Unknown, 1694
d. Unknown, 1760

RYAN, Mary (Mrs. Sam Forrest)
Actress
b. Brooklyn, NY, Nov. 11, 1885
d. Cranford, NJ, Oct. 2, 1948, Age 62

RYAN, Robert
Actor
b. Chicago, IL, Nov. 11, 1909
d. New York, NY, July 11, 1973, Age 63

RYAN, T. E.
Scenic artist
b. Unknown
d. Unknown, Oct. 21, 1920

RYDER, Arthur W.
Educator, Play translator
b. Oberlin, OH, Unknown
d. Berkeley, CA, March 21, 1938, Age 61

RYERSON, Florence (Mrs. Colin Clements, née Florence Willard)
Playwright, Screenwriter
b. Glendale, CA, Sept. 20, 1892
d. Mexico City, Mexico, June 8, 1965, Age 72

RYLEY, J. H.
Actor
b. Unknown
d. Unknown, July 28, 1922, Age 81

RYLEY, Madeleine Lucette
Actress, Playwright
b. London, England, Dec. 26, 1865
d. London, England, Feb. 17, 1934, Age 68

RYLEY, Samuel William
Actor, Author
b. Unknown
d. Unknown, Sept. 12, 1837, Age 82

S

SAAVEDRA, Angel de (Duke of Rivas)
Playwright
b. Cordova, Spain, 1791
d. Unknown, 1865

SABATINI, Rafael
Playwright, Novelist
b. Jesi, Italy, April 29, 1875
d. Unknown, Feb. 13, 1950, Age 74

SABBATTINI, Nicola
Architect, Designer
b. Unknown, 1574
d. Unknown, 1654

SABEL, Josephine
Actress
b. Lawrence, MA, Unknown
d. Unknown, Dec. 24, 1945, Age 79

SABU, (Sabu Dastagir)
Actor
b. Karapur Jungle, Mysore, India, Unknown
d. Chatsworth, CA, Dec. 2, 1963, Age 39

SACHS, Hans
Playwright, Singer
b. Nuremberg, Germany, Nov. 5, 1494
d. Nuremberg, Germany, Jan. 20, 1576, Age 81

SACKS, Joseph Leopold
Theatre manager
b. Russia, Feb. 17, 1881
d. Unknown, May 18, 1952, Age 71

SADOVSKY (ERMILOV), Prov Michailovich
Actor
b. Moscow, Russia, 1818
d. Unknown, 1872

SAGARRA Y CASTALLARNAU, Jose Maria de
Playwright
b. Unknown
d. Barcelona, Spain, Oct. 25, 1961, Age 67

SAINT-DENIS, Michel Jacques
Director
b. Beauvais, France, Sept. 13, 1897
d. London, England, July 31, 1971, Age 73

SAINTE-BEUVE, Charles Augustin
Critic
b. Boulogne-sur-Mer, France, Dec. 23, 1804
d. Paris, France, Oct. 13, 1869, Age 64

SAINT-EVREMOND, Sieur de (Charles de Marguetel de Saint-Denis)
Critic
b. Château de Saint-Denis-le-Guast, France, 1610
d. London, England, 1703

SAINT GELASIUS (Gelasinus) OF HELIOPPOLIS
Attributed actor and patron saint of actors
b. Unknown
d. Heliopolis, 297 A.D.

SAINT GENESIUS THE COMEDIAN
Attributed actor and patron saint of actors
b. Unknown
d. Rome, Italy, c286 A.D.

SAINT-SAENS, (Charles) Camille
Composer
b. Paris, France, Oct. 3, 1835
d. Algiers, Dec. 16, 1921, Age 86

SAINTSBURY, H. A.
Actor, Playwright
b. Chelsea, London, England, Dec. 18, 1869
d. Unknown, June 19, 1939, Age 69

SAKALL, S. Z. (Szoke Szakall)
Actor
b. Budapest, Hungary, Unknown
d. Hollywood, CA, Feb. 12, 1955, Age 67

SAKER, Annie
Actress
b. Unknown, March 13, 1882
d. Unknown, Oct. 8, 1932, Age 50

SAKER, Edward
Actor, Producer
b. Unknown
d. Unknown, March 29, 1883, Age 52

SAKER, Horace
Actor
b. Unknown
d. Unknown, April 2, 1861, Age 34

SAKER, Horatio
Actor
b. Unknown
d. Unknown, Oct. 19, 1902, Age 54

SAKER, Maria
Actress
b. Unknown
d. Unknown, Sept. 1, 1902

SAKER, Mrs. Edward
Actress
b. Unknown
d. Unknown, Feb. 6, 1912, Age 64

SAKER, Richard Henry
Actor, Producer
b. Unknown
d. Unknown, April 26, 1870, Age 28

SAKER, Rose
Actress
b. London, England, Unknown
d. Unknown, Sept. 22, 1923

SAKER, William
Actor
b. Unknown
d. Unknown, June 22, 1849, Age 59

SALA, George Augustus
Playwright, Journalist
b. Unknown
d. Unknown, Dec. 8, 1895, Age 67

SALAMAN, Malcolm C.
Critic
b. Unknown
d. Unknown, Jan. 22, 1940, Age 84

SALBERG, Leon
Producer
b. Unknown
d. Unknown, Sept. 29, 1937, Age 62

SALE, Charles ("Chic")
Comedian, Author
b. Huron, SD, Aug. 25, 1885
d. Los Angeles, CA, Nov. 7, 1936, Age 51

SALINGER, Conrad
Composer
b. Unknown
d. Hollywood, CA, June 18, 1962, Age 59

SALISBURY, Leah
Literary representative
b. Joplin, MO, Unknown
d. New York, NY, Nov. 2, 1975, Age 82

SALMOND, Norman
Actor
b. Unknown
d. Unknown, April 28, 1914, Age 56

SALSBURY, "Nate" Nathan
Playwright, Producer
b. Freeport, IL, Feb. 28, 1846
d. Long Beach, NJ, Dec. 24, 1902, Age 56

SALVINI, Alexander or Alessandro
Actor
b. Rome, Italy, Dec. 21, 1860
d. Unknown, Dec. 15, 1896, Age 35

SALVINI, Gustavo
Actor
b. Civita Vecchia, Italy, May 24, 1859
d. Pisa, Italy, Dec. 20, 1930, Age 71

SALVINI, Tommaso
Actor, Producer
b. Milan, Italy, Jan. 1, 1829
d. Florence, Italy, Jan. 1, 1916, Age 87

SALZER, Eugene
Musical director, Conductor
b. Unknown
d. Brooklyn, NY, Jan. 29, 1964, Age about 80

SAMARY, Jeanne
Actress
b. Unknown
d. Unknown, Sept. 18, 1890, Age 33

SAMARY, Marie
Actress
b. Unknown
d. Paris, France, June 1941, Age 93

SAMMIS, George W.
Manager
b. Unknown
d. Sound Beach, CT, April 1927, Age 72

SAMPSON, William
Actor
b. Unknown
d. New York, NY, April 6, 1922, Age 63

SAMSON, Ivan
Performer
b. Brighton, England, Aug. 28, 1894
d. London, England, May 1, 1963, Age 68

SAMSON, Joseph Isidore
Actor, Teacher, Playwright
b. Unknown, 1793
d. France, 1871

SANCHEZ, Florencio
Journalist, Playwright
b. Montevideo, Uruguay, 1875
d. Unknown, 1917

SAND, George (Mme. Amandine Lucile Aurore Dudevant, née Dupin)
Playwright, Novelist
b. Paris, France, July 1, 1804
d. Nohant, France, June 8, 1876, Age 71

SANDERS, Scott
Performer
b. Unknown
d. Unknown, Dec. 2, 1956, Age 68

SANDERSON, Julia
Actress, Singer
b. Springfield, MA, Aug. 20, 1887
d. Springfield, MA, Jan. 27, 1975, Age 87

SANDISON, Gordon H.
General sec'y. of British Actors' Equity Association
b. Newcastle-on-Tyne, England, April 17, 193
d. Unknown, July 3, 1958, Age 45

SANDROCK, Adele
Actress
b. Unknown
d. Unknown, Aug. 30, 1937, Age 73

SANDS, Diana
Actress
b. New York, NY, Aug. 22, 1934
d. New York, NY, Sept. 21, 1973, Age 39

SANGER, Fred
Performer
b. Unknown
d. Newcastle-on-Tyne, England, 1923, Age 72

SANTLEY, Fredric
Actor
b. Unknown
d. Los Angeles, CA, May 14, 1953, Age 65

SANTLEY, Kate
Actress, Producer
b. U.S.A., Unknown
d. Brighton, England, Jan. 18, 1923, Age 86

SANTLOW, Hester (Mrs. Barton Booth)
Actress
b. Unknown
d. Unknown, Jan. 15, 1778, Age 93

SANTLY, Joseph H. ("Banjo")
Performer, Songwriter
b. New York, NY, Aug. 21, 1886
d. New York, NY, Aug. 28, 1962, Age 76

"SAPPER"
(Lt.-Col. Cyril McNeile), Playwright, Novelist
b. Unknown
d. Unknown

SARCEY, Francisque
Critic
b. Unknown, 1827
d. Unknown, May 15, 1899, Age 71

SARDOU, Victorien
Playwright
b. Paris, France, Sept. 7, 1831
d. Paris, France, Nov. 8, 1908, Age 77

SARGENT, Epes Winthrop (Chic)
Drama critic
b. Nassau, Bahamas, Unknown
d. Brooklyn, NY, Dec. 6, 1938, Age 66

SARGENT, Franklin H.
Educator, Producer
b. Unknown
d. Plattsburg, NY, Aug. 29, 1923

SARNER, Alexander
Actor
b. London, England, Dec. 17, 1892
d. Unknown, Jan. 6, 1948, Age 55

SARRACINI, Gerald
Actor
b. Unknown
d. New York, NY, Dec. 26, 1957, Age 30

SASS, Edward
Actor
b. Unknown
d. Unknown, Nov. 15, 1916, Age 58

SASS, Enid
Actress
b. London, England, Jan. 11, 1889
d. Unknown, Feb. 12, 1959, Age 70

SATIKOV-SHCHEDRIN, Mikhail Evgrafavich
Essayist, Playwright
b. Unknown, 1826
d. Unknown, 1889, Age 63

SAUNDERS, Charlotte
Actress
b. Unknown
d. Unknown, March 31, 1899, Age 73

SAUNDERS, E. G.
Producer
b. Unknown
d. Unknown, May 19, 1913

SAUNDERS, Florence
Actress
b. Valparaiso, Chile, Unknown
d. Unknown, Jan. 24, 1926, Age 35

SAUNDERS, John
Playwright
b. Unknown
d. Unknown, March 29, 1895, Age 84

SAVAGE, Henry Wilson
Manager
b. New Durham, NH, March 21, 1859
d. Boston, MA, Nov. 29, 1927, Age 68

SAVAGE, Richard
Playwright, Poet
b. Unknown
d. Unknown, Aug. 1, 1743, Age 46

SAVILLE, Edmund Faucit
Actor
b. Unknown, 1811
d. London, England, Nov. 20, 1857, Age 46

SAVILLE, J. Faucit
Actor
b. Unknown
d. Unknown, Dec. 31, 1855, Age 48

SAVILLE, Kate
Actress
b. Unknown
d. Unknown, May 7, 1922

SAVILLE, Mrs. E. Faucit
Actress, Producer
b. Unknown
d. Unknown, Aug. 25, 1879

SAVILLE, Mrs. J. Faucit
Actress, Producer
b. Unknown
d. Unknown, March 31, 1889, Age 77

SAVILLE, T. G.
Actor
b. Unknown
d. London, England, May 30, 1934, Age 31

SAVINA, Maria
Actress
b. Unknown
d. Unknown, Sept. 21, 1915, Age 61

SAVO, Jimmy (Sava)
Actor
b. Bronx, NY, 1895
d. Terni, Italy, Sept. 6, 1960, Age 64

SAVOIR, Alfred (Alfred Poznanski)
Playwright
b. Lodz, Poland, Unknown
d. Paris, France, June 26, 1934, Age 51

SAWYER, Charles P.
Music and drama critic
b. Newbury, MA, Unknown
d. New York, NY, May 8, 1935, Age 80

SAXE, Templar (Templar Edward Edeveain)
Actor
b. Redhill, Surrey, England, 1866
d. Unknown, April 17, 1935, Age 70

SAXE-MEININGEN, Georg II Duke of
Producer, Director
b. Meiningen, Germany, April 2, 1826
d. Meiningen, Germany, 1914, Age 88

SAXON, Marie
Actress
b. Lawrence, MA, Unknown
d. Harrison, NY, Nov. 12, 1941, Age 37

SAYERS, Dorothy L.
Playwright, Novelist
b. Oxford, England, June 13, 1893
d. Unknown, Dec. 17, 1957, Age 64

SAYERS, Harry
Producer, Songwriter
b. Unknown
d. Unknown, 1934, Age 77

SAYLOR, Oliver Martin
Playwright, Critic
b. Huntington, IN, Oct. 23, 1887
d. Mamaroneck, NY, Oct. 19, 1958, Age 71

SAYLOR, Syd
Performer
b. Unknown
d. Hollywood, CA, Dec. 21, 1962, Age 67

SCALIGER, Julius Ceasar
Critic
b. Unknown, 1484
d. Unknown, 1588

SCAMOZZI, Vincenzo
Architect
b. Unknown, 1552
d. Unknown, 1616

SCANLAN, W. James
Performer, Songwriter
b. Springfield, MA, Feb. 14, 1856
d. White Plains, NY, Feb. 19, 1898, Age 42

SCARDON, Paul
Actor, Director
b. Unknown
d. Fontana, CA, Jan. 17, 1954, Age 79

SCHADER, Freddie (Frederic F.)
Press representative, Journalist
b. Unknown
d. Bronx, NY, April 2, 1962, Age 77

SCHARF, Herman
Performer
b. Unknown
d. Hollywood, CA, April 8, 1963, Age 62

SCHAUFFLER, Elsie T.
Playwright
b. Baltimore, MD, Unknown
d. New York, NY, Oct. 24, 1935, Age 47

SCHEERER, Maud
Actress, Teacher
b. Unknown
d. New York, NY, Sept. 12, 1961, Age 80

SCHEFF, Fritzi (née Anna Scheff Yager)
Actress, Singer
b. Vienna, Austria, Aug. 30, 1879
d. New York, NY, April 8, 1954, Age 74

SCHENCK, Joe (Joseph T. Schenck)
Singer
b. Brooklyn, NY, Unknown
d. Detroit, MI, June 28, 1930, Age 39

SCHEPP, Dieter
Acrobat
b. Germany, Unknown
d. Detroit, MI, Jan. 28, 1962, Age 23

SCHERTZINGER, Victor
Composer, Conductor, Film director
b. Mahanoy City, PA, April 8, 1890
d. Hollywood, CA, Oct. 26, 1941, Age 52

SCHILDKRAUT, Joseph
Actor
b. Vienna, Austria, March 22, 1895
d. New York, NY, Jan. 21, 1964, Age 68

SCHILDKRAUT, Rudolph
Actor
b. Wallachia, Unknown
d. Los Angeles, CA, July 15, 1930, Age 65

SCHILLER, Johann Christoph Friedrich von
Playwright, Poet
b. Marbach, Wurtemberg, Germany, Nov. 10, 1759
d. Weimar, Germany, May 9, 1805, Age 45

SCHILLER, Leon
Director, Producer
b. Unknown, 1887
d. Unknown, 1954

SCHLANGER, Ben
Architect
b. New York, NY, Nov. 20, 1904
d. New York, NY, May 3, 1971, Age 66

SCHLEGEL, August Wilhelm von
Playwright, Critic, Author, Translator
b. Hanover, Germany, 1767
d. Unknown, 1845

SCHLEGEL, Johann Elias von
Playwright
b. Unknown, 1719
d. Unknown, 1749

SCHLENTER, Dr. Paul
Producer, Actor
b. Unknown
d. Unknown, May 1916, Age 62

SCHLESINGER, Isidore
Theatre owner, Producer
b. Unknown
d. Unknown, March 11, 1949, Age 78

SCHLETTER, Annie
Actress
b. Unknown
d. Unknown, Dec. 27, 1944

SCHMIDTBONN, Wilhelm (ne' Wilhelm Schmidt)
Playwright
b. Bonn, Germany, Feb. 6, 1876
d. Bad Goolesberg, Germany, July 3, 1952, Age 76

SCHMITT-SENTNER, Willy
Composer
b. Unknown
d. Vienna, Austria, Feb. 14, 1964, Age 70

SCHNHERR, Karl
Playwright
b. Axams, Tyrol, Austria, Feb. 4, 1867
d. Vienna, Austria, March 15, 1943, Age 76

SCHNITZLER, Arthur
Playwright
b. Vienna, Austria, May 15, 1862
d. Vienna, Austria, Oct. 21, 1931, Age 69

SCHOFIELD, Johnny
Actor, Minstrel
b. Unknown
d. Unknown, Dec. 21, 1921, Age 65

SCHONEMANN, Johann Friedrich
Actor, Producer
b. Unknown, 1704
d. Unknown, 1782

SCHRADER, Frederich Franklin
Journalist, Critic, Playwright
b. Hamburg, Germany, Oct. 27, 1857
d. New York, NY, March 1943, Age 85

SCHRAT, Katharina
Actress
b. Unknown
d. Unknown, April 17, 1940, Age 84

SCHREYVOGEL, Joseph
Producer
b. Unknown, 1768
d. Unknown, 1832, Age 64

SCHRODER, Friedrich Ludwig
Actor, Producer
b. Unknown, 1744
d. Holstein, Germany, Sept. 3, 1816, Age 72

SCHROEDER, Sophia Charlotta (né e Biereichel)
Actress, Producer
b. Unknown, 1714
d. Unknown, 1792, Age 78

SCHUBERT, Franz Peter
Composer
b. Himmelpfortgrund, Vienna, Austria, Jan. 31, 1797
d. Vienna, Austria, Nov. 19, 1828, Age 31

SCHUDY, Frank
Theatre manager
b. Unknown
d. Kansas City, MO, May 19, 1963, Age 59

SCHUENZEL, Reinhold
Actor, Director
b. Hamburg, Germany, Nov. 7, 1886
d. Munich, Germany, Sept. 11, 1954, Age 67

SCHULBERG, B. P. (Benjamin Percival)
Producer
b. Bridgeport, CT, Jan. 19, 1892
d. Key Biscayne, FL, Feb. 25, 1957, Age 65

SCHUMANN, Walter
Composer, Conductor
b. New York, NY, Oct. 8, 1913
d. Minneapolis, MN, Aug. 21, 1958, Age 44

SCHWAB, Laurence
Playwright, Producer
b. Boston, MA, Dec. 17, 1893
d. Southampton, L.I., NY, May 29, 1951, Age 57

SCHWARTZ, Abe
Composer, Conductor
b. Unknown
d. New York, NY, May 7, 1963, Age 75

SCHWARTZ, Jean
Composer, Performer
b. Budapest, Hungary, Nov. 4, 1878
d. Los Angeles, CA, Nov. 30, 1956, Age 78

SCHWARTZ, Maurice
Actor, Producer
b. Sedikor, Russia, June 18, 1890
d. Petah Tikva, Israel, May 10, 1960, Age 69

SCOTT, Clement William
Critic, Poet, Playwright
b. Unknown, 1841
d. Unknown, June 25, 1904, Age 62

SCOTT, Cyril
Actor
b. Banbridge, County Down, Ireland, Feb. 9, 1866
d. Flushing, NY, Aug. 16, 1945, Age 79

SCOTT, Gertrude
Actress
b. . . .near Sevenoaks, Kent, England, Unknown
d. Unknown, Dec. 23, 1951

SCOTT, Harold
Actor
b. Unknown
d. London, England, April 15, 1964, Age 73

SCOTT, Harry (Scott and Whaley)
Performer
b. Unknown
d. Unknown, June 22, 1947, Age 67

SCOTT, Ivy
Actress
b. Unknown
d. New York, Ny, Feb. 4, 1947, Age 61

SCOTT, John R.
Actor
b. Unknown
d. Unknown, April 4, 1856, Age 46

SCOTT, Malcolm
Comedian
b. Unknown
d. Unknown, Sept. 7, 1929, Age 57

SCOTT, Noel
Playwright
b. Manchester, England, Dec. 25, 1889
d. Unknown, Nov. 20, 1956, Age 66

SCOTT, Richard L.
Performer
b. Unknown
d. Hollywood, CA, May 5, 1962, Age 36

SCOTT, Zachary Thomson
Actor
b. Austin, TX, Feb. 21, 1914
d. Austin, TX, Oct. 3, 1965, Age 51

SCOTT-GATTY, Alexander
Actor
b. Ecclesfield, Yorkshire, England, Oct. 3, 1876
d. Unknown, Nov. 6, 1937, Age 61

SCRIBE, (Augustine) Eugè ne
Playwright
b. Paris, France, Dec. 25, 1791
d. Paris, France, Feb. 20, 1861, Age 69

SCRIBNER, Samuel A.
Theatrical manager
b. Brookville, PA, Unknown
d. Bronxville, NY, July 8, 1941, Age 82

SCUDAMORE, Frank A.
Playwright, Actor
b. Unknown
d. Unknown, Nov. 1, 1904, Age 58

SCUDAMORE, Margaret
Actress
b. Portsmouth, England, Nov. 13, 1884
d. Unknown, Oct. 5, 1958, Age 73

SCULLION, James H. J.
Theatre treasurer
b. Unknown
d. New York, NY, July 14, 1920

SEABROOKE, Thomas Q. (Thomas James Quigley)
Performer
b. Mount Vernon, NY, Oct. 20, 1860
d. Chicago, IL, April 3, 1913, Age 52

SEAGRAM, Wilfrid
Actor
b. Finchley, England, Jan. 10, 1884
d. New York, NY, May 28, 1938, Age 54

SEAMAN, Isaac
Critic, Journalist
b. Unknown
d. Unknown, Dec. 16, 1923, Age 88

SEAMAN, Julia
Actress
b. Unknown
d. Unknown, Jan. 30, 1909, Age 71

SEAMAN, Sir Owen
Critic, Editor
b. Unknown, Sept. 18, 1861
d. Unknown, Feb. 2, 1936, Age 74

SEARS, Zelda (née Paldi)
Actress, Playwright
b. Brockway, MI, Jan. 21, 1873
d. Hollywood, CA, Feb. 19, 1935, Age 62

SEASTROM, Victor (Sjoestroem)
Actor, Film director
b. Varmland, Sweden, Sept. 21, 1879
d. Stockholm, Sweden, Jan 3, 1960, Age 80

SEBASTIAN, Dorothy
Actress
b. Birmingham, AL, Unknown
d. Hollywood, CA, April 8, 1957, Age 52

SEDLEY, Sir Charles
Playwright
b. Unknown, c1639
d. Unknown, Aug. 20, 1701

SEDLEY-SMITH, William Henry
Actor, Theatre manager
b. England, 1806
d. San Francisco, CA, 1872

SEEBOHM, E. V.
Playwright
b. Unknown
d. Unknown, Sept. 11, 1888

SEELEY, Blossom
Actress
b. San Francisco, CA, Unknown
d. New York, NY, April 17, 1974, Age 82

SEELEY, James L.
Actor
b. Rushville, IL, Unknown
d. New York, NY, Feb. 15, 1943, Age 76

SEFTON, Ernest
Actor
b. Unknown
d. Unknown, Dec. 5, 1954, Age 71

SEGER, Lucia Backus
Actress
b. Unknown
d. New York, NY, Jan. 17, 1962, Age 88

SEILER, Lewis
Film director
b. Unknown
d. Hollywood, CA, Jan. 8, 1964, Age 73

SELBY, Charles
Actor, Playwright
b. Unknown
d. London, England, March 21, 1963, Age 62

SELBY, Mrs. Charles
Actress
b. Unknown
d. Unknown, Feb. 8, 1873, Age 76

SELBY, Percival M.
Producer
b. London, England, April 19, 1886
d. Unknown, Nov. 25, 1955, Age 69

SELDES, Gilbert
Playwright, Critic
b. Alliance, NJ, Jan. 3, 1893
d. New York, NY, Oct. 1, 1970, Age 77

SELIG, William Nicholas
Performer, Film producer
b. Chicago, IL, 1864
d. Hollywood, CA, July 16, 1948, Age 84

SELIGMANN, Lilias Hazewell MacLane
Dancer
b. Unknown
d. New York, NY, Aug. 22, 1964, Age 71

SELLAR, Robert J. B.
Playwright, Journalist
b. Unknown
d. Edinburgh, Scotland, Oct. 10, 1960, Age 67

SELTEN, Morton (Morton Richard Stubbs)
Actor
b. Unknown, Jan. 6, 1860
d. London, England, July 27, 1939, Age 79

SELWYN, Archibald ("Arch")
Producer
b. Toronto, CAN, Unknown
d. Los Angeles, CA, June 21, 1959, Age 82

SELWYN, Edgar
Actor, Playwright, Producer
b. Cincinnati, OH, Oct. 20, 1875
d. Hollywood, CA, Feb. 13, 1944, Age 68

SELWYN, Ruth
Producer, Actress
b. Unknown
d. Hollywood, CA, Dec. 13, 1954, Age 49

SELZNICK, Lewis J.
Film executive
b. New York, NY, Unknown
d. Los Angeles, CA, Jan. 25, 1933, Age 62

SELZNICK, Myron
Talent representative
b. Pittsburgh, PA, Unknown
d. Santa Monica, CA, March 23, 1944, Age 45

SEMENOVA, Ekaterina Semenovna
Actress
b. Unknown, 1786
d. Unknown, 1849

SENECA, Lucius Annaeus
Playwright, Philosopher, Tutor
b. Cordoba, Spain, c3 B.C.
d. Unknown, 65 A.D.

SENSENDERFER, Robert E. P.
Drama critic
b. Philadelphia, PA, Unknown
d. Ivyland, PA, Jan. 2, 1957, Age 73

SERGINE, Vera
Actress
b. Unknown
d. Unknown, Aug. 22, 1946, Age 62

SERJEANTSON, Kate (née Morris)
Actress
b. Unknown
d. Unknown, Feb. 16, 1918

SERLE, T. J.
Actor, Playwright
b. Unknown
d. Unknown, March 20, 1889, Age 90

SERLIN, Oscar
Producer
b. Yalowa, Poland, Jan. 30, 1901
d. New York, NY, Feb. 27, 1971, Age 70

SERLIO, Sebastiano
Architect, Painter, Critic
b. Unknown, c1473
d. Unknown, 1554

SERRANO, Vincent
Actor
b. New York, NY, Feb. 17, 1870
d. New York, NY, Jan. 10, 1935, Age 64

SERVANDONY, Jean Nicolas
Scene designer
b. Lyons, France, 1695
d. Unknown, 1766

SETH, Will (née William Bullock)
Performer
b. Unknown
d. Leicester, England, July 1964

SETTLE, Elkanah
Playwright, Poet
b. Unknown, 1648
d. London, England, Feb. 12, 1724, Age 76

SEVERIN-MARA, M.
Actor
b. Unknown
d. Unknown, July 17, 1920

SEWELL, Hetty Jane (Mrs. Wayne P. Sewell, née Dunaway)
Actress, Playwright
b. Arkansas, Unknown
d. Newman, GA, Dec. 12, 1961

SEYMOUR, Clarine
Actress
b. Unknown, 1900
d. Unknown, 1919

SEYMOUR, (Cunningham) James
Actor
b. Belfast, Ireland, 1823
d. Unknown, 1864

SEYMOUR, Jane (Mrs. John W. Lair, née Marjorie Seymour Fitz-patrick)
Actress
b. Hamilton, Ontario, CAN, Unknown
d. New York, NY, Jan. 29, 1956, Age 57

SEYMOUR, May Davenport
Stage historian, Archivist, Actress
b. Boston, MA, Dec. 5, 1883
d. New York, NY, Oct. 5, 1967, Age 83

SEYMOUR, Mrs. Laura
Actress, Producer
b. Unknown
d. Unknown, Sept. 25, 1879, Age 59

SEYMOUR, William Gorman
Actor, Director
b. New York, NY, Dec. 19, 1855
d. Plymouth, MA, Oct. 2, 1933, Age 77

SHACKLETON, Robert W.
Actor
b. Lawrence, MA, Unknown
d. Jacksonville, FL, June 21, 1956, Age 42

SHADE, Lillian
Performer
b. Unknown
d. Beverly Hills, CA, May 8, 1962, Age 51

SHADWELL, Charles
Playwright
b. Unknown
d. Unknown, Aug. 12, 1726

SHADWELL, Thomas
Playwright
b. Weeting, Norfolk, England, 1642
d. Unknown, Nov. 19, 1692, Age 50

SHAIRP, (Alexander) Mordaunt
Playwright
b. Totnes, Devon, England, March 13, 1887
d. Unknown, Jan. 18, 1939, Age 51

SHAKESPEARE, William
Playwright, Poet
b. Stratford-upon-Avon, England, April 22 or 23, 1564
d. Stratford-upon-Avon, England, April 23, 1616, Age 52

SHAKHOVSKY, Alexander Alexandrovich
Playwright
b. . . . near Smolensk, Russia, 1777
d. Unknown, 1846

SHALE, Thomas Augustin
Actor
b. Birmingham, England, Sept. 10, 1867
d. Unknown, 1953

SHAND, John
Critic, Journalist
b. Clifton, Bristol, England, Jan. 30, 1901
d. Unknown, Oct. 27, 1955, Age 54

SHANNON, Effie
Actress
b. Cambridge, MA, May 13, 1867
d. Bay Shore, NY, July 23, 1954, Age 87

SHANNON, Harry
Actor
b. Unknown
d. Hollywood, CA, July 27, 1964, Age 74

SHANNON, Peggy
Actress
b. Pine Bluff, AR, Jan. 10, 1907
d. North Hollywood, CA, May 11, 1941, Age 34

SHANNON, Winona (Mrs. Albert G. Andrews)
Actress
b. Boston, MA, Unknown
d. New York, NY, Oct. 17, 1950, Age 76

SHARLAND, Reginald
Actor
b. Southend-on-Sea, England, Nov. 19, 1886
d. Unknown, Aug. 21, 1944, Age 57

SHARP, Henry (Henry Schacht)
Actor, Teacher
b. Unknown
d. Brooklyn, NY, Jan. 10, 1964, Age 77

SHARPHAM, Edward
Playwright
b. Unknown
d. Unknown, April 23, 1608, Age 32

SHATTUCK, Ethel (Greenman)
Performer
b. Unknown
d. Hollywood, CA, Jan. 25, 1963, Age 73

SHATTUCK, Truly (Claire Etrulia)
Performer
b. San Miguel, CA, July 27, 1876
d. Unknown, Dec. 6, 1954, Age 78

SHAW, Arthur W.
Actor
b. New York, NY, Unknown
d. Washington, DC, March 22, 1946, Age 65

SHAW, George Bernard
Playwright, Essayist, Critic
b. Dublin, Ireland, July 26, 1856
d. Ayot St. Lawrence, England, Nov. 2, 1950, Age 94

SHAW, Mary
Actress
b. Boston, MA, 1854
d. New York, NY, May 18, 1929, Age 75

SHAW, Mrs. George Bernard (née Charlotte Frances Payne-Townshend)
Playwright
b. Derry, County Cork, Ireland, 1857
d. London, England, Sept. 12, 1943, Age 86

SHAW, Robert Gould
Curator of Harvard College Theatrical Collection
b. Unknown
d. Unknown, April 10, 1931, Age 80

SHCHEPKIN, Mikhail Semenovich
Actor
b. Kursk Province, Russia, 1788
d. Unknown, 1863, Age 75

SHCHUKIN, Boris Vasilievich
Actor
b. Unknown, 1894
d. Moscow, U.S.S.R., Oct. 7, 1939, Age 45

SHEA, Thomas E.
Actor, Playwright
b. East Cambridge, MA, Unknown
d. Cambridge, MA, April 23, 1940, Age 79

SHEAN, Al (Schonberg)
Actor
b. Dornum, Germany, May 12, 1868
d. New York, NY, Aug. 12, 1949, Age 81

SHEEHAN, Jack (John Sheehan, Jr.)
Actor
b. Manchester, NH, Oct. 22, 1890
d. New York, NY, Dec. 11, 1958, Age 68

SHEFFIELD, Leo
Actor
b. Malton, Yorkshire, England, Nov. 15, 1873
d. Unknown, Sept. 3, 1951, Age 77

SHEFFIELD, Nellie
Actress
b. Unknown
d. Unknown, Feb. 23, 1957, Age 84

SHEFFIELD, Reginald
Actor
b. London, England, Feb. 18, 1901
d. Pacific Palisades, CA, Dec. 8, 1957, Age 56

SHEIL, Richard Lalor
Playwright
b. Unknown
d. Unknown, Nay 25, 1851, Age 59

SHELDON, Edward Brewster
Playwright
b. Chicago, IL, Feb. 4, 1886
d. New York, NY, April 1, 1946, Age 60

SHELDON, Harry Sophus
Playwright
b. Copenhagen, Denmark, Unknown
d. New York, NY, March 18, 1940, Age 63

SHELDON, Herb
Performer
b. Brooklyn, NY, Unknown
d. Manhasset, L.I., NY, July 21, 1964, Age 51

SHELDON, Jerome
Actor
b. Unknown
d. Hollywood, CA, April 15, 1962, Age 71

SHELDON, Jerry (Charles H. Patton)
Actor
b. Unknown
d. Hollywood, CA, April 11, 1962, Age 61

SHELDON, Marie (Mrs. R. B. Mantell)
Actress
b. Edinburgh, Scotland, Unknown
d. Bronx, NY, April 11, 1939, Age 83

SHELDON, Suzanne (Mrs. Henry Ainley)
Actress
b. Vermont, Jan. 24, 1875
d. Unknown, March 21, 1924, Age 49

SHELLEY, Herbert
Actor, Author, Producer
b. Unknown
d. Unknown, Feb. 28, 1921, Age 50

SHELLEY, Percy Bysshe
Poet, Playwright
b. Horsham, Sussex, England, Aug. 4, 1792
d. Via Reggio, Italy, July 8, 1822, Age 29

SHELTON, George
Actor
b. Manchester, England, Jan. 26, 1852
d. Unknown, Sept. 17, 1932, Age 80

SHELTON, Kenneth E.
Performer
b. Unknown
d. Santa Barbara, CA, Aug. 16, 1962, Age 37

SHELVING, Paul
Designer, Artist
b. Rowley, England, Unknown
d. Warwick, England, June 5, 1968, Age 79

SHENBURN, Archibald A.
Producer
b. London, England, Jan. 17, 1905
d. Unknown, July 12, 1954, Age 49

SHEPHARD, Firth
Producer, Playwright, Director
b. London, England, April 27, 1891
d. London, England, Jan. 3, 1949, Age 57

SHEPLEY, Michael
Actor
b. Plymouth, England, Sept. 29, 1907
d. Unknown, Sept. 28, 1961, Age 54

SHEPLEY, Ruth (Mrs. Beverly Chew Smith)
Actress
b. Providence, RI, May 29, 1892
d. New York, NY, Oct. 15, 1951, Age 59

SHERBROOKE, Michael
Actor
b. Unknown, Dec. 15, 1874
d. Unknown, April 3, 1957, Age 82

SHEREK, Henry
Producer, Director
b. London, England, April 23, 1900
d. Venice, Italy, Sept. 23, 1967, Age 67

SHERIDAN, Elizabeth Ann (Linley)
Singer
b. Unknown, 1754
d. Unknown, June 28, 1792, Age 37

SHERIDAN, Frances Chamberlayne
Playwright
b. England, 1724
d. Blois, France, Sept. 1766, Age 42

SHERIDAN, Frank
Actor
b. Boston, MA, Unknown
d. Hollywood, CA, Nov. 24, 1943, Age 74

SHERIDAN, Richard Brinsley
Playwright, Producer
b. Dublin, Ireland, Oct. 30, 1751
d. London, England, July 7, 1816, Age 64

SHERIDAN, William Edward
Actor
b. Unknown, 1840
d. Australia, 1887, Age 47

SHERINGHAM, George
Designer, Artist
b. London, England, Nov. 13, 1885
d. Unknown, Nov. 11, 1937, Age 52

SHERMAN, John K.
Critic
b. Sioux City, IA, April 19, 1898
d. Minneapolis, MN, April 18, 1969, Age 70

SHERMAN, Lowell J.
Actor, Film director
b. San Francisco, CA, Oct. 11, 1885
d. Hollywood, CA, Dec. 28, 1934, Age 49

SHERRIFF, Robert C.
Playwright
b. Kingston-on-Thames, England, June 6, 1896
d. London, England, Nov. 13, 1975, Age 79

SHERWIN, Jeannette (née Gorlitz)
Actress
b. Unknown
d. Unknown, July 8, 1936, Age 42

SHERWOOD, Garrison P.
Actor, Director, Critic
b. New York, NY, March 30, 1902
d. New York, NY, Feb. 12, 1963, Age 60

SHERWOOD, Robert Emmet
Playwright
b. New Rochelle, NY, Aug. 4, 1896
d. New York, NY, Nov. 14, 1955, Age 59

SHIELDS, Helen
Actress
b. British Honduras, Unknown
d. New York, NY, Aug. 7, 1963

SHIELDS, Sydney
Actress
b. New Orleans, LA, Unknown
d. Elmhurst, Queens, NY, Sept. 19, 1960, Age 72

SHIELS, George
Playwright
b. County Antrim, Ireland, June 24, 1886
d. Ballymoney, Ireland, Sept. 19, 1949, Age 63

SHILKRET, Jack
Composer, Bandleader
b. New York, NY, Unknown
d. New York, NY, June 16, 1964, Age 67

SHINE, John L.
Actor
b. Unknown, March 28, 1854
d. Unknown, Oct. 17, 1930, Age 76

SHINE, Wilfred E.
Actor
b. Manchester, England, July 12, 1864
d. Unknown, March 14, 1939, Age 74

SHIPMAN, Louis Evan
Playwright, Novelist
b. Brooklyn, NY, Aug. 2, 1869
d. Boury-en-Vexin, France, Aug. 2, 1933, Age 64

SHIPMAN, Samuel
Playwright
b. New York, NY, Dec. 25, 1883
d. New York, NY, Feb. 9, 1937, Age 53

SHIPP, Cameron
Biographer, Author
b. Dallas, TX, Unknown
d. Glendale, CA, Aug. 20, 1961, Age 57

SHIPP, Julia Lowande
Performer
b. Unknown
d. New York, NY, Jan. 9, 1962, Age 91

SHIRLEY, Arthur
Playwright
b. London, England, Feb. 17, 1853
d. Unknown, Aug. 22, 1925, Age 72

SHIRLEY, James
Playwright
b. Unknown, 1596
d. London, England, Oct. 29, 1666, Age 70

SHIRLEY, Thomas P. (Tom)
Actor, Announcer
b. Unknown
d. New York, NY, Jan. 24, 1961, Age 62

SHIRLEY, Walter Sr.
Performer
b. Unknown
d. Palm Beach, FL, Jan. 31, 1963, Age 67

SHIRLEY, William
Playwright
b. Unknown, 1739
d. Unknown, 1780

SHIRRA, Edmonston
Actor
b. Unknown
d. Unknown, June 28, 1861

SHORT, Ernest Henry
Historian, Author, Journalist
b. Unknown
d. London, England, Aug. 29, 1959, Age 78

SHORT, Frank Lea
Actor, Director
b. Kansas City, MO, Unknown
d. Yonkers, NY, June 14, 1949, Age 75

SHORT, Hassard
Director, Actor, Producer
b. Eddington, England, Oct. 15, 1877
d. Nice, France, Oct. 9, 1956, Age 79

SHOTWELL, Marie
Actress
b. New York, NY, Unknown
d. Long Island City, NY, Sept. 18, 1934, Age 54

SHRADER, Frederick P.
Critic, Editor
b. Unknown
d. Unknown, March 1943, Age 85

SHREVE, Tiffany (née Carol Everson)
Actress
b. Unknown
d. Hollywood, CA, April 2, 1964, Age 31

SHRINER, Herb
Humorist
b. Toledo, OH, May 29, 1918
d. Unknown, Apr. 24, 1976, Age 51

SHUBERT, Jacob J.
Producer, Theatre proprietor
b. Syracuse, NY, Aug. 15, 1880 (?)
d. New York, NY, Dec. 26, 1963, Age 86

SHUBERT, John
Producer, Theatre proprietor
b. New York, NY, Dec. 13, 1908
d. Florida, Nov. 17, 1962, Age 53

SHUBERT, Lee
Producer, Theatre proprietor
b. Syracuse, NY, March 15, 1875
d. New York, NY, Dec. 25, 1953, Age 78

SHUBERT, Milton I. (né Isaacson)
Producer, Theatre executive
b. Syracuse, NY, Unknown
d. Boynton, FL, March 7, 1967, Age 66

SHUBERT, Sam S.
Producer, Theatre proprietor
b. Syracuse, NY, 1875
d. Harrisburg, PA, May 12, 1905, Age 30

SHUTER, Edward (Ned)
Actor
b. St. Giles, London, England, 1728
d. London, England, Nov. 2, 1776, Age 48

SHY, Gus
Performer
b. Unknown
d. Hollywood, CA, June 15, 1945, Age 51

SIBELIUS, Jean (Johan Julius Christian Sibelius)
Composer
b. Hämeenlinna, Tavastehus, Finland, Dec. 8, 1865
d. Järvenpää, Finland, Sept. 20, 1957, Age 91

SIBLEY, Lucy
Actress
b. Isle of Wight, England, Unknown
d. Unknown, Dec. 30, 1945

SICKERT, Walter Richard
Artist, Actor
b. Unknown
d. Unknown, Jan. 22, 1942, Age 81

SIDDONS, Henry
Actor, Author
b. Unknown
d. Unknown, April 12, 1815, Age 40

SIDDONS, Mrs. Harriett
Actress
b. Unknown
d. Unknown, Dec. 2, 1844, Age 61

SIDDONS, Mrs. Sarah (Kemble)
Actress
b. Brecon, Wales, July 5, 1755
d. London, England, June 8, 1831, Age 75

SIDNEY, George
Actor
b. Hungary, Unknown
d. Hollywood, CA, April 29, 1945, Age 68

SIEGEL, Max
Producer
b. Unknown
d. New York, NY, Nov. 16, 1958, Age 57

SIENKIEWICZ, Henryk
Playwright, Novelist
b. Volla Okrejska, Lithuania, May 4, 1846
d. Vevey, Switzerland, Nov. 16, 1916, Age 71

SIGNORET, Gabriel
Actor
b. Marseilles, France, Nov. 15, 1878
d. Paris, France, March 16, 1937, Age 58

SILETTI, Mario G.
Actor
b. Unknown
d. Los Angeles, CA, April 19, 1964, Age 60

SILL, William Raymond
Press representative, Drama editor
b. Hartford, CT, Unknown
d. Flushing, NY, Dec. 1, 1922, Age 53

SILLS, Milton
Actor
b. Chicago, IL, Jan. 12, 1882
d. Los Angeles, CA, Sept. 15, 1930, Age 48

SILLWARD, Edward
Actor, Impersonator
b. Unknown
d. Unknown, April 1930

SILVA, António José da
Playwright
b. Rio de Janiero, Brazil, 1705
d. Portugal, 1739

SILVAIN, Eugène Charles Joseph
Actor
b. Bourg, Ain, France, Jan. 17, 1851
d. Saint Cyr les Secques, Var, France, Aug. 21, 1930, Age 79

SIL-VARA, G.
Playwright
b. Vienna, Austria, Unknown
d. Unknown, April 5, 1938, Age 62

SILVERA, Frank
Actor, Director, Producer
b. Kingston, Jamaica, July 24, 1914
d. Pasadena, CA, June 11, 1970, Age 56

SILVERMAN, Sid (Sidne)
Publisher
b. New York, NY, Dec. 11, 1898
d. Harrison, NY, March 10, 1950, Age 51

SILVERMAN, Sime
Editor, Publisher
b. Cortland, NY, May 19, 1872
d. Los Angeles, CA, Sept. 22, 1933, Age 61

SILVERS, Louis
Composer
b. New York, NY, Unknown
d. Hollywood, CA, March 26, 1954, Age 64

SIMON, Charles
Playwright
b. Unknown
d. Unknown, May 31, 1910, Age 60

SIMONS, Seymour
Songwriter
b. Unknown
d. Detroit, MI, Feb. 12, 1949, Age 53

SIMONSON, Lee
Scene designer, Artist, Editor
b. New York, NY, June 26, 1888
d. Yonkers, NY, Jan. 23, 1967, Age 78

SIMPSON, Cheridah
Actress
b. Unknown
d. New York, NY, Dec. 26, 1922, Age 58

SIMPSON, Edmund Shaw
Actor, Producer
b. Unknown, 1784
d. Unknown, 1848

SIMPSON, Ivan
Actor
b. Hargate, England, Unknown
d. New York, NY, Oct. 12, 1951, Age 76

SIMPSON, J. Palgrave
Playwright
b. Unknown
d. Unknown, Aug. 19, 1887, Age 82

SIMPSON, Ronald
Actor
b. Acton, Middlesex, England, Sept. 27, 1896
d. Unknown, Sept. 23, 1957, Age 61

SIMPSON, Russell
Actor
b. Unknown
d. Woodland Hills, CA, Dec. 12, 1959, Age 81

SIMS, George Robert
Playwright, Novelist
b. Unknown, Sept. 2, 1847
d. London, England, Sept. 4, 1922, Age 75

SINCLAIR, Arthur (née McDonnell)
Actor
b. Dublin, Ireland, Aug. 3, 1883
d. Belfast, Ireland, Dec. 14, 1951, Age 68

SINCLAIR, Hugh
Actor
b. London, England, May 19, 1903
d. Slapton, England, Dec. 29, 1962, Age 59

SINCLAIR, Moray
Actor, Press representative
b. Prince Albert, Saskatchewan, CAN, Unknown
d. Vancover, British Columbia, CAN, Jan. 27, 1964, Age 63

SINCLAIR, Robert B. Broadway-Film Director
Toledo, OH
b. May 24, 1905, Montecito, CA
d. Jan. 2, 1970, 65

SINGER, John
Actor, Playwright
b. Unknown, 1594
d. Unknown, 1602

SIPPERLEY, Ralph
Actor
b. Unknown
d. Bangor, ME, Jan. 1928, Age 38

SIRE, Henry B.
Producer
b. Unknown
d. Unknown, Jan. 17, 1917

SITGREAVES, Beverly
Actress
b. Charleston, SC, April 17, 1867
d. New York, NY, July 14, 1943, Age 76

SKEFFINGTON, Sir Lumley
Playwright
b. Unknown
d. Unknown, Nov. 10, 1850, Age 79

SKINNER, Frank
Composer, Film director
b. Meredosia, IL, Dec. 31, 1897
d. Hollywood, CA, Oct. 11, 1968, Age 69

SKINNER, Harold Otis
Actor
b. Unknown
d. San Diego, CA, Sept. 1922, Age 33

SKINNER, Otis
Actor, Producer, Author
b. Cambridge, MA, June 28, 1858
d. New York, NY, Jan. 4, 1942, Age 83

SKINNER, Richard
Producer
b. Watertown, MA, Feb. 27, 1900
d. New York, NY, Aug. 3, 1971, Age 71

SKIPWORTH, Alison
Actress
b. London, England, July 25, 1863
d. New York, NY, July 5, 1952, Age 88

SKOURAS, George P.
Theatre executive
b. Skourohorion, Greece, Unknown
d. New York, NY, March 16, 1964, Age 68

SKULNIK, Menasha
Actor
b. Warsaw, Poland, May 15, 1892
d. New York, NY, June 4, 1970, Age 78

SLADE, Olga
Actress
b. Unknown
d. Unknown, April 24, 1949

SLATER, George M.
Actor, Producer
b. Unknown
d. Unknown, Aug. 26, 1949, Age 79

SLATER, Hartley
Performer
b. Unknown
d. Morecambe, Lancashire, England, Feb. 1964, Age 63

SLATKIN, Felix
Arranger, Conductor, Composer
b. Unknown
d. Hollywood, CA, Feb. 8, 1963, Age 47

SLATTERY, Daniel G.
Manager
b. Unknown
d. Piscataway Township, NJ, June 28, 1964, Age 91

SLAUGHTER, N. Carter ("Tod")
Actor, Producer
b. Newcastle-on-Tyne, England, March 19, 1885
d. Unknown, Feb. 19, 1956, Age 70

SLAUGHTER, Walter
Composer
b. Unknown
d. Unknown, March 2, 1908, Age 48

SLAVIN, John C.
Actor
b. New York, NY, Unknown
d. New York, NY, Aug. 27, 1940, Age 71

SLEATH, Herbert (Herbert Sleath Skelton)
Actor, Producer
b. Unknown, Oct. 8, 1870
d. Unknown, Sept. 26, 1921, Age 51

SLOAN, Alfred Baldwin
Playwright, Composer
b. Baltimore, MD, Aug. 28, 1872
d. Red Bank, NJ, Feb. 21, 1925, Age 52

SLOANE, Everett
Actor
b. New York, NY, Oct. 1, 1909
d. Brentwood, CA, Aug. 6, 1965, Age 55

SLOUS, A. R.
Playwright
b. Unknown
d. Unknown, March 28, 1883, Age 71

SLY, William
Actor
b. Unknown
d. Unknown, (buried) Aug. 16, 1608

SMALL, Jack
Theatre manager, Booker
b. New York, NY, Unknown
d. Gibralter, Spain, April 27, 1962, Age 52

SMALL, Lillian Schary
Talent representative
b. Unknown
d. Los Angeles, CA, Dec. 16, 1961, Age 60

SMALL, Paul
Talent representative
b. Brooklyn, NY, Unknown
d. New York, NY, Aug. 6, 1954, Age 45

SMART, Christopher
Playwright, Poet
b. Unknown
d. Unknown, May 21, 1771, Age 49

SMEDLEY, Morgan T.
Actor, Teacher
b. Philadelphia, PA, Unknown
d. New York, NY, May 7, 1964, Age 46

SMITH, Albert
Playwright, Performer, Novelist
b. Unknown, 1816
d. London, England, May 23, 1860, Age 44

SMITH, Arthur Corbett
Playwright, Composer
b. Unknown
d. Unknown, Jan. 17, 1945, Age 65

SMITH, Beasley
Composer
b. McEwen, TN, Sept. 27, 1901
d. Nashville, TN, May 14, 1968, Age 67

SMITH, Betty (née Elizabeth Keogh)
Writer - Playwright
b. Brooklyn, NY, Dec. 6, 1906
d. Shelton, CT, Jan. 17, 1972, Age 75

SMITH, Billy ("Little Billy Smith")
Performer
b. Unknown
d. New York, NY, March 13, 1963, Age 60

SMITH, Bruce
Scenic artist
b. Unknown
d. Unknown, Nov. 8, 1942, Age 87

SMITH, Chris
Composer
b. Charleston, SC, Oct. 12, 1879
d. New York, NY, 1949, Age 70

SMITH, Cyril
Performer
b. Peterhead, Scotland, April 4, 1892
d. London, England, March 5, 1963, Age 70

SMITH, Eddie
Talent representative
b. Unknown
d. Mesa, AZ, Feb. 5, 1964, Age 70

SMITH, Edgar McPhail
Librettist, Playwright, Actor
b. Brooklyn, NY, Dec. 9, 1857
d. Bayside, Queens, NY, March 8, 1938, Age 80

SMITH, Elmer
Performer
b. Unknown
d. Philadelphia, PA, Jan. 18, 1963, Age 71

SMITH, Elsie Linehan (Mrs. A. A. Southwick)
Actress
b. Unknown
d. Cleveland, OH, March 26, 1964, Age 86

SMITH, Frank L.
Press representative, Theatre manager
b. Brooklyn, NY, Unknown
d. New York, NY, Feb. 8, 1953, Age 67

SMITH, Frederick Wilson
Actor
b. Unknown
d. Miami, FL, July 13, 1944, Age 64

SMITH, G. Albert
Actor
b. Louisville, KY, Unknown
d. New York, NY, Sept. 3, 1959, Age 61

SMITH, George T.
Producer
b. Unknown
d. Unknown, May 21, 1947, Age 45

SMITH, Harry Bache
Librettist, Lyricist
b. Buffalo, NY, Dec. 28, 1860
d. Atlantic City, NJ, Jan. 1, 1936, Age 75

SMITH, Howard I.
Actor
b. Attleboro, MA, Aug. 12, 1894
d. Hollywood, CA, Jan. 10, 1968, Age 73

SMITH, J. Sebastian
Actor
b. Southwell, Nottinghamshire, England, Oct. 3, 1869
d. Unknown, Jan. 15, 1948, Age 78

SMITH, Jack ("Whispering Jack Smith")
Singer
b. New York, NY, May 31, 1898
d. New York, NY, May 13, 1950, Age 52

SMITH, Joe
Performer
b. Unknown
d. Unknown, 1952

SMITH, Mark (Marcus)
Actor
b. New Orleans, LA, Jan. 7, 1829
d. Paris, France, Aug. 11, 1874, Age 45

SMITH, Mark III
Actor
b. New York, NY, Unknown
d. New York, NY, May 9, 1944, Age 57

SMITH, Moses
Music critic, Biographer
b. Unknown
d. Boston, MA, July 27, 1964, Age 63

SMITH, Paul G.
Playwright, Actor, Director
b. Omaha, NE, Sept. 14, 1894
d. San Diego, CA, April 4, 1968, Age 73

SMITH, Richard Penn
Playwright
b. Unknown, 1799
d. Unknown, 1854, Age 55

SMITH, Robert B.
Librettist, Songwriter
b. Chicago, IL, Unknown
d. New York, NY, Nov. 6, 1951, Age 76

SMITH, Sir C. (Charles) Aubrey
Actor
b. Brighton or London, England, July 21, 1863
d. Beverly Hills, CA, Dec. 20, 1948, Age 85

SMITH, Sol (Solomon Franklin Smith)
Actor, Lawyer
b. Norwich, NY, April 20, 1801
d. St. Louis, MO, 1869, Age 67

SMITH, Sydney
Business manager, Director of Drury Lane
b. Unknown
d. Unknown, July 9, 1935, Age 80

SMITH, Wentworth
Playwright
b. Unknown, 1601
d. Unknown, 1620

SMITH, William ("Gentleman Smith")
Actor
b. Unknown, 1730
d. Unknown, 1819, Age 89

SMITH, William Henry
Actor, Playwright
b. Unknown
d. Unknown, Jan. 17, 1872, Age 66

SMITH, Winchell
Actor, Producer, Director, Playwright
b. Hartford, CT, April 5, 1872
d. Mill Stream, Farmington, CT, June 10, 1933, Age 61

SMITHSON, Florence
Actress
b. Leicester, England, March 13, 1884
d. Unknown, Feb. 11, 1936, Age 51

SMITHSON, Frank
Actor, Director
b. Tralee, Ireland, Unknown
d. New York, NY, Jan. 15, 1949, Age 88

SMITHSON, Henrietta Constance (Mme. Berlioz)
Actress
b. Ennis, County Clare, Ireland, March 18, 1800
d. Unknown, March 3, 1854, Age 53

SMITHSON, Will
Producer
b. Unknown
d. Unknown, Feb. 9, 1927, Age 67

SMOLLETT, Tobias George
Playwright, Novelist
b. Dalquhurn, Dumbartonshire, Scotland, 1721
d. Leghorn, Italy, Sept. 17, 1771, Age 50

SMYTHE, James Moore
Playwright
b. Unknown
d. Unknown, Oct. 18, 1734, Age 32

SMYTHE, William G.
Producer, Manager
b. Unknown
d. New York, NY, Sept. 15, 1921, Age 66

SNOW, Marguerite
Actress
b. Unknown
d. Woodland Hills, CA, Feb. 17, 1958, Age 69

SNOW, Valaida
Singer, Dancer
b. Unknown
d. Unknown, May 29, 1956, Age 42

SNYDER, Gene
Dance Director
b. Fairfax, MN, Unknown
d. New York, NY, April 15, 1953, Age 45

SOANE, George
Playwright
b. Unknown
d. Unknown, July 13, 1860, Age 69

SOBEL, Bernard
Press representative, Historian, Author
b. Attica, IN, March 13, 1887
d. New York, NY, March 12, 1964, Age 77

SOBOL, Edward
Producer
b. Unknown
d. Santa Monica, CA, March 11, 1962, Age 70

SOBOTKA, Ruth
Costume designer, Actress, Dancer
b. Vienna, Austria, Unknown
d. New York, NY, June 17, 1967, Age 42

SOHLKE, Gus (Augustus)
Director
b. Unknown, Aug. 21, 1865
d. Unknown, June 7, 1924, Age 58

SOKOLOFF, Vladimir
Actor, Musician
b. Moscow, Russia, Dec. 25, 1889
d. Hollywood, CA, Feb. 14, 1962, Age 72

SOLAR, Willie
Performer
b. Unknown
d. Unknown, Dec. 17, 1956, Age 65

SOLDENE, Emily
Performer
b. Islington, England, 1840
d. London, England, April 8, 1912, Age 72

SOLOMON, Edward
Composer
b. Unknown
d. Unknown, Jan. 22, 1895, Age 36

SOLSKI, Ludwik
Actor
b. Poland, March 20, 1854
d. Cracow, Poland, Dec. 1954, Age 100

SOMAN, Claude
Producer
b. London, England, Oct. 29, 1897
d. Unknown, Oct. 1960, Age 63

SOMERSET, C. W.
Actor
b. Unknown, 1847
d. London, England, Feb. 5, 1929, Age 82

SOMMERS, Harry G.
Theatre manager
b. Cairo, IL, Unknown
d. New York, NY, May 15, 1953, Age 80

SOMNES, George
Producer, Director, Actor
b. Boston, MA, Unknown
d. Denver, CO, Feb. 8, 1956, Age 68

SOPHOCLES
Playwright
b. Colonus, Greece, 495 B.C.
d. Unknown, 406 B.C., Age 88

SORIN, Louis
Actor
b. New York, NY, 1893
d. New York, NY, Dec. 14, 1961, Age 68

SORMA (ZAREMBA), Agnes (Countess Agnes Minotto)
Actress
b. Germany, 1865
d. Crown King, AZ, Feb. 10, 1927, Age 62

SOTHERN, E. A. (Edward Askew, née Douglas Stewart)
Actor
b. Liverpool, England, April 1, 1826
d. London, England, Jan. 20, 1881, Age 54

SOTHERN, Edward Hugh
Actor
b. New Orleans, LA, Dec. 6, 1859
d. New York, NY, Oct. 28, 1933, Age 73

SOTHERN, Harry
Actor
b. London, England, April 26, 1883
d. New York, NY, Feb. 22, 1957, Age 73

SOTHERN, Hugh (a/k/a Roy Sutherland)
Actor
b. Unknown
d. Hollywood, CA, April 13, 1947, Age 65

SOTHERN, Jean
Actress
b. Unknown
d. Lancaster, PA, April 14, 1964

SOTHERN, Sam
Actor
b. England, Unknown
d. Los Angeles, CA, March 21, 1920, Age 55

SOUDEIKINE, Serge
Designer
b. Tiflis, Russia, Unknown
d. Nyack, NY, Aug. 12, 1946, Age 64

SOUPER, G. Kay
Actor
b. Unknown
d. Unknown, Jan. 2, 1947

SOUSA, John Philip
Composer, Bandmaster
b. Washington, DC, Nov. 6, 1854
d. Reading, PA, March 6, 1932, Age 77

SOUTAR, Andrew
Playwright, Novelist
b. Unknown
d. Saint Austell, Cornwall, England, Nov. 24, 1941, Age 61

SOUTAR, Robert
Actor, Playwright
b. Unknown
d. Unknown, Sept. 28, 1908, Age 81

SOUTH, Eddie
Musician
b. Louisiana, MO, 1904
d. Chicago, IL, April 25, 1962, Age 57

SOUTHERNE, Thomas
Playwright
b. . . . near Dublin, Ireland, 1660
d. Unknown, May 26, 1746, Age 85

SOVEY, Raymond
Scene designer
b. Torrington, CT, 1897
d. Columbus, OH, June 25, 1966, Age 72

SOWARDS, Len
Actor, Stuntman
b. Unknown
d. Sawtelle, CA, Aug. 20, 1962, Age 69

SPARKS, Ned (Edward A. Sparkman)
Actor
b. Guelph, Ontario, CAN, Unknown
d. Victorville, CA, April 3, 1957, Age 73

SPEAKS, Oley
Composer, Singer
b. Canal Winchester, OH, June 28, 1874
d. New York, NY, Aug. 27, 1948, Age 74

SPENCE, Edward F.
Critic
b. Liverpool, England, 1860
d. Unknown, May 28, 1932, Age 71

SPENCE, Ralph
Director
b. Unknown
d. Unknown, Dec. 22, 1949, Age 59

SPENCER, Gabriel
Actor
b. Unknown
d. Haxton Fields, England, Sept. 22, 1598

SPENCER, Kenneth
Singer
b. Los Angeles, CA, Unknown
d. New Orleans, LA, (airline crash), Feb. 25, 1964, Age 51

SPENCER, Willard
Composer
b. Cooperstown, NY, July 7, 1852
d. Philadelphia, PA, Dec. 16, 1933, Age 81

SPEWACK, Samuel
Playwright
b. Bachmut, Russia, Sept. 16, 1899
d. New York, NY, Oct. 14, 1971, Age 71

SPIKER, Ray (Ray Faust)
Actor, Stuntman
b. Unknown
d. Hollywood, CA, Feb. 23, 1964, Age 62

SPILLER, Emily
Actress
b. Unknown
d. Unknown, Jan. 14, 1941, Age 81

SPONG, Hilda
Actress
b. London, England, May 14, 1875
d. Norwalk, CT, May 16, 1955, Age 80

SPONG, W. B.
Scenic artist
b. Unknown
d. Unknown, March 2, 1929, Age 79

SPOONER, Edna May
Actress
b. Centerville, IA, Unknown
d. Sherman Oaks, CA, July 14, 1953, Age 78

SPOTTSWOOD, James
Actor
b. Washington, DC, Unknown
d. New York, NY, Oct. 11, 1940, Age 58

SPRY, Henry
Playwright
b. Unknown
d. Unknown, Feb. 17, 1904, Age 69

SQUIRE, Ronald
Actor
b. Tiverton, Devonshire, England, March 25, 1886
d. London, England, Nov. 16, 1958, Age 72

STAGG, Charles
Actor, Dancing instructor
b. Unknown
d. Williamsburg, VA, 1735

STAHL, Rose
Actress
b. Montreal, CAN, Oct. 29, 1875 (?)
d. Flushing, L.I., NY, July 16, 1955, Age 84

STALLINGS, Laurence
Playwright, Screenwriter
b. Macon, GA, Nov. 25, 1894
d. Pacific Palisades, CA, Feb. 28, 1968, Age 73

STAMMERS, Frank
Composer
b. Unknown
d. New York, NY, June 27, 1921

STAMPER, David
Composer, Musician
b. New York, NY, Nov. 10, 1883
d. Poughkeepsie, NY, Sept. 18, 1963, Age 79

STAMPER, F. Pope
Actor
b. Richmond, Surrey, England, Nov. 20, 1880
d. Unknown, Nov. 12, 1950, Age 70

STANDING, Ellen
Actress
b. Unknown
d. Unknown, March 23, 1906, Age 50

STANDING, Emily
Actress
b. Unknown
d. Unknown, March 9, 1899

STANDING, Herbert
Actor
b. Peckham, England, Nov. 13, 1846
d. Los Angeles, CA, Dec. 5, 1923, Age 77

STANDING, Herbert
Actor
b. London, England, Unknown
d. New York, NY, Sept. 23, 1955, Age 71

STANDING, Sir GUY
Actor
b. London, England, Sept. 1, 1873
d. Hollywood, CA, Feb. 24, 1937, Age 63

STANFIELD, Clarkson
Scenic artist, Painter
b. Unknown, 1793
d. Unknown, 1867

STANFORD, Henry
Actor
b. Ramleh, Egypt, Jan. 22, 1872
d. Great Kills, NY, Feb. 19, 1921, Age 49

STANGE, Stanislaus
Playwright, Actor
b. Liverpool, England, Unknown
d. Unknown, Jan. 2, 1917, Age 56

STANISLAUS, Frederick
Composer, Conductor
b. Unknown
d. Unknown, Nov. 22, 1891, Age 47

STANISLAVSKY, Constantin Sergeivich (C. S. Alexeyev)
Actor, Producer, Director, Teacher
b. Moscow, Russia, 1863
d. Moscow, U.S.S.R., Aug. 7, 1938, Age 75

STANLEY, Alma
Actress
b. Unknown
d. Unknown, March 8, 1931, Age 78

STANLEY, Lilian
Actress
b. Unknown
d. Unknown, Nov. 10, 1943, Age 65

STANLEY, S. Victor
Actor
b. Clun, Salop, England, Feb. 17, 1892
d. Unknown, Jan. 29, 1939, Age 46

STANMORE, Frank
Actor
b. London, England, March 10, 1878
d. Unknown, Aug. 15, 1943, Age 65

STANTLEY, Ralph
Actor, Editor-Publisher
b. Unknown
d. Williamsburg, VA, June 5, 1964, Age 67

STAPLETON, Sir Robert
Playwright
b. Unknown
d. Unknown, July 10, 1669

STARLING, Lynn
Playwright
b. Hopkinsville, KY, Unknown
d. Hollywood, CA, March 1955, Age 67

STARR, Frances
Actress
b. Oneonta, NY, June 6, 1881
d. New York, NY, June 11, 1973, Age 92

STARR, Muriel (née Muriel MacIver)
Actress
b. near Montreal, CAN, Feb. 20, 1888
d. New York, NY, April 19, 1950, Age 62

ST. AUDRIE, Stella
Actress
b. Unknown
d. Unknown, May 11, 1925, Age 49

STAYTON, Frank
Playwright
b. Unknown
d. Unknown, Jan. 29, 1951, Age 76

ST. DENIS, Ruth
Dancer
b. Newark, NJ, Jan. 20, 1877
d. Hollywood, CA, July 21, 1968, Age 88-91

STEARNS, Edith Bond
Producer
b. Unknown
d. Mount Clements, MI, Nov. 15, 1961, Age 77

STEARNS, Myron Morris
Writer, Editor, Producer
b. Unknown
d. Palm Beach, FL, April 19, 1963, Age 78

STEBBINS, Rowland
Producer, under name of Laurence Rivers
b. New York, NY, 1882
d. New York, NY, Dec. 12, 1948, Age 66

STECK, Olga
Singer
b. California, Unknown
d. San Francisco, CA, Dec. 18, 1935, Age 38

STEDMAN, Lincoln
Actor, Producer
b. Unknown
d. Hollywood, CA, March 22, 1948, Age 41

STEDMAN, Myrtle (née Lincoln)
Actress
b. Chicago, IL, 1888
d. Hollywood, CA, Jan. 8, 1938, Age 50

STEEL, Susan
Actress
b. Unknown
d. Washington, DC, Nov. 11, 1959, Age 54

STEELE, Blanche (Mrs. W. H. Hallatt)
Actress
b. Unknown
d. Unknown, Feb. 15, 1944, Age 80

STEELE, Sir Richard
Playwright, Journalist
b. Dublin, Ireland, baptized March 12, 1672
d. Carmarthen, Wales, Sept. 1, 1729, Age 57

STEELE, Vernon (née Antonietti)
Actor
b. Santiago, Chile, Sept. 18, 1882
d. Los Angeles, CA, July 23, 1955, Age 72

STEELE, Wilbur Daniel
Writer - Playwright
b. Greensboro, NC, March 17, 1886
d. Essex, CT, May 26, 1970, Age 84

STEEVENS, George
Shakespearean authority
b. Unknown
d. Unknown, Jan. 22, 1800, Age 63

STEFAN, Virginia
Actress
b. Unknown
d. New York, NY, May 5, 1964, Age 38

STEFFEN, Albert
Playwright, Poet, Novelist
b. Bern, Switzerland, 1884
d. Dornach, Switzerland, July 13, 1963, Age 78

STEGER, Julius
Actor, Singer
b. Vienna, Austria, Unknown
d. Vienna, Austria, March 1959

STEGUWEIT, Heinz
Playwright, Novelist
b. Unknown
d. Halver, Germany, May 20, 1964, Age 67

STEHLI, Edgar
Actor
b. Lyon, France, July 12, 1884
d. Upper Montclair, NJ, July 25, 1973, Age 89

STEIN, Gertrude
Librettist, Lyricist, Playwright, Author
b. Allegheny, PA, Feb. 3, 1874
d. Neuilly, Paris, France, July 27, 1946, Age 72

STEINBECK, John
Playwright, Novelist
b. Salinas, CA, Feb. 27, 1902
d. New York, NY, Dec. 20, 1968, Age 66

STEINBERG, Amy
Actress
b. Unknown
d. Unknown, Nov. 4, 1920, Age 70

STEINER, Max (né Maximilian Raoul Steiner)
Theatre and Film Music Composer
b. Vienna, Austria, May 10, 1888
d. Hollywood, CA, Dec. 28, 1971, Age 83

STEPHENS, George
Playwright
b. Unknown
d. Unknown, Oct. 15, 1851

STEPHENS, H. Pottinger
Playwright
b. Unknown
d. Unknown, Feb. 13, 1903

STEPHENS, J. Frank
Publisher
b. Unknown
d. New York, NY, Jan. 18, 1950, Age 72

STEPHENS, Mrs. W. H. ("Granny")
Actress
b. Unknown
d. Unknown, Jan. 15, 1896, Age 83

STEPHENS, Yorke
Actor, Producer
b. London, England, Sept. 26, 1862
d. Unknown, Feb. 5, 1937, Age 74

STEPHENSEN, B. C.
Playwright
b. Unknown
d. Unknown, Jan. 22, 1906, Age 67

STEPHENSON, Henry (née Garraway)
Actor
b. Grenada, British West Indies, April 16, 1871
d. San Francisco, CA, April 24, 1956, Age 85

STEPHENSON, James
Actor
b. Unknown
d. Unknown, July 29, 1941, Age 52

STEPHENSON, John
Performer, Producer
b. Unknown
d. Dublin, Ireland, June 1, 1963, Age 74

STERLING, Edythe
Actress
b. Unknown
d. Hollywood, CA, June 4, 1962, Age 75

STERLING, Ford (George F. Stitch)
Actor
b. LA Crosse, WI, c1884
d. Unknown, Oct. 15, 1939, Age 55

STERLING, Richard (née Albert G. Leggatt)
Actor
b. New York, NY, Aug. 30, 1880
d. Douglaston, NY, April 15, 1959, Age 78

STERN, Ernest
Stage designer
b. Bucharest, Romania, 1876
d. Unknown, Aug. 28, 1954, Age 78

STERN, Joseph W.
Songwriter, Music publisher
b. New York, NY, Jan. 11, 1870
d. Brightwater, L.I., NY, March 31, 1934, Age 64

STERNAD, Rudolph
Art director
b. Unknown
d. Knoxville, TN, April 21, 1963, Age 57

STERNDALE-BENNETT, T. C.
Composer, Performer
b. Unknown
d. Unknown, May 16, 1944

STERNHEIM, Carl
Playwright
b. Germany, 1878
d. Switzerland, March 1943, Age 65

STERNROYD, Vincent
Actor
b. Highgate, London, England, Oct. 8, 1857
d. Unknown, Nov. 3, 1948, Age 91

STETTHEIMER, Florine
Designer, Artist
b. Unknown
d. New York, NY, May 12, 1944

STETTITH, Olive
Actress
b. Unknown
d. Unknown, Nov. 15, 1937

STEVENS, Ashton
Critic
b. San Francisco, CA, Aug. 11, 1872
d. Chicago, IL, July 11, 1951, Age 78

STEVENS, Charles
Actor
b. Unknown
d. Hollywood, CA, Aug. 22, 1964, Age 71

STEVENS, Emily
Actress
b. New York, NY, Feb. 27, 1882
d. New York, NY, Jan. 2, 1928, Age 45

STEVENS, George Alexander
Actor, Author
b. Unknown
d. Unknown, Sept. 6, 1784, Age 74

STEVENS, Inger (nee Inger Stensland)
Actress
b. Stockholm, Sweden, Oct. 18, 1934
d. Los Angeles, CA, April 30, 1970, Age 35

STEVENS, John A.
Playwright, Actor
b. Unknown
d. Unknown, June 2, 1916, Age 73

STEVENS, Morton L.
Performer
b. Unknown
d. Marlboro, MA, Aug. 5, 1959, Age 69

STEVENS, Robert
Actor, Director
b. Unknown
d. Lauderdale-by-the-Sea, FL, Dec. 3, 1963, Age 83

STEVENS, Thomas Wood
Author, Director
b. Daysville, IL, Unknown
d. Tucson, AR, Jan. 29, 1942, Age 62

STEVENS, Victor
Actor, Playwright
b. Unknown
d. Unknown, Dec. 14, 1925, Age 72

STEVENSON, Charles A.
Actor
b. Dublin, Ireland, Unknown
d. New York, NY, July 2, 1929, Age 77

STEVENSON, Douglas
Actor
b. Versailles, KY, Unknown
d. Versailles, KY, Dec. 31, 1934, Age 52

STEVENSON, William
Teacher, Playwright
b. Unknown
d. Unknown, 1575

STEWART, Anita
Actress
b. Brooklyn, NY, Unknown
d. Beverly Hills, CA, May 4, 1961, Age 65

STEWART, Athole
Actor, Director
b. Ealing, England, June 25, 1879
d. Unknown, Oct. 18, 1940, Age 61

STEWART, Danny (Danny Kalauawa Stewart)
Actor, Musician, Composer
b. Unknown
d. Honolulu, HI, April 15, 1962, Age 55

STEWART, David J. (né Abe J. Siegel)
Actor
b. Omaha, NE, 1919
d. Cleveland, OH, Dec. 23, 1966, Age 52

STEWART, Fred
Actor, Director
b. Atlanta, GA, Dec. 7, 1906
d. New York, NY, Dec. 5, 1970, Age 63

STEWART, Grant
Actor, Playwright
b. England, Unknown
d. Woodstock, NY, Aug. 18, 1929, Age 63

STEWART, John
Founder and Director of Pillochry Festival Theatre
b. Unknown
d. Glasgow, Scotland, May 23, 1957, Age 58

STEWART, Katherine
Actress
b. Unknown
d. New York, NY, Jan. 24, 1949, Age 81

STEWART, Nellie
Actress
b. Melbourne, Austrlia, 1860
d. Unknown, June 10, 1931, Age 71

STEWART, William G.
Singer, Director
b. Cleveland, OH, Unknown
d. Glendale, CA, July 16, 1941, Age 74

ST. GEORGE, Julia
Actress
b. Unknown
d. Unknown, Nov. 11, 1903, Age 79

STILL, Dr. John
Playwright
b. Unknown
d. Unknown, Feb. 26, 1607, Age 63

STILLMAN, David B.
Lawyer, Film executive
b. Unknown
d. Westport, CT, April 25, 1963, Age 57

STILLMAN, Marsha (Mrs. Harry Joe Brown, Jr.)
Actress
b. Unknown
d. New York, NY, Nov. 22, 1962, Age 23

STIRLING, Edward (Edward Lambert)
Actor, Playwright
b. Thame, Oxfordshire, England, April 19, 1809
d. Unknown, Aug. 14, 1894, Age 85

STIRLING, Fanny (Mary Anne Hehl, Lady Gregory)
Actress, Teacher
b. London, England, July 1813
d. London, England, Dec. 28, 1895, Age 80

STIRLING, W. Edward
Actor, Producer, Playwright
b. Birmingham, England, May 26, 1891
d. Paris, France, Jan. 12, 1948, Age 56

ST. JOHN, Al
Actor
b. Unknown
d. Vidalia, GA, Jan. 21, 1963, Age 70

ST. JOHN, Christopher Marie
Playwright
b. Unknown
d. Smallhythe, England, Oct. 20, 1960

ST. JOHN, Florence
Actress, Singer
b. Unknown
d. Unknown, Jan. 30, 1912, Age 57

ST. JOHN, Howard
Actor
b. Chicago, IL, Oct. 9, 1905
d. New York, NY, March 13, 1974, Age 68

ST. JOHN, Marguerite
Actress
b. London, England, Unknown
d. New York, NY, Oct. 16, 1940, Age 79

ST. JOHN, Norah
Performer
b. Unknown
d. London, England, April 28, 1962, Age 58

STOCK, Jack
Actor
b. Unknown
d. Unknown, Feb. 2, 1954, Age 60

STODDART, J. H.
Actor
b. Unknown, 1827
d. Unknown, Dec. 9, 1907, Age 80

STOEPEL, Richard
Composer, Conductor
b. Unknown
d. Unknown, Oct. 1, 1887

STOKER, Bram
Producer, Novelist
b. Unknown
d. England, April 20, 1912, Age 64

STOKES, Ernest L.
Actor
b. Unknown
d. Wilson, NC, May 26, 1964, Age 57

STOLL, Sir Oswald (Gray)
Theatre proprietor, Producer
b. Australia, 1866
d. Unknown, Jan. 9, 1942, Age 75

STOLZ, Robert
Composer, Conductor
b. Graz-Styria, Austria, Aug. 25, 1880
d. West Berlin, Germany, June 27, 1975, Age 94

STONE, Dorothy
Actress
b. Brooklyn, NY, June 3, 1905
d. Santa Barbara, CA, Sept. 24, 1974, Age 69

STONE, Florence Oakley (Mrs. Lewis Stone née Pryor)
Actress
b. Unknown
d. Hollywood, CA, Sept. 26, 1956, Age 65

STONE, Fred Andrew
Actor
b. Longmont, CO, Aug. 19, 1873
d. North Hollywood, CA, March 6, 1959, Age 85

STONE, John Augustus
Playwright, Actor
b. Unknown, 1801
d. Philadelphia, PA, May 29, 1834, Age 33

STONE, Lewis
Actor
b. Worcester, MA, Nov. 15, 1879
d. Beverly Hills, CA, Sept. 12, 1953, Age 73

STONEHOUSE, Ruth (Mrs. Felix Hughes)
Actress
b. Unknown, 1894
d. Hollywood, CA, May 12, 1941, Age 47

STORDAHL, Axel
Composer, Arranger, Conductor
b. Staten Island, NY, Unknown
d. Encino, CA, Aug. 30, 1963, Age 50

STOREY, Fred
Actor, Dancer, Scenic Artist
b. London, England, June 20, 1861
d. Unknown, Dec. 4, 1917, Age 56

STOREY, Sylvia Lilian (Countess Poulett)
Actress
b. England, Unknown
d. Unknown, July 20, 1947

STORM, Lesley
Playwright
b. Maud, Aberdeenshire, Scotland, Dec. 1903
d. Unknown, Oct. 19, 1975, Age 71

STORMONT, Leo
Actor
b. Unknown
d. Unknown, Jan. 28, 1923

STORY, Aubrey
Literary representative
b. Unknown
d. Hontion, England, 1963, Age About 75

STOTHART, Herbert P.
Composer
b. Milwaukee, WI, Unknown
d. Hollywood, CA, Feb. 1, 1949, Age 64

STOWE, Harriet Elizabeth Beecher
Novelist
b. Litchfield, CT, June 14, 1811
d. Hartford, CT, July 1, 1896, Age 85

STRADNER, Rose (Mrs. Joseph Mankiewicz)
Actress
b. Vienna, Austria, 1913
d. Mt. Kisco, NY, Sept. 27, 1958, Age 45

STRANACK, Wallace
Actor, Business manager
b. Unknown
d. Unknown, Aug. 14, 1950, Age 78

STRANGE, Michael (née Blanche Oelrichs)
Actress, Author, Poet
b. New York, NY, 1890
d. Boston, MA, Nov. 5, 1950, Age 60

STRASBERG, Paula (née Paulina Miller)
Actress, Coach
b. New York, NY, Unknown
d. New York, NY, April 29, 1966, Age 55

STRATTON, Eugene (Eugene Augustus Ruhlmann)
Performer
b. Buffalo, NY, 1861
d. Unknown, Sept. 15, 1918, Age 57

STRAUS, Oscar
Composer
b. Vienna, Austria, March 6, 1870
d. Bad Ischl, Austria, Jan. 11, 1954, Age 83

STRAUSS, Johann (the Elder)
Composer, Conductor
b. Vienna, Austria, March 14, 1804
d. Vienna, Austria, Sept. 25, 1849, Age 45

STRAUSS, Johann (the Younger)
Composer, Conductor
b. Vienna, Austria, Oct. 25, 1825
d. Vienna, Austria, June 3, 1899, Age 73

STRAUSS, Johann (the third)
Composer, Conductor
b. Vienna, Austria, Unknown
d. Berlin, Germany, Jan. 14, 1939, Age 72

STRAUSS, Joseph
Composer
b. Unknown
d. Unknown, July 22, 1870, Age 42

STRAUSS, Richard
Composer
b. Munich, Germany, June 11, 1864
d. Garmish-Partenkirken, Germany, Sept. 8, 1949, Age 85

STRAUSS, Robert
Actor
b. New York, NY, Nov. 8, 1913
d. New York, NY, Feb. 20, 1974, Age 61

STRICKLAND, Enfield "Rube"
Performer
b. Unknown
d. Unknown, Jamestown, NY, Age Aug. 7, 1964

STRICKLAND, Helen
Actress
b. Boston, MA, Unknown
d. New York, NY, Jan. 11, 1938, Age 75

STRINDBERG, (Johan) August
Playwright
b. Stockholm, Sweden, Jan. 22, 1849
d. Stockholm, Sweden, May 14, 1912, Age 63

STROLLO, Angie
Costumer
b. Unknown
d. New York, NY, June 29, 1964

STROMBERG, John ("Honey")
Composer
b. Unknown, 1853
d. New York, NY, July 1902

STRONG, Austin
Playwright
b. San Francisco, CA, Unknown
d. Nantucket Island, MA, Sept. 17, 1952, Age 71

STRONG, Jay
Actor, Director, Producer
b. Unknown
d. New York, NY, Dec. 1, 1953, Age 57

STROOCK, James E.
Costumer
b. Boston, MA, Sept. 4, 1891
d. New York, NY, July 22, 1965, Age 73

STUART, Cora
Actress
b. Unknown
d. Unknown, Jan. 5, 1940, Age 83

STUART, Leslie (Thomas Augustine Barrett)
Composer
b. Southport, England, March 15, 1864
d. Unknown, March 27, 1928, Age 64

STUART, Otho (Otto Stuart Andreae)
Actor, Producer
b. Unknown, Aug. 9, 1865
d. Unknown, May 1, 1930, Age 64

STUART, Philip P.
Playwright
b. Ootacamund, India, Aug. 10, 1887
d. Unknown, June 18, 1936, Age 48

STUDHOLM, Marie
Actress
b. Eccleshill, Yorkshire, England, Sept. 10, 1875
d. London, England, March 10, 1930, Age 54

STURGESS, Arthur
Librettist, Playwright
b. Unknown
d. Unknown, May 8, 1931

STYLES, Edwin
Actor
b. Chiswick, London, England, Jan. 13, 1899
d. Unknown, Dec. 20, 1960, Age 61

SUDERMANN, Herman
Playwright, Poet
b. Matziken, East Prussia, Germany, Sept. 30, 1857
d. Berlin, Germany, Nov. 21, 1928, Age 71

SUDLOW, Bessie
Actress
b. Unknown
d. Unknown, Jan. 28, 1928, Age 78

SUESSENGUTH, Walther
Actor
b. Unknown
d. Berlin, Germany, May 1964, Age 64

SUGDEN, Charles
Actor
b. Cambridge, England, Dec. 24, 1850
d. Unknown, Aug. 3, 1921, Age 70

SULLAVAN, Margaret
Actress
b. Norfolk, VA, May 16, 1911
d. New Haven, CT, Jan. 1, 1960, Age 48

SULLIVAN, Elliott
Actor, Director, Producer
b. San Antonio, TX, July 4, 1907
d. Los Angeles, CA, June 2, 1974, Age 66

SULLIVAN, Francis L.
Actor
b. London, England, Jan. 6, 1903
d. New York, NY, Nov. 19, 1956, Age 53

SULLIVAN, John A.
Ticket broker
b. Unknown
d. Spring Lake, NJ, Sept. 1, 1964, Age Late 70s

SULLIVAN, Mella
Voice-Drama coach
b. Unknown
d. Hollywood, CA, Jan. 11, 1963, Age 87

SULLIVAN, Sir Arthur Seymour
Composer
b. Lambeth, London, England, May 13, 1842
d. London, England, Nov. 22, 1900, Age 58

SULLIVAN, Thomas Russell
Playwright
b. Unknown, 1849
d. Unknown, 1916

SULLIVAN, (Thomas) Barry
Actor, Producer
b. Ireland, 1821
d. Unknown, May 3, 1891, Age 69

SULLY, Daniel (Sullivan)
Actor, Playwright
b. Newport, RI, Nov. 6, 1855
d. Unknown, June 25, 1910, Age 54

SUMAROKOV, Alexei Petrovich
Playwright
b. Unknown, 1718
d. Unknown, 1777

SUMMERS, Dorothy
Actress
b. Unknown
d. London, England, Jan. 13, 1964, Age 70

SUMMERS, Rev. (Alphonsus Joseph-Mary Augustus Montague)
Historian, Editor
b. Clifton, Bristol, England, April 10, 1880
d. Unknown, Aug. 10, 1948, Age 68

SUMMERVILLE, Slim (George J. Summerville)
Actor
b. Albuquerque, NM, Unknown
d. Laguna Beach, CA, Jan. 5, 1946, Age 54

SUMNER, Mary
b. London, England, Oct. 7, 1888
d. Unknown, 1956, Age 68

SUNDERLAND, Nan
Actress
b. Fresno, CA, Unknown
d. New York, NY, Nov. 23, 1973

SUNSHINE, Marion (Mary Tunstall Ijames)
Performer, Songwriter
b. Unknown
d. New York, NY, Jan. 25, 1963, Age 66

SUTER, W. E.
Playwright
b. Unknown
d. Unknown, May 31, 1882, Age 70

SUTHERLAND, Anne
Actress
b. Washington, DC, March 1, 1867
d. Brentwood, NY, June 22, 1942, Age 75

SUTHERLAND, Birdie (Mrs. Montague Grahame-White)
Actress
b. Unknown
d. England, Dec. 1955, Age 81

SUTHERLAND, Evelyn Greenleaf (née Baker)
Playwright
b. Cambridge, MA, Sept. 15, 1855
d. Unknown, Dec. 24, 1908, Age 53

SUTHERLAND, Robert C.
Theatre operator
b. Unknown
d. Weyburn, Saskatchewan, CAN, Sept. 30, 1962, Age 79

SUTRO, Alfred
Playwright
b. London, England, Aug. 7, 1863
d. London, England, Sept. 11, 1933, Age 70

SWAFFER, Hannen
Critic, Journalist
b. Lindfield, Sussex, England, Nov. 1, 1879
d. London, England, Jan. 16, 1962, Age 82

SWALLOW, Margaret
Actress
b. Hampstead, London, England, Nov. 18, 1896
d. Unknown, Dec. 16, 1932, Age 36

SWAN, Lew
Performer, Film projectionist
b. Unknown
d. South Bend, IN, Aug. 6, 1964, Age 69

SWAN, Mark Elbert
Playwright, Actor
b. Louisville, KY, 1871
d. Unknown, Jan. 26, 1942, Age 70

SWANBOROUGH, Ada
Actress
b. Unknown
d. Unknown, Dec. 12, 1893, Age 48

SWANBOROUGH, Mrs.
Actress, Producer
b. Unknown
d. Unknown, Jan. 6, 1889, Age 85

SWEARS, Herbert
Playwright
b. Unknown
d. Unknown, March 6, 1946, Age 77

SWEET, Sam
Performer
b. Unknown
d. Midwest plane crash, Jan. 9, 1948, Age 27

SWETS, E. Lyall
Actor, Director, Playwright
b. Wrington, Somerset, England, July 25, 1865
d. Unknown, Feb. 19, 1930, Age 64

SWINBURNE, Algernon Charles
Playwright, Poet
b. London, England, April 5, 1837
d. Putney, London, England, April 10, 1909, Age 72

SWINLEY, Ion
Actor, Playwright
b. Barnes, England, Oct. 27, 1891
d. Unknown, Sept. 16, 1937, Age 45

SWITZER, Carl "Alfalfa"
Actor
b. Unknown
d. Sun Valley, CA, Jan. 21, 1959, Age 33

SYDNEY, Basil
Actor
b. St. Osyth, Essex, England, April 23, 1894
d. London, England, Jan. 10, 1968, Age 73

SYKES, Jerome
Performer
b. Unknown
d. Unknown, Dec. 29, 1903, Age 35

SYLE, Edwin A.
Manager, Press representative
b. Unknown
d. New York, NY, July 30, 1964, Age 86

SYLVA, Marguerita (Marguerite Alice Helene Smith)
Actress, Opera singer
b. Brussels, Belgium, Unknown
d. Glendale, CA, Feb. 21, 1957, Age 81

SYLVAIN, Louise
Actress
b. Unknown
d. Unknown, Oct. 20, 1930, Age 56

SYLVAINE, Vernon
Actor, Playwright
b. Manchester, England, Aug. 9, 1897
d. Unknown, Nov. 22, 1957, Age 60

SYMONS, Arthur
Critic, Author
b. Unknown
d. Unknown, Jan. 22, 1945, Age 79

SYMS, Algernon
Actor
b. Unknown
d. Unknown, Feb. 11, 1915, Age 71

SYNGE, (Edmund) John Millington
Playwright
b. Newton Little, Ireland, 1871
d. Dublin, Ireland, March 24, 1909, Age 38

SZIGLIGETI, Ede
Playwright
b. Unknown, 1814
d. Unknown, 1878

SZOMORY, Dezsö
Playwright
b. Unknown
d. 1869, Unknown, Age 1945

T

TABBERT, William
Singer, Actor
b. Chicago, IL, Oct. 5, 1921
d. New York, NY, Oct. 18, 1974, Age 53

TABER, Richard
Actor, Playwright
b. Long Branch, NJ, Unknown
d. New York, NY, Nov. 16, 1957, Age 72

TABER, Robert Schell
Performer
b. Staten Island, NY, Jan. 24, 1865
d. Saranac Lake, NY, March 8, 1904, Age 39

TABOADA, Julio Jr.
Performer
b. Unknown
d. Mexico City, Mexico, Sept. 15, 1962, Age 36

TABOR, Disiree (Mrs. Gerado Pettigrew)
Actress
b. Canada, Unknown
d. Buenos Aires, Argentina, May 12, 1957, Age 57

TAGLIONI, Filippo
Dancer, Choreographer
b. Unknown, 1777
d. Unknown, Feb. 11, 1871, Age 94

TAGLIONI, Marie
Dancer, Choreographer
b. Stockholm, Sweden, April 23, 1804
d. Unknown, April 24, 1884, Age 80

TAGLIONI, Paul
Dancer, Choreographer
b. Unknown
d. Unknown, Jan. 6, 1884, Age 75

TAGORE, Rabindranath
Playwright, Poet
b. Calcutta, India, May 6, 1861
d. Calcutta, India, Aug. 7, 1941, Age 80

TAILLADE, Paul
Actor
b. Unknown
d. Unknown, Jan. 26, 1898, Age 72

TAIROV, Alexander Yakovlevich
Director, Producer
b. Russia, 1885
d. Moscow, U.S.S.R., Sept. 1950, Age 65

TAIT, E. J.
Producer
b. Unknown
d. Unknown, July 12, 1947, Age 69

TAKEDA, Izumo
Playwright, Producer
b. Unknown, 1688
d. Unknown, 1756

TALBOT, Howard (Munkittrick)
Composer, Conductor
b. New York, NY, March 9, 1865
d. Unknown, Sept. 12, 1928, Age 63

TALFOURD, Frances
Playwright
b. Unknown
d. Unknown, March 9, 1862, Age 35

TALFOURD, Sir Thomas Noon
Playwright, Lawyer
b. Reading, England, 1795
d. Unknown, March 13, 1854, Age 59

TALIAFERRO, Edith
Actress
b. Richmond, VA, Dec. 21, 1893
d. Newton, CT, March 2, 1958, Age 64

TALLIS, Sir George
Producer
b. Unknown, 1867
d. Unknown, Aug. 16, 1948, Age 80

TALLMAN, Ellen
Performer
b. Unknown
d. Northfield, NJ, June 1963, Age 73

TALMA, François Joseph
Actor
b. Paris, France, Jan. 15, 1763
d. Paris, France, Oct. 19, 1826, Age 63

TALMADGE, Norma
Actress
b. Jersey City, NJ, 1897
d. Las Vegas, NV, Dec. 24, 1957, Age 60

TAMARA, (Tamara Swann, née Drasin)
Actress, Singer
b. Sorochintzy, Russia, Unknown
d. Lisbon, Portugal, Feb. 22, 1943

TAMAYO Y BAUS, Manuel
Playwright, Actor
b. Madrid, Spain, 1829
d. Unknown, 1898

TAMIRIS, Helen (née Helen Becker, Mrs. Danie Nagrin)
Choreographer, Dancer
b. New York, NY, April 24, 1905
d. New York, NY, Aug. 4, 1966, Age 61

TAMIROFF, Akim
Actor
b. Baku, Russia, Oct. 17, 1901
d. Palm Springs, CA, Sept. 17, 1972, Age 70

TANGUAY, Eva
Actress, Singer
b. Marbleton, Quebec, CAN, Aug. 1878
d. Hollywood, CA, Jan. 11, 1947, Age 68

TANNER, Annie Louise
Singer
b. Unknown
d. New York, NY, Feb. 28, 1921, Age 65

TANNER, James T.
Playwright, Librettist, Lyricist
b. Unknown
d. Unknown, June 18, 1915, Age 56

TAPPING, Alfred B.
Actor, Producer
b. Unknown
d. Unknown, Dec. 31, 1928, Age 77

TAPPING, Mrs. Alfred B. (Florence Cowell)
Actress
b. Unknown, April 1, 1852
d. Unknown, March 26, 1926, Age 73

TARKINGTON, Newton Booth
Playwright, Novelist
b. Indianapolis, IN, July 29, 1869
d. Indianapolis, IN, May 19, 1946, Age 76

TARKINGTON, William O.
Talent representative, Manager
b. Unknown
d. Kokomo, IN, Feb. 3, 1962, Age 89

TARLETON, Richard
Actor
b. Unknown
d. Unknown, 1588

TARRI, Suzette
Performer
b. Unknown
d. Unknown, Oct. 10, 1955, Age 74

TASHMAN, Lilyan
Actress
b. Brooklyn, NY, Oct. 23, 1899
d. New York, NY, March 21, 1934, Age 34

TASSO, Torquato
Poet, Playwright
b. Sorrento, Italy, 1544
d. Rome, Italy, 1595, Age 51

TATE, Henry (Ronald Macdonald Hutchison)
Performer
b. Scotland, July 4, 1872
d. Unknown, Feb. 14, 1940, Age 67

TATE, James W.
Composer, Producer
b. Unknown
d. Unknown, Feb. 5, 1922, Age 46

TATE, Nahum
Playwright, Poet laureate
b. County Cavan, Ireland, 1652
d. Unknown, Aug. 12, 1715, Age 63

TATE, Reginald
Actor
b. Garforth, Yorkshire, England, Dec. 13, 1896
d. Unknown, Aug. 23, 1955, Age 58

TATHAM, John
Playwright, Poet
b. Unknown, 1632
d. Unknown, 1664

TAUBER, Richard
Actor, Singer, Composer, Conductor
b. Linz, Austria, May 16, 1891
d. London, England, Jan. 8, 1948, Age 56

TAYLEUR, Clifton W.
Actor, Playwright, Editor
b. Unknown, 1831
d. Unknown, 1887

TAYLOR, Charles A.
Producer, Playwright
b. South Hadley, MA, Unknown
d. Glendale, CA, March 20, 1942, Age 78

TAYLOR, Charles H.
Playwright, Lyricist
b. Unknown
d. Unknown, June 27, 1907, Age 46

TAYLOR, Deems (né Joseph Deems Taylor)
Composer, Author, Critic
b. New York, NY, Dec. 22, 1885
d. New York, NY, July 3, 1966, Age 80

TAYLOR, Enid Stamp
Actress
b. Whitley Bay, England, June 12, 1904
d. Unknown, Jan. 13, 1946, Age 41

TAYLOR, Estelle (Ida Taylor)
Actress
b. Wilmington, DE, May 20, 1899
d. Hollywood, CA, April 15, 1958, Age 58

TAYLOR, Ethel Corintha
Artist
b. Schroon Lake, NY, April 26, 1885
d. Salinas, CA, Feb. 16, 1963, Age 77

TAYLOR, John
Playwright
b. Unknown
d. Unknown, Dec. 1, 1653, Age 73

TAYLOR, John
Critic
b. Unknown
d. Unknown, May 1832, Age 74

TAYLOR, Joseph
Actor, Patentee
b. Unknown, 1586
d. Unknown, Nov. 4, 1653, Age 67

TAYLOR, Laurette (née Cooney)
Actress
b. New York, NY, April 1, 1884
d. New York, NY, Dec. 7, 1946, Age 62

TAYLOR, Nellie
Actress
b. Sutton Coldfield, England, June 7, 1894
d. Unknown, Oct. 16, 1932, Age 38

TAYLOR, Sam
Director
b. Unknown
d. Santa Monica, CA, March 6, 1958, Age 62

TAYLOR, Sir Henry
Playwright
b. Unknown
d. Unknown, March 27, 1886, Age 85

TAYLOR, Tom
Playwright, Editor
b. Sunderland, Durham, England, 1817
d. Wandsworth, England, July 12, 1880, Age 63

TAYLOR, William
Critic, Poet
b. Unknown
d. Unknown, March 5, 1836, Age 70

TCHEKOV, Anton See Chekhov, Anton
Playwright, Author

TEAL, Ben
Stage manager, Director
b. Unknown
d. Unknown, April 20, 1917, Age 55

TEARLE, Conway
Actor
b. New York, NY, May 17, 1878
d. Hollywood, CA, Oct. 1, 1938, Age 60

TEARLE, Edmund
Actor, Producer
b. England, Oct. 24, 1856
d. Brighton, England, Feb. 4, 1913, Age 56

TEARLE, (George) Osmond
Actor, Producer
b. Plymouth, England, 1852
d. Newcasle-on-Tyne, England, Sept. 7, 1901, Age 49

TEARLE, Malcolm
Actor
b. Unknown
d. London, England, Dec. 6, 1935, Age 47

TEARLE, Sir Godfrey
Actor
b. New York, NY, Oct. 12, 1884
d. London, England, June 8, 1953, Age 68

TEIXEIRA DE MATTOS, Alexander Louis
Play translator
b. Amsterdam, Holland, April 9, 1865
d. Unknown, Dec. 5, 1921, Age 56

TELBIN, William
Scenic artist
b. Unknown, 1813
d. St. John's Wood, London, England, Dec. 25, 1873, Age 60

TELBIN, William Lewis
Scenic artist
b. Unknown, 1846
d. Twyford Abbey, Park Royal, England, Dec. 3, 1931, Age 85

TELESHOVA, Elizabeth (Mme. S. M. Eisenstein)
Actress
b. Unknown
d. Moscow, U.S.S.R., July 10, 1943

TELL, Alma
Actress
b. New York, NY, 1892
d. San Fernando, CA, Dec. 30, 1937, Age 45

TELL, Olive (Mrs. Henry M. Hobart)
Actress
b. New York, NY, 1894
d. New York, NY, June 8, 1951, Age 56

TELLEGEN, Lou (Isador Louis Bernard van Dammeler)
Actor
b. Holland, Nov. 26, 1881
d. Los Angeles, CA, Oct. 29, 1934, Age 52

TEMPLE, Edward P.
Director
b. New York, NY, Unknown
d. New York, NY, June 22, 1921, Age 60

TEMPLE, Madge (Mrs. Herman Darewski)
Actress
b. Unknown
d. Sheffield, England, Dec. 8, 1943

TEMPLETON, Alec Andrew
Composer, Performer, Musician
b. Cardiff, Wales, July 4, 1910
d. Greenwich, CT, March 28, 1963

TEMPLETON, Fay
Actress
b. Little Rock, AR, Dec. 25, 1865
d. San Francisco, CA, Oct. 3, 1939, Age 73

TEMPLETON, John
Actor, Producer
b. Unknown
d. Unknown, Dec. 10, 1907, Age 69

TENNENT, Henry M.
Theatre manager, Producer
b. Unknown, 1879
d. London, England, June 10, 1941, Age 62

TENNY, Marion H.
Performer, Actress
b. Unknown
d. South Weymouth, MA, June 23, 1964, Age 73

TENNYSON, Alfred Lord
Playwright, Poet laureate
b. Somersby, Lincolnshire, England, Aug. 6, 1809
d. Aldeworth, England, Oct. 6, 1892, Age 83

TERENCE, (Publius Terentius Afer)
Playwright
b. Carthage (?), c190 B.C.
d. Unknown, 159 B.C.

TERMINI, Joe
Performer
b. Unknown
d. Miami Beach, FL, March 20, 1964, Age 72

TERNAN, Thomas
Actor, Playwright
b. Unknown
d. Unknown, Oct. 17, 1846, Age 47

TERRAUX, L. H. du
Playwright
b. Unknown
d. Unknown, March 31, 1878

TERRISS, Mrs. William (Amy Fellowes)
Actress
b. Unknown
d. Unknown, Aug. 12, 1898

TERRISS, William (William Charles James Lewin)
Actor
b. London, England, Feb. 20, 1847
d. London, England, Dec. 16, 1897, Age 50

TERRY, Benjamin
Actor
b. Portsmouth, England, 1818
d. Unknown, May 22, 1896, Age 77

TERRY, Charles
Business manager
b. Unknown
d. Unknown, March 4, 1933, Age 73

TERRY, Dame Ellen Alice
Actress
b. Coventry, Warwickshire, England, Feb. 27, 1848
d. Small Hythe, Kent, England, July 21, 1928, Age 80

TERRY, Daniel
Actor, Playwright
b. Unknown, 1789
d. Unknown, June 24, 1829, Age 40

TERRY, Dennis
Actor
b. Unknown, 1895
d. South Africa, 1932

TERRY, Edward O'Connor
Actor, Producer
b. London, England, March 10, 1844
d. Unknown, April 2, 1912, Age 68

TERRY, Eliza
Actress
b. Unknown
d. Unknown, Dec. 21, 1878, Age 61

TERRY, Florence (Floss)
Actress
b. Unknown, 1854
d. Unknown, March 15, 1896, Age 42

TERRY, Fred
Actor, Producer
b. London, England, Nov. 9, 1863
d. London, England, April 17, 1933, Age 69

TERRY, George
Producer
b. Unknown
d. Unknown, May 22, 1928

TERRY, J. E. Harold
Playwright
b. York, England, Sept. 21, 1885
d. Unknown, Aug. 10, 1939, Age 53

TERRY, Kate (Mrs. Arthur Lewis)
Actress
b. England, April 21, 1844
d. London, England, Jan. 5, 1924, Age 79

TERRY, Marion
Actress
b. London, England, Oct. 16, 1852
d. Unknown, Aug. 21, 1930, Age 77

TERRY, Mrs. Benjamin (Sarah Ballard)
Actress
b. Unknown, 1819
d. Unknown, March 1, 1892

TERRY, Walter
Editor, (THE ERA)
b. Unknown
d. Unknown, April 1932

TERRY-LEWIS, Mabel
Actress
b. London, England, Oct. 28, 1872
d. Unknown, Nov. 28, 1957, Age 85

TEVERNER, William
Playwright
b. Unknown
d. London, England, Jan. 8, 1731

THALBERG, T. B. (Thalberg Corbett)
Actor
b. Aylburton, Gloucestershire, England, Unknown
d. Unknown, Jan. 15, 1947, Age 82

THEILMANN, Helen
Actress
b. Unknown
d. Unknown, Aug. 18, 1956, Age 41

THEOBALD, Lewis
Playwright, Shakespearean authority
b. Unknown
d. Unknown, Sept. 18, 1944, Age 56

THESIGER, Ernest
Actor
b. London, England, Jan. 15, 1879
d. London, England, Jan. 14, 1961, Age 82

THESPIS
Performer, Playwright, Poet, (fl. 6th Century B.C.)
b. Icaria, Attica, Greece
d. Unknown

THIERRY, Edouard
Director of Comédie Française
b. Unknown
d. Unknown, Nov. 27, 1894, Age 81

THIRER, Irene (Mrs. Zac Freedman)
Editor, Film critic
b. London, England, Unknown
d. New York, NY, Feb. 19, 1964, Age 59

THOMA, Ludwig
Playwright, Novelist
b. Oberammergau, Germany, 1867
d. Unknown, 1921

THOMAS, A. Goring
Composer
b. Unknown
d. Unknown, March 20, 1892, Age 40

THOMAS, Albert Ellsworth
Playwright, Author
b. Chester, MA, Sept. 16, 1872
d. Wakefield, RI, June 18, 1947, Age 74

THOMAS, Ambroise
Composer
b. Metz, France, Aug. 5, 1811
d. Paris, France, Feb. 12, 1896, Age 84

THOMAS, Augustus
Playwright
b. St. Louis, MO, Jan. 8, 1857
d. Nyack, NY, Aug. 12, 1934, Age 77

THOMAS, Basil
Playwright
b. Edgbaston, Birmingham, England, Sept. 29, 1912
d. Unknown, Feb. 28, 1957, Age 44

THOMAS, Brandon
Playwright, Producer, Actor, Composer
b. Liverpool, England, Dec. 25, 1856
d. Unknown, June 19, 1914, Age 57

THOMAS, Charles Henry
Theatre business manager
b. Unknown
d. London, England, Sept. 8, 1941, Age 76

THOMAS, Dylan
Playwright, Poet
b. Carmarthenshire, Wales, Oct. 22, 1914
d. New York, NY, Nov. 9, 1953, Age 39

THOMAS, J. W.
Publisher, Editor
b. Unknown
d. Unknown, April 7, 1878

THOMAS, Jamieson
Actor
b. Unknown
d. Unknown, Jan. 10, 1939, Age 45

THOMAS, John Charles
Actor, Singer
b. Meyersdale, PA, Unknown
d. Apple Valley, CA, Dec. 13, 1960, Age 68 or 69

THOMAS, Olive (Mrs. Jack Pickford)
Actress
b. Unknown, 1898 (?)
d. Paris, France, Sept. 10, 1920, Age 25

THOMAS, Stephen
Director of Drama, British Council
b. Unknown
d. Unknown, Feb. 23, 1961, Age 63

THOMAS, W. Moy
Critic
b. Unknown
d. Unknown, July 21, 1910, Age 81

THOMASHEFSKY, Bessie (Mrs. Boris Thomashefsky)
Actress
b. Unknown
d. Hollywood, CA, July 6, 1962, Age 88

THOMASHEFSKY, Boris
Actor, Playwright, Impressario, Producer
b. Kiev, Russia, May 12, 1868
d. New York, NY, July 9, 1939, Age 71

THOME, Francis
Composer
b. Unknown
d. Unknown, Nov. 16, 1909, Age 59

THOMPSON, Alexander M.
Playwright, Journalist
b. Carlsruhe, Germany, May 9, 1861
d. Unknown, March 25, 1948, Age 86

THOMPSON, Alfred
Playwright, Designer
b. Unknown
d. Unknown, Aug. 31, 1895

THOMPSON, Benjamin
Playwright
b. Unknown
d. Unknown, May 26, 1816, Age 40

THOMPSON, Denman (a/k/a Joshua Whitcomb)
Playwright, Actor, Producer
b. Beechwood, Erie County, PA, Oct. 15, 1833
d. West Swanzey, NH, April 14, 1911, Age 77

THOMPSON, Fred
Librettist
b. London, England, Jan. 24, 1884
d. London, England, April 10, 1949, Age 65

THOMPSON, Frederick W.
Producer
b. Nashville, TN, 1872
d. Unknown, June 6, 1919, Age 47

THOMPSON, Gerald Marr
Critic
b. London, England, 1856
d. Unknown, March 2, 1938, Age 81

THOMPSON, Lydia
Actress, Dancer, Producer
b. London, England, 1836
d. Unknown, Nov. 17, 1908, Age 72

THOMPSON, Madeleine
Screenwriter
b. Unknown
d. Hollywood, CA, July 20, 1964

THOMPSON, W. T.
Actor
b. Unknown
d. Unknown, Jan. 17, 1940

THOMPSON, William H.
Actor
b. Scotland, April 24, 1852
d. New York, NY, Feb. 4, 1923, Age 70

THOMPSON, Woodman
Stage designer
b. Pittsburgh, PA, Unknown
d. New York, NY, Aug. 26, 1955, Age 66

THOMSON, James
Playwright, Poet
b. Ednam, Scotland, Sept. 11, 1700
d. Richmond, England, Aug. 27, 1748, Age 47

THORBURN, H. M.
Producer
b. London, England, June 11, 1884
d. Unknown, Jan. 14, 1924, Age 39

THORN, Geoffrey
Playwright
b. Unknown
d. Unknown, June 3, 1905, Age 62

THORNDIKE, Dame Sybil
Actress
b. Gainsborough, England, Oct. 24, 1882
d. London, England, June 9, 1976, Age 93

THORNDIKE, Eileen
Actress, Director
b. Rochester, Kentshire, England, Jan. 31, 1891
d. Unknown, April 17, 1954, Age 63

THORNE, Charles Robert Jr.
Actor
b. Unknown, 1840
d. Unknown, Feb. 10, 1883, Age 42

THORNE, Clara
Actress
b. Unknown
d. Unknown, Dec. 25, 1915, Age 63

THORNE, Eric
Actor
b. Unknown
d. Unknown, Nov. 26, 1922, Age 60

THORNE, George Tyrrel
Actor, Playwright
b. Unknown, 1856
d. Unknown, July 22, 1922, Age 66

THORNE, Mrs. Thomas (Amelia Newton)
Actress
b. Unknown
d. Unknown, April 18, 1884

THORNE, Sarah (Mrs. Sarah Macknight)
Actress, Producer
b. England, May 10, 1836
d. Chatham, England, Feb. 27, 1899, Age 62

THORNE, Sylvia
Singer
b. Unknown
d. New York, NY, May 9, 1922, Age 55

THORNE, Thomas
Actor, Producer
b. London, England, Nov. 23, 1841
d. Unknown, Dec. 26, 1918, Age 77

THORNTON, Frank
Actor
b. Unknown
d. Unknown, Dec. 18, 1918, Age 73

THORNTON, James
Actor, Songwriter
b. Liverpool, England, Dec. 5, 1861
d. Astoria, NY, July 27, 1938, Age 76

THROCKMORTON, Cleon
Scenic designer
b. Atlantic City, NJ, Oct. 8, 1897
d. Atlantic City, NJ, Oct. 23, 1965, Age 68

THROPP, Clara
Actress
b. Unknown
d. New York, NY, Feb. 29, 1960, Age 88

THUMB, General Tom (Charles Sherwood Stratton)
Performer
b. Bridgeport, CT, Jan. 4, 1838
d. Middleborough, MA, July 15, 1883, Age 45

THURBER, James Grover
Playwright, Author, Artist
b. Columbus, OH, Dec. 8, 1894
d. New York, NY, Nov. 2, 1961, Age 66

THURNER, Georges
Playwright
b. Unknown
d. Unknown, Sept. 1910, Age 32

THURSTON, Ernest Temple
Playwright, Novelist
b. Cork, Ireland, Sept. 23, 1879
d. London, England, March 19, 1933, Age 53

THURSTON, Harry (Marcus Cowan)
Actor, Writer
b. London, England, Unknown
d. Rumson, NJ, Sept. 2, 1955, Age 81

THURY, Ilona
Actress
b. near Budapest, Hungary, Unknown
d. New York, NY, April 1, 1953, Age 77

TIBBETT, Lawrence
Actor, Opera singer
b. Bakersfield, CA, Nov. 16, 1896
d. New York, NY, July 15, 1960, Age 63

TICKELL, Richard
Playwright
b. Unknown
d. Unknown, Nov. 4, 1793, Age 42

TICKLE, Frank
Actor
b. London, England, June 25, 1893
d. Unknown, Oct. 18, 1955, Age 62

TIDEN, Fritz
Actor
b. Unknown
d. Liberty, NY, Nov. 12, 1931, Age 54

TIDMARSH, Vivian
Playwright, Critic
b. Clacton-on-Sea, Essex, England, Aug. 13, 1896
d. Unknown, May 10, 1941, Age 44

TIECK, Ludwig
Playwright, Director, Critic
b. Unknown, 1773
d. Unknown, 1853

TIERNEY, Harry Austin
Composer
b. Perth Amboy, NJ, May 21, 1890
d. New York, NY, March 22, 1965, Age 74

TIETJENS, Paul
Composer, Conductor
b. St. Louis, MO, Unknown
d. St. Louis, MO, Nov. 25, 1943, Age 66

TIGHE, Harry
Actor
b. New Haven, CT, Unknown
d. Old Lyme, CT, Feb. 10, 1935, Age 50

TILBURY, Zeffie
Actress
b. London, England, Nov. 20, 1863
d. Unknown, July 24, 1950, Age 86

TILDEN, Bill (William Tatem Tilden, II)
Actor, Tennis champion
b. Germantown, PA, Feb. 10, 1893
d. Hollywood, CA, June 4, 1953, Age 60

TILDEN, Milano C.
Performer
b. Paris, France, Unknown
d. Grant City, S.I., NY, Sept. 30, 1951, Age 73

TILDSLEY, Peter (Hadden)
Performer, Author, Theatre Manager
b. Unknown
d. London, England, Sept. 7, 1962, Age 64

TILLER, John
Dancing master, Director, Designer
b. Manchester, England, Unknown
d. New York, NY, Oct. 22, 1925, Age 73

TILLEY, John
Actor
b. Unknown
d. Unknown, Aug. 3, 1935, Age 35

TILLEY, Vesta (Lady de Frece née Matilda Ball or Powles)
Performer
b. Worcester, England, May 13, 1864
d. London, England, Sept. 16, 1952, Age 88

TIMBLIN, Slim
Performer
b. Unknown
d. Fort Worth, TX, Dec. 19, 1962, Age 70

TINNEY, Frank
Performer
b. Philadelphia, PA, March 29, 1878
d. Northport, NY, Nov. 28, 1940, Age 62

TITHERADGE, Dion
Actor, Playwright, Producer
b. Melbourne, Australia, March 30, 1889
d. London, England, Nov. 16, 1934, Age 45

TITHERADGE, George S.
Actor
b. Portsmouth, England, Dec. 9, 1848
d. Unknown, Jan. 22, 1916, Age 67

TITHERADGE, Lily
Actress
b. Unknown
d. Unknown, May 21, 1937

TITHERADGE, Madge
Actress
b. Melbourne, Australia, July 2, 1887
d. Fetcham, Surrey, England, Nov. 13, 1961, Age 74

TITMUSS, Phyllis
Actress
b. Unknown
d. Unknown, Jan. 6, 1946, Age 45

TITTELL, Charlotte
Actress
b. Unknown
d. Unknown, Dec. 21, 1941, Age 60

TOBIN, John
Playwright
b. Unknown
d. Unknown, Dec. 7, 1804, Age 34

TOCHE, Raoul
Playwright
b. Unknown
d. Unknown, Jan. 17, 1895, Age 45

TODD, Michael (Michael Goldbogen)
Producer
b. Minneapolis, MN, June 22, 1907
d. Grants, NM, March 22, 1958, Age 50

TODD, Thelma
Actress
b. Massachusetts, 1905
d. near Santa Monica, CA, Dec. 16, 1935, Age 30

TODHUNTER, Dr. John
Playwright
b. Unknown
d. Unknown, Oct. 1916, Age 76

TOLER, Sidney
Actor, Author
b. Warrenburg, MO, April 28, 1874
d. Hollywood, CA, Feb. 12, 1947, Age 72

TOLLER, Ernst
Playwright
b. Samotschin, Posen, Prussia, Dec. 1, 1893
d. New York, NY, May 22, 1939, Age 45

TOLSTOY, Alexie Nikolayevich
Playwright, Novelist
b. Unknown, 1882
d. Unknown, Feb. 24, 1945, Age 62

TOLSTOY, Count Leo Nikolayevich
Playwright, Novelist
b. Yasnaya Lolyana, Tula, Russia, 1828
d. Astapovo, Russia, Nov. 20, 1910, Age 82

TOMACK, Sid
Performer
b. Brooklyn, NY, Unknown
d. Palm Springs, CA, Nov. 12, 1962, Age 55

TOMKIS, Thomas
Playwright, fl. 1615

TOMLINS, Frederick Guest
Critic, Journalist
b. Unknown
d. Unknown, Sept. 21, 1867, Age 63

TOMPKINS, Eugène
Producer
b. Unknown
d. Unknown, Feb. 22, 1909, Age 58

TONE, Franchot
Actor
b. Niagara Falls, NY, Feb. 27, 1905
d. New York, NY, Sept. 18, 1968, Age 63

TONGE, H. Asheton
Actor
b. Unknown
d. New York, NY, April 2, 1927, Age 55

TONGE, Philip
Actor
b. London, England, April 26, 1892
d. Hollywood, CA, Jan. 28, 1959, Age 66

TONSON, Jacob
Play publisher
b. Unknown
d. Unknown, April 2, 1736, Age 80

TOOHEY, John Peter
Press representative, Author
b. Binghamton, NY, Unknown
d. New York, NY, Nov. 7, 1947, Age 66

TOOLE, John Laurence
Actor, Producer
b. London, England, 1830
d. Brighton, England, July 30, 1906, Age 76

TOOLEY, Nicholas (Wilkinson)
Actor, Patentee
b. Unknown, c1575
d. Unknown, buried June 5, 1623

TOPHAM, Edward
Playwright
b. Unknown
d. Unknown, April 26, 1820, Age 69

TORELLI, Giacomo
Designer, Mechanic
b. Fano, Italy, 1608
d. Unknown, 1678, Age 70

TOREN, Marta (Mrs. Leonardo Bercovici)
Actress
b. Sweden, Unknown
d. Stockholm, Sweden, Feb. 19, 1957, Age 30

TORRENCE, Ernest (Thayson)
Actor, Singer
b. Edinburgh, Scotland, June 26, 1878
d. New York, NY, May 15, 1933, Age 54

TOSCANINI, Arthuro
Conductor
b. Parma, Italy, March 25, 1867
d. Riverdale, NY, Jan. 16, 1957, Age 89

TOTTEN, Joseph Byron
Actor, Playwright
b. Brooklyn, NY, Unknown
d. New York, NY, April 29, 1946, Age 70

TOULMOUCHE, Frédéic
Composer
b. Unknown
d. Unknown, Feb. 23, 1909, Age 58

TOURNEUR, Cyril
Playwright, Poet
b. Unknown, c1575
d. Unknown, 1626

TOURS, Frank E.
Conductor, Composer
b. London, England, Sept. 1, 1877
d. Santa Monica, CA, Feb. 2, 1963, Age 85

TOUTAIN, Blanche
Actress
b. Unknown
d. Unknown, July 9, 1932

TOWER, Allen (John Allen Coggeshall)
Performer
b. Boston, MA, Unknown
d. New York, NY, May 28, 1963

TOWERS, Johnson
Playwright
b. Unknown
d. Unknown, July 8, 1891, Age 78

TOWNE, Charles Hanson
Writer, Editor, Actor
b. Louisville, KY, Feb. 2, 1877
d. New York, NY, Feb. 28, 1949, Age 72

TOWNLEY, Rev. James
Playwright
b. Unknown
d. Unknown, July 15, 1778, Age 64

TOWNSEND, Aurelian
Writer of Masques, fl. 1601-43

TOWNSEND, Thompson
Playwright
b. Unknown
d. Unknown, May 16, 1870, Age 64

TOWSE, John Ranken
Drama critic, Jounalist
b. Streatham, Surrey, England, April 2, 1845
d. Streatham, Surrey, England, April 11, 1933, Age 88

TOY, Beatrice
Actress
b. Unknown
d. Unknown, June 3, 1938, Age 64

TOYNE, Gabriel
Actor, Producer
b. Unknown
d. Ibiza, Spain, Dec. 29, 1963, Age 58

TOZERE, Frederic
Actor
b. Brookline, MA, June 19, 1901
d. New York, NY, Aug. 5, 1972, Age 71

TRACEY, Thomas F. (Thomas W. Flynn)
Actor
b. County Cork, Ireland, Unknown
d. New York, NY, Aug. 27, 1961, Age 86

TRACY, Lee
Actor
b. Atlanta, GA, April 11, 1898
d. Santa Monica, CA, Oct. 18, 1968, Age 70

TRACY, Spencer
Actor
b. Milwaukee, WI, April 5, 1900
d. Beverly Hills, CA, June 10, 1967, Age 67

TRACY, Virginia
Actress, Author
b. New York, NY, Unknown
d. New York, NY, March 4, 1946, Age 72

TRAVERSE, Madlaine (Madlaine Businsky)
Actress
b. Cleveland, OH, Unknown
d. Cleveland, OH, Jan. 7, 1964, Age 88

TREACHER, Arthur
Actor
b. Brighton, England, July 23, 1894
d. Manhasset, NY, Dec. 14, 1975, Age 81

TREADWAY, Charlotte
Actress
b. Unknown
d. Hollywood, CA, Feb. 26, 1963, Age 68

TREE, Lady (Helen Maud Holt)
Actress
b. London, England, Oct. 5, 1863
d. London, England, Aug. 7, 1937, Age 73

TREE, Maria (Mrs. Bradshaw)
Actress
b. Unknown
d. Unknown, Feb. 18, 1862, Age 60

TREE, Sir Herbert Draper Beerbohm (Herbert Beerbohm)
Actor, Producer, Playwright
b. London, England, Dec. 17, 1853
d. Unknown, July 2, 1917, Age 63

TREE, Viola
Actress, Playwright, Singer
b. London, England, July 17, 1884
d. London, England, Nov. 15, 1938, Age 54

TRENCH, Herbert
Playwright, Poet, Producer
b. Avoncore, County Cork, Ireland, Nov. 1865
d. June 11, 1923, 57

TRENHOLME, Helen
Actress
b. Montreal, CAN, June 23, 1911
d. New York, NY, Jan. 30, 1962, Age 50

TRENT, Sheila
Actress
b. Unknown
d. New York, NY, May 26, 1954, Age 46

TRENTINI, Emma
Actress, Opera singer
b. Italy, Unknown
d. Milan, Italy, April 12, 1959, Age about 76

TRERSAHAR, John
Actor
b. Unknown
d. Unknown, April 19, 1936, Age 76

TREVELYAN, Hilda (née Tucker)
Actress
b. Unknown, Feb. 4, 1880
d. Henley-on-Thames, England, Nov. 10, 1959, Age 79

TREVOR, Leo
Playwright
b. Unknown
d. Unknown, Nov. 27, 1927, Age 62

TREVOR, Norman
Actor
b. Calcutta, India, June 23, 1877
d. Unknown, Oct. 31, 1929, Age 52

TREVOR, Spencer
Actor
b. Biarritz, France, May 29, 1875
d. Unknown, May 22, 1945, Age 70

TRIMBLE, Jessie
Playwright
b. Toledo, OH, Unknown
d. New York, NY, April 14, 1957, Age 83

TRIMBLE, Lawrence
Director
b. Unknown
d. Woodland Hills, CA, Feb. 8, 1954, Age 69

TRIMMINGHAM, Ernest
Actor
b. Unknown
d. Unknown, Feb. 6, 1942, Age 63

TRIX, Helen
Actress
b. Unknown
d. Unknown, Nov. 18, 1951, Age 59

TROSPER, Guy
Screenwriter
b. Unknown
d. Sherman Oaks, CA, Dec. 20, 1963, Age 52

TROUNCER, Cecil
Actor
b. Southpart, Lancashire, England, April 5, 1898
d. Unknown, Dec. 15, 1953, Age 55

TRUEBA, Don
Playwright
b. Unknown
d. Unknown, Oct. 12, 1835

TRUESDELL, (George) Frederick
Actor, Writer
b. Unknown
d. New York, NY, May 3, 1937, Age 64

TRUEX, Ernest
Actor
b. Kansas City, MO, Sept. 19, 1889
d. Fallbrook, CA, June 27, 1973, Age 84

TRUJILLO, Lorenzo L. ("Chel")
Actor
b. Unknown
d. Mexico City, Mexico, 1962, Age 56

TRUSSELL, Fred
Producer, Conductor
b. Unknown
d. Unknown, July 21, 1923, Age 64

TSCHAIKOWSKY, Peter
Composer
b. Votkinsk, Viatka, Russia, May 7, 1840
d. Unknown, Nov. 6, 1893, Age 53

TUCKER, George Loane
Actor, Director
b. Chicago, IL, Unknown
d. Los Angeles, CA, June 21, 1921, Age 49

TUCKER, Sophie (née Sophie Kalish Abuza)
Performer
b. Russia, Jan. 13, 1887
d. New York, NY, Feb. 9, 1966, Age 79

TUCKERMAN, Maury (né Ludlow Maury Tuckerman)
Director, Stage manager, Actor
b. Bronx, NY, Oct. 31, 1905
d. Denver, CO, Oct. 23, 1966, Age 61

TUERK, John
Producer
b. New York, NY, Unknown
d. New York, NY, May 25, 1951, Age 59

TULLY, George F.
Actor
b. Balla, County Mayo, Ireland, Nov. 22, 1876
d. Unknown, July 2, 1930, Age 53

TULLY, May
Actress, Author
b. Victor, British Columbia, Unknown
d. New York, NY, March 9, 1924, Age 40

TULLY, Richard Walton
Playwright, Producer
b. Nevada City, CA, May 7, 1877
d. New York, NY, Jan. 31, 1945, Age 67

TUNBRIDGE, Joseph A.
Composer, Conductor
b. London, England, Jan. 21, 1886
d. Orpington, England, Dec. 28, 1961, Age 75

TUPPER, Mary (Mary Tupper Jones)
Actress
b. Fresno, CA, Unknown
d. Poughkeepsie, NY, July 2, 1964, Age 86

TURGENEV, Ivan Sergeyevich
Playwright, Novelist
b. Orel, Russia, Oct. 28, 1818
d. Bougival, France, Aug. 23, 1883, Age 64

TURLUPIN, (Henri Legrand)
Actor, Farceur
b. Unknown, c1587
d. Unknown, 1637

TURNBULL, John
Actor
b. Dunbar, Scotland, Nov. 5, 1880
d. Unknown, Feb. 23, 1956, Age 75

TURNBULL, Stanley
Actor
b. Whitby, Yorkshire, England, Unknown
d. Unknown, May 8, 1924, Age 43

TURNER, Alfred
Theatre manager
b. London, England, July 29, 1870
d. Unknown, May 12, 1941, Age 70

TURNER, Cicely (Mrs. W. H. Leverton)
Actress
b. Unknown
d. Unknown, March 13, 1940

TURNER, Eardley
Actor, Journalist
b. Unknown
d. Unknown, Jan. 23, 1929

TURNER, Florence
Actress
b. New York, NY, 1877
d. Woodland Hills, CA, Aug. 28, 1946, Age 59

TURNER, George
Actor
b. Fundon Manor, England, Feb. 19, 1902
d. New York, NY, July 27, 1968, Age 66

TURNER, Harold
Dancer, Ballet master, Teacher
b. Manchester, England, Dec. 2, 1909
d. London, England, July 2, 1962, Age 52

TURNER, J. W.
Singer, Producer
b. Unknown
d. Unknown, Jan. 17, 1913, Age 68

TURNER, Maidel (Mrs. Maidel Turner Thomas)
Actress
b. Sherman, TX, Unknown
d. Ocean Springs, MS, April 12, 1953, Age 72

TURNER, W. J.
Author, Poet, Critic
b. Unknown
d. Unknown, Nov. 18, 1946, Age 57

TURPIN, Ben
Actor
b. New Orleans, LA, 1874
d. Hollwyood, CA, July 1, 1940, Age 66

TWAIN, Mark (Samuel Langhorne Clemens)
Playwright, Humorist, Writer, Lecturer
b. Florida, MO, Nov. 30, 1835
d. Hartford, CT, April 21, 1910, Age 74

TWAITS, William
Actor
b. Unknown
d. New York, NY, 1814

TWELVETREES, Helen (Mrs. Conrad Payne née Helen Jurgen)
Actress
b. Unknown
d. Harrisburg, PA, Feb. 13, 1958, Age about 50

TYARS, Frank
Actor
b. Kent, England, July 26, 1848
d. Unknown, May 11, 1918, Age 69

TYLER, George Crouse
Producer, Director
b. Circleville, OH, April 13, 1867
d. Yonkers, NY, March 13, 1946, Age 78

TYLER, Judy
Performer
b. Unknown
d. Billy The Kid, WY, July 3, 1957, Age 24

TYLER, Odette (Mrs. R. D. Shepherd)
Actress
b. Savannah, GA, Sept. 26, 1869
d. Hollywood, CA, Dec. 8, 1936, Age 67

TYLER, Royall
Playwright
b. Boston, MA, July 18, 1757
d. Brattleboro, VT, Aug. 26, 1826, Age 69

TYLER, Tom
Actor
b. Unknown
d. Hamtramek, MI, May 1, 1954, Age 50

TYNDALL, Kate
Actress
b. Unknown
d. Unknown, Aug. 1919

TYRRELL, Rose
Dancer
b. Unknown
d. Unknown, April 5, 1934, Age 75

U

UDALL, Nicholas
Playwright, Teacher
b. Hampshire, England, 1505 or 1506
d. London, England, buried Dec. 23, 1556, Age 51

ULMAR, Geraldine
Actress
b. Boston, MA, June 23, 1862
d. Unknown, Aug. 13, 1932, Age 70

UNAMUNOY, Jugo Miguel de
Philosopher, Author, Poet, Playwright
b. Bilbao, Spain, Sept. 29, 1864
d. Salamanca, Spain, Dec. 31, 1936, Age 72

UNDERHILL, Edward
Actor
b. Unknown
d. London, England, March 8, 1964, Age 65

UNDERHILL, John Garrett
Playwright
b. Brooklyn, NY, Unknown
d. Brooklyn, NY, May 15, 1946, Age 70

UNDERWOOD, Franklyn
Actor
b. Denver, CO, Unknown
d. New York, NY, Dec. 22, 1940, Age 63

UNGER, Gladys Buchanan
Playwright
b. San Francisco, CA, Unknown
d. New York, NY, May 25, 1940, Age 55

UNRUH, Walter
Stage Designer, Writer, Teacher
b. Dresden, Germany, Jan. 10, 1898
d. Wiesbaden, West Germany, Aug. 28, 1973, Age 75

UPSHER, Peter
Performer
b. Unknown
d. London, England, 1963, Age 70

URBAN, Joseph
Artist, Architect, Scene designer
b. Vienna, Austria, 1872
d. New York, NY, July 10, 1933, Age 61

URE, Mary
Actress
b. Glasgow, Scotland, Feb. 18, 1933
d. London, England, Apr. 3, 1975, Age 42

URQUHART, Isabelle
Actress
b. New York, NY, Dec. 9, 1865
d. Rochester, NY, Feb. 7, 1907, Age 41

V

VACHELL, Horace Annesley
Novelist, Playwright
b. Sydenham, Kent, England, Oct. 30, 1861
d. Unknown, Jan. 10, 1955, Age 93

VAIL, Lester
Actor, Director
b. Unknown
d. Los Angeles, CA, Nov. 28, 1959, Age 59

VAJDA, Ernest
Playwright
b. Komaron, Hungary, 1887
d. Woodland Hills, CA, April 3, 1954, Age 67

VAKHTANGOV, Eugen V.
Actor, Director, Producer
b. Russia, 1883
d. U.S.S.R., May 29, 1922, Age 39

VAL, Paul
Actor, Producer
b. Unknown
d. Hollywood, CA, March 23, 1962, Age 75

VALDARE, Sunny Jim (James Mulligan)
Performer
b. Plattsmouth, NB, Unknown
d. Columbus, OH, Aug. 16, 1962, Age 88

VALENTINE, Paul
Dancer, Ballet master
b. Unknown
d. Unknown, May 29, 1924, Age 85

VALENTINE, Sydney
Actor
b. Unknown, Feb. 14, 1865
d. Unknown, Dec. 23, 1919, Age 54

VALENTINO, Rudolph (Rudolph Alfonzo Raffaelo Pierre Filbert Guglielmi di Valentina d'Antonguolla)
Actor, Dancer
b. Martina Franca, Lecce, Italy, May 6, 1895
d. New York, NY, Aug. 23, 1926, Age 31

VALERIO, Theresa
Performer
b. Unknown
d. Spring Lake, NJ, May 23, 1964, Age 70's

VALK, Frederick
Actor
b. Germany, Unknown
d. London, England, July 23, 1956, Age 55

VAN, Billy B.
Actor
b. Pottstown, PA, Unknown
d. Newport, NH, Nov. 16, 1950, Age 72

VAN, Charley
Performer
b. Unknown
d. Chicago, IL, Jan. 21, 1963, Age 80

VAN, Gus (Van and Schenck)
Performer
b. Brooklyn, NY, Unknown
d. Miami Beach, FL, March 12, 1968, Age 80

VAN ALSTYNE, Egbert Aanson
Songwriter
b. Marengo, IL, March 5, 1882
d. Chicago, IL, July 9, 1951, Age 69

VAN BIENE, Auguste
Actor, Musician, Composer
b. Holland, May 16, 1850
d. Unknown, Jan. 23, 1913, Age 62

VANBRUGH, Dame Irene
Actress
b. Exeter, England, Dec. 2, 1872
d. London, England, Nov. 30, 1949, Age 76

VANBRUGH, Sir John
Playwright, Architect
b. England, 1664
d. London, England, March 26, 1726, Age 61

VANBRUGH, Violet Augusta Mary (Mrs. Artyur Bourchier)
Actress
b. Exeter, England, June 11, 1867
d. London, England, Nov. 10, 1942, Age 75

VAN BUREN, Mabel
Actress
b. Unknown
d. Hollywood, CA, Nov. 4, 1947, Age 69

VANDAMM, Florence (Mrs. George Robert Thomas)
Photographer
b. London, England, Unknown
d. New York, NY, March 15, 1966, Age 83

VAN DAMM, Vivian
General Mgr. of the Windmill Theatre
b. Unknown
d. London, England, Dec. 14, 1960, Age 71

VANDENHOFF, Charles H.
Actor
b. Unknown
d. Unknown, April 29, 1890

VANDENHOFF, Charlotte Elizabeth (Mrs. Swinbourne)
Actress
b. England, 1818
d. near Birmingham, England, July 26, 1860, Age 42

VANDENHOFF, George C.
Actor
b. Unknown, 1813
d. Unknown, Aug. 10, 1884, Age 62

VANDENHOFF, Henry
Actor
b. Unknown
d. Unknown, Oct. 7, 1888

VANDENHOFF, John M.
Actor
b. Salisbury, England, March 31, 1790
d. London, England, Oct. 4, 1861, Age 71

VANDENHOFF, Kate
Actress
b. Unknown
d. Unknown, Sept. 27, 1942, Age 73

VANDENHOFF, Mrs. Henry
Actress
b. Unknown
d. Unknown, March 27, 1870

VANDERBILT, Gertrude
Actress
b. Brooklyn, NY, Unknown
d. New York, NY, Feb. 18, 1960, Age 72

VANDERCOOK, John W.
Writer, Newscaster
b. London, England, Unknown
d. Delhi, NY, Jan. 6, 1963, Age 60

VAN DRUTEN, John
Playwright, Director
b. London, England, June 1, 1901
d. Indio, CA, Dec. 19, 1957, Age 56

VANE, Dorothy
Actress
b. Unknown
d. Unknown, March 4, 1947, Age 76

VANE, Helen (Mrs. Charles Sugden)
Actress
b. Unknown
d. Unknown, Jan. 18, 1840, Age 79

VANE, Sutton
Playwright
b. Unknown
d. Unknown, Feb. 16, 1913

VANE, Sutton (Vane Sutton-Vane)
Playwright, Actor
b. Unknown, 1888
d. Hastings, England, June 17, 1963, Age 74

VANE-TEMPEST, Francis Adolphus
Actor
b. Unknown, Jan. 4, 1863
d. Unknown, Dec. 11, 1932, Age 69

VAN HORN, Rollin Weber
Costumer
b. Unknown
d. Miami Beach, FL, Feb. 3, 1964, Age 83

VAN LENNEP, Dr. William
Curator Harvard Theatre Collection
b. Philadelphia, PA, May 2, 1906
d. Bay Head, NJ, Aug. 20, 1962, Age 56

VANLOO, Albert
Playwright
b. Unknown
d. Unknown, March 4, 1920

VAN ROOY, Anton
Singer
b. Rotterdam, Holland, Unknown
d. Munich, Germany, Nov. 27, 1932, Age 62

VAN SAHER, Mrs. Lilla Alexander
Author, Actress
b. Budapest, Hungary, March 10, 1912
d. New York, NY, July 15, 1968, Age 56

VAN SICKLE, Raymond
Actor, Playwright
b. Unknown
d. Kobe, Japan, July 10, 1964, Age 79

VAN SLOAN, Edward
Actor
b. San Francisco, CA, Unknown
d. San Francisco, CA, March 6, 1964, Age 82

VAN STUDDIFORD, Grace (Quivey)
Singer
b. North Manchester, IN, Jan. 8, 1873
d. Fort Wayne, IN, Jan. 29, 1927, Age 54

VAN TULY, Helen
Actress, Educator
b. Unknown
d. Hollywood, CA, Aug. 22, 1964, Age 73

VAN VECHTEN, Carl
Critic, Author, Photographer
b. Cedar Rapids, IA, June 17, 1880
d. New York, NY, Dec. 21, 1964, Age 84

VARDEN, Evelyn (née Hall, Mrs. William J. Quinn)
Actress
b. Adair, OK, June 12, 1895
d. New York, NY, July 11, 1958, Age 63

VARLAMOV, Konstantin Alexandrovitch
Actor
b. Unknown
d. Aug. 15, 1915, 65

VARNEL, Marcel (Marcel le Bozec)
Director
b. Paris, France, Oct. 16, 1894
d. Unknown, July 13, 1947, Age 53

VARREY, Edwin
Actor
b. Unknown
d. Unknown, May 5, 1907, Age 80

VASSAR, Queenie
Actress
b. Glasgow, Scotland, Unknown
d. West Los Angeles, CA, Sept. 11, 1960, Age 89

VAUCAIRE, Maurice
Playwright
b. Versailles, France, 1865
d. Unknown, Feb. 1918, Age 53

VAUGHAN, Kate (Catherine Candelin)
Actress, Dancer
b. Unknown, c1852
d. Unknown, Feb. 21, 1903, Age 47

VAUGHAN, Susie (Susan Mary Charlotte Candelin)
Actress
b. Hoxton, New Town, Middlesex, England, Feb. 21, 1853
d. Unknown, Dec. 17, 1950, Age 97

VAUGHAN, T. B.
Producer
b. Unknown
d. Unknown, June 28, 1928

VAUGHN, Hilda
Actress
b. Baltimore, MD, Unknown
d. Baltimore, MD, Dec. 28, 1957, Age 60

VEDRENNE, John E.
Producer
b. Unknown, July 13, 1867
d. Unknown, Feb. 12, 1930, Age 62

VEGA CARPIO, Lope Felix de
Playwright, Poet
b. Madrid, Spain, Nov. 25, 1562
d. Madrid, Spain, Aug. 27, 1635, Age 72

VEIDT, Conrad
Actor
b. Berlin, Germany, 1893
d. Los Angeles, CA, April 3, 1943, Age 50

VEILLER, Bayard
Playwright
b. Brooklyn, NY, Jan. 2, 1869
d. New York, NY, June 16, 1943, Age 74

VELEZ, Lupe (Guadeloupe Velez de Villabos)
Actress, Dancer
b. San Luis de Potosi, Mexico, July 18, 1908
d. Beverly Hills, CA, Dec. 14, 1944, Age 36

VENESS, Amy
Actress
b. Unknown
d. Saltdean, England, Sept. 22, 1960, Age 84

VENIER (Vernier), Marie
Actress
b. Unknown, 1590
d. Unknown, 1619

VENNE, Lottie
Actress
b. Unknown, May 28, 1852
d. Unknown, July 16, 1928, Age 76

VERMILYEA, Harold
Actor
b. New York, NY, Oct. 10, 1889
d. New York, NY, Jan. 8, 1958, Age 68

VERNEUIL, Louis
Playwright, Actor
b. Paris, France, May 14, 1893
d. Paris, France, Nov. 3, 1952, Age 59

VERNON, Frank
Playwright, Producer, Director
b. Bombay, India, March 6, 1875
d. Unknown, March 17, 1940, Age 65

VERNON, Harriett
Actress
b. Unknown
d. Unknown, July 11, 1923, Age 71

VERNON, Ida (Mrs. I. V. Taylor)
Actress
b. "The South," U.S.A., 1843
d. New York, NY, Feb. 22, 1923, Age 80

VERNON, Kate Olga
Actress
b. Unknown
d. Unknown, Dec. 13, 1939, Age 71

VERTES, Marcel
Scene designer, Painter
b. Budapest, Hungary, Aug. 10, 1895
d. Paris, France, Oct. 31, 1961, Age 66

VESTOFF, Floria (Mrs. Gordon Andrews)
Choreographer, Dancer, Writer
b. Russia, Unknown
d. Hollywood, CA, March 18, 1963, Age about 43

VESTRIS, Madame (Lucia Elizabeth Mathews) Bartolozzi
Actress, Producer
b. London, England, Jan. 1797
d. Unknown, Aug. 8, 1856, Age 59

VEZIN, Hermann
Actor
b. Philadelphia, PA, 1829
d. London, England, June 12, 1910, Age 81

VEZIN, Mrs. Hermann (Jane Elizabeth Thomson)
Actress
b. Bath, England, Unknown
d. England, 1902

VIARDOT, Pauline
Actress
b. Unknown
d. Unknown, May 18, 1910, Age 89

VICTOR, Benjamin
Historian, Producer
b. Unknown
d. Unknown, Dec. 3, 1778

VICTOR, Lionel
Actor
b. Unknown
d. Unknown, Dec. 15, 1940

VICTOR, Mary Anne
Actress
b. Unknown
d. Unknown, March 13, 1907, Age 76

VICTORIA, Vesta (Mrs. Victoria Terry née Lawrence)
Performer
b. London, England, Unknown
d. London, England, April 7, 1951, Age 77

VIDAL, Henri
Actor
b. Unknown
d. Paris, France, Dec. 10, 1959, Age 40

VIE, Florence
Actress
b. Unknown
d. Unknown, April 12, 1939, Age 63

VIGARANI, Gaspare
Designer, Mechanic
b. Italy, 1586
d. Unknown, 1663

VIGNOLA, Robert G.
Actor, Director
b. Italy, Unknown
d. Hollywood, CA, Oct. 25, 1953, Age 71

VIGNY, Alfred Victor, Comte de
Author, Playwright
b. Loches, France, March 27, 1797
d. Paris, France, Sept. 17, 1863, Age 66

VILAR, Jean
Actor
b. Sète, France, March 25, 1912
d. Sète, France, May 28, 1971, Age 59

VILLETARD, Edmond
Playwright
b. Unknown
d. Unknown, Aug. 18, 1890, Age 78

VILLIERS, Edwin
Actor, Producer
b. Unknown
d. Unknown, April 29, 1904, Age 73

VILLIERS, George (Duke of Buckingham)
Playwright
b. Unknown, 1628
d. Unknown, April 16, 1687, Age 59

VINCENT, Charles T.
Actor, Playwright
b. Bristol, England, Unknown
d. Glen Cove, NY, March 21, 1935, Age 76

VINCENT, James
Actor, Director
b. Springfield, MA, Unknown
d. New York, NY, July 12, 1957, Age 74

VINCENT, Mary Ann (née Farley, Mrs. J. R. Vincent)
Actress
b. Portsmouth, England, Sept. 18, 1818
d. Boston, MA, Sept. 4, 1887, Age 68

VINCENT, Ruth
Actress
b. Yarmouth, Norfolk, England, March 22, 1877
d. Unknown, July 4, 1955, Age 78

VINCENT, Walter
Actor, Producer, Writer
b. Lake Geneva, WI, Aug. 10, 1868
d. New York, NY, May 10, 1959, Age 90

VINING, Fanny (Mrs. E. L. Davenport)
Actress
b. Unknown
d. Unknown, July 20, 1891, Age 62

VINING, Frederick
Actor
b. Unknown
d. Unknown, June 2, 1871, Age 81

VINING, George J.
Actor, Producer
b. Unknown
d. Unknown, Dec. 17, 1875, Age 51

VINTON, Arthur R.
Actor
b. Brooklyn, NY, Unknown
d. Guadalajara, Mexico, Feb. 26, 1963

VIOLINSKY, Solly Sol Ginsberg
Performer, Writer, Songwriter
b. Unknown
d. Binghampton, NY, May 5, 1963, Age 77

VITRUVIUS POLLIO, Marcus
Historian, (fl. 70-15 B.C.)
b. Unknown, 1st Century B.C.

VIVIAN, Percival
Actor, Director
b. England
d. Burbank, CA, Jan. 14, 1961, Age 70

VIVIAN, Robert
Actor
b. London, England, Unknown
d. New York, NY, Jan. 31, 1944, Age 85

VIVIAN, Ruth
Actress
b. England, Unknown
d. New York, NY, Oct. 24, 1949, Age 66

VIVIAN, Violet (Mrs. Charles Robert Hopkins)
Actress
b. England, Unknown
d. New York, NY, Dec. 24, 1960, Age 74

VOGEL, Henry
Actor
b. Unknown
d. New York, NY, June 17, 1925, Age 60

VOKES, F. M. T.
Pantomimst, Dancer
b. Unknown
d. Unknown, June 4, 1890, Age 74

VOKES, Frederick Mortimer
Pantomimist, Dancer
b. Unknown, 1846
d. Unknown, June 3, 1888, Age 42

VOKES, Harry
Comedian
b. Unknown
d. Lynn, MA, April 15, 1922, Age 56

VOKES, John Russell
Performer
b. Australia, Unknown
d. Minneapolis, MN, April 21, 1924, Age 52

VOKES, May (Mrs. Robert Lester)
Actress
b. Unknown
d. Stamford, CT, Sept. 13, 1957, Age 70's

VOKES, Robert
Pantomimist, Dancer
b. Unknown
d. Unknown, March 2, 1912, Age 56

VOKES, Rosina
Actress
b. Unknown, 1854
d. Unknown, Jan. 27, 1894, Age 39

VOKES, Victoria
Actress, Dancer
b. Unknown, 1853
d. Unknown, Dec. 2, 1894, Age 41

VOLKOV, Fedor Gregoryevich
Actor
b. Kostroma, Russia, 1729
d. Moscow, Russia, 1763

VOLLMER, Lula
Playwright
b. Keyser, NC, 1898
d. New York, NY, May 2, 1955, Age 57

VOLLMOELLER, Karl
Playwright
b. Stuttgart, Germany, Unknown
d. Hollywood, CA, Oct. 17, 1948, Age 69

VOLPE, Frederick
Actor
b. Liverpool, England, July 31, 1865
d. Unknown, March 6, 1932, Age 66

VOLTAIRE, Francois Marie Aronet de
Playwright, Author, etc.
b. Paris, France, 1694
d. Paris, France, May 30, 1778, Age 84

VOLTERRA, Leon
Producer, Director
b. Unknown
d. Unknown, June 5, 1949, Age 61

VON BUSING, Fritzi (Mrs. Forrest Huff)
Performer
b. Nyack, NY, Unknown
d. New York, NY, March 6, 1948, Age 64

VON HOFMANNSTAHL, Hugo
Playwright, Poet, See Hofmannstahl, Hugo von

VON LER, Sarah (Mrs. J. M. Hardie)
Actress, Producer
b. Unknown
d. Unknown, June 29, 1916

VONNEGUT, Walter
Actor, Director
b. Indianapolis, IN, Unknown
d. Culver, IN, Dec. 23, 1940, Age 56

VON TILZER, Albert (Albert Gumm)
Composer, Song publisher, Performer
b. Indianapolis, IN, March 29, 1878
d. Los Angeles, CA, Oct. 1, 1956, Age 78

VON TILZER, Harry (Harry Gumm)
Composer, Song publisher, Performer
b. Detroit, MI, July 8, 1872
d. New York, NY, Jan. 10, 1946, Age 73

VON TWARDOWSKI, Hans Heinrich
Actor, Director
b. Germany, Unknown
d. New York, NY, Nov. 19, 1958, Age 60

VOSPER, Frank
Actor, Playwright
b. London, England, Dec. 15, 1899
d. at sea, March 6, 1937, Age 37

VROOM, Lodewick
Producer, Press representative
b. St. John, N.B., CAN, Unknown
d. New York, NY, July 5, 1950, Age 66

W

WADE, Allan
Actor, Business manager, Director
b. Unknown, May 17, 1881
d. Unknown, July 12, 1955, Age 74

WADE, Philip
Actor
b. Unknown
d. Unknown, Dec. 3, 1950, Age 54

WADE, Walter
Performer, Songwriter
b. Unknown
d. London, England, Jan. 10, 1963, Age 52

WADSWORTH, Handel
Director
b. Yorkshire, England, Unknown
d. Cleveland, OH, May 19, 1964

WAGENHALS, Lincoln A.
Producer
b. Lancaster, OH, April 11, 1869
d. Montrose-on-Hudson, NY, Sept. 11, 1931, Age 62

WAGNER, Charles L.
Producer, Director
b. Unknown
d. New York, NY, Feb. 25, 1956, Age 87

WAGNER, Wilhelm Richard
Composer, Librettist, Producer, Director
b. Leipzig, Germany, 1813
d. Venice, Italy, Feb. 13, 1883, Age 70

WAGNER, William
Actor
b. Unknown
d. Hollywood, CA, March 11, 1964, Age 79

WAINWRIGHT, John
Actor, Producer
b. Unknown
d. Unknown, March 13, 1911, Age 69

WAINWRIGHT, Marie
Actress
b. Philadelphia, PA, May 8, 1853
d. Scranton, PA, Aug. 17, 1923, Age 70

WAKEFIELD, Douglas
Performer
b. Sheffield, England, Aug. 28, 1899
d. Unknown, April 14, 1951, Age 51

WAKEMAN, Keith
Actress
b. Oakland, CA, April 6, 1866
d. Unknown, Oct. 17, 1933, Age 67

WALBROOK, Anton (né Adolph Anton Wilhelm Wohlbrück)
Actor
b. Vienna, Austria, Nov. 19, 1900
d. Munich, West Germany, Aug. 9, 1967, Age 66

WALBROOK, Henry Mackinnon
Critic, Playwright
b. Unknown
d. Brighton, England, Feb. 10, 1941, Age 77

WALBURN, Raymond
Actor
b. Plymouth, IN, Sept. 9, 1887
d. New York, NY, July 26, 1969, Age 81

WALCOT, Charles Melton
Actor
b. London, England, 1816
d. Unknown, 1868

WALCOT, Charles Melton Jr.
Actor
b. Boston, MA, July 1, 1840
d. New York, NY, Jan. 1, 1921, Age 80

WALDEN, Harry
Actor
b. Berlin, Germany, Oct. 22, 1875
d. Berlin, Germany, June 4, 1921, Age 45

WALDORF, Wilella
Drama critic
b. South Bend, IN, Unknown
d. New York, NY, March 12, 1946, Age 46

WALDOW, Ernst
Actor
b. Unknown
d. Hamburg, Germany, June 5, 1964, Age 70

WALDRON, Charles D.
Actor
b. Waterford, NY, Dec. 23, 1874
d. Hollywood, CA, March 4, 1946, Age 71

WALDRON, Francis Godolphin
Actor, Playwright
b. Unknown
d. Unknown, March 1818, Age 64

WALDRON, Georgia (Mrs. Edward Emery)
Actress
b. Salt Lake City, UT, 1872
d. Los Angeles, CA, Jan. 9, 1950, Age 77

WALDRON, Jack
Actor, Writer
b. Brooklyn, NY, Feb. 3, 1893
d. New York, NY, Nov. 21, 1969, Age 76

WALDRON, James A.
Editor of N. Y. Dramatic Mirror
b. Unknown
d. Unknown, June 3, 1931, Age 79

WALENN, Charles R.
Actor
b. Unknown
d. Unknown, May 30, 1948

WALKER, Bob (Robert Hudson Walker)
Actor
b. Salt Lake City, UT, Oct. 13, 1918
d. Pacific Palisades, CA, Aug. 28, 1951, Age 32

WALKER, Charlotte
Actress
b. Galveston, TX, Dec. 29, 1878
d. Kerrville, TX, March 23, 1958, Age 79

WALKER, Danton
Columnist, Journalist, Actor
b. Marietta, GA, Unknown
d. Hyannis, MA, Aug. 8, 1960, Age 61

WALKER, Johnny
Actor
b. Unknown, 1894
d. New York, NY, Dec. 5, 1949, Age 55

WALKER, June
Actress
b. Chicago, IL, June 14, 1899
d. Los Angeles, CA, Feb. 3, 1966, Age 66

WALKER, Laura
Actress
b. Unknown
d. New York, NY, May 17, 1951, Age 57

WALKER, Martin
Actor
b. Harrow, Middlesex, England, July 27, 1901
d. Unknown, Sept. 18, 1955, Age 54

WALKER, Robert
See Walker, Bob

WALKER, Stuart
Actor, Playwright, Producer, Director
b. Augusta, KY, March 4, 1888
d. Hollywood, CA, March 13, 1941, Age 53

WALKER, Syd
Actor
b. Salford, Manchester, Lancashire, England, March 22, 1886
d. Unknown, Jan. 13, 1945, Age 58

WALKER, Thomas
Actor
b. Unknown
d. Unknown, June 5, 1744, Age 46

WALKES, W. R.
Playwright
b. Unknown
d. Unknown, Feb. 2, 1913

WALKLEY, Arthur Bingham
Critic, Essayist
b. Bristol, England, Dec. 17, 1855
d. Unknown, Oct. 8, 1926, Age 70

WALLACE, David
Playwright
b. Syracuse, NY, Unknown
d. New York, NY, June 15, 1955, Age 66

WALLACE, Edgar (Richard Edgar Horatio Wallace)
Playwright, Producer, Novelist, Journalist
b. Deptford, London, England, April 1, 1875
d. Beverly Hills, CA, Feb. 10, 1932, Age 56

WALLACE, Gen. Lewis
Lawyer, Soldier, Diplomat, Novelist
b. Brookville, IN, April 10, 1827
d. Crawfordsville, IN, Feb. 15, 1905, Age 77

WALLACE, Louise Chapman
Actress
b. Unknown
d. Hollywood, CA, May 20, 1962, Age 80

WALLACE, Morgan
Actor
b. California, Unknown
d. Tarzana, CA, Dec. 12, 1953, Age 72

WALLACE, Mrs. Edgar
Producer
b. Unknown
d. Unknown, April 8, 1933, Age 36

WALLACE, Nellie (Mrs. Christopher Landry)
Actress
b. Edinburgh, Scotland, Unknown
d. Bowdoinham, ME, Nov. 28, 1933, Age 53

WALLACE, Nellie (Mrs. Eleanor Jane Liddy)
Performer
b. Glasgow, Scotland, March 18, 1870
d. Unknown, Nov. 24, 1948, Age 78

WALLACH, Edgar
Theatre manager
b. Washington, DC, Unknown
d. New York, NY, April 10, 1953, Age 68

WALLACK, Arthur J.
Theatre manager
b. Unknown
d. Stapelton, L.I., NY, July 21, 1940, Age 91

WALLACK, Henry John
Actor
b. London, England, 1790
d. Unknown, Aug. 30, 1870, Age 79

WALLACK, James William
Actor, Producer
b. Lambeth, London, England, 1791
d. New York, NY, Dec. 25, 1864, Age 73

WALLACK, James William Jr.
Actor
b. Hull, Yorkshire, England, Feb. 24, 1818
d. Unknown, May 24, 1873, Age 55

WALLACK, Lester (John Johnstone Wallack)
Actor-Manager
b. New York, NY, Dec. 31,1819
d. near Stamford, CT, Sept. 6, 1888, Age 68

WALLACK, Mrs. Henry J. (Miss Turpin)
Actress
b. Unknown
d. London, England, June 19, 1860

WALLACK, Mrs. J. W. Jr. (Ann Duff)
Actress
b. Unknown
d. Unknown, Feb. 11, 1879, Age 64

WALLACK, Mrs. Lester
Actress
b. Unknown
d. Unknown, March 28, 1909, Age 84

WALLACK, Mrs. William (Elizabeth Granger)
Actress
b. Unknown
d. Unknown, March 6, 1850, Age 90

WALLENDA, Yetta (Mrs. Grotofent)
Performer
b. Unknown
d. Omaha, NB, April 18, 1963, Age 42

WALLER, D. W. (née Daniel Wilmarth)
Actor
b. New York, NY, Unknown
d. New York, NY, Jan. 30, 1882, Age 58

WALLER, "Fats"
(Thomas Waller), Composer, Musician
b. New York, NY, May 21, 1904
d. Kansas City, MO, Dec. 15, 1943, Age 39

WALLER, J. Wallet
Director
b. Unknown
d. Unknown, March 19, 1951, Age 69

WALLER, Jack
Producer, Director, Composer, Actor
b. London, England, April 2, 1885
d. Unknown, July 28, 1957, Age 72

WALLER, Lewis (William Waller Lewis)
Actor, Producer
b. Bilbao, Spain, Nov. 3, 1860
d. Unknown, Nov. 1, 1915, Age 55

WALLER, Mrs. D. W. (Emma)
Actress, Teacher
b. Unknown, 1820
d. Unknown, Feb. 28, 1899

WALLER, Mrs. Lewis (Florence West)
Actress, Producer
b. Unknown, Dec. 15, 1862
d. Unknown, Nov. 14, 1912, Age 49

WALLING, Roy
Playwright, Actor
b. Oregon, Unknown
d. Stanfordville, NY, May 7, 1964, Age 75

WALLIS, Bella (Mrs. Hugh Moss)
Actress
b. Unknown
d. England, April 26, 1960

WALLIS, Bertram
Actor
b. London, England, Feb. 22, 1874
d. Unknown, April 11, 1952, Age 78

WALLIS, Gladys
Actress
b. New York, NY, Unknown
d. Chicago, IL, Sept. 23, 1953, Age 80

WALLS, Tom
Actor, Producer
b. Kingsthorpe, Northants, England, Feb. 18, 1883
d. Unknown, Nov. 27, 1949, Age 66

WALPOLE, Sir Hugh Seymour
Playwright, Novelist
b. Auckland, New Zealand, 1884
d. Brackenburn, Keswick, Scotland, June 1, 1941, Age 57

WALSH, Blanche
Actress
b. New York, NY, Jan. 4, 1873
d. Unknown, Oct. 31, 1915, Age 42

WALSH, Lionel
Actor
b. Woolwich Common, Kent, England, Jan. 28, 1876
d. London, England, July 1, 1916, Age 40

WALSH, Sam
Actor
b. Unknown
d. Unknown, Jan. 12, 1920, Age 42

WALSH, Thomas H.
Actor
b. Unknown
d. New York, NY, April 25, 1925, Age 62

WALSH, Thomas J.
Theatre executive
b. Unknown
d. Portland, OR, Nov. 12, 1962, Age 59

WALTER, Bruno
Conductor
b. Berlin, Germany, Sept. 15, 1876
d. Beverly Hills, CA, Feb. 17, 1962, Age 85

WALTER, Edwin
Actor
b. Passaic, NJ, Unknown
d. New York, NY, Nov. 23, 1953, Age 82

WALTER, Eugene
Playwright, Press representative
b. Cleveland, OH, Nov. 27, 1874
d. Hollywood, CA, Sept. 26, 1941, Age 66

WALTER, Wilfrid
Actor, Playwright
b. Ripon, Yorkshire, England, March 2, 1882
d. Unknown, July 9, 1958, Age 76

WALTHALL, Henry B.
Actor
b. Shelby City, AL, 1878
d. Monrovia, CA, June 17, 1936, Age 60

WALTON, Douglas (J. Douglas Duder)
Actor, Painter
b. Toronto, CAN, Unknown
d. New York, NY, Nov. 15, 1961, Age 51

WALTON, Fred
Performer
b. Unknown
d. Unknown, Dec.28, 1936, Age 71

WALTON, Herbert
Actor
b. Unknown
d. Unknown, Jan. 16, 1954, Age 74

WALTON, J. K.
Actor
b. Unknown
d. Unknown, April 5,1928, Age 79

WARAM, Percy Carne
Actor
b. Kent, England, Unknown
d. Huntington, L.I., NY, Oct. 5, 1961, Age 80

WARBURTON, Charles M.
Actor
b. Huddersfield, England, Oct. 20, 1887
d. Flushing, NY, July 19, 1952, Age 64

WARD, Albert
Actor
b. Unknown
d. Unknown, Dec. 9, 1956, Age 86

WARD, Annie
Actress
b. Unknown
d. Unknown, Dec. 31, 1918, Age 72

WARD, Dame (Lucy) Genevieve Teresa
Actress
b. New York, NY, March 27, 1834
d. Hampstead, London, England, Aug. 18, 1922, Age 88

WARD, Ethel
Actress
b. Unknown
d. Unknown, April 1, 1955, Age 75

WARD, Fannie
Actress
b. St. Louis, MO, June 22, 1872
d. New York, NY, Jan. 27, 1952, Age 79

WARD, Fleming
Actor
b. Unknown
d. Bronx, NY, Aug. 2, 1962, Age 75

WARD, Hap (John O'Donnell)
Performer, Producer
b. Cameron, PA, Unknown
d. New York, NY, Jan. 3, 1944, Age 76

WARD, Hugh J.
Producer, Actor
b. Philadelphia, PA, 1871
d. Sydney, Australia, April 1941, Age 70

WARD, Mary (née Mary Ward Holton)
Press representative, Actress
b. Maysville, Mason County, KY, Unknown
d. New York, NY, May 2, 1966, Age 78

WARD, Sir A. W.
Historian
b. Unknown
d. Unknown, June 19, 1924, Age 86

WARD, Solly
Actor
b. Unknown
d. Unknown, May 17, 1942, Age 51

WARDE, Ernest C.
Actor, Stage manager
b. Unknown
d. Los Angeles, CA, Sept. 9, 1923, Age 49

WARDE, Frederick Barkham
Actor, Lecturer
b. Warrington, Oxfordshire, England, Feb. 23,1851
d. Brooklyn, NY, Feb. 7, 1935, Age 83

WARDE, George
Actor
b. Unknown
d. Unknown, Nov. 12, 1917, Age 80

WARDE, Willie
Actor, Dancer
b. Great Yarmouth, England, 1857
d. Unknown, Aug. 18, 1943, Age 86

WARDEN, Fred. W.
Actor, Producer
b. Unknown
d. Unknown, June 4, 1929, Age 68

WARDWELL, Geoffrey
Actor, Director
b. York, England, July 30, 1900
d. Unknown, Aug. 9, 1955, Age 55

WARE, Harriet (Mrs. Hugh M. Krumbhaar)
Composer, Musician
b. Waupun, WI, Unknown
d. New York, NY, Feb. 10, 1962, Age 84

WARE, Helen
Actress
b. San Francisco, CA, Oct. 15, 1877
d. Carmel, CA, Jan. 25, 1939, Age 61

WAREING, Alfred
Producer
b. Greenwich, England, Oct. 26, 1876
d. Unknown, April 11, 1942, Age 65

WARFAZ, Georges de
Actor
b. Spa, Belgium, Dec. 2, 1889 (?)
d. London, England, Oct. 14, 1959, Age 74

WARFIELD, David
Actor
b. San Francisco, CA, Nov. 28, 1866
d. New York, NY, June 27, 1951, Age 84

WARING, Herbert
Actor
b. London, England, Nov. 17, 1857
d. London, England, Jan. 31, 1932, Age 74

WARING, Mary
Actress
b. Unknown
d. Washington, DC, Jan. 10, 1964, Age 72

WARMINGTON, Stanley J.
Actor
b. Herts, England, Dec. 16, 1884
d. Unknown, May 10, 1941, Age 56

WARNER, Charles (Charles Lickfold)
Actor
b. England, 1846
d. USA, 1909

WARNER, Grace
Actress, Producer
b. London, England, Feb. 26, 1873
d. Unknown, Nov. 14, 1925, Age 52

WARNER, Henry Byron (Henry Byron Lickfold)
Actor
b. London, England, Oct. 26, 1876
d. Woodland Hills, CA, Dec. 21, 1958, Age 82

WARREN, F. Brooke
Actor
b. Unknown
d. Unknown, Aug. 5, 1950, Age 83

WARREN, Mrs. Mercy Otis
Playwright
b. Unknown, 1728
d. Unknown, 1814

WARREN, T. Gideon
Actor, Playwright
b. Unknown
d. Unknown, May 1919, Age 65

WARREN, William (the elder)
Actor-Manager
b. England, 1767
d. Philadelphia, PA, Oct. 19, 1832, Age 65

WARREN, William Jr.
Actor-Manager
b. Philadelphia, PA, Nov. 17,1812
d. Boston, MA, Sept. 21, 1888, Age 75

WARRENDER, Harold
Actor
b. London, England, Nov. 15, 1903
d. Unknown, May 6, 1953, Age 49

WARRENER, Warren
Actor
b. Unknown
d. Chicago, IL, Dec. 4, 1961, Age 73

WARWICK, Ethel
Actress
b. London, England, Oct. 13, 1882
d. Unknown, Sept. 12, 1951, Age 68

WARWICK, Robert (Robert Taylor Bien)
Actor
b. Sacramento, CA, Oct. 9, 1878
d. Hollywood, CA, Dec. 3, 1944, Age 66

WARWICK, Robert
Actor
b. Unknown
d. Hollywood, CA, June 6, 1964, Age 85

WASHBURN, Bryant
Actor
b. Chicago, IL, April 28, 1889
d. Woodland Hills, CA, April 30, 1963, Age 74

WASHINGTON, Dinah (Ruth Jones)
Singer
b. Tuscaloosa, AL, Aug. 8, 1924
d. Detroit,MI, Dec. 14, 1963, Age 39

WATERLOW, Marjorie
Actress
b. Teddington, England, June 7, 1888
d. Unknown, Sept. 20, 1921, Age 33

WATERMAN, Ida
Actress
b. Unknown
d. Unknown, May 22, 1941, Age 89

WATEROUS, Herbert
Actor
b. Flint, MI, Unknown
d. Kingston, NY, Aug. 29, 1947, Age 78

WATERS, James
Critic, Journalist
b. Unknown
d. Unknown, Jan. 14, 1923, Age 68

WATHALL, Alfred G.
Composer
b. England, Unknown
d. Chicago, IL, Nov. 14, 1938, Age 58

WATKIN, Pierre
Actor
b. Unknown
d. Hollywood, CA, Feb. 3, 1960

WATKINS, Harry
Actor, Playwright
b. Texas, Unknown
d. Unknown, Feb. 5, 1894, Age 69

WATSON, A. E. T.
Critic, Journalist
b. Unknown
d. Unknown, Nov. 8, 1922, Age 73

WATSON, Billy (Isaac Levie)
Performer, Producer
b. New York, NY, Unknown
d. Asbury Park, NJ, Jan. 14, 1945, Age 78

WATSON, E. Bradlee
Educator, Editor
b. Boston,MA, Unknown
d. Anacortes, WA, Dec. 6, 1961, Age 82

WATSON, Elizabeth
Actress
b. Dundee,Scotland, Unknown
d. Unknown, Dec. 1, 1931

WATSON, Horace
Producer
b. London, England, 1867
d. Unknown, Sept. 16, 1934, Age 67

WATSON, Lucile (Mrs. Louis E. Shipman)
Actress
b. Quebec, CAN, May 27, 1879
d. New York, NY, June 24, 1962, Age 83

WATSON, Malcolm
Critic, Playwright
b. Glasgow, Scotland, Oct. 22, 1853
d. Unknown, Aug. 8, 1929, Age 75

WATSON, Margaret
Actress
b. Unknown
d. Unknown, Oct. 31, 1940, Age 65

WATSON, Minor
Actor
b. Marianna, AR, Unknown
d. Alton, IL, July 28, 1965, Age 75

WATSON, Rosabel Grace
Conductor, Musical director
b. Unknown
d. London, England, Oct. 6, 1959, Age 94

WATSON, Stuart
Producer
b. Unknown
d. London, England, Sept. 1956, Age 64

WATSON, Thomas M.
Playwright, Critic
b. Unknown
d. Glasgow, Scotland, March 18, 1963, Age 62

WATSON, Vernon ("Nosmo King")
Performer
b. Unknown
d. Unknown, Jan. 14, 1949, Age 62

WATTERS, George Manker
Playwright, Producer
b. Rochester, NY, Unknown
d. Los Angeles, CA, March 14, 1943, Age 52

WAXMAN, Morris D.
Actor
b. Unknown
d. Unknown, Nov. 10, 1931, Age 55

WAYBURN, Ned
Director, Producer, Actor
b. Pittsburgh, PA, March 30, 1874
d. New York, NY, Sept. 2, 1942, Age 68

WAYNE, Rollo
Designer
b. Louisville, KY, March 5, 1899
d. Unknown, March 18, 1954, Age 55

WEADON, Percy (Frank Preston)
Producer, Press representative
b. Greensburg, IN, Unknown
d. Long Island, NY, May 29, 1939, Age 79

WEATHERSBY, Helen
Actress
b. Unknown
d. Unknown, Nov. 26, 1943, Age 80

WEAVER, Affie
Actress
b. Unknown
d. Unknown, Nov. 18, 1940, Age 85

WEAVER, John
Introduced Pantomines to England
b. Unknown
d. Unknown, Sept. 24, 1760, Age 87

WEAVER, John Van Alstyn
Playwright, Critic, Novelist, Poet
b. Charlotte, NC, July 17, 1893
d. Colorado Springs, CO, June 15, 1938, Age 44

WEBB, Clifton (né Webb Parmelee Hollenbeck)
Actor, Singer, Dancer
b. Indianapolis, IN, Nov. 19, 1893
d. Beverly Hills, CA, Oct. 13, 1966, Age 72

WEBB, Jack
Theatre manager
b. Unknown
d. Unknown, Feb. 25, 1954, Age 65

WEBB, John
Scene designer, Philologist
b. Unknown, 1611
d. Unknown, 1672

WEBB, John
Actor
b. Unknown
d. Unknown, Feb. 21, 1913, Age 49

WEBB, Nella
Actress
b. Atlanta, GA, Unknown
d. New York, NY, Dec. 1, 1954, Age 78

WEBB, Sidney F.
Producer
b. Unknown
d. London, England, Feb. 22, 1956, Age 64

WEBER, Henry William
Play editor
b. Unknown
d. Unknown, June 1818, Age 35

WEBER, Joseph M.
Performer, Manager
b. New York, NY, Aug. 11, 1867
d. Los Angeles, CA, May 10, 1942, Age 74

WEBER, L. Lawrence
Producer
b. New York, NY, Unknown
d. New York, NY, Feb. 22, 1940, Age 68

WEBER, Mrs. Joe (Lillian Friedman)
Actress
b. Unknown
d. New York, NY, Nov. 10, 1951, Age 76

WEBSTER, Ben (Benjamin)
Actor
b. London, England, June 2, 1864
d. Hollywood, CA, Feb. 26, 1947, Age 82

WEBSTER, Benjamin Nottingham
Actor, Producer, Playwright
b. England, Sept. 3, 1797
d. England, July 8, 1882, Age 84

WEBSTER, Florence Ann (Mrs. George Lupino)
Actress, Dancer
b. Unknown, 1860
d. Unknown, 1899

WEBSTER, Frederick
Stage manager
b. Unknown, 1802
d. Unknown, 1878

WEBSTER, Jean (Mrs. Glen Ford McKinney)
Playwright, Novelist
b. Fredonia, NY, July 24, 1876
d. New York, NY, June 11, 1916, Age 39

WEBSTER, John
Playwright, (fl. 1602-24)
b. Unknown, c1580
d. Unknown, c1635

WEBSTER, Margaret
Actress - Director
b. New York, NY, March 15, 1905
d. London, England, Nov. 13, 1972, Age 67

WEBSTER-GLEASON, Lucile
Actress
b. Pasadena, CA, Feb. 6, 1888
d. Unknown, May 17, 1947, Age 59

WEDEKIND, Frank (Benjamin Franklin)
Playwright, Producer, Actor
b. Hanover, Germany, July 24, 1864
d. Munich, Germany, March 9, 1918, Age 53

WEEDE, Robert (né Robert Wiedefeld)
Singer - Actor
b. Baltimore, MD, Feb. 22, 1903
d. Walnut Creek, CA, July 9, 1972, Age 69

WEEKS, Barbara
Actress
b. Binghamton, NY, Unknown
d. New York, NY, July 4, 1954, Age 47

WEEMS, Ted
Bandleader
b. Pitcairn, PA, Unknown
d. Tulsa, OK, May 6, 1963, Age 62

WEGENER, Paul
Actor, Producer
b. Unknown
d. Berlin, Germany, Sept. 13, 1948, Age 73

WEIL, Mrs. Leonard D. (Grace Fisher)
Theatre operator, Puppet collector
b. Unknown
d. Stony Creek, CT, Aug. 30, 1963, Age 62

WEILL, Kurt
Composer
b. Dessau, Germany, March 2, 1900
d. New York, NY, April 3, 1950, Age 50

WEIMAN, Rita (Mrs. Maurice Marks)
Playwright, Novelist
b. Philadelphia, PA, Unknown
d. Hollywood, CA, June 23, 1954, Age 71

WEINBERG, Gus (Gustav C. Weinberg)
Actor, Playwright
b. Milwaukee, WI, Unknown
d. Portland, ME, Aug. 11, 1952, Age 86

WEINER, Lawrence A.
Theatrical advertising executive
b. Unknown
d. New York, NY, Nov. 15, 1961, Age 62

WEINTRAUB, Frances
Theatre treasurer
b. Unknown
d. New York, NY, Jan. 18, 1963, Age 62

WEINTRAUB, Milton
Stage labor leader
b. Brooklyn, NY, Unknown
d. New York, NY, Nov. 17, 1968, Age 70

WEIR, George R.
Actor
b. Unknown
d. Unknown, March 2, 1909, Age 56

WEISBERG, Sylvia
Actress
b. Unknown
d. Philadelphia, PA, Jan. 12, 1962

WEISE, Christian
Playwright, Teacher
b. Unknown, 1642
d. Unknown, 1708

WEISSE, Christian Felix (also Weisze)
Playwright, Translator
b. Annaberg, Germany, 1726
d. Unknown, 1804

WEITZENKORN, Louis
Playwright, Journalist
b. Wilkes-Barre, PA, May 1893
d. Wilkes-Barre, PA, Feb. 7, 1943, Age 49

WELCH, Constance
Educator
b. Spencer, WI, Unknown
d. New Haven, CT, June 20, 1976, Age 77

WELCH, Deshler
Drama critic & founder - Theatre Mag.
b. Unknown
d. Unknown, Buffalo, NY, Age Jan. 7, 1920

WELCH, James
Actor, Producer
b. Liverpool, England, Nov. 6, 1865
d. Unknown, April 10, 1917, Age 51

WELCH, Lew
Actor
b. Unknown
d. Miami, FL, June 22, 1952, Age 67

WELCH, Mary
Actress
b. Charleston, SC, Unknown
d. New York, NY, May 31, 1958, Age 35

WELCH, Robert Gilbert
Drama critic
b. Unknown
d. Bermuda (drowned), July 22, 1924, Age 45

WELFORD, Dallas
Actor
b. Liverpool, England, May 23, 1874(?)
d. Santa Monica, CA, Sept. 28, 1946, Age 74

WELLER, Bernard
Critic, Editor The Stage
b. Unknown
d. July 19, 1870, London, England, Aug. 23, 1943, Age 73

WELLER, Carrie
Actress
b. La Porte, IN, Unknown
d. Central Islip, L.I., NY, June 6, 1954, Age 84

WELLMAN, Emily Ann
Actress
b. Kiddersfield, England, Unknown
d. New York, NY, March 19, 1946

WELLS, Charles B.
Actor
b. Unknown
d. Bayside, NY, Oct. 14, 1924, Age 73

WELLS, Herbert George
Playwright, Novelist, Historian, etc.
b. Bromley, Kent, England, Sept. 21, 1866
d. London, England, Aug. 13, 1946, Age 79

WELLS, Marie
Actress
b. Unknown
d. Hollywood, CA, July 2, 1949, Age 55

WELLS, Roxanna (Mrs. Eugene J. Anspach)
Lecture bureau executive, Booking agent
b. Unknown
d. New York, NY, July 15, 1964, Age 70

WELLS, William (Billy K.)
Actor, Writer
b. New York, NY, Unknown
d. New York, NY, April 17, 1956, Age 72

WEMYSS, Francis Courtney
Actor, Manager, Editor
b. England, 1797
d. USA, Jan. 5, 1859, Age 61

WENMAN, Henry N.
Actor
b. Leeds, England, Sept. 7, 1875
d. Unknown, Nov. 6, 1953, Age 78

WENMAN, T. E.
Actor
b. Unknown
d. Unknown, Feb. 4, 1892, Age 47

WENNING, Thomas H.
Critic
b. New York, NY, Unknown
d. New York, NY, Dec. 1, 1962, Age 59

WENRICH, Percy
Composer, Performer
b. Joplin, MO, Jan. 23, 1887
d. New York, NY, March 17, 1952, Age 65

WENTWORTH, Fanny (Fanny Wentworth Osborn Porteus, née Evans)
Actress, original Topsy in Uncle Tom's Cabin
b. Long Beach, NJ, Unknown
d. Watertown, SD, May 14, 1934, Age 85

WENTWORTH, Stephen
Actor
b. Unknown
d. Unknown, March 20, 1935

WENTZ, John K.
Educator, Critic
b. Unknown
d. Philadelphia, PA, April 23, 1964, Age 40

WERBA, Louis F.
Producer, Director
b. Unknown
d. Unknown, Nov. 16, 1942

WERFEL, Franz V.
Author, Composer, Poet
b. Prague, Czechoslovakia, Sept. 10, 1890
d. Beverly Hills, CA, Aug. 26, 1945, Age 54

WERGELAND, Henrik Arnold
Poet, Playwright
b. Norway, 1808
d. Unknown, 1845

WERNER, Friedrich Ludwig Zacharias
Poet, Playwright
b. Koenigsberg, Germany, 1768
d. Unknown, 1823

WESFORD, Susan
Actress
b. Chicago, IL, Unknown
d. Bayshore, L.I., NY, Unknown, Age 79

WEST, Edna Rhys
Performer
b. Greenup, KY, Unknown
d. Middletown, NY, Feb. 7, 1963, Age 76

WEST, Henry St. Barbe
Actor
b. London, England, Feb. 7,1880
d. Unknown, May 10, 1935, Age 55

WEST, Will
Actor
b. Unknown, Sept. 22, 1867
d. Unknown, Feb. 5, 1922, Age 52

WESTCOTT, Netta (née Lupton)
Actress
b. London, England, Unknown
d. Unknown, Aug. 9, 1953, Age 60

WESTERN, Helen
Performer
b. Unknown, 1843
d. Unknown, 1868

WESTERN, Kenneth
Performer
b. Unknown
d. Bedford, England, Jan. 24, 1963, Age 62

WESTERN, (Pauline) Lucille
Actress
b. Unknown, 1843
d. Unknown, Jan. 11, 1877, Age 34

WESTERTON, Frank H.
Actor
b. London, England, Unknown
d. New York, NY, Aug. 25, 1923

WESTFORD, Susanne (Mrs. Susan Westford Allen née Susan Leonard)
b. Chicago, IL, April 25, 1865
d. Bay Shore, L.I., NY, June 13, 1944, Age 79

WESTLAND, Henry
Actor
b. Unknown
d. Unknown, Dec. 27, 1906, Age 68

WESTLEY, Helen
Actress
b. Brooklyn, NY, March 1879
d. Middlebush, NJ, Dec. 12, 1942, Age 63

WESTLEY, John
Actor
b. Unknown
d. Hollywood, CA, Dec. 26, 1948, Age 70

WESTMAN, Nydia
Actress
b. New York, NY, Feb. 19, 1902
d. Burbank, CA, May 23, 1970, Age 68

WESTON, Robert P.
Librettist, Songwriter
b. Islington, England, March 7, 1878
d. Unknown, Nov. 6, 1936, Age 58

WESTON, Ruth (Mrs. Reginald Mead née Ruth West Shillaber)
Actress
b. Boston, MA, Aug. 31, 1908
d. East Orange, NJ, Nov. 5, 1955, Age 47

WESTOVER, Robert
Actor
b. Unknown
d. Unknown, 1916

WETHERALL, Frances
Actress
b. Greenwich, England, Unknown
d. Unknown, Nov. 13, 1923

WEWITZER, Ralph
Actor, Author
b. Unknown
d. London, England, Jan. 1, 1825

WHARTON, Anthony P. (Alister M'Allister)
Playwright
b. Dublin, Ireland, 1877
d. Unknown, Aug. 6, 1943, Age 65

WHARTON, Edith
Author
b. New York, NY, Jan. 24, 1862
d. Pavilion Colombes, France, Aug. 11, 1937, Age 75

WHATMORE, A. R.
Actor, Director
b. Much Marcle, Gloucestershire, England, May 30, 1889
d. Unknown, Oct. 15, 1960, Age 71

WHEATCROFT, Adeline Stanhope
Actress
b. Unknown
d. Unknown, June 18, 1935, Age 82

WHEATCROFT, Nelson Actor
Teacher
b. London, England, Feb. 15, 1852
d. New York, NY, March 3, 1897, Age 45

WHEATLEY, Emma
Actress
b. Unknown, 1822
d. Unknown, 1854

WHEATLEY, Frederick
Actor
b. Ireland, Unknown
d. USA, 1836

WHEATLEY, Jane (Jane Simpson)
Actress
b. Roslyn, NY, Aug. 28, 1881
d. New York, NY, Feb. 17, 1935, Age 53

WHEATLEY, Sarah Ross
Actress
b. Unknown, 1790
d. Unknown, 1872

WHEATLEY, William
Actor, Producer
b. Unknown, 1816
d. Unknown, Nov. 3, 1876, Age 59

WHEATON, Anna (Mrs. Ann Wheaton Collins)
Actress
b. Savannah, GA, Unknown
d. Pasadena, CA, Dec. 25, 1961, Age 65

WHEELER, Andrew Carpenter ("Nym Crinkle")
Critic
b. Unknown
d. Unknown, March 10, 1903, Age 67

WHEELER, Benjamin F.
Producer
b. Unknown
d. Unknown, Oct. 26, 1934, Age 74

WHEELER, Bert
Performer
b. Paterson, NJ, April 17, 1895
d. New York, NY, Jan. 18, 1968, Age 73

WHELAN, Tim
Actor, Screenwriter, Film director
b. Cannelton, IN, Unknown
d. Beverly Hills, CA, Aug. 12, 1957, Age 63

WHIFFEN, Blanche (Mrs. Thomas Whiffen née Galton)
Actress
b. London, England, March 12, 1845
d. near Montvale, VA, Nov. 25, 1936, Age 91

WHIFFEN, Thomas
Actor
b. England, Unknown
d. USA, Oct. 10, 1897

WHINCOP, Thomas
Historian
b. Unknown
d. Unknown, Aug. 1730

WHISTLER, Rex
Designer, Artist
b. London, England, June 24, 1905
d. Unknown, July 18, 1944, Age 39

WHITBECK, Frank L.
Press representative
b. Unknown
d. Hollywood, CA, Dec. 23, 1963, Age 81

WHITBREAD, J. W.
Playwright, Journalist
b. Unknown
d. Unknown, June 9, 1916, Age 68

WHITBY, Arthur
Actor
b. Ottery St. Mary, Devonshire, England, 1869
d. Unknown, Nov. 29, 1922, Age 53

WHITBY, Mrs. Arthur
(Cissie Saumarez), Actress
b. Unknown
d. Unknown, July 23, 1930

WHITE, Beatrice (a/k/a Beatrice Curtis)
Performer
b. Unknown
d. Los Angeles, CA, March 26, 1963, Age 62

WHITE, Charles
Songwriter, Song publisher
b. Boston, MA, 1830
d. Boston, MA, 1892, Age 62

WHITE, Elmore
Performer, Songwriter
b. Unknown
d. Brooklyn, NY, Jan. 15, 1964, Age 75

WHITE, George (George Weitz)
Dancer, Producer, Director
b. Toronto, Canada, 1890
d. Hollywood, CA, Oct. 11, 1968, Age 78

WHITE, J. Fisher
Actor
b. Clifton, Bristol, England, May 1, 1865
d. Unknown, Jan. 14, 1945, Age 79

WHITE, James
Producer
b. Unknown
d. Unknown, June 29, 1927, Age 49

WHITE, Josh (Tom Pinewood)
Folk singer, Performer
b. Greenville, SC, 1908
d. Manhasset, NY, Sept. 5, 1969, Age 61

WHITE, Lee
Actress
b. Louisiana, MO, March 26, 1886
d. Unknown, Dec. 4, 1927, Age 41

WHITE, Pearl (Pearl Fay White)
Actress
b. Greenridge, MO, March 4, 1889
d. Paris, France, April 4, 1938, Age 49

WHITE, Rev. James
Playwright
b. Unknown
d. Unknown, March 28, 1862, Age 77

WHITE, Ruth
Actress
b. Perth Amboy, NJ, Unknown
d. Perth Amboy, NJ, Dec. 3, 1969, Age 55

WHITE, Sammy
Actor
b. Unknown
d. Beverly Hills, CA, March 3, 1960, Age 65

WHITEHEAD, John
Actor
b. Unknown
d. Hollywood, CA, March 21, 1962, Age 89

WHITEHEAD, William
Playwright, Poet laureate
b. Unknown
d. Unknown, April 14, 1785, Age 70

WHITEHOUSE, Esther
Actress
b. Unknown
d. Unknown, June 24, 1946, Age 51

WHITESIDE, Walker
Actor
b. Logansport, IN, March 16, 1869
d. Hastings-on-Hudson, NY, Aug. 17, 1942, Age 73

WHITING, Jack
Actor
b. Philadelphia, PA, June 22, 1901
d. New York, NY, Feb. 15, 1961, Age 59

WHITING, John
Playwright
b. Salisbury, England, Nov. 15, 1917
d. London, England, June 16, 1963, Age 45

WHITING, Richard A.
Composer
b. Peoria, IL, Nov. 12, 1891
d. Beverly Hills, CA, Feb. 10, 1938, Age 46

WHITLING, Townsend
Actor
b. Oxford, England, Oct. 21, 1869
d. Unknown, June 24, 1952, Age 82

WHITLOCK, Billy (Frederick Essex)
Composer, Performer
b. Unknown
d. Birkenhead, England, Jan. 26, 1951, Age 76

WHITLOCK, Mrs. (Elizabeth Kemble)
Actress
b. Unknown, 1761
d. Unknown, Feb. 27, 1836, Age 74

WHITMAN, Essie
Performer
b. Unknown
d. Chicago, IL, May 7, 1963, Age 81

WHITMAN, John P.
Performer
b. Unknown
d. Boston, MA, Feb. 10, 1963, Age 91

WHITNER, Edwin
Actor
b. Unknown
d. New York, NY, Jan 5, 1962, Age 53

WHITNEY, Bert C.
Manager
b. Detroit, MI, Unknown
d. Toronto, CAN, Oct. 26, 1929, Age 60

WHITNEY, Fred C.
Theatrical manager
b. Unknown
d. Unknown, June 4, 1930, Age 65

WHITTAKER, Arthur
Producer
b. Unknown
d. Unknown, Nov. 1, 1914

WHITTAKER, James
Journalist, Critic
b. Unknown
d. New York, NY, March 19, 1964, Age 73

WHITTLE, Charles R.
Performer
b. Unknown
d. Unknown, Nov. 27, 1947, Age 73

WHITTLESEY, (Charles) White
Actor
b. Danbury, CT, Unknown
d. New York, NY, Dec. 6, 1940, Age 79

WHITTY, Dame May (Mrs. Ben Webster)
Actress
b. Liverpool, England, June 19, 1865
d. Hollywood, CA, May 29, 1948, Age 82

WHITWORTH, Geoffrey
Director of the British Drama League
b. London, England, April 7, 1883
d. Unknown, Sept. 9, 1951, Age 68

WHORF, Richard
Actor, Director, Producer, Designer
b. Winthrop, MA, June 4, 1906
d. Santa Monica, CA, Dec. 14, 1966, Age 60

WHYTAL, A. Russ
Actor, Playwright
b. Boston, MA, June 20, 1860
d. New York, NY, June 24, 1930, Age 70

WHYTE, Frederic
Biographer, Playwright
b. Unknown
d. Unknown, May 14, 1941, Age 74

WHYTE, Harold
Playwright, Actor
b. Unknown
d. Unknown, Feb. 14, 1919, Age 73

WHYTE, Robert Jr
Actor
b. Blackheath, England, Feb. 7, 1874
d. Unknown, Nov. 10, 1916, Age 42

WICKHAM, Tony (Anthony Wickham-Jones)
Actor
b. Croydon,Surrey, England, Jan. 15, 1922
d. Unknown, March 2, 1948, Age 26

WICKMAN, Sally (Mrs. Rudolph Samson)
Dancer, Choreographer, Producer
b. Chicago, IL, Unknown
d. San Francisco, CA, Jan. 25, 1963, Age 49

WICKWIRE, Nancy
Actress
b. Harrisburg, PA, Nov. 20, 1925
d. San Francisco, CA, July 10, 1974, Age 48

WIDDICOMBE, Harry
Actor
b. Unknown
d. Unknown, April 6, 1868, Age 55

WIDDICOMBE, Victor
Actor
b. Unknown
d. Unknown, Feb. 27, 1912

WIED, Gustav
Playwright
b. Unknown, 1858
d. Unknown, 1914

WIELEPP, Kurt O.
Performer
b. Berlin, Germany, Unknown
d. Toledo, OH, Dec. 4, 1962, Age 80

WIETH, Mogens
Actor
b. Denmark, Unknown
d. London, England, Sept. 10, 1962, Age 42

WIGAN, Alfred
Actor, Producer
b. Unknown
d. Unknown, Nov. 29, 1878, Age 61

WIGAN, Horace
Actor, Producer
b. Unknown
d. Unknown, Aug. 7, 1885, Age 67

WIGAN, Mrs. Alfred
Actress
b. Unknown
d. Unknown, April 17, 1884, Age 79

WIGNELL, Thomas
Actor, Producer
b. Unknown, 1753
d. Philadelphia, PA, Feb. 21, 1803, Age 50

WILBRAHAM, Edward (3rd Earl of Lathom)
Playwright
b. London, England, May 16, 1895
d. Unknown, Feb. 6, 1930, Age 34

WILCOX, Robert
Actor
b. Rochester, NY, Unknown
d. Rochester, NY, June 11, 1955, Age 44

WILD, George
Actor, Producer
b. Unknown
d. Unknown, March 29, 1856, Age 51

WILDBERG, John J.
Producer
b. New York, NY, Sept. 4, 1902
d. London, England, Feb. 8, 1959, Age 56

WILDE, Oscar Fingal O'Flahertie Wills
Playwright, Poet, Author
b. Dublin, Ireland, Oct. 16, 1854
d. Paris, France, Nov. 30, 1900, Age 46

WILDE, Percival
Playwright
b. New York, NY, March 1, 1887
d. New York, NY, Sept. 19, 1953, Age 66

WILDENBRUCH, Ernst von
Playwright, Novelist, Poet
b. Beirut, 1845
d. Unknown, Jan. 15, 1909, Age 64

WILDER, Thornton
Playwright, Novelist
b. Madison, WI, Apr. 17, 1897
d. New Haven, CT, Dec. 7, 1975, Age 78

WILEY, John A.
Actor
b. Unknown
d. San Antonio, TX, Sept. 30, 1962, Age 78

WILHELM, C. (William John Charles Pitcher)
Designer, Artist
b. Unknown
d. Unknown, March 2, 1925, Age 66

WILKE, Hubert
Singer, Actor
b. Stettin, Germany, Unknown
d. Yonkers, NY, Oct. 22, 1940, Age 85

WILKERSON, William R. (Billy)
Publisher
b. Springfield, TN, Unknown
d. Hollywood, CA, Sept. 2, 1962, Age 72

WILKES, Thomas Egerton
Playwright
b. Unknown
d. Unknown, Sept. 18, 1854, Age 42

WILKINS, George
Playwright
b. Unknown, fl. 1607

WILKINS, John
Actor, Playwright
b. Unknown
d. Unknown, Aug. 28, 1853, Age 26

WILKINSON, H. Spenser
Critic
b. Unknown
d. Unknown, Jan. 31, 1937, Age 83

WILKINSON, Norman
Scenic artist, Designer
b. Unknown, 1882
d. Unknown, Feb. 14, 1934, Age 51

WILKINSON, Tate
Producer
b. England, 1734
d. England, Aug. 25, 1803, Age 69

WILKS, Robert
Actor, Producer
b. Unknown, 1665
d. Unknown, 1732, Age 67

WILLA, Suzanne
Actress
b. Unknown
d. New York, NY, March 24, 1951, Age 58

WILLARD, Catherine Livingston
Actress
b. Dayton, OH, Unknown
d. New York, NY, Nov. 4, 1954, Age 54

WILLARD, Edmund
Performer
b. Brighton, England, Unknown
d. Kingston, Surrey, England, Oct. 6, 1956, Age 71

WILLARD, Edward Smith
Actor-Manager
b. Brighton, England, Jan. 9, 1853
d. London, England, Nov. 9, 1915, Age 62

WILLARD, John (Clawson)
Playwright, Actor
b. San Francisco, CA, Nov. 28, 1885
d. Unknown, Aug. 30, 1942, Age 56

WILLIAM, Robert
Actor
b. Morgantown, NC, Unknown
d. Hollywood, CA, Nov. 3, 1931, Age 34

WILLIAM, Warren
Actor
b. Aitkin, MN, Dec. 2, 1895
d. Encino, CA, Sept. 24, 1948, Age 52

WILLIAMS, A. B. "Racehorse"
Performer
b. Unknown
d. Unknown, Boston, MA, Age July 24, 1964

WILLIAMS, Arthur
Actor
b. London, England, Dec. 9,1844
d. Unknown, Sept. 15, 1915, Age 70

WILLIAMS, Barney (Bernard O'Flaherty)
Actor
b. Cork, Munster, Ireland, June 19, 1824
d. New York, NY, April 25, 1876, Age 51

WILLIAMS, Bert (Egbert Austin Williams)
Performer
b. New Providence, Nassau, B. W. Indies, c1876
d. New York, NY, March 4, 1922, Age 46

WILLIAMS, Bransby
Actor
b. Hackney, England, Aug. 14, 1870
d. London, England, Dec. 3, 1961, Age 91

WILLIAMS, Dick
Journalist, Drama editor
b. Unknown
d. Los Angeles, CA, Jan. 5, 1962, Age 46

WILLIAMS, Earle
Actor
b. Sacramento, CA, 1880
d. Hollywood, CA, April 25, 1927, Age 46

WILLIAMS, (Ernest George) Harcourt
Actor, Director
b. Croyden, England, March 30, 1880
d. London, England, Dec. 13, 1957, Age 77

WILLIAMS, Evelyn M.
Deputy Director of British Drama Council
b. Unknown
d. Unknown, April 13, 1959, Age 63

WILLIAMS, Frances (Frances Jellinek)
Performer
b. St. Paul, MN, 1903
d. New York, NY, Jan. 27, 1959, Age 56

WILLIAMS, Fritz (Frederick Williams)
Actor
b. Boston, MA, Aug. 23, 1865
d. New York, NY, April 1, 1930, Age 64

WILLIAMS, Guinn (Big Boy)
Actor
b. Decatur, TX, Unknown
d. Van Nuys, CA, June 6, 1962, Age 62

WILLIAMS, Gus
Performer
b. New York, NY, July 19, 1847
d. Yonkers, NY, Jan. 16, 1915, Age 67

WILLIAMS, Gwen
Performer
b. Unknown
d. Worthing, England, May 27, 1962

WILLIAMS, Hattie
Actress
b. Boston, MA, Unknown
d. New York, NY, Aug. 17, 1942, Age 72

WILLIAMS, Herb (Herbert Schussler Billerbeck)
Comedian
b. Philadelphia, PA, Unknown
d. Freeport, NY, Oct. 1, 1936, Age 52

WILLIAMS, Hugh
Actor, Author
b. Bexhill-on-Sea, Sussex, England, March 6, 1904
d. London, England, Dec. 7, 1969, Age 65

WILLIAMS, Ina
Performer
b. Australia, Unknown
d. Santa Monica, CA, June 9, 1962, Age 65

WILLIAMS, Jesse Lynch
Playwright, Composer
b. Stirling, IL, Aug. 17, 1871
d. Unknown, Sept. 14, 1929, Age 58

WILLIAMS, John (Anthony Pasquin)
Playwright
b. Unknown
d. Unknown, Nov. 23, 1818, Age 57

WILLIAMS, John D.
Producer, Director
b. Boston, MA, Unknown
d. Riverdale, NY, March 22, 1941, Age 55

WILLIAMS, Kathlyn
Actress
b. Unknown
d. Hollywood, CA, Sept. 23, 1960, Age 72

WILLIAMS, Le Roy A.
Performer
b. Newburgh, NY, Unknown
d. Elkhart, IN, 1962, Age 70

WILLIAMS, Malcolm
Actor
b. Spring Valley, MN, Unknown
d. New York, NY, June 10, 1937, Age 67

WILLIAMS, Montague
Playwright
b. Unknown
d. Unknown, Dec. 23, 1892, Age 58

WILLIAMS, Mrs. Barney
Actress
b. New York, NY, Unknown
d. Unknown, May 6, 1911, Age 85

WILLIAMS, Percy G.
Vaudeville manager
b. Baltimore, MD, 1857
d. East Islip, L.I., NY, July 21, 1923, Age 66

WILLIAMS, Rhys
Actor
b. Glamorganshire, Wales, Dec. 31, 1897
d. Santa Monica, CA, May 28, 1969, Age 71

WILLIAMS, Robert
Actor
b. North Carolina, Unknown
d. Hollywood, CA, Nov. 3, 1931, Age 34

WILLIAMS, Stephen
Critic
b. Flixton, Lancashire, England, June 15, 1900
d. Unknown, July 13, 1957, Age 57

WILLIAMS, Thomas J.
Playwright
b. Unknown
d. Unknown, Sept. 8, 1874, Age 50

WILLIAMS, Walter
Actor
b. London, England, Oct. 15, 1887
d. Unknown, Oct. 29, 1940, Age 53

WILLIAMSON, James Cassius
Actor, Producer
b. Mercer, PA, Aug. 26, 1845
d. Paris, France, July 6, 1913, Age 67

WILLING, James
Playwright
b. Unknown
d. Unknown, July 26, 1915, Age 77

WILLIS, Nathaniel Parker
Playwright
b. Portland, ME, 1806
d. Unknown, 1867

WILLNER, A. M.
Librettist
b. Unknown
d. Unknown, Nov. 4, 1929, Age 71

WILLS, Beverly (Mrs. Martin Colbert)
Actress
b. Unknown
d. Palm Springs, CA, Oct. 24, 1963, Age 29

WILLS, Brember (Le Conteur)
Actor
b. Reading, England, Unknown
d. Unknown, Dec. 1, 1948, Age 65

WILLS, Drusilla
Actress
b. London, England, Nov. 14, 1884
d. Unknown, Aug. 6, 1951, Age 66

WILLS, Nat M. (Edward McGregor)
Performer
b. Fredericksburg, VA, July 11, 1873
d. Woodcliff-on-Hudson, NJ, Dec. 9, 1917, Age 44

WILLS, Tommy
Performer
b. Unknown
d. Darien, CT, Nov. 1962, Age 59

WILLS, W. G.
Playwright
b. Unknown, 1828
d. Unknown, Dec. 13, 1891, Age 63

WILLY, (Henry Gauthier-Villars)
Playwright
b. Villiers-sur-Orge, France, Aug. 10, 1859
d. Unknown, Jan. 12, 1931, Age 71

WILMOT, Charles
Actor, Producer
b. Unknown
d. Unknown, Nov. 18, 1896, Age 57

WILMOT, Robert
Playwright, Fl. 1568-16--

WILMOTT, Charles
Songwriter
b. Unknown
d. Unknown, Jan. 18, 1955, Age 95

WILSON, Albert Edward
Critic
b. London, England, Oct. 1, 1885
d. Balham, England, Jan. 22, 1960, Age 74

WILSON, Arthur
Playwright, Historian
b. Unknown
d. Unknown, Oct. 1652

WILSON, Beatrice
Actress, Director
b. Dalhousie, India, Unknown
d. Unknown, Jan. 20, 1943, Age 63

WILSON, Charles
Producer, Director
b. Unknown
d. Unknown, July 25, 1909, Age 49

WILSON, Christopher
Composer, Conductor
b. Unknown
d. Unknown, Feb. 17, 1919, Age 43

WILSON, Diana (Hunt)
Actress
b. Patricroft, Lancashire, England, Aug. 31, 1897
d. Unknown, Oct. 26, 1937, Age 40

WILSON, Francis
Actor, Playwright
b. Philadelphia, PA, Feb. 7, 1854
d. New York, NY, Oct. 7, 1935, Age 81

WILSON, Frank H.
Actor, Playwright
b. New York, NY, Unknown
d. Jamaica, NY, Feb. 16, 1956, Age 70

WILSON, George W.
Actor
b. Boston, MA, Sept. 24, 1849
d. Boston, MA, Dec. 24, 1931, Age 82

WILSON, Harry Leon
Playwright, Novelist
b. Oregon, IL, May 1, 1867
d. Carmel, CA, June 29, 1939, Age 72

WILSON, John
Playwright
b. Unknown
d. Unknown, 1696

WILSON, John Chapman
Director, Producer
b. Lawrenceville, NJ, Aug. 19, 1899
d. New York, NY, Oct. 29, 1961, Age 62

WILSON, John Dover
Shakespeare scholar
b. London, England, July 13, 1881
d. Balerno, Scotland, Jan. 15, 1969, Age 87

WILSON, Joseph
Actor, Producer
b. Dublin, Ireland, Feb. 16, 1858
d. Unknown, Dec. 4, 1940, Age 83

WILSON, Joseph Maria
Designer, Architect, Illustrator
b. Unknown, 1872
d. Unknown, 1933, Age 61

WILSON, Mrs. C. Baron
Biographer, Playwright
b. Unknown
d. Unknown, Jan. 12, 1846, Age 49

WILSON, Ray
Writer, Director, Producer
b. Unknown
d. Detroit, MI, Jan. 16, 1963, Age 56

WILSON, Robert (the elder)
Actor, Playwright
b. Unknown, 1550
d. Unknown, buried Nov. 20, 1600

WILSON, Robert (the younger)
Playwright
b. Unknown
d. Unknown, Oct. 22, 1610, Age 39

WILSON, W. Cronin
Actor, Playwright
b. Unknown
d. London, England, Feb. 16, 1934

WILSON, Walter M.
Actor, Director
b. Unknown
d. New Haven, CT, Nov. 13, 1926, Age 52
WILSON, William J.
Director
b. Scotland, Unknown
d. Cleveland, OH, March 2, 1936, Age 62
WILSTACH, Frank Jenners
Author, Manager
b. Lafayette, IN, 1865
d. New York, NY, Nov. 28, 1933, Age 68
WILSTACH, Paul
Playwright
b. Lafayette, IN, July 1, 1870
d. Washington, DC, Feb. 9, 1952, Age 81
WILTON, Augusta
Actress
b. Unknown
d. Unknown, Feb. 5, 1926
WILTON, Robb
Performer
b. Liverpool, England, Unknown
d. London, England, May 1, 1957, Age 75
WIMAN, Anna Deere
Producer, Actress
b. Moline, IL, Unknown
d. Southampton, Bermuda, March 22, 1963, Age 40
WIMAN, Dwight Deere
Producer
b. Moline, IL, Aug. 8, 1895
d. Hudson, NY, Jan. 20, 1951, Age 55
WIMPERIS, Arthur
Lyricist, Playwright
b. London, England, Dec. 3, 1874
d. Unknown, Oct. 14, 1953, Age 78
WINANT, Forest
Actor
b. New York, NY, Feb. 21, 1888
d. Alameda, CA, Jan. 30, 1928, Age 39
WINCHELL, Walter
Columnist - Newscaster
b. New York, NY, Apr. 7, 1897
d. Los Angeles, CA, Feb. 21, 1972, Age 74
WINDEATT, George (Alan)
Composer, Musical director
b. Kingston Hill, Surrey, England, Jan. 21, 1901
d. Hampton, Middlesex, England, Sept. 25, 1959, Age 58
WINDERMERE, Charles
Actor, Producer
b. Occold Rectory, Eye, Suffolk, England, Dec. 23, 1872
d. Unknown, Oct. 8, 1955, Age 82
WINDUST, Bretaigne
Actor, Director
b. Paris, France, Jan. 20, 1906
d. New York, NY, March 18, 1960, Age 54
WINGFIELD, Conway
Performer
b. Unknown
d. New York, NY, Feb. 9, 1948, Age 81
WINGFIELD, Hon. Lewis
Designer
b. Unknown
d. Unknown, Nov. 12, 1891, Age 49
WINKLER, Frank
Performer
b. Unknown
d. Hollywood, CA, May 24, 1964, Age 64
WINNER, Septimus
Songwriter, Teacher
b. Philadelphia, PA, May 11, 1827
d. Philadelphia, PA, Nov. 22, 1902, Age 75
WINNINGER, Charles
Actor
b. Athens, WI, May 26, 1884
d. Palm Springs, CA, Jan. 19, 1969, Age 84

WINSLOW, Herbert Hall
Playwright
b. Keokuk, IA, 1865
d. Hastings-on-Hudson, NY, June 1, 1930, Age 64
WINSTON, C. Bruce
Actor, Designer
b. Liverpool, England, March 4, 1879
d. Unknown, Sept. 27, 1946, Age 67
WINSTON, James
Actor, Author
b. Unknown, 1773
d. Unknown, July 9, 1843, Age 70
WINSTON, Jane
Actress
b. Unknown
d. New York, NY, Sept. 22, 1959, Age 51
WINTER, Banks
Balladist
b. Unknown
d. Reseda, CA, Dec. 13, 1936, Age 81
WINTER, Percy Campbell
Actor, Stage manager
b. Toronto, CAN, Nov. 16, 1861
d. Boonton, NJ, May 4, 1928, Age 66
WINTER, William
Critic, Biographer, Author
b. Gloucester, MA, July 15, 1836
d. Unknown, June 30, 1917, Age 80
WINTER, Winona
Actress
b. Huntsville, AL, 1888
d. Hollywood, CA, April 27, 1940, Age 52
WINTHROP, Adelaide
Actress
b. Unknown
d. New York, NY, Oct. 13, 1923, Age 32
WISE, Thomas A.
Actor
b. Faversham, Kent, England, March 23, 1865
d. New York, NY, March 21, 1928, Age 63
WISHENGRAD, Morton
Playwright
b. New York, NY, Unknown
d. New York, NY, Feb. 12, 1963, Age 50
WITHEE, Mable
Actress
b. Detroit, MI, Unknown
d. Bayside, NY, Nov. 3, 1952, Age 55
WITHERS, Charles
Actor
b. Louisville, KY, Unknown
d. Bayside, L.I., NY, July 10, 1947, Age 58
WITHERS, Grant
Actor
b. Pueblo, CO, Unknown
d. North Hollywood, CA, March 27, 1959, Age 55
WITHERSPOON, Cora
Actress
b. New Orleans, LA, Jan. 5, 1890
d. Las Cruces, NM, Nov. 17, 1957, Age 67
WITHERSPOON, Herbert
Actor, Manager
b. Buffalo, NY, July 21, 1873
d. New York, NY, May 10, 1935, Age 61
WOFFINGTON, Margaret ("Peg")
Actress
b. Dublin, Ireland, c1720
d. London, England, March 28, 1760, Age 40
WOLF, Rennold
Playwright, Drama editor
b. Ithaca, NY, April 4, 1872
d. New York, NY, Jan. 2, 1922, Age 49
WOLFE, Clarence (Monty)
Performer
b. Unknown
d. Jersey City, NJ, March 20, 1963, Age 75

WOLFE, Humbert
Playwright, Poet
b. Milan, Italy, Jan. 5, 1886
d. London, England, Jan. 5, 1940, Age 54
WOLFF, William
Performer
b. Germany, 1858
d. Los Angeles, CA, Dec. 13, 1936, Age 78
WOLF-FERRARI, Ermanno
Composer
b. Venice, Italy, Jan. 12, 1876
d. Venice, Italy, Jan. 21, 1948, Age 72
WOLFIT, Donald
Actor-Manager
b. Newark-on-Trent, England, April 20, 1902
d. London, England, Feb. 17, 1968, Age 65
WOLFSON, Martin
Actor
b. New York City, NY, Apr. 4, 1904
d. Unknown, Sept. 11, 1973, Age 69
WOLHEIM, Louis Robert
Actor
b. New York, NY, 1881
d. Los Angeles, CA, Feb. 18, 1931, Age 50
WOLLHEIM, Eric
Impresario
b. Unknown, Dec. 13, 1879
d. Unknown, April 7, 1948, Age 68
WOLSELEY-COX, Garnet
Composer
b. Unknown
d. Unknown, Nov. 11, 1904, Age 32
WOLZOGEN, Ernst von
Playwright, Novelist
b. Unknown
d. Unknown, July 30, 1934, Age 79
WONG, Anna May (Wong Liu Tsong) "Frosted Yellow Willows"
Actress
b. Los Angeles, CA, Jan. 3, 1907
d. Santa Monica, CA, Feb. 3, 1961, Age 54

WONTNER, Arthur
Performer
b. London, England, Jan. 21, 1875
d. Buckinghamshire, England, July 10, 1960, Age 85
WOOD, Arthur
Conductor, Composer
b. Heckmondwike, England, Jan. 24, 1875
d. Unknown, Jan. 18, 1953, Age 78
WOOD, Arthur Augustus
Actor
b. Unknown
d. Unknown, Feb. 7, 1907, Age 83
WOOD, Frank Motley
Actor
b. Unknown
d. Unknown, June 30, 1919, Age 75
WOOD, J. Hickory
Pantomime, Author
b. Unknown
d. Unknown, Aug. 25, 1913, Age 54
WOOD, Marjorie
Actress
b. London, England, Sept. 5, 1887
d. Hollywood, CA, Nov. 8, 1955, Age 68
WOOD, Mrs. John (née Matilda Charlotte Vining)
Actress, Producer
b. Liverpool, England, 1831
d. Unknown, Jan. 10, 1915, Age 83
WOOD, William Burke
Actor-Manager
b. USA, 1779
d. Unknown, Sept. 23, 1861, Age 82
WOODBURN, James
Actor
b. Edinburgh, Scotland, Jan. 17, 1888
d. Unknown, Nov. 26, 1948, Age 60

WOODBURY, Clare
Actress
b. Philadelphia, PA, Unknown
d. New York, NY, March 13, 1949, Age 69

WOODFALL, William
Critic
b. Unknown
d. Unknown, Aug. 1, 1803, Age 57

WOODHOUSE, Vernon
Critic, Playwright
b. London, England, July 2, 1874
d. Unknown, June 12, 1936, Age 61

WOODRUFF, Edna (Mrs. Edna W. Montague)
Actress, Writer
b. Unknown
d. Los Angeles, CA, Oct. 16, 1947, Age 73

WOODRUFF, Henry Ingott
Actor
b. Hartford, CT, June 1, 1869
d. Unknown, 1916, Age 46

WOODS, Albert Herman ("A. H.") (né Aladore Herman)
Producer, Playwright
b. Budapest, Hungary, Jan. 3, 1870
d. New York, NY, April 24, 1951, Age 81

WOODWORTH, Samuel
Playwright, Journalist
b. Unknown, 1785
d. Unknown, 1842

WOOLER, J. P.
Playwright
b. Unknown
d. Unknown, Sept. 18, 1868, Age 44

WOOLF, Edgar Allan
Actor, Playwright, Librettist, Lyricist
b. New York, NY, Unknown
d. Beverly Hills, CA, Dec. 9, 1943, Age 62

WOOLF, Kitty
Actress
b. Unknown
d. Unknown, June 13, 1944, Age 73

WOOLF, Stanley
Producer, Performer
b. Unknown
d. on board liner Homeric, Feb. 28, 1959, Age 59

WOOLLCOTT, Alexander
Author, Actor, Drama critic, Commentator
b. Phalanx, NJ, Jan. 19, 1887
d. New York, NY, Jan. 23, 1943, Age 56

WOOLLEY, Monty (Edgar Montillion Woolley)
Actor, Director, Educator
b. New York, NY, Aug. 17, 1888
d. Albany, NY, May 6, 1963, Age 74

WOOLSEY, Robert
Performer
b. Oakland, CA, Aug. 14, 1889
d. Malibu Beach, CA, Oct. 31, 1938, Age 49

WORK, Henry Clay
Songwriter
b. Middletown, CT, Oct. 1, 1832
d. Hartford, CT, June 8, 1884, Age 51

WORKMAN, Charles Herbert
Actor
b. Bottle, Lancashire, England, May 5, 1873
d. Unknown, May 1, 1923, Age 50

WORLOCK, Frederick
Actor
b. London, England, Dec. 14, 1886
d. Woodland Hills, CA, Aug. 1, 1973, Age 87

WORM, A. Toxen
Producer, Press representative
b. Unknown
d. Unknown, Jan. 12, 1922, Age 55

WORMS, Gustave Hippolyte
Actor, Teacher
b. Unknown, 1836
d. Unknown, Nov. 19, 1910, Age 74

WORMSER, Andre
Composer
b. Unknown
d. Unknown, Nov. 4, 1926, Age 75

WORTHING, Frank
Actor
b. Edinburgh, Scotland, Oct. 12, 1866
d. Detroit, MI, Dec. 27, 1910, Age 44

WORTHING, Helen Lee
Actress
b. New York, NY, Unknown
d. Hollywood, CA, Aug. 26, 1948, Age 43

WRAY, John
Actor
b. Philadelphia, PA, Feb. 13, 1888
d. Unknown, April 5, 1940, Age 52

WREN, Sam
Actor, Director
b. Brooklyn, NY, Unknown
d. Hollywood, CA, March 15, 1962, Age 65

WREN, Sir Christopher
Architect, Mathematician, Scientist
b. East Knoyle, Wiltshire, England, Oct. 20, 1632
d. Unknown, Feb. 26, 1723, Age 90

WRIGHT, Cowley
Actor
b. Anerley, England, Oct. 6, 1889
d. Unknown, Jan. 18, 1923, Age 33

WRIGHT, Dr. G. Harry
Educator, Theatre historian
b. Carbon, IN, Aug. 9, 1901
d. Cleveland, OH, Dec. 14, 1964, Age 63

WRIGHT, Fanny
Actress
b. Unknown
d. Unknown, Dec. 24, 1954

WRIGHT, Fred Sr.
Actor, Producer
b. Unknown, 1826
d. England, Oct. 19, 1911, Age 85

WRIGHT, Fred Jr.
Actor
b. Dover, England, March 8, 1871
d. New York, NY, Dec. 12, 1928, Age 57

WRIGHT, Georgie (Georgina Henley)
Actress
b. Vauxhall, London, England, Unknown
d. Mitcham, England, April 20, 1937, Age 79

WRIGHT, Haidée
Actress
b. London, England, Jan. 13, 1868
d. London, England, Jan. 29, 1943, Age 75

WRIGHT, Hugh E.
Actor, Playwright
b. Cannes, France, April 13, 1879
d. Unknown, Feb. 12, 1940, Age 60

WRIGHT, Huntley
Actor
b. London, England, Aug. 7, 1868
d. Bangor, Wales, July 10, 1943, Age 74

WRIGHT, Lawrence
Music publisher, Songwriter
b. Unknown
d. Blackpool, England, May 16, 1964, Age 76

WRIGHT, Lloyd Jr.
Lawyer
b. Unknown
d. Los Angeles, CA, Aug. 12, 1965, Age 45

WRIGHT, Marie
Actress
b. Unknown
d. Unknown, May 1, 1949, Age 87

WRIGHT, Mrs. Fred (Jessie F.)
Actress
b. Unknown
d. Unknown, Feb. 21, 1919, Age 72

WRIGHT, Mrs. Theodore (Alice Austin)
Actress
b. Unknown
d. Unknown, Sept. 1922

WRIGHT, Richard
Novelist, Playwright
b. near Natchez, MS, Sept. 4, 1908
d. Paris, France, Nov. 28, 1960, Age 52

WRIGHT, Will
Actor
b. California, Unknown
d. Hollywood, CA, June 19, 1962, Age 68

WYATT, Agnes (Mrs. John Ernest Hill)
Actress
b. Unknown
d. London, England, March 2, 1932

WYATT, Frank Jr.
Producer
b. Unknown, 1890
d. Unknown, May 1, 1933, Age 43

WYATT, Frank Gunning
Actor, Producer, Playwright
b. Unknown, 1852
d. Unknown, Oct. 5, 1926, Age 74

WYCHERLEY, William
Playwright
b. Clive, Shropshire, England, 1640
d. London, England, Jan. 1, 1716, Age 75

WYCHERLY, Margaret
Actress
b. London, England, Oct. 26, 1881
d. New York, NY, June 6, 1956, Age 74

WYES, William
Actor
b. Unknown
d. Unknown, Sept. 22, 1903, Age 46

WYKE, Byam
Pantomime author
b. Unknown
d. Unknown, Nov. 24, 1944, Age 84

WYLIE, James
Critic
b. Unknown
d. Unknown, Feb. 9, 1941, Age 65

WYLIE, Julian (Samuelson)
Playwright, Producer, Director
b. Southport, Lancashire, England, Aug. 1, 1878
d. London, England, Dec. 6, 1934, Age 56

WYNDHAM, Fred W.
Producer
b. Unknown
d. Unknown, April 30, 1930, Age 77

WYNDHAM, Howard
Theatre Manager, Producer
b. England, April 4, 1865
d. Welwyn, Hertfordshire, England, March 16, 1947, Age 81

WYNDHAM, Louise Isabella (Mrs. F. W. Wyndham)
Actress
b. Unknown
d. Unknown, Dec. 25, 1942

WYNDHAM, R. H.
Actor, Producer
b. Unknown
d. Unknown, Dec. 16, 1894, Age 81

WYNDHAM, Sir Charles
Actor, Producer, Playwright
b. Liverpool, England, March 23, 1837
d. Unknown, Jan. 12, 1919, Age 81

WYNN, Ed (né Isaiah Edward, or Edwin, Leopold)
Performer, Actor
b. Philadelphia, PA, Nov. 9, 1886
d. Beverly Hills, CA, June 19, 1966, Age 79

WYNNE, Wish
Actress
b. Croydon, England, Feb. 9, 1882
d. London, England, Nov. 11, 1931, Age 49

WYNYARD, Diana CBE (née Dorotyy Isobel Cox)
Actress
b. London, England, Unknown
d. London, England, May 13, 1964, Age 58

WYSPIANSKI, Stanislaw
Poet, Playwright, Painter, Architect
b. Cracow, Poland, Jan. 15, 1869
d. Cracow, Poland, Nov. 28, 1907, Age 38

Y

YABLOCHKINA, Alexandra
Actress
b. Unknown
d. Moscow, U.S.S.R, Mar. 20, 1964, Age 97

YALE, Charles H.
Manager
b. Unknown
d. Rochester, NY, March 23, 1920, Age 64

YARBOROUGH, Bertram
Director
b. Unknown
d. New York, NY, Dec. 2, 1962, Age 58

YARDE, Margaret
Actress
b. Dartmouth, England, April 2, 1878
d. Unknown, March 11, 1944, Age 65

YARDLEY, William
Playwright
b. Unknown
d. Oct. 26, 1900, 51

YATES, Edmund
Playwright, Journalist
b. Unknown, 1832
d. Unknown, May 20, 1894, Age 62

YATES, Frederick Henry
Actor, Producer
b. Unknown, 1795
d. Unknown, June 21, 1842, Age 47

YATES, Mary Ann Graham
Actress
b. Unknown, 1728
d. Unknown, 1787

YATES, Mrs. Frederick (Elizabeth Brunton)
Actress
b. Unknown
d. Unknown, Aug. 30, 1860, Age 61

YATES, Richard
Actor
b. Unknown, 1706
d. Pimlico, London, England, 1796

YATES, Theodosia (Mrs. Richard Stewart)
Actress
b. Unknown
d. Unknown, July 1904, Age 89

YAVOROSKA, Lydia
Actress
b. Kiev, Russia, Aug. 3, 1874
d. Unknown, Sept. 3, 1921, Age 47

YEAMANS, Annie (Annie Griffiths)
Actress
b. Isle of Man, England, Nov. 19, 1835
d. New York, NY, March 3, 1912, Age 76

YEAMANS, Jennie (Eugenia Marguerite Yeamans)
Actress
b. Sydney, Australia, 1862
d. Unknown, Nov. 28, 1906, Age 44

YEARSLEY, Claude
Music publisher, Composer, Producer
b. Unknown
d. Gibralter, Spain, Nov. 10, 1961, Age 76

YEATS, William Butler
Playwright, Poet
b. Sandymount, Ireland, June 13, 1865
d. Roquebrune, France, Jan. 28, 1939, Age 73

YERMOLOVA, Maria Nikolaievna
Actress
b. Russia, 1853
d. U.S.S.R, 1928

YOHÉ, May
(Mrs. John A. Smuts), Actress
b. Bethlehem, PA, April 6, 1869
d. Boston, MA, Aug. 28, 1938, Age 69

YOKEL, Alex (Alexander)
Producer, Director
b. Chicago, IL, Jan. 25, 1889
d. Lawrence, L.I., NY, Nov. 27, 1947, Age 61

YORKE, Augustus
Actor
b. Unknown
d. Hollywood, CA, Dec. 27, 1939, Age 79

YORKE, Dallas
Performer
b. Unknown
d. Birmingham, England, June 1963

YORKE, Oswald
Actor
b. London, England, Unknown
d. New York, NY, Jan. 25, 1943, Age 76

YOST, Herbert Alms
Actor
b. Harrison, OH, Unknown
d. New York, NY, Oct. 24, 1945, Age 65

YOULL, Jim
Stage manager
b. Unknown
d. Preston, England, 1962

YOUMANS, Vincent Millie
Composer
b. New York, NY, Sept. 27, 1898
d. Denver, CO, April 4, 1946, Age 48

YOUNG, Arthur
Actor
b. Bristol, Gloucestershire, England, Sept. 2, 1898
d. Unknown, Feb. 24, 1959, Age 60

YOUNG, Charles
Actor
b. Unknown
d. Sydney, Australia, Jan. 24, 1874

YOUNG, Charles Mayne
Actor
b. Unknown, Jan. 10, 1777
d. Brighton, England, June 29, 1856, Age 79

Young, Clara Kimball
Actress
b. Chicago, IL, 1890
d. Woodland Hills, CA, Oct. 15, 1960, Age 70

YOUNG, Florence
Actress
b. Unknown
d. Unknown, Nov. 10, 1920

YOUNG, J. Arthur
Actor
b. Chicago, IL, Unknown
d. Kew Garden, NY, Sept. 14, 1943, Age 63

YOUNG, Rida Johnson
Playwright
b. Baltimore, MD, Feb. 28, 1875
d. Southfield Point, CT, May 8, 1926, Age 51

YOUNG, Roland
Actor
b. London, England, Nov. 11, 1887
d. New York, NY, June 5, 1953, Age 65

YOUNG, Sir Charles
Playwright
b. Unknown, April 1839
d. Unknown, Sept. 11, 1887, Age 48

YOUNG, Stark
Playwright, Author, Critic
b. Como, MS, Oct. 11, 1881
d. Fairfield, CT, Jan. 6, 1963, Age 81

YOUNG, Victor
Composer, Conductor, Pianist
b. Bristol, TN, April 9, 1889
d. Ossining, NY, Sept. 2, 1968, Age 79

YOUNG, Victor
Composer, Conductor
b. Chicago, IL, Aug. 8, 1900
d. Palm Springs, CA, Nov. 10, 1956, Age 56

YOUNG, William
Playwright
b. Unknown
d. Burkhaven, NH, Oct. 2, 1920, Age 73

YOUNG, Winfred
Actor
b. Unknown
d. New York, NY, June 30, 1964, Age 86

YOW, Joe
Performer
b. Tulare, CA, Unknown
d. San Francisco, CA, March 8, 1964, Age 70

YULE, Joe
Actor
b. Scotland, Unknown
d. North Hollywood, CA, March 30, 1950, Age 61

YURGEV, Yuri
Actor
b. Unknown
d. Unknown, March 1948, Age 77

YURKA, Blanche
Actress, Coach
b. Czechoslovakia, Unknown
d. New York, NY, June 5, 1974, Age 86

Z

ZACCHINI, Ildebrando
Performer
b. Spain, Unknown
d. Tampa, FL, July 17, 1948, Age 79

ZACCONI, Ermete
Actor, Producer
b. Montecchio di Reggio Emilia, Italy, Sept. 14, 1857
d. Viareggio, Italy, Oct. 14, 1948, Age 91

ZALUD, Sam
Costume and Set designer
b. Unknown
d. Margate, FL, March 27, 1963, Age 77

ZANFRETTI, Francesca
Dancer
b. Unknown
d. Unknown, June 4, 1952, Age 90

ZANGWILL, Isreal
Playwright, Novelist, Critic
b. London, England, Feb. 14, 1864
d. Midhurst, Sussex, England, Aug. 1, 1926, Age 62

ZEMACH, Nahum L.
Producer, Director
b. Bialostock, Grodno, Russia, Aug. 9, 1887
d. New York, NY, Sept. 8, 1939, Age 52

ZENO, Apostolo
Poet, Librettist, Playwright
b. Unknown, 1668
d. Unknown, 1750

ZERBINI, Carlotta
Actress
b. Unknown
d. Unknown, April 15, 1912, Age 69

ZIEGFELD, Florenz Jr.
Producer
b. Chicago, IL, March 21, 1867
d. Santa Monica, CA, July 22, 1932, Age 65

ZIEGLER, Clara
Actress, Playwright
b. Unknown, April 27, 1844
d. Unknown, Dec. 20, 1909, Age 65

ZIEGLER, Edward
Music critic, Manager
b. Baltimore, MD, March 25, 1870
d. New York, NY, Oct. 25, 1947, Age 77

ZIEGLER, Jules Morton
Talent representative & manager
b. Botosian, Rumania, April 12, 1900
d. New York, NY, Aug. 21, 1967, Age 67

ZIMBALIST, Sam
Producer
b. Unknown
d. Rome, Italy, Nov. 4, 1958, Age 54

ZIMMERMAN, J. Fred
Manager
b. Unknown
d. Philadelphia, PA, March 24, 1925, Age 84

ZIMMERMAN, J. Fred Jr.
Director, Producer
b. Unknown
d. Palm Springs, CA, Dec. 12, 1948, Age 77

ZOLA, Emile Edouard Charles Antoine
Playwright, Novelist
b. Paris, France, April 2, 1840
d. Paris, France, Sept. 29, 1902, Age 62

ZORILLA Y MORAL, Jose
Playwright, Poet
b. Valladolid, Spain, 1817
d. Unknown, 1893

ZUCCO, George
Actor
b. Manchester, England, Jan. 11, 1886
d. Hollywood, CA, May 28, 1960, Age 74

ZWEIG, Stefan
Playwright, Novelist, Poet
b. Vienna, Austria, Nov. 28, 1881
d. Petropolis, Brazil, Feb. 23, 1942, Age 60

Notable Names in the American Theatre

A

AARON, PAUL. Director. Mr. Aaron's credits include *Salvation* (Jan Hus Th., N.Y.C., Sept. 24 1969); *Paris Is Out!* (Brooks Atkinson Th., Jan. 19, 1970); *A Dream Out of Time* (Promenade, Nov. 8, 1970); *70 Girls 70!* (Broadhurst, May 15, 1971); *Love Me, Love My Children* (Mercer Arts Ctr., Nov. 3, 1971); *That's Entertainment* (Edison, Apr. 14, 1972); the world premiere of *Ring-a-levio* (Studio Arena Buffalo, N.Y., Jan. 4, 1973); and *The Burnt Flower Bed* (Roundabout Th. Co., N.Y.C., July 2, 1974).

He is a former casting director for the Center Th. Group (Los Angeles).

ABBOTT, GEORGE. Director, actor, producer, playwright. b. George Francis Abbott, June 25, 1887, Forestville, N.Y., to George B. and May (McLaury) Abbott. Father, county supervisor; mother, teacher. Grad. Hamburg (N.Y.) H.S., 1907; Univ. of Rochester. B.A. 1911; attended Harvard Univ., 1912–13. Married July 9, 1914, to Ednah Levis (dec. 1930); one daughter, Judy Abbott, director, casting director, actress; married Mar. 27, 1946, to Mary Sinclair, actress (marr. dis 1951). Member of AEA; SSD&C; Dramatists Guild; AMPAS; ALA; AFTRA; WGA; SDG; Psi Upsilon; Coffee House Club. Address: One Rockefeller Plaza, New York, NY 10020, tel. (212) JU 2-0600.

Pre-Theatre. Western Union runner, cowboy, steel worker, salesman, swimming instructor at boys' camp, and basketball coach.

Theatre. Mr. Abbott wrote *The Head of the Family,* a one-act play presented by the Harvard Dramatic Club in 1912; his *Man in the Manhole* (Bijou Art Th., Boston, Mass., 1912) won a local playwriting contest. He first appeared as an actor, as Babe Merrill in *The Misleading Lady* (Fulton Th., N.Y.C., Nov. 25, 1913). He played Henry Allen in *Daddies* (Belasco, Sept. 5, 1918); Sylvester Cross in *The Broken Wing* (48 St. Th., Nov. 29, 1920); Texas in *Zander the Great* (Empire, Apr. 9, 1923); Sverre Peterson in *White Desert* (Princess, Oct. 18, 1923); Sid Hunt in *Hellbent fer Heaven* (Klaw, Jan. 4, 1924); Steve Tuttle in *Lazybones* (Vanderbilt, Sept. 22, 1924); and Dynamite Jim in *Processional* (Garrick, Jan. 12, 1925).

He wrote, with James Gleason, *The Fall Guy* (Eltinge, N.Y.C., Mar. 10, 1925); subsequently, with Winchell Smith, wrote *A Holy Terror,* in which he played Dirk Yancey (George M. Cohan Th., Sept. 28, 1925); with John V. A. Weaver, he wrote and directed *Love 'Em and Leave 'Em* (Harris Th., Feb. 3, 1926); and, with Philip Dunning, wrote and directed *Broadway* (Broadhurst, Sept. 16, 1926). He directed *Chicago* (Music Box, Dec. 30, 1926); *Spread Eagle* (Martin Beck Th., Apr. 4, 1927); wrote, with Dana Burnet, and directed *Four Walls* (John Golden Th., Sept. 19, 1927); and wrote, with Ann Preston Bridgers, and directed *Coquette* (Maxine Elliott's Th., Nov. 8, 1927). With John Meehan, he directed *Bless You, Sister* (Forrest, Dec. 26, 1927); directed *Gentlemen of the Press* (Henry Miller's Th., Aug. 27, 1928); wrote, with Edward E. Paramore, Jr., and directed *Ringside* (Broadhurst, Aug. 29, 1928); and directed *Poppa* (Biltmore, Dec. 24, 1928).

Mr. Abbott wrote, with S. K. Lauren, and directed *Those We Love,* in which he played Frederick Williston (John Golden Th., Feb. 19, 1930); directed *Louder, Please* (Masque, Nov. 12, 1931); and, with Philip Dunning, wrote, produced (Abbott-Dunning, Inc.), and directed *Lilly Turner* (Morosco, Sept. 19, 1932). He directed *The Great Magoo* (Selwyn, Dec. 2, 1932); produced, with Philip Dunning, and directed *Twentieth Century* (Broadhurst, Dec. 29, 1932); with Dunning, he produced *Heat Lightning* (Booth, Sept. 15, 1933), which he wrote with Leon Abrams and which he directed; and, with Dunning, he also produced *The Drums Begin* (Shubert, Nov. 24, 1933), which he directed. He produced and directed *John Brown* in which he played the title role (Ethel Barrymore Th., Jan. 22, 1934). He produced, with Dunning (Abbott-Dunning, Inc.), and directed *Kill That Story* (Booth, Aug. 29, 1934); directed *Small Miracle* (John Golden Th., Sept. 26, 1934); wrote and directed *Ladies' Money* (Ethel Barrymore Th., Nov. 1, 1934); directed *Page Miss Glory* (Mansfield, Nov. 27, 1934); and wrote, with John Cecil Holm, and directed *Three Men on a Horse* (Playhouse, Jan. 30, 1935).

He directed the book of *Jumbo* (Hippodrome, Nov. 16, 1935); produced and directed *Boy Meets Girl* (Cort, Nov. 27, 1935); and, in collaboration with Richard Rodgers and Lorenz Hart, wrote the book for *On Your Toes* (Imperial, Apr. 11, 1936). He produced, directed, and wrote *Sweet River* (51st St. Th., Oct. 28, 1936); produced and directed *Brother Rat* (Biltmore, Dec. 16, 1936), and *Room Service* (Cort., May, 19, 1937). He produced and directed *Angel Island* (National, Oct. 20, 1937); *Brown Sugar* (Biltmore, Dec. 2, 1937); and *All That Glitters* (Biltmore, Jan. 19, 1938).

He wrote the book, produced, and directed the musical *The Boys from Syracuse* (Alvin, Nov. 23, 1938); produced and directed *The Primrose Path* (Biltmore, Jan. 4, 1939); and *Mrs. O'Brien Entertains* (Lyceum, Feb. 8, 1939); and produced *See My Lawyer* (Biltmore, Sept. 27, 1939). He produced and directed *Too Many Girls* (Imperial, Oct. 18, 1939); *Ring Two* (Henry Miller's Th., Nov. 22, 1939); *The White-Haired Boy* (opened Plymouth, Boston, Mass., Oct. 28, 1940; closed there Nov. 2, 1940); *The Unconquered* (Biltmore, N.Y.C., Feb. 13, 1940); *Goodbye in the Night* (Biltmore, Mar. 18, 1940); *Pal Joey* (Ethel Barrymore Th., Dec. 25, 1940); and *Best Foot Forward* (Ethel Barrymore Th., Oct. 1, 1941).

Mr. Abbott produced *Jason* (Hudson, Jan. 21, 1942); wrote the book, with George Marion, Jr., produced and directed *Beat the Band* (46 St. Th., Oct. 14, 1942); directed *Sweet Charity* (Mansfield, Dec. 28, 1942); produced and directed *Kiss and Tell* (Biltmore, Mar. 17, 1943); *Get Away Old Man* (Cort, Nov. 24, 1943); *A Highland Fling* (Plymouth, Apr. 28, 1944); and *Snafu* (Hudson, Oct. 25, 1944). He directed *On the Town* (Adelphi, Dec. 28, 1944); produced, with Richard Myers, and directed *Mr. Cooper's Left Hand* (opened Wilbur, Boston, Mass., Sept. 25, 1945; closed there Oct. 6, 1945); directed *Billion Dollar Baby* (Alvin, N.Y.C., Dec. 21, 1945); produced and directed *One Shoe Off* (opened Nixon, Pittsburgh, Pa., Feb. 18, 1946; closed Shubert, New Haven, Conn., Mar. 2, 1946); and produced *Twilight Bar* (opened Ford's, Baltimore, Md., Mar. 12, 1946; closed Walnut St. Th., Philadelphia, Pa., Mar. 23, 1946). He produced *The Dancer* (Biltmore, N.Y.C., June 5, 1946); produced, with Richard Oldrich, and directed *It Takes Two* (Biltmore, Feb. 3, 1947); produced and directed *Barefoot Boy with Cheek* (Martin Beck Th., Apr. 3, 1947); directed *High Button Shoes* (Century, Oct. 9, 1947); produced and directed *Look, Ma, I'm Dancin'* (Adelphi, Jan. 29, 1948); wrote the book for and directed *Where's Charley?* (St. James, Oct. 11, 1948); and produced and directed *Mrs. Gibbons' Boys* (Music Box, May 4, 1949).

Mr. Abbott produced *Touch and Go* (Broadhurst, Oct. 13, 1949); directed *Call Me Madam* (Imperial, Oct. 12, 1950); and gave additional direction to *Out of This World* (New Century, Dec. 21, 1950). He wrote the book, with Betty Smith, and produced and directed *A Tree Grows in Brooklyn* (Alvin, Apr. 19, 1951); directed *The Number* (Biltmore, Oct. 30, 1951); produced, with Jule Styne, and directed *In Any Language* (Cort, Oct. 7, 1952); directed *Wonderful Town* (Winter Garden, Feb. 25, 1953); directed *Me and Juliet* (Majestic, May 28, 1953); wrote the book, with Richard Bissell, and directed with Jerome Robbins, *The Pajama Game* (St. James, May 13, 1954); produced and directed a revival of *On Your Toes* (46 St. Th., Oct. 11, 1954); and wrote the book, with Douglass Wallop, and directed *Damn Yankees* (46 St. Th., May 5, 1955). He appeared as Mr. Antrobus in *The Skin of Our Teeth* (Th. Sarah Bernhardt, Paris, Fr., June 1955; ANTA, N.Y.C., Aug. 17, 1955).

He wrote the book for, and directed *New Girl in Town* (46 St. Th., May 14, 1957); directed *Drink to Me Only* (54 St. Th., Oct. 8, 1958); directed *Once Upon a Mattress* (Phoenix, May 11, 1959; moved to Alvin, Nov. 25, 1959); wrote the book, with Jerome Weidman, and directed *Fiorello!* (Broadhurst, Nov. 23, 1959); and wrote the book with Weidman, and directed *Tenderloin* (46 St. Th., Oct. 17, 1960). He directed *A Call on Kuprin* (Broadhurst, May 25, 1961); *Take Her, She's Mine* (Biltmore, Dec. 21, 1961); *A Funny Thing Happened on the Way to the Forum* (Alvin, May 8, 1962); *Never Too Late* (Playhouse, Nov. 27, 1962); and *Fade Out — Fade In* (Mark Hellinger Th., May 26, 1964; re-opened, Mark Hellinger Th., Feb. 15, 1965).

Mr. Abbott directed and, with Robert Russell, wrote the book for *Flora, the Red Menace* (Alvin Th., May 11, 1965); directed and, with Guy Bolton, wrote the book for *Anya* (Ziegfeld Th., Nov. 29, 1965); directed *The Well-Dressed Liar* (Royal Poinciana Playhouse, Palm Beach, Fla., Mar. 7, 1966; Cocoanut Grove Playhouse, Miami, Fla., May 31, 1966); directed *Help Stamp Out Marriage* (Booth Th., N.Y.C., Sept. 29, 1966); *Agatha Sue I love you* (Henry Miller's Th., Dec. 14, 1966); *How Now, Dow Jones* (Lunt-Fontanne Th., Dec. 7, 1967); *The Education of H*Y*M*A*N K*A*P*L*A*N* (Alvin Th., Apr. 4, 1968); *The Fig Leaves Are Falling* (Broadhurst, Jan. 2, 1969); and a revival of *Three Men on a Horse* (Lyceum, Oct. 16, 1969). He also directed *Norman, Is That You?* (Lyceum, Feb. 19, 1970); *Not Now, Darling* (Brooks Atkinson Th., Oct. 29, 1970); and revivals of *The Pajama Game* (Lunt-Fontanne Th., Dec. 9, 1973) and *Life with Father* (Seattle Repertory Th., Seattle, Wash., Dec. 6, 1974).

Films. Mr. Abbott directed *The Bishop's Candlesticks* (Par., 1928); *Why Bring That Up?* (Par., 1929); *Manslaughter* (Par., 1930); *All Quiet on the Western Front* (U, 1930); *Secrets of a Secretary* (Par., 1931); *Stolen Heaven* (Par., 1931); *My Sin* (Par., 1931); *Too Many Girls* (RKO, 1940); *Kiss and Tell* (Col., 1945); *Pajama Game* (WB, 1957); and *Damn Yankees* (WB, 1958).

Television. Mr. Abbott directed and was emcee for the US Royal Showcase (NBC, Jan. 13, 1952–June 29, 1952); and appeared as Mr. Antrobus in *The Skin of Our Teeth* (NBC, Sept. 11, 1955).

Awards. *Fiorello!* of which Mr. Abbott was author with Jerome Weidman, and director, won a Pulitzer Prize (1960), and also received a NY Drama Critics Circle Award (1961), *Wonderful Town*, which he directed, was voted the best musical by the NY Drama Critics Circle (1953); and five musical productions that he directed have received Antoinette Perry (Tony) awards: *Wonderful Town* (1953), *The Pajama Game* (1955), *Damn Yankees* (1956), *Fiorello!* (1960), and *A Funny Thing Happened on the Way to the Forum* (1963). In addition, Mr. Abbott received Tony awards as best director of a musical play for *Fiorello!* and *A Funny Thing Happened on the Way to the Forum* and a Tony nomination as best director of a musical play (1968) for *How Now, Dow Jones*. Mr. Abbott received the Donaldson Award for his direction of *Billion Dollar Baby*, (1946), *High Button Shoes* (1948), *Wonderful Town* (1953) and, with Jerome Robbins, for *The Pajama Game* (1955). In 1965, Mr. Abbott received the first annual Award of Merit given by the Society of Stage Directors and Choreographers; at the same time, the 54th St. Th., N.Y.C., was renamed the George Abbott Th.

Recreation. Golf, dancing, swimming, travel.

ABBOTT, JOHN. Actor. b. June 5, 1905, London, England. Educated privately in England. Served British diplomatic service as honorary attaché, Stockholm, Sweden, 1939–40. Member of AEA; AFTRA; SAG; Drama Society, Inc. (pres., 1951–58). Address: 6424 Ivarene Ave., Hollywood, CA 90068.

Pre-Theatre. Art student.

Theatre. Mr. Abbott made his Bway debut as Count Mancini in *He Who Gets Slapped* (Booth, Mar. 20, 1946); followed by Juan Salcedo Alvarez in *Montserrat* (Fulton, Oct. 29, 1949); Dr. Bonant in *The Waltz of the Toreadors* (Coronet, Jan. 17, 1957); in stock, the title role in *Doctor Knock* (Gate, Hollywood, Apr. 25, 1944); Eloi in *Auto da Fe* (Stage Society, Hollywood, June 1950); Malvolio in *Twelfth Night* (Huntington Hartford Th., Hollywood, 1950); Gayev in *The Cherry Orchard* (Royal Poinciana Playhouse, Palm Beach, Fla., Jan. 1960; Sombrero Playhouse, Phoenix, Ariz., Feb. 6, 1960); and Peter Sorin in *The Seagull* (Theatre Group of the Univ. of Southern California, Jan. 10, 1964).

He made his stage debut in amateur productions of *The School for Scandal* and *The Last of Mrs. Cheyney* (1930); subsequently appeared in amateur productions (St. Pancras Peoples' Th., London, 1931–34); wrote *Driftwood* (Festival Th., Sept. 1932); and *Clash* (St. Pancras Peoples' Th., Nov. 10, 1934).

He made his professional debut in London as Solyman in *Aurengzebe* (Westminster Th., May 13, 1934); followed by Chiba in *Two Kingdoms* (Savoy, Oct. 28, 1934); appeared in repertory (Palace Th., Watford, Eng., Jan.-May 1935; New Th., Crewe, June-Sept. 1935); in *Redemption* (Arts, London, Sept. 1935); toured in *Man of Yesterday* (Oct.-Dec. 1935); played Jensen in *Repayment* (Arts, Jan. 5, 1936); Fletcher in *Bitter Harvest* (Arts, Jan. 29, 1936); Sir Thomas Lovell in *Henry VIII* (Open Air Th., June 22, 1936).

Mr. Abbott joined the Old Vic Co., appearing as Sir Nathaniel in *Love's Labour's Lost* (Old Vic, Sept. 14, 1936); William Prynne and Tench in *Charles the King* (Lyric, Oct. 9, 1936); the Justice in *The Witch of Edmonton* (Old Vic, Dec. 8, 1936); Claudius in *Hamlet* (Old Vic, Jan. 5, 1937; Elsinore Castle, Den., June 1937); the Friar in *Much Ado About Nothing* (Ring Blackfriars, London, Jan. 17, 1937); Malvolio in *Twelfth Night* (Old Vic, Feb. 23, 1937); and Shakespeare in *The Dark Lady of the Sonnets* (Old Vic, Apr. 23, 1937).

He played Joseph Chamberlain in *Mr. Gladstone* (Gate, Sept. 30, 1937); Seth Beckwith in *Mourning Becomes Electra* (Westminster, Nov. 19, 1937); Karl the Clown in *The Painted Smile* (New, Apr. 22, 1938); Fydor in *The Last Train South* (St. Martin's, Sept. 6, 1938); Dr. Rank in *Nora* (Duke of York's, Feb. 3, 1939); and Zariloff in *Progress in Paradise* (Richmon, May 22, 1939).

Films. Mr. Abbott made his film debut in *Mademoiselle Docteur* (1937); subsequently appeared in *The Return of the Scarlet Pimpernel* (UA, 1938); *Algiers* (UA, 1938); *This Man Is News* (Par., 1939); *The Saint in London* (RKO, 1939); *The Shanghai Gesture* (UA, 1941); *Missing Ten Days* (Col., 1941); *London Blackout Murders* (Rep., 1942); *This Above All* (20th-Fox, 1942); *The Gorilla Man* (WB, 1942); *Joan of Paris* (RKO, 1942); *Rubber Racketeers* (Mono., 1942); *Get Hep to Love* (U, 1942); *Nightmare* (U, 1942); *Mission to Moscow* (WB, 1943); *They Got Me Covered* (RKO, 1943); *U-Boat Prisoner* (Col., 1944); *The Mask of Dimitrius* (WB, 1944); *The Falcon in Hollywood* (RKO, 1944); *Once Upon a Time* (Col., 1944); *Jane Eyre* (20th-Fox, 1944); *Summer Storm* (UA, 1944); *The End of the Road* (Rep., 1944); *The Vampire's Ghost* (Rep., 1945); *Saratoga Trunk* (WB, 1945); *The Crime Doctor's Warning* (Col., 1945); *Scotland Yard Investigator* (Rep., 1945); *A Thousand and One Nights* (Col., 1945); *Deception* (WB, 1946); *The Bandit of Sherwood Forest* (Col., 1946); *Anna and the King of Siam* (20th-Fox, 1946); *Humoresque* (WB, 1946); *Adventure Island* (Par., 1947); *The Web* (U, 1947); *If Winter Comes* (MGM, 1947); *Time Out of Mind* (U, 1947); *The Woman in White* (WB, 1948); *The Return of the Whistler* (Col., 1948); *Danger, Blondes* (Col., 1948); *Madame Bovary* (MGM, 1949); *Sideshow* (Mono., 1950); *Her Wonderful Lie* (Col., 1950); *Public Pigeon Number One* (U, 1951); *Thunder in the East* (Par., 1953); *Navy Bound* (Mono., 1951); *Crosswinds* (Par., 1951); *The Merry Widow* (MGM, 1952); *The Rogues March* (MGM, 1952); *The Steel Lady* (UA, 1953); *Sombrero* (MGM, 1953); *Omar Khayyam* (Par., 1957); *Gigi* (MGM, 1958); *Who's Minding the Store* (Par., 1953); *The Greatest Story Ever Told* (UA, 1964); *Gambit* (U, 1966); and *Two Thousand Years Later* (WB-7 Arts, 1969).

Television. In England, Mr. Abbott has appeared on TV in *The Harmfulness of Tobacco* (BBC, June 1937); as Ernest in *The Importance of Being Earnest* (BBC, Nov. 1937); as Akhnaton in *The Beautiful One* (BBC, Feb. 1938); and as Prospero in *The Tempest* (BBC, Feb. 1939).

In the US, Mr. Abbott has appeared in *The Harmfulness of Tobacco* (Par-TV, 1944); *International Incident* (Ray Milland Show, Feb. 1955); *Outward Bound* (Front Row Center, CBS, Feb. 1955); *Tender Is the Night* (Front Row Center, CBS, Mar. 1955); *Professor Lostbone* (Gunsmoke, CBS, Sept. 1955); *One for the Road* (Matinee Th., NBC, Sept. 1955); *Life of a Ballerina* (General Electric Th., CBS, Dec. 1955); *The Optimist* (Crusader, Feb. 1956); *The Sainted General* (Campbell Soup Show, Feb. 1956); The Wally Cox Show (July 1956); *The Glorious Gift of Molly Malone* (General Electric Th., CBS, Aug. 1956); *Marriage Royal* (Matinee Th., NBC, Sept. 1956); *Billings* (Climax, CBS, Sept. 1956); *Sight Unseen* (Matinee Th., NBC, Oct. 1956); *The Tell-Tale Heart* (NBC, Oct. 1956); *Johnny Moves Up* (Ann Sothern Show, Nov. 1956); *Pay Now, Kill Later* (Peter Gunn, Jan. 1957); *Child of Virtue* (Philip Marlowe, Feb. 1957); *Kind Mother* (Philip Marlowe, Mar. 1957); *Poor Lillie* (Philip Marlowe, Mar. 1957); *Story Without a Moral* (Alcoa, NBC, May 1957); *Shot By Request* (Have Gun, Will Travel, CBS, July 1957); *The Richest Man in the World* (Matinee Th., NBC, July 1957); and *The Jewel Box* (Matinee Th., NBC, Aug. 1957).

Also, *Cold Ice* (Tightrope, Aug. 1957); *The Power of Positive Thinking* (Dobie Gillis, Sept. 1957); *The Song of David* (General Electric Th., CBS, Oct. 1957); *The Tragedian* (Gunsmoke, CBS, Nov. 1957); *The Makropoulos Secret* (Matinee Th., NBC, Jan. 1958); *The Suicide Club* (Matinee Th., NBC, Feb. 1958); *Washington Square* (Matinee Th., NBC, June 1958); *Bellingham* (Studio One, CBS, Sept. 1958); *Accused* (ABC, Aug. 1959); *The Waltz of the Toreadors* (Play of the Week, WNTA, Dec. 1959); *The House with the Seven Gables* (Shirley Temple Show, NBC, Oct. 1960); *Shangri-La* (Hallmark Hall of Fame, NBC, Oct. 1960); *Day for a Scoundrel* (Four Star, June Allyson Show, Dec. 1960); *Arabian Nights* (Jim Backus Show, Jan. 1961); *Trio for Terror* (Thriller, Feb. 1961); *First Class Honeymoon* (Alfred Hitchcock Presents, CBS, May 1961); *The Purple Cow* (Ichabod and Me, June 1961); *Mr. Arcularis* (Great Ghost Stories, NBC, Aug. 1961); *Gabrielle* (Bonanza, CBS, Aug. 1961); *The Detectives* (Four Star Th., Dec. 1961); *The Prison* (Dick Powell Show, Dec. 1961); *The Old Man* (Outlaws, NBC, Dec. 1961); *The Forgery* (Dupont, NBC, Feb. 1962); *Days of Glory* (Four Star Dick Powell Show, Feb. 1962); *The Case of the Stolen Books* (Perry Mason, CBS, Aug. 1962); *The Betrayal* (Dupont, NBC, Nov. 1962); *Six Feet Under* (77 Sunset Strip, Nov. 1962); *Mr. Smith Goes to Washington* (Four Star Th., Jan. 1963); *The Meeting of the Minds* (Steve Allen Show, May 1963); *One Day in the Life of Ivan Denisovich* (Bob Hope Presents, NBC, July 1963); and *Deputy For a Day* (Destry, ABC, 1964).

Also, *Mr. Marvello* (Flipper, July 1964); *Dr. Jekyll* (Beverly Hillbillies, CBS, Aug. 1964); Great Profiles (Oct. 1964); Wendy and Me (Oct. 1964); The Living Doll (Nov. 1964); Burke's Law (Aug. 1965); Laredo (Oct. 1965); Get Smart (Oct. 1965); I Spy (Oct. 1965); Man from Uncle (Dec. 1965); The John Forsythe Show (Mar. 1966); Lost in Space (Sept. 1966); Gideon (NBC, Oct. 1966); Rango

(Jan. 1967); Star Trek (Jan. 1967); Garrison's Gorillas (ABC, Aug. 1967); *Run, Sheep, Run* (Mannix, Oct. 1967); *Samantha's Da Vinci Affair* (Bewitched, ABC, Oct. 1967); Wild, Wild West (Jan. 1968); Land of the Giants (Feb. 1968); *Witchcraft* (Medical Center, MGM, Sept. 1970); McMillan and Wife (U, Aug. 1971); *How Many Carats in a Grapefruit?* (The Partners, U, Aug. 1971); O'Hara (Dec. 1971); *The Upper Depths* (Cool Million, U, Sept. 1972); *No Margin for Error* (Medical Center, MGM, Jan. 1973); and *The Cat Creature* (Screen Gems, TV Film of the Week, Nov. 1973). In addition to the preceding, Mr. Abbott has made several television commercials.

Recreation. Music, painting.

ABBOTT, JUDITH. Casting director, actress, director. b. Judith Ann Abbott, Mar. 17, Rochester, N.Y., to George and Ednah (Levis) Abbott. Father, director, playwright; mother, school teacher. Grad. Harley Sch., Rochester, N.Y.; attended AADA. Married Mar. 18, 1946, to Tom Ewell, actor (marr. dis. Jan. 1947); married Feb. 18, 1949, to Richard Clark (marr. dis. June 1960); one son, two daughters. Relative in theatre: cousin, Carl Fisher, business manager. Member of AEA. Address: (home) 160 E. 81st St., New York, NY 10028; (bus.) 630 Fifth Ave., New York, NY 10020, tel. (212) JU 2-0600.

Theatre. Miss Abbott made her N.Y.C., debut as successor to Helen Walker in the role of Lisa Otis in *Jason* (Hudson Th., Jan. 21, 1942); subsequently appeared as Helen in *Alice in Arms* (National, Jan. 31, 1945); succeeded Phyllis Thaxter in the role of Anne Michaelson in *Take Her, She's Mine* (Biltmore, Dec. 21, 1961).

She was casting director for *The Pajama Game* (St. James, May 13, 1954); *Damn Yankees* (46 St. Th., May 5, 1955); *New Girl in Town* (46 St. Th., May 14, 1957); *Drink to Me Only* (54 St. Th., Oct. 8, 1958); *Once Upon a Mattress* (Phoenix, May 11, 1959); *Fiorello!* (Broadhurst, Nov. 23, 1959); *Tenderloin* (46 St. Th., Oct. 17, 1961); *A Funny Thing Happened on the Way to the Forum* (Alvin, May 8, 1962); *Never Too Late* (Playhouse, Nov. 27, 1962); and *Fade Out, Fade In* (Mark Hellinger Th., May 26, 1964). She was one of the producers of *Agatha Sue I love you* (Henry Miller's Th., Dec. 14, 1966).

In stock, she directed *Fiorello!* (summer tour, 1962); *Take Her, She's Mine* (Palm Beach Playhouse, Fla., and Coconut Grove Playhouse, Miami, Fla., Summer 1963); *Never Too Late* (Coconut Grove Playhouse, Miami, Fla., 1963); *Golden Fleecing* (Coconut Grove Playhouse, Miami, Fla., Fall 1963); touring productions of *Thursday Is a Good Night* and *Take Her, She's Mine* (Summer 1964); *Warm Heart, Cold Feet* (Falmouth Playhouse, Falmouth, Mass., Aug. 24, 1964); and *Sunday in New York* (Palm Beach Playhouse, Fla., Winter 1964).

Miss Abbott directed the London production of *Never Too Late* (Prince of Wales's Th., Sept. 24, 1963).

Television and Radio. She was casting director for Arthur Godfrey Talent Scouts (CBS, 1948) and acted in The Aldrich Family (NBC and CBS, 1943–52). On television, she appeared on Girl Talk (ABC, 1966–67).

ABBOTT, PHILIP. Actor. b. Philip Abbott Alexander, Mar. 20, 1924, Lincoln, Neb., to John M. and Helen B. (Boggs) Alexander. Father, realtor. Grad. Beverly Hills H.S., 1940; Pasadena Jr. Coll., 1942. Studied acting with Sanford Meisner, N.Y.C., 1949–53. Married Apr. 29, 1950, to Jane DeFrayne; two sons, one daughter. Served WW II, USAAF, ETO; rank, 1st Lt.; received Distinguished Flying Cross, four air medals, four battle stars. Member of SAG; AEA; AFTRA. Address: c/o Ashley Famous Agency, Inc., 9255 Sunset Blvd., Los Angeles, CA 90069, tel. (213) CR 3-8811.

Theatre. Mr. Abbott first appeared on Bway as Jules Bromark in *Harvest of Years* (Hudson Th., Jan. 12, 1948) which he had also played in a summer tryout (Tanglewood, Falmouth, Mass., Aug. 25, 1947); played at Eastern Slope Playhouse (North Conway, N.H., Summer 1948); toured as general understudy in *Detective Story* (1948–49); played John Tucker in *The Square Root of Wonderful* (National, N.Y.C., Oct. 30, 1957); was standby for Henry Fonda in the role of Jerry Ryan in *Two for the Seesaw* (Booth, Jan. 16, 1958), playing the role for one week (Jan. 20, 1958).

In stock, he played Juror 8 in *Twelve Angry Men* (Bucks County Playhouse, New Hope, Pa., Summer 1960) and Jerry Ryan in *Two for the Seesaw* (Bucks Co. Playhouse, New Hope, Pa.; Cape Playhouse, Dennis, Mass., Summer 1960). He played Antanas in *Five Posts in the Market Place* (Gate, N.Y.C., Mar. 5, 1961), and he became an active member of Theatre West, Los Angeles, Calif., in 1964.

Mr. Abbott dramatized, co-directed, and played the Poet in *Robert Frost: Promises to Keep* (Humanities Bldg. Aud., UCLA, Los Angeles, July 7, 1965); dramatized and directed *The Web and the Rock* (Actors Th., Los Angeles, 1967); and was in *Spoon River* (Th. West, Los Angeles, May 19, 1972).

Films. Mr. Abbott appeared in *Bachelor Party* (UA, 1957); *The Invisible Boy* (MGM, 1957); *Sweet Bird of Youth* (MGM, 1962); *The Spiral Road* (U, 1962); *The Miracle of the White Stallions* (Buena Vista, 1963); and *Those Calloways* (Buena Vista, 1964).

Television. Following his television debut in Crisis (1949), Mr. Abbott appeared in both New York and Hollywood on such major network shows as Philco Playhouse (NBC), Goodyear Playhouse (NBC), Climax! (CBS), and Playhouse 90 (CBS). He was in Man Against Crime (CBS, 1949–54); starred in *Shadow of Suspicion* (Kraft Th., NBC, Nov. 1956); in *A Doll's House* (CBS, Apr. 1959); played John Collier in The House on High Street (NBC, 1964); was Assistant Director Arthur Ward in The F.B.I. (ABC, 1964–70); Ed Barrett in *Kilroy* (Walt Disney's World, NBC, Mar. 13, 21, 28 and Apr. 4, 1965); and appeared on many other programs, including Eleventh Hour (NBC, 1964); Slattery's People (CBS, 1964); Rawhide (CBS, 1964); Fugitive (ABC, 1964); Perry Mason (CBS, 1965); Ben Casey (ABC, 1965); Outer Limits (Ind., 1966); Twilight Zone (Ind., 1966); and Dr. Kildare (Ind., 1967).

ABBOTT, RICHARD. Actor. b. Simon Vandenberg, May 22, 1899, Antwerp, Belg., to Brahm and Bertha (Delden) Vandenberg. Father, pianist, conductor; mother, pianist, opera coach. Grad. private school, Antwerp, 1910; grad. DeWitt Clinton H.S., N.Y.C., 1915; attended Columbia Univ., 1918–19; the Univ. of Paris (de la Sorbonne), Paris, Fr., 1920–21; AADA (scholarship), studied with Gelevjer; Nelidoff of the Moscow Art Th. (1924). Married May 20, 1921, to Sara Haden, actress (marr. dis. 1948); married June 5, 1952, to Virginia Howard, singer (marr. dis. 1955); married Sept. 9, 1957, to Pearl Eaton (marr. dis. 1959). Relatives in theatre: third cousin, Sarah Bernhardt; grandmother, Jean Vandenberg, Flemish actress. Member of AEA; SAG; AFTRA; AFM. Address: (home) 315 W. 94th St., New York, NY 10025, tel. (212) UN 5-1414; (bus.) tel. (212) LE 2-1100.

Pre-Theatre. Musician, teacher.

Theatre. Mr. Abbott's first appearance in the theatre was as Tarver in the touring company of *Green Stockings* (1916); subsequently played David in the touring company of *The Melting Pot* (1917); made his first N.Y.C. appearance as the Office Boy in *Success* (Harris Th., Jan. 28, 1918); played in the touring company of *The Auctioneer* (1918); appeared in Theatre Guild productions at the Garrick Th. (N.Y.C.), as Chikara in *The Faithful* (Oct. 13, 1919); Charles Bellingham in *The Rise of Silas Lapham* (Nov. 25, 1919), and a Police Officer in *Powers of Darkness* (Jan. 15, 1920); appeared in Walter Hampden's Shakespearean repertory, as the Ghost in *Hamlet*, Tybalt in *Romeo and Juliet*, Ross in *Macbeth*, Lorenzo in *The Merchant of Venice* (Broadhurst, Spring 1921), and on tour; portrayed Andre in *The Masked Woman* (Eltinge, N.Y.C., Dec. 22, 1922); and played a season of stock in Woonsocket, R.I. (1923), and Providence, R.I. (1924).

He appeared as Aryka in *The Little Clay Cart* (Neighborhood Playhouse, N.Y.C., Dec. 5, 1924); Vanderbluff in *Polly* (Cherry Lane, Oct. 10, 1925); co-produced and acted in the US premiere of three plays by Roswitha, *Abraham, Dulcitus,* and *Gallicanus* (in a studio on 12th St., 1925); appeared in *Jakob Slovak* (Greenwich Village Th., Oct. 5, 1927); played a season of stock in Keene, N.H. (1927), and Dallas, Tex., (1929); played the Dentist in *First Mortgage* (Broadhurst, N.Y.C., Oct. 10, 1929); Jimmy Hollister in *Winterbound* (Garrick, Nov. 13, 1930); Harris in *The Last Mile* (Harris, Feb. 13, 1930); appeared in *Youth* (Cherry Lane, 1931); played a Disciple and a High Priest in *The Dark Hours* (New Amsterdam, Nov. 14, 1932); appeared in *Candide* (Booth, May 15, 1933); and Joe Morgan in a stock production of *Ten Nights in a Barroom* (Locust Valley, L.I., N.Y., 1933).

From 1933–48, he appeared as Jed Harris in *The Terrible Turk* and the Bishop of Beauvaise in *Saint Joan* (Pasadena Playhouse, Calif., 1934); John the Baptist and Caiaphas in the *Pilgrimage Play* (Pilgrimage Bowl, Hollywood, Calif., 1945); performed in the *Mission Play* (Mission Th., Alhambra, Calif., 1946); *The Three Musketeers* (Los Angeles and San Francisco, Calif., 1946); Father Nordraak and Henrik Ibsen in a cross-country tour of *Song of Norway* (1947); Kent in *King Lear,* Benedick in *Much Ado About Nothing,* and the title role in *Henry VIII* (West Hollywood Th., Calif., Summer 1948).

Mr Abbott appeared in an ELT production of *The Good Fairy* (Lenox Hill Playhouse, N.Y.C., 1948); succeeded Ralph Bunker as a Professor in *Goodbye, My Fancy* (Morosco, Nov. 17, 1948); played a Preacher in an ELT production of *Sister Oakes* (Lenox Hill Playhouse, Apr. 23, 1949); in stock, portrayed Dr. Chausable in *The Importance of Being Earnest* (Stockbridge Th., Mass., Summer 1949); and the Bishop of Beauvaise in *Joan of Lorraine* (Nyack Festival, N.Y., Summer 1949); played the Doctor in *Now I Lay Me Down to Sleep* (Broadhurst, N.Y.C., Mar. 2, 1950); and in stock, performed in *The Vagabond King* and *Song of Norway* (Hyannis, Mass., Summer 1950), *Desert Song* (Toronto, Can., Summer 1951), *Song of Norway* (Starlight Th., Kansas City, Mo., Summer 1951), *Kiss Me, Kate* (Dallas State Fair Music Hall, Summer 1953).

He appeared as the Owner of the park in the pre-Bway tryout of *By the Beautiful Sea;* the Squire in *The Corn Is Green* (Fred Miller Th., Milwaukee, Wis., 1954); adapted, directed, composed music, and played Captain Ahab in *Moby Dick* (Kaufmann Aud., N.Y.C., Mar. 1955); appeared as General Wetjoen in *The Iceman Cometh* (Circle in the Sq., N.Y.C., 1956); in stock, played the Sheriff in *Show Boat,* and the Owner of the team in *Damn Yankees* (Th. Under the Stars, Vancouver, B.C., Can., Summer 1958); Abernathy in *Guys and Dolls* (Melody Fair, Toronto, Ont., Can., 1959); appeared in *Towards Zero,* and as the Senator in *Deep Are the Roots* (North Jersey Playhouse, Fort Lee, N.J., 1960); and as the Soviet Commissar in *Five Posts in the Market Place* (Gate, N.Y.C., Mar. 5, 1961). He appeared with the American Shakespeare Festival, Stratford, Conn., 1966.

Films. Mr. Abbott appeared in *Battle in the North Atlantic* (1943); *The Moon Is Low* (20th-Fox, 1943); *Happy Land* (20th-Fox, 1943); *Appointment in Berlin* (Col., 1943); *Wilson* (20th-Fox, 1944); *The Story of Dr. Wassell* (Par., 1944); *Adventure* (MGM, 1945); *The Exile* (U, 1947); *Green Dolphin Street* (MGM, 1947); *The Hucksters* (MGM, 1949); *Roman Holiday* (Par., 1953); *The Hustler* (20th-Fox, 1961); *Splendor in the Grass* (WB, 1961); *The Manchurian Candidate* (UA, 1962); *The Cardinal* (UA, 1963); *The Pawn Broker* (Ely Landau, 1964); *The World of Henry Orient* (UA, 1964); *Cast a Giant Shadow* (UA, 1966); *A Man Could Get Killed* (U, 1966).

Television. He has appeared on The Defenders (CBS, 1962); Philco Television Playhouse (NBC); Studio One (CBS); Robert Montgomery Presents (NBC); Catholic Hour (NBC); Lux Video Th. (NBC); Jackie Gleason Show (CBS); and Milton Berle Show (NBC).

Recreation. Writing, music, literature, sports.

ABEGGLEN, HOMER N. Educator, director. b. Apr. 5, 1901, Albia, Iowa, to John F. and Nora (Ensley) Abegglen. Father, lawyer. Grad. Albia H.S., 1918; Grinnell Coll., B.A. 1923; attended Univ. of Washington, 1926–27; Yale Univ., 1927–28; grad. Teachers Coll., Columbia Univ., M.A. 1932; Western Reserve Univ., Ph.D. 1943. Married Aug. 16, 1937, to Henrietta Pulskamp, French instructor. Member of ATA, NTC. Address: (home) Coulter Lane, Oxford, OH 45056, tel. (513) 523-5112; (bus.) Fisher Hall, Miami University, Oxford, OH 45056, tel. (513) 523-2161, ext. 275.

Mr. Abegglen retired from Miami University as professor emeritus of speech in 1968. He had been a member of the faculty from 1928; assistant professor of speech (1928–39), associate professor of speech (1939–46), professor of speech (1946–68), director of the Miami University Th. (1960–68). He also taught at the Albia H.S. (1923–26).

Awards. He received an honorary D. Litt. from Wilmington College, Wilmington, Ohio (1966).

Recreation. Horseback riding.

ABEL, LIONEL. Educator, playwright, critic, translator. b. Nov. 28, 1910, New York City, to Alter and Anna (Schwartz) Abelson. Educ. St. Johns Univ., Brooklyn, N.Y. (1926–28); Univ. of North Carolina (1928–29). Married 1939 to Sherry Goldman (marr. dis.); one daughter (deceased, 1964); married 1970 to Gloria Becker. Address: Dept. of English, State University, Buffalo, NY 14222.

Mr. Abel became professor of English at the State Univ. of NY (Buffalo) in 1970. His previous academic posts included visiting professorships in drama at Columbia Univ. (1961), Rutgers (1964), and at Buffalo (1965, 1967); and he was visiting professor of aesthetics at Pratt Institute (1962).

Theatre. Mr. Abel wrote *The Death of Odysseus* (Amato Opera Th., N.Y.C., Nov. 3, 1953); *Absalom* (Artists Th., May 1956; Carl Fischer Concert Hall, Sept. 27, 1956); *The Pretender* (Cherry Lane Th., May 24, 1960); translated Michael de Ghelderode's *Escurial*, which was presented off-Bway (Gate Th., July 21, 1960); and wrote *The Wives* (Stage 73, May 17, 1965).

Published Works. Mr. Abel wrote *Metatheatre* (1963), a book of criticism; *Moderns on Tragedy* (1967); and his articles have appeared in various periodicals. His translations include *Some Poems of Rimbaud* (1939); Camille Pissarro's *Letters to His Son Lucien* (1943); John Rewald's *Georges Seurat* (1943); Guillaume Apollinaire's *The Cubist Painters* (1944); Jean Paul Sartre's *Three Plays* (1949); Michael Seuphor's *Piet Mondrian: Life and Work* (1956); and Racine's *Andromaque* (published in *Genius of the French Theatre*, 1961).

Awards. Mr. Abel was awarded a Guggenheim Fellowship (1958–59); a Longview Foundation Award (1960); and a Rockefeller Foundation grant (1966). He received a National Institute of Arts and Letters Award in 1964.

ABEL, WALTER. Actor. b. June 6, 1898, St. Paul, Minn., to Richard Michael and Christine (Becker) Abel. Attended AADA, N.Y.C., 1917–18. Married Sept. 24, 1926, to Marietta Bitter, two sons. Address: (home) 167 E. 71st St., New York, NY 10021, tel. (212) TR 9-9444; (bus.) Ashley Famous Agency, Inc., 555 Madison Ave., New York, NY 10022, tel. (212) MU 8-8330.

Theatre. While a student at the American Academy of Dramatic Art, Mr. Abel appeared in *A Woman's Way, Harvest, Nocturne*, and *Garside's Career* (Lyceum Th., Mar. 1, 1918); subsequently was engaged by David Belasco to play in a benefit performance, by Lewis and Gordon for a vaudeville playlet, and by Henry Miller for a road tour of *Come Out of the Kitchen* (Wilmington, Del., Sept. 25, 1918); toured in *Friendly Enemies* (one-night stands, Dec. 25, 1918–May 1919); and in *Toby's Bow*; during the actor's strike, was stage manager for all-star Equity benefits (Tomaschefsky's Playhouse, N.Y.C., Aug.–Sept. 1919).

He appeared as Vincent Moretti in *Forbidden* (Manhattan Opera House, N.Y.C., Dec. 20, 1919); was engaged by the Jessie Bonstelle New Stock Company for the summer (Detroit, Mich., May 20, 1920); was stage manager for *Wake Up, Jonathan!* (Henry Miller's Th., N.Y.C., Jan. 17, 1921); played Acis in *Back to Methuselah* (Garrick Th., Feb. 27, 1922); Eugene Huckins in *A Square Peg* (Punch and Judy Th., Jan. 27, 1923); a Lord and Jacques in *As You Like It* (44 St. Th., Apr. 23, 1923); the Student in *The Spook Sonata* (Provincetown Playhouse, Jan. 5, 1924); Colonel Howard in *Fashion* (Provincetown Playhouse, Feb. 3, 1924); Romeo in a stock production of *Romeo and Juliet* (Mariarden, N.H., July 19, 1924).

Mr. Abel played Ted in *The Crime in the Whistler Room* (Provincetown Playhouse, N.Y.C., Oct. 9, 1924); Olson in *S.S. Glencairn* (Provincetown Playhouse, Nov. 3, 1924); a Sheriff in *Desire Under the Elms* (Greenwich Village Th., Nov. 11, 1924); Raul in *Beyond* (Provincetown Playhouse, Jan. 26, 1925); Armand Blondeau in *Michel Auclair* (Provincetown Playhouse, Mar. 4, 1925); Sir Sampson Legend in *Love for Love* (Greenwich Village Th., Mar. 31, 1925); Carl Behrend in *The Enemy* (Times Square Th., Oct. 20, 1925); Hortensio in *The Taming of the Shrew* (Klaw, Dec. 18, 1925); and Dermot McDermot in *Hangman's House* (Forrest, Dec. 16, 1926); followed Donn Cook (Dec. 1926) as John Roberts in *Seed of the Brute* (Little, Nov. 1, 1926); succeeded Robert Keith (Jan. 1927) as Robert Mayo in *Beyond the Horizon* (Mansfield, Nov. 20, 1926); played Henry Bascom in *The House of Women* (Maxine Elliott's Th., Oct. 3, 1927); Wayne Trenton, III, in *Skidding* (Bijou, May 21, 1928); Olson in *S.S. Glencairn* (Provincetown Playhouse, Jan. 9, 1929); played Trigorin in *The Seagull* (Comedy, Apr. 9, 1929); and made his London debut as Michael Jeffery in *Coquette* (Apollo, June 3, 1929).

He played Elmer Gray in *First Mortgage* (Royale, N.Y.C., Oct. 10, 1929); Vaska in *At the Bottom* (Waldorf, Jan. 9, 1920); Trigorin in *The Seagull* (Waldorf, Feb. 25, 1930); George in *I Love an Actress* (Times Square Th., Sept. 17, 1931); Orrin Mannon in *Mourning Becomes Electra* (Alvin, May 9, 1932); Jimmie Lee in *When Ladies Meet* (Royale, Oct. 26, 1933); Andre Roussel in *The Drums Begin* (Shubert, Nov. 24, 1933); Morgan Chadwick in *Wife Insurance* (Ethel Barrymore Th., Apr. 12, 1934); Dr. Linton in *Invitation to a Murder* (Masque, May 17, 1934); Jonathan Crale in *Merrily We Roll Along* (Music Box, Sept. 29, 1934); and Nathaniel McQuestion in *The Wingless Victory* (Empire, Dec. 23, 1936).

Mr. Abel portrayed John Shand in *What Every Woman Knows* (County Th., Suffern, N.Y., Sept. 1938); David Hudson in *The Birds Stopped Singing* (Princeton, N.J., Jan. 1939); toured as Cedric Trent in *West of Broadway* (Mar. 1939); played Benjamin de Wolfe in *No Code to Guide Her* (Playhouse, N.Y.C., Nov. 1939); Clement Waterlow in *The Mermaids Singing* (Empire, Nov. 28, 1945); Charles Burnett in *Parlor Story* (Biltmore, Mar. 4, 1947); and Dr. Jay Stewart in *The Biggest Thief in Town* (Mansfield, Mar. 30, 1949).

He played Claudius in *Hamlet* (Kronborg Castle, Elsinore, Denmark; toured Germany, June 1949); Gavin Leon Andree in *The Wisteria Trees* (Martin Beck Th., Mar. 29, 1950); Capt. Mike Dorgan in *The Long Watch* (Lyceum, Mar. 20, 1952); was Narrator for the Philadelphia Orchestra's production of *King David* (Carnegie Hall, Apr. 18, 1952); played the title role in *Noah* (Parkland Coll., Seattle, Wash., May 14, 1953); and appeared in *Under Milk Wood* (Kaufmann Aud., N.Y.C., Feb. 8, 1954).

He played Jim Dougherty in *The Pleasure of His Company* (Longacre, Oct. 22, 1958); Nat Miller in *Take Me Along* (State Fair Music Hall, Dallas, Tex., July 6, 1962); Lew in *Night Life* (Brooks Atkinson Th., N.Y.C., Oct. 23, 1962); Malvolio in *Twelfth Night* (State Coll., Fresno, Calif., Dec. 1, 1963); Argan in *The Imaginary Invalid* (Univ. of Delaware, Newark, Del., Feb. 29, 1964); Bill Hastings in *The Ninety-Day Mistress* (Biltmore, N.Y.C., Nov. 6, 1972); Chief Justice Harry Griffin in *A Conflict of Interest* (Arena Th., Washington, D.C., Feb. 4, 1972); in which he also toured (Summer 1972); in *Saturday, Sunday, Monday* (1974); and toured as Mark Walters in *In Praise of Love* (Summer 1975).

Films. Mr. Abel has appeared in *Three Musketeers* (RKO, 1935); *The Witness Chair* (RKO, 1936); *Racket Busters* (WB, 1938); *Arise, My Love* (Par., 1940); *Holiday Inn* (Par., 1942); *Star Spangled Rhythm* (Par., 1942); *13 Rue Madeleine* (Fox, 1946); *The Kid from Brooklyn* (RKO, 1946); *So This Is Love* (WB, 1953); *Island in the Sky* (WB, 1953); *Night People* (20th-Fox, 1954); *Indian Fighter* (UA, 1955); *The Steel Jungle* (WB, 1956); *Bernadine* (20th-Fox, 1957); and *Raintree County* (MGM, 1957).

Television. Mr. Abel first appeared on television for General Electric Co. (Schenectady to Elmira Network, Apr. 1944); performed on *Gaslight* (NBC, 1948); *The Enchanted* (NBC, 1961); East Side/West Side (CBS, 1964); and starred in the Natl. Council of Senior Citizens' *We've Come of Age* (1973).

ABELES, JOSEPH. Theatrical photographer. b. July 7, 1911, New York City, to Samuel and Anna Abeles. Father, salesman. Attended New Utrecht H.S., Brooklyn, N.Y. Served WW II, ATC, CBI. Address: (home) 333 W. 56th St., New York, NY 10019, tel. (212) 581-3244; (bus.) 351 W. 54th St., New York, NY 10019, tel. (212) 245-7465.

Theatre. Mr. Abeles established in 1935 his own photography studio, Talbot Studio, and with Leo and Sy Friedman formed Friedman-Abeles (1957), photographers of stage productions and personalities, as well as magazine photo stories about theatrical subjects.

Recreation. Reading, swimming, music.

ABELSON, HOPE. Producer. b. Hope Janice Altman, Sept. 21, 1919, Chicago, Ill., to Gilbert and Sadie (Lesem) Altman. Father, manufacturer. Grad. Hyde Park H.S., Chicago, 1936; attended Northwestern Univ., 1936–37; Univ. of Chicago, 1937–38; Art Inst. of Chicago, 1939–40. Studied acting with drama coaches in Chicago. Married Jan. 15, 1939, to Lester S. Abelson, business executive; one son, one daughter. Served Amer. Red Cross, Chicago Chapter, as entertainment chairman, WW II. Member of League of New York Theatres. Address: 75 Maple Mill Rd., Glencoe, IL 60022, tel. (312) 835-1476.

Theatre. Mrs. Abelson's first assignment in the theatre was as associate producer of the Chevy Chase Summer Th. (Wheeling, Ill., Summers 1948–50); subsequently she was associate producer of the Music Th. (Highland Park, Ill., Summers 1950–51); and executive producer (Summer 1952).

Her first N.Y.C. assignment was as production assistant to Cheryl Crawford for *Camino Real* (National, Mar. 19, 1953); followed by production assistant for *Madam, Will You Walk?* (Phoenix, Dec. 1, 1953), and *The Golden Apple* (Phoenix, Mar. 11, 1954). Ethel Linder Reiner, in association with Mrs. Abelson, produced *The Rainmaker* (Cort, Oct. 28, 1954); Mrs. Abelson was producer of *The Egghead* (Ethel Barrymore Th., Oct. 9, 1957); and co-producer of *The Royal Hunt of the Sun* (ANTA Th., Oct. 26, 1965).

Recreation. Skiing, tennis, collecting art and antiques.

ABEND, SHELDON. Literary representative. b. June 13, 1929, New York City, to Morris and Betty (Rosonoff) Abend. Father, union executive; mother, real estate broker. Grad. William Howard Taft H.S., N.Y.C., 1946. Married June 1, 1952, to Dorothy Mulnick (marr. dis. 1960); one son. Served US Merchant Marine. Member of Authors Research Co. (pres., chmn. of bd., 1957, exec. dir. 1960); Million Dollar Play Library (fdr., 1961); Guild for Authors Heirs (fdr., pres., 1962; 1970–72); AR; Natl. Showmens Assn. Address: 52 Vanderbilt Ave., New York, NY 10017, tel. (212) MU 6-6333.

Pre-Theatre. Tugboat fireman, marine engineer, maritime union organizer, union negotiator.

Theatre. Mr. Abend was vice-president of the Rosecroft Music Circus, Maryland, where he also co-directed and co-produced *Du Barry Was a Lady*,

Brigadoon, Show Boat, The Pajama Game, Jamaica, Li'l Abner and *Ziegfeld Follies Revue* (June–Sept. 1959).

He has been president of the American Play Co., Inc., a literary agency in N.Y.C.; serves as copyright clearance specialist for major film studios and motion picture and television packagers; was consultant to the Zane Grey Corp. (1969–72); special literary and production consultant to Romer Zane Grey on theatrical developments of Zane Grey properties; and literary consultant and product negotiator for Robert Fryer (1972).

Recreation. Riding, hunting, fishing, collects rare literary documents and manuscripts.

ABLE, WILL B. Actor, comedian, choreographer, singer, dancer, mime. b. Nov. 21, 1923, Providence, R.I., to William and Rebecca (Lyman) Able. Grad. Mt. Pleasant H.S., Providence; studied at Lavoie Sch. of Dance; and with Emilo de Petrillo, Providence; studied drama with Betty Cashman; dance at the Amer. Sch. of Ballet; Lou Wills Sch. of Acrobatics, N.Y.C. Also trained in tap, Spanish, Oriental, modern-jazz, eccentric-legomania. Married Nov. 30, 1953, to Graziella, acrobatic and can-can dancer; one daughter. Member of AEA; AGVA; AFTRA; SAG. Address: 420 W. 58th St., New York, NY 10019, tel. (212) CI 6-7466.

Pre-Theatre. Farmer.

Theatre. Mr. Able made his professional debut in *Hit the Deck* (State Fair Music Hall, Dallas, Tex., 1941); and played Jacob Yoder in *Plain and Fancy* (Mark Hellinger Th., Jan. 27, 1955); the Usher in the pre-Bway tour of *Midgie Purvis* (1960–61); appeared in five roles in *Bella* (Gramercy Arts, N.Y.C., Nov. 16, 1961); understudied Ray Bolger and Fritz Weaver in *All American* (Winter Garden, Mar. 19, 1962); was in *Hellza-Poppin' '67* (Garden of Stars, Expo '67, Montreal, Quebec, Canada); played Dwight Berkwit in *Coco* (Mark Hellinger Th., Dec. 18, 1969) and on tour (1970–71); and was in *Snow White Goes West* (Mark Taper Forum, Los Angeles, Calif., 1971).

In stock, Mr. Able first appeared as Charley in *Where's Charley?* at Indianapolis, Ind., in 1955 and has since played the part in theatres throughout the US, as well as directing many productions of the musical. He also played Bill Delroy in *Rosalie* (Indianapolis, 1956); Bilge in *Hit the Deck* (Indianapolis, 1957); Silas in *Naughty Marietta* (Pittsburgh Civic Light Opera, Pa., 1958); Will Parker in *Oklahoma!* (Indianapolis, 1958; Casa Mañana, Fort Worth, Tex., 1959; Starlight Th., Kansas City, Mo., 1960); the Scarecrow in *The Wizard of Oz* (Casa Mañana, 1961; St. Louis Municipal Opera, 1962; Starlight Th., 1963); an Ugly Sister in *Cinderella* (St. Louis Municipal Opera, 1961; Mineola Th., N.Y., Dec. 11, 1965); Boris in *Can-Can* (Pittsburgh Civic Light Opera, 1962; Pocono Playhouse, Mountainhome, Pa.); directed and staged dances for *The Wizard of Oz* (Hawaii, 1968); played Captain Hook and Mr. Darling in the NBC Arena Production of *Peter Pan* throughout the US and Canada (1973–74); the Parson in *The Wayward Way* (Meadowbrook Dinner Th., N.J., July 1974 and pre-Bway tour). He has also appeared on stages in many cities and in summer theatres in *The Red Mill, The Fortune Teller, Babes in Toyland, Dame Wiggins' Dilemma, Show Boat, Irma La Douce,* and *Follies 68, Follies 69,* and *Follies 70.*

Films. Mr. Able played the role of Clyde in *The Night They Raided Minsky's* (UA, 1968) and was Harvey in *Agnes,* for which he also wrote two songs.

Television. Mr. Able has appeared on Chance of a Lifetime (1952); as Blooper the Clown on Super Circus (ABC, 1955); Suspense (1955); as Hannigan on the Sergeant Bilko Show (NBC, 1955–56); on the Arthur Murray Dance Party (1955, 1956, 1958); played in *He Who Gets Slapped* (Play of the Week, WNTA, 1956); *High Button Shoes* (1957); appeared on Omnibus (1958); played in *Mister Broadway* (1958); appeared on Your Hit Parade (1958–59); *The Taming of the Shrew* (Hallmark Hall of Fame, NBC, 1959); Agnes de Mille's *Gold Rush* (1959); *Hansel and Gretel* (1959); Jackie Gleason Show (CBS, 1960); and Steve Allen Show (1960).

As a member of the Prince Street Players (CBS), Mr. Able played Antonio in *Pinocchio* (Dec. 26, 1965); the Giant in *Jack and the Bean Stalk* (Apr. 8, 1966); the Emperor in *The Emperor's New Clothes* (Sept. 4, 1967); and the Genie in *Aladdin and the Magic Lamp* (Dec. 1967). He appeared in the television film *Carnival,* on the Kraft and Alcoa Aluminum shows (both NBC), on Truth or Consequences and various panel and talk shows; as Funshine on Funshine Saturday Morning (ABC); as the Reverend Felcher on All in the Family (CBS); on the special *Hellzapoppin'* (ABC Comedy Hour, Mar. 1972); as Gordon on the Doris Day Show (CBS 1973); and on Everything Goes (Toronto, Canada, 1974).

Night Clubs. He has appeared at the following N.Y.C. hotels: Plaza, Waldorf, and New Yorker; as well as hotels and clubs throughout the US, in Canada and England, both as solo performer and with his wife.

Awards. Mr. Able received the Casa Mañana Award for his portrayal of the Scarecrow in *The Wizard of Oz* (1961). The Prince Street Players won a Congressional award for the best children's show on television.

Recreation. Art, carpentry, gardening, swimming.

ABORN, LOUIS H. Executive. b. Louis Henry Aborn, Feb. 28, 1912, New York City, to Sargent and Hattie (Anthony) Aborn. Father, co-owner Aborn Opera Co. Grad. Fieldston Sch., N.Y.C., 1930; Columbia Univ., Certificate in Bus. Studies 1933. Married June 23, 1946, to Hermine Friedman; one son, one daughter. Relative in theatre: uncle, Milton Aborn. Served US Army, Signal Corps, 1942–46; rank, Tech. Sgt. Member of Natl. Panel of Amer. Arbitration Assn.; Society of Authors Representatives (member board of dir., 1961–63). Address: (home) 46 Wilshire Rd., Greenwich, CT 06830, tel. (203) 661-4046; (bus.) 757 Third Ave., New York, NY 10017, tel. (212) MU 8-2525.

Mr. Aborn has been associated with the Tams-Witmark Music Library, Inc., since 1930, and has been president since 1956.

The Tams-Witmark Music Library, Inc. represents authors and composers of Bway musicals; licenses stage, radio, television, and foreign language presentations; creates and adapts literary materials; and supplies necessary musical and dialogue material in connection with such licenses.

Mr. Aborn was manager of the Arthur W. Tams Costume Co. (1930–42).

ABRAMS, DOLORES. Teacher, theatre administrator. b. Dolores May Abrams, Apr. 18, 1927, Santa Cruz, Calif., to Hyman L. and Mildred Lawrence Abrams; father, merchant; mother, housewife. Grad. Univ. of California at Berkeley, B.A. 1949; Stanford Univ., M.A. 1956; Univ. of North Carolina, L.D.A. 1958. Studied directing with Henry Schnitzler and Arthur Luce Klein, both at Berkeley, with F. Cowles Strickland at Stanford, and with Samuel Selden at Univ. of North Carolina. Member of ATA (natl. chmn., Two-Year College Project, 1962–69; dir., 1966–69; exec. comm., 1967–69); Natl. Assn. of Schools of Theatre (secy., 1970–74); Univ. and College Theatre Assn. (vice-pres. for theatre administration, research and development, 1970–73); Northern California chapter of ATA (pres., 1971–72; secy., 1967–69); California Educational Theatre Assn. (exec. comm., 1971–72); Northern California Junior College Theatre Assn. (founding pres., 1963–65); Delta Kappa Gamma. Address: (home) 1036 Laurent St., Santa Cruz, CA 95060, tel. (408) 423-2892; (bus.) Dept. of Drama, Cabrillo College, Aptos, CA 95003, tel. (408) 475-6000.

Theatre. Miss Abrams's first theatrical work was done in college, when she appeared as a lady in waiting in a production of *Saint Joan* at Berkeley in 1947; two years later she directed scenes from *Liliom,* also at Berkeley. During the summer of 1950 she was an acting apprentice with the Peterborough (N.H.) Players, appearing as Diana Dream and Dolores D. Dolores in *On the Town.* In 1953, she was stage manager and understudy for a production of *The Glass Menagerie* put on by The Players and sponsored by the US State Dept. and Eleanor Roosevelt. Miss Abrams toured the Scandinavian countries with this company (Sept.–Dec. 1953). She performed with the Holiday Summer Theatre in California in 1954, appearing as Ruth in *Dear Ruth,* Alison in *Lady in the Dark,* and Liserl in *Candle-Light.* In 1954–55, Miss Abrams was a director for the Santa Cruz Community Theatre under the city adult education program and for the Santa Cruz Children's Theatre. In 1956–57, she taught speech and drama at the Helen Bush-Parkside School, Seattle, Wash., and in 1957–58 she was managing director, The Thalian Association, Wilmington, N.C., where she directed *Ah, Wilderness!* and *The Desperate Hours.*

In 1959, with the establishment of Cabrillo College, Aptos, Calif., Miss Abrams became teacher of acting and theatre management in the Dept. of Drama, of which she is chairman. Productions she has directed at Cabrillo include *The Diary of Anne Frank* (1960), *Our Town* (1961), *The Lark* (1963), *Ondine* (1963), *Look Homeward, Angel* (1964), *The Taming of the Shrew* (1964), *The Lady's Not for Burning* (1965), *Antigone* of Sophocles (1965), *Rhinoceros* (1966), *Inherit the Wind* (1966), *As You Like It* (1967), *Becket* (1968), *The Madwoman of Chaillot* (with guest artist-in-residence Lilia Skala, 1968), *The Marriage of Mr. Mississippi* (1969), *We Bombed in New Haven* (regional finalist, American College Theatre Festival, 1970), *School for Scandal* (1971), *The Crucible* (with guest artist-in-residence Carl Vetz, 1971), *The Prime of Miss Jean Brodie* (1972), *Twelfth Night* (regional finalist, American College Theatre Festival, 1972), *A Flea in Her Ear* (1973), and *Indians* (1973).

Other Activities. Miss Abrams has been speech coach for Miss California since 1965.

Published Works. Miss Abrams is author of *Theatre in the Junior College* (ATA, 1965), articles that have appeared in *UCTA Newsletter* and *Western Speech,* and drama reviews and travel articles published in the Santa Cruz *Sentinel* since 1955.

Recreation. She is "an avid duplicate bridge player" and a member of the American Contract Bridge League with the rank of senior master. Travel and writing are her other recreations.

ABRAMSON, CHARLES H. Producer. b. Charles Harrison Abramson, Feb. 2, 1902, Buffalo, N.Y., to Simon and Dora Abramson. Father, builder. Grad. Cornell Univ., LL.B. 1922. Served US Army, Field Artillery; rank, Lt. Address: 44 W. 44th St., New York, NY 10036, tel. (212) MU 2-8060.

Pre-Theatre. Attorney, newspaper publisher, book publisher.

Mr. Abramson is an associate, and the American representative, of Paris Film Production (1968–to date). Previously, he was an associate (1944–1968) of Charles K. Feldman's Famous Artists Agency, and Famous Artists Productions.

Theatre. Mr. Abramson produced *Collette* (Forrest, Philadelphia, Feb. 9, 1927); and *Taza* (Jamaica Cort Th., Brooklyn, Jan. 30, 1928); with Harry L. Cort, produced *Veneer* (Sam H. Harris Th., N.Y.C., Nov. 12, 1929); with Jess Smith, *The Web* (Morosco, June 27, 1932); with Mr. Cort, by arrangement with E. Steuart-Tavant, *All the King's Horses* (Shubert, Jan. 30, 1934); and independently, *Orchids Preferred* (Imperial, May 11, 1937).

Films. While with Famous Artists Productions, he was associated with the production of *The Group* (UA, 1966); *The 7th Dawn* (UA, 1964); *What's New, Pussycat* (UA, 1965); and *Casino Royale* (Col. 1967). Recent releases of Paris Film Production include *Belle de Jour* (Allied Artists, 1968); and *The Loves of Isadora* (U, 1969).

ABRAVANEL, MAURICE. Musical director, conductor, educator. b. Maurice de Abravanel, Jan. 6, 1903, Salonica, Greece, to Edouard and Rachel (Bitty) de Abravanel. Attended Gymnasium, Lausanne, Switz., 1917–19; Univ. of

Lausanne, 1919–21; Univ. of Zurich, 1921–22. Studied music with E. Masson, Zurich; Kurt Weill, Berlin. Married 1947, to Lucy Carasso. Address: 1235 E. 7th St., Salt Lake City, UT 84105.

Theatre. Mr. Abravanel was the musical director of *Knickerbocker Holiday* (Ethel Barrymore Th., N.Y.C., Oct. 19, 1938); *Lady in the Dark* (Alvin, Jan. 23, 1941); *One Touch of Venus* (Imperial, Oct. 7, 1943); *The Seven Lively Arts* (Ziegfeld, Dec. 7, 1944); *The Firebrand of Florence* (Alvin, Mar. 22, 1945); *The Day Before Spring* (Natl., Nov. 22, 1945); *Street Scene* (Adelphi, Jan. 9, 1947) and *Regina* (46 St., Th., Oct. 31, 1949).

Mr. Abravanel has worked with opera and concert symphony music for many years, beginning in Europe. He was a musician in Zwickau, Ger. (Stadttheater, 1924–26); Lausanne, Switz. (Altenburg, 1926–29) and in Kassel, Ger. (1929–32). He has conducted all over Europe in such cities as Berlin, Ger.; Paris, Fr.; London, Eng.; and Rome, It.

With the British Natl. Opera Co. he toured Melbourne and Sydney (Austl.) as their musical director (1935), after which he went to the US where he became a conductor with the Metropolitan Opera Co. (N.Y.C., 1936–37); and subsequently for the Chicago (Ill.) Opera Co. (1940). During this time he was guest conductor in such US cities as N.Y.C.; Washington (D.C.); Pittsburgh (Pa.); and Cleveland (Ohio).

He became associated with the Natl. Opera Co. (Mexico City, 1945); became musical director of the Symphony Society (Sydney, Austl., 1946); returned to the US to be musical director and conductor of the Utah Symphony (Salt Lake City, 1947), and during the subsequent years he remained there, making many guest conducting appearances with orchestras in both the US and Europe.

Other Activities. Mr. Abravanel is a member of the National Council on the Arts, appointed by Pres. Nixon in 1970.

Discography. Mr. Abravanel conducted the Utah Symphony in the complete cycle of Mahler symphony recordings (Vanguard), the first American orchestra to have recorded the complete cycle.

Awards. He received the Antoinette Perry (Tony) Award for his musical direction of *Regina* (1950).

ACKLAND, RODNEY. Playwright, actor, screenwriter. b. May 18, 1908, to Edward and Diana (Lock) Ackland. Attended school, London, England. (Salesian College, 1915–1916; Balham Grammar Sch., 1916–1923; studied acting at the Central Sch. of Speech Training and Dramatic Art.) Married 1951 to Mab Lonsdale (dec. 1972). Member of British AEA. Address: c/o Eric Glass, Ltd., 28 Berkeley Sq., London, W.1, England.

Theatre. Mr. Ackland made his stage debut as Medvedieff in *The Lower Depths* (Gate Th. Studio, London, 1924); subsequently appeared with such repertory companies as J. B. Fagan's Oxford Players; played Lubin, Zozim, and the He-Ancient in *Back to Methuselah* (Masque, Edinburgh, Scotland); toured England in the title role in *Young Woodley* (1929); wrote *Improper People* (1929); *Marion-Ella* (1930); *Dance with No Music* (1930); *Strange Orchestra* (Embassy, London, June 30, 1931; revived St. Martin's, Sept. 27, 1932; Playhouse, N.Y.C., Nov. 28, 1933); and toured England in *Recipe for Murder* (Nov. 1932), and as Joseph in *Musical Chairs* (1933).

He adapted *Ballerina*, in which he played Paul (Gaiety, London, Oct. 1933); wrote *Birthday* in which he played Tony Willow (Cambridge, Feb. 1934); adapted *The White Guard* (Ambassadors', Mar. 11, 1934; revived Phoenix, Oct. 6, 1938); appeared as Tony in *Battle Royal* (Embassy, Apr. 1934); toured as Paul in *Ballerina* (1934); adapted *The Old Ladies* from Hugh Walpole's novel (New, Apr. 3, 1935; revived Lyric, Hammersmith, Oct. 4, 1950); retitled *Night in the House* for the N.Y.C. production (Booth, Nov. 7, 1935); wrote *After October*, in which he appeared as Oliver Nashwick (Arts, London, Feb. 21, 1936); *Plot Twenty-One* (1936); and adapted *Yes, My Darling Daughter* (1937), *Remembrance of Things Past* (1938), *Sixth Floor* (1939), and *Blossom Time* (Lyric, Mar. 17, 1942).

He directed *The Belle of New York* (Coliseum, Sept. 16, 1942); wrote *The Dark River*, which he also directed (Whitehall, Oct. 19, 1943); adapted *Crime and Punishment* (New, London, June 26, 1946; National, N.Y.C., Dec. 22, 1947); wrote with Robert Newton, *Cupid and Mars* (Arts, London, Oct. 1, 1947); adapted *The Diary of a Scoundrel* (Arts, London, Oct. 19, 1948; Phoenix, N.Y.C., Nov. 4, 1956); wrote *Before the Party*, based on Somerset Maugham's story (St. Martin's, London, Oct. 26, 1949); wrote with Robert Newton, *A Multitude of Sins* (1951); wrote *The Pink Room* or, *The Escapists* (Lyric, Hammersmith, June 18, 1952); wrote *A Dead Secret* (Piccadilly, May 30, 1957); and adapted *Farewell, Farewell Eugene* (Garrick, London, June 5, 1959; Helen Hayes Th., N.Y.C., Sept. 27, 1960).

Films. Mr. Ackland appeared in *The Case of Gabriel Perry* (British Lion, 1935). He wrote, with Emeric Pressburger, the scenario for *The Invaders* (Col., 1942), and collaborated on the screenplays for *Number 17* (BIP Wardour, 1932); *Bank Holiday* (Gainsborough, 1938; released in the US as *Three On a Weekend; The Silent Battle* (Pinebrook, 1939, released in the US as *Continental Express*); *George and Margaret* (WB, 1940); *49th Parallel* (Ortus, 1941); *Love Story* (Gainsborough, 1944; released in the US as *A Lady Surrenders*); *Uncensored* (20th-Fox, 1944); *Wanted for Murder* (20th-Fox, 1946); *Hatter's Castle* (Par., 1948); *Temptation Harbour* (Mono., 1949); *Bond Street* (Stratford, 1950); *Queen of Spades* (Stratford, 1950); *The Seddons; A Dead Secret;* and *The Other Palace* (1965).

ADAIR, YVONNE. Singer, actress, dancer. b. Yvonne Vivienne Bornshine, July 13, 1925, Plainfield, N.J., to Carl and Agnes (MacAndrew) Bornshine. Father, engineer, Grad. Nutley (N.J.) H.S.; attended Feagin Sch. of Dramatic Art, N.Y.C.; studied with Leola Carter, 1936–37; attended Boston (Mass.) Conservatory of Music, 1939–41; studied with Herb Green 1960–61. Married Apr. 30, 1950, to Harold J. Patterson. Member of AEA; AGVA; SAG; Eastern Star. Address: 11 Clyde Ct., Bergenfield, NJ tel. (201) DU 4-6046.

Theatre. Miss Adair first appeared on stage at the age of four in a vaudeville act, *Sunshine Kids* (Keith Circuit, 1929); subsequently toured Europe and Japan in *Hellzapoppin* (1942); and was understudy to Mary Martin as Annie Oakley in the national tour of *Annie Get Your Gun* (1947–48).

She made her N.Y.C., debut in the revue, *Lend an Ear* (National, Dec. 16, 1948); subsequently played Dorothy Shaw in *Gentlemen Prefer Blondes* (Ziegfeld, Dec. 8, 1949; Palace, Chicago, Ill., Sept. 20, 1951); toured in *On Your Toes* and *Girl Crazy* (Summer 1951); played Janice Dayton in the pre-Bway tour of *Silk Stockings* (Imperial, N.Y.C., Feb. 24, 1955); and appeared in stock productions at Swampscott, Mass. (1962).

Television. Miss Adair made guest appearances on the Milton Berle Show (NBC, 1948); Ed Sullivan Show (CBS, 1949); and Fred Waring Show (1949).

Night Clubs. Since 1942, Miss Adair has performed at the Cocoanut Grove (Boston, Mass.); Palmer House (Chicago); Zimmerman's, Carnaval, and Leon and Eddie's (N.Y.C.); and Bar of Music, 5 O'Clock Club, Clover Club, Olympia, and Saxony Hotel (Miami Beach, Fla.).

Awards. Miss Adair received the Donaldson Award for her performance in *Lend an Ear* (1948).

Recreation. Swimming, riding, painting.

ADAMS, BRET. Talent representative, literary agent. b. John Wallace Adams, Apr. 10, 1930, Memphis, Tenn., to Hugh Edward and Johnie Catherine (Wallace) Adams. Father, businessman. Grad. Castle Hts. Military Acad., Lebanon, Tenn., 1947; attended Emerson Coll., 1947; National Classic Acad., Pleasantville, N.Y., 1948. Served in US Army, 1951–53. Address: (home) 30 Fifth Ave., New York, NY 10011, tel. (212) GR 5-2055; (bus.) Bret Adams Ltd., 36 E. 61st St., New York, NY 10021, tel. (212) 752-7864; Bret Adams Ltd., 8440 Sunset Blvd., Los Angeles, CA 90069.

Pre-Theatre. Newspaperman.

Theatre. Mr. Adams was briefly an actor in the early 1950s; toured with Clare Tree Major Children's Th., National Classic Th. In the army, he was attached to the Public Information Office, Berlin, Germany, where he publicized Berlin Festival productions of *Porgy and Bess* and the NY City Ballet.

Later, he was associate producer, with Sanford Leigh, of John Gielgud's *Ages of Man* (46 St. Th., N.Y.C., Dec. 28, 1958), which subsequently toured the US and Canada and was recorded. In the mid-1960s, Mr. Adams left the theatrical agent field and was producer of the Corning (N.Y.) Summer Th., production manager of American Conservatory Th., now situated in San Francisco, and operated the first musical tent theatre outside of the US, Bret Adams's Warringah Mall Festival, Sydney, Australia.

Returning to the US in 1966, Mr. Adams was associated with personal manager Glenn Rose on the West Coast; he then returned to New York, where he opened his own literary and talent agency in 1972.

Films. He appeared in *Desperate Moments* (Rank, 1952).

ADAMS, EDIE. Actress, singer, entertainer. b. Edith Adams Enke, Apr. 16, Kingston, Pa., to Sheldon and Ada (Adams) Enke. Father, real estate broker. Attended Juilliard Sch. of Music, N.Y.C., 1946–50; Columbia Univ., N.Y.C., 1947–48; Traphagen Sch. of Fashion Design, N.Y.C., 1956. Married Sept. 12, 1954, to Ernie Kovacs, actor, performer (dec. Jan. 13, 1962); three daughters; married Aug. 16, 1964, to Martin Hager Mills, music publisher (marr. dis. Apr. 1972); one daughter; married June 5, 1972, to M. Pete Candoli, musician. Member of SAG; AEA; AGVA; AFTRA; WGA; Designers Guild; ASCAP; AFM. Address: c/o William Morris Agency, 1350 Ave. of the Americas, New York, NY.

Theatre. Miss Adams made her professional debut in a stock production of *Blithe Spirit* (Chapel Th., Ridgewood, N.J., July 1947); first appeared on Bway as Eileen in *Wonderful Town* (Winter Garden, Feb. 25, 1953); played Daisy Mae in *Li'l Abner* (St. James, Nov. 15, 1956); appeared in stock productions of *The Merry Widow* (Packard Music Hall, Warren, Ohio, June 1959), *Sweet Bird of Youth* and *Free as a Bird* (N.J., 1960), and *Rain* (Packard Music Hall, Warren, Ohio, July–Aug. 1963).

She appeared in *Eccentricities of a Nightingale: The Sun That Warms the Dark* (Tappan Zee Playhouse, Nyack, N.Y., June 25, 1964); played La Mome Pistache in *Can-Can* (Starlight Musicals, Indianapolis, Ind., July 19, 1965); Ella Peterson in *Bells Are Ringing* (Chastain Memorial Amphitheatre, Atlanta, Ga., July 26, 1966); appeared in *Mame* and played Billie Dawn in *Born Yesterday* (both Colonie Summer Th., Latham, N.Y.; Shady Grove Music Fair, Washington, D.C., Summer 1969); played the title role in *La Périchole* (Opera House, Seattle, Wash., Oct. 1972); and toured summer music fairs as Reno Sweeney in *Anything Goes* (Summer 1973).

Films. She appeared in *The Apartment* (UA, 1960); *Lover, Come Back* (U, 1961); *Call Me Bwana* (UA, 1962); *Under the Yum Yum Tree* (Col., 1963); *Love with the Proper Stranger* (Par., 1963); *It's a Mad, Mad, Mad, Mad World* (UA, 1963); *The Best Man* (UA, 1964); *Made in Paris* (MGM, 1966); *The Oscar* (Embassy, 1966); and *The Honey Pot* (UA, 1967).

Television. Miss Adams made her television debut in Talent Scouts (CBS, 1949); subsequently appeared on the Ernie Kovacs Show (NBC, CBS, Dumont, 1951–56); *Cinderella* (CBS, Mar. 31, 1957); *The Falling Angel* (GE Th., CBS, Nov. 16, 1958); her own shows, Here's Edie (ABC, 1962) and Edie Adams Show (ABC, 1963); the Bob Hope (CBS), Perry Como (NBC), Dinah Shore (NBC), Ed Sullivan (CBS), Jack Paar (NBC), Red Skelton (CBS), Sammy Davis (ABC), Danny Kaye (CBS), Johnny Carson (NBC), Mike Douglas (Ind.), Pat Boone (NBC), and Dean Martin (NBC) shows; in *Wonderful World of Burlesque* (Danny Thomas Special, NBC, Mar. 14, 1965); and the Colgate Comedy Hour (NBC, May 11, 1967).

Night Clubs. Miss Adams made her first night club appearance at the One Two Club (Toronto, Canada, 1951); subsequently appeared at the Persian Room (Plaza Hotel, N.Y.C., 1955); the Tropicana (Las Vegas, Nev., 1957); Harrah's Club (Lake Tahoe, Nev., 1958); the Thunderbird (Las Vegas, Nev., 1960); and the Hotel Riviera (Las Vegas, Nev., 1963). Other night club appearances include The Latin Quarter (N.Y.C., May 6, 1965); Americana Hotel (N.Y.C., June 1966); Cork Club (Houston, Tex., Oct. 22, 1966); Desert Inn (Las Vegas, Nev., Mar. 1967); Copacabana (N.Y.C., Apr. 1967); Palmer House (Chicago, Ill., Oct. 1969); Empire Room (Chicago, Ill., Jan. 1973); and Blue Room (Shoreham Hotel, Washington, D.C., Apr. 1973).

Awards. She received the *Theatre World* Award for her performance as Eileen in *Wonderful Town* (1953).

Recreation. Dressmaking, interior decorating.

ADAMS, LEE. Lyricist. b. Aug. 14, 1924, Mansfield, Ohio, to Leopold and Florence (Ellis) Adams. Father, physician. Grad. Mansfield H.S., 1941; Ohio State Univ., B.A. 1949; Columbia Univ., M.Sc. (journalism) 1950. Married July 21, 1957, to Rita Reich; one daughter. Served US Army, 1943–46; 14th Armored Div., ETO; rank, Cpl. Member of ASCAP, AGAC, Dramatists Guild. Address: 35 E. 85th St., New York, NY 10028.

Pre-Theatre. Edited and wrote articles for *Pageant, This Week* and local radio programs.

Theatre. Mr. Adams contributed material to the *Shoestring Revue* (President Th., Feb. 28, 1955); additional lyrics to *The Littlest Revue* (Phoenix, May 22, 1956); sketches to *Shoestring '57* (Barbizon-Plaza, Nov. 5, 1956); sketches to the revue *Kaleidoscope* (Provincetown Playhouse, June 13, 1957); wrote the lyrics for *Bye Bye Birdie* (Martin Beck Th., N.Y.C., Apr. 14, 1960); *All American* (Winter Garden, Mar. 19, 1962); *Golden Boy* (Majestic, 1964); *It's a Bird, It's a Plane, It's Superman* (Alvin, 1966); *Applause* (Palace, 1970); and *I and Albert* (Piccadilly Th., London, England, 1972).

Films. *Bye Bye Birdie* (Col., 1963).

Awards. He won Antoinette Perry (Tony) Awards for *Bye Bye Birdie* (1961) and for *Applause* (1970).

Recreation. Reading.

ADAMS, ROBERT K. Producer, actor, director. b. Oct. 29, 1909, Flint, Mich., to Lynne and Josephine Adams. Father, salesman. Grad. Flint H.S., 1926; Univ. of Michigan, A.B. 1930, M.A. (Speech) 1931, Ph.D. studies, 1932–33. Married Jan. 5, 1942, to Rosalind Gould; two daughters. Served USN, 1942–46; rank, Lt. Comdr. Member of AEA; SAG; AFTRA; Beta Theta Pi. Address: (home) 506 E. 89th St., New York, NY 10028, tel. (212) RE 7-7291; (bus.) tel. (212) RE 7-7125.

Pre-Theatre. Teacher of speech and drama at Flint Jr. College; owner and operator of a dairy and a machine shop.

Theatre. Mr. Adams made his theatre debut as a walk-on with the Wright Players in *Lombardi, Ltd.* (Palace Th., Flint, Mich., May 1925); played an Officer in *Arms and the Man* (Ann Arbor Drama Festival, Mich., Apr. 1928); appeared in summer stock at the Northport (Mich.) Playhouse (1930); with the Bonstelle Players in Detroit; and toured in *Murder in the Old Red Barn* and others, in repertory with the Jitney Players (Summer 1934).

He made his first N.Y.C. appearance as Green in *Richard II* (St. James Th., Feb. 5, 1937); subsequently played a Banished Duke in *As You Like It* (Ritz, Oct. 30, 1937); directed *Fanny's First Play* (Amateur Comedy Club, N.Y.C., 1940); the revue, *Around in Circles* (Hexagon Players, Washington, D.C., 1940); was actor-manager for the Eaglesmere (Pa.) Players (1940, 1941); played the Policeman in *First Stop to Heaven* (Windsor, N.Y.C., Jan. 5, 1941); directed the Univ. of Michigan Mimes Opera male revue (Ann Arbor, Dec. 1941); was producer-manager of the Flint (Mich.) Musical Tent Th. (Summers 1954, 1958); producer for the Detroit Music Circus (Summers 1957, 1958); assistant producer for the Lyric Circus Light Opera Assn. (Skaneateles, N.Y., Summer 1959); producer for *Say, Darling* (Summer tour, 1959); directed *The Tattooed Countess* (Barbizon-Plaza, N.Y.C., Apr. 13, 1961); and adapted and produced *Tom Sawyer* for children (Flint, Mich.); and has directed children's theatre productions for the Junior League (Montclair, N.J.; Flint and Lansing, Mich.).

Mr. Adams was president of Harnick-Adams Productions, producers of such children's theatre plays as *Young Abe Lincoln, Young Tom Edison, Young Jefferson* and *Magic in King Arthur's Court.* He is president of the Masque and Mime Theatre Foundation, presenting educational musicals for jr. and sr. high schools. He is also on the board of directors of the Producers Association for Young America, a company that presents plays and musicals for elementary grades.

Films. Mr. Adams made film shorts on Long Island, N.Y., including *Christie Comedies.*

Television and Radio. He wrote and directed the radio programs, Meet Your Navy (ABC), Skyhigh (NBC), and Meet the Admiral (CBS); and wrote for the series, Stories of Escape (NBC). Mr. Adams played Patrick Briggs in the radio serial, Life and Loves of Dr. Susan (CBS, 1938–41); played in Duffy's Tavern (NBC); The Goldbergs (CBS); Norman Corwin Presents (CBS); Hilltop House (NBC); and Author's Playhouse. From 1946–50, he was associated with the NBC production department. In 1951, he became associated with the Gale Agency, N.Y.C., where he was in charge of the radio and television department. One of the programs he developed for radio was Star Playhouse (NBC); for television, the Jane Pickens Show (NBC, 1951–53) and the Lili Palmer Show (1953). In 1953, he formed the Robert K. Adams Productions Co. which produced dramatic and variety television package programs.

Other Activities. Mr. Adams taught a course in radio production and in radio acting in the University Extension Division, Columbia Univ. (1947–48).

Awards. Mr. Adams' production, *The Best Plays* radio series, which he developed while at NBC, won the Radio Critics Award for best dramatic series (1950).

ADAMS, ROGER. Composer. b. Roger Robert Adams, Sept. 11, 1917, Maidenhead, Eng., to Bob and Odette (Myrtil) Adams. Father, entertainer; mother, actress. Grad. Fessenden Sch., West Newton, Mass., 1932; attended Phillips Andover Acad., 1934–36. Studied music with Felix Fox, Boston; Jacques Gordon, N.Y.C.; Olga Steeb Music Sch. and Henry Mancini, Los Angeles, Calif. Served US Army, Special Services, 1942–46; rank, PFC. Member of AFM, Locals 47 and 802. Address: c/o Chez Odette, New Hope, PA 18938, tel. (215) VO 2-2432.

Theatre. Mr. Adams composed incidental music for the US Army Special Services (Honolulu, Hawaii), for the following productions: in 1943, *Macbeth, Hey Mac!,* and *Free for All;* in 1944, *Hamlet* and *Night Must Fall;* and in 1945, *Jumpin' Jupiter.* At the Honolulu (Hawaii) Community Th., he composed the musical scores for *Alice in Wonderland* (1947), *The Bluebird* (1948), and *49th St. Revue* (1949).

He made his N.Y.C. debut as the composer of incidental music for Maurice Evans's *Hamlet* (Columbus Circle Th., Dec. 13, 1945); arranged the dance music for *Three Wishes for Jamie* (Mark Hellinger Th., Mar. 21, 1952); composed and arranged the dance music for *Buttrio Square* (New Century, Oct. 14, 1952); composed the dance music for *Me and Juliet* (Majestic, May 28, 1953); *Carnival in Flanders* (New Century, Sept. 8, 1952); did the dance music arrangements for *The Pajama Game* (St. James, May 13, 1954); with Donald Pippin, devised dance music for *Ankles Aweigh* (Mark Hellinger Th., April 18, 1955); composed dance music for *Damn Yankees* (46 St. Th., May 5, 1955); *Happy Hunting* (Majestic, Dec. 6, 1956); *New Girl in Town* (46 St. Th., May 14, 1957); *Redhead* (46 St. Th., Feb. 5, 1959); composed and arranged dance music for *Once Upon a Mattress* (Alvin, Nov. 25, 1959); composed and arranged dance music with Trude Rittman for *Peter Pan* (Mary Martin) (Winter Garden, Oct. 20, 1954); composed and arranged dance music for *Ben Franklin in Paris* (Lunt-Fontanne Th., Oct. 27, 1964); *Mame* (Winter Garden, May 24, 1966); *Illya Darling* (Mark Hellinger Th., Apr. 11, 1967); *Mata Hari* (National, Washington, D.C., Nov. 18, 1967); and *A Mother's Kisses* (Shubert Th., New Haven, Conn., Sept. 23, 1968).

Films. Mr. Adams composed the dance music for *My Sister Eileen* (Col., 1955); *The Pajama Game* (WB, 1957); *Looking for Love* (MGM, 1963); and *Damn Yankees* (WB, 1958).

Television. He composed the musical score for Maurice Evans's *Hamlet* (Hallmark Hall of Fame, NBC, 1952); wrote the dance music for *Our Town* (NBC); and subsequently wrote dance music and special material for Arthur Godfrey Special; Producers Showcase (NBC); Ed Sullivan Show (CBS); Hollywood Palace; Red Skelton Show (CBS); Steve Allen Show; Kate Smith Hour; Colgate Comedy Hour (NBC, 1955); Frankie Laine Time (CBS, 1955); Rosalind Russell Special (NBC); Hit Parade (NBC, 1958); Mary Martin Special (NBC, 1959); Garry Moore Show (ABC, 1961–62); and the Perry Como Show (NBC, 1963).

Night Clubs. He was conductor-pianist and arranger in night clubs in Hawaii (1948–49); worked in the same capacity at major supper clubs for the Statler Hilton chain (1950–51); and was conductor-pianist and composed the dance music for the Cyd Charisse Act at various supper clubs (1963); wrote special material for club and hotel acts of Dora Maugham (1949–51); toured with Odette Myrtil and created act for her (1949–50); at present managing Chez Odette Restaurant, New Hope, Pa., and playing club dates with Roger Adams Trio.

Recreation. Tennis, weightlifting, playwriting.

ADAMS, STANLEY. Composer, lyricist, executive. b. Aug. 14, 1907, New York City, to Henry Charles and Nan (Josephs) Adams. Grad. New York Univ., LL.B. 1929. Married Sept. 28, 1940, to Janice Schwartz (marr. dis. 1947); one daughter; married Dec. 2, 1955, to Berenice Halperin. Member of ASCAP; AGAC (honorary member, council), (formerly Songwriters' Protective Assn., vice-pres., 1943–44); Musicians' Aid Society, Inc. (member, advisory board); AFM (mbr., admin. adv. bd.); President's Music Comm. (mbr., exec. bd.); Natl. Music Council (vice-pres.); Music for the Blind, Inc. (bd. of dir.); Music Committee of N.Y.C.; Natl. Culture Center (adv. committee); Delta Beta Phi; The Friars. Address: (home) 3 Woodland Place, Great Neck, NY 10022; (bus.) c/o ASCAP, 575 Madison Ave., New York, NY 10022.

Theatre. Mr. Adams wrote songs for *The Show Is On* (Winter Garden Th., N.Y.C., Dec. 25, 1936; return engagement Winter Garden, Sept. 18, 1937); and *A Lady Says Yes* (Broadhurst, Jan. 10, 1945).

Films. He wrote songs for *Everyday's a Holiday* (Par., 1937); *Duel in the Sun* (Selznick, 1946); and *Strategic Air Command* (Par., 1955).

Published Works. He wrote lyrics for the songs "Little Old Lady" (1937), "My Shawl" (1934), "What a Diff'rence a Day Makes" (1934), and "There Are Such Things" (1942).

Awards. In 1961, Mr. Adams received the Share Your Knowledge Award from the Philadelphia, Pa., Club of Printing House Craftsmen. In 1963, he was awarded a citation by the Natl. Federation of Music Clubs and a plaque from Music for the Blind, Inc. In 1964, he received the Veterans Hospital Radio and Television Guild Award.

ADDINSELL, RICHARD. Composer. b. Jan. 13, 1904, London, England, to William Arthur and Anne Beatrice (Richards) Addinsell. Father, company director. Attended Hertford Coll., Oxford, England, 1922–25. Member of Composers Guild of Great Britain; Song Writers Guild; Performing Right Society (member of council). Address: 1 Carlyle Mansions, Cheyne Walk, London, S.W. 3, England.

Theatre. Mr. Addinsell's first work for the theatre was half the score for the revue, *The Charlot Show of 1926* (Prince of Wales's Th., London, Oct. 5, 1926); subsequently composed music to Clemence Dane's libretto for *Adam's Opera* (Old Vic, 1928); incidental music for *Alice in Wonderland* (Civic Repertory Th., N.Y.C., Dec. 12, 1932); in collaboration with Clemence Dane, music for *Come of Age* (Maxine Elliott's Th., Jan. 12, 1934); and *L'Aiglon* (Broadhurst, Nov. 3, 1934).

In London, he wrote music scores for *The Happy Hypocrite* (His Majesty's, Apr. 8, 1936); *The Taming of the Shrew* (New, Mar. 23, 1937); *Alice in Wonderland* (Scala, Dec. 24, 1943); *Trespass* (Globe, 1947); and *Ring Around the Moon* (Globe, Jan. 26, 1950); *All Clear* (Queen's, Dec. 20, 1939); *Tuppence Coloured* (Lyric, Hammersmith, Sept. 4, 1947); *Penny Plain* (St. Martin's, Sept. 4, 1947); *The Lyric Revue* (Lyric, Hammersmith, May 24, 1951); *The Globe Revue* (Globe, July 10, 1952); *Joyce Grenfell Requests the Pleasure. . .* (Fortune, London, June 2, 1954; Bijou, N.Y.C., Oct. 5, 1955); *Joyce Grenfell* (Lyric, Hammersmith, London, Oct. 8, 1957; Lyceum, New York, Apr. 17, 1958); and wrote music for Arthur Macrae's *Living for Pleasure* (Garrick, London, July 10, 1958).

Films. Mr. Addinsell wrote film scores for *Fire Over England* (UA, 1937); *Dark Jorney* (UA, 1937); *South Riding* (UA, 1938); *Goodbye, Mr. Chips* (MGM, 1939); *The Lion Has Wings* (UA, 1940); *Dangerous Moonlight* (RKO); *Blithe Spirit* (UA, 1945); *Under Capricorn* (UA, 1949); *The Black Rose* (20th-Fox, 1950); *Highly Dangerous* (Lippert, 1951); *Tom Brown's Schooldays* (UA, 1951); *The Prince and the Showgirl* (WB, 1957); *Loss of Innocence* (Col. 1961); *The Roman Spring of Mrs. Stone* (WB, 1961); *The Waltz of the Toreadors* (Col., 1962); and *The War Lover* (Col., 1962).

During WW II, he wrote music for documentaries, including *We Sail at Midnight* and *The Siege of Tobruk.*

Television. For television, he composed the scores for *Macbeth* (Hallmark Hall of Fame, NBC, Nov. 20, 1960); in London, *Will Shakespeare* (BBC); *The Canterville Ghost* (BBC); *Southern Rhapsody* (Southern TV); and *Ring Round the Moon* (BBC, Apr. 1964).

ADDISON, JOHN. Composer. Grad. Royal Coll. of Music, London.

Theatre. Mr. Addison wrote the score for the revue *Cranks* (Bijou, N.Y.C., Nov. 26, 1956); incidental music for *The Entertainer* (Royal Court, London, England, Apr. 10, 1957; Royale, N.Y.C., Feb. 12, 1958); for *The Chairs* and *The Lesson* (Phoenix, Jan. 9, 1958); composed and arranged music for *Luther* (Royal Court, London, July 27, 1961; St. James, N.Y.C., Sept. 25, 1963; composed music for *Saint Joan of the Stockyards* (Queen's Th., London, June 11, 1964); was musical advisor for *A Patriot for Me* (Royal Court, June 30, 1965); and, with David Heneker, wrote music for *Popkiss* (Globe, Aug. 22, 1972).

Films. He composed the background scores for *Seven Days to Noon* (Mayer-Kingsley, 1950); *The Man Between* (UA, 1953); *High and Dry* (U, 1954); *Cockleshell Heroes* (Col., 1956); *Private's Progress* (DCA, 1956); *Reach for the Sky* (Rank, 1957); *Guns at Batasi* (20th-Fox, 1964); *The Loved One* (MGM, 1965); *The Amorous Adventures of Moll Flanders* (Par., 1965); *A Fine Madness* (WB, 1966); *I Was Happy Here* (Rank, 1966); *Torn Curtain* (U, 1966); *The Honey Pot* (UA, 1967); *The Charge of the Light Brigade* (UA, 1968); *Brotherly Love* (MGM, 1970); *Start the Revolution without Me* (WB, 1970); *Sleuth* (20th-Fox, 1972); *Luther* (Amer. Film Th., 1974); and *Dead Cert* (London Pavilion, A, 1974).

Other Activities. He is a professor at the Royal Coll. of Music (London).

ADDY, WESLEY. Actor. b. August 4, 1913, Omaha, Neb., to John R. and Maren S. Addy. Attended Univ. of California at Los Angeles, B.A. 1934. Served US Army, Field Artillery, 1941–45; rank, Maj. Member of AEA; AFTRA; SAG.

Theatre. Mr. Addy made his Bway debut playing one of the unemployed in *Panic* (Imperial, Mar. 14, 1935); subsequently appeared as a Wedding Guest in *How Beautiful with Shoes* (Booth, Nov. 28, 1935); as Marcellus in Leslie Howard's *Hamlet* (Imperial, Nov. 10, 1936); the Earl of Salisbury in Maurice Evans' production of *King Richard II* (St. James, Sept. 15, 1937); Bernardo and Fortinbras in Maurice Evans' *Hamlet* (St. James, Oct. 12, 1938); Hotspur in *Henry IV, Part 1* (St. James, Jan. 30, 1939); and Melvin Lockhart in *Summer Night* (St. James, Nov. 2, 1939).

Mr. Addy played Benvolio in the Laurence Olivier-Vivien Leigh production of *Romeo and Juliet* (51 St. Th., May 9, 1940); Orsino, Duke of Illyria, in the Evans-Hayes production of *Twelfth Night* (St. James, Nov. 19, 1940); Haemon in *Antigone* (Cort, Feb. 18, 1946); James Mavor Morell in Katharine Cornell's *Candida* (Cort, Apr. 3, 1946); and succeeded (Feb. 1947) Leo Genn as Benjamin Hubbard in *Another Part of the Forest* (Fulton, Nov. 20, 1946).

He played the Old Cardinal in the ANTA Experimental Th. production of *Galileo* (Maxine Elliott's Th., Dec. 7, 1947); Harry in *The Leading Lady* (National, Oct. 18, 1948); Professor Allen Carr (the title role) in The Traitor (48 St. Th., Apr. 4, 1949); the Supervisor of Weights and Measures in *The Enchanted* (Lyceum, Jan. 18, 1950); Edgar in Louis Calhern's *King Lear* (Natl., Dec. 25, 1950); Ladislaus Oros, S.J., in *The Strong Are Lonely* (Broadhurst, Sept. 29, 1953); Mr. Henry Brougham in *The First Gentleman* (Belasco, Apr. 25, 1957); Mihail Alexandrovitch Rakitin in *A Month in the Country* (Maidman Playhouse, May 28, 1963); and toured in *With Love and Laughter* (Summer 1963).

He played George Henderson in *Affairs of State* (La Jolla Playhouse, Calif., June 29, 1964); appeared in *The Grass Is Greener* (Ivanhoe Th., Chicago, Ill., Aug. 2, 1966); in 1966–67 made a world tour in *An Evening of the Theater in Concert,* appeared at Pasadena (Calif.) Playhouse in *Captain Brassbound's Conversion* and as George Henderson in *Affairs of State,* and at Ivanhoe Th. in *Not Even in Spring.* He played Mr. Joseph Chamberlain in *The Right Honourable Gentleman* (Huntington Hartford Th., Los Angeles, Calif., Mar. 13, 1967); again played James Mavor Morrell in *Candida* (Great Lakes Shakespeare Festival, Lakewood, Ohio, July 31, 1969; Longacre, N.Y.C., Apr. 6, 1970); was Papa in *Mama* (Studio Arena Th., Buffalo, N.Y., Jan. 6, 1972); and Pastor Manders in *Ghosts* (Roundabout Th., N.Y.C., Mar. 13, 1973).

Films. Mr. Addy made his debut as Father Fulton in *The First Legion* (UA, 1951); subsequently appeared in *Kiss Me Deadly* (UA, 1955); *The Big Knife* (UA, 1955); *Timetable* (UA, 1956); *The Garment Jungle* (Col., 1957); *Ten Seconds to Hell* (UA, 1959); and *What Ever Happened to Baby Jane?* (WB, 1962); in *Hush. . .Hush, Sweet Charlotte* (20th-Fox, 1964); in *Mister Budwing* (MGM, 1966); *Seconds* (Par., 1966); *Tora! Tora! Tora!* (20th-Fox, 1970); and *The Grissom Gang* (Natl. Genl., 1971).

Television. Mr. Addy narrated *The Brick and the Rose* (TV Workshop, CBS, Jan. 24, 1960); and appeared on Slattery's People (CBS, 1965); Fugitive (ABC, 1965); Perry Mason (CBS, 1966); I Spy (NBC, 1966); was Mr. Smith in *Meet Me in St. Louis* (Summer Fun, ABC, Sept. 2, 1966); was on 12 O'-Clock High (ABC, 1966); Love on a Rooftop (ABC, 1967); Edge of Night (CBS, 1972); and The Days of Our Lives (NBC, 1973).

ADIX, VERN. Educator, director, designer. b. LaVern Adix, May 3, 1912, Boone, Iowa, to Albert and Katie (Kumpf) Adix. Father, manufacturer, hotel owner. Grad. Boone H.S., 1931; attended Boone Junior Coll., 1933; grad. State Univ. of Iowa, B.A. 1937; Univ. of Minnesota, M.A. 1943; graduate study at Univ. of Utah, 1944–47. Married Apr. 5, 1946, to Marjorie Clegg (marr. dis. 1955); married Mar. 1, 1957, to Shauna McLatchy; one son, one daughter. Member of NCP; ATA; CTC; AAUP; Theta Alpha Phi. Address: (home) 1532 Michigan Ave., Salt Lake City, UT 84105, tel. (801) 363-2139; (bus.) Pioneer Memorial Theatre, Univ. of Utah, Salt Lake City, UT tel. (801) 581-6222.

Mr. Adix, professor of theatre and supervising director of the Young Peoples Theatre at the Univ. of Utah, has been active in educational theatre for more than 35 years as a director, designer, actor and teacher (theatre and speech). He previously was a member of the faculty at the Univ. of Minnesota (1939–43); taught design and stagecraft at the Banff (Canada) School of Fine Arts (Summers 1949, 1952); was technical director and designer at the Cain Park Th., Cleveland, Ohio (Summers 1943, 1944).

Mr. Adix designed, staged and acted in *Annie Get Your Gun* (South American tour, Summer 1962); *Papa Is All* and *But Not Goodbye* (Utah tour, 1947).

Published Works. Mr. Adix contributed articles to *Educational Theatre Journal* and *Players Magazine.* He is the author of the textbook *Theatre Stagecraft* (1956), and many children's plays, which have been produced.

Recreation. Photography, puppetry, gardening.

ADLER, JERRY. Director, production supervisor. Grad. Syracuse (N.Y.) Univ., 1950.

Theatre. Mr. Adler directed off-Bway productions of *Light Up the Sky* (Lenox Hill Playhouse, N.Y.C., Oct. 11, 1958) and *A View from the Bridge* (1959). He produced, with Samuel Liff, Orson Welles's *Moby Dick* (Ethel Barrymore Th., Nov. 28, 1962); was stage manager for *Jack Benny* (Ziegfeld Th., Feb. 27, 1963); *The Girl Who Came to Supper* (Broadway Th., Dec. 8, 1963); and for *Oh! What a Lovely War* (Broadhurst, Sept. 30, 1964). He produced, with Norman Rosemont, *Drat! The Cat!* (Martin Beck Th., Oct. 10, 1965); was production supervisor for *A Time for Singing* (Broadway Th., May 21, 1966); production stage manager for *The Apple Tree* (Sam S. Shubert Th., Oct. 18, 1966); and production supervisor for *Black Comedy* (Ethel Barrymore Th., Feb. 12, 1967).

He was production supervisor for *Little Murders* (Broadhurst, Apr. 25, 1967); *The Unknown Soldier and His Wife* (Vivian Beaumont Th., July 6, 1967; London, Eng., July 11, 1973); *Halfway Up the Tree* (Brooks Atkinson Th., N.Y.C., Nov. 6, 1967); production stage manager for *Dear World* (Mark Hellinger Th., Feb. 6, 1969); directed *The Ofay Watcher* (Stage 73, Sept. 15, 1969); was production stage manager for *Coco* (Mark Hellinger Th., Dec. 18, 1969); production supervisor for *Home* (Morosco, Nov. 17, 1970); and for the pre-Bway tryout of *Prettybelle* (Shubert Th., Boston, Feb. 1–Mar. 6, 1971). He directed a revival of *The Homecoming* (Bijou, N.Y.C., May 18, 1971); directed *Charlie Was Here and Now He's Gone* (Eastside Playhouse, June 6, 1971); *Fun City* (Morosco, Jan. 2, 1972); *A Conflict of Interest* (Arena Stage, Washington, D.C., Feb. 4, 1972); was production supervisor for *6 Rms Riv Vu* (Helen Hayes Th., N.Y.C., Oct. 17, 1972); directed *Good Evening* (Plymouth, Nov. 14, 1973); and was production supervisor for a revival of *Ulysses in Nighttown* (Winter Garden, Mar. 10, 1974).

Television. Mr. Adler was production supervisor for the telecast of Hal Holbrook's *Mark Twain Tonight!* (CBS, Mar. 6, 1967), and as of 1973 he had been production supervisor of all seven national Antoinette Perry (Tony) Award telecasts.

ADLER, LARRY. Musician, performer, composer. b. Lawrence Cecil Adler, Feb. 10, 1914, Baltimore, Md., to Louis and Sadie (Hack) Adler. Father, plumber. Attended Peabody Sch. of Music, Baltimore, Md.; Baltimore City Coll., 1925–28. Married Apr. 11, 1938, to Eileen Walser, model; one son, two daughters. Relative in theatre: brother, Jerry Hilliard (Hilliard Adler), performer.

Theatre. Mr. Adler appeared first in vaudeville, playing the harmonica, with the Paramount touring units (1928); subsequently played Larry in *Smiles* (Ziegfeld, N.Y.C., Nov. 18, 1930); appeared as one of the principals in *Flying Colors* (Imperial, Sept. 15, 1932); and played at the Palace in a vaudeville act (N.Y.C., 1934). Mr. Adler appeared in *Streamline* (Palace, London, Sept. 28, 1934); performed in a vaudeville act (Holborn Empire, Mar. 1936); *Tune In* (1937); and produced and appeared in *In Town*

Tonight (Stratford Empire, Sept. 20, 1937); and toured South Africa and Australia (1938–39). He appeared in a Gus Edwards revue (N.Y.C., 1939); in *Keep Off the Grass* (Broadhurst, May 23, 1940); in vaudeville (Roxy Th., Apr. 1948) and in vaudeville acts in Europe (1951); in *Ad-Lib* (Fortune Th., London, England, Feb. 2, 1966); and in *Six O'Clock Holiday Show* (Arts, London, Jan. 10, 1967).

Films. Mr. Adler has appeared in *Many Happy Returns* (Par., 1934); *The Big Broadcast of 1937* (Par., 1936); *Singing Marine* (WB, 1937); *Sidewalks of London* (Par., 1940); *Music for Millions* (MGM, 1944); was composer for *Genevieve* (U, 1954); appeared in *The Birds and the Bees* (Par., 1956); and was composer for *The Camp* (United Nations); *A Cry from the Streets* (Tudor, 1959); and *The Hook* (MGM, 1963).

Television and Radio. On radio he performed on the Rudy Vallee Show (WEAF, June 1936). On television he appeared on a BBC program, for which he was the composer and commentator (telecast in London and N.Y.C., June 21, 1957); Camera Three (CBS, Mar. 8, 1959); and One Night Stand (WNTA, Mar. 24, 1959). He composed the score for *The Midnight Man* (BBC, London, Summer 1964) and appeared on the Mike Douglas Show (Ind., 1967–68).

Night Clubs. His night club appearances, many of them with Paul Draper, include The Heigh-Ho Club (N.Y.C., 1927); the Versailles (N.Y.C., Feb. 1937); *Lew Brown's Varieties* (French Casino, N.Y.C., Jan. 1940); at the Village Gate (N.Y.C., Nov. 1962); and with the Second City Company, Square East (N.Y.C., July 7, 1964).

Concerts. Playing the harmonica, he gave many concerts with the dancer, Paul Draper, which included appearances at the Civic Opera House (Chicago, Ill., Dec. 22, 1941); at Carnegie Hall (N.Y.C., Dec. 28, 1941); and at NY City Ctr. (Dec. 31, 1943; Dec. 25, 1944; Dec. 25, 1945; Dec. 1946; Dec. 21, 1947). Mr. Adler has appeared as soloist with piano and with orchestra in both Europe and America, and played a suite especially composed for him, for harmonica and orchestra, with the Philadelphia (Pa.) Orchestra (Nov. 16, 1945). He appeared in a concert at the Salle Pleyel (Paris, France, May 27, 1947); at Town Hall (N.Y.C., May 3, 1952); made a world tour (1964–65); appeared at the Edinburgh (Scotland) Festival (Aug. 1965); and played in the Third Annual Harpsichord Festival (Carnegie Hall, N.Y.C., June 17, 1975).

Published Works. Mr. Adler is the author of an autobiography, *From Hand to Mouth; How I Play* (1936); edited *Harmonica Favorites* (1943); and has written articles for publications including the Chicago *Sun* and *Collier's* Magazine.

Discography. Mr. Adler has recorded for Columbia and Decca labels.

Awards. He was the winner of a harmonica contest sponsored by the Baltimore *Sun* (1927); received the Outstanding Young American Award from the Natl. Chamber of Commerce (1944); and the Grand Prix du Disque (France) for his recording of "Touchez pas au Grisbi" (1954).

ADLER, LUTHER. Actor, director. b. Lutha Adler, New York City, May 4, 1903, to Jacob P. and Sarah (Levitskaya) Adler. Father, actor, director, producer; mother, actress. Attended Lewis Inst., Chicago, Ill. Married Aug. 13, 1938, to Sylvia Sidney, actress (marr. dis. 1947); one son; married Apr. 24, 1959, to Julia Hadley Roche. Relatives in theatre: brother, Jay Adler, actor; sisters, Julia Adler, Stella Adler, Celia Adler, Frances Adler, actresses; cousin, Francine Larrimore, actress. Member of AEA; SAG; AFTRA. Address: (home) R.D. 3, Box 196, Kutztown, PA 19530; (bus.) c/o AEA, 45 W. 47th St., New York, NY 10036.

Theatre. Mr. Adler made his stage debut in the Yiddish theatre at the age of five in *Schmendrick* (Thalia Th., Bowery, N.Y.C., 1908); subsequently appeared with his parents, Jacob P. and Sarah Adler, in *Resurrection* and *The Kreutzer Sonata* (Novelty, Bklyn., 1912–13); under the name Lutha Adler, with the Provincetown Players, as Joe and Samuel Elkas in *The Hand of the Potter* (Provincetown Playhouse, N.Y.C., Dec. 5, 1921); and toured in *Sonya* (1922).

As Luther Adler, the name he has used ever since, he made his Bway debut as Leon Kantor in *Humoresque* (Vanderbilt Th., Feb. 27, 1923); appeared as Zizi in *The Monkey Talks* (Harris, Dec. 28, 1925); Sam Madorsky in *Money Business* (National Jan. 20, 1926); Phil Levine in *We Americans* (Harris, Oct. 12, 1926); the Old Man in *John* (Klaw, Nov. 2, 1927); performed in *The Music Master, Is Zat So?* and *Give and Take* on a tour of South Africa and Eng. (1927); played Piotr in *Red Rust* (Martin Beck Th., N.Y.C., Dec. 17, 1929); succeeded (Dec. 1929) Horace Braham as Samuel Kaplan in *Street Scene* (Playhouse, Jan. 10, 1929); and appeared with the Yiddish theatre in *Millions* and *The Wild Man* (1930–31).

As a member of the Group Th., he appeared as Don Fernando in its production of *Night Over Taos* (48 St. Th., Mar. 9, 1932); and as Sol Ginsberg in *Success Story* (Maxine Elliott's Th., Sept. 26, 1932); and played Julian Vardaman in Katharine Cornell's production of *Alien Corn* (Belasco, Feb. 20, 1933). With the Group Th., Mr. Adler appeared as Dr. Gordon in *Men in White* (Broadhurst, Sept. 26, 1933), Emperor Norton and Tang Sing in *Gold Eagle Guy* (Morosco, Nov. 28, 1934), Moe Axelrod in *Awake and Sing!* (Belasco, Feb. 19, 1935), Dr. Benjamin in *Waiting for Lefty* (Belasco, Sept. 9, 1935), Marcus Katz in *Paradise Lost* (Longacre, Dec. 9, 1935), the Doctor in *The Case of Clyde Griffiths* (Ethel Barrymore Th., Mar. 13, 1936), an English Sergeant, a Belgian Major-General and Brother Henry in *Johnny Johnson* (44 St. Th., Nov. 19, 1936), Joe Bonaparte in *Golden Boy* (Belasco, Nov. 4, 1937; St. James's, London, June 21, 1938); Mr. Prince in *Rocket to the Moon* (Belasco, N.Y.C., Nov. 24, 1938); and Charleston in *Thunder Rock* (Mansfield, Nov. 14, 1939).

He appeared as Lawrence Ormont in *Two on an Island* (Broadhurst, Jan. 22, 1940); in *No Time for Comedy* at Amherst (Mass.) Coll. (June 24, 1940); *Accent on Youth* (Windsor, Bronx, N.Y., July 8, 1941); Globa in *The Russian People* (Guild, N.Y.C., Dec. 29, 1942); directed the touring production of *Jane Eyre*, in which he played Mr. Rochester (1943–44); played the title role in *Uncle Harry* (Great Northern, Chicago, Ill., Apr. 1944); Capt. Angelini in *Common Ground* (Fulton, N.Y.C., Apr. 25, 1945); Noll Turner in *The Beggars Are Coming to Town* (Coronet, Oct. 27, 1945); Miguel Riachi in *Dunnigan's Daughter* (John Golden Th., Dec. 26, 1945); and Glowworm in the pre-Bway tryout of *Twilight Bar* (opened Ford's Th., Baltimore, Md., Mar. 12, 1946; closed Walnut St. Th., Philadelphia, Pa., Mar. 23, 1946).

Mr. Adler staged *A Flag Is Born* (Alvin, N.Y.C., Sept. 5, 1946), and later succeeded Paul Muni as Tevya; appeared as Commissar Gorotchenko in *Tovarich* (NY City Ctr., May 14, 1952); Almady in *The Play's the Thing* (Boston, Mass., Aug. 1952); Shylock in *The Merchant of Venice* (NY City Ctr., Mar. 4, 1953); Renato di Rossi in *Time of the Cuckoo* (Biltmore, Miami, Fla., July 6, 1954); directed a stock production of *Angel Street*, in which he played Mr. Manningham (Quarterdeck, Atlantic City, N.J., June 29, 1955; Northland Playhouse, Detroit, Mich., Aug. 7, 1956); played Ignaty Illyich Shpichelsky, the Doctor, in *A Month in the Country* (Phoenix, N.Y.C., Apr. 3, 1956); Lucas Edgerton in *Reclining Figure* (Roosevelt, Miami Beach, Fla., June 1956); Mr. Manningham in *Angel Street* (Northland Playhouse, Detroit, Mich., Aug. 7, 1956); Casale in *A Very Special Baby* (Playhouse, N.Y.C., Nov. 14, 1956); Eddie Carbone in *A View from the Bridge* (Studebaker, Chicago, Ill., Feb. 19, 1957), and in a touring production which he directed (1958–59).

In stock at the Playhouse-in-the-Park (Philadelphia, Pa.), Mr. Adler played Willie Loman in *Death of a Salesman* (June 20, 1960); Henry Drummond in *Inherit the Wind* (June 26, 1961): Uncle Louis in *The Happy Time* (June 25, 1962); Chris Christopherson in *Anna Christie* (July 30, 1962); Caesario Grimaldi in *Tchin-Tchin* (Aug. 26, 1963); and appeared in *Brecht on Brecht* (Playhouse-on-the-Mall, Paramus, N.J.; Guild Hall, East Hampton, L.I., N.Y., Summer 1963); played Lenin in *The Passion of Josef D.* (Ethel Barrymore Th., N.Y.C., Feb. 11, 1964); Chebutykin in the Actors Studio Th. production of *The Three Sisters* (Morosco, June 16, 1964). He replaced (Jan. 18–30, 1965) Zero Mostel as Tevye in *Fiddler on the Roof* (Imperial, Sept. 22, 1964) and again (beginning Aug. 15, 1965); played in *The Tenth Man* (Mineola Th., Mineola, N.Y., Jan. 18, 1966); and toured as Tevye in *Fiddler on the Roof* (opened San Diego, Calif., Apr. 11, 1966).

Films. Mr. Adler made his film debut in *Lancer Spy* (20th-Fox, 1937); subsequently appeared in *Cornered* (RKO, 1945); *Saigon* (Par., 1948); *The Loves of Carmen* (Col., 1948); *Wake of the Red Witch* (Rep., 1948); *House of Strangers* (20th-Fox, 1949); *D.O.A.* (UA, 1949); *South Sea Sinner* (U, 1950); *Under My Skin* (20th-Fox, 1950); *Kiss Tomorrow Goodbye* (WB, 1950); *M* (Col., 1951); *The Magic Face* (Col., 1951); *The Desert Fox* (20th-Fox, 1951); *Hoodlum Empire* (Rep., 1952); *The Tall Texans* (Lippert, 1953); *The Miami Story* (Col., 1954); *Crashout* (Filmmakers, 1955); *The Girl in the Red Velvet Swing* (20th-Fox, 1955); *Hot Blood* (Col., 1956); *The Last Angry Man* (Col., 1959); *Crazy Joe* (Col., 1974); and *Murph the Surf* (Amer. Intl., 1975).

Television. Mr. Adler has appeared in *Hedda Gabler* (US Steel Hour, CBS, June 10, 1954); *The Day Before Atlanta* (Center Stage, ABC, Sept. 7, 1954); *Billy Budd* (ABC, Mar. 1955); *The Killer* (Robert Montgomery Presents, NBC, June 6, 1955); *Man with a Vengeance* (GE Th., CBS, July 24, 1955); *The Unholy Trio* (Crossroads, ABC, Oct. 21, 1955); *The Partners* (US Steel Hour, CBS, July 18, 1956); *The Sainted General* (Star Stage, NBC, Aug. 10, 1956); *The Cauliflower Heart* (Studio One, CBS, Sept. 10, 1956); *The Last Clear Chance* (Playhouse 90, CBS, Sept. 11, 1958); *The Plot to Kill Stalin* (Playhouse 90, CBS, Sept. 25, 1958); *The Rank and File* (Playhouse 90, CBS, May 28, 1959); and *The Lincoln Murder Case* (Dupont Show-of-the-Month, CBS, Feb. 18, 1961).

He appeared on Naked City (Ind., 1964); *Meeting at Appalachin* (Desilu Playhouse, NBC, 1965); Twilight Zone (ABC, 1965); Ben Casey (ABC, 1965; 1966); The Untouchables (Ind., 1965; narrator for the special *A Symphony for Finland* (NET, Dec. 10, 1965); appeared in *The Actor's Studio Th.* (BBC-2, London, England, 1965); Mission: Impossible (CBS, 1970); Name of the Game (NBC, 1970); The Psychiatrist (NBC, 1970–71); and Hawaii Five-O (CBS, 1972).

ADLER, RICHARD. Composer, producer, lyricist. b. Aug. 3, 1921, New York City, to Clarence and Elsa Adrienne (Richard) Adler. Father, pianist, teacher. Married Sept. 4, 1951, to Marion Hart (marr. dis. Jan. 3, 1958); two sons; married Jan. 3, 1958, to Sally Ann Howes, actress, singer (marr. dis. Feb., 1966); married Dec. 1968, to Ritchey Farrell Barker. Grad. Columbia Grammar Sch., N.Y.C. 1939; Univ. of North Carolina, A.B. 1943. Served USN 1943–46, rank Lt. (jg). Member of ASCAP (bd. of dir.; exec. comm.); AGAC (exec. council); Dramatists Guild (exec. council); North Carolina Sch. of the Arts Advisory Council (1952); board of trustees, John F. Kennedy Center for the Performing Arts (1964–to date; exec. comm., 1975); National Outdoor Regional Theatre Advisory Council (1966); ANTA (bd. of dir., 1973–to date); and New Dramatists (bd. of dir., 1974–to date). Address: (home) 19 E. 72nd St., New York, NY 10021; (bus.) tel. (212) 988-9766.

Theatre. Mr. Adler's first music and lyrics, written in collaboration with Jerry Ross, were for the revue, *John Murray Anderson's Almanac* (Imperial Th., Dec. 10, 1953); followed by *The Pajama Game* (St. James, May 13, 1954); and *Damn Yankees* (46 St. Th., May 5, 1955).

Since Mr. Ross's death (Nov. 11, 1955), Mr. Adler has worked without a collaborator; he was the composer-lyricist for *Kwamina* (54 St. Th., Oct. 23, 1961); producer-director of *New York's Salute to President Kennedy* (Madison Square Garden, May 19, 1962); producer-director of the *Inaugural Anni-*

versary Salute to President Kennedy (Natl. Guard Armory, Wash., D.C., Jan. 18, 1963); and director and master of ceremonies at the invitation of President and Mrs. Johnson for the first State Dinner entertainment of the new administration (Jan. 14, 1964) and many other State Dinner entertainments during both the Kennedy and Johnson administrations. He was producer-director of two salutes to President Johnson (Madison Sq. Garden, 1965 and Natl. Guard Armory, Washington, D.C., 1966); and the Inaugural Gala for President Johnson at the Natl. Guard Armory (Washington, D.C., Jan., 18, 1965).

Films. Film adaptations were made of *The Pajama Game* (WB, 1957) and *Damn Yankees* (WB, 1958).

Television. Mr. Adler was composer-lyricist and co-producer for *Little Women* (CBS, Nov. 1959); *Gift of the Magi* (CBS, Dec. 1959); and Stage '67 Series "Olympus 7-0000" (ABC, 1967).

Awards. Mr. Adler received the Antoinette Perry (Tony) Award, the Donaldson Award, and won the *Variety* NY Drama Critics Poll for *The Pajama Game* (1954) and *Damn Yankees* (1955); and was nominated for the Antoinette Perry (Tony) Award for *Kwamina* (1961); and received *The Evening Standard* Award for *The Pajama Game* (London, 1956).

ADLER, STELLA. Actress, director, teacher of acting. b. New York City, to Jacob P. and Sarah (Lewis) Adler. Father, actor-manager; mother, actress-manager. Attended New York Univ. Studied for the theatre with her father, Maria Ouspenskaya, and Richard Boleslavsky, all at the Amer. Laboratory Th.; and with Constantin Stanislavsky. Married 1943, to Harold Clurman, director (marr. dis. 1960). Relatives in theatre: sisters, Frances, Celia, and Julia, actresses; brothers, Luther and Jay, actors; cousin, Francine Larrimore, actress. Member of AEA. Address: (home) 1016 Fifth Ave., New York, NY 10028, tel. (212) RH 4-4494; (bus.) Stella Adler Theatre Studio, 130 West 56th St., New York, NY 10019, tel. (212) 246-1195-6.

Theatre. Miss Adler, as a member of her father's Yiddish theatre company, first appeared on stage at age four in *Broken Hearts* (Grand Th., N.Y.C.). She made other appearances with her father's (repertory) company in N.Y.C.; and made her London debut at the Pavillion Th. (Winter 1919).

Under the name, Lola Adler, she first appeared on Bway as Apatura Clythia in *The World We Live In (The Insect Comedy)* (Jolson Th., Oct. 31, 1922); subsequently appeared with the American Laboratory Th., as the Baroness Creme de la Creme in *The Straw Hat* (Oct. 14, 1926), using her real name, Stella Adler, which she has used ever since; as Elly in *Big Lake* (Apr. 11, 1927); and Beatrice in *Much Ado About Nothing* (Nov. 18, 1927). She played in productions of the Yiddish Art Theatre in New York, on tour in the US and in Europe (1927–31).

In 1931, Miss Adler joined the Group Theatre, and with it appeared as Geraldine Connelly in *The House of Connelly* (Martin Beck Th., Sept. 28, 1931); in *1931* (Mansfield, Dec. 10, 1931); Doña Josefa in *Night Over Taos* (48 St. Th., Mar. 9, 1932); Sarah Glassman in *Success Story* (Maxine Elliott's Th., Sept. 26, 1932); and Myra Bonney in *Big Night* (Maxine Elliott's Th., Jan. 17, 1933). She played the title role in *Hilda Cassidy* (Martin Beck Th., May 4, 1933); and with the Group Theatre, appeared as Gwyn Ballantine in *Gentlewoman* (Cort, Mar. 22, 1934); Adah Menken in *Gold Eagle Guy* (Morosco, Nov. 28, 1934); Bessie Berger in *Awake and Sing* (Belasco, Feb. 19, 1935); and Clara in *Paradise Lost* (Longacre, Dec. 9, 1935).

She appeared as Catherine Carnrick in *Sons and Soldiers* (Morosco, May 4, 1943); staged *Manhattan Nocturne* (Forrest, Oct. 26, 1943); appeared as Clotilde in *Pretty Little Parlor* (Natl., Apr. 17, 1944); directed *Polonaise* (Alvin, Oct. 6, 1945); appeared as Zinaida in *He Who Gets Slapped* (Booth, Mar. 20, 1946); directed *Sunday Breakfast* (Coronet, May 28, 1952), and *Johnny Johnson* (Carnegie Hall Playhouse, Oct. 21, 1956). In London, she appeared as Madame Rosepettle in the premiere of *Oh Dad, Poor Dad, Mamma's Hung You in the Closet and I'm Feelin' So Sad* (Lyric, Hammersmith, July 5, 1961).

Films. Under the name of Stella Ardler, she made her film debut in *Love on Toast* (Par. 1938); subsequently was associate producer of *Du Barry Was a Lady* (MGM, 1943); appeared in *The Thin Man* (MGM, 1944); and *My Girl Tisa* (UA, 1948).

Other Activities. Since 1949, Miss Adler has been director of the Stella Adler Theatre Studio in N.Y.C. Previously, she taught technique of acting at the Dramatic Workshop of the New School for Social Research (1940–42). She was head of the acting department, Yale Drama School, Yale University New Haven, Conn. (1967–68), was associated with the New School for Social Research (1970–72) and now teaches in the NY Univ. Undergraduate Drama Dept., holding the classes at her own studio.

AGHAYAN, RAY. Costume designer. b. Reymond Aghayan in Teheran, Iran.

Theatre. Mr. Aghayan designed costumes for a production of *The Lady's Not for Burning*, which he also directed (Carnegie Hall Playhouse, N.Y.C., Feb. 21, 1957); for *Vintage '60*, with Ret Turner (Brooks Atkinson Th., Sept. 12, 1960); *The Egg* (Cort, Jan. 8, 1962); *Eddie Fisher at the Winter Garden* (Oct. 2, 1962); *Applause* (Palace, Mar. 30, 1970); and, with Bob Mackie, for *On the Town* (Imperial, Oct. 31, 1971) and for Carol Channing in *Lorelei* (Palace, Jan. 27, 1974).

Films. Mr. Aghayan designed clothes and costumes for *Father Goose* (U, 1964); *Our Man Flint* (20th-Fox, 1966); *Caprice* (20th-Fox, 1967); *Dr. Doolittle* (20th-Fox, 1967); and *Gaily, Gaily* (UA, 1969).

Television. Mr. Aghayan has been designer for the Carol Burnett Show (CBS) and for programs of Carol Channing, Lucille Ball, Julie Andrews, and Diana Ross.

Other Activities. In addition to designing clothes for stage, screen, television, and nightclub acts, often in association with Bob Mackie, Mr. Aghayan designs clothing for sale in retail stores, also with Mr. Mackie.

Awards. With his partner, Bob Mackie, Mr. Aghayan has received three NATAS (Emmy) awards for costume design on television.

AHERNE, BRIAN. Actor. b. Brian de Lacy Aherne, May 2, 1902, King's Norton, Worcestershire, England, to William de Lacy and Louise (Thomas) Aherne. Attended Edgbaston Sch., Birmingham, and Malvern Coll., England. Studied with Italia Conti. Married 1939 to Joan Fontaine, actress (marr. dis. 1943); married 1946 to Eleanor de Liagre Labrot. Relative in theatre: brother-in-law, Alfred de Liagre, producer and manager. Member of AEA; British AEA (founding member, on council, 1930–34); SAG; AFTRA. Address: Chemin des Charmettes 7, Lausanne, Switzerland.

Pre-Theatre. Architect (Liverpool, England, 1921–22).

Theatre. Mr. Aherne made his first stage appearance at the age of eight with the Pilgrim Players in *Fifinella* (Birmingham, Eng., April 5, 1910); his London debut in *Where the Rainbow Ends* (Garrick Th., Dec. 26, 1913); subsequently appeared as Jack O'Hara in *Paddy, the Next Best Thing* (Savoy, Dec. 26, 1923); toured England as Hugo in *The Flame* (opened Feb. 1924); and played Langford in *White Cargo* (Playhouse, London, May 15, 1924).

In 1926, he toured Australia as Valentine Brown in *Quality Street*, John Shand in *What Every Woman Knows*, Crichton in *The Admirable Crichton*, Simon and Harry in *Mary Ross*, and Willocks in *Aren't We All?* He repeated his role as Langford in *White Cargo* (Strand, London, March 7, 1927); played David in *The Silver Cord* (St. Martin's, Sept. 13, 1927); Gerald in *Let's All Talk About Gerald* (Arts, May 1928); Young Marlow in *She Stoops to Conquer* (Lyric, Hammersmith, Aug. 16, 1928); Walter Craig in *Craig's Wife* (Fortune) Wyndham Brandon in *Rope* (Ambassadors', April 1929); Lt. St. Aubyn in *Tunnel Trench* (Duchess, Nov. 1929); Bastien in *S.S. Tenacity* (Arts, July 1930); succeeded Godfrey Tearle as Francis Archer in *The Beaux' Stratagem* (Royalty, June 11, 1930); Marquis de Presles in *An Object of Virtue* (Duchess, Nov. 1930); and Alan Varrey in *A Marriage Has Been Disarranged* (Royalty, Dec. 1930).

He made his N.Y.C. debut as Robert Browning in *The Barrets of Wimpole Street* (Empire, Feb. 9, 1931); followed by Tarquin in *Lucrece* (Belasco, Dec. 20, 1932); appeared as Mark in *Birthday* (Cambridge, London, Feb. 1934); Mercutio in Katharine Cornell's *Romeo and Juliet* (Martin Beck Th., N.Y.C., Dec. 20, 1934); repeated the role of Browning in a revival of *The Barretts of Wimpole Street* (Martin Beck Th., Feb. 25, 1935); played the Earl of Warwick in Katharine Cornell's *Saint Joan* (Martin Beck Th., Mar. 9, 1936); and Iago in *Othello* (New Amsterdam, Jan. 6, 1937); repeated his role of Browning in *The Barretts of Wimpole Street* (Ethel Barrymore Th., Mar. 26, 1945) and played the same role in the production that toured the ETO (July 1944–Feb. 1945), under the auspices of the Amer. Th. Wing.

Mr. Aherne played Roublard in *The French Touch* (Cort, N.Y.C., Dec. 8, 1945). In July–Sept. 1948, Mr. Aherne toured as Archer in *The Beaux' Stratagem;* played Young Marlow in *She Stoops to Conquer* (NY City Ctr., Dec. 28, 1949); John Middleton in *The Constant Wife* (Natl., Dec. 8, 1951); John Hampden in *Escapade* (48 St. Th., Nov. 18, 1953); and the Marquis of Heronden in *Quadrille* (Coronet, Nov. 3, 1954). In 1957–58, he toured as Henry Higgins in the national company of *My Fair Lady;* played George Bernard Shaw in *Dear Liar* (Billy Rose Th., N.Y.C., Mar. 17, 1960).

Films. Mr. Aherne made his film debut in England where he appeared in several silent films. He made his American film debut in *Song of Songs* (Par., 1933); followed by his role as John Shand in *What Every Woman Knows* (MGM, 1934); *The Constant Nymph* (20th-Fox, 1934); *Sylvia Scarlett* (RKO, 1935); *I Live My Life* (MGM, 1935); *Beloved Enemy* (UA, 1936); *The Great Garrick* (WB, 1937); *Captain Fury* (UA, 1939); Maxmillian in *Juarez* (WB, 1939); *Lady in Question* (Col., 1940); *Hired Wife* (U, 1940); *My Son, My Son* (UA, 1940); *Skylark* (Par., 1941); *My Sister Eileen* (Col., 1942); *Smilin' Through* (MGM, 1942); *Forever and a Day* (RKO, 1943); *What a Woman* (Col., 1943); *The Locket* (RKO, 1946); *Smart Woman* (Allied, 1948); *I Confess* (WB, 1953); Capt. Smith in *Titanic* (20th-Fox, 1953); *Prince Valliant* (20th-Fox, 1954); *A Bullet Is Waiting* (Col., 1954); *The Swan* (MGM, 1956); *The Best of Everything* (20th-Fox, 1959); *Susan Slade* (WB, 1961); King Arthur in *Sword of Lancelot* (U, 1963); Johann Strauss, Sr., in *The Waltz King* (Disney, 1963); and General Braithwaite in *The Cavern* (U, 1964).

Other Activities. He is a founder of the Aircraft Owners' and Pilots' Assn., and has held a flying license since 1934.

Awards. Mr. Aherne was nominated for an Academy (Oscar) Award for his portrayal of Maximillian in *Juarez* (1938). He is an honorary Texas Ranger, and received the honorary degree of LL.D. from Baylor Univ. (Texas, 1951).

AIDMAN, CHARLES. Actor, director. b. Charles L. Aidman, Jan. 31, 1925, Indianapolis, Ind., to George and Etta (Kwitny) Aidman. Father, veterinarian. Grad. Frankfort (Ind.) H.S., 1942; Indiana Univ., B.A. 1948. Studied with Sanford Meisner at the Neighborhood Playhouse Sch. of the Th., 1949–51. Married 1957 to Frances Gasman, model. Served WW II, USN. PTO; rank, Ensign. Member of AEA; SAG; AFTRA; SSD&C; ASCAP; Theatre West. Address: 11720 Laurelcrest Dr., Studio City, CA 91604, tel. (213) PO 3-7512.

Theatre. Mr. Aidman first appeared as Theseus in *The Cretan Woman* (Provincetown Playhouse, N.Y.C., July 7, 1954), followed by Marc Antony in the NY Shakespeare Festival production of *Julius Caesar* (E. River Park Amphitheatre, June 29, 1956); and Sam Lawson in *Career* (Seventh Ave. So. Th., Apr. 20, 1957).

Mr. Aidman adapted, wrote songs for, directed and appeared in *Spoon River Anthology* (Booth, Sept. 29, 1963), retitled *Spoon River* after its opening;

opened Royal Court, London, England, Feb. 13, 1964); appeared in *King Lear* (Th. Group, Univ. of California, Los Angeles, June 5, 1964); toured as Quentin in the national company of *After the Fall* (opened Playhouse, Wilmington, Del., Oct. 21, 1964; closed Shubert Th., Boston, Mass., May 29, 1965); directed *The Hemingway Hero* (pre-Bway: opened Shubert Th., New Haven, Conn., Feb. 21, 1967; closed Wilbur Th., Boston, Mass., Mar. 4, 1967); appeared in *The Adventures of Jack and Max* (Schoenberg Hall, Univ. of California, Los Angeles, 1967); in *Spoon River* (Th. West, Los Angeles, May 19, 1972); was Fred in *Caesarean Operations* (Th. West, Oct. 6, 1972); and directed *Some People, Some Other People and What They Finally Do* (Stage 73, N.Y.C., June 5, 1974).

Films. Mr. Aidman played in *Pork Chop Hill* (UA, 1959) and *War Hunt* (UA, 1962).

Television. Mr. Aidman appeared on approximately 150 television shows, including Philco Television Playhouse (NBC, 1957–59); Studio One (CBS, 1958–59); GE Th. (CBS, 1960); Playhouse 90 (CBS, 1961); The Defenders (CBS, 1962); Dr. Kildare (NBC, 1962); The Nurses (CBS, 1963); US Steel Hour (CBS, 1956, 1963); DuPont Show of the Week (CBS, 1964).

AILEY, ALVIN. Choreographer, actor, director, dancer, dance coach. b. Alvin Ailey, Jr., Jan. 5, 1931, Rogers, Tex., to Alvin, Sr., and Lula E. (Cliff) Ailey. Father, laborer. Grad. Thomas Jefferson H.S., Los Angeles, Calif., 1948; attended Univ. of California at Los Angeles 1949–50; Los Angeles City Coll., 1950–51; San Francisco State Coll., 1952–53. Studied dancing at the Lester Horton Dance Th., Los Angeles, 1949–51; 1953; in N.Y.C., with Hanya Holm, 1954–55; Martha Graham, 1956; Anna Sokolow, 1956; Karel Shook, 1954–56; Charles Weidman, 1957; acting, in N.Y.C., with Stella Adler, 1960–62; Milton Katselas, 1961. Member of AEA; AFTRA; AGVA; AGMA. Address: Dance Theatre Foundation, Inc., 229 East 59th St., New York, NY 10022, tel. (212) 832-1740.

Pre-Theatre. Office clerk, busboy, baggage handler, counterman.

Theatre. Mr. Ailey made his debut as a dancer with the Lester Horton Dance Th. (Los Angeles, Calif., 1950–51); became choreographer for this company in 1953; and appeared with them and had two of his ballets performed at the Jacob's Pillow Dance Festival (Lee, Mass., Summer 1954).

He made his N.Y.C. debut as Alvin in *House of Flowers* (Alvin, Dec. 3, 1954); subsequently danced and played the Purple Bandit in *The Carefree Tree* (Phoenix, Oct. 11, 1955); toured with Harry Belafonte's *Sing, Man, Sing* (1956); and danced in the Jones Beach (N.Y.) Marine Th. production of *Show Boat* (Summer 1957). He was the lead dancer in *Jamaica* (Imperial, N.Y.C., Oct. 31, 1957), which he subsequently choreographed for the Lambertville (N.J.) Music Circus (Summer 1959).

During the run of *Jamaica*, he formed his own dance company, the Alvin Ailey Dance Th. (1958), which in its initial appearance at Kaufmann Concert Hall (YMHA, N.Y.C., Mar. 30, 1958) presented two new works choreographed by Mr. Ailey: *Cinco Latinos* and *Blues Suite*. He choreographed *Carmen Jones* (Theatre-in-the-Park, Aug. 17, 1959); the ELT production of *Dark of the Moon* (Lenox Hill Playhouse, May 13, 1960); and directed the tour of *African Holiday* (Apollo, N.Y.C.; Howard, Washington, D.C., Feb.–May 1960). His dance company performed at the World Dance Festival (Central Park, N.Y.C., 1959); Jacob's Pillow Dance Festival (Lee, Mass., Summers 1959–60); premiered Mr. Ailey's *Revelations* (Kaufmann Concert Hall, YMHA, N.Y.C., Jan. 31, 1960), *Three for Now*, and *Knoxville: Summer 1915* (both Clark Center, West Side YWCA, N.Y.C., Nov. 27, 1960); and at the Boston (Mass.) Arts Festival (June 1961) Mr. Ailey and Carmen De Lavallade presented Mr. Ailey's new creation, *Roots of the Blues;* (N.Y.C. premiere, Lewisohn Stadium, July 1, 1961).

Mr. Ailey made his acting debut as Paul in *Call Me by My Rightful Name* (One Sheridan Sq. Th., Jan. 31, 1961); appeared as a Negro Political Leader in *Ding Dong Bell* (Westport Country Playhouse, Conn., Summer 1961); Blackstone Boulevard in *Talking to You*, part of a double bill with *Across the Board on Tomorrow Morning*, called *Two by Saroyan* (East End, N.Y.C., Oct. 22, 1961); and Clarence Morris in *Tiger, Tiger, Burning Bright* (Booth, Dec. 22, 1962).

For the US State Dept., the Ailey Dance Th. toured Australia and Southeast Asia (Jan.–May 1962). Mr. Ailey also choreographed a ballet, *Feast of Ashes* (previewed NY Fashion Institute of Technology, Sept. 30, 1962; first perf., Teatro San Carlos, Lisbon, Portugal, Nov. 30, 1962) that was performed by the Robert Joffrey Co. Mr. Ailey's company appeared at the American Dance Festival, New London, Conn., July 1962 and at the Delacorte Th., N.Y.C., Sept. 1962; appeared in the revue, *My People* (McCormick Place, Chicago, Ill., Sept. 1963); presented another new work by Mr. Ailey, *Hermit Songs* (Library of Congress, Washington, D.C., Oct. 1963); danced at the International Music Festival (Rio de Janiero and Sao Paulo, Braz., Sept. 1963).

Mr. Ailey also staged with William Hairston, the production, *Jerico-Jim Crow* (The Sanctuary, N.Y.C., Jan. 12, 1964). His dance company appeared at the Delacorte Th. (N.Y.C., Sept. 1, 1964); followed by a three-month tour of Europe (opened Th. des Champs-Elysées, Paris, Fr., Sept. 7, 1964).

His company went on European tours in 1965 and 1966; toured Australia in 1965; appeared at the World Festival of Negro Arts, Dakar, Senegal, in 1966; and toured East and West Africa in 1967. He did the choreography for the new opera *Anthony and Cleopatra* to open the Metropolitan Opera House at Lincoln Center, N.Y.C. (Sept. 16, 1966). The Harkness Ballet presented for the first time Mr. Ailey's *Ariadne* (Paris Opera Comique, Mar. 12, 1965) and his *Macumba* (Gran Teatro del Liceo, Barcelona, Spain, May 11, 1966); the latter received its American premiere as *Yemanja* (Chicago Opera House, Mar. 1967). Mr. Ailey's company first presented his *Quintet* at the Edinburgh (Scotland) Festival in 1968 (Church Hill Th., Aug. 28) and gave the first N.Y.C. performance (Billy Rose Th., Jan. 27, 1969). The company performed at the American Dance Festival, New London, Conn., in 1969, where *Masekela Language* was introduced (Aug. 16), and the N.Y.C. premiere followed (Brooklyn Academy of Music, Nov. 21, 1969).

The spring 1970 engagement of Mr. Ailey's company at the Brooklyn Academy of Music included premieres of *Streams* (Apr. 15) and *Gymnopédies* (Apr. 23), and the American Ballet Theatre first presented *The River* (NY State Th., June 25, 1970). Under US State Dept. sponsorship, the Ailey company toured Africa again (Summer 1970) and made a six-week (Sept. 23–Nov. 1) visit to the USSR.

In 1971, Mr. Ailey's company gave first performances of his work *Flowers* (ANTA Th., Jan. 25), *Choral Dances* (NY City Ctr., Apr. 28), and *Cry* (NY City Ctr., May 4). He collaborated on the staging of *Mass* for the opening of the John F. Kennedy Center for the Performing Arts, Washington, D.C. (Sept. 8), and the City Center Joffrey Ballet presented a new production of *Feast of Ashes* (NY City Ctr., Oct. 7) and the premiere of Mr. Ailey's *Mingus Dances* (NY City Ctr., Oct. 13). In its own NY City Ctr., engagement, the Ailey company introduced two additional new works by Mr. Ailey: *Mary Lou's Mass* (Dec. 9) and *Myth* (Dec. 15).

Mr. Ailey staged a full-length ballet for the world premiere of the opera *Lord Byron* (Juilliard School of Music, N.Y.C., Apr. 20, 1972). At the NY City Ctr., the Ailey company introduced Mr. Ailey's *Song for You* and *The Lark Ascending* (both Apr. 25). During the summer of 1972 the company became known as the Alvin Ailey City Center Dance Theater and officially became part of the NY City Ctr. of Music and Drama. At the 10th New York Dance Festival (Delacorte Th., N.Y.C., Sept. 7–17, 1972), Mr. Ailey's *Shaken Angels* was given its first performance by Bonnie Mathis and Dennis Wayne. For the Metropolitan Opera's new *Carmen*, Mr. Ailey created choreography (Sept. 19, 1972). The American Ballet Th. presented for the first time *Sea-Change* (Kennedy Center Opera House, Washington, D.C., Oct. 26, 1972) and gave the work its N.Y.C. premiere (NY City Ctr., Jan. 9, 1973). Mr. Ailey's company introduced his *Love Songs* (NY City Ctr., Nov. 18, 1972) and *Hidden Rites* (NY City Ctr., May 17, 1973), and he staged *Four Saints in Three Acts* for the Piccolo Met (N.Y.C., Feb. 26, 1973).

Films. Mr. Ailey made his debut as a dancer in *Lydia Bailey* (20th-Fox, 1952) and subsequently danced in *Carmen Jones* (20th-Fox, 1954). A number of works he has created have been recorded on film, including *Blues Suite, Masekela Language, Streams*, and the dances for the opera *Lord Byron*.

Television. Mr. Ailey was choreographer and dancer with the Horton Co. on Party at Ciro's (July–Aug. 1954); and the Red Skelton Show (CBS, 1954). He staged dances for the Jack Benny Show (CBS, 1954); and with his own company has appeared on the Dave Garroway Today Show (NBC, 1959); Camera Three (CBS, Sept. 1962–July 1963); and Look Up and Live (CBS, Mar. 1962). He choreographed *Parade* (CBC, Can., 1964). *Alvin Ailey: Memories and Visions* was televised as a WNET Special (PBS, May 6, 1974).

Other Activities. In 1966, Mr. Ailey joined with Merce Cunningham, Murray Louis, and Alwyn Nikolais to form the National Dance Foundation, a nonprofit public foundation. Mr. Ailey conducts a school, the American Dance Center, which, with his company, operates under the Dance Theatre Foundation, Inc. In 1974, Mr. Ailey was appointed to the advisory council for the City College of New York Leonard Davis Center for the Performing Arts.

Published Works. Articles by Mr. Ailey on his company and his work have appeared in such publications as *Dance* magazine and *Dance and Dancers*.

Awards. Mr. Ailey received the honorary degree of D.F.A. from Cedar Crest College and Princeton Univ., both in 1972.

Recreation. Writing, collecting art objects related to the history of dance and religion.

ALBEE, EDWARD. Playwright, director, producer. b. Mar. 12, 1928, Washington, D.C., adopted and named Edward Franklin Albee III by Reed and Frances (Cotter) Albee. Attended Lawrenceville; Valley Forge (Pa.) Military Acad.; grad. Choate Sch. 1946; attended Trinity Coll. 1946–47. Relative in the theatre: grandfather (adoptive), Edward F. Albee, vaudeville theatre manager. Member of P.E.N., Dramatists Guild. Address: c/o The Dramatists Guild, 6 E. 39th St., New York, NY 10016.

Theatre. Mr. Albee's first play, *The Zoo Story*, was first produced in Berlin (Schiller Th. Werkstatt, Sept. 28, 1959); played in N.Y.C. (Provincetown Playhouse, Jan. 14, 1960), and in London (Arts, Aug. 25, 1960). He wrote *The Death of Bessie Smith*, which also had its first performance in Berlin (Schlosspark Th., Apr. 21, 1960) and was later produced in N.Y.C. (York Playhouse, Mar. 1, 1961). Albee's *The Sandbox* appeared on a program of four one-act plays, entitled *4 in 1* (Jazz Gallery, May 15, 1960), and his *Fam and Yam* was produced in summer theatre (White Barn, Westport, Conn., Aug. 27, 1960). His play *The American Dream* and William Flanagan's opera, *Bartleby*, of which Mr. Albee was librettist with James Hinton, Jr., were presented (York Playhouse, Jan. 24, 1961); Albee's *The Death of Bessie Smith* replaced *Bartleby* (York Playhouse, Feb. 28, 1961); *The American Dream* opened in London on a double bill with *The Death of Bessie Smith* (Royal Court, Oct. 24, 1961).

Mr. Albee's first three-act play, *Who's Afraid of Virginia Woolf?*, was his first Bway production (Billy Rose Th., Oct. 13, 1962), and was produced in London (Piccadilly, Feb. 6, 1964); followed by an adaptation of Carson McCullers' novel, *The Ballad of the Sad Cafe* (Martin Beck Th., N.Y.C., Oct. 30, 1963); *Tiny Alice* (Billy Rose Th., Dec. 29, 1964); an adaptation of James Purdy's novel *Malcolm* (Sam S. Shubert Th., Jan. 11, 1966); and *A Delicate Balance*

(Martin Beck Th., Sept. 22, 1966). Mr. Albee succeeded Abe Burrows as book author for the musical based on Truman Capote's *Breakfast at Tiffany's* (closed during previews: Majestic, Dec. 12–14, 1966); he adapted *Everything in the Garden,* based on a play by Giles Cooper (Plymouth, Nov. 29, 1967); wrote *Box* and *Quotations from Chairman Mao Tse-Tung* (Billy Rose Th., Sept. 30, 1968); *All Over* (Martin Beck Th., Mar. 28, 1971); and *Seascape,* which he also directed (Sam S. Shubert Th., Jan. 26, 1975).

As a member, with Richard Barr and Clinton Wilder, of Theater 1964, Mr. Albee produced *Corruption in the Palace of Justice* (Cherry Lane, Oct. 8, 1963); *Play* and *The Lover* (Cherry Lane, Jan. 4, 1964); *Funnyhouse of a Negro* (East End Th., Jan. 14, 1964); *Three at the Cherry Lane* (Cherry Lane, Mar. 23, 1964); and a double bill consisting of a revival of *The American Dream* and *Dutchman* (Cherry Lane, Apr. 21, 1964). Theater 1964 also organized the Playwrights Unit, which presented twenty-five plays by new playwrights at the Village South Th., N.Y.C. (1963–64).

Theater 1965 (Messrs. Albee, Barr, and Wilder) presented three programs of one-act plays (all Cherry Lane Th.): *Up to Thursday, Balls,* and *Home Free!* (Feb. 10, 1965); *Pigeons* and *Conerico Was Here To Stay* (Mar. 3, 1965); and *Hunting the Jingo Bird* and *Lovey* (Mar. 25, 1965); and the play *Do Not Pass Go* (Cherry Lane, Apr. 19, 1965).

Mr. Albee also participated with Mr. Barr and Mr. Wilder in Theater 1967 (at Cherry Lane Th.) presentations of three Thornton Wilder revivals: *The Long Christmas Dinner, Queens of France,* and *The Happy Journey to Trenton and Camden* (Sept. 6, 1966); of a revival of *The Butter and Egg Man* (Oct. 17, 1966); of *Night of the Dunce* (Dec. 28, 1966); *The Rimers of Eldritch* (Feb. 20, 1967); and *The Party on Greenwich Avenue* (May 10, 1967).

He was associated with Mr. Barr in Theater 1969 Playwrights Repertory programs (at the Billy Rose Th., N.Y.C.): *Box* and *Quotations from Chairman Mao Tse-Tung* (Sept. 30, 1968); *The Death of Bessie Smith* and *The American Dream* (Oct. 2, 1968); *Krapp's Last Tape* and *The Zoo Story* (Oct. 9, 1968); and *Happy Days* (Oct. 12, 1968); with Richard Barr and Charles Woodward, in Theater 1969's revival of *The Front Page* (Ethel Barrymore Th., May 10, 1969); and, again with Messrs. Barr and Woodward, in Theater 1971's production of *All Over* (Martin Beck Th., Mar. 28, 1971).

Films. Mr. Albee's *Who's Afraid of Virginia Woolf?* was the basis for a film (WB, 1966).

Television. Works by Mr. Albee seen on television include *The Death of Bessie Smith* (ITV, London, Eng., June 28, 1965) and *The American Dream* (ITV, London, July 5, 1965).

Awards. Mr. Albee received the Berlin Festival Award for the best new foreign play (*The Zoo Story,* 1959, and *The Death of Bessie Smith,* 1961). For *The Zoo Story,* he also received the Vernon Rice Award for outstanding contribution to the off-Bway theatre and the *Village Voice* Off-Bway (Obie) Award (1960); the Lola D'Annunzio Award for *The American Dream* (1961); the Foreign Press Assn. Award for the best American play of the year (1961); and the Argentine Critics' Award for the best foreign play of the year (1961). For *Who's Afraid of Virginia Woolf?,* he received (1963) the NY Drama Critics Circle Award for the best play of the year; the Outer Circle Award for outstanding American playwright of a Bway production; the Antoinette Perry (Tony) Award for best play of the season; the Annual ANTA Award; and the Foreign Press Assn. Award for the best American play of the year. Mr. Albee shared with Richard Barr and Clinton Wilder in the fourth annual Margo Jones Award (Feb. 1965) for encouraging new plays and playwrights; he was elected to the National Institute of Arts and Letters (1966); and he received Pulitzer prizes for drama for *A Delicate Balance* (1967) and *Seascape* (1975).

ALBERG, MILDRED FREED. Producer. b. Jan. 15, 1920, Montreal, Canada, to Harry and Florence (Goldstein) Freed. Father, president Freed Paper Box Co. Educated in Montreal, Canada. Married Jan. 28, 1940, to Somer Alberg, insurance broker, former actor. Member of NATAS (bd. of gov.; N.Y.C. natl. awards comm., 1961–63; elected natl. trustee, 1964). Address: R.R. 2, Box 104, Pound Ridge, NY 10576, tel. (914) 764-4395.

Pre-Theatre. Director of information for CARE; wrote for NY *Post* and other newspapers.

Theatre. Mrs. Alberg produced *Little Moon of Alban* (Longacre Th., N.Y.C., Dec. 1, 1960), which was based on the original script she had commissioned for television.

Films. Mrs. Alberg produced *Hot Millions* (MGM, 1967).

Television and Radio. She was writer-producer of public service programs for radio (1940–47); associate producer of a weekly series, Where Are You From (1940–47); and producer of the dramatic series We Care (ABC, 1947). For the Hallmark Hall of Fame (NBC), she was associate producer to Maurice Evans and adapter of his production of *Hamlet;* as executive producer (1953–59); she presented *Little Moon of Alban, Macbeth, Cradle Song, Kiss Me Kate, The Green Pastures, The Corn Is Green,* and *Hans Brinker.* She produced the series Our American Heritage (NBC, 1959–61) and the television films *The Going-Up of David Lev* (NBC, Apr. 25, 1973) and *The Story of Jacob and Joseph* (ABC, Apr. 7, 1974).

Awards. As president of and producer for Milberg Enterprises, Inc., Mrs. Alberg received the George Foster Peabody Award (1957) for the best non-musical television entertainment, given to the Hallmark Hall of Fame; the Hallmark presentation of *The Green Pastures* won the Sylvania Award (1957); in 1959, *Little Moon of Alban* received a NATAS (Emmy) Award, and Mrs. Alberg received the *McCall's Magazine* Golden Mike Award as "the woman of the year in broadcasting." Mrs. Alberg also received the Canadian Theatre Exhibitors Award for *Hot Millions* (1968).

ALBERGHETTI, ANNA MARIA. Singer, actress. b. May 15, 1936, Pesaro, Italy, to Daniele and Vittoria (Ricci) Alberghetti. Father, cellist and singer; mother, pianist. Attended school in Italy 1941–50; private school at Paramount Studio 1951–53 received vocal coaching from father 1941–56. Married Sept. 12, 1964 to Claudio Guzman, television producer, director; one daughter. Relative in theatre: sister, Carla Alberghetti, singer, actress.

Theatre. Miss Alberghetti made her Bway debut as Lili in *Carnival!* (Imperial Th., Apr. 13, 1961), then toured with the national company from April 1962 to March 1963 (opened Rochester Aud., N.Y., Dec. 7, 1961).

She made her US debut as a soloist at Carnegie Hall (N.Y.C., Apr. 28, 1950); subsequently sang with symphony orchestras at the Robin Hood Dell (Philadelphia, Pa., June 21, 1950; July 2, 1951); Lewisohn Stadium (N.Y.C., June 29, 1950; July 9, 1951); Red Rocks Theatre (Denver, Colo., Aug. 12, 1954); Hollywood Bowl (Los Angeles, Calif., July 1955; Sept. 5, 1959); and the Birmingham Symphony (Ala., 1959).

In summer theatres, she appeared in *Rose Marie* (Dallas, Tex., 1957; Warwick, R.I., Wallingford, Conn., and Framingham, Mass., 1959; Kansas City, Mo., and Warren, Ohio, 1960); *Fanny* (Framingham, Mass., 1958; Warren and Columbus, Ohio, 1959); *The Firefly* (Kansas City Mo., 1959; Wallingford, Conn., Framingham, Mass., and Warwick, R.I., 1960; Pittsburgh, Pa., Anaheim, Calif. 1963); and as Maria in *West Side Story* (Framingham, Mass., Wallingford, Conn., Warwick, R.I., and Tonawanda, N.Y., 1963; Mineola, N.Y., and other US theatres, 1965); and she toured in *The Fantasticks* (June–Aug. 1968). In addition, she has appeared at many nightclubs (see below), music fairs, and tents throughout her career.

Films. Miss Alberghetti appeared in *The Medium* (Scalera Studios, 1950); *Here Comes the Groom* (Par., 1951); *The Stars Are Singing* (Par., 1953); *The Last Command* (Rep., 1955); *Ten Thousand Bedrooms* (MGM, 1957); and *CinderFella* (Par., 1960).

Television. She made her TV debut on Ed Sullivan's Toast of the Town (CBS, 1950); subsequently appeared 12 times on the Ed Sullivan Show; performed on the Eddie Fisher Show (NBC, 1953–54); Red Skelton Show (CBS, 1954); Make Room for Daddy (ABC, 1954); Shower of Stars (CBS, 1955); Colgate Hour (NBC, 1955); Ford Th. (CBS, 1955); Jimmy Durante Show (1955–56); Loretta Young Show (CBS, 1955–56); GE Theatre (CBS, 1956); Ford Star Jubilee (CBS, 1956); Climax! (CBS, 1956–59); Schlitz Playhouse (CBS, 1956); Pat Boone Show (1957); Gisele MacKenzie Show (NBC, 1957); Chevrolet Show (NBC, 1957); Dupont Show (NBC, 1957); Wagon Train (NBC, 1957), Masquerade Party (1957); Steve Allen Show (NBC, 1957); Eddie Fisher (NBC, 1957–58); What's My Line? (CBS, 1957–61); Perry Como Show (NBC, 1957–62); Person to Person (CBS, 1958); Bob Hope Buick Show (NBC, 1958); Westinghouse-Desilu Playhouse (CBS, 1959); Voice of Firestone (CBS, 1959); Garry Moore Show (1959–60, 1961); Jerry Lewis (NBC, 1959; ABC, 1963); I've Got a Secret (CBS, 1961); Andy Williams Show (1963); and in *Kismet* (ABC, Oct. 1967).

Night Clubs. Miss Alberghetti appeared at the Sahara Hotel, Las Vegas, Nev. (1953–54); Royal Nevada, Las Vegas (1955); Flamingo, Las Vegas (1957); Waldorf-Astoria, N.Y.C. (1957); Americana, Miami, Fla. (1957); Latin Quarter, N.Y.C. (1958); Moulin Rouge, Los Angeles, Calif. (1958); Desert Inn, Las Vegas (1958–62); Eden Roc, Miami (1959); Stardust, Las Vegas (1960); Cocoanut Grove, Los Angeles (1960); Deauville Hotel, Miami (1960); New Arena, Pittsburgh, Pa. (1960); Casino Royal, Washington, D.C. (1960); Palumbo's, Philadelphia, Pa. (1960); Palmer House, Chicago, Ill. (1960); and the Shamrock, Houston, Tex. (1968).

Awards. She received the Antoinette Perry (Tony) Award for her performance as Lili in *Carnival!* (1962).

ALBERT, ALLAN. Director, producer, playwright, educator. b. Allan Praigrod Albert, June 29, 1945, New York City, to Irving Shelbourne and Ferda (Praigrod) Albert. Father, restaurant and hotel food supplier; mother, former actress. Educ. Miami Beach (Fla.) H.S. Grad. Amherst Coll., B.A. (magna cum laude, Phi Beta Kappa) 1968; Yale School of Drama, D.F.A. Professional training with Robert Brustein, Richard Gilman, Stanley Kauffmann, Gordon Rogoff, Nikos Psacharopoulos, Paul Sills. Member of SSD&C (1971–to date); NETC (dir., 1969–71; advisory bd., 1971–to date); (Mass.) Governor's Task Force on the Arts (1972–74); Boston Metropolitan Cultural Alliance (trustee, 1972–73); Walnut Hill (Boston, Mass.) School for the Performing Arts (trustee, 1972–73); Mercer Arts Ctr. (trustee, 1972–73). Address: (home) 205 W. 57th St., New York, NY 10019, tel. (212) 581-3137; (bus.) 202 Hampshire St., Cambridge, MA 02139, tel. (617) 661-1776.

Theatre. Mr. Albert conceived, produced, and directed *The Proposition* (Cambridge, Mass., June 1969), which toured colleges and regional theatres (Sept. 1969–to date) and opened in N.Y.C. (Gramercy Arts, Mar. 24, 1971). He was artistic director, Charles Playhouse, Boston, Mass. (1972), and The Proposition Workshop, Cambridge (1973); director of *Downtown Holy Lady* (Greenwich Mews, N.Y.C., Fall 1972); producer and director of *The Boston Tea Party* (The Performance Ctr., Cambridge, Oct. 1973; Grendel's Lair, Philadelphia, Pa., Nov. 25, 1975) and touring production; directed *The King of the United States* (Cambridge, May 1974; St. Clements, N.Y.C., Nov. 1974); and *The Extension* (Ann Arbor, Mich., Summer 1974).

Mr. Albert wrote and directed *Corral* (Cambridge, May 1975; Jan Hus, N.Y.C., Jan. 1976); *The Wanted Wagon* (Grand Opera House, Wilmington, Del., Summer 1975); and *The Whale Show* (Cambridge, Dec. 16, 1975).

Television. Mr. Albert directed the educational series How Can I Teli You? (21" Classroom, WGBH-TV, Boston, 1970) and the children's special *A Kid's Proposition* (Westinghouse, Ch. 4, Boston, 1971).

Other Activities. Mr. Albert edited *Yale/Theatre* (1968–69); is a contributing editor to *Architectural Digest;* a consultant to CBS, Inc.; and has taught at Amherst Coll., NY Univ., Queens Coll., Hunter Coll., the New School, and the State Univ. of NY at Stony Brook.

Awards. Mr. Albert received (1968–71) NDEA, Wood, and Lay fellowships for graduate study; a NETC Regional Award (1970) for contributions to New England theatre; and the Mayor's Award (Boston, Mass.) for his contributions.

ALBERT, EDDIE. Actor. b. Edward Albert Heimberger, Apr. 22, 1908, Rock Island, Ill., to Frank Daniel and Julia (Jones) Heimberger. Father, realtor. Grad. Central H.S., Minneapolis, Minn.; attended Univ. of Minnesota. Married Dec. 5, 1945, to Margo, actress and singer; one son, one daughter. Served WW II, USN, PTO; rank, Lt. Member of AEA; SAG; AFTRA. Address: c/o John Crosby, International Famous Agency, 9255 Sunset Blvd., Los Angeles, CA 90069, tel. (213) 273-8811.

Theatre. Mr. Albert began in the theatre in 1933 in Minneapolis, where he paid his school expenses at the Univ. of Minnesota by singing at amateur nights and helping to manage local theatres. He later joined a singing trio called the "Threesome" that performed on radio and in St. Louis, Mo.; Cincinnati, Ohio; and Chicago, Ill.; followed by engagements in small night clubs in N.Y.C. He formed an act with Grace Bradt known on radio as "The Honeymooners—Grace and Eddie" (1935).

He made his Bway debut as Bing Edwards in *Brother Rat* (Biltmore Th., Dec. 16, 1936); subsequently appeared as Leo Davis in *Room Service* (Cort, May 19, 1937); Antipholus in *The Boys from Syracuse* (Alvin, Nov. 23, 1938); Horace Miller in *Miss Liberty* (Imperial, July 15, 1949); the title role in the pre-Bway tryout of *Reuben Reuben* (opened Shubert, Boston, Oct. 10, 1955; closed there Oct. 22, 1955); succeeded David Wayne in *Say, Darling* (ANTA, Apr. 3, 1958); and succeeded (1960) Robert Preston as Harold Hill in *The Music Man* (Majestic, Dec. 19, 1957).

Films. Mr. Albert made his film debut in *Brother Rat* (WB, 1938); followed by *On Your Toes* (WB, 1939); *Four Wives* (WB, 1939); *Brother Rat and a Baby* (WB, 1940); *An Angel from Texas* (WB, 1940); *My Love Came Back* (WB, 1940); *A Dispatch from Reuters* (WB, 1940); *Four Mothers* (WB, 1941); *Wagons Roll at Night* (WB, 1941); *Thieves Fall Out* (WB, 1941); *Out of the Fog* (WB, 1941); *Great Mr. Nobody* (WB, 1941); *Treat 'Em Rough* (U, 1942); *Eagle Squadron* (U. 1942); *Lady Bodyguard* (Par., 1943); *Ladies's Day* (RKO, 1943); *Bombardier* (RKO, 1943); *Strange Voyage* (Mono., 1945); *Rendezvous with Annie* (Rep., 1946); *The Perfect Marriage* (Par., 1946); *The Hit Parade of 1947* (Rep., 1947); *Time Out of Mind* (U, 1947); *The Dude Goes West* (AA, 1948); *You Gotta Stay Happy* (U, 1948); *The Fuller Brush Girl* (Col., 1950); *You're in the Navy Now* (20th-Fox, 1951); *Meet Me After the Show* (20th-Fox, 1951); *Actors and Sin* (UA, 1952); and *Roman Holiday* (Par., 1953).

Also, *The Girl Rush* (Par., 1955); *Oklahoma!* (MTC, 1955); *I'll Cry Tomorrow* (MGM, 1955); *Attack!* (UA, 1956); *Teahouse of the August Moon* (MGM, 1956); *The Sun Also Rises* (20th-Fox, 1957); *The Joker Is Wild* (Par., 1957); *The Gun Runners* (UA, 1958); *Roots of Heaven* (20th-Fox, 1958); *Orders to Kill* (UMP, 1958); *Beloved Infidel* (20th-Fox, 1959); *Madison Avenue* (20th-Fox, 1962); *The Teddy Bears* (20th-Fox, 1961); *The Young Doctors* (UA, 1961); *The Longest Day* (20th-Fox, 1962); *Who's Got the Action* (Par., 1962); *The Miracle of the White Stallions* (Disney, 1962); *Captain Newman, M.D.* (U, 1963); *McQ* (Batjac, 1973); *The Longest Yard* (Par., 1973); *Escape To Witch Mountain* (Disney, 1974); *Whiffs* (Brut Prods., 1974); and *Birch Interval* (Radnitz-Mattel, 1974).

Television. Mr. Albert appeared in *1984* (Studio One, CBS) and *The Chocolate Soldier.* He has also performed on Climax! (CBS), Playhouse 90 (CBS), US Steel Hour (CBS), The Virginian (NBC), Dupont Show of the Week (NBC), Wagon Train (NBC), Sam Benedict (NBC), Wide Country (NBC), The Naked City (ABC), Dr. Kildare (NBC), The Lieutenant (NBC), Green Acres (CBS), Ben Franklin (CBS, 1974), and has acted as spokesman for the Institute of Life Insurance, and Imperial Savings and Loan.

Other Activities. He was Special World Envoy (1963) of "Meals for Millions," a philanthropic project which makes nutritious meals at low cost available to the underprivileged around the world.

He is on the board of trustees of the National Recreation and Parks Assoc., and served as special consultant for Gov. Schapp of Pennsylvania at the U.N. Food Conference in Rome (Nov. 1974).

Recreation. Organic gardening, reading philosophical works; playing the guitar; beachcombing; designing and making mobiles and glass paintings; field trips with son, Edward.

ALBERTSON, JACK. Actor. b. Malden, Mass., to Leo and Flora (Craft) Albertson. Educ. Malden public schools. Married Oct. 31, 1952, to Wallace Thomson, model; one daughter. Member of AEA; SAG; AFTRA; AGVA. Address: 8947 Rosewood Ave., Los Angeles, CA 90048.

Theatre. Mr. Albertson made his first appearance on the NY stage in *Meet the People* (Mansfield Th., Dec. 25, 1940). He played Eddie in *Strip for Action* (National, Sept. 30, 1942); Caswell in *Allah Be Praised* (Adelphi, Apr. 20, 1944); the Photographer in *Champagne for Everybody* (pre-Bway, opened National Th., Washington, D.C., Sept. 4, 1944; closed Walnut St. Th., Philadelphia, Pa., Sept. 16, 1944); and Doctor Bartoli in *A Lady Says Yes* (Broadhurst, N.Y.C., Jan. 10, 1945). He replaced (1946) Eddie Foy, Jr., as Kid Conner in a revival of *The Red Mill* (Ziegfeld Th., Oct. 16, 1945); was Yasha in a revival of *The Cradle Will Rock* (Mansfield Th., Dec. 26, 1947); replaced (1948) Joey Faye as Mr. Pontdue in *High Button Shoes* (Shubert Th., Oct. 9, 1947); and was a replacement in *Make Mine Manhattan* (Broadhurst, Jan. 15, 1948).

He was in the revue *Tickets, Please* (Coronet, Apr. 27, 1950); played Vic David in *Top Banana* (Winter Garden, Nov. 1, 1951), also touring in the part (opened Shubert Th., Philadelphia, Pa., Oct. 6, 1952; closed Biltmore, Los Angeles, Calif., June 27, 1953); and in Los Angeles appeared in productions of *Waiting for Godot* (1957) and *Conversation at Midnight* and with The Theatre Group (UCLA) played various roles in *Mother Courage* (Schoenberg Hall, Jan. 14, 1963) and was Skid in *Burlesque* (Schoenberg Hall, Jan. 14, 1963). He appeared on Bway as John Cleary in *The Subject Was Roses* (Royale, N.Y.C., May 25, 1964) and toured (1965–1966) in the part; was Frederic René Saint-Claude in *The Marriage of Mr. Mississippi* (Mark Taper Forum, Los Angeles, Calif., Aug. 25, 1967); and was Willie Clark in *The Sunshine Boys* (Broadhurst, N.Y.C., Dec. 20, 1971), also touring in the part (1973).

Films. Mr. Albertson's films include *Miracle on 34th Street* (20th-Fox, 1947); *Top Banana* (UA, 1954); *Bring Your Smile Along* (Col., 1955); *You Can't Run Away from It* (Col., 1956); *The Harder They Fall* (Col., 1956); *Man of a Thousand Faces* (U, 1957); *Don't Go Near the Water* (MGM, 1957); *Monkey on My Back* (UA, 1957); *Teacher's Pet* (Par., 1958); *Never Steal Anything Small* (U, 1959); *The George Raft Story* (Allied Artists, 1961); *Convicts Four* (Allied Artists, 1962); *Lover Come Back* (U, 1962); *Days of Wine and Roses* (WB, 1963); *Kissin' Cousins* (MGM, 1964); *Roustabout* (Par., 1964); *How to Murder Your Wife* (UA, 1965); *How to Save a Marriage and Ruin Your Life* (Col., 1968); *The Subject Was Roses* (MGM, 1968); *Changes* (Cinerama, 1969); *Justine* (20th-Fox, 1969); *Rabbit, Run* (WB, 1970); *Willie Wonka and the Chocolate Factory* (Par., 1971); and *The Poseidon Adventure* (20th-Fox, 1972).

Television. Mr. Albertson appeared on The Hour Glass (NBC, 1946); Colgate Comedy Hour (NBC, 1950–54); The Thin Man (NBC, 1958); Ensign O'Toole (NBC, 1962–63); Jack Benny Show (CBS); Red Skelton Show (NBC); Playhouse 90 (CBS); Dick Van Dyke Show (CBS); I Love Lucy (Ind.); The Defenders (CBS); Dr. Simon Locke (1972); and Chico and the Man (NBC, 1974–75).

Awards. Mr. Albertson was awarded an Antoinette Perry (Tony) Award (1965) as best supporting actor for his performance in *The Subject Was Roses,* and he received an AMPAS (Oscar) for playing the same role in the motion picture of the play. He received a Tony nomination and a Drama Desk Award (both 1973) for his performance in *The Sunshine Boys.*.

ALBERY, DONALD. Producer. b. Donald Arthur Rolleston Albery, June 19, 1914, London, Eng., to Sir Bronson James and Una Gwynn (Rolleston) Albery. Father, director, producer. Attended Alpine Coll., Switz. Married 1946, to Heather Boys. Member of executive council of the Society of West End Managers. Address: c/o Albery Theatre, St. Martin's Lane, London, W.C.2, England tel. 240-1691, 836-5650.

Theatre. Since 1950, Mr. Albery has been managing director of Wyndham Theatres Ltd., in London. He has also been managing director of Donmar Productions Ltd., Piccadilly Theatre Ltd., Calabash Productions Ltd., a director of Independent Plays Ltd., and Anglia Television Ltd., and director and administrator, London's Festival Ballet (1964–68). Previously, he was general manager of the Sadler's Wells Ballet (1941–45).

He has produced *Birthday Honours* ("Q" Th., London, Feb. 17, 1953); *The Living Room* (Wyndham's, Apr. 16, 1953); and *I Am a Camera* (New, Mar. 12, 1954).

His first production in N.Y.C. was *The Living Room,* which he presented in association with Gilbert Miller (Henry Miller's Th., Nov. 17, 1954); subsequently in London, he presented *Lucky Strike* ("Q" Th., Apr. 11, 1955); *The Remarkable Mr. Pennypacker* (New, May 18, 1955); *Waiting for Godot* (Arts, Aug. 3, 1955); *The Waltz of the Toreadors* (Arts, Feb. 24, 1956); *Gigi* (New, May 23, 1956); *Grab Me a Gondola* (Lyric, Hammersmith, Nov. 27, 1956); *Zuleika* (Saville, Apr. 11, 1957); *Tea and Sympathy* (Comedy, Apr. 25, 1957); *Paddle Your Own Canoe* (Criterion, Dec. 4, 1957); *Dinner with the Family* (New, Dec. 10, 1957); *The Potting Shed* (Globe, Feb. 5, 1958); *Epitaph for George Dillon* (Royal Court, Feb. 11, 1958), retitled *George Dillon* (Comedy, May 29, 1958); and *Irma La Douce* (Lyric, July 17, 1958).

Mr. Albery produced *The Rose Tattoo* (New, Jan. 15, 1959); *A Taste of Honey* (Wyndham's, Feb. 10, 1959); *The Hostage* (Wyndham's, June 11, 1959); *The Complaisant Lover* (Globe, June 18, 1959); *One to Another* (Lyric, Hammersmith, July 15, 1959); *The Ring of Truth* (Savoy, July 16, 1959); *The World of Suzie Wong* (Prince of Wales's, Nov. 17, 1959); *Make Me an Offer* (New, Dec. 16, 1959); *Fings Ain't Wot They Used T' Be* (Garrick, Feb. 11, 1960); *A Passage to India* (Comedy, Apr. 20, 1960); *Call It Love* (Wyndham's, June 22, 1960); *Oliver!* (New, June 30, 1960); and *The Art of Living* (Criterion, Aug. 18, 1960).

In N.Y.C., *The Hostage* was produced by Leonard S. Field and Caroline Burke Swann by arrangement with Donald Albery and Oscar Lewenstein Ltd. (Cort, Sept. 20, 1960); *Irma La Douce* was produced by David Merrick, in association with Mr. Albery and H. M. Tennent Ltd., and by arrangement with Henry Hall (Plymouth, Sept. 29, 1960); *A Taste of Honey* was presented by David Merrick, by arrangement with Mr. Albery and Oscar Lewenstein Ltd. (Lyceum, Oct. 4, 1960).

In London, Mr. Albery produced *The Tinker* (Comedy, Dec. 7, 1960) in association with H. H. Wingate for New Watergate Presentations Ltd.; *The Miracle Worker,* by arrangement with Fred Coe (Royalty, Mar. 9, 1961); and *Beyond the Fringe* (Fortune, May 10, 1961–Mar. 21, 1964; reopened Mayfair, Apr. 15, 1964). In N.Y.C., *The Complaisant Lover* was presented by Irene Mayer Selznick in association with Mr. Albery, H. M. Tennent Ltd.

and F.E.S. Plays Ltd. (Ethel Barrymore Th., Nov. 1, 1961); *A Passage to India* was presented by the Theatre Guild Productions, Inc., Robert Fryer, Lawrence Carr and John Herman by arrangement with Mr. Albery and Tennent Productions Ltd. (Ambassador, Jan. 31, 1962).

In London, Mr. Albery produced *Blitz!* (Adelphi, May 8, 1962). In N.Y.C., *Beyond the Fringe* was presented by Alexander H. Cohen by arrangement with Mr. Albery and William Donaldson (John Golden Th., Oct. 27, 1962); and *Oliver!* was presented by David Merrick and Mr. Albery (Imperial, Jan. 6, 1963). In London, Mr. Albery produced *A Severed Head* (Criterion, June 27, 1963); with Richard Barr and Clinton Wilder, *Who's Afraid of Virginia Woolf?* (Piccadilly, Feb. 6, 1964); produced *Poker Session* (Globe, Feb. 11, 1964); and *Entertaining Mr. Sloane* (New Arts, May 6, 1964).

Other 1964 London presentations from Mr. Albery were *Instant Marriage* (Piccadilly) and *The Diplomatic Baggage* (Wyndham's), both in association with Brian Rix, and Graham Greene's *Carving a Statue* was produced by H. M. Tennent in association with Mr. Albery. In N.Y.C., David Merrick and Mr. Albery produced *A Severed Head* (Royale, Oct. 28, 1964). In 1965, Mr. Albery's London productions were *Jorrocks* (New) and, in association with H. Clay Blaney, *Portrait of a Queen* (Vaudeville). In N.Y.C., Mr. Albery and David Merrick produced a return engagement of *Oliver!* (Martin Beck Th., Aug. 2, 1965), and Slade Brown, Tanya Chasman, and E. A. Gilbert in association with Michael Codron and Mr. Albery produced *Entertaining Mr. Sloane* (Lyceum, Oct. 12, 1965). In 1966, Mr. Albery produced in London *The Prime of Miss Jean Brodie* (Wyndham's), by arrangement with Whitehead Stevens Productions, Inc., and in 1967 *Mrs. Wilson's Diary* (Criterion), in association with Perry Raffles; *Spring and Port Wine* (New); and David Storey's *The Restoration of Arnold Middleton* (Criterion). Mr. Albery's 1968 London productions included *The Italian Girl* (Wyndham's) and, by arrangement with Albert W. Selden and Hal James, *Man of La Mancha* (Piccadilly). Later London productions were *Conduct Unbecoming* (Queen's Th., July, 1969) and in 1970 *It's a Two Foot Six Inches Above the Ground World* (Wyndham's), presented by Michael Codron in association with Mr. Albery; *Poor Horace* (Lyric), in association with Knightsbridge Theatrical Productions; and *Mandrake* (Criterion). In N.Y.C., Mr. Albery presented *Conduct Unbecoming* (Ethel Barrymore Th., Oct. 12, 1970), in association with Roger Stevens; and in London in 1972 he produced *Popkiss* (Globe).

ALBRIGHT, H. DARKES. Educator, writer, editor. b. Harry Darkes Albright, July 24, 1907, Lebanon, Pa., to Harry S. and Bertha (Darkes) Albright. Father, clerk. Grad. Lebanon H.S., 1924; Lebanon Valley Coll., A.B. 1928; Cornell Univ., A.M. 1931; Ph.D. 1935. Married June 24, 1936, to Elizabeth O. Nelson; one son, one daughter. Member of AETA (vice-pres., 1947; pres., 1948); SAA; NTC; ANTA; AAUP (pres. of local chapter, 1960–62); Phi Kappa Phi. Address: (home) 129 N. Sunset Dr., Ithaca, NY 14850, tel. AR 3-6635; (bus.) 107 Lincoln Hall, Cornell Univ., Ithaca, NY 14850, tel. AR 5-5256.

Since 1972, Mr. Albright has been emeritus professor of speech and drama at Cornell Univ., where he was previously an instructor (1936–39), assistant professor (1940–46), associate professor (1946–58) and professor (1958–72). He was also chairman of the Dept. of Speech and Drama (1949–57). He was instructor of English at Iowa State Teachers Coll. (1934–36).

Mr. Albright was associate editor (1949–51) and editor (1952–54) of the *Educational Theatre Journal* and since 1962, general editor of *Books of the Theatre.*

Published Works. Mr. Albright is the author of *Working Up a Part* (1947; rev. ed., 1959); *Principles of Theatre Art* (1955), written in collaboration with Lee Mitchell and William Halstead; and a translation of Adolphe Appia's *The Work of Living Art* (1960). He edited *The Story of Meininger* (1963), *Memories of the Theatre Libre* (1964), and Meyerhold's Theatre of the Grotesque (1971); and has contributed articles to *Theatre Arts, Virginia Journal of Education, Quarterly Journal of Speech* and *Studies in Speech and Drama in Honor of Alexander M. Drummond* (1944).

ALDA, ALAN. Actor, director, writer. b. Alphonso D'Abruzzo, Jan. 28, 1936, New York City, to Robert and Joan (Browne) D'Abruzzo. Father, actor, known as Robert Alda. Grad. Cardinal Stepinac H.S., White Plains, N.Y., 1952; Fordham Univ., B.S. 1956. Attended Paul Sills' Improvisational Workshop at Second City, N.Y.C., 1963. Married Mar. 15, 1957, to Arlene Weiss, musician, teacher; three daughters. Served ROTC, Fordham Univ.; rank 2nd Lt., Reserves. Member of AEA; SAG; AFTRA.

Theatre. Mr. Alda made his debut at the Hollywood (Calif.) Canteen, playing Costello to his father's Abbott in various Abbott and Costello sketches; subsequently, he played Jack Chesney in a stock production *Charley's Aunt* (Barnesville, Pa., Summer 1953); Leo Davis in *Room Service* (Teatro Del 'Eliseo, Rome, Italy, 1955); was understudy to Don Murray as Clarence "Lefty" McShane in *The Hot Corner* (John Golden Th., N.Y.C., Jan. 25, 1956); in a stock tour, appeared as Wade in *Roger the Sixth,* Artie in *Compulsion,* Irwin Trowbridge in *Three Men on a Horse,* Horace in *The Little Foxes* (Summer 1957); played Billy Turk in *Nature's Way* (Valley Playhouse, Chagrin Falls, Ohio, Summer 1958); appeared at the Cleveland (Ohio) Play House in his own adaptation of *The Book of Job,* as David Williams in *Who Was That Lady I Saw You With?,* in *Monique,* Toni in *To Dorothy, a Son* (Winter, 1958–59); and played Sky Masterson in *Guys and Dolls* (Grand Th., Sullivan, Ill., July, 1959), a role his father, Robert Alda, created on Bway.

He made his Bway debut as the Telephone Man in *Only in America* (Cort, Nov. 19, 1959); subsequently played the title role in *L'il Abner* (Grand Th., Sullivan, Ill., July, 1960); appeared in the revue *Darwin's Theories* (Madison Ave. Playhouse, N.Y.C., Oct. 19, 1960), to which he contributed sketches; played David in *The Woman with Red Hair* (Teatro Dei Servi, Rome, Italy, Jan. 1961); Fergie Howard in a stock production of *Golden Fleecing* (Southbury Playhouse, Conn., June, 1961); Fleider and was understudy to Jean Pierre Aumont in the title role of *Anatol* (Boston Arts Center, Mass., July 31, 1961).

Mr. Alda appeared as Charlie Cotchipee in *Purlie Victorious* (Cort, N.Y.C., Sept. 28, 1961); Howard Mayer in *A Whisper in God's Ear* (Cricket, Oct. 11, 1962); Willie Alvarez in the pre-Bway tour of *Memo* (opened Shubert, New Haven, Conn., Feb. 27, 1963; closed Wilbur, Boston, Mass., Mar. 19, 1963); toured in stock as Francis X. Dignan in *King of Hearts* (Lakes Region Playhouse, Laconia, N.H.; Bucks County Playhouse; Coconut Grove Playhouse, Miami, Fla.; Playhouse-on-the-Mall, Paramus, N.J., Summer 1963); played Benny Bennington in *Fair Game for Lovers* (Cort, N.Y.C., Feb. 10, 1964); and Dr. Gilbert in *Cafe Crown* (Martin Beck Th., Apr. 7, 1964).

He was Woodrow O'Malley in a tryout tour of *Watch the Birdie!* (Summer 1964); Mike Mitchell in *Sunday in New York* (Bucks County Playhouse, New Hope, Pa., Aug. 24, 1964); F. Sherman in *The Owl and the Pussycat* (ANTA Th., N.Y.C., Nov. 18, 1964); and directed the pre-Bway tryout of *The Midnight Ride of Alvin Blum* (Westport Country Playhouse, Conn., July 4, 1966; Playhouse on the Mall, Paramus, N.J., Aug. 23, 1966). He played Adam in *The Diary of Adam and Eve,* Captain Sanjar in *The Lady or the Tiger?,* and The Prince Charming in *Passionella,* the three parts of *The Apple Tree* (Sam S. Shubert Th., N.Y.C., Oct. 18, 1966); and was in *There's a Girl in My Soup* (Playhouse on the Mall, Paramus, N.J., Oct. 1968).

Films. He played Charlie Cotchipee in *Gone Are the Days!* (Hammer, 1963), film version of *Purlie Victorious;* was in *Paper Lion* (UA, 1968); *Jennie* (Cinerama, 1970); *The Moonshine War* (MGM, 1970); *The Mephisto Waltz* (20th-Fox, 1971); and *To Kill a Clown* (20th-Fox, 1972).

Television. Mr. Alda appeared on Secret Files, U.S.A. (synd., 1955); the Phil Silvers Show (CBS, 1957); Naked City (ABC, 1962); Dupont Show of the Week (NBC, 1962); The Nurses (CBS, 1962); Route 66 (CBS, 1962); The Shari Lewis Show (CBS, 1963); East Side, West Side (CBS, 1963); and This Was the Week That Was (NBC, 1964). He was in *The Tree and the Cross* (Directions '64, ABC, June 28, 1964); was a guest on Memory Lane (Ind., 1964–65); on the Today Show (NBC, 1964–65); Match Game (NBC, 1965–66); Trials of O'Brien (CBS, 1965); in *Out of the Flying Pan* and *It's Almost Like Being* (NY Television Th., NET, Feb. 7, 1966); in the pilot *Where's Everett?* (CBS, Apr. 18, 1966); and in *The Glass House* (CBS, Feb. 4, 1972).

He has written some scripts for, directed segments of, and starred as Hawkeye in M*A*S*H (CBS, 1972–to date); appeared in the pilot *Lily* (CBS, Nov. 1973); in *6 Rms Riv Vu* (CBS, Mar. 17, 1974), which he also directed; and created, wrote, and co-produced *We'll Get By* (CBS, Mar. 1975).

Night Clubs. Mr. Alda performed in the improvisational revues, *Compass* (Yachtsman Hotel, Hyannis, Mass., Summer 1962); and *Second City* (Second City at Square East, N.Y.C., Oct. 1963).

Other Activities. In 1963, Mr. Alda began teaching at the Compass School of Improvisation, N.Y.C. On Apr. 14, 1975, he was appointed by Pres. Ford to the Commission on the Observance of International Women's Year.

Discography. Mr. Alda is on the Marlo Thomas album *Free To Be . . . You and Me* (Bell Records, 1973).

Awards. Mr. Alda received a *Theatre World* Award for his performance as Benny Bennington in *Fair Game for Lovers* (1964).

ALDA, ROBERT. Actor. b. Alphonso Giovanni Giusseppe Roberto D'Abruzzo, Feb. 26, New York City, to Anthony and Frances (Tumillo) D'Abruzzo. Father, barber. Grad. Stuyvesant H.S., N.Y.C., 1928; attended Architectural Sch., New York Univ., 1929–31. Married Dec. 1935 to Josephine Brown (marr. dis. 1955); one son; married Sept. 1956 to Flora Marino; one son. Relative in theatre: son, Alan Alda, actor. Member of AEA; SAG; AFTRA; AGVA.

Pre-Theatre. Junior draftsman in architectural firm in N.Y.C. (1928–31).

Theatre. Mr. Alda made his debut as a singer in vaudeville in an act called *Charlie Ahearn and His Millionaires* (RKO, N.Y.C., 1933), and toured in it (RKO Th. circuit); subsequently appeared in burlesque as a singer and straight man in N.Y.C. (Republic, Oct. 1935), and on tour (1935–1940); in Summer hotel-theatre productions, in the Catskill Mountain (N.Y.) resort area, of *Waiting for Lefty, Golden Boy, Of Mice and Men, Men in White, Three Men on a Horse, Love from a Stranger, Tobacco Road, Boy Meets Girl, Room Service, The Jazz Singer, The Postman Always Rings Twice* and *The Time of Your Life* (Summers 1935–40); appeared in *There Goes the Bride* (La Jolla Playhouse, Calif., 1947); in *The Male Animal* (Beverly Th., Mass., Summer 1948); and toured in vaudeville in *A Hollywood Revue* (Dec. 1949–Mar. 1950).

He made his Bway debut as Sky Masterson in *Guys and Dolls* (46 St. Th., Nov. 24, 1950); repeated the role in a night club version (Riviera Hotel, Las Vegas, Nev., Summer 1955); in Italy, appeared in *La Padrona di Raggio di Luna,* the only American in the cast (Eliseo Th., Rome; Lirico Th., Milan; La Fenice Th., Naples; Palermo, Catania, and Messina, Sicily, 1955–56).

Mr. Alda appeared as Chris in *Harbor Lights* (Playhouse, N.Y.C., Oct. 5, 1956); in a stock tour of *Roger the VI* (Summer 1957); in *Fair Game* (Long Beach, N.Y., Summer 1958); *Three Men on a Horse* (Cleveland, Ohio, Summer 1958); toured in a stock production of *Can-Can* (June–Aug. 1963); played Al Manheim in *What Makes Sammy Run?* (54 St. Th., N.Y.C., Feb. 27, 1964); toured as Fred Sumner in *Riverwind* (Summer 1966); appeared in *The Odd Couple* (Pittsburgh Playhouse, Pittsburgh, Pa., Apr.

3, 1968); was Arthur Gordon in *My Daughter, Your Son* (Booth Th., N.Y.C., May 13, 1969); and replaced (Jan. 27, 1970) James Flavin as Murphy in a revival of *The Front Page* (Ethel Barrymore Th., Oct. 18, 1969).

Films. Mr. Alda made his debut as George Gershwin in *Rhapsody in Blue* (WB, 1945); subsequently appeared in *Cinderella Jones* (WB, 1946); *Beast with Five Fingers* (WB, 1946); *The Man I Love* (WB, 1946); *Cloak and Dagger* (WB, 1946); *Nora Prentiss* (WB, 1947); *April Showers* (WB, 1948); *Tarzan and the Slave Girl* (RKO, 1950); *Hollywood Varieties* (LIP, 1950); *Mister Universe* (Eagle-Lion, 1951); *Two Gals and a Guy* (Eagle-Lion, 1951); *Beautiful but Dangerous* (20th-Fox, 1958); *Imitation of Life* (U, 1959); in Italy, in *Un Militaire e Mezzo* (Titanus, 1959); *Sepulchre dei Rei* (Cinecitta, 1960); *Vendetta dei Barbari* (Titanus, 1961); *Mosschettiere dei Mare* (Titanus, 1962); *Toto e Peppino* (Cinecitta, 1962); and in the US, *Force of Impulse* (SPC, 1961).

Television and Radio. Mr. Alda made his radio debut as a singer (WHN, 1934); subsequently appeared on WOV and WNEW (1934–35); Lux Radio Th. (CBS, 1945); Th. of Romance (CBS, 1945); the Rudy Vallee Show; and the Jack Carson Show (NBC, 1947–48).

He made his television debut on a variety program in Grand Central Station, entitled *Alda and Henry* (CBS, 1937); appeared as emcee on By Popular Demand (CBS, Summer 1950); on the Milton Berle Show (NBC, 1950, 1951); as emcee of What's Your Bid (Dumont, 1952); the Robert Alda Show (ABC, 1953); on the filmed series Secret File U.S.A. (1954); was emcee of Can-Do (NBC, 1956–57); appeared on To Tell the Truth (CBS, 1964–65); the Merv Griffin Show (Ind., 1965–66); Match Game (NBC, 1965–66); The Millionaire (Ind., 1966); Love of Life (CBS, 1966–67); Ironside (NBC, 1967, 1968, 1969); Judd for the Defense (ABC, 1967); N.Y.P.D. (ABC, 1968); and Here's Lucy (CBS, 1970, 1971).

In Italy, Mr. Alda has been in *Raggio di Luna* (RAI) and *Il Musichiere* (RAI); and on radio, in *Rosso e Nero* (Rome), *Il Disco D'Oro,* (Ischia) and *L'Ospite d'Onore* (Milan).

Night Clubs. Mr. Alda made his night-club debut at the Paradise Restaurant (N.Y.C., 1935); subsequently appeared at the Strand Th. (N.Y.C., 1946, 1948, 1949); Warner's Th. (Pittsburgh, Pa., 1948, 1949); Chicago Th. (Ill., 1948, 1949, 1952); Hippodrome (Baltimore, Md., 1949, 1953); Riviera Hotel (Las Vegas, Nev., 1955); and El Rancho Vegas (Las Vegas, Nev., 1956).

Awards. Mr. Alda received the Antoinette Perry (Tony) Award, the Donaldson Award, and the *Variety* NY Drama Critics Poll for his performance as Sky Masterson in *Guys and Dolls* (1951); and the Golden Wing in Italy for his performances in the play, *La Padrona di Raggio di Luna* and in the film *La Donna Piu Bella del Monda,* released in US as *Beautiful but Dangerous* (1956).

Recreation. Reading, writing.

ALDEN, HORTENSE.

Actress. b. Feb. 12, Dallas, Tex. Member of AEA; AFTRA.

Theatre. Miss Alden made her stage debut in summer stock in Erie, Pa., and Rochester, N.Y.; first appeared on Bway as Maria in *Liliom* (Garrick Th., Apr. 20, 1921); followed by Audrey in *As You Like It* (44 St. Th., Apr. 23, 1923); Laila in *Arabesque* (National, Oct. 20, 1925); Amelia in *The Firebrand* (Morosco, Oct. 15, 1924); followed (June 1927) Margalo Gillmore as Jenny in *Ned McCobb's Daughter* (John Golden Th., Nov. 29, 1926) and temporarily succeeded (Apr. 1927) Phyllis Connard in the role of Dina in *Right You Are If You Think You Are* (Guild, Mar. 2, 1927).

Miss Alden toured (1927–28) in the Theatre Guild productions of *Mr. Pim Passes By, The Silver Cord, The Guardsman,* and *Arms and the Man;* played Katia in *A Month in the Country* (Guild, N.Y.C., Mar. 17, 1930); Myrrhina in *Lysistrata* (44 St. Th., June 5, 1930); Flaemmchen in *Grand Hotel* (National, Nov. 13, 1930); Joyce Clyde in *Thunder on the Left* (Maxine Elliott's Th., Oct. 31, 1933); Lois Dodd in *But Not for Love* (Empire, Nov. 26, 1934); Crysis in *Arms for Venus* (John Golden Th., Mar. 11, 1937); Gert Marble in *Here Come the Clowns* (Booth, Dec. 7, 1938); and Mary Baker Eddy in *Battle for Heaven* (Educational Alliance, May 18, 1948). In the double-bill, *Garden District,* she played Grace Lancaster in *Something Unspoken* and Violet Vanable in *Suddenly Last Summer* (York Playhouse, Jan. 7, 1958); she was in *Pigeons* (Village South Th., Dec. 1, 1963); and on the program *Triple Play,* she was Laura Langston in *The Late Late Show* (Cherry Lane, Nov. 3, 1968).

Television. Miss Alden appeared on the television serials, From These Roots (NBC, 1962) and The Doctors and the Nurses (CBS, 1964).

ALDREDGE, THEONI V.

Costume designer. b. Theoni Athanasiou Vachlioti, Salonika, Greece, to Athanasios and Merope Vachliotis. Father, Surgeon-General, Greek Army, member of Greek Parliament. Attended The American Sch., Athens; Goodman Sch. of the Theatre, Chicago, Ill., 1949–52. Married Dec. 10, 1953 to Tom Aldredge, actor. Member of United Scenic Artists. Address: c/o William Morris Agency, 1350 Ave. of Americas, New York, NY 10019.

Theatre. The first play for which Mrs. Aldredge designed costumes was *The Distaff Side* (Goodman Memorial Th., Chicago, 1950); subsequently designed costumes for a stock production of *The Importance of Being Earnest* (Tower Ranch Tenthouse Th., Rhinelander, Wis., Summer 1953); costumes for *A Month in the Country* (Studebaker Th., Chicago, Oct. 22, 1956); followed by other designing assignments for costumes at the Studebaker Th., *The Immoralist* (Dec. 26, 1956), *Much Ado About Nothing* (Jan. 22, 1957), *A View from the Bridge* (Feb. 19, 1957), *Lysistrata* (Mar. 12, 1957), and *The Guardsman* (Apr. 3, 1957).

She designed costumes for *Heloise* (Gate, N.Y.C., Sept. 24, 1958); *The Golden Six* (York Playhouse, Oct. 25, 1958); and *The Saintliness of Margery Kempe* (York Playhouse, Feb. 2, 1959); for Geraldine Page in *Sweet Bird of Youth* (Martin Beck Th., Mar. 10, 1959); was costume designer for *The Geranium Hat* (Orpheum, Mar. 19, 1959); *The Nervous Set* (Henry Miller's Th., May 12, 1959); *Chic* (Orpheum, May 19, 1959); *Flowering Cherry* (Lyceum, Oct. 21, 1959); *Silent Night, Lonely Night* (Morosco, Dec. 31, 1959); *A Distant Bell* (Eugene O'Neill Th., Jan. 13, 1960).

She created costumes for *The Best Man* (Morosco, Mar. 31, 1960); *Measure for Measure* (NY Shakespeare Festival, Belvedere Lake Th., July 25, 1960); *Hedda Gabler* (Fourth St. Th., Nov. 9, 1960); *Rosemary and the Alligators* (York Playhouse, Nov. 14, 1960); *Mary, Mary* (Helen Hayes Th., Mar. 8, 1961); *The Devil's Advocate* (Billy Rose Th., Mar. 9, 1961); *Under Milk Wood* (Circle in the Square, Mar. 29, 1961); *Smiling, the Boy Fell Dead* (Cherry Lane, Apr. 19, 1961); *Much Ado About Nothing* NY Shakespeare Festival, Wollman Memorial Rink, July 5, 1961); *Ghosts* (Fourth St. Th., Sept. 21, 1961); *First Love* (Morosco, Dec. 25, 1961); *I Can Get It for You Wholesale* (Shubert, Mar. 22, 1962); and *Rosmersholm* (Fourth St. Th., Apr. 11, 1962).

Mrs. Aldredge designed costumes for the NY Shakespeare Festival productions of *The Merchant of Venice* (Delacorte Th.) (June 19, 1962), *the Tempest* (July 16, 1962) and *King Lear* (Aug. 13, 1962); also for *Who's Afraid of Virginia Woolf?* (Billy Rose Th., Oct. 13, 1962); *Mr. President* (St. James, Oct. 20, 1962); *Tchin-Tchin* (Plymouth, Oct. 25, 1962); and *Strange Interlude* (Hudson, Mar. 11, 1963); with the NY Shakespeare Festival (Delacorte Th.) was costume designer for *Antony and Cleopatra* (June 20, 1963), *As You Like It* (July 16, 1963) and *The Winter's Tale* (Aug. 14, 1963); followed by costumes for *The Trojan Women* (Circle in the Square, Dec. 23, 1963); *Any Wednesday* (Music Box, Feb. 18, 1964); *But for Whom Charlie* (ANTA Washington Square Th., Mar. 12, 1964); *Anyone Can Whistle* (Music Box, Apr. 1, 1964); *The Knack* (Establishment Th., May 19, 1964); was costume designer with Ray Diffen for the Actors Studio production of *The Three Sisters* (Morosco, June 22, 1964); and created costumes for the NY Shakespeare Festival productions (Delacorte Th.) of *Hamlet* (June 10, 1964), *Othello* (July 8, 1964) and *Electra* (Aug. 5, 1964).

She also designed costumes for *Luv* (Booth Th., Nov. 11, 1964); *P.S. I Love You* (Henry Miller's Th., Nov. 19, 1964); *Poor Richard* (Helen Hayes Th., Dec. 2, 1964); *Ready When You Are, C.B.!* (Brooks Atkinson Th., Dec. 7, 1964); and for NY Shakespeare Festival productions (Delacorte Th.) of *Love's Labour's Lost* (June 9, 1965), *The Taming of the Shrew* (June 28, 1965), *Coriolanus* (July 7, 1965), and *Troilus and Cressida* (Aug. 4, 1965). She designed costumes for *Hot September* (Shubert Th., Boston, Sept. 14, 1965); *Minor Miracle* (Henry Miller's Th., Oct. 7, 1965); *The Porcelain Year* (Locust, Philadelphia, Oct. 11, 1965); *Skyscraper* (Lunt-Fontanne Th., N.Y.C., Nov. 13, 1965); *The Playroom* (Brooks Atkinson Th., Dec. 5, 1965); and *Cactus Flower* (Royale, Dec. 8, 1965).

Also for *U.T.B.U.* (Helen Hayes Th., Jan. 4, 1966); *First One Asleep, Whistle* (Belasco Th., Feb. 26, 1966); *Serjeant Musgrave's Dance* (Th. de Lys, Mar. 8, 1966); *Happily Never After* (Eugene O'Neill Th., Mar. 10, 1966); NY Shakespeare Festival productions (Delacorte Th.) of *All's Well That Ends Well* (June 15, 1966), *Measure for Measure* (July 12, 1966), and *Richard III* (Aug. 9, 1966); and costumes for *A Delicate Balance* (Martin Beck Th., Sept. 22, 1966). She also designed costumes for *You Know I Can't Hear You When the Water's Running* (Ambassador, Mar. 13, 1967); *That Summer — That Fall* (Helen Hayes Th., Mar. 16, 1967); *Illya Darling* (Mark Hellinger Th., Apr. 11, 1967); *Little Murders* (Broadhurst, Apr. 25, 1967); NY Shakespeare Festival (Delacorte Th.) productions of *The Comedy of Errors* (June 7, 1967), *King John* (July 5, 1967), and *Titus Andronicus* (Aug. 2, 1967); costumes for *Daphne in Cottage D* (Longacre, Oct. 15, 1967); *Hair* (NY Shakespeare Festival, Public Th., Oct. 29, 1967); *The Trial of Lee Harvey Oswald* (ANTA, Nov. 5, 1967); and for *Hamlet* (NY Shakespeare Festival, Public Th., Dec. 26, 1967).

Mrs. Aldredge also created costumes for *Before You Go* (Henry Miller's Th., Jan. 11, 1968); *I Never Sang for My Father* (Longacre, Jan. 25, 1968); *Portrait of a Queen* (Henry Miller's Th., Feb. 28, 1968); *Ergo* (NY Shakespeare Festival, Public Th., Mar. 3, 1968); *Weekend* (Broadhurst, Mar. 13, 1968); *The Memorandum* (NY Shakespeare Festival, Public Th., Apr. 23, 1968); *The Only Game in Town* (Broadhurst, May 23, 1968); NY Shakespeare Festival (Delacorte Th.) productions of *King Henry IV, Part 1* (June 11, 1968), *King Henry IV, Part 2* (June 18, 1968), and *Romeo and Juliet* (Aug. 8, 1968); costumes for *King Lear* (Vivian Beaumont Th., Nov. 7, 1968); *Huui, Huui* (NY Shakespeare Festival, Public Th., Nov. 24, 1968); and *Ballad for a Firing Squad* (Th. de Lys, Dec. 11, 1968). Also for *Cities in Bezique* (NY Shakespeare Festival, Public Th., Jan. 4, 1969); *Zelda* (Ethel Barrymore Th., Mar. 5, 1969); *Invitation to a Beheading* (NY Shakespeare Festival, Public Th., Mar. 8, 1969); *Billy* (Billy Rose Th., Mar. 22, 1969); *The Gingham Dog* (John Golden Th., Apr. 23, 1969); NY Shakespeare Festival's *Peer Gynt* (Delacorte Th., July 15, 1969), *Electra* (Mobile Th., Aug. 5, 1969), *Twelfth Night* (Delacorte Th., Aug. 12, 1969), and *No Place To Be Somebody* (Public Th., Dec. 30, 1969).

She also created costumes for NY Shakespeare Festival productions (Delacorte Th.) of *King Henry VI, Part 1* (June 23, 1970), *King Henry VI, Part 2* (June 24, 1970), and *Richard III* (June 25, 1970); and, at the Public Th., for *The Happiness Cage* (Oct. 4, 1970) and *Trelawney of the Wells* (Oct. 11, 1970); costumes for *Colette* (Ellen Stewart Th., Oct. 14, 1970); and for the one-man show *Jack MacGowran in the Works of Samuel Beckett* (Public Th., Nov. 19, 1970). She designed costumes for NY Shakespeare Festival productions (Public Th.) of *Subject to Fits* (Feb. 14, 1971), *Here Are Ladies* (Feb. 22, 1971), *Blood* (Mar. 7, 1971), *Underground* (Apr. 18, 1971), *The Basic Training of Pavlo Hummel* (May 19, 1971); and, at the Delacorte Th., of *Timon of Athens* (June 30, 1971), *The Two Gentlemen of Verona* (July 27, 1971), and *The Tale of Cymbeline* (Aug. 17, 1971). She designed costumes for *The Incomparable Max*

(Royale, Oct. 19, 1971); *Sticks and Bones* (Public Th., Nov. 7, 1971; John Golden Th., Mar. 1, 1972); *Two Gentlemen of Verona* (St. James Th., Dec. 1, 1971); and *The Wedding of Iphigenia* (Public Th., Dec. 16, 1971).

Mrs. Aldredge also designed costumes for *The Sign in Sidney Brustein's Window* (Longacre, Jan. 26, 1972); *Voices* (Ethel Barrymore Th., Apr. 4, 1972); NY Shakespeare Festival productions of *That Championship Season* (Public Th., May 2, 1972; Booth Th., Sept. 14, 1972); *Older People* (Public Th., May 14, 1972); *The Hunter* (Public Th., May 23, 1972); *Hamlet* (Delacorte Th., June 20, 1972); *The Corner* (Public Th., June 22, 1972); *Ti-Jean and His Brothers* (Delacorte, July 19, 1972); *Much Ado About Nothing* (Delacorte, Aug. 16, 1972; Winter Garden, Nov. 11, 1972); and *The Children* (Public Th., Dec. 17, 1972).

Later productions for which she designed costumes include *The Cherry Orchard* (NY Shakespeare Festival, Public Th., Jan. 11, 1973); *No Hard Feelings* (Martin Beck Th., Apr. 8, 1973); *The Orphan* (NY Shakespeare Festival, Public Th., Apr. 18, 1973); *Nash at Nine* (Helen Hayes Th., May 17, 1973); NY Shakespeare Festival productions of *As You Like It* (Delacorte Th., June 21, 1973); *King Lear* (Delacorte Th., July 26, 1973); *Two Gentlemen of Verona* (Mobile Th., July 31, 1973); *Boom Boom Room* (Vivian Beaumont Th., Nov. 8, 1973); and *The Au Pair Man* (Vivian Beaumont Th., Dec. 27, 1973). Also for *Find Your Way Home* (Brooks Atkinson Th., Jan. 2, 1974); *The Killdeer* (NY Shakespeare Festival, Public Th., Mar. 28, 1974); *The Dance of Death* (NY Shakespeare Festival, Vivian Beaumont Th., Apr. 4, 1974); *Music! Music!* (NY City Ctr., Apr. 11, 1974); *An American Millionaire* (Circle in the Square — Joseph E. Levine Th., Apr. 20, 1974); *In Praise of Love* (Morosco, Dec. 10, 1974); *Mert and Phil* (NY Shakespeare Festival, Vivian Beaumont Th., Oct. 30, 1974); *A Doll's House* (NY Shakespeare Festival, Vivian Beaumont Th., Mar. 5, 1975); *Kid Champion* (Public Th., Jan. 28, 1975); *Little Black Sheep* (Public Th., May 7, 1975); and *A Chorus Line* (Public Th., Apr. 5, 1975).

Films. Mrs. Aldredge designed the costumes for *Girl of the Night* (WB, 1960); *You're a Big Boy Now* (7 Arts, 1967); *No Way To Treat a Lady* (Par., 1968); *Up Tight* (Par., 1966); *Promise at Dawn* (Avco, 1971); *I Never Sang for My Father* (Col., 1970); *The Great Gatsby* (Par., 1974); for Faye Dunaway in *Three Days of the Condor* (Par., 1975); and costumes for *Harry and Walter Go to New York* (Col., 1975).

Awards. Mrs. Aldredge was nominated for Antoinette Perry (Tony) awards for costume design for her costumes for *The Devil's Advocate* (1961) and for *Much Ado About Nothing;* received the Maharam Award for her costumes for *Peer Gynt* (1969); and for her designs for the film *The Great Gatsby* received an Academy (Oscar) Award (1974), the Society of Film and Television Arts (England) Award (1974), and an American Fashion Award (1975).

ALDREDGE, THOMAS. Actor, director, producer. b. Thomas Ernest Aldredge, Feb. 28, 1928, Dayton, Ohio, to W. J. and Lucienne Juliet (Marcillat) Aldredge. Father, Col., USAF (ret.). Grad. Oakwood H.S., Dayton, Ohio, 1946; attended Univ. of Dayton, 1947–49; studied acting with Maurice Gnesin, Mary Agnes Doyle, David Itkin at the Goodman Memorial Sch. of the Th., Chicago, Ill., B.F.A. 1953. Married Dec. 10, 1953, to Theoni Vachliotti, costume designer, known as Theoni V. Aldredge. Served US Army, A.G.D., PTO, 1946–47; rank 1st Sgt. Member of AEA; SAG; AFTRA. Address: c/o William Morris Agency, 1350 Ave. of the Americas, New York, NY.

Theatre. Mr. Aldredge first appeared on stage in the title role of a school production of *Rip Van Winkle* (Belmont Jr. H.S., Dayton, Ohio, 1939); followed by his first speaking role as a Messenger in *Hamlet* (Goodman Mem. Th., Chicago, Ill., Jan. 1950); and his professional debut as Chester (Bud) Norton in a stock production of *Personal Appearance* (Summer 1950).

At the Tower Ranch Tenthouse Th. (Rhinelander, Wis.) he performed in *Jason, The Corn Is Green, Summer and Smoke, The Play's the Thing, Death of a Salesman, The Hasty Heart, Blood Wedding, The Drunkard, The Glass Menagerie, Private Lives, Tovarich, Our Town, The Little Foxes, Laura, Blithe Spirit* and *Inherit the Wind* (Summers 1951–53); directed *The Fourposter,* played in and directed *Here Today, Saturday's Children, The Rope, Arms and the Man, The Guardsman, A Streetcar Named Desire, The Heiress, Shadow and Substance* and *Years Ago* (Summer 1954); appeared in and directed *I Am a Camera, My Three Angels, Sabrina Fair, The Moon Is Blue, The Immoralist, Mister Roberts, The Rainmaker,* and *The Lady's Not for Burning* (Summer 1955); and played in *Will Success Spoil Rock Hunter?, Inherit the Wind, Cat on a Hot Tin Roof, Teahouse of the August Moon, No Time for Sergeants,* and directed *A Member of the Wedding* (Summer 1958).

He made his N.Y.C. debut as the Messenger in *Electra* (Jan Hus House, May 9, 1958); appeared at the Crystal Palace (St. Louis, Mo.) as Vladimir (Didi) in *Waiting for Godot* (Jan. 27, 1958), Hamm in *Endgame* (1959) and Danny in *The Nervous Set* (Mar. 10, 1959); repeated his role in *The Nervous Set* (Henry Miller's Th., N.Y.C., May 12, 1959); played David in *Between Two Thieves* (York Playhouse, Feb. 11, 1960); the Dauphin in the NY Shakepeare Festival production of *Henry V* (Belvedere Lake Th., June 29, 1960); and performed in *The Premise,* improvisational theatre (Premise Th., Nov. 22, 1960; Shoreham Hotel, Washington, D.C., Jan. 1962; Comedy Th., London, Sept. 1962; Ivar, Los Angeles, Calif., May 1964).

He played Boyet in *Love's Labour's Lost* (Delacorte Th., N.Y.C., June 9, 1965); Nestor in *Troilus and Cressida* (Delacorte Th., Aug. 4, 1965); Eugene Boyer in *UTBU* (Helen Hayes Th., Jan. 4, 1966); Bernie in *Slapstick Tragedy* (Longacre, Feb. 22, 1966); Angelo in *Measure for Measure* (Delacorte Th., July 12, 1966); the Second Murderer in *King Richard III* (Aug. 9, 1966); and Jack McClure in *The Butter and Egg Man* (Cherry Lane, Oct. 17, 1966).

In 1967, he appeared at the American Shakespeare Festival, Stratford, Conn., as Quince in *A Midsummer Night's Dream* (June 17), the Chorus in *Antigone* (June 18), Gratiano in *The Merchant of Venice* (June 20), and Macduff in *Macbeth* (June 25). He played Gilbert in *Everything in the Garden* (Plymouth, N.Y.C., Nov. 29, 1967); McKeating in *Stock Up on Pepper 'Cause Turkey's Going to War* (Ellen Stewart Th., 1967); was Wurz in Ego (Public Th., Mar. 3, 1968); and Tybalt in *Romeo and Juliet* (Delacorte Th., June 25, 1968).

He was Emory in *The Boys in the Band* (Wyndham's Th., London, England, Feb. 1969); Sir Andrew Aguecheek in *Twelfth Night* (Delacorte Th., N.Y.C., Aug. 19, 1969); Senator Logan in *Indians* (Brooks Atkinson Th., Oct. 13, 1969); Victor Bard in *The Engagement Baby* (Helen Hayes Th., May 21, 1970); directed *The Happiness Cage* (Public Th., Oct. 4, 1970); and played William Detweiler in *How the Other Half Loves* (Royale, Mar. 29, 1971).

He appeared as Cymbeline in *The Tale of Cymbeline* (Delacorte Th., Aug. 17, 1971); was Ozzie in *Sticks and Bones* (Public Th., Nov. 7, 1971; Royale, Mar. 1, 1972); the Second Gravedigger in *Hamlet* (Delacorte Th., June 20, 1972); Calchas in *The Orphan* (Public Th., Apr. 18, 1973); the Fool in *King Lear* (Delacorte Th., July 26, 1973); Jimmy Tomorrow in *The Iceman Cometh* (Circle in the Square/-Joseph E. Levine Th., Dec. 13, 1973); and Amy Spettigue in *Where's Charley?* (Circle in the Square/-Joseph E. Levine Th., Dec. 19, 1974).

Films. Mr. Aldredge appeared in *The Mouse on the Moon* (UA, 1962); *The Troublemaker* (Seneca, 1964); *Who Killed Teddy Bear?* (Magna, 1965); and *The Rain People* (WB, 1969).

Television. For the Chicago Educational TV Association, Mr. Aldredge was producer-director (1955–57) and producer-host of the Curious One (1956). He was in *Seasons of Youth* (Timex Special, ABC); N.Y.P.D. (WPIX-Ind.); *The Threepenny Opera* (PBS); *Ten Blocks on the Camino Reale* (PBS); Candid Camera; Love of Life (CBS); *The Spy Who Returned from the Dead* (ABC Mystery Movie); *Sticks and Bones* (CBS Special, 1972); and *King Lear* (PBS, 1973).

Awards. Mr. Aldredge received Village Voice off-Bway (Obie) awards in 1967 for his distinguished performances in *Measure for Measure* and *Stock Up on Pepper 'Cause Turkey's Going to War;* the Drama Desk Award in 1972 for his performance in *Sticks and Bones;* and Antoinette Perry (Tony) nominations for *Sticks and Bones* (1972) for best actor and for *Where's Charley?* (1975) for best supporting actor in a musical.

Recreation. Sailing, boat design.

ALEXANDER, C. K. Actor, director, composer. b. Charles K. Alexander, May 4, 1923, Cairo, Egypt. Attended Fuad Univ., 1938–39 and American Univ., 1940–41, Cairo. Married Apr. 22, 1950, to Margaret Frances Kachur, social worker; three sons, four daughters. Member of AEA; SAG; AFTRA; Dramatists Guild; English Speaking Union; Amer. Guild of Authors and Composers; League of Off-Broadway Theatres.

Theatre. Mr. Alexander made his professional debut in the theatre in *The Merry Widow* (Royal Opera House, Cairo, Egypt, 1942); made his Bway debut, billed as Charles Alexander, as Steward in *Hidden Horizon* (Plymouth, Sept. 19, 1946); directed a season of stock (Duxbury Summer Th., Mass., Summer 1947); understudied Kurt Kasznar as Uncle Louis in *The Happy Time* (Plymouth, N.Y.C., Jan. 24, 1950); using the name C. K. Alexander, which he used thereafter, he appeared as Karim Effendi in *Flight Into Egypt,* for which he wrote the incidental music (Music Box, Mar. 18, 1952); played Joe and Turnkey in *Mr. Pickwick* (Plymouth, Sept. 17, 1952); Judge Paul Barriere in *Can-Can* (Shubert, May 7, 1953); and Ali Hakim in *Oklahoma!* (Th. of Nations Festival, Paris, France, Rome, Naples, Milan, and Venice, Italy, 1955).

He understudied (Fall 1955) Walter Slezak as Panisse in *Fanny* (Majestic, Nov. 4, 1954), and during the same period, understudied Loring Smith as Vendergelder in *The Matchmaker* (Royale, Dec. 5, 1955); played Khadja in *The Merry Widow* (NY City Ctr., Apr. 10, 1957); Warden Bastiand in the pre-Bway tryout of *The Gay Felons* (opened Wilmington, Del., Feb. 12, 1959; closed Ford's Th., Baltimore, Md., Mar. 14, 1959); was a stage manager and understudy (1959) in *La Plume de Ma Tante* (Royale, N.Y.C., Nov. 11, 1958); a stage manager and succeeded Joseph Bernard as the Café Proprietor in *Rhinoceros* (Longacre, Jan. 9, 1961); was stage manager in *Carnival!* (Imperial, Apr. 13, 1961); stage manager and played M. Chauffourier-Dubieff in *Tovarich* (Bway Th., Mar. 18, 1963); played the Burgomaster in *The Dragon* (Phoenix, Apr. 9, 1963); and Croz in *Corruption in the Palace of Justice* (Cherry Lane, Oct. 8, 1963); played Pedro Juarez in *Not in the Book* (Playhouse-on-the-Mall, Paramus, N.J.; Mineola Playhouse, N.Y.; Paper Mill Playhouse, Millburn, N.J., 1964); played Mr. Peachum in *The Threepenny Opera* (Playhouse in the Park, Cincinnatti, Ohio, 1964); played Vulture/Mirabeau in *Poor Bitos* (Cort, N.Y.C., 1964); directed *Francesca Da Rimini* and *The Campbells of Boston* for The Company of Twelve (Library & Museum of the Performing Arts, Lincoln Ctr., 1967); directed *As Happy As Kings* (New Th., N.Y.C., 1968); again played Mr. Peachum in *The Threepenny Opera* (Arena Stage, Washington, D.C., 1969); directed *Harlequinades for Mourners* (New Th., N.Y.C., 1970); played Mandria, the Greek, in *Ari* (Shubert Th., Philadelphia, Pa.; National Th., Washington, D.C.; Mark Hellinger Th., N.Y.C., 1970–71); produced *The Justice Box* (Th. de Lys, N.Y.C., 1971); directed *Love One Another* (The New Dramatists, Inc., N.Y.C., 1974); played the Rev. Dr. Lloyd in *Life with Father,* directed by George Abbott (Seattle Repertory Th., Seattle, Wash., 1974–75); played the Lecturer in Chekhov's *The Harmfulness of Tobacco* and Chubukov in *The Marriage Proposal* (Syracuse Stage, Nov. 1975); and Mr. Peachum in *The Threepenny Opera* (Vivian Beaumont Th., Lincoln Ctr., Apr. 21, 1976). Under his own name, or the pseudonyms Mario Quimber or Basheer Qadar, he composed the music for *Francesca Da Rimini, The Campbells of Boston, As Happy As Kings, Harlequinades for Mourners, The Justice Box,* and *Love One Another.*

Television and Radio. Mr. Alexander has appeared on television on Studio One (CBS, 1947, 1958); Dupont Show-of-the-Week (NBC 1963); Armstrong Circle Th. (NBC, 1963); The Defenders (CBS, 1964); Hallmark Th. (NBC, 1966); *N.Y.P.D.* (CBS, 1968); and was a member of the playwrights unit of the CBS Television Workshop (1960); and played Dutch Banker in The Adams Chronicles (PBS).

ALEXANDER, CRIS. Actor, photographer. b. Jan. 14, 1920, Tulsa, Okla., to Allen Ticer and Mary Hunt (Murry) Smith. Father, musician. Attended Univ. of Oklahoma, 1937; Feagin Sch., N.Y.C., 1938–39. Member of AEA. Address: (home) 134 E. 61st St., New York, NY 10021, tel. (212) TE 2-9324; (bus.) 144 W. 57th St., New York, NY 10019, tel. (212) JU 2-1404.

Pre-Theatre. Radio announcer.

Theatre. Mr. Alexander appeared as Chip in *On the Town* (Adelphi Th., N.Y.C., Dec. 28, 1944); Roland Maule in *Present Laughter* (Plymouth, Oct. 29, 1946); Frank Lippincott in *Wonderful Town* (Winter Garden, Feb. 25, 1953); Raymond, Mr. Loomis, and understudied Robert Higgins in the role of Patrick Dennis in *Auntie Mame* (Broadhurst, Oct. 31, 1956); performed in the revue *Parade* (Players, Jan. 20, 1960); and as Leslie Bright in *The Madness of Lady Bright* (Th. East, Mar. 22, 1966). He also designed projections for *Two by Two* (Imperial, Nov. 10, 1970).

ALEXANDER, JANE. Actress. b. Jane Quigley, Oct. 28, 1939, Boston, Mass., to Dr. and Mrs. Thomas Bart Quigley. Father, physician. Grad. Beaver Country Day Sch. (Boston); Sarah Lawrence Coll., 1961; attended Univ. of Edinburgh (Scotland). Married to Robert Alexander, theatre executive (marr. dis.).

Theatre. Miss Alexander has appeared in *The Madwoman of Chaillot* (Charles Playhouse, Boston, Mass., Feb. 3, 1965); played Eleanor in *The Great White Hope* (Alvin, N.Y.C., Oct. 3, 1968); for the Amer. Shakespeare Festival (Stratford, Conn., Summer 1971), played Lavinia Mannon in *Mourning Becomes Electra,* appeared in *The Merry Wives of Windsor,* and subsequently played the title role in *Major Barbara* (May 8, 1972); played Ann in *6 Rms Riv Vu* (Helen Hayes Th., N.Y.C., Oct. 17, 1972); Jacqueline Harrison in *Find Your Way Home* (Brooks Atkinson Th., Jan. 2, 1974); and appeared in *Present Laughter* (Eisenhower Th., Kennedy Ctr., Washington, D.C., Apr. 27, 1975).

Films. Miss Alexander recreated the role of Eleanor in *The Great White Hope* (20th-Fox, 1970); and played Dorothy in *The New Centurions* (Col., 1972).

Awards. She received the Antoinette Perry (Tony) Award for best supporting actress (1969) for her performance in *The Great White Hope.*

ALEXANDER, JOHN. Actor. b. John Smith Alexander, Nov. 29, 1897, Newport, Ky., to Capt. James S. and Olive (Jones) Alexander. Father, steamboat owner and captain; mother, telegraph operator. Grad. Highland H.S., Fort Thomas, Ky., 1915; Schuster-Martin Dramatic Sch., Cincinnati, Ohio, 1916; studied 11 years with Helen Schuster, Mrs. Tyrone Power, Sr., and Rachel Barton Butler. Married Oct. 20, 1928, to Genevieve Hamper, actress. Served WW I, US Field Artillery; rank, Cpl. Member of AEA (council 1938–54); SAG; AFTRA; The Players; The Lambs.

Theatre. Mr. Alexander made his stage debut at 11 in the title role in *Elmer Brown, the Only Boy in Town* (Oddfellows Hall, Cincinnati, Nov. 1908). He made his professional debut in 1913 with a Cincinnati stock company, appearing as Carribeniere in *The Man from Home* (Orpheum Th., Nov. 30, 1913), followed by *The Little Minister* (Opheum, Dec. 1913).

In 1916, he joined the Margaret Anglin Repertory Co. on tour and played Peter in *The Taming of the Shrew* (Colonial, Cleveland, Ohio, Mar. 1916) and Charles the Wrestler in *As You Like It* (Forest Park, St. Louis, Mo., June 1916). From 1916–19, he toured with the Robert B. Mantell and Genevieve Hamper Co., playing various Shakespearean roles in repertory for seasons ranging from 18 to 42 weeks. As a member of the company he made his N.Y.C. debut in the role of Solanio in *The Merchant of Venice* (44 St. Th., Apr. 16, 1917).

He toured for ten weeks (commencing June 1920), as Bronson in *It Pays to Advertise;* rejoined the Mantell-Hamper Co., playing Shakespearean roles in repertory (Fall 1920–May 1923); toured as Mariano in *The Man from Home* (Summer 1921); Sam Martin in *Turn to the Right* (Summer 1922); and Matt Peasley in *Cappy Ricks* (Summer 1923); and appeared as the Musketeer in Walter Hampden's *Cyrano de Bergerac* (National, N.Y.C., Nov. 1, 1923).

On tour, Mr. Alexander played Richard Loring in *The First Year* (June 1924; 12 weeks); appeared with the Fritz Leiber Shakespearean repertoire (Sept. 1924; 30 weeks); as Daniel Gilchrist in *The Fool* (June 1925; 13 weeks); and Tom Gibney in *White Collars* (Sept. 1925; 18 weeks). In N.Y.C., he played Montfleury in *Cyrano de Bergerac* (Hampden Th., Feb. 18, 1926).

On tour, he portrayed Chico in *Seventh Heaven* (May 1926; 17 weeks); played with the Robert B. Mantell and Genevieve Hamper Co. in Shakespearean repertory (Sept. 1926; 32 weeks) and (Sept. 1927; 27 weeks); Allie in *Puffy* (Long Branch and Asbury Park, N.J.; July 1928; two weeks); appeared in *The Legacy* (Sept. 1928; two weeks); and performed with Genevieve Hamper in Shakespearean repertory (Jan. 1929; 18 weeks) and (Sept. 1929; 30 weeks).

In stock, he appeared in *The Green Bottle* (Vine St. Th., Hollywood, Calif., Nov. 1930); *Elmer the Great* (El Capitan, Hollywood, Dec. 1930); *The Butter and Egg Man* (El Capitan, Hollywood, Feb. 1931); *Elmer the Great* (Alacazar, San Francisco, Calif., Apr. 1931); on tour, as Le Brey in *Cyrano de Bergerac* (Belasco, Los Angeles, Calif., Feb. 1932); and Peter in an outdoor production of *Pilgrimage Play* (Pilgrimage, Hollywood, July 1932).

Mr. Alexander appeared in N.Y.C. as Bull in *Jamboree* (Vanderbilt, Nov. 24, 1932), and in *Tragedy of the Ages* (Mecca Temple, Apr. 1933); on tour, played Pee Wee Moore in *Sailor Beware* (San Francisco and Los Angeles, Dec. 1933), and J. B. in *She Loves Me Not* (San Francisco and Los Angeles, May 1934).

He appeared as Pee Wee Moore in *Sailor Beware* (Lyceum, N.Y.C., Sept. 28, 1933), in which he subsequently toured (Mar. 1935; ten weeks); Dobbs in *Nowhere Bound* (Imperial, N.Y.C., Jan. 22, 1935); Big Wash Rowell in *Mid-West* (Booth, Jan. 7, 1936); Murphy in *The Devil of Pei-ling* (Adelphi, Feb. 20, 1936); Joe Skopopoulus in *Swing Your Lady* (Booth, Oct. 18, 1936); Sergeant Bennett in *Red Harvest* (National, Mar. 30, 1937); the Rajah in *The Greatest Show on Earth* (Playhouse, Jan. 5, 1938); Garde in *All the Living* (Fulton, Mar. 24, 1938); and Madison Breed in *Kiss the Boys Goodbye* (Henry Miller's Th., Sept. 28, 1938).

He portrayed Henry Bolton in *Mornings at Seven* (Longacre, Nov. 30, 1939); Joe Parker in *Out from Under* (Biltmore, May 4, 1940); Teddy Brewster in *Arsenic and Old Lace* (Fulton, Jan. 10, 1941); succeeded (May 1948) Paul Douglas in the role of Harry Brock in *Born Yesterday* (Lyceum, Feb. 4, 1946); at the Ann Arbor (Mich.) Drama Festival (May 1950), played Caliban in *The Tempest,* and Harry Brock in *Born Yesterday;* appeared as Henry Ottwel in *Hilda Crane* (Coronet, N.Y.C., Nov. 1, 1950); Auguste in *Ondine* (46 St. Th., Feb. 18, 1954).

He toured as Colonel Purdy in *Teahouse of the August Moon* (opened Hartman, Columbus, Ohio, Oct. 5, 1955; closed San Diego Aud., Calif., Oct. 1, 1956), which he repeated on Bway (NY City Ctr., Nov. 8, 1956); succeeded (Dec. 1957) Edward Andrews in the role of General Powers in *Visit to a Small Planet* (Booth, Feb. 7, 1957), in which he later toured (opened Playhouse, Wilmington, Del., Feb. 5, 1958; closed Geary, San Francisco, Calif., June 28, 1958); toured as Rodney Aspinwall in *An Adventure* (July 1959; two weeks); played Reverend Brock in *Tenderloin* (Dunes, Las Vegas, May 1961), and Mayor Crane in *Never Too Late* (Playhouse, N.Y.C., Nov. 27, 1962).

Films. Mr. Alexander made his film debut as Teddy Brewster in *Arsenic and Old Lace* (WB, 1944), and has appeared in more than 35 films including *The Doughgirls* (WB, 1944); *Mr. Skeffington* (WB, 1944); *A Tree Grows in Brooklyn* (20th-Fox, 1945); *Junior Miss* (20th-Fox, 1945); *Horn Blows at Midnight* (WB, 1945); *The Jolson Story* (Col., 1946); *New Orleans* (UA, 1947); *Cass Timberlane* (MGM, 1947); *Night Has a Thousand Eyes* (Par., 1948); *Summer Holiday* (MGM, 1948); *Winchester "73"* (U, 1950); *The Sleeping City* (U, 1950); *Fancy Pants* (Par., 1950); *The Model and the Marriage Broker* (20th-Fox, 1951); *Untamed Frontier* (U, 1952); and *The Marrying Kind* (Col., 1952).

Television. He first appeared in *Dead on the Vine* (Ford Th., CBS, 1951); subsequently appeared in approximately 30 plays on such programs as Philco Television Playhouse (NBC), Gulf Th. (NBC), Omnibus (CBS), Phil Silvers Show (NBC), You'll Never Get Rich (CBS), Inner Sanctum (NBC), and Kraft Television Th. (NBC). He also appeared on *Arsenic and Old Lace* (CBS, 1955).

ALEXANDER, KATHERINE. Actress. b. Sept. 22, 1901, Fort Smith, Ark. Studied violin, nine years. Married 1925 to William A. Brady, Jr., producer, director (dec. Sept. 21, 1935); one daughter. Member of AEA; SAG.

Theatre. Miss Alexander made her stage debut as Julie Partington in *A Successful Calamity* (National, Washington, D.C., Jan. 21, 1917); repeated the role for her Bway debut (Booth, Feb. 5, 1917); subsequently played Rose Ingleby in *Good Morning, Judge* (Shubert, Feb. 6, 1919); Beverly Phillips in *Love Laughs* (Bijou, May 20, 1919); Leila Archibald in *Bab* (Hollis St. Th., Boston, Mass., Apr. 19, 1920); appeared with the Jessie Bonstelle stock company as Theodora Gloucester in *Nice People* (Providence Opera House, R.I., Oct. 2, 1922), in *The Man Who Came Back* (Providence Opera House, Nov. 27, 1922), and in the title role in *Peter Pan* (Shubert, Detroit, Mich., Dec. 31, 1933).

She appeared as Grace in *Chains* (Playhouse, N.Y.C., Sept. 19, 1923); Barbara McAlpin in *The New Way* (Longacre, Dec. 4, 1923); Sophie Chaponniere in *Leah Kleschna* (Lyric, Apr. 21, 1924); Peggy O'Neal Eaton in *That Awful Mrs. Eaton* (Morosco, Sept. 29, 1924); Martha Winslow in *The Youngest* (Gaiety, Dec. 22, 1924); Susanne in *The Stork* (Cort, Jan. 26, 1925); Kit Charlton in *Ostriches* (Comedy, Mar. 20, 1925); Shirley Lane in *It All Depends* (Vanderbilt, Aug. 10, 1925); Catherine in *The Call of Life* (Comedy, Oct. 9, 1925); succeeded (Jan. 1926) Lynn Fontanne as Raina in *Arms and the Man* (Guild, Sept. 14, 1925); played Sally in *Grand Grafters* (Music Box, Oct. 27, 1926); Connaught O'Brien in *Hangman's House* (Forrest, Dec. 16, 1926); Ethel Mills in the pre-Bway tryout of *Among the Married* (closed Auditorium, Baltimore, Md., Oct. 24, 1927); Princess Anne in *The Queen's Husband,* (Playhouse, N.Y.C., Jan. 25, 1928); Isabel Drury in *Little Accident* (Morosco, Oct. 9, 1928).

She played Dorothea Fenway in *The Boundary Line* (48 St. Th., Feb. 5, 1930; Ann Field in *Hotel Universe* (Martin Beck Th., Apr. 14, 1930); Kit Evans in *Stepdaughters of War* (Empire, Oct. 6, 1930); Jo Costello in a stock production of *The Whistler* (Elitch Gardens, Denver, Colo., July 1931); Claire Shelby in *The Left Bank* (Little, N.Y.C., Oct. 5, 1931); Cora Davis in *Best Years* (Bijou, Sept. 7, 1932); Mrs. Leslie Taylor in *Honeymoon* (Little, Dec. 23, 1932); Mrs. Patricia Henley in *The Party's Over* (Vanderbilt, Mar. 27, 1933); in stock, appeared in *There's Always Juliet* (Elks' Aud., Elizabeth, N.J., June 26, 1933), *Forsaking All Others* and *The Party's Over* (Spring Lake, N.J., July 1933), and *Love Flies in the Window* (Berkshire Playhouse,

Stockbridge, Mass., Aug. 1933).

Miss Alexander appeared as Kathryn Darrow in *Honor Bright* (New Haven, Conn., Sept. 1937); Melba Greene in *The Best Dressed Woman in the World* (Berkshire Playhouse, Stockbridge, Mass., July 1938); Paula in *Music at Evening* (Ridgeway Th., White Plains, N.Y., Aug. 1938); Harriet Farnsworth in *Mirror for Children* (Westport Th., Conn., Aug. 1938); Mrs. Hunter in *Letters to Lucerne* (Cort, N.Y.C., Dec. 23, 1941); Mrs. Archer in the touring company of *Kiss and Tell* (1943); Anne Fawcett in a pre-Bway tryout of *I'll Be Waiting* (opened Playhouse, Wilmington, Del., Mar. 29, 1945; closed Walnut St. Th., Philadelphia, Pa., Apr. 14, 1945); Mrs. Cooper in the pre-Bway tryout of *Mr. Cooper's Left Hand* (opened Wilbur, Boston, Mass., Sept. 25; closed there Oct. 6, 1945); Irene Haskell in *Little Brown Jug* (Martin Beck Th., N.Y.C., Mar. 6, 1946); and Kay Davis in *Time for Elizabeth* (Fulton, Sept. 27, 1948).

She made her London debut as Linda in *Death of a Salesman* (Phoenix, July 28, 1949); and appeared as Mary Tyler in *Summersault* (Cape Playhouse, Dennis, Mass., July, 1951).

Films. She first played in *Should Ladies Behave?* (MGM, 1933); followed by *Death Takes a Holiday* (Par., 1934); *Operator 13* (MGM, 1934); *The Barretts of Wimpole Street* (MGM, 1934); *Enchanted April* (RKO, 1935); *The Girl from 10th Avenue* (1st Natl., 1935); *Ginger* (20th-Fox, 1935); *She Married Her Boss* (Col., 1935); *Alias Mary Dow* (U, 1935); *Splendor* (UA, 1935); *Anna Karenina* (MGM, 1935); *Moonlight Murder* (MGM, 1936); *Stage Door* (RKO, 1937); *Double Wedding* (MGM, 1937); *The Great Man Votes* (RKO, 1939); *Broadway Serenade* (MGM, 1939); *In Name Only* (RKO, 1939); *The Hunchback of Notre Dame* (RKO, 1939); *Three Sons* (RKO, 1939); *Now, Voyager* (WB, 1942); *The Human Comedy* (MGM, 1943); *Kiss and Tell* (Col., 1945); and *John Loves Mary* (WB, 1949).

ALEXANDER, ROBERT. Director, teacher. Mr. Alexander is the director of Living Stage, an off-shoot of the (Washington, D.C.) Arena Stage. An improvisational theatre company involving extensive audience participation, the group plays primarily to children and young adults, touring throughout the country in addition to having an intensive schedule concentrated in the Washington inner city.

He joined Arena Stage (1966) as director of the newly developed Children's Th., producing traditional plays; subsequently added a school program (1967); expanded their programming to include teenagers while developing the company's improvisational approach (1968), culminating (1969) in the three-fold program which includes teacher training, improvisational workshops and a musical theatre for children and youth.

Each year, Mr. Alexander participates in numerous teacher-training workshops and seminars, including summer sessions in the Netherlands. Address: Living Stage, 6th and M Sts., S.W., Washington, DC 20024, tel. (202) 347-0931.

Other Activities. In 1970, Mr. Alexander organized "You and Me," a free school offering an alternative to traditional education.

ALEXANDER, ROD. Educator, actor, director. b. Apr. 23, 1919, Spokane, Wash., to Russell Edward and Ruth (Wilson) Alexander. Grad. West Valley H.S., Millwood, Wash.; Whitman Coll., B.A. (music) 1941; Columbia Univ., M.A. (dramatic arts) 1953. Studied voice with Elnora C. Maxey, Whitman Coll., 1939–41; and Mary March, Philadelphia, 1945; musical composition with Frederick Schlieder, N.Y.C., 1946–48; and modern dance at the New Dance Group, N.Y.C., 1947. Married Sept. 11, 1942, to Marilyn Maxey; two daughters. Served USNAF, 1941–46; rank, Lt. (AUC). Member of Wash. State Drama Assn. (pres., 1956); ANTA (Wash. delegate to Natl. Convention, 1952); AETA (Northwest Drama Assn.); Beta Theta Pi; Kiwanis Club; Jr. Chamber of Commerce; Chamber of Commerce; Inquiry Club. Address: c/o Dept. of Drama, Dartmouth College, Hanover, NH 03755.

Theatre. Mr. Alexander is professor of drama and director of theatre (Hopkins Center) at Dartmouth College (1967–to date). He made his acting debut as a member of the ANTA-sponsored Th. Project, which performed plays in N.Y.C. and East Stroudsburg, Pa. (Summer, Fall 1947), where he played Father in *Happy Journey*, the Stage Manager in *Our Town*, the Major in *Home of the Brave*, Algernon in *The Importance of Being Earnest*, the President in *Christopher Blake*, and David in *The Silver Cord;* was co-producer and actor for his own company, Th. Unlimited, which produced *The Comedy of Errors*, in which he played Dromio of Syracuse (Barbizon-Plaza, N.Y.C., Feb. 1948).

He was a faculty member of Whitman Coll. (1948–67), where he was professor of drama, senior professor of drama, and director of theatre (1950–67). He designed and helped construct the former and present Whitman Th., established the major study of drama in curriculum, directed and appeared in Whitman Coll. productions. During 1965–66, he taught courses in directing and acting, and was guest director at the Univ. of California at Santa Barbara. He was also guest director at the Univ. of Missouri Kansas City Repertory Co. and Center Stage Repertory Co., Baltimore, Md. (both 1966); and at Syracuse Repertory Co., N.Y. (1966–67). During the summers of 1967–68 he was producer and director at Dartmouth Repertory Th.

With Nagle Jackson, Mr. Alexander wrote the book for the musical *Popoff* (1960–61); he has been active in community theatre (1949–to date), acting and directing for the Walla Walla Little Th. (1949–60); directing and producing productions at the Summer Circle, Inc. (1955–58); and directing at the Pendleton Civic Th. (1964); for the Southeastern Washington Fair Assn., directed *The Magic Musket* (Colfax, Wash., Sept. 1953) and a pageant based on the Stevens Treaties of 1855 (Sept. 1955); for the Walla Walla Symphony Orchestra, narrated *Peter and the Wolf* (1949), *Tubby the Tuba* (1952), and the oratorio *King David* (Dec. 1963).

From 1961 to 1964, Mr. Alexander was a company member of the Oregon Shakespearean Festival, and became a member of the production staff (1962). He appeared as Bottom in *A Midsummer Night's Dream*, in the title role in *Henry IV, Part 1*, as the King of France in *All's Well That Ends Well*, and in several small roles in *Hamlet* (1961), directing *The Comedy of Errors*, and playing Menenius in *Coriolanus*, (1962), directing *Love's Labour's Lost*, playing the prince Escalus in *Romeo and Juliet*, the Constable of France in *Henry V* (1963), and directing *The Merchant of Venice* (1964).

Television and Radio. The Theatre Unlimited production of *Comedy of Errors* was produced by CBS-TV (1948); Mr. Alexander played the Young Man in *My Beloved Father* (CBS, 1948); provided character and animal voices for several puppet shows and commercials (CBS, 1948); and presented his own weekly radio program of book reviews, *Bookshelf* (KUZ-CBS, 1958–63).

Awards. He received (1953) an Award of Merit from the Jr. Chamber of Commerce (Walla Walla, Wash.); has been honored by the Inst. of Renaissance Studies for roles played at the Oregon Shakespearean Festival (1961); and for his direction of *The Comedy of Errors* (1962).

ALEXANDER, RONALD. Playwright, actor. b. Ronald George Alexander, Feb. 16, 1917, West New York, N.J., to Walter Ungerer and Florence (Finnegan) Alexander. Father, welder; mother, factory worker. Attended St. Joseph Sch., West New York, 1925–33. Married Mar. 8, 1954, to Mary Hartig (marr. dis. 1964); three daughters. Member of Dramatists Guild. Address: 215 E. 68th St., New York, NY 10021, tel. (212) YU 8-6649.

Pre-Theatre. Factory worker.

Theatre. Mr. Alexander made his Bway debut as Mr. Fenno in *The Patriots* (Natl. Th., Jan. 29, 1943); subsequently played Capt. Birkenbach in *The Day Will Come* (Natl., Sept. 7, 1944); Capt. Thornton Scudder in *Sophie* (Playhouse, Dec. 25, 1944); Detective Dennis Marsh in *Lady in Danger* (Broadhurst, Mar. 29, 1945); Henry Barlow in *Little Brown Jug* (Martin Beck Th., Mar. 6, 1946); the Bailiff in *Christopher Blake* (Music Box, Nov. 30, 1946); Dr. Tom Morrisey in *Doctor Social* (Booth, Feb. 11, 1948); and a Plainclothesman in *Light Up the Sky* (Royale, Nov. 18, 1948).

Mr. Alexander wrote *Time Out for Ginger* (Lyceum, Nov. 26, 1952); *The Grand Prize* (Plymouth, Jan. 26, 1955); *Holiday for Lovers* (Longacre, Feb. 14, 1957); *Nobody Loves an Albatross* (Lyceum, Dec. 19, 1963); and *A Gift for Cathy* (opened Maurice Mechanic Th., Baltimore, Md., Apr. 3, 1972; closed Hanna Th., Cleveland, Ohio, Apr. 22, 1972).

Films. He wrote the screenplay for *Return to Peyton Place* (20th-Fox, 1961) and, based on his play *Time Out for Ginger*, the scenario for *Billie* (VA, 1965).

Recreation. Writing.

ALFORD, WALTER. Press representative. b. Harold Walter Alford, Nov. 14, 1912, Ottawa, Ontario, Canada, to Dr. John Harold and Muriel Grace (Odell) Alford. Grad. Lisgar Collegiate Inst., Ottawa, 1929; Queen's Univ., B.A. 1933; grad. studies, McGill Univ., 1933–34. Member of ATPAM.

Pre-Theatre. Able-bodied seaman, Canadian Merchant Marine (Summers 1931–32); teacher of English, French and history, Albert Coll., Canada (1934–35); reporter, Montreal *Herald* (1933–34); and reporter, Ottawa *Journal* (1935–38).

Theatre. Mr. Alford's first assignment in theatre was as press representative for the Surry (Me.) Theatre (June–Aug. 1939); his first N.Y.C. assignment was as apprentice press agent in the Shubert press dept. for *The Straw Hat Revue, Hellzapoppin, The Streets of Paris, Keep Off the Grass, Three After Three, Sons o' Fun*, and *Count Me In* (1939–42); was press representative (Summers) for the North Shore Players (Marblehead, Mass., 1941) and the Maplewood (N.J.) Th. (1942); press representative for *The Three Sisters* (1942–43); *Ballet Russe de Monte Carlo* (Spring 1943); advance press representative for the coast-to-coast tour of *Sons o' Fun* (Oct. 1943–Aug. 1944); prepared publicity for the tour of the Mia Slavenska Dance Group (Fall 1944); associate press representative in the Shubert press dept. for *Ten Little Indians, Song of Norway, Dark of the Moon, The Wind Is Ninety* (Oct. 1944–May 1945); and press representative for the touring production of *Ten Little Indians* (May–Aug. 1945).

Mr. Alford became associate press representative for the Playwrights Co., and remained until the organization was disbanded (1945–60), working on *Dream Girl* (1945); *Joan of Lorraine* (1946); *Street Scene* (1947); *Anne of the Thousand Days* (1948); *Lost in the Stars* (1949); *Darkness at Noon* (1951); *Barefoot in Athens* (1951); *The Fourposter* (1951); *Mr. Pickwick* (1952); *Tea and Sympathy* (1953); *Sabrina Fair* (1953); *Ondine* (1954); *The Winner* (1954); *All Summer Long* (1954); *The Traveling Lady* (1954); *The Bad Seed* (1954); *Cat on a Hot Tin Roof* (1955); *Island of Goats* (1955); *A Quiet Place*, which closed on its pre-Bway tryout (1955); *The Lovers* (1956); *The Ponder Heart* (1956); *A Clearing in the Woods* (1957); *Small War on Murray Hill* (1957); *Time Remembered* (1957); *Nude with Violin* (1957); *The Rope Dancers* (1957); *The Country Wife* (1957); *Present Laughter* (1958); *Summer of the Seventeeth Doll* (1958); *Howie* (1958); *The Pleasure of His Company* (1958); *Edwin Booth* (1958); *Cue for Passion* (1958); *The Gazebo* (1958); *Listen to the Mocking Bird*, which closed on its pre-Bway tryout (1959); *Juno* (1959); *Look After Lulu* (1959); *Cheri* (1959); *Flowering Cherry* (1959); *Five Finger Exercise* (1959); *Silent Night, Lonely Night* (1959); *Motel*, which closed on its pre-Bway tryout (1960); *Duel of Angels* (1960); was press representative for the productions of the Ballet Th. on Bway and on tour (1945–61).

Mr. Alford also worked as press representative for *Pygmalion* (1945); the Old Vic Co. productions (1946); *The Playboy of the Western World* (1946); Michael Redgrave's *Macbeth* (1947); *The Big People*, which closed on its pre-Bway tryout (1947); *How I Wonder* (1947); Dublin Gate Th. Repertory Co. (1948); *The Leading Lady* (1948); *Goodbye My Fancy*

(1948); *Miss Liberty* (1948); *Caesar and Cleopatra* (1949); Les Ballets de Paris (1950); *Peter Pan* (1950); *Lily Henry,* which closed on its pre-Bway tryout (1950); *Let's Make an Opera* (1950); José Greco Dance Co. (1951); Congress for Cultural Freedom Exposition, Paris, France (Apr.–May 1952); The Boston Symphony Orchestra's Tanglewood Music Festival, Lenox, Mass. (Summers 1953–56); *The Dark Is Light Enough* (1954); the national touring production of *Cat on a Hot Tin Roof* (1956); *Happy Hunting* (1956); *Visit to a Small Planet* (1957); Ballet Russe de Monte Carlo (1957); a summer-theatre tryout production of *The Saturday Night Kid* (Westport Country Playhouse, Conn., 1957); on Bway, the Shanta Rao Dancers of India (1957); *Miss Lonelyhearts* (1957); *The Firstborn* (1958); Joyce Grenfell (one-woman show) (1958); a summer-theatre touring production of *The Gazebo* (1959); the national touring production of *Duel of Angels* (1960); on Bway, *A Lovely Light* (1960); *Julia, Jake and Uncle Joe* (1960); the overseas repertory tour of *The Skin of Our Teeth, The Glass Menagerie* and *The Miracle Worker* (1961); the pre-Bway tryout tour of *Sail Away* (1961); on Bway, *Milk and Honey* (1961); *The Gay Life* (1961); *General Seeger* (1962); *Great Day in the Morning* (1962); pre-Bway tryouts of *Bravo Giovanni* (1962), *Come on Strong* (1962), and *Nowhere To Go But Up* (1962); and the national touring production of *How To Succeed in Business without Really Trying* (1963).

Mr. Alford was also a press representative for *One Flew Over the Cuckoo's Nest* (Cort, N.Y.C., Nov. 13, 1963); *Funny Girl* (Winter Garden, Mar. 26, 1964); a revival of *The Glass Menagerie* (Brooks Atkinson Th., May 4, 1965); *Square in the Eye* (Th. de Lys, May 19, 1965); *The World of Ray Bradbury* (Orpheum, Oct. 8, 1965); *The Mad Show* (New, Jan. 9, 1966); Rooms (Cherry Lane, Jan. 27, 1966); *Jonah* (American Place Th., St. Clement's Church, Feb. 15, 1966); *Monopoly* (Stage 73, Mar. 5, 1966); *Serjeant Musgrave's Dance* (Th. de Lys, Mar. 8, 1966); *The Journey of the Fifth Horse* (American Place Th., St. Clement's Church, Apr. 21, 1966); *The Office* (Henry Miller's Th., Apr. 30, 1966); *Who's Got His Own* (American Place Th., St. Clement's Church, Oct. 12, 1966); *The Displaced Person* (American Place Th., St. Clement's Church, Dec. 29, 1966); and *La Turista* (American Place Th., St. Clement's Church, Mar. 4, 1967).

Films. Mr. Alford was press representative for films at the 55th St. Playhouse (N.Y.C., Oct.–Dec. 1938); and researcher and press writer for the Tri-Natl. Films (N.Y.C., Jan.–Mar. 1939). He was a press representative for Franco Zeffirelli's *Romeo and Juliet* (Par., 1968) and for *Promise at Dawn* (Avco-Embassy, 1971).

Recreation. Swimming, traveling, theatre, cinema, ballet, "long-hair" music.

ALFRED, WILLIAM. Playwright, educator. b. Aug. 16, 1922, New York City, to Thomas Allfrey and Mary (Bunyan) Alfred. Father, bricklayer. Ed. St. Anne's Acad., St. Francis Preparatory Sch., N.Y.C.; Brooklyn Coll., B.A. 1948; Harvard Univ., M.A. 1949, Ph.D. 1954. Served U.S. Army, 1943–46. Member of Mediaeval Acad. of America; Modern Language Assn.; Dramatists Guild. Address: 31 Athens St., Cambridge, MA 02138.

Theatre. Mr. Alfred wrote *Hogan's Goat* (Amer. Place Th., N.Y.C., Nov. 11, 1965; moved to East 74 St. Th., Jan. 7, 1966); with T. Albert Marre, wrote the book, and with Phyllis Robinson, wrote the lyrics for *Cry for Us All* (Broadhurst, Apr. 8, 1970) the musical version of *Hogan's Goat*; and wrote *Agamemnon* (McCarter Th., Princeton, N.J., Oct. 27, 1972).

Television. Mr. Alfred's television credits include *Hogan's Goat* (PBS, 1971); and appearances as a guest on talk shows.

Other Activities. Mr. Alfred is Professor of English and Drama (1963–to date) at Harvard Univ. (Cambridge, Mass.) where he joined the faculty in 1954.

Published Works. Mr. Alfred was associate editor of *American Poet* Magazine (1942–44); wrote *The Annunciation Rosary* (1948); was co-editor of *Reformation, The Prose Works of John Milton* (1954); and *Agamemnon* (1954). He has also contributed to such periodicals as *Commonweal* and *Hudson Review.*.

Awards. He has been the recipient of the Atlantic Coll. Monthly Poetry Prize (1947); Harvard Monthly Poetry Prize (1951); a National Institute of Arts and Letters Grant; the Amy Lowell Travelling Poetry Scholarship (1956); Creative Arts Grant, Brandeis Univ. (1960); and the Th. Club Gold Medal for *Hogan's Goat* (Best Play, 1966).

ALLEN, ADRIANNE. Actress. b. Feb. 7, 1907, Manchester, England, to Charles D. and Ethel (Mapleston) Allen. Father, financier. Attended schools in Belgium and Switzerland. Studied at RADA, London, 1925–27. Married 1929 to Raymond Massey, actor (marr. dis. 1939); one son, Daniel Massey, actor; one daughter, Anna Massey, actress; married July 20, 1939, to William Dwight Whitney, lawyer. Served WW II, ENSA; rank, 2nd Lt. Member of British AEA; AEA. Address: Glion sur Montreux, Switzerland.

Theatre. Miss Allen made her first professional stage appearance as Nina Vansittart in *Easy Virtue* (Duke of York's, London, June 9, 1926); subsequently appeared in repertory, as Martha in *Made in Heaven,* Ruby Raymond in *The Rat Trap,* Mrs. Squeamish in *The Country Wife,* and Miss Meadows in *Br'er Rabbit* (Everyman, Oct.–Dec. 1926).

She played Leah in *Lost Property* (Duke of York's, Jan. 17, 1927); Ena Gossett in *Common People* (Everyman, Apr. 12, 1927); the Soubrette in *Might Have Beens* (Prince's, May 22, 1927); Cicely Hodder in *Faithful Philanderers* (Strand, June 12, 1927); Sondra Finchley in *An American Tragedy* (Apollo, June 26, 1927); Mabel Worthington in *Potiphar's Wife* (Globe, Aug. 17, 1927); Madge Carson in *The Devil's Host* (Comedy, Aug. 22, 1928); Dorothy Allitsen in *Always Afternoon* (Lyric, Feb. 5, 1929); the Hon. Audrey Findon in *The Stag* (Globe, Apr. 2, 1929); Stella Brice in *Why Drag in Marriage?* (Strand, May 31, 1929); Fay Willoughby in *Happy Families* (Garrick, Oct. 1, 1929); Mavis in *Cut Grass* (Lyceum Club, May 23, 1930); Sybil Chase in *Private Lives* (Phoenix, Sept. 24, 1930); and Audrey Carlisle in *Five Farthings* (Haymarket, Apr. 8, 1931).

She made her N.Y.C. debut as Doris Lea in *Cynara* (Morosco, Nov. 2, 1931); subsequently played Mary Linkley in *Never Come Back* (Phoenix, London, Oct. 28, 1932); Judy Linden in *The Shining Hour* (Booth, N.Y.C. Feb. 13, 1934; St. James's, London, Sept. 4, 1934); Elizabeth Bennett in *Pride and Prejudice* (Music Box, N.Y.C., Nov. 5, 1935); Joan Forrester in *'Til the Cows Come Home* (St. Martin's, London, Oct. 27, 1936); Griselda Taunton in *Plans for a Hostess* (St. Martin's, Mar. 10, 1938), and later toured in it; Helen in *We at the Cross Roads* (Globe, Mar. 7, 1939); and Countess Skriczevinsky in *Flare Path* (Apollo, Aug. 12, 1942).

During World War II, she toured the Middle East and Italy appearing before troops as Olivia in *Night Must Fall,* Doris in *Flare Path,* and Ruth in *Blithe Spirit* (1944).

She played Ann Proctor in *Guest in the House* (Embassy, London, May 21, 1946); Mrs. Frail in *Love for Love* (Royale, N.Y.C., May 26, 1947); Helen Gainsford in *Point to Point* (St. Martin's, London, June 1948); succeeded (Nov. 1948) Peggy Ashcroft as Evelyn Holt in *Edward, My Son* (Martin Beck Th., N.Y.C., Sept. 30, 1948); played Joan Lewis in *Bold Lover* (Royal, Brighton, Eng., Dec. 1951); Helen Saville in *The Vortex* (Lyric, Hammersmith, London, Mar. 4, 1952); Mrs. Rose Hardynge in *The Wedding Ring* (Opera House, Manchester, Aug. 1952); Lady Coniston in *Lord Arthur Savile's Crime* (Arts, London, Oct. 23, 1952); Mrs. Tilton in *Gossip Column* ("Q," Apr. 14, 1953); Vera in *Someone Waiting* (Globe, Nov. 25, 1953); Ruth Fleming in *The Pet Shop* (St. Martin's, Sept. 7, 1954); Sheila Broadbent in *The Reluctant Debutante* (Henry Miller's Th., N.Y.C., Oct. 10, 1956); and Louise Harrington in *Five Finger Exercise* (Comedy, London, July 17, 1958).

Films. Miss Allen made her first appearance in *Loose Ends* (British Intl., 1930); and has since appeared in *Merrily We Go to Hell* (Par., 1932); *The Night of June 13* (Par., 1932); *The Morals of Marcus* (Gaumont, 1936); *The October Man* (Elstree, 1948); *Bond Street* (Stratford, 1950); and *The Final Test* (Rank, 1954).

Recreation. Cooking, golf, interior decorating.

ALLEN, ELIZABETH. Actress, singer. b. Elizabeth Ellen Gillease, Jan. 25, 1934, Jersey City, N.J., to Joseph and Viola (Mannion) Gillease. Grad. St. Aloysius H.S., Jersey City, N.J., 1950. Studied at Traphagen Sch. of Design, N.Y.C., 1952–54. Married Oct. 23, 1952, to Baron Carl von Vietinghoff-Scheel (marr. dis. 1955). Member of AEA; SAG; AFTRA; AGVA. Address: (home) 205 E. 78th St., New York, NY 10021, tel. (212) RE 4-1740; (bus.) c/o Eric Schepard, General Artists Corp., 640 Fifth Ave., New York, NY 10019, tel. (212) CI 7-7563.

Pre-Theatre. Fashion design student, model.

Theatre. Miss Allen made her professional debut touring as Julie in a stock production of *The Tender Trap* (Summer 1955); subsequently toured as a showgirl in an industrial show, Motorama (1956); and appeared as Ophelia in *Hamlet* (Brooklyn Acad. of Music, N.Y., 1956); Viola in *Twelfth Night* (YMHA, N.Y.C., 1956); and Portia in *The Merchant of Venice* (NY City Ctr., July 10, 1957).

She played Jane in a stock presentation of *The Reluctant Debutante* (Ivy Tower Playhouse, Spring Lake, N.J., Summer 1957); toured as a show girl and singer in the Pontiac (industrial) show (1957); and appeared as Juliet in *Romanoff and Juliet* (Plymouth, N.Y.C., Oct. 10, 1957).

She played Irene in *Say, Darling* (Coconut Grove, Miami, Fla., 1959; Oakdale Musical Th., Wallingford, Conn., 1959; Warwick Musical Th., R.I., 1959); Kitty in *Where's Charley?* (Coconut Grove, 1959); appeared in the revue, *Lend an Ear* (Renata, N.Y.C., Sept. 24, 1959); played Babe in *The Pajama Game* (Starlight Th., Kansas City, Mo.; Music Circus, Sacramento, Calif.; Civic Opera, Seattle, Wash., 1960); Nellie Forbush in *South Pacific* (Oakdale Musical Th., Wallingford, Conn.; Warwick Musical Th., R.I., 1960); and Frenchy in *Destry Rides Again* (Starlight Th., Kansas City, Mo., 1961).

She played Magda in *The Gay Life* (Shubert, Nov. 18, 1961); Julie in *Show Boat* (Stadium Th., Columbus, Ohio; Kenley Players, Warren, Ohio, 1963); Nellie Forbush in *South Pacific* (St. Louis Municipal Opera, Mo.; Starlight Th., Kansas City, 1963); Lois and Bianca in *Kiss Me, Kate* (Civic Light Opera, Los Angeles, Calif.; San Francisco, Calif., Apr. 20–Aug. 1, 1964); repeated her performance as Nellie Forbush in *South Pacific* (Civic Arena, Pittsburgh, Pa., Aug. 17, 1964); was Leona Samish in *Do I Hear a Waltz?* (46 St. Th., N.Y.C., Mar. 18, 1965); Annie Oakley in *Annie Get Your Gun* (Music Circus, Sacramento, Calif., July 4, 1966); toured as Nancy in *Oliver!* (Summer 1966); played Maggie Cutler in *Sherry!* (Alvin Th., N.Y.C., Mar. 28, 1967); and toured as Stephanie in *Cactus Flower* (1967).

Films. Miss Allen appeared in *From the Terrace* 20th-Fox, 1960); *Diamond Head* (Col., 1962); *Donovan's Reef* (Par., 1963); and *Cheyenne Autumn* (WB, 1964).

Television. She made her debut as the "Away We Go" Girl on the Jackie Gleason Show (CBS, 1955–56); subsequently appeared on the Jack Paar Show (NBC, 1959); Wells Fargo (1960); Twilight Zone (CBS, 1960); played Betty Compton in *The Jimmy Walker Story* (CBS, 1960); appeared in The Naked City (ABC, 1960, 1963, 1966); Checkmate (NBC, 1960); Thriller (NBC, 1960); Bachelor Father (NBC, 1960, 1964); The Hunters (1961); Alcoa Hour (ABC, 1960); 77 Sunset Strip (ABC, 1961); Route 66 (CBS, 1961); Alfred Hitchcock Presents (CBS, 1962); Ed Sullivan Show (CBS, 1962); Ben Casey (ABC, 1963, 1965); Combat (ABC, 1963); Stoney Burke (ABC, 1963, 1965); Burke's Law (ABC, 1963); Girl Talk (ABC, 1963); Chan Canasta (WNEW, 1963); Tonight Show (NBC, 1963); Fugitive (ABC, 1964, 1966); Slattery's People (CBS, 1964); The Man from U.N.C.L.E. (NBC, 1966); and

Dr. Kildare (NBC, 1966).

Night Clubs. Miss Allen has sung at the Stork Club (N.Y.C., 1956).

Awards. She was nominated for the Antoinette Perry (Tony) Award (1962) for her performance as Magda in *The Gay Life;* received the Laurel Award as outstanding new female personality (1963); and for her performance in *Do I Hear a Waltz?* tied for first place in the NY Drama Critics *Variety* poll for best performance by a female lead in a musical (1965).

Recreation. Swimming, sailing, guitar playing, sewing, cooking.

ALLEN, JAY PRESSON. Playwright, novelist. b. Texas. Married March 1955 to Lewis M. Allen, theatrical producer; one daughter.

Theatre. Mrs. Allen wrote *The Prime of Miss Jean Brodie,* a dramatization adapted from Muriel Spark's novel of the same title (world premiere, Princess Th., Torquay, England, Apr. 5, 1966; Wyndham's, London, May 5, 1966; Helen Hayes Th., N.Y.C., Jan. 16, 1968); *Forty Carats,* adapted from the French of Pierre Barillet and Jean-Pierre Gredy (Morosco, Dec. 26, 1968); and the book for the musical *I and Albert* (world premiere, Piccadilly Th., London, Nov. 6, 1972).

Films. Mrs. Allen wrote scripts for *Marnie* (U, 1964); *The Prime of Miss Jean Brodie* (20th-Fox, 1969); *Cabaret* (Allied Artists, 1972); and *Funny Lady* (Col., 1975).

Television. Mrs. Allen has written scripts for Philco Playhouse (NBC) and Playhouse 90 (CBS). She wrote the television script for *The Borrowers* (Hallmark Hall of Fame, NBC, Dec. 14, 1973).

Published Works. Mrs. Allen wrote the novel *Just Tell Me What You Want* (1975).

ALLEN, LEWIS. Producer, author. b. Lewis Maitland Allen, Jr., June 27, 1922, Berryville, Va., to Lewis M. Allen, Sr., and Dorothy (Gilpin) Allen. Father, physician. Grad. Episcopal H.S., Alexandria, Va., 1940; Univ. of Virginia, B.A. (Phi Beta Kappa) 1946. Married March 1955, to Jay Presson, writer; one daughter. Served US Army, ETO, N. Africa, Middle East, 1942–45; awarded Polish Cross with Palms. Address: (home) 146 Central Park West, New York, NY 10023; (bus.) c/o Allen-Hodgdon, Inc., 165 W. 46th St., New York, NY 10036, tel. (212) LT 1-1670.

Pre-Theatre. Business executive.

Theatre. Mr. Lewis began as an assistant to Mr. Whitehead of the Robert Whitehead Production office (1950); became assistant managing director to Mr. Whitehead for the ANTA Play Series (1952); and associate producer with the Producers' Theatre, Inc. (1954–60).

In 1960, he formed, with Dana Hodgdon, the firm of Allen-Hodgdon, Inc., of which he was president. Mr. Allen presented, with Ben Edwards, in association with Joseph I. Levine, *Big Fish, Little Fish,* (ANTA Th., N.Y.C., Mar. 15, 1961). In London, he produced *A Time To Laugh* (1962); subsequently, with Ben Edwards, *The Ballad of the Sad Cafe* (Martin Beck Th., N.Y.C., Oct. 30, 1963).

He was one of the producers of *The Physicists* (Martin Beck Th., Oct. 13, 1964); of *Slow Dance on the Killing Ground* (Plymouth, Nov. 30, 1964); and of *Half a Sixpence* (Broadhurst, Apr. 25, 1965).

Films. Mr. Allen was co-producer of *The Connection* (FAW, 1962) and *The Balcony* (Cont., 1963) and producer of *Lord of the Flies* (Cont., 1963).

Other Activities. Mr. Allen was co-founder of Thaibok Fabrics (1949); served as chairman of the board (1949–60); and after 1960 as a member of the board of directors.

Published Works. Mr. Allen wrote *American Plays and Playwrights* (1965) and a play, *La Guerre, Yes Sir* (1971).

ALLEN, RAE. Actress, director. b. Rafaella Julia Teresa Abruzzo, July 3, Brooklyn, N.Y., to Joseph and Julia (Riccio) Abruzzo. Father, garage owner; mother, businesswoman. Grad. St. Brendan's H.S., N.Y.C.; attended Hunter Coll., 1945; grad. School of the Arts, New York Univ., B.F.A. 1969; M.F.A. 1970. Studied at AADA, N.Y.C., 1947; acting with Stella Adler, N.Y.C., 1949; Morris Carnovsky, N.Y.C., 1950–53; Harold Clurman, N.Y.C., 1954–57; Hiram Sherman, N.Y.C., 1959; Uta Hagan, N.Y.C., 1963–64; Jerzy Grotowski. Married Jan. 1949 to John M. Allen, producer, writer (marr. dis. 1954); married Nov. 10, 1957, to Herbert J. Harris, musician, businessman (marr. dis. 1973). Member of AEA; AFTRA; SAG. Address: 2 W. 67th St., New York, NY 10023, tel. (212) 874-2212.

Theatre. Miss Allen first performed as a singer and understudy in *Where's Charley?* (St. James Th., N.Y.C., Oct. 11, 1948); subsequently performed in the revue *Alive and Kicking* (Winter Garden, Jan. 17, 1950); appeared at the Falls Church (Va.) Th. (Summers 1951–52); played Poopsie in *The Pajama Game* (St. James, N.Y.C., May 13, 1954); Gloria in *Damn Yankees* (46 St. Th., May 5, 1955); conceived, produced, with Paul Shyre, and appeared in readings of Sean O'Casey's autobiography, *Pictures in the Hallway* (YMHA, N.Y.C., 1956; moved Playhouse, Sept. 16, 1956); and O'Casey's *I Knock at the Door* (YMHA, N.Y.C., 1956; moved Belasco, Sept. 29, 1957).

She appeared as Ninotchka in *Silk Stockings* (North Shore Music Th., Beverly, Mass., Summer 1957; Miami Musical Tent, Fla., Winter 1958; North Tonawanda Music Tent, N.Y., Summer 1958); Bianca in *Kiss Me, Kate* (Oakdale Music Th., Wallingford, Conn., Summer 1957); Lorna in *Cock-a-Doodle-Dandy* (Carnegie Hall Playhouse, N.Y.C., Nov. 12, 1958); joined (Dec. 1958) as Marfa the tour of *Romanoff and Juliet* (opened Royal Alexandra, Toronto, Ont., Can., Sept. 15, 1958; closed Blackstone, Chicago, Ill., Jan. 3, 1959); played Pearl in *The Summer of the Seventeenth Doll* (Players, N.Y.C., Oct. 13, 1959); toured as Miss Krantz in the pre-Bway tryout of *Sweet Love Remembered* (opened Shubert, New Haven, Conn., Dec. 28, 1959; closed there Dec. 31, 1959); and appeared in Dos Passo's *U.S.A.* (Martinique, N.Y.C., Feb. 1960).

For the American Shakespeare Festival (Stratford, Conn.), she played Ceres in *The Tempest* (June 19, 1960) and Charmion in *Antony and Cleopatra* (July 31, 1960), and toured as Paulina in *The Winter's Tale* (1960–61) and Hippolyta in *A Midsummer Night's Dream* (1960–61). She portrayed the Nurse in *The Death of Bessie Smith* (York, N.Y.C., Feb. 28, 1961); title role in *St. Joan* (Princeton Repertory Th., N.J., Oct. 1961); Tekla in *The Creditors* (Mermaid, N.Y.C., Jan. 25, 1962), and repeated the role in the Univ. of California's (Extension) Professional Theatre Group production (Los Angeles, May 1962).

Also for the Theatre Group, she appeared in *'Tis Pity She's a Whore* and *Peribanez* (July–Sept. 1962); was standby (Jan.–June 1963) for Georgia Brown as Nancy in *Oliver!* (Imperial, N.Y.C., Jan. 6, 1963); succeeded (Jan. 1964) Marian Seldes as Miss Frost in *The Ginger Man* (Orpheum, Nov. 21, 1963); directed her own adaptation of *American Women in Poetry* for ELT (Spring 1964); played Goneril in *King Lear* (UCLA Th. Group, Summer 1964); and Juliette in *Traveller without Luggage* (ANTA, N.Y.C., Sept. 17, 1964).

She was in *I Knock at the Door* (Th. de Lys, Nov. 24, 1964) and *Pictures in the Hallway* (Th. de Lys, Dec. 15, 1964); played Rosaline in *Love's Labour's Lost* (NY Shakespeare Festival, Delacorte Th., June 9, 1965); and was Mrs. Hatch in *On a Clear Day You Can See Forever* (Mark Hellinger Th., Oct. 17, 1965). She appeared with the APA Repertory Co. at the Huntington Hartford Th., Los Angeles, Calif., as Essie in *You Can't Take It with You* (July 11, 1966); as Lady Sneerwell in *School for Scandal* (July 25, 1966); and in *Right You Are* (Aug. 1, 1966). She was Doll Tearsheet in *Henry IV, Part 2* (NY Shakespeare Festival, Delacorte Th., June 11, 1968); succeeded (July 15, 1968) Dolores Wilson as Golde in *Fiddler on the Roof* (Imperial, Sept. 22, 1964); directed *A View from the Bridge* (Sterling Forest Th., N.Y., Summer 1969); played Anne in *A Cry of Players* (Center Stage, Baltimore, Md., Oct. 23, 1970); directed for the New Dramatists (1970); played Fleur in *And Miss Reardon Drinks a Little* (Morosco, N.Y.C., Feb. 25, 1971); the Old Lady in the San Francisco and Los Angeles Civic Light Opera associations' revival of *Candide* (Los Angeles and San Francisco, Calif., 1971; Opera House, John F. Kennedy Ctr., Washington, D.C., Oct. 26, 1971). She directed *The Country Girl* (Barter Th., Abingdon, Va., June 20, 1972); played Reba in *Dude* (Broadway Th., N.Y.C., Oct. 9, 1972); Clytemnestra in *The Orphan* (Public Th., Mar. 30, 1973); staged a reading of *We Can't Have Strangers Here* (St. Clement's Church, N.Y.C., 1974) and of *Lilly Plum* (Women's Program, Town Hall, N.Y.C., 1974); directed *Private Lives* (Barter Th., Abingdon, Va. 1974); and directed *Hothouse* (Chelsea Theatre Ctr., Brooklyn, N.Y., Oct. 23, 1974).

Films. She appeared as Gloria in *Damn Yankees!* (WB, 1958) and was in *The Tiger Makes Out* (Col., 1967); *Taking Off* (U, 1971); and *Where's Papa?* (UA, 1970).

Television. Miss Allen has appeared on Camera Three (CBS); Look Up and Live (CBS); Car 54, Where Are You? (NBC); The Untouchables (ABC); in *The Little Moon of Alban* (Hallmark Hall of Fame, NBC); on two episodes of All in the Family (CBS, 1972–73); played the female lead in a pilot, Grant's Tomb (ABC, 1972); appeared on the *Marlo Thomas Special* (1973); Madigan (1973); in one episode of a Universal mini-series (1973); in the Screen Gems pilot Look After Lisa (1973); in an MTM pilot for the Bob Crane Show (CBS, 1974); and in *Legacy of Fear,* a Playhouse 90 daytime special (CBS, 1974).

Other Activities. In addition to her directing in the commerical theatre, Miss Allen directed approximately forty projects from 1967 to 1970 for the N.Y. Univ. School of the Arts.

Awards. She received Antoinette Perry (Tony) Award nominations for her performances as Gloria in *Damn Yankees!* (1955) and as Juliette in *Traveller without Luggage* (1964); *The Village Voice* Off-Bway (Obie) Award nominations for her performances as the Nurse in *The Death of Bessie Smith* (1961) and Tekla in *The Creditors* (1962); and the Tony Award as best supporting actress for her performance as Fleur in *And Miss Reardon Drinks a Little* (1971).

Recreation. Painting, swimming, cooking, language study, living.

ALLEN, REGINALD. Theatre administrator, writer. b. Alfred Reginald Allen, Jr., Mar. 22, 1905, Philadelphia, Pa., to Alfred Reginald and Helen Johnson (Warren) Allen. Father, neurologist. Grad. William Penn Charter H.S., Philadelphia, Pa., 1920; Philips Exeter Acad. (cum laude), 1922; Harvard Univ., B.A. 1926. Married May 31, 1946, to Helen Howe, monologuist, novelist. Served USNR, 1942–45. Member of President's Advisory Comm. to the Natl. Cultural Center (1958–63); NY State Council on the Arts (1961–65); Shakespeare Anniversary Comm., 1564–1964 (exec. committee); D'Oyly Carte Opera Trust (trustee); Pierpont Morgan Library (life fellow, council of Fellows, 1954–56); The Century Assn.; Grolier Club. Address: (home) 1158 Fifth Ave., New York, NY 10029, tel. (212) EN 9-7075; (bus.) Pierpont Morgan Library, 29 E. 36th St., New York, NY 10016, tel. (212) 685-0008.

Mr. Allen is curator, Gilbert and Sullivan Collection, Pierpont Morgan Library (1971–to date). He was a member of the board of directors of the Philadelphia Orchestra (1933–35) and manager of the orchestra (1935–39). He was first associated with the Metropolitan Opera as assistant manager, business administrator, and secretary to the board of directors (1949–57); was executive director of operations, Lincoln Center for the Performing Arts (1957–62); and returned to the Metropolitan Opera as special assistant to the president and general manager (1963–69). He was executive vice-president, American Academy in Rome (1969–71), acting director in Rome (1969–70).

Films. He was head of the story dept., Universal Pictures (1939–42), and Pacific Coast representative for J. Arthur Rank Organization (1946–49).

Published Works. Mr. Allen is the author of *The First Night Gilbert and Sullivan* (1958); and *W. S. Gilbert, an Anniversary Survey and Exhibition Checklist* (1963).

Awards. Mr. Allen was awarded a Guggenheim Fellowship for Gilbert and Sullivan research in 1973–74.

Recreation. Field collecting in ornithology and entomology; collecting material on Gilbert and Sullivan.

ALLEN, VERA. Actress. b. Vera Klopman, Nov. 27, 1897, New York City, to William and Lillian (Allen) Klopman. Father, business executive. Grad. Barnard Coll., B.A. (Phi Beta Kappa) 1919. Studied with Maria Ouspenskaya, Howard Barlow and Laura Elliott at the Neighborhood Playhouse, N.Y.C., 1924–28. Married July 3, 1921, to John Malcom Schloss, engineer; one son. Relative in theatre: aunt, Florence Vincent, actress. Member of AEA (council mbr., 1945–49); SAG; AFTRA; ANTA (bd. mbr., 1947–49). Address: 510 E. 77th, New York, NY 10021, tel. (212) 861-7219.

Pre-Theatre. Secretary, researcher.

Theatre. Miss Allen made her first stage appearance in *Grand Street Follies* (Neighborhood Playhouse, June 18, 1925); subsequently played Ann Rigordan in *Slaves All*(Bijou, Dec. 6, 1926); Estelle Pemberton in *Sinner*(Klaw, Feb. 7, 1927); Christina in the touring production of *The Silver Cord* (1927–28); and performed in another edition of *Grand Street Follies* (Booth, May 28, 1928).

She joined the Jessie Bonstelle Stock Company in Detroit, Mich., where she played (forty weeks) in *Candida, The Constant Wife, Interference, Samson and Delilah, Hedda Gabler, This Thing Called Love, The Queen's Husband, You Never Can Tell, Baby Cyclone, Ghost Train, The Jest and Liliom* (Bonstelle Playhouse, 1928–29). She played (1930) with the Fritz Leiber Shakespeare (repertory) Company, appearing as Portia in *The Merchant of Venice,* Rosalind in *As You Like It,* Viola in *Twelfth Night,* Lady Anne in *Richard III,* Goneril in *King Lear,* Emilia in *Othello,* Bianca in *The Taming of the Shrew*and in *Othello,* the Player Queen in *Hamlet* and the Gentlewoman in *Macbeth.*

In N.Y.C., she appeared as Celia Hardman in *Lean Harvest* (Forrest, Oct. 30, 1931); Penelope in *Money in the Air*(Ritz, Mar. 7, 1932); Zillah Carrington in *Strange Gods*(Ritz, Apr. 15, 1933); Madeleine in *I Was Waiting for You* (Booth, Nov. 13, 1933); in the revue *At Home Abroad*(Winter Garden, Sept. 19, 1935); and in *The Show Is On* (Winter Garden, Dec. 25, 1936). She played Irene in *Susan and God*(Plymouth, Oct. 7, 1937); Christine Foster in *A Woman's a Fool to Be Clever*(National, Oct. 18, 1938); Ann in *Glorious Morning* (Mansfield, Nov. 26, 1938); Margaret Lord in *The Philadelphia Story* (Shubert, Mar. 28, 1939); Cornelia Lauren in *The Burning Deck* (Maxine Elliott's Th., Mar. 1, 1940); Miss Eloise in *The Moon Vine*(Morosco, Feb. 11, 1943); Harriet in *The Two Mrs. Carrolls* (Booth, Aug. 3, 1943); Alma Deen in *Strange Fruit* (Royale, Nov. 29, 1945); and Mrs. Lauterbach in *Ladies of the Corridor*(Longacre, Oct. 21, 1953).

Television and Radio. Miss Allen has performed on radio with Beatrice Lillie (NBC, 1933–34); and with Helen Hayes (CBS, 1941), and on many daytime programs.

On television, she has appeared as Kass in the series From These Roots (NBC, June 1958–Dec. 1961) and as Ida in Search for Tomorrow (CBS, Sept. 1968–June 1972).

Other Activities. Miss Allen was a co-founder of the American Theatre Wing (1940), vice-president (1940–June 1946), and chairman of the board (June 1946–Oct. 1947); director of the Speakers' Bureau (1941); founder of the Victory Players (1942), later called Community Plays; and vice chairman of Plays for Living, an outgrowth of Community Plays, now a department of the Family Service Association of America (1962–to date).

She was a member of the US National Commission for UNESCO and the US Centre of International Theatre Institute (1948–49).

Awards. She received a special citation, an Antoinette Perry (Tony) Award for her services with the American Theatre Wing during and after World War II (1948).

Recreation. Gardening.

ALLEN, WOODY. Playwright, actor, director. b. Allen Stewart Konigsberg, Dec. 1, 1935, Brooklyn, N.Y., to Martin and Nettie (Cherry) Konigsberg. Mr. Allen attended N.Y.C. public schools, NY Univ. (1953), and the Coll. of the City of NY (1953). Married Feb. 2, 1966, to Louise Lasser (marr. dis. 1969).

Pre-Theatre. As a high-school student, Mr. Allen sold jokes that he had made up to newspaper columnists, and he was hired by a public relations firm to write humorous material for prominent people to use in their public appearances.

Theatre. Mr. Allen wrote *Don't Drink the Water* (Morosco, N.Y.C., Nov. 17, 1966) and *Play It Again, Sam,* in which he also played the part of Allan Felix (Broadhurst, Feb. 12, 1969).

Films. Mr. Allen wrote the original story and the screenplay for and played a small part in *What's New, Pussycat?* (UA, 1965); he supervised and helped write English dialogue for the Japanese film *What's Up, Tiger Lily?*(Amer. Intl., 1966); appeared briefly in *Casino Royale* (Col., 1967); was co-author of the original story and screenplay for and directed and starred in *Take the Money and Run* (Cinerama, 1969); and appeared in the film version of *Don't Drink the Water* (Avco-Embassy, 1969). He wrote, directed, and performed in *Bananas*(UA, 1971); *Everything You Always Wanted To Know About Sex*(UA, 1972); *Sleeper*(co-author) (UA, 1973); and *Love and Death* (UA, 1975).

Television. Mr. Allen wrote for such performers as Herb Shriner (1953), Sid Caesar (1957), Art Carney (1958–59), Jack Paar, and Carol Channing. He was a writer for the Tonight Show (NBC) and the Garry Moore Show (CBS).

Night Clubs. Mr. Allen made his debut as a performer in 1961 at the Duplex in N.Y.C.'s Greenwich Village. This was followed by appearances at the Bitter End (Nov. 1962) and the Blue Angel (1964), both also in N.Y.C. Other night clubs where he has performed include Mister Kelly's (Chicago); the hungry i (San Francisco); Crystal Palace (St. Louis, Mo.); Crescendo (Los Angeles); the Shadows (Washington, D.C.); and the Village Gate, Basin St. East, and the Hotel Americana's Royal Box (all in N.Y.C.).

Published Works. Mr. Allen wrote *Getting Even* (1971), and his articles have appeared in *The New Yorker* and other magazines.

ALLERS, FRANZ. Conductor. b. Aug. 6, 1905, Carlsbad, Czechoslovakia, to Dr. Carl and Paula (Kellner) Allers. Came to US in 1938, naturalized. Father, lawyer. Attended Acad. of Music, Prague, 1921–23; grad. Hochschule f. Musik, Berlin, M.o.M. 1926. Studied violin with Marak, Schweyda, 1920–23; Haveman, 1923–26; piano with Burgstaller 1923–26; composition with Schrattenholz, 1923–26; and conducting with Pruwer, 1924–26. Married Aug. 20, 1941, to Carolyn Shaffer, sociologist (marr. dis. 1961); one daughter; married May 30, 1963, to Janina Furch, author. Member of AFM; Bohemians; N.Y. Musicians Club; Actors' Fund of America. Address: 139 W. 94th St., New York, NY 10025; Papageno-Platz 1, 8033 Krailling, Munich, Germany tel. Munich 857-1559.

Mr. Allers began as conductor at the Municipal Opera House (Wuppertal, Germany, 1926–33); was a musical assistant at the Bayreuth Wagner Festival (1927) and the Paris Wagner Festival (1929); musical director at the Opera House of Aussig, Czechoslovakia (1933); and was guest conductor of the Czech Philharmonic Orchestra (1936–37).

He came to the US in 1938 and served as conductor for the Ballet Russe de Monte Carlo Repertory Co. until 1944. He first conducted for Bway musical theatre with *The Day Before Spring* (Natl. Th., Nov. 22, 1945); followed by *Brigadoon*(Ziegfeld, Mar. 13, 1947); *Paint Your Wagon* (Shubert, Nov. 12, 1951); *My Darlin' Aida* (Winter Garden, Oct. 27, 1952); *Plain and Fancy*(Mark Hellinger Th., Jan. 27, 1955); *My Fair Lady* (Mark Hellinger Th., Mar. 15, 1956); and *Camelot* (Majestic, Dec. 3, 1960). He also conducted the national touring production of *South Pacific*(1950–51), and the foreign tour of *My Fair Lady* (Moscow, Leningrad, Kiev, 1960; Berlin, 1961; Munich, 1962; and Vienna, 1963). He was musical director, Music Th. of Lincoln Center (NY State Th.) of *The King and I* (July 6, 1964); *The Merry Widow* (Aug. 17, 1964); *Kismet* (June 22, 1965); *Carousel* (Aug. 10, 1965); *Annie Get Your Gun* (May 31, 1966); and *Show Boat* (July 19, 1966). He was also musical director, Grand Opera, Geneva, Switz. (1967–72) and the Amsterdam (Neth.) Opera (1973–75), and since 1973, he has been music director, State Opera Comique (Staatstheater am Gaertnerplatz), Munich, Ger.

For the NY City Opera Co., he conducted *Die Fledermaus* (NY City Ctr., Oct. 13, 1957), and *The Merry Widow* (NY City Ctr., Oct. 27, 1957); for the American Opera Society, *The Merry Widow* (1962) and *Countess Maritza* (1963); and for the Metropolitan Opera Co., *Die Fledermaus*(1963, 1966), *La Perichole* (1965, 1970–71), *Der Rosenkavalier* (1969), *Hansel and Gretel* (1967–68, 1971–72), and *Martha* (1967–68), all at the Metropolitan Opera House.

Films. Mr. Allers was musical conductor for the film, *Hansel and Gretel* (RKO, 1954).

Television and Radio. He was guest conductor for the Prague Radio Symphony (1935–37); conductor for the Radio Orchestra of Hamburg (1958, 1959, 1962, and 1964); the Radio Orchestra of Zurich (1959); Radio Orchestra of Stuttgart (1959); the Symphony of the Air (1961, 1962); Radio Orchestra of Oslo (1962); since 1962, has made regular appearances with the Radio Orchestra of Munich; and since 1967, with Radio Hilversum (Netherlands).

For television, he has been conductor for such Hallmark Hall of Fame (NBC) productions as *Alice in Wonderland* (1955), *Yeoman of the Guard* (1957), *Kiss Me Kate* (1958), *Hans Brinker* (1958), and a *Christmas Show* (1958). Since 1957, he has also conducted for Omnibus (NBC) and Robert Saudek Productions (ABC). Other programs for which he has conducted include David Susskind's production of *Meet Me in St. Louis* (CBS, 1959); Leland Heyward's production of *The Fabulous Fifties* (CBS, 1960); the Voice of Firestone (ABC, Nov. 1962); and *The Broadway of Lerner and Loewe* (NBC, 1962).

For European television, Mr. Allers conducted music for the opera, *Czar and Carpenter* (NDR-TV, 1959); scenes from Handel operas (South German TV, 1959); *A Streetcar Named Desire* (South German TV, 1959); the series, Music Made in U.S.A. (Bavaria TV, 1962–64); *The Nutcracker Suite* (Bavaria TV, 1963); two productions based on the music of Offenbach (Bavaria TV, 1963); productions with Anneliese Rothenberger (1968–70); Hermann Prey (1966–73); and Anna Moffo in *La Belle Helene* (1974), all for Bavaria TV.

Other Activities. Mr. Allers has conducted for the leading symphony orchestras in Europe and America.

Discography. Among Mr. Allers's recordings are original cast albums of *Brigadoon* (RCA), *Camelot* (Columbia), *My Fair Lady* (Columbia), *Paint Your Wagon* (RCA), *Plain and Fancy* (Capitol), and the following revivals (all Columbia): *Show Boat, The Merry Widow, The Student Prince,* and *Annie Get Your Gun.* With the Music Theatre of Lincoln Center, he recorded *The King and I, The Merry Widow, Kismet, Carousel, Annie Get Your Gun,* and *Show Boat.* In Europe, he recorded *The Beggar Student, Gypsy Baron, Night in Venice* (all EMI) and *La Vie Parisienne* (Eurodisc).

Awards. He received the Antoinette Perry (Tony) Award as distinguished musical director-conductor of the season for *My Fair Lady* (1957) and *Camelot* (1961). He is a member of the Wisdom Hall of Fame.

Recreation. Historical research, traveling, outdoor life, hiking, swimming.

ALLINSON, MICHAEL. Actor. b. John Michael Anthony Allinson, London, England, to Adrian and Joan (Buckland) Allinson. Father, artist; mother, interior decorator. Grad. Ryeford Hall, Stonehouse, Gloustershire, 1934; Wycliffe Coll., Stonehouse, 1937; attended Lausanne Univ., Switzerland, 1937–38; Institut Ribeaupierre, Lausanne, 1937–38. Studied for the theatre at RADA, 1940. Married May 10, 1959, to Judith Lee Schriver, dancer; two sons. Served British Army, Royal Corps of Signals, 1941–46; rank, Capt. Member of AEA; SAG; AFTRA. Address: (home) 11 Knollwood Dr., Larchmont, NY 10538, tel. (914) 834-0645; (bus.) c/o William Morris Agency, 1350 Ave. of the Americas, New York, NY 10019, tel. (212) JU 6-5100.

Theatre. Mr. Allinson's first engagement in the US was as standby for Michael Evans (June 30, 1958) in the role of Henry Higgins for the national touring company of *My Fair Lady* (opened Rochester Aud., N.Y., Mar. 18, 1957); succeeded (Feb. 10, 1960) Edward Mulhare as Higgins in the N.Y.C. production (Mark Hellinger Th., Mar. 15, 1956); appeared in Lerner and Loewe concerts, repeating Higgins' songs (Hollywood Bowl, Calif., Sept. 1960; Aug. 1961; 1963); played John Worthing in *The Importance of Being Ernest* (Madison Ave. Playhouse, N.Y.C., Feb. 25, 1963); toured for Time, Inc., in an industrial show, *All About Life* (June 3, 1963–Aug. 1963); and toured as Philip Clair in *Kind Sir* (Mineola, N.Y., Millburn, N.J., and Yonkers, N.Y., Dec.–Apr. 1964).

Mr. Allinson made his stage debut in England as Mabel Dancy in a Wycliffe Coll. Drama Club production of *Loyalties* (1935); first appeared in London as a Servant and understudy to Max Adrian in *The Country Wife* (Little Th., Apr. 9, 1940); subsequently toured for two weeks in *Under One Roof* (May 1940): played Karl Tausig in *Till the Day I Die* (Threshold, London, July 25, 1940); toured as Willie Ainsley in *Smilin' Through* (opened Grand Th., Leeds, Aug. 1940); and performed in repertory at the Garrick Playhouse (Altringham, Cheshire, Oct. 1940–Oct. 1941).

Mr. Allinson played Robert Brown in *Just William* (Granville, London, Dec. 17, 1946); in repertory at Tunbridge Wells (Mar.–Apr. 1947), Watford, and Richmond (July 1947–Jan. 1949); appeared as Hounslow and was understudy to John Clements as Francis Archer in *The Beaux' Stratagem* (Phoenix, London, May 5, 1949); produced a season of plays in weekly stock ("Q" Th., London, July 18, 1950–Jan. 1951), playing Brian Cudlippe in *A Pig in a Poke* (Oct. 17, 1950); Geoffrey Sims in *Who Goes Home?* (Oct. 31, 1950); in *Celestial Fire* (Nov. 28, 1950); *Quay South* (Dec. 5, 1950); and *Red Dragon* (Dec. 12, 1950); and appeared in repertory at Leatherhead (Feb. 1951–July 1952).

Mr. Allinson played a French waiter and understudied Alfred Lunt in *Quadrille* (Phoenix, London, Sept. 12, 1952); in repertory at Leatherhead and Canterbury (Sept.–Oct. 1953; Jan.–Mar. 1954); and at the Camberwell Th. (London, Apr.–May 1954); was understudy to Arthur Macrae (June 1954) as Tom Davenport in *Both Ends Meet* (Apollo, June 9, 1954); played in repertory with the Bristol Old Vic (Sept. 1954–Aug. 1955); was understudy to Rupert Davis as Hercules and played other roles in the Edinburgh Festival production of *A Life in the Sun* (Assembly Hall, Edinburgh, Scotland, Aug. 1955).

Mr. Allinson played Francisco and a Captain in *Hamlet* (Moscow Arts Th., U.S.S.R., Nov. 1955; Phoenix, London, Dec. 5, 1955); performed in repertory (Hornchurch, May 1956); toured in *Ring for Catty* (July 1956); played in repertory at Leatherhead (Nov.–Dec. 1956; Jan.–Feb. 1957); toured concurrently in leading roles in *Love's a Luxury* (Feb. 25, 1957) and *We Must Kill Toni* (Mar. 11, 1957); performed in repertory at Leatherhead, Richmond, and Windsor (May–Sept. 1957); and at Leatherhead (Nov.–Dec. 1957, and Mar. 1958); and appeared as Bamboo in *Imperial Nightingale* (Arts, London, Apr. 7, 1958).

Mr. Allinson appeared as Higgins in stock productions of *My Fair Lady* (Kansas City, Mo.; Atlanta, Ga.; St. Paul, Minn.; San Bernardino, Calif., 1964); was in a stock production of *Beekman Place* (Palm Beach, Fla., Feb. 1965); appeared at the Westport (Conn.) Country Playhouse as Higgins in *Pygmalion;* as Lord Summerhays in *Misalliance;* as Bill Walker in *Major Barbara* (May–June 1965); did Higgins in *My Fair Lady* (Chicago, Ill. and Milwaukee, Wis., July 1965); King Arthur in *Camelot* (Indianapolis, Ind., Aug. 1965); and Roy Collier in *Signpost to Murder* (Paramus, N.J., Nov. 1965). He appeared on Bway as Sir Peter Crossman in *Hostile Witness* (Music Box Th., Feb. 17, 1966); toured in stock as Higgins in *My Fair Lady* (Summer 1966); returned to Bway as Hawkins in *Come Live with Me* (Billy Rose Th., Jan. 23, 1967); and did more stock, appearing again as Higgins in *My Fair Lady* (Kansas City, Mo., July 1967); and as King Arthur in *Camelot* (Coconut Grove Playhouse, Fla., Aug. 1967). He toured as Elyot Chase in *Private Lives* (Summer 1968); appeared as the Captain in *The Sound of Music* (Dallas, Tex., Aug. 1968); played Lord Melbourne in the tryout of *Love Match* (Ahmanson Th., Los Angeles, Calif., Nov. 19, 1968); replaced Douglas Campbell in *The Adventures of the Black Girl in Search of God* (Mark Taper Forum, Los Angeles, Calif., Apr. 1969); again played Higgins in stock productions of *My Fair Lady* (Warren, Dayton, and Columbus, Ohio; Wichita, Kans., Summer 1969; Miami, Fla., Winter 1969–70); and returned to Bway as understudy to Anthony Quayle playing Andrew Wyke in *Sleuth* (Music Box Th., Nov. 1970). He went on tour with the national company of *Sleuth* as Andrew Wyke (opened Toronto, Can., Oct. 6, 1971) and returned to the N.Y.C. company of the play as understudy to Paul Rogers (Jan. 1, 1972); played Andrew Wyke in stock (Fort Lauderdale and Palm Beach, Fla., Feb.–Mar. 1972); returned again to the N.Y.C. company of *Sleuth* as understudy (Mar. 13, 1972); and rejoined the national company of the play as Andrew Wyke (May 22, 1972–Jan. 13, 1973).

He played Andrew Wyke abroad (Garrick Th., London, England, Mar. 6, 1973–Apr. 28, 1973); appeared in the US once more as Higgins in *My Fair Lady* (San Bernardino, Calif., May 1973; Atlanta, Ga., and Norfolk, Va., July 1973); and returned to England, where he played Bernard Kersal in *The Constant Wife* (Albery, London, Sept. 19, 1973–May 4, 1974) and Lord Illingworth in *A Woman of No Importance* (Leatherhead, Surrey, May 1974). He toured in the US, playing the first male role in *Oh, Coward!* (Summer 1974) and appearing again as Higgins in *My Fair Lady* (Sacramento, Calif., July 1974).

Television. Mr. Allinson made his television debut in England, playing Robert in *Shop at Sly Corner* (BBC, Nov. 1953); subsequently appeared in *Once in a Lifetime* (BBC, Dec. 1953); as George in *Stolen Waters* (BBC, Mar. 1954); Gen. D'Arblay in *Juniper Hall* (BBC, Apr. 1956); Maxim, Duke of Willenstein, in *Two Headed Eagle* (ATV, Jan. 9, 1957); *Peaceful Inn* (BBC, Nov. 7, 1957); *The Wishing Well* (BBC, Dec. 17, 1957); Banquo in *Macbeth* (A/R, Jan. 22, 1958), and worked as a specialist in the series Emergency Ward 10 (ABC, Feb. 11, 1958).

For US television, he appeared as Piggy Franklin for an episode of the series The New Breed (ABC, Aug. 1961); sang Higgins'songs on PM East (WNEW-TV, Jan. 5, 1962); was narrator for Alexander's Fashion Show, N.Y.C. (CBS, Mar. 1963); and for one episode of Lamp Unto My Feet (CBS, Feb. 1963).

He played Sir Walter Raleigh in *Elizabeth the Queen* (Hallmark Hall of Fame, NBC, 1968); appeared in England as Roderick Alleyne in *Artists in Crime* (BBC, 1968); and in the US made guest appearances on Family Affair (1970) and Young Rebels (1970); and was featured in the television film *Three into Two Won't Go* (1970).

Awards. He received the French Prize from RADA (1940).

Recreation. Skiing, swimming, golf, bridge, chess.

ALSWANG, RALPH. Designer, director, producer. b. Apr. 12, 1916, Chicago, Ill., to Hyman and Florence Alswang. Father, tanner. Grad. Senn H.S., Chicago, Ill.; Goodman Th., Chicago Art Inst., Diploma 1936. Studied with Robert Edmund Jones. Married Aug. 19, 1944, to Betty Taylor, interior designer and author; two daughters; one son. Served WW II, USAAF, Special Services. Member of United Scenic Artists. Address: (home) 295 North Ave., Westport, CT 06880, tel. (203) 227-2135; (bus.) 1564 Broadway, New York, NY 10036, tel. (212) 265-4720.

Theatre. Mr. Alswang made his N.Y.C. debut as designer of the setting for *Comes the Revelation* (Al Jolson's Th., May 26, 1942); was designer for Moss Hart's *Winged Victory,* produced by the USAAF for the benefit of Army Emergency Relief (44 St. Th., Nov. 20, 1943); designed the costumes for *Beggars Are Coming to Town* (Coronet, N.Y.C., Oct. 27, 1945); settings and lighting for *Home of the Brave* (Belasco, Dec. 27, 1945); setting for *I Like It Here* (John Golden Th., Mar. 22, 1946); setting and lighting for the pre-Bway tryout of *Crescendo* (opened Bushnell Memorial Aud., Hartford, Conn., Jan. 18, 1946; closed Shubert, Philadelphia, Pa., Feb. 16, 1946), which opened in N.Y.C. as *Swan Song* (Booth, May 15, 1946); settings for the pre-Bway tryout of *Barnaby and Mr. O'Malley* (opened Playhouse, Wilmington, Del., Sept. 6, 1946; closed Ford's Th., Baltimore, Md., Sept. 14, 1946); *Lysistrata* (Belasco, N.Y.C., Oct. 17, 1946); setting for the pre-Bway tryout of *Darling, Darling, Darling* (opened McCarter Th., Princeton, N.J., Jan. 31, 1947; closed Wilbur, Boston, Mass., Feb. 8, 1947); settings and costumes for *The Whole World Over* (Biltmore, N.Y.C., Mar. 27, 1947); scenery and lighting for *A Young Man's Fancy* (Plymouth, Apr. 29, 1947); settings and lighting for *Our Lan'* (Royale, Sept. 27, 1947); setting and lighting for *The Gentleman from Athens* (Mansfield, Dec. 9, 1947); *Strange Bedfellows* (Morosco, Jan. 14, 1948); settings and costumes for *The Last Dance* (Belasco, Jan. 27, 1948); setting for *To Tell You the Truth* (New Stages, Apr. 18, 1948); lighting for *The Play's the Thing* (Booth, Apr. 28, 1948); designed *Seeds in the Wind* (Empire, May 25, 1948); scenery and lighting for *Small Wonder* (Coronet, Sept. 15, 1948); settings for *A Story for Strangers* (Royale, Sept. 21, 1948); *Set My People Free* (Hudson, Nov. 3, 1948); setting for *Jenny Kissed Me* (Hudson, Dec. 23, 1948); setting and lighting for *Blood Wedding* (New Stages, Feb. 6, 1949); lighting for *Me, the Sleeper* (Lenox Hill Playhouse, May 14, 1949); settings for S. M. Chartock's Gilbert & Sullivan Co. productions of *The Mikado, The Pirates of Penzance, Trial by Jury, and H.M.S. Pinafore* (Mark Hellinger Th., commencing Oct. 4, 1949); settings for *How Long Till Summer* (Playhouse, Dec. 27, 1949); settings for Jean Arthur's *Peter Pan* (Imperial, Apr. 24, 1950); sets for *Tickets, Please!* (Coronet, Apr. 27, 1950); designed *Julius Caesar* (Arena Th., Edison Hotel, June 20, 1950); settings for *Legend of Sarah* (Fulton, Oct. 11, 1950); setting for *Pride's Crossing* (Biltmore, Nov. 20, 1950); sets for *Let's Make an Opera* (John Golden Th., Dec. 13, 1950); and Louis Calhern's *King Lear* (Natl., Dec. 25, 1950).

He designed the scenery and lighting for the musical, *Courtin' Time* (Natl., June 14, 1951); *Out West of Eighth* (Ethel Barrymore Th., Sept. 20, 1951); for the touring company of Veronica Lake's *Peter Pan* (opened Lyric, Baltimore, Md., Oct. 10, 1951; closed Great Northern, Chicago, Ill., Nov. 24, 1951); setting for *Love and Let Love* (Plymouth, N.Y.C., Oct. 19, 1951); settings for *The Number* (Biltmore, Oct. 30, 1951); scenery and lighting for *Conscience* (Booth, May 15, 1952); setting for the pre-Bway tryout of *The Suspects* (opened McCarter Th., Princeton, N.J., Oct. 10, 1952; closed Plymouth, Boston, Mass., Nov. 8, 1952); settings for S. M. Chartock's Gilbert & Sullivan Co. productions of *The Mikado, The Pirates of Penzance, Trial by Jury, H.M.S. Pinafore,* and *Iolanthe* (Mark Hellinger Th., N.Y.C., commencing Oct. 20, 1952); scenery and lighting for the revue, *Two's Company* (Alvin, Dec. 15, 1952); setting for *Be Your Age* (48 St. Th., Jan. 14, 1953); setting and lighting for *The Bat* (Natl., Jan. 20, 1953); setting and lighting for *The Pink Elephant* (Playhouse, Apr. 22, 1953); lighting for *Anna Russell's Little Show* (Vanderbilt, Sept. 7, 1953); settings and lighting for *The Ladies of the Corridor* (Longacre, Oct. 21, 1953); *Sing Till Tomorrow* (Royale, Dec. 28, 1953); and produced with Alex Cohen, and designed the setting for *The Magic and the Loss* (Booth, Apr. 9, 1954).

Mr. Alswang designed the scenery and lighting for *Fragile Fox* (Belasco, Oct. 13, 1954); setting and lighting for *The Rainmaker* (Cort, Oct. 28, 1954); *The Troublemakers* (President, Dec. 30, 1954); *The Southwest Corner* (Holiday, Feb. 3, 1955); settings for the revue, *Catch a Star!* (Plymouth, Sept. 7, 1955); designed *Deadfall* (Holiday, Oct. 27, 1955); *Time Limit!* (Booth, Jan. 24, 1956); scenery and lighting for *The Hot Corner* (John Golden Th., Jan. 25, 1956); designed *Affair of Honor* (Ethel Barrymore Th., Apr. 6, 1956); scenery and lighting for *The Best House in Naples* (Lyceum, Oct. 26, 1956); *Uncle Willie* (John Golden Th., Dec. 20, 1956); designed *The Tunnel of Love* (Royale, Feb. 13, 1957) and two subsequent touring companies; setting and lighting for *Hide and Seek* (Ethel Barrymore Th., N.Y.C., Apr. 1, 1957); *The First Gentleman*, which he produced with Alex H. Cohen in association with Arthur C. Twitchell, Jr. (Belasco, Apr. 25, 1957); designed *Sunrise at Campobello* (Cort, Jan. 30, 1958), and two subsequent touring companies; scenery for *Love Me Little* (Helen Hayes Th., N.Y.C., Apr. 15, 1958); supervised the scenery and lighting for *Epitaph for George Dillon* (John Golden Th., Nov. 4, 1958); staged and designed the lighting for three touring productions of *An Evening with Harry Belafonte* (1958, 1959, 1960); supervised the scenery and lighting for the American tour and N.Y.C. engagement of *Les Ballets Africains de Keita Fodeba* (Martin Beck Th., Feb. 16, 1959); designed *A Raisin in the Sun* (Ethel Barrymore Th., Mar. 11, 1959), and on tour; designed the scenery for *Detour After Dark* (Fortune, London, June 8, 1959); scenery and lighting for *The Girls Against the Boys* (Alvin, N.Y.C., Nov. 2, 1959); designed the lighting for the pre-Bway tryout of *Goodwill Ambassador* (opened Shubert, New Haven, Conn., Mar. 16, 1960; closed Wilbur, Boston, Mass., Mar. 26, 1960); supervised the scenery and lighting for *Les Ballets Africains de La République de Guinée (Alvin, N.Y.C., Sept. 26, 1960); lighting for the touring company of At the Drop of a Hat* (opened Playhouse, Wilmington, Del., Oct. 26, 1960; closed O'Keefe Ctr., Toronto, Can., Mar. 11, 1961); setting and lighting for *Come Blow Your Horn* (Brooks Atkinson Th., N.Y.C., Feb. 2, 1961), and on tour, staged and designed the lighting for the pre-Bway tryout of "Impulse!" (opened O'Keefe Ctr., Toronto, Can., Mar. 20, 1961; closed there Mar. 25, 1961); staged and designed the lighting for the pre-Bway tryout of *Lena Horne and Her Nine O'Clock Revue* (opened O'Keefe Ctr., Oct. 16, 1961; closed Shubert, New Haven, Conn., Nov. 18, 1961); staged and designed the lighting for *Music for Tonight* (Greek Th., Los Angeles, Calif.); designed the lighting for *Beyond the Fringe* (John Golden Th., N.Y.C., Oct. 27, 1962), and on tour; staged and designed the lighting for the touring production, *The Belafonte Show* (opened 1962); was lighting supervisor for *The School for Scandal* (Imperial, N.Y.C., Jan. 24, 1963); designed the stage for Second City (Sq. East, N.Y.C.), which opened with *To the Water Tower* (Apr. 4, 1963); directed and designed the lighting for the touring production of *The Robert Goulet Revue* (1963); was technical director for *Rugantino* (Mark Hellinger Th., N.Y.C., Feb. 6, 1964); and designed *Fair Game for Lovers* (Cort, Feb. 10, 1964).

Other Activities. Mr. Alswang also served as designer and consultant for the restoration of the Palace Theatre, N.Y.C., and for such new structures as the Garden State Arts Center, N.J.; the Pine Knob Pavilion, Detroit, Mich. (1971); the Uris Th., N.Y.C. (1972); the Multi-Media Th., School of Visual Arts, N.Y.C.; the Miami Beach (Fla.) Th., of Performing Arts; the Priemer Th., Westchester County, N.Y.; and the Children's Center, Teheran, Iran. He also designed Broadway's Theatre Hall of Fame in the Uris Th.; has been designer for such performers as Barbra Streisand (road tour), Maurice Chevalier, Judy Garland, Charles Aznavour, and Andy Williams; designed the Bahamas' Independence Day Celebration (Fall 1973); and designed the production for the celebration of Paul Robeson's 75th birthday at Carnegie Hall, N.Y.C., in 1973.

Awards. Mr. Alswang received a Ford Foundation Grant for the development of a theatre technique called Living Screen, which combines motion picture and live stage action. He has produced a musical show entitled *Is There Intelligent Life on Earth?* (Eng.), using this technique; and holds three patents in the field of stage and screen technique. He is presently working on productions for the industrial field and legitimate theatre using the Living Screen technique.

ALTMAN, FRIEDA. Actress. b. Aug. 18, 1904, Boston, Mass., to Samuel and Bella Altman. Father, real estate broker. Grad. Girls Latin Sch., Boston, 1920; Wellesley Coll., Mass., B.A. 1924. Attended Amer. Lab Th. Sch., N.Y.C., 1925–26; studied drama with Benno Schneider, c.1939, Robert Lewis, 1953, and Harold Clurman, N.Y.C., 1959–64. Member of AEA; AFTRA; SAG. Address: 311 W. 24th St., New York, NY 10011, tel. (212) 243-8350.

Theatre. Miss Altman appeared in various character roles in little theatres (1924–25); made her professional debut as Juno in *Juno and the Paycock* (Univ. Players, Falmouth, Mass., 1930); made her N.Y.C. debut as Mrs. Gloyd in *Carry Nation* (Biltmore, Oct. 29, 1932); appeared as a walk-on in *We the People* (Empire, Jan. 20, 1933); played Mrs. Miller in *Hilda Cassidy* (Martin Beck Th., May 4, 1933); Mrs. Hallam, succeeding Margaret Wycherly, in the return engagement of *Another Language* (Waldorf, May 8, 1933); joined as the Housekeeper in *Amourette* (Henry Miller's Th., Sept. 27, 1933); appeared as the Maid in *I Was Waiting for You* (Booth, Nov. 13, 1933); the French Governess in *Picnic* (National, May 2, 1934); and Tillie Solomon in *Spring Song* (Morosco, Oct. 1, 1934).

Miss Altman played Bertha Katz in *Paradise Lost* (Longacre, Dec. 9, 1935); Alvina Gloucester in *Timber House* (Longacre, Sept. 19, 1936); Cora Rodman in *Days to Come* (Vanderbilt, Dec. 15, 1936); Jenny Russell in *Marching Song* (Nora Bayes Th., Feb. 17, 1937); Podd in *Yr. Obedient Husband* (Broadhurst, Jan. 10, 1938); the Maid in the pre-Bway tryout of *The Birds Stop Singing* (closed Philadelphia, Pa., 1939); and Sara Tenbrock in *Pastoral* (Henry Miller's Th., N.Y.C., Nov. 1, 1939).

At the Bucks County Playhouse (New Hope, Pa.), she appeared as Prossy in *Candida* and played in *The Late Christopher Bean* (Summer 1940); appeared in *Morning's at Seven* (Berkshire Playhouse, Stockbridge, Mass., Summer 1940); as Frau Spatz in *Gabrielle* (Maxine Elliott's Th., N.Y.C., Mar. 25, 1941); succeeded Enid Markey as Lily Miller for final few performances of *Ah, Wilderness!* (Guild, Oct. 2, 1941); and toured in the role; as Miss Rhodes in *Guest in the House* (Plymouth, N.Y.C., Jan. 24, 1942); played Goldie Rindskoff in *Counsellor-at-law* (Royale, Nov. 24, 1942); Mrs. Davis in *The Naked Genius* (Plymouth, Oct. 21, 1943); and Mrs. Pessolano in *Hickory Stick* (Mansfield, May 8, 1944).

Miss Altman played Aunt Susan in the pre-Bway tryout of *Mr. Cooper's Left Hand* (opened Wilbur, Boston, Mass., Sept. 25, 1945; closed there Oct. 6, 1945); Mrs. Tillery in *A Joy Forever* (Biltmore, N.Y.C., Jan. 7, 1946); Lydia in *Little Brown Jug* (Martin Beck Th., Mar. 6, 1946); Miss Penrose in *Land's End* (Playhouse, Dec. 11, 1946); Madam Endor in *The Wanhope Building* (Princess, Feb. 9, 1947); Mrs. Gimble in *Strange Bedfellows* (Morosco, Jan. 14, 1948); Emmy Foster in *The Young and Fair* (Fulton, Nov. 22, 1948); Miriam in the pre-Bway tryout of *Exodus* (opened Brighton Beach, N.Y., Apr. 14, 1949; closed there Apr. 24, 1949); and Miss Kearney in *Hilda Crane* (Coronet, N.Y.C., Nov. 1, 1950).

She appeared as Hattie Carew in *The Southwest Corner* (Holiday, Feb. 3, 1955); Eugenie in *The Waltz of the Toreadors* (Coronet, Jan. 17, 1957); Frau Burgomaster and Frau Schill in *The Visit* (Lunt-Fontanne, May 5, 1958); Madame Valerie Aldonza in *Chéri* (Morosco, Oct. 13, 1960); Mrs. Kovacs in *Shadow of Heroes* (York Playhouse, Dec. 5, 1961); and Madame Delachaume in *Rendezvous at Senlis* (Gramercy Arts, Feb. 27, 1961).

Films. Miss Altman made her debut in *Go, Man, Go* (UA, 1954).

Television. She made her debut as the Daughter-in-Law in *Another Language* (NBC, 1939); subsequently appeared in over 150 productions, including Studio One (CBS), Hallmark Hall of Fame (NBC), Pulitzer Prize Th. (ABC), Armstrong Circle Th. (CBS), and US Steel Hour (CBS).

ALTMAN, RICHARD. Director, actor. b. Richard Charles Altman, Mar. 3, 1932, Los Angeles, Calif., to Harry I. and Ida (Hirschhorn) Altman. Father, retailer. Grad. Beverly Hills (Calif.) H.S., 1949; Univ. of California, Los Angeles, B.A. (theatre arts) 1953. Served US Army, 1953–55; rank, SP/4. Member of Actors Studio (Directors Unit); SSD&C; AEA; AGMA; Zeta Beta Tau. Address: (home) 45 W. 10th St., New York, NY 10011, tel. (212) 260-5680; (bus.) c/o SSD&C, New York, NY.

Theatre. Mr. Altman first appeared on stage as Floyd Allen in *Dark of the Moon* (Players' Ring Th., Los Angeles, Calif., Sept. 5, 1951); subsequently played the Shore Patrol Officer in *Mister Roberts* (Las Palmas Th., Hollywood, Calif., Aug. 15, 1953); at the Wingspread Th. (Colon, Mich., directed *The Taming of the Shrew* (June 24, 1957); *Idiot's Delight* (July 8, 1957); *Angel in the Pawnshop* (July 15, 1957); *Tiger at the Gates* (July 29, 1957); and *Tobias and the Angel* (Aug. 19, 1957); these productions were also presented at the Wagon Wheel Playhouse (Warsaw, Ind., Summer 1957).

From 1957–62, Mr. Altman was an instructor and director at the American Academy of Dramatic Arts, N.Y.C.

He directed *Triad* (Th. Marquee, N.Y.C., Nov. 21, 1958); *Chic* (Orpheum, May 19, 1958); under a Ford Foundation Grant, was observer-director, with George Abbott, for *Tenderloin* (46 St. Th., Oct. 17, 1960); staged the double-bill *Mrs. Dally Has a Lover* and *Whisper into My Good Ear* (Cherry Lane, Oct. 1, 1962); *The Saving Grace* (Writers Stage, Apr. 18, 1963); co-directed, with Ernest Flatt, *Calamity Jane* (State Fair Music Hall, Dallas, Tex., June 24, 1963); staged *Corruption in the Palace of Justice* (Cherry Lane, N.Y.C., Oct. 8, 1963); and was assistant to director, Jerome Robbins, for *Fiddler on the Roof* (Imperial Th., Sept. 22, 1964).

Subsequently, he staged *Fiddler on the Roof* in Tel Aviv (June 1965), Amsterdam (Dec. 1966), London (Feb. 1967), and Paris (Nov. 1969). He directed *Man of La Mancha* in the Netherlands (Amsterdam, Dec. 1968) and West Germany (Hamburg, Feb. 1969); and *Small Craft Warnings* (Truck and Warehouse Th., N.Y.C., Apr. 1972).

Films. He was casting consultant for motion picture version of *Fiddler on the Roof* (UA, 1970).

Television. Mr. Altman was director of the book for the musical, *Calamity Jane* (CBS, Nov. 12, 1963).

Other Activities. He created the course The Actor in New York: The Art of Survival at the New School, N.Y.C. (Jan. 1973). He is artist-in-residence in drama at Duke Univ. (1974–75).

Published Works. He was co-author, with Merryn Kaufman, of the book *The Making of a Musical: Fiddler on the Roof* (1971).

ALVAREZ, CARMEN. Dancer, actress, singer. b. Carmencita Louise Alvarez, July 2, Hollywood, Calif., to Don Mario and Jeanne Alvarez. Father, musician, writer, teacher; mother, musician, cellist. Grad. Classical H.S., Providence, R.I., 1953; studied dance with Annette Van Dyke and Lucille Flint at Millikin Conservatory (at age 3 1/2); Eva

Handy Hall and Lydia Sch. of Ballet, Providence; studied ballet in N.Y.C., with Mme. Swoboda, 1952–54; Mme. Kraske, Metropolitan Ballet, 1955–56; studied character ballet with Anton Vilzac, N.Y.C., 1953–55; studied voice in N.Y.C., with Colin Romoff, 1956; Gian-Carlo Menotti, 1959; Carmen Gagliardi, 1961–64; David Craig, 1964; modern dance and jazz in N.Y.C., with Peter Gennaro, 1955–56; Frank Wagner, 1956–57; Matt Mattox, 1964; and Luigi, 1964; drama with Uta Hagen and Herbert Berghof, N.Y.C., 1961–62. Married 1958 to Chad D. Block, dancer, singer, actor; two sons. Member AEA; SAG; AGVA.

Pre-Theatre. Child model.

Theatre. Miss Alverez made her stage debut at age three, singing "Jesus Loves Me" before a Sunday school congregation (Presbyterian Church, Decatur, Ill.); subsequently, as a high-school student, danced in a stock production of *Pal Joey* (Matunuck-Th.-by-the-Sea, R.I., Summer 1951); danced in a corps de ballet production at Radio City Music Hall (N.Y.C., Spring 1953); at the State Fair Music Hall (Dallas, Tex., 1953); played Maggie in *Brigadoon,* appeared in *Kiss Me, Kate, Paint Your Wagon, Girl Crazy, Best Foot Forward,* and *The New Moon;* and played the Flower Girl in *Cyrano de Bergerac* (NY City Ctr., Nov. 11, 1953).

She made her Bway debut as a dancer, singer, and actress in *The Pajama Game* (St. James, May 13, 1954), succeeding Shirley MacLaine as first understudy to Carol Haney as Gladys and appeared several times in the role in Miss Haney's absence, and replaced Rae Allen as Poopsie. From 1955–63, Miss Alvarez appeared in all the Spring Millikin (industrial) Shows; played Moonbeam McSwine in *Li'l Abner* (St. James, N.Y.C., Nov. 15, 1956); succeeded Chita Rivera as Anita in *West Side Story* (Winter Garden, Sept. 26, 1957); was standby to Miss Rivera as Rose Grant in *Bye Bye Birdie* (Martin Beck Th., Apr. 14, 1960), succeeding Miss Rivera as a vacation replacement in this role; also played the role in stock (Kenley Players, Warren, Ohio; Columbus, Ohio; Ovens Aud., Charlotte, N.C., Summer 1963). She danced in a Buick Industrial Show (Detroit, Mich.; Chicago, Ill., 1960); played Rosita in the pre-Bway tryout of *We Take the Town* (opened Shubert, New Haven, Conn., Feb. 19, 1962; closed Shubert, Phildelpia, Pa., Mar. 17, 1962); and played Anita in *West Side Story* (Kenley Players, Warren, Ohio; Columbus, Ohio, Sept. 1963–July 1964); joined as a dancer in *To Broadway with Love* (Texas Pavilion, NY World's Fair, Apr. 22, 1964); and appeared in *That Hat* (Th. Four, N.Y.C., Sept. 14, 1964).

She was in *The Decline and Fall of the Entire World as Seen Through the Eyes of Cole Porter revisited* (Square East, Mar. 30, 1965); was Twink in *The Yearling* (Alvin Th., Dec. 10, 1965); Nadjira in *The Lady or the Tiger?,* part of *The Apple Tree* (Sam S. Shubert Th., Oct. 18, 1966); assumed (Aug. 16, 1967) the female lead at matinees in all three parts of *The Apple Tree;* played the Widow in *Zorba* (Imperial, Nov. 17, 1968); Rosita in *Look to the Lilies* (Lunt-Fontanne Th., Mar. 29, 1970); and Helen McFudd in a revival of *Irene* (Minskoff, Mar. 13, 1973).

Films. Miss Alvarez played Moonbeam McSwine in *Li'l Abner* (Par., 1959); and in a GE industrial film (N.Y.C., 1959).

Television and Radio. She sang "Yankee Doodle" on a children's radio show (Decatur, Ill.); was a child guest on Believe It or Not—Ripley (N.Y.C., Mar. 1941); and on the Horn and Hardart's Children's Hour (N.Y.C., Summer 1941).

On television, she has danced on Omnibus (CBS, 1955); Odyssey (CBS, 1955); appeared as the Flower Girl in *Cyrano de Bergerac* (NBC, 1955); Herridge Th. (1961); Arthur Murray Dance Party (NBC, 1961); American Bandstand Review (1961); Colgate Comedy Hour (NBC, 1962); the Ernie Kovacs Show (NBC, 1962); and has also appeared in commercials.

Night Clubs. She danced in *Arabian Nights* (Versailles, N.Y.C., 1956); between the shows at the Versailles, was guest performer at Roseland Ballroom; also has appeared at the Palladium (N.Y.C., 1956).

Recreation. Swimming, water skiing, horseback riding, knitting, piano, reading.

AMES, LEON. Actor. b. Leon Wycoff, Jan. 20, 1903, Portland, Ind., to Charles Elmer and Cora Alice (De Masse) Wycoff. Father, banker and merchant. Attended Univ. of Indiana. Married June 25, 1938, to Christine Gossett; one son, one daughter. Served USN, 113th Observation Squadron. Member of AEA (councillor, 1942); SAG (pres., 1957); Motion Picture Relief Fund (dir.).

Pre-Theatre. Barnstorming flyer, shoe salesman.

Theatre. Mr. Ames Em his professional debut with the Charles K. Champlin Players, a stock company (Landsford, Pa., 1925–27); subsequently appeared in touring productions of *The Cat and the Canary* (1927); *Love 'Em and Leave 'Em* (1928); and *Broadway* (1929); appeared with the Stuart Walker Stock Co. (Cincinatti, Ohio, 1929–30) in *Tomorrow and Tomorrow* (Los Angeles, 1931); and as Lov Bensey in a touring production of *Tobacco Road* (1934–36).

He made his N.Y.C. debut as Gordon Reese in *Bright Honor* (48 St. Th., Sept. 27, 1936); appeared as Mac in *A House in the Country* (Vanderbilt, Jan. 11, 1937); Luke Warner in *Thirsty Soil* (48 St. Th., Feb. 3, 1937); Joe Ferguson in *The Male Animal* (Cort, Jan. 9, 1940); as Grant Kincaid in *The Land Is Bright* (Music Box, Oct. 28, 1941); Douglas Proctor in *Guest in the House* (Plymouth, Feb. 24, 1942); Kenneth Brown in *Little Darling* (Biltmore, Oct. 27, 1942); Safonov in *The Russian People* (Guild, Dec. 29, 1942); Brian Quin in *Slightly Married* (Cort, Oct. 25, 1943); David Slater in the National (Chicago) Co. of *The Moon Is Blue* (opened Cass, Detroit, Apr. 19, 1951; closed Harris, Chicago, 1952); Professor George Appleton in *The Paradise Question* (opened Shubert, New Haven, Sept. 17, 1953); Dr. Reefy in *Winesburg, Ohio* (National, N.Y.C., Feb. 5, 1958); William Russell in the national tour of *The Best Man* (opened Lobero, Santa Barbara, Calif., Aug. 5, 1960; closed Alcazar, San Francisco, Calif., Oct. 15, 1960); Walter Simms in *Howie* (46 St. Th., N.Y.C., Sept. 17, 1958); and Father in *Life with Father* (Pasadena Playhouse, Pasadena, Calif., 1966; City Ctr. Drama Co., NY City Ctr., N.Y.C., Oct. 19, 1967).

Films. Mr. Ames made his debut in *Murders in the Rue Morgue* (U, 1932); subsequently appeared in *Alimony Madness* (Mayfair, 1933); *The Man Who Dared* (Fox, 1933); *Forgotten* (Invincible, 1933); *Ship of Wanted Men* (Showmen's Pictures, 1933); *I'll Tell the World* (U, 1934); *Reckless* (MGM, 1935); *Stowaway* (20th-Fox, 1936); *Charlie Chan on Broadway* (20th-Fox, 1937); *Dangerously Yours* (20th-Fox, 1937); *Forty-Five Fathers* (20th-Fox, 1937); *Murder in Greenwich Village* (Col., 1937); *International Settlement* (20th-Fox, 1938); *Suez* (20th-Fox, 1938); *Walking Down Broadway* (20th-Fox, 1938); *Island in the Sky* (20th-Fox, 1938); *Mysterious Mr. Moto* (20th-Fox, 1938); *Come On, Leatherneck* (Rep., 1938); *Cipher Bureau* (Grand Natl., 1938); *Strange Faces* (U, 1938); *Risky Business* (U, 1939); *Code of the Streets* (U, 1939); *Legion of Lost Fliers* (U, 1939); *I Was a Convict* (Rep., 1939); *Calling All Marines* (Rep., 1939); *Fugitive at Large* (Col., 1939); *Panama Patrol* (Grand Natl., 1939); and *Man of Conquest* (Rep., 1939).

Also *The Marshall of Mesa City* (RKO, 1940); *East Side Kid* (Mono., 1940); *No Greater Sin* (Univ. Film Products, 1940); *Ellery Queen and the Murder Ring* (Col., 1941); *Crime Doctor* (Col., 1943); *The Iron Major* (RKO, 1943); *Meet Me in St. Louis* (MGM, 1944); *Thirty Seconds over Tokyo* (MGM, 1944); *Son of Lassie* (MGM, 1945); *Week-End at the Waldorf* (MGM, 1945); *They Were Expendable* (MGM, 1945); *Yolanda and the Thief* (MGM, 1945); *Anchors Aweigh* (MGM, 1945); *The Postman Always Rings Twice* (MGM, 1956); *No Leave, No Love* (MGM, 1946); *The Cockeyed Miracle* (MGM, 1946); *Lady in the Lake* (MGM, 1946); *The Show Off* (MGM, 1946); *The Song of the Thin Man* (MGM, 1947); *Merton of the Movies* (MGM, 1947); *Maisie* (MGM, 1947); *On an Island with You* (MGM, 1948); *The Velvet Touch* (RKO, 1948); *A Date with Judy* (MGM, 1948); *Alias a Gentleman* (MGM, 1948); *Little Women* (MGM, 1949); *Battleground* (MGM, 1949); *Any Number Can Play* (MGM, 1949); *Ambush* (MGM, 1949); *Scene of the Crime* (MGM, 1949); and *The Big Hangover* (MGM, 1950).

Also *Dial 1119* (MGM, 1950); *The Happy Years* (MGM, 1950); *Crisis* (MGM, 1950); *Watch the Birdie* (MGM, 1950); *Cattle Drive* (U, 1951); *On Moonlight Bay* (WB, 1951); *It's a Big Country* (MGM, 1951); *Angel Face* (RKO, 1953); *By the Light of the Silvery Moon* (WB, 1953); *Let's Do It Again* (Col., 1953); *Sabre Jet* (UA, 1953); *Peyton Place* (20th-Fox, 1957); *The Absent-Minded Professor* (Buena Vista, 1961); *Son of Flubber* (Buena Vista, 1963); *Misadventures of Merlin Jones* (Buena Vista, 1964); *The Monkey's Uncle* (Buena Vista, 1965); *On a Clear Day You Can See Forever* (Par., 1960); *Tora! Tora! Tora!* (20th-Fox, 1970); and *Toklat* (Sun Inter., 1971).

Television. Mr. Ames has appeared as Father Day in the series Life with Father (CBS, Nov. 22, 1953); and was in *Adam Had Four Sons* (Apr. 4, 1957); *Tongues of Angels* (CBS, Mar. 17, 1958); the series Father of the Bride (CBS, 1962); and *Want Ad Wedding* (NBC). Other programs on which he appeared include Mr. Ed (CBS); Please Don't Eat the Daisies (NBC, 1966); Beverly Hillbillies (CBS, 1966); the Andy Griffith Show (CBS, 1966); Bewitched (ABC, 1970); The Ghost and Mrs. Muir (ABC, 1970); and Name of the Game (NBC, 1971).

AMMIDON, HOYT. Executive. b. June 30, 1909, Lutherville, Md., to Daniel Clark and Estelle (Hoyt) Ammidon. Father, manufacturer. Attended Gilman Country Sch., Baltimore, Md.; The Loomis Sch., Windsor, Conn., 1923–24, 1926–28; Yale Univ., B.A. 1932. Married May 19, 1933, to Elizabeth MacIntosh Callaway; one son, one daughter. Member of Amer. Acad. in Rome (of finance comm.); The Loomis Sch. (pres., board of trustees); Council on Foreign Relations, Inc., Citizens Advisory Comm., N.Y. Public Library; Chi Psi; Cold Spring Harbor Beach Club; Elihu (Yale, grad. pres., 1958–60); The Grad. Club Assn. (New Haven); Racquet and Tennis Club; The Pierpont Morgan Library (fellow). Address: 45 Wall St., New York, NY 10005.

In 1963, Mr. Ammidon was appointed to the board of directors of Lincoln Center for the Performing Arts and also, at that time, became chairman of the Music Theater of Lincoln Center.

He joined the Central Hanover Bank and Trust Company, becoming assistant secretary in 1937, and assistant vice-president in the Trust Dept. (1943); he moved to the Banking Dept. (1950), and became vice-president and general banking officer of the Banking Dept. (1952).

In 1953, Mr. Ammidon joined the Vincent Astor Organization as chief executive officer, also serving as vice-president and a trustee of the Vincent Astor Foundation, and a partner of Astor & Co. In 1957, he was elected president and a trustee of the US Trust Company of New york, subsequently became chairman of the executive committee, and in 1962, chairman of the board and chief executive officer.

AMRAM, DAVID. Composer, conductor, musician. b. David Werner Amram III, Nov. 17, 1930, Philadelphia, Pa., to Philip and Emilie (Weyl) Amram. Father, attorney, writer. Grad. Putney (Vt.) Sch., 1948; attended Oberlin Conservatory of Music (1948–49); grad. George Washington Univ., B.A. (European History) 1952; attended Manhattan Sch. of Music, 1955–56. Studied composition with Vittorio Giannini; horn with Gunther Schuller, N.Y.C. Served US Army, Bremerhaven (Germany) Band; Seventh Army Sym. 1952–54; rank, PFC. Member of AFM, Local 802. Address: (home) 461 Sixth Ave., New York, NY 10011, tel. (212) OR 5-8456; (bus.) c/o Barna Ostertag, 501 Fifth Ave., New York, NY 10017, tel. (212) OX 7-6339.

Pre-Theatre. Truck driver, gym teacher, symphonic musician, jazz musician, carpenter's helper, short order cook.

Theatre. Mr. Amram's first stage assignment was composing incidental music for the NY Shakespeare Festival production of *Titus Andronicus* (Emanuel Presbyterian Church, Nov. 1956); subsequently composed incidental music for their productions of *Romeo and Juliet* and *The Two Gentlemen from Verona* (Belvedere Lake Th., June, July 1957); *Richard III* (Heckscher, Nov. 25, 1957) and *As you Like It* (Heckscher, Jan. 20, 1958); composed music for *The Sign of Winter* (Theatre 74, May 7, 1958); the NY Shakespeare Festival production of *Othello* and *Twelfth Night* (Belvedere Lake Th., July, Aug. 1958); *Deathwatch* (Theatre East, Oct. 9, 1958); and *The Family Reunion* (Phoenix, Oct. 20, 1958).

His first Bway score was incidental music for *Comes a Day* (Ambassador, Nov. 6, 1958); followed by *The Power and the Glory* (Phoenix, Dec. 10, 1958); the NY Shakespeare Festival production of *Antony and Cleopatra* (Heckscher, Jan. 13, 1959); *J.B.* (ANTA, Dec. 11, 1958); *The Rivalry* (Bijou, Feb. 7, 1959); *The Beaux' Stratagem* (Phoenix, Feb. 24, 1949); and *Kataki* (Ambassador, Apr. 9, 1959).

He composed the incidental music for *Romeo and Juliet* (American Shakespeare Festival Th., Stratford, Conn., June 12, 1959); *Julius Caesar* (NY Shakespeare Festival, Belvedere Lake Th., N.Y.C., Aug. 3, 1959); *The Great God Brown* (Coronet, Oct. 6, 1959); *Lysistrata* (Phoenix, Nov. 24, 1959); *Peer Gynt* (Phoenix, Jan. 12, 1960); *Caligula* (54 St. Th., Feb. 16, 1960); *Henry IV, Part 1* (Phoenix, Apr. 18, 1960).

He composed incidental music for the NY Shakespeare Festival productions of *Henry V* (Belvedere Lake Th., June 29, 1960), *Measure for Measure* (Belvedere Lake Th., July 25, 1960), and *Taming of the Shrew* (Belvedere Lake Th., Aug. 18, 1960); for *Hamlet* (Phoenix, Mar. 16, 1961); the American Shakespeare Festival Th. productions of *As You Like It* (Stratford, Conn., June 27, 1961) and *Macbeth* (Stratford, Conn., June 28, 1961); the NY Shakespeare Festival productions of *Much Ado About Nothing* (Wollman Skating Rink, July 31, 1961), *A Midsummer Night's Dream* (Wollman Skating Rink, July 31, 1961), and *Richard I* (Wollman Skating Rink, Aug. 28, 1961); at the Delacorte Th., *The Tempest* (July 16, 1962), *King Lear* (Aug. 13, 1962) and *The Merchant of Venice* (June 14, 1962); *Macbeth* (Heckscher, Nov. 12, 1962); and *The Winter's Tale* (Delacorte Th., July 19, 1963).

Mr. Amram was musical director for the Repertory Theatre of Lincoln Center and wrote the music for *After the Fall* (ANTA Washington Sq. Th., Jan. 23, 1964); and also for *The Passion of Joseph D.* (Ethel Barrymore Th., Feb. 11, 1964). He composed music and conducted for *That Summer—That Fall* (Helen Hayes Th., Mar. 16, 1967).

Films. Mr. Amram wrote incidental music for *Echo of an Era* (1957); *Pull My Daisy* (1958); *Harmful Effects of Tobacco* (1959); *The Young Savages* (UA, 1959); *Splendor in the Grass* (WB, 1961); *The Manchurian Candidate* (UA, 1962); and *The Arrangement* (WB, 1969).

Television. He has composed music for *The American* (Purex Special, NBC, 1960); *The Fifth Column* (CBS, 1960); *Something Special* (NBC, 1959); and *Turn of the Screw* (Ford Startime, NBC, Oct. 20, 1959).

Other Activities. Mr. Amram composed orchestral music for *The American Bell* (Independence Hall, Philadelphia, Pa., June 1962). Additional works, for orchestra, voice, or instrumental groups include: for narrator and orchestra—*Autobiography for Strings, Shakespearean Concerto;* for chamber groups—*Dirge and Variation, Discussion for Flute, Cello, Piano and Percussion, Overture and Allegro, Sonata for Unaccompanied Violin, Sonata for Violin and Piano, Three Songs for Marlboro, String Quartet, Trio* and *The Wind and the Rain;* for choral groups—*May the Worlds of Our Lord, Shir L'Erev Shabat* and *Thou Shalt Love the Lord, Thy God; A Piano Sonata;* and the opera *Twelfth Night.* He was guest composer at the Marlboro (Vt.) Music Festival (1961).

Awards. He received the *Village Voice* Off-Bway (Obie) Award for his compositions for the Phoenix Theatre and the NY Shakespeare Festival (1959).

Recreation. Kayaking in the ocean, sailing, skiing, running track, playing jazz, learning languages.

ANDERS, GLENN. Actor. b. Charles Glenn Anders, Sept. 1, 1889, Los Angeles, Calif., to Charles Gustave and Etta Arvilla (Slade) Anders. Father, contractor. Attended Los Angeles (Calif.) H.S., 1904–08; Columbia Univ., 1919–21. Member of AEA, Delta Upsilon, Columbia Univ. Club, NYAC.

Theatre. Mr. Anders made his first appearance on the stage as Lennox in *Macbeth* (Los Angeles, 1910); in N.Y.C. at the Academy of Music (1912); toured with Sothern and Marlowe's Shakespearean Co. (1912); and toured on the Keith and Orpheum Circuits (1913–15).

He made his Bway debut as Harry Wattles in *Just Around the Corner* (Longacre, Feb. 5, 1919); subsequently played Billy Awkwright in *Civilian Clothes* (Morosco, Sept. 12, 1919); Larry McLeod in *Scrambled Wives* (Fulton, Aug. 5, 1920); Richard Hunt in *The Ghost Between* (39 St. Th., Mar. 22, 1921); Wally Dean in *The Demi-Virgin* (Times Sq. Th., Oct. 18, 1921); Dr. Harry Nolles in *Cold Feet* (Fulton, May 21, 1923); Gerald Warner in *What's Your Wife Doing?* (49 St. Th., Oct. 1, 1923); Andy Lowry in *Hell-Bent fer Heaven* (Klaw, Jan. 4, 1924); John Buckmaster in *So This Is Politics* (Henry Miller's Th., June 16, 1924); the Aviator in *Bewitched* (National, Oct. 1, 1924); and Joe in *They Knew What They Wanted* (Garrick, Nov. 24, 1924), which he repeated for his London debut (St. Martin's, May 18, 1926).

He appeared as Lewis Dodd in *The Constant Nymph* (Selwyn, N.Y.C., Dec. 9, 1926); Worthington Smythe in *Murray Hill* (Bijou, Sept 29, 1927); Edmund Darrell in *Strange Interlude* (John Golden Th., Jan. 30, 1928); Reuben Light in *Dynamo* (Martin Beck Th., Feb. 11, 1929); Pat Farley in *Hotel Universe* (Martin Beck Th., Apr. 4, 1930); Lt. Frederick Henry in *A Farewell to Arms* (National, Sept. 22, 1930); Bob Nolan in *Midnight* (Guild, Dec. 29, 1930); Julian Fichtner in a touring production of *The Lonely Way* (Feb. 1931); succeeded (June 1931) Herbert Marshall as Nicholas Hay in *Tomorrow and Tomorrow* (Henry Miller's Th., N.Y.C., Jan. 13, 1931); appeared as Victor Hallam in *Another Language* (Booth, Apr. 8, 1933); Leo in *Design for Living* (Ann Arbor Dramatic Festival, Lydia Mendelssohn Th., Univ. of Michigan, June 1933); Carl in *Love and Babies* (Cort, N.Y.C., Aug. 22, 1933); Pierre in *I Was Waiting for You* (Booth, Nov. 13, 1933); Eugene Cabot in *False Dreams, Farewell* (Little, Jan. 15, 1934); Branwell Bronte in *Moor Born* (Playhouse, Apr. 3, 1934); Charles Cameron in *A Sleeping Clergyman* (Guild, Oct. 8, 1934); and Chester Digges in *On to Fortune* (Fulton, Feb. 4, 1935).

In stock, he appeared as Turner in *If This Be Treason* (Westport Playhouse, Conn., July 1935) and at the same theatre as Lucien Goddard in *Dame Nature* (July 1935); played Tony Cooke in *There's Wisdom in Women* (Cort, N.Y.C., Oct. 30, 1935); Kornoff in *The Masque of Kings* (Shubert, Feb. 8, 1937); Karl Brenner in *Three Waltzes* (Majestic, Dec. 25, 1937); Dr. Thomas Held in a summer-theatre touring production of *I Am Different* (Aug. 1938); Bill Blake in *Skylark* (Morosco, N.Y.C., Oct. 11, 1939); and appeared in *Vincent Youman's Ballet Revue* (Lyric, Baltimore, Md., 1943).

He played Sam in *Get Away Old Man* (Cort, N.Y.C., Nov. 24, 1943); the Angel Guardian in *Career Angel* (Natl., May 23, 1944); Alexander Craig in *Soldier's Wife* (John Golden Th., Oct. 4, 1944); Miguel Riachi in a tryout of *Dunnigan's Daughter* (McCarter Th., Princeton, N.J., Oct. 1945); Carleton Fitzgerald in *Light Up the Sky* (Royale, N.Y.C., Nov. 18, 1948); Arthur Mitchell in *One Bright Day* (Royale, Mar. 19, 1952); Dr. Fifield in *The Remarkable Mr. Pennypacker* (Coronet, Dec. 30, 1953); Dr. Gerald Lyman in the national tour of *Bus Stop* (opened Central City, Colo., Aug. 15, 1955; closed Shubert, New Haven, Conn., May 5, 1956); Lord Hector in *Time Remembered* (Morosco, N.Y.C., Nov. 12, 1957); and Prof. Muller in *The Visit* (NY City Ctr., Mar. 8, 1960), in which he also toured.

ANDERSON, DAME JUDITH. Actress. b. Frances Margaret Anderson-Anderson, Feb. 10, 1898, Adelaide, South Australia, to James and Jessie Margaret (Saltmarsh) Anderson-Anderson. Attended Rose Park Sch., Adelaide, 1908–12; Norwood H.S., Adelaide, 1913–16. Married May 18, 1937, to Benjamin Harrison Lehman, educator (marr. dis. Aug. 23, 1939); married July 11, 1946, to Luther Greene, producer, director, (marr. dis. June 26, 1951). During WW II, made USO tours, entertaining Armed Forces in Hawaii, New Guinea, and the Caribbean. Member of AEA; AFTRA; SAG. Address: c/o Actors Equity Assn., 165 W. 46th St., New York, NY 10036.

Theatre. Miss Anderson made her stage debut in Australia, as Stephanie in *A Royal Divorce* (Theatre Royal, Sydney, 1915); followed by two years touring Australia in *Monsieur Beaucaire, The Scarlet Pimpernel,* and *David Garrick* (1915–17).

She came to the US in 1918, and joined the Emma Bunting Stock Co. (14 St. Th., N.Y.C., 1918–19); toured in *Dear Brutus* (1920); played in stock companies in Albany, N.Y., and in Boston, Mass. (1921).

Billed as Frances Anderson, she made her Bway debut as Mrs. Bellmore in *On the Stairs* (Playhouse, Sept. 25, 1922); subsequently, billed as Judith Anderson, appeared as Jessie Weston in *Peter Weston* (Harris, Sept. 18, 1923); Elise Van Zile in *Cobra* (Hudson, Apr. 22, 1924); and Dolores Romero in *The Dove* (Empire, Feb. 11, 1925).

She returned to Australia (Jan. 1927) and repeated the role of Elise in *Cobra,* and later played the wife in *Tea for Three* and Iris March in *The Green Hat;* appeared as Antoinette Lyle in *Behold the Bridegroom* (Cort, N.Y.C., Dec. 26, 1927); Anna Plumer in *Anna* (Lyceum, May 15, 1928); succeeded (July 1928) Lynn Fontanne as Nina Leeds in *Strange Interlude* (John Golden Th., Jan. 30, 1928), and toured with the production.

Miss Anderson toured as the Unknown One in *As You Desire Me* (1930–31) and opened with the play in N.Y.C. (Maxine Elliott's Th., Jan. 28, 1931); played Lavinia Mannon in *Mourning Becomes Electra* (Alvin, May 9, 1932), and toured in the role; appeared as Karola Lovasdy in *Firebird* (Empire, N.Y.C., Nov. 21, 1932); Helen Nolte in *Conquest* (Plymouth, Feb. 18, 1933); Savina Grazia in *The Mask and the Face* (Guild, May 18, 1933); Valerie Latour in *The Drums Begin* (Shubert, Nov. 24, 1933); the Woman in *Come of Age* (Maxine Elliott's Th., Jan. 12, 1934); and Minea Sheller in a stock production of *The Female of the Species* (Pittsburgh, Pa., Aug. 1, 1934).

She appeared as Lila in *Divided by Three* (Ethel Barrymore Th., Oct. 2, 1934); Delia Lovell in *The Old Maid* (Empire, Jan. 7, 1935), and toured with it (1935–36); played Gertrude in John Gielgud's *Hamlet* (Empire, N.Y.C., Oct. 8, 1936); Lady Macbeth in Laurence Olivier's *Macbeth* (Old Vic, London, Nov. 26, 1937); appeared as Mary in *Family Portrait* (Morosco, N.Y.C., Mar. 8, 1939); repeated the role (Carmel Forest Th., Calif., 1940), and at the same theatre, played Clytemnestra in *The Tower Beyond Tragedy,* which she also directed (1940); played Lady Macbeth in Maurice Evans' *Macbeth* (National, N.Y.C., Nov. 11, 1941); and Olga in *The Three Sisters* (Ethel Barrymore Th., Dec. 21, 1942).

Miss Anderson played the title role in *Medea* (National, Oct. 20, 1947; N.Y. City Ctr., May 2, 1949); Clytemnestra in *The Tower Beyond Tragedy* (ANTA, Nov. 26, 1950); the title role in *Medea* (Hebbel Th., Berlin, Germany, Sept. 13, 1951); the Woman in *Come of Age* (NY City Ctr., Jan. 23, 1952); appeared in the dramatic reading of *John Brown's Body* (New Century, Feb. 14, 1953); and played Gertrude Eastman-Cuevas in *In the Summer House* (Playhouse, Dec. 29, 1953).

She played the title role in *Medea* for the Salute to France Festival (Th. Sarah Bernhardt, Paris, France, June 14, 1955); the 1st Applicant (Miss Madrigal) in the national tour of *The Chalk Garden* (opened Lobero, Santa Barbara, Calif., Sept. 6, 1956; closed McCarter, Princeton, N.J., Feb. 16, 1957); and Isabel Lawton in *Comes a Day* (Ambassador, N.Y.C., Nov. 6, 1958).

With the Old Vic Co., she played Irina Arkadina in *The Seagull* (Edinburgh Festival, Scotland, Aug. 1960; Old Vic, Sept. 1, 1960); toured the US in scenes from *Macbeth, The Tower Beyond Tragedy,* and *Medea* (1961–63); and appeared as Alice Christie in *Black Chiffon* (Sombrero Playhouse, Phoenix, Ariz., Jan. 28, 1964).

She appeared in a program of dramatic readings (Elder Hall, Adelaide, Australia, Mar. 12, 1966); played Clytemnestra in the three-part *The Oresteia* (Ypsilanti Greek Th., Ypsilanti, Mich., June 28, 1966); the title role in a revival of *Elizabeth the Queen* (NY City Ctr., Nov. 3, 1966); and played the title role in *Hamlet* (Lobero Th., Santa Barbara, Calif., Jan. 21, 1968; Civic Th., Chicago, Ill., Dec. 27, 1970; Carnegie Hall, N.Y.C., Jan. 14–15, 1971).

Films. Miss Anderson appeared in *Blood Money* (UA, 1933); *Rebecca* (UA, 1940); *Forty Little Mothers* (MGM, 1940); *Lady Scarface* (RKO, 1941); *Free and Easy* (MGM, 1941); *Kings Row* (WB, 1941); *All Through the Night* (WB, 1942); *Edge of Darkness* (WB, 1943); *Stage Door Canteen* (UA, 1943); *Jane Eyre* (20th-Fox, 1944); *Laura* (20th-Fox, 1944); *And Then There Were None* (20th-Fox, 1945); *The Diary of a Chambermaid* (UA, 1946); *Specter of the Rose* (Rep., 1946); *The Strange Love of Martha Ivers* (Par., 1946); *The Red House* (UA, 1947); *Pursued* (WB, 1947); *Tycoon* (RKO, 1947); *The Furies* (Par., 1950); *Don't Bother To Knock* (20th-Fox, 1952); *Salomé* (Col., 1953); *The Ten Commandments* (Par., 1956); *Cat on a Hot Tin Roof* (MGM, 1958); *CinderFella* (Par., 1960); and *A Man Called Horse* (Natl. Gen., 1970).

Television and Radio. On radio, Miss Anderson performed in *Mary of Scotland* (Lux Th., CBS, May 1937).

On television, she appeared in *Black Chiffon* (ABC, Apr. 1954); *Macbeth* (Hallmark Hall of Fame, NBC, Nov. 28, 1954); *Yesterday's Magic* (Elgin Hour, ABC, Dec. 14, 1954); *Caesar and Cleopatra* (Showcase, NBC, Mar. 4, 1956); *The Cradle Song* (Hallmark Hall of Fame, NBC, May 6, 1956); *The Circular Staircase* (Climax, CBS, June 21, 1956); *The Clouded Image* (Playhouse 90, CBS, Nov. 7, 1957); *Abby, Julia and the 7 Pet Cows* (Telephone Time, ABC, Jan. 7, 1958); *The Bridge of San Luis Rey* (Dupont Show of the Month, CBS, Jan. 21, 1958); *Medea* (Play of the Week, WNTA, Oct. 12, 1959); *The Moon and Sixpence* (NBC, Oct. 30, 1959); and a repeat of *Macbeth* (Hallmark Hall of Fame, NBC, Nov. 20, 1960).

Miss Anderson was in *Abby, Julia and the Seven Pet Cows* (Star Th., Ind., Jan. 15, 1965); repeated her performance in *Medea* (Play of the Week, NET, Oct. 5, 1966); was on the Creative Person series (NET, 1967–68); and appeared again on the Hallmark Hall of Fame in the title role of *Elizabeth the Queen* (NBC, Jan. 21, 1968) and in *The Borrowers* (NBC, Dec. 14, 1973).

Awards. She was created Dame Commander of the Most Excellent Order of the British Empire (D.B.E.) in the Queen's Birthday Honours (July 12, 1960); received the honorary degree of Doctor of Fine Arts from Northwestern Univ. (1953); the Dickinson College Art Award (1960); and an honorary L.H.D. from Fairfield (Conn.) Univ. (May 16, 1964).

She received the Donaldson Award for her performance in the title role in *Medea* (1948); was named the "first lady of the theatre" by the General Federation of Woman's Clubs (1948); received the American Academy of Arts and Sciences Award for her diction (1948); and two NATAS (Emmy) awards for her portrayal of Lady Macbeth (1954, 1960).

Recreation. Music, gardening, riding, reading.

ANDERSON, LEROY. Composer, conductor. b. Franklin Leroy Anderson, June 29, 1908, Cambridge, Mass., to Brewer A. and Anna M. (Johnson) Anderson. Father, post office clerk. Grad. Cambridge High and Latin Sch., 1925; Harvard Univ., B.A. (magna cum laude, Phi Beta Kappa) 1929, M.A. (Elkan Naumberg Fellowship) 1930; also studied Germanic languages, Harvard Univ. 1930–34. Studied piano at New England Conservatory, Boston; composition with Walter Raymond Spalding and Walter Piston at Harvard Univ. Married Oct. 31, 1942, to Eleanor Jane Firke; three sons, one daughter. Served with NY Natl. Guard, 101 Cavalry, 1937–39. Served with US Army, 1942–46; translator, interpreter, Iceland Base Command; Military Intelligence Service, Washington, D.C.; rank, Capt. Served Korean War, 1951–52, translation officer. Member of ASCAP (board of review, 1960–64); Dramatists Guild; AFM, Local 802. Address: (home) Woodbury, CT 60798; (bus.) c/o Woodbury Music Corp., Woodbury, CT 60798, tel. (203) 263-2288.

Theatre. Mr. Anderson composed the music for *Goldilocks* (Lunt-Fontanne, Oct. 11, 1958).

Films. His composition, *The Typewriter,* was used as background music for the film, *But Not for Me* (Par., 1959).

Other Activities. Mr. Anderson was choirmaster and organist of the East Congregational Church (Milton, Mass., 1929–35); orchestrator and arranger for the Boston Pops Orchestra (1936–50) during which time he composed such works as *Jazz Pizzicato* (1937), *Fiddle-Faddle* (1947), *The Syncopated Clock* (1945), *Blue Tango* (1951), *Sleigh Ride* (1947), *Serenata* (1948), and *Waltzing Cat* (1950). He has been guest conductor of many symphony orchestras in the US and Canada. He was a member of the visiting committee to the Department of Music, Harvard Univ. (1962–68) and is a director of the New Haven (Conn.) Symphony Orchestra (1969–to date) and the Hartford (Conn.) Symphony Orchestra (1971–to date).

Recreation. Carpentry, home repairs.

ANDERSON, LINDSAY. Director. b. Apr. 17, 1923, Bangalore, India, to Alexander Vass and Estelle Bell (Gasson) Anderson. Educ. Cheltenham Coll.; Windham Coll., Oxford Univ. Address: c/o Royal Court Th., Sloane Sq., London S.W. 1, England.

Theatre. Mr. Anderson directed *The Waiting of Lester Abbs* (Royal Court Th., London, June 1957); *The Long and the Short and the Tall* (Royal Court, Jan. 7, 1959); *Jazzetry* (Royal Court, May 3, 1959); *Dispersal* (Belgrade Th., Coventry, Eng., June 29, 1959); *Serjeant Musgrave's Dance* (Royal Court, Oct. 22, 1959); *The Lily White Boys* (Royal, Brighton, Eng., Jan. 18, 1960; Royal Court, London, Jan. 27, 1960); *Billy Liar* (Royal, Brighton, Sept. 1, 1960; Cambridge Th., London, Sept. 13, 1960); *Trials,* two one-act plays by Christopher Logue: *Antigone* and *Cob and Leach* (Royal Court, Nov. 23, 1960); and *The Diary of a Madman,* which, with Richard Harris, he also adapted (Royal Court, Mar. 7, 1963).

He also directed the National Th. production of *Andorra* (Old Vic, London, Jan. 28, 1964); *Julius Caesar* (Royal Court, Nov. 26, 1964); played Reg Parsons in *Miniatures* (Royal Court, Apr. 25, 1965); directed (Contemporary Th., Warsaw, Pol., 1966) the first Polish production of *Inadmissible Evidence (Nie do Obrony);* and directed *The Cherry Orchard* (Chichester Festival, Eng., July 19, 1966).

He was co-artistic director (1969–70) of the Royal Court, where he directed *In Celebration* (Apr. 22, 1969), *The Contractor* (Oct. 20, 1969), and *Home* (June 17, 1970; also the N.Y.C. production: Morosco, Nov. 15, 1970); *The Changing Room* (Nov. 9, 1971), *The Farm* (Sept. 26, 1973), and *Life Class* (Apr. 9, 1974).

Films. The first film directed by Mr. Anderson was the documentary *Meet the Pioneers* (1948); followed by the documentaries *Thursday's Children,* on which Guy Brenton was his collaborator in direction and writing of the screenplay; *Every Day Except Christmas; O Dreamland; Three Installations; Pleasure Garden; March to Aldermaston;* and *The Singing Lesson* (Documentary Studio, Warsaw, Pol.). Other films directed by Mr. Anderson include *This Sporting Life* (Reade, 1963); *The White Bus* (UA, 1967), which, with Oscar Lewenstein, he also produced; *If . . .* (Par., 1969), which, with Michael Medwin, he also produced; and *O Lucky Man* (WB, 1973).

Awards. Mr. Anderson received the Hollywood Short Subject Award (1954); his documentary *Every Day Except Christmas* won the Venice Grand Prix (1957); and for his direction of the N.Y.C. production of *Home,* he was nominated for an Antoinette Perry (Tony) Award (1970–71) and named in the *Variety* poll of NY drama critics.

ANDERSON, RICHARD. Actor. b. Richard Norman Anderson, Aug. 8, 1926, Long Branch, N.J., to Henry and Olga (Lurie) Anderson. Father, hat manufacturer. Grad. Univ. H.S., Los Angeles, Calif., 1944; studied at Actor's Lab., Los Angeles (1946–47) with Elza Shdanoff, Los Angeles. Married Oct. 1961, to Katharine; three daughters. Served WW II US Army, 1944–46; camp newspaper correspondent; rank, t/4 Sgt. Member of AEA; SAG; AFTRA; Ephebian Society, Los Angeles. Address: (home) 10120 Cielo Dr., Beverly Hills, CA 90210, tel. (213) 278-4614; (bus.) Diamond Artists Ltd., 8400 Sunset Blvd., West Hollywood, CA 90069.

Pre-Theatre. Theatre usher, marquee boy, salesman, movie studio messenger boy and guide, publicity writer.

Theatre. Mr. Anderson first appeared on the stage as a walk-on in *Volpone* (Actor's Lab., Los Angeles, Sept. 10, 1947); in stock, appeared in *Kind Lady* and in *Dear Ruth* (Lobero Th., Santa Barbara, Calif., July 1948); played Rudolph in *Anna Lucasta* and in *Peg o' My Heart* (Laguna Beach Playhouse, July-Aug. 1949); and Caleb Cornish in *The Highest Tree* (Longacre, N.Y.C., Nov. 4, 1959).

Films. Mr. Anderson made his film debut in *The Vanishing Westerner* (Rep., 1950); followed *A Life of Her Own* (MGM, 1950); *Grounds for Marriage* (MGM, 1951); *The Magnificient Yankee* (MGM, 1950); *Across the Wide Missouri* (MGM, 1951); *Payment on Demand* (RKO, 1951); *Cause for Alarm (MGM, 1951); Go for Broke* (MGM, 1951); *Rich, Young and Pretty* (MGM, 1951); No Questions Asked (MGM, 1951); *The Unknown Man* (MGM, 1951); *The People Against O'Hara* (MGM, 1951); *Just This Once* (MGM, 1952); *Fearless Fagan* (MGM, 1952); *Scaramouche* (MGM, 1952); *I Love Marvin* (MGM, 1953); *Dream Wife* (MGM, 1953); *The Story of Three Loves* (MGM, 1953); *Give a Girl a Break* (MGM, 1953); *Escape from Fort Bravo* (MGM, 1953); *The Student Prince* (MGM, 1954); *Hit the Deck* (MGM, 1955); *It's a Dog's Life* (MGM, 1955); *Forbidden Planet* (MGM, 1956); *The Buster Keaton Story* (Par., 1957); *Three Brave Men* (20th-Fox, 1957); *Paths of Glory* (UA, 1957); *The Long Hot Summer* (20th-Fox, 1958); *Compulsion* (Fox, 1959); *The Wackiest Ship in the Army* (Col., 1960); *Gathering of Eagles* (U, 1963); *Johhny Cool* (UA, 1963); *Seven Days in May* (Par., 1964); Seconds (Par., 1966); *Tora, Tora, Tora* (20th-Fox, 1970); *Doctors' Wives* (Col. 1971); *Play It As It Lays* (U, 1972); *The Honkers* (UA, 1972); and *Macho Callohan* (Avco Embassy, 1969).

Television. Mr. Anderson made his debut in 1950, appearing in 20 live shows; subsequently in *Eighty-Yard Run* (Playhouse 90, CBS, 1958); Zane Grey Theatre (CBS, 1959); Wagon Train (CBS, 1959); Rifleman (CBS, 1960); Thriller (NBC, 1960); Checkmate (NBC, 1960); Target The Corrupters (ABC, 1962); Kraft Television Th. (NBC, 1962); The Virginian (NBC, 1963); Dr. Kildare (NBC, 1963); Eleventh Hour (NBC, 1963); Alfred Hitchcock Show (CBS, 1964); The Untouchables (ABC); Ironside (NBC); FBI (ABC); Gunsmoke (CBS); Mod Squad (ABC); Bonanza (NBC). He has been a series regular on *Bus Stop* (ABC, 1961); Lieutenant (NBC, 1963); Perry Mason; Dan August; The Six Million Dollar Man; and Movie of the Week (CBS; ABC). Other shows in which he appeared include Longstreet; Owen Marshall; Cannon; Columbo; Jigsaw; Barnaby Jones; Fugitive; Wanted Dead or Alive; Big Valley; Felony Squad; My Friend Tony; Mannix; Bracken's World; Death Valley Days; Land of the Giants; Invaders; Alias Smith and Jones; and Target The Corrupters.

Recreation. Fishing, tennis, photography.

ANDERSON, ROBERT. Playwright. b. Robert Woodruff Anderson, Apr. 28, 1917, New York City, to James H. and Myra (Grigg) Anderson. Father, businessman; mother, schoolteacher. Grad. Phillips Exeter Academy, N.H., 1935; Harvard Univ., B.A. (magna cum laude) 1939; M.A. 1940; grad. study, Harvard Univ., 1940–42; studied with John Gassner at The Dramatic Workshop of New Sch. for Social Research, on a playwriting fellowship awarded by NTC, 1946. Married June 24, 1940, to Phyllis Stohl (dec. Nov. 28, 1956); married Dec. 11, 1959, to Teresa Wright, actress; one stepson, one stepdaughter. Served USNR, PTO, 1942–46; rank, Lt.; Bronze Star Medal. Member of New Dramatists Committee (one of founders; pres., 1959–60); Dramatists Guild (council, 1954–to date; pres., 1971–73); Dramatists Guild Fund (board of dir., 1962–to date); *Dramatists Bulletin* (edit. comm., 1964); Amer. Playwrights Theatre (board of governors, 1964–to date); Authors League Fund (board of dir., 1966–to date); Authors League Council (1969–to date); Authors Guild (1970–to date). WGA, West; Harvard Club of N.Y.C.; Century Association; Coffee House Club. Address: Bridgewater, CT 06752.

Theatre. Mr. Anderson made his stage debut as a Troll in a seventh-grade school production of *Three Billy Goats Gruff* (New Rochelle, N.Y., 1929); appeared in Harvard Univ. productions; and in stock productions with the South Shore Players (Cohasset, Mass., Summers 1937–38).

His first play produced was a musical comedy, *Hour Town*, staged at Harvard Univ. (Dunster House, Dec. 1938), for which he wrote the book, lyrics, and music, directed the production, and performed in it.

His first play to be produced in N.Y.C. was *Come Marching Home* (Blackfriars Guild, May 18, 1946), after its premiere at State Univ. of Iowa (Univ. Th., 1945); his play, *The Eden Rose*, was first presented by the Theatre Workshop of Ridgefield (Conn.), Inc. (July 27, 1949).

Mr. Anderson's first Bway production was the revue, *Dance Me a Song* (Royale, Jan. 20, 1950), for which he wrote the sketch, "The Lunts Are the Lunts"; wrote *Love Revisited* (Westport Country Playhouse, Conn., June 25, 1951); *All Summer Long* (Arena Stage, Washington, D.C., premiere Jan. 13, 1953).

His first full-length play produced on Bway was *Tea and Sympathy* (Ethel Barrymore Th., Sept. 30, 1953), which toured and was staged in London (Comedy, Apr. 25, 1957); subsequently wrote *All Summer Long* (Coronet, N.Y.C., Sept. 23, 1954); followed by *Silent Night, Lonely Night* (Morosco, Dec. 3, 1959); *The Days Between* (world premiere, Dallas Theatre Center, Dallas, Tex., May 19, 1965), played under American Playwrights Theatre plan in fifty college and community theatres throughout the country; *You Know I Can't Hear You When the Water's Running* (Ambassador Th., N.Y.C., Mar. 13, 1967); *I Never Sang for My Father* (Longacre, Jan. 25, 1968); and *Solitaire/Double Solitaire* (Long Wharf Th., New Haven, Conn., Feb. 12, 1971; Edinburgh Festival, Scotland, Sept. 6, 1971; John Golden Th., N.Y.C., Sept. 30, 1971).

Films. Mr. Anderson adapted *Tea and Sympathy* (MGM, 1956); subsequently wrote *Until They Sail* (MGM, 1957); *The Nun's Story* (WB, 1959); *The Sand Pebbles* (20th C-Fox, 1966); *Night of the Generals* (Col., 1967); and *I Never Sang for My Father* (Col., 1970).

Television and Radio. He adapted for radio, *The Petrified Forest* (Th. Guild on the Air, 1948); and adapted about 30 other plays for Th. Guild on the Air, and Cavalcade of America.

His first television assignment was an adaptation of *Biography* (Kraft Television Th., NBC, Oct. 27, 1956); followed by adaptations of *The Old Lady Shows Her Medals* (U.S. Steel Hour, CBS, May 23, 1956; Dec. 19, 1956; June 12, 1963); *All Summer Long* (Goodyear Playhouse, NBC, Oct. 28, 1956); *Rise Up and Walk* (Robert Montgomery Presents, NBC, Feb. 4, 1952); Goodyear Playhouse, NBC, Jan. 1, 1956); *Double Solitaire* (Hollywood Television Th., P.B.S., Jan. 16, 1973); and original works and adaptations for Schlitz Playhouse, Studio One, Celanese Th., and Cosmopolitan Th.

Other Activities. Mr. Anderson taught playwriting at the Amer. Theatre Wing (N.Y.C., 1946–50); was a member of the Playwrights Co., and producing organization of playwrights (1953–60); set up and taught a playwriting group at Actors Studio (1955–56); was a member of the faculty, Salzburg (Austria) Seminar in Amer. Studies (1968); writer-in-residence, Univ. of North Carolina (1969); chmn., Harvard Bd. of Overseers' Comm. to visit the performing arts (1972–to date).

Published Works. Mr. Anderson is the author of a novel, *After* (1973).

Awards. Mr. Anderson won an NTC citation for his play, *Come Marching Home* (1945); the *Variety* NY Drama Critics Poll for his play, *Tea and Sympathy* (1954); and was nominated for an Academy (Oscar) Award for his screenplay *The Nun's Story* (1960) and *I Never Sang for My Father* (1970). He was also nominated for a Screen Writer's Award for *The Nun's Story* (1960) and *The Sand Pebbles* (1966) and won the Screen Writer's Award for *I Never Sang for My Father* (1970). He also won the University of Southern California Gerontology Center Humanities Award for *I Never Sang for My Father* in 1974.

ANDES, KEITH. Actor, singer. b. John Charles Andes, July 12, 1920, Ocean City, N.J., to William G. and Elsie (Metzger) Andes. Father, lawyer. Grad. Upper Darby (Pa.) H.S., 1938; attended St. Edwards Sch., Oxford, England, 1938; grad. Temple Univ., B.S. (Education), 1943. Studied voice with Dr. Clyde Dengler, Philadelphia, Pa.; Luigi Guiffrida and Rosalie Snyder, N.Y.C.; and J. Mebane Beasley, Hollywood, Calif. Married, two sons. Served WW II, USAAF, 3-1/2 yrs.; rank, Sgt. Member of SAG; AFTRA; AEA.

Theatre. Mr. Andes made his N.Y.C. debut as a singer and understudy to Barry Nelson in the role of Bobby Grills in *Winged Victory* (44 St. Th., Nov. 20, 1943) and on tour subsequently appeared as Bumerli in *The Chocolate Soldier* (Century, Mar. 12, 1947) and on tour; followed (June, 1950) Alfred Drake as Petruchio in *Kiss Me, Kate* (Century, Dec. 30, 1948) in which he toured in the national company (1949–50); played John Shand in *Maggie* (Natl., Feb. 18, 1953); Joe Dynamite in *Wildcat* (Alvin, Dec. 16, 1960); repeated his role in *Wildcat* (New Circle Arts Th., San Diego, Calif., May 28, 1963); and toured as Don Quixote in *Man of La Mancha* (1967).

Films. Mr. Andes made his debut in the film adaptation of *Winged Victory* (20th-Fox, 1944); subsequently appeared in *The Farmer's Daughter* (RKO, 1947); *Project X* (Four Continents, 1949); *Clash By Night* (RKO, 1952); *Blackbeard the Pirate* (RKO, 1952); *Split-Second* (RKO, 1953); *Key Man* (1954); *The Second Greatest Sex* (U, 1955); *Away All Boats* (U, 1956); *Pillars of the Sky* (U, 1956); *Interlude* (U, 1957); *The Girl Most Likely* (U, 1957); *Back from Eternity* (RKO, 1956); *Damn Citizen* (U, 1958); *Surrender, Hell!* (Allied, 1959); *Model for Murder* (1958).

Television and Radio. Mr. Andes first appeared on Philadelphia, Pa., radio stations in small roles on various shows (WHAT, 1934); played small roles and sang on Singing Master (WFIL, 1940); and sang on the Doris Havens Show (KYW, 1941).

He first appeared on television as a singing guest star on the Steve Allen Spectacular (NBC, July 2, 1955); subsequently played in *The Great Waltz* (NBC, Nov. 5, 1955); *Bloomer Girl* (NBC, May 28, 1956); *Holiday* (NBC, June 9, 1956); *Homeward Borne* (Playhouse 90, CBS, Sept. 1956); *Blind Drop-Warsaw* (Conflict, NBC, 1957); *Tribute to Ethel Barrymore* (Alcoa Playhouse, NBC, Nov. 23, 1957); the series, This Man Dawson (Syndicated, 1959–60; Bell Telephone Hour (NBC, Jan. 6, 1961); and Crimes at Sea (ABC, July, 1961). In addition, he appeared on Have Gun, Will Travel (CBS, 1961); The Rifleman (ABC, 1962); Follow the Sun (ABC, 1962); Perry Mason (CBS, 1963, 1964); the Lucy Show (CBS, 1963, 1964, 1965); Glynis Johns Show (CBS, 1963); 77 Sunset Strip (ABC, Dec. 1963); Daniel Boone (NBC, 1967); I Spy (NBC, 1967); Star Trek (NBC, 1967); Dan August (ABC, 1971); and Cannon (CBS, 1972).

ANDREWS, ANN. Actress. b. Oct. 13, 1895, Los Angeles, Calif., to Josias J. and Ann (Anthony) Andrews. Studied at Egan's Dramatic Sch., Los Angeles, Calif. (1916). Member of AEA. Address: (home) 675 Madison Ave., New York, NY 10021; (bus.) c/o Actors Equity Association, 226 W. 47th St., New York, NY 10036, tel. (212) Plaza 7-7660.

Theatre. Miss Andrews made her stage debut in the title role of *Nju* (Little Th., Los Angeles, Calif., Oct. 31, 1916, and repeated the role for her N.Y.C. debut (Bandbox, Mar. 22, 1917); subsequently played Lady Mary Heather in *Seven Days Leave* (Majestic, Boston, Mass., Oct. 1917); the Author's Muse in *Josephine* (Knickerbocker, N.Y.C., Jan. 28, 1918); Katherine in *The Master* (Hudson, Feb. 19, 1918); toured N.Y. State as Connie in *Blind Youth* (Sept. 1918); appeared as Chloe in *Papa* (Little, N.Y.C., Apr. 10, 1919); Edith in *Up from Nowhere* (Comedy, Sept. 8, 1919); Mrs. Chadwick in *The Hottentot* (George M. Cohan Th., Mar. 1, 1920); Lady Elizabeth Galten in *The Champion* (Longacre, Jan. 3, 1921); in stock (Lyceum, Rochester, N.Y., Summers 1921–23); Blanche Ingram in *Her Temporary Husband* (Frazee, N.Y.C., Aug. 31, 1922); Eve Devant in *Two Married Men* (Longacre, Jan. 13, 1925); in stock (Lyceum, Rochester, N.Y., Summer 1925); Françoise Meillant in *The Captive* (Empire, N.Y.C., Sept. 29, 1926); Rita Landers in *The Dark* (Lyceum, Feb. 1, 1927); Margaret Heal in *The Fanatics* (49 St. Th., Nov. 7, 1927); and Julie Cavendish in *The Royal Family* (Selwyn, Dec. 28, 1927).

Miss Andrews played Patricia Tulliver Browne in *Recapture* (Eltinge, Jan. 29, 1930); Isabelle de Corquefon in *A Kiss of Importance* (Fulton, Dec. 1, 1930); Millicent Jordan in *Dinner at Eight* (Music Box, Oct. 22, 1932); Constance Oakshot in *Oliver Oliver* (Playhouse, Jan. 5, 1934); Alden Blaine in *Dark Victory* (Plymouth, Nov. 7, 1934); Lady Daisy Dantry in *De Luxe* (Booth, Mar. 5, 1935); appeared in a stock production of *First Love* (Jackson Heights, L.I., N.Y., Aug. 1936); played Miss Sloane in *Reflected Glory* (Morosco, N.Y.C., Sept. 21, 1936); Baroness de Launey in *Three Waltzes* (Majestic, Dec. 25, 1937); appeared in a stock production of the *Texas Nightingale* (Berkshire Playhouse, Stockbridge, Mass., 1938); played Elsie in *Miss Swan Expects* (Cort, N.Y.C., Feb. 20, 1939); and Clara Soppitt in *When We Are Married* (Lyceum, Dec. 25, 1939).

In stock, Miss Andrews appeared in *Our Betters* (Cape Playhouse, Dennis, Mass., July 1940); *Yes, My Darling Daughter* (Bucks County Playhouse, New Hope, Pa., 1940); *Serena Blandish* (Westport Country Playhouse, Conn., 1940); *Tonight at 8:30* (Royal Alexandra Th., Toronto, Can.; His Majesty's Th., Montreal, Oct. 1940); and *Seraphina* (Paper Mill Playhouse Millburn, N.J., July 1941).

She played Edith Weybright in *Spring Again* (Henry Miller's Th., N.Y.C., Nov. 10, 1941), and toured in it; Anita Sawyer in *Public Relations* (Mansfield, N.Y.C., Apr. 6, 1944); Ruth in *Blithe Spirit* (Queens, L.I., N.Y., June 1944; Martha's Vineyard Playhouse, Mass., July 1944; Sayville Playhouse, L.I., N.Y., July 24, 1944); Portia in *The Merchant of Venice* (Royal Alexandra, Toronto, Can., Aug. 1944); Minerva in the pre-Bway tryout of *Laughing Water* (opened Shubert, New Haven, Conn., Nov. 16, 1944; closed Plymouth, Boston, Mass., Dec. 1944); and in the national company of *Dream Girl* (opened Cass, Detroit, Mich., 1946; closed Selwyn, Chicago, Ill., 1947).

Films. Miss Andrews appeared in *The Cheat* (Par. 1931).

Television. Her TV credits include When We Were Married.

Recreation. Cats.

ANDREWS, EDWARD. Actor. b. Oct. 9, 1914, Griffin, Ga., to Edward Bryan Andrews, clergyman. Attended Univ. of Virginia, 1932–35. Married Aug. 23, 1955, to Emily Barnes; two daughters, one son. Served US Army, 1941–46; highest rank, Captain.

Theatre. Mr. Andrews first appeared on stage at the age of eight in *The Shannons of Broadway* (George Sharp Stock Co., Pittsburgh, Pa.). He made his Bway debut in a walk-on role in *How Beautiful with Shoes* (Booth Th., N.Y.C., Nov. 28, 1935); was understudy for Broderick Crawford as Lenny in *Of Mice and Men* (Music Box, Nov. 23, 1937), later touring as Lenny; played Tom in *The Time of Your Life* (Booth Th., Oct. 25, 1939), and later toured with the play until he entered military service. He toured with the national company of *The Glass Menagerie* (1946); played Clive Mortimer in *I Am a Camera* (Empire, N.Y.C., Nov. 28, 1951); Mr. Monroe in *Three by Thurber* (Th. de Lys, Mar. 7, 1955); took over (June 1957) the role of Gen. Tom Powers in *A Visit to a Small Planet* (Booth Th., Feb. 7, 1957); played Harlow Edison in *The Gazebo* (Lyceum, Dec. 12, 1958); and appeared in *The Marriage of Mr. Mississippi* (Center Th. Group, Los Angeles, Calif., Aug. 25, 1967).

Films. Mr. Andrews made his motion-picture debut in *The Phenix City Story* (Allied Artists, 1955). Among his many other films are *Tea and Sympathy* (MGM, 1956); *Elmer Gantry* (UA, 1960); and *Advise and Consent* (Col., 1962).

Television. Mr. Andrews first appeared on television in *Boy Meets Girl* (Studio One, CBS, 1949). Included among numerous other television appearances were co-starring roles on Broadside and Mr. Terrific. He has also been on the US Steel Hour (CBS); Kraft Th. (NBC); Alfred Hitchcock Presents (NBC); Gunsmoke (CBS); Eleventh Hour (NBC); Dr. Kildare (NBC); and Bonanza (NBC).

ANDREWS, JULIE. Actress, singer. b. Julia Elizabeth Wells, Oct. 1, 1935, Walton-on-Thames, Surrey, England, to Edward C. Wells and Barbara (Ward) Andrews. Father, schoolteacher; mother, pianist. Tutored privately in England. Married May 10, 1959, to Tony Walton, theatrical designer and producer; one daughter. Member of AEA; SAG; AFTRA. Address: c/o Chasin-Park-Citron Agency, 9255 Sunset Blvd., Los Angeles, CA 90069, tel. (213) 273-7190.

Theatre. Miss Andrews made her N.Y.C. debut in *The Boy Friend* (Royale Th., Sept. 30, 1954); followed by Eliza in *My Fair Lady* (Mark Hellinger Th., N.Y.C., May 15, 1956; Drury Lane, London, Apr. 30, 1958) and Guinevere in *Camelot* (Majestic, N.Y.C., Dec. 3, 1960).

Miss Andrews made her stage debut in England, in the revue, *Starlight Roof* (Hippodrome, London, Oct. 23, 1947); subsequently appeared at the Royal Command Performance (Palladium, London, Nov. 1, 1948); played the title role in *Humpty Dumpty* (Casino, London, Dec. 21, 1948); appeared in a revue (Hippodrome, Blackpool, June 27, 1949); played the title role in *Red Riding Hood* (Theatre Royal, Nottingham, Dec. 23, 1950); Princess Balroulbadour in *Aladdin* (Casino, London, Dec. 19, 1951); performed in the pantomime, *Jack and the Beanstalk* (Hippodrome, Coventry, Dec. 23, 1952); and played the title role in *Cinderella* (Palladium, London, Dec. 7, 1953). She appeared in the revue, *Cap and Belles* (Empire Th., Nottingham, May 25, 1953); and in *Mountain Fire* (Royal Court Th., Liverpool, May 18, 1954).

Films. Miss Andrews has appeared in *Mary Poppins* (Disney Studios, 1963); *Americanization of Emily* (1963); *Sound of Music* (1964); *Hawaii* (1965); *Torn Curtain* (1966); *Thoroughly Modern Millie* (1967); *Star* (1968); *Darling Lilli* (1970); and *The Tamarind Seed* (1973).

Television. Miss Andrews played the title role of *Cinderella* (CBS, 1947) and performed in Julie Andrews and Carol Burnett at Carnegie Hall (CBS, 1962); the *Julie Andrews Show* (1966); *An Evening with Julie Andrews and Harry Belafonte* (1969); *The World of Walt Disney* (1971); Julie Andrews Hour (series) (1972–73); *Julie on Sesame Street* (1973); *Julie Andrews Christmas Special* (1973); *Julie and Dick in Covent Garden* (1974); *Julie Andrews and Jackie Gleason Together* (1974); and *Julie Andrews–My Favorite Things* (1975).

Published Works. She is the author of *Mandy* (1971) and *The Last of the Really Great Whangdoodles* (1973).

Discography. Her recordings include *Tell It Again, Broadway's Fair Julie, Lion's Cage, Julie Andrews and Carol Burnett at Carnegie Hall,* and the original cast albums of *My Fair Lady* and *Camelot.*.

Recreation. Theatre, music, tennis.

ANDREWS, NANCY. Actress, singer. b. Nancy Currier Andrews, Dec. 16, 1924, Minneapolis, Minn., to James Currier and Grace (Gerrish) Andrews. Father, hotel owner and grain executive; mother, drama coach. Grad. Beverly Hills (Calif.) H.S., drama award, 1938; Los Angeles City Coll., 1940; attended Pasadena Playhouse Coll. of Theatre Arts, 1940–42; studied piano with Dean Fletcher, Minneapolis; drama with Ethel Chilstrom, Minneapolis. Married 1945, to Parke N. Bossart (marr. dis. 1952); one daughter. Member of AEA; AFTRA; AGVA; SAG; AFM, Local 802; Veterans Hospital Radio and Television Guild (bd. of dir., Bedside Network); NATAS (events comm.); Pasadena Playhouse Alumni Assn. (secy., vice-pres.). Address: 302 W. 12th St., New York, NY 10014, tel. (212) CH 2-5378.

Theatre. Miss Andrews made her debut as Mistress Ford in a high-school production of *The Merry Wives of Windsor* (Beverly Hills, Calif., 1938); subsequently wrote the music and lyrics for *Bright Champagne* (Melrose Th., Los Angeles, Calif., 1943); and was a singer-pianist with USO shows touring the Caribbean (1943–45).

She made her Bway debut in the revue *Touch and Go* (Broadhurst, Oct. 13, 1949); played Nicki in a stock production of *Break It Up* (Theatre-by-the-Sea, Matunuck, R.I., Summer 1950); Dorothy in *Gentlemen Prefer Blondes* (Greek Th., Los Angeles, Calif.; Curran, San Francisco, Calif., 1950); was stand-by for Ethel Merman as Mrs. Sally Adams in *Call Me Madam* (Imperial, N.Y.C., Oct. 12, 1950); appeared as Julie in a stock production of *Show Boat* (Lambertville Music Circus, N.J., 1951); succeeded (June 1953) Benay Venuta as Laura Carew in *Hazel Flagg* (Mark Hellinger Th., N.Y.C., Feb. 11, 1953); and played Sister Bessie in *Tobacco Road* (La Cienega Playhouse, Los Angeles, Calif., 1953).

Miss Andrews toured in a one-woman show, *Songs and Laughter* (Germany; Italy; Austria; France; England, Mar. 1–Aug. 1, 1954); played Sister Bessie in *Tobacco Road* (Grist Mill Playhouse, Andover, N.J., Aug. 1954); Emma Miller in *Plain and Fancy* (Mark Hellinger Th., N.Y.C., Jan. 27, 1955); succeeded (June 11, 1956) Helen Traubel as Fauna in *Pipe Dream* (Shubert, Nov. 30, 1955); appeared at the Sacramento (Calif.) Music Circus in the title role in *Panama Hattie* and in *Hit the Deck* (Summer, 1956); as Grace in *Bus Stop* (Robin Hood Th., Arden, Del., Summer 1957); Mrs. Brady in *Juno* (Winter Garden, N.Y.C., Mar. 9, 1959); Mother Grieg in *Song of Norway* (St. Louis Municipal Opera, Mo., Summer 1959); Amanda in *The Glass Managerie* (Totem Pole Playhouse, Fayetteville, Pa., Summer 1959); and toured in stock as Mrs. Livingston in *Happy Hunting* (Summer 1959).

She joined (Dec. 1959) the cast of *The Threepenny Opera* (Th. de Lys, N.Y.C., Sept. 20, 1955), as Mrs. Peachum; played Auntie in *Christine* (46 St. Th., Apr. 28, 1960); toured in stock as Bloody Mary in *South Pacific* (Summer 1960); and returned (Sept. 1960) to *The Threepenny Opera* as Mrs. Peachum (Th. de Lys, N.Y.C., Sept. 20, 1955).

Miss Andrews appeared as Mother Cadman, Mme. Spig-Eye, and the Irish Washerwoman in *The Tiger Rag* (Cherry Lane, Feb. 16, 1961); played Mrs. Peachum in *The Threepenny Opera* (Feb. 1961); succeeded (Mar. 1961); Juanita Hall as Madam Liang in the national touring company of *Flower Drum Song* (opened Riviera, Detroit, Mich., May 10, 1960).

She played the title role in *Madame Aphrodite* (Orpheum, N.Y.C., Dec. 29, 1961); Helen in *A Taste of Honey,* Mrs. Peachum in *The Threepenny Opera,* and Emma in *Look Out, Sailor* (Red Barn Th., Northport, L.I., N.Y., Summer 1962); Belle Poitrine, Today, in *Little Me* (Lunt-Fontanne, N.Y.C., Nov. 17, 1962); toured as Mrs. Peachum in *The Threepenny Opera* (opened McAllister Aud., San Antonio, Tex., Oct. 25, 1963); and played Belle Poitrine, Today, in the national touring company of *Little Me* (opened Rochester, N.Y., Aud., Jan. 30, 1964; closed Civic Aud., Pasadena, Calif., Aug. 1, 1964).

She played Mrs. Mister in *The Cradle Will Rock* (Th. Four, N.Y.C., Nov. 8, 1964); Mrs. Baines in *Say Nothing* (Jan Hus Th., Jan. 27, 1965); Belle Poitrine, Today in *Little Me* (Mineola Playhouse, Mineola, L.I., N.Y., Apr. 22–May 23, 1965) and summer tour (St. Louis Municipal Opera; Pittsburgh Music Fair; Starlight Th., Indianapolis, July–Aug. 1965); Rosie Brice in national company of *Funny Girl* (Mar. 15–Sept. 30, 1966); Dragoon in *The Day the Lid Blew Off* (Jan Hus Th., N.Y.C., Jan. 5, 1968); Mrs. Venzenzio in *A Likely Story* (Kennebunkport, Me., July 22–Aug. 3, 1968); Inez in *In the Summer House* (Southampton College, L.I., N.Y., Aug. 8–25, 1968); Marian in *Don't Drink the Water* (Bucks County Playhouse, New Hope, Pa., June 25–July 19, 1969); Inez in *In the Summer House* (Dublin International Festival, Dublin, Ireland, Sept. 23–Oct. 5, 1969); Peggy Monash in *How Much, How Much?* (Provincetown Playhouse, N.Y.C., Mar. 16, 1970); Marion in *Don't Drink the Water* (Warren, Dayton, and Columbus, Ohio, June 15–July 19, 1970); Sister Bessie in *Tobacco Road* (Alhambra Dinner Th., Jacksonville, Fla., Sept. 20–Nov. 1, 1970); Ida in *70, Girls, 70* (Starlight Th., Kansas City, July 12–26, 1971); Esther in *Two by Two* (St. Louis Municipal Opera; Dallas State Fair; Starlight Th., Kansas City, July 27–Sept. 5, 1971; North Shore Music Th., Beverly, Mass., July 16–29, 1972); and Aunt Demetria in *On Borrowed Time* (Bucks County Playhouse, June 24–July 15, 1973).

Films. Miss Andrews played Mrs. Hudson in *Pigeons* (MGM, 1970); Dr. Seaton in *Made for Each Other* (20th-Fox, 1971); Mrs. Captree in *The Werewolf of Washington* (Diplomat Pictures, 1973); Mrs. Hungerford in *Summer Wishes, Winter Dreams* (Col., 1973); and Rosie in *W. W. and The Dixie Dance Kings* (20th-Fox, 1974).

Television. Miss Andrews made her debut on the Ed Sullivan Show (CBS, 1950); followed by appearances on the Perry Como Show (NBC, 1950); the Ray Milland series (1954); the Spike Jones Show (1954); the Betty White Show (1954); Kraft Television Th. (NBC, 1954); the TV Telethon (Cincinnati, 1962); Girl Talk (ABC, 1963); the Tonight Show (NBC, 1963); Mike Douglas Show (ABC, 1964); Queen for a Day (ABC, 1964); and Girl Talk (ABC, Nov. 5, 1965). She was Maggie Baker in The Hawk (ABC, Dec. 1965); Mrs. Potts in Pistols and Petticoats (CBS, July 1966); Aunt Hagatha in Bewitched (ABC, 1966); and was on *E. E. Cummings' Fairy Tales* on Camera Three (CBS, May 1968); the Joe Franklin Show (WOR-TV, Nov. 26, 1968 and Nov. 11, 1969); Girl Talk (ABC, Feb. 7, 1969). She appeared also as Miss Peterson ("Pete") on As the World Turns (CBS, Feb. 22–May 1, 1971); and as Mrs. Johnson in Faith For Today (1971).

Night Clubs. Miss Andrews sang and played the piano in her club debut at the Windsor House (San Fernando Valley, Calif., 1941); subsequently was a singing comedienne at Number One Fifth Ave. (N.Y.C., 1948); appeared at the Blue Angel (N.Y.C., 1950); the Embassy Club (London, 1951); the Thunderbird Hotel (Las Vegas, Nev., 1952); the Hotel Radisson (Minneapolis, Minn., 1952); the Bar of Music (Los Angeles, Calif., 1952); the Colony (London, 1954); the Bon Soir (N.Y.C., 1954); Le Ruban Bleu (N.Y.C., 1957); the Emerald Beach Hotel (Nassau, Bahamas, 1959); and Gotham Hotel (N.Y.C., 1967, 1968).

Awards. Miss Andrews received a *Theatre World* Award for her performance in the revue, *Touch and*

Go (1950); and a State of Israel Bonds Award.
Recreation. Archaeology, painting, writing.

ANOUILH, JEAN. Playwright. b. Jean Marie Lucien Pierre Anouilh, June 23, 1910, Bordeaux, France, to François and Marie-Magdeleine (Soulue) Anouilh. Father, tailor; mother, violinist. Grad. Colbert Sch., Bordeaux; Coll. Chaptal, baccalaureate; attended Univ. of Paris, Faculty of Law, 1931–32. Married to Monelle Valentin, actress (marr. dis.); one daughter; married July 30, 1953, to Nicole Lançon; one son, two daughters.

Pre-Theatre. Advertising copy writer, secretary to Louis Jouvet, assistant to Georges Pitoëff.

Theatre. Mr. Anouilh's first play, *Humulus le Muet* (1929; pub. 1945), was a brief skit written in collaboration with Jean Aurenche. His first play to be performed in Paris was *L'Hermine* (Th. de l'Oeuvre, Apr. 26, 1932); followed by *Mandarine* (Th. de l'Athénée, 1933) and *Y avait un prisonnier* (Th. des Ambassadeurs, Mar. 21, 1935), which was also presented by the French-Language Co., Théâtre des Quatre Saisons (Barbizon-Plaza, N.Y.C., Nov. 28, 1938). *Le voyageur sans bagages* (Th. des Mathurins, Paris, Feb. 16, 1937) was translated by John Whiting as *Traveller without Luggage* (Arts, London, Jan. 29, 1959); and by Lucienne Hill under the same title (ANTA, N.Y.C., Sept. 17, 1964); *La sauvage* (Th. des Mathurins, Jan. 10, 1938), translated by Lucienne Hill, was produced in London as *The Restless Heart* (St. James's, May 8, 1957); *Le bal des voleurs* was first produced in Paris (Th. des Arts, Sept. 17, 1938), followed by the French-Language Co., Théâtre des Quatre Saisons production in N.Y.C. (Barbizon-Plaza, Nov. 28, 1938) and also presented in English, adapted by Lucienne Hill, as *Thieves' Carnival* (Cherry Lane, Feb. 1, 1955).

Subsequently, Mr. Anouilh's *Léocadia* was produced in Paris (Th. de la Michodière) and in N.Y.C., as *Time Remembered,* the English version by Patricia Moyes (Morosco, Nov. 12, 1957); *Le rendez-vous de Senlis* was first produced in Paris (Th. de l'Atelier, 1940); translated into English by Edward Owen Marsh, it was presented in London as *Dinner with the Family* (New, Dec. 10, 1957) and in N.Y.C. as *Rendezvous at Senlis* (Gramercy Arts, Feb. 27, 1961). *Eurydice* was presented in Paris (Th. de l'Atelier, Dec. 18, 1941), in the US translated and adapted by Mel Ferrer (Coronet, Hollywood, Calif., Oct. 15, 1948); translated by Kitty Black, it was presented in London as *Point of Departure* (Lyric, Hammersmith, Nov. 1, 1950) and in N.Y.C. as *Legend of Lovers* (Plymouth, Dec. 26, 1951).

Antigone, an adaptation of Sophocles' play, was written and produced in occupied Paris during WW II (Th. de l'Atelier, Feb. 4, 1944), and presented in N.Y.C. in an adaptation by Lewis Galantière (Cort, Feb. 18, 1946); *Roméo et Jeannette* was performed in Paris (Th. de l'Atelier, Dec. 3, 1946), in London, adapted by Donagh MacDonagh as *Fading Mansion* (Duchess, Aug. 31, 1949), and in N.Y.C., as *Jeannette,* translated by Miriam John (Maidman Playhouse, Mar. 24, 1960).

L'Invitation au château (Th. de l'Atelier, Nov. 4, 1947), translated and adapted by Christopher Fry, was presented with music as *Ring Round the Moon* (Globe, London, Jan. 26, 1950; Martin Beck Th., N.Y.C., Nov. 23, 1950).

Anouilh wrote *Épisode de la vie d'un auteur,* presented on the same bill as *Ardèle ou la Marguerite* (Comédie des Champs-Elysées, Paris, Nov. 3, 1948). *Ardèle,* adapted by Cecil Robson as *The Cry of the Peacock,* was produced in N.Y.C. (Mansfield, Apr. 11, 1950) and revived in a new adaptation by Lucienne Hill as *Ardèle* (Cricket, N.Y.C., Apr. 8, 1958). *Cécile, ou L'École des pères* was presented in Paris (Comédie des Champs-Elysées, 1949).

La répétition ou L'Amour puni (Th. Marigny, Paris, Oct. 25, 1950), was presented in N.Y.C. in a French-language production by Jean-Louis Barrault (Ziegfeld, Nov. 27, 1952), and revived as *The Rehearsal,* adapted by Pamela Hansford Johnson and Kitty Black (Royal, London, Apr. 6, 1961; Royale, N.Y.C., Sept. 23, 1963). *Colombe* (Th. de l'Atelier, Feb. 11, 1951) was adapted by Louis Kronenberger as *Mademoiselle Colombe* (Longacre, N.Y.C., Jan. 6, 1954) and by Denis Cannan as *Colombe* (Garrick Th., N.Y.C., Feb. 23, 1965).

Anouilh also wrote *La valse des toréadors* (Comédie des Champs-Elysées, Paris, Jan. 9, 1952), subsequently presented in an English version by Lucienne Hill as *The Waltz of the Toreadors* (Coronet, N.Y.C., Jan. 17, 1957); *Medée* (Th. de l'Atelier, Paris, Mar. 26, 1953); *L'Alouette* (Th. Montparnasse, Oct. 14, 1953), translated by Christopher Fry as *The Lark* (Lyric, Hammersmith, London, May 11, 1955) and adapted by Lillian Hellman as *The Lark* (Longacre, N.Y.C., Nov. 17, 1955); and *Ornifle, ou Le courant d'air* (Comédie des Champs-Elysées, Nov. 4, 1955).

Anouilh's *Pauvre Bitos, ou Le diner de têtes* (Th. Montparnasse, Oct. 11, 1956), translated by Lucienne Hill as *Poor Bitos,* was presented in London (Arts Th. Club, Nov. 13, 1963; Duke of York's Th., Jan. 7, 1964) and in N.Y.C. (Cort, Nov. 14, 1964). *Madame de. . .,* Anouilh's adaptation of a story by Louise de Vilmorin was translated by John Whiting and presented in London on the same bill as *Traveller without Luggage* (Arts, Jan. 29, 1959); the French premiere was in 1971.

Anouilh wrote *L'Hurluberlu, ou Le réactionnaire amoureux* (Comédie des Champs-Elysées, Feb. 5, 1959), adapted by Lucienne Hill as *The Fighting Cock* (ANTA Th., N.Y.C., Dec. 8, 1959); *Becket, ou L'Honneur de Dieu,* which he produced with Roland Pietri (Th. Montparnasse-Gaston Baty, Paris, Oct. 1, 1959), translated by Lucienne Hill as *Becket* (St. James, N.Y.C., Oct. 5, 1960); and he wrote *La petite Molière,* which he produced with Roland Laudenbeck (Festival of Bordeaux, June 1, 1960).

The one-act play *La foire d'empoigne* received its premiere performances in Germany under the title *Majestäten* (Recklinghausen Festival, July 1960; Renaissance Th., Berlin, Oct. 1960) and was first presented in Paris on a double bill with Anouilh's one-act *L'Orchestre,* both staged, with Roland Pietri, by the author (Comédie des Champs-Elysées, Jan. 10, 1962); *La foire d'empoigne,* translated by Lucienne Hill as *Animal Grab,* was first presented in English on television (BBC-3, July 3, 1962); *L'Orchestre* was given in the US on a double-bill with Anouilh's *Épisode de la vie d'un auteur,* both translated by Miriam John (Studio Arena, Buffalo, N.Y., Sept. 16, 1969). Anouilh also wrote *La grotte,* which, with Roland Pietri, he staged Th. Montparnasse-Gaston Baty, Paris, Oct. 5, 1961); translated by Lucienne Hill as *The Cavern,* it was presented in England (Nottingham Playhouse, May 5, 1965; Strand, London, Nov. 11, 1965) and in the US (Playhouse in the Park, Cincinnati, Ohio, June 8, 1967).

Anouilh also adapted Kleist's *Käthchen von Heilbronn* as *L'Ordalie, ou La petite Catherine d'Heilbron* (Th. Montparnasse, Sept. 30, 1966); wrote *Le boulanger, la boulangère, et le petit mitron (The Baker, the Baker's Wife, and the Baker's Apprentice* (Comédie des Champs-Elysées, Paris, Nov. 1968); and *Cher Antoine* (Comédie des Champs-Elysées, Oct. 1, 1969), translated by Lucienne Hill as *Dear Antoine* and presented in England (Chichester Festival, May 19, 1971; Piccadilly London, Nov. 3, 1971). He also wrote and, with Roland Pietri, staged *Les poissons rouges (The Goldfish)* (Th. de L'Oeuvre, Feb. 1, 1970); *Ne reveillez pas madame (Don't Waken Madame)* (Comédie des Champs-Elysées, Oct. 21, 1970); and *Tu étais si gentil quand tu étais petit* (Th. Antoine, Jan. 18, 1972), translated by Lucienne Hill as *You Were So Sweet When You Were Little* and presented in London (Theatre at New End, Hampstead, April 1974); and *Le directeur de l'Opéra* (Comédie des Champs-Elysées, Oct. 1, 1972).

Anouilh has also translated plays of Shakespeare and Oscar Wilde for French production, and he has written stories for ballets performed by Roland Petit's Les Ballets de Paris.

Films. He directed the film version of his play *Le voyageur sans bagages,* which was released in the US as *Identity Unknown* (Rep., 1945); wrote an original screenplay, *Monsieur Vincent* (Lopert, 1949). Other of his plays made into films were: *Madame de . . .*(1959), and *Waltz of the Toreadors* (Continental, 1962). He wrote the screenplay for *The End of Belle,* reviewed as *The Passion of Slow Fire* (Trans-Lux, 1962); and directed Roger Vitrac's film *Victor* (1963). *Becket* (Par., 1964) was based on Anouilh's play of the same name, and *Circle of Love* (Reade-Sterling, 1965) was adapted by Anouilh from Arthur Schnitzler's *La ronde.* Other films written by Anouilh include *Deux sous les violettes; Richard III; Anna Karenine; Pattes blanches;* and *Caroline cherie.*

Television and Radio. M. Anouilh wrote the radio play *Point of Departure* (Home Network, London, England, May 3, 1965). Television productions based on his work include *The Lark* (Hallmark Hall of Fame, NBC, Feb. 10, 1957); *Time Remembered,* based on *Léocadia* (Hallmark Hall of Fame, NBC, Feb. 7, 1961); *Animal Grab,* based on *La foire d'empoigne* (BBC-3, England, July 3, 1962); *Traveller Without Luggage* (BBC-1, London, England, Aug. 19, 1965); *Festival* (CBC, Toronto, Ontario, Canada, Oct. 6, 1965); and *Antigone* (Playhouse New York, PBS, Oct. 1, 1972).

Awards. The film *Monsieur Vincent* received the Grand prix du cinéma français; *The Waltz of the Toreadors* was voted best foreign play of 1956–57 by the NY Drama Critics Circle; and in 1959 M. Anouilh received the Prix Dominique.

ANTHONY, JOSEPH. Director, actor, playwright. b. Joseph Deuster, May 24, 1912, Milwaukee, Wis., to Leonard and Sophie (Herz) Deuster. Attended West Allis (Milwaukee) H.S.; Univ. of Wisconsin; Pasadena Playhouse Sch. Studied at Tamara Daykarhanova Sch. for the Stage, N.Y.C., 1935–38. Married Perry Wilson, actress; one son, one daughter. Served with US Army, Signal Corps, Intelligence, 1942–46. Member of AEA; AFTRA; SAG; AGVA, SSD&C (pres., 1963–64); DGA; Actors Studio. Address: Winding Rd. Farm, Ardsley, NY 10502, tel. (914) OW 3-3099.

Theatre. Mr. Anthony made his debut in stock, playing several roles at the Rice Playhouse (Martha's Vineyard, Mass., 1935). He was co-founder, director and actor with the American Actors Co., at its off-Bway studio and summer theatre at Branford, Conn., (1937–42). He directed such experimental plays, as *Indiana Sketches, Saturday Night, Minnie Fields, Roadside,* and a series of one-act plays by Horton Foote.

He made his Bway debut with the Federal Theatre (WPA), playing Rolf Mamlock in *Professor Mamlock* (Daly's Th., Apr. 13, 1937) and David Chavender in *On the Rocks* (Daly's Th., June 15, 1938); subsequently appeared as Agnes de Mille's partner in a series of dance concerts (1940–41); and as one of the Seven in *Liberty Jones* (Shubert, Feb. 5, 1941).

Under the name of Joseph Adams, played the Second Man and was understudy in *Truckline Cafe* (Belasco, Feb. 27, 1946); directed his own play, *Return at Night* (Peterborough Playhouse, N.H., 1947); and appeared in stock at the Westchester Playhouse (Summers 1946–48).

As Joseph Anthony, he portrayed Richters in *Skipper Next to God* (Maxine Elliot's Th., Jan. 13, 1948); for the Six O'Clock Th., of which he was a co-founder, he directed *Celebration* (Maxine Elliot's Th., Apr. 11, 1948); played Rothschild in a pre-Bway tryout of *Exodus* (opened Brighton, Brighton Beach, N.Y., April 14, 1949; closed there April 24, 1949); was an understudy in *Montserrat* (Fulton, Oct. 29, 1949); and appeared at the Cecil Wood Playhouse (Fishkill, N.Y., Summers 1949–51).

He succeeded Louis Veda Quince as Phil Cook in *The Country Girl* (Lyceum, N.Y.C., Nov. 10, 1950); directed *Candy Store* (Hunter College, 1950); appeared as Solveig's Father, Dr. Begriffenfeldt, and Monsieur Ballon in *Peer Gynt* (ANTA, Jan. 28, 1951); performed at the Pocono Playhouse (Mountainhome, Pa., Summer 1952); played Ghoulos in *Flight into Egypt* (Music Box, Mar. 18, 1952); and a Gentleman of Fortune in *Camino Real* (Natl., Mar. 19, 1953).

Mr. Anthony directed *Bullfight* (Th. de Lys, Jan. 12, 1954); *The Rainmaker* (Cort, Oct. 28, 1954); appeared as Prince Bounine in *Anastasia* (Lyceum, Dec. 29, 1954); directed *Once Upon a Tailor* (Cort, May 23, 1955), *The Lark* (Longacre, Nov. 17, 1955), *The Most Happy Fella* (Imperial, May 3, 1956), *A Clearing in the Woods* (Belasco, Jan. 10, 1957), the pre-Bway tryout of *Maiden Voyage* (opened Forrest, Philadelphia, Pa., Feb. 28, 1957; closed there Mar. 9, 1957); *Winesburg, Ohio* (Natl., N.Y.C., Feb. 5, 1958); *The Marriage-Go-Round* (Plymouth, Oct. 29, 1958); and the pre-Bway tryout of *The Pink Jungle* (Alcazar, San Francisco, Calif., Oct. 14, 1959; closed Shubert, Boston, Mass. Dec. 12, 1959).

He also directed *The Best Man* (Morosco, N.Y.C., Mar. 31, 1960); *Under the Yum-Yum Tree* (Henry Miller's Th., Nov. 16, 1960); *Rhinoceros* (Longacre, Jan. 9, 1961); *Mary, Mary* (Helen Hayes Th., Mar. 8, 1961); *The Captains and the Kings* (Playhouse, Jan. 2, 1962); *Romulus* (Music Box, Jan. 10, 1962); *The Dragon* (Phoenix, Apr. 9, 1963); *110 in the Shade* (Broadhurst, Oct. 24, 1963); *The Chinese Prime Minister* (Royale, Jan. 2, 1964); *The Last Analysis* (Belasco Th., Oct. 1, 1964); *Slow Dance on the Killing Ground* (Plymouth, Nov. 30, 1964); and *The Taming of the Shrew* (American Shakespeare Festival, Stratford, Conn., June 22, 1965).

He also directed *Mrs. Dally* (John Golden Th., N.Y.C., Sept. 22, 1965); *The Playroom* (Brooks Atkinson Th., Dec. 5, 1965); *Happily Never After* (Eugene O'Neill Th., Mar. 10, 1966); *Falstaff (Henry IV, Part 2)* (American Shakespeare Festival, Stratford, Conn., June 18, 1966); and played Frank Elgin in a revival of *The Country Girl* (NY City Ctr., Sept. 29, 1966). He directed *Breakfast at Tiffany's*, which closed during previews (Majestic, N.Y.C., Dec. 12–14, 1966); directed *Weekend* (Broadhurst, Mar. 13, 1968); *The Homecoming* (Tyrone Guthrie Th., Minneapolis, Minn., July 8, 1969); *Jimmy* (Winter Garden, N.Y.C., Oct. 23, 1969); and *Finishing Touches* (Plymouth, Feb. 8, 1973).

Films. Mr. Anthony appeared in *Hat, Coat and Glove* (RKO, 1934); *She* (RKO, 1935); *Shadow of the Thin Man* (MGM, 1941); *Joe Smith, American* (MGM, 1942). He directed *The Rainmaker* (Par., 1956); *The Matchmaker* (Par., 1958); *Career* (Par., 1959); *All in a Night's Work* (Par., 1961); and *Captive City* (Maxima Films, Italy, 1963). He directed *Conquered City* (Amer. International, 1965) and *Tomorrow* (Filmgroup, 1972).

Television. His play, *Return at Night*, was produced on Lights Out (NBC, 1953). He has appeared on Danger (CBS), Suspense (CBS), Kraft Theatre (NBC), You Are There (CBS).

Other Activities. He taught acting at the Amer. Theatre Wing (1946–49) and at the Tamara Daykarhanova Sch. for the Stage (1946–64), where he has been co-director with Mme. Daykarhanova (1963–64).

Recreation. Gardening, collecting antique glass.

ANTONIO, LOU. Actor, director. b. Louis Demetrios Antonio, Jan. 23, 1934, Oklahoma City, Okla., to James Demetrios and Lucille (Wright) Antonio. Father, restaurant owner; Mother, cashier. Grad. Central H.S., Oklahoma City, 1951; Univ. of Oklahoma, B.A. 1955. Studied with Lee Strasberg, Lonny Chapman, Curt Conway, and at Actors Studio (mbr., 1958–to date). Member of AEA; SAG; AFTRA.

Pre-Theatre. Sports reporter, chef, waiter, ranch-hand, bricklayer's helper, junk and manure dealer, swimming-pool inspector, Fuller Brush Man.

Theatre. Mr. Antonio made his stage debut in stock, playing David Slater in *The Moon Is Blue*, Sidney Black in *Light Up the Sky*, Lord Byron, A. Ratt, Nursie and the Pilot in *Camino Real*, Preacher Haggler in *Dark of the Moon*, and John Goronwyn Jones in *The Corn Is Green* (White Barn, Terre Haute, Ind., Summer, 1955); followed by the role of Hotspur in *Richard II* and a Soldier in *The Secret Concubine* (McCarter Th., Princeton, N.J., Summer 1956).

He was understudy to George Peppard as Mickey Argent and to John Harkins as Tommy Brookman in *Girls of Summer* (Longacre, Nov. 19, 1956); in stock, played Larrup Rule in *Saddle Tramps* and Polo in *A Hatful of Rain* (Cecilwood Th., Fishkill, N.Y., Summer 1957); Will Stockdale in *No Time for Sergeants*, Sgt. Gregovich in *Teahouse of the August Moon*, Brick in *Cat on a Hot Tin Roof*, Cornelius in *The Matchmaker* and the Musician-Husband in *Middle of the Night* (Cecilwood Th., Fishkill, N.Y., Summer 1958).

Mr. Antonio played Woody in *The Buffalo Skinner* (Th. Marquee, N.Y.C., Feb. 19, 1959); at the Festival of Two Worlds (Spoleto, Italy), appeared as Jake Latta in the premiere production of *Night of the Iguana* (Teatro Caio Melisso, July 2, 1959), and in the revue *Album Leaves* (Summer 1959); played Cliff Lewis in *Look Back in Anger* (Capri Th., Atlantic Beach, L.I., N.Y., Summer 1959); Nikita in *The Power of Darkness* (York, N.Y.C., Sept. 29, 1959); the Shady One, the Third Patron and Lecasse in *The Good Soup* (Plymouth, Mar. 2, 1960).

At the Cecilwood Th. (Fishkill, N.Y., Summer 1960); appeared as Lt. Ferguson Howard in *The Golden Fleecing*, Jack in *Amazing Grace*, Clay in *Cry of the Raindrop*, directed *Missouri Legend*.

He repeated his role in *Cry of the Raindrop* (Hedgerow Th., Moylan, Pa., Summer 1960; Th. Club, Washington, D.C. June 3, 1960; St. Mark's Playhouse, N.Y.C., Mar. 7, 1961); played Stavros in *The Garden of Sweets* (ANTA, Oct. 31, 1961); joined the company (June 12, 1962) of *Brecht on Brecht* (Th. de Lys, Jan. 3, 1962); directed a stock production of *The Chalk Garden* (Elmwood, Nyack, N.Y., Winter, 1962); played in *Brecht on Brecht* (Playhouse-on-the-Mall, Paramus, N.J.; John Drew Th., East Hampton, L.I., N.Y., Summer 1963); portrayed the Sergeant in *Andorra* (Biltmore, N.Y.C., Feb. 9, 1963); Gaston in *The Lady of the Camellias* (Winter Garden, Mar. 20, 1963); Marvin Macy in *The Ballad of the Sad Cafe* (Martin Beck Th., Oct. 30, 1963); Faustus in a revival of Christopher Marlowe's *Tragical History of Doctor Faustus* (Phoenix, Oct. 5, 1964); Jonas in *Ready When You Are, C.B.!* (Brooks Atkinson Th., Dec. 7, 1964); and he produced *Hootsudie* (Merle Oberon Playhouse, Actors Studio West, Los Angeles, Calif., Apr. 28, 1972).

Films. Mr. Antonio made his debut as a Cadet in *The Strange One* (Col., 1957); followed by a Roustabout in *Splendor in the Grass* (WB, 1961); Abdul in *America, America* (WB, 1963); Rev. Abraham Hewlett in *Hawaii* (UA, 1966); and Koko in *Cool Hand Luke* (WB, 1967).

Television. Mr. Antonio has appeared on the US Steel Hour (CBS); Studio One (CBS); Suspicion (NBC); Have Gun—Will Travel (CBS); *The Wendigo* (Great Ghost Tales, CBS, 1961); *The Pure Horse* (Tallahassee 7000, CBS, 1959); Love of Life (CBS, 1958, 1960); Naked City (ABC, 1959, 1963); a pilot film, *Road to Reality* (ABC, 1960); *A Piece of Blue Sky* (Play of the Week, WNTA, 1960); *The Power and the Glory* (CBS, 1961); My True Story (CBS, 1959–61); The Defenders (CBS, 1961, 1962, 1963); Route 66 (CBS, 1963); Breaking Point (ABC, 1963); The Fugitive (ABC, 1963, 1964, 1965, 1966); Camera Three (CBS, 1963); For the People (CBS, 1965); 12 O'Clock High (ABC, 1965); Gunsmoke (CBS, 1965); The Virginian (NBC, 1966); The Wackiest Ship in the Army (NBC, 1966); and The Road West (NBC, 1967).

Awards. He received the *Theatre World* Award for his performance as Woody in *The Buffalo Skinner* (1959).

Recreation. Softball, basketball, reading, writing.

ANTOON, A. J. Director. b. Alfred Joseph Antoon, Methuen, Mass.

Theatre. Mr. Antoon directed *Subject to Fits* (Public, N.Y.C., Feb. 14, 1971); *The Tale of Cymbeline* (Delacorte Th., Aug. 12, 1971); *Subject to Fits* (Royal Shakespeare Co. at the Place, London, England, Oct. 21, 1971); *That Championship Season* (Public, N.Y.C., May 2, 1972; Booth Th., Sept. 14, 1972); *Much Ado About Nothing* (Delacorte Th., Aug. 10, 1972; Winter Garden, Nov. 11, 1972); wrote some of the lyrics for *Please Don't Let It Rain!* (Delacorte Th., July 13, 1973); directed *The Good Doctor* (Eugene O'Neill Th., Nov. 27, 1973); and directed and adapted *The Dance of Death* (Vivian Beaumont Th., Apr. 4, 1974).

Television. Mr. Antoon directed the NY Shakespeare Festival–CBS special *Much Ado About Nothing* (CBS, Feb. 2, 1973).

Awards. For his direction of *That Championship Season*, Mr. Antoon received a 1972 Drama Desk Award as outstanding director and an Antoinette Perry (Tony) Award (1973) as best director.

APPELBAUM, GERTRUDE. Personal manager. b. Gertrude H. Appelbaum, Feb. 20, Brooklyn, N.Y., to David and Celia (Cohen) Appelbaum. Father, clothing manufacturer. Grad. Bushwick H.S., Brooklyn, N.Y.; attended City Coll. During WW II, worked at Stage Door Canteen, Merchant Seaman Canteen. Member of Amer. Th. Wing; Actors' Fund; Amer. Jewish Congress. Address: 55 Central Park West, New York, NY 10023, tel. (212) 362-4392.

Theatre. Miss Appelbaum (known by many in the profession as "Apple") was business manager for the Theatre Guild (Apr. 6, 1964 through 1965).

She was first a secretary to the literary department of the A. & S. Lyons Agency; subsequently became secretary to the casting director, Margaret Linley, and, in 1936, her assistant. In 1946, she worked for Howard Lindsay and Russel Crouse as production assistant for the third touring company of *State of the Union*, and for *Detective Story* (Hudson Th., N.Y.C., Mar. 23, 1949); was engaged as casting and production assistant by Theron Bamberger (Bucks County Playhouse, New Hope, Pa., 1949); was production secretary-assistant for *The Liar* (Broadhurst, N.Y.C., May 18, 1950); for Courtney Burr and Malcolm Pearson's production of *Season in the Sun* (Cort, Sept. 28, 1950); and for their production of *Out West of Eighth* (Ethel Barrymore Th., Sept. 20, 1951); and *The Seven Year Itch* (Fulton, Nov. 20, 1952); worked on productions for the Cornell-McClintic office (1952) and also took dictation from Guthrie McClintic for his autobiography, *Me and Kit;* worked as casting and production assistant for Ben Boyar, general manager for *The Bat* (Natl., Jan 20, 1953); worked as casting and production assistant for Manning Gurian's production of *The Warm Peninsula* (Helen Hayes Th., Oct. 20, 1959) and worked for two years with the Arena Managers' Assn.

With the production of *Finian's Rainbow* (46 St. Th., Jan. 10, 1947), she formed an investment syndicate comprised of a group of investors with small sums of money to invest in Bway productions. Other productions included *Detective Story, Medea, Roomful of Roses, The Happiest Millionaire* and *The Owl and The Pussycat*.

In 1965, she produced, with Stella Holt, Pauline Myers in her one-woman show *The World of My America* (Greenwich Mews Th.), and she is now personal manager for Miss Myers and others.

Recreation. Tennis, walking, swimming, knitting, needlepoint work.

APSTEIN, THEODORE. Playwright. b. Tevyeh Apstein, July 3, 1918, Kiev, Russia, to Marcos and Eugenia (Tcherniavsky) Apstein. Father, textile manufacturer. Grad. Amer. Sch., Mexico City, Mexico, 1934; attended Natl. Univ. of Mexico, 1935–36; grad. Univ. of Texas, B.A. 1939; M.A. 1940; Ph.D. 1945. Married June 1, 1947, to Patricia Elliott; three sons, two daughters. Member of WGA, East (council, 1959–61; 2nd vice-pres., 1963–65); WGA, West (1965–to date); WGA-TV Credits Committee (chmn., 1969–to date); New Dramatists' Comm. (assoc. member, advisory board). Address: 623 No. Walden Dr., Beverly Hills, CA 90210.

Theatre. Mr. Apstein wrote in collaboration with Dwight Morris, the play, *Mañana Is Another Day* (Palace of Fine Arts, Mexico City, 1940). From 1941–47, he wrote plays that were produced in such community theatres as Pasadena (Calif.) Playhouse, and at the Univ. of Texas. He wrote *Breve Kermesse* (Teatro de la Comedia, Mexico City, 1955); *Sell Me Down the River, Darling* (Barn Theatre, Augusta, Mich., July 6, 1965); *Slight of Hand* (Ralph Freud Playhouse, UCLA, Apr. 27, 1972).

He first wrote for Bway, *The Innkeepers* (John Golden Th., Feb. 2, 1956); followed by *Come Share My House* (Actors' Playhouse, Feb. 18, 1960).

Mr. Apstein has taught dramatic arts at Columbia Univ. and the American Theatre Wing and playwriting at UCLA (1966–to date).

Films. He wrote the screenplays for *Without Each Other* (III Trask Productions, 1961) and *What Ever Happened to Aunt Alice?* (Cinerama, 1969).

Television. Since 1954, he has written for many programs, including Lamp Unto My Feet (CBS), GE Th. (CBS), Hallmark Hall of Fame (NBC), Studio One (CBS), Danger (CBS), Alcoa Playhouse (NBC), US Steel Hour (NBC), Ben Casey (ABC), Dr. Kildare (NBC), Eleventh Hour (CBS), Channing (ABC), and The Nurses (CBS). He adapted *Time Remembered* for Hallmark Hall of Fame (NBC, Feb. 7, 1961) and in 1974 was head writer for *Search for Tomorrow* (CBS).

Published Works. Seven of his one-act plays were published in Margaret Mayorga's *Best Short Plays of the Year* (1946–47, 1947–48, 1948–49, 1951–52, 1952–53, 1953–54, 1960–61, 1957 20th Anniversary Edition); each have been performed frequently in the US and abroad. His play, *Come Share My House*, was published in 1960.

Recreation. Traveling.

ARCHER, OSCEOLA. Director, actress, teacher. b. Osceola Marie Macarthy, June 13, 1890, Albany, Ga., to Charles H. and Julia Anne (Johnson) Macarthy. Father, life insurance executive. Educ. Albany Normal and Fisk Univ, Preparatory schools; grad. Howard Univ., A.B. 1913; NY Univ., M.A. 1936. Professional training: Hatcher Hughes (playwriting); Repertory Playhouse Associates, 1932–34; RPA Summer Th., Putney, Vt., 1934; Amer. Th. Wing, 1955; Robert Lewis Workshop, 1960; Actors' Studio, 1965. Married Sept. 13, 1915, to Numa P. G. Adams, dean (1929–40), Howard Univ. Medical School; one son. Member of AEA (council, 1954; Ethnic Minorities Comm.; Regional Th. Comm.; Equity Library Th. comm.; Paul Robeson Citation Comm.); AFTRA (Equal Employment Comm.; Membership Activities Comm.); SAG; SSD&C; NATAS (Blue Ribbon panelist for Emmy awards). Address: 66 W. 88th St., 5-B, New York, NY 10024, tel. (212) 724-2273.

Pre-Theatre. Miss Archer held a variety of jobs while her husband was in medical school; she studied at the Master School of Design; was assistant designer at J. Reinhardt & Co., Chicago.

Theatre. Miss Archer made her stage debut as Pauline in *The Lady of Lyons* (Howard Univ. Players, Washington, D.C., Feb. 2, 1913; her professional debut was in summer stock as a factory worker in *Strange House* (RPA Summer Th., Putney, Vt., Aug. 1934); and her Bway debut was as Rose Hennaford in *Between Two Worlds* (Belasco Th., N.Y.C., Oct. 26, 1934). She appeared as the Native Woman in *Emperor Jones* (Westport (Conn.) Country Playhouse, Aug. 5, 1940), later touring summer theatres with the production (July–Sept. 1941). She was Michaela in *The Cat Screams* (Martin Beck Th., N.Y.C., June 16, 1942); directed American Negro Th. productions of *Our Town* (May 1944) and *On Strivers' Row* (Mar. 1945); played Mary in *Family Portrait* (Ethical Culture Soc., N.Y.C., Apr. 1946); directed *Days of Our Youth* (Amer. Negro Th., June 24–29, 1946); and, at the Putnam County (NY) Playhouse (Summer 1947) directed *The Octoroon* (July 23), played Sophrone in *The Arbitration* (July 29), and directed *Hedda Gabler* (Aug. 5) and *Lady Precious Stream* (Aug. 12).

She also directed *Sojourner Truth* (Amer. Negro Th., N.Y.C., Apr. 26, 1948); directed, at the Putnam Co. Playhouse (Summer 1948) *The New York Idea* (Aug. 3), *The Glass Menagerie* (Aug. 10), and *For Love or Money* (Aug. 31); played the Nurse in *Hippolytus* (ANTA Experimental Th., Nov. 21, 1948); Maurya in *Riders to the Sea* (Amer. Negro Th., Feb. 3, 1949); and directed, again at the Putnam Co. Playhouse, *A Doll's House* (July 19, 1949) and *Dear Brutus* (Aug. 9, 1949). She played Maude in *Bayou Legend* (Hunter Coll., N.Y.C., May 13, 1950); at Putnam Co. Playhouse was Helen in *Born Yesterday* (July 1, 1950) and Harmony Blue Blossom in *Beautiful People* (Aug. 15, 1950) and directed *The Two Mrs. Carrolls* (Aug. 22, 1950). She directed *Soledara* (Equity Library Th., N.Y.C., Nov. 2, 1950); and, again at Putnam Co. Playhouse, directed *Amphitryon 38* (June 30, 1951), played Florence in *The Curious Savage* (July 17, 1951), directed *A Streetcar Named Desire* (July 24, 1951), *Angel Street* (Aug. 21, 1951), *The Rose Tattoo* (July 3, 1952), *Clutterbuck* (July 15, 1952), *Lo and Behold* (July 22, 1952), *The Lady's Not for Burning* (July 29, 1952), and *The Children's Hour* (Aug. 5, 1952).

She was artistic coordinator, Greenwich Mews Th., N.Y.C. (1953–54); returned (Summer 1953) to Putnam Co. Playhouse, where she directed *Bell, Book and Candle* (July 3), played Miss Prism in *The Importance of Being Earnest* (July 17), Anaxo in *Too Much Amphitryon* (July 28); returned (Summer 1954) to Putnam Co. Playhouse, where she directed *The Member of the Wedding* (July 13), *My Three Angels* (Aug. 3), and *The Country Girl* (Aug. 10). She directed *The Bad Seed* (Long Beach Th., N.Y., Aug. 21, 1956); returned (Summer 1958) to Putnam Co. Playhouse, where she directed *The Diary of Anne Frank* (June 27), *Time of Storm* (July 21), *The Seven Year Itch* (July 28), and *The Loud Red Patrick* (Aug. 6). She also played Tita in *Juniper and the Pagans* (Colonial, Boston, Mass., Dec. 19, 1959; Forrest, Philadelphia, Pa., Dec. 22, 1959); the Fortune Teller in *The Skin of Our Teeth* (Olney, Md., July 20, 1960); and the Nurse in *Romeo and Juliet* (Hecksher Th., N.Y.C., and high school and college tour, Jan. 2–May 6, 1961).

From Aug. 6, 1963 to May 2, 1964, Miss Archer toured with the National Repertory Th., appearing as Capulat in *Ring Round the Moon*, Tituba in *The Crucible*, and Paulina in *The Seagull*. She directed *A Raisin in the Sun* (Prospect Park, N.Y., July 13, 1965); in 1966 at Penn State Univ. Th. played Marta Ball in *The Physicists* (July 12) and the Servant Woman in *Blood Wedding* (Aug. 2); was Anfisa in *Three Sisters* (Hartford Stage Co., Hartford, Conn., Dec. 15, 1966); directed *This Bird of Dawning Singeth All Night Long* (Chelsea Th., N.Y.C., Nov. 24, 1967); played a Villager in *The Guide* (Hudson Th., N.Y.C., Mar. 9, 1968); directed *The Silver Box* (Harlem School of the Arts Community Th., July 2, 1971); and played Ommu in *The Screens* (Chelsea Th., Dec. 1, 1971).

Films. Miss Archer appeared in *People's Enemy* (1934) and *An Affair of the Skin* (1963).

Television and Radio. Miss Archer played on radio in the mid–1940s on Mystery Th. (NBC) and as Celia in Joyce Jordan, M.D. (NBC), and in 1975 she read *Miss MacIntosh, My Darling* (WBAI, May 1975). On television, she appeared in *Panama Hattie* (CBS, Nov. 10, 1954); was in *Tower of Babel* (NBC, Jan. 27, 1957); Big Story (NBC, June 21, 1957); *The Power and the Glory* (Play of the Week, NET, Oct. 19, 1959); *Rashomon* (Play of the Week, Dec. 12, 1960); *Saint Maker's Christmas Eve* (ABC, Dec. 24, 1961); *The Teahouse of the August Moon* (Hallmark Hall of Fame, NBC, Oct. 26, 1962); and *Pygmalion* (Hallmark Hall of Fame, NBC, Feb. 6, 1963).

Other Activities. Miss Archer was director of the training program and teacher of acting, American Negro Th., N.Y.C. (1941–46), and she taught acting at the American Th. Wing School (1953–55).

Awards. Miss Archer was cited by the American Th. Wing, United Seamen's Service, and the USO for her club and servicemen's canteen activities during World War II; in 1974, the mayor of Detroit issued a special proclamation honoring her for her contributions to the theatre.

Recreation. Painting; designing and making her own clothes.

ARDEN, EVE. Actress. b. Eunice Quedens, Apr. 30, 1912, Mill Valley, Calif., to Charles Peter and Lucille (Frank) Quedens. Attended Tamalpais H.S., Mill Valley, 1924–28. Married June 28, 1939, to Edward G. Bergen, insurance agent, literary agent (marr. dis. July 27, 1947); two daughters; married Aug. 24, 1951, to Brooks West, actor; two sons. Member of AEA; SAG; AFTRA. Address: (home) Westhaven Ranch, Hidden Valley, Ventura County, CA 91360; (bus.) Box 1065, Studio City, CA 90164.

Theatre. Miss Arden made her stage debut as a walk-on in *Alias the Deacon* and played in *The Patsy* (Henry Duffy Stock Co., San Francisco, Calif., 1928); subsequently appeared in the revue *Low and Behold* (Pasadena Playhouse, Calif., 1933); and toured with the Bandbox Repertory Th. as Amanda in *Private Lives* and Matilda in *On Approval* (1933).

She made her Bway debut in *Ziegfeld Follies* (Winter Garden, Jan. 4, 1934); appeared in *Parade* (Guild, May 20, 1935); *Ziegfeld Follies* (Winter Garden, Jan. 30, 1936); played Winnie Spofford in *Very Warm for May* (Alvin, Nov. 17, 1939); appeared in *Two for the Show* (Booth, Feb. 8, 1940); played Maggie Watson in *Let's Face It* (Imperial, Oct. 29, 1941); in stock, appeared as Marion in *Biography*, Amytis in *The Road to Rome*, and Mary Hilliard in *Here Today* (The Gryphon Players, La Jolla, Calif., Summer 1945); on tour, played Paula Wharton in *Over 21* (Summer 1950); and Mary Hilliard in *Here Today* (Olney Summer Th., Md., June 1951); appeared in the title role in a national tour of *Auntie Mame* (opened Russ Aud., San Diego, Calif., Aug. 4, 1958; closed Geary, San Francisco, Calif., Dec. 13, 1958); Charlie in *Goodbye, Charlie* (Paper Mill Playhouse, Millburn, N.J., Aug. 1960); and Constant Deauville in *The Marriage-Go-Round* (The Gristmill Playhouse, Andover, N.J., July 1961).

She toured as Pamela Piper in *Beekman Place* (Summer 1965); substituted (Shubert Th., Chicago, Ill., June 13–Oct. 8, 1966) for Carol Channing as Dolly Gallagher Levi in the national touring production of *Hello, Dolly!* (opened Community Concourse, San Diego, Calif., Sept. 7, 1965); toured as Mrs. Banks in *Barefoot in the Park* (Winter 1967); and played Mrs. Baker in the national company of *Butterflies Are Free* (Los Angeles, Calif., May 19–Oct. 1970).

Films. Miss Arden made her debut in *Oh, Doctor* (U, 1937); subsequently appeared in *Stage Door* (RKO, 1937); *Letter of Introduction* (U, 1938); *Cocoanut Grove* (Par., 1938); *Having Wonderful Time* (RKO, 1938); *Forgotten Woman* (U, 1939); *At the Circus* (MGM, 1939); *Eternally Yours* (UA, 1939); *The Women* (MGM, 1939); *Women in the Wind* (WB, 1939); *A Child Is Born* (WB, 1940); *No, No, Nanette* (RKO, 1940); *Slightly Honorable* (UA, 1940); *Comrade X* (MGM, 1940); *She Couldn't Say No* (WB, 1941); *She Knew All the Answers* (Col., 1941); *Manpower* (WB, 1941); *Last of the Duanes* (20th-Fox, 1941); *Whistling in the Dark* (MGM, 1941); *Sing for Your Supper* (Col., 1941); *San Antonio Rose* (U, 1941); *Bedtime Story* (Col., 1941); *Obliging Young Lady* (RKO, 1941); *Ziegfeld Girl* (MGM, 1941); *That Uncertain Feeling* (UA, 1941); and as Maggie Watson in *Let's Face It* (Par., 1943).

Also, *Cover Girl* (Col., 1944); *The Doughgirls* (WB, 1944); *Road to Utopia* (Par., 1945); *Mildred Pierce* (WB, 1945); *Patrick the Great* (U, 1945); *Pan-Americana* (RKO, 1945); *Earl Carroll Vanities* (Rep., 1945); *My Reputation* (WB, 1946); *The Kid from Brooklyn* (RKO, 1946); *Night and Day* (WB, 1946); *The Unfaithful* (WB, 1947); *Voice of the Turtle* (WB, 1947); *One Touch of Venus* (U, 1948); *Whiplash* (WB, 1948); *My Dream Is Yours* (WB, 1949); *The Lady Takes a Sailor* (WB, 1949); *Tea for Two* (WB, 1950); *Three Husbands* (UA, 1950); *Paid in Full* (Par., 1950); *Curtain Call at Cactus Creek* (U, 1950); *Goodbye, My Fancy* (WB, 1951); *We're Not Married* (20th-Fox, 1952); *Our Miss Brooks* (WB, 1956); *Bitter Victory* (Col., 1958); *Anatomy of a Murder* (Col., 1959); and *The Dark at the Top of the Stairs* (WB, 1960); *The Beauty Jungle* (Rank, 1964); and *Sergeant Deadhead* (Amer. Intl., 1965).

Television and Radio. Miss Arden made her radio debut on the Ken Murray Show (ABC, 1936);

subsequently performed on the Russ Morgan Show (NBC, 1938); Jack Haley's Village Store (NBC, 1945); as Miss Brooks in Our Miss Brooks (CBS, 1948–52), a role she repeated on television (CBS, 1952–56; 1964–66). Also on radio, she performed on the Danny Kaye Show (CBS) and the Jack Carson series (NBC, 1952).

On television, she has appeared on the Perry Como Show (NBC); the Dinah Shore Show (CBS); was on the Eve Arden Show (CBS, 1957); *Meet Cyd Charisse* (Startime, NBC, Dec. 29, 1959); was in *Take Him, He's All Yours* (Vacation Playhouse, CBS, July 20, 1964); on I Love Lucy (CBS, Aug. 11, 1964); was a guest on the Red Skelton Show (CBS, 1964–65; 1966–67); the Johnny Carson Show (NBC, 1965–66); and Laredo (NBC, 1965). She was on Girl Talk (ABC, 1965–66); Bewitched (ABC, 1966); Run for Your Life (NBC, 1966); The Man from U.N.C.L.E. (NBC, 1966); on the Pat Boone Show (NBC, 1966–67); Hollywood Squares (NBC, 1966–67); in *A Very Missing Person* (ABC Movie of the Week, Mar. 4, 1972); and in *Mother of the Bride* (ABC Afternoon Playbreak, Jan. 9, 1974).

Awards. She received a NATAS (Emmy) Award for her role in Our Miss Brooks (1953) and the Sarah Siddons Award in Chicago for her performance in *Hello, Dolly!*.

Recreation. Antiques, interior decorating, mosaics, painting, sculpting, writing, raising children.

ARDEN, JOHN. Playwright. b. Oct. 26, 1930, Barnsley, England, to Charles Alwyn and Annie (Layland) Arden. Educ. Sedbergh; Edinburgh (Scotland) Coll. of Art; grad. King's Coll., Cambridge (England) Univ., B.A. 1953. Served in Intelligence Corps. Married May 1, 1957, to Margaretta Ruth D'Arcy, actress, playwright; four sons. Address: c/o Ramsay Ltd., 14a Goodwin's Court, London, W.C. 2, England.

Pre-Theatre. Mr. Arden, a trained architect, worked in an architect's office.

Theatre. Productions in the US of Mr. Arden's plays include *Live Like Pigs* (Th. Co. of Boston, Boston, Mass., Jan. 28, 1965); *The Waters of Babylon* (New Th. Workshop, N.Y.C., Nov. 8, 15, 12, 1965); *Serjeant Musgrave's Dance* (Th. de Lys, Mar. 8, 1966); *The Happy Haven* (Long Wharf Th., New Haven, Conn., Aug. 8, 1966); *Armstrong's Last Good Night* (Th. Co. of Boston, Dec. 1, 1966); *Left-Handed Liberty* (Th. Co. of Boston, Jan. 3, 1968); *The Business of Good Government* (Spencer Memorial Ch., N.Y.C., Dec. 24, 1969); and *The True History of Squire Jonathan and His Unfortunate Treasure* (AMDA Th., N.Y.C., Dec. 1974).

Premieres in Great Britain of the preceding and other works by Mr. Arden, some in collaboration with his wife as indicated, include *The Waters of Babylon* (Royal Court Th., London, Oct. 20, 1957); *When Is a Door Not a Door?* (Central School of Speech and Drama, London, 1958); *Live Like Pigs* (Royal Court Th., Sept. 30, 1958); *Serjeant Musgrave's Dance* (Royal Court Th., Oct. 22, 1959); and *The Happy Haven,* which he wrote with his wife (Royal Court Th., Sept. 14, 1960).

Also *The Business of Good Government* (Brent Knoll Ch., Somerset, Dec. 1960); *The Workhouse Donkey* (Chichester Festival, July 8, 1963); *Ironhand,* adapted from Goethe's *Goetz von Berlichingen* (Th. Royal, Bristol, England, Nov. 12, 1963); *Armstrong's Last Good Night* (Citizen's Th., Glasgow, Scotland, May 5, 1964); *Ars Longa, Vita Brevis,* which he wrote with his wife (Aldwych, London, 1964); *Friday's Hiding,* also with his wife, and also called *Word Watching* (London, 1965); *Left-Handed Liberty* (Mermaid Th., London, June 14, 1965); and *The Royal Pardon,* written with his wife (Beaford Arts Centre, Devon, England, Sept. 1, 1966; Arts, London, Dec. 21, 1967).

Other works include *The True History of Squire Jonathan and His Unfortunate Treasures* (Ambiance Lunch-Hour Th. Club, London, June 17, 1968); with his wife and the Cartoon Archetypical Slogan Th., *Harold Muggins Is a Martyr* (Unity Th. Club, London, June 1968); and, all with his wife, *The Hero Rises Up* (Round House, London, Nov. 8, 1968); *The Ballygombeen Bequest* (Belfast, N. Ireland, May 1972; Edinburgh Festival Fringe, Aug. 1972; Bush Th., London, Sept. 11, 1972); and *The Island of the Mighty* (Alwych, London, Dec. 5, 1972).

Television and Radio. Mr. Arden's first professional production was his radio play *The Life of Man* (1956). Also for radio, he wrote *The Bagman; or The Impromptu of Muswell Hill* (BBC Radio 3, Mar. 27, 1970). His television plays include *Soldier, Soldier* (BBC, Mar. 1960) and *Wet Fish* (1961).

Awards. Mr. Arden received the BBC Northern Region Prize (1956) for *The Life of Man* and *Soldier, Soldier* won a prize at the Trieste Festival. In 1959–60, he held a fellowship in playwriting at Bristol (Eng.) Univ.; and in 1960 he received the London *Evening Standard* "most promising playwright" award.

ARDREY, ROBERT. Playwright, scenarist, author. b. Oct. 16, 1908, Chicago, Ill., to R. L. and Marie (Haswell) Ardrey. Father, editor and publisher. Grad. Hyde Park H.S., Chicago, 1927; Univ. of Chicago, Ph.B. (Phi Beta Kappa), 1930. Studied writing with Thornton Wilder, Chicago, 1930–35. Married June 12, 1938, to Helen Johnson (marr. dis. 1960); two sons; married Aug. 11, 1960, to Berdine Grunewald, South African actress. Member of WGA, West; Dramatists Guild. Address: 25 Piazza dei Mercanti, Trastavere, Rome, Italy.

Theatre. Mr. Ardrey wrote *Star Spangled* (John Golden Th., N.Y.C., Mar. 10, 1936); *How To Get Tough About It* (Martin Beck Th., Feb. 8, 1938); *Casey Jones* (Fulton, Feb. 19, 1938); *Thunder Rock* (Mansfield, Nov. 14, 1939); *Jeb* (Martin Beck Th., Feb. 21, 1946); *Sing Me No Lullaby* (Phoenix, Oct. 14, 1954); *Shadow of Heroes* which was first produced in London (Piccadilly, Oct. 7, 1958), and was later presented in N.Y.C. (York Playhouse, Dec. 5, 1961).

Films. Mr. Ardrey wrote the screenplays for *They Knew What They Wanted* (RKO, 1940); *A Lady Takes a Chance* (RKO, 1943); *The Green Years* (MGM, 1946); *The Three Musketeers* (MGM, 1948); *The Secret Garden* (MGM, 1949); *Madame Bovary* (MGM, 1949); *Quentin Durward* (MGM, 1955); *The Power and the Prize* (MGM, 1956); *The Wonderful Country* (U, 1959); *Khartoum* (UA, 1966); and *Out of Africa* (U, 1969).

Published Works. His novels include *World's Beginning* (1944) and *Brotherhood of Fear* (1952). He also wrote *African Genesis* (1961), a scientific work concerned with human evolution; *The Territorial Imperative* (1966), dealing with human and animal behavior and instinct; and *The Social Contract* (1970), also dealing with behavior and with human ecology.

Awards. He received a fellowship from the Guggenheim Memorial Foundation (1937); the Sidney Howard Memorial Award for *Thunder Rock* (1940); the Theresa Helburn Memorial Award for *Shadow of Heroes* (1961); and a grant by the Willkie Brothers Foundation (1963) to continue research in anthropology for the following ten years.

ARKIN, ALAN. Actor, director, composer, writer. b. Mar. 26, 1934, New York City, to David and Beatrice Arkin. Father, artist; mother, teacher. Grad. Benjamin Franklin H.S., Los Angeles, Calif., 1951; attended Los Angeles City Coll., 1951–52; Los Angeles State Coll., 1952–53; Bennington Coll., 1953–55. Studied with Benjamin Zemach, Los Angeles, 1952–55. Married June 16, 1964, to Barbara Dana, actress; one son; two sons by previous marriage. Member of AEA; SAG; AFTRA; AFM; ASCAP. Address: 200 W. 57th St., New York, NY 10019, tel. (212) JU 6-6553.

Theatre. Mr. Arkin made his professional debut in improvisational theatre with the Compass Players (Crystal Palace, St. Louis, 1959), and the following year appeared with the Second City (Chicago, 1960).

He appeared in N.Y.C. as a singer in *Heloise* (Gate, Sept. 24, 1958); in *From the Second City* (Royale, Sept. 26, 1961); was Jimmy in *Man Out Loud, Girl Quiet,* for which he also wrote the music (Cricket, Apr. 3, 1962); played David Kolowitz in *Enter Laughing* (Henry Miller's Th., Mar. 13, 1963), in which he later (1964) toured; was in *A View from Under the Bridge* (Square East, Aug. 5, 1964); played Harry Berlin in *Luv* (Booth Th., Nov. 11, 1964). He directed (under the name Roger Short) *Eh?* (Circle in the Square, Oct. 16, 1966); directed *Hail Scrawdyke!* (Booth Th., Nov. 28, 1966); a revival of *Little Murders* (Circle in the Square, Jan. 5, 1969); *The White House Murder Case* (Circle in the Square, Feb. 18, 1970); *The Sunshine Boys* (Broadhurst, Dec. 20, 1972); *Molly* (Alvin Th., Nov. 1, 1973); and *The Soft Touch* (opened Wilbur Th., Boston, Mass., Aug. 30, 1975; closed there Sept. 13, 1975).

Films. Mr. Arkin made his motion picture debut in *The Russians Are Coming, The Russians Are Coming* (UA, 1966); and he appeared in *Woman Times Seven* (Embassy, 1967); *Wait Until Dark* (WB-Seven Arts, 1967); *The Heart Is a Lonely Hunter* (WB-7 Arts, 1968); *Inspector Clouseau* (UA, 1968); *Popi* (UA, 1969); *Catch-22* (Par., 1970); *Little Murders* (20th-Fox, 1971); *Last of the Red Hot Lovers* (Par., 1972); *Freebie and the Bean* (WB, 1975); and *Rafferty and the Gold Dust Twins* (WB, 1975).

Television. He has appeared with the Second City group on the David Susskind Show (1962); in *The Beatnik and the Politician* (East Side/West Side, CBS, June 29, 1964); on the Les Crane Show (ABC, 1964–65); and in *The Love Song of Barney Kempinski* (Stage ABC, Sept. 14, 1966).

Discography. Mr. Arkin recorded *The Babysitters* (1958); *Songs and Fun with the Babysitters* (1960); *The Family Album* (1965); and *The Babysitters Menagerie* (1968).

Awards. In 1963, for his performance in *Enter Laughing,* he received the Antoinette Perry (Tony) Award; the *Theatre World* Award; and won the *Variety* NY Drama Critics Poll. He received the Golden Globe Award (1967) for his performance in *The Russians Are Coming, The Russians Are Coming;* a *Village Voice* off-Bway (Obie) for distinguished direction and a Drama Desk Award as an outstanding director (both 1970) for *The White House Murder Case;* and an Antoinette Perry (Tony) Award nomination (1973) for direction of *The Sunshine Boys.*.

ARLEN, HAROLD. Composer. b. Hyman Arluck, Feb. 15, 1905, Buffalo, N.Y., to Samuel and Celia (Orlin) Arluck, Father, cantor. Attended Hutchison Central H.S., Buffalo, N.Y. Elementary piano instruction with mother. Married Jan. 8, 1937, to Anya Taranda. Relative in theatre: brother, Jerry Arlen, conductor. Member of ASCAP, Hillcrest Country Club. Address: c/o A. L. Berman, 551 Fifth Ave., New York, NY 10019, tel. (212) MU 2-7930.

Pre-Theatre. Cafe pianist, organized jazz ensemble, night club performer, arranger, singer.

Theatre. Mr. Arlen was, at first, a rehearsal pianist for *George White's Scandals* (Apollo Th., N.Y.C., July 2, 1928), and *Great Day* (Cosmopolitan, Oct. 17, 1929). His first song to appear in a Bway musical was "Get Happy," from the *9:15 Revue* (George M. Cohan Th., Feb. 11, 1930); subsequently contributed music to *Earl Carroll's Vanities* (New Amsterdam, July 1, 1930); and wrote his first Bway score, *You Said It* (46 St. Th., Jan. 19, 1931).

He appeared in vaudeville with Lou Holtz and Lyda Roberti (Palace Th.); wrote two songs for *Earl Carroll's Vanities* (Bway Th., Sept. 27, 1932); and contributed music to *Americana* (Shubert, Oct. 5, 1932). His song, "If You Believe in Me," appeared in the play *The Great Magoo* (Selwyn, Dec. 2, 1932); was a contributor to *George White's Music Hall Varieties* (Casino, Jan. 2, 1933); toured the Loew's vaudeville circuit with his chorus in a program of his own songs (1933); and composed the score for the revue *Life Begins at 8:40* (Winter Garden, N.Y.C., Aug. 27, 1934).

Mr. Arlen wrote two songs for *The Show Is On* (Winter Garden, Dec. 25, 1936); composed the scores for *Hooray For What?* (Winter Garden, Dec. 1, 1937); *Bloomer Girl* (Shubert, Oct. 5, 1944); *St. Louis Woman* (Martin Beck Th., Mar. 30, 1946); *House of Flowers* (Alvin, Dec. 30, 1954); *Jamaica*

(Imperial, Oct. 31, 1957); and *Saratoga* (Winter Garden, Dec. 7, 1959). On a commission from Robert Breen (1954), Mr. Arlen reworked his score for *St. Louis Woman*, adding songs from his other productions to create an opera version, entitled *Free and Easy* (opened Carre Th., Amsterdam, Netherlands, Dec. 22, 1959).

Mr. Arlen also wrote the music and contributed lyrics to songs used in *The Harold Arlen Songbook* (Stage 73, N.Y.C., Feb. 28, 1967); composed five new songs for a revival of *House of Flowers* (Th. de Lys, Jan. 28, 1968); and composed music for the marionette show *The Wizard of Oz* (Bil Baird Th., Nov. 27, 1968).

Films. Mr. Arlen first wrote the song "It's Only a Paper Moon," for *Take a Chance* (Par., 1933); subsequently wrote the score and title song for *Let's Fall in Love* (Col., 1934); the title song for the film version of *Strike Me Pink* (UA, 1936); contributed to *The Singing Kid* (1st Natl., 1936); *Stage Struck* (1st Natl., 1936); *Gold Diggers of 1937* (1st Natl., 1936); and *Artists and Models* (Par., 1937). He wrote the scores for *Love Affair* (RKO, 1939); and *The Wizard of Oz* (MGM, 1939); contributed to *At the Circus* (MGM, 1939); wrote "This Time the Dream's on Me" for *Blues in the Night* (WB, 1941); contributed to *Captains of the Clouds* (WB, 1942); and *Rio Rita* (MGM, 1942); and wrote the score for *Star Spangled Rhythm* (Par., 1942).

Mr. Arlen wrote the score for *Cabin in the Sky* (MGM, 1943); and *The Sky's the Limit* (RKO, 1943); contributed to *They Got Me Covered* (RKO, 1943); *Up in Arms* (RKO, 1944); and *Kismet* (MGM, 1944); composed the score for *Here Come the Waves* (Par., 1944); and *Out of This World* (Par., 1945); contributed to *Casbah* (U, 1948); *My Blue Heaven* (20th-Fox, 1950); *The Petty Girl* (Col., 1950); *Mr. Imperium* (MGM, 1951); *Down Among the Sheltering Palms* (20th-Fox, 1953); and *The Farmer Takes a Wife* (20th-Fox, 1953); wrote "The Man That Got Away" for *A Star Is Born* (WB, 1954); was composer for *The Country Girl* (Par., 1954); and contributed to *Gay Purr-ee* (WB, 1962); and *I Could Go on Singing* (1963).

Television. Mr. Arlen's works were featured on *Happy with the Blues* (NBC, 1962) and *The Songs of Harold Arlen* (Twentieth Century, CBS, 1964), and he appeared on the latter program.

Night Clubs. Collaborating with Ted Koehler, Mr. Arlen contributed music to eight editions of the Harlem revue, *Cotton Club Parade* (1930–34), including the songs, "Stormy Weather," "I Love a Parade," "I've Got the World on a String," "Kickin' the Gong Around," and "I Gotta Right to Sing the Blues.".

Published Works. Mr. Arlen's first songs were "My Gal, My Pal" and "I Never Knew What Love Could Do" (1924). His first published work was *Minor Graff*, a "blues fantasy" for piano (1926), written with Dick George. His concert works include *Mood in Six Minutes* (1935), *American Minuet* (1939), *American Negro Suite* (1940), *Blues Opera* (1957–58), *Ode and Bon-Bon* (1960). He has also contributed an article to a book on George Gershwin.

Awards. He received an Academy (Oscar) Award (1939) for "Over the Rainbow" from *The Wizard of Oz;* the *Variety* NY Drama Critics Poll (1955) for *House of Flowers;* and was nominated for an Academy (Oscar) Award (1955) for "The Man That Got Away" from *A Star Is Born*. .

Recreation. Painting, photography.

ARNOTT, PETER.

Educator, author, puppeteer. b. Peter Douglas Arnott, Nov. 21, 1931, Ipswich, Suffolk, England, to George William and Audrey (Smith) Arnott. Father, civil servant. Grad. Ipswich Sch., England, 1949; Exeter Coll., Oxford, B.A., 1954; Univ. Coll. of North Wales, B.A., 1952; M.A. 1956, Ph.D. 1958. Married July 26, 1958, to Eva Charlotte Schenkel; one son, one daughter. Member of ATA; Society for Promotion of Hellenic Studies; Classical Association of Midwest and South; Kiwanis. Address: 6 Herrick St., Winchester, MA 01890.

Mr. Arnott came to the US in 1958 and joined the faculty of the State Univ. of Iowa as a visiting lecturer in classics. At Iowa, he was assistant professor of classics and dramatic art, 1959–61, associate professor, 1961–68, and professor, 1968–69. Since 1969 he has been professor of drama at Tufts Coll. and since 1970 also director of graduate studies, Drama Department. He was visiting professor at the Univ. of Mississippi in 1961 and at Monmouth Coll. in 1963, taught at the Univ. of Colorado during the summers of 1960 and 1962, and taught in Japan in 1967. He teaches history of the theatre and Greek and Oriental drama and has directed plays in university theatres.

He operates the Marionette Theatre of Peter Arnott, producing Greek tragedy and comedy, Renaissance drama, and French neo-classical tragedy in repertoire. He has performed with his marionettes throughout Great Britain, Canada, and the US, including two tours of Canada under the auspices of the Canada Council; appearances at the Folger Shakespeare Library (Washington, D.C., 1960), the Amer. Council of Learned Societies (N.Y.C., 1961), seasons at the Oregon Shakespeare Festival (1963–64), and at universities.

Published Works. Mr. Arnott translated and edited *Two Classical Comedies: The Birds by Aristophanes and the Brothers Menaechmi by Plautus* (1958); wrote *An Introduction to the Greek Theatre* (1959); translated *Antigone* (1960) and *Oedipus the King* (1960); translated and edited *Three Greek Plays for the Theatre: Medea, Cyclops, and The Frogs* (1961); wrote *Greek Scenic Conventions in the Fifth Century B.C.* (1962); translated and edited Aeschylus' *Oresteia* (1965); wrote *Plays without People: Puppetry in Modern and Serious Drama* (1965), *The Theatres of Japan* (1969), *The Romans and Their World* (1970), *The Ancient Greek and Roman Theatre* (1971), *Ballet of Comedians* (a novel based on the life of Molière, 1971), and *The Byzantine World* (1973).

Awards. He was the winner of the San Diego State Coll. Playwriting contest with the comedy *The Devil My Brother*. .

Recreation. Oil painting, collecting historical miniatures.

ARONSON, BORIS.

Scenic designer, costume designer. b. Boris Solomon Aronson, Oct. 15, 1900, Kiev, Russia, to Solomon and Deborah (Turfsky) Aronson. Father, rabbi. Attended State Art Sch., Kiev, 1912–18; studied with Ilya Mashkov, Sch. of Modern Painting, Moscow; Alexandra Exter, Sch. of the Theatre, Kiev; in Germany and France. Married July 15, 1945, to Lisa Jalowetz; one son. Member of United Scenic Artists. Address: 1 W. 89th St., New York, NY 10024, tel. (212) EN 2-1547.

Theatre. Mr. Aronson's first assignment was as designer of sets and costumes for the N.Y.C. Yiddish theatre productions *Day and Night* (Unser Theater, Bronx, Dec. 1924); followed by *The Final Balance* (Unser, Jan. 1925); *Bronx Express* (Schildkraut Th., Sept. 1925); *Tenth Commandment* (Yiddish Art Th., Nov. 1926); *Tragedy of Nothing* (Irving Place Th., Jan. 18, 1927); sets for *2 × 2 = 5* (Civic Repertory Th., Nov. 28, 1927), and for the Yiddish Art Th. productions of *Stempenyu the Fiddler* (1929), *Jew Suss* (Nov. 25, 1929), *Angels on Earth* (Dec. 16, 1929) and *Roaming Stars* (Jan. 23, 1930).

He designed sets for *Walk a Little Faster* (St. James, Dec. 7, 1932); *Small Miracle* (John Golden Th., Sept. 26, 1934); *Ladies' Money* (Ethel Barrymore Th., Nov. 1, 1934); *Battleship Gertie* (Lyceum, Jan. 18, 1935); *Three Men on a Horse* (Playhouse, Jan. 30, 1935); *Awake and Sing* (Belasco, Feb. 19, 1935); *The Body Beautiful* (Plymouth, Oct. 31, 1935); *Weep for the Virgins* (46 St. Th., Nov. 30, 1935); *Paradise Lost* (Longacre, Dec. 9, 1935); and the Radio City Music Hall stage productions (1935); sets and costumes for *Western Waters* (Hudson, Dec. 28, 1937); and *The Merchant of Yonkers* (Guild, Dec. 28, 1938); sets for *The Gentle People* (Belasco, Jan. 5, 1939) and *Ladies and Gentlemen* (Martin Beck Th., Oct. 17, 1939).

Mr. Aronson designed sets and costumes for the Ballet Th. production of *The Great American Goof* (NY City Ctr., world premiere, Jan. 11, 1940); sets for *The Unconquered* (Biltmore, Feb. 13, 1940); sets and costumes for *Heavenly Express* (Natl., Apr. 18, 1940) and *Cabin in the Sky* (Martin Beck Th., Oct. 25, 1940); sets for *The Night Before Christmas* (Morosco, Apr. 10, 1941); *Clash by Night* (Belasco, Dec. 27, 1941) and *Cafe Crown* (Cort, Jan. 23, 1942); sets and costumes for the ballet, *The Snow Maiden* (Metropolitan Opera House, world premiere, Oct. 12, 1942); sets for *R.U.R.* (Ethel Barrymore Th., Dec. 2, 1942), *The Russian People* (Guild, Dec. 29, 1942) and *The Family* (Windsor, Mar. 30, 1943); sets and costumes for the ballet, *Red Poppy*, performed by the Ballet Russe de Monte Carlo (Music Hall, Cleveland, world premiere, Oct. 9, 1943); sets for *What's Up* (Natl., N.Y.C., Nov. 11, 1943) and *South Pacific* (Cort, Dec. 29, 1943); sets and costumes for the Ballet Th. production of *Pictures at an Exhibition* (Internations, world premiere, Nov. 3, 1944).

He created sets for *Sadie Thompson* (Alvin, Nov. 16, 1944); *The Stranger* (Playhouse, Feb. 12, 1945), *The Desert Song* (Los Angeles Phil. Aud., Calif., May 1, 1945); *The Assassin* (Natl., N.Y.C., Oct. 17, 1945); *Truckline Cafe* (Belasco, Feb. 27, 1946); *The Gypsy Lady* (Century, Sept. 17, 1946); the pre-Bway tryout of *Sweet Bye and Bye* (opened Shubert, New Haven, Conn., Oct. 10, 1946; closed Erlanger, Philadelphia, Pa., Nov. 4, 1946); and the pre-Bway tryout of *The Big People* (opened Lyric, Bridgeport, Conn., Sept. 20, 1947; closed Locust St. Th., Philadelphia, Pa., Sept. 27, 1947).

Mr. Aronson designed the sets for *Skipper Next to God* (Maxine Elliott's Th., N.Y.C., Jan. 4, 1948); *The Survivors* (Playhouse, Jan. 29, 1948); *Love Life* (46 St. Th., Oct. 7, 1948); *Detective Story* (Hudson, Mar. 23, 1949); *The Bird Cage* (Coronet, Feb. 22, 1950); *Season in the Sun* (Cort, Sept. 28, 1950); *The Country Girl* (Lyceum, Nov. 10, 1950); *The Rose Tattoo* (Martin Beck Th., Mar. 3, 1951); *Barefoot in Athens* (Martin Beck Th., Oct. 31, 1951); *I Am a Camera* (Empire, Nov. 28, 1951); sets and costumes for the ballet, *Ballade*, performed by the N.Y.C. Ballet (NY City Ctr., world premiere, Feb. 14, 1952); sets for *I've Got Sixpence* (Ethel Barrymore Th., Dec. 2, 1952); *The Crucible* (Martin Beck Th., Jan. 22, 1953); *My 3 Angels* (Morosco, Mar. 11, 1953); *The Frogs of Spring* (Broadhurst, Oct. 20, 1953); *Mademoiselle Colombe* (Longacre, Jan. 6, 1954); *The Master Builder* (Phoenix, Mar. 1, 1955); *Bus Stop* (Music Box, Mar. 2, 1955); *Once Upon a Tailor* (Cort, May 23, 1955); the twin bill of *A View from the Bridge* and *A Memory of Two Mondays* (Coronet, Sept. 29, 1955); and *The Diary of Anne Frank* (Cort, Oct. 5, 1955).

He created sets for the pre-Bway tryout of *Dancing in the Chequered Shade* (opened McCarter, Princeton, N.J., Dec. 20, 1955; closed Wilbur, Boston, Mass., Dec. 31, 1955); *Girls of Summer* (Longacre, N.Y.C., Nov. 19, 1956); *Small War on Murray Hill* (Ethel Barrymore Th., Jan. 3, 1957); *A Hole in the Head* (Plymouth, Feb. 28, 1957); *Orpheus Descending* (Martin Beck Th., Mar. 21, 1957); *The Rope Dancers* (Cort, Nov. 20, 1957); and the pre-Bway tryout of *This Is Goggle* (opened McCarter, Princeton, N.J., Jan. 23, 1958; closed Shubert, Washington, D.C., Feb. 1, 1958); *The Firstborn* (Coronet, N.Y.C., Mar. 30, 1958); *The Cold Wind and the Warm* (Morosco, Dec. 8, 1958); *J.B.* (ANTA, Dec. 11, 1958); *Coriolanus* (Shakespeare Memorial Th., Stratford-upon-Avon, Eng., July 7, 1959); *The Flowering Cherry* (Lyceum, N.Y.C., Oct. 21, 1959); *A Loss of Roses* (Eugene O'Neill Th., Nov. 28, 1959); *Semi-Detached* (Martin Beck Th., Mar. 10, 1960); *Do Re Mi* (St. James, Dec. 26, 1960); *Garden of Sweets* (ANTA, Oct. 31, 1961); *A Gift of Time* (Ethel Barrymore Th., Feb. 22, 1962); *Judith* (Her Majesty's Th., London, July 2, 1962); *Andorra* (Biltmore, N.Y.C., Feb. 9, 1963); *Fiddler on the Roof* (Imperial, Sept. 22, 1964); *Incident at Vichy* (ANTA Washington Sq., Dec. 3, 1964. He did the set for a special performance in honor of Igor Stravinsky of *L'Histoire du Soldat* on the occasion of the America-Israel Cultural Foundation's 25th anniversary (Grand Ballroom of the Waldorf-Astoria, N.Y.C., Jan. 24, 1965); *Cabaret*(Broadhurst, Nov. 20, 1966); and the world premiere of the opera *Mourning Becomes Electra*(Metropolitan Opera, Mar. 17, 1967). He did the sets and the costumes for *The Price* (Morosco, Feb. 7, 1968) and sets for *Zorba* (Imperial, Nov. 17, 1968) and *Company*(Alvin Th., Apr. 26, 1970). He designed sets and costumes also for the Metropolitan Opera Association's new production of *Fidelio* (Metropolitan Opera, Dec. 16, 1970); and sets for *The Creation of the World and Other Business*(Sam S. Shubert Th., Nov. 30, 1972); *The Great God Brown* (Lyceum, Dec. 10, 1972); and *A Little Night Music* (Sam S. Shubert Th., Feb. 25, 1973). For the Eliot Feld Ballet he created sets and costumes for the ballet *The Tzaddik* (Newman Th., world premiere, June 2, 1974).

Other Activities. Mr. Aronson has exhibited his theatre designs and his paintings: designs for the Yiddish theatre (Anderson Galleries, N.Y.C., Dec. 1927; Paris, France, 1928); followed by exhibitions at New Art Circle (N.Y.C., 1931, 1938), The Guild Art Gallery (N.Y.C., 1935), Boyer Gallery (N.Y.C., 1937), Stendhall Galleries (Los Angeles, Calif., 1941), Nierendorf Galleries (Los Angeles, 1945), Bertha Schaefer (N.Y.C., 1958), Saidenberg Gallery (N.Y.C., 1962), a retrospective at Storm King Art Center (Mountainville, N.Y., 1963), and a one-man show at the Wright/Hepburn/Webster Gallery (London, 1968).

His technique of creating settings with color slides was demonstrated at the Museum of Modern Art (N.Y.C., 1947). He designed the interior of Temple Sinai, Washington, D.C. (1959) and the interior and sanctuary of the Community Center Synagogue, Sands Point, Long Island, N.Y. (1959).

Mr. Aronson wrote (in Russian) *Marc Chagall* (Petropolis, Berlin, 1923) and *Modern Graphic Art* (Petropolis, Berlin, 1924).

Awards. Mr. Aronson received a Guggenheim Fellowship (1950); an American Theatre Wing Award for stage design (1950–51); the Antoinette Perry (Tony) Award for his set designs for *The Rose Tattoo, The Country Girl,* and *Season in the Sun* (1951); a Ford Foundation grant (1962); the Tony award and the Joseph Maharam Award for his designs for *Cabaret*(1967); and Tony awards for his designs for *Zorba* (1969), *Company* (1971), and *Follies*(1972).

ARONSTEIN, MARTIN.

Lighting designer. b. Martin Henry Aronstein, Nov. 2, 1936, Pittsfield, Mass., to Milton and Selma F. (Iacomini) Aronstein. Father, glazier; mother, cosmetician. Educated public schools, Albany, N.Y., New York City, and Queens College, N.Y.C. Member of United Scenic Artists, Local 829. Address: 91-30 84th St., Woodhaven, NY 11421, tel. (212) 296-8568.

Pre-Theatre. Consultant to architects.

Theatre. Mr. Aronstein began his professional career as a lighting designer for the N.Y. Shakespeare Festival in 1960. The following year, he lighted his first off-Bway production, *Electra*(Players Th., Sept. 19, 1961), and his first Bway production was *Arturo Ui* (Lunt-Fontanne, Nov. 11, 1963). From then through the 1973–74 season he was lighting designer for sixty-eight productions, including *The Milk Train Doesn't Stop Here Anymore* (Brooks Atkinson Th., Jan. 1, 1964); *Tiny Alice*(Billy Rose Th., Dec. 29, 1964); *The Impossible Years* (Playhouse, Oct. 13, 1965); *Royal Hunt of the Sun* (ANTA Th., Oct. 26, 1965); and *Cactus Flower* (Royale, Dec. 8, 1965). Other productions were *Slapstick Tragedy* (Longacre, Feb. 22, 1966); *How Now, Dow Jones* (Lunt-Fontanne Th., Dec. 7, 1967); *George M!* (Palace, Apr. 10, 1968); *Promises, Promises* (Shubert, Dec. 1, 1968); *Forty Carats* (Morosco, Dec. 26, 1968); *Play It Again, Sam* (Broadhurst, Feb. 12, 1969); and *The Gingerbread Lady* (Plymouth, Dec. 13, 1970). Also *And Miss Reardon Drinks a Little* (Morosco, Feb. 25, 1971); *Ain't Supposed to Die a Natural Death*(Ethel Barrymore Th., Oct. 20, 1971); *Sugar*(Majestic, Apr. 9, 1972); *Nash at Nine*(Helen Hayes Th., May 17, 1973); *The Boom Boom Room* (Vivian Beaumont Th., Nov. 8, 1973); *Au Pair Man* (Vivian Beaumont Th., Dec. 27, 1973); *What the Wine Sellers Buy* (Vivian Beaumont Th., Feb. 4, 1974); *My Fat Friend* (Brooks Atkinson Th., Mar. 31, 1974); and *Music! Music!*(NY City Ctr., Apr. 11, 1974).

Awards. Mr. Aronstein was nominated for Antoinette Perry (Tony) awards for *Ain't Supposed to Die a Natural Death*(1972), *Much Ado About Nothing* (1973), and *Boom Boom Room*(1974).

ARRICK, LAWRENCE.

Director. b. Sept. 12, 1928, New York City, to Harold and Alyce Lawrence. Attended Bennington Coll., Bard Coll., studied at Herbert Berghof Sch., Dramatic Workshop (N.Y.C.), Stella Adler Sch. Married Nov. 2, 1952, to Rose Arrick. Member of Actor's Studio Directors Unit. Address: 1200 Fifth Ave., New York, NY 10029.

Theatre. Mr. Arrick directed *The Journey of the Fifth Horse* (American Place Th., N.Y.C., Apr. 21, 1966); and *Fragments* (Cherry Lane Th., N.Y.C., Oct. 2, 1967); was named artistic director to Yale Repertory Th. (New Haven, Conn., 1968); directed *My Daughter, Your Son* (Booth, N.Y.C., May 13, 1969); and, for the Yale Rep. Th. (John Drew Th., East Hampton, N.Y., Summer 1970), directed *Conversion of the Jews, Defender of the Faith,* and *Epstein.*

ARROWSMITH, WILLIAM.

Translator, editor, educator. b. William Ayres Arrowsmith, Apr. 13, 1924, Orange, N.J., to Walter Weed and Dorothy (Ayers) Arrowsmith. Father, businessman. Grad. Hill Sch., Pottstown, Pa., 1941; Princeton Univ., B.A. (Phi Beta Kappa) 1974; Ph.D. 1954; Oxford Univ., England, B.A. 1951, M.A. 1958. Married Jan. 10, 1945, to Jean Reiser; two daughters. Served US Army Military Intelligence (Japanese), 1943–46. Member of P.E.N. Address: (home) R.D. 1, Box 311, Lincoln, VT 05443, tel. (802) 453-2298; (bus.) The University Professors, Boston University, 270 Bay State Rd., Boston, MA 02212, tel. (617) 353-4020.

Since 1972, Mr. Arrowsmith has been University Professor and professor of classics, Boston Univ. He has been instructor in classics at Princeton Univ. (1951–53), instructor at Wesleyan Univ. (1953–54), assistant professor at the Univ. of California at Riverside (1954–56), associate professor (1958–59) and professor (1959–70) in the Classics Dept. at the Univ. of Texas. He was also honors professor at the Univ. of Michigan (Summer 1962) and visiting professor of humanities at Massachusetts Institute of Technology (1971).

He was the founding editor of the literary quarterly, *The Chimera* (1942–44); founding editor of *The Hudson Review*(1948–60); an advisory editor of the *Tulane Drama Review* (1960–67); founding editor of *Arion* (1962–to date), a journal of classical culture; editor of *Delos*(1968–70); advisory editor of *Mosaic* (1967–to date); and contributing editor for *Change* (1970–72) and *American Poetry Review* (1972–to date).

Other Activities. Mr. Arrowsmith has been a member of the board of the National Translation Center (1965–69); a fellow at the Center for Advanced Studies at Wesleyan Univ. (1967–68) and a fellow at Battelle Memorial Institute (1968). He has been also a member of the National Book Awards jury (1967; 1972) and a member of the board, National Professions Foundation (1969–to date). He has been an American Specialist, US State Dept. (Middle East) (1969), and a trustee, National Humanities Faculty (1972–to date) and commissioner, National Study Commission on Education (1972–to date).

He is a member of the Phi Beta Kappa Nominating Committee.

Published Works. Mr. Arrowsmith translated Euripides' *Hecuba, Orestes, Bacchae, Cyclops,* and *Heracles,* which were included in *The Complete Greek Tragedies,* edited by Lattimore and Grene (1960). His other published translations include *Satyricon of Petronius* (1959); Aristophanes' *The Birds* and *The Clouds* (1960); *The Knights* (1964); and, with D. S. Carne-Ross, *Dialogues with Leucc* (1964).

Mr. Arrowsmith edited, with Roger Shattuck, *The Craft and Context of Translation* (1961); *Image of Italy* (1961); *Complete Greek Comedy;* and *Six Modern Italian Novellas* (1964). He is general editor of *The New Greek Tragedy* (in process of appearance, 1973–) and of *The Complete Greek Comedy* (forthcoming).

Awards. Mr. Arrowsmith received a Woodrow Wilson Fellowship (Princeton Univ., 1947); Rhodes Scholarship (Florida and Queens, 1948–51); Prix de Rome (Senior Research Fellowship American Academy in Rome, 1956–57); Guggenheim Fellowship (1957–58); the Longview Award for his article "The Criticism of Greek Tragedy" (Tulane Drama Review, 1960); and the Morris Ernst Excellence in Teaching Award (Univ. of Texas, 1962). He was appointed a national Phi Beta Kappa Visiting Scholar for 1964–65. He has received honorary degrees from Loyola Univ., Chicago (LL.D. 1968); St. Michael's College, Burlington, Vt. (L.H.D. 1968); Westminster College (D. Litt. 1969); Dartmouth College (D. Litt. 1970); Dickinson College (LL.D. 1971); Lebanon Valley College (D. Litt. 1973); Univ. of Detroit (L.H.D. 1973); Grand Valley State College (L.H.D. 1973); Carnegie-Mellon Univ. (L.H.D. 1974).

Recreation. Travel, music.

ARTHUR, BEATRICE.

Actress. b. Bernice Frankel, New York City, to Philip and Rebecca Frankel. Attended Cambridge (Md.) H.S.; grad. Linden Hall H.S., Liberty, Pa.; attended Blackstone Coll., two years; grad. Franklin Inst. of Science and Arts, M.T. Studied acting with Erwin Piscator at the Dramatic Workshop of the New Sch. for Social Research, N.Y.C. two years. Married May 28, 1950, to Gene Saks, actor, director; two sons. Member of AEA; SAG; AFTRA.

Theatre. Miss Arthur's first stage appearance was in the title role in *Lysistrata* (Dramatic Workshop of the New Sch. for Social Research, 1947). She made her professional debut at the Cherry Lane Th., where she appeared in the chorus of *Dog Beneath the Skin* (July 21, 1947), and *Gas* (1947), as Yerma in *Yerma* (1947), Inez in *No Exit* (1948), Kate in *The Taming of the Shrew*(1948), the Mother in *Six Characters in Search of an Author* (1948), the Mother in *The Owl and the Pussycat*(1948), the Marchioness in *Le Bourgeois Gentilhomme* (1949), Constance in *Yes Is for a Very Young Man* (1949), Tekla in *The Creditors*(1949) and Hesione in *Heartbreak House*(1949).

She played stock at the Circle Th. (Atlantic City, N.J., Summer, 1951), appearing as Jessie in *Personal Appearance,* the Baroness in *Candle Light,* Nita in *Love or Money* and Olive in *The Voice of the Turtle.*

She also appeared as Clotilde Lombaste in *The New Moon* (State Fair Music Hall, Dallas, Tex., 1953); Dorothy in *Gentlemen Prefer Blondes* (Music Circus, Lambertville, N.J., 1953); and was resident comedienne at the Tamiment (Pa.) Theatre (1953).

She played Lucy Brown in *The Threepenny Opera* (Th. de Lys, Mar. 10, 1954; Sept. 20, 1955) and was a comedienne in *Shoestring Revue* (President Th., Feb. 28, 1955); appeared as Mme. Suze in *Seventh Heaven* (ANTA, May 26, 1955); and in the pre-Bway tour of *The Ziegfeld Follies* (Shubert, Boston, Mass., Apr. 16, 1956); closed Shubert, Philadelphia, Pa., 1956); *What's the Rush?* (Summer tour, 1956); and as Mirandolina in *Mistress of the Inn* (Bucks County Playhouse, New Hope, Pa., 1957).

She played Nadine Fesser in *Nature's Way*(Coronet, N.Y.C., Oct. 16, 1957); Bella-Bello in *Ulysses in Nighttown* (Rooftop Th., June 5, 1958); in the revue, *Chic* (Orpheum, May 19, 1959); Hortense in *Gay Divorce* (Cherry Lane, Apr. 3, 1960); Mrs. Miller in the pre-Bway tryout of *A Matter of Position* (opened Walnut, Philadelphia, Pa., Sept. 29, 1962; closed there Oct. 13, 1962); Yente, the Matchmaker in *Fiddler on the Roof* (Imperial, N.Y.C., Sept. 22, 1964); Vera Charles in *Mame* (Winter Garden, May 24, 1966); and Meg in *A Mother's Kisses* (pre-Bway: opened Shubert Th., New Haven, Conn., Sept. 23, 1958; closed Morris A. Mechanic Th., Baltimore, Md., Oct. 19, 1968).

Films. Miss Arthur appeared in *That Kind of*

Woman (Par., 1959); *Lovers and Other Strangers* (Cinerama, 1970); and repeated her performance as Vera Charles in the film version of *Mame* (WB, 1974).

Television. She appeared as a singer in *Once Upon a Time* (1948); a comedienne on the George Gobel Show (CBS, 1958); and has been on the Steve Allen Show (NBC); Sid Caesar Show (ABC); Jack Paar Show (NBC); Art Carney Show; and Wayne and Shuster. She first appeared as Maude on All in the Family (CBS, Sept. 1971), followed by a pilot for the show Maude, consisting of a complete episode of All in the Family (Spring 1972); Maude premiered as an independent series, starring Miss Arthur on Sept. 12, 1972 (CBS).

Night Clubs. Miss Arthur has performed her own act at Number One Fifth Avenue (N.Y.C.), Ruben Bleu (N.Y.C.), and the Blue Angel (N.Y.C.).

Awards. Miss Arthur was nominated for the Donaldson Award for her performance in *Shoestring Revue* (1955) and received an Outer Circle Award and an Antoinette Perry (Tony) Award for her performance in *Mame*, both 1966.

ARTHUR, CAROL. Actress, comedienne, singer. b. Carol Jane Arata, Aug. 4, 1935, Hackensack, N.J., to Peter and Mildred (Foehl) Arata. Father, police lieutenant. Grad. East Rutherford (N.J.) H.S., 1953. Studied at Feagin Sch. of Drama and Radio, N.Y.C., 1953–54; AADA, 1954–55; coached at Actors Center, N.Y.C., by Mervyn Nelson (one year); voice with Bob Kobin, Herbert Berghof Studio, N.Y.C.; scene study with Lee Grant and James Welch, N.Y.C. Relatives in theatre: grandfather, Henry C. Foehl, and uncle Julius Witzig, vaudeville team (Short and Sweet). Member AEA; AGVA.

Pre-Theatre. Secretary, airlines reservation agent, department store credit writer.

Theatre. Miss Arthur's first speaking role was at four in a Sunday School play (East Rutherford, N.J., 1939); and at eleven she served as producer, director and end man in a children's minstrel show (Gillooly's Barn, East Rutherford, N.J., 1946).

From 1955 to 1959, she played 80 roles in summer stock with the Caravan Th., Dorset, Vt., and Pinehurst, N.C., initially as apprentice, later as resident actress.

She appeared as Sue in *Bells Are Ringing* (Gateway Playhouse, Sommers Point, N.J., Summer 1960); subsequently toured as the Nightingale of Samarkand in *Once Upon a Mattress* (opened Erlanger Th., Chicago, Ill., Sept. 1, 1960; closed Colonial, Boston, Mass., Mar. 18, 1961); appeared as the Waitress in the pre-Bway tryout of *Kicks and Co.* (opened Arie Crown Th., Chicago, Ill., Sept. 1961; closed there Oct. 14, 1961); Miss Marmelstein in the national tour of *I Can Get It for You Wholesale* (Rochester, N.Y., Nov. 1, 1962); and Hildy in the London production of *On the Town* (Prince of Wales's, Mar. 1963).

Miss Arthur directed *The Happiest Millionaire* and *The Marriage-Go-Round* (Caravan Players, Dorset, Vt., Aug. 1963); played Edith in *High Spirits* (Alvin, N.Y.C., Apr. 7, 1964); Patty in *Quality Street* (Bucks Co. Playhouse, New Hope, Pa., Aug. 23, 1965); appeared in *Oh, What a Lovely War* (Studio Arena Th., Buffalo, N.Y., Oct. 28, 1965); in Ben Bagley's *New Cole Porter Revue* (Square East, N.Y.C., Dec. 22, 1965); and toured as Luce in *The Boys from Syracuse* (Summer 1966).

Night Clubs. She appeared as comedienne-singer in *Tongue in Cheek* (Upstairs at the Duplex, N.Y.C., Dec. 1961); *Summer and Smirk* (Madeira Club, Provincetown, Mass., June 1962); and *No Shoestrings* (Upstairs at the Downstairs, N.Y.C., Sept. 1962).

Recreation. Caricatures, violin, coin collecting.

ARTHUR, JEAN. Actress. b. Gladys Georgianna Greene, Oct. 17, 1905, New York City, to Hubert Sidney and Johanna Augusta (Neilson) Greene. Father, photographer. Attended Ft. Washington H.S., N.Y.C., summer sessions at Stephens Coll., Bennington Coll. Married 1928, to Julian Anker (marr. dis. 1928); married June 11, 1932, to Frank J. Ross, Jr., film producer (marr. dis. 1949). Address: (home) Carmel, CA; (bus.) c/o Actor's Equity Assn., 165 W. 46th St., New York, NY 10036.

Pre-Theatre. Illustrator's model.

Theatre. Miss Arthur appeared in summer stock (Red Bank, N.J., 1932), in *Coquette, Let Us Be Gay,* and *The Road to Rome;* and toured as Kalonika in *Lysistrata* (1932).

She made her N.Y.C. debut as Ann in *Foreign Affairs* (Avon Th., Apr. 13, 1932); followed by Adele Vernin in *The Man Who Reclaimed His Head* (Broadhurst, Sept. 8, 1932); Lucy in *$25 An Hour* (Masque, May 10, 1933); Elsa Karling in *The Curtain Rises* (Vanderbilt, Oct. 19, 1933); Klari in *The Bride of Torozko* (Henry Miller's Th., Sept. 13, 1934); Billie Dawn in the pre-Bway tour of *Born Yesterday* (1946); the title role in *Peter Pan* (Imperial, N.Y.C., Apr. 24, 1950); the title role in the pre-Bway tryout of *Saint Joan* (opened Natl., Washington, D.C., Sept. 20, 1954; closed Hartman, Columbus, Ohio, Nov. 6, 1954); the title role in *The Freaking Out of Stephanie Blake* (Eugene O'Neill Th., N.Y.C., Oct. 30, 1967); and the female lead in *First Monday in October* (Cleveland Play House, Oct. 17, 1975).

Films. Miss Arthur appeared in two-reel comedies and westerns (1923); made her debut in *The Temple of Venus* (Fox, 1923); followed by *Sins of the Father* (Par., 1923); *Warming Up* (Par., 1928); *Canary Murder Case* (Par., 1929); *Mysterious Dr. Fu Manchu* (Par., 1929); *Green Murder Case* (Par., 1929); *Half Way to Heaven* (Par., 1929); *Saturday Night Kid* (Par., 1929); *Return of Dr. Fu Manchu* (Par., 1930); *Street of Chance* (Par., 1930); *Ex-Bad Boy* (U, 1931); *Virtuous Husband* (U, 1931); *Paramount on Parade* (Par., 1930); *The Whirlpool* (Col., 1934); *Defense Rests* (Col., 1934); *Most Precious Thing in Life* (Col., 1934); *The Whole Town's Talking* (Col., 1935); *Public Hero Number One* (MGM, 1935); *Diamond Jim* (U, 1935); *The Public Menace* (Col., 1935); *Party Wire* (Col., 1935); and *If You Could Only Cook* (Col., 1935).

Also *Mr. Deeds Goes to Town* (Col., 1936); *Adventure in Manhattan* (Col., 1936); *The Ex Mrs. Bradford* (RKO, 1936); *More Than a Secretary* (Col., 1936); *The Plainsman* (Par., 1936); *History Is Made at Night* (UA, 1937); and *Easy Living* (Par., 1937); *You Can't Take It with You* (Col., 1938); *Only Angels Have Wings* (Col., 1939); *Mr. Smith Goes To Washington* (Col., 1939); *Too Many Husbands* (Col., 1940); *Arizona* (Col., 1940); *The Devil and Miss Jones* (RKO, 1941); *The Talk of the Town* (Col., 1942); *The More the Merrier* (Col., 1943); *A Lady Takes a Chance* (RKO, 1943); *The Impatient Years* (Col., 1944); *A Foreign Affair* (Par., 1948); and *Shane* (Par., 1953).

Television and Radio. Miss Arthur was in the Lux Radio Th. production of *Mr. Deeds Goes to Town* (WABC, Feb. 1, 1937); made her television debut on Gunsmoke (CBS, Mar. 6, 1965); played Patricia Marshall on the Jean Arthur Show (CBS, 1966–67).

Other Activities. Miss Arthur has been an instructor of drama at Vassar College and was instructor in drama and acting, North Carolina School of Arts, in 1973.

ASHCROFT, DAME PEGGY. Actress. b. Edith Margaret Emily Ashcroft, Dec. 22, 1907, Croydon, London, England, to William Worsley and Violet Maud (Bernheim) Ashcroft. Father, estate agent. Attended Woodford Sch., Croydon, 1913–23; grad. from Central Sch. of Dramatic Art, London, diploma in dramatic art, 1925. Studied acting with Elsie Fogerty. Married Dec. 23, 1929, to Rupert Charles Hart-Davis (marr. dis. June 1931); married Nov. 1934 to Theodore Komisarjevsky, actor, director (marr. dis. June 14, 1937); married Sept. 14, 1940, to Jeremy Nicolas Hutchinson, barrister (marr. dis. 1966); one son, one daughter. Member of British AEA; English Stage Co. (councillor, Jan. 1957); English Arts Council (1962); The Apollo (poetry reading) Society (founder, 1943); Worcester's Society for the Advancement of Music and the Arts (pres., 1961). Address: 40 Frognal Lane, Hampstead, London N.W.3, England tel. Hampstead 4260.

Theatre. Miss Ashcroft first appeared on the Bway stage as Lise in *High Tor* (Martin Beck Th., Jan. 9, 1937); and played Evelyn Holt in *Edward, My Son* (Martin Beck Th., Sept. 30, 1948).

She made her stage debut as Margaret in *Dear Brutus* (Birmingham Repertory Th., May 22, 1926); her London debut as Bessie in *One Day More* (Playroom Six, May 1927); followed by Mary Dunn in *The Return* (Everyman, May 30, 1927); Eve in *When Adam Delved* ("Q," July 18, 1927); Joan Greenleaf in *Bird in Hand* (Birmingham Repertory Th., Sept. 3, 1927); Betty in *The Way of the World* (Wyndham's, London, Nov. 15, 1927); in a double bill, played Anastasia Vulliamy in *The Fascinating Foundling* and Mary Bruin in *The Land of Heart's Desire* (Arts, Jan. 28, 1928); Hester in a touring production of *The Silver Cord* (Spring 1928); Edith Strange in *Earthbound* ("Q," London, Sept. 10, 1928); Kristina in *Easter* (Arts, Oct. 10, 1928); and Eulalia in *A Hundred Years Old* (Lyric, Hammersmith, Nov. 21, 1928).

She played Lucy Deren in *Requital* (Everyman, Apr. 23, 1929); Sally Humphries in *Bees and Honey* (Strand, May 12, 1929); Constance Neville in a touring production of *She Stoops to Conquer* (June 1929); Naomi in *Jew Süss* (Duke of York's, London, Sept. 19, 1929); Desdemona in *Othello* (Savoy, May 19, 1930); Judy Battle in *The Breadwinner* (Vaudeville, Sept. 30, 1930); Pervanah in the Oxford Univ. Dramatic Society's production of *Hassan* (Oxford, Feb. 1931); Angela in *Charles the Third* (Wyndham's, London, Apr. 7, 1931); Anne in *A Knight Passed By* (Ambassadors', June 6, 1931); Fanny in *Sea Fever* (New, June 30, 1931); Marcela in *Take Two from One* (Haymarket, Sept. 16, 1931); Juliet in the Oxford Univ. Dramatic Society's production of *Romeo and Juliet* (Oxford, Feb. 1932); Stella in *Le cocu magnifique* (Globe, London, May 22, 1932); and Salome Westaway in *The Secret Woman* (Duchess, June 15, 1932).

Miss Ashcroft made her first appearance with the Old Vic Co. playing the roles of Cleopatra in *Caesar and Cleopatra* (Old Vic, Sept. 18, 1932); followed by Imogen in *Cymbeline* (Old Vic, Oct. 10, 1932); and Rosalind in *As You Like It* (Old Vic, Oct. 31, 1932); the title role in *Fräulein Elsa* (Kingsway, Nov. 23, 1932); with the Old Vic Co., as Portia in *The Merchant of Venice* (Old Vic, Dec. 12, 1932); Kate Hardcastle in *She Stoops to Conquer* (Old Vic, Jan. 2, 1932); Perdita in *The Winter's Tale* (Old Vic, Jan. 23, 1933); the title role in *Mary Stuart* (Old Vic, Feb. 13, 1933); Juliet in *Romeo and Juliet* (Old Vic, Mar. 6, 1933); Lady Teazle in *The School for Scandal* (Old Vic, Mar. 27, 1933); and Miranda in *The Tempest* (Old Vic, Apr. 17, 1933).

She appeared as Inken Peters in *Before Sunset* (Shaftesbury, Sept. 28, 1933); Vasantesena in *The Golden Toy* (Coliseum, Feb. 28, 1934); Lucia Maubel in *The Life That I Gave Him* (Little, Oct. 4, 1934); Therese Paradis in a Glasgow (Scot.) production of *Mesmer* (King's, May 1935); repeated Juliet in a London production of *Romeo and Juliet* (New, Oct. 17, 1935); and played Nina in *The Seagull* (New, May 20, 1936). After she made her Bway debut in *High Tor* (see above), she was engaged by the John Gielgud Co. to play the Queen in *Richard II* (Queen's, London, Sept. 6, 1937); Lady Teazle in *The School for Scandal* (Queen's, Nov. 25, 1937); Irina in *The Three Sisters* (Queen's, Jan. 28, 1938); and Portia in *The Merchant of Venice* (Queen's, Apr. 21, 1938).

Miss Ashcroft played Yeleina Talberg in *The White Guard* (Phoenix, Oct. 6, 1938); Viola in *Twelfth Night* (Phoenix, Dec. 1, 1938); Isolde in a touring production of *Weep for the Spring* (May–June 1939); Cecily Cardew in *The Importance of Being Earnest* (Globe, London, Aug. 16, 1939); Dinah Sylvestor in *Cousin Muriel* (Globe, Mar. 7, 1940); followed Jessica Tandy (June 1940) in the role of Miranda in *The Tempest* (Old Vic, May 29, 1940); portrayed Mrs. de Winter in a touring production of *Rebecca* (Jan.–Mar. 1941); repeated the role of Cecily in *The Importance of Being Earnest*

(Phoenix, London, Oct. 14, 1942); appeared as Catherine Lisle in *The Dark River* (Whitehall, Oct. 19, 1943); Ophelia in a tour of *Hamlet* (Aug. 1944), and repeated the role in the subsequent London production (Haymarket, Oct. 13, 1944); played Titania in *A Midsummer Night's Dream* (Haymarket, Jan. 25, 1945); the title role in *The Duchess of Malfi* (Haymarket, Apr. 18, 1945); and Evelyn Holt in *Edward, My Son* (His Majesty's, May 30, 1947), later repeating the role in the Bway production (see above).

She portrayed Catherine Sloper in the London production of *The Heiress* (Haymarket, Feb. 1, 1949); at the Shakespeare Memorial Th. (Stratford-upon-Avon), played Beatrice in *Much Ado About Nothing* and Cordelia in *King Lear* (July 18, 1950); at the inauguration of the newly constructed Old Vic Th. (London), appeared as Viola in *Twelfth Night* (Nov. 14, 1950), the title role in *Electra* (Mar. 13, 1951), and Mistress Page in *The Merry Wives of Windsor* (May 13, 1951); played Hester Collyer in *The Deep Blue Sea* (Duchess, Mar. 6, 1952); at the Shakespeare Memorial Th. (Stratford-upon-Avon), appeared as Portia in *the Merchant of Venice* (Mar. 17, 1953), and Cleopatra in *Antony and Cleopatra* (Apr. 28, 1953), repeated the latter role for the Company's engagement in London (Prince's, Nov. 4, 1953), and on the subsequent tour (Neth., Belg., Fr., 1953–54).

Miss Ashcroft appeared in the title role in *Hedda Gabler* (Lyric, Hammersmith, London, Sept. 8, 1954), and repeated her role on tour (Holland; Den.; New Th., Oslo, Nor., Mar. 16, 1955); with the Shakespeare Memorial Th. Co. (Stratford-upon-Avon), toured as Beatrice and Cordelia in *Much Ado About Nothing* (Aust.; Switz.; Holland; Mar.–June 1955), and repeated the role of Beatrice in the London production (Palace, July 21, 1955); appeared as Miss Madrigal in *The Chalk Garden* (Haymarket, Apr. 12, 1956); Shen Te in *The Good Woman of Setzuan* (Royal Court, Oct. 31, 1956); at the Shakespeare Memorial Th. (Stratford-upon-Avon), Rosalind in *As You Like It* (Apr. 2, 1957), and Imogen in *Cymbeline* (July 2, 1957); at the Edinburgh (Scot.) Festival, appeared in the monologue *Portraits of Women* (Lyceum, Sept. 1958); Julia Raik in *Shadow of Heroes* (Piccadilly, London, Oct. 7, 1958); Eva Delaware in a touring production of *The Coast of Coromandel* (Jan.–Mar. 1959); Rebecca West in *Rosmersholm* (Royal Court, London, Nov. 18, 1959); at the Shakespeare Memorial Th. (Stratford-upon-Avon), Katherina in *The Taming of the Shrew* (June 21, 1960), and Paulina in *The Winter's Tale* (Aug. 30, 1960).

As a member of the Royal Shakespeare Th. Co., formerly the Shakespeare Memorial Th. Co., Miss Ashcroft appeared in the title role in *The Duchess of Malfi* (Aldwych, London, Dec. 15, 1960); performed in *The Hollow Crown* (Aldwych, London, Dec. 15, 1960); at the Royal Shakespeare Th. (Stratford-upon-Avon) played Emilia in *Othello* (Oct. 10, 1961), and Madame Ranevsky in *The Cherry Orchard* (Dec. 2, 1961); toured in *The Hollow Crown* (Geneva, Switz.; Amsterdam, The Hague, Neth.; Paris, Fr., May–June 1962); repeated her role in *The Cherry Orchard* (Aldwych, London, Dec. 17, 1962); appeared as Margaret of Anjou in the historical trilogy *The Wars of the Roses,* comprised of Shakespeare's *Henry VI, Edward IV* (compression of *Henry VI, Parts 1, 2, & 3),* and *Richard III* (Royal Shakespeare Th., July 3–Dec. 1963); repeated the role of Margaret of Anjou (Aldwych, London, Jan. 11–Feb. 5, 1964); played Madame Arkadina in *The Seagull* (New, Oxford, Mar. 2, 1964; Queen's, London, Mar. 12, 1964); and repeated her role in a revival of *The Wars of the Roses* (Royal Shakespeare Th. July 29–Aug. 12, 1964).

She toured Europe and Israel in *Women and Words* in 1965; was the Mother in *Days in the Trees* (Aldwych, London, June 1966); Mrs. Alving in *Ghosts* (Aldwych, London, June 1967); Agnes in *A Delicate Balance* (Aldwych, London, Jan. 14, 1969); Beth in *Landscape* (Royal Shakespeare Th., Stratford-upon-Avon, July 1969); Queen Katherine in *Henry VIII* (Royal Shakespeare Th., Stratford-upon-Avon, Oct. 1969); Volumnia in *The Plebians Rehearse the Uprising* (Aldwych, London, July 1970); repeated her role in *Henry VIII* (Aldwych, London, Dec. 1970); played the part of Clair Lannes in *Lovers of Viorne* (Royal Court Th., London, July 5, 1971); was the Wife in *All Over* (Aldwych, Jan. 31, 1972); Lady Boothroyd in *Lloyd George Knew My Father* (Savoy, London, July 4, 1972); toured in Europe as Beth in *Landscape* and as Flora in *A Slight Ache* (1973), and toured in America in *The Hollow Crown* (1973); and repeated her roles in *Landscape* and *A Slight Ache* (Aldwych, London, Oct. 17, 1973).

Films. Miss Ashcroft appeared in *The Wandering Jew* (Olympic, 1935); *The 39 Steps* (Gaumont-British, 1935); *Rhodes* (Gaumont-British, 1936); *Channel Incident* (Denham & Pinewood, 1940); *Quiet Wedding* (U, 1942); *The Nun's Story* (WB, 1959).

Television and Radio. Miss Ashcroft made her television debut in *Shadow of Heroes* (BBC, London, July 1959). She has also appeared many times on British radio (BBC).

Awards. She received the Ellen Terry Theatre Award for her role as Evelyn Holt in *Edward, My Son* (1947); the King's Medal from King Haakon of Norway for her performance in the title role in *Hedda Gabler* (1955); the *Evening Standard* Drama Award for her performance as Miss Madrigal in *The Chalk Garden* (1956); the Paris Festival Théâtre des Nations Award for her role in *The Hollow Crown* (1962); the London *Evening Standard* drama award and the Variety Club of Great Britain award as the best actress of 1964 for her *Wars of the Roses* performance; and the *Plays and Players* London Theatre Critics award and the *Evening Standard* drama award as the best actress of 1971 for her performance in *Lovers of Viorne.*

She was made a Commander of the Order of the British Empire (C.B.E., 1951); was made Dame Commander of the Order of the British Empire (D.B.E., 1956); and received an honorary D.Litt. from Oxford Univ. (1961); from Leicester Univ. (1963); from London Univ. (1965); and from Cambridge Univ. (1972).

ASHLEY, CELESTE. Theatre librarian. b. Mabel Celeste Ashley, Aug. 11, 1930, Baltimore, Md., to Edward L. and Mabel C. (Almony) Ashley. Grad. Johns Hopkins Univ., B.S. (English) 1947; Univ. of California at Berkeley, B.S. (librarianship) 1948; Stanford Univ., graduate study 1951–53, M.A. (theatre) 1967. Member of Johns Hopkins Club, Inc.; Palo Alto (Calif.) Community Theatre. Address: (home) 1077 Stanford Ave., Palo Alto, CA 94302, tel. (415) 325-4637; (bus.) Stanford University Libraries, Stanford, CA 94305, tel. (415) 321-2300.

Miss Ashley was librarian in the catalogue division of Johns Hopkins Univ. Library (1946–47); continued in the same division of the Univ. of California Library at Santa Barbara (1948–51). Since 1953, she has specialized in theatre film, and television at Stanford Univ. Libraries, and has been a reference librarian and curator for the Theatre Arts Collection there.

ASHLEY, ELIZABETH. Actress. b. Aug. 30, Ocala, Fla. Grad. University H.S., Baton Rouge, La., 1957; attended Louisiana State Univ., 1958. Studied ballet with Tatiana Semenova, Baton Rouge; acting at Neighborhood Playhouse Sch. of the Th., N.Y.C., 1958–59. Married Sept. 1962 to James Farentino, actor (marr. dis.); married 1966 to George Peppard, actor (marr. dis.); one son. Member of AEA; SAG; AFTRA.

Pre-Theatre. Fashion model, cover girl.

Theatre. Miss Ashley first appeared in N.Y.C. as Esmeralda in a student performance of *Camino Real;* followed by the role of Abigail in *The Crucible* (Neighborhood Playhouse, 1959). Off-Bway, she played Jessica in Sartre's *Dirty Hands* (June 1959) and in stock appeared in *Marcus in the High Grass* (Westport Country Playhouse, Conn., Aug. 1959).

She made her debut on Bway in *The Highest Tree* (Longacre Th., Nov. 4, 1959); subsequently was understudy to Inga Stevens in the role of Elizabeth Brown in *Roman Candle* (Cort, Feb. 3, 1960); appeared in stock at the Green Mansions Th. (Warrensburg, N.Y., Summer 1960); was understudy to Barbara Bel Geddes as Mary in *Mary, Mary* (Helen Hayes Th., Mar. 8, 1961); played Mollie Michaelson in *Take Her, She's Mine* (Biltmore, Dec. 21, 1961) and Corie Bretter in *Barefoot in the Park* (Biltmore, Oct. 23, 1963).

She played Maggie Train in *Ring Round the Bathtub* (Martin Beck Th., Apr. 29, 1972); was in *The Enchanted* (Eisenhower Th., John F. Kennedy Ctr., Washington, D.C., Mar. 2, 1973); played Maggie in *Cat on a Hot Tin Roof* (American Shakespeare Th., Stratford, Conn., July 10, 1974; ANTA Th., N.Y.C., Sept. 24, 1974); and Sabina in *The Skin of Our Teeth* (Eisenhower Th., Kennedy Ctr., Washington, D.C., July 9, 1975; Mark Hellinger Th., N.Y.C., Sept. 9, 1975).

Films. She appeared in *The Carpetbaggers* (Par., 1964); *Ship of Fools* (Col., 1965); and *The Third Day* (WB, 1965).

Television. Miss Ashley appeared in *Heaven Can Wait* (Dupont Show of the Month, NBC, 1960); The Defenders (CBS); US Steel Hour (CBS); The Nurses (CBS); Ben Casey (ABC); Stoney Burke (ABC); Sam Benedict (CBS); Ed Sullivan Show (CBS); Jack Paar Show (NBC); Mike Wallace's PM East (WNEW); and Route 66 (CBS).

Other shows on which she appeared include Run for Your Life (NBC, 1966); *The File on Devlin* (Hallmark Hall of Fame, NBC, Nov. 21, 1969); *Happy* (CBS, Mar. 13, 1971); *Second Chance* (ABC, Feb. 8, 1972); and *Your Money or Your Wife* (CBS, Dec. 19, 1972).

Other Activities. Miss Ashley was appointed a member of the newly created National Council of the Performing Arts (1965) and a trustee of the American Film Institute (1967).

Awards. For her performance as Mollie Michaelson in *Take Her, She's Mine,* she received the Antoinette Perry (Tony) Award, *Theatre World* Award and the Southern Woman's Achievement Award (1962).

ASHLEY, TED. Business executive, talent representative. Father, tailor. Attended night courses in accounting at City Coll. of New York. Married Dec. 19, 1963, to Linda Palmer, photographer (marr. dis.). Served US Army.

Mr. Ashley was, at first, an office boy, later a talent representative, at the William Morris Agency in N.Y.C. (1936–46); was a personal manager (1947–50); was founder with Ira Steiner, of the Ashley-Steiner Agency (1950); and, upon the merger of the firm with Famous Artists, became president of Ashley-Steiner-Famous Artists, Inc. (1962); which was changed to Ashley Famous Agency, Inc. (1964).

Warner Communications, Inc. (WCI) acquired Ashley Famous in 1967, at which time Mr. Ashley became a director and chairman of the executive committee of WCI. In 1969, WCI acquired Warner Brothers-Seven Arts, Ltd., and Mr. Ashley became chairman of the board and chief executive officer of the latter, continuing until 1974, when he resigned all his posts. Mr. Ashley was also elected to the board of the Motion Picture Association of America in 1969.

Awards. Mr. Ashley received the Pioneer of the Year Award (1973) of the Foundation of Motion Picture Pioneers.

ASTAIRE, ADELE. Dancer, actress. b. Adele Austerlitz, Sept. 11, 1898, Omaha, Nebr., to Frederick E. and Anna (Geilus) Austerlitz. Father, traveling salesman, brewer. Attended Highwood Park Sch., Weehawken, N.J., 1905–7. Studied dancing at Chambers Dancing Acad., Omaha, Nebr., 1902; Alvienne Sch., N.Y.C., 1904; with Ned Wayburn, N.Y.C., 1907; Alberieri, Metropolitan Ballet Sch., N.Y.C. Married May 9, 1932, to Lord Charles Cavendish (dec. 1944); married 1947 to Kingman Douglass, investment banker (dec. Oct. 8, 1971). Relative in theatre: brother, Fred Astaire, dancer, actor. Address: Middleburg, VA.

Theatre. Miss Astaire made her professional debut with her brother, Fred, in their vaudeville dance act, playing the Orpheum and Keith circuits (1906–16). Fred Astaire was her dancing partner for twenty-five years and appeared with her in all the productions listed.

She first appeared in N.Y.C., in the musical revue, *Over the Top* (44 St. Roof Th., Nov. 28, 1917), and on tour. She performed in *The Passing Show of 1918* (Winter Garden, July 25, 1918) and in the subsequent tour; played Molly in *Apple Blossoms* (Globe, Oct. 7, 1919), touring the US; appeared as Aline Moray in *The Love Letter* (Globe, Oct. 4, 1921); Suzanne Hayden in *For Goodness Sake* (Lyric, Feb. 20, 1922); and Judy Jordan in *The Bunch and Judy* (Globe, Nov. 28, 1922).

She made her London debut, playing Suzanne Hayden in *For Goodness Sake,* retitled *Stop Flirting* (Shaftesbury, May 30, 1923), which later toured England; appeared as Susie Trevor in *Lady Be Good* (Liberty, N.Y.C., Dec. 1, 1924; Empire Th., London, Apr. 14, 1926); Frankie Wynne in *Funny Face* (Alvin, N.Y.C., Nov. 22, 1927; Prince's Th., London, Nov. 8, 1928); Dot Hastings in *Smiles* (Ziegfeld, N.Y.C., Nov. 18, 1930); and in the revue *The Bandwagon* (New Amsterdam, June 3, 1931).

Miss Astaire retired permanently from the stage in 1931.

Television. Miss Astaire appeared on Girl Talk (ABC, 1965–66) and on *Musicals of the '30's* (New York Illustrated, NBC, Apr. 8, 1967).

ASTAIRE, FRED. Dancer, actor, producer, composer, singer. b. Frederic Astaire, May 10, 1899, Omaha, Nebr., to Frederick and Ann (Geilus) Astaire. Father, brewer. Attended public school in Highwood Park, N.J.; subsequent private tutoring. Married July 12, 1933, to Phyllis Livingston Baker (dec. Sept. 13, 1954); two sons, one daughter. Served USO, 1946. Relative in theatre: sister, Adele, dance partner. Member of SAG; AFTRA; ASCAP; Racquet & Tennis Club; Brook Club; The Lambs; Bel-Air Country Club (Los Angeles, Calif.).

Theatre. Mr. Astaire made his professional debut at seven with his sister Adele in a featured vaudeville act, *Fred and Adele Astaire,* playing the Orpheum and Keith circuits (1906–16); subsequently danced with Adele (1906–31).

Mr. Astaire made his Bway debut in the musical revue *Over the Top* (44 St. Roof Th., Nov. 28, 1917), then toured cross-country; performed in *Passing Show of 1918* (Winter Garden, July 25, 1918), and on tour; as Johnny in *Apple Blossoms* (Globe, Oct. 7, 1919), and on tour; and as Richard Kolnar in *The Love Letter* (Globe, Oct. 4, 1921).

He played Teddy Lawrence in *For Goodness Sake* (Lyric, N.Y.C., Feb. 20, 1922), in London where it was retitled *Stop Flirting* (Shaftesbury, May 30, 1923), and on tour throughout England; played Gerald Lane in *The Bunch and Judy* (Globe, N.Y.C., Nov. 28, 1922); Dick Trevor in *Lady, Be Good* (Liberty, N.Y.C., Dec. 1, 1924; Empire, London, Apr. 14, 1926); Jimmy Reeve in *Funny Face* (Alvin, N.Y.C., Nov. 22, 1927; Princess, London, Nov. 8, 1929); Bob Hastings in *Smiles* (Ziegfeld, N.Y.C., Nov. 18, 1930); played in the revue *The Band Wagon* (New Amsterdam, June 3, 1931), which also toured the US; and played Guy in *Gay Divorce* (Ethel Barrymore Th., Nov. 29, 1932; Palace, London, Nov. 2, 1933).

Films. Mr. Astaire made his film debut in *Dancing Lady* (MGM, 1933); subsequently appeared in *Flying Down to Rio* (RKO, 1933); *Gay Divorcee* (RKO, 1934); *Roberta* (RKO, 1935); *Top Hat* (RKO, 1935); *Follow the Fleet* (RKO, 1936); *Swingtime* (RKO, 1936); *Shall We Dance* (RKO, 1937); *Damsel in Distress* (RKO, 1937); *Carefree* (RKO, 1938); *The Story of Vernon and Irene Castle* (RKO, 1939); *Broadway Melody* (MGM, 1940); *Second Chorus* (Par., 1940); *You'll Never Get Rich* (Col., 1941); *Holiday Inn* (Par., 1942); *The Sky's the Limit* (RKO, 1943); *Yolanda and the Thief* (MGM, 1945); *Ziegfeld Follies* (MGM, 1946); *Blue Skies* (Par., 1946); *Easter Parade* (MGM, 1948); *The Barkleys of Broadway* (MGM, 1949); *Three Little Words* (MGM, 1950); *Let's Dance* (Par., 1950); *Royal Wedding* (MGM, 1951); *Belle of New York* (MGM, 1950); *The Band Wagon* (MGM, 1953); *Daddy Long Legs* (20th-Fox, 1955); *Funny Face* (Par., 1957); *Silk Stockings* (MGM, 1957); *On the Beach* (UA, 1959); *The Pleasure of His Company* (Par., 1961); *Notorious Landlady* (Col., 1962); *Finian's Rainbow* (WB, 1968); *The Midas Run* (Cinerama, 1969); *That's Entertainment* (UA, 1974); and *Towering Inferno* (20th-Fox, 1974).

Television. Mr. Astaire made his television debut in *Imp on a Cobweb Leash* (GE Th., CBS, 1957); followed by *Man on a Bicycle* (CBS, 1958); produced and appeared on *An Evening with Fred Astaire* (NBC, 1958), *Another Evening with Fred Astaire* (NBC, 1959), and *Astaire Time* (NBC, 1960); and was host and occasional performer on Alcoa Premiere Th. (ABC, 1961–63).

He was in *Think Pretty* (Bob Hope Presents, NBC, Oct. 2, 1964); host on segments of Hollywood Palace (ABC, 1965–66); appeared as Joe Quinlan in segments of Dr. Kildare (NBC, 1965); was on the *Fred Astaire Show* (NBC, Feb. 7, 1968); in It Takes a Thief (ABC, 1969); *The Over the Hill Gang Rides Again* (ABC, Nov. 17, 1970); and his voice was on *Santa Claus Is Coming to Town* (ABC, Dec. 3, 1971).

Other Activities. Mr. Astaire is technical advisor to the Fred Astaire Dance Studios Corp.; president of Ava Records; and the composer of "Blue Without You," "I'm Building Up to an Awful Let-Down," "I'll Never Let You Go," "Just One More Dance, Madame," "Sweet Sorrow," "Just Like Taking Candy from a Baby," "If Swing Goes, I Go Too," and "Oh, My Achin' Back.".

Published Works. He is the author of *Steps in Time* (1959), his autobiography.

Discography. Among Mr. Astaire's recordings are *The Fred Astaire Story; Mr. Top Hat; Easy to Dance With; Now, Fred Astaire; Three Evenings with Fred Astaire;* and numerous sound track recordings for MGM Records.

Awards. Mr. Astaire received a special Academy (Oscar) Award for "unique artistry and contribution to musical motion pictures" (1949) and the George Eastman House annual George Award "for outstanding contributions to motion pictures" (1965). Mr. Astaire and his various television specials together have received nine NATAS (Emmy) awards, and he has received many other awards, including the Peabody, *Look* magazine, *Dance Magazine,* and *TV Guide* citations. On Apr. 30, 1973, the Film Society of Lincoln Ctr., N.Y.C., honored Mr. Astaire with a special showing of excerpts from his films.

Recreation. Thoroughbred racing, golf.

ASTOR, RICHARD. Talent representative. b. Feb. 19, 1927, Chicago, Ill., to Albert and Sarah Astor. Father, manufacturer. Grad. Northwestern Univ., B.S. 1945. Member of TARA.%

Mr. Astor has been a talent representative since 1958 and opened his own agency with offices in N.Y.C. (Sept. 1960); worked with Kaplan-Veidt (Feb. 1957–Sept. 1958) and with the H. C. Brown agency (Sept. 1958–Sept. 1960). Address: (home) 27 W. 86th St., New York, NY 10024, tel. (212) SC 4-3684; (bus.) 119 W. 57th St., New York, NY 10019, tel. (212) LT 1-1970.

ATIENZA, EDWARD. Actor. b. Edward Vincent Atienza, Jan. 27, 1924, London, England, to Alvaro V. and Dulce M. (Laws) Atienza. Grad. Sutton Valence Sch., Eng., 1942; attended King's Coll., Univ. of London, 1942–43; Lamda, 1947–48. Served in the Queen's Royal Regiment, England and East Africa; rank, Lt. Member of AEA; AFTRA; SAG; British AEA. Address: 14 Ripplevale Grove, London N.1., England.

Theatre. Mr. Atienza made his stage debut as Raskolnikoff in a Univ. of London Dramatic Society production of *Crime and Punishment* (1943); and made his professional debut as the Butler in The Richmond Players' production of *Up in Mabel's Room* (Scala Th., Dartford, England, 1949); became a member of the Shakespeare Memorial Repertory Th. Co. (Stratford-upon-Avon, England), and performed with them in 1950–52 and 1954–55, and toured Germany (1950), New Zealand and Australia (1953).

He made his London debut as Mr. Mole in *Toad of Toad Hall* (Prince's, Dec. 23, 1954); played the East Wind in *Listen to the Wind* (Arts, Dec. 16, 1955); Dromio in a musical version of *The Comedy of Errors* (Oxford Playhouse, Mar. 28, 1956); the Archbishop in *Romanoff and Juliet* (Piccadilly, London, May 17, 1956); the Clown in *Titus Andronicus* (Stoll, July 1, 1957), and on tour; made his N.Y.C. debut as the Archbishop in *Romanoff and Juliet* (Plymouth, Oct. 10, 1957), and on tour (1957); toured as Wash in the national company of *Destry Rides Again* (July 1960); appeared as the Pope in *Becket* (St. James, N.Y.C., Oct. 5, 1960); toured the US, Canada, Europe, and the Middle East with the Old Vic Co., as Mercutio in *Romeo and Juliet,* the Porter in *Macbeth,* and d'Estiret in *St. Joan* (1961–62); played Professor Gay in *The Affair* (Henry Miller's Th., N.Y.C., Sept. 20, 1962); and the Sorcerer in *The Boys from Syracuse* (Drury Lane, London, Nov. 1963).

Mr. Atienza appeared at the Open Air Th., Regent's Park, London, England, as the Dauphin in *Henry V* (June 5, 1964), Biondello in *The Taming of the Shrew* (July 15, 1964), and Touchstone in *As You Like It* (June 10, 1965). He played Count Shabelsky in *Ivanov* (Yvonne Arnaud Th., Guildford, Eng., Aug. 30, 1965; Phoenix, London, Sept. 30, 1965; Sam S. Shubert Th., N.Y.C., May 3, 1966); and Ward V. Evans in *In the Matter of J. Robert Oppenheimer* (Hampstead Th. Club, Oct. 17, 1966; Fortune, London, Nov. 1966). He toured as Potter in *Brother and Sister* (Apr. 1967); played Firs in *The Cherry Orchard* (Queens Th., London, Oct. 5, 1967); Alphonso Santospirito in *Climb the Greased Pole* (Mermaid, London, Nov. 23, 1967); and the Barber in *Man of La Mancha* (Piccadilly, London, Apr. 24, 1968).

He was Foehn in *The Eagle Has Two Heads* (Yvonne Arnaud Th., Guildford, Apr. 1969); Dr. Rank in *A Doll's House* (Gardner Centre, Brighton, England, Jan. 1970); and at the 1970 Chichester (England) Festival played Solveig's father in *Peer Gynt* (May 13), de Quadra in *Vivat! Vivat! Regina!* (May 20), and Subtle in *The Alchemist* (July 22). He repeated his performance as de Quadra in London (Piccadilly, Oct. 8, 1970); was in a revival of *Geneva* (Mermaid, London, Nov. 1971); and appeared at the Stratford (Ontario, Canada) Shakespeare Festival; in 1972 as Touchstone in *As You Like It* (June 5) and the Fool in *King Lear* (June 7) and in 1973 as Grumio in *The Taming of the Shrew* and Gower in *Pericles* (July 24). At the National Arts Ctr., Ottawa, Ontario, Canada, he played Malvolio in *Twelfth Night* (Nov. 22, 1973) and the title role in *Arturo Ui* (Jan. 10, 1974); and he toured Australia (Feb. 15–Apr. 6, 1974) with the Stratford National Th. of Ontario in *The Imaginary Invalid.*

Mr. Atienza returned again to the Stratford (Ont.) Festival (Summer 1974), repeating his performance as Gower in *Pericles* (June 4), and playing Boyet in *Love's Labour's Lost* (June 5), and the title role in *King John* (July 23); and he was at the Shaw Festival, Niagara-on-the-Lake, Ontario, Canada (Summer 1975), where he played Col. Pickering in *Pygmalion* (June 9) and Caesar in *Caesar and Cleopatra* (July).

Films. In England, he was seen as Pop the Gaucho in *Battle of the River Plate* (1955), which was shown in the US as *Pursuit of the Graf Spée* (1957).

Television. Mr. Atienza made his television debut as Leonardo da Vinci in *Sword of Freedom* on British television (1957), played Shabelsky in *Ivanov* (CBS, May 30, 1967), and has performed on various programs in N.Y.C., Hollywood, (Calif.), and Toronto (Can.).

Recreation. Classical guitar, collecting folk songs.

ATKINS, EILEEN. Actress. b. June 16, 1934, London, England, to Arthur Thomas and Annie Ellen (Elkins) Atkins. Father, meter reader; mother, bar-maid. Attended Latymers Grammer Sch., Edmonton, England. Studied acting at Guildhall Sch. of Music and Drama. Married to John Glover, actor (marr. dis.). Member of AEA; British AEA. Address: (home) 65 Ennismore Gardens, London, S.W. 7, England; (bus.) c/o Peggy Thompson, 110 Jermyn St., London, S.W. 1, England tel. 01-839-7589.

Theatre. Miss Atkins made her theatrical debut as the Nurse in *Harvey* (Repertory Th., Bangor, Ireland, June 1952); subsequently played Jacquenetta in *Love's Labour's Lost* (Open Air Th., Regents Park, London, June 1953); joined the Memorial Th. Co., Stratford-upon-Avon (1957–59) during which time she played Diana in *Pericles, Prince of Tyre;* Beattie in *Roots* (Bristol Old Vic., Mar. 1960); and appeared in *The Girl in the Square* (Bromley, Apr. 1961). She joined the Old Vic Company (Jan.–May 1962) playing Viola in *Twelfth Night,* Lady Anne in *Richard III,* and Miranda in *The Tempest;* subsequently played Eileen Midway in *Semi Detached* (Saville, Dec. 1962); Lady Brute in *The Provok'd Wife* (Vaudeville, July 1963); and Juliette in *Exit the King* (Royal Court, Sept. 1963; and Edinburgh Festival). She made her US debut as Viola in *Twelfth Night* and Ophelia in *Hamlet* (Ravinia, Ill., Festival, Aug. 1964); subsequently played Childie in *The Killing of Sister George* (Bristol Old Vic, Apr. 1965; transferred to Duke of York's Th., London, June 1965; and Belasco, N.Y.C., Oct. 5, 1966) making her Bway debut; Joan Middleton in *The Restoration of Arnold Middleton* (Royal Court, London, July 1967); Lika in *The Promise* (Henry Miller's Th., N.Y.C., Nov. 14, 1967); Celia Coplestone in *The Cocktail Party* (Chichester Festival, May 1968; transferred to Wyndham's Th., London, Nov. 1968; and Haymarket); Joan Shannon in *The Sleeper's Den* (Royal Court's Th. Upstairs, Nov. 1969); Elizabeth I in *Vivat! Vivat Regina!* (Chichester Festival, May 1970; transferred to Piccadilly Th., London, Oct. 8, 1970; and Broadhurst, N.Y.C., Jan. 20, 1971); the title role in *Suzana Adler* (pre-West End tryout, Wimbledon, England, Th.); Rosalinde in *As You Like It* (Stratford-upon-Avon, 1973); appeared in *The Duchess of Malfi* (Mark Taper Forum, Los Angeles, Jan. 22, 1975); and played Hesione Hushabye in *Heartbreak House* (National Th., London, Feb. 25, 1975).

Films. Miss Atkins' appearances include *Inadmissible Evidence* (Par., 1968); and *The Baby.*

Television. A frequent television performer since 1959, Miss Atkins' appearances include *The Age of Kings* (BBC/PBS); *The Three Sisters* (BBC/PBS); *The Heiress; The Trigon* (BBC); *Major Barbara* (BBC); *Hilda Lessways; The Duchess of Malfi* (BBC/PBS); *The Lady's Not for Burning* (BBC); *A Midsummer Night's Dream* (BBC); *Electra; The Lady from the Sea; Party Games; Double Bill; Olive;* Omnibus; The Jean Rhys Program; and *The Letter.*

Other Activities. With Jean Marsh, she is co-creator of the television series, Upstairs-Downstairs (BBC/PBS).

Awards. Miss Atkins is the recipient of the Clarence Derwent Award (1963) for her performance in *Exit the King;* and the Evening Standard Award for Best Actress (1965) for her performance in *The Killing of Sister George.*

ATKINSON, BROOKS. Drama critic, journalist. b. Justin Brooks Atkinson, Nov. 28, 1894, Melrose, Mass., to Jonathan Henry and Garafelia (Taylor) Atkinson. Father, newspaperman. Grad. Melrose H.S., 1913; Harvard Univ., A.B. 1917. Married Aug. 18, 1926, to Oriana A. (Torrey) MacIlveen; one stepson. Served US Army, 1918; rank, Cpl. Member of the American Academy of Arts and Sciences (fellow); The Players; NY Drama Critics Circle (1st pres.). Address: Durham, NY 12422.

Mr. Atkinson was drama critic for the NY *Times* (1925–60), with a leave of absence to serve as overseas war correspondent in China (1942–44) and in Moscow (1945–46). After his retirement as drama critic, he wrote a bi-weekly column, "Critic at Large," for the NY *Times* until 1965, when he retired from the *Times.*

He was a reporter for the *Daily News* (Springfield, Mass., 1917); joined the staff of the Boston *Evening Transcript* as a police reporter, assistant to drama critic, H. T. Parker (1919–22); and joined the NY *Times* as editor of the book review section (1922–25).

Mr. Atkinson was an instructor of English at Dartmouth College (1917).

Television. He appeared on Play of the Week to introduce *The Iceman Cometh* (WNTA, Nov. 1960).

Published Works. His published works include *Skyline Promenades* (1925), *Henry Thoreau, the Cosmic Yankee* (1927), *East of the Hudson* (1931), *The Cingalese Prince* (1934), *Cleo for Short* (1940), *Broadway Scrapbook* (1947), *Tuesdays and Fridays* (1963), *Brief Chronicles* (1966), *Broadway* (1970), *This Bright Land* (1972), and *The Lively Years* (1973). He also edited and wrote the introduction to *Walden and Other Writings of Henry David Thoreau* (1936), *The Complete Essays and Other Writings of Ralph Waldo Emerson* (1940), edited *College in a Yard* (1957), and wrote the foreword to Meyer Berger's *New York* (1960).

Awards. For his contribution to the theatre, Mr. Atkinson was honored by a citation from AEA (1958); an honorary life membership in AEA (1960); a testimonial by the League of Off-Bway Theatres (Mar. 1960); the dedication of the Brooks Atkinson Th. (Sept. 1960), at which time he received a placque for "35 years of selfless devotion to the theatre . . ."; a citation from The Lambs (1960); a citation from the Shakespeare Festival, Stratford, Ontario (June 1960); and a citation from ANTA (1960). He was also honored by the League of NY Theatres (1960) and received a special citation from the *Village Voice* Off-Bway (Obie) Award (1960); and Antoinette Perry (Tony) Award (Silver Medal, 1962) for "distinguished achievement in theatre."

Mr. Atkinson received a Pulitzer Prize for Journalism (1947), for his reporting on the Soviet Union.

Recreation. Birds, reading.

ATKINSON, DAVID. Actor, singer. b. David Anthony Stuart Atkinson, Oct. 20, 1921, Montreal, Canada, to W. Stuart and Marjorie (Burke) Atkinson. Father, executive. Grad. Bishop Coll. Sch., Lennoxville, Quebec, 1938; attended Univ. of Hawaii, 1943; McGill Univ., 1946; studied voice with Florence Easton, Herbert Jansen, Paul Althouse; acting with Uta Hagen, Stella Adler, and at Pasadena (Calif.) Playhouse. Married Apr. 2, 1949, to Carol Zane, authors' representative. Relative in theatre: uncle, Edmund Burke, Metropolitan Opera basso. Served WW II, RCAF, RAF; rank, Pilot Officer. Member of AEA; AFTRA; AGVA; AGMA.

Theatre. Mr. Atkinson made his stage debut with the Montreal (Can.) Opera Guild as the High Priest in *Samson and Delilah* (Jan. 7, 1948), where he also sang in *Rigoletto* (May 4, 1948), Nilakantha in *Lakme,* and Escamillo in *Carmen.*

He made his N.Y.C. debut joining the cast (Majestic, Sept. 1948) of the revue, *Inside U.S.A.* (Century, Apr. 30, 1948), and on tour for two years. He played Clyde Hallam in *The Girl in Pink Tights* (Mark Hellinger Th., N.Y.C., Mar. 5, 1954); Billy Bigelow in *Carousel* (NY City Ctr., June 2, 1954); John Sorel and the Chief of Police in the opera *The Consul* (Montreal Opera Guild, Canada, Jan. 1955); Oliver J. Oxheart in *The Vamp* (Winter Garden, N.Y.C., Nov. 10, 1955); Fred Graham in *Kiss Me, Kate* (NY City Ctr., May 9, 1956); Gaylord Ravenal in *Show Boat* (Marine Th., Jones Beach, L.I., N.Y., Summers 1956–57); Tommy Albright in *Brigadoon* (NY City Ctr., Mar. 27, 1957; moved to Adelphi, Apr. 9, 1957) and Frank Butler in *Annie Get Your Gun* (NY City Ctr., Feb. 19, 1958).

He appeared as Dr. Gregg in the opera *Gallantry* (Columbia Univ. Th., world premiere, Feb. 1958); played Petruchio in the opera *The Taming of the Shrew* (NY City Ctr., Mar. 1958); Sam in the opera *Trouble in Tahiti* (NY City Ctr., world premiere, Apr. 6, 1958); and Billy Bigelow in the Brussels (Belgium) World's Fair production of *Carousel* (Summer 1958).

He appeared as Rudy Lorraine in *Say, Darling* (NY City Ctr., Feb. 25, 1959); Lieutenant Lukash in the opera, *The Good Soldier Schweik* (NY City Ctr., world premiere, Feb. 1959); He was in the opera *He Who Gets Slapped* (NY City Ctr., premiere, Apr. 2, 1959); Heathcliff in the opera, *Wuthering Heights* (Chatauqua Opera, N.Y., July 1959); Judge Aristide Forestier in *Can-Can* (Theatre-in-the-Park, N.Y.C., Aug. 25, 1959); and in the title role in *Macbeth* (Rollins Coll., Winter Park, Fla., 1960).

He played Larry Forman in the opera, *The Cradle Will Rock* (NY City Ctr., Feb. 11, 1960); succeeded (April 19, 1960) Scott Brady as Kent in *Destry Rides Again* (Imperial, Apr. 23, 1959); succeeded (Mar. 1961) James Mitchell as Mack the Knife in *The Threepenny Opera* (Th. de Lys, Sept. 20, 1955); and played Jack Absolute in *All in Love* (Martinique, Nov. 10, 1961).

At the Vanguard Th. (Detroit, Mich.), Mr. Atkinson played El Gallo in *The Fantasticks* (Dec. 1962); and the title role in Ibsen's *The Master Builder* (Jan. 1963), and in e. e. Cummings' *him* (Mar. 1963).

In Sept. 1963, he appeared in a one month guest engagement as Miles Gloriosus in *A Funny Thing Happened on the Way to the Forum* (Alvin, N.Y.C., May 8, 1962); at the Vanguard Th., played the title role in Pirandello's *Henry IV* (Mar. 1964); and Strindberg's *St. Pete* (Apr. 1964); followed by appearances at the Marine Th., Jones Beach, N.Y., as Phileas Fogg in *Around the World in 80 Days* (June 27, 1964) and as John Laffity, Jean Lafitte, and Lucky Laffity in *Mardi Gras* (June 26, 1965; return engagement: July 8, 1966).

Mr. Atkinson also appeared in *Man of La Mancha,* touring as Dr. Carrasco in the national company (opened Shubert Th., New Haven, Conn., Sept. 24, 1966); he substituted (July 14, 1967) for Jose Ferrer in the title role of the original N.Y.C. production (ANTA Washington Sq. Th., Nov. 22, 1965); toured in the title role (Sept. 27, 1968–Apr. 26, 1969); again played the role in N.Y.C. (Sept. 8–21, 1969), toured again (Sept. 27, 1969–June 1, 1970); and played the title role in a revival (Vivian Beaumont Th., June 22–Oct. 21, 1972). Mr. Atkinson also played Clive Champion-Cheney in a revival of *The Circle* (Roundabout Th., N.Y.C., Mar. 26, 1974).

Television. Mr. Atkinson has appeared on the Colgate Comedy Hour (NBC, 1951); Broadway Television Th. (1952); his own show, TV Town Topics with David Atkinson (WOR, 1952); played in *Mayerling* (NBC, 1956); made guest appearances on the Ed Sullivan Show (CBS); the Jack Paar Show (NBC); played in *The Importance of Being Earnest* (US Steel Hour, CBS); and on Studio One (CBS). He has also appeared on the Gypsy Rose Lee Show; Musical Comedy Hour; and The Stork Club. With the NBC-TV Opera Co., he played King Melchoir in *Amahl and the Night Vistors,* Escamillo in *Carmen,* and Sam in *Trouble in Tahiti.* .

Night Clubs. Mr. Atkinson appeared for eight months at the Caucus Club (Detroit, Mich., Feb. 1963).

Discography. He has recorded *David Atkinson Sings* (Montreal Record Club); *Trouble in Tahiti* (MGM); *All in Love* (Mercury); and *The Girl in Pink Tights* (Col.).

Recreation. Painting, writing, wild life conservation, ornithology.

ATLEE, HOWARD. Press representative. b. Howard Atlee Heinlen, May 14, 1926, Bucyrus, Ohio, to Howard Ezra and Blanche Lena (Newmann) Heinlen. Father, miller, cab owner, railroader, real estate broker. Grad. Bucyrus H.S., 1944; attended Ohio State Univ., 1944; grad. Emerson Coll., A.B. 1950. Served USNR, 1944–46. Member of ATPAM. Address: 165 W. 46 St., New York, NY 10036, tel. (212) 575-9415.

Theatre. Mr. Atlee was an actor in summer stock at Duxbury (Mass.) Playhouse (Summer 1950); subsequently was an actor and assistant manager at Olney (Md.) Th. (Summer 1952); actor, manager and press representative at the Mountaintop Th.

(Frederick, Md., Summer 1953); production assistant for *By the Beautiful Sea* (Majestic Th., N.Y.C., Apr. 8, 1953); press representative for Ogunquit (Me.) Playhouse (Summers 1954–55); and press assistant to Marian Byram and Phyllis Perlman for *Wonderful Town* (Winter Garden, N.Y.C., Feb. 25, 1953); and *The Seven Year Itch* (Fulton, Nov. 20, 1952).

He was assistant press representative to Michael Mok for *Pipe Dream* (Shubert, Nov. 30, 1955); press representative for the playhouse at Camden, N.J. (1956); assistant to Misses Byram and Perlman for *The Happiest Millionaire* (Lyceum, N.Y.C., Nov. 20, 1956), *Speaking of Murder* (Royale, Dec. 19, 1956) and The Irish Players production of the triple-bill *On the Shadow of the Glen, The Tinker's Wedding* and *Riders to the Sea* (Th. East, Mar. 6, 1957); and press representative for the Lakeside Playhouse (Barnesville, Pa., Summer 1957).

From 1958–60, Mr. Atlee was press representative for the N.Y.C. productions of *She Shall Have Music, The Legend of Lizzie, The Playboy of the Western World, Triad, Season of Choice, Shadow and Substance, The Tempest, Krapp's Last Tape, The Zoo Story, Shakespeare in Harlem, Absolutely Time, The Ignorants Abroad, Darwin's Theories, John Brown's Body, Call Me by My Rightful Name, The Sudden End of Anne Cinquefoil, A Banquet for the Moon, The American Dream, Bartleby* and *The Death of Bessie Smith* and for The Circle in the Square Theatre.

In 1961, Mr. Atlee represented *Hedda Gabler, A Worm in Horseradish, Krapp's Last Tape, The Zoo Story, The Moon in the Yellow River, Happy as Larry, Philoktetes, Women at the Tomb, Young Abe Lincoln, The Sap of Life, The Opening of a Window, The Cockeyed Kite, Ghosts, The Golden Apple, Sharon's Grave, The Cantilevered Terrace, A Stage Affair, Black Nativity* and *Fly Blackbird.*

During 1962, he was press representative for *The Theatre of the Absurd, 4 × 4, A Toy for the Clowns, Wretched the Lion Hearted, Anything Goes, Sweet Miani, Who's Afraid of Virginia Woolf?*, the double-bill *Whisper Into My Good Ear* and *Mrs. Dally Has a Lover, The Laundry, The Coach with the Six Insides,* and *Brecht on Brecht,* also for the APA Repertory and the American Savoyards.

In 1963, he represented *Strange Interlude, Save Me a Place at Forest Lawn, The Last Minstrel, Andorra, The American Dream, The Zoo Story, Tour de Four, Brecht on Brecht, The Ballad of the Sad Cafe, Corruption in the Palace of Justice, The Streets of New York, Play* and *The Lover.*

In 1964, he represented *Funnyhouse of a Negro, Dutchman, The Two Executioners, Naughty Marietta, The Brig, Tiny Alice, That Hat!, The Giants' Dance,* and the double-bill *Play* and *The Lover;* and, with Bonnard Productions, produced the double-bill *Dark Corners* and *Mr. Grossman* (Actors Playhouse, May 5, 1964).

In 1965, he represented Theater 1965's New Playwrights Series, the double-bill *The Fourth Pig* and *The Fisherman, Friday Night, A Sound of Silence, Do Not Pass Go, That Thing at the Cherry Lane, Troubled Waters,* a double-bill of *Krapp's Last Tape* and *The Zoo Story, Happy Days,* the double-bill *Good Days* and *The Exhaustion of Our Son's Love,* and the double-bill *Happy Ending* and *Day of Absence.*

In 1966, he was representative for a revival of *Winterset,* for *Malcolm, Laughwind, A Delicate Balance,* for a program of revivals consisting of *The Long Christmas Dinner, Queens of France,* and *The Happy Journey to Trenton and Camden,* for *The Butter and Egg Man, America Hurrah, Three Hand Reel,* and *Night of the Dunce.*

In 1967, he represented *The Rimers of Eldritch, The Experiment, The Party on Greenwich Avenue,* and *Johnny No-Trump;* and in 1968, he was representative for *Song of the Lusitanian Bogey,* the double-bill *The Indian Wants the Bronx* and *It's Called the Sugar Plum, The Bench, Two Camps, Frère Jacques, Walk Down Mah Street!,* for *Another City, Another Land,* for *The Young Master Dante, The Grab Bag,* the double bill *Sweet Eros* and *Witness,* for *"God Is a (Guess What?)", The Firebugs, How to Steal an Election,* and *Yes Yes, No No.*

In 1969, he represented *Get Thee to Canterbury, Adaptation/Next, Ceremonies in Dark Old Men, The Triumph of Robert Emmet,* American Conservatory Th. revivals of *Tiny Alice, A Flea in Her Ear,* and *Three Sisters;* a revival of *The Front Page, Man Better Man, The Reckoning, The American Hamburger League, Mercy Street, Crimes of Passion,* and *The Harangues.*

In 1970, he represented *Gloria and Esperanza,* a revival of *The Cherry Orchard, The Memory Bank,* a revival of *Hedda Gabler, Nature of the Crime,* a revival of *Endgame* a revival of *Hay Fever,* a revival of *Johny Johnson, Sunday Dinner,* and *Ododo;* and in 1971, he represented *Ride a Black Horse, In New England Winter, Things That Almost Happen, Kiss Now, Black Girl, The Sty of the Blind Pig,* and *Fingernails Blue as Flowers.*

In 1972, he represented *Uhuruh, Jamimma, The Contrast,* and *The River Niger;* in 1974, *The Great Macdaddy* and *In the Deepest Part of Sleep;* and in 1975, *Bette Midler's Clams on the Half Shell Revue, Salome,* and *The First Breeze of Summer.* .

Recreation. Raising, breeding and showing pure-bred dogs, particularly dachshunds.

ATTAWAY, RUTH. Actress. b. Greenville, Miss., to William and Florence Attaway. Father, physician; mother, school teacher. Grad. Hyde Park H.S., Chicago, Ill., 1930; Univ. of Illinois, B.A. 1933; attended Univ. of Chicago, 1933–34. Married June 1942 to Allan Morrison, writer, editor (marr. dis. Aug. 1954). Served Amer. Red Cross, England, 1942–45. Relative in theatre: brother, William Attaway, writer. Member of AEA; SAG; AFTRA; Delta Sigma Theta. Address: 448 W. 54th St., New York, NY 10019, tel. (212) JU 6-2999.

Theatre. Miss Attaway made her N.Y.C. debut as Rheba in *You Can't Take It with You* (Booth, Dec. 14, 1936); subsequently played Catherine Greek in *The Grass Harp* (Circle in the Square, Apr. 27, 1953); Anna Hicks in *Mrs. Patterson* (National, Dec. 1, 1954); Mother in *Mister Johnson* (Martin Beck Th., Mar. 29, 1956); Essie in *The Egghead* (Ethel Barrymore Th., Oct. 9, 1957); and with the Repertory Th. of Lincoln Ctr., portrayed Carrie in *After the Fall* (ANTA Washington Square, Jan. 23, 1964) and in Repertory Th. productions at the Vivian Beaumont Th. appeared as one of the Women at the Scaffold in *Danton's Death* (Oct. 21, 1965), as Maro, the Nurse, and a Villager in *The Caucasian Chalk Circle* (Mar. 24, 1966), the First Neighbor in *Yerma* (Dec. 8, 1966), as standby for Beah Richards as Addie in *The Little Foxes* (Oct. 26, 1967), a Servant in *King Lear* (Nov. 7, 1968), and one of the Townspeople in *A Cry of Players* (Nov. 14, 1968).

Films. She made her debut as Moll in *The President's Lady* (20th-Fox, 1953); subsequently played in *The Young Don't Cry* (Col., 1957); *Raintree County* (MGM, 1957); and *Porgy and Bess* (Col., 1959).

Television. Miss Attaway has appeared on Harlem Detective (1953, 1955); High Tension (WOR, 1954); and Kraft Television Th. (NBC, 1955).

Awards. Miss Attaway received a citation from the Co-ordinating Council for Negro Performers for her contribution to the theatrical profession (1953).

Recreation. Tennis.

ATTLES, JOSEPH. Actor. b. Joseph Egbert Attles, Apr. 7, 1903, James Island, S.C., to Joseph Elias and Victoria Attles. Grad. Avery Normal Institute, Charleston, S.C., 1924. Professional training Harlem Conservatory (Vocal), N.Y.C. Member AEA; SAG. Address: 240 W. 65th St., New York, NY 10023, tel. (212) 874-4834.

Theatre. As a student, Mr. Attles belonged to a quartet that gave summer concerts at Congregational gatherings throughout South Carolina. In 1926, he sang with the Hall Johnson Choir in N.Y.C. (Lafayette Th.). His first professional work in the theatre was as a song and dance man and as the character of Porgy in a sketch in *Blackbirds of 1928* (Liberty Th., N.Y.C., May 9, 1928), in which he also toured (Moulin Rouge, Paris, 1929; London and British Isles, 1934–35). He played Sam and Bad Stacker Lee in *John Henry* (44 St. Th., Jan. 10, 1940); was Calcus in *La Belle Helene* (Westport, Conn., 1941); and understudied Cab Calloway as Sportin' Life in a revival of *Porgy and Bess* (Ziegfeld Th., N.Y.C., Mar. 10, 1953), in which he toured North and South America, Europe, Africa, and USSR (1952–56).

He played Akufo in *Kamina* (54 St. Th., Oct. 23, 1961); Chicken-Crow-for-Day in *Tambourines to Glory* (Little, Nov. 2, 1963); the Father in *Jerico-Jim Crow* (The Sanctuary, Jan. 12, 1964); Brother Green and John Henry in *Cabin in the Sky* (Greenwich Mews Th., Jan. 21, 1964); and appeared on a double-bill, as the Innkeeper in *The Exception and the Rule* and as the Exhorter in *The Prodigal Son* (Greenwich Mews Th., May 20, 1965).

He was Pious in *The Day of Absence* (St. Mark's Playhouse, Nov. 15, 1965); appeared in *King Lear* (Vivian Beaumont Th., Nov. 7, 1968); *A Cry of Players* (Vivian Beaumont Th., Nov. 14, 1968); was Josh in *The Reckoning* (St. Mark's Playhouse, Sept. 4, 1969); and appeared off-Bway in a one-man show, *The World of Paul Lawrence Dunbar* (1970). He was Sweets in *No Place to Be Somebody* (Hartford Stage Co., Hartford, Conn., Oct. 15, 1971); Pops in *The Duplex* (Forum Th., Mar. 9, 1972); Henry in *The Last of Mrs. Lincoln* (ANTA Th., Dec. 12, 1972); and toured for nine months (1975) as Checkers Clark in *Bubbling Brown Sugar* prior to N.Y.C. opening (ANTA Th., Mar. 2, 1976).

Films. Mr. Attles's motion pictures include *The Swimmer* (Col., 1968); *LBJ* (1969); *Pursuit of Happiness* (Col., 1971); *Going Home* (MGM, 1971); *The Gang That Couldn't Shoot Straight* (MGM, 1971); *Across 110th Street* (UA, 1972); *The Gambler* (Par., 1974); and *The Taking of Pelham 1-2-3* (UA, 1974).

Television. Mr. Attles appeared on television in *Weddin' Band* (ABC, 1974); *Bad Girl* (1974); *Love's Sweet Song* (1974); *Harriet Tubman* (1974); and *Beacon Hill* (CBS, 1975).

Night Clubs. Mr. Attles appeared at the Plantation Club (N.Y.C., 1929); Kit Kat Club (N.Y.C., 1938); the new Planatation Club (N.Y.C., 1938–39); Vecchia Roma (Rome, It., 1956); and Copacabana (N.Y.C., 1960).

Awards. In 1975, Mr. Attles was named a life member of the Actors Fund of America and received an award for distinguished achievement in the performing arts from the Uptown Musicians, N.Y.C.

ATWATER, EDITH. Actress. b. Apr. 22, 1911, Chicago, Ill., to Henry and Adeline (Pynchon) Atwater. Father, contracting engineer; public relations executive. Grad. Holmquist H.S., New Hope, Pa. 1928; attended Amer. Lab. Th., 1928–29; AADA, 1929–30. Married Nov. 23, 1940, to Hugh Marlowe, actor (marr. dis. 1944); married Aug. 20, 1950, to Joseph Allen, Jr. (marr. dis. 1952); married Mar. 10, 1962, to Kent Smith, actor. Member of AEA (council member 1940–53); AFTRA; SAG.

Theatre. Miss Atwater first appeared on stage as a Concubine in *This Queen of Sheba* (Atlantic City, N.J., 1929); subsequently played an Amazon in *The Black Crook* (Lyric, Hoboken, N.J., 1929); appeared in repertory with the Goodman Players (Chicago, Ill., 1930–31); in stock productions at the Woodstock (N.Y.) Playhouse (Summer 1929) and at the Cape May (N.J.) Playhouse (1931).

She made her Bway debut as Miss Jones in *Springtime for Henry* (Bijou Th., Dec. 9, 1931); followed by Helen Hunt in *Brittle Heaven* (Vanderbilt, Nov. 13, 1934); Beatrice Cenci in *This, Our Home* (58 St. Th., Dec. 10, 1935); Mrs. Dainty Fidget in *The Country Wife* (Henry Miller's Th., Dec. 1, 1936); succeeded (Feb. 1937) Claudia Margan as the Countess Larisch in *The Masque of Kings* (Shubert, Feb. 8, 1937); played Leonora Stubbs in *Susan and God* (Plymouth, Oct. 7, 1937), and on tour; at the Ridgeway Th. (White Plains, N.Y., Summer 1939), appeared in *Fashion, Goodbye Again* and *Kind Lady;* portrayed Maggie Cutler in *The Man Who Came to Dinner* (Music Box, N.Y.C., Oct. 16, 1939); Norah Galligan in *Retreat to Pleasure* (Belasco, Dec. 17, 1940); Julie Glynn in *Johnny on a Spot* (Plymouth, Jan. 8, 1942); Christina Landers in *Broken*

Journey (Henry Miller's Th., June 23, 1942); Helena Glory in *R.U.R.* (Ethel Barrymore Th., Dec. 3, 1942).

Miss Atwater appeared at Elitch Gardens (Denver, Colo., Summer 1944) in *Without Love, Theatre, Uncle Harry*, and *It's a Wise Child*; played Leno Richards in *Tomorrow the World* (Chicago, Ill., 1944–45); succeeded (Nov. 1946) Kay Francis as Mary Matthews in *State of the Union* (Hudson, N.Y.C., Nov. 14, 1945); toured as Alice Langon in *Deep Are the Roots* (Selwyn, Chicago, Ill., Feb. 1946); appeared as Marian Burnett in *Parlor Story* (Biltmore, N.Y.C., Mar. 4, 1947); Lee Kilpatrick in *The Gentleman from Athens* (Mansfield, Dec. 9, 1947); Miss Harrington in *Metropole* (Lyceum, Dec. 6, 1949); Goneril in *King Lear* (National, Dec. 25, 1950); and K. T. Pettigrew in *Flahooley* (Broadhurst, May 14, 1951).

She appeared as Agnes Carol in the national tour of *Time Out for Ginger* (opened Shubert, New Haven, Conn., Oct. 1, 1953); Mary Winter in a stock production of *Love Is a Two-Way Street* (Sharon Playhouse, Conn., Aug. 1956); toured cross-country with Albert Dekker in concert readings, *Two's a Company* (1955–56) and appeared in London (Arts Th., July 1959); in stock played the Woman in *The Inseparables* (Southern Tier Playhouse, Binghamton, N.Y., Sept. 1957); portrayed Countess Louise de Clerambard in *Clerambard* (Rooftop, N.Y.C., Nov. 7, 1957); Gertrude Bequpre in *Physicians for Fools* (Margo Jones Th., Dallas, Tex., Oct. 1959); succeeded Leora Dana (Dec. 13, 1962) as Alice Russell in the national tour of *The Best Man* (opened Hanna Th., Cleveland, Ohio, Sept. 18, 1961; closed Forrest Th., Philadelphia, Pa., Feb. 3, 1962); and played in *Ah, Wilderness!* (Pasadena Playhouse, Calif., 1966).

Films. Miss Atwater made her film debut in *We Went to College* (MGM, 1936); followed by roles in *Sweet Smell of Success* (UA, 1958); *Take Me to the Fair* (MGM, 1963); *Straight Jacket* (Col., 1963); and *Strange Bedfellows* (UU, 1964).

Television and Radio. Miss Atwater's television appearances include Eleventh Hour (NBC, 1963); Stoney Burke (WNEW, 1963); and Dr. Kildare (NBC, 1964).

AUBERJONOIS, RENE.

Actor. b. June 1, 1940, New York City, to Fernand and Laura (Murat) Auberjonois. Father, foreign correspondent. Grad. Carnegie Tech. (1963). Trained at Arena Stage (Washington, D.C.), 1962. Married 1963 to Judith Mihalyi; one daughter. Member of AEA; SAG.

Theatre. Mr. Auberjonois made his debut with the Washington (D.C.) Arena Stage; with the Lincoln Ctr. Rep. Co., played The Fool in *King Lear* (Vivian Beaumont Th., N.Y.C., Nov. 7, 1968); Marco in *Fire* (Longacre, N.Y.C., Jan. 28, 1969); appeared in *Chemin de Fer* (Mark Taper Forum, Los Angeles, 1969); played Sebastian Baye in *Coco* (Mark Hellinger Th., N.Y.C., Dec. 18, 1969); appeared in *The Good Doctor* (Eugene O'Neill Th., N.Y.C., Sept. 27, 1973); and, with ACT, played Earl in *The Ruling Class* (Geary, San Francisco, Mar. 18, 1975).

Films. He played Dago Red in *M*A*S*H* (20th-Fox, 1970); the Lecturer in *Brewster McCloud* (MGM, 1970); and Sheehan in *McCabe and Mrs. Miller* (WB, 1971).

Television. He has appeared on Mod Squad (ABC); and McMillan and Wife (NBC).

Awards. Mr. Auberjonois received the Antoinette Perry (Tony) Award for best supporting actor (1969) for his performance in *Coco*.

AUBUCHON, JACQUES.

Actor. b. Oct. 30, 1924, Fitchburg, Mass. Attended Assumption Coll., Worcester, Mass.; Amer. Th. Wing. Served U.S. Army, W.W. II, assigned to liaison duty with the French Army. Member of AEA; SAG.

Theatre. Mr. Aubuchon made his Bway debut as the replacement for James Westerfield in the role of the Sewer Man in *The Madwoman of Chaillot* (Belasco, N.Y.C., Dec. 27, 1948); replaced Kurt Kazner (Apr. 30, 1950) as Uncle Louis in *The Happy Time* (Plymouth, Jan. 24, 1950); repeated his performance as the Sewer Man in *The Madwoman of Chaillot* (NY City Ctr., June 13, 1950); again played Uncle Louis in *The Happy Time* (tour, opened Cass, Detroit, Oct. 22, 1951; closed Blackstone, Chicago, Jan. 1, 1952); played Mr. Bugfuz in *Mr. Pickwick* (Plymouth, N.Y.C., Sept. 12, 1952); again toured in *The Happy Time* (1953); played Ragueneau in *Cyrano de Bergerac* (NY City Ctr., Nov. 11, 1953); John Ankoritis in *The Shrike* (NY City Ctr., Nov. 25, 1953); and Stephen Spettigue in *Charley's Aunt* (NY City Ctr., Dec. 23, 1953). In 1967, he became a member of the company of the Center Th. Group (Mark Taper Forum, Los Angeles), appearing in various productions, including *In the Matter of J. Robert Oppenheimer* (world premiere, May 24, 1968); and *Chemin de Fer* (American premiere, June 5, 1969).

Films. Mr. Aubuchon has appeared in *Beneath the Twelve-Mile Reefe* (20th-Fox, 1953); *So Big* (WB, 1953); *Operation Manhunt* (1954); *The Silver Chalice* (WB, 1954); *The Scarlet Hour* (Par., 1956); *The Big Boodle* (UA, 1957); *The Way to the Gold* (20th-Fox, 1957); *Gun Glory* (MGM, 1957); *Short Cut to Hell* (Par., 1957); *Thunder Road* (UA, 1958); *The Shaggy Dog* (BV, 1959); *Twenty Plus Two* (AA, 1961); *Wild and Wonderful* (U, 1964); *McHale's Navy Joins the Air Force* (U, 1965); *The Love God?* (U, 1969); and *Doppelganger* (1969).

Television. Among Mr. Aubuchon's extensive television appearances are Zane Grey Th. (CBS); Walter Winchell File (ABC); You Are There (CBS); Hiram Holliday (NBC); Telephone Time (CBS); Studio One (CBS); *Cyrano de Bergerac* (Producers' Showcase, NBC); and Suspense (CBS).

AUDRÉ.

Costume designer. Attended Syracuse Univ.; Traphagen Sch. of Fashion. Address: 215 E. 64th St., New York, NY 10021, tel. (212) TE 8-0190.

Theatre. The Studio of Audré, operated by Miss Audré, has designed costumes for *Three to Make Ready* (Adelphi Th., N.Y.C., Mar. 7, 1946); *Topaze* (Morosco, Dec. 27, 1947); *Arms and the Girl* (46 St. Th., Feb. 2, 1950); *The Starcross Story* (Royale, Jan. 13, 1954); *The Wayward Saint* (Cort, Feb. 17, 1955); *A Roomful of Roses* (Playhouse, Oct. 17, 1955); *The Happiest Millionaire* (Lyceum, Nov. 20, 1956); *The Righteous Are Bold* (Holiday, Dec. 22, 1955); *Conversation Piece* (Barbizon-Plaza, Nov. 18, 1957); *Miss Isobel* (Royale, Dec. 26, 1957); the double bill of *Harlequinade* and *Electra* (Rita Allen Th., Feb. 13, 1959); *Put It in Writing* (Th. de Lys, May 13, 1963); *Once for the Asking* (Booth, Nov. 20, 1963); and *A Very Rich Woman* (Belasco Th., Sept. 30, 1965).

Audré designed costumes for some 100 musicals in ten years for the St. Louis Municipal Opera Co.; approximately 200 musicals in 18 years for the Kansas City (Mo.) Starlight Th.; was associate costume designer for the Metropolitan Opera Co.'s production of *Tosca* and *Andrea Chénier*.

Audré created the costumes for the industrial shows, Motorama (General Motors, 1953); for Oldsmobile, *Aida* (1963) and *Faust* (1964); and for Coca-Cola, Delco, and Collegiate Cap and Gown. She designed costumes for ice shows and for such night club revues as the Diamond Horseshoe (New York) and The Happy Medium (Chicago). The Studio of Audré currently designs uniforms/costumes for restaurants, motels, hotels, banks, and so on, worldwide.

Television. As department head of costume design for four years at ABC-TV, Audré designed for the Paul Whiteman Show, The Don Ameche Show, Celanese Th., Pulitzer Playhouse; and was under personal contract (5½ years) for the Perry Como Show (NBC); Mindy Carson Show (NBC); Helen O'Connell Show (CBS); Patti Page Show (ABC); Pat Boone Show (ABC); Patrice Munsel Show (ABC); Music Box Th. (ABC); and Andy Williams (ABC).

Published Works. Audré is the author of *To Take a Giant Step Up a Glass Ladder* (1964), a book for high-school and college students contemplating a career in costume design for the theatre.

AUERBACH, LEONARD.

Educator, stage manager.

Theatre. Mr. Auerbach became chairman, Theatre Arts Dept., SUNY (Stony Brook) in 1972. Mr. Auerbach was, at first, stage manager for *First Lady* (NY City Ctr., May 28, 1952); subsequently was stage manager for *Mrs. Patterson* (National, Dec. 1, 1954); *The Hot Corner* (John Golden Th., Jan. 25, 1956); *New Faces of '56* (Ethel Barrymore Th., June 14, 1956); production stage manager for *Holiday for Lovers* (Longacre, Feb. 14, 1957); *A Raisin in the Sun* (Ethel Barrymore Th., Mar. 11, 1959); *Semi-Detached* (Martin Beck Th., Mar. 10, 1960); stage manager for *Purlie Victorious* (Cort, Sept. 28, 1961); *The Heroine* (Lyceum, Feb. 19, 1963); and *The Dragon* (Phoenix, Apr. 19, 1963); production stage manager for *Nobody Loves an Albatross* (Lyceum, Dec. 19, 1963); *The Owl and the Pussycat* (ANTA, Nov. 18, 1964; also director for the nat'l co., 1965–66); the Moscow Art Theatre (NY City Ctr., Feb. 4–28, 1965); Théâtre National Populaire on tour (1965); *Nathan Weinstein, Mystic, Connecticut* (Brooks Atkinson Th., Feb. 25, 1966); *What Do You Really Know About Your Husband?* (pre-Bway tryout, Shubert Th., New Haven, Conn., Mar. 9–11, 1967); *The Ninety-Day Mistress* (Biltmore, Nov. 6, 1967); *Does a Tiger Wear a Necktie?* (Belasco Th., Mar. 29, 1969); *A Teaspoon Every Four Hours* (ANTA, June 14, 1969); and *Purlie* (Broadway, Mar. 15, 1970).

AUGUSTINE, LARRY D.

Educator, producer. b. Larry Dean Augustine, Sept. 4, 1940, Meyersdale, Penn. Educated Meyersdale Joint High School; Potomac State College (1958–60); West Virginia Univ. (1960–64; B.A., M.A.). Member of ATA; IATSE; American Forensics Assn. (natl. council, 1968–72); SCA; SCA of Penn.; Debating Assn. of Penn. Colleges (pres., 1971–72); Eastern Forensics Assn. (pres., 1968–72); Alpha Psi Omega; Delta Sigma Rho—Tau Kappa Alpha. Address: (home) 612 South Front St., Selinsgrove, PA 17870, tel. (717) 373-4430; (bus.) Susquehanna Univ., Selinsgrove, PA 17870, tel. (717) 374-2345.

Mr. Augustine became instructor in theatre arts, West Virginia Institute of Technology, Montgomery, W.Va., in 1964. He was instructor in communication, Pennsylvania State Univ., Uniontown, Pa., in 1965 and instructor in speech and theatre arts, West Liberty (W.Va.) State College and technical director, West Virginia Univ., Morgantown, in 1965–66. In 1966, he became assistant professor of speech, Susquehanna Univ., Selinsgrove, Pa., and in 1969 assistant professor of communication and theatre arts and acting chairman of the department. He became chairman of the Dept. of Communication and Theatre Arts in 1970 and associate professor in 1971. In addition, he has been producer of Susquehanna Univ. Theatre (1969–to date), director of forensics (1966–to date), and advisor (1968–69) and general manager (1969–to date) of radio station WQSU.

Mr. Augustine became producer and general manager with the West Virginia Historical Drama Association, Beckley, W.Va. in 1972. Previously, he was property master (1961), lighting master electrician (1962), lighting designer (1966–70), technical supervisor (1967), production supervisor and assistant to the general manager (1967–68), assistant to the producer (1970), and associate producer (1971). During his occupancy of those posts, Mr. Augustine helped mount such productions of the association as *Honey in the Rock* and *The Hatfields and the McCoys* (Cliffside Amphitheatre, Beckley, W.Va.). Mr. Augustine was also stage manager, technical director, and co-captain of the West Virginia Dept. of Natural Resources showboat "Rhododendron" (Charleston, W.Va., 1964–65); stage manager for Pennsylvania State Univ., summer of professional theatre (Pavillion Th., Univ. Park, Pa., 1965) and theatre manager and consultant to the producer for the Smoky Mountain Passion Play (Maryville-Alcoa, Tenn., 1974).

Published Works. Mr. Augustine is author of "The Physical Facilities and Architectural Design of the Edwin Booth Theatre in New York City" (1964).

Awards. Mr. Augustine was named outstanding student in theatre at West Va. Univ. (1964).

Recreation. Music, reading, cooking.

AUMONT, JEAN PIERRE. Actor, playwright. b. Jan. 5, 1913, Paris, France. Married July 13, 1943, to Maria Montez, actress (dec. Sept. 7, 1951); one daughter; married Mar. 27, 1956, to Marisa Pavan, actress; two sons. Served WW II, Free French Forces; awarded Legion of Honor. Member of AEA; SAG; AFTRA.

Theatre. M. Aumont made his stage debut as Oedipus in Jean Cocteau's *La machine infernale* (Comédie Champs-Elysées, Paris, Fr. Apr. 10, 1934); subsequently appeared in *Le coeur* (Gymnase, 1937); and as Pelléas in *Pelléas et Mèlisande* (Th. des Champs-Elysées, 1938); Orlando in *As You Like It* (Th. des Champs-Elysées, 1939).

He made his US debut as Pierre in a tour of *Rose Burke* (Curran Th., San Francisco, Calif., Jan. 19, 1942); performed as Pierre Renault in his own play, *L'Empereur de Chine* (Th. des Mathurins, Paris, Jan. 1948); Otto in a stock production of *Design for Living* (Westport Country Playhouse, Conn., 1948); Pierre Renault in the Philip Barry adaptation of *L'Empereur de Chine*, entitled *My Name Is Aquilon* (Lyceum, N.Y.C., Feb. 9, 1949), originally entitled *Figure of a Girl* in the pre-Bway tour.

He appeared as Mark Antony in *Julius Caesar*, performed in the Roman arenas of Arles, France (1953); both Henri and Pierre Belcourt in *The Heavenly Twins* (Booth, N.Y.C., Nov. 4, 1955); Jupiter in *Amphitryon 38* (Comédie des Champs-Elysées, Paris, 1957); played in *Mon pére avait raison* (Th. de la Madeleine, 1960); as Farou in *Second String* (Eugene O'Neill Th., N.Y.C., Apr. 13, 1960); the title role in *The Affairs of Anatol* (Boston Arts Festival, Mass., July 31, 1961); in *Flora* (Th. des Variétés, Paris, 1962); and as Mikail in *Tovarich* (Broadway, N.Y.C., Mar. 18, 1963), in which he also toured (Summer 1964). He played Gaston Lachaille in *Gigi* (Community Playhouse, Atlanta, Ga., Jan. 26, 1965) and toured in the production (Summer 1965); was Emile de Becque in *South Pacific* (Meadowbrook Dinner Th., Cedar Grove, N.J., Feb. 25, 1965); played Paul in *Madame Mousse*, which he also wrote (pre-Bway: Westport Country Playhouse, Conn., Aug. 16, 1965); played Von Berg in *Incident at Vichy* (Huntington Hartford Th., Los Angeles, Calif., Oct. 25, 1965); was in *Jacques Brel Is Alive and Well and Living in Paris* (Playhouse on the Mall, Paramus, N.J., June 6, 1972); Jacques Casanova in a revival of *Camino Real* (Vivian Beaumont Th., N.Y.C., Jan. 8, 1970); and Dag Hammarskjold in *Murderous Angels* (Playhouse, N.Y.C., Dec. 20, 1971) and in the French version, *Les Anges meurtriers* (Th. National Populaire, May 1971).

M. Aumont is the author of *L'Ile heureuse* (Th. Edouard VII, Paris, Jan. 23, 1951); *Un beau dimanche* (Th. de la Michodière, June 25, 1952), based on the novel, *Rencontre*, by Pierre Corthomas; *Ange le bienheureux* (Th. Municipal, Nice, Dec. 21, 1956); *Farfada* (Comédie Wagram, Paris, Nov. 12, 1957), and *Lucy Crown*, adapted from Irwin Shaw's novel of the same name (Th. de Paris, Sept. 22, 1958).

Films. He made his debut as Eric in *Lac aux dames* (1936); followed by *L'Equipage* (1936); *Cheri-Bibi* (1937); *Maria Chapdelaine* (1937); *Drôle de drame* (1938); *Hôtel du Nord* (1938); *Le Deserteur* (1939); *Assignment in Brittany* (MGM, 1943); *The Cross of Lorraine* (MGM, 1943); *Scherezade* (U, 1945); *Atlantis* (1945); *Heartbeat* (RKO, 1946); *Lili* (MGM, 1953); *Charge of the Lancers* (Col., 1954); *Hilda Crane* (20th-Fox, 1956); *The Seventh Sin* (MGM, 1957); *Royal Affairs in Versailles* (Times, 1957); *L'Homme de joie* (France, 1959); *John Paul Jones* (WB, 1959); *Domenica d'estate* (Italy, 1961); *The Devil at 4 O'Clock* (Col., 1961); *The Blonde of Buenos Aires* (Argentina, 1962); *The Horse without a Head* (Buena Vista, 1962); *Les sept péchés capitaux* (France, 1960), released in the US as *7 Capital Sins* (Embassy, 1962); *Castle Keep* (Col., 1969); *The Happy Hooker* (Cannon, 1975); and *Mahogany* (Par., 1975).

Television. His television appearances include *No Time for Comedy* (1951); *Arms and the Man* (1952); *Crime and Punishment* (1953); the Perry Como Show (NBC, 1954); Sid Caesar Show (CBS, 1954); Nanette Fabray Show (1959); *Intermezzo* (1960); April in Paris Ball (1962); *The Plague* (1962); and The Patty Duke Show (1962).

He was in *The Horse Without a Head* (Walt Disney's World, NBC, June 14 and 21, 1964); the *Aumont and Pavan* special (ABC, Dec. 11, 1965); *Integrity* (Mystery Th., Ind., Sept. 4, 1966); and appeared on various talk and variety shows, including Merv Griffin (Ind., 1966–67); Hollywood Palace (ABC, 1966–67); Center Stage (Ind., 1966–67); Dateline: Hollywood (ABC, 1967–68); and Mike Douglas (Ind., 1967–68).

Night Clubs. M. Aumont appeared with his wife, Marisa Pavan, in a supper club act (Drake Hotel, Chicago, Ill., May 1965; Nov. 1966; Persian Room, Plaza Hotel, N.Y.C., July 1966; Princess Hotel, Hamilton, Bermuda, Apr. 1967).

Awards. M. Aumont was nominated by the *Variety* N.Y. Drama Critics Poll for his performance as Mikail in *Tovarich* (1963).

Recreation. Swimming, horseback riding.

AURTHUR, ROBERT ALAN. Playwright, producer. b. June 10, 1922, New York City, to William and Margaret (Brock) Aurthur. Father, painter; mother, school principal. Grad. Freeport H.S., N.Y., 1938; Univ. of Pennsylvania, B.A. 1942. Married Mar. 8, 1947, to Virginia Lea; two sons, one daughter. Served USMC, infantry, 1942–46, PTO; rank, 1st Lt. Member of WGA, East; Dramatists Guild; ALA.

Pre-Theatre. Novelist, short-story writer.

Theatre. Mr. Aurthur's first play to be produced on Bway was *A Very Special Baby* (Playhouse Th., Nov. 14, 1956); he subsequently wrote the libretto for *Kwamina* (54 St. Th., Oct. 23, 1961); and the play *Carry Me Back to Morningside Heights* (John Golden Th., Feb. 27, 1968).

Films. He wrote the screenplay for *Edge of the City*, which he also co-produced (MGM, 1957); adapted *Warlock* (20th-Fox, 1959) and *Lilith* (Col., 1964); and wrote the screenplays for *Grand Prix* (MGM, 1966) and *For Love of Ivy* (Cinerama, 1968).

Television. Mr. Aurthur produced and wrote plays for the Philco Television Playhouse (NBC), including *Birth of the Movies* (Apr. 1951), *The Sisters* (Dec. 1951), *The Basket Weaver* (Apr. 1952), *A Man's Game* (June 1952), *The Witness* (Aug. 1952), *The Darkness Below* (Nov. 1952), *The Winter of the Dog* (Nov. 1952), *Medal in the Family* (Feb. 1953), *A Long Way Home* (Mar. 1953), *The Baby* (Sept. 1953), *Spring Reunion* (Apr. 1954), *Shadow of the Champ* (May 1954), *Man on a Mountaintop* (Sept. 1954), *A Man Is Ten Feet Tall* (Sept. 1955), and an adaptation of *Darkness at Noon* (May 1955).

He produced, with Fred Coe, and wrote, with David Shaw, the series Bonino (CBS, Sept.–Dec. 1953); was writer and script editor for the Mr. Peepers series (NBC, 1953–54); wrote *Tale of the Comet* (Studio One, CBS, Mar. 1957); *A Sound of Different Drummers* (Playhouse 90, CBS, Sept. 1957), and *The Thundering Wave* (CBS, Dec. 1957).

He produced for the Sunday Showcase series (NBC) *What Makes Sammy Run?* (Sept. 1959), *People Kill People Sometimes* (Sept. 1959), *Murder of the Androids* (Oct. 1959), *The Invincible Mr. Gore* (Nov. 1959), *The Margaret Bourke-White Story* (Dec. 1959), *One Loud Clear Voice* (Jan. 1960), *The American* (Mar. 1960), *Turn the Key Deftly* (Mar. 1960), *The Sacco-Vanzetti Story* (June 1960), *John Brown's Raid* (Oct. 1960), *The Guiliano Story* (Dec. 1960).

As vice-president of Talent Associates, Ltd.-Paramount (1961–62), he produced a pilot film of *The Truman Years*, and has subsequently produced television series for United Artists-TV.

Published Works. He wrote *The History of the 3rd Marine Division Infantry* (1947); a novel, *The Glorification of Al Toolum* (1952); and short stories and articles in *The New Yorker, Harpers, Colliers, The Saturday Evening Post,* and *Esquire.*.

Awards. Mr. Aurthur's television play *Man on a Mountaintop* received the Sylvania Award as best original teleplay of 1954; his play *A Man Is Ten Feet Tall*, won a Sylvania Award (1955), the National Conference of Christians and Jews Brotherhood Award (1955), and a NATAS (Emmy) Award nomination for best original teleplay writing (1955). Philco Television Playhouse, which he produced, received NATAS awards (1950, 1954), as well as *The Sacco-Vanzetti Story*, which he produced for Sunday Showcase (1961).

AUSTIN, LYN. Producer. b. Evelyn Page Austin, Jan. 14, 1922, Glen Ridge, N.J., to Chellis A. and Edna (Pope) Austin. Father, banker. Grad. Milton (Mass.) Acad., 1940; Vassar Coll., B.A. 1944; Columbia Univ., M.A. (Dramatic Arts) 1948. Address: 112 E. 55th St., New York, NY 10022, tel. (212) 371-9610.

Pre-Theatre. Teacher.

Theatre. Miss Austin was producer, with Thomas Noyes, of *Take a Giant Step* (Lyceum Th., N.Y.C., Sept. 24, 1953); subsequently was associate to Roger L. Stevens for *Tea and Sympathy* (Ethel Barrymore Th., Sept. 30, 1953); producer, with Thomas Noyes, and in association with Robert Radnitz and Robert Sagalyn, of *The Frogs of Spring* (Broadhurst, Oct. 20, 1953); associate producer of *In the Summer House* (Playhouse Dec. 29, 1953); producer, with Thomas Noyes, of the summer tryout of *Blue Denim* (Westport Country Playhouse, Conn., July 18, 1955); and producer, with Thomas Noyes and The Producers Theatre, of *Joyce Grenfell Requests the Pleasure. . .* (Bijou, N.Y.C., Oct. 10, 1955).

Miss Austin produced the first two plays, for Roger L. Stevens' New Directors' Series, *The Terrible Swift Sword* (Phoenix, Nov. 15, 1955) and *The Adding Machine* (Phoenix, Feb. 9, 1956); produced, with Thomas Noyes, and in association with Anderson Lawler, *Copper and Brass* (Martin Beck Th., Oct. 17, 1957); was associate producer of *The Best Man* (Morosco, Mar. 31, 1960); *Rosemary and the Alligators* (York Playhouse, Nov. 14, 1960); *Mary, Mary* (Helen Hayes Th., Mar. 8, 1961); *A Far Country* (Music Box, Apr. 4, 1961); *Blood, Sweat and Stanley Poole* (Morosco, Oct. 5, 1961); *Romulus* (Music Box, Jan. 10, 1962); *Oh Dad, Poor Dad, Mama's Hung You in the Closet and I'm Feelin' So Sad* (Phoenix, Feb. 26, 1962); *Calculated Risk* (Ambassador, Oct. 21, 1963); *Tiger, Tiger Burning Bright* (Booth, Dec. 22, 1962); *The Milk Train Doesn't Stop Here Anymore* (Morosco, Jan. 16, 1963); *The Private Ear and the Public Eye* (Morosco, Oct. 9, 1963); and *The Chinese Prime Minister* (Royale, Jan. 2, 1964).

Miss Austin was also an associate producer for *The Last Analysis* (Belasco Th., Oct. 1, 1964); *Beekman Place* (Morosco, Oct. 7, 1964); *Poor Richard* (Helen Hayes Th., Dec. 2, 1964); producer of *UTBU* (Helen Hayes Th., Jan. 4, 1966); one of the producers of *The Coop* (Actors Playhouse, Mar. 1, 1966); *Stephen D* (E. 74 St. Th., Sept. 24, 1967); *The Niggerlovers* (Orpheum, Oct. 1, 1967); *The Exercise* (John Golden Th., Apr. 24, 1968); *Collision Course* (Cafe Au Go Go, May 8, 1968); *Adaptation* and *Next* (Greenwich Mews, Feb 10, 1969); *Indians* (Brooks Atkinson Th., Oct. 13, 1969); and the Manhattan Project production of *Alice in Wonderland* (The Extension, Oct. 8, 1970; revived Performing Garage, Mar. 1, 1972).

She was also a producer of *Doctor Selavy's Magic Theatre* (Mercer-O'Casey Th., Nov. 23, 1972); a revival of the opera *The Mother of Us All* (Guggenheim Museum, Nov. 26, 1972); one of the producers for Lenox Arts Center/Music Theatre Performing Group of *Mourning Pictures* (Lyceum, Nov. 10, 1974); and a producer of *Hotel for Criminals* (Exchange Th., Dec. 30, 1974). Miss Austin has also been producer for The Manhattan Project and produced, under a guest residency of the NY Shakespeare Festival (Public Th.), their productions of *The Sea Gull* (Jan. 8, 1975), *Our Late Night* (Jan. 9, 1975), another revival of *Alice in Wonderland* (Apr. 15, 1975), and *Endgame* (Apr. 29, 1975). She has been in addition operator of The Loft Th., an off-off Bway showcase.

AXELROD, GEORGE. Playwright, director, producer, writer. b. June 9, 1922, New York City, to Herman and Beatrice (Carpenter) Axelrod. Married Feb. 28, 1942, to Gloria Washburn, actress (marr. dis. June 1954); two sons; married Oct. 1954 to Joan Stanton; one daughter. Served WW II, US Army Signal Corps. Member of Dramatists Guild; ALA; SWG.

Theatre. Mr. Axelrod was, at first, assistant stage manager for *Kind Lady* (Playhouse, N.Y.C., Sept. 3, 1940); subsequently contributed sketches to *Small Wonder* (Coronet, Sept. 15, 1948); wrote *The Seven Year Itch* (Fulton, Nov. 20, 1952); wrote and directed *Will Success Spoil Rock Hunter?* (Belasco, Oct. 13, 1955); produced, with Clinton Wilder, *Visit to a Small Planet* (Booth, Feb. 7, 1957); directed *Once More, With Feeling* (National, Oct. 21, 1958); wrote and directed *Goodbye, Charlie* (Lyceum, Dec. 16, 1959); directed *The Star-Spangled Girl* (Plymouth Th., Dec. 21, 1966).

Films. He was scenarist for *Phffft* (Col., 1954); co-adapted *The Seven Year Itch* (20th-Fox, 1955); was scenarist for *Bus Stop* (20th-Fox, 1956); *The Catbird Seat;* and *Breakfast at Tiffany's* (Par., 1961); scenarist and producer, with John Frankenheimer, of *The Manchurian Candidate* (UA, 1962); and scenarist and co-producer of *Paris When It Sizzles* (Par., 1964). *Goodbye Charlie* (20th-Fox, 1964) was based on Mr. Axelrod's play of the same title. Mr. Axelrod was author of the screenplay for and one of the producers of *How To Murder Your Wife* (UA, 1965); he wrote, with Larry H. Johnson, *Lord Love a Duck* (UA, 1966), which he also produced and directed; and wrote, produced, and directed *The Secret Life of an American Wife* (20th-Fox, 1968).

Television and Radio. Mr. Axelrod was a writer for the radio program, Midnight in Manhattan (1940); and wrote comedy material for Grand Ole Opry (NBC, 1950–52).

For television, he has written for Celebrity Time (CBS, 1950).

Night Clubs. He was co-author of *All About Love* (Versailles, N.Y.C., 1951).

Published Works. Mr. Axelrod wrote *Beggar's Choice* (1947), *Blackmailer,* (1952), and *Where Am I Now When I Need Me?* (1971).

AYERS, DAVID H. Executive, director, educator. b. David Hugh Ayers, Feb. 26, 1924, Cincinnati, Ohio, to Walter E. and Thelma (Runyan) Ayers. Father, farmer. Attended Union Township H.S., West Chester, Ohio, 1939–42; Ohio State Univ., 1942–43; Miami Univ., Oxford, Ohio, 1946–47; Hedgerow Th. Sch., Philadelphia, Pa., 1947 (four months); grad. Ohio State Univ., B.A. 1949; M.A. 1951; Ph.D. 1969. Married Dec. 30, 1948, to Jean Yeager; one son, three daughters. Served USN and Fleet Marine Force, 1943–46; rank, Pharmacist's Mate 2/c. Member of AETA; NATAS. Address: (home) 178 Glencoe Rd., Columbus, OH 43214, tel. (614) 267-7079; (bus.) American Playwrights Theatre, 1849 Cannon Dr., Columbus, OH 43210, tel. (614) 422-4205.

Since Dec. 1963, Mr. Ayers has been executive director of the American Playwrights Theatre at Ohio State Univ.

At educational station WOSU in Columbus, Ohio, he was radio and television producer, director and program director (Nov. 1951–July 1958) and program director (July 1958–Dec. 1963). He produced the National Educational Television and Radio Center series, Essentials of Freedom, won the George Washington Freedom Foundation Award, and was producer-director of the children's series, Sports Studio, for NETRC.

AYLMER, FELIX. Actor, writer. b. Felix Edward Alymer-Jones, Feb. 21, 1889, Corsham, Wiltshire, England, to Thomas Edward and Lilian (Cookworthy) Aylmer-Jones. Father, military officer (Lt. Col., R.E.); mother, music instructor. Attended Magdalen Coll., Oxford, England, 1901–08; grad. Exeter Coll., Oxford, B.A. 1911; studied acting with Rosina Filippi, London, two years. Married 1915 to Cecily Byrne, actress; two sons, one daughter. Served RNVR, 1916–19; rank, Lt. Relative in theatre: daughter, Jennifer. Member of British AEA (pres., 1949–69); RADA (pres., 1955–56); Garrick Club; Green Room Club; Beefsteak Club.

Theatre. Mr. Aylmer made his N.Y.C. debut as General Canynge in *Loyalties* (Gaiety Th., Sept. 22, 1922); followed by Lord Elton in *The Last of Mrs. Cheney* (Fulton, Nov. 9, 1925); Walter Harrowby in *The Flashing Stream* (Biltmore, Apr. 10, 1939), which he had previously played in London (see below); and Sir Audley-Marriott in *The Prescott Proposals* (Broadhurst, Dec. 16, 1953).

He made his stage debut as the Italian in *Cook's Man* (Coliseum, London, Mar. 1911); subsequently appeared in minor roles in Fred Terry and Sir Herbert Tree's productions (London, 1911); and performed in *The Winter's Tale* (Savoy, Sept. 21, 1912); and *Twelfth Night* (Savoy, Nov. 15, 1912). From 1913–16, he played the following roles with the Birmingham (England) Repertory Co.: Gurville in *The Tragedy of Man,* Kira in *The Faithful,* Orsino and Malvolio in *Twelfth Night,* Prospero in *The Tempest,* Bassanio in *The Merchant of Venice,* Jaques in *As You Like It,* Morell in *Candida,* Valentine and Bohun in *You Never Can Tell,* Sergius in *Arms and the Man,* Inca in *The Inca of Perusalem,* Lord Illingworth in *A Woman of Importance,* and Henry in *The Return of the Prodigal.*

He appeared as the Messenger in *Judith* (Kingsway, London, Apr. 1919); Sir Moran Tremayne in *Saint George and the Dragons* (Kingsway, June 1919); Paul de Musset in *Madame Sand* (Duke of York's, June 1919); toured as Dalman in *The Choice* (Fall, 1920); and played William Seward in *Abraham Lincoln* (Lyceum, London, July 6, 1921).

Mr. Aylmer appeared in a series of Shaw revivals (Everyman Th., London) as Bohun in *You Never Can Tell* (Jan. 24, 1921); Morell in *Candida* (Feb. 7, 1921); Ridgeon in *The Doctor's Dilemma,* the Husband in *How He Lied to Her Husband* (Mar. 14, 1921); the Sheriff in *The Shewing-Up of Blanco Posnet* (Mar. 14, 1921); Cusins in *Major Barbara* (Apr. 18, 1921); and Hector in *Man and Superman* (May 23, 1921). He played Capt. Jonathan Taliboys in *Old Jig* (Strand, Jan. 19, 1922); the Bishop in *Getting Married* (Everyman, Mar. 27, 1922); Summerhays in *Misalliance* (Everyman, Apr. 18, 1922); and Sir Mortimer Isleworth in *The Green Cord* (Royalty, June 2, 1922).

Following his US appearance in *Loyalties* (see above), played the title role in *Robert E. Lee* (Regent, London, June 20, 1923); succeeded (Oct. 1923) Allan Jeayes as Devizes in *The Will* and as George Miles in *The Likes of Her* (St. Martin's, Aug. 15, 1923); played Conan in *Gruach* (St. Martin's, Jan. 20, 1924); Paul Revere and Samenda in *The Forest* (St. Martin's, Mar. 6, 1924); Lord Leonard Alcar in *The Great Adventure* (Haymarket, June 5, 1924); Lord Summerhays in *Misalliance* (Everyman, Oct. 27, 1924); Dr. Paramore in *The Philanderer* (Everyman, Dec. 26, 1924); and Colonel Roland in *The Show* (St. Martin's, July 1, 1925).

After appearing in the N.Y.C. production of *The Last of Mrs. Cheney* (see above), he played Sir Colenso Ridgeon in *The Doctor's Dilemma* (Kingsway, London, Nov. 17, 1926); William Goodman in *The Terror* (Lyceum, May 11, 1927); Ambrose Godolphin in *Bird in Hand* (Royalty, Apr. 18, 1928); Sir John Ames in *The Garey Hotel Case* (Court, Apr. 1929); Councillor Weissensee in *Jew Süss* (Duke of York's, Sept. 19, 1929); Mr. Butler in *Badger's Green* (Prince of Wales's, Nov. 10, 1930); and Robert Woking in *The Man Who Kissed His Wife* (Prince of Wales's, Nov. 10, 1930).

He appeared as Count Sturm in *The Rocklitz* (Duke of York's, Feb. 4, 1931); toured as Michael Adye in *The Ware Case* (Aug.–Dec. 1931); played Lord Duncaster in *The Nelson Touch* (St. Martin's, Dec. 16, 1931); Evelyn Arthur in *Wings Over Europe* (Globe, Apr. 27, 1932); the Specialist in *The Scion* (Embassy, July 11, 1932); Sherlock Holmes in *The Holmeses of Baker Street* (Lyric, Feb. 15, 1933); Baron de Courlay in *Rose Giralda* ("Q," Apr. 24, 1933); Frederic Wilder in *Strife* (Little, May 15, 1933); Hannenfeldt in *Before Sunset* (Shaftesbury, Sept. 28, 1933); William Goodman in *The Terror* (Lyceum, Nov. 10, 1933); Mr. Voysey in *The Voysey Inheritance* (Sadler's Wells, May 3, 1934); Lord James Stuart in *Queen of Scots* (New, June 8, 1935); and the Earl of Warwick in *Saint Joan* (Old Vic, Nov. 26, 1935).

He appeared as Dr. Porthal in *Mesmer* (King's, Glasgow, Scotland, May 6, 1935); Dr. Van Lesser in *Out of the Dark* (Ambassadors', London, Feb. 12, 1936); Sir Edward Pakenham in *Heroes Don't Care* (St. Martin's, June 10, 1936); Cyril Horsham in *Waste* (Westminster, Dec. 1, 1936); Rev. Richard Jarrow in *Yes and No* (Ambassadors', Oct. 26, 1937); Professor Sigelius in *Power and Glory* (Savoy, Apr. 8, 1938); the Rt. Hon. Walter Harrowby in *The Flashing Stream* (Lyric, Sept. 1, 1938), and repeated the latter role (Biltmore, N.Y.C., Apr. 10, 1939).

He played Rev. Josiah Crawley in *Scandal at Barchester* (Lyric, London, Oct. 5, 1944); Sir Joseph Pitts in *Daphne Laureola* (Wyndham's, Mar. 23, 1949); Henry Fanshaw Beringer in *First Person Singular* (Duke of York's, Feb. 20, 1952); appeared in *The Prescott Proposals* (see above); Sir Rowland Delahaye in *Spider's Web* (Savoy, London, Dec. 13, 1954); and the Judge in *The Chalk Garden* (Haymarket, Apr. 12, 1956).

Films. Mr. Aylmer made his first appearance as the Public Prosecutor in *The Temporary Widow* (UFA, 1930); subsequently appeared in *Tudor Rose; Victoria the Great* (RKO, 1937); *This Demi-Paradise* (Two Cities Films, 1942); *Mr. Emmanuel* (UA, 1945); *Henry V* (UA, 1946); *The Ghosts of Berkeley Square* (British Natl., 1946); *Hamlet* (U, 1948); *Prince of Foxes* (20th-Fox, 1949); *Quo Vadis* (MGM, 1951); *The Master of Ballantrae* (WB, 1953); *Angel Who Pawned Her Harp* (1953); *Knights of the Round Table* (MGM, 1953); *Anastasia* (20th-Fox, 1956); *Saint Joan* (UA, 1957); *Captain Dreyfus* (MGM, 1957); *Separate Tables* (UA, 1958); *The Doctor's Dilemma* (MGM, 1958); *The Mummy* (U, 1959); *From the Terrace* (20th-Fox, 1960); *Exodus* (UA, 1960); *Never Take Sweets from a Stranger* (Sutton, 1961); *The Boys* (WB, 1962); *Becket* (Par., 1964); *The Chalk Garden* (MGM, 1964); and *Masquerade* (UA, 1965).

Television. He made his first appearance as Lord Leonard Alcar in *The Great Adventure* (BBC, London, 1938); then appeared as Dr. Dotheright in *The Golden Cuckoo* (A.R., 1956); and the Judge in *Ten Little Niggers* (A.R., 1959).

He played Sir Howard Hallam in *Captain Brassbound's Conversion* (Hallmark Hall of Fame, NBC, US, 1960); and also for Hallmark Hall of Fame, (NBC, 1961), appeared as Melbourne in *Victoria Regina* and the Doctor in *Macbeth;* played General Canynge in *Loyalties* (BBC, London, 1962); Edwin St. Clair in *The Round Dozen* (A.R., 1962); the Master in *The Affair* (BBC, 1962); Sir Peter Teazle in the BBC production of *The School for Scandal* (June 3, 1964); Mr. Quilt in *The Walrus and the Carpenter* (BBC, 1964–65); David Anson in *A Day by the Sea* (BBC-2, Dec. 10, 1964); and he appeared in *Nelson* (Play of the Week, ATV, Mar. 1966); and as the Prior in *Oh, Brother!* (1968–69).

Published Works. He is the author of *Dickens Incognito* (1959); and *The Drood Case* (1964).

Awards. Mr. Aylmer received the Order of the British Empire (O.B.E.) in the Birthday Honours (1950) and was Knighted in the Birthday Honours (1965).

B

BACALL, LAUREN. Actress. b. Betty Joan Perske, Sept. 16, 1924, New York City, to William and Natalie (Bacall) Perske. Grad. Julia Richman H.S., N.Y.C., 1940; grad. AADA, 1941. Married May 21, 1945, to Humphrey Bogart, actor (dec. Jan. 14, 1957); one son, one daughter; married July 4, 1961, to Jason Robards, Jr., actor (marr. dis. Sept. 10, 1969); one son. Member of SAG; AFTRA; AEA.

Pre-Theatre. Model.

Theatre. Miss Bacall made her N.Y.C. debut as a walk-on in *Johnny 2 × 4* (Longacre Th., Mar. 16, 1942); played the ingenue in the pre-Bway tryout of *Franklin Street* (opened Wilmington, Del.; closed Washington, D.C., Fall 1942); subsequently played Charlie in *Goodbye, Charlie* (Lyceum, N.Y.C., Dec. 16, 1959); Stephanie in *Cactus Flower* (Royale, Dec. 8, 1965); and Margo Channing in *Applause* (Palace, Mar. 30, 1970), which she repeated on tour (opened Toronto, Canada, Nov. 29, 1971) and in the English company (London, Nov. 16, 1972).

Films. Miss Bacall made her film debut in *To Have and Have Not* (WB, 1944); followed by *Confidential Agent* (WB, 1945); *The Big Sleep* (WB, 1946); *Dark Passage* (WB, 1947); *Key Largo* (WB, 1948); *Young Man with a Horn* (WB, 1950); *Bright Leaf* (WB, 1950); *How To Marry a Millionaire* (20th-Fox, 1953); *A Woman's World* (20th-Fox, 1954); *Blood Alley* (WB, 1955); *The Cobweb* (MGM, 1955); *Written on the Wind* (U, 1956); *Designing Woman* (MGM, 1957); *Gift of Love* (20th-Fox, 1958); *Flame Over India* (Rank, 1960); *Shock Treatment* (20th-Fox, 1964); *Sex and the Single Girl* (WB, 1964); *Harper* (WB, 1966); and *Murder on the Orient Express* (Par., 1974).

Television and Radio. She performed on dramatic radio shows (WNEW, 1942), and was the star of Bold Venture for one year.

On television, she appeared in *The Petrified Forest* (Producer's Showcase, NBC, 1955); *Blithe Spirit* (Hallmark Hall of Fame, NBC, 1956); on Dupont Show of the Month (NBC, 1963); Dr. Kildare (NBC, 1963); Stage 67 (ABC, Feb. 1967); *Applause* (CBS, Mar. 15, 1973).

Awards. She received the Award for Achievement from the American Academy of Dramatic Arts (1963) and a medallion of recognition from *Harper's Bazaar* magazine for her contribution to international fashion (July 1966). For her performance in *Applause,* she won the *Variety* NY Drama Critics Poll (1969–70) as best female lead in a musical and received the Drama Desk and Antoinette Perry (Tony) awards.

Recreation. Tennis, swimming, needlepoint.

BACHARACH, BURT. Composer, conductor, pianist, performer. b. May 12, 1929 Kansas City, Mo., to Bert and Irma (Freeman) Bacharach. Father, newspaper columnist; mother, painter and singer. Educ. Forest Hills (N.Y.) H.S.; McGill Univ., Montreal, Canada; New School for Social Research, N.Y.C. (composition with Darius Milhaud); Music Acad. West, Santa Barbara, Calif. (composition with Henry Cowell). US Army, 1950–52. Married to Paula Stewart (marr. dis.); married to Angie Dickinson, actress; one daughter. Address: 166 E. 61st St., New York, NY 10021.

Theatre. Mr. Bacharach composed arrangements and conducted the orchestra for Marlene Dietrich's one-woman show *Marlene Dietrich* (Lunt-Fontanne Th., Nov. 18, 1967); did arrangements for a return engagement of the same (Mark Hellinger Th., Oct. 3, 1968); and wrote the music (words by Hal David) for *Promises, Promises* (Sam S. Shubert Th., Dec. 1, 1968).

Films. Motion Pictures for which Mr. Bacharach composed scores include *The Man Who Shot Liberty Valance* (Par., 1962); *After the Fox* (UA, 1966); *The April Fools* (Natl. Gen. 1969); *Butch Cassidy and the Sundance Kid* (20th-Fox, 1969); and *Lost Horizon* (Col., 1973).

With Hal David, he wrote the title songs for the films *The Man Who Shot Liberty Valance; Wives and Lovers* (Par., 1963); *Send Me No Flowers* (U, 1964); *A House Is Not a Home* (Embassy, 1964); and *What's New, Pussycat?*

(UA, 1965), a film for which they also wrote the songs "Anyone Who Had a Heart" and "My Little Red Book." They also wrote title songs for *Alfie* (Par., 1966); *Promise Her Anything* (Par., 1966); the song "The Look of Love" for *Casino Royale* (Col., 1967); and "Raindrops Keep Fallin' on My Head" for *Butch Cassidy and the Sundance Kid.*

Television. Mr. Bacharach appeared on the *Burt Bacharach Special* (CBS, Mar. 14, 1971); *Another Evening with Burt Bacharach* (1971); *Burt Bacharach—Close to You* (1972); and *Burt Bacharach!* (1972).

Night Clubs. Mr. Bacharach began his career in 1952 as an accompanist for Vic Damone, a night-club singer. Other performers he accompanied, chiefly in night-club appearances, include Joel Gray, the Ames Brothers, Polly Bergen, and Georgia Gibbs, all in the early and mid-1950s, and he composed arrangements and toured the US and abroad (1958–61) with Marlene Dietrich in club and concert engagements.

Concerts. Mr. Bacharach has conducted concerts at several music theatres, and he conducted for Dionne Warwick in concert (Philharmonic Hall, N.Y.C., Oct. 1966).

Published Works. Mr. Bacharach began collaborating with the lyricist Hal David in 1957, when they wrote "Magic Moments" and "The Story of My Life." In addition to the film songs referred to above, other songs written by Mr. Bacharach and Hal David, many of which were introduced by the singer Dionne Warwick, include "Don't Make Me Over" (1962), "Only Love Can Break a Heart" (1962), "Reach Out for Me" (1963), "Message to Michael" (1963), "Walk on By" (1964), "Trains and Boats and Planes" (1964), "Here I Am" (1965), "Don't Go Breakin' My Heart" (1965), "What the World Needs Now Is Love" (1965), "Do You Know the Way to San Jose?" (1967), "I Say a Little Prayer" (1967), and "This Guy's in Love with You" (1968). Words and music for many of the songs are contained in *The Bacharach and David Song Book,* introduction by Dionne Warwick (1970).

Discography. Mr. Bacharach's "Mexican Divorce" (1960) led to a 1962 contract for Mr. Bacharach, Hal David, and the singer Dionne Warwick with Scepter Records, a label on which many Bacharach-David songs were released as sung by Dionne Warwick. Mr. Bacharach has also recorded the albums *Reach Out* (A & M) and *Burt Bacharach—Man* (Kapp). *Promises, Promises* was recorded by the original cast (UA, 1969) and by Dionne Warwick (Scepter, 1969).

Awards. *Promises, Promises* was nominated (1969) for an Antoinette Perry (Tony) Award as best musical, and Mr. Bacharach was named (1970) in the *Variety* NY Drama Critics poll as best composer for the same show. Mr. Bacharach and Hal David shared an AMPAS (Oscar) Award for "Raindrops Keep Fallin' on My Head," named as best song (1970), and Mr. Bacharach received a second Oscar award for his scoring of the film from which the song came, *Butch Cassidy and the Sundance Kid.* His television program *Another Evening with Burt Bacharach* won a NATAS (Emmy) Award in 1971 as best musical program.

BADEL, ALLAN. Actor, director, producer. b. Alan Fernand Badel, Sept. 11, 1923, Rusholme, Manchester, England, to Auguste and Elizabeth Olive (Durose) Badel. Father, city office manager. Grad. Burnage H.S., Manchester, G.C.E. 1939; attended RADA, London, 1939–41. Married 1942 to Marie Yvonne Owen; one daughter, Sarah Badel, actress. Served British Paratroopers, 1942–47; rank, Platoon Sgt.; awarded 1939–45 Star and Defence Medal. Member of AEA; British AEA; RADA (hon. mbr. of council). Address: (home) 38 Cleaver St., London, S.E.11, England tel. REL-3598; (bus.) c/o London Artists Ltd., 25 Gilbert St., London, W.1, England tel. MAY-8721.

Theatre. Mr. Badel made his first stage appearance in a Burnage H.S. production of *The Anatomist* (1938); subsequently appeared as George in the Oxford Repertory Co.'s production of *The Black Eye* (1940).

He made his professional debut as Pierrot in *L'Enfant Prodigue* (Mercury, London, Aug. 18, 1941), and toured in the same part; followed by Lennox and the Servant in *Macbeth* (Piccadilly, July 8, 1942), in which he subsequently toured.

During his military service, he appeared with the Army Play Unit, playing the title role in *Othello* (Egypt and the Middle East and Joe Rock in *Exercise Bowler* (Germany). He subsequently played Morgan Evans in the Farnham (Eng.) Repertory production of *The Corn Is Green* (Apr.–May 1947); Stevie in *Peace in Our Time* (Lyric, London, July 22, 1947); Sandman in *Frenzy* (St. Martin's, Apr. 21, 1948); at the Birmingham Repertory Th. (Feb.–July 1949), played Everyman in *The Modern Everyman,* the title role in *Richard III,* the Fool in *The Marvellous History of St. Bernard,* and the Scoundrel in *Diary of a Scoundrel.*

At the Shakespeare Memorial Th. (Stratford-upon-Avon), appeared as Ratty in *Toad of Toad Hall* (Dec. 1949); Don John in *Much Ado About Nothing* (1950); Claudio in *Measure for Measure* (Mar. 9, 1950); the Lord Chamberlain in *Henry VIII* (May 28, 1950); Octavius Caesar in *Julius Caesar* (May 2, 1950); the Fool in *King Lear* (July 18, 1950); Poins and Justice Shallow in *Henry IV, Part 2* (May 8, 1951); Ariel in *The Tempest* (June 26, 1951); the Dauphin in *Henry V* (July 31, 1951); the title role in *Hamlet* (Apr. 10, 1956); Berowne in *Love's Labour's Lost* (July 3, 1956); and Lucio in *Measure for Measure* (Aug. 14, 1956).

Mr. Badel played the Prince in *Beauty and the Beast* (Westminster, Dec. 1950); and Quince in *A Midsummer Night's Dream* (Old Vic, Dec. 26, 1951); François Villon in *The Other Heart* (Old Vic, Apr. 15, 1952); and Romeo in *Romeo and Juliet* (Old Vic, Sept. 15, 1952); Eilert Lovborg in *Hedda Gabler* (Lyric, Hammersmith, Sept. 8, 1954); and Fouquier-Tinville in *The Public Prosecutor* (Arts, Oct. 15, 1957), which he also directed.

Mr. Badel formed (1958) Furndel Productions, Ltd., with Viscount Furness, presenting *Ulysses in Nighttown,* in which he played Stephen Dedalus (Arts, May 21, 1959), which subsequently toured for seven wks. (Th. Sarah Bernhardt, Paris; Opera House, Amsterdam; Opera House, The Hague, 1959). Furndel Productions also presented *The Ark* (Westminster, London, Sept. 9, 1959); *Visit to a Small Planet,* in which Mr. Badel played Kreton (Westminster, Feb. 25, 1960); *Roger the Sixth* (Westminster, May 24, 1960); and the Voodoo Dancers (1960).

He played Hero in *The Rehearsal* (Royal, Dec. 7, 1961), which he repeated on Bway (Royale, Sept. 23, 1963); John Tanner in *Man and Superman* (New Arts, London, Nov. 23, 1965); and, at the Playhouse, Oxford, he played the title roles in *Kean* (Sept. 1970) and *Othello* (Oct. 1970). He later played *Kean* in London (Globe, Jan. 28, 1971).

Films. Mr. Badel made his first appearance as the English Lord in *The Young Mr. Pitt* (20th-Fox, 1942); followed by *The Stranger Left No Card* (Windsor, 1952); *Salome* (Col., 1953); *Three Cases of Murder* (Shepperton, 1953); *Magic Fire* (Rep., 1956); *This Sporting Life* (Beaconsfield, 1962); and *Children of the Damned* (1963); and *Arabesque* (U, 1966).

Television. He made his first appearance as Rawdon Crawley in *Vanity Fair* (BBC); followed by Mr. D'Arcy in *Pride and Prejudice* (BBC, 1957); Don Juan in *Don Juan in Hell* (ITV, 1962); in *The Complaisant Lover* (BBC, 1961); the Cardinal in *The Prisoner* (BBC, 1963); the Husband in *The Lover* (ATV, 1963). He was also in *A Couple of Dry Martinis* (Play of the Week, Rediff., June 1965) and played the title role in *Gordon of Khartoum* (BBC-1, Jan. 1966).

Awards. He received the Bancroft Gold Medal from the Royal Academy of Dramatic Art (1941), and an actor of the year award from the guild of television producers and directors (1963). For his performance in *Kean,* he tied with Paul Scofield for best male performance in the 1971 *Variety* poll of London theatre critics.

Recreation. Gardening, bricklaying.

BAGLEY, BEN. Producer, director. b. Benjamin James Bagley, Oct. 18, 1933, Burlington, Vt., to James and Madeline (Beaupre) Bagley. Father, railroad clerk; mother, music teacher. Attended Holy Family H.S., Burlington, Vt., 1948–52. Address: (home) 147-46 84 Rd., Jamaica, NY 11435, tel. (212) OR 8-8416; (bus.) Painted Smiles Records, 1860 Bway, New York, NY 10023.

Pre-Theatre. Copywriter; wrote obituaries and a news-brief column for *Engineering News Record* (1952–54).

Theatre. Mr. Bagley directed in association with Mr. and Mrs. Judson S. Todd and produced *Shoestring Revue* (President Th., Feb. 28, 1955); assembled and produced *The Littlest Revue* (Phoenix Th., May 22, 1956); and produced and assembled *Shoestring '57* (Barbizon-Plaza, Nov. 5, 1957).

Mr. Bagley directed stock production of *Shoestring Texas* (Casa Mañana, Ft. Worth, Tex., Summer 1958); and presented The Paul Taylor Modern Dance Co. in Paris (Th. de Lutèce, Apr. 11, 1962).

In 1965, he created and directed in N.Y.C. *The Decline and Fall of the Entire World as Seen Through the Eyes of Cole Porter* (Square East, Mar. 30, 1965); *New Cole Porter Review* (Square East, Dec. 22, 1965) was a second edition. A combined version of both shows, using the title of the first, opened at the Little Fox, San Francisco, Calif., in 1966. The show has been produced also in London, England, and many US cities.

Films. Mr. Bagley played in *Chafed Elbows* (Robert Downey, 1967); *Putney Swope* (Cinema 5, 1969); *The Corpse Has Traces of Carnal Violence* (Italian); and an industrial for UPI, *It's Been a Good Year.*

Television. He produced and co-directed *Shoestring Revue* (WABD, 1955); appeared on the Armstrong Circle Th. (CBS, 1957), and From These Roots (NBC, 1960); and assembled the television production of Rodgers and Hart Revisited (CBS, Mar. 26, 1964).

Night Clubs. In clubs and cafes, he produced and directed *The Little Revue* (1960), *Seven Come Eleven* (1962), and *Broadcast of 1963.* He replaced Julius Monk at Upstairs at the Downstairs with a revue he assembled and directed, *No Shoestrings* (Oct. 1962).

Discography. Starting with *Rodgers and Hart Revisited* (RIC), Mr. Bagley recorded for MGM, RCA Victor, and Columbia a series of "revisited" albums composed of little-known songs of such famous theatre composers as Cole Porter, Jerome Kern, Irving Berlin, George Gershwin, Arthur Schwartz, Noel Coward, and Vernon Duke. He subsequently bought these back from the recording companies and reissued them under his own label, "Painted Smiles Records.".

Recreation. Theatre, music, writing, films.

BAGNOLD, ENID. Playwright, writer. b. Oct. 27, 1889, Rochester, Kent, England, to Col. A. H. and Ethel (Alger) Bagnold. Father, Royal Engineers. Attended schools in Priors Field, Godalming, Surrey, Eng., Marburg, Ger., and Paris, Fr. (1901–07). Married July 8, 1920, to Sir Roderick Jones, K.B.E., chairman, managing director, Reuters (dec. Jan. 1962); three sons, one daughter. Served WW I, French Army, driver. Member of Dramatists Guild. Address: North End House, Rottingdean, Sussex, England.

Theatre. Miss Bagnold's first work presented in N.Y.C. was the adaptation by S. N. Behrman of her novel, *Serena Blandish* (Morosco, Jan. 23, 1929), which was presented in London (Gate, Sept. 13, 1938), as were her own adaptations of her novels, *Lottie Dundass* (Vandeville, July 21, 1943), and *National Velvet* (Embassy, Apr. 20, 1946).

She also wrote *Poor Judas* (Arts, London, July 18, 1951); *Gertie* (Plymouth, N.Y.C., Jan. 30, 1952), retitled *Little Idiot* for the London production ("Q" Th., Nov. 10, 1953); *The Chalk Garden* (Ethel Barrymore Th., N.Y.C., Oct. 26, 1955; Haymarket, London, England, Apr. 12, 1956); *The Chinese Prime Minister* (Royale, N.Y.C., Jan. 2, 1964; Globe, London, England, May 20, 1965); and *Call Me Jacky* (premiere: Oxford Playhouse, Oxford, England, Feb. 27, 1968).

Films. Screen adaptations were made of Miss Bagnold's *National Velvet* (MGM, 1944), and *The Chalk Garden* (U, 1964).

Published Works. Miss Bagnold's works include *Sailing Ships,* a collection of poems (1912); *a Diary Without Dates* (1918); *The Happy Foreigner* (1920); *Serena Blandish* (1924); *Alice and Thomas and Jane,* a children's book (1930); *National Velvet* (1935); *Alexander of Asia,* a translation of Princess Marthe Bibesco's *Alexandre Asiatique* (1935); *The Squire* (1938), US title, *The Door of Life; Lottie Dundass* (1941); *The Girl's Journey* (reprint of *The Squire* and *The Happy Foreigner,* 1954); and *Enid Bagnold's Autobiography* (1969).

Awards. For her play, *Poor Judas,* Miss Bagnold received the Arts Theatre Prize (1951); and for *The Chalk Garden,* she received the Award of Merit Medal for drama from the American Academy of Arts and Letters (1956).

Recreation. Gardening.

BAILEY, PEARL. Actress, singer. b. Pearl Mae Bailey, Mar. 29, 1918, Newport News, Va., to Joseph James and Pearl Bailey. Father, minister. Attended William Penn H.S., 1933. Married Aug. 31, 1948, to John Randolph Pinkett, Jr. (marr. dis. Mar. 20, 1952); married Nov. 19, 1952, to Louis Bellson, Jr., drummer; one son, one daughter. Relative in theatre: brother, Bill Bailey, tap dancer and minister. Member of AGVA; AEA; SAG; AFTRA; AGMA. Address: 109 Bank St., New York, NY 10014.

Theatre. Miss Bailey first appeared as a singer in vaudeville (Pearl Th., Philadelphia, 1933); in N.Y.C., appeared as Butterfly in *St. Louis Woman* (Martin Beck Th., Mar. 30, 1946); Connecticut in *Arms and the Girl* (46 St. Th., Feb. 2, 1950); in the revue, *Bless You All* (Mark Hellinger Th., Dec. 14, 1950); Madame Fleur in *House of Flowers* (Alvin, Dec. 30, 1954); was Sally Adams in a production of *Call Me Madam* (Melodyland, Berkeley, Calif., Aug. 1966); went on tour (Oct. 11, 1967) as Mrs. Dolly Gallagher Levi in *Hello, Dolly!,* played the same role in the N.Y.C. production (St. James, Nov. 12, 1967–Dec. 1969), then toured with the production again until May 1970. She returned to Bway as Dolly in a limited engagement revival of *Hello, Dolly!* (Minskoff Th., Nov. 6–Dec. 14, 1975).

Films. Miss Bailey appeared in *Variety Girl* (Par., 1947); *Isn't It Romantic?* (Par., 1948); *Carmen Jones* (20th-Fox, 1954); *That Certain Feeling* (Par., 1956); *St. Louis Blues* (Par., 1958); *Porgy and Bess* (MGM, 1959); *All the Fine Young Cannibals* (MGM, 1960); and *The Landlord* (UA, 1970).

Television. Miss Bailey has appeared on all the major talk and variety shows, including Johnny Carson Show (NBC), Danny Kaye Show (CBS), Jack Paar (NBC), the Milton Berle Show (NBC), Ed Sullivan Show (CBS), Ed Wynn Show (NBC), What's My Line? (CBS), Perry Como Show (NBC), Mike Douglas Show (CBS), on *Carol Channing and Pearl Bailey on Broadway* (ABC, Mar. 16, 1966); and the Pearl Bailey Show (ABC, 1970–71).

Night Clubs. She appeared in such night clubs as the Village Vanguard (1941); the Blue Angel (1942); La Vie en Rose (1945); Cafe Zanzibar (1950); the Empire Room (Waldorf-Astoria Hotel, 1956); the Royal Box (Americana Hotel, 1963); Cafe Pompeii (Eden Roc Hotel, Miami Beach, Fla., Jan. 1966); The Flamingo (Las Vegas, Nev., Sept. 1966); and The Talk of the Town (London, England, Sept. 1966); as well as others in the US and abroad. She has also performed in her night club act at the Apollo Th. (N.Y.C.).

Concerts. Miss Bailey appeared in *An Evening with Pearl Bailey* for the benefit of the Youth Welfare and Community Service Fund, Albany (N.Y.) Jr. Chamber of Commerce (Albany, N.Y., Mar. 1966); she appeared in concert with Al Hirt (O'Keefe Ctr., Toronto, Canada, May 30, 1966); and at Philharmonic Hall, Lincoln Ctr., N.Y.C. (Mar. 1966; Feb. 17, 1967).

Other Activities. In Nov. 1975, Pres. Gerald R. Ford appointed Miss Bailey a special advisor to the US Mission of the UN General Assembly, 30th session, and she was sworn in on Dec. 1, 1975.

Published Works. Miss Bailey wrote *The Raw Pearl* (1968) and *Pearl's Kitchen* (1973).

Discography. Miss Bailey has recorded on the Coral, Decca, and Columbia labels such popular songs as "Row, Row, Row," "That's Good Enough for Me," "Takes Two to Tango," "Nothin' for Nothin'," "There Must Be Something Better Than Love," "What Is a Friend For?," "Legalize My Name," "A Woman's Prerogative," "Birth of the Blues," and for RCA-Victor a *Hello, Dolly!* album.

Awards. Miss Bailey received the Donaldson Award for her performance as Butterfly in *St. Louis Woman* (1946); was named entertainer of the year by *Cue* magazine (1967); received the March of Dimes Award (1968); a special Antoinette Perry (Tony) Award (Apr. 1968) for her performance in *Hello, Dolly!;* and the 27th annual Barter Th. Award (Nov. 1969).

Recreation. Cooking.

BAILEY, ROBIN. Actor. b. William Henry Mettam Bailey, Oct. 5, 1919, Hucknall, Nottingham, England, to George Henry and Thirza Ann (Mettam) Bailey. Father, china dealer. Grad. Henry Mellish Sch., Nottingham, England, 1936. Married Sept. 6, 1941, to Patricia Mary Weekes; three sons. Served British Army, 1940–45; rank Lt. RASC. Member of AEA; British AEA. Address: (home) 19 Chartfield Ave., Putney, London, S.W. 15, England tel. PUT 5061; (bus.) c/o Derek Glynne, 115 Shaftesbury Ave., London, W.C.2, England tel. TEM 5224.

Pre-Theatre. Postal Service.

Theatre. Mr. Bailey made his N.Y.C. debut as Christopher in *Jennie* (Majestic, Oct. 17, 1963) and also appeared there as Martin Lynch-Gibbon in *A Severed Head* (Royale, Oct. 28, 1964).

He first appeared professionally with the Court Players as George in *The Barretts of Wimpole Street* (Theatre Royal, Nottingham, England, Sept. 1938); appeared in repertory at the Playhouse (Newcastle-on-Tyne, July 1940); as Bassanio in *The Merchant of Venice* and Dubedat in *The Doctor's Dilemma.*

During 1944–45, he played in repertory at the Alexandra Th. (Birmingham, England, and toured in Italy; subsequently appeared in repertory (Worthing, England, 1945–46); toured Europe as Ludovico in an English Arts Th. production of *Othello* (English Arts Th., 1946–47), and made his London debut in this role (Piccadilly, Mar. 26, 1947). He appeared with the Birmingham Repertory Th. Co. (1947–48) as Edmund in *King Lear,* played the title role in *Peer Gynt,* Reggie in *The Banbury Nose,* Faulkland in *The Rivals,* and Pip in *Great Expectations;* played Robert Lawn in *Love in Albania* (Lyric, Hammersmith, June 7, 1949); Alexander MacColgie Gibbs in *The Cocktail Party* (New, May 3, 1950); Terrence Sullivan in *The Gentle Gunman* (Arts, Aug. 2, 1950); Ludolph in *Otho the Great* (St. Martin's Nov. 26, 1950); Prof. Henry Higgins in *Pygmalion* (Embassy, Jan. 23, 1951); and Robin Colquhoun in *Winter Sport* (Hippodrome, Golders Green, Mar. 26, 1951).

Mr. Bailey also appeared as Gustave in *Thieves' Carnival* (Arts, Jan. 3, 1952); Henry Winger in *Sweet Madness* (Vaudeville, May 21, 1952); Marc Antony in *Julius Caesar* (Old Vic, Feb. 24, 1953); the 2nd Knight in *Murder in the Cathedral* (Old Vic, Mar. 31, 1953); Sergius in *Arms and the Man* (Arts, June 25, 1953); Lord Basingstoke in *No Sign of the Dove* (Savoy, Dec. 3, 1953); Jack Hokinshaw in *No News from Father* (Streatham Hill, Aug. 30, 1954); and toured with the Old Vic Co. in Australia (1955), as Lucio in *Measure for Measure,* Tranio in *The Taming of the Shrew,* and Gratiano in *The Merchant of Venice.*

He played Captain Hawtree in *She Smiled at Me* (St. Martin's, London, Feb. 2, 1956); Juggins in the Edinburgh (Scotland) Festival production of *Fanny's First Play* (Lyceum, Edinburgh, Sept. 1956); Mr. Justice Blanchard in *Duel of Angels* (Apollo, Apr. 24, 1958); Prof. Henry Higgins in *My Fair Lady* (Her Majesty's, Melbourne, Australia, Jan. 1959); Gerald in *The Formation Dancers* (Arts, London, Mar. 18, 1964).

He appeared at the Edinburgh (Scotland) Festival as Theseus and Oberon in *A Midsummer Night's Dream* (Sept. 1967), which transferred to London (Saville, Sept. 26, 1967), and Haakon Werle in *The Wild Duck* (Aug. 1969); toured Australia repeating his performance as Henry Higgins in *My Fair Lady* (1970); played Harry Branksome in *Parents' Day* (Globe, London, July 12, 1972); and appeared in *Edward G., Like the Film Star* (London, 1974).

Films. Mr. Bailey made his debut in *Private Angelo* (ABC, 1949); subsequently appeared in *Portrait of Clare* (Stratford, 1951); *Folly to Be Wise* (Brit. Lion, 1952); *The Gift Horse* (1952), which was released in the US as *Glory at Sea* (Independent Film Distributors, 1953); *Single-Handed* (1953), released in the US as *Sailor of the King* (20th-Fox, 1953); *Having a Wild Weekend* (WB, 1965); and *The Spy with a Cold Nose* (Embassy, 1966).

Television. Mr. Bailey was in *The Edwardians—Olive Latimer's Husband* (ITV, London, England, May 17, 1965) and has appeared on other English television programs, including Armchair Th.; The Wednesday Play; Newcomers; and Power Game.

Awards. He received the Clarence Derwent Award (London) for his performance as Falkland in *The Rivals* (1948).

Recreation. Painting; tennis; gardening.

BAILEY, RUTH. Producer, actress. b. Ruth Robison, Pittsburgh, Pa., to L. A. and Mira (Greenough) Robison. Father, railroad traffic manager; mother, artist. Attended Briarcliff (N.Y.) Sch.; Vassar Coll.; Goodman Sch. of Theatre, Chicago, Ill., 1934; Pasadena (Calif.) Playhouse, 1935. Married Apr. 12, 1939, to Eugene Swigart; one son. Member of AEA; SAG; AFTRA. Address: (home) Spring Hill Lane, Cincinnati, OH 45226, tel. (513) 871-0049; (bus.) Cherry County Playhouse, Traverse City, MI 49684, tel. (616) WI 7-9560.

Pre-Theatre. Professional social worker, school teacher, model, and radio actress.

Theatre. Miss Bailey made her acting debut as the White Queen and the Cheshire Cat in *Alice in Wonderland* (Punch and Judy Th., Nov. 1935); subsequently appeared in stock as Donna Lucia in *Charley's Aunt* (Chevy Chase Th., Wheeling, Ill., Summer 1952), Mrs. Biddle in *There's Always a Murder* (Drury Lane Th., Evergreen Park, Ill., 1954), and Margaret Munson in *Kind Sir* (Drury Lane, 1962).

In 1955, Miss Bailey organized the Cherry County Playhouse in Traverse City, Mich., where she has produced, managed, and appeared in such one-week summer stock productions as Myra in *Hay Fever* (1956); Janice Revere in *Anniversary Waltz* (1957); Agatha Reed in *Goodbye, My Fancy* (1957), Miss Preen in *The Man Who Came to Dinner* (1958); Margot in *Dial 'M' for Murder* (1958); and Mable Crossthwaite in *The Reluctant Debutante* (1958). In 1974, Cherry County Playhouse observed its twentieth season with Miss Bailey as producer.

Television and Radio. On radio Miss Bailey played (1936–42) in such serials as Guiding Light, Woman in White, Right to Happiness, and Arnold Grimm's Daughter. During this period, she also appeared on Chicago networks in First Nighter, Chicago Theatre of the Air, Lights Out and Helen Trent.

On television, she played (1948–52) in *Leave It to Kathy* (WLWT, Cincinnati, 6 mos.) and appeared in Rod Serling's series, The Storm (WKRC, Cincinnati).

Recreation. Swimming, tennis, reading, dancing.

BAIN, CONRAD. Actor. b. Conrad Stafford Bain, Feb. 4, 1923, Lethbridge, Alberta, Canada, to Stafford Harrison and Jean Agnes Bain. Father, wholesaler. Grad. Western Canada H.S., Calgary, Alberta, 1940; attended Banff (Alberta) Sch. of Fine Arts, 1941; grad. AADA, N.Y.C., 1948. Married Sept. 4, 1945, to Monica Sloan, artist; two sons, one daughter. Served Canadian Army, 1943–46, Canada; rank, Sgt. Member of AEA (council member 1962–67); SAG; AFTRA; AFM, Local 802; Actors Federal Credit Union (founder, pres.); The Players. Address: 175 W. 72nd St., New York, NY 10023, tel. (212) TR 4-2139.

Pre-Theatre. Farmer.

Theatre. Mr. Bain's first assignment was as stage manager in *Our Town* (Western Canada H.S., Calgary, Alberta, 1939); subsequently made his first professional appearance as Albert Kummer in a stock production of *Dear Ruth* (Ivoryton Playhouse, Conn., Summer 1947); toured as Alfred Moulton-Barrett in *The Barretts of Wimpole Street* (Sept. 1949); performed in stock productions at the Barnstormers (Tamworth, N.H., Summers 1948–50), the North Shore Playhouse, (Marblehead, Mass., Summers 1951–52, July 1953, July 1955), the British Colonial Th. (Nassau, Bahamas, B.W.I., Mar.–Apr. 1953), the Warren (Ohio) Civic Th. (Apr. 1954), the Grist Mill Playhouse (Andover, N.J., July–Aug. 1954), and the Mutual Hall Th. (Boston, Mass., Aug. 1955).

He made his N.Y.C. debut as Larry Slade in *The Iceman Cometh* (Circle in the Square, May 8, 1956); followed by Dr. Peter Hoenig in *Sixth Finger in a Five Finger Glove* (Longacre, Oct. 8, 1956); the King of Hesse, the Captain, and the Very, Very Old Inquisitor in *Candide* (Martin Beck Th., Dec. 1, 1956); played in stock productions at the South Shore Music Circus, Cohasset, Mass. (July–Aug. 1957); appeared as Vitek in *The Makropoulos Secret* (Phoenix, N.Y.C., Dec. 3, 1957); Uncle Smelicue in *Dark of the Moon* (Carnegie Hall Playhouse, Feb. 26, 1958); and Mark Eland in *Lost in the Stars* (NY City Ctr., Apr. 19, 1958). At the Stratford (Ontario) Shakespeare Festival of Canada, he portrayed the Earl of Northumberland in *Henry IV, Part 1*, Antonio in *Much Ado About Nothing* and Antigonus in *The Winter's Tale* (June 23–Sept. 13, 1958); subsequently played Dr. Warburton in *The Family Reunion* (Phoenix, N.Y.C., Oct. 20, 1958); and appeared in *A Shaw Festival* as Mr. Juno in *Overruled*, the Solicitor in *Buoyant Billions* and Gen. Bridgenorth in *Getting Married* (Provincetown Playhouse, May 26, 1959).

Mr. Bain played in the pre-Bway tryout of *One for the Dame* (opened Ford's, Baltimore, Md., Mar. 26, 1960; closed Colonial Th., Boston, Mass., Apr. 2, 1960); Nicholas in *A Country Scandal* (Greenwich Mews, May 5, 1960); Lt. General Dayton in a stock production of *Roman Candle* (Spa Music Th., Saratoga, N.Y., July 1960); Sen. Winthrop in the N.Y.C. production of *Advise and Consent* (Cort, Nov. 17, 1960); the Gunner in *The Interpreter* (Bucks County Playhouse, New Hope, Pa., July 1961); appeared in repertory in *A Pair of Pairs* as Mr. Norah in *It's All Yours*, the second play of one of the *Pairs*, entitled *Deuces Wild*, and appeared as Daddy Jack in *A Summer Ghost*, the second play of the other *Pair*, entitled *Charlatans* (Van Dam, N.Y.C., Apr. 24, 1962); toured as Mr. Nicklebush in *Rhinoceros* (Westport Country Playhouse, Conn.; Playhouse in the Park, Philadelphia, Pa., July 1962); portrayed the Older Man in the ANTA Matinee series production of *Lunatic View* (Th. de Lys, N.Y.C., Nov. 27, 1962); George Higgins in *Hot Spot* (Majestic, Apr. 19, 1963); and was in *The Kitchen* (New, May 1963).

At the Seattle (Wash.) Repertory Th., he appeared as the Duke of Cornwall in *King Lear* (Nov. 13, 1963); Biedermann in *The Firebugs* (Nov. 14, 1963); Howard in *Death of a Salesman* (Feb. 12, 1964); and as Rakosi in *Shadow of Heroes* (Apr. 1, 1964).

He played Patsy Murphy in *Hogan's Goat* (St. Clement's Church, N.Y.C., Nov. 11, 1965); was the American Tourist in *Scuba Duba* (New, Oct. 10, 1967); was the Old Timer in *Steambath* (Truck and Warehouse Th., June 30, 1970); played Swede in *Celia*, one of the one-act plays comprising *Twigs* (Broadhurst, Nov. 14, 1971); played Aslaksen in *An Enemy of the People* (Vivian Beaumont Th., Mar. 11, 1971); Kurt in *Play Strindberg* (Forum, June 5, 1971); and Ilya Telyegin in *Uncle Vanya* (Circle in the Square, June 4, 1973).

Films. Mr. Bain appeared in *Coogan's Bluff* (U, 1968); *A Lovely Way to Die* (U, 1968); *Star!* (20th-Fox, 1968); *Jump* (Cannon, 1971); *The Anderson Tapes* (Col., 1971); *Bananas* (UA, 1971); *Who Killed Mary What's 'Ername* (Cannon, 1972); and *Up the Sandbox* Natl. Gen., 1973).

Television. Mr. Bain appeared on Studio One (CBS), in *A Chance for Happiness*, *Little Women*, and *The Last Dictator*. He also performed on The Defenders (CBS); Look Up and Live (CBS); the Anne Bancroft Special (1971); and plays Dr. Arthur Harmon on Maude (CBS).

Recreation. Swimming, sailing, sculpture, music (guitar).

BAIRD, BILL. Puppeteer, designer, composer, writer. b. William Britton Baird, Aug. 15, 1904, Grand Island, Nebr., to William Hull and Louise Baird. Father, chemical engineer, playwright. Grad. Mason City (Iowa) H.S., 1922; State Univ. of Iowa, B.A. 1926; Chicago Acad. of Fine Arts, diploma 1927. Married Evelyn Schwartz (marr. dis.); married Jan. 13, 1937, to Cora Burlar, puppeteer (dec. Dec. 7, 1967); one son, one daughter; married Dec. 29, 1974, to Susanna Lloyd. Served US Army reserve, 1925; rank, 2d Lt. Member of AFTRA; AGVA; AGMA; SAG; AEA; AFM; IATSE; NATAS (board of governors); Sigma Chi Fraternity (Alpha Eta Chapter); Omicron Delta Kappa; The Firehorses. Address: 59 Barrow St., New York, NY 10014, tel. (212) YU 9-9840.

Pre-Theatre. Steeplejack.

Theatre. Mr. Baird built scenery and appeared in dramatic productions at the State Univ. of Iowa (1924–26); subsequently joined Tony Sarg as a principal puppeteer for his touring production of *Ali Baba and the 40 Thieves* (1927–28); and choreographed Tony Sarg's touring productions of *Rip Van Winkle* and *Alice in Wonderland* (1931–32).

Mr. Baird was contracted by Tony Sarg to build the puppets, assist in rewriting, and direct the puppeteers for A&P Show (Chicago World's Fair, Ill., 1933); produced *Bil Baird's Marionettes* for Swift and Co. (Chicago World's Fair, Ill., 1934); presented his marionettes at industrial shows for Shell Oil, Atlantic Refining Co., De Beers, and the *Philadelphia Bulletin* (1935–40); in the Federal Th. (WPA) Project productions of *Horse Eats Hat* (Maxine Elliott's Th., N.Y.C., Sept. 22, 1936) and *Dr. Faustus* (Maxine Elliott's Th., Jan. 8, 1937), at which time he met his wife, then known as Cora Burlar.

The Bil and Cora Baird Marionettes appeared in the *Ziegfeld Follies* (Winter Garden, Apr. 1, 1943); *Nellie Bly* (Adelphi, Jan. 21, 1946); *Flahooley* (Broadhurst, May 14, 1951), in which Mr. Baird played Clyde; *Ali Baba and the 40 Thieves*, written by Alan Stern and with songs by George Kleinsinger, Joe Darion, and Mr. Baird (Phoenix, Dec. 26, 1955); *Pageant of Puppet Variety* (Apr. 19, 1957); on tour of the US; and in their marionette theatre production *Davy Jones' Locker*, based on a story by Mr. Baird, with a book by Arthur Bernkrant and Waldo Salt, and music and lyrics by Mary Rodgers (Morosco, N.Y.C., Mar. 28, 1959), with which they made a 17-week tour (1962) of India, Nepal, and Afghanistan and a 10-week tour (1963) of the USSR as part of the US Cultural Exchange Program under US State Dept. sponsorship. They presented their marionette theatre in *Man in the Moon* (Biltmore, N.Y.C., Apr. 11, 1963); performed on the concert stage with Thomas Scherman's Little Orchestra in *Carnival of Animals* and *Surprise Box*; and appeared in the "Diamond Jubilee Parade" number in the musical *Baker Street* (Broadway Th., Feb. 16, 1965).

Mr. Baird and his wife opened their own theatre, the Bil Baird Th., in 1966, starting with a series of free matinees (July 28–Aug. 9) for children in Operation Headstart. They revived *Davy Jones' Locker* (Dec. 24, 1966), and Mr. Baird subsequently expanded the repertory with a number of new productions, staged at his theatre together with revivals of earlier work. Presentations included *People Is the Thing That the World Is the Fullest Of* (Feb. 20, 1967), which was conceived by Mr. Baird and directed by Burt Shelelove; *Winnie the Pooh*, also conceived by Mr. Baird, book by A. J. Russell, and music by Jack Brooks (Nov. 23, 1967); *The Wizard of Oz*, with music by Harold Arlen and lyrics by E. Y. Harburg (Nov. 27, 1968); and they appeared with Andre Kostelanetz and the NY Philharmonic in *L'Histoire du Soldat* (Philharmonic Hall, Summer 1969).

Other shows at the Bil Baird Th. were *The Whistling Wizard and the Sultan of Tuffet,* book and lyrics by Alan Stern, music by Mr. Baird (Dec. 20, 1969); *Holiday on Strings,* created and designed by Mr. Baird and written by Alan Stern (Dec. 26, 1970); *Peter and the Wolf,* book by A. J. Russell, music by Sergei Prokofiev, and lyrics by Ogden Nash (Dec. 18, 1971); *The Magic Onion,* written by Mr. Baird (July 1972); *Band Wagon,* a varieties program (Mar. 16, 1973); *Pinocchio,* with book by Jerome Coopersmith, music by Mary Rodgers, and lyrics by Sheldon Harnick (Dec. 15, 1973); and *Alice in Wonderland,* co-produced by Susanna Baird, with book by A. J. Russell, music by Joe Raposo, and lyrics by Sheldon Harnick (Mar. 14, 1975).

Films. The Baird Studio has filmed more than 200 commercials, including *Adventure in Telezonia* (AT&T); *Party Lines* (AT&T); *The King Who Came to Breakfast* (Nabisco); *Adventures in Number and Space* (Westinghouse); has participated in the Heath-De Rochemont series *Parlons Français;* and Mr. Baird appeared with his puppets in *The Sound of Music* (20th-Fox, 1965).

Television. The Baird marionettes have performed many times on such programs as the Ed Sullivan Show (CBS) and the Jack Paar Show (NBC). They appeared with Sid Caesar (CBS); Mike Douglas (CBS); on their own series, Life with Snarky Parker (CBS, 1949–50); The Whistling Wizard (CBS, 1952–53); The Morning Show (CBS, 1954–55); Babes in Toyland (NBC, 1954–55); the special *Heidi* (NBC, 1955); the special *Art Carney Meets Peter and the Wolf* (ABC, three times, 1958); the special *The Sorcerer's Apprentice* (ABC, 1959); *Bairdseye View* (1961); *Discovery Visits the Baird Marionettes* (Discovery '65, ABC, Jan. 3, 1965); Wonderama (Ind., 1965–66); Book Talk (NET, 1966–67); and New York Illustrated (NBC, 1966–67). The Baird marionettes also appeared in space simulations on NBC.

Night Clubs. The Baird Marionettes have appeared in Le Ruban Bleu (N.Y.C.), The French Casino Lounge and The Persian Room (N.Y.C.).

Published Works. Mr. Baird is author of *The Art of the Puppet* (1965).

Awards. *Art Carney Meets Peter and the Wolf* was nominated for a NATAS (Emmy) Award (1958), and the Bairds together received the Outer Circle Award (1967) for having founded a permanent puppet theatre.

Recreation. Sailing, collecting old musical instruments.

BAKER, DAVID. Composer, pianist. b. David Keith Baker, June 6, 1926, Portland, Me., to Richard Mason and Theodora (Cooper) Baker. Father, tax consultant. Grad. Cape Elizabeth (Me.) H.S., 1943; attended Juilliard Sch. of Music, 1943–44, 1947–49. Served USNR, 1944–46; rank, Yeoman 2/c. Member of Dramatists Guild; AFM, Local 802; BMI.

Theatre. Mr. Baker started as a concert pianist (Portland City Hall, Me., 1940); subsequently composed music for the Children's Th. (Portland, Me., 1943); was pianist for a summer opera production of *Cosi fan Tutti* (Deertrees, Harrison, Me., 1946); for a summer stock tour of *Best Foot Forward* (1948); and was musical director and pianist for a tour of *Gay Divorce* (1949).

He was pianist for the N.Y.C. production of *Gentlemen Prefer Blondes* (Ziegfeld, Dec. 8, 1949); rehearsal pianist for *Alive and Kicking* (Winter Garden, Jan. 17, 1950); arranger, pianist, and musical director for a stock tour of *Pal Joey* (Summer 1950); and rehearsal and audition pianist for the Rogers and Hammerstein office at the Majestic Th. (1950–51).

He arranged the dance music for the pre-Bway tryout of *A Month of Sundays* (opened Shubert, Boston, Mass., Dec. 25, 1951; closed Forrest, Philadelphia, Pa., June 26, 1952); and *Of Thee I Sing* (Ziegfeld, N.Y.C., May 5, 1952); composed two songs in *It's About Time* (Brattle, Cambridge, Mass., 1952); arranged the dance music for the revue *Two's Company* (Alvin, N.Y.C., Dec. 15, 1952); and composed the music for two songs in *Sticks and Stones* (John Drew Th., East Hampton, L.I., N.Y., 1954).

He composed the music for *Horatio* (Th. 54, Dallas, Tex., 1954); two songs in *Shoestring Revue* (President, N.Y.C., Feb. 28, 1955); music for *Phoenix '55* (Phoenix, Apr. 23, 1955); one song in *Shoestring '57* (Barbizon-Plaza, Nov. 5, 1956); one song in *Kaleidoscope* (Provincetown Playhouse, June 13, 1957); and music for *Copper and Brass* (Martin Beck Th., Oct. 17, 1957).

He composed the music for *Dig We Must* (John Drew Th., East Hampton, L.I., N.Y., 1959); and *Petticoat Fever* (Bucks County Playhouse, New Hope, Pa., 1960); was musical arranger for *Gay Divorce* (Cherry Lane, N.Y.C., Apr. 3, 1960; Royal Poinciana Playhouse, Palm Beach, Fla., 1963); composed the music for two songs in *Vintage '60* (Ivar Th., Hollywood, Calif., 1960; Brooks Atkinson Th., N.Y.C., Sept. 12, 1960); and arranged the dance music for *Do Re Mi* (St. James, Dec. 26, 1960).

He composed the music and was pianist for *Prior to Broadway* (Hilltop Th., Owings Mills, Md., 1960); composed the music for *Smiling the Boy Fell Dead* (Cherry Lane, N.Y.C., Apr. 19, 1961); the music for one song and was musical director of *Put It in Writing* (Royal Poinciana Playhouse, Palm Beach, Fla., 1962); and composed new dance music for *I Married an Angel* (Royal Poinciana Playhouse, Mar. 16, 1964).

He was arranger, pianist, and musical director for a West Coast tour of the Chevy Show (1957); Nabisco Show (St. Louis, Mo., 1959); Sportswear Assn. (N.Y.C., 1959–62); *Esquire* Magazine (Barbizon-Plaza Th., N.Y.C., 1961); *Sports Illustrated* (Shamrock Hotel, Houston, Tex., 1962); and Neiman-Marcus (Dallas, Tex., 1962).

Mr. Baker did the dance arrangements for *Flora, the Red Menace* (Alvin, N.Y.C., May 11, 1965); *The Yearling* (Alvin, Dec. 10, 1965); contributed special material to *The Carol Burnett Show* (Greek Th., Los Angeles, Aug. 8, 1966); arranged the dance music for *Cabaret* (Broadhurst, N.Y.C., Nov. 20, 1966); and wrote the music for *Come Summer* (Lunt-Fontanne Th., Mar. 18, 1969).

Television. Mr. Baker composed dance music for Caesar's Hour (NBC, 1952); was pianist for the Ford Anniversary Show (NBC, 1953); and composed dance music for the Garry Moore Show (CBS, 1958).

Night Clubs. He was pianist for Nancy Walker's Act (Carman Th., Philadelphia, Pa., 1950; Sans Souci Hotel, Miami Beach, Fla., 1950); composed the music for one song in *Taboo Revue* (Show Place, N.Y.C., 1959); and one song in *Medium Rare* (Happy Medium, Chicago, Ill., 1960).

BAKER, HOWARD. Playwright, educator. b. Howard Wilson Baker, Jr., Apr. 5, 1905, Philadelphia, Pa., to Howard Baker, Sr., and Bertha Baker. Father, orange grower. Grad. Strathmore H.S., Calif., 1923; Whittier Coll., B.A. 1927; Stanford Univ., M.A. 1928; Univ. of Paris (de la Sorbonne), 1929–31; Univ. of California at Berkeley, Ph.D. 1936. Married 1931 to Dorothy Dodds (dec. 1968); married 1969 to Virginia De Camp Beattie; two daughters. Member of Lindsay Cooperative Ripe Olive Assn.; Grandview Heights Citrus Assn. (bd. of dir., 1958–to date; pres. of bd., 1960–to date). Address: Rt. 1, Box 11, Terra Bella, CA 93270, tel. (209) KE 5-4648.

Theatre. Mr. Baker and his wife, Dorothy Dodds, wrote *Trio* (Belasco Th., N.Y.C., Dec. 29, 1944; Arts Club, London, England, 1948; San Francisco Repertory Th., Calif., 1950); and *The Ninth Day* (Gate Th., Dublin, Ireland, 1961).

Television. *The Ninth Day* was presented on Playhouse 90 (CBS, 1957), and in London (BBC, 1959).

Other Activities. Mr. Baker has taught at Harvard Univ. and at the Univ. of California.

Published Works. Chapters from Mr. Baker's book on the civilization of ancient Greece were published in *The Sewanee Review* beginning in 1969.

Awards. He received a Guggenheim Fellowship (1944).

BAKER, LENNY. Actor. Member of AEA; SAG.

Theatre. At the Actor's Th. of Louisville (Ky.), Mr. Baker appeared in *Charley's Aunt* (Oct. 20, 1966), *The Knack* (Dec. 15, 1966), *Nathan Weinstein's Daughter* (Mar. 9, 1967), *The Hostage* (Nov. 2, 1967), *The Firebugs* (Dec. 7, 1967), *Long Day's Journey into Night* (Jan. 4, 1968), *Misalliance* (Feb. 8, 1968), the double bill *Strip-Tease* and *Endgame* (Mar. 7, 1968), and *Night of the Dunce* (Apr. 4, 1968); subsequently appeared in *Boy Meets Girl* (Center Stage, Baltimore, Sept. 27, 1968); played the Young Man in *Frank Gagliano's City Scene,* which included *City Scene I: Paradise Gardens East* and *City Scene II: Conerico Was Here to Stay* (Fortune Th., N.Y.C., Mar. 10, 1969); the Young Man in *Summertree* (Players Th., Dec. 9, 1969); and appeared in *The Survival of Saint Joan* (Anderson Th., Feb. 28, 1971). He was a member of the acting company at the Eugene O'Neill Playwrights Conference (Waterford, Conn., summers 1971, 1972, 1973); where he performed in some seventeen works-in-progress; played Fitzgerald in *The Freedom of the City* (Goodman Memorial Th., Chicago, Oct. 9, 1973); Mike Lovett in *Barbary Shore* (Public/Anspacher, N.Y.C., Dec. 18, 1973); Skinner in *The Freedom of the City* (Alvin, Feb. 17, 1974); Thailiard and Knight of Ephesus in *Pericles, Prince of Tyre* (Delacorte, June 20, 1974); Slender in *The Merry Wives of Windsor* (Delacorte, July 25, 1974); Hatch in *The Sea* (Goodman Memorial Th., Chicago, Nov. 15, 1974); and Mathews in *Life Class* (Manhattan Th. Club, N.Y.C., Dec. 14, 1975).

Films. Mr. Baker has appeared in *Hospital* (UA, 1971); *The Paper Chase* (20th-Fox, 1973); and *Next Stop, Greenwich Village* (20th-Fox, 1976).

BAKER, MARK. Actor. b. Oct. 2, 1946, Cumberland, Md. Educ. Northwestern Univ.; Carnegie-Mellon Univ. (costume design); Wittenberg Univ. Professional training at Neighborhood Playhouse, N.Y.C. Member of AEA; AFTRA; SAG.

Theatre. Mr. Baker made his professional debut as Linus in a touring company of *You're a Good Man, Charlie Brown.* He toured also in *The Fantasticks* and appeared in *Here Today* and *Hello, Dolly!* His N.Y.C. debut was in the off-Bway *Love Me, Love My Children* (Mercer-O'Casey Th., Nov. 3, 1971), and he first played on Bway as one of the Blue People in *Via Galactica* (Uris Th., Nov. 28, 1972). He was in an off-Bway production of *Godspell* and played the title role in the Chelsea Th. Ctr. revival of *Candide* (Brooklyn Acad. of Music, Dec. 11, 1973; moved to Broadway Th., Mar. 5, 1974).

Awards. For his performance in *Candide,* Mr. Baker received a 1974 Theater World Award and an Antoinette Perry (Tony) Award nomination as best supporting actor in a musical.

BAKER, PAUL. Producer, director, educator. b. July 24, 1911, Hereford, Tex., to William Morgan and Retta (Chapman) Baker. Father, minister. Attended Univ. of Wisconsin; grad. Trinity Univ., B.A. 1932; Yale Univ. Sch. of Drama, M.F.A., 1939. Studied with Elsie Fogarty at Central Sch. of Speech, London, England, 1932; studied and observed theatre in England, Germany, Russia, Manchuria, Korea, and Japan 1936. Married Dec. 21, 1936, to Sallie Kathryn Cardwell; three daughters. Relatives in theatre: daughters, Robyn Baker Flatt, actress, and Sallie Baker Laurie, actress. Served WW II, US Army, Chief of Entertainment Branch, ETO; rank, Maj.; Legion of Merit for reorganization of Entertainment Branch 1945. Member of NTC (pres., 1958–62); SWTC (pres.); Texas Inst. of Letters; American Playwrights Theater (bd. of governors). Address: (home) 455 E. Rosebud, San Antonio, TX 78212, tel. (915) 828-3976; (bus.) c/o Dallas Theater Center, 3636 Turtle Creek Blvd., Dallas, TX 75219, tel. (214) 526-0107; c/o Ruth Taylor Theater, Trinity University, 715 Stadium Dr., San Antonio, TX 78284, tel. (915) 736-8511.

Theatre. Since 1959, Mr. Baker has been director of the Dallas (Tex.) Th. Center, where he has produced and directed such plays as *Of Time and the*

River, The Cross-Eyed Bear, Our Town, The Matchmaker, Waltz in the Afternoon, The Visit, Joshua Bean and God, The Crossing, Naked to Mine Enemies, Journey to Jefferson, Hamlet ESP, Macbeth, The Homecoming, and *Jack Ruby, All-American Boy.* Mr. Baker is one of the nation's major producers of new plays. At the Dallas Theater Center some sixty new scripts and American premieres have been introduced since 1959. In 1974, he organized the highly successful "Dallas Playmarket '74", which brought theatre people from America and abroad to see new shows by Dallas Theater Center writers.

Mr. Baker has been professor and chairman of the Dept. of Speech and Drama, Trinity Univ. (1963–to date).

Published Works. Mr. Baker's *Integration of Abilities: Exercises for Creative Growth* and his *Hamlet ESP* have been published.

Awards. Mr. Baker received grants from the Rockefeller Foundation for study at Yale Univ. (1937–39); and for Baylor Th. (1941), to write on his war experiences (1946) and to study leisure time problems as related to the community (1959). He received, with Eugene McKinney, the Chris Award for their production of the Baylor Theatre's *Hamlet* film (1957); a prize at the Brussels World Fair Film Festival for best short-run fiction film (1958); an honorary Doctor of Fine Arts degree from Trinity Univ. (1958); and the first Rodgers and Hammerstein Award for theatrical contribution in the Southwest (1961). In 1968, he was presented the Margo Jones Award for "daring and continuous new play production"; in 1974, Mr. Baker received the San Diego National Shakespeare Festival Award for outstanding contribution to classic theatre.

Recreation. Writing, ranching.

BAKER, WORD. Director, producer. b. Charles William Baker, Mar. 21, 1923, Honey Grove, Fannin County, Texas, to Dan and Maggie (Word) Baker. Father, druggist; mother, music teacher. Grad. Honey Grove H.S., 1940; attended North Texas State Univ., 1940–42; grad. Univ. of Texas, B.F.A. (summa cum laude), 1951; studied with B. Iden Payne, Univ. of Texas, 1948–51. Married Oct. 24, 1942 to Joanna Alexander (dec. 1966); three daughters. Served with US Army, PTO. Member of AEA; SSD&C.

Pre-Theatre. Bookkeeper.

Theatre. Mr. Baker first appeared on stage at nine as Lear in a school production of *King Lear* (Honey Grove, Tex., 1932); danced in a university revue, *College Capers* (Interstate Theatres, Tex., 1942); and was director, designer, choreographer, and actor in productions at Auburn Coll. and Texas Western Coll., where he served as drama instructor (1951–55).

He designed sets for summer theatre productions at the Grist Mill (N.J.) Playhouse (1956) and at the Montclair (N.J.) Playhouse (1956); designed the costumes for the ELT producton of the double bill, *The Admirable Bashville, The Dark Lady of the Sonnets* and *Liliom* (Lenox Hill Playhouse, N.Y.C., Dec. 14, 1955). He was casting director for Jo Mielziner and stage manager for *Happy Hunting* (Majestic, Dec. 6, 1956).

Mr. Baker and Paul Libin, with Mouzon Law and Franchot Productions produced *The Crucible,* a revival which Mr. Baker also directed (Martinique, Mar. 11, 1958). He was associate director and producer, as well as costume designer, for a cabaret revue, *Demi-Dozen* (Upstairs at the Downstairs, N.Y.C., Sept., 1958); directed and choreographed *Ride a Pink Horse* (Crest Th., Toronto, Canada, May 1959); directed student productions of *The Mall, The Gay Apprentice* and the premiere of *The Fantasticks* in its original short version (Minor Latham Th., N.Y.C., Summer, 1959); co-produced, and designed the costumes for two revues, *Pieces of Eight* and *Four Below Strikes Back* (Upstairs at the Downstairs, 1959–60).

Mr. Baker directed *The Fantasticks* (Sullivan St. Playhouse, May 3, 1960); *The Tragical History of Dr. Faustus* (Boston Univ. Th., Dec. 7, 1960); directed *The Fantasticks* (Royal Poinciana Playhouse, Palm Beach, Fla., 1960); *As You Like It* for the American Shakespeare Festival (Stratford, Conn., Summer 1961); *The Fantasticks* again for the London production (Apollo, Sept., 1961); directed and choreographed *Guys and Dolls* (Bradford Roof, Boston), and *Maggie* (Paper Mill Playhouse, Millburn, N.J.; Westport Country Playhouse, Conn., Summer 1962).

At the Festival of Two Worlds (Spoleto, Italy, he directed *The American Dream, Rosemary, Ginger Anne, The Exhaustion of Our Son's Love* and scenes from Shakespeare, which he also designed (Teatro-Tenda, Summer 1962). He directed *The Fantasticks* (Dec. 5, 1962), and *A Comedy of Errors* (Dec. 26, 1962) for the Fred Miller Th. (Milwaukee, Wis.); *A Plumb Line* (Village South Th., N.Y.C., Nov. 24, 1963); *The Bell Telephone Show* (NY World's Fair, 1964); *The Tragical Historie of Doctor Faustus* (Phoenix, Oct. 5, 1964); *The Room* and *A Slight Ache* (Writers Stage Th., Dec. 9, 1964); *Venus Is* (Billy Rose Th., Apr. 5, 1966); *Now Is the Time for All Good Men* (Th. de Lys, Sept. 26, 1967); *The Odd Couple* (Hamlet St. Th., Pittsburgh, Apr. 3, 1968); *The Last Sweet Days of Isaac* (East Side Playhouse, N.Y.C., Jan. 26, 1970); and the world premiere of *Dracula* by Leon Katz (Lab. Playhouse, Purdue Univ., Lafayette, Ind., Feb. 24, 1970).

At Playhouse in the Park (Cincinnati, Ohio), where he was artistic director (Sept. 1970–Nov. 1972), he directed, and with Ken Jansen, co-choreographed *Man Happy Returns: A Re-View of Revues* (June 18, 1970); with Dan Early, co-directed *Tobacco Road* (Sept. 24, 1970); with Michael Flanagan, co-directed *As You Like It* (Oct. 27, 1970); directed *The Last Sweet Days of Isaac* (June 1, 1971); the world premieres of *Caravaggio* (July 1, 1971), and *Shelter* (June 1, 1972; *The Play's the Thing* (July 2, 1972); the world premiere of *Sensations of the Bitten Partner* (Aug. 3, 1972); with Donald Brooks, co-directed *The Rivals* (Sept. 7, 1972); with Dan Early, co-directed *The Crucible* (Sept. 21, 1972); conceived, directed and, with Dan Early, Maria Irene Fornes, Milburn Smith, Sherman F. Warner and the company, co-wrote *Baboon!!!* (Oct. 5, 1972); and directed *Kiss Me, Kate* (June 21, 1973).

Elsewhere, he has directed *The Soft Core Pornographer* (Stage 73, N.Y.C., Apr. 11, 1972); at the Trinity Square Playhouse (Providence, R.I.), *Lady Audley's Secret* (Nov. 21, 1972; re-opened Mar. 22, 1973), the world premiere of *For the Use of the Hall* (Jan. 2, 1974), and *Jumpers* (Dec. 12, 1974); *The Matchmaker* (Seattle, Wash., Repertory Th., Mar. 5, 1975); and, again, *The Matchmaker* (Queens Community Coll., N.Y.C., Feb. 1976).

Television. Mr. Baker staged *The Grass Harp* and *New York Scrapbook* (Play of the Week, WNTA, 1960, 1961).

Other Activities. Mr. Baker has taught at the HB (Herbert Berghof) Studio, N.Y.C., since 1962.

Awards. The revival of *The Crucible,* which he directed and co-produced, received a *Village Voice* Off-Bway (Obie) Award (1958); and he was given a Ford Foundation Grant to travel in Europe (Summer 1960).

BALCH, MARSTON. Educator, writer, director. b. Marston Stevens Balch, Nov. 21, 1901, Detroit, Mich., to Ernest Alanson and Bertha Lou (Stevens) Balch. Father, history professor, mayor of Kalamazoo, Mich. Grad. Central H.S., Kalamazoo, 1919; Kalamazoo Coll., A.B. 1923; Harvard Univ., M.A. 1925; Ph.D. 1931; research in theatre history, British Museum, Oxford Univ. and Cambridge Univ., Summer 1929, and Paris, Summers 1931, 1932. Married Sept. 6, 1925, to Germaine Cornier, French professor; one daughter. Served OWI, N. Africa, 1943–44; USIS, Paris, 1944–46. Member of NTC (exec. secy., 1961–67); New England Th. Conf. (co-founder, 1950; member of bd. and advisory council, to date); ASTR (delegate to 1973 Prague congress of Internat. Fed. Th. Research); ATA; AAUP; The French Center in New England, Inc. (co-founder, 1946; vice-pres., 1946–74); The French Library in Boston, Inc. (co-founder, 1946; trustee and secy., to date). Address: 50 Sawyer Ave., Medford, MA 02155, tel. (617) 623-6775.

He was instructor of English, Williams Coll. (1925–27); instructor of English and tutor, Division of Modern Languages, Harvard Univ. (1928–33); and instructor of English, Phillips Exeter Acad. (1933–34). Since 1934, Mr. Balch has been a member of the faculty of arts and sciences, Tufts Univ. (asst. prof. of English, 1934–37; prof. of drama, 1937–71; chmn., dept. of drama and speech, 1940–66; prof. emeritus, 1971–to date). As exec. dir. of Tufts Univ. Th. (1935–66), he staged over a hundred major productions, including many new plays, also his own translations from the French of Charles Vildrac's *The Steamship Tenacity* (1948), Gaston-Marie Martens' *Beggars in Paradise* (1949), Nicholas Evreinoff's *The Chief Thing* (1952), Jules Romains' *Doctor Knock* (1957), and Molière's *The Would-Be Gentleman* (1960).

At Tufts, in collaboration with John R. Woodruff, Mr. Balch began experimenting as early as 1940 with various forms of nonproscenium staging, and together they developed in the mid-forties "the first permanent arena theater east of Seattle." They also created a small but influential "occasional periodical" of the Tufts University Theater called *Prologue* (1945–to date), portions of which have often been reprinted in national and international publications.

Since 1961, Mr. Balch has been making a critical study of the changing state of the American theatre. One product of this evaluation, conducted in collaboration with Robert E. Gard, was the book, *Theater in America: Appraisal and Challenge* (1968). Since that publication, Mr. Balch has been making a survey of the present state of playwriting in America.

Published Works. *The Dramatic Legacy of Thomas Middleton* (1931); editor of *Modern Short Biographies* (1935); co-editor of *The College Omnibus* (1936 and 1939); co-author of *You and College* (1936); editor of *Modern Short Biographies and Autobiographies* (1940); co-author (with Robert E. Gard) of *Theater in America: Appraisal and Challenge* (1968); contributed articles to *The Dictionary of American Biography, The World Book Encyclopedia,* other reference works and U.S. government documents on theatre; and also to *Theatre Arts Monthly, Theatre Arts* magazine, *La Revue Théâtrale* (Paris), *Conferences d'Alger, Modern Language Review, Dramatists Guild Quarterly, Cue,* and numerous other American and foreign periodicals.

Awards. He is a recipient of the French Republic's Médaille de la Reconnaissance (1947) and is a chevalier in the Légion d'Honneur (1953). He received the honorary degree of Doctor of Humane Letters (L.H.D.) from Kalamazoo College (1960); a special award for distinguished service from the Tufts Alumni Council (1960); citations for long and distinguished service to the theatre from the New England Th. Conf. (1960 and 1972); the Margo Jones Award (1955); and, on the occasion of his retirement from Tufts University, numerous tributes from ATA, NTC, Amer. Coll. Th. Fest., Nat. Assoc. of Schools of Th., and other organizations, institutions, and causes he has served.

BALDWIN, JAMES. Author, playwright. b. James Arthur Baldwin, Aug. 2, 1924, New York City, to David and Berdis Emma (Jones) Baldwin. Father, clergyman. Grad. De Witt Clinton H.S., N.Y.C., 1942. Member of Congress of Racial Equality (natl. adv. bd.); Natl. Com. for Sane Nuclear Policy; Actors Studio; Natl. Institute of Arts and Letters.

After graduation from high school, Mr. Baldwin did defense work in Belle Meade, N.J., and was a general handyman, dishwasher, restaurant waiter, and office boy in Greenwich Village, N.Y.C. He was also writing at this period and in 1945 received a Eugene F. Saxton Memorial Trust Award and in 1948 a Rosenwald Fellowship. From 1948 to 1958 he lived in Europe, mainly in Paris, and completed three books: *Go Tell It on the Mountain* (1952), *Notes of a Native Son* (1955), and *Giovanni's Room* (1956). Later works by Mr. Baldwin are *Another Country* (1961); *Nobody Knows My Name: More Notes of a Native Son* (1961), a collection of his magazine articles; *The Fire Next Time* (1963); with Richard Avedon, *Nothing Personal* (1964); *Tell Me How Long the Train's Been Gone* (1968); with Margaret Mead, *A Rap on Race* (1971); *No Name in the Streets* (1971); *One Day, When I Was Lost: A Scenario Based on "The Autobiography of Malcolm X"* (1972); and *If Beale Street Could Talk* (1973).

Theatre. Mr. Baldwin's plays are *The Amen Corner* (Howard Univ., Washington, D.C., 1953; Robertson Playhouse, Los Angeles, Calif., Mar. 4, 1964; Ethel Barrymore Th., N.Y.C., Apr. 15, 1965); *Blues for Mr. Charlie* (ANTA Th., Apr. 23, 1964); and *A Deed from the King of Spain* (Amer. Ctr. for Stanislavski Th. Art., Jan. 24, 1974).

Other Activities. Mr. Baldwin has been active in civil rights work.

Awards. In addition to the fellowships referred to above, Mr. Baldwin received a Guggenheim Fellowship (1954); a *Partisan Review* Fellowship (1956); a National Institute of Arts and Letters Award (1956); and a Ford Foundation grant (1959). *Nobody Knows My Name* was named by the American Library Association as an outstanding book of 1961 and was given a certificate of honor by the Natl. Conference of Christians and Jews.

BALL, ROBERT HAMILTON. Educator, theatre historian. b. May 21, 1902, New York City, to Dr. George Martin and Flora Cristene (Hill) Ball. Father, physician. Grad. Phillips Exeter Acad., N.H., arts degree; Princeton Univ., B.A. 1923, M.A. 1924, Ph.D. 1928. Married June 26, 1928, to Esther Marshall Smith; one daughter. Member of AAUP (past chapter pres.); Princeton Club of N.Y.; ASTR (exec. committee to 1973; chmn., program committee, 1958–63); Intl. Federation for Th. Research, TLA (former chmn., Theatre Documents Board; exec. committee); Shakespeare Assn. of Amer., Modern Humanities Research Assn. (Amer. exec. comm., 1958–67); MLA (former secy., chmn. of English Drama Section). Address: (home) 11 N. Washington St., Port Washington, NY tel. (516) PO 7-1157; (bus.) Dept. of English, Queens College of the City Univ. of N.Y., Flushing, NY 11367, tel. (212) HI 5-7500.

He became a member of the faculty, Dept. of English, Queens College, in 1939, serving as assistant professor until 1943, associate professor (1944–51), professor (1951–71), and professor emeritus (1971–to date). he was in addition chairman of the Dept. of English (1941–47; 1960–65) and of the Arts Division (1949–55).

He was instructor (1927–31) and assistant professor (1931–39) of English and dramatic art, and curator (1936–39) of the William Seymour Theatre Collection at Princeton Univ.; professor at the Univ. of Ankara, Turkey (1955–56); and visiting professor at the Univ. of Colorado (1939), New York Univ. (1948–49), and the Univ. of California at Los Angeles (1949).

Published Works. Mr. Ball is the author of *The Amazing Career of Sir Giles Overreach* (1939); has edited *The Plays of Henry C. DeMille* (1941); served on the advisory board of editors for *America's Lost Plays*, 20 vols. 1939–42); wrote, with T. M. Parrott, *A Short View of Elizabethan Drama* (1943; rev. ed. 1960), and, with W. P. Bowman, *Theatre Language* (1961); and was sole author of *Shakespeare on Silent Film* (1968). He has also contributed articles to *Collier's Encyclopedia, Encyclopedia Americana, University of Colorado Studies, Pacific Spectator, Quarterly of Film, Radio and Television, Shakespeare Quarterly, Theatre Survey, Players* magazine, *Shakespeare Newsletter*, and *Literature/Film Quarterly*. .

Awards. Mr. Ball received a Fellowship in English, Princeton Univ. (1925–26); Charlotte Elizabeth Proctor Fellowship, Princeton Univ. (1926–27); Guggenheim Fellowship (1946–47); Rockefeller Foundation Grant (1955–56).

Recreation. Fishing, collecting glass cup plates and theatrical memorabilia.

BALL, WILLIAM. Director. b. Apr. 29, 1931, Chicago, Ill., to Russell and Catherine (Gormaly) Ball. Attended Iona (N.Y.) Preparatory Sch., 1944–48; Fordham Univ., 1948–50; grad. Carnegie Inst of Tech., B.A. (acting and design) 1953, M.A. (directing) 1955. Member of SSD&C; AEA. Address: American Conservatory Theatre, 450 Geary St., San Francisco, CA 94102, tel. (415) 771-3880. of San Francisco (1973).

Theatre. Mr. Ball made his stage debut as an actor while a student at Carnegie Tech., performing in *Uncle Vanya, Candida,* and *Hamlet* (1948); joined Margaret Webster's Shakespeare touring company as assistant designer and as an actor, playing minor roles (1948–50); subsequently appeared with the Oregon Shakespeare Festival as Mark Antony in *Julius Caesar*, Feste in *Twelfth Night*, Lorenzo in *The Merchant of Venice*, Ariel in *The Tempest*, and Claudio in *Much Ado About Nothing* (Ashland, Ore., 1950–53).

He played Richard in *Ah, Wilderness!* (Pittsburgh Playhouse, Pa., 1952); with the Pittsburgh Symphony, appeared as Puck in *A Midsummer Night's Dream* and as the Devil in *L'Histoire du Soldat* (1954). At the Antioch Shakespeare Festival, he played Romeo in *Romeo and Juliet*, Trinculo in *The Tempest*, Old Gobbo in *The Merchant of Venice*, Puck in *A Midsummer Night's Dream*, Vincentio in *The Taming of the Shrew*, and Montano in *Othello;* and directed *As You Like It* (Yellow Springs, Ohio, Summer 1954).

With the San Diego (Calif.) Shakespeare Festival, he performed the title role in *Hamlet* (Summer 1955); with the Group 20 Players, appeared as the Lion in *Androcles and the Lion*, as Gonzales in *The Tempest*, as the Witch in *Faust* (Wellesley, Mass., 1955–56); and at the Antioch Shakespeare Festival, directed *Twelfth Night* (Yellow Springs, Ohio, 1957).

Mr. Ball played Acaste in *The Misanthrope* (Th. East, N.Y.C., Nov. 12, 1956); the voice of Rosencrantz in Siobhan McKenna's *Hamlet* (Th. de Lys, Jan. 28, 1957); Nicholas Devise in *The Lady's Not for Burning* (Carnegie Hall Playhouse, Feb. 21, 1957); Mr. Horner in *The Country Wife* (Renata, June 26, 1957); toured as Conrad in *Visit to a Small Planet* (Summer 1957); appeared as Dubedat in *The Doctor's Dilemma* (Arena Stage, Washington, D.C., 1957–58); and was stage manager for *Back to Methuselah* (Ambassador, N.Y.C., Mar. 26, 1958).

He directed *Ivanov* (Renata, Oct. 7, 1958); *Once More, With Feeling* (Alley Th., Houston, Tex., 1958); *Henry IV, Part 1* and *Julius Caesar* for the San Diego (Calif.) Shakespeare Festival (1958–59); directed *The Devil's Disciple* (Actor's Workshop, San Francisco, Calif., 1958); *A Month in the Country* (Arena Stage, Washington, D.C., 1959); for the NY City Opera (NY City Ctr.,) directed *Six Characters in Search of an Author* (Apr. 26, 1959) and *Cosi Fan Tutti* (Oct. 8, 1959); directed *The Tempest* for the American Shakespeare Festival (Stratford, Conn., July 19, 1960); for the NY City Opera, directed *The Inspector General* (NY City Ctr., Oct. 19, 1960); directed *Under Milkwood* (Circle in the Square, Mar. 29, 1961); for the NY City Opera directed *Porgy and Bess* (NY City Ctr., Mar. 31, 1962); directed and played Hal, Prince of Wales, in *Henry IV, Part 2* (San Diego Shakespeare Festival, Calif., June 20, 1962); directed *Six Characters in Search of an Author* (Martinique, N.Y.C., Mar. 7, 1963; Mayfair, London, June 17, 1963); directed *Don Giovanni* for the NY City Opera (NY City Ctr., Spring 1963); directed *The Yeoman of the Guard* (Festival Th., Stratford, Ontario, Canada, July 3, 1964); directed *Tartuffe* for Lincoln Center Repertory Th. (ANTA Washington Square Th., Jan. 14, 1965).

Awards. Mr. Ball received a Fulbright Scholarship Award (1953–54) to study repertory theatre in England and Europe; an NBC/RCA Directors Fellowship (1955–56) from Carnegie Tech.; and a Ford Foundation Grant (1958–59) for directing. For his direction of *Ivanov*, he received a Village Voice (Obie) Award (1959) and a Vernon Rice Award (1959). He has received two Lola D'Annunzio Awards: for his direction of *Under Milkwood* (1961), and *Six Characters in Search of an Author* (1963). He won the Outer Circle Critics Award (N.Y.) for his direction of *Tartuffe* for Lincoln Center Repertory Theatre (1965).

BALLANTYNE, PAUL. Actor. b. Paul Ardivon Ballantyne, July 18, 1909, Moorhead, Iowa, to James Carl and Inez Mae (Adams) Ballantyne. Grad. Lamoni (Iowa) H.S., 1926; Sherwood Music Sch., Chicago, Ill., teacher's certificate, 1931. Studied acting for three years with Mrs. Luella Canterbury, Chicago. Served US Army Infantry, 1940–46; rank, Maj. Member of AEA; AFTRA; SAG.

Theatre. Mr. Ballantyne first appeared on stage as an apprentice with the Eva Le Gallienne Civic Repertory Co., playing the Eight of Hearts in *Alice in Wonderland* (Civic Repertory Th., N.Y.C., Dec. 12, 1932); followed by a tour in *Dark Tower* (1934), and a season at the Cape Playhouse, where he played Fred in Rachel Crother's *Talent* (Dennis, Mass., Summer 1934). With the Federal Th. (WPA) Project, Mr. Ballantyne played Captain Jack Absolute in *The Rivals*, Everyman in *Everyman*, and Young Marlowe in *She Stoops to Conquer* (1935–37); and appeared as Bing in the national tour of *Brother Rat* (Feb. 1937–June 1938).

He played Heinrich Wertheimer in *Mrs. O'Brien Entertains* (Lyceum, N.Y.C., Feb. 8, 1939); Johann in *Brown Danube* (Lyceum, May 17, 1939); a Student in *The Unconquered* (Biltmore, Feb. 13, 1940); Kurt in *Goodbye in the Night* (Biltmore, Mar. 18, 1940); appeared in *Biography* (Summer 1940); and played Charles Owen in *Suzanna and the Elders* (Morosco, Oct. 29, 1940).

Mr. Ballantyne appeared at the Brattle Th. (Cambridge, Mass.), where he portrayed Brutus in *Julius Caesar*, Ferovius in *Androcles and the Lion*, Frank in *The Little Blue Light*, the Reverend Davidson in *Rain*, Northumberland in *Henry IV, Part II*, Tchebutykin in *The Three Sisters*, the Burglar in *Heartbreak House*, Costard in *Love's Labour's Lost* and Cleante in *Tartuffe* (Summers 1950–51).

He returned to New York to play La Hire in the Th. Guild production of *Saint Joan* (Cort, Oct. 4, 1951); portrayed William Clark, S.J., in *The Strong Are Lonely* (Broadhurst, Sept. 29, 1953); Brackenbury in *Richard III* (NY City Ctr., Dec. 9, 1953); and De Baudricourt in *Saint Joan* (opened National Th., Washington, D.C., Sept. 20, 1954; closed Hartman Th., Columbus, Ohio, Nov. 6, 1954).

For the American Theatre Repertory Company's tour of Europe made in association with the US State Dept., he played Fred Bailey and a Professor in *The Skin of Our Teeth*, understudied Leif Erickson in the role of the Gentleman Caller in *The Glass Menagerie*, and played Mr. Keller in *The Miracle Worker* (Mar.–June 1961).

With the National Repertory Theatre, he toured as the Earl of Shrewsbury in *Mary Stuart*, and Sir Walter Raleigh in *Elizabeth the Queen* (opened Acad. of Music, Northampton, Mass., Oct. 19, 1961; closed, Rochester, N.Y., Apr. 14, 1962).

As an original member of the Minnesota Th. (repertory) Co. (Tyrone Guthrie Th., Minneapolis, Minn., 1963–to date), Mr. Ballantyne played Marcellus in *Hamlet* (May 7, 1963), La Fleche in *The Miser* (May 8, 1963), and Charley in *Death of a Salesman* (July 16, 1963); returned to play Williams in *Henry V* (May 11, 1964), Chaplain de Stogumber in *Saint Joan* (May 12, 1964), and the First Avocatore and to understudy Douglas Campbell in the title role in *Volpone* (June 29, 1964). He subsequently appeared there in *Richard III, The Way of the World, The Cherry Orchard,* and *The Caucasian Chalk Circle* (1965); *The Dance of Death,* and *S. S. Glencairn* (1966); *The House of Atreus, Shoemaker's Holiday, Thieves, Carnival, Harper's Ferry, She Stoops To Conquer, Tango,* and *Man with a Flower in His Mouth* (1967); *Twelfth Night, Sergeant Musgrave's Dance, Arturo Ui,* and *The House of Atreus* (1968).

During the Minnesota Th. Co.'s N.Y.C. engagement (Billy Rose Th.), he appeared in *The House of Atreus* (Dec. 17, 1968), and *Arturo Ui* (Dec. 22, 1968).

Returning to the Tyrone Guthrie Th., he appeared in *The Beauty Part, Uncle Vanya,* and *Ardele* (1969); *The Venetian Twins, The Tempest, A Man's a Man,* and *A Play* (1970), written by Alexander Solzhenitsyn; and *Misalliance* and *A Touch of the Poet* (1971–72). In addition, Mr. Ballantyne played Crysalde in *The School for Wives* (Lyceum, N.Y.C., Feb. 16, 1971); and appeared as a guest artist at the Meadowbrook Th. (Rochester, Mich., 1971–72).

Films. Mr. Ballantyne appeared in *The Andromeda Strain* (U, 1971).

Television and Radio. Mr. Ballantyne has appeared on all radio networks, including Th. Guild of the Air (CBS); Pet Milk Show (NBC); Junior G-Men (Mutual); Ave Maria Hour (WMCA, NYC); and Ma Perkins (CBS).

On television, he has appeared on Hallmark Hall of Fame (NBC); Play of the Week (WNDT); You Are There (CBS); The Catholic Hour (NBC); and Westinghouse Th. (CBS).

BALLARD, KAYE. Actress, singer. b. Catherine Gloria Balotta, Nov. 20, 1926, Cleveland, Ohio, to Vincent and Lena (Nacarato) Balotta. Grad. West Technical H.S., Cleveland, 1944. Member of AEA; AFTRA; AGVA; SAG. Address: c/o Singer & Tiano, 9595 Wilshire Blvd., Beverley Hills, CA 90212.

Theatre. Miss Ballard first appeared on stage in a USO production of *Stagedoor Canteen* (Cleveland, 1941); and made her first professional appearance touring cross-country in vaudeville (RKO circuit, 1943).

She made her NYC debut in the revue *Three to Make Ready* (Adelphi Th., Mar. 7, 1946); subsequently appeared in stock productions of *Once in a Lifetime* (Duxbury, Mass., 1946); *Wonderful Town* (Tenthouse Th., Highland Park, Ill.; Kenley Players, Warren, Ohio, 1946); *Annie Get Your Gun* (Asbury Park, N.J., 1946); and in *Look Ma, I'm Dancing* (State Fair Music Hall, Dallas, Tex., 1946).

Miss Ballard appeared in *That's the Ticket* (opened Shubert, Philadelphia, Pa., Sept. 24, 1948; closed there Oct. 2, 1948); in the London production of *Touch and Go* (Prince of Wales, May 19, 1950); *Top Banana* (Winter Garden, N.Y.C., Nov. 1, 1951); played Helen of Troy in *The Golden Apple* (Phoenix, Mar. 11, 1954); the Countess in *Reuben, Reuben* (Shubert, Boston, Mass., Oct. 22, 1955); and *Pleasure Dome* (1956).

She appeared in the national tour of *Ziegfeld Follies* (opened Royal Alexandra, Toronto, Canada, Sept. 12, 1957; closed Shubert, Cincinnati, Oct. 12, 1957); played the Incomparable Rosalie in *Carnival!* (Imperial, Apr. 13, 1961); Rose in *Gypsy* (State Fair Music Hall, Dallas, Tex., 1962); Ruth in *Wonderful Town* (NY City Ctr., Feb. 13, 1963); and appeared in the revue *The Beast in Me* (Plymouth, May 16, 1963); *Cole Porter Revisited* (Square East Th., March 19, 1966); *Molly* (Alvin Th., Sept. 11, 1973); and appeared in *Sheba* (First Chicago Center, Chicago, July 14, 1974).

Films. Miss Ballard appeared in *The Girl Most Likely* (RKO, 1956); *A House Is Not a Home* (Par., 1964); and *Which Way to the Front?* (WB, 1971).

Television. Miss Ballard made her first television appearance on the Mel Torme Show (CBS, 1952); played the Step-Sister in the Rodgers and Hammerstein special, *Cinderella* (CBS, 1952); and has since appeared on the Garry Moore Show (CBS), Ed Sullivan Show (CBS), John Conte Show (CBS), Password (CBS), and Arthur Godfrey Show (CBS).

She also appeared on Nothing But the Best (NBC), Colgate Comedy Hour (NBC), Perry Como Show (NBC), Jack Paar Show (NBC), Alcoa-Goodyear Show (NBC), Kraft Television Th. (NBC), Steve Allen Show (NBC), Andy Williams Show (NBC), Today (NBC), Patrice Munsel Show (ABC), and Girl Talk (ABC).

She has appeared on Laugh-In (NBC); Merv Griffin (CBS); Tonight Show (NBC); Here's Lucy (CBS); Love, American Style (ABC); Hollywood Squares (NBC); Celebrity Sweepstakes (NBC); Match Game (NBC); The Doris Day Show (CBS); Dinah Shore Show (CBS); Carol Burnett Show (CBS); Flip Wilson Show (NBC); Leslie Uggams Show (CBS); Bi-Centennial (CBC); and on the Penny Fuller Special (1975). Miss Ballard also appeared as a regular in the Mothers-in-Law (NBC, 1968 and 1969).

Night Clubs. Miss Ballard appeared at the Plaza Hotel, N.Y.C.; Blue Angel, N.Y.C.; Bon Soir, N.Y.C.; Mr. Kelly's, Chicago, Ill.; Palmer House, Chicago; Fontainebleau Hotel, Miami, Fla.; Monteleone Hotel, New Orleans, La.; hungry i, San Francisco, Calif.; and the Cocoanut Grove, Los Angeles; Flamingo, Hilton, Desert Inn, Fremont and Thunderbird, Las Vegas, Nev.; Disney World, Los Angeles; Bermuda Princess, South Hampton, Bermuda; and New Orleans Pop Concerts, New Orleans, La.

Awards. Miss Ballard has received the Italian American Award (1963); the Ometa Award; Dallas State Fair Award for *Gypsy;* and the Jefferson Award nomination in Chicago, Ill.

Recreation. Sketching, painting, playing the flute.

BALLARD, LUCINDA. Costume designer, scenic designer. b. Lucinda Davis Goldsborough, Apr. 3, 1906, New Orleans, La., to Richard Francis and Anna Girault (Farrar) Goldsborough. Father, lawyer; mother, political cartoonist, known as Doré. Grad. Miss McGehee's Sch., New Orleans, La., 1922; attended Art Students' League, N.Y.C., 1923–35; Fontainebleau, France, Summers 1927, 1929–31; Sorbonne, Paris, 1928–29; Beaux Arts and Chaumière, Paris, 1928–30; studied true fresco painting under Paul Baudoin and La Montagne St., Hubert, France. Married Feb. 6, 1930, to William F. R. Ballard (marr. dis. 1938); one son, one daughter; married July 31, 1951, to Howard Dietz, lyricist. During WW II, worked for British Information Services; was an initial member of The Stage Door Canteen; painted mural for Canteen; designed scenery and costumes for *Stage Door Follies.* Member of United Scenic Artists, Local 829; Regency Club. Address: 1 Lincoln Plaza, New York, NY 10023.

Pre-Theatre. Assistant to Tony Sarg and Norman Bel Geddes; mural painter (ceiling of Congregational Church, Kalamazoo, Mich.; Princeton Univ., N.J.); designer of book jackets and textiles; book illustrator.

Theatre. Miss Ballard began as costume and scenic designer for Dwight Deere Wilman's production of *As You Like It* (Ritz, N.Y.C., Oct. 30, 1937); subsequently designed costumes for *Great Lady* (Majestic, Dec. 1, 1938); costumes for the NY World's Fair production of *American Jubilee* (1939); *The Three Sisters* (Longacre, Oct. 14, 1939); and *Morning's at Seven* (Longacre, Nov. 30, 1939).

When the Ballet Theatre was formed in 1940, Miss Ballard was appointed technical director for all costumes, and designed costumes for *Les Sylphides* (premiere, Center Th., Jan. 11, 1940); scenery and costumes for *Giselle* (premiere, Center, Jan. 12, 1940); and *Peter and the Wolf* (world premiere, Center, Jan. 13, 1940); costumes for *Swan Lake* (premiere, Center, Jan. 16, 1940); scenery and costumes for *Quintet* (world premiere, Center, Feb. 1, 1940); and supervised and reconstructed the foreign ballets and the Bakst-designed ballets.

She created costumes for *Higher and Higher* (Shubert, Apr. 4, 1940); *Solitaire* (Plymouth, Feb. 27, 1942); scenery and costumes for *The Moon Vine* (Morosco, Feb. 11, 1943); designed *Beggar on Horseback* (Berkshire Playhouse, Stockbridge, Mass., July 1943); designed costumes for *My Dear Public* (46 St. Th., N.Y.C., Sept. 9, 1943); and *Listen, Professor!* (Forrest, Dec. 22, 1943); scenery and costumes for the pre-Bway tryout of *Stove Pipe Hat* (opened Shubert, New Haven, Conn., 1944; closed Shubert, Boston, Mass., 1944); costumes for *Sing Out, Sweet Land* (International, N.Y.C., Dec. 27, 1944); *I Remember Mama* (Music Box Th., Oct. 19, 1944); *The Glass Menagerie* (Playhouse, Mar. 31, 1945); *A Place of Our Own* (Royale, Apr. 2, 1945); and *Memphis Bound* (Bway Th., May 24, 1945).

She designed costumes for new productions of *Show Boat* (Ziegfeld, Jan. 5, 1946; NY City Ctr., Sept. 7, 1948); for the pre-Bway tryout of *One Shoe Off* (opened Nixon, Pittsburgh, Pa., Feb. 18, 1946; closed Shubert, New Haven, Conn., Mar. 2, 1946); *Annie Get Your Gun* (Imperial, N.Y.C., May 16, 1946) and subsequent national touring productions; *Happy Birthday* (Broadhurst, Oct. 31, 1946); *Another Part of the Forest* (Fulton, Nov. 20, 1946); *Street Scene* (Adelphi, Jan. 9, 1947); *John Loves Mary* (Booth, Feb. 4, 1947).

She created costumes for *The Chocolate Soldier* (Century, March 12, 1947); *Allegro* (Majestic, Oct. 10, 1947); *A Streetcar Named Desire* (Ethel Barrymore Th., Dec. 3, 1947), and subsequent touring productions; *Alice Sit by the Fire* (Olney Th., Md., Summer 1948); *The Glass Menagerie* (Haymarket, London, England, July 28, 1948); *Love Life* (46 St. Th., N.Y.C., Oct. 7, 1948); scenery and costumes for *Make Way for Lucia* (Cort, Dec. 22, 1948); and designed, with Joseph Fretwell III, costumes for *The Rat Race* (Ethel Barrymore Th., Dec. 22, 1949).

Miss Ballard designed costumes for *The Fourposter* (Ethel Barrymore Th., Oct. 24, 1951), the subsequent national tour (opened Civic Aud., Pasadena, Calif., July 25, 1952; closed National, Washington, D.C., May 30, 1953), and the NY City Ctr. production (Jan. 5, 1955); *Mrs. McThing* (Martin Beck Th., Feb. 20, 1952), and the subsequent national tour (opened Colonial, Boston, Mass., Jan. 13, 1953; closed Nixon, Pittsburgh, Pa., May 30, 1953); *My Three Angels* (Morosco, N.Y.C., Mar. 11, 1953); and *Carnival in Flanders* (Century, Sept. 8, 1953).

She created costumes for *The Time of Your Life* (NY City Ctr., Jan. 19, 1955); *The Wisteria Trees* (NY City Ctr., Feb. 13, 1955); *Silk Stockings* (Imperial, Feb. 24, 1955), and the subsequent national tour (opened Curran, San Francisco, Calif., Apr. 23, 1956); *Cat on a Hot Tin Roof* (Morosco, Mar. 24, 1955), and the following national tour (opened National, Washington, D.C., Nov. 26, 1956); *A Clearing in the Woods* (Belasco, N.Y.C., Jan. 10, 1957); *Orpheus Descending* (Martin Beck Th., March 21, 1957); *The Dark at the Top of the Stairs* (Music Box Th., Dec. 5, 1957), and subsequent national tours (opened Playhouse, Wilmington, Del., Jan. 21, 1959; closed Pabst, Milwaukee, Wis., May 16, 1959; opened Veterans Memorial Aud., Providence, R.I., Sept. 21, 1959; closed National, Washington, D.C., Apr. 23, 1960).

She designed costumes for *Handful of Fire* (Martin Beck Th., N.Y.C., Oct. 1, 1958); *The Girls in 509* (Belasco, Oct. 15, 1958), and the following national tour (opened Hanna, Cleveland, Ohio, Jan. 26, 1959; closed Nixon, Pittsburgh, Pa., May 9, 1959); *J.B.* (ANTA, N.Y.C., Dec. 11, 1958) and the following national tours (opened Shubert, New Haven, Conn., Oct. 28, 1959; closed Locust St. Th., Philadelphia, Pa., Mar. 29, 1960; opened Playhouse, Wilmington, Del., Oct. 19, 1960; closed Camp, Camp LeJeune, N.C., Apr. 15, 1961); *The Sound of Music* (Lunt-Fontanne, N.Y.C., Nov. 16, 1959), and subsequent national tours (opened Riviera, Detroit, Mich., Feb. 27, 1961; opened Community, Hershey, Pa., Sept. 17, 1962), and the London production (Palace, May 18, 1961); *A Loss of Roses* (Eugene O'Neill Th., N.Y.C., Nov. 28, 1959); *Invitation to a March* (Music Box, Oct. 29, 1960); *The Gay Life* (Sam S. Shubert Th., Nov. 18, 1961); *Romulus* (Music Box, Jan. 10, 1962); *Lord Pengo* (Royale, Nov. 19, 1962); and *Tiger, Tiger Burning Bright* (Booth, Dec. 22, 1962).

Films. Miss Ballard designed the costumes for *Portrait of Jenny* (Selznick, 1948), and *A Streetcar Named Desire* (WB, 1951).

Night Clubs. She has designed costumes for the Copacabana revues (1941).

Awards. Miss Ballard received the Donaldson Award for her designs for *I Remember Mama* (1945); the Antoinette Perry (Tony) Award for her designs for *Happy Birthday, Another Part of the Forest, Street Scene, John Loves Mary,* and *The Chocolate Soldier* (1947); and was nominated for the Academy (Oscar) Award for her designs for *A Streetcar Named Desire* (1951). For her designs for *The Gay Life,* she received an Antoinette Perry (Tony) Award, and tied for the *Variety* NY Drama Critics' Poll (1962).

Recreation. Bridge, swimming.

BALLET, ARTHUR H. Dramaturg, educator. b. Hibbing, Minn. Grad. Univ. of Minnesota, B.A.; M.A.; Ph.D.

Mr. Ballet is professor of theatre and founder

(1964) and head of the Univ. of Minn. Advanced Drama Research Office, a project designed to facilitate experimental productions of works-in-progress in regional theatres throughout the country. He has served as dramaturg for the Eugene O'Neill Playwrights Conference (Waterford, Conn.) since 1969. At the Univ. of Minn., he has directed over seventy-five plays.

Published Works. Mr. Bal et has published over a dozen volumes of *Playwrights for Tomorrow,* has been contributing editor to *Theatre Quarterly* and *Oxford Companion to the Theatre;* and has contributed articles to *Dramatics,* and *The World Theatre.*.

Awards. For the ADRO project, he has received the Margo Jones "University" Award; and funding from the Rockefeller and Andrew Mellon foundations and the National Endowment for the Arts.

BALLEW, LEIGHTON M. Educator. b. Leighton Milton Ballew, Feb. 17, 1916, Des Arc, Ark., to Laurence Durant and Allie (Schnebly) Ballew. Father, postmaster. Grad. Tulsa (Okla.) Central H.S., 1933; Memphis State Coll., B.S. 1937; Western Reserve Univ., M.S. (fellowship) 1941; Univ. of Illinois, Ph.D. (Rockefeller Foundation Fellowship) 1955. Studied history of the theatre with George Kernodle and Bernard Hewitt; play direction with Edwin Duerr; and dramatic literature with T. W. Baldwin. Married Mar. 19, 1949, to Despy Karlas; one son. Served USAAF 1942–45. Member of SETC (pres. 1956–57); NTC; ATA (member of bd. of dir., 1962–64; chmn., ATA Production Lists Project, 1968–to date); Ga. Speech Assn. (member of bd. of dir., 1952–64; and former president); Southern Speech Assn. (member of bd. of dir.); SAA; Alcone Drama Fund, Inc. (chmn., 1962–to date). Address: (home) 175 Duncan Springs Rd., Athens, GA 30601, tel. (404) 546-6050; (bus.) c/o The Dept. of Speech and Drama, Univ. of Georgia, Athens, GA 30601, tel. (404) 542-2836.

Mr. Ballew has been chairman of the Dept. of Drama and Theatre, Univ. of Georgia, since 1946. He joined the faculty as assistant professor (1942) then left for military service during World War II. In 1945–46 he was assistant professor of English at South Dakota State Coll. of Agriculture and Mechanic Arts, and he returned in 1946 to the Univ. of Georgia. He became a professor and supervising director of the university theatre in 1956. Mr. Ballew founded the Junior Artist Fellowship program in 1950 to bring two or more young theatre artists from foreign countries to the Univ. of Georgia each year, and in 1957 he founded the Visiting Professorship Program to bring internationally known professional directors and designers to the Univ. of Georgia.

Theatre. Mr. Ballew made his first professional appearance in the opera *La Boheme* (San Carlo Opera Co., 1937); played leading comic roles in *The Red Mill, The Merry Widow,* and other musicals (Memphis Open Air Th., Tenn., Summers 1940–42); and he has acted in, directed, and produced over 300 productions in community and university theatres (1933–to date).

Television. Mr. Ballew appeared as host and interviewer on educational programs with visiting scholars and lecturers (WGTV, Univ. of Georgia, 1960–to date).

Other Activities. In 1974, Mr. Ballew represented SETA, ATA, and USITT as official delegate to the Bergen (Norway) International Festival, and in the same year he was selected as Drama Adjudicator for the first Arts Festival in the Republic of the Bahamas, sponsored by the Ministry of Education and Culture.

Recreation. Swimming, tennis, chess.

BALSAM, MARTIN. Actor. b. Martin Henry Balsam, Nov. 4, 1919, New York City, to Albert and Lillian (Weinstein) Balsam. Father, manufacturer. Grad. DeWitt Clinton H.S., Bronx, N.Y., 1937; attended the New School for Social Research, 1946–48. Married Oct. 1952 to Pearl L. Somner, actress (marr. dis. 1954); married Aug. 1959 to Joyce Van Patten, actress (marr. dis. 1962); one daughter; married Nov. 1963, to Irene Miller, television production assistant. Served US Army, 1941–45; combat engineers, 1941; Air Force, 1943. Member of AEA; AFTRA; SAG; Actors' Studio (member 1948–to date). Address: c/o Lazarow, 119 W. 57th St., New York, NY 10019, tel. (212) JU 6-5930.

Pre-Theatre. Salesman; radio operator; mechanic; commentator; waiter; usher; announcer, New York World's Fair (1940).

Theatre. Mr. Balsam first appeared on stage as the Villain in *Pot Boiler* (N.Y.C. Playground, 1935). He made his first professional appearance as Johann in *The Play's the Thing* (Red Barn, Locust Valley, N.Y., Aug. 1941); and made his N.Y.C. debut as Mr. Blow in *Ghost for Sale* (Daly's Th., Sept. 29, 1941); subsequently, performed with the Town Hall Players (Newbury, Mass., Summer 1947); appeared as Sizzi in *Lamp at Midnight* (New Stages, N.Y.C., Dec. 21, 1947); Eddie in *The Wanhope Building* (Princess, Feb. 9, 1947); performed in *High Tor* (1945–46); *A Sound of Hunting* (ELT, 1946–47); appeared as one of the Three and a Murderer in Michael Redgrave's *Macbeth* (Natl., Mar. 31, 1948); Merle and an understudy in *Sundown Beach* (Belasco, Sept. 7, 1948); and the Ambulance Driver in *The Closing Door* (Empire, Dec. 1, 1949).

In stock, he played in *Three Men on a Horse* (Monticello Playhouse, Kiamesha Lake, N.Y., 1949); *Home of the Brave* (Straw Hat Players, West Newbury, Mass., 1949); and in *A Letter from Harry* (Putnam County Playhouse, N.Y., 1949); a Servingman and an understudy in *The Liar* (Broadhurst, N.Y.C., May 18, 1950), a Man in *The Rose Tattoo* (Martin Beck Th., Mar. 3, 1951); and a Bum in a Window, one of the Fiesta People, and a Pilot of the Fugitivo in *Camino Real* (Natl., Mar. 19, 1953).

Mr. Balsam played Bernie Dodd in a stock production of *The Country Girl* (Westchester Playhouse, Mt. Kisco, N.Y., July 1953); a Gangster in *Detective Story* (Westchester Playhouse, Mt. Kisco, N.Y.; Playhouse-in-the-Park, Philadelphia, Pa., 1953); Bernie Dodd in *The Country Girl* (John Drew Th., East Hampton, L.I., N.Y., 1954); and Golux in *Thirteen Clocks* (Westport Country Playhouse, Conn., 1954); the Son-in-Law in *Middle of the Night* (ANTA, N.Y.C., Feb. 8, 1956); toured as Norman with *Wedding Breakfast* (Chicago, Ill.; Westport Country Playhouse, Conn., 1955); appeared in stock in *With Respect to Joey* (Westport Country Playhouse, 1957); as Eddie Carbone in *A View from the Bridge* (La Jolla Playhouse, Calif., 1958); was Hickey in *The Iceman Cometh* (Theatre Group, Univ. of Calif. at Los Angeles, Oct. 23, 1961); Moe Smith in *Nowhere to Go But Up* (Winter Garden, N.Y.C., Nov. 10, 1962); Jules Walker in *The Porcelain Year* (opened Locust St. Th., Philadelphia, Pa., Oct. 11, 1965; closed Shubert Th., New Haven, Conn., Nov. 13, 1965); and played Richard Pawling, George, and Chuck in *You Know I Can't Hear You When the Water's Running* (Ambassador, N.Y.C., Mar. 13, 1967).

Films. He made his debut as the Investigator in *On the Waterfront* (Col., 1954); subsequently appeared as the Foreman of the Jury in *12 Angry Men* (UA, 1957); the Sergeant in *Time Limit* (UA, 1957); the Doctor in *Marjorie Morningstar* (WB, 1957); Matt Keely in *Al Capone* (Allied, 1959); the Son-in-Law in *Middle of the Night* (Col., 1959); the Investigator in *Psycho* (Par., 1960); the Soldier in *All at Home* (*Tutti a Casa*) (De Laurentis, Rome, Italy, 1960); the Agent in *Breakfast at Tiffany's* (Par., 1961); a Friend in *Ada* (MGM, 1961); the Sheriff in *Cape Fear* (U, 1962); a Soldier in *The Captive City* (Maxima Prod., Rome, Italy, 1962); the Psychiatrist in *Who's Sleeping in My Bed?* (Par., 1963); the Press Secretary in *Seven Days in May* (Par., 1963); and the Producer in *The Carpetbaggers* (Par., 1963).

He played Everett Redman in *Harlow* (Par., 1965); Lt. Cmdr. Chester Potter in *The Bedford Incident* (Col., 1965); Arnold Burns in *A Thousand Clowns* (UA, 1965); appeared in *Conquered City* (Amer. Intl., 1965); was Harry in *After the Fox* (UA, 1966); Mendez in *Hombre* (20th-Fox, 1967); appeared in *2001: A Space Odyssey* (MGM, 1968); was Uncle Harold in *Me, Natalie* (Natl., Genl., 1969); Col. Cathcart in *Catch-22* (Par., 1970); Admiral Kimmel in *Tora, Tora, Tora* (20th-Fox, 1970); Merriweather in *Little Big Man* (Natl. Genl., 1970); Haskins in *The Anderson Tapes* (Col., 1971); Harry Walden in *Summer Wishes, Winter Dreams* (Col., 1973); Vescari in *The Stone Killer* (Col., 1973); Green in *The Taking of Pelham, 1, 2, 3* (UA, 1974); and Bianchi in *Murder on the Orient Express* (Par., 1974).

Television. Mr. Balsam first appeared on the Philco Television Playhouse (NBC, Oct. 1948); subsequently performed on Actors Studio Theatre (CBS); T-Men in Action (NBC); The Goldbergs (CBS); Captain Video (ABC); Crime Photographer (CBS); Danger (CBS); Mr. Peepers (NBC); Search for Tomorrow (CBS); Valiant Lady (CBS); Col. Flack (NBC); Inner Sanctum (NBC); Magic Cottage (CBS); Robert Montgomery Presents (NBC); The Eternal Light (NBC); The Stranger (NBC); American Inventory (NBC); US Steel Hour (ABC, CBS, NBC); Greatest Gift (CBS); Frontiers of Faith (NBC); Alcoa Playhouse (NBC); Ed Sullivan Show (CBS); Studio One (CBS); Alfred Hitchcock Presents (CBS); Father Knows Best (CBS); Desilu Playhouse (NBC); The Untouchables (ABC); Playhouse 90 (CBS); Have Gun, Will Travel (CBS); Rawhide (CBS); The Naked City (ABC); Ellery Queen (NBC); Westinghouse Theatre (CBS); Twilight Zone (CBS); Rendezvous (CBS); Hallmark Hall of Fame (NBC); 5 Fingers (NBC); Cain's Hundred (ABC); Dr. Kildare (NBC); Target Corruptors (WNEW); Zane Grey Theatre (CBS); The New Breed (ABC); Route 66 (CBS); Eleventh Hour (NBC); Breaking Point (ABC); Arrest and Trial (NBC); Espionage (NBC); Chrysler Show (NBC); and Armstrong Circle Theatre (NBC).

Also on The Defenders (CBS); Mr. Broadway (CBS); Decoy (CBS); as Doc Delaney in *Come Back, Little Sheba* (ITV, London, Eng., Mar. 8, 1965); on The Man from U.N.C.L.E. (NBC); Fugitive (ABC); and *Among the Paths to Eden* (ABC, Dec. 17, 1967); *Hunters Are for Killing* (CBS, Mar. 12, 1970); and *The Old Man Who Cried Wolf* (ABC, Oct. 10, 1972).

Night Clubs. He first appeared in *The Skeptics* (Cafe Society Uptown, Cafe Society Downtown, Spivy's Roof, The Blue Angel, N.Y.C., 1947).

Awards. Mr. Balsam received an Outer Circle Award and a *Variety* poll citation for his performance in *You Know I Can't Hear You When the Water's Running.*

Recreation. Golf, photography.

BANCROFT, ANNE. Actress. b. Anna Maria Luisa Italiano, Sept. 17, 1931, Bronx, N.Y., to Michael and Mildred (DiNapoli) Italiano. Father, dress-pattern maker; mother, telephone operator. Attended Christopher Columbus H.S., Bronx, N.Y.; AADA, 1947–48. Studied acting with Herbert Berghof; Actors' Studio (mbr., 1958–to date). Married July 1, 1953, to Martin A. May, building contractor (marr. dis. Feb. 13, 1957); married 1964 to Mel Brooks, comedian; one son. Member of AEA; SAG; AFTRA. c/o David Cogan, 350 Fifth Ave., New York, NY 10001.

Pre-Theatre. Saleslady, English tutor, receptionist.

Theatre. Miss Bancroft made her N.Y.C. debut as Gittel Mosca in *Two for the Seesaw* (Booth, Jan. 6, 1958); subsequently appeared as Annie Sullivan in *The Miracle Worker* (Playhouse, Oct. 19, 1959); and as Mother Courage in *Mother Courage and Her Children* (Martin Beck Th., Mar. 28, 1963).

Films. She made her debut in *Don't Bother to Knock* (20th-Fox, 1952); subsequently played in *Treasure of the Golden Condor* (20th-Fox, 1953); *Tonight We Sing* (20th-Fox, 1953); *The Kid from Left Field* (20th-Fox, 1953); *Demetrius and the Gladiators* (20th-Fox, 1954); *The Raid* (20th-Fox, 1954); *Gorilla at Large* (20th-Fox, 1954); *New York Confidential* (WB, 1955); *A Life in the Balance* (20th-Fox, 1955); *The Naked Street* (UA, 1955); *The Last Fron-*

tier (Col., 1955); *Nightfall* (Col., 1956); *Walk the Proud Land* (U, 1956); *The Girl in Black Stockings* (UA, 1957); *The Restless Breed* (20th-Fox, 1957); appeared in the role of Annie Sullivan in the film version of *The Miracle Worker* (UA, 1962); played Mrs. Robinson in *The Graduate* (Embassy, 1967); Lady Randolph Churchill in *Young Winston* (Col., 1972); and Edna Edison in *The Prisoner of Second Avenue* (Warner, 1975).

Television. Miss Bancroft made her first appearance in *The Torrents of Spring* (Studio One, CBS, 1950); appeared regularly as Anne Marno in The Goldbergs (CBS, 1950–51); performed on Danger (CBS); Suspense (CBS); Lux Video Th. (CBS); and Climax! (CBS). She also played in *So Soon To Die* (Playhouse 90, CBS, 1957); *Invitation to a Gunfighter* (Playhouse 90, CBS, 1957); *Hostages to Fortune* (Alcoa Hour, NBC, 1957); *A Time To Cry* (Frank Sinatra Show, ABC, 1958); appeared on the Perry Como Show (NBC, 1960, 1961); the Bob Hope Show (NBC, 1964); and specials entitled *Annie, the Women in the Life of a Man* (CBS, 1970); and *Annie and the Hoods* (CBS, 1974).

Awards. For her performance as Gittel Mosca in *Two for the Seesaw,* Miss Bancroft received (1958) the Antoinette Perry (Tony) Award, and won the *Variety* NY Drama Critics Poll. For her portrayal of Annie Sullivan in *The Miracle Worker,* she received (1960) an Antoinette Perry (Tony) Award, the ANTA Award, and the NY Philanthropic League Award. She also received an Academy (Oscar) Award (1962) for her performance as Annie Sullivan in the film version of *The Miracle Worker,* and the NATAS (Emmy) Award for *Annie, the Women in the Life of a Man* (1970).

BARAGREY, JOHN.

Actor. b. Apr. 15, 1918, Haleyville, Ala., to John and Nora (Godsey) Baragrey. Father, mining engineer. Grad. Haleyville H.S., 1935; Massey Coll., 1939. Married July 23, 1948, to Louise Larabee, actress. Member of AEA; SAG; AFTRA. Address: 21 W. 16th St., New York, NY 10011, tel. (212) OR 5-7794.

Theatre. Mr. Baragrey was a member of the resident acting company at Grove Th., Nuangola, Pa. (Summer 1942); subsequently toured as Mortimer Brewster in *Arsenic and Old Lace* (1942–43); was understudy to Gregory Peck in the role of Andrew Talbot in *Sons and Soldiers* (Morosco Th., May 4, 1943); toured the South Pacific as Dascom Dinsmora in a USO production of *Petticoat Fever* (1943–45); appeared in the pre-Bway tour of *Twilight Bar* (opened Ford's Th., Baltimore, Md., Mar. 12, 1946; closed Walnut St. Th., Philadelphia, Pa., Mar. 23, 1946); played in summer stock productions of *Richard III, The Bad Men* and *Design for Living* (Royal Alexandria, Toronto, Canada, 1946).

He appeared as the Young One in *A Flag Is Born* (Alvin, N.Y.C., Sept. 5, 1946); was a resident actor at the Lakewood Th., Skowhegan, Me. (Summer 1947); played a Juvenile in *Life of the Party* (June–Aug. 1949); portrayed the Ghost in *The Enchanted* (Lyceum, Jan. 18, 1950); appeared in a stock production of *The Road to Rome* (Playhouse in the Park, Philadelphia, Pa., Summer 1951); succeeded John Emery (Jan. 11, 1951) as Anthony Cavendish in *The Royal Family* (NY City Ctr., Jan. 10, 1951), and subsequently toured in the same role (Bucks County Playhouse, New Hope, Pa., Summer 1951); and played Lowell Markey in *One Eye Closed* (Bijou, Nov. 24, 1954).

At the Playhouse in the Park (Philadelphia, Pa.), Mr. Baragrey played in *Detective Story* (1955), *Sabrina Fair* (1957), *Tonight at 8:30* (1957), *The Crucible* (1958), *The Disenchanted* (1959), *The Marriage-Go-Round* (1960) and *The Happy Time* (1962). He appeared as the Ragpicker in *The Madwoman Of Chaillot* (Royal Poinciana Playhouse, Palm Beach, Fla., Feb. 1961); and toured as Cosmo Constantine in *Call Me Madam* (South Shore Music Circus, Cohasset, Mass.; Cape Cod Melody Tent, Hyannis, Mass., Summer 1963). He was Casanova in *Camino Real* (Mark Taper Forum, Los Angeles, Calif., 1968); Judge Cool in *The Grass Harp* (Martin Beck Th., N.Y.C., Nov. 2, 1971); and the Ambassador of the United States in *Murderous Angels* (Playhouse, Dec. 20, 1971).

Films. Mr. Baragrey made his film debut in *The Loves of Carmen* (Col., 1948); subsequently, appeared in *The Saxon Charm* (U, 1948); *Shockproof* (Col., 1949); *Four Days' Leave* (Film Classics, 1950); *Tall Man Riding* (WB, 1955); and *The Fugitive Kind* (UA, 1960).

Television and Radio. He made his debut in *Ring on Her Finger* (NBC, 1945); subsequently appeared on Philco Television Playhouse (NBC); Studio One (CBS); Kraft Television Th. (NBC); Robert Montgomery Presents (NBC); Danger (CBS); Suspense (CBS); GE Th. (CBS); Alfred Hitchcock Presents (CBS); Schlitz Playhouse (NBC); Jane Wyman Th. (NBC); Climax! (CBS); Playhouse 90 (CBS); Dupont Show of the Month (NBC); American Heritage (NBC); The Defenders (CBS); Naked City (ABC); The Secret Storm (CBS); and he was on Radio Mystery Th.

Recreation. Tennis, reading, singing.

BARAKA, IMAMU AMIRI.

Playwright, author, poet, political leader. b. Everett LeRoi Jones, Oct. 7, 1934, Newark, N.J., to Coyette LeRoi and Anna Lois (Russ) Jones. Father, postal supervisor; mother, social worker. Educ. Newark public schools; grad. Barringer H.S., Newark, 1949; attended Rutgers Univ. Grad. Howard Univ., B.A. (English) 1954; Columbia Univ., M.A. Served in USAF, 1954–57. Married Oct. 13, 1958, to Hettie Roberta Cohen (marr. dis. Aug. 1965); two daughters; Aug. 1966 to Sylvia Robinson (later called Bibi Amina Baraka); two sons. Member of Black Acad. of Arts and Letters; Spirit House, Newark, N.J. (fdr. & dir., 1966); Cong. of African Peoples (mbr., Intl. Coordinating Comm.); Cong. of Afrikan People (chmn.); Natl. Black Political Assembly (secy.-gen.). Address: c/o Hobbs Agency, 211 E. 43rd St., New York, NY 10017.

Theatre. Imamu Baraka's first play produced was *A Good Girl Is Hard to Find* (Montclair, N.J., 1958); his first play produced in N.Y.C. was *Dante* (1961), produced again as *The Eighth Ditch* (New Bowery Th., 1964). *Dutchman* opened on a Playwrights Unit double-bill with Eric Hughes's *The Empty Room* (Village South Th., Jan. 12, 1964), then ran on a bill with plays by Samuel Beckett and Fernando Arrabal under the title *Three at the Cherry Lane* (Mar. 23, 1964), and continued as half of the double-bill *Two at the Cherry Lane,* first with *The American Dream* (Apr. 21, 1964) and then with *The Zoo Story* (Nov. 1964). Other plays include *The Baptism* (Writers Stage, May 1, 1964); *The Slave* and *The Toilet* (St. Marks Playhouse, Dec. 16, 1964); a street production in Harlem, N.Y.C., of *J-E-L-L-O* (Black Arts Repertory Th. School, 1965); *Experimental Death Unit 1* (St. Marks Playhouse, Mar. 1965); *Black Mass* (Newark, N.J., 1966); *Arm Yourself and Harm Yourself* (Newark, 1967); and *Slave Ship* (Newark, 1967; Chelsea Th. Ctr., Brooklyn Acad. of Music, N.Y.C., Nov. 19, 1969; transferred to Washington Square Methodist Ch., N.Y.C., Jan. 13, 1970).

Other productions of his works include *Mad Heart* (San Francisco, Calif., 1967); *Home on the Range* (Newark, N.J., and N.Y.C., 1968); *Great Goodness of Life (A Coon Show),* part of the bill *A Black Quartet* (Tambellini's Gate Th., N.Y.C., July 30, 1969; transferred to Frances Adler Th., Oct. 7, 1969); *Junkies Are Full of (SHHH. . .)* and *Bloodrites* (Newark, N.J., 1970); *Junkies. . .* was later performed in repertory with *Experimental Death Unit 1* and *Great Goodness of Life* (Afro-American Studio for Acting and Speech, Oct. 1, 1972); *A Recent Killing* (New Federal Th., Henry St. Settlement, Jan. 1973); and *Sidnee Poet Heroical,* which he also directed (New Federal Th., May 15, 1975).

Films. Imamu Baraka wrote the screenplay for *Dutchman,* based on his play (Walter Reade, 1967).

Other Activities. Imamu Baraka taught at the New School for Social Research, N.Y.C. (1961–64); the Univ. of the State of NY at Buffalo (Summer 1964); Columbia Univ. (1964; 1966–67); and at San Francisco (Calif.) State Coll. (1967–68).

He founded the American Theatre for Poets (1961); the Black Arts Repertory Th. School, Harlem, N.Y.C. (1965); and, at Spirit House, The Spirit House Movers, a drama group (Newark, N.J., 1966). Becoming active in Newark politics, he was an organizer of United Brothers (1967); the Committee for a United Newark (1968); and was a founder (1968) of the Black Community Development and Defense Organization, Newark, to promote racial pride among American blacks. This group embraced the Muslim faith, took Arabic personal names, and used the Swahili language as well as English. As a Muslim minister, the former Mr. Jones prefixed the Swahili title Imamu (religious leader) to his new name, Amiri Baraka.

Published Works. In addition to the plays that have been produced, Imamu Baraka wrote *Police (Drama Review,* Summer 1968); *The Death of Malcolm X (New Plays from the Black Theatre,* 1969); and *BA-RA-KA (Spontaneous Combustion: Eight New American Plays,* 1972). He wrote the novel *The System of Dante's Hell* (1965); his short stories were collected in *Tales* (1967); and his poetry has appeared in *Poetry, The Nation, Yale Literary Magazine, The Village Voice* and such little magazines as *Big Table, Evergreen Review,* and *Niagara Frontier Review.* His volumes of published poetry include *Preface to a Twenty-Volume Suicide Note* (1961); *The Dead Lecturer* (1964); *Black Art* (1966); *Black Magic: Poetry 1961–67* (1969); *It's Nationtime* (1970); and *Spirit Reach* (1972).

Other works include *Blues People: Negro Music in White America* (1963); *Home: Social Essays* (1966); *Black Music* (1967); *In Our Terribleness* (1970); *A Black Value System* (1970); *Raise Race Rays Raze: Essays Since 1965* (1971); *The Life and Times of John Coltrane* (1971); and *The Creation of the New-Ark* (1972). He edited *Four Young Lady Poets* (1962); *The Moderns: New Fiction in America* (1964); with Larry Neal, *Black Fire: An Anthology of Afro-American Writing* (1968); and *African Congress: A Documentary of the First Pan-African Congress* (1972).

With his first wife, he founded Totem Press and the magazine *Yugen* (both 1958) and, with Diane DiPrima, he edited (1961–63) the magazine *Floating Bear.* His jazz criticism appeared in *Downbeat, Metronome,* and other music periodicals.

Awards. Imamu Baraka received a Whitney Fellowship (1961); a Guggenheim Fellowship (1965); his play *Dutchman* received a *Village Voice* off-Bway (Obie) Award (1964) as best American play off-Bway; he received a Dakar (Senegal) Festival Prize (1966); and a National Endowment for the Arts grant (1966).

BARAL, ROBERT.

Writer. b. Apr. 2, 1910, Fort Wayne, Ind., to John G. and Bertha (Tremelling) Baral. Grad. Central H.S., Fort Wayne; attended Indiana Univ. 1930. Served OWI, 1945–46. Member of Author's Guild; Delta Upsilon; Ziegfeld Club (adv. bd.).

Mr. Baral was a staff member of *Variety* and then wrote for it as a roving reporter.

He has also worked on special film assignments for Sam Goldwyn, Metro-Goldwyn-Mayer, Warner Bros., Columbia Pictures and Walt Disney.

He has written articles for magazines, including *Harper's Bazaar, Photoplay* and *Dance,* and the books *Revue—A Nostalgic Reprise of The Great Broadway Period* (1962) and *Turn West on 23rd; A Toast to New York's Old Chelsea* (1966).

Recreation. Collecting old-time theatre memorabilia, show music.

BARASCH, NORMAN.

Playwright. b. Feb. 18, 1922, Rockville Centre, N.Y., to Michael and Eva (Bogotsky) Barasch. Father, salesman. Grad. South Side Rockville Centre H.S., 1939. Married June 5, 1947, to Gloria Rosenberg, two sons, one daughter. Served WW II USAAF; rank, Pfc. Relatives in theatre: cousin, William B. Williams, disc jockey; cousin, Jack Barry, producer and emcee. Member of Dramatists Guild; ALA; WGA East.

Pre-Theatre. Page boy, NBC.

Theatre. Mr. Barasch wrote, with Carroll Moore, *Make a Million* (Playhouse Th., Oct. 23, 1958) and *Send Me No Flowers* (Brooks Atkinson Th., Dec. 5, 1960).

Films. Messrs. Barasch and Moore wrote the original scenario for *That Funny Feeling* (U, 1963).

Television. In 1961, Mr. Barasch became a staff writer for the Garry Moore Show (CBS).

Awards. For his contribution to the Garry Moore Show, Mr. Barasch received a NATAS (Emmy) Award (1962).

Recreation. Tennis, golf.

BARCELO, RANDY. Costume designer. b. Sept 10, 1946, Havana, Cuba, to Ramón and Ondina (Lopez) Barcelo. Father, architect; mother, architect. Educ. Univ. of Puerto Rico. Professional training with Lester Polakov School of Design (1967–68). Member of United Scenic Artists, Local 829. Address: 200 W. 90th St., N.Y.C., NY 10024, tel. (212) 877-1083.

Pre-Theatre. Elevator operator, dancer.

Theatre. Mr. Barcelo's first costume designing in the theatre was done between 1967 and 1970 for stock productions of such plays as *The Unsinkable Molly Brown, Cabaret, Man of La Mancha, Gypsy,* and *The King and I.* He designed costumes for the first off-off-Bway production of *Gloria and Esperanza* (La Mama ETC, N.Y.C., Apr. 3, 1969), and this was followed by costumes for *The Moon Dreamers* (Ellen Stewart Th., Dec. 8, 1969); New Troupe productions of *The Holy Ghostly, Melodrama Play,* and *Gammer Gurton's Needle* (touring the US and Europe, 1970); *Lenny* (Brooks Atkinson Th., May 26, 1971); *Jesus Christ Superstar* (Mark Hellinger Th., Oct. 12, 1971; also Amphitheater, Universal Studios, June 26, 1972); *Dude* (Bway Th., Oct. 9, 1972); *Lady Day: A Musical Tragedy* (Chelsea Theatre Center of Brooklyn, Academy of Music, Brooklyn, N.Y., Oct. 17, 1972); *Mary C. Brown and the Hollywood Sign* (Shubert Th., Los Angeles, Cal., Oct. 1972); the Street Theatre production of *Noah's Flood* (1972); university theatre productions of *The Amorous Flea, Long Day's Journey into Night,* and *Romeo and Juliet* (all 1973); special costumes for Bette Midler's act (1973); and costumes for *The Magic Show* (Cort, May 28, 1974); and for *Sgt. Pepper's Lonely Hearts Club Band on the Road* (Beacon Th., N.Y.C., Nov. 17, 1974).

Other Activities. Since 1971, Mr. Barcelo has been a guest lecturer at the Lester Polakov School of Design (Studio and Forum of Stage Design), N.Y.C., and in 1973 he was assistant professor of costume design at Purdue Univ.

Awards. Mr. Barcelo received the Antoinette Perry (Tony) Award nomination for best costume designer for his costumes for *Jesus Christ Superstar,* and he was cited in the *Variety* poll of NY Drama critics for the same work.

Recreation. Quiltmaking, painting, etching.

BARER, MARSHALL. Lyricist, director, playwright. b. Marshall Louis Barer, Feb. 19, 1923, Long Island City, N.Y., to Frank and Sadie Barer. Father, contractor. Grad. Palm Beach H.S., Fla., 1938; Cavanagh Art Sch., N.Y.C., 1941. Served US Army, 1941, Special Services. Member of ASCAP; AGAC; ALA; Dramatists Guild.

Pre-Theatre. Commercial artist, 1941–50; editor and staff lyricist for Golden Records, 1950–55.

Theatre. Mr. Barer made his debut as a performer and lyricist for *Walk Tall* (Playhouse, Houston, Tex., Aug. 1953) in which he subsequently toured (northeastern states, July 1954); at Tamiment, Pa. (six summers) was lyricist, sketch writer and performer for revues and book shows, including *The Emperor's New Clothes, The Princess and the Pea,* which served as the basis for *Once Upon a Mattress* (see below) and *The Happy Medium.*

He made his N.Y.C. debut as lyricist for *Once Over Lightly* (Barbizon-Plaza Th., Jan. 1955); wrote the lyrics for six of the songs in *New Faces of '56* (Ethel Barrymore Th., June 1956); wrote the lyrics for four songs in *Ziegfeld Follies* (Winter Garden, Mar. 1957); wrote lyrics and was author, with Jay Thompson and Dean Fuller, of the book for *Once Upon a Mattress* (Phoenix, May 11, 1959; moved Alvin, Nov. 25, 1959); wrote the lyrics for the pre-Bway tryout of *La Belle* (opened Shubert, Philadelphia, Pa., Aug. 13, 1962; closed there Aug. 25, 1962); contributed lyrics to the revue *From A to Z* (Plymouth, Apr. 20, 1960); wrote, with Larry Sigel and Steven Vinaver, lyrics for *The Mad Show* (New, Jan. 10, 1966); and wrote lyrics, with Fred Tobias, for *Pousse-Café* (46 St. Th., Mar. 18, 1966).

Television. Mr. Barer wrote lyrics for a Mohawk Thanksgiving Special (NBC).

Recreation. Science fiction, old movies.

BARNES, BILLY. Lyricist, composer, singer. b. William Christopher Barnes, Jr., Jan. 27, 1927, Los Angeles, Calif., to William C. and Leoma (Lee) Barnes. Father, mechanic; mother, bookkeeper. Grad. Susan M. Dorsey Sch., Los Angeles, 1944; attended Univ. of Calif. at Los Angeles, 1947–50. Studied piano with Mary McMillan, fourteen years; studied theatre with Estelle K. Harman, two years. Served USNR, 1945–46. Married Nov. 10, 1952, to Joyce Jameson, actress (marr. dis. 1956); one son. Member of AEA; ASCAP; AFM, Local 47.

Theatre. Mr. Barnes' first produced work was *Footprints on the Ceiling,* for which he was composer and lyricist (Univ. of California at Los Angeles, Mar. 1948). He played the title role in *Baby Face O'Flynn,* for which he wrote the book, lyrics, and music (Gallery Stage, Los Angeles, Aug. 13, 1952); and was lyricist and composer of *Foolin' Ourselves* (Lobero, Santa Barbara, Calif., Jan. 1958).

He was lyricist and composer for *The Billy Barnes Revue* (hungry i, San Francisco, Calif., Winter 1956; Crescendo, Los Angeles, Winter 1957; Cabaret Concert Th., Los Angeles, Aug. 1958; Las Palmas Th., Los Angeles, Oct. 15, 1958; York Playhouse, N.Y.C., June 9, 1959; John Golden Th., N.Y.C., Aug. 4, 1959; on tour, England-Scotland, Mar. 1960; Lyric, Hammersmith, London, Apr. 4, 1960); followed by a second edition of this revue, *Billy Barnes' People* (Royale, N.Y.C., June 13, 1961; Las Palmas Th., Los Angeles, Dec. 27, 1961). He wrote, composed the music, and appeared in *Billy Barnes Party* (Cabaret Concert Th., Los Angeles, Sept. 1961); *Billy Barnes L.A.* (Coronet, Los Angeles, Oct. 10, 1961); *Billy Barnes Summer Revue* (Playhouse-in-the-Park, Philadelphia, Pa., May 28, 1962, June 7, 1963); *The Best of Billy Barnes* (Coronet, Los Angeles, Aug. 5, 1963); and *Billy Barnes' Hollywood* (Las Palmas, Los Angeles, May 26, 1964).

Television. Mr. Barnes wrote special material for the Colgate Comedy Hour (NBC, Aug. 1957) and became a writer for the Danny Kaye Show (CBS) in 1964.

Night Clubs. He was lyricist, composer, and appeared in *The Personalities* (Chi-Chi, Palm Springs, Calif., June 1950); *Something Cool* (Cabaret Concert Th., Los Angeles, Feb. 1957); and *Be My Guest* (Mocambo, Los Angeles, June 1957).

Recreation. Swimming, painting, dancing.

BARNES, CLIVE. Dance and drama critic, writer, lecturer. b. Clive Alexander Barnes, May 13, 1927, London, England, to Arthur Lionel and Freda Marguerite (Garratt) Barnes. Grad. Oxford Univ., B.A. 1951. Married 1946 (marr. dis. 1956); July 26, 1958, to Patricia Amy Evelyn Winckley; one son, one daughter. Served in RAF, 1946–48. Member of Critics Circle, London (past secy., chmn. ballet section); NY Drama Critics Circle. Address: (home) 344 W. 72nd St., New York, NY 10023; (bus.) NY *Times,* 229 W. 43rd St., New York, NY 10036.

Mr. Barnes has been dance critic (1965–to date) and daily drama critic (1967–to date) for the NY *Times;* he replaced Walter Kerr in the latter post when Mr. Kerr became critic for the Sunday *Times.*

Mr. Barnes began his career as journalist and critic in 1950 as co-editor of Oxford Univ. Ballet Club's *Arabesque* and has been on the staff of *Dance and Dancers* as assistant editor (1950–58), associate editor (1958–61), executive editor (1961–65), and N.Y.C. editor (1965–to date). In addition, he was dance reviewer for newspapers in London, England (1956–65); wrote on music, dance, drama, and films for the London *Daily Express* (1956–65); and was dance critic for *The Spectator,* London (1959–65). He began contributing to the NY *Times* in 1963.

Radio. Mr. Barnes reads his reviews on WQXR, the NY *Times* radio station each weekday morning.

Other Activities. Mr. Barnes gives lectures, and he has been associate professor of journalism at NY Univ.

Published Works. Mr. Barnes wrote *Ballet in Britain Since the War* (1953); *Frederick Ashton and His Ballets* (1961); with others, *Ballet Here and Now* (1961); and *Dance Scene, U.S.A.: America's Greatest Ballet and Modern Dance Companies* (1967); and writes for various magazines.

BARNES, MAE. Singer, actress, dancer. b. Edith Mae Stith, Jan. 23, 1907, New York City, to Edmond and Emma Stith. Father, longshoreman. Attended public schools, N.Y.C. Married March 16, 1924, to Rufus Walker (dec. 1930); one daughter; married June 20, 1940, to David Small. Member of AEA; AFTRA; AGVA; SAG.

Theatre. Miss Barnes made her Bway debut as a singer-dancer, in *Running Wild* (Colonial Th., Oct. 29, 1923); followed by *Lucky Sambo* (Colonial, June 6, 1925); subsequently danced in the national tour of *Shuffle Along* (1926); appeared in the revue *Rang Tang* (Royale, N.Y.C., July 12, 1927); *The Rainbow* (Gallo, Nov. 21, 1928); played the Keith Circuit in the variety show, *Ebony Scandals* (1932–33); appeared in the revue *Hot Rhythm* (Times Square Th., N.Y.C., Aug. 21, 1930); as Ruby Monk in *By The Beautiful Sea* (Majestic, April 8, 1954); and in the revue *Ziegfeld Follies* (opened Shubert, Boston, Mass., April 16, 1956; closed Shubert, Philadelphia, Pa., May 12, 1956).

Films. Miss Barnes made her debut in *Odds Against Tomorrow* (UA, 1959).

Television. She has appeared on the Steve Allen Show (NBC); the Garry Moore Show (CBS); the Today Show (NBC); the Merv Griffin Show; Dupont Show of the Month (NBC); the Kitty Foyle series; and America, Be Seated (Ed Sullivan Show, CBS, 1964).

Night Clubs. Miss Barnes has performed at the Village Vanguard, the Blue Angel, Bon Soir (all N.Y.C.), and numerous other clubs in the US.

Recreation. Baseball, basketball, music, piano, drums, reading.

BARNEY, JAY. Actor, stage manager. b. John Bernhardt Vander Kleine Schmide, Mar. 14, Chicago, Ill., to Edwin Walter and Evelyn (Stowell) Schmide. Father, businessman; mother, pianist, lecturer. Grad. Proviso H.S., Maywood, Ill. 1935; Univ. of Chicago, B.S. (political science) 1938; studied acting at Amer. Th. Wing, N.Y.C., 1946–50; with Robert Lewis, 1947–52; Marian Rich, 1947–52; Lee Strasberg, 1948–50; Joseph Anthony, 1948–50; William Hansen, 1948–50; Sydney Lumet, 1948–50; Daniel Mann, 1949–50; Harold Clurman, 1949; Fanny Bradshaw, 1949; Eva Brown, 1949–56; Tad Danielewski, 1954–55. Served US Army, 1941–47; rank, Lt. Col. Member of AEA; AFTRA; SAG; New Stages; Actors Studio.

Pre-Theatre. Store manager.

Theatre. Mr. Barney made his first stage appearance in high school, playing the director in *Merton of the Movies* (Proviso Aud., Maywood, Ill.). He made his N.Y.C. debut succeeding (Jan. 1938) Robert J. Mulligan as Detective Stark in *Many Mansions* (Biltmore, Oct. 27, 1937); and played Al in *On Borrowed Time* (Longacre, Feb. 3, 1938), and in the national tour (opened Selwyn, Chicago, Nov. 1939).

He was stage manager for productions of the Paper Mill Playhouse (Millburn, N.J.), and appeared there as Father Chu in *Flight into China,* and Dr. Levine in *Men in White* (Summer 1939). During 1939, he also served as lecturer for the NY World's Fair Ford Exhibition. He played the title role in an ELT production of *Jason* (Hudson Park Branch, NY Public Library, Nov. 1945); and Wellborne in *A New Way To Pay Old Debts* (ELT, Dec. 1945).

He portrayed the Rector in *Land's End* (Playhouse, Dec. 11, 1946); Tremoille in *Joan of Lorraine* (Ridgefield Playhouse, N.J., Summer 1947); and Dr. Cobb in *Shining Threshold* (Falmouth Playhouse, Mass., Summer 1947). He played Cardinal Borgia and Cesare in *Lamp at Midnight* (New Stages, N.Y.C., Dec. 21, 1947); Rev. Morrell in an ELT production of *Candida* (Lenox Hill Playhouse, Mar. 13, 1948); succeeded (Apr. 10, 1948) Martin Tarby as Lynch Mob Leader in *The Respectful Prostitute*, and Don McLoughlin (June 1948) as Pa Kirby in *The Happy Journey to Trenton and Camden* (Cort, Mar. 16, 1948); and played Doc in *Hope Is the Thing with Feathers* (Cort, May 11, 1948).

He played the Bride's Father in *Blood Wedding* (New Stages, Feb. 6, 1949); Albert in an ELT production of *Brooklyn, U.S.A.* (Lenox Hill Playhouse, Mar. 18, 1949), Bassanio in an ELT production of *The Merchant of Venice* (Lenox Hill Playhouse, Apr. 9, 1949); Georgie Porgie in *Don't Go Away Mad* (Master Th., May 9, 1949); toured as Doc in *Hope Is the Thing with Feathers* and Lynch Mob Leader in *The Respectful Prostitute* (opened Harris, Chicago, May 11, 1949). While on tour, Mr. Barney played Henderson in *You Can't Take it with You* (Las Palmas Th., Hollywood, Calif., May 29, 1950); Schwartz in *The Front Page*, Alin Stimson in *Our Town* (La Jolla Playhouse, Calif., Summer 1950).

Mr. Barney toured the N.Y.C. Subway Circuit as Lt. Monaghan in *Detective Story* (Windsor, Flatbush, Brighton Beach, Long Beach, opened Aug. 22, 1950); played Hasdrubal in an ELT production of *The Road to Rome* (Lenox Hill Playhouse, Jan. 19, 1951); Franklin in *Southern Wild* (New Stages, Feb. 7, 1951); Si in *The Number* (Biltmore, Oct. 1951); the Postmaster in *The Grass Harp* (Martin Beck Th., Mar. 17, 1952); Dr. Schiller in an ELT production of *The World We Make* (Lenox Hill, Dec. 10, 1952); succeeded (June 20, 1953) Frederick Downs as Judge Cool in a revival of *The Grass Harp* (Circle in the Square, Apr. 17, 1953); played Odysseus in the Artists and Poets Th. production of *Death of Odysseus* (Amato Th., Nov. 3, 1953); Lord Ratcliff in *Richard III* (NY City Ctr., Dec. 9, 1953); the Major in *Stockade* (President, Jan. 31, 1954); and succeeded (Mar. 1, 1954) Louis Jourdan as Michel in *The Immoralist* (Royale, Feb. 8, 1954).

Mr. Barney played Anthony in *The Homeward Look* (Th. de Lys, May 8, 1954); York in *Henry IV* (Shakespearewrights, P.S. 154, Jan. 24, 1955); Masters in an ELT production of *Joan of Lorraine* (Lenox Hill Playhouse, Mar. 15, 1955); succeeded (July 30, 1955) Richard Kronold as Titorelli in *The Trial* (Provincetown Playhouse, June 14, 1955); played Mr. Perry in *The Young and the Beautiful* (Longacre, Oct. 1, 1955); and succeeded (Oct. 1955) Richard Kronold as Prof. Sonnenstitch in *Spring's Awakening* (Provincetown Playhouse, Oct. 9, 1955).

He played Robert Acton in *Eugenia* (Ambassador, Jan. 30, 1957); was emcee for a Coca-Cola industrial show (N.Y.C.; Washington, D.C.; Los Angeles, 1957); appeared as Jackson Thorpe in *Sign of Winter* (Th. 74, N.Y.C., May 7, 1958); and as the District Manager in a Chevrolet industrial show (Detroit, Mich., July 16, 1958). He played Walter Burns in an ELT production of *The Front Page* (Lenox Hill Playhouse, Jan. 3, 1961); Mr. Coldfacts in a Coca-Cola industrial show (McCormick Pl., Chicago, May 1961); Reverdy Johnson in an ELT production of *The Story of Mary Surratt* (Lenox Hill Playhouse, Dec. 9, 1961); and the Sales Manager in an Oldsmobile industrial show (Cobo Hall, Detroit, Aug. 3, 1962).

He played Hiram Griswold in *The Anvil* (Maidman, N.Y.C., Oct. 30, 1962); succeeded (Mark Hellinger Th., Jan. 21, 1963) John Randolph as Franz in *The Sound of Music* (Lunt-Fontanne Th., Nov. 16, 1959); and toured as Forbes in the pre-Bway tryout of *Thursday Is a Good Night* (opened Playhouse on the Mall, Paramus, N.J., July 7, 1964). He was Rev. Flap in *Blastoma City*, one of two plays billed as *Route 1* (One Sheridan Square, N.Y.C., Nov. 17, 1964); succeeded (Jan. 20, 1965) John Alexander as Mayor Crane in *Never Too Late* (Playhouse, Nov. 27, 1962); played Claude Dancer in a stock tryout of *Anatomy of a Murder* (Mill Run Playhouse, Niles, Ill., Aug. 17, 1965); Miller in *Enemies* on the double bill *Friends and Enemies* (Th. East, N.Y.C., Sept. 16, 1965); George Masters, Jr. in *The Parasite* (Renata Th., Dec. 16, 1965); and Mayor Muller in *Beyond Desire* (Th. Four, Oct. 10, 1967).

He was Charlie Danvers in *A Certain Young Man* (Stage 73, Dec. 26, 1967); the Administrator in *Goa* (Martinique, Feb. 22, 1968); Samuel in *The David Show* (Players Th., Oct. 31, 1968); Mr. Mittleman in *The Fig Leaves Are Falling* (Broadhurst, Jan. 2, 1969); and Angel Rodriguez in *All the Girls Came Out To Play* (Cort, Apr. 20, 1972).

Films. Mr. Barney made his debut in *711 Ocean Drive* (Col., 1950); followed by *The Killer that Stalked New York* (Col., 1950); *Convicted* (Col., 1950); *Visa* (MGM, 1950); *Spy Hunt* (U, 1950); *The Fuller Brush Girl* (Col., 1950); *Wyoming Mail* (U, 1950); *The Return of Jesse James* (Lippert, 1950); *The Jackpot* (20th-Fox, 1950); *Battle Taxi* (UA, 1955); *The Shrike* (U, 1955); *Mister Rock and Roll* (Par., 1957); *The Big Fisherman* (Buena Vista, 1959); and *Blueprint for Murder* (Par., 1961).

He also produced and directed 28 US Army Signal Corps training films (1941–47).

Television and Radio. Mr. Barney has performed on such radio shows as Th. Guild on the Air (NBC); Treasury Hour (NBC); The March of Time (ABC); School of the Air (CBS); The Falcon (CBS); Believe It or Not (NBC); Michael Shayne (NBC); Rosemary (CBS); House of Glass (NBC); Ma Perkins (CBS); Inheritance (NBC); Doctor's Wife (NBC); The Eternal Light (NBC); The Romance of Helen Trent (CBS); Ave Maria Hour (NBC); Five Star Final (NBC); True Confessions (NBC); The Couple Next Door (CBS); My True Story (NBC); and *Birthright, Our Town, Ethan Frome, Mr. Roberts, Beyond the Blue Horizon, Abe Lincoln in Illinois* and *The Heiress* (Voice of America).

His television appearances include You Be the Jury (NBC, 1949); Your Witness (ABC, 1950); Armchair Detective (NBC, 1950); Ed Wynn Show (NBC, 1950); *My Heart's in the Highlands* (Silver Th., NBC, 1950); State's Attorney (CBS, 1950); Big Town (NBC, 1950); Big Story (NBC, 1950, 1951, 1958); Hands of Mystery (Dumont, 1950); Billy Rose Show (ABC, 1950); *Macbeth* (NBC, 1950); Plainclothesman (Dumont, 1950); Pilgrim's Progress (CBS, 1950); Casey, Crime Photographer (CBS, 1951); *The Moon and Sixpence* (ABC, Apr. 30, 1951); Treasury Men in Action (NBC, 1951, 1952); Pulitzer Prize Th. (ABC, 1951); *The Greatest Story Ever Told* (NBC, June 16, 1951); *Rodeo* (Armstrong Circle Th., CBS, June 26, 1951); *Shadow of the Cloak* (Dumont, July 11, 1951); Assignment Manhunt (NBC, 1951); Police Story (ABC, 1951); A Date with Judy (ABC, 1951, 1952, 1953); Rogue's Gallery (NBC, 1951); Nero Wolfe (NBC, 1951); and Captain Video (Dumont, 1951, 1952, 1953, 1954).

Also *John Wilkes Booth* (Kraft Television Th., NBC, Aug. 16, 1951); *Madame Liu-Tsong* (Dumont, 1951); *Signal 32* (Studio One, CBS, 1951); *Flying Tigers* (Dumont, 1951); Cameo Th. (NBC, 1952); Danger (CBS, 1952, 1953); *Paper Box Kid* (Suspense, CBS, 1952); Crime Syndicated (NBC, 1952); The Fix (NBC, 1952); Top Guy (CBS, 1952); Rocky King (Dumont, 1952); Lamp Unto My Feet (CBS, 1952, 1953, 1954); The Web (CBS, 1952); and Studio One (CBS, 1952, 1953).

Also You Are There (CBS, 1953, 1954); Martin Kane (CBS, 1953); City Hospital (CBS, 1953); Johnny Jupiter (Dumont, 1953); Rookie Cop (Dumont, 1953); Revlon Th. (NBC, 1953); *Parakeet* (Inner Sanctum, NBC, July 16, 1953); Doorway to Danger (NBC, 1953); Kate Smith Show (NBC, 1953); Philip Morris Playhouse (CBS, 1953); Sound Stage (Dumont, 1953); *John Paul Jones* (Hallmark Hall of Fame, NBC, July 4, 1954); *Saint Joan* (Omnibus, CBS, Jan. 2, 1955); Mama (CBS, 1955); and *The Adams Family* (Omnibus, CBS, Jan. 23, 1955).

Also, The Goldbergs (1955); You'll Never Get Rich (NBC, 1955); First Love (NBC, 1955); *Silent Gun* (Studio One, CBS, Feb. 6, 1956); *The Architect* (Faith for Today, NBC, Feb. 6, 1956); *The Constitution* (Omnibus, CBS, Feb. 19, 1956); *The Court Martial of Billy Mitchell* (Omnibus, CBS, Apr. 1, 1956); Valiant Lady (CBS, 1956); *Honest in the Rain* (US Steel Hour, CBS, May 9, 1956); Ethel and Albert (ABC, May 25, 1956); *The Janitor* (Robert Montgomery Presents, NBC, June 21, 1956); *Election Returns* (Alcoa Presents, NBC, Aug. 19, 1956); *Soldier from the Wars Returning* (NBC, Sept. 10, 1956); Frontiers of Faith (NBC, 1957); Brighter Day (CBS, 1958); Search for Tomorrow (CBS, 1958); Love of Life (CBS, 1958); Ed Sullivan Show (CBS, 1958); *Kidnap: Hold for Release* (Armstrong Circle Th., CBS, June 11, 1958); New York Confidential (Dumont, 1958); Edge of Night (CBS, 1958); Man with a Camera (NBC, Nov. 25, 1958); Ellery Queen (NBC, 1958); and *Sound of Violence* (Armstrong Circle Th., CBS, Apr. 29, 1959).

Also, *Body and Soul* (Dupont Show of the Month, CBS, Sept. 27, 1959); *Boy on Page One* (Armstrong Circle Th., CBS, Dec. 23, 1959); As the World Turns (CBS, 1960); The Catholic Hour (NBC, 1960); *Gentlemen's Agreement* (American Heritage, NBC, Mar. 2, 1961); *Andrew Carnegie Story* (American Heritage, NBC, Mar. 27, 1960); Search for Tomorrow (CBS, Sept. 11, 1961); Lonely Woman (NBC, 1961); Perry Mason (CBS, 1962; 1964; 1965); Car 54, Where Are You? (NBC, 1962); *Mutiny* (Dupont Show of the Month, NBC, Nov. 19, 1962); and Secret Storm (CBS, 1962–64).

Awards. Mr. Barney received first prize for his film, *Schistosomiasis (Snail Fever)*, produced for the US Army Signal Corps (Intl. Film Festival, Venice, Italy, 1947); and an Academy (Oscar) Award nomination for his Signal Corps documentary, *Shades of Gray* (1957).

Recreation. Reading, scooter riding.

BARNHILL, JAMES. Educator, actor, director. b. James Orris Barnhill, May 23, 1922, Sumner, Miss., to James Arthur and Louise (Sullivan) Barnhill. Father, minister. Grad. Hattiesburg (Miss.) H.S., 1940; attended Mississippi Coll., 1940–42; grad. Yale Univ., A.B. 1947, M.F.A. 1954; New York Univ., M.A. 1949. Studied acting with Constance Welch at Yale Univ., three years; speech with Dorothy Mulgrave at New York Univ., two years; voice with J. Lagana, one year; acting and directing with Frank Corsaro, one year; Actors' Studio (observer, 1962–64). Served USN, 1942–46, PTO; rank, Lt. (jg). Member of ATA; RIETA; ASTR; SCA; TLA; NETC (vice-pres., 1959–61; adv. council, 1961–to date); AEA; AFTRA; IASTA; University Club, Providence, R.I.; The Players Club, Providence, R.I.; Brown Club, N.Y.C. Address: (home) 81 Transit St., Providence, RI 02906, tel. (401) 331-4266; (bus.) Dept. of English, Brown Univ., Providence, RI 02912, tel. (401) 863-2838.

Mr. Barnhill is Professor of English and director of theatre at Brown Univ.; he has been a member of the faculty since 1954. As assistant director of Sock and Buskin from 1954–63, he staged forty productions at Brown Univ. He was on sabbatical leave from the university during 1963–64, working professionally as an actor and director in N.Y.C. In 1972, Mr. Barnhill was appointed visiting professor, Tagore Chair, at M.S. University of Baroda, Baroda, Gujarat, India.

Mr. Barnhill appeared as Snobson in the ELT production of *Fashion* (Lenox Hill Playhouse, Feb. 1948); in *Stalag 17* (Norwich Summer Th., Conn., July 1953); in over 100 productions in 15 seasons of summer stock; and joined (Feb. 1964) *Six Characters in Search of an Author* (Martinique Th., N.Y.C., Mar. 7, 1963).

He was associated with the founding of Trinity Square Repertory Th., Providence, and was in the resident company during the first two seasons (1964–66), playing roles in *Twelfth Night, Uncle Vanya*, and *The Rehearsal*. In April 1972, he appeared at the Cafe La Mama, N.Y.C., in *The American Fantasies*. .

Television. Mr. Barnhill first appeared as the Jailor in *The French, They Are So French* (Chronicle, CBS, Oct. 1963); followed by Dr. Mudd in *Weather or Not* (Look Up and Live, CBS, Dec. 1963).

Awards. Mr. Barnhill was the recipient of a Brown University Fellowship for study of European theatre (Summer 1962), and a Rockefeller Grant in directing at IASTA (1964). He received an honorary M.A. degree from Brown Univ. (1961).

Recreation. Swimming, painting, calligraphy.

BARON, ROBERT ALEX. Company manager, director, writer, general manager, press representative. b. Robert H. Barimbaum, Sept. 2, 1920, Chicago, Ill., to Morris and Emma (Bagus) Barimbaum. Father, dairy technologist. Grad. Marshall H.S., Chicago, 1938; attended YMCA Coll. (Chicago), 1938–39; grad. Univ. of Illinois, B.A. (cum laude) 1943; Smith Coll., M.A. 1949. Studied at Amer. Theatre Wing, N.Y.C., 1950–51. Married Dec. 2, 1956, to Joan DeKeyser, theatre administrator; one daughter. Served US Army Medical Corps and Special Services, 1944–46; rank T/5. Member of ATPAM (bd. of gov., 1962–65); Gamma Sigma Delta; Alpha Zeta. Address: 150 West End Ave., New York, NY 10023, tel. (212) 873-2626.

Pre-Theatre. Public Health Service.

Theatre. Mr. Baron made his first appearance on stage as Miles Standish in a third-grade play (LaFayette Grammar School, Chicago, Ill., 1928); subsequently, for the Actors Company Experimental Th., he appeared as Gustave in *Out of This World* (Foresters Th., Chicago, Nov. 10, 1943), and as the Postman in *They Knew What They Wanted* (Foresters Th., Feb. 1944).

During 1947–48, he served as theatre business manager at Smith Coll., Northampton, Mass., and at the Monticello (N.Y.) Playhouse. At the Community Th. (Longmeadow, Mass., 1948–49), he directed *Years Ago, The Male Animal* and *The Winslow Boy.*

Mr. Baron was press representative for *Right You Are If You Think You Are* (Kaufmann Th., YMHA, N.Y.C., May 1950); assistant to the press representative for *The Medium* and *The Telephone* (Arena Th., Edison Hotel, N.Y.C., Aug. 1950); press representative for the concerts at the Music Festival, Locust Valley, N.Y. (Aug. 1950); assistant stage manager for *Razzle Dazzle* (Arena Th., Edison Hotel, N.Y.C., Jan. 1951); stage manager for the N.Y.C. production of *Hook 'n Ladder* (Royale, Apr. 29, 1952); and director of stock productions of *Joan of Lorraine* and *Born Yesterday* (Pine Bush, N.Y., June 1952).

He was advance director for a stock tour of *I Am a Camera* (July 1953); treasurer for the Westport (Conn.) Country Playhouse (July 1954); director and production manager at the Norwich (N.Y.) Summer Th. (Aug. 1954); company manager for *The Threepenny Opera* (Th. de Lys, N.Y.C., Sept. 20, 1955); company and general manager for *The First Gentleman* (Belasco, Apr. 25, 1957); company manager for *Summer of the Seventeenth Doll* (Coronet, Jan. 22, 1958); general manager for *Love Me Little* (Helen Hayes Th., Apr. 14, 1958); company manager for *The Man in the Dog Suit* (Coronet, Oct. 30, 1958), *The Gazebo* (Lyceum, Dec. 12, 1958), for the Bway tryout of *Listen to the Mocking Bird* (opened Colonial, Boston, Mass., Dec. 27, 1958; closed Shubert, Washington, D.C., Jan. 29, 1959), and for *Look After Lulu* (Henry Miller's Th., N.Y.C., Mar. 3, 1959).

Mr. Baron was company manager for *Oedipus Rex* (Carnegie Hall Playhouse, Apr. 1959), and *Destry Rides Again* (Imperial, Apr. 23, 1959); general manager for *A Mighty Man Is He* (Cort, Jan. 6, 1960), and *At the Drop of a Hat* (John Golden Th., N.Y.C., Oct. 8, 1959); company manager for *Becket* (St. James, Oct. 5, 1960); *An Evening with Yves Montand* (John Golden Th., Oct. 8, 1961); company and general manager for *Seidman and Son* (Belasco, Oct. 15, 1962); general manager for *Strange Interlude* (Hudson, Mar. 11, 1963); company manager for *Bicycle Ride to Nevada* (Cort, Sept. 24, 1963), *A Case of Libel* (Longacre, Oct. 10, 1963), and *The Deputy* (Brooks Atkinson Th., Feb. 26, 1964); and house manager of the Blackstone Th., Chicago (Aug. 5–Sept. 6, 1974) and the Ethel Barrymore Th., N.Y.C. (season of 1974–75).

Television. Mr. Baron appeared (1952–53) on The Big Story (NBC), Big Town (CBS), Treasury Men in Action (NBC), and Suspense (CBS). He was a guest on the Johnny Carson Tonight Show (NBC), the Merv Griffin Show (Ind.), the Today Show (NBC), and Not for Women Only (NBC).

Other Activities. Mr. Baron is a pioneer noise abatement advocate (1966–to date). In N.Y.C., he formed Citizens for a Quiet City and became a member of Mayor John V. Lindsay's Task Force on Noise Control. With Ford Foundation funding, he conducted Project Quiet City (1970–72), a survey of urban noise pollution and a study of ways to reduce such noise.

Published Works. He researched and co-authored "Report to the Legitimate Theatre Industry" (American Theatre Guild Society and the Council of the Living Theatre, 1952–55); wrote "2001 Opening Nights" (*Theatre Arts,* 1953); "Actor in Search of Contract" (*Equity Magazine,* 1953); "Modern Theatre" (*Inquiry,* Fordham Univ. 1963); and *The Tyranny of Noise* (1970).

BARR, RICHARD. Producer, director. b. Richard Alphonse Baer, Sept. 6, 1917, Washington, D.C., to David and Ruth (Israel) Baer. Father, builder, Grad. Western H.S., Washington, D.C., 1934; Princeton Univ., A.B. 1938. Served USAAF, 1941–46; rank, Capt. Member of AEA; SAG; SSD&C; League of NY Theatres (pres., Feb. 1967 to date); ANTA (dir., 1969–71); League of Off-Bway Theatres. Address: (home) 26 W. 8th St., New York, NY 10011, tel. (212) OR 4-3861; (bus.) 226 W. 47th St., New York, NY 10036, tel. (212) 354-7470.

Theatre. Mr. Barr began his career as an actor with Orson Welles' Mercury Th. Co., as a "convention attendant" in *Danton's Death* (Mercury, N.Y.C., Nov. 2, 1938), remaining with the company until 1941. After his discharge from the service, he directed (1946–49) various summer stock productions; directed, and co-adapted (with Richard Whorf and José Ferrer) *Volpone* (NY City Ctr., Jan. 8, 1948); directed *Angel Street* (NY City Ctr., Jan. 22, 1948); directed *The Bear* (one of four one-act plays, NY City Ctr., Feb. 5, 1948); directed and designed lighting for *Richard III* (Booth, Feb. 8, 1949); directed the US premiere of Synge's *Deirdre of the Sorrows* (Master Inst. Th., Dec. 14, 1949); directed *Arms and the Man* (Arena, Oct. 19, 1950); produced, packaged, and directed various shows (1950–1952); produced with Charles Bowden *At Home With Ethel Waters,* which he also directed (48 St. Th., Sept. 22, 1953); *Ruth Draper* (Vanderbilt, Jan. 25, 1954); dir. *The Boy with a Cart* (Bway Tabernacle Church, Apr. 4, 1954); produced, with Mr. Bowden, *Ruth and Paul Draper* (Bijou, Dec. 26, 1954); *All in One,* a triple-bill consisting of *Trouble in Tahiti, Paul Draper,* and *27 Wagons Full of Cotton* (Playhouse, Apr. 19, 1955); and another *Ruth Draper* production (Playhouse, Dec. 25, 1956).

With Mr. Bowden and H. Ridgely Bullock, he produced *Fallen Angels* (Playhouse, Jan. 17, 1956); and with Mr. Bowden, H. Ridgely Bullock, Richard Myers, and Julius Fleischmann, *Hotel Paradiso* (Henry Miller's Th., Apr. 11, 1957). Messrs. Bowden, Barr, and Bullock produced two national tours of *Auntie Mame,* the first starred Constance Bennett (opened Hanna, Cleveland, Ohio, Oct. 30, 1957; closed Erlanger, Chicago, Ill., Jan. 17, 1959), the second starred Sylvia Sydney (opened Amer. Shakespeare Festival, Stratford, Conn., Apr. 19, 1958; closed Civic Aud., Pasadena, Calif., Feb. 4, 1959); and they produced *Season of Choice* (Barbizon-Plaza Th., Apr. 13, 1959).

In 1960, Mr. Barr and H. B. Lutz formed "Theatre 1960," to produce experimental plays Off Bway. The produced, with Harry J. Brown, Jr., two one-act plays, *Krapp's Last Tape* and *The Zoo Story* (Provincetown Playhouse, Jan. 14, 1960); and *The Killer* (Seven Arts Th., Mar. 22, 1960), directed by Mr. Barr. For the ANTA Matinee Series, Mr. Barr also directed three one-act plays: *Nekros, Embers,* and *Fam and Yam* (Th. de Lys, Oct. 25, 1960).

in 1961, Mr. Barr produced as "Theater 1961" *The Sudden End of Anne Cinquefoil* (East End, Jan. 10, 1961); subsequently, with Clinton Wilder, produced as "Theater 1961" the double-bill, *The American Dream* and *Bartleby* (York, Jan. 24, 1961). *Bartleby* was replaced by *The Valerie Bettis Dance Theatre* (Feb. 7, 1961–Feb. 28, 1961), which was replaced by *The Death of Bessie Smith.* Messrs. Barr and Wilder next presented *Gallows Humor* (Gramercy Arts, Apr. 18, 1961).

As "Theatre 1962", they produced *Happy Days* (Cherry Lane, Sept. 17, 1961); and a program of works in repertory entitled *The Theatre of the Absurd* (Cherry Lane, Feb. 11, 1962), which included *Endgame, Bertha, Gallows Humor, The Sandbox, Deathwatch, Picnic on the Battlefield, The American Dream, The Zoo Story,* and *The Killer.* Mr. Barr also directed *The Zoo Story* and *The Killer* in this presentation.

As "Theater 1963", they presented the double-bill, *Mrs. Dally Has a Lover* and *Whisper into My Good Ear* (Cherry Lane, Oct. 1, 1962); *Who's Afraid of Virginia Woolf?* (Billy Rose Th., Oct. 13, 1962); *Like Other People* (Village South, Mar. 29, 1963); and *The American Dream* and *The Zoo Story,* a double-bill (Cherry Lane, May 29, 1963).

Mr. Barr, Mr. Wilder, and Edward Albee formed "Theater 1964" for which they leased the Cherry Lane Th. through June 1967. They produced *Corruption in the Palace of Justice* (Oct. 8, 1963), and a double-bill: Samuel Beckett's *Play* and, by arrangement with Michael Codron in association with David Hall, Harold Pinter's *The Lover* (Jan. 4, 1964). At the East End Th., they presented *Funnyhouse of a Negro* (Jan. 14, 1964). They produced the London company production of *Who's Afraid of Virginia Woolf?* (Picadilly, Feb. 6, 1964); "Theater 1964" presented a triple-bill of *Play, The Two Executioners,* and *The Dutchman* (Cherry Lane, Mar. 24, 1964); Mr. Barr, with Mr. Wilder and Sometimes, Inc., produced the bus and truck tour of *Who's Afraid of Virginia Woolf?* (opened Westport Country Playhouse, Conn., Aug. 17, 1964; closed Royal Alexandra, Toronto, Canada, Apr. 3, 1965); he produced, with Mr. Wilder, *The Giants' Dance* (Cherry Lane, N.Y.C., Nov. 16, 1964); and "Theater 1964" presented *The Zoo Story* and *The Dutchman* (Cherry Lane, Nov. 24, 1964).

"Theater 1965" (Messrs. Barr, Albee, and Wilder) presented *Tiny Alice* (Billy Rose Th., Dec. 29, 1964); the New Playwrights Series I, II, and III, at the Cherry Lane Th., including: (Series I) Sam Shepard's *Up to Thursday,* Paul Foster's *Balls,* and Lanford Wilson's *Home Free!* (Feb. 10, 1965); (Series II) Lawrence Osgood's *Pigeons* and Frank Gagliano's *Conerico Was Here To Stay* (Mar. 3, 1965); and (Series III) Kenneth Pressman's *Hunting the Jingo Bird* and Joseph Morgenstern's *Lovey* (Mar. 25, 1965); "Theater 1965," with Frith Banbury, presented *Do Not Pass Go* (Cherry Lane, Apr. 19, 1965); Mr. Barr and Mr. Wilder produced a revue, *That Thing at the Cherry Lane* (Cherry Lane, May 18, 1965); and "Th. 1965" presented *The Zoo Story* and *Krapp's Last Tape* (Cherry Lane, June 8, 1965).

"Th. 1966" (Messrs. Barr, Albee, and Wilder) presented *Happy Days* (Cherry Lane, Sept. 14, 1965); and *Malcolm* (Shubert, Jan. 11, 1966). "Th. 1967" (Messrs. Barr, Albee and Wilder) presented *A Delicate Balance* (Martin Beck Th., Sept. 22, 1966; national company opened Coconut Grove Playhouse, Miami, Fla., Jan. 17, 1967); and "Th. 1967," a project of Albarwild Th. Arts, Inc., presented at the Cherry Lane, three one-act plays by Thornton Wilder: *The Long Christmas Dinner, Queens of France,* and *The Happy Journey to Trenton and Camden* (Sept. 6, 1966); a revival of George S. Kaufman's *The Butter and Egg Man* (Oct. 17, 1966); *Night of the Dunce* (Dec. 28, 1966); *The Rimers of Eldritch* (Feb. 20, 1967); and *The Party on Greenwich Avenue* (May 10, 1967); "Th. 1967" (Messrs. Barr, Mr. Wilder, and Michael Kasdan) presented a double-bill, *Match-Play* and *A Party for Divorce* (Provincetown Playhouse, Oct. 11, 1966); "Th. 1967" (Messrs. Barr, Wilder, and Albee) presented the Paul Taylor Dance Co. (ANTA Th., Dec. 26, 1966); "Th. 1968" (Messrs. Barr, Wilder and Charles Woodward, Jr.) presented *Johnny No-Trump* (Cort, Oct. 8, 1967);

and "Th. 1968" (Messrs. Barr and Wilder) presented *Everything in the Garden* (Plymouth, Nov. 29, 1967).

Mr. Barr produced, with Charles Woodward, Jr., *The Boys in the Band* (Th. Four, Apr. 14, 1968; first national company opened Huntington Hartford Th., Los Angeles, Mar. 10, 1969; second national company opened Wilbur, Boston, May 5, 1969); he directed *Private Lives* (Th. de Lys, May 19, 1968); the "Th. 1969 Playwrights Rep."0 (Mr. Barr and Mr. Albee) presented four programs in repertory: *Box* and *Quotations from Chairman Mao Tse-Tung* (Sept. 30, 1968), *The Death of Bessie Smith* and *The American Dream* (Oct. 2, 1968), *Krapp's Last Tape* and *The Zoo Story*, directed by Mr. Barr (Oct. 9, 1968), and *Happy Days* (Oct. 12, 1968), all four of which programs were first presented at the Studio Arena Th., Buffalo, N.Y. (from Sept. 10, 1968); and "Th. 1969" (Messrs. Barr, Albee and Woodward) presented a revival of *The Front Page* (Ethel Barrymore Th., May 10, 1969).

ANTA produced the "Playwrights Unit of Th. 1970" (Messrs. Barr, Albee and Woodward) production of *Watercolor* and *Criss-Crossing*, a double-bill (ANTA Th., Jan. 21, 1970); "Th. 1971" (Messrs. Barr, Woodward and Albee) presented *All Over* (Martin Beck Th., Mar. 27, 1971); "Th. 1972" (Messrs. Barr, Woodward and Michael Harvey) presented *The Grass Harp* (Martin Beck Th., Nov. 2, 1971); "Th. 1972" (Messrs. Barr and Woodward) presented *Drat!* (McAlpin Rooftop Th., Oct. 18, 1971); Mr. Barr was co-director, with Edward Albee, of the John Drew Th., Guild Hall, East Hampton, L.I., N.Y., for a season of stock (Summer 1972); "Th. 1973" (Messrs. Barr and Woodward) presented, with ANTA, *The Last of Mrs. Lincoln* (ANTA Th., N.Y.C., Dec. 12, 1972); and a pre-Bway revival of *Detective Story* (opened Paramus, N.J., Playhouse, Feb. 18, 1973; closed Shubert, Philadelphia, Mar. 24, 1973).

Mr. Barr produced, with Mr. Woodward, *Noel Coward in Two Keys* (Ethel Barrymore Th., N.Y.C., Feb. 28, 1974; and a subsequent tour); produced, with Messrs. Woodward and Wilder, *Seascape* (Shubert, Jan. 26, 1975; and a subsequent Los Angeles production); produced, with Mr. Woodward and Terry Spiegel, *P.S.: Your Cat Is Dead!* (John Golden Th., Apr. 7, 1975; after a try-out at the Studio Arena Th., Buffalo, N.Y.).

In 1963, Mr. Barr founded (with Messrs. Albee and Wilder), The Playwright's Unit, dedicated to the production of works by new playwrights. The Unit's first home was The Village South Th., 15 Van Dam St., N.Y.C.; in the fall, 1969, under the guidance of Messrs. Barr, Albee and Woodward, it moved to 83 E. 4th St., N.Y.C. (formerly the home of the New Dramatists Comm.), and through Apr. 1971, it presented 94 plays, many of which went on to Bway or Off-Bway productions.

Films. Mr. Barr served as an executive assistant to Orson Wells on *Citizen Kane* (RKO, 1941); made military training films, while serving with the USAAF (1941–46), becoming head of its motion picture unit; and in 1947, was a dialogue director for several Hollywood films.

Television and Radio. He was an actor on various Mercury Th. radio programs.

Awards. Messrs. Barr and Wilder received the Vernon Rice Award for their "Theater 1961" productions (1962); the Antoinette Perry (Tony) Award and the NY Drama Critics Circle Award for *Who's Afraid of Virginia Woolf?* (1963); "Th. 1965" (Messrs. Barr, Albee and Wilder) received the fourth annual Margo Jones Award, for encouragement given to new plays and playwrights (Feb. 1965); *A Delicate Balance* won the Antoinette Perry (Tony) Award as Best Play (1967), and a Pulitzer Prize in drama (1967); and *Seascape* won a Pulitzer prize in drama (1975).

BARRANGER, M. S. Educator, theatre administration. b. Milly Hilliard Slater, Feb. 12, 1937, Birmingham, Ala., to C. C. and Mildred C. (Hilliard) Slater. Father, engineer; mother, teacher. Grad. Univ. of Montevallo, B.A. (English) 1958; Tulane Univ., M.A. (English) 1959; Ph.D. (theatre) 1964. Married 1961 to Garic Kenneth Barranger; one daughter. Member of ATA (vice-chmn. and area coordinator in theatre administration of 1974 convention program comm.; recorder for 1974 convention; Standards Comm., 1974; chmn. of 1975 convention program comm.); UCTA (chmn., program for chief administrators of theatre programs, 1973–74); Speech Communication Assn., Southern Speech Communication Assn.; Southwest Theatre Conference, Theatres of Louisiana. Address: Dept. of Theatre & Speech, Tulane Univ., New Orleans, LA 70118, tel. (504) 865-6205.

Mrs. Barranger was special lecturer in English, Univ. of New Orleans (1964–69) and joined the Tulane Univ. faculty in 1969 (asst. prof. of theatre, 1969–73; assoc. prof. of theatre and chmn., Dept. of Theatre & Speech, 1973–to date); mng. dir., Tulane Center Stage, a professional summer repertory theatre (1973–to date).

Published Works. Mrs. Barranger is the author of *Henrik Ibsen* (1969) and co-editor of *Generations: An Introduction to Drama* (1971). She wrote nine critical articles on modern and Renaissance drama (1969–74), thirteen book reviews (1969–74), and contributed twenty-three entries to the *Dictionary of Church History* (1971).

Recreation. Film, music, and travel.

BARRIE, BARBARA. Actress. b. Barbara Ann Berman, May 23, 1931, Corpus Christi, Tex., to Louis and Frances (Boruszak) Berman. Father, insurance man. Educ. Corpus Christi (Tex.) grammar and high schools; Delmar Jr. Coll., Corpus Christi; grad. Univ. of Texas, B.F.A. Professional training with Uta Hagen, Nina Gonaroff, Walt Witcover, David Craig. Married July 23, 1964, to Jay Malcolm Harnick, producer, director; one daughter; one son. Relative in theatre: brother-in-law, Sheldon Harnick, lyricist, composer. Member of AEA; SAG; AFTRA. Address: 465 West End Ave., New York, NY 10024, tel. (212) 787-8497.

Theatre. In 1953, Miss Barrie played Sloth in an Equity Library Theatre (ELT) production of *Dr. Faustus* (Lenox Hill Playhouse, N.Y.C., Apr. 1953) and appeared at the Corning (N.Y.) Summer Theatre in *The Moon Is Blue, The Happy Time,* and *Be Your Age.* She played at the Rochester (N.Y.) Arena Th. (Spring 1954) and returned to Corning (Summer 1954), where she played Celia Coplestone in *The Cocktail Party* (July 13); Nellie Ewell in *Summer and Smoke* (July 20); Mabel in *Three Men on a Horse* (July 27); Nancy Stoddard in *The Country Girl* (Aug. 3); Marie Louise Ducotel in *My 3 Angels* (Aug. 10); Hilda Manney in *Room Service* (Aug. 17); and Sibyl Chase in *Private Lives* (Aug. 31).

She played Ilse in an ELT production of *Maedchen in Uniform* (Lenox Hill Playhouse, N.Y.C., Apr. 21, 1955); made her Bway debut as Janey Stewart in *The Wooden Dish* (Booth Th., Oct. 6, 1955); was Goodie Proctor in *The Crucible* (Martinique, Mar. 11, 1958); and appeared at the American Shakespeare Festival, Stratford, Conn., as the Player Queen in *Hamlet* (June 19, 1958), Hermia in *A Midsummer Night's Dream* (June 20, 1958), and Dorcas in *The Winter's Tale* (July 20, 1958). She played Cherry in *The Beaux' Stratagem* (Phoenix Th., N.Y.C., Feb. 24, 1959); returned to Stratford, Conn. (Summer 1959), where she played Anne Page in *The Merry Wives of Windsor* (July 8) and Diana in *All's Well That Ends Well* (Aug. 1); and appeared at the NY Shakespeare Festival as Bianca in *The Taming of the Shrew* (Belvedere Lake, N.Y.C., Aug. 18, 1960). As Annie Sullivan in *The Miracle Worker,* she toured Europe and the Middle East with the Theatre Guild's American Repertory Co. (Mar.–June 1961). She played again in N.Y.C. as Joan Mills in *Happily Never After* (Eugene O'Neill Th., Mar. 10, 1966); as Intellect in *Horseman, Pass By* (Fortune Th., Jan. 15, 1969); Viola in the NY Shakespeare Festival *Twelfth Night* (Delacorte Th., Aug. 6, 1969); Sarah in *Company* (Alvin Th., Apr. 26, 1970); Grace Mason in *The Selling of the President* (Shubert Th., Mar. 22, 1972); replaced (June 5, 1972) Lee Grant as Edna Edison in *The Prisoner of Second Avenue* (Eugene O'Neill Th., Nov. 11, 1971); and played Sparky in *The Killdeer* (Public Th.—Newman Th., Mar. 28, 1974).

Films. Miss Barrie's first motion picture appearance was in *Giant* (WB, 1956), and she was in *The Caretakers* (UA, 1963) and *One Potato, Two Potato* (Cinema V, 1964).

Television. Miss Barrie was on Kraft Television Th. (NBC) in the mid-1950s and has been a guest on many other major network shows, including Armstrong Circle Th. (NBC), US Steel Hour (NBC), Robert Montgomery Presents (NBC), Alfred Hitchcock Presents (NBC), Rawhide, Mr. Novak, The Invaders, Love of Life (CBS), The Defenders (CBS), Dr. Kildare (NBC), Ironsides (NBC), The Fugitive (ABC), Naked City (ABC), Route 66 (CBS), and Ben Casey (ABC). She was in *Lorraine Hansberry: To Be Young, Gifted, and Black* (PBS, Jan. 20, 1972); played Mrs. Brodnik in the series Diana (NBC, 1973); and was Charlotte in *For the Use of the Hall* (Hollywood TV Theatre, PBS, Jan. 3, 1975).

Awards. Miss Barrie won the Cannes (France) Festival Award as best actress for her performance in *One Potato, Two Potato* (1964); was nominated for a 1970–71 Antoinette Perry (Tony) Award as best supporting actress in a musical for her performance in *Company;* and was nominated in 1974 for a *Village Voice* Off-Bway (Obie) Award for her performance in *The Killdeer.*

Recreation. Tennis, decorating, cooking, caring for her country house.

BARROW, BERNARD. Educator, writer, actor, director. b. Bernard Elliott Barrow, Dec. 30, 1927, New York City, to Samuel and Sophie (Halpern) Barrow. Father, laundry operator. Grad. Stuyvesant H.S., N.Y.C., 1944; Syracuse Univ., B.A. 1947; Columbia Univ., M.A. 1948; Yale Univ., Ph.D. 1957. Studied acting with Lee Strasberg, 1960–61. Married June 1948, to Jane Mabbott (marr. dis. 1953); married Feb. 1954 to Joyce Gitelman (marr. dis. 1962), one son, one daughter; married Feb. 1963 to Joan Kahn (Kaye), actress. Member of AETA; ASTR; SAG; AFTRA; AEA. Address: (home) 14 Sutton Pl. So., New York, NY 10022, tel. (212) 371-5160; (bus.) Brooklyn College, Brooklyn, NY 11210, tel. (212) 780-5666.

Since 1955, Mr. Barrow has taught speech and theatre at Brooklyn Coll., serving as assistant professor (1960–65); and associate professor (1965–to date). He served as visiting lecturer in the Program in the Arts at Columbia Univ. (1961–63); and was instructor and director of drama in the English Dept. at Lincoln Univ., Pa. (1948–1951); lecturer at the Yale Shakespeare Institute (Summer 1955); visiting assistant professor of theatre history and criticism at the Yale Univ. Sch. of Drama (Spring 1963); and visiting assistant professor of dramatic art at Univ. of California at Berkeley (Summer 1964).

Theatre. Mr. Barrow played Jonah Goodman in the N.Y.C. production of *The Gentle People* (Provincetown Playhouse, July 1947); Major Davis in the Cherokee Historical Assn. production of *Unto These Hills* (Cherokee, N.C., 1950); appeared in stock at the Coconut Grove Playhouse (Miami, Fla., Winter 1953); was production stage manager at the Sacandaga Summer Th. (Sacandaga Park, N.Y., Summers 1957–59); played Claggert in ELT's production of *Billy Budd* (Lenox Hill Playhouse, N.Y.C., Feb. 17, 1958); was the Narrator in the NY Pro Musica's production of *The Play of Daniel* (Cloisters, N.Y.C., Feb. 1959); and was stage manager for *Carousel* and *South Pacific* (Oakdale Musical Th., Wallingford, Conn.; Warwick Musical Th., R.I. Summer 1960).

Off-Bway, he played the Tourist in *Scuba Duba* (New Th., 1966); John in *Molly's Dream* (Stage 73, Summer 1973); Dr. Astrov in *Uncle Vanya* (Martinique, 1973); and the Rabbi in *Meegan's Game* (Cricket Th., 1974). He directed *Spiro Who* (Gate Th., 1968); and *Stag Movie* (Gate Th., 1970).

Films. He appeared in featured roles in *Rachel, Rachel* (WB-Seven Arts, 1968); *Glass Houses* (Col., 1972); *Serpico* (Par., 1973); and *Claudine* (20th-Fox, 1974).

Television. He has appeared on *The Defenders* (CBS); *Car 54, Where Are You?* (NBC); *Edge of Night* (CBS); *East Side/West Side* (CBS); *Get Smart* (NBC); *N.Y.P.D.* (ABC); and in featured roles on *Where the Heart Is* (CBS); *The Secret Storm* (CBS); *The Waltons* (CBS); *Kojak* (CBS); *The Rookies* (ABC); and *Rhoda* (CBS).

Published Works. He has written articles for *AETA Journal, Theatre Notebook* and *ANTA Newsletter.*

Recreation. Tennis.

BARRY, PAUL. Producer, actor, director. Grad. Wayne State Univ., B.A. Married to Ellen Barry, actress, public relations director.

Theatre. Mr. Barry is founder (1963) and artistic director of The NJ Shakespeare Festival (Drew Univ., Madison, N.J., 1972–to date), a professional repertory company originally housed at the Cape May (N.J.) Playhouse, where Mr. Barry had served as producer-director and actor since 1963. Other directing credits include the New Orleans Repertory Co.; Bucks County Playhouse (New Hope, Pa.); Little Th.-on-the-Square (Sullivan, Ill.); The Showboat (Rochester, N.Y.); Equity Library Th. (N.Y.C.); and the Keweenaw Playhouse (Calumet, Mich.), of which he was founder-producer.

He made his acting debut with the Ashland (Ore.) Shakespeare Festival (1952); subsequently appeared off-Bway in *The Last Mile* (Lennox Hill Playhouse, N.Y.C., Nov. 1, 1956), and *Enemy of the People* (Provincetown Playhouse, Feb. 25, 1958); played in the NY Shakespeare Festival production of *Romeo and Juliet;* made his Bway debut as Mr. Keres in *Tiger, Tiger Burning Bright* (Booth, Dec. 22, 1962); and appeared with the Barter Th. (Abingdon, W.Va.).

Films. He appeared in *About Mrs. Leslie* (Par., 1954), *Brigadoon* (MGM, 1954); *Bridges at Toko-Ri* (Par., 1954); and *Battle Cry* (WB, 1955).

Television. Mr. Barry's credits include The Catholic Hour (NBC); Alcoa Th.; and *Cyrano de Bergerac.*

Other Activities. He has been a guest lecturer at Marymount Coll., the Univ. of Toledo; Yale; Rutgers; Princeton; and Drew Univ.; and has served as a consultant to the NY State Council on the Arts.

Awards. For his work with the NJ Shakespeare Festival, Mr. Barry received the NJ Drama Critics Assn. awards (1973) for "best production of a play," "best New Jersey production during a season," and "best actor.".

BART, LIONEL. Lyricist, director, playwright, composer. b. Lionel Begleiter, Aug. 1, 1930, London, England, to Maurice and Yetta Begleiter. Father, tailor. Attended St. Martin's Sch. of Art, London, 1944–48. Served, WW II, RAF. Member of Performing Right Society; Music Publishers Assn.; Song-Writers Guild of Great Britain (gen. council); Dramatists Guild.

Pre-Theatre. Managing director and chairman of silk-screen printing works and commercial art studios.

Theatre. Mr. Bart made his debut in London as composer and lyricist of *Fings Ain't Wot They Used T'Be* (Th. Royal, Stratford, Feb. 17, 1959; revived in revised form, Th. Royal, Dec. 22, 1959; moved Garrick, Feb. 11, 1960). He wrote the lyrics for *Lock Up Your Daughters* (Mermaid, May 28, 1959; in U.S.: opened Shubert Th., New Haven, Conn., Apr. 27, 1960; closed Shubert Th., Boston, Mass., May 7, 1960; in London, revived at Mermaid, May 17, 1962, and Mar. 31, 1969).

He wrote book, music and lyrics for *Oliver!* (New London, June 30, 1960; Stockholm, 1961; Australia, 1961–62; Rotterdam, 1963; Imperial, N.Y.C., Jan. 6, 1963; revived Piccadilly, London, Apr. 26, 1967); wrote book, music, and lyrics for and directed *Blitz!* (Adelphi, May 8, 1962); wrote, with Harvey Orkin, the book for and wrote music and lyrics for *Maggie May* (Adelphi, Sept. 22, 1964); directed and wrote lyrics for *Twang!* (Shaftesbury, Dec. 20, 1965); wrote music and lyrics for *La Strada* (Lunt-Fontanne Th., N.Y.C., Dec. 14, 1969); wrote, with Stephen Lewis, *The Londoners* (Th. Royal, Stratford East, London, Eng., 1971); and wrote songs for *Costa Packet* (Th. Royal, 1972).

Films. Mr. Bart composed the music and lyrics for *Serious Charge* (1957); music, lyrics and screenplay for *The Duke Wore Jeans* (1958); music and lyrics for *The Tommy Steele Story* (1957) and *Tommy the Toreador* (1959); title song and theme music for *Sparrows Can't Sing* (1963) and *From Russia With Love* (UA, 1964). A motion picture version was made of *Oliver!* (U, 1968).

Television. Mr. Bart wrote *The Golden Year* (BBC, London, 1957), which was the life story of singer Tommy Steele, appeared on That Was the Week That Was (BBC, 1963); and appeared on David Susskind's Open End (WNEW-TV, N.Y.C., 1963).

Awards. Mr. Bart received Ivor Novello Awards, presented by the British Songwriters Guild, for "Handful of Songs" outstanding song of the year (1957); "Water, Water," outstanding novelty song of the year (1957); *The Tommy Steele Story,* outstanding score of the year (1957); for "Living Doll," best-selling work of the year (1959); "Little White Bull," outstanding novelty song of the year (1959); *Lock Up Your Daughters,* outstanding score of the year (1959); outstanding personal services to British music (1959); "As Long as He Needs Me" from *Oliver!* best-selling song and outstanding song of the year (1960); *Oliver!,* outstanding score of the year; *Blitz!,* outstanding contribution to British music (1962); and *Maggie May,* outstanding score of the year (1964). The last-named musical also won first place in the annual London critics poll as best new British musical (1964–65).

Recreation. Entertaining.

BARTENIEFF, GEORGE. Actor, director, teacher. b. George Michael Bartenieff, Jan. 24, 1933, Berlin, Ger., to Michael and Irmgard Bartenieff. Father, physiotherapist, dance teacher; mother, physiotherapist, dance teacher. Attended public schools, Pittsfield, Mass., and N.Y.C.; Professional Children's School, N.Y.C. Professional training at Katherine Dunham's School of Dance; American School of Ballet; Royal Academy of Dramatic Art, London; Guildhall School of Music and Drama, London; Paul Mann Actors Workshop, N.Y.C.; with Morris Carnovsky; Lloyd Richards; Frederica Schmitz Svevo. Married Jan. 27, 1963, to Crystal Field, actress; one son. Member of Equity; AFTRA; SAG. Address: (home) 190 Riverside Dr., New York, NY 10024, tel. (212) 362-8911; (bus.) Theater for the New City, 113 Jane St., New York, NY 10014, tel. (212) 691-2220.

Pre-Theatre. Busboy, dishwasher, sportswear salesman, soda jerk.

Theatre. He made his stage debut with Maria Piscator's Jr. Dramatic Workshop in the title role of *Pinocchio* (Master's Institute, N.Y.C., Nov. 1945); subsequent Jr. Dramatic Workshop roles were the Prince in *The Prince Who Learned Everything Out of Books* (1946) and the title role in *Tom Sawyer* (Theatre of the Engineering Societies Bldg., Dec. 26, 1947).

He first appeared on Bway as Vanya Shopolyanski in *The Whole World Over* (Biltmore, Mar. 27, 1947). He was in summer stock at the Greenwood Garden Playhouse, Portland, Me., in 1949 and returned to Bway as Ricardo in *Montserrat* (Fulton Th., Oct. 29, 1949). In 1955, he appeared in England at the Perranporth (Cornwall) Playhouse (June–Aug.) and the Royal Theatre, Surrey. His first off-Bway role was Leader of the Chorus in *Antigone* (Provincetown Playhouse, Oct. 1955). He was the Friar in *The Lady's Not for Burning* (Arena Th., Washington, D.C., 1958) and returned to the off-Bway stage as Krapp in *Krapp's Last Tape* and Peter in *The Zoo Story* (Cricket, Sept. 1960), then touring in these roles.

He played Prisoners 8 and 6 and the Guard in The Living Theatre's *The Brig* (Midway, May 15, 1963); and in *Home Movies* he was the floor model TV set in "Softly, and Consider the Nearness" and Mr. Verdun in "Home Movies " (Provincetown Playhouse, May 11, 1964). He was the Madman in *The Changeling* (ANTA Washington Sq., Oct. 29, 1964); Ariel in the Hartford (Conn.) Stage Co. production of *The Tempest* (May 7, 1965); in a revival of the *Krapp's Last Tape/Zoo Story* double bill (Cherry Lane, June 8, 1965); and he was the King of France in *All's Well That Ends Well* (NY Shakespeare Festival, Delacorte Th., June 15, 1966). In 1966–67, he performed with the Theater of the Living Arts, Philadelphia, Pa., in the title role of *Poor Bitos* (Feb. 8, 1966); in *A Dream of Love* (Sept. 13, 1966); in *U.S.A.* (Mar. 28, 1967); as Faker Englund in *Room Service;* as Kit Carson in *The Time of Your Life.* He toured in *Room Service* in 1967 and returned to N.Y.C. as Ralph in *Walking to Waldheim* (Forum Th., Nov. 10, 1967); was in the Judson Poets' Theater's *The Line of Least Existence* (Judson Memorial Ch., Mar. 15, 1968); played Pillar in *The Memorandum* (NY Shakespeare Festival, Public Th., May 5, 1968); toured as the Psychiatrist in *Scuba Duba;* and appeared as the Minister in *Quotations from Chairman Mao Tse-Tung* (Billy Rose Th., Sept. 30, 1968) and the Father in *Death of Bessie Smith* (Billy Rose Th., Oct. 2, 1968). He was Steve in *The Expressway* (NY Shakespeare Festival, Public Th., Oct. 1968).

He appeared as Peter in a workshop production of *Romainia, That's the Old Country* (The Other Stage, Public Th., Jan. 1, 1969; Catchpole in the "Home Fires" half of *Cop-Out* (Cort, Apr. 7, 1969); Cadmus in *The Bacchae* (Yale Repertory, New Haven, Conn., May 15, 1969); and Mr. Beck in *The Increased Difficulty of Concentration* (Forum Th., Dec. 4, 1969). He appeared also as Faker Englund in another revival of *Room Service* (Edison Th., May 12, 1970); as Sir William Gower in *Trelawny of the "Wells"* (Public Th., Oct. 11, 1970); as Major Leo Ben Ezra in "Defender of the Faith" and Artie in "The Fanatic," the two parts of *Unlikely Heroes* (Plymouth, Oct. 26, 1971); and in *The Thing Itself,* a Theater for the New City experimental production (Nov. 30, 1972).

Mr. Bartenieff and his wife became directors in 1970 of an experimental group, Theater for the New City, funded by the National Endowment for the Arts and Humanities, the New York State Council on the Arts, and private foundations. The company has produced at least seven new plays each season and tours through N.Y.C. boroughs in the summer with Free Street Theater. Mr. Bartenieff manages the company, acts in its productions, and gives acting lessons. Two New City plays —*The Children's Army Is Late* and *Chile '73*—were selected for the International Theater Festival, Parma, Italy (Parma Opera House, April 1974).

Films. Mr. Bartenieff made his film debut as Yorgo in *America! America!* (WB, 1963). He played also as Prisoner 8 in *The Brig* (Mekas Bros., 1964), the Prospector in *The Double-Barreled Detective Story* (Mekas Bros., 1964), Rodriguez Wedikind in *Zero in the Universe* (Jock Livingston, 1967), a Museum Guard in *Hot Rock* (20th Cent-Fox, 1972), and the Drunk in *The Effect of Gamma Rays on Man-in-the-Moon Marigolds* (20th-Fox, 1972).

Television. Mr. Bartenieff first appeared on television as the reporter in *The Great Adventure* (Theatre Guild Hour, 1956). He was a waiter in *Snap Your Fingers* (U.S. Steel Hour, CBS, 1957) and did comedy improvisations on the Mike Douglas Show (CBS, 1965) and in *The Overnight Bag,* a CBS special (1969).

Awards. In 1973 he was nominated for a *Village Voice* Off-Bway (Obie) Award for his performance in *The Thing Itself.* .

Recreation. Tennis, sketching, swimming, travel.

BARTON, LUCY. Costume designer, educator. b. Sept. 26, 1891, Ogden, Utah, to Jesse Billing and Lucy Eudora (Thomas) Barton. Father, lawyer. Grad. Natl. Cathedral Sch., Washington, D.C., 1910; Anna Morgan Sch. of Expression, Chicago, certificate, 1913; Carnegie Inst. of Tech., B.A. 1917; attended Yale Univ. Sch. of Drama, 1938–39; attended New York Univ. Inst. of Fine Arts, M.A. 1941. Studied oral interpretation in Chicago, with Jessie Harding (1905–13) and Winifred Woodside-Just (1913–14); at Carnegie Inst. of Technology (1914–17). Member of AETA; NETC; Coll. Art

Assn.; Renaissance Society. Address: Terrace Apartments, Apt. 129, 1005 South Congress, Austin, TX 78704.

From 1947, until her retirement in 1961 when she became professor emeritus, Miss Barton was professor of costume design and costumer for the University Th. at the Univ. of Texas.

After working in Philadelphia, Pa., for Van Horne and Son, Costumers (1919–20), Miss Barton began teaching (1921). She taught courses in theatre arts and costume design at Knox Sch. for Girls, Cooperstown, N.Y. (1921–23), the State Univ. of Iowa (1929–31), and the Univ. of Michigan (Summers 1939–51). At the Univ. of Arizona, she was associate professor of dramatic arts, acting head of the Dept. of Dramatic Arts, and director of the University Th. (1943–47); she taught costume design and costumed the plays at the Univ. of Washington (Summers 1947–51).

Miss Barton has served as costume designer for plays and pageants. In Apr. 1917, she played the role of Truth in the WW I recruiting masque, *The Drawing of the Sword*, produced by Thomas Wood Stevens. She repeated her performance and designed costumes when this masque was incorporated into a Red Cross pageant (Long Island; Metropolitan Opera House, N.Y.C.; and Carnegie Hall, N.Y.C., Sept. 1917). In 1918, the masque was incorporated into a St. Louis civic pageant, *Freedom* in which she again played Truth and designed the costumes (July 4, 1918). She directed historical pageants at Cherry Valley, N.Y., and Jamestown, N.Y.; wrote and directed *The Interpreter*, a pageant for the Va. Council of Parents and Teachers (1928), and designed costumes for a historical pageant in New Brunswick, N.J. (Aug. 1929).

During the 1930's, Miss Barton worked with the Federal Theatre (WPA) Project in Chicago, and was designer and workshop supervisor of the costumes for the Old Globe Shakespearean Repertory Group at the English Village (Century of Progress Exposition, Chicago, 1934). She designed the masque costumes for the *Pageant of Old Fort Niagara* (Niagara Falls, N.Y., 1934), and for *The Entrada of Coronada*, presented at the Coronado Quarto Centennial that toured the Southwest (Dec. 6, 1940–Aug. 16, 1941).

Miss Barton was the costume editor for *Players Magazine* (1939–50), and wrote a series of articles on costume design for *Dramatics Magazine* (1944–45).

Published Works. Miss Barton is the author of *Historic Costumes for the Stage* (1935); *Costuming the Biblical Play* (1937; rev. 1962); *Costumes by You: Eight Essays from Experience* (1940); *Period Patterns* with Doris Edson (1942), and *Appreciating Costume* (1969). She wrote the chapter, "Costume Design," for the book *Arts of the United States* (1960), and the section on "Costume Design: Theatrical" for the *Encyclopaedia Britannica*.

Awards. She received the Merit Award from the Southwest Theatre Conference (1957) for "service to the visual eloquence of the theatre"; the AETA Senior Eaves (Costume) Award (1960); and the Merit Award from the Alumni Federation of Carnegie Institute of Technology (1960).

BASEHART, RICHARD. Actor. b. Aug. 31, 1919, Zanesville, Ohio, to Harry T. and Mae (Wetherald) Basehart. Attended school in Zanesville, Ohio. Married Jan. 14, 1940, to Stephanie Klein (dec. July 28, 1950); married Mar. 24, 1951, to Valentina Cortese (marr. dis.); one son; married to Diana Lotery. Member of AEA; SAG; AFTRA.

Theatre. Mr. Basehart first appeared on stage at the age of thirteen with the Wright Players Stock Co. (Zanesville, Ohio, 1932); subsequently played in stock productions in repertory (Hedgerow Th., Moylan, Pa., 1938–42) before making his Bway debut as Weiler in *Counterattack* (Windsor, Feb. 3, 1943). He played Sgt. Hauptmann in *Land of Fame* (Belasco, Sept. 21, 1943); joined Margaret Webster's production of *Othello* (Shubert, Oct. 19, 1943); appeared as Kip in *Take It as It Comes* (48 St. Th., Feb. 10, 1944); Steven Ames in *Hickory Stick* (Mansfield, May 8, 1944); Lachlen in *The Hasty Heart* (Hudson, Jan. 3, 1945); Steve Decker in *The Survivors* (Playhouse, Jan. 19, 1948); Charles Morrow in *The Day the Money Stopped* (Belasco, Feb. 20, 1958); the title role in the American Shakespeare Festival production of *Richard II* (Stratford, Conn., June 13, 1962); and played several previews in the title role of the Lincoln Ctr. Rep. Co. production of *Cyrano de Bergerac*, withdrawing before the official opening (Vivian Beaumont Th., N.Y.C., Apr. 25, 1968).

Films. Mr. Basehart made his first screen appearance in *Cry Wolf* (WB, 1947); and subsequently played in *Repeat Performance* (Eagle-Lion, 1947); *He Walked by Night* (Eagle-Lion, 1948); *Region of Terror* (Eagle-Lion, 1949; retitled 'The Black Book); (Eagle-Lion, 1949); *Roseanna McCoy* (Goldwyn, 1949); *Tension* (MGM, 1949); *Outside the Wall* (U, 1950); *Two Flags West* (20th-Fox, 1950); *The House on Telegraph Hill* (20th-Fox, 1951); *Fourteen Hours* (20th-Fox, 1951); *Fixed Bayonets* (20th-Fox, 1951); *Decision Before Dawn* (20th-Fox, 1952); *Titanic* (20th-Fox, 1953); *The Good Die Young* (UA, 1955); *The Stranger's Hand* (DCA, 1955); *Canyon Crossroads* (UA, 1955); *Il bidone* (Italian, 1955; released in US as *The Swindlers*, 1964); *Moby Dick* (WB, 1956); *La Strada* (Trans-Lux, 1956); *Finger of Guilt* (RKO, 1957); *Cartouche* (RKO, 1957); *Time Limit* (UA, 1957); *The Brothers Karamazov* (MGM, 1958); *Five Branded Women* (Par., 1960); *Portrait in Black* (U, 1960); *For the Love of Mike* (20th-Fox, 1960); *Passport to China* (Col., 1961); *Hitler* (Allied, 1962); *The Savage Guns* (MGM, 1962); *Kings of the Sun* (UA, 1963); *The Climbers* (1964); narrated *Four Days in November* (UA, 1964); appeared in *The Satan Bug* (UA, 1965); *Rage* (WB, 1972); and *Chato's Land* (UA, 1972).

Television and Radio. On radio, Mr. Basehart played in *Shangri-La* (Hollywood Star Time, 1946). His first television appearance was in *So Soon To Die* (Playhouse 90, CBS, Jan. 17, 1957); subsequently, he appeared in *A Dream of Treason* (Playhouse 90, CBS, Jan. 21, 1960); *The Hiding Place* (CBS, Mar. 22, 1960); *Men in White* (Dupont Show of the Month, CBS, Sept. 30, 1960); *Shangri-La* (Hallmark Hall of Fame, NBC, Oct. 24, 1960); as *He Who Gets Slapped* (Play of the Week, WNTA, Jan. 30, 1961); in *The Light That Failed* (Family Classics, CBS, Mar. 16, 1961); narrated *D-Day* (Dupont Show of the Month, CBS, June 3, 1962); appeared in *The Paradine Case* (NBC, Mar. 11, 1962); and narrated *The Yanks Are Coming* (Nov. 11, 1963). He starred as Admiral Harriman Nelson on the series *Voyage to the Bottom of the Sea* (ABC, 1964–1968).

Mr. Basehart's other television appearances include *Hans Brinker* (NBC, Dec. 13, 1969); *The Andersonville Trial* (made by KCET, Hollywood, for PBS; shown on WNET, May 17, 1970); *The Case Against Milligan* (CBS, Jan. 28, 1975); the ABC telefilms *City Beneath the Sea, Assignment: Munich, The Birdmen*, and *The Bounty Man;* and many other network dramatic shows.

Awards. For his performance in *The Hasty Heart*, Mr. Basehart won the *Variety* NY Drama Critics Poll (1945); and for his performance in the film *Fourteen Hours*, he received the Natl. Board of Review Award (1951).

BASS, GEORGE HOUSTON. Playwright, director, educator. b. Apr. 23, 1938, Murfreesboro, Tenn., to Clarence Cornelius and Mabel (Dixon) Bass. Father, minister; mother, teacher. Educ. Fisk Univ., B.A. 1959; NY Univ., M.A. 1964; Yale Univ. School of Drama, 1966–68. Professional training with John Gassner (Yale) and Robert Gessner (NY Univ.). Married Jan. 15, 1972, to Ramona Wilkins. Address: (home) 11 Poplar St., Providence, RI 02906; (bus.) Brown Univ., Providence, RI 02912.

Mr. Bass became an associate professor in the theatre arts program, English Dept., Brown Univ., in 1970. He had previously been associate director and playwright in residence, Urban Arts Corps, NY City (1969–70).

Theatre. Mr. Bass was director, Black Arts Th., New Haven, Conn. (1967–68) and artistic director, (Third Party) Long Wharf Summer Th., New Haven (Summer 1968) and Jacob Riis Amphitheatre, N.Y.C. Summer (1966). In the last, he produced forty-eight shows for a performing arts series, using professional and amateur talent under a grant from the Astor Foundation to the N.Y.C. Parks Dept.

Among his plays are *Games* (street theatre prod., N.Y.C. Mobilization for Youth, June 1966); *A Trio for the Living* (Yale Univ., New Haven, Conn., Apr. 1968); *The Fun House* (Long Wharf Th., New Haven, Conn., Sept. 1968); *How Long Suite* (Onyx Arts Festival, N.Y.C., Nov. 1968); *Oh Lord, This World* (Queen of Angels Players, Newark, N.J., Dec. 1969); *Black Masque* (Brown Univ., Apr. 1971); and *The Providence Garden Blues* (Brown Univ., Mar. 1975).

Television. Mr. Bass was a script writer for Voices, Inc., N.Y.C. (1960–63), an organization that performed his first play on television — *A Voice of the People* (WNBC, Sept. 1962). He was also associate producer (story editor) and director for the series On Being Black, original teleplays (WGBH, Boston, Nov. 1968–Aug. 1969).

Awards. Mr. Bass received a John Hay Whitney Fellowship in playwriting (1963–64); the Rosenthal Award given by the American Society of Cinematologists for the most creative film script by a young American writer (1964); the John Golden Fellowship in playwriting (1966–68) at Yale Univ. School of Drama; and a Harlem Cultural Council grant for writing two children's plays (1969). *The Game*, a screen adaptation of one of his original stage plays, won the Plaque of the Lion of St. Mark at the 1967 Venice (Italy) Film Festival.

BATCHELDER, WILLIAM H. Lighting designer, production manager, projection consultant. b. William Henry Batchelder, June 27, 1937, New York City, to Edward T. and Wilma H. Batchelder. Father, advertising executive. Educ. North Tarrytown (N.Y.) H.S.; Hackley School, Tarrytown, N.Y.; Harvard Univ., B.A. 1958. Professional training Yale School of Drama; studied stagecraft with Harry Feldman. Married Apr. 12, 1960, to Eleanor Olds; two sons; one daughter (marr. dis.); married April 18, 1970, to Anne McKay, casting director and stage manager. Member of United Scenic Artists, Local 829; AEA; AGMA. Address: 173 Riverside Dr., New York, NY 10024, tel. (212) 724-5132.

Theatre. Mr. Batchelder began his work in the theatre as a technician with the Group 20 Players, Wellesley, Mass. (1958–59). He spent three summers (1960–62) as lighting designer for the Theatre-by-the-Sea, Matunuck, R.I.; was lighting designer and stage manager at the Woodstock (N.Y.) Playhouse in 1963; and in the following year was lighting designer at the Boston (Mass.) Arts Festival and stage manager for the touring Chrysler-Dodge show.

From 1964 to 1966, he was stage manager for productions of the NY City Center Light Opera Co. at the NY City Ctr.: *Brigadoon* (Dec. 23, 1964); *Kiss Me, Kate* (May 12, 1965); and *Where's Charley?* (May 25, 1966). In the meantime, he had stage managed his first Bway show, *The Right Honourable Gentleman* (Billy Rose Th., Oct. 19, 1965). He was stage manager, production manager, and lighting designer for the Martha Graham Dance Co. for N.Y.C. engagements and on tour in the US, Europe, Asia, and Mexico during the period from 1963 to 1974. From 1966 to 1972, he was a theatre consultant with Jean Rosenthal Associates, working with such organizations as the State Univ. of N.Y.; Juilliard Th. and Alice Tully Hall, both in N.Y.C.; and the Music Center, Los Angeles, Calif. He was Miss Rosenthal's assistant for a touring production of *Fiddler on the Roof; Cabaret* (Broadhurst, Nov. 20, 1966); *The Happy Time* (Broadway Th., Jan. 18, 1968); *Plaza Suite* (Plymouth, Feb. 14, 1968); and *Dear World* (Mark Hellinger Th., Feb. 6, 1969); and five productions of the Metropolitan Opera.

He was production manager and lighting designer for Eliot Feld's American Ballet Co. at Spoleto, Italy (June 1969). He was projection consultant for *Company* (Alvin Th., Apr. 26, 1970) and lighting designer for the touring company (1971); projection consultant for *Two by Two* (Imperial, Nov. 10, 1970); lighting designer for *Captain Brassbound's Conversion* (Ethel Barrymore Th., Apr. 17, 1972); projection consultant for *An Evening with Richard Nixon And. . .* (Sam S. Shubert Th., Apr. 30, 1972); and production manager for *The Daughter of the Regiment* (Wolf Trap, Va., July 1974).

Television. Mr. Batchelder was assistant producer for the television dance presentation *3 by Martha Graham* (NBC, 1969).

Night Clubs. Mr. Batchelder was lighting designer for the John Davidson Show (Empire Room, Waldorf-Astoria Hotel, N.Y.C., May 1970).

Recreation. Sailing, model making.

BATCHELLER, JOSEPH D. Educator, director. b. Joseph Donald Batcheller, Mar. 7, 1915, Portland, Me., to Clifford Eaton and Mildred (Parker) Batcheller. Father, social work administrator; mother, teacher. Grad. Lewistown (Pa.) H.S., 1932; Carnegie Inst. of Tech., A.B. 1936; Univ. of Minn., M.A. 1938, Ph. D. 1942. Married Sept. 3, 1937, to Frances Norton, costume and scenic designer; one son, one daughter. Relative in theatre: cousin, Walter Pritchard Eaton, drama critic and teacher. Member of ANTA; ATA; SAA; SCA; NETC (pres., 1956; advisory board, 1958); NESA (pres., 1963); Council of the Arts (1957); NCP (former advisor); Tau Kappa Alpha (former advisor). Address: (home) 11 Rosemary Lane, Durham, NH 03824, tel. 868-2465; (bus.) Dept. of Speech and Drama, University of New Hampshire, Durham, NH 03824, tel. (603) 868-5511 ext. 370.

Since 1950, Mr. Batcheller has been associate professor, Dept. of Speech and Drama, Univ. of New Hampshire (asst. professor and director of theatre, 1944–50; dept. chmn., 1960–72). From 1939–41, he was instructor and director of theatre at Occidental Coll.; and, from 1941–44, was instructor, stage director and in charge of theatre publicity at Ohio Univ.

Theatre. Mr. Batcheller was an actor and taught scenic design at the Gloucester School of Little Th. (Mass., Summer 1936); was acting technical director at the Univ. of Minnesota Th. (1936–37); for the Russell Crouse Prize Play Contest at the Cape Ann Festival of the Arts, directed *Gloucester Story* (1954) and *The Witch of Dogtown* (1955); and was director at Annisquam Community Th. (Mass., Summers 1947–53).

Awards. He received a NETC Regional Citation (1962).

Recreation. Photography, woodworking, gardening.

BATES, ALAN. Actor. b. Alan Arthur Bates, Feb. 17, 1934, Allestree, Derbyshire, England, to Harold Arthur and Florence Mary (Wheatcroft) Bates. Attended Herbert Strut Grammar Sch., Belper, Derbyshire; RADA, London, England. Studied acting with Claude W. Gibson, Derbyshire, two years; voice with Gladys Lea, N.Y.C. Married Victoria Ward; twin sons. Served RAF, two years. Member of AEA; British AEA. Address: c/o William Morris Agency, 4 Saville Row, London W.1, England tel. 734-9361.

Theatre. Mr. Bates made his stage debut with the Midland Theatre Co. in *You and Your Wife* (Coventry, England, 1955); first appeared in London as Simon Fellowes in *The Mulberry Bush* (Royal Court, Apr. 2, 1956); subsequently played Hopkins in *The Crucible* (Royal Court, Apr. 9, 1956); Cliff Lewis in *Look Back in Anger* (Royal Court, May 8, 1956); Stapleton in *Cards of Identity* (Royal Court, June 26, 1956); Mr. Harcourt in *The Country Wife* (Royal Court, Dec. 12, 1956); Monsieur le Cracheton in *The Apollo de Bellac* (Royal Court, May 14, 1957); and Dr. Brock in *Yes—and After* (Royal Court, June 9, 1957).

He made his N.Y.C. debut as Cliff Lewis in *Look Back in Anger* (Lyceum, Oct. 1, 1957); appeared as Edmund Tyrone in the Edinburgh (Scotland) Festival's production of *Long Day's Journey into Night* (Lyceum, Edinburgh, Sept. 1, 1958), and repeated the role in London (Globe, Sept. 24, 1958); appeared as Mick in *The Caretaker* (Arts, London, Apr. 27, 1960) and repeated the role in N.Y.C. (Lyceum, Oct. 4, 1961); Adam in *The Four Seasons* (Saville, London, Aug. 1965); returned to N.Y.C. as Richard Ford in *Poor Richard* (Helen Hayes Th., Dec. 2, 1964); performed at the Canadian Shakespeare Festival, Stratford, Ontario, Canada, in the title role in *Richard III* (Avon, June 12, 1967) and as Ford in *The Merry Wives of Windsor* (Avon, June 14, 1967); returned to England, where he appeared with the Bristol Old Vic as Jaffeir in *Venice Preserved* (Th. Royale, Spring 1969); played in London as Andrew Shaw in *In Celebration* (Royal Court Th., Apr. 22, 1969); in the title role of *Hamlet* (1970); and as Ben Butley in *Butley* (Criterion, July 14, 1971), repeated in N.Y.C. (Morosco, Oct. 31, 1972).

Films. Mr. Bates played Frank Rice in *The Entertainer* (Cont., 1960); the Man in *Whistle Down the Wind* (Pathé America, 1962); Vic in *A Kind of Loving* (Governor, 1962); Stephen in *The Running Man* (Col., 1963); Mick in *The Caretaker* (Janus, 1963); released in the US as *The Guest*, 1964); James Brewster in *Nothing But the Best* (Elstree, 1964); Basil in *Zorba the Greek* (20th-Fox, 1964); Jos in *Georgy Girl* (Col., 1966); in *King of Hearts* (Lopert, 1967); as Gabriel Oak in *Far from the Madding Crowd* (MGM, 1967); Yakov Bok in *The Fixer* (MGM, 1968); Birkin in *Women in Love* (UA, 1970); Vershinin in *The Three Sisters* (Brandon, 1969); Bri in *A Day in the Death of Joe Egg* (Col., 1972); Ted Burgess in *The Go-Between* (Col., 1971); and Harry in *Impossible Object* (Franco London-Euro Intl., 1973).

Television. In the US, he appeared in *The Thug* (ABC, 1959); *Three on a Gas Ring* (ABC, 1959); and *Duel for Love* (ABC, 1959); and in England, in *A Memory of Two Mondays* (Granada-TV, 1959); *The Juke Box* (AR-TV, 1959); *The Square Ring* (AR-TV, 1959); and *The Wind in the Rain* (Granada, 1959).

Awards. He received the Forbes Robertson Award from RADA and the Clarence Derwent Award for his portrayal of Edmund Tyrone in the London production of *Long Day's Journey into Night* (1959); won the (London) *Evening Standard* award, an Antoinette Perry (Tony) Award, and Drama Desk Award (1973) for *Butley;* and was nominated for Academy Award as best actor for his performance in *The Fixer.*

Recreation. Tennis, squash, swimming, traveling, driving.

BATES, LULU. Singer, actress. b. New York City, to George and Carolyn Ries. Father, singing coach; mother, dress designer. Grad. Girls H.S., Brooklyn, N.Y., 1917. Studied acting with Claudia Franke. Member of AEA; SAG; AFTRA; AGVA.

Theatre. Miss Bates made her debut as the Tavern Owner in *Set 'em Up Tony* (1946); subsequently appeared in stock as Dame Durbin in *Robin Hood*, and as Lavinia in *Hit the Deck* (Victor Morley Th., Memphis, Tenn., Summer 1946); toured cross-country in *The Wizard of Oz* (1947); and in *Showboat Party* (1949).

She played Blodgett in *Great to Be Alive* (Winter Garden, N.Y.C., Mar. 23, 1950); Elsa Bullinger in *Flahooley* (Broadhurst, May 14, 1951); Lily in *New Girl in Town* (46 St. Th., May 14, 1957); the Maid in *The Gazebo* (Lyceum, Dec. 12, 1958); and Mother Lederer in *A Family Affair* (Billy Rose Th., Jan. 27, 1962).

Television and Radio. Her first professional broadcasting experience was singing for a small radio studio (Staten Island, N.Y.C., 1920); subsequently sang for a broadcasting company (Lincoln Hotel, now the Manhattan Hotel, N.Y.C.). During the late 1920s, Miss Bates appeared for two years with Jerry Baker on the Sally Studio radio program, and then became the singing star of the All Time Hit Parade, and the Lower Basin Street Chamber of Music. Between broadcasting engagements she sang in night clubs and in vaudeville.

In 1941 she appeared on her first television show with Danton Walker; subsequently performed on the Steve Allen Show (NBC); Battle of the Ages; and the Dinah Shore Show (NBC).

Awards. Miss Bates received the Silver Dollar Award from the US Treasury Dept., and placques for making personal appearances and performing in defense plants and hospitals during WW II.

Recreation. Swimming, interior decorating.

BATSON, GEORGE. Playwright. b. George Donald Batson, Feb. 13, 1918, Brooklyn, N.Y., to Donald A. and Vera Melvin (Freystadt) Batson. Father, oil business. Attended Erasmus Hall H.S., Brooklyn, 1933; grad. Summit (N.J.) H.S., 1934. Served US Army Signal Corps, ETO, 1942–46. Member of Dramatists Guild.

Theatre. Mr. Batson wrote *Treat Her Gently*, which was presented by a touring company traveling through the South and Midwest (1941); *Punch and Julia*, which was presented in a pre-Bway tryout (Baltimore, Md.; Washington, D.C., 1942); *Ramshackle Inn* (Royale Th., N.Y.C., Jan. 4, 1944), which later toured cross-country, and was produced in Holland and Germany; *Magnolia Alley* (Lakewood Th., Skowhegan, Me., 1948), which opened in N.Y.C. (Mansfield, Apr. 18, 1949); *A Date with April* (Royale, Apr. 15, 1953). For stock, he has written *Celia* (Bucks County Playhouse, New Hope, Pa., 1954), *Miss Private Eye* (1955), and *House on the Rocks* (1958).

He also wrote *Murder on Arrival* (Westminster, London, June 19, 1959); his next plays, *Murder at Midnight* (1960), *Two Faces of Murder* (1961), and *House on the Cliff* (1963) are performed in repertory.

Television. Mr. Batson has written scripts for such television shows as Colgate Theatre (NBC), Suspense Theatre (CBS), and Climax (CBS).

Published Works. He has written 24 three-act plays, published by Samuel French and the Dramatist's Play Service, for community theatres and schools.

Recreation. Golf, swimming, reading, traveling.

BAUERSMITH, PAULA. Actress. b. July 26, 1909, Oakmont, Pa., to William Robinson and Susan (Paul) Bauersmith. Father, member of stock exchange. Attended St. Mary's Hall, Burlington, N.J.; grad. Miss Ellis' Sch., Pittsburgh, Pa., 1927; Carnegie Inst. of Tech., B.A. 1931. Married 1934 to Barnett M. Warren, dentist (dec. 1953); one son, one daughter. Relatives in theatre: daughter, Jennifer Warren, actress; brother-in-law, Jacob Ben Ami, actor. Member of AEC; SAG; AFTRA; Alpha Kappa Psi. Address: 213 W. 21st St., New York, NY 10011, tel. (212) 675-8990; PL 7-6300.

Theatre. Miss Bauersmith made her first stage appearance in *The Bronze Woman* (George Sharp Stock Co., Pittsburgh, Pa., 1929); subsequently appeared at the Ann Arbor (Mich.) Drama Festival, playing in *The Guardsman, Close Harmony*, and *The Constant Wife* (1930); played Tanja in *Russian Dressing* (County Center Rep. Co., White Plains, N.Y., Aug. 24, 1931); and made her first N.Y.C. appearance as Carmen in *Lean Harvest* (Forrest Th., Oct. 13, 1931); followed by her role as Lora McDonald in *East of Broadway* (Belmont, Jan. 26, 1932); the First Sergeant in *The Warrior's Husband* (Morosco, Mar. 11, 1932); Mary Paterson in *The Anatomist* (Bijou, Oct. 24, 1932); Jenny in *Three-Cornered Moon* (Cort, Mar. 16, 1933); Big Marge in *Mahogany Hall* (Bijou, Jan. 17, 1934); Miss Moorhead in *All Good Americans* (Henry Miller's Th., Dec. 5, 1933); Emma Martin in *Let Freedom Ring* (Broadhurst, Nov. 6, 1935); Martha Webster in *Bury the Dead* (Ethel Barrymore Th., Apr. 18, 1936); and Jennie Walters in *Two Hundred Were Chosen* (48 St. Th., Nov. 20, 1936); as Andrée in *By Your Leave* (Provincetown, Mass., Aug. 23, 1937); and Laura Starling in *Rhyme without Reason* (Aug. 26, 1938).

Miss Bauersmith appeared as a Russian Farmer in *Winter Soldiers* (New Sch. of Social Research, N.Y.C., 1943); *It's Up to You* (Amer. Th. Wing, Mar.

31, 1934); and as the Proprietress in *Paths of Glory* (Equity Library Th., 92 St. and 145 St. library branches, Feb. 1947). She played Dr. Johnson in *Twentieth Century* (ANTA, Dec. 24, 1950); the Grand Duchess in *You Can't Take It with You* (Pocono Playhouse, Mountainhome, Pa., Aug. 2, 1954), and Ring One in *The Other Devil* (Aug. 30, 1954); a Neighbor in *Jenny Kissed Me* (John Drew Th., East Hampton, L.I., N.Y., July 30, 1956); and Señora Amaranta in *Fortunata* (Club Cinema, N.Y.C., Mar. 22, 1956). She appeared as the Maid in *The Lesson* (Tempo Playhouse, Oct. 2, 1956); Anna in *Thor with Angels* (Bway Congregational Church, Oct. 14, 1956); and at the Ann Arbor (Mich.) Drama Festival in *The Member of the Wedding, The Chalk Garden, Tiger at the Gates* and *The Solid Gold Cadillac* (May 21, 1956).

She played in *Grand Guignol* (Actors' Playhouse, N.Y.C., July 1957); played Miss Margaret in *A Box of Watercolors* (Bway Congregational Church, Feb. 17, 1957); returned to East Hampton to play in *Witness for the Prosecution* (July 15, 1957), and *The Old Maid* (July 22, 1957); and played Anna in *Tobias and the Angel* (Bway Congregational Church, Oct. 20, 1957).

She played the Maid in *The Lesson* (Phoenix, Jan. 9, 1958); Bernoline in *The Marvelous History of Saint Bernard* (Bway Congregational Church, Feb. 23, 1958); appeared as Swart in *Swim in the Sea* (Winter Park and Palm Beach, Fla., Apr. 21 and 28, 1958); played Mrs. Railton-Bell in *Separate Tables* and Miss Casewell in *The Mouse Trap* (Stockbridge, Mass., June–July 1958); and Miss Connelly in *The Potting Shed* (Bway Congregational Church, N.Y.C., Nov. 2, 1958), a role she repeated in Philadelphia (43 St. Th., Jan. 11, 1950).

She played Hecuba in the ELT production of *Tiger at the Gates* (Feb. 8, 1960); toured as Essie Miller in *Take Me Along* (June–July 1961); played Mrs. Sweeney in *Sail Away* (Broadhurst, N.Y.C., Oct. 3, 1961); Dr. Liz Wooley in *Write Me a Murder* (Olney Playhouse, Md., July 30, 1962); appeared in *Sweet of You To Say So* (Th. de Lys, Apr. 9, 1962); and in *Write Me a Murder* (Playhouse-on-the-Mall, Paramus, N.J., Nov. 13, 1962; Royal Poinciana Playhouse, Palm Beach, Fla., Feb. 11, 1963); *Damn Yankees* and *Bells Are Ringing* (Starlight Th., Indianapolis, Ind., July 1963); *Anything Goes* (Westchester Town House, Yonkers, N.Y., Nov. 19, 1963); *Tunnel of Love* (Paramus, N.J., July 14, 1964); Miss Julia Tessan in *Hedda Gabler*, Mrs. Hardcastle in *She Stoops to Conquer*, and Mother Hollunder in *Liliom* (National Repertory tour, August 10, 1964–March 28, 1965). She played Sheila Fezzonetti in *Breakfast at Tiffany's* (Majestic, Dec. 3, 1966); Ellyat's mother in *John Brown's Body* and Luce in *Comedy of Errors* (National Repertory tour, Sept. 4, 1967–Dec. 17, 1967; and at Ford's Th., Jan. 21, 1968); and appeared in *The Long Christmas Dinner* (John Drew Th., Summer 1972).

Television and Radio. Miss Bauersmith first performed on radio in 1934 on such programs as Big Sister (NBC, ABC, CBS, 1930–40); and True Story (NBC, ABC, CBS, 1930–40); Inside America (WMCA, 1951); New World a Comin' (WMCA, 1952).

She made her first television appearance on Studio One (CBS, 1951); and has appeared on the US Steel Hour (ABC, 1954; 1955; 1956; 1959); Kraft Television Th. (NBC, 1954; 1955); Producers Showcase (NBC, 1954; 1955); The Eternal Light (NBC, 1958); *Tom Sawyer* (US Steel Hour, CBS, Nov. 1956); *Orestes* (Omnibus, NBC, 1959); *Deadline for Action* (ABC, CBS, Sept. 1959); *Tobias and the Angel* (CBS Television Workshop, CBS, 1960); *Down the Road* (Hallmark Hall of Fame, NBC, 1961); and on East Side/West Side (CBS, 1963).

Awards. She received the Otto Kahn Award for best actress from Carnegie Inst. of Technology (1931).

Recreation. Word games, crossword puzzles.

BAXLEY, BARBARA. Actress. b. Jan. 1, 1925, Porterville, Calif., to Bert and Emma (Tyler) Baxley. Father, insurance salesman; mother, teacher. Grad. Coll. of the Pacific, B.A. (with honors) 1946. Studied acting with Sanford Meisner at Neighborhood Playhouse, N.Y.C., 1947–48; Elia Kazan and Lee Strasberg at Actors' Studio, N.Y.C. (member 1949–to date); voice with Henry Jacobi, N.Y.C., 1948–to date. Married Apr. 30, 1961, to Douglas Taylor, writer. Member of AEA; AFTRA; SAG. Address: 150 W. 87th St., New York, NY 10024, tel. (212) SU 7-7156.

Theatre. Miss Baxley made her first appearance on a stage as Gretel in a grammar school production of *Hansel and Gretel* (Manteca, Calif.). She made her professional debut taking over Buff Cobb's role as Sybil Chase in Chicago during the cross-country tour of *Private Lives* (opened Harris Th., Chicago, Ill., July 22, 1947), and repeated the role with this company in N.Y.C. (Plymouth, Oct. 4, 1948).

She understudied Jean Arthur in the title role of *Peter Pan*, later succeeding Miss Arthur in this role (Imperial, Apr. 24, 1950); played Marie in *Come Back, Little Sheba* (Bucks County Playhouse, New Hope, Pa., Summer 1951); Virginia in *Out West of Eighth* (Ethel Barrymore Th., N.Y.C., Sept. 20, 1951); understudied Julie Harris as Sally Bowles, played the role during Miss Harris' vacation (June 2, 1952), and succeeded her in *I Am a Camera* (Empire, Nov. 28, 1951); played Esmeralda in *Camino Real* (Natl., Mar. 19, 1953); Virginia Belden in *The Frogs of Spring* (Broadhurst, Oct. 20, 1953); succeeded (May 29, 1954) Anne Jackson as Mildred Turner in *Oh Men! Oh Women!* (Henry Miller's Th., Dec. 17, 1953); Goldie in *The Flowering Peach* (Belasco, Dec. 28, 1954); and succeeded (Sept. 1955) Kim Stanley as Cherie in *Bus Stop* (Music Box, Mar. 2, 1955).

She played Barbara Parris in *A Palm Tree in a Rose Garden* (Cricket, Nov. 26, 1957); toured as Cora in *The Dark at the Top of the Stairs* (opened Playhouse, Wilmington, Del., Jan. 21, 1959; closed Pabst, Milwaukee, Wisc., May 16, 1959); played Beatrice in *Much Ado About Nothing* (Studebaker, Chicago, Ill.); Cherie in a summer touring production of *Bus Stop;* Isabel Haverstick in *Period of Adjustment* (Helen Hayes Th., N.Y.C., Nov. 10, 1960); appeared in *Brecht on Brecht* (Th. de Lys, Jan. 3, 1962); played Miss Ritter in *She Loves Me* (Eugene O'Neill Th., Apr. 23, 1963); and Natasha in the Actors' Studio production of *The Three Sisters* (Morosco, June 22, 1964), making her London debut in the same role and production at the World Th. Season (Aldwych, May 12, 1965).

Miss Baxley played Ilona in *Anatol* (Milwaukee Rep. Th., Wis., Mar. 31, 1965); Katherine in *The Taming of the Shrew* (Univ. of Oklahoma, Norman, Okla., Oct. 24, 1965); Celimene in *The Misanthrope* (Univ. of Chicago, Feb. 5, 1966); Isabel in *Measure for Measure* (NY Shakespeare Fest., Delacorte Th., N.Y.C., July 12, 1966); Dollyheart Talbo in a musical version of *The Grass Harp* (Trinity Square Rep. Co., Providence, R.I., Dec. 26, 1966); Portia in *The Merchant of Venice* (Amer. Shakespeare Fest., Stratford, Conn., June 20, 1967); succeeded (Feb. 1969) Maureen Stapleton in various roles in *Plaza Suite* (Plymouth, N.Y.C., Feb. 14, 1968); appeared in the dramatic revue *To Be Young, Gifted, and Black* (Cherry Lane, Jan. 2, 1969); played Juliet in her husband's play, *Oh, Pioneers* (ANTA Matinee Series, Th. de Lys, Nov. 10–11, 1969); Madame Hortense in the national tour of *Zorba* (opened Forrest, Philadelphia, Dec. 26, 1969); Catherine Reardon in *And Miss Reardon Drinks a Little* (Summer tour, 1972); and in *The Scarecrow* (Eisenhower Th., Kennedy Ctr., Washington, D.C. Aug. 10, 1975).

Films. She made her debut as The Nurse in *East of Eden* (WB, 1955); and has appeared in *The Savage Eye* (Trans., 1960); *All Fall Down* (MGM, 1962); *Countdown* (WB, 1968); *No Way to Treat a Lady* (Par., 1968); and *Nashville* (Par., 1975).

Television. Miss Baxley has made nearly a hundred appearances on all major dramatic shows, including a re-creation of her original Bway role in *A Palm Tree in a Rose Garden* (Play of the Week, WNTA, Apr. 4, 1960); and an appearance in *Ladies of the Corridor* (Hollywood Television Th., PBS, Apr. 1975).

Awards. She received the Best Actress Award from the Philadelphia critics for her performance as Isabel Haverstick in *Period of Adjustment* (1960).

Recreation. Reading.

BAXTER, ANNE. Actress. b. May 7, 1923, Michigan City, Ind., to Kenneth Stuart and Catherine (Wright) Baxter. Father, distilleries sales manager. Attended public sch., White Plains, Chappaqua, and Bronxville, N.Y.; Theodora Irvine's Sch. of the Theatre, N.Y.C., 1934–36; The Lenox Sch., N.Y.C., 1937; The Brearley Sch., N.Y.C., 1938–39; The 20th-Century Fox Studio Sch., Westwood, Calif., 1940. Studied acting with Maria Ouspenskaya, N.Y.C., three years (c. 1937–40). Married July 7, 1946, to John Hodiak, actor (marr. dis. Feb. 9, 1953; dec. Oct. 9, 1955); one daughter; married Feb. 18, 1960, to Randolph Galt, rancher (marr. dis. 1970); two daughters. Member of AEA; SAG; AFTRA. Address: c/o Chasin-Park-Citron Agency, 10889 Wilshire Blvd., Los Angeles, CA 90024.

Theatre. Miss Baxter made her N.Y.C. debut as Elizabeth Winthrop in *Seen But Not Heard* (Henry Miller's Th., Sept. 17, 1936); followed by the role of Lita Hammond in *There's Always a Breeze* (Windsor, Mar. 2, 1938); in stock, she appeared in *Susan and God* (Cape Playhouse, Dennis, Mass., Summer 1938); played Rosalie in *Madame Capet* (Cort, N.Y.C., Oct. 25, 1938); and at the Cape Playhouse played in *Spring Meeting* (Dennis, Mass., July 17, 1939).

She toured in *John Brown's Body* (1954); played Mollie Lovejoy in *The Square Root of Wonderful* (Natl., Oct. 30, 1957); Louise Shaeffer in the London production of *The Joshua Tree* (Duke of York's Th., July 9, 1958); replaced (July 19, 1971) Lauren Bacall as Margo Channing in *Applause* (Palace, N.Y.C., Mar. 30, 1970); played Maude and Carlotta in *In Two Keys* on tour (Dec. 1973–Jan. and Feb. 1974) and in N.Y.C. (Ethel Barrymore Th., Feb. 28, 1974).

Films. Miss Baxter made her debut in *20 Mule Team* (MGM, 1940); subsequently appeared in *The Great Profile* (20th-Fox, 1940); *Charley's Aunt* (20th-Fox, 1941); *Swampwater* (20th-Fox, 1941); *The Magnificent Ambersons* (RKO, 1942); *The Pied Piper* (20th-Fox, 1942); *Crash Dive* (20th-Fox, 1943); *Five Graves to Cairo* (Par., 1943); *The North Star* (RKO, 1943); *The Sullivans* (20th-Fox, 1944); *Sunday Dinner for a Soldier* (20th-Fox, 1944); *A Royal Scandal* (20th-Fox, 1945); *The Razor's Edge* (20th-Fox, 1946); *Smoky* (20th-Fox, 1946); *Angel on My Shoulder* (UA, 1946); *Blaze of Noon* (Par., 1947); *Homecoming* (MGM, 1948); *The Walls of Jerico* (20th-Fox, 1948); *The Luck of the Irish* (20th-Fox, 1948); *Yellow Sky* (20th-Fox, 1948); *You're My Everything* (20th-Fox, 1949); *Ticket to Tomahawk* (20th-Fox, 1950); *All About Eve* (20th-Fox, 1950); *Follow the Sun* (20th-Fox, 1951); *The Outcasts of Poker Flat* (20th-Fox, 1952); *O. Henry's Full House* (20th-Fox, 1952); *My Wife's Best Friend* (20th-Fox, 1952); *I Confess* (WB, 1953); *The Blue Gardenia* (WB, 1953); *Carnival Story* (RKO, 1954); *The Spoilers* (U, 1955); *Bedevilled* (MGM, 1955); *One Desire* (U, 1955); *The Come On* (Allied, 1956); *Three Violent People* (Par., 1956); *The Ten Commandments* (Par., 1956); *Chase a Crooked Shadow* (WB, 1958); *Summer of the Seventeenth Doll* (UA, 1960); *Cimarron* (MGM, 1960); *Walk on the Wild Side* (Col., 1962); *Mix Me a Person* (Blackton, 1962); *The Busy Body* (Par., 1966); *Stranger on the Run* (U, 1967); *Companions in Nightmare* (U, 1968); *The Tall Women* (Allied Artists); *Fools' Parade* (Col., 1970); and *The Late Liz* (1971).

Television. She has appeared in *Right Hand Man* (Playhouse 90, CBS, Mar. 20, 1958), *Stop-Over* (Television Th., CBS, Apr. 1958); Dr. Kildare (NBC, 1964); Columbo (NBC); Marcus Welby (ABC); *Lisa, Bright and Dark* (Hallmark, NBC); Cannon (CBS); *Love Story; Banacek;* Mannix (CBS); and Name of the Game.

Awards. Miss Baxter received an Academy (Oscar) Award as best supporting actress and the Foreign Press Award for her performance in *The Razor's Edge* (1947).

BAXTER, KEITH. Actor. b. Keith Stanley Baxter Wright, Apr. 29, 1935, Newport Monmouthshire, Wales, to Capt. Stanley Baxter and Emily Marian (Howell) Wright. Father, dockmaster. Newport (Monmouthshire) H.S. 1944; Barry (Glamorganshire) Grammar School, 1951. Studied at RADA, London, 1952–53; 1955–56. Served British Army, Korea and Hong Kong, 1953–55; rank, Sgt. Member of AEA; SAG. Address: (home) 56 Duncan Terrace, Islington, London, N.1, England; (bus.) c/o IFA, 1301 Avenue of the Americas, New York, NY 10019, tel. (212) 956-5800; c/o IFA, 11-12 Hanover St., London W.1, England tel. 01-629-8080.

Theatre. Mr. Baxter appeared in repertory productions in Worthing and Oxford, England, and played Sanyamo in the post-London tour of *South Sea Bubble;* made his London debut as Ralph in *Tea and Sympathy* (Comedy, Apr. 25, 1957); followed by Hippolytus in *Phèdre* (Theatre-in-the-Round, Nov. 10, 1957); John-Pierre Vasse in *Change of Tune* (Strand, May 13, 1953); Prince Hal in *Henry IV, Part 1,* and *Henry IV, Part 2* (Opera House, Belfast, Ireland, Feb. 23, 1960); Roger Balion in *Time and Yellow Roses* (St. Martin's, London, May 11, 1961); and David Owen in *Unfinished Journey* (Pembroke Th., Croydon, England, Sept. 4, 1961).

He made his N.Y.C. debut as Henry VIII in *A Man for All Seasons* (ANTA, Nov. 22, 1961); played Donald Howard in *The Affair* (Henry Miller's Th., Sept. 20, 1962). He appeared in London as Gino in *Where Angels Fear to Tread* (St. Martin's, July 9, 1963) and Charles in *The Trigon* (New Arts, May 27, 1964) and played the role of the Inspector in *Torpe's Hotel* at Guildford, England (Yvonne Arnaud Th., Oct. 10, 1965). In London he played at the Th. Royal, Haymarket, as Valentine in *You Never Can Tell* (Jan. 17, 1966) and Bob Acres in *The Rivals* (Oct. 12, 1966). He returned to N.Y.C. as Baldassare Pantaleone in *Avanti* (Booth Th., Feb. 1, 1968) and, returning to England was Mr. Horner in *The Country Wife* and Octavius Caesar in *Antony and Cleopatra* (Chichester Festival Th., June 9–Sept. 13, 1969); Milo Tindle in *Sleuth* (St. Martin's, London, Feb. 12, 1970, transferring in same production to the Music Box Th., N.Y.C., Nov. 12, 1970); Macbeth in *Macbeth* (Birmingham Repertory Th., Oct. 12, 1972); Vershinin in *Three Sisters* (Greenwich Th., Jan. 17, 1973); Benedick in *Much Ado About Nothing* (Lyceum Th., Edinburgh, Scotland, 30, 1973); the leading actor in *Tonight We Improvise* (Chichester Festival Th., May 15–July 14, 1974).

Films. Mr. Baxter played Charles Moulton-Barrett in *The Barretts of Wimpole Street* (MGM, 1956); Alexander in *Family Doctor* (20th-Fox, 1957); the Young Detective in *Peeping Tom* (Rank, 1959); Prince Hal in *Chimes at Midnight* (Welles, 1965); Tony in *With Love in Mind* (Associated British, 1969); and David in *Ash Wednesday* (Par., 1973).

Television. He played Thomas in *She Stoops to Conquer* (BBC, London, Mar. 17, 1956). *Man and Superman* (ATV, 1958); *The Reward of Silence* (BBC, 1963); *For Tea on Sunday* (BBC, 1963); Dunois in *St. Joan* (BBC, 1968); *Love Story* (ITV, 1968); *Orson Welles Great Mysteries* (Anglia, 1973); *The Vineyard* (BBC, 1974).

Awards. Mr. Baxter received the Bronze Medal from the Royal Acad. of Dramatic Art (1956); the *Theatre World* Award (1962); the Fanny Kemble Award (Philadelphia, Pa., 1962); and the Drama Desk and Outer Circle awards (both 1971) for *Sleuth.*

BAY, HOWARD. Setting and lighting designer. b. May 3, 1912, Centralia, Wash., to William D. and Bertha (Jenkins) Bay. Father and mother, teachers. Attended Chappel Sch. of Art (Denver), 1928; Univ. of Colorado, 1929; Marshall Coll. 1929–30; Carnegie Inst. of Technology, 1930–31; Westminster Coll. 1931–32. Married Ruth Jonas, Nov. 23, 1932; one son, one daughter. Member United Scenic Artists of America (pres., 1940–46; 1952–63); Natl. Soc. of Interior Designers (bd. mem., 1960–62); Soc. of Motion Picture Art Directors; International Theatre Institute (National Advisory Board). Address: 236 Marlborough St., Boston, MA 02116, tel. (617) 267-2743.

Theatre. Mr. Bay has designed settings and lighting for more than 150 productions in New York, beginning in 1933 with *There's a Moon Tonight;* and designed settings and lighting for a winter stock company in Atlanta, Ga. (1934). For the Federal Th. (WPA) Project (N.Y.C.), he designed settings for the following productions: *Chalk Dust* (Experimental Th., Mar. 4, 1936); *Battle Hymn* (Experimental Th., May 22, 1936); *Power* (Ritz, Feb. 23, 1937); *Native Ground* (Venice, Mar. 23, 1937); "*. . . one-third of a nation*" (Adelphi, Jan. 17, 1938); *Trojan Incident* (St. James, Apr. 21, 1938); and *Life and Death of an American* (Maxine Elliott's Th., May 19, 1939). While still working for the Federal Th. (WPA) Project, he designed the settings for the Th. Union production of *Marching Song* (Bayes Th., Feb. 17, 1937); Bway productions of *Sunup to Sundown* (Hudson, Feb. 1, 1938); and *The Little Foxes* (Natl., Feb. 15, 1939).

Mr. Bay designed settings and lighting for four operas at Carnegie Hall: *Pagliacci, Gianni Schicchi, Suor Angelica,* and *The Abduction from the Seraglio* (1939–40); for *The Fifth Column* (Alvin, N.Y.C., Mar. 6, 1940); *Morning Star* (Longacre, Apr. 16, 1940); *The Corn Is Green* (Natl., Nov. 26, 1940); *The Man With Blond Hair* (Belasco Th., Nov. 4, 1941); *Brooklyn, U.S.A.* (Forrest, Dec. 21, 1941), *Johnny 2 × 4* (Longacre, Mar. 16, 1942); *The Moon Is Down* (Martin Beck Th., Apr. 7, 1942); *The Strings, My Lord, Are False* (Royale, May 19, 1942); *Uncle Harry* (Broadhurst, May 20, 1942); for the Bucks County Playhouse (New Hope, Pa., Summer 1942); *The Eve of St. Mark* (Cort, N.Y.C., Oct. 7, 1942); *Count Me In* (Ethel Barrymore Th., Oct. 8, 1942); *The Great Big Doorstep* (Morosco, Nov. 26, 1942); *Something for the Boys* (Alvin, Jan. 7, 1943); *The Patriots* (Natl., Jan. 29, 1943); *The Merry Widow* (Majestic, Aug. 4, 1943); and *A New Life* (Royale, Sept. 15, 1943).

He designed settings and lighting for *One Touch of Venus* (Imperial, Oct. 7, 1943); *Carmen Jones* (Bway, Dec. 2, 1943); *Listen, Professor!* (Forrest, Dec. 22, 1943); settings only for *Storm Operation* (Belasco, Jan. 11, 1944), and *Peep Show* (Fulton, Feb. 3, 1944); settings and lighting for *Chicken Every Sunday* (Henry Miller's Th., Apr. 5, 1944); *Follow the Girls* (Century, Apr. 8, 1944); *The Searching Wind* (Fulton, Apr. 12, 1944); *Ten Little Indians* (Broadhurst, June 27, 1944); *Catherine Was Great* (Shubert, Aug. 2, 1944); the pre-Bway tryout of *Franklin Street* (closed Playhouse, Wilmington, Dec., 1944); the pre-Bway tryout of *Spring in Brazil* (closed 1944); and for a US Dept. of Agriculture touring production of *It's Up to You* (1944); designed the settings and lighting for *Men to the Sea* (Natl., Oct. 3, 1944); *The Visitor* (Henry Miller's Th., N.Y.C., Oct. 17, 1944); *Violet* (Belasco, Oct. 24, 1944); the pre-Bway tryout of *Glad to See You* (opened Shubert, Philadelphia, Pa., Nov. 13, 1944; closed Opera House, Boston, Mass., Jan. 6, 1945); *Up in Central Park* (Century, N.Y.C., Jan. 27, 1945); *Marinka* (Winter Garden, July 18, 1945); *Devils Galore* (Royale, Sept. 12, 1945); *Deep Are the Roots* (Fulton, Sept. 26, 1945); *Polonaise* (Alvin, Oct. 6, 1945); and produced, directed, and designed a USO touring production of *Up in Central Park* (ETO, 1945).

Mr. Bay designed settings and lighting for *Show Boat* (Ziegfeld, N.Y.C., Jan. 5, 1946); *The Would-Be Gentleman* (Booth, Jan. 9, 1946); and *Woman Bites Dog* (Belasco Th., Apr. 17, 1946). He designed the settings and lighting for *Magdalena* (Philharmonic Aud., Los Angeles, Calif., 1948); directed and designed *As the Girls Go* (Winter Garden, Nov. 13, 1948); *The Big Knife* (Natl., N.Y.C., Feb. 24, 1949); *Montserrat* (Fulton, Oct. 29, 1949); *Come Back Little Sheba* (Booth, Feb. 15, 1950); *Michael Todd's Peep Show* (Winter Garden, June 28, 1950); *Parisienne* (Fulton Th., July 24, 1950); *Hilda Crane* (Coronet, Nov. 1, 1950); *The Autumn Garden* (Coronet, Mar. 7, 1951); *Flahooley* (Broadhurst, May 14, 1951); *Two on the Aisle* (Mark Hellinger Th., July 19, 1951); *The Grand Tour* (Martin Beck Th., Dec. 10, 1951); *The Shrike* (Cort, Jan. 15, 1952); *The Children's Hour* (Coronet, Dec. 18, 1952); settings, lighting, and costumes for a production of *Les Noces* (Brandeis Univ., Boston, Mass., 1952); settings and lighting for *Mid-Summer* (Vanderbilt Th., Jan. 21, 1953); settings for *Show Boat* (NY City Ctr., May 5, 1954); *Sandhog* (Phoenix, Nov. 23, 1954); settings and lighting for *The Desperate Hours* (Ethel Barrymore Th., Feb. 10, 1955); and *Finian's Rainbow* (NY City Ctr., May 5, 1955).

He directed and designed a production of *Crimes and Crimes* (Brattle Th., Cambridge, Mass., 1955); settings and lighting for *Top Man* (opened Shubert, New Haven, Conn., Nov. 16, 1955; closed Locust St. Th., Philadelphia, Pa., Nov. 26, 1955); *Red Roses for Me* (Booth, N.Y.C., Dec. 28, 1955); *Carmen Jones* (NY City Ctr. May 31, 1956); *Build With One Hand* (opened Shubert, New Haven, Conn., Nov. 7, 1956; closed Ford Th., Baltimore, Md., Nov. 27, 1956); *A Very Special Baby* (Playhouse, N.Y.C., Nov. 14, 1956); the pre-Bway tryout of *A Certain Joy* (opened Wilmington, Del.; closed Philadelphia, Pa., 1956); *Night of the Auk,* (Playhouse, N.Y.C., Dec. 3, 1956); *Interlock* (ANTA, Feb. 6, 1958); *Jolly Anna* (Philharmonic Aud., Los Angeles, Calif., 1959); *A Desert Incident* (John Golden Th., Mar. 24, 1959); *Cut of the Axe* (Ambassador, Feb. 1, 1960); *The Cool World* (Eugene O'Neill Th., N.Y.C., Feb. 22, 1960); *Toys in the Attic* (Hudson, Feb. 25, 1960); *The Wall* (Billy Rose Th., Oct. 11, 1960); *Pal Joey* (NY City Ctr., May 31, 1961); *Milk and Honey* (Martin Beck Th., Oct. 10, 1961); *Carmen* (San Francisco Opera, Calif., 1961); settings and lighting for *Isle of Children* (Cort, N.Y.C., Mar. 16, 1962); *My Mother, My Father and Me* (Plymouth, Mar. 23, 1963); *Bicycle Ride to Nevada* (Cort, Sept. 24, 1963); and *Never Live Over a Pretzel Factory* (Eugene O'Neill Th., Mar. 28, 1964).

He did the scenery and lighting for the NY City Ctr. Light Opera Company's revival of *The Music Man* (NY City Ctr., June 16, 1965) and for two operas of the NY City Opera Company, both at the City Center: *Natalia Petrovna* (Oct. 8, 1964) and *Capriccio* (Oct. 27, 1965). He did settings, costumes, and lighting for *Man of La Mancha* (ANTA, Nov. 22, 1965); *Chu Chem* (Locust, Philadelphia, Nov. 15, 1966; closed Nov. 19); and he did scenery and lighting for the Lincoln Center Repertory revival of *The Little Foxes* (Vivian Beaumont Th., Oct. 26, 1967). He designed settings and lighting also for *Fire!* (Longacre, Jan. 28, 1969); *Cry for Us All* (Broadhurst, Apr. 8, 1970); *Knickerbocker Holiday* (Curran Th., San Francisco, Calif., 1971); and *Halloween* (Bucks County Playhouse, New Hope, Pa., Sept. 20, 1972; closed Oct. 1).

Films. Mr. Bay designed the puppets and settings for an industrial film, *Pete Roleum and His Cousins* (1939). He was art director for *The Exile* (U, 1947); *Up in Central Park* (U, 1948); *Go, Man, Go!* (UA, 1955); and *Midsummer Night's Dream* (Col., 1962).

Television. He has been art director for television productions including the Fred Waring Show (CBS, 1953–55) the Somerset Maugham Theatre (CBS and NBC, 1954–56); *Peer Gynt* (Hallmark Hall of Fame, NBC, 1956); Mr. Broadway series (1963–64); and *The Pueblo Incident* (ABC, 1973).

Other Activities. Mr. Bay was an instructor in the Drama Dept. of the Univ. of Michigan (Summer 1941); instructor at the Circle in the Square School of the Th., N.Y.C. (1962–63); guest lecturer and instructor in drama at Purdue Univ. (1962); the Andrew W. Mellon guest director in the Drama Dept. of Carnegie Inst. of Technology (1963); drama lecturer at the Univ. of Oregon Festival of Contemporary Arts (1963); director-designer-instructor at the Univ. of Ohio (1964), where he directed and designed the US premiere of *The Cage* (Apr. 22, 1964); and guest instructor at Yale Univ. (1966–67).

He went to Brandeis Univ., Waltham, Mass., in 1965 as professor of theatre arts (chmn., 1966–69) and directed productions at the Spingold Th.: *Ping Pong* (1966); *Workhouse Donkey* (May 1967); *Co-*

lombe (Dec. 6, 1967); and *Eh?* (Dec. 4, 1968).

Published Works. He is a contributor to *Navy on Stage* (1945) and *Scene Design for Stage and Screen* (1961), to the "Staging and Stage Design" section of the Enclyclopaedia Britannica, and wrote *Stage Design* (1974).

Awards. Mr. Bay won the *Variety* NY Drama Critics Poll for his settings in *Brooklyn, USA* (1942); he received two Donaldson Awards, one for his settings and lighting for *Carmen Jones* (1944), and one for *Up in Central Park* (1945); and received the Antoinette Perry (Tony) Award for his settings and lighting in *Toys in the Attic* (1960) and a Tony and the Maharam Award for his settings and lighting for *Man of La Mancha* (1966).

He received a Guggenheim Fellowship for research in scenic design (1939–40).

BAYLIES, EDMUND. Production stage manager, actor, director. b. July 11, 1904, Taunton, Mass., to Walter and Charlotte (Upham) Baylies. Father, cotton broker. Grad. St. Marks Sch., Southborough, Mass., 1923. Served Amer. Field Service, ambulance driver attached to British Army, 1942–44. Member of AEA; SAG; The Players. Address: 406 Harbor Rd., Southport, CT 06490, tel. (203) 255-4677.

Theatre. Mr. Baylies, billed as Edmund George, made his debut as a Policeman in *Justice* (Copley Th., Boston, Mass., Nov. 1923).

He played a Clerk, was understudy to Deering Wells as Bob Pillin, was assistant stage manager for *Old English* (Ritz, N.Y.C., Dec. 23, 1924); toured as Sidney Armstead in *Mrs. Partridge Presents* (1925); Clint Blackburn in *Is Zat So?* (1925); appeared in stock at the Copley Th. (Boston, 1926); played Clem Durward in *The Banshee* (Daly's, N.Y.C., Dec. 5, 1927); and appeared in stock at the Copley Th. (Boston, 1928).

He played Tom Arnott in *Whispering Gallery* (Forrest, N.Y.C., Feb. 11, 1929); Geoffrey Rawson in *Mrs. Bumpstead-Leigh* (Klaw, Apr. 1, 1929); Horace Parker in *Family Affairs* (Maxine Elliott's Th., Dec. 10, 1929); Richard Sibley in *Milestones* (Empire, June 2, 1930); succeeded (Aug. 1930) Roger Pryor as Daniel Curtis in *Apron Strings* (48 St. Th., Feb. 17, 1930); played Prescott Barrington in *The Great Barrington* (Avon, Feb. 19, 1931); and toured as Daniel Curtis in *Apron Strings* (1931).

Mr. Baylies played Ralph in *After All* (Booth, N.Y.C., Dec. 3, 1931); appeared in *Love Flies in the Window* (Berkshire Playhouse, Stockbridge, Mass., Aug., 1933); was stage manager and performer with stock companies (1933–40); succeeded (Dec. 1936) William Brisbane as Mr. Omansetter in *Reflected Glory* (Morosco, Sept. 21, 1936), and toured in it (June 1937); played Harvey Van Ingen in *I Know What I Like* (Hudson, N.Y.C., Nov. 24, 1939); and joined Music Corporation of America (MCA) as casting agent for legitimate theatre (1944–48).

Billed as Edmund Baylies, he was production stage manager for *Private Lives* (Plymouth, Oct. 4, 1948), and its tour (June 1950); *Romeo and Juliet* (Broadhurst, N.Y.C., Mar. 10, 1951); productions at the Westport (Conn.) Country Playhouse (Summers 1951–52); *Lo and Behold!* (Booth, N.Y.C., Dec. 12, 1951); the tour of *The Constant Wife* (opened Ford's Th., Baltimore, Md., Oct. 13, 1952; closed Drama Festival, Ann Arbor, Mich., May 16, 1963); *The Prescott Proposals* (Broadhurst, N.Y.C., Dec. 16, 1953); *Dear Charles*, which he also directed (Morosco, Sept. 15, 1954); *Fallen Angels* (Playhouse, Jan. 10, 1956); *Hotel Paradiso* (Henry Miller's Th., Apr. 11, 1957); the Constance Bennett tour of *Auntie Mame* (opened Hanna, Cleveland, Ohio, Oct. 30, 1957; closed Riviera, Detroit, Mich., Dec. 15, 1957); *Interlock* (ANTA, N.Y.C., Feb. 6, 1958); and for the Sylvia Sidney tour of *Auntie Mame* (opened Amer. Shakespeare Festival Th., Stratford, Conn., Apr. 19, 1958).

He played David Bascombe in the State Dept. production of *Carousel* (Brussels World's Fair, Belg.); was technical director for the London production of *Auntie Mame* (Adelphi, N.Y.C., Sept. 10, 1958); directed the Australian presentation of *Auntie Mame* (Princess, Melbourne, Feb., 1959); was production stage manager for *Dear Liar* (Billy Rose Th., N.Y.C., Mar. 17, 1960); *Midgie Purvis* (Martin Beck Th., Feb. 1, 1961); played Capt. Brackett in *South Pacific* (NY City Ctr., Apr. 26, 1961), and repeated the role in summer stock (Carter Barron Th., Washington, D.C., 1961).

He played the Star Keeper in *Carousel* (Carter Barron Th., Aug. 1961); joined (Dec. 1961) the staff of *The Unsinkable Molly Brown* as production stage manager (Winter Garden, Nov. 3, 1960), and for its tour (opened Bushnell Memorial Aud., Hartford, Conn., Feb. 13, 1962; closed Shubert, Boston, Mass., Oct. 1962); joined (Oct. 1962) as production stage manager, the staff of *Camelot* (Majestic, N.Y.C., Dec. 3, 1960), and for its tour (opened Fisher, Detroit, Mich., Jan. 8, 1963; closed Opera House, San Francisco, Calif., July 13, 1963); was production stage manager for the national tour of *Little Me* (opened Aud., Rochester, N.Y., Jan. 30, 1964; closed Civic Aud., Pasadena, Calif., Aug. 1, 1964; and was stage manager (Oct. 1965–Oct. 1969) of the N.Y.C. Company of *Fiddler on the Roof* (Imperial Th.).

Television. Mr. Baylies played the College Dean in the television pilot film of Cheers for Miss Bishop (MGM, 1959).

Recreation. Building completely detailed miniature opera house.

BAYNE, DONALD S. Director, actor, business manager, stage manager. b. Donald Storm Bayne, Apr. 20, 1949, San Antonio, Tex., to John Marr Bayne and Jean (Eaton) Bayne. Father, attorney; mother, elementary school teacher. Grad. Alamo Heights H.S., 1967; Rice Univ., B.A., 1973. Attended director's workshop, Roger Glade, Playwright's Showcase; Mime and Mask Workshop, Jacques LeCoq, Rice Univ. Address: (home) 219 Rosemary Ave., San Antonio, TX 78209, tel. (512) 824-5156; (bus.) c/o Fine Arts Dept., Rice Univ., Houston, TX 77001, tel. (713) 528-4141.

Theatre. Mr. Bayne made his acting debut as General Bullmoose in *Li'l Abner* (Alamo Heights H.S., Nov. 1967), and first directed a production of *Krapp's Last Tape* (Rice Players, Dec. 1969). While an undergraduate, he appeared with the Rice Players as Jacques Roux in *Marat/Sade* (Feb. 1969); Father Barre in *The Devils* (Feb. 1970); Isaac Newton in *The Physicists* (Mar. 1970); and Lt. Practice in *The Little Murders* (Oct. 1970). He appeared as Baptista in *The Taming of the Shrew* (Baker Coll. Th., Apr. 1970); with the Rice Players, played Arnolphe in *The School for Wives* (Apr. 1971); Harry Bailey in *Canterbury Tales* (Oct. 1971); Tobias in *A Delicate Balance* (Jan. 1972); and Face in *The Alchemist* (Apr. 1972).

He has appeared with the First Repertory Company (San Antonio) as the Duke of Milan in *Two Gentlemen of Verona* (Sept. 1972): Polonius in *Hamlet* (Sept. 1972); Major Thompson in *Boy Meets Girl* (Nov. 1972); the Envoy in *The Balcony* (Jan. 1973); Sir in *The Roar of the Greasepaint, the Smell of the Crowd* (Aug. 1973); the Male Player in *Adaptation* (Apr. 1974); and Malvolio in *Twelfth Night* (June 1974).

While a student, he directed *The Taming of the Shrew* (Baker Coll. Th., Mar. 1970); *Exit the King* (Dec. 1970), *A Midsummer Night's Dream* (Feb. 1971), and *The Short, Sacred Rite of Search and Destruction* (Dec. 1971) for the Rice Players; and *Arsenic and Old Lace* (Weiss Tabletop Th., Nov. 1972). For the First Repertory Co., he has directed *America, Hurrah* (June 1971); *Summertree* (July 1971); *Promenade* (Aug. 1971); *Cabaret* (Aug. 1972); *The Canterbury Tales* (Feb. 1973); *A Midsummer Night's Dream* (Oct. 1973); and *Feiffer's People* (Jan. 1974), and has served as managing director (Summer 1971), business manager (June 1972–Apr. 1973), and artistic director (Apr. 1973–Aug. 1974) for that company.

As acting director of the Rice Players (1974–75), Mr. Bayne staged productions of *The Real Inspector Hound, Who's Afraid of Virginia Woolf?*, an original musical adaptation of Aristophanes' *The Birds*, and *Enrico IV*.

He has been employed as a make-up artist by the Plaza Dinner Th. (San Antonio) for their production of *Sleuth*.

BEAL, JOHN. Actor, director, portrait artist. b. James Alexander Bliedung, Aug. 13, 1909, Joplin, Mo., to Edmund A. and Agnes (Harragan) Bliedung. Father, businessman; mother, pianist. Grad Joplin H.S., 1926; Wharton Sch. of Finance and Commerce, Univ. of Pennsylvania, B.S. 1930; attended Art Students League of NY, 1930–63. Chouinard Art Sch., Los Angeles, Calif., 1935–36. Studied drawing and painting with Nicolai Fechin, George Bridgeman, Richard Munsell, John Groth, Robert Brackman, Howard Sanden, and Dimitri Romanovsky. Studied acting with Josephine Hull and Jasper Deeter. Married July 13, 1934, to Helen Craig, actress; two daughters; Tita Beal, writer and puppeteer; Tandy Beal, dancer, choreographer, and teacher. Other relatives in theatre: sister Theodora Bliedung (dec.), violinist; sister, Dorothea (Mrs. David) Hoover (dec.), director, actress. Served USAAF, 1942–45; rank, S/Sgt. Member of AEA (rec. secy., 1940–47); SAG; AFTRA; The Players; Catholic Actors Guild; Mask and Wig Club. Address: (home) 123 Parker Hill Rd., R.R. 2, Killingworth, CT; (bus.) c/o Actors' Equity Association, 165 W. 46th St., New York, NY 10036.

Pre-Theatre. Drawing, painting.

Theatre. Mr. Beal made his stage debut in school plays, most significantly as Mephistopheles in a Mask and Wig Club musical, *John Faust, Ph.D.*, presented by the Univ. of Pennsylvania (Philadelphia, 1930), and on tour in Eastern cities, including N.Y.C. (Metropolitan Opera House, 1930); his first professional appearance as Horace in *Inheritors* at the Hedgerow Th. (Moylan, Pa., Summer 1930), where he also appeared in *Captain Brassbound's Conversion, When We Dead Awake, Liliom, Mr. Pim Passes By, The Hairy Ape, Mask and the Face, Roadside, Emperor Jones, Solitaire Man* and *Merry-Go-Round*.

Mr. Beal was an understudy in *That's Gratitude* (John Golden Th., Sept. 11, 1930); appeared with the Hedgerow Players, as Sample Swichel in *Ten Nights in a Barroom* (Lyric, Philadelphia, Pa., Feb. 1931); was a walk-on, understudy and assistant stage manager for *Give Me Yesterday* (Charles Hopkins Th., N.Y.C., Mar. 4, 1931); appeared as Jerry Hallam in *Hallam Wives* (tryout title of *Another Language)* (Greenwich Civic Th., Conn., Summer 1932); as Flint Bailey, 2nd, in *No More Frontier* (Provincetown Playhouse, N.Y.C., Oct. 22, 1931); as John Duffy in *Wild Waves* (Times Sq. Th., N.Y.C., Feb. 19, 1932); repeated his role of Jerry Hallam in *Another Language* (Booth, Apr. 25, 1932), and on tour; appeared as Rex Garrison in a stock production of *Solid South* (Berkshire Playhouse, Stockbridge, Mass., Aug. 1932).

Mr. Beal appeared as Paul Lawton in *She Loves Me Not* (46 St. Th, N.Y.C., Nov. 20, 1933); John Galt in *Russet Mantle* (Masque, Jan. 16, 1936); Jimmy Mimms and Jimmy's Thoughts in *Soliloquy* (Empire, Nov. 28, 1938); Bert in *Miss Swan Expects* (Cort, Feb. 20, 1939); Karl Hedstrom in *I Know What I Like* (Hudson, Nov. 24, 1939); Kenneth Bixby in *Goodbye Again* (Theatre-by-the-Sea, Matunuck, R.I., Summer 1940); Alan Squier in *The Petrified Forest* (Berkshire Playhouse, Stockbridge, Mass., Summer 1940); and Gaylord Easterbrook in *No Time for Comedy* (Casino Th., Newport, R.I., Ivoryton Playhouse, Conn., Summer 1940).

He appeared as Commander Tom Smith in *Liberty Jones* (Shubert, N.Y.C., Feb. 5, 1941); succeeded (Jan. 1946) Elliott Nugent as Bill Page in *The Voice of the Turtle* (Morosco, Dec. 8, 1943); appeared as Kit Trevor in the pre-Bway tryout of *Carrot and Club* (opened Shubert, New Haven, Conn., Jan. 30, 1947; closed Walnut St. Th., Philadelphia, Pa., Feb. 8, 1947); succeeded (Fall 1949) William Eythe in the revue *Lend an Ear* (National, N.Y.C., Dec. 16, 1948; moved Broadhurst, Feb. 22, 1949; moved Mansfield Oct. 31, 1949), and played in it on tour.

Mr. Beal appeared as M. Henri in *Eurydice* (Coronet, Hollywood, Calif., 1949); the Chorus in Anouilh's *Antigone* (Circle Th., Hollywood, Calif., May 1949); played the title role in *Ivanov* (Brattle Th., Cambridge, Mass., Jan. 1952); and the Genie in *Jollyanna* (Philharmonic Aud., Los Angeles, Calif., 1952; Curran Th., San Francisco, Aug. 1952).

He staged the sketches for *New Faces of 1952* (Royale, May 16, 1952); played Ludie Watts in a summer-theatre tryout of *The Trip to Bountiful* (Westport Country Playhouse, Conn., 1953); Michael in a touring production of *The Fourposter* (1954); Frank Elgin in a stock production of *The Country Girl* (John Drew Th., East Hampton, N.Y., 1954); succeeded (May 2, 1955) John Forsythe as Capt. Fisby in *The Teahouse of the August Moon* (Martin Beck Th., N.Y.C., Dec. 15, 1953); appeared in *Heartland, U.S.A.* (Old Cathedral, St. Louis, Mo., Sept. 1956); in the title role of a stock production of *Mister Roberts* (Garden Center Th., Ontario, Canada, July 1958); in *Everyman Today* (Coll. of Wooster, Ohio, Nov. 1958); and as Sheriff Hawes in *The Chase* (Fred Miller Th., Milwaukee, Wis., Jan. 1959).

Mr. Beal appeared as the Stage Manager in *Our Town* (Circle in the Square, N.Y.C., Mar. 23, 1959); substituted (July 1962) for Art Carney as Frank Michaelson in *Take Her, She's Mine* (Biltmore, Dec. 21, 1961); played Harrison Bellowes in *Calculated Risk* (Ambassador, Oct. 31, 1962); toured (1965) as Sir Thomas More in *A Man for All Seasons;* was in a reading of *The White Rose and the Red* (Kaufmann Auditorium, YM-YWHA, N.Y.C., Jan. 1966); was the Narrator in *Come Slowly, Eden* (White Barn, Westport, Conn., July 1966); appeared in revivals of three one-act plays by Thornton Wilder: as Roderick in *The Long Christmas Dinner,* M. Cahusac in *Queen of France,* and Pa Kirby in *The Happy Journey to Trenton and Camden* (Cherry Lane, N.Y.C., Sept. 6, 1966); toured as Horace Giddens in *The Little Foxes (Mar.–Sept. 1968); and played in the first productions of the Plumstead Playhouse, Mineola (N.Y.) Th., as Simon Stimson in Our Town* (Sept. 24, 1968) and as Murphy in *The Front Page* (Oct. 5, 1968).

He appeared in *To Be Young, Gifted and Black* (Cherry Lane, N.Y.C., Jan. 2, 1969); played Dansker in *Billy* (Billy Rose Th., Mar. 22, 1969); Gordon Gray in *In the Matter of J. Robert Oppenheimer* (Vivian Beaumont Th., June 26, 1969); Simon Stimson in a revival of *Our Town* (ANTA, Nov. 27, 1969); appeared in summer stock (1970) as the Stage Manager in *Our Town;* was Tom McGrath in *Candyapple* (Edison Th., N.Y.C., Nov. 23, 1970); succeeded (July 20, 1971) Robert Ryan as James Tyrone in *Long Day's Journey into Night* (Promenade, Apr. 2, 1971); played Ed Mosher in *The Iceman Cometh* (Long Wharf Th., New Haven, Conn., Apr. 14, 1972); and played Danny Crosby several times and was standby for five roles in *The Changing Room* (Morosco, N.Y.C., Mar. 6, 1973).

Films. Mr. Beal made his film debut in *Another Language,* recreating his role of Jerry Hallam (MGM, 1933); subsequently appeared in *Hat, Coat and Glove* (RKO, 1934); *The Little Minister* (RKO, 1934); *Laddie* (RKO, 1935); *Les Miserables* (UA, 1935); *Break of Hearts* (RKO, 1935); *M'Liss* (RKO, 1936); *We Who Are About To Die* (RKO, 1936); *The Man Who Found Himself* (RKO, 1937); *Danger Patrol* (RKO, 1937); *Beg, Borrow or Steal* (MGM, 1937); *Border Cafe* (RKO, 1937); *Double Wedding* (MGM, 1937); *Madame X* (MGM, 1937); *Port of Seven Seas* (MGM, 1938); *I Am the Law* (Col., 1938); *The Arkansas Traveler* (Par., 1938); *The Cat and the Canary* (Par., 1939); *The Great Commandment* (20th-Fox, 1939); *Ellery Queen and the Perfect Crime* (Col., 1941); *Doctors Don't Tell* (Rep., 1941); *Atlantic Convoy* (Col., 1942); *One Thrilling Night* (Mono., 1942); *Stand By All Networks* (Col., 1942); *Edge of Darkness* (WB, 1942); *Let's Have Fun* (Col., 1943); and directed and narrated training films for the USAAF (1942–45).

He appeared in *Key Witness* (Col., 1947); narrated *So Dear to My Heart* (RKO, 1948); appeared in *Song of Surrender* (Par., 1949); *Alimony* (Eagle Lion, 1949); *Chicago Deadline* (Par., 1949); *The Country Parson* (Astor, 1950); *My Six Convicts* (Col., 1952); *Remains to Be Seen* (MGM, 1953); *The Vampire* (UA, 1957); *That Night* (U, 1957); *The Sound and the Fury* (20th-Fox, 1959); *Ten Who Dared* (Buena Vista, 1960); and *The Bride* (Unisphere, 1973).

Television and Radio. Mr. Beal performed in radio on the Lux Radio Th. (CBS, 1934); the Favorite Story series, (1947–49); US Steel Hour of Mystery (1947); Cavalcade of America (1947); Columbia Workshop (1947); Suspense (CBS); The Whistler (1948); Prudential Playhouse (1948–49); Crime Doesn't Pay (1948–49); The Eternal Light (1947–48–49); The Amazing Mr. Tutt (CBS, 1948); University Th. of the Air (NBC, 1948–49); Best Plays (NBC, 1956); and has appeared on CBS Radio Mystery Th. (1973–74).

Mr. Beal made his television debut as master of ceremonies on the Darts for Dough series (NBC, 1948); followed by appearances on Your Show Time; Chicago Mysteryland Players (1949); the Kate Smith Show (NBC, 1950); *The Trip to Bountiful* (Goodyear-Philco Hour, NBC, 1953); was emcee on Freedom Rings series (CBS, 1953); appeared on Philip Morris Playhouse, (1954) Campbell Sound Stage (1953); Inner Sanctum (1953); Kraft Television Th. (1953).

Omnibus (CBS, 1954); GE Th. (1954); in *Twelve Angry Men* (Studio One, CBS, 1954); on the Elgin Hour (ABC, 1954); was narrator and host on Horizons (1954); appeared in *As the Twig Is Bent* (Lamp Unto My Feet, CBS, 1955); on Montgomery Presents (NBC, 1956; 1957); Studio One (CBS, 1957); US Steel Hour (CBS, 1957); Suspicion (1958); The Millionaire (WOR-TV, 1958); The Verdict Is Yours (CBS, 1958); the Loretta Young Show (NBC, 1959); Alcoa Presents (NBC, 1959); The Alaskans (1959); as host, interviewer and commentator on Hollywood's Best (WHNC, New Haven, Conn., 1957–58); as Dr. Lewis on Road to Reality (ABC, 1960–61); on The Lieutenant (NBC, 1964); Kojak (CBS, 1974); Hawkins (CBS, 1974); played Senator Fogelson in *Mrs. Lincoln's Husband* (Carl Sandburg's Lincoln, Sept. 6, 1974); on The Waltons (CBS, 1974); and was Dr. Bowen in *The Legend of Lizzie Borden* (ABC Monday Night Movie, Feb. 10, 1975).

Other Activities. Mr. Beal founded and managed the Actor's Hobby Market in Hollywood and Beverly Hills (1948–50).

Recreation. Riding, Swimming, drawing.

BEAN, ORSON. Actor, producer, educator, writer. b. Dallas Frederick Burrows, July 22, 1928, Burlington, Vt., to George and Marian (Pollard) Burrows. Father, policeman. Attended Cambridge (Mass.) High and Latin, 1943–46. Married July 2, 1956, to Jacqueline De Sibour (marr. dis. 1962), one daughter; married 1965 to Carolyn Maxwell, designer. Served US Army, 1946–47. Member of AEA; AFTRA; SAG.

Pre-Theatre. Soda clerk, waiter.

Theatre. Mr. Bean was a boy magician, and made his first professional appearance as a night club performer at the Blue Angel (N.Y.C., June 1952). He made his first stage appearance in *The Spider* at the Cambridge (Mass.) Summer Th. (1945); was the Bellboy in *Goodbye Again* (Boston, Mass., Summer Th., 1948); toured as Sonny Dorrence in *Josephine* (opened Playhouse, Wilmington, Del., Jan. 8, 1953; closed Selwyn, Chicago, Ill., Feb. 7, 1953); appeared in *The School for Scandal,* and *The Scarecrow* (Th. de Lys, N.Y.C., June 1953).

He appeared as Edgar Grassthal in *Men of Distinction* (48 St. Th., Apr. 30, 1953); subsequently played in John Murray Anderson's revue, *Almanac* (Imperial, Dec. 10, 1953); Charlie in *Will Success Spoil Rock Hunter?* (Belasco, Oct. 13, 1955); Ensign Pulver in *Mister Roberts* (NY City Ctr., Dec. 5, 1956); Billy Turk in *Nature's Way* (Coronet, Oct. 16, 1957); Jack Jordan in *Say, Darling* (NY City Ctr., Feb. 25, 1959); Charlie Smith in *Subways Are for Sleeping* (St. James, Dec. 27, 1961); Charlie in *Never Too Late* (Playhouse, Nov. 27, 1962); Tom Considine in *I Was Dancing* (Lyceum, Nov. 8, 1964); succeeded (Nov. 22, 1965) Anthony Newley as Cocky in *The Roar of the Greasepaint— The Smell of the Crowd* (Sam S. Shubert Th., May 16, 1965); played Homer Thrace in *Illya Darling* (Mark Hellinger Th., Apr. 11, 1967); was in *A Round with Ring* (ANTA Matinee Th. Series, Th. de Lys, Oct. 27, 1969); and *The Odd Couple* (Meadowbrook Th. Restaurant, Cedar Grove, N.J., Feb. 1970).

Mr. Bean's company Orson Bean Productions, Inc., produced, in association with Judson Poets' Th., *Home Movies* and *Softly, and Consider the Nearness* (Provincetown Playhouse, May 11, 1964).

Films. Mr. Bean made his film debut in *How To Be Very, Very Popular* (20th-Fox, 1955) and appeared in *Anatomy of a Murder* (Col., 1959).

Television. Among television plays in which Mr. Bean appeared are *Three Men on a Horse* and *Nothing But the Truth* (both Broadway Television Th., NET, 1952); *The Square Peg* (Studio One, CBS, Sept. 1952); *Joye* (Studio One, CBS, Nov. 1954); *Arsenic and Old Lace* (Best of Broadway, CBS, Jan. 1955); *A Christmas Surprise* (Studio One, CBS, Dec. 1956); *Charley's Aunt* (Playhouse 90, CBS, Mar. 1957); *The Man in the Dog Suit* (NBC, Jan. 1960); *Miracle on 34th Street* (NBC, Nov. 1960); *The Star Wagon* (NET Playhouse, June 1967); and the pilots *The Bean Show* (CBS, Sept. 1964) and *Ghostbreaker* (NBC, Sept. 1967). He has also appeared at various times on such programs as the Ed Sullivan Show (CBS); Steve Allen Show (NBC); Jack Paar Show (NBC); Phil Silvers Show (CBS); Twilight Zone (CBS); Naked City (ABC); Love, American Style (ABC); To Tell the Truth (CBS); Password (CBS); and Match Game (NBC).

Other Activities. Mr. Bean founded (1964) and is administrative director of the Fifteenth Street School for children in N.Y.C., an institution utilizing the methods of the Summerhill School in England.

Published Works. Mr. Bean wrote *Me and the Orgone* (1971).

Awards. Mr. Bean was nominated (1962) for an Antoinette Perry (Tony) Award for his performance in *Subways Are for Sleeping.* .

Recreation. Collecting Laurel and Hardy movies.

BEATON, SIR CECIL. Designer, photographer, painter, costume designer, writer. b. Jan. 14, 1904, London, England, to Ernest and Esther (Sisson) Beaton. Father, timber merchant. Grad. Harrow Sch., England, 1922; attended St. John's Coll., Cambridge, England, 1922–25. Served as official war photographer to Ministry of Information, Near East and Far East (1939–45). Member of Costume Designers Guild (US); United Scenic Artists (US); Assn. of Cinematography, Television and Allied Technicians (England); Society of Film and Television Arts (England). Address: (home) Reddish House, Broadchalke, Salisbury, Witshire, England; (bus.) 8 Pelham Place, London, S.W.7, England.

Theatre. Sir Cecil Beaton designed sets and costumes for *Follow the Sun* (Adelphi, London, 1935); for the Sadler's Wells production of the ballet *Apparitions* (Sadler's Wells, 1936); for the Ballets Russes de Monte Carlo (Covent Garden, 1937); designed the sets and lighting for *Lady Windermere's Fan* (Haymarket, Aug. 21, 1945), and for the N.Y.C. production, his first Bway assignment, in which he also played Cecil Graham (Cort, Oct. 14, 1946). Thereafter, he divided his time, in the main, working in London and New York. He designed the sets and costumes for *The Return of the Prodigal* (Covent Garden, London, Nov. 24, 1948); and *Charley's Aunt* (Piccadilly, Dec. 22, 1949); for *Cry of the Peacock* (Mansfield, N.Y.C., Apr. 11, 1950); and for *The Second Mrs. Tanqueray* (Haymarket, London, Aug. 29, 1950). He wrote a play, *The Gainsborough Girls* (London, 1951).

He designed the sets and costumes for *The Grass Harp* (Martin Beck Th., N.Y.C., Mar. 27, 1952); for *Quadrille* (Phoenix, London, Sept. 12, 1952); *Aren't We All?* (Haymarket, Aug. 6, 1953); *Love's Labour's Lost* (Old Vic, Oct. 19, 1954); for *Quadrille* (Coronet, N.Y.C., Nov. 3, 1954); designed the costumes for *Portrait of a Lady* (ANTA, Dec. 21, 1954); sets and costumes for *The Chalk Garden* (Ethel Barrymore Th., Oct. 26, 1955); for *My Fair Lady* (Mark Hellinger Th., Mar. 15, 1956); for the opera *Vanessa* (Metropolitan Opera House, Jan. 15, 1958); *My Fair Lady* (Drury Lane, London, Apr. 30, 1958); *Saratoga* (Winter Garden, N.Y.C., Dec. 7, 1959); the opera *Turandot* (Metropolitan Opera House, Feb. 24, 1961); *The School for Scandal* (Comédie Française, Paris, 1962); the ballet, *Marguerite and Armand* (Covent Garden, London, 1963; Winter Garden, N.Y.C., 1963; and the opera *La Traviata* (Metropolitan Opera House, Sept. 25, 1966).

Films. Sir Cecil Beaton designed the sets and costumes for *Gigi* (MGM, 1958); *The Doctor's Dilemma* (MGM, 1958); and the film version of *My Fair Lady* (MGM, 1964).

Other Activities. His photographs have appeared in magazines; he had his first photographic exhibition at the Cooling Gallery (London, 1930). He has had exhibitions of his paintings and stage designs at the Redfern Gallery (London, 1936; 1958; 1965); the Sagittarius Gallery (N.Y., 1956); the Lefevre Gallery (London, 1966); an exhibition of photographs at the National Portrait Gallery (London, 1968); and an exhibition of fashions at the Victoria and Albert Museum (London, 1971).

Published Works. Sir Cecil Beaton has written *The Book of Beauty* (1930); *Cecil Beaton's Scrapbook* (1937); *Portrait of New York* (1938); *My Royal Past* (1939); *Time Exposure*, in collaboration with Peter Quennell (1941); *Air of Glory* (1941); *Winged Squadrons* (1942); *Near East* (1943); *British Photographers* (1944); *Far East* (1945); *Ashcombe* (1949); *Photobiography* (1951); *Persona Grata*, with Kenneth Tynan (1953); *The Glass of Fashion* (1954); *It Gives Me Great Pleasure (I Take Great Pleasure*, US ed.) (1955); *The Face of the World* (1957); *Japanese* (1959); *The Wandering Years*, the first volume of his diaries (1961); *Quail in Aspic* (1962); *Royal Portraits* (1963); *Images* (1963); *Fair Lady* (1964); *The Best of Beaton* (1968); *My Bolivian Aunt* (1971); and three additional volumes of diaries —*The Years Between* (1965); *The Happy Years* (1972; US ed. 1963, *Memories of the 40's)*; and *The Strenuous Years* (1973).

Awards. Sir Cecil Beaton was made Commander of the Most Honourable Order of the British Empire (C.B.E.) (1957); was awarded the Legion d'Honneur (Chevalier de la Légion d'Honneur, 1960); received the Academy of Motion Picture Arts and Sciences (Oscar) Award for his costume designs in *Gigi* (1958) and again for his costume designs and for his art direction of *My Fair Lady* (1964); and he was awarded a knighthood in New Year's Honours List, Jan. 1972.

Recreation. Diaries, scrapbooks, decoration, traveling, gardening, collecting modern paintings.

BEAUFORT, JOHN.

Drama critic, editor, news correspondent. b. Sept. 23, 1912, Edmonton, Alberta, Canada, to Ernest and Margaret (Crawley) Beaufort. Father, journalist. Attended Ottawa, Ontario, Canada; and Newton, Mass., public schools; Winnwood School, Long Island, N.Y.; Rollins College, Winter Park, Fla.; Boston Univ. Married June 28, 1940, to Francesca Bruning, actress. Member of NY Drama Critics Circle (treas., 1972–to date); Drama Desk (past pres.); The Players; The Garrick Club. Address: The Christian Science Monitor, 588 Fifth Ave., New York, NY 10036, tel. (212) 757-1222.

Mr. Beaufort joined *The Christian Science Monitor* as a copy clerk in 1930 and later became a junior reporter, at the same time attending Boston University at night. He was on leave-of-absence in 1933–34 and 1934–35 to attend Rollins College. From 1935 to 1939 he had varied news, feature, and reviewing assignments, and from 1939 to 1942 he was the *Monitor's* film and theatre critic in N.Y.C. During WW II, he served the paper as a war correspondent, chiefly in the Pacific (1943–45). He has been chief of the NY bureau (1946–50); arts and magazine editor in Boston (1951); arts editor and theatre and film critic based in N.Y.C. (1952–62); chief of the London bureau (1962–65); feature editor in Boston (1965–70); and NY drama critic (1970–to date).

Awards. Mr. Beaufort received the Directors Guild of America Award in 1961.

Recreation. Reading, walking, travel.

BEAUMONT, RALPH.

Choreographer, dancer. b. Ralph Wallace Bergendorf, Mar. 5, 1926, Pocatello, Idaho, to Nels Peter and Florence Marie (Feldsted) Bergendorf. Father, painter. Attended Commerce H.S., San Francisco, Calif., 1941–43; grad. Pocatello (Idaho) H.S., 1944; attended San Francisco City Coll., 1946–48; studied dance, acting, and speech at the Amer. Th. Wing, 1948–50. Served US Army, 1944–46; rank, Sgt. Member of SSD&C; AEA; SAG; AFTRA; AGVA; Beta Phi Beta.

Theatre. Mr. Beaumont made his debut as a dancer and actor (Hanna Th., Cleveland, Ohio, 1949), in the national touring company of *Inside U.S.A.;* subsequently was dancer and assistant choreographer for musical productions at the Starlight Operetta (Dallas, Tex., Summer 1950); dancer and dance captain in the national company of *Guys and Dolls* (opened Curran, San Francisco, Calif., June 4, 1951).

He made his Bway debut as a dancer in *Can-Can* (Shubert, May 7, 1953); subsequently was dancer and assistant choreographer in *Shangri-La* (Winter Garden, June 13, 1956); received his first assignment as choreographer in N.Y.C. for *Wonderful Town* (NY City Ctr., Mar. 5, 1958), which he also choreographed at the Brussels World's Fair (Belgium, July 1958); was choreographer for *Saratoga* (Winter Garden, N.Y.C., Dec. 7, 1959); *The Most Happy Fella* (Coliseum, London, Apr. 21, 1960); *Pal Joey* (NY City Ctr., May 31, 1961); *Rinaldo in Campo* and *Enrico* (Teatro Sistina, Rome, Italy, 1961); *Gentlemen Prefer Blondes* (Prince's, London, 1962); *Babilonia* (Teatro Sistina, Rome, Italy, 1962); and *Enrico* (London, 1963); choreographed and staged the musical numbers for *Babes in the Wood* (Orpheum Th., N.Y.C., Dec. 28, 1964); choreographed *The Yearling* (Alvin, Dec. 10, 1965); directed and choreographed *The Most Happy Fella* (NY City Ctr., May 11, 1966); *Guys and Dolls* (NY City Ctr., June 8, 1966) ; *A Funny Thing Happened on the Way to the Forum* (Playhouse, Pennsylvania State Univ., State College, Pa., July 7, 1966); staged the musical numbers and dances for *Wonderful Town* (NY City Ctr., N.Y.C., May 17, 1967); choreographed *A Funny Thing Happened on the Way to the Forum* (Lunt-Fontanne Th., Mar. 30, 1972); and was production administrator for The Center Theatre Group (Ahmanson Th., Los Angeles, Oct. 16, 1973–May 11, 1974).

Films. Mr. Beaumont has been dancer and assistant choreographer for *April in Paris* (WB, 1952); *She's Back on Broadway* (WB, 1952); *The Band Wagon* (MGM, 1952); and *Gentlemen Prefer Blondes* (20th-Fox, 1952).

Television. Mr. Beaumont has appeared as a dancer and an assistant choreographer for Holiday Hotel (ABC, 1950); the Martha Raye Show (NBC, 1954); Sid Caesar Show (NBC, 1955); Milton Berle Show (NBC, 1956); Ed Sullivan Show (CBS, 1952); choreographer for *Wonderful Town* (CBS, 1958); for Senore Della Venturo (Mr. Nine O'Clock), an Italian television series (RAI, Rome, 1962); and the Jack Paar Show (NBC, 1963).

Night Clubs. He appeared as dancer and singer in the Imogene Coca Show (Americana, Miami, Fla.); Sahara (Las Vegas, Nev.); Beverly Hilton (Beverly Hills, Calif.); and Adolphus Hotel (Dallas, Tex.).

BECHER, JOHN C.

Actor. b. John Conrad Becher, Milwaukee, Wis., Jan. 13, 1915, to John and Katherine (Schmidt) Becher. Father, carpenter. Grad. Custer H.S., Milwaukee, 1933; Milwaukee State Teachers Coll., B.S. 1938; Goodman Sch. of Drama, B.F.A. 1941. Married Aug. 7, 1945, to Margaret Williams, theatrical accountant. Served WW II, US Army, head of Soldier Shows Dept., Sch. for Special Service, Washington and Lee Univ.; rank, Capt. Member of AEA; SAG; AFTRA. Address: 43 Greenwich Ave., New York, NY 10014, tel. (212) WA 4-8944.

Pre-Theatre. Elementary school teacher (1938).

Theatre. Mr. Becher made his stage debut in a school production of *Tony's Wife* (1929); subsequently played a Coffinbearer and First Murderer in a touring production of *Richard III* (Cambria and West Bend, Wis., Oct. 1934); Sganarelle in *The Doctor in Spite of Himself* (Lake Zurich Playhouse, Ill., 1938); performed in stock at the Putnam County Playhouse (Lake Mahopac, N.Y., 1947); Ridgefield Summer Th. (Conn., 1947); Cape Playhouse (Dennis, Mass., 1948, 1957, 1960); Olney Th., (Md., 1950–51); St. Louis Municipal Opera (Mo., 1950, 1955, 1963); Paper Mill Playhouse (Millburn, N.J., 1952–3, 1959); Westport Country Playhouse (Conn., 1954, 1957, 1958); Ogunquit Playhouse (Me., 1957); Lakes Region Playhouse (Glendale-Laconia, N.H., 1957); Bucks County Playhouse (New Hope, Pa., 1957, 1960); the Ivoryton Playhouse (Conn., 1957); and Royal Poinciana Playhouse (Palm Beach, Fla., 1958).

With the Amer. Repertory Th. at the International Th., N.Y.C., he played Lord Sands in *Henry VIII* (Nov. 6, 1946); a Villager in *What Every Woman Knows* (Nov. 8, 1946); The Lion in *Androcles and the Lion* (Dec. 19, 1946); Brinkerhof in *Yellow Jack* (Feb. 27, 1947); and the Queen of Hearts in *Alice in Wonderland* (Apr. 5, 1947).

Mr. Becher played Mate Meyer in *Skipper Next to God* (Maxine Elliott's Th., Jan. 13, 1948; moved Playhouse, Jan. 30, 1948); toured as Mr. Lundie in the national company of *Brigadoon* (Sept. 6, 1948–Sept. 12, 1949); appeared as Dumpsty in *Idiot's Delight* (NY City Ctr., May 28, 1951); succeeded (Mar. 29, 1954) Arthur O'Connell as Howard in *Picnic* (Music Box, Feb. 19, 1953), and played the role on tour (Apr. 19, 1954 to Oct. 9, 1954); played Mr. Henderson in *Teach Me How To Cry* (Th. de Lys, N.Y.C., Apr. 5, 1955); toured as Cliff Snell in *The Solid Gold Cadillac* (June 28, 1955–Nov. 26, 1955).

He succeeded (Aug. 8, 1956) Bern Hoffman as Draft Man, and was standby for Myron McCormick as Sergeant King in *No Time for Sergeants* (Alvin, N.Y.C., Oct. 20, 1955); played Mr. Lundie in *Brigadoon* (NY City Ctr., Mar. 27, 1957; moved Adelphi, Apr. 9, 1957); and appeared in an ANTA program sponsored by the US State Dept. in one-act plays by Thornton Wilder, William Saroyan and Tennessee Williams (Congress Hall, West Berlin, Ger., Sept. 1, 1957).

Mr. Becher played Daddy in *The American Dream* (York, N.Y.C., Jan. 24, 1961; moved Cherry Lane, May 23, 1961); took over (May 23, 1961) the role of Father in *The Death of Bessie Smith* (York, Jan. 24, 1961; moved Cherry Lane, May 23, 1961); played Willie in *Happy Days* (Cherry Lane, Sept. 17, 1961), and on tour (McCarter Th., Princeton, N.J., Jan. 12, 1962; Kaufmann Aud., N.Y.C., Jan. 15, 1962).

In repertory at Cherry Lane, under the title, *Theatre of the Absurd*, he played Nagg in *Endgame;* Old Man in *Bertha;* Daddy in *Sandbox;* Father in *Picnic on the Battlefield;* Daddy in *The American Dream;* and Old Man in *The Killer* (Feb. 11, 1962–Mar. 25, 1962).

He played Mr. Lundie in *Brigadoon* (NY City Ctr., May 30, 1962); Gus in *The Dumbwaiter*, one of a double bill, entitled *The Pinter Plays* (Cherry Lane, Nov. 26, 1962); his role as Mr. Lundie in *Brigadoon* (NY City Ctr., Jan. 30, 1963); Stumpy in *The Ballad of the Sad Café* (Martin Beck, Oct. 30, 1963); Gus in *The Dumbwaiter* (Provincetown Playhouse, May 14, 1963); and Voyolko in *The Child Buyer* in the Univ. of Michigan Professional Th. program (Trueblood Aud., Ann Arbor, Michigan, Mar. 3–8, 1964; Garrick Th., N.Y.C., Dec. 21, 1964); was in the revue *That Thing at the Cherry Lane* (Cherry Lane, May 18, 1965); repeated his performance as Willie in the English version of a French-English revival of *Happy Days* (Cherry Lane, Sept. 28, 1965); was Mr. Upson in *Mame* (Winter Garden, May 24, 1966); played Judge Gaffney in a revival of *Harvey* (ANTA Th., Feb. 24, 1970); and was the Detective in *Status Quo Vadis* (Brooks Atkinson Th., Feb. 18, 1973).

Films. Mr. Becher appeared in *March of Time*

(1946); *Kiss of Death* (20th-Fox, 1947); and *The Wrong Man* (WB, 1957).

Television. He has appeared on Philco Television Playhouse (NBC); Goodyear Th. (NBC); Schlitz Playhouse (CBS); in *Louis the Louse* (Phil Silvers' Special, NBC, 1959); in *The Sacco-Vanzetti Story* (Sunday Showcase, June 1960); in episodes from *Sandbox* (Omnibus, CBS, 1961); in scenes from *The American Dream* and *The Dumbwaiter* (Open End, Ind., 1963); on US Steel Hour (CBS); The Defenders (CBS); and The Nurses (CBS); For the People (CBS); The Trials of O'Brien (CBS); and Car 54, Where Are You? (ABC). On NY Television Th. (NET), he appeared in *Gallows Humor* (Oct. 18, 1965) and was George Gordon in *The Immovable Gordons* (Nov. 14, 1966).

Recreation. Philately, photography.

BECK, GORDON. Educator, editor, director. b. Gordon Eugene Beck, Mar. 23, 1929, Goshen, Ind., to Ralph L. and Lydia (Greenlee) Beck. Parents, educators. Grad. Goshen H.S., 1947; attended Purdue Univ., 1947–49; Indiana Univ., 1949; Bowling Green State Univ., B.A. 1951; Western Reserve Univ., M.A. 1952; Univ. of Ill., 1954–57. Served US Army, Occupational Therapy Spec., 1952–54; rank, Cpl. Married Mar. 22, 1951, to Elizabeth Arnholt; one son, two daughters. Member of AETA; SAA; Central States Speech Assn.; ASTR; NCP (exec. council, 1961–to date); AAUP; Society for Theatre Research; Intl. Federation for Theatre Research; Société d'Histoire du Théâtre.

Mr. Beck began teaching courses in theatre at the Univ. of Kansas in 1957. He had previously held positions at the Univ. of Illinois (1954–56) and at Bowling Green State Univ. (1956–57).

He has directed *Salome* (Bowling Green State Univ., Apr. 1951); *The Curious Savage* (Fairview Community Th., Ohio, Jan. 1952); and *Picnic* (Bowling Green State Univ., Mar. 1957); at the Univ. of Kansas, directed *The Cave Dwellers* (June 1958), *Under Milk Wood* (Oct. 1958), *An Italian Straw Hat* (Feb. 1959), *Tartuffe* (July 1959), *The Crucible* (Mar. 1960), *The Caucasian Chalk Circle* (Mar. 1961), *Twelfth Night* (Apr. 1962), *Maria Stuart* (Feb. 1963), and *Period of Adjustment* (Apr. 1964).

Mr. Beck edited *Players Magazine* beginning in 1961) while that periodical was published at the Univ. of Kansas.

Recreation. Golf, photography, book collecting.

BECK, JULIAN. Director, actor, producer, scenic designer. b. Julian D. Beck, May 31, 1925, New York City, to Irving and Mabel (Blum) Beck. Father, businessman; mother, elementary school teacher. Grad. Horace Mann H.S., N.Y.C., 1942; attended Yale Univ., 1942–43; City Coll. of N.Y., 1946–49. Married Oct. 30, 1948, to Judith Malina, actress, director, producer; one son; one daughter. Member of AEA; NY Committee for General Strike for Peace; IWW. Address: c/o M. L. Beck, 800 West End Ave., New York, NY 10025.

Theatre. Mr. Beck is co-director of The Living Theatre, which he founded (1947) with Judith Malina; his first assignment in N.Y.C. was as designer of *The Thirteenth God* (Cherry Lane Th., Mar. 20, 1951); he designed and, with his wife, Judith Malina, presented a series of plays in the living room of their home, playing Regisseur in *Childish Jokes;* the Teacher in *He Who Says Yes and He Who Says No;* directing *Ladies' Voices;* and playing the Young Man in *Dialogue of the Young Man and the Manikin* (Aug. 15, 1951).

With Judith Malina, Mr. Beck produced and designed the Living Theatre presentations at the Cherry Lane Th., *Doctor Faustus Lights the Lights* (Dec. 2, 1951); *Beyond the Mountains* (Dec. 30, 1951), which he also directed; *An Evening of Bohemian Theatre,* a triple bill including *Ladies' Voices,* which he also directed, *Desire,* and *Sweeney Agonistes* (Mar. 2, 1952); *Faustina* (May 25, 1952); and a double-bill, *The Heroes,* in which he also played Theseus, and *Ubi Roi* (Aug. 5, 1952).

Mr. Beck designed *R.U.R.* for the Dramatic Workshop (Capitol Th. Studio, Apr., 1953); *Ticklish Acrobat* for the Artists' Theatre (Amato Opera Th., Mar. 8, 1954); produced and designed at the Living Th. Studio, at 2641 Bway, *The Age of Anxiety* (Mar. 18, 1954), in which he played Quant; *The Spook Sonata* (June 3, 1954), in which he played the Colonel; *Orpheus* (Sept. 30, 1954), in which he played Azrael; *The Idiot King* (Dec. 2, 1954), in which he played the title role, *Tonight We Improvise* (Feb. 17, 1955), which he directed and in which he played the Director; *Phaedra* (May 27, 1955), in which he played Theramenes; and *The Young Disciple* (Oct. 12, 1955), which he directed; and designed a double bill of operas, *Voices for a Mirror* and *The Curious Fern* (Master Inst. Th., June 5, 1957); and *Dances Before a Wall* (Henry St. Playhouse, Mar. 30, 1958).

Mr. Beck and Judith Malina produced in repertory at the Living Theatre's new quarters, 530 Sixth Ave., *Many Loves* (Jan. 13, 1959), which he designed and directed; *The Cave at Machpelah* (June 30, 1959), which he designed and directed; *The Connection,* which he designed (July 15, 1959); *Tonight We Improvise* (Nov. 6, 1959), which he designed and directed and in which he played the Director; *Madrigal of War* (Nov. 11, 1959); a triple-bill, *All that Fall, Embers,* and *Act Without Words, I & III* (Dec. 7, 1959); another triple-bill, *Bertha, Theory of Comedy* and *Love's Labour* (Dec. 28, 1959); *The Devil's Mother* (Feb. 1, 1960); *Faust Foutu* (May 2, 1960); a double-bill, *The Marrying Maiden* and *The Women of Trachis,* which he designed and directed (June 22, 1960); a triple-bill, *The Herne's Egg, Purgatory,* and *A Full Moon in March* (Sept. 19, 1960); *The Election* (Nov. 4, 1960), in which he played the Director; *In the Jungle of Cities* (Dec. 20, 1960), which he designed and in which he succeeded (Feb. 14, 1961), Khigh Diegh in the role of Shlink, *The Mountain Giants* (Apr. 3, 1961), which he designed; *Many Loves* (May 15, 1961), which he designed and in which he played Peter; *The Apple* (Dec. 7, 1961), which he designed and in which he played Ajax; *Man Is Man* (Sept. 18, 1962), which he designed and directed; and *The Brig,* which he designed (May 15, 1963).

Mr. Beck and Judith Malina took the Living Theatre's productions of *The Connection, Many Loves,* and *In the Jungle of Cities* on tour in Italy, France, and Germany (June 1961); *The Connection, The Apple,* and *In the Jungle of Cities* on tour of France, Germany, Switzerland, the Netherlands, and Belgium (Apr.–May 1962). In 1964, they went with the Living Theatre to London, where they presented *The Brig* (Mermaid, Sept. 2–26), subsequently touring Europe (1964–68) and producing the following new works: *Mysteries and Smaller Pieces,* created collectively by the company under direction of Mr. Beck and Judith Malina (American Students and Artists Center, Paris, Oct. 26, 1964); *The Maids,* directed by Judith Malina with Mr. Beck playing Claire (Forum Th., Berlin, Feb. 26, 1965); *Frankenstein,* created collectively by the company under the direction of Judith Malina and Mr. Beck (Teatro La Perla, Venice, Sept. 26, 1965); Sophocles' *Antigone,* a translation by Judith Malina from the Bertolt Brecht version, with Miss Malina as Antigone and Mr. Beck as Creon (Stadttheater, Krefeld, Germany, Feb. 18, 1967); and *Paradise Now,* created collectively by the company under the direction of Mr. Beck and Judith Malina (Cloître des Carmes, Festival d'Avignon, France, July 20, 1968). The Becks then toured the US coast to coast with the Living Theatre productions *Mysteries, Antigone, Frankenstein,* and *Paradise Now* (tour opened Yale University Th., New Haven, Conn., Sept. 16, 1968; closed Brooklyn Acad. of Music, N.Y.C., Mar. 28–29, 1969); followed by return to Europe for tour.

The Living Theatre changed its form in Jan. 1970 to concentrate on productions for street and non-theatre environments. Judith Malina and Mr. Beck went with the Living Theatre to Brazil (July 1970) and began production of the play cycle *The Legacy of Cain,* producing *Favela Project 1: Christmas Cake for the Hot Hole and the Cold Hole* (São Paulo, Dec. 1970); *Plaza Project 1: Rituals and Transformations* (Embu, Dec. 1970); *School Project 1: A Critical Examination of Six Dreams About Mother* (Saramenha, Brazil, May 1971). Further work on *The Legacy of Cain* cycle continued after the return of Judith Malina and Mr. Beck to the US (Sept. 1971) with production of *University Project 1: Seven Meditations on Political Sado-Masochism* (Chapel Hill, N.C., Apr. 1972) and *Strike Support Play 1: Strike Support Oratorium* (Brooklyn, N.Y., Mar. 1974).

Films. Mr. Beck and members of the Living Theatre company have appeared in *Narcissus* (1957); *The Connection* (Allen-Hogdon, 1961); *The Brig* (White Line, 1964); *Living and Glorious,* excerpts from *The Brig* and *Mysteries* (1965); *Amore, Amore* (1966); *Agonia,* part of *Vangelo 70* (1967); *Le Compromis,* scenes from *Mysteries* and *Antigone* (1968); *Etre Libre* (1968); and *Paradise Now* (1969; 1970). Mr. Beck appeared in the film *Edipo Re* (1967).

Television. In the US, scenes from *The Brig* have been televised (Look Up and Live, CBS, Aug. 2, 1964); and from *Mysteries* (WQED, Mar. 8, 1969). In Europe, telecasts included *The Brig* (Nov. 1, 1964) and *Frankenstein* (Oct. 17, 1965), both from Berlin, Germany; *The Maids* (Amsterdam, The Netherlands, Dec. 6, 1966); and *Mysteries* (Copenhagen, Denmark, Dec. 30, 1965; Laren, Netherlands, Dec. 12, 1966; Paris, France, Oct. 13, 1967).

Published Works. Mr. Beck has published *Songs of the Revolution 1–35* (1963); *Living Theatre Poems* (1968); *21 Songs of the Revolution* (1969); *Conversations with Julian Beck and Judith Malina* (1969); *We, the Living,* with Judith Malina (1970); *The Life of the Theatre* (1972); and *Songs of the Revolution 36–89* (1974). His articles have appeared in *Tulane Drama Review* (later *The Drama Review*), the *NY Times, City Lights Journal,* and he wrote an introductory essay on The Living Theatre in the published edition of *The Brig* and an introduction to Michael Smith's *Theatre Trip* (1969).

Awards. The Living Theatre received the Lola D'Annunzio Award (1959); the Newspaper Guild of NY, Page One Award (1960); *The Village Voice* Off-Bway (Obie) Award for *The Connection* (1960); the Brandeis Univ. Creative Arts Award Th. Citation (1961); the Grand Prix de Théâtre de Nations, Paris, (1961); the Medallion from the Paris Th. Critics Circle (1961); the Prix de l'Université, Paris (1961); the New England Th. Conference Award (1962); *The Village Voice* Off-Bway (Obie) Awards for stage design and production for *The Brig* (1964); the Olympia Prize, Taormina, Italy, for *Antigone* (1967); two *Village Voice* Off-Bway (Obie) awards in 1969 — for best new play, *Frankenstein,* and for acting, Creon in *Antigone;* and the Maharam Award (1969) for stage design, for *Frankenstein.*

BECKER, WILLIAM. Executive, actor, director, writer. b. Arthur William John Becker III, May 23, 1927, St. Louis, Mo., to Arthur William John and Margaret (Heath) Becker. Father, business executive. Grad. Clayton (Mo.) H.S., 1943; attended Washington Univ., 1943–44; Duke Univ., 1944; grad. Harvard Univ., A.B. (Phi Beta Kappa) 1948; Oxford (Eng.) Univ., D. Phil. (Rhodes Scholar) 1953. Married July 19, 1952, to Patricia Birch, actress, dancer, choreographer; two sons; one daughter. Served USN, submarine forces, South Pacific, 1945–46. Member of Racquet and Tennis Club; Harvard Club (N.Y.C.); Brook Club (N.Y.C.); Society of Colonial Wars. Address: (home) 320 E. 72nd St., New York, NY 10021, tel. (212) BU 8-6261; (bus.) Janus Films, Inc., 745 Fifth Ave., New York, NY 10022, tel. (212) PL 3-7100.

Mr. Becker is chairman of the board of Janus Films, Inc., which he bought in 1965, and of City Entertainment Corp., also a film company, which he bought in 1972.

Theatre. For the USO, Mr. Becker toured Missouri and Illinois as Duke Weatherby in *Sixteen in August* and George in *Our Town* (1943), and North and South Carolina as Dexter in *Kiss and Tell* and Robert in *The Silver Cord* (1944).

While a student at Harvard Univ., he was a founder of the Veterans' Th. Workshop (1946), which became the Brattle Th. Co. (1951), and appeared in summer productions at the Windham (N.Y.) Playhouse (1951); played the Archangel Uriel in *I Was a King in Babylon* (Veterans' Th. Workshop, 1946); Dan Jordan Knockem in *Barthol-*

omew Fair (Eliot House, Cambridge, Mass., 1947); the Stage Manager in *The Happy Journey to Trenton and Camden*, and Larry Toms in *Boy Meets Girl* (Mordan Hall, Oxford, Eng., 1948); played Hubert de Burgh in *King John*, for which he was also production manager (Clarendon Press Inst., Oxford, 1948); Caliban in *The Tempest* (Worcester Gardens, Oxford, 1949); and The Thin Man in *Peer Gynt*, for which he was also stage manager (Oxford Playhouse, 1949).

He assisted as stage manager for productions given by French and Italian companies at the Internationale Theaterfestspiele (Salzburg, Austria), where he also appeared as the Doctor in *Him* (1950); was director, Eric Bentley's assistant for the following plays prepared for the American tour of the Young Ireland Th. Co. of Dublin: *The Player Queen, Purgatory, The Rising of the Moon, In the Shadow of the Glen, The Words Upon the Window-Pane, Shadow of a Gunman*, and *Riders to the Sea* (1951).

At the Windham (N.Y.) Playhouse, he appeared as Steve in *A Streetcar Named Desire*, and Sergius Saranoff in *Arms and the Man* (1951); and was faculty director and appeared in student productions at the Experimental Th. (Vassar Coll., 1952).

Mr. Becker was associated with Roger L. Stevens Productions (N.Y.C.) from 1954 to 1964.

Radio. He played various roles in Saturday morning broadcasts for children (WEW, St. Louis, 1938–40); was an announcer for Navy radio programs in Guam, Marianas Islands (1946); and performed on programs with the Harvard Radio Players (1947–48).

Other Activities. He lectured for the Arts Council of Great Britain on "Theatre in America" (1949) and on "Yeats as a Playwright" at the Salzburg (Austria) Seminar in American Studies (1950); was a director of Intl. Th. Exchange (1950–51); drama critic for *The Hudson Review* (1951–56); book reviewer for *The New Republic* (1952–56); founder and chairman of the board of Theatre Trains and Planes, Inc. (1954–56); chairman of the board and president of Playbill, Inc. (1956–60) and has been a consultant (1960–to date); advisory director of the New Dramatists Committee (1957–67); a director for Stein and Day, Inc. (1962–to date); and on the editorial board of "Paris Review" editions, which he helped organize in 1966 and which is an affiliate of Doubleday & Co.

Published Works. Mr. Becker contributed articles to *The Harvard Advocate* (1947); *The Isis* (1949, 1950); *Mercury* (1949, 1950); *La Revue Théâtrale* (1950); *Theatre der Zeit* (1950); *Il Dramma* (1950); *Tribune* (1950); *Theatre Arts* (1951); *Vassar Miscellany News* (1951); and translated Andre Obey's "Venus and Adonis" in *From the Modern Repertoire, Series Two* (1952); also wrote for *The Hudson Review* (1952, 1953, 1954, 1955, 1956); *The Dublin Magazine* (1952); *The New Republic* (1952, 1953); *The Sewanee Reveiw* (1953); *Poetry* Magazine (1953); and *Harper's Bazaar* (1954).

Awards. Mr. Becker received (1959) the Merit Award from the Actors Fund of America.

BECKERMAN, BERNARD. Educator, lecturer, writer, director. b. Sept. 24, 1921, New York City, to Morris and Elizabeth (Scheftel) Beckerman. Father, photographer. Grad. City Coll. of New York, B.S.S. 1942; Yale Univ. Sch. of Drama (Fellowship), M.F.A. 1943; Columbia Univ., Ph.D. 1956. Married Aug. 21, 1940, to Gloria Brim; two sons. Served US Army, 1943–45, overseas; rank, Sgt. Member AETA (regional rep., 1962; dir., 1967–70); AAUP; ASTR (exec. comm., 1972–73; chmn. exec. comm., 1973–76); ANTA (dir., 1964–68); NTC (trustee, 1972–75); Long Island Arts Center (trustee; exec. comm., 1964). Address: (home) 27 W. 67th St., New York, NY 10023; (bus.) School of the Arts, Columbia Univ., New York, NY 10027.

In 1947, Mr. Beckerman joined the teaching staff of Hofstra Univ., where he was chmn., Dept. of Drama and Speech. He was special lecturer in drama, Columbia Univ. (Sept. 1957–June 1960); Fulbright Lecturer, Tel Aviv (Israel) Univ. (1960–61); theatre consultant to the program in the arts, Columbia Univ. (1964); and chmn., Theatre Arts Div., Columbia Univ. (1965–72). In 1972, he became dean, Sch. of the Arts, Columbia Univ. He has directed more than 50 productions, including 15 of the Hofstra Shakespeare Festival productions, among them *Twelfth Night* with Stella Andrews, *Macbeth* with Ian Keith, and *Hamlet* with William Hutt.

In N.Y.C., he directed ELT's production of *The Shining Hour* (Lenox Hill Playhouse, Nov. 1946); and for the Nassau County Jubilee Exposition, the pageant, *Nassau County Story* (Roosevelt Field, Oct. 1949).

Published Works. Mr. Beckerman wrote *Shakespeare at the Globe, 1599–1609* (1962) and *Dynamics of Drama* (1970). His articles include "The Globe Playhouse: Notes for Direction" (*ETJ*, Mar. 1953); "Shakespearean Production in New York, 1906–1956" (*Speech Assoc. of Eastern States*, 1959); "Shakespearean Production in America" (*Enciclopedia dello Spettacolo*); "Shakespeare's Theatre" in *The Complete Pelican Shakespeare* (1969); "Philip Henslowe" in *The Theatrical Manager in England and America* (1971); "Dramatic Analysis and Literary Interpretation" in *New Literary History, II* (Spring 1971); and major articles on theatre history in the *Encyclopedia Americana* and theatre art in the *Encyclopaedia Britannica* (1974). From 1965 to 1968, he was reviewer for *Shakespeare Quarterly* of American Shakespeare Festival Productions. He edited, with Joseph Papp, *Troilus and Cressida* (1967) and *Love's Labour's Lost* (1968) and, with Howard Siegman, *On Stage: Selected Theatre Reviews from The New York Times* (1973). In 1973, he became a member of the editorial boards of *Shakespeare Quarterly* and *Twentieth Century Literature*.

Awards. For his book, *Shakespeare at the Globe, 1599–1609*, Mr. Beckerman received the Seventh Annual Award from the American Shakespeare Festival Theatre and Academy (1962). He was elected a fellow of the American Theatre Association (1973).

BECKETT, SAMUEL. Playwright, author. b. Samuel Barclay Beckett, Apr. 13, 1906, Dublin, Ireland, to William Frank and Mary (Roe) Beckett. Father, quantity surveyor; mother, interpreter for Irish Red Cross. Graduated Portora Royal School, Enniskillen, Ireland; Trinity Coll., Dublin, B.A. 1927 (Foundation Scholarship in modern languages, 1926; prize and gold medal for outstanding performance in finals, 1927); M.A. 1932. Married to Suzanne Dumesnil. During World War II served in French Resistance, 1941–42, and with Irish Red Cross, 1945. Address: c/0 Grove Press, Inc., 53 E. 11 St., New York, NY 10003, tel. (212) 677-2400.

Theatre. Mr. Beckett's first play produced was *En attendant Godot* (Th. de Babylone, Paris, France, Jan. 5, 1953), in English as *Waiting for Godot* (Arts Th. Club, London, England, Aug. 3, 1955). The first US production (Coconut Grove Playhouse, Miami Beach, Fla., Jan. 3, 1956) was followed by a Bway production (John Golden Th., Apr. 19, 1956). Subsequent premieres of other works by Mr. Beckett include *Fin de partie* (*Endgame*), in French, on a double bill with the mime *Acte sans paroles I* (*Act Without Words I*) (Royal Court Th., London, Apr. 3, 1957); *Endgame* in English (Cherry Lane Th., N.Y.C., Jan. 28, 1958); *Krapp's Last Tape* (Royal Court Th., London, Oct. 28, 1958; Provincetown Playhouse, N.Y.C., Jan. 14, 1960); *Act Without Words* (Living Th., Dec. 14, 1959); *Act Without Words II* (Institute of Contemporary Arts, London, Jan. 25, 1960); *La dernière bande*, the first production in French of *Krapp's Last Tape* (Th. Récamier, Paris, France, Mar. 22, 1960); and *Happy Days* (Cherry Lane Th., N.Y.C., Sept. 17, 1961), presented in France as *Oh, les beaux jours* (Odéon-Th. de France, Paris, Oct. 29, 1963).

Mr. Beckett's *Play* was first produced in West Germany as *Spiel* (Ulmer Th., Ulm, June 14, 1963), then in the US (Cherry Lane Th., N.Y.C., Jan. 4, 1964) and in France, as *Comédie* (Pavillon de Marsan, Paris, June 14, 1964). *Come and Go*, a three-minute sketch, was also first produced in West Germany, as *Kommen und Gehen* (Werkstatt des Schiller-Theaters, Berlin, Sept. 1965, followed by a French production, *Va et vient*, directed by Mr. Beckett (Odéon-Th. de France, Paris, Feb. 28, 1966); the first English-language production was staged in Ireland (Peacock Th., Dublin, Feb. 28, 1968). Mr. Beckett's brief sketch *Breath*, about half a minute in length, was written for the revue *Oh, Calcutta!* (Eden Th., N.Y.C., June 16, 1969) and first produced by itself in Scotland (Glasgow, Oct. 1969). The world premiere of Mr. Beckett's *Not I* was presented during a N.Y.C. Beckett festival (Forum Th., Lincoln Ctr., Nov. 22, 1972) and was followed by the British premiere (Royal Court Th., London, Jan. 16, 1973).

Films. Mr. Beckett wrote the scenario for the motion picture *Film* (Evergreen Th., 1965).

Television and Radio. Mr. Beckett wrote in English three radio plays, all of which were first broadcast in England on the BBC: *All That Fall* (Jan. 13, 1957), *Embers* (June 24, 1959), and *Words and Music* (Nov. 13, 1962). In French, he wrote the radio play *Cascando*, first broadcast in France (O.R.T.F., Oct. 13, 1963). His television play *Eh Joe* was first produced in West Germany as *He, Joe* (Süddeutscher Rundfunk, Apr. 13, 1955), directed by Mr. Beckett; the first production in English was on the BBC (July 4, 1966).

Other Activities. Mr. Beckett taught at Campbell Coll., Belfast (1927–28); was English lecturer at the Ecole Normale Supérieure, Paris (1928); and assistant lecturer in French at Trinity Coll., Dublin (1930–32). He also did secretarial work for James Joyce.

Published Works. In addition to plays, Mr. Beckett's works include poems, criticism, short stories, and novels. He wrote the essay "Dante. . . Bruno, Vico. . . Joyce," which appeared in *Our Exagmination round His Factification for Incamination of Work in Progress* (1929); the critical study *Proust* (1931); a collection of short stories, *More Pricks Than Kicks* 1934); a collection of poems, *Echo's Bones and Other Precipitates* (1935); and the novel *Murphy* (1938). These were written in English. After World War II, Mr. Beckett wrote in French, and his first published works in that language were three novels: *Molloy* (1951; English translation, 1955); *Malone meurt* (1951; translated as *Malone Dies*, 1956); and *L'Innommable* (1953; translated as *The Unnamable*, 1958). The novel *Watt*, also published in 1953, had been written in English by Mr. Beckett in 1942.

Other published works include *Nouvelles et textes pour rien* (1955; translated as *Stories and Texts for Nothing*, 1967); the novel *Comment C'est* (1961; translated as *How It Is*, 1964); *Sans* (1969; translated as *Lessness*, 1970); and the novel *Mercier et Camier* (1970; English translation, 1974); the last of these had been written by Mr. Beckett in 1946, his first work in French. He also wrote *Premier Amour* (1970; English translation *First Love and Other Shorts*, 1974) and *Le Dépeupleur* (1971; English translation *The Lost Ones*, 1972). Mr. Beckett also translated on commission from UNESCO *Anthology of Mexican Poetry* (1949–50) and translated, alone or in collaboration, most of his works from the original English or French into French or English, respectively.

Awards. Mr. Beckett was awarded the Nobel Prize for Literature in 1969, and he shared with Jorge Luis Borges the first International Publishers' Prize (1961). Plays of his that have received *Village Voice* off-Bway (Obie) awards include: *Endgame* (1958), *Krapp's Last Tape* (1960), *Happy Days* (1962), *Play* (1964), and *Not I* (1973). *Film* received the Diploma of Merit at the 1965 Venice Film Festival, was named one of the outstanding films of the year at the 1965 London Film Festival, received the prize for film shorts at the 1966 Oberhausen (W. Germany) Film Festival, and received a special jury prize at the 1966 Tours (France) Film Festival. Mr. Beckett was awarded the honorary degree of D.Litt. by Trinity Coll., Dublin, in 1959.

BEDELIA, BONNIE. Actress. b. Bonnie Bedelia Culkin, Mar. 25, 1948, New York City, to Philip Harley and Marian (Wagner) Culkin. Attended Hunter Coll., N.Y.C., 1965–66. Member of AEA; AFTRA; SAG. Address: c/o Lew Sherrell, 8961 Sunset Blvd., Los Angeles, CA 90069.

Theatre. Miss Bedelia made her Bway debut as Kathy Lanen in *Isle of Children* (Cort, May 16, 1962). She replaced (Mar. 1964) Barbara Dana as Wanda in *Enter Laughing* (Henry Miller's Th., Mar. 13, 1963), playing the role for the last two weeks of the play's N.Y.C. engagement; was Pauline in *The Playroom* (Brooks Atkinson Th., Dec. 5, 1965); and Marlene Chambers in *My Sweet Charlie* (Longacre, Dec. 6, 1966). As a member of the Inner City Repertory Co., Los Angeles, she appeared as Laura Wingfield in *The Glass Menagerie* (1967), Nina in *The Seagull* (1968), and was in *A Midsummer Night's Dream* (1968).

Films. Miss Bedelia's films include *The Gypsy Moths* (MGM, 1968); *They Shoot Horses, Don't They?* (Cinerama, 1969); and *Lovers and Other Strangers* (ABC Pictures, 1970).

Television. Miss Bedelia was in *My Father and My Mother* (CBS Playhouse, Feb. 13, 1968) and has appeared on such programs as Judd for the Defense (ABC, Nov. 1968); High Chaparral (NBC, Nov. 1968); Then Came Bronson (NBC, Mar. 1969); Bonanza (NBC, 1969, 1972); and *Sandcastles* (CBS, Oct. 1972).

BEDFORD, BRIAN. Actor. b. Brian Anthony Bedford, Feb. 16, 1935, Morley, Yorkshire, England, to Arthur and Ellen (O'Donnell) Bedford. Father, postal clerk. Attended St. Bede's Sch., Bradford, England, 1946–51; grad. RADA, 1955. Member of AEA; British AEA. Address: c/o Peter Witt Associates, Inc., 37 W. 57th St., New York, NY 10019.

Theatre. Mr. Bedford first appeared on stage as the Virgin Mary in a school nativity play (1946); subsequently played Decius Brutus in *Julius Caesar* (Bradford Civic Playhouse, Eng., Sept. 1951); made his professional debut as a Neighbor in *Desire Under the Elms* ("Q" Th., London, Mar. 9, 1955); Travis de Coppet in *The Young and the Beautiful* (Arts Th., London, Aug. 15, 1956); joined (1956) the Liverpool Repertory Co., playing Paul D'Argenson in *Sabrina Fair,* Hugo and Frederic in *Ring Round the Moon,* Capt. Absolute in *The Rivals,* and the title role in *Hamlet.*

At the Shakespeare Memorial Th., Stratford-upon-Avon, he played Arviragus in *Cymbeline* (July 2, 1957), and Ariel in *The Tempest* (Aug. 13, 1957); appeared as Rodolpho in *A View from the Bridge* (Comedy Th., London, Oct. 11, 1957); and Clive Harrington in *Five Finger Exercise* (Comedy Th., July 17, 1958), which he also played in N.Y.C. (Music Box Th., Dec. 2, 1959), and on the subsequent US tour (opened Walnut St. Th., Philadelphia, Pa., Oct. 3, 1960; closed Hartman Th., Columbus, Ohio, Apr. 22, 1961).

Mr. Bedford appeared as David Rodingham in *Write Me a Murder* (Lyric, London, May 13, 1962); Derek Pengo in *Lord Pengo* (Royale, N.Y.C., Nov 19, 1962); Louis Dubedat in *The Doctor's Dilemma* (Haymarket Th., London, Apr. 2, 1963); Tchaik in *The Private Ear* and *The Public Eye* (Morosco, N.Y.C., Oct. 9, 1963); and as Tom in *The Knack* (New Th., May 27, 1964), also in Los Angeles, Calif. (Huntington Hartford Th.) in a production that he also directed.

He was James in *The Astrakhan Coat* (Helen Hayes Th., N.Y.C., Jan. 12, 1967); the General in *The Unknown Soldier and His Wife* (Vivian Beaumont Th., July 6, 1967); Lot in *The Seven Descents of Myrtle* (Ethel Barrymore Th., Mar. 27, 1968); Edward in *The Cocktail Party* (Lyceum, Oct. 7, 1968); Acaste in *The Misanthrope* (Lyceum, Oct. 9, 1968); appeared at the American Shakespeare Festival, Stratford, Conn., playing the title role in Hamlet (June 18, 1969) and as Tusenbach in *The Three Sisters* (July 23, 1969); played Elyot Chase in *Private Lives* (Billy Rose Th., N.Y.C., Dec. 4, 1969); Arnolphe in *The School for Wives* (Lyceum, Feb. 16, 1971) and on the subsequent national tour (opened Huntington Hartford Th., Los Angeles, Calif., Aug. 23, 1971; closed O'Keefe Center, Toronto, Ontario, Canada, Jan. 15, 1972); appeared at the Academy Playhouse, Lake Forest, Ill., in *The Tavern* and as Charles Condomine in *Blithe Spirit* (Summer 1972); toured (1973) as Ben in *Butley;* repeated his performance as the General in *The Unknown Soldier and His Wife* (London, England, Jan. 11, 1973); and played the role of George in *Jumpers* (Eisenhower Th., John F. Kennedy Center, Washington, D.C., Feb. 18, 1974; Billy Rose Th., N.Y.C., Apr. 22, 1974).

Films. Mr. Bedford made his screen debut in *Man of the Moment* (Pinewood, 1955); subsequently appeared in *Miracle in Soho* (Rank, 1957); *The Angry Silence* (VAT, 1960); *Number Six* (Merton Park, 1961); *The Punch and Judy Man* (Elstree, 1962); *The Pad (and How to Use It)* (U, 1966); and *Grand Prix* (MGM, 1966).

Television. He first appeared as Johnny in *The Appleyards* (BBC, London, 1955); subsequently played in *Madeleine* (BBC, 1955); *Winterset* (ATV, 1957); *Squaring the Circle* (ATV, 1958); *As the Twig Is Bent* (ATV, 1958); *The Secret Thread* (BBC, 1961); Sir Francis Drake series (1961); and *The Judge and His Hangman* (BBC, 1962). Mr. Bedford also appeared in *Lady with a Lamp* (Hallmark); as Shakespeare in *The Dark Lady of the Sonnets* (PBS, 1966); and in the musical version of *Androcles and the Lion* (NBC, Nov. 15, 1967). He has been on the Dick Cavett (ABC), Merv Griffin, and David Frost shows; was a regular on the series Coronet Blue; and has appeared in episodes of Judd for the Defense; Ben Casey; The Name of the Game; and Nanny and the Professor.

Awards. Mr. Bedford received from RADA the H. M. Tennent Award (two-year contract with Tennent Productions) and The Liverpool Playhouse Award (one-year contract with the Liverpool Repertory Co.). He was cited by the Obie Award committee (1965) for his performance in *The Knack;* received (1969) a Drama Desk Award for his performance in *The Misanthrope;* the Los Angeles Critics', Outer Circle, and Drama Desk awards (1970) for his performance in *Private Lives;* and the Los Angeles Critics', Drama Desk, and Tony awards (1971) for his performance in *The School for Wives.*

Recreation. For recreation, Mr. Bedford says he enjoys going to movies; "dabbling" in real estate; and "living in the country and cooking.".

BEHN, NOEL. Producer, author. b. Jan. 6, 1928, Chicago, Ill., to Jack and Dorothy (Polakow) Behn. Father, food broker. Grad. Highland Park (Ill.) H.S., 1946; attended Univ. of Wyoming, 1946–47; grad. Stanford Univ., B.A. 1950; studied at Univ. of Paris (Fr.), 1950–51. Served US Army, CIC, 1952–54. Married 1956 to Jo Ann Lecompte (marr. dis. 1961). Relative in theatre: Lester Polakov, stage designer. Member of League of Off-Bway Theatres (co-fdr. and dir., 1958–62); Musical and Dramatic Th. Acad., pres., until 1962).

Theatre. Mr. Behn produced *The Plough and the Stars* (Cherry Lane, N.Y.C., 1953; East Chop Playhouse, Martha's Vineyard, Mass., Summer 1953); presented *In the Zone, Liliom, The Time of Your Life, An Inspector Calls, Boy Meets Girl, Hay Fever,* and *The Plough and the Stars* (East Chop Playhouse, Martha's Vineyard, Mass., Summer 1954); was company manager (Flint Musical Tent Th., Mich., Summer 1955); in N.Y.C., operated the Cherry Lane Th.; produced Hal Holbrook's one-man show, *Mark Twain Tonight,* as a Monday night special (Cherry Lane); and with Paul Shyre, Howard Gottfried, and Lewis Marilow, presented *Purple Dust* (Cherry Lane, Dec. 27, 1956).

He was producer of *The Circus of Dr. Lao, My Three Angels, The Affairs of Anatol, Father of the Bride* and *The Matchmaker* (Edgewater Beach Playhouse, Chicago, Ill., Summer 1957); produced with Rooftop Productions, *Endgame* (Cherry Lane, N.Y.C., Jan. 28, 1958); presented *The Remarkable Mr. Pennypacker, The Little Hut, Sweet and Sour, Kind Sir* and *Uncle Willie* (Edgewater Beach Playhouse, Chicago, Ill., Summer 1958); and *Caesar and Cleopatra, Tall Story, Time for Elizabeth, Once More, With Feeling,* and *Law and Mr. Simon* (Edgewater Beach Playhouse, Chicago, Ill., Summer 1959); was producer, with the New Princess Co., of *Gay Divorce* (Cherry Lane, N.Y.C., Apr. 3, 1960); producer, with Robert Kamlot of *Ernest in Love* (Gramercy Arts, May 4, 1960); and producer of a Monday night special, *A Curious Evening with Gypsy Rose Lee* (Cherry Lane); presented *Not in the Book, Good-bye Again, Craig's Wife, Two for the Seesaw,* and *Make a Million* (Edgewater Beach Playhouse, Chicago, Ill., Summer 1960); and presented, with Robert Costello, *"Elsa Lanchester—Herself"* (41 St. Th., N.Y.C., Feb. 4, 1961).

Published Works. Mr. Behn wrote *The Kremlin Letter* (1966) and *The Shadow Boxer* (1969).

Awards. His production of *Endgame* won the *Village Voice* Off-Bway (Obie) Award (1958).

BEIN, ALBERT. Playwright. b. May 18, 1902, Kishinev, Romania, to Louis and Sarah Bein. Father, watchmaker. Member of Dramatists Guild.

Theatre. Mr. Bein wrote *Little Ol' Boy* (Playhouse, Apr. 24, 1933); *Let Freedom Ring,* which he also produced, with Jack Goldsmith (Broadhurst, Nov. 6, 1935); *Heavenly Express* (National, Apr. 18, 1940); and wrote, with Mary Bein, and produced, with Frederick Fox, *Land of Fame* (Belasco, Sept. 1, 1943).

Films. He wrote the film script for *Boy Slaves* (RKO, 1939).

Awards. Mr. Bein was awarded a Guggenheim Fellowship (1936).

Recreation. Chess.

BEL GEDDES, BARBARA. Actress. b. Barbara Geddes, Oct. 31, 1922, New York City, to Norman Bel and Helen Belle (Sneider) Geddes. Father, designer, producer, architect. Grad. Andebrook Sch., Tarrytown, N.Y., 1940. Married Jan. 24, 1944, to Carl Schreuer, engineer (marr. dis. 1951); one daughter; married Apr. 15, 1951, to Windsor Lewis, producer, director; one daughter. Member of AEA; SAG; AFTRA.

Theatre. Miss Bel Geddes first appeared on stage as a walk-on in a stock production of *The School for Scandal* (Clinton Playhouse, Conn., July 1940); also at the Clinton Playhouse (1940), appeared in *Tonight at 8:30, The World We Make,* and played Amy in *Little Women.*

She made her N.Y.C. debut as Dottie Coburn in *Out of the Frying Pan* (Windsor, Feb. 11, 1941); subsequently toured military camps as Judy in a USO production of *Junior Miss* (1942); played Cynthia Brown in *Little Darling* (Biltmore, N.Y.C., Oct. 27, 1942); Alice in *Nine Girls* (Longacre, Jan. 13, 1943); at the Newport (R.I.) Casino (Summer 1943), appeared as Ellen Murray in *Yes, My Darling Daughter* and played the title role in *Claudia;* played Wilhelmina in *Mrs. January and Mr. X* (Belasco, N.Y.C., Mar. 31, 1944); Genevra Langdon in *Deep Are the Roots* (Fulton, Sept. 26, 1945); Mordeen in *Burning Bright* (Broadhurst, Oct. 18, 1950); and Patty O'Neill in *The Moon Is Blue* (Henry Miller's Th., Mar. 8, 1951).

At the Robin Hood Th. (Wilmington, Del.), Miss Bel Geddes appeared in plays produced by her husband, Windsor Lewis: Julie in *Liliom,* Billie Dawn in *Born Yesterday,* Lizzie McKaye in *The Respectful Prostitute* (Summer 1952); the title role in *Claudia,* Sally Middleton in *The Voice of the Turtle,* and appeared in *The Winter Palace* (Summer 1953). She toured summer theatres as Susan in *The Little Hut* (1954); played Rose Pemberton in *The Living Room* (Henry Miller's Th., N.Y.C., Nov. 17, 1954); Maggie in *Cat on a Hot Tin Roof* (Morosco, Mar. 24, 1955); Mary in *The Sleeping Prince* (Coronet, Nov. 1, 1956); Katherine Johnson in *Silent Night, Lonely Night* (Morosco, Dec. 3, 1959); and Mary McKellaway in *Mary, Mary* (Helen Hayes Th., Mar. 8, 1961).

She toured as Constance Middleton in *The Constant Wife* (Summer 1964); was in *Love and Marriage* (Tappan Zee Playhouse, Nyack, N.Y., Aug. 31, 1964); repeated her performance as Mary McKellaway in *Mary, Mary* (Warwick Musical Th., Warwick, R.I., July 26, 1965); played Alice Potter in the pre-Bway tryout of *The Porcelain Year* (opened Locust St. Th., Philadelphia, Pa., Oct. 11, 1965; closed Shubert Th., New Haven, Conn., Nov. 13, 1965); Ellen Manville in *Luv* (Royal Poinciana Playhouse, Palm Beach, Fla., Jan. 17, 1966); succeeded (Mar. 2, 1966) Anne Bancroft in that part in the N.Y.C. production of *Luv* (Booth Th., Nov. 11, 1964); was Jenny in *Everything in the Garden* (Plymouth, Nov. 29, 1967); and Katy Cooper in *Finishing Touches* (Plymouth, Feb. 8, 1973; Ahmanson Th., Los Angeles, Calif., Dec. 4, 1973).

Films. Miss Bel Geddes made her first appearance in *The Long Night* (RKO, 1947); followed by roles in *I Remember Mama* (RKO, 1948); *Blood on the Moon* (RKO, 1948); *Caught* (MGM, 1949); *Panic in the Streets* (20th-Fox, 1950); *14 Hours* (20th-Fox, 1951); *Vertigo* (Par., 1959); *The Five Pennies* (Par., 1959); *Five Branded Women* (Par., 1960); *By Love Possessed* (UA, 1961); and *Summertree* (1971).

Television. She appeared in *Isn't Everything* (Campbell Television Soundstage, NBC, 1954); *The Morning Face* (Studio One, CBS, 1957); *French Provincial* (Schlitz Playhouse, CBS, 1957); *The Desperate Age* (Studio One, CBS, 1958); *Lamb to the Slaughter* (Alfred Hitchcock Presents, CBS, 1958); *Rumors of Evening* (Playhouse, NBC, 1958); *Midsummer* (US Steel Hour, CBS, 1958); *The Hasty Heart* (Dupont Show of the Month, NBC, 1958); *Miracle for Margaret* (Dr. Kildare, NBC, 1965); and *Foghorn* and *Lamb to the Slaughter* (both Alfred Hitchcock, Ind., 1967).

Awards. She received the Clarence Derwent Award (1946) for her performance as Genevra Langdon in *Deep Are the Roots.*

Recreation. Painting, animals, travel.

BEL GEDDES, EDITH LUTYENS. Costume designer, producer, writer, costumier. b. Edith Addams de Habbelinck, Aug. 1, 1917 to Robert Francis Addams and Eliza de Habbelinck. Studied at private schools in England and Germany; attended Univ. of Brussels, Belg. Married to Archibald Charles Thacker Lutyens (marr. dis.); married to Moseley Taylor (dec.); married 1954 to Norman Bel Geddes, designer, producer, architect (dec.). Member of Theatrical Garment Workers Union; Ladies Garment Union (A.F.L.); Theatrical Designers Union; ALA. Address: 125 E. 57th St, New York, NY 10022.

Pre-Theatre. Translator.

Theatre. Mrs. Lutyens Bel Geddes executed the costumes for the Ballet Theatre production of *Dim Lustre, Tally-Ho,* and *Fancy Free* (Metropolitan Opera House, N.Y.C., Oct. 20, 1943). In association with Chandler Cowles and Efrem Zimbalist, Jr., she produced *The Medium* and *The Telephone* Ethel Barrymore Th., May 1, 1947), which, by arrangement with Mrs. Lutyens Bel Geddes and Messrs. Cowles and Zimbalist, was presented at NY City Ctr. (Dec. 7, 1948).

She executed costumes for *Anne of the Thousand Days* (Shubert, Dec. 8, 1948); *Gentlemen Prefer Blondes* (Ziegfeld, Dec. 8, 1948); *South Pacific* (Majestic, Apr. 7, 1949); *The Liar* (Broadhurst, May 18, 1950); *Ring Round the Moon* (Martin Beck Th., Nov. 23, 1950); designed the costumes for *The Shrike* (Cort, Jan. 15, 1952); for *The Crucible* (Martin Beck Th., Jan. 22, 1953); and for *A Girl Can Tell* (Royale, Oct. 29, 1953); and supervised, executed, and co-designed costumes for *Ondine* (46 St. Th., Feb. 18, 1954).

She did the costumes for the Ringling Bros. and Barnum and Bailey's combined circus (Madison Square Garden, N.Y.C., Spring 1954); designed the costumes for *Wedding Breakfast* (48 St. Th., Nov. 20, 1954); executed the costumes for The Hollywood Ice Revue and its tour (1955); designed the costumes for *Kicks and Co.* (opened Arie Crown Th., Chicago, Ill., Oct. 11, 1961; closed Oct. 14, 1961); *Do You Know the Milky Way!* (Billy Rose Th., N.Y.C., Oct. 16, 1961); *A Gift of Time* (Ethel Barrymore Th., Feb. 22, 1962); *Dear Me, the Sky Is Falling* (Music Box, Mar. 2, 1963); *Too True To Be Good* (54 St. Th., Mar. 12, 1963); *Bicycle Ride to Nevada* (Cort, Sept. 24, 1963); *The Deputy* (Brooks Atkinson Th., Feb. 26, 1964); *The Web and the Rock* (Th. de Lys, Mar. 19, 1972); and *The Divorce of Judy and Jane* (Bijou, Apr. 26, 1972).

Mrs. Lutyens Bel Geddes has also been artistic consultant for the Robert Joffrey ballet company and designed costumes for the Joffrey's *The Clowns;* has served as president of Ballet Hispanico, for which she has also designed costumes; and she designed costumes for the Alvin Ailey ballet *The Road of Phoebe Snow.*

Films. Mrs. Lutyens Bel Geddes designed the costumes for *So Young, So Bad* (UA, 1950); and *The Trouble with Harry* (Par., 1955).

Other Activities. She was a member of the Belgium Women's Fencing Team in the Olympic Games; publisher of *Theatre Arts* Magazine (1958–60); and has been a contributing editor for *Theatrical Costume.*

Awards. Mrs. Lutyens Bel Geddes received the George J. Nathan Award for her costumes in *The Crucible* (1953); and with Richard Whorf, the Antoinette Perry (Tony) Award for the costumes in *Ondine* (1954).

Recreation. Fencing, fishing, traveling, cooking, snorkeling.

BELKIN, JEANNA. Assistant stage manager, choreographic assistant, dancer, dance teacher. b. Apr. 13, 1924, New York, N.Y., to Sam and Ida (Lukin) Belkin. Father, dental mechanic; mother, underwear manufacturer. Educ. Samuel J. Tilden H.S., Roosevelt Coll., and Brooklyn Coll., all in N.Y.C. Professional training at School of American Ballet, Emily Frankel (ballet); Hanya Holm School (modern dance); Matt Mattox, Frank Wagner, Luigi's American Dance Center (jazz). Married Apr. 16, 1950, to Sidney Klein, surgical supply manufacturer; one daughter. Member of AEA (chorus councillor, 1955–65; 2nd vice-pres., 1965–70; 4th vice-pres., 1970–73; 3rd vice-pres., 1973–to date; delegate to Associated Actors and Artistes of America, 1970–to date); AGMA; AFTRA; SAG; Assoc. of Amer. Dance Companies. Address: 941 Washington Ave., Brooklyn, NY 11225, tel. (212) 287-9655.

Theatre. Miss Belkin began her theatrical career in Jan. 1945 touring as a dancer in the chorus of the national company of *One Touch of Venus.* She was a dancer in *A Flag is Born* (Alvin Th., N.Y.C., Sept. 5, 1946); went on tour as a chorus dancer in the national company of *Call Me Mister* (Oct. 21, 1946); danced in the Lemonade Opera Co's. *Down in the Valley* and *Man in the Moon* (N.Y.C., 1948); toured as a chorus dancer in *Make Mine Manhattan* (Feb. 14, 1949); was a dancer in *Two's Company* (Alvin Th., N.Y.C., Dec. 15, 1952); appeared in summer stock as the lead dancer in *One Touch of Venus* (Cape Cod Melody Tent, Hyannis, Mass., Aug. 31, 1953); danced in *Girl in Pink Tights* (Mark Hellinger Th., N.Y.C., Mar. 5, 1954); *Sandhog* (Phoenix, Nov. 29, 1954); *Hit the Trail* (Mark Hellinger Th., Dec. 2, 1954); a revival of *Guys and Dolls* (NY City Ctr., Apr. 20, 1955); *Reuben, Reuben* (pre-Bway, Sept. 8, 1955, closed Boston); and was dancer-captain at the Oakdale Music Th., Wallingford, Conn. (Summer 1956). She toured in the Chevrolet show as a dancer (Sept. 1956); was dancer-captain in a revival of *Brigadoon* (NY City Ctr., Mar. 27, 1957); was choreographic assistant at the Westbury (N.Y.) Music Fair (Summer 1957); danced in *Body Beautiful* (Bway Th., N.Y.C., Jan. 23, 1958); was dancer-captain at the Colonie Music Fair, Latham, N.Y. (Summer 1958); and danced in *Whoop-Up* (Shubert Th., Dec. 22, 1958).

She was a dancer in *Fiorello!* (Broadhurst, N.Y.C., Nov. 23, 1959); was dancer-captain at the South Shore Music Circus, Cohasset, Mass. (Summer 1960); of the touring Chevrolet show (Aug. 9, 1961); danced in a revival of *Fiorello!* (NY City Ctr., June 13, 1962); was dancer-captain of the touring Chevrolet show (July 1962); danced in and played the Second Girl off-Bway in *The Dragon* (Phoenix, N.Y.C., Apr. 9, 1963); toured as Maggie in a stock production of *Brigadoon* (Summer 1963); danced in a dinner theatre production of *Can-Can* (Meadowbrook, N.Y., Mar. 1964); in *That Hat!* (Th. Four, N.Y.C., Sept. 23, 1964); and danced in and was assistant to the choreographer for *The Most Happy Fella* (Paper Mill, Millburn, N.J.; Mineola, N.Y., Mar. 1965); was assistant to the choreographer for *Brigadoon* (Pabst Th., Milwaukee, Wis., Dec. 1965); for *Tenth Man* (Mineola, N.Y., Jan. 1966); and for appearances of the Sophie Maslow Dance Co. at Brooklyn Coll. (Apr. 30, 1966). She was also assistant stage manager for a revival of *Annie Get Your Gun* (Broadway Th., Sept. 21, 1966); assistant to the choreographer for *On a Clear Day* (Paper Mill, Millburn, N.J., Mar. 1967); assistant stage manager for *Love Match* (pre-Bway, opened Nov. 3, 1968; closed Ahmanson Th., Los Angeles, Calif., Jan. 4, 1969); for *Jimmy* (Winter Garden, N.Y.C., Oct. 23, 1969); and for the Philadelphia Drama Guild, Walnut St. Th., Philadelphia, Pa., for *The Imaginary Invalid, Born Yesterday,* and *The Rivals* (1971–72); *Volpone, Tartuffe, The Waltz of the Toreadors,* and *Ceremonies in Dark Old Men* (1972–73); and *Juno and the Paycock, Death of a Salesman,* and *The Little Foxes* (Feb. 1974).

Television. On television, Miss Belkin appeared in *The Dragon* (Dupont Show of the Week, NBC, Mar. 18, 1963).

Concerts. Miss Belkin has appeared in concert as a dancer with Betty Lind and was assistant to Sophie Maslow in appearances at the YMHA, N.Y.C. She was assistant to the choreographer for the Chanukah Festivals (Madison Square Garden, N.Y.C., 1967–71).

Other Activities. Miss Belkin has taught jazz dance at the Matt Mattox School of Dance and the International School of Dance.

BELL, MARY HAYLEY. Actress, playwright, novelist. b. Jan. 22, 1914, Shanghai, China, to Francis Hayley and Agnes (MacGowan) Bell. Attended Sherborne Sch., Malvern Girls' Coll., England. Studied for the theatre at RADA, London. Married to John Mills, actor, producer, singer; one son, two daughters. Relatives in theatre: daughters, Hayley and Juliet, actresses. Address: The Wick, Richmond Hill, London, England.

Theatre. Miss Bell made her stage debut as Henrietta in *The Barretts of Wimpole Street* (Shanghai, China, 1932); made her London debut as Lissa in *Vintage Wine* (Daly's Th., May 29, 1934); played Daisy Hawkins in *Summer's Lease* (Vaudeville, Feb. 1935); and appeared with the Manchester Repertory Co. (1935). In London, she again played Lissa in *Vintage Wine* (Victoria Palace, June 22, 1935) and Carter in *The Composite Man* (Daly's, Sept. 1936).

She toured England as Lissa in *Vintage Wine* and appeared in *It's You I Want* (1936–37) and toured Australia in *Victoria Regina, Tonight at 8:30* and *George and Margaret* (1937–38). She played Agnes in *Tony Draws a Horse* (Criterion, London, Jan. 26, 1939) and succeeded (1939) Diana Churchill in the role of Clare Fleming. When the same play was produced in the US as *Billy Draws a Horse,* Miss Bell made her N.Y.C. debut as Clare (Playhouse, N.Y.C., Dec. 21, 1939).

She played Marion Fisher in *The Peaceful Inn* (Duke of York's, London, May 1940).

Miss Bell wrote *Men in Shadow* (Vaudeville, London, Sept. 3, 1942; Morosco, N.Y.C., Mar. 10, 1943); *Duet for Two Hands* (Lyric, London, June 27, 1945; Booth, N.Y.C., Oct. 7, 1947); and *Angel* (Strand, London, June 6, 1947), which was produced in N.Y.C. as *Dear Enemy* (Intimate, May 2, 1949); *The Uninvited Guest* (St. James's, London, May 27, 1953); and *Foreign Field* (Glasgow, Scotland, Sept. 15, 1953).

Films. The film, *Whistle Down the Wind* (Pathe-American Dist., 1962), was based on Miss Bell's novel of the same name.

Published Works. Miss Bell wrote the plays *Feather on the Water* (1953) and *Treble Key* (1956) and the novels *Avolena* (1957), *Whistle Down the Wind* (1959), and *Far Morning* (1962).

BELLA, JOSEPH F. Costume designer, instructor in costume design and execution. b. Joseph Francis Bella, Aug. 12, 1940, Greensburg, Pa., to Joseph Albert and Frances (Dengg) Bella. Father, cost clerk. Educ. Cathedral Catholic School, Greensburg; Greensburg High School; Carnegie Mellon Univ., B.F.A.; and Catholic Univ. of America. Member of United Scenic Artists. Address: (home) 305 W. 18th St., Apt 5G, New York, NY 10011, tel. (212) 675-6399; (bus.) Montclair State College, Normal Ave. and Valley Rd., Upper Montclair, NJ 07043, tel. (201) 893-5130.

Pre-Theatre. Mr. Bella was a dress designer for Aremis Fashions and a pattern maker with Spartan Industries.

Theatre. Mr. Bella was a costume designer for productions at Catholic Univ. Of America, Washington, D.C. (Sept. 1962–May 1965), including *Medea* (Jan. 1963) and *Good Morning, Miss Dove* (Jan. 1964); instructor of costume design and costume supervisor for thirty productions at Carnegie Mellon Univ., Pittsburgh, Pa. (Sept. 1965–May 1968); and adjunct assistant professor in theatre arts, Hunter College, N.Y.C. (Sept. 1970–May 1973); and became assistant professor of costume design, Montclair State College, Upper Montclair, N.J., in Sept. 1973.

In summer theatre, Mr. Bella's first work was as an apprentice at William Penn Playhouse, Delmont, Pa. (June 1958). Later, he was costume designer for Olney (Md.) Theatre (June 1963–Aug. 1967) productions, including *Plays from Bleeker Street* (June 1963) and *Mother Courage* (July 1964), and for seven productions at the Great Lakes Shakespeare Festival, Lakewood, Ohio (June–Aug. 1966; June–Aug. 1967). For opera, he designed costumes for nine Baltimore (Md.) Opera Co. productions (Jan. 1969–Jan. 1973), including *Manon Lescaut* (Feb. 1969); for Opera Society of Washington (D.C.) productions of *La Bohème* (Mar. 1970), *Koanga* (American premiere, Dec. 1970), and *Falstaff* (Dec. 1971); and for the Lake George (N.Y.) Opera Co. production of *La Bohème* (July 1970).

Mr. Bella was costume designer for the off-Bway *Philosophy in the Boudoir* (Gramercy Arts, N.Y.C., May 21, 1969); he was stage, costume, and lighting designer for the productions by the National Players, Washington, D.C., of *King Lear* and *The Lady's Not for Burning* (Sept. 1969); costume designer for ten productions at Walnut St. Th., Philadelphia, Pa. (Sept. 1971–Jan. 1974), including *The Imaginary Invalid, Born Yesterday, Tartuffe, The Rose Tattoo,* and *The Taming of the Shrew;* for *The Fourposter* (Windmill Dinner Th., Dallas, Tex., May 1972); and for *The Waltz of the Toreadors* (John F. Kennedy Ctr., Washington, D.C., June 19, 1973; Circle in the Square/Joseph E. Levine Th., N.Y.C., Sept. 13, 1973).

Films. Mr. Bella designed costumes for *The House That Screamed Murder* (Golden Gate Films, 1972).

Awards. At Carnegie Mellon Univ., Mr. Bella received the Boettcher Scholarship for professional promise.

Recreation. Music, painting.

BELLAMY, RALPH. Actor. b. June 17, 1904, Chicago, Ill., to Rexford and Lilla Louise (Smith) Bellamy. Father, advertising executive. Grad. New Trier H.S., Winnetka, Ill., 1922. Married Nov. 27, 1949, to Alice Murphy. Member of AEA (vice-pres., 1949–52; pres., 1952–1964); SAG; AFTRA; The Players (bd. of dir., 1959–63); The Lambs (bd. of dir., 1950–54); Dutch Treat Club. Address: c/o Milton Grossman, 8730 Sunset Blvd., Los Angeles, CA, 90069.

Theatre. Mr. Bellamy made his professional debut as Old Matt and Wash Gibbs in *The Shepherd of the Hills* (Chautauqua Circuit, Midwest tour, May 1922); and subsequently was stage manager for stock companies in Madison, Wis., and Evansville, Ind. (1922–23). From 1924–30, he appeared with the Beach and Jones and John Wininger traveling repertory companies, and as leading man with stock companies in Terre Haute, Ind.; St. Joseph, Mo.; Waterloo, Iowa; Jamestown, N.Y.; Rochester, N.Y.; Fort Wayne, Ind.; and Freeport, N.Y.; and with his own stock companies in Des Moines, Iowa; Nashville, Tenn.; and Evanston, Ill.

Mr. Bellamy made his Bway debut as Ben Davis in *Town Boy* (Belmont, Oct. 4, 1929); played Texas in *Roadside* (Longacre, Sept. 25, 1930); Michael Frame in *Tomorrow the World* (Ethel Barrymore Th., Apr. 14, 1943); directed *Pretty Little Parlor,* which he produced with John Moses (Natl., Apr. 17, 1944); appeared as Grant Matthews in *State of the Union* (Hudson, Nov. 14, 1945); Detective McLeod in *Detective Story* (Hudson, Mar. 23, 1949); and Franklin D. Roosevelt in *Sunrise at Campobello,* (Cort, Jan. 30, 1958), which he also played on tour (opened Blackstone, Chicago, Ill., Sept. 21, 1959; closed, Tower Th., Atlanta, Ga., Jan. 30, 1960).

Films. Among the ninety-six films that Mr. Bellamy has made to date are *Secret Six* (MGM, 1931), in which he made his motion picture debut. He subsequently appeared in *The Magnificent Lie* (Par., 1931); *Surrender* (20th-Fox, 1931); *Forbidden* (Col., 1931); *West of Broadway,* (MGM, 1932); *Wild Fire* (RKO, 1932); *Dishonorable Discharge* (20th-Fox, 1932); *Air Mail* (U, 1932); *Young America* (20th-Fox, 1932); *Picture Snatcher* (WB, 1933); *This Man Is Mine* (RKO, 1934); *Hands Across the Table* (Par., 1935); *Wedding Night* (UA, 1935); *The Man Who Lived Twice* (Col., 1936); *The Awful Truth* (Col., 1937); *Trade Winds* (UA, 1938); *Boy Meets Girl* (WB, 1938); *Rebecca of Sunnybrook Farm* (20th-Fox, 1938); *Carefree* (RKO, 1938); *Blind Alley* (Col., 1939); *His Girl Friday* (U, 1940); *Dive Bomber* (WB, 1941); *Great Impersonation* (U, 1942); *Lady in a Jam* (U, 1942); *Guest in the House* (UA, 1944); *Lady on a Train* (U, 1945); *The Court-Martial of Billy Mitchell* (WB, 1955); *Delightfully Dangerous* (UA, 1955); and *Sunrise at Campobello* (WB, 1960); *The Professionals* (Col., 1966); *Rosemary's Baby* (Par., 1968); *Doctors' Wives* (Col., 1971); and *Cancel My Reservation* (WB, 1972).

Television and Radio. Mr. Bellamy has appeared on many radio and television programs, including the Phillip Morris Show; the Rudy Vallee Fleischmann Hour (NBC); the Kate Smith Show; the Gertrude Lawrence Show; Armstrong Th. of the Air; Cresta Blanca Show; International Silver Show; Helen Hayes Th. (CBS); Th. of Romance; Th. Wing; the Martin and Lewis Show; the Barry Wood-Patsy Kelly Show; the Bing Crosby Show (NBC); Inner Sanctum; the Cecil B. de Mille Show; and Suspense.

He was master of ceremonies on Stage Door Canteen and appeared also as a guest star on Screen Directors Show; the Donald O'Connor Show; To Tell the Truth; World Premiere; Th. Guild—US Steel; Four Star Th.; Bell Telephone Hour (NBC); Perry Como Show (NBC); Armstrong Circle Th. (NBC); the Sid Caesar Show (ABC); What's My Line? (CBS); The F.B.I. (ABC); the Dick Powell Show (NBC); Person to Person (CBS); Route 66 (CBS); Man Against Crime (CBS, 1949–54); US Steel Hour (ABC, 1954, 1956, 1957); Hallmark Hall of Fame (NBC, 1955); GE Th. (CBS, 1955); Philco Playhouse (NBC, 1955, 1956); Studio One (CBS, 1955, 1957); Zane Grey Th. (CBS), 1956); Ford Th. (NBC and ABC, 1956); Playhouse 90 (CBS, 1956); Climax (CBS, 1956, 1957); Kraft Th. (NBC, 1957); the Barbara Stanwyck Show (NBC, 1960); the Dinah Shore Show (NBC, 1961); the documentary film *The Good Ship Hope* (NBC, 1961); Rawhide (CBS, 1961, 1965); Alcoa Premiere (ABC, 1963); Dr. Kildare (NBC, 1963); Death Valley Days (ABC, 1963); Eleventh Hour (NBC, 1963–64); Bob Hope Chrysler Th. (NBC, 1967); Run for Your Life (NBC, 1967); Gunsmoke (CBS, 1967); 12 O'Clock High (ABC, 1967); CBS Playhouse (CBS, 1968); The Survivors (ABC, 1969); and Most Deadly Game (ABC, 1970).

Other Activities. Mr. Bellamy was on the national board of Project Hope (1964); a member of the California State Arts Commission (1964–67); and he became a director of Theatre Vision in 1971.

Awards. Mr. Bellamy was nominated for an Academy (Oscar) Award for his performance in *The Awful Truth* (1937); received an Academy of Radio and Television Arts and Sciences Award for his performance on Man Against Crime (1950); and the Antoinette Perry (Tony) Award, the Delia Austrian Award, and won the *Variety* NY Drama Critics Poll (1958), for his performance as Franklin D. Roosevelt in *Sunrise at Campobello.*

BELLAVER, HARRY. Actor. b. Enrico Bellaver, Feb. 12, 1905, Hillsboro, Ill., to Matteo and Maria (Cora) Bellaver. Father, coal miner. Attended elementary sch., Hillsboro, 1911–18; Brookwood Labor Coll., 1926–28; studied with A. J. Muste, Tom Tippett, Arthur Calhoun, and Jasper Deeter. Married Jan. 7, 1932, to Gertrude Dudley, actress; two daughters, Lee Bellaver, actress and singer; Vaughan Allentuck, actress. Served WW II, USO, North Africa and Italy. Member of AEA; SAG; AFTRA.

Pre-Theatre. Coal miner, farmer.

Theatre. Mr. Bellaver made his stage debut as a Coal Miner in *What Price Coal?* (Miners Hall, Hillsboro, Ill., June, 1925); his professional debut as Yank in *The Hairy Ape* (Hedgerow Th., Moylan, Pa., July 1928); and appeared there (1928–31, 1938) as Major Paul Petkoff in *Arms and the Man,* the Idiot Brother in *The Devil's Disciple,* Robert de Baudricourt in *St. Joan,* Jackson in *He Who Gets Slapped,* James Mayo in *Beyond the Horizon,* Lem in *The Emperor Jones,* Mark Sheffield in *The First Man,* Senator Lewis in *The Inheritors,* the title role in *Liliom,* Sam in *Lucky Sam McCarver,* Shipbuilder Aune in *The Pillars of Society,* Nils Krogstad in *A Doll's House,* Ulfheim in *When We Dead Awaken,* the Salvation Army Man in *From Morn to Midnight,* C. Rogers Forbes in *Dulcy,* Mr. Pim in *Mr. Pim Passes By,* Julius Bickel in *Rancor,* Papa in *Uncle's Been Dreaming,* the Man in *White Man,* the Stage Hand in *Cast Up By the Sea,* George in *Merry-Go-Round,* the Guy in *Pinwheel,* Walter in *Thunder on the Left,* the Dall Glic in *The Dragon,* the King in *Alice in Wonderland,* Michael James Flaherty in *Playboy of the Western World,* the title role in *The Prisoner,* the Landlord in *In Abraham's Bosom,* a Man in *The Mask and the Face,* and the Union Organizer in *The Frodi.*

He made his Bway debut as a Farmer in *The House of Connelly* for the Group Th. (Martin Beck Th., Sept. 28, 1931); with the Group Th., appeared in *1931* (Mansfield, Dec. 13, 1931), and as Diego in *Night Over Taos* (48 St. Th., Mar. 9, 1932); played Butch and Beachley in *Merry-Go-Round* (Provincetown Playhouse, Apr. 22, 1932); and in stock, appeared as Esteban in *The Great Fambombo* (Beechwood, Scarborough, N.Y., Aug. 1932).

Mr. Bellaver played the Landlord in *Carry Nation* (Biltmore, N.Y.C., Oct. 29, 1932); Mike Ramsey in *We, the People* (Empire, Jan. 21, 1933); Walter in *The Threepenny Opera* (Empire, Apr. 13, 1933); Abe (Frogface) Matz in *The Sellout* (Cort, Sept. 6, 1933); Petey in *Page Miss Glory* (Mansfield, Nov. 27, 1934); and Ham in *Noah* (Longacre, Feb. 13, 1935), a role he repeated at the Central Sch. (Glencoe, Ill., July 1935); and succeeded Vincent Sherman as Barolla in *The Black Pit* (Civic Repertory Th., Mar. 20, 1935).

Mr. Bellaver played Ruby Herter in *How Beautiful with Shoes* (Booth, Nov. 28, 1935); Pablo in *Russet Mantle* (Masque, Jan. 16, 1936), which he also played in stock (Ogunquit Playhouse, Me., July 1936); the Abbe Vignali in *St. Helena* (Lyceum, N.Y.C., Oct. 6, 1936); Horseface in the pre-Bway tryout of *Glory for All* (opened Erlanger, Philadelphia, Pa., Feb. 1937); Comrade Patayo in *To Quito and Back* (Guild, Oct. 6, 1937); Pablo Sanchez in *Tortilla Flat* (Henry Miller's Th., Jan. 12, 1938); Al in the pre-Bway tryout of *Once Upon a Night* (opened Playhouse, Wilmington, Del., Sept. 1938).

He played Domino in *Tell My Story* (Mercury, N.Y.C., Mar. 15, 1939); appeared in the pre-Bway tryouts of *She Had To Say Yes* (opened Forrest Philadelphia, Pa., 1940) and *The King's Maid* (opened Baltimore, Md., 1941); played Knuckles Kelton in *Johnny 2 × 4* (Longacre, N.Y.C., Mar. 16, 1942); Mr. Fink in *Mr. Sycamore* (Guild, Nov. 18, 1942); and Sgt. Snyder in *The World's Full of Girls* (Royale, Dec. 6, 1943).

Mr. Bellaver served with the USO as stage manager of *Over Twenty-One* (Italy and North Africa, Apr. 1944), in which he also played the role of Joel L. Nixon.

He played Chief Sitting Bull in *Annie Get Your Gun* (Imperial, May 16, 1946); and, in stock, played Eddie Carbone in *A View from the Bridge* (Rockland County Playhouse, Blauvelt, N.Y., July 1957); again played Chief Sitting Bull in a revival of *Annie Get Your Gun* (NY State Th., May 31, 1966; transferred to Broadway Th., Sept. 21, 1966); and replaced (Feb. 25–Mar. 20, 1974) Pat Hingle as the Coach in *That Championship Season* (Public Th., May 2, 1972).

Films. Mr. Bellaver made his film debut as Creeps in *Another Thin Man* (MGM, 1939); subsequently appeared in *The House on 92nd Street* (20th-Fox, 1945); in *Side Street* (MGM, 1949); *Perfect Strangers* (WB, 1950); *No Way Out* (20th-Fox, 1950); *Something to Live For* (Par., 1952); *Lemon Drop Kid* (Par., 1952); *The Stage to Tucson* (Col., 1952); *The Great Diamond Robbery* (MGM, 1952); *From Here to Eternity* (Col., 1953); *Miss Sadie Thompson* (Col., 1953); *Love Me or Leave Me* (MGM, 1955); *The Birds and the Bees* (Par., 1956); *Serenade* (WB, 1956); *Slaughter on Tenth Avenue* (U, 1957); *The Brothers Ricco* (Col., 1958); *The Old Man and the Sea* (WB, 1958); *One Potato, Two Potato* (Brit. Lion, 1964).

Television. Mr. Bellaver made his television debut as Jack Armstrong in *Abe Lincoln in Illinois* (NBC, 1942); subsequently appeared on the premiere of Studio One (CBS); Naked City (ABC); Suspense (CBS); the premiere of Omnibus (CBS); Westinghouse Th. (CBS); Philco Television Playhouse (NBC); Kraft Television Th. (NBC); Climax (CBS); Alfred Hitchcock Presents (CBS); Danger (CBS); Robert Montgomery Presents (NBC); The Somerset Maugham Th. (NBC); You Are There (CBS); Navy Log (ABC); Tight Rope (ABC); US Marshall (CBS); Track Down (ABC); Wanted, Dead or Alive (ABC); Rescue 8 (ABC); The Twilight Zone (CBS); The Millionaire (CBS); Ziv Productions; Revue Productions; and Four Star Productions.

BELLIN, OLGA.

Actress. b. Olga Helena Bielinski, Aug. 18, 1935, to Walter and Helena Bielinski. Grad. South Division H.S., Milwaukee, Wis. (valedictorian); attended Northwestern Univ.; grad. Milwaukee-Downer Coll., B.A. Studied piano and viola at the Wisconsin Coll. of Music. In N.Y.C., studied acting at the Herbert Berghof (HB) Studio; speech with Alice Hermes; dance with Martha Graham. Married Aug. 24, 1961, to Paul Roebling. Member of AEA; AFTRA; SAG.

Theatre. Miss Bellin made her first appearance on a stage in a dancing recital (1941). From 1948 to 1953, she acted in the resident companies of three little theatre groups in Milwaukee, Wis.: the Van Buren Players, the Norman Players, and the West Milwaukee Players. She was resident leading lady of the Tower Ranch Th. (Rhinelander, Wis., 1948–54), where she made her professional debut as Mrs. Bramson in *Night Must Fall* (June 1948). She appeared in a season of productions at the Garden Center Th. (Vineland, Ontario, Canada).

She understudied Kim Stanley as Georgette Thomas in *The Traveling Lady* (Playhouse, N.Y.C., Oct. 27, 1954); played Sabrina in *Sabrina Fair* (Fred Miller Th., Milwaukee, Wis., Jan. 1955); Mary in *Four Fingers of Pride* (Ogunquit Playhouse, Me., 1955); was understudy in *Once Upon a Tailor* (Cort, N.Y.C., May 23, 1955); appeared as a Widow in *The Carefree Tree* (Phoenix, Oct. 11, 1955); Vera in *A Month in the Country* (Phoenix, Apr. 3, 1956); and toured summer theatres as Miriam in *The Fifth Season* (1956).

Miss Bellin played Helen in *Protective Custody* (Ambassador, N.Y.C., Dec. 28, 1956); Joan in *The Lark* (Tower Ranch Th., July 1957); toured as Maggie in *Cat on a Hot Tin Roof* (1958); played Betty in *Middle of the Night* (Bucks County Playhouse, New Hope, Pa., July 1958); Sister Francois in *Port Royal* (Charity Church, N.Y.C., May 1960); Gretchen in *Faust* (HB Studio, Oct. 1960); Ruth in *Sodom and Gomorrah* (Vancouver, B.C., Canada, Aug. 1961); and Margaret in *A Man for All Seasons* (ANTA, N.Y.C., Nov. 22, 1961).

Television and Radio. She performed on such radio programs as Johnny Dollar, Indictment and Best Seller.

Since 1955, she has appeared on US Steel Hour (CBS); Armstrong Circle Th. (NBC); Play of the Week (WNTA); *A Month in the Country;* Camera Three (CBS); *Crime and Punishment;* and *Notes to the Underground.* She has also appeared on the daytime serial Edge of Night (CBS, 1959).

Awards. Miss Bellin received the Fanny Kemble Award from the Charlotte Cushman Club (Philadelphia, Pa., 1962).

BELLOW, SAUL.

Writer, teacher, playwright. b. June 10, 1915, Lachine, Quebec, Can., to Abraham and Liza (Gordon) Bellow. Educ. Univ. of Chicago, 1933–35; grad. Northwestern Univ., B.S. (honors) 1937. Served in US Merchant Marine, 1944–45. Married 1937 to Anita Goshkin (marr. dis.); one son; 1956 to Alexandra Tschacbasov (marr. dis.); one son; 1961 to Susan Glassman; one son. Member Natl. Institute of Arts and Letters; P.E.N. Address: Committee on Social Thought, Univ. of Chicago, 1126 E. 59th St., Chicago, IL 60637.

In 1962, Mr. Bellow became a professor, Committee on Social Thought, Univ. of Chicago. His previous teaching posts were at the Pestalozzi-Froebel Teachers Coll., Chicago (1938–42); at the Univ. of Minnesota, Minneapolis, where he was an instructor (1946) and then assistant professor of English (1948–49); NY Univ., where he was a visiting lecturer (1950–52); Princeton Univ., where he was a fellow in creative writing (1952–53); Bard Coll., Annandale-on-Hudson, N.Y., where he taught English (1953–54); Univ. of Minnesota, where he was associate professor of English (1954–59); and the Univ. of Puerto Rico, Rio Piedras, where he was a visiting professor of English (1961).

Theatre. Mr. Bellow's first work presented in the theatre was his play *The Last Analysis* (Belasco Th., N.Y.C., Oct. 1, 1964). His three one-act plays—*Out from Under, A Wen,* and *Orange Soufflé*— were produced in London under the title *The Bellow Plays* (Fortune, June 28, 1966); *A Wen* and *Orange Soufflé* were presented soon after at the Festival of the Two Worlds, Spoleto, It. (July 14, 1966); and this was followed by the US production of all three plays, billed as *Under the Weather* (Mineola Th., Mineola, N.Y., Oct. 4–16, 1966; Cort, N.Y.C., Oct. 27–Nov. 5, 1966).

Television. Mr. Bellow's play *The Wrecker* was televised in 1964.

Other Activities. Mr. Bellow was on the editorial staff of the *Encyclopedia Britannica* in Chicago from 1943 to 1946 and was a founding editor (1960) of *The Noble Savage.* .

Published Works. Mr. Bellow's first novel, *Dangling Man* (1944), was followed by *The Victim* (1945); *The Adventures of Augie March* (1953); *Henderson the Rain King* (1959); *Herzog* (1964); *Mr. Sammler's Planet* (1970); and *Humboldt's Gift* (1975). His other published work includes *Seize the Day* (1956), a collection of short stories and a one-act play (1956); the text, with C. Zervos, for Jess Reichek's *Dessins* (1960); *Recent American Fiction: A Lecture* (1963); *Like You're Nobody* (1966); *Mosby's Memoirs and Other Stories* (1968); and *The Future of the Moon* (1970). In addition, he was one of the translators of Isaac Bashevis Singer's *Gimpel the Fool and Other Stories* (1957) and edited *Great Jewish Short Stories* (1963).

Awards. Mr. Bellow received a Guggenheim grant (1948); a National Institute of Arts and Letters grant (1952); Ford Foundation grants (1959, 1960); the National Book Award for fiction in 1954, 1965, and 1971; the Friends of Literature Award (1960); the James L. Dow Award (1964); the Prix International de Littérature (1965); and the Jewish Heritage Award (1968). He was awarded honorary D. Litt. degrees by Northwestern Univ. (1962) and Bard Coll. (1963).

BELT, ELMER.

Physician, art curator. b. Apr. 10, 1893, to Charles Elmer and Minnie (Drier) Belt. Grad Univ. of California, A.B. 1916; Hooper Inst. for Medical Research, San Francisco, Calif., M.S. 1918; Univ. of California Medical Sch., San Francisco, M.D. 1920; Pacific Coll. of Law, Los Angeles, LL.D. 1930. Married, June 9, 1918, to Mary Ruth Smart; two sons. Address: (home) 2201 Ferndell Place, Los Angeles, CA 90028; (bus.) 1893 Wilshire Blvd., Los Angeles, CA 90057, tel. (213) HU 3-6830.

Dr. Belt collected the Elmer Belt Library of Vinciana, which he donated to the Univ. of California at Los Angeles, Division of Fine Arts (1961).

Concerned primarily with Leonardo da Vinci and the Renaissance, it contains special studies, publications and films, among which is a film of Leonardo da Vinci's theatrical drawings, stage, and pageantry designs. The library also contains books of the Renaissance theatre, and has exhibited a theatre model based on the drawings of Leonardo at Prof. Jacquot's exhibition entitled *La Vie Théâtrale au Temps de la Renaissance* (Institut Pédagogique National, Paris, Fr., Mar.-May, 1963).

Awards. Dr. Belt received an honorary Doctor of Laws degree from the Univ. of California (June 8, 1962). On May 2, 1964, the Alumni Association of the University awarded Dr. and Mrs. Belt its 1964 Distinguished Service Award of the Univ. of California at Los Angeles.

BEN-AMI, JACOB.

Actor, director, producer. b. Jacob Shtchirin, Nov. 23, 1890, Minsk, Russia. Father, merchant. Member of AEA; AFTRA; Hebrew Actors Guild. Address: 50 W. 97th St., New York, NY 10031, tel. (212) 222-7511.

Pre-Theatre. Choir boy in Synagogue.

Theatre. Mr. Ben-Ami began acting with the Russian theatre in Minsk (c. 1907); subsequently appeared in the Yiddish theatre production of *Sam Adler* (Minsk, 1908) and *Peretz Hirshbein* (Odessa, 1910); performed first in the Yiddish theatre (London, England, 1914), before residing in the US (1914); performed in Yiddish with various companies on national tours (1914–18), in addition to playing in *The Kreutzer Sonata* (Novelty, Brooklyn, N.Y., c. 1914); and was associated with the Neighborhood Playhouse (N.Y.C., 1917–18).

He joined the Jewish Art Th. (N.Y.C.); and appeared in *The Abandoned Nook, Devious Paths of Love, A Doll's House, The Battle of the Butterflies, Samson and Delilah,* and *The Power of Darkness* (Irving Place Th., 1918–19). He played in *Lonely Lives;* appeared in *Samson and Delilah,* played Eisik in *The Idle Inn* (Madison Square Th., 1919–20); *The Bronx Express* (Madison Square Th., Jan. 2, 1920); Levi Itzchok in *Green Fields* (Madison Square Th., Mar. 25, 1920); and Alexander in *The Mute* (Madison Square Th., Apr. 13, 1920).

Mr. Ben-Ami's first English-speaking role was Peter Krumback in *Samson and Delilah* (Greenwich Village Th., Nov. 17, 1920); followed by Eisik in *The Idle Inn* (Plymouth, Dec. 20, 1921); the title role in *Johannes Kreisler* (Apollo, Dec. 20, 1922); He in *The Failures* (Garrick, Nov. 19, 1923); a Stranger in *The Race with the Shadow* (Garrick, Jan. 20, 1924), Michael Cape in *Welded* (39 St. Th., Mar. 17, 1924); the Nameless One in *Man and the Masses* (Garrick, Apr. 14, 1924); directed *The Goat Song* (Guild, Jan. 25, 1926); played Franz Schweiger in *Schweiger* (Mansfield, Mar. 23, 1926); John the Baptist in *John* (Klaw, Nov. 2, 1927); Michael Orloff in *Diplomacy* (Erlanger's, May 28, 1928); and toured in *Jim, the Penman* (Spring 1929).

In Sept. 1929, he became a member of Eva Le Gallienne's Civic Repertory Co. at the Civic Repertory Th. (N.Y.C.), with whom he played Trigorin in *The Seagull,* Ephidov in *The Cherry Orchard* (Sept. 23, 1929), Feyda in *The Living Corpse* (Dec. 6, 1929), Escalus in *Romeo and Juliet* (Apr. 21, 1930), Henri in *The Green Cockatoo* (Oct. 9, 1930), the title role in *Siegfried* (Oct. 20, 1930), and M. Duval in *Camille* (Jan. 26, 1931). He traveled with the company when it performed in Buenos Aires, Argentina (Fall 1931).

In Chicago, Ill. he played Peter Krumback in *Samson and Delilah* (Adelphi, Jan. 1932); played William Marble in a touring production of *Payment Deferred;* appeared as Arthur Kober in *Evensong* (Selwyn, N.Y.C., Jan. 31, 1933); directed, with Isaac Van Grove, the pageant, *The Romance of a People* (Polo Grounds, Sept. 14, 1933); played Dr. Victor Bard in *A Ship Comes in* (Morosco, Sept. 19, 1934); directed, with Charles Friedman, *Bitter Stream* (Civic Repertory Th., Mar. 30, 1936); and toured South America (1936).

For the Jewish Drama Society of Chicago (Ill.), he directed and played the title role in *Yegor Bulitchev* (People's Playhouse, Chicago, 1937); for the Yiddish Art Th. (N.Y.C.), appeared as Zachary Mirkin in *Three Cities* (Yiddish Art, Oct. 10, 1938); and in *Who is Who* (Al Jolson's Th., Dec. 1938). He played in *Awake and Sing* (Parkway, Bklyn., Apr. 25, 1939); directed and portrayed the title role in *Chavar Nachman* (Downtown Natl., Sept. 30, 1939); and played in *Life Marches On* (Downtown Natl., Dec. 29, 1939).

In South America, he toured in plays performed both in Yiddish and English (Spring and Summer 1941); and in N.Y.C., played in *The Day of Judgement* (Yiddish Art, Oct. 1, 1941); *Abe Lincoln in Illinois* (S. America, 1944); and for the New Jewish Folk Th. (N.Y.C.), appeared in *The Miracle of the Warsaw Ghetto* (Phoenix Yiddish Art, Oct. 1944).

In South Africa, he played Willy Loman in a touring production of *Death of a Salesman* (1951–52); portrayed Detective McLeod in *Detective Story* (Parkway, Bklyn., N.Y., Oct. 5, 1952); in *The World of Sholom Aleichem* (Chicago, Ill., 1954); in stock, played Mr. Bonaparte in *Golden Boy* (Playhouse-in-the-Park, Philadelphia, Pa., July 1954); portrayed Noah in *The Flowering Peach* (Cathay Circle, Los Angeles, Calif., Summer 1956); played Pyotr Nikolayevitch Sorin in *The Seagull* (Fourth St. Th., N.Y.C., Oct. 22, 1956); Papa in a pre-Bway tryout of *With Respect to Joey* (opened Westport Country Playhouse, Conn., July 22, 1957); the Old Shepherd in *The Infernal Machine* (Phoenix, N.Y.C., Feb. 3, 1958); toured as Bonche Schweig in *The World of Sholom Aleichem* (1959) and at the Barbizon-Plaza, (N.Y.C., 1959); played Forman in *The Tenth Man* (Booth, Nov. 5, 1959); Mr. Frank in a tour of *The Diary of Anne Frank;* Dr. Joseph Breuer in the national touring company of *A Far Country* (opened Playhouse, Wilmington, Del., Oct. 24, 1962; closed Hanna, Cleveland, Ohio, Jan. 12, 1963); and appeared in *Hamlet, Beethoven* and *Liliom.*

Mr. Ben-Ami was Eddie Bromberg in *Walking to Waldheim* (Forum, N.Y.C., Nov. 10, 1967); joined the Folksbiene Players Organization in 1971, appearing with that group as the Rabbi in *In My Father's Court* (Nov. 10, 1971); and he played the Rabbi from Krakow in *Yoshe Kalb* (Eden Th., Oct. 22, 1972).

Films. Mr. Ben-Ami appeared in *The Wandering Jew* (Jewish-Am. Film Arts, 1933), and was co-director, for *Green Fields* (Collective Film Producers, 1937).

Television. He has played in *Assassin!* (Playhouse, NBC, Feb. 20, 1955), *Rudy* (Studio One, CBS, Aug. 19, 1957). *The Song of Freedom* (Look Up and Live, CBS, Mar. 30, 1958); and *Three Deeds* (Fed. of Jewish Philanthropies, NBC).

BENCHLEY, NATHANIEL. Writer. b. Nathaniel Goddard Benchley, Nov. 13, 1915, Newton, Mass., to Robert and Gertrude (Darling) Benchley. Father, writer, actor. Grad. Phillips Exeter Acad., N.H., 1934; Harvard Univ., B.S. 1938. Married May 19, 1939, to Marjorie Bradford; two sons. Served USNR, 1941–45, ETO, PTO, Caribbean; rank, Lt. Comdr. Member of ALA; WGA, West; The Coffee House, N.Y.; The Century Assn., N.Y.; The Pacific Club, Nantucket, Mass. Address: Box 244, Siasconset, MA 02564, tel. (617) 257-6534.

Pre-Theatre. Newspaper work, free-lance writing.

Theatre. Mr. Benchley wrote *The Frogs of Spring* (Broadhurst Th., Oct. 30, 1953).

Films. He wrote the original screenplay for *The Great American Pastime* (MGM, 1956), and appeared in *Act One* (WB, 1964). His novel, *The Off-Islanders,* was made into the film *The Russians Are Coming! The Russians Are Coming!* (UA, 1966).

Published Works. Mr. Benchley's writings include *Side Street* (1950), *Robert Benchley; A Biography* (1955), *One To Grow On* (1958), *Sail a Crooked Ship* (1960), *The Off-Islanders* (1951), *Catch a Falling Spy* (1963), *A Winter's Tale* (1964), *The Visitors* (1965), *A Firm Word or Two* (1965), *The Monument* (1966), *Welcome to Xanadu* (1968), *The Wake of the Icarus* (1969), *Lassiter's Folly* (1971), *The Hunter's Moon* (1972).

BENDER, JACK E. Educator. b. Jack Earl Bender, Dec. 6, 1918, Ann Arbor, Mich., to Frank and Mary (Reeve) Bender. Grad. Central H.S., Grand Rapids, Mich., 1937; Univ. of Michigan, B.A. 1941, M.A. 1942, Ph.D. 1954. Married Aug. 20, 1949, to Jane Grothaus; one son. Member of Zeta Psi; AETA; ANTA; AAUP. Address: (home) 1620 Hillridge Blvd., Ann Arbor, MI 48103, tel. (313) 662-9603; (bus.) Univ. of Michigan, Ann Arbor, MI 48104, tel. (313) 663-1511.

Since 1965, Mr. Bender has been professor of speech and drama at the Univ. of Michigan, where he has designed and directed many student productions. He was an instructor at New York Univ. (1942–45).

Published Works. He has contributed articles to *Education Theatre Journal.*

BENEDICT, PAUL. Actor, director. b. Sept. 17, 1938, Silver City, New Mexico. Grad. Suffolk Univ., Boston, Mass., A.B. 1960.

Theatre. Mr. Benedict first appeared professionally as the Chaplain in *The Lady's Not for Burning* (Image Th., Boston, Mass., 1962) and later played at the same theatre in *The Underpants* (Jan. 2, 1964). He was a member (1963–68) of the Theatre Company of Boston and appeared in more than fifty of their productions, including *Waiting for Godot* (June 25, 1964); *The Caretaker; Live Like Pigs* (US premiere: Jan. 28, 1965); *Yes Is for a Very Young Man* (Nov. 11, 1965); *Measure for Measure* (Dec. 9, 1965); *The Fear and Misery of the Third Reich* (Jan. 6, 1966); and *The Birthday Party* (Feb. 3, 1966. Also for the Theatre Co. of Boston, he directed *The Investigation* (Apr. 28, 1966) and *Ivy Day* (May 9, 1966), in which he also appeared; and he was in the company's productions of *The Way Out of the Way In* (May 18, 1966); *Tiny Alice* (Jan. 3, 1967); *The Dwarfs* (Nov. 30, 1967); *Left-Handed Liberty* (US premiere, Jan. 3, 1968); and *Who's Afraid of Virginia Woolf?* (Jan. 18, 1968).

In N.Y.C., Mr. Benedict made his debut off-Bway as Sailor Sawney in *Live Like Pigs* (Actors Playhouse, June 7, 1965), following with a performance as the Mother in *The Infantry* (81st St. Th., Nov. 14, 1966); and in 1967 he appeared at the Cincinnati (Ohio) Playhouse in the Park as Stanley in *The Birthday Party* and Leon in *The Cavern.* He made his Bway debut as Matt Killigrew in *Leda Has a Little Swan* (closed during previews: Cort, Mar. 29–Apr. 10, 1968); then played Rev. Dupas in *Little Murders* (Circle in the Square, Jan. 5, 1969); several parts in a presentation of seven short Harold Pinter Plays billed as *The Local Stigmatic* (Actors' Playhouse, Nov. 3, 1969); was Stiles in *The White House Murder Case* (Circle in the Square, Feb. 18, 1970); and returned to Cincinnati to play in *He Who Gets Slapped* (Playhouse in the Park, Aug. 27, 1970).

At Arena Stage, Washington, D.C., Mr. Benedict was in *Pantagleize* (Oct. 22, 1971) and played Eberhard Stausch in *Uptight* (US premiere, Mar. 17, 1972). He was also in *Old Times* (Trinity Square Repertory Co., Providence, R.I., Sept. 24, 1972); and, again with the Theatre Co. of Boston, in *Play Strindberg* (Dec. 5, 1972), *Richard III,* (Feb. 3, 1973), and *Old Times* (Mar. 6, 1973). Mr. Benedict also appeared with Center Stage, Baltimore, Md., in *The Hot l Baltimore* (Oct. 26, 1973) and *Uncle Vanya* (Nov. 30, 1973); and in N.Y.C. appeared off-Bway in two plays billed as *Bad Habits,* playing Jason Pepper, M.D. in *Ravenswood* and Hugh Gumbs in *Dunelawn* (Astor Place Th., Feb. 4, 1974); when *Bad Habits* moved to Bway (Booth Th.) Mr. Benedict played (May 5–May 11, 1974) Hiram Spane in *Ravenswood* and Mr. Ponce in *Dunelawn.* .

Television. Mr. Benedict has appeared on television as Henri in *Yes Is for a Very Young Man* and Pete in *The Dwarfs* (both NET).

BENLINE, ARTHUR J. Architect, engineer. b. Arthur Jay Benline, Oct. 30, 1902, New York City, to Harry C. and Margaret M. (von Pfalzgraf) Benline. Father, builder, song writer, performer. Grad. Sch of Industrial Arts, Mount Vernon, N.Y., Architectural Engineering Cert. 1921; attended New York Univ., 1926–32; Univ. of the State of New York, 1925. Married May 17, 1951, to Peggy Cornell, actress, dancer, singer. Served USN, Civil Engineer Corps, ETO, PTO, 1942–46; rank, Capt.; awarded Bronze Star with Combat V; Purple Heart; combat commendation ribbons, NY State Distinguished Service Cross. Member of TMAT; US Inst. of Theatre Technicians (dir., 1960–65; first vice-pres., 1969); ANTA (mbr., board of planning); Building Officials Conference of Amer. (pres., 1955–56); Eastern States Building Officials Federation (exec. vice pres., 1951–to date); Municipal Engineers of City of N.Y. (pres., 1969); Amer. Society of Civil Engineers; Natl. Society of Professional Engineers; NY Society of Architects; American Legion; VFW; Disabled Amer. Veterans; Navy vice pres., Reserve Officers Assn., Manhattan, and Retired Officers Assn., Manhattan. Address: 2107 Broadway, New York, NY 10023.

Mr. Benline is an architect and engineer specializing in theatre construction. From 1925 to 1930, as supervising engineer for Loew's Theatres and MGM Studios, he directed the design and construction of motion picture theatres in Yonkers, Syracuse, New Rochelle, Brooklyn, N.Y.C., N.Y.; Pittsburgh, Pa.; Baltimore, Md.; and Providence, R.I. He supervised the reconstruction of the Cosmopolitan Studios (N.Y.C., 1926) for the first sound movies, and installed the first sound and air conditioning systems in the Loew's circuit. Mr. Benline performed similar duties for Twentieth-Century Fox theatres (1930–32); and for RKO Radio Theatres (1932–34). During this period he contributed to the organization of Radio City Music Hall (N.Y.C.) and set up its budget.

From 1934–40, he was associated with Harold B. Franklin and Arch Selwyn, as executive manager for *Lady Jane* (Plymouth Th., Sept. 10, 1934); *Continental Varieties* (Little, Oct. 3, 1934); *Conversation Piece* (44 St. Th., Oct. 23, 1934); *L'Aiglon* (Broadhurst, Nov. 3, 1934); and *Revenge with Music* (New Amsterdam, Nov. 28, 1934). During 1935–40, he was executive aide to Ben F. Stein, for *Jumbo* (NY Hippodrome, Nov. 16, 1935); *One Good Year* (Lyceum, Nov. 27, 1935); *Mainly for Lovers* (48 St., Th., Feb. 11, 1936); and *Bet Your Life* (John Golden Th., Apr. 5, 1937).

From 1940–1952, he was superintendent of the Dept. of Housing and Buildings (N.Y.C.) with supervision over all city theatres; was director of the NY State building construction code (1952–60), governing performance regulations, theatre construction and design; was Commissioner of the Dept. of Air Pollution Control, N.Y.C. (1960–66); and thereafter had a consulting practice as architect and engineer.

Awards. Mr. Benline's awards include the Strauss Medal and Award of the NY Society of Architects (1957) for service to the profession; the Society of Construction Superintendents Distinguished Service Award (1957) for Professional Attainment; the NY State Society of Professional Engineers Distinguished Engineer in Public Service Award (1966); the Underwriters Laboratories Fire Council Recognition Award for Distinguished Service in the Interest of Public Safety; and the Building Officials and Code Administrators (BOCA) International Walker S. Lee Award for service to BOCA.

BENNETT, ALAN. Writer, actor. b. May 9, 1934, Leeds, Yorkshire, England, to Walter and Lilian Mary (Peel) Bennett. Father, butcher. Grad. Leeds Modern Sch., 1952; Exeter Coll., Oxford Univ., B.A. 1958, M.A. 1962. Member of British AEA; AEA; AFTRA. Served British Army, Intelligence Corps., 1952–54; rank, Pvt.

Pre-Theatre. Taught medieval history.

Theatre. Mr. Bennett first appeared in the revue *Better Late,* presented by the Oxford Theatre Group (Cranston St. Hall, Edinburgh, Scotland, Aug. 1949). He was author with Jonathan Miller, Dudley Moore and Peter Cook, and a performer in *Beyond the Fringe,* commissioned by the Edinburgh Festival authorities (Lyceum Th., Edinburgh, Aug. 1959); an expanded version of it was presented in London (Fortune, May 10, 1961) and in N.Y.C. (John Golden Th., Oct. 27, 1962).

Mr. Bennett was also author, with Dudley Moore, Peter Cook, and Paxton Whitehead, and a performer in *Beyond the Fringe 1964* (John Golden Th., Jan. 18, 1964); wrote and played Tempest in *Forty Years On* (Apollo Th., London, Oct. 1968); wrote *Getting On* (London, 1971); and *Habeas Corpus* (Lyric, London, May 10, 1973; Martin Beck Th., N.Y.C., Nov. 25, 1975).

Television. Mr. Bennett appeared in *Beyond the Fringe* (BBC, London, Dec. 19, 1964); played six roles in *My Father Knew Lloyd George* (BBC, Dec. 18, 1965); was in *Streets Ahead* (BBC, 1966); *On the Margin* (BBC, 1966); was host of the Alan Bennett series (BBC, 1966–67); appeared in *Alice in Wonderland* (BBC, Jan. 1967); and *A Day Out* (BBC, 1972).

Awards. For *Beyond the Fringe,* Mr. Bennett and his colleagues received the (London) *Evening Standard* Award for best revue or musical (1961); the Antoinette Perry (Tony) Special Citation Award (1963); and the NY Drama Critics Circle special citation (1963).

Recreation. Medieval history.

BENNETT, MICHAEL. Choreographer, director, dancer, author. b. Michael Bennett Di Figlia, about 1943, Buffalo, N.Y., to Salvatore and Helen Di Figlia. Father, machinist; mother, secretary.

Theatre. Mr. Bennett began his professional career as a dancer in the national company of *West Side Story* when he was sixteen years old. He made his N.Y.C. debut as a dancer in *Subways Are for Sleeping* (St. James Th., Dec. 27, 1961) and was a dancer in *Here's Love* (Sam S. Shubert Th., Oct. 3, 1963) and *Bajour* (Sam S. Shubert Th., Nov. 23, 1964). He was choreographer for *A Joyful Noise* (Mark Hellinger Th., Dec. 15, 1966); *Henry, Sweet Henry* (Palace, Oct. 23, 1967); *Promises, Promises* (Sam S. Shubert Th., Dec. 1, 1968); *Coco* (Mark Hellinger Th., Dec. 18, 1969); and *Company* (Alvin Th., Aug. 26, 1970).

Mr. Bennett was choreographer and co-director of *Follies* (Winter Garden, Apr. 4, 1971); director of *Twigs* (Broadhurst, Nov. 14, 1971); author, director, and co-choreographer of *Seesaw* (Uris Th., Mar. 18, 1973); director of *God's Favorite* (Eugene O'Neill Th., Dec. 11, 1974); and he conceived, directed, and choreographed *A Chorus Line* (Newman Th., May 21, 1975; transferred to Sam S. Shubert Th., July 25, 1975).

Films. Mr. Bennett did the choreography for *What's So Bad About Feeling Good?* (U, 1968).

Television. Mr. Bennett has done choreography for such shows as Hullaballoo, the Dean Martin Show, Hollywood Palace, the Ed Sullivan Show, and others.

Awards. Mr. Bennett received two Antoinette Perry (Tony) awards for *Follies*—as best choreographer and best director; and for *Seesaw,* he received a Tony as best choreographer and a Tony nomination for writing the best book for a musical.

BENNETT, ROBERT RUSSELL. Composer, conductor, orchestrator. b. June 15, 1894, Kansas City, Mo., to George Robert and May (Bradford) Bennett. Father, farmer, musician; mother, musician. Attended public school in Freeman, Mo., 1909–12. Studied composition with Carl Busch, Kansas City, 1912–15; Nadia Boulanger, Paris, 1926–31. Married Dec. 26, 1919, to Louise Edgerton Merrill; one daughter. Served US Army, 1917–18; rank, Pvt. Member of AFM, Locals 802, 47, 34; American Society of Musical Arrangers (pres., 1937–40); Composers and Lyricists Guild; Amer. Music Center; ASCAP; NATAS; NARAS; NAACC (pres., 1947–54); The Bohemians (vice-pres., 1951; pres., 1965); West Side Tennis Club; Los Angeles Tennis Club. Address: (home) 140 E. 56th St., New York, NY 10022, tel. EL 5-2291; (bus.) c/o NBC, 30 Rockefeller Plaza, New York, NY 10020, tel. CI 7-8300; 65 W. 54th St., New York, NY 10019.

Pre-Theatre. Played in dance bands and orchestras. Worked as a copyist and arranger for G. Schirmer (N.Y.C., 1916).

Theatre. Mr. Bennett made his first stage appearance at age three when Julia Marlowe carried him across the stage of the Grand Opera House, (Kansas City, Mo., 1897). He made his professional debut as a pianist, violinist, and brass player in 1910, and first appeared as a composer-pianist, in the performance of "Trio," his own composition written for violin, cello, and piano (Kansas City, Mo., 1914). In 1919, he was commissioned by George Moody of the T. B. Harms Co. to orchestrate several songs, the first of which was "An Old Fashioned Garden," composed by Cole Porter.

He also orchestrated *Daffydill* (Long Beach, L.I., N.Y., Aug. 1922); orchestrated *Wildflower* (Casino, N.Y.C., Feb. 7, 1923); *Mary Jane McKane* (Imperial, Dec. 25, 1923); *Sitting Pretty* (Fulton, Apr. 8, 1924); *Stepping Stones* (Globe, Sept. 1, 1924); *Rose-Marie* (Imperial, Sept. 2, 1924); *Sunny* (New Amsterdam, Sept. 22, 1925); *One Damn Thing After Another* (London Pavilion, May 20, 1927); *Show Boat* (Ziegfeld, N.Y.C., Dec. 27, 1927); *Sweet Adeline* (Hammerstein's, Sept. 3, 1929); and about 200 others.

Mr. Bennett composed the operetta-ballet, *Endymion* (Eastman Sch., Rochester, N.Y.C., c.1932); wrote the opera, *Maria Malibran,* produced by the Juilliard Sch. of Music (N.Y.C., Apr. 8, 1935); was commissioned by the League of Composers to compose "Hollywood," a symphonic scherzo (1936); was commissioned by CBS to write "Eight Etudes for Symphony Orchestra" (1938); and composed music for six 15-minute spectacles for the Lagoon of Nations (NY World's Fair, 1939).

He orchestrated *Oklahoma!* (St. James, N.Y.C., Mar. 31, 1943); *Carmen Jones* (Bway Th., Dec. 2, 1943); composed the one-act opera, *The Enchanted Kiss* (1944); orchestrated *Three to Make Ready* (Adelphi, Mar. 7, 1946); composed incidental music for *Happy Birthday* (Broadhurst, Oct. 31, 1946); *If the Shoe Fits* (Century, Dec. 5, 1946); *Finian's Rainbow* (46 St. Th., Jan. 10, 1947); the pre-Bway tryout of *In Gay New Orleans* (opened Colonial, Boston, Mass., Dec. 25, 1946; closed there Jan. 31, 1947); *Louisiana Lady* (Century, N.Y.C., June 2, 1947); *Allegro* (Majestic, Oct. 10, 1947); *Inside U.S.A.* (Century, Apr. 30, 1948); was commissioned by the Louisville (Ky.) Orchestra to compose "Variations for Violin and Orchestra" (1949); orchestrated *South Pacific* (Majestic, N.Y.C., Apr. 7, 1949); *The King and I* (St. James, Mar. 29, 1951); *Paris '90* (Booth, Mar. 4, 1952); *Three Wishes for Jamie* (Mark Hellinger Th., Mar. 21, 1952); *By the Beautiful Sea* (Majestic, Apr. 8, 1954); and *Pipe Dream* (Shubert, Nov. 30, 1955).

Mr. Bennett orchestrated, with Phil Lang, *My Fair Lady* (Mark Hellinger Th., Mar. 15, 1956); orchestrated *Bells Are Ringing* (Shubert, Nov. 29, 1956); *The Ziegfeld Follies* (Winter Garden, Mar. 1, 1957); with Mr. Lang, *New Girl in Town* (46 St. Th., May 14, 1957); orchestrated *Flower Drum Song* (St. James, Dec. 1, 1958); with Mr. Lang, *Redhead* (46 St. Th., Feb. 5, 1959); with Messrs. Blitzstein and Kay, *Juno* (Winter Garden, Mar. 9, 1959); orchestrated *The Sound of Music* (Lunt-Fontanne, Nov. 16, 1959); with Mr. Lang, *Camelot* (Majestic, Dec. 3, 1960); with Mr. Kay, the pre-Bway tryout of *We Take the Town* (opened Shubert, New Haven, Conn., Feb. 19, 1962; closed Shubert, Philadelphia, Pa., Mar. 17, 1962); and orchestrated *The Girl Who Came to Supper* (Bway Th., N.Y.C., Dec. 8, 1963); *On a Clear Day You Can See Forever* (Mark Hellinger, Oct. 17, 1965); *Mata Hari* (National Th., Washington, D.C., Nov. 18, 1967).

Films. Mr. Bennett orchestrated the music for *Men of the Sky* (20th-Fox, 1931); and for *Oklahoma!* (Magna, 1955); and others.

Television and Radio. He has been conductor (1941–to date) on such radio programs as Russell Bennett's Notebook (Mutual).

On television, he composed, arranged, and conducted music for Project 20 (NBC, 1951), including such works as "Victory at Sea" (1952), "Nightmare in Red" (1954), "Twisted Cross" (1956), and "Call to Freedom" (1958).

Published Works. He has composed the following premiered works: "The Four Freedoms Symphony" (1944); "Concerto for Violin and Orchestra" (London, Eng.); "Three Marches for Two Pianos or Orchestras" (Los Angeles, Calif.); "Overture to an Imaginary Drama" (Toronto, Can.); "Concerto for Piano and Orchestra" (Helsinki, Fin.); "Suite of Old American Dances" (N.Y.C.); "Mademoiselle" (N.Y.C.); "Rose Variations" (N.Y.C.); "Mississippi Overture" (Indianapolis, Ind.); "Kansas City Album" (Kansas City, Mo.); "Ohio River Suite for Wind Symphony" (Pittsburgh, Pa.); "Concerto Grosso for Woodwind Quintet and Wind Symphony" (Pittsburgh, Pa.); "Symphonic Songs for Band" (Houston, Tex.); "Charleston Rhapsody" (N.Y.C.); "Adagio Eroico" (Rochester, N.Y.); "Organ Sonata" (Paris, Fr.); "Water Music for String Quartet" (N.Y.C.).

He has also composed the chamber music, "A Song Sonata" (1947); "Hexapoda" (N.Y.C., c. 1940); "Four Dances for Violin, Cello and Piano"; "Five Improvisations for Flute, Cello, and Piano" (N.Y.C.); "Sonatine for Soprano and Harp" (N.Y.C.); "A Commemoration Symphony" (Pittsburgh Symphony Orchestra, Pa., Dec. 30, 1959); "Concerto for Harp, Cello, and Orchestra" (Naumburn Concerts, N.Y.C., July 31, 1960); "Concerto for Violin, Piano, and Orchestra" (Portland, Ore., Mar. 17, 1962); "Symphony" (to Fritz Reiner) Chicago Symphony, Ill. (Apr. 1, 1962); "Quintet for Accordion and String Quartet" (Kansas City, Mo., June 10, 1962); and "A West Virginia Epic for Wind Symphony" (Fairmont, W.Va., June, 1963).

Discography. Mr. Bennett has recorded "Armed Forces Suite" (RCA Victor, Sept. 1960); "An Adventure in High Fidelity" (RCA Victor); three albums from Victory at Sea; two albums with Marion Anderson; and five with the Robert Shaw Chorale.

Awards. In 1926, Mr. Bennett won honorable mention for a symphony he submitted to the *Musical America* Contest. In 1930, he won a prize for two symphonic works he submitted to the RCA Victor contest, "Abraham Lincoln" and "Sights and Sounds." In 1928–29, he was awarded a Guggenheim Fellowship to study in Paris, London, and Berlin. Mr. Bennett received an Academy (Oscar) Award (1955) for his orchestration of *Oklahoma!* He also received a NATAS (Emmy) Award (1963) for original music composed for television; was named Doctor of Humane Letters (Franklin and Marshall College, 1965); received the George Frederick Handel Medallion (N.Y., 1967); and was awarded the Henry Hadley Medal of the National Assn. for American Composers and Conductors (1969).

Recreation. Tennis, baseball.

BENSON, GEORGE. Actor. b. George Frederick Percy Benson, Jan. 11, 1911, Cardiff, South Wales, England, to Leslie Bernard Gilpin and Isita Lenora (Waddington) Benson. Father, architect. Grad. Blundell's Sch., Tiverton, Devonshire School Certificate, Keats Medalist 1927 and 1928. Studied acting at RADA, 1928–30. Served WW II, Officer in Royal Artillery, 1941–46. Married Feb. 27, 1937, to Jane Ann Sterndale Bennett; two daughters (marr. dis. 1949); married Apr. 24, 1950, to Pamela Enid White; one son. Member of British AEA; Society for Theatre Research (committee member; chmn., 1969–73). Address: 20 Makepeace Ave., Highgate West Hill, London N. 6, England tel. Mountview 0991.

Theatre. Mr. Benson made his N.Y.C. debut as Desmond Curry in *The Winslow Boy* (Empire Th., Oct. 29, 1947), which he repeated on tour.

He made his first appearance in England as a Roman Soldier in *Caesar and Cleopatra* at the Malvern Festival (Aug. 24, 1929). He made his London debut in *Charlot's Masquerade* (Cambridge, Sept. 4, 1930); subsequently appeared as Willie in *Wonder Bar* (Savoy, Dec. 5, 1930); and at the Festival Th., Cambridge, in the following productions: *Love for Love, Bastos the Bold, Alison's House, The Knight of the Burning Pestle, Marco Millions,* and *Will You Play With Me?* (Jan.–Mar. 1932). He played George Pelham in *Faces* (Comedy, London, Apr. 19, 1932); Ben and Trapland in *Love for Love* (Faculty of Arts, May 22, 1932); and Sam Gerridge in *Caste* (Embassy, Oct. 1932). He then toured Egypt and Australia with the Nicholas Hannen and Athene Seyler repertory co. (Dec. 1932–Apr. 1933).

He appeared in the revue, *Please* (Savoy, London, Nov. 16, 1933); as the Courtier in *The Golden Toy* (Coliseum, Feb. 28, 1934); Snyde in *Mary Read* (His Majesty's Th., Nov. 21, 1934); in *Shall We Reverse?* (Comedy, May 10, 1935); *Stop-Go!* (Vaudeville, Sept. 1935); as King Hildebrand in *What a Witch!* (Vaudeville, Dec. 1935); in *The Town Talks* (Vaudeville, Mar. 11, 1936); as Socrates in *No More Peace* (Gate, June 11, 1936); Edward Gill in *The Two Boquets* (Ambassadors', Aug. 13, 1936); Dromio of Ephesus in *Comedy of Errors* (Open Air, Sept. 6, 1937); and Vlas Fillipovich in *Distant Point* (Gate, Nov. 25, 1937). He also appeared in the revue, *Nine Sharp* (Little, Jan. 26, 1938); as Gus Michaels in *Paradise Lost* (Wyndham's, Dec. 11, 1938); Tony Lumpkin in *She Stoops to Conquer* (Old Vic, Jan. 24, 1939); in *The Little Revue* (Little, Apr. 21, 1939); as Sir Jasper Fidget in *The Country Wife* (Little, Apr. 9, 1940); appeared in and directed the revue, *Diversion* (Wyndham's, Oct. 28, 1940); *Better Late* (Garrick, Apr. 24, 1946); and *Between Ourselves* (Playhouse, Dec. 16, 1946).

Mr. Benson appeared with the Old Vic Co. as Costard in *Love's Labour's Lost* (New, Oct. 11, 1949); Bolshintsov in *A Month in the Country* (New, Nov. 30, 1949); Marcellus and First Gravedigger in *Hamlet* (New, Feb. 2, 1950); and in *The Miser* (New, Jan. 17, 1950). He played Poupart in *Music at Midnight* (His Majesty's Th., Nov. 10, 1950); appeared in *The Lyric Revue* (Globe, Sept. 26, 1951); *The Globe Revue* (Globe, July 10, 1952); as Pasqualino in *The Impresario from Smyrna* (Arts, May 26, 1954); and Mr. Potter in *The Diary of a Nobody* (Arts, Sept. 1, 1954). From May–Nov. 1955, he toured Australia with the Old Vic Co., appearing as Pompey in *Measure for Measure,* Gremio in *The Taming of the Shrew,* and Launcelot Gobbo and the Prince of Arragon in *The Merchant of Venice.*

He appeared as Percival in *Jubilee Girl* (Victoria Palace, London, June 14, 1956); at the Edinburgh Festival, as Mr. Gilby in *Fanny's First Play* (Lyceum, Sept. 3, 1956); in London, as Siblot in *Nekrassov* (Royal Court, Sept. 17, 1957); the Magistrate in *Lysistrata* (Royal Court, Dec. 27, 1957); Wellington Potts in *Caught Napping* (Piccadilly, May 22, 1959); Arthur Groomkirby in *One Way Pendulum* (Royal Court, Dec. 22, 1959); Dr. Crippin in *Belle* (Strand, May 4, 1961); Bolt in *August for the People* (Royal Court, Sept. 12, 1961); Boss Mangan in *Heartbreak House* (Wyndham's, Nov. 1, 1961); and Rupert Tilling in *The Tulip Tree* (Haymarket, Nov. 29, 1962).

He also played the part of Henry Carter in *The Excursion* (Ashcroft, Croydon, Feb. 1964); Thring in *The Man Who Let It Rain* (Theatre Royal, Stratford, England, May 1964); Lord Loam in *Our Man Crichton* (Shaftesbury Th., Dec. 1964); Count Bodo in *The Marriage of Mr. Mississippi* (Hampstead Th. Club, Sept. 1965); Dudley in *A Family and a Fortune* (Yvonne Arnaud Th., Guildford, July 1966); Lord Pilco in *The Last of Mrs. Cheyney* (Yvonne Arnaud Th., June 1967); Simon, Fred, and Reginald in *The Adventures of Tom Random* (Yvonne Arnaud Th., Sept. 1967); Steward, Carpenter, and January in *Canterbury Tales* (Phoenix, Oct. 1968–Jan. 1970); Justice Shallow in *Henry IV, Part 2* (Mermaid, May 1970); Gonzalo in *The Tempest* (Mermaid, June 1970); the Inquisitor in *St. Joan* (Mermaid, Sept. 1970); the Secretary of the League of Nations in *Geneva* (Mermaid, Oct. 1971); Dean Judd in *Dandy Dick* (Birmingham Repertory Th., July 1972); Rev. Harold Davidson in *The Vicar of Soho* (Gardner Centre, Sussex Univ., Aug. 1972); Christopher Glowry in *Nightmare Abbey* (Yvonne Arnaud Th., Guildford, Nov. 1972); Squire Trelawney in *Treasure Island* (Mermaid, Dec. 1972); the Waiter in *You Never Can Tell* (on tour, Feb. 1973); and Polonius in *Hamlet* (Theatre Royal, Windsor, Sept. 1973).

Films. Mr. Benson's film appearances include *Dracula* (U, 1931); *The Man from Toronto* (Gainsborough, 1937); *The October Man* (Eagle Lion, 1948); *Executioner* (20th-Fox, 1948); *The Man in the White Suit* (U, 1952); *The Captain's Paradise* (UA, 1953); *Value for Money* (Rank, 1957); and *The Pure Hell of St. Trinian's* (Continental, 1961); *For He's a Jolly Bad Fellow; The Best of Both Worlds; A Home of Your Own* (U, 1964); *The Great St. Trinian's Train Robbery* (U, 1966); *The Strange Affair* (Par., 1968); and *The Creeping Flesh* (Col., 1972).

Television. From 1936–40, Mr. Benson appeared in pioneer entertainment programs, transmitted by the British Broadcasting Corporation from Alexandra Palace, London. Since 1945, he has appeared on television both for the B.B.C. and I.T.V. companies on *Green Fingers; Tons of Money; Bardell v. Pickwick; Love for Love; Rosmersholm: The Light of Heart; Here and Now; Mrs. Moonlight; The Lilac Domino: My Wife's Sister; Mayor's Nest; Sandcastle; Arsenic and Old Lace; And So To Bed; The Mulberry Bush; The One Who Came Back; Charles and Mary; Call Me A Liar: The Fourth Wall; Badgers Green; The Lower Depths; Life and Death of Sir John Falstaff; Sam Weller and His Father; Movement of Troops; David and Broccoli; Mr. Nobody; Full Circle; The Ring of Truth; Coach 7, Seat 15; The Lady and the Clerk; Roll out the Barrel; The Rag Trade; Dentist on the Dyke; No Hiding Place; Comedy Playhouse; The Avengers; Girl in the Garden; The Case of Oscar Brodski; Danger Man; The Man in Room 17; The Regulator; The Dead Past; David Copperfield; Adam Adamant; Before the Fringe; The Forsythe Saga; The Mock Doctor; Half Hour Story; The World of Beachcomber; The Fireplace Firm; Canterbury Tales (The Canon's Yeoman's Tale); The Misfit; Jackanory; Albert and Victoria; The Double Deckers; The Goodies; Kate; The Last of the Baskets; Misleading Cases; Casanova; Six Days of Justice; A Warning to the Curious; Harriet's Back in Town.*

Recreation. Theatre, reading, gardening.

BENTLEY, ERIC. Playwright, critic, educator, translator. b. Eric Russell Bentley, Sept. 14, 1916, Bolton, England, to Fred and Laura (Evelyn) Bentley. Oxford Univ., B.A. 1938; B.Litt. 1939; Yale Univ., Ph.D. 1941. Married 1953 to Joanne Davis. Member of ASCAP. Address: 711 West End Ave., New York, NY 10025.

Mr. Bentley was Brander Matthews prof. of dramatic literature, Columbia Univ. (1954–69) and was Norton prof. of poetry, Harvard Univ. (1960–61).

Theatre. From 1952 to 1956, Mr. Bentley served as drama critic for *The New Republic.*

He adapted and directed *Good Woman of Setzuan* (Phoenix Th., Dec. 18, 1956); adapted *The Private Life of the Master Race* (City College Aud., N.Y.C., June 11, 1945); *A Man's a Man* (Masque, Sept. 19, 1962); *Mother Courage and Her Children* (Martin Beck Th., Mar. 28, 1963); *Baal* (Martinique Th., May 6, 1965); *The Exception and the Rule* (Greenwich Mews Th., May 30, 1965); and *Edward II* (Marine Memorial Th., San Francisco, Oct. 22, 1965). Mr. Bentley wrote *Commitments* (HB Playwrights Th., Mar. 27, 1967), later retitled *A Time to Die and A Time to Live; The Red, White, and Black* (La Mama E.T.C., Feb. 24, 1971); *Are You Now or Have You Ever Been* (Yale Repertory, New Haven, Conn., Nov. 11, 1972); and *The Recantation of Galileo Galilei* (Wayne State Univ. Th., Oct. 19, 1973).

Published Works. Mr. Bentley's books include *A Century of Hero Worship* (1944), *The Playwright as Thinker* (1946), *Bernard Shaw* (1947), *In Search of Theatre* (1953), *The Life of the Drama* (1964), *The Theatre of Commitment* (1967), and *The Theatre of War* (1972). *The Dramatic Event* (1954) and *What Is Theatre?* (1956) are collections of his drama reviews.

He edited *The Importance of Scrutiny* (1948), *The Play: Critical Anthology* (1951), *From the Modern Repertoire* (three vols., 1949–56), *Shaw on Music* (1955), *The Modern Theatre* (six vols., 1955–60), *Let's Get a Divorce and Other Plays* (1958), *The Classic Theatre* (four vols., 1958–61), *Seven Plays by Bertolt Brecht* (1961), *The Storm Over the Deputy* (1964), *The Brecht-Eisler Song Book, The Theory of the Modern Stage* (1968), *The Great Playwrights* (1970), *Thirty Years of Treason* (1971), and *The Genius of the Italian Theatre* (1972). Mr. Bentley was also editor for the *Dramabook* series and the Grove Press edition of *Bertolt Brecht.* .

Discography. Mr. Bentley was editor and performer for the recordings of *Bentley on Brecht* (Riverside Records, 1963), *Brecht Before the HUAC* (Folkways, 1963), *A Man's a Man* (Spoken Arts, 1963), *Songs of Hanns Eisler* (Folkways, 1964), *The Exception and the Rule, The Elephant Calf* (Folkways-Asch, 1967), *Bentley on Biermann* (Folkways-Broadside, 1968), and *The Queen of 42nd Street* (Pacifica, 1969).

Awards. Mr. Bentley received two Guggenheim fellowships (1948–49 and 1967–68), a Rockefeller grant (1949–50), the Longview Award for criticism (1961), and the George Jean Nathan Award (1966).

BERGEN, POLLY. Actress, singer, writer. b. Nellie Paulina Burgin, July 14, 1930, Knoxville, Tenn., to William and Lucy Burgin. Father, construction engineer. Attended Compton Junior Coll. Married to Jerome Cortland, actor (marr. dis. 1955); one daughter; married 1956 to Frederic Fields, talent representative. Member of AEA; SAG; AFTRA.

Theatre. Miss Bergen appeared in the N.Y.C. revue, *John Murray Anderson's Almanac* (Imperial, Dec. 10, 1953); played Allyn Macy in *Champagne Complex* (Cort, Apr. 12, 1955); and Elizabeth Bennett in *First Impressions* (Alvin, Mar. 19, 1959).

Films. She appeared in *At War with the Army* (Par., 1950); *Warpath* (Par., 1951); *That's My Boy* (Par., 1951); *The Stooge* (Par., 1952); *Half a Hero* (MGM, 1953); *Cry of the Hunted* (MGM, 1953); *Arena* (MGM, 1953); *Fast Company* (MGM, 1953); *Escape from Fort Bravo* (MGM, 1953); *Cape Fear* (U, 1962); and *A Guide for the Married Man* (20th-Fox, 1967).

Television and Radio. Miss Bergen performed on radio programs for WKBU, Richmond, Ind. (1944). She appeared on television in the title role in *The Helen Morgan Story* (Playhouse 90, CBS, Apr. 16, 1957); in *Just Polly and Me* (CBS, Aug. 11, 1964); in *The Loving Cup* (Bob Hope Presents (NBC, Jan. 29, 1965); did a special, *The Polly Bergen Show* (CBS, June 1968); and she has appeared at various times on variety and talk shows, including the Allan Young Show; Pepsi Cola Show; To Tell the Truth (CBS); Steve Allen Show (NBC); Ed Sullivan Show (CBS, 1965–66); Tonight Show (NBC, 1965–66); Dean Martin Show (NBC, 1965–66); Mike Douglas Show (ABC, 1966–67); and Red Skelton Show (CBS, 1967–68).

Night Clubs. She has performed at the Thunderbird Hotel (Las Vegas, Nev.); and the Persian Room (Hotel Plaza, N.Y.C.).

Published Works. Miss Bergen wrote *Polly's Principles* (1974).

BERGER, SIDNEY L. Teacher, actor, director. b. Jan. 25, 1936, New York City, to Sam and Pauline Berger. Father, leather goods manufacturer; mother, housewife. Graduated Brooklyn College, B.A. 1957; Univ. of Kansas, M.A. 1960; Univ. of Kansas, Ph.D. 1964. Professional training with Jose Quintero, the Directing Studio, and Jack Garfein. Married Mar. 2, 1964, to Helen Sandra Hopkins; one son; one daughter. Member ATA (regional chmn., 1967–69); American College Theatre Festival (regional chmn., 1968–69). Address: (home) 4711 Imogene, Houston, TX 77035, tel. (713) 664-9703; (bus.) Drama Dept., Univ. of Houston, Cullen Blvd., Houston, TX 77035, tel. (713)

749-4708.

Mr. Berger since 1969 has been professor and chairman of the Univ. of Houston Drama Dept. He was an assistant instructor at the Univ. of Kansas during 1958–63 and assistant professor at Michigan State Univ. during 1964–69.

Theatre. Mr. Berger appeared first on stage while an undergraduate at Brooklyn College, where he was in a 1953 production of *Street Scene* at the college's George Gershwin Theatre. Subsequently, he played at the Gershwin as Tavy in *Man and Superman* (Feb. 1954), Azrael in *The Dybbuk* (Apr. 1954), Brown in *The Great God Brown* (Sept. 1955), and Jerry Boyle in *Juno and the Paycock* (Feb. 1955). He was the author also of two Gershwin Th. productions at Brooklyn College: *That Caveman Touch* (Apr. 1956) and *Hell of an Angel* (Apr. 1957).

His first activity in the professional theatre was as a general understudy in the Off-Bway *Johnny Summit* (Renata Th., Sept. 1958). He began directing with productions for USO units touring in the Far East: *Brigadoon* (Sept. 1959), in which he played the role of Jeff, and *The Boy Friend* (Apr. 1960). In Feb. 1960, he directed *Tea and Sympathy* at the Univ. of Kansas, where he appeared also as Azdak in *The Caucasian Chalk Circle* (Sept. 1960), Truffaldino in *Servant of Two Masters* (Apr. 1962), and Face in *The Alchemist* (Sept. 1962). For the US State Dept., he made concert tours of the theatre to Eastern Europe and Germany in May 1963 and May 1964.

At Michigan State Univ., he directed *Long Day's Journey into Night* (Sept. 1964), *Slow Dance on the Killing Ground* (Mar. 1965), *West Side Story* (Nov. 1965), *Oh, What a Lovely War!* (Jan. 1966), and *Marat/Sade* (Sept. 1966). For a USO tour of Iceland, Greenland, and Labrador, he directed *The Boys from Syracuse* (June 1966) and for a USO tour of Western Europe, he directed *Sweet Charity.* He directed *Threepenny Opera* at the Univ. of Houston (Sept. 1969) and directed previews of the operas *The Marriage of Figaro, Macbeth,* and Gounod's *Romeo and Juliet* for the Houston Grand Opera (Jan. 1970; Jan. 1971). Later, at the Univ. of Houston, he directed *Richard III* (Apr. 1972), *The Homecoming* (Sept. 1972), *The Time of Your Life* (Feb. 1973), and *Fiddler on the Roof* (Apr. 1973).

Films. Mr. Berger played the role of John Linden in *Carnival of Souls* (Harcourt Prod., 1962).

Television and Radio. Mr. Berger was a panelist on the radio show Between the Teens (CBS, Jan. 1957), and he made his television debut as narrator for On the Carousel (CBS, Dec. 1957).

Published Works. Mr. Berger has written articles for the *Bulletin of Education Players,* and *Jewish Book Annual,* and his book reviews have appeared in *American Theatre Journal.* .

Awards. In 1968, Mr. Berger was appointed a member of the Michigan Council on the Arts by Governor Romney, and in 1973 he became a director of the Texas Opera Theatre. The National Foundation for Jewish Culture awarded him a grant for the study of Yiddish theatre. He is a member of the screening committee for Fulbright-Hays awards in theatre.

Recreation. Collecting books, classical music.

BERGERSEN, BALDWIN. Composer, musical director, musician. b. Louis Baldwin Bergersen, Feb. 20, 1914, Vienna, Austria, to Louis Edward and Beatrice (Rice) Bergersen. Grad. Cathedral Choir Sch. of St. John the Divine, N.Y.C., 1929; Trinity Sch., N.Y.C., 1933. Member of AFM, Local 802; Dramatists Guild; ASCAP. Address: 865 First Ave., New York, NY 10017, tel. (212) MU 8-4395.

Theatre. Mr. Bergersen composed the music for *Calling All Men* (Cape Playhouse, Dennis, Mass., 1936); subsequently contributed songs to the N.Y.C. revue *Who's Who* (Hudson, Mar. 1, 1938); composed the music for *Allah Be Praised* (Adelphi, Apr. 20, 1944); *Carib Song* (Adelphi, Sept. 27, 1945); contributed songs to the revue *Small Wonder* (Coronet, Sept. 15, 1948); was arranger and musical director for the touring revue *Musical Americana* (1953); composed the music for *The Crystal Heart* (Saville, London, Feb. 19, 1957 and E. 74 St. Th., N.Y.C., Feb. 15, 1960); was musical director for the revue *Double Dublin* (Little, Dec. 26, 1963), and accompanist for *The Hostage* (The Club House, Apr. 24, 1967).

Night Clubs. Mr. Bergersen composed the music and was musical director for the revue *Prickly Pear* (Show Place, 1961); and played the piano interludes for the Plaza 9 Music Hall productions of *Dames at Sea* (Plaza Hotel, Sept. 22, 1970) and *Cooler Near the Lake* (Plaza Hotel, Feb. 7, 1971).

Discography. He was the pianist for the album of *Carib Song* (1946); and composed the music for *Where's the Boy I Saved for a Rainy Day?* (1959) and *Hunger* (1959).

Recreation. Swimming, skiing.

BERGHOF, HERBERT. Actor, director, coach. b. Sept. 13, 1909, Vienna, Austria, to Paul and Regina Berghof. Father, railroad station-master. Attended Univ. of Vienna. Studied for the theatre at Vienna State Acad. of Dramatic Art (1927); studied acting with Alexandre Moissi and Max Reinhardt; Actors Studio (charter member); Lee Strasberg, N.Y.C. Married to Alice Hermes, coach (marr. dis.); married to Uta Hagen, actress. Member of AEA; AFTRA; SAG. Herbert Berghof Studio, 120 Bank St., New York, NY 10014, tel. (212) OR 5-2370.

Theatre. Mr. Berghof first appeared on the stage in Vienna (Aust.) in a production of *Don Carlos* (Deutsches Volkstheater, Sept. 1927). He became a resident member of the St. Gallen (repertory) Co. (Zurich, Switzerland, 1927–29); a member of the Volles Th. (Vienna, Austria, 1929–30); performed in Berlin, Germany, (Deutsches Th., Volksbühne, 1930–33); and at the Salzburg (Austria) Festivals (1933–38); played Romeo in *Romeo and Juliet,* performed in *Journey's End,* Louis Dubedat in *The Doctor's Dilemma* (Vienna); the title role in *Hamlet* (Vienna); and directed *The Melody That Got Lost* (Vienna); in Berlin (Germany), appeared in *All God's Chillun Got Wings, Crime for Crime, Six Characters in Search of an Author,* and *An American Tragedy,* Death in *Everyman* (Salzburg Festival, Austria); Oswald in *Ghosts;* Orlando in *As You Like It;* and Marchbanks in *Candida.*

Mr. Berghof made his N.Y.C. debut as the Fool in *King Lear* (New Sch. for Social Research, Studio Th., 1941); also at the New Sch., played Kummerer in *The Criminals* (Studio Th., Dec. 20, 1941). His first Bway production was *From Vienna* which he directed for the Refugee Artists Group (Music Box, June 20, 1939); appeared in and directed, with Ezra Stone, *Reunion in New York,* a revised version of *From Vienna* (Little, Feb. 21, 1940); and played Captain Milder in *Somewhere in France,* which closed on its pre-Bway tour (Natl., Washington, D.C., Apr. 28, 1941).

He appeared in the title role in *Nathan the Wise* (Shubert, N.Y.C., Apr. 3, 1942); as Milosh Kraussnig in a tryout production of *Twelve Midnight* (Scarsdale, N.Y., Sept. 1, 1942); Tieck in *Winter Soldiers* (New Sch. for Social Research, Studio Th., Nov. 29, 1942); subsequently played Panin in *The Russian People* (Guild, Dec. 29, 1942); Otto in *The Innocent Voyage* (Belasco, Nov. 15, 1943); succeeded Joseph Buloff as Ali Hakim in *Oklahoma!* (St. James, March 31, 1943); succeeded Oscar Karlweiss as Jacobowsky in *Jacobowsky and the Colonel* (Martin Beck Th., Mar. 14, 1944); played Gustav Ebertson in *The Man Who Had All The Luck* (Forrest, Nov. 23, 1944); Professor Bhaer in *Little Women* (NY City Ctr., Dec. 12, 1944); Maurice in *The Beggars Are Coming to Town* (Coronet, Oct. 27, 1945); Jean, Jr., and Jean, Sr., in a touring production of *St. Lazare's Pharmacy* (opened His Majesty's Th., Montreal, Quebec, Canada, Dec. 6, 1945; closed Harris, Chicago, Ill., Mar. 2, 1946); Pedro Crespo in a special Sunday performance of *The Mayor of Zalemia* (Majestic, N.Y.C., Jan. 27, 1946); Captain Karel Palivec in *Temper the Wind* (Playhouse, Dec. 27, 1946); directed *The Key* (Old Knickerbocker Music Hall, Jan. 6, 1947); succeeded (May 1947) Stephen Bekassy as Dmitri Savelev in *The Whole World Over* (Biltmore, Mar. 27, 1947); directed *Rip Van Winkle* (NY City Ctr., July 15, 1947); appeared as the Rev. Mr. Manders in *Ghosts* (Cort, Feb. 16, 1948); Judge Brack in *Hedda Gabler* (Cort, Feb. 24, 1948); Bartholdi in *Miss Liberty* (Imperial, July 15, 1949); the title role of *Torquato Tasso* (Barbizon-Plaza Th., Nov. 20, 1949); as Dr. Wangel in *The Lady from the Sea* (Fulton, Aug. 7, 1950); the Critic in a production of *The Guardsman* (Erlanger, Buffalo, N.Y., Jan. 1951); Prince Mikhail Alexandrovitch Ouratieff in *Tovarich* (NY City Ctr., May 25, 1952); and Mr. Miller in *The Deep Blue Sea* (Morosco, Nov. 5, 1952). In stock, he appeared in *Michael and Lavinia* (Theatre-by-the Sea, Matunuck, R.I., Aug. 30, 1954); and played M. Prunelles in *Cyprienne* (Norwich Summer Th., Conn., June 3–27, 1955).

Mr. Berghof directed *Waiting for Godot* (John Golden Th., N.Y.C., Apr. 19, 1956); *Protective Custody* (Ambassador, Dec. 28, 1956); and a production of *Waiting for Godot* with an all Negro cast (Ethel Barrymore Th., Jan. 21, 1957).

At the Ann Arbor (Mich.) Dramatic Festival, he directed and performed in *The Affairs of Anatol* (Lydia Mendelssohn Th., 1957); directed *The Infernal Machine* (Phoenix, N.Y.C., Feb. 3, 1958); for the Cambridge (Mass.) Drama Festival, directed *Twelfth Night* (July 1959); and *The Queen and The Rebels* (Bucks County Playhouse, New Hope, Pa., Aug. 24, 1959). He appeared as Henry Wirz in *The Andersonville Trial* (Henry Miller's Th., N.Y.C., Dec. 29, 1959); succeeded (Dec. 27, 1960); Henderson Forsythe as Krapp in *Krapp's Last Tape* (Provincetown Playhouse, Jan. 14, 1960).

He directed *Do You Know the Milky Way?* (Billy Rose Th., Oct. 16, 1961); *This Side of Paradise* (Sheridan Sq. Playhouse, Feb. 21, 1962; played the title role in *Enrico IV* (Arena Stage, Washington, D.C., Apr. 22, 1964); and Edward Teller in *In the Matter of J. Robert Oppenheimer* (Vivian Beaumont Th., N.Y.C., Mar. 6, 1969).

Films. Mr. Berghof appeared in *Assignment Paris* (Col., 1952); *Diplomatic Courier* (20th-Fox, 1952); *Five Fingers* (20th-Fox, 1952); *Red Planet Mars* (UA, 1952); *Fraülein* (20th-Fox, 1958); *An Affair of the Skin* (1963); *Cleopatra* (20th-Fox, 1963); and *Harry and Tonto* (20th-Fox, 1974).

Television and Radio. On radio, he has performed on Report to the Nation, The Goldbergs, and Norman Corwin Presents. On television, he played in *For Whom the Bell Tolls* (Playhouse 90, CBS, Mar. 19, 1959); appeared on Producer's Showcase (NBC); Kraft Television Th. (NBC); in *Chez Rouge* (Desilu Playhouse, NBC, Aug. 8, 1965); and *And the Bones Come Together* (ABC, Feb. 15, 1973).

Other Activities. Mr. Berghof has taught acting at Columbia Univ.; the New Sch. for Social Research; the Neighborhood Playhouse, and The American Theatre Wing (1949). He founded (1946) the Herbert Berghof (HB) Studio (of acting), which he directs with his wife, Uta Hagen, and (1964) the HB Playwrights Foundation.

BERGMAN, INGRID. Actress. b. Aug. 29, 1915, Stockholm, Sweden, to Justus and Friedel (Adler) Bergman. Father, painter, photographer. Attended Lyceum Sch. for Girls, 1922–32; studied for theatre at Royal Dramatic Th. Sch., Stockholm, 1933–34. Married July 10, 1937, to Peter Lindstrom, physician (marr. dis. 1950), one daughter, Pia Lindstrom, actress; married May 24, 1950, to Roberto Rossellini, director (marr. dis.); one son, twin daughters; married Dec. 21, 1958 to Lars Schmidt, producer.

Theatre. Miss Bergman made her N.Y.C. debut as Julie in *Liliom* (44 St. Th., Mar. 25, 1940); appeared as Anna Christopherson in *Anna Christie* (Lobero, Santa Barbara, Calif., 1941) and on tour in southern Calif., appeared in the title role of *Joan of Lorraine* (Alvin, N.Y.C., Nov. 18, 1946); played Joan, a non-singing role, in the opera *Joan of Arc at the Stake* (San Carlo Opera House, Naples, It., Dec. 1953; Stoll, London, England, Oct. 20, 1954; and Opera House, Stockholm, Sweden, Feb. 1955). She appeared as Laura Reynolds in *Tea and Sympathy* (Th.

de Paris, Paris, France, Dec. 10, 1956); and the title role in *Hedda Gabler* (Th. Gaston Baty-Montparnasse, Dec. 11, 1962).

She played Natalia Petrovna in *A Month in the Country* (opening production Yvonne Arnaud Th., Guilford, England, May 1965; Cambridge Th., London, Sept. 1965); Deborah in the first production of *More Stately Mansions* (Ahmanson Th., Los Angeles, Calif., Sept. 12, 1967; Broadhurst, N.Y.C., Oct. 31, 1967); Lady Cicely Waynflete in *Captain Brassbound's Conversion* (Cambridge, London, England, Feb. 1971; Opera House, John F. Kennedy Ctr., Washington, D.C., Mar. 13, 1972; Ethel Barrymore Th., N.Y.C., Apr. 17, 1972); and Constance Middleton in *The Constant Wife* (Albery, London, England, Sept. 19, 1973; Opera House, John F. Kennedy Ctr., Mar. 1975; Sam S. Shubert Th., N.Y.C., Apr. 14, 1975).

Films. During 1936-14 37, Miss Bergman appeared in several films in Sweden, including *Intermezzo* (SCA, 1937). She made her American film debut in an English-speaking version of the same film, entitled *Intermezzo: A Love Story* (UA, 1939). She also appeared in *Adam Had Four Sons* (Col., 1941); *Rage in Heaven* (MGM, 1941); *Dr. Jekyll and Mr. Hyde* (MGM, 1941); *Casablanca* (WB, 1942); *For Whom the Bell Tolls* (Par., 1943); *Gaslight* (MGM, 1944); *Saratoga Trunk* (WB, 1945); *The Bells of St. Mary's* (RKO, 1945); *Spellbound* (UA, 1945); *Notorious* (RKO, 1946); *Arch of Triumph* (UA, 1948); *Joan of Arc* (RKO, 1948); *Under Capricorn* (WB, 1949); *Stromboli* (RKO, 1950); *The Greatest Love* (Ital. Films Export, 1954); *A Trip to Italy* (1955); *Fear* (Astor, 1956); *Paris Does Strange Things* (WB, 1956) *Anastasia* (20th-Fox, 1957); *The Inn of the Sixth Happiness* (20th-Fox, 1958); *Indiscreet* (WB, 1958); *Goodbye Again* (UA, 1961); *The Visit* (20th-Fox, 1963); in "The Necklace" segment of *Stimulantia* (Sweden, 1967); *The Yellow Rolls-Royce* (MGM, 1965); *Cactus Flower* (Col., 1969); and *Murder on the Orient Express* (Par., 1974).

In 1943, Miss Bergman appeared in the OWI documentary film *Swedes in America.* .

Television. She appeared in *The Turn of the Screw* (CBS, Oct. 20, 1959); *Hedda Gabler* (CBS, Sept. 20, 1963); and *Twenty-Four Hours in a Woman's Life* (CBS, Mar. 20, 1961).

Awards. Miss Bergman received Academy (Oscar) Awards as best actress for her performances in *Gaslight* (1944) and *Anastasia* (1956) and as best supporting actress (1975) for her performance in *Murder on the Orient Express.* She also received (1957) the NY Film Critics Award for her performance in *Anastasia* and the Stella Award of the Society of British Film and Television Arts for her performance in *Murder on the Orient Express.* She was voted one of the ten best money-making stars by the Motion Picture Herald Fame Poll (1946–48).

For her performance in the television production of *The Turn of the Screw,* she received a NATAS (Emmy) Award (1960) and the Sylvania Award.

BERGNER, ELISABETH. Actress. b. Aug. 22, 1900, Vienna, Austria, to Emil and Anna Rosa (Wagner) Bergner. Studied for the theatre at Vienna Conservatory. Married 1933 to Dr. Paul Czinner, producer-director. Member of AEA; SAG. Address: 42 Eaton Square, London, S.W. 1, England.

Theatre. Miss Bergner's first professional appearance was with the City Th. (Zurich, Switzerland, 1919). In Zurich, she also played Ophelia in Moissi's *Hamlet* (1919) and Rosalind in *As You Like It* (1920), a role she later repeated in Vienna, Munich, and Berlin.

She appeared in the Berlin production of Julius Berstl's *The Wicked Mr. Chu;* appeared at the Deutches Th. under the direction of Max Reinhardt, as Katherine in *The Taming of the Shrew;* the Queen in *Richard II;* Rosalind in *As You Like It;* the title role in *Miss Julie;* played in *Hannele;* Nora in *A Doll's House;* Viola in *Twelfth Night;* Juliet in *Romeo and Juliet;* in 1924, she played the title role in *Saint Joan;* Marguerite in *The Lady of the Camellias;* and Rosalind in *As You Like It;* in 1925, she appeared in *The Circle of Chalk* and in Nestroy's *He Wants to Have His Fun.*

She played Mrs. Cheyney in *The Last of Mrs. Cheyney* (Koeniggraetzer Th., Berlin, Germany, 1927); Tessa in *The Constant Nymph* (Koeniggraetzer Th., Berlin, 1927); and Portia in *The Merchant of Venice* (Staattheater, Berlin, 1927).

In 1928, Miss Bergner toured Holland, Switzerland, Denmark, Sweden, Germany, and Austria in *Hannele, Kaiser Karl's Geisel, Einsame Menschen, The Taming of the Shrew, Richard II, Queen Christina, The Circle, Miss Julie, Lanzelot and Sanderein, The Circle of Chalk, As You Like It, The Last of Mrs. Cheyney, Saint Joan,* and *Amphitryon 38.*

In Berlin, she played Nina Leeds in *Strange Interlude* (1929); Juliet in *Romeo and Juliet* (1930); and Alkmena in *Amphitryon 38* (1931).

She made her debut in England as Gemma Jones in *Escape Me Never* (Opera House, Manchester, Nov. 21, 1933; Apollo, London, Dec. 8, 1933); and made her N.Y.C. debut in it (Shubert, Jan. 21, 1935).

She played David in J. M. Barrie's *The Boy David* (His Majesty's, London, Dec. 14, 1936), Joan in *Saint Joan* (Malvern, England, Aug. 1938), Sally in *The Two Mrs. Carrolls* (Booth, N.Y.C., Aug. 3, 1943), and also toured in it (1945).

She directed *The Overtons* (Booth, N.Y.C., Feb. 6, 1945); played the title role in *The Duchess of Malfi* (Ethel Barrymore Th., Oct. 15, 1946); the title role in *Miss Julie* (Forrest, Philadelphia, Pa., Jan. 21, 1947); Ellen Croy in *The Cup of Trembling* (Music Box, N.Y.C., Apr. 20, 1948); and repeated her role as Alkmena in *Amphitryon 38* (June 1949).

Miss Bergner toured Australia in *The Two Mrs. Carrolls* (1950); played Toinette in *The Gay Invalid* (Opera House, Manchester, England, Nov. 1950; Garrick, London, Jan. 1951); appeared in Berlin as Hester in *The Deep Blue Sea,* and also toured Europe in it.

She appeared in the pre-Bway tryout of *First Love* (1961); appeared in Berlin and toured Europe as Stella Patrick Campbell in *Dear Liar;* and as Mary Cavan Tyrone in *A Long Day's Journey into Night* (1963).

She repeated her *Dear Liar* role in N.Y.C. (Barbizon-Plaza, May 3, 1963); played the title role in *The Madwoman of Chaillot* (Oxford, England; Berlin and Dusseldorf, Germany; European tour; (1968); was Deborah in *More Stately Mansions* (Berlin, 1970; Germany and European tour, 1971–72); and appeared in *Catsplay* (Greenwich, London, 1973).

Films. Miss Bergner has appeared in *Nju; Geiger of Florence; Donna Juana; Love; Miss Else; Catherine of Russia* (UA, 1934); *Ariane* (Biue Ribbon, 1934); *As You Like It* (20th-Fox, 1936); *Dreaming Lips* (UA, 1937); *Stolen Life* (Par., 1939); *Paris Calling* (U, 1941); and *Escape Me Never* (WB, 1947).

Awards. She received the Schiller Prize "for outstanding contributions to the cultural life in Germany" (1963); and the Gold Ribbon for best female acting achievement in Germany during the Berlin Film Festival (1963).

BERKOWITZ, SOL. Composer, writer. b. Apr. 27, 1922, Warren, Ohio, to Jacob and Lillie Berkowitz. Father, painter. Grad. John Adams H.S., N.Y.C., 1938; Queens Coll., B.A. 1942; Columbia Univ., M.A. 1947. Studied music with Karol Rathaus (1939–42); Otto Leuning (1945–46); and Abby Whiteside (1934–1938). Married June 9, 1945, to Pearl, psychologist, educator. Relative in theatre: brother, David, musician. Served US Army, radar technician with Signal Corps, 1942–45; rank, Staff Sgt., Special Services. Member of Dramatists Guild; AFM; ASCAP. Address: 46-36 Hanford St., Douglaston, NY 11363, tel. (212) BA 5-8944.

Theatre. Mr. Berkowitz composed songs for *The Littlest Revue* (Phoenix Th., May 22, 1956); composed the score for *Miss Emily Adam* (Th. Marquee, Mar. 29, 1960); incidental music for *The Unsinkable Molly Brown* (Winter Garden, Nov. 3, 1960); wrote the music for *Nowhere to Go But Up* (Winter Garden, Nov. 10, 1962); and the ballet and incidental music for *Mornin' Sun* (Phoenix, Oct. 6, 1963).

Television and Radio. Several of his songs were included on the radio program Song Cycle (WNYC, Feb. 1947). For television, he wrote music for *Jazz of This Hotel* (ABC, Feb. 1952); and was staff composer for the Garry Moore Show (CBS, 1963–64 season) and for the Carol Burnett Show (CBS, 1964–65 season).

Night Clubs. Mr. Berkowitz composed and orchestrated *Diamond Fair* (Latin Quarter, N.Y.C., Nov. 1963).

Other Activities. Some of his works that have been performed in programs on the concert stage are "Duo Concertanta for Two Pianos" (Carnegie Hall, NYC, Jan. 1947); "Scherzo for Piano" (Carnegie Hall, Nov. 1948); "Sonata for Piano" (Brooklyn Museum, Feb. 1948); "Concerto for Oboe" (Amer. Festival of Music, Feb. 1950); "Suite for Piano" (NY City Ctr., Mar. 1949); and "Quintet for Winds" (Town Hall, NYC, Nov. 1951). He also composed music for Jazz Ballet (92 St. YM-YWHA, NYC, Dec. 1952); and the opera *Fat Tuesday* (Tamiment Playhouse, Pa., Aug. 1956).

Mr. Berkowitz was professor of music at Queens College from 1945 to 1959 and has held this position at Queens College of the City University of New York since 1967.

Published Works. He is the author of *New Approach to Sight Singing* (1960) and *Improvisation Through Keyboard Harmony* (1974). His published compositions include *The Jazz of This Hotel,* for mixed chorus (1954); *Drinking Song,* for chorus (1956); *Without Words,* suite for chorus (1963); *Five Sad and Humorous Songs in Jazz Rock,* for chorus (1970); *27 Jazzettes,* for piano (1971); *Three Tongue Twisters,* for chorus (1972); *Diversion,* for orchestra (1972); *Nine Folk Song Preludes,* for piano (1972); *Ten Duets,* for treble instruments (1971); *Game of Dance,* for concert band (1956; 1971); *Two Letters from Lincoln,* for chorus (1974); and *Introduction and Scherzo,* for viola and piano (1974).

Awards. Mr. Berkowitz received a Ford Foundation Grant for composition (1955–56).

Recreation. Baseball, football, sculpture, painting.

BERLE, MILTON. Actor, producer, lyricist, writer. b. Milton Berlinger, July 12, 1908, New York, City, to Moses and Sarah (Glantz) Berlinger. Father, painter decorator. Attended Professional Children's Sch., N.Y.C., 1916. Married 1941 to Joyce Matthews, show girl (marr. dis. Oct. 1947); one daughter; married June 16, 1949 to Joyce Matthews (marr. dis. 1950); married Dec. 9, 1953, to Ruth Cosgrove Rosenthal, press agent; one son. Relatives in theatre: mother, performer, manager; brother, Frank, performer, manager. Member of AEA; AFTRA; AGVA; SAG; AFL, Local 802; The Friars (Abbot, 1939; hon. Abbot emeritus, 1968); Milton Berle Foundation; National Children's Cardiac Home (chmn. of bd.); Grand Street Boys' Club; Jewish Theatrical Guild (pres., 1961); Hillcrest Golf Club.

Theatre. Mr. Berle made his N.Y.C. debut in *Floradora* (Century, Apr. 5, 1920). He spent a twelve-year period in vaudeville, making his first appearance in *Melody of Youth* (Nixon's Grand, Philadelphia, Pa., 1921); appeared in N.Y.C., as half of the comedy team, Kennedy and Berle (Palace, 1921); and as a single, in addition to touring the various vaudeville circuits with his own company.

Mr. Berle appeared in *Earl Carroll Vanities* (Bway Th., N.Y.C., Sept. 27, 1932); as "Windy" Walker in *Saluta!* (Imperial, Aug. 28, 1934); and toured in *Life Begins at 8:40* (1935).

He appeared in vaudeville (Loew's State, N.Y.C., 1938); in stock, played Alvin Roberts in *Blessed Event* (Maplewood Th., N.J., May 8, 1939); played Arthur Lee in *See My Lawyer* (Biltmore, N.Y.C., Sept. 27, 1939); appeared in *The Ziegfeld Follies* (Winter Garden, Apr. 1, 1943); was producer with Clifford Hayman, of *I'll Take the High Road* (Ritz, Nov. 9, 1943); produced, with Andrew Billings, *Same Time Next Week,* which closed on its pre-Bway tour (Shubert, New Haven, Conn., May 4, 1944); toured as Walter Gribble, Jr. in *Spring in Brazil* (Oct. 1945); produced, in association with Sammy Lambert and Bernie Foyer, *Seventeen* (Broadhurst, N.Y.C., June 2, 1951); appeared at the Roxy Th., N.Y.C. (Aug. 1951); made a tour of summer theatres as Jerry Biffle in *Top Banana* (Guber-Ford-Gross Circuit, Summer 1963); played Dr. Jack Kingsley in *The Impossible Years* (Parker Playhouse, Fort Lauderdale, Fla., Mar. 27, 1967; Coconut Grove Playhouse, Miami, Fla., Apr. 4, 1967) and was Max Silverman in *The Goodbye People* (Ethel Barrymore Th., N.Y.C., Dec. 3, 1968).

Films. As a child, Mr. Berle appeared in *The Perils of Pauline* (Pathé, 1914); *Tillie's Punctured Romance* (1914); *Easy Street* (Mutual, c. 1916); *Little Brother* (Ince-Triangle, 1917); *Humoresque* (Par., 1920); *The Mark of Zorro* (UA, 1920); *Divorce Coupons* (Vitagraph, 1922); and *Lena Rivers* (Arrow, 1925). Later films include *Sparrows* (UA, 1926); *New Faces of 1937* (RKO, 1937); *Radio City Revels* (RKO, 1938); *Sun Valley Serenade* (20th-Fox, 1941); *Rise and Shine* (20th-Fox, 1941); *Tall, Dark and Handsome* (20th-Fox, 1941); *A Gentleman at Heart* (20th-Fox, 1942); *Over My Dead Body* (20th-Fox, 1943); *Margin for Error* (20th-Fox, 1943); *Always Leave Them Laughing* (WB, 1949); *The Dolly Sisters* (20th-Fox, 1960); *Let's Make Love* (20th-Fox, 1960); *It's a Mad, Mad, Mad, Mad World* (UA, 1963); *The Loved One* (MGM, 1965); *The Oscar* (Embassy, 1966); *The Happening* (Col., 1967); *Who's Minding the Mint?* (Col., 1967); *Where Angels Go—Trouble Follows* (Col., 1968); *Can Hieronymus Merkin Ever Forget Mercy Humppe and Find True Happiness?* (U, 1969).

Television and Radio. On radio, Mr. Berle performed regularly on The Rudy Vallee Hour (WEAF, 1934–36); Shell Chateau (WEAF, 1935); Ziegfeld Follies of the Air (1936); Community Sing (WABC, 1937); Stop Me If You've Heard This One (NBC, 1939); Three Ring Time (WOR, 1941); Let Yourself Go (Blue Network, 1944); Milton Berle Show (NBC, 1947); and the Texaco Star Th. (ABC, 1948). Mr. Berle was also on the radio special *The Chase and Sanborn 101st Anniversary Presents Fred Allen* (NBC, Nov. 14, 1965).

On television, Mr. Berle appeared on the Texaco Star Th. (NBC, 1948); and the Damon Runyon Cancer Memorial Fund Telethon (NBC, Apr. 9–10, 1949). He was in *State of Confusion* (NBC, Oct. 18, 1955); on the Kraft Music Hall (NBC, 1958–59); in *Material Witness* (Kraft Television Th., NBC, Feb. 19, 1958); the City of Hope Telethon (Dumont, May 15–16, 1959); the Lucille Ball-Desi Arnez Show (CBS, Sept. 25, 1959); Sunday Showcase (NBC, Oct. 11, and Nov. 1, 1959); played in *Doyle Against the House* (Dick Powell Th., NBC, Oct. 24, 1961); appeared on the Chrysler Television Special (NBC, Mar. 9, 1962); played in *The Candidate* (Bob Hope Presents, NBC, Dec. 6, 1963); *Die Laughing* (CBS, Apr. 1964); and produced the series My Favorite Martian (CBS, 1963–64).

He was in *Milton Berle Hides Out at the Ricardos* (Lucy-Desi, CBS, July 25, 1964); in *That He Should Weep For Her* (Kraft Suspense Th., NBC, Nov. 5, 1964); in *Dead End on Flugel Street* (Trials of O'Brien, CBS, Dec. 3, 1965); and was host of the Milton Berle Show (ABC, 1966–67). Other appearances include F Troop (ABC, 1966); *Murder at NBC* (Bob Hope, NBC, Oct. 19, 1966); *Seven in Darkness* (ABC, Sept. 23, 1969); Here's Lucy (CBS, 1969); Love, American Style (ABC, 1971); Mod Squad (ABC, 1971); Mannix (CBS, 1971); The Bold Ones (ABC, 1972); and *Evil Roy Slade* (NBC, Feb. 18, 1972).

In addition, Mr. Berle appeared on many talk and variety series, including the Bob Hope Show (NBC, 1964–65); Johnny Carson Show (NBC, 1964–65); Andy Williams Show (NBC, 1964–65); Jack Benny Show (NBC, 1964–65); Hollywood Palace (ABC, 1964–67); Ed Sullivan Show (CBS, 1965–66), Dean Martin Show (NBC, 1965–66); Mike Douglas Show (Ind. 1965–66); Lucille Ball Show (CBS, 1965); Sammy Davis, Jr. Show (NBC, 1965–66); and Dateline: Hollywood (ABC, 1967–68).

Night Clubs. Mr. Berle made his first appearance at the Embassy Club (Atlantic City, N.J., 1926). Among his subsequent engagements are The Carnival (N.Y.C., 1946–47); the Latin Quarter (Miami Beach, Fla., 1957–58); and the Desert Inn (Las Vegas, Nev., Jan. 1963); The Flamingo (Las Vegas, Dec. 1965); Cafe Pompeii (Eden Roc, Miami Beach, Fla., Feb. 1966); the Deauville (Miami Beach, Fla., Jan. 1967); and Caesar's Palace (Las Vegas, June 1967).

Published Works. Mr. Berle's published songs include: "Gotta Darn Good Reason," "We Incorporated," "Just Say the Word," "What Do I Have To Do to Make You Love Me?," "Moon Magic," "What's Gonna Be (with You and Me)," "I'm Living in the Past," "Here Comes the Girl," "Let's Begin Again," "Your Eyes Are Bigger Than Your Heart," "For the First Time in My Life," "I Hate to Say Goodnight," "Violins and Violets," "Sorry Dear," "Ain't That Something Now," "You Took Me Out of This World," "I'd Give a Million Tomorrows (for Just One Yesterday)," "Li'l Abner," "Sam, You Made the Pants Too Long," "Let's Keep It That Way," "I'll Be Hanging Round Your Doorstep," "Save Me a Dream," "Sunkissed Days and Moonkissed Nights," "Never Break a Promise," "There's Green Grass Under the Snow," "I'm So Happy I Could Cry," "Shave and a Haircut-Shampoo," "It's Just a Mile from Treasure Isle," "Give Her My Love," "I Wuv a Wabbit," "You're Not Fooling Anyone But Yourself," "Leave the Dishes in the Sink, Ma," "Lucky Lucky Lucky Me," and "Always Leave Them Laughing."

Mr. Berle also wrote *Laughingly Yours* (1939); and *Out of My Trunk* (1945); was co-author of *Earthquake* (1959), and *I, The People;* and wrote, with Haskel Frankel, *Milton Berle: An Autobiography* (1974). He has also contributed a column "of humorous chit-chat" to *Variety*. .

Awards. Mr. Berle received the Humanitarian Award from The Yiddish Theatrical Alliance (1951) and was named NATAS "Man of the Year" (1959).

BERLIN, IRVING. Composer, lyricist. b. Israel Baline, May 11, 1888, Temun, Russia, to Moses and Leah (Lipkin) Baline. Father, cantor. Attended NYC public sch., two years. Married Jan. 4, 1926, to Ellin Mackay; three daughters. Served US Army, 1917–18, Infantry; rank, Sgt. Member of ASCAP (charter member, director 1914–18); Mason (Shriner); Elks; The Lambs; The Friars. Address: 1290 Avenue of the Americas, New York, NY 10019, tel. (212) CI 7-4200.

Pre-Theatre. Singing waiter.

Theatre. Mr. Berlin made his first N.Y.C. appearance singing his own songs in the revue, *Up and Down Broadway* (Casino, July 18, 1910); subsequently contributed songs to *The Ziegfeld Follies* (Jardin de Paris, June 26, 1911). His first complete score, music and lyrics, was for *Watch Your Step* (New Amsterdam, Dec. 8, 1914); subsequently he wrote 15 songs for the revue, *Stop! Look! Listen!* (Globe, Dec. 25, 1915), which was presented as *Follow the Crowd* (Empire, London, Feb. 19, 1916); and six songs for Victor Herbert's *The Century Girl* (Century, Nov. 6, 1916); and contributed songs to *The Cohan Revue of 1918* (New Amsterdam, Dec. 31, 1917).

He wrote the book, lyrics and music, and produced the WW I all-soldier show *Yip Yip Yaphank* (Century, Aug. 19, 1918); he wrote songs for the musical, *The Canary* (Globe, Nov. 4, 1918); and contributed songs to two editions of *The Ziegfeld Follies* (New Amsterdam, June 16, 1919; June 22, 1920).

With producer Sam H. Harris, Mr. Berlin built the Music Box Th. (1921), where four editions of the annual *Music Box Revue* were presented, for which he wrote the lyrics and music (Music Box, Sept. 22, 1921; Oct. 23, 1922; Sept. 22, 1923; and Dec. 1, 1924). He wrote the lyrics and music for *The Cocoanuts* (Lyric, Dec. 8, 1925); contributed an interpolated number, "Blue Skies," to the musical, *Betsy* (New Amsterdam, Dec. 28, 1926); wrote the lyrics and music for the *Ziegfeld Follies* (New Amsterdam, Aug. 16, 1927); wrote the music and lyrics of "Begging for Love," for the revue, *Shoot the Works* (George M. Cohan Th., July 21, 1931); *Face the Music* (New Amsterdam, Feb. 17, 1932); for the revue, *As Thousands Cheer* (Music Box, Sept. 30, 1933).

He wrote both lyrics and music for *Louisiana Purchase* (Imperial, May 28, 1940); *This Is the Army* (Bway Th., July 4, 1942) in which he also sang his song, "Oh How I Hate to Get Up in the Morning"; *Annie Get Your Gun* (Imperial, May 16, 1946); *Miss Liberty* (Imperial, July 15, 1949), which he produced with Robert E. Sherwood and Moss Hart; *Call Me Madam* (Imperial, Oct. 12, 1950); and *Mr. President* (St. James, Oct. 20, 1962).

Films. Mr. Berlin has composed music for *Top Hat* (RKO, 1935); *Follow the Fleet* (RKO, 1936); *On the Avenue* (20th-Fox, 1937); *Alexander's Ragtime Band* (20th-Fox, 1938); *Care Free* (RKO, 1938); *Second Fiddle* (20th-Fox, 1939); *Louisiana Purchase* (Par., 1941); *Holiday Inn* (Par., 1942); *This Is the Army* (WB, 1943); *Blue Skies* (Par., 1946); *Easter Parade* (MGM, 1948); *Annie Get Your Gun* (MGM, 1950); *Call Me Madam* (20th-Fox, 1953); *White Christmas* (Par., 1954); and *There's No Business Like Show Business* (20th-Fox, 1954).

Other Activities. Since 1919, Mr. Berlin has been president of Irving Berlin Music Corp.

Published Works. Mr. Berlin's first published song was "Marie from Sunny Italy" (1907) for which he wrote the lyrics; he wrote both lyrics and music for "Alexander's Ragtime Band" (1911) and since that time has written approximately 800 songs which include: "Say It with Music"; "All Alone"; "What'll I Do?"; "Always"; "Remember"; "Blue Skies"; "The Song Is Ended"; "Marie"; "How Deep Is the Ocean"; "Say It Isn't So"; "Easter Parade"; "God Bless America"; "Isn't This a Lovely Day"; "White Christmas"; "They Say It's Wonderful"; "You're Just in Love.".

Discography. The following musicals have been recorded: *Annie Get Your Gun* (Decca, Capitol, MGM); *Miss Liberty* (Columbia); *Call Me Madam* (RCA Victor, Decca); and *Mr. President* (Columbia).

Awards. Mr. Berlin has received a Medal for Merit, for *This Is the Army;* the Legion of Honor, France; Congressional Gold Medal for "God Bless America"; and has received an Academy (Oscar) Award for his song, "White Christmas" from *Holiday Inn* (1942). He holds honorary D.Mus. degrees from Bucknell Univ. and Temple Univ. and the Honorary Degree of Doctor of Humane Letters from Fordham Univ.

BERLINGER, WARREN. Actor. b. Aug. 31, 1937, Brooklyn, N.Y., to Elias and Frieda Berlinger. Father, building contractor. Grad. Professional Children's Sch., N.Y.C., 1955; attended Columbia Univ. Married Feb. 18, 1960, to Betty Lou Keim; one son, one daughter. Member of AEA; SAG; AFTRA; AMPAS; ATAS. Address: (home) Chatsworth, CA 91311; (bus.) c/o Kumin-Olenick, 400 South Beverly Dr., Beverly Hills, CA 94712, tel. (213) 553-8561.

Theatre. Mr. Berlinger made his N.Y.C. debut at age nine playing a Little Boy, an Indian, and understudying the role of Little Jake in *Annie Get Your Gun* (Imperial Th., May 16, 1946); subsequently played Bibi in *The Happy Time* (Plymouth, Jan. 24, 1950), and toured cross-country in it (opened Cass Th., Detroit, Mich., Oct. 22, 1951; closed Blackstone, Chicago, Ill., Jan. 1, 1952).

He played Dave Gibbs in *Bernadine* (Playhouse, N.Y.C., Oct. 16, 1952); Johnny Reynolds in *Take a Giant Step* (Lyceum, Sept. 24, 1953); Okkie in *Anniversary Waltz* (Broadhurst, Apr. 7, 1954); made his first stock appearance in *The Other Foot* (East Hampton Th., Andover, Mass., Summer 1955); played Dick in *A Roomful of Roses* (Playhouse, N.Y.C., Oct. 17, 1955); Ernie in *Blue Denim* (Playhouse, Feb. 27, 1958); Buddy in *Come Blow Your Horn* (Brooks Atkinson Th., Feb. 22, 1961), and in stock (Bucks County Playhouse, New Hope, Pa., Summer 1961), and toured in it (opened Moore Th., Seattle, Wash., Oct. 8, 1962; closed Civic Th., Chicago, Ill., Feb. 2, 1963).

Mr. Berlinger made his London debut as J. Pierpoint Finch in *How to Succeed in Business Without Really Trying* (Shaftesbury, 1963). He appeared in the US as Richard Hallen in *Who's Happy Now?* (Mark Taper Forum, Los Angeles, Nov. 3, 1967).

Films. He made his first motion picture appearance in *Teenage Rebel* (20th-Fox, 1956); subsequently appeared in *Three Brave Men* (20th-Fox, 1957); *Blue Denim* (20th-Fox, 1959); *The Wackiest Ship in the Army* (Col., 1960); *Platinum High School* (MGM, 1960); *All Hands on Deck* (20th-Fox, 1961); *Thunder Alley* (Amer. Internat., 1967); *The Long Goodbye* (UA, 1973); and *Lepke* (Ind., 1974).

Television. Mr. Berlinger has appeared on Secret Storm (CBC, Can., 1956); the Joey Bishop Show (NBC, 1962); Bracken's World (NBC, 1971); Funny Side (NBC, 1972); and Touch of Grace (ABC, 1973).

Awards. He received the *Theatre World* Award (1958) for his performance as Ernie in *Blue Denim*, and in 1969 he was honorary mayor of Chatsworth, Calif.

BERMAN, SHELLY.

Comedian, actor. b. Sheldon Berman, Feb. 3, 1926, Chicago, Ill., to Nathan and Irene Berman. Grad. Manley H.S., 1943; Goodman Memorial Theatre and Sch. of Drama, 1947. Studied acting with Uta Hagen, N.Y.C., 1953-54. Married Apr. 19, 1947, to Sarah Herman. Served US Navy, 1943. Member of AEA; AGVA; AFTRA; SAG; WGA.

Theatre. Mr. Berman made his N.Y.C. debut in the revue, *Girls Against the Boys* (Alvin Th., Nov. 2, 1959); subsequently appeared in stock, as Applegate in *Damn Yankees* (Melody Top, Chicago, Ill., Summer 1959) and as Charley Wykeham in *Where's Charley* (Carousel, Framingham, Mass.; Oakdale Musical Th., Wallingford, Conn., Summer 1960); in N.Y.C., played Alfie Nathan in *A Family Affair* (Billy Rose Th., Jan. 27, 1962); appeared as Applegate in *Damn Yankees* (Circle Arts Th., San Diego, Calif., June 1963).

Mr. Berman was Elihu Good in *A Perfect Frenzy* (Bucks County Playhouse, New Hope, Pa., June 29, 1964); Oscar Madison in *The Odd Couple* (Coconut Grove Playhouse, Miami, Fla., Dec. 27, 1966); and Simon Wabash in *The Unemployed Saint* (Parker Playhouse, Fort Lauderdale, Fla., Mar. 13, 1967). He toured as Noah in *Two by Two* (Sept. 1972–Mar. 1973); played Mayer Rothschild in *The Rothschilds* (North Shore Music Th., Mass., Aug. 1973); toured as Mel Edison in a roadshow production of *The Prisoner of Second Avenue* (opened: Baltimore, Md., Sept. 15, 1973; closed Boston, Mar. 1974); and appeared in *Room Service* (Queens Playhouse, Flushing Meadows, N.Y.C., July–Aug. 1974).

Mr. Berman was the first comedian to appear in Carnegie Hall, N.Y.C. and Orchestra Hall, Chicago, Ill., and has given comedy concerts throughout the US, Canada and Australia.

Films. Mr. Berman made his debut in *The Best Man* (UA, 1964) and appeared in *Divorce American Style* (Col., 1967).

Television. Mr. Berman has appeared on all the major variety shows as well as on Peter Gunn (NBC), Rawhide (ABC), GE Theatre (CBS), Twilight Zone (CBS) and Breaking Point (ABC). He was in *The Comedian Backstage* (DuPont Show of the Week, NBC, 1963) and was co-producer, with Robert Kline, of the comedy segments of Comedy Tonight (CBS, July 1970).

Night Clubs. He has performed in all major clubs in the US and Canada, and toured New Zealand and Australia (Summer 1963).

Published Works. Mr. Berman wrote *A Hotel Is a Place* (1973).

Discography. Mr. Berman's recordings include *Inside Shelley Berman, Outside Shelley Berman, The Edge of Shelley Berman, Personal Appearance* and *New Sides of Shelley Berman.*

Awards. Mr. Berman received the NARAS (Grammy) Award for best nonmusical recording (1958), the AGVA (Joey) Award for most promising comedian (1959), and three Gold Records.

Recreation. Astronomy, mountain climbing, reading, "temperamental fits.".

BERNARD, KENNETH.

Educator, playwright, short story writer. b. May 7, 1930. Father, Otis Bernard. Mr. Bernard was graduated B.A. from City College of New York and M.A. and Ph.D. from Columbia Univ. Married Sept. 1962 to Elaine Ceil Reiss; two sons, one daughter. Served US Army, 1953-55. Address: 788 Riverside Drive, New York, NY 10032, tel. (212) WA 6-6579.

Mr. Bernard has been professor of English, Long Island Univ., since 1969. In 1972, he joined with other playwrights to form the New York Theatre Strategy and became 2nd vice-pres. of the organization. Among plays he has written that have been staged are *The Moke-Eater* (Max's Kansas City, N.Y.C., Sept. 1968); *Night Club* (LaMama E.T.C., Nov. 1970); *The Giants in the Earth* (Yale Repertory Th., Sunday Experiments, Mar. 7, 1971); *The Unknown Chinaman* (Omaha, Nebr., June 1971); *The Magic Show of Dr. Ma-Gico* (LaMama E.T.C., Apr. 1973); *Mary Jane*, directed also by Mr. Bernard (Manhattan Theater Club, May 1973); and *How We Danced While We Burned* (Antioch College, Ohio, Dec. 1973).

Published Works. Mr. Bernard has published *Night Club and Other Plays* (1971) and *Two Stories* (1973).

Awards. He received a grant from the Office for Advanced Drama Research (1971), a Guggenheim fellowship in playwriting (1972–73), and a NY State Creative Artist Public Service grant (1973).

BERNARDI, HERSCHEL.

Actor, singer. b. 1923, New York City, to Bernard and Helen Bernardi, actors. Married to Cynthia Griffith; one son; two daughters.

Theatre. Mr. Bernardi began his career in the theatre at the age of three and by the time he was nine he was a child star at the Yiddish Theatre on 2nd Ave., N.Y.C. Later he worked for two summers with the Stanley Woolf Players in the Catskill Mts. of New York, and this was followed by five years during which he combined acting and working as a social director at resort hotels.

He succeeded Howard da Silva as Mendele, the Book Seller, in *The World of Sholom Aleichem* (Barbizon-Plaza Hotel, N.Y.C., May 1, 1953); toured (1961) as Harry Golden in *Only in America;* toured (1962) as Willy Loman in *Death of a Salesman;* made his debut on Bway as Johnny Dembo in *Bajour* (Sam S. Shubert Th., Nov. 23, 1964); succeeded (Nov. 8, 1965) Luther Adler as Tevye in *Fiddler on the Roof* (Imperial, Sept. 22, 1964), continuing until Aug. 13, 1967, and again playing the role (Sept. 18–Nov. 5, 1967); co-produced *Nathan Weinstein, Mystic, Connecticut* (Brooks Atkinson Th., Feb. 25, 1966); and played the title role in *Zorba* (Imperial, Nov. 17, 1968).

Films. Mr. Bernardi appeared in *Love with the Proper Stranger* (Par., 1963); *Irma La Douce* (UA, 1963); and *The Honey Pot* (UA, 1967).

Television. Mr. Bernardi played Lt. Jacoby in the Peter Gunn series (NBC) from 1958 to 1961. He appeared also on many other television shows, including *Much Ado About Nothing* (Matinee Th., NBC, May 20, 1958); *Their Own Executioner* (Kraft Suspense Th., NBC, Apr. 23, 1964); *A Hatful of Rain* (ABC, Mar. 3, 1968); *But I Don't Want To Get Married* (ABC, Oct. 6, 1970); *No Place To Run* (ABC, Sept. 19, 1972); and *Sandcastles* (CBS, Oct. 17, 1972). In addition, he appeared on episodes of such programs as Bonanza (NBC, 1961); Dr. Kildare (NBC, 1961; 1962; 1966); The Untouchables (ABC, 1962); Dick Powell Th. (NBC, 1962; 1963); Route 66 (CBS, 1962; 1964); Naked City (ABC, 1962); Profiles in Courage (NBC, 1965); and others. He has also done the Charlie the Tuna commercial and the "ho-ho-ho" voice-over for the Jolly Green Giant commercial.

Discography. Mr. Bernardi's recordings include *Show Stopper* (Col., 1970) and *Bernardi Sings Fiddler* (Col.).

Awards. Mr. Bernardi was awarded the March of Dimes "Star of the Year" Award (1967) and was nominated for an Antoinette Perry (Tony) Award (1968–69) for best musical actor for his performance as Zorba.

BERNHAGEN, ROLAND F.

Setting and lighting designer, teacher, theatre designer, musician, engineer. b. Roland Frederick Bernhagen, Mar. 26, 1933, Milwaukee, Wis., to George and Frieda Patten. Father, accountant; mother, housewife. Educated Rufus King H.S., Milwaukee; Univ. of Wisconsin (Milwaukee and Madison); Phoenix College; Cooper Union, N.Y.C. Professional training Phoenix College (John Paul); Univ. of Wisconsin (Fred Berkee); Shorewood (Wis.) Opportunity School (Bernard Greeson); Goodman Memorial Th., Chicago, Ill.; Cooper Union. Married 1967 to Bernice Loren. Served 1954–56 in US Air Force. Member AAAS; Instrument Society of America. Address: 350 W. 55th St., New York, NY 10019, tel. (212) 586-8604.

In addition to his theatrical work, Mr. Bernhagen is a mechanical and structural engineer, artist, and teacher of art and classical guitar.

Theatre. Mr. Bernhagen's first experience with theatre began when he was in grade school, and he appeared in about fifteen school plays from 1940 to 1950. From 1950 to 1954, he did technical work for approximately twenty productions of the Shorewood (Wis.) Players and the Shorewood Light Opera Co. and in 1955–56 for three productions of the Sombrero Th., Phoenix, Ariz. From 1956 to 1958, he was technical worker for the Tuppence Players and the Fred Miller Th., both in Milwaukee, and the Elm Grove (Wis.) Players. He worked on a production of *Gaslight* for the first; *Annie Get Your Gun* for the last; and did various variety and benefit shows in the Chicago, Ill., and Milwaukee areas.

Mr. Bernhagen's association with the Shorewood Players and the Shorewood Light Opera Co. continued also during the 1956–58 periods, with Mr. Bernhagen doing special work for the Shorewood Players on the lighting of their productions of *Death of a Salesman; Picnic;* and *Black Sheep of the Family;* he worked also on set design of the Shorewood Players' presentation of *Voice of the Turtle* and *The Solid Gold Cadillac* and for the Shorewood Light Opera *Pirates of Penzance.* And, also during the 1956–58 period, Mr. Bernhagen did set design for the Whitefish Bay (Wis.) Players' productions of *Bus Stop* and *Desk Set* and setting and lighting design for the Univ. (of Wisconsin) Players (Milwaukee) presentation of *Dr. Knock.*

In Sept. 1958, Mr. Bernhagen was appointed part-time instructor in theatre production at the Univ. of Wisconsin, Milwaukee, and he supervised all aspects of the design and execution of the following productions: *Time Limit* (Nov. 1958); *The Emperor's New Clothes* (Dec. 1958); *The Winter's Tale* (Mar. 1959); and the opera *Dido and Aeneas* (May 1959). From June to August, 1959, he was with the Putnam County Playhouse, Lake Mahopac, N.Y., where he was setting and lighting designer and technical director for productions of *Mame; Third Best Sport; Blue Denim; Drink to Me Only; Tunnel of Love; Cat on a Hot Tin Roof; Fair Game; Look Back in Anger;* and *Mr. Roberts.*

In May 1972, Mr. Bernhagen became the founder and director of Expressions, with Bernice Loren and Marilyn Lief Kramberg. Expressions, a nonprofit center for the arts, includes a theatre and a school of the theatre and designs and constructs theatres, including light and sound systems. Its presentations have included guitar concerts directed by Mr. Bernhagen (May, June, and Dec. 1973) and *Aspects of Theatre* (June 1973), for which he was technical director and for which he did set and lighting designs.

Concerts. Mr. Bernhagen has appeared in concert as a classical guitarist (Philharmonic Hall Cafe, N.Y.C., Nov. 1971).

Awards. Mr. Bernhagen has received various local awards for scenic design and lighting in community theatres.

Recreation. Electronics, photography, woodworking, reading, old movies.

BERNSTEIN, KARL. Press representative. b. Brooklyn, N.Y. Relatives in theatre: son, Ira Bernstein, general manager, producer; daughter-in-law, Florence Henderson, actress. Member of ATPAM, Actors' Fund of Amer. Address: 136 West 55th St., New York, NY 10019.

Theatre. Mr. Bernstein served as press representative for *Oh, Kay!* (1926); *Funny Face* (1927); *Hold Everything!* (1929); *Heads Up!* (1930); *Girl Crazy* (1930); *Anything Goes* (1934); *Red, Hot and Blue!* (1936); *Leave It to Me* (1938); *Cabin in the Sky* (1940); *Liliom* (1940); *Let's Face It* (1941); *Banjo Eyes* (1942); *Rosalinda* (1942); *One Touch of Venus* (1943); *On the Town* (1944); *Billion Dollar Baby* (1946); *High Button Shoes* (1947); *Where's Charley?* (1948); *Me and Molly* (1948); *The Father* (1949); *Affairs of State* (1950); *Guys and Dolls* (1950); *Don Juan in Hell* (1951); *King Lear* (1951); *John Brown's Body* (1953); *Can-Can* (1953); Victor Borge's *Comedy in Music* (1953); *The Caine Mutiny Court-Martial* (1954); *The Boy Friend* (1954); *Silk Stockings* (1955); *3 for Tonight* (1955); *Tiger at the Gates* (1955); *A Hatful of Rain* (1955); *Major Barbara* (1956); *The Marriage-Go-Round* (1958); *Lord Pengo* (1962); *Wait Until Dark* (1966); and *Golden Rainbow* (1967).

BERNSTEIN, LEONARD. Conductor, composer, lecturer, writer, pianist. b. Aug. 25, 1918, Lawrence, Mass., to Samuel Joseph and Jennie (Resnick) Bernstein. Grad. Boston Latin Sch., 1935; Harvard Coll., A.B. (Music, cum laude) 1939. Studied at Curtis Inst. of Music 1939–41; orchestration with Randall Thompson at Curtis Inst.; music courses at Harvard Univ. with Walter Piston, Arthur Tillman Merritt, and Edward Burlingame Hill; piano with Helen Coates, Heinrich Gebhard, Isabelle Vengerova; conducting with Fritz Reiner, Serge Koussevitzky (Berkshire Music Ctr., Tanglewood, Mass.). Married Sept. 9, 1951, to Felicia Montealegre Cohn, actress; one son, two daughters. Member of ASCAP; Natl. Inst. of Arts and Letters; AFTRA; Royal Society of Arts; and The Institute of Arts and Sciences. Address: 205 West 57th St., New York, NY 10019.

Theatre. Mr. Bernstein first wrote the music for the ballet *Fancy Free* for the Ballet Theatre (Metropolitan Opera House, N.Y.C., Apr. 18, 1944); this ballet by Jerome Robbins was expanded into the musical *On the Town* (Adelphi, Dec. 28, 1944), for which Mr. Bernstein wrote the music and additional lyrics. He composed the score for the ballet *Facsimile* for the Ballet Theatre (Bway Th., Oct. 24, 1946); wrote music for *Peter Pan* (Imperial, Apr. 24, 1950); and the music for *Wonderful Town* (Winter Garden, Feb. 25, 1953).

Mr. Bernstein's first opera, *Trouble in Tahiti*, a one-act work, for which he also wrote the libretto, was presented as part of a triple bill, *All in One* (Playhouse, Apr. 19, 1955), and later performed by the NY City Opera Co. (NY City Ctr., Apr. 6, 1958). He composed incidental music for *The Lark* (Longacre, Nov. 17, 1955); the score and, with Hershy Kay, the orchestrations for *Candide* (Martin Beck Th., Dec. 1, 1956); the music and, with Sid Ramin and Irwin Kostal, the orchestrations for *West Side Story* (Winter Garden, Sept. 26, 1957); and songs for *The Firstborn* (Coronet, Apr. 29, 1958). *West Side Story* was also produced in London (Her Majesty's Th., Dec. 12, 1958) and revived at the NY City Ctr. (Apr. 8, 1964).

In 1969, Mr. Bernstein was named Laureate Conductor of the NY Philharmonic, following his resignation as music director of the orchestra, a post he had held since 1958. He previously conducted with Dimitri Mitropoulos (1957–58); conducted major orchestras in the US and Europe, including the Israel Philharmonic Orchestra (1947–57); was conductor of the NY City Symphony (1945–48); assistant conductor of the NY Philharmonic Symphony (1943–44); was piano soloist with most of the leading orchestras of the world; and has conducted opera at La Scala (Milan, It.) and the Metropolitan Opera, N.Y.C., where he conducted *Falstaff* (Mar. 6, 1964) and *Carmen* (Sept. 19, 1972).

Films. Mr. Bernstein first wrote the music for *On the Town* (MGM, 1949); subsequently composed background music for *On the Waterfront* (Col., 1954). A film version was made of *West Side Story* (UA, 1961).

Television. Mr. Bernstein's Young People's Concerts (New York Philharmonic) and the series Leonard Bernstein and the New York Philharmonic have been televised (CBS). He has also appeared as a lecturer on Omnibus (ABC).

Published Works. Mr. Bernstein's musical works include *Jeremiah Symphony* (1942); sonata for piano and clarinet (1942); *I Hate Music*, song cycle (1943); *Seven Anniversaries* for piano (1943); *Five Pieces for Brass* (1947); *Four Anniversaries* for piano (1948); *La Bonne Cuisine*, song cycle (1949); *The Age of Anxiety*, symphony (1949); *Serenade* for violin solo, strings, and percussion (1954); Symphony No. 3, "Kaddish" (1963); *Chichester Psalms* (1965); and *Mass*, a theatre piece for singers, players, and dancers (commissioned for the opening of the John F. Kennedy Center for the Performing Arts, Washington, D.C., Sept. 8, 1971).

His books include *The Joy of Music* (1959), *Leonard Bernstein's Young People's Concerts* (1962), and *The Infinite Variety of Music* (1966).

Awards. The musical, *Wonderful Town*, for which he wrote the music, received the NY Drama Critics' Circle Award, the Donaldson Award, and the Antoinette Perry (Tony) Award (1953). Mr. Bernstein received a citation from ANTA for "his outstanding contribution to the art of the living theatre."

He has won two NATAS (Emmy) awards for the best musical contribution to television (1956), for conducting and composing; and for "conducting and analyzing music of Johann Sebastian Bach" (Omnibus, ABC, 1957).

His *Jeremiah Symphony* won the Music Critics Circle of NY Award as the "most outstanding orchestral work by an American composer introduced during the 1943–44 season." He received the Alice M. Ditson Award (1958) for distinguished service to American Music; the Albert Einstein Commemorative Award (1960) for furthering the cause of international understanding through music; the Page One Award (1960); the American Symphony Orchestra League Award for distinguished service to music in America; and a citation from the National Federation of Music Clubs (1961); and for his book, *The Joy of Music*, the Christopher Award (1959) and the Secondary Education Award (1959).

BEROLZHEIMER, HOBART F. Librarian. b. Oct. 25, 1921, Chicago, Ill., to Milton and Edna (Barnett) Berolzheimer. Father, engineer. Grad. Bloom Township H.S., Chicago Heights, 1938; Woodrow Wilson Jr. Coll., 1940; Univ. of Illinois, B.A. (magna cum laude, Phi Beta Kappa) 1942, M.A. 1943; Univ. of Chicago, B.L.S. 1945; attended Univ. of Chicago, 1950–52. Member of Theatre Library Assn. (bd. mbr., 1967–to date; vice-pres. and program chmn., 1972–to date); Philadelphia Regional Writers Conference (exec. bd. 1954–to date; pres., 1956–58); Philadelphia District Library Assn. (vice-pres., 1962; pres.-elect, 1962; pres., 1963–65; Ziegfeld Club, Inc. (advisory board, 1961–to date); Pi Delta Phi. Address: (home) The Philadelphian, 2401 Pennsylvania Ave., Philadelphia, PA 19130, tel. (215) CE 2-4323; (bus.) Literature Dept., Free Library of Philadelphia, Logan Sq., Philadelphia, PA 19103, tel. (215) MU 6-5356.

Since 1953, Mr. Berolzheimer has been head of the literature dept. and curator of the theatre collection of the Philadelphia Free Library.

His first position was with the Chicago Public Library as reference assistant (1943–45), then as first assistant, book selection division (1945–48); and subsequently was with the Univ. of California at Santa Barbara, as acquisitions librarian (1948–53).

Recreation. Collecting books and records, walking.

BERRY, ERIC. Actor. b. Eric George William Berry, Jan. 9, 1913, London, England, to Frederick William and Anna Lovisa (Danielson) Berry. Father, paper merchant. Grad. City of London Sch., 1930; RADA (winner of Silver Medal) 1932. Served British Army, Royal West African Frontier Force and with ENSA, Cairo, 1940–1946; emigrated to the US in 1954; became naturalized citizen in 1964. Member of AEA; AFTRA; SAG; The Players; Green Room Club, London.

Theatre. Mr. Berry made his stage debut in *Spilt Milk* (Everyman Th., Hampstead, England, Apr. 1931); subsequently appeared in productions at the Embassy Th. (Hampstead, 1932); and joined the St. Martin Players (Edinburgh, Glasgow, Scotland, 1932).

He first appeared in London as Falk Brandon in *The Cathedral* (New, Dec. 7, 1932); followed by the role of Fahnrich in *The Ace* (Lyric, Aug. 24, 1933); Hugh Bennett in *Dark Horizon* (Daly's, Apr. 20, 1934); played a season with the Hull Repertory Co. (1934–35); Scipio in *The Road to Rome* (Savoy, London, Mar. 15, 1937); George Khitov in *Judgment Day* (Strand, June 2, 1937); toured Scandinavia as John Worthing in *The Importance of Being Earnest* (1938); and, in London, played Guido von Allmen in *Juggernaut* (Richmond, May 8, 1939).

In 1944, while serving with the British Army in Egypt, Mr. Berry directed and acted in several productions; subsequently appeared at the Playhouse (Liverpool, England, 1946–1948); played Lopahin in *The Cherry Orchard* (St. James's, London, June 1, 1948); Charles Appleby in *Eden End* (Duchess, Aug. 26, 1948); toured Germany as Claudius in *Hamlet* (1949); played Mameav in *The Diary of a Scoundrel* (Arts, London, Oct. 19, 1949); Sir George Crofts in *Mrs. Warren's Profession* (Arts, Jan. 25, 1950); Arnold Littlejohn in *The Platinum Set* (Saville, Mar. 30, 1950); Banquo in *Macbeth*, (Arts, June 8, 1950); Ugo Praga in *The Mask and the Face* (Arts, Sept. 19, 1950); Lord Burleigh in *Queen Elizabeth* (Arts, Oct. 10, 1950); the Lefthand Property Man in *Lady Precious Stream* (Arts, Dec. 13, 1950); George Tesman in *Hedda Gabler* (Arts, Jan. 17, 1951); and toured in *Frou-Frou* (1951).

Mr. Berry appeared as Dame Gladys Flagpole in *Puss in Red Riding Breeches* (Watergate, London, Dec. 29, 1951); performed in the revue *See You Again* (Watergate, Feb. 21, 1952; Edinburgh Festival, Scotland, 1953); played Mr. Toobad in *Nightmare Abbey* (Westminster, London, Feb. 27, 1952); appeared in *The Magistrate* (Bermuda, 1952); played in the revue, *At the Lyric* (Lyric, Hammersmith, London, Dec. 23, 1953) and in its revised version, entitled *Going to Town* (St. Martin's, May 20, 1954).

Mr. Berry made his N.Y.C. debut as Percival Browne in *The Boy Friend* (Royale, Sept. 30, 1954), which he repeated on the national tour (opened Shubert, New Haven, Conn., Nov. 28, 1955; closed Shubert, Philadelphia, Pa., Jan. 5, 1957); subsequently appeared with the Stratford Shakespeare Festival of Canada as Thurio in *Two Gentlemen of Verona* and as Major Clovell in *The Broken Jug* (Royal Alexandra Th., Toronto, Feb. 1958); repeated his role in *Two Gentlemen of Verona* (Phoenix, N.Y.C., Mar. 18, 1958); and in *The Broken Jug* (Phoenix, Apr. 1, 1958).

He also played the Hon. Charles Piper in *The Family Reunion* (Phoenix, Oct. 2, 1958); Tench in *The Power and the Glory* (Phoenix, Dec. 10, 1958); Squire Sullen in *The Beaux' Stratagem* (Phoenix, Feb. 24, 1959); the Client in *The Great God Brown* (Coronet, N.Y.C., Oct. 6, 1959); in *Pictures in the Hallway* (Phoenix, Dec. 26, 1959); the Troll King in *Peer Gynt* (Phoenix, Jan. 12, 1960); Falstaff in *Henry IV, Part 1* (Phoenix, Mar. 1, 1960) and *Henry IV, Part 2* (Phoenix, Apr. 18, 1960); Charles Gringoire in *Turn on the Night* and Drinkwater in *Captain Brassbound's Conversion* (Playhouse in the Park, Philadelphia, Aug. 1961); Shillem in *Gideon* (Plymouth, N.Y.C., Nov. 9, 1961); and Falstaff in the American Shakespeare Festival production of *Henry IV, Part 1* (Stratford, Conn., June 12, 1962).

He played several roles in *The White House* (Henry Miller's Th., N.Y.C., May 19, 1964), which he repeated in a subsequent stock tour (Summer 1964); played The Cardinal in *Tiny Alice* (Billy Rose Th., Dec. 29, 1964); Charles in a stock tour of *The Public Eye* (Summer 1965); toured in *An Evening with Hermione Gingold and Eric Berry* (Summer

1965); played Cardinal Monticelso in *The White Devil* (Circle in the Square, N.Y.C., Dec. 6, 1965); directed and played Inspector Hubbard in *Dial "M" for Murder* (winter stock, Feb. 1966); toured as Lord Porteus in *The Circle* (1966); and directed *The Pleasure of His Company* (Coconut Grove Playhouse, Miami, Fla., Aug. 2, 1966). He acted with the John Fernald Co. at the Meadow Brook Th. (Rochester, Mich., seasons 1966–69), playing the title roles in *King Lear* and *John Gabriel Borkman*, James Tyrone, Sr. in *Long Day's Journey into Night*, and appearing in *The Caucasian Chalk Circle* (Jan. 1967), *You Never Can Tell* (Mar. 1967), and *The Seagull*, among others; and played The Host in the national tour of *Canterbury Tales* (opened Playhouse, Wilmington, Del., Dec. 29, 1969; closed National, Washington, D.C., Apr. 11, 1970).

Mr. Berry played Stephen Spettigue in a revival of *Charley's Aunt* (Brooks Atkinson Th., N.Y.C., July 4, 1970); Sir Toby Belch in *Twelfth Night* (Goodman Th., Chicago, Fall 1970); Max in a revival of *The Homecoming* (Bijou, N.Y.C., May 18, 1971); Sir Howard Hallam in *Captain Brassbound's Conversion* (toured before arriving at the Ethel Barrymore Th., Apr. 17, 1972); and Charles in *Pippin* (Imperial, Oct. 23, 1972).

Films. Mr. Berry has performed in the British-made films, *Escape by Night* (Rep., 1937); *The Edge of the World* (Rock Studios, 1937); *The Red Shoes* (Eagle Lion, 1948); *Miss Robin Hood* (Group Three, 1952); *Operation Diplomat* (Nettleford, 1953); *Gilbert and Sullivan* (UA, 1953); *The Diamond* (Gibraltar, 1954; released in US as *The Diamond Wizard* by UA, 1954); *The Constant Husband* (Br. Lion, 1955); and in the US-made *To Trap a Spy* (MGM, 1966).

Television. Mr. Berry has appeared in *The Scarlet Letter; Billy Budd; Medea; Vanity Fair; The Light That Failed* (Family Classics, CBS, Mar. 16, 1961); played Sir Robert Peel in *The Invincible Mr. Disraeli* (Hallmark Hall of Fame, NBC, 1963); and on Bob Hope Presents (NBC); The Man from UNCLE (NBC); Directions '65 (ABC); Lamp Unto My Feet (CBS); and in *Barefoot in Athens* (Hallmark Hall of Fame, NBC, Nov. 11, 1966).

BERUH, JOSEPH. Producer, director, general manager. b. Sept. 27, 1924, Pittsburgh, Pa., to William I. and Clara (Friedman) Beruh. Father, dry cleaner. Grad. Schenley H.S., Pittsburgh, 1942; Carnegie Inst. of Tech., B.F.A. (drama) 1950; studied acting and directing with Lee Strasberg (1950–56); attended Amer. Theatre Wing, N.Y.C. (1951–52). Married 1955 to Kathleen Murry, actress (dec. Aug. 1969); two sons. Served US Army, 1943–46; administration and Special Services. Member of ATPAM; AEA; AFTRA; SAG. Address: (home) 31 W. 93rd St., New York, NY 10025, tel. (212) 222-9687; (bus.) 1650 Broadway, New York, NY 10019, tel. (212) 765-5910.

Theatre. Mr. Beruh made his stage debut as Teddy Brewster in a stock production of *Arsenic and Old Lace* (Rabbit Run Th., Madison, Ohio, Summer 1946); made his N.Y.C. debut with the Loft Players, as Friend Ed in *Burning Bright* (Circle in the Square, Nov. 1951); subsequently directed *A Sound of Hunting* (Cherry Lane, Apr. 1953); was stage manager and played a Prison Guard, a Drugstore Clerk, a Waiter, and Danny Mines in *Compulsion* (Ambassador, Oct. 24, 1957).

He was owner with Philip Minor and Gigi Cascio of the Sheridan Square Playhouse (1958–73); with Peter Kent produced, *Leave It to Jane* (Sheridan Sq. Playhouse, May 25, 1959); and directed *Missouri Legend, The Male Animal, Harvey, Peg o' My Heart, A Streetcar Named Desire, The Hasty Heart, Of Mice and Men,* and *Born Yesterday* (Grand Teton National Th., Jackson Hole, Wy., Summer 1953).

Mr. Beruh was general manager of *The Goose* (Sullivan St. Playhouse, N.Y.C., Mar. 15, 1960); business manager of the South Shore Music Circus (Hyannis, Mass., Summer 1960); producer, with Lawrence Carra, of *Kittiwake Island* (Martinique, N.Y.C., Oct. 12, 1960); general manager of "*Elsa Lanchester—Herself*" (41 St. Th., Feb. 4, 1961); director of *The Seven at Dawn* (Actors Playhouse, Apr. 17, 1961); general manager of *Hi, Paisano!* (York, Sept. 30, 1961) and of the twin bill, *The Long Voyage Home* and *Diff'rent* (Mermaid, Oct. 17, 1961); company manager (Feb. 1962) of *Sunday in New York* (Cort, Nov. 29, 1961); general manager (Aug. 1962) of *Brecht on Brecht* (Th. de Lys, Jan. 3, 1962); company manager of *Moon on a Rainbow Shawl* (East 11 St. Th., Jan. 15, 1962); general manager of *Creditors* (Mermaid, Jan. 25, 1962); company manager (Apr. 1962) of *I Can Get It for You Wholesale* (Shubert, Mar. 22, 1962); general manager (May, shortly after the opening) of *Anything Goes* (Orpheum, May 15, 1962); and producer, under the title P.G.J. Productions, of *The Cats' Pajamas* (Sheridan Sq. Playhouse, May 31, 1962).

Mr. Beruh was general manager of *Riverwind* (Actors Playhouse, Dec. 12, 1962); the twin bill, *The Typist* and *The Tiger* (Orpheum, Feb. 4, 1963); *Yes Is for a Very Young Man* (Players, Mar. 4, 1963); general manager and co-producer of musical productions at the Gladiators Music Arena (Totowa, N.J., Summer 1963); and general manager of *A Time of the Key* (Sheridan Sq. Playhouse, Sept. 11, 1963), *Jo* (Orpheum, Feb. 12, 1964), *Cindy* (Gate, Mar. 19, 1964), and *The Subject Was Roses* (Royale, May 25, 1964); *The Alchemist* (Gate Th., Sept. 14, 1964); *Gogo Loves You* (Th. de Lys, Oct. 9, 1964); *I Knock at the Door* (Th. de Lys, Nov. 25, 1964); *Pictures in the Hallway* (Th. de Lys, Dec. 16, 1964); *A View from the Bridge* (Sheridan Sq. Playhouse, Jan. 28, 1965); and the double bill *The Day the Whores Came Out to Play Tennis* and *Sing to Me Through Open Windows* (Players Th., Mar. 15, 1965).

He was general manager for the national tour of *The Subject Was Roses* (began Sept. 13, 1965); the pre-Bway tryout of *The Porcelain Year* (opened Locust Th., Philadelphia, Pa., Oct. 11, 1965; closed New Haven, Conn., Nov. 13, 1965); general manager of *First One Asleep, Whistle* (Belasco Th., Feb. 26, 1966); the visit of the Bavarian State Theater, which presented *Die Mitschuldigen* and *Woyzeck* (NY City Ctr., Apr. 5–10, 1966) and *Die Ratten* (NY City Ctr., Apr. 12–17, 1966); *That Summer—That Fall* (Helen Hayes Th., Mar. 16, 1967); *Arms and the Man* (Sheridan Sq. Playhouse, June 22, 1967); *Fragments* (Cherry Lane, Oct. 2, 1967); *In Circles* (Cherry Lane, Nov. 5, 1967); *Love and Let Love* (Sheridan Sq. Playhouse, Jan. 3, 1968); *Who's Who, Baby?* (The Players Th., Jan. 29, 1968); *Saturday Night* (Sheridan Sq. Playhouse, Feb. 25, 1968); *The Only Game in Town* (Broadhurst, May 23, 1968); and *Woman Is My Idea* (Belasco Th., Sept. 25, 1968).

Mr. Beruh was also general manager of *To Be Young, Gifted, and Black* (Cherry Lane, Jan. 2, 1969); *A Way of Life* (ANTA Th., Jan. 18, 1969); *God Bless You, Harold Fineberg* (Actors' Playhouse, Mar. 30, 1969); produced, with Edgar Lansbury, *Promenade* (Promenade Th., June 4, 1969); was general manager of *Fireworks* (Village South Th., June 11, 1969); *Love Your Crooked Neighbor* (Cherry Lane, Dec. 29, 1969); produced *Instructions for the Running of Trains, Etc., on the Erie Railway to Go into Effect January 1, 1862* (Sheridan Sq. Playhouse, Jan. 6, 1970); was general manager of *Look to the Lilies* (Lunt-Fontanne Th., Mar. 29, 1970); *The Engagement Baby* (Helen Hayes Th., May 21, 1970); *Golden Bat* (Sheridan Sq. Playhouse, July 21, 1970); a revival of *Waiting for Godot*, which he also produced, with Edgar Lansbury and Mark Wright in association with Stuart Duncan and H. B. Lutz (Sheridan Sq. Playhouse, Feb. 3, 1971); *Do It Again* (Promenade Th., Feb. 18, 1971); a revival of *Long Day's Journey into Night*, which he also produced with Edgar Lansbury, Jay H. Fuchs, and Stuart Duncan (Promenade Th., Apr. 21, 1971); produced, with Edgar Lansbury and Stuart Duncan, *Godspell* (Cherry Lane, May 17, 1971); *Louis and the Elephant* (previews, Sheridan Sq. Playhouse, Nov. 2, 1971); *Godspell* (London, Nov. 17, 1971); *Elizabeth I* (Lyceum, N.Y.C., Apr. 5, 1972); *Godspell* (Washington, D.C., Apr. 7, 1972; Toronto, Canada, June 1, 1972; San Francisco, Calif., July 18, 1972; Chicago, Sept. 18, 1972; Toledo, Ohio, Sept. 21, 1972; Pittsburgh, Pa., Oct. 27, 1972); *Comedy* (Colonial Th., Boston, Mass., Nov. 6–18, 1972); a revival of *Gypsy* (London, Apr. 1973; Winter Garden, N.Y.C., Sept. 23, 1974); and *The Magic Show* (Cort, N.Y.C., May 28, 1974).

Recreation. Baseball, football, basketball.

BETHENCOURT, FRANCIS. Actor, writer. b. Francis Edward John de Bethencourt, Sept. 5, 1926, London, Eng., to Baron Charles and Dorothy de Bethencourt. Attended Mayfield Coll., Sussex, Eng., 1937–42. Married June 6, 1950, to Judy Hall, actress (marr. dis. 1951); married Dec. 8, 1952, to Nancy Nugent, actress (marr. dis. 1954). Served WW II, British RAF; rank, Pilot Officer. Member of AEA; SAG; AFTRA. Address: c/o AEA, 165 West 46th St., New York, NY 10036, tel. (212) PL 7-7660.

Theatre. Mr. Bethencourt made his debut as the Servant in the London production of *The Recruiting Officer* (Arts, Nov. 23, 1943); subsequently appeared in production with the Melville Players (1944–46); toured Great Britain as Danny in *Night Must Fall*, Clive in *See How They Run*, Favell in *Rebecca*, Nigel in *No Medals*, and Henry in *Is Your Honeymoon Really Necessary?* (1946–47); appeared in *Partners in Crime* (Savoy, London, Apr. 1948); joined the cast of *The Lady Asks for Help* (Garrick, June 14, 1948); played Heathcliff in *Wuthering Heights* (Hammersmith, 1948); and appeared in *The Cherry Tree* (Casino, Aug. 1948).

He made his N.Y.C debut as Henry Norris in *Anne of the Thousand Days* (Shubert, Dec. 8, 1948); toured as Desmonde in the national company of *The Happy Time* (opened Cass, Detroit, Mich., Oct. 22, 1951; closed Blackstone, Chicago, Ill., Jan. 1, 1952); toured in this role with the West Coast company (opened Sombrero Playhouse, Phoenix, Ariz., Feb. 6, 1952; closed Geary, San Francisco, Calif., Apr. 5, 1952); played Captain Lesgate in *Dial 'M' for Murder* (Plymouth, N.Y.C., Oct. 29, 1952); appeared in *Libel* (Westport Country Playhouse, Conn., Aug. 1954); and with the Amer. Shakespeare Festival, played Benedick in *Much Ado About Nothing* (Stratford, Conn., Summer 1955; Olney Playhouse, Md., Summer 1956).

Mr. Bethencourt played the Leading Man in *Six Characters in Search of an Author* (Phoenix, N.Y.C., Dec. 11, 1955); toured summer theatres as Tom Mackensie in *The Seven Year Itch* (June–Aug. 1956); appeared in and directed *Murder Without Crime* (Bucks County Playhouse, New Hope, Pa., Summer 1956); played a Friend in *Visit to a Small Planet* (Booth, N.Y.C., Feb. 7, 1957); Dickinson in *Ross* (Eugene O'Neill Th., Dec. 26, 1962); appeared in *Dream Girl* (Playhouse-in-the-Park, Philadelphia, Pa., June 1963); toured summer theatres as Leonard Vole in *Witness for the Prosecution* (June–July 1963); appeared in productions for the Stroller's Club (N.Y.C., Oct. 1963–Mar. 1964); and with Eva Le Gallienne's Natl. Repertory Co., toured as Judge Brack in *Hedda Gabler* and Hastings in *She Stoops to Conquer* (1964–65 season).

He played Leonard Vole again in *Witness for the Prosecution* and Hector in *Heartbreak House* (Manitoba Theatre Center, Winnipeg, Canada, 1965) and returned to N.Y.C. as Capt. Forster in *The Right Honourable Gentleman* (Billy Rose Th., Oct. 19, 1965). Off-Bway, he played Capt. O'Sullivan in *Hamp* (Renata Th., Mar. 9, 1967) and on Bway he was Warder Whitbread in *Borstal Boy* (Lyceum, Mar. 31, 1970), repeated in Toronto (Royal Alexandra Th., 1971). In 1971, he repeated his performance in *Heartbreak House* at Urbana, Ill. (Krannert Center), and was Victor in *Private Lives* (Barat College, Lake Forest, Ill.). He played the role of Colonel Pickering in *Pygmalion* (Queens Playhouse, N.Y.C., Oct. 30, 1972) and again played Victor in *Private Lives* (Arlington Park Th., Chicago, 1973).

Films. Mr. Bethencourt has appeared in *Royal Wedding* (MGM, 1951); *Rogue's March* (MGM, 1952); *This Earth is Mine* (U, 1959); and wrote *Mr. Clavicle and the Horsefly* (1960).

Television. He played Rawdon in *Becky Sharpe* (Philco Television Playhouse, NBC, 1949); wrote *Borgia Lamp* (Lights Out, NBC, 1951); and *The Ascent of Alfred Fishkettle* (Lux Video Th., CBS, 1953); played Rosencrantz in *Hamlet* (Hallmark Hall of

Fame, NBC, 1953); appeared in *Tonight at 8:30*(Producers Showcase, NBC, 1954); and on two Jackie Gleason shows (CBS, 1967); narrated *King Tutankamen* (PBS, 1973); performed on Studio One (CBS), Suspense (CBS), Lights Out (CBS), Robert Montgomery Presents (NBC), and You Are There (CBS). Mr Bethencourt has also made numerous appearances on camera and done "voice-overs" for many commerical products.

Recreation. Riding, photography, flying.

BETTIS, VALERIE. Dancer, choreographer, actress, director. b. Valerie Elizabeth Bettis, Houston, Tex., to Royal Holt and Valerie Elizabeth (McCarthy) Bettis. Father, dealer in oil well supplies. Attended Sidney Lanier Jr. H.S., Houston; grad. San Jacinto Sr. H.S., Houston; attended Univ. of Texas. Studied dance with Hanya Holm, N.Y.C., 1937–40. Married Sept. 20, 1943, to Bernardo Segall, pianist-composer (marr. dis. Aug. 24, 1955); married Sept. 26, 1959, to Arthur A. Schmidt, public relations. Member of AEA; AFTRA; SSD&C. Address: 16 E. 11th St., New York, NY 10003.

Theatre. Miss Bettis first performed on the concert stage in N.Y.C., and on tour, as a member of the Hanya Holm (dance) Co. (Dec. 1937–40); and subsequently danced in *Railroads on Parade* (New York World's Fair, Apr.–Oct. 1939; Apr.-Oct. 1940); and as a soloist in a concert which she choreographed and presented (Carnegie Chamber Music Hall, N.Y.C., Nov. 27, 1941); also was director of modern dance at the Perry-Mansfield Sch., Steamboat Springs, Colo., and dancer-choreographer at the Colorado Springs Dance Festival (Summers 1942–43). Her dance, *And the Earth Shall Bear Again*, had its first performance in N.Y.C. (Kaufmann Concert Hall, Dec. 6, 1942); followed by her solo work, *The Desperate Heart* (Studio Th.; Mar. 24, 1943). In 1943–44, she toured the US as dancer-choreographer, including appearances in N.Y.C. (Kaufmann Concert Hall, Jan. 23, 1944; Mar. 5, 1944).

She staged the musical numbers and appeared as leading dancer in the pre-Bway tryout of *Glad to See You* (opened Shubert, Philadelphia, Pa., Nov. 13, 1944; closed Opera House, Boston, Mass., Jan. 6, 1945); danced in her own works of *Theatrics, Facts and Figures* and *Dramatic Incident* (Adelphi, May 13, 1945); later appeared as dancer-choreographer in N.Y.C. (New York Times Hall, Dec. 28, 1945), in Washington, D.C. (Cafritz Aud., Feb. 24, 1946), and again in N.Y.C. (Barbizon-Plaza Concert Hall, June 25, 1946). She was dancer-choreographer at the Jacob's Pillow Dance Festival (Lee, Mass., July 12, 1946); and toured South America as dancer-choreographer in a series of solo concerts (Aug.-Sept. 1946).

She was choreographer for *Beggar's Holiday* (Bway Th., N.Y.C., Dec. 26, 1946); danced the leading role in her work, *Virginia Sampler* for the Ballet Russe de Monte Carlo (NY City Ctr., Mar. 4, 1947); appeared with her company in Greensboro, N.C. (Aycook Aud., Mar. 22, 1947) and in N.Y.C. (Central H.S. of Needle Trades, Apr. 19, 1947; Kaufmann Concert Hall, May 4, 1947); returned to the Jacob's Pillow Dance Festival (Lee, Mass., July 4, 1947); appeared in N.Y.C. with her company (New York Times Hall, Dec. 28, 1947), when her *Status Quo* and *Figure '47* were first presented, and in *An Evening on American Dance* (Museum of Modern Art Aud., Jan. 5, 1948).

Miss Bettis appeared as Tiger Lily and as solo dancer in "Haunted Heart" in the revue, *Inside USA* (Century, Apr. 30, 1948) and on tour (1949); her next work was *A° I Lay Dying*, which had its first performance in Baltimore, Md. (Museum of Art, Dec. 12, 1948), and was then presented in N.Y.C. (Hunter Coll. Playhouse, Dec. 19, 1948). At the Connecticut College Dance Festival, she appeared with her company in the premiere of *Domino Furioso* (Aug. 14, 1949) and *It's Always Farewell* (Aug. 18, 1949); subsequently appeared as dancer-choreographer of her own works with the N.Y.C. Dance Th. (NY City Ctr., Dec. 14, 17, 24, 1949); with her own company (Kaufmann Aud., YMHA, Jan. 22, 1950); as Kitty in *Great to Be Alive!* (Winter Garden, Mar. 23, 1950); as dancer-choreographer with her own company in concert (Kaufmann Aud., May 14, 1950); and in *Crimes and Crimes* (Cambridge Summer Th., Boston, Mass., Aug. 29, 1950).

She appeared in the revue, *Bless You All* (Mark Hellinger Th., N.Y.C., Dec. 14, 1950), and as choreographer for *Peer Gynt* (ANTA, Jan. 28, 1951); for the Slavenska-Franklin Co., choreographed the ballet, *A Streetcar Named Desire* (Her Majesty's Th., Montreal, Can., Oct. 9, 1952); played in a stock production of *Frogs of Spring* (Falmouth Playhouse, Mass., July 27, 1953; Ogunquit Playhouse, Me., Aug. 8, 1953); staged for Amer. Ballet Th., her ballet, *A Streetcar Named Desire*, in which she danced the leading role (McCarter Th., Princeton, N.J., Oct. 26, 1954); and was dancer-choreographer of her own works in the American Dance Festival (ANTA, May 3, 1955), where her solo work, *The Golden Round*, in which she portrayed Lady Macbeth, had its premiere (May 8, 1955). She played Leona Samish in a Univ. of Michigan production of *The Time of the Cuckoo* (Lydia Mendelssohn Th., Ann Arbor, Mich., June 6, 1955).

With her own dance company, she was dancer-choreographer of *Circa '56* (Kaufmann Aud., YMHA, Apr. 21, 1956); appeared in a concert-reading of *Children of the Ladybug* (Kaufmann Aud., YMHA, Nov. 18, 1956); and in the opera, *The Soldier* (Carnegie Hall, Nov. 25, 1956); played Calypso in *Maiden Voyage* (Forrest, Philadelphia, Pa., Feb. 28, 1957–Mar. 9, 1957); choreographed *The Past Perfect Hero* (NY Acad. of Music, Jan. 19, 1958); played both the Serpent Fusima and Chlow in *Back to Methuselah* (Ambassador, N.Y.C., Mar. 26, 1958); was choreographer for *Ulysses in Nighttown* (Rooftop, June 5, 1958); played Ninotchka in *Silk Stockings* (Rye Music Th., N.Y., June 24, 1958); and in a program of her own works, danced in the premiere of *Closed Door* (Juilliard Concert Hall, N.Y.C., May 9, 1959).

She choreographed and also played both Mrs. Thornton and Bella-Bello in *Ulysses in Nighttown* (Arts Th. Club, London, May 21, 1959; Th. Sarah Bernhardt, Paris, July 8, 1959; The Hague and Amsterdam, Neth., July–Aug. 1959); restaged for the Dallas (Tex.) Civic Ballet, and danced the leading role in her work, *Virginia Sampler* (Civic Aud., Mar. 27, 1960); was dancer-choreographer with her company, the Valerie Bettis Dance Th., at Castle Hill (Ipswich, Mass., July 23, 1960), and at Jacob's Pillow Dance Festival (Lee, Mass., Aug. 2–6, 1960), where her *Early Voyages* received its first performance (Aug. 2).

Miss Bettis choreographed, directed, and was the narrator in *Domino Furioso Columbine* (York, N.Y.C., Feb. 7, 1961); appeared with her own company in concert in Bloomington, Ind. (Indiana Univ. Aud., Apr. 9, 1961), and Chicago (Goodman Th., Apr. 10, 1961); played Camilla Jablonski in *Invitation to a March* (Playhouse-in-the-Park, Philadelphia, Pa., July 17, 1961); staged *If Five Years Pass* (Stage 73, N.Y.C., May 10, 1962); and appeared (July 1962) in *Brecht on Brecht* (Th. de Lys, Jan. 3, 1962). *Early Voyagers* was presented by the National Ballet (Washington, D.C., Jan. 3, 1963); Brooklyn College, N.Y.C., Feb. 16, 1963). Miss Bettis was co-narrator for the tour of *America Dances* (Feb. 28–Mar. 3, 1963), and at the Dancers Studio Concert, she choreographed *Songs and Precessions, He Who Runs* and choreographed and danced in *Inventions in Darkness* (Kaufmann Concert Hall, YMHA, N.Y.C., May 3, 1964). In 1965, she revived *As I Lay Dying* for American Dance Theater's Mar. 2–7 season (NY State Th.).

Films. Miss Bettis was dancer and choreographer for "The Desperate Heart," a part of the "Dance of Life" sequence in *An American Dance Trilogy* (UI, 1951); arranged dances for Rita Hayworth and appeared in *Affair in Trindad* (Col., 1952); choreographed the "Dance of Seven Veils" in *Salome* (Col., 1953); choreographed and staged production numbers and appeared in *Let's Do It Again* (Col., 1953); and choreographed *Athena* (MGM, 1954). She has appeared also in dance training and demonstration films.

Television. Miss Bettis was dancer-choreographer on the series, Valerie Bettis Dancers (CBS, Feb. 8, 1946); appeared on the Texaco Star Th. (NBC, June 15, 1948); *Holiday* (Studio One, CBS, Feb. 20, 1949); *The Stronger* (Fireside Th., NBC, June 1949); and in *Unguarded Moment* (NBC, Oct. 3, 1949). She directed ensembles for the Paul Whitman Revue (ABC, Sept.–Dec. 1949); played the title role in *Kitty Doone* (Philco Television Playhouse, NBC, Feb. 11, 1951); was dancer-choreographer for *An Evening with Richard Rodgers* (America Applauds, NBC, Mar. 4, 1951), and *All Star Revue* (NBC Comedy Hour, Mar. 18, 1951); appeared as dancer-choreographer on the General Electric Guest House (CBS, July 15 and Sept. 2, 1951); and again in *All Star Revue* (NBC Comedy Hour, Sept. 8 and Sept. 22, 1951); appeared in *Wings on My Feet* (Philco Television Playhouse, NBC, Feb. 22, 1953); choreographed the Gershwin opera, *135th Street* (Omnibus, CBS, Mar. 29, 1953); appeared in *The Shining Hour* (Kraft Television Th., ABC, Aug. 19, 1954); *The Women* (Producers Showcase, NBC, Feb. 7, 1955); choreographed *Our Town* (NBC, Sept. 1955); appeared in *The Sound and the Fury* (Playwrights '56, NBC, Dec. 6, 1955); *The Investigators* (NBC, July 22, 1958); *Music Hath Charms* (Bell Telephone Hour, NBC, Jan. 20, 1961); and on special programs for Christmas 1965, Easter 1966, and Christmas 1966, all for ABC. *As I Lay Dying* was presented on Camera Three (CBS, Mar. 1965), and she choreographed *Histoire du Soldat* for Sunday Showcase (PBS, 1967).

Other Activities. Since Mar. 1963, Miss Bettis has taught dancing in her own studio.

In Apr. 1963, she was instrumental in forming the Dancers' Studio, a group of professional dancers and choreographers who study and work together, and in 1964 she founded Dancers' Studio Foundation, Inc.

Awards. Miss Bettis received the John Martin New York *Times* Award for her choreography in *The Desperate Heart* (1943); for her dancing performance in *Inside USA*, she received the Donaldson Award and the *Theatre World* Award (1948), the *Mademoiselle* Magazine Award for Signal Achievement (1948); and the *Dance* Magazine Award for her choreography in *As I Lay Dying* (1949).

Recreation. Painting.

BETTMANN, OTTO L. Archivist, writer. b. Oct. 15, 1903, Leipzig, Germany, to Dr. Hans I. and Charlotte Bettmann. Attended Freiburg Univ., Germany, 1926; grad. Leipzig Univ., Germany, Ph.D. 1928; studied art history in Paris, London and Florence. Married Anne Gray, decorator and antique dealer. Address: Bettmann Archive, 136 E. 57th St., New York, NY 10022.

In 1935, Mr. Bettmann went to N.Y.C. as a refugee and founded the Bettmann Archive, Inc., a photograph research library with a special section on the theatre including theatrical history, costume studies and early history of the motion-picture industry.

Published Works. Mr. Bettmann is the author of *A Pictorial History of Medicine* (1962). He also wrote, with Van Wyck Brooks, *Our Literary Heritage: A Pictorial History of the Writer in America* (1956); and, with Paul Henry Lang, *A Pictorial History of Music* (1960).

BEVAN, DONALD. Artist, playwright. b. Joseph Donald Bevan, Jan. 16, 1920, Holyoke, Mass., to Walter L. and Edna (Stebbins) Bevan. Father, mechanical engineer. Attended Holyoke H.S., Mass., 1936; Commerce H.S., Springfield, Mass., 1937–38. Studied at Grand Central Art Sch., N.Y.C., 1941–42. Married Nov. 1948 to Patricia Kirkland, actress; three sons, one daughter. Relatives in theatre: father-in-law, Jack Kirkland, playwright; mother-in-law, Nancy Carroll, actress. Served WW II, USAF, ETO; rank, Sgt. Member of Dramatists Guild. Address: 610 West End Ave., New York, NY 10024, tel. (212) EN 2-6255.

Mr. Bevan is primarily an artist, whose caricatures of theatrical celebrities are displayed in Sardi's Restaurant, N.Y.C.

Recreation. Most sports.

BHASKAR. Dancer, actor, choreographer, singer. b. Bhaskar Roy Chowdhury, Feb. 11, 1930, Madras, India, to D. P. Roy and Charlotte (Banerjee) Chowdhury. Father, sculptor, painter. Grad. Doveton Corrie Boys H.S., Madras, 1947; Christian Coll., Madras, B.A. 1950; attended Bard Coll., 1955–56. Married May 25, 1957, to Joan Wells Harper (marr. dis. Apr. 18, 1963). Relative in theatre: aunt, Shupraba Mukherjee, actress. Member of AEA; AFTRA; SAG; AGVA. Address: 203 Columbus Ave., New York, NY 10023, tel. (212) EN 2-1288.

Pre-Theatre. Professional boxer.

Theatre. Bhaskar made his debut as a concert dancer with his own company in Madras, India (Victoria Public Hall, 1950), and toured India with his group (1950–53).

He made his first N.Y.C. appearance as choreographer and dancer with his company (Kaufmann Concert Hall, 1956); subsequently the company performed at Carnegie Recital Hall (1956); Boston (Mass.) Univ. (1956); George Washington Univ. (Washington, D.C., May 1956); and Brooklyn (N.Y.) Acad. of Music (Dec. 15, 1956). Bhaskar and his troupe appeared at the Kaufmann Concert Hall (N.Y.C., May 18, 1958); Newport (R.I.) Jazz Festival (1958); Philadelphia (Pa.) Welcome House (1958); Jacob's Pillow Dance Festival (Lee, Mass., 1959); International World Trade Fair (Chicago, Ill., 1959); Arundel Opera (Kennebunkport, Me., 1959); and in Catskill Mt. (N.Y.) resorts (Summer 1959).

He appeared as a Roman Soldier in *Caligula* (54 St. Th., N.Y.C., Feb. 16, 1960); Rainath in *Christine,* for which he was also a dancer and assistant choreographer (46 St. Th., Apr. 28, 1960); as solo dancer at Radio City Music Hall (June 17, 1960); and toured South America and the Caribbean with his company (Aug. 15–30, 1960).

He was choreographer for *King of the Dark Chamber,* in which he played Thakurdada and the King's Cosmic Dancer (Jan Hus House, N.Y.C., Feb. 9, 1961), toured South Africa with the production as the King of Konchi (1961–62); was producer, writer, choreographer, and dancer in his company's concert presentation of *Life of Buddha* (Kaufmann Concert Hall, N.Y.C., 1962); played Garcilaso and choreographed *We're Civilized* (Jan Hus House, Nov. 8, 1962); and choreographed *Showgirls of 1964* (May 1964).

He made three tours of southern and midwestern US with his company (1969, 1970, 1971); traveled from coast to coast giving school and college concerts and toured South and Central America with his company (1972, 1973); toured India (Summer 1973), giving his final concert at Theatre Center, Calcutta (Aug. 28); gave educational shows for children in Connecticut, New Jersey, and New York state (Winter 1973–74); appeared in concert, Internatl. Dance Festival, Los Angeles, Calif. (Mar. 23, 1974).

Bhaskar choreographed *The Way* (YM-YWHA, N.Y.C., Feb. 1973) and *Kali Mother* (Actors Playhouse, N.Y.C., Sept. 1973).

Films. Bhaskar's Indian film appearances include *Nava Jeevan* (Gemini, 1945); *Swapna Sundari* (Vauhani, 1945); *Varzan* (Shoba Nachala, 1948) and *Sakkubai* which he also choreographed (Star Combines, 1949). For Gemini Studios, he choreographed *Dodula* (1949), *Bhaut Dinhue,* in which he also appeared (1954), and *In San Yat* (1955).

He appeared as a dancer in the short subject *Fabrics* (MPO, 1956); choreographed and appeared in *The Creation of Woman* (Trident, 1960); played Pedro in *Instant Love* (1963); played a cameo role as himself in *Leap into Hell* (Jomar Productions, 1970); danced in *Dances of India* (WLB Productions, 1969); and played the lead role, Horace Bones, in *I Drink Your Blood* (Cinemation Industries, 1972).

Television. He made his debut as a featured player and dancer on the Max Liebman Spectacular, *Marco Polo* (NBC, 1956); appeared on the Arlene Francis Home Show (NBC, 1958); played Agi in *The Letter* (Alcoa Playhouse, NBC, 1958); and appeared in *The Protégé* (NBC, 1958). He has also appeared with his company on the Dave Garroway Show (NBC, 1959); Exploring (NBC, 1962); Johnny Carson's Tonight Show (CBS, 1962); was featured dancer on the Mike Douglas Show (CBS, 1969); and had a featured role in *Gandhi* (ABC, 1972). His film *Dances of India* was shown as a supplementary feature to Louis Malle's *Phantom India,* (NET, 1973). Bhaskar has also appeared in a number of television commericals.

Night Clubs. Bhaskar has appeared at the Alpine Village (Cleveland, Ohio, Feb. 1956); the Golden Slipper (N.Y.C., 1957); and was dancer, choreographer, and director of *Oriental Inferno* (New Frontier, Las Vegas, Nev., 1963). With his partner Anjali Devi, he performed at Chacun (Petionville, Haiti, Dec. 1973).

Awards. He received the Pandit Nehru Award for his contribution to Indian Art (Madras, India, 1954); and his short subject, *The Creation of Woman,* was nominated (1960) for an Academy (Oscar) Award. His *Dances of India* won a citation at the Cannes (France) International Film Festival (1970).

Recreation. Swimming, body-building, painting, sculpting, costume design, interior design, reading, especially science fiction.

BIEBER, MARGARETE. Writer, educator. b. July 31, 1879, Schoenau Kreis Schwets, West Prussia, Germany, to Jacob and Wally (Bukotzer) Bieber. Father, industrialist. Grad. Univ. of Berlin, 1903; Univ. of Bonn, Ph.D. 1907. Member of Archaeological Inst. of America; American Academy of Arts and Sciences. Address: 605 W. 113th St., Apt. 33, New York, NY 10025, tel. (212) MO 3-4454.

Dr. Bieber was visiting lecturer at Barnard Coll. (1934–36) and at Columbia Univ. Graduate Sch. in Fine Arts, where she was associate professor (1937–48). From 1948 to 1956, she lectured at the School of General Studies, Columbia Univ., summer school; Princeton University; and the New Sch. for Social Research.

Published Works. Miss Bieber, a research scholar in archaeology and the history of the ancient theatre, is the author of *Das Dresdener Schauspieler-Relief* (1907), a work dealing with costume in Greek tragedy; *Skenika Kuchenform mit Tragoedienszene, Programm zum Winckelmanns-Feste 75* (1915), a work on masks; *Denkmäler zum Theaterwesen* (1920), on monuments relating to theatre; *Griechische Kleidung* (1928), on Greek dress; and *Entwicklungsgeschiichte der griechishchen Tracht* (1934), a history of Greek fashion; and *History of the Greek and Roman Theatre* (1939; revised 1961).

Since 1912, she has contributed articles to *Theatre Arts* magazine, the *American Journal of Archaeology,* and others.

Awards. Miss Bieber received an honorary Litt.D. from Columbia Univ. (1954), and was named *Ehrensenator* (honorary senator) of Giessen Univ., Germany (1959).

Recreation. Theatre, reading, music.

BIKEL, THEODORE. Actor, musician, singer. b. May 2, 1924, Vienna, Austria, to Joseph and Miriam (Riegler) Bikel. Father, former rector, Israel Public Health Service. Attended agricultural college (Israel), one year; apprentice Habimah Th., Tel Aviv, 1942–43; RADA, London, 1946–48. Member of AEA (council mbr., 1961–64; 1st vice-pres., 1964–73; pres., 1973–to date); AFTRA; SAG; AFM; American Jewish Congress (pres., arts chapter, 1961–64; natl. vice-pres., 1964–71; cochmn. governing council, 1971–to date); Acad. of Television Arts and Sciences (bd. of gov., 1962–65). Address: Georgetown, CT.

Pre-Theatre. Worked on Israeli agricultural commune.

Theatre. Mr. Bikel first appeared on stage as an apprentice with the Habimah Theatre (Tel Aviv, Israel, 1943–44); helped form the Tel Aviv Chamber Th. (1944), where he remained for two years as an actor; followed by his London debut as Pablo Gonzales in *A Streetcar Named Desire* (Aldwych Th., Oct. 11, 1949), in which he succeeded Bernard Braden as Howard Mitchell; and appeared as Col. Ikonenko in *The Love of Four Colonels* (Wyndham's, May 28, 1951).

He made his N.Y.C. debut as Inspector Massoubre in *Tonight in Samarkand* (Morosco, Feb. 16, 1955); followed by Robert de Baudricourt in *The Lark* (Longacre, Nov. 17, 1955); Dr. Jacobson in *The Rope Dancers* (Cort, Nov. 20, 1957); Captain Georg Von Trapp in *The Sound of Music* (Lunt-Fontanne, Nov. 16, 1959); *Brecht on Brecht* (Th. de Lys, Jan. 3, 1962); and appeared as Samuel Cole in *Cafe Crown* (Martin Beck Th., Apr. 17, 1964).

He appeared as Tevye in the national company of *Fiddler on the Roof* (Caesar's Palace, Las Vegas, Nev., Dec. 1967–June 1968) and later in summer theatres (1969; 1971–72) and as Mayer with the national company of *The Rothschilds* (Toronto; Washington, D.C.; and Baltimore, Sept.-Nov. 1972) and in summer theatres (1972). He played also in *Jacques Brel Is Alive and Well and Living in Paris* in summer theatres (1972; 1974); as Paul Delville in *The Marriage Go Round* (Miami, Apr. 1973; Dallas, Aug.-Sept. 1973); as Al Lewis in *The Sunshine Boys* (Miami, Dec. 1973–Jan. 1974); and as Michael in *I Do, I Do* (Miami, Mar.-Apr. 1974).

Films. Following his film debut in *The African Queen* (UA, 1952), Mr. Bikel appeared in many motion pictures, including *Moulin Rouge* (UA, 1953); *Desperate Moment* (U, 1953); *Never Let Me Go* (MGM, 1953); *Melba* (UA, 1953); *Love Lottery* (Ealing, 1954); *The Little Kidnappers* (UA, 1954); *Forbidden Cargo* (Fine Arts, 1956); *The Vintage* (MGM, 1957); *The Pride and the Passion* (UA, 1957); *The Enemy Below* (20th-Fox, 1957); *Fraulein* (20th-Fox, 1958); *I Want to Live! (UA, 1958); The Defiant Ones* (UA, 1958); *The Blue Angel* (20th-Fox, 1959); *Woman Obsessed* (20th-Fox, 1959); *The Angry Hills* (MGM, 1959); *Chance Meeting* (Par., 1960); *Dog of Flanders* (20th-Fox, 1960); *My Fair Lady* (WB, 1964); *Sands of the Kalahari* (Par., 1965); *The Russians Are Coming! The Russians Are Coming!* (UA, 1966); *The Desperate Ones* (David Films, 1966); *Sweet November* (WB, 1968); *My Side of the Mountain* (Par., 1969); *Darker Than Amber* (Cinema Ctr., 1969); *The Little Ark* (Cinema Ctr., 1970); and *200 Motels* (UA, 1971).

Television and Radio. On radio, Mr. Bikel had his own program, At Home with Theodore Bikel (1957–62).

He has made numerous television appearances, including the US Steel Hour (CBS); Studio One (CBS); Kraft Television Th. (NBC); Producers Showcase (NBC); Climax! (CBS); Alcoa Hour (NBC); Mod Squad (ABC) the Danny Thomas Hour; Wagon Train; The Trials of O'Brien; Dick Powell Th. (NBC); Chrysler Th.; Gunsmoke (CBS); Playhouse 90 (CBS); Combat (ABC); Hawaii Five-0 (CBS); Alfred Hitchcock Presents (CBS); appeared in *Bridge of San Luis Rey* (Dupont Show of the Month, CBS, Jan. 20, 1958); *The Dybbuk* (Play of the Week, Oct. 3, 1960); on Naked City (ABC, 1961); Twilight Zone (CBS, 1962); Dr. Kildare (NBC, 1962); Sam Benedict (NBC, 1962); East Side/West Side (CBS, 1963); in *Who Has Seen the Wind?* (ABC, Feb. 19, 1965); *Noon Wine* (ABC Stage 67, Nov. 23, 1966); *The Diary of Anne Frank* (ABC, Nov. 26, 1967); *Saint Joan* (Hallmark Hall of Fame, NBC, Dec. 4, 1967); on Mission: Impossible (CBS, 1968); Ironside (NBC, 1971); in *Killer by Night* (CBS, Jan. 7, 1972); and on Cannon (CBS, 1972).

Mr. Bikel wrote and performed on The Eternal Light (NBC, 1958–60); and Look Up and Live (CBS, 1958–60); and was host-editor of Directions 61 (ABC, 1961). He made his foreign television debut in *The Cherry Orchard* (BBC, London, 1948).

Other Activities. He made his N.Y.C. concert debut at Carnegie Recital Hall (1956) in a folk song program; each year subsequent he has appeared in concerts throughout the US, Canada, and Europe, including an extensive tour of New Zealand and

Australia (1963), in addition to frequent concert appearances at Town Hall and Carnegie Hall in N.Y.C.

He has had an exhibition of his photographs at the Bank Street Gallery (N.Y.C., 1961) and has contributed to *U.S. Camera* and *Popular Photography.* The author of *Folksongs and Footnotes* (1960), he is also a frequent contributor of articles concerning the arts and Judaic affairs to various magazines and newspapers in the US and abroad.

Active in the reform wing of the Democratic Party, he was an elected delegate to the 1968 Democratic National Convention.

Discography. Mr. Bikel has recorded the following albums for Elektra, *Israeli Folk Songs* (1955), *An Actor's Holiday* (1958), *Jewish Folk Songs* (1958), *Folk Songs of Israel* (1958), *Songs of a Russian Gypsy* (1958). *A Young Man and a Maid* (1958), *Folk Songs from Just About Everywhere* (1959), *More Jewish Folk Songs* (1959), *Bravo Bikel* (1959), *Songs of Russia, Old and New* (1960), *From Bondage to Freedom* (1961), *A Harvest of Israeli Folk Songs* (1962), *Poetry and Prophecy of the Old Testament* (1962), *The Best of Bikel* (1962), *Theodore Bikel on Tour* (1963), *A Folksinger's Choice* (1964), *Yiddish Theatre and Folk Songs, Songs of the Earth* (1967), and *Theodore Bikel Is Tevye* (1968). For Columbia, he recorded *The Sound of Music* (1960), with the original cast, and *The King and I* (1964). His later releases include *A New Day* (Reprise, 1970), *Silent No More,* Soviet Jewish underground songs (Star/American Jewish Congress, 1972), and *Theodore Bikel for the Young* (Ambassador, 1973).

Awards. Mr. Bikel was nominated for Antoinette Perry (Tony) awards for his role as Dr. Jacobson in *The Rope Dancers* (1958) and his performance as Captain Georg Van Trapp in *The Sound of Music* (1960); and was nominated for an Academy (Oscar) Award for his role in *The Defiant Ones* (1959).

Mr. Bikel has also been the recipient of a number of civic awards, including the Brandeis University Women's Committee citation as "Citizen of the World and Friend of Humanity" (1960). In the same year, a collection of books in Brandeis Library was dedicated to him; the National Jewish Hospital, Denver, Colo., cited him for distinguished philanthropic service; and Mt. Sinai Hospital, N.Y.C., named him man of the year. In 1961, the Joint Defense Appeal of the American Jewish Committee and the Anti-Defamation League cited him for distinguished service in the cause of human rights, and he received the Mar Mitzvah Award of Israel Bonds and the New York Jewish War Veterans Public Service Award. He received also the Arts Chapter citation, American Jewish Congress, in 1964 and the "Morim" award of the Jewish Teacher's Association. In 1965 he was the recipient of the Combined Jewish Philanthropies (Boston) Appreciation Award for his television special, "Birthday of an Idea," and in 1966 he received the Israel Bonds (Detroit) annual award. Goodwill Industries of Philadelphia gave him its distinguished achievement award in 1966, and he was named man of the year by B'nai B'rith in 1967. The Southern California division, American Jewish Congress, gave him its Man of Conscience award in 1967, and the following year he received the Women's Division Keynoters Award of the United Jewish Welfare Fund (Los Angeles). Other awards include the Hebrew University of Jerusalem certificate of honor (1969), the Mizrachi Women's Organization of America (West Coast) bronze medallion award (1970), the National Press Club certificate of appreciation (1972), the certificate of honor from the city and county of San Francisco (1973), and the Jewish Heritage Award of Farband Labor Zionist Organization (1973).

BILOWIT, IRA J. Producer, writer. b. Ira Jacob Bilowit, Sept. 12, 1925, New York City, to Isidor and Fanny Bilowit. Father, restaurateur. Attended DeWitt Clinton H.S., Bronx, N.Y., 1939–42; City Coll. of New York, B.S.S. 1947. Married Mar. 11, 1956, to Alice Spivak, actress; two sons; (div.). Member of Drama Desk (chmn., membership comm.). Address: 240 W. 10th St., New York, NY 10014, tel. (212) 929-7723.

Theatre. Mr. Bilowit was off-Bway editor and reviewer for the weekly newspaper, *Show Business* (1953–58), and managing editor (Jan. 1961–Nov. 1963; July 1972–April 1975).

He participated in his college theatre group, as actor, publicist, and manager, as well as working in production and publicity capacities with summer theatre and off-Bway groups. He taught courses in theatre production at the City Coll. of N.Y. (1947–51). Mr. Bilowit produced, in association with Unicorn Productions, a musical version of *Of Mice and Men,* for which he wrote the adaptation and lyrics (Provincetown Playhouse, N.Y.C., Dec. 4, 1958). He produced, with Terese Hayden and Elaine Aiken, *The Secret Concubine* (Carnegie Hall Playhouse, Mar. 21, 1960); and wrote and directed *For Love of Candy* (Forestburgh Summer Th., Monticello, N.Y., Aug. 1971).

He has been stage manager, production manager and general manager for children's theatre, dance presentations, and off-Bway, community and summer stock productions.

Films. He has been producer with film properties under option and has written and produced television spots, training films, and documentary films, as well as dramatic shorts (Pancosmas Productions, 1963–70).

Published Works. He is editor of an ANTA publication on off-Bway theatre.

Awards. Mr. Bilowit won second prize in an Inter-Collegiate Play Contest (1947).

BIRCH, PATRICIA. Choreographer, actress, dancer. b. about 1934, Scarsdale, N.Y. Professional training with Merce Cunningham; Martha Graham; School of American Ballet. Married to William Becker; two sons, one daughter.

Theatre. Miss Birch began her career as a dancer with the Martha Graham Co.; she was also a teacher and rehearsal director with the same organization. She made her debut on the musical stage as a dancer in *Goldilocks* (Lunt-Fontanne Th., N.Y.C., Oct. 11, 1958); was Anybodys in a revival of *West Side Story* (Winter Garden, Apr. 27, 1960); danced in NY City Ctr. Light Opera Co. revivals of *Brigadoon* (Mar. 27, 1957), *Carousel* (Sept. 11, 1957), and *Oklahoma!* (Mar. 19, 1958); and played constance in *Fortuna* (Maidman, Jan. 3, 1962).

Miss Birch did choreography for *You're a Good Man, Charlie Brown* (Th. 80, St. Mark's, Mar. 7, 1967); musical staging for *Up Eden* (Jan Hus Th., Nov. 27, 1968) staged special sequences for *Fireworks* (Village South Th., June 11, 1969); musical numbers for *The Me Nobody Knows* (Orpheum, May 18, 1970); for *F. Jasmine Adams* (Circle in the Square, Oct. 27, 1971); musical and dance numbers for *Grease* (Eden, Feb. 14, 1972); was choreographer for the double-bill *The Real Inspector Hound* and *After Magritte* (Th. Four, Apr. 23, 1972); for *A Little Night Music* (Sam S. Shubert Th., Feb. 25, 1973); for a revival of *Candide* (Chelsea Th. Ctr., Brooklyn Acad. of Music, Dec. 11, 1973; transferred to Broadway Th., Mar. 5, 1974); staged musical and dance numbers for *Over Here!* (Sam S. Shubert Th., Mar. 6, 1974); and did choreography for *Pacific Overtures* (Winter Garden, Jan. 11, 1976). Miss Birch also staged the opera *Falstaff* at the Kennedy Ctr., Washington, D.C.

Television. Miss Birch has done choreography for The Electric Company (PBS).

Awards. Miss Birch received Drama Desk awards for her choreography for *Grease* and *Over Here!* and was also nominated for Antoinette Perry (Tony) awards as best choreographer for the same productions.

BIRNEY, DAVID. Actor. b. David Edwin Birney, Washington, D.C., to Edwin B. and Jeanne (McGee) Birney. Father, special agent, FBI. Grad. high school, Cleveland, Ohio; Dartmouth Coll. (A.B. in English literature with high distinction); UCLA (M.A. in theatre arts). Professional training with Henry Williams and Warner Bentley at Dartmouth; with Ralph Freud, Henry Goodman, Dora Folger, and Edward Hearn at UCLA. Married to Jean Concannon 1961 (marr. dis.); to Meredith Baxter, actress, 1974. Served in US Army, 1963–65 and was director and performer with Second US Army Showmobile touring US; received honorable discharge with certificate of outstanding achievement. Member of AEE; AFTRA; SAG. Address: MAB Productions, Ltd., c/o Zeiderman, 625 Madison Ave., New York, NY 10022, tel. (212) 688-5333.

Theatre. Mr. Birney's first stage appearances were as the Captain in *H.M.S. Pinafore* at the West High School, Cleveland, Ohio, and as Percy in *The Little Red School House,* Brooklyn High School, Cleveland. He made his professional debut as Simon in *Hay Fever* (Barter Th., Abingdon, Va., July 6, 1965). Other Barter Theatre appearances were made by Mr. Birney in 1965: as the Street Singer in *The Threepenny Opera* (June 22); Damis in *Tartuffe* (July 27); the Narrator in *Pictures in the Hallway* (July 30); Cristoforov in *The Public Eye* (Aug. 10); in *Never Too Late* (Sept. 7); and as Tolan in *The Knack* (Sept. 21). In 1966, he performed with the Barter Theatre as Orsino in *Twelfth Night* (Apr. 15) and as Tony in *You Can't Take It with You* (Apr. 28). Mr. Birney has appeared also with the Hartford Stage Co., Hartford, Conn., as Deschamps in *Poor Bitos* (Oct. 7, 1966); Clove in *Endgame* (Nov. 11, 1966); Fedotik in *Three Sisters* (Dec. 16, 1966); the Chorus in *Under the Gaslight* (Jan. 20, 1967); Di Nolli in *Enrico IV* (Feb. 24, 1967); and Silvio in *The Servant of Two Masters* (Mar. 31, 1967).

In the summer of 1967, he was with the New York Shakespeare Festival, Delacorte Th.: as Antipholus of Syracuse in *The Comedy of Errors* (June 7); as the Dauphin in *King John* (July 5); and as Chiron in *Titus Andronicus* (Aug. 2). He toured with Viveca Lindfors' Strolling Players in an anthology of Brecht and Strindberg (Sept.–Oct. 1967) and was Egg of Head and the Chrous in *MacBird!* (Village Gate, Nov. 1967). He played Edmund in *The Ceremony of Innocence* (American Place Th., Jan. 1968); the Young Man in *Summertree* (Forum, Mar. 3, 1968); Cleanthes in *The Miser* (Vivian Beaumont Th., May 8, 1969); and appeared off-Bway as Andocides in *The Long War* (Triangle, July 1969) and as Wilson and Kenny in *Crimes of Passion* (Astor Place Th., Sept. 1969). In July and August 1970, he appeared as Hamlet at the State Univ. of Pennsylvania. He was with the Repertory Th. of Lincoln Center, Vivian Beaumont Th., as the Flyer in *The Good Woman of Setzuan* (Nov. 5, 1970); Christy Mahon in *The Playboy of the Western World* (Jan. 7, 1971); Hovstad in *An Enemy of the People* (Mar. 11, 1971); and Haemon in *Antigone* (May 13, 1971). He appeared in Los Angeles with the Center Th. Group as Cusins in *Major Barbara* (Mark Taper Forum, Aug. 26, 1971) and in Buffalo, N.Y., as Mercutio in *Romeo and Juliet* (Studio Arena Th., Mar. 2, 1972); in Chicago as Valentine in *You Never Can Tell* (Arlington Park Th., Jan. 1973); and toured in Ohio and Michigan with the Kenley Players as Sky Masterson in *Guys and Dolls* (May–July 1973). He played Romeo at the American Shakespeare Festival, Stratford, Conn. (June 1974), and for the Festival's new playwrights series directed *Yanks 3, Detroit 0, Top of the Seventh* (July 1974).

Films. Mr. Birney's film debut was in the starring role of Bowman in *Caravan to Vaccares* (Rank, 1974).

Television. Mr. Birney made his first appearance on television as Brother Martin in *St. Joan* (Hallmark Hall of Fame, NBC, Dec. 4, 1967). He played the role of Mark Elliot in *Love Is a Many Splendored Thing* (CBS, 1969–70); in 1971 was guest star on Hawaii Five-0, The F.B.I. and Canon (all CBS); and was the star of Ghost Story (NBC pilot series, Jan. 1972). He performed as Bernie in Bridget Loves Bernie (CBS, 1972) and was a special guest star in Murder or Mercy (CBS pilot, Feb. 1974).

Discography. Mr. Birney has recorded for Caedmon, reading the part of Cleanthes in *The Miser* (1969) and that of Hovstad in *An Enemy of the People* (1971).

Awards. In 1965, Mr. Birney won a national acting competition and received the Barter Theatre

Award, which includes an Equity contract to appear at the Barter Theatre. He was the winner in 1968 of the Clarence Derwent Award and the Theatre World Award for his role in *Summertree*, and in 1972 his performance as Mercutio in *Romeo and Juliet* was named as the best of the season at the Studio Arena Theatre, Buffalo, by the Buffalo *Courier-Express*. *Photoplay* magazine and *Sixteen* magazine gave him awards in 1973 for his performance as Bernie on the television series Bridget Loves Bernie.

Recreation. Poetry, guitar, skiing, and sailing.

BISHOP, DAVID. Managing director, actor. b. Mar. 4, 1931, Macon, Ga. Educ. Univ. of South Carolina; Columbia Univ. Professional training American Th. Wing, N.Y.C.; Actors Studio (Lee Strasberg).

Theatre. In 1971, Mr. Bishop joined the staff of the Memorial Arts Ctr., Atlanta, Ga., where he subsequently became managing director of the center's theatrical productions. He began his career in the theatre under the name Joe, or Joseph, Bishop; was assistant stage manager for *The Desperate Hours* (Ethel Barrymore Th., N.Y.C., Feb. 10, 1955); appeared in *The Ponder Heart* (Music Box, Feb. 16, 1956); and was Charlie Taylor in *The Happiest Millionaire* (Lyceum, Nov. 20, 1956), later touring with the production in the part of Tony Biddle. Mr. Bishop was also at various times stage manager for *How To Succeed in Business without Really Trying* (46th St. Th., Oct. 14, 1961); production stage manager for the American Shakespeare Festival, Stratford, Conn.; and managing director of the Meadow Brook Th., Rochester, Mich.

Television. Mr. Bishop appeared on Playhouse 90 (CBS); Studio One (CBS); Philco Playhouse (NBC); and As the World Turns (CBS).

BISSELL, RICHARD. Playwright, writer. b. Richard Pike Bissell, June 27, 1913, Dubuque, Iowa, to Frederick Ezekiel and Edith Mary (Pike) Bissell. Father, industrialist, Grad. Phillips Exeter Acad., 1932; Harvard Univ. B.S. 1936. Married Feb. 5, 1938, to Marian Van Patten Grilk, editor, writer; three sons, one daughter. Relatives in theatre: cousin, Mary James, actress; Mae "Bubbles" Bellew, burlesque performer. Member of Dramatists Guild; SWG; Mississippi Valley Assn.; Sons and Daughters of Pioneer Rivermen; Masters, Mates and Pilots Assn.; Amalgamated Tugboat Owners; The Lambs; Harvard Club of New York; Poesta Boat Club; Bowfin Yacht Club; Rockdale Athenaeum. Address: (home) 6 Rocky Point Rd., Bell Island, Rowayton, CT 06853; (summer), 15 Roads End, Boothbay Harbor, ME 04538; (bus.) c/o Harold Matson, 22 East 40th St., New York, NY 10016.

Pre-Theatre. Anthropologist, steamboat pilot, licensed mate, factory superintendent.

Theatre. Mr. Bissell wrote with George Abbott, the book for *The Pajama Game* (St. James Th., May 13, 1954), based on his novel *7 ½ Cents;* served as an assistant to George Abbott & Douglas Wallop on the book for *Damn Yankees* (46 St. Th., May 5, 1955); and wrote with Abe Burrows and Marian Bissell the book for *Say, Darling* (ANTA, May 3, 1958), based on his novel of the same name.

Films. He was co-author of *The Pajama Game* (WB, 1957).

Other Activities. Mr. Bissell is the president of Bissell Towing and Transportation Co., Dubuque, Iowa (1958–to date).

Published Works. Mr. Bissell has written *A Stretch on the River* (1950), *The Monongahela* (1952), 7½ Cents (1953), *High Water* (1954), *Say, Darling* (1957), *Goodbye Ava* (1960), *You Can Always Tell a Harvard Man* (1962), *Still Circling Moose Jaw* (1965), *How Many Miles to Galena?* (1968), *Julia Harrington* (1969), and *My Life on the Mississippi* (1973).

Awards. In 1954, he received the Antoinette Perry (Tony) and Donaldson Awards for the *The Pajama Game.*

Recreation. Mountaineering, boating, history.

BITTNER, JACK. Actor, singer. b. 1917, Omaha, Neb. Grad. Univ. of Nebraska, B.A. (drama 1940); studied at Dramatic Workshop of the New School, N.Y.C., 1940–42. Member of AEA; AFTRA; SAG; AGMA.

Theatre. Mr. Bittner made his professional debut as a monk in *Nathan the Wise* (Studio Th. of the New School, N.Y.C., 1942) and first appeared on Bway in the same production (Belasco Th., Apr. 3, 1942). He followed this with a performance as Mr. Frey in *All the King's Men* (President Th., Jan. 14, 1948); replaced (Jan. 1951) Nehemiah Persoff as the Duke of Cornwall in *King Lear* (National Th., Dec. 25, 1950); played Senator Blake in a revival of *Room Service* (The Playhouse, Apr. 6, 1953); the Second Murderer in *Richard III* (NY City Ctr., Dec. 9, 1953); a Citizen in *Coriolanus* (Phoenix, Jan. 19, 1954); the Foreman of the Jury in *Witness for the Prosecution* (Henry Miller's Th., Dec. 16, 1954); Topman in *Tiger at the Gates* (Plymouth, Oct. 3, 1955); and Father Baussan in *The Hidden River* (The Playhouse, Jan. 23, 1957).

He spent three summers (1957–59) at the American Shakespeare Festival, Stratford, Conn., where his roles included Montano in *Othello* (June 22, 1957), Tubal in *The Merchant of Venice* (July 10, 1957), Borachio in *Much Ado About Nothing* (Aug. 3, 1957), Tybalt in *Romeo and Juliet* (June 12, 1959), the Host in *The Merry Wives of Windsor* (July 8, 1959), and the Clown in *All's Well That Ends Well* (Aug 1, 1959). Mr. Bittner also played Thibaut in *The Carefree Heart* (pre-Bway: opened Cass Th., Detroit, Mich., Sept. 30, 1957; closed Hanna Th., Cleveland, Ohio, Oct. 26, 1957); Borkin in *Ivanov* (Renata Th., N.Y.C., Oct. 7, 1958); the Deputy in *Rashomon* (Music Box, Jan. 27, 1959); Oscar in *The Sap of Life* (Apollo, Oct. 2, 1961); Rinaldi in *First Love* (Morosco, Dec. 25, 1961); Mick Mandelbaum in *Venus at Large* (Morosco, Apr. 12, 1962); Mentor Graham and Stephen A. Douglas in a revival of *Abe Lincoln in Illinois* (Anderson Th., Jan. 21, 1963); and Sean O'Loughlin in *Nobody Loves an Albatross* (Lyceum, Dec. 19, 1963).

In 1962, Mr. Bittner became a member of the NY City Opera Co., where his roles included George Jones in *Street Scene* (State Th., Feb. 24, 1966) and Assan in *The Consul* (State Th., Mar. 17, 1966; Oct. 6, 1966); and with the City Ctr. Gilbert & Sullivan Co. (NY City Ctr.) he was the Sergeant of Police in *The Pirates of Penzance* (Apr. 25, 1968) and Wilfred Shadbolt in *The Yeomen of the Guard* (May 8, 1968). Mr. Bittner also played the role of the Marquess of Queensberry in *Dear Oscar* (Playhouse Th., Nov. 16, 1972); was Mr. Hardcastle in *Chips 'n' Ale* (Actors Th. of Louisville, Louisville, Ky., Apr. 25, 1974); and was the Bartender in *By Bernstein* (Westside Th., N.Y.C., Nov. 23, 1975).

Films. Mr. Bittner was in *Dreams That Money Can Buy* (1948).

Television. Mr. Bittner has appeared on Armstrong Circle Th. (NBC); Hallmark Hall of Fame (NBC); The Defenders (CBS); and other programs.

BLACK, DAVID. Producer. b. David Goldmark Black, Nov. 20, 1931, New York City, to Algernon D. and Elinor (Goldmark) Black. Father and mother, educators. Grad. Fieldston Sch., Riverdale, N.Y., 1949; Harvard Univ., B.A. 1952. Also studied for the opera. Married Dec. 21, 1951, to Linda Cabot; two sons, one daughter. Address: 251 E. 51st St., New York, NY 10022, tel. (212) 753-1188; 192 Olmstead Hill Rd., Wilton, CT 06897, tel. (203) 762-9671.

Pre-Theatre. Investment business.

Theatre. Mr. Black's first Bway production was *Look: We've Come Through!* (Hudson Th., Oct. 25, 1961), presented in association with Saint Subber and Frank Prince. Subsequently he produced *The Aspern Papers* (Playhouse, Feb. 7, 1962); *Semi-Detached* (Music Box Th., Oct. 7, 1963); in London, *The Ides of March* (Haymarket, Aug. 8, 1963); The Establishment Th. Co. produced, by arrangement with David Black, *The Knack* (New Th., N.Y.C., May 27, 1964); *Cambridge Circus* (Plymouth, Oct. 6, 1964), with Sol Hurok; *Ready When You Are, C. B.!* (Brooks Atkinson Th., Dec. 7, 1964); *The Impossible Years* (Playhouse, Oct. 13, 1965); *To Clothe the Naked* (Sheridan Square Playhouse, Apr. 27, 1967); *Those That Play the Clowns* (ANTA, Nov. 24, 1966); *The Natural Look* (Longacre, Mar. 11, 1967); *George M!* (Palace, Apr. 10, 1968); *Fire!* (Longacre, Jan. 28, 1969); *Salvation* (Jan Hus House, Sept. 24, 1969); *Paris Is Out!* (Brooks Atkinson Th., Jan. 19, 1970); *Earl of Ruston* (Billy Rose Th., May 5, 1971); *A Funny Thing Happened on the Way to the Forum* (Lunt-Fontanne Th., Mar. 30, 1972); *Lysistrata* (Brooks Atkinson Th., Nov. 13, 1972).

Recreation. Music, tennis, chess, horseback riding.

BLACK, EUGENE R. Theatre executive, banker. b. Eugene Robert Black, May 1, 1898, Atlanta, Ga., to Eugene Robert and Gussie (Grady) Black. Father, banker. Grad. Univ. of Ga., 1917. Married Jan. 25, 1930, to Susette Heath; two sons, one daughter. Served WW I, U.S.N. Address: (home) 178 Columbia Heights, Brooklyn, NY 11201, tel. (212) UL 5-7881; (bus.) 65 Broadway, New York, NY 10006.

Mr. Black is a trustee and former pres. of the American Shakespeare Th., Stratford, Conn., with offices in N.Y.C. He was chmn. of the Shakespeare Anniversary Comm. of America (1964), and was appointed a life-time trustee of the Shakespeare Birthplace Trust at Stratford-on-Avon, England (Apr. 29, 1964).

Other Activities. Mr. Black became a member of Harris, Forbes & Co., Atlanta, Ga., 1931, where he was named vice-pres., 1933. He joined the Chase National Bank, N.Y.C., 1933, serving as second vice-pres. (1933–37) and vice-pres. (1937–47); for the US Intl. Bank for Reconstruction and Devel., Washington, D.C., was exec. dir. (1947–49) and pres., chmn. exec. dirs. (1949–62). He was chmn. and pres. of the Intl. Finance Corp. (1961–62); dir. and consultant to the Chase Manhattan Bank (1963–70); consultant to American Express Co. (1970 to date); dir., Boise Cascade Corp; mbr. of adv. bd., Colonial Fund, Inc., Colonial Growth Shares, Inc., and Colonial Income Fund, Inc.; dir., Hartford Fire Ins. Co., Hartford Accident Indemnity Co.; special financial consultant to Secretary General of the UN; mbr. perm. adv. comm. to evaluate US foreign aid programs; dir., Chase Internat. Investment Corp.; chmn., dir., Howmet Corp., Intl. Tel. & Tel. Co., NY *Times* Co., Cummins Engine Co., Inc., Trust Co. of Ga.; trustee, Bowery Savings Bank; mbr., World Bank Pension Fund; financial adv. to Shaikh of Kuwait; trustee, chmn. of bd., Pierpont Morgan Library, Johns Hopkins; trustee, Conservation Fdtn., Population Council, Inc.; dir., Atlantic Council, Project Hope, Intl. Exec. Service Corp.; mbr., Nat. Comm. for Intl. Devel., Dag Hammarskjold Found.; mbr. bd. of overseers of the visiting comm. of Harvard Univ. Ctr. Intl. Affairs; mbr., Phi Beta Kappa.

Published Works. Mr. Black is the author of *The Diplomacy of Economic Development.*

Awards. Mr. Black has received honorary degrees from Univ. of Chattanooga, 1951; Columbia Univ., 1954; Oglethorpe Univ., 1955; Syracuse Univ., 1957; Macalester Coll., 1959; Univ. of Ark., 1959; Rutgers Univ., 1959; Yale Univ., 1960; Princeton Univ., 1960; Harvard Univ., 1960; Williams Coll., 1960; Manchester Univ., England, 1961; Oxford Univ., England; Univ. of Sussex, England; Univ. of Hamburg, 1962; and Northeastern U., 1962.

BLACK, MALCOLM. Director, producer, teacher. b. Malcolm Charles Lamont Black, May 13, 1928, Liverpool, England, to Kenneth and Althea Black. Father, oil company sales representative. Grad. Bryanston Sch., Blandford, Dorset, England (Oxford and Cambridge Sch. Certificate) 1946. Studied at Old Vic Sch., London, 1948–50, with Michel Saint-Denis, Glen Byam Shaw and George Devine. Married Aug. 6, 1955, to Diane Forhan, dancer. Married June 9, 1967, to Charla Doherty, actress; two sons. Served British Army, 1946–48; rank, 2nd Lt. Member of AEA; SSD&C.

Address: Chairman, Dept. of Theatre, York University, Downsview, Ontario, Canada tel. (416) 667-6266.

Theatre. Mr. Black made his stage debut with the Old Vic Theatre Co. (London, May 1953). Between 1950–53, he appeared in provincial repertory companies, and was actor-stage manager for the Arts Council of Great Britain Drama Dept. (1950, 1952 tours with Arts Council Regional Companies), the Arts Th. Salisbury, and the West of England Company. From Jan. 1957–Mar. 1959, he was stage director and production manager for the Crest Th. (Toronto, Canada).

Mr. Black came to the US to serve as administrator and instructor of acting for the American Shakespeare Festival Th. and Acad. (Apr. 1959–Apr. 1961), and was assistant director for *The Winter's Tale* (Apr. 25, 1960). He directed *The Thracian Horses* (Orpheum Th., N.Y.C., Sept. 27, 1961); *The Curate's Play* (St. George's Church, Dec., 1961). (Gramercy Arts, Jan. 6, 1964).

For summer theatre, Mr. Black directed *The Pleasure of His Company* (Hunterdon Hills Playhouse, Clinton, N.J., June 1961); *Five Finger Exercise* (Playhouse-in-the-Park, Philadelphia, Pa., June 1961, and on tour); *Sweet Bird of Youth* (Hunterdon Hills Playhouse, Aug., 1961); *Critic's Choice* (Playhouse-in-the-Park, Philadelphia, Pa.; Colonie Th., Latham, N.Y., June 1962); *Write Me a Murder* (Grist Mill Playhouse, Andover, N.J., June 1962). He directed *Janus* (Grist Mill Playhouse, July 1962); *Champagne Complex* (Hunterdon Hills Playhouse, Clinton, N.J., July 1962); *Blithe Spirit* (Colonie, Latham, N.Y., Aug. 1962); *The Best Man* (Playhouse-in-the-Park, Philadelphia, Pa., Aug. 1962); *A Thousand Clowns* (Royal Poinciana Playhouse, Palm Beach, Fla.; Coconut Grove, Miami, Fla., Mar. 1963); *Julius Caesar* (North Shore Th., Beverly, Mass., May, 1963); *Sunday in New York* (Playhouse-in-the-Park, Philadelphia, Pa., June 1963); summer tours of *Lord Pengo* (June 1963). He directed a summer tour of *Romanoff and Juliet* (July 1963), and *A Shot in the Dark* (Aug. 1963).

Mr. Black directed *Have I Got a Girl for You* (Biltmore, Los Angeles, Feb. 1963); *The Hostage*, as the opening production of the Playhouse Theatre Company's first repertory season (Queen Elizabeth Playhouse, Vancouver, B.C., Canada, Oct. 1963).

He directed the musical *Pimpernel* (Gramercy Arts, N.Y.C., Jan. 6, 1964); was appointed artistic director of the Playhouse Th. Co., and, for them, directed *The Caretaker, Charley's Aunt* and *Ring 'Round the Moon* (Queen Elizabeth Playhouse, Vancouver, B.C., Canada, Feb.–Mar. 1964); directed productions of *A Thousand Clowns* (Paper Mill Playhouse, Millburn, N.J., Apr. 1964); *The Play's the Thing* (Bucks County Playhouse, New Hope, Pa., May 1964); a summer tour of *Take Her, She's Mine* (June 1964); and a season of musicals for the Rainbow Stage (Winnipeg, Manitoba, Canada, June 1964).

He directed *The Seagull; Stop the World, I Want to Get Off;* and *The Knack* (Playhouse Th. Co., Vancouver, B.C., Canada, 1965); *The Most Happy Fella* (Vancouver Festival, 1965); a season of musicals (Melodyland, Berkeley, Calif., Summer 1966); *Like Father, Like Fun, Lock Up Your Daughters* and *Countdown to Armageddon* (Playhouse Th. Co., Vancouver, B.C., Canada, 1966–67); *Next Time I'll Sing for You* and *Poor Bitos* (UCLA Th. Group, Summer 1967); *Peer Gynt, How To Run the Country* and *Anything Goes* (Playhouse Th. Co., 1967–68); *All's Well that Ends Well* (Old Globe, San Diego, Calif., Summer 1968); *The Marriage of Mr. Mississippi* (Mark Taper Forum, Los Angeles, Calif., Summer, 1968); *Lock Up Your Daughters* (Pasedena Playhouse, Summer 1968); *Life with Father* (Santa Barbara (Calif.) Summer Th., Summer 1968); *Philadelphia, Here I Come, Walking Happy* and *The Fourth Monkey* (Playhouse Th. Co., Vancouver, B.C., Canada, 1968–69); *Lock Up Your Daughters* (Florida tour, Summer 1969); *A Midsummer Night's Dream* (Inner City Rep. Co., Los Angeles, Calif., Summer, 1969); *Tosca* (Seattle (Wash.) Opera Co., Summer 1969); *Crab Dance* (ACT, San Francisco, Calif., Summer 1969); *Oedipus Rex* (National Shakespeare Co., Stratford, Ont., Canada, 1970); *Hobson's Choice* and a season of musical stock (Winnipeg, Manitoba, Canada); *The Way of the World* (Longwharf Th., New Haven, Conn., 1972); *The Sound of Music* (St. Louis Municipal Opera Co., Mo., Summer 1972); *Pillar of Sand* (National Arts Center, Ottawa, Ontario, Canada, 1973); *The House of Blue Leaves* (Juilliard Drama Division, N.Y.C., 1973); *The Taming of the Shrew* (Walnut Street Th., Philadelphia, Pa., 1974); *Black Comedy*, and *Indian* (Manitoba Th. Co., Canada, 1974); and *Bitter Sweet* (St. Louis Municipal Opera Co., Mo., Summer 1974).

Television. Mr. Black acted in 15 BBC shows (London, 1950–53); was a BBC studio manager and handled light entertainment, drama and children's programs (Feb. 1954–Nov. 1956). He adapted *Volpone* for Canadian Broadcasting Corporation's Special Programmes Department; wrote comedy material for CBC-TV (Vancouver); was associated with Sheldon Leonard Productions (1967); and directed Room 222 (NBC, 1969).

Other Activities. He has been professor of drama at the Univ. of Wash. (1968–70); professor of drama and theatre at Queens College (CUNY, 1970–74); and chairman of the Theatre Dept. of York Univ. (Toronto, Ontario, Canada, 1974–to date).

He has written numerous articles on theatre for newspapers and magazines. Recently, the Univ. of Washington commissioned a book from him entitled *What I Really Want to Do Is Direct* . . . .

BLACKBURN, DOROTHY. Actress. b. Dorothy Loraine Blackburn Smith, Buffalo, N.Y., to William Loren and Pauline (Blackburn) Smith. Father, hotel manager; mother, composer, lyricist. Attended public school, Yonkers, N.Y.; Mrs. Leslie Morgan's Sch., N.Y.C.; the Misses Hunters Sch., N.Y.C. Studied dancing at the Metropolitan Opera Ballet Sch., N.Y.C.; acting at the Yorska Conservatoire, N.Y.C. Married June 24, 1926, to Edward May, Jr., stock broker (marr. dis. 1952); one son. Member of AEA; SAG; AFTRA; Episcopal Actors Guild (recording secy., 1951–to date); The Woman's Club of Rye, N.Y. (pres., 1941–42). Address: 903 Park Ave., New York, NY 10021.

Theatre. While a student at the Metropolitan Opera Ballet Sch., Miss Blackburn made her debut in *Aida* (Metropolitan Opera House); and during this period also danced with the Diaghileff Ballet Co.

She appeared as Miss D'Arcy in a vaudeville sketch, "In the Dark" (Orpheum Circuit; Keith's 58 St. Th.); followed by appearances with the Jessie Bonstelle Stock Co. (Garrick, Detroit, Mich., 1923); and with stock companies in Worcester, Mass.; Yonkers, N.Y.; Oakland, Calif. (1923); and Dayton, Ohio (1924).

She made her N.Y.C. debut as Florence Wheeler in *New Brooms* (Fulton, Nov. 17, 1924), also toured in it (Feb.–June 1925); played Sally in *Service for Husbands* (La Salle, Chicago, Ill., Sept. 1925); and Mrs. Pymbrook in *If I Was Rich* (La Salle, Chicago, May 1926).

She appeared in stock productions at the Empress Th. (St. Louis, Mo., 1926); Cox Th. (Cincinnati, Ohio, 1926); and the B. F. Keith Theatres (Lowell and Walden, Mass., 1927–28).

She succeeded (Jan. 16, 1928) Mary Kennedy as Mrs. Chase in *The Nineteenth Hole* (George M. Cohan Th., N.Y.C., Oct. 11, 1927), also toured in it; Mrs. Molly Richards in *Sweet Land of Liberty* (Knickerbocker, Sept. 23, 1929); toured as the Duchess of Devonshire in *Berkeley Square* (Selwyn, Chicago, Ill.; Belasco, Los Angeles, Calif., 1930); and as Winkie in *The Vinegar Tree* (Belasco, Los Angeles; Curran, San Francisco, Calif., 1930).

She was a member of the resident acting companies at Elitch Gardens (Denver, Colo., 1933); Cape Playhouse (Dennis, Mass., 1935, 1936, 1937); and the Ann Arbor (Mich.) Drama Festival (1941).

She played Miss Russell in *Pick-Up Girl* (48 St. Th., N.Y.C., May 3, 1944); succeeded (Mar. 1945) Ivy Troutman as Lydia Leyton in *The Late George Apley* (Lyceum, Nov. 23, 1944); played Myrtle Keller in *The Male Animal* (Music Box, May 15, 1952); Nancy Lawson in *High Named Today* (Th. de Lys, Dec. 10, 1954); Peg Costello in *The Desk Set* (Broadhurst, Oct. 24, 1955); Doris Upson in *Auntie Mame* (Broadhurst, Oct. 31, 1956); and Mrs. Horton in *A Desert Incident* (John Golden Th., Mar. 24, 1959).

She appeared as the Grand Duchess Sophie in *Call Me Madam* (St. Louis Municipal Opera, Mo., Summer 1959); Mrs. Callendar in *A Passage to India* (Ambassador, N.Y.C., Jan. 31, 1962); and appeared in stock at Elitch Gardens (Denver, Colo., 1963). She was Mrs. Butcher in *The Loves of Cass McGuire* (Helen Hayes Th., N.Y.C.; Oct. 6, 1966); Mrs. McGlone in *The Unsinkable Molly Brown* (St. Louis Municipal Opera, Mo., 1967); Mrs. Chauvinet in a revival of *Harvey*, (ANTA Th., N.Y.C., Feb. 24, 1970; national tour 1971) was in *The Torch-Bearers* (Meadow Brook Th., Rochester, Mich., Dec. 7, 1972); played Mrs. DeFries in *Cocktails with Mimi*, (Barter Th., Abingdon, Va., 1973); Old Margaret in *The Father* (Roundabout Th., N.Y.C., 1973); and was Mrs. Fisher in *The Show-Off* (Stage West, West Springfield, Mass., 1974).

Films. Miss Blackburn has appeared in *The Tiger Makes Out* (1966) and was the Neighbor in *The Boston Strangler* (20th-Fox, 1968).

Television. Miss Blackburn made her debut as the Nurse on the first one-hour telecast, *Post Road* (NBC, 1940); and has appeared on Studio One (CBS); Lux Th. (CBS); Armstrong Circle Th. (NBC); American Heritage (NBC); Hallmark Hall of Fame (NBC); Naked City (ABC); Robert Montgomery Presents (NBC); The Defenders (CBS); The Nurses (CBS); Theatre '62 (NBC); *Intermezzo* (CBS Workshop); Young Doctor Malone (NBC); played Nurse Brown on the series The Doctors (NBC, 1964–66); Luella Watson on the series Another World (NBC, 1968–71); and Mrs. Chauvinet in *Harvey* (Hallmark Hall of Fame, NBC, 1972).

BLACKMAN, EUGENE J. Educator. b. Eugene Joseph Blackman, Nov. 8, 1922, Malden, Mass., to Jacob and Lillian (Orloff) Blackman. Grad. Malden (Mass.) H.S., 1940; Boston Univ., B.S. 1944, M.A. 1947, doctoral studies, 1947. Married July 5, 1945, to Edna Ruth Feldman; one son, one daughter. Served US Army, Med. Dept., 1943–46; rank, Sgt. Major. Member of ATA; AAUP; NTC; ANTA; CTC; Society of Stage Directors & Choreographers; NETC (exec. bd., 1957–63; secy., 1957–60; pres., 1960–63; vice-pres., 1967; pres., 1968; chmn., New Scripts Committee, 1963; advisory council, 1969–to date; a trustee as of 1974); SAA; Speech Assn. of Eastern States. Address: (home) 51 Sumner St., Milton, MA 02186, tel. (617) 696-8929; (bus.) Northeastern Univ., 360 Huntington Ave., Boston, MA 02115, tel. (617) 437-2244.

Mr. Blackman has been chairman of the Dept. of Drama, Speech, and Music at Northeastern Univ. (1959–to date), where he has been a member of the faculty since 1947 (instructor of English, 1947–51; assistant professor of English, 1951–57; associate professor of English, 1957–61; and professor of drama, 1961–to date).

Since 1952, he has directed or produced more than 200 plays for the Northeastern Univ. Th. He adapted from the French and directed *The Imaginary Invalid* and *Tartuffe;* adapted and directed *Lysistrata;* and adapted Racine's *Phèdre*. Mr. Blackman directed the Tufts Univ. Th. production of *Caste* (Medford, Mass., Summer 1955). He is a director of the Charles Playhouse, Boston.

Other Activities. Mr. Blackman has been a guest drama critic for the Boston *Herald Traveler* and the Quincy (Mass.) *Patriot Ledger*.

Published Works. Mr. Blackman edited, with Elliot Norton, *The Actor in America* and, with Mr. Norton and Mort Kaplan, *The Playwright in America*, both works being done for the New England Theatre Conference.

BLACKTON, JAY. Musical director, conductor, composer, pianist, arranger. b. Jacob Schwartzdorf, Mar. 25, 1909, New York City, to Samuel and Jennie (Sporn) Schwartzdorf. Father, dry goods merchant. Grad. Eastern District H.S., Brooklyn, N.Y., 1927; attended Juilliard Sch. of Music, diploma in piano, 1930; in conducting, 1939. Studied piano with Henrietta Cammeyer, 1924–31; Ignace Hilsberg, 1927; conducting with Willy Collin, Berlin Opera, 1930–33; Cohen, Opéra-Comique, Paris, 1931; composition with Bernard Wagenaar, 1935–39. Married Feb. 8, 1936, to Eleanor Falk, artist (marr. dis. Mar. 13, 1940); married May 20, 1941, to Louise Holt, pianist; one son, William, a journalist; one daughter, Jennie Lou Blackton, actress. Member of Amer. Soc. of Musical Arrangers; ASCAP; AFM, Local 802 (N.Y.C.), Local 47 (Los Angeles), St. Cecile Lodge (Masons); The Players. Address: 4645 Rubio Ave., Encino, CA 91316, tel. (213) 981-2929.

Theatre. Mr. Blackton began his career as musical director for the St. Louis (Mo.) Municipal Opera (1937–42), where he conducted approximately sixty musicals.

He was musical director of *Sunny River* (St. James Th., N.Y.C., Dec. 4, 1941); *Oklahoma!* (St. James, Mar. 31, 1943); *Annie Get Your Gun* (Imperial, May 16, 1946); his own adaptation of Strauss' *The Chocolate Soldier* (Century, Mar. 12, 1947); *Inside USA* (Century, Apr. 30, 1948); *Miss Liberty* (Imperial, July 15, 1949); *Call Me Madam* (Imperial, Oct. 12, 1950); musical supervisor for *A Tree Grows in Brooklyn* (Alvin, Apr. 19, 1951); musical director for *Wish You Were Here* (Imperial, June 25, 1952); *By the Beautiful Sea* (Majestic, Apr. 8, 1954); *New Faces of '56* (Ethel Barrymore Th., June 14, 1956); *Happy Hunting* (Majestic, Dec. 6, 1956); *Oh, Captain!* (Alvin, Feb. 4, 1958); and the Los Angeles (Calif.) Civic Light Opera Assn. production of *At the Grand* (opened Philharmonic Aud., Los Angeles, July 7, 1958; closed Curran, San Francisco, Calif., Sept. 13, 1958).

Mr. Blackton was musical director of *Redhead* (46 St. Th., N.Y.C., Feb. 5, 1959); *Christine* (46 St. Th., Apr. 28, 1960); *Let It Ride* (Eugene O'Neill Th., Oct. 12, 1961); *Mr. President* (St. James, Oct. 20, 1962); *Fiorello* (NY City Ctr., June 13, 1962); *Pal Joey* (NY City Ctr., May 29, 1963); *The Girl Who Came to Supper* (Bway Th., Dec. 8, 1963); the international company of *Hello Dolly* (Orpheum, Minneapolis, Minn., Apr. 19, 1965); *A Time for Singing* (Broadway, May 21, 1966); *Sherry* (Alvin, Mar. 28, 1967); *George M!* (Palace, Apr. 9, 1968); *Two by Two* (Imperial, Nov. 10, 1970); *The King and I* (Jones Beach Th., July 1972); *Oliver!* and *Gone with the Wind* (Los Angeles Civic Light Opera, 1973 season); *Fiddler on the Roof* (Jones Beach Th., July 1974).

He was musical director of the Delaware Philharmonic Orchestra (1947–48); has conducted the Utah State Symphony (1947); the Houston (Tex.) Lyric Th. (1949); and the opera, *La Traviata*, for the Lyric Arts Opera, Inc. (N.Y.C., 1961).

Films. Mr. Blackton was musical director for *The Merry Widow* (MGM, 1951); *Oklahoma!* (MTC, 1955); and *Guys and Dolls* (MGM, 1955).

Television and Radio. Mr. Blackton served as musical director of the weekly radio program Broadway Showtime (CBS, 1944); and the RCA Victor Radio Show (NBC, 1944). On television, he was musical director of Inside U.S.A. (CBS, 1949); the Mary Martin-Ethel Merman segment of the Ford Anniversary Show (CBS, 1952); The Fabulous Fifties (CBS, 1960); *Shangri-La* (Hallmark Hall of Fame, NBC, 1960); The Good Years (CBS, 1961); Mary Martin Easter Show (NBC, 1965); Androcles and the Lion (NBC, 1969); and was music supervisor for The Gershwin Years (CBS, 1962).

Other Activities. Mr. Blackton is a composer, arranger, orchestrator, concert pianist, vocal instructor, and coaches operatic roles in Italian, French, and German. In 1970 he was commissioned by Walt Disney to write a stage version of the Disney movie *Snow White.* He added ten new songs to the original score and it was produced at the St. Louis Municipal Opera and the Kansas City Starlight Th. At New York's Philharmonic Hall he has arranged and presented many special concerts of our leading composers of the American Theatre —Gershwin, Kern, Youmans, Coward, Arlen, Friml and Rodgers—featuring Howard Keel, Fred Astaire, Judy Garland, Benny Goodman, Dinah Shore, Andy Williams, Peggy Lee, and many more.

Discography. Mr. Blackton has conducted the original cast recordings of most of the Bway musicals he was associated with and has made recordings of a number of other musicals, and conducted the orchestras for recordings by many major popular and classical singers.

Awards. Mr. Blackton received an Academy (Oscar) Award for his musical direction of *Oklahoma!* (1956); and was nominated for the same award for *Guys and Dolls* (1956).

Recreation. Swimming, chess, carpentry, photography.

BLACKWELL, EARL. Publisher, author. b. Samuel Earl Blackwell, Jr., May 3, 1914, Atlanta, Ga., to Samuel Earl and Carrie (Lagomarsino) Blackwell. Father, cotton broker. Grad. Oglethorpe Univ., B.A. (journalism) 1933; attended Columbia Univ., 1935. Address: (home) 171 W. 57th St., New York, NY 10019, tel. (212) PL 7-8187; (bus.) 171 W. 57th St., New York, NY 10019, tel. (212) PL 7-7979.

Theatre. Mr. Blackwell wrote, with Caroline North and Sydney Sanders, *Aries Is Rising* (John Golden Th., N.Y.C., Nov. 21, 1939).

Other Activities. In 1939, Mr. Blackwell founded Celebrity Service, Inc., a firm that provides information about prominent persons and publishes the daily *Celebrity Bulletin*, the weekly *Theatrical Calendar*, and the annual *Contact Book*. He is editor of *Celebrity Register* and contributes to other magazines.

He was celebrity director for the NY World's Fair (1939–40); coordinator of American celebrities at the Cannes and Venice Film Festivals (1954–55); and commentator on the radio program, Celebrity Table (ABC, 1955–56). In 1972 he organized and was first chairman of the Theater Hall of Fame (located in New York's Uris Theater), honoring outstanding contributors to the Bway theatre. The annual election to the Theater Hall of Fame is made by the nation's leading drama critics and drama editors.

BLAINE, VIVIAN. Actress, singer. b. Vivian S. Stapleton, Nov. 21, 1923, Newark, N.J., to Lionel Pierre and Wilhelmina (Tepley) Stapleton. Father, theatrical booking agent. Attended Southside H.S., Newark; AADA. Married Jan. 10, 1945, to Manuel George Frank, talent representative (marr. dis. Dec. 10, 1956); married May 9, 1959, to Milton R. Rackmil, film executive (marr. dis. July 25, 1961); married Dec. 14, 1973, to Stuart Clark. Toured during WW II for U.S.O. Member of AEA; SAG; AFTRA; AGVA; AMPAS.

Theatre. Miss Blaine, at age three, was performing on the vaudeville stage at the Branford Th. (Newark N.J.). She sang with several local bands when she was 14, and eventually sang in N.Y.C. at the Café de la Paix (1940) and at The Glass Hat (1941).

She appeared several times at the Roxy Th. (1945–50); in a variety show at the Casino Th. (London, England, June 1947); elsewhere in Great Britain (1947–48); at the Copacabana (N.Y.C., Apr. 6, 1948); in a stock production of *One Touch of Venus* (Dallas Starlight Th., Tex., Summer 1948); at the Oriental Th. (Chicago, Ill., Dec. 23, 1948); in a stock production of *Light Up the Sky* (Lakeside Summer Th., Lake Hopatcong, N.J., July 1949); and in a stock tour of *Bloomer Girl* (Summer 1949).

Miss Blaine made her N.Y.C. debut as Miss Adelaide in *Guys and Dolls* (46 St. Th., Nov. 24, 1950), a role which she repeated in London (Coliseum, May 28, 1953); appeared in *Panama Hattie* (Dallas Starlight Th., Tex., Summer 1955); succeeded (June 25, 1956) Shelley Winters in the role of Celia Pope in *A Hatful of Rain* (Lyceum, N.Y.C., Nov. 9, 1955), which she played on the national tour (opened Selwyn, Chicago, Ill., Oct. 15, 1956; closed Plymouth, Boston, Mass., May 4, 1957); appeared as Irene Lovelle in *Say, Darling* (ANTA, Apr. 3, 1958); Rose in a stock production of *Gypsy* (Shady Grove Music Fair, Washington, D.C., Summer 1962); repeated her role of Adelaide for a stock engagement of *Guys and Dolls* (Milwaukee, Wis., Nov. 1962); and appeared as Angela in *Enter Laughing* (Henry Miller's Th., N.Y.C., Mar. 13, 1963). Miss Blaine played Nell Henderson in a stock production of *Mr. President* (Civic Arena, Pittsburgh, Pa., July 27, 1964); repeated her role of Miss Adelaide in *Guys and Dolls* (NY City Ctr., revived Apr. 22, 1965, and June 8, 1966; also, Paper Mill Playhouse, Millburn, N.J., Nov. 23, 1965; Candlewood Th., New Fairfield, Conn., July 1966); played Edith Lambert in a stock tour of *Never Too Late* (Summer 1965); played Stephanie in a stock tour of *Cactus Flower* (Winter 1967–68); toured as Marion Hollander in *Don't Drink the Water* (opened Nixon, Pittsburgh, Oct. 7, 1968); toured in *Hello, Dolly!*; played Mme. Hortense in a national tour of *Zorba* (opened Bushnell Aud., Hartford, Conn., Sept. 11, 1970; closed Memorial Aud., Worcester, Mass., May 18, 1971); Frances Black in a tour of *Light Up the Sky* (opened Fisher, Detroit, Aug. 17, 1971); succeeded Jane Russell, who succeeded Elaine Stritch, as Joanne in *Company* (Alvin, N.Y.C., Apr. 26, 1970); and toured in *Follies*, and *Twigs* (1973).

Films. For 20th-Fox, Miss Blaine appeared in *It Happened in Flatbush* (1942), *Girl Trouble* (1942), *Through Different Eyes* (1942), *Jitterbugs* (1943), *He Hired the Boss* (1943), *Something for the Boys* (1944), *Greenwich Village* (1944), *Nob Hill* (1945), *State Fair* (1945), *Doll Face* (1945), *Three Little Girls in Blue* (1946), and *If I'm Lucky* (1946); as well as appearing in *Skirts Ahoy!* (MGM, 1952); as Miss Adelaide in *Guys and Dolls* (MGM, 1955); and in *Public Pigeon No. 1* (U, 1957).

Television and Radio. On radio, she performed on The Fitch Bandwagon.

On television, she has appeared in *Those Two* (NBC, Nov. 26, 1951); *Double Jeopardy* (Philco Television Playhouse, NBC, Jan. 4, 1953); *Heart of a Clown* (Elgin Hour, ABC, Sept. 20, 1954); *Pick the Winner* (Damon Runyon Th., CBS, Apr. 16, 1955); *Dream Girl* (Hallmark Hall of Fame, NBC, Dec. 11, 1955); *The Awful Truth* (Bob Hope Show, NBC, Mar. 20, 1956); *Ray Bolger's Washington Square Show* (NBC, June 4, 1956); and in *The Undesirable* (Lux Video Th., NBC, Feb. 7, 1957). She has also appeared on the Ford Th. (CBS); the Jimmy Durante Show; the Milton Berle Show (NBC); the Jackie Gleason Show (CBS); and Route 66 (CBS).

Night Clubs. Miss Blaine's recent N.Y.C. appearances include engagements at Brothers and Sisters (1975), and Grand Finale (1976).

Awards. She was named "Musical Comedy Star of the Year" by the NY Theatre Goers (1951), and received the Donaldson Award (1951), for her performance in *Guys and Dolls;* was elected by the Fashion Academy as Best Dressed Woman (1952); by presidential request, played Miss Adelaide, in excerpts from *Guys and Dolls*, at the White House (Mar. 19, 1967).

BLAIR, WILLIAM. House manager, press representative. b. William Thomas Blair, Jr., June 25, 1896, Cincinnati, Ohio, to William Thomas and Katherine (Snodgrass) Blair. Father, building contractor. Grad. Glenville H.S., Cleveland, Ohio, 1914; Cleveland Bus. Coll., night classes, 1917. Married Oct. 30, 1917, to Effie Wilma Froelk (dec. July 29, 1963); two sons, one daughter. Relatives in theatre: uncles, Arthur and Paul Algrim, known as Musical Bells, in vaudeville and burlesque (1900–20); sister-in-law Dorothy Townes, musical comedienne; brother-in-law, Arthur Froelk, theatre manager and treasurer, Cleveland, Ohio (1917–26); sister-in-law Marion Froelk, Ziegfeld Follies show-girl, past president Ziegfeld Follies Club. Member of ATPAM, Local 18032; Meridian Lodge F&AM 610; Ancient Accepted Scottish Rite Valley of Cleveland (32nd degree); Al Koran Temple A.A.O.

N. M.S. (pres., Al Koran Patrol, 1937); Royal Order of Jesters, Court 14. Address: 3910 Monticello Blvd., Cleveland Heights, OH 44121, tel. (216) 392-7892.

Pre-Theatre. Building contractor.

Theatre. From 1951 to 1964, Mr. Blair was house manager of the Nixon Th., Pittsburgh, Pa.; he also served as advance press representative on tour for the musical *Brigadoon,* and as company manager for other touring Bway shows. He was company manager for eight seasons with the Civic Light Opera in Pittsburgh. He retired in 1968.

He began his theatrical career in the 1920's in Cleveland, Ohio, associated with the Hanna Th. for sixteen seasons, serving as house manager for the final eight seasons. He also worked in production capacities for summer stock companies; and, during WW II, toured the South Pacific Islands as manager of a USO camp show, *Three's a Family,* which featured Charles Butterworth, Luella Gear, and Ann Mason (1944–45).

Awards. Mr. Blair received life membership in Al Koran Temple (1936) for "services rendered on the entertainment committee.".

Recreation. Hunting, fishing, woodworking with power and hand tools.

BLAKE, BETTY. Publisher, editor. b. Aug. 16, 1920, New York City, to Frederic and Violet (Fisher) Gibbs. Father, actor; mother, actress. Attended Columbia Univ., 1941–42. Married May 31, 1947, to Glyn Lewis, artist. Relatives in theatre: great-grandfather, Alexander Fisher, actor; grandfather, Charles E. Fisher, actor. Member of the Drama Desk; Outer Circle (treas., 1961–to date). Address: (home) 61 Jane St., New York, NY 10014, tel. (212) Chelsea 3-9167; 6 Weymouth St., Nantucket, MA; (bus.) Proscenium Publications, 4 Park Ave., New York, NY 10016, tel. (212) LE 2-2570.

Pre-Theatre. Editorial staff of *Newsweek.* .

Theatre. Since 1944, Miss Blake, with her partner, Joan Marlowe, has been co-editor and publisher of *Theatre Information Bulletin,* and since Jan. 1964, of *Theatre Critics Review.* .

Published Works. With Miss Marlowe, Miss Blake has written *The Keys to Broadway* (1951), and *Broadway—Inside the Last Decade* (1954).

Recreation. Collecting antiques, art, theatre.

BLAKE, CHARLES. Producer, choreographer, stager, consultant. b. Charles Hibbitt Blake, Louisville, Ky., to Blanche (Messick) and Joseph Woods Blake. Father, merchant; mother, artist. Relative in the theatre: Virginia Blake Ward. Educ. public schools Louisville; grad. Washington and Lee Univ. (A.B. in psychology); graduate work in theatre at Cornell. Studied ballet with Kobelef, Svoboda, Preobrazhinska, Mordkin; diploma from Chalif and Shawn; studied acting with Benno Schneider; mime with Etienne de Croux. Member of AEA; AGVA; SAG; AGMA. Served in US Army 1942–45 in Special Service unit presenting Irving Berlin's *This Is the Army;* co-author of and performer in *Bonds Away,* fund raising for Army relief; 4th Air Force intelligence. Address: Suite 1527, 250 W. 57th St., New York, NY 10019, tel. (212) JU 2-1757.

Pre-Theatre. Interest in human behavior related to dance led to development of choreokinesthetic system as basis for body language for dancers and actors.

Theatre. Mr. Blake's first stage experience was in college plays and musicals and little theatre presentations. He made his professional debut in 1935 with the Ruth Page Ballet at the Chicago Opera House as the preacher in *Gold Standard.*

He made his Bway debut as a sailor and an understudy to the Dead End kids in *Dead End* (Belasco Th., N.Y.C., Oct. 28, 1935). In 1936 he toured with a Univ. of Indiana repertory group, appearing as Death in *Everyman* and as Hodge in *Gammer Gurton's Needle,* and in 1937 he starred as Aska, the Magician, in a travelling magic show. He was in the London production of *Dead End* (Covent Garden, July 1938) and in Fall 1938, was in the ten-week pre-Bway tour of *Right This Way* as a dance soloist. He was the dancing magician in the touring *Crazy with the Heat* (Summer and Fall 1940), and he performed in and sang the title song of *This Is the Army* (Bway Th., April 1942) and toured with the show for six months.

From 1949 to 1964, Mr. Blake produced and staged some two hundred charity and industrial shows all over the US for a variety of organizations, including Litton Industries, Chrysler Corp., General Electric, and the US Navy. From 1950 to 1955, he was director of choreography and then producer of the Harvard Univ. Hasty Pudding shows. He produced *On the Town* for the Chicago musical theatre (Music in the Round, Chicago Lakefront Fair, Apr.–Sept. 1950); musicals at Asheville, N.C. (Forest Amphitheatre, July–Aug. 1950); and the *Sesquicentennial Show* at Toledo, Ohio (Amphitheatre, June–July 1953). He was consultant and administrator for the International Ballet (Chicago Opera House and tour, Nov. 1968–Apr. 1969) and manager of the national tour of the second company of *Fiddler on the Roof* (Aug.–Dec. 1969). He was choreographer for a German production of *Showboat* (Theatre am Goethe Platz, Bremen, March 1972) and consultant for the European tour of *Carmen Jones* (June–July 1973).

Films. Mr. Blake's first film appearance was in *This Is the Army* (WB, 1943). He was also in *The Master Key* (U, 1946); *Her Sister's Secret* (Intl., 1946); and played the role of a returning veteran in *The Red Wagon* (Amer. Film Center, 1947). He also directed and staged the movement for the industrial documentary *The Eighth Lively Art* (1957).

Television. Mr. Blake's television debut was as a magician on the Hollywood Saturday Night Review. His other television work includes direction of choreography for the Pee Wee King Show (1956).

Night Clubs. Mr. Blake made his night club debut doing impressions and starring in *Charles Blake Entertains* at the Trianon Room (Hotel Ambassador, N.Y.C., Jan. 1939). He appeared also in N.Y.C. at the Greenwich Village Inn (Oct. 1939) and as a dancing magician at the Rainbow Room (Jan. 1940).

Other Activities. Mr. Blake was consultant to the African pavilion at the NY World's Fair (Apr.–Oct. 1964) and was producer-manager and choreographer and consultant to the Belgian village and the Polynesian village at the World's Fair (Apr.–Oct. 1965). He was a consultant to Expo 67, Montreal, Canada (Oct. 1966–Oct. 1967).

Awards. Mr. Blake received the 1956 award of the Hollywood Writers Club for his outstanding contributions to community theatre. In 1957, *The Eighth Lively Art* received an award at the Milan Festival, and Mr. Blake was made an *honoré* of the Province of Quebec at the Champlain-Hudson Festival of 1957–58.

Recreation. International economics.

BLAKEMORE, MICHAEL. Director, actor, novelist. b. Michael Howell Blakemore, June 18, 1928, Sydney, Australia, to Conrad and Una (Heyworth) Blakemore. Father, eye surgeon. Educ. Cranbrook School; The King's School; St. Paul's College, Univ. of Sydney, Australia. Professional training at R.A.D.A., London, England (1950–52). Married 1960 to Shirley Blakemore; one son. Member of AEA; SSD&C. Address: (home) 15 Gardnor Mansions, Church Row, London N.W.3, England tel. 435-9951; (bus.) National Theatre, 10a Aquinas St., London S.E.1, England tel. 928-2033.

Pre-Theatre. Medical student, Univ. of Sydney, 1948–49.

Theatre. Mr. Blakemore's first professional appearance was as the Doctor in *The Barretts of Wimpole Street* (Th. Royal, Huddersfield, England, 1952). This was followed by several years of repertory in such cities as Birmingham, Bristol, and Coventry. He made his London debut as Jack Poyntz in *School* (Princes Th., Mar. 1958); played several small parts at the Memorial Th., Stratford, during the 1959 season; appeared at the Open Air Regent's Park, London, in 1962 as Sir Toby in *Twelfth Night* and Holofernes in *Love's Labour's Lost* and in 1963 as Dogberry in *Much Ado About Nothing* and Theseus in *A Midsummer Night's Dream;* was Badger in *Toad of Toad Hall* (Comedy Th., London, Dec. 1963); and toured Australia as Palmer Anderson in *A Severed Head* (1965).

In 1966–67, Blakemore was with the Citizens', Glasgow, Scotland, where his parts included George in *Who's Afraid of Virginia Woolf?* and Maitland in *Inadmissible Evidence.* He directed, both at the Citizens' and the Close, such plays as *The Investigation; Little Malcolm; Stephen D;* and *Nightmare Abbey* (all 1966); *The Visions of Simone Machard; A Choice of Wars;* and *Rosmersholm* (all 1967). The first play he directed for the London stage was *A Day in the Death of Joe Egg* (Comedy Th., July 20, 1967), and it was also the first play he directed on Bway, where it was known as *Joe Egg* (Brooks Atkinson Th., N.Y.C., Feb. 1, 1968).

Since then, Mr. Blakemore has been active in London, where he directed *The Strange Case of Martin Richter* (Hampstead Th. Club, Nov. 4, 1968); *The Resistible Rise of Arturo Ui* (Saville, July 1, 1969); *The National Health* (Old Vic, Oct. 16, 1969); *Widowers' Houses* (Royal Court, Apr. 14, 1970); and *Forget-Me-Not Lane* (1971). Mr. Blakemore became associate director of the National Theatre in 1971; his productions there include *Long Day's Journey into Night* (1972); *Macbeth* (1972); *The Cherry Orchard;* and *The Front Page* (Old Vic, July 6, 1972). Outside of his work at the National Th., Mr. Blakemore's recent work includes direction of *Knuckle* (Comedy Th.) and a revival of *Design for Living* (Phoenix).

Television. Mr. Blakemore directed, with Peter Wood, *Long Day's Journey into Night* (ATV, 1973).

Published Works. Mr. Blakemore is author of the novel *Next Season* (1968).

Awards. Mr. Blakemore was nominated for an Antoinette Perry (Tony) Award for *Joe Egg;* he received the Scottish TV award for the best stage production for *Arturo Ui;* won the Variety critics poll for *Forget-Me-Not Lane;* and received the *Plays and Players* award as best director for *The Front Page* and *Long Day's Journey into Night.*

Recreation. Architecture, surfing.

BLANE, RALPH. Composer, actor, director, producer, playwright, singer, vocal arranger. b. Ralph Uriah Hunsecker, July 26, 1914, Broken Arrow, Okla., to Tracey Mark and Florence Hazel (Wilborn) Hunsecker. Father, merchant; mother, composer. Attended Kemper Military Sch., Boonville, Mo., 1928–29; Tulsa Central H.S., 1929–1932; Northwestern Univ., 1932–33. Studied piano in Tulsa with John Knowles Weaver, two years; Thelma Johnson, two years; Wade Hamilton, one year; dancing with Lew Miller, two years; voice with Robert Boice Carson, one year; in N.Y.C., voice with Estelle Liebling, eight years. Married Oct. 5, 1947, to Emajo Stage; one son. Member of ASCAP; Dramatists Guild; AGAC; AEA; AFTRA; AMPAS. Address: 1115 Kenwood Ave., Broken Arrow, OK 74012, tel. (918) 251-3712.

Theatre. Mr. Blane first appeared in the pre-Bway tryout of *The Moon Rises* (opened Shubert Th., Philadelphia, Pa., Jan. 1934; closed Shubert, Boston, Mass., Feb. 1934); during the St. Louis Municipal Opera's 1934 season, played several supporting roles as a singer-dancer in 13 productions.

He appeared in the revue *New Faces of 1936* (Vanderbilt, N.Y.C., May 19, 1936); toured South America on the Holland-America Line for WOR Artists Bureau (1936); appeared as a singer-dancer in *Frederika* (Imperial, N.Y.C., Feb. 4, 1937); sang with Radio City Music Hall's Male Glee Club (1937); and toured with the Leonardi Singers (1937). As a member of the Martins Quartet, Mr. Blane appeared in the pre-Bway tryout of *Walk with Music,* then called *Three After Three* (Shubert, Chicago, Ill., 1941); *Louisiana Purchase* (Imperial, N.Y.C., May 23, 1940); and *The Lady Comes Across* (44 St. Th., Jan. 9, 1942); and appeared in several vaudeville shows (1941).

He collaborated with Hugh Martin in music and lyrics for *Best Foot Forward* (Ethel Barrymore Th., Oct. 1, 1941; revived Stage 73, Apr. 2, 1963); composed music and lyrics for *Three Wishes for Jamie* (Mark Hellinger Th., Mar. 21, 1952); toured in a concert with music from *Three Wishes for Jamie* (1962–63); toured in a concert, *Ralph Blane—Songs from a Musician's Trunk* (1964); wrote *Tattered Tom;* composed the score for *Something About Anne* (world premiere, Clark Th., Birmingham, Ala., Oct. 15, 1973); and, with James Gregory and Peter Garey, composed the score for *Don't Flash Tonight (Mother Dear, the Fuzz Is in the House, the Patch Ain't Here).*

Films. Mr. Blane, with Hugh Martin, composed the music and lyrics for the song, "Three Cheers for the Yanks," in *For Me and My Gal* (MGM, 1942); complete score for *Best Foot Forward* (MGM, 1943); partial score for *Thousands Cheer* (MGM, 1943); complete score for *Meet Me in St. Louis* (MGM, 1944); partial score for *Broadway Rhythm* (MGM, 1944); complete score for *Abbott and Costello in Hollywood,* and *Spreadin' the Jam* (MGM, 1945); partial scores for *Ziegfeld Follies of 1946* (MGM, 1946); *No Leave, No Love* (MGM, 1946); *Two Smart People* (MGM, 1946); *Easy to Wed* (MGM, 1946); and *Good News* (MGM, 1947).

With Harry Warren, he composed the complete score for *My Dream Is Yours* (WB, 1949); *My Blue Heaven* (20th-Fox, 1950); and *Skirts Ahoy!* (MGM, 1952). With Harold Arlen, he composed the complete score for *Down Among the Sheltering Palms* (20th-Fox, 1953); and with Joe Myron, the complete score for *The French Line* (RKO, 1954). Again with Mr. Martin, he composed complete scores for *The Girl Rush* (Par., 1955); *The Girl Most Likely* (U, 1957); and *Who Is Sylvia?* (Col., 1958).

Radio. Mr. Blane was known as NBC's "Young Man of Melody" (1938–40), appearing on Port of Missing Hits; The Royal Crown Cola Show; with The Martins Quartet, on the Mary Martin-Walter O'Keefe Radio Show; and regularly on The Fred Allen Show.

Night Clubs. Mr. Blane has performed at Number One Fifth Avenue (N.Y.C., 1939, 1959); and The Night Owl Club (N.Y.C., 1959).

Other Activities. He has produced and directed the Miss Oklahoma Pageant and since 1956 has judged the National Miss America Pageant in Atlantic City, N.J., as well as many state and local pageants throughout the US. His first song, "How Warm It Is the Weather," was composed in 1939 and was subsequently published by Irving Berlin. Mr. Blane has composed a symphony "A Prayer by Voltaire" (premiere, Thanksgiving Choral Festival, Oklahoma State Univ., Stillwater, premiere Nov. 20, 1956); and "Duty, Honor, Country," a musical setting of Gen. Douglas MacArthur's 1962 farewell address to West Point cadets (premiere, Constitution Hall, Washington, D.C., Apr. 29, 1963).

Awards. He was nominated (1944) for an Academy (Oscar) Award for "The Trolley Song" from *Meet Me in St. Louis;* won (1945) the *Tune Dex Digest* Award for "The Trolley Song"; and was nominated (1947) for an Academy (Oscar) Award for "Pass That Peace Pipe" from *Good News.*.

Recreation. Scuba diving, golf, world travel.

BLANKFORT, MICHAEL.

Playwright, writer. b. Seymour Michael Blankfort, Dec. 10, 1907, New York City, to Henry and Hannah Blankfort. Father, manufacturer. Grad. DeWitt Clinton H.S., N.Y.C., 1925; Univ. of Pennsylvania, B.A. 1929; Princeton Univ., M.A. 1931. Married June 7, 1931 to Laurette Spingarn, artist (marr. dis. 1948); two daughters; married July 22, 1950, to Dorothy V. Stiles, writer. Served USMC (1942–45); rank, Capt. Member of Dramatists Guild; ALA; WGA (natl. chmn., 1971–73); WGA, West (member of council, 1962–64; treas. 1963–64; pres., 1967–69); Academy of Motion Picture Arts and Sciences (vice-pres., gov., 1967–to date); Los Angeles County Museum of Art (trustee, 1971–to date). Address: 1636 Comstock Ave., Los Angeles, CA 90024.

Pre-Theatre. Educator, prison psychologist.

Theatre. Mr. Blankfort produced, with Walter Hart, *Merry-Go-Round* (Provincetown Playhouse, N.Y.C., Apr. 22, 1932); subsequently was assistant director of *Peace on Earth* (Civic Repertory Th., Nov. 29, 1933; moved to 44 St. Th., March 31, 1934); directed *Stevedore* (Civic Repertory, Apr. 18, 1934); adapted *Sailors of Cattaro* (Civic Repertory, Dec. 10, 1934); contributed a sketch to *Parade* (Guild, May 20, 1935); wrote *The Crime* (Civic Repertory, Mar. 1, 1936); wrote, with Michael Gold, the Federal Th. (WPA) Project production of *Battle Hymn* (Experimental Th., May 22, 1936); wrote *The Brave and the Blind* (Labor, Stage, Mar. 21, 1937); wrote *The Spaniard* (1954); and wrote, with his wife, Dorothy V. Stiles, *Monique* (John Golden Th., Oct. 22, 1957).

Films. Mr. Blankfort made his film debut in *Blind Alley* (Col., 1939); *Adam Had Four Sons* (Col., 1941); *Texas* (Col., 1941); *Flight Lieutenant* (Col., 1942); *Dark Past* (Col., 1949); *Act of Murder* (UI, 1938); *Broken Arrow* (20th-Fox, 1950); *Halls of Montezuma* (20th-Fox, 1950); *My Six Convicts* (Col., 1952); *Lydia Bailey* (20th-Fox, 1952); *The Juggler* (Col., 1953); *The Caine Mutiny* (Col., 1954); *Untamed* (20th-Fox, 1955); *Tribute to a Bad Man* (MGM, 1956); *The Vintage* (MGM, 1957); and *The Plainsman* (U, 1965).

Television. He wrote *A Pelican in the Wilderness* (Breaking Point, ABC, 1963); *The Other Man* (NBC, 1968); and *See How They Run.*.

Other Activities. Mr. Blankfort was an Intercollegiate Playwriting judge (ATA) in 1974.

Published Works. Mr. Blankfort has published the following novels: *I Met a Man* (1937); *The Brave and the Blind* (1940); *A Time to Live* (1943); *The Widow Makers* (1946); *The Big Yankee* (1947); *The Juggler* (1952); *The Strong Hand* (1956); *Goodbye, I Guess* (1962); *Behold the Fire* (1965); *I Didn't Know I Would Live So Long* (1973); plays: *The Crime, The Brave and the Blind, Battle Hymn, Monique.*

Awards. He received the Samuel Daroff Award for the best Jewish novel of the year, *The Juggler* (1952); The Gold Medal of the Commonwealth Club for *Behold the Fire* (1965) as best novel by a Californian.

BLAU, HERBERT.

Director, producer, playwright, educator. b. May 3, 1926, Brooklyn, N.Y., to Joseph and Yetta Blau. Father, plumber. Grad. New York Univ. B.S.; Stanford Univ. M.A. (speech and drama) 1949; Ph.D. (English literature) 1954. Married to Beatrice Manley, actress; two sons; one daughter. Served US Army, 1944–46; rank, PVT.

Theatre. In Jan. 1952, Mr. Blau and Jules Irving founded the San Francisco (Calif.) Actor's Workshop. Mr. Blau was managing director until 1965, when he and Mr. Irving were appointed joint directors of the Repertory Theater of Lincoln Center, N.Y.C., effective Mar. 1 of that year. Mr. Blau resigned as co-director at Lincoln Center on Jan. 13, 1967.

The first play Mr. Blau directed at the Actor's Workshop was *Playboy of the Western World* (Feb. 26, 1953); followed by *Summer and Smoke* (Apr. 3, 1953); *Venus Observed* (Dec. 25, 1953); *The Cherry Orchard* (June 25, 1954); *Oedipus Rex* and *The Farce of Master Pierre Patelin* (Oct. 8, 1954); *Camino Real* (July 10, 1954); *Captive at Large* (Aug. 25, 1955); *Mother Courage* (Jan. 13, 1956); *The Plough and the Stars* (Oct. 12, 1956); *Waiting for Godot* (Feb. 28, 1957), which played in N.Y.C. (York Th., July 1957), and at the Brussels World's Fair (Amer. Pavilion, Belgium, Aug. 1957).

With Dan Danforth, Mr. Blau directed *The Bloody Tenet* (Church for the Fellowship of All Peoples, San Francisco, Calif.); at the Actor's Workshop, staged *A Gift of Fury,* which he wrote (Mar. 14, 1958); *The Iceman Cometh* (July 11, 1958); *The Waltz of the Toreadors* (Sept. 26, 1958); a concert reading of *The River Line* (1958); *Endgame* (May 10, 1959); *Cock-a-Doodle Dandy* (June 19, 1959); *The Marriage of Mr. Mississippi* (May 13, 1960); *A Touch of the Poet* (Dec. 7, 1960); *King Lear* (Mar. 29, 1961); *Serjeant Musgrave's Dance* (Oct. 13, 1961); and *Galileo* (Dec. 14, 1962).

For the Actor's Workshop, he wrote *Telegraph Hill,* staged by Jules Irving (Jan. 18, 1963); directed *The Balcony* (Mar. 29, 1963); *Major Barbara* (May 3, 1963); a double-bill, *The Master* and *There! You Died* (Nov. 29, 1963); *The Firebugs* (Feb. 28, 1964); *The Birds* (May 15, 1964); and *Uncle Vanya* (Jan. 1, 1965).

Under the directorship of Mr. Blau and Jules Irving, the Repertory Theater of Lincoln Center presented (all at the Vivian Beaumont Th.) *Danton's Death* (Oct. 21, 1965), for which Mr. Blau wrote a new version and which he directed; *The Country Girl* (Dec. 9, 1965); *The Condemned of Altona* (Feb. 3, 1966), which Mr. Blau directed; *The Caucasian Chalk Circle* (Mar. 24, 1966); *The Alchemist* (Oct. 13, 1966); and *Yerma* (Dec. 8, 1966).

Television and Radio. Mr. Blau was host for a series of dramatic readings (KQED-TV, San Francisco, Calif.), and in N.Y.C., he appeared as a guest on discussion programs about Lincoln Center (Community Dialogue, Ind., Apr. 18, 1965; Eye on New York, CBS, May 18 and Oct. 23, 1965).

Other Activities. As professor of English and world literature at San Francisco State Coll. until 1965, Mr. Blau taught creative writing and literature courses. He was appointed professor of English at City Coll. of New York in 1967 and vice-president of the California Institute of Arts in 1968.

Published Works. Mr. Blau wrote the book *The Impossible Theater: A Manifesto* (1964), and his articles have appeared in such periodicals as *Kenyon Review, Theatre Arts Encore* (British); *Tulane Drama Review, Educational Theatre Journal, Modern Language Quarterly, Journal of Aesthetics and Art Criticism, Western Humanities Review, New England Quarterly,* and *Saturday Review.*

Awards. He received a Ford Foundation Grant for theatre directors, a Guggenheim Fellowship, and the first San Francisco State College Presidential Award for Distinguished Services (1965).

BLEY, MAURICE.

Community theatre director, producer. b. Maurice George Bley, Dec. 7, 1910, Hamburg, N.Y., to Lawrence H. and Matilda (Schummer) Bley. Father, architect. Grad. Hamburg (N.Y.) H.S., 1928; attended Albright Art Sch., Buffalo, N.Y., 1928–29; Carnegie Inst. of Technology, B.A. 1933. Studied acting with Jane Keeler, at Studio Theatre Sch., Buffalo, N.Y., 1935–39. Married Oct. 14, 1942, to Anna Kowalska, concert pianist, educator. Served US Army, 1942–45; rank, T/Sgt. Member of Delta Tau Delta. Address: (home) 140 S. Lake St., Hamburg, NY 14075, tel. (716) 649-5101; (bus.) c/o MSN Co., Inc., 703 Seneca St., Buffalo, NY 14210, tel. (716) 853-1960.

Theatre. Starting in 1959, Mr. Bley was a member of the NY State Community Theatre Assn. (area representative, mbr. of bd., 1959–60; vice-pres., 1960–61; pres., 1961–63; mbr. of bd., ex-officio, 1963–64); recalled 1965–66 to serve as vice-pres. on emergency basis as chmn. of annual state conference. Beginning in 1928, Mr. Bley was active in community theatre, as an actor, director, and producer. He was producer and director of the Hamburg (N.Y.) Little Th., where he designed, directed, and produced approximately 35 plays (1949–62).

Other Activities. In 1937, Mr. Bley became designer engineer for the Meyer Equipment Co. (later part of MSN Co., Inc.), Buffalo, N.Y.

Recreation. Music, gardening, nature study, travel.

BLISS, HELENA.

Singer, actress. b. Helen Louise Lipp, Dec. 31, 1917, St. Louis, Mo., to Albert and Augusta (Clemens) Lipp. Father, realtor; mother, singer. Grad. Hosmer Hall, St. Louis, 1935; attended Washington Univ., 1935–36. Studied singing with Luigi Giuffrida, N.Y.C., five years; Rossini Opera Sch., N.Y.C., five years; Muriel O'Mally, Irvington, N.J., three years. Married 1947 to John Tyers; one son. Member of AEA. Address: 15100 Fawndale Rd., Los Gatos, CA 95030, tel. (408) 356-5332.

Theatre. Miss Bliss made her debut in the chorus of *Very Warm for May* (Alvin, Nov. 17, 1939); subsequently appeared in *Du Barry Was a Lady* (46 St. Th., Dec. 6, 1939); and with the Philadelphia (Pa.) Opera Company (1942), sang in *Rosalinda, Faust,* and *La Boheme.*

She appeared in *Let's Face It* (Imperial, N.Y.C., Aug. 17, 1942); played Nina in *Song of Norway* (Imperial, Aug. 21, 1944); Musetta in *Gypsy Lady* (Century, Sept. 17, 1946); and repeated her role in the London production, retitled *Romany Love* (His Majesty's, Mar. 7, 1947); played Julie in *Show Boat* (NY City Ctr., May 5, 1954); appeared in *Song of Norway* (Starlight Th., Kansas City, Mo., 1948); *The Chocolate Soldier* and *Song of Norway* (Pittsburgh Civic Light Opera, Pa., 1950); and at the NY City Ctr. appeared in *Troubled Island* (1950), *Pagliacci* (1950), and *La Boheme* (1950).

She played Kate in *Kiss Me, Kate* (Coliseum, London, England, Mar. 8, 1951); Vera in a stock production of *Pal Joey* (Music Circus, Cleveland, Ohio); Nadina in *The Chocolate Soldier* and *Music in the Air* (Lambertville Music Circus, N.J.); *The Merry Widow* and *The Great Waltz* (Houston, Tex., 1952); *The Firefly* (Miami, Fla., 1952); *Kiss Me, Kate* (1962); *Pal Joey* (1962); *Take Me Along* (1962); and *Gypsy* (Music Circus, Sacramento, Calif., 1963); and *Show Boat* and *Gypsy* (Starlight Th., Vancouver, B.C., Canada, 1963).

Miss Bliss has appeared in concerts at the Robin Hood Dell, Philadelphia, Pa. (1944), the Hollywood Bowl (1947), and at the NY Stadium (1953).

Recreation. Golf, horses, gardening.

BLOCH, BERTRAM. Playwright, novelist. b. Apr. 5, 1892, New York City, to Meyer and Meda Bloch. Father, butcher. Grad. DeWitt Clinton H.S., N.Y.C., 1909; New York Law Sch., LL.B. 1913. Married 1915, to Sara Koenigsberger (marr. dis. 1946); one son, one daughter; married 1946, to Edythe Latham, novelist. Member of Dramatists Guild. Address: 50 E. 72nd St., New York, NY 10021, tel. (212) BU 8-1650.

Theatre. Mr. Bloch wrote, with Thomas Mitchell, *Glory Hallelujah* (Broadhurst, Apr. 6, 1926); subsequently wrote *Joseph* (Liberty, Feb. 12, 1930); *Jewel Robbery,* adapted from a work by Lazlo Fodor, (Booth, Jan. 13, 1932); wrote with George Brewer, Jr., *Dark Victory* (Plymouth, Nov. 7, 1934); and with Isabel Leighton, *Spring Again* (Henry Miller's Th., Nov. 10, 1941).

Other Activities. Mr. Bloch was head of the Eastern Story Dept. for MGM (1928–39) and for 20th Century-Fox (1941–56).

Published Works. Mr. Bloch is the author of *Mrs. Hulett* (1953), *The Little Laundress and the Fearful Knight* (1954), and *The Only Nellie Fayle* (1960).

BLOFSON, RICHARD. Film maker, producer, lighting designer, stage manager. b. Richard S. Blofson, Jan. 13, 1933, Philadelphia, Pa., to Albert and Adeline Blofson. Father, printer. Grad. Central H.S., Philadelphia, 1949; Antioch Coll., B.F.A. 1954; one son. Served US Navy; rank, PO-2. Member of AEA. Address: (home) 21 Cornelia St., New York, NY 10014, tel. (212) 675-2780; (bus.) 66 Witherspoon St., Princeton, NJ 08540, tel. (609) 924-2340.

Theatre. Mr. Blofson was lighting designer for *The Devil's Disciple* (Antioch Area Th., Ohio, 1950); lighting designer at Rice Playhouse (Martha's Vineyard, Mass., Summer 1950); and lighting director and production manager at the Antioch (Ohio) Area Th. (Summers 1951–53).

In N.Y.C., Mr. Blofson was stage manager for the Phoenix Theatre productions of *Sing Me No Lullaby,* (Oct. 14, 1954), *Sandhog* (Nov. 23, 1954), *The Doctor's Dilemma* (Jan. 11, 1955), *The Master Builder* (Mar. 14, 1955), and *The Carefree Tree* (Oct. 11, 1955); lighting designer for the Phoenix Theatre's "Sideshow" productions of *The White Devil* (Mar. 17, 1955), *L'Histoire du Soldat* (Mar. 28, 1955), and *Moby Dick* (Apr. 25, 1955); and stage manager for the NY City Ctr. productions of *Guys and Dolls* (Apr. 20, 1955), *South Pacific* (May 4, 1955), and *Finian's Rainbow* (May 18, 1955).

He was stage manager for the American Shakespeare Festival Th. (Stratford, Conn.) touring production of *Much Ado About Nothing* (Dec. 30, 1957–Mar. 1, 1958); the N.Y.C. production of *The Firstborn* (Coronet, Apr. 30, 1958); the American Shakespeare Festival Th. (Stratford, Conn.) productions of *Hamlet* (June 19, 1958), *A Midsummer Night's Dream* (June 20, 1958) and *The Winter's Tale* (July 21, 1958); was stage manager for *The Rivalry* (Bijou, N.Y.C., Feb. 7, 1959); for the American Shakespeare Festival Th. (Stratford, Conn.) productions of *Romeo and Juliet* (June 12, 1959), *Merry Wives of Windsor* (July 8, 1959) and *All's Well That Ends Well* (Aug. 1, 1959).

Mr. Blofson was production stage manager for *The Great God Brown* (Coronet, N.Y.C., Oct. 6, 1959); *Lysistrata* (Phoenix, Nov. 24, 1959); *Pictures in the Hallway* (Phoenix, Dec. 26, 1959); *Peer Gynt* (Phoenix, Dec. 12, 1960); *Henry IV, Part 1* (Phoenix, Mar. 1, 1960); *Henry IV, Part 2* (Phoenix, Apr. 18, 1960); produced, with Gordon Davidson and Richard Jackson, *Borak* (Martinique, Dec. 13, 1960); was production stage manager for *Period of Adjustment* (Helen Hayes Th., Nov. 10, 1960); *The Garden of Sweets* (ANTA, Oct. 31, 1961); *I Can Get It for You Wholesale* (Shubert, Mar. 22, 1962); *Strange Interlude* (Hudson, Mar. 11, 1963); *Tambourines to Glory* (Little, Nov. 2, 1963); *Baby Want a Kiss* (Little, Apr. 9, 1964); production coordinator for the Actors Studio Theatre; and production stage manager for *The Freaking Out of Stephanie Blake* (previews, Eugene O'Neill Th., Oct. 30–Nov. 1, 1967).

Films. Between 1968 and 1971, Mr. Blofson was cameraman for educational and industrial films for Westinghouse and for Visual Educational Corp., Princeton, N.J.; production manager and sound technician for the US Information Agency films *Champion* and *Better Than Before;* and sound technician for the United Church of Christ film *Search.* Films he made as producer-director with Arden Productions (1968–72) include *Continuum* (Maryland State Dept. of Education); *The Giants in Us* (also cameraman), a documentary on the professional school for deaf theatre personnel; *The Love of Don Perlimplin and Belisa in the Garden,* as performed by the National Theatre of the Deaf; and *The Starting Line,* a documentary on the National Theatre of the Deaf; *Street Theatre,* on N.Y.C.'s Phoenix Theatre; and *Shakespeare in New York* and *I Want Youth,* both for the NY Shakespeare Festival. For British-Leyland Motors, he produced *The Devil You Say* and *A Touch of the Devil* (both 1974).

Television. Mr. Blofson engaged in sound and camera work for CBS sports spectaculars (Summer 1963), and independent documentary films (NBC, Fall, Winter 1964), and was cameraman for *The Making of the President—1968* (CBS); production manager and sound technician for Wolper Productions' television specials *Wall Street, Blondes, Untamed World,* and *Robert Kennedy.* He was an associate on *Tommy—Kids and Drugs* (Westinghouse, 1971). At Arden Productions, he was producer-director of *Rabbit Suite* (NET), and as a partner in The Production Staff, Princeton, N.J., he produced the PBS documentaries *The Vanishing Family Farm* (1973), *Wherever You Go, There You Are* (1974), and *Steel Town—Company Town* (1974), for all of which he was director and cameraman.

Awards. *Tommy—Kids and Drugs* was winner of a 1971 Dupont award for television journalism.

Recreation. Mountaineering, bicycling.

BLOMQUIST, ALLEN. Educator, director. b. Allen Palmer Blomquist, Jan. 15, 1928, Pocatello, Idaho, to Allen A. and Hanna C. (Hellsten) Blomquist. Father, machinist. Grad. Pocatello H.S., 1946; Idaho State Coll., B.A. 1950; Univ. of Wisconsin, M.S. (Speech) 1951; attended Univ. of Stockholm, Sweden, 1951–1953; Western State Coll., Colo., 1953–1954; Univ. of Minnesota, Ph.D. 1967. Married May 20, 1954, to Charlotte Jean Tooley, journalist; two sons, one daughter. Member of ATA; Rocky Mountain Th. Conference (college representative, 1959–60; editor newsletter, 1960–63; pres., 1963–65). Address: (home) 95 Harvard, Pocatello, ID 83201, tel. (208) 232-9254; (bus.) Theatre ISU, Idaho State Univ., Pocatello, ID 83209, tel. (208) 236-3695.

He was director, actor, and technical director for the Baraboo (Wis.) Summer Th. (1951–52); stage technician for the Royal Opera, Stockholm, Sweden; stage manager for *Summer Review,* Stockholm, (1952); directional observant for the film *Barabbas,* in Stockholm (1951); director, designer, and costume designer for more than sixty productions (1951–to date) at Univ. of Wisconsin, Baraboo Summer Theatre, Western State College, Univ. of Minnesota, Univ. of Wyoming, and American-Swedish Institute, Minneapolis, Minn. In addition, Mr. Blomquist has been producer-director of summer theatre with a semi-professional troupe, Idaho State Univ. (1969–to date) and stage director of the city of Pocatello summer musical (1969–73).

Awards. Mr. Blomquist received a senior scholarship from Alpha Psi Omega (Idaho State Coll. 1949); a Tozer Foundation grant (1958); was Out-of-State Scholar at the Univ. of Wisconsin (1951); was King Gustav V Fellow (American-Scandinavian Foundation, 1952–53); received a travel grant from Förningen Norden (1953); and was Theatre Scholar at the Univ. of Minnesota (1957–58).

Recreation. Gardening, ceramics.

BLONDELL, JOAN. Actress. b. Aug. 30, 1912, New York City, to Edward and Kathryn (Cain) Blondell. Father and mother, vaudevillians. "Only attended school when Geery Society demanded it," says Miss Blondell. Schools attended included Venice (Calif.) Grammar Sch.; Erasmus H.S., Brooklyn, N.Y.; Santa Monica H.S., Calif. Married to George Barnes, cameraman (dec.); one son; married to Dick Powell, actor (marr. dis.); one daughter; married Mike Todd, producer (marr. dis.). Relatives in theatre; sister, Gloria Blondell, actress; brother, Edward Blondell, Jr., motion picture and television electrician; son, Norman Powell, television and motion picture producer. Member of AEA; SAG; AFTRA; AGVA. Address: 1416 Havenhurst, Los Angeles, CA 90046.

Theatre. Miss Blondell made her first stage appearance in vaudeville at age three in her parents' act (Sydney, Australia), and remained with the act until 1926, at which time she joined a stock company.

She made her N.Y.C. debut as Etta in *Maggie, the Magnificent* (Cort, Oct. 1929); subsequently played Myrtle in *Penny Arcade* (Fulton, Mar. 1930); Honey Bee Carrol in *The Naked Genius* (Plymouth, Oct. 21, 1943); appeared in touring productions of *Call Me Madam* (1952); played Cissy in *A Tree Grows in Brooklyn* (opened Klein Aud., Bridgeport, Conn., Oct. 10, 1952); appeared in *Come Back Little Sheba, The Time of the Cuckoo, Happy Birthday, New Girl in Town, Watch the Birdie,* and *Copper and Brass.* She played Mrs. Farrow in *The Rope Dancers* (Cort, N.Y.C., Nov. 20, 1957); appeared in *Crazy October; A Palm Tree in a Rose Garden;* played Lottie Lacey in a touring production of *The Dark at the Top of the Stairs* (opened Veterans Memorial Aud., Providence, R.I., Sept. 21, 1959; closed Natl., Washington, D.C., Apr. 23, 1960); Mae Peterson in the national touring production of *Bye Bye Birdie* (opened Curran, San Francisco, Calif., Apr. 24, 1961); replaced (Sept. 28, 1971) Carolyn Coates as Beatrice in *The Effect of Gamma Rays on Man-in-the-Moon Marigolds* (Mercer-O'Casey Th., N.Y.C., Apr. 7, 1970).

Films. Miss Blondell's films include *Sinners' Holiday* (WB, 1930); *Steel Highway* (WB, 1930); *Office Wife* (WB, 1930); *Big Business Girl* (1st Natl., 1930); *Blonde Crazy* (WB, 1931), *God's Gift to Women* (WB, 1931); *Illicit* (WB, 1931); *Local Boy Makes Good* (1st Natl., 1931); *Millie* (RKO, 1931); *My Past* (WB, 1931); *Night Nurse* (WB, 1931); *Reckless Hour* (1st Natl., 1931); *Other Men's Women* (WB, 1931); *Larceny Lane* (WB, 1931); *Public Enemy* (WB, 1931); *Central Park* (1st Natl., 1932); *Crowd Roars* (WB, 1932); *Big City Blues* (WB, 1932); *Famous Ferguson Case* (1st Natl., 1932); *Lawyer Man* (WB, 1932); *Make Me a Star* (Par., 1932); *Miss Pinkerton* (1st

Natl., 1932); *Greeks Had a Word for Them* (UA, 1932); *Three on a Match* (1st Natl., 1932); *Union Depot* (1st Natl., 1932); *Blondie Johnson* (1st Natl., 1933); *Convention City* (1st Natl., 1933); *Footlight Parade* (WB, 1933); *Gold Diggers of 1933* (WB, 1933); *Broadway Bad* (20th-Fox, 1933); *Goodbye Again* (1st Natl., 1933); *Havana Widows* (1st Natl., 1933); *Dames* (WB, 1934); *He Was Her Man* (WB, 1934); *I've Got Your Number* (WB, 1934); *Kansas City Princess* (WB, 1934); *Merry Wives of Reno* (WB, 1934); *Smarty* (WB, 1934); *Maybe It's Love* (1st Natl., 1934); *Broadway Gondolier* (WB, 1935); *Miss Pacific Fleet* (WB, 1935); *Traveling Saleslady* (1st Natl., 1935); *We're in the Money* (WB, 1935); *Sons o' Guns* (WB, 1936); *Stage Struck* (1st Natl., 1936); *Bullets or Ballots* (1st Natl., 1936); *Colleen* (WB, 1936); *Gold Diggers of 1937* (1st Natl., 1936); *Three Men on a Horse* (1st Natl., 1936); *Perfect Specimen* (1st Natl., 1937); *Stand In* (UA, 1937); *Back in Circulation* (WB, 1937); *The King and the Chorus Girl* (WB, 1937).

Also, in *There's Always a Woman* (Col., 1938); *The Amazing Mr. Williams* (Col., 1939); *East Side of Heaven* (U, 1939); *Good Girls Go to Paris* (Col., 1939); *Kid from Kokomo* (WB, 1939); *Off the Record* (WB, 1939); *I Want a Divorce* (Par., 1940); *Two Girls on Broadway* (MGM, 1940); *Lady for a Night* (Rep., 1941); *The Nurse's Secret* (WB, 1941); *Model Wife* (U, 1941); *Three Girls About Town* (Col., 1941); *Topper Returns* (UA, 1941); *Cry Havoc* (MGM, 1943); *A Tree Grows in Brooklyn* (20th-Fox, 1945); *Don Juan Quilligan* (20th-Fox, 1945); *Adventure* (MGM, 1945); *Christmas Eve* (UA, 1947); *The Corpse Came C.O.D.* (Col., 1947); *Nightmare Alley* (20th-Fox, 1947); *Without Honor* (UA, 1949); *For Heaven's Sake* (20th-Fox, 1950); *The Blue Veil* (RKO, 1951); *The Opposite Sex* (MGM, 1956); *Desk Set* (20th-Fox, 1957); *Lizzie* (MGM, 1957); *This Could Be the Night* (MGM, 1957); *Will Success Spoil Rock Hunter?* (20th-Fox, 1957); *Angel Baby* (Allied, 1961); *Sunday in New York* (MGM, 1964); *Advance to the Rear* (MGM, 1964); *The Cincinnati Kid* (MGM, 1964); *Paradise Road* (Par., 1965); *Ride Beyond Vengeance* (Col., 1966); *Waterhole #3* (Par., 1967); *Kona Coast* (WB, 1968); *Stay Away, Joe* (MGM, 1968); *The Phynx* (WB, 1970); and *Support Your Local Gunfighter* (UA, 1971).

Television. Miss Blondell has played in *Burlesque* (Kraft Television Th., NBC, 1954); *Sgt. Sullivan Speaking* (1954); *Child of Trouble* (1957); *The Funny-Looking Kid* (1958); *Marriage of Strangers* (Playhouse 90, CBS, 1959); appeared on Person to Person (CBS, 1959); Shower of Stars (CBS); Playhouse 90 (CBS, 1961); played in *The Witness* (Studio One, CBS, 1961); appeared on The Real McCoys (NBC, 1961); The Virginian (NBC, 1963); Wagon Train (NBC, 1963); Burke's Law (ABC, 1963); Studio One; the Pontiac Show; Kraft Music Hall; Fireside Th.; Alcoa Hour; GE Th.; Banyon; Westinghouse Th.; Colgate Comedy Hour; Twilight Zone; Bonanza; Dr. Kildare; Death Valley Days; The Greatest Show on Earth; Hooray for Hollywood; the Bob Hope Show; And Baby Makes Three; the Lucy Show; My Three Sons; Name of the Game; Will Sonnett; Family Affair; Petticoat Junction; McCloud; the Merv Griffin Show; the Dick Cavett Show; the Jack Paar Show; the Johnny Carson Show; the Rookies; Love American Style; Medical Center; the Carroll O'Connor Special; the New Dick Van Dyke Show; and The Snoop Sisters.

She has also performed in such plays as *Snow Job, Star in the House, Tango, The Pussy-footin' Rocks, Vacancy for Death* and *White Gloves.*

Published Works. Miss Blondell wrote the novel *Center Door Fancy* (1972).

Awards. Miss Blondell received a Presidential Gold Medal Award honoring her for entertaining members of the armed forces in 1943, during World War 11; an Academy (Oscar) Award (1951) nomination for her performance in *The Blue Veil* (1951), and two NATAS (Emmy) Award nominations for her performance in *Here Come the Brides.*

Recreation. Writing, painting.

BLOOM, CLAIRE. Actress. b. Patricia Claire Bloom, Feb. 15, 1931, London, England, to Edward and Elizabeth (Grew) Blume. Father, executive. Attended Badminton Sch., Bristol and Fern Hill Manor, New Milton, England. Studied at Guildhall Sch. of Music and Drama, London, 1946–47; acting with Eileen Thorndike, London, 1946–47; Central Sch. of Speech Training and Dramatic Art, London, 1947–48. Married Sept. 19, 1959, to Rod Steiger, actor (marr. dis. 1969); one daughter; married Aug. 14, 1969, to Hillard Elkins, producer, director. Relative in theatre: aunt, Mary Grew, actress. Member of AEA; SAG; AFTRA.

Theatre. Miss Bloom made her first N.Y.C. appearance with the Old Vic Co., playing the Queen in *Richard II* (Winter Garden, Oct. 23, 1956), Juliet in *Romeo and Juliet* (Winter Garden, Oct. 24, 1956); subsequently toured the US in both roles (1957); and appeared as the Wife in *Rashomon* (Music Box, N.Y.C., Jan. 27, 1959).

She made her debut with the Oxford Repertory Th. (Oct. 1946), appearing as Private Jessie Killigrew in *It Depends What You Mean,* followed by Helen in *An Italian Straw Hat* and Jessie in *Pink String and Sealing Wax.*

She made her London debut as a walk-on in *The White Devil* (Duchess, Mar. 6, 1947); subsequently appeared in *He Who Gets Slapped* (Duchess, June 17, 1947); and as Erinna in *The Wanderer* (His Majesty's, Sept., 1947).

At the Shakespeare Memorial Th. (Stratford-upon-Avon), she played Lady Blanche in *King John* (Apr. 15, 1948); Ophelia in *Hamlet* (Apr. 23, 1948), and Perdita in *The Winter's Tale* (June 4, 1948); in London, Daphne Randall in *The Damask Cheek* (Lyric, Feb. 2, 1949); Alizon Eliot in *The Lady's Not for Burning* (Globe, May 11, 1949); and Isabelle in *Ring 'Round the Moon* (Globe, Jan. 26, 1950). Miss Bloom portrayed Juliet in *Romeo and Juliet* (Old Vic, Sept. 1, 1952); Jessica in *The Merchant of Venice* (Old Vic, Jan. 6, 1953); Ophelia in *Hamlet* (Old Vic, Sept. 14, 1953); Helena in *All's Well That Ends Well* (Old Vic, Sept. 15, 1953); Viola in *Twelfth Night* (Old Vic, Jan. 6, 1954); Virgilia in *Coriolanus* (Old Vic, Feb. 23, 1954); Miranda in *The Tempest* (Old Vic, Apr. 13, 1954); and Cordelia in *King Lear* (Shakespeare Memorial Th., Stratford-upon-Avon, 1956).

After she appeared in the US with the Old Vic Co. (see above), she played Lucile in *Duel of Angels* (Apollo Th., Apr. 24, 1958); returned to Bway to play in *Rashomon* (see above); in London, portrayed Johanna in *Altona* (Royal Court, Apr. 1961); and at the Spoleto Festival of the Two Worlds, played Andromache in *The Trojan Women* (Teatro Caio Melisso, July 12, 1963).

She appeared as Sasha in *Ivanov* (Yvonne Arnaud Th., Guildford, England, Aug. 30, 1965; Phoenix, London, Sept. 30, 1965); played Nora in *A Doll's House* (Playhouse, N.Y.C., Jan. 13, 1971); Hedda in *Hedda Gabler* (Playhouse, Feb. 17, 1971); repeated her performance as Nora for the opening of the Eisenhower Th., Kennedy Ctr., Washington, D.C. (Oct. 16, 1971); was Mary Queen of Scots in *Vivat! Vivat Regina!* (Broadhurst, N.Y.C., Jan. 20, 1972); again played Nora (Criterion, London, Feb. 20, 1973); and was Blanche Du Bois in *A Streetcar Named Desire* (Piccadilly Th., London, Mar. 14, 1974).

Films. Miss Bloom made her first motion picture appearance as Teresa in *Limelight* (UA, 1952); followed by *The Man Between* (UA, 1953); *Richard III* (Lopert, 1956); *Alexander the Great* (UA, 1956); *The Brothers Karamazov* (MGM, 1958); *The Buccaneer* (Par., 1958); *Look Back in Anger* (WB, 1959); *Royal Game* (Ufa, 1960); Brainwashed (AA, 1961); *The Brothers Grimm* (MGM, 1962); *The Chapman Report* (WB, 1962); *The Haunting* (MGM, 1963); *Alta Infedelita* (De Laurentiis, 1963); *Il Maestro di Vigedano* (De Laurentiis, 1963); *The Outrage* (MGM, 1964); *The Spy Who Came in from the Cold* (Par., 1965); *Charley* (Cinerama, 1968); *The Illustrated Man* (WB-7 Arts, 1969); *Three into Two Won't Go* (U, 1969); *A Severed Head* (Col., 1971); *Red Sky at Morning* (U, 1971); and *A Doll's House* (Par., 1973).

Television. Miss Bloom appeared as Roxanne in *Cyrano de Bergerac* (Producers Showcase, NBC, 1956); Cleopatra in *Caesar and Cleopatra* (Producers Showcase, 1956); Juliet in *Romeo and Juliet* (NBC, 1957); in *Misalliance* (Playhouse 90, CBS, Oct. 29, 1959); in London the title role in *Anna Karenina* for the 25th Anniversary of BBC-TV (1961); Kathy in *Wuthering Heights* (BBC, 1962). She appeared on *Claire Bloom Reads Poetry* (Camera Three, CBS, Dec. 27, 1964); played Margaret Chapman in *A Time to Love* (Bob Hope, NBC, Jan. 11, 1967); Queen Anne in *Soldier in Love* (Hallmark Hall of Fame, NBC, Apr. 26, 1967); and Sasha in *Ivanov* (CBS, May 30, 1967).

Awards. Miss Bloom received for her performance as Teresa in *Limelight* both the British Film and Elle awards (1952), and for her performance as Hedda she received the Drama Desk and Outer Circle awards.

Recreation. Walking, music.

BLUM, EDWARD. Personal manager, casting director. b. Edward Allen Blum, May 23, 1928, New York City, to J. J. and Sabina Blum. Father, actor, known as J. J. Bloom. Relative in theatre: cousin, Ross Elliot, actor. Grad. George Washington H.S., N.Y.C., 1945; City Coll. of New York, 1946–48. Married Oct. 11, 1957, to Nancy G. Woodruff, casting director; two daughters. Address: Bulls Mill Rd., Chester, NY 10918, tel. (914) 783-4659.

Theatre. Mr. Blum joined the William Morris Agency, first in the stockroom, then as secretary to Ira Steiner. He was head of the Transportation and Special Services Dept. for three years, and subsequently was a talent representative in the Theatre Dept., where he was primarily responsible for casting Bway musicals (1946–54).

From 1954–56, he was casting director for producers Kollmar and Gardiner, for whom he cast *Plain and Fancy* (Mark Hellinger Th., Jan. 27, 1955), and the pre-Bway tryout of *The Ziegfeld Follies* (opened Shubert Th., Boston, Mass., Apr. 16, 1956; closed Shubert, Philadelphia, Pa., May 12, 1956).

In 1956, he became a partner of the Wallace A. Ross Enterprises, in charge of the Talent Dept.; subsequently, he became variety and musical casting director for CBS (1956–58).

From 1958 to 1967, he was casting director for Rodgers and Hammerstein and general assistant to Mr. Rodgers; from 1967 to 1970, he was a legitimate agent at Creative Management Associates; and in 1971, he became personal manager for Joel Grey.

BLYDEN, LARRY. Actor, director, producer. b. Ivan Lawrence Blieden, June 23, 1925, Houston, Tex., to Adolph and Marian (Davidson) Blieden. Father, exterminator. Grad. Lamar H.S., 1942; attended Univ. of Houston, 1942–43; Southwestern Louisiana Inst., 1943–44; grad. Univ. of Houston, B.S. 1948. Studied acting with Stella Adler, N.Y.C., 2 yrs.; singing with Ethel Meyers, 6 yrs.; dancing with Frank Wagner, 2 yrs.; Matt Mattox, N.Y.C., 6 mos. Married Apr. 17, 1954, to Carol Haney, actress, dancer, choreographer, director (marr. dis., June 1961; dec. May 10, 1964); one son, one daughter. Served USMC, 1943–46; rank, 2nd Lt.; USMCR, 1946–61; rank, 1st Lt. Member of AEA, AFTRA, SAG, SDG, The Players. c/o International Business Management, 641 Lexington Ave., New York, NY 10022, tel. (212) HA 1-6161.

Theatre. Mr. Blyden first performed as Capt. Andy in *Show Boat* (Wharton Sch., Houston, Tex., May 1930); subsequently played the Bank Examiner in *Kind Lady* (Interstate Players, Austin, Tex., Sept. 1946).

He made his N.Y.C. debut succeeding (July 1949) Rufus Smith as the Southern Shore Patrol Officer in *Mr. Roberts* (Alvin, Feb. 18, 1948); subsequently succeeded Dick Van Patten as Ensign Pulver in the same production, and played on tour (opened Klein Aud., Bridgeport, Conn., Sept. 13, 1951).

He appeared as Valere in *The Miser* (Walt Whitman Sch., N.Y.C. Dec. 1950); as Schmutz, and understudied Sydney Armus as Itchy Flexner in *Wish*

You Were Here (Imperial, June 25, 1952), and succeeded (June 1953) Mr. Armus as Itchy in the same production; played Grant Cobbler in *Oh Men! Oh Women!* (Henry Miller's Th., Dec. 17, 1953); and Fadinard in *Italian Straw Hat* (Fourth St. Th., Sept. 30, 1957).

Mr. Blyden succeeded Ray Walston as Michael Haney in *Who Was That Lady I Saw You With?* (Martin Beck Th., Mar. 3, 1958); played the Cop in *The Time of Your Life* (Brussels World's Fair, Bldg., Oct. 1958); Sammy Fong in *The Flower Drum Song* (St. James, N.Y.C., Dec. 1, 1958); and Doc Mosk in *Foxy* (Palace, Dawson City, Yukon, Can., June 30, 1962).

Mr. Blyden directed *Harold* (Cort, N.Y.C. Nov. 29, 1962); and repeated the role of Doc Mosk in *Foxy* (Ziegfeld, Feb. 13, 1964).

Mr. Blyden made his London debut in *Blues for Mr. Charlie* with Actors' Studio at the World Th. Season (Aldrwych Th., London, England, May, 1965); replaced Eli Wallach in *Luv* (Booth Th., Feb., 1966); replaced Martin Balsam in *You Know I Can't Hear You When the Water's Running* (Ambassador Th., Mar. 13, 1967); played the Devil in *The Apple Tree* (Shubert Th., Oct. 18, 1966). He directed *Race of Hairy Men* (Henry Miller Th., Apr. 29, 1965), and *Mother Lover* (Booth Th., Feb. 1, 1969) and played the role of the son. He opened in *A Funny Thing Happened on the Way to the Forum* (Ahmanson Th., Los Angeles, Calif., Oct. 21, 1971, and Lunt-Fontanne Th., N.Y.C., Mar. 30, 1972); appeared in a limited engagement of *The Frogs* (Yale Rep. Th. Co., New Haven, Conn., May 20, 1974); and played Sidney Hopcroft in *Absurd Person Singular* (Music Box Th., Oct. 8, 1974).

Films. He has appeared in *Bachelor Party* (UA, 1957); *Kiss Them for Me* (20th-Fox, 1957); and *On a Clear Day You Can See Forever* (Par., 1970).

Television. Mr. Blyden has performed on the Philco Television Playhouse (NBC); in *What Makes Sammy Run?* (NBC, Oct. 1960); as Joe in Joe and Mabel (CBS, 1954); and as Harry in the series, Harry's Girls (NBC, 1963).

He has hosted the game shows *Personality* and *Movie Game,* and is currently hosting *Waht's My Line?.*

Awards. Mr. Blyden won the Antoinette Perry (Tony) award for best supporting actor (1972) in *A Funny Thing Happened on the Way to the Forum.*

BOCK, JERRY. Composer. b. Jerrold Lewis Bock, Nov. 23, 1928, New Haven, Conn., to George Joseph and Rebecca (Alpert) Bock. Grad. P.S. 32, Flushing, N.Y.; Flushing H.S., 1945; attended Univ. of Wisconsin, Sch. of Music, 1945–49. Married May 28, 1950, to Patti Faggen; one son, one daughter. Member of Dramatists Guild, BMI.

Theatre. Mr. Bock first wrote a high school musical comedy entitled *My Dream* (Flushing H.S., 1945); subsequently wrote the score for a college musical, *Big as Life* (Univ. of Wisconsin, 1948); composed weekly revues at Camp Tamiment (Pa., Summers 1950, 1951, 1953); contributed three songs to the revue *Catch a Star!* (Plymouth, N.Y.C., Sept. 6, 1955); and three songs to *The Ziegfeld Follies* (Winter Garden, Mar. 1, 1957). His first complete Bway score was for *Mr. Wonderful* (Bway Th., Mar. 22, 1956), with lyrics by Sheldon Harnick. The pair continued to collaborate on *The Body Beautiful* (Bway Th., Jan. 23, 1958); *Fiorello!* (Broadhurst, Nov. 23, 1959; revived NY City Ctr., June 13, 1962), which later toured (opened State Fair Music Hall, Dallas, Tex., Aug. 8, 1960; closed Erlanger, Philadelphia, Pa., Mar. 31, 1962), and in London (Piccadilly, Oct. 8, 1962); *Tenderloin* (46 St. Th., Oct. 17, 1960); *She Loves Me* (Eugene O'Neill Th., Apr. 23, 1963), subsequently presented in London (Lyric, Apr. 29, 1964); and *Fiddler on the Roof* (Imperial, N.Y.C., Sept. 22, 1964; Her Majesty's Th., London, Feb. 16, 1967).

Mr. Bock wrote the score and co-authored the book for *The Apple Tree* (Shubert, N.Y.C., Oct. 18, 1966) and composed the score for *The Rothschilds* (Lunt-Fontanne, Oct. 19, 1970). He wrote the "Never Too Late Cha-Cha" for the play of the same name (Playhouse, Nov. 27, 1962); the incidental music for *Generation* (Morosco, Oct. 6, 1965); and songs for *Hello, Solly* (Henry Miller's Th., Apr. 4, 1967) and *The Mayor's Rebuttal* (NY Hilton, Mar. 5, 1973 only).

Films. Mr. Bock composed the background score for *Wonders of Manhattan* (Col., 1956).

Television. With Larry Holofcener, Mr. Bock wrote songs for Admiral Broadway Revue and Show of Shows (1949–51); wrote continuity and sketches for the Mel Torme Show (CBS, 1951–52); and was a member of the writing staff for the Kate Smith Hour (1953–54). With Sheldon Harnick, he wrote lyrics and music for *The Canterville Ghost* (ABC, Nov. 2, 1966). He has appeared on the Musical Theatre series (CBS, June 14, 1964) and The Today Show (NBC, 1966).

Awards. For *Fiorello!,* Mr. Bock received the Pulitzer Prize for Drama, the NY Drama Critics' Award, and the Antoinette Perry (Tony) Award (1960). The film, *Wonders of Manhattan,* for which he composed the background music, received Honorable Mention at the Cannes Film Festival (1956). For *Fiddler On the Roof,* he won the Annual Variety NY Drama Critics' Poll (Best Score, 1964–65); the B'nai B'rith Music and Performing Arts Lodge Award for "exceptional creative achievement" (June 16, 1965); the Antoinette Perry (Tony) Award (composer, 1965); and the Ny Drama Critics' Circle Award (best musical, 1964–65).

BOGARD, TRAVIS. Educator. b. Jan. 25, 1918, San Francisco, Calif., to Verner E. and Gertrude (Travis) Bogard. Father, businessman; mother, teacher. Grad. Univ. of California at Berkeley, A.B. 1939, M.A. 1940; Princeton Univ., Ph.D. 1946. Married June 21, 1947, to Jane Malmgren; one son, one daughter. Served US Army, 1942–45; rank, Staff Sgr. Member of AFTRA; AETA; MLA; AAUP. Address: (home) 7 W. Parnassus Ct., Berkeley, CA 94708; (bus.) Dept. of Dramatic Art, Univ. of California, Berkeley, CA 94720, tel. (415) 642-1677.

Mr. Bogard joined the staff of the Dept. of English at the Univ. of California at Berkeley in 1947. He served as chmn. of the Dept. of Dramatic Art (1960–67) and joined the staff of that department in 1966. In 1966, he served as director of the Univ. of California Study Center for Classical Drama at Delphi, Greece. He was an instructor of English at Yale University (1941–42).

Published Works. He is the author of *The Tragic Satire of John Webster* (1955) and *Contour in Time, the Plays of Eugene O'Neill* (1972). He has edited *The Later Plays of Eugene O'Neill* (1967) and, with William I. Oliver, *Modern Drama, Essays in Criticism* (1965).

Awards. Mr. Bogard received a Guggenheim Fellowship (1957–58) and a Commonwealth Club of California award for *Contour in Time* (1973).

BOGIN, ABBA. Musical director, musical arranger. b. Nov. 24, 1925, New York City, to Morris and Anna (Pinson) Bogin. Father, post office clerk; mother, writer and poet. Grad. Bronx (N.Y.) High School of Science; Curtis Institute of Music, Philadelphia, Pa., 1949; studied with Mme. Isabella Vengerova (piano); Alexander Hilsberg (conducting); Samuel Barber and Gian-Carlo Menotti (orchestration); additional conducting studies with Pierre Monteux, 1947–52. Served US Army, 1944–46, including eight months of combat duty in Europe with 78th Infantry Div. Married 1952 to Silvana Casti, painter and artist (marr. dis. 1966); one daughter, one son; married 1966 to Suzanne Cogan, actress and singer (marr. dis. 1970); married in 1971 to Masako Yanagita, concert violinist. Member of Local 802, AFM; AGMA (natl. treas. and bd. mbr., 1950–55; permanent trustee of AGMA Relief Fund, 1953–to date); American Symphony Orchestra League; NY Musicians Club; Natl. Assn. of Composers and Conductors. Address: (home) 838 West End Ave., New York, NY 10025, tel. (212) 663-4198; (bus.) American Symphony Orchestra, 119 W. 57th St., New York, NY 10019, tel. (212) 581-1365.

Theatre. Mr. Bogin's first work in the theatre was as conductor for a bus and truck tour of *Finian's Rainbow* (Sept. 1952). He has conducted musicals in many stock theatres throughout the US, beginning with his work as conductor of *Kiss Me, Kate* (Woodstock, N.Y., Playhouse, July 1953). He did his first work off Bway as musical director for *The Threepenny Opera* (Th. de Lys, Mar. 10, 1954) and made his Bway debut as musical director of *Mrs. Patterson* (National, Dec. 1, 1954). He was musical director for a revival of *The Most Happy Fella* (NY City Ctr., Feb. 10, 1959); for *Greenwillow* (Alvin Th., Mar. 8, 1960); *Send Me No Flowers* (Brooks Atkinson Th., Dec. 5, 1960); *How To Succeed in Business without Really Trying* (46 St. Th., Oct. 14, 1961); musical director and arranger for *Another Evening with Harry Stoones* (Gramercy Arts, Oct. 21, 1961); musical director for *New Faces of 1962* (Alvin, Feb. 1, 1962); *The Fun Couple* (Lyceum, Oct. 26, 1962); musical arranger for *Riverwind* (Actors Playhouse, Dec. 11, 1962); musical director for *The Beauty Part* (Music Box Th., Dec. 26, 1962); and *The Megilla of Itzak Manger;* musical director and arranger for *That Thing at the Cherry Lane* (Cherry Lane Th., May 18, 1965); and musical director and supervisor for NY City Ctr. Light Opera Co. revivals of *How To Succeed in Business without Really Trying* (Apr. 20, 1966), *The Most Happy Fella* (May 11, 1966), *Where's Charley?* (May 25, 1966), and *Guys and Dolls* (June 8, 1966). He was also musical arranger for *By Jupiter* (Th. Four, Jan. 19, 1967); musical director for *The Fig Leaves Are Falling* (Broadhurst, Jan. 1969); and musical arranger for *Blood Red Roses* (John Golden Th., Mar. 22, 1970).

Films. Mr. Bogin was musical director of *A Time to Play,* the official US film for showing at the US Pavilion, Expo '67, Montreal, Canada (May 1967).

Television. Mr. Bogin was musical director and arranger for the NET production of *The Beggar's Opera* (PBS, 1968).

Concerts. Mr. Bogin made his N.Y.C. debut as a concert pianist at Town Hall (Oct. 1947), and since then he has given recitals in more than 200 civic, community, and college music associations in the US and Canada, as well as touring in Mexico, Europe, and the Far East. He has appeared as soloist in concert with many major symphonies, including the NY Philharmonic, Philadelphia, Chicago, Houston, Kansas City, National, and San Francisco orchestras, and the Little Orchestra Society of NY.

Mr. Bogin was musical director of the GI Symphony (Europe, 1945) and the Wiesbaden (Germany) Symphony (1946). He made his debut as an opera conductor at a performance of *Cosi fan Tutte* (Wiesbaden Opera House, Mar. 1946). He was founder (1946) and musical director of the YMHA Community Orchestra, Philadelphia, Pa. (1946–48); on the musical staff of the NY City Opera and the NY City Ballet (1953–55); musical director of the After Dinner Opera Co., N.Y.C. (1970–73); musical director of the Queens (N.Y.C.) Opera (1971–72); of the summer concerts of the Hudson Valley (N.Y.) Philharmonic Symphony (1972); of the Tappan Zee Concert Society, Nyack, N.Y. (1972–to date); and musical director, Cosmopolitan Opera Co., N.Y.C. (1974). In addition, Mr. Bogin has been guest conductor of the Boston Pops Orchestra, for three concerts (Symphony Hall, Boston, Mass., 1968); musical director of the Haiti-American Opera Co., (Port-au-Prince, Haiti, 1969); artistic coordinator and conductor, Lake George (N.Y.) Opera, with whom he made his US operatic debut conducting a performance of *Don Giovanni* (July 1970); and conductor of American Symphony Orchestra's Special Projects concerts (1974).

Other Activities. Mr. Bogin has been an associate and consultant with the music staff, NY State Council on the Arts (1970–to date) and a board member and assistant treasurer of the American Symphony Orchestra (1973–to date).

Discography. Mr. Bogin was conductor and musical director of the cast albums for *Mrs. Patterson* and *Greenwillow;* arranger and conductor of the cast album for *Riverwind;* and arranger of the cast album of

By Jupiter. His classical recordings include the complete sonatas for cello and piano of Beethoven and Brahms (both with Janos Starker, cellist); the piano trios of Mozart and Beethoven (the Boston Trio: Ruth Posselt, violin; Samuel Mayes, cello; Abba Bogin, piano); and Swanson's *Sonata* for cello and piano (with Carl Stern, cellist).

Awards. Mr. Bogin received the Naumburg Award (1947), the Philadelphia Orchestra Award (1948), and the Chamber Music Guild (Washington, D.C.) Award (1948).

Recreation. Mr. Bogin is a "hi-fi nut (tape editing and copying)" and has an "enormous collection of old 78 rpm recordings (mostly classical)"; other recreations include bridge, poker, and swimming.

BOLASNI, SAUL. Costume designer. b. Saul Harold Bolasny, Cleveland, Ohio, to Bernard and Bertha (Bodner) Bolasny. Father, businessman; mother, nurse, professional swimmer. Attended Cleveland public schools. Relative in theatre: sister, Eleanor Boleyn, dancer, actress. Member of United Scenic Artists, Local 829 (pres., costume designer membership, 1953–54). Address: 57 W. 69th St., New York, NY 10023, tel. (212) SU 7-9117.

Theatre. Mr. Bolasni was a dancer and appeared in concerts with Valerie Bettis' Co.; performed in *Up in Central Park* (Century Th., N.Y.C., Jan. 27, 1945); and danced in Italy (Verona), Vicenza, Venice, Summer 1949) with Compagnia Salvine, at the Festival of Antique Classics.

He designed costumes for *Courtin' Time* (Natl., N.Y.C., June 13, 1951); *The Rainmaker* (Cort, Oct. 28, 1954); *The Threepenny Opera* (Th. de Lys, Mar. 10, 1954); *The Duchess of Malfi* (Phoenix, Mar. 19, 1957); *A Minor Adjustment* (Brooks Atkinson Th., Oct. 6, 1967); and *Of Love Remembered* (ANTA, Feb. 18, 1967).

Mr. Bolasni has designed ballet costumes for The American Ballet Theatre's *Nimbus, Rodeo,* and *Pas de Deux Tropicale;* Valerie Bettis' various solo and group concert pieces; the American Negro Theatre of Dance's *Italian Concerto* and *Les Preludes;* Mata & Hari's, *The Silent Screen;* The Franklin-Shavenska Co.'s. *Streetcar Named Desire* (1952); A.B.C. Theatre's *Les Ballets Ho* (Paris, Fr., 1956); the Tamaris-Nagrin Co.; the Natl. Ballet Co. (Washington, D.C., 1963); and for the Cellomatic Industrial Show (Apr. 1963).

Television. Mr. Bolasni has designed costumes for Hallmark Hall of Fame (NBC, 1951–52); Chesterfield Suspense dramas (NBC, 1952); Salute to Baseball (NBC Spectacular, 1956); the Martha Raye Show (NBC, 1956); *La Boheme* (NBC, 1956); Omnibus (ABC, 1956–57; NBC 1958–61); Crescendo (CBS Spectacular, 1957); the Polly Bergen Show (NBC, 1957–58); Leonard Bernstein's Christmas Special (CBS, 1959), and all of Mr. Bernstein's Philharmonic telecasts (1959–Feb., 1962); the Dow Mystery series (NBC 1960); Bell Telephone Hour (NBC, 1960–61); Thanksgiving specials (ABC, 1961, 1963); The Nurses (CBS, 1963); for the continuing series *Love of Life* (CBS, 1966–70); and he was guest designer for *Another World* (NBC, 1973).

Other Activities. Mr. Bolasni has done art work for *Town and Country; Mademoiselle; The Ladies's Home Journal; The New Yorker, Glamour;* and advertising art work for Columbia Records, Ponds, Hattie Carnegie, Vanguard Press, Lenthéric, Moore-McCormack Lines, Kayser Hosiery, Stendahl Cosmetics, Lippincott Press, Rosemarie De Paris, and Galey & Lord. He also paints portraits, many of which are in the permanent exhibit of C. C. Price Portrait Gallery, 30 West 57th St., N.Y.C.

Recreation. Dance, languages, piano.

BOLGER, RAY. Actor, dancer. b. Raymond Wallace Bolger, Jan. 10, 1904, Boston, Mass., to James E. and Anne (Wallace) Bolger. Father, painter. Grad. Dorchester (Mass.) H.S., 1920. Married July 9, 1929, to Gwendolyn Rickard. Served in USO Camp Shows (Oct. 1941–July 1943). Member of AEA; AFTRA; SAG; AGVA; The Players; Bohemian Club; Burlingame Country Club; Valley Club of Montecito; Bel-Air Country Club; Desert Inn Country Club. Address: (home) 618 N. Beverly Dr., Beverly Hills, CA 90210, tel. (213) CR 6-8331; (bus.) c/o Julius Lefkowitz & Co., B&R Enterprises Inc., 9171 Wilshire Blvd., Beverly Hills, CA 90210, tel. (213) CR 5-0111.

Pre-Theatre. Employed by the First National Bank of Boston; New England Mutual Life Insurance Co.; Kelly Peanut Co.

Theatre. Mr. Bolger made his first stage appearance as a soloist in Rusakoff's dance recital (Jordan Hall, Boston, Mass., 1922); first appeared professionally with the Bob Ott Musical Comedy Repertoire Company as a comedian and dancer in *One Hour from Broadway* (Moose Home, Lykens, Pa., 1923), and toured with the company in various musicals until he joined Ralph Sanford in vaudeville in *A Pair of Nifties* (Central Square Th., Cambridge, Mass., 1925); appeared as dancing comedian at the Rialto Th. in New York (1925); in *The Merry World* (Imperial, June 8, 1926); in the second edition of *A Night in Paris* (44 St. Th., July, 1926); played in Gus Edwards' *Ritz-Carlton Nights* (Palace, 1926), with which he toured the Keith-Albee and Orpheum circuits (1927–28); and appeared in several miniature revues in movie houses throughout the country (1928–29).

He played Georgie in *Heads Up* (Alvin, Nov. 11, 1929); appeared in *George White's Scandals* (Apollo, Sept. 14, 1931); in the inaugural program dedicating Radio City Music Hall (Dec. 27, 1932); in *Life Begins at 8:40* (Winter Garden, Aug. 27, 1934); *On Your Toes* (Imperial, Apr. 11, 1936); *Keep Off the Grass* (Broadhurst, May 23, 1940); played Sapiens in *By Jupiter* (Shubert, June 3, 1942); and appeared in *Three To Make Ready* (Adelphi, Mar. 7, 1946); as Charley in *Where's Charley?* (St. James, Oct. 11, 1948); and as Prof. Fodorski in *All American* (Winter Garden, Mar. 19, 1962).

Films. Mr. Bolger first appeared in *The Great Ziegfeld* (MGM, 1936); subsequently in *Rosalie* (MGM, 1937); *Sweethearts* (MGM, 1938); *The Wizard of Oz* (MGM, 1939); *Four Jacks and a Jill* (RKO, 1941); *Sunny* (RKO, 1941); *The Harvey Girls* (MGM, 1946); *Look for the Silver Lining* (WB, 1949); *Where's Charley?* (WB, 1952); *April in Paris* (WB, 1952); and *Babes in Toyland* (Buena Vista, 1961).

Television. He first appeared on the Colgate Comedy Hour (NBC, 1952); and later in the series Where's Raymond? (ABC, 1953–54); the Ray Bolger Show (ABC, 1955–56); and Washington Square (NBC, 1958). His guest appearances include the London Palladium TV Hour (1957).

Night Clubs. Mr. Bolger appeared in the premiere performance at the opening of the Hotel Sahara (Las Vegas, Nev., 1952) and has since played night clubs throughout the country.

Awards. He received a Newspaper Guild of NY Page One Award for his performance as Sapiens in *By Jupiter* (1943); for his performance in *Three To Make Ready* he received two Donaldson Awards (1946) and won a *Variety* NY Drama Critics Poll (1946); for his performance as Charley in *Where's Charley?* he received the Antoinette Perry (Tony) Award (1949), the Donaldson Award (1949), and the Newspaper Guild of NY Page One Award (1950). He also received The Lamb's Distinguished Achievement Award (1957), the medallion of valor of the state of Israel (1960), a Distinctive Contribution Award from the Dance Educators of America (1962), and the "Decency of Entertainment" Award given by the Notre Dame University Club of Chicago (1967).

Recreation. Golf, racing.

BOLIN, SHANNON. Actress, singer. b. Shannon Ione Bolin, Jan. 1, 1917, Spencer, S.D., to Harry and Grace (Elsie) Bolin. Father, hotel owner. Grad. Spencer H.S., 1934; South Dakota Wesleyan, B.S. 1938; attended Univ. of Maryland, 1940. Studied singing with Myron Whitney; with Harold Clurman and Sanford Meisner. Married Oct. 7, 1946, to Milton Kaye, conductor, composer, pianist. Member of AFTRA; SAG; AEA. Address: 171 W. 57th St., New York, NY 10019, tel. (212) JU 6-2779.

Pre-Theatre. Teacher.

Theatre. Miss Bolin made her Bway debut as a member of the chorus and understudy to Rosalind Nadell as Juno in *Helen Goes to Troy* (Alvin, Apr. 24, 1944); subsequently played Adah in *Naughty Marietta* (Pittsburgh Civic Light Opera, Pa., Summer 1949); alternated with Jane Pickens in the title role in *Regina* (46 St. Th., N.Y.C., Oct. 31, 1949); and succeeded Geraldine Viti as Mrs. Jupiter in the Phoenix production of *The Golden Apple* (Alvin, Apr. 20, 1954).

She appeared as Countess Zedlau in *Waltz Down the Aisle* (Lambertville Music Circus, N.J., July 1954); Meg in *Damn Yankees* (46 St. Th., N.Y.C., May 5, 1955); Ninotchka in *Silk Stockings* (Columbus and Dayton, Ohio, July 1958); Mrs. Kate Golden in *Only in America* (Cort, N.Y.C., Nov. 19, 1959); Lily in *Take Me Along* (State Fair Music Hall, Dallas, Tex., 1961; Coconut Grove Playhouse, Miami, Fla., July 25, 1961); and Zampa in *The Student Gypsy* (54 St. Th., N.Y.C., Sept. 30, 1963). She has appeared in a Rodgers and Hammerstein Evening (St. Louis Municipal Opera, Mo.), and she was the Mother in *Promenade* (Promenade Th., N.Y.C., June 4, 1969).

Films. She appeared as Meg in *Damn Yankees* (WB, 1958).

Television and Radio. On radio, Miss Bolin was a staff singer in Washington, D.C. (CBS), and a soloist on the Woolworth Hour (CBS).

On television, she has appeared as Principessa in *Sour Angelica* (NBC Opera, Dec. 1954); Jackie Gleason's Wife on the Jackie Gleason Show (CBS, 1961); the Patty Duke Show (ABC, 1964); Armstrong Circle Th. (CBS); Edge of Night (CBS); and Music for a Summer Night (ABC).

Night Clubs. She has performed at the Normandy Room (Mt. Royal Hotel, Montreal, Can., 1950), and the Flame Room (Radisson Hotel, Minneapolis, Minn., 1951).

Awards. Miss Bolin received the Blue Bonnet Award for her performance as Lily in *Take Me Along* (1961).

Recreation. Trout fishing, archaeology, antiques.

BOLOGNA, JOSEPH. Actor, author, producer of television commercials. b. Brooklyn, N.Y. Educ. Brown Univ. Married 1965 to Renee Taylor, actress. Served in USMC.

Theatre. With his wife, Mr. Bologna wrote *Lovers and Other Strangers* (Brooks Atkinson Th., Sept. 18, 1968).

Films. The Bolognas collaborated on a film short called *2,* which was shown at the 1966 NY Film Festival. They also wrote, with David Goodman, the screenplay for *Lovers and Other Strangers* (ABC Pictures, 1970), which was based on their play, and the screenplay for *Made for Each Other* (20th-Fox, 1971), in which Mr. Bologna appeared as Giggy and his wife as Pandora. Mr. Bologna also acted in *Cops and Robbers* (UA, 1973) and *Mixed Company* (UA, 1974).

Television. Mr. Bologna has produced television commercials. He and his wife wrote and played leading roles in *Paradise* (CBS, Mar. 12, 1974), and they wrote *Acts of Love and Other Comedies.*

Awards. Mr. Bologna and his wife won a NATAS (Emmy) Award for *Acts of Love and Other Comedies.*

BOLT, ROBERT. Playwright. b. Robert Oxton Bolt, Aug. 15, 1924, Sale, Manchester, England, to Ralph and Leah (Binnion) Bolt. Father, shopkeeper; mother, teacher. Attended Manchester Univ., B.A. (history), 1950. Married Nov. 6, 1950, to Celia Anne Roberts (marr. dis. 1967); one son, two daughters; married 1967 to Sarah Elizabeth Miles (actress); one son. Served RAF, 1943–44; Royal West African Frontier Force, 1944–46. c/o Margaret Ramsay Ltd., 14 Goodwins Court, London, W.C. 2, England.

Pre-Theatre. Office boy in insurance office (Manchester, 1941–42); teaching.

Theatre. Mr. Bolt's first produced play in the US was *Flowering Cherry* (Lyceum, N.Y.C., Oct. 21, 1959); followed by *A Man for All Seasons* (ANTA, Nov. 22, 1961).

His first produced play in England was *The Critic and the Heart* (Oxford Playhouse, 1957); followed by *Flowering Cherry* (Haymarket, London, Nov. 21, 1957); *The Tiger and the Horse* (Queen's, Aug. 24, 1960); *A Man for All Seasons* (Globe, July 1, 1960); *Gentle Jack* (Queen's, Nov. 28, 1963); *The Thwarting of Baron Bolligrew* (Aldwych Th., London, Dec. 1965); and *Vivat! Vivat Regina!* (Broadhurst Th., N.Y.C., Jan. 20, 1972).

Films. Mr. Bolt wrote the screenplay for *Lawrence of Arabia* (Col., 1962); *Dr. Zhivago* (MGM, 1965); *A Man for All Seasons* (Col., 1966); *Ryan's Daughter* (MGM, 1970); and *Lady Caroline Lamb*, which he also directed (UA, 1972).

Awards. He received the *Evening Standard* Award (1957) for *Flowering Cherry;* the NY Drama Critics' Circle Award (1962) for *A Man for All Seasons;* and received an Academy (Oscar) Award nomination (1962) for his screenplay, *Lawrence of Arabia.* He received Academy Awards for his screenplays for *Dr. Zhivago* (1965) and *A Man for All Seasons* (1966).

BOLTON, GUY. Playwright, novelist. b. St. George Guy Reginald Bolton, Nov. 23, 1886, Broxbourne, Herts., England, to Reginald Pelham and Katherine (Behenna) Bolton. Father, consulting engineer. Attended Hudson Military Acad., Nyack, N.Y.; Pratt Inst.; Atelier Masquerey, and other architectural schools. Married 1910 to Julie Alexander Currie (marr. dis. 1915, dec. 1945); one son, one daughter; married 1917 to Marquerite Namara (marr. dis. 1927); one daughter; married 1927 to Marion Redford (marr. dis. 1939, dec. 1956); one son; married 1939 to Virginia De Lanty, playwright, known as Stephen Powys. Member of Sons of the American Revolution. Address: (home) Shore Road, Remsenburg, NY 11960, tel. (516) EA 5-0206; (bus.) 46 Onslow Square, London, S.W.7, England.

Theatre. Mr. Bolton wrote *The Drone*, with Douglas J. Wood, (Daly's Th., N.Y.C., Dec. 30, 1912); wrote *The Rule of Three* (Sam H. Harris Th., Feb. 16, 1914); *The Fallen Idol* (Comedy, Jan. 23, 1915); *90 in the Shade* (Knickerbocker, Jan. 25, 1915); with Paul Ruben, *Nobody Home* (Princess, Apr. 20, 1915); and *Her Game* (Teck Th., Buffalo, N.Y., June 22, 1915).

He collaborated with George Middleton on *Hit-the-Trail-Holiday* (Astor, N.Y.C., Sept. 13, 1915); with Phillip Bartholomae, wrote the book for *Very Good, Eddie* (Princess, Dec. 23, 1915); with Tom Carleton, *Children*, which was included in the repertoire of the Washington Square Players (Bandbox, Oct. 4, 1915–May 20, 1916); and, with George Middleton, *Thought* (Colonial, Cleveland, Ohio, June 26, 1916). He wrote the book for *Miss Springtime* (New Amsterdam, N.Y.C., Sept. 25, 1916).

With P. G. Wodehouse, Mr. Bolton wrote the book and lyrics for *Have a Heart* (Liberty, Jan. 11, 1917); *Oh, Boy* (Princess, Feb. 20, 1917); *Leave It to Jane*, based on *The College Widow*, by George Ade (Longacre, Aug. 28, 1917; Sheridan Square Playhouse, May 25, 1959); with George Middleton, he collaborated on the comedy, *Polly with a Past* (Belasco, Sept. 6, 1917); with Mr. Wodehouse, wrote the book and lyrics for *The Riviera Girl* (New Amsterdam, Sept. 24, 1917), *Miss 1917* (Century, Nov. 5, 1917), *Oh, Lady! Lady!* (Princess, Feb. 1, 1918), *See You Later* (Acad. of Music, Baltimore, Md., Apr. 15, 1918), *The Girl Behind the Gun* (New Amsterdam, Sept. 24, 1917) *Miss* and *Oh, My Dear!* (Princess, Nov. 27, 1918).

Mr. Bolton wrote with Frank Mandel, *The Five Million* (Lyric, July 8, 1919); with George Middleton, *Adam and Eva* (Longacre, Sept. 13, 1919); wrote, with Mr. Wodehouse, the book and lyrics for *The Rose of China* (Lyric, Nov. 25, 1919); with George Middleton, the drama, *The Light of the World*, under the joint pseudonym of Pierre Saisson (Lyric, Jan. 6, 1920); also with Mr. Middleton, *The Cave Girl* (Longacre, Aug. 18, 1920); wrote the book for *Sally* (New Amsterdam, Dec. 21, 1920; revived Martin Beck Th., May 6, 1948); the book, with Philip Bartholomae, for *Tangerine* (Casino, Aug. 9, 1921); with Max Marcin, *The Night Cap* (39 St. Th., Aug. 15, 1921); adapted from the French, the book for *The Hotel Mouse* (Shubert, Mar. 13, 1922); with Oscar Hammerstein, II, the book for *Daffy Dill* (Apollo, Aug. 22, 1922); *Polly Preferred* (Little, Jan. 11, 1923); *Chicken Feed or Wages for Wives* (Little, Sept. 24, 1923); with Frank Mandel, *Nobody's Business* (Klaw, Oct. 22, 1923); with Mr. Wodehouse, the book for *Sitting Pretty* (Fulton, Apr. 8, 1924); and *Grounds for Divorce*, adapted from Ernest Vejda's *Fata Morgana* (Empire, Sept. 23, 1924).

Mr. Bolton wrote with George Grossmith, the book for the musical, *Primrose* (Winter Garden, London, Sept. 11, 1924); with Fred Thompson, wrote the book for the musicals, *Lady, Be Good* (Liberty, N.Y.C., Dec. 1, 1924), and *Tip-Toes* (Liberty, Dec. 1, 1925); collaborated with Bert Kalmar and Harry Ruby on the book for *The Ramblers* (Lyric, Sept. 20, 1926); with Mr. Wodehouse, wrote the book and lyrics for *The Nightingale* (Al Jolson's, Jan. 3, 1927); with Mr. Thompson the book and lyrics for *Rio Rita* (Ziegfeld, Feb. 2, 1927), and the book for *5 O'Clock Girl* (44 St. Th., Oct. 10, 1927); with Mr. Wodehouse, the book for *Oh, Kay!* (Imperial, Nov. 9, 1928); and with Messrs. Kalmar and Ruby, the book for *She's My Baby* (Globe, Jan. 3, 1928); with William Anthony McGuire, the book for *Rosalie* (New Amsterdam, Jan. 10, 1928); he collaborated with Graham John on the book for *Blue Eyes* (Piccadilly, London, Apr. 27, 1928).

With Mr. Middleton, he wrote the book for *Polly*, which was based on Belasco's *Polly with a Past* (Lyric, N.Y.C., Jan. 8, 1929); with Messrs. Kalmar and Ruby, wrote the book and lyrics, and produced *Top Speed* (46 St. Th., Dec. 25, 1929). He collaborated with Ed Wynn on *Simple Simon* (Ziegfeld, Feb. 18, 1930); with John McCowan, the book for *Girl Crazy* (Alvin, Oct. 14, 1930); with Mr. Thompson, the book for *The Song of the Drum* (Drury Lane, London, Jan. 9, 1931); with R. P. Weston and Bert Lee *Give Me a Ring* (Hippodrome, June 22, 1933); wrote *Seeing Stars* (Gaiety, Oct. 31, 1935); with Mr. Thompson, *This'll Make You Whistle* (Palace, Sept. 15, 1936); with Mr. Thompson and Douglas Furber, *Swing Alone* (Gaiety, Sept. 2, 1936); *Going Greek* (Gaiety, Sept. 16, 1937), and *Hide and Seek* (Hippodrome, Oct. 14, 1937); and with Messrs. Thompson and Lee, *The Fleet's Lit Up* (Hippodrome, Aug. 17, 1938). The book for *Running Riot* was written by Douglas Furber, from a plot by Mr. Bolton and Firth Shephard (Gaiety, Aug. 31, 1938). Mr. Bolton collaborated with Messrs. Thompson and Lee on the book for *Bobby Get Your Gun* (Adelphi, Oct. 7, 1938); with Gerald Fairlee, *Number Six*, which was adapted from Edgar Wallace's novel (Aldwych, Dec. 21, 1938); with Mr. Thompson and Eric Maschwitz, adapted *Paprika*, for the book for *Magyar Melody*, (His Majesty's, Jan. 20, 1939); and with Vernon Sylvaine, *Nap Hand*, originally titled *Two and Two Make Five* (Aldwych, Apr. 1, 1940).

He wrote, with Mr. Wodehouse, the book for *Anything Goes* (Alvin, N.Y.C., Nov. 21, 1934); and, with his wife, Stephen Powys, *Wise Tommorrow* (Biltmore, Oct. 15, 1937).

Mr. Bolton collaborated, with Parke Levy and Alan Lipscott, on the book for *Walk with Music*, based on Stephen Powys' comedy, *Three Blind Mice* (Ethel Barrymore Th., June 4, 1940); with Matt Brooks and Eddie Davis, on the book for *Hold on to Your Hats* (Shubert, Sept. 11, 1940); with Somerset Maugham, on the play *Theatre* based on Maugham's novel of the same name (Hudson, Nov. 12, 1941); with William Jay, on the drama *Golden Wings* (Cort, Dec. 8, 1941); with John Golden, *Another Heaven*, which closed on its pre-Bway tour (Royal Alexandra, Toronto, Ontario, Canada, Aug. 30, 1943); with Sidney Sheldon and Ben Roberts on the book for *Jackpot* (Alvin, N.Y.C., Jan. 13, 1944); and with Eddie Davis on the book for *Follow the Girls* (Century, Apr. 8, 1944).

He revised the American version of *The Chocolate Soldier* (Century, Mar. 12, 1947); wrote *The Shelley Story* (Mercury, London, Aug. 11, 1947); and *Humoresque* ("Q", Oct. 26, 1948); adapted *Don't Listen Ladies*, which was translated by Stephen Powys from the French by Sacha Guiltry (Booth, N.Y.C., Dec. 28, 1948); adapted *Larger Than Life* from Maugham's novel (Duke of York's, London, Feb. 7, 1950); wrote the book for *Music at Midnight* (His Majesty's, Nov. 10, 1950); and with Harold Purcell, the book and lyrics for *Rainbow Square* (Stoll, Sept. 21, 1951).

He wrote *Anastasia*, adapted from the French of Marcelle Maurette (Lyceum, N.Y.C., Dec. 29, 1954); with Eddie Davis, the book for *Ankles Aweigh* (Mark Hellinger Th., Apr. 18, 1955); *Child of Fortune*, adapted from Henry James' *Wings of the Dove* (Royale, Nov. 13, 1956). His play *Theatre*, was adapted by Mr. Silva and Renato Alvin, and presented in Paris under the title, *Adorable Julia* (1956). He also wrote *Fireworks in the Sun* (Connaught Th., Worthing, England, Sept. 29, 1958); and, with George Abbott, the book for *Anya* (Ziegfeld Th., N.Y.C., Nov. 29, 1965), which was based on *Anastasia* by Mr. Bolton and Marcelle Maurette.

Films. Mr. Bolton wrote, with Joseph Noel, the screenplay for *The Sea Wolf* (Par., 1920); wrote the screenplay for *Going Places* (WB, 1938); with Pat Wallace, *The Sun Never Sets* (Par., 1939); and *The Long Arm*, released in the US as *The Third Key* (Rank, 1957). *When the Boys Meet the Girls* (MGM, 1965) was based on the stage musical *Girl Crazy* (1930) with book by Mr. Bolton and John McCowan.

Published Works. He wrote the novels *The Olympians* (1961) and *The Enchantress* (1964).

Recreation. Work, travel.

BOND, EDWARD. Playwright. b. 1935, London, England. Address: c/o Margaret Ramsey, 14a Goodwins Court, St. Martin's Lane, London, W.C. 2, England.

Theatre. Mr. Bond's plays (all of which received their first performances at the Royal Court, London, except where otherwise noted) include *The Pope's Wedding* (Dec. 9, 1962); *Saved* (Nov. 3, 1965; first public performance premiere, US premiere, Chelsea Th. Ctr. of Brooklyn, Brooklyn Acad. of Music, Oct. 20, 1970; moved to Cherry Lane Th., Nov. 13, 1970); *Early Morning* (1968; US premiere, La Mama E.T.C., N.Y.C., Nov. 18, 1970); *Narrow Road to the Deep North* (Belgrade Th., Coventry, England, June 1968; US premiere, Charles Playhouse, Boston, Mass., Oct. 30, 1969); *Black Mass* (1970); *Passion* (1971; US premiere, Yale Repertory Th., New Haven, Conn., Feb. 1, 1972); *Lear* (1971; US premiere, Yale Rep. Th., Apr. 13, 1973); *The Sea* (May 22, 1973; American premiere, Goodman Memorial Th., Chicago, 1974); *Bingo* (Aug. 1974; American premiere, Cleveland Playhouse, Cleveland, Ohio, Nov. 1975); and a translation for the National Th. of Frank Wedekind's *Spring Awakening* (Old Vic., London, May 28, 1974).

Awards. Mr. Bond received the George Devine Award (1968) for *Early Morning.*

BOND, RUDY. Actor. b. Rudolph R. Bond, Philadelphia, Pa., Oct. 1, 1913, to Louis and Frieda (Halbert) Bond. Father, chemist. Attended Univ. of Pennsylvania, 1933–35. Married Feb. 1, 1948, to Alma Bond; two sons, one daughter. Served US Army, ETO 1942–45; rank, Cpl. Member of AEA; AFTRA; SAG; DAV; Actors' Studio (1947). Address: 800 West End Ave., New York, NY 10025, tel. (212) MO 3-4518.

Pre-Theatre. Newspaperman.

Theatre. Mr. Bond made his N.Y.C. debut in the role of a Bartender in the Experimental Theatre's production of *O'Daniel* (Princess, Feb. 23, 1947); subsequently played Steve Hubbel in *A Streetcar Named Desire* (Ethel Barrymore Th., Dec. 3, 1947); Mr. Mack in *The Bird Cage* (Coronet, Feb. 22, 1950); succeeded Robert Pike as Commander Thomas Jellico in *Two Blind Mice* (Cort, Mar. 2, 1949); played Gregory in *Romeo and Juliet* (Broadhurst, Mar. 10, 1951); Gus Kennedy in *Glad Tidings* (Lyceum, Oct. 11, 1951); Roxy Gottlieb in *Golden Boy* (ANTA, Mar. 12, 1952); Mitch in *A Streetcar Named Desire* (NY City Ctr., Feb. 15, 1956); Andre (Leadhead) in the pre-Bway tryout of *The Gay Felons* (opened Wilmington, Del., Feb. 12, 1959; closed Ford's Baltimore, Md., Mar. 14, 1959); Ben in the national tour of *Fiorello!*(State Fair Music Hall, Dallas, Tex., Aug. 8, 1960); toured as the Father in *After the Fall* (opened Oct. 21, 1964, Wilmington, Del.; closed Shubert, Boston, Mass., May 29, 1965); appeared in *Incident at Vichy;* played Al Pecter in *Big Man* (Cherry Lane, N.Y.C., May 19, 1966); Mr. Gillman in *Match Play* (Provincetown Playhouse, Oct. 11, 1966); the Captain in *Illya Darling* (Mark Hellinger Th., Apr. 11, 1967); Salamandro in *A Mother's Kisses* (pre-Broadway tryout, opened Shubert, New Haven, Sept. 23, 1968; closed Mechanic, Baltimore, Oct. 19, 1968); Mak in *Papp* (American Place Th., N.Y.C., May 17, 1969); Legislator and Triballos in *The Birds* (Actors Studio Th., Oct. 19, 1972); in *Twelve Angry Men* (Queens Playhouse, Dec. 3, 1972); Lou in *Bread* (American Place Th., Jan. 28, 1974); Bertrand de Poulengy and Father Massieu in *Joan of Lorraine* (Good Shepherd/Faith Church, Mar. 18, 1974). Mr. Bond was an understudy for the pre-Bway tryout of *Turtlenecks* (title changed to *One Night Stand;* opened Fisher, Detroit, Aug. 6, 1973; closed Forrest, Phila., Sept. 22, 1973).

Films. Mr. Bond's film appearances include *With These Hands* (ILGWU, 1950); *A Streetcar Named Desire* (WB, 1951); *On the Waterfront* (Col., 1954); *Miss Sadie Thompson* (Col., 1954); *Twelve Angry Men* (UA, 1957); *Nightfall* (Col., 1957); *A Way of Life; Run Silent, Run Deep* (UA, 1958); *Middle of the Night* (Col., 1959); and *The Mountain Road* (Col., 1960).

Television. Mr. Bond has appeared on many television shows, including The Defenders (CBS); Empire (ABC); The Nurses (CBS); Naked City (Ind.); Directions '66 (ABC); Playhouse 90 (CBS); Brenner (CBS); and NYPD (ABC).

Awards. Mr. Bond received the John Golden Auditions Best Actor Award, and an award from Jasper Deeter (Hedgerow Th., Moylan, Pa.) as an amateur.

Recreation. Writing.

BOND, SHEILA. Dancer, actress, singer. b. Sheila Phylis Berman, Mar. 16, 1928, New York City, to Samuel and Yetta Berman. Father, construction foreman. Attended New Utrecht H.S., Brooklyn, N.Y.; grad. Children's Professional Sch., N.Y.C., 1954. Married Mar. 19, 1947, to Leo Peter Coff (marr. dis. Apr. 28, 1953); married Mar. 15, 1957, to Barton Lawrence Goldberg; one son, one daughter. Relatives in theatre: sister, Francine Bond, actress, dancer, singer; niece, Sheri Bond, actress, dancer, singer. Member of AEA; AGVA; SAG; TV Acad. Address: 5 Tudor City Place, New York, NY 10017, tel. (213) OX 7-1574.

Theatre. Miss Bond made her Bway debut in the chorus of *Let Freedom Sing* (Longacre Th., Oct. 5, 1942); subsequently she appeared in the chorus of *Artists and Models* (Bway Th., Nov. 5, 1943); danced and played the role of the Clerk in *Allah Be Praised* (Adelphi, Apr. 20, 1944); sang, danced, and played Mae Jones in *Street Scene* (Adelphi, Jan. 9, 1947); appeared as a comedienne in the revue *Make Mine Manhattan* (Broadhurst, Jan. 15, 1948); played Ursula Poe in *The Live Wire* (Playhouse, Aug. 17, 1950); Fay Fromkin in *Wish You Were Here* (Imperial, June 25, 1952); Sable Wellington in *Lunatics and Lovers* (Broadhurst, Dec. 13, 1954); substituted (two weeks) for Gwen Verdon as Lola in *Damn Yankees* (46 St. Th., May 5, 1955); Billie Devine in *Deadfall* (Holiday, Oct. 27, 1955); and Gladys in *Pal Joey* (NY City Ctr., May 31, 1961).

Films. She played a comedy role in *The Marrying Kind* (Col. 1952).

Television. Miss Bond has appeared on the Ed Sullivan Show (CBS, 10 appearances, 1947–55); Arthur Murray Show (NBC, 1952); Schlitz Playhouse (CBS, 1952); Playhouse 90 (CBS, 1956); Jack Paar Show (NBC, 1957); and Inside U.S.A.

Night Clubs. She has performed at the Versailles, N.Y.C. (1943); Belmont Plaza, N.Y.C. (1944); La Martinique, N.Y.C. (1945); and the Latin Quarter, N.Y.C. (1946).

Awards. She received the Antoinette Perry (Tony) Award for her performance as Fay Fromkin in *Wish You Were Here* (1953).

Recreation. Tennis, golf, cards, reading.

BOND, SUDIE. Actress, dancer. b. Sudie Stuart Bond, July 13, 1928, Louisville, Ky., to James Roy and Carrie (Showers) Bond. Father, lawyer. Grad. Fassifern Sch., Hendersonville, N.C.; attended Virginia Intermont Coll.; grad. Rollins Coll., B.A. 1950. Grad. studies, New York Univ., 1954. Studied acting with Uta Hagen and Herbert Berghof, N.Y.C., 1954–56; dance with José Limón (1955) Martha Graham (1955), Merce Cunningham (1956) N.Y.C. Married Jan. 5, 1954, to Massen Cornelius Noland, writer (marr. dis. 1958); one son. Member of AEA; SAG; AFTRA; Theta Alpha Phi (pres. 1950). Address: 441 E. 20th St., Apt. 1B, New York, NY 10010, tel. (212) WA 9-8559.

Pre-Theatre. Nursery school teacher.

Theatre. Miss Bond appeared as Mrs. Winemiller in *Summer and Smoke* (Circle in the Square, N.Y.C., Apr. 24, 1952); Olga in *Tovarich* (NY City Ctr., May 25, 1952); Estelle in *Waltz of the Toreadors* (Coronet Th., Jan. 17, 1957); Agnes Gooch in *Auntie Mame* (NY City Ctr., Aug. 11, 1958), and on tour (opened Amer. Shakespeare Th., Stratford, Conn., Apr. 19, 1958; closed Civic Aud., Pasadena Calif., Feb. 4, 1959); Lily in a summer tour of *A Piece of Blue Sky* (June–Aug. 1959); Justine in *The Egg* (Cort, N.Y.C., Jan. 8, 1962).

She appeared as Grandma in *The American Dream* (York, Jan. 24, 1961), which she repeated, and also played Grandma in *The Sandbox,* Nell in *Endgame,* and the title role in *Bertha* in the program entitled *Theatre of the Absurd* (Cherry Lane, Feb. 11, 1962). She played Miss Prose in *Harold* (Cort, Nov. 29, 1962); Mrs. Lazar in *My Mother, My Father, and Me* (Plymouth, Mar. 23, 1963); Vivienne in *Home Movies* and Nona in *Softly, and Consider the Nearness,* which were on the same program (Provincetown Playhouse, May 11, 1964).

She played the Matron in *The Great Western Union* (Bouwerie Lane, Feb. 4, 1965); Miss Hammer in *The Impossible Years* (Playhouse, Oct. 13, 1965); Betsy Jane in *Keep It in the Family* (Plymouth, Sept. 27, 1967); Hana in *The Memorandum* (Anspacher, May 5, 1968); the Old Woman in *Quotations from Chairman Mao-Tse Tung* (Spoleto Festival, Italy, Summer 1968; Billy Rose Th., N.Y.C., Oct. 1968); Grandma in *The American Dream* (Billy Rose Th., Oct. 1968); and various roles in seven short plays by Harold Pinter, presented under the title of *The Local Stigmatic* (Actors Playhouse, Nov. 9, 1969). She succeeded (May 4, 1970) Polly Rowles as Mrs. Margolin in *Forty Carats* (Morosco, Dec. 26, 1968); played Clara in *Hay Fever* (Helen Hayes Th., Nov. 9, 1970); succeeded (1973) Dorothy Leon as Miss Lynch in *Grease* (Eden, Feb. 14, 1972); played the Lady in *Thieves* (Broadhurst, Apr. 7, 1974); as the Mother, joined the cast of *Over Here* (Shubert, Mar. 6, 1974); and played Alma Stone in *The Mind with the Dirty Man* (Bucks County Playhouse, New Hope, Pa., Summer 1974).

Films. Miss Bond appeared in *Andy; A Thousand Clowns* (UA, 1965); Samuel Beckett' *Film; The Tiger Makes Out* (Col., 1967); *They Might Be Giants* (U, 1971); *Cold Turkey* (UA, 1971); *Tomorrow* (Filmgroup, 1972); and *Where the Lilies Bloom* (UA, 1974).

Television. Miss Bond repeated her role of Grandma in *The American Dream* (Camera Three, CBS); *Lily in A Piece of Blue Sky* (Play of the Week, WNTA); Nell in *Endgame* (Camera Three, CBS); and Grandma in *The Sandbox* (Omnibus, NBC). She has also appeared on The Defenders (CBS); Route 66 (CBS); East Side/West Side (CBS); Philco Television Playhouse (NBC); Alcoa Presents (NBC); Armstrong Circle Th., (NBC); Junior Jamboree (CBS); *Saroyan Short Plays* and excerpts from *Home Movies* (both PBS); was Wilma in *The Borgia Stick,* the NBC Saturday Night Movie (Feb. 4, 1967); and appeared as the Mother in the series The New Temperature's Rising (1973).

Night Clubs. She appeared in the revue *Seven Come Eleven* (The Upstairs at the Downstairs, N.Y.C.).

Other Activities. She has appeared as a dancer at the YMHA, Hunter College, and Cooper Union (N.Y.C.); and was one of the four founders of The Paper Bag Players, a children's theatre group.

Awards. Miss Bond received the *Village Voice* off-Bway (Obie) Award for her performances in the plays of the *Theatre of the Absurd* (1962).

Recreation. Swimming, painting.

BONDI, BEULAH. Actress. b. Beulah Bondy, May 3, 1892, Chicago, Ill., to A. O. and Eva M. Bondy. Father, realtor. Attended Convent of the Holy Name of Jesus and Mary, Montreal, Canada, 1907; attended Frances Skinner Acad., 1908; grad. Hyde Park H.S., Chicago, 1909; grad. Valparaiso Univ., B. Oratory, M. Oratory, 1913. Studied at Chicago Little Th. During WW II, served with American Red Cross as Grey Lady, 1942–45; USO hostess; entertained troops with Brentwood Players, six months. Member of AEA; SAG; AFTRA; The Cosmopolitan Club (N.Y.C.) Los Angeles Art Assn.; Motion Picture Mothers Assn. (hon.); Theatre Alliance (N.Y.C., a founder, 1935); Phi Beta (hon.); member of the board: Motion Picture Relief Fund; Motion Picture Relief Fund and Motion Picture Country House, and California Junior Symphony Assn., Inc.

Theatre. Miss Bondi appeared with stock companies in the Midwest (1919–29); Stuart Walker's (Indianapolis, Ind., 1919); and stock companies in Cincinnati and Toledo (1921), Dayton, Ohio (1922), Baltimore, Md. (1924), and Elitch Gardens (Denver, Col., Summers 1926–27).

She made her N.Y.C. debut as Maggie in *One of the Family* (49 St. Th., Dec. 21, 1925); subsequently played Miss Pym in *Mariners* (Plymouth, Mar. 28, 1927); appeared in a tryout of *My Princess* (opened Shubert, Boston, Mass., Oct. 6, 1927); portrayed Mrs. Gorlik in *Saturday's Children* (Booth, N.Y.C., Jan. 26, 1927); Maria Scott in *Cock Robin* (48 St. Th., Jan. 12, 1928); Emma Jones in *Street Scene* (Playhouse, Jan. 10, 1929); Gertrude Rhead in *Milestones* (Empire, June 2, 1930); Mrs. Pike in *Distant Drums* (Belasco, Jan 18, 1932); Mrs. Haggett in *The Late Christopher Bean* (Henry Miller's Th., Oct. 31, 1932); Mrs. Kate Hawkins in *Mother Lode* (Cort, Dec. 22, 1934); Mrs. Crane in *Hilda Crane* (Coronet, Nov. 1, 1950); and Nellie (Granny) in a revival of *On Borrowed Time* (48 St. Th., Feb. 10, 1953).

Films. Miss Bondi appeared in *Street Scene* (UA, 1931); *Arrowsmith* (UA, 1931); *Rain* (UA, 1932); *Stranger's Return* (MGM, 1933); *Christopher Bean* (MGM, 1933); *Finishing School* (RKO, 1934); *Two Alone* (RKO, 1934); *Registered Nurse* (1st Natl., 1934); *Ready for Love* (Par., 1934); *Bad Boy* (20th-Fox, 1935); *The Good Fairy* (U, 1935) *The Invisible Ray* (U, 1936); *The Moon Is Our Home* (Par., 1936) *Hearts Divided* (1st Natl., 1936); *The Gorgeous Hussy* (MGM, 1936); *The Trail of the Lonesome Pine* (Par., 1936; *The Case Against Mrs. Ames* (Par., 1936); *Maid of Salem* (Par., 1937); *Make Way for Tomorrow* (Par., 1937); *Of Human Hearts* (MGM, 1938); *The Sisters* (WB, 1938); *Vivacious Lady* (RKO, 1938); *The Buccaneer* (Par., 1938); *On Borrowed Time* (MGM, 1939); *The Under Pup* (U, 1939); *Mr. Smith Goes to Washington* (Col., 1939); *Remember the Night* (Par., 1940); *The Captain Is a Lady* (MGM, 1940); *Our Town* (UA, 1940); *The Shepherd of the Hills* (Par., 1941); *Penny Serenade* (Col., 1941); *One Foot in Heaven* (WB, 1941); *Tonight We Raid Calais* (20th-Fox, 1943); and *Watch on the Rhine* (WB, 1943).

Also, *She's a Soldier, Too* (Col., 1944); *Our Hearts Were Young and Gay* (Par., 1944); *And Now Tomorrow* (Par., 1944); *The Very Thought of You* (WB, 1944); *I Love a Soldier* (Par., 1944); *The Southerner* (UA, 1945); *Back to Bataan* (RKO, 1945); *Breakfast in Hollywood* (UA, 1946); *Sister Kenny* (RKO, 1946); *It's a Wonderful Life* (RKO, 1946); *High Conquest* (Mono., 1947); *So Dear to My Heart* (Disney, 1948); *The Snake Pit* (20th-Fox, 1948); *The Sainted Sister* (Par., 1948); *Life of Riley* (U, 1949); *Reign of Terror* (Lion-Wanger, 1949); *Mr. Soft Touch* (Col., 1949); *The Baron of Arizona* (Lippert, 1950); *The Furies* (Par., 1950); *Lone Star* (MGM, 1952); *Latin Lovers* (MGM, 1953); *Track of the Cat* (WB, 1954); *Back from Eternity* (RKO, 1956); *The Unholy Wife* (U, 1957); *The Big Fisherman* (Buena Vista, 1959); *A*

Summer Place (WB, 1959); *Tammy Tell Me True* (U, 1961); and *The Wonderful World of the Brothers Grimm* (MGM, 1962).

Television. Miss Bondi appeared on Medallion Th. (CBS, Oct. 1953); Alfred Hitchcock Presents (CBS, Nov. 1955); Climax (CBS, 1956, 1957); Zane Grey Th. (CBS, Apr. 1957); *On Borrowed Time* (Hallmark Hall of Fame, NBC, Nov. 1957); Wagon Train (NBC, 1961); Route 66 (CBS, 1961); *The Hands of Danofrio* (Alcoa Premiere, ABC, Nov. 1962); Perry Mason (CBS, 1962); *She Waits* (CBS, Jan. 1972); The Waltons (CBS, 1973); Dirty Sally (1974); and *Crossing Fox River* (Carl Sandburg's Lincoln, NBC, 1976).

BOOKE, SORRELL. Actor. b. Jan. 4, 1930, Buffalo, N.Y. Grad. Columbia Coll., A.B.; Yale School of Drama, M.F.A. Member of AEA; AFTRA; SAG. Address: c/o Joan Scott, Inc., 162 W. 56th St., New York, NY tel. (212) 246-9029.

Theatre. As a child, Mr. Booke performed on Mutual radio in Buffalo, N.Y. He made his professional stage debut in *Right You Are, If You Think You Are* (July 1950), and his first appearance on stage in N.Y.C. was as Doctor Julio in *The White Devil* (Phoenix, Mar. 14, 1955). This was followed by his performance as the Duke of Albany in *King Lear* (NY City Ctr., Jan. 12, 1956); as a Footman in *A Month in the Country* (Phoenix, Apr. 3, 1956), a production in which he later replaced Luther Adler as Dr. Shpichelsky; Baron Schwarz in *The Sleeping Prince* (Coronet, Nov. 1, 1956); Rip Voorhees in *Nature's Way* (Coronet, Oct. 16, 1957); Abramovitch in *Winkelberg* (Renata Th., Jan. 14, 1958); and the Burglar in *Heartbreak House* (Billy Rose Th., Oct. 18, 1959).

He played Darling in *Caligula* (54 St. Th., Feb. 16, 1960); Sen. Billboard Rawkins in a revival of *Finian's Rainbow* (NY City Ctr., Apr. 27, 1960); was in *Evenings with Chekhov* (Key Th., Apr. 20, 1961); played Ol' Cap'n Cotchipee in *Purlie Victorious* (Cort, Sept. 28, 1961); the title role in a revival of *Fiorello!* (NY City Ctr., June 13, 1962); several roles in *The White House* (Henry Miller's Th., May 19, 1964); Milton Rademacher in *Come Live with Me* (Billy Rose Th., Jan. 26, 1967); and was Updike, Cecil, and Fibber Kidding in *Morning, Noon, and Night* (Henry Miller's Th., Nov. 28, 1968).

Films. Mr. Booke's films include *Gone Are the Days* (Hammer Bros., 1963); *Black Like Me* (Reade, 1964); *Fail Safe* (Col., 1964); *Joy House* (MGM, 1965); and *A Fine Madness* (WB, 1966).

Television. Mr. Booke was in *The Life of Samuel Johnson* (Omnibus, NBC, Dec. 15, 1957); *Little Moon of Alban* (Hallmark Hall of Fame, NBC, Mar. 24, 1958); *The Iceman Cometh* (Play of the Week, WNTA, Nov. 1960); and *Père Goriot* (Masterpiece Th., PBS, June 1971). He has also appeared on Dr. Kildare (NBC); Bob Hope Chrysler Th. (NBC); Twelve O'Clock High (ABC); Slattery's People (CBS); Route 66 (CBS); The Great Adventure (CBS); Naked City (ABC); and DuPont Show of the Week (NBC).

BOOKMAN, LEO. Talent representative. b. Leo Charles Bookman, May 17, 1932, Jersey City, N.J., to Charles and Martha (Beech) Bookman. Grad. Bayonne (N.J.) H.S., 1950; Columbia Univ., B.A., 1953; Columbia Dental Sch., 1953–55. Address: (home) 414 E. 52nd St., New York, NY 10022, tel. (212) PL 5-8823; (bus.) Creative Management Assocs., 600 Madison Ave., New York, NY 10022, tel. (212) 935-4000.

Mr. Bookman was a talent representative with the Baum-Newborn Agency (1955–57) and with MCA (1957–62). From 1962 to 1969, he was a partner in Hesseltine, Bookman and Seff, Ltd. (HBS, Ltd.), talent and literary representatives, which in the latter year merged with Creative Management Associates (CMA). At that time, Mr. Bookman became a vice-pres. in the motion picture dept. of CMA.

BOOTH, JOHN ERLANGER. Writer. b. Aug. 23, 1919, Dobbs Ferry, N.Y. to Aimee (Erstein) Booth. Attended Lawrenceville (N.J.) Sch.; Columbia Univ., 1946–47; and Sorbonne, Paris, 1949. Married 1948 to Janet Pomeroy; one son. Served US Army, 1941–45, two years overseas. Member of Drama Desk (secy., 1962–64). Address: (home) 4 Ploughman's Bush, Riverdale, NY 10471, tel. (212) KI 9-4633; (bus.) c/o Twentieth Century Fund, 41 E. 70th St., New York, NY 10021, tel. (212) LE 5-4441.

Mr. Booth is associate director with the Twentieth Century Fund. He is the author of a report for the Rockefeller Brothers Fund on government support to the performing arts in Western Europe (1964).

Published Works. He wrote, with Lewis Funke, the book, *Actors Talk About Acting* (1961). As a free-lance writer he has contributed articles on theatre to *Theatre Arts* magazine, *Show, Plays and Players,* the New York *Times* Magazine, and the New York *Times.*.

BOOTH, SHIRLEY. Actress. b. Thelma Booth Ford, Aug. 30, 1907, in New York City, to Albert James and Virginia (Wright) Ford. Father, sales manager for I.B.M. Grad. Erasmus Hall H.S., Brooklyn, N.Y. Married 1931 to Edward F. Gardner, actor, producer (marr. dis. 1944; dec. 1963); married 1946 to William H. Baker, investment counselor (dec. 1950). Member of AEA; SAG; AFTRA.

Theatre. Miss Booth first appeared on the stage at the age of twelve, playing small roles with the Poli Stock Co. (Hartford, Conn., 1919). Her NYC debut was as Nan Winchester in *Hell's Bells* (Wallack's Th., Jan. 26, 1925); followed by Betty Hamilton in *Buy, Buy, Baby* (Princess, Oct. 7, 1926); Peggy Bryant in *Laff That Off* (Wallack's, Nov. 2, 1926); Mary Marshall in *High Gear* (Wallack's, Oct. 6, 1927); Emily Rosen in *The War Song* (National, Sept. 24, 1928); Marg in *The School for Virtue* (Longacre, Apr. 21, 1931); Bobby Marchante in *The Camels Are Coming* (President, Oct. 2, 1931); Annie Duval in *Coastwise* (Provincetown Playhouse, Nov. 30, 1931); and Elisa Zanotti in *The Mask and the Face* (Guild, May 8, 1933). She appeared as a principal in a series of comedy vignettes, *After Such Pleasures* (Bijou, Feb. 7, 1934), in the revue, *Sunday Nights at Nine* (Barbizon-Plaza Th., Nov. 11, 1934), and as Mabel in the farce *Three Men on a Horse* (Playhouse, Jan. 30, 1935).

She played Mrs. Loschavio in *Excursion* (Vanderbilt, Apr. 9, 1937); Carrie Nolan in *Too Many Heroes* (Hudson, Nov. 15, 1937); Elizabeth Imbrie in *The Philadelphia Story* (Shubert, Mar. 28, 1939); Ruth Sherwood in *My Sister Eileen* (Biltmore, Dec. 26, 1940); Leona Richards in *Tomorrow the World* (Ethel Barrymore Th., Apr. 14, 1943); Louhedda Hopsons in *Hollywood Pinafore* (Alvin, May 31, 1945); Susan Pengilly in *Land's End* (Playhouse, Dec. 11, 1946); appeared in the pre-Bway tryout of *Heartsong* (opened Shubert, New Haven, Conn., Feb. 27, 1947; closed Walnut St. Th., Philadelphia, Pa., Mar. 29, 1947); was in a revival of *The Cradle Will Rock* (Mansfield Th., N.Y.C., Dec. 26, 1947); played Maggie Welch in *The Men We Marry* (Mansfield, Jan. 16, 1948); Grace Woods in *Goodbye, My Fancy* (Morosco, Nov. 17, 1948); Abby Quinn in *Love Me Long* (48 St. Th., Nov. 7, 1949); and Lola in *Come Back, Little Sheba* (Booth Th., Feb. 15, 1950).

She played Cissy in her first musical, *A Tree Grows in Brooklyn* (Alvin, Apr. 19, 1951); Leona Samish in *The Time of the Cuckoo* (Empire, Oct. 15, 1952); Lottie Gibson in the musical *By the Beautiful Sea* (Majestic, Apr. 8, 1954); Bunny Watson in *The Desk Set* (Broadhurst, Oct. 24, 1955), in which she toured (1956–57); Mrs. Ackroyd in *Miss Isobel* (Royale, N.Y.C., Dec. 26, 1957); Juno Boyle in the musical, *Juno* (Winter Garden, Mar. 9, 1959); the title role in *Nina* (Summer 1959); Fanny in *A Second String* (Eugene O'Neill Th., N.Y.C., Apr. 13, 1960); Mother Maria in *Look to the Lilies* (Lunt-Fontanne Th., Mar. 29, 1970); Judith Bliss in a revival of *Hay Fever* (Helen Hayes Th., Nov. 9, 1970); and as Veta Louise Simmons in *Harvey* (Amer. Conservatory Th., San Francisco, Calif., Sept. 1971).

Films. Miss Booth played Lola in *Come Back, Little Sheba* (Par., 1952); appeared in *About Mrs. Leslie* (Par., 1954); *The Matchmaker* (Par., 1958); and *Hot Spell* (Par., 1958).

Television and Radio. Miss Booth was Miss Duffy on Duffy's Tavern (NBC, 1940–42). On television, she appeared in *The Perle Mesta Story;* in the title role in the series Hazel (NBC, 1961–68); and as Amanda in *The Glass Menagerie* (CBS, Dec. 8, 1966).

Awards. Miss Booth received the Antoinette Perry (Tony) Award for her performance in *Goodbye, My Fancy* (1949); *Come Back, Little Sheba* (1950); and *The Time of the Cuckoo* (1953); for her performance in the film *Come Back, Little Sheba* she received the National Board of Review and NY Film Critics' awards, an Academy (Oscar) Award (1953), and was named "best actress" at the Cannes (France) International Film Festival (1953); for her performance in *The Time of the Cuckoo,* she was awarded the Drama League of New York's Delia Austrian Medal (1953); and for her performance in *The Desk Set,* the Sarah Siddons Award (Chicago, 1957). For her performance in the television series Hazel, she received 28 awards, among them a NATAS (Emmy) Award as best continuing performance by an actress in a series (1962).

Recreation. Painting, knitting, needlework, gardening, interior decorating.

BORCHERS, GLADYS. Educator. b. Gladys Louise Borchers, July 4, 1891, LaValle, Wis., to August and Sophie (Gross) Borchers. Father, farmer; mother, teacher. Grad. public school, LaValle, 1906; Whitewater State Coll., diploma, 1918; Univ. of Wisconsin, Madison, B.A. 1921; M.A. 1925; Ph.D. 1927. Member of SCA; Central States Speech Assn.; Wisconsin Speech Assn.; National Retired Teachers; Intl. Inst. of Arts & Letters; AAUW; AAUP; Delta Sigma Rho; Civics Club; Drama Club; Zeta Phi Eta; Natl. Collegiate Players; Unitarian Church. Address: (home) 1812 Kendall Ave., Madison, WI 53705, tel. (608) 238-1393; (bus.) Univ. of Wisconsin, Dept. of Communication Arts, Madison, WI 53706, tel. (608) 262-2277.

Since 1961, Miss Borchers has been professor emeritus in the Dept. of Communication Arts, Univ. of Wisconsin, where she joined the faculty in 1927 (asst. prof., 1927–34; assoc. prof., 1934–46; prof., 1946–61). She was visiting professor at Louisiana State Univ. (1946–47), Univ. of Hawaii (1949–50), Univ. of Colorado (1961–63), Univ. of Wisconsin Laboratory School (first semester, 1963–64), Brigham Young Univ. (second semesters, 1964–65 and 1969–70) and Illinois State Univ., Normal (second semester, 1965–66). She was visiting professor and distinguished consultant at Taylor Univ. (first semesters, 1964–65 and 1966–67), visiting lecturer at Western Washington State Univ., Bellingham, Wash. (first quarter, 1965–66), and scholar in residence for the humanities, Univ. of Wisconsin, Whitewater (Oct. 1973). In addition she was visiting professor on summer session faculties at Northwestern Univ., Univ. of Utah, Univ. of Colorado, Eastern Washington Univ., Pullman (1966, 1967, 1968), Univ. of Minnesota (1968), and was a consultant at the Univ. of Wisconsin, Stevens Point (1970).

Published Works. Miss Borchers wrote *The New Better Speech* (1937); *English Activities* (1939); *Speech* (1946); *Modern Speech* (1948); *Living Speech* (rev. ed., 1949); author, with A. G. Weaver and D. Smith, of *The Teaching of Speech* (1952); and author of *Speaking and Listening* (1956). She contributed to *Women in College and University Teaching,* Joseph Totaro, ed. (1963); *Communicative Arts and Sciences of Speech,* Keith Brooks, ed. (1967); *History of Speech Education in America,* Karl Wallace, ed. (1967); and a volume in honor of Harry Caplan, John Wilson, ed. In addition, she was editor (1959–63) of *The Speech Teacher,* a publication of the Speech Assn. of America.

Awards. Miss Borchers received the Distinguished Alumni Award, Whitewater Coll. (1958) and the

Andrew T. Weaver Award as Outstanding Speech Teacher for 1973–74, awarded by the Wisconsin Communication Association. She is an honorary member of the German Speech Association, West Germany.

BORETZ, ALLEN. Playwright, composer. b. Aug. 31, 1900, New York City, to Moishe M. and Hanah (Sobel) Boretz. Attended New York City schools; City Coll. of New York; New York Univ. Married 1921, to Elsie Karlen (marr. dis. 1931); married 1931 to Sarah Manney (marr. dis. July 13, 1950); married July 19, 1950, to Ruby Sully, playwright (marr. dis. Apr. 1960). Member of Dramatists Guild; ASCAP (since 1941); AGAC; WGA.

Pre-Theatre. Businessman.

Theatre. Mr. Boretz contributed lyrics to the Bway musicals *Garrick Gaieties* (Guild Th., June 4, 1930); *Garrick Gaieties* (Oct. 16, 1930), which then toured; *Sweet and Low* (46 St. Th., N.Y.C., Nov. 17, 1930); *Night Cruise* (Radio City Music Hall, 1934); with Ned Glass, wrote *The School Teacher* (Provincetown Playhouse, 1936); with John Murray, wrote *Room Service* (Cort, May 19, 1937); with Max Liebman, *Off to Buffalo* (Ethel Barrymore Th., Feb. 21, 1939); contributed material to the Federal Th. (WPA) Project production of *Sing for Your Supper* (Adelphi, Apr. 24, 1939); was producer, with Alfred Bloomingdale, of *Ring Around Elizabeth* (Playhouse, Nov. 17, 1941); wrote and co-produced *The Hard Way* (opened Plymouth, Boston, Mass., Dec. 26, 1940; closed there); with Ruby Sully, wrote *The Hot Corner* (John Golden Th., N.Y.C., Jan. 25, 1956); wrote *The Only Game in Town* (Ivar, Hollywood, Calif., 1959); *Artist in Residence* (Barn Th., Augusta, Mich., Aug. 30, 1964); *Here Come the Butterflies* (Barn Th., Augusta, Mich., July 21, 1964); and *The Hermit's Cock* (Eastside Playhouse, N.Y.C., 1970).

Films. Mr. Boretz co-authored the films *Trouble for Two* (MGM, 1936); *It Ain't Hay* (U, 1943); *Bathing Beauty* (MGM, 1944); *The Princess and the Pirate* (RKO, 1944); *Up in Arms* (RKO, 1944); *Where There's Life* (Par., 1947); *It Had To Be You* (Col., 1947); *Copacabana* (UA, 1947); *Two Guys from Texas* (WB, 1948); and wrote *My Girl Tisa* (UA, 1948).

Television. Mr. Boretz has written for Studio One (CBS); Faith Baldwin Theatre of Romance (ABC); and wrote sketches for Stop the Music.

Published Works. He wrote the songs "Whistling in the Dark"; "So Shy"; "Dark Clouds"; "Got It Again"; "Love Is Like That"; "Beauty"; "Ten Minutes in Bed"; "You're Grand"; "Faces"; and "You're Something To Write Home About.".

Recreation. Playing the piano and the violin, art collecting, reading, traveling.

BORGE, VICTOR. Pianist, humorist. b. Jan. 3, 1909, Copenhagen, Denmark, to Bernhardt and Frederikke (Lichtinger) Borge. Immigrated to the US, 1940; naturalized, 1948. Attended Borgerdydskolen. Studied music at Conservatory of Copenhagen, 1925; piano with Egon Petri, Vienna, Aust.; Frederic Lammond, Berlin, Germany. Married Mar. 17, 1953, to Sarabel Sanna Scraper; one son, two daughters; one son, one daughter by previous marriage. Member of AEA; AFTRA; AGVA; AGMA. Address: Greenwich, CT 06830.

Theatre. Mr. Borge made his debut at thirteen as a concert pianist in Copenhagen (Dec., 1922). In 1934, he wrote, directed, and performed in his own musical revues. In the US, he performed in supper clubs, on radio, and in concert halls. Mr. Borge opened his one-man show *Comedy in Music* (Seattle, Wash.), which subsequently opened on Bway (John Golden Th., Oct. 2, 1953); appeared in this show in London (Palace, 1957); and toured with it throughout Britain, Australia, Scandinavia, Europe, and the US. *Comedy in Music* returned to NY (John Golden Th., Nov. 9, 1964).

Films. Mr. Borge made his debut in Denmark in 1937 and appeared in a number of Danish films for which he also wrote music and scripts.

Television and Radio. On radio, Mr. Borge performed on the Kraft Music Hall, the Victor Borge Show, and Lower Basin Street. He appeared in his one-man show, *Comedy in Music* (1956); repeated his performance in England (BBC, July 31, 1956); and in Australia. He has also appeared in *Victor Borge's Copenhagen*, and in a series of US TV specials in the 1950's and 1960's. He also appeared in a six-part series for BBC-TV in 1974 as well as two BBC-TV specials in 1972 and 1973.

Other Activities. Mr. Borge has been a guest conductor for numerous symphony orchestras around the world.

Published Works. Mr. Borge is the author of *My Favorite Intermissions*, with Robert Sherman (1971).

Discography. Mr. Borge's recordings include the original cast album of *Comedy in Music* (Col.); *Piccolo, Saxie and Company* (Col.); *Victor Borge Plays and Conducts Favorites; Caught in the Act* (Col.); and *Borge's Back* (MGM).

Awards. King Frederik IX of Denmark dubbed Mr. Borge, Knight of the Royal Order of Dannebrog. He is an honorary member of the class of 1961, Univ. of Connecticut; and has been named top personality in British television; Funniest Man in Music (1951); Comedian of the Year (1954); and TV Father of the Year (1958). In 1957, he won the Brotherhood Award. In 1973, the Gold Award was presented to Mr. Borge for Best Public Service TV Commercial, for the Heart Fund, from the International Film and TV Festival of New York; he was awarded the Royal Norwegian Order of St. Olav–Knight First Class, 1973; and he was decorated with the Order of Vasa, Sweden.

BORST, STEPHEN. Director, performer, theatre manager. b. Stephen Earl Borst, Dec. 19, 1944, Philadelphia, Pa., to Maurice and Jane (Richards) Borst. Father, U.S. Naval officer; mother, executive secretary. Educated at Norwich (Vt.) Free Academy; grad. Univ. of Rochester, B.A. (English). Professional training: School of the Arts, N.Y. Univ. (M.F.A. program, acting); Peter Kass; Lloyd Richards; Kristen Linklater. Member of AEA. Address: (home) 455 Hudson St., New York, NY 10014, tel. (212) 691-8239; (bus.) The Performance Group, 33 Wooster St., New York, NY 10013, tel. (212) 966-3651.

Theatre. Mr. Borst first appeared on stage with the Submarine Base Players, New London, Conn., as Ali Hakim in *Oklahoma!* (Sept. 1960) and as Patrick Dennis in *Auntie Mame* (Mar. 1961); and his first professional appearances were at the Warwick (R.I.) Playhouse (July 1967) as Rudolfo in *A View from the Bridge* and Lord Summerhays in *Misalliance*.

While at the Univ. of Rochester, he appeared as John Gay in *Dreaming Dust* (Oct. 1962); Egon in *Tiger at the Gates* (Mar. 1963); Ben in *Fiorello!* (Oct. 1963); Andrei in *The Icicle* (Apr. 1964); several characters in *Danton's Death* (June 1964); Henry in *The Fantasticks* (Feb. 1965); Bassanio in *The Merchant of Venice* (Apr. 1965); the Father in *Look Back in Anger* (Aug. 1965); Krapp in *Krapp's Last Tape* (Oct. 1965); and George in *Who's Afraid of Virginia Woolf?* (May 1966). At Rochester, Borst directed also a production of *The Bald Soprano* (July 1965). At New York Univ., he appeared in *Tartuffe* (Mar. 1967); as the Governor in *The Tavern* (Mar. 1968); and as Lord Foppington in *The Relapse* (Mar. 1969).

In 1969, Mr. Borst joined The Performance Group, an off-Bway organization started by Richard Schechner in 1967, and he first appeared with the group as Macduff in *Makbeth* (Aug. 1969). This was followed by appearances as David Angel in *Commune* (July 1970), repeated at the International Festival, Wroclaw, Poland (Aug. 1970); Galactic Max in *The Tooth of Crime* (Nov. 1972); and the Chaplain in *Mother Courage* (Apr. 1974). Mr. Borst directed The Performance Group's *The Beard* (May 1973). He became co-executive director of The Performance Group in 1972.

Recreation. Travel, cooking.

BORUFF, JOHN. Actor, playwright. b. John Perry Boruff, Jr., Dec. 31, 1910, Mt. Vernon, N.Y., to John Perry and Alice (Sawyer) Boruff. Father, architect's solicitor. Grad. Scarborough Sch., N.Y.C., 1926; attended Blair Acad., Blairstown, N.J., 1926–28; grad. Yale Univ., B.A. 1932. Studied directing, Yale Univ. Sch. of Drama, with Alexander Dean, 1931. Married June 21, 1938, to Helen Shields, actress (marr. dis. 1950); married May 19, 1951, to Vivian Wolfert; one son, one daughter. Served USN, 1942–45; rank, Lt. Cmdr.; served military government in Japan, 1945. Member of AEA; SAG; AFTRA; Dramatists Guild; WGA, East; Alpha Delta Phi.

Theatre. Mr. Boruff made his stage debut as Captain Brassbound in *Captain Brassbound's Conversion* (Yale Univ. Sch. of Drama, New Haven, Conn., 1929); subsequently appeared in *It's a Wise Child* (Westchester Playhouse, Mt. Kisco, N.Y., Summer 1932); made his professional debut as Stephen Hamill, Max, and the Radio Announcer in *Peace on Earth* (Civic Repertory Th., N.Y.C., Nov. 29, 1933); appeared as Gustav Stanewski in *Sailors of Cattaro* (Civic Repertory Th., Dec. 10, 1934), Pavel Vlasov in *Mother* (Civic Repertory Th., Nov. 19, 1935), the Stranger in *Bitter Stream* (Civic Rep. Th., Mar. 30, 1936); and played Buzz, a radio operator, in *Ceiling Zero* (Music Box, Apr. 10, 1935).

Mr. Boruff wrote *Timber House* (Longacre, Sept. 19, 1936); played Vortigern in *The Daughters of Atreus* (44 St. Th., Oct. 14, 1936); and succeeded (March 1937) Donald Randolph as Sir Stephen Scroop in *Richard II* (St. James, Feb. 5, 1937).

He wrote, with Walter Hart, *Washington Jitters* (Guild, May 2, 1938); played Josef Straub in *Waltz in Goose Step* (Hudson, Nov. 1, 1938); Baron Nikolai Vovitch Tusenbach in *The Three Sisters* (Longacre, Oct. 14, 1939); the Newspaper Reporter in *The Male Animal* (Cort, Jan. 9, 1940); wrote *Bright Boy* (Playhouse, Mar. 2, 1944); was understudy to Richard Whorf as Johnny Goodwin in *The Fifth Season* (Cort, Jan. 23, 1953); wrote *The Loud Red Patrick* (Ambassador, Oct. 3, 1956); played Mr. Barrett in the pre-Bway tryout of *One Foot in the Door* (opened Locust St. Th., Philadelphia, Pa., Nov. 6, 1957; closed Shubert, Boston, Mass., Nov. 23, 1957); succeeded (Apr. 1958) Victor Kilian as Dr. McGuire in *Look Homeward, Angel* (Ethel Barrymore Th., N.Y.C., Nov. 28, 1957); played Rabbi Ansbacher in *The 49th Cousin* (Ambassador, Oct. 27, 1960); and appeared as Bentley in *Bicycle Ride to Nevada* (Cort, Sept. 24, 1963).

Films. Mr. Boruff appeared in *Never Love a Stranger* (Allied, 1958).

Television. He made his debut on the series Lights Out (CBS, 1949); subsequently appeared in the serials As the World Turns (CBS, 1958–60); The Brighter Day (CBS, 1960–61); as Henry Benedict in The Guilding Light (CBS, 1962–to date); performed on Studio One (CBS), Philco Television Playhouse (NBC), Kraft Television Th. (NBC), Robert Montgomery Presents (NBC), and the Th. Guild.

BOSCO, PHILIP. Actor. b. Philip Michael Bosco, Sept. 26, 1930, Jersey City, N.J., to Philip Lupo Bosco and Margaret Raymond (Thek) Bosco. Father, carnival worker; mother, policewoman. Grad. St. Peter's Prep. Sch., 1948; Catholic Univ. of Amer., A.B. 1957. Married Jan. 2, 1957, to Nancy Ann Dunkle; two sons, three daughters. Served US Army, Signal Corps, Special Services, ETO, 1951–53; rank, Pvt. Member of AEA; AFTRA; SAG; Catholic Actors Guild. Address: (home) 935 Warren Parkway, Teaneck, NJ tel. (201) 833-0717; (bus.) Hesseltine, Bookman and Seff, Ltd., 200 W. 57th St., New York, NY 10019, tel. (212) LT 1-8850.

Pre-Theatre. Carnival worker, trailer truck driver.

Theatre. Mr. Bosco made his debut as Machiavelli, the Cat, in *The Fairy Cobbler* (St. John's Aud., Jersey City, N.J., 1943); followed by his professional debut as Bohun in a stock production of *You Never Can Tell* (Olney Th., Md., Summer 1954); subsequently appeared in 20 productions (Olney Th., Md., Summers 1954–58); was a resident actor at the Arena Stage (Washington, D.C., Winters 1958–60); appeared as Brian O'Bannion in a touring production of *Auntie Mame* (opened American Shakespeare Festival Th., Stratford, Conn., Apr. 19, 1958; closed

Civic Aud., Pasadena, Calif., Feb. 4, 1959); repeated his role in *Auntie Mame* (NY City Ctr., Aug. 11, 1958); played Angelo in the NY Shakespeare Festival production of *Measure for Measure* (Belvedere Lake Th., July 25, 1960).

He made his Bway debut as Heracles in *The Rape of the Belt* (Martin Beck Th., Nov. 5, 1960); followed by Will Danaher in *Donnybrook!* (46 St. Th., May 18, 1961); and Hawkshaw in *The Ticket-of-Leave Man* (Midway, Dec. 22, 1961). At the American Shakespeare Festival Th. (Stratford, Conn.), he played Bolingbroke in *Richard II* (June 16, 1962), appeared in the title role in *Henry IV, Part 1* (June 17, 1962); played the Earl of Kent in *King Lear* (June 9, 1963), Pistol in *Henry V* (June 12, 1963), Ruffo in *Caesar and Cleopatra* (July 30, 1963), Benedick in *Much Ado About Nothing* (June 9, 1964), Claudius in *Hamlet* (June 16, 1964); and alternated with Stephen Joyce in the title role in *Coriolanus* (June 19, 1965). With the NY Shakespeare Festival, he played the Duke of Buckingham in *King Richard III* (Delacorte, N.Y.C., Aug. 9, 1966).

As a member (1966–73) of the Lincoln Center Repertory Co. (Vivian Beaumont Th.), he played Lovewit in *The Alchemist* (Oct. 13, 1966); Jack in *The East Wind* (Feb. 9, 1967); Sagredo in *Galileo* (Apr. 13, 1967); Dunois in *Saint Joan* (Jan. 4, 1967); Hector in *Tiger at the Gates* (Feb. 29, 1968); Comte de Guiche in *Cyrano de Bergerac* (Apr. 25, 1967); the Earl of Kent in *King Lear* (Nov. 7, 1968); Curtis Moffat, Jr., in *In the Matter of J. Robert Oppenheimer* (Mar. 6, 1969); Zelda and Mr. Gray in *A Great Career,* on a double-bill entitled and including *An Evening for Merlin Finch* (Forum, Dec. 26, 1968); again at the Vivian Beaumont Th., Anselme in *The Miser* (May 8, 1969); Nick in *The Time of Your Life* (Nov. 6, 1969); Baron de Charlus in *Camino Real* (Jan. 8, 1970); Captain Bovine in *Operation Sidewinder* (Mar. 12, 1970); Jupiter in *Amphitryon* (Forum, May 28, 1970); at the Vivian Beaumont Th., First God in *The Good Woman of Setzuan* (Nov. 5, 1970); Jimmy Farrell in *The Playboy of the Western World* (Jan. 7, 1971); Peter Stockmann in *An Enemy of the People* (Mar. 11, 1971); Creon in *Antigone* (May 13, 1971); Robert Dudley in *Mary Stuart* (Nov. 1, 1971); the Prime Minister in *Narrow Road to the Deep South* (Jan. 6, 1972); Antonio in *Twelfth Night* (Mar. 2, 1972); Rev. John Hale in *The Crucible* (Apr. 27, 1972); Mikhail Skrobotov in *Enemies* (Nov. 9, 1972); Cpl. Stoddart in *The Plough and the Stars* (Jan. 4, 1973); Gratiano in *The Merchant of Venice* (Mar. 1, 1973); and Harold Mitchell in *A Streetcar Named Desire* (Apr. 26, 1973).

Films. He played Fuller in *A Lovely Way To Die* (U, 1968).

Television. Mr. Bosco has appeared in *Prisoner of Zenda* (Dupont Show of the Month, CBS, 1960); The Nurses (CBS); The Defenders (CBS); and Armstrong Circle Th. (CBS); For the People (CBS); The Doctors/The Nurses (CBS); Esso Repertory Theater (Ind.); Trials of O'Brien (CBS); Directions '66 (ABC); Art in Our Times (NET); Hawk (ABC); *An Enemy of the People* (NET); *A Nice Place To Visit* (NET); and others.

Awards. Mr. Bosco received the Shakespeare Society of Washington, D.C., Award (1957); won the *Variety* NY Drama Critics' Poll for his performance as Heracles in *The Rape of the Belt* (1961); and was nominated for an Antoinette Perry (Tony) Award (1961) for his performance as Heracles in *The Rape of the Belt.* .

Recreation. All sports (NY Yankee and Cleveland Brown fan), reading, music, movies.

BOSLEY, TOM. Actor. b. Thomas Edward Bosley, Oct. 1, 1927, Chicago, Ill., to Benjamin and Dora (Heyman) Bosley. Father, Lt. Col., US Army (ret.), realtor; mother, saleslady. Grad. Lakeview H.S., 1945; attended De Paul Univ., 1946; Radio Inst. of Chicago, 1947–48. Studied acting with Lee Strasberg (1952). Married Mar. 8, 1962, to Jean Eliot, dancer, singer, actress. Served USN, 1945–46; rank, Seaman 1/c, Radioman. Member of AEA (governing council, 1961–to date); SAG; AFTRA.

Theatre. Mr. Bosley made his stage debut as Simon Stimson in the Canterbury Players production of *Our Town* (Fine Arts Th., Chicago, Ill., 1946); subsequently played Papa Bonaparte in *Golden Boy* (R.I.C. Players, 11 St. Th., Chicago, Ill., June 1947); and appeared at the Woodstock (Ill.) Summer Playhouse (1947–48).

He played Dupont-Dufour Junior in *Thieves Carnival* (Cherry Lane, N.Y.C., Feb. 1, 1955); followed by Homer Bolton in *Morning's At Seven* (Cherry Lane, June 22, 1955); Yakov in *The Seagull* (Fourth St. Th., Oct. 10, 1956); a Villager, a Prisoner, and an Indian in *The Power and the Glory* (Phoenix, Dec. 10, 1956); and Scrub in *The Beaux' Stratagem* (Phoenix, Feb. 24, 1959).

Mr. Bosley made his Bway debut as Fiorello La Guardia in *Fiorello!* (Broadhurst, Nov. 23, 1959); played Izzy Einstein in *Nowhere to Go But Up* (Winter Garden, Nov. 10, 1962); Vince Brinkman in *Natural Affection* (Booth, Jan. 31, 1963); Cabouche in *A Murderer Among Us* (Morosco, Mar. 25, 1964); Inspector Levine in *Catch Me If You Can* (Playhouse in the Park, Philadelphia, Aug. 24, 1964; and Morosco, N.Y.C., Mar. 9, 1965); Milt Manville in the national tour of *Luv* (opened Playhouse, Wilmington, Del., Sept. 6, 1965); Sid in *Take Me Along* (Paper Mill Playhouse, Millburn, N.J., Nov. 15, 1966); the title role in *The Education of H*Y*M*A*N K*A*P*L*A*N* (Alvin, N.Y.C., Apr. 4, 1968); and appeared in *A Shot in the Dark* (Ivanhoe, Chicago, 1970–71 season).

Films. Mr. Bosley made his debut in *Love with the Proper Stranger* (Par., 1963); appeared in *The World of Henry Orient* (Pan-Arts, 1964); played Farley Fronter in *Divorce, American Style* (Col., 1967); the Doctor in *Yours, Mine, and Ours* (UA, 1968); Gen. Pennypacker in *The Secret War of Henry Frigg* (U, 1968); and appeared in *To Find a Man* (Col., 1972); and *Mixed Company* (UA, 1974).

Television. Mr. Bosley made his debut in *Alice in Wonderland* (Hallmark Hall of Fame, NBC, 1953). Subsequent appearances include Teddy in *Arsenic and Old Lace* (Hallmark Hall of Fame, NBC, 1962); Fred in *Focus* (NBC, 1961); Throttle-bottom in *Of Thee I Sing* (CBS); *The Right Man;* Naked City (ABC); The Nurses (CBS); Route 66 (CBS); the Perry Como Show (NBC); The Doctors/The Nurses (CBS); Dr. Kildare (NBC); Car 54, Where Are You? (ABC); Ben Casey (ABC); The Defenders (CBS); Jericho (CBS); The Girl from U.N.C.L.E. (NBC); and his own series, Happy Days (ABC).

Awards. Mr. Bosley won the Antoinette Perry (Tony) Award, the ANTA Award, the Newspaper Guild Page One Award, the *Variety* NY Drama Critics Poll for his performance as Fiorello La Guardia in *Fiorello!* (1960); and the Festival of Leadership Award (Chicago, Ill.).

Recreation. Golf, football, baseball.

BOUGHTON, WALTER. Educator, director. b. Walter Leroy Boughton, Dec. 27, 1918, Toledo, Ohio, to Solon James and Theodora Ferguson (Prince) Boughton. Father, patent attorney. Grad. Shaker Heights (Ohio) H.S., 1937; Brown Univ., A.B. (English) 1941, M.A. (English) 1949; Yale Univ. Sch. of Drama, M.F.A. (play production) 1951; attended the Shakespeare Inst. at Stratford-upon-Avon (England) as a Fulbright Scholar (1951–52). Married June 9, 1950, to Georgia Dagmar Aune; three sons. Relatives in theatre: brother-in-law, Will Hussung, actor; sister-in-law, Allene Aune, producer. Served USAAF, Radar Intelligence Officer, 1941–46; rank, Capt. Member of AEA; ATA (chmn., summer th. project, 1959–61); ANTA; NTC (trustee, 1962). Address: (home) 326 Shays St., Amherst, MA 01002, tel. (413) 253-5844; (bus.) Kirby Memorial Theater, Amherst, MA 01002.

Since 1957, Mr. Boughton has been chairman of the Dept. of Dramatic Arts and director of the Kirby Memorial Th. at Amherst Coll., directing more than 50 plays at the college. He has held academic positions at Brown Univ. (instructor in speech and drama, English Dept. 1947–49); Ripon Coll. (chmn., Drama Dept., 1953–56).

He was visiting director at the Univ. of California at Berkeley, where he directed *The Lower Depths,* and *Camille* (1956–57). Mr. Boughton directed four seasons at Keuka Summer Th. (Keuka Coll., 1950–53); and *Picnic* (Casino Th., Holyoke, Mass., 1960). He became the producer-director of the Weston (Vt.) Playhouse, a summer theatre, in 1972. Since 1950, he has acted in fourteen seasons of summer stock, including the roles of Willy Loman in *Death of a Salesman* (Casino-in-the-Park Playhouse, Holyoke, Mass., July 1962); the Husband in *The Fourposter* (Old Log Th., Excelsior, Minn., June 1954); and a tour as Big Daddy in *Cat on a Hot Tin Roof* with Veronica Lake (Summer 1958).

Mr. Boughton played Landulph in *The Angelic Doctor* (Blackfriars', N.Y.C., 1952–53).

Films. Mr. Boughton had a supporting role in the film *Silent Night, Lonely Night* (U, 1969).

Recreation. Philately, upholstering.

BOURNEUF, PHILIP. Actor. b. Philip Hilaire Bourneuf, Somerville, Mass., to Ambrose F. and Josephine (Comeau) Bourneuf. Father, engineer, draftsman. Grad. Melrose (Mass.) H.S. Married June 27, 1940, to Frances Reid, actress. Served with USAAF, Apr. 1943–Sept. 1945. Member of AEA (council, 1941–43; 1946–54); AFTRA; SAG. Address: 235 Oceano Dr., Los Angeles, CA 90049.

Theatre. Mr. Bourneuf first appeared on stage as an Old Man in a school play (Melrose, Mass.); made his professional debut as the Landlord in a vaudeville sketch entitled "Meadowbrook Lane" (Natl., Boston, Mass., 1930); followed by the role of Count La Ruse in *Children of Darkness* (Peabody Playhouse, Boston, 1930); Lingley in a stock production of *Outward Bound* (Turk's Head Playhouse, Rockport, Mass., Summer 1932); a small role in *The Squeaker* (Copley, Boston, 1932); appeared in stock productions at the Barnstormer's Th. (Tamworth, N.H., Summers 1933–35, 1937), and the Peabody Playhouse (Boston, Winters 1933, 1934).

He made his Bway debut as a walk-on in *The Farmer Takes a Wife* (46 St. Th., Oct. 30, 1934); subsequently played Joe, a Drunk, in *The Night Remembers* (Playhouse, Nov. 27, 1934); an Intern in *Dead End* (Belasco, Oct. 28, 1935); Lessay in *Ten Million Ghosts* (St. James, Oct. 23, 1936); Adolphus Vanderpool in *The Fireman's Flame* (American Music Hall, Oct. 9, 1937); Sir Arthur Chavender in *On the Rocks* (Daly's, June 15, 1938); replaced (two weeks, Summer 1938) Leslie French as Edward Gill in *The Two Bouquets* (Windsor, May 31, 1938); and performed in the revue *One for the Money* (Booth, Feb. 4, 1939).

Mr. Bourneuf appeared in stock at the Ridgefield (Conn.) Playhouse (Summer 1939); toured cross-country as the Lord in the Lunts' *The Taming of the Shrew* (1939–40) and repeated this role in N.Y.C. (Alvin, Feb. 5, 1940); played Jackson in *Medicine Show* (New Yorker, Apr. 12, 1940); appeared in stock at the Ridgefield (Conn.) Playhouse (Summer 1940); played Buckley in *Native Son* (St. James, N.Y.C., Mar. 24, 1941); appeared in stock productions of *Arms and the Man, The Play's the Thing,* and *Biography* (Bucks County Playhouse, New Hope, Pa., Summer 1941); Jaques in *As You Like It* (Mansfield, Oct. 20, 1941); Sir Lucius O'-Trigger in *The Rivals* (Shubert, Jan. 14, 1942), which he repeated on tour (1942); succeeded (June 1942) Allyn Joslyn as Mortimer Brewster in *Arsenic and Old Lace* (Fulton, N.Y.C., Jan. 10, 1941); played Ovid in *The Moon Vine* (Morosco, Feb. 11, 1943); and Buckingham in *Richard III* (Forrest, Mar. 24, 1943).

He appeared as Col. Gibney in the USAAF production of *Winged Victory* (44 St. Th., N.Y.C., Nov. 20, 1943), which he repeated in the cross-country tour (1944–45); played Count Dorante in the pre-Bway tour of *The Would-Be Gentleman* (1945); Dan Curtis in *Flamingo Road* (Belasco, N.Y.C., Mar. 19, 1946); for the American Repertory Th. (Intl. Th.), read the prologue in *Henry VIII* (Nov. 6, 1946), played David Wylie in *What Every Woman Knows* (Nov. 8, 1946), Jerry in *Pound on Demand* and Caesar in *Androcles and the Lion* (Dec. 19,

1946), Dr. Carlos Finlay in *Yellow Jack* (Feb. 27, 1937), and the White Knight in *Alice in Wonderland* (Apr. 5, 1947).

Mr. Bourneuf played the title role in *Rip Van Winkle* (NY City Ctr., July 15, 1947); Curtis in *The Last Dance* (Belasco, Jan. 27, 1948); appeared in stock at the Bucks County Playhouse (New Hope, Pa., Summer 1948); played Captain Shotover in a repertory production of *Heartbreak House* (Copley, Boston, Mass., 1948); Buckingham in *Richard III* (Copley, 1949), which he repeated in N.Y.C. (Booth, Feb. 8, 1949); Joseph Pulitzer in *Miss Liberty* (Imperial, N.Y.C., July 15, 1949); and toured cross-country as Pastor Anderson in *The Devil's Disciple* (1950).

He played Dr. Peter Wilson in *Faithfully Yours* (Coronet, N.Y.C., Oct. 18, 1951); in stock, played Professor Higgins in *Pygmalion* (Bucks County Playhouse, New Hope, Pa., Summer 1952); at NY City Ctr., appeared as Holofernes in *Love's Labour's Lost* (Feb. 4, 1953), and Antonio in *The Merchant of Venice* (Mar. 4, 1953); toured summer theatres as Captain Shotover in *Heartbreak House* (Summer 1953); in repertory, repeated the role of Captain Shotover and played Ludovisi in *Right You Are If You Think You Are* (Brattle Th., Cambridge, Mass., 1953); portrayed Lorenzo Quirini in *The Strong Are Lonely* (Broadhurst, N.Y.C., Sept. 29, 1953); appeared in stock as Edward in *The Cocktail Party* (Bucks County Playhouse, Summer 1954); again played David Wylie in *What Every Woman Knows* (NY City Ctr., Dec. 22, 1954); Dr. Paddy Cullen in *The Doctor's Dilemma* (Phoenix, Jan. 11, 1955); and played Macbeth in the Ann Arbor Festival production of *Gentlemen, the Queens* (Lydia Mendelssohn Th., Univ. of Michigan, 1955), which included *The Great Catherine* and the Jubilee scene from *Victoria Regina*, narrated by Mr. Bourneuf.

He appeared as Mr. Antrobus in *The Skin of Our Teeth* (Boston Arts Festival, 1955); Caesar in a Chicago (Ill.) Th. Society production of *Androcles and the Lion* (Studebaker, 1956); Roberto in a tryout production of *Leave on Love* (Columbia Univ., N.Y.C.; Bucks County Playhouse, Summer 1957); Gremio in *The Taming of the Shrew* (Phoenix, N.Y.C., Feb. 20, 1957); the High Priest in *The Infernal Machine* (Phoenix, Feb. 3, 1958); Dr. Bonfant in a tour of *The Waltz of the Toreadors* (Summer 1958); the Cardinal in two benefit performances of the US premiere of *Port Royal* (Grace Church, N.Y.C., 1959); Prince Nieou in *Lute Song* (NY City Ctr., Mar. 12, 1959); Stephen in a tour of *Hilary* (Summer 1959); narrated and played a variety of roles in a summer tryout of *Mirror Under the Eagle* (Bucks County Playhouse, Summer 1960); played Cherea in *Caligula* (54 St. Th., N.Y.C., Feb. 16, 1960); in repertory, at the Actor's Workshop (San Francisco, Calif.), he played Cornelius Melody in *A Touch of the Poet* and the King of France in *King Lear* (1960); and John Tarleton in *Misalliance* (1961); appeared as Russell in *Best Man* (Playhouse-in-the-Park, Philadelphia, Pa., Summer 1962); Brutus in *Julius Caesar* (North Shore Th., Beverly, Mass., Summer 1963); Enoch Drury in a tour of *Lord Pengo* (Summer 1963); Col. Douglas in *A Case of Libel* (Longacre, N.Y.C., Oct. 10, 1963); Pope Pius XII in *The Deputy* (Theatre Group, Gordon Davidson, Schoenberg Hall, U.C.L.A. Campus, Westwood, L.A., Calif., Aug. 13, 1965); toured as Harry in *A Delicate Balance* (1967); appeared in *A Resounding Tinkle* (Beckman Auditorium Series, Calif. Inst. of Technology, Pasadenia, Calif., 1969); and in *The Greatest Glory* (North Texas State Univ., 1973).

Films. Mr. Bourneuf made his debut as Col. Gibney in *Winged Victory* (20th-Fox, 1944); and has since appeared as d'Estivet in Ingrid Bergman's *Joan of Arc* (RKO, 1948); in *Big Night* (UA, 1951); as a Sikh Chieftain in *Thunder in the East* (Par., 1953); the Prosecutor in *Beyond a Reasonable Doubt* (RKO, 1956); the Mayor in *Everything But the Truth* (U, 1956); the Editor in *Adventure of a Young Man* (20th-Fox, 1962); the Chief Inspector in *Chamber of Horrors* (WB, 1965); Father O'Connor in *The Molly Maguires* (Par., 1967); the Yankee Judge in *The Arrangement* (WB, 1967); the Supreme Court Chief Justice in *The Man* (UA, 1970); and Dr. Willett in *Pete and Tilly* (U, 1972).

Television. Mr. Bourneuf's debut was as Mark Antony in *Julius Caesar* (Studio One, CBS, 1949); since 1949, has appeared on Philco Television Playhouse (NBC), Suspense (CBS), Omnibus (CBS), Hallmark Hall of Fame (NBC), Armstrong Circle Th. (CBS), US Steel Hour (NBC), You Are There (CBS), Danger (CBS), Cameo Th. (NBC), Dupont Show of the Month (NBC), Playhouse 90 (CBS), Matinee Th. (NBC), Alfred Hitchcock Presents (CBS), Alcoa Premiere (ABC), Climax (CBS), Wagon Train (ABC), Gunsmoke (CBS), One Step Beyond (Ind.), Ben Casey (ABC), Dr. Kildare (NBC), Thriller (Ind.), The Defender (CBS), and Perry Mason (CBS). He appeared also in such television film specials as *Istanbul Express* (U); *The Day They Took the Babies Away* (ABC); *Frankenstein* (ABC); *Search; Hec Ramsay; Big Valley;* and *Petticoat Junction* (U). Mr. Bourneuf also did the narration for the bicentennial exhibition in Paris (Charles Eames) in 1973.

Awards. Mr. Bourneuf received a special citation from the NY Drama Critics' Circle (1947), for his performances with the American Repertory Th.

Recreation. Boating, deep-sea fishing, gardening.

BOVA, JOSEPH. Actor. b. Joseph A. Bova, May 25, Cleveland, Ohio, to Anthony and Mary Bova. Father, produce manager. Grad. Northwestern Univ., B.S. (Theatre) 1948; studied acting, at Cleveland Play House, 1953–55; with Lee Strasberg, N.Y.C., 1958–60. Served WW II, US Army, Signal Corps, PTO; rank, Sgt. Member of AEA; SAG; AFTRA. Address: (home) 132 E. 70th St., New York, NY 10021, tel. (212) SU 7-5400; (bus.) c/o Geoffrey Barr, 865 First Ave., New York, NY 10017, tel. (212) PL 1-2441.

Theatre. Mr. Bova appeared as David in a Federal Theatre (WPA) Project production of *It Can't Happen Here* (Cleveland, Ohio, 1938); subsequently appeared in *Stalag 17* (Cleveland Playhouse, Ohio, 1953); played Francis X. Dignan in *King of Hearts* (Cleveland Playhouse, Ohio, 1954); Sakini in *Teahouse of the August Moon* (Chagrin Valley Playhouse, Cleveland, Ohio, 1957).

He made his first N.Y.C. appearance as Chip in *On the Town* (Carnegie Hall Playhouse, Jan. 15, 1959); followed by Prince Dauntless in *Once Upon a Mattress* (Phoenix, May 11, 1959; moved Alvin, Nov. 25, 1959); Tranio in the NY Shakespeare Festival's *The Taming of the Shrew* (Delacorte, Aug. 18, 1960); Theseus in *Rape of the Belt* (Martin Beck Th., Nov. 5, 1960); succeeded (Aug. 1961) Clive Revill as Bob-le-Hotu in *Irma La Douce* (Plymouth, Sept. 29, 1961), and in the subsequent national tour (opened Colonial Th., Boston, Mass., Jan. 4, 1962); appeared as Shim in *Hot Spot* (Majestic, Apr. 19, 1963); and for one week (Oct. 1963) substituted for Orson Bean as Charlie in *Never Too Late* (46 St. Th., Nov. 27, 1962).

Mr. Bova played Louie in *Thursday Is a Good Night* (tour, Summer 1964); Junior Mister in *The Cradle Will Rock* (Th. Four, N.Y.C., Nov. 11, 1964); The Common Man in *A Man for All Seasons* (Royal Poinciana Playhouse, Palm Beach, Fla., Feb. 8, 1965; and Paper Mill Playhouse, Millburn, N.J., Feb. 16, 1965); Costard in *Love's Labour's Lost* (Delacorte, N.C., June 9, 1965); Thersites in *Troilus and Cressida* (Delacorte, Aug. 4, 1965); Charlie Bickle in *The Well-Dressed Liar* (Royal Poinciana Playhouse, Palm Beach, Fla., Mar. 7, 1966; and Coconut Grove Playhouse, Miami, Fla., May 31, 1966); the title role in *King Richard III* (Delacorte, N.Y.C., Aug. 3, 1966); Stanley Tibbets in the pre-Bway production of *The Unemployed Saint* (Parker Playhouse, Fort Lauderdale, Fla., Mar. 13, 1967); Antipholus of Ephesus in *A Comedy of Errors* (Delacorte, N.Y.C., Summer 1967); Mercutio in *Romeo and Juliet* (Delacorte, N.Y.C., Summer 1968); Monsieur Pierre in *Invitation to a Beheading* (Public Th., Mar. 8, 1969); Mr. Lee in *The Chinese* (Ethel Barrymore Th., Mar. 10, 1970); appeared in *House of Blue Leaves* (Truck and Warehouse Th., Feb. 10, 1971); Coviello in the pre-Bway production of *Comedy* (Colonial Th., Boston, Nov. 6–18, 1972); and Jake Jackson in *An American Millionaire* (Circle in the Square/Joseph E. Levine Th., N.Y.C., Apr. 20, 1974).

Films. Mr. Bova appeared in *The Young Doctors* (UA, 1961); and *Pretty Poison* (20th-Fox, 1968).

Television and Radio. He was director of radio programs and producer-writer-actor of Children's TV programs (NBC, Cleveland, Ohio, 1951–54); producer-writer-actor on Time for Fun and Little Rascals (ABC, 1955–58).

He repeated his role in *Once Upon a Mattress* (CBS, June 3, 1964); played Kook in *The Good Old Days* (Vacation Playhouse, CBS, 1966); appeared in Hawk (ABC, 1966); and played Oscar in *The World of Günter Grass* (NY Television Th., Educ., 1967).

Awards. Mr. Bova received the Edgar Bergen Scholarship to Northwestern Univ.; the Northwestern Acting Award (1948); and the AFTRA Award for best written and produced children's program (1954).

Recreation. Swimming, golf, bridge.

BOVASSO, JULIE. Actress, director, producer, playwright. b. Aug. 1, 1930, Brooklyn, N.Y., to Bernard Michael and Angela (Padovani) Bovasso. Father, truck driver. Grad. H.S. of Music and Art, N.Y.C., 1948; attended City Coll. of New York, 1948–51. Studied acting in N.Y.C., with Herbert Berghof, 1950–51; Uta Hagen, 1951–53; Mira Rostova, 1953–55; and Harold Clurman, 1961. Married Feb. 4, 1951, to George Ortman, painter (marr. dis. 1958), married Aug. 12, 1959, to Leonard Wayland, actor (marr. dis. 1964). Member of AEA; AFTRA; SAG; Dramatists' Guild; Author's League of America. Address: 14 W. 10th St., New York, NY 10011, tel. (212) 228-4377.

Theatre. Miss Bovasso made her debut at age 13 as a Maid in *The Bells* (Davenport Free Th., N.Y.C., Aug. 3, 1943). For The Rolling Players (N.Y.C.), she played Gwendolyn in *The Importance of Being Earnest,* and the title roles in *Salome* and *Hedda Gabler* (1947–49).

She played Belissa in *Don Perlimplin* (Studio Th. of Komissarjevski, May 21, 1949); Lona Hessel in *Pillars of Society* (Globe Repertory Th., July 18, 1949); at the Provincetown Playhouse, played Emma in *Naked* and Countess Geschwitz in *Earth Spirit* (June 6, 1950); Zinida in *He Who Gets Slapped* (Th. Workshop, Oct. 10, 1950); the title role in the Living Theatre's production of *Faustina* (Cherry Lane, May 25, 1952); and with the San Francisco (Calif.) Repertory Co., played Anna Petrovna in *Ivanov* (Nov. 28, 1952).

In 1953, Miss Bovasso established the Tempo Th. (N.Y.C.), serving as manager-actress, introducing to the US the works of Genet, Ionesco and de Ghelderode, and appearing there as Margot in *The Typewriter* (Aug. 4, 1953); Madeleine in *Amedée* (Oct. 31, 1954); Claire in *The Maids* (May 6, 1955), and Solange in its revival (May 18, 1956); the Student in *The Lesson;* and produced and directed *Escurial* (Oct. 2, 1956).

She played Henriette in *Monique* (John Golden Th., Oct. 22, 1957); Luella in *Dinny and the Witches* (Cherry Lane, Dec. 9, 1959); the Wife in *Victims of Duty* (ANTA Matinee Series, Jan. 19, 1960); Lucy and Martha in *Gallows Humor* (Gramercy Arts, Apr. 18, 1961); at the American Shakespeare Festival, Mistress Quickly in *Henry IV, Part 1* (Stratford, Conn., June 11, 1962); and Madame Rosepettle in *Oh Dad, Poor Dad, Mamma's Hung You in the Closet and I'm Feelin' So Sad* (Playhouse-in-the-Park, Cincinnati, Ohio, Apr. 22, 1964). She wrote and directed *The Moon Dreamers* (La Mama E.T.C., 1968; Ellen Stewart Th., Dec. 8, 1969); wrote, directed, and played Gloria B. Gilbert in *Gloria and Esperanza* (La Mama E.T.C., 1969; ANTA Th., Feb. 4, 1970); wrote and directed *Schubert's Last Serenade* (La Mama E.T.C., 1971; Manhattan Th. Club, 1973); *Monday on the Way to Mercury Island* (La Mama E.T.C., 1971); appeared as the Mother in *The Screens* (Brooklyn Acad. of Music, N.Y.C., Dec. 7, 1971); and wrote *Down by the River Where Waterlilies Are Disfigured Every Day* (Trinity Square Rep. Th., Providence, R.I., Dec. 20, 1971; Circle Rep. Co.,

N.Y.C., Mar. 24, 1975). Miss Bovasso was briefly connected with the NY Shakespeare Festival in 1973, at that time becoming the first woman director at Lincoln Center, where she directed *The Boom Boom Room* (Vivian Beaumont Th.) until Joseph Papp dismissed her during previews of the play.

Television. Miss Bovasso has appeared on From These Roots (NBC, 1958–60); played in *The Iceman Cometh* (Play of the Week, WNTA, 1960); *Man on a Mountain* and *Two Black Kings* (US Steel Hour, CBS, 1961); and *The Colossus* (The Defenders, CBS, 1963).

Other Activities. Miss Bovasso was on the Theatre Dept. faculty New School for Social Research (1967–72) and was a faculty associate, Theatre Dept., Sarah Lawrence College (1969–74).

Awards. Miss Bovasso received two *Village Voice* off-Bway (Obie) awards in 1956: for her performance as Claire in *The Maids* and for the best experimental theatre, Tempo. She received three Obies in 1970—for writing, directing, and acting in *Gloria and Esperanza.* In 1972, she received the Drama Desk Award and the Outer Circle Critics Award for her performance in *The Screens,* and she received the Public Broadcasting Award for *Schubert's Last Serenade.* For playwriting, she received a Rockefeller Foundation Award in 1970, NY State Council on the Arts Public Service grants in 1971 and 1973, and a Guggenheim Fellowship in 1972.

BOWDEN, CHARLES. Producer, actor, director, lecturer. b. Charles Francis Bowden, Aug. 7, Somerville, Mass., to John and Elizabeth (Rose) Bowden. Father, contractor. Grad. Harvard Univ., B.A. 1935. Married Feb. 22, 1953, to Paula Laurence, actress. Served US Army, 1941–45; rank, Capt.; awarded commendation and Bronze Star. Member of AEA; League of NY Theatres; SSD&C; Catholic Actors Guild (vice-pres.); St. Jude Apostolate (life member); Actors Fund of America (auction committee). Address: (home) 263 West End Ave., New York, NY 10023, tel. (212) 873-8994; (bus.) 230 W. 41st St., Suite 1300, New York, NY 10036, tel. (212) 736-2762.

Theatre. Mr. Bowden began as an actor in a production of *The Drunkard* (Wharf Players, Provincetown, Mass., Summer 1929); subsequently appeared with the New London (N.H.) Players in *Ah, Wilderness!, Meet the Prince, Hedda Gabler, In Any Language,* and *Dr. Knock* (Summers 1930–32); with the Ford Hall Forum, played in *The Three Sisters, Gold in Them Hills, or The Dead Sister's Secret,* and *The Proposal* (Boston, Mass., 1930–32).

He made his N.Y.C. debut as an orderly in *Ten Million Ghosts* (St. James, Oct. 23, 1936); played several walk-ons in *The Eternal Road* (Manhattan Opera House, Jan. 7, 1937); Demetrius in Tallulah Bankhead's *Antony and Cleopatra* (Mansfield Th., Nov. 10, 1937); walk-ons in the Maurice Evans production of *Hamlet* (St. James, Oct. 12, 1938); Shadow in Mr. Evans' *Henry IV, Part 1* (St. James, Jan. 30, 1939); toured as Pantaloon and the Tailor in the Lunt-Fontanne production of *The Taming of the Shrew* (1940); and was stage manager for the touring company of *There Shall Be No Night* (1941).

He was technical director for *O Mistress Mine* (Empire, Jan. 23, 1946); played Reilly in *I Know My Love* (Shubert Th., Nov. 2, 1949); was managing director at Westport (Conn.) Country Playhouse (1948–53); owned and operated the British Colonial Th. (Nassau, B.W.I., 1950–52); and the New Parsons Th. (Hartford, Conn., 1952–54).

With Philip Langner, in association with Peter Cookson, he produced *Seagulls Over Sorrento,* which he also directed (John Golden Th., N.Y.C., Sept. 11, 1952); produced *At Home with Ethel Waters* (48 St. Th., Sept. 22, 1953); presented Ruth Draper (Vanderbilt, Jan. 25, 1954); he presented Ruth and Paul Draper (Bijou, Dec. 26, 1954); *All in One,* which included Paul Draper, Leonard Bernstein's *Trouble in Tahiti* and Tennessee William's *27 Wagons Full of Cotton* (Playhouse, Apr. 19, 1955); *Fallen Angels,* which he also directed (Playhouse, Jan. 17, 1956); *Ruth Draper and Her Company of Characters* (Playhouse, Dec. 25, 1956); was a producer of *Hotel Paradiso* (Henry Miller's Th., Apr. 11, 1957); was a producer and director for three touring companies of *Auntie Mame* (1957–59); directed and produced a touring company of *Romanoff and Juliet* (opened Topeka, Kans., 1959); produced and directed *Season of Choice* (Barbizon-Plaza, N.Y.C., Apr. 13, 1959); produced *Caligula* (54 St. Th., Feb. 16, 1960); and produced and directed *The Night of the Iguana* (Royale, Dec. 28, 1961); he produced *Slapstick Tragedy* (Longacre, Feb. 22, 1966); directed *Song of the Grasshopper* (ANTA, Sept. 28, 1967); produced a tour of *Streetcar Named Desire* (1969–70); produced *The Changing Room* (Morosco, Mar. 6, 1973); and has been associated with the Tony awards telecast since 1971.

Other Activities. Mr. Bowden has lectured on various aspects of the theatre, at schools and colleges, women's clubs, and civic organizations.

BOWERS, FAUBION. Author. b. Jan. 29, 1917, Miami, Okla., to Powell Clayton and Emily Robinson (Brouk) Bowers. Father, insurance salesman; mother, schoolteacher. Attended Univ. of Oklahoma, 1933–34; Columbia Univ., 1935–36; Université de Poitiers, France, 1937; Juilliard Grad. Sch. of Music, 1939; studied music with Katherine Ruth Heyman, 1935; Alfred Cortot, 1936; and Alexander Ziloti, 1939. Married Oct. 20, 1951, to Santha Rama Rau, playwright, author (marr. dis. 1968); one son. Served WW II, US Army, PTO; civilian censor of the Japanese theatre, 1945–49, ADC to Gen. D. MacArthur; rank, Major; awarded Bronze Star and Oak Leaf Cluster. Member of Scriabin Circle (founder, 1932). Address: 205 E. 94th St., New York, NY 10028, tel. (212) 876-4390.

Theatre. Mr. Bowers is the author of the play *The Daytime Moon* (Actors Studio, N.Y.C., 1962).

Television and Radio. Mr. Bowers frequently appears on Camera Three (CBS) in cultural programs on Bali, Kabuki, Bunraku, and music programs devoted to such composers as Liszt, Scriabin, and Mahler. He has done frequent radio series in the US and Canada on Scriabin, Rachmaninoff, and other musicians.

Published Works. He is the author of *Japanese Theatre* (1952); *Dance in India* (1952); *Broadway: U.S.S.R.* (1958); *Theatre in the East* (1960); *Scriabin, A Biography of the Russian Composer 1871–1915* (1969); *Japan: Islands of the Rising Sun* (1973); *The New Scriabin* (1974); and is a frequent contributor of articles, reviews, and criticisms to *The New Yorker, Theatre Arts, Holiday, Harper's, The Nation,* and *The New Republic.*

Works in progress include *The Unuttered Code* and *Frogs from the Well.*

BOWLES, PAUL. Composer, writer. b. Paul Frederick Bowles, Dec. 30, 1910, Jamaica, N.Y., to Dr. Claude Dietz and Rena (Winnewisser) Bowles. Father, dentist. Attended Sch. of Design and Liberal Arts, N.Y.C., 1928; Univ. of Va., 1928–30. Studied composition with Aaron Copland. Married Feb. 21, 1938, to Jane Sidney Auer, playwright, novelist (dec.). Member of ASCAP. Address: (home) Itesa, Campoamor, Tangier, Morocco; (bus.) c/o William Morris Agency, 1740 Broadway, New York, NY 10019, tel. (212) JU 6-5100.

Theatre. Mr. Bowles' first Bway score was the incidental music for the Federal Theatre Project's production of *Horse Eats Hat* (Maxine Elliott's Th., Sept. 26, 1936); followed by his music for FTP's production of *Dr. Faustus* (Maxine Elliott's Th., Jan. 8, 1937). He composed a ballet score, *Yankee Clipper* (1937); and an opera, *Denmark Vesey* (1937); incidental music for *My Heart's in the Highlands* (Guild, Apr. 13, 1939); *Love's Old Sweet Song* (Plymouth, May 2, 1940); *Twelfth Night* (St. James, Nov. 19, 1940); *Liberty Jones* (Shubert, Feb. 5, 1941); and *Watch on the Rhine* (Martin Beck Th., Apr. 1, 1941).

He wrote a ballet score, *Pastorelela* (1941); the opera *The Wind Remains* (Museum of Modern Art, 1943); incidental music for the play *South Pacific* (Cort, Dec. 29, 1943); and *Jacobowsky and the Colonel* (Martin Beck Th., Mar. 14, 1944); composed the score for the ballet *Sentimental Colloquy* (world premiere, International, Oct. 30, 1944); music for *The Glass Menagerie* (Playhouse, Mar. 31, 1945); *Twilight Bar* (Ford's, Baltimore, Md., Mar. 12, 1946) which closed during its pre-Bway tour (Walnut St. Th., Philadelphia, Pa., Mar. 23, 1946); *On Whitman Avenue* (Cort, N.Y.C., May 8, 1946); *The Dancer* (Biltmore, June 5, 1946); and a revival of *Cyrano de Bergerac* (Alvin, Oct. 8, 1946).

He wrote the English adaptation of Sartre's *No Exit* (Biltmore, Nov. 26, 1946); composed incidental music for *Land's End* (Playhouse, Dec. 11, 1946); *Summer and Smoke* (Music Box, Oct. 6, 1948); the NY City Ctr. production of *Cyrano de Bergerac* (Nov. 11, 1953); *In the Summer House* (Playhouse, Dec. 29, 1953); and the revival of *The Glass Menagerie* (NY City Ctr., Nov. 21, 1956). He wrote the music for the song "Heavenly Grass" in *Orpheus Descending* (Martin Beck Th., Mar. 21, 1957); and the ballet score *Blue Roses* (1957); composed incidental music for *Edwin Booth* (46 St. Th., Nov. 24, 1958); *Sweet Bird of Youth* (Martin Beck Th., Mar. 10, 1959); and the first Bway production of *The Milk Train Doesn't Stop Here Anymore* (Morosco, Jan. 16, 1963).

Films. Mr. Bowles has written music for the Dept. of Agriculture film *Roots in the Soil* (1940); and for *Congo* (1944), produced by the Belgian government in exile.

Published Works. He is author of *The Sheltering Sky* (1949), *The Delicate Prey and Other Stories* (1950), *Let It Come Down* (1952), *The Spider's House* (1955), *Their Heads Are Green and Their Hands Are Blue* (1963), *The Time of Friendship* (1967), and *Without Stopping* (1972).

Awards. He received a Guggenheim Fellowship (1941) and a Rockefeller Grant (1959).

BOWMAN, WALTER P. Educator, writer. b. Walter Parker Bowman, Nov. 13, 1910, New Haven, Conn., to Isaiah and Cora (Goldthwait) Bowman. Father, university president; mother, educator. Grad. Yonkers (N.Y.) H.S., 1927; Bowdoin Coll., A.B. 1931; attended Univ. of Cambridge, England, 1931–32; grad. Columbia Univ., M.A. 1933, Ph.D. 1942; attended Univ. of Paris (de la Sorbonne), 1936–37. Married June 28, 1946, to Erna Henschke, social worker; one son. Served USAAF, 1942–46; rank, Capt. Member of Modern Language Assn. (chmn., comparative literature group, Anglo-French lit. relations, 1951); Milton Society of Amer. (treas., 1952–61; exec. comm., 1962–64); American Name Society; ASTR; Natl. Council of Teachers of English; AAUP; Montgomery, Md., Light Opera Assn. (business mgr., 1960); Lake Wentworth (N.H.) Assn. (dir.; pres. 1963–to date); Schools Comm., Montgomery County Civic Fed. (chmn., 1960–61); Orchardale (Md.) Civic Assn. (pres., 1958–59); Boy Scouts (counselor). Address: (home) 107 West Ave., Brockport, NY 14420, tel. (716) NE 7-5411; (bus.) Dept. of English, State University College, Brockport, NY 14420, tel. (716) NE 7-3161.

Since 1963, Mr. Bowman has been professor of English at the State Univ. Coll., Brockport, N.Y. He began his academic career as an instructor at Arden School, Staten Island, N.Y. (1933–34); was assistant in the English Dept. at Lycée Malherbe, Caen, France (1934–35); instructor of English at Lafayette Coll., Pa., (1935–36). Other academic positions include Hopkins Sch., New Haven, Conn. (instructor, 1937–39); Marietta Coll., Ohio (assistant professor, 1946–47); Western Reserve Univ. (associate professor 1947–50); Amer. Univ., Washington, D.C. (professor, 1950–53); Amer. Language Inst., Baghdad, Iraq (director, 1957); Amer. Language Ctr., Washington, D.C. (lecturer, 1958–61). During 1961–63, he was assistant supervisor of research, Montgomery County, Md., public schools.

Published Works. Mr. Bowman wrote, with Robert H. Ball, *Theatre Language, A Dictionary of Terms in English of the Drama and Stage from Medieval to Modern Times* (1961). He has contributed articles to *Theatre Arts, Modern Language Notes,* and *French Review;* and served as advisor to the publishers and authors of *English Literature and Its Background* (1949).

Awards. At Bowdoin Coll., Mr. Bowman received the Pray Prize as best student in English, the Poetry Prize, and the Hawthorne Short Story Prize.

Recreation. Swimming, sailing, music, civic work, Boy Scout work.

BOWMAN, WAYNE. Educator, writer, director, designer. b. Wayne Eno Bowman, July 28, 1914, Rouses Point, N.Y., to Harold E. and Evalina (Marshall) Bowman. Father, immigration inspector. Grad. Kempsville H.S., Princess Anne, Va., 1931; Elon Coll., A.B. 1937; Univ. of North Carolina, A.M. (English) 1940; A.M. (dramatic art) 1947. Married July 30, 1944, to Jean V. Dudley, commercial artist; three sons. Served USNR, 1941–45; rank, Lt. (sg). Member of AETA; SETC; AAUP. Address: (home) 1800 St. Denis Ave., Norfolk, VA 23509, tel. (804) MA 3-4561; (bus.) Dept. of English, Old Dominion College, Norfolk, VA 23508, tel. MA 7-8651.

Since 1962, Mr. Bowman has been associate professor of English at Old Dominion Coll., where he has been a member of the faculty since 1954 (lecturer, 1954–55; assistant professor, 1955–62). He has held academic positions in the North Carolina public schools (instructor of English, mathematics and band director, 1937–40); No. Georgia Coll. (instructor of English, director of dramatics, 1940–41); and the Women's Coll. of the Univ. of North Carolina (assistant professor of English and dramatics, technical director of the theatre, 1947–54), where he designed and directed approximately twenty one productions. He was lighting director for the Roanoke Island Historical Association's production of *The Lost Colony* (July 1947).

Published Works. Mr. Bowman wrote *Modern Theatre Lighting* (1957), and has contributed articles and reviews to *Players* Magazine.

Recreation. Music, reading.

BOWMER, ANGUS L. Educator, director, producer. b. Angus Livingston Bowmer, Sept. 25, 1904, Bellingham, Wash., to Charles C. and Flora Bowmer. Father, printer and newspaper editor. Grad. Oak Harbor H.S., Wash., 1922; Western Washington Coll. of Education, Life Teaching Cert. 1926; Univ. of Washington, B.A. 1930, M.A. 1934. Married Dec. 30, 1940, to Gertrude M. Served US Army, 1942–43. Member of AEA; ATA; ANTA; Northwest Drama Conf. (bd. of dir., 1960–63); International Inst. of Arts and Letters (life fellow). Address: (home) 1280 Madrone, Ashland, OR 97520, tel. (503) 482-0292; (bus.) Box 27, Ashland, OR 97520, tel. (503) 482-2111.

From 1935 to 1970, Mr. Bowmer, as producing director of the Oregon Shakespearean Festival which he founded, produced thirty-seven Shakespearean plays in a total of ninety-one productions; directed twelve Shakespearean plays in twenty-nine productions; and played thirty different characters in forty-three productions, including Shylock in *The Merchant of Venice* in nine productions.

Mr. Bowmer was a teacher and administrator in the public schools of the State of Washington (1924–30); and has been a professor of drama at Southern Oregon Coll., where he has taught courses in theatre and lectured on Shakespearean and Elizabethan theatre (1931–to date).

Other Activities. In 1974, President Ford appointed Mr. Bowmer to the National Council on the Arts.

Awards. Mr. Bowmer received the distinguished service awards from the Univ. of Oregon (1961) and from Oregon State Univ. (1967); a special award for his contribution to the arts in the Northwest from the Washington State Arts Commission (1966); Western Washington State College Distinguished Alumnus award (1974); and the Edith Knight Hill Memorial Award for "outstanding contribution to Oregon" given by the Portland professional chapter of Theta Sigma Phi (1964). Honorary D.F.A. degrees were conferred on him by the Univ. of Portland (1964) and Lewis and Clark Coll. (1967).

BOYD, SAM, JR. Educator. b. Aug. 22, 1915, Pittsburgh, Pa., to Sam and Mary (O'Neil) Boyd. Grad. Taylor Alderdice H.S., Pittsburgh, 1934; Carnegie Inst. of Tech., B.F.A. 1940; M.F.A. 1949. Married Feb. 9, 1947, to Frances Bason; one son, one daughter. Member of Speech Assn. of Eastern States (Editor of Newsletter, 1957–59; vice-pres., 1959–60; pres., 1960–61); SAA; AETA; Delta Tau Delta (faculty adviser). Address: (home) 249 Grandview Ave., Morgantown, WV 26505, tel. (304) LI 2-5493; (bus.) Division of Drama, West Virginia University, Morgantown, WV 26505, tel. (304) LI 9-3411.

Since 1943, Mr. Boyd has been director of drama at West Virginia Univ., where he has been instructor (1943); assistant professor (1947); associate professor (1951); professor (1960); chairman of the Division of Drama in the Creative Arts Center (1964); and director of more than 100 productions in university theatre.

Mr. Boyd appeared with the Chatauqua Players (N.Y., 1938, 1939); the Fox Chapel Playhouse (Pittsburgh, Pa., 1940); and directed a medical drama for the AMA National Convention (Pittsburgh, Pa., 1941).

Radio. Mr. Boyd appeared in the African explorer series (NBC, 1938); and a series on the postal service (CBS, Pittsburgh, Pa.).

Awards. Mr. Boyd received a West Virginia Faculty Summer Fellowship to study European modes of theatre education (1961); the West Virginia Univ. Outstanding Teaching Award (1973); the university's Division of Drama's Outstanding Service Award; and the West Virginia State High School Drama Festival Award for originating and contributing to this activity.

Recreation. Boating, deep sea fishing.

BOYLE, E. ROGER. Educator, director. b. Eldridge Roger Boyle, Jr., May 10, 1907, Washington, D.C., to Eldridge Roger and Louise (Dixon) Boyle. Father, civil engineer. Grad. Sidwells Friends Sch., Washington, D.C., 1924; Univ. of Virginia, B.S. 1930; attended Yale Sch. of Drama, 1930–31; grad. Univ. of North Carolina, M.A. 1939. Married Dec. 27, 1932, to Sarah Patton; two sons. Member of ANTA; AETA; SAA; SSA; SETC; (chairman coll. & univ. section 1963–64), Va. Speech & Drama Assn. (pres., 1951–52), Farmington Country Club, Colonnade Club. Address: (home) Box 3138, University of Virginia, P.O., Charlottesville, VA 22903, tel. (804) 293-8683; (bus.) 144 Cabell Hall, University of Virginia, Charlottesville, VA 22903, tel. (804) 295-2166.

Since 1960, Mr. Boyle has been chairman of the Dept. of Speech and Drama at the Univ. of Virginia, where he has taught since 1930.

He is the director of the Virginia Players; was associate director of the outdoor historical drama *The Common Glory* (Williamsburg, Va., 1947), and director of the same play (1948).

Recreation. Photography.

BOYT, JOHN. Designer, producer, writer. b. John Thomas Boyt, Apr. 19, 1921, Newark, N.J., to Alexander and Marjorie W. Boyt. Father, consulting marine engineer, surveyor. Grad. Bloomfield (N.J.) H.S., 1938; attended Union Coll., 1938–41; grad. Univ. of Iowa, B.A. 1942; attended Northwestern Univ., 1943. Studied at Mohawk Drama Festival, Schenectady, N.Y., 1939–40. Member of United Scenic Artists, Local 829. Address: 423 Madison Ave., New York, NY 10017, tel. (212) MU 8-9140.

Pre-Theatre. Educator.

Theatre. Mr. Boyt designed costumes for *A Flag Is Born* (Alvin, N.Y.C., Sept. 5, 1946); sets and costumes for *The Playboy of the Western World* (Booth, Oct. 26, 1946); costumes for *Years Ago* (Mansfield, Dec. 3, 1946); the men's costumes for *Antony and Cleopatra* (Martin Beck Th., Nov. 26, 1947); and directed an ELT production of *Richard III* (Lenox Hill Playhouse, Feb. 13, 1948).

During 1951, he was a member of the Brattle Th. Co. (Cambridge, Mass.). He designed the setting for *Misalliance* (NY City Ctr., Feb. 18, 1953; moved to Ethel Barrymore Th., Mar. 6, 1953); costumes for NY City Opera's productions of Aaron Copland's *The Tender Land* (NY City Ctr., world premiere, Apr. 1, 1954) and sets and costumes for its production of *Falstaff* (NY City Ctr., Apr. 14, 1954); and costumes for *Carousel* (NY City Ctr., June 2, 1954).

He designed the setting for NY City Ballet's production of *Western Symphony* (NY City Ctr., Sept. 7, 1954); costumes for *The Wooden Dish* (Martin Beck Th., Oct. 6, 1955); settings and costumes for NY City Opera's production of *Troilus and Cressida* (NY City Ctr., Oct. 20, 1955); setting and costumes for *Debut* (Holiday, Feb. 22, 1956); costumes for *The Lovers* (Martin Beck Th., May 10, 1956); designed *Exiles* (Renata, Mar. 12, 1957); setting and lighting for *The Girl of the Golden West* (Phyllis Anderson Th., Nov. 5, 1957); sets for the tour of *Look Homeward, Angel* (opened Playhouse, Wilmington, Del., Oct. 21, 1959); lighting for *Sweet Confession*, presented on a double-bill with *I Rise in Flame, Cried the Phoenix* (ANTA Matinee Th. Series, Th. de Lys, Apr. 14, 1959); scenery for the pre-Bway tryout of *Odd Man In* (opened Playhouse, Wilmington, Del., Oct. 1, 1959); closed Memorial Aud., Burlington, Iowa, Mar. 5, 1960); the settings for the London production of *Come Blow Your Horn* (Prince of Wales's, Mar. 1962); the sets and lighting for *The Queen and the Rebels* (Th. Four, N.Y.C., Feb. 25, 1965); supervised the costumes for *Danton's Death* (Vivian Beaumont Th., Oct. 21, 1965); designed *Private Lives* (Studio Arena Th., Buffalo, N.Y., July 7, 1966); designed the costumes for a tour of *Dear Love* (opened Alley, Houston, Tex., Sept. 17, 1970; closed Shubert, New Haven, Conn., Jan. 16, 1971); and designed sets and costumes for the Center Stage Company of Baltimore, Md., in their 1972–1973 season.

Television. Mr. Boyt was art director for WENR-TV, Chicago (ABC, 1948–51), also wrote mystery and dramatic plays for this network (1949), and directed and produced dramatic and musical shows (1949–51). During 1952, he was head of the costume dept. of NBC Television (N.Y.C.).

Recreation. History, cuisine, seashore.

BRACKEN, EDDIE. Actor, director, singer, writer. b. Edward Vincent Bracken, Feb. 7, 1920, Astoria, N.Y., to Joseph L. and Catherine (D.) Bracken. Father, foreman, East River Gas Co.; mother, saleslady, demonstrator for Con Edison. Attended The Professional Sch. for Actors, N.Y.C. Studied with the Homer Sisters, Astoria, two years; yrs.; Katherin Billamann, N.Y.C., four years; Harriet Lee, Hollywood, Calif., three years. Married Sept. 25, 1939, to Connie Nickerson, actress; two sons, three daughters. Member of AEA; SAG; AFRA; AGVA; The Lambs.

Theatre. Mr. Bracken first appeared on a stage at age six, as the Purser in *The Good Ship Leviathan* for the Knights of Columbus (Astoria, N.Y.). He made his professional debut on Bway as a Western Union Boy in *The Man on Stilts* (Plymouth, Sept. 9, 1931); subsequently played Hank Parkes in *The Lady Refuses* (Bijou, Mar. 7, 1933); a Boy in *The Drunkard* (American Music Hall, Mar. 10, 1934); Alfred in *Life's Too Short* (Broadhurst, Sept. 20, 1935); Cadet Brown in *So Proudly We Hail* (46 St. Th., Sept. 22, 1936); and a Plumber in *Iron Men* (Longacre, Oct. 19, 1936).

He succeeded (June 1937) Frank Albertson as Billy Randolph in *Brother Rat* (Biltmore, Dec. 16, 1936); appeared as Bill in *What a Life* (Biltmore, Apr. 13, 1938); Henry Aldrich in the national touring company of the latter play; played Henry Aldrich and directed a summer theatre production of *What a Life* for the Bass Rocks Th. (Aug. 1939); and played Jo Jo Jordan in *Too Many Girls* (Imperial, N.Y.C., Oct. 18, 1939).

During WW II, he entertained the servicemen in camps and hospitals throughout the South Pacific and in the US; subsequently played Richard Sherman in the national touring company of *The Seven*

Year Itch (opened Cass, Detroit, Mich., Sept. 7, 1953); repeated the latter role in N.Y.C. (Fulton, May 28, 1955); succeeded (Apr. 1956) Burgess Meredith as Sakini in the national touring company of *The Teahouse of the August Moon* (opened Hartman, Columbus, Ohio, Dec. 16, 1954; closed Colonial, Boston, Mass., June 23, 1956); appeared in summer theatre tours, as Richard Sherman in *The Seven Year Itch* and as Charlie Reader in *The Tender Trap* (Summer 1956); toured as George MacCauley in *Will Success Spoil Rock Hunter?* (1956–57); and appeared as Archy in *Shinbone Alley* (Bway Th., N.Y.C., Apr. 13, 1957).

Mr. Bracken played Erwin Trowbridge in *Three Men on a Horse* (Drury Lane Th., Chicago, Ill., Sept. 1957); Charley Wykeham in *Where's Charley?* (Music Th., Columbus, Ohio, June 1958); and as Kreton in *Visit to a Small Planet* (Grist Mill Playhouse, Andover, N.J., July 1958). He played Augie Poole in the national company of *Tunnel of Love* (opened Veterans War Memorial Aud., Columbus, Ohio, Oct. 4, 1958; closed Coliseum, Evansville, Ind., Dec. 6, 1958); made winter stock and summer theatre appearances as Richard Sherman in *The Seven Year Itch,* and Jack Jordan in *Say, Darling* (1959); played Pistol in *Beg, Borrow or Steal,* which he produced, with Carroll and Harris Masterson (Martin Beck Th., Feb. 10, 1960); and made various stock appearances, as Fergie Howard in *The Golden Fleecing,* the Leprechaun in *Finian's Rainbow,* in *The Shemansky Affair,* and as Ensign Pulver in *Mr. Roberts* (1960).

Mr. Bracken directed *How to Make a Man* (Brooks Atkinson Th., N.Y.C., Feb. 2, 1961); in subsequent winter stock and summer theatre appearances, repeated the roles of Sakini in *The Teahouse of the August Moon* and Charlie Reader in *The Tender Trap* (1962); performed in *Come Blow Your Horn* (1963).

He played Richard Sherman in *The Seven Year Itch* (Little Th., Sullivan, Ill., June 16, 1964); appeared in *Damn Yankees* (Municipal Th., St. Louis, Mo., July 27, 1964); played the First Man in *A Thurber Carnival* (Bucks County Playhouse, New Hope, Pa., June 28, 1965); Mr. Kris Kringle in *Here's Love* (Charlotte, N.C., Summer Th., July 27, 1965); Pseudolus in *A Funny Thing Happened on the Way to the Forum* (Piccolo Playhouse, Joliet, Ill., Aug. 3, 1965); succeeded (Oct. 25, 1965) Paul Dooley in the role of Felix Ungar in *The Odd Couple* (Plymouth Th., N.Y.C., Mar. 10, 1965); and played Harvard Bevans in *Hot September* (Shubert Th., Boston, Sept. 14, 1965).

Mr. Bracken is a co-owner of Staircase Theater, N.Y.C., and produces under the auspices of Eddie Bracken Ventures, Inc.

Films. He made his debut as the Rich comedies in a series of four *Our Gang* comedies (Hal Roach, 1920's); appeared in six episodes of the *Kiddie Troupers* series (20th-Fox, 1920's); subsequently performed as Dizzy in *Life with Henry* (Par., 1941); Jo Jo Jordan in *Too Many Girls* (RKO, 1940); *Reaching for the Sun* (Par., 1941); Bert in *Caught in the Draft* (Par. 1941); *Sweater Girl* (Par., 1942); *The Fleet's In* (Par., 1942); Jimmy Webster in *Star Spangled Rhythm* (Par., 1942); Wally Case in *Happy Go Lucky* (Par., 1943); George Bodell in *Young and Willing* (UA, 1943); Jones in *The Miracle of Morgan's Creek* (Par., 1944); Woodrow Truesmith in *Hail the Conquering Hero* (Par., 1944); Toby Smith in *Rainbow Island* (Par., 1944); Herbie Fenton in *Out of This World* (Par., 1944); J. Newport Bates in *Bring On the Girls* (Par., 1945); "Himself" in *Duffy's Tavern* (Par., 1945); Ogden Spencer Trulow III in *Hold That Blonde* (Par., 1945); Henry Haskell in *Ladies Man* (Par., 1947); Paterson Price Porterhouse III in *Fun on a Weekend* (UA, 1947); *The Girl From Jones Beach* (WB, 1949); *Summer Stock* (MGM, 1950); *Two Tickets to Broadway* (RKO, 1951); *We're Not Married* (20th-Fox, 1952); *About Face* (WB, 1952); and *A Slight Case of Larceny* (MGM, 1953); narrated *Wild, Wild World* (Sokoler, 1965); and provided the voice of archy in *Shinbone Alley* (AA, 1971).

Television and Radio. Mr. Bracken was, at first, a radio gag writer for The Bob Hope Show (NBC, 1934–36). As an actor, he made his debut as Dizzy on The Henry Aldrich Show (NBC, 1939). He has had his own show in Hollywood, Calif., The Eddie Bracken Radio Show (NBC, CBS, Feb. 1945–47); and in Bay Shore, L.I., N.Y., (WB-IC, Sept. 1963–to date).

He made his television debut in *Front Row Center* (CBS, Jan. 1956); subsequently appeared in *Finley's Fan Club* (Climax, CBS, Jan. 1956); was emcee for Masquerade Party (NBC, Apr. 1957); appeared on Studio One (CBS, Aug. 1957); The General Motors 50th Anniversary Show (NBC, Nov. 1957); the Dinah Shore Show (NBC, 1959); and in *Strawberry Blonde* (NBC, 1959); archy the Cockroach, in *Archy and Mehitabel* (Play of the Week, WNTA, May 1960); The Roaring 20's (ABC, 1961); Rawhide (CBS, 1962, 1963); and Burke's Law (ABC, 1963); Showcase (NBC, 1964); Creative Person (Educ., 1965); was a guest on the Ernie Ford Show (ABC, 1964–65); Memory Lane (Ind., 1965–66); and Step This Way (Ind., 1966–67).

Night Clubs. He has appeared at The Boulevard (Queens, N.Y.C., 1931); and The Last Frontier (Las Vegas, Nev., 1953).

Other Activities. For the Sunrise Press, which owns a chain of 12 Long Island newspapers, he has written a syndicated column, *Crackin' with Bracken* (July 1963–to date). He has made sketches of members of the Lambs which are exhibited in the club.

Awards. He has received awards from the American Cancer Society, The Chicago Heart Association, and Mount Sinai Hospital. He was winner of the "Out of this World" Baseball Series Award (Hollywood C. of C.); the National Box Office Awards; the Red Book Award; the *Box Office Digest* "Honor Box"; and received the Centennial (television) Club Award (1959).

Recreation. Golf, chess, baseball, football, boxing.

BRADEN, WALDO W. Educator. b. Waldo Warder Braden, Mar. 11, 1911, Ottumwa, Iowa, to W. C. and Stella (Warder) Braden. Father, insurance agent. Grad. Oskaloosa (Iowa) H.S., 1929; William Penn Coll., B.A. 1932; State Univ. of Iowa, M.A. 1938; Ph.D. 1942. Married 1938, to Dana Crane; one daughter. Served US Army, 1943–45. Member of SAA (exec. secy., 1954–57; pres., 1962); SSA; SSCA (pres., 1969–70); Amer. Studies Assn. Address: (home) 535 Ursuline Dr., Baton Rouge, LA 70808, tel. (504) 766-5671; (bus.) Department of Speech, Louisiana State University, Baton Rouge, LA 70803, tel. (504) 388-4172.

Since 1958, Mr. Braden has been chairman of the Dept. of Speech at Louisiana State Univ., where he has been on the faculty since 1946 and where he was appointed Boyd Professor of Speech in 1973. He was held academic positions at Fremont (Iowa) H.S. (1933–35); Mt. Pleasant (Iowa) H.S. (1933–38); and Iowa Wesleyan Coll. (1938–46).

Other Activities. Lecturer.

Published Works. Mr. Braden has contributed articles to the journals, *The Forensic, The Speech Teacher, Quarterly Journal of Speech, Speech Monographs, Dramatics* Magazine, *The Southern Speech Journal, F.D.R. Collector, The Kansas Historical Quarterly,* and *The Journal of Illinois State Historical Society.* He wrote with G. W. Gray, *Public Speaking, Principles and Practices* (1951; rev. ed. 1963); with Earnest Brandenburg, *Oral Decision-Making* (1955); with Mary Louise Gehring, *Speech Practices, A Resource Book for the Student of Public Speaking* (1958); and was editor and author of four and a half chapters of *Speech Methods and Resources, A Textbook for the Teaching of Speech* (1961; 2nd ed., 1972). In addition, he wrote with John H. Pennybacker, *Broadcasting and the Public Interest* (1969); *Public Speaking: The Essentials* (1966); edited with Dorothy I. Anderson, *Lectures Read to the Seniors in Harvard College* by Edward T. Channing (1968); wrote with Lester Thonssen and A. Craig Baird, *Speech Criticism* (1970); and edited *Oratory in the Old South* (1970); He contributed a chapter, "Research for Debate," to *Argumentation and Debate* (1954); a chapter, "Franklin Roosevelt," written with Earnest Brandenburg, for *History and Criticism of American Public Address* (1955); a chapter, "The Political Speaking of William E. Borah," to *American Public Address, Studies in Honor of Albert Craig Baird* (1961); and a chapter, "The Campaign for Memphis, 1860" to *Anti-Slavery and Disunion* (1963). He also edited *Representative American Speeches* (1971, 1972, and 1973).

BRADY, LEO B. Educator, actor, director, playwright. b. Leo Bernard Brady, Jan. 23, 1917, Wheeling, W.Va., to Joseph and Nannie (Beans) Brady. Father, bookbinder. Attended Central Catholic H.S., Wheeling, 1929–31; grad. St. Paul's Acad., Washington, D.C., 1933; Catholic Univ., Washington, D.C., A.B. (Phi Beta Kappa) 1941, M.A. 1942. Studied playwriting with Walter Kerr, 1941; speech with Josephine Callan, 1941; and directing with Alan Schneider, 1942. Married Apr. 17, 1945, to Eleanor Buchroeder; four sons, four daughters. Served US Army, 1942–46. Member of WGA; AAUP; AEA. Address: (home) 3605 Dunlop St., Chevy Chase, MD 20015, tel. (301) OL 2-6512; (bus.) Department of Speech and Drama, Catholic University, Washington, DC 20017, tel. (202) LA 9-6000, ext. 351.

In 1957, Mr. Brady became a professor in the Dept. of Speech and Drama, Catholic Univ., Washington, D.C., where he had been an instructor (1946–47); assistant professor (1947–52); and associate professor (1952–57).

Theatre. Mr. Brady was co-author, with Walter Kerr and Nancy Hamilton, of *Count Me In* (Ethel Barrymore Th., N.Y.C., Oct. 8, 1942). At the Olney (Md.) Theatre, he played Hector Malone in *Man and Superman* and Jack Jordan in *Say Darling* (1953); directed *The Cocktail Party* (1954); *Ondine* (1958); *Electra* (1960); *Arms and the Man* and *The Matchmaker* (both 1962); *Romulus* (1963); wrote and directed *The Bum's Rush* (1964); directed *Hay Fever* (June 1, 1971) and *Child's Play* (Aug. 24, 1971). He also directed *Juno and the Paycock* (Hartke Th., Catholic Univ., Washington, D.C., Jan. 7, 1972); and, again at the Olney Th., directed *The Effect of Gamma Rays on Man-in-the-Moon Marigolds* (June 20, 1972); *The Patrick Pearse Motel* (Aug. 22, 1972); *Private Lives* (June 5, 1973); and *The Tavern* (Aug. 28, 1973).

Television. Mr. Brady wrote *Luck of Luke McTrigger* (Studio One, CBS, 1956); adapted *Oresteia* (Omnibus, NBC, 1959); and wrote *Broken Pitcher* (Look Up and Live, CBS, 1963).

Published Works. He wrote *The Edge of Doom* (1949), for which he received the Catholic Writers Best Fiction Award (1959); *Brother Orchid;* and *Signs and Wonders.* He has contributed reviews of the Washington, D.C., theatrical season to several of the annual *Best Plays* volumes edited by Otis Guernsey.

BRAMLEY, RAYMOND. Actor. b. July 19, 1891, Independence, Ohio, to George H. and Alice (Rose) Bramley. Father, contractor. Grad. Central H.S., Cleveland, 1906; Shenandoah Coll., 1910; AADA, 1913; studied voice with Homer Mowe, N.Y.C., 1935. Married Aug. 3, 1920, to Edith Speare, actress. Served US Army, 1918–19; rank, PFC. Member AEA; AFTRA; SAG; The Lambs. Address: (home) 347 West 55 St., New York, NY 10019, tel. (212) CI 5-4979; (bus.) c/o The Lambs, 130 West 44 St., New York, NY 10036, tel. (212) 265-9495.

Theatre. Mr. Bramley made his stage debut in minor roles with the Louise Coleman Players in summer theatre productions (Shubert, Rochester, N.Y., June–Aug. 1913); subsequently toured in a vaudeville sketch, *The Common Law,* on the Keith circuit (1914); and played in such stock companies as the Palace Players (Palace Th., Houston, Tex., 1923), and the St. Charles Players (New Orleans, La., 1925).

His first appearance on Bway was as Tracy Sutton in *Not Herbert* (52 St. Th., Jan. 26, 1926); followed by the pre-Bway tryout of *The Pushover* (closed Brooklyn, N.Y., 1926); on Bway, succeeded Fred Irving Lewis (Oct. 1926) as George Hildreth in *If I Was Rich* (Mansfield, Sept. 2, 1926); appeared in the pre-Bway tryout of *Please Stand By* (closed

Hartford, Conn., 1927); appeared as Doc Rice in the N.Y.C. production of *The Barker*(Biltmore, Jan. 28, 1927); Higgins in *The House Unguarded* (Little, Jan. 15, 1929); and in the pre-Bway tryout of *The Crooks' Convention* (Atlantic City, N.J., 1929); and played a season of summer stock (Elitch Gardens, Denver, Colo., 1930).

In N.Y.C., he appeared as Judge Gohagan in *This Is New York* (Plymouth, Nov. 28, 1930); played in stock with the National Players (National Washington, D.C., Spring 1931); appeared as Joe Day in a N.Y.C. production of *The Man on Stilts* (Plymouth, Sept. 9, 1931); Papa Gouli in *East Wind*(Manhattan, Oct. 27, 1931); and Inspector Quick in *The Black Tower* Harris, Jan. 11, 1932); played in stock with the National Players (National, Washington, D.C., Spring 1932); on Bway, portrayed De Witt C. Rubensohn in *Keeping Expenses Down* (National, Oct. 20, 1932); succeeded Stanley Ridges (Fulton, 1933) as Charles Stanton in *Dangerous Corner* (Empire, Oct. 27, 1932); appeared as Jacot in *Her Man of Wax* (Shubert, Oct. 11, 1933); Mathard in *Three and One* (Longacre, Oct. 25, 1933); and Marcus in *Theodora, the Queen* (Forrest, Jan. 31, 1934).

Also, he played in stock with the National Players (National, Washington, D.C., Spring 1934); appeared on Bway as Dr. Panayot Tsankov in *Judgment Day* (Belasco, Sept. 12, 1934); Wilbur Hanley in *Cross Ruff* (Masque, Feb. 19, 1935); and in stock with the National Players (National, Washington, D.C., Spring 1935); played the Radio Announcer in a Bway production of *Whatever Goes Up* (Biltmore, Nov. 25, 1935); Ernesto Trivelli in *Tomorrow's a Holiday* (Golden, Dec. 30, 1935); Sorrel Freely in *The Golden Journey* (Booth, Sept. 15, 1936); Inspector Laker in *The Holmeses of Baker Street* (Masque, Dec. 9, 1936); and in a pre-Bway tryout of *In a Nutshell* (closed Cleveland, Ohio, 1938).

Also, Mr. Bramley appeared as Dr. Humphreys and understudied the role of Father in a touring production of *Life with Father* (opened Hartford, Conn., 1942); in N.Y.C., appeared as George Slater in *Sleep No More* (Cort, Aug. 31, 1944); played Sir Lawrence Wargrave in a USO touring production of *Ten Little Indians* (ETO, 1945), and subsequently toured the play in the US and Canada; on Bway, portrayed Cleasy in *Hear That Trumpet* (Playhouse, Oct. 7, 1946); Oliver Crandell in *A Young Man's Fancy* (Plymouth, Apr. 29, 1947); Major John Groh in *Two Blind Mice* (Cort, Mar. 2, 1949); Frederick Newberry in *One Bright Day* (Royale, Mar. 19, 1952); Chauffourier-Dubieff in *Tovarich* (NY City Ctr., May 14, 1952); Thomas Putnam in *The Crucible* (Martin Beck Th., Jan. 22, 1953); and Granville Prescott in *Wake Up, Darling* (Ethel Barrymore Th., May 2, 1956).

He also appeared as Vanhattan in *The Apple Cart* (Plymouth, Oct. 18, 1956); Laurent in the pre-Bway tryout of *The Gay Felons* (opened Playhouse, Wilmington, Del., Feb. 12, 1959; closed Locust St. Th., Philadelphia, Pa., Mar. 14, 1959); in N.Y.C., appeared as Purdy in *Tenderloin* (46 St. Th., Oct. 17, 1960); and succeeded Rufus Smith as the Senator in *Fiorello!* (Broadhurst, Nov. 23, 1959).

Films. Mr. Bramley played in *Vagabond King* (Par., 1930); Col. Bernal in *Broken Arrow* (20th-Fox, 1950); *Outside the Wall* (U, 1950); and *The Sun Sets at Dawn* (Ind., 1950).

Television. His TV credits include Playhouse 90 (CBS), Kraft Television Th. (NBC), Robert Montgomery Presents (NBC), Armstrong Circle Th. (CBS), Studio One (CBS), Philco Playhouse (NBC), The Defenders (CBS), Th. Guild (CBS), and You'll Never Get Rich (NBC).

Recreation. Reading, acting.

BRAND, OSCAR. Author, performer, playwright, composer. b. Feb. 7, 1920, Winnipeg, Manitoba, Canada, to I. Z. and Beatrice (Shulman) Brand. Father, Indian interpreter for Hudson's Bay Co. Educ. Erasmus Hall H.S., N.Y.C.; grad. Brooklyn College, B.A. (psychology) 1942. Married May 10, 1955, to Rubyan Antonia Schwaeber (marr. dis.); three children; married June 14, 1970, to Karen Lynn Grossman. Served US Army (psychologist, 1942–44; newspaper editor, 1944–45); unit citation; special merit citation. Member of AFM; AFTRA; ACTRA (Canada); SAG; Newport Festival Foundation (dir., trustee, 1964–to date); Songwriters Hall of Fame (1970–to date). Address: 141 Baker Hill, Great Neck, NY 11023, tel. (516) 487-5979.

Theatre. Mr. Brand was music director for *In White America* (Sheridan Square Playhouse, N.Y.C., May 31, 1964). With Paul Nassau, he wrote the music and lyrics for *A Joyful Noise* (Mark Hellinger Th., Dec. 15, 1966) and for *The Education of H*Y*M*A*N K*A*P*L*A*N* (Alvin, Apr. 4, 1968); wrote, with W. V. Brown, music and lyrics for *How To Steal an Election* (Oct. 13, 1968); wrote the book, music, and lyrics for *The Bridge* (Greenwich Mews Th., Nov. 28, 1972). He has appeared in summer stock at Schroon Lake, N.Y., in such presentations as *Carousel; Oklahoma!; HMS Pinafore;* and *Fall of the City.*

Films. Mr. Brand has made eighty-eight industrials and documentaries, and he wrote the songs for *The Fox* (Claridge, 1968).

Television. Among the many television programs on which Mr. Brand has appeared are Whistlestop (CBS, 1947); the Kate Smith Hour and Americana (both NBC, 1948); Presidential Timber (CBS, 1952); the Longines Hour (ABC, 1955); and Draw Me a Laugh (ABC, 1956). He was host on the Bell Telephone Hour (CBC, 1963); music director of Exploring (NBC, 1964); appeared on The Right Man (CBS, 1964); on Sunday (NBC, 1965); and was star and host of Let's Sing Out (CBC, 1966); Brand New Scene (CBC, 1967); and American Odyssey (NET, 1970). He is currently host of CBC's Touch the Earth and the NPR series Voices in the Wind and critic-reviewer for CBC's Arts in Review. In addition to his many network appearances, Mr. Brand served as a member of the board that created Sesame Street (NET) in 1968.

Radio. On radio, Mr. Brand was host of Folk Song Festival (WNYC, 1945–74; played the lead on Dr. Christian (CBS, 1948); and was soloist on Citizen of the World (CBS, 1949). He has been on many other radio programs.

Night Clubs. Mr. Brand has played engagements in many night clubs, including the Troubadour, Exodus, Village Gate, and the Bitter End, all in N.Y.C.

Concerts. Mr. Brand's first stage appearance was as narrator for a performance of *Peter and the Wolf* (Midwood Auditorium, N.Y.C., 1938). Since that time he has given many concerts throughout the US and Canada.

Other Activities. Mr. Brand has been on the faculties of the New School for Social Research (1968–to date) and Hofstra Univ. (1969–to date).

Published Works. Mr. Brand has published *Singing Holidays* (1957); *Bawdy Songs* (1958); *Folk Songs for Fun* (1962); *Counting's a Pleasure* (1963); *The Ballad Mongers* (1964); *Songs of '76* (1972); and *When I First Came to This Land* (1974). He has also issued ten song folios (1945–to date).

Discography. Mr. Brand has made fifty-seven long-playing records.

Awards. Mr. Brand was made gaudete at Fairfield (Conn.) Univ. in 1973. Among the numerous honors he has received throughout his career are awards at the Venice and Edinburgh festivals; the Golden Reel; the Golden Lion; Emmy award; Thomas Alva Edison Award; Freedoms Foundation award; *Scholastic* award; the Peabody award; and Ohio State award.

Recreation. Sailboating, carpentry.

BRAND, PHOEBE. Actress, director, teacher. b. Phoebe Elizabeth Brand, Nov. 27, 1907, Syracuse, N.Y., to George and Inez (Trowbridge) Brand. Father, engineer; mother, school teacher. Attended Ilion (N.Y.) H.S., 1920; Stamford (Conn.) H.S., 1921–22; grad. The Low and Heywood Sch., Stamford, Conn., 1924; attended Clare Tree Major's Sch. of the Th., N.Y.C., 1924–25; studied Shakespeare with Isabelle Manson (1926–27); singing with Dudley Buck (1927–28); dancing with Michael Mordkin (1926–27), Michio Ito (1927–28) and Lotte Goslar (1939–42); speech with Elizabeth Merson (1926–28); singing with Keith Davis (1962–63); coached by Milton Shafer (1962); studied at the Group Th. with Lee Strasberg, Stella Adler, Morris Carnovsky, Helen Tamiris (1930–40). Married Sept. 17, 1941, to Morris Carnovsky, actor; one son. Member of AEA; SAG; AFTRA. Address: (home) 309 W. 104th St., New York, NY 10025, tel. (212) UN 5-5560; (bus.) American Academy of Dramatic Arts, 120 Madison Ave., New York, NY 10016.

Theatre. Miss Brand made her stage debut as a Princess in a Clare Tree Major children's production of *The Golden Apple;* followed by Veronika in *The Piper*and Luciana in *The Comedy of Errors* (Princess Th., N.Y.C., Apr. 1926); was understudy and appeared (in repertory) at the Royale Th. in the chorus of Gilbert and Sullivan's *The Mikado* (Sept. 17, 1927), *Iolanthe* (Nov. 14, 1927) and *The Pirates of Penzance* (Nov. 24, 1927); at the Actors Playshop, Inc. (Stamford, Conn.), played Lady Jane Walton in *Spring Cleaning* (July 1928) and See Fah in *The Blue Butterfly* (Aug. 1928); toured with the Th. Guild as the Little Singer in *Volpone* and a Lady-in-Waiting in *Marco Millions* (Oct. 1928); appeared in the chorus of *The Silver Swan* during its pre-Bway tour (Boston, Summer 1929); toured as Dame Van Winkle in the Tony Sarg marionette production of *Rip Van Winkle* (1929–30); and played Ellen in *Elizabeth the Queen* (Guild, N.Y.C., Nov. 2, 1930).

As a member of the Group Th., Miss Brand played one of the Serenaders in *The House of Connelly* (Martin Beck Th., Sept. 28, 1931); the Girl in *1931* (Mansfield, Dec. 10, 1931); and Nuna in *Night Over Taos* (48 St. Th., Mar. 9, 1932); and portrayed Nina in *The Seagull* (Hollis St. Th., Boston, Mass., May 17, 1932).

With the Group Th., she appeared as Winnie Murphy in *Big Night* (Maxine Elliott's Th., N.Y.C., Jan. 17, 1933); Barbara Dennin in *Men in White* (Broadhurst, Sept. 26, 1933); one of the girls of the "Mantic" and Elizabeth Jolais in *Gold Eagle Guy* (Morosco, Nov. 28, 1934); Hennie Berger in *Awake and Sing* (Belasco, Feb. 19, 1935; reopened Belasco, Sept. 9, 1935); Violet Jobes in *Weep for the Virgins* (46 St. Th., Nov. 30, 1935); Roberta Alden in *The Case of Clyde Griffiths* (Ethel Barrymore Th., Mar. 13, 1936); Minnie Belle Tompkins in *Johnny Johnson* (44 St. Th., Nov. 19, 1936); and Anna Banana in *Golden Boy* (Belasco, Nov. 4, 1937; St. James's, London, June 21, 1938).

Miss Brand played Colomba in the Actors Laboratory production of *Volpone* (Las Palmas Th., Hollywood, Calif., July 9, 1945); directed the Negro Art Th. production of *Golden Boy* (1950); played Rifkele in *The World of Sholem Aleichem* (Barbizon-Plaza, N.Y.C., Sept. 1953); was stand-by for Lillian Roth in *I Can Get It for You Wholesale* (Shubert, Mar. 22, 1962); adapted and directed the double-bill *A Portrait of the Artist as a Young Man* and *The Bar Room Monks* (Martinique, May 28, 1962); directed, for the Th. in the Street, *The Shoemaker's Prodigious Wife* (Sept. 1962), *The Bear* (Summer 1963), and *The Doctor in Spite of Himself* (July 1964).

Other Activities. Miss Brand has taught at Piscator's Dramatic Workshop, N.Y.C. (1939); the Actors Laboratory, Hollywood, Calif. (1942–50); the Master Institute, N.Y.C. (1954–56); the American Shakespeare Festival Th. and Academy, Stratford, Conn. (1958–61); Amer. Th. Wing, N.Y.C. (1961–62); and the Amer. Acad. of Dramatic Arts (1962–64). She and Patricia Reynolds founded (1962) Th. in the Street for free outdoor performances in N.Y.C.

BRANDON, PETER. Actor. b. July 11, 1926, Berlin, Germany, to Norbert and Marianne (Winkler) Brandon. Father, physician. Grad. Mt. Hermon (Mass.) H.S., 1944; attended Neighborhood Playhouse Sch. of the Theatre, N.Y.C., 1947–49. Married Dec. 9, 1950, to Jane Hopkins Clark; one son, one daughter. Served US Army, 1945–47; rank, T/3. Member of AEA; SAG; AFTRA.

Theatre. Mr. Brandon first appeared on the stage in *Nobody's Girl,* which toured school auditoriums (Mar. 1947). He made his professional debut in the role of Michael Barnes in *The Male Animal* (East Hampton Summer Th., L.I., N.Y., July 1949).

He appeared as Nicholas in *Cry of the Peacock* (Mansfield, N.Y.C., Apr. 11, 1950); Dupont in *Tovarich* (NY City Ctr., May 14, 1952); Bertram in *Ondine* (46 St. Th., Feb. 18, 1954); Travis de Coppet in *The Young and Beautiful* (Longacre, Oct. 1, 1955); and Francis in *The Hillen River* (Playhouse, Jan. 23, 1957). In stock, he toured as Leonard Vole in *Witness for the Prosecution* (Summer 1957); played a Young Soldier in *The Infernal Machine* (Phoenix, N.Y.C., Feb. 3, 1958); Will Roper in *A Man for All Seasons* (ANTA, Nov. 22, 1961); and Rupert of Hentzau in the pre-Bway tour of *Zenda* (opened Curran, San Francisco, Calif., Aug. 5, 1963; closed Philharmonic Aud., Los Angeles, Calif., Nov. 9, 1963).

He was one of The Accused in *The Investigation* (Ambassador, N.Y.C., Oct. 4, 1966); appeared with the Oakland Univ. Professional Theater Program in *The Crucible* (Meadow Brook Th., Rochester, Minn., Jan. 7, 1971; Detroit Institute of Art, Detroit, Mich., Jan. 27, 1971), *Who's Afraid of Virginia Woolf?* (Meadow Brook Th., Apr. 1, 1971; Detroit Institute of Art, Apr. 21, 1971), and in *A Doll's House* (Meadow Brook Th., Mar. 2, 1972); and he was in *An Evening With the Poet-Senator* (Playhouse 2, N.Y.C., Mar. 21, 1973).

Television. Mr. Brandon appeared on Our Private World (CBS, 1965–66); was Love in *Dante: The Man* (Look Up and Live, CBS, Sept. 12, 1965); and Stark in *The Investigation* (NBC, Apr. 14, 1967).

BRANDT, ALVIN. Executive, editor, writer. b. Alvin George Brandt, Jan. 3, 1922, Union City, N.J., to Henry W. and Mabel Brandt. Grad. Emerson H.S., Union City, 1939; ANTA on-the-job training program, 1947–48. Married Oct. 21, 1950, to Josephine Baldessari; one son, one daughter. Served US Army, 1942–46, PTO. Member of Episcopal Actors Guild. Address: 33 Columbia St., Wharton, NJ 07885, tel. (201) 361-1682.

Since 1969, Mr. Brandt has been on the staff of Dover General Hospital, Dover, N.J., as personnel director and outpatient accounts manager.

From 1949 to 1969, Mr. Brandt was employed by AGVA where he was executive head of the Minutes, Meetings and Elections Dept. (1952–69); editor of *AGVA News* (1957–66); and where he produced ten variety shows for agents and producers as auditions coordinator (1957–59).

From 1947 to 1949, Mr. Brandt was on the staff of ANTA as correspondent, writer, publicist, and playreader for the ANTA Experimental Theatre.

For little theatres and church drama groups in New Jersey, Mr. Brandt has been an actor, singer, composer, writer, and director, most recently director of Chancel Players of St. John's, Dover; and previously president of The Giles Players and administrative director of Two-by-Four Playshop, Union City.

He is the author of *Drama Handbook for Churches* (1964), and has contributed articles to several theatre publications.

BRASMER, WILLIAM. Educator, director. b. Oct. 22, 1921, Evanston, Ill., to William O. and Hildegarde P. Brasmer. Grad. Northwestern Univ. (B.S. 1946, M.A. 1948); attended RADA, London, 1946. Married Aug. 31, 1948, to Constance Alice Fuller; one daughter, one son. Served in US Army, 1942–46, rank, Sgt. Address: (home) 17 Sunset Hill, Granville, OH 43023; (bus.) Dept. of Theatre and Film, Denison Univ., Granville, OH 43023, tel. (614) 587-0810.

Mr. Brasmer has taught at Denison Univ. since 1948 and been managing director of Denison Summer Theatre since 1952. At present he is professor and chairman, Dept. of Theatre and Film.

Published Works. He is the author of *Black Drama* (1970); the definitive text of John O'Keeffe's *The Poor Soldier,* and numerous articles. At present he is writing on Matthew Sommerville Morgan, 19th-century illustrator and scene designer, Buffalo Bill, and Nate Salsbury.

BREAUX, MARC. Choreographer, director, actor, dancer. b. Marc Charles Breaux, Nov. 3, Carenco, La., to Camille and Camilla Breaux. Father, railroad engineer. Attended Cathedral H.S., Lafayette, La.; Southwestern La. Inst.; Loyola Univ.; Tulane Univ. Married Sept. 11, 1955, to Deedee Wood, dancer, choreographer; two sons. Served USNAF, 1942–45; rank, Lt. (jg). Member of AEA; AFTRA; SAG. Address: (home) P.O. Box 256, Cave Creek, AZ 85331; (bus.) c/o L. K. Strauss, 440 E. 57th St., New York, NY 10022, tel. (212) PL 3-7651.

Theatre. Mr. Breaux made his debut as a dancer, touring with the Charles Weidman Concert Co. (1947–48); subsequently appeared as a dancer in *Ballet Ballads* (Music Box Th., N.Y.C., May 18, 1948); a dancer in the pre-Bway tryout of *That's the Ticket* (opened Shubert, Philadelphia, Pa., Sept. 24, 1948; closed there Oct. 2, 1948); appeared as the Tailor in *Kiss Me, Kate* (Century, N.Y.C., Dec. 30, 1948); danced Young Norwood in *The Barrier* (Broadhurst, Nov. 2, 1950); played Jim in *Fire Exit* (D'Amato, 1953); toured as a dancer in *Il Terrone Corressul Filo* (Italy, 1954); performed in the revue *Catch a Star!* (Plymouth, N.Y.C., Sept. 6, 1956); was assistant to Michael Kidd and played Romeo Scragg and Dr. Schleifitz in *Li'l Abner* (St. James, Nov. 15, 1956), and on tour (opened Riviera, Las Vegas, Nev., Sept. 1, 1958; closed Royal Alexandra, Toronto, Canada, Jan. 3, 1959); played Gyp Watson in *Destry Rides Again* (Imperial, N.Y.C., Apr. 23, 1959); with Deedee Wood, choreographed *Do Re Mi* (St. James, Dec. 26, 1960); was associate choreographer, with Michael Kidd, for *Subways Are for Sleeping* (St. James, Dec. 27, 1961); and choreographed *Minnie's Boys* (Imperial, Mar. 26, 1970), and a revival of *A Funny Thing Happened on Way to the Forum* (Lunt-Fontanne, Mar. 30, 1972).

Films. Mr. Breaux choreographed *Mary Poppins* (Buena Vista, 1964), *The Sound of Music* (20th-Fox, 1965), *The Happiest Millionaire* (Buena Vista, 1967), *Chitty, Chitty, Bang, Bang* (UA, 1968), and *Huckleberry Finn* (UA, 1974).

Television. Mr. Breaux has choreographed the Ed Sullivan Show (CBS, 1959); *Shubert Alley* (Bing Crosby Show, ABC, 1960); the Andy Williams Show (NBC, 1961); Jimmy Durante Special (1962); Judy Garland Show (CBS, 1963); Dick Van Dyke Show (CBS, 1963); and Jack Benny Show (CBS, 1963). He directed Hollywood Palace for one year, the King Family Show for one year, a Debbie Reynolds special, *Carol+2* (Carol Burnett special), *Goldilocks* (the Bing Crosby family), and choreographed *Of Thee I Sing.* .

Recreation. Painting, riding.

BREEN, ROBERT. Director, producer, actor. b. Dec. 26, 1914, to Henry James and Marie Therese (Cody) Breen. Attended St. John's Academy, Collegeville, Minn.; Cathedral H.S., St. Cloud, Minn.; Univ. of Iowa; Coll. of St. Thomas. Married Sept. 11, 1946, to Wilva Davis, actress, executive; two sons. Served USAAF, 1942–45; rank, Sgt. Member of AEA; NCP; ANTA (1st exec. secy., 1946–51; life member). Address: 139 W. 44th St., New York, NY 10036.

Theatre. Mr. Breen made his debut as Romaine in a Univ. of Iowa production of *Ten Nights in a Bar Room* (1931), and also toured in it (opened Wis., June 1931; closed Mich., Aug. 1931); for the Old Minneapolis Repertory Co., he appeared as Captain Hook in *Peter Pan,* Baptista in *The Taming of the Shrew,* the Chancellor in *The Ivory Door,* Louis XI in *If I Were King,* Brian de b. Guilbert in *Ivanhoe,* Winterset in *Monsieur Beaucaire,* Antony in *Julius Caesar,* and Osvald in *Ghosts* (1931–32); at the Univ. of Minnesota, he played Lord Dilling in *The Last of Mrs. Cheyney* (June 1932), and Gregers Werle in *The Wild Duck* (July 1932); at the College Art Th. (St. Paul, Minn.) he directed *R.U.R., Everyman, Liliom, Monsieur Beaucaire,* and *Urfaust,* in which he played Mephistopheles, and *Hamlet,* in which he played the title role (1932–33); and directed and appeared in the title role in *Hamlet* (Shubert, Minneapolis, Minn., June 1933).

With the Univ. of Minnesota group, he toured as Lord Gresham in *Aren't We All?* and in *Young Woodley* (July–Aug. 1933); for the St. Cloud (Minn.) Th. Guild, appeared in *The Enemy, The Fool, The Cat and the Canary,* and directed *Dr. Jekyll and Mr. Hyde* and *Romeo and Juliet* (Paramount and Grand theatres, Oct. 1933–Apr. 1934). With Wilva Davis producing, he directed the following repertory productions on tour: *The Ivory Door,* in which he played the Chancellor; *Romeo and Juliet,* in which he played Mercutio; *Urfaust,* in which he played Mephistopheles; and *Hamlet* (opened Birmingham, Ala., Oct. 1934; closed Chicago, Ill., May 1935). Under the auspices of the Chicago (Ill.) Park Administration, at the Hamilton Park Th. (Chicago, Ill.), he played the Chancellor in *The Ivory Door,* Mephistopheles in *Urfaust,* and the Chairman in *Amaco,* which he also directed (July–Sept. 1935).

In Oct. 1935, Hallie Flanagan appointed Mr. Breen and Miss Davis to conduct a survey of Chicago's needs for a Federal Th. allocation. In Jan. 1936, they organized the Chicago (Ill.) Federal Th. (WPA) Project, serving as associate director and administrator of Federal Theatre No. 1, which served the Chicago area.

He directed *Faust,* in which he played Mephistopheles (Great Northern Th., Chicago, Ill., Apr. 1936); *Technique* (Los Angeles, Calif., Feb. 1938); and *Speak of the Devil,* in which he played Mephistopheles (Nora Bayes Th., N.Y.C., May and Oct. 1939); and studio productions of *The Zeal of Thy House* (N.Y.C., Dec. 1939), *Adam the Creator* (N.Y.C., Feb. 1940), and *Winesburg, Ohio* (Irving Place Th., N.Y.C., Oct. 1940).

From 1941 to 1946, Mr. Breen and Miss Davis (joined by Robert Porterfield in 1945) promulgated The National Theatre Foundation plan. In 1946, the Congressionally chartered (1935) American National Theatre & Academy (ANTA) voted to commence operation, based on this National Theatre Foundation plan, and appointed Mr. Breen ANTA's first executive secretary, with Miss Davis as assistant. He served five years, creating and administering ANTA's national and international programs.

Mr. Breen was a founder and served as general director of the ANTA Experimental Th., which produced plays in its Subscription and Invitational Series. The Subscription Series included *The Wanhope Building* (Princess, Feb. 9, 1947); *O'Daniel* (Princess, Feb. 23, 1947); *As We Forgive Our Debtors* (Princess, Mar. 9, 1947); *The Great Campaign* (Princess, Mar. 30, 1947); *Virginia Reel* (Princess, Apr. 3, 1947); *Galileo* (Maxine Elliott's Th., Dec. 7, 1947); *Skipper Next to God* (Maxine Elliott's Th., Jan. 4, 1948); *A Long Way from Home* (Maxine Elliott's Th., Feb. 8, 1948); *A Temporary Island* (Maxine Elliott's Th., Mar. 14, 1948); a triple-bill, *Celebration, Afternoon Storm,* and *Hope Is a Thing with Feathers* (Maxine Elliott's Th., Apr. 11, 1948); *Ballet Ballads* (Maxine Elliott's Th., May 9, 1948); *Talent '48* (Maxine Elliott's Th., May 19, 1948) and the Martha Graham Company (Maxine Elliott's Th., May 25, 1948). The Invitational Series included *Seeds in the Wind* (Lenox Hill Playhouse, Apr. 24, 1948); *Danny Larkin* (May 8, 1948); *Battle for Heaven* (Educational Alliance, May 18, 1948); *These Tender Mercies* (Lenox Hill Playhouse, June 4, 1948); *E = MC²* (Brander Matthews Th., Columbia Univ., June 15, 1948); *Hippolytus* (Lenox Hill Playhouse, Nov. 20, 1948); *Uniform of Flesh* (Lenox Hill Playhouse, Jan. 29, 1949); *Cock-a-Doodle-Doo* Lenox Hill Playhouse, Feb. 26, 1949); *The 19th Hole of Europe* (Lenox Hill Playhouse, Mar. 26, 1949); *Sister Oakes* (Lenox Hill Playhouse, Apr. 23, 1949); *Me, The Sleeper* (Lenox Hill Playhouse, May 14, 1949); *The Fifth Horseman* (Lenox Hill Playhouse, June 14, 1949).

For the State of Utah Centennial, he organized productions (May 1947) of Orson Welles's *Macbeth* and Katharine Cornell's *The Barretts of Wimpole Street.*

He directed and played the title role in the State Theatre of Virginia's "Anniversary" touring production of *Hamlet* (Aug. 21, 1948–Apr. 20, 1949); and, at the invitation of the Danish government (Intl. Hamlet Festival, Kronborg Castle, Elsinore, Denmark, June 1949), and also toured Germany in it (July 1949).

He produced *ANTA Album* (Ziegfeld, N.Y.C., Jan. 1950), and arranged a European tour for the American Ballet Th., which marked the first such tour by a US ballet company (Aug. 7, 1950–Dec. 10, 1950).

Assisted by Wilva Davis, he created and served as general director of the first ANTA play series, which were produced at the ANTA Th. (N.Y.C.). The series included *The Tower Beyond Tragedy* (Nov. 26, 1950); *The Cellar and the Well* (Dec. 10, 1950); *Twentieth Century* (Dec. 24, 1950); *The House of Bernarda Alba* (Jan. 7, 1951); *Peer Gynt* (Jan. 28, 1951); *L'Ecole des femmes,* which was performed by Louis Jouvet and his Théâtre de l'Athénée Co. (Mar. 18, 1951); *Night Music* (Apr. 8, 1951); *The Little Blue Light* (Apr. 29, 1951); *Mary Rose* (May 4, 1951); and *Getting Married* (May 7, 1951).

With Wilva Davis, he organized ANTA's first National Theatre Assembly (N.Y.C., Jan. 2–5, 1951), attended by representatives from professional, community, and educational theatres nationwide. He arranged with the US Dept. of State for American participation in the first Berlin (Germany) Festival, marking the first instance of US financial sponsorship of international cultural exchange (1951). Under the auspices of ANTA, the following productions were presented at this festival: *Oklahoma!, Medea,* the Hall Johnson Choir, the Juilliard String Quartet and Angna Enters (Sept. 1951).

He conducted negotiations which led to the Katina Paxinou-Alexis Minotis productions at the Mark Hellinger Th. (N.Y.C.), of *Electra* (Nov. 19, 1952) and *Oedipus Tyrannus* (Nov. 24, 1952).

Mr. Breen produced, with Blevins Davis, and directed *Porgy and Bess* (opened State Fair Music Hall, Dallas, Tex., June 9, 1952); toured the US (Civic Opera, Chicago, Ill., June 25, 1952; Nixon, Pittsburgh, Pa., July 22; and Natl., Washington, D.C., Aug. 6); and in Europe (Volksoper, Vienna, Austria, Sept. 7, 1952; Titania Palast Th., Berlin, Germany, Sept. 18; Stoll, London, England, Oct. 9; and Th. de l'Empire, Paris, France, Feb. 16, 1953); opened in N.Y.C. (Ziegfeld, Mar. 10, 1953); again toured the USA (opened Forrest, Philadelphia, Pa., Dec. 1, 1953; Natl., Washington, D.C., Dec. 21; Mosque, Richmond, Va., Jan. 18, 1954; Nixon, Pittsburgh, Pa., Jan. 25; Taft, Cincinnati, Ohio, Feb. 1; American, St. Louis, Mo., Feb. 8; Music Hall, Kansas City, Mo., Feb. 22; Civic Opera, Chicago, Ill., Mar. 2; Lyceum, Minneapolis, Minn., Mar. 24; Royal Alexandra, Toronto, Ontario, Canada, Apr. 6; Cass, Detroit, Mich., Apr. 19; Hanna, Cleveland, Ohio, May 10; Hartman, Columbus, Ohio, May 24; Denver Aud., Colo., June 1; Curran, San Francisco, Calif., June 14; Philharmonic Aud., Los Angeles, Calif., July 12; Shubert, Boston, Mass., Aug. 20; Royal Alexandra, Toronto, Ontario, Canada, Aug. 31; and Her Majesty's Montreal, Quebec, Canada, Sept. 13); toured Europe, Africa, and the Near East (Teatro la Fenice, Venice, Italy, Sept. 22, 1954; Th. de l'Empire, Paris, France, Sept. 30; Th. de l'Opera, Zagreb, Yugoslavia, Dec. 11; Th. de l'Opera, Belgrade, Yugoslavia, Dec. 16; Th. Mohamed Aly, Alexandria, Egypt, Dec. 31; Th. de l'Opera, Cairo, Egypt, Jan. 7, 1955; Royal National Th., Athens, Greece, Jan. 17; Habimah Th., Tel Aviv, Israel, Jan. 26; Concert Hall, Casablanca, Morocco, Jan. 31; Gran Teatro del Liceo, Barcelona, Spain, Feb. 3; Teatro di San Carlo, Naples, Italy, Feb. 15; Teatro Alla Scala, Milan, Italy, Feb. 23; Teatro Carlo Felice, Genoa, Italy, Mar. 1; Teatro Comunale, Florence, Italy, Th. de Beaulieu, Lausanne, Switzerland, Mar. 16; Opera Municipal, Marseilles, France, Mar. 26; Teatro Alfieri, Turin, Italy, Apr. 9; Teatro Quattro Fontana, Rome, Italy, Apr. 21; Hallenstadion, Zurich, Switzerland, June 3; Th. Royal de la Monnaie, Brussels, Belgium, June 15; and Hippodrome Th., Antwerp, Belgium, June 23). The production then toured Latin America under sponsorship of ANTA and Dept. of State (Teatro Municipal, Rio De Janeiro, Brazil, July 7, 1955; Teatro Santana, Sao Paulo, Brazil, July 16; Teatro Solis, Montevideo, Uruguay, July 26; Teatro Astral, Buenos Aires, Argentina, Aug. 3; Teatro Municipal, Santiago, Chile, Aug. 25; Teatro Municipal, Lima, Peru, Sept. 3; Teatro Colombia, Bogota, Colombia, Sept. 13; Teatro Municipal, Cali, Colombia, Sept. 21; Teatro Municipal, Caracas, Venezuela, Sept. 27; Teatro Nacional, Panama City, Panama, Oct. 6; Teatro Bellas Artes, Mexico City, Mexico, Oct. 11); and returned to Europe (Th. Hippodrome, Antwerp, Belgium, Nov. 9, 1955; Apollo Th., Duesseldorf, Germany, Nov. 18; Grosses Haus der Stadtischen Buhnen, Frankfort, Germany, Nov. 25; Deutsches Th., Munich, Germany, Dec. 1; Titania Palast, Berlin, Germany, Dec. 9; Palace of Culture, Leningrad, USSR, Dec. 26; Stanislavsky Th., Moscow, USSR, Jan. 10, 1956; National Opera Th., Warsaw, Poland, Jan. 24; Wyspianski Th., Stalinogrod, Poland, Feb. 4; Karlin Th., Prague, Czechoslavakia, Feb. 11; Deutsches Th., Munich, Germany, Feb. 22; Staats Th., Stuttgart, Germany, Mar. 1; Staatsoper, Hamburg, Germany, Mar. 7; Th. Royal de La Monnaie, Brussels, Belgium, Mar. 25; Gebouw Voor Kunsten en Wetenschappen, The Hague, Holland, Apr. 2; Luxor Th., Rotterdam, Holland, Apr. 13; Volks Th., Oslo, Norway, Apr. 25; Aarhushallen, Aarhus, Denmark, May 9; and Th. Carre, Amsterdam, Holland, May 19–June 3, 1956).

For the American Theatre Wing's "*Command Performance—Serenade to the White House,*" Mr. Breen directed Sammy Davis, Jr., in *Porgy and Bess,* Jan. 27, 1957. He directed *Free and Easy,* a "blues opera," by Harold Arlen (Amsterdam, Holland, Dec. 7, 1959; Brussels, Belgium, and Utrecht, Holland, Dec. 1959–Jan. 1960; Paris, France, Feb. 1960).

Films. Mr. Breen played Bolus in *The Pentagram (Faust),* Kalmar Prods. Ltd., Berlin Film Festival (Germany) 1964. Since 1970, he has been co-executive director (with Wilva Davis) of Crucible, Inc.

Television. Mr. Breen was executive producer of, ANTA *Television Playhouse* (NBC, 1947–48) and executive director of, *Theatre U.S.A.* (ABC, 1949–50). He played the role of the Cardinal-Inquisitor in *Lamp at Midnight,* (Hallmark Hall of Fame, NBC, 1965) and Elijah in *Inherit the Wind,* (Hallmark Hall of Fame, NBC 1966). He was on the National Academy of Television Arts and Sciences (NATAS) Blue Ribbon Panel for New York "Emmy" Awards (1969, 1970).

Radio. He played Dr. Stockmann in *An Enemy of the People,* Metternich in *L'Aiglon,* and others (KSTP, St. Paul, Minn., 1931–33).

Other Activities. Since 1952, he has been vice-president of Everyman Opera, Inc.

Discography. ANTA *Album of Stars* series, vols. I & II, Decca Records, associate to Wilva Davis, producer, 1950–51.

Awards. Mr. Breen received the Danish Hamlet Medal (1949).

BRENNAN, EILEEN.

BRENNAN, EILEEN. Actress. b. Verla Eileen Brennan, Sept. 3, 1935, Los Angeles, Calif., to Jerry and Regina (Menehan) Brennan. Grad. Mt. St. Gertrude Acad., Boulder, Colo., 1953; AADA, 1958. Two sons, Samuel and Patrick Lampson. Member of AEA; AFTRA; AGVA. Address: 3966 Alcove Ave., Studio City, CA 91604.

Theatre. Miss Brennan made her N.Y.C. debut in the title role of *Little Mary Sunshine* (Orpheum, Nov. 18, 1959); played Annie Sullivan in the national company of *The Miracle Worker* (opened Playhouse, Wilmington, Del., Apr. 12, 1961; closed Veterans Memorial Aud., Providence, R.I., Mar. 31, 1962); Anna Leonowens in *The King and I* (NY City Ctr., June 10, 1963); Merry May Glockenspiel in *The Student Gypsy or the Prince of Liederkranz* (54 St. Th., Sept. 30, 1963); and Irene Molloy in *Hello, Dolly!* (St. James, Jan. 16, 1964).

Films. Miss Brennan played Genevieve in *The Last Picture Show* (Col., 1971); Billie in *The Sting* (U, 1973); Mrs. Walker in *Daisy Miller* (Par., 1973); and Elizabeth in *At Long-Last Love* (20th-Fox, 1975).

Awards. For her performance in the title role of *Little Mary Sunshine,* Miss Brennan received the Newspaper Guild Page One Award, the *Theatre World* Award, the *Village Voice* Off-Bway (Obie) Award, and the Kit-Kat Artists and Models Award.

She received a nomination for Best Supporting Actress from the British Academy Awards (1972) for her role in *The Last Picture Show.*.

BRENT, ROMNEY.

BRENT, ROMNEY. Actor, director, playwright. b. Romulo Larralde, Jr., Jan. 26, 1902, Saltillo, Mexico, to Romulo and Juanita (Hagueman) Larralde. Father, banker, diplomat. Grad. Chauncy Hall H.S., Boston, Mass., 1920; attended New York Univ., 1920–22. Studied acting with Theodore Kommissarjevski, N.Y.C., 1922. Married 1937 to Gina Malo, actress; one daughter. Served Canadian Army, 1943–46; rank, Capt. Member of AEA; SAG; ALA. Assn. de Actores Mexicanos. Address: 234 W. 14th St., New York, NY 10011, tel. (212) WA 9-7637.

Theatre. Mr. Brent made his N.Y.C. debut playing an acrobat in *He Who Gets Slapped* (Garrick Th., Jan. 9, 1922); subsequently appeared as Tommy Todd in *The Lucky One* (Garrick, Nov. 20, 1922); the Thief in *Peer Gynt* (Garrick, Feb. 5, 1923); on Theatre Guild tours, as the Bridegroom in *Peer Gynt,* Tilly in *He Who Gets Slapped,* and the Idiot Brother in *The Devil's Disciple* (Aug.–Dec. 1924).

He played the Chancellor in *The Wild Duck* (48 St. Th., N.Y.C., Feb. 24, 1925); appeared in the revue *The Garrick Gaieties* (Garrick, June 8, 1925); played the Lion in *Androcles and the Lion* (Klaw, Nov. 25, 1925); Petronicus in *The Chief Thing* (Guild, Mar. 22, 1926); Finito in *The Squall* (32 St. Th., Nov. 11, 1926); Johnny Dunn in *Loud Speaker* (32 St. Th., Mar. 7, 1927); Carlo in *Katy Did* (Daly's, May 7, 1927); Gobbo in *The Merchant of Venice* (Broadhurst, Jan. 16, 1928); Leguerche in *The Phantom Lover* (49 St. Th., Sept. 4, 1928); Dr. Gage in *Be Your Age* (Belmont, Feb. 4, 1929); appeared in the revue *The Little Show* (Music Box, Apr. 30, 1929); Hlesttakoff in *The Inspector General* (Hudson, Dec. 23, 1929); and Cecil Sykes in *Getting Married* (Guild, Mar. 30, 1931).

At the Westport (Conn.) Country Playhouse, Mr. Brent appeared in six plays (Summer 1931); performed, in repertory, as Badger in *The Streets of New York,* and Hellmar in *The Pillars of Society* (48 St. Th., N.Y.C., Oct. 6; Oct. 14, 1931); and as Sappy in *The Warrior's Husband* (Morosco, Mar. 11, 1932). He wrote the play *The Mad Hopes* (Curran, San Francisco, Calif., July 1932); made his London debut in the revue, *Words and Music* (Adelphi, Sept. 16, 1932); directed his own play, *Nymph Errant* (Adelphi, Oct. 6, 1933); played Iddy in *The Simpleton of the Unexpected Isles* (Guild, N.Y.C., Feb. 18, 1935); toured as Oswald in *Ghosts* (July 1935); and wrote *Tomorrow's Holiday* (John Golden Th., N.Y.C., Dec. 30, 1935).

Mr. Brent played Erwin Trowbridge in *Three Men on a Horse* (Wyndham's, London, Feb. 18, 1936); Tobias in *Tobias and the Angel* (St. Martin's, Sept. 6, 1938); Levi in *Scandal in Assyria* (Globe, Apr. 30, 1939); Bottom in *A Midsummer Night's Dream* (Open Air Th., July 4, 1939); Jeremy in *Love for Love* (Players Club, N.Y.C., June 3, 1940); Cyril in *Bird in Hand* (Morosco, Oct. 19, 1942); Cyril in *The Deep Mrs. Sykes* (Booth, Mar. 19, 1945); Autolycus in *The Winter's Tale,* which he also directed (Cort, Jan. 15, 1946); directed a tour of *The Merry Wives of Windsor,* in which he played Dr. Caius (June 1946); appeared as the Dauphin in *Joan of Lorraine* (Alvin, N.Y.C., Nov. 18, 1946); Adolphe in *Parisienne* (Fulton, July 24, 1950); appeared in *Springboard to Nowhere* (Garrick, Chicago, Ill., Oct. 1950); played Charles Dupont in *Tovarich* (NY City Ctr., May 14, 1952); and succeeded (Dec. 1952) Hume Cronyn as Michael in *The Fourposter* (Ethel Barrymore Th., Oct. 24, 1951).

Mr. Brent performed in and directed stock at the British Colonial Hotel (Nassau, B.W.I., Winters 1951, 1955); played in *The Little Hut* (Bermuda, Jan. 1954); for the Los Angeles (Calif.) Civic Light Opera Assn., directed *Brigadoon* (Philharmonic

Aud., Apr. 1954); directed *One Eye Closed* (Bijou, N.Y.C., Nov. 24, 1954); a Spanish-language production of *The Teahouse of the August Moon* (Insurgentes, Mexico City, May 1955), and its State Dept. sponsored tour of South America (Apr. 1956); toured as Denny in *Janus* (opened Aud., Rochester, N.Y., Sept. 27, 1956; closed Ford's Th., Baltimore, Md., Mar. 16, 1957); staged *Lady Windermere's Fan* (Fabregas, Mexico City, May 1958); and *Picara Ladrona* (Sala Chopin, Aug. 1958); and directed and performed in stock (Palm Beach Playhouse, Fla., Jan. 1959; Westport Country Playhouse, Conn., June 1959; No. Shore Music Th., Beverly, Mass., June 1960; Elitch Gardens, Denver, Colo., Summer 1961).

During 1961, he played Homer in *The Skin of Our Teeth*, and the Doctor in *The Miracle Worker* on a State Dept. tour (Europe, the Near East, and South America). He appeared as Francisco Indero in the pre-Bway tryout of *We Take the Town* (opened Shubert, New Haven, Conn., Feb. 19, 1962; closed Shubert, Philadelphia, Pa., Mar. 17, 1962); and directed the Summer tryout of *No Bed of Roses* (Bucks County Playhouse, New Hope, Pa., June 1963). From Nov. 1965 to Jan. 1966 he toured again for the US State Dept.'s Div. of Americans Abroad, performing in the Far East. Subsequently, he staged *Finders in the Dark* (Inst. for Adv. Studies in the Th. Arts, N.Y.C.) and directed Blanche Yurka in *These I Have Loved* for the Monday Nights in Concert series (Stage 73 Th.).

Films. Mr. Brent made his debut in *East Meets West* (Gaumont-British, 1930); subsequently appeared in *Dreaming Lips* (UA, 1937); *The Dominant Sex* (Gainsborough, 1937); *School for Husbands* (Hoffberg, 1939); *His Lordship Goes to Press* (1939); *Let George Do it* (Film Alliance, 1940); *The Adventures of Don Juan* (WB, 1948); *Singoalla* (Sandref, 1950); *The Virgin Queen* (20th-Fox, 1955); *Don't Go Near the Water* (MGM, 1957); *Screaming Mimi* (Col., 1958); and *The Sign of Zorro* (Buena Vista, 1960).

Television. Mr. Brent has appeared on Armstrong Circle Th. (NBC); Billy Rose's Playbill (Ind.); Somerset Maugham Th. (NBC); CBS Summer Th.; *King Lear* (Omnibus, CBS); *The Trial of St. Joan* (Omnibus, CBS); *Camille* (Studio One, CBS); Schlitz Playhouse of Stars (CBS); the Loretta Young Show (NBC); Playhouse 90 (CBS); and *Ten Little Indians* (NBC).

BRICE, CAROL. Singer, actress. b. Carol Lovette Hawkins Brice, Apr. 16, 1918, Indianapolis, Ind., to John and Ella (Hawkins) Brice. Father, minister, teacher; mother, teacher. Grad. Palmer Memorial Inst. (H.S.), Sedalia, N.C.; Talladega (Ala.) Coll., B.Mus. (1939); Juilliard Grad. Sch., 1944; studied with Vera Covert, N.Y.C., eight years. Married Dec. 24, 1942, to Neil Scott, Sr.; one son, one daughter. Relatives in theatre: Jonathan Brice, accompanist and coach; Eugene Brice, singer and teacher. Member of AEA; AGMA; AFTRA; Alpha Kappa Alpha.

Pre-Theatre. Concert singer.

Theatre. She first appeared in N.Y.C. as Kakou in *Saratoga* (Winter Garden, Dec. 7, 1959); followed by Maude in *Finian's Rainbow* (NY City Ctr., Apr. 27, 1960); Queenie in *Show Boat* (Apr. 12, 1961); Maria in *Porgy and Bess* (May 17, 1961); and Harriet Tubman in *Gentlemen Be Seated* (Oct. 10, 1963).

In NY City Ctr. Light Opera Co. revivals, she played Maria in *Porgy and Bess* (NY City Ctr., May 6, 1964) and Maude in *Finian's Rainbow;* and she was Catherine Creek in the musical version of *The Grass Harp* (Martin Beck Th., Nov. 2, 1971).

Concerts. Miss Brice sang at The Chaplet, N.Y.C. (1941); Town Hall, N.Y.C. (1944); and appeared with symphony orchestras, including the Kansas City Symphony (1944); Pittsburgh Symphony (1945–46); Boston Symphony (1947; 1948); and San Francisco Symphony (1948). She sang at the Marc Blitzstein Memorial Concert (Philharmonic Hall, N.Y.C., Apr. 19, 1964).

Discography. Miss Brice's recordings include Gustav Mahler's *Lieder eines Fahrenden Gesellen*, with the Pittsburgh Symphony, and Manuel De Falla's *El Amor Brujo* (both Columbia, 1946); *Sacred Arias of Bach* with the Daniel Saidenburg Orchestra; and *A Carol Brice Recital Album.*

Awards. Miss Brice was made an Honorary L.H.D. by Talladega College (1959); received the Naumburg Award, an all-expense paid Town Hall Recital debut (1944); and was chosen Woman of the Year in Music by the National Council of Negro Women.

BRICKER, HERSCHEL. Educator, writer. b. Herschel Leonard Bricker, May 22, 1905, Earlham, Iowa, to Augustus Melvin and Mary Ella (Taylor) Bricker. Father, farmer. Grad. Earlham H.S., 1924; Coe Coll., A.B. 1928. Studied directing methods with Broadway producer-directors, including Brock Pemberton, Antoinette Perry, George Abbott, Arthur Hopkins, and Marc Connelly (1936); at Cleveland (Ohio) Play House, at Pasadena (Calif.) Playhouse, and at Univ. of Washington (Seattle), (1937). Married Nov. 10, 1944, to Cecelia Kohl; one son. Member of ATA (formerly AETA; pres., 1944–45); ANTA (bd. of dir., 1961–63); NTC; NETC; Phi Kappa Phi. Address: (home) Corner Main and Anson, Farmington, ME 04938, tel. (207) 778-3475; (bus.) Univ. of Me. at Farmington, Fine Arts Dept., Farmington, ME tel. (207) 778-3501, ext. 334.

Mr. Bricker was director of the Maine Masque Th. at the Univ. of Maine at Orono (1938–70). He was scene designer and assistant director there (1928–38). In 1970, he became professor emeritus at Orono and was made visiting professor of theatre at the Univ. of Maine at Farmington and director of the theatre there.

Other Activities. Mr. Bricker served as a member of the Civilian Advisory Committee on Entertainment for the War Dept. (1944–45); head of the theatre branch of the US Army's Shrivenham-American Univ., England (1945); theatre consultant for the US Armed Forces in Europe (1946), and directed the Army Day Show under Gen. Mark Clark's command in Vienna, Austria (1946).

He founded the Camden Hills Th. (1947), also serving as director-manager (Summers 1947–56); was chairman of the International Theatre Celebration (1948–60); chairman of the Rosamond Gilder Awards (1958); was chosen by AETA-USO to tour a Univ. of Maine Masque Th. company to entertain US servicemen in West Germany and Italy (1959); and by ANTA-AETA to tour a Univ. of Maine Masque Th. company throughout India and East and West Pakistan under the auspices of the State Dept. (1962).

Mr. Bricker was a member of the Governor's Arts and Humanities Council (1966–67); State of Maine Commission for the Arts and Humanities (1967–70); and is a member of the Maine State Ballet (bd. of dir., 1968–to date); Theatre Association of Maine (bd. of dir., 1968–to date); the Fine Arts Advisory Comm. for Schools (1974–to date); and World Mime (Tony Montanaro) (1973–to date).

Published Works. Mr. Bricker edited *Our Theatre Today* (1936); wrote the chapter, "Staging the Classic Play," for Ronald B. Levinson's *The College Journey* (1938); and contributed articles to educational and international theatre publications.

Awards. He received a Rockefeller Foundation Grant to study directing (1936–37) and the New England Theatre Conference (NETC) citation for contribution to theatre (1958).

Recreation. Gardening and cooking.

BRICUSSE, LESLIE. Composer, lyricist, writer. b. about 1931 in England. Married to Yvonne Romain, actress; one son.

Theatre. Mr. Bricusse made his London debut in 1954 as co-author and director of the Cambridge Univ. Footlights review *Out of the Blue.* He was leading man in the show *An Evening with Beatrice Lillie* (Globe Th., London, Nov. 24, 1954). He wrote, with Anthony Newley, the book, music, and lyrics for *Stop the World—I Want to Get Off* (Queen's Th., July 20, 1961; Sam S. Shubert Th., N.Y.C., Oct. 3, 1962); wrote the lyrics for *Pickwick* (London 1963; American premiere, San Francisco, Calif., Apr. 1965; 46 St. Th., N.Y.C., Oct. 4, 1965); and, with Anthony Newley, book, music, and lyrics for *The Roar of the Greasepaint—The Smell of the Crowd* (Sam S. Shubert Th., May 16, 1965) and *The Good Old Bad Old Days* (London, Feb. 1973).

Films. Mr. Bricusse wrote, with Anthony Newley, the title song for *Goldfinger* (UA, 1964); wrote the screenplay, based on his own story, for *Three Hats for Lisa* (Warner-Pathé, 1965), for which he also provided the songs; collaborated with Anthony Newley on the screenplay for *Stop the World—I Want to Get Off* (WB, 1966); wrote, with Jerry Goldsmith, the title song for *In Like Flint* (20th-Fox, 1967); wrote lyrics for the title song for *A Guide for the Married Man* (20th-Fox, 1967); collaborated on songs for *Gunn* (Par., 1967); and wrote the screenplay, music, and lyrics for *Dr. Doolittle* (20th-Fox, 1967).

Awards. In 1962, Mr. Bricusse won an Ivor Novello Award for his song "My Kind of Girl" and shared Ivor Novello awards with Mr. Newley for "What Kind of Fool Am I?" (best song) and for best score, for *Stop the World.* "What Kind of Fool Am I?" also received the 1962 Broadcast Music Inc. Award as best popular song of the year. In 1965, Mr. Bricusse and Mr. Newley received a Whitbread Anglo-American Theatre Award for their score of *The Roar of the Greasepaint—The Smell of the Crowd.*

BRIGGS, WALLACE NEAL. Educator, director. b. Mar. 1, 1914, Meridian, Miss., to W. R. and Mary (Neal) Briggs. Grad. Holmes H.S., Covington, Ky., 1933; Univ. of Kentucky, A.B. 1936, M.A. 1944; attended Western Reserve Univ., 1938; Sorbonne, 1939; Yale Univ. Sch. of Drama, 1953–54. Married June 24, 1942, to Olive Terrill. Served US Army Counter Intelligence Corps, 1942–43; rank, Cpl. Member of Ky. Speech Assn., SETC (committee on The Architecture, 1956–58); ATA (curriculum committee, 1967–68); Lexington (Ky.) Children's Theatre (pres., 1969–70); Living Arts and Science Center (dir., 1970–to date); Lexington (Ky.) Musical Theatre (dir.); Omicron Delta Kappa; Phi Kappa Tau; Kappa Delta Pi. Address: (home) 3013 Windermere Rd., Lexington, KY 40502, tel. (606) 258-4678; (bus.) Fine Arts Bldg., Guignol Theatre, Univ. of Kentucky, Lexington, KY 40506.

Mr. Briggs became a member of the faculty, Univ. of Kentucky, as an instructor in 1941. He later became assistant professor (1949), associate professor (1960–to date), and was chairman, Dept. of Theatre Arts (1968–69).

Theatre. Since 1944, Mr. Briggs has been director of the Guignol Theatre at the Univ. of Kentucky. He was the director of the Paul Green musical drama *The Stephen Foster Story* (Bardstown, Ky., 1964); director, Shakespeare in the Park, Louisville, Ky. (1973); and director-actor, Shakertown Summer Theatre (1972–73).

Other Activities. Mr. Briggs was a reporter for the Cincinnati (Ohio) *Enquirer* (1937–38) and a teacher at Lloyd H. S., Erlanger, Ky. (1938–41).

Published Works. His poetry has appeared in *Poets of America* (1940) and his articles in *Accent Magazine* and *Kentucky Journal of Communication Arts.*.

Awards. Mr. Briggs received the Outstanding Teacher Award, Univ. of Kentucky (1968), and the university's Great Teaching Award (1971).

Recreation. Bridge, gardening, swimming.

BRIGGS, WILLIAM A. Architect, theatre architectural consultant, product designer. b. William Adolphus Briggs, Jan. 8, 1915, Asheville, N.C., to Henry Harrison and A. Lillian (Briggs) Briggs. Father, physician. Grad. Asheville School for Boys, 1933; Yale Univ., B.F.A. 1939. Served USNR, 1943–44. Married 1935 to Harriet Durstine (marr. dis. 1947); three sons; married Dec. 24, 1949, to Eloise McPherson; one son, two daughters. Member of AETA; AIA; USITT (bd. mbr., 1964); Acoustical Society of Amer.; Historic Richmond Foundation (trustee); Rotunda Club, Richmond, Va. Address: 3014 Seminary Ave., Richmond, VA

23227, tel. (804) 358-9008.

Mr. Briggs has been a member of the Natl. Committee on auditorium and theatre architecture of the AIA since its formation in 1961; was president of the Richmond (Va.) chapter of the AIA (1962–63); was architectural consultant on theatres in Maryland and Virginia, including the Richmond (Va.) Civic Center; and is a professional advisor for the nation's largest AIA approved competition, the Birmingham-Jefferson Civic Activities Complex (Birmingham, Ala.), which includes a theatre, a music hall, an auditorium, and a convention center.

He received his early training as draftsman and designer with the architectural firms Anthony Lord, Asheville, N.C., and Baumann & Baumann, Knoxville, Tenn.; was assistant to Henry Dreyfus, industrial designer (N.Y.C., 1942–43); and designed rocket factories for the USN during WW II, after which he directed the Keeble Associates Consulting Division (1948–53).

In 1953, Mr. Briggs formed his own consulting firm with offices in Nashville, Tenn.; Washington, D.C.; and Richmond, Va. (1960), receiving consulting and design commissions from the Dept. of Defense and state, city, and corporate clients.

Since 1960, Mr. Briggs has specialized in architectural programming and the design of major structures.

Other Activities. Mr. Briggs holds patents on machinery and many household and furniture items.

Published Works. He wrote *Night and Day, Richmond, Va.* (1962), a survey on cultural facilities in the US and outline of techniques for pre-programming theatres and auditoriums.

Awards. He received a USN Bureau of Ordnance Commendation for Machinery Design (1944); and a layout contest award from *Automation* (1961).

BRINCKERHOFF, BURT. Actor, director, producer. b. Burton Field Brinckerhoff, Oct. 25, 1936, Pittsburgh, Pa., to Rev. J. Howard and Marion (Field) Brinckerhoff. Grad. Horace Mann H.S., N.Y.C., 1954. Studied with Wendell K. Phillips, N.Y.C., three years; Milton Katselas, two years; and Brian Shaw, three years. Married Dec. 26, 1959, to Zina Jasper (marr. dis.). Received USAR training. Member of AEA; AFTRA; SAG. Address: 365 West End Ave., New York, NY 10024, tel. (212) TR 3-2370.

Theatre. Mr. Brinckerhoff first appeared on the stage as Lachie in a high-school production of *The Hasty Heart* (N.Y.C., Mar. 1954); followed by his professional debut as Richard in *Ah, Wilderness!* (Boston Arts Festival, Mass.; Playhouse-in-the-Park, Philadelphia, Pa., June 1954); Arthur Bartley in a summer tryout of *Blue Denim* (Westport Country Playhouse, Conn., July 1955); Eddie Davis in *Time Out for Ginger* (Playhouse-in-the-Park, Philadelphia, Pa., Aug. 1955); and Tom Lee in *Tea and Sympathy* (Summer tour, 1956).

He repeated the role of Arthur Bartley in *Blue Denim* (Playhouse Th., N.Y.C., Feb. 27, 1958; Feb. 1959); appeared as Paul Ormos in the N.Y.C. production of *Answered the Flute* (Th. Guild's Studio Three, Mar. 1960) and in the title role of *Marcus in the High Grass* (Greenwich Mews, Nov. 21, 1960); played Marchbanks in *Candida* (Sombrero Playhouse, Phoenix, Ariz., Jan. 1961); Clive Harrington in *Five Finger Exercise* (Summer tour, 1961); and served as producer (Windham Playhouse, N.H., Summers 1962–63). He played Simon Bliss in *Hay Fever* (Bucks County Playhouse, New Hope, Pa., June 14, 1965); Igor in *Cactus Flower* (Royale, N.Y.C., Dec. 8, 1965); and Michael Brady in *Keep It in the Family* (Plymouth, Sept. 27, 1967).

In 1964, he founded, with Tony LoBianco the Triangle Theatre at the Church of the Holy Trinity, N.Y.C., where he subsequently produced and directed a variety of plays, classical and new (1964–to date).

Films. Mr. Brinckerhoff appeared in *The Goddess* (Col., 1958) and as the Apostle Andrew in *The Greatest Story Ever Told* (UA, 1964).

Television. Mr. Brinckerhoff made his television debut in *Crime without Motive* (Philco Television Playhouse, NBC, Nov. 1954); followed by appearances in more than sixty shows, including Studio One (CBS); Armstrong Circle Th. (NBC); US Steel Hour (CBS); Hong Kong (ABC); Route 66 (CBS); Naked City (ABC); The Defenders (CBS); *John Brown's Body* (CBS Special); Ben Casey (ABC); *Inherit the Wind* (Hallmark Hall of Fame, NBC); Gunsmoke (CBS); and Eternal Light (NBC).

He has directed episodes of Beacon Hill (CBS) and Search for Tomorrow (CBS) among other shows, and is currently a regular alternating director for Love of Life (CBS).

Awards. Mr. Brinckerhoff was nominated for a Sylvania Award for his role in *Five Dollar Bill* (Studio One, CBS, 1957); and won the *Variety* NY Drama Critics Poll (1957), for his performance in *Blue Denim.*.

BRISSON, FREDERICK. Producer. b. Carl Frederick Brisson, Mar. 17, 1913, Copenhagen, Denmark, to Carl and Cleo Brisson. Father, stage and film actor (knighted by the kings of Denmark and Sweden). Grad. Rossall Coll., Fleetwood, Lancashire, England, 1930. Married Oct. 25, 1941, to Rosalind Russell, actress; one son. Served USAAF, 1942–45; rank, Lt. Col. Member of Screen Producers Guild; AMPAS; Hollywood Foreign Press Assn.; Air Force Assn.; Eldorato Country Club; Bel Air Country Club; St. Ansgar's Scandinavian Catholic League; Racquet & Tennis Club. Address: 745 Fifth Ave., New York, NY 10022, tel. (212) PL 2-2220; 615 South Flower St., Los Angeles, CA 90017, tel. (213) 625-2121.

Theatre. Mr. Brisson's first theatrical assignment was in a managerial capacity for the London productions of *Wonder Bar* (Savoy, Dec. 5, 1930), and *The Merry Widow* (Hippodrome, Sept. 29, 1932); subsequently he was co-producer of the American musical, *Transatlantic Rhythm* (Adelphi, London, 1937). He became a talent representative in 1936, establishing offices in London and Paris; and a junior partner in the Frank Vincent agency in Hollywood (1939–June 1942).

He produced with Robert E. Griffith and Harold S. Prince, *The Pajama Game* (St. James, N.Y.C., May 13, 1954), *Damn Yankees* (46 St. Th., May 5, 1955), *New Girl in Town* (46 St. Th., May 1, 1957); with the Playwrights' Co., *The Pleasure of His Company* (Longacre, Oct. 22, 1958), *The Gazebo* (Lyceum, Dec. 12, 1958), and *Five Finger Exercise* (Music Box, Dec. 2, 1959); with Roger L. Stevens, *Under the Yum-Yum Tree* (Henry Miller's Th., Nov. 16, 1960); with Mr. Stevens and Gilbert Miller, *The Caretaker* (Lyceum, Oct. 4, 1961); with Mr. Stevens, in association with Samuel Taylor, *First Love* (Morosco, Dec. 25, 1961). In London, he produced *Alfie* (Mermaid, June 19, 1963) and the musical *Passion Flower Hotel* (Prince of Wales Th., Aug. 24, 1965) and in N.Y.C. *Generation* (Morosco, Oct. 6, 1965); *The Flip Side* (Booth Th., Oct. 10, 1968); *Coco* (Mark Hellinger Th., Dec. 18, 1969); and *Twigs* (Broadhurst, Nov. 14, 1971).

Films. Mr. Brisson's first film assignment was as associate producer with Gaumont-British where he was associated with *Two Hearts in Three-Quarter Time* and *Prince of Arcadia;* subsequently, he produced independently *Moonlight Sonata* (UA, 1938); formed Independent Artists Pictures, Inc. in Hollywood, Calif.; and produced *The Velvet Touch* (RKO, 1948) and *Never Wave at a Wac* (RKO, 1952); was a co-producer of the screen adaptation of *The Pajama Game* (WB, 1957); and *Under the Yum-Yum Tree* (Col., 1963). His later films were *Generation* (Avco-Embassy, 1969); and *Mrs Pollifax, Spy* (UA, 1971).

Awards. Mr. Brisson was awarded the U.S. Legion of Merit, and the King Christian X Medal of Denmark.

Recreation. Golf, tennis, swimming, boating, photography (16-mm home movie and still shots).

BROCKETT, O. G. Educator, writer. b. Oscar Gross Brockett, Mar. 18, 1923, Hartsville, Tenn., to Oscar H. and Minna (Gross) Brockett. Father, farmer. Grad. Trousdale County H.S., Hartsville, 1940; Peabody Coll., 1940–43, B.A. 1947; Stanford Univ., M.A. 1949; Ph.D. 1953. Married Sept. 4, 1951, to Lenyth Spenker, copywriter and editor; one daughter. Served USNR, 1943–46; rank, Lt. (j.g.). Member of ATA (vice-pres. for program, 1973–75); ASTR (executive comm., 1970–73); SCA (administrative council, 1966–69); International Federation for Theatre Research; Modern Language Association; Central States Speech Association. Address: Dept. of Theatre and Drama, Indiana Univ., Bloomington, IN 47401.

Mr. Brockett has taught theatre courses and directed and designed plays at Univ. of Kentucky (1949–50), Stanford Univ. (1950–52), Stetson Univ. (1952–56), Univ. of Iowa (1956–63), Univ. of Southern California (Summer 1959), Univ. of Illinois (1963) and Indiana Univ. (1963–to date). He was a Fulbright Lecturer on American Theatre at the Univ. of Bristol, England (1963–64).

Published Works. Mr. Brockett has served as editor of the *Educational Theatre Journal,* and has published articles in the *Educational Theatre Journal, TDR, Theatre Research, Shakespeare Quarterly, Modern Philology, Quarterly Journal of Speech, Classical Journal, Civil War History, Southern Speech Journal, Cue, New Theatre Magazine, Encyclopaedia Britannica, Encyclopedia Americana,* and *World Book Encyclopedia.* He is the author of the following books: *A Bibliographical Guide to Research in Speech and Dramatic Art* (1963); *The Theatre: An Introduction* (1964; 2d ed. 1969; 3d ed. 1974); *Plays for the Theatre* (1967; 2d ed. 1974); *History of the Theatre* (1968; 2d ed. 1974); *Perspectives on Contemporary Theatre* (1971); *Studies in Theatre and Drama* (1972); and *Century of Innovation: A History of European and American Theatre and Drama Since 1870* (1973).

Awards. Fulbright Fellowship; Guggenheim Fellowship; Fellow, ATA; excellence in research, SCA.

BRODERICK, JAMES. Actor. b. Mar. 7, 1929, Manchester, N.H. Father, James Broderick, letter carrier. Educ. Univ. of New Hampshire (pre-medical). Professional training at Neighborhood Playhouse, N.Y.C. Served in US Navy, 1945–47. Married to Patricia; two daughters. Member of AEA; AFTRA; SAG.

Theatre. Mr. Broderick made his theatrical debut in summer stock at Duxbury, Mass., and first appeared on Bway as James Wylie in *Maggie* (National Th., Feb. 18, 1953). He was understudy for the role of Kenneth in *A Memory of Two Mondays,* one of the two plays making up the program *A View from the Bridge* (Coronet, Sept. 29, 1955); played the title role in a revival of *Johnny Johnson* (Carnegie Hall Th., Oct. 21, 1956); was Mickey Maloy in *A Touch of the Poet* (Helen Hayes Th., Oct. 2, 1958); replaced (1960) William Windom in *U.S.A.* (Martinique, Oct. 28, 1959); and played Tom in *The Glass Menagerie* and the Announcer in *The Skin of Our Teeth* on the US State Dept.—ANTA European tour (1960–61).

Mr. Broderick also played the Tiger in *Talking to You* and Harry Mallory in *Across the Board on Tomorrow Morning,* two William Saroyan plays billed as *Two by Saroyan* (East End Th., N.Y.C., Oct. 22, 1961); played Sepp Schmitz in *The Firebugs* (Maidman Th., Feb. 27, 1963); in 1965 was a member of the company at the Charles Playhouse, Boston, Mass., where he was in *The Madwoman of Chaillot* (Feb. 3), *The Plough and the Stars* (Mar. 10), and a Harold Pinter double-bill, *The Lover* and *The Collection* (Apr. 14); was on the double-bill *Rooms* (Cherry Lane, N.Y.C., Jan. 27, 1966), playing William Foster in *Better Luck Next Time* and Dr. Robert Palmer in *A Walk in Dark Places;* and played Alexander Edwards in *Johnny No-Trump* (Cort, Oct. 8, 1967).

He appeared in *Exiles* (Trinity Square Rep., Providence, R.I., Apr. 24, 1969); was Joe in *The Time of Your Life* (Vivian Beaumont Th., N.Y.C., Nov. 6, 1969); appeared in *The World of Carl Sandburg* (Alley Th., Houston, Tex., Apr. 16, 1970); played Dan Train in *Ring Round the Bathtub* (Alley Th., Dec. 3, 1970); was in *Scenes from American Life* (Forum, N.Y.C., Mar. 25, 1971); played Jerry Ryan in *Two for the Seesaw* (Olney Th., Olney, Md., July 13, 1971); was in *Lemon Sky* (Washington Th. Club,

Washington, D.C., Jan. 12, 1972); played Herman in *The Wedding Band* (Public Th., N.Y.C., Sept. 26, 1972); Deeley in *Old Times* (Hartford Stage Co., Hartford, Conn., Apr. 6, 1973); played in *The Front Page* (Cleveland Play House, Cleveland, Ohio, Oct. 19, 1973); in *Twelfth Night* (McCarter Th., Princeton, N.J., Feb. 14, 1974); and was James Tyrone in *Long Day's Journey into Night* (Kreeger Th., Arena Stage, Washington, D.C., Oct. 17, 1975).

Films. Mr. Broderick was in *The Group* (UA, 1966).

Television. Mr. Broderick has appeared on Hallmark Hall of Fame (NBC); ABC Stage 67; Walt Disney Presents (NBC); The F.B.I. (ABC); The Defenders (CBS); Play of the Week; and other programs.

BROEDER, RAY. General manager. b. Raymond Louis Broeder, Aug. 28, 1898, Potoch, Austria-Hungary, to Adolph and Pauline (Heck) Broeder. Father, farmer; mother, music teacher. Grad. H.S. of Commerce, N.Y.C., 1916; attended Pace & Pace Sch., N.Y.C., 1916–18. Served US Army, 1942–43; rank, Staff Sgt. Member of ATPAM (vice-pres., 1955); The Lambs; NY Athletic Club.

In 1943, Mr. Broeder became general manager of City Playhouses, Inc., operators of five legitimate theatres in N.Y.C. and the National Th. in Washington, D.C.

He was assistant auditor and manager for producer Charles B. Dillingham (1916–28); was general manager to composer Vincent Youmans (1928–34); and New York representative for Associated Talking Pictures, Ltd. (1934–36).

Mr. Broeder was company manager for *Elmer the Great* (Lyceum, N.Y.C., Sept. 24, 1928); *Yokel Boy* (Majestic, July 6, 1939); and *Margin for Error* (Plymouth, Nov. 3, 1939).

BRONNER, EDWIN. Playwright, editor-writer, theatre historian. b. Jan. 21, 1926, New York City, to Edwin H. and Joyce (Maduro) Bronner. Father, advertising executive. Attended Thomas Jefferson H.S., Elizabeth, N.J.; Middlebury Coll.; Columbia Univ.; The New Sch. for Social Research. Studied playwriting with Hatcher Hughes and John Gassner. Served US Army, Special Services.

Theatre. Mr. Bronner wrote *A Young American,* first presented at the Blackfriars Guild Th. (N.Y.C.), and on tour; and *The Intruder,* which was presented on tour. He conceived, assembled, and produced, with Gene Adrewski, a "revue of revues" entitled *One Damn Thing After Another* (Lyric Th., Oklahoma City, Okla., Sept. 30, 1964).

Television and Radio. Mr. Bronner was writer, producer, and narrator of the nationally syndicated radio programs Musical Comedy Memories (1950) and Hollywood Memories (1950).

For television, he was writer and producer of *Salute to Eugene O'Neill.*

Published Works. Mr. Bronner was author, with George Freedley, of *The Broadway Almanac;* and has contributed articles to *Saturday Review, Variety, Theatre Arts, Life* Magazine and many other publications.

Recreation. Collecting rare show-tune recordings and sheet-music.

BROOK, PETER. Director, designer. b. Peter Stephen Paul Brook, Mar. 21, 1925, London, England, to Simon and Ida (Jansen) Brook. Father, pharmaceuticals manufacturer; mother, chemist. Grad. Gresham's Sch., Holt, Eng., 1941; Magdalen Coll., Oxford Univ., B.A. 1944. Married Nov. 3, 1951, to Natasha Parry; one daughter. Member of SSD&C; Assn. of Cinematographers and Allied Technicians.

Theatre. Mr. Brook directed *Dr. Faustus* (Torch Th., London, 1943); subsequently at the Birmingham Repertory Th., directed *Man and Superman, King John,* and *The Lady from the Sea* (1945); directed an ENSA tour of *Pygmalion* for the British armed forces (1945); *The Barretts of Wimpole Street* ("Q," Th., London, 1945); *The Infernal Machine* (Chanticleer, 1945); *The Brothers Karamazov* (Lyric, Hammersmith, June 4, 1946); and at the Shakespeare Memorial Th., *Love's Labour's Lost* (Stratford-upon-Avon, 1946).

He directed *Man without Shadows* and *The Respectable Prostitute* (Lyric, Hammersmith, July 17, 1947); the opera, *Boris Godounov* (Covent Garden, 1948); *Dark of the Moon* (Ambassador's, Apr. 12, 1949); and at Covent Garden, directed three operas, *The Marriage of Figaro, The Olympians,* and *Salome* (1949).

Mr. Brook also directed *Romeo and Juliet* (Shakespeare Memorial Th., Stratford-upon-Avon, 1947); *Ring 'Round the Moon* (Globe, London, Jan. 26, 1950); *The Little Hut* (Lyric, Aug. 23, 1950); *Measure for Measure* (Shakespeare Memorial Th., Stratford-upon-Avon, Mar. 9, 1950); *Penny for a Song* (Haymarket, London, 1951); and *The Winter's Tale* (Phoenix, June 27, 1951).

He directed *Figure of Fun* (Aldwych, Oct. 16, 1951); *La mort d'un commis voyageur* (Th. National, Brussels, Bel., 1951); *Colombe* (New, London, Dec. 13, 1951); *Venice Preserved* (Lyric, Hammersmith, May 13, 1953); and his first assignment in the US was as director of *Faust* (Metropolitan Opera House, N.Y.C., Nov. 16, 1953).

He directed *The Dark Is Light Enough* (Aldwych, London, Apr. 30, 1954); *Both Ends Meet* (Apollo, June 9, 1954); *House of Flowers* (Alvin, N.Y.C., Dec. 30, 1954); *The Lark* (Lyric, Hammersmith, London, May 11, 1955); *Titus Andronicus* (Shakespeare Memorial Th., Stratford-upon-Avon, Aug. 16, 1955); and Paul Scofield's *Hamlet* (Phoenix, London, Dec. 8, 1955; and Mayakovsky Th., Moscow, U.S.S.R., Nov. 1955).

He directed *The Power and the Glory* (Phoenix, London, Apr. 5, 1956); *The Family Reunion* (Phoenix, June 7, 1956); directed and designed *A View from the Bridge* (Comedy, Oct. 11, 1956); directed and designed *La chatte sur un toit brulant (Cat on a Hot Tin Roof)* (Th. Antoine, Paris, Fr., 1956).

He directed and designed *The Tempest* (Shakespeare Memorial Th., Stratford-upon-Avon, Aug. 13, 1957); directed *Eugene Onegin* (Metropolitan Opera House, N.Y.C., 1957); *The Visit* (Lunt-Fontanne, N.Y.C., May 5, 1958; Royalty, London, June 23, 1960); and directed and designed *Vu du pont (A View from the Bridge)* (Th. Antoine, Paris, 1958).

He directed *Irma La Douce* (Lyric, London, July 17, 1959; Plymouth, N.Y.C., Sept. 29, 1960); *The Fighting Cock* (ANTA, Dec. 8, 1959); directed and designed *Le Balcon (The Balcony)* (Gymnase, Paris, 1960); became a co-director of the Royal Shakespeare Co. (June 1962); directed *King Lear* (Royal Shakespeare Th., Stratford-upon-Avon, Eng., Nov. 6, 1962; Aldwych, London, Dec. 12, 1962; NY State Th., N.Y.C., May 18, 1964); with Clifford Williams directed *The Tempest* Royal Shakespeare Th., Stratford-upon-Avon, Eng., Apr. 2, 1963); directed and designed *Serjeant Musgrave's Dance* (Th. de l'Athénée, Paris, 1963); and directed the Royal Shakespeare Company's *The Persecution and Assassination of Marat as Performed by the Inmates of the Asylum of Charenton under the Direction of the Marquis de Sade* (Aldwych, London, Aug. 20, 1964; Martin Beck Th., N.Y.C., Dec. 27, 1965).

He directed *The Physicists* (Martin Beck Th., Oct. 13, 1964); a reading of *The Investigation* (Aldwych, London, Nov. 14, 1965); the revue *US* (Aldwych, Oct. 13, 1966), parts of which he wrote; Seneca's *Oedipus,* which he also designed (Old Vic, London, Mar. 19, 1968); *The Tempest* (Round House, London, 1968); and the Royal Shakespeare Company's *A Midsummer Night's Dream* (Stratford-upon-Avon, Aug. 27, 1970; Billy Rose Th., N.Y.C., Jan. 20, 1971).

Mr. Brook founded (Fall 1970) the International Centre of Theatrical Research at the Galerie Mobilier National, Paris, Fr., a company to explore new uses of sound and language in the theatre. With this company and the poet Ted Hughes, Mr. Brook produced and directed *Orghast,* staged at the site of ancient Persepolis, near Shiraz, Iran (Summer 1971) and *The Conference of the Birds* (Th. Bouffes du Nord, Paris, 1972); the latter toured five West African countries (Nov. 1972–Jan. 1973) and was included in presentations made by the International Centre during a five-week visit in N.Y.C. (Brooklyn Acad. of Music, Sept.–Oct. 1973). In Paris, Mr. Brook and his group staged (all at Th. Bouffes du Nord) *Kaspar* (1972), *Timon of Athens* (Fall 1974), and *Les Iks* (Jan. 12, 1975).

Films. Mr. Brook directed *Sentimental Journey* (Oxford Univ. Film Society, Eng., 1944); *The Beggar's Opera* (WB, 1953); *Moderato Cantabile* (France, 1960); *Lord of the Flies* (Continental, 1963); *Tell Me Lies* (Continental, 1968); the film version of *Marat/-Sade* (UA, 1967); and *King Lear* (Col., 1969).

Television. He wrote *Box for One* (BBC, London, 1949); directed *King Lear* (Ford Foundation Program, 1953); and *Heaven and Earth* (ABC, 1957). He appeared on a television program about his work, *The Magic of Peter Brook* (Camera Three, CBS, Feb. 28 and Mar. 7, 1971).

Published Works. Mr. Brook wrote *The Empty Space* (1968).

Awards. Mr. Brook was made Commander of the British Empire and Chevalier de l'Ordre des Arts et des Lettres (both in 1965). For his direction of the play *Marat/Sade,* he won first place in the London Critics' Poll (best director, 1964–65); received an Antoinette Perry (Tony) Award as best play director (1966); was named first in the annual *Variety* NY Drama Critics Poll (best direction, 1965–66); and received the Outer Circle Award (1965–66). For his direction of *A Midsummer Night's Dream,* he was named by the Drama Desk outstanding director (1970–71); received a second Tony as best director; and won the *Variety* poll as best director for a second time. In 1973, he was given the Freiherr von Stein Foundation Shakespeare Award.

Recreation. Traveling.

BROOKE, IRIS. Educator, writer, costume designer, painter, book illustrator. b. 1908, to Isaac and Emily Evelina Brooke. Grad. Royal Coll. of Art, South Kensington, Eng., 1930. Married Nov. 14, 1931, to Patrick Macdowell (marr. dis.); one son; married June 4, 1944, to Hugh Giffard. During WW II, served as ambulance driver in London. Address: 15 Braemar House, Manor Rd., Teddington, Middlesex, England tel. 01-977-7735.

Iris Brooke has lectured on historic and theatrical costume throughout the US, England, Norway, and Japan; and in Paris, Jamaica, Canada, Stockholm, and Athens. She has designed both costume and settings for theatres, theatre schools, and universities. She has been a special lecturer in the Dept. of Drama at Bristol Univ. (1955–69) and a free-lance author and artist since 1931.

Television and Radio. She has lectured on costume design, historical subjects, architecture, and the history of art on radio and television in England (BBC, London; BBC, Bristol) and the US.

Other Activities. Miss Brooke was art critic for *Sphere* magazine (1936–39); and editor at Oldhams Press Book Dept. (1943–46). She has had exhibitions of her paintings and designs in the Royal Academy, London, and West of England Academy, Bristol.

Published Works. Miss Brooke's first published work was *English Costume of the Nineteenth Century* (1929) written from her notes by James Laver; wrote *English Children's Costume since 1775* (1930), *English Costume of the Eighteenth Century* (1931), *English Costume in the Age of Elizabeth* (1933), *English Costume of the Seventeenth Century* (1934), *English Costume of the Later Middle Ages* (1935), *English Costume of the Early Middle Ages* (1936), *History of English Costume* (1937), *Western European Costume and Its Relation to the Stage, Parts 1 & 2* (1939), 1940, 1963), *A History of English Footwear* (1949), *English Costume, 1900–1950* (1952), *Four Walls Adorned* (1952), *Pleasures of the Past* (1955), *Dress and Undress* (1958), *Costume in Greek Classic Drama* (1962), *Medieval Theatre Costume* (1967), *Footwear* (1971), and magazine and encyclopedia articles.

Awards. In 1958, Miss Brooke was granted a Coulson research award by Bristol Univ. for study in Greece. She was a Fulbright Scholar (1960–61).

BROOKES, JACQUELINE. Actress. b. Jacqueline Victoire Brookes, July 24, 1930, Montclair, N.J., to Frederick J. and Maria V. (Zur Haar) Brookes. Father, accountant. Grad. Hunter Coll. H.S., N.Y.C., 1947; State Univ. of Iowa, B.F.A. (magna cum laude) 1951. Studied at RADA, London, as a Fulbright scholar, 1953; acting with Michael Howard, N.Y.C., two years; singing with Raymond J. D. Buckingham, N.Y.C., one year. Member of AEA; SAG; AFTRA; Actors Studio (1971). Address: (home) 182 Waverly Place, New York, NY 10014, tel. (212) YU 9-4269; (bus.) c/o Oscar Assocs., 19 W. 44th St., New York, NY 10019, tel. (212) YU 6-8470.

Theatre. Miss Brookes made her stage debut at age thirteen as a supernumerary in *La Bohème* (Metropolitan Opera House, N.Y.C., 1943); subsequently appeared as Emilia in the Shakespeare Guild's *Othello* (Jan Hus House, Oct. 14, 1953); Phaedra in *The Cretan Woman* (Provincetown Playhouse, July 7, 1954); was understudy to Marion Winters as Gelda in *The Dark Is Light Enough* (ANTA Th., Feb. 25, 1955), and on tour; and played Vittoria Corombona in *The White Devil* (Phoenix, Mar. 17, 1955).

For ANTA's Salute to France, she played the Second Woman in *Medea* (Th. Sarah Bernhardt, Paris, June 14, 1955); at the Antioch Shakespeare Festival (Yellow Springs, Ohio, July 1955) played Lady Macbeth in *Macbeth,* the Queen in *Cymbeline,* and the Jailer's Daughter in *Two Noble Kinsmen;* appeared as a Woman and was understudy to Leueen McGrath as Cassandra in *Tiger at the Gates* (Plymouth, N.Y.C., Oct. 3, 1955); at the American Shakespeare Festival (Stratford, Conn.), she played Blanche of Spain in *King John* (June 26, 1956), Juliet in *Measure for Measure* (June 27, 1956), and succeeded Mildred Dunnock as Constance in *King John* later that season.

She appeared as Celimene in *The Misanthrope* (Th. East, N.Y.C., Nov. 12, 1956); the title role in *The Duchess of Malfi* (Phoenix, Mar. 19, 1957); at the American Shakespeare Festival (Stratford, Conn.) played Desdemona in *Othello* (June 22, 1957), Ursula, and was standby for Katherine Hepburn as Beatrice in *Much Ado About Nothing* (Aug. 7, 1957), and in the national tour (opened Dec. 30, 1957; closed Mar. 1, 1958); appeared as Sheila in *Dial 'M' for Murder* (Cape Playhouse, Dennis, Mass., Aug. 1958); and Anna Petrovna in *Ivanov* (Renata, N.Y.C., Oct. 7, 1958).

At the Univ. of Michigan Drama Festival, she played Lady Macbeth in *Macbeth* (Lydia Mendelssohn Th., Ann Arbor, Mich., May 1959); for the Ford Foundation, appeared as the Mother in *Kinderspiel* (Boston Univ., Oct. 1959); and for the San Diego National Shakespeare Festival, played Portia in *Julius Caesar,* Rosalind in *As You Like It,* and Gertrude in *Hamlet* (Old Globe Th., San Diego, Calif., Summer 1960).

She joined the Association of Producing Artists (APA) (McCarter Th., Princeton, N.J., Winter 1960), and appeared as Ilona in *Anatol,* Zerbinette in *Scapin,* Goneril in *King Lear,* Helena in *A Midsummer Night's Dream,* and Ophelia in *Hamlet;* returned to the Old Globe Th. (Summer 1961) to play Viola in *Twelfth Night,* Portia in *The Merchant of Venice,* and Elizabeth in *Richard III;* at the Fred Miller Th. (Milwaukee, Wis., Winter 1961–62), played Mrs. Molloy in *The Matchmaker,* the Stepdaughter in *Six Characters in Search of an Author,* Katherine in *The Taming of the Shrew,* Elizabeth Proctor in *The Crucible,* and Dona Lucia in *Charley's Aunt.*

At the Univ. of Kansas, Miss Brookes played Madame Ranevsky in *The Cherry Orchard* (Feb. 1963); subsequently appeared as the Stepdaughter in *Six Characters in Search of an Author* (Martinique, N.Y.C., Mar. 7, 1963); at the San Diego (Calif.), National Shakespeare Festival, she played Helena in *A Midsummer Night's Dream,* Hermione in *The Winter's Tale,* and Cleopatra in *Antony and Cleopatra* (Old Globe, Summer 1963); and appeared as Joan in the opera *Joan of Arc at the Stake* (NY City Ctr., Oct. 3, 1963).

She appeared at the American Shakespeare Festival, Stratford, Conn., in 1964 as Beatrice in *Much Ado About Nothing* (June 3) and Elizabeth in *King Richard III* (May 30) and the same year was Katherina in *The Taming of the Shrew* (Queen Elizabeth Th., Vancouver, B.C.). She returned to San Diego's National Shakespeare Festival in 1965 as Mistress Page in *The Merry Wives of Windsor* (June 15), Katherine of Aragon in *King Henry VIII* (June 23), and Volumnia in *Coriolanus* (July 13). She created the role of Elinor Frost in the Univ. of Michigan premiere of *An Evening's Frost* (Lydia Mendelssohn Th., Ann Arbor, 1965), repeated in N.Y.C. (Th. de Lys, Oct. 11, 1965). In 1966, she played the title role in the premiere of *White Widow* (Florida State Univ.) and was Athene and the Leader of the Chorus in the Ypsilanti (Mich.) Greek Festival presentation of *The Oresteia* (June 28). She played also in the ANTA Matinee Theater Series presentation of *Come Slowly, Eden* (Th. de Lys, N.Y.C., Dec. 5, 1966).

Miss Brookes appeared in 1967 in the ANTA Regional Conference presentation of *Dear Liar* (St. Paul, Minn.), followed by a tour in the play for the Minnesota Arts Council. She was at the San Diego Shakespeare Festival as Helena in *All's Well That Ends Well,* Maria in *Twelfth Night,* and Emilia in *Othello* (Old Globe, Summer 1967) and was a standby for *More Stately Mansions* (Ahmanson Th., Los Angeles, Sept. 12, 1967), repeated in N.Y.C. (Broadhurst, Oct. 31, 1967). In 1968, she appeared at Southampton as Gertrude Eastman Quevas in *In the Summer House* and in *Immortal Husband* (both repeated at the Dublin Festival, 1969); played the title role in *Mother Courage* (Morehead State Univ., Morehead, Ky.); and was in the Actors Studio presentation of *The Plebians Rehearse the Uprising.*

In 1969, Miss Brookes was a standby for the N.Y.C. production of *In the Bar of a Tokyo Hotel* (Eastside Playhouse, May 11); played in *American Roulette;* and appeared with Lincoln Center Repertory, as Renata in *The Increased Difficulty of Concentration* (Forum, Dec. 4). Her 1970 performances included Diane in *Watercolor* (ANTA Th., Jan. 21); Atossa in *The Persians* (St. George's Church, N.Y.C., Apr. 15); the title role in the Little Orchestra Society's presentation of *Herodiade* (Alice Tully Hall); and Estella in the American Place's production, *Sunday Dinner* (St. Clement's Church, N.Y.C., Oct. 16. She was the Abbess of Argenteuil in *Abelard & Heloise* (Brooks Atkinson Th., Mar. 10, 1971); appeared at the Eugene O'Neill Th. Ctr., Waterford, Conn., as Countess Tolstoy in *Body and Soul* (July 16, 1971) and as Elizabeth Bruce in *Bruce* (July 30, 1971); and took over (Nov. 17, 1971) the role of Bunny in *The House of Blue Leaves* (Truck and Warehouse Th., Feb. 10, 1971).

She created the role of Carrie in *Silent Partner* (Actors Studio, May 8, 1972); returned to the Eugene O'Neill Th. Ctr., where she was Julie English in *And the Old Man Had Two Sons* (July 15, 1972), and Lena and the Old Woman in *Tales of the Revolution and Other American Fables* (Aug. 3, 1972); and appeared in the Phoenix Sideshow production, *Meeting by the River* (Dec. 1972). She played Marion in *Owners* (Mercer-Shaw Th., May 14, 1973); was standby for the role of Josie in *A Moon for the Misbegotten* (Kennedy Ctr., Washington, D.C., and Morosco, N.Y.C., 1973–74); and appeared as Kath in the U.R.G.E.N.T. revival of *Entertaining Mr. Sloane* (1974).

Films. Miss Brookes has appeared in the following films for Paramount: *Hospital* (1971), *Werewolf of Washington* (1972), and *Gambler* (1973).

Television. Miss Brookes made her debut on Adventure (NBC, 1955); subsequently appeared in *Elizabethan Miscellany* (Camera Three, CBS, 1956); in the title role in *Antigone* (Look Up and Live, CBS, 1956); as Mary Magdalene on Frontiers of Faith (CBS, 1958); on Lamp Unto My Feet (CBS, 1958); as Athena in *The Oresteia* (Omnibus, CBS, 1959); the Second Woman in *Medea* (Play of the Week, NTA, 1959); for ten months played Liz Conroy on Love of Life (CBS, 1962); and appeared as a Citizen in *Fall of a City* (Accent, CBS, 1962). She was on Time for Us (ABC, 1964); Direction (CBS, 1968–70); played Miss Thompson on As the World Turns (CBS, 1970); appeared on You Are There (CBS, 1971), Look Up and Live (1971), Sit Down, Shut Up, or Get Out (NBC, 1971); and was Ursula Winthrop on Secret Storm (1972).

Other Activities. Miss Brookes taught (1973–74) at the Circle in the Square, N.Y.C.

Awards. Miss Brookes, while attending RADA, won the Temperly Prize for the most promising performance (1953). She received the *Theatre World* Award for her performance as Phaedra in *The Cretan Woman* (1955); and the *Village Voice* Off-Bway (Obie) Award for her performance as the Stepdaughter in *Six Characters in Search of an Author* (1963); and she was named actress of the year in 1969 by the Dublin (Ireland) *Times* for her performance in *In the Summer House.*.

Recreation. Tennis, bridge.

BROOKS, DAVID. Actor, director, producer, singer. b. Henry David Berger, Sept. 24, 1920, Portland, Ore., to Henry and Grace (Von Gruenwald) Berger. Father, photographer; mother, concert pianist. Attended Univ. of Washington, 1937–40; studied with Steward Wilson, Curtis Inst. of Music, Philadelphia, 1940–42; studied with Sylvan Levin, Philadelphia, 1943–44; attended Columbia Univ., 1945–46; studied with Signora Zinetti, Milan, Italy, 1950–52. Married June 4, 1960, to Grace Cavender Van Dyke, magazine editor. Member of AEA; AFTRA.

Pre-Theatre. Photography.

Theatre. Mr. Brooks made his stage debut as Octavian in the opera *Der Rosenkavalier* (Philadelphia Acad. of Music, Pa., Dec. 1942); was lead baritone with the Philadelphia Opera Co. for two seasons (1942–44); made his N.Y.C. debut as Jeff Calhoun in *Bloomer Girl* (Shubert, Oct. 5, 1944); subsequently appeared as Tommy Albright in *Brigadoon* (Ziegfeld, Mar. 13, 1947); Robert Burns in *Comin' Thro' the Rye* (Olney Th., Olney, Md., Aug. 19, 1952; Westport Country Playhouse, Conn., Aug. 31, 1953); Clyde Hallam in *The Girl in Pink Tights* (Shubert Th., New Haven, Conn., Jan. 25, 1954; Mark Hellinger Th., N.Y.C., Feb. 27, 1954); Tim Cavanaugh in *Sandhog* (Phoenix Th., Nov. 23, 1954); directed the opera *Trouble in Tahiti,* included in the program *All in One* (Playhouse, Apr. 19, 1955); sang Macheath in the world premiere of the Marc Blitzstein translation of *The Threepenny Opera* (Brandeis Univ. Th., Boston, Mass., Sept. 1957); co-produced (Rooftop Productions) *Endgame* (Cherry Lane, N.Y.C, Jan. 28, 1958); directed *The Bald Soprano* and *Jack* (Sullivan St. Playhouse, June 3, 1958); and co-produced (Rooftop Productions) *Ulysses in Nighttown* (Rooftop, June 5, 1958).

He staged *The Shepherd's Chameleon* (Th. de Lys, Nov. 29, 1960); played Governor Bardal in *Mr. President* (St. James, Oct. 20, 1962); played Jim in *The Sunday Man* (Morosco, May 13. 1964); the Man in *Park* (Center Stage, Baltimore, Md., Feb. 25, 1970; John Golden Th., N.Y.C., Apr. 22, 1970); Winkleman in *The Last Analysis* (Circle in the Square, June 23, 1971); and directed *Sally, George and Martha* (Th. de Lys, Dec. 20, 1971).

Television. Mr. Brooks was a staff director for CBS (1960–61).

Recreation. Farming, horses.

BROOKS, DONALD. Costume designer. b. Donald Marc Brooks, Jan. 10, 1928, New York City, to Harrison and Miriam (Goodwin) Brooks. Father, hotel executive. Attended Syracuse Univ., 1946–49; Parsons Sch. of Design, 1949–51. Member of United Scenic Artists; Council of Fashion Designers of America.

Theatre. Mr. Brooks designed Diahann Carroll's costumes for *No Strings* (54 St. Th., N.Y.C., Mar. 15, 1962); was costume designer for *Barefoot in the Park* (Biltmore, Oct. 23, 1963); *The Amorous Flea* (E. 78 St. Playhouse, Feb. 17, 1964); *Fade Out—Fade In* (Mark Hellinger Th., May 26, 1964); designed clothes for Arlene Francis in *Beekman Place* (Morosco, Oct. 7, 1964); costumes for *Rich Little*

Rich Girl (pre-Bway, opened Walnut St. Th., Philadelphia, Pa., Oct. 26, 1964; closed there Nov. 7, 1964); *Poor Bitos* (Cort, N.Y.C., Nov. 14, 1964); *Diamond Orchid* (Henry Miller's Th., Feb. 10, 1965); *Flora, the Red Menace* (Alvin Th., May 11, 1965); *Promises, Promises* (Sam S. Shubert Th., Dec. 1, 1968); *Last of the Red Hot Lovers* (Eugene O'Neill Th., Dec. 28, 1969); *Minnie's Boys* (Imperial, Mar. 26, 1970); and *Night Watch* (Morosco, Feb. 28, 1972).

He designed costumes for the New Phoenix Repertory Co. revival of *Holiday* (Ethel Barrymore Th., Dec. 26, 1973); for Jane Powell, replacing (Feb. 6, 1974) Debbie Reynolds in the title role of the revival of *Irene* (Minskoff Th., Mar. 13, 1973); for the revival of *Good News* (St. James Th., Dec. 23, 1974); for Alexis Smith in *Summer Brave* (ANTA Th., Oct. 26, 1975); and for *A Musical Jubilee* (St. James Th., Nov. 13, 1975).

Films. Mr. Brooks designed the costumes for *The Cardinal* (Col., 1963); *The Third Day* (WB, 1965); *Star* (20th-Fox, 1968); *Darling Lili* (Par., 1970); and *The Drowning Pool* (WB, 1975).

Television. Mr. Brooks designed costumes for *An Evening with Carol Channing* (CBS, Feb. 19, 1966) and for Mia Farrow's special (ABC, Feb. 8, 1974).

Other Activities. Mr. Brooks designs men's and women's clothing; shoes; home furnishings fabrics; is a design consultant; and has lectured at Parsons School of Design since 1964.

Awards. Mr. Brooks received the American Fashion Critics (Coty) Award (1958, 1962, 1970); the National Cotton Award (1960, 1970); the Parsons School of Design Medal (1974); won the *Variety* NY Drama Critics Poll for his costumes in *No Strings* (1962); and was nominated for an Academy (Oscar) Award for his costumes in *The Cardinal* (1964).

Recreation. Theatre, concerts, opera, ballet, art, reading.

BROOKS, LAWRENCE. Actor, singer. b. Emile Huard, Aug. 7, 1912, Westbrook, Me., to Emile Eli and Anna (Duchaine) Huard. Father, storekeeper. Grad. Westbrook H.S., 1932; studied voice with Estele Liebling, N.Y.C., 1942. Married Apr. 12, 1956, to Pauline Burnham. Member of AEA; AFTRA; AGVA; Catholic Actors' Guild of America (vice-pres., 1964).

Theatre. Mr. Brooks made his first appearances on stage with the Portland (Me.) Players in *Kind Lady, Double Door, The Gondoliers,* and *Yeomen of the Guard* (1939); made his N.Y.C. debut as Edvard Grieg in *Song of Norway* (Imperial, Aug. 21, 1944); subsequently played Bishop Tom Armstrong in *My Romance* (Shubert, Oct. 19, 1948); Joey in a touring company of *The Most Happy Fella* (Summer 1958); was standby for Alfred Drake in *Kean* (Bway Th., Nov. 2, 1961); appeared as Dr. Sumner in *Riverwind* (Actors' Playhouse, Dec. 12, 1962); was standby for Alfred Drake in the pre-Bway tryout of *Zenda* (opened Curran, San Francisco, Aug. 5, 1963; closed Civic Aud., Pasadena, Calif., Nov. 16, 1963); appeared in *Meet Me in St. Louis* (Municipal Th., St. Louis, Mo., June 7, 1965); played Col. Drivinitz in *Anya* (Ziegfeld Th., Nov. 29, 1965), in which he was an alternate for Michael Kermoyan in the role of Bounine; and has appeared at the Brunswick (Me.) Summer Playhouse in musicals such as *The Sound of Music* and *Silk Stockings.*

Recreation. Golf, building models of airplanes which fly by radio control, photography.

BROUN, HEYWOOD HALE. Television and radio announcer, actor, author. b. Mar. 10, 1918, New York City, to Heywood Campbell and Ruth (Hale) Brown. Father, journalist, critic, actor; mother, journalist, theatrical press representative. Grad. Horace Mann Sch., 1936; Swarthmore Coll., B.A. (Phi Beta Kappa) 1940. Studied acting with Joseph Leon, N.Y.C., 1955–56. Married 1949 to Jane Lloyd-Jones, actress; one son. Relative in theatre: uncle, Richard Hale, actor. Served WW II, US Army; rank, T/Sgt. Member of AEA; SAG; AFTRA; Amer. Newspaper Guild; The Coffee House Club. Address: (home) 35 W. 81st St., New York, NY 10024, tel. TR 7-8872; (bus.) c/o Julie Leonard, 11 W. 42nd St., New York, NY 10036.

Pre-Theatre. Columnist, book critic, sports writer, co-proprietor of record company.

Theatre. Mr. Broun made his stage debut as Mr. Thorkelson in *I Remember Mama* at the Woodstock (N.Y.) Playhouse (July 1949) where he appeared (1950–58) in *Anna Lucasta, Joy to the World, A Sound of Hunting, The Live Wire, The Enchanted, Mr. Roberts, Finian's Rainbow, Picnic, Sabrina Fair, My Three Angels, Look Homeward Angel, The Disenchanted, The Solid Gold Cadillac, The Bad Seed, Tovarich,* and *The Rainmaker.* At the Lakeside Th. (Putnam, Conn.), he played Mr. Hawkes in *Peg O' My Heart* and the Vicar in *Yes and No* (Summer 1949).

He made his N.Y.C. debut as the Phone Man in *Love Me Long* (48 St. Th., Nov. 7, 1949); played Mr. Ripley in *The Bird Cage* (Coronet, Feb. 22, 1950); Harry Holland in *The Live Wire* (Playhouse, Aug. 17, 1950); the Great Chesterton in *The Small Hours* (Natl. Feb. 15, 1951); and the bank clerk in *Point of No Return* (Alvin, Dec. 13, 1951).

He played Bluntschli in *Idiot's Delight* (Westport Country Playhouse, Conn., 1952); Ed Glennon in *The Pink Elephant* (Playhouse, N.Y.C., Apr. 22, 1953); appeared in *The Frogs of Spring* in Ogunquit (Me.) and at the Falmouth (Mass.) Playhouse; appeared as "Her Lawyer" in *His and Hers* (48 St. Th., N.Y.C., Jan. 8, 1954); in stock, as the Inspector in *Dial 'M' for Murder* (Westchester County Playhouse, Mt. Kisco, N.Y., 1954); and the following year there, played the psychiatrist in *The Seven Year Itch,* Leroy in *The Bad Seed,* and the insurance man in *Affair of Murder.*

He played the Postman in *The Gimmick* at the Westport (Conn.) Country Playhouse (1956); succeeded (June 21, 1958) Jack Weston as Francis in *The Bells Are Ringing* (Shubert, N.Y.C., Nov. 29, 1956); appeared in *Janus* (Bucks County Playhouse, New Hope, Pa., 1958); played the Clerk in *The Andersonville Trial* (Henry Miller's Th., N.Y.C., Dec. 29, 1959); and Mr. Akins in *Send Me No Flowers* (Brooks Atkinson Th., Dec. 5, 1960), a role he also played at the Pocono Playhouse (Mountainhouse, Pa.); Falmouth, (Mass.) Playhouse; Cape Playhouse (Dennis, Mass.); the Ogunquit (Me.) Playhouse; Lakewood Th. (Skowhegan, Me.); Playhouse-on-the-Mall (Paramus, N.J.); Clinton, N.J.; and the Royal Poinciana Playhouse (Palm Beach, Fla.).

Mr. Broun appeared as Mr. Whitmyer in *Take Her, She's Mine* (Biltmore, N.Y.C., Dec. 21, 1961); in *Love Among the Platypi* (Bucks County Playhouse, New Hope, Pa., 1962); as Mr. Kelly in *My Mother, My Father, and Me* (Plymouth, N.Y.C., Mar. 23, 1963); Man in Periwig in *My Kinsman, Major Molineux,* Part 1 of *The Old Glory* (American Place Th., Nov. 1, 1964); Dr. Franklin Dugmore in *The Man with the Perfect Wife* (Royal Poinciana Playhouse, Palm Beach, Fla., Mar. 22, 1965; Coconut Grove Playhouse, Miami, Fla., Mar. 30, 1965); Michael Wellspot in *Xmas in Las Vegas* (Ethel Barrymore Th., N.Y.C., Nov. 4, 1965); William Tracy in *The Philadelphia Story* (Royal Poinciana, Mar. 14, 1966); and Carol Newquist in *Little Murders* (Broadhurst, N.Y.C., Apr. 25, 1967).

Films. Mr. Broun appeared in *It Should Happen to You* (Col., 1952); *All the Way Home* (Par., 1963); and *Black Like Me* (Reade-Sterling, 1964).

Television and Radio. Mr. Broun made his debut on Phil Silvers' Arrow Television Th. (NBC, Feb. 1949); appeared in *Bloomer Girl* (Producer's Showcase, NBC, 1956); *Ethan Frome* (Dupont Show of the Month, CBS, 1960); and was moderator for *The Poet Looks at the 20th Century* (Under Discussion, WNEW-TV, Sept. 1964). He appeared on The Nurses (CBS, 1964); Car 54, Where Are You? (ABC, 1965); The Defenders (CBS, 1965, 1966); The Today Show (1965); the Quote Unquote panel series (Ind., 1966–67); the Patty Duke Show (ABC); and the US Steel Hour (CBS).

On radio, he performed in The Eternal Light series and was guest critic for Invitation to Learning (1960–62). From 1965 through 1975, he has been a CBS-TV news and sports commentator.

Published Works. Mr. Broun edited a book of his father's newspaper columns, entitled *The Collected Edition of Heywood Brown* (1940). He also wrote *A Studied Madness* (1965).

BROWN, ARVIN. Director, artistic director. b. Los Angeles, Calif., 1940. Educ. Los Angeles public schools. Grad. Stanford Univ., B.A.; Harvard Univ., M.A. Studied at Univ. of Bristol, England (Fulbright scholarship). Professional training, Yale Univ. School of Drama, 1963–65. Married to Joyce Ebert, actress. Member of Theatre Communications Group (co-pres.); Natl. Endowment for the Arts (theatre panel). Address: c/o Long Wharf Theatre, 222 Sargent Drive, New Haven, CT 06511.

Theatre. Mr. Brown began his directing career at the Univ. of Bristol, England, where he directed August Strindberg's one-act play *The Stronger.* He joined the Long Wharf Th., New Haven, Conn., when it began operations (Summer 1965) as a supervisor of the apprentice program and within a year directed his first full-length play there, *Long Day's Journey into Night* (May 6, 1966). In 1967, he became artistic director of the entire Long Wharf program, holding that post at present. Plays he has personally directed at Long Wharf include: *Misalliance* (Jan. 13, 1967); *The Glass Menagerie* (Oct. 20, 1967); *The Rehearsal* (Nov. 17, 1967); *A Whistle in the Dark* (Amer. premiere, Feb. 9, 1968); *Don Juan in Hell* (May 3, 1968); *The Lion in Winter* (Oct. 18, 1968); the double-bill *The Indian Wants the Bronx* and *It's Called a Sugar Plum* (Mar. 7, 1969); *Ghosts* (May 2, 1969); and *Tango* (Nov. 14, 1969).

Also *Country People* (American premiere, Jan. 9, 1970); *Spoon River Anthology* (Apr. 3, 1970); *Yegor Bulichov* (American premiere, Dec. 18, 1970); *Solitaire/Double Solitaire* (world premiere, Feb. 12, 1971); *You Can't Take It with You* (Oct. 22, 1971); *The Contractor* (American premiere, Nov. 19, 1971); *Hamlet* (Jan. 21, 1972); *A Swan Song,* part of a program billed as *Troika* (Mar. 17, 1972); *The Iceman Cometh* (Apr. 14, 1972); *What Price Glory?* (Oct. 22, 1972); *The Changing Room* (Amer. premiere, Nov. 17, 1972); *Juno and the Paycock* (Mar. 2, 1973); *Forget-Me-Not Lane* (American premiere, Apr. 6, 1973); *The Widowing of Mrs. Holroyd* (American premiere, Nov. 16, 1973); *The Seagull* (Mar. 1, 1974); *The National Health* (Apr. 5, 1974); *Ah, Wilderness!* (Dec. 20, 1974); and *Artichoke* (world premiere, Oct. 17, 1975).

In addition to his work at the Long Wharf Th., Mr. Brown has directed productions in other cities. He made his London debut as director of *The Indian Wants the Bronx* (1967). In N.Y.C., productions directed by Mr. Brown include *A Whistle in the Dark* (Mercury, Oct. 8, 1969); *Hay Fever* (Helen Hayes Th., Nov. 3, 1970); *Long Day's Journey into Night* (Promenade Th., Apr. 21, 1971); *Solitaire/Double Solitaire* (John Golden Th., Sept. 30, 1971); *The National Health* (Circle in the Square/Joseph E. Levine Th., Oct. 10, 1974); and *Ah, Wilderness!* (Circle in the Square/Joseph E. Levine Th., Sept. 18, 1975). In Los Angeles, he directed *Forget-Me-Not Lane* (Mark Taper Forum, May 31, 1973) and *Saint Joan* (Ahmanson Th., Jan. 29, 1974). He also directed a musical version of *Juno and the Paycock* at the Williamstown (Mass.) Th. (Summer 1974).

Films. In 1973, Mr. Brown directed *Cold Sweat.* .

Television. Mr. Brown's staging of *The Widowing of Mrs. Holroyd* was televised (Theatre in America, PBS, 1974).

Awards. For his direction of the N.Y.C. revival of *Long Days's Journey Into Night* (1971), Mr. Brown received the Vernon Rice Award and was named in the 1970-71 *Variety* poll as best off-Bway director.

BROWN, DEMARCUS. Educator, director. b. May 13, 1900, Woodland, Calif., to DeMarcus and Margaret (Phillips) Brown. Father, farmer. Grad. Woodland H.S., 1923; Coll. of the Pacific, A.B. 1923; studied with Hedwiga Reicher and Irving Pichel at AADA, Summer 1923; with Maurice Browne, Ellen Von Volkenburg at San Francisco Sch. of the Th., 1923–24; Coll. of the Pacific, M.A. 1934. Married June 20, 1926, to Lucy Woodhouse, drama coach; one daughter. Member of Theta Alphia Phi. Address: (home) 142 W. Knoles Way, Stockton, CA 95204, tel. (209) HO 2-7771; (bus.) Univ. of the Pacific, Stockton, CA 95204, tel. (209) HO 2-8676.

Until his retirement in 1968, Mr. Brown was Chairman of the Drama Dept. of the Univ. of the Pacific, where he had been teaching since 1924.

He became director of the Pacific Th. in 1926, where he produced and directed over 300 plays, including the American premiere of Maurice Browne's *Tomorrow's Sun* (Apr. 1946). He founded Fallon Th., Columbia State Park, Columbia, Calif., where he was producer-director (1949–69) for a summer repertory program and produced over a hundred plays.

BROWN, GEORGIA. Actress, singer. b. Lillian Claire Laizer Getel Klot, Oct. 21, 1933, London, England, to Mark and Anne (Kirshenbaum) Klot. Father, furrier. Attended Central Foundation Sch. for Girls, London, 1944–50. Studied singing with Keith Davis, N.Y.C., one year; acting with Curt Conway, N.Y.C., one year. Married Nov. 7, 1974, to Gareth Wigan. Member of AEA; AFTRA; AGVA.

Pre-Theatre. Night Clubs.

Theatre. Miss Brown first appeared on stage in a girls' club pageant in London (1950); first appeared professionally in a variety show (Empire Th., London, 1951); and later toured England in variety shows (Moss Empire Tour, 1954).

She appeared as Lucy Brown in *The Threepenny Opera* (Royal Court, London, Feb. 9, 1956), and succeeded (June 1957) Beatrice Arthur in the same role (Th. de Lys, N.Y.C., Sept. 20, 1955); played Jeanie in *The Lily White Boys* (Royal Court, London, Jan. 27, 1960); Nancy in *Oliver* (New, London, June 30, 1960; Imperial, N.Y.C., Jan. 6, 1963).

Miss Brown succeeded (Mar. 1, 1965) Rachel Roberts in the title role of *Maggie May* (Adelphi, London, Sept. 22, 1964); she appeared in *Artists Against Apartheid* (Prince of Wales Th., Mar. 22, 1965); and played Widow Begbick in *Man Is Man* (Royal Court, Mar. 1971).

Films. Miss Brown appeared in *A Study in Terror* (Col., 1965); *Fog* (Col., 1966); and *The Fixer* (MGM, 1968).

Television. Miss Brown appeared on Tophat (BBC, London, 1950); Show Time (BBC, 1954); played Yvette Pottier in *Mother Courage* (BBC, 1960); and has appeared as a guest on numerous programs, including Password (CBS, 1964–65); Get the Message (ABC, 1964–65); the Ed Sullivan Show (CBS, 1964–65); and Girl Talk (ABC, 1964–65). She was in the musical special *Take a Sapphire* (BBC, London, England, Fall 1965); on David Jacobs' Words and Music (Rediffusion, Oct. 3, 1966); *The Heart of Show Business* (ATV, Apr. 1967); and *Shoulder to Shoulder* (WNET, 1975).

Night Clubs. Miss Brown first appeared as a singer in the Stork Room (London, 1950); subsequently appeared in the American Army Service Clubs in Germany with the USO; in clubs in Paris and Monte Carlo; the Casina Della Rosa (Rome, It.); and at the Mocambo (Hollywood, Calif.).

Discography. Miss Brown recorded *The Many Shades of Georgia Brown* (Capitol, 1965) and *Georgia Brown Sings Kurt Weill* (Capitol, 1970).

Awards. Miss Brown received the *Variety* Critics Poll Award (England) (1961) for her performance as Nancy in *Oliver* and was nominated for the Antoinette Perry (Tony) Award (1963) for her role in *Oliver!* in N.Y.C.

BROWN, IRVING. Educator, director, administrator. b. Irving Marsan Brown, Apr. 15, 1922, Cambridge, Mass., to Irving Menzies and M. (Vertene) Brown. Father, civil engineer. Grad. Arlington (Mass.) H.S., 1939; Antioch Coll., A.B. 1948; State Univ. of Iowa, M.A. 1950; Ohio State Univ., Ph.D. 1961. Married Sept. 29, 1946, to Eleanor Taylor; one son, one daughter. Served USNR, 1943–46; rank, Lt. (j.g.). Member of AETA; ACTA; ANTA; AAUP; Maryland Arts Council (mbr., dance and theatre panels, 1970–72); Greater Baltimore Arts Council (pres., 1971–72); Maryland Dance Theatre (bd. of dir., 1972–73). Address: Office of the Dean of Fine and Performing Arts, State University of New York, New Paltz, NY 12561.

Mr. Brown taught theatre courses and was associate director at Antioch (Ohio) Area Th. (1948–49); technical director at Univ. of Connecticut (1950–51); acting director (1951–52) and production supervisor (1953–54) at Ohio State Univ.; and associate director (1954–55) and director (1955–66) at Lake Erie College-Community Th.

He was theatre and dance education specialist for the arts and humanities program of the US Office of Education 1966–68); professor of fine arts and director of the fine arts program at the Univ. of Maryland, Baltimore (1968–70); and director of the arts program at Antioch Coll. (1970–73). Since 1973, he has been dean of fine and performing arts at the State Univ. of New York College at New Paltz.

In 1967, his translation (co-authored) of Carlo Goldoni's *The Servant of Two Masters* was produced at McCarter Theatre, Princeton Univ.

He directed and acted at the Antioch (Ohio) Area Th. (Summer 1961); directed *A View from the Bridge* (Greek-Cypriote Natl. Th., Nicosia, Cyprus, 1963); and was lecturer-consultant in Theatre Arts for the U.S. Educational Foundation in Cyprus (1962–63).

He has appeared as an actor in industrial films for Industrial Motion Pictures, Inc. (Cleveland, Ohio, 1955–59) and on KYW-TV (Cleveland, Ohio, 1958–59).

He has written articles on theatre for the *Lake Erie College Bulletin* and the U.S. Information Agency.

Awards. For his play *Help Wanted,* written with Marjorie Watson, Mr. Brown received a citation from the Mental Health Federation, Inc., the Ohio Division of the National Assn. for Mental Health.

BROWN, KELLY. Dancer, actor. b. Elford Cornelious Kelly Kingman Brown, Sept. 24, 1928, Maysville, Ky., to Arnold Elmore and Sue (Taylor) Brown. Father, salesman; mother, dancing teacher. Grad. Maysville H.S., 1946; attended Brown Dance Studio, Maysville, 1946; Stone-Camryn Sch. of Ballet, Chicago, Ill., 1946–49. Studied voice with Ken Welch, one year; acting with Wynn Handman, three years; voice with Raoul Querze, five years. Married July 15, 1951, to Isabel Mirrow, dancer, two sons, two daughters. Member of SAG; AFTRA; AEA; AGVA. Address: 250 W. 94th St., New York, NY 10025, tel. (212) MO 6-5676.

Pre-Theatre. Newspaper boy, busboy, assistant dancing teacher.

Theatre. Mr. Brown first performed in a dancing school recital (1940); and made his professional debut as a member of the corps de ballet in *Carmen* (Chicago Civic Opera House, Nov. 1947). He toured in the chorus and played Enoch, Jr., in *Carousel* (1947–48); was soloist with the Chicago Opera Ballet (Southern Univ., 1949), understudied Ken Leroy in the role of Harry Beaton in the touring company of *Brigadoon* (1949); appeared as soloist with Ballet Th. Metropolitan Opera House, N.Y.C., 1949–53, Covent Garden, London, England, 1950), and on tour (1950); and danced as a sailor in *Fancy Free* (Jacob's Pillow, Lee, Mass., 1950).

He appeared in *That's Life* (Las Palmas, Hollywood, Calif., 1954); toured Europe in the dancing role of Curly in *Oklahoma!* (Paris, France; Rome, Naples, Italy, 1955); appeared as Tommie in *Annie Get Your Gun* (Dallas State Fair, Tex., 1956); danced in *Shinbone Alley* (Bway, N.Y.C., Apr. 14, 1957); appeared in the revue, *Chic* (Orpheum, May 19, 1959); danced in *Goldilocks* (Lunt-Fontanne, Oct. 11, 1958); performed in the revue, *From A to Z* (Plymouth, Apr. 20, 1960); and as Buggo and understudied Elliot Gould in the role of Harry Bogen in *I Can Get It for You Wholesale* (Shubert, Mar. 22, 1961). He also played Bill Calhoun (Lucentio) in *Kiss Me, Kate* (NY City Ctr., revived May 12, 1965); and appeared in *Meet Me in St. Louis* (Municipal, St. Louis, Mo., June 7, 1965).

Films. Mr. Brown has appeared in *Seven Brides for Seven Brothers* (MGM, 1954); *Oklahoma!* (MTC, 1955); *Daddy Long Legs* (20th-Fox); and *The Girl Most Likely* (U, 1957).

Television. He appeared as the Pitcher in the opera, *The Mighty Casey* (Omnibus, CBS, Mar. 6, 1955); and as Lon, Jr., in *Meet Me in St. Louis* (CBS, Mar. 26, 1959).

Night Clubs. He was dance soloist at the Last Frontier (Las Vegas, Nev., 1952).

Recreation. Golf, bridge, springboard diving, horseback riding, thoroughbred handicapping.

BROWN, KENNETH H. Playwright. b. about 1937, Brooklyn, N.Y. Educ. at Columbia Univ. Married to Tammy Boettcher.

Theatre. Mr. Brown wrote *The Brig* (The Living Th., N.Y.C., May 13, 1963); *The Happy Bar* (1967); *The Green Room* (Univ. of Iowa, 1971); *Nightlight* (world premiere, Hartford Stage Co., Hartford, Conn., Jan. 12, 1973); and *The Cretan Bull* (world premiere, Eugene O'Neill Th. Ctr., Waterford, Conn., July 29, 1972; Manhattan Th. Club, N.Y.C., Feb. 1, 1974).

Awards. Mr. Brown received a National Endowment for the Arts $5,000 fellowship on May 29, 1973.

BROWN, L. SLADE. Producer. b. Lutcher Slade Brown, Nov. 3, 1922, Orange, Tex., to E. W. and Gladys (Slade) Brown, Jr. Father, industrialist. Attended Ashville (N.C.) Sch., 1938–40; Midwestern Univ., 1940–42, 1944–46. Studied piano with Dalies Frantz; organ with Nita Akin, Paul Koch, and Dr. Charles Courbois; voice with Solon Alberti; dance with Mary Alice Callahand; drama with Margo. Married Dec. 5, 1942, to Jane Robbins (dis.); one son, two daughters. Served USCG, 1942–44; director of USCG Orchestra. Member of Amer. Guild of Organists. Address: (home) P. O. Box 908, Orange, TX 17630, tel. (713) TU 6-4107; (bus.) 1175 York Ave., New York, NY 10021, tel. (212) 755-4880.

Pre-Theatre. Business executive.

Theatre. Mr. Brown, in association with Edward Padula, produced *Bye Bye Birdie* (Martin Beck Th., N.Y.C., Apr. 14, 1960), which toured (opened Curran Th., San Francisco, Calif., Apr. 24, 1961; closed Orpheum, Minneapolis, Minn., Mar. 19, 1962); *All American* (Winter Garden, N.Y.C., Mar. 19, 1962); produced *Entertaining Mr. Sloan* (Lyceum Th., Oct. 12, 1965); *Hotel Passionata* (E. 74 St. Th., Oct. 22, 1965); *Until the Monkey Comes* (Martinique Th., June 20, 1966); the musical revue *Six* (Cricket Playhouse, Apr. 12, 1971); and co-produced *Miss Moffat* (opened Shubert, Philadelphia, Pa., Oct. 7, 1974; closed Oct. 18, 1974).

BROWN, RICHARD PEYRON. Educator. b. Aug. 25, 1936. Grad. Tulane Univ., B.A. 1957; Ph.D. 1964; Indiana Univ., M.A. 1960. Professional training with Richard Schechner, The Performance Group (1970); Omar Shapli (1971). Member of ATA (dir., The Acting Ctr., 1971–72); AEA; SAA; Inst. for Acting Rsch. (exec. dir.); The Players; ACLU. Address: (home) 3439 Anderson Ave., Apt. E, Riverside, CA 92507, tel. (714) 784-0149; (bus.) Theatre Dept., Univ. of California, Riverside, CA 92502, tel. (714) 787-3343.

In 1972, Mr. Brown became chairman and head of the acting program, Univ. of California, Riverside. He had previously been a teaching associate at Indiana Univ. (1957–59); a member of the faculty at Louisiana State Univ., New Orleans (1959–64); Wayne State Univ. (1964–68); Rutgers Univ. (1968–70); and from 1970 to 1972 was director of the theatre at SUNY, New Paltz, N.Y. During his academic career, he has taught courses in many aspects of theatre, including school and community play production, theatre history, drama theory, directing, and acting. In addition, he has directed over thirty productions and performed in over forty roles.

He was head of and a teacher in the acting program at La Petite Theatre, New Orleans (1959–60); at Wayne State, was director of the mime workshop

(1965), of "Theatre of the Thirties," the American Studies Conference (1966), and curator of the Malbin Th. Library. He was a consulting lecturer, Project EAST (1967), and he was chairman, professional theatre comm. for southern Michigan (1968).

Published Works. Mr. Brown has delivered numerous papers on theatrical subjects at meetings of ATA (formerly AETA); the Southwest Th. Conference; the Michigan Speech Assn.; and other professional organizations. He contributed a chapter, "Italian Drama," to *A Digest of 500 Plays* (1963) and is author of *Actor Training I* (1973).

Awards. Mr. Brown received two NY State Council on the Arts grants in (1971); a grant from the Research Foundation, State Univ. of N.Y. (1972) and a grant from the Univ. of California (1974).

BROWNE, CORAL. Actress. b. July 23, 1913, in Melbourne, Australia, to Leslie Clarence and Victoria Elizabeth (Bennett) Browne. Attended schools in Melbourne. Married June 26, 1950, to Philip Westrope Pearman (dec. 1964). Member of British and American AEA; SAG. Address: 16 Eaton Place, London, S.W.1, England.

Theatre. Miss Browne first appeared on Bway as Zambina in *Tambourlaine the Great* (Winter Garden Th., Jan. 19, 1956); subsequently appeared with the Old Vic Co. as Lady Macbeth in *Macbeth* (Winter Garden, Oct. 29, 1956); and Helen in *Troilus and Cressida* (Winter Garden, Dec. 26, 1956); and played the Countess in *The Rehearsal* (Royale, Sept. 23, 1963).

She made her stage debut as Mary Orme in *Loyalties* (Comedy, Melbourne, Australia, May 2, 1931); and subsequently played in Australia such roles as Wanda in *The Calendar*, Mimi in *A Warm Corner*, Myra in *Hay Fever*, Madge in *Let Us Be Gay*, Mrs. Murdo Fraser in *The First Mrs. Fraser*, Suzy in *Topaze*, Manuela in *The Command to Love*, Diane in *The Quaker Girl*, Orinthia in *The Apple Cart*, Fraulein von Bernberg in *Children in Uniform*, Hedda in *Hedda Gabler*, and Mrs. Dearth in *Dear Brutus*.

She made her London debut as understudy and then as successor to Nora Swinburne in the role of Helen Storer in *Lover's Leap* (Vaudeville, Oct. 25, 1934); followed by Concordia del Urbino in *Mated* (Arts, Feb. 17, 1935); Lady Amerdine in *Basalik* (Arts, Apr. 7, 1935); Mary Penshott in *This Desirable Residence* (Embassy, May 27, 1935); Victoria Buest in *The Golden Gander* (Embassy, Jan. 6, 1936); Connie Crawford in *Heroes Don't Care* (St. Martin's, June 10, 1936); Lydia Latimer in *Death Asks a Verdict* (Royalty, Dec. 13, 1936); the Widow in *The Taming of the Shrew* (New, Mar. 23, 1937); Adah Isaacs Menken in *The Great Romancer* (Strand, May 9, 1937); and Ida Ferrier in *The Great Romancer* (New, June 15, 1937).

She also played Jacqueline in *The Gusher* (Prince's, July 31, 1937); Empress Poppaea in *Emperor of the World* (Strand, Mar. 19, 1939); Madeleine in *Believe It or Not* (New, Jan. 23, 1940); Maggie Cutler in *The Man Who Came to Dinner* (Savoy, Dec. 4, 1941); Ruth Sherwood in *My Sister Eileen* (Savoy, Sept. 22, 1943); Mrs. Cheyney in *The Last of Mrs. Cheyney* (St. James's, June 15, 1944); Lady Frederick Berolles in *Lady Frederick* (Savoy, Nov. 21, 1946); Elma Melton in *Canaries Sometimes Sing* (Garrick, Nov. 18, 1947); Bathsheba in *Jonathan* (Aldwych, July 29, 1948); "Boss" Trent in *Castle in the Air* (Adelphi, Dec. 7, 1949); Emilia in *Othello* (Old Vic, Oct. 31, 1951); Regan in *King Lear* (Old Vic, Mar. 3, 1952); Constance Russell in *Affairs of State* (Cambridge, Aug. 28, 1952); Laura Foster in *Simon and Laura* (Strand, Nov. 25, 1952); and Nina Tessier in *Nina* (Haymarket, July 27, 1955).

After she appeared in the N.Y.C. production of *Tambourlaine the Great* (see above), she returned to London to play Lady Macbeth in *Macbeth* (Old Vic, May 22, 1956), which she repeated on Bway (see above) as well as *Troilus and Cressida* (see above); appeared as Gertrude in *Hamlet* (Old Vic, Dec. 18, 1957); Helena in *A Midsummer Night's Dream* (Old Vic, Dec. 23, 1957); Goneril in *King Lear* (Old Vic, Feb. 19, 1958); Gertrude in the Shakespeare Memorial Theatre touring production of *Hamlet* (Moscow, U.S.S.R., Dec. 1958); in London, appeared as Katherine Dougherty in *The Pleasure of His Company* (Haymarket, Apr. 23, 1959); Albertine Prine in *Toys in the Attic* (Piccadilly, Nov. 10, 1960); Marie-Paul in *La Bonne Soupe* (Comedy, Sept. 19, 1962); and in the N.Y.C. production of *The Rehearsal* (see above).

She played in London as Mrs. Rossiter in *The Right Honorable Gentleman* (Her Majesty's Th., May 1964), repeated in N.Y.C. (Billy Rose Th., Oct. 19, 1965); Mrs. Prentice in *What the Butler Saw* (Queens Th., Mar. 1969); Daisy, Countess of Warwick, in *My Darling Daisy* (Lyric, June 22, 1970); Mrs. Warren in *Mrs. Warren's Profession* (Natl., Dec. 30, 1970); Mrs. Raffi in *The Sea* (Royal Court, May 1973); and Emily in *The Waltz of the Toreadors* (Haymarket, Feb. 14, 1974).

Films. Miss Browne has appeared in *Auntie Mame* (WB, 1958); *The Roman Spring of Mrs. Stone* (WB, 1961); *Dr. Crippen* (WB, 1963); *The Legend of Lylah Clare* (MGM, 1968); *The Killing of Sister George* (Cinerama, 1969); *The Ruling Class* (Avco-Embassy, 1972); *The Theatre of Blood* (UA, 1973).

Recreation. Needlepoint.

BROWNE, E. MARTIN. Director, actor, lecturer. b. Elliott Martin Browne, Jan. 29, 1900, Wiltshire, England, to Percival John and Bernarda Gracia (Lees) Browne. Father, colonel in British Army. Attended Eton Coll., 1913–18; grad. Christ Church, Oxford Univ., B.A. 1921; M.A. 1923. Studied speech with Elsie Fogerty, London, 1926–27. Married Dec. 20, 1924, to Henzie Raeburn, actress (dec. 1973); two sons. Served in Grenadier Guards, S.R., 1918–19; rank, 2nd Lt. Member of British AEA; British Drama League (director); Royal Society of Literature (fellow); Religious Drama Society of Great Britain (pres.). Address: 20 Lancaster Grove, London, N.W.3, England tel. 01-794-1.

Pre-Theatre. Mr. Browne was director of religious drama, Diocese of Chichester, 1930–34, and worked in adult education at the Doncaster Folkhouse, 1924–26.

Theatre. Mr. Browne first appeared on stage as the Elder in *David* (Regent, London, May 22, 1927); subsequently came to the US (1927) as assistant professor of speech and drama at the Carnegie Inst. of Technology; and first appeared in the US in *So This Is London* (Ann Arbor Dramatic Festival, Univ. of Michigan, June 1928), and appeared at Ann Arbor in other works; performed in *The Beautiful Sabine Women*, and as Paolo in *Paolo and Francesca* (Manhattan Th. Camp, Peterboro, N.H., July–Aug. 1929).

He directed *Murder in the Cathedral* and played the Fourth Tempter and Knight (Mercury, London, Nov. 1, 1935); appeared in *Mutiny* (1936); as the Skeleton in *Cranmer of Canterbury* (Canterbury Festival, 1936); repeated his role in *Murder in the Cathedral* (Duchess, London, Oct. 30, 1936); at the Mercury Th., directed *Panic* (1936) and *In Theatre Street* (1937); staged *The Virgin and the Clerk* (Tewkesbury Festival, 1937); and *A Midsummer Night's Dream* (Stratford-on-Avon, 1937).

He made his N.Y.C. debut as the Fourth Tempter and Knight in *Murder in the Cathedral*, which he also directed (Ritz, Feb. 16, 1938); appeared as Prof. Strassman and the Rev. Tyndal-Morgan in *Trumpeter Play!* (Garrick, London, June, 1938); Liam Poer in *Blind Man's Buff* (Arts, Sept. 1938); directed *The Last Day* (Croydon Rep. Th., 1938); *Sanctity* (Piccadilly, 1938); and *The Family Reunion*, in which he played the Hon. Charles Piper (Westminster, Mar. 21, 1939). He directed the Pilgrim Players, in association with the Arts Council (1939–48), in such productions as *The Way of the Cross* (1940), *The Dragon and the Dove* (1942), and *A Change for the Worse* (1942), that toured throughout England.

In 1945, Mr. Browne became director of the Mercury Th., where he staged plays in verse, titled "New Plays by Poets" (1945–48), combining this position with his direction of the Pilgrim Players. He directed the verse plays, *The Old Man of the Mountains* (Mercury, Sept. 13, 1945), *This Way to the Tomb* (Mercury, Oct. 11, 1945), *The Shadow Factory* (Mercury, Dec. 19, 1945), *The Resurrection* and *A Phoenix Too Frequent* (Mercury, Apr. 25, 1946), *Kate Kennedy* (Mercury, Dec. 15, 1947), and *A Change for the Worse*, in which he played St. Eloi (Mercury, Jan. 14, 1948).

For the Old Vic Co., he directed *Coriolanus* (New, Mar. 31, 1948); at the Edinburgh (Scotland) Festival, staged *The Firstborn* (Gateway, Aug. 1948), directed *The Cocktail Party* (Edinburgh Festival, Aug. 1949; Henry Miller's Th., N.Y.C., Jan. 21, 1950; New, London, May 3, 1950). He also directed the first full-scale revival of the York Cycle of Mystery Plays (York Festival, June 3, 1951); directed *Don Juan* (Devon Festival, Summer 1953); *The Confidential Clerk* (Edinburgh Festival, Aug. 1953; Lyric, London, Sept. 16, 1953; Morosco, N.Y.C., Feb. 11, 1954). He again directed the York Cycle of Mystery Plays at the York (England) Festival, where he also staged *The Flood* (Summer 1954). He staged a production of *Murder in the Cathedral*, in which he played Becket (Gloucester Cathedral, July 20, 1955); *A Man Named Judas* (Lyceum, Edinburgh, (Scotland, 30, 1956); again directed the York Cycle of Mystery Plays (York, Summer 1957); staged *Christ's Comet*, in which he played the Angel of the Tree (Canterbury Festival, June 1958); directed *The Elder Statesman* (Edinburgh Festival, Aug. 1958; Cambridge, London, Sept. 25, 1958); and *The Play of Daniel* (Westminster Abbey, June 6, 1960).

In the fall of 1956, Mr. Browne was appointed visiting professor in Religious Drama at Union Theological Seminary, N.Y.C., and thereafter divided his time (approximately half of each year) between England and the US. At Union Seminary, he directed *Christ in the Concrete City* (Oct. 31, 1956); directed a reading of *The Firstborn* (Kaufmann Aud., YMHA, Jan. 1, 1957); at Union Seminary, directed *The House by the Stable* and *Grab and Grace* (Jan. 15, 1957), *The Mystery of the Finding of the Cross* (Jan. 15, 1959), *Cranmer of Canterbury* (Dec. 1, 1959), *Cry Dawn in Dark Babylon* (Jan. 28, 1960); at Saint Mary's College, Notre Dame, he compiled and directed *The Mystery of Mary* from the medieval Hegge Mystery Cycle (Mar. 23, 1960).

He and his wife were Danforth visiting lecturers for the Assn. of Amer. Coll. Arts Program, 1962–65; in England, during these years he was honorary adviser on drama to the new Coventry Cathedral. In 1966, he again directed the York Cycle of Mystery Plays. Since 1967 he has been a lecturer for Tufts-in-London. After Yvonne Arnaud Th., Guildford, he directed *Murder in the Cathedral* (1967), *The Family Reunion* (1968), *Our Town* (1969), *Everyman*, and *The Long Christmas Dinner* (1970). He revived *Murder in the Cathedral* in Canterbury Cathedral for the 800th anniversary of Becket's martyrdom (1970).

Television. Mr. Browne directed *Prince Orestes* (Omnibus, CBS, Jan. 1959).

Published Works. *The Making of T. S. Eliot's Plays* (1969).

Awards. The rank of Commander of the British Empire (C.B.E.) was conferred upon him in 1952. The Archbishop of Canterbury made him Hon. D.Litt (Lambeth) 1971.

Recreation. Reading, walking.

BROWNE, ROSCOE LEE. Actor. b. 1925, Woodbury, N.J. Attended Lincoln Univ.; Middlebury Coll.; Columbia Univ. Member of AEA; SAG; AFTRA.

Pre-Theatre. Teacher at Lincoln Univ.

Theatre. Mr. Browne made his N.Y.C. debut as a Soothsayer and Pindarus in the NY Shakespeare Festival production of *Julius Caesar* (East River Park Amphitheatre); subsequently played a walk-on role in *The Taming of the Shrew* (East River Park Amphitheatre, 1956); Aaron in *Titus Andronicus* (Emmanuel Presbyterian Church); Balthazar in *Romeo and Juliet* (Metropolitan N.Y.C. Area school tour, opened June 27, 1957); and understudied the title role in *Othello* (Belvedere Lake Th., July 2, 1958).

He played Cothurnus in *Aria da Capo* (Th. Marquee, June 26, 1958); Archibald Wellington in *The Blacks* (St. Mark's Playhouse, May 4, 1961); understudied Ossie Davis in the title role in *Purlie Victorious* (Cort, Sept. 28, 1961); appeared in *Brecht on Brecht* (Th. de Lys, Jan. 3, 1962); played a Corporal in *General Seeger* (Lyceum, Feb. 28, 1962); Deacon Sittre Morris in *Tiger, Tiger Burning Bright* (Booth, Dec. 22, 1962); for the NY Shakespeare Festival, played the Fool in *King Lear* (Delacorte, Aug. 13, 1962); and, at the Arena Th. (Washington, D.C.), appeared in *Brecht on Brecht* and played the Street Singer in *The Threepenny Opera* (May 14, 1963).

He again appeared in the staged reading *Brecht on Brecht* (Sheridan Square Playhouse, N.Y.C., July 9, 1963); was Autolycus in the NY Shakespeare Festival *The Winter's Tale* (Delacorte Th., Aug. 14, 1963); appeared as the Narrator in *The Ballad of the Sad Cafe* (Martin Beck Th., Oct. 30, 1963); played the male lead in *the Empty Room* (Village South Th., Jan. 12, 1964); participated in a program of readings from Sartre and Brecht, *Hell Is Other People* (Carnegie Hall, May 9, 1964); was Babu in *Benito Cereno*, the second of two one-act plays on the program *The Old Glory* (St. Clements Church Th., Nov. 1, 1964; revived Th. de Lys, Jan. 14, 1965); Ulysses in the NY Shakespeare Festival *Troilus and Cressida* (Delacorte Th., Aug. 4, 1965); and St. Just in *Danton's Death* (Vivian Beaumont Th., Oct. 21, 1965).

At the Playhouse in the Park, Cincinnati, Ohio, he was Mendoza in *Man and Superman* (Apr. 6, 1966), repeated his role in *Benito Cereno* (Apr. 28, 1966), and played the Gardener in *Sodom and Gomorrah* (May 25, 1966). He appeared in *Beyond the Fringe* (Goodspeed Opera House, East Haddam, Conn., June 27, 1966); arranged, directed, contributed material to, and appeared in *An Evening of Negro Poetry and Folk Music* (Delacorte Th., N.Y.C., Aug. 15, 1966), later revived as *A Hand Is on the Gate* (Longacre, Sept. 21, 1966); was Sheridan Whiteside in *The Man Who Came to Dinner* (Long Wharf Th., New Haven, Conn., Dec. 9, 1966); Mosca in *Volpone* (NY Shakespeare Festival Mobile Th., June 22, 1967); and appeared in several productions with the New Theater for Now Workshop, Mark Taper Forum (Los Angeles, Calif., 1969–70). He was Makak in *The Dream on Monkey Mountain* (Center Th. Group, Mark Taper Forum, Los Angeles, Aug. 27, 1970; St. Marks Playhouse, N.Y.C., Mar. 9, 1971); appeared in *As You Like It* (Pilgrimage Th., Los Angeles, Sept. 3, 1973); and, with Anthony Zerbe, selected and presented a poetry program, *Behind the Broken Words* (Washington Th. Club, Washington, D.C., Mar. 8, 1974).

Films. He appeared in *The Connection* (FAW, 1962); *Black Like Me* (Walter Reade, 1964); *The Cool World; Uptight* (Par., 1968); *The Liberation of L. B. Jones* (Col., 1970); *The Cowboys* (WB, 1971); *Superfly* (WB, 1972); *Superfly T.N.T.* (Par., 1973); and *The World's Greatest Athlete* (Buena Vista, 1973).

Television. He appeared in *Green Pastures* (Hallmark Hall of Fame, NBC, Oct. 17, 1952); on Espionage (NBC, 1963); repeated his performance as Babu in *Benito Cereno* (Festival of the Arts, NET, Oct. 11, 1965); and played W.E.B. Du Bois in *Free at Last* (History of the Negro People, NET, Nov. 9, 1965). He was on Mannix (CBS, 1968); Name of the Game (NBC, 1969); Bonanza (NBC, 1972); and has also been on The Defenders (CBS) and East Side/West Side (CBS).

Awards. Mr. Browne received a *Village Voice* off-Bway (Obie) Award (1964–65) for his performance in *The Old Glory.*

BRUCE, CAROL. Actress, singer. b. Nov. 15, Great Neck, L.I., N.Y., to Harry and Beatrice Bruce. Grad. Erasmus H.S., Brooklyn, N.Y. Married June 17, 1945, to Milton Nathanson, manufacturers' representative (marr. dis. May 1963); one daughter. Member of AEA; AFTRA; AGVA. Address: 211 E. 53rd St., New York, NY 10022, tel. (212) PL 9-8625.

Theatre. Miss Bruce appeared in vaudeville (Roxy, Atlanta, Ga., Apr. 1939); *George White's Scandals* (Boston, Mass., Aug. 1939). She left the show to join the company of *Nice Goin'!*, which closed out of town (Shubert, Boston, Mass., Sept. 1939).

She made her Bway debut as Beatrice in *Louisiana Purchase* (Imperial Th., May 28, 1940); followed by her appearance in the vaudeville show *New Priorities of 1943* (46 St. Th., Sept. 15, 1942); played Julie in *Show Boat* (Louisville Summer Light Opera, Ky., June 1943), a role which she repeated with Los Angeles Civic Light Opera Assn. (Philharmonic Aud., Los Angeles, Calif.; Curran, San Francisco, Calif., June 1944), on Bway (Ziegfeld, Jan. 5, 1946), and with the Civic Light Opera Assn. of Greater Pittsburgh (Civic Arena, Pittsburgh, Pa., May 1948); and played Evalina in *Bloomer Girl* (Starlight Operetta Co., Dallas, Tex., July, 1948).

She played Julie in *Show Boat* (NY City Ctr., Sept. 7, 1948); appeared in the revue, *Along Fifth Avenue* (Broadhurst, Jan. 13, 1949); played Liza Elliott in the stock production of *Lady in the Dark* (Chapel Playhouse, Guilford, Conn., July 1949; Seacliff Summer Th., N.Y., July 1949); Julie in *Show Boat* (Starlight Operetta Co., Dallas, Tex., Aug. 1949); Evalina in *Bloomer Girl* and Venus in *One Touch of Venus* (Lyric Th., Houston, Tex., June–July 1950); and Annie Oakley in *Annie Get Your Gun* (Starlight Operetta Co., Dallas, Tex., Aug. 1950).

Miss Bruce appeared as Vera Simpson in *Pal Joey* on a tour of eleven stock theatres in the East (June–Sept. 1951); sang Julie in *Show Boat* (Lewisohn Stadium, N.Y.C., July 1952); and toured six stock theatres as Venus in *One Touch of Venus* (July–Aug. 1952); played two performances as Vera Simpson at the end of the N.Y.C. run of *Pal Joey* (Broadhurst, Jan. 3, 1952), toured in the national company (opened Shubert, Washington, D.C., Apr. 20, 1953; closed Pittsburgh, Pa., Dec. 1953), and played the role in the London production (Princes, Mar. 31, 1954).

She toured US stock theatres as Mother Goddam in *Shanghai Gesture* (Summer 1955); Alice Walten in *Anniversary Waltz* (Summer 1956); Celia in *A Hatful of Rain* and Liza Elliot in *Lady in the Dark* (Summer 1957); in *Fallen Angels* (Summer 1958); Vera Simpson in *Pal Joey* and Irene Lovelle in *Say, Darling* (Summer 1959); appeared in the revue, *Angel in the Wings* (Miami, Fla., Feb.–Mar. 1960); and in *Petticoat Fever* (Summer 1960).

She played Vera Simpson in *Pal Joey* (NY City Ctr., May 31, 1961), and toured in the role in stock (Summer 1961); succeeded (Feb. 1962) Eileen Heckart as Tilly Siegal in *A Family Affair* (Billy Rose Th., N.Y.C., Jan. 27, 1962); played Vera Simpson in *Pal Joey* (Charlotte Music Th., N.C., June 1962), and on tour (Summer 1963); Signora Fioria in *Do I Hear a Waltz?* (46 St. Th., N.Y.C., Mar. 18, 1965); Verena Talbo in a musical version of *The Grass Harp* (Trinity Square Rep. Co., Providence, R.I., Dec. 26, 1966); and Mrs. Boyd in *Henry, Sweet Henry* (Palace, N.Y.C., Oct. 1967).

Films. Miss Bruce appeared in *This Woman Is Mine* (U, 1941); *Keep 'Em Flying* (U, 1941); and *Behind the Eight Ball* (U, 1942).

Television and Radio. She appeared on the weekly Ben Bernie radio program (NBC, Oct. 1941); the Al Jolson-Colgate Radio Show (CBS, Oct. 1942); the Raleigh Carton of Cheer Show (NBC, Sept. 1944); and the MGM Musical Comedy Th. production of *Honolulu* (Jan. 1951).

She made her television debut on Holiday Hotel (ABC, Dec. 1950); appeared in *Miss Liberty* (Musical Comedy Time, NBC, Jan. 1951); Studio One (CBS, Nov. 1951); Texaco Star Th. (NBC, May 1952); *The Promise* (Curtain Call, NBC, June 1952); The Armstrong Circle Th. (CBS, Dec. 1954); narrated Voice of the Hurricane (Armstrong Circle Th., CBS, Oct. 1955); appeared in the serial Modern Romances (NBC, Jan. 1956); and *The Shark* (Dupont Show of the Month, NBC, 1963).

Miss Bruce has made guest appearances on Memory Lane (Ind. 1964–65); The Herb Gardiner Show (Ind. 1964–65); and Girl Talk (ABC, 1965–66).

Night Clubs. Miss Bruce made her debut as a vocalist at the Normandie Roof (Royal Hotel, Montreal, Canada, June 1937); subsequently appeared at the Manhattan Room (Hotel New Yorker, N.Y.C., Apr. 1938); Arcadia Ballroom (Philadelphia, Pa., May 1938); The Mayfair (Boston, Mass., July 1938); Nils T. Granlund's Midnight Sun (N.Y.C., Sept. 1938); Hi Hat Club (Chicago, Ill., Dec. 1938); Billy Rose's Casa Manana (N.Y.C., Dec. 1938); Jack Lynch's Roof (Philadelphia, Pa., Feb. 1939); Dempsey-Vanderbilt (Miami Beach, Mar. 1939); The Shalimar (Newark, N.J., Jan. 1940); Cafe Pierre (N.Y.C., June 1941); the Sert Room (Waldorf-Astoria Hotel, N.Y.C., Oct. 1941).

She sang at Chez Paree (Chicago, Mar. 1942); Copacabana and Paramount Th. (N.Y.C., Apr. 1942); Ritz Carlton Roof (Boston, Aug. 1942); Persian Room (Hotel Plaza, N.Y.C., Jan. 1943); Roxy Th. (N.Y.C., Feb. 1943); State Th. (Hartford, Conn., Mar. 1943); Earle Th. (Philadelphia, Pa., Mar. 1943); Adams Th. (Newark, N.J., May 1943); RKO Th. (Cleveland, Ohio, May 1943); RKO Palace Th. (Columbus, Ohio, May 1943); RKO Th. (Boston, Mass., June 1943); Starlight Roof (Chase Hotel, St. Louis, Mo., Aug. 1943); Oval Room (Copley-Plaza Hotel, Boston, Mass., Sept. 1943); and Central Th. (Passaic, N.J., Nov. 1943).

Miss Bruce sang at the Roxy (N.Y.C., Mar. 1944); Earle (Philadelphia, Pa., Apr. 1944); Copacabana (N.Y.C., Dec. 1944); Mayfair Room (Hotel Blackstone, Chicago, Ill., Jan. 1945); Plymouth (Worcester, Mass., Feb. 1945); Wedgewood Room (Waldorf-Astoria Hotel, N.Y.C., Apr. 1945); Crystal Terrace (Park Plaza Hotel, St. Louis, Mo., May 1945); Flame Room (Radisson Hotel, Minneapolis, Minn., June 1945); Earle (Philadelphia, Pa., Sept. 1945); Copacabana (N.Y.C., Sept. 1950); Strand Th. (N.Y.C., Nov. 1950); Hotel Thunderbird (Las Vegas, Nev., Nov. 1950); appeared with Jackie Gleason in Monte Proser's production *Billion Dollar Baby* (The Gilded Cage, N.Y.C., Mar. 1951); performed at Hotel Thunderbird (Las Vegas, Nev., Oct. 1951); Roxy (N.Y.C., Dec. 1951); Ciro's (Miami Beach, Fla., Feb. 1952); Chez Paree (Chicago, Ill., Mar. 1952); Latin Casino (Philadelphia, Pa., Apr. 1952); Shamrock Hotel (Houston, Tex., June 1952); Nicollet Hotel (Minneapolis, Minn., Dec. 1952); in *A Night with Harold Arlen* (Cafe Pierre, N.Y.C., Dec. 1959); at Statler Hilton (Dallas, Tex., Apr. 1960); Langford Hotel (Orlando, Fla., Sept. 1960); The Beverly Hills (Cincinnati, Ohio, Sept. 1961); and The Living Room (N.Y.C., Dec. 1962); the Living Room (N.Y.C., 1964); and the St. Regis Maisonette (Paris, 1966).

Other Activities. Miss Bruce sang at President Franklin D. Roosevelt's Birthday Ball (The White House, Washington, D.C., Jan. 1942); and on a US War Bond tour of New England for the Boston and Maine Railroad (1944).

Discography. Miss Bruce has recorded *Thrill to the Fabulous Carol Bruce* (Topps Records 1958); *Show Boat* (Columbia); and *Showtime Series* (RCA Victor).

Awards. Carol Bruce Day was celebrated on July 18, 1940, at the NY World's Fair. She was cited for entertaining troops and participating in war bond drives during WW II; and received the Donaldson Award for her performance as Julie in *Show Boat* (1946).

BRUNING, FRANCESCA. Actress. b. Mar. 13, 1907, Miles City, Mont., to Louis and Evelyn (Houg) Bruning. Father, physician; mother, teacher. Grad. Univ. Sch. for Girls, Chicago, Ill., 1925; attended Chateau de Groslay, France, 1925–26. Studied with Mrs. Elsa D. Mower, Chicago, 1922–25; Mme. Jeanne Grumbach, Paris, France, 1925–26; Mrs. Laura Elliot, 1927–31. Married June 28, 1940, to John Beaufort, newspaperman. Member of AEA; AFTRA. Address: c/o Actors Equity Assn., 226 W. 47th St., New York, NY 10036.

Theatre. Miss Bruning's first appearance was as a walk-on and understudy in Mrs. Fiske's production of *The Merry Wives of Windsor* (Broad St. Th., Newark, N.J., Oct. 1927); played Poppy in *Captain Applejack* (Berkshire Playhouse, Stockbridge, Mass., Summer 1928); toured with the Jitney Players (1929); appeared as Dolly in *You Never Can Tell*

(Berkshire Playhouse, Stockbridge, Mass., Summer 1929); Cecily Cardew in *The Importance of Being Earnest* (Surrey Playhouse, Me., Summer 1929); Vera in the Theatre Guild touring production of *A Month in the Country* (opened Blackstone Th., Chicago, Ill., 1930–31); Anya in *The Cherry Orchard* (White Plains, N.Y., 1932); and in a season of winter stock at the Palm Beach (Fla.) Playhouse (1932).

She made her N.Y.C. debut as Amy in *One Sunday Afternoon* (Little, Feb. 15, 1933); played the title role in *Amourette* (Henry Miller's Th., Sept. 27, 1933); Laura and Vivienne in *The House of Ramsen* (Henry Miller's Th., Apr. 2, 1934); Amy in *One Sunday Afternoon,* and Princess Beatrice in *The Swan* (Westchester Playhouse, Mt. Kisco, N.Y., Summer 1934); Sylvia in *Spring Freshet* (Plymouth, N.Y.C., Oct. 4, 1934); Helen Pettigrew in *Berkeley Square* (Berkshire Playhouse, Stockbridge, Mass., Summer 1935); Nora Trinell in *Remember the Day* (National, N.Y.C., Sept. 25, 1935); Barbara Denny in *Men in White* (Berkshire Playhouse, Aug. 1936); Frances Newberry in *Sunkissed* (Little, Mar. 10, 1937); succeeded (Jan. 1938) Flora Campbell as Joan Hollis in *Many Mansions* (Biltmore, Oct. 27, 1937); played Sally Turner in *Escape This Night* (44 St. Th., Apr. 22, 1938); Annabella in *Bright Rebel* (Lyceum, Dec. 27, 1938); the Lady in Spectacles in *Autumn Crocus* (Berkshire Playhouse, Summer 1940); and Ellen Curtis in *Junior Miss* (Lyceum, N.Y.C., Nov. 18, 1941).

Other summer theatre appearances included Catherine Slopes in *The Heiress* (Berkshire Playhouse, 1949); Maggie Wylie in *What Every Woman Knows* (Bass Rocks Th., Gloucester, Mass., 1950) and at the Berkshire Playhouse, the title role in *Jane* (1953); Eliza Doolittle in *Pygmalion* (1954); Charlotte Lovell in *The Old Maid* (1955); and Nancy Fallon in *A Roomful of Roses* (1956).

Television. Miss Bruning's television appearances include the Colgate Th. (NBC, 1948); Ford Th. (CBS, 1949); Studio One (CBS, 1957); and The Verdict Is Yours (CBS, 1958–59).

Recreation. Travel, reading, walking.

BRUSTEIN, ROBERT. Educator, critic. b. Robert Sanford Brustein, Apr. 21, 1927, Brooklyn, N.Y., to Max and Blanche (Haft) Brustein. Father, textile merchant. Attended H.S. of Music and Art, N.Y.C., 1940–42; Grad. Columbia Grammar Sch., N.Y.C., 1943; attended Merchant Marine Acad., 1945–47; grad. Amherst Coll., B.A. 1948; attended Yale Univ. Sch. of Drama, 1948–49; grad. Columbia Univ., M.A. 1950; attended Univ. of Nottingham, England, (Fulbright Fellowship) 1953–55; grad. Columbia Univ., Ph.D. 1957. Married March 25, 1962, to Norma Cates; one son, one stepson. Member of AEA; AFTRA; MLA. Address: (home) 10 St. Ronan Terrace, New Haven, CT 06511; (bus.) Yale School of Drama, New Haven, CT 06520, tel. (203) 436-1586.

Mr. Brustein became dean, Yale School of Drama, and artistic director, Yale Repertory Theatre, in 1966. Since that time he has also been professor of English, Yale Univ. Previously he was at Columbia Univ. as lecturer in drama (1957), assistant professor of dramatic literature (1958–62), associate professor of English and dramatic literature (1963–65), and full professor (1965–66). He was also an instructor of English at Cornell Univ. (1955–56) and instructor in drama at Vassar College (1956–57).

Theatre. From 1950–57, Mr. Brustein played some seventy roles in summer and winter stock with such companies as Studio 7, N.Y.C.; Group 20, Theatre-on-the-Green, Wellesley, Mass.; and the Ellenville (N.Y.) Music Festival; and appeared in productions with ELT and the 92nd Street YMHA, N.Y.C.

Mr. Brustein has supervised over sixty productions of the Yale Repertory Theatre (YRT), New Haven, Conn., which he founded in 1966 and which he has since served as artistic director. He played in the YRT production of *The Rivals* (Oct. 16, 1969) and directed *Don Juan, or the Enemy of God* (world premiere, May 15, 1970); *The Revenger's Tragedy* (Nov. 19, 1970); *Macbeth* (Feb. 18, 1971); and *the Big House* (Oct. 21, 1971). Mr. Brustein is also one of the authors of YRT's satirical revue *Watergate Classics* (Nov. 20, 1973), in which he appeared as Richard M. Nixon.

Television. Mr. Brustein appeared on dramatic television programs from 1950 to 1957. He was author and host of a Channel 13 (N.Y.C.) series, *The Opposition Theatre* (NET), and he appeared in Great Britain on programs of the BBC.

Other Activities. Mr. Brustein was a panel member (1970–72) of the National Endowment for the Arts and has been (1974–to date) a panel member of the National Endowment for the Humanities.

Published Works. Books by Mr. Brustein include *The Theatre of Revolt* (1964); *Seasons of Discontent* (1966); *The Third Theatre* (1968); *Revolution as Theatre* (1971); and he edited *The Plays of Strindberg* (1964). He was drama critic and drama editor of *The New Republic* (1957–67); cultural critic of the *New York Review of Books* (1964–65); and is advisory editor of *Yale/Theatre* and *Theatre Quarterly.* He has contributed articles to *Hudson Review; Partisan Review; Harper's; Tulane Drama Review; Theatre Arts; Encounter;* New York *Times; New York Review of Books; Yale/Theatre;* and *The* (London) *Observer.*

Awards. Mr. Brustein received honorary doctor of humanities degrees from Lawrence College (1967) and Amherst College (1972). He received a Fulbright Fellowship (1953–55); a Guggenheim Fellowship (1960–61); and a Ford Fellowship (1964–65); the George Jean Nathan Award for drama criticism (1962); the George Polk Award in criticism (1965); and the Jersey City (N.J.) *Journal* Award for criticism (1966). He is a member of Phi Beta Kappa (1948).

BRYANT, MARY. Press representative, former actress. b. Mary Elizabeth Bryant, Oct. 17, 1936, Apopka, Fla., to Theodore A. and Mabel (Eddy) Bryant. Father, building contractor. Grad. Jackson H.S., Miami, Fla., 1952; attended Wesleyan Coll., 1952–53; grad. Univ. of Miami, B.A. 1955; studied with Jasper Deeter, Hedgerow Th., Moylan, Pa., 1955–57. Member of ATPAM; AFTRA; Zeta Tau Alpha. Address: (home) 230 Central Park South, New York, NY 10019, tel. (212) LT 1-2549; (bus.) 165 W. 46th St., New York, NY 10036, tel. (212) 575-1166.

Theatre. Miss Bryant made her stage debut at five as Mother Goose in an elementary school production of *Mother Goose's Birthday Party* (Fla., 1941); her professional debut as Maria in *The House of Bernarda Alba* at the Hedgerow Th. (Moylan, Pa., Oct. 1955), where she appeared in repertory (1955–57) as Regina in *Ghosts,* Jacqueline in *The Physician in Spite of Himself,* a Martyr in *Androcles and the Lion,* Mrs. Harkness in *The Man Who Corrupted Hadleyburg,* Mercy Lewis in *The Crucible,* Doris in *The Inheritors,* Rosalie in *Unfinished Portrait,* Lady India in *Ring Around the Moon,* and Señora Cinni in *Right You Are.*

She appeared in stock at the Coconut Grove Playhouse (Miami, Fla.), as Geraldine in *A Soft Touch* (Jan. 1958), Mrs. McClain in *Inherit the Wind* (Jan. 1958), Miss Mills in *Simon and Laura* (Feb. 1958), and the Nurse in *Chalk Garden* (Feb. 1958); succeeded Mary Gower as Mercy Lewis in *The Crucible* (Martinique, N.Y.C., Mar. 11, 1958); and appeared as a Gypsy in the ANTA Matinee Series play, *Song of Songs* (Th. de Lys, Oct. 28, 1958).

As assistant to Sol Jacobson, press representative, she was associated with *Flower Drum Song* (1958); *West Side Story* (1959), *Tall Story* (1959), *Sweet Bird of Youth* (1959), *Fiorello!* (1959), *Toys in the Attic* (1960), *Tenderloin* (1960), *Donnybrook* (1961), *A Call on Kuprin* (1961), *Write Me a Murder* (1961), *Take Her, She's Mine* (1961), *The Aspern Papers* (1962), and *A Funny Thing Happened on the Way to the Forum* (1962).

Miss Bryant opened her own office (1962) and has served as press representative for the Bucks County Playhouse, New Hope, Pa. (June 1962); and in N.Y.C., has represented *Never Too Late* (1962), *She Loves Me* (1963), *The Amorous Flea* (1964), *Home Movies* (1964), *Poor Bitos* (1964), National Repertory Theatre (1964–67), *Flora, the Red Menace* (1965), *Anya* (1965), *Mating Dance* (1965), *Superman* (1966), *Agatha Sue* (1966), *Cabaret* (1966), *Girl in the Freudian Slip* (1967), *Zorba* (1968), *Angela* (1969), *Jeremy Troy* (1969), *Company* (1970), *Dear Janet Rosenberg* (1970), *Grin and Bare It* (1970), *Follies* (1971), *Abelard and Heloise* (1971), *All the Girls* (1972), *A Little Night Music* (1973), New Phoenix Repertory Company (1973).

BULGAKOV, BARBARA. Actress, director, teacher, coach. b. Russia. Married to Leo Bulgakov, actor, director (dec. July 20, 1948). Studied with Constantin Stanislavsky (1918–24).

Theatre. Mme. Bulgakov was a member of the Moscow Art Th. (Russia). She came to the US with the Moscow Art Th. (c. 1923).

She played in a special matinee performance of *The Cricket on the Hearth* (Neighborhood Playhouse, N.Y.C., May 1925); followed by the title role in *Princess Turandot* (Greenwich Village, Nov. 12, 1926); Natasha in *Love Is Like That* (Cort, Apr. 18, 1927); succeeded (May 1927) Suzanne Caubet in the role of Nubi in *The Squall* (48 St. Th., Nov. 11, 1926); appeared as Luz la Mar in *Hot Pan* (Provincetown Playhouse, Feb. 15, 1928); appeared as Lise in *Goin' Home* (Hudson, Aug. 23, 1928); Nina in *The Seagull* (Comedy, Apr. 9, 1929); Nastya in *At the Bottom (Lower Depths)* (Waldorf, Jan. 9, 1930); Tanya Savelov in *Devil in the Mind* (Fulton, May 1, 1931); Tatyana Mirova in *Wonder Boy* (Alvin, Oct. 23, 1931); and appeared in *The Cherry Orchard.*

In stock, she appeared in *Tempest Calm* (Litchfield, Conn., July 10, 1933); and directed *Escape into Glory* (Master Inst., N.Y.C., c. 1941).

She played Auntie in *Lovely Me* (Adelphi, Dec. 25, 1946); and directed a Russian-language production of *Uncle Vanya* (Master Inst., Feb. 12, 1960).

Other Activities. Mrs. Bulgakov was a teacher at the American Theatre Wing, N.Y.C. (1948–59).

BULL, PETER. Writer, actor, producer. b. Peter Cecil Bull, Mar. 21, 1912, London, England, to the Rt. Hon. Sir William James, Bt., and Lady Lilian (Brandon) Bull. Father, politician and lawyer. Grad. The Coll., Winchester, England, Sch. Certificate, 1930; attended Univ. of Tours, France, 1930. Studied with Elsie Fogerty; Central Sch. of Drama; Royal Albert Hall, London. Served British Royal Naval Volunteer Reserve, 1940–46; rank, Lt. Comdr.; awarded Distinguished Service Cross, 1945; Relative in theatre: aunt, Nora Gray, actress. Member British AEA; AEA; SAG; AFTRA; Theatre Mgrs. Assn. of England. Address: (home) 149 King's Rd., Chelsea, London S.W.3, England tel. FLA 4384; (bus.) Barclays Bank Chambers, Hebden Bridge, Yorkshire, England.

Pre-Theatre. Journalist.

Theatre. Mr. Bull made his New York debut as the Waiter in *Escape Me Never* (Shubert Th., Jan. 21, 1935); followed by the role of Edward Tappercoom in *The Lady's Not for Burning* (Royale, Nov. 8, 1950); Tetzel in *Luther* (St. James, Sept. 25, 1963).

In London, he first appeared as the Janitor in *If I Were You* (Shaftesbury, June 15, 1933); subsequently, played the Doctor in *As You Desire Me* (Gate, Sept. 19, 1933); the Waiter in *Escape Me Never* (Apollo, Dec. 8, 1933); Ammon in *The Boy David* (His Majesty's, Dec. 14 1936); produced and acted at the Perranporth Summer Th. (Cornwall, Summers 1936–37); produced *Goodness, How Sad!* (Vaudeville, Oct. 18, 1938); appeared as Kurt Schneider in *Judgement Day* (Phoenix, Nov. 21, 1939); produced a tour of *Cage Me a Peacock* (1946); played Edward Tappercoom in the London production of *The Lady's Not for Burning* (Arts, Mar. 10, 1948), which he repeated (Globe, May 11, 1949); appeared as Pandar and Antiochus in *Pericles* (Rudolf Steiner Hall, July 2, 1950); and Jacques Lambert in *Figure of Fun* (Aldwych, Oct. 16, 1951).

Also, he portrayed the General in *Under the Sycamore Tree* (Aldwych, Apr. 23, 1952); Squire Simon Lummie in *Second Best Bed* (Arts, May 20, 1953); M. Onyx in *The Man with Expensive Tastes* (Vaudeville, July 23, 1953); Kassel in *The Dark Is Light*

Enough (Aldwych, Apr. 30, 1954); Pozzo in *Waiting for Godot* (Arts, Aug. 3, 1955); Hartmann in *The Restless Heart* (St. James, May 8, 1957); Captain von Schmettau in *Man of Distinction* (Princess, Oct. 17, 1957); Tetzel in *Luther* (Th. Royal, Nottingham, June 26, 1961; later, Royal Court, London); Sgt. Buzfuz in *Pickwick* (Saville, London, July 4, 1963), repeated in N.Y.C. (46th St. Th., Oct. 4, 1965); and Colonel Melkett in *Black Comedy* (Ethel Barrymore Th., Feb. 12, 1967). He was on tour in the US with *An Evening of Bull* (Oct. and Nov. 1973).

Films. Mr. Bull has played in *The African Queen* (UA, 1951); *Oliver Twist* (UA, 1951); *The Old Dark House* (Col., 1963); *Tom Jones* (Woodfall, 1963); *Doctor Strangelove* (Col., 1964); *Doctor Dolittle* (20th-Fox, 1968); *Lady Caroline Lamb* (Pulsar, 1971); *Alice's Adventures in Wonderland* (Amer. Natl., 1972); and *Up the Front* (Associated London, 1972).

Television. He appeared with Merv Griffin (1967–68), Johnny Carson (1967–68), Dick Cavett (1968–70), and Jack Paar (1973).

Published Works. He is the author of *To Sea in a Sieve* (1956); *Bulls in the Meadows* (1957); *I Know the Face But—* (1955); *Not on Your Telly!* (1961); *I Say, Look Here!* (1965); *It Isn't All Greek to Me* (1967); *Bear With Me* (1969); *The Teddy Bear Book* (1970); and *Life Is a Cucumber* (1973).

Recreation. Swimming, food, travel.

BULLINS, ED. Playwright, producer. b. July 2, 1934, Philadelphia, Pa., to Bertha Marie Queen Bullins, power machine operator. Member of the Dramatists Guild; P.E.N. Address: 932 E. 212th St., Bronx, NY 10469, tel. (212) 691-2966.

Theatre. Among over thirty plays written by Mr. Bullins are *Dialect Determinism* and *Clara's Ole Man* (both produced at Firehouse Repertory Th., San Francisco, Calif., Aug. 5, 1965). *Clara's Ole Man* was presented in N.Y.C. with Mr. Bullins's *A Son, Come Home* and *The Electronic Nigger*, as part of a program billed as *The Electronic Nigger and Others* (American Place Theatre, St. Clement's Church, Mar. 6, 1968), which, as *Three Plays by Ed Bullins*, moved to the Martinique Th. (Mar. 28, 1968). Other productions of Mr. Bullins's work include *In the Wine Time* (New Lafayette, Dec. 10, 1968), the first of a projected twenty-play cycle about Afro-Americans bearing the overall title *20th Century Cycle; The Corner* (Theatre Co. of Boston, 1968); *The Gentleman Caller*, one of four one-act plays by Mr. Bullins and others, on the program *A Black Quartet* (Tambellini's Gate Th., N.Y.C., July 30, 1969); *The Pig Pen* (American Place Th., St. Clement's Church, Apr. 29, 1970); *The Duplex* (New Lafayette, May 22, 1970); *It Bees Dat Way* (Ambiance Lunch-Hour Th. Club, London, Sept. 21, 1970); *Death List* (Th. Black, N.Y.C., Oct. 16, 1970); *Street Sounds* (La Mama E.T.C., Oct. 22, 1970); the second cycle play, *In New England Winter* (Henry St. Playhouse, Jan. 26, 1971; *The Fabulous Miss Marie* (New Lafayette, Mar. 11, 1971); *Goin' a Buffalo* (Workshop of the Players' Art, Feb. 15, 1972); and *House Party* (American Place Th., Oct. 29, 1973).

Other Activities. Mr. Bullins has taught writing and English at Fordham Univ., Columbia Univ., the Univ. of Massachusetts at Boston, Bronx Community Coll., and Manhattan Community Coll. He has lectured at such institutions as Dartmouth Coll., Talladega Coll., Clark Coll., and Univ. of California at Berkeley.

Published Works. Mr. Bullins's published works include *The Hungered One* and *The Reluctant Rapist.* Articles and criticism by him have appeared in such publications as the NY *Times, Black World, The Drama Review,* and *Performance.*

Awards. Mr. Bullins received the Drama Desk-Vernon Rice Award (1967–68) for *Three Plays by Ed Bullins;* the *Village Voice* Off-Bway (Obie) Award (1970–71) for distinguished playwriting for *The Fabulous Miss Marie* and *In New England Winter;* a Guggenheim Fellowship; the Rockefeller Playwriting Grant; the Creative Artists Program Service (CAPS) grant for playwriting; and a National Endowment for the Arts (NEA) grant for playwriting.

BULOFF, JOSEPH. Actor, director. b. Dec. 6, 1907, Vilno, Lithuania, to Benjamin and Sarah (Rotlast) Buloff. Father, fur dealer. Married to Luba Kadison; one daughter. Member of AEA; AFTRA; SAG. Address: 40 W. 67th St., New York, NY 10023, tel. (212) TR 7-3088.

Theatre. Mr. Buloff made his N.Y.C. debut as Sam Stern in *Don't Look Now* (Bayes, Nov. 2, 1936); followed by Sidney Castle in *Call Me Ziggy* (Longacre, Feb. 12, 1937); Zamiano in *To Quito and Back* (Guild, Oct. 6, 1937); Istvan in *The Man from Cairo* (Broadhurst, May 4, 1938); Aaron Greenspan in *Morning Star* (Longacre, Apr. 16, 1940); William Auchinchloss in *Spring Again* (Henry Miller's Th., Nov. 10, 1941); Ali Hakim in *Oklahoma!* (St. James, Mar. 31, 1943); and Feodor Vorontsov in *The Whole World Over* (Biltmore, Mar. 27, 1947).

He directed *Mrs. McThing* (ANTA, Feb. 20, 1952); played Max Pincus in *The Fifth Season* (Cambridge, London, Feb. 24, 1954); toured South Africa in the same role (1954) and repeated it in the US national tour (opened Shubert, Washington, D.C., Oct. 25, 1954); succeeded (Dec. 15, 1958) Walter Matthau as Maxwell Archer in *Once More, With Feeling* National, N.Y.C., Oct. 21, 1958); played Detective Inspector Petrov in *Moonbirds* (Cort, Oct. 9, 1959); and Fishel Shpunt in *The Wall* (Billy Rose Th., Oct. 11, 1960); and in *A Chekhov Sketchbook,* played the title role in *The Vagrant,* Siveli in *The Witch,* and Ivan in *The Music Shop* (Gramercy Arts, Feb. 15, 1962).

Mr. Buloff directed and appeared in a revival of *A Chekhov Sketchbook* (Harper Th., Chicago, Ill., Jan. 19, 1965); was Paul Hirsch in *Dear Me, The Sky Is Falling* (Harper Th., Jan. 1965); played Glas in *Slow Dance on the Killing Ground* (Playhouse in the Park, Philadelphia, Pa., June 1965); Friedrich Welt in *Fidelio* (Playhouse on the Mall, Paramus, N.J., July 20, 1965; Town and Country Playhouse, E. Rochester, N.Y., Aug. 10, 1965); toured the US as Gregory Solomon in *The Price* (Feb. 2–Mar. 26, 1970); directed and played Simkhe Meyer in a Yiddish version of *The Brothers Ashkenazi* (Folksbiene, N.Y.C., Nov. 16, 1970); directed and played Sheyne/Yoshke in *Yoshke Musikant* (Folksbiene, Nov. 4, 1972); played David Shapiro in *Hard to Be a Jew,* which, with David Licht, he also adapted (Eden Th., Oct. 28, 1973); presented a one-man show based on the dramatic writings of I. L. Peretz and Sholem Aleichem (Apr. 1975); and staged and played Max Pincus in a revival of *The Fifth Season* (Eden Th., N.Y.C., Oct. 12, 1975).

Mr. Buloff has produced, directed, and acted in more than 200 plays in Russian, English, and Yiddish in Europe, England, Argentina, Brazil, South Africa, and Israel.

Films. He made his motion picture debut in *Let's Make Music* (RKO, 1940); subsequently appeared in *They Met in Argentina* (RKO, 1941); *To the Victor* (WB, 1948); *The Loves of Carmen* (Col., 1948); *Somebody Up There Likes Me* (MGM, 1956); and *Silk Stockings* (MGM, 1957).

Television. He has appeared on television as Pincus Pines in The Goldbergs (NBC); performed in *Anything Can Happen* (Philco Playhouse, NBC, June 18, 1950); in *Justice and Mr. Pleznik* (Philco Playhouse, May 20, 1951); was the Cantor in *Holiday Song* (Goodyear Playhouse, NBC, Sept. 14, 1952); appeared in the special *Wonderful Town* (CBS, Nov. 30, 1958); was on The Untouchables (ABC, Nov. 12, 1959); Ben Casey (CBS, Jan. 18, 1964); and Medical Center (CBS, Oct. 8, 1969).

Awards. For his performance in *Hard to Be a Jew,* Mr. Buloff received *Village Voice* Off-Bway (Obie) and Drama Desk awards.

Recreation. Stamp collecting.

BURIAN, JARKA M. Educator, actor, director. b. Jaroslav Marsano Burian, Mar. 10, 1927, Passaic, N.J., to Jaroslav V. and Olga (Marsanova) Burian. Father, textile worker, bookbinder, actor; mother, piano accompanist and teacher. Grad. Rutgers Univ., B.A. 1949; Columbia Univ., M.A. 1950; Cornell Univ., Ph.D. 1955. Studied with Mrs. Jane Inge, New Brunswick, N.J., four years. Married June 1951, to Grayce Susan De Leon. Served US Army, ETO, 1946–47, 1950–51; rank, Staff Sgt., Adjutant General's Dept. Address: (home) 7 MacPherson Terrace, Albany, NY 12206, tel. (518) 465-4409; (bus.) c/o Dept. of Theatre, State University of New York, Albany, NY 12203, tel. (518) 457-8360.

Since 1971, Mr. Burian has been chairman of the Dept. of Theatre, State Univ. of N.Y., where he has been assistant professor (1955–59), associate professor (1959–63), and professor (1963–to date). He taught English at Cornell Univ. (1951–55).

At the University Th., State Univ. of N.Y., he directed *Diary of a Scoundrel* (1956); his own translation of *Insect Comedy* (Mar. 1957); *A View from the Bridge* (Nov. 1957); *Tiger at the Gates* (Nov. 1958); *Queen and the Rebels* (Feb. 1960); *The Iceman Cometh* (Nov. 1960), presented also at Cornell Univ., for the N.Y. State Community Th. Conference (Oct. 1960); *The Maids* (Feb. 1963); *The Good Woman of Setzuan* (Nov. 1963); *Dr. Faustus* (Nov. 1964); *J.B.* (Mar. 1966); *The Memorandum* (Dec. 1966, an English language premiere, in his own translation); *Hamlet*, 1st Quarto (Apr. 1968); *A Scent of Flowers* (Nov. 1970); *The Measures Taken* (Apr. 1971); *Marat/Sade* (Nov. 1972); *Antigone* (Feb. 1974, his own adaptation).

He was producer-director of the Arena Summer Theatre (Albany, N.Y.), where he directed *Too True To Be Good* (1959), *Uncle Vanya* (1959), *Emperor Jones* (1963), *Three Sisters* (1963), *The Tempest* (1964), *The Ghost Sonata* (1964), *The Birthday Party* (1966), *The Sea Gull* (1967), *Hughie* and *The Dumbwaiter* (1967), *Endgame* (1968), and *The Cherry Orchard* (1973). He was visiting professor at the Univ. of California at Berkeley, where he directed *A Raisin in the Sun* (University Th., Dec. 1961); and for the State Univ. of N.Y., he directed *Murder in the Cathedral* (Cathedral of All Saints, Albany, N.Y., Nov. 1962). He directed a Czech language production of *The Glass Menagerie* at the regional theatre in Kladno, Czechoslovakia, in Nov. 1965, while on a lecture tour in that country.

Mr. Burian's first acting role was Agamemnon in *Daughters of Atreus* (Little Theatre, Rutgers Univ., Feb. 1945); subsequently played Earnest in *The Importance of Being Earnest* (Tufts Univ. Summer Arena Th., July 1949); and made his professional debut as Lawyer Colline in *The Doctored Wife* and as the Doctor in *The Son* (Circle Th., N.Y.C., July 1950). He played Tsali in the outdoor historical drama, *Unto These Hills* (Mountainside Th., Cherokee, N.C., Summers 1956–58, 1960–62); conducted acting classes for the cast of *Unto These Hills* (1961–62); and directed *The Dumbwaiter* (Mountainside Th., Cherokee, N.C., Summer 1962).

Published Works. Mr. Burian's books include *Central Staging: New Force in the Theatre* (1950); an unpublished adaptation of *The Good Soldier Schweik; O Americkem Dramatu a Divadelnictvi (American Drama and Theatre),* lectures delivered in Czechoslovakia in 1965 (Prague, 1966); *The Scenography of Josef Svoboda* (Middletown, Conn., 1971). Among his articles are "Challenge of the Absurd," *New York State Community Theatre Journal* (Jan. 1964); "A Case for Arena Theatre: 1966," *The Theatre Annual: 1965–1966* (1966); "Art and Relevance: The Small Theatres of Prague 1958–1970," *Educational Theatre Journal* (Oct. 1971); and "Post-War Drama in Czechoslovakia," *Educational Theatre Journal* (Oct. 1973).

Awards. On a research grant from the Inter-University Committee on Travel Grants, Mr. Burian spent eleven months in 1968–69 in Czechoslovakia. He held State University of N.Y. summer research fellowships in 1970, 1971, and 1974 and an NEH summer stipend in 1974. He received an IREX Fellowship for theatre research in Czechoslovakia in 1974–75.

Recreation. High fidelity, swimming, travel.

BURKE, GEORGIA. Actress. b. Gracie Maedell Burke, Feb. 27, 1906, La Grange, Ga., to Stakes and Mahala Burke. Father, minister; mother, practical nurse. Grad. Clafin Univ., Orangeburg,

S.C., 1930; attended New York Univ., 1932–34. Relative in theatre: sister, Lulu B. King, actress. Member of AEA; AFTRA; SAG; Negro Actors Guild. Address: 465 W. 152nd St., New York, NY 10031, tel. (212) WA 6-1774.

Pre-Theatre. Teacher.

Theatre. Miss Burke made her Bway debut as Mrs. Wood in *They Shall Not Die* (Royale, Feb. 21, 1934); followed by Eva in *Mamba's Daughters* (Empire, Jan. 3, 1939); succeeded Gee Gee Williams as Clementine in *No Time for Comedy* (Ethel Barrymore Th., Apr. 17, 1939); in stock, appeared in *Coquette* (Bucks County Playhouse, New Hope, Pa., 1934); as Virgie in *Decision* (Belasco, N.Y.C., Feb. 2, 1944); and Theresa in *Anna Lucasta* (Mansfield, Aug. 30, 1944; His Majesty's, London, Oct. 29, 1947; Scotland).

She appeared as Cassie in *The Wisteria Trees* (Martin Beck Th., N.Y.C., Mar. 27, 1952); Catherine Greek in *The Grass Harp* (Martin Beck Th., Mar. 27, 1952); Maria in *Porgy and Bess* (Stoll, London, Oct. 9, 1952; and Ziegfeld, N.Y.C., Mar. 10, 1953), and toured Europe, USSR, and South America (1952–56); appeared in a stock production of *Tambourines to Glory* (Westport Country Playhouse, Conn., 1958); as Lucille in *Interlock* (ANTA, N.Y.C., Feb. 6, 1958); Mrs. Peep in *The Killer* (Seven Arts Playhouse, Mar. 22, 1960); and in a stock production of *Two Queens of Love and Beauty* (Bucks County Playhouse, New Hope, Pa., 1961).

She appeared as Lucretia Borgia in *Mandingo* (Lyceum, N.Y.C., May 22, 1961); Sister Moore in *The Amen Corner* (Lyceum, Edinburgh, Scotland, Aug. 23, 1965; Saville, London, Oct. 12, 1965); Aunty Mom in *Bohikee Creek* (Stage 73, N.Y.C., Apr. 28, 1966); and as Mrs. Harding in *A Dream of Love* (Th. of the Living Arts, Philadelphia, Pa., Sept. 13, 1966).

Films. *Anna Lucasta* (UA, 1959); *The Cool World* (Cinema V, 1964).

Television and Radio. On radio, Miss Burke played the role of Lilly for fourteen years on the serial When a Girl Marries (NBC); she also acted regularly on the serials Our Gal Sunday, One Man's Family, and Big Story (NBC, 1932).

On television she has appeared on Goodyear Th. (NBC, 1950); *The Little Foxes* (Hallmark Hall of Fame, NBC, 1957); and *The Grass Harp* (Play of the Week, WNTA, 1960).

Awards. She received the Donaldson Award for her performance as Virgie in *Decision* (1944).

Recreation. Tennis, fishing, bridge.

BURNIM, KALMAN A.

BURNIM, KALMAN A. Educator, scholar, director, theatre historian. b. March 7, 1928, Malden, Mass., to Jack K. and Sadie Burnim. Father, business executive. Grad. Revere (Mass.) H.S.; Tufts Coll., B.A. 1950; Indiana Univ., M.A. 1951; Yale Univ., Ph.D. 1958. Married Sept. 12, 1948, to Verna Lesser; two daughters; one son. Served US Army, 1945–46, as an actor with Special Services in the Far East command. Member of Phi Beta Kappa (1950); American Society for Theatre Research (exec. comm.); American Theatre Assn.; Society for Theatre Research (England); University Resident Theatre Assn. (exec. bd.); Modern Language Assn.; Shakespeare Assn. of America; International Federation for Theatre Research; American Assn. of University Professors. Address: (home) 22 Cranmore Lane, Melrose, MA 02176, tel. (617) 662-9588; (bus.) Tufts University, Medford, MA 02155, tel. (617) 628-5000, ext. 484.

Pre-Theatre. From 1951 to 1955, Dr. Burnim was general manager for the New England Adding Machine Co., Boston, Mass.

Theatre. Dr. Burnim is chairman of the dept. (1966–to date); and Fletcher professor of drama (1971–to date) at Tufts Univ., where he has previously served as professor (1965–71); associate professor (1961–65); and assistant professor (1960–61). He has also served as managing director (1960–66), and is currently executive director (1966–to date) of the Tufts University Theatre.

Prior to 1960, he was assistant professor of drama at the Univ. of Pittsburgh (1959–60); and at Valparaiso (Ind.) Univ. (1958–59). He also directed numerous plays at the theatres connected with these institutions.

Published Works. In addition to many articles on theatre history, he has written *David Garrick, Director* (1961); *Aaron Hill's The Prompter* (1966); *A Biographical Dictionary of Actors, Actresses, Musicians, Dancers, Managers, and Other Stage personnel in London 1660–1800* (Vols. 1 and 2, 1974; Vols. 3–12 in process of publication).

Awards. For research into theatre history, Dr. Burnim has received a Guggenheim Fellowship (1964–65); grants from ACLS (1966 and 1973); and from the National Endowment for the Humanities (1968 and 1974); and Folger Library Fellowships (1957, 1969, 1971, and 1973).

BURR, DONALD.

BURR, DONALD. Actor, director. b. July 31, 1907, Cincinnati, Ohio, to Frederick and Edna Burr. Father, dentist. Grad. Withrow H.S., Cincinnati, 1925; attended Univ. of Cincinnati, 1925–28; Conservatory of Music, Cincinnati, 1925–30; studied voice with Dan Beddoe, 1928–29; Coll. of Music, Cincinnati, studied drama with John Redhead Froome (1929–30), Dramatic Arts diploma, 1930. Married Oct. 24, 1935, to Billie Worth, actress, singer; one son, one daughter. Served US Army, Coast Artillery and Infantry, 1943–45. Member of AEA; SAG; AFTRA; Sigma Alpha Epsilon. Address: RD, Long Valley, NJ tel. (201) 876-3342.

Theatre. Mr. Burr made his N.Y.C. debut as a singing juvenile in *Garrick Gaieties* (Guild Th., Oct. 16, 1930); subsequently appeared as Sasha Sachalow in *Marching By* (46 St. Th., Mar. 3, 1932); played in *Walk a Little Faster* (St. James, Dec. 7, 1932); toured cross-country with *Earl Carroll's Vanities* (Oct. 1934); toured England and Scotland as Billy in *Anything Goes* (Apr. 1936), and in *Darling You* (Dec. 1936).

He made his London debut as Tony Luffington in *Certainly Sir* (Hippodrome, Sept. 17, 1936); toured Australia and New Zealand in *Over She Goes, Jill Darling, Swing Along, Nice Going* and *No! No! Nanette!* (1937–38); in N.Y.C., appeared in *Walk with Music* (Ethel Barrymore Th., June 14, 1940); portrayed Feste in *Twelfth Night* (St. James, Nov. 19, 1940); played in *Sweethearts* and *The Three Musketeers* (St. Louis Municipal Opera, June 1941); appeared as Captain Absolute in *The Rivals* (Shubert, N.Y.C., Jan. 14, 1942); played in *Girl Crazy, Too Many Girls* and *Wildflower* (St. Louis Municipal Opera, June 1942); portrayed Gardefeu in *La Vie Parisienne* (Bway, Nov. 10, 1942); followed Gene Barry (March 1943) as Falke in *Rosalinda* (44 St. Th., Oct. 28, 1942); played the Music Master in *The Would-Be Gentleman* (Booth, Jan. 9, 1946); appeared in musicals (Iroquois Amphitheatre, Louisville, Ky., Summers 1946–47); played Charlie Davenport in the national tour of *Annie Get Your Gun* (opened State Fair Music Hall, Dallas, Tex., Oct. 1947; closed Shubert-Lafayette, Detroit, Mich., May 1949); and repeated the role in the same play (Greek Th., Los Angeles, Calif., June 1949).

Mr. Burr was resident director of the St. Louis Municipal Opera (Summer 1950); followed Richard Hart (Oct. 1950) as Uncle Desmonde in *The Happy Time* (Plymouth, Jan. 24, 1950); directed musicals (Bradford Roof Dinner Th., Boston, Mass., Spring 1951); played Pemberton Maxwell, later followed Anton Walbrook in the role of Cosmo Constantine in *Call Me Madam* (Coliseum, March 15, 1952); performed in the resident company of the Detroit Civic Light Opera Co. (Winter 1953–54); played Cosmo Constantine in *Call Me Madam* (Starlight Th., Kansas City, Mo., Summer 1954); and Gus Esmond in *Gentlemen Prefer Blondes* (St. Louis Municipal Opera, Mo., Summer 1954).

Mr. Burr was resident director of the Sacramento (Calif.) Light Opera, (1955–63) where he also appeared in *Anything Goes, The Boy Friend, Guys and Dolls, Music in the Air, Song of Norway, Rosalie, Fanny, Show Boat, Rosalinda* and *Chocolate Soldier;* and played Charley Davenport in *Annie Get Your Gun* (San Francisco and Los Angeles Light Opera Co., Calif., Fall 1957; directed *Annie Get Your Gun* (N.Y.City Ctr., Feb. 1958); *Guys and Dolls* (Meadowbrook Dinner Th., N.Y., Spring 1958); and other musicals (Lambertville Music Circus, N.J., 1959; Westchester Town House, N.Y., Spring 1962; Vogue Terrace, Pittsburgh, Pa., 1963).

At the Meadowbrook Dinner Th. (Cedar Grove, N.J.), Mr. Burr played Panisse in *Fanny* (Apr. 2, 1964); directed, and played the Governor in, *The Red Mill* (Apr. 26, 1964); played Col. Pickering in *My Fair Lady* (July 8, 1964; Oct. 8, 1964); appeared as the Police Inspector in *Irma La Douce* (Aug. 5, 1964); directed *Flower Drum Song* (Nov. 4, 1964); played Pellinore in *Camelot* (Jan. 28, 1965); directed, staged the musical numbers, and appeared as Capt. Brackett in *South Pacific* (Feb. 25, 1965); played Mr. MacAfee in *Bye Bye Birdie* (Apr. 21, 1965; and directed, and played Hilaire Jussac in, *Can-Can* (June 2, 1965).

He played Mr. Allerton in *Skyscraper* (Lunt-Fontanne, N.Y.C., Nov. 13, 1965); and Ernest W. Stanley in *Sherry!* (Alvin, Mar. 28, 1967).

Television. Mr. Burr has appeared on dramatic and variety shows including Schlitz Playhouse (CBS); *Dearest Enemy* (NBC); A Date with Judy (ABC); Man Against Crime (CBS); Paul Winchell Show (ABC); and *Annie Get Your Gun* (NBC, Nov. 1957).

Recreation. Tennis, golf.

BURRIS-MEYER, HAROLD.

BURRIS-MEYER, HAROLD. Theatre planning consultant, writer, educator, director. b. Apr. 6, 1902, Madison, N.J. Grad. City Coll. of New York, B.S. 1923; Columbia Univ., M.A. 1926; attended Columbia Univ., 1926–32. Married Apr. 12, 1945, to Anita Mersfelder, actress; one son, one daughter. Served WW II, USN; rank, Comdr. Member and former director of ANTA; USITT (exec. comm.); Accoustical Society of America (exec. comm., 1942–45; fellow); currently a director of ACAIE; member of Audio Engineering Society (fellow); ATA; Amer. Inst. of Physics; Amer. Physical Society. Mr. Burris-Meyer belongs also to the Army-Navy Club, Washington, D.C., and the Golden Harbour Yacht Club, Boca Raton, Fla. Address: (home) 3165 N. Quincy St., Arlington, VA 22207, tel. (703) JA 7-7123; (bus.) 1629 K St., N.W., Washington, DC 20006, tel. (202) 296-8228..

Mr. Burris-Meyer was asst. dir. of the Washington (Pa.) Drama League and asst. prof. of speech and drama, Washington and Jefferson Coll. (1927–29); asst. prof. and prof. of dramatic arts (1929–54); and dir. (1930–54) of the theatre, Stevens Inst. of Technology, Hoboken, N.J. He became a theatre consultant in 1954, specializing in acoustics, sound systems, and theatre planning. He was prof. and dir. of the theatre (1965–72) and prof. emeritus (1972–to date), Florida Atlantic Univ., Boca Raton, Fla.

Theatre. Mr. Burris-Meyer was sound consultant for a pageant entitled *Control* (Stevens Inst. of Technology, Hoboken, N.J., (1930); *Hamlet* (Broadhurst Th., N.Y.C., Nov. 5, 1931; Imperial, Nov. 19, 1936); subsequently was consultant on sound and other production problems for the Living Newspaper productions of *Ethiopia* (1935); *Triple A Plowed Under* (1935); *One-Third of a Nation* (Adelphi, Jan. 17, 1938); the pageants *Railroads on Parade* (NY World's Fair, 1939), and *Founders* (Williamsburg, Va.); *Two on an Island* (Broadhurst, N.Y.C., Jan. 22, 1940); and *Night Music* (Broadhurst, Feb. 22, 1940). He designed sound control systems for the Metropolitan Opera productions of *Alceste, Un Ballo in Mascera, La Nozzach de Figaro, Die Walküre, The Magic Flute, Faust,* and *Tannhäuser* (1940–42); and directed experimental productions using various new electronic and mechanical devices for *Hamlet, The Tempest, A Midsummer Night's Dream, Macbeth, Lazarus Laughed, The Adding Machine,* and *Faust* (Stevens Inst. of Technology, Hoboken, N.J., 1940–41).

He was sound consultant for *Yankee Point* (Longacre, N.Y.C., Nov. 23, 1942); *Lute Song* (Plymouth, Feb. 6, 1946); *Happy Birthday* (Broadhurst,

Oct. 31, 1946); *The Rat Race* (Ethel Barrymore Th., Dec. 22, 1949); *Tower Beyond Tragedy* (ANTA, Nov. 26, 1950); *Twentieth Century* (ANTA, Dec. 24, 1950); *King Lear* (Natl., Dec. 25, 1950); *Peer Gynt* (ANTA, Jan. 28, 1951); *Mary Rose* (ANTA, May 4, 1951); *Come of Age* (NY City Ctr., Jan. 23, 1952); the pre-Bway tryout of *Saint Joan* (opened Natl., Washington, D.C., Sept. 20, 1954; closed Hartman, Columbus, Ohio, Nov. 6, 1954); and the Playwrights production of *Madam, Will You Walk* (opened Ford's Th., Baltimore, Md.), and the Phoenix production of the same play (Phoenix, N.Y.C., Dec. 1, 1953).

Mr. Burris-Meyer was the theatre planning and acoustical consultant for new theatres such as the Lynchburg Fine Arts Center at the Univ. of Connecticut (Storrs); Howard Univ. (Washington, D.C.); Sweet Briar (Va.) Coll.; Temple Univ. (Philadelphia, Pa.); the Paper Mill Playhouse (Millburn, N.J.); Atlanta Cultural Center (Ga.), as well as for many churches, auditoriums, and night clubs.

Other Activities. From 1938–47, Mr. Burris-Meyer was consultant to, and later vice-president of Muzak Corp. He was also a director of Associated Program Service (1945–47); vice-president and director of Magnetic Programs, Inc. (1948–57); and director of ENCABULATOR Corp. (1970–to date). In 1943, he was a member of the US War Dept. Planning Board. Mr. Burris-Meyer has done research on equipment and techniques for control of sound in the theatre; psycho-acoustics; psychophysical measurements; functional music; non-verbal communication; and unconventional weapons and weapons systems under grants from Stevens Institute of Technology; Stevens Research Foundation; Research Corp.; Rockefeller Foundation; US Office of Education; National Defense Research Committee; US Army; and US Air Force Systems Command.

Published Works. He wrote, with Edward Cole, *Scenery for the Theatre* (1938; rev. ed. 1971); *Theatres and Auditoriums* (1949; 2nd ed. 1964); with Lewis S. Goodfriend, *Acoustics for the Architect* (1957); and, with Vincent Mallory, *Sound in the Theatre* (1959). He has contributed articles to *Theatre Arts, Journal of the Society of Motion Picture Engineers*, and *Journal of the Acoustical Society of America.*

Discography. In 1941, he directed the first stereophonic recordings, dramatic episodes from *The Emperor Jones* and *Cyrano de Bergerac*, for the Bell Telephone Laboratories.

Awards. Mr. Burris-Meyer received a USN commendation "for development of new and unconventional military devices and techniques" (1945) and the first USITT Founders Award (1973).

BURROUGHS, ROBERT C. Educator. b. Robert Clark Burroughs, Mar. 1, 1923, Milwaukee, Wis., to S. Dillon and Matta (Smith) Burroughs. Father, sales manager. Grad. Carl Schurz H.S., Chicago, Ill., 1939; Hanover Coll., B.A. 1943; State Univ. of Iowa, M.A. 1947; attended Cornell Univ., Summers 1961–62. Married Dec. 29, 1951, to Patricia Genematas, theatrical costumer, decorator; two sons. Served US Army, Special Services, 1943–46; rank, Sgt. Member of SAA; USITT; ANTA; NCP; CTC; AETA (chmn., stage design and technical developments project, 1960–62); Sigma Chi; Univ. Players. Address: (home) 5810 N. Williams Dr., Tucson, AZ 85702, tel. (602) CY 7-1625; (bus.) c/o Drama Dept., Coll. of Fine Arts, Univ. of Arizona, Tucson, AZ 85702, tel. (602) 887-6277.

Since 1947, Mr. Burroughs has been professor of drama as well as art director and designer for the University Th., at the Univ. of Arizona.

He was an actor and stage manager for a USO tour of *The Doughgirls* (Alaskan Dept., 1944); designer, stage manager, and actor for the US Army Special Services tour of the revue, *Take a Break* (Alaskan Dept. 1944–45); designed *The Skin of Our Teeth* (San Diego State Univ., Calif., Summer 1948); played Argon in a Town Hall Players production of *The Imaginary Invalid* (Brewster-on-the-Cape, Mass., 1948); designed both and portrayed the Actor in *The Guardsman* and Arnold Holt in *Edward, My Son* (Univ. of Ala., 1950); was designer for the Tucson (Ariz.) Children's Th. (1950–70); technical director and actor at the Wagon Wheel Playhouse (Rockton, Ill., Summer 1955); appeared as Warren Gillie in *The Solid Gold Cadillac* (Wagon Wheel Playhouse, Rockton, Ill., Summer 1955); serves as drama dept. chairman of the National Music Camp, a camp-school, and as director (Grunow Th., Interlochen, Mich., Summers 1957–to date); director of Imperial Players, Cripple Creek, Col. (1968–to date); guest director, Arizona Civic Theatre; narrator, San Xavier Pageant (1959–to date); director and designer of *Misalliance*, one of the ten best college plays in the 1969 American College Theatre Festival; author of numerous international magazine articles.

Television. Mr. Burroughs was narrator for the Christmas program (KOLD-TV, Tucson, Ariz., 1954).

Recreation. Swimming, reading, and travel.

BURROWS, ABE. Playwright, director. b. Abram S. Burrows, Dec. 18, 1910, New York City, to Louis and Julia (Salzberg) Burrows. Father, retailer, wall paper and paints. Grad. New Utrecht H.S., Brooklyn, N.Y., 1928; attended Coll. of the City of New York, 1928–29; New York Univ., 1929–32. Married Dec. 2, 1950, to Carin Elsie Marie Smith; one son, one daughter. Member of Dramatists Guild; WGA, West; DGA; SSD&C; ASCAP; AFTRA; AGVA: Musicians Union.

Pre-Theatre. Worked for accounting firm and on Wall Street.

Theatre. Mr. Burrow's first assignment was writer, with Jo Swerling, of the book of *Guys and Dolls* based on characters from Damon Runyon's stories (46 St. Th., N.Y.C., Nov. 24, 1950); subsequently directed *Two on the Aisle* (Mark Hellinger Th., July 19, 1951); directed and collaborated on the book with Charles O'Neal for *Three Wishes for Jamie* (Mark Hellinger Th., Mar. 21, 1952); wrote the book and directed *Can-Can* (Shubert, May 7, 1953); directed *Reclining Figure* (Lyceum, Oct. 7, 1954); wrote the book with George S. Kaufman and Leueen MacGrath, for *Silk Stockings* (Imperial, Feb. 24, 1955); directed *Happy Hunting* (Majestic, Dec. 6, 1956); directed and wrote the book with Richard and Marion Bissell, for *Say, Darling* (ANTA, Apr. 3, 1958); wrote the book and directed *First Impressions* (Alvin, Mar. 19, 1959); directed *Golden Fleecing* (Henry Miller's Th., Oct. 15, 1959); directed and wrote the book, with Jack Weinstock and Willie Gilbert, for *How To Succeed in Business without Really Trying* (46 St. Th., Oct. 14, 1961); and directed *What Makes Sammy Run?* (54th St. Th., Feb. 27, 1964).

Mr. Burrows directed *Cactus Flower*, which he also wrote, basing it on a French play by Pierre Barillet and Jean-Pierre Gredy (Royale, Dec. 8, 1965; Lyric, London, Mar. 6, 1967); withdrew during the pre-Bway engagement (Shubert Th., Boston, Mass., Nov. 1, 1966) as director and book author of *Holly Golightly*, which closed (Dec. 14, 1966) during N.Y.C. previews under the title *Breakfast at Tiffany's* (Majestic Th.); directed *Forty Carats* (Morosco, Dec. 26, 1968); wrote and directed a program of four one-act plays, *Four on a Garden* (Broadhurst, Jan. 30, 1971); and directed *No Hard Feelings* (Martin Beck Th., Apr. 8, 1973).

Films. Mr. Burrows adapted *The Solid Gold Cadillac* (Col., 1956).

Television and Radio. Mr. Burrows was on the writing staff of the radio programs, This Is New York (CBS, 1938); Texaco Star Theatre (CBS, 1939); the Rudy Vallee-John Barrymore Program (NBC, 1940); Duffy's Tavern (CBS and NBC, 1941–45); the Dinah Shore Show (CBS, 1945); the Joan Davis Show (CBS, 1946); and he wrote and appeared on the Abe Burrows Show (CBS, 1946–47) and Breakfast with Burrows (CBS, 1949).

On television, he was on This Is Show Business (CBS, 1949–50); Abe Burrows' Almanac (CBS, 1950), which he also wrote; and We Take Your Word (CBS, 1950), which was also on radio. He appeared as a guest on PM East (1961–62); To Tell the Truth (CBS, 1964–65); Get the Message (ABC, 1964–65); Musical Th. (CBS, 1964–65) and Match Game (NBC, 1964–68); and he has also appeared on such shows as What's My Line? (CBS); Password (CBS); and the Mike Douglas Show (Ind.).

Published Works. Mr. Burrows published *Abe Burrows' Song Book* (1955).

Discography. Mr. Burrows recorded the albums *The Girl with the Three Blue Eyes*, for which he wrote words and, with Frank Loesser, music (Decca, 1945) and *Abe Burrows Sings* (Columbia, 1950).

Awards. He received the Radio Critics Award for the Abe Burrows Show; NY Drama Critics' Circle Award and the Antoinette Perry (Tony) Award for *Guys and Dolls* (1951); NY Drama Critics' Award, Antoinette Perry (Tony) Award, and the Pulitzer Prize in Drama for *How To Succeed in Business without Really Trying* (1962).

Recreation. Painting, music.

BURTON, PHILIP. Teacher, director. b. Philip Henry Burton, Nov. 30, 1904, Mountain Ash, Glamorgan, Wales, to Henry and Emma Burton. Grad. Grammar Sch., Mountain Ash, 1921; Univ. of Wales, Cardiff, Wales, B.A. (double honors) 1925. Served WW II, RAF; rank, Flight Lt.; awarded M.B.E. by King George VI. Relative in theatre: foster son, Richard Burton, actor. Member of SSD&C (exec. vice-pres., 1962–to date); Dramatists Guild; AEA. Address: (home) 350 W. 22nd St., New York, NY 10011; (bus.) 245 E. 23rd St., New York, NY 10011, tel. (212) OR 9-2730.

From 1962 until his retirement in 1971 Mr. Burton was the director of the American Musical and Dramatic Academy, N.Y.C. and taught acting for Shakespearean works (1956–to date). He was chief instructor with the British Broadcasting Company (1945–52).

Theatre. Mr. Burton directed *Purple Dust* (Cherry Lane Th., N.Y.C., Dec. 27, 1956); a stock production of *Back to Methuselah* (Summer tour, 1957); in N.Y.C., *Interlock* (ANTA, Feb. 6, 1958); *Cock-a-Doodle Dandy* (Carnegie Hall Playhouse, Nov. 12, 1958); *Harlequinade* (Rita Allen Th., Feb. 13, 1959); *A Shaw Festival* (Provincetown Playhouse, May 26, 1959); presented *A Poetry Reading* (Lunt-Fontanne, June 21, 1964); was resident director of The Music Hall (Clinton, N.J.), where he played Sheridan Whiteside in *The Man Who Came to Dinner* (July 27, 1965); was director, narrator, and arranger for *Four and Twenty Women* (Guild Hall, East Hampton, N.Y., Aug. 21, 1966); directed *Comedy Through the Ages* (Town Hall, N.Y.C., Nov. 19, 1967); and directed for the Washington (D.C.) Shakespeare Festival (Sylvan Th., 1967–68).

Television. Mr. Burton was host for The Human Stage (Ind., 1965); and has made guest appearances on The Merv Griffin Show (Ind., 1965); and The Today Show (NBC, 1966).

Published Works. Mr. Burton is the author of *Early Doors* (Dial, 1969; and *The Sole Voice* (Dial, 1970).

Awards. He received a Guild of Graduates Fellowship for the study of dramatic training in the US (1939).

BURTON, RICHARD. Actor. b. Richard Walter Jenkins, Jr., Nov. 10, 1925, Pontrhydyfen, South Wales, to Richard Walter and Edith (Thomas) Jenkins. Father, coal miner. Grad. Port Talbot Secondary Sch., Wales, 1943; attended Exeter Coll., Oxford Univ., 1943–44. Served RAF, 1944–47. Married Feb. 5, 1949, to Sybil Williams, actress (marr. dis. Dec. 16, 1963); two daughters; married Mar. 15, 1964, to Elizabeth Taylor, actress (marr. dis. June 26, 1974). Relative in theatre: foster father, Philip Burton, teacher, director. Member of AEA; British AEA; SAG. Address: c/o Weissberger and Frosch, 120 E. 56th St., New York, NY 10022, tel. (212) PL 8-0800.

Theatre. Mr. Burton made his first stage appearance as Glan in *Druid's Rest* (Royal Court Th., Liverpool, Nov. 1943), the role in which he made his London debut (St. Martin's, Jan. 26, 1944); subsequently played Mr. Hicks in *Castle Anna* (Lyric,

Hammersmith, Feb. 24, 1948); Richard in *The Lady's Not for Burning* (Globe, May 11, 1949); Cuthman in *The Boy with a Cart* (Lyric, Hammersmith, Jan. 19, 1950); and Tegeus in *A Phoenix Too Frequent* (Brighton, Mar. 1950).

He made his N.Y.C. debut as Richard in *The Lady's Not for Burning* (Royale, Nov. 8, 1950); played the Young Musician in *Legend of Lovers* (Plymouth, Dec. 26, 1951); the title role in *Montserrat* (Lyric, Hammersmith, London, Apr. 8, 1952); at the Edinburgh (Scotland) Festival (1953), played the title role in *Hamlet* with the Old Vic Co., with whom he remained for the 1953–54 London season, playing the title role in *Hamlet;* Philip, the Bastard, in *King John* (Oct. 26, 1953); Sir Toby Belch in *Twelfth Night* (Jan. 6, 1954); Caius Marcius in *Coriolanus* (Feb. 23, 1954); and Caliban in *The Tempest* (Apr. 13, 1954); and alternated with John Neville as Othello (Feb. 21, 1956) and Iago (Feb. 22, 1956) in *Othello.*

He played Albert in *Time Remembered* (Morosco, N.Y.C., Nov. 12, 1957); King Arthur in *Camelot* (Majestic, Dec. 3, 1960); the title role in *Hamlet* (Lunt-Fontanne, Apr. 9, 1964); and, with his wife, gave an evening of poetry readings (Lunt-Fontanne, June 21, 1964).

Films. Mr. Burton made his screen debut in *Dolwyn* (London Films, 1948); and has since appeared in *Now Barrabas Was a Robber* (WB, 1949); *Waterfront* (GFD, 1950); *The Woman with No Name* (Rank, 1952); *My Cousin Rachel* (20th-Fox, 1952); *The Desert Rats* (20th-Fox, 1953); *The Robe* (20th-Fox, 1953); *The Prince of Players* (20th-Fox, 1955); *The Rains of Ranchipur* (20th-Fox, 1955); *Alexander the Great* (UA, 1956); *Sea Wife* (20th-Fox, 1957); *Bitter Victory* (Col., 1958); *Look Back in Anger* (WB, 1959); *The Bramble Bush* (WB, 1960); *Ice Palace* (WB, 1960); *The Longest Day* (20th-Fox, 1962). He played Marc Antony in *Cleopatra* (20th-Fox, 1963); Paul Andros in *The VIP's* (MGM, 1963); the title role in *Becket* (Par., 1964); Shannon in *Night of the Iguana* (MGM, 1964); and the title role in *Hamlet* (WB, 1964).

His other films include *The Sandpiper* (MGM, 1965); *The Spy Who Came in from the Cold* (Par., 1965); *Who's Afraid of Virginia Woolf?* (WB, 1966); *The Taming of the Shrew* (Col., 1967); *The Comedians* (MGM, 1967); *Doctor Faustus* (Col., 1968); *Boom!* (U, 1968); *Candy* (Cinerama, 1968); *Where Eagles Dare* (MGM, 1969); *Staircase* (20th-Fox, 1969); *Anne of the Thousand Days* (U, 1969); *Raid on Rommel* (U, 1971); *Villain* (MGM, 1971); *Hammersmith Is Out* (Cinerama, 1972); *The Assassination of Trotsky* (Cinerama, 1972). Mr. Burton spoke the narration for *A Wall in Jerusalem* (Eyr, 1972) and appeared also in *Bluebeard* (Cinerama, 1972); *Under Milkwood* (Ind., 1973); *Massacre in Rome* (Natl. Gen., 1973); *Tito* (Ind., 1973); and *The Klansman* (Par., 1974).

Television. Mr. Burton appeared in *Wuthering Heights* (CBS, May 1958); The Broadway of Lerner and Loewe (NBC, Feb. 11, 1960); and *A Subject of Scandal and Concern* (BBC, London, Nov. 6, 1960); and *The Tempest* (Hallmark Hall of Fame, NBC). He also performed several times in poetry readings on the BBC.

Awards. Mr. Burton won the *Theatre World* Award (1951). For his performance in *Camelot,* he received the Antoinette Perry (Tony) Award (1961).

Recreation. Rugby, swimming, boxing, chess, piano.

BURY, JOHN. Stage designer, costume designer, lighting designer, consultant in designing theatres. b. Jan. 27, 1925, Aberystwyth, Wales, to Charles Rugely and Emily Frances Margaret (Adams) Bury. Father, chemistry professor, University College, Wales; mother, botanist. Educated Hereford Cathedral School and University College, London, England. Married 1947 to Margaret Leila Greenwood (marr. dis. 1965); one son; married 1966 to Elizabeth Rebecca (Duffield) Blackborrow; three children. Served in Royal Navy, 1942–46, as observer, Fleet Air Arm. Member of Associations of British Theatre Designers (chmn., 1971–to date), British Theatre Lighting Designers (exec. comm., 1968–to date), British Theatre Technicians (exec. comm., 1969–to date), United Scenic Artists; Society of British Theatre Consultants; Organisation Internationale de Scenographie et Théâtre Technicians (steering comm., 1968–to date). Address: (home) 14 Woodlands Dr., Barnes, London S.W. 13, England tel. (01) 876-1865; (bus.) The National Theatre of Great Britain, South Bank, London, England tel. (01) 928-2033.

Theatre. Mr. Bury was appointed head of design, National Theatre of Great Britain, London, England, in 1973. From 1947 to 1962, he was associated with over sixty productions of Joan Littlewood's Theatre Workshop, London, first as lighting designer, then designer, and finally with full technical control. From 1962 to 1969, he was associate designer and then head of designing, Royal Shakespeare Theatre, Stratford-upon-Avon, England, for which he did over twenty-five productions. In addition to his theatre work, Mr. Bury has free-lanced in the films and opera, notably at the Royal Opera House, Covent Garden, and Glyndebourne Opera House.

His first N.Y.C. production was the Off-Bway *Blood Knot* (Cricket, Mar. 1, 1964), and his first Bway production was *Oh What a Lovely War,* for which he did the setting and the lighting (Broadhurst, Sept. 30, 1964). He then did scenery, lighting, and costumes for *The Physicists* (Martin Beck Th., Oct. 13, 1964). Later Bway productions with which he was associated include *The Homecoming* (Music Box Th., Jan. 5, 1967), which he designed; *Old Times* (Billy Rose Th., Nov. 16, 1971), for which he did scenery and lighting); *The Rothschilds* (Lunt-Fontanne Th., Oct. 19, 1970), for which he did scenery and costumes; *A Doll's House* (Playhouse, Jan. 13, 1971) and *Hedda Gabler* (Playhouse, Feb. 17, 1971), for both of which he did scenery, costumes, and lighting; and *Via Galactica* (Uris Th., Nov. 28, 1972), for which he did the scenery and the costumes.

Awards. Mr. Bury was elected a fellow of the Royal Society of Arts in 1968.

Recreation. Sailing, gardening, travel, and stamp collecting.

BUTLER, JAMES H. Educator. b. James Harmon Butler, Dec. 16, 1908, Cathlamet, Wash., to Don Carlos and Maude K. Butler. Father, contractor, builder; mother, school-teacher, principal. Grad. Buckley (Wash.) H.S., 1927; attended Univ. of Wash., 1929–30; Pasadena (Calif.) Playhouse, certif. 1935; grad. Western Washington Coll. of Educ.; Univ. of Southern California, M.A. 1939, Ph.D. 1948. Married June 1937 to Etta Willena, schoolteacher. Served US Army, 1942–43. Member of ANTA; ATA (pres., Southern Calif. district, 1948–49; dir., 1958–63; exec. comm., 1963–64; pres., 1968); NCP (natl. pres., 1958–63); ATA-USO Overseas Touring Comm., 1957–68; NTC; AAUP; International Federation for Theatre Research; American Society for Theatre Research; Society for Theatre Research (England); Theatre Library Assn.; US Institute for Teacher Technology; Phi Beta Kappa (pres., USC chap., 1960–61); Phi Delta Kappa; Phi Kappa Phi; Alpha Psi Omega. Address: (home) 5030 W. Slauson Ave., Los Angeles, CA 90056, tel. (213) AX 4-1703; (bus.) Dept. of Drama, Univ. of Southern California, Los Angeles, CA tel. (213) RI 8-2311.

Mr. Butler taught in public school systems of Kelso, Wash., and Tulare, Calif., at the elementary and secondary levels (1934–40). He was assistant professor of speech and drama, West Texas State College, Canyon, Tex. (1940–42) and head of the speech department (1943–44), then becoming assistant professor of speech and drama, San Jose (Calif.) State College (1945–46). He went to the Univ. of Southern California in 1946, where he was successively asst. prof. of drama (1946–48); assoc. prof. of drama (1948–51); prof. of drama (1951–to date); and chmn., Dept. of Drama and de Mille Professor of Drama (1953–70).

Theatre. Mr. Butler was director, Longview (Wash.) Community Players (1935–38) and directed at the Pasadena (Calif.) Playhouse in the summer of 1935. He subsequently directed plays at the colleges where he was teaching and in 1946 founded the Experimental Theatre at the Univ. of Southern California, serving as its supervising director until 1961.

Films. Mr. Butler acted in and narrated the college film *Let Me See It,* winner of the Screen Producers Academy Award (1953). In addition, he appeared in several short films produced at USC.

Other Activities. An authority on production of ancient Greek and Roman plays, Mr. Butler has toured in Italy, France, England, Greece, Spain, and Turkey studying ancient theatres. From 1965 to 1967, he was on an Office of Education team drawing up guidelines for theatre teaching and research; from 1967 to 1971 he was a member of the California Fine Arts and Humanities Program establishing a framework for teaching theatre in California public schools. He was a member of the advisory and executive committee of the American College Theatre Festival held in Washington, D.C., Spring 1969 and 1970. Mr. Butler is also a member of the national advisory board for the Aesthetic Education Program being developed by the Central Midwestern Regional Educational Laboratory, Inc. (CEMREL), St. Ann, Mo., and he is educational advisor and consultant for Olesen Filmstrips.

Published Works. Mr. Butler is author of the book *The Theatre and Drama of Greece and Rome* (1972) and of articles that have appeared in such periodicals as *Western Speech Journal, California Journal of Secondary Education, Educational Theatre Journal, Educational Theatre News, Theatre Survey, Theatre Research/Recherches Théâtrales, Players Magazine, The Independent Shavian,* and *Dramatics.* He also wrote the section "The University Begins to Come of Age: 1925–1969" in *The American Theatre: A Sum of Its Parts* (1971).

In addition, Mr. Butler has written educational materials, including *A Production Manual* (1950), used in the Experimental Theatre Class, USC, and *A Bibliography for Theatre History* (1962), used in USC theatre history classes, and numerous filmstrips, including *Electra* (1955); *Roman Circuses, Amphitheatres, and Naumachiae* (1959); *English Playhouses* (1963); *Italian Renaissance Theatres* (1964); *History of the Physical Theatre* (1965); and *The American Theatre to 1850* (1965), all distributed by Comma. He is also author and photographer of five filmstrips on the ancient Greek and Roman theatre (Comma, 1957).

Awards. In 1972, Mr. Butler was named an Outstanding Educator of America, and he received the American Oil Company's Award of Excellence for his work in the performing arts at the college and university level. He received the ATA Award of Merit in 1973.

Recreation. Book collecting, swimming.

BYRAM, JOHN. Press representative, drama editor, producer. b. Nov. 4, 1901, Indianapolis, Ind., to John and Bertha (Campbell) Byram. Grad. Shortridge H.S., Indianapolis, 1919; attended Butler Univ., 1919–20; Indiana Univ., 1922. Married Apr. 30, 1932, to Marian Miller, press representative. Member of The Players. Address: 482 Second Ave., South, P.O. Box 65, Naples, FL 33940, tel. (813) MI 2-4210.

Pre-Theatre. Newspaper reporter for the Indianapolis *Star* (1921).

Theatre. Mr. Byram was a press representative for the Keith Vaudeville circuit in New York (1922–23); the New York Hippodrome (1923–26); assistant drama editor (1926) and drama editor of the NY *Times* (1926–33); play editor of Paramount Pictures, handling the company's interests in the theatre in N.Y.C. and Europe (1933–53); and script editor of ABC (1953–54).

He was associated with Courtney Burr in his theatrical productions (1951–56); and with Mr. Burr and Elliot Nugent, produced *The Wayward Saint* (Cort, N.Y.C. Feb. 17, 1955).

Recreation. Reading, walking on the beach, and travel.

BYRAM, MARIAN. Press representative. b. Marian Miller, Feb. 22, 1904, Columbus, Ohio, to Ad F. and Irene (Bliss) Miller. Father, co-owner of Valentine Co. and manager of English Opera House, Indianapolis, Ind.; mother, press representative. Grad. Shortridge H.S., Indianapolis, 1920; attended Butler Coll., 1920–22; grad. Lasell Seminary, Auburndale, Mass., 1923; attended Ohio State Univ., 1923; grad. Butler Univ., B.A. 1924; John Heron Art Inst., Indianapolis, 1925; Ethel Traphagen Sch. of Fashion, N.Y.C., 1928. Married Apr. 30, 1932, to John Byram, drama editor, NY *Times* (1926–33). Relative in theatre: brother, Addison B. Miller, theatre manager. Member of ATPAM. Address: 482 Second Ave., S., Naples, FL 33940, tel. (813) MI 2-4210.

Pre-Theatre. Reporter on the Miami *Herald.* .

Theatre. Mrs. Byram's first assignment was as press representative for the Shuberts, working on productions that included *The Street Singer, Young Sinners,* and *Death Takes a Holiday* (1928–30); subsequently, she handled publicity for the Playwrights' Co., the Th. Guild, Jed Harris, Sam Harris, Eddie Dowling and George Abbott; entered into partnership with Phyllis Perlman, handling publicity for such productions as *An Inspector Calls, The Hallams, Season in the Sun, The Seven Year Itch, Wonderful Town, By the Beautiful Sea, The Desperate Hours, The Wayward Saint, The Happiest Millionaire,* and *Hotel Paradiso* (1946–57).

Recreation. Riding, swimming, shelling, travel, "extreme interest and curiosity in people," photography, dogs.

C

CACOYANNIS, MICHAEL. Director, actor, producer, writer. b. Limassol, Cyprus, to Sir Panayotis and Angeliki Cacoyannis. Father, lawyer. Educ. Greek gymnasium: Gray's Inn, London (barrister at law). Professional training Central School of Dramatic Art, London (acting); Old Vic School, London (directing); Henryka Suffrian, acting coach. Member of SSD&C; Dramatists Guild. Address: 96 Blvd. Montparnasse, Paris 14$_e$, rance.

Theatre. Mr.Cacoyannis made his debut in the theatre as an actor, playing Herod in a London production of *Salome* (1945), and his first theatre work in Athens was as director of *A Woman of No Importance* (1954). He made his US debut as director of *The Trojan Women* (Circle in the Square, N.Y.C., Dec. 23, 1963), a play he also directed in Paris (Théâtre Nationale Populaire, 1965). His first directing on Bway was *And Things That Go Bump in the Night* (Royale, Apr. 26, 1965), followed by *The Devils* (Broadway Th., Nov. 16, 1965); the opera *Mourning Becomes Electra* (world premiere, Metropolitan Opera House, Mar. 17, 1967); *Iphigenia in Aulis* (Circle in the Square, Nov. 21, 1967); a Paris production of *Romeo and Juliet* (Théâtre Nationale Populaire, 1968); the *Beckett—Billetdoux Evening* (Spoleto, Italy, 1968); the opera *La Bohem* (Juilliard American Opera Center, N.Y.C., Feb. 11, 1972); *Lysistrata,* also adapter (Brooks Atkinson Th., N.Y.C., Nov. 13, 1972); and *King Oedipus* (Abbey Th., Dublin, Ireland, 1973).

Films. Mr. Cacoyannis began writing and directing films in Greece in 1954 with *Windfall in Athens,* which was followed by *Stella* (1955); *A Girl in Black* (1956); *A Matter of Dignity* (1957); and *Our Last Spring* (1959), which he also produced. He wrote and directed *The Wastrel* (1960) in Italy and returned to Greece, where he wrote, produced, and directed *Electra* (1962); *Zorba the Greek* (20th-Fox, 1964); and *The Day the Fish Came Out* (International Classica, 1969). In Spain he wrote, produced, and directed *The Trojan Women* (Cinerama, 1971).

Television and Radio. Mr. Cacoyannis was a BBC producer in London from 1940 to 1950. He directed for television *The Story of Jacob and Joseph* (ABC, 1974).

Awards. Mr. Cacoyannis has received the Order of the Phoenix and received awards for many of his films: diploma of merit, Edinburgh Festival, for *Windfall in Athens;* Golden Globe for *Stella* and for *A Girl in Black;* Moscow Gold Medal for *A Girl in Black;* and the English Critics' Award for *A Matter of Dignity. Our Last Spring* was named best film and he best director at the Salonica Festival; *Electra* won the Cannes Grand Jury Prize and twenty-seven other international awards; and *Zorba the Greek* received seven nominations and three Academy (Oscar) awards. In the theatre, *The Trojan Women* received a special citation from the NY Drama Critics' Circle.

Recreation. Painting, composing lyrics.

CAESAR, IRVING. Lyricist, composer, publisher. b. Isaac Caesar, July 4, 1895, New York City, to Morris and Sifia (Selinger) Caesar. Father, teacher, book dealer. Attended Chappaqua (N.Y.) Mountain Inst., 1908–9; grad. Townsend Harris Hall H.S., N.Y.C., 1914; attended Coll. of the City of New York, 1915. Member of ASCAP (board of dir., 1930–46; 1949–to date); AFTRA; Dramatists Guild; The Friars (bd. of gov.); AGVA: AGAC (formerly Songwriters Protective Assn., pres.); Grand St. Boys; P.S. 20 Alumni (bd. mbr.). Address: 1619 Broadway, New York, NY 10019, tel. (212) CO5-7868.

Pre-Theatre. Stenographer with the Ford Peace Expedition (1915), press correspondent.

Theatre. Mr. Caesar wrote first, with George Gershwin, the song, "Swanee," which was sung by Al Jolson in *Sinbad* (Winter Garden Th., N.Y.C., Feb. 14, 1918); subsequently wrote the lyrics, with John Murray Anderson, for *The Greenwich Village Follies* (Shubert, Sept. 12, 1922); was lyricist for Here's Howe (Broadhurst, May 1, 1923); with Mr. Anderson, wrote lyrics for *The Greenwich Village Follies* (Winter Garden, Sept. 20, 1923); with Cole Porter and Mr. Anderson, lyrics for *The Greenwich Village Follies* (Winter Garden, Nov. 24, 1924); with Otto Harbach, lyrics for *Betty Lee* (44th St. Th., Dec. 25, 1924); with Mr. Harbach, lyrics for *No, No, Nanette* (Globe, Sept. 16, 1925); with Ballard Macdonald and Harry B. Smith, lyrics for *Sweetheart Time* (Imperial, Jan. 19, 1926); with David Freedman, dialogue for *Betsy* (New Amsterdam, Dec. 28, 1926); contributed lyrics to *Hit the Deck* (Belasco, Apr. 25, 1927); wrote lyrics for *Talk About Girls* (Waldorf, June 14, 1927); *Yes, Yes, Yvette* (Sam H. Harris Th., Oct. 3, 1927); with J. P. McEvoy, lyrics for *Americana* (Mansfield, Oct. 30, 1928); was lyricist for *New Americana* (Liberty, Nov. 29, 1928); *Polly* (Lyric, Jan. 8, 1929); *Nice to See You;* the London production of *The Bamboula* (Royale, June 26, 1929); contributed sketches and lyrics for the 10th edition of *George White's Scandals* (Apollo Th., N.Y.C., Sept. 23, 1929); with Graham John, lyrics for *Ripples* (New Amsterdam, Feb. 11, 1930); contributed lyrics to Ruth Selwyn's *9:15 Revue* (George M. Cohan Th., Feb. 11, 1930); wrote lyrics for *Nina Rosa* (Majestic, Sept. 20, 1930); adapted, with Aben Kandel, and wrote lyrics for *The Wonder Bar* (Bayes, Mar. 17, 1931); contributed songs to *George White's Music Hall Varieties* (Casino, Nov. 22, 1932); contributed lyrics for *Thumbs Up* (St. James, Dec. 27, 1934); wrote lyrics for *White Horse Inn* (Center, Oct. 1, 1936); produced a revue, written with Chuno Gottefeld, and with songs by Sam Lerner, Gerald Marks, and Mr. Caesar, *My Dear Public* (46th St. Th., Sept. 9, 1943). He has also appeared in vaudeville.

Later presentations of Mr. Caesar's work were in *One-Man Show* (Palm Beach Spa Playhouse, Fla., Feb. 16, 1970); a revival of *No, No, Nanette* (46 St. Th., N.Y.C., Dec. 19, 1970); and *A Bio in Song* (Th. de Lys, Dec. 6, 1971).

Published Works. Mr. Caesar's songs include "Tea for Two" (with Vincent Youmans); "I Want to be Happy" (with Mr. Youmans, 1924); "Sometimes I'm Happy" (with Mr. Youmans); "Crazy Rhythm" (with Joseph Meyer & Roger Kahn, 1928); "Lady Play Your Mandolin" (with Oscar Levant); "And Still I Love You" (with Rudolph Friml); "Yankee Doodle Blues" (with George Gershwin); "Just a Gigolo" (with Lionello Casucci); "Is It True What They Say About Dixie?" (Sammy Lerner-Gerald Marks, 1936); "Umbriago" (with Jimmy Durante); "Oh Donna Clara" (with Mr. Petersburski); "Oh Suzanna, Dust Off that Old Pianna," "If I Forget You," "Frosty Mornin'," and "Saskatchewan" (with Messrs. Lerner and Marks); and "That's What I Want for Christmas" (with Mr. Marks); and wrote the children's songs, Sing a Song of Safety (1938), Sing a Song of Friendship, and Songs of Health, which have been sung in classrooms throughout the country; and a Suite for Piano, Orchestra and Chorus, *Pilgrim of 1940.* .

Awards. Mr. Caesar wrote music for the Pledge of Allegiance which was accepted by the US Govt. and made an official document by Congressional resolution.

CAGE, RUTH. Press representative. b. Ruth Sylvia Cage, Sept. 25, 1923, Portland, Ore., to Harry and Hazel Cage. Father, businessman. Grad. Thomas Jefferson H.S., Los Angeles, Calif., 1941; Univ. of California at Los Angeles, B.A. 1946. Member of ATPAM.

In 1956, Miss Cage was assistant press representative for *Middle of the Night;* in 1957, for *Measure for Measure* and *The Taming of the Shrew;* in 1958, for *The World of Suzie Wong* and *La plume de ma tante;* in 1959, for *The Miracle Worker, U.S.A., Saratoga,* and was associate press representative for the Oakdale Musical Th. (Wallingford, Conn., Summer).

She was associate press representative in 1960 for *Roman Candle, Caligula, Come Share My House, Oh, Kay!, Rosemary and the Alligators, Farewell, Farewell Eugene,* and that summer for the Oakdale Music Th. In 1961, she publicized *Ballet Ballads, The American* Dream, Double Entry, Gallows Humor, Happy as *Larry,* a double-bill of *Philoktetes* and *The Women at the Tomb, Sharon's Grave,* and with Samuel J. Friedman was press representative for the Canadian tour of *The Threepenny Opera.*

In 1962, she was press representative for *A Pair of Pairs, If Five Years Pass,* and the Oakdale Music Th. (Summer); in 1963, for *Andorra, The Laundry, Strange Interlude, The Purple Canary, Bicycle Ride to Nevada, The Private Ear and The Public Eye,* and *A Rainy Day in Newark.*

In 1964, Miss Cage publicized *The Chinese Prime Minister, Dark Corners, Mr. Grossman,* and The New Dramatists Committee; in 1965, *Drat! The Cat;* in 1966, *The Lion in Winter, Hooray! It's a Glorious Day. . .and all that,* and *Under the Weather;* in 1967, *Halfway Up the Tree;* in 1968, *How To Be a Jewish Mother,* and *The Prime of Miss Jean Brodie;* in 1969, *Cop-Out, Hamlet, In the Bar of a Tokyo Hotel, Oklahoma!,* and *The Mundy Scheme;* in 1970, *Unfair to Goliath, Nobody Hears a Broken Drum, The Moths,* and *Candaules, Commissioner;* in 1972, *We Bombed in New Haven,* and *Halloween;* and, in 1973, *Irene* and *Veronica's Room.*

Pre-Theatre. Social work.

Films. She was press representative for The Dynamic Films, Theatre Vision (Rochester, N.Y., 1962).

Night Clubs. She was press representative for the Harry Belafonte Show (Donnelly Aud., Boston, Mass., 1962); The Establishment (Strollers Th. Club, N.Y.C., (1963); and the Miss Connecticut Pageant (1963).

Other Activities. She was public relations consultant for product Services Advertising Co. (N.Y.C., 1962).

CAGNEY, JEANNE. Actress. b. Jeanne Carolyn Cagney, Mar. 25, New York City, to James and Carolyn (Nelson) Cagney. Father, insurance. Grad. Hunter College H.S., N.Y.C., 1934; Hunter College, B.A. (cum laude) 1938; attended Univ. of California at Los Angeles, 1949–50, 1951–52. Married June 6, 1953, to Jack Morrison, educator (marr. dis. 1973); two daughters. Relatives in theatre: brother, James Cagney, actor; brother, William Cagney, motion picture producer. Member of AEA;

SAG; AFTRA; Phi Beta Kappa; German Honor Fraternity; Radio and TV Women of Southern Calif.; AETA; Rancho San Antonio Guild; UCLA Women's Club.

Theatre. Miss Cagney made her stage debut as Kate in *Brother Rat* (Pasadena Playhouse, Calif., 1939); subsequently played Harriet Winter in *Family Album,* one of the one-act plays in *Tonight at 8:30* (Curran, San Francisco, Calif., Feb. 26, 1940); and Alice in *Meet the Wife* (Mar. 27, 1941) with which she later toured; appeared in the title role of *Claudia* (Temple of Music and Arts, Tucson, Ariz., Nov. 1942); and at the Cambridge (Mass.) Summer Th. (July–Aug., 1943) played Isabelle Parry in *Strictly Dishonorable,* Cynthia Brown in *Little Darling,* and played in *Personal Appearance, Front Page, Ladies in Retirement,* and *Biography.*

She made her Bway debut as Judy Budd in *I'll Take the High Road* (Ritz, Nov. 9, 1943); in stock, appeared as Lottie Disenhower in *Marriage Is for Single People* (Cambridge Summer Th., Mass., Aug. 25, 1944); played Angelika in *The Streets Are Guarded* (Henry Miller's Th., N.Y.C., Nov. 20, 1944); Nancy Monroe in *A Place of Our Own* (Royale, Apr. 2, 1945); and Margie in *The Iceman Cometh* (Martin Beck Th., Oct. 9, 1946).

Miss Cagney appeared as Miss Darling in *Accent on Youth* (El Patio, Hollywood, Calif., 1949); Addie in *Happy Birthday* (Albuquerque Little Th., N.M., 1950); Sally Middleton in *The Voice of the Turtle* (Winter Park, Fla., 1952); at the La Jolla (Calif.) Playhouse, appeared as Content Lowell in *The Marriage-Go-Round* (July 1961), and in *The World of Carl Sandburg* (July 1962).

Films. Miss Cagney made her debut in *All Women Have Secrets* (Par., 1939); subsequently appeared as *Queen of the Mob* (Par., 1940); *Golden Gloves* (Par., 1940); *Rhythm on the River* (Par., 1940); *Yankee Doodle Dandy* (WB, 1942); *The Time of Your Life* (UA, 1948); *Quicksand* (UA, 1950); *A Lion Is in the Streets* (WB, 1953); *Kentucky Rifle* (UA, 1954); *Man of a Thousand Faces* (U, 1957); and *Town Tamer* (Par., 1965).

Television and Radio. Miss Cagney performed on radio as Lou on *Ceiling Zero* (1939); Kraft Music Hall (1939); Silver Th.; and on various daytime serials (NBC, CBS, ABC, 1942–47).

On television she appeared in *A Capture* (1949); *The Big Hello* (1951); Wild Bill Hickock (1951); *Legal Tender;* Mr. and Mrs. North; *Story of St. Patrick* (1952); as Mary Magdalen in *Hill No. 1* (Feb. 1953); in a burlesque of Dr. Jekyll and Mr. Hyde on The Jack Benny Show (CBS, 1953); Red Skelton Show (CBS, 1955); Mr. and Mrs. North (1956); was the interviewer for the opening of the Ice Follies (1960–63); and she was fashion commentator on Queen for a Day (ABC, 1953).

Recreation. Swimming, horseback riding, sculpture.

CAHLMAN, ROBERT.

Director, producer, lecturer. b. Bernard Kalman, Jan. 23, Chicago, Ill., to Abraham H. and Mabelle (Cahlman) Kalman. Father, dentist; mother, interior designer. Grad. Nicholas Senn H.S., Chicago, 1942. Married June 1947 to Margaret Furman (marr. dis. July 1948). Member of ANTA (dir. of membership, 1958–64); USITT (founding bd. mem.; bd. of dir., 1960–64); SSD&C (founding mem.); ACTA (bd. of dir., 1961–62); ATA; CTC; SWTC; SSTC; Publicity Club of N.Y.; New Orleans Music and Drama Foundation (bd. of dir.); Louisiana Council, Music and Performing Arts; NTC (hon.). Address: (home) 1 W. 67th St., New York, NY 10023, tel. (212) EN 2-6700; 1433 Melpomene, New Orleans, LA 70130, tel. (504) 525-1728; (bus.) MGM Costume Rental Co., 1726 St. Charles Ave., New Orleans, LA 70130, tel. (504) 581-3999.

Theatre. From 1939 to 1947, Mr. Cahlman was an actor and technician with Margo Jones, Paul Stephanson, Nina Vance and Ralph Mead; was a director at the Players Guild (Houston, Tex., 1941–45), and one of the founders when it was renamed the Alley Th. In 1947, he organized the Gallery Circle Th., New Orleans, La., of which he was executive director until 1955 and again in 1965–66 and where he produced and directed fifty-three plays, including *Personal Appearance* (1947); *Spring Again, The Silver Cord, Hay Fever* and *Rope* (1948); the original *Monkey on My Back, Foolish Notion, Pygmalion, The Hasty Heart* and *The Importance of Being Earnest* (1949); *The Children's Hour, The Enchanted Cottage, Kind Lady, Suspect, Out of the Frying Pan, Mr. Barry's Etchings, The Heiress* and *Seventh Heaven* (1950); *The Curious Savage, Gayden, Billy Budd, Dark of the Moon, Black Chiffon, See How They Run* and *Gramercy Ghost* (1951); *Home of the Brave, Ladies in Retirement,* produced *Clutterbuck, Joan of Lorraine,* directed and produced *Bell, Book and Candle* and *Room Service* (1952); *Voice of the Turtle,* the original *Strange Duel, Amphitryon 38, The Young and Fair,* produced *Dark Victory,* directed and produced *I Am a Camera, The Moon Is Blue, Bernadine,* an original musical revue *Summertime* (1953); *The Innocents,* produced *He Ran All the Way* (1954); produced and directed *Picnic, Time Out for Ginger, Light Up the Sky, Arsenic and Old Lace, End as a Man,* and *The Man Who Came to Dinner* (1955); and, in 1965–66, *A Funny Thing Happened on the Way to the Forum, Two for the Seesaw, How To Succeed in Business without Really Trying,* and *A Streetcar Named Desire.* For the Royal Comedy Co., New Orleans, he produced and directed *A Funny Thing Happened on the Way to the Forum* (1973).

He directed the opera, *Amelia Goes to the Ball* (Experimental Opera Th. of America, New Orleans, Nov. 1955; repeat 1966); for the Joe Jefferson Players (Mobile, Ala.) was producer and director of *Rope, The Women* (1955); *The Moon Is Blue, The Country Girl, The Solid Gold Cadillac, A Roomful of Roses, The Tender Trap* and *The Bad Seed* (1956); *The Rainmaker* and *The Seven Year Itch* (1957); and for the Edison Electric Institute produced and directed *An Evening with Al Hirt, Pete Fountain, and the Dukes of Dixieland* (1967).

Television and Radio. Mr. Cahlman developed Theatre 6, a weekly dramatic series (WDSU-TV, New Orleans, La.) in which he directed dramatic and musical productions (1949–54). He was an account and production executive for commercials and trailers with Motion Picture Advertising (MPA) Co., Inc., New Orleans (1953–55, 1957), for which he produced Television Court, a series of half-hour musical comedies; he produced for ANTA *Wide Wide World* and *The American Theatre* (NBC, 1958); and he was host and producer of Theatre Dialog (1963–64), a taped radio series of theatre conversations from Sardi's, N.Y.C. He was also executive producer, cultural affairs, WYES-TV, New Orleans (1965–73), where he produced and directed Speakeasy, Places Please, City in Crisis, Pieces of Eight, Garden Show, and other regular local programs and specials, and he also appeared on the Tonight Show, To Tell the Truth, and Who Do You Trust?.

Other Activities. From 1958 to 1964, Mr. Cahlman was director, special projects, American National Theatre and Academy (ANTA), N.Y.C.; he conceived and directed the ANTA Assembly and organized a department to increase national services and development, including membership. Since 1961, he has been producer and narrator of *Exits and Entrances,* a pageant featuring the original costumes worn by stage and screen stars. The costume collection was exhibited at the Metropolitan Museum of Art, N.Y.C. (1974–75) and at Lincoln Center, N.Y.C. Mr. Cahlman has also been president since 1971 of Mardi Gras Masquerade Co., Inc. (MGM Costume Rental Co.), New Orleans, which handles productions for conventions, and he was director of regional services for Brooks Costume Co., N.Y.C. (1959–61) and handled theatre public relations for Capezio, Inc., N.Y.C. (1962–63). He served as supervisor of Project Genesis, New Orleans Board of Education, a program in the arts in association with the US Dept. of Health, Education and Welfare (Summer 1966).

Awards. He received a Certificate of Merit from New Orleans, La. (1950); the Blue Book Award, New Orleans (1953); the Medal of Paris (1950); and was made an Honorary Colonel of the Governor's Staff, Louisiana (1950).

Recreation. Photography, reading.

CAHN, SAMMY.

Lyricist, performer. b. Samuel Cohen June 18, 1913, New York City, to Edmund Joseph and Myrtle Ellen (Perdue) Cohen. Educ. N.Y.C. public schools. Married Sept. 5, 1945, to Gloria Delson (marr. dis. May 1964); one son, one daughter; Aug. 2, 1970, to Tita Basile (Curtis). Member of ASCAP. Address: Edward Traubner & Co., 1901 Ave. of the Stars, Los Angeles, CA 90067.

A violinist since boyhood, Mr. Cahn later organized a band with Saul Chaplin, the first musician with whom he collaborated when he began writing lyrics for popular songs in 1933.

Theatre. Mr. Cahn's first work for the Bway stage was lyrics for the musical *High Button Shoes* (Century, N.Y.C., Oct. 9, 1947); followed by *Skyscraper* (Lunt-Fontanne Th., Nov. 13, 1965); *Walking Happy* (Lunt-Fontanne, Nov. 26, 1966); *Look to the Lilies* (Lunt-Fontanne Th., Mar. 29, 1970); and *Words and Music* (John Golden Th., Apr. 16, 1974), for which he was also host, narrator, and performer.

Films. Among the many films for which Mr. Cahn wrote song lyrics are *Anchors Aweigh* (MGM, 1945); *Romance on the High Seas* (WB, 1948); *Three Sailors and a Girl* (WB, 1953), which he also produced; *Three Coins in the Fountain* (20th-Fox, 1954); *The Joker Is Wild* (Par., 1957); *Say One for Me* (20th-Fox, 1959); *The Road to Hong Kong* (Par., 1962); *Robin and the Seven Hoods* (WB, 1964); *The Second Best Secret Agent in the Whole Wide World* (Embassy, 1965); and *Thoroughly Modern Millie* (U, 1967). Mr. Cahn also wrote the screenplay for *Rookies on Parade* (Republic) and wrote the story on which the screenplay for *Two Tickets to Broadway* (RKO, 1951) was based.

Television. In collaboration with James Van Heusen, Mr. Cahn wrote songs for a musical version of *Our Town* (NBC Producers' Showcase, Sept. 18, 1955); *High Button Shoes,* on which he had collaborated with Jule Styne, was adapted for television (Garry Moore Show, CBS, Nov. 2, 1966); and with Mr. Van Heusen he wrote songs for *Jack and the Beanstalk* (NBC, Feb. 26, 1967). Mr. Cahn appeared on Musical Theatre (CBS, 1964–65); the Hy Gardner Show (Ind., 1964–65); House Party (CBS, 1964–65); on the Today Show (NBC, 1965–66; 1966–67).

Other Activities. Mr. Cahn has been a consultant for Brut Productions.

Published Works. Mr. Cahn wrote both words and music for his first published song, "Shake Your Head from Side to Side" (1933), and for "Bei Mir Bist Du Schoen" (1933) he wrote English words to a Yiddish song. Among nearly 80 other songs that he wrote are, in collaboration with the composer Saul Chaplin, "Rhythm Is Our Business" (1935), "Shoeshine Boy" (1936), and "Please Be Kind" (1938); with Paul Weston and Alex Stordahl, "I Should Care" (1944) and "Day by Day" (1945); with Jule Styne, "I've Heard That Song Before" (1942), "I'll Walk Alone" (1944), "It's Been a Long, Long Time" (1945), "Five Minutes More" (1946), "It's Magic" (1948), "The Christmas Waltz" (1954), and "Three Coins in the Fountain" (1954); and, with James Van Heusen, on such songs as "The Tender Trap" (1955), "All the Way" (1957), "High Hopes" (1959), "Pocket Full of Miracles" (1959), "Walking Happy" (1962), "Call Me Irresponsible" (1962), and "Thoroughly Modern Millie" (1967). Many of Mr. Cahn's songs were introduced and recorded by Frank Sinatra. Mr. Cahn also wrote his autobiography, *I Should Care* (1975).

Awards. "Love and Marriage," one of the songs that Mr. Cahn wrote for the televising of *Our Town* received NATAS (Emmy) and Christopher awards; "Three Coins in the Fountain," "All the Way," "High Hopes," and "Call Me Irresponsible" received AMPAS (Oscar) awards as best songs of their years, and "My Kind of Town" and "Where Love Has Gone," both with lyrics by Mr. Cahn, received Oscar nominations in 1964. In April 1968,

Mr. Cahn was given the Henry Street Settlement's Man of the Year Award.

CAIN, JAMES M. Novelist, playwright. b. James Mallahan Cain, July 1, 1892, to Mr. and Mrs. James William Cain. Father, college president and businessman. Grad. Washington Coll., A.B. 1910, A.M. 1917. Married Sept. 19, 1947, to Florence Macbeth, opera singer. Served USAEF in France, 1918–19; editor-in-chief of division newspaper, *The Lorraine Cross*, 1919. Member of Dramatists Guild.

Theatre. Mr. Cain wrote the play, based upon his novel, *The Postman Always Rings Twice*, produced on Bway (Plymouth Th., Feb. 25, 1936).

Other Activities. Mr. Cain was a professor of journalism at St. John's Coll., Annapolis, Md. (1923–24). He was also a reported for *The Baltimore American* (1917–18) and the *Baltimore Sun* (1918–23), an editorial writer for the New York World (1924–31) and sub-editor for *The New Yorker* Magazine (1931).

Published Works. He is the author of *Our Government* (1930); *The Postman Always Rings Twice* (1934); *Double Indemnity* (1936); *Serenade* (1937); *Two Can Sing* (1938); *The Embezzler* (1940); *Mildred Pierce* (1941); *Love's Lovely Counterfeit* (1942); *Three of a Kind* (1943); *Past All Dishonor* (1946); *The Butterfly* (1947); *The Moth* (1948); *Galatea* (1953); *Mignon* (1962); *The Magician's Wife* (1965); and *Rainbow's End* (1975).

Awards. He received the Public Service Award, Univ. of Maryland (1963).

CALDERON, IAN. Lighting designer, producer, educator, production supervisor, theatre consultant. b. Ian Rodney Calderon, July 20, 1948, to Samuel and Marion (Barocas) Calderon. Father, artist-designer and jewelry manufacturer; mother, teacher's aide. Educ. N.Y.C. public schools. Grad. Hunter Coll., B.A. 1970; Yale School of Drama, M.F.A. 1973. Professional training with Max Perlman, (stage design), Donald Oenslager, and Ming Cho Lee. Member of Local 829, United Scenic Artists; IES; ITT; ATA; Soc. of British Theatre Designers, London. Address: Ian Calderon Associates, Inc., 125 E. 71st St., New York, NY 10021, tel. (212) 988-7040.

Theatre. Mr. Calderon made his debut as a lighting designer with a high school production of *The Father of the Bride* (Oswald Aud., Brooklyn, N.Y., May 1964), and this was followed by lighting design for two plays at Brooklyn Community Th.: *Bells Are Ringing* (Dec. 10, 1965) and *Milk and Honey* (Apr. 12, 1966). He did his first professional work for La Mama ETC (N.Y.C.), designing lighting for *The Missing Scorpion* (June 16, 1967), *The Sunday Agreement* (Oct. 21, 1967), *Fergusson* (Nov. 18, 1967), and *The Moondreamers* (Dec. 4, 1967). He was lighting designer for *A Christmas Carol* (Beacon Th., N.Y.C., Dec. 4, 1968; Dec. 12, 1969); was lighting technician for the NY Shakespeare Festival's *Black Electra* (Mobile Th. tour, 1969); was lighting designer for *Ballet Brave* (ANTA Th., Apr. 7, 1970); and for the tour of *Street Theatre* (Mobile Unit, May 10, 1970).

Mr. Calderon was also lighting designer for *Rosmersholm* (Yale Experimental Th., New Haven, Conn., Nov. 21, 1970); *Subject to Fits* (Public, N.Y.C., Feb. 14, 1971); *Life Is a Dream* (Yale Repertory Th., New Haven, Conn., Feb. 28, 1971); *The Life and Times of J. Walter Smintheus* (Public, N.Y.C., Mar. 16, 1971); *Jazznite* (Public, Mar. 21, 1971); *Sticks and Bones* (Public, Nov. 7, 1971; moved to Golden Th., Mar. 1, 1972); *That Championship Season* (Public, Mar. 21, 1972; moved to Booth Th., Sept. 14, 1972); *Slaughterhouse Play* (Public, Mar. 18, 1972); *The Corner* (Public, June 20, 1972); *Andrew* (Public, June 21, 1972); *His First Step* (Public, June 22, 1972); *The Cherry Orchard* (Public, Jan. 11, 1973); and *The Siamese Connections* (Public, Jan. 25, 1973).

He was also lighting designer for *More Than You Deserve* (Public, Apr. 21, 1973) and *I Love Thee Freely* (Astor Place Th., Sept. 17, 1973); for a touring production of *That Championship Season* (Royal Alexandra Th., Toronto, Ontario, Canada, Sept. 21, 1973); Shubert Th., Los Angeles, Calif., Oct. 1, 1973); for *The Foursome* (Astor Place Th., N.Y.C., Nov. 17, 1973); *Troilus and Cressida* (Newhouse Th., Dec. 7, 1973); *The Dance of Death* (Vivian Beaumont Th., Apr. 4, 1974); and for the English production of *That Championship Season* (Garrick Th., London, Apr. 11, 1974). He designed lighting for *Jacques Brel Is Alive and Well and Living in Paris* (Astor Place Th., N.Y.C., May 17, 1974); *Waiting for Godot* (St. Clements Ch., Sept. 10, 1974); *The Last Days of British Honduras* (Public, Nov. 5, 1974); *How To Get Rid of It* (Astor Place Th., Nov. 17, 1974); *Fishing* (Public, Feb. 12, 1975); and *The Dubliners* (Roundabout Th., Feb. 25, 1975).

Mr. Calderon became associate producer, Roundhouse Co. (Mar. 1975) and production supervisor, Roundabout Th. Co. (Oct. 1975) and Shirtsleeves Th. Co. (Dec. 1975). Additional productions for which he was lighting designer include *The Lieutenant* (Lyceum, Mar. 9, 1975); *What Every Woman Knows* (Roundabout Th., Mar. 28, 1975); *Summer and Smoke* (Roundabout Th., Sept. 14, 1975); *Awake and Sing* (Hartford Stage Co., Hartford, Conn., Sept. 20, 1975); *Trelawney of the Wells* (Vivian Beaumont Th., Oct. 21, 1975); *Corfax* (La Mama ETC, Nov. 18, 1975); *Clarence* (Roundabout Th., Nov. 28, 1975); and *Old Times* (Center Stage Co., Baltimore, Md., Mar. 23, 1976).

Concerts. Mr. Calderon was lighting designer for a Janis Joplin concert (Hunter Coll., Oct. 1967); Duke Ellington concert (Woolsey Hall Th., New Haven, Conn., Oct. 6, 1972); Odetta concert (Woolsey Hall Th., Oct. 7, 1972); Dizzy Gillespie jazz concert (Woolsey Hall Th., Oct. 8, 1972); Marian Williams concert (Woolsey Hall Th., Oct. 9, 1972); and Dick Shawn concert (Carnegie Hall, N.Y.C., Dec. 28, 1975).

Other Activities. Ian Calderon Associates, Inc., architectural lighting and theatrical consultants, began business June 20, 1973. Mr. Calderon was also lighting system consultant for Ellen Stewart's Second Ave. Th., Cafe La Mama (June 1967) and Lafayette H.S., Brooklyn, N.Y. (June 1970). He was also a consultant on stage and lighting facilities for Hunter Coll. Playhouse (Sept. 1973); Queens Playhouse in the Park, N.Y.C. (June 1974); Little Th., Hunter Coll., (Sept. 1974); Roundhouse Co., Queens, N.Y. (June 1975); Bicentennial Committee, Cultural Affairs Office of New York (July 1975); and Roundabout Th. Co. (Aug. 1975).

Awards. Mr. Calderon was nominated for Antoinette Perry (Tony) awards for best lighting design for *That Championship Season* (1973) and *Trelawney of the Wells* (1976).

Recreation. Travel, flying, auto racing, photography, collecting rare books, horseback riding, and "being a good uncle.".

CALDWELL, ZOE. Actress. b. Zoe Ada Caldwell, Sept. 14, 1933, Hawthorn, Australia, to A. E. and Zoe Caldwell. Father, plumber; mother, singer and dancer. Educ. Methodist Ladies' Coll., Melbourne, Australia. Married May 9, 1968, to Robert Whitehead, producer; two sons. Address: c/o Robert Whitehead Productions, 1564 Bway, New York, NY 10036.

Pre-Theatre. Perfume salesgirl; pickle bottler.

Theatre. Miss Caldwell appeared on stage, dancing and singing, when three years old and began professional acting at nine in Melbourne, Australia. In 1953, with the Union Repertory Co., Melbourne, she was in several Shakespeare plays and played the lead in *Major Barbara*. As a member of the Elizabethan Theatre Trust, which she joined in 1954, she played various roles, including Bubba in *The Summer of the Seventeenth Doll* and Ophelia in *Hamlet*.

She first performed with the Royal Shakespeare Co., Stratford-upon-Avon, England, in walk-on roles in *Twelfth Night* (Apr. 22, 1958) and *Hamlet* (June 3, 1958), then appeared as the daughter of Antiochus in *Pericles* (July 8, 1958); Margaret in *Much Ado About Nothing* (Aug. 1958); Bianca in *Othello* (Apr. 7, 1959); Cordelia in *King Lear* (Apr. 1959); Helena in *All's Well That Ends Well* (Apr. 21, 1959); and on tour with the company (1959) in the USSR she played in *Hamlet, Twelfth Night*, and *Romeo and Juliet*.

Miss Caldwell made her London stage debut at the Royal Court Th. as the Whore in *Cob and Leach*, part of the bill *Trials by Logue* (Nov. 1960), following this with performances at the same theatre as Ismene in *Antigone* (Nov. 1960); Isabella in *The Changeling* (Feb. 21, 1961); and Jacqueline in *Jacques* (Mar. 22, 1961). Her first role at the Stratford (Ontario, Canada) Shakespeare Festival was that of Rosaline in *Love's Labour's Lost* (June 19, 1961), and she then played Sonja Downfahl in *The Canvas Barricade* (Aug. 1961). She was Pegeen Mike in *The Playboy of the Western World* (Manitoba Th. Ctr., Winnipeg, Canada, Summer 1961); played the title role in *Saint Joan* at the Adelaide (Australia) Festival of the Arts (Mar. 1962), in which she also toured; appeared in *The Ham Funeral* (Elizabethan Th. Trust, Sydney, Australia, July 1962); and played Nola Boyle in *The Season at Sarsaparilla* (Union Th. Rep. Co., Melbourne, Oct. 1962).

Joining Tyrone Guthrie's Minnesota Th. Co., Minneapolis, Minn., in 1963, she was Frosine in *The Miser* (May 8, 1963); Natalia in *The Three Sisters* (June 18, 1963); and The Woman in *Death of a Salesman* (July 16, 1963); and in Australia she repeated her performance as Saint Joan for the Adelaide Festival (Mar. 1964). She was Elizabeth von Ritter in *A Far Country* (Crest Th., Toronto, Ontario, 1964); played the title role in *Mother Courage* (Manitoba Th. Ctr., 1964); Countess Aurelia in *The Madwoman of Chaillot* (Goodman Memorial Th., Chicago, Ill., Oct. 23, 1964); and returned to the Minnesota Th. Co. to play Millamant in *The Way of the World* (May 11, 1965); Grusha Vashnadze in *The Caucasian Chalk Circle* (Aug. 3, 1965); and, again, Frosine in *The Miser* (Sept. 7, 1965).

Miss Caldwell first appeared on Bway as Sister Jean in *The Devils* (Broadway Th., Nov. 16, 1965), when she replaced Anne Bancroft on two occasions (Dec. 1965; Jan. 1966) in that role; this was followed by her performance as Polly in *The Gnadiges Fraulein* segment of *Slapstick Tragedy* (Longacre, Feb. 22, 1966). She was at the Shaw Festival, Niagara-on-the-Lake, Ontario, as Orinthia in *The Apple Cart* and Lena Szczepanowska in *Misalliance* (both Summer 1966) and at the Stratford (Ontario) Festival (Avon Th.) as Lady Ann in *Richard III* (June 12, 1967); Mrs. Page in *The Merry Wives of Windsor* (June 14, 1967); and Cleopatra in *Antony and Cleopatra* (July 31, 1967).

She played the title role in *The Prime of Miss Jean Brodie* (Helen Hayes Th., N.Y.C., Jan. 16, 1968); the title role in *Colette* (Ellen Stewart Th., May 6, 1970); was Lady Hamilton in *A Bequest to the Nation* (Haymarket Th., London, England, Sept. 30, 1970); was Eve in *The Creation of the World and Other Business* (Sam S. Shubert Th., N.Y.C., Nov. 30, 1972); played the female role in the two-character arrangement of sections dealing with love in the writings of William Shakespeare, *Love and Master Will* (Opera House, John F. Kennedy Ctr., Washington, D.C., Sept. 11, 1973); was Alice in *The Dance of Death* (Vivian Beaumont Th., Lincoln Ctr., N.Y.C., Apr. 4, 1974); and was Mary Tyrone in *Long Day's Journey Into Night* (Eisenhower Th., Kennedy Ctr., Washington, D.C., Dec. 17, 1975; Brooklyn Acad. of Music, N.Y.C., Jan. 27, 1976).

Television. Plays in which Miss Caldwell has appeared on television include *The Apple Cart, Macbeth*, and *The Lady's Not for Burning*.

Awards. Miss Caldwell won an Antoinette Perry (Tony) Award (1966) as best supporting actress for her performance in *Slapstick Tragedy* and was also named first in the *Variety* NY Drama Critics Poll for the same role; in 1968, she won a second Tony, as best actress, for her performance in *The Prime of Miss Jean Brodie* and was also named first in the *Variety* poll for that role. For her performance as Colette, she received the Drama Desk Award for most outstanding performance by an actress in 1970.

CALHOUN, ROBERT. Production and stage manager, production supervisor, director, producer. b. Robert Peter Calhoun, Nov. 24, 1930, New York City, to John Caldwell and Alice Grace (Van Pelt) Calhoun. Father, restaurateur. Grad. Cardinal Farley Military Acad., Rhinecliff, N.Y., 1948; Univ. of Maryland, B.A. 1957. Served USN, Medical Corps, 1951–55. Member of AEA; AFTRA; AGMA; Phi Delta Theta.

Theatre. Mr. Calhoun first was assistant stage manager for the National Phoenix Th. touring production of *Mary Stuart* (opened Sacramento H.S. Aud., Calif., Oct. 2, 1959; closed National, Washington, D.C., May 7, 1960); was stage manager for the national touring company of *Once Upon a Mattress* (opened Erlanger, Chicago, Ill., Sept. 1, 1960); and production stage manager of a second touring company of *Once Upon a Mattress* (opened Veterans Memorial Aud., Providence, R.I., Oct. 21, 1960).

He was production stage manager at the American Festival (Boston, Mass., for the opera, *Turn of the Screw* (July 1961) and f0r *Anatol* (Aug. 1961). He was technical director for the National Repertory Company's touring productions of *Mary Stuart* and *Elizabeth the Queen* (opened Acad. of Music, Northampton, Mass., Oct. 19, 1961); and stage manager for the Dallas (Tex.) Civic Opera season (State Fair Music Hall, Nov.–Dec. 1961).

Mr. Calhoun was stage manager for *New Faces of '62* (Alvin, N.Y.C., Feb. 1, 1962); *Turn of the Screw* (NY City Ctr., Mar. 25, 1962); Martyn Green's Gilbert and Sullivan productions at the Boston (Mass.) Arts Festival (June 1962); stage manager for the Dallas Civic Opera season (State Fair Music Hall, Oct.–Nov. 1962); and stage manager for Martyn Green's Gilbert and Sullivan touring productions (opened Forrest, Philadelphia, Pa., Apr. 1963).

He became associate producer and production supervisor for the National Repertory Th. touring productions of *The Seagull, The Crucible,* and *Ring 'Round the Moon* (opened Greensboro, N.C., Oct. 10, 1963); and for its N.Y.C. productions of *The Seagull* (Belasco, Apr. 5, 1964), and *The Crucible* (Belasco, Apr. 6, 1964).

From 1968 to 1970, Mr. Calhoun was at the New Th. for Now Workshop, Los Angeles, Calif., where he directed *Private Private* (June 3, 1968), *Movie, Movie on the Wall* (Oct. 28, 1968), *Tilt (Formerly Untitled)* (May 13, 1969), and other plays.

Television and Radio. Mr. Calhoun was on the staff of WRAMC-TV (Washington, D.C.) as operations manager and program director (Oct. 1957 –May 1959).

Recreation. Skin diving, water skiing, island hopping.

CALLAWAY, PAUL. Musician, conductor, educator. b. Paul Smith Callaway, Aug. 16, 1909, Atlanta, Ill., to Ralph V. and Mattie (Cubbage) Callaway. Father, clergyman. Grad. Missouri Military Acad., Mexico, Mo., 1927; attended Westminster Coll., 1927–29. Studied music with T. Tertius Noble, N.Y.C., 1930–35; Leo Sowerby, Chicago, Ill., 1936; and Marcel Dupré, Paris, Fr. 1938. Served US Army, 1942–46; rank, Warrant Officer (jg) and bandleader. Member of AF of M; Amer. Guild of Organists (fellow). Address: (home) 2230 Decatur Place, N.W., Washington, DC 20013, tel. (202) HO 2-7136; (bus.) c/o Washington Cathedral, Mt. St. Alban, Washington, DC 20013, tel. (202) WO 6-3500.

Mr. Callaway has been organist and choirmaster of the Washington (D.C.) Cathedral since 1939; conductor of The Cathedral Choral Society of Washington, D.C. (1942–to date); and musical director of the Opera Society of Washington, conducting most of its productions since its founding in 1956. He was music director and conductor, Lake George Opera Festival, Glen Falls, N.Y. (1966).

Awards. He received the honorary degree of doctor of music from Westminster College in 1959 and from Washington College, Chestertown, Md., in 1967.

CAMBRIDGE, GODFREY. Comedian, actor, writer. b. Godfrey MacArthur Cambridge, Feb. 26, 1933, New York, N.Y., to Alexander and Sarah Cambridge. Educ. Hofstra Coll. (later Univ.), Hempstead, N.Y.; City Coll. of N.Y. Married 1962 to Barbara Anne Teer (marr. dis.).

Theatre. Mr. Cambridge made his debut playing a bartender in an off-Bway revival of *Take a Giant Step* (Jan Hus House, Sept. 25, 1956). His Bway debut, as the Butler in *Nature's Way* (Coronet, Oct. 16, 1957), was followed by appearances as Johannes in a revival of *Lost in the Stars* (NY City Ctr., Apr. 10, 1958); Detective Lou Brody in an Equity Library production of *Detective Story* (Lenox Hill Playhouse, Dec. 16, 1960); and as Diouf in *The Blacks* (St. Mark's Playhouse, May 4, 1961). He played Gitlow Judson in *Purlie Victorious* (Cort, Sept. 28, 1961); various roles in *The Living Premise* (The Premise, June 13, 1963); toured as Prologus and Pseudolus in *A Funny Thing Happened on the Way to the Forum* (Summer 1965); and played all the roles except the Jewish Mother in *How To Be a Jewish Mother* (Hudson, Dec. 28, 1967).

Mr. Cambridge is also a stand-up comedian who has frequently performed on college campuses and in night-club engagements (see Night Clubs).

Films. Mr. Cambridge's films include *The Last Angry Man* (Col., 1959); *Gone are the Days!* (Hammer Films, 1963); *The Troublemaker* (Janus, 1964); *The President's Analyst* (Par., 1967); *The Busy Body* (Par., 1967); *The Biggest Bundle of Them All* (MGM, 1968); *Bye, Bye, Braverman* (WB-7 Arts, 1968); *The Night the Sun Came Out* (Col., 1969); and *Cotton Comes to Harlem* (UA, 1970).

Television. Mr. Cambridge made his television debut on the Jack Paar Show (NBC, 1964), later appearing regularly on that program. His other television appearances include the Garry Moore Show (CBS); Johnny Carson Tonight Show (NBC); Dick Van Dyke Show (CBS); Danny Kaye Show (CBS); Hollywood Palace (ABC); Red Skelton Show (CBS); Sgt. Bilko (CBS); Night Gallery (NBC); US Steel Hour (CBS); Naked City (ABC); and I've Got a Secret (CBS).

Night Clubs. Mr. Cambridge's numerous night club engagements, for which he writes his own material, include appearances at the Blue Angel, Village Vanguard, Village Gate, and Basin Street East, all in N.Y.C. Also at the Diplomat Hotel, Miami, Fla.; The Cave, Vancouver, Brit. Col., Can.; The Troubadour, Los Angeles, Calif.; the Cellar Door, Washington, D.C.; Act IV, Detroit, Mich.; Cal-Neva Lodge, Lake Tahoe; Crescendo, Hollywood, Calif.; Basin Street West, San Francisco, Calif.; and the Aladdin Hotel, Las Vegas, Nev.

Concerts. Mr. Cambridge appeared at Philharmonic Hall, Lincoln Ctr., N.Y.C., (Sept. 30, 1966).

Other Activities. Mr. Cambridge has been an active worker in the civil rights movement.

Published Works. Mr. Cambridge has contributed to *Monocle* magazine and wrote *Put-Downs and Put-Ons* (1967).

Discography. Mr. Cambridge began recording for Epic, and his releases include *Ready or Not, Here's Godfrey Cambridge* (1964); *Them Cotton Pickin' Days Is Over; Godfrey Cambridge Toys With the World;* and *The Godfrey Cambridge Show.*

Awards. Mr. Cambridge received a *Village Voice* off-Bway (Obie) award (1961) for his distinguished performance in *The Blacks,* and he was nominated for an Antoinette Perry (Tony) Award (1962) as the best feature actor on Bway for his performance in *Purlie Victorious.*

Recreation. Photography.

CAMPANELLA, JOSEPH. Actor. b. Joseph Mario Campanella, Nov. 21, 1927, New York City, to Philip and Mary O. Campanella. Father, musician. Grad. George Washington H.S., N.Y.C., 1943; Manhattan Coll., B.A. 1948; attended Holy Cross Coll., 1944; Columbia Univ., 1948–49. Studied acting with Steffen Zacharias, N.Y.C., two years; with Lee Strasberg, four years. Married May 30, 1964, to Jill Bartholomew, singer, dancer; one son. Served USNR, PTO 1944–46; rank, Lt. (jg). Relatives in theatre: brother, Frank Campanella, actor; cousin, Ralph Maero, operatic baritone. Member of AEA; SAG; AFTRA.

Theatre. Mr. Campanella made his professional debut as Angelo in the pre-Bway tour of *Tonight in Samarkand* (McCarter Th., Princeton, N.J.; Colonial, Boston, Mass., Jan. 1954). At Westport (Conn.) Country Playhouse, he appeared as John O'Brien in *Detective Story* (Summer 1954), Apollo in *The Empress* and Valere in *The Doctor in Spite of Himself* (both Summer 1955).

He appeared as the Fuller Brush Man in *Mr. and Mrs. North* (Finch Coll. Aud., N.Y.C., Oct. 1954); was understudy to Pat Hingle as Jules Taggart in *Girls of Summer* (Longacre, Nov. 19, 1956); and toured as Jack Marins in *House on the Rocks* (Summer 1958). At the North Jersey Playhouse (Fort Lee, N.J.), he played Lt. Marek in *The Caine Mutiny Court Martial* and Captain Fisby in *The Teahouse of the August Moon* (Summer 1958); appeared as Turk in *Come Back, Little Sheba* (Tappan Zee, Nyack, N.Y., Sept. 1958); played Pierre in *Hilary* (Summer 1959); at the Paper Mill Playhouse (Millburn, N.J.), appeared in *The Country Girl* and *A View from the Bridge* (Summer 1961); and at the Bergen (N.J.) Mall Playhouse, appeared as Paul Verrall in *Born Yesterday* (Sept. 1961).

He played Commander Carl Romano in *The Captains and the Kings* (Playhouse, N.Y.C., Jan. 2, 1962); Daniel Stein in *A Gift of Time* (Ethel Barrymore Th., Feb. 22, 1962); Gabriel Snapper in *Hot Spot* (Majestic, Apr. 19, 1963); Herbie in *Gypsy* (Summer tour, 1962); Robert Baker in *Wonderful Town* (Summer 1963); and toured as Dirk Winston in *Mary, Mary* (Summer 1965).

Films. Mr. Campanella appeared in *Murder, Inc.* (20th-Fox, 1961); *The Young Lovers* (MGM, 1964); and *The Saint Valentine's Day Massacre* (20th-Fox, 1967).

Television and Radio. He was a radio announcer on the Voice of America (1951) and on WQXR (N.Y.C., 1951).

On television, Mr. Campanella appeared on Robert Montgomery Presents (NBC, 1955, 1957); Kraft Th. (NBC, 1956); US Steel Hour (CBS, 1957); The Guiding Light (CBS, 1958–61); Armstrong Circle Th. (CBS, 1959); Ford Star Time (NBC, 1960); Alcoa Premiere (ABC, 1962); The Untouchables (ABC, 1962); Combat (ABC, 1962, 1963, 1964); The Nurses (CBS, 1962–63, 1964–65, 1965–66); Route 66 (CBS, 1963); The Virginian (NBC, 1963, 1964); Bob Hope Chrysler Th. (NBC, 1963, 1964); Espionage (NBC, 1964); Eleventh Hour (NBC, 1964); East Side/West Side (CBS, 1964); The Fugitive (ABC, 1964, 1965, 1967); For the People (CBS, 1965); FBI (ABC, 1966, 1968); 12 O'Clock High (ABC, 1966); Mission: Impossible (CBS, 1967, 1968); Mannix (CBS, 1967, 1972); The Name of the Game (NBC, 1968, 1970); Gunsmoke (CBS, 1968, 1972); *The Whole World Is Watching* (NBC, Mar. 1969); Ironside (NBC, 1969, 1970); Marcus Welby, M.D. (ABC, 1970, 1971); *A Clear and Present Danger* (NBC, 1970); and Night Gallery (NBC, 1970, 1971).

Recreation. Golf, softball, football, directing little theatre.

CAMPBELL, DOUGLAS. Actor, director. b. June 11, 1922, Glasgow, Scotland, to Dugald and Ethel (Sloan) Campbell. Father, post office worker. Attended public school, 6 yrs. Married 1947 to Ann Casson, actress; four sons, one daughter. Relatives in theatre: mother-in-law, Dame Sybil Thorndyke, actress; father-in-law, Sir Lewis T. Casson, actor. Member of AEA; ACTRA; AFTRA.

Theatre. Mr. Campbell was first engaged in the theatre as a truck driver for the Old Vic Co. (England) working also as assistant stage manager for the company in a touring production of *Jacob's Ladder* (1942); with the Old Vic, he played a season at Liverpool, appearing in *Androcles and the Lion, Six Characters in Search of an Author,* and *Abraham Lincoln.* He has performed in repertory at the Glasgow Citizens Th., and the Birmingham Midland Th. Co.;

in London, appeared in *The Merchant of Venice*, and as the boy, Scott in *Abraham Lincoln*; and has toured with the C.E.M.A. as actor and stage manager (1944).

He played Wanton-ness in the Tyrone Guthrie production of *The Three Estates* which inaugurated the Edinburgh (Scotland) Festival (Summer 1948); again appeared at the festival (Summers 1949, 1950), and later played John the Commonweal in *The Three Estates*.

He rejoined the London Old Vic Co., playing Cadi of Kintafi and Capt. Learney, USN in *Captain Brassbound's Conversion* (Old Vic, Apr. 17, 1951); Master Page in *The Merry Wives of Windsor* (Old Vic, May 31, 1951), which toured Belgium and The Netherlands; subsequently at the Old Vic, the title role in *Othello* (Oct. 31, 1951); Theseus in *A Midsummer Night's Dream* (Dec. 26, 1951); Casin in *The Other Heart* (Apr. 15, 1952); toured South Africa with the Old Vic, repeating his role in *Othello* and appearing in the title role in *Macbeth* (1952).

At the Old Vic in London, played Antonio in *The Merchant of Venice* (Jan. 6, 1953), Julius Caesar and Octavius Caesar in *Julius Caesar* (Feb. 24, 1953), and the 2nd Tempter in *Murder in the Cathedral* (Mar. 31, 1953).

In the first season of the Stratford (Canada) Shakespearean Festival, Mr. Campbell appeared as Parolles in *All's Well That Ends Well* and as Hastings in *Richard III* (Summer 1953); subsequently joined the Bristol (England) Old Vic Co., playing Antony in *Antony and Cleopatra* (Oct. 1953), and Robert Bailey I in *Old Bailey* (Nov. 1953); with the Stratford Shakespearean Festival, played Baptista in *The Taming of the Shrew*, Pompey in *Measure for Measure*, and the Man from Corinth in *King Oedipus* (Summer 1954). Later in Toronto, Canada, at the Crest Th., he directed *Antony and Cleopatra*, played the Cardinal in *The Prisoner*, and Ormonroyd in *When We Are Married*.

He subsequently organized the Canadian Players, and for their first season, directed and appeared as Cauchon and DeBaudricourt in their tour of *Saint Joan* (1954); at Stratford (Canada), played Casca in *Julius Caesar*, the title role in *King Oedipus* (1955); with the Canadian Players, directed and played the title role in a touring company of *Macbeth* (1955); at Stratford (Canada), appeared as Falstaff in *The Merry Wives of Windsor*, and as Pistol in *Henry V* (Summer 1956); at the Edinburgh Festival, repeated his roles in *Henry V* and *King Oedipus* (Aug. 1956); directed *Peer Gynt* for The Canadian Players' tour (Winter 1956); at Stratford (Canada), played Sir Toby Belch in *Twelfth Night* and Claudius in *Hamlet* (Summer 1957); and with the Canadian Players, directed a tour of *Othello* and appeared as John Tanner in *Man and Superman* (1957).

Mr. Campbell made his N.Y.C. debut as the Earl of Leicester in *Mary Stuart* (Phoenix Th., Oct. 8, 1957); subsequently played with the Stratford Festival Co. of Canada as the Duke of Milan in *The Two Gentleman of Verona* (Phoenix, Mar. 18, 1958) and Judge Adam in *The Broken Jug* (Phoenix, Apr. 1, 1958).

At Stratford (Canada), he played Falstaff in *Henry IV, Part 1* and directed *The Winter's Tale* (Summer 1958); appeared as Touchstone in *As You Like It* and in the title role in *Othello* (Summer 1959); with the Canadian Players, played General Burgoyne in *The Devil's Disciple* (1959); and at Stratford (Canada), directed *A Midsummer Night's Dream* and played the Boatswain in *H.M.S. Pinafore* (Summer 1960). He repeated his role in *H.M.S. Pinafore* and choreographed the production (Phoenix, N.Y.C., Sept. 7, 1960); and with the London Old Vic Co., played Bottom in *A Midsummer Night's Dream* (Old Vic, Dec. 20, 1960).

At Stratford, he played Menenius Agrippa in *Coriolanus* and the title role in *Henry VIII* (opened, June 19 and 20, 1961, respectively); in N.Y.C., he played the title role in *Gideon* (Plymouth, Nov. 9, 1961), later succeeding Fredric March as the Angel in the same production; again at Stratford, he was Don Alhambra del Bolero in *The Gondoliers* (Summer 1962); and in N.Y.C., directed and appeared in *The Golden Age* (Lyceum, Nov. 18, 1963).

From 1963 to 1965, Mr. Campbell was associate artistic director of the Minnesota Th. Co. at the Tyrone Guthrie Th., Minneapolis, Minn., where he directed *The Miser* (May 8, 1963), *Death of a Salesman* (July 16, 1963), *Saint Joan* (May 12, 1964), in which he also played the roles of De Baudricourt and an English soldier; played the title role in *Volpone* (June 29, 1964); arranged the fights for Richard III (May 10, 1965); and directed *The Way of the World* (May 11, 1965). At the Stratford Shakespearean Festival, he played Hotspur in *Henry IV, Part 1* (June 14, 1965); directed *Julius Caesar* (June 16, 1965); and played Lopahin in *The Cherry Orchard* (July 26, 1965).

Mr. Campbell succeeded (Oct. 1965) Sir Tyrone Guthrie as artistic director of the Minnesota Th. Co., continuing in the post until 1967, and during the 1966 season presented *The Skin of Our Teeth* (May 31, 1966), which he directed; *The Dance of Death* (June 1, 1966), which he directed; *As You Like It* (June 2, 1966); *The Doctor's Dilemma* (Sept. 6, 1966), which he directed; and *S.S. Glencairn* (Sept. 7, 1966), which he co-directed with Edward Payson Call. In 1967, he directed, with John Olon-Scrymgeour, *The Shoemaker's Holiday* (June 1, 1967), in which he also appeared, and he played Clytemnestra and Atreus in *The House of Atreus* (July 21, 1967).

At the Stratford Festival, he directed *Romeo and Juliet* (June 10, 1968) and the opera *La Cenarentola* (1968); and in N.Y.C. repeated his performances as Clytemnestra and Atreus in *The House of Atreus* (Billy Rose Th., Dec. 17, 1968). He appeared in *The Adventures of the Black Girl in Her Search for God* (Mark Taper Forum, Los Angeles, Calif., Mar. 20, 1969); played Alfred S. Doolittle in *My Fair Lady* (Los Angeles Music Ctr., Calif., June 1969); directed the opera *Macbeth* for the Chicago (Ill.) Lyric Opera; and appeared at the Goodman Memorial Th., Chicago, as Winston Churchill in *Soldiers* (Oct. 24, 1969); Prospero in *The Tempest* (Jan. 23, 1970); was in the Pinter double bill *The Basement* and *Tea Party* (Mar. 6, 1970); and played Captain Shotover in *Heartbreak House* (May 29, 1970).

At the Stratford Festival, he played the title role in *Vatzlav* (Avon Th., Aug. 11, 1970); at the Goodman Memorial, Chicago, he was Emerson in *The Night Thoreau Spent in Jail* (Jan. 18, 1971); appeared in *Marching Song* (Mar. 1, 1971); directed *Poor Bitos* (Apr. 12, 1971); and, returning again to Stratford, played the Baron of Gondremarck in *Life in Paris* (Avon Th., June 27, 1974).

Films. He appeared in the Tyrone Guthrie production of *Oedipus Rex* (Motion Pic. Dist., 1957) and directed an educational film on *Hamlet, Macbeth*, and *Oedipus* (E.B.F.), which he also narrated.

Television. For Canadian television, Mr. Campbell has appeared in *Julius Caesar, The Queen's Ring, The Gentle Gunman*, and *The Colonel and the Lady*; and in the US, in scenes from *Hamlet* (Omnibus, NBC). He directed *Peer Gynt* (CBS, 1958); appeared in *John Brown's Body* (CBS, Jan. 14, 1962); *The Prince and the Pauper; The Crucible* and *Billy Budd*; played John Quincy Adams in Profiles in Courage (NBC, Apr. 11, 1965); and appeared on The Defenders (CBS, July 1965).

Recreation. Talking.

CAMPBELL, PATTON. Costume designer, stage designer, educator. b. Sept. 10, 1926, Omaha, Neb., to Ralph and Frances (Patton) Campbell. Father, insurance executive. Grad. Central H.S., Omaha, 1944; Yale Univ., B.A. 1950; Yale Univ. Sch. of Drama, M.F.A. 1952. Served USNR, 1944–46; rank, Pharmacist's Mate 3rd Class. Member of United Scenic Artists, Local 829; Yale Club. Address: 46 W. 95th St., New York, NY 10025, tel. (212) 866-1757.

Theatre. Mr. Campbell was assistant scenic designer at the Cape Playhouse, Dennis, Mass. (Summers 1948–50); was scenic designer at the Barnstormers, Tamworth, N.H. (Summer 1951) and at the Famous Artists' Country Playhouse, Fayetteville, N.Y. (Summer 1954).

In N.Y.C., he was scenic designer for *The Grand Prize* (Plymouth Th., Jan. 26, 1955); costume designer for the *All in One* double-bill of *Trouble in Tahiti* and *27 Wagons Full of Cotton* (Playhouse, Apr. 19, 1955); designed costumes for *Fallen Angels* (Playhouse, Jan. 17, 1956); and for *A Hole in the Head* (Plymouth, Feb. 28, 1957); and assisted Rouben Ter-Arutunian in the production design of *New Girl in Town* (46 St. Th., May 14, 1957).

During the summers of 1957–59, Mr. Campbell was the scenic, costume and lighting designer at the Sante Fe (N.M.) Opera for *Barber of Seville, Ariadne auf Naxos, The Rake's Progress, Falstaff, Cinderella, La Bohème, Die Fledermaus, Abduction from the Seraglio, Anne Boleyn* and *Capriccio*.

He designed the costumes for the N.Y.C. production of *The Makropoulos Secret* (Phoenix, Dec. 3, 1957); designed the costumes for the operas *Wuthering Heights* (NY City Ctr., Apr. 9, 1959); and *The Mikado* (NY City Ctr., Oct. 3, 1959); assisted Mr. Ter-Arutunian on set and costume designs for *Redhead* (46 St. Th., Feb. 5, 1959) and William and Jean Eckart for *Fiorello!* (Broadhurst, Nov. 23, 1959).

He designed the costumes for *There Was a Little Girl* (Cort, Feb. 29, 1960) and *The Pirates of Penzance* (NY City Ctr., Jan. 16, 1961); assisted Cecil Beaton for *Tenderloin* (46 St. Th., Oct. 17, 1960); designed costumes for the opera *The Inspector General* (NY City Ctr., Oct. 19, 1960); was scenic and costume designer for *H.M.S. Pinafore* (NY City Ctr., 1961); costume designer for *The Conquering Hero* (ANTA, Jan. 16, 1961); assistant to Mr. Ter-Arutunian for *Donnybrook* (46 St. Th., May 18, 1961); costume designer for the opera *The Wings of the Dove* (NY City Ctr., Oct. 12, 1961); associate costume designer for *Kean* (Bway Th., Nov. 2, 1961); costume designer for *All American* (Winter Garden, Mar. 19, 1962), *A Month in the Country* (Maidman, May 28, 1963); for the opera *Katya Kabanova* (world premiere, Juilliard School of Music, May 1, 1964); and for the 1964 Central City (Colo.) Opera Festival productions of *Madame Butterfly* (June 27) and *The Lady from Colorado* (world premiere, July 3).

He also designed costumes for the opera *Natalia Petrovna* (world premiere, NY City Ctr., Oct. 8, 1964); for national companies of *After the Fall* (opened Playhouse, Wilmington, Del., Oct. 16, 1964) and *Oliver!* opened Hershey, Pa., Nov. 1964); for the opera *Lizzie Borden* (world premiere, NY City Ctr., Mar. 25, 1965) for a 25th anniversary revival of *The Glass Menagerie* (Brooks Atkinson Th., May 4, 1965); for a musical version of *Purple Dust* (Goodspeed Opera House, East Haddam, Conn., July 22, 1965); for *Great Scot!* (Th. Four, N.Y.C., Oct. 10, 1965); for the operas (both at NY City Ctr.) *Miss Julie* (Nov. 4, 1965) and *Capriccio* (Fall 1965); and, with Howard Bay, for *Man of La Mancha* (ANTA Washington Sq., Nov. 22, 1965).

He designed costumes for the operas (both NY State Th.) *The Ballad of Baby Doe* (Spring 1966) and *La Traviata* (1966); for the national company of *On a Clear Day You Can See Forever* (1966); for the play *Gone with the Wind* (New Imperial Th., Tokyo, Japan, Nov. 3, 1966); for *Agatha Sue, I love you* (Henry Miller's Th., N.Y.C., Dec. 14, 1966); and *Come Live with Me* (Billy Rose Th., Jan. 28, 1967). Also for *The Natural Look* (Longacre, Mar. 11, 1967); for the London, (England, production of *Man of La Mancha* (Piccadilly Th., 1968); *Loot* (Biltmore, N.Y.C., Mar. 18, 1968); for NY City Ctr. Gilbert & Sullivan productions (all at NY City Ctr., 1968) of *Pirates of Penzance* (Apr. 25), *H.M.S. Pinafore* (Apr. 27), and *The Mikado* (May 1); and for Santa Fe (N.M.) Opera productions of *Der Rosenkavalier* (1968), *Cosi fan tutte* (1969), and *Tosca* (1969).

He also designed costumes for the NY City Opera's *Carry Nation* (NY State Th., 1969); for the Opera Co. of Boston (Mass.) production *The Fisherman and His Wife* (1970); and for *Scarlett*, a musical version of *Gone with the Wind* (New Imperial Th., Tokyo, Japan, Jan. 1, 1970). He designed costumes for the NY City Opera productions (both NY State Th.) of *The Makropoulos Affair* (Nov. 10, 1970) and *Susannah* (1971); for *Mama* (world premiere, Studio Arena Th., Buffalo, N.Y., Jan. 6, 1972); and for the musical *Gone with the Wind* (Theatre Royal, Drury

Lane, London, England, May 3, 1972; Amer. premiere: Dorothy Chandler Pavilion, Los Angeles, Calif., Aug. 28, 1973).

Television. Mr. Campbell designed costumes for the television productions of the operas *Lizzie Borden* (NET, Jan. 25, 1967); *The Fisherman and His Wife* (NET, Spring 1970); *Between Time and Timbuktu* (NET, Spring 1972); and *The Ballad of Baby Doe* (NET, Apr. 21, 1976).

Other Activities. Mr. Campbell also taught stage design at Barnard Coll. Drama Workshop (1955–57); NY Univ. (1962–64); was on the staff of the opera theatre of Juilliard School of Music (1963–64); was an associate professor at Columbia Univ. (1967–72); and was appointed associate professor, State Univ. of NY (Purchase) in 1975.

CANDLER, PETER. General manager, educator. b. Mar. 21, 1926, New York City, to F. B. and Caroline K. (Mills) Candler. Father, salesman. Grad. Kent (Conn.) Sch., 1944; Williams Coll., B.A. 1949; attended Univ. of Virginia Law Sch., 1949–50; Columbia Univ., 1950–51. Served USAAF, 1944–45; rank, Aviation Cadet. Relative in theatre: cousin, Wolcott Gibbs, drama critic (dec. 1958). Member of MATA; ETA; Kappa Alpha (secy., Williams Chap.); Phi Alpha Delta. Address: Lodge, Lawrenceville School, Lawrenceville, NJ 08648, tel. (609) 896-1490.

Since 1960, Mr. Candler has been instructor of English, drama, and film and director of drama at Lawrenceville (N.J.) Sch., where he is also director of the Kirby Arts Center. From 1952 to 1960, he was instructor of English and director of drama at Taft Sch. (Watertown, Conn.).

From 1949 to 1952, Mr. Candler was lighting designer for Monomoy Th. (Chatham, Mass.). He was business manager for Cape Playhouse (Dennis, Mass., Summer 1953), general manager for Cape Playhouse (Summers 1954–59); general manager for the Cape Code Melody Tent (Hyannis, Mass., Summers 1960–64); and director, Lawrenceville Summer Th. Workshop (1966–70).

Awards. Mr. Candler was awarded a Ford Foundation grant in theatre in 1965.

Recreation. Crew, soccer, music, touring by car, old bookshops, water sports.

CANFIELD, CURTIS. Educator, writer, director. b. Fayette Curtis Canfield, July 29, 1903, Bridgeport, Conn., to Andrew A. and Elizabeth M.C.V. (O'Connor) Canfield. Grad. Amherst Coll., A.B. 1925. Married May 21, 1927, to Katharine Fitz Randolph Newbold; one daughter. Served USNR, 1943–46; rank, Lt. Comdr.; received Secretary of Navy Commendation Ribbon. Member of NTC (trustee, 1958–1962; pres., 1964–65); Theatre Inc. (bd. of dir., 1954–62); Fulbright Fellowship Screening Comm., 1958–61 (chairman, 1961); President's Comm. for Cultural Exchange (Drama Advisory Panel, 1957–62); President's Comm. for Shakespeare's 400th Anniversary (exec. comm., 1963); Century Assn. (1953–72); Elizabethan Club; fellow of Saybrook Coll. (Yale). Address: 36 Dana St., Amherst, MA 01002.

Mr. Canfield was University Professor of Theatre Arts, Univ. of Pittsburgh, from 1968 to 1973, when he retired as University Professor Emeritus. He began his academic career as instructor of dramatics at Amherst College in 1927 and advanced through the ranks to professor and director of Kirby Memorial Th. (1938); he was named Stanley King Professor of Dramatics in 1952. He left Amherst in 1954 to head the Yale Univ. Dept. of Drama as professor of drama and director of Yale Univ. Th. In 1955, he was named the first dean of the Drama School, which had heretofore been administered by the Dept. of Fine Arts, and continued in this post until 1965. He resigned from Yale in 1968 to accept appointment at the Univ. of Pittsburgh.

He directed *J. B.* for the American theatre exhibit at the World's Fair (Brussels, Belgium, 1958); and an off-Bway revival of *John Brown's Body* (Martinique Th., June 20, 1960).

Published Works. Mr. Canfield is the author of *Plays of the Irish Renaissance* (1929), *Plays of Changing Ireland* (1936), *The Seed and the Sowers* (1955) and *The Craft of Play Directing* (1963). He has also published acting versions of *Fashion* by Anna Cora Mowatt and *John Brown's Body* by Stephen Vincent Benét, as well as articles and reviews.

Awards. He has been awarded three honorary degrees: M.A. (Yale Univ., 1954), L.H.D. (Amherst Coll., 1955) and LL.D. (Emerson Coll., 1956). In 1974, he was named honorary president of the Society of the Alumni of Amherst College.

CANNON, J. D. Actor. b. John Donovan Cannon, Apr. 24, 1922, Salmon, Idaho, to William J. and Bessie (Moore) Cannon. Father, miner. Grad. Salmon H.S., 1940. Studied acting at AADA, 1940–42; Amer. Theatre Wing, 1949–50. Married Feb. 27, 1947, to Alice McCamley, known as Alice Cannon, playwright. Served US Army, 1942–45; rank, T/Sgt. Member of AEA; SAG; AFTRA.

Pre-Theatre. Ranch hand, sheepherder, guide, restaurant cashier.

Theatre. Mr. Cannon was associated with the Artists' Th., and appeared with this company in *Try, Try, The Heroes, The Screen,* and *The Ticklish Acrobat.* With the New York Shakespeare Festival, at the Emanuel Presbyterian Church, he played Don John and Dogberry in *Much Ado About Nothing* (Apr. 1955), Jacques in *As You Like It* (Oct. 20, 1955), Mercutio in *Romeo and Juliet* (Dec. 1955), and De Flores in *The Changeling* (Apr. 1956). With this company, at the East Side Amphitheatre, he appeared as Cassius in *Julius Caesar* (June 29, 1956), and Petruchio in *The Taming of the Shrew* (July 1956). At their Belvedere Lake Th., he played Speed in *Two Gentlemen of Verona* (July 1957); and Ross in *Macbeth* (Aug. 15, 1957); Mercutio in *Romeo and Juliet* there and on the NY Shakespeare Festival tour (June 27, 1957); and played Tyrrel in *Richard III* (Heckscher Th., Nov. 25, 1957).

He played Count La Ruse in *Children of Darkness* (Circle in the Sq., Feb. 28, 1958); at the NY Shakespeare Festival, appeared as Touchstone in *As You Like It* (Heckscher, July 20, 1958); played the Schoolmaster in *The Power and the Glory* (Phoenix, Dec. 10, 1958); Charles Morell in *Masquerade* (John Golden Th., Mar. 16, 1959); Mr. Anthony in *The Great God Brown* (Coronet, Oct. 6, 1959); Phaidrias and a Spartan Commissioner in *Lysistrata* (Phoenix, Nov. 24, 1959); appeared in the staged reading, *Pictures in the Hallway* (Phoenix, Dec. 26, 1959); played the Button Moulder and a Strange Passenger in *Peer Gynt* (Phoenix, Jan. 12, 1960); and Poins in *Henry IV, Parts I and II* (Phoenix, Mar. 1, 1960; Apr. 18, 1960). With the NY Shakespeare Festival he played Petruchio in *The Taming of the Shrew* (Belvedere Lake, Aug. 19, 1960), Benedick in *Much Ado About Nothing* (Wollman Rink, Central Park, July 5, 1961), Bolingbroke in *Richard II* (Wollman Rink, Aug. 28, 1961); Joe McAnany in *Great Day in the Morning* (Henry Miller's Th., Mar. 28, 1962); toured as the King in summer stock production of *The King and I* (Guber-Ford-Gross Circuit, Summer 1963); played Morris Pieterson in *The Blood Knot* (Cricket, N.Y.C., Mar. 1, 1964); Stolts in *The Umbrella* (Bouwerie Lane Th., May 26, 1965); Oscar Davenport in *Mating Dance* (Eugene O'Neill Th., Nov. 3, 1965); and Parolles in *All's Well That Ends Well* (Delacorte, June 15, 1966).

Films. Mr. Cannon's appearances include *An American Dream* (WB, 1966); *Cool Hand Luke* (WB, 1967); *Heaven with a Gun* (MGM, 1969); *Cotton Comes to Harlem* (UA, 1969); *The Thousand Planes Raid* (UA, 1969); *Krakatoa, East of Java* (Cinerama, 1969); *Lawman* (UA, 1971); and *Scorpio* (UA, 1973).

Television. Mr. Cannon has appeared on Omnibus (CBS), US Steel Hour (CBS), Camera Three (CBS), The Catholic Hour (NBC), The Defenders (CBS), The Nurses (CBS), Play of the Week (NTA), The Untouchables (ABC), Stoney Burke (ABC), Wagon Train (NBC), Combat (ABC), Great Adventure (CBS), and the Chrysler Hour (NBC); Naked City (Ind.); *Wedding Band* (ABC); and McCloud (NBC).

Awards. Mr. Cannon received a *Village Voice* off-Bway (Obie) Special Citation for distinguished performances with the N.Y. Shakespeare Festival (1958); and has received the Ian Keith Knight for Benedick in *Much Ado About Nothing,* and Bolingbroke in *Richard II* (NY Shakespeare Festival, 1961).

Recreation. Horseback riding.

CANTOR, ARTHUR. Producer, press representative. b. March 12, 1920, Boston, Mass., to Samuel S. Cantor and Lillian (Landsman) Cantor. Grad. Harvard Coll., B.A. 1940. Married Nov. 18, 1951, to Deborah Rosmarin (dec. Sept. 22, 1970); two sons, one daughter. Served WW I, USAF. Member of ATPAM; Harvard Club; The Players; League of New York Theatres (bd. of govs., 1967).

Theatre. Mr. Cantor was first an assistant to the press representative of the Playwright's Company (1945). He became an independent press representative for *Hook 'n' Ladder* (Royale Th., Apr. 29, 1952); *Inherit the Wind* (Natl. Th., Apr. 21, 1955); *The Most Happy Fella* (Imperial, May 3, 1956); *Auntie Mame* (Broadhurst, Oct. 31, 1956); *Long Day's Journey into Night* (Helen Hayes Th., Nov. 7, 1956); *Two for the Seesaw* (Booth, Jan. 16, 1958); and *The Miracle Worker* (Playhouse, Oct. 19, 1959).

He produced, with Saint Subber, *The Tenth Man* (Booth, Nov. 5, 1959); and, with Fred Coe, *All the Way Home* (Belasco, Nov. 30, 1960), *Gideon* (Plymouth, Nov. 9, 1961), and *A Thousand Clowns* (Eugene O'Neill Th., Apr. 5, 1962; and national tour, 1963–64); and was co-producer and press agent for *Three Cheers for the Tired Businessman* (tour, 1963–64); co-produced the national tour of *Camelot* (1963–64); co-produced *The Golden Age* (Lyceum, N.Y.C., Nov. 18, 1963); and co-produced *The Passion of Josef D* (Ethel Barrymore Th., Feb. 11, 1964).

Mr. Cantor was general press agent for *Follies Bergere* (Broadway Th., N.Y.C., June 2, 1964); co-produced with Henry Guettel, the bus and truck touring productions of both *Camelot* (1964) and *Oliver!* (1965); produced, in association with Committee Productions, *The Committee* (Henry Miller's Th., N.Y.C., Sept. 16, 1964); with Artie Solomon, was press representative for *The Great Western Union* (Bouwerie Lane, Feb. 9, 1965) and *Matty and the Moron and Madonna* (Orpheum, Mar. 29, 1965); supervised stage arrangements for a US Department of State tour (1965) made by Florence Eldridge and Frederic March (Italy, Greece, Turkey, Syrian Arab Republic, Lebanon, United Arab Republic, Iran, and Afghanistan): produced and directed *The Trigon* (Stage 73, N.Y.C., Oct. 9, 1965); was one of the press representatives for *Bugs* and *Veronica* (Pocket, Nov. 18, 1965); with Artie Solomon, was press representative for *Man of La Mancha* (ANTA Washington Square, Nov. 22, 1965); associate producer and press representative for *La Grosse Valise* (54 St. Th., Dec. 14, 1965); co-produced and was press representative for *The World of Günter Grass* (Pocket, Apr. 26, 1966); was one of the press representatives for *Fitz* and *Biscuit* (Circle in the Square, May 16, 1966); company manager for the Stockholm Marionette Theatre of Fantasy production of *The Threepenny Opera* (Billy Rose Th., Oct. 27, 1966); press representative for *Kicking the Castle Down* (Gramercy Arts, Jan. 18, 1967); with Nicholas Vanoff, co-produced *Of Love Remembered* (ANTA Th., Feb. 18, 1967); press agent and producer of *People Is the Thing that the World Is Fullest Of* (Bil Baird Th., Feb. 20, 1967); press representative for *Diary of a Madman* (Orpheum, Mar. 23, 1967); co-produced *By George* (Lyceum, Oct. 12, 1967); directed *The Tenth Man* (NY City Ctr., Nov. 8, 1967); press representative for *Darling of the Day* (George Abbott Th., Jan. 27, 1968); by arrangement with the Theatre of Genoa, presented *The Venetian Twins* (Henry Miller's Th., May 28, 1968); press representative for the concurrent presentation (Barbizon-Plaza Th.) of *Le Tartuffe* (Apr. 18, 1968) and *Waiting for Godot* (Apr. 22, 1968); with Mortimer Levitt, presented the Daytop Th. Co. in *The Concept* (Sheridan Sq. Playhouse, May 6, 1968); press representative for *The House of Atreus* (Dec. 17, 1968), and *Arturo Ui* (Dec. 22, 1968) presented in repertory; presented the Bil and Cora Baird Marionettes (Bil Baird Th.) in *Win-*

nie the Pooh (Mar. 7, 1969) and *The Wizard of Oz* (Nov. 27, 1968); co-produced *Tango* (Pocket Th., Jan. 18, 1969); co-produced a revival of *The Concept* (Gramercy Arts, Aug. 21, 1969; moved to Pocket Th., Mar. 4, 1970); press representative for *The Picnic on the Battlefield* and *Guernica*, billed as *Two Plays by Fernando Arrabal* (Barbizon-Plaza Th., Apr. 23, 1969); co-produced *Golden Bat* (Sheridan Square Playhouse, July 21, 1970); press agent for *L'Amante Anglaise* (Barbizon-Plaza Th., Apr. 14, 1971); with David Merrick, produced *Vivat! Vivat Regina!* (Broadhurst, Jan. 20, 1972); co-produced *Promenade, All!* (Alvin, Apr. 16, 1972); co-produced a revival of *Captain Brassbound's Conversion*, starring Ingrid Bergman (Ethel Barrymore Th., Apr. 17, 1972); produced *The Little Black Book* (Helen Hayes Th., Apr. 25, 1972); as executive producer of The American Puppet Arts Council, presented the Bil Baird Marionettes (Bil Baird Th.) productions of *Winnie the Pooh* (Oct. 29, 1972), *Davy Jones' Locker* (Dec. 24, 1972), *Band Wagon* (Mar. 16, 1973); *The Whistling Wizard*, and *The Sultan of Tuffet* (Oct. 17, 1973), and *Pinocchio* (Dec. 15, 1974); presented *Forty-two Seconds from Broadway* (Playhouse, Mar. 11, 1973); and, in association with H. M. Tennent Ltd., presented *In Praise of Love* (Morosco, Dec. 10, 1974); *Private Lives* (46 St. Th., Feb. 6, 1975); and *The Constant Wife* (Shubert, Apr. 14, 1975).

Television. Mr. Cantor has made guest appearances on the Today Show (NBC); All Things Considered (NET); and produced *The Thirteen Stars* variety special (NET).

Awards. He is a recipient of the Amer. Jewish Congress Award (1969).

CAPALBO, CARMEN. Director, producer, writer. b. Carmen Charles Capalbo, Nov. 1, 1925, Harrisburg, Pa., to Joseph and Concetta (Riggio) Capalbo. Father, merchant. Grad. William Penn H.S., Harrisburg, 1943; attended Yale Univ. Sch. of Drama, 1945–46. Married July 9, 1950, to Patricia McBride, ballet dancer (marr. dis. June 23, 1961); one son, one daughter. Served US Army, 1944–45; rank, Sgt.; awarded Bronze Star, Purple Heart. Member of League of Off-Bway Theatres (co-founder, 1958; member of exec. board, 1958–60); League of New York Theatres; SSD&C (contract negotiating comm., 1962); Dramatists Guild. Address: 21 E. 11th St., New York, NY 10003.

Theatre. Mr. Capalbo first appeared as the Jester in a William Penn H.S. production of *The Forest Prince* (1941).

He produced, with Leo Lieberman, and directed *Juno and the Paycock* (Cherry Lane, N.Y.C., July 2, 1946); produced and played in *Awake and Sing* (Cherry Lane, Aug. 1946); produced *Dear Brutus* (Cherry Lane, Aug. 1946); directed and produced *Shadow and Substance* (Cherry Lane, Sept. 1946); and directed *A Connecticut Yankee* (summer tour, 1951).

He was stage manager for *Emlyn Williams as Charles Dickens* (John Golden Th., N.Y.C., Feb. 4, 1952), which then toured, and returned to N.Y.C. (Bijou, Apr. 20, 1953); production stage manager for the Jean-Louis Barrault-Madeleine Renaud Co. (Ziegfeld, Nov. 12, 1952); produced, with Stanley Chase, and directed *The Threepenny Opera* (Th. de Lys, Mar. 9, 1954; revived Sept. 20, 1955), which was produced in California (opened Marines Memorial Th., San Francisco, Calif., Sept. 13, 1960; closed Music Box, Los Angeles, Calif., Dec. 15, 1960), and in Canada (Royal Alexandra, Toronto, Sept. 19, 1961).

At the Bijou Th., N.Y.C., he produced, with Stanley Chase, and directed *The Potting Shed* (Jan. 29, 1957), *A Moon for the Misbegotten* (May 2, 1957), and *The Cave Dwellers* (Oct. 19, 1957); directed *The Good Soldier Schweik* (NY City Ctr., Apr. 23, 1958); directed and co-produced *The Threepenny Opera* (Paper Mill Playhouse, Millburn, N.J., Sept. 4, 1961); directed *Seidman and Son* (Belasco, N.Y.C., Oct. 15, 1962); directed *The Strangers* (Westport Country Playhouse, Conn., Nov. 5, 1963); directed *Enter Solly Gold* (Paramus Playhouse, Paramus, N.J., 1965); and co-produced and directed *The Rise and Fall of the City of Mahagonny* (Anderson Th., N.Y.C., April 28, 1970).

Television and Radio. Mr. Capalbo wrote, directed, and produced 200 radio plays (WKBO, Harrisburg, Pa., 1941–45).

He served as story editor for Studio One (CBS, 1951–52); and he directed *The Power and the Glory* (Play of the Week, WNTA, 1959).

Awards. Mr. Capalbo received the Antoinette Perry (Tony) Award and the *Village Voice* off-Bway (Obie) Award for *The Threepenny Opera* (1956).

Recreation. Piano, reading, baseball, painting, philately.

CAPERS, VIRGINIA. Actress, singer. b. Sept. 25, 1925, Sumter, S.C. Educ. Howard Univ., Washington, D.C.; Juilliard School of Music, N.Y.C.

Theatre. Miss Capers began her professional career in the theatre playing in Yiddish vaudeville on Second Ave., N.Y.C. She was understudy for Adelaide Hall as Grandma Obeah in *Jamaica* (Imperial, Oct. 31, 1957) and later replaced Miss Hall; played the Charwoman in *Saratoga* (Winter Garden, Dec. 7, 1959); appeared in *Sister Sadie and the Sons of Sam* (New Th. for Now Workshop, Mark Taper Forum, Los Angeles, Calif., Nov. 25, 1968); and played Lena Younger in *Raisin* (Arena Stage, Washington, D.C., May 23, 1973; 46 St. Th., N.Y.C., Oct. 18, 1973).

Miss Capers has also been a featured member of the Los Angeles Civic Light Opera.

Films. Miss Capers appeared in *Lady Sings the Blues* (Par., 1972); *Trouble Man* (20th-Fox, 1972); and *Five on the Black Hand Side* (UA, 1973).

Television. Miss Capers has appeared on Mannix (CBS) and other television programs.

Awards. In 1973, Miss Capers was nominated for a NATAS (Emmy) Award for best supporting actress for her appearance on Mannix, and in 1974 she received an Antoinette Perry (Tony) Award for best actress in a musical for her performance in *Raisin*..

CAPLIN, GERTRUDE. Producer. b. Trudi Michel, May 17, 1921, New York City, to Isadore and Esther (Goodman) Michel. Father, doctor; mother, known as Ruth Powell, The Dancing Violinist, vaudeville performer. Grad. Walton H.S., Bronx, N.Y.C., 1939, attended Columbia Univ., 1946–48. Married Oct. 21, 1939, to Paul Caplin, manufacturer. Relatives in theatre: brother, Scott Michel, playwright; uncle, Jack Powell, blackface drummer and vaudeville performer; uncle, Walter "Mousie" Powell, orchestra leader; uncle, Archie Powell, trombonist. Member of League of N.Y. Theatres; Theatre Life Co. (pres.). Address: 130 E. 63rd St., New York, NY 10021, tel. (212) 832-7676.

Theatre. Mrs. Caplin produced *Angels Kiss Me* (National Th., N.Y.C., Apr. 17, 1951); produced, with Herbert L. Berger, the pre-Bway tryout of *Rise by Sin* (opend Shubert, New Haven, Conn., Aug. 1952; closed Shubert, Washington, D.C., Sept. 1952); produced, with Thelma Fingar, *Sixth Finger in a Five Finger Glove* (Longacre, N.Y.C., Oct. 8, 1956); and produced *The Murder of Me* (Maidman, May 14, 1962).

Published Works. Mrs. Caplin, as Trudi Michel, wrote the autobiographical novel *Inside Tin Pan Alley* (1948). She has also written approximately 35 popular songs, including "Strange and Sweet" (1947).

Awards. She received a USO award in 1952 for supplying theatre ticket and book distribution to the armed forces.

Recreation. Bowling, painting, swimming.

CAPOTE, TRUMAN. Writer. b. Truman Streckfus Persons, Sept. 30, 1924, New Orleans, La., to Julian A. and Nina (Faulk) Persons; stepfather, Joseph Garcia Capote. Member of ASCAP; ALA; Natl. Inst. of Arts & Letters; Dramatists Guild.

Theatre. Mr. Capote is the author of *The Grass Harp* (Martin Beck Th., Mar. 27, 1952; revived Circle in the Square, Apr. 27, 1953). He also wrote the book and, with Harold Arlen, the lyrics for *House of Flowers* (Alvin, Dec. 30, 1954), which was adapted from his own short story; his story "Breakfast at Tiffany's" was the basis for the musical *Holly Golightly* (opened Forrest Th., Philadelphia, Pa., Oct. 10, 1966), retitled *Breakfast at Tiffany's* (closed during previews: Majestic, N.Y.C., Dec. 14, 1966); his novel *The Grass Harp* was made into a musical (Trinity Square Playhouse, Providence, R.I., Dec. 26, 1966; Martin Beck Th., N.Y.C., Nov. 2, 1971); Mr. Capote wrote lyrics for songs in *The Harold Arlen Songbook* (Stage 73, Feb. 28, 1967); and his novel *Other Voices, Other Rooms* was dramatized by Anna Marie Barlow (Studio Arena, Buffalo, N.Y., Oct. 4, 1973).

Films. With John Huston, Mr. Capote wrote the screenplay for *Beat the Devil* (UA, 1954); and with William Archibald, the screenplay for *The Innocents* (20th-Fox, 1962). *Breakfast at Tiffany's* (Par., 1961) was adapted from his novella; *In Cold Blood* (Col., 1967) was based on Mr. Capote's book of the same title; *Truman Capote's Trilogy* (Allied Artists, 1969) consisted of dramatizations of three of Mr. Capote's stories, previously on television (see below).

Television. Mr. Capote appeared on *The Nonfiction Novel* (U.S.A. Novel, NET, Feb. 1966) and on such talk and variety shows as the Johnny Carson *Tonight Show* (NBC, 1968, 1969, 1972) and the *David Frost Show* (Ind., 1971). With Eleanor Perry, he dramatized three of his own stories for television: *A Christmas Memory* (ABC, Stage 67, Dec. 21, 1966); *Among the Paths to Eden* (ABC, Dec. 17, 1967); and *Miriam* (ABC, 1970); dramatized, also with Mrs. Perry, his story *The Thanksgiving Visitor* (ABC, Nov. 28, 1968); wrote, with Wyatt Cooper, the story on which *The Glass House* (CBS, Feb. 4, 1972) was based; and appeared interviewing prisoners in *Truman Capote Behind Prison Walls* (ABC, Dec. 7, 1972).

Published Works. Mr. Capote wrote *Other Voices, Other Rooms* (1948); *Tree of Night* (1949); *Local Color* (1950); *The Grass Harp* (1953); *The Muses Are Heard* (1956); *Breakfast at Tiffany's* (1958); with Richard Avedon, *Observations* (1959); and *Selected Writings* (1963); *In Cold Blood* (1965); *A Christmas Memory* (1966); *The Thanksgiving Visitor* (1969); and *The Dogs Bark* (1973), a collection of some of the articles Mr. Capote had written for *The New Yorker, Harper's Bazaar, Cosmopolitan*, and other magazines.

Discography. Mr. Capote recorded excerpts from *In Cold Blood* (RCA, 1966).

Awards. Mr. Capote received O. Henry Memorial Awards for his short stories (1946, 1948, 1951, 1952); an award for his prose from the National Institute of Arts and Letters (1959); and an Edgar Award (1966) for *In Cold Blood* from the Mystery Writers of America for the best fact crime book. *A Christmas Memory* received a Peabody Award (1967); won first prize at the Monte Carlo International Television Festival; was cited by the US Television Critics Assn. as best program of the year; and Mr. Capote and Mrs. Perry received NATAS (Emmy) awards for their script. In addition, the film *Trilogy* was chosen as an official American entry at the 1968 Cannes Film Festival.

Recreation. Skin-diving, skiing, fast cars, collecting small art objects.

CAPPY, TED. Choreographer, director. b. July 9, Brooklyn, N.Y., to Nicolo Antonio and Nicoletta (Capozza) Capuozzo. Father, contractor. Grad. Franklin K. Lane H.S., Brooklyn, N.Y., 1928. Studied ballet with Nanette Charisse, two years; Aubrey Hitchins, two years; modern dance with Hanya Holm, two years; tap dancing with Carlos, two years. Served US Army, 1941–45; rank, Sgt. Member of AEA; SSD&C. Address: 163 W. 48th St., New York, NY 10036, tel. (212) CI 5-7202.

Theatre. Mr. Cappy was first a dancer in night clubs. While serving in the army he appeared in *This Is the Army* (Bway Th., N.Y.C., July 4, 1942).

He was choreographer for *Ring Around the Moon* (Martin Beck Th., N.Y.C., Nov. 23, 1950); *Idiot's Delight* (NY City Ctr., May 23, 1951); *Two on the Aisle* (Mark Hellinger Th., July 19, 1951); *Remains to be Seen* (Morosco, Oct. 3, 1951); *Three Wishes for Jamie* (Mark Hellinger Th., Mar. 21, 1952); was assistant choreographer for *Two's Company* (Alvin, Dec. 15, 1952); and choreographed *Hit the Deck* (Marine Stadium, Jones Beach, N.Y., Summer 1960).

He choreographed for the St. Louis (Mo.) Municipal Opera (Summers 1952, 1953, 1958, 1959, 1962); the Omaha (Nebr.) centennial show (1954); a revue called *Festival* (Teatro Nuovo, Milan, Italy, Sept. 1954); and has staged the dance numbers in industrial shows for Milliken (Astor Hotel, N.Y.C., 1960–61). Clothing Manufacturers of Amer. (Hotel New Yorker, N.Y.C., 1960), Brunswick (Concord Hotel, N.Y.C., 1961); Tobacco Manufacturers of America (Chicago, Ill., 1963). He also served as director and choreographer for two Buick industrials (Flint, Mich., Aug. and Sept. 1963).

Mr. Cappy was associate choreographer, with Stuart Hodis, to Donald Saddler for *To Broadway with Love* (Music Hall at the Texas Pavillion, NY World's Fair, Apr. 22, 1964). He choreographed again for the St. Louis Municipal Opera, in particular *Cavalcade of America* (Summer 1971) and *Anything Goes* (1972), for which he created an all-tap choreography.

Films. He was assistant choreographer for the film version of *This Is the Army* (WB, 1943).

Television. Mr. Cappy was assistant choreographer for the spectacular Salute to America (NBC, 1951); choreographer for Kate Smith Presents (NBC, 1954); the ANTA closed-circuit spectacular, All Star Revue (NBC, 1955); Caesar Presents (NBC, 1955); Sid Caesar's Hour (NBC, 1955–56–57); Guy Mitchell Show (ABC, 1958); Sid Caesar-Jose Ferrar spectacular (NBC, 1959); Art Carney spectacular, *O'Halloran's Luck* (NBC, 1961). He also choreographed commercials for Phillip Morris, RCA, Ford, Griffin, Pepsodent, and Revlon.

Other Activities. Mr. Cappy held tap dancing classes for adult theatrical performers at the Don Farnsworth and Hauer Studios, N.Y.C., in 1970–71.

Awards. Mr. Cappy has received awards for ballroom dancing (Roseland, N.Y.C.).

Recreation. Swimming, handyman around the house.

CAREW, HELEN. Actress. Member of AEA; AFTRA; SAG.

Theatre. Miss Carew first appeared on stage as Josephine in a high school production of *H.M.S. Pinafore* (Mason Opera House, Los Angeles, Calif., 1910). A member of the Holden Players, she appeared in their production of *Darkest Russia* (Cleveland Th., Ohio, Oct. 6, 1914).

She made her N.Y.C. debut as the School Teacher in *The Flame* (Lyric, Sept. 4, 1916); subsequently appeared as Jane Wade in *Kempy* (Belmont, May 15, 1922); a Salesgirl in *Roger Bloomer* (48 St. Th., Mar. 1, 1923); Madge in *The Rising Son* (Klaw, Oct. 27, 1924); Flo Alden in *Thrills* (Comedy, Apr. 16, 1925); Mrs. Langdon in *Human Nature* (Sept. 24, 1925); Mary Millett in *The Trouper* (52 St. Th., Mar. 8, 1926); Agatha Bloom in *Wooden Kimono* (Martin Beck Th., Dec. 27, 1926); and Jane in *The Breaks* (Klaw, Apr. 16, 1928).

She played Emma Heller in *The Family Upstairs* (Biltmore, Oct. 27, 1933); and succeeded (Feb. 1934) Elizabeth Risdon as Elizabeth Kalness in *Big Hearted Herbert* (Biltmore, Jan. 1, 1932); played Attie Brant in *Dream Child* (Vanderbilt, Sept. 27, 1934); Mrs. Webb in *Our Town* (Henry Miller's Th., Feb. 4, 1938); appeared in the pre-Bway tours of *Battle of Angels* (1940), *Broken Dishes*, and *Lonely Way;* played Mrs. Matilda Martin in *Hope for a Harvest* (Guild, N.Y.C., Nov. 26, 1941); Essie in *Broken Journey* (Henry Miller's Th., June 23, 1942); Mrs. Hobbs in *Harriet* (Henry Miller's Th., Mar. 3, 1943); Miss Belle in *Mrs. January and Mr. X* (Belasco, Mar. 31, 1944); Mrs. Brandt in *A Place of Our Own* (Royale, Apr. 2, 1945); Mathilda Rockwood in *January Thaw* (Golden, Feb. 4, 1946); and Clara Breedlove in *The Traveling Lady* (Playhouse, Oct. 27, 1954).

Since 1934, she has appeared extensively in summer theatres, including Ivoryton Playhouse, Conn.; Cape Playhouse, Dennis, Mass.; Berkshire Playhouse, Stockbridge, Mass.; Falmouth Playhouse, Mass.; Westport (Conn.) Country Playhouse.

Films. Miss Carew appeared in *All the Way Home* (Par., 1964).

Television and Radio. She first appeared on radio in 1929, subsequently on numerous daytime serials and dramatic programs including the Helen Hayes Th., the Texaco Star Th., the Th. Guild of the Air, and US Steel Hour, and Arthur Hopkins Presents.

She has made guest appearances on television on the Philco Television Playhouse (NBC), US Steel Hour (CBS) and Robert Montgomery Presents (NBC).

CAREY, DENIS. Director, actor. b. Aug. 3, 1909, London, England, to William Denis and May (Wilkinson) Carey. Attended St. Paul's Sch., London; Trinity Coll., Dublin, Ireland. Married to Yvonne Coulette, actress. Member of AEA; Garrick Club.

Pre-Theatre. Clerk in income tax office.

Theatre. He made his N.Y.C. debut as the Second Priest in *Murder in the Cathedral* (Ritz Th., Feb. 16, 1938); played Michael Byrne in *Spring Meeting* (Morosco, Dec. 8, 1938); and was the first director (1955) of the Amer. Shakespeare Festival (Stratford, Conn.), directing *Julius Caesar* (July 12) and *The Tempest* (Aug. 11).

He made his debut as Micky in a Christmas pantomine, *The Great Big World* (Royale Court Th., London, Dec. 26, 1921); and appeared in productions at the Gate and Abbey theatres in Dublin. At the Abbey, he appeared in *Deirdre, Is Life Worth Living,* as the Greek in *The Resurrection* (Aug. 1934); in the title role of *Parnell of Avondale* (Oct. 1, 1934); and appeared in *Summer's Day* (Dec. 9, 1935).

He played the Second Priest in *Murder in the Cathedral* (Duchess, London, Oct. 30, 1936); took over the role of Michael Byrne in *Spring Meeting* (Ambassadors', May 31, 1938); toured England with the Pilgrim Players (1940–43); played Dermot Francis O'Flingsley in *Shadow and Substance* (Duke of York's, London, May 25, 1943); appeared in productions with the Glasgow (Scotland) Citizens' Th. (1943–45); with the Arts Council Th., (Coventry, England, 1945–46); played Jack Manders in *Galway Handicap* (Lyric, Hammersmith, London, Feb. 4, 1947); and Clochet in *Men without Shadows* (Lyric, Hammersmith, July 17, 1947).

Mr. Carey directed a double-bill, *A Pound on Demand* and *Happy as Larry* (Mercury, Sept. 19, 1947); *The Playboy of the Western World* (Mercury, Mar. 11, 1948); and *Georgia Story* (New Lindsay, July 1, 1948); and was associate director of the Salisbury Arts Th. (1948–49).

He was director of the Bristol Old Vic Co. (1949–54), staging *The Cocktail Party, Traveller without Luggage,* and the following, many of which were also presented in London, *Two Gentlemen of Verona* (Old Vic, June 30, 1952); *Henry V* (Old Vic, Oct. 17, 1957); *Waiting for Godot* (Bristol Old Vic, Winter 1957); a musical adaptation of *The Playboy of the Western World,* entitled *The Heart's a Wonder* (Westminster, London, Sept. 18, 1958); and *Mr. Fox of Venice* (Piccadilly, Apr. 15, 1959).

He directed *The Cherry Orchard* and *The Taming of the Shrew* (Ottawa, Canada, 1959); *Follow That Girl* (Vaudeville, London, Mar. 17, 1960); and *Othello* (Th. Nationale de Belgique, Brussels, Belgium, 1960); *The Truth About Billy Newton* (Playhouse Th., Salisbury, England, Jan. 18, 1960); *Hooray for Daisy* (Lyric, Hammersmith, Dec. 20, 1960); *Mam'zelle Nitouche* (Nottingham Playhouse, Apr. 11, 1961); *The Golden Years* (Royal Court, Liverpool, June 26, 1961); and *Twelfth Night* (Ludlow Festival, June 26, 1962; Open Air Th., Regent's Park, London, July 11, 1962).

In 1963, Mr. Carey was appointed artistic director of the Bristol Old Vic for a fourteen-week tour that took the company to India, Pakistan, and Ceylon giving performances of *Hamlet* and *A Man for All Seasons,* both directed by Mr. Carey. Following return to England, Mr. Carey directed *The Golden Rivet* (Royal, Bristol, Oct. 22, 1963); *The Life in My Hands* (Nottingham Playhouse, 1964); *Armstrong's Last Goodnight* (Citizens', Glasgow, Scotland, May 5, 1964); *A Scent of Flowers* (Old Vic, Bristol, England, 1965); *The Cherry Orchard* (Nottingham Playhouse, 1965); *Volpone* (Nottingham Playhouse, 1965); *When the Saints Go Cycling In* (Gate Th., Dublin Festival, Ireland, Sept. 27, 1965); and *The Happiest Days of Your Life* (Old Vic, Bristol, England, 1965).

He also directed *Juno and the Paycock* (Gaiety, Dublin, Aug. 1, 1966); and for the Bristol Old Vic *The Playboy of the Western World* (1966); *Hedda Gabler* (Royal, Bristol, England, Sept. 28, 1966); *I'll Get My Man* (Royal, Dec. 26, 1966); *The Way of the World* (1967); and *D. P.* (Little Th., Bristol, Apr. 25, 1967). He directed *Hobson's Choice* (Alhambra, Bradford, England, Sept. 2, 1968); played Telyegin in *Uncle Vanya* (Royal Court, London, Feb. 24, 1970); and played Gunga Din in *Chez Nous* (Globe, London, Feb. 6, 1974).

Recreation. Walking, drinking.

CAREY, JOYCE. Actress, playwright. b. Joyce Lilian Carey, Mar. 30, 1905, London, England, to Gerald Lawrence and Lilian (Braithwaite) Carey. Father, actor; mother, actress. Attended Waterside Sch., Westgate-on-Sea; Queen's Gate Sch. London. Studied acting with Kate Rorke at Florence Eltinger Drama Sch. Member of AEA; SAG; Dramatists Guild. Address: (home) 12 Chesham St., London S.W.1, England tel. Belgravia 7106; (bus.) "Essanay," National House, 60 Wardour St., London W.1, England tel. Gerard 5158.

Theatre. Miss Carey made her debut playing Katherine in an all-woman cast of *Henry V* (Queen's, London, June 30, 1916); followed by Hilda Gregory in *Mr. Wu* (Strand, Oct. 14, 1916); Jacqueline in *The Aristocrat* (St. James's, Jan. 25, 1917); Miss Hooker in *Sheila* (St. James's, June 1917); Miss Phelps in *One Hour of Life* (Kingsway, Oct. 1917); Hildegrade Culver in *The Title* (Royalty, July 20, 1918); Gwendolyn Ralston in *Nothing But the Truth* (Savoy, Apr. 1919).

During Aug. 1919, at the Shakespeare Memorial Th., (Stratford-upon-Avon), she played Anne Page in *The Merry Wives of Windsor,* Perdita in *The Winter's Tale, Titania in A Midsummer Night's Dream,* Miranda in *The Tempest,* and Juliet in *Romeo and Juliet.*

Miss Carey appeared as Meg in *Little Women* (New, London, Nov. 10, 1910); Leonora in *The Young Person in Pink* (Prince of Wales's, Feb. 10, 1920), and also appeared in its revivals (Haymarket, Mar. 29, 1920; Adelphi, July 13, 1923); Jessica in *The Merchant of Venice* (Duke of York's, Mar. 1920); Posario in *The Romantic Young Lady* (Royalty, Sept. 1920); Miranda in *The Tempest* (Aldwych, Feb. 1, 1921); and Elsie Challoner in *The Charm School* (Prince of Wales's, Mar. 1921), also touring in it.

She again appeared as Katherine in an all-woman cast of *Henry V* (Strand, London, Apr. 26, 1921); played Joanna Trout in *Dear Brutus* (Wyndham's May 6, 1922); Hattie Friedman in *Partners Again* (Garrick, Feb. 28, 1923); Lady Angela Vale in *Good Luck* (Drury Lane, Sept. 27, 1923; Perdita in *The Winter's Tale* (Lyric, Hammersmith, Sept. 30, 1923); Hermia in *A Midsummer Night's Dream* (Kingsway, Nov. 13, 1923); Freda Fortnum in *Far Above Rubies* (Comedy, Mar. 1924); Celia in *As You Like It* (Regent, July 6, 1924); and Phyllis Burton in *Six Cylinder Love* (Garrick, Dec. 1924).

She played Sarah Hurst in the Bway production of *Easy Virtue* (Empire, Dec. 7, 1925), also playing this role in London (Duke of York's, June 9, 1926); played Meta in *The Road to Rome* (Playhouse, N.Y.C., Jan. 31, 1927); Vermilia in *The Jealous Moon* (Majestic, Nov. 20, 1928); Nita in *Paolo and Francesca* (Forrest, Apr. 1, 1929); Olivia in *Twelfth Night* (Maxine Elliott's Th., Oct. 15, 1930); Sonia

Tippett in *Art and Mrs. Bottle* (Maxine Elliott's Th., Nov. 18, 1930); Arabel Moulton Barrett in *The Barretts of Wimpole Street* (Empire, Feb. 9, 1931); Chrysothemis in *Electra* (Selwyn, Jan. 8, 1932); Emilia in *Lucrece* (Belasco, Dec. 20, 1932); and toured as Mary Howard in *When Ladies Meet* (Aug. 1933).

Miss Carey played Celia in *As You Like It* (Phoenix, London, Nov. 6, 1933); Julia Melville in *The Rivals* (Ambassadors', Jan. 18, 1934); and Lady Farrington in *Sweet Aloes,* which she also wrote, using the pseudonym of Jay Mallory (Wyndham's, Oct. 31, 1934); appeared in *The Shining Hour* (San Francisco, Calif., Jan. 1935); played Arabel Moulton-Barrett in *The Barretts of Wimpole Street* (Martin Beck Th., N.Y.C., Feb. 25, 1935); returned to London to resume her role of Lady Farrington in *Sweet Aloes,* and also played it on Bway (Booth, Mar. 4, 1936).

She played Mrs. Wadhurst in *Hands Across the Sea,* Barbara Faber in *The Astonished Heart* and Mabel Grace in *Red Peppers,* which were presented as *Tonight at 8:30* (Phoenix, London, Apr. 1936); and also these roles in N.Y.C. (National, Nov. 24, 1936). She played Joan Furze in *Spring Meeting* (Ambassadors', London, May 31, 1938); Gwendolen Fairfax in *The Importance of Being Earnest* (Globe, Jan. 31, 1939); toured with John Gielgud for ENSA (1940); toured in *Fumed Oak* and *Tonight at 8:30* (1941); and as Ruth in *Blithe Spirit,* Liz Essendine in *Present Laughter,* and Sylvia in *This Happy Breed* (1942); repeated her role in *Present Laughter* (Haymarket, London, Apr. 29, 1943; Apr. 16, 1947) and her role in *This Happy Breed* (Haymarket, Apr. 30, 1943).

She toured for ENSA as Ruth in *Blithe Spirit* (1943); played Rose Hardynge in *Marriage Playground* ("Q," Sept. 27, 1949); Dora Middleton in *The Watchman* ("Q," Feb. 6, 1951); Alice Winter in *The White Sheep of the Family* (Piccadilly, Oct. 11, 1951); Lady Harriet Ripley in *Quadrille* (Phoenix, Sept. 12, 1952); the title role in *The Duenna* (Westminster, July 28, 1954); Cuckoo Honey in *South Sea Bubble* (Lyric, Apr. 25, 1956); Isabel Sorodin in *Nude with Violin* (Globe, Nov. 7, 1956), and also played this role in N.Y.C. (Belasco, Nov. 14, 1957).

She played Liz Essendine in *Present Laughter* (Belasco, Jan. 31, 1958); Mrs. Walsworth in *Speaking of Murder* (St. Martin's, London, June 4, 1958); the Duchess Dupont-Dufour in *Traveller Without Luggage* (Arts, Jan. 29, 1959); Mrs. Lee in *The Wrong Side of the Park* (Cambridge, Feb. 3, 1960); was in *Dazzling Prospect* (Globe, 1961); *The Cupboard* (Arts, 1961); played Mrs. Sedley in a musical version of *Vanity Fair* (Queens Th., 1962); Lady Markby in *An Ideal Husband* (Garrick Th., Dec. 13, 1966); Aunt Juley in *Howards End* (New, Feb. 28, 1967); Belle Shlessinger in *Dear Octopus* (Haymarket, Dec. 7, 1967); May Beringer in *The Old Ladies* (Westminster Th., Nov. 4, 1969); and was in the musical *Trelawny* (Sadler's Wells, 1972).

Films. Miss Carey has appeared in such films as *In Which We Serve* (UA, 1942); *Blithe Spirit* (UA, 1945); *The Way to the Stars; Brief Encounter* (U, 1946); *Cry, the Beloved Country* (UA, 1952); and *Drabble* (1973).

Television. She has appeared in such British television plays as *Greyfriars Bobbie; The Family First; Before the Party; Naked Edge;* and *Not Many Mansions* (all 1960); *Barchester Towers; Top Secret* (both 1961); *No Hiding Place* (1962); *Take the Plunge* and *The Scissors* (both 1963); *Sergeant Cork; Man at St. Marks; Silas Marner; Sally; Tarnish on a Golden Boy;* and *Gideon's Way* (all 1964); *Wings of the Dove; Maigret* (both 1965); a repeat of *Sergeant Cork* (1966); *Only a Scream Away* (1967); *Father, Dear Father* (1968–73); *Avengers* and *Randall and Hopkirk* (both 1968); *Tropical Wednesdays* and *Hadleigh* (both 1970); *The Shopper; The Last Witness;* and *Pandora* (all 1971); and *The Coffee Lace* and *Barbara's Wedding* (both 1973).

CARIOU, LEN. Actor, director, artistic director. b. Sept. 30, 1939, Winnipeg, Manitoba, Canada. Educ. Holy Cross School and St. Paul's Coll., Winnipeg; professional training at Stratford (Ont.) Festival; Guthrie Th., Minneapolis, Minn.; Kristin Linklater, Fan Bennett, Judith Liebowitz. Address: Manitoba Th. Ctr., Winnipeg, Manitoba, Canada.

Theatre. On Apr. 1, 1975, Mr. Cariou became artistic director of the Manitoba Th. Ctr., Winnipeg, succeeding Edward Gilbert in that post.

Mr. Cariou began his theatrical career performing at Rainbow Stage, Winnipeg, first in the chorus of a production of *Damn Yankees* (June 1959), later in *the Boy Friend, Irma La Douce,* and other musicals. He appeared at the Manitoba Th. Ctr. for the first time in 1961, in the title role of *Mr. Roberts.* His later roles there included Orlando in *As You Like It,* Ralph in *The Shoemakers' Holiday,* Henry in *The Skin of Our Teeth;* he also appeared in *Mother Courage, The Taming of the Shrew, Who's Afraid of Virginia Woolf?, The Hostage, Andorra, The Tempest,* and *The Threepenny Opera.*

As a member of the Stratford (Ontario) Shakespeare Festival acting company (1961–65), he had roles in *The Tempest, Macbeth, Cyrano de Bergerac, The Taming of the Shrew,* and other plays. He was the Servant in *Troilus and Cressida* (June 17, 1963), appeared in *The Comedy of Errors* (June 19, 1963), played Servilius in *Timon of Athens* (July 29, 1963), Bushy in *Richard III* (June 15, 1964), Cléonte in *Le bourgeois gentilhomme* (June 16, 1964), and had several roles in *The Country Wife.*

At the 1964 Chichester (England) Festival, Mr. Cariou played Longaville in *Love's Labour's Lost* (Apr. 6, 1964), Cléonte in *Le bourgeois gentilhomme* (Apr. 7, 1964), and Servilius in *Timon of Athens* (Apr. 8, 1964). He became a member of the Tyrone Guthrie Th., Minneapolis, Minn., in 1966 and appeared there in *The Skin of Our Teeth, S. S. Glencairn,* as Orlando in *As You Like It* (June 2, 1966), as Ralph in *The Shoemaker's Holiday* (June 1, 1967), as Orestes in *The House of Atreus* (July 21, 1967), in *The Visit* (Sept. 11, 1967), and as Feste in *Twelfth Night.* He played Iago in *Othello* (Goodman Th., Chicago, Ill., Feb. 16, 1968); made his N.Y.C. debut as Orestes in the Guthrie Th. production of *The House of Atreus* (Billy Rose Th., Dec. 17, 1968); and appeared at the American Shakespeare Festival, Stratford, Conn., in *Much Ado About Nothing* (June 18, 1969); in the title role of *Henry V* (June 19, 1969); and in *The Three Sisters* (July 23, 1969). He repeated his performance in *Henry V* in N.Y.C. (ANTA Th., Nov. 10, 1969).

Mr. Cariou played (Mar. 30, 1970–May 1971) Bill Sampson in *Applause* (Palace, N.Y.C., Mar. 30, 1970); returned to the Guthrie Th. where he played the title role in *Cyrano de Bergerac* (matinee July 22, 1971), Petruchio in *The Taming of the Shrew* (evening July 22, 1971), and was in *The Diary of a Scoundrel* (Nov. 9, 1971). He returned to Bway as John Wheeler in *Night Watch* (Morosco, Feb. 28, 1972); became associate artistic director at the Guthrie Th. in 1972, where he directed *Of Mice and Men* (July 10, 1972) and played the title role in Sophocles' *Oedipus the King* (Oct. 24, 1972); again appeared (Feb. 25, 1973–Feb. 1974) on Bway, as Frederik Egerman in *A Little Night Music* (Sam S. Shubert Th., Feb. 25, 1973); directed *The Petrified Forest* (Th. at St. Clements, Jan. 22, 1974); played the title role in *King Lear* (Guthrie Th., Minneapolis, July 1, 1974); directed *The Crucible* (Guthrie Th., Aug. 20, 1974); and directed *Don't Call Back* (Helen Hayes Th., N.Y.C., Mar. 18, 1975).

Television. Mr. Cariou made his television debut as Ragnar Brovik in *The Master Builder* (CBC, Nov. 1965).

Awards. Mr. Cariou was nominated for Antoinette Perry (Tony) awards in 1970 and 1973, respectively, best actor in a musical for his performances in *Applause* and *A Little Night Music.*.

CARLINO, LEWIS JOHN. Playwright, screen writer. b. 1932, New York, N.Y. Attended El Camino Coll., Calif.; grad. Univ. of Southern Calif., Los Angeles, B.A.; M.A. (drama). Married; three children. Served in US Air Force. Member Playwrights Unit, Actors Studio, New Dramatists Comm.

Theatre. The Los Angeles, Calif., chapter of ANTA produced Mr. Carlino's *The Brick and the Rose: A Collage for Voices* (1957) and has also produced his *Used Car for Sale.* Mr. Carlino's other plays include *Junk Yard* (1959); *Piece and Precise* consisting of two one-act plays, *Objective Case* and *Mr. Flannery's Ocean* (White Barn Th., Westport, Conn., July 23, 1961; N.Y.C., 1962); *The Beach People* (Madison, Ohio, 1962); *High Sign* (1962); *Cages: Snowangel* and *Epiphany* (York Playhouse, N.Y.C., June 13, 1963); *Telemachus Clay: A Collage for Voices* (Writers' Stage, Nov. 15, 1963); *Doubletalk: Sarah and the Sax* and *The Dirty Old Man* (Th. de Lys, May 14, 1964); and *The Exercise* (Berkshire Festival, Stockbridge, Mass., Summer 1967; John Golden Th., N.Y.C., Apr. 24, 1968).

Films. Mr. Carlino wrote film scripts for *Seconds* (Par., 1966); *The Fox* (Claridge Pic., 1968); *The Brotherhood* (Par., 1968); *The Mechanic* (UA, 1972); and *Crazy Joe* (Col., 1974).

Television. Mr. Carlino wrote the script for *In Search of America* (ABC, 1971).

Awards. Mr. Carlino was awarded the British Drama League Prize (1960); the Vernon Rice Award (1964) as most promising off-Bway playwright; Huntington Hartford and Yaddo fellowships; and a Rockefeller Foundation grant.

CARLISLE, KITTY. Actress, singer. b. Catharine Conn, Sept. 3, 1915, New Orleans, La., to Dr. Joseph and Hortense (Holzman) Conn. Father, physician. Attended Newman Sch., New Orleans; Miss McGehee's Sch., New Orleans; Chateau Mont Choisi, Lausanne, Switz.; studied with Princess Mestchersky in Paris, Fr.; attended RADA, London, Eng. Married Aug. 10, 1946, to Moss Hart, playwright and director (dec. Dec. 20, 1961); one son, one daughter. Member of AEA; AFTRA. Address: (home) 32 E. 64th St., New York, NY 10020; (bus.) c/o Hyman & Hart, 1501 Broadway, New York, NY, 10036.

Theatre. Miss Carlisle made her New York debut in the title role of a "tabloid" version of *Rio Rita* (Capitol, 1932); subsequently appeared as Prince Orlofsky in *Champagne, Sec* (Morosco, Oct. 14, 1933); Katarina in *White Horse Inn* (Center, Oct. 1, 1936); Marie Hiller, Charlotte, and Franzi in *Three Waltzes* (Majestic, Dec. 25, 1937); Pamela Gibson in *Walk with Music* (Ethel Barrymore Th., June 14, 1940); Lucretia in *The Rape of Lucretia* (Ziegfeld, Dec. 29, 1948); Alice Walters in *Anniversary Waltz* (Broadhurst, Apr. 7, 1954); and Katherine in *Kiss Me, Kate* (NY City Ctr., May 9, 1956).

She appeared as Diana Lake in *French without Tears* (Ridgeway, White Plains, N.Y., July 1938); Sonia in *The Merry Widow* (Boston Opera House, Mass., May 1943); Gilda in *Design for Living* (Cleveland, Ohio, July 1943); Leonora in *There's Always Juliet* (Philadelphia, Pa., June 1944); played in a stock production of *The Man Who Came to Dinner* (Bucks County Playhouse, New Hope, Pa.; Olney Playhouse, Md., 1949); Liza in *Lady in the Dark* (Bucks County Playhouse, 1952); Prince Orlowsky in *Die Fledermaus* (Metropolitan Opera, N.Y.C., 1966–67 season and in the 1972 Summer Parks program); *Light Up the Sky* (summer stock tour, 1969–72); and *Don't Frighten the Horses* (summer stock tour, 1973).

Films. Miss Carlisle made her debut in *Murder at the Vanities* (Par., 1934); subsequently appeared in *She Loves Me Not* (Par., 1934); *Here Is My Heart* (Par., 1934); and *A Night at the Opera* (MGM, 1936).

Television. She has been a panelist on several television shows, including I've Got a Secret (CBS) and To Tell the Truth (CBS); and played in Women on the Move (NBC).

Other Activities. Miss Carlisle is vice-chairman of the New York State Council of the Arts; and a member of the Overseers Visiting committee for the Music Dept. and Associate Fellow at Yale Univ.

Recreation. Winter sports, swimming, horseback riding.

CARMINES, AL. Minister, performer, director, playwright, composer, lyricist. b. Alvin Allison Carmines, Jr., July 25, 1936, Hampton, Va., to Alvin Allison and Katherine (Graham) Carmines. Grad. Swarthmore Coll., B.A. 1958; Union Theological Seminary, B.D. 1961; S.T.M. 1963. Address: (home) 237 Thompson St., New York, NY 10012; (bus.) 55 Washington Square South, New York, NY 10012.

Theatre. Mr. Carmines, associate minister of Judson Memorial Church, N.Y.C., formed the Judson Poets' Th. in 1961 at the request of the church's minister, Rev. Howard R. Moody, as part of the church's general effort to bring together creativity in the arts and the act of religious worship. The first program was a double-bill, *The Great American Desert* and *The Breasts of Tiresias* (Nov. 18, 1961). Mr. Carmines composed his first music for a Judson production with *Vaudeville Skit* (Aug. 24, 1962); he wrote songs for *The Wax Engine* (June 13, 1963); music for *What Happened*, in which he also appeared (Sept. 19, 1963); and *An Old Tune* (Dec. 19, 1963). He composed music for and appeared as Father Shenanagan in *Home Movies* (Mar. 19, 1964; transferred to Provincetown Playhouse, May 11, 1964); wrote songs for *Patter for a Soft Shoe Dance* (July 9, 1964); *Sing Ho for a Bear* (Dec. 17, 1964); and the score for *Promenade* (Apr. 8, 1965).

He also wrote music for *A Beautiful Day* (Dec. 16, 1965); *Pomegranada* (Mar. 4, 1966); *San Francisco's Burning* (Jan. 1, 1967); *Song of Songs* (Feb. 1967); and, with Robert Cosmos Savage, for *Gorilla Queen* (Mar. 10, 1967; transferred to Martinique, Apr. 24, 1967); wrote music for *Successful Life of 3* (May 18, 1967); *Celebrations* (June 15, 1967); *In Circles*, in which he also played Dole (Oct. 6, 1967; transferred to Cherry Lane, Nov. 5, 1967); *Untitled Play* (1967); wrote the opera *The Sayings of Mao Tse-tung*, in which he also appeared (Jan. 26, 1968); music for *The Line of Least Existence* (Mar. 15, 1968); appeared in a one-man show, *Songs by Carmines* (Gramercy Arts Th., June 25, 1968); wrote music and played the piano for *Peace* (Nov. 7, 1968; tranferred to Astor Place Th., Feb. 27, 1969); and wrote music for *The Poor Little Match Girl* (Dec. 22, 1968).

Mr. Carmines wrote *The Urban Crisis* (Oct. 9, 1969); the oratorio *Christmas Rappings*, which he also directed (Dec. 14, 1969); wrote, with Theo Barnes, *About Time* (Apr. 12, 1970); wrote *The Playful Tyrant* (Oct. 18, 1970); the oratorio *The Journey of Snow White* (Feb. 26, 1971); and composed music for and wrote, with David Epstein, lyrics for *Wanted* (Sept. 17, 1971). He wrote the book, music, and lyrics for and directed *Joan* (Nov. 19, 1971; transferred to Circle in the Square, June 19, 1972); *A Look at the Fifties* (Apr. 14, 1972); wrote words and music for and directed *The Life of a Man* (Sept. 29, 1972); composed music for *The Making of Americans*, in which he also appeared (Nov. 10, 1972); wrote words and music for, appeared in, and directed *The Faggot* (Apr. 13, 1973; transferred to the Truck and Warehouse Th., June 18, 1973); wrote, directed, and appeared in *Religion* (Oct. 28, 1973); wrote book, lyrics, and music for and directed *The Future* (Mar. 25, 1974); wrote book, lyrics, and music for *The Duel* (Brooklyn Acad. of Music, Apr. 24, 1974); music for *Listen to Me* (Oct. 18, 1974); conceived and directed *Christmas '74* (Dec. 1974); wrote and directed *Sacred and Profane Love* (Feb. 1975); and wrote music and lyrics for *Why I Love New York* (Oct. 1975).

Night Clubs. Mr. Carmines appeared at the Upstairs at the Downstairs, N.Y.C. (Feb. 1972).

Other Activities. Mr. Carmines preaches, lectures, teaches, and has written film criticism for the magazine *Motive*.

Discography. Recordings have been made of *In Circles* (Avant-Garde), *Promenade* (RCA-Victor), *Peace* (Metromedia), and *Joan* (Judson).

Awards. In 1964, *What Happened* received a *Village Voice* off-Bway (Obie) Award as best musical production off-Bway (1963–64), *Home Movies* was awarded an Obie as a distinguished off-Bway play, and the Judson Memorial Church received a special Obie citation for innovativeness and sponsorship of experimentation in the theatre. In 1968, *In Circles*, received an Obie as best off-Bway musical, and Mr. Carmines received a Drama Desk–Vernon Rice Award for composing the score for that production. Mr. Carmines also received a Drama Desk Award in 1969 for composing the score for *Peace*, and in 1974 he was named outstanding composer by the Drama Desk for *The Faggot*..

CARNEY, ART. Actor. b. Arthur William Carney, Nov. 4, 1918, Mount Vernon, N.Y., to Edward M. and Helen (Farrell) Carney. Father, newspaperman. Grad. A.B. Davis H.S., Mt. Vernon, 1937. Married Aug. 15, 1940, to Jean Myers (marr. dis. 1966); two sons, one daughter; married Dec. 22, 1966, to Barbara Isaac. Relative in theatre: son, Brian, musician. Served US Army, Infantry, ETO, 1944–45; awarded Purple Heart; rank, Pfc. Member of AFTRA; SAG; AEA; The Players.

Theatre. Mr. Carney toured New England summer theatres as Richard Sherman in *The Seven Year Itch* (1956), and played Elwood P. Dowd in *Harvey* (Ivoryton Playhouse, Conn., Summer).

He made his N.Y.C. debut as James Hyland in *The Rope Dancers* (Cort, Nov. 20, 1957); played Frank Michaelson in *Take Her, She's Mine* (Cort, Dec. 21, 1961); and toured New England theatres as Harold Carol in *Time Out for Ginger* (1963). He was Felix Ungar in *The Odd Couple* (Plymouth, Mar. 10, 1965); F.D.R.'s voice in *Flora, the Red Menace* (Alvin, May 11, 1965); Andy Tracey in *Lovers* (Vivian Beaumont Th., July 25, 1968; and on tour, Feb.–June 1969); replaced (June 5, 1972) Peter Falk as Mel Edison in *The Prisoner of Second Avenue* (Eugene O'Neill Th., Nov. 11, 1971); and played Mel Edison in California (Ahmanson Th., Los Angeles, Oct. 17, 1972).

Films. He appeared in *Pot o' Gold* (UA, 1941); *The Yellow Rolls Royce* (MGM, 1965); *Harry and Tonto* (20th-Fox, 1974), which originated as a television film (ABC, 1973); *W. W. and the Dixie Dancekings* (20th-Fox, 1975); and *Won Ton Ton, The Dog Who Saved Hollywood* (Par., 1976).

Television. Mr. Carney made his debut on the Morey Amsterdam Show, playing the Doorman in "The Golden Goose" and Newton the Waiter in "Silver Swan" (1948).

He appeared as Ed Norton in "The Honeymooners" segment of the Jackie Gleason Show (CBS, 1950–59).

He appeared in *Uncle Harry* (1954); *Panama Hattie* (1954); *Burlesque* (Kraft Television Th., NBC, 1954); *The Incredible World of Horace Ford* (CBS, 1955); Omnibus (1955); *Charley's Aunt* (Playhouse 90, CBS, 1957); played Robert Briscoe, the Jewish Lord High Mayor of Dublin, Ireland, in *Incredible Irishman* (Playhouse 90, CBS, 1957); appeared on the Sid Caesar Show (NBC, 1958); in *Harvey* (1958); *Safety for the Witness* (Alfred Hitchcock Presents, CBS, 1958); and narrated *Peter and the Wolf* (ABC, 1958, 1959).

He performed with Sid Caesar on the Art Carney Show (NBC, 1959); appeared in *Art Carney Meets the Sorcerer's Apprentice* (ABC, 1959); *America Pauses for May* (CBS, 1959); *Small World Isn't It?* (NBC, 1959); *Our Town* (NBC, 1959); *The Velvet Alley* (CBS, 1959); *Very Important People* (NBC, 1959); *The Man in the Dog Suit* (NBC, 1960); *Three in One* (NBC, 1960); *Victory* (NBC, 1960); *Full Moon Over Brooklyn* (NBC, 1960); *Call Me Back*, a one-man show (NBC, 1960); *The Right Man* (CBS, 1960); *The Triumph of Gerald Q. West* (DuPont Show, NBC, 1963); *A Day Like Today* (DuPont Show, NBC, 1964); *The Timothy Heist* (Bob Hope Chrysler Th., NBC, 1964); and the Carol Channing Special (NBC, Sept. 9, 1970). He also appeared on episodes of Twilight Zone (CBS, 1960); Mr. Broadway (CBS, 1964); Batman (ABC, 1966); Men from Shiloh (NBC, 1970); and was in the pilot for the series The Snoop Sisters (NBC, Dec. 1972); on the special *Happy Anniversary & Goodbye* (CBS, Nov. 19, 1974); and was narrator on *Middle Age Blues* (Ind., July 13, 1975).

He has also appeared on a number of variety and talk shows, including the Ed Sullivan Show (CBS); the Dinah Shore Show (NBC); the Perry Como Show (NBC); and the Tonight Show (NBC).

Awards. For his performance as Ed Norton in "The Honeymooners" on the Jackie Gleason Show, Mr. Carney (with Jackie Gleason who played Ralph Kramden in the sketches), received three NATAS (Emmy) Awards (1953–54–55) and the Sylvania Award as "Outstanding Comedy Team" (1954).

He also received Sylvania awards for his narration of *Peter and the Wolf* (1958) and *Very Important People* (1959); was nominated for an Antoinette Perry (Tony) Award (1958–59) as best actor for his performance in *Lovers;* and received an Academy (Oscar) Award (1975) as best actor for his performance in *Harry and Tonto*.

Recreation. Bowling, ping-pong, horse shoes, music, photography, pool.

CARNEY, FRANK. Playwright, actor, producer. b. John Francis Carney, Apr. 13, 1904, Westport, County Mayo, Ireland, to Patrick Joseph and Sarah (King) Carney. Father, trader. Grad. St. Jarlath's Coll., Tuam, Ireland, 1921; St. Patrick's Coll., Maynooth, Ireland, B.A. (with first honors) 1924. Married Mar. 18, 1934, to Sheilah Eileen O'-Brien; one daughter. Member of Dramatists Guild; Authors Guild, Ireland; P.E.N., Dublin. Address: Murrisk, Greenfield Park, Ballsbridge, Dublin, Ireland.

Pre-Theatre. Civil servant.

Theatre. Mr. Carney wrote *They Went by the Bus* (Abbey, Dublin, Oct. 19, 1939); *Peeping Tom* (Abbey, Nov. 25, 1940); *House of Cards* (Olympia, Mar. 13, 1944); *Doctor's Boy* (Gaiety, Mar. 16, 1945); *The Righteous Are Bold* (Abbey, July 29, 1946); and *The Man Who Climbed the Hill* (Damar, June 29, 1959).

The Righteous Are Bold has also been produced in Scotland (Glasgow Citizens Th., Feb. 3, 1947); London (Embassy, Mar. 22, 1948); N.Y.C. (Holiday, Dec. 22, 1955); and other theatres in Great Britain, Australia, South Africa, Canada, New Zealand, and at US universities.

Radio. Mr. Carney has written, produced and acted in plays and documentaries (Radio Eireann, Dublin, 1935–40).

Recreation. Golf; swimming; gardening; collecting rare books, pictures, horse-brasses, old silver and china; European travel; Siamese cats; plus chit-chat with literary-artistic people in front of Irish turf fires complete with whiskey punch.

CARNOVSKY, MORRIS. Actor, director, teacher. b. Sept. 5, 1897, St. Louis, Mo., to Isaac and Jennie Carnovsky. Father, grocer. Grad. Teatman H.S., St. Louis; Washington Univ., A.B. (Phi Beta Kappa) 1920. Studied acting with Emanuel Reacher, 1922; Florence Lasersohn, Michael Chekhov, 1935. Married 1922 (marr. dis. 1933); married 1941 to Phoebe Brand, actress, teacher, director; one son. Served SATC, 1918–19; rank, Pvt. Member of AEA; AFTRA; SAG. Address: 309 W. 104th St., New York, NY 10025, tel. (212) UN 5-5560.

Theatre. Mr. Carnovsky made his first stage appearance in the title role of his high-school production of *Disraeli* (June 1914); appeared at the St. Louis (Mo.) Artists' Guild Th. as a Minimalist in *A Bunch of Bolsheviki* and The Chamberlain in *The Tents of the Arabs* (Mar. 20, 1918); subsequently appeared in productions with the Henry Jewitt Players and the E. E. Clive Co. (Boston, Mass.); and made his N.Y.C. debut as Reb Aaron in *The God of Vengeance* (Provincetown Playhouse, Dec. 20, 1922).

As a member of the Th. Guild Acting Co. (1924–30), he played the Commissioner of Police and the Magistrate in *The Failures* (Garrick, Nov. 19, 1923); La Hire and Brother Martin in Winifred Lenihan's *Saint Joan* (Garrick, Dec. 28, 1923); Philip Speed in *The Creeking Chair* (Lyceum, Feb. 22, 1926); a General and a Priest in *Juarez and Maximilian* (Guild, Oct. 11, 1926); the Second Federal Man in *Ned McCobb's Daughter* (John Golden Th.,

Nov. 29, 1926); Alypsha in *The Brothers Karamazov* (Guild, Jan. 3, 1927); Centuri and Aggazi in *Right You Are, If You Think You Are* (Guild, Mar. 2, 1927); Dr. Schutzmacher in *The Doctor's Dilemma* (Guild, Nov. 21, 1927); Kublai the Great Khan in *Marco Millions* (Guild, Jan. 9, 1928); the Judge in *Volpone* (Guild, Apr. 8, 1928); Bezchyba in *Camel Through the Needle's Eye* (Martin Beck Th., Apr. 14, 1929); the title role in *Uncle Vanya* (Morosco, May 24, 1929); The Cabinet Minister in *The Apple Cart* (Martin Beck Th., Feb. 24, 1930); the Grandfather in *Hotel Universe* (Martin Beck Th., Apr. 14, 1930); and Francis Bacon in *Elizabeth the Queen* (Guild, Nov. 3, 1930).

Mr. Carnovsky appeared as Uncle Bob in *The House of Connelly* (Martin Beck Th., Sept. 28, 1931); played various roles in the revue *1931* (Mansfield, Dec. 10, 1931); Father Martinez in *Night Over Taos* (48 St. Th., Mar. 9, 1932); Rufus Sonnenberg in *Success Story* (Maxine Elliott's Th., Sept. 26, 1932); Levering in *Both Your Houses* (Royale, Mar. 6, 1933); Dr. Levine in *Man in White* (Broadhurst, Sept. 26, 1933); Dr. Lewis Golden in *Gentlewoman* (Cort, Mar. 22, 1934); Will Parrot in *Gold Eagle Guy* (Morosco, Nov. 28, 1934); Jacob in *Awake and Sing* (Belasco, Feb. 19, 1935); Mr. Gordon in *Paradise Lost* (Longacre, Dec. 9, 1935); the Speaker in *The Case of Clyde Griffiths* (Ethel Barrymore Th., Mar. 13, 1936); Dr. Mahodan in *Johnny Johnson* (44 St. Th., Nov. 19, 1936); Mr. Bonaparte in *Golden Boy* (Belasco, N.Y.C., Nov. 4, 1937; St. James's, London, June 21, 1938); played Ben Stark in *Rocket to the Moon* (Belasco, N.Y.C., Nov. 24, 1938); Captain Joshua in *Thunder Rock* (Mansfield, Nov. 14, 1939); and Rosenberger in *Night Music* (Broadhurst, Feb. 22, 1940).

As a member of the Actors Lab. Th. (Hollywood, Calif., 1940–50), he directed *Volpone; The Dragon; Monday's Heroes;* and *Distant Isles.* He appeared as John Adams Kent in *Suzanna and the Elders* (Morosco, N.Y.C., Oct. 29, 1940); Mr. Appopolous in *My Sister Eileen* (Biltmore, Dec. 26, 1940); David Cole in *Cafe Crown* (Cort, Jan. 23, 1942); Kulkov in *Counterattack* (Windsor, Mar. 3, 1943); Sam Blumenfield in *Joy to the World* (Plymouth, Mar. 18, 1948); Mayor Stockman in *An Enemy of the People* (Broadhurst, Dec. 28, 1950); Aaron Katz and the Presiding Angel in *The World of Sholom Aleichem* (Barbizon-Plaza, May 1953); Tzaddik in *The Dybbuk* (4th St. Th., Oct. 26, 1954); Audrey in *The Three Sisters* (4th St. Th., Feb. 25, 1955); Priam in *Tiger at the Gates* (Plymouth, Oct. 3, 1955); and Probus in *The Lovers* (Martin Beck Th., May 10, 1956).

At the Amer. Shakespeare Festival (Stratford, Conn.), he played the Earl of Salisbury in *King John* (June 26, 1956); Provost in *Measure for Measure* (June 27, 1956); and Gremio in *The Taming of the Shrew* (Aug. 5, 1956); at the Phoenix Th., N.Y.C., he played Provost in *Measure for Measure* (Jan. 22, 1957); and Gremio in *The Taming of the Shrew* (Feb. 20, 1957); Shylock in *The Merchant of Venice* (Amer. Shakespeare Festival, July 10, 1957); the Connoisseur in *Nude with Violin* (Belasco, N.Y.C., Nov. 14, 1957); and at the Amer. Shakespeare Festival (Stratford, Conn.), Claudius in *Hamlet* (June 19, 1958), and Quince in *Twelfth Night* (June 20, 1958).

He appeared as the Father in *The Cold Wind and the Warm* (Morosco, N.Y.C., Dec. 8, 1958); at the Amer. Shakespeare Festival, Capulet in *Romeo and Juliet* (June 12, 1959) and Dr. Caius in *The Merry Wives of Windsor* (July 8, 1959); at the Goodman Memorial Th. (Chicago, Ill.), Shylock in *The Merchant of Venice* (Oct. 1959); and at the Amer. Shakespeare Festival (Stratford, Conn.), Feste in *Twelfth Night* (June 8, 1960), Prospero in *The Tempest* (July 19, 1960), and Lepidus in *Antony and Cleopatra* (July 31, 1960).

He played the Logician in *Rhinoceros* (Longacre, N.Y.C., Jan. 9, 1961); Mr. Baker in *Come Blow Your Horn* (Brooks Atkinson Th., Feb. 22, 1961); and at the San Diego (Calif.) Summer Festival, Malvolio in *Twelfth Night* (June 27, 1961), Shylock in *The Merchant of Venice* (July 5, 1961), and King Edward IV in *Richard III* (July 26, 1961).

He played Morris Siegal in *A Family Affair* (Billy Rose Th., N.Y.C., Jan. 27, 1962); Adzac in *The Caucasian Chalk Circle* (Goodman Memorial Th., Chicago, Ill., May 11, 1962); the title role in *King Lear* (Amer. Shakespeare Festival, June 9, 1963), and repeated this role for the Theatre Group productions (Schoenberg Hall, Univ. of California at Los Angeles, June 6, 1964; Pilgrimage Th., Hollywood, Calif., July 10, 1964).

He was Dr. Max Faessler in *The Man With the Perfect Wife* (Royal Poinciana Playhouse, Palm Beach, Fla., Mar. 22, 1965; Coconut Grove Playhouse, Miami, Fla., Mar. 30, 1965); again played the title role in *King Lear* (Amer. Shakespeare Festival, June 23, 1965; Spingold Th., Brandeis Univ., Waltham, Mass., Feb. 3, 1966); and played the title role in *Galileo* (Goodman Memorial Th., Chicago, Ill., May 6, 1966). He appeared at the Amer. Shakespeare Festival in 1967 as Creon in Jean Anouilh's *Antigone* (June 18) and Shylock in *The Merchant of Venice* (June 20); played the lead in *Schewyk in the Second World War* (Spingold Th., Brandeis Univ., Nov. 1, 1967); toured (Jan.–May 1969) as Galileo in *Lamp at Midnight;* and returned to the Amer. Shakespeare Festival, where he played Polonius in *Hamlet* (June 18, 1969) and Chebutikin in *The Three Sisters* (July 23, 1969). He played the title role in *Yegor Bulichov* (Long Wharf Th., New Haven, Conn., Dec. 18, 1970; Prospero in *The Tempest* (Amer. Shakespeare Festival, June 12, 1971); directed *the Country Woman* and *The Wedding* and acted in *A Swan Song,* three short Russian plays, which he also adapted and which were billed as *Troika: An Evening of Russian Comedy* (Long Wharf Th., Mar. 17, 1972); and again played *King Lear* (Amer. Shakespeare Festival, May 17, 1975).

Films. Mr. Carnovsky made his first appearence as Anatole France in *The Life of Emile Zola* (WB, 1937); followed by *Edge of Darkness* (WB, 1943); *Address Unknown* (Col., 1944); *Rhapsody in Blue* (WB, 1945); *Our Vines Have Tender Grapes* (MGM, 1945); *Dead Reckoning* (Col., 1947); *Saigon* (Par., 1948); *Man-Eater of Kumaon* (U, 1948); *Cyrano de Bergerac* (UA, 1950); and *A View from the Bridge* (Continental, 1962).

Television. He appeared as Creon in *Medea* (Play of the Week, WNTA, 1961); as the Rabbi, Presiding Angel, and Mr. Katz in *The World of Sholom Aleichem* (Play of the Week, WNTA, 1961); and as Judge Julius Hoffman in *The Chicago Eight Conspiracy Trial* (BBC, England, Oct. 1970; later in US on PBS).

Other Activities. Mr. Carnovsky was a founder (1935) and a member of the Group Th., N.Y.C., until 1939. He taught at the American Shakespeare Festival, Stratford, Conn. (1956–63), as well acted there, and he was an adjunct professor on the faculty of the Theatre Arts Dept., Brandeis Univ., Waltham, Mass. (1966–69).

CARO, WARREN. Production executive, author, lecturer. b. Feb. 24, 1907, Brooklyn, N.Y., to Arthur B. and Madeline (Davidsburg) Caro. Father, manufacturer of costume jewelry. Grad. Boys' H.S., N.Y.C., 1923; Cornell Univ., B.A. 1927, LL.B. 1929. Married Nov. 25, 1955, to Nancy Kelly, actress (marr. dis. 1967); one daughter. Relative in theatre: cousin, Jo Mielziner, scenic designer. Served with USCGR, 1942–45; rank, Lt. Comdr. Member of Board of Governors of League of N.Y. Theatres; National Academy of the Living Theatre (dir.); Independent Book Office (bd. of dir.); New Dramatists Comm. (adv. bd.); AADA (trustee); NATAS (founder NY chapter); Amer. TV Society (a founder; 1st pres.); Radio and Television Executives' Society; Shaw Society of America (a founder); NY Bar Assn. Address: (home) 159 W. 53rd St., New York, NY 10019; (bus.) 234 W. 44th St., New York, NY 10036, tel. (212) 246-9500.

Pre-Theatre. Lawyer.

Theatre. Since 1967, Mr. Caro has been director of theatre operations for the Shubert organization, in charge of the booking and supervision of seventeen theatres in New York and six across the country. Prior to his association with the Shubert organization, Mr. Caro was executive director of the Theatre Guild-American Th. Society, the Guild's national subscription affiliate. As vice-president of the Theatre Guild Productions, Inc., he served as director of the production company, with Armina Marshall and Philip Langner.

Mr. Caro served at the request of the State Dept., as chairman of the US delegation to the first Congress of ITI sponsored by UNESCO, at Prague, Czechoslovakia, participating in the drafting of its charter and by-laws and in the formulation of plans for the exchange of theatrical productions throughout the world (1948); and represented the US, with Clarence Derwent and Rosamond Gilder of ANTA, at the annual ITI Congress at Zurich (1949).

Mr. Caro has been a member of the advisory committee of the John F. Kennedy Center for the Performing Arts (Washington, D.C.).

Awards. Mr. Caro received a special Antionette Perry (Tony) Award for inaugurating and producing, with Lawrence Langner and Armina Marshall the Theatre Guild-American Repertory Co. (1961), an organization that toured abroad under US State Dept. auspices and that included Helen Hayes, June Havoc, Leif Erickson, and Helen Mencken.

Recreation. Music.

CARPENTER, CARLETON. Actor, composer. b. Carleton Upham Carpenter, II, July 10, 1926, to Carleton Upham and Marjorie (Main) Carpenter. Father, builder; mother, bridge expert. Grad. Bennington (Vt.) H.S., 1944. Served USN, 1943–45, PTO. Member of AEA; SAG; AFTRA; ASCAP; Dramatists Guild. Address: Chardavoyne Road, Warwick, NY 10990.

Theatre. Mr. Carpenter made his stage debut at four as a singer in a variety show (State Armory, Bennington, Vt., 1930); his professional debut as a magician in a touring show (Gen. Stark Th., Bennington, Vt., 1935); worked in carnivals; made his Bway debut as Tittman in *Bright Boy* (Playhouse Th., Mar. 2, 1944); subsequently appeared as Rinn in *Career Angel* (Natl., May 23, 1944); in the revue *Three to Make Ready* (Adelphi, Mar. 7, 1946); Larry Masters in *The Magic Touch* (International, Sept. 3, 1947); the First Sailor in the pre-Bway tryout of *The Big People* (opened Lyric, Bridgeport, Conn., Sept. 20, 1947; closed Locust St. Th., Philadelphia, Pa., Sept. 27, 1947); and Raunchy in the pre-Bway tryout of *Out of Dust* (1949).

Mr. Carpenter has appeared in stock and on tour in *Remains To Be Seen,* (La Jolla Playhouse, Calif., 1952); *Mr. Roberts* (Salt Creek, Chicago, Ill., 1953); *The Rainmaker* (Hampton Playhouse, N.H., 1955); *King of Hearts* (Somerset, Mass., 1955); *Where's Charley?* (Summer 1956); and *Here's Music* (Corning, N.Y., 1956).

Mr. Carpenter appeared in *John Murray Anderson's Almanac* (Imperial, N.Y.C., Dec. 10, 1953); played Lee in *A Box of Watercolors* (Bway Cong. Church, Feb. 17, 1957); Maxime in *Hotel Paradiso* (Henry Miller's Th., Apr. 11, 1957); appeared in *The Milky Way* (Barnsville, Pa., 1957); *Beachcomber* (Royal Poinciana Playhouse, West Palm Beach, Fla., 1959); *French Postcards* (Civic, Los Angeles, Calif., 1960); *The Boy Friend* and *Cinderella* (Light Opera, Sacramento, Calif., 1961); *Little Mary Sunshine* (Le Grande, Los Angeles, Calif., 1961); played David Greenfield in *A Stage Affair* (Cherry Lane, N.Y.C., Jan. 16, 1962); toured as Albert Peterson in *Bye Bye Birdie* (1962); was an understudy for cast members of *Boeing-Boeing* (Cort, N.Y.C., Feb. 2, 1965); toured as Cornelius Hackl in *Hello Dolly!* with international company, then played in N.Y.C. company (St. James Th.), and toured with national company (1965–66); was standby for William Redfield in *A Minor Adjustment* (Brooks Atkinson Th., N.Y.C., Oct. 6, 1967); toured with *Lock Up Your Daughters* (1968), *Oklahoma!,* and *How to Succeed in Business Without Really Trying,* and directed two companies of the last; was in *Your Own Thing* (Wilbur Th., Boston, 1969); replaced (Nov. 11, 1969) David Daniels as Michael in *The Boys in the Band* (Th. Four, N.Y.C., Apr. 15, 1968); appeared in *Lyle* (McAlpin Rooftop Th., Mar. 20, 1970); in *Oh Men,*

Oh Women (Louisville, Ky., 1971); in *Curse You, Spread Eagle* (world premiere, Washington Th. Club, Washington, D.C., Dec. 8, 1971); as Brinnin in *Dylan* (Mercer O'Casey Th., N.Y.C., Feb. 7, 1972); toured in *Light Up the Sky* (1972); appeared in *The Greatest Fairy Story Ever Told* (St. Clements Church, N.Y.C., 1973); and in *What Is Turning Gilda So Grey?* (Village Gate, Oct. 1, 1974).

Films. Mr. Carpenter made his debut in *Lost Boundaries* (Film Classics, 1949); subsequently appeared in *Three Little Words* (MGM, 1950); *Two Weeks with Love* (MGM, 1950); *Summer Stock* (MGM, 1950); *Vengeance Valley* (MGM, 1951); *Whistle at Eaton Falls* (Col., 1951); *Fearless Fagan* (MGM, 1952); *Sky Full of Moon* (MGM, 1952); *Take the High Ground* (MGM, 1953); *Up Periscope* (WB, 1959); *Cauliflower Cupids* (Savage, 1968); *Some of My Best Friends Are* (Am. Int., 1971); and *That's Entertainment!* (UA, 1974).

Television and Radio. Since 1944, Mr. Carpenter has appeared on more than 300 radio programs, including My True Story, Mr. District Attorney and The Aldrich Family. He made his television debut in *Campus Hoop-La* (NBC, 1946); subsequently performed on more than 2,500 live and filmed productions.

Night Clubs. Mr. Carpenter appeared in *New Faces Revue* (Persian Room, Hotel Plaza, N.Y.C., 1948).

Other Activities. Mr. Carpenter composed the songs "Christmas Eve," "Cabin in the Woods", "Come Away, Ev'ry Other Day," "Loving' Time," and "I Wouldn't Mind." He wrote most of the material for *Curse You, Spread Eagle,* a revue at the Washington (D.C.) Theatre Club.

Published Works. Mr. Carpenter is author of the following mysteries: *Games Murderers Play; Cat Got Your Tongue?; Only Her Hairdresser Knew; Pinecastle; Deadhead;* and *Sleight of Deadly Hand.*

Discography. Mr. Carpenter has recorded several singles for MGM, including "Aba Daba Honeymoon"; "Row, Row, Row"; "Oh By Jingo"; and *"No Two People";* his albums include *Reynolds and Carpenter Sing; Million Dollar Vaude Show;* and *Two Weeks with Love; Lady in the Dark* (RCA Victor); and *That's Entertainment!* (MCA).

Awards. Mr. Carpenter won the Laurel Award, Exhibitor Mag.; Topliner New Male Screen Personality (1951); Modern Screen Award; Box Office Award; and a Gold Record for sale of over 1,000,000 records of his recording of *Aba Daba Honeymoon.*.

Recreation. Bridge, bowling, beer.

CARPENTER, CONSTANCE.

Actress, singer. b. Apr. 19, 1906, Bath, England, to Harold and Mabel Anne (Cotrell) Carpenter. Attended Harley Street Schools, Bath. Married to Paul Ord Hamilton (marr. dis.); married to Commander J.H.S. Lucas-Scudamore, R.N. (marr. dis.); married to Capt. James Kennedy. Member of AEA; SAG. Address: c/o Stephen Draper Agency, 37 W. 57th St., New York, NY 10019.

Theatre. Miss Carpenter appeared in the chorus of *Seven Days Leave* (Lyceum, London, Feb. 14, 1917), and in *Fun of the Fayre* (London Pavilion, Oct. 17, 1921).

She made her N.Y.C. debut in *Andre Charlot's Revue of 1924* (Times Square Th., Jan. 9, 1924); appeared in *Charlot Revue, 1926* (Selwyn, Nov. 10, 1925); played Mae in *Oh, Kay* (Imperial, Nov. 8, 1926); Alice Carter in *A Connecticut Yankee* (Vanderbilt, Nov. 3, 1927); and succeeded (Mar. 1929) Mary Lawlor as Connie Block in *Hello Daddy* (Lew Fields' Th., Dec. 26, 1928).

She played Alice Carter in *A Yankee at the Court of King Arthur* (Daly's, London, Oct. 1929); succeeded (Apr. 1930) Ada May in *Cochran's 1930 Revue* (London Pavilion, Mar. 27, 1930); appeared in *Charlot's Masquerade* (Cambridge, Sept. 1930); played Polly Perkins in *Robinson Crusoe* (Lyceum, Dec. 1930); appeared in *The Third Little Show* (Music Box, N.Y.C., June 1931); played Evie Wynne in *Dirty Work* (Aldwych, London, Mar. 7, 1932); and Joy Armstrong in *All for Joy* (Piccadilly, Oct. 1932).

She played Giaconda and Marella in *Music Hath Charms* (Majestic, N.Y.C., Dec. 29, 1934); Jack in the English production of *Jack and the Beanstalk* (King's, Southsea, Dec. 1935); Lucille Phelps in *Baby Austin* (Strand, London, Apr. 1936); toured the US in the title role of *Lady Precious Stream* (Sept. 1936); played Princess Elaine in *Humpty Dumpty* (Golder's Green, London, Dec. 1937); appeared in *Happy Returns* (Adelphi, May 1938); played Diana Lake in *French without Tears* (Criterion, Nov. 6, 1938); Ann Perryman in *The Flying Squad* (Coliseum, July 1939); toured in *Other People's Houses* (1939); appeared in *Almost a Honeymoon* (1939); and in *Wild Violets* (1940).

During WW II, Miss Carpenter toured the Middle East with ENSA (1940), Holland and Germany (1945), India and Burma (1946); joined Alice Delysia's company in Cairo, Egypt, to play Gabrielle in *The French for Love* (1943); and toured England with the Amer. Red Cross (1944).

She toured as Mrs. Dunne in *Castle in the Air* (1950); succeeded (Aug. 1952) Gertrude Lawrence as Anna Leonowens in *The King and I* (St. James, N.Y.C., Mar. 29, 1951); appeared in *An Evening with Beatrice Lillie* (Globe, London, Nov. 24, 1954); and played the title role in *Auntie Mame* (Corning Summer Th., N.Y., July 1959).

She appeared in *Roar Like a Dove* (Booth Th., 1964); toured as the Wife of Bath with the national company of *Canterbury Tales* (1970); and succeeded Ruth Warrick as Emmeline Marshall in the national company of *Irene* (Jan. 1975).

Films. Miss Carpenter made her debut in *Just for a Song* (World Wide, 1931).

CARPENTER, THELMA.

Singer, actress. b. Jan. 15, 1922, to Fred and Mary (Jordan) Carpenter. Attended Girls Commercial H.S., Brooklyn, N.Y., 1935–38. Studied voice with Bernie Thall, 1942–52. Member of AEA; AFTRA; AGVA; SAG. Address: 864 Broadway, New York, NY 10003, tel. (212) AL 4-7604.

Theatre. Miss Carpenter made her singing debut as Henry Paradise in *Memphis Bound* (Bway Th., N.Y.C., May 24, 1945); subsequently appeared as the Race Track Girl in *Inside U.S.A.* (Century, Apr. 30, 1948); Corporal Betty Lee in *Shuffle Along* (Bway, May 8, 1952); Chipolate in *Ankles Aweigh* (Mark Hellinger Th., Apr. 18, 1955); and Dolly Gallagher Levi in *Hello, Dolly!* (St. James, Nov. 10, 1968–Dec. 13, 1969).

Television and Radio. Miss Carpenter first performed on radio at age ten on the Jack Darrell Kiddie Hour (WNYC, 1932); sang on the Major Bowes program (1934); the J. C. Flippen program (WHN); and on the *Eddie Cantor Show* (NBC, 1945–46).

On television, she has appeared on the Ed Sullivan Show (CBS); the Steve Allen Show (NBC); the Jackie Gleason Show (CBS); the first television show in Rome (ITA, 1953); and performed in London (BBC, 1957).

Miss Carpenter's first performance in a non-singing role was in the weekly television series, Barefoot in the Park (ABC, 1970–71), in which she starred. Other straight acting roles include those she played on Call Her Mom (ABC, 1972); the Paul Lynde Show (ABC, 1972); Love, American Style (ABC, 1972–73); and The Devil's Daughter (ABC, 1973).

Night Clubs. Miss Carpenter has appeared at the Copacabana (N.Y.C.); Ruban Bleu (N.Y.C.); Cafe Society (N.Y.C.); Zanzibar (N.Y.C.); Rio Cabana (Chicago, Ill.); Le Papillon (Hollywood, Calif.); Copocabana (England, 1953; Rome, 1953, 1957, 1959); Fenimina Renard Bleu (Athens); Dinarzard (Paris, 1953, 1957, 1959); the Maisonette, St. Regis Hotel (N.Y.C., 1969); and Downbeat (N.Y.C., 1973).

Other Activities. Miss Carpenter has appeared with the orchestras of Teddy Wilson (1939–40), Coleman Hawkins (1940–41), Count Basie (1942–44), and Duke Ellington. She made her N.Y.C. concert debut at Town Hall in 1973.

Awards. Miss Carpenter won the Esquire Award as a vocalist on radio (1945–46).

CARRA, LAWRENCE.

Educator, director. b. Lorenzo Carra, Jan. 20, 1909, Malfa, Isole Eolie, Italy, to Domenico and Angela (Lazzaro) Carra. Father, wine merchant. Grad. Somerville (Mass.) H.S. 1927; Harvard Coll., B.A. 1931; Yale Univ., M.F.A. 1937. Married Nov. 27, 1935, to Marguerita Carmosino; three sons. Member AEA; ANTA; Variety Club. Dept. of Drama, Carnegie-Mellon Univ., 5066 Forbes Ave., Pittsburgh, PA 15213.

Since 1956, Mr. Carra has been professor of play directing and director in the Drama Dept. of Carnegie-Mellon Univ., where he has been a faculty member since 1946. Previously, he was assistant professor of drama (1940–46) and acting head of the department (1942–46) at the Univ. of Texas; director of drama at Shimer Coll. (1939–40); and instructor at Northwestern Univ. (1938–39).

In addition to staging university theatre productions, Mr. Carra has directed at the Shimer Summer Th. (Mt. Carroll, Ill., 1940–43); operas and musical comedies for the Civic Opera of San Antonio, Tex., (Sunken Garden Th., 1944–47); three operas for the Houston (Tex.) Symphony Society (City Aud., 1944–45); plays at the Interstate Th. (Dallas, Tex.), which also toured the southwest (1946–47); directed 30 works for the Mill Playhouse (Hammonton, N.J., 1953–55); musicals for the South Shore Music Circus (Cohasset, Mass., Summers 1956–58); directed a touring production of *Sudden Spring* (New England states, 1956); and musical productions for the Civic Light Opera (Pittsburgh, Pa., 1959–63).

In N.Y.C., he directed *Leave It to Jane* (Sheridan Sq. Playhouse, May 25, 1959); and *Kittiwake Island,* which he produced with Joseph Beruh (Martinique, Oct. 12, 1960).

He has been a guest lecturer and director at Stanford Univ. (1945); Indiana Univ. (1951); the Arena Th. (Washington, D.C., 1953); and Columbia Univ. (1956).

Television and Radio. For radio, Mr. Carra wrote The Great Magician (NBC, 1938–1939). For television he produced for the Pulitzer Prize Playhouse (ABC): *The Skin of Our Teeth* (Dec. 19, 1951), *Alison's House* (Feb. 2, 1951), *The Town* (Jan. 16, 1952), *Years of Grace* (Jan. 30, 1952), *Hill 346* (Feb. 13, 1952), *Melville Goodwin, U.S.A.* (Feb. 27, 1952), *The Jungle* (Mar. 9, 1952), *Monsieur Beaucaire* (Mar. 12, 1952), *Robert E. Lee* (Mar. 26, 1952), *Fascinating Stranger* (Apr. 23, 1952), *Return of Dr. Moto* (May 7, 1952), *American Leonardo* (May 31, 1952), and *Daily Mayme* (June 4, 1952).

Published Works. Mr. Carra is co-author of the book *Fundamentals of Play Directing* (1974); and contributed to *The American Theatre* (1971).

CARROLL, DIAHANN.

Singer, actress. b. New York City, July 17. Grad. H.S. of Music and Art; attended New York Univ. Married to Monte Kay, casting director (marr. dis.), one daughter; married Feb. 21, 1973, to Frederick Glusman (marr. dis.); married May 1975 to Robert De Leon, public relations executive. Member of AEA; SAG; AFTRA.

Theatre. Miss Carroll made her N.Y.C. debut as Ottilie in *House of Flowers* (Alvin Th., Dec. 30, 1954); subsequently appeared as Barbara Woodruff in *No Strings* (54 St. Th., Mar. 15, 1962). She has given concerts at Philharmonic Hall (Lincoln Ctr. for the Peforming Arts, 1962); and at Kennedy Center (Washington, D.C., Oct. 8, 1971).

Films. Miss Carroll made her debut in *Carmen Jones* (20th-Fox, 1954); followed by *Porgy and Bess* (Col., 1959); *Paris Blues* (UA, 1961); *Goodbye Again* (UA, 1961); *Hurry Sundown* (Par., 1967); *The Split* (MGM, 1968); and *Claudine* (20th-Fox, 1974).

Television. She has appeared on Naked City (ABC), Eleventh Hour (NBC), the Jack Paar Show (NBC), Ed Sullivan Show (CBS), Garry Moore Show (CBS), Danny Kaye Show (CBS); Judy Garland Show (CBS); Bill Cosby Show; Hollywood Palace (ABC); *Cole Porter in Paris* (NBC); *Jack Lemmon—Get Happy* (NBC); specials entitled *The Diahann Carroll* (NBC), and *The Diahann Carroll*

Show (CBS); and played the title role in the series Julia.

Night Clubs. Miss Carroll has sung at the Persian Room (Plaza Hotel, N.Y.C.); the Royal Box (Americana Hotel, N.Y.C.); the Sands Hotel (Las Vegas, Nev.); Harold's (Reno, Nev.); The Ambassador (Los Angeles); the Palmer House (Chicago); and the Dunes (Las Vegas).

Awards. She received the *Cue* "entertainer of the year" Award (1961); the Antoinette Perry (Tony) Award for her performance as Barbara Woodruff in *No Strings* (1962); and was nominated for a NATAS (Emmy) Award for her role in Naked City.

CARROLL, HELENA. Actress, producer. b. Helena Winifred Carroll, Glasgow, Scotland, to Paul Vincent and Helena (Reilly) Carroll. Father, playwright. Grad. Convent de Notre Dame de Mamur, Scot., 1947; attended Webber-Douglas Sch. of Drama, London, 1948–1949. Member of AEA; AFTRA; SAG.

Theatre. Miss Carroll made her stage debut in a small part and as understudy in *a Babble of Green Fields* (Glasgow Citizens' Th., Scotland, Nov. 1949), where she played a season in repertory; subsequently played various roles in repertory in Worthing, England (1949); Croyden, England (1951); and Southport, England (1950); appeared in London in *Riders to the Sea* (Watergate, 1949), *The Monkey Puzzle* (New Lindsay, 1950); and *The Common Property* (Embassy, 1951).

She toured the US with the Dublin players as Brigid in *Shadow and Substance* and Cecily in *The Importance of Being Earnest* (1952–1953); made her N.Y.C. debut as Una in *The Wise Have Not Spoken* (Cherry Lane, Feb. 1954); followed by a tour as Marie What-Ever-Her-Name-Was in *The Seven Year Itch* (Summer 1956); made her Bway debut as Doreen in *Separate Tables* (Music Box, Oct. 25, 1956); with Dermot McNamara, formed the Irish Players and produced *Three by Synge* (Th. East, Mar. 6, 1957); and played Pegeen Mike in the Company's production of *Playboy of the Western World* (Tara, May 8, 1956).

Miss Carroll was understudy to Kim Stanley as Sara Melody in *A Touch of the Poet* (Helen Hayes Th., Oct. 2, 1958); played Brigid in the Irish Players production of *Shadow and Substance* (Tara, Nov. 3, 1959), and repeated the role (Tappia Th., Puerto Rico, 1958); played the Young Widow in *Happy as Larry* (Martinique, N.Y.C., 1961); appeared as Sister Theresa and was standby for Julie Harris as Brigid Mary Mangan in *Little Moon of Alban* (Longacre, Dec. 1, 1960); played Meg Dillon in the touring company of *The Hostage* (opened O'Keefe Center, Toronto, Canada, Jan. 30, 1961; closed Geary, San Francisco, Calif., May 13, 1961); played Thrassy in the Irish Players production of *Sharon's Grave* (Maidman, N.Y.C., Nov. 8, 1961); and Miss Sowerberry in *Oliver!* (Imperial, Jan. 6, 1963).

She played Rachel in *Pickwick* (46 St. Th., Oct. 4, 1965); appeared in a program of three one-act plays billed as *Three Hand Reel:* as Una Whitton in *The Frying Pan,* Mary Cummins in *Eternal Triangle,* and Miss Regan in *The Bridal Night* (Red Barn Th., Northport, N.Y., Aug. 30, 1966; Renata Th., N.Y.C., Nov. 7, 1966); was Rose Keller in *Something Different* (Cort, N.Y.C., Nov. 28, 1967); appeared in *A Man's a Man* (Goodman Memorial Th., Chicago, Ill., Mar. 29, 1968); was Peg in *Georgy* (Winter Garden, N.Y.C., Feb. 26, 1970); appeared at the Syracuse (N.Y.) Repertory Th. in *Juno and the Paycock* (Apr. 3, 1970); was Alice Boyd in *Pictures in the Hallway* (Forum, Apr. 29, 1971); and Leona Dawson in *Small Craft Warnings* (Truck and Warehouse Th., Apr. 2, 1972).

Films. Miss Carroll did the narration for a travel film, entitled *The Spell of Ireland* (1953); and appeared in *Midnight Episode* (Fine Arts, 1955).

Television. She appeared in *The White Steed* (Play-of-the-Week, WNTA, 1960); on Camera 3 (CBS); in *A Night to Remember* (NBC); *The Prince and the Pauper* (NBC); on Lamp Unto My Feet (CBS); Look Up and Live (CBS); and the Donna Reed Show (1962).

Recreation. Browsing around cut-rate liquor stores on tour in US cities.

CARROLL, JUNE. Singer, actress, lyricist. b. June Betty Sillman, June 22, Detroit, Mich., to Morton and May (Grosslight) Sillman. Father, jeweler. Grad. Russell H.S. for Girls, Los Angeles, Calif; attended Cunmock Jr. Coll. Studied singing with T. Francis Smith, Los Angeles, 1935; Richard Amber, White Plains, N.Y., 1960. Married 1935 to Leonard Reich (marr. dis. 1937); one son; married Aug. 30, 1940, to Sidney Carroll, writer; two sons, one daughter. Relative in theatre: brother, Leonard Sillman, producer, performer, author. Member of AEA; AFTRA; AGVA; SAG; ASCAP. Address: 1 W. 72nd St., New York, NY 10021, tel. (212) 877-5018; Cedar Lane Remsenburg, Long Island, NY.

Theatre. As June Sillman, Miss Carroll made her stage debut at five, singing at the Fox Th. (Detroit, Mich.); subsequently appeared as a singer and dancer in *11:15 Revue* (Hollywood, Calif., 1927); in *Lo and Behold* and *Hullabaloo* (Pasadena Playhouse, Calif., 1933).

She made her Bway debut as a general understudy and lyricist for *New Faces of 1934* (Fulton Th., Mar. 15, 1934); subsequently wrote lyrics for *Fools Rush In* (Playhouse, Dec. 25, 1935); *New Faces of 1936* (Vanderbilt, May 19, 1936; contributed lyrics to and appeared in *Who's Who* (Hudson, Mar. 1, 1938); in stock, appeared in *Calling All Men* and *New Faces* (Cape Playhouse, Dennis, Mass., Summer 1938); and *Meet the People* (Assistance League Playhouse, Hollywood, Calif., Dec. 25, 1939).

As June Carroll, she wrote music and lyrics for *All in Fun* (Majestic, N.Y.C., Dec. 27, 1940); sketches and lyrics for *New Faces of 1943* (Ritz, Dec. 22, 1942); *If the Show Fits* (Century, Dec. 5, 1946); appeared in *New Faces of 1952,* for which she also wrote lyrics (Royale, May 16, 1952); appeared at the Tenthouse Th., (Highland Park, Ill.), as Mrs. Sally Adams in *Call Me Madam* and Julie in *Show Boat* (Summer 1955), Liza Elliott in *Lady in the Dark* (Summer 1956), Vera in *Pal Joey* (Summer 1957), and Liz Livingstone in *Happy Hunting* (Summer 1958).

Miss Carroll contributed music and lyrics to *New Faces of 1956* (Ethel Barrymore Th., N.Y.C., June 14, 1956); *Mask and Gown* (John Golden Th., Sept. 10, 1957), which toured (opened Curran, San Francisco, Calif., June 21, 1958; closed Great Northern, Chicago, Ill., Oct. 4, 1958); played Aunt Lily in *Take Me Along* (Cape Cod Melody Top, Hyannis, Mass., Summer 1960); wrote lyrics for *Hi Paisano!* (York, N.Y.C., Sept. 30, 1961); played Rose in *Gypsy* (Cape Cod Melody Top, Hyannis, Mass.; South Shore Music Circus, Cohasset, Mass., Summer 1962); and contributed music and lyrics to *New Faces of 1962* (Alvin, N.Y.C., Feb. 1, 1962).

Films. Miss Carroll was a screenwriter for Republic Pictures (1942) and appeared in *An Angel Comes to Brooklyn* (Rep., 1943); and *New Faces* (20th-Fox, 1954).

Television and Radio. Miss Carroll performed on radio on the Rudy Vallee Show (1937); New Faces on the Air (NBC, 1949), for which she also wrote lyrics; and made her television debut on the Jack Paar Show (NBC, 1955). For the television special *Miracle on 34th St.* (CBS, Dec. 1973), she wrote lyrics for the song "Open Your Eyes and Dream.".

Night Clubs. Miss Carroll made her night club debut as a child with the Ted Lewis Band (Addison Hotel, Detroit, Mich.); subsequently performed (1936–37) in N.Y.C. at the Tria Room, Ambassador Hotel, the Versailles, Victor Hugo, and the Roosevelt Hotel; she was lyricist for the *New Faces Revue* at the Plaza Hotel (N.Y.C., 1949); and performed in the revue *Come as You Are* at the Versailles (N.Y.C., 1955).

Awards. Miss Carroll received an ASCAP Award (1963).

Recreation. Cooking, "chauffering," gardening, knitting.

CARROLL, PAT. Actress, comedienne. b. Patricia Ann Carroll, May 5, 1927, Shreveport, La., to Maurice Clifton and Kathryn Angela (Meagher) Carroll. Father, with Los Angeles Dept. of Water & Power; mother, businesswoman. Grad. Immaculate Heart H.S., Hollywood, Calif., 1944; attended Immaculate Heart Coll., 1945–47; Catholic Univ., 1949. Married Jan. 2, 1955, to Lee Karsian, theatrical and personal manager; one son, one daughter. Member of AEA; AFTRA; SAG; AGVA.

Pre-Theatre. Teacher, secretary.

Theatre. Miss Carroll made her professional debut in *A Goose for the Gander* (Lynn Summer Th., Mass., Aug. 1947); and has since appeared in the following stock productions: *Opal, The Desk Set, The Unsinkable Molly Brown, Once Upon a Mattress, Two for the Seesaw, Gypsy, Oh, Men! Oh, Women!, Who Was That Lady I Saw You With?, Dream Girl,* and *Once More, With Feeling.*

She appeared in the N.Y.C. revues *Come What May* (Charles Weidman Studio, May 1950) and *Catch a Star!* (Plymouth, Sept. 6, 1956); and played Hildy in *On the Town* (Carnegie Hall Playhouse, Jan. 15, 1959). She was one of the People of Paris in *Artists for the Revolution* (Eugene O'Neill Th. Ctr., Waterford, Conn., July 22, 1972); appeared in a dinner theatre production of *Everybody Loves Opal* (Minnesota Music Hall, Minneapolis, Minn., May 1974); in her own one-woman show, *An Evening with Who?* (Coachlight Dinner Th., Warehouse Point, Conn., July 17, 1974); in *Irene* (Parker Playhouse, Fort Lauderdale, Fla., Mar. 1975; Royal Poinciana Playhouse, Palm Beach, Fla., Mar. 1975); and toured in a production of *Something's Afoot* Summer 1975) prior to presentation in the Professional Theatre Program, Univ. of Michigan, Ann Arbor (Power Ctr., Sept. 19, 20, 21, 1975).

Television. She appeared on the Red Buttons Show (CBS, Sept. 1952); Kraft Television Th. (NBC, 1955); Caesar's Hour (NBC), 1956); Keep Talking (CBS, NBC, ABC, 1958–61); Producer's Showcase (NBC, 1959); the Danny Thomas Show (CBS, 1961–64); Password (CBS, 1962–64); The Price Is Right (CBS, ABC, 1962–64); First Impressions (NBC, 1963–64); You Don't Say (NBC, 1964); the Danny Kaye Show (CBS, 1964); in *Cinderella* (CBS, 1965); on The Interns (CBS, 1971); My Three Sons (CBS, 1971); and Love, American Style (ABC, 1971).

Night Clubs. She made her debut at the Ruban Bleu (N.Y.C., Feb. 1951); and has performed at the Village Vanguard, One Fifth Avenue, and the Blue Angel.

Awards. Miss Carroll received the NATAS (Emmy) Award for her performance on Caesar's Hour (1956).

Recreation. Reading, tennis, swimming, sailing.

CARROLL, VINNETTE. Actress, director. b. Vinette Justine Carroll, Mar. 11, 1922, New York City, to Edgar E. and Florence (Morris) Carroll. Father, dentist. Grad. Wadleigh H.S., N.Y.C.; Long Island Univ., B.A. 1944; New York Univ., M.A. 1946; attended Columbia Univ. Grad. Sch., 1945–46. Studied with Erwin Piscator at Dramatic Workshop, N.Y.C., two years; Lee Strasberg, N.Y.C., 1948–50; Stella Adler, N.Y.C., 1954–55; Actors' Studio (member, directors unit). Member of AEA; SAG; AFTRA. Address: 26 West 20th St., New York, NY 10011, tel. (212) 924-7820.

Pre-Theatre. Clinical and industrial psychologist.

Theatre. Miss Carroll first appeared on stage in plays presented at the New Sch. for Social Research (N.Y.C., 1948–50), as Clytemnestra in *Agamemnon,* the Nurse in *Romeo and Juliet,* the Duchess in *Alice in Wonderland,* and the River Elbe in *Outside the Door.*

She made her professional debut in stock at the Southhold Playhouse (L.I., N.Y.), as Addie in *The Little Foxes* (Summer 1948), subsequently played Bella in *Deep Are the Roots* (Summer 1949); Ftatateetah in a touring company of *Caesar and Cleopatra* (opened Olney Th., Md., June 1950); toured the US and British West Indies in a one-woman show (1952–57); appeared in *A Streetcar Named Desire*

(NY City Ctr., Feb. 15, 1956); and played Catherine in *The Grass Harp* (Lakewood Summer Th., N.J., 1956).

She played Amelie in *Small War on Murray Hill* (Ethel Barrymore Th., N.Y.C., Jan. 3, 1957); Tituba in *The Crucible* (Martinique, Mar. 11, 1958); Sophia Adams in *Moon on a Rainbow Shawl* (Royal Court, London, Dec. 4, 1958); and Dora in *Jolly's Progress* (Longacre, N.Y.C., Dec. 5, 1959).

Miss Carroll directed the ELT production of *Dark of the Moon* (Lenox Hill Playhouse, May 13, 1960); played Dido in *The Octoroon* (Phoenix, Jan. 27, 1961); directed *Ondine* for ELT (Masters Institute, Apr. 25, 1961); *Black Nativity* (41 St. Th., Dec. 11, 1961); *The Disenchanted* for the ELT (Masters Institute, Jan. 6, 1962); played Sophia Adams in *Moon on a Rainbow Shawl* (E. 11 St. Th., Jan. 15, 1962); narrated and directed *Black Nativity* (Criterion, London, 1962), and for the Spoleto Festival of Two Worlds (Teatro Caio Melisso, 1962).

Miss Carroll was director of the Ghetto Arts Program, NY State Council on the Arts when she organized the Urban Arts Corps in N.Y.C. in 1967 and became its artistic director. The Corps began operation in Summer 1967 with twenty-five black and Puerto Rican performers who presented their own programs of songs, poetry, and dramatic readings to audiences of minority groups. Members of the corps also taught young urban dwellers how to create their own dramatic programs. In 1968, the program expanded to a year-round operation.

Miss Carroll created and directed *But Never Jam Today*, a musical version of *Alice in Wonderland*, first presented by Urban Arts in 1969 and revived in 1970, when it toured N.Y.C., appearing in playgrounds and schools throughout the city. Other productions created and directed by Miss Carroll for the organization and first presented at the Urban Arts Corps Th., N.Y.C., include *Don't Bother Me, I Can't Cope* (Oct. 1970); with Micki Grant, *Croesus and the Witch* (Aug. 24, 1971) and *Step Lively, Boy* (Feb. 7, 1973); and *The Flies* (1974).

Films. Miss Carroll appeared as Mother in *A Morning for Jimmy* (Hyman Brown, 1960); as Martha in *One Potato Two Potato* (Bawalco, 1963); as the Mother in *Up the Down Staircase* (Alan J. Pakula, 1967); and as the Recruiting Officer in *Alice's Restaurant* (UA, 1969).

Television. She played Bernice in *A Member of the Wedding* (Granada, London, 1960); was narrator and director of *Black Nativity* (Westinghouse Th., CBS, US, 1962); conceived, adapted, and supervised *Beyond the Blues* (Stage 2, CBS, 1964), and *Jubilation* (Repertoire Workshop, CBS, 1964); and was Sojourner Truth in *We, the Women* (CBS, 1974).

Other Activities. Since 1955, Miss Carroll has taught drama at the High School of Performing Arts, N.Y.C.

Awards. She received a Ford Foundation Grant for directors (1960–61); the *Village Voice* Off-Bway (Obie) Award for her performance as Sophia Adams in *Moon on a Rainbow Shawl* (1961); an Emmy Award for her direction of *Beyond the Blues* (1964); Outer Circle Critics awards for direction (1971, 1972); Los Angeles Drama Critics Circle Award (1972) for her distinguished direction of *Don't Bother Me, I Can't Cope;* the Harold Jackman Memorial Award (1973); and she was nominated (1973) for an Antoinette Perry (Tony) Award for her direction of *Don't Bother Me, I Can't Cope.*.

Recreation. Sports cars, horseback riding, building furniture, and "my Great Dane.".

CARSON, WILLIAM G. B. Writer, educator. b. William Glasgow Bruce Carson, Sept. 1, 1891, St. Louis, Mo., to Norman Bruce and Susan (Glasgow) Carson. Father, surgeon. Grad. Smith Acad., St. Louis, 1909; Wash. Univ., A.B. (Phi Beta Kappa) 1913, M.A. 1916; attended Columbia Univ., 1925–26. Married June 12, 1923, to Elizabeth Chapin; two sons. Member of Omicron Delta Kappa; Sigma Delta Chi; Natl. Collegiate Theatre; Theatre Library Assoc.; Amer. Society for Theatrical Research; Missouri Historical Society (bd. mbr., 1930–60; secy., 1944–50)%

Since 1919, Mr. Carson has been a member of the faculty at Washington Univ. and is presently professor emeritus. From 1916–19, he was instructor in English at State Univ. of Iowa.

He was co-founder (1927), then president, of the Little Theatre of St. Louis (later called Community Playhouse, now defunct). Address: 7006 Maryland Ave., St. Louis, MO 63155, tel. (314) PA 7-1050.

Published Works. He is the author of *The Theatre on the Frontier* (1932), *The Letters of Mr. and Mrs. Charles Kean* (1945), *Managers in Distress* (1949), *Dear Josephine, the Theatrical Life of Josephine Hull* (1963), and an adventure story, *Peter and Brownie Follow the Trace.* His one-act plays include *Tea, The Wedding Present,* and *Five for Bad Luck.*

CARVER, JAMES. Theatre manager, director. b. James Caleb Carver, Jan. 30, 1932, Kalamazoo, Mich., to Norman F. and Louise (Blackaller) Carver. Father, theatre manager; mother, actress and TV personality. Grad. Kimball Union Academy, Meriden, N.H., 1950; Michigan State Univ., B.A. 1954; M.A. 1965. Married Mar. 5, 1955, to Nancy Ann Organ, Detroit, Mich.; two sons. Served US Army; rank, Capt. Member of ATA; Michigan Council for the Arts (theatre advisory comm.); Michigan Artrain; Community Theatre Assn. of Mich. (pres., 1964–66; vice-pres., 1962–64); Kalamazoo Arts Council (vice-pres.); Theta Chi; Torch Club; BPOE; Kalamazoo Country Club. Address: (home) 5624 Lovers Lane, Portage, MI 49081, tel. (616) 349-6366; (bus.) The Kalamazoo Civic Players, 329 S. Park St., Kalamazoo, MI 49006, tel. (616) 343-1313.

Mr. Carver is business manager of the Kalamazoo Civic Players and manager of the Kalamazoo Civic Auditorium (1968–to date). From 1959 to 1968, he was assistant business manager of the Civic Players and chairman of the theatre dept., Nazareth College.

Recreation. Golf, skiing, tennis.

CARVER, NORMAN. Theatre manager. b. Norman Francis Carver, June 16, 1899, Newburyport, Mass., to John Hermann and Grace (Estes) Carver. Father, journalist. Grad. Newburyport H.S., 1917; Dartmouth Coll., B.S. 1921; Univ. of Michigan, M.S. 1922. Married May 22, 1925, to Helen Louise Blackaller, actress; three sons. Served WW I, US Army; rank, Sgt. Relative in theater: father-in-law, Arthur Blackaller, actor. Member of Community Theatre Assn. of Mich., Natl. Assn. of Community Theatres, Alpha Chi Rho (pres., Dartmouth Chapter, 1920–21), Kalamazoo Rotary Club, Kalamazoo Country Club. Address: (home) 5770 Parkview Ave., Kalamazoo, MI 49001, tel. (616) FI 4-7512; (bus.) The Kalamazoo Civic Players, 329 S. Park St., Kalamazoo, MI 49006, tel. (616) FI 3-1313.

Mr. Carver was a founder and the first president of the Community Theatre Association of Michigan (1946), and a founder and the first president of the National Association of Community Theatres (1955). He was business and theatre manager of the Kalamazoo Civic Players from 1929 until his retirement in 1968.

Carver Center, an addition to Kalamazoo's cultural buildings complex (1958), was named in recognition of his service to the community.

Recreation. Golf, acting.

CASEY, ROSEMARY. Playwright. b. Dec. 21, 1904, Pittsburgh, Pa., to John Francis and Mary (Lee) Casey. Father, contractor. Attended Ursuline Acad., Pittsburgh, Pa., 1918–20; Brownson Sch., N.Y.C., 1921–22; St. Elizabeth's Coll., 1922–24; grad. Barnard Coll., B.A. 1926; Columbia Univ., M.A. 1929. Member of Dramatists Guild; ALA; Amer. Red Cross (secy., Pittsburgh chapter, 1942–60); Nurses Aid Corps (chmn., 1942–46); Fight for Freedom Comm. (vice-chmn., 1941). Address: (home) Park Mansions, Pittsburgh, PA 15213, tel. (412) 621-7232; (bus.) c/o International Famous Agency, 1301 Avenue of Americas, New York, NY 10019.

Theatre. Miss Casey produced the pre-Bway tryout of *Agatha Calling* (opened Philadelphia, Pa., Sept. 30, 1935; closed Binghamton, N.Y., Oct. 9, 1935); subsequently wrote, with B. Iden Payne, *Mary Goes To See* (Haymarket Th., London, Feb. 17, 1938); wrote *The Velvet Glove* (Booth, N.Y.C., Dec. 26, 1949); and *Late Love* (Natl., Oct. 13, 1953).

Films. An unproduced play she wrote with James L. Shute and Nancy Hamilton was the basis for the film *Fools for Scandal* (WB, 1938).

Published Works. She has written short stories for magazines.

Awards. Miss Casey received the Christopher Award for her play *Mother Hildebrand* (1949), which was later titled *The Velvet Glove.*

CASHMAN, BETTY. Drama coach, actress, director, author. b. May 15, New York City, to Jack and Anna (Safchick) Cashman. Father, business executive. Attended Lincoln Private Sch., N.Y.C.; grad. Amer. Acad. of Dramatic Arts, 1937; attended Juilliard Sch. of Music, 1942–43; Columbia Univ., 1945–46. Studied directing with Harry Wagstaff Gribble, N.Y.C., 1946. Member of AEA; SAG; AFTRA. Address: 1860 Broadway, New York, NY 10023, tel. (212) CI 5-8784.

Theatre. Since 1947, Miss Cashman has been director of the Betty Cashman Drama Studios in N.Y.C.

She made her stage debut at the age of four in *Mrs. Wiggs of the Cabbage Patch* (Poughkeepsie Players, N.Y.); and her N.Y.C. debut as Lillian Piccichanti in *Honor Code* (Vanderbilt, May 13, 1931); followed by Giovanna Baccolini in *Moon Over Mulberry Street* (Lyceum, Sept. 4, 1935); and for the Professional Players Guild, played Lyska in *Preferred,* and Jenny in *The Torchbearers* (McDowell Club Th.).

She toured New England and the Southern states as Miss Caza in *Bitter Road,* Eloise Vander in *The Little Fixer;* and with the Mansfield Players, toured as Portia in *The Merchant of Venice,* and Katherine in *The Taming of the Shrew* (1940–42).

Miss Cashman directed *God Strikes Back* (Concert Th., N.Y.C., Feb. 26, 1943); was acting coach for *Anna Lucasta* (Mansfield, Aug. 30, 1944); *Rhapsody* (Century, Nov. 22, 1944); and *Polonaise* (Alvin, Oct. 6, 1945).

Radio. During 1941–53, Miss Cashman performed on Mr. District Attorney; Philip Morris Playhouse; Aunt Jenny's Real Life Story; True Detective Story; Famous Jury Murder Trials; Hop Harrigan; The Cisco Kid; Bright Horizons; The Romance of Helen Trent; Modern Romances; Molly Picon Th. of the Air; and Eye Witness Stories.

Published Works. Miss Cashman wrote *The Exercise* (1950), *Betty Cashman and You in—Personality, Acting and Public Speaking* (1950), *Successful Self-Expression Course* (1954), and *Thoughts for Actors and You* (1958).

Awards. She was awarded honorary membership in the Intl. Mark Twain Society for "contribution to literature" for her book, *Betty Cashman and You in—Personality, Acting and Public Speaking* (1950); and received the Show Business Award for "outstanding development of new talent in the theatre" (1955–58).

CASPARY, VERA. Novelist, playwright. b. Nov. 18, 1904, Chicago, Ill., to Paul and Julia (Cohen) Caspary. Father, department store buyer. Married Oct. 5, 1949, to Isadore G. Goldsmith, film producer (dec.). Member of SWG; Dramatists Guild; ALA; Authors Guild. Address: 55 E. 9th St., New York, NY 10003.

Theatre. Miss Caspary wrote, with Winifred Lenihan, *Blind Mice* (Times Square Th., N.Y.C., Oct. 15, 1930); with Samuel Ornitz, wrote *Geraniums in My Window* (Longacre, Oct. 26, 1924); with George Sklar, *Laura,* based on her novel of the same title (Cort, June 26, 1947); and the book for the musical, *Wedding in Paris* (Hippodrome, London, England, Apr. 3, 1954).

Films. For the screen, Miss Caspary has written *Night of June 13* (Par., 1932); *Such Women Are Dangerous* (20th-Fox, 1934); *Easy Living* (Par., 1937);

Laura (20th-Fox, 1944); *Claudia and David* (20th-Fox, 1946); *Bedelia* (Eagle-Lion, 1947); *Letter to Three Wives* (20th-Fox, 1948); *Three Husbands* (UA, 1950); *I Can Get It for You Wholesale* (20th-Fox, 1951); *The Blue Gardenia* (WB, 1953); *Give a Girl a Break* (MGM, 1953); *Les Girls* (MGM, 1957); *Out of the Blue* (Eagle-Lion, 1960); and *Bachelor in Paradise* (MGM, 1961).

Other Activities. Miss Caspary was editor of *Dance* magazine from 1926–28.

Published Works. She wrote the following novels: *The White Girl* (1929), *Ladies and Gents* (1929), *Music in the Street* (1930), *Thicker Than Water* (1932), *Laura* (1942), *Bedelia* (1944), *Stranger Than Truth* (1946), *The Weeping and the Laughter* (1950), *Thelma* (1952), *The Husband* (1957), *Evvie* (1960), *A Chosen Sparrow* (1964), *The Man Who Loved His Wife* (1966), *The Rosecrest Cell* (1967), and *Final Portrait* (London, 1971).

CASS, PEGGY. Actress. b. Mary Margaret Cass, May 21, 1926, Boston, Mass., to Raymond James and Margaret (Loughlin) Cass. Father, sports promoter. Attended Cambridge Latin Sch.; Fordham Univ.; studied acting with Uta Hagen; Mira Rostova; and Tamara Daykarhanova. Married Dec. 4, 1948, to Carl Fisher, general manager. Member of AEA (council 1958–62); SAG; AFTRA.

Theatre. Miss Cass was understudy to Jan Sterling in the role of Billie Dawn in a touring production of *Born Yesterday* (Erlanger, Chicago, Ill., Winter 1947); she succeeded (1948) Ann Thomas as Maisie in *Burlesque* (Belasco, N.Y.C., Dec. 25, 1946); appeared in the revue, *Touch and Go* (Broadhurst, Oct. 13, 1949); in stock, played in *A Month in the Country* (Westport County Playhouse, Conn., 1949); appeared as Helen in *Bernadine* (Playhouse, N.Y.C., Oct. 16, 1952); and succeeded Barbara Baxley in *Oh, Men! Oh, Women!* (Henry Miller's Th., Dec. 17, 1953); played a season of Shakespeare at the Brattle Th. (Cambridge, Mass., Summer 1955), appearing as Mistress Quickly in *Henry IV, Part 2* and Bianca in *Othello;* and in the revue, *Phoenix '55* (Phoenix Th., N.Y.C., Apr. 23, 1955).

Miss Cass repeated the role of Bianca in *Othello* (NY City Ctr., Sept. 7, 1955); and that of Mistress Quickly in *Henry IV, Part 2* (NY City Ctr., Sept. 15, 1955); played Madame Velda in the pre-Bway tryout of *The Amazing Adele* (opened Shubert, Boston, Mass., Dec. 26, 1955); Agnes Gooch in *Auntie Mame* (Broadhurst, N.Y.C., Sept. 30, 1956); Ella in *Bells Are Ringing* (State Fair Music Hall, Dallas, Tex., Summer 1959); performed in *A Thurber Carnival* (ANTA, N.Y.C., Feb. 26, 1960); played Wildcat Jackson in *Wildcat* (State Fair Music Hall, Dallas, Tex., Summer 1962); appeared as Vera von Stovel in *Children from their Games* (Morosco, N.Y.C., Apr. 11, 1963); toured as Eadie in *Bachelor's Wife* (Summer 1964); was Edith (Mrs. Phelps Popper) in *The Women* (Paper Mill Playhouse, Millburn, N.J., Mar. 22, 1966); appeared in the Milliken Breakfast Show (Waldorf-Astoria Hotel, N.Y.C., June 1966); succeeded (June 19, 1967) Kay Medford as Marion Hollander in *Don't Drink the Water* (Morosco, Nov. 17, 1966); played Mollie Malloy in a revival of *The Front Page* (Ethel Barrymore Th., May 10, 1969: reopened Oct. 18, 1969); and replaced (Jan. 5, 1970) Maureen Stapleton as Karen, Muriel, and Norma in *Plaza Suite* (Plymouth, Feb. 14, 1968).

Films. Miss Cass made her film debut in *The Marrying Kind* (Col., 1952); appeared in *Auntie Mame* (WB, 1956); and in *If It's Tuesday, This Must Be Belgium* (UA, 1969).

Television and Radio. Miss Cass was on radio as hostess of the Peggy Cass Show (WNEW-FM, N.Y.C., commencing May 24, 1967). On television she has appeared on Ford Theatre (CBS); Magic Cottage (Dumont); Robert Montgomery Presents (CBS); Keep Talking (ABC); To Tell the Truth (CBS); The Hathaways (ABC); Password (CBS); Match Game (CBS); and Missing Links (CBS). She appeared at various times on To Tell the Truth (CBS, 1964, 1965, 1966, 1967); Girl Talk (ABC; Ind.; 1964–68); Match Game (NBC, 1964–65); Password (CBS, 1964–65); on other panel shows; as a guest on the Mike Douglas Show (Ind., 1966–67); and on Generation Gap (ABC, May 16, 1969).

Awards. For her performance as Agnes Gooch in *Auntie Mame,* Miss Cass received the Antoinette Perry (Tony) Award (1956–57); and the *Theatre World* Award (1957). She also received an Academy (Oscar) Award nomination for the same role in the film version of *Auntie Mame* (1958).

Recreation. Swimming, skiing, cooking, collecting antiques.

CASSIDY, CLAUDIA. Drama and music critic. b. Shawneetown, Ill., to George Peter and Olive (Grattan) Cassidy. Grad. Univ. of Illinois, B.A. Married June 15, 1929, to William John Crawford.

Theatre. Miss Cassidy began her career with the Chicago *Journal of Commerce,* writing a daily column, "On the Aisle," on theatre, music, ballet, books, people, places, painting and other topics (1925–41); subsequently joined the Chicago *Sun* to organize its drama department and to become its theatre and music critic, continuing her column "On the Aisle" (1941–42). In 1942, she joined the Chicago *Tribune* as its theatre and music critic, continuing until her retirement in 1965. She wrote six to seven columns a week; and, during the summer, when she was abroad, her column was titled "Europe on the Aisle."

Miss Cassidy served on the 1970–71 committee for the Joseph Jefferson awards. In 1971, The Goodman Memorial Th., Chicago, engaged her to help select plays.

Published Works. Miss Cassidy has published a collection of her writings under the title of *Europe on the Aisle* (1954).

CASSIDY, JACK. Actor. b. John Cassidy, Mar. 5, 1927, Richmond Hill, N.Y., to William and Charlotte (Kohler) Cassidy. Father, railroad engineer. Grad. Richmond Hill H.S., 1944; studied singing with Polly Robertson, 1945–57. Married Oct. 31, 1948, to Evelyn Ward (marr. dis. 1956); one son; married Aug. 5, 1956, to Shirley Jones, actress (marr. dis.); two sons. Relative in theatre: cousin, Ben Dova Spah, acrobat. Member of AEA; AFTRA; SAG; AGVA; AGMA.

Pre-Theatre. Bellhop; counterman; dishwasher; chauffeur; clothing salesman; postal clerk, hotel clerk; stable boy; coal and ice truck handler.

Theatre. Mr. Cassidy first performed in the chorus of *Something for the Boys* (Alvin Th., N.Y.C., Jan. 7, 1943); subsequently appeared in the chorus of *Sadie Thompson* (Alvin, Mar. 22, 1945); *Marinka* (Winter Garden, July 18, 1945); the pre-Bway tryout of *Spring in Brazil* (opened Shubert, Boston, Mass., Oct. 1, 1945; closed Great Northern, Chicago, Ill., Jan. 12, 1946); *Around the World* (Adelphi, N.Y.C., May 31, 1946); *The Red Mill* (Ziegfeld, Oct. 16, 1945); the pre-Bway tryout of *Three Indelicate Ladies* (opened Shubert, New Haven, Conn., Apr. 10, 1947; closed Wilbur, Boston, Mass., Apr. 19, 1947); *Music in My Heart* (Adelphi, N.Y.C., Oct. 10, 1947); *Inside USA* (Century, Apr. 30, 1948); in the revue, *Small Wonder* (Coronet, Sept. 16, 1948); as Rocky Barton in *Billion Dollar Baby* (Monte Proser Cafe Th., 1949); in *Alive and Kicking* (Winter Garden, Jan. 17, 1949); and in *South Pacific* (Majestic, Apr. 7, 1949).

Mr. Cassidy played Chick Miller in *Wish You Were Here* (Imperial, June 25, 1952); Johnny O'Sullivan in *Sandhog* (Phoenix, Nov. 23, 1954); under US State Dept. sponsorship, Curley in *Oklahoma!* (Paris, France; Rome, Italy, 1955); appeared at the Bucks County Playhouse (New Hope, Pa.) in *Wedding Breakfast, Mistress of the Inn, The Importance of Being Earnest,* and *Witness for the Prosecution* (Summer 1955). He appeared as Charles Mallinson in *Shangri-La* (Winter Garden, N.Y.C., June 13, 1956); and at the Cambridge Drama Festival as Macheath in *The Beggar's Opera* (1956); performed in *Wonderful Town* (Brussels, Bel., London, Eng. 1959); *Epitaph for George Dillon* (Players Ring, Los Angeles, Calif., 1959); *The Vagabond King* (Westbury Music Fair, N.Y., 1961); *Gypsy* (State Fair Music Hall, Dallas, Tex., 1962); as Mr. Kodaly in *She Loves Me* (Eugene O'Neill Th., N.Y.C., Apr. 23, 1963); and Byron Prong in *Fade Out–Fade In* (Mark Hellinger Th., May 26, 1964).

Mr. Cassidy replaced (Mar. 28, 1965) Alfred Marks as Potemkin in the pre-Bway tryout of *Pleasures and Palaces* (Fisher Th., Detroit, Mich., Mar. 11–Apr. 10, 1965); played Lancelot in *Camelot* (Starlight Musicals, Indianapolis, Ind., Aug. 16, 1965); Max Mencken in *It's a Bird! It's a Plane! It's Superman!* (Alvin Th., N.Y.C., Mar. 29, 1966); toured as Harry Roat, Jr., in *Wait Until Dark* (1967); played Phineas in *Maggie Flynn* ANTA Th., N.Y.C., Oct. 23, 1968); and Mick Moloney in *The Mundy Scheme* (Royale, Dec. 11, 1969).

Films. Mr. Cassidy appeared in *Look in any Window* (Allied, 1961), and *The Chapman Report* (WB, 1962).

Television. He has performed on This Is Show Business (CBS); the Ed Sullivan Show (CBS); US Steel Hour (CBS); Lux Video Th. (NBC); Gunsmoke (CBS); Richard Diamond (CBS); Wagon Train (NBC); Alfred Hitchcock Presents (CBS); Chevy Mystery Th. (NBC); the Dick Powell Th. (NBC); The Real McCoy's (CBS); Bell Telephone Hour (NBC); Hennessey (CBS); 77 Sunset Strip (ABC); Cheyenne (ABC); Surfside 6 (ABC); Hawaiian Eye (ABC). In London, he performed on his own series with his wife, Date with Shirley and Jack (ATV, London, 1959).

Among his other television appearances, Mr. Cassidy was Allan in *The He-She Chemistry* (Mr. Broadway, CBS, Oct. 31, 1964); the voice of Bob Cratchit in *Mr. Magoo's Christmas Carol* (NBC, Dec. 18, 1964; Dec. 17, 1965); Floy in a television adaptation of *High Button Shoes* (Garry Moore Show, CBS, Nov. 20, 1966); and was on the Mike Douglas Show (Ind., 1965–66); the Johnny Carson Show (NBC, 1966–67); and others.

Night Clubs. Mr. Cassidy appeared with the Milton Berle Show as a featured singer (Carnival Room, N.Y.C., 1955); in *One Thousand and One Nights* (Versailles, N.Y.C., 1955–56); and in his own act (Cocoanut Grove, Los Angeles, Calif., 1958).

Discography. Mr. Cassidy has recorded the Columbia albums, *Boys from Syracuse, On Your Toes, Babes in Arms, Oh, Kay!, Roberta;* and with his wife, *With Love from Hollywood, Speaking of Love, Brigadoon,* and *Wish You Were Here.* .

Awards. Mr. Cassidy won the *Variety* NY Drama Critics Poll, *Saturday Review* Critics Poll; won an Antoinette Perry (Tony) Award (1963–64) as best supporting actor in a musical for his performance as Mr. Kodaly in *She Loves Me;* For his performance as Phineas in *Maggie Flynn,* he received a Tony nomination (1968–69) as best musical actor and a *Variety* poll citation.

Recreation. Tennis, handball, sculpture, decorating, fishing, hunting.

CATES, GILBERT. Producer, director. b. Gilbert Katz, June 6, 1934, New York City, to Nathan and Nina Katz. Father, dress manufacturer. Grad. DeWitt Clinton H.S., Bronx, N.Y., 1949; Syracuse Univ., B.A. 1954. Studied at Neighborhood Playhouse Sch. of the Th., N.Y.C., summer session 1953; with Robert Lewis, N.Y.C., 1959. Married Feb. 9, 1957, to Jane; three sons, one daughter. Relatives in theatre: brother, Joseph Cates, producer; brother-in-law, Gerald Adler, producer; sister, Kit Adler, producer. Member of DGA (exec. council); NATAS; Amer. Acad. of Television Arts and Sciences; AEA (eastern regional bd. of dir., 1962–63); The Friars; Tau Delta Phi; Syracuse Univ. Drama Dept. Advisory Committee. Address: (home) 6 Penn Blvd., Scarsdale, NY 10583; (bus.) 119 W. 57th St, New York, NY 10019, tel. (212) CI 7-6130.

Pre-Theatre. Instructor of Speech and Drama at Syracuse Univ. (1955).

Theatre. Mr. Cates was stage manager for *Shinbone Alley* (Bway Th., N.Y.C., Apr. 13, 1957); associate producer with his brother, Joseph Cates, of *Spoon River Anthology,* which was later retitled *Spoon River* (Booth, Sept. 29, 1963), also was associated with its

London production (Royal Court, Feb. 13, 1964); was associated with the production of *What Makes Sammy Run?* (54 St. Th., N.Y.C., Feb. 27, 1964); produced *You Know I Can't Hear You When the Water's Running* (Ambassador, Mar. 13, 1967), national and London companies (1968); *I Never Sang For My Father* (Longacre, Jan. 25, 1968); *The Chinese and Dr. Fish* (Ethel Barrymore Th., Mar. 10, 1970); *Solitaire/Double Solitaire* (Golden Th., Sept. 30, 1971); directed *The Price* as guest director (Long Wharf Th., New Haven, Conn., 1971); and directed *Voices* (Ethel Barrymore Th., Apr. 3, 1972).

Films. He produced and directed a short film, *The Painting* (Union Films, 1962); produced and directed *Rings Around the World* (Col., 1966) and *I Never Sang For My Father* (Col., 1970); and directed *Summer Wishes, Winter Dreams* (Col., 1973).

Television. Mr. Cates was producer and director of Camouflage (ABC, 1962); Hootenanny (ABC, 1963); and executive producer, director, and brother-in-law, Gerald, in Showtime (NBC, 1963–64); directed and produced Electric Showcase and specials featuring the Ice Follies, the World's Fair, and Aquacade (all ABC, 1965); directed a Timex special (NBC, 1971); produced and directed *To All My Friends on Shore* (CBS, 1972); directed *The Affair*, feature Movie of the Week (ABC, 1973); and produced and directed *After the Fall*, a dramatic special (NBC, 1974).

Awards. Mr. Cates received the Edinburgh (Scotland) Film Festival Citation Award; the San Francisco (Calif.) Film festival Citation for *The Painting* (1963); and the TV Scout Award for excellence in television and the NAACP Image Award for *To All My Friends on Shore* (1972).

Recreation. Fencing, photography.

CATES, JOSEPH. Producer, director. b. New York City, Aug. 10, 1924. Attended New York Univ., 1946. Married to Lily Valentine; one son, three daughters. Relatives in theatre: brother, Gilbert Cates, producer, director; brother-in-law, Gerald Adler, theatrical attorney; sister, Kit Adler, producer. Served WW II, USAAF, pilot; rank, 1st Lt. Address: 157 W. 57th St., New York, NY 10019, tel. (212) 765-1300.

Theatre. Mr. Cates produced *Spoon River* (Booth, N.Y.C., Sept. 29, 1963); *What Makes Sammy Run?* (54 St. Th., Feb. 27, 1964); *A Day in the Death of Joe Egg* (Brooks Atkinson Th., Feb. 1, 1968); *Her First Roman* (Lunt-Fontanne Th., Oct. 8, 1968); and *Elmer Gantry* (George Abbott Th., Feb. 12, 1970).

Films. He directed *Girl of the Night* (WB, 1960); and *Who Killed Teddy Bear?* (Magna, 1965).

Television. Mr. Cates produced and directed more than 30 special programs including *The Bachelor* (NBC); the first Gene Kelly Special (NBC); the Victor Borge Show (ABC); Yves Montand on Broadway (ABC); *High Button Shoes* (NBC); Accent on Love (NBC); was the executive producer of International Showtime (NBC, 1961–64); and produced *The Canterville Ghost* (NBC); *Dames at Sea* (NBC); the *CMA Awards* (CBS); *Country Comes Home* (NBC); *Country Music Hit Parade* (CBS); *Married is Better* (NBC); and *George M!* (NBC).

Awards. Mr. Cates received Emmy Awards for the Anne Bancroft Special (CBS, 1970), and the George Gershwin Special, *S'Wonderful, S'Marvelous, S'Gershwin* (NBC, 1972).

CHAIKIN, JOSEPH. Director, actor. b. 1935, Brooklyn, N.Y. Attended Drake Univ. Professional training at Herbert Berghof Studio; Nola Chilton; Mira Rostiva. Relative in theatre, sister, Shami Chaikin, actress.

Theatre. Mr. Chaikin played roles in a number of productions of the Living Theatre, of which he was a member (1959–63), including Leach in *The Connection* (July 15, 1959), also on European tours with Living Theatre (1961, 1962); Mangini in *Tonight We Improvise* (Nov. 6, 1959); Serafina's boy Friend and the Real Estate Agent in *Many Loves* (May 15, 1961); and Galy Gay in *Man Is Man* (Sept. 18, 1962).

He was founder and a leader (1963–73) of the Open Theatre, an experimental group, many of whose productions were created by actors and director collaborating and using only a framework supplied by the playwright; many Open Theatre performances were open only by invitation. Mr. Chaikin played Hamm in Open Theatre's presentation of *Endgame* (Washington Sq. Methodist Ch., N.Y.C., May 30, 1970); productions developed by the group under Mr. Chaikin's direction include *Terminal*, with Roberta Sklar (Washington Sq. Methodist Ch., May 26, 1970; Th. at St. Clements, Sept. 15, 1973); *The Serpent: A Ceremony* (Washington Sq. Methodist Ch., May 29, 1970); *The Mutation Show*, with Roberta Sklar (1972; Th. at St. Clements, Sept. 19, 1973); and *Nightwalk* (April 1973; Th. at St. Clements, Sept. 8, 1973).

Additional work by Mr. Chaikin in the theatre includes performances as the Second Furniture Mover in *The New Tenant* and the Detective in *Victims of Duty* (Writers' Stage Th., May 24, 1964); the Clown in *Sing to Me Through Open Windows* (Players Th., Mar. 15, 1965); the Coolie in *The Exception and the Rule* (Greenwich Mews, May 20, 1965); and he was in *Captain Fantastic Meets the Ectomorph* (New Th. Workshop, Mar. 1966). He directed *Interview*, part of *America Hurrah* (Pocket Th., Nov. 6, 1966); collaborated in creating *Electra* (Th. at St. Clements, May 27, 1974); directed *The Seagull* (Manhattan Th. Club, Jan. 29, 1975); sponsored, with the Theatre of Latin America, the collaborative work *Chile, Chile* (Washington Sq. Methodist Ch., May 23–June 8, 1975); directed the collaborative *A Fable* (Exchange Th. at Westbeth, Oct. 1975); and played the title role in *Woyzeck* (Public Th., Mar. 5, 1976).

Films. Mr. Chaikin appeared in Robert Frank's film *Me and My Brother* (1968).

Published Works. Mr. Chaikin wrote *The Presence of the Actor* (1972).

Awards. In 1963, Mr. Chaikin received a *Village Voice* off-Bway (Obie) Award for his distinguished performances in *The Connection* and *Man Is Man;* in 1969, Open Theatre received an Obie for *The Serpent*, and Open Theatre and Mr. Chaikin received the Vernon Rice Award for outstanding contributions to the Bway theatre; *The Mutation Show* was named (1972) by the Obie committee as best theatre piece of the season, and for his direction of it Mr. Chaikin received (1973) the Drama Desk Award.

CHAMBERS, WILLIAM. Stage manager, actor, director. b. William Hall Chambers, June 8, 1910, New York City, to Walter B. and Elizabeth M. F. Chambers. Father, architect. Attended Allen-Stevenson Sch., N.Y.C., 1920–27; grad. Prep Sch., Lake Mohonk, N.Y., 1928; Colgate Univ., B.A. 1932. Married May 25, 1947, to Frances Hammond, actress. Served WW II, US Army, awarded Bronze Star, Silver Star, Purple Heart, four invasion stars; rank, Capt. Relatives in theatre: brother, Peter Chambers, singer; uncle, Robert W. Chambers, novelist, playwright. Member of AEA; AFTRA; SAG; Dramatists Guild; Alpha Tau Omega.

Pre-Theatre. Sailor, newspaper reporter.

Theatre. Mr. Chambers first performed as an actor in stock productions at the Mt. Kisco (N.Y.) Playhouse (Summer 1936); subsequently played Riley in *200 Were Chosen* (48 St. Th., N.Y.C., Nov. 20, 1936); Pat Sloan in *Excursion* (Vanderbilt, Apr. 9, 1937); and appeared in *Never Trouble Trouble* (Subway Circuit, Summer 1937).

He played Bill Adams and served as assistant stage manager of *Great Lady* (Majestic, N.Y.C., Dec. 1, 1938); played Sylvestra in *Tell My Story* (Mercury, Mar. 15, 1939); played a Customer and was stage manager of *Billy Draws a Horse* (Playhouse, Dec. 21, 1939); appeared as Defense Counsel McVail in *Johnny Belinda* (Belasco, Sept. 18, 1940); Private Edward Freling in *Skydrift* (Belasco, Nov. 13, 1945); was stage manager and understudy for two companies of *The Voice of the Turtle* (1945–47); played the Doorman, 2nd Prospector, 3rd Reporter, understudied the Ragpicker, and was stage manager of *The Madwoman of Chaillot* (Belasco, Dec. 27, 1948, natl. tour 1949–50); was stage manager of the pre-Bway tryout of *A Month of Sundays* (opened Shubert, Boston, Mass., Dec. 25, 1951; closed Forrest, Philadelphia, Pa., Jan. 26, 1952); stage manager of *Deep Blue Sea* (Morosco, N.Y.C., Nov. 5, 1952); *Escapade* (48 St. Th., Nov. 18, 1953); stage manager and assistant director of *Thracian Horses* (Brandeis Univ., Waltham, Mass., June 1953); and for a tour of *The Sudden Spring* (July–Aug. 1953).

Mr. Chambers was production stage manager and assistant director of *Ondine* (46 St. Th., N.Y.C., Feb. 18, 1954); production stage manager of *Quadrille* (Coronet, Nov. 3, 1954); *Janus* (Plymouth, Nov. 24, 1955); and its tour (opened Rochester Aud., N.Y., Sept. 27, 1956; closed Ford's Th., Baltimore, Md., Mar. 16, 1957); production stage manager of *Nature's Way* (Coronet, N.Y.C., Oct. 16, 1957); *The Girls in 509* (Belasco, Oct. 15, 1958); *The Tumbler* (Helen Hayes Th., Feb. 24, 1960); *Period of Adjustment* (Helen Hayes Th., Nov. 10, 1960); *The Golden State* (Fulton, Nov. 25, 1960); and produced *A Wreath for Udomo* (Hammersmith, London, Eng., Nov. 2, 1962).

He was also stage manager for *Of Love Remembered* (ANTA Th., N.Y.C., Feb. 18, 1967); stage manager for *Keep It in the Family* (Plymouth, Sept. 27, 1967), for which he also was understudy for Patrick Magee, playing the role of Frank Brady; stage manager for the City Ctr. Drama Co. revival of *The Tenth Man* (NY City Ctr., Nov. 8, 1967); and stage manager for a revival of *The Venetian Twins* (Henry Miller's Th., May 28, 1968).

Recreation. Football, college hockey, horses, small boats.

CHAMPION, GOWER. Director, actor, choreographer, dancer. b. Geneva, Ill., June 22, 1921, to John W. and Beatrice (Carlisle) Champion. Father, advertising executive. Attended Fairfax H.S., Los Angeles, Calif., 1933–36. Married Oct. 5, 1947, to Marjorie Belcher, dancer, actress, (marr. dis. 1973); two sons. Served WW II, US Coast Guard; rank, ordinary seaman. Member of SDG; SSD&C; SAG; AGVA; AEA.

Theatre. Mr. Champion made his debut as a dancer in 1936 in supper clubs, appearing with Jeanne Tyler as "Gower and Jeanne" (1936–41). Subsequently the team appeared in *Streets of Paris* (Broadhurst, N.Y.C., June 19, 1939); *The Lady Comes Across* (44 St. Th., Jan. 9, 1942); and *Count Me In* (Ethel Barrymore Th., Oct. 8, 1942); and while in the Coast Guard, Mr. Champion toured in *Tars and Spars* (1943–44).

In 1946, he formed a dance team with Marge Belcher, billed as "Gower and Bell," and after their marriage, were known as "Marge and Gower Champion." In N.Y.C., they appeared in *Three for Tonight* (Plymouth, Apr. 6, 1955).

Mr. Champion choreographed *Small Wonder* (Coronet, Sept. 15, 1948); choreographed and directed *Lend an Ear* (National, Dec. 16, 1948); choreographed *Make a Wish* (Winter Garden, Apr. 18, 1951); directed and choreographed *Bye Bye Birdie* (Martin Beck Th., Apr. 14, 1960) and *Carnival!* (Imperial, Apr. 13, 1961); directed *My Mother, My Father and Me* (Plymouth, Mar. 23, 1963); and choreographed and directed *Hello, Dolly!* (St. James, Jan. 16, 1964; Th. Royal, Drury Lane, London, Eng., Dec. 2, 1965).

He directed *3 Bags Full* (Henry Miller's Th., N.Y.C., Mar. 6, 1966), which he also co-produced; directed *I Do! I Do!* (46th St. Th., Dec. 5, 1966); directed, filmed, and choreographed *The Happy Time* (Broadway Th., Jan. 18, 1968); directed *A Flea in Her Ear* (American Conservatory Th., San Francisco, Calif., Dec. 10, 1968; ANTA Th., N.Y.C., Oct. 3, 1969); produced *Prettybelle*, which he also directed (pre-Bway tryout: Shubert Th., Boston, Mass., Feb. 1–Mar. 6, 1971); directed and choreographed *Sugar* (Majestic, Apr. 9, 1972); directed a revival of *Irene* (Minskoff Th., Mar. 13, 1973); directed another production of *I Do! I Do!* (Huntington Hartford Th., Los Angeles, Calif., June 20, 1973); and directed *Mack and Mabel* (Majestic, N.Y.C., Oct. 6, 1974).

Films. Mr. Champion made his film debut in *Till the Clouds Roll By* (MGM, 1946); followed by dancing roles, with his wife, in *Mr. Music* (Par., 1950); *Show Boat* (MGM, 1951); *Lovely to Look At* (MGM, 1952); *Give a Girl a Break* (MGM, 1953); *Everything I Have Is Yours* (MGM, 1952); *Three for the Show* (Col., 1955); *Jupiter's Darling* (MGM, 1955); and *The Girl Most Likely* (RKO, 1956).

Television. Mr. Champion made many television appearances with his wife (see Champion, Marge); appeared as a guest star on the Gene Kelly Show (CBS, 1965); was on the Merv Griffin Show (Ind., 1965–66); Today Show (NBC, 1965–66); the *New York, New York* special (CBS, Feb. 14, 1966); and he produced and directed the special *Mary Martin at Eastertime* (NBC, Apr. 3, 1966).

Night Clubs. Mr. Champion and Miss Tyler appeared at the Rainbow Room, N.Y.C.; the Empire Room, Waldorf-Astoria Hotel, N.Y.C.; and at the Cocoanut Grove, Ambassador Hotel, Los Angeles, Calif.

Marge and Gower Champion made their N.Y.C. debut at the Persian Room, Plaza Hotel (Oct. 1947), followed by appearances together at the Cocoanut Grove, Ambassador Hotel, Los Angeles, Calif., and many other places (*see* Champion, Marge). Mr. Champion choreographed and directed the night club version of *Hello, Dolly!* (Riviera, Las Vegas, Nev., Dec. 23, 1965).

Awards. For *Lend an Ear*, Mr. Champion received the Antoinette Perry (Tony) (1949) and the Donaldson awards for choreography (1949); for *Bye Bye Birdie*, he received two Antoinette Perry (Tony) Awards for direction and choreography (1961); for *Hello, Dolly!*, he received two Antoinette Perry (Tony) Awards for direction and choreography (1964); for *The Happy Time* he received Antoinette Perry (Tony) awards for direction and choreography (1968); and he was in addition nominated twice for Tony's for best director of a musical, for *I Do! I Do!* and for *Irene*. .

Recreation. Swimming, sailing, photography.

CHAMPION, MARGE. Actress, dancer. b. Marjorie Celeste Belcher, Sept. 2, 1925, Hollywood, Calif., to Ernest and Gladys (Baskette) Belcher. Father, ballet teacher. Attended Berkeley Hall, Beverly Hills, Calif.; grad. Bancroft Jr. H.S., Hollywood; Hollywood H.S. Studied dance with her father; acting with Helena Sorrell, Beverly Hills, Maria Ouspenskaya, Hollywood; in N.Y.C., ballet with Vincenzo Celli, modern dance with Hanya Holm and in Hollywood, tap dancing with Nick Castle. Married Oct. 5, 1947, to Gower Champion, director, choreographer (marr. dis. 1973); two sons. Member of AEA; AFTRA; SAG.

Pre-Theatre. Dance instructor.

Theatre. Mrs. Champion first appeared on the stage, billed as Marjorie Belle, as the Spirit of the Night in the ballet *Carnival in Venice* (Hollywood Bowl, Calif., Aug. 1935). She made her professional debut in three roles in a West Coast touring production of *Tonight at 8:30* (Biltmore Th., Los Angeles, Calif., 1939); subsequently appeared as a dancer with The Three Stooges in vaudeville (1939); in the Bway tryout of *Little Dog Laughed* (1940); and in a pre-Bway tryout of *Portrait of a Lady* (1941). She played in a summer-theatre production of *Sally* (Paper Mill Playhouse, Millburn, N.J., July 1943).

She made her N.Y.C. debut as a dancer in *What's Up* (Natl., Nov. 11, 1943); subsequently played the Fair Witch in *Dark of the Moon* (46th St. Th., Apr. 14, 1945); and appeared as the First Girl and performed as a dancer in *Beggar's Holiday* (Bway Th., Dec. 26, 1946). In 1947 she began the first of many appearances with her husband Gower Champion, as a dance team in night clubs; appeared as Crete with her husband in *Dancing Years* (St. Louis Municipal Opera Th., Mo., June 1947); billed as Marge Champion, appeared with her husband in *3 for Tonight* (Plymouth, N.Y.C., Apr. 6, 1955), and in the West Coast production (Claremont, Calif., 1955); and they also performed in an Ed Sullivan Variety program presented in the USSR (Green Th., Gorky Park, Moscow, Aug. 1958).

In 1959, she appeared in summer-theatre productions, playing Cloris in *Hemingway and All Those People* and the title role in *Sabrina Fair* (Avondale Playhouse, Indianapolis, Ind.); Essie Sebastian in *The Great Sebastians* and Camilla in *Invitation to a March* (La Jolla Playhouse, Calif.).

She was a special assistant to her husband, the director and choreographer of *Hello, Dolly!* (St. James Th., N.Y.C., Jan. 16, 1964); played Marietta Joy in the pre-Bway tryout of *Everybody Out, the Castle Is Sinking* (opened and closed: Colonial Th., Boston, Mass., Dec. 26, 1964–Jan. 9, 1965); and appeared in *High Button Shoes* (Municipal, St. Louis, Mo., Aug. 2, 1965). In 1969–70, she was a member of the acting company of the Los Angeles (Calif.) Center Th. Group's New Theater for Now Workshop of the Mark Taper Forum, where she appeared in *Slivovitz* (May 15, 1969); and in 1970 she taught acting at the Mafundi Institute in Watts, Los Angeles.

Films. Mrs. Champion began as a cartoon model for Walt Disney, performing as Snow White in *Snow White and the Seven Dwarfs* (RKO, 1937); the Blue Fairy in *Pinocchio* (RKO, 1940); and various dance roles in *Fantasia* (RKO, 1940). Also in *Mr. Music* (Par., 1950); in *Show Boat* (MGM, 1951); *Lovely to Look At* (MGM, 1952); *Everything I Have Is Yours* (MGM, 1952); *Give a Girl a Break* (MGM, 1953); *Jupiter's Darling* (MGM, 1955); *Three for the Show* (Col., 1955); *The Swimmer* (Col., 1966).

Television. She appeared with her husband on the Milton Berle Show (NBC, Oct. 1947); played Gower and Bell on a New Year's Eve Show (NBC, Jan. 1948); as Marge and Gower Champion, they appeared on the Admiral Broadway Review (NBC, 1949); the Perry Como Show (NBC); the Dinah Shore Show (NBC); the Ed Sullivan Show (CBS); Accent on Love; the Standard Oil Show; the Eddie Fisher Show (NBC); the Jack Benny Show (CBS); Shower of Stars (CBS); the Bell Telephone Hour (NBC); Toast of the Town (CBS); General Electric Th. (CBS); and the Sid Caesar Show (ABC). In 1957, they had their own program, the Marge and Gower Champion Show (CBS); she appeared on the Mike Douglas Show (Cleveland, Ohio, 1963); on Candid Camera (CBS, 1963); at various times on Girl Talk (ABC, Ind., 1964–67); on Step This Way (Ind., 1965–66); and Memory Lane (Ind., 1965–66).

Night Clubs. When she and her husband first appeared together as a team they were billed as *Gower and Bell* at the Normandie Roof (Montreal, Quebec, Canada, Apr. 1947); subsequently played in Boston (Apr. 1947); the Park Plaza (St. Louis, Mo., May 1947); and the Palmer House (Chicago, Ill., July 1947). Billed as Marge and Gower Champion, they performed at the Plaza Hotel (N.Y.C., Oct. 1947); Mayflower Hotel (Washington, D.C., Nov. 1947); Statler hotels (1948); Miami Beach (Fla., Jan. 1949); the Riviera (Fort Lee, N.J., June 1949; July 1959); Mocambo (Hollywood, Calif., Aug. 1949); Fairmont Hotel (San Francisco, Calif., Oct. 1949); and the Flamingo (Las Vegas, Nev., 1949).

CHANNING, CAROL. Actress, singer. b. Carol Elaine Channing, Jan. 31, 1921, Seattle, Wash., to George and Adelaide (Glaser) Channing. Father, Christian Science lecturer, writer, newspaper editor. Attended Bennington Coll., 1938. Married 1942 to Theodore Nadish (marr. dis. 1944); married Dec. 12, 1948, to Al Carson (marr. dis. Sept. 1955); married Sept. 5, 1956, to Charles F. Lowe, television producer, writer; one son. Member of AEA; SAG; AFTRA; AGVA. Address: Charles Lowe Productions, Inc., 8749 Sunset Boulevard, Hollywood, CA 90046.

Theatre. Miss Channing made her stage debut in the opera, *No for an Answer* (Mecca Temple, N.Y.C., Jan. 5, 1941); subsequently understudied Eve Arden as Maggie Watson in *Let's Face It* (Imperial Th., Oct. 29, 1941); playing the role at one performance (July, 1942); appeared as Steve in *Proof Through the Night* (Morosco, Dec. 25, 1942); in the revue, *Lend an Ear* (Las Palmas Th., June 12, 1948; National, N.Y.C., Dec. 16, 1948); Lorelei Lee in *Gentlemen Prefer Blondes* (Ziegfeld, Dec. 8, 1949), in which she toured for two years (opened Palace, Chicago, Ill., Sept. 20, 1951); toured as Eliza Doolittle in *Pygmalion* (opened Ivoryton Playhouse, Conn., Aug. 1953); succeeded (Mar. 1954) Rosalind Russell as Ruth Sherwood in *Wonderful Town* (Winter Garden, N.Y.C., Feb. 25, 1953), in which she toured (opened Shubert, Chicago, Ill., July 7, 1954).

Miss Channing appeared as Flora Weems in *The Vamp* (Winter Garden, N.Y.C., Nov. 10, 1955); in a one-woman show, entitled *Show Biz* (Curran, San Francisco, Calif., Oct. 19, 1959), in which she toured; appeared in the same show retitled *Show Girl* (Eugene O'Neill Th., Jan. 12, 1961), and on tour. She performed in a concert tour (Jan.–May 1962); and a touring production, *The George Burns, Carol Channing Show* (opened Orpheum, Seattle, Wash., June, 1962); played Epifania in a touring production of *The Millionairess* (opened Brown Th., Louisville, Ky., June 1963); Mrs. Dolly Gallagher Levi in *Hello, Dolly!* (St. James Th., N.Y.C., June 16, 1964), in which she also toured (Sept. 7, 1965–June 13, 1966; Oct. 12, 1966–June 11, 1967); appeared in *Carol Channing and Her Ten Stout-Hearted Men* (Drury Lane, London, England, Apr. 1970); played the female lead in a program of four one-act plays, *Four on a Garden* (Broadhurst, N.Y.C., Jan. 30, 1971); and was Lorelei Lee in *Lorelei* (National Th., Washington, D.C., May 15, 1973; Palace, N.Y.C., Jan. 27, 1974).

Films. Miss Channing appeared in *The First Traveling Saleslady* (RKO, 1956) and *Thoroughly Modern Millie* (U, 1967).

Television. Miss Channing was a guest on Women on the Move (NBC, 1964–65); Password (CBS, 1964–65; 1965–66); To Tell the Truth (CBS, 1964–65); What's My Line? (CBS, 1964–65; 1965–66); I've Got a Secret (CBS, 1964–65); Girl Talk (ABC & Ind., 1964–65; 1965–66); Hy Gardner Show (Ind., 1964–65); Merv Griffin Show (Ind., 1964–65; 1965–66); Hollywood Backstage (Ind., 1966–67); and she has made numerous appearances on the Ed Sullivan Show (CBS), Perry Como Show (NBC), Dinah Shore Show (CBS), Red Skelton Show (NBC), Garry Moore Show (CBS), and Jack Paar Show (NBC).

She was also in *Svengali and the Blonde* (NBC, July 30, 1955); *Three Men on a Horse* (Playhouse 90, CBS, Apr. 18, 1957); *Crescendo* (CBS, Sept. 29, 1957); *The Christmas Tree* (NBC, Dec. 1959); the World's Fair Spectacular (1964); *Best on Record* special (NBC, May 18, 1965); *Today on Broadway* (Today, NBC, May 21, 1965); *Stars Salute* (Ind., Oct. 24, 1965); *An Evening with Carol Channing* (CBS, Feb. 18, 1966); *Wonderful World of Burlesque: III* (NBC, Dec. 11, 1966); and was the subject of *Carol Channing — Interview* (NET, July 24, 1967). Her other television shows include *Carol Channing and 101 Men* (ABC, Feb. 29, 1968); *Carol Channing and Pearl Bailey on Broadway* (ABC, Mar. 16, 1969); *Carol Channing Proudly Presents the Seven Deadly Sins* (ABC, Apr. 14, 1969); *Carol Channing's Mad English Tea Party* (NBC, Sept. 16, 1970); and *I'm a Fan* (CBS, Jan. 25, 1972).

Night Clubs. Miss Channing has performed in her own musical revue at the Tropicana Hotel, Las Vegas, Nev. (July–Oct. 1958); Plaza Hotel, N.Y.C. (1957–58); toured night clubs in major cities (July 1958–Oct. 1959); appeared at the Waldorf-Astoria, N.Y.C. (1961–63); in an act with George Burns at the Dunes Hotel, Las Vegas, Nev. (July–Nov. 1962); at the Cork Club, Houston, Tex. (Aug. 1968); and at the Latin Casino, Cherry Hill, N.J. (1969). Miss Channing also performed for Pres. John F. Kennedy (Jan. 28, 1963) and, by presidential request, at the Inaugural Gala for Pres. Lyndon B. Johnson (Natl. Guard Armory, Washington, D.C., Jan. 18, 1965).

Awards. Miss Channing won an Antoinette Perry (Tony) Award and the *Variety* Drama Critics Poll (both 1964) for best female lead in a musical for her performance in *Hello, Dolly!*; she received a Golden Globe Award (1967) as best supporting actress for her role in *Thoroughly Modern Millie*; received a special Tony award in 1968; was voted best musical actress in the annual *Variety* poll of London theatre critics for her performance in *Carol Channing and Ten Stout-Hearted Men;* was awarded Harvard University's Hasty Pudding Theatrical Award as "Woman of the Year" (Feb. 1971); and was nominated for a Tony for best actress in a musical (1974) for *Lorelei.*

CHAPLIN, SYDNEY. Actor. b. Sidney Earl Chaplin, Mar. 30, 1926, Los Angeles, Calif., to Charles Spencer and Lita (Gray) Chaplin. Father, actor, director, producer, writer, composer; mother, actress. Attended Blach Fox Military Acad., Los Angeles; Lawrenceville Sch., N.J.; North Hollywood H.S., Calif. Married Mar. 1960 to Noelle Adam, actress. Served US Army Inf. Relative in theatre: brother, Charles Chaplin, Jr., actor. Member of AEA; SAG; AFTRA.

Theatre. From 1947–51, Mr. Chaplin produced with Jerry Epstein, at the Circle Th. (Hollywood, Calif.), where he also appeared as Lt. Charles in *The Adding Machine;* John Shand in *What Every Woman Knows;* Sgt. O'Hara in *Rain;* appeared in *Hindle Wakes;* played the Housemover's Brother in *Sam Ego's House* (Oct. 30, 1947); and Nick in *The Time of Your Life.*

He made his N.Y.C. debut as Jeff Moss in *Bells Are Ringing* (Shubert, Nov. 29, 1956); subsequently appeared as George Tracy in *Goodbye Charlie* (Lyceum, Dec. 16, 1959); Tom Bailey in *Subways Are for Sleeping* (St. James, Dec. 27, 1961); Woody Hartman in *In the Counting House* (Biltmore, Dec. 13, 1962); and as Nick Arnstein in *Funny Girl* (Winter Garden, Mar. 26, 1964).

Films. Mr. Chaplin made his debut in *Limelight* (UA, 1952); followed by *Land of the Pharoahs* (WB, 1955); *Pillars of the Sky* (U, 1956); *Quantez* (U, 1958); *Four Girls in Town* (U, 1956); *A Countess from Hong Kong* (U, 1967); and *The Sicilian Clan* (20th-Fox, 1970).

Television. Mr. Chaplin appeared in *Wonderful Town* (CBS, Nov. 30, 1958); *Keep in Step* (CBS); *Kings Row* (ABC); and on the Phil Silvers Show (CBS).

Other Activities. Mr. Chaplin is co-owner, with Moustache, of the Chez Mous' restaurant in Paris.

Awards. Mr. Chaplin received an Antoinette Perry (Tony) Award (1957) for his performance as Jeff Moss in *Bells Are Ringing.*

CHAPMAN, LONNY. Actor, director, playwright. b. Lon Leonard Chapman, Oct. 1, 1920, Tulsa, Okla., to Elmer and Eunice (Presley) Chapman. Father, truck mechanic. Grad. Joplin (Mo.) H.S., 1938; Univ. of Okla., B.A. 1947. Studied at the Actors Studio (member, 1949–to date). Married Feb. 13, 1944, to Erma Dean; one son. Served WW II, USMC, PTO; rank, 2nd Lt. Member of AEA; AFTRA; Writer's Guild of America; SAG. Address: 240 W. 98th St., New York, NY 10025, tel. MO 2-9924; 3973 Goodland Ave., Studio City, CA 91604, tel. (213) 980-9118.

Theatre. Mr. Chapman's first theatrical assignment was as stage manager of *A House Possessed* (Henry St. Playhouse, N.Y.C., Nov. 21, 1947); subsequently appeared as Wiley in the touring production of *Mister Roberts* (Erlanger Th., Chicago, Ill., Sept. 1948); made his Bway debut as the Guard in *The Closing Door* (Empire, Dec. 1, 1949); appeared as Turk in *Come Back, Little Sheba* (Booth, Feb. 15, 1950); Knub McDermott in *The Chase* (Playhouse, Apr. 15, 1952); succeeded Walter Matthau as Charlie Hill in *In Any Language* (Cort, Oct. 7, 1952); played Eddie in *Whistler's Grandmother* (President, Dec. 11, 1952); Harry in *The Ladies of the Corridor* (Longacre, Oct. 21, 1953); Henry Thomas in *The Traveling Lady* (Playhouse, Oct. 26, 1954); Tom in *The Time of Your Life* (NY City Ctr., Jan. 19, 1955); and the Gentleman Caller in *The Glass Menagerie* (NY City Ctr., Nov. 21, 1956).

Mr. Chapman wrote *The Buffalo Skinner* (Th. Marquee, Feb. 19, 1958), which he also staged; was managing director and producer of the Cecilwood Th. (Fishkill, N.Y., 1959–63); wrote *Cry of the Raindrop* (St. Mark's Playhouse, N.Y.C., Mar. 7, 1961). He played Lt. Col. Bonney in *General Seeger* (Lyceum, Feb. 28, 1962); and Mr. Dankle, the Dance Marathon Promoter, in *Marathon '33* (ANTA, Dec. 22, 1963).

He directed, for Inner City Rep. Co. (Los Angeles, CA), *The Glass Menagerie* (1968), *The Fantasticks* (1969), and *West Side Story* (1969). He directed *Nature of the Crime* (Bouwerie Lane Th., N.Y.C., Mar. 23, 1970); directed and wrote, for Actor's Studio Th. (Los Angeles, Calif.), *Echoes* (1970) and *Hootsudir* (1972); and was artistic director, Group Repertory Theatre (Los Angeles, Calif.), where he directed *La Ronde* (1973) and *Born Yesterday* (1974) and wrote and directed *Go Hang the Moon* (1973).

Films. Mr. Chapman has appeared in *Young at Heart* (WB, 1954); *East of Eden* (WB, 1955); *Baby Doll* (WB, 1956); and *The Birds* (U, 1963); *Covenant with Death* (WB, 1965); *Hour of the Gun* (UA, 1966); *The Stalking Moon* (WB, 1969); *I Walk the Line* (Col., 1971); *Run Wild* (Ind., 1972); *Where the Red Fern Grows* (CMI, 1973); *Earthquake* (U, 1974); and *Witch Who Came Out of the Sea* (Ind., 1974).

Television. Mr. Chapman has performed (1950–to date) on Studio One (CBS); Philco Television Playhouse (NBC); Goodyear Television Playhouse (NBC); Dupont Show-of-the-Month (NBC); Ben Casey (ABC); Gunsmoke (CBS); Alfred Hitchcock Presents (CBS); directed *The Windows* (CBS, 1956); and appeared in the title role of the series The Investigator (NBC, 1958).

He was a series regular on For the People (CBS, 1963) and has appeared on such television series as The Defenders (CBS); Bonanza (NBC); Name of the Game (NBC); The Virginian (NBC); The Fugitive (ABC); Mod Squad (ABC); Medical Center (CBS); Lucas Tanner (NBC); and McCloud (NBC).

CHAPMAN, ROBERT H. Educator, director, playwright. b. Robert Harris Chapman, Apr. 14, 1919, Highland Park, Ill., to Paul W. and Joanna H. Chapman. Father, banker. Grad. Princeton Univ., B.A. 1941; Harvard Univ. Served USN; rank, Lt. Member of Dramatists Guild. Address: (home) Eliot House, C-31, Cambridge, MA; (bus.) Loeb Drama Center, Harvard Univ., 64 Brattle St., Cambridge, MA 02138.

Since 1960, Mr. Chapman has been Director of Loeb Drama Center, Harvard Univ., where he has been a member of the faculty since 1950 (instructor, 1950–52; asst. professor, 1952–56; assoc. professor, 1956–67 professor, 1967–to date). He has also held academic positions at Princeton Univ. (1946–48); and the Univ. of California at Berkeley (1948–50).

He has been director of the Princeton Triangle Club (1947–48) and the University Players (Princeton, N.J., 1949–50).

He wrote, with Louis Coxe, an adaptation of *Billy Budd* (Biltmore Th., N.Y.C., Feb. 10, 1951). He was a consultant to the Rockefeller Foundation (1954–56); the National Arts Foundation (1966–68); the Juilliard Sch. of Drama, Lincoln Center for the Performing Arts (1966–68), and was script writer for and consultant to David O. Selznick (1956).

Published Works. Mr. Chapman wrote the prefatory comment for the Laurel edition of Shakespeare's *Measure for Measure.*

Awards. He holds an honorary M.A. from Harvard Univ. (1956).

CHARNIN, MARTIN. Director, producer, lyricist. b. Martin Jay Charnin, Nov. 24, 1934, New York City, to William and Birdie (Blakeman) Charnin. Father, singer with Metropolitan Opera Co. Grad. H.S. of Music and Art, N.Y.C., 1951; Cooper Union, B.A. 1956. Married Mar. 2, 1958, to Lynn Ross, dancer (marr. dis. 1961); one son; married Jan. 8, 1962, to Genii Prior, dancer; one daughter. Member of Dramatists Guild; ASCAP; WGA; SSDC; NYTAS; AGAC; DGA. Address: (home) 48 Jane St., New York, NY 10014, tel. (212) OR 5-2638; (bus.) Beam One Ltd., 157 W. 57th St., New York, NY 10019, tel. (212) 489-1012.

Theatre. Mr. Charnin's first professional assignment was as contributor of lyrics to the revue *Kaleidoscope* (Provincetown Playhouse, N.Y.C., Sept. 17, 1957); subsequently he appeared as Big Deal in *West Side Story* (Winter Garden, Sept. 26, 1957); was lyricist and sketch writer for *Fallout Revue* (Renata, May 8, 1959); appeared in the revue *The Girls Against the Boys* (Alvin, Nov. 2, 1959); as Big Deal in the return engagement of *West Side Story* (Winter Garden, Apr. 27, 1960); was lyricist for *Hot Spot* (Majestic, Apr. 19, 1963); the touring production of *Zenda* (opened Curran, San Francisco, Calif., Aug. 5, 1963; closed Civic Aud., Pasadena, Calif., Nov. 16, 1963); *Mata Hari* (closed in pre-Bway tryout at National, Washington, D.C., Dec. 9, 1967); was lyricist and director of *Ballad for a Firing Squad* (off-Bway revival of *Mata Hari;* Th. de Lys, N.Y.C., Dec. 13, 1968); lyricist for *Two by Two* (Majestic, Nov. 10, 1970); conceived and directed *Nash at Nine* (Helen Hayes Th., May 17, 1973); and directed *Music! Music!* (NY City Ctr., April 1974).

Television. Mr. Charnin was lyricist for the television special *Feathertop* (ABC, Oct. 15, 1961) and for the Jackie Gleason Show (CBS, 1961). He conceived and produced *Annie, the Women in the Life of a Man* (CBS, Feb. 18, 1970); conceived, produced, and directed the television special *George M!* (NBC, 1970); conceived, produced, wrote, and directed *Jack Lemmon in 'S Wonderful, 'S Marvelous, 'S Gershwin* (NBC, Jan. 17, 1972); conceived, produced, and directed *Dames at Sea* (NBC, 1972); *Cole Porter in Paris* (NBC, 1973); *Jack Lemmon in Get Happy— The Music of Harold Arlen* (NBC, 1973); and produced a two-hour variety pilot for Children's Television Workshop on adult health (Summer 1973).

Night Clubs. He contributed lyrics to Julius Monk's revue, *Pieces of Eight* (Upstairs at the Downstairs, N.Y.C., Sept. 1959); Ben Bagley's touring *Little Revue* (May 1960); wrote and staged material for Anna Maria Alberghetti, Leslie Uggams, Nancy Wilson, Larry Kert, Dionne Warwicke, Abbe Lane, José Ferrer, Jack Cassidy, and Shirley Jones.

Discography. Mr. Charnin wrote music and lyrics for the Barbra Streisand recording "The Best Thing You've Ever Done" (1972), and he wrote the lyrics for "Maman," issued on many recordings, including a dozen in foreign languages.

Awards. Television productions on which Mr. Charnin has worked and that have received NATAS (Emmy) awards or nominations include: *Annie, the Women in the Life of a Man* (Mr. Charnin won an Emmy); *'S Wonderful, 'S Marvelous, 'S Gershwin* (best program, best director, and nomination for best writing); *George M!* (nomination for best directing); and *Jack Lemmon in Get Happy* (nomination for best directing).

CHASE, ILKA. Actress, author. b. Apr. 8, New York City, to Francis Dane and Edna Alloway (Woolman) Chase. Father, hotel manager; mother, former editor of *Vogue.* Attended Mrs. Dow's Sch., Briarcliff, N.Y.; private schools in France. Married 1926, to Louis Calhern (marr. dis. 1926); married July 13, 1935, to William Murray (marr. dis. 1946); married Dec. 7, 1946, to Dr. Norton Brown. Member of AEA; SAG; AFTRA. Address: 333 E. 57th St., New York, NY 10022.

Theatre. Miss Chase made her professional debut as Polly Carter in *The Proud Princess* (Cox Th., Cincinnati, Ohio, Nov. 1924); her Bway debut as Sister Francesca and the Maid in *The Red Falcon* (Broadhurst, Oct. 7, 1924); appeared as Mrs. Castro in *Shall We Join the Ladies?,* one of a double-bill (Empire, Jan. 13, 1925); with the Henry Miller Co., appeared in San Francisco, Calif., in *Embers, The Swan,* and *The Grand Duchess and the Waiter* (Apr.–May 1925); played Lia in *Antonia* (Empire, N.Y.C., Oct. 20, 1925); Madame Cleremont in *Embers* (Henry Miller Th., Feb. 1, 1926); succeeded (Sept. 1926) Leonore Sorsby as Frances Drayton in *Loose Ankles* (Biltmore, Aug. 16, 1926); and played Consuelo Pratt in *The Happy Husband* (Empire, May 7, 1928).

Miss Chase played Grace Macomber in *The Animal Kingdom* (Broadhurst, Jan. 12, 1932); adapted, with William S. Murray, *We Are No Longer Children* (Booth, Mar. 31, 1932); played Elinor Branch in

Forsaking All Others (Times Square Th., Mar. 1, 1933); Lucy Hillman in *Days without End* (Henry Miller's Th., Jan. 8, 1934); Marion Langdon in *Wife Insurance* (Ethel Barrymore Th., Apr. 12, 1934); and Lady Cattering in *While Parents Sleep* (Playhouse, June 4, 1934).

She appeared as Sylvia Temple in *Small Miracle* (John Golden Th., Sept. 26, 1934); Dona Isabella in *Revenge with Music* (New Amsterdam, Nov. 28, 1934); Eleanor Sloan in *On to Fortune* (Fulton, Feb. 4, 1935); Sylvia Farren in *Co-Respondent Unknown* (Ritz, Feb. 11, 1936); Sylvia Fowler in *The Women* (Ethel Barrymore Th., Dec. 26, 1936); in *Keep Off the Grass* (Broadhurst, May 23, 1940); Jean Harding in *Beverly Hills* (Fulton, Nov. 7, 1940); toured in stock as Carlotta in *Love in Our Time* (Summer 1943); and as Marion Froude in *Biography* (Summer 1943).

Miss Chase appeared as Devon Wainwright in her own play, *In Bed We Cry* (Belasco, Nov. 14, 1944); Susan in a stock production of *Susan and God* (Summer 1945); in *Laughter From a Cloud* (Boston, Mass., Aug. 1947); in *The First Lady* (Empress, St. Louis, Mo., Oct. 1952); in the Farewell Tribute to the Empire Theatre (May 24, 1953); and she succeeded (May 23, 1966–Apr. 1967) Eileen Heckart as Mrs. Banks in *Barefoot in the Park* (Biltmore, Oct. 23, 1963).

Films. Miss Chase made her debut in *Paris Bound* (Pathé, 1929); subsequently appeared in *Red Hot Rhythm* (Pathé, 1929); *The Careless Age* (1st Natl., 1929); *South Sea Rose* (20th-Fox, 1929); *Why Leave Home?* (20th-Fox, 1929); *On Your Back* (20th-Fox, 1930); *The Big Party* (20th-Fox, 1930); *Let's Go Places* (20th-Fox, 1930); *Rich People* (Pathé, 1930); *The Floradora Girl* (MGM, 1930); *The Lady Consents* (RKO, 1936); *Soak the Rich* (Par., 1936); *Stronger Than Desire* (MGM, 1939); *Now, Voyager* (WB, 1942); *No Time for Love* (Par. 1943); *Miss Tatlock's Millions* (Par., 1948); *Johnny Dark* (U, 1954); *It Should Happen to You* (Col., 1954); *The Big Knife* (UA, 1955); and *Oceans 11* (WB, 1960).

Television. Miss Chase has appeared on Masquerade Party; the Ilka Chase Program; and 90 Bristol Court. She also was on Silver Theatre (CBS, Mar. 20, 1950); in *Robert E. Lee* (Pulitzer Prize Playhouse, ABC, Mar. 26, 1952); *Cinderella* (CBS, Mar. 31, 1957); *Spell of the Tigress* (Kraft Th., NBC, Feb. 5, 1958); The Defenders (CBS, 1961); I Remember Murder (ABC, 1961); the Patty Duke Show (ABC, Sept. 1963); Trials of O'Brien (CBS, Sept. 18, 1965); and Cool Million (NBC, Nov. 22, 1972).

Published Works. Miss Chase wrote *Past Imperfect* (1941); *In Bed We Cry* (1943); *I Love Miss Tilli Bean* (1946); *Free Admission* (1948); *New York 22* (1951); with Edna Woolman Chase, *Always in Vogue* (1954); *The Island Players* (1956); *Three Men on the Left Hand* (1960); *The Carthaginian Rose* (1961); *Elephants Arrive at Half Past Five* (1963); *Second Spring and Two Potatoes* (1965); *Fresh From the Laundry* (1967); and *The Varied Airs of Spring* (1969).

CHASE, MARY. Playwright. b. Mary Coyle, Feb. 25, 1907, West Denver, Colo., to Frank and Mary (McDonough) Coyle. Father, flour salesman. Grad. West Denver H.S., 1922; attended Univ. of Denver, 1922–24; Univ. of Colorado, 1924–25. Married June 7, 1920, to Robert L. Chase; three sons. Member of Amer. Newspaper Guild; Dramatists Guild.

Pre-Theatre. Reporter for *Rocky Mountain News* (1925).

Theatre. Mrs. Chase's first produced play was for the Federal Th. (WPA) Project, *Me Third* (Denver, Colo., 1936), which was presented in N.Y.C. as *Now You've Done It* (Henry Miller's Th., Mar. 5, 1937).

She wrote *A Slip of a Girl* for a US Infantry Unit (Camp Hale, Colo., 1941); followed by *Harvey* (48th St. Th., N.Y.C., Nov. 1, 1944; Prince of Wales', London, Jan. 5, 1949); *The Next Half Hour* (Empire, N.Y.C., Oct. 29, 1945); *Mrs. McThing* (ANTA, Feb. 20, 1952); *Bernadine* (Playhouse, Oct. 16, 1952); *Lolita* (Barter Th., Abingdon, Va., Aug. 30, 1954); *Midgie Purvis* (Martin Beck Th., N.Y.C., Feb. 1, 1961); and *Cocktails with Mimi* (world premiere, Barter Th., Abingdon, Va., July 3, 1973).

Published Works. She wrote a short story, *He's Our Baby*, for *Ladies Home Journal* (Apr. 1945), and a children's book, *Loretta Mason Potts* (1959).

Awards. Mrs. Chase received the Pulitzer Prize for *Harvey* (1945).

CHASE, STANLEY. Producer. b. May 3, 1928, New York City, Grad. New Utrecht H.S., Brooklyn, N.Y., 1944; New York Univ., B.A. 1949; studied drama with Dr. Milton Smith at Columbia Univ., 1949–50. Married May 17, 1955, to Dorothy Rice, actress. Served USN, PTO, 1944–45; won Presidential Citation. Member of League of NY Theatres; NATAS.

Theatre. Mr. Chase was co-producer with Carmen Capalbo of *The Threepenny Opera* (Th. de Lys, N.Y.C., Mar. 10, 1954); at the Bijou Th., was producer with Mr. Canalbo of *The Potting Shed* (Jan. 29, 1957); *A Moon for the Misbegotten* (May 2, 1957); *The Cave Dwellers* (Oct. 19, 1959); and presented *Free and Easy*, a blues opera (Th. Alhambra, Paris, France, Jan. 7, 1960), which toured Europe.

Films. Mr. Chase was producer of *The Forbin Project* (U, 1970).

Television. He founded the television trade weekly *Tele-Talent* in 1950; has been associated with CBS-TV story department and has been an associate producer and writer for Startime (NBC); was director of network programs (ABC, 1962); and produced *A Time To Love* (Bob Hope Chrysler Th., NBC, Jan. 1967).

Awards. *The Threepenny Opera* was cited by the American Th. Wing (1956).

Recreation. Horseback riding, traveling, poker.

CHAVEZ, EDMUND M. Teacher, director. b. Nov. 29, 1926, San Antonio, Tex., to Edward M. and Stella G. Chavez. Educated at Brackenridge H.S., San Antonio; Southwest Texas State Coll., San Marcos, Tex., B.A. (history, drama, and speech), 1949; Univ. of Texas, Austin, M.F.A. 1951; Stanford Univ., Cal., Ph.D. 1958. Served in US Navy (1944–46); USNR (1946–54). Married June 11, 1951, to Joan Coble; three sons, one daughter. Member of ATA (secy. of Design Proj., natl. conv., 1962; chmn. of same, 1963); SCA; Pi Kappa Delta; Alpha Psi Omega; Phi Mu Alpha Sinfonia. Dept. of Theatre Arts, Univ. of Idaho, Moscow, ID 83843, tel. (208) 885-6465; 1416 Chinook, Moscow, ID 83843, tel. (208) 882-2636.

Mr. Chavez is an associate professor at the Univ. of Idaho, where he has been head of the Dept. of Theatre Arts since 1969. He began his teaching career as an undergraduate assistant for two years in the history department, Southwest Texas Coll., then for two years he was a graduate assistant in drama at the Univ. of Texas. He was artist-in-residence at Stanford Univ. in 1951 and in the same year was appointed an instructor at the Univ. of Idaho, where he was subsequently appointed assistant professor (1954), associate professor (1966), and chairman of drama (1968). Mr. Chavez was also a graduate teaching assistant at Stanford Univ. (1957–58).

In addition to the preceding, Mr. Chavez was a lecturer at the Institute of Renaissance Studies, Oregon Shakespeare Festival, Ashland, Ore. (1953–58), where he lectured on swordplay in 1957–58, and he was technical director of the Oregon Shakespeare Festival (1953–58). He was co-developer of the summer theatre program that began at Moscow in 1952, and in 1959 he became director of the summer theatre. He has also developed a technical theatre program, a children's theatre program, and a touring theatre that uses federal/state matching funds. In 1972, he was given responsibility for planning Phase 1 of the Performing Arts Center, and he played a central role in the architectural planning and in practical matters of building.

Other Activities. Mr. Chavez lectured at Washington State Univ. (1963), and was senior guest lecturer, Univ. of Manchester, England, where he spoke on Victorian theatre, Chekhov, Ibsen, and contemporary American theatre. He studied physical theatres in Europe, including Roman and Renaissance theatres in France and Italy, and he studied production and directing techniques in London.

Published Works. Mr. Chavez has written numerous articles that have been published in *Players Magazine*. In 1967, he began editing a quarterly newsletter for high schools in Idaho and eastern Washington, and he edits *Curtain Call*, news quarterly of the Rocky Mountain Theatre Association.

Recreation. Research on stage fencing; sailing ship models.

CHAYEFSKY, PADDY. Playwright, director, producer. b. Sidney Chayefsky, Jan. 29, 1923, New York City, to Harry and Gussie (Stuchevsky) Chayefsky. Father, milk company executive. Grad. DeWitt Clinton H.S., 1939; City Coll. of N.Y., B.S.S. 1943. Married Feb. 24, 1949, to Susan Sackler; one son. Served WW II, US Army, Infantry; rank, Pfc.; awarded Purple Heart. Member of WGA; Dramatists Guild (member of council, 1962–to date); SWG; AGVA; SAG; P.E.N.; AGAC; Songwriters Protective Assn.; New Dramatists Committee (1952–53). Address: 850 Seventh Ave., New York, NY 10019, tel. (212) CI 5-5663.

Pre-Theatre. Printer's apprentice.

Theatre. Mr. Chayefsky is the author of *Fifth from Garibaldi* (unproduced); *Middle of the Night* (ANTA Th., Feb. 8, 1956); *The Tenth Man* (Booth, Nov. 5, 1959); *Gideon* (Plymouth, Nov. 9, 1961); *The Passion of Josef D.* (Ethel Barrymore Th., Feb. 11, 1964), which he also directed; and *The Latent Heterosexual* (Aldwych, London, 1968).

Films. He wrote the screenplay for *The Great American Hoax* (20th-Fox); was both writer of the screenplay and associate producer of *Marty* (UA, 1955) and *The Bachelor Party* (UA, 1957); wrote the screenplays for *The Goddess* (Col., 1958); *Middle of the Night* (Col., 1959); *The Americanization of Emily* (MGM, 1964); and *The Hospital* (UA, 1971).

Television and Radio. For radio, Mr. Chayefsky adapted for Theatre Guild of the Air (1951–52), *The Meanest Man in the World, Tommy* and *Over 21.*

For television, he has written for Suspense (CBS, 1952); Manhunt (1952); *Holiday Song* (Philco Television Playhouse, NBC, Sept. 14, 1952); *Printer's Measure* (Goodyear Playhouse, NBC, Apr. 26, 1953); *Marty* (Goodyear Playhouse, NBC, May 24, 1953); *The Big Deal* (Goodyear Playhouse, NBC, July 19, 1953); *The Bachelor Party* (Goodyear Playhouse, NBC, Oct. 11, 1953); *The Sixth Year* (Philco Television Playhouse, NBC, Nov. 20, 1953); *Catch My Boy on Sunday* (Philco Television Playhouse, NBC, 1953); *The Mother* (Philco Television Playhouse, NBC, Apr. 4, 1954); the television version of *Middle of the Night* (Philco Television Playhouse, NBC, Sept. 19, 1954); and *The Catered Affair* (Goodyear Playhouse, NBC, May 22, 1955).

Other Activities. He has served as pres. of Sudan Corp. (1956–to date); Carnegie Products (1957–to date); and S.P.D. Corp.

Awards. Mr. Chayefsky received an Academy (Oscar) Award for *Marty* (1955), the Critic's Prize at the Brussels Film Festival for *The Goddess* (1958), and an Academy (Oscar) Award for *The Hospital* (1971).

CHENEY, SHELDON. Writer, lecturer, editor. b. Sheldon Warren Cheney, June 29, 1886, Berkeley, Calif., to Lemuel Warren and May Lucretia (Shepard) Cheney. Father, editor, writer, businessman; mother, executive at Univ. of California at Berkeley. Grad. Berkeley H.S., 1904; Univ. of California at Berkeley, B.A. 1908; graduate work in drama with George P. Baker at Harvard Univ., 1913; studied at art schools in San Francisco and Berkeley, Calif. Married Apr. 2, 1910, to Maud Meurice Turner (dec.); two sons, one daughter; married Nov. 27, 1934, to Martha Candler, writer. Served in War Camp Community Service, 1918–19. Member of Society of American Historians; The Players. Address: 12 Stony Hill Rd., New Hope, PA 18938, tel. (215) 862-2348.

In 1916, Mr. Cheney founded *Theatre Arts Magazine*, and was its editor until 1921. He was a member of the advisory committee of the Theatre Guild

(1919–20); was play reader, press representative and assistant director with the Actors' Theatre, originally called Equity Players (48 St. Th., N.Y.C., 1922–25); was manager for producer-director Augustin Duncan (1925–26); and was director of the Independent Theatres Clearing House, N.Y.C. (1926).

He spent five years in Europe, writing and studying theatres from Sicily to Leningrad; subsequently was lecturer with the Drama League tour of Europe (1930) and conducted the Drama League tour of Russian theatres (1931).

Mr. Cheney was associated with the Arts and Crafts Th. in Detroit (1916–17), Berkeley (Calif.) Playhouse (1932–33) and Mohawk Drama Festival (1937–38). His single acting experience was as a Supernumerary in Margaret Anglin's productions of *Antigone* and *Electra* (Greek Th., Berkeley, Calif., 1907).

Published Works. He is the author of *The New Movement in the Theatre* (1914); *The Art Theatre* (1917, revised and enlarged 1925); *The Open-Air Theatre* (1918); *Stage Decoration* (1928); and *The Theatre: 3,000 Years of Drama, Acting and Stagecraft* (1929, revised and enlarged 1952 and 1972).

He has also written *The New World Architecture* (1930); *Expressionism in Art* (1934); *Art and the Machine* (1936); *A World History of Art* (1937); *The Story of Modern Art* (1941); *Men Who Have Walked with God* (1945); *A New World History of Art* (1956); and *Sculpture of the World* (1968).

Mr. Cheney is a contributor on theatre subjects to *Encyclopaedia Britannica* and other encyclopedias. He collected and edited Isadora Duncan's writings, published as *The Art of the Dance* (1928).

Awards. Mr. Cheney received an honorary fellowship in the arts from Union Coll. (1937–40), and a Benjamin Franklin fellowship from the Royal Society of Arts in London, (1960–to date).

Recreation. Traveling, reading, studying the arts and religion.

CHERNUCK, DOROTHY. Director, producer, educator. b. Nov. 3, New York City, to William and Mary Alice (Mulligan) Chernuck. Father, policeman. Grad. Cathedral H.S., N.Y.C. Coll. of Mount St. Vincent, B.A. (magna cum laude), 1942; Catholic Univ. of Amer., M.A. 1943; studied at Columbia Univ., 1944. Member of AEA; SSD&C; ANTA; COST; ATA: CORST; Theatre Festival Assn. (pres. 1963, vice-pres. 1962); Chairman NY State Th. Festival, 1962; Kappa Gamma Pi. Corning Summer Theatre, Box 51, Corning, NY; 220 E. 52nd St., New York, NY 10022, tel. (212) 752-8437.

Theatre. Since 1953, Miss Chernuck has been producer-director of the Corning (N.Y.) Summer Th., where she has staged about 75 productions and supervised over 50 additional works, including ballets and touring productions. Summer touring productions prepared by Miss Chernuck include: (all 1970) *Barefoot in the Park* and *Never Too Late,* which both originated at Painters Mills, Md., and *The Prime of Miss Jean Brodie;* and (all 1972–to date) *The Last of the Red Hot Lovers; No, No, Nanette; Irene; The Price;* and *1776.*

In N.Y.C., Miss Chernuck directed *The Family Affair* (New Dramatists Committee, 1957); was assistant to the director of *Caligula* (54 St. Th., Feb. 16, 1960); directed *Rate of Exchange* (Players, Apr. 1, 1968); *Fashion* (American Th. Co., Feb. 1, 1973); and *Dear Piaf* (Mama Gail's Restaurant, Dec. 19, 1975).

In Rochester, N.Y., Miss Chernuck was artistic director at Theater East (1966–67), where the following were staged: *Long Day's Journey into Night; Life with Father; She Loves Me; Hay Fever; Twelfth Night; The Birthday Party; Major Barbara; Under the Yum-Yum Tree;* and *The Glass Menagerie.* Of the preceding, Miss Chernuck personally directed all but *She Loves Me; Twelfth Night;* and *The Birthday Party.*

Miss Chernuck also was artistic director (1950–56) of the Rochester Arena Th., of which she was a founder and later a co-producer, and where she staged more than 40 productions, including the following original works: *The Little Woman,* by Irene Cowan and Jay Looney, (1952); *Once an Actor,* by Rosemary Casey, (1954); and *Kilgo Run,* by Arnold Sundgaard, (1953); and directed the *Page One* show for the Rochester Newspaper Guild (1952–54). Previously, she directed productions at the Barn Th., Adrian, Mich. (Summer 1948), and at the Henrietta Hayloft, Rochester, N.Y., of which she was cofounder and producer (1949–50).

Other Activities. Miss Chernuck was a lecturer at Hunter Coll., N.Y.C. (1965–67); was assistant professor of drama at Skidmore Coll. (1960–63) and acting chairman of the theatre dept. there (1962–63); previously, was a guest director at the General Theological Seminary, N.Y.C. (1957); instructor of acting at the Sch. of Radio and TV, Rochester, N.Y. (1953–54); speech consultant instructor of English at the Catholic Univ. of America (1946–47); instructor in speech and drama at Trinity Coll., Washington, D.C. (1946–49); and teacher of English and drama at the Northport (N.Y.) H.S. (1945–46).

Awards. In 1951 and 1953, Miss Chernuck was named Citizen of the Day by the Rochester *Times-Union.*

CHESKIN, IRVING. Theatre executive. b. Irving W. Cheskin, July 19, 1915, New York City, to Henry A. and Bertha L. Cheskin. Grad. Brooklyn Coll., B.A. 1936; Graduate Faculty of Political and Social Sciences, New Sch. for Social Research, M.S.S. 1938; attended Univ. of Pennsylvania, graduate studies, 1936–37. Married Oct. 25, 1941, to Mildred Estrin, social worker; one son. Address: (home) 189 Cleveland Dr., Croton-on-Hudson, NY 10520, tel. (914) CR 1-8216; (bus.) League of N.Y. Theatres and Producers, Inc., 226 W. 47th St., New York, NY 10036, tel. (212) JU 2-4455.

Mr. Cheskin has been executive director of the League of New York Theatres (1960–to date). Prior to his joining the League, he was a professor of economics at the Univ. of the State of New York and was executive director of the Film Producers Association.

CHILDRESS, ALICE. Playwright, actress, director. b. Charleston, S.C. Educ. N.Y.C. Studied acting with Venzella Jones and Nadja Romonov.

Theatre. Mrs. Childress first appeared on stage in junior high school theatricals and later in amateur presentations by such groups as the Urban League Players and the Negro Youth Th. After joining the American Negro Th. (ANT) as an actress and member of its technical staff, she appeared in such ANT productions as *On Strivers' Row* (Library Th., Sept. 11, 1940); was Sistuh Bessie in *Natural Man* (Library Th., May 7, 1941); appeared in *Three's a Family* (Library Th., Nov. 18, 1943); was Blanche in *Anna Lucasta* (Library Th., June 8, 1944; transferred to Mansfield Th., Aug. 30, 1944); Sadie in *Rain* (ANT Playhouse, Dec. 26, 1947); and played in *Almost Faithful* (ANT Playhouse, June 2, 1948). She was in *The Candy Story* (New Playwright's, Feb. 24, 1951); played the Mother in *The Emperor's Clothes* (Greenwich Mews Th., Oct. 22, 1953); and Mrs. Thurston in *The Cool World* (Eugene O'Neill Th., Feb. 22, 1960).

The first play she wrote, *Florence* (ANT, 1949), was followed by *Just a Little Simple* (Club Baron, Sept. 1950), which she adapted from Langston Hughes's novel *Simple Speaks His Mind; Gold Through the Trees* (Club Baron, 1952); *Trouble in Mind* (Greenwich Mews Th., Nov. 3, 1955); *Wedding Band* (PTP, Univ. of Michigan, Ann Arbor, Dec. 1966), later produced in N.Y.C. (Public Th., Sept. 26, 1972), where, with Joseph Papp, she directed it; and *String* (Negro Ensemble Co., St. Marks Playhouse, Mar. 25, 1969). Her other plays include *A Man Bearing a Pitcher; Wine in the Wilderness* (1969); *The African Garden* (1971); and *When the Rattlesnake Sounds* (1975).

Other Activities. From 1966 to 1968, Mrs. Childress lectured under a Harvard appointment at the Radcliffe Institute.

Published Works. In addition to her plays, Mrs. Childress wrote *Like One of the Family,* sketches of black life; *A Hero Ain't Nothin' But a Sandwich* (1973); and she edited *Black Scenes* (1971), an anthology of excerpts from dramas by black writers.

Awards. *Trouble in Mind* received a *Village Voice* Off-Bway (Obie) Award (1956) as the best original off-Bway play of its season.

CHILDRESS, ALVIN. Actor. Grad. Meridian (Miss.) H.S.; attended Rust Coll.; New York Univ.

Theatre. Mr. Childress made his Bway debut in *Savage Rhythm* (John Golden Th., Jan. 1, 1932); and, with the Federal Th. Project (Lafayette Th. N.Y.C.), appeared in *Sweet Land* (Jan. 19, 1937), *The Case of Philip Laurence* (June 8, 1937), and *Haiti* (Feb. 2, 1937).

He played Slim in *Brown Sugar* (Biltmore, N.Y.C., Dec. 2, 1937); appeared in *Two on an Island* (Broadhurst, Jan. 22, 1940); toured the "subway circuit" in *Native Son* (circa 1941); with the Amer. Negro Th. (Library Th.), played Rev. Alfred Davidson in *Rain,* Captain Tom in *Natural Man* (May 7, 1941), appeared in *On Strivers' Row,* played Noah in *Anna Lucasta* (1944; moved to Mansfield Th., Aug. 30, 1944), and Edwin M. Stanton in *The Washington Years* (Mar. 11, 1948). He has also appeared in *The Amen Corner* (Th. of Being, Los Angeles, 1966–67 season).

Films. Mr. Childress made his film debut in *Anna Lucasta* (UA, 1959); and appeared in *The Man in the Net* (UA, 1959).

Television and Radio. Mr. Childress made frequent appearances on the Amer. Negro Th.'s series of radio dramas on WNEW (N.Y.C.); and taught radio technique for that group.

On television, he was a regular performer on Amos 'n' Andy (CBS).

CHINOY, HELEN KRICH. Educator, director. b. Helen Krich, Sept. 25, 1922, Newark, N.J., to Ben and Anne Krich. Father, automobile dealer. Relative in theatre: sister-in-law, Toby Cole, talent representative. Grad. South Side H.S., Newark, 1939; New York Univ., B.A. 1943, M.A. 1945; attended Univ. of Birmingham, Barford-on-Avon, England, summer sch., certificate, 1947; Columbia Univ., Ph.D. 1963. Married June 6, 1948, to Ely Chinoy; one son, one daughter. Member of AETA; ASTR; AAUW. Address: 230 Crescent St., Northampton, MA 01060, tel. (413) JU 4-5348.

In 1965, Mrs. Chinoy became a member of the faculty, Department of Theatre and Speech, Smith College. She was chairman of this department (1968–71) and then associate professor. 1945;

In 1963, she was a member of the faculty of the Univ. of Leicester, England. She has held academic positions at New York Univ. (1944–45); Queens Coll., N.Y.C. (Fall 1945; Summer 1950); Rutgers Univ. (1946–48); and an earlier appointment at Smith (1952–60).

Published Works. Mrs. Chinoy has edited, with Toby Cole, three books concerning the American theatre, *Actors on Acting* (1949; 2nd ed. 1970); *Directing the Play* (1953); and its revised edition *Directors on Directing* (1963); and she wrote "The Profession and the Art—Directing in America, 1860–1920" in *The American Theatre: A Sum of Its Parts* (1971). She has also contributed articles to the Encyclopaedia Britannica (*Production and Direction* and *Talma,* 1958); and *Enciclopedia dello Spettacolo,* Rome, It. (*American Views of Acting and Directing* plus 20 biographies of American actors and directors).

Awards. She has received fellowships from both New York Univ. (1943–44) and the AAUW (1962–63) and has been elected a member of the National Theatre Conference.

Recreation. Cooking.

CHOATE, EDWARD. Theatre manager, producer. b. Edward Austin Choate, Jr., Nov. 23, 1908, New York City, to Edward Austin and Olive (Allison) Choate. Father, contractor. Grad. Hotchkiss Sch., Lakeville, Conn., 1926; Yale Univ., M.A. 1930. Married June 24, 1948, to Jane Ann Shirk (marr. dis. Oct. 1961); one son, one daughter; married Nov. 13, 1961, to Judith Newkirk; one son. Member of ATPAM. Address: (home) 11 W. 84th St., New York, NY 10024, tel. (212) TR 7-5171; (bus.) Music Box Theatre, 239 West 45th St., New York, NY 10036, tel. (212) JU 6-1363.

Theatre. Mr. Choate made his stage debut with the Univ. Players (Southampton, L.I., N.Y., Summer 1928); joined the staff of Herman Shumlin as assistant to the press agent and company manager for *The Last Mile* (Harris Th., N.Y.C., Feb. 13, 1930) and *Grand Hotel* (National, Nov. 13, 1930); was casting director and play reader for Mr. Shumlin (1931–32); opened his own production office with John Krimsky (1933); and was producer with Robert Ross at Old Silver Beach Th. (Falmouth, Mass., Summer 1933). (National,

Mr. Choate's first Bway production was *I Was Waiting for You* (Booth, Nov. 13, 1933); he was a member of the Shubert staff and served as house and company manager, press agent, play reader, casting director, and producer (1934–45); produced for Messrs. Shubert, *Frederika* (Imperial, Feb. 4, 1937) and *Between the Devil* (Imperial, Dec. 22, 1937); with Arthur Shields, produced *Kindred* (Maxine Elliott's Th., Dec. 26, 1939); with Mr. Shields, in association with Robert Edmond Jones, presented *Juno and the Paycock* (Mansfield, Jan. 16, 1940); produced independently *The Flying Gerardos* (Playhouse, Dec. 29, 1940); presented, in association with Alexander Kirkland and John Sheppard, Jr., *The Strings, My Lord, Are False* (Royale, May 19, 1942); produced, with Marie Louise Elkins, *Yankee Point* (Longacre, Nov. 23, 1942); presented *Decision* (Belasco, Feb. 2, 1944); produced, with Marie Louise Elkins, *Alice in Arms* (National, Jan. 31, 1945); presented, for Messrs. Shubert, *Dark of the Moon* (46 St. Th., Mar. 14, 1945); produced *Common Ground* (Fulton, Apr. 25, 1945); and was general manager for the Old Vic Co. productions (Century, May 1946); *Medea* (National, Oct. 20, 1947), and *Crime and Punishment* (National, Dec. 22, 1947).

Mr. Choate was business manager of the Pittsburgh Light Opera Co. (1948); managing director and partner with Margaret Webster of the Margaret Webster Shakespeare Company, which made two bus-and-truck tours of the US and Can. (1949–50); and with Miss Webster, operated the Woodstock (N.Y.) Playhouse (Summer 1950).

He raised one half financing with Miss Webster and acted as general manager for the second Theatre Guild production of *Saint Joan* (Cort, N.Y.C., Oct. 4, 1951); for the Theatre Guild production of *Venus Observed* (Century, Feb. 13, 1952); was general manager for *Time Out for Ginger* (Lyceum, Nov. 25, 1952); co-produced, with Gilbert Miller and Donald Oenslager, *Horses in Midstream* (Royale, Apr. 2, 1953); and produced, with George Ross, *Gently Does It* (Playhouse, Oct. 28, 1953), which he and Wauna Paul had previously produced in London under the title *Murder Mistaken* (Ambassadors', Nov. 4, 1952).

Mr. Choate took over (Dec. 1952) production rights from Gilbert Miller of *Gigi* while it was on tour (opened Nixon, Pittsburgh, Pa., Oct. 13, 1952; closed Alcazar, San Francisco, Calif., May 16, 1953); was general manager of *King of Hearts* (Lyceum, N.Y.C., Apr. 1, 1954) and *Anastasia* (Lyceum, Dec. 29, 1954); and produced a tour of *Harvey* (opened Dec. 1954; closed Mar. 1955).

Mr. Choate, with Albert H. Rosen, acquired (1956) production rights from Elaine Perry of *Anastasia* while it was on tour (opened Ford's, Baltimore, Md., Sept. 26, 1955; closed Huntington Hartford, Los Angeles, Calif., July 1956); produced with Mr. Rosen, a tour of *The Chalk Garden* (opened Lobero, Santa Barbara, Calif., Sept. 6, 1956; closed McCarter, Princeton, N.J., Feb. 16, 1957); and produced, with Mr. Rosen and Huntington Hartford, a West Coast tour of *The Sleeping Prince* (opened Huntington Hartford Th., Hollywood, Calif., Nov. 22, 1956; closed Geary, San Francisco, Calif., Jan. 12, 1957).

Mr. Choate was general manager for *Jane Eyre* (Belasco, N.Y.C., May 1, 1958); *The Fighting Cock* (ANTA, Dec. 8, 1959); *A Thurber Carnival* (ANTA, Feb. 26, 1960); and *13 Daughters* (54 St. Th., Mar. 2, 1961); business manager for the West Coast tour of *Rhinoceros* (opened Alcazar, San Francisco, Calif., Oct. 3, 1961; closed Huntington Hartford Th., Hollywood, Calif., Nov. 11, 1962).

Mr. Choate was house manager for the Royale Th. (N.Y.C., Nov. 1961–May 1962); general manager for Dore Schary productions (Nov.–Dec. 1962); general business manager for *Love & Kisses* and for The Music Theatre of Lincoln Center, Inc. (N.Y.C.) of the New York State Theatre at Lincoln Center. Since 1970, he has been manager of the Music Box Theatre (N.Y.C.).

Recreation. Photographer, gardening.

CHODOROV, EDWARD. Playwright, director, producer, scenarist. b. Apr. 17, 1914, New York City, to Harry and Lena (Simmons) Chodorov. Father, actor, businessman. Grad. Erasmus Hall, Brooklyn, N.Y.; attended Brown Univ., Providence, R.I. Married June 16, 1954, to Rosemary Pettit; one son, two daughters. Relatives in theatre: brother, Jerome Chodorov, playwright, director; son, Stephen Chodorov, playwright. Member of Dramatists Guild.

Pre-Theatre. Motion Picture publicity.

Theatre. Mr. Chodorov wrote first *Wonder Boy* (Alvin Th., N.Y.C., Oct. 23, 1931); followed by *Kind Lady* (Booth, Apr. 23, 1935); and wrote, with H. S. Kraft, *Cue for Passion* (Royale, Dec. 19, 1940).

Mr. Chodorov directed first productions of his plays, *Those Endearing Young Charms* (Booth, June 16, 1943); *Decision* (Belasco, Feb. 2, 1944); *Common Ground* (Fulton, Apr. 25, 1945); *Oh, Men! Oh, Women!* (Henry Miller's Th., Dec. 17, 1953); the pre-Bway tryout *Listen to the Mocking Bird* (opened Colonial, Boston, Mass., Dec. 27, 1958; closed Shubert, Washington, D.C., Jan. 29, 1959); and *M. Lautrec* (Belgrade Civic Th., Coventry, England, 1959).

Mr. Chodorov wrote the unproduced plays, *Erskine; The Clubwoman;* and the *Irrational Knot.* .

Films. Mr. Chodorov wrote and produced *The World Changes* (1st Natl., 1933); *Mayor of Hell* (WB, 1933); *Captured* (WB, 1933); *Gentlemen Are Born* (1st Natl., 1934); *Madame Du Barry* (WB, 1934); *The Story of Louis Pasteur* (WB, 1935); *Living on Velvet* (1st Natl., 1935); *Sweet Adeline* (WB, 1935); *Craig's Wife* (Col., 1936); *Yellow Jack* (MGM, 1938); *Woman Against Woman* (MGM, 1938); *Rich Man, Poor Girl* (MGM, 1938); *Spring Madness* (MGM, 1938); *The Man from Dakota* (MGM, 1940); *The Hucksters* (MGM, 1947); and *Road House* (20th-Fox, 1948).

Television. Mr. Chodorov wrote for the Billy Rose Show (ABC, 1952).

Published Works. He wrote two plays for amateur production, *Signor Chicago* (1947); and *The Spa* (1955).

CHODOROV, JEROME. Playwright, director, screen-writer. b. Aug. 10, 1911, New York City, to Harry and Lena (Simmons) Chodorov. Father, actor, businessman. Attended Geo. Washington H.S., N.Y.C. Married Nov. 19, 1932, to Rhea Grand; one daughter. Served USAAF, 1942–45; rank, Capt. Relatives in theatre: brother, Edward Chodorov, playwright; nephew, Stephan Chodorov, playwright. Member of AEA; Dramatists Guild (council member, 1949–55); SWG (council member, 1938–39); DGA. Address: Dramatists Guild of America, 234 W. 44th St., New York, NY 10036.

Pre-Theatre. Journalist, publicity.

Theatre. Mr. Chodorov wrote, with Joseph Fields, *Schoolhouse on the Lot* (Ritz Th., N.Y.C., Mar. 22, 1938); *My Sister Eileen* based on the stories of Ruth McKenney (Biltmore, Dec. 26, 1940); *Junior Miss* (Lyceum, Nov. 18, 1941); *The French Touch* (Cort, Dec. 8, 1945); the books for the musicals *Pretty Penny* (Bucks County Playhouse, New Hope, Pa., Summer 1949), *Wonderful Town* (Winter Garden, N.Y.C., Feb. 25, 1953), and *The Girl in Pink Tights* (Mark Hellinger Th., Mar. 5, 1954); the plays *Anniversary Waltz* (Broadhurst, Apr. 7, 1954) and *The Ponder Heart,* adapted from the novel by Eudora Welty (Music Box, Feb. 16, 1956).

Mr. Chodorov directed *Make a Million* (Playhouse, Oct. 23, 1958); *The Gazebo* (Lyceum, Dec. 12, 1958); *Blood, Sweat and Stanley Poole* (Morosco, Oct. 5, 1961); and wrote *The Happiest Man Alive* (Falmouth Playhouse, Mass., July 1962); wrote *I Had a Ball* (Martin Beck Th., Dec. 15, 1964); *3 Bags Full* (Henry Miller's Th., Mar. 6, 1966); prepared material as indicated for productions of the Los Angeles (Calif.) Civic Light Opera: new book for revival of *The Great Waltz* (Music Center, July 27, 1965); book revisions for revival of *The Student Prince* (Dorothy Chandler Pavilion, July 26, 1966); original book for *Dumas and Son* (world premiere, Dorothy Chandler Pavilion, 1967); and he wrote and directed *A Community of Two* (six-month tour began Dupont Th., Wilmington, Del., Dec. 1973).

Films. Mr. Chodorov wrote, with Mr. Fields, the screenplays of *Rich Man, Poor Girl* (MGM, 1938); *Two Girls on Broadway* (MGM, 1940); *Louisiana Purchase* (Par., 1941); *My Sister Eileen* (Col., 1942); *Junior Miss* (20th-Fox, 1945); *Happy Anniversary* (UA, 1959); and he prepared the English adaptation of *Re: Lucky Luciano* (Titanus, 1973).

Television. Mr. Chodorov, with Mr. Fields, wrote the book for the television version of *Wonderful Town* (CBS, 1959).

Awards. The musical *Wonderful Town,* with a book by Messrs. Chodorov and Fields, was awarded the NY Drama Critics' Circle Award and the Outer Critic's Circle Award (1953).

CHRISTIE, AUDREY. Actress. b. June 27, 1912, Chicago, Ill., to Charles and Florence (Ferguson) Christie. Attended Lakeview H.S., Chicago. Studied acting with Bertha Iles; dance with Marie Veatch, Chicago. Married to Guy Robertson (marr. dis.); married to Donald Briggs. Address: 1425 Queen's Rd., Los Angeles, CA 90052, tel. (213) 656-0421.

Theatre. Miss Christie first appeared as a dancer in the vaudeville production of *Six Chicago Steppers* (Keith-Orpheum Circuit, 1926); repeated her performance at the Palace, N.Y.C. (1928); in Chicago performed in the chorus of *Castles in the Air* (1926) and *Oh, Please* (1927), and followed Dorothy McNulty as Babe O'Day in *Good News* (1928–29).

She made her N.Y.C. debut as Olive in *Follow Thru* (46 St. Th., Jan. 9, 1929); appeared in *Sons o' Guns* (Imperial, Nov. 26, 1929); followed Hannah Williams in the revue *Sweet and Low* (44 St. Th., Nov. 17, 1930); played in *Of Thee I Sing* (Music Box, Dec. 26, 1931); appeared as Billie "Stonewall" Jackson in *Sailor, Beware!* (Lyceum, Sept. 28, 1933); Jean Wakes in *Alley Cat* (48 St. Th., Sept. 17, 1934); Nellie Quinn in *Geraniums in My Window* (Longacre, Oct. 26, 1934); played with the St. Louis (Mo.) Municipal Opera in such works as *No, No, Nanette!, A Connecticut Yankee* and *The Red Mill* (Summers 1935, 1936); appeared as Miriam Aarons in *The Women* (Ethel Barrymore Th., N.Y.C., Dec. 26, 1936); Anna Murphy in *I Married an Angel* (Shubert, May 11, 1938); Ruth Conway in *Return Engagement* (John Golden Th., Nov. 1, 1940); and as Ruth in the Chicago company of *My Sister Eileen* (Harris Th., Chicago, Ill., Feb. 1941).

Miss Christie played Mabel in *Banjo Eyes* (Hollywood, N.Y.C., Dec. 25, 1941); Kitty Trimble in the Theatre Guild production of *Without Love* (St. James, Nov. 10, 1942); Olive Lashbrooke in *The Voice of the Turtle* (Morosco, Dec. 8, 1943); and subsequently made her London debut in the same role (Piccadilly, July 9, 1947). She appeared as Crystal Shalimar and the Duchess of Alba in *The Duchess Misbehaves* (Adelphi, N.Y.C., Feb. 13, 1946); Frances Black in *Light Up the Sky* (Royale, Nov. 18, 1948); Liz Kendall in *Buy Me Blue Ribbons* (Empire, Oct. 17, 1951); and was standby for Rosalind Russell as Ruth in *Wonderful Town* (Winter Garden, Feb. 25, 1953).

She followed (June 1956) Shirley Booth as Bunny Watson in *The Desk Set* (Broadhurst, N.Y.C., Oct. 24, 1955); played Connie McDougall in *Holiday for Lovers* (Longacre, Feb. 14, 1957), Mrs. Fawcett in *Nature's Way* (Coronet, Oct. 16, 1957), and Lillian Anders in *The Pink Burro* (Playhouse, Palm Springs, Calif., Jan. 1958); followed (Dec. 1953) Eileen Heckart as Lottie Lacey in *The Dark at the Top of the Stairs* (Music Box, N.Y.C., Dec. 5, 1957), a role which she repeated on tour (opened Playhouse, Wilmington, Del., Jan. 21, 1959; closed Pabst, Milwaukee, Wis., May 16, 1959); appeared in *Lady in the Dark* (Pasadena, Calif., Playhouse, 1966–67 season); replaced Beatrice Arthur (Apr. 1, 1968) as Vera Charles in *Mame* (Wintergarden, N.Y.C., May 24, 1966); and played Maude Hayes in the first national company of *Forty Carats* (tour, opened Cincinnati, Ohio, Sept. 29, 1969).

Films. Miss Christie appeared in *Keeper of the Flame* (MGM, 1942); *Deadline, U.S.A.* (20th-Fox, 1952); *Carousel* (20th-Fox, 1956); *Splendor in the Grass* (WB, 1961); *The Unsinkable Molly Brown* (MGM, 1964); *Frankie and Johnny* (UA, 1966); *The Ballad of Josie* (U, 1968); and *Mame* (WB, 1974).

Television. Since 1948, Miss Christie has appeared in dramatic and variety programs, one of which was the series Fair Exchange (CBS, July 1962–Dec. 1963).

CHURCH, SANDRA. Actress. b. Sandra Lee Church, Jan. 13, San Francisco, Calif., to Charles J. and Muriel Lee (Denton) Church. Father, importer; mother, nurse. Attended Immaculate Heart H.S., Hollywood, Calif. Studied acting with Lee Strasberg, N.Y.C.; voice with Ray McDermott, N.Y.C. Member of AEA; SAG; AFTRA. Married Nov. 1964 to Norman Twain, producer.

Theatre. Miss Church made her N.Y.C. debut succeeding (1954) Janice Rule as Madge Owens in *Picnic* (Music Box Th., Feb. 19, 1953), also playing this role in the national company; succeeded (Aug. 7, 1956) Peggy McCay as Sofia Alexandrovna in *Uncle Vanya* (Fourth St. Th., N.Y.C., Jan. 31, 1956); played Betsy Dean in *Holiday for Lovers* (Longacre, Feb. 14, 1957); Helen White in *Winesburg, Ohio* (National, Feb. 5, 1958); Louise in *Gypsy* (Bway Th., May 21, 1959); Robin Austin in *Under the Yum-Yum Tree* (Henry Miller's Th., Nov. 16, 1960); and Maude in the pre-Bway tryout of *Conversations in the Dark* (opened Walnut St. Th., Philadelphia, Pa., Dec. 23, 1963; closed there Jan. 4, 1964).

Films. She appeared in *The Ugly American* (U, 1963).

Television. She appeared in *All Summer Long* (1957); *Years Ago* (Dupont Show of the Month, CBS, 1960); and on The Eleventh Hour (NBC, 1963); *A Hero for Our Times* (Kraft Suspense Th., NBC, 1963); and The Nurses (CBS, 1964).

Awards. Miss Church was nominated for the Antoinette Perry (Tony) Award for her performance as Louise in *Gypsy* (1960).

Recreation. Painting, travel.

CHUTE, MARCHETTE. Playwright, biographer, poet, novelist. b. Aug. 16, 1909, Wayzata, Minn., to William Young and Edith Mary (Pickburn) Chute. Father, realtor. Grad. Central H.S., Minneapolis, 1925; Minneapolis Sch. of Art (one year); Univ. of Minn., B.A. (magna cum laude, Phi Beta Kappa) 1930. Member of Royal Soc. of Arts; Natl. Inst. of Arts and Letters; P.E.N.; Soc. of Amer. Historians; and Natl. Book Comm. Address: 450 E. 63rd St., New York, NY 10021, tel. (212) TE 8-8920.

Theatre. Miss Chute was co-author, with M. G. Chute, of *Sweet Genevieve*, which she produced with M. G. Chute, Joy Chute, and Mina Cole (President Th., Mar. 20, 1956); and was co-author, with Ernestine Perrie, of *The Worlds of Shakespeare* (Carnegie Recital Hall, Dec. 3, 1963).

Published Works. Miss Chute's books include *Shakespeare of London* (1950); for young readers, *An Introduction to Shakespeare* (1951), and *The Wonderful Winter* (1954); *Stories from Shakespeare* (1956); and *The Worlds of Shakespeare* (1963), written with Ernestine Perrie.

She has also written *Rhymes About Ourselves* (1932); *The Search for God* (1941); *Rhymes About the Country* (1941); *Geoffrey Chaucer of England* (1943); *Rhymes About the City* (1946); *The End of the Search* (1947); *Ben Jonson of Westminster* (1953); *Innocent Wayfaring* (1955); *Around and About* (1957); *Two Gentle Men* (1959); *Jesus of Israel* (1961); *The First Liberty* (1969); *The Green Tree of Democracy* (1971); and *Rhymes About Us* (1974).

Awards. She holds three honorary Litt.D. degrees from Western Coll. (1952), Carleton Coll. (1957), and Dickinson Coll. (1963). She received the Author Meets the Critics Award for *Shakespeare of London* (1950); the NY Shakespeare Club Award (1954); Chap-Book Award from the Poetry Society of America (1954); Outstanding Achievement Award from the Univ. of Minnesota (1958); and Constance Lindsay Skinner Award (1959).

CILENTO, DIANE. Actress, author. b. Oct. 5, 1933, Brisbane, Australia, to Sir Raphael Cilento. Father, tropical surgeon. Attended AADA, N.Y.C., 1950; RADA, London. Married Feb. 1955 to Andrea Volpe, writer (marr. dis. Oct. 1962); one daughter; married 1962 to Sean Connery, actor (marr. dis. 1973). Member of British AEA; AEA.

Theatre. Miss Cilento appeared as Helen in *Tiger at the Gates* (Plymouth Th., N.Y.C., Oct. 3, 1955); Ellie in *Heartbreak House* (Billy Rose Th., Oct. 18, 1959); and Marie-Paul II in *The Good Soup* (Plymouth, Mar. 2, 1960).

She made her professional debut with the Manchester Repertory Co. (England); made her London debut as Dixie Evans in *The Big Knife* (Wimbledon, Nov. 30, 1953; moved Duke of York's, Jan. 1, 1954); subsequently played the title role in the musical *Zuleika;* Carole Cutrere in *Orpheus Descending* (Royal Court, May 14, 1959); and the title role in *Miss Julie* (Lyric, Hammersmith, July 28, 1960). She was Beatrice in *The Four Seasons* (Saville Th., London, Sept. 21, 1965; Ludmilla in *Marya* (Royal Court, London, 1967); Sarah in *I've Seen You Cut Lemons* (Fortune, Dec. 1969); and Nastasya in *The Idiot* (Old Vic, July 1970).

Films. Miss Cilento made her debut in *The Angel Who Pawned Her Harp;* followed by roles in *The Admirable Crichton* (Col., 1957); *The Truth About Women* (Continental, 1958); *Stop Me Before I Kill!* (Col., 1961); *The Naked Edge* (UA, 1962); *I Thank a Fool* (MGM, 1962); *Tom Jones* (UA, 1963); *The Breaking Point* (1964); *Rattle of a Simple Man* (Continental, 1964); *The Agony and the Ecstasy* (20th-Fox, 1965); *Hombre* (20th-Fox, 1967); and *Negatives* (Continental, 1968).

She also appeared in *Passage Home, The Woman for Joe, The Passing Strangers, Jet Storm,* and *The Full Treatment.*

Television. Miss Cilento has appeared on *The Small Servant* (NBC, Oct. 30, 1955); played Bianca in *The Taming of the Shrew* (Hallmark Hall of Fame, NBC, Mar. 18, 1956); and Sadie Thompson in *Rain* (ABC, Eng., Dec. 1960). She played Lina in *Festival of Pawns* (Espionage, NBC, June 3, 1964); was Geraldine in *Once Upon a Tractor* (UN Drama, ABC, Sept. 9, 1965); was in *Cut Yourself a Slice of Throat* (Blackmail, ITV, Oct. 15, 1965); was Prince Boriarsi in a segment of The Girl from U.N.C.L.E. (NBC, 1967); and was in *The Kiss of Blood* (BBC-2, May 1968).

Published Works. Miss Cilento wrote *The Manipulator* (1967) and *Hybrid* (1971).

Awards. Miss Cilento won the *Variety* NY Drama Critics' Poll (1956) for her performance as Helen in *Tiger at the Gates.*

CIMBER, MATT. Producer, director. b. Thomas Ottaviano, Jan. 12, 1936, New York City, to Thomas and Fannie Ottaviano. Attended Poly Prep Country Day Sch., Brooklyn, N.Y., 1952–54; Syracuse Univ., 1955. Studied acting with Vera Soloviova. Married to Jayne Mansfield (marr. dis. 1966); one son. Relative in theatre: brother-in-law, Jerry Lo Monaco, singer. Member of AEA; Sigma Phi Epsilon.

Theatre. Mr. Cimber's first theatrical assignment was as director of *The Young and the Beautiful* (Th. East, N.Y.C., May 1959); subsequently directed *Burning Bright* (Th. East, Oct. 1960); *Ignorants Abroad* (Th. East, June 1960); *Walk-Up* (Provincetown Playhouse, Feb. 23, 1961); at the 41 St. Th., *The Voice of the Turtle* (June 27, 1961); *Susan Slept Here* (July 11, 1961); *The Little Hut* (July 25, 1961); *The Moon is Blue* (Aug. 8, 1961); *The Tender Trap* (Aug. 25, 1961); was producer-director of *Intimate Relations* (Mermaid, Nov. 1, 1962); two one-act plays, *Orphée* and *Antigone* (Midway, Dec. 27, 1962); at the Yonkers (N.Y.) Playhouse, produced *Milk and Honey* (Feb. 7, 1964); *Carnival!* (Mar. 10, 1964); *Kind Sir* (Mar. 24, 1964); *Bus Stop* which he also directed (May 26, 1964); directed a touring production of *Bus Stop* (Summer 1964); directed and appeared in *Champagne Complex* (Mineola, N.Y., Playhouse, Jan. 20, 1965); directed and played Billy Turk in a touring production of *Nature's Way* (Summer, 1965); and directed *The Rabbit Habit* (pre-Bway tour, Dec. 1965).

CISNEY, MARCELLA. Theatre administrator, actress, director. b. Marcella Ruth Abels, Altoona, Pa., to M. J. and Anne E. Abels. Grad. New Utrecht H.S., Brooklyn, N.Y. Studied at AADA, N.Y.C., 1931–32; Bennington Coll. Arts Festival (fellowship in theatre arts) 1940; New York Univ. Radio-TV Workshop, Summer 1943; Neighborhood Playhouse of the Th., N.Y.C., Directors Seminars, Summer 1945; Actors Studio (member of directors unit). Married June 7, 1953, to Robert C. Schnitzer, theatre administrator. Member of AEA; SSD&C; NTC; ATA; ANTA; Amer. Playwrights Th. (bd. of govs.).

Theatre. From 1964 to 1973, Miss Cisney was associate director of the Professional Theatre Program at the Univ. of Michigan.

She made her N.Y.C. debut as Lilli Von Kattner in *Girls in Uniform* (Booth, Dec. 30, 1932); and played Silver Stream in *Lady Precious Stream* (Booth, Jan. 27, 1936).

She was director of the Hillsdale (Mich.) College-Community Th. (1939–42); executive director of the Civic Th. (Jacksonville, Fla., 1942–44); was a faculty member and producer-director at the Pasadena (Calif.) Playhouse (1944–46); and was producer and director at the Laguna (Calif.) Playhouse (1947) and the Las Palmas Th. (Hollywood, Calif., 1948).

In 1956, Miss Cisney administered the Rockefeller Foundation Emergency Project for Hungarian Artists. She directed three operas for the NY City Opera Co. at NY City Center: *Mignon* (Sept. 25, 1956), *Susannah* (Sept. 27, 1957), and *L'Histoire du Soldat* (Oct. 16, 1957). She was administrator and associate coordinator of performing arts, in charge of assembling the music, theatre, and dance attractions for the American Pavilion at the Brussels (Belgium) World's Fair (1957–58).

She directed the tryout of *I Hear You Singing* (Saratoga, N.Y., Playhouse, Summer 1958); and directed *Whisper to Me* (Summer 1958), and *Ferryboat* (Summer 1959) at the White Barn (Westport, Conn.); and was artistic director of the Theatre Guild American Repertory Company's productions of *The Skin of Our Teeth,* and *The Glass Menagerie,* which toured Europe and Latin America (1960).

For the New Play Project at the Univ. of Michigan (1963–70), she produced and staged premiers of *The Child Buyer, Amazing Grace, The Conjuror, The Castle, Wedding Band, Ivory Tower* (also staged at Dennis, Mass., and East Hampton, N.Y.), *Siamese Connections, An Evening's Frost* (also at Th. de Lys, N.Y.C., Oct. 11, 1965; ACT, San Francisco; and on national tour, 1967); and produced *Last Respects,* and *The Union* (Ann Arbor, Mich.).

Films. Miss Cisney was head of talent development at Warner Brothers Studio (1949), where she coached such stars as Gary Cooper, Lauren Bacall, Debbie Reynolds, and Patricia Neal.

Television and Radio. She performed in radio dramas for CBS and NBC (1932–36).

For television she was a CBS staff director (1950–54).

Awards. Miss Cisney is the recipient of the Belgian Music Critics Gold Medal (1958). She was awarded the Bronze Medal of the Israeli Ministry of Culture by Abba Eban (1960), and the Presidential Award of the Univ. of Michigan (1972).

CLAIRE, INA. Actress. b. Oct. 15, 1895, Washington, D.C., to Joseph Fagan. Attended Holy Cross Acad., Washington, D.C. Married to James Whitaker (marr. dis.); married May 9, 1929, to John Gilbert, actor (marr. dis.); married Mar. 16, 1939, to William Ross Wallace, lawyer. Member of AEA; SAG. Address: 1100 Sacramento St., San Francisco, CA.

Theatre. Miss Claire made her first stage appearance in vaudeville (1907), and her N.Y.C. debut in an impersonation of Sir Harry Lauder (American Music Hall, Mar. 13, 1909). For the next two years, she toured in vaudeville on the Orpheum Circuit and in Keith and Proctor theatres. Subsequently she appeared as Molly Febbleford in *Jumping Jupiter* (New York Th., N.Y.C., Mar. 6, 1911); Prudence in *The Quaker Girl* (Park, Oct. 23, 1911); and in vaudeville (Hammerstein's Music Hall, July 1913).

She made her London debut as Una Trance in *The Girl from Utah* (Adelphi, Oct. 18, 1913); subsequently played Winnie Harborough in *The Belle of Bond Street* (Adelphi, June 8, 1914); Eloise Van Cuyler in *Lady Luxury* (Casion, N.Y.C., Dec. 25, 1914); and appeared in vaudeville (Palace, Feb. 1915); in the revues *The Ziegfeld Follies* (New Amsterdam, June 21, 1915, and *June 12, 1916); played Polly in Polly with a Past* (Belasco Th., Sept. 6, 1917); Jerry Lamar in *The Gold Diggers* (Lyceum, Sept. 30, 1919); Monna in *Bluebeard's Eighth Wife* (Ritz Th., Sept. 19, 1921); Lucy Warringer in *The Awful Truth* (Henry Miller's Th., Sept. 18, 1922); Denise Sorbier in *Grounds for Divorce* (Empire, Sept. 23, 1924); and Mrs. Cheyney in *The Last of Mrs. Cheyney* (Fulton, Nov. 9, 1925), in which she later toured; appeared as Pearl Grayston in *Our Betters* (Henry Miller's Th., N.Y.C., Feb. 20, 1928).

She appeared as Elena in the touring production of *Reunion in Vienna*, which role she relinquished in Boston, Mass. (Sept. 19, 1932); Marion Froude in *Biography* (Guild Th., N.Y.C., Dec. 12, 1932; on tour, 1933–34; and in London, Globe, Apr. 25, 1934); Madeleine in *Ode to Liberty* (Lyceum, N.Y.C., Dec. 21, 1934); played Hilda Seidler in the pre-Bway tryout of *Love Is Not So Simple* (opened Chestnut St. Th., Philadelphia, Pa., Nov. 4, 1935; closed there Nov. 16, 1935); Leonie Frothingham in *End of Summer* (Guild, N.Y.C., Feb. 17, 1936); Madeline Neroni in *Barchester Towers* (Martin Beck Th., Nov. 30, 1937); the Duchess of Hampshire in *Once Is Enough* (Henry Miller's Th., Feb. 15, 1938); Lorinda Bleeker in a pre-Bway tryout of *Yankee Fable* (opened Colonial, Boston, Mass., Oct. 19, 1938; closed Washington, D.C., Nov. 5, 1938); Enid Fuller in *The Talley Method* (Henry Miller's Th., N.Y.C., Feb. 24, 1941); Mrs. Paul Espenshade in *The Fatal Weakness* (Royale, Nov. 19, 1946), and on tour (1946–47); and Lady Elizabeth Mulhammer in *The Confidential Clerk* (Morosco, Feb. 11, 1954).

Films. Miss Claire first appeared in *The Awful Truth* (Pathé, 1929); subsequently played in *The Royal Family of Broadway* (Par., 1930); *Rebound* (Pathé, 1931); *The Greeks Had a Word for Them* (UA, 1932); *Ninotchka* (MGM, 1939); and *Claudia* (20th-Fox, 1943).

Awards. She was awarded the gold medal for diction by American Academy of Arts and Letters (Nov. 1936).

CLAIRE, LUDI. Actress. b. Edilou Bailhé, Apr. 15, 1922, Fort Wayne, Ind., to Georges Laurent and Edith (Nickell) Bailhé. Father, pianist; mother, singer. Grad. Central H.S., Fort Wayne, Ind., 1938. Studied with Lee Strasberg, N.Y.C., 1938–40. Married May 22, 1940, to John Claar, director (marr. dis., 1949). Member of AEA; AFTRA; SAG; WGA. Address: 244 E. 23rd St., New York, NY 10010, tel. (212) JU 6-6300.

Theatre. Miss Claire was understudy to Claire Luce as Tanis Talbot in *Portrait in Black* (Booth, N.Y.C., May 14, 1947); to Joan Tetzel as Clarissa Blynn Cromwell in *Strange Bedfellows* (Morosco, Jan. 14, 1948); and to Ruth Ford as Deborah Pomfred and Ruth Matteson as Jane Pugh in *Clutterbuck* (Biltmore, Dec. 3, 1949).

She appeared as Leucippe in *Tower Beyond Tragedy* (ANTA, Nov. 26, 1950); played a Girl and succeeded Polly Rowles as Lucy McLean in *The Small Hours* (Natl., Feb. 15, 1951); at the Berlin (Germany) Arts Festival, played the Third Woman in Robinson Jeffers' adaptation of *Medea* (Hebbel Th., 1951); appeared as Another Actress in *Legend of Lovers* (Plymouth, N.Y.C., Dec. 26, 1951); and succeeded Joan Hay Thorne as Rosabel in *Venus Observed* (Century, Feb. 13, 1952).

Miss Claire played the French Saleslady and understudied Hildegarde Neff as Ninotchka in *Silk Stockings* (Imperial, Feb. 24, 1955); played Miss Lennie in *Someone Waiting* (Golden, Feb. 14, 1956); understudied Polly Rowles as Anne Rogers in *Goodbye Again* (Helen Hayes Th., Apr. 24, 1956); played Mrs. Griffiths in *The First Gentleman* (Belasco, Apr. 25, 1957); and Mrs. Dainty Fidget in *The Country Wife* (Adelphi, Nov. 27, 1957).

She appeared for a season at Elitch Gardens (Denver, Colo.); played summer stock at the Ann Arbor (Mich.) Drama Festival, Berkshire Playhouse (Stockbridge, Mass.), Straight Wharf Th. (Nantucket, R.I.), Sea Cliff Th. (N.Y.), and Panama City (Fla.), appearing in *Biography, Blithe Spirit, Rain, The Fourposter, Ring Round the Moon, Goodbye My Fancy, Clutterbuck, A Streetcar Named Desire, Charley's Aunt, Three's a Family, Present Laughter, Springtime for Henry, The Happy Time, Glad Tidings, The Potting Shed, Third Best Sport*, and *Once More, With Feeling.*

Miss Claire played Eugenie in *Duel of Angels* (Helen Hayes Th., N.Y.C., Apr. 19, 1960); in stock, played Vinnie in *Life With Father* (Olney Playhouse, Md., Summer 1960); at the San Diego (Calif.) Shakespeare Festival, appeared as Nerissa in *The Merchant of Venice*, Olivia in *Twelfth Night*, and Lady Anne in *Richard III* (Old Globe, 1961); performed in Racine's *Phèdre* (Catholic Univ., Washington, D.C., 1961); in stock, appeared in *The Gazebo* and in *The Madwoman of Chaillot* (Palm Beach, Fla., 1962); in stock tour, played Angie in *Critic's Choice* (Summer 1962); in stock, appeared in *Take Her, She's Mine* (Royal Poinciana Playhouse, Palm Beach, Fla., Winter 1962); and played Mme. Lemaitre in *The Lady of the Camellias* (Winter Garden, N.Y.C., Mar. 20, 1963).

She was standby for Rosemary Harris as Eleanor of Aquitaine in *Lion in Winter* (Ambassador, Mar. 3, 1966); played in *The Entertainer* (Th. of the Living Arts, Philadelphia, Pa., Nov. 1, 1967); again played Vinnie in *Life with Father* on the road (Westport, Conn.; Easthampton and Mineola, N.Y.; Philadelphia, Pa.); toured in *There's a Girl in My Soup* (Skowhegan and Ogunquit, Me.; Dennis, Mass.; Pocono Playhouse); appeared as Claire in *A Delicate Balance* (Manitoba Th. Ctr., Winnipeg, Canada); repeated her performance as Vinnie in *Life with Father* (Robert S. Marx Th., Cincinnati, Ohio, Nov. 1, 1971; Walnut Street Th., Philadelphia; Barter Th., Abingdon, Va., July–Aug. 1973); played Goneril in *King Lear;* toured as Queen Gertrude in Judith Anderson's *Hamlet* (1971); played Esther Franz in *The Price* (Neptune Th., Halifax, Nova Scotia, Canada, Mar. 9, 1972); was a replacement (1973) in the cast of *The Prisoner of Second Avenue* (Eugene O'Neill Th., N.Y.C., Nov. 11, 1971).

Films. Miss Claire appeared in *North Star* (RKO, 1943); *Since You Went Away* (UA, 1944); and was the original writer for the screenplay of *Cleopatra* (20th-Fox, 1963).

Television. She has appeared on Danger (CBS), Suspense (CBS), U.S. Steel Hour (CBS), Hallmark Hall of Fame (NBC), Armstrong Circle Th. (NBC), Kraft Television Th. (NBC), Catholic Hour (NBC), Desilu Playhouse (CBS), The Nurses (CBS), Bus Stop (CBS, ABC); was Girl of the Week for the Today Show (NBC); appeared on Edge of Night (CBS); adapted *The Bridge of San Luis Rey* (Dupont Show of the Month, NBC, 1958); *Bernadette* (Desilu Playhouse, CBS, 1958); and Meredith Willson's *And Then I Wrote The Music Man;* and appeared on Hidden Faces (NBC) and Guiding Light (CBS, 1973).

Awards. Miss Claire received the Sylvania and Christopher awards for her television adaptation of Thornton Wilder's *The Bridge of San Luis Rey* (1958).

CLANCY, JAMES. Educator, director. b. James Harvey Clancy, May 1, 1912, Oakland, Calif., to James Lawrence and Edna Estelle Clancy. Father, salesman. Grad. San Jose State Coll., B.A. 1935; Stanford Univ., M.A., Ph.D. 1947. Married Sept. 10, 1949, to Stella Pinoris; two sons, one daughter. Served USAAF, 1940–42; rank, Capt. Member of ATA (formerly AETA). Address: (home) 107 Ellis Hollow Creek Road, Ithaca, NY 14850, tel. (607) 272-5695; (bus.) Dept. of Theatre Arts, Cornell Univ., Ithaca, NY 14850, tel. (607) 256-4060.

Since 1967, Mr. Clancy has been professor of theatre at Cornell Univ. He served as chairman of the Theatre Arts Dept. there from 1968 to 1973. In 1968 he added a professional training program in acting/directing to the other more traditional activities of the department. He was responsible, in 1970, for the formation of the Ithaca Summer Repertory Company, now participated in by Cornell Univ., Ithaca College, and the Center for the Arts at Ithaca.

Before 1967, Mr. Clancy had been instructor of dramatic literature and history of the theatre, as well as director of the theatre at San Jose (Calif.) State College (1936–57); professor of dramatic literature, director of the theatre and founder of the experimental theatre at the State Univ. of Iowa (1957–60); professor of dramatic literature, director of the theatre, and director of graduate study in theatre at Stanford (Calif.) Univ. (1961–62); and professor of drama at Dartmouth College and director of the theatre at Dartmouth's Hopkins Center (1962–67).

Mr. Clancy was the editor of the *Education Theatre Journal* (1957–59).

Awards. He was one of ten directors chosen to receive a Ford Foundation grant-in-aid (1960).

CLARK, ALEXANDER. Actor. b. May 2, 1901, New York City, to Alexander and Amy (Ashmore) Clark. Father, comedian; mother, composer and advertising executive. Grad. Burroughs Sch., Great Neck, N.Y., 1916. Married Jan. 8, 1945, to Frances Tannehill, actress; one daughter. Member of AEA; AFTRA; SAG; The Players; The Lambs; Escholier Club of N.Y. (secy., 1943–to date). Address: 175 W. 79th St., New York, NY 10024, tel. (212) TR 7-9306.

Theatre. Mr. Clark made his first professional appearance as Charlie Mason in *Golden Days* (Powers Th., Chicago, Ill., Mar. 22, 1920); and played Charles Phillips in *Shavings* (Powers, Chicago, Feb. 21, 1921), also touring in it.

He made his N.Y.C. debut as Charlie Mason in *Golden Days* (Gaiety, Nov. 1, 1921); toured New England states as Willie Parker in *Dulcy* (Spring 1922); played Harold Parmalee in *Merton of the Movies* (Cort, N.Y.C., Nov. 13, 1922), also touring in it (1923–24); Ted Burton in *The Comedienne* (Bijou, Oct. 21, 1924); Clifford Pendleton in *Jack in the Pulpit* (Princess, Jan. 6, 1925); Harry Fitch in *The Judge's Husband* (49 St. Th., Sept. 27, 1926); Elmer Dixon in *Fog* (National, Feb. 7, 1927); Laertes in a modern-dress version of *Hamlet* (Casino, Newport, R.I., July 1927); succeeded (Apr. 1928) Herbert Clark as Val D' Errico in *Excess Baggage* (Ritz, N.Y.C., Dec. 26, 1927); also playing this role in the Chicago company and in stock (1928); and played Roy Lane in *Broadway* (Rialto, Hoboken, N.J., 1928).

He made his London debut as Tony in *The Patsy* (Apollo, Dec. 19, 1928); played Sam in *The Tiger in Men* (Vaudeville, Aug. 6, 1929); took over Warren William's role as Paul Rana in *Out of a Blue Sky* (Booth, N.Y.C., Feb. 8, 1930); played Johnnie Case in *Holiday* (Vine St. Th., Hollywood, Calif.; President, San Francisco, Calif., 1930); the Doctor in *Too*

True To Be Good (Guild, N.Y.C., Apr. 4, 1932); Warwick Wilson in *Biography* (Guild, Dec. 12, 1932); The Young Norman in *Lady Godiva* (Westport Country Playhouse, Conn., Summer 1933); Tom Courtney in *American—Very Early* (Vanderbilt, N.Y.C., Jan. 30, 1934); toured as Damon Wells in *The Dark Tower* (Mar.–May 1934); as Otto in *Design for Living* (Nov.–Dec. 1934); played Wade Hamlin in *Spring Freshet* (Plymouth, N.Y.C., Oct. 4, 1934); and appeared in stock as Hansi in *Ode to Liberty* (San Francisco, Los Angeles, Calif., July –Aug. 1935).

He played Peter Santard in *Kind Lady* (Queen's, London, June 12, 1936); P. De Quincey Devereux in *Naughty Naught '00* (Amer. Music Hall, N.Y.C., Jan. 1, 1937); appeared in stock at the Berkshire Playhouse (Stockbridge, Mass., Summer 1937); played Prince Ernst in the national tour of *Victoria Regina* (1937–38); and also during this period played Bassanio in Helen Hayes' special performance of *The Merchant of Venice* (Chicago, Ill.; Los Angeles, San Francisco, Calif.).

He repeated his role as Prince Ernst in *Victoria Regina* (Martin Beck Th., N.Y.C., Oct. 3, 1938); took over Louis Martin's role as Ninian Edwards in *Abe Lincoln in Illinois* (Plymouth, Nov. 15, 1938); played the Team Manager in a tryout of *Elmer the Great* which closed during its pre-Bway tour (opened Wilbur, Boston, Mass., 1940); toured as Otto Horst in *Margin for Error* (Sept.–Oct. 1939); took over this role from Philip Collidge in its N.Y.C. production (Plymouth, Nov. 3, 1939); and appeared in a stock production at the Cape Playhouse (Dennis, Mass., Summer 1940).

He appeared on the subway circuit (theatres in the N.Y.C. metropolitan area) as Teck de Broncovis in *Watch on the Rhine* (1941); played Buckley in *Native Son* (Majestic, N.Y.C., Oct. 23, 1942); Roy Darwin in *Counsellor-at-Law* (Royale, Nov. 24, 1942); Dr. Tumansky in *Listen Professor* (Forrest, Dec. 22, 1943); and toured as Stevens in a USO production of *The Night of January 16th* (ETO, Apr. 1, 1945–Oct. 1, 1945).

Mr. Clark played Mr. Bolton in *Sheppey* (Playhouse, N.Y.C., April 18, 1944); Victor in a summer theatre tour of *Private Lives* (Toronto and Montreal, Canada; Boston, Mass., 1946); the title role in an ELT production of *Richard III* (Feb. 17, 1948); appeared in summer productions at the Casino Th. (Newport, R.I., 1949); played Seth Lord in the national company of *The Philadelphia Story* (1949–50); appeared in stock at the Nassau (B.W.I.) Playhouse (1950); and as Smallwood in a summer theatre tour of *Miss Mable* (1951).

He played Vincent in *Legend of Lovers* (Plymouth, N.Y.C., Dec. 26, 1951); Perriton Maxwell in a cross-country tour of *Call Me Madam* (1952–53); Alamady the Actor in summer theatre productions of *The Play's the Thing* (1953); played the Earl of Moray in *Mary of Scotland* and the Brother in *The Wisteria Tree* in the Helen Hayes Festival (Falmouth Playhouse, Mass., (Summer 1954); toured as Philo in *No Time for Comedy* (Summer 1955); and took over Clarence Derwent's role as Prof. Serebriakoff in *Uncle Vanya* (Fourth St. Th., N.Y.C., Jan. 31, 1956).

He appeared as the Duke in a tryout of *The Dazzling Hour* (Pocono Playhouse, Mountainhome, Pa.; Theatre-in-the-Park, Philadelphia, Pa., Aug. 1957); Dr. Adams in *A Soft Touch* (Coconut Grove Playhouse, Miami, Fla., Dec. 1957–Jan. 1958); Richard Hackett in *Say, Darling* (NY City Ctr., Feb. 25, 1959); the Senator in *John Loves Mary* (Warwick, R.I., June 1960; Wallingford, Conn., Detroit, Mich., July 1960); the Publisher in *An Adventure* (Nyack Playhouse, N.Y., 1960); Petkoff in *Arms and the Man* (Westport Country Playhouse, Conn., 1960); Dickinson Wadsworth in *Julia, Jake and Uncle Joe* (Booth, N.Y.C., Jan. 28, 1961); Andrew MacLaren in *Brigadoon* (NY City Ctr., May 30, 1961); Admiral Hall in *The Captains and the Kings* (Playhouse, Jan. 2, 1962); and Augustus in a tour of *The Vinegar Tree* (July–Sept. 1962).

He played James McQueen in *Calculated Risk* (Ambassador, N.Y.C., Oct. 31, 1962); took over Frank Conroy's role as Clyde Norman in the same play; Oscar Nelson in a national tour of *Mary, Mary* (opened Fisher, Detroit, Mich., July, 1963); and James Baldwin in *A Case of Libel* (Longacre, N.Y.C., Oct. 10, 1963).

He repeated his role as MacLaren in *Brigadoon* (NY City Ctr., Dec. 2, 1964); appeared as Baptista in *Kiss Me, Kate* (NY City Ctr., May 12, 1965); and made a fourteen-week tour as King Pellinor in *Camelot* (Summer 1965). He played in the 1966 American Shakespeare Festival, Stratford, Conn., as the Lord Chief Justice in *Falstaff* (June 18) and Third Tempter in *Murder in the Cathedral,* (June 19); he toured as the Professor in *The Male Animal* (Summer 1967); and he played Pa Fisher in *The Show-Off* (Lyceum, N.Y.C., Sept. 13, 1968; touring also for fourteen weeks).

Television and Radio. Mr. Clark wrote the scripts and performed with Gertrude Lawrence in *Broadway Calling,* a radio program which was broadcast to British Troops by ENSA (Entertainment's Natl. Services Assn.). On television, he has appeared on US Steel Hour (CBS), Robert Montgomery Presents (NBC), Camera Three (CBS), Kraft Television Th. (NBC), Ethel and Albert (ABC), I Remember Mama (CBS), Three Steps to Heaven (NBC), As the World Turns (CBS), The Brighter Day (CBS), Claudia Storm (CBS), Edge of Night (CBS), and he played Captain Mullen in *The Man without a Country* (Rosemont Prods., 1972).

He also appeared on Rodgers and Hammerstein's *Cinderella* (CBS, 1957) and Cole Porter's *Aladdin.*.

Other Activities. Mr. Clark was a co-founder of Friends of Richard III, Inc., "a NY State educational project for the purpose of helping to clear the maligned name of that monarch" (1954). In Sept. and Oct. 1970, he led a five-week Theatre Guild tour of Dublin, London, Stockholm, Leningrad, and Moscow.

Published Works. He wrote articles on the theatre for *Vanity Fair,* for which he was also drama editor (1931); and has also written articles for *The New Yorker.*.

Recreation. Swimming, collecting original drawings by Max Beerbohm.

CLARK, F. DONALD. Educator. b. Frank Donald Clark, July 15, 1913, Wellington, Kan., to Frank Dan and Nancy Clark. Father, railway yardmaster. Relative in theatre: brother, Dort Clark, actor. Grad. Wellington H.S., 1931; attended Friends Univ., 1931–32; Kansas State Teachers Coll., B.S. (education) 1936; State Univ. of Iowa, M.A. (theatre) 1938. Married June 28, 1939, to Evelyn Lorene Madison; one daughter. Member of SWTC (vice-pres., 1960–61; pres., 1961–62). Address: (home) 505 Foreman Ave., Norman, OK 73069, tel. (405) 321-7299; (bus.) Coll. of Fine Arts, Univ. of Oklahoma, Norman, OK 73069, tel. (405) 325-2771.

Since 1961, Mr. Clark has served as both professor of drama and dean of the Coll. of Fine Arts, Univ. of Oklahoma, where he was assistant professor of broadcasting (1946–55); associate professor of drama (1955–61); and acting dean of the Coll. of Fine Arts (1959–61).

Mr. Clark made his stage debut with the Globe Theatre Repertory Co., Dallas, Tex., playing minor roles in *As You Like It, Twelfth Night, Dr. Faustus, Comedy of Errors, Julius Caesar, Taming of the Shrew* (Summer 1936). He was instructor of speech and drama (1936–38) at Kansas State Teachers Coll.; director of Dramatic Productions, Parsons (Kan.) Junior Coll. (1938–40); head of the Dept. of Speech and Drama, Amarillo (Tex.) Coll. (1940–44); and radio news editor, KFDA, Amarillo, Tex. (1944–46).

CLARK, KENDALL. Actor. b. Feb. 5, 1912, Chicago, Ill., to Kendall and Margaret (Jordan) Clark. Grad. Univ. of Wisconsin, B.A. 1933. Served US Army, 1941–45; rank, Capt. Member of AEA; SAG; AFTRA. Address: 6650 Whitley Terrace, Hollywood, CA 90068.

Theatre. Mr. Clark made his Bway debut as Gustave in Eva Le Gallienne's production of *Camille* (Shubert, Dec. 4, 1935); subsequently played Juanito in the curtain raiser, *A Sunny Morning,* presented with *The Women Have Their Way* (Shubert, Dec. 7, 1935), which was also presented by Miss Le Gallienne.

He played Robert in *End of Summer* (Guild, Feb. 17, 1936); Junior Counsel in *Storm Over Patsy* (Guild, Mar. 8, 1937); succeeded (Dec. 1937) Richard Carlson as Martin Holme in *The Ghost of Yankee Doodle* (Guild, Nov. 22, 1937); appeared as Jerry in *Washington Jitters* (Guild, May 2, 1938); Wade Barnett in *The Big Blow* (Maxine Elliott's Th., Oct. 1, 1938); and in stock, in *Olympia* (No. Shore Players, Marblehead, Mass., July 3, 1939).

Mr. Clark played Robert and succeeded Franchot Tone (spring 1940) in the role of Philip Rawlings in *The Fifth Column* (Alvin, N.Y.C., Mar. 6, 1940); appeared as Steve Eldridge in *George Washington Slept Here* (Lyceum, Oct. 18, 1940); Major Dennis Robinson, Jr., in *Home of the Brave* (Belasco, Dec. 27, 1945); Maxim, Duke of Willenstein, in *The Eagle Has Two Heads* (Plymouth, Mar. 19, 1947); Murdo Fraser in *The First Mrs. Fraser* (Shubert, Nov. 5, 1947); was stage manager for *Private Lives* (Plymouth, Oct. 4, 1948); played Petruchio in *Taming of the Shrew* and Marc Antony in *Julius Caesar* with the Margaret Webster Shakespeare Co. (Oct. 1949 to Apr. 1950); and in stock, toured as Morrell in *Candida* (Summer 1951).

He played Brother Martin Ladvenu in *Saint Joan* (Cort, Oct. 4, 1951); Dr. Bellman in *The Shrike* (Cort, Jan. 15, 1952); in stock, George Henderson in *Affairs of State* (Ogunquit Playhouse, Me., July 6, 1953); repeated his role in *The Shrike* (NY City Ctr., Nov. 25, 1953); played Sir James Tyrell in *Richard III* (NY City Ctr., Dec. 9, 1953); and David Carson in *The Desperate Hours* (Ethel Barrymore Th., Feb. 10, 1955).

At the American Shakespeare Festival (Stratford, Conn.), he played Cardinal Pandulph in *King John* (June 26, 1956); and Hortensio in *The Taming of the Shrew* (Aug. 5, 1956); repeated his role in *The Taming of the Shrew* (Phoenix, Feb. 20, 1957); toured as M. Lindsay Woolsey in *Auntie Mame* (opened Hanna, Cleveland, Ohio, Oct. 30, 1957; closed Erlanger, Chicago, Ill., Jan. 17, 1959); and, at the American Shakespeare Festival (Stratford, Conn.), played Gratiano in *Othello* (June 22, 1957) and Solanio in *The Merchant of Venice* (July 10, 1957).

He appeared as Valere in *Dr. Willy Nilly* (Barbizon-Plaza, N.Y.C., June 4, 1959); Very Reverend Thomas Canon Skerritt in *Shadow and Substance* (Tara, Nov. 3, 1959); was understudy to Richard Derr in the role of Tucker Grogan in *Invitation to a March* (Music Box Th., Oct. 29, 1960); at the Arena Stage (Washington, D.C.), played Ulysses in *Tiger at the Gates* (Mar. 7, 1961); Mendoza (and the Devil) in *Man and Superman* (May 2, 1961); Governor—one of the Iron-Shirts—and a lawyer in *The Caucasian Chalk Circle* (Oct. 20, 1961); the President in *The Madwoman of Chaillot* (Dec. 26, 1961); Dobelle in *The Moon in the Yellow River* (Jan. 23, 1962); Lord Summerbeys in *Misalliance* (Feb. 20, 1962); Blick in *The Time of Your Life* (May 15, 1962); the Bishop in *Once in a Lifetime* (Oct. 23, 1962); Mog Edwards, Butcher Beynon, and Organ Morgan in *Under Milkwood* (Nov. 20, 1962); Corvino in *Volpone* (Dec. 18, 1963); Juror Four in *Twelve Angry Men* (Jan. 15, 1963); Monsewer in *The Hostage* (Feb. 12, 1963); the Bishop of Limoux in *The Burning of the Lepers* (Mar. 20, 1962); Alexander Vladimirovich Voinitskaya in *Uncle Vanya* (Apr. 17, 1962); Lodovico in *Othello* (Apr. 10, 1963); and Smith, a Warden, in *The Threepenny Opera* (May 14, 1963).

He played George in the national company of *Who's Afraid of Virginia Woolf?* (Sept. 1963 to Apr. 1965); James Tyrone in *Long Day's Journey into Night* (American Repertory Th., Portland, Ore., Feb. 1968); and Lear in *King Lear* (Univ. of Calif. at Davis, Feb. 5, 1969).

At the Alley Th., in Houston, Tex., Mr. Clark appeared as the Grandfather in *All the Way Home* (June 1969); General Wallace in *The Andersonville Trial* (Jan. 1970); Charles in *Blithe Spirit* (May 1970); Emerson in *The Night Thoreau Spent in Jail* (Jan. 1971); and Mr. Webb in *Our Town* (March

1971).

Films. Mr. Clark appeared in *The Shrike* (U, 1955); *Away All Boats* (U, 1956); *Daddy's Gone A'Hunting* (20th-Fox, 1969); and *Johnny Got His Gun* (Cinemation, 1971).

Television. Mr. Clark appeared (1966, 1967) on West Coast television.

CLARK, PEGGY. Lighting designer and scenic designer, costume designer. b. Margaret Brownson Clark, Sept. 30, 1915, Baltimore, Md., to Eliot and Eleanor (Linton) Clark. Father, retired professor of anatomy. Grad. Phebe Anna Thorne Sch., Bryn Mawr, Pa., 1931; Smith Coll., A.B. (cum laude) 1935; Yale Univ., M.F.A. (scenic design) 1938. Married Jan. 28, 1960, to Lloyd R. Kelley, (dec. June 3, 1972), theatre electrician. Member of United Scenic Artists, Local 829 (recording secy., 1942–47; trustee, 1948–51, 1953–54; pres., 1968–69; pension and welfare trustee, 1971–75); US Institute of Theatrical Technology (dir., 1969–72; vice commissioner of engineering, 1974); Illuminating Engineering Society; ANTA; International Theatre Institute (advisory comm., 1969–72); Smith College Alumnae Th. Comm. (chmn., 1961–69; bd. of counsellors, 1961–69); Smith College class of '35 (pres., 1970–75); Brooklyn (N.Y.) Smith Club (dir. of community calling, 1972–74); New York Smith Club; Yale Drama Alumnae Assn. (Eastern vice-pres., 1970–74); French Bulldog Club of America (1958–to date; vice-pres., 1972–to date); Woods Hole (Mass.) Yacht Club. Address: 36 Cranberry St., Brooklyn, NY 11201, tel. (212) UL 2-2597.

Theatre. Miss Clark first designed the costumes for *The Girl from Wyoming* (American Music Hall, N.Y.C., Oct. 29, 1938); was subsequently technical supervisor for *Wuthering Heights* (Longacre Th., Apr. 27, 1939); set and lighting designer for *Gabrielle* (Maxine Elliott's Th., Mar. 25, 1941); costume designer for *Uncle Harry* (Broadhurst, May 20, 1942); the US Dept. of Agriculture's touring production of *It's Up to You* (1942); *The Great Big Doorstep* (Morosco, N.Y.C., Nov. 26, 1942); and for *Counterattack* (Windsor, Mar. 3, 1943); was co-designer of the American Th. Wing's *Stage Door Canteen* (1942) and technical director of the *Lunchtime Follies* (1942–43).

She was technical supervisor for *A Connecticut Yankee* (Martin Beck Th., Nov. 17, 1943); *The Innocent Voyage* (Belasco, Nov. 15, 1943); costume designer for *Ramshackle Inn* (Royale, Jan. 5, 1944); technical supervisor for *Laffing Room Only* (Winter Garden, Dec. 23, 1944); technical supervisor and stage manager (Dec. 1944–June 1945) for *On the Town* (Adelphi, Dec. 28, 1944); costume designer for *Dark of the Moon* (46 St. Th., Mar. 14, 1945); *Devils Galore* (Royale, Sept. 12, 1945); technical supervisor for *Billion Dollar Baby* (Alvin, Dec. 21, 1945); the pre-Bway tryout of *Twilight Bar* (opened Ford's Th., Baltimore, Md., Mar. 12, 1946; closed Walnut St. Th., Philadelphia, Pa., Mar. 23, 1946); lighting designer and 2nd technical supervisor for *Beggar's Holiday* (Bway Th., N.Y.C., Dec. 26, 1946); lighting designer and technical supervisor for *Brigadoon* (Ziegfeld, Mar. 13, 1947); lighting designer for *High Button Shoes* (Century, Oct. 9, 1947); *Medea* (Natl., Oct. 20, 1947); the pre-Bway tryout of *Bonanza Bound!* (opened Shubert, Philadelphia, Pa., Dec. 26, 1947; closed there, Jan. 3, 1948); and technical supervisor of *Topaze* (Morosco, N.Y.C., Dec. 27, 1947).

She was technical supervisor of *Look Ma, I'm Dancin'* (Adelphi, Jan. 29, 1948); and lighting designer for the pre-Bway tryout of *That's the Ticket* (opened Shubert, Philadelphia, Pa., Sept. 24, 1948; closed there, Oct. 2, 1948); as well as *Love Life* (46 St. Th., N.Y.C., Oct. 7, 1948); *The Rape of Lucretia* (Ziegfeld, Dec. 29, 1948); *Along Fifth Avenue* (Broadhurst, Jan. 13, 1949); *Miss Liberty* (Imperial, July 15, 1949); *Touch and Go* (Broadhurst, Oct. 13, 1949); *Gentlemen Prefer Blondes* (Ziegfeld, Dec. 8, 1949); *All You Need Is One Good Break* (Mansfield, Feb. 9, 1950); *Cry of the Peacock* (Mansfield, Apr. 11, 1950); and for *Bless You All* (Mark Hellinger Th., Dec. 14, 1950).

She designed the setting, costumes, and lighting for *The High Ground* (48 St. Th., Feb. 20, 1951); was lighting designer for *Paint Your Wagon* (Shubert, Nov. 12, 1951); *Pal Joey* (Broadhurst, Jan. 3, 1952); designed the setting and lighting for the pre-Bway tryout of *Curtain Going Up* (opened Forrest, Philadelphia, Pa., Feb. 15, 1952; closed there Apr. 1, 1952); designed lighting for *Of Thee I Sing* (Ziegfeld, N.Y.C., May 5, 1952); *The Song of Norway* (Philharmonic Aud., Los Angeles, Calif., Summer 1952); *Jollyanna* (Curran, San Francisco, Summer 1952); *Maggie* (Natl., N.Y.C., Feb. 18, 1953); *Wonderful Town* (Winter Garden, Feb. 25, 1953); was technical supervisor for *Carnival in Flanders* (New Century, Sept. 8, 1953); lighting designer for *The Trip to Bountiful* (Henry Miller's Th., Nov. 3, 1953); *Kismet* (Ziegfeld, Dec. 3, 1953); and scenic and lighting designer for the touring production of the Agnes de Mille Dance Th. (1952–53).

She was lighting designer for *In the Summer House* (Playhouse, N.Y.C., Dec. 29, 1953); *Bullfight* (Th. de Lys, Jan. 12, 1954); *The Threepenny Opera* (Th. de Lys, Mar. 10, 1954); *Brigadoon* (Philharmonic Aud., Los Angeles, Calif., Summer 1954); *On Your Toes* (46 St. Th., N.Y.C., Oct. 11, 1954); *Peter Pan* (Winter Garden, Oct. 20, 1954); *Plain and Fancy* (Mark Hellinger Th., Jan. 27, 1955); *Kiss Me, Kate* (Philharmonic Aud., Los Angeles, Calif., Summer 1955); the national touring production of *Plain and Fancy* (Summer 1955); *Will Success Spoil Rock Hunter?* (Belasco, N.Y.C., Oct. 13, 1955); *No Time for Sergeants* (Alvin, Oct. 20, 1955); *The Righteous Are Bold* (Holiday, Dec. 22, 1955); the pre-Bway tryout of *The Amazing Adele* (opened Shubert, Philadelphia, Pa., Dec. 26, 1956; closed Shubert, Boston, Mass., Jan. 21, 1956); *Mr. Wonderful* (Bway Th., N.Y.C., Mar. 22, 1956); the pre-Bway tryout of *The Ziegfeld Follies* (opened Shubert, Boston, Mass., Apr. 16, 1956; closed Shubert, Philadelphia, Pa., May 12, 1956); *New Faces of 1956* (Ethel Barrymore Th., N.Y.C., June 14, 1956); *Rosalinda* (Philharmonic Aud., Los Angeles, Calif., Summer 1956); the national touring production of *No Time for Sergeants* (Summer 1956); *Auntie Mame* (Broadhurst, N.Y.C., Oct. 31, 1956); and for *Bells Are Ringing* (Shubert, Nov. 29, 1956).

Miss Clark was lighting designer for the national touring production of *Auntie Mame* (1957); and at the NY City Ctr., for *Brigadoon* (Mar. 27, 1957); *The Merry Widow* (Apr. 10, 1957); *South Pacific* (Apr. 24, 1957); and *The Pajama Game* (May 15, 1957). She designed lighting for *South Pacific* and *Annie Get Your Gun* (Curran, San Francisco, Calif.; Philharmonic Aud., Los Angeles, Calif., Summer 1957); *Carousel* (NY City Ctr., Sept. 11, 1957); the pre-Bway tryout of *The Carefree Heart* (opened Cass, Detroit, Mich., Sept. 30, 1957; closed Hanna, Cleveland, Ohio, Oct. 26, 1957); *Nude with Violin* (Belasco, N.Y.C., Nov. 14, 1957); and three NY City Ctr. productions: *Annie Get Your Gun* (Feb. 19, 1958), *Wonderful Town* (Mar. 5, 1958), and *Oklahoma!* (Mar. 19, 1958); and for *Say, Darling* (ANTA, Apr. 3, 1958).

At the Brussels (Belgium) World Exposition (US Pavilion, Summer 1958), Miss Clark was lighting designer for *Carousel, Susannah,* and *Wonderful Town.* She designed lighting for *Flower Drum Song* (St. James, N.Y.C., Dec. 1, 1958); *Juno* (Winter Garden, Mar. 9, 1959); *Oklahoma!* (Calif., Summer 1959); the *Billy Barnes Revue* (York, N.Y.C., June 9, 1959); *Cheri* (Morosco, Oct. 12, 1959); and *Goodbye, Charlie* (Lyceum, Dec. 16, 1959).

Subsequent productions for which she has designed lighting include *A Distant Bell* (Eugene O'Neill Th., Jan. 13, 1960); *Bye Bye Birdie* (Martin Beck Th., Apr. 14, 1960); *The Unsinkable Molly Brown* (Winter Garden, Nov. 3, 1960); *Under the Yum-Yum Tree* (Henry Miller's Th., Nov. 16, 1960); *Showgirl* (Eugene O'Neill Th., Jan. 12, 1961); *Mary, Mary* (Helen Hayes Th., Mar. 8, 1961); *Paradise Island* (Marine Th., Jones Beach, L.I., N.Y., Summers 1961, 1962); *The Merry Widow* (Philharmonic Aud., Los Angeles, Calif., Summer 1961); *Guys and Dolls* (Philharmonic Aud., Summer 1961); *Sail Away* (Broadhurst, N.Y.C., Oct. 3, 1961); *Romulus* (Music Box Th., Jan 10, 1962); *The Song of Norway* (Philharmonic Aud., Los Angeles, Calif., Summer 1962); *Kismet* (Curran, San Francisco, Calif., Summer 1962); three national touring productions of *Mary, Mary* (1962–63); *Eddie Fisher at the Winter Garden* (N.Y.C., Oct. 2, 1962); five NY City Ctr. productions: *Brigadoon* (Jan. 30, 1963); *Wonderful Town* (Feb. 13, 1963); *Oklahoma!* (Feb. 27, 1963); *Pal Joey* (May 29, 1963); and *The King and I* (June 10, 1963); for *Carousel* (Curran, San Francisco, Calif., Summer 1963); *Around the World in 80 Days* (Marine Th., Jones Beach, L.I., N.Y., Summers 1963, 1964); for 1964 Chevrolet industrial show (Masonic Temple, Detroit, Mich., Aug. 1963); the pre-Bway tryout of *The Time of the Barracudas* (opened Geary, San Francisco, Calif., Oct. 21, 1963; closed out of town); *Kiss Me, Kate* (Philharmonic Aud., Los Angeles, Calif., Apr. 20, 1964); and for *Bajour* (Shubert, N.Y.C., Nov. 19, 1964).

Other productions for which she has designed lighting include *Poor Richard* (Helen Hayes Th., Dec. 2, 1964); four productions for the NY City Ctr. Light Opera Co.: *Brigadoon* (Dec. 23, 1964); *Guys and Dolls* (Apr. 28, 1965); *Kiss Me, Kate* (May 12, 1965); and *South Pacific* (June 2, 1965); *The Great Waltz* (Los Angeles Civic Light Opera Association, Music Ctr., Los Angeles, Calif., July 27, 1965); five productions for the NY City Ctr. Light Opera Co.: *Oklahoma!* (Dec. 15, 1965); *How to Succeed in Business Without Really Trying* (Apr. 20, 1966); *The Most Happy Fella* (May 11, 1966); *Where's Charley?,* also settings (May 25, 1966); and *Guys and Dolls* (June 8, 1966); *The Best Laid Plans* (Brooks Atkinson Th., Mar. 25, 1966); *Mardi Gras!* (Marine Th., Jones Beach, L.I., N.Y., July 8, 1966); *The Student Prince* (Los Angeles Civic Light Opera Association, Music Ctr., Los Angeles, Calif., 1966); *The Rose Tattoo* (NY City Ctr. Drama Co., Oct. 20, 1966); four productions for the NY City Ctr. Light Opera Co.: *Finian's Rainbow* (Apr. 5, 1967); *The Sound of Music* (Apr. 26, 1967); *Wonderful Town* (Mary 17, 1967); and *Brigadoon* (Dec. 13, 1967); *Dumas and Son* (Los Angeles Civic Light Opera Association, 1967); *Arabian Nights* (Marine Th., Jones Beach, L.I., N.Y., Summer 1967); *Show Boat* (Los Angeles Civic Light Opera Association, 1967); *People Is the Thing That the World Is Fullest Of,* consultant (Bil Baird Th., Feb. 20, 1967); *Darling of the Day* (George Abbott Th., Jan. 27, 1968); *Rosalinda* (Los Angeles Civic Light Opera Association, 1968); *South Pacific* (Marine Th., Jones Beach, L.I., N.Y., Summers 1968 and 1969); *Jimmy* (Winter Garden, Oct. 23, 1969); *Last of the Red Hot Lovers* (Eugene O'Neill Th., Dec. 28, 1969); two productions for the Los Angeles Civic Light Opera Association: *My Fair Lady* and *1491* (1969); *The Sound of Music* (Marine Th., Jones Beach, L.I., N.Y. (Summers 1970 and 1971); *Cavalcade of Musical Theatre* (Los Angeles Civic Light Opera Association, 1970); *How the Other Half Loves* (Royale, Mar. 29, 1971); *Candide* (Opera House, John F. Kennedy Ctr., Washington, D.C., Oct. 26, 1971); two productions at Marine Th., Jones Beach, L.I., N.Y.: *The King and I* (Summer 1972) and *Carousel* (Summer 1973); and three productions at the Bil Baird Th., N.Y.C., of Bil Baird's Marionettes: *The Whistling Wizard and the Sultan of Tuffet* (1973); *Pinocchio* (1973); and *Band-Wagon* (Mar. 16, 1973).

Other Activities. Miss Clark has been an instructor in lighting design (1965–74) at the Studio and Forum of Stage Design, Inc. She was a lecturer in 1967 and 1969 on lighting design, Theatre Dept., Smith College, Northampton, Mass., where she did the lighting for the 1969 presentation of *The Crucible* at Smith's Center for the Performing Arts. In 1969–70, she was visiting critic at the Yale Drama School, New Haven, Conn.

Published Works. Miss Clark has had articles published in *Theatre 2, The American Theatre, 1968–69* and *Theatre Crafts.*

CLARKE, DAVID. Actor. b. David Gainey Clarke, Aug. 30, 1908, Chicago, Ill., to Charles Milton and Nora (Coakley) Clarke. Father, clergyman. Grad. Arsenal Tech. H.S., Indianapolis, Ind., 1926; attended Butler Univ., 1926–29. Studied speech with Margaret Prendergast McLean, Hollywood, Calif, one yr. Married Dec. 21, 1946, to Nora

Dean Dunfee, actress; two daughters, Katharine and Susan Dunfee, actresses. Served USNR, 1942; rank, hospital apprentice 1/C; USMC, PTO, 1942–45; rank, Pharmacist's Mate 2/C. Member of AEA; SAG; AFTRA. Address: (home) 225 Central Park West, New York, NY tel. (212) EN 2-1807; (bus.) Actors' Equity Association, 1500 Bway, New York, NY 10036.

Theatre. Mr. Clarke made his debut at age five as the Groom in *Tom Thumb's Wedding* (Verona, Wis., 1913); his professional debut as Barabbas in the American version of the *Frieburg Passion Play* (Chicago, Ill.; West Coast, 1929); and appeared in stock productions at the Ivoryton (Conn.) Playhouse (June 29, 1930–Aug. 1930).

His first N.Y.C. assignment was as stage manager for *Roadside* (Longacre Th., Sept. 26, 1930); subsequently appeared in stock at the Ivoryton (Conn.) Playhouse (June 1–Sept. 1, 1934); and the Saybrook (Conn.) Th. (June 1–Sept. 1935); succeeded (May 1936) Anthony Ross as Private Webster in *Bury the Dead*, part of a double-bill with *Prelude* (Ethel Barrymore Th., N.Y.C., Apr. 18, 1936); played Hannan in *200 Were Chosen* (48 St. Th., Nov. 20, 1936); was assistant stage manager for *The Cradle Will Rock* (Windsor, Jan. 4, 1938); appeared as Jack in *The Journeyman* (Fulton, Jan. 29, 1938); the Guide, Second Senator, Jed and McGinty in *Washington Jitters* (Guild, May 2, 1938); Feargus in *Abe Lincoln in Illinois* (Plymouth, Oct. 15, 1938), and Bill Herndon in the national touring production (1939–40).

He appeared (Hollywood, Calif., 1945–50) in *The Sound of Hunting, All My Sons, Galileo, Portrait of a Madonna, The Stone Jungle* and *Awake and Sing;* played Yetter in *See the Jaguar* (Cort, N.Y.C., Dec. 3, 1952); The Man without Shoes in *The Emperor's Clothes* (Ethel Barrymore Th., Feb. 9, 1953); Justice Merton in *The Scarecrow* (Th. de Lys, June 16, 1953); Alderman Doyle in *Madam Will You Walk?* (Phoenix, Dec. 1, 1953); Second Citizen in *Coriolanus* (Phoenix, Jan. 19, 1954); the Sheriff in *Front Page* and Tokyo in *Golden Boy* (Playhouse-in-the-Park, Philadelpia, Pa., 1954).

Mr. Clarke played Raymond in *A Memory of Two Mondays* and Louis in *A View from the Bridge*, a double bill (Coronet, N.Y.C., Sept. 29, 1955); Owen Wister in a stock production of *The Magnificent Yankee* (Bucks County Playhouse, New Hope, Pa., Summer 1956); Dog Hamma in *Orpheus Descending* (Martin Beck Th., N.Y.C., Mar. 21, 1957); Helmesberger in *The Visit* (Lunt-Fontanne, N.Y.C., May 5, 1958), and on tour (1959); Joshua Speed in *The Last Days of Lincoln* (Florida State Univ., Tallahassee, 1959); Helmesberger in *The Visit* (NY City Ctr., Mar. 8, 1960); played Henry Ford Crimp in *The Ballad of the Sad Cafe* (Martin Beck Th., Oct. 30, 1963), and succeeded (Jan. 11, 1964) William Prince as Henry Macy in the same play.

He was Jack Norbit in *Christy* (American Place Th., Mar. 19, 1964); the Chef in *The Kitchen* (81 St. Th., June 13, 1966); Mr. Shortley in *The Displaced Person* (American Place Th., St. Clement's Ch., Dec. 29, 1966); Mr. Elmstead in *Rose* (Provincetown Playhouse, Oct. 28, 1969); a Reporter in *Inquest* (Music Box, Apr. 23, 1970); the Boss in *Of Mice and Men* (Brooks Atkinson Th., Dec. 18, 1974); and he wrote *Never a Snug Harbor* (New Dramatists, Oct. 13, 1974).

Films. Mr. Clarke made his debut in *The Long Night* (RKO, 1947); subsequently appeared in *Killer McCoy* (MGM, 1947); *The State of the Union* (MGM, 1948); *The Man from Colorado* (Col., 1948); *The Boy with the Green Hair* (RKO, 1948); *The Doolins of Oklahoma* (Col., 1949); *The Set-Up* (RKO, 1949); *Red Canyon* (U, 1949); *The Asphalt Jungle* (MGM, 1950); *The Gunfighter* (20th-Fox, 1950); *The Red Badge of Courage* (MGM, 1951); *The Narrow Margin* (RKO, 1952); *Edge of the City* (MGM; 1957); and *The St. Louis Bank Robbery* (UA, 1957).

Television. He made his debut on the Somerset Maugham Th. (ABC, 1950); and has performed on Suspense (CBS); Casey, Crime Photograher (CBS); Route 66 (CBS); Naked City (ABC); and Tallahassee 7000.

Recreation. Experimentation with puppets, writing poetry.

CLAYTON, JAN. Actress, singer. b. Jane Byral Clayton, Aug. 26, 1917, Alamogordo, N.M., to G. Verner and Vera (Carter) Clayton. Father, rancher, teacher; mother, teacher. Attended Gulf Park Jr. Coll., 1935–37. Studied drama with Nadine Shepardon, two years; piano with Albert Davies, two years; voice with Lillian Sloane, ten years. Married 1938, to Russell Hayden, actor (marr. dis. 1940); one daughter; married 1945, to Robert W. Lerner, producer (marr. dis. 1958); one son, three daughters; married 1965 to George Greeley, musician (marr. dis. 1967). Appeared in USO productions during WW II. Member of SAG; AFTRA; AGVA; AEA; Phi Theta Kappa. Address: 9018 Elevado Ave., Los Angeles, CA 90069.

Theatre. Miss Clayton made her debut in California, where she appeared in the musicals, *Meet the People* (Hollywood, 1939), *Music in the Air* (Los Angeles), *They Can't Get You Down* (Hollywood), *Hopalong Cassidy* (Hollywood), and *Sailor Beware* (San Francisco).

She played Julie Jordan in *Carousel* (Majestic Th., N.Y.C., Apr. 9, 1945), also in Los Angeles and San Francisco, and at the Brussel's (Belg.) World's Fair, (1958); played Magnolia in *Show Boat* (Ziegfeld, N.Y.C., Jan. 5, 1946); the title role in *Rose Marie* (Greek Th., Hollywood); Sarah Brown in the national company of *Guys and Dolls* (opened Curran, San Francisco, June 4, 1951); Anna Leonowens in *The King and I* (NY City Ctr., Apr. 18, 1956); and succeeded Terry Saunders as Christine Crane in *Follies* on Feb. 27, 1972, and later opened in *Follies* in St. Louis at Century City.

In stock she has appeared at Elitch Gardens (Denver, Colo.) in *Auntie Mame, The Best Man, A Majority of One, Write Me a Murder, Kiss Me, Kate, The Marriage-Go-Round*, and *Once More, With Feeling.*

Television. She appeared four years on the Lassie series (CBS).

Other Activities. In addition to her WW II work with the USO, she held membership on the USO National Council (1972–76) and toured Germany and the Netherlands as a USO entertainer (1973). Miss Clayton is also a counsellor and speaker for the National Council for Alcoholism in New York and Los Angeles.

Recreation. Real estate.

CLIMENHAGA, JOEL RAY. Educator. b. Apr. 9, 1922, Bulawayo, So. Rhodesia, Africa, to John and Emma (Smith) Climenhaga. Parents, missionaries. Grad. Pottstown (Pa.) H.S., 1939; attended Messiah Coll., 1939–41; Chaffey Coll., A.A. 1950; Claremont Coll., Summer 1950; Univ. of California at Los Angeles, B.A. 1953, M.A. 1958; graduate study at Stanford Univ., 1962. Married Dec. 21, 1955, to Zoe Lenore Motter; one son, two daughters. Relatives in theatre: mother-in-law, Opal Euard, actress; sister-in-law, Charlotte Motter, director-teacher. Served US Army 1945–46. Member of AETA; Intl. Liaison Project, 1963; Latin-American Theatre Project, 1963; Amer. Poetry League; World Poetry Soc. Intercontinental. Address: Dept. of Speech, Kansas State University, Manhattan, KS 66506.

Pre-Theatre. Newspaperman, warehouse worker.

Theatre. From 1968–to date, Mr. Climenhaga has been associate professor of speech at Kansas State Univ. Previously, he has been chairman of the Dept. of Speech and Drama at Culver-Stockton Coll. (1963–68), and general chairman of the AETA's Playwrights' Program (1960–65). He formerly had been chairman of AETA's committee on evaluation of the Manuscript Play Project (1961).

He was instructor of English and director of drama at the Central Dauphin H.S., Harrisburg, Pa. (1956–57); assistant professor of English and director of creative writing, Wilmington Coll. (1958–61), and director of the Southern Ohio Writers Workshop, Wilmington Coll. (Summer 1961); a visiting associate professor of dramatic art at the Univ. of North Carolina (1962–63); and visiting lecturer in playwriting at the Southern Writers Workshop (Univ. of Georgia, Summer 1963).

He has written the following plays which have been produced by the Univ. of California at Los Angeles One-Act Play Program: *Cracked Bells* (1951); *Marriage for Michael* (1952; and at Durham Th. Guild, Durham, N.C., 1963); *Mother Love* (1952); *Heathen Pioneer* (Univ. of California at Los Angeles, 1952); *Only One Fish in the Water* (1952; and Durham Th. Guild, 1963); *The Lesser Joy* (1952); *The Jesus-Cop* (1953); and *The Man Who Came Again* (1953). The Univ. of California at Los Angeles New Play Program produced his play, *Marriage Wheel* (1954), which has since been produced by leading community and university theatre groups.

The UCLA One-Act Play Program has presented the premieres of several of his plays: *The Death of God* (1953); *Water Hole* (1953); *The Playmates*, written with Julian Burton (1954); *Prairie Dog* (1954); The Durham Theatre Guild premiered *Night's End* in 1963.

Mr. Climenhaga has acted and directed for the Upland California Community Players; Chaffey Coll. Little Th.; Caravan Th. for Children, Los Angeles, Calif.; Pacific Palisades (Calif.) Community Players; Central Dauphin H.S., Harrisburg, Pa.; Univ. of North Carolina; the Valley Community Players, Claremont, Calif.; Bam Price Productions, Hollywood, Calif.; Stanford Univ.; and Culver-Stockton Coll.

Films. He was host interviewer for a film entitled *Writers Today* (National Educational Television Inc.).

Television. He has appeared on the Jana Demas Show (WHIO-TV, Dayton, Ohio, 1960–61).

Published Works. He has published the plays *Heathen Pioneer* (1956) and *Marriage Wheel* (1963); and two books of poetry, *Hawk and Chameleon* (1972), and *Belief in Chaos* (1973).

Awards. He received from UCLA the Best Playwright Award, (1952), Best Director Award (1952); and has received the Samuel Goldwyn 1st Prize Award for creative writing (1955) for *Marriage Wheel;* the Samuel French National Collegiate One-Act Play Competition (1st prize, 1955) for *Heathen Pioneer;* a Rockefeller Playwriting Grant to UCLA (1955–56); the Theatre Americana Best Play of the Season Award (1956); and the Field-Hotaling Fellowship, Stanford Univ. (1961–62).

CLURMAN, HAROLD. Director, critic, author, lecturer. b. Harold Edgar Clurman, Sept. 18, 1901, New York City, to Samuel M. and Bertha (Saphir) Clurman. Father, doctor. Attended Columbia Univ., 1921; grad. Univ. of Paris (Sorbonne), diplomé 1923; attended Sch. of the Vieux-Colombier Th., Paris, France, where he studied with Jacques Copeau (1923–1924); Amer. Laboratory Th., N.Y.C., where he studied direction with Richard Boleslavsky, 1927. Married 1943 to Stella Adler, actress (marr. dis. 1960); one daughter; married Apr. 28, 1960, to Juleen Compton, actress. Member of SSD&C (exec. board). Address: (home) 205 W. 57th St., New York, NY 10019, tel. (212) CI 7-5420; (bus.) 165 W. 46th St., New York, NY 10036, tel. (212) PL 7-5100.

Theatre. Mr. Clurman made his professional debut in N.Y.C. as a walk-on in *The Saint* (Greenwich Village Th., Oct. 11, 1924); subsequently was assistant stage manager and appeared as a Market Porter in *Caesar and Cleopatra* (Guild, Apr. 13, 1925); played a Clerk in *Goat Song* (Guild, Jan. 25, 1926); Mariano Escobedo and Polyhemio in *Juarez and Maximilian* (Guild, Oct. 11, 1926); was a walk-on in *Spread Eagle* (Martin Beck Th., Apr. 4, 1927); and stage manager for *The Garrick Gaieties* (Garrick, May 10, 1925).

He was a founder (1931) of the Group Theatre, Inc., executive director (1937–41), and directed the following productions for it: *Awake and Sing*, which was the first play he directed on Bway (Belasco, N.Y.C., Feb. 19, 1935); *Paradise Lost* (Longacre, Dec. 9, 1935); *Golden Boy* (Belasco, Nov. 4, 1937);

Rocket to the Moon (Belasco, Nov. 24, 1938); *The Gentle People* (Belasco, Jan. 5, 1939); *Night Music* (Broadhurst, Feb. 22, 1940); and *Retreat to Pleasure* (Belasco, Dec. 17, 1940).

He directed *Beggars Are Coming to Town* (Coronet, Oct. 27, 1945); directed and produced with Elia Kazan, in association with the Playwrights Co., *Truckline Café* (Belasco, Feb. 27, 1946); produced with Elia Kazan and Walter Fried, in association with Herbert H. Harris, *All My Sons* (Coronet, Jan. 29, 1947); directed *The Whole World Over* (Biltmore, Mar. 27, 1947); *The Young and Fair* (Fulton, Nov. 22, 1948); *Montserrat* (Tel-Aviv, Israel, June 1949); *The Member of the Wedding* (Empire, N.Y.C., Jan. 5, 1950); *The Bird Cage* (Coronet, Feb. 22, 1950); *The Autumn Garden* (Coronet, Mar. 7, 1951); *Desire Under the Elms* (ANTA, Jan. 16, 1952); *The Time of the Cuckoo* (Empire, Oct. 15, 1952); *The Emperor's Clothes* (Ethel Barrymore Th., Feb. 9, 1953); *The Ladies of the Corridor* (Longacre, Oct. 21, 1953); *Mademoiselle Colombe* (Longacre, Jan. 6, 1954); and *Bus Stop* (Music Box, Mar. 2, 1955).

He staged *Tiger at the Gates* (Apollo, London, Eng., June 6, 1955; Plymouth, N.Y.C., Oct. 3, 1955); directed *Pipe Dream* (Shubert, Nov. 30, 1955); *The Waltz of the Toreadors* (Coronet, Jan. 17, 1957); a touring production of *The Waltz of the Toreadors* (opened McCarter Th., Princeton, N.J., Sept. 26, 1957; moved to Coronet, Mar. 4, 1958); *Orpheus Descending* (Martin Beck Th., Mar. 21, 1957); *The Day the Money Stopped* (Belasco, Feb. 20, 1958); *A Touch of the Poet* (Helen Hayes Th., Oct. 2, 1958); and *The Cold Wind and the Warm* (Morosco, Dec. 8, 1958).

He directed *Heartbreak House* (Billy Rose Th., Oct. 18, 1959); *Sweet Love Remember'd* (Shubert, New Haven, Conn., Dec. 28, 1959; closed there Dec. 31, 1959); *Jeannette* (Maidman, N.Y.C., Mar. 24, 1960); *A Shot in the Dark* (Booth, Oct. 18, 1961); *Judith* (Her Majesty's, London, June 20, 1962); *Incident at Vichy* (ANTA, Dec. 3, 1964); *A Long Day's Journey into Night* (Tokyo, Japan, 1965); *Where's Daddy?* (Billy Rose Th., Mar. 2, 1966); *The Iceman Cometh* (Tokyo, Japan, 1968); and *Uncle Vanya* (Center Th. Group, Mark Taper Forum, Los Angeles, Calif., Aug. 21, 1969).

Since October 1963, Mr. Clurman has been executive consultant of the Repertory Theatre of Lincoln Center, N.Y.C.

Films. Mr. Clurman directed *Deadline at Dawn* (RKO, 1946).

Other Activities. Since 1953, Mr. Clurman has been theatre critic for the *Nation.* Previously, he was a guest theatre critic for the London *Observer* (1959-63); theatre critic for the *New Republic* (1949–53); critic of the arts for *Tomorrow* Magazine (1946–52); and reader for the Theatre Guild (1929–31).

He was the Andrew Mellon lecturer at Carnegie Inst. of Tech. (1962–63) on "The World of the Theatre." Since 1954, he has conducted classes for professional actors. From 1969 to 1973, he was play selector for the Theatre Development Fund, N.Y.C., and he is a member of the executive board.

Published Works. Mr. Clurman has contributed articles to magazines, including *Harper's Bazaar, Theatre Arts, New York* magazine, and the NY *Times* Magazine.

His published books include *The Fervent Years; The Story of the Group Theatre* (1945); *Lies Like Truth: Theatre Reviews and Essays* (1958); *The Naked Image: Observations on Modern Theatre* (1966); *On Directing* (1973); *The Divine Pastime: Theatre Essays* (1974); and *All People Are Famous: Instead of an Autobiography* (1974). He selected the works and wrote the introduction to *Famous Plays of the 1930's* (1959); and contributed a chapter entitled, "Principles of Interpretation" to *Directing the Play* (1953).

Awards. Mr. Clurman received the George Jean Nathan Award (1959) for his book, *Lies Like Truth: Theatre Reviews and Essays;* and Donaldson Award (1950) for his direction of *The Member of the Wedding*

He was made a Chevalier of the French Legion of Honor (1959); was awarded an honorary D.Litt. by Bard Coll. (1959), and an honorary D.F.A. by Carnegie Inst. of Tech. (1963). Other institutions that have awarded him honorary doctorates are Ripon College and Boston University.

Recreation. Travel.

COAD, ORAL SUMNER. Educator, writer, editor. b. Dec. 27, 1887, Mt. Pleasant, Iowa, to Laurel Evan and Sarah (Baldwin) Coad. Father, farmer, lawyer, evangelist. Educated in public schools of Eldon and Galesburg, Ill.; grad Knox College (B.A.) and Columbia Univ. (M.A. and Ph.D.). Married Dec. 29, 1915, to Lucy Virginia Fitzwater (dec. Oct. 9, 1973); one son. Member of Modern Language Assoc. Address: 13 Sandford St., New Brunswick, NJ 08902, tel. (201) 545-2318.

Mr. Coad was instructor in English at Ohio Wesleyan (1911–14) and Columbia Univ. (1916–23), then was at Douglass Coll., New Brunswick, N.J., as assist. prof. of English (1923–26), assoc. prof. of English (1926–27), and prof. and dept. chmn. (1927–58); he became prof. emeritus in 1958.

Published Works. Mr. Coad is author of *William Dunlap: A Study of His Life and Works and of His Place in Contemporary Culture* (1917; 1962) and, in collaboration with Edwin Mims, Jr., *The American Stage* (1929). He wrote also twenty-two biographical sketches, chiefly of theatre figures, in *Dictionary of American Biography;* "The New York Theater" in Vol. IX of *History of the State of New York*, edited by Alexander C. Flick (1937); *New Jersey in Travelers' Accounts 1524–1971: A Descriptive Bibliography* (1972); and many articles and book reviews, mostly dealing with American drama and theatre, that appeared in scholarly publications. Mr. Coad is editor also of *The Autobiography of Benjamin Franklin* (1927); *False Shame and Thirty Years: Two Plays by William Dunlap* (1940); and *Edgar Poe and His Critics* by Sarah Helen Whitman (1949).

Recreation. Music.

COCA, IMOGENE. Actress. b. c. 1909, Philadelphia, Pa., to Joseph Coca (family surname was Fernandez y Coca) and Sadie (Brady) Coca. Father, orchestra conductor; mother, dancer, actress. Married Jan. 7, 1935, to Robert Burton, actor, musician (dec. 1955); married 1960 to King Donovan, actor, director; two sons, one daughter. Member of AEA; AFTRA; AGVA.

Theatre. At age nine, Miss Coca appeared in vaudeville as a tap dancer; at 11, as a singer (Dixie, Philadelphia, Pa.); and at 14, as a dancer.

She appeared as a chorus girl, Imogene, in *When You Smile* (National, N.Y.C., Oct. 5, 1925); toured as Jan, the Maid, in *Bubbling Over* (Werba's Brooklyn Th., Oct. 4, 1926); appeared as a dancer in the vaudeville production of *Snow and Columbus;* and with Leonard Sillman (Palace Th., N.Y.C.); toured as Jimmy, the Office Assistant, in *Queen High* (Mayfair, Brooklyn, Oct. 8, 1928); and in *Garrick Gaieties* (Guild, June 4, 1930); *Garrick Gaieties*, second edition (Guild, Oct. 16, 1930); and *Shoot the Works* (George M. Cohan Th., July 21, 1931); was understudy to Patsy Kelly and appeared in the revue *Flying Colors* (Imperial, Sept. 15, 1932); performed in vaudeville with Solly Ward; appeared in *New Faces* (Fulton, Mar. 15, 1934); *Fools Rush In* (Playhouse, Dec. 25, 1934); in stock, played the Comique Star in *Up to the Stars* (Lydia Mendelssohn Th., Ann Arbor, Mich., June 3, 1935); appeared in *New Faces of 1936* (Vanderbilt, N.Y.C., May 19, 1936); played in a tryout of *Spring Dance* (Cape Playhouse, Dennis, Mass., July 6, 1936); played Priscilla Paine in a tryout of *Calling All Men* (Cape Playhouse, Dennis, Mass., July 5, 1937); appeared in stock (Tamiment Lodge, Bush Kill, Pa., Summers 1938–42); played in *Straw Hat Revue* (Ambassador, N.Y.C., Sept. 29, 1939); toured in *A Night at the Folies Bergère* (1940); appeared in the stock production of *Tonight at 8:30* (Community Playhouse, Spring Lake, N.J., July 1940); performed in *All in Fun* (Majestic, N.Y.C., Dec. 27, 1940); *Concert Varieties* (Ziegfeld, June 1, 1945); and in stock, played Addie in *Happy Birthday* (Music Hall, Clinton, N.J., Aug. 1948); and Ruth in *Wonderful Town* (State Fair Music Hall, Dallas, Tex., Aug. 23, 1954).

She succeeded (June 11, 1956) Claudette Colbert in the role of Jessica in *Janus* (Plymouth, N.Y.C., Nov. 24, 1955); in stock, played Essie Sebastian in *The Great Sebastians* (Summer 1957); was Mimsy in *The Girls in 509* (Belasco, N.Y.C., Oct. 15, 1958; and in national tour, opened Hanna, Cleveland, Ohio, Jan. 26, 1959; closed Nixon, Pittsburgh, Pa., May 9, 1959); in stock, played Agnes in *The Fourposter* (Playhouse at Deep Well, Palm Springs, Calif., Winter 1960); toured as princess Winnifred in *Once Upon a Mattress* (opened Veterans Memorial Aud., Providence, R.I., Oct. 21, 1960; closed National, Washington, D.C., May 27, 1961); toured in *A Thurber Carnival* (opened Norfolk, Va., Sept. 22, 1961; closed Music Hall, Kansas City, Mo., Apr. 28, 1962); played the Queen in a stock production of *Under the Sycamore Tree* (Pasadena Playhouse, Calif., Sept. 1962); and Ella Peterson in a summer stock production of *Bells Are Ringing* (1963).

She toured as Ellen Manville in *Luv* (1967); toured with Sid Caesar in the *Caesar-Coca Revue* (Summer 1968); toured in *You Know I Can't Hear You When the Water's Running* (Oct. 1968–Mar. 1969); appeared in *You Can't Take It with You* (Loretto-Hilton Repertory Th., St. Louis, Mo., 1969); played Mr. Alden and Aunt Veronica in *Why I Went Crazy* (Westport Country Playhouse, Conn., July 14, 1969; Falmouth Summer Th., Mass., July 21, 1969); appeared as Penny Moore in *A Girl Could Get Lucky* (Playhouse on the Mall, Paramus, N.J., Feb. 1970); Agnes in *The Fourposter* (Showboat Dinner Th., St. Petersburg, Fla., Dec. 12, 1972); and toured as Edna Edison in *The Prisoner of Second Avenue* (Oct. 1973–Apr. 1974).

Films. Miss Coca appeared in the short subject, *Bashful Ballerina* (Educational Pictures, 1937); subsequently in *Under the Yum-Yum Tree* (Col., 1963); *Promise Her Anything* (Par., 1966); and in *Ten from Your Show of Shows* (Walter Reade, 1973), a collection of sketches from the television program.

Television. Miss Coca performed on the Admiral Broadway Revue (Jan. 1949); Your Show of Shows (NBC, Feb. 24, 1950–June 5, 1954); Imogene Coca Show (NBC, Oct. 2, 1954); Panorama (NBC, Feb. 26, 1956); played in *The Funny Heart* (CBS, Apr. 11, 1956); *Helpmate* (NBC, Dec. 4, 1956); *Made in Heaven* (Playhouse 90, CBS, Dec. 6, 1956); *Ruggles of Red Gap* (NBC, Feb. 3, 1957); *The Cab Driver* (GE Th., CBS, Apr. 14, 1957); appeared on English television (1958); performed on Sid Caesar Invites You (ABC, Jan. 26, 1958); the Shirley Temple Show (NBC, Oct. 16, 1960); and appeared in the title role in the series Grindl (NBC, 1963–64).

She appeared on It's About Time (CBS, 1966); *Sid Caesar, Imogene Coca, Carl Reiner, Howard Moss Special* (CBS, Apr. 5, 1967); the Jackie Gleason Show (CBS, 1968); the Carol Burnett Show (CBS, 1969); Bewitched (ABC, 1971); Night Gallery (NBC, 1971); Love, American Style (ABC, 1972); and on the Dick Cavett Show (CBS, Aug.–Sept. 1975).

Night Clubs. Miss Coca has performed at the Silver Slipper (N.Y.C., c. 1926); Fifth Avenue Club (N.Y.C.); New Yorker Club (N.Y.C.); Jay C. Flippen Club (N.Y.C.); Piccadilly Club (Philadelphia, Pa.); Rainbow Room (N.Y.C., 1937); toured with George Olsen's orchestra (1938); appeared at La Martinque (N.Y.C., 1940, 1942); Le Ruban Bleu (N.Y.C., 1944, 1954); Cafe Society Uptown (N.Y.C., 1945); Cafe Society Downtown (N.Y.C., 1945); Blue Angel (N.Y.C., Oct. 1948); Palmer House (Chicago, Ill.); Park Plaza (St. Louis, Mo.); and the Sahara (Las Vegas, Nev., Nov. 1, 1955).

Awards. She received an Award of Merit (1950) from the Women's Division of the Federation of Jewish Philanthropies; the Saturday Review Poll (Tops in TV) Award (1951); and the Peabody Award (1953). The Show of Shows special *Sid Caesar, Imogene Coca, Carl Reiner, Howard Moss Special* received a NATAS (Emmy) Award (1967) as outstanding variety special.

Recreation. Dogs and other animals.

COCO, JAMES. Actor. b. Mar. 21, 1930, New York City, to Felice and Ida Coco. Educ. Evander Childs H.S., Bronx, N.Y.C. Professional training with Uta Hagen at Berghof Studios. Member of AEA; SAG; AFTRA.

Theatre. Soon after graduating from high school, Mr. Coco began his theatrical career, touring the US as a member of the Clare Tree Major Children's Theatre. He played also in summer and winter stock organizations, appearing in such roles as Willy Loman in *Death of a Salesman* and Uncle Louis in *The Happy Time.* He appeared in N.Y.C. as Herod in *Salome* (Davenport Th., Feb. 2, 1956); Tabu in *Hotel Paradiso* (Henry Miller's Th., Apr. 11, 1957); Tausch in *The Moon in the Yellow River* (East End Th., Feb. 6, 1961); the Doctor in *Everybody Loves Opal* (Longacre, Oct. 11, 1961); and Mr. Hamidullah in *Passage to India* (Ambassador, Jan. 31, 1962). He toured (until June 1963) in *A Shot in the Dark;* was in the pre-Bway tryout of *The Shemansky Affair* (Summer 1963); played O'Casey in *Arturo Ui* (Lunt-Fontanne Th., N.Y.C., Nov. 11, 1963); Stanley Mintey in *Squat Betty* and Leslie Edwards in *The Sponge Room* (East End Th., Feb. 24, 1964); Mr. Andrikos in *The Irregular Verb to Love* (Bucks County Playhouse, New Hope, Pa., Summer 1964) and on tour; the First in *That 5 A.M. Jazz* (Astor Place Th., Oct. 19, 1964); Roger Varnum in *Lovey* (Cherry Lane Th., Mar. 25, 1965); the Sewer Man in *The Devils* (Broadway Th., Nov. 16, 1965); replaced (July 1966) Gino Conforti as the Barber in *Man of La Mancha* (ANTA Washington Square Th., Nov. 22, 1965); was Inspector Rogers in *The Astrakhan Coat* (Helen Hayes Th., Jan. 12, 1967); Leo in *The Basement* and Max in *Fragments* (Cherry Lane Th., Oct. 2, 1967); Lee in *Here's Where I Belong* (Billy Rose Th., Mar. 3, 1968); Marion Cheever in *Next* (Berkshire Theatre Festival, Stockbridge, Mass., Summer 1968); the Window Washer in *Witness* (Gramercy Arts Th., Nov. 21, 1968); repeated his performance as Marion Cheever in *Next* (Greenwich Mews Th., Feb. 10, 1969); and played Barney Cashman in *The Last of the Red Hot Lovers* (Eugene O'Neill Th., Dec. 28, 1969).

Films. Mr. Coco was in *Ensign Pulver* (WB, 1964); *Tell Me That You Love Me, Junie Moon* (Par., 1970); *Strawberry Statement* (MGM, 1970); *End of the Road* (Allied Artists, 1970); *Such Good Friends* (Par., 1971); *A New Leaf* (Par., 1971); and played Sancho Panza in the motion-picture version of *Man of La Mancha* (UA, 1972).

Television. Mr. Coco has been on the Mike Douglas Show (CBS); has made twelve guest star appearances on the Alan King Show; and has been on the Johnny Carson Show over fifty times. He appeared on Studio One (CBS); Kraft Th. (NBC); Hallmark Playhouse; Goodyear Playhouse (NBC); Plainclothes Man; Man Behind the Badge; You Are There (CBS); Armstrong Circle Th. (NBC); Frontiers of Faith (NBC); and Marcus Welby, M.D. (CBS). He was in *The Power and the Glory* (CBS, Oct. 1961); played Falstaff in *Henry IV, Part 1* and *Part 2* (Camera Three, CBS); played Gonorrhea in *VD Blues* (PBS, Oct. 9, 1972); was in *The Greasy Diner* sketch on *The Trouble with People* (NBC, Nov. 12, 1972); and had his own television show, *Calucci's Department* (CBS, 1973).

Awards. Mr. Coco was nominated for an Antoinette Perry (Tony) Award for his performance in *The Last of the Red Hot Lovers* and for a Golden Globe Award for his performance in *Man of La Mancha.* He received *Village Voice* off-Bway (Obie) awards for his performances in *The Moon in the Yellow River* and *Fragments* and the Drama Critics Award and *Show Business* magazine's grand award for his performance in *Next.*

COE, FRED. Producer, director. b. Fred H. Coe, Alligator, Miss., to Fred and Annette (Harold) Coe. Father, lawyer; mother, nurse. Grad. Peabody Democratic Sch., Nashville, Tenn.; Peabody Coll.; attended Yale Univ. Sch. of Drama. Married to Joyce Beeler; two sons, two daughters. Address: 234 W. 44th St., New York, NY 10036, tel. (212) OX 5-9262.

Theatre. At age 18, Mr. Coe directed for the Nashville Community Th., Tenn.; and shortly thereafter he became director of the Civic Th., Columbia, S.C.

With the Theatre Guild, he co-produced his first N.Y.C. play, *The Trip to Bountiful* (Henry Miller's Th., Nov. 3, 1953); subsequently produced *Two for the Seesaw* (Booth, Jan. 16, 1958); *The Miracle Worker* (Playhouse, Oct. 19, 1959); with Arthur Cantor, produced *All the Way Home* (Belasco, Nov. 30, 1960); *Gideon* (Plymouth, Nov. 9, 1961); and *A Thousand Clowns,* which he also directed (Eugene O'Neill Th., Apr. 5, 1962).

Mr. Coe produced *Fiddler on the Roof* (Imperial, N.Y.C., Sept. 22, 1964); directed and co-produced *Xmas in Las Vegas* (Ethel Barrymore Th., Nov. 4, 1965); in association with Hiller Productions, he presented *Wait Until Dark* (Ethel Barrymore Th., Feb. 2, 1966; and on tour, 1967); presented *Georgy* (Winter Garden, Feb. 15, 1970); and co-produced *Promenade, All!* (Alvin, Apr. 16, 1972).

Films. Mr. Coe produced *The Left Handed Gun* (WB, 1958); *The Miracle Worker* (UA, 1962); produced and directed *A Thousand Clowns* (UA, 1965); co-authored the screenplay for *This Property Is Condemned* (Par., 1966); and produced *Me Natalie* (Natl. Gen., 1969).

Television. Mr. Coe was on the staff of NBC-TV, as producer of the Philco Television Playhouse, the Goodyear Playhouse, Producer's Showcase, *Mister Peepers* (1945–56); and produced *The Final War of Olly Winter* (CBS Playhouse, 1967).

Awards. *All the Way Home,* which he co-produced, received the Pulitzer Prize and the NY Drama Critics' Circle Award (1961).

COE, PETER. Director, playwright. b. Peter Leonard Coe, Apr. 18, 1929, London, England, to Leonard and Gladys (Frith) Coe. Father, grocer. Grad. Latymer Upper Sch., 1946; Coll. of St. Mark and St. John, Teacher's Certificate, 1948; London Acad. of Music and Dramatic Art, Teachers Certificate 1952. Married 1952 to Maria Caday, actress (marr. dis., 1958); married 1959 to Tsai Chin, actress (marr. dis., 1962); married Mar. 2, 1962, to Suzanne Fuller, actress; one daughter. Served RAF, 1948–50.

Theatre. Mr. Coe directed a university production of *Sweeny Agonistes* (1947); made his acting debut as St. John Rivers in a touring production of *Jane Eyre* (England, 1955); directed *The Correspondence Course* (Royal Court, London, May 26, 1957); *Miss Julie* (Edinburgh, Scotland, Festival, Summer 1958); *The Importance of Being Earnest* (St. Pierre, Geneva, Switzerland, 1958); *The World of Suzie Wong* (Prince of Wales's Th., London, Nov. 17, 1959); *Lock Up Your Daughters* (Mermaid, May 28, 1959); and *Treasure Island* (Mermaid, Dec. 14, 1959).

He directed *Twelfth Night* (Assembly Hall, Madras, India, 1959); *Oliver!* (New, London, June 30, 1960); *The Miracle Worker* (Wyndham's, 1961); *Oliver!* (Imperial, Melbourne, Aust., 1961; Princes's, Sydney, 1961); *Julius Caesar* (Habimah Th., Israel, July 2, 1961); and *Castle in Sweden* (Piccadilly, London, June 1962).

Mr. Coe directed the Bway production of *Oliver!* (Imperial, Jan. 1, 1963); *Macbeth* at the Stratford (Ontario, Canada) Shakespeare Festival (June 1962); *Pickwick* (Saville, London, July 4, 1963; 46 St. Th., N.Y.C., Oct. 4, 1965); the opera *The Love of Three Oranges* (Sadler's Wells, Apr. 1963); *The Rehearsal* (Royale, N.Y.C., Sept. 23, 1963); *Next Time I'll Sing to You* (Phoenix, Nov. 27, 1963); and *Caligula* (Phoenix, London, Apr. 1964).

Mr. Coe also directed *In White America* (New Arts Th. Club, London, England, Nov. 16, 1964); the opera *Angel of Fire* (English premiere, Sadler's Wells, July 27, 1965); *The King's Mare* (Garrick Th., July 6, 1966); *In the Matter of J. Robert Oppenheimer* (Hampstead Th., Club, Oct. 17, 1966); *The Silence of Lee Harvey Oswald* (Hampstead Th. Club, Nov. 23, 1966); and *World War 2½* (New Apr. 13, 1967). At the Chichester (England) Festival, he directed *An Italian Straw Hat* (Aug. 8, 1967), *The Skin of Our Teeth* (July 31, 1968), *The Caucasian Chalk Circle* (May 14, 1969), and *Peer Gynt* (May 13, 1970).

He also directed *Six* (Cricket, N.Y.C., Apr. 12, 1971); *Woman in the Dunes* (Cleveland Play House, Cleveland, Ohio, Nov. 19, 1971); *Hamlet* (Bankside Globe, London, July 1972); and he wrote *Decameron '73* (London, July 1973).

COE, RICHARD L. Drama and film critic. b. Richard Livingston Coe, Nov. 8, 1916, New York City, to Elmer James Secor and Lillie Isabel (Musgrave) Coe. Father, banker; mother, writer. Grad. Cathedral Choir Sch., N.Y.C., 1930; St. James Sch., Washington County, Md., 1934; attended George Washington Univ., 1934. Married May 4, 1946, to Christine Sadler, writer. Served USAAF, Middle East 1942–43; editor, middle east edition of *Stars and Stripes* (1943–46); rank, S/Sgt. Member of Amer. Newspaper Guild; Natl. Press Club, Washington, D.C.; Variety Club, Tent 11, Washington, D.C.; Overseas Press Club, N.Y.C.; ANTA (mbr. of drama panel, 1955–63). Address: (home) 2713 Dumbarton Ave., N.W., Washington, D.C. 20007, tel. (202) HU 3-8580; (bus.) The Washington Post, 1515 L St., N.W., Washington, D.C. 20005, tel. (202) RE 7-1234.

Since 1946, Mr. Coe has been drama and film critic for the Washington *Post.* Previously, he was assistant drama and film critic (1938–42).

He also has written articles for magazines and newspapers, including *Theatre Arts,* the NY *Times,* the NY *Herald Tribune,* and *Amerika;* and has served as a US correspondent for Reynolds, now *Citizen's News* (London, Eng., 1947–63), and the Egyptian *Gazette* (Cairo, Egypt, 1943–52).

Other Activities. Mr. Coe has been a guest lecturer at the American Univ. (Cairo, Egypt), speaking on American government and culture (1943–46), and (Washington, D.C.), on theatre and films at the American Univ. (1959–to date); and has been on the staff of the President's Program for Cultural Exchange (1955–to date).

Awards. Mr. Coe received the Newspaper Guild Award for criticism (1949); an award from the Washington, D.C., Board of Trade for public service (1957); an award for criticism from the General Federation of Women's Clubs (1957); an award for "distinguished citizenship" from the District of Columbia Board of Commissioners (1957); and was named critic of the year by the Directors Guild of America (1963).

Recreation. Travel, working for the John F. Kennedy Memorial Center, collecting paintings by players.

COGAN, DAVID J. Producer, theatre owner, artists' and literary representative. b. David Joseph Cogan, July 24, 1923, Rumania, to Morris and Helen (Meyers) Cogan and brought to the US the same year; naturalized, 1928. Father, manufacturer. Grad. St. John's Univ., B.B.S. 1945. Married 1946 to Ferne; two daughters. Served WW II, US Army, Special Services. Member of Actors Studio; League of NY Theatres; NY Theatre Owners Assn.; Family Institute, N.Y.C. (dir. and treas., 1961–to date); National Soc. of Public Accountants; NY Chapter of American Red Cross (chmn., legitimate theatre section, 1964–to date); and a director of Young Childrens Music School and Dance, N.Y.C. (1959–to date), the Berkshire Theatre Festival, and the Eugene O'Neill Foundation. Address: 350 Fifth Ave., New York, NY 10001, tel. (212) 594-3335.

Mr. Cogan is owner of the Biltmore Th. (since 1960), the Eugene O'Neill Th. (since 1964), and the Plaza Th., all in N.Y.C., and the Viking Th. in Philadelphia. He has been a personal and business manager of artists and literary personalities since 1956. He has been also an instructor in theatrical production and management at the New School for Social Research, N.Y.C., since 1971.

Theatre. He produced, with Philip Rose, *A Raisin in the Sun* (Ethel Barrymore Th., Mar. 11, 1959); with Howard Erskine and Joseph Hayes, the pre-Bway tryout of *The Midnight Sun* (Shubert Th., New Haven, Conn., Nov. 4, 1959; closed Wilbur Th., Boston, Mass., Nov. 28); and *In the Counting House* (Biltmore, Dec. 13, 1962).

Films. Mr. Cogan produced *Run Across the River* (1954).

Other Activities. Mr. Cogan is a partner (1955–to date) in Cogan & Bell & Co., N.Y.C.; president (1955–to date) of the David J. Cogan Agency; and president (1968–to date) of Cogan Management, Inc. In addition to his theatres, he owns real estate in New Jersey, Georgia, Ohio, and California.

Awards. The NY Drama Critics Circle Award for best American play went to *A Raisin in the Sun* in 1959.

COHEN, ALEXANDER H. Producer. b. July 24, 1920, New York City, to Alexander H. and Laura (Tarantous) Cohen. Grad. Dwight Prep. Sch., N.Y.C., 1937; attended New York Univ., 1937–40. Married Jan. 11, 1942, to Jocelyn Newmark (marr. dis. Feb. 1, 1956); one daughter; married Feb. 25, 1956, to Hildy Parks, actress; two sons. Served US Army, 94th Infantry Division, 1942–43. Member of League of NY Theatres (board of gov.); Independent Booking Office (dir); ATPAM; SSD&C; Council of the Living Theatre; Jewish Theatrical Guild of Amer.; Actors' Fund of Amer. (bd. of trustees); The Lambs; The Friars. Address: (home) Trinity Pass, Pound Ridge, NY 10576; (bus.) 225 W. 44th St., New York, NY 10036, tel. (212) 757-1200.

Theatre. Since 1941 Mr. Cohen has been a Bway producer. Among his productions are *Ghost for Sale* (Daly's Th., N.Y.C., Sept. 29, 1941); produced with Shepard Straube, *Angel Street* (John Golden Th., Dec. 5, 1941); *Of "V" We Sing* (Concert, Feb. 11, 1942); produced with Sam H. Grisman, *They Should Have Stood in Bed* (Mansfield, Feb. 13, 1942); and *Bright Lights of 1944* (Forrest, Sept. 16, 1943).

He produced with Joseph Kipness, *The Duke in Darkness* (Playhouse, Jan. 24, 1944); with James Russo and Michael Ellis, in association with Clarence M. Shapiro, *Jenny Kissed Me* (Hudson, Dec. 23, 1948); with Robert L. Joseph, *King Lear* (Natl., Dec. 25, 1950); with Jule Styne and Harry Rigby, *Make a Wish* (Winter Garden, Apr. 18, 1951); with Michael Ellis and James Russo, *Courtin' Time* (Royale, June 13, 1951); produced *Be Your Age* (48 St. Th., Jan. 14, 1953); produced, with Ralph Alswang, in association with Arthur C. Twitchell, Jr., *The Magic and the Loss* (Booth, Apr. 9, 1954); produced *The First Gentleman* (Belasco, Apr. 25, 1957); and *Love Me Little* (Helen Hayes Th., Apr. 15, 1958).

Mr. Cohen produced a series of intimate reviews at the John Golden Th., N.Y.C., which included *At the Drop of a Hat,* in association with Joseph L. Levine (Oct. 8, 1959); *An Evening with Mike Nichols and Elaine May* (Oct. 8, 1960); *An Evening with Yves Montand,* in association with Norman Granz and Jacques Canetti (Oct. 24, 1961); and *Beyond the Fringe,* which he also directed (Oct. 27, 1962). He produced *Lena Horne's Nine O'Clock Revue* (opened O'Keefe Ctr., Toronto, Canada, Oct. 16, 1961; closed Shubert, New Haven, Conn., Nov. 18, 1961); *The School for Scandal* (Majestic, N.Y.C., Jan. 24, 1963); *An Evening with Maurice Chevalier* (Ziegfeld, Jan. 28, 1963); *Lorenzo* (Plymouth, Feb. 14, 1963); a return engagement of John Gielgud's *The Ages of Man* (Lyceum, Apr. 14, 1963); the *Karmon Israeli Dancers* (Royale, May 21, 1963); *The Doctor's Dilemma* (Th. Royal, Haymarket, London, England, May 23, 1963); in association with H. M. Tennent Ltd., *Man and Boy* (Brooks Atkinson Th., N.Y.C., Nov. 12, 1963); *Beyond the Fringe 1964* (John Golden Th., Jan. 8, 1964); in association with Jack Hylton, *The Roses Are Real* (Vaudeville, London, England, Jan. 22, 1964) and *Rugantino* (Mark Hellinger Th., N.Y.C., Feb. 6, 1964); and, with Frenman Productions, Richard Burton's *Hamlet* (Lunt-Fontanne Th., Apr. 9, 1964).

He produced the revue *Comedy in Music Opus 2* (John Golden Th., Nov. 9, 1964); produced and directed *Beyond the Fringe '65* (Ethel Barrymore Th., Dec. 15, 1964); produced, in association with Gabriel Katzka, *Baker Street* (Broadway Th., Feb. 16, 1965); produced *Maurice Chevalier at 77* (Alvin Th., Apr. 1, 1965); produced, in association with Arthur Whitelaw, *Ken Murray's Hollywood* (John Golden Th., May 10, 1965); with Tennent Productions, *Ivanov* (Yvonne Arnaud Th., Guildford, Eng., Aug. 30, 1965; Phoenix, London, England, Sept. 30, 1965); and he produced *The Devils* (Broadway Th., N.Y.C., Nov. 16, 1965).

He presented, with Tennent Productions and by arrangement with Frederick Harrison Trust Ltd., *You Never Can Tell* (Haymarket, London, England, Jan. 12, 1966); presented the Tennent production of *Ivanov* (Sam. S. Shubert Th., N.Y.C., May 3, 1966); produced *A Time for Singing* (Broadway Th., May 21, 1966); with Tennent Productions Ltd., *The Importance of Being Oscar* (Haymarket, London, Sept. 19, 1966); presented, with Tennent Productions, *The Rivals* (Haymarket, Oct. 6, 1966); presented *At the Drop of Another Hat* (Booth Th., N.Y.C., Dec. 27, 1966); in association with Gerry Geraldo, presented the Royal Shakespeare Co. production of *The Homecoming* (Music Box, Jan. 5, 1967); presented *Black Comedy* and *White Lies* (Ethel Barrymore Th., Feb. 12, 1967); *Little Murders* (Broadhurst, Apr. 25, 1967); *Hellzapoppin' '67* (Garden of Stars, Expo 67, Montreal, Quebec, Canada, July 1, 1967); and he produced *The Unknown Soldier and His Wife* (Vivian Beaumont Th., N.Y.C., July 6, 1967; transferred to George Abbott Th., Sept. 18, 1967).

He presented Marlene Dietrich in a one-woman show called *Marlene Dietrich* (Lunt-Fontanne Th., Oct. 9, 1967); produced, with Tennent Productions Ltd., *The Merchant of Venice* (Haymarket, London, Sept. 7, 1967); produced *Halfway Up the Tree* (Brooks Atkinson Th., N.Y.C., Nov. 7, 1967); presented a return engagement of *Marlene Dietrich* (Mark Hellinger Th., Oct. 3, 1968); produced *Dear World* (Mark Hellinger Th., Feb. 6, 1969); presented *We Who Are About To . .* (Hampstead Th. Club, London, England, Feb. 10, 1969; transferred as *Mixed Doubles* to Comedy Th., Apr. 9, 1969); presented *Plaza Suite* (Lyric, Feb. 18, 1969); *The Price* (Duke of York's Th., Mar. 4, 1969); and, with Murray MacDonald and John Stevens Ltd., *His, Hers, and Theirs* (Apollo, Dec. 2, 1969).

He produced, with Allan Davis, *Come As You Are!* (New, Jan. 27, 1970; transferred to Strand, June 1, 1970); with Eddie Kulukundis, *The Happy Apple* (Apollo, Mar. 11, 1970); with Bill Freedman, *Who Killed Santa Claus?* (Piccadilly, Apr. 2, 1970); and *1776* (New, June 16, 1970); He presented the Royal Court Th. production of *Home* (Morosco, N.Y.C., Nov. 17, 1970); produced *Prettybelle* (pre-Bway: Shubert Th., Boston, Mass., Feb. 1–Mar. 6, 1971); with Rocky H. Aoki, *Fun City* (Morosco, N.Y.C., Jan. 2, 1972); and, all with Bernard Delfont, *Applause* (Her Majesty's Th., London, Nov. 16, 1972); *6 Rms Riv Vu* (Helen Hayes Th., N.Y.C., Oct. 17, 1972); *Good Evening* (Plymouth, Nov. 14, 1973); and a revival of *Ulysses in Nighttown* (Winter Garden, Mar. 10, 1974). He also produced, with Harvey Granat, the Sammy Cahn revue *Words and Music* (John Golden Th., Apr. 16, 1974); with Bernard Delfont, *Who's Who in Hell* (Lunt-Fontanne Th., Dec. 9, 1974); and he produced *We Interrupt This Program* (Ambassador, Apr. 1, 1975).

Television. Mr. Cohen has produced television coverage of the annual Antoinette Perry (Tony) Awards presentation ceremonies (1967–to date), and for UNICEF he produced the special *A World of Love* (CBS, 1970). He also appeared as a guest on Musical Th. (CBS, 1964–65); Hy Gardner Show (Ind., June 5, 1965); The Scene (Ind., 1966–67); and other programs.

Awards. Mr. Cohen received a special citation (1963) from the Outer Circle for "innovation befitting the development of the intimate review in N.Y.C. through the production of the Nine O'Clock Theatre"; the Sam S. Shubert Foundation Award (1963) for his "outstanding contribution to the legitimate theatre" during the 1962–63 season; was named "Showman of the Year" by the Bway ticket brokers (N.Y.C., Apr. 20, 1967); received an Outer Circle Award (1967) for producing *The Homecoming* and *Black Comedy* and for his contribution to the Tony Awards; received a Tony Award (1967) for *The Homecoming* and a Tony nomination for producing *Black Comedy;* was nominated for a Tony (1971) for producing *Home;* received a special *Theatre World* award (1973) for his television productions of the annual Tony Award ceremonies; and his production of *Ulysses in Nighttown* received a Tony nomination (1974) as best play.

COHEN, MARTIN B. Company manager, director, producer. b. Apr. 23, 1923, New York City, to Morris and Fannie (Steinbalm) Cohen. Grad. Franklin K. Lane H.S., Queens, N.Y., 1940; City Coll. of New York, B.B.A. (public accounting) 1948. Served WW II, USAAF; rank Lt.

Theatre. Mr. Cohen produced, with Oscar Lerman and Alexander Carson, *The Vamp* (Winter Garden Th., N.Y.C., Nov. 10, 1955); produced *Christine* (46 St. Th., Apr. 28, 1960); directed *We're Civilized?* (Jan Hus House, Nov. 8, 1962); produced *One in a Row* (Playhouse on the Mall, Paramus, N.J., Aug. 18, 1964); *Kindly Monkeys* (New Arts Th., N.Y.C., Mar. 17, 1965); and was business manager for *Pousse-Café* (46 St. Th., Mar. 18, 1966). He was company manager for *Agatha Sue I love you* (Henry Miller's Th., Dec. 14, 1966); *Of Love Remembered* (ANTA Th., Feb. 18, 1967); *By George* (Lyceum, Oct. 12, 1967); *The Trial of Lee Harvey Oswald* (ANTA Th., Nov. 5, 1967); *New Faces of 1968* (Booth Th., May 7, 1968); was a member of the press staff for *Just for Love* (Provincetown Playhouse, Oct. 17, 1968); and company manager for the tour of *The Apple Tree* (1968–69).

He was company director for *South Pacific* (Jones Beach Th., Long Island, N.Y., July 3, 1969); company manager for the tour of *Hadrian VII* (Aug. 1969–May 1970); for *Sleuth* (Music Box, N.Y.C., Nov. 12, 1970); *The Sound of Music* (Jones Beach Th., Long Island N.Y., July 1, 1970); and *Veronica's Room* (Music Box, N.Y.C., Oct. 25, 1973).

Films. He produced *Instant Love* (1963).

Television. Mr. Cohen has worked in various phases of production for NBC on such shows as the Philco Television Playhouse; Goodyear Th.; the Kay Kayser Show; Man Against Crime; the Kate Smith Show; American Inventory; NBC Opera; and Wide, Wide World (1950–57).

Recreation. Basketball, horses, golf.

COHEN, SELMA JEANNE. Educator, writer, editor. b. Sept. 18, 1920, Chicago, Ill., to Frank A. and Minna (Skud) Cohen. Father, businessman. Grad. Univ. of Chicago, A.B. 1941; M.A. 1942; Ph.D. 1946. Studied dancing with Edna McRae, Eugene Loring, Martha Graham, José Limon, Hanya Holm. Member of ASTR (exec. comm., 1967–70, 1973–to date); Modern Language Assn.; National Association for Regional Ballet (dir., 1963–72); Amer. Society for Aesthetics (trustee, 1963–65, 1973–to date); National Endowment for the Arts (advisory dance panel, 1966–70). Address: 29 E. 9th St., New York, NY 10003, tel. (212) SP 7-1594.

In 1974, Miss Cohen founded and was director of the Dance History Workshop, Univ. of Chicago. Miss Cohen was teacher of dance history, Connecticut College (1963–69), founder-director of the Connecticut College Dance Critics' Conference (1970) and director (1971–72), a project supported by NEA. Previously she taught dance history at the School of Performing Arts, N.Y.C. (1953–56); was a reporter for the NY *Times* (1955–58); and was a technical assistant at the NY Public Library (1960–62; Emily E. F. Skeel Fellow, 1961–62).

Miss Cohen has been guest teacher or lecturer at several institutions, including Mount Holyoke College, Princeton Univ., York Univ., the Univ. of Wisconsin, the Univ. of California, the Modern Language Assn., and the American Soc. for Aesthetics. Her lecture subjects are theatrical dancing in England, 1660–1760; dance in America in the 18th and 19th centuries; and dance aesthetics.

Published Works. Miss Cohen was co-editor (1958–64) and then editor (1965–to date) of *Dance Perspectives.* She was the American editor of *Dictionary of Modern Ballet* (1959); author, with I. K. Fletcher, of *Famed for Dance* (1960); author of *Stravinsky and the Dance* (1962); editor of *The Modern*

Dance: Seven Statements of Belief (1966), and *Dance as a Theatre Art: Source Readings in Dance History* (1974); author of *Doris Humphrey: An Artist First* (1972); and contributor of articles to *The Ballet Annual; Journal of Aesthetics; Dance* Magazine; *Dance News; Theatre Arts; Dancing Times* (London); and the *Encyclopaedia Britannica*. .

Awards. Miss Cohen was awarded a Rockefeller Foundation research grant in 1969.

Recreation. Travel, "seeing plays that have no dancing in them.".

COLBIN, ROD. Actor, fencing master. b. Irving Herbert Lichenstein, Dec. 23, 1923, New Haven, Conn., to Samuel and Bess (Silverdollar) Lichenstein. Father, memorial dealer. Grad. New Haven H.S., Conn., 1941; attended Central Sch. of Speech and Drama, London, 1945–46; Columbia Univ., 1946; American Theatre Wing, 1946–48; Stella Adler Studio, 1950–52; studied with F. Komisarjevsky, New Haven; Harold Clurman, N.Y.C. Married 1965 to Annemarie Polonyi; two daughters. Served US Army, Special Services, 1942–46, ETO; rank, Sgt. Member of SAG; AFTRA; AEA; Natl. Fencing Coaches Assn. of Amer. Address: 330 E. 48th St., New York, NY 10017, tel. (212) 371-3746.

Mr. Colbin has been fencing master for the Neighborhood Playhouse, N.Y.C., since 1957 and for the Musical and Dramatic Theatre Academy, N.Y.C., since 1963.

Pre-Theatre. Salesman; interviewer.

Theatre. Mr. Colbin made his debut as Scrooge in *A Christmas Carol* (Ivy Street Sch., New Haven, Conn., 1932); appeared as a Newsboy in *Town Topics Musical* (College Theatre, New Haven, Conn., 1936); as the Doctor in *The Journey to Heaven* (Lincoln, New Haven, Conn., 1940).

He made his N.Y.C. debut as the Visiting Soldier in *Janie* (Henry Miller's Th., Sept. 10, 1942); followed by Tommy Arbuckle in the national tour of *Junior Miss* (Philadelphia, Pa., 1942); appeared as a monologuist in a salute to England and America (Royal Albert Hall, London, 1945); appeared as Valvert in *Cyrano de Bergerac* (Alvin, N.Y.C., Oct. 8, 1946); in stock, appeared as Rough in *Angel Street* (summer tour 1947); and Lt. Lenny Archer in *Kiss and Tell* (Pompton Lakes Playhouse, N.Y., Summer 1948).

He played Curtis in *The Taming of the Shrew* and Hubert de Burgh in *King John* (American Shakespeare Festival, Stratford, Conn., Summer 1957); Officer Meade in *Legend of Lizzie* (54 St. Th., N.Y.C., Feb. 9, 1959); Harry Doe in *Machinal* (Gate, Apr. 7, 1960); played Schrank in *West Side Story* (Summer tour, 1960); played Fifty in *Madame Aphrodite* (Orpheum, N.Y.C., Dec. 29, 1961) and appeared in stock as Schrank in *West Side Story* (O'-Keefe Center, Toronto, Ont., Summer 1961).

As fencing master, Mr. Colbin staged the dueling scenes for *Julius Caesar* (ASFTA, Stratford, Conn., July 12, 1955); *Macbeth* (Rooftop, N.Y.C., Oct. 7, 1955); *The Taming of the Shrew* (ASFTA, Stratford, Conn., Aug. 5, 1956); *King Lear* (Players, Jan. 2, 1959); *The Fighting Cock* (ANTA, Dec. 8, 1959); *Hamlet* (McCarter Th., Princeton, N.J., 1961); *Henry IV, Part I* (ASFTA, Stratford, Conn., June 17, 1962); and *Othello* (Arena Stage, Washington, D.C., 1963).

He played Uwe Sievers in *The Physicists* (Martin Beck Th., Oct. 13, 1964); toured with his own show, *Touche* (1966–68); staged the duels for the APA-Phoenix *Hamlet* (Lyceum, Mar. 3, 1969) and for *A Patriot for Me* (Imperial, Oct. 5, 1969); and was a standby in *Twigs* (Broadhurst, Nov. 14, 1971).

Films. Mr. Colbin has appeared in *Stage Door Canteen* (UA, 1943), and in *The Captain* (US Navy, 1952). He dubbed voices for the English soundtracks of *The Castillians* (WB, 1961), and *Processo di Verona, I, Semiramis* and *II Boia de Verona* (1963).

Television. Mr. Colbin first appeared on television as Robin (The Magic Cottage, Dumont, 1950); subsequently appeared in 35 roles on The Magic Cottage (Dumont); performed on All Star Revue (NBC, 1951); The Al Capp Show (NBC, 1952); Strike It Rich (NBC, 1952); The Hunter (NBC, 1953); *Hamlet* (Hallmark Hall of Fame, NBC, 1953); The Detective (NBC, 1953); *Macbeth* (Hallmark Hall of Fame, NBC, 1954); Captain Video (Dumont, 1955); The Wendy Barrie Show (Dumont, 1955); Mr. Citizen (ABC, 1955).

He played Carl Whipple for one year on the serial As the World Turns (CBS, 1958); appeared on Wonderama (Dumont, 1959); in The Great Impersonator (NBC, 1960); Young Dr. Malone (NBC, 1961, 1963); Edge of Night (CBS, 1961, 1974); Richard Carvelle (NBC); Naked City (NBC, 1962); and Dupont Show of the Month (NBC, 1963).

He staged dueling scenes for television productions of *The Art of the Ballet* (Omnibus, CBS, 1956); *The Three Musketeers* (Family Classics, CBS, 1960); and *The Prisoner of Zenda* (CBS, 1960).

Recreation. Folk and flamenco guitar.

COLBY, ETHEL. Drama and film critic, actress, singer. b. Ethel Duckman, Sept. 15, 1908, New York City, to Dr. M. Duckman and Rebecca (Scharlin) Duckman. Father, physician. Attended Girls H.S., Brooklyn, N.Y.; Columbia Univ. Married Sept. 25, 1929, to Julius J. Colby, advertising director of *Variety*; one son. Member of AEA; AFTRA (honorable withdrawals); NY Drama Critics Circle (treas.; Keeper of the Scrolls; chmn., membership comm.); The Drama Desk; Newspaperwomen's Club. Address: 10300 West Bay Harbor Dr., Bay Harbor Island, FL 33154, tel. (305) 861-1576.

Miss Colby has been critic-at-large for the New York *Journal of Commerce* since 1971. From 1939 to 1971, she was film and drama reviewer for the *Journal*. Her reviews were syndicated in the Twin Coast (Ridder Chain) newspapers.

Under the billing, Ethel Dallon, she appeared as a child in vaudeville acts with Gus Edwards and Pat Rooney, Jr. (1917), and as a singer on the RKO-Keith circuit; played in vaudeville, with Leonard Sillman. She made her Bway debut succeeding (1927) Violet Carlson in the role of Gretchen in *The Student Prince* (Jolson Th., Dec. 2, 1924); toured with Joe Besser as a singing comedienne on the Paramount Theatre circuit (1929); appeared in *Maytime, Blossom Time* and *The Red Robe*, presented by the Shuberts (Long Beach, N.Y.); using the name Ethel Colby, she appeared in *The Fabulous Invalid* (Broadhurst, N.Y.C., Oct. 8, 1938); *It Shouldn't Happen to a Dog* (Masonic Th., Long Beach, N.Y., July 24, 1939); and *The Moorings* (Masonic Th., Long Beach, N.Y., Aug. 14, 1939).

Television and Radio. Miss Colby was heard on the radio programs, Miss Hollywood, Mr. and Mrs. Go to the Theatre (with her husband), and Broadway Busybody (WMCA, 1941–57). For television, she produced and appeared on Broadway Matinee (Dumont, 1950–51), consisting of critique, commentary, and celebrity interviews; and Curtain Call.

COLE, EDWARD C. Educator. b. Edward Cyrus Cole, Mar. 26, 1904, Pawtucket, R.I., to Washington Leverett and Fanny Ethel (Nicholson) Cole. Father, merchant; mother, accountant. Grad. Pawtucket H.S., R.I., 1922; Dartmouth Coll., A.B. 1926; Yale Univ. Sch. of Drama, M.F.A. 1942. Married Sept. 6, 1930, to Alice Sylvia Crawford, interior designer; one son, one daughter. From 1955 to 1957, was civilian advisor to special services officer, First Army; awarded US Treasury Citation for war bond sales. Member of ATA (bd. mbr., 1954–61; vice-pres., 1957; pres., 1958); ANTA (bd. mbr., 1953–68; 2nd vice-pres., 1962; secy., 1967–68); NETC (exec. comm., 1951–55; vice-pres., 1951–to date; advisory council, 1955–to date); USITT (bd. mbr., 1961); Amer. Coll. Th. Festival (central comm., 1962–71; dept. nat. coordinator, 1969–71); American Playwrights Th. (bd. of gov., 1963–65); Theatre Haven, Inc. (bd. of dir., 1972–to date); Yale Univ. Dramatic Assn. (adv. bd., 1946–61); Theatre-in-the-Rink, Yale Univ. (adv. bd., 1964). Also, Natl. Council of the Arts in Education (delegate at large, 1962–72; exec. secy., 1962–68); American Council for the Arts in Education (delegate at large, 1972–to date; chmn., Committees on Awards and Recognitions, 1972–to date); AAUP; USPS; Zeta Psi; Dartmouth Coll. Club, New Haven, (pres., 1946); Yale Club, New Haven; Yacht Club, Branford, Conn.; Appalachian Mountain Club, Hutmen's Assn.; Mystic Seaport, Mystic, Conn.; Connecticut Conservation Assn.; US Yacht Racing Union; Branford Historical Soc.; Natl. Trust for Historic Preservation; Arts Council of Greater New Haven; Yale Alumni Fund (dir., 1959–69; advisor, Drama Fund, 1953–71; chmn., Drama Fund, 1972–to date); New Haven Power Squadron (commander, 1956); US Power Squadrons (educational officer, district one, 1955; Amer. Cancer Society, New Haven Chapter (dir., 1952–56). Yale Univ. School of Drama, Box 1903–A, Yale Station, New Haven, CT 06520, tel. (203) 436-3166; 17 Parker Place, Branford, CT 06405, tel. (203) 488-6287.

Mr. Cole became emeritus professor, Yale Univ. School of Drama in 1971. He had joined the faculty as an instructor in 1930 and then was assistant professor (1934–46) and associate professor (1946–71). He was in addition an assistant technical director in the School of Drama (1930–32); technical director (1939–46); production manager (1946–66); executive officer (1959–64); acting dean (1965–66); and a senior faculty fellow (1966–67).

Mr. Cole was Associate Fellow of Timothe Dwight College, Yale Univ. (1944–59), Fellow (1959–71), and Emeritus Associate Fellow (1974–to date). He conducted seminars at William and Mary College (Summer 1948).

He was stage manager and acted in productions of the Pawtucket (R.I.) Community Players (1926); technical director of the Hampton Players, Southampton, N.Y. (1928–32); business and production manager of the Wellesley (Mass.) Summer Th. (1947).

Mr. Cole was theatre planning consultant for the Amer. Shakespeare Festival Theatre; Hopkins Center (Dartmouth Coll.); Pickard Th. (Bowdoin Coll., Brunswick, Me.); Virginia Museum of Fine Arts Th. (Richmond, Va.); Ohio Univ. Th. (Athens, Ohio); Bates Coll. Th. (Lewiston, Me.); Wheelock Coll. Th. (Boston, Mass.); O'Keefe Center (Toronto, Canada); and the Civic Aud. and Th. (Vancouver, Canada).

Television. In 1944, Mr. Cole was production consultant at WRGB, the General Electric Company's experimental television station in Schenectady, N.Y. Thereafter, until 1964, he introduced courses in television production and writing for television to the Yale drama curriculum; was liaison and production coordinator of experiments with plays, musical acts, and documentaries prepared at Yale and presented over WRGB; and assisted in the production of operas in the Hartt College of Music on WRGB. He was a charter member and director of the American Television Society and a director of the Television Broadcasters Association.

Published Works. Mr. Cole wrote, with Alexander Dean, *Syllabus of Play Production* (1934, 1935), which was privately published; *Stage Manager's Manual* (1937), also privately published; with Harold Burris-Meyer, *Scenery for the Theatre* (1938; rev. 1971); and *Theatres and Auditoriums* (1949; rev. 1964; augmented, 1975). He wrote definitions for theatre terms, *American College Dictionary* (1947); has written many articles on theatre organization and theatre planning; and has lectured widely on these subjects and on television production.

Awards. Mr. Cole received the Theta Alpha Phi Award (1958) for distinguished service to the American theatre; ATA Award of Merit (1964); was made a charter fellow of ATA (1965); received NETC regional citation (1971); USITT Founders Award (1971); the ACTF/Amoco Gold (1972) and Silver (1973) medals; became a founding fellow of ACAE (1973); and a life member of USPS (1973).

Recreation. Skiing, sailing.

COLE, TOBY. Actors' and playwrights' representative, editor. b. Jan. 27, 1916, Newark, N.J., to Jacob and Bess Cholodenko. Father, builder.

Grad. South Side H.S., Newark, 1933; New Jersey Junior Coll., 1935; attended New Theatre Sch., N.Y.C., 1936–38; Cornell Univ., 1942. Married Aug. 3, 1946, to Dr. Aron Krich, author and psychologist; one son. Relative in theatre: Helen Krich Chinoy, educator, editor. 234 W. 44th St., New York, NY 10036, tel. (212) BR 9-7770.

Since 1957 Ms. Cole has had her own agency.

Published Works. Ms. Cole edited *Acting: A Handbook of the Stanislavsky Method* (1947), and *Playwrights on Playwriting* (1960); with Helen Krich Chinoy, edited *Actors on Acting* (1949), *Directing the Play* (1953), and *Directors on Directing* (1962), a revision of *Directing the Play.*

COLE, WENDELL. Educator, scene designer. b. Wendell Gordon Cole, May 15, 1914, Chicago, Ill., to Herbert and Susan B. (Richards) Cole. Father, accountant; mother, teacher. Grad. Carl Schurz H.S., Chicago, Ill., 1932; Albion Coll., A.B. 1936; Univ. of Michigan, M.A. (medieval history) 1937; Stanford Univ., Ph.D. 1951. Married Dec. 14, 1948, to Charlotte Klein, librarian. Member of ATA; ANTA; SAA; Western Speech Assn.; CTC. Address: (home) 853 Esplanada Way, Stanford, CA 94305; (bus.) Memorial Hall, Stanford Univ., Stanford, CA 94305, tel. (415) 321-2300.

Since 1951, Mr. Cole has been a professor in the Dept. of Speech and Drama at Stanford Univ. He was previously assistant professor of speech at Alma Coll. (1943–45); instructor, Stanford Univ. (1945–51); assistant professor (1951–54); associate professor (1954–63); professor (1963–to date); acting executive head, Dept. of Speech and Drama (1956–57; 1957–58; 1959–60; 1960–61; 1963–64); and acting chairman, Dept. of Drama (1967–69; 1972–73). He was a scene designer for the Stanford Players (1945–65).

Awards. He received the American Council of Learned Societies Scholarship in 1936, 1937, and 1938.

Recreation. Architecture.

COLEMAN, CY. Composer. Studied with Adele Mavus, New York Coll. of Music, piano. Member of Dramatists Guild; ASCAP; AFM.

Theatre. Mr. Coleman composed the music for the "Tin Pan Alley" number in *John Murray Anderson's Almanac* (Imperial, N.Y.C., Dec. 10, 1953); composed the incidental music and was musical director for *Compulsion* (Ambassador, Oct. 24, 1957); composed the scores for *Wildcat* (Alvin, Dec. 16, 1960); *Little Me* (Lunt-Fontanne, Nov. 17, 1962); *Sweet Charity* (Palace, Jan. 29, 1966); and *Seesaw* (Uris, Mar. 18, 1973); and contributed songs to the revue, *Straws in the Wind* (Amer. Place Th., Feb. 21, 1975).

Films. Mr. Coleman wrote the scores for *Spartacus* (U, 1960); *Father Goose* (U, 1965); music for *The Art of Love* (U, 1965); additional songs for his original score for *Sweet Charity* (U, 1969); and the title song for *The Heartbreak Kid* (20th-Fox, 1972).

Television. Mr. Coleman was associated, as a composer, with Date in Manhattan (NBC, 1950–53); the Kate Smith Show (NBC, 1955–56); and Art Ford's Greenwich Village Party (WNEW, N.Y.C., 1960).

Night Clubs. A popular society pianist, Mr. Coleman has played throughout the country in appearances including The Rainbow Grill (N.Y.C.); The Sherry Netherlands (N.Y.C.); London House (Chicago); Sheraton Cadillac (Detroit); Sahara (Las Vegas); Eden Roc (Miami); the Copacabana; Raleigh Room; the Embers; the Little Club; the Waldorf; and his own club, the Playroom (N.Y.C.).

Published Works. He has written such songs as "Witchcraft," "Firefly," "The Best Is Yet to Come," "Playboys Theme," "I'm Gonna Laugh You Out of My Life," "It Amazes Me," "Hey! Look Me Over," "I've Got Your Number," "The Riviera," and "You Fascinate Me So.".

Discography. His recordings include *Cy Coleman Sings Cy Coleman* (Col.) and *The Party's on Me* (RCA, 1976).

COLEMAN, FAY R. Puppeteer. b. Fay Ross Coleman, Aug. 7, 1918, Milledgeville, Ill., to Henry R. and Emma L. (Stein) Coleman. Father, insurance-real estate business. Grad. Milledgeville (Ill.) Community H.S., 1932–36; attended Goodman Sch. of Theatre, 1936–37; Ashland Coll., 1938–40; grad. Univ. of Wisconsin, B.A. (Phi Beta Kappa) 1947. Married Nov. 4, 1945, to Barbara Jeanne Foxwell; two sons, one daughter. Served USAAF, 1941–45, ETO; Weather Observer. Member of Puppeteers of America; Chicagoland Puppetry Guild (past secy., treas., pres.); Scribes; Alpha Psi Omega; Union Internationale des Marionettes. Address: 1516 South Second Ave., Maywood, IL 60153, tel. (312) 344-2920.

Mr. Coleman has produced puppet shows in the Chicago area for schools and children's theatres, with premieres as follows: *The Lilliput Revue* (Sept. 1948); *Tom Sawyer* (Feb. 1950); *Cinderella* (May 1951); *Aladdin* (Sept. 1951); *A Christmas Carol* (Dec. 1951); *Pinocchio* (Jan. 1953); *Hans Brinker* (Oct. 1953); *Snow White and the Seven Dwarfs* (Sept. 1954); *The Amazing Voyage of Nicky Noodle* (Sept. 1955); *Rumpelstiltskin* (Oct. 1956); *The Magic Dog of Fuji* (Oct. 1957); *The Elves and the Shoemaker* (Sept. 1960); *The Snow Queen* (Jan. 1962); *Ali Baba and the Forty Thieves* (Jan. 1963); *Cinderella* (Jan. 1964); *Androcles and the Lion* (Nov. 1970); *The Alligator's Eggs* (Apr. 1972); *Silly Saburo* (Oct. 1972); *The Magic Nutcracker* (Dec. 1972); *Mark My Words, Sam* (May 1973); *Stone Soup* (Aug. 1974); *Pierre* (Nov. 1974); and *Hansel and Gretel* (Dec. 1974). Some of his productions have toured extensively in the US and Canada.

Recreation. Reading, music.

COLEMAN, LONNIE. Playwright, novelist. b. Lonnie William Coleman, Aug. 2, 1920, Bartow, Ga., to John Aldine and Lily Delle (Williams) Coleman. Grad. Univ. of Alabama, B.A. 1942. Served USN, 1942–46, gunnery officer; rank, 1st Lt. Member of Dramatists Guild. Address: c/o Miriam Howell, Ashley Famous Agency, Inc., 555 Madison Ave., New York, NY 10022, tel. (212) MU 8-8330.

Theatre. Mr. Coleman wrote *Next of Kin* (Hyde Park Playhouse, N.Y., Aug. 1955); *Jolly's Progress* (Longacre, N.Y.C., Dec. 5, 1959); *She Didn't Say Yes* (Summer stock tour, 1963); *A Warm Body* (Cort, N.Y.C., Apr. 15, 1967); and *A Place for Polly* (Ethel Barrymore Th., Apr. 18, 1970).

Films. *Hot Spell* (Par., 1958) was adapted for the screen from Mr. Coleman's play *Next of Kin.* .

Published Works. He wrote the novels *Sam* (1959), *The Golden Vanity* (1962), *Beulah Land* (1973), and *Orphan Jim* (1975).

COLEMAN, NANCY. Actress. b. Nancy Katherine Coleman, Dec. 30, 1917, Everett, Wash., to Charles S. and Grace (Sharpless) Coleman. Father, newspaper managing editor. Grad. Everett H.S.; Univ. of Washington, B.A. Studied acting with Reginald Travers, San Francisco, Calif., two years; Benno Schneider, N.Y.C., one year. Married Sept. 16, 1943, to Whitney Bolton, drama critic, radio commentator, columnist (dec.); two daughters. Member of AEA; AFTRA; SAG; Kappa Alpha Theta; Phi Mu Gamma. Address: 888 8th Ave., New York, NY 10019, tel. (212) 765-3187; service (212) JU 6-3700; tel. service (212) JU 6-3700.

Theatre. Miss Coleman made her N.Y.C. debut when she succeeded to the role of Blossom Trexel in *Susan and God* (Plymouth, Apr. 1938), repeated the role in stock and played Kay in *Stage Door* (Theatre-by-the-Sea, Matunuck, R.I., Summer 1939). She appeared as Lovely Mary in *Mrs. Wiggs of the Cabbage Patch* (Mohawk Drama Festival, Schenectady, N.Y., July 1940); played the title role in *Liberty Jones* (Shubert, N.Y.C., Mar. 5, 1941); and appeared in five productions at Elitsche Gardens (Denver, Colo., 1951).

Miss Coleman played the Nurse in *The Sacred Flame* (President, N.Y.C., Oct. 7, 1952); succeeded to the role of Ellen Turner in *The Male Animal* (Music Box, May 15, 1952); played Eleanor Hilliard in *The Desperate Hours* (Ethel Barrymore Th., Feb. 10, 1955), and on tour. She played Roda in *The Damask Cheek* (Fred Miller Th., Milwaukee, Wis., Jan. 1956); Maggie in *Cat on a Hot Tin Roof* (Capri, Atlantic Beach, N.Y., July 1957); Georgie in *The Country Girl* (San Juan Drama Festival, P.R., Feb. 1958); and Ruth Gray in *Epitaph for George Dillon* (Capri, Atlantic Beach, N.Y., July 1958).

She appeared in two productions for the State Dept. as Laura in *The Glass Menagerie* (Europe and Middle East, Jan. 1961), and Kate Keller in *The Miracle Worker* (Latin Americas, Aug. 1961); appeared in *U.S.A.* (Fred Miller Th., Milwaukee, Wis., Fall 1962); toured South Africa as Edith in *Never Too Late* (1964); played Birdie in *The Little Foxes* (Ivanhoe Th., Chicago, 1969); played Lavinia in *Another Part of the Forest* (Ivanhoe Th., Chicago, 1971); Miss Prism in *The Importance of Being Earnest* (Goodman Th., Chicago, 1971); was standby for Gloria Swanson as Mrs. Baker in *Butterflies Are Free* on national tour and played the role at Barter Th., Abingdon, Va. (1972); appeared with the Indiana Repertory Co., Indianapolis, Ind., as Bananas in *House of Blue Leaves,* Amanda in *Glass Managerie,* and Sybil in *Count Dracula* (all 1972); and was Cora in *Morning's at Seven* (Long Wharf Th., New Haven, Conn., 1973).

Films. Miss Coleman has appeared in *Kings Row* (WB, 1941); *Dangerously They Live* (WB, 1941); *The Gay Sisters* (WB, 1942); *Desperate Journey* (WB, 1942); *Edge of Darkness* (WB, 1943); *In Our Time* (WB, 1944); *Devotion* (WB, 1946); *Her Sister's Secret* (PRC, 1946); *Mourning Becomes Electra* (RKO, 1947); and *The Slaves* (1968).

Television and Radio. She has performed on such radio series as Death Valley Days (NBC, 1940), Hawthorne House (NBC, 1940), played Alice Hughes in Young Doctor Malone (NBC, 1940), and various Saints on the Ave Maria Hour (WMCA, 1940).

On television, she appeared as Helen in *The Valiant Lady* (CBS, 1953); Henrietta in *The Barretts of Wimpole Street* (NBC, 1956); appeared in *Black Monday* (1960); and has performed on Robert Montgomery Presents (NBC); Kraft Television Th. (NBC); US Steel Hour (CBS); Philco Television Playhouse (NBC); Lux Th.; Edge of Night; You Are There; and Colgate Th.

Recreation. Interior decorating, world traveling, archaeology.

COLEMAN, SHEPARD. Musical director. b. Shepard David Coleman, Apr. 24, 1924, New York City, to Albert P. and Etta Coleman. Father, merchant. Grad. Samuel J. Tilden H.S., Brooklyn, N.Y., 1941; Juilliard Sch. of Music, 1946. Studied cello with Willem Willeke, Frank Miller; conducting with Leon Barzin, N.Y.C., 1950–57. Married June 18, 1956, to Gretchen Wyler, singer, dancer, actress. Relative in theatre: brother, Avron Coleman, cellist. Member of AFM, Local 802.

Theatre. Mr. Coleman was cellist in the orchestra of ten N.Y.C. musicals (1946–60), cellist with the NY Philharmonic, and staff cellist at Stations WQXR and WMCA (N.Y.C., 1962–63).

He joined (American Th., St. Louis, Mo.) the national tour, as musical director, of *Destry Rides Again* (opened Riviera, Las Vegas, Nev., July 31, 1960; closed O'Keefe Centre, Toronto, Canada, Jan. 29, 1961); took over (Shubert, N.Y.C., July 1961) as musical director of *Bye Bye Birdie* (Martin Beck Th., Apr. 14, 1960), and for its national tour (opened Shubert, Boston, Mass., Oct. 9, 1961; closed Forrest, Philadelphia, Pa., Mar. 31, 1962); returned to N.Y.C. as musical director of *The Student Gypsy, or The Prince of Liederkranz* (54 St. Th., Sept. 30, 1963); *Hello, Dolly! (St. James, Jan. 16, 1964), for which he made the vocal arrangements; and Oh What a Lovely War* (Broadhurst, Sept. 30, 1964). He was musical director for *Mardi Gras! (Marine Th., Jones Beach, Long Island, N.Y., July 8, 1966) and for Henry, Sweet Henry* (Palace, N.Y.C., Oct. 23, 1967), for which he made the vocal arrangements.

Awards. For his musical direction of *Hello Dolly!, Mr. Coleman received an Antoinette Perry (Tony)*

Award (1964).

Recreation. Literature, collecting rare instruments, horses, Great Danes.

COLEMAN, WILLIAM S.E. Educator, director, playwright. b. William Samuel Edward Coleman, June 7, 1926, Parnassus, Pa., to William Robert and Ila Fern (Philips) Coleman. Father, electrical engineer. Educated Virginia Military Institute; Slippery Rock (Pa.) State College, B.S. 1949; Pennsylvania State Univ., M.A. 1953; Univ. of Pittsburgh, Ph.D. 1965. Professional training Cleveland Playhouse, Chautauqua, N.Y., Summer 1949. Served US Army, 1944–46; rank, Technician 4th grade. Married in 1953 to Jane McNair Howland (dec. 1955); one son; married 1957 to Phyliss Young (marr. dis. 1974); one son. Member ATA (chmn., Liaison Comm. for International Educational Theatre Projects, 1970–71; asst. administrative vice-pres., 1970–72; co-chmn., Playwriting Project, 1971–72; Planning Comm. for annual convention, 1971–72; advisory comm. new playwrights' program, 1972–73); SCA; West Virginia Intercollegiate Speech Assoc. (pres., 1960–61, 1962–63). Address: (home) 1334 31st St., Des Moines, IA 50311, tel. (515) 277-8893; (bus.) Dept. of Theatre Arts, Drake Univ., Des Moines, IA 50311, tel. (515) 271-2186.

Mr. Coleman has been department chairman and professor of theatre arts and director of the Drake Univ. Theatre since 1966. Previously, he was assistant professor of theatre and speech, SUNY at Buffalo, N.Y. (1965–66); assistant professor of theatre, speech, and English, Slippery Rock (Pa.) State College (1963–65); head of the department and associate professor of theatre, speech, and English, Glenville (W. Va.) State College (1955–63); and instructor of English and journalism, Grove City (Pa.) High School (1949–52).

Theatre. Mr. Coleman's first theatrical experience occurred while he was in the US Army, when he performed in the review *ERC-Sa-Poppin'* (May 1944). He made his professional debut at the Pennsylvania State Univ. summer theatre in 1951 and 1952. In 1958, he founded the drama division, West Virginia State Folk Festival and was chairman (1958–63). He was a member of the planning committee for the West Virginia centennial showboat "Rhododendron" and later touring director (1962–63). In N.Y.C., Mr. Coleman directed the off-Bway production *The Living Knife* (41 St. Th., May 6, 1965), for which he also designed settings, and he directed the Theatre Fabulous of Des Moines production of *Guys and Dolls* (June 12, 1973).

Mr. Coleman has been active in the American College Theatre Festival. He was co-author (with Michael Frisbie) and director of *Saturn's Feast,* a national finalist in the first festival (1969); he directed *A Funny Thing Happened on the Way to the Forum* (1971), finalist in the Region VI (Iowa, Nebraska, Missouri, and Kansas) competition; he directed and devised additional material for the English-language premiere of Raphael Alberti's *Night and War in the Prado,* 1972 Region VI finalist; and in 1972 he founded the Region VI New Playwrights' Showcase.

As chairman, Dept. of Theatre Arts at Drake, he originated a continuing guest artist production, and he made Drake the first Midwestern university to affiliate with the Eugene O'Neill Theatre Festival, leading to Drake being the first American university to produce plays in the O'Neill Theatre Festival's Second Step Program (Oct. 1973).

Mr. Coleman has written a number of original plays, fifteen of which have been produced in colleges, universities, community theatres, high schools, and on regional radio and television stations.

Television. Mr. Coleman created an educational series of television programs on elementary arithmetic, presented on WQED, Pittsburgh, Pa., in 1955.

Published Works. Mr. Coleman wrote, with Ned A. Bowman and Glorianne Engel, *Planning for the Theatre* (1965; repr. 1972), and he is author of articles and book reviews that have appeared in *Players Magazine, Theatre Survey, Marquee,* and *West Virginia Speech Journal.*

Awards. Mr. Coleman received Danforth Teacher Study grants in 1963–64 and 1964–65, a SUNY Foundation grant for research, and Drake Univ. research grants in 1967, 1968, 1969, 1970, and 1974. In the 1955 Arts of the Theatre Foundation Playwriting Contest, Mr. Coleman's play *Pillars in the Night* won third place. His play *A Ballad for John Hardy* won first prize in the West Virginia Centennial Folk Play Contest in 1963, and in the 1962 Naugatuck Footlighters One-Act Play Contest his play *Rondo* won third prize and his play *Courtship and Early Death* won honorable mention.

Recreation. Research in history of the American West; collecting motion picture soundtrack albums; cartooning.

COLICOS, JOHN. Actor. b. Dec. 10, 1928, Toronto, Ontario, Canada. Married January 1957 to Mona McHenry; two sons.

Theatre. Mr. Colicos made his professional debut as Shakespeare in a production of Clemence Dane's *Will Shakespeare* (Montreal Repertory Co., 1947); appeared at the Canadian Drama Festival (1951) as Charles II in *In Good King Charles's Golden Days;* and was a member of the Old Vic Co., London, England (1951–52). On tour with the Old Vic, he played the title role in *King Lear* (Helsinki, Finland) and in the London production of the same play (opened Old Vic, Mar. 3, 1952) he was the Captain and also understudy to Stephen Murray, whom he replaced as Lear on several occasions.

He played Rick Martell in *The Square Ring* (Lyric, Hammersmith, Oct. 21, 1952); toured as Sir Claude in *The Confidential Clerk,* replacing Robert Speaight (Oct. 1954); and was Ralph Sherman in *The Ghost Writers* (Arts, London, Feb. 9, 1955). Mr. Colicos made his US debut as Edmund in Orson Welles's *King Lear* (NY City Ctr., Jan. 12, 1956); appeared at the American Shakespeare Festival, Stratford, Conn., as Lodovico in *Othello* (June 22, 1957), Gratiano in *The Merchant of Venice* (July 10, 1957), and Leonato in *Much Ado About Nothing* (Aug. 3, 1957). He was Mortimer in *Mary Stuart* (Phoenix, N.Y.C., Oct. 8, 1957); in Washington, D.C., replaced (Feb. 10, 1958) Alfred Drake as Benedick in the American Shakespeare Festival touring production of *Much Ado About Nothing;* and returned to the American Shakespeare Festival to play Laertes in *Hamlet* (June 19, 1958), Lysander in *A Midsummer Night's Dream* (June 20, 1958), and Leontes in *The Winter's Tale* (July 20, 1958). He appeared for the NY Theatre Society as Cuchulain in *The Death of Cuchulain* and *On Baile's Strand* (Beekman Tower Hotel Th., N.Y.C., Apr. 12, 1959).

At the Canadian Shakespeare Festival, Stratford, Ontario (Festival Th.), Mr. Colicos was Tullus Aufidius in *Coriolanus* (June 19, 1961), Berowne in *Love's Labour's Lost* (June 21, 1961), Caliban in *The Tempest* (June 1962), the Comte de Guiche in *Cyrano de Bergerac* (1962), Petruchio in *The Taming of the Shrew* (June 10, 1962), Hector in *Troilus and Cressida* (June 17, 1963), in the title role of *Cyrano de Bergerac* (June 18, 1963), and in the title role of *Timon of Athens* (July 29, 1963). At the Chichester (England) Festival, he repeated his performances as Berowne in *Love's Labour's Lost* (Apr. 6, 1964) and Timon in *Timon of Athens* (Apr. 8, 1964); then returned to Stratford, Ontario, where he played the title role in *King Lear* (June 17, 1964) and was Mr. Horner in *The Country Wife* (July 27, 1964).

He played Brother Julian in *Tiny Alice* (Playhouse in the Park, Philadelphia, Pa., Summer 1965); the title role in *Poor Richard* (Olney Th., Olney, Md., June 1, 1965); De Laubardemont in *The Devils* (Broadway Th., N.Y.C., Nov. 16, 1965); the title role in *Serjeant Musgrave's Dance* (Th. de Lys, Mar. 8, 1966); appeared at the Olney (Md.) Th. as Sir Thomas More in *A Man for All Seasons* (July 13, 1966) and Matthew Stanton in *Hogan's Goat* (Sept. 14, 1966); was the Monseigneur in *The Drummer Boy* (Th. Toronto, Ontario, Canada, Jan. 1968); and appeared as Winston Churchill in *Soldiers* (Royal Alexandra Th., Feb. 28, 1968; Billy Rose Th., N.Y.C., May 1, 1968; New, London, England, Dec. 12, 1968).

Films. Mr. Colico's films include *War Paint* (UA, 1953); *Bond of Fear* (Eros, 1956); and *Passport to Treason* (Eros, 1956).

Television. Mr. Colicos has repeated on television his performance as Petruchio in *The Taming of the Shrew* (Studio One, NBC). Other programs on which he has appeared include Star Trek (NBC); Secret Storm; Mission: Impossible (CBS); Mannix (CBS); Hallmark Hall of Fame (NBC); The Defenders (CBS); Omnibus; Profiles in Courage (NBC); and Armstrong Circle Th. (NBC). On Canadian television, he appeared in *Galileo, The Wild Duck, The Critic, The Man Born To Be King, The Queen of Spades, Hamlet,* and *Richard III.*

Awards. Mr. Colicos received the Canadian Drama Festival Award (1951) as best actor for his performance as Charles II in *In Good King Charles's Golden Days.*

COLLIER, GAYLAN JANE. Educator. b. July 23, 1924, Fluvanna, Tex., to Ben V. and Narcis N. (Smith) Colier. Father, stock farmer. Grad. Fluvanna H.S., 1941; Abilene Christian Coll., B.A. 1946; State Univ. of Iowa, M.A. 1949; Univ. of Denver, Ph.D. 1957. Member of CTC (gov. of region four; editor of regional *Newsletter,* 1962–63); Rocky Mountain Th. Conf. (vice-pres., 1962–63); AETA (committee on academic and production standards); SAA; SWTC; Alpha Psi Omega (secy., vice-pres., pres., college chap.); Zeta Phi Eta. Address: Dept. of Theatre Arts, Texas Christian University, Fort Worth, TX 76129.

Since 1967, Ms. Collier has been professor of theatre arts at Texas Christian Univ. Previously she had been associate professor of drama at Sam Houston State Coll. (1963–65). She was instructor of speech and drama at Woman's Coll., Univ. of North Carolina (1947–48); assistant professor and acting head of the drama dept. at Greensboro Coll. (1949–50), and assistant professor of speech and drama (1950–55); associate professor and director of theatre at Abilene Christian Coll. (1955–60); and associate professor of drama, Idaho State Univ. (1960–63).

She lectured on drama at Idaho State Univ. (Summers 1958–59) and Wisconsin State Univ., Whitewater (Summer 1965). During 1964–65, she was chairman and editor of Children's Theatre Directory for the US under the auspices of the Children's Theatre Conf. (AETA).

She directed *Ten Little Indians* and appeared in *The Taming of the Shrew* (Parkway Playhouse, Burnsville, N.C., July–Aug. 1951); produced *The Man Who Married a Dumb Wife* (Abilene Christian Coll., Tex., 1958; Higher Education Ctr., State Fair of Texas, Oct., 1958); was guest director for the summer theatre festival at the Univ. of Denver, Colo., where she staged *Once in a Lifetime* (Summer 1962); directed *The Imaginary Invalid* (Texas Christian Univ., Summer 1970); and *The Rainmaker* (Fort Worth Repertory Th., Summer 1972).

Published Works. Ms. Collier has contributed articles to *Harper, Southern Speech Journal,* and *Western Speech.* .

Awards. Miss Collier was three times voted the best undergraduate actress at Abilene Christian Coll. (1943–46); and has received awards for poetry reading, and in radio speech contests.

Under a Ford Foundation Grant, she is a member of the staff for Research in Frontier Theatre, sponsored by the Univ. of Denver (1962–to date).

COLLINS, ALLEN FREDERICK. Theatrical book dealer, actor, stage manager. b. Dec. 18, 1915, Indianapolis, Ind., to Fred C. and Dora M. Collins. Father, salesman. Grad. South Side H.S., Fort Wayne, Ind., 1933; attended Valparaiso Univ., 1933–34. Married Mar. 30, 1940, to Dorothy Hosier, two daughters. Relative in theatre: brother, Fred C. Collins, radio and television announcer. Served Merchant Marine, 1944–45; rank, Seaman. Member of AEA; SAG; AFTRA. Address:

(home) 382 Central Park West, New York, NY 10025, tel. (212) UN 6-2485; (bus.) c/o Drama Book Shop, Inc., 150 W. 52nd St., New York, NY 10019, tel. (212) JU 2-1037.

Pre-Theatre. Insurance claims agent.

Theatre. Since 1946, Mr. Collins has been co-owner with Arthur Seelen of The Drama Book Shop, Inc., N.Y.C., specialists in plays and books relating to the theatre. Previously, he had worked on the theatre as an actor and stage manager.

His first appearance on stage was in a community theatre production, playing "Magpie" Welch in *The Poor Nut* (Fort Wayne Civic Th., Ind., Sept. 1933). During 1934–43, he was with the Fort Wayne Civic Theatre as actor and stage manager.

Mr. Collins made his professional debut on tour as Nym in *The Merry Wives of Windsor* (opened Playhouse, Wilmington, Del., Mar. 15, 1946; closed His Majesty's, Montreal, Canada, Sept. 14, 1946); was stage manager for *Lovely Me* (Adelphi, N.Y.C., Dec. 25, 1946); appeared in stock at Yardley, Pa. (Summer 1946), and at Clinton, N.J. (Summer 1947); was assistant stage manager for *As You Like It,* later succeeded Bill Owen as Touchstone (Cort, N.Y.C., Jan. 26, 1950), and was stage manager for the subsequent tour (opened Hershey, Pa., Sept. 1950); closed Buffalo, N.Y., Apr. 1951); stage manager for *Buy Me Blue Ribbons* (Empire, N.Y.C., Oct. 17, 1951); appeared as Wilson in *Jane* (Coronet, Feb. 1, 1952); directed *The Voice of the Turtle* and *Glad Tidings* (Maplewood, N.J., Summer 1951); appeared as Ferelli in *The Fifth Season* (Cort, N.Y.C., Jan. 23, 1953), and on tour (opened Shubert, Washington, D.C., Oct. 25, 1954; closed Montreal, Canada, May 1955).

Mr. Collins was a member of the cast with Dylan Thomas in the premiere of a concert reading of *Under Milk Wood* (Kaufman Concert Hall, N.Y.C., May 14, 1953); directed *The Fifth Season* (Cathay Circle, Los Angeles, Calif., July 1955); succeeded (Jan. 26, 1959) Spofford Beadle as the Bellboy in *Third Best Sport* (Ambassador, N.Y.C., Dec. 30, 1958); and played Arturi in *A Cook for Mr. General* (Playhouse, Oct. 19, 1961).

Films. Mr. Collins made his film debut in *A Big Hand for the Little Lady* (WB, 1966).

COLÓN, MIRIAM.

Actress. b. 1945, Ponce, Puerto Rico. Professional training at Erwin Piscator's Dramatic Workshop, N.Y.C. (special scholarship from Univ. of Puerto Rico); Actors Studio, N.Y.C. Married 1966 to George P. Edgar. Trustee of Amer. Mus. of Natural History, N.Y.C. (1971–74). Address: 141 W. 94th St., New York, NY tel. (212) 749-8535.

Theatre. Miss Colón made her N.Y.C. debut as Frederica in *In the Summer House* (The Playhouse, Dec. 29, 1953); was Erperanza in *The Innkeepers* (John Golden Th., Feb. 2, 1956); Adelita Gomez in *Me, Candido* (Greenwich Mews, Oct. 15, 1956); was in *The Puppet Theater of Don Cristobal* and *The Shoemaker's Prodigious Wife* (Delacorte Mobile Th., Sept. 1, 1964); played Maria Esposito in *Matty and the Moron and the Madonna* (Orpheum, Mar. 29, 1965); and Juanita in *The Ox Cart* (Greenwich Mews, Dec. 19, 1966).

In 1965, Miss Colón founded the Puerto Rican Traveling Th. to present shows throughout N.Y.C. With this group she appeared in *The Eagle and the Serpent;* repeated her performance as Juanita in *The Ox Cart* (1967); and played Miriamne in *Winterset* (1968). She appeared on Bway as Dolores Gonzales in *The Wrong Way Light Bulb* (John Golden Th., Mar. 4, 1969); and for Puerto Rican Traveling Th. produced and directed *The Golden Streets* (Aug. 10, 1970) and played the title role in *The Passion of Antigona Perez* (May 18, 1972).

Films. Miss Colón's motion pictures include *Thunder Island* (20th-Fox); *One-Eyed Jacks* (Par., 1961); *Harbor Lights* (20th-Fox, 1964); and *The Appaloosa* (U, 1966).

Television. Miss Colón has appeared on the Dick Van Dyke Show (CBS); Ben Casey (ABC); Dr. Kildare (NBC); Alfred Hitchcock Presents (CBS); Gunsmoke (CBS); Bonanza (NBC); and other shows.

COLT, ALVIN.

Costume and set designer. b. July 15, 1915, Louisville, Ky. Attended Yale Univ., Sch. of Fine Arts and Dept. of Drama, 1934–37. Studied with Donald Oenslager, Frank Poole Bevan, Pavel Tchlitchew. Member of United Scenic Artists. Address: 90 Riverside Dr., New York, NY 10024, tel. (212) 799-5380.

Theatre. Mr. Colt designed the costumes for the ballet, *Charade,* and costumes and scenery for the ballet, *Pastorale,* for the Amer. Ballet Caravan (now the NY City Ballet Co.) in 1940; costumes for the Ballet Russe de Monte Carlo production of *Saratoga* (Met. Opera House, N.Y.C, Oct. 19, 1941); for the Ballet Th., designed sets and costumes for *Slavonika* (44 St. Th., Nov. 21, 1941); and created costumes for the ballet, *Waltz Academy* (Boston Opera House, Oct. 5, 1944). His first Bway designs were costumes for *On the Town* (Adelphi Th., N.Y.C., Dec. 28, 1944); followed by sets and costumes for the ballets *On Stage!* (Boston Opera House, Oct. 4, 1945) and Graziana (Met. Opera House, N.Y.C., Oct. 25, 1945); costumes for *Around the World in Eighty Days* (Adelphi, May 31, 1946); *Barefoot Boy with Cheek* (Martin Beck Th., Apr. 3, 1947); *Music in My Heart* (Adelphi, Oct. 2, 1947); *Clutterbuck* (Biltmore, Dec. 3, 1949); *Guys and Dolls* (46 St. Th., Nov. 24, 1950; NY City Ctr., Apr. 20, 1955); sets and costumes for *The Miraculous Mandarin* (NY City Ctr., Sept. 6, 1951); costumes for *Top Banana* (Winter Garden, Nov. 1, 1951); costumes for the NY City Ballet Co. production of *Kaleidoscope* (NY City Ctr., Dec. 18, 1952); *The Frogs of Spring* (Broadhurst, Oct. 20, 1953); *Madam, Will You Walk* (Phoenix, Dec. 1, 1953); *Coriolanus* (Phoenix, Jan. 19, 1954); *The Golden Apple* (Phoenix, Mar. 11, 1954; moved Alvin, Apr. 20, 1954); *The Seagull* (Phoenix, May 11, 1954); *Sing Me No Lullaby* (Phoenix, Oct. 14, 1954); and *Fanny* (Majestic, Nov. 4, 1954).

Also, costumes for *The Doctor's Dilemma* (Phoenix, Jan. 11, 1955); *The Master Builder* (Phoenix, Mar. 1, 1955); *Phoenix '55* (Phoenix, Apr. 23, 1955); *Finian's Rainbow* (NY City Ctr., May 18, 1955); *The Carefree Tree* (Phoenix, Oct. 11, 1955); *The Lark* (Longacre, Nov. 17, 1955); *Pipe Dream* (Shubert, Nov. 30, 1955); *Six Characters in Search of an Author* (Phoenix, Dec. 11, 1955); *Miss Julie* and *The Stronger* (Phoenix, Feb. 21, 1956); *A Month in the Country* (Phoenix, Apr. 3, 1956); *Kiss Me, Kate* (NY City Ctr., May 9, 1956); *The Littlest Revue* (Phoenix, May 22, 1956); *The Sleeping Prince* (Coronet, Nov. 1, 1956); *The Diary of A Scoundrel* (Phoenix, Nov, 4, 1956); *Li'l Abner* (St. James, Nov. 15, 1956); and the pre-Bway tryout of *Maiden Voyage* (opened Forrest, Philadelphia, Pa., Feb. 28, 1957; closed there Mar. 9, 1957).

Also, costumes for *Livin' the Life* (Phoenix, Apr. 27, 1957); *Mary Stuart* (Phoenix, Oct. 8, 1957); *Copper and Brass* (Martin Beck Th., Oct. 17, 1957); *Rumple* (Alvin, Nov. 6, 1957); *The Infernal Machine* (Phoenix, Feb. 3, 1958); *Blue Denim* (Playhouse, Feb. 27, 1958); *Say, Darling* (ANTA, Apr. 3, 1958); *Hamlet* (Amer. Shakespeare Fest., Stratford, Conn., June 19, 1958); the pre-Bway tryout of *Crazy October* (opened Shubert, New Haven, Conn., Oct. 8, 1958; closed Geary, San Francisco, Calif., Jan. 3, 1959); *First Impressions* (Alvin, N.Y.C., Mar. 19, 1959); *Destry Rides Again* (Imperial, Apr. 23, 1959); *Greenwillow* (Alvin, Mar. 8, 1960); *Christine* (46 St. Th., Apr. 28, 1960); *Wildcat* (Alvin, Dec. 16, 1960); *13 Daughters* (54 St. Th., Mar. 2, 1961); the Natl. Repertory Th. touring productions of *Mary Stuart* and *Elizabeth the Queen* (opened Academy of Music, Northampton, Mass., Oct. 19, 1961; closed Rochester, N.Y., Apr. 14, 1962); the opera, *The Turn of the Screw* (NY City Opera, NY City Ctr., 1962); *The Aspern Papers* (Playhouse, Feb. 7, 1962); and *The Beauty Part* (Music Box, Dec. 26, 1962); *Abe Lincoln in Illinois* (Phoenix, Jan. 21, 1963); *Here's Love* (Shubert, Oct. 3, 1963); and the Natl. Repertory Th. tour (opened Aycock Aud., Greensboro, N.C., Oct. 10, 1963), of *Ring 'Round the Moon, The Seagull* (Belasco, N.Y.C., Apr. 5, 1964), and *The Crucible* (Belasco, Apr. 6, 1964).

Mr. Colt designed costumes for the City Center Gilbert & Sullivan Co. production of *The Yeoman of the Guard* (NY City Ctr., premiere Mar. 18, 1964); *Wonderworld* (NYC World's Fair, 1964); the Natl. Rep. Th. tour of *Lilliom, She Stoops to Conquer,* and *Hedda Gabler* (opened Amer. Th., St. Louis, Mo., Oct. 19, 1964; closed Blackstone, Chicago, Mar. 27, 1965); *Something More!* (Eugene O'Neill Th., N.Y.C., Nov. 10, 1964); *Anna Karenina* (Goodman Mem. Th., Chicago, May 7, 1965); the Natl. Rep. Th. tour of *The Rivals* and *The Trojan Women* (opened Nov. 8, 1965; closed Los Angeles, Mar. 26, 1966); the Milliken industrial show (N.Y.C., Summer 1966); *The Paisley Convertible* (Henry Miller's Th., Feb. 11, 1967); and *Henry, Sweet Henry* (Palace, Oct. 23, 1967).

He designed costumes for the Natl. Rep. Th. tour (1966–67) of *The Imaginary Invalid* (including N.Y.C. engagement at the ANTA Th., May 1, 1967), *A Touch of the Poet* (ANTA, May 2, 1967), and *Tonight at 8:30* (ANTA, May 3, 1967); and the following year for their tour of *John Brown's Body* and *She Stoops to Conquer* (opened Aycock Aud., Univ. of N.C., Greensboro, N.C., Oct. 16, 1967; closed Civic Th., Chicago, Dec. 16, 1967; played extended engagement at Ford's Th., Washington D.C., from Feb. 12, 1968); the pre-Bway tryout of *A Mother's Kisses* (opened Shubert, New Haven, Sept. 23, 1968; closed Mechanic, Baltimore, Oct. 19, 1968); *The Goodbye People* (Ethel Barrymore Th., N.Y.C., Dec. 3, 1968); *The Ballad of Johnny Pot* (Th. Four, Apr. 26, 1971); *Sugar* (Majestic, Apr. 9, 1972); and *Lorelei* (began natl. tour Civic Center, Oklahoma City, Feb. 26, 1973; opened Palace, N.Y.C., Jan. 27, 1974).

Films. Mr. Colt designed costumes for *Top Banana* (UA, 1954); *Li'l Abner* (Par., 1959); and *Stiletto* (Avco-Embassy, 1969).

Television. He designed costumes for *The World of Lerner and Loewe* (NBC, 1964); *The Enchanted Nutcracker* (ABC); The Adams Chronicles series (WNET, 1976); etc.

Other Activities. He has designed costumes for the NY World's Fair presentations of the Ford Motor Show (1939); for night clubs; and for industrial shows.

Awards. Mr. Colt received the Antoinette Perry (Tony) Award for his costume designs for *Pipe Dream* (1956).

COLT, ETHEL BARRYMORE.

Actress, singer. b. Apr. 30, 1912, Mamaroneck, N.Y., to Russell G. and Ethel Barrymore Colt. Father, stock broker; mother, actress. Attended Lenox Sch., N.Y.C.; Acad. of Notre Dame, Philadelphia, Pa.; Villa Gazzola, Verona, Italy; ext. divs. of Columbia and NY universities. Studied singing with Queena Mario, Povla Frijish, Emil Cooper, Rosalie Snyder and Maggie Teyte. Studied acting with Betty Cashman, Robert Lewis, Uta Hagen and Herbert Berghof. Relatives in theatre: mother, Ethel Barrymore, actress; grandparents, Maurice and Georgie Drew Barrymore; uncles, John and Lionel Barrymore and great-uncles John and Sidney Drew, actors; great-grandmother, Mrs. John Drew and great-great grandmother, Eliza Kinlock, actresses. Married Dec. 1, 1944, to Romeo Miglietta; one son, John Drew Miglietta, actor. Member of Actors Equity; AFTRA; AGMA; Natl. Board of Family Service Assn. of America (1972–75); Plays for Living (vice-chmn., 1976). Address: (home) 333 E. 68th St., New York, NY 10021; (bus.) Plays for Living, 44 E. 23rd St., New York, NY 10010, tel. (212) OR 4-6100.

Theatre. Miss Colt made her professional debut as Seraphine in *Scarlet Sister Mary* (Ethel Barrymore Th., N.Y.C., Nov. 25, 1930); and subsequently played the Fiancée in a national tour of *The Love Duel* (1931); Harriet in *Bittersweet* (St. Louis Municipal Opera, 1933) and Sydney in a regional production of *Bill of Divorcement* (Skowhegan, Me., 1933). She was Stephanie Pell in *Under Glass* (Ambassador, Oct. 30, 1933; Fanny Ellsler in L'Aiglon (Broadhurst, Nov. 3, 1934); appeared in *Cradle Song* (Broadhurst, 1934); played Grace Harkaway in *Lon-*

don Assurance, which she adapted and for which she wrote lyrics (Vanderbilt Th., Feb. 18, 1937); was Pheasant in *Whiteoaks* (Hudson Th., Mar. 23, 1938); and appeared with Judith Anderson in *Come of Age* (NY City Ctr., Jan. 23, 1952).

In addition to apparing on Bway during 1936–41, Miss Colt toured in stock with and was manager of the Jitney Players, playing roles in *The Little Foxes, Private Lives, Tonight or Never,* and *Tonight at 8:30.* She decided to become a singer and appeared throughout the US and Canada in opera, notably as Micaela in *Carmen* and Musetta in *La Bohème,* both with the Columbia Opera Co. (Baltimore, 1938). She sang with the NY City Opera as Lady Harriet in *Martha* (NY City Ctr., Feb. 22, 25, 26, 1944); as Violetta in *La Traviata* with the NY Opera Guild (1945–46); as Marguerite in *Faust* and again as Violetta in *La Traviata* with the Cincinnati Zoo Opera (1953). She performed in her one-woman show, *Curtains Up,* an evening of songs from American musicals (Th. de lys, 1957; Day Tuttles E. 74 St. Th., 1959), and toured with it (1962) in Austria, Italy, France and Germany for the US State Dept.

Miss Colt returned to the Bway stage as Christine Crane in *Follies* (Winter Garden, Apr. 4, 1971) and to the NY City Opera as the Duchess of Krackenthrop in *Daughter of the Regiment* (State Th., Sept. 7, 1975).

Since 1964, she has been executive producer of Plays for Living, producing one-act plays on social, health and educational problems.

Television. She appeared as Rosalinda in *Fledermaus* (NBC Opera, 1951).

COMDEN, BETTY. Playwright, lyricist, performer. b. May 3, 1919, Brooklyn, N.Y. to Leo and Rebecca (Sadvoransky) Comden. Attended Ethical Culture Sch., Brooklyn; Grad. Erasmus Hall H.S., Brooklyn; New York Univ., B.S. Married Jan. 4, 1942, to Steven Kyle, designer; one son, one daughter. Member of AEA; AFTRA; AGVA; ASCAP; WGA East; WGA West; SWG; Dramatists Guild (council member). Address: c/o Ronald S. Korecky, 300 Park Ave., New York, NY 10022.

Theatre. Miss Comden wrote, with Adolph Green, the lyrics and book for and played Claire in *On the Town* (Adelphi, Dec. 28, 1944). She collaborated with Mr. Green on all future works; they wrote the book and lyrics for *Billion Dollar Baby* (Alvin, Dec. 21, 1945); sketches and lyrics for *Two on the Aisle* (Mark Hellinger Th., July 19, 1951); lyrics for *Wonderful Town* (Winter Garden, Feb. 25, 1953); and *Peter Pan* (Winter Garden, Oct. 20, 1954); book and lyrics for *Bells Are Ringing* (Shubert, Nov. 29, 1956); and the lyrics for the songs in *Say, Darling* (ANTA, Apr. 3, 1958).

With Mr. Green, she appeared in N.Y.C. in the revue *A Party,* composed of songs and sketches from their previous works in Monday night performances (Cherry Lane, Nov. 10, Nov. 17, 1958), expanded into *A Party with Betty Comden and Adolph Green* (Golden, Dec. 23, 1958–Jan. 24, 1959; reopened, Apr. 16, 1959). She wrote, with Mr. Green, the lyrics for *Do Re Mi* (St. James, Dec. 26, 1960); the book and lyrics for *Subways Are for Sleeping* (St. James, Dec. 27, 1961); for *Fade-Out, Fade-In* (Mark Hellinger Th., May 26, 1964); the lyrics for *Hallelujah, Baby!* (Martin Beck Th., Apr. 26, 1967); the book for *Applause* (Palace, March 30, 1970); and lyrics for *Lorelei* (Palace, Jan. 27, 1974).

Films. Miss Comden wrote, in collaboration with Adolph Green, the screenplays for *Good News* (MGM, 1947), and *The Barkleys of Broadway* (MGM, 1949); screenplay and lyrics for *On the Town* (MGM, 1949); lyrics for *Take Me Out to the Ball Game* (MGM, 1949); screenplay and lyrics for *Singin' in the Rain* (MGM, 1952), *The Band Wagon* (MGM, 1953), and *It's Always Fair Weather* (MGM, 1955); screenplay for *Auntie Mame* (WB, 1958); lyrics and screenplay for *Bells Are Ringing* (MGM, 1960), and *What A Way to Go* (20th-Fox, 1964).

Night Clubs. Miss Comden first appeared in N.Y.C. as a member of *The Revuers,* a group (two other members were Adolph Green and Judy Holliday) who wrote and performed their own material at the Village Vanguard (1939), and later at the Rainbow Room, the Blue Angel (1940–44), and Cafe Society Downtown.

Awards. Miss Comden and Mr. Green received the Donaldson Award for their lyrics in *Wonderful Town* (1953); the Screen Writers Branch of WGA Award for *On the Town* (1949), *Singin' in the Rain* (1952), and *It's Always Fair Weather* (1955); *The Village Voice* Off-Bway (Obie) Award for *A Party with Betty Comden and Adolph Green* (1959); and the Antoinette Perry (Tony) Award for the lyrics in *Hallelujah, Baby!* (1968) and for the book of *Applause* (1970). *Wonderful Town* was awarded a Tony in 1953 as best musical play.

COMEGYS, KATHLEEN. Actress. b. Kathleen Foster Comegys, July 25, 1895, Shreveport, La., to Thomas M. and Elinor (Foster) Comegys. Father, dentist; mother, dramatic reader. Attended public schools, Shreveport; Sch. of Educ., Chicago, Ill. Relative in theatre: sister, Claiborne Foster, actress. Member of AEA; SAG (council, 1954–1956); AFTRA. Address: 2991 Cortez Blvd., Fort Myers, FL 33901, tel. (813) 334-8578.

Theatre. Miss Comegys made her professional debut in 1912 as Grace in a coast-to-coast touring production of *A Night Out;* made her N.Y.C. debut as Coquette in *Prunella* (Little Th., Oct. 27, 1913); played in Jessie Bonstelle's stock companies (Buffalo, N.Y.C., and Detroit, Mich., Summer 1914); in the touring company of *In the Vanguard* (Fall 1914); in stock companies in Portland, Me. (Spring 1915), and in San Francisco, Calif. (Alcazar Th., Summer 1915); succeeded (Nov. 1915) Claiborne Foster as Irma in *Abe and Mawruss* (Lyric, N.Y.C., Oct. 20, 1915), retitled *Potash and Perlmutter in Society* (Jan. 24, 1916); played in stock in Syracuse, N.Y. (Summer 1916); in the touring production of *Bosom Friends* (1917); in a touring production of *The Thirteenth Chair* (1917–18); in *Thirty Days* (Chicago, Ill., 1918–19); and as Ethel in *First Is Last* Maxine Elliott's Th., N.Y.C., Sept. 17, 1919).

Miss Comegys appeared as Peggy Gibbs in *The Famous Mrs. Fair* (Henry Miller's Th., Dec. 22, 1919), and on tour (1921); Grace Whiting in *The Man in the Making* (Hudson, Sept. 25, 1921); toured in vaudeville (1922); played stock in Harrisburg, Pa. (Summer 1922); appeared as Anne in the touring production of *The Dover Road* (Fall 1922); played in stock in Louisville, Ky. (1923); appeared as Leola in *Roseanne* (Greenwich Village Th., N.Y.C., Dec. 29, 1923); played stock in Russell Fillmore's stock company (Birmingham, Ala., 1924); played Sally Morgan in the touring production of *The Nervous Wreck* (1924); played stock in Omaha, Neb. (1925); appeared as Ann Harper in *Loose Ankles* (Biltmore, N.Y.C., Aug. 16, 1926); in stock engagements in Richmond, Va. (1927); in W. H. Wright's stock companies (Dayton, Ohio, 1928; Cincinnati, Ohio, 1929); and in Russell Fillmore's company (Birmingham, Ala., 1929). She played Alice Hale in the pre-Bway tryout of *Dread* 1929); and played stock in Birmingham, Ala. (1929–30). She played Sister Marcella in *The Cradle Song* (Westport Country Playhouse, Conn., Summer 1931–32).

Miss Comegys appeared as Mrs. Haron in *Chrysali* (Martin Beck Th., N.Y.C., Nov. 14, 1932); was the understudy to Eleanor Hicks in the role of Comfort Kirkland in *The Pursuit of Happiness* (Avon, Oct. 9, 1933); played another season at the Westport (Conn.) Country Playhouse (Summer 1934); Fairdy Tabor in *Tight Britches* (Avon, N.Y.C., Sept. 11, 1934); Mrs. Condos in *Lost Horizons* (St. James, Oct. 15, 1934); Mrs. Bane in *If This Be Treason* (Music Box, Sept. 23, 1935); succeeded (May 1936) Frances Williams as Ethel Frances in *Call It a Day* (Morosco, Jan. 28, 1935) and on tour; appeared as Sister Emmy in the pre-Bway tryout of *Love Is Not So Simple* (Fall 1935); played in stock at the Eastport (Conn.) Playhouse and the Westchester Playhouse (Mt. Kisco, N.Y., Summer 1936); appeared as Doris Garrison in *The Ghost of Yankee Doodle* (Guild, N.Y.C., Nov. 22, 1937); as Nellie (Granny) in the national touring production of *On Borrowed Time* (1938); played in stock at the Clinton (Conn.) Playhouse (Summer 1941); appeared as Miss Austin in *Craig's Wife* (Playhouse, N.Y.C., Feb. 12, 1947); played stock at the Lakewood Th. (Skowhegan, Me., Summer 1947); appeared as Mrs. Sampler in *The Silver Whistle* (Biltmore, N.Y.C., Nov. 24, 1948); as Mrs. Coade in the touring production of *Dear Brutus* (Summer 1949); as Aunt Lavinia in a touring production of *The Heiress* (Summer 1950); as Mrs. Tillman in *The Traveling Lady* (Playhouse, N.Y.C., Oct. 27, 1954); Mrs. Touchett in *Portrait of a Lady* (ANTA, Dec. 21, 1954); Mrs. Louisa Stoddard in *The Man in the Dog Suit* (Coronet, Oct. 30, 1958); and as Aunt Ev in *The Miracle Worker* (Playhouse, Oct. 19, 1959).

Films. Miss Comegys made her film debut as the doctor's wife, Mrs. Wilson, in *Birth of a Baby* (Jack H. Skirboll, 1938). She was Mrs. Sampler in *Mr. Belvedere Rings the Bell,* the film adaptation of *The Silver Whistle* (20th-Fox, 1951); appeared in *The First Time* (Col., 1952); and played Aunt Ev in *The Miracle Worker* (UA, 1962).

Television and Radio. On radio she performed on Theatre Guild on the Air (Jan. 18, 1953); Grand Central Station (Feb. 7, 1953); Aunt Jenny (March 27, 1953; Apr. 4–10, 1953; Apr. 16, 1953; July 11–16, 1953; Aug. 8–26, 1953); Woman with a Past (Feb. 11, 1954); Aunt Jenny (March 8, 9, 1954; Feb. 10, 11, 17, 1955); City Hospital (June 19, 1956); Star Matinee (Aug. 29, 1956); Nora Drake (Sept. 12, 1956); City Hospital (Dec. 20, 1956); Five-Star Matinee (Oct. 22, 1957); City Hospital (Oct. 24, 1957); Five-Star Matinee (Dec. 31, 1957); The Couple Next Door (Apr. 17, 1958); Five-Star Matinee (May 23, 1958); and The Couple Next Door (June 9, 1958).

Her television appearances include Studio One (CBS, Jan. 5, 1953); Goodyear (NBC, Feb. 1, 1953); Studio One (CBS, Mar. 23, 1953); Kraft Television Th. (NBC, May 8, 1953); Robert Montgomery Presents (NBC, May 21, 1953); Ethel and Albert (ABC, May 27, 1953); Hallmark Hall of Fame (NBC, June 4, 1953); Ethel and Albert (ABC, June 18, 1953); Goodyear Playhouse (NBC, June 27, 1953); Kraft Television Th. (NBC, July 29, 1953); Robert Montgomery Presents (NBC, Aug. 31, 1953); Kraft Television Th. (NBC, Sept. 23, 1953); Philco Television Playhouse (NBC, Nov. 29, 1953); Lamp Unto My Feet (CBS, Dec. 20, 1953); The World of Mr. Sweeney (NBC, Jan. 13, 1954); Armstrong Circle Th. (CBS, Jan. 19, 1954); Martin Kane (CBS, Jan. 28, 1954); Jaimie McPheeters (ABC, Feb. 8, 1954); Ethel and Albert (ABC, Feb. 20, 1954); Danger (CBS, Mar. 6, 1954); Kraft Television Th. (NBC, Mar. 24, 1954); Jaimie McPheeters (ABC, Mar. 29, 1954); Robert Montgomery Presents (NBC, Apr. 26, 1954); Brighter Day (CBS, June 5–Aug. 1, 1954); Concerning Miss Marlowe (Nov.–Dec. 1954; Jan. 5–May 20, 1955); Robert Montgomery Presents (NBC, Feb. 7, 1955); *His Honor, Judge Bell* (Feb. 25, 1955); Star Tonight (ABC, Sept. 15, 1955); Theatre Guild, US Steel Hour (CBS, Oct. 10, 1955); Star Stage; Star Tonight (Jan. 1956); General Electric Th. (CBS, Mar. 1956); The Goldbergs; G.E. Th. (CBS, Apr. 22, 1956); Armstrong Circle Th. (CBS, May 29, 1956); Kraft Television Th. (ABC, July 18, 1956); Look Up and Live (CBS, Sept. 2, 1956); Armstrong Circle Th. (CBS, Sept. 18, 1956); Lamp Unto My Feet (CBS, Oct. 7, 1956); Love of Life (CBS, Nov. 28, 1956); The Verdict Is Yours (CBS, Oct. 2, 1957); Matinee Th. (Nov. 15, 1957; Dec. 2, 1957); The Verdict Is Yours (CBS, Dec. 23, 1957); Suspicion (NBC, Mar. 10, 1958); Love of Life (CBS, May 2, 7, 16, 19, 1958); and The Investigator (June 3, 1958).

Recreation. Swimming, gardening, foreign travel.

COMPTON, FAY. Actress. b. Sept. 18, 1894, London, England, to Edward and Virginia (Bateman) Compton. Attended Leatherhead Court Sch., Surrey. Married to H. G. Pelissier (dec. 1913); married to Lauri de Frece (dec. 1921); married to Leon Quartermaine (marr. dis.); married to Ralph Michael (marr. dis.). Member of AEA; British AEA.

Theatre. Miss Compton made her debut in *Sir Philomir, or Love's Victory* (Royal Albert Hall, London, Jan. 10, 1906); subsequently appeared in *The Follies* (Apollo, Aug. 20, 1911); played Denise in *Who's the Lady?* (Garrick, Nov. 22, 1913); succeeded Iris Hoey (Mar. 1914) as Miranda Reploe in *The Pearl Girl* (Shaftesbury, Sept. 25, 1913); and played Cissie in *The Cinema Star* (Shaftesbury, June 4, 1914).

She made her Bway debut as Victoria in *Tonight's the Night* (Shubert, Dec. 24, 1914); then played Ruth Wilson in *The Only Girl* (Apollo, London, Sept. 25, 1915); Lady Di in *Follow the Crowd* (Empire, Feb. 19, 1916); Virginia Xelva in *The Boomerang* (Queen's, May 11, 1916); Annabel in *Innocent and Annabel* (Coliseum, June 26, 1916); Lucy White in *The Professor's Love Story* (Savoy, Sept. 7, 1916); Annette in *The Bells* (Savoy, May 19, 1917); Sheila West in *Sheila* (St. James's, June 7, 1917); Helen Bransby in *The Invisible Foe* (Savoy, Aug. 23, 1917); the title role in *Peter Pan* (New, Dec. 24, 1917); Blanche Wheeler in *Fair and Warmer* (Prince of Wales's, May 14, 1918); Sylvia in *The Harbury Pearls* (Victoria Palace, Dec. 1, 1918); Violet Little in *Caesar's Wife* (Royalty, Mar. 27, 1919); Silvia in *Summertime* (Royalty, Oct. 30, 1919); The Wife in *Tea for Three* (Haymarket, Feb. 3, 1920); and the title role in *Mary Rose* (Haymarket, Apr. 22, 1920).

At a special performance, Miss Compton played Juliet in the Balcony Scene from *Romeo and Juliet* (His Majesty's, Nov. 1920); appeared as Elizabeth in *The Circle* (Haymarket, Mar. 3, 1921); Phoebe Throssel in *Quality Street* (Haymarket, Aug. 11, 1921); both Mary and Lady Carlton in *Secrets* (Comedy, Sept. 7, 1922); Loyse in *The Ballad Monger* (His Majesty's, Feb. 26, 1923); Princess Flavia in *The Prisoner of Zenda* (Haymarket, Aug. 23, 1923); Lady Babbie in *The Little Minister* (Queen's, Nov. 8, 1923); Diana Tunstall in *The Claimant* (Queen's, Sept. 11, 1924); and Madeleine in *Orange Blossom* (Queen's, Dec. 4, 1924).

Miss Compton played Ophelia in *Hamlet* (Haymarket, Feb. 19, 1925); Ariadne Winter in *Ariadne, or Business First* (Haymarket, Apr. 22, 1925); The Lady in *The Man with a Load of Mischief* (Haymarket, June 16, 1925); the title role in *Mary Rose* (Haymarket, Jan. 21, 1926); Crawford in *This Woman Business* (Haymarket, Apr. 15, 1926); Jenny Bell in *The White Witch* (Haymarket, Sept. 29, 1926); Julie in *Liliom* (Duke of York's, Dec. 23, 1926); Constance Middleton in *The Constant Wife* (Strand, Apr. 6, 1927); Lisa Mordaunt in *The Bridge* (Arts, May 31, 1927); Gianella in *The Wandering Jew* (Drury Lane, May 23, 1927); La Femme de Chambre in *Other Men's Wives* (St. Martin's, Apr. 9, 1928); and Suzanne de Tournai in *The Scarlet Pimpernel* (Palace, May 14, 1928).

Miss Compton played the title role in *Olympia* (Empire, N.Y.C., Oct. 16, 1928); Mary Marlowe in *Secrets* (Comedy, London, Sept. 16, 1929); toured as Julia March in *Virtue for Sale* (Jan. 1930); Madeleine Cary in *Dishonoured Lady* (Playhouse, May 8, 1930); the title role of the pantomime, *Dick Whittington* (Palace, Manchester, Dec. 1930); Fanny Grey in *Autumn Crocus* (Lyric, London, Apr. 6, 1931); and Ophelia in *Hamlet* (Haymarket, May 3, 1931).

In Glasgow, Scotland, she repeated the title role in *Dick Whittington* (Th. Royal, Dec. 1931); toured in *Autumn Crocus;* appeared as Camilla Graham in *Once a Husband* (Haymarket, London, Oct. 26, 1932); the title role in *Dick Whittington* (London Hippodrome, Dec. 26, 1932); toured in the revue *This, That and the Other* (Mar. 1933); played Norma Matthews in *Proscenium* (Globe, June 14, 1933); Christina in *Indoor Fireworks* (Aldwych, Mar. 29, 1934); Mary Ventyre in *Murder in Mayfair* (Globe, Sept. 5, 1934); The Duchess of Shires in *Harvey House* (His Majesty's, May 17, 1935); Titania in *A Midsummer Night's Dream* (Open Air Th., July 30, 1935); Rosaline in *Love's Labour's Lost* (Open Air Th., Sept. 3, 1935); and Dorothy Hilton in *Call It a Day* (Globe, Oct. 30, 1935).

She appeared at the Open Air Th. as Titania in *A Midsummer Night's Dream* (June 21, 1937), Calpurnia in *Julius Caesar* (July 5, 1937), The Lady in *Comus* (July 19, 1937), and Paulina in *The Winter's Tale* (Aug. 2, 1937); toured Australia and New Zealand in the title role in *Victoria Regina* in *Tonight at 8:30,* and as Margaret in *George and Margaret* (1937–38). She played Robin Hood in *Babes in the Wood* (Drury Lane, London, Dec. 23, 1939); performed music hall songs at the Coliseum (Feb. 1939); played Mrs. Philips in *Drawing Room* (Golder's Green; Streatham Hill, Mar.–June 1939); Ophelia in *Hamlet* (Lyceum, June 28, 1939), which she repeated at Elsinore Castle (Den., June–July, 1939); toured as Sanchia Carson in *Robert's Wife* (Aug. 1939); appeared as Regan in *King Lear* (Old Vic, London, Apr. 15, 1940); toured as the Virgin Mary in *Family Portrait* (June 1940), and as Doris Gow in *Fumed Oak* (1940).

Miss Compton played the Prince in the pantomime, *Cinderella* (Palace, Manchester, Dec. 1940); Ruth in *Blithe Spirit* (Piccadilly, London, July 2, 1941); Regina Giddens in *The Little Foxes* (Piccadilly, Oct. 21, 1942); the Prince in *Cinderella* (Stoll, Dec. 24, 1942); toured as Madame Sans-Gene in *The Duchess of Dantzig* (1943); Hannah Kernahan in *The Last of Summer* (Phoenix, London, June 7, 1944); and Martha Dacre in *No Medals* (Vaudeville, Oct. 4, 1944).

On a tour of Belgium, Holland, France, and Switzerland, she played Emilia in *Othello,* the title role in *Candida,* and Ophelia in *Hamlet* (Sept. 1946); portrayed Emilia in *Othello* (Piccadilly, London, Mar. 26, 1947); the title role in *Candida* (Piccadilly, Mar. 27, 1947); the Virgin Mary in *Family Portrait* (Strand, Feb. 17, 1948); Gina Ekdal in *The Wild Duck* (St. Martin's, Nov. 3, 1948); Sister Mary Bonaventure in *Bonaventure* (Vaudeville, Dec. 6, 1949); Yvonne in *Intimate Relations* (Arts, Mar. 21, 1951); Lora Sutherland in *Red Letter Day* (Garrick, Feb. 21, 1952); Esther Ledoux in *The Holy Terrors* (Arts, Nov. 20, 1952); and Martha in *Out of the Whirlwind* (Westminster Abbey, June 10, 1953).

With the Old Vic Co., at the Edinburgh Scot. Festival, she appeared as Gertrude in *Hamlet* (Summer 1953); repeated the role of Gertrude in *Hamlet* (Old Vic, London, Sept. 14, 1953); played the Countess of Rossillion in *All's Well That Ends Well* (Old Vic, Sept. 15, 1953); Constance of Bretagne in *King John* (Old Vic, Oct. 27, 1953); Volumnia in *Coriolanus* (Old Vic, Feb. 23, 1954); Juno in *The Tempest* (Old Vic, Apr. 13, 1954); Gertrude Blunt in *Witch Errant* ("Q," Sept. 7, 1954); toured as Ruth Prendergast in *Tabitha* (Sept. 1955), and as Lydia Sheridan in *Starlight* (Mar. 1956); played Queen Margaret in *Richard III* (Old Vic, London, May 29, 1957); toured as Mrs. St. Maugham in *The Chalk Garden* (Jan. 1958); Kate Murphy in *God and Kate Murphy* (54th St. Th., N.Y.C., Feb. 26, 1959); Lady Bracknell in *The Importance of Being Earnest* (Old Vic, Oct. 13, 1959); and the Comtesse de la Briere in *What Every Woman Knows* (Old Vic, Apr. 12, 1960).

She appeared at the Chichester Festival as Grausis in *The Broken Heart* (July 9, 1962) and Marya in *Uncle Vanya* (July 16, 1962); played Mrs. Malaprop in *The Rivals* (Lyric, Hammersmith, London, Apr. 24, 1963); appeared again at the Chichester Festival, repeating her performance as Marya in *Uncle Vanya* (July 1, 1963), and Mrs. Boocock in *The Workhouse Donkey* (July 8, 1963); and toured (Sept. 1963) as Mrs. Caution in *The Gentleman Dancing Master.* She also played in the premiere production at the Yvonne Arnaud Th., Guildford, Eng., as Anna Semyonovna Yslaeva in *A Month in the Country* (June 2, 1965), repeating this performance in London (Cambridge Th., Sept. 23, 1965); and was the Chorus in *Samson Agonistes* (Yvonne Arnaud Th., June 16, 1965).

Films. Miss Compton's films include *A Woman of No Importance* (Selznick, 1922); *The Old Wives' Tale* (Ideal, 1922); *Diana of the Crossways* (Ideal, 1922); *This Freedom* (Fox, 1923); *The Loves of Mary, Queen of Scots* (Ideal, 1923); *Claude Duval* (Gaumont, 1924); *Happy Ending* (Gaumont, 1925); *Settled Out of Court* (Gaumont, 1925); *Somehow Good* (Pathe, 1927); *Cape Forlorn* (Wardour, 1931); *Tell England* (Wardour, 1931); *The Eleventh Commandment* (AP, 1938); *A Bill of Divorcement* (RKO, 1940); *So This Is London* (20th-Fox, 1940); *The Prime Minister* (WB, 1941); *Nicholas Nickleby* (U, 1947); *Odd Man Out* (U, 1947); *Sin of Esther Waters* (Intl. Releasing, 1951); *Laughter in Paradise* (Stratford, 1951); *Lady Possessed* (Rep., 1952); *Othello* (UA, 1955); and *The Virgin and the Gypsy* (Chevron, 1970).

Television. Miss Compton appeared in a segment of Our Man at St. Mark's (Rediffusion, London, England, July 5, 1965); was in *Uncle Vanya* (NET Playhouse, Feb. 10, 1967); appeared in the series Sanctuary (Rediffusion, London, 1967–68); and was Aunt Ann in *The Forsythe Saga* (BBC-2, 1967).

Published Works. Miss Compton wrote *Rosemary* (1926), a book of reminiscenses.

Recreation. Golf, tennis.

CONKLE, E. P. Playwright, educator. b. Ellsworth Prouty Conkle, July 10, 1899, Peru, Nebr., to Elza and Mary Estella Conkle. Grad. Univ. of Nebraska (A.B. 1921; A.M. 1923); Univ. of Iowa, Ph.D. 1936; first Ph.D. in playwriting granted in the US. Studied in George Pierce Baker's 47 Workshop, Yale Univ., 1926–28; awarded Guggenheim Fellowship, 1929–30; Rockefeller Fellowships, 1934–36. Married July 19, 1934, to Virginia McNeal; one son, one daughter. Member of ATA, Southwest Th. Assn.; Dramatists Guild. Address: (home) 510 Cater Drive, Austin, TX 78704, tel. (512) HI 2-7683; (bus.) The University of Texas, Austin, TX 78712.

Since 1946, Mr. Conkle has been professor of drama at the Univ. of Texas, where he has been a member of the faculty since 1939. Previously, he was assistant professor of speech and drama at the Univ. of Iowa (1937–39); assistant professor of English at the Univ. of Delaware (1928–29); and instructor in English at the Univ. of North Dakota (1923–26).

He has taught drama at the Banff School of Fine Arts, Canada, during summer sessions (1945–49; 1954–60).

Mr. Conkle wrote *200 Were Chosen* (48 St. Th., N.Y.C., Nov. 20, 1936); *Prologue to Glory* (Maxine Elliott's Th., Mar. 17, 1938); *Afternoon Storm* (Maxine Elliott's Th., Apr. 11, 1948); and *Don't Lose Your Head* (Saville, London, Eng., Aug. 5, 1950).

Television and Radio. Mr. Conkle wrote a half-hour weekly radio series, Honest Abe (CBS, 1940–41). His play, *Prologue to Glory,* has been produced on radio and on television, including Theatre Guild of the Air (Feb. 10, 1946; May 11, 1952); Cavalcade of America (Feb. 7, 1950); and Kraft Television Th. (NBC, May 2, 1952).

Published Works. His published plays include *In the Shadow of a Rock; Five Plays* consisting of *Paul and the Blue Ox, The Delectable Judge, Bill and the Widowmaker, Johnny Appleseed,* and *49 Dogs in the Meathouse;* Minnie Field; Sparkin'; Madge; Chickadee; Hawk a-Flyin'; Gold Is Where You Don't Find It; Afternoon Storm; China-Handled Knife; Muletail Prime; The Least One; Arbie, the Bug Boy; Poor Old Bongo; No More Wars But the Moon; The Reticent One; Son-of-a-Biscuit-Eater; Heaven Is Such a Long Time to Wait; Granny's Little Cheery Room; Kitten in the Elm Tree; Lavender Gloves; No Time for Heaven; and two collections, *Crick Bottom Plays* and *Loolie and Other Plays.* .

Awards. Mr. Conkle received an honorary degree of D.Litt. from the Univ. of Nebraska in 1970.

CONKLIN, PEGGY. Actress. b. Margaret Eleanor Conklin, Nov. 2, 1912, Dobbs Ferry, N.Y., to George and Gertrude (Pfeil) Conklin. Grad. Dobbs Ferry Sch. Married Aug. 7, 1935, to James D. Thompson, advertising executive; one son, one daughter. Member of AEA; AFTRA; SAG. Address: 142 E. 71st St., New York, NY 10021, tel. (212) RH 4-6396.

Theatre. Miss Conklin made her N.Y.C. debut in the chorus of *Treasure Girl* (Alvin Th., Nov. 8, 1928); subsequently appeared in *The Little Show* (Music Box, Apr. 30, 1929); as Mitzi in *His Majesty's Car* (Ethel Barrymore Th., Oct. 23, 1930); Yvonne in *Purity* (Ritz, Dec. 25, 1930); Elinor Murphy in *Old Man Murphy* (Royale, May 18, 1931); Helen Wilson in *Hot Money* (George M. Cohan Th., Nov. 17, 1931); Christine Galvosier in *Mademoiselle*

(Playhouse, Oct. 18, 1932); Phyllis Blakely in *The Party's Over* (Vanderbilt, Mar. 27, 1933); Peggy Winston in *The Ghost Writer* (Masque, June 19, 1933); and Prudence Kirkland in *The Pursuit of Happiness* (Avon, Oct. 9, 1933), repeating the role in the London production (Vaudeville, May 30, 1934).

She played Gabby Maple in *The Petrified Forest* (Broadhurst, N.Y.C., Jan. 7, 1935); played Hattie La Forge in *Co-respondent Unknown* (Ritz, Feb. 11, 1936); Ellen Murray in *Yes, My Darling Daughter* (Playhouse, Feb. 9, 1937); Portsmouth Jones in *Casey Jones* (Fulton, Feb. 19, 1938); Josie Swan in *Miss Swan Expects* (Cort, Feb. 20, 1939); Mrs. North in *Mr. and Mrs. North* (Belasco, Jan. 12, 1941); and Annabelle Hallock in *Feathers in a Gale* (Music Box, Dec. 21, 1943). Miss Conklin played Alice in *Alice in Arms* (National, Jan. 31, 1945), which had, on its pre-Bway tryout, been titled *Star in the Window*, a production in which she played Jo. In 1947, she played in stock appearing as Georgina Allerton in *Dream Girl* (Berkshire Playhouse, Stockbridge, Mass.), and as Lucy Gade in *Act of Darkness* (Theatre-in-the-Dale, New Milford, Conn.).

She played Martha in *The Wisteria Trees* (Martin Beck Th., N.Y.C., Mar. 29, 1950); Flo Owens in *Picnic* (Music Box, Feb. 19, 1953); Olivia Brown in a stock production of *O Mistress Mine* (Berkshire Playhouse, Stockbridge, Mass., July 1955); and Edith Simms in *Howie* (46 St. Th., N.Y.C., Sept. 19, 1958).

Films. Miss Conklin has appeared in *The President Vanishes* (Par., 1934); *One Way Ticket* (Col., 1935); *Her Master's Voice* (Par., 1936); *The Devil Is a Sissy* (MGM, 1936); and *Having Wonderful Time* (RKO, 1938).

Television and Radio. On radio she has performed on the US Steel Hour (CBS); on such programs as *Pride and Prejudice* (Nov. 18, 1945); *Second Man* (Feb. 3, 1946); and *The Male Animal* (Jan. 12, 1947). She also played on Big Sister and Grand Central Station. On television she has appeared in *Years of Grace* (Elgin Hour, ABC, Feb. 11, 1955); and *Years Ago* (Dupont, NBC, 1960).

Recreation. Tennis, sailing, music.

CONNELL, GORDON. Actor, musical director, dramatic coach, pianist. b. William Gordon Connell, Mar. 19, 1923, Berkeley, Calif., to Charles James and Mamie (Smith) Connell. Father and mother, teachers. Grad. Berkeley (Calif.) H.S., 1939; Univ. of California, B.A. 1946; attended New York Univ., 1956–61; studied musicology at Univ. of California with Dr. Manfred Bukofzer; drama with Fred and Mary Harris, Henry Schnitzler. Married Aug. 15, 1948, to Jane Bennett, actress (known as Jane Connell): two daughters. Member of AEA; AFTRA; SAG; AFM, Local 802; Dramatic Honor Societies at Univ. of California; Hammer and Coffin, College Humor Society.

Pre-Theatre. Salesman, window dresser.

Theatre. Mr. Connell first performed on stage in San Francisco, Calif., with the Straw Hat Revue Co. (June 1947), also serving as composer and musical director for 10 productions.

He was performer, composer, and musician for *49th State Revue* (Roosevelt H.S., Honolulu, Hawaii, Apr. 1948); appeared in *Out of Order* (Las Palmas, Hollywood, Calif., Feb. 1949); and toured in *One Thing After Another* (Summer 1953); was a pianist for a touring production of *Where's Charley* (Aug. 1956); rehearsal pianist and performer in revues and musical comedy (Tamiment Th., Pa., May–Sept. 1957); pianist and performer in musical tent productions of *Oklahoma! The King and I, The Mikado, Happy Hunting, Girl Crazy* and *Rose Marie* (Musical Tents, Flint and Detroit, Mich., June 1958); assistant musical director of nine productions at the Sacramento (Calif.) Music Circus (June 1959), in which he also performed; played the King in *All Kinds of Giants* (John Drew Th., East Hampton, L.I., N.Y., June–July 1961); toured with a Chevrolet Industrial Show (Aug.–Sept. 1961); and made his Bway debut as Mr. Pitman in *Subways Are for Sleeping* (St. James, Dec. 27, 1961). He appeared as Dr. Kitchell in *Bells Are Ringing* and Percival Browne in *The Boy Friend* (Sheraton-Palace Dinner Th., San Francisco, Calif., Summer 1962); toured as pianist and performer in Celeste Holm's concert production, *With Love and Laughter* (Nov. 1962).

He was musical director for *Young Tom Jefferson* (Greenwich News Th., N.Y.C., Apr. 1963); and for *Put It in Writing* (Th. de Lys, May 13, 1963); appeared as the Judge and was understudy to David Burns in the role of Horace Vandergelder in *Hello, Dolly! (St. James, Jan. 16, 1964); was Mr. Peachum in The Beggar's Opera* (Chelsea Th. Ctr. of Brooklyn, Acad. of Music, Mar. 21, 1972); and Phi-Chi in *Lysistrata* (Brooks Atkinson Th., N.Y.C., Nov. 13, 1972).

Films. Mr. Connell appeared in the documentary, *Primer for Survival* (Robert Saudek Productions, 1963).

Television and Radio. He first appeared on radio as Billy Sherwood in the serial, Hawthorne House (NBC, Sept. 1943), and, on the same network, played a variety of roles in Standard Sch. Broadcast, a weekly series (Spring 1944).

He made his television debut as a pianist in *Son of Four Below* (Eye on New York, Dec. 1956); appeared on Kraft Television Th. (NBC, May 1957; Nov. 1957); as accompanist-performer on the Garry Moore Show (CBS, July 1957); as pianist-accompanist on the Jack Paar Show (NBC, Nov. 1958; Dec. 1959); on the Ed Sullivan Show (CBS, Jan. 1962); and on *As Caesar Sees It* (ABC, 1962).

Night Clubs. He has appeared in the *Jane and Gordon Connell* act at the Purple Onion (San Francisco, Calif., Feb. 1, 1954); at Le Ruban Bleu (N.Y.C., Mar. 1955); Number One Fifth Ave. (N.Y.C., Oct. 1955); the hungry i (San Francisco, Calif., Dec. 1955–Feb. 1956); in the act, *Four Below* at the Downstairs Room (N.Y.C., July 1956); *Son of Four Below* at the Downstairs Room (N.Y.C., Oct. 1956); *Take Five* at Downstairs at the Upstairs (N.Y.C., Oct. 1957); *Demi-Dozen* at the Upstairs at the Downstairs (N.Y.C., Sept. 1958); *Pieces of Eight* (Sept. 1959) and *Dressed to the Nines* (Sept. 1960), Upstairs at the Downstairs (N.Y.C.); and *Dime a Dozen* at Plaza 9 (Plaza Hotel, N.Y.C., June 1963).

Other Activities. Mr. Connell has also been active as a coach for musical comedy, revue, and night club performers.

Recreation. Decorating his own home.

CONNELL, JANE. Actress. b. Jane Sperry Bennett, Oct. 27, 1925, Oakland, Calif., to Louis Wesley and Mary (Sperry) Bennett. Father, attorney. Grad. Anna Head Sch., Berkeley, 1943; Univ. of California at Berkeley, B.A. 1946. Married Aug. 15, 1948 to (William) Gordon Connell, actor, musician; two daughters. Relatives in theatre: brothers, Louis W. Bennett, Jr., actor; and Jack Bennett, television writer. Member of AEA; AFTRA; AGVA; SAG; Kappa Alpha Theta; Mask and Dagger; Hammer and Dimmer; Thalian; Prytanean; Panile.

Theatre. From 1947–53, Miss Connell appeared in the intimate musical revues presented by Straw Hat-Revue company in the San Francisco (Calif.) Bay area and on tour (Westport, Conn.; Bucks County, Pa.; Skowhegan, Me.; Newport, R.I.; Boston, Mass.; Ogunquit, Me.; Los Angeles, Calif.; and Berkeley, Calif.; 1955).

She played in the Honolulu Community Theatre production of *The 49th State Revue* (Roosevelt H.S. Aud., Hawaii, Apr. 1948); in the Alice Ghostley roles in Leonard Sillman's *New Faces of 1952* (Music Circus, Sacramento, Calif., Summer 1954); appeared as a replacement for Beatrice Arthur in *Shoestring Revue* (President Th., N.Y.C., Apr., 1955); played Mrs. Peacham in *Threepenny Opera* (Th. de Lys, Sept. 20, 1955), returning to the role intermittently for seven yrs.; and appeared in *New Faces of '56* (Ethel Barrymore Th., June 14, 1956).

In stock, she performed in revues and musical comedies (Camp Tamiment, Pa., Summer 1957); appeared at the Flint and Detroit Music Tents. (Mich., Summer 1958) in the roles of Kate in *Girl Crazy;* Katisha in *The Mikado;* Aunt Eller in *Oklahoma!*, Maud in *Happy Hunting;* and Lady Jane in *Rose Marie;* at the Sacramento (Calif.) Music Circus, played Adelaide in *Guys and Dolls* (Summer 1959); Mammy Yokum in *L'il Abner;* Agnes Gooch in *Auntie Mame;* La Lume in *Kismet;* and Sue in *Bells Are Ringing.*

She appeared as Princess Winifred in *Once Upon a Mattress* (Adelphi, London, Eng., Sept., 1960); as Mrs. Spencer in the one-act musical, *The Oldest Trick in the World* (Martinique, N.Y.C., Feb. 20, 1961), part of a double bill called *Double Entry;* in stock, repeated her role in *Once Upon A Mattress* (Melody Fair, N. Tanawanda, N.Y., Aug. 1961); appeared as Christina, in the musical, *Fortuna* (Maidman, N.Y.C., Jan. 3, 1962); as Lovey Mars in *The Golden Apple* (York, Feb. 12, 1962; Summer 1962); at the Music Circus Sacramento (Calif.) played Mae Petersen in *Bye Bye Birdie;* Mrs. Spofford in *Gentlemen Prefer Blondes;* and Sue in *Bells Are Ringing;* and appeared as Mme. Dubonnet in *The Boy Friend* (Sheraton-Plaza Hotel, San Francisco, Calif., July–Aug. 1962); appeared in the revue, *Put It in Writing* (Th. de Lys, N.Y.C., May 3, 1963); and as Miss Ramphere in *The Peacock Season* (Playhouse-on-the Mall, Paramus, N.J., May 5, 1964).

Miss Connell played Queen Fredrika in *Royal Flush* (opened Shubert Th., New Haven, Conn., Dec. 31, 1964); which closed during its pre-Bway tryout (Shubert, Philadelphia, Jan. 23, 1965); Matilda Van Guilder in *Drat! The Cat!* (Martin Beck Th., N.Y.C., Oct. 10, 1965); Agnes Gooch in *Mame* (Winter Garden, May 24, 1966; and national company, opened Curran Th., San Francisco, Apr. 30, 1968); Gabrielle in *Dear World* (Mark Hellinger Th., Feb. 6, 1969); Mrs. Hardcastle in *She Stoops to Conquer* (Roundabout, Apr. 25, 1971); Widow Merryweather in *Drat!* (McAlpine Rooftop Th., Oct. 18, 1971); on a double bill, Mother in *After Magritte* and Mrs. Drudge in *The Real Inspector Hound* (Theatre Four, Apr. 23, 1972); appeared with the Long Wharf Th. (New Haven, Conn., 1971–72 season); played Gamma in *Lysistrata* (Brooks Atkinson Th., Nov. 13, 1972); and appeared in *Cyrano de Bergerac* (Ahmonson Th., Los Angeles, 1973–74 season).

Films. She made her film debut as Miss Maxton in *Ladybug, Ladybug* (UA, 1963); and played Mrs. Connolly in *Trilogy* (AA, 1969); Miss Roberts in *Kotch* (Cinerama, 1971); and Agnes Gooch in *Mame* (WB, 1974).

Television and Radio. From 1952–56, Miss Connell was known as the "sweetheart of musical comedy" in the San Francisco Standard School NBC radio shows. In 1947, she acted on the Standard Hour, broadcast from San Francisco Opera House; performed on 4 telecasts on the Stanley Show (ABC, 1956); Kraft Theatre (NBC, Sept., 1957); has made guest appearances on the Jack Paar Show (NBC, 1958) and Ed Sullivan Show (CBS, Jan. 1962). She has appeared in *Baby Love Dallas* (WNTA, Play-of-the-Week, 1960); *The Grass Harp;* NY Scrapbook (Jan., 1961); on *As Caesar Sees It* (ABC, 1962–63); The Nut House (CBS, 1964); Bewitched (ABC, 1967); and *A Nice Place to Visit* (NET, 1967).

Night Clubs. Miss Connell first appeared, with her husband, at The Purple Onion (San Francisco, Calif., Feb. 1954); has since appeared at Le Ruban Bleu (N.Y.C., Mar. 1955); Number One Fifth Avenue (N.Y.C., Oct. 1955); and the hungry i (San Francisco, Dec. 1955).

She has performed in 3 original revues at Upstairs at the Downstairs (N.Y.C.), and joined (July 1963) the cast of Julius Monk's *Dime a Dozen* (Plaza 9, N.Y.C.).

Discography. Miss Connell has recorded *New Faces of '56* (Victor, 1956); Demi-Dozen (Off Beat, 1958); Pieces of Eight (Off Beat, 1959); *Once Upon a Mattress* (London Cast, His Master's Voice, 1960); Mrs. Mister's role in Marc Blitzstein's *The Cradle Will Rock* (Spoken Arts, 1956); and sang Abbe's Spinning Song in *Johnny Johnson* (MGM, 1956).

Recreation. Family activities, housekeeping.

CONNELL, LEIGH. Producer. b. May 5, 1926, Wartrace, Tenn., to Maurice L. and Elizabeth (Chamberlain) Connell. Father, physician. Grad. Wartrace (Tenn.) H.S., 1944; Southwestern at Memphis, B.A. 1949; attended Columbia Univ., 1950–51; George Peabody Coll., M.A., 1961–62. Member of Sigma Alpha Epsilon. Address: Wartrace, TN.

Theatre. Mr. Connell began as an assistant to the producer, Walter P. Chrysler, Jr., in his productions of *The Hanging Judge* (Globe Th., London, Sept. 23, 1952); *Camino Real* (National, N.Y.C., Mar. 19, 1953); and *The Strong Are Lonely* (Broadhurst, Sept. 29, 1953). From 1955–61, Mr. Connell was producer, with José Quintero and Theodore Mann, of the Circle in the Square (N.Y.C.), and has served as assistant director, and casting director.

Productions with which Mr. Connell was associated at the Circle in the Square include *La Ronde* (June 27, 1955), *The King and the Duke* (1955), *The Cradle Song* (Dec. 1, 1955), *The Iceman Cometh* (May 8, 1956), *Children of Darkness* (Feb. 28, 1958), *Our Town* (Mar. 23, 1959), and *The Balcony* (Mar. 3, 1960).

Messrs. Connell, Mann, and Quintero produced *Long Day's Journey into Night* (Helen Hayes Th., N.Y.C., Nov. 7, 1956), and on tour (opened Hanna, Cleveland, Ohio, Dec. 13, 1957; closed Biltmore, Los Angeles, Calif., May 17, 1958), and with Messrs. Quintero and Hugh Beaumont, produced the London production (Globe, Sept. 24, 1958).

Other Activities. Since 1962, Mr. Connell has been an instructor at George Peabody Coll. (Nashville, Tenn.).

Awards. With Messrs. Mann and Quintero, he received an Antoinette Perry (Tony) Special Award (1957) for their production of *Long Day's Journey into Night.*

Recreation. Music.

CONNELLY, MARC. Playwright, actor, director, educator. b. Marcus Cook Connelly, Dec. 13, 1890, McKeesport, Pa., to Patrick Joseph and Mabel Louise Connelly. Attended Trinity Hall, Washington, Pa. Member of Dramatists Guild (council member, since 1920); ALA; AEA; AFTRA; SAG; The Players; Natl. Institute of Arts and Letters (pres., 1953–56); Savage Club (London, Eng.). Address: 25 Central Park West, New York, NY 10023, tel. (212) CI 7-2147.

Pre-Theatre. Reporter for the Pittsburgh *Gazette-Times* and other newspapers.

Theatre. Mr. Connelly was first engaged on Bway as the writer of lyrics for *The Amber Express* (Globe Th., Sept. 19, 1916); subsequently wrote a revised version of *Erminie* (Park, Jan. 3, 1921); in collaboration with George S. Kaufman, wrote *Dulcy* (Frazee, Aug. 13, 1921); *To the Lawies* (Liberty, Feb. 20, 1922); *The '49ers* (Punch and Judy, Nov. 7, 1922); *Merton of the Movies* (Cort, Nov. 13, 1922); the book for *Helen of Troy, New York* (Selwyn, June 19, 1923); *The Deep Tangled Wildwood* (Frazee, Nov. 5, 1923); *Beggar on Horseback* (Broadhurst, Feb. 12, 1924); and *Be Yourself* (Harris, Sept. 3, 1924).

He wrote *The Wisdom Tooth* (Little, Feb. 15, 1926); collaborated with Herman J. Mankiewicz in writing *The Wild Man of Borneo,* which he also staged (Bijou, Sept. 13, 1927); *The Green Pastures,* which he directed (Mansfield, Feb. 26, 1930); with Frank B. Elser, wrote and directed *The Farmer Takes a Wife,* adapted from the novel *Rome Haul* by Walter D. Edmonde (46 St. Th., Oct. 30, 1934); directed *Till the Cows Come Home* (St. Martin's, London, Eng., 1936); directed and, with Bela Blau, produced *Having Wonderful Time* (Lyceum, N.Y.C., Feb. 20, 1937); and *The Two Bouquets* (Windsor, May 31, 1938); with Arnold Sundgaard, wrote and directed *Everywhere I Roam* which he reproduced with Bela Blau (National, Dec. 29, 1938).

He staged *The Happiest Days* (Vanderbilt, Apr. 11, 1939); wrote and staged *The Flowers of Virtue* (Royale, Feb. 5, 1942); made his first N.Y. appearance as an actor in the role of the Stage Manager in *Our Town* (NY City Ctr., Jan. 10, 1944; New, London, England, Apr. 30, 1946); directed and, with Jean Dalrymple, produced *Hope for the Best* (Fulton, N.Y.C., Feb. 7, 1945); wrote and directed *Story for Strangers* (Royale, Sept. 21, 1948); directed *The Green Pastures* (Bway, Mar. 15, 1951); wrote and directed *Hunter's Moon* (Winter Garden, London, England, Feb. 26, 1958); and appeared as Charles Osman in *Tall Story* (Belasco, N.Y.C., Jan. 29, 1959).

Films. Mr. Connelly has written the screenplays for *Cradle Song* (Par., 1933); *Captains Courageous* (MGM, 1934); and *I Married a Witch* (Par., 1936). He appeared as Father Hussman in *The Spirit of St. Louis* (WB, 1957); and Charles in *Tall Story* (WB, 1960).

Television. His play *The Green Pastures* was presented on Hallmark Hall of Fame (NBC, Oct. 1957).

Mr. Connelly has appeared in segments of The Defenders (CBS); New York Illustrated (NBC); The Trials of O'Brien (CBS); played Davenport in *The Borgia Stick* (NBC); and has made guest appearances on the Today Show (NBC); and the Merv Griffin Show (Ind.).

Other Activities. He was professor of playwriting at the Yale Univ. Sch. of Drama (1946–50); and since 1948, has conducted seminars and lectures at universities and colleges.

Published Works. Mr. Connelly wrote *A Souvenir from Qam* (Holt, Rinehart, and Winston, July 1965); and *Voice Offstage* (Holt, Rinehart, and Winston, Nov. 1968).

Awards. Mr. Connelly received the Pulitzer Prize (1930) for *The Green Pastures;* and O. Henry short story awards (1930) for *Coroner's Inquest.* He received the honorary degree of Litt.D. from Bowdoin College (1952), and from Baldwin-Wallace College (1962).

CONNOR, WHITFIELD. Actor. b. Dec. 3, 1916, Rathdowney, Ireland, to James and Eleanor (Wilde) Connor. Father, engineer. Grad. Lincoln H.S., Ferndale, Mich., 1935; Wayne Univ. B.A. 1940; Univ. of Michigan, M.A. 1941. Married 1956 to Haila Stoddard, actress and producer. Served USCG Reserve, 1942-46; rank, Lt. Member of AFTRA; SAG; AEA; Council of Stock Theatres (pres., 1968–72). Address: 5 Ladder Hill Road South, Weston, CT 06880, tel. (203) 227-8227.

Theatre. Mr. Connor made his debut as Horatio in Maurice Evans' GI version of *Hamlet* (Columbus Circle Th., N.Y.C., Dec. 13, 1945); subsequently played Antonio Bologna in *The Duchess of Malfi* (Ethel Barrymore Th., Oct. 15, 1946); Lt. Aengus Macogue in *Kathleen* (Mansfield, Feb. 3, 1948); Macduff in Michael Redgrave's *Macbeth* (Natl., Mar. 31, 1948); David Browning in *The Winner* (Playhouse, Feb. 17, 1954); succeeded Arthur O'-Connell in the role of Will Harrison in *Lunatics and Lovers* (Broadhurst, Dec. 13, 1954).

He appeared as the Father in *Six Characters in Search of an Author* (Phoenix, Dec. 11, 1955); the Suitor in *The Makropolous Secret* (Phoenix, Dec. 3, 1957); Victor Milgrim in *The Disenchanted* (Coronet, Dec. 3, 1958); Mr. Newton in *There Was a Little Girl* (Cort, Feb. 29, 1960); Chuck in *Everything in the Garden* (Plymouth, Nov. 29, 1967); and Thomas A. Morgan in *In the Matter of J. Robert Oppenheimer* (Vivian Beaumont Th., Mar. 6, 1969). In addition, he played in six seasons of stock at Elitch Gardens (Denver, Colo., Summer), where he has been producer since 1964, and has made tours of summer theatres in *Janus* and *The Complaisant Lover.*

Films. Mr. Connor has appeared in *Tap Roots* (U, 1948); *The Scarlet Angel* (U, 1952); *The President's Lady* (20th-Fox, 1953); *Prince of Pirates* (Col., 1953); *City of Bad Men* (20th-Fox, 1953); *The Saracen Blade* (Col., 1954); and *Butterfield 8* (MGM, 1960).

Television. Mr. Connor has appeared on the programs Omnibus (CBS), Studio One (CBS), and The Guiding Light (CBS). He was spokesman for Gulf Oil Corp. (1960–64).

Radio. He made his radio debut while a student at Wayne Univ., on The Lone Ranger (Station WXYZ, 1937).

Awards. Mr. Conner received the *Theatre World* Award (1948) for his performance as Macduff in *Macbeth.*

Recreation. Tennis, swimming, reading, Irish poetry.

CONREID, HANS. Actor. b. 1917, Baltimore, Md., to Hans, Jr., and Edith Conreid. Grad. H.S. of Commerce, N.Y.C., 1935; attended Columbia Univ. Married 1942 to Margaret; two sons, two daughters. Served US Army, program director Armed Forces Radio in occupied Japan. Member of AEA; SAG; AFTRA. Address: c/o Sid Gold Agency, 8961 Sunset Blvd., Hollywood, CA 90048.

Theatre. Mr. Conreid made his Bway debut as Boris Adzinidzinadze in *Can-Can* (Sam S. Shubert Th., May 8, 1953); subsequently played Leon Solomon in *Tall Story* (Belasco, Jan. 29, 1959); appeared in *70, Girls, 70* (Broadhurst, Apr. 15, 1971); and succeeded George S. Irving (June 1974) as Madame Lucy in *Irene* (Minskoff, N.Y.C.; and on national tour, opened Aerie Crown Th., Chicago, Sept. 13, 1974; closed Shubert, Boston, May 3, 1974).

Mr. Conreid's extensive appearances in summer stock and touring productions include *Absence of a Cello* (Summer 1965); *Generation* (Jan.–Apr. 1967); *Take Her, She's Mine* (Summer 1968); *Don't Drink the Water* (Summer 1968); *Spofford!* (Sept. 1969 –Mar. 1970); *Critic's Choice; Tall Story; The Pleasure of His Company;* and *How the Other Half Loves* (Winter 1974).

Films. His appearances in films include *Dramatic School* (MGM, 1938); *It's a Wonderful World* (MGM, 1939); *Dulcy* (MGM, 1940); *Week-End for Three* (RKO, 1941); *Nightmare* (UI, 1942); *The Wife Takes a Flyer* (Col., 1942); *Journey into Fear* (RKO, 1942); *The Big Street* (RKO, 1942); *A Lady Takes a Chance* (RKO, 1942); *Hitler's Children* (RKO, 1943); *Hostages* (Par., 1943); *Crazy House* (UI, 1943); *Mrs. Parkington* (MGM, 1944); *Passage to Marseilles* (WB, 1944); *The Senator Was Indiscreet* (UI, 1947); *Variety Time* (RKO, 1948); narrated *Design for Death* (RKO, 1948); played in *My Friend Irma* (Par., 1949); *Summer Stock* (MGM, 1950); *Nancy Goes to Rio* (MGM, 1950); *Too Young to Kiss* (MGM, 1951); *Rich, Young and Pretty* (MGM, 1951); *Behave Yourself* (RKO, 1951); *Big Jim McLain* (WB, 1952); *Three for Bedroom C* (WB, 1952); *The World in His Arms* (UI, 1952); *The Twonky* (UA, 1952); *The 5000 Fingers of Dr. T* (Col., 1953); supplied the voices of Mr. Darling and Captain Hook in *Peter Pan* (RKO, 1953); appeared in *Siren of Bagdad* (Col., 1953); *The Affairs of Dobie Gillis* (MGM, 1953); *Davy Crockett, King of the Wild Frontier* (BV, 1955); *You're Never Too Young* (Par., 1955); *Birds and the Bees* (Par., 1956); *Bus Stop* (20th-Fox, 1956); *The Monster that Challenged the World* (UA, 1957); *Jet Pilot* (U, 1957); *The Big Beat* (U, 1958); *Rockabye Baby* (Par., 1958); *Juke Box Rhythm* (Col., 1959); supplied voices for *1001 Arabian Nights* (Col., 1962); and appeared in *Magic Fountain* (Aguila, 1962); *My Six Loves* (Par., 1963); *The Patsy* (Par., 1964); and *The Brothers O'Toole* (CVD, 1973).

Television and Radio. Mr. Conreid began his career in 1936 acting in radio adaptations of Shakespeare's plays. His subsequent work in the medium includes Orson Welles' Mercury Radio Th. Co.; Life with Luigi; My Friend Irma; Lassie; The Great Gildersleeve; and Monitor.

Among his extensive television work are appearances on My Friend Irma; Hansel and Gretel (NBC); the Charlie Weaver Show (1960); the George Gobel Show; Disneyland (NBC); Four Star Playhouse; Playhouse of the Stars; The Line Up; I Love Lucy (CBS); the Danny Thomas Show (CBS); *The Ransom of Red Chief;* Fractured Flickers (synd.); Lost in Space; Please Don't Eat the Daisies; Stump the Stars; the Tonight Show (NBC); the Merv Griffin Show (synd.); *The Alphabet Conspiracy* (NBC); Maverick (ABC); Omnibus (CBS); Pantomime Quiz; the Red Skelton Show (CBS); What's It For? (NBC); and US Steel Hour.

Other Activities. With Jerry Hauser, Mr. Conreid made a seventeen-day tour of military hospitals in Japan, Guam, and the Philippines (1970). He frequently lectures at colleges and high schools.

Discography. Mr. Conreid recorded "Peter Meets the Wolf in Dixieland".

Recreation. Collects oriental objets d'art and furniture.

CONVY, BERT. Actor. b. Bernard Whalen Convy, July 23, 1936, St. Louis, Mo., to Bert Fleming and Monica (Whalen) Convy. Grad. North Hollywood (Calif.) H.S., 1954; Univ. of California, at Los Angeles, B.A. 1955; studied acting with Jeff Corey, Los Angeles, Calif., 1957–59. Married Oct. 10, 1959, to Anne Anderson; one daughter. Member of AEA; AFTRA; SAG.

Pre-Theatre. Professional baseball player.

Theatre. Mr. Convy made his first stage appearance with the Player's Ring (Hollywood, Calif.) in *The Matchmaker; A Tree Grows in Brooklyn;* and *Liliom.* He made his Bway debut in *Billy Barnes Revue* (John Golden Th., Aug. 4, 1959); subsequently appeared as Tommy Dee in *Nowhere to Go But Up* (Winter Garden, Nov. 10, 1962); and in the revue, *The Beast in Me* (Plymouth, May 16, 1963); succeeded Jean Rupert as El Gallo in *The Fantasticks* (Sullivan St. Playhouse, May 3, 1960); appeared as Rome in *Mornin' Sun* (Phoenix, Oct. 6, 1963); and in *Love and Kisses* (Music Box, Dec. 18, 1963); and *Damn Yankees* (St. Louis Municipal Th., July 27, 1964).

He played Perchik, the Student, in *Fiddler on the Roof* (Imperial, N.Y.C., Sept. 22, 1964); Richard Merrick in *The Impossible Years* (Playhouse, Oct. 13, 1965); Clifford Bradshaw in *Cabaret* (Broadhurst, Nov. 20, 1966); Peter in *Shoot Anything that Moves* (Provincetown Playhouse, Feb. 2, 1969); Hildy Johnson in *The Front Page* (Ethel Barrymore Th., May 10, 1969; and (in a second Bway production) Oct. 18, 1969); and conceived and directed *Do It Again!* (Promenade, Feb. 18, 1971).

Films. Mr. Convy has appeared in *Gunman's Walk* (Col., 1958); *Susan Slade* (WB, 1961); *Act One* (WB, 1964); and *Give Her the Moon* (UA, 1970).

Television. Mr. Convy appeared on *The Untouchables* (ABC); *Alfred Hitchcock Presents* (CBS); *Perry Mason* (CBS); *77 Sunset Strip* (ABC); *Hawaiian Eye* (ABC); Hennessey (NBC); *Father of the Bride* (CBS); *Alcoa Hour* (ABC); *You'll Never Get Rich* (CBS); *One Step Beyond* (NBC); *The Defenders* (CBS); *The Nurses* (CBS); and *East Side/West Side* (CBS).

He has appeared on East Side/West Side (CBS, 1964); The Memory Lane Show (Ind., 1965); The Mike Douglas Show (Ind., 1965–66); Harrigan and Son (Ind., 1965); The Untouchables (Ind., 1966); Hawk (ABC, 1966); *The Cave Dwellers* (ABC, 1966); Perry Mason (Ind., 1967); Silent Force (ABC, 1970); The Most Deadly Game (ABC, 1971); Night Gallery (1971); *Death Takes a Holiday* (ABC, 1971); Mission: Impossible (CBS, 1972); Keep the Faith (CBS, 1972); The Mary Tyler Moore Show (CBS, 1972); Hawaii Five-O (CBS, 1975); and is the host on the game show, Tattletales (CBS, 1974–to date).

Discography. As a member of the group, "The Cheers," he recorded *Black Denim Trousers* (Capitol); and *I Need Your Lovin'* (Capitol).

CONWAY, JOHN ASHBY. Educator, art director. b. Jan. 15, 1905, Pittsburgh, Pa., to John and Alberta D. (Dixon) Conway. Father, businessman; mother, businesswoman. Grad. Schenley H.S., 1923; Carnegie Inst. of Tech., 1927. Married June 22, 1942, to Dorothy Manchester. Member of AAUP; ANTA; ATA; Society for Theatre Research (London, Eng.) and La Societe d'Histoire du Théâtre (Paris, Fr.); The Players. Address: (home) 4625 22nd St., N.E., Seattle, WA 98105; (bus.) School of Drama, Univ. of Washington, Seattle, WA 98105.

Since 1931, Mr. Conway has been art director of the Univ. Theatre, and since 1950, professor in the School of Drama at the Univ. of Washington. Previously, at the University, he was associate professor (1943–49), assistant professor (1930–42), and an associate (1927–29). He has introduced courses in Japanese, Chinese and East Indian theatre and drama.

Since 1927, he has designed scenery and costumes for university and other local productions. He has also designed five theatres in Seattle, Wash.: the Studio Theatre, the Penthouse (arena) Theatre, the Playhouse, the Center Theatre, and the Showboat Theatre; and has also designed the Tacoma Little Theatre (Tacoma, Wash.); and the Lakewood Playhouse (Lakewood Center, Wash.). He designed an Elizabethan style stage that was used for 30 years at the Oregon Shakespearean Festival, Ashland, Or., and for many years he has specialized in the design of scenery for opera productions.

Other Activities. Mr. Conway was appointed by the Governor of Washington to the Washington State Arts Commission (chmn., 1961); was a member of the Governor's Art Council (chmn., 1958–60); appointed by the Mayor of Seattle to the Seattle Arts Commission (vice-chmn., 1955); and a founding member and past president of Allied Arts, Inc. (Seattle, Wash.).

CONWAY, SHIRL. Actress. b. Shirley Elizabeth Crosman, June 13, 1916, Franklinville, N.Y., to William Clark and Elizabeth (Thomas) Crosman. Father, merchant. Grad. Ten Broeck Acad., Franklinville, 1934; Univ. of Michigan, B.A. 1938. Married Sept. 1943 to William Johnson (marr. dis. 1951; dec. 1956); married Nov. 1960 to Gordon P. Larson. Relative in theatre: great-aunt, Henrietta Crossman, actress. Member of AEA; AFTRA; AGVA; SAG.

Pre-Theatre. Assistant merchandise buyer.

Theatre. Miss Conway first appeared on Bway in the chorus of *Banjo Eyes* (Hollywood Th., Dec. 25, 1941); and succeeded Frances Mercer in the role of Melanie Walker in *Something for the Boys* (Alvin, Jan. 7, 1943).

She made her London debut as Lisa Marvin in *Carissima* (Palace, Mar. 10, 1948); succeeded Yvonne Adair as Dorothy Shaw in *Gentlemen Prefer Blondes* (Palace, Chicago, Ill., Sept. 20, 1951); appeared as Ruth Winters in *Plain and Fancy* (Mark Hellinger Th., N.Y.C., Jan. 27, 1955); continued in the same role for the London production (Drury Lane, Jan. 2, 1956); toured in the Australian company, in the title role of *Auntie Mame* (Melbourne, Adelaide, Sydney, and Brisbane, 1959); toured with the same play (Summer 1959); appeared in stock in *Pal Joey; A Roomful of Roses; The Time of the Cuckoo; The Primrose Path; Sunrise at Campobello; The King and I;* and *Plain and Fancy;* and, for the Seattle (Wash.) Repertory Th., appeared in *Waltz of the Toreadors* (Jan. 8, 1975), and played Dolly Gallagher in *The Matchmaker* (Mar. 5, 1975).

Television. Miss Conway has appeared as Liz Thorpe in The Nurses (CBS, 1962); The Defenders (CBS, 1961); Naked City (ABC, 1961); Route 66 (CBS, 1961); the Ed Sullivan Show (CBS, 1955); the Sid Caesar Show (NBC, 1956–57); Joe and Mabel (CBS, 1956); and *The Beggar's Opera* (Ind.).

Awards. For her performance as Ruth Winters in *Plain and Fancy,* Miss Conway received the *Theatre World* Award (1955); the NATAS (Emmy) Award nomination for her performance as Liz Thorpe in The Nurses (1963).

Recreation. Gardening, cooking, golfing, singing.

COOK, BARBARA. Actress, singer. b. Barbara Nell Cook, Oct. 25, 1927, Atlanta, Ga., to Charles Bunyan and Nell (Harwell) Cook. Father, salesman. Grad. Girls H.S., Atlanta, 1945. Studied singing with Robert Kobin, N.Y.C., 1954; acting with David LeGrant, N.Y.C., 1958. Married Mar. 9, 1952, to David LeGrant, acting teacher, (marr. dis.); one son. Member of AEA; AFTRA.

Pre-Theatre. Typist.

Theatre. Miss Cook, as a member of the entertainment staff of the Tamiment (Pa.) Playhouse, appeared in musical revues (Summer 1950–51); made her N.Y.C. debut as Sandy in *Flahooley* (Broadhurst, May 14, 1951); played Ado Annie in *Oklahoma!* (NY City Ctr., Aug. 31, 1953), and repeated her role in a cross-country tour; Carrie in *Carousel* (NY City Ctr., June 3, 1954); Hilda Miller in *Plain and Fancy* (Mark Hellinger Th., Jan. 27, 1955); Cunegonde in *Candide* (Martin Beck Th., Dec. 1, 1956); Julie in *Carousel* (NY City Ctr., Sept. 11, 1957); Marion Paroo in *The Music Man* (Majestic, Dec. 19, 1957); Anna Leonowens in *The King and I* (NY City Ctr., May 11, 1960); Leisl in *The Gay Life* (Shubert, Nov. 18, 1961); Amalia Balash in *She Loves Me* (Eugene O'Neill Th., Apr. 23, 1963).

Miss Cook played Molly Tobin in *The Unsinkable Molly Brown* (Charlotte, N.C., Summer Th., June 30, 1964); Carol Deems in *Something More!* (Eugene O'Neill Th., N.Y.C., Nov. 10, 1964); succeeded (Feb. 22, 1965) Sandy Dennis in the role of Ellen Gordon in *Any Wednesday* (Music Box, Feb. 18, 1965); appeared in *George Gershwin's Theatre* (Philharmonic Hall, Jan. 23, 1966); played Polly Browne in *The Boy Friend* (Paper Mill Playhouse, Millburn, N.J., Mar. 1, 1966); Magnolia in *Show Boat* (NY State Th., N.Y.C., July 19, 1966); Patsy Newquist in *Little Murders* (Broadhurst Th., Apr. 25, 1967); Fanny in *Funny Girl* (tour, 1967); Dolly Talbo in *The Grass Harp* (Martin Beck Th., Nov. 2, 1971); with the Repertory Th. of Lincoln Center, played Kleopatra in *Enemies* (Vivian Beaumont Th., Nov. 9, 1972); and appeared in concert at Carnegie Hall (Jan. 26, 1975).

Television. Miss Cook has appeared on Kraft Television Th. (NBC, 1956); played Evalina in *Bloomer Girl* (NBC, 1956); Elsie in *Yeoman of the Guard* (Hallmark Hall of Fame, NBC, 1956); appeared on the Alfred Hitchcock series (CBS, 1957); in *In the Garden* (Play of the Week, NTA, 1961); US Steel Hour (CBS, 1962); the Perry Como Show (NBC, 1963); To Tell the Truth (CBS); Get the Message (ABC); The Bell Telephone Hour (NBC); *Careerathon* (ABC): Girl Talk (ABC); and The Today Show (NBC).

Night Clubs. Miss Cook has sung in supper clubs in Boston, Mass., and Chicago, Ill., and the Blue Angel and other clubs in N.Y.C.

Awards. Miss Cook received the Antoinette Perry (Tony) Award for *The Music Man* (1958); and won the *Variety* NY Drama Critics Poll for her performance as Amalia Balash in *She Loves Me* (1963).

Recreation. Photography, painting, knitting, gardening, swimming.

COOK, DOUGLAS. Scenic designer, actor, director, producer, educator. b. Douglas N. Cook, Sept. 22, 1929, Phoenix, Ariz., to Neil E. and Louise N. Cook. Father, rancher, writer, professor; mother, teacher. Educ. Phoenix College, Univ. of Chicago, Univ. of California (Los Angeles), Univ. of Arizona, Stanford Univ. Professional training at Polakov Studio of Design, Los Angeles Art Institute (Peter Marroney, F. Cowles Strickland, Lester Polakov, Hubert Heffner, Robert Burroughs, Robert Loper, Milford Zornes). Married Joan Buechner Compton; three sons. Member of ATA; USITT; ASTR; ANTA (vice-pres., 1973–74); URTA; Theatre Assn. of Penn. (vice-pres., 1973–74). Address: (home) 526 Westview Ave., State College, PA tel. (814) 237-0006; (bus.) Dept. of Theatre and Film, College of Arts and Architecture, The Pennsylvania Univ., University Park, PA 16802, tel. (814) 865-7588.

Mr. Cook became head of the Dept. of Theatre and Film, College of Arts and Architecture, The Pennsylvania State Univ., in 1970. Previously he had been scenic artist, Dept. of Drama Stanford Univ. (1955–57); instructor, San Mateo (Cal.) College (1955–57); and instructor and then associate professor, Dept. of Theatre, Univ. of California (Riverside) (1957–70).

Theatre. Mr. Cook began acting as a member of the Phoenix (Ariz.) Community Th.; made his professional debut as the Bartender in *Three Men on a Horse* (Corral Th., Tucson, Ariz., May 1953); made his summer stock debut as Sir Toby Belch in *Twelfth Night* and Joe in *Ten Nights in a Barroom* (Orleans Arena Th., Orleans, Mass., June–Sept. 1953). The first play he directed was *Our Hearts Were Young and Gay* (Palo Alto Th., Palo Alto, Cal., Oct. 1953), followed by *The Girl of the Golden West* (Little Th., Stanford, Cal., May 1955). He was artistic director for *Dial 'M' for Murder, Ladies in Retirement,* and *The*

Solid Gold Cadillac (Millbrae Community Th., Millbrae, Cal., Sept. 1955–June 1957); scenic designer for *The Duchess of Malfi, Burnt Flowerbed, The Good Woman of Setzuan, The Seagull,* and *As You Like It* (Theatre 100, Riverside, Cal., Sept. 1957–June 1961); and he directed *The Crucible* (National Music Camp, Interlochen, Mich., Aug. 1961).

He was scenic designer for *The Alchemist, The Fighting Cock, The Time of Your Life, The Threepenny Opera, The Glass Menagerie,* and *Juno and the Paycock* (UCR Th., Riverside, Cal., Sept. 1961–June 1966); staff designer for *The Taming of the Shrew, Hamlet,* and *The Comedy of Errors* (Utah Shakespeare Festival, Cedar City, Utah, June–Sept. 1966); and technical director for *The Emperor Jones* (O'Neill Memorial Th., New London, Conn., May 1967). He was scenic designer for *The Skin of Our Teeth* and *Medea* (UCR Th., Riverside, Cal., Sept. 1967–June 1968); directed *Oh Dad, Poor Dad. . .* (Studio Th., Riverside, Cal., Apr. 1968); was staff designer and associate producer for *As You Like It, The Merchant of Venice,* and *Romeo and Juliet* (Utah Shakespeare Festival, Cedar City, Utah, June–Sept. 1968); and scenic designer for *The Marriage Contest* (Kiki-Kai Opera Co., Tokyo, Japan, Sept. 1968). He was scenic designer for *The Knack* and *The Revenger's Tragedy* (UCR Th., Riverside, Cal., Sept. 1968–June 1969); director of *Isabel* (Studio Th., Riverside, Cal.); and staff designer and associate producer for *A Midsummer Night's Dream, Othello,* and *Love's Labour's Lost* (Utah Shakespearean Festival, Cedar City, Utah, June–Sept. 1969); and scenic designer for *The Trial* (UCR Th., Riverside, Cal., Mar. 1970).

In 1971, Mr. Cook became producer for the Festival of American Theatre at Pennsylvania State Univ. (June–Sept. annually), where his programs have included *Captain Jinks, Sidewinder, The Little Foxes, Anna Christie, Plaza Suite, Merton of the Movies, Carousel, Anything Goes, Damn Yankees, Most Happy Fella, A Streetcar Named Desire, Little Murders, Brigadoon, Harvey, Death of a Salesman, Finian's Rainbow,* and *Kiss Me Kate.* He continued as associate producer at the Utah Shakespearean Festival, where the programs included *Much Ado About Nothing, A Midsummer Night's Dream,* and *Macbeth* (June–Sept. 1972) and *Henry VIII, Hamlet,* and *As You Like It* (June–Sept. 1974).

Television. Mr. Cook made his first appearance on television in *The Silver Lieutenant* (KPIX-TV, San Francisco).

Other Activities. Mr. Cook designed the Adams Memorial Th., Utah Shakespearean Festival (1970–74). He directed a Univ. of California intercampus study on early California theatres in 1965, and he taught a special course on American scenic design and designers for the Humanities Institute, Univ. of California (1966–67).

Recreation. Watercolor painting, drums, camping.

COOK, ELISHA. Actor. b. Dec. 26, 1906, San Francisco, Calif., to Helen (Henry) Cook. Mother, actress. Attended St. Alban's School, Chicago, Ill. Married 1929 to Mary Cook (marr. dis. 1942). Member of AEA; AFTRA; SAG.

Theatre. Mr. Cook played Felix in *The Crooked Friday* (Bijou, N.Y.C., Oct. 8, 1925); Joe Bullitt in *Hello, Lola* (Eltinge, Jan. 12, 1926); appeared in the revue *Great Temptations* (Winter Garden, May 18, 1926); played Dick Wilton in *Henry—Behave* (Nora Bayes Th., Aug. 23, 1926); Jimmie in *Gertie* (Nora Bayes Th., Nov. 15, 1926); Algernon Simpson in *Jimmy's Women* (Biltmore, Sept. 26, 1927); and Stewart Kennedy in *Her Unborn Child* (Eltinge, Mar. 5, 1928).

He appeared as Felix in *The Kingdom of God* (Ethel Barrymore Th., Dec. 20, 1928); Francis Demarco in *Lost Boy* (Mansfield, Jan. 5, 1932); Ed Martin in *Merry-Go-Round* (Provincetown Playhouse, Apr. 22, 1932); Honey Rogers in *Chrysalis* (Martin Beck Th., Nov. 15, 1932); Ed Rumplegar in *Three-Cornered Moon* (Cort, Mar. 16, 1933); appeared in a stock production of *Goodbye Again* (Grossinger Playhouse, Ferndale, N.Y., May 1933); Richard in *Ah, Wilderness!* (Guild, N.Y.C., Oct. 2, 1933); Russell Gibbons in *Crime Marches On* (Morosco, Oct. 23, 1935); succeeded Robert Lowes as the Reporter in *Lightin'* (John Golden Th., Sept. 15, 1938); and played Guiseppe Givola in *Arturo Ui* (Lunt-Fontanne Th., Nov. 11, 1963).

Films. Mr. Cook appeared in *Two in a Crowd* (U, 1936); *Pigskin Parade* (20th-Fox, 1936); *They Won't Forget* (WB, 1937); *Love Is News* (20th-Fox, 1939); *Dillinger* (Mono., 1945); *Cinderella Jones* (WB, 1946); *The Big Sleep* (WB, 1946); *The Long Night* (RKO, 1947); *Don't Bother to Knock* (20th-Fox, 1952); *Shane* (Par., 1953); *I, the Jury* (UA, 1953); *Thunder Over the Plains* (WB, 1953); *Drum Beat* (WB, 1954); *The Outlaw's Daughter* (20th-Fox, 1954); *Timberjack* (Rep., 1955); *The Indian Fighter* (UA, 1955); *The Killing* (UA, 1956); *Voodoo Island* (UA, 1957); *Papa's Delicate Condition* (Par., 1963); *The Haunted Palace* (AI, 1963); *Black Zoo; Johnny Cool* (UA, 1963); *Blood on the Arrow* (AA, 1964); *The Glass Cage; Welcome to Hard Times* (MGM, 1967); *Rosemary's Baby* (Par., 1968); *The Great Bank Robbery* (WB, 1969); *El Condor* (Natl. Gen., 1970); *The Great Northfield Minnesota Raid* (U, 1972); *Blacula* (AI, 1972); *Emperor of the North Pole* (20th-Fox, 1973); *Pat Garrett and Billy the Kid* (MGM, 1973); *Electra Glide in Blue* (UA, 1973); and The Outfit (MGM, 1973).

Television. He has appeared as Charles Pulaski in *Emergency No Warning* (NBC, 1958) and on TV Hour (ABC); Treasury Men in Action (ABC); Alfred Hitchcock Presents (CBS); TV Reader's Digest (ABC); The Millionaire (CBS); Wyatt Earp (ABC); GE Th. (CBS); Trackdown (CBS); No Warning (NBC); Perry Mason (CBS); Bat Masterson (NBC); Rawhide (CBS); Johnny Ringo (CBS); Gunsmoke (CBS); Tightrope (CBS); Wagon Train (NBC); Ford Star Time (NBC); Rebel (ABC); Thriller (NBC); The Real McCoys (ABC); Surfside 6 (ABC); The Outlaws (NBC); The Fugitive (ABC); Destry (ABC); Perry Mason (CBS); Bonanza (NBC); *McNab's Lab* (ABC); The Road West (NBC); Batman (ABC); *Night Chase* (CBS); and The Chicago Teddy Bears (CBS).

COOK, PETER. Writer, actor, producer. b. Peter Edward Cook, Nov. 17, 1937, Devonshire, England, to Alexander E. and Margaret Cook. Father, in Colonial Service. Grad. St. Bedes (preparatory school, England); Radley Coll. (public school, England, Cambridge Univ., B.A. Married Oct. 28, 1963, to Wendy Snowden, artist (marr. dis); one daughter; married Feb. 14, 1974, to Judy Huxtable. Member of AEA; AFTRA; AGVA.

Theatre. Mr. Cook contributed material for the revues, *Pieces of Eight* (Apollo, N.Y.C., Sept. 23, 1959), and *One Over the Eight.* With Alan Bennett, Jonathan Miller, and Dudley Moore, he wrote and performed in *Beyond the Fringe,* first presented at the Edinburgh (Scot.) Festival (Aug. 1959); an expanded version was shown in London (Fortune, May 10, 1961) and in N.Y.C. (John Golden Th., Oct. 27, 1962). With Messrs. Moore, Bennett, and Paxton Whitehead, Mr. Cook also wrote and performed in *Beyond the Fringe 1964* (John Golden Th., Jan. 18, 1964).

Mr. Cook was a writer and, with John Krimsky, producer of *The Establishment* (Strollers Theatre-Club, N.Y.C., Jan. 23, 1963), as well as a 1963–64 edition bearing the same title (Strollers Theatre-Club, Oct. 31, 1963); and, again with Mr. Krimsky, producer of *The Muffled Report* (Strollers Theatre-Club, Apr. 8, 1964). With John Bird, he wrote *The Establishment: 1964 Edition* (Lindy Opera House, Los Angeles, Calif., Sept. 7, 1964); and he performed in *Artists Against Apartheid* (Prince of Wales Th., London, Eng., Mar. 22, 1965).

He was a director of The Establishment Theatre Co., Inc., which presented *Square in the Eye,* by arrangement with Lucille Lortel Productions, Inc. (Th. de Lys, N.Y.C., May 19, 1965); *The Mad Show* (New Th., Jan. 9, 1966); *Monopoly* (Stage 73, Mar. 3, 1966); *Serjeant Musgrave's Dance,* by arrangement with Lucille Lortel (Th. de Lys, Mar. 8, 1966); presented, with Rita Fredricks and Paul Stoudt, *The Kitchen* (81st St. Th., June 13, 1966); and, with Rita Fredricks, *A Hand Is on the Gate* (Longacre, Sept. 21, 1966).

With Dudley Moore, Mr. Cook wrote and performed in *Beyond the Fringe* (Cambridge Th., London, Nov. 21, 1972), which was presented in N.Y.C. as *Good Evening* (Plymouth, Nov. 14, 1973).

Films. Mr. Cook appeared in *The Wrong Box* (Col., 1966); *Bedazzled* (20th-Fox, 1967); *A Dandy in Aspic* (Col., 1968); *The Bed Sitting Room* (UA, 1969); and *The Rise and Rise of Michael Rimmer* (WB, 1970).

Television and Radio. On radio, Mr. Cook was on the Let's Find Out series (Light Network, London, Eng., 1965–66). On television, he repeated his *Beyond the Fringe* performance (BBC, Dec. 19, 1964); contributed to and appeared on Not Only. . . But Also (BBC, 1964–65, 1965–66); performed on the New London Palladium Show (Associated TV, Oct. 3, 1965); on the Laughter Makers (Rediffusion, 1965–66); Merv Griffin Show (Ind., N.Y.C., 1965–66); in *Alice in Wonderland* (BBC, London, Jan. 1967); and *Where Do I Sit?,* also on British television.

Awards. He received the London *Evening Standard* Award (1962) for the best revue or musical; the Antoinette Perry (Tony) Award (1963); and a Special Citation by the NY Drama Critics' Circle (1963) for *Beyond the Fringe.* Mr. Cook and Dudley Moore were named comedians of the year by the Guild of Television Producers and Directors in 1973, and they received a special Antoinette Perry (Tony) Award in 1974 for their contributions to the theatre of comedy.

COOKE, RICHARD P. Critic. b. Richard Platt Cooke, July 5, 1904, Bloomfield, N.J., to Frederick P. and Jennie M. Cooke. Father, corporation executive. Grad. Bloomfield H.S., 1922; attended Phillips Exeter Acad., N.H., 1922–23; grad. Princeton Univ., B.S. 1927. Married Nov. 22, 1931, to Mary Ford Haggart (marr. dis. 1937); married July 1, 1939, to Ruth Seder Rowe; one son. Served with US Field Artillery Res., 1927–32. Address: Cove Neck Rd., R.D. 311, Oyster Bay, NY 11771.

Mr. Cooke was drama critic for *The Wall Street Journal* (1939–69). He also has written on aviation for the *Journal* and for *Barrons* financial weekly.

Recreation. Sailing.

COOKSON, PETER. Actor, producer. b. Peter W. Cookson, May 8, 1913, Milwaukie, Ore., to Gerald and Helen (Willis) Cookson. Father, Major, British Army; mother, nurse. Attended public schools in Calif., 1927–31; Pasadena Playhouse, 1932–33. Married June 1937 to Maurine Gray (marr. dis. 1948); one son, one daughter; married June 2, 1949, to Beatrice Straight, actress; two sons. Served US Army, 1944; rank, Pvt. Member of AEA; AFTRA. Address: (home) R.F.D., Canaan, CT tel. (413) 229-6841; (bus.) Kaplan and Veidt, 667 Madison Ave., New York, NY 10021, tel. (212) PL 5-2214.

Theatre. Mr. Cookson first performed in 1935 at the Old Globe Shakespeare Th. (San Diego, Calif.), playing Laertes in *Hamlet,* and other Shakespearean roles; and appeared in stock (Dallas, Tex., 1936).

He made his N.Y.C. debut in an ELT production of *The Constant Nymph* (Lenox Hill Playhouse, Fall 1946); and his Bway debut as Robert Chalcot in *Message for Margaret* (Plymouth Th., Apr. 16, 1947); subsequently played Morris Townsend in *The Heiress* (Biltmore, Sept. 29, 1947); with his wife Beatrice Straight, produced *The Innocents* (Playhouse, Feb. 1, 1950); appeared as Ellis in *The Little Blue Light* (ANTA, Apr. 29, 1951); Judge Aristide Forestier in *Can-Can* (Shubert, May 7, 1953); Garrett Scott in *Four Winds* (Cort, Sept. 25, 1957); and Robert Baker in *Wonderful Town* (NY City Ctr., Mar. 5, 1958).

Published Works. Mr. Cookson has published a novel, *Henderson's Head* (1973).

Recreation. Traveling, boating, building a home, reconverting barns.

COOPER, ANTHONY KEMBLE. Actor. b. Francis Anthony (Kemble) Cooper, Feb. 6, 1908, London, Eng., to Frank Kemble and Alice May (Taunton) Cooper. Father, actor; mother, oratorio singer. Attended Ampleforth Coll., Yorkshire, Eng.; Berkeley-Irving Sch., N.Y.C. Married 1934, to Dorothy Lucille Henkle. Relatives in theatre: sisters, Greta, Lilian, and Violet, actresses; descendant of John Philip Kemble, Fanny Kemble, and Sarah Siddons. Member of AEA; AFTRA. Address: 5 E. 82nd St., New York, NY 10028, tel. (212) LE 5-1905; Casa de S. Jorge, Linho-Sintra, Portugal tel. 98-98-31.

Theatre. Mr. Cooper made his N.Y.C. debut as a walk-on in The Players Club production of *The School for Scandal* (Lyceum, June 4, 1923); followed by the role of Decius Brutus in the Robert B. Mantell Repertory Co. production of *Julius Caesar* (Davenport Th., Stamford, Conn., 1923); and the Hon. Ian Maxwell in *Lass o' Laughter* (Comedy, N.Y.C., Jan. 8, 1925).

With the Robert B. Mantell Repertory Co., he toured the US and Canada in the roles of Osric in *Hamlet*, Lorenzo in *The Merchant of Venice*, Le Beau in *As You Like It*, and the Fool in *King Lear* (1925); and played Trip in *The School for Scandal* (Knickerbocker, N.Y.C., Dec. 6, 1925).

In stock he played Capt. Smollet in *Treasure Island*, Bobby in *Fanny's First Play*, juvenile roles in *The Farmer's Wife* and *Mr. Pim Passes By*, the male lead in *Caesar's Wife*, Bannister in *Lord Richard in the Pantry*, Charles Murdock in *The Ghost Train*, and Charles Windsor in *Loyalties* (Empire, Toronto, Can., Winter 1926).

Mr. Cooper played Fernand Lagardes in *The Thief* (Ritz, N.Y.C., Apr. 22, 1927); Emile Ardillot in *The Command to Love* (Longacre, Sept. 20, 1927); the King in *His Majesty's Car* (Ethel Barrymore Th., Nov. 23, 1930); Anthony Howard in *Silent Witness* (Morosco, Mar. 23, 1931); Simon Bliss in *Hay Fever* (Avon, Dec. 29, 1931); and Claude Hope in *The Mad Hopes* (Ann Arbor Drama Festival, Mich., Summer 1932). He directed and played Marchbanks in *Candida* (Griswold Th., Eastern Point, Conn., Summer 1933); appeared as Lord Darnley in *Mary of Scotland* (Alvin, N.Y.C., Nov. 27, 1933); the Lord in a touring company of *The Taming of the Shrew* (opened Nixon, Pittsburgh, Pa., Apr. 1935); played Shelley in *Aged 26* (Lyceum, N.Y.C., Dec. 21, 1936); the Earl of Southampton in *Gloriana* (Little, Nov. 25, 1938); and Henry Dakin in *Quiet Please* (Guild, Nov. 8, 1940).

With the Chapel Players, he played Billy Ross in *Nancy's Private Affair* and Mr. Code in *Dear Brutus* (Chapel Playhouse, Guilford, Conn., Summer 1941); played Capt. Vanbrugh in *Anne of England* (St. James, N.Y.C., Oct. 7, 1941); Wallace Grainger in a stock tour of *Let Us Be Gay* (Summer 1942); Lord Hastings in *Richard III* (Forrest, N.Y.C., Mar. 24, 1943); Ernest Turner in *Sheppey* (Playhouse, Apr. 18, 1944); Anthony Marston in *Ten Little Indians* (Broadhurst, June 27, 1944); and the Hon. Butterfield Slingsby in *Sweethearts* (Shubert, Jan. 21, 1947).

He toured summer theatres as the Prince in *The Swan* (1949); played Arnold Champion-Cheney, M.P., in *The Circle* (Jersey Th., Morristown, N.J., Summer 1949); Desmond Curry in *The Winslow Boy* (League Th., Univ. of Michigan, Summer 1950); Lord Tillbrook in the Th. Guild's summer tryout of *Traveller's Joy* (Westport Country Playhouse, Conn., July 1950); Snodgrass in *Mr. Pickwick* (Plymouth, N.Y.C., Sept. 17, 1952); both Capt. Arthur Ford and Carl Houtzman in the summer tryout of the two-character melodrama, *And Two Make Four* (Berkshire Playhouse, Stockbridge, Mass., June 1953); and Richard in *On Approval* (John Drew Memorial Th., East Hampton, L.I., N.Y., 1954).

Mr. Cooper appeared as Don Pedro in the American Shakespeare Festival (Stratford, Conn.) production of *Much Ado About Nothing* (Summer 1955); the Critic in *The Guardsman* (Studebaker Th., Chicago, Ill., Apr. 1957); toured as the Coroner in the pre-Bway tryout of *Listen to the Mocking Bird* (opened Colonial, Boston, Mass., Dec. 27, 1958; closed Shubert, Washington, D.C., Jan. 29, 1959); played Dr. Looke in the stock tryout of *Not in the Book* (1960); Lord Bottingham in *Foxy* (Ziegfeld, N.Y.C., Feb. 16, 1964); and the prosecutor, Mr. Naylor in *Hostile Witness* (Music Box, N.Y.C., Feb. 17, 1966).

Films. Mr. Cooper made his debut as William Shakespeare in *Milestones in the Theatre: Life of the Bard* (MGM, 1936); followed by roles in *The Hound of the Baskervilles* (20th-Fox, 1939); and *I Was an Adventuress* (20th-Fox, 1940).

Television. Mr. Cooper made his debut in the role of Prince Alexandrovitch in *The Chess Game* (NBC, 1937). He has also appeared on the US Steel Hour (CBS); Lucky Strike Hour; Danger (CBS); Suspense (CBS); Playhouse of the Stars; Studio One (CBS); Ford Th. (CBS); Pulitizer Prize Th. (ABC); You Are There (CBS); DuPont Show of the Month (NBC); Lux Video Th. (CBS); Kraft Television Th. (NBC); and Broadway Television Th.

Recreation. Restoring antiques, book collecting, writing.

COOPER, THEODORE GLESTON. Educator, writer, actor, director, producer. b. Aug. 14, 1939. Grad. Howard Univ., B.F.A. 1970 (drama); Univ. of Miami, M.A. 1971 (directing/theatre management); Financial Progress, Denver, Col. Married July 17, 1971, to Grace Cooper; two children. Address: (home) 7975 Riggs Rd., #10, Adelphi, MD 20783, tel. (301) 431-1148; (bus.) Dept. of Drama, College of Fine Arts, Howard Univ., Washington, DC 20001, tel. (202) 636-7050.

Mr. Cooper became professor and acting chairman, Dept. of Drama, Howard Univ., in 1972. He taught previously at Booker T. Washington H.S. and Miami-Dade Junior College, both in Miami, Fla., and as a volunteer at Roosevelt H.S., Washington, D.C., and during 1971–72 he was a professor at Miami-Dade Junior College, Miami, Fla.

Theatre. Mr. Cooper founded in 1971 and was director of the M. Ensemble Company, a theatre group in Miami, Fla., and he was president and chairman of the board of UCAPT, Inc., a nonprofit corporation that received funds for the operation of the theatre. Among the plays directed by Mr. Cooper are his own works—*Strawman* (Howard Univ., Washington, D.C., 1970); *A Town Called Tobyville* (Univ. of Miami, Coral Gables, Fla., 1972); *Portrait of a Woman* (Playboy Plaza, Miami Beach, Fla., 1972; Howard Univ., 1973); and *Goodnight Mary Beck* (Howard Univ., 1974).

He has produced and directed at many places in Florida, at universities in Alabama and Tennessee; at the Black Arts Festival, Lincoln Univ., Pa.; and in Washington, D.C., proper. Mr. Cooper has directed productions of *The Trial of Mary Dugan; This Property is Condemned; A Christmas Carol; The Night of January 16th;* and *Twelve Angry Men.* Plays that he has produced as well as directed are *Gangsters Over Harlem; Ornette; Purlie Victorious; Sister Sonji; A Day in Germ City; Big Hit; Contribution; Ourside*s*; The Prayer Meeting; God's Trombones;* and *A Dress for Annalee.* Parts that he has acted include Edwards in *Fear;* Scrooge in *A Christmas Carol;* Holly in *Of Being Hit;* Man #2 in *Ornette;* Chauncey in *Doctor B.S. Black;* the Rebel in *Winterset;* the Defense Attorney in *Night of January 16th;* Cliff Dawson in *In The Wine Time;* Baker in *Otis in Doughnut Land;* Lee Mack in *A Town Called Tobyville;* and the Slave in *The Slave with Two Faces.*

Television and Radio. Mr. Cooper was director-producer of the radio play *Searchlight* (WMBM, Miami, Fla.) and of the television show *Black Is* (Ch. 11, Miami, Fla.).

Other Activities. Mr. Cooper was president of Soulbook International, Washington, D.C., a company that promoted cabarets and concerts, managed local talent, and raised funds for local organizations. At various times he was also director of public relations for the Dr. Martin Luther King Boulevard Development Corp., Miami, Fla., and an account executive with Fianancial Programs, Denver, Col. Mr. Cooper worked also with the Office of Economic Opportunity (OEO), where he was an employee development specialist and career development officer, a community organizer and evaluator of OEO programs in such localities as Watts, Los Angeles, Calif.; Gary, Ind.; Chicago, Ill.; and Washington, D.C. He also served OEO as an information officer and developed the agency's Information Center.

Published Works. Mr. Cooper wrote "The Black Playwright" (*On Stage* Magazine, 1973).

COOTE, ROBERT. Actor. b. Feb. 4, 1909, London, England. Father, Bert Coote, comedian, director; mother, dancer. Professional training with Manchester (England) Repertory Co. Served in Royal Canadian Air Force, 1940–46; highest rank, Squadron Leader.

Theatre. Mr. Coote appeared in the English provinces as John in *The Private Secretary* (1925); toured (1926–27) throughout England with the Charles Doran Shakespeare Co. and the D. Basil Gill Shakespeare Co.; appeared with the Rusholme Repertory Th., Manchester, England (1927–29); toured (1929) South Africa in *Just Married* and *77 Park Lane;* and toured (1930–34) England in *Frederica, For the Love of Mike, Mother of Pearl,* and *Private Lives.*

His first London appearance, as the King in *The Windmill Man* (Victoria Palace, Dec. 1931), was followed by his portrayal of Horace Bream in *Sweet Lavender* (Lyric, Hammersmith, June 18, 1932). He was on tour (1934) in Australia as a member of a musical comedy company and appeared in productions of *Anything Goes; Yes, Madam;* and *Waltzes from Vienna.*

Mr. Coote was active in films (see below) before and after World War II, then returned to the London stage. He replaced Cempbell Cotts as John Nedlow in *Someone Waiting* (Globe Th., Nov. 25, 1953); made his Bway debut as Col. Rinder-Sparrow in *The Love of Four Colonels* (Shubert Th., Jan. 15, 1953); played Sir Michael Anstruther in *Dear Charles* (Morosco, Sept. 15, 1954); and created the role of Col. Pickering in *My Fair Lady* (Mark Hellinger Th., Mar. 15, 1956; Drury Lane, London, Apr. 30, 1958; Army Th., Moscow, USSR, 1959).

He was Pellinore in *Camelot* (Majestic, N.Y.C., Dec. 3, 1960); played Col. Lukyn in a revival of Pinero's *The Magistrate* (Cambridge, London, Sept. 18, 1969); and was Col. Sir Robert Richardson in *The Jockey Club Stakes* (Vaudeville Th., Sept. 30, 1970; Eisenhower Th., Washington, D.C., Nov. 14, 1972; Cort, N.Y.C., Jan. 24, 1973). He appeared also as the Farmer in *Birds of Paradise* (Garrick, London, June 19, 1974) and repeated his performance as Col. Pickering in a 20th-anniversary revival of *My Fair Lady* (St. James Th., N.Y.C., Mar. 25, 1976).

Films. Mr. Coote's numerous motion pictures include *The Prisoner of Zenda* (UA, 1937); *A Yank at Oxford* (MGM, 1938); *Gunga Din* (RKO, 1939); *Forever Amber* (20th-Fox, 1947); *Stairway to Heaven* (U, 1947); *The Ghost and Mrs. Muir* (20th-Fox, 1947); *Othello* (UA, 1955); *The Swan* (MGM, 1956); *Merry Andrew* (MGM, 1958); *The Horse's Mouth* (UA, 1958); *The Golden Head* (Cinerama, 1965); *A Man Could Get Killed* (U, 1966); *The Swinger* (Par., 1966); *The Cool Ones* (WB, 1967); and *Prudence and the Pill* (20th-Fox, 1968).

Television. Mr. Coote played Timmy St. Clair on The Rogues (NBC, 1964–65); was the Red King in *Alice Through the Looking Glass* (NBC, Nov. 6, 1966); appeared on the Jackie Gleason Show (CBS, Nov. 12, 1966); *The Whitehall Warriors* (BBC, London, England, Jan. 1967); and in Best of Enemies (England).

COOTS, J. FRED. Composer. b. May 2, 1897, Brooklyn, N.Y., to William Jerome and Annie (Dent) Coots. Father, shipping inspector; mother, pianist. Grad. P.S. 118, Bay Ridge, 1912. Member of ASCAP, Dramatists Guild, ALA. Address: 150 E. 69th St., New York, NY 10021, tel. (212) YU 8-4060.

Pre-Theatre. Banking house clerk, stock boy.

Theatre. Mr. Coots began his career as a song plugger for the McKinley Publishing Co. (N.Y.C.,

1918–19); contributed music to vaudeville productions (1918–19) one of which was a song for Sophie Tucker, entitled "There's a Little Bit of Devil in Your Angel Eyes," which he wrote with Jack Little (RKO Palace, N.Y.C., 1920); and contributed special music material to the team of (Bert) Savoy and (Jay) Brennan for their acts in *The Greenwich Village Follies of 1920* (Greenwich Village Th., Aug. 30, 1920), and *The Greenwich Village Follies* (Shubert, Sept. 12, 1922).

He composed the music for the Bway production of *Sally, Irene and Mary* (Casino, Sept. 4, 1922); *Bal Tabarin* (Shubert, 1924); *Spice of 1922* (Winter Garden, July 6, 1922); composed the music, with Sigmund Romberg, for *Artists and Models* (Astor, Oct. 15, 1924); the return engagement of *Sally, Irene and Mary* (44 St. Th., Mar. 23, 1925); with Alfred Goodman and Maurice Rubents; for the 1925 edition of *Artists and Models* (Winter Garden, June 24, 1925); and composed the music for *June Days* (Astor, Aug. 6, 1925).

He composed the music with Alfred Goodman and Maurice Rubens for *Gay Paree* (Shubert, Aug. 18, 1925); with Maurice Rubens for *A Night in Paris* (Casino de Paris, Jan. 5, 1926); contributed music to *The Merry World* (Imperial, June 8, 1926); composed the music for *White Lights* (Ritz, Oct. 11, 1927); and *Sons O'Guns* (Imperial, Nov. 26, 1929).

He composed the music for three editions of the *Cotton Club Revues* (1936, 1937, 1938), for Cab Calloway, Bill "Bojangles" Robinson, Ethel Waters, Lena Horne, and "Fats" Waller.

Films. His music for the song "A Precious Little Thing Called Love" was used as the theme for *Shopworn Angel* (Par., 1929).

Night Clubs. Mr. Coots wrote the music for tabloid musicals performed at such N.Y.C. cabarets as the Moulin Rouge, Tokio, Pekin, and the Marlborough.

Other Activities. He has delivered 200 lectures entitled *Melody and Memories* and *Broadway Is My Home.*

Published Works. He has written such songs as "Santa Claus Is Coming to Town" (translated into 12 languages); "Love Letters in the Sand"; "You Go to My Head"; "I Still Get a Thrill"; "For All We Know"; "One Minute to One"; and "A Beautiful Lady in Blue".

COPELAND, JOAN. Actress, singer. b. Joan Maxine Miller, New York City, to Isidore and Augusta (Barnett) Miller. Father, manufacturer of women's wear. Grad. Abraham Lincoln H.S., Brooklyn; Brooklyn Coll. Studied Actors' Studio (charter member, 1947); singing with Jack Harrold; John Wallowitch. Married to George Kupchik, engineer; one son. Relative in theatre: brother, Arthur Miller, playwright. Member of AEA; AFTRA; SAG.

Pre-Theatre. Secretary; concert pianist.

Theatre. Miss Copeland made her stage debut as Juliet in *Romeo and Juliet* (Brooklyn Acad. of Music, 1945); and subsequently played in ELT productions of *The Servant of Two Masters* (1946); Othello (1946); and *There's Always Juliet* (1947). She appeared in the title role in *Claudia* (Hempstead, N.Y., Summer 1946); and understudied Meg Mundy in the role of Lisa in *How I Wonder* (Hudson Th., N.Y.C., Sept. 30, 1947).

Her first Bway appearance was as Nadine in *Sundown Beach* (Belasco Th., Sept. 7, 1948). She subsequently appeared as Susan Carmichael in *Detective Story* (Hudson Th., N.Y.C., March 23, 1949); as Evangeline Orth in *Not for Children* (Coronet, N.Y.C., Feb. 13, 1951); as Ann Deever in *All My Sons* (Robin Hood Th., Arden, Del., Summer 1953); understudied roles in *The Tender Trap* (Longacre, N.Y.C., Sept., 1954); and *The Diary of Anne Frank* (Cort Th., N.Y.C., Oct. 1955); and appeared with the Maurice Schwartz Co. in *The Grass Is Always Greener,* and *The Miser* (1955). She played Melanie in *Conversation Piece* (Barbizon-Plaza, N.Y.C., Nov. 18, 1957); Maria in *Handful of Fire* (Martin Beck Th., N.Y.C., Oct. 1, 1958); in stock, Raina in *Arms and the Man* (Westport Country Playhouse, Conn., July 1959); Mrs. Erlynne in *Delightful Season* (Gramercy Arts, N.Y.C., Sept. 1960); and was the standby for Vivien Leigh in *Tovarich* (Broadway Th., N.Y.C., Mar. 18, 1963). She co-starred as Eliza Doolittle in *My Fair Lady* (Guber-Ford Circuit, Summer 1964); and as Marchesa Valentina Crespi in *Something More* (Eugene O'Neill Th., Nov. 10, 1964); understudied the role of Esther Franz in *The Price* (46 St. Th., N.Y.C., Feb. 1969); and stood by for Katherine Hepburn in *Coco* (Mark Hellinger Th., N.Y.C., Nov. 12, 1969). She appeared as Esther in *Two by Two* (Imperial, N.Y.C., Nov. 1970); and starred as Leonie in the revival of S. N. Behrman's *End of Summer* (Manhattan Th. Club, N.Y.C., Nov. 1974).

Films. Miss Copeland appeared in *The Goddess* (Col., 1958) and *Middle of the Night* (Col., 1959).

Television. She has appeared as Cora in *The Iceman Cometh* (Play-of-the-Week, WNTA); as Maggie Porter in Love of Life (CBS); as Andrea Whiting in Search for Tomorrow (CBS); and as Monica Courtland in How to Survive a Marriage (NBC).

Night Clubs. She has appeared at the Upstairs at the Duplex; The Showcase (1963); and sang in concert at Town Hall (1964).

Recreation. Tennis, sewing, piano, swimming, snorkeling.

COPPOLA, ANTON. Musical director, conductor. b. Mar. 21, 1918, New York City, to Augostino and Maria (Zasa) Coppola. Father, toolmaker. Grad. Stuyvesant H.S., N.Y.C., 1934; Juilliard Sch. of Music, 1936; in N.Y.C., studied opera and symphonic repertoire with Fulgenzio Guerrieri, 1931–39; composition and orchestration with Rosalino De Maria, 1938–40; opera and symphonic repertoire with Paul Breisach, 1946–51. Grad. Manhattan Sch. of Music, B. Mus. (composition) 1964. Married Mar. 21, 1950, to Almerinda Drago; one son, one daughter. Served US Army, 1942–45, assigned to USAAF Band; rank, Warrant Officer Bandmaster. Member of AFM. Address: 75 Central Park West, New York, NY 10023, tel. (212) TR 3-8254.

Theatre. Mr. Coppola first performed as principal oboist at Radio City Music Hall, (N.Y.C., 1936); and for the next six years, as oboist on radio programs and recordings; subsequently conducted for the San Carlo Opera on cross-country tours in the US and Canada (1946–48); for opera companies (Hartford, Conn.; Cincinnati, Ohio; and San Francisco, Calif.; 1947–62); and was associate conductor at Radio City Music Hall (N.Y.C., 1948–51).

He was the musical director of *New Faces of 1952* (Royale Th., N.Y.C., May 16, 1952); *The Boy Friend* (Royale, Sept. 30, 1954); and succeeded Jay Blackton as musical director of *New Faces of '56* (Ethel Barrymore Th., June 14, 1956); was musical director for summer-theatre productions (Dayton, Ohio; Oakdale Musical Th., Wallingford, Conn.; Summer 1957); became musical director of the national touring production of *The Most Happy Fella* (opened Riviera, Detroit, Mich., Dec. 23, 1957; closed Philharmonic Aud., Los Angeles, Calif., June 22, 1958); and for a touring production of *My Fair Lady* (1958–59).

He was musical director of *Bravo Giovanni* (Broadhurst, N.Y.C., May 19, 1962); a touring production of *Irma La Douce* (Summer 1963); for *Rugantino* (Mark Hellinger Th., N.Y.C., Feb. 8, 1964); for a revival of *My Fair Lady* (NY City Ctr., May 20, 1964); and for *Camelot* (Carousel Th., Framingham, Mass., July 20 and Aug. 24, 1964). He conducted the opera *Lizzie Borden* (world premiere, NY City Ctr., N.Y.C., Mar. 25, 1965); was musical director for a revival of *South Pacific* (NY City Ctr., June 2, 1965); for touring productions of *The King and I* and *Guys and Dolls* (Summer 1965); for a revival of *How To Succeed in Business without Really Trying* (NY City Ctr., Apr. 20, 1966); touring productions of *Oliver!* (Summer 1966) and *West Side Story* (Summer 1967); for another revival of *My Fair Lady* (NY City Ctr., June 13, 1968); and for a revival of *The Most Happy Fella* (Wolf Trap Farm Park, Vienna, Va., July 19, 1973).

Television. Mr. Coppola conducted *Lizzie Borden* (WNET, Jan. 25, 1967).

Recreation. Flying airplanes.

CORRIGAN, ROBERT W. Educator. b. Robert Willoughby Corrigan, Sept. 23, 1927, Portage, Wis., to Daniel and Elizabeth (Waters) Corrigan. Father, bishop. Grad. Cornell Univ., B.A. 1950; Johns Hopkins Univ., M.A. 1952; Univ. of Minnesota, Ph.D. 1955. Married July 2, 1949, to Elaine L. Beagle (marr. dis. 1953); married Dec. 17, 1953, to Mary K. Kolling (marr. dis. 1960); two sons; married June 15, 1963, to Elizabeth T. Seneff (marr. dis. 1969); married Aug. 1, 1969, to Jane Langley. Member of ATA (chmn.) publications comm., 1957–63); ANTA; ASTRA; NTC; NCAE; NCP; Sigma Phi; Sigma Delta Chi. Address: 500 Highland Rd., Ann Arbor, MI 48104, tel. (313) 663-7952.

Mr. Corrigan was visiting professor of English and theatre, Univ. of Michigan (1973–74). He has held positions at the Gilman School, Baltimore, Md. (instr. in English and dir. of drama, 1950–52); the Univ. of Minnesota (instr. in theatre and classics, 1952–54); Carleton College, Northfield, Minn. (assist. prof. of drama, 1954–57); Tulane Univ., New Orleans, La. (assoc. prof. of theatre, 1957–61); Carnegie-Mellon Univ., Pittsburgh, Pa. (Andrew Mellon prof. and head of the Dept. of Drama, 1961–64); New York Univ. (first dean of the School of the Arts and prof. of dramatic literature, 1964–68); California Institute of the Arts, Valencia, Calif. (1st pres., 1968–72). He was also visiting professor of drama at the Univ. of Southern California (Summer 1961); visiting lecturer at Bennington (Vt.) College (1967–68); visiting Regents Lecturer, State Univ. of Virginia (1968); Avery Hopwood lecturer at the Univ. of Michigan (1973); and a member of the faculty of the Univ. for Presidents, Young Presidents Organization (1973).

Other Activities. Mr. Corrigan founded the *Tulane Drama Review* (later *The Drama Review*) in 1957 and was its editor until 1961. He was general editor in drama, Chandler Publishing Co. (1960–72) and advisory editor in theatre, communications, and the arts for Dell Publishing Co. (1961–70); *Modern International Drama* (1964–to date); *Arts in Society* (1965–to date); McGraw-Hill Co. and *Glamour* magazine (both 1965–68); and Houghton Mifflin Co. (1968–70); and contributing editor, *Michigan Quarterly* (1974–to date). In addition to his academic and publishing activities, Mr. Corrigan directed 40 plays in N.Y.C. and in university and regional theatres (1951–1962). He served as a member of the President's Council, Vassar College (1964–68), was a director of the Critics Program, National Endowment for the Humanities (1966–68), and was an associate trustee, Univ. of Pennsylvania (1967–72). In 1970–71, he was chairman, International Council of Fine Arts Deans (ICFAD) and ICFAD representative to the National Council on the Arts. He has been a director, National Choral Council (1966–to date), consultant to the Samuel Rubin Foundation (1973–to date), and chairman of the trustees, Space for International Development, New York City (1974–to date).

Published Works. He has translated *Chekhov: Six Plays* (1962), for which he also wrote the introduction; edited and wrote the introduction to a translation of Euripides' *Hippolytus* (1962); with Mary Dirks, he translated Adolphe Appia's *Music and the Art of the Theatre* (1962); and edited and wrote the introductions to *New Theatre of Europe* (Vol. 1, 1962; Vol. 2, 1964; Vol. 3, 1968); *The Theatre in the Twentieth Century* (1963); *The Modern Theatre* (1964), *The Art of the Theatre* (1964), *The Context and Craft of Drama* (1964), *New American Plays* (Vol. 1, 1965), *Laurel British Drama: 20th Century* (1965), *Laurel British Drama: 19th Century* (1967), *Masterpieces of the Modern Theatre* (9 vols., 1967), *Arthur Miller* (Twentieth Century View Series, 1969); *Comedy: A Critical Anthology* and *Tragedy: A Critical Anthology,* both with Glenn M. Loney (both 1971) and *The Forms of Drama,* with Glenn M. Loney (1972). Mr. Corrigan's other books include *Tragedy: Vision and Form* (1965), *Comedy: Vision and Form* (1965), and *The Theatre in Search of a Fix* (1973). Mr. Corrigan is also the author of over 100 articles on theatre, literature, education, and the arts.

Awards. Mr. Corrigan received an honorary citation of merit from Niagara Univ. (1967).

CORSARO, FRANK. Director, actor, playwright, teacher. b. Francesco Andrea Corsaro, Dec. 22, 1924, to Joseph and Marie (Quirino) Corsaro. Father, tailor. Grad. DeWitt Clinton H.S., 1944; attended Yale Univ. School of Drama, 1945–47. Studied at Actors Studio (1954–67). Married 1971 to Mary Cross Lueders; one son. Member of AGMA; SDG; SSD&C; AEA. Address: 33 Riverside Drive, New York, NY 10023, tel. (212) 874-1058.

Theatre. Mr. Corsaro made his first appearance on stage as Merlin in a school production of *A Connecticut Yankee* (DeWitt Clinton H.S., 1942); subsequently directed his first production, *No Exit* (Cherry Lane Th., June 1947); staged *Family Reunion* (Cherry Lane, Dec. 1947); appeared as the Professor of Philosophy in *The Would-Be Gentleman* (Cherry Lane, Aug. 1949); directed *Creditors* (Cherry Lane, Nov. 1949); *Heartbreak House* (Bleecker St. Playhouse, Mar. 1950); *Naked,* which he also adapted (Provincetown Playhouse, Sept. 1950); appeared as Tapster and one of Petruchio's Servants in *The Taming of the Shrew* (NY City Ctr., Apr. 25, 1951); and directed *The Curtain Rises* (Olney Th., Md., July 1951), and *Rain* (Pocono Playhouse, Mountainhome, Pa., Aug. 1951).

He directed a touring production of *Peter Pan* (opened Lyric, Baltimore, Md., Oct. 10, 1951; closed Great Northern, Chicago, Ill., Nov. 24, 1951); at the Rooftop Th., Atlanta, Ga., staged productions of *The Voice of the Turtle, For Love or Money, Legend of Sarah,* and *Holiday* (Oct.–Nov. 1951); succeeded Irwin Corey (Apr. 1952) as Dirty Joe in *Mrs. McThing* (ANTA, N.Y.C., Feb. 20, 1952); played Launcelot Gobbo in *The Merchant of Venice* (NY City Ctr., Mar. 4, 1953); and directed *The Scarecrow* (Th. de Lys, July 1953).

He directed *The Honeys* (Longacre, Apr. 28, 1955); *A Hatful of Rain* (Lyceum, Nov. 9, 1955); the opera, *Susannah* (NY City Ctr., N.Y.C., premiere Sept. 27, 1926); which was later presented at the Brussels World's Fair (Aug 1958); staged *The Making of Moo* (Rita Allen Th., N.Y.C., June 11, 1958); *The Night Circus* (John Golden Th., Dec. 2, 1958); and at the Spoleto (Italy) Festival of Two Worlds, staged the world premieres of *The Night of the Iguana* and *The Tiny Closet* (Teatro Caio Melisso, July 2, 1959), and directed an opera, *Angel of Fire* (July 1959).

He directed a tryout production of *The Night of the Iguana* (Coconut Grove Playhouse, Miami, Fla., Sept. 1960); the world premiere of *Oh Dad, Poor Dad, Mama's Hung You in the Closet and I'm Feelin' So Sad* (Lyric, Hammersmith, London, July 5, 1961); the pre-Bway tryout of *A Short, Happy Life* (opened Moore Th., Seattle, Wash., Sept. 12, 1961; closed, Hartford Th., Los Angeles, Calif., Oct. 21, 1961); *The Night of the Iguana* (Royale, Dec. 28, 1961); and *Baby Want a Kiss* (Little, Apr. 13, 1964).

Mr. Corsaro has been active in opera since 1966, directing for the NY City Opera (State Th., Lincoln Ctr. for the Performing Arts) productions of *La Traviata* (Oct. 23, 1966), *Madama Butterfly* (Mar. 5, 1967), *Cavalleria Rusticana* and *Pagliacci* (Feb. 24, 1968), *The Crucible* (Mar. 8, 1968), *Carry Nation* (N.Y.C. premiere, Mar. 28, 1968), *Faust* (Oct. 17, 1968), *Prince Igor* (Feb. 27, 1969), *Rigoletto* (Mar. 20, 1969), *Pelléas et Mélisande* (Mar. 18, 1970), *The Makropoulos Case* (Nov. 10, 1970), *Don Giovanni* (Sept. 15, 1972), and *Medea* (Mar. 7, 1974). Mr. Corsaro also directed the world premieres of the operas *Of Mice and Men* (Seattle, Wash., 1970); *Summer and Smoke* (St. Paul, Minn., Summer 1971), also first N.Y.C. production (NY City Opera, State Th., Mar. 20, 1972); and *The Sea Gull* (Houston, Tex., Mar. 5, 1974); for the Opera Society of Washington (D.C.), he directed *Koanga* (Lisner Aud., Dec. 18, 1970), *A Village Romeo and Juliet* (Opera House, Kennedy Ctr., Apr. 26, 1972), and *The Coronation of Poppea* (Opera House, Kennedy Ctr., Apr. 10, 1973); and for the Atlanta (Ga.) Municipal Opera, he directed *La Bohème.*.

Films. Mr. Corsaro made his motion picture debut performing in *Rachel, Rachel* (WB, 1968).

Television. Mr. Corsaro directed his own play *A Piece of Blue Sky* (Play of the Week, WNEW, 1960); directed *On the Outskirts of Town* (Bob Hope Chrysler Theatre, NBC, 1964); and a television production of the opera *Prince Igor* (Cincinnati Acad. of Music, 1966).

Other Activities. Mr. Corsaro has taught acting since 1955..

Recreation. Piano, tennis, ice-skating, painting.

CORSON, RICHARD. Actor, writer, educator, make-up artist. b. Dec. 27, Genoa, Ill., to V. J. and Myrna (Long) Corson. Grad. Elgin H.S., Ill.; DePauw Univ., B.A.; La. State Univ., M.A. Address: 121 Lincoln Pl., Brooklyn, NY 11217, tel. (212) UL 7-5812.

Mr. Corson was technical director of the Workshop Th. and instructor in stage make-up at Louisiana State Univ. Subsequently he was technical director of the University Th. and instructor in theatre at the Women's Coll. of the Univ. of North Carolina; later, technical director of the Experimental Th. at Vassar Coll.; artist-professor-in-residence, California State University at Long Beach; and adjunct professor of theatre, Southern Methodist University. He has been a guest lecturer at the Univ. of Minnesota, Denison University, Eastern Washington State College, Ohio State Univ., and State Univ. of New York.

Mr. Corson made his debut as actor-author in a performance of original character sketches (Brooklyn Acad. of Music, Jan. 18, 1956). He has subsequently given several thousand one-man performances of his sketches throughout the US; Canada; and England, where he first appeared at the Crane Th., Liverpool (Sept. 1963).

His first N.Y.C. engagement was as make-up consultant for *Johnny Johnson* (Carnegie Th., Oct. 21, 1956).

Television. Mr. Corson performed his character sketches on local television (Peoria, Ill., May 1955). His one-act play, The Sisters McIntosh, was produced by NBC-TV.

Published Works. He wrote *Stage Makeup* (1960; 5th ed. 1974); *Monologs for Men* (1960); *Fashions in Hair: The First 5000 Years* (1964); *Fashions in Eyeglasses* (1967); and *Fashions in Makeup* (1973).

He was make-up editor for *Players* Magazine, contributing monthly articles; and has contributed articles to *Theatre Arts, Dramatics Magazine,* and the *Quarterly Journal of Speech.*

CORWIN, NORMAN. Playwright, director, producer. b. May 3, 1910, Boston, Mass., to Samuel H. and Rose (Ober) Corwin. Father, printer; mother, artist. Attended public schools in Boston and Winthrop, Mass. Married Mar. 17, 1947, to Katherine Locke, actress; one son, one daughter. Member of SWG; ALA; Dramatists Guild; Filmex (trustee); WGA, West (director). Address: 10401 Wellworth Ave., Los Angeles, CA 90024.

Pre-Theatre. Journalist, radio writer.

Theatre. Mr. Corwin wrote the libretto for the opera *The Warrior* (Metropolitan Opera House, N.Y.C., Nov. 1947); narrated Stravinsky's *Oedipus Rex* (NY City Ctr., Nov. 1946); wrote and directed the cantata *The Golden Door* (Music Hall, Cleveland, Ohio, Mar. 23, 1955); first wrote and directed for Bway *The Rivalry* (Bijou Th., Feb. 7, 1959), which had previously toured (opened Georgia Aud., Vancouver, Can., Sept. 23, 1957; closed Shubert, New Haven, Jan. 25, 1958); subsequently wrote and directed *The World of Carl Sandburg* (Henry Miller's Th., Sept. 14, 1960), which had also previously toured (opened State Th., Portland, Me., Oct. 12, 1959; closed Alcazar, San Francisco, Calif., Apr. 23, 1960).

At the Univ. of California at Los Angeles, he narrated the cantata *Joshua* (Royce Hall, June 1961); and for the Theatre Group there, he directed *The Chinese Wall* (Schoenberg Hall, July 31, 1962). He wrote and directed *Overkill and Megalove* (invitational performances, Desilu Th., Hollywood, Calif., July 24–26, 1964; public performances, Festival Th., San Anselmo, Calif., Feb. 24–Apr. 2, 1967); wrote and performed *Jerusalem Printout* for opening of "Jerusalem Fair" (Los Angeles Convention Center Aud., Nov. 22, 1972); wrote and directed *The Odyssey of Runyon Jones* (Valley Music Th., Los Angeles, Dec. 16, 1972); and wrote *Cervantes,* (American Th., Washington, D.C., Sept. 6, 1973).

Films. Mr. Corwin wrote the screenplays for *The Blue Veil* (RKO, 1951); *Scandal at Scourie* (MGM, 1953); *Lust for Life* (MGM, 1956); and *The Story of Ruth* (20th-Fox, 1961). The film *Once Upon a Time* (Col., 1944) was based upon his *My Client Curley.* He was chairman of the Documentary Awards Committee of the Motion Picture Academy (1964–74) and co-chairman of the Scholarship Committee of the Academy (1970–to date).

Television and Radio. Mr. Corwin wrote, directed, and/or produced the following radio series and special broadcasts: Words Without Music (CBS, 1938); They Fly Through the Air (CBS, 1939); Ballad for Americans (CBS, 1939); Pursuit of Happiness (CBS, 1939–40); Showcase (CBS, 1940); 26 by Corwin (CBS, 1941); We Hold These Truths (all networks, Dec. 15, 1941); and One World Flight (CBS, 1947).

He was director and a contributing writer for the series This Is War! (all networks, 1942); writer and director of the series An American in England (CBS, BBC, 1942); writer, director, and producer of Transatlantic Call (CBS, BBC, 1943); Passport for Adams (CBS, 1943); and Columbia Presents Corwin (CBS, 1944, 1945); director and producer of The Lonesome Train (CBS, 1944); writer, director, and producer of On a Note of Triumph (CBS, May 1945); Word from the People (CBS, May 1945); Stars in the Afternoon (CBS, Sept. 1945); and writer-director of Citizen of the World (CBS, 1949).

He was writer, director, and producer for the UN radio specials: Could Be (NBC, BBC, Oct. 1949); Fear Itself (NBC, BBC, May 1950); Document A/777 (NBC, BBC, CBS, Mar. 1950); Windows on the World (NBC, BBC, ABC, Australia, Nov. 1951); The Charter in the Saucer (BBC, Apr. 1955).

For television, Mr. Corwin wrote two works (1 and 26) for the series, F.D.R. (1963); and wrote Inside the Movie Kingdom (NBC, 1964). He was co-narrator of the series The Seven Seas (1969); wrote Guest of Honor CATV series of twenty-six programs (1971); wrote thirteen, directed five, appeared as on-camera host in all twenty-six of the TV series Norman Corwin Presents (Westinghouse Broadcasting Group W, 1971–72); wrote a segment and appeared in The Last GI's (PBS, 1971); wrote and directed The Plot to Overthrow Christmas (PBS, 1970; repeated annually through 1974); and wrote The Trial of Yamashita for Judgment (ABC, 1974).

Other Activities. Mr. Corwin taught a course, "Creative Man in the Lively Arts," at UCLA (1967–69) and a course in telecommunications at USC in 1970. He served also as a judge for the Norman Corwin One-Act Playwriting Contest, San Diego (Calif.) State College in 1968 and 1970. He lectured on the documentary film at the Univ. of North Carolina in 1972.

Published Works. He is the author of *They Fly Through the Air* (1940), *Thirteen by Corwin* (1942), *More by Corwin* (1944), *On a Note of Triumph* (1945), *Untitled and Other Plays* (1947), *The Plot to Overthrow Christmas* (1952), *Dog in the Sky* (1952), *The Rivalry* (1960), *The World of Carl Sandburg* (1961), *Prayer for the Seventy's,* (1969), *Gettysburg and The Few Appropriate Remarks,* (1971), and the monthly department, *Corwin On Media,* Westways.

Awards. Mr. Corwin received the Metropolitan Opera Award for the libretto of *The Warrior* (1946); and for the screenplay, *Lust for Life,* the Film Critics Circle of the Foreign Language Press Award for best screenplay of the year (1957), and an Academy (Oscar) Award nomination (1957). He received the first award of the Women's American ORT for his screenplay of *The Story of Ruth* (1960).

For his radio work, Mr. Corwin has received the first award of the Institute for Education by Radio for his series *Words Without Music* (1939), for his verse drama They Fly Through the Air (1939), and for his Pursuit of Happiness (1940).

He was awarded the American Writers Congress Award for *26 by Corwin* (1941); The Bok Medal "for distinguished service to radio," (1942); the Peabody Medal for *We Hold These Truths* (1942); the American Academy of Arts and Letters Award "for the high standards that mark his work" (1942); the Page One Award "for using his journalistic talents to create a unique literature of the air" (1944); the Distinguished Merit Award of the Natl. Conf. of Christians and Jews for *Untitled* (1945); the Inter-Racial Film and Radio Guild Unity Award "for contributions to universal understanding through the medium of radio" (1945).

For his V-E Day broadcast, *On a Note of Triumph*, Mr. Corwin received the first citation in radio by the Natl. Council of Teachers of English (1945), first citation in radio by the Assn. of Teachers of Social Studies of NY, the Page One Award (1945), first place in *Billboard's* national poll of radio editors (1946), and the first award of the Inst. for Education by Radio (1946).

He also received the Award of the American Schools and Colleges Assn. "for distinguished radio writing" (1946); the Wendell Willkie One World Award "for his writing for radio and other media" (1946); first radio award of the Speakers Research Comm. of the UN "for distinguished service in presenting the UN to the peoples of the world" (1950); the first radio and television award of the Natl. Conf. of Christians and Jews for *Document A/777* (1951); the Honor Medal of the Freedom Foundation for the television production of *Between Americans* (1950); and the American Jewish Committee Citation "for contributions to better human understanding" (1959).

He was elected a fellow of the American Coll. of Radio Arts, Crafts and Sciences, and became the first writer admitted to the Radio Hall of Fame, at Chicago, Ill. (July 27, 1962). In 1972, he received the Artist of the Year Award, University of Judaism, and the Valentine Davies Award, Writers Guild of America.

COSTIGAN, JAMES. Playwright, actor. b. Mar. 31, 1928, Belvedere Gardens, Calif., to Thomas Patrick and Joan Rose (Sullivan) Costigan. Father, electrical manufacturer. Attended Professional Children's Sch., Hollywood, Calif., 1940–41 and N.Y.C., 1943; Hollywood (Calif.) H.S., 1941–43; Mar-Ken Sch., Los Angeles, Calif., 1943–44; L'Alliance Française, Paris, France, 1954. Served US Army, 1944–45; rank, Pvt.; Anti-Aircraft Batt. Member of AEA; SAG; AFTRA; WGA, West. Address: Ashley Famous Agency, Inc., 555 Madison Ave., New York, NY 10022, tel. (212) MU 8-8330.

Theatre. Mr. Costigan began as an actor at age 12, playing the title role in *Tom Sawyer* (Wilshire-Ebell Th., Los Angeles, Calif., 1940); made his N.Y.C. debut as Keith Morehouse in *Slightly Married* (Cort, Oct. 25, 1943), which was performed as *Mother's Day* during its pre-Bway tour (opened Geary, San Francisco, Calif., Sept. 25, 1943). He played Seton, the Third Murdered, and the voice of the Third Witch in the Lionel Stander-Richard Barr production of *Macbeth* (El Patio Th., Hollywood, Calif., 1945). He appeared in stock at the Gretna Playhouse (Mt. Gretna, Pa., 1948–49); toured local schools and colleges in N.Y.C. in the ELT "Scrapbook" Productions as Trepleff in *The Seagull*, Algy in *The Importance of Being Earnest*, and Max in *Anatole* (Winter 1950–51); also played Gustave in the ELT production of *Camille* (Lenox Hill Playhouse, 1951). He played Happy in *Death of a Salesman* (Niagara Falls Summer Th., N.Y., 1952); Donald Duffy in the pre-Bway tour of *The Fig Leaf* (opened Empress Playhouse, St. Louis, Mo., Sept. 30, 1952; closed Selwyn, Chicago, Ill., Oct. 18, 1952); and Donald Gresham in a tour of *The Moon Is Blue* (N.Y., N.J., Summer 1953).

Mr. Costigan's first play to be produced on Bway was *Little Moon of Alban* (Longacre, Dec. 1, 1960); subsequently wrote the lyrics for the tryout production of *The Beast in Me*, a revue based on Thurber's *Fables for Our Time* (Nash's Barn Th., Westport, Conn., 1962), and contributed both lyrics and sketches for its Bway production, appearing in both productions (Plymouth, May 16, 1963). He wrote *Baby Want a Kiss*, produced by the Actors Studio Th., in which he played Edward (Little, Apr. 19, 1964).

Films. Mr. Costigan played the role of Everett in *Happy Land* (20th-Fox, 1943); and Peanuts in *The Trouble with Women* (Par., 1947).

Television. Mr. Costigan wrote *Rain No More*, in which he played the role of John Falvey (Kraft Television Th., NBC, Apr. 15, 1953); adapted *A Cup of Kindness* from a play by Aleen Leslie, in which he also appeared (1945). For the series The Web (CBS), he wrote and played in *The Bells of Damon* (1953) and *The World, My Cage* (1954). For the Hallmark Hall of Fame (NBC), he adapted *Cradle Song* (1956, 1960), *The Lark* (Feb. 10, 1957), *On Borrowed Time* (1957), and *A Doll's House* (1959); also his original play *Little Moon of Alban* was presented (Mar. 1958). For the Dupont Show of the Month (CBS), he adapted *Wuthering Heights* (1958). For Ford Startime (NBC), he adapted *The Turn of the Screw* (Oct. 20, 1959).

COTSWORTH, STAATS. Actor. b. Staats Jennings Cotsworth, Jr., Feb. 17, 1908, Oak Park, Ill., to Staats Jennings and Dorothy (Bodley) Cotsworth. Father, steel executive. Grad. West Philadelphia (Pa.) H.S., 1927; Pennsylvania Museum Sch. of Industrial Art, 1929. Studied painting with Thornton Oakley, 1927–29; acting with Eva Le Gallienne at the NY Civic Repertory Th., (apprentice scholarship), N.Y.C., 1932–33, and with May Sarton and Santelli, N.Y.C., 1932–33. Married May 24, 1936, to Muriel Kirkland, actress (deceased); married Josephine Hutchinson, actress. Member of AEA (council, 1957–62); AFRA (vice-pres., NY Local 1949); AFRA-AFTRA (natl. boards, 1947–54); SAG; The Players (bd. of dir., chmn. art comm.); Amer. Water Color Soc.; Audubon Artists; Natl. Society of Painters (Casein); Connecticut Acad. of Fine Arts. Address: (home) 360 E. 55th St., New York, NY 10022, tel. EL 5-5645; (bus.) tel. SU 7-5400.

Theatre. Mr. Cotsworth made his stage debut as Gervase in an amateur production of *The Romantic Age* (Belmont Mansion, Philadelphia, Pa., June 1929); subsequently played Dick Dudgeon in the Main Line Repertory Company's production of *The Devil's Disciple* (Bala-Cynwyd, Pa., May 1930); made his N.Y.C. debut as a walk-on with the Civic Repertory Co., in *Liliom* (Civic Rep. Th., Oct. 26, 1932); remaining with them, succeeded Burgess Meredith (Apr. 1933) as Tweedledee in *Alice In Wonderland and Through the Looking Glass* (Civic Rep. Th., Dec. 12, 1932); and toured as Benvolio in *Romeo and Juliet* (Sept. 1933–May 1934).

He appeared as Tony and in other roles in *She Stoops to Conquer* (Community House Th., Springlake, N.J., Summer 1934); succeeded (Majestic, Oct. 1934) Ben Lackland as Billy Slade in *Murder at the Vanities* (New Amsterdam, N.Y.C., Sept. 8, 1933); played Philip Kahn in *First Episode*, title later changed to *College Sinners* (Ritz, Sept. 17, 1934); Clendon Wyatt in *Rain from Heaven* (John Golden Th., Dec. 24, 1934), and on national tour (Spring 1935); played in stock productions of *Private Lives* and *On Approval* (Oceanside Th., Magnolia, Mass., Summer 1935); the Second Gentleman in Philip Merivale's *Othello* (Ethel Barrymore Th., N.Y.C. Sept. 27, 1935); Donalbain and a Messenger in Mr. Merivale's, *Macbeth* (Ethel Barrymore Th., Oct. 7, 1935); succeeded (Feb. 1936) Edward Marr as George Bowman in *Moon Over Mulberry Street* (44 St. Th., Jan. 13, 1936); toured as Vasya in *Squaring the Circle* (Baltimore, Md.; Philadelphia, Pa.; Washington, D.C., Mar. 1936); in stock, played Mattie Matthews in *Sailor Beware* (Brighton Th., Brooklyn, N.Y., July 1936); Arthur Brown in *Happy Ending* (Greenwich, Conn., July 1936); and Jim Reed in *Suddenly a Stranger* (Beechwood Th., Scarborough, N.Y., Summer 1936); and toured for 30 weeks in Max Gordon's production of *Pride and Prejudice* (Oct. 1936).

Mr. Cotsworth appeared as Georges Dupont in *Damaged Good* (48 St. Th., N.Y.C., May 17, 1937); and in stock as Geoffrey in *The Two Mrs. Carrolls*, Elyot Chase in *Private Lives*, and in other roles (Playhouse, Southampton, N.Y., July–Aug. 1937); as Oliver in the Surrey Players *As You Like It* (Ritz, N.Y.C., Oct. 30, 1937); Dick McKernan in *Stop-Over* (Lyceum, Jan. 11, 1938); appeared as Elyot Chase in *Private Lives*, Geoffrey in *The Two Mrs. Carrolls*, Mr. Jelliwell in *Springtime for Henry*, and as Colin Derwent in *Ten Minute Alibi* (Playhouse, Southampton, N.Y., June–July 1938); and as Chaveau-Lagarde and Count De Vaudreuil in *Madame Capet* (Cort, N.Y.C., Oct. 25, 1938); for the Ann Arbor (Mich.) Festival, played Ajax in *No War in Troy;* Tom, the Press Agent, in *Here Come the Clowns*, Capt. Kearny in *Captain Brassbound's Conversion*, and appeared in *The White Steed* (Apr., May 1939); and performed in *The Master's Servants* (Stony Creek Th., Conn., July 1939).

He played Tom Prior in a Kanawha Players production of *Outward Bound* (Charleston, W. Va., Jan. 1940); toured as Eilert Lovborg in *Hedda Gabler* (Apr. 1940); appeared with the South Shore Players (Cohasset, Mass., Summer 1940) as Andre in *Her Cardboard Lover*, Gay in *No Time for Comedy*, and Gail in *Tomorrow and Tomorrow;* played Gaylord in *Boudoir* (John Golden Th., N.Y.C., Feb. 7, 1941); toured as Rudd Kendall in *Old Acquaintances* (Apr. 1941); with the South Shore Players (Summer 1941), portrayed Rudd Kendall in *Old Acquaintances*, Mr. North in *Mr. and Mrs. North*, Tom Prior in *Outward Bound*, and in *Hay Fever;* Banquo in Maurice Evans' *Macbeth* (Natl., N.Y.C., Nov. 11, 1941), and on tour (until Apr. 1942); at the Bucks County Playhouse (New Hope, Pa., Summer 1942), played Lord Essex in *Elizabeth the Queen*, Barrie Trexel in *Susan and God*, Mr. North in *Mr. and Mrs. North*, and Henry Higgins in *Pygmalion;* and repeated his role in a touring production of *Pygmalion* (Oct.–Dec. 1942).

Mr. Cotsworth played Hastings in *She Stoops to Conquer* (NY City Ctr., Dec. 28, 1949); Clarence in José Ferrer's *Richard III* (NY City Ctr., Dec. 9, 1953); Rev. Jeremiah Brown in *Inherit the Wind* (Natl., Apr. 21, 1955); was the Narrator for *Pictures in the Hallway* (Playhouse, Sept. 16, 1956), and for *I Knock at the Door* (Belasco, Sept. 29, 1957). For the double bill of Jean Giraudoux plays, he played Matamua in *The Virtuous Island*, and the President in *The Apollo of Bellac* (Carnegie Hall Playhouse, Apr. 9, 1957); appeared in the title role in the NY Shakespeare Festival production of *Julius Caesar* (Belvedere Lake Th., Aug. 3, 1959); toured for the Natl. Phoenix Th. as Lord Burleigh in *Mary Stuart* (Oct. 1959–May 1960); appeared as Mr. Manningham in *Angel Street*, and "He" in *The Fourposter* for a USO tour of 68 military installations in France and Germany (March–June 1959); at the South Shore Music Tent (Cohasset, Mass.), played Old Strauss in *The Great Waltz*, (July 1960), wang Chi Yang in *Flower Drum Song* (July 1961), and Ben in *Fiorello!* (July 1962).

He appeared as William A. Huntington in *Advise and Consent* (Cort, N.Y.C., Nov. 17, 1960); Larry Burnett in the pre-Bway tryout of *Banderol* (opened Forest Th., Philadelphia, Pa., Sept. 17, 1962; closed there Sept. 22, 1962); Pastor Manders in *Ghosts* (4th St. Th., N.Y.C., Sept. 21, 1961); and as Polonius in the NY Shakespeare Festival production of *Hamlet* (Delacorte, N.Y.C., June 16, 1964).

He was the Narrator for the revival of *Pictures in the Hallway* (Th. de Lys, Dec. 15, 1964); played Menenius in *Coriolanus* (NY Shakespeare Festival, Delacorte Th., July 7, 1965); Sir James in *The Right Honorable Gentleman* (Billy Rose Th., Oct. 19, 1965); Lafew in *All's Well That Ends Well* (NY Shakespeare Festival, Delacorte Th., June 15, 1966); Cardinal Pandulph in *King John* (NY Shakespeare Festival, Delacorte Th., July 5, 1967); Senator Andrews in *Weekend* (Broadhurst, Mar. 13,

1968); Lt. Col. Ludwig von Mohl in *A Patriot for Me* (Imperial, Oct. 5, 1969); played in a revival of *The Madwoman of Chaillot* (Sokol Th., Mar. 22, 1970); was Mr. Kirby in *You Can't Take It With You* (Long Wharf Th., New Haven, Conn., Oct. 22, 1971); and the Judge in a revival of *Lost in the Stars* (Imperial, Apr. 18, 1972).

Films. Mr. Cotsworth made his debut as Charles Partidge in *Peyton Place* (20th-Fox, 1957).

Television and Radio. He first performed on radio on the serial, Big Sister (CBS, 1943); subsequently appeared on Pepper Young's Family (NBC, 1943); the March of Time (NBC, 1943–45); Cavalcade of America (NBC, 1943–44); Amanda of Honeymoon Hill (CBS, 1944–45); Casey, Crime Photographer (CBS, 1944–55); Theatre Guild on the Air (NBC, 1944–45); Front Page Farrell (NBC, 1943); narrated These Are Our Men (NBC, 1947); appeared on Great Plays (NBC, 1948–49); played the title role of *Macbeth* (NBC, 1949); Manley Halliday in *The Disenchanted* (NBC, 1949); Wolfe Bennett in *Lone Journey* (NBC, 1950); and narrated You Make the News (Mutual, 1947–48).

On television, he first performed in *Hay Fever* (NBC, 1937); subsequently as Banquo in Maurice Evans' *Macbeth* (Hallmark Hall of Fame, NBC, 1954); as Abraham Lincoln in *Abe Lincoln in Illinois* (Hallmark Hall of Fame, NBC); and on such dramatic series as The Defenders (CBS); Dr. Kildare (NBC); G.E. Th. (CBS); The Nurses (CBS); Alfred Hitchcock Presents (CBS); and Bonanza (NBC, 1971).

Other Activities. Mr. Cotsworth is also a painter (one-man show, Hammer Gallery, N.Y.C., 1954) and illustrator, and has received the Connecticut Academy of Fine Arts Penrose Award (1959) and the Knickerbocker Artists' Oil Painting Award (1962).

Awards. He recieved the Sylvania Achievement Award (1949) for his performance of the title role in Casey, Crime Photographer; the West Philadelphia High School Award of Merit (1954); and the Actor's Fund Award of Merit (1960).

Recreation. Swimming, sketching, reading, writing.

COTTEN, JOSEPH. Actor. b. Joseph Cheshire Cotten, May 15, 1905, Petersburg, Va., to Joseph and Sally (Willson) Cotten. Father, assistant postmaster. Attended Robert Nugent Hickman Sch. of Expression, Washington, D.C., 1923. Married Oct. 18, 1931, to Lenore Kipp (dec. Jan. 7, 1960), one step-daughter; married Oct. 20, 1960, to Patricia Medina, actress. Member of AEA; SAG (director, 1945–48); AFTRA.

Theatre. Mr. Cotten was assistant stage manager and understudy to Lynne Overman as Lord Robert Brummel in *Dancing Partner* (Belasco, N.Y.C., Aug. 5, 1930); assistant stage manager and understudy to Melvyn Douglas as the Unknown Gentleman in *Tonight or Never* (Belasco, Nov. 18, 1930); played a season of stock at the Copley Th. (Boston, Mass., 1931–32); appeared as Larry (Lawrence Carter Boyden) in *Absent Father* (Vanderbilt, N.Y.C., Oct. 17, 1932); Dick Ashley in *Jezebel* (Ethel Barrymore Th., Dec. 19, 1933); Ralph Merdes in *Loose Momets* (Vanderbilt, Feb. 4, 1935); succeeded (May 1935) Theodore Newton as Dickie Reynolds in *Accent on Youth* (Plymouth, Dec. 25, 1934); and played a Policeman in *The Postman Always Rings Twice* (Lyceum, Feb. 25, 1936).

For the Federal Theatre (WPA) Project, he played Freddie Hooper in *Horse Eats Hat* (Maxine Elliott's Th., Sept. 26, 1936), and a Scholar in *Dr. Faustus* (Maxine Elliott's Th., Jan. 8, 1937); for the Mercury Th. of which he was president (1938–40), played Publius in *Julius Caesar* (Mercury, Nov. 11, 1937), Rowland Lacy in *The Shoemaker's Holiday* (Mercury, Jan. 1, 1938); and Augustus Billings in the pre-Bway tryout of *Too Much Johnson* (Stony Creek Th., Conn., Aug. 16, 1938).

He played C.K. Dexter Haven in *The Philadelphia Story* (Shubert, Mar. 28, 1939); Linus Larrabee, Jr., in *Sabrina Fair* (Natl., Nov. 11, 1953); Victor Fabian in *Once More, With Feeling* (Natl., Oct. 21, 1958); Dr. Roy Flemming in the pre-Bway tryout of *Prescription: Murder* (opened Curran, San Francisco, Calif., Jan. 15, 1962; closed Shubert, Boston, Mass., May 26, 1962); Julian Armstone in *Calculated Risk* (Ambassador, N.Y.C., Oct. 31, 1962); toured in *Seven Ways of Love* (Jan.–May 1964); played Paul Delville in *The Marriage-Go-Round* (Drury Lane Th., Chicago, May 1971); and Jimmy Broadbent in *The Reluctant Debutant* (touring production, 1974–75).

Films. Mr. Cotten appeared in industrial shorts (1933–34); in *Citizen Kane* (RKO, 1941); *Lydia* (UA, 1941); *The Magnificent Ambersons* (RKO, 1942); wrote, with Orson Welles, and appeared in *Journey into Fear* (RKO, 1942); played in *Shadow of a Doubt* (U, 1943); *Hers to Hold* (U, 1943); *Gaslight* (MGM, 1944); *Since You Went Away* (UA, 1944); *I'll Be Seeing You* (UA, 1944); *Love Letters* (Par., 1945); *The Farmer's Daughter* (RKO, 1947); *Duel in the Sun* (Selznick, 1946); *Portrait of Jenny* (Selznick, 1948); *Under Capricorn* (WB, 1949); *Beyond the Forest* (WB, 1949); *The Third Man* (Selznick, 1950); *Walk Softly, Stranger* (RKO, 1950); *September Affair* (Par., 1950); *Two Flags West* (20th-Fox, 1950); *Half Angel* (20th-Fox, 1951); *Peking Express* (Par., 1951); *The Man with a Cloak* (MGM, 1951); *Untamed Frontier* (U, 1952); *The Steel Trap* (20th-Fox, 1952); *Niagara* (20th-Fox, 1953); *A Blueprint for Murder* (20th-Fox, 1953); *Special Delivery* (Col., 1955); *The Bottom of the Bottle* (20th-Fox, 1956); *The Killer Is Loose* (UA, 1956); *The Halliday Brand* (UA, 1957); *From the Earth to the Moon* (WB, 1958); *Frankenstein's Daughter* (Astor, 1958); *The Last Sunset* (U, 1961); *The Angel Wore Red* (MGM, 1960); *Hush, Hush, Sweet Charlotte* (20th-Fox, 1965); *The Money Trap* (MGM, 1966); *Petulia* (WB, 1968); *Grasshopper* (National General, 1970); *Latitude Zero* (National General, 1970); *Dr. Phibes Rises Again!* (AI, 1972); *Baron Blood* (Amer. Internat., 1972); *A Delicate Balance* (American Film Th., 1973); and *Timber Tramp.*

Television and Radio. On radio, Mr. Cotten was a writer and actor for Mercury Theatre of the Air (1938–39); performed on American-Ceiling Unlimited (Lockheed Aircraft, 1943–44); was narrator and actor with Philco Radio Playhouse (ABC, 1953); and performed on The Private Files of Dr. Matthew Bell (MBS, 1953).

On television, he was host and narrator for 20th-Century-Fox Television Hour (CBS, 1955–56); appeared in *State of the Union* (NBC, 1955); *Man Without Fear* (Ford Th., NBC, Mar. 1, 1956); *Broadway* (CBS, May 4, 1956); *H.M.S. Marlborough* (GE Th., CBS, Apr. 29, 1956); *The Enemies* (CBS, Oct. 14, 1956); the series, On Trial (NBC, 1957–58); *The Case of the Jealous Bomber* (NBC, July 26, 1957); *The Edge of Innocence* (Playhouse 90, CBS, Oct. 31, 1957); *Command Appearance* (NBC, Nov. 23, 1957); Wagon Train (1961); was narrator for Hollywood and the Stars (NBC, 1963–64); and appeared on 77 Sunset Strip (ABC, Nov. 15, 1963).

Awards. Mr. Cotten received the Venice Film Festival Award for his performance in *Portrait of Jenny* (1949).

COULOURIS, GEORGE. Actor. b. Oct. 1, 1903, Manchester, Eng., to Nicholas and Abigail (Redfern) Coulouris. Father, merchant. Grad. Manchester Grammar Sch. Studied with Elsie Fogerty at Central School of Speech Training and Dramatic Art. Married to Louise Franklin. Member of AEA, British AEA, AFTRA. Address: Chestnut Cottage, Vale of Health, London, N.W.3, England tel. Hempstead 8647.

Theatre. Mr. Coulouris first performed on stage as Rev. William Duke in *Outward Bound* (Rusholme Repertory, Manchester, Eng., May 1926); made his London debut as Sir Thomas Grey in *Henry V* (Old Vic, Oct. 18, 1926); continued with the Old Vic company in small roles; subsequently appeared as Giuseppe in *Sirocco* (Daly's, Nov. 1927); joined (Oct. 1928) the Cambridge Festival Th., playing Yank in *The Hairy Ape,* Mercutio in *Romeo and Juliet,* and Jaques in *As You Like It;* appeared as Petronius in *The Theatre of Life* (Arts, London, Apr. 1929) and Jacques Bonalie in *The Black Ace* (Globe, May 1929).

He made his Bway debut as Friar Peter in *The Novice and the Duke,* a modern dress version of *Measure for Measure* (Assembly, Dec. 9, 1929); succeeded Rex O'Malley as Sempronius (Apr. 1930) in *The Apple Cart* (Martin Beck Th., Feb. 24, 1930); played Tallant in *The Late Christopher Bean* (Henry Miller's Th., Oct. 31, 1932); Tybalt in *Romeo and Juliet* (Embassy, London, Feb. 1932); the Bank Manager in *From Morn to Midnight* (Gate, May 1932); Julian Mosca in *Best Sellers* (Morosco, N.Y.C., May 3, 1933); Lord Burleigh in *Mary of Scotland* (Alvin, Nov. 27, 1933); Lt. Cutting in *Valley Forge* (Guild, Dec. 10, 1934); Dr. Shelby in *Blind Alley* (Booth, Sept. 24, 1935); John de Stogumber in *Saint Joan* (Martin Beck Th., Mar. 9, 1936); and Zacharey in *Ten Million Ghosts* (St. James, Oct. 23, 1936).

With the Mercury Th., N.Y.C. Mr. Coulouris appeared as Marc Antony in *Julius Caesar* (Nov. 11, 1937), the King in *Shoemaker's Holiday* (Jan. 1, 1938), and Boss Mangan in *Heartbreak House* (Apr. 29, 1938); subsequently played Mirabeau in *Madame Capet* (Cort, Oct. 25, 1938); Father Shaughnessy in *The White Steed* (Jan. 10, 1939); John Elliott in *Cue for Passion* (Royale, Dec. 19, 1940); Teck de Brancois in *Watch on the Rhine* (Martin Beck Th., Apr. 1, 1941), in which he also toured; produced, directed, and appeared in the title role of *Richard III* (Forrest, Mar. 24, 1943); performed in *Blind Alley* (Hollywood, Calif.); appeared as Waldo Cruikshank in the pre-Bway tryout of *Bonanza Bound* (opened Shubert, Philadelphia, Dec. 26, 1947; closed there Jan. 3, 1948); and with the New York City Th. Co. (NY City Ctr., 1948), appeared as Subtle in *The Alchemist* (May 6–16), The Donkey Man in *The Moon of the Caribees* (May 20–30), and the Vagrant in *The Insect Comedy (or The World We Live In)* (June 3–13).

He joined the Bristol (Eng.) Old Vic Co. (Jan. 1950) to play Jaques in *As You Like It,* the title role in *Tartuffe,* in *The Admirable Crichton,* Brutus in *Julius Caesar,* and Sir John Brute in *The Provok'd Wife;* played the title role in *Tartuffe* (Lyric, Hammersmith, London, June 27, 1950); Ulric Brendel in *Rosmersholm* (St. Martin's Aug. 22, 1950); at the Edinburgh (Scot.) Festival, performed in *The Man in the Overcoat* (1950); and played the title role in *King Lear* (Glasgow Citizens' Th. Scot., 1952).

He portrayed King James I in *Fool's Mate* (Criterion, London, Jan. 11, 1953); Clumber Holmes in *The Full Treatment* ("Q," Feb. 3, 1953); Malvolio in *Twelfth Night* (Embassy, May 20, 1953); Claudius in *Hamlet* (Embassy, May 26, 1953); Smiley Coy in *The Big Knife* (Wimbledon, Nov. 30, 1953); toured as the General in *The Soldier and the Lady* (Spring, 1954); appeared as Paul Finch in *The Ghost Writers* (Arts, London, Feb. 9, 1955); Charles Touchdown in *Moonshine* ("Q," Oct. 10, 1955); Hawkshaw in *The Ticket-of-Leave Man* (Arts, Cambridge, Dec. 20, 1956); John Pope in *A Hatful of Rain* (Prince's, Mar., 1957; return engagement Prince's, Aug. 12, 1958); Dr. Stockmann in Arthur Miller's version of *The Enemy of the People* (Arts, Cambridge, Feb. 1959); Squeezum in *Lock Up Your Daughters* (Mermaid, Aug. 1962); Peter Flynn in *The Plough and the Stars* (Mermaid, Sept. 25, 1962); performed in scenes from *Tartuffe* and *The Way of the World* (Georgian Th., Richmond, Yorkshire, May 1963); and as Shylock in *The Merchant of Venice* (Flora Robson, Newcastle-on-Tyne, 1963).

He appeared in N.Y.C. as Sam Holt in *Beekman Place* (Morosco, Oct. 8, 1964) and as the Father in *The Condemned of Altona* (Vivian Beaumont Th., Feb. 3, 1966); and in Los Angeles as Voltaire in *The Sorrows of Frederick* (Mark Taper Forum, June 23, 1967). In London he played the Earl of Theign in *The Outcry* (Arts, Mar. 20, 1968); Sikorski in *The Soldiers* (New, Dec. 12, 1968); and at Derby, England, he appeared as Philip Bummidge in *The Last Analysis* (Theatre Royal, 1970). He was in London as Big Daddy in *Cat on a Hot Tin Roof* (Richmond Th., 1970) and was at Brighton as Shylock in *The Merchant of Venice* (Gardiner Arts Th., Aug. 1973).

Films. Since 1933, Mr. Coulouris has appeared in

nearly 50 pictures, including *Lady in Question* (Col., 1940); *All This and Heaven Too* (WB, 1940); *Citizen Kane* (RKO, 1941); *This Land is Mine* (RKO, 1943); *Assignment in Brittany* (MGM, 1943); *For Whom the Bell Tolls* (Par., 1943); *Watch on the Rhine* (WB, 1943); *Between Two Worlds* (WB, 1944); *Mr. Skeffington* (WB, 1944); *None But the Lonely Heart* (RKO, 1944); *Master Race* (RKO, 1944); *A Song to Remember* (Col., 1945); *Confidential Agent* (WB, 1945); *The Verdict* (WB, 1946); *Lady on a Train* (U, 1945); *Hotel Berlin* (WB, 1945); *California* (Par., 1946); *Sleep My Love* (UA, 1948); *Southern Yankee* (MGM, 1948); *Kill or Be Killed* (Eagle Lion, 1950); *Island Rescue* (Rep., 1952); *Outcast of the Islands* (UA, 1952); *The Assassin* (Gaumont, 1952); *The Heart of the Matter* (Brit. Lion, 1953); *Doctor in the House* (Rep., 1955); *Doctor at Sea* (Rep., 1956); *St. Joan* (UA, 1957); *Doctor at Large* (U, 1957); *I Accuse!* (MGM, 1958); *Law and Disorder* (Brit. Lion, 1958); *Conspiracy of Hearts* (Rank, 1960); *Surprise Package* (Col., 1960); *Bluebeard's Ten Honeymoons* (WPD, 1960); *The Boy Who Stole a Million* (Bryanston, 1961); *The Crooked Road* (Gala, 1964); *Arabesque* (U, 1966); *The Horror on Snape Island* (Fanfare, 1972); *Papillon* (Allied Artists, 1973); *The Final Program* (Gladiole, 1973); *Mahler Lives* (Goodtimes Enterprises, 1974); *Percy's Progress* (Box and Thomas, 1974); *Murder on the Orient Express* (1974).

Recreation. Tennis, music.

COWLES, CHANDLER. Producer, actor. b. Sept. 29, 1917, New Haven, Conn., to Walter B. and Mrs. Cowles. Father, pianist, teacher. Attended Yale Univ., Bennington Theatre Sch.; Dramatic Workshop of the New Sch. for Social Research, c. 1940. Married to Lenore Lonergan, actress. Served USN, 1941–45.

Theatre. Mr. Cowles made his N.Y.C. debut as a principal in the revue, *Call Me Mister* (Natl., Apr. 16, 1946). He produced, with Efrem Zimbalist, Jr., in association with Edith Lutyens, *The Telephone* and *The Medium* (Ethel Barrymore Th., May 1, 1947), which was revived by David Heilweil and Derrick Lynn-Thomas, in association with Mr. Cowles (Arena Th., Edison Hotel, N.Y.C., July 19, 1950); played Dauber in *The Cradle Will Rock* (Mansfield, Dec. 26, 1947); and was a principal in the revue *Small Wonder* (Coronet, Sept. 15, 1948).

He produced, with Efrem Zimbalist, Jr., *The Consul* (Ethel Barrymore Th., Mar. 15, 1950); produced, with Anthony B. Farrell, *Billy Budd* (Biltmore, Feb. 10, 1951); produced, with Ben Segal, *Fancy Meeting You Again* (Royale, Jan. 14, 1952), and *Of Thee I Sing* (Ziegfeld, May 5, 1952); produced, with Martin Gabel, and played the role of Carleton Pelter in *Men of Distinction* (48 St. Th., Apr. 30, 1953); and produced *The Saint of Bleeker Street* (Bway Th., Dec. 27, 1954). At the American Shakespeare Festival (Stratford, Conn.), Mr. Cowles was executive producer for *Julius Caesar, The Tempest,* and *Much Ado About Nothing* (July 12–Sept. 3, 1955).

T. Edward Hambleton and Norris Houghton presented on two consecutive Monday evenings Mr. Cowles' production of *The Transposed Head* (Phoenix, N.Y.C., Feb. 10, 1958). He produced, with Charles Bowden and Ridgely Bullock, *Caligula* (54 St. Th., Feb. 16, 1960).

Television. Mr. Cowles was general manager of the NBC Opera tour (1956).

Other Activities. He is the model for the comic strip character Steve Canyon.

COXE, LOUIS O. Educator, playwright. b. Louis Osborne Coxe, Apr. 15, 1918, Manchester, N.H., to Charles S. and Helen (Osborne) Coxe. Father, insurance executive. Grad. St. Paul's Sch., Concord, N.H., 1936; Princeton Univ., B.A., 1940. Married June 28, 1946, to Edith Winsor; three sons, one daughter. Served USN, PTO (1942–46); rank Lt. Member of ALA; Dramatists Guild. Address: (home) RD #2, Adams Rd., Brunswick, ME 04011, tel. (207) 443-5385; (bus.) c/o Bowdoin College, Brunswick, ME 04011.

Mr. Coxe teaches English and American literature at Bowdoin College (1955–to date). Mr. Coxe also held academic positions at Lawrenceville Sch. (1946–48); Harvard Coll. (Briggs-Copeland Fellow, 1948–49); Univ. of Minnesota (assistant professor, 1949–52; associate professor, 1952–55); Trinity Coll., Dublin, Ire., (visiting lecturer, 1959–60); Princeton Univ. (visiting professor, 1961–62); Bread Loaf School of English (Summer 1963); State Univ. of New York at Buffalo (Summer 1967); Univ. d'Aix, Marseille, France (visiting lecturer, 1971–72); Harvard Univ. (Summer 1973).

Mr. Coxe adapted, with Robert Chapman, *Billy Budd* (Biltmore Th., Feb. 10, 1951); and has written *The General* (Harvard Univ. and Univ. of Minnesota, Minneapolis, 1954); *The Witchfinders* (Rochester, Minn., and Univ. of Minnesota, 1955; Cornell Univ., 1957; Provincetown Playhouse, N.Y.C., 1958); *Decoration Day* (Bowdoin Coll., 1965); *Birth of a State,* sesquicentennial play, state of Maine (Portland, Me., 1970); and *Hare and Hounds* (Conn. State Coll., Willimantic, Conn.).

Television. Mr. Coxe's *Birth of a State* was telecast on Portland, Me., educational television (1970–71).

Published Works. He has written the following volumes of poetry: *The Sea Faring and Other Poems* (1947), *The Second Man and Other Poems* (1955), *The Wilderness and Other Poems* (1958), *The Middle Passage* (1960), *The Last Hero and Other Poems* (1965); *Nikal Seyn and Decoration Day* (1966), and *Edwin Arlington Robinson: The Life of Poetry* (1969).

Awards. Mr. Coxe has received, with Mr. Chapman, the Donaldson Award for *Billy Budd* (1952); a *Sewanee Review* Fellowship (1956); Vachel Lindsay Prize, *Poetry* Magazine; the Brandeis Award (1961); and State of Maine Humanities Award (1972).

Recreation. Sailing, birdwatching.

CRABTREE, PAUL. Writer, actor, director, producer. b. Paul Joyce Crabtree, Nov. 17, 1918, Pulaski, Va., to Robert Thomas and Mollie (Smith) Crabtree. Father, telephone company manager. Grad. Pulaski H.S., 1937; attended Syracuse Univ., 1938–42. Married Nov. 19, 1944, to Mary Ducey; four sons, three daughters. Member of WGA; SDG; AEA; ASCAP; Phi Kappa Psi. Address: Holliday Hills, Crossville, TN 38555, tel. (615) 484-5776.

Theatre. Mr. Crabtree performed at age three as a singer-dancer in a firemans' minstrel show in Pulaski, Va.; later played Pvt. Francis Marion in *The Eve of St. Mark* (Cedarhurst Playhouse, L.I., N.Y., July 1943); Pvt. Earheart in a touring company of *Kiss and Tell* (opened Shubert, New Haven, Sept. 7, 1943).

He made his Bway debut as Harry in *Men to the Sea* (National, Oct. 3, 1944); followed by Sgt. Winters in *The Streets Are Guarded* (Henry Miller's Th., Nov. 20, 1944); succeeded Lee Dixon as Will Parker in *Oklahoma!* (St. James, Dec. 25, 1944); and played Sulfa in *Skydrift* (Belasco, Nov. 12, 1945).

Mr. Crabtree was special assistant to Lawrence Langner and Theresa Helburn, directors of the Th. Guild (1946–1950); also for the Guild, he appeared as Dan Parritt in *The Iceman Cometh* (Martin Beck Th., Oct. 9, 1946); and produced and directed *This Time Tomorrow* (Ethel Barrymore Th., Nov. 24, 1948) and *The Silver Whistle* (Biltmore Th., Nov. 25, 1948).

For Studio Productions, Inc. and A. B. Farrell, he produced and directed *Texas Li'l Darlin'* (Mark Hellinger Th., Nov. 25, 1949); and for Trio Productions and Milo Thomas, wrote, produced and directed *A Story for a Sunday Evening,* and also appeared as David (Playhouse, Nov. 17, 1950); appeared as Jack McDougal in *Lo and Behold!* (Booth, Dec. 12, 1951); produced, with Frank J. Hale, and directed *Mid-Summer* (Vanderbilt, Jan. 21, 1953).

He directed a stock production of *Devil Take a Whittler* (Westport Country Playhouse, Conn., July 29, 1946). He has been affiliated, as actor, director, and associate managing director with Martin Manulis, with the Westport (Conn.) Country Playhouse (1946–49); managing director of the Famous Artists Playhouses (Syracuse, Rochester, and Watkins Glen, N.Y., 1949–51); managing director (1951–53) and producing director of the Palm Beach (Fla.) Playhouse (1952–55); producing director of the Royal Poinciana Playhouse (Palm Beach, Fla. 1957–60); producing director, Cumberland County Playhouse (Crossville, Tenn., 1965–to date), where his musical *Tennessee U.S.A.!* has been presented each season; and executive writer, producer, and director of all live shows Theme Park, *Opryland U.S.A.!* including *I Hear America Singing.*

Films. Mr. Crabtree wrote screenplays for *Johnny Tiger* (U, 1966) and *Country Boy* (Ambassador, 1967) and appeared as Jackson in the latter.

Television and Radio. For radio, Mr. Crabtree has written for the Th. Guild of the Air and NBC Monitor. He was also an actor on Theatre Guild programs and played David in the radio serial Claudia.

He has written scripts for Studio One (CBS); the Pilot (CBS, 1956); Kraft Television Playhouse (NBC); American Heritage Series (1958); My Three Sons (1962); The New Loretta Young Show (CBS, 1962); and Death Valley Days (1963).

He has performed on television since April, 1946, on the Armstrong Circle Th. (NBC); Philco Television Playhouse (NBC); and the Loretta Young Show (CBS), for which he also directed several programs.

Recreation. Tennis, basketball, baseball (fan), carpentry, training young people in the theatre.

CRAIG, DAVID. Coach, lyricist, librettist. b. David Krangel, Mar. 12, 1923, New York City, to Samuel and Belle Krangel. Father, tax consultant. Grad. DeWitt Clinton H.S., New York City, 1938; attended City Coll. of New York, 1938–39; Juilliard Sch. of Music, 1939–41. Married Jan. 29, 1951, to Nancy Walker, actress; one daughter. Served USAAF, SAC, Far East, 1942–46. Member of ASCAP.

Theatre. Mr. Craig made his N.Y.C. debut as lyricist of the revue, *Phoenix '55* (Phoenix Th., Apr. 23, 1955). He also wrote the lyrics and, with Ellen Violett, the book for *Copper and Brass* (Martin Beck Th., Oct. 17, 1957).

Since 1960, he has been engaged in training actors, singers and dancers for the musical theatre.

Recreation. Reading, living in the Virgin Islands.

CRAIG, HELEN. Actress, teacher. b. May 13, San Antonio, Tex., to Edward J. and Emily (Cauthorn) Craig. Father, mining engineer; mother, painter. Grad. Scarborough Sch., N.Y.; attended AADA. Studied with Jasper Deeter, Hedgerow Th., Moylan, Pa., 1929–32; Lee Strasberg, N.Y.C., 1936; Josephine Dillon Gable, Hollywood, 1936; Dame May Whitty, Hollywood, 1941; and Fanny Bradshaw, N.Y.C., 1952. Married July 13, 1934, to John Beal, actor, director; two daughters: Tita Beal, writer and puppeteer; Tandy Beal, dancer, choreographer, and teacher. Relative in theatre: sister-in-law, Valentine Vernon, actress. Member of AEA; SAG; AFTRA. Address: c/o Actors' Equity Association, 165 W. 46th St., New York, NY 10036.

Theatre. Miss Craig first appeared on a stage as an Old Woman in a school production of *Will o' the Wisp;* and first appeared professionally as a Maid in *A Doll's House* at the Hedgerow Th. (Moylan, Pa., 1929), where she subsequently appeared (1929–1932) in over 40 roles in repertory, including Masha in *The Seagull,* Elsa in *Alison's House,* Mary Fitton in *Will Shakespeare,* Joyce in *Thunder on the Left,* Nida in *Son of Perdition,* Nurse Guinness in *Heartbreak House,* and Lina Szczepanowska in *Misalliance.* She appeared as Hortense in *Nellie the Beautiful Cloak Model* (Lyric, Philadelphia, Pa., Winter 1931); and at the Pasadena (Calif.) Playhouse, appeared as Mellisinde in *La Princesse Lointaine,* Bossy in *The Texas Steer,* and Regina in *Ghosts* (1934–35).

She made her N.Y.C. debut as Manuelita in *Russet Mantle* (Masque, Jan. 16, 1936), and later succeeded (Spring 1936) Martha Sleeper as Kay Rowley; subsequently played Lottie of the Liberati and other roles in the revue, *New Faces of 1936* (Vanderbilt, May 19, 1936); Olive in *American Primitive* (Lobero Th., Santa Barbara, Calif., Summer 1937); succeeded (May 1938) Polly Rowles as Calpurnia in

Julius Caesar (Mercury, Nov. 11, 1937), and repeated it on tour (1938); played Ann Jenkins in *Soliloquy* (Empire, Nov. 28, 1938); succeeded Margaret Webster as Mary of Magdala in *Family Portrait* (Morosco, Mar. 8, 1939); in stock, appeared as Elizabeth in *The Circle* and Jane Moonlight in *Mrs. Moonlight* (Montclair, N.J., Summer 1939); Kira Argounova in *The Unconquered* (Biltmore, N.Y.C., Feb. 13, 1940); in stock, played Linda in *No Time for Comedy* (Community Playhouse, Stamford, Conn.), and Sophie Baumer in *Margin for Error* (Maplewood, N.J., Summer 1940).

Miss Craig appeared as Belinda McDonald in *Johnny Belinda* (Belasco, N.Y.C., Sept. 18, 1940); Rosalind in *As You Like It* (Mansfield, Oct. 20, 1941); Princess Nieou-Chi in *Lute Song* (Plymouth, Feb. 6, 1946); Ellen in *Land's End* (Playhouse, Dec. 11, 1947); the title role in Anouilh's *Antigone* (Circle, Hollywood, Calif., May 1949); Mattie in *Out of the Dust* (Westport Country Playhouse, Conn., Summer 1949); repeated her role in *Antigone* with a student cast at the Coll. of Wooster (Mass., Nov. 1949); and appeared as Mrs. Dearth in *Dear Brutus* (Cape Playhouse, Dennis, Mass.; Boston, Mass.; Olney Th., Md.).

She appeared as Angustias in *The House of Bernarda Alba* (ANTA, N.Y.C., Jan. 7, 1951); and in stock, played in *Murder in the Family* (Berkshire Playhouse, Stockbridge, Mass., Summer 1952); appeared as Bella in *Maya* (Th. de Lys, N.Y.C., June 10, 1953); and in stock, appeared at Heritage Th., Stonington, Conn., as Dona Ana in *Don Juan in Hell* (July 1955) and in *John Brown's Body* (July 1957); played Clytemnestra in *Tower Beyond Tragedy* (Kaufmann Aud., YMHA, N.Y.C., 1956), which was repeated for the Poetry Society of America, N.Y.C., and the Library of Congress, Washington, D.C.; Mama in *Diamond Orchid* (Henry Miller's Th., Feb. 10, 1965); was in *Some Winter Games* (Red Barn, Northport, N.Y., Aug. 1965); the Nurse in *Medea* (Martinique, N.Y.C., Nov. 28, 1965); Mrs. Onoria in *To Clothe the Naked* (Sheridan Square Playhouse, Apr. 27, 1967); Nora Melody in *More Stately Mansions* (American premiere, Ahmanson Th., Los Angeles, Calif., Sept. 12, 1967; Broadhurst, N.Y.C., Oct. 31, 1967); and played Countess Aurelia in *The Madwoman of Chaillot* (Bucks Co. Playhouse, New Hope, Pa., 1968).

Films. Miss Craig made her film debut as Rosa in *The Keys of the Kingdom* (20th-Fox, 1944); followed by Mattie in *They Live by Night* (RKO, 1948); and Nurse Davis in *The Snake Pit* (20th-Fox, 1948). She dubbed the role of the Countess in the Russian *War and Peace* (Mosfilm, 1968); was Mrs. Olds in *The Sporting Club* (Avco Embassy, 1971); and Mrs. Castle in *Rancho De Luxe*. .

Television and Radio. Miss Craig first played on radio as Patricia Layton in *Wickford Point* (1939); subsequently in *Crime Does Not Pay* (1938); and in *Those Who Dance* (Star Spangled Theatre of the Air, 1940) and was the star of many Favorite Story programs, including *Jane Addams of Hull House* and *Peter Ibbetson.*

She made her television debut as Ruth Linsey in *The Donovan Affair* (NBC, 1938); appeared as Olwen Peel in *The Dangerous Corner* (NBC, 1939); the first Mrs. Carroll in *The Two Mrs. Carrolls* (Broadway Television Th.); was in *Susan and God* (Celanese Th.); *The Clock* (Boris Karloff Show); *As the Twig Is Bent* (Lamp Unto My Feet, CBS, 1955); and played Abby Borden in *The Legend of Lizzie Borden* (ABC Monday Night Movie, Feb. 10, 1975).

Other Activities. Miss Craig has taught acting at the Lenox School, N.Y.C. (1951–53); at the Country Sch., North Madison, Conn. (1957–60), and at the Day Prospect Hill Sch., New Haven, Conn. (1960–62).

Awards. For her performance as Belinda McDonald in *Johnny Belinda,* Miss Craig received the Bronze Medallion by Commedia Club (1941), and the Delia Austrian Medal by the Drama League of New York (1941).

Recreation. Swimming, dancing, reading.

CRAIN, HAROLD. Educator. b. Harold Cleveland Crain, Jan. 9, 1911, Gilmore City, Iowa, to Grover C. and Ida E. Crain. Father, farmer, carpenter. Grad. Humboldt (Iowa) H.S., 1928; Morningside Coll., A.B. 1935; Syracuse Univ., M.A. 1937; State Univ. of Iowa, Ph.D. 1947. Studied with Robert W. Blaylock, Des Moines, Iowa (1930); Addison Pitt, Syracuse, N.Y. (1936). Married Sept. 7, 1937, to Dorothy E. Cross; one son, one daughter. Member of ATA; Western Speech Assn.; Northwest Drama Conference; CTC. Address: (home) 1736 St. Anthony Dr., San Jose, CA 95125, tel. (408) 264-5110; (bus.) San Jose State Univ., San Jose, CA 95114, tel. (408) 294-6414.

Since 1955, Mr. Crain has been professor of drama, head of the Dept. of Speech and Drama, and chairman of the fine arts area at San Jose State Univ. In 1972, he became associate dean, Humanities and the Arts, at the university. He was a member of the faculty at State Univ. of Iowa in the Dept. of Speech and Dramatic Art (assist. prof., 1947–49; assoc. prof., 1949–55), and visiting prof., Univ. of Kansas.

Mr. Crain toured in *Smilin' Through* for United Chautauquas (Summer 1929); was director for the National Producing Company (Kansas City, Mo., 1930–31); acted with the Federal Theatre Stock Co. (Syracuse, N.Y., 1936); and adapted and directed *Elijah* for the NY World's Fair (1939).

Published Works. Crain wrote *Projects in Oral Interpretation* (1959) and translated Georges Feydeau's *La Dame de Chez Maxim* for production at San Jose State Univ., 1970.

Awards. Mr. Crain won a fellowship from the Ford Foundation's Fund for the Advancement of Education for study of the theatre in New York and London (1953).

Recreation. Camping, gardening, weaving.

CRAVEN, ROBIN. Actor. b. Robin Harry Salaman Cohen, Sept. 20, 1906, London, Eng., to Herman Joseph and Bessie (Salaman) Cohen. Father, lawyer, author. Grad. Eastbourne Coll., Sussex, 1925; Oxford Univ., B.A. 1929. Studied at RADA, London, 1929–30. Married May 17, 1948, to Babette Carolyn Krauss. Served WW II, with British Army as a member of the American Field Service, N. Africa, Italy. Relatives in theatre: cousin, Alec Guiness, actor; cousin, Jonathan Miller, performer. Member of AEA (council, 1953–75); AFTRA; SAG; The Players; The Lambs; Green Room Club (London); Stage Golfing Society (London); British Universities and Schools Club (N.Y.C.). Address: 360 E. 55th St., New York, NY 10022.

Theatre. Mr. Craven made his debut as Georges in the French language production of *La Prisonière* (Arts Th. Club, London, Nov. 1929); subsequently appeared as a walk-on in *Othello* (Savoy, May 19, 1930); toured as El Moro in *The Squall* (July 1930–Jan. 1931); appeared in Shakespearean roles at the Old Vic Th., London (1931); in repertory productions at the Sheffield (Eng.) Repertory Th. (Sept. 1932–May 1933); and the Croydon (Eng.) Repertory Th. (1933–34); toured England as the Inspector in *For the Defense* (1934); played Shindler in *Vicky* (Garrick, London, Jan. 1935); the Hotel Manager in *Golden Arrow* (Whitehall, May 1935); Captain Nicholson in *St. Helena* (Daly's, Mar. 19, 1936); and Victor Beamish in *Housemaster* (Apollo, Nov. 12, 1936).

He made his N.Y.C. debut as Kenneth Harvey in *Dear Octopus* (Broadhurst, Jan. 11, 1939); followed by the Englishman in *Foreigners* (Belasco, Dec. 5, 1939); Sir Hubert Towyn in *Glamour Preferred* (Booth, Nov. 15, 1940); Jerry Seymoure in the Chicago (Ill.) Co. of *Claudia* (Selwyn, Sept. 1941), on tour (1941–42), and in the return engagement in N.Y.C. (St. James, May 24, 1942); played the Sergeant in *Hand in Glove* (Playhouse, Dec. 4, 1944); appeared in stock as the Bishop in *The Bishop Misbehaves,* Colonel Foley in *Over 21,* and the Duke of Roxburgh in *While the Sun Shines* (Casino Th., Newport, R.I., Summer 1945); played Master Page in a national touring company of *The Merry Wives of Windsor* (Feb. 1946–Sept. 1946); Hugo Lyppiatt in *Present Laughter* (Plymouth, N.Y.C., Oct. 29, 1946); Gifford in *Strange Bedfellows* (Morosco, Jan. 14, 1948); and in stock appeared as Ernest Friedman in *Design for Living* and Rough in *Angel Street* (Pocono Playhouse, Mountainhome, Pa., Summer 1948).

Mr. Craven toured as the Squire in the production of *The Corn Is Green* (Summer 1949); played Titus Jaywood in *Yes, My Darling Daughter* (Bucks County Playhouse, New Hope, Pa., Summer 1949); and repeated the role of the Squire in *The Corn Is Green* (NY City Ctr., Jan. 11, 1950). He played Harris in the pre-Bway tryout of *The Heart of the Matter* (closed Wilbur, Boston, Mass., 1950); was understudy in *Cry of the Peacock* (Mansfield, N.Y.C., Apr. 11, 1950); succeeded (June 1950) Ernest Clark in the role of Alexander MacCoigie Gibbs in *The Cocktail Party* (Henry Miller's Th., Jan. 21, 1950); and played Sir Edward Ramsey in *The King and I* (St. James, Mar. 29, 1951). He played Sir Michael in a pre-Bway tour of *Dear Charles* (opened Cape Playhouse, Dennis, Mass., Summer 1954); Mr. Mayhew in *Witness for the Prosecution* (Henry Miller's Th., N.Y.C., Dec. 16, 1954); Zoltan Karpathy in *My Fair Lady* (Mark Hellinger Th., Mar. 15, 1956); Mr. Turton in *A Passage to India* (Ambassador, Jan. 31, 1962); Lord Rottingham in *Foxy* (Palace Grande Th., Dawson City, Alas., July 2, 1962); and Colonel Pickering in a summer touring production of *My Fair Lady* (opened Mineola Playhouse, L.I., N.Y., Mar. 31, 1964).

Television. Mr. Craven's many roles include Torp in *The Light That Failed* (Studio One, CBS, 1948).

Other Activities. Mr. Craven became president of Equity Library Theatre in 1971.

Recreation. Golf, collecting cricket prints and other cricket memorabilia.

CRAWFORD, CHERYL. Producer, director. b. Sept. 24, 1902, Akron, Ohio, to Robert K. and Luella Elizabeth (Parker) Crawford. Father, realtor. Attended Buchtel Coll.; grad. Smith Coll., B.A. (cum laude), 1925. Member of AEA. Address: c/o The Actors Studio, 432 W. 44th St., New York, NY 10036, tel. (212) PL 7-0870.

Theatre. Miss Crawford first performed in a high school production as Lady Macbeth in *Macbeth* (Central H.S. 1917); became a secretary for the Theatre Guild (N.Y.C., 1925); and appeared in its productions; made her Bway debut as Madame Barrio in *Juarez and Maximilian,* the first production of the Theatre Guild Acting Company (Guild Th., Oct. 11, 1926), in which she was also assistant stage manager; appeared as a walk-on in *The Brothers Karamazov* (Guild Th., Jan. 3, 1927); and was casting director at the Theatre Guild (1928–30).

She was a founding member of the Group Theatre in 1930 and a director of that organization until 1937; with Lee Strasberg, directed the Group Theatre's first production, *The House of Connelly* (Martin Beck Th., Sept. 28, 1931); directed their productions of *Big Night* (Maxine Elliott's Th., Jan. 17, 1933); *Till the Day I Die,* which was performed on a double-bill with *Waiting for Lefty* (Longacre, Mar. 26, 1935); and *Weep for the Virgins* (46 St. Th., Nov. 30, 1935).

She produced, in association with John Stillman, Jr., *All the Living* (Fulton, Mar. 24, 1938); in association with Day Tuttle and Richard Skinner, produced *Family Portrait* (Morosco, Mar. 8, 1939); and *Another Sun* (National, Feb. 23, 1940); with John Wildberg, founded the Maplewood (N.J.) Th., where she presented weekly productions, including *Porgy and Bess* (Summer 1941; Majestic, N.Y.C., Jan. 22, 1942).

Miss Crawford produced *The Flowers of Virtue* (Royale, Feb. 5, 1942); produced, with Richard Krakeur, in association with John Wildberg and Horace Schmidlapp, *A Kiss for Cinderella* (Music Box, Mar. 10, 1942); presented, in association with John Wildberg, *Porgy and Bess* (44 St. Th., Sept. 13, 1943) and *One Touch of Venus* (Imperial, Oct. 7, 1943); and, in association with John Wildberg, presented *Porgy and Bess* (NY City Ctr., Feb. 7, 1944); produced *The Perfect Marriage* (Ethel Barrymore Th., Oct. 26, 1944); *The Tempest* (Alvin, Jan. 25, 1945; NY City

Ctr., Nov. 12, 1945).

She founded, with Eva Le Gallienne and Margaret Webster, the American Repertory Th.; was managing director of the following American Repertory Th. works at the International Theatre (N.Y.C.); *Henry VIII* (Nov. 6, 1946); *What Every Woman Knows* (Nov. 8, 1946); *John Gabriel Borkman* (Nov. 12, 1946); and a double-bill of *Androcles and the Lion* and *Pound on Demand* (Dec. 19, 1946); and the last work produced by the American Repertory Th., *Alice in Wonderland* and *Through the Looking Glass* (International, Apr. 5, 1947; Majestic, May 28, 1947).

She presented *Brigadoon* (Ziegfeld, Mar. 13, 1947); founded, with Elia Kazan, Lee Strasberg, and Robert Lewis (1947), the Actors Studio, where she is a member of the board of directors and executive producer of the producing unit, the Actors Studio Th.

She presented independently and supervised the production of *Skipper Next to God* (Maxine Elliott's Th., Jan. 13, 1948); produced, with T. Edward Hambleton, *A Temporary Island* (Maxine Elliott's Th., Mar. 14, 1948); produced *Love Life* (46 St. Th., Oct. 7, 1948); presented, in association with Clinton Wilder, *Regina* (46 St. Th., Oct. 31, 1949); produced *The Closing Door* (Empire, Dec. 1, 1949) and *Brigadoon* (NY City Ctr., May 2, 1950).

In 1950, she became general director, with Robert Breen, of the ANTA play series. The first presentation was *The Tower Beyond Tragedy* (ANTA, Nov. 26, 1950); subsequently produced, with Roger L. Stevens, *Peer Gynt* (ANTA, Jan. 28, 1951); presented *The Rose Tattoo* (Martin Beck Th., Feb. 3, 1951); produced, in association with E. Y. Harburg and Fred Saidy, *Flahooley* (Broadhurst, May 14, 1951); presented *Paint Your Wagon* (Shubert, Nov. 12, 1951); *Camino Real* (National, Mar. 19, 1953) which she produced with Ethel Reiner, in association with Walter P. Chrysler, Jr.; produced, in association with Anderson Lawler, *Oh, Men! Oh, Women!* (Henry Miller's Th., Dec. 17, 1953); produced *The Honeys* (Longacre, Apr. 28, 1955); the pre-Bway tryout of *Reuben Reuben* (opened Shubert, Boston, Mass., Oct. 10, 1955; closed there, Oct. 22, 1955); produced, with Robert Lewis, *Mister Johnson* (Martin Beck Th., N.Y.C., Mar. 29, 1956); produced *Girls of Summer* (Longacre, Nov. 19, 1956); with William Myers, *Good as Gold* (Belasco, Mar. 7, 1957); with Alan Pakula, *Comes a Day* (Ambassador, Nov. 6, 1958); with Joel Schenker, by arrangement with the Actors Studio, *The Shadow of a Gunman* (Bijou, Nov. 19, 1958); with Joel Schenker, *The Rivalry* (Bijou, Feb. 7, 1959); presented *Sweet Bird of Youth* (Martin Beck Th., Mar. 10, 1959); with Mr. Schenker, in association with October Productions, *The Long Dream* (Ambassador, Feb. 17, 1960); with Mr. Schenker, presented *Kukla, Burr and Ollie* (Hotel Astor, Oct. 31, 1960); and produced *Period of Adjustment* (Helen Hayes Th., Nov. 10, 1960).

The Greater N.Y. Chapter of ANTA presented her production of *Brecht on Brecht* (Th. de Lys, N.Y.C., Jan. 3, 1962); she presented, with Roger L. Stevens, *Andorra* (Biltmore, Feb. 9, 1963); with Jerome Robbins, *Mother Courage and Her Children* (Martin Beck Th., Mar. 28, 1963); with Richard Halliday, *Jennie* (Majestic, Oct. 17, 1963); with Roger L. Stevens, the double-bill *Double Talk* (Th. de Lys, May 4, 1964). She produced, with Mitch Leigh, *Chu Chem* (opened Locust Th., Philadelphia, Pa., Nov. 15, 1966; closed there Nov. 19, 1966); with Carl Schaeffer, *The Freaking Out of Stephanie Blake* (previews, Eugene O'Neill Th., N.Y.C., Oct. 30–Nov. 1, 1967); with Richard Chandler, *Celebration* (Ambassador, Jan. 22, 1969); in association with Mary W. John, *Colette* (Ellen Stewart Th., May 6, 1970; return engagement Oct. 14–18, 1970); with Konrad Matthaei, Hale Matthews, and Robert Weinstein, *The Love Suicide at Schofield Barracks* (ANTA Th., Feb. 9, 1972); and, with Jean Dalrymple, *The Web and the Rock* (Th. de Lys, Mar. 19, 1972).

Awards. Miss Crawford received an Antoinette Perry (Tony Award (1951) for her production of *The Rose Tattoo.*

In 1962, she received an honorary Ph.D. from Smith Coll. and in 1964 the Brandeis Univ. Achievement Medal.

Recreation. Reading books.

CRISS, LOUIS. Artistic director, director, casting director. b. May 8, 1925, Philadelphia, Pa., to Boris and Pauline Criss. Father, upholsterer. Educated at Central High School, Philadelphia; Temple Univ.; Dramatic Workshop at New School for Social Research, N.Y.C.; Columbia Univ. Professional training at Dramatic Workshop; Amer. Th. Wing; studied with Harold Clurman, Paul Mann, Joseph Anthony, Al Saxe. Served in US Army, Infantry (1943–45). Member of AEA. Address: Box 209, Ranchos de Taos, NM 87557, tel. (505) 758-2677.

Theatre. Mr. Criss made his theatrical debut playing a small part in a Philadelphia presentation of *No for An Answer* (1941). He bowed in summer stock as Sir Andrew Aguecheek in *Twelfth Night* (Chapel Th., Great Neck, L.I., N.Y., July 1947) and made his first off-Bway appearance as Alan Norman in *Dog Beneath the Skin* (Cherry Lane Th., N.Y.C., July 21, 1948). During the summer and fall of 1948 he appeared at the Cherry Lane Th. as Johnny Boyle in *Juno and the Paycock* and Landolph in Pirandello's *Henry IV.* In the summer, fall, and winter of 1949–50 he was in Interplayers presentations as Oedipus in *The Infernal Machine* (Provincetown Playhouse); as the Sales Manager in *The Silver Tassie* (Carnegie Recital Hall); and he was associate director of *The Beggar's Opera* (Carnegie Recital Hall).

His first Bway work (Oct. 1951) was as the Shore Patrolman in *Mister Roberts* (Alvin Th., Feb. 18, 1948), and on tour. He was subsequently assistant stage manager for and played Casey in *Ladies of the Corridor* (Longacre Th., Oct. 21, 1953); assistant stage manager for and played the Messenger and a Sailor in *Tiger at the Gates* (Helen Hayes Th., Oct. 3, 1955); assistant to the director and production manager for *Major Barbara* (Martin Beck Th., Oct. 30, 1956); and stage manager for *The Cool World* (Eugene O'Neill Th., Feb. 22, 1960). He began working in professional regional theatre in Boston, Mass., as director of *Major Barbara* (Charles Playhouse, Dec. 15, 1965) and was director-in-residence (1967–69) at the Alley Th., Houston, Tex., where he directed *The Physicists* (Jan. 11, 1967) and *A Delicate Balance* (Oct. 5, 1967).

Mr. Criss has directed many other productions, including *A Thousand Clowns* (Manitoba Th. Ctr., Winnipeg, Canada, Mar. 1968); *Everything in the Garden* (Charles Playhouse, Boston, Mass., Jan. 1969); *Charlie* and *Out at Sea* (both Alley Th., Apr. 1969); *Narrow Road to the Deep North* (American premiere, Charles Playhouse, Oct. 30, 1969); and *In the Jungle of Cities* (Charles Playhouse, Feb. 12, 1970). He was artistic advisor to the Charles Playhouse in 1969–71 and during the same period directed *The Rose Tattoo* (American Conservatory Th., San Francisco, Calif., May 26, 1970); *Cymbeline* (Old Globe Th., San Diego, Calif., July 9, 1970); *The Homecoming* (McCarter Th., Princeton, N.J., Apr. 2, 1971); and *The Interrogation of Havana* (Chelsea Theatre Center, Brooklyn, N.Y., Dec. 27, 1971).

He was artistic director, McCarter Th., Princeton, N.J., from 1972 to 1974, during which he directed *The Tooth of Crime* (American premiere, Nov. 9, 1972); *The Tempest* (Mar. 1, 1973); *Rosmersholm* (Mar. 29, 1973); *The Seagull* (Oct. 1973); and *Twelfth Night* (Feb. 1974).

Mr. Criss is visiting professor at the Univ. of Denver; in the fall of 1974 he was artist-in-residence at the Univ. of New Mexico.

CROMWELL, JOHN. Director, actor, producer. b. Elwood Dager Cromwell, Dec. 23, 1887, Toledo, Ohio, to George Oliver and Helen (Sheeler) Cromwell. Father, businessman. Grad. Howe (Ind.) Sch., 1905. Married Jan. 23, 1914, to Alice Indahl, actress (dec. Nov. 17, 1918); married May 8, 1920, to Marie Goff, actress (marr. dis. Feb. 12, 1922); married Nov. 23, 1928, to Kay Johnson, actress (marr. dis. July 1, 1946); one son; married Aug. 21, 1946, to Ruth Nelson, actress. Served WW I, US Army. Member of AEA; SAG; DGA (pres. 1944). Address: Checken St., Wilton, CN 06897, tel. (203) PO 2-3097.

Theatre. Mr. Cromwell made his first stage appearance as a Clerk in a school play, entitled *His Excellency, the Governor* (June 20, 1900). Billed as E. D. Cromwell, he played the Corporal in *The Dictator* and played three roles in a tour of *Dorothy Vernon of Haddon Hall* (1906).

He toured as Rene de Montigny in *If I Were King* (Jan. 1907); appeared in and was stage manager for stock productions (Colonial, Cleveland, Ohio, 1907); toured in *The Girl Who Looks Like Me* (1907–1908); appeared in stock at the Lakewood Th. (Skowhegan, Me., Summer 1908); toured in *Classmates* (1908–1909); and appeared in stock at Skowhegan, Me. (Summer 1909). As actor and stage manager, he toured in *A Woman's Way* (1909–1910); and played again at Skowhegan, Me. (Summer 1910).

He made his first N.Y.C. appearance as the Policeman in *Baby Mine* (Playhouse, Aug. 23, 1910); as actor and stage manager, he toured in *Sauce for the Goose,* and appeared in it in N.Y.C. (Playhouse, Apr. 15, 1911); toured in *Baby Mine* (1911); was stage manager and took over the role of Jimmy in *Bought and Paid For* (Playhouse, N.Y.C., Sept. 26, 1911); and, billed for the first time as John Cromwell, played John Brooke in *Little Women* (Playhouse, Oct. 14, 1912).

His first assignment as a director was for *The Painted Woman* (Playhouse, Mar. 5, 1913). Subsequently, he directed *The Family Cupboard* (Playhouse, Aug. 21, 1913); *The Things That Count* (Maxine Elliott's Th., Dec. 8, 1913); appeared as Frank Andrews and directed, with the author, Frank Craven, *Too Many Cooks* (39 St. Th., Feb. 24, 1914). With William A. Brady and Frank Hatch, he directed *Life* (Manhattan Opera House Oct. 24, 1914); and appeared as Joe Garfield in *Sinners* (Playhouse, Jan. 7, 1915).

For the New York Repertory Co., he appeared as William Ludley in *The New York Idea* (Playhouse, Sept. 28, 1915); as Archibald Coke in *The Liars* (Playhouse, Nov. 9, 1915); Charles Lomax in *Major Barbara* (Playhouse, Dec. 9, 1915); Roger Moorish in *The Earth* (Playhouse, Feb. 15, 1916); and as Capt. Hamlin Kearney in *Captain Brassbound's Conversion* (Playhouse, Mar. 29, 1916). He directed *The Man Who Came Back* (Playhouse, Sept. 2, 1916); *L'Elevation* (Playhouse, Nov. 14, 1917); appeared as Paul Brooks and directed *The Indestructible Wife* (Hudson, Jan. 30, 1918); directed *At 9:45* (Playhouse, June 28, 1919); and directed and appeared as Frank Gower in *She Would and She Did* (Vanderbilt, Sept. 11, 1919).

Mr. Cromwell directed the London productions of *The Man Who Came Back* (Oxford, Mar. 1920); and *The "Ruined" Lady* (Comedy, June 25, 1920); directed and appeared as Mr. Tackaberry in *Immodest Violet* (48 St. Th., N.Y.C., Aug. 30, 1920); staged *The Young Visitors* (39 St. Th., Nov. 29, 1920); directed and appeared as Roddy Caswell in *The Teasers* (Playhouse, July 27, 1921); appeared as Simpson in *Personality* (Playhouse, Aug. 7, 1921); and staged and appeared as Walter Homer in *The Law Breaker* (Booth, Feb. 1, 1922). He produced and directed *Manhattan* (Playhouse, Aug. 15, 1922); directed *The World We Live In (The Insect Comedy)* (Jolson, Oct. 31, 1922); directed *Tarnish* (Belmont, Oct. 1, 1923); produced and directed *Bewitched* (National, Oct. 1, 1924); produced with William A. Brady, Jr., *It All Depends on You* (Vanderbilt, Aug. 10, 1925); produced and appeared as Julian Rhenal in *Oh! Mama!* (Playhouse, Aug. 19, 1925); produced, in association with the Shuberts, *Harvest* (Belmont, Sept. 19, 1925), which he also directed; appeared as Sam McCarver in *Lucky Sam McCarver,* which he produced in association with William A. Brady, Jr., and Dwight Deere Wiman (Playhouse, Oct. 21, 1925); appeared as Engineer Borgheim in *Little Eyolf* at special matinees (Guild, Feb. 2, 1926); directed and appeared as Matthew Dibble in *Devils* (Maxine Elliott's Th., Mar. 17, 1926); directed with Bobby Connolly, *Kitty's Kisses* (Playhouse, May 26, 1926); and appeared as Ned McCobb in *Ned McCobb's Daughter* (Princess, Chicago, Ill., Mar. 1926).

Mr. Cromwell appeared as "Gyp" Gradyear in *Fanny* (Lyceum, N.Y.C., Sept. 21, 1926); for the Th. Guild, directed *The Silver Cord* (John Golden Th., Dec. 20, 1926); with Mr. Brady, Jr., and Mr. Wiman (Playhouse, Oct. 21, 1925); which he directed (Forrest, Sept. 7, 1927); appeared as Capt. McQuigg in *The Racket* (Ambassador, Nov. 22, 1927); directed *The Queen's Husband* (Playhouse, Jan. 25, 1928); appeared as Wick Snell in *Gentlemen of the Press* (Henry Miller's Th., Aug. 27, 1928); directed *The Ghost of Yankee Doodle* (Guild, Nov. 22, 1937); directed *Yr. Obedient Husband,* which he produced with Fredric March (Broadhurst, Jan. 10, 1938); directed and appeared as Bob Adams in *Yankee Point* (Longacre, Nov. 23, 1942); directed *The Moon Vine* (Morosco, Feb. 11, 1943); appeared as John Gray in *Point of No Return* (Alvin, Dec. 13, 1951); appeared as the Rev. Gerald Harmston in *The Climate of Eden* (Martin Beck Th., Nov. 13, 1952); and appeared as Linus Larrabee in *Sabrina Fair* (National, Nov. 11, 1953), and repeated his role and directed the production in London (Palace, Aug. 4, 1954).

He appeared as Mr. Venables in *What Every Woman Knows* (NY City Ctr., Dec. 22, 1954); directed the original company of *The Desk Set* in Boston (1955); appeared as Oscar Nelson in *Mary, Mary* (Helen Hayes Th., N.Y.C., Mar. 8, 1961); directed *The Aspern Papers* (Cleveland Play House, Ohio, Feb. 1963); with the Minnesota Th. Co. (Tyrone Guthrie Th., Minneapolis), appeared as The Player King in *Hamlet* (May 7, 1963); Anselme in *The Miser* (May 8, 1963); Uncle Ben in *Death of a Salesman* (July 16, 1963); directed *The Madwoman of Chaillot* (Cleveland Play House, Ohio, Jan. 1964); and appeared at the Tyrone Guthrie Th. (Minneapolis, Minn.) as Exeter in *Henry V* (May 11, 1964); De Courcelles in *Saint Joan* (May 12, 1964); as Avocatore in *Volpone* (June 29, 1964); Sir Robert Brakenbury in *Richard III* (May 10, 1965); Aleko Bereshwili and Lavrenti's servant in *The Caucasian Chalk Circle* (Aug. 3, 1965); Sir Patrick Cullen in *The Doctor's Dilemma* (Sept. 6, 1966); and the Donkeyman in *The Moon of the Caribees* in *S. S. Glencairn* (Sept. 7, 1966). he appeared with the Yale Repertory Th., New Haven, Conn., as Don Luis in Molière's *Don Juan* (May 15, 1970); played the roles of Mr. Potter and Father in *Solitaire/Double Solitaire* (Long Wharf Th., New Haven, Conn., Feb. 12, 1971; John Golden Th., N.Y.C., Sept. 30, 1971); and wrote *Split Lip* (Gene Frankel Th. Workshop, N.Y.C., May 14, 1974.

Films. Mr. Cromwell made his first appearance in *The Dummy* (Par., 1929). He directed *Tom Sawyer* (Par., 1930); *The Silver Cord* (RKO, 1933); *Ann Vickers* (RKO, 1933); *Sweepings* (RKO, 1933); *Of Human Bondage* (RKO, 1934); *Little Lord Fauntleroy* (UA, 1936); *Prisoner of Zenda* (UA, 1937); *Algiers* (UA, 1938); *Abe Lincoln in Illinois* (RKO, 1940); *So Ends Our Night* (UA, 1941); *Son of Fury* (20th-Fox, 1942); *Since You Went Away* (UA, 1944); *The Enchanted Cottage* (RKO, 1945); *Anna and the King of Siam* (20th-Fox, 1946); *Night Song* (RKO, 1947); *The Company She Keeps* (RKO, 1950); *Caged* (UA, 1950); *The Racket* (RKO, 1951); and *The Goddess* (Independent, 1956).

Television. He made his debut as the Politician in *State of the Union* (NBC, Apr. 1954). He wrote *Opening Night* (NY Television Th., NET, Jan. 24, 1966).

Awards. Mr. Cromwell received the US Treasury Award for patriotic service (1941–45); and the Antoinette Perry (Tony) Award for his performance as John Gray in *Point of No Return* (1952).

Recreation. Riding, tennis, golf.

CRONYN, HUME. Actor, director, writer. b. July 18, 1911, London, Ontario, Canada, to Hume Blake and Frances Amelia (Labatt) Cronyn. Grad. Ridley Coll., St. Catherines, Ontario, 1930; studied art at McGill Univ., 1930–31; acting under auspices of NY Sch. of the Theatre; with Harold Kreutzberg, Mozarteum, Salzburg, Austria, Summers 1932, 1933; and at AADA, 1932–34. Married Sept. 27, 1942, to Jessica Tandy, actress; one son, one daughter, one step-daughter. Past director of SSD&C, SAG, Theatre Development Fund; past council member of AEA, Yale Univ. School of Drama; trustee of the American Academy of Dramatic Arts; member of board of directors of Guthrie Theatre Foundation. Address: Route 137, Box 85A, Pound Ridge, NY 10576.

Theatre. While a student at McGill Univ., Mr. Cronyn appeared with the Montreal Repertory Th. and the McGill Player's Club in productions which included *The Adding Machine, Dr. Faustus, From Morn to Midnight, The Road to Rome, Alice in Wonderland,* and the *Red and White Revue* (1930–31).

He made his professional debut with Cochran's Stock Co. in *Up Pops the Devil* (Natl., Washington, D.C., Spring 1931); joined Robert Porterfield's Barter Th. Co. as production director and played Austin Lowe in *The Second Man,* Dr. Haggett in *The Late Christopher Bean,* Jim Hipper in *He Knew Dillinger* (later entitled *Hipper's Holiday),* and Doke Odum in *Mountain Ivy* (Summer 1934). His first appearance on Bway was as a Janitor and understudy to Burgess Meredith in the role of Jim Hipper in *Hipper's Holiday* (Maxine Elliott's Th., Oct. 18, 1934); subsequently joined the Jitney (touring) Players, appearing as Stingo and Sir Charles Marlowe in *She Stoops to Conquer* and as Gideon Bloodgood in *The Streets of New York* (Mar.–Sept. 1935).

He played Erwin Trowbridge in the national (touring) production of *Three Men on a Horse* (Oct. 1935–June 1936); succeeded (Sept. 1936) Garson Kanin as Green in *Boy Meets Girl* (Cort, N.Y.C., Nov. 27, 1935), and played it on tour; appeared as Elkus and understudied Burgess Meredith in the role of Van Van Dorn in *High Tor* (Martin Beck Th., N.Y.C., Jan. 9, 1937); succeeded (Aug. 1937) Eddie Albert as Leo Davis in *Room Service* (Cort, May 19, 1937), continuing in the role on tour.

He appeared as Abe Sherman in *There's Always a Breeze* (Windsor, N.Y.C., Mar. 2, 1938); Steve in *Escape This Night* (44 St. Th., Apr. 22, 1938); Harry Quill in *Off to Buffalo* (Ethel Barrymore Th., Feb. 21, 1939); and played two seasons with the Lakewood Th. (Skowhegan, Me.), in roles which included Hutchens Stubbs in *Susan and God,* Toby Cartwright in *Ways and Means,* George Davies in *We Were Dancing* from *Tonight at 8:30,* Francis O'-Connor in *Shadow and Substance,* Christy Dudgeon in *The Devil's Disciple,* Lloyd Lloyd in *Kiss the Boys Goodbye,* Judas in *Family Portrait,* the Stage Manager in *Our Town,* Denis Dillon in *The White Steed,* Karl Baumer in *Margin for Error,* and Joe Bonaparte in *Golden Boy* (May–Sept. 1939; May–Sept. 1940).

He played Andrei Prozoroff in *The Three Sisters* (Longacre, N.Y.C., Oct. 14, 1939); Peter Mason in *The Weak Link* (John Golden Th., Mar. 4, 1940); Lee Tatnall in the Group Th. production of *Retreat to Pleasure* (Belasco, Dec. 17, 1940); produced and appeared in a revue for the Canadian Active Service Canteen (May 1941); played Joe Bonaparte in *Golden Boy* (Bucks County Playhouse, New Hope, Pa., July 1941); played Harley L. Miller in *Mr. Big* (Lyceum, N.Y.C., Sept. 30, 1941); for the USO, produced *Junior Miss* (Jan. 1942); co-produced and appeared in a USO revue, *It's All Yours* (Mar. 1942); appeared as Tommy Turner in an Actor's Laboratory Th. production of *The Male Animal,* which toured military installations in Calif. (May 1944); and in a vaudeville sketch in Canada for the Victory Loan (Oct. 1944).

Mr. Cronyn directed an Actor's Laboratory Th. production of *Portrait of a Madonna* (Las Palmas Th., Los Angeles, Calif., Summer 1946); played Jodine Decker in *The Survivors* (Playhouse, N.Y.C., Jan. 19, 1948); the title role in an ANTA touring production of *Hamlet* (Mar.–May 1949); directed *Now I Lay Me Down to Sleep* (Stanford Univ., Calif., July 1949) and in N.Y.C. (Broadhurst, Mar. 2, 1950); appeared in *The Little Blue Light* (Brattle Th., Cambridge, Mass., Aug. 1950); directed *Hilda Crane* (Coronet, N.Y.C., Nov. 1, 1950); and played Michael in *The Fourposter* (Ethel Barrymore Th., Oct. 24, 1951).

With Norman Lloyd, he staged the initial Phoenix Th. (N.Y.C.) production, *Madam, Will You Walk,* in which he played Dr. Brightlee (Phoenix, Dec. 1, 1953); with his wife, Jessica Tandy, appeared in concert readings, titled *Face to Face,* on a cross-country tour (Sept.–Dec. 1954); played Michael in *The Fourposter* (NY City Ctr., Jan. 5, 1955); played Curtis and Bennett Honey in *The Honeys* (Longacre, Apr. 28, 1955); Julian in *A Day by the Sea* (ANTA, Sept. 26, 1955); and Oliver Walling in a touring production of *The Man in the Dog Suit* (June–Sept. 1957).

Mr. Cronyn directed *The Egghead* (Ethel Barrymore Th., N.Y.C., Oct. 9, 1957); directed and toured with Miss Tandy in *Triple Play,* a bill of three one-act plays and a monologue, in which he appeared as the Doctor in *Portrait of a Madonna,* Jerry in *A Pound on Demand,* John Jo Mulligan in *Bedtime Story,* and as "Professor" Ivan Ivanovitch Nyukhin in the monologue, *Some Comments on the Harmful Effects of Tobacco* (Summer 1958); appeared as Oliver Walling in *The Man in the Dog Suit* (Coronet, N.Y.C., Oct. 30, 1958); directed and repeated his roles in *Triple Play* (Playhouse, Apr. 15, 1959); and appeared as Jimmy Luton in *Big Fish, Little Fish* (ANTA, N.Y.C., Mar. 15, 1961); Duke of York's, London, Sept. 18, 1962).

He appeared with the Minnesota Theatre Co. (Tyrone Guthrie Th., Minneapolis, Minn.), in its first season, as Harpagon in *The Miser* (May 8, 1963); Tchebutkin in *The Three Sisters* (June 18, 1963); and Willie Loman in *Death of a Salesman* (July 16, 1963). He played Polonius in Richard Burton's *Hamlet* (Lunt-Fontanne, N.Y.C., Apr. 9, 1964); Newton in *The Physicists* (Martin Beck Th., Oct. 7, 1964); and produced *Slow Dance on the Killing Ground* (Plymouth, Dec. 1, 1964).

In Feb. 1965, together with his wife, Jessica Tandy, Mr. Cronyn appeared at the White House, Washington, D.C., at the request of the President and Mrs. Johnson in *Hear America Speaking.* He returned to Minneapolis, Minn., for the third season of the Minnesota Theatre Co. in 1965 and appeared at the Tyrone Guthrie Th. in the title role of *Richard III* (May 10); as Yephikodov in *The Cherry Orchard* (June 15); and as Harpagon in *The Miser* (Sept. 7). He appeared as Tobias in *A Delicate Balance* at Martin Beck Th., N.Y.C., (Sept. 22, 1966) and in US tour (Jan.–June 1967). He appeared again as Harpagon in a revival of *The Miser* (Mark Taper Forum, Los Angeles, Calif., Mar. 17, 1968) and played Frederick William Rolfe in *Hadrian VII* with the Stratford National Theatre Co. of Canada (Stratford, Ont., Aug. 5, 1969) and in national tour (Sept. 4, 1969–May 1970); played Capt. Queeg in *Caine Mutiny Court Martial* (Ahmanson Th., Los Angeles, Calif., Nov. 30, 1971); appeared in *Promenade, All!* (pre-Broadway tour Jan. 31, 1972); Alvin Th., N.Y.C., Apr. 16, 1972; summer tour Aug. 14, 1972, and winter tour, Jan. 24, 1973; portrayed Krapp in *Krapp's Last Tape,* Willie in *Happy Days,* and the Player in *Act without Words I* in a limited engagement with his wife, Jessica Tandy, as part of a "Samuel Beckett Festival" in N.Y.C. at The Forum of Lincoln Center, (Nov. 20, 1972); appeared again in the title role of *Krapp's Last Tape* at the St. Lawrence Theatre Center, Toronto, Canada; Arena Stage, Washington, D.C.; and universities in the east (Sept. 4, 1973); and appeared as Verner Conklin and Sir Hugo Latymer in the double bill of Noel Coward's *In Two Keys* pre-Broadway tour and at Ethel Barrymore Th., N.Y.C., (Dec. 1973–June 1974).

Films. Mr. Cronyn made his debut as Herbie Hawkins in *Shadow of a Doubt* (U, 1943); subsequently appeared in *The Cross of Lorraine* (MGM, 1943); *The Seventh Cross* (MGM, 1944); *Main Street After Dark* (MGM, 1944); *Lifeboat* (20th-Fox, 1944); *A Letter for Evie* (MGM, 1945); *The Sailor Takes a Wife* (MGM, 1945); *The Green Years* (MGM, 1946); *The Postman Always Rings Twice* (MGM, 1946); *The Ziegfeld Follies* (MGM, 1946); as Dr. Robert Oppenheimer in *Beginning of the End* (MGM, 1947); *Brute Force* (U, 1947); *The Bride Goes Wild* (MGM, 1948); wrote the screenplays for *Rope* (WB, 1948) and *Under Capricorn* (WB, 1949); appeared in *Top o' the*

Morning (Par., 1949); *People Will Talk* (20th-Fox, 1951); *Crowded Paradise* (Tudor, 1956); as Louis Howe in *Sunrise at Campobello* (WB, 1960); in *Cleopatra* (20th-Fox, 1963); in *Gaily Gaily* (UA, 1969); *The Arrangement* (WB, 1969); *There Was a Crooked Man* (WB, 1970); *Conrack* (20th-Fox 1974); and *Parallox View* (Par., 1974).

Television. Mr. Cronyn's first appearance was as Ned Farrar in *Her Master's Voice* (NBC, 1939). He produced and directed *Portrait of a Madonna* (Actor's Studio, ABC, Sept. 26, 1948); produced and appeared with Jessica Tandy in their own series, The Marriage, on radio and television (NBC, 1953, 1954). He appeared on Omnibus (CBS); the Ed Sullivan Show (CBS); played Michael in *The Fourposter* (NBC, 1955); performed in *The Great Adventure* (CBS, 1956); *The Confidence Man* (NBC, 1956); *The Big Wave* (NBC, 1956); *The $5 Bill* (CBS, 1957); *Member of the Family* (CBS, 1957); *The Bridge of San Luis Rey* (DuPont Show of the Month, CBS, Jan. 1958); *The Moon and Sixpence* (NBC, Oct. 30, 1959); *A Doll's House* (NBC, 1959); *Juno and the Paycock* (Play of the Week, WNTA, 1960); the John F. Kennedy Memorial Broadcast (NBC, 1963); and played Polonius in *Hamlet* (Electronovision, Fall 1964).

Awards. Mr. Cronyn was nominated for an Academy (Oscar) Award (1944) for his performance in *The Seventh Cross.* He and his wife received the Comoedia Matinee Club's Award (1952) for their performances in *The Fourposter.* He received the Barter Th. Award (1961) "for outstanding contribution to the theatre"; was nominated for the Antoinette Perry (Tony) Award (1961) and received the Delia Austria Medal from the NY Drama League (1961) for his performance as Jimmy Luton in *Big Fish, Little Fish;* received the Tony Award and won the *Variety* NY Drama Critics' Poll (1964) for his performance as Polonius in *Hamlet;* received the American Academy of Dramatic Arts ninth annual award for achievement for alumni (Dec. 1964); was nominated for the Tony Award (1967) and received the Herald Theatre Award for his performance as Tobias in *A Delicate Balance;* received the Los Angeles Drama Critics Circle Award for best actor for his performance in *Caine Mutiny Court Martial* (1972); received the fourth annual Straw Hat Award for best director (1972) for direction of *Promenade, All!;* and received the Obie Award (1972–73) for outstanding achievement in off-Broadway theatre for distinguished performance in *Krapp's Last Tape.*

CROSWELL, ANNA.

CROSWELL, ANNA. Lyricist, writer. b. Mary Ann Pearson, Dec. 12, Tuscaloosa, Ala., to John Hale and Eudora (Yerby) Pearson. Father, Methodist minister. Attended George Washington H.S., Danville, Va.; grad. Maury H.S., Norfolk, Va.; Randolph-Macon Woman's Coll., B.A.; Strayer Business Coll., Washington, D.C.; attended Sch. of Radio and Television Technique, N.Y.C.; New York Univ. Married Sept. 4, 1954, to Volney R. Croswell, Jr., artist-writer (separated 1971). Member of ASCAP; Dramatists Guild. Address: 201 W. 89th St., New York, NY 10024, tel. (212) 362-7959.

Pre-Theatre. Free-lance radio, newspaper, and jingle writer; advertising copywriter with J. Walter Thompson Co.; television production assistant with Leo Burnett Co.; specializing in jingle writing with both companies.

She wrote the lyrics for the National Democratic Party Campaign Song, *Believe in Stevenson.* .

Theatre. Ms. Croswell is author of the book and lyrics for the musical *Ernest in Love,* based on Oscar Wilde's *The Importance of Being Earnest* (Gramercy Arts Th., N.Y.C., May 5, 1960); and wrote the lyrics for *Tovarich* (Bway Th., Mar. 18, 1963). She was lyricist and co-author of the book for *I'm Solomon* (Mark Hellinger Th., Apr. 1958) and wrote lyrics for a number of songs in concert at Carnegie Hall, *Gershon Kingsley's First Moog Quartet,* and at Philharmonic Hall, both 1970. In 1974, Ms. Croswell wrote the lyrics and was co-author of the book for *Chips 'n Ale,* a musical version of Goldsmith's *She Stoops to Conquer,* presented at the Actors Theatre of Louisville, April 25, 1974.

Television. Ms. Croswell wrote the lyrics of the theme song and original numbers for *Washington Square* (NBC, 1956–57); the book and lyrics for the musical *Who's Earnest?* (US Steel Hour, CBS, Oct. 9, 1957); and the book for the musical, *Huck Finn* (US Steel Hour, CBS, Nov. 20, 1957).

Discography. Original cast albums were made of *Ernest in Love* (Col., 1960) and *Tovarich* (Cap., 1963), and *Gershon Kingsley's First Moog Quartet* (Audio Fidelity, 1970) has been recorded. Other works of Ms. Croswell's have been recorded on *Learning the ABC's and How to Count* (Col.) and *Firestone Christmas Album — The Bells of Christmas* (twice recorded by Julie Andrews and others). Ms. Croswell's songs have also been recorded by Andy Williams, Johnny Mathis, Tennessee Ernie Ford, Nanette Fabray, Ray Bolger, and others.

Recreation. Skiing, sailing, remodeling brownstone houses, raising Siamese cats, studying astrology.

CROUCH, JACK H.

CROUCH, JACK H. Educator. b. Jack Herbert Crouch, Aug. 13, 1918, Montpelier, Idaho, to James Herbert and Georgia Ruth (Jones) Crouch. Father, railroad engineer; mother, teacher. Grad. Univ. of California at Los Angeles, B.A. 1939; Cornell Univ., M.A. 1941, Ph.D. 1951. Married Oct. 23, 1939, to Shirley Schuh; two sons, one daughter. Served USN, 1944–46. Member of NTC; MLA; AAUP; Lambda Chi Alpha. Address: (home) 3020 Pennsylvania Ave., Boulder, CO 80302, tel. (303) 443-4027; (bus.) University of Colorado, Boulder, CO 80302.

Since 1960, Mr. Crouch has been professor of English at the Univ. of Colorado, where he has been an instructor in English and Speech (1946–48), assistant professor of English and Speech (1948–52), and associate professor of English (1952–60). He was a founder (1958) and was executive director of the Colorado Shakespeare Festival (1958–60).

Mr. Crouch was instructor in drama at Mills College (1941–42); guest lecturer at the Carleton (Coll.) Drama Festival (1953); and guest professor and director at the Greystone Th., Univ. of Saskatchewan, Canada (1959–60).

CROWLEY, MART.

CROWLEY, MART. Playwright. b. Aug. 21, 1935, Vicksburg, Miss. Educ. Vicksburg public schools; Catholic Univ., Washington, D.C.; Univ. of California at Los Angeles. Address: c/o Farrar Straus and Giroux, Inc., 19 Union Sq. W., New York, NY 10003.

Theatre. Mr. Crowley wrote *The Boys in the Band* (Th. Four, N.Y.C., Apr. 14, 1968); *Remote Asylum* (Center Th. Group, Los Angeles, 1970); and *A Breeze from the Gulf* (Eastside Playhouse, N.Y.C., Oct. 15, 1973).

Films. Mr. Crowley was co-author of the script for *Fade-in* (Par.) and wrote the script for the motion picture version of *The Boys in the Band* (Natl. Gen., 1970).

CRYER, DAVID.

CRYER, DAVID. Actor, producer, singer. b. Mar. 8, 1936, Evanston, Ill. Grad. De Pauw Univ.; Boston Univ., M.A. (directing); attended Yale Divinity School (Rockefeller scholarship). Served in US Army. Married to Gretchen Kiger, actress, writer (marr. dis. 1968); two sons. Member of AEA; AFTRA; AGVA.

Theatre. Mr. Cryer appeared in high school productions of *The Desert Song* and *Kiss Me, Kate.* His first professional appearance, made when he was studying at Yale, was as Curly in *Oklahoma!* (Polka Dot Playhouse, Bridgeport, Conn.). In 1963, he first played in N.Y.C., replacing Don Stewart as El Gallo in *The Fantasticks* (Sullivan St. Playhouse, May 3, 1960). He toured as Tony in *West Side Story* (Summer 1963); appeared in stock productions of *Carousel, The Threepenny Opera, The Boy Friend, The King and I, Irma La Douce, The Teahouse of the August Moon,* and *Summer and Smoke;* was Mark Livingstone in the off-Bway *The Streets of New York* (Maidman Th., Oct. 29, 1963); was a baritone soloist at Radio City Music Hall; made his Bway debut succeeding (1964) Robert Horton as Bill Starbuck in *110 in the Shade* (Broadhurst, Oct. 24, 1963); toured (1964) as Phil Mackey in the National Rep. Th. production of *110 in the Shade;* and appeared for three months as a Cowboy Extra in *Fade Out—Fade In* (Mark Hellinger Th., May 26, 1964).

Mr. Cryer was a member of the first American Conservatory Th. company in Pittsburgh, Pa., where he played Valère in *Tartuffe* (July 15, 1965), the Messenger in Jean Anouilh's *Antigone* (Aug. 1, 1965), Jack Hunter in *The Rose Tattoo* (Aug. 6, 1965), John Brown, Woodrow Wilson, and others in *In White America* (Aug. 31, 1965), Oswald in *King Lear* (Sept. 3, 1965), Silvio in *The Servant of Two Masters* (Sept. 9, 1965), and Theseus in *A Midsummer Night's Dream.* He produced, with Albert Poland, and played El Gallo in *The Fantasticks* for a ten-week college tour (1966); appeared off-Bway as Mike Butler in *Now Is the Time for All Good Men,* which he also co-produced with Albert Poland (Th. de Lys, N.Y.C., Sept. 26, 1967); and was an associate producer of *Futz* (Th. de Lys, June 9, 1968).

He played Jude Scribner in *Come Summer* (O'-Keefe Ctr., Toronto, Ontario, Canada, Jan. 27, 1969; Lunt-Fontanne Th., N.Y.C., Mar. 18, 1969); replaced (May 30, 1969) Clifford David as Edward Rutledge in *1776* (46 St. Th., Mar. 16. 1969), continuing until May 1970; was the Narrator in *Whispers on the Wind* (Th. de Lys, June 3, 1970); Ari Ben Canaan in *Ari* (Mark Hellinger Th., Jan. 15, 1971); sang the role of the Celebrant in Leonard Bernstein's *Mass* (Metropolitan Opera House, June 28, 1972); played the dual role of the Red Baron/Pierre Birabeau in *The Desert Song* (Uris Th., Sept. 5, 1973); was in *Brecht: Sacred and Profane* (Mark Taper Forum, Los Angeles, Calif., Nov. 1, 1973); and in *Portfolio Revue* (Portfolio Studio, N.Y.C., Dec. 6, 1974).

Television. Mr. Cryer appeared on the Bell Telephone Hour (NBC, 1962–63) and in Where The Heart Is (CBS, 1969–73).

CULLMAN, MARGUERITE.

CULLMAN, MARGUERITE. Author, lecturer, investor. b. Marguerite Virginia Henry Sanders. Father, wine merchant. Attended St. Catherine's Acad. and Columbia Univ. Sch. of Journalism. Married June 7, 1935, to Howard S. Cullman (dec. June 29, 1972); three sons, one daughter. Member of Authors' League of America. Address: 480 Park Ave., New York, NY 10022, tel. (212) PL 5-0882.

Theatre. Mrs. Cullman has been an assistant to a playwright, a play reader for the movies, an associate editor of *Stage Magazine,* and a lecturer on drama at various colleges, universities, and the women's clubs.

Mrs. Cullman and her husband invested in approximately 300 Broadway productions, among which are *Life With Father, Arsenic and Old Lace, The Voice of the Turtle, South Pacific, Death of a Salesman, Abe Lincoln in Illinois, I Remember Mama, Mister Roberts, The Teahouse of the August Moon, Music Man, Sound of Music,* and *Toys in the Attic.* .

Other Activities. In addition to her work in the theatre, Mrs. Cullman was associate editor to McNaught Syndicate; operated her own public relations office; was public relations director for Bonwit Teller (N.Y.C.); and in N.Y.C. has done charity work for the Lighthouse and the Spence-Chapin Adoption Service, having been a director of both, and for the High School of the Performing Arts, which she served as chairwoman of an advisory commission.

Published Works. She wrote two books, *Ninety Dozen Glasses,* dealing with experiences with the Brussels (Belgium) World's Fair (1960); and *Occupation: Angel,* concerning their experiences investing in the NY theatre (1963). She has written a series of feature articles on various aspects of the theatre for the NY *Times* Magazine.

Awards. She received the Order of Leopold Award from King Baudouin of Belgium, as well as the Cross Pro Ecclesia and Pontifica from Pope Pius. XII.

CULLUM, JOHN.

CULLUM, JOHN. Actor, singer. b. Mar. 2, 1930, Knoxville, Tenn. Grad. Univ. of Tennessee. Served US Army (Korea), 1953–55. Married 1959 to Emily Frankel. Member of AEA; AFTRA; SAG.

Theatre. Mr. Cullum was Sir Dinadan in *Camelot*

(Majestic, Dec. 3, 1960), understudy to Richard Burton as Arthur in the same production, performing that role on a few occasions, and he succeeded Roddy McDowell as Mordred. He was Cyril Bellamy in *The Saving Grace* (Writers' Stage, Apr. 18, 1963); understudy to Keith Michell as the Count and Alan Badel as Hero in *The Rehearsal* (Royale, Sept. 23, 1963); played Timothy in *Thistle in My Bed* (Gramercy Arts, Nov. 19, 1963); was in *Come to the Palace of Sin* (ANTA Matinee Th. Series, Th. de Lys, Dec. 10, 1963); and played Laertes in Richard Burton's *Hamlet* (Lunt-Fontanne Th., Apr. 9, 1964).

He played Oliver and Jaques in a musical version of *As You Like It* (White Barn Th., Westport, Conn., Sept. 6, 1964); King Arthur in *Camelot* (Paper Mill Playhouse, Millburn, N.J., Nov. 3, 1964); Dr. Mark Bruckner in *On a Clear Day You Can See Forever* (Mark Hellinger Th., N.Y.C., Oct. 17, 1965); Cheviot Hill in *Engaged, or Cheviot's Choice* (Goodspeed Opera House, East Haddam, Conn., July 18, 1966); and on the program *Three Hand Reel* was Father Jerome Fogarty in *The Frying Pan,* Tom Dorgan in *Eternal Triangle,* and Denis Sullivan in *The Bridal Night* (Renata Th., Nov. 7, 1966). Mr. Cullum replaced (Feb. 24–Apr. 10, 1967) José Ferrer as Don Quixote in *Man of La Mancha* (ANTA Washington Square Th., Nov. 22, 1965); replaced (May 19, 1970) David Cryer as Edward Rutledge in *1776* (46 St. Th., Mar. 16, 1969); replaced (Mar. 25, 1972) Lee Richardson as Lord Bothwell in *Vivat! Vivat Regina!* (Broadhurst, Jan. 20, 1972); was the King in *The King and I* (Jones Marine Beach Th., Wantagh, Long Island, N.Y., June 28, 1972); Shakespeare in *The Elizabethans* (New Dramatists, N.Y.C., Oct. 14, 1972); appeared in *The Lady's Not for Burning* (Goodman Memorial Th., Chicago, Ill., Apr. 1, 1973); played Billy Bigelow in *Carousel* (Jones Beach Marine Th., Long Island, N.Y., June 22, 1973); was in *Gris-Gris* (New Phoenix Rep. Co. Side Show, Playhouse II, N.Y.C., Apr. 19, 1974); and was Charlie Anderson in *Shenandoah* (Alvin Th., Jan. 7, 1975).

Films. Mr. Cullum's films include *All the Way Home* (Par., 1963); *Hamlet* (WB, 1964); and *Hawaii* (UA, 1966).

Television. Among the telvision shows on which Mr. Cullum has appeared are The Defenders (CBS); Bell Telephone Hour (NBC); and the Joe Franklin Show (Ind.).

Awards. Mr. Cullum received a *Theatre World* Award (1966) as most promising Bway actor; an Antoinette Perry (Tony) nomination (1966) for best musical star for his performance in *On a Clear Day You Can See Forever;* and Tony and Drama Desk awards (1975) for best actor in a musical for his performance in *Shenandoah.*

CULVER, ROLAND. Actor, director, playwright. b. Aug. 31, 1900, London, England, to Edward and Florence (Tulledge) Culver. Father, optician. Attended Highgate Coll., London, 1914–16. Studied at RADA, London, 1923–24. Married Aug. 13, 1934, to Daphne Rye (marr. dis. 1946); two sons, Robin and Michael Culver, actors; married Oct. 11, 1947, to Marjorie Anne Stanton Hopkins. Served RAF, 1918–19; rank, Pilot Officer. Member of British AEA; AEA; Garrick Club (London); Green Room Club (London).

Theatre. Mr. Culver made his first appearance on Bway as Philip in *The Little Hut* (Coronet, Oct. 7, 1953); subsequently played Stanley Harrington in *Five Finger Exercise* (Music Box, Dec. 2, 1959) and toured in it (opened Walnut St. Th., Philadelphia, Pa., Oct. 3, 1960; closed Hartman, Columbus, Ohio, Apr. 22, 1961); and was Lebedev in *Ivanov* (Sam S. Shubert Th., N.Y.C., May 3, 1966).

He first appeared on stage as Paul in *Peter and Paul* (Hull Repertory Th., Hull, England, Sept. 1924); and first appeared in London with the Greater London Players in the Sunday Night Experimental Theatre (Century, 1925).

He played Jeff Weems in *Forbidden Fluids* (Scala, May 3, 1925); Jack Harding in a satirical skit, *Behind the Beyond* (St. Martin's, Dec. 1926); Lord Byron in *Nathaniel Bendersnap* (Arts, Dec. 3, 1927); Harry in *Gentlemen Prefer Blondes* (Prince of Wales's, Apr. 2, 1928); George Penguard in *77 Park Lane* (St. Martin's, Oct. 25, 1928); Andrew Hardy in *The Stranger Within* (Garrick, June 20, 1929); Anthony Musgrave in *Beau Austin* (Lyric, Hammersmith, Oct. 31, 1929); Corporal Brown in *Suspense* (Duke of York's, Apr. 8, 1930); Denis in *Dance with No Music* (Arts, July 23, 1930); Clotaire in *John O'Dreams* (Little, Aug. 27, 1930); Ma in *The Circle of Chalk* (Arts, Jan. 22, 1931); Casmir in *The Rocklitz* (Duke of York's, Feb. 4, 1931); and Captain Hastings in *Black Coffee* (St. Martin's, Apr. 9, 1931).

Mr. Culver played Sharper in *The Old Bachelor* (Lyric, Hammersmith, Sept. 18, 1931); Gilbert Lester in *An Average Man* (Q, May 23, 1932); Carol Shaw in *Vacant Possession* (Fortune, Oct. 2, 1933); Franco Spina in *The Mask and the Face* (Royalty, Apr. 14, 1934); Eliot Vines in *Distinguished Gathering* (Embassy, Oct. 7, 1935); Lt. Comm. Rogers in *French without Tears* (Criterion, Nov. 6, 1936); Ford in *Believe It or Not* (New, Jan. 23, 1940); Viscount Goring in *An Ideal Husband* (Westminster, Nov. 16, 1943); George Wayne in *Another Love Story* (Phoenix, Dec. 13, 1944); Ronald Knight in *Master of Arts* (Strand, Sept. 1, 1949); Oscar in *Who Is Sylvia?* (Criterion, Oct. 24, 1950); William Collyer in *Deep Blue Sea* (Duchess, Mar. 5, 1952); and directed *Aren't We All?* (Haymarket, Aug. 16, 1953).

After he made his Bway debut in *The Little Hut* (see above), he returned to London to play Simon Foster in *Simon and Laura* (Strand, Nov. 25, 1954); Colonel George Ferring in *A River Breeze,* which he also wrote (Phoenix, 1955); Stanley Harrington in *Five Finger Exercise* (Comedy, July 17, 1958), which he repeated in N.Y.C. and on tour of the US.

He played Dr. Parker in *Carving a Statue* (Haymarket Th., London, Sept. 17, 1964); Pavel Kirillych Lebedev in *Ivanov* (Yvonne Arnaud Th., Guildford, England, Aug. 30, 1965; Phoenix, London, Sept. 30, 1965), which he repeated in N.Y.C.; succeeded (May 1967) Hugh Williams as the Bishop in *Getting Married* (Strand, London, Apr. 19, 1967); played David Bliss in a revival of *Hay Fever* (O'-Keefe Th., Toronto, Ontario, Canada, Jan. 1968; Duke of York's Th., London, Feb. 1968); joined the cast of *His, Hers and Theirs* as Rupert Cardew (Apollo, London, Dec. 1969); and was Lord Stamfordham in *My Darling Daisy* (Lyric, June 1970).

Films. Mr. Culver has appeared in *Term of Trial* (Romulus, 1936); *To Each His Own* (Par., 1946); *Down to Earth* (Col., 1947); *Emperors Waltz* (Par., 1948); *Singapore* (U, 1947); *Isn't It Romantic* (Par., 1948); *The Great Lover* (Par., 1949); *The Hour of 13* (MGM, 1952); *Folly To Be Wise* (British Lion, 1952); *The Iron Maiden* (Rank, 1962); *The Yellow Rolls-Royce* (MGM, 1965); *Thunderball* (UA, 1965); *A Man Could Get Killed* (U, 1966); and *The Magic Christian* (Commonwealth United, 1970).

Television. He appeared in *Affairs of State* (BBC, London, 1961); *The Back of the Beyond* (Associated, Rediffusion, 1962); *Spread of the Eagle* (BBC, 1963); *Loop* (Associated Television, 1963); *Castle in Spain* (Espionage Series, Dec. 1963); *Gideon's Way* (The "V" Men, Associated Television, 1964); on The Spread of the Eagle (Ind., N.Y.C., 1964–65); in his role as Lebedev in *Ivanov* (CBS, May 30, 1967); and in The Caesars (Granada Television, 1968).

Awards. Mr. Culver was nominated for an Antoinette Perry (Tony) Award as best actor (1966) for his performance as Lebedev in *Ivanov.*

Recreation. Swimming, golf, riding, painting, bridge.

CUMMINGS, CONSTANCE. Actress. b. Constance Halverstadt, May 15, Seattle, Wash., to Dallas Vernon and Kate Logan (Cummings) Halverstadt. Father, lawyer. Attended St. Nicholas Sch., Seattle; Coronado (Calif.) H.S. Married 1933 to Benn Wolfe Levy, playwright (dec. 1973); one son, one daughter. Member of AFTRA; AEA; British AEA (exec. comm. council); SAG.

Theatre. Miss Cummings made her stage debut as the Prostitute in a Savoy Stock Co. production of *Seventh Heaven* (San Diego, Calif., 1926); subsequently appeared there in *Silence* (1927); and toured in the chorus of *Oh, Kay! (1928). She made her Bway debut in the chorus of Treasure Girl* (Alvin, Nov. 8, 1928); appeared in the revue *The Little Show* (Music Box, Apr. 30, 1929); played Carrie in *This Man's Town* (Ritz, Mar. 10, 1930); and joined the cast (Summer 1930) of *June Moon* (Broadhurst, Oct. 9, 1929).

She made her London debut as Alice Overton in the Repertory Players production of *Sour Grapes* (Comedy, July 22, 1934); played Linda Brown in *Accent on Youth* (Plymouth, N.Y.C., Dec. 25, 1934); Regina Conti in *Young Madame Conti* (Savoy, London, Nov. 1936), and repeated this role in N.Y.C. (Music Box, Mar. 31, 1937); played Penelope Marsh in *Three Set Out* (Embassy, London, June 22, 1937); Emma Bovary in *Madame Bovary* (Broadhurst, N.Y.C., Nov. 16, 1937); Nellie Blunt in *If I Were You* (Mansfield, Jan. 24, 1938); Katherine in *Goodbye, Mr. Chips* (Shaftesbury, London, Sept. 23, 1938); for the Oxford Univ. Dramatic Society (O.U.D.S.), she played Katherine in *The Taming of the Shrew* (July 1938); played Dorothy Shaw in *What a Husband Should Do* (Th. Royal, Brighton, Feb. 1939); with the Old Vic, played Juliet in *Romeo and Juliet,* Miss Richland in *The Good-Natured Man* and the title role in *Saint Joan* (Buxton Festival, England, Aug. 1939); and at Streatham Hill, London, repeated her roles in *Romeo and Juliet* (Oct. 2, 1939), *The Good-Natured Man* (Oct. 5, 1939), and *Saint Joan* (Oct. 10, 1939).

During WW II, Miss Cummings toured as Helen Hayle in *On Approval,* for the armed forces; played Lydia in *Skylark* (Duchess, London, Mar. 26, 1942); Gabby Maple in *The Petrified Forest* (Globe, Dec. 16, 1942); Racine Gardner in *One-Man Show* (Ethel Barrymore Th., N.Y.C., Feb. 8, 1945); Jane Pugh in *Clutterbuck* (Wyndham's, London, Aug. 14, 1946); Annaluise Klopps in *Happy with Either* (St. James's, Apr. 22, 1948); and Madeleine in *Don't Listen Ladies!* (St. James's, Sept. 2, 1948). She performed in a concert reading of the Oratorio, *St. Joan at the Stake* (Albert Hall, Dec. 7, 1949); played Laura Whittingham in *Before the Party* (St. Martin's, Oct. 26, 1949); Martha Cotton in *Return to Tyassi* (Duke of York's, Nov. 29, 1950); succeeded (Oct. 1952) Googie Withers as Georgie Elgin in *Winter Journey (The Country Girl)* (St. James's, Apr. 3, 1952); appeared as Ann Downs in *The Shrike* (Prince's, Feb. 13, 1953); Andrea in *Trial and Error* (Vaudeville, Sept. 17, 1953); Theodora Effington in *Not for Children* (Gate, Dublin, Ireland, 1954); narrated *Peter and the Wolf* (Albert Hall, London, Nov. 5, 1955); played the title role in *Lysistrata* (Oxford Playhouse, England, Mar. 1957); and played Antiope in *The Rape of the Belt* (Piccadilly, London, Dec. 12, 1957).

With the Bristol Old Vic, she played Sylvia in *The Edwardians* (May 17, 1960); again played Antiope in *The Rape of the Belt* (Martin Beck Th., N.Y.C., Nov. 5, 1960); played Mrs. J. B. in *J. B.* (Phoenix, London, Mar. 23, 1961); Inez in *In Camera* (Oxford, England, Feb. 7, 1962), and appeared there in *A Social Success;* played Katey Maartins in *The Genius and the Goddess* (Comedy, London, June 29, 1962); played "C" in the stock tryout of *The Strangers* (Westport Country Playhouse, Conn., Nov. 1963); and succeeded (Globe, London, May 1964) Uta Hagen in *Who's Afraid of Virginia Woolf?* (Piccadilly, Feb. 6, 1964).

Miss Cummings played Liza Foote in *Public and Confidential* (Festival Th., Malvern, England, July 26, 1966; Duke of York's Th., London, Aug. 1966); Julia Stanford in *Justice Is a Woman* (Vaudeville, London, Nov. 16, 1966); Jane Banbury in *Fallen Angels* (Vaudeville, Apr. 4, 1967); Queen Gertrude in Nicol Williamson's *Hamlet* (Roundhouse, Apr. 1969; Lunt-Fontanne Th., N.Y.C., May 1, 1969); Flora Goforth in *The Milk Train Doesn't Stop Here Anymore* (Citizens', Glasgow, Scotland, Sept. 1969); Claire in *The Visit* (Belgrade Th., Coventry, England, Oct. 1970); and appeared with the National Th. (New Th., London as Volumnia in *Coriolanus* (May 1971), Leda in *Amphitryon 38* (June 1971), Mary Tyrone in *Long Day's Journey into Night* (Dec. 21, 1971); and Madame Ranevskaya in *The Cherry Orchard* (May 24, 1973); and Agave in Wole Soyinka's adaptation of Euripides' *The Bacchae*

(July 31, 1973).

Films. Miss Cummings made her debut in *Movie Crazy* (Par., 1932); and has since appeared in *Doomed Cargo; Behind the Mask* (Col., 1932); *Washington Merry-go-round* (Col., 1932); *Broadway Thru a Keyhole* (UA, 1933); *Glamour* (U, 1934); *Looking for Trouble* (UA, 1934); *Heads We Go* (B.I.P., 1934); *Channel Crossing* (Gaumont-British, 1934); *Remember Last Night* (U, 1935); *Seven Sinners* (Gaumont-British, 1936); *The Northing Tramp* (Ealing, 1936); *The Wrecker* (Ealing, 1936); *Strangers on a Honeymoon* (Gaumont-British, 1937); *Busman's Honeymoon* (MGM, 1940); *Blithe Spirit* (UA, 1940); *This England* (World, 1941); *The Foreman Went to France* (Ealing, 1942); *Into the Blue* (Wilcox, 1950); *Three's Company* (1953); *Finger of Guilt* (RKO, 1956); *With All My Heart* (1956); *The Intimate Stranger* (Anglo-Amalgamated, 1956); *John and Julie* (DCA, 1957); *The Battle of the Sexes* (Continental, 1960); *Sammy Going South* (Seven Arts, 1963); *In the Cool of the Day* (MGM, 1963); and *A Boy Ten Feet Tall* (Par., 1965).

Television and Radio. On radio, Miss Cummings has performed on Showmen of England (1938); in *The White Cliffs* (1941); played the title role in *Saint Joan* (1941); in *The Rebirth of Venus* (1941); *Man's Company* (1942); Amy in *They Knew What They Wanted* (1942); Cleopatra in *Antony and Cleopatra* (1942); participated in a discussion on Women on the Stage (1949); played the title role in *Hedda Gabler* (1952); Georgie Elgin in *Winter Journey* (1954); Emma Bovary in *Madame Bovary* (1955); and performed on Variety Playhouse (1955); and Call the Tune (1957).

Her television appearances include the roles of Roxanne in *Cyrano de Bergerac* (1938); Martha in *Return to Tyassi* (1956); Mary in *The Trial of Mary Dugan* (1957); Harriet Craig in *Craig's Wife* (1957); Kathleen in *The Last Tycoon* (1959); Jane in *Clutterbuck* (1959); the title role in *Ruth* (1962); and Helga in *Late Summer* (1963).

Awards. Miss Cummings was made a Commander of the Order of the British Empire (C.B.E.) in the 1974 New Year's honors (Jan. 15, 1974).

Recreation. Anthropology.

CURTIS, KEENE. Actor, production stage manager. b. Keene Holbrook Curtis, Feb. 15, 1923, Salt Lake City, Utah, to Ira Charles and Polley (Holbrook) Curtis. Father, civil service employee; mother, teacher. Grad. Davis H.S., Kaysville, Utah, 1940; Univ. of Utah, B.A. 1943; M.S. 1947. Served USN, 1943–46; rank, Lt. (jg). Member of AEA; AGMA; SAG; AFTRA. Address: 6363 Ivarene Ave., Hollywood, CA 90068, tel. (213) 466-6688.

Theatre. Mr. Curtis first served as understudy to Jay Robinson in the role of Archie in *The Shop at Sly Corner* (Booth, N.Y.C., Jan. 18, 1949); subsequently was stage manager for a cross-country tour of the Martha Graham Dance Co. (1949–50); *The Constant Wife* (Boston, Mass., engagement of tour, 1953); and the national company tour of *The Male Animal* (opened Nixon, Pittsburgh, Pa., Mar. 9, 1953; closed Blackstone, Chicago, Ill., May 2, 1953).

He served as stage manager for the European tour of the Martha Graham Dance Co. (1954); *Mrs. Patterson* (Natl., N.Y.C., Dec. 1, 1954); production stage manager for *The Dark Light Is Enough* (ANTA, Feb. 23, 1955); *Medea* (Th. Sarah Bernhardt, Paris, France, June 1955); and general manager for the world concert tour of Eleanor Steber (Dec. 30, 1956–Apr. 21, 1957).

He was production stage manager for *Four Winds* (Cort, N.Y.C., Sept. 25, 1957); *Nude with Violin* (Belasco, Nov. 14, 1957); *Present Laughter* (Belasco, Jan. 31, 1958); *The Firstborn* (Coronet, Mar. 30, 1958), and toured Israel (June 26, 1958–July 16, 1958); *Look After Lulu* (Henry Miller's Th., N.Y.C., Mar. 3, 1959); *Twelfth Night* (Boston Drama Festival, Mass., 1959); *Much Ado About Nothing* (Cambridge Drama Festival, Mass., 1959; Lunt-Fontanne, N.Y.C., Sept. 17, 1959); and for *Silent Night, Lonely Night* (Morosco, Dec. 3, 1959).

Mr. Curtis, a charter member of the Association of Producing Artists (APA) upon its formation in 1960, appeared in the following APA productions: at City Hall Th., Hamilton, Bermuda, as Franz in *Anatol* (May 12, 1960), Henry Straker in *Man and Superman* (May 18, 1960), Medvedenko in *The Seagull* (May 31, 1960), and, at Outdoor Th., Hamilton, appeared as Julian Froth, and later Biondello, in *The Taming of the Shrew* (July 4–23, 1960); he then toured summer theatres in the US with APA (Bucks County Playhouse, New Hope, Pa., Aug. 1–13, 1960; Theatre-by-the-Sea, Matunuck, R.I., Aug. 22–27, 1960; John Drew Th., East Hampton, N.Y., Aug. 30–Sept. 4, 1960).

At the McCarter Th., Princeton, N.J., he repeated his roles in *Man and Superman* (Sept. 28, 1960) and *Anatol* (Sept. 28, 1960); was Tyson in *The Lady's Not for Burning* (Oct. 6, 1960), Agazzi in *Right You Are If You Think You Are* (Oct. 13, 1960), Stevens in *The Tavern* (Oct. 20, 1960), again played Medvedenko in *The Seagull* (Oct. 27, 1960), played the title role in *Scapin* (Nov. 3, 1960), was Lane in *The Importance of Being Earnest* (Nov. 10, 1960), Oswald in *King Lear* (Feb. 3, 1961), Bottom in *A Midsummer Night's Dream* (Feb. 9, 1961), Feste in *Twelfth Night* (Feb. 23, 1961), a Page in *As You Like It* (Mar. 4, 1961), and Lucianus in *Hamlet* (Mar. 23, 1961).

He appeared in repertory with APA (June 21–Sept. 3, 1961) at Boston (Mass.) Arts Festival; Highfield Th., Falmouth, Mass.; Bucks County Playhouse, New Hope, Pa.; John Drew Th., East Hampton, N.Y.; and Olney (Md.) Th., repeating his roles in *Twelfth Night* and *The Seagull* and playing Sir Oliver Surface in *The School for Scandal* and the Sheriff in *The Tavern;* he appeared also with APA at the Fred Miller Th., Milwaukee, Wis., as Bottom in *A Midsummer Night's Dream* (Oct. 17, 1961), Dorn in *The Seagull* (Oct. 19, 1961), and repeated his roles in *The Tavern* (Nov. 3, 1961) and *The School for Scandal* (Nov. 17, 1961); and he toured Australia and the Far East as stage manager for the Ailey–de Lavallade American Dance Co. (Jan.–May 1962).

He toured (Summer 1962) with APA, playing George Selincourt in *A Penny for a Song* (Bucks County Playhouse, New Hope, Pa., Aug. 6–18, 1962; John Drew Th., East Hampton, N.Y., Aug. 20–25, 1962); and appeared with APA in the Univ. of Michigan Professional Theatre Program (PTP) at the Lydia Mendelssohn Th., Ann Arbor, Mich., as Sir Benjamin Backbite in *The School for Scandal* (Oct. 2, 1962), and repeated his roles in *The Tavern* (Oct. 17, 1962) and *A Penny for a Song* (Oct. 31, 1962), and, at the Trueblood Th., as Bottom (Feb. 13, 1963), Salarino in *The Merchant of Venice* (Feb. 20, 1963), and Sir William Bagot in *King Richard II* (Feb. 27, 1963). With APA, he again played Bottom (Boston Arts Festival, Boston, Mass., July 8, 1963) and, at Trueblood Th., Ann Arbor, Mich., played Conrad in *Much Ado About Nothing* (Oct. 8, 1963), the title role in *Scapin* (Oct. 17, 1963), Sirelli in *Right You Are* (Nov. 7, 1963), the Tartar in *The Lower Depths* (Nov. 21, 1963); and, also with APA, at the Phoenix, N.Y.C., repeated his roles in *Right You Are* (Mar. 4, 1964), *The Tavern* (Mar. 5, 1963), *Scapin* (Mar. 9, 1964), played Du Croisy in *Impromptu at Versailles* (also Mar. 9, 1964), and repeated his role in *The Lower Depths* (Mar. 30, 1964).

Mr. Curtis appeared with APA at the Lydia Mendelssohn Th., Ann Arbor, Mich., as Napoleon in *War and Peace* (Sept. 24, 1964), Henry Straker in *Man and Superman* (Sept. 30, 1964), Rio Rita in *The Hostage* (Oct. 14, 1964), and Egon in *Judith* (Oct. 28, 1964), then repeating at the Phoenix, N.Y.C., his performances in *Man and Superman* (Dec. 6, 1964), *War and Peace* (Jan. 11, 1965), and *Judith* (Mar. 24, 1965). He appeared with APA at the Lydia Mendelssohn Th. as Kolenkov in *You Can't Take It with You* (Sept. 29, 1965), Molvik in *The Wild Duck* (Oct. 6, 1965), and the Guide in *Herakles* (Oct. 27, 1965), repeating his performance as Kolenkov in N.Y.C. (Lyceum Th., Nov. 23, 1965).

He appeared with APA in repertory: at Huntington Hartford Th., Hollywood, Calif. (beginning July 11, 1966) as Sir Oliver Surface in *The School for Scandal,* Sirelli in *Right You Are,* and Kolenkov in *You Can't Take It with You;* at the Greek Th., Los Angeles, Calif., as Pierre in *War and Peace* (Aug. 31, 1966); and at the Lydia Mendelssohn Th., Ann Arbor, he repeated his performances as Sir Oliver (Sept. 20, 1966) and Sirelli (Oct. 11, 1966) and directed *Sweet of You To Say So* (Sept. 27, 1966). He appeared with APA at the Royal Alexandra Th., Toronto, Ontario, Canada (beginning Nov. 8, 1966) in his roles in *The School for Scandal* and *Right You Are;* then, at the Lyceum, N.Y.C., repeated both of these (Nov. 21 and 22, respectively), alternated at various performances as Molvik and Balle in *The Wild Duck,* played Boris in *You Can't Take It with You* (Feb. 10, 1967), and Napoleon in *War and Peace* (Mar. 21, 1967), in which he alternated also as Pierre.

He appeared with APA in repertory at the Huntington Hartford Th., Hollywood, Calif., as the Anarchist in *Pantagleize* (July 31, 1967); at the Lydia Mendelssohn Th., Ann Arbor, Mich., in the same role (Sept. 19, 1967), as Kolenkov in *You Can't Take It with You* (Oct. 3, 1967), and as Sirelli in *Right You Are* (Oct. 6, 1967); at the Royal Alexandra Th., Toronto, Ontario, Canada (beginning Oct. 17, 1967) as Kolenkov, Sirelli, and the Anarchist; at the Lyceum, N.Y.C., as the Anarchist (Nov. 30, 1967) and as Epihodov in *The Cherry Orchard* (Mar. 19, 1968); at Memorial Aud., Stanford Univ., Calif. (beginning July 8, 1968), as the Anarchist and as Alex in *The Cocktail Party;* at the Royal Alexandra Th., Toronto (beginning Aug. 12, 1968) as Oronte in *The Misanthrope* and again as Alex; at the Lyceum, N.Y.C., as the Anarchist (Sept. 3, 1968); at the Lydia Mendelssohn Th., Ann Arbor, as Oronte (Sept. 17, 1968) and again as Alex; and at the Lyceum, N.Y.C., again as Alex (Oct. 7, 1968), Oronte (Oct. 9, 1968), the Sergeant in *Cock-a-Doodle Dandy* (Jan. 20, 1969), and as the Player King in *Hamlet* (Mar. 3, 1969).

He played various roles in *Collision Course* (Pavilion Th., Pennsylvania State Univ., State Coll., Penn., July 23, 1969); was Oblensky in *A Patriot for Me* (National Th., Washington, D.C., Sept. 15, 1969; Imperial, N.Y.C., Oct. 5, 1969); replaced (Dec. 8, 1969) Charles Durning as Ned Buntline in *Indians* (Brooks Atkinson Th., Oct. 13, 1969); played the Captain, Max, George Wague, and a Reporter in *Colette* (Ellen Stewart Th., May 6, 1970); was Prince William, Fouché, Lord Herries, and Prince Metternich in *The Rothschilds* (Fisher Th., Detroit, Mich., Aug. 11, 1970; Forrest Th., Philadelphia, Pa., Sept. 17, 1970; Lunt-Fontanne Th., N.Y.C., Oct. 19, 1970); was in *The Ride Across Lake Constance* (Forum Th., N.Y.C., Jan. 13, 1972); played Curtis Appleby in *Nightwatch* (Morosco, Feb. 28, 1972); and appeared at the John Drew Th., East Hampton, N.Y. (Summer 1972) as Dr. Rance in *What the Butler Saw* and Dr. Oates in *Guttman Ordinary Scale.* He also played Death in *Ratfink* (Portfolio Th., N.Y.C., Spring 1972); Dr. Isaacs in *Via Galactica* (Uris Th., Nov. 28, 1972); the Inquisitor in *Saint Joan* (Ahmanson Th., Los Angeles, Calif., Jan. 29, 1974); President Wilson in *President Wilson in Paris* (Forum Lab Th., Los Angeles, Calif., Jan. 14, 1975); and Joshua in *Ring 'Round the Moon* (Ahmanson Th., Los Angeles, Calif., Apr. 1, 1975).

Films. Mr. Curtis played Lennox in *Macbeth* (Rep., 1947) and appeared in *Blade* (Joseph Green Pictures, 1973) and *The Wrong Damn Film* (Carson Davidson, 1975).

Television. Mr. Curtis appeared in the pilot for The Magician (NBC, Dec. 1972–Jan. 1973) and subsequently in the first eleven episodes of the series. He was a guest star in *Killer at Sea* (Hawaii Five-O, CBS, Dec. 1973); played Kiever in the *Whirlwind* episode of the four-part Benjamin Franklin series (CBS, Jan. 1974); was Hebble Tyson in *The Lady's Not for Burning* (Hollywood Television Th., PBS, May 1974); played Col. Wortman in *Iron Guts Kelly* (M*A*S*H., CBS, 1974); Uri Lazlo in *The Cloning of Mr. Swimmer* (ABC Movie of the Week, June 1974); McCone in *The Missiles of October* (ABC, 1974); Estes in *Stowaway to the Moon* (CBS Movie of the Week, 1974); Dobbs Burke in *Bones of Contention* (Hawaii Five-O, CBS, Oct. 1974); William Scott in the pilot *Strange New World* (ABC, Oct.–Nov. 1974); Lowell Bates in the Karen Valentine Show (NBC, Nov. 1974); and a Doctor on Sanford and Son (NBC, Jan. 1975).

Awards. For his performance in *The Rothschilds,* Mr. Curtis won an Antoinette Perry (Tony) Award (1971) as best supporting actor in a musical.

Recreation. Carpentry, photography.

CURTIS, PAUL J. Mime. b. Aug. 29, 1927, Boston, Mass. Professional training at Dramatic Workshop, the New Sch. for Social Research, N.Y.C. Founder and director of The American Mime Theatre; American Mime, Inc. (pres.); International Mimes & Pantomimists (administrator). Address: c/o The American Mime Theatre, 192 Third Ave., New York, NY 10003, tel. (212) 777-1710.

Theatre. Mr. Curtis founded the American Mime Theatre in 1952. Concerts have been given by the group in many parts of the country, including the Univ. of Vermont, Bard College, Cornell Univ., Syracuse Univ., Amherst College, Baltimore Museum of Art, Pennsylvania State Univ., and Springfield College. In N.Y.C., American Mime Theatre has appeared at such places as Kaufmann Auditorium, YMHA; Cooper Union; Brooklyn Academy; NY Shakespeare Festival Public Theatre; Pratt Institute; Bronx Community College; and Equity Library Theatre.

Films. Films of American Mime Theatre are *Environment; Whitescope; Abstraction;* and *The American Mime Theatre.* .

Television. Mr. Curtis and his group have been seen on such programs as Today Show (NBC); Montage IV (NBC); the Jackie Gleason Show (CBS); Look Up and Live (CBS); Lamp Unto My Feet (NBC); and Profile on the Arts (NBC).

Other Activities. American Mime Theatre conducts a training school, which has trained over 5,000 performers. In 1970, American Mime, Inc., was incorporated as a nonprofit public foundation and chartered by the State of New York, thereby becoming eligible for funding from state and federal agencies. Mr. Curtis has lectured or given courses on mime at many colleges and other institutions, including Jacob's Pillow; Sarah Lawrence College; the Guggenheim Museum; Circle in the Square; Johns Hopkins Univ.; and the American Conservatory Theatre, San Francisco, Calif.

Published Works. Mr. Curtis's published works are *American Mime Textbook; Twenty-Five American Mime Plays;* and *Directory of International Mimes & Pantomimists.*

Awards. Mr. Curtis has received grants from the New York State Council on the Arts; the Rockefeller Foundation; and the Capezio Foundation.

CURVIN, JONATHAN W. Educator. b. Jonathan Wadhams Curvin, July 14, 1911, Brockport, N.Y., to Francis Gilbert and Mabel (Wadhams) Curvin. Father, storekeeper. Grad. Medina (N.Y.) H.S., 1928; Cornell Univ., B.A. 1932, M.A. 1934, Ph.D. 1941. Married Aug. 24, 1935, to Helen Champlin; one son, one daughter. Served USNR 1944–46, PTO; rank, Lt. Member of SAA; AETA. Address: (home) 2125 Chadbourne Ave., Madison, WI 53705, tel. (608) 233-9629; (bus.) Dept. of Theatre and Drama, Univ. of Wisconsin, Madison, WI 53706, tel. (608) 263-3352.

Since 1954, Mr. Curvin has been professor of speech and associate director of the Wisconsin Players at the Univ. of Wisconsin; was chairman of the Dept. of Speech and Theatre at Hobart Coll. (1934–41); and chairman of the Dept. of Speech and Theatre at Vanderbilt Univ. (1941–43).

He was guest faculty member and director at the Univ. of Colorado (Summer 1955); guest lecturer at the Centro Sperimentale di Cinematografia (Rome, Italy, Apr. 1956); and Fulbright research grantee in Theatre Arts in Finland (1957–58).

Other Activities. Since 1963, Mr. Curvin has been editor of the *Educational Theatre Journal;* was chairman of the editorial board (1954); assistant editor (1955); and associate editor (1956); and is currently (1974) associate editor, *Quarterly Journal of Speech.*

He was US delegate to the Intl. Theatre Congress (Helsinki, Finland, June 1959).

Published Works. He has written articles for the *Quarterly Journal of Speech,* the *National Theatre Conference Bulletin, Western Speech,* and *World Theatre,* and has contributed an article, "The Stage Yankee," to the book *Studies in Speech and Drama* (1944).

Recreation. Golf, photography.

CUSACK, CYRIL. Actor, producer, playwright. b. Cyril James Cusack, Nov. 26, 1910, Durban, Natal, Africa, to James W. and Moira (Cole) Cusack. Father, member of Natal Mounted Police; mother, actress. Attended Dominican Coll., Droichead Nua, Ire., 1922–26; Natl. Univ. of Ireland, Univ. Coll., 1928–32. Married Apr. 5, 1945, to Maureen Kiely, actress; two sons, three daughters. Relative in theatre: step-father, Brefni O'Rorke, actor. Member of British AEA; Irish AEA; AFTRA; SAG; United Arts Club (Dublin); Irish Club (London).

Theatre. Mr. Cusack made his N.Y.C. debut as Phil Hogan in *The Moon for the Misbegotten* (Bijou Th., May 2, 1957); subsequently appeared as Seumas O'Beirne in the pre-Bway tryout of *Goodwill Ambassador* (opened Shubert, New Haven, Conn., Mar. 16, 1960; closed Wilbur, Boston, Mass., Mar. 26, 1960), in which he had appeared earlier in Dublin (see below).

He made his stage debut at age six as Little Willie in a touring production of *East Lynne,* in which his parents also appeared (Clonmel, Ire., 1916); toured theatres and halls throughout Ireland with his step-father in Dion Boucicault's *Arrah-na-Pogue* (1918), *The Sign of the Cross, Shot at Dawn,* the Cat in *Dick Whittington* (1920); the Donkey in *Ali Baba* (1922), and Babe in *The Babes in the Wood* (1922). With his parents, he also toured the English theatre circuits as the Boy in *Irish and Proud of It* (1924); with the Norwich (Eng.) Repertory Co., played the Indian Student in *Tilly of Bloomsbury,* Carruthers in *Mr. Wu,* appeared in *Milestones, The Promised Land, Ambrose Applejohn's Adventure* (1928); and toured England in *The Terror* (1928).

In 1932, Mr. Cusack joined the Abbey Th. (Dublin), and was intermittently associated with it until 1945, appearing in about 65 productions, in such roles as the Boy in *The Vigil* (Oct. 24, 1932); Hughie Boyle in *Wrack* (Nov. 21, 1932); Michael in *Drama at Inish* (Feb. 6, 1933); *Margaret Gillan* (July 17, 1933); an Irish Countryman in *Parnell of Avondale* (Oct. 1, 1934); Malcolm in *Macbeth* (Oct. 25, 1934); *Gallant Cassian* (Nov. 12, 1934); the Son in *Six Characters in Search of an Author* (Dec. 3, 1934); Colin Langford in *At Mrs. Beams'* (Dec. 26, 1934); *The King of Spain's Daughter* (Apr. 29, 1935); *The Silver Tassie* (Aug. 12, 1935); *A Deuce of Jacks* (Sept. 16, 1935); Marchbanks in *Candida* (Sept. 30, 1935); Japhet in *Noah* (Nov. 4, 1935); performed in *A Saint in a Hurry* (Dec. 2, 1935); played Curran in *Summer's Day* (Dec. 9, 1935); Titus Larius in *Coriolanus* (Jan. 13, 1936); *The Grand House in the City* (Feb. 3, 1936); Andy in *Boyd's Shop* (Feb. 24, 1936); Jo Mahony in *Katie Roche* (Mar. 16, 1936); and Hind in *The Passing Day* (Apr. 13, 1936).

He made his London debut as Richard in *Ah, Wilderness!* (Westminster, May 4, 1936); at the Abbey Th., appeared as John Joseph Barrett in *The Silver Jubilee* (Sept. 14, 1936); Mr. Bunton in *The Jailbird* (Oct. 12, 1936); performed in *Blind Man's Buff* (Dec. 12, 1936); played O'Flingsley in *Shadow and Substance* (Jan. 25, 1937); Quin in *Quin's Secret* (Mar. 29, 1937); Loftus de Lury in *Killycreggs in Twilight* (Apr. 19, 1937); Dan Cusack in *The Patriot* (Aug. 15, 1937); Mangan in *The Man in the Cloak* (Sept. 27, 1937); Kelly in *The Invincibles* (Oct. 18, 1937); Cartney in *Cartney and Kevney* (Nov. 8, 1937); Neddy in *She Had to Do Something* (Dec. 27, 1937); Adam in *Neal Maquade* (Jan. 17, 1938); appeared in *A Spot in the Sun* (Feb. 14, 1938); played Ned Hegarty in *Moses Rock* (Feb. 28, 1938); Hyacinth in *Bird's Nest* (Sept. 12, 1938); appeared in *The Great Adventure* (Sept. 19, 1938); and *Pilgrims* (Oct. 10, 1938). During the Abbey Th. Festival of 1938, he played the Fool in *On Baile's Strand,* the Covey in *The Plough and the Stars,* Christopher Mahon in *The Playboy of the Western World,* and O'Flingsley in *Shadow and Substance.*

Mr. Cusack repeated his roles in *The Playboy of the Western World* (Mercury, London, Jan. 27, 1939); *The Plough and the Stars* ("Q", June 1939); played Michel in *Les parents terribles* (Gate, May 17, 1940); at the Abbey Th. (Dublin), portrayed Pat Hooey in *Give Him a House* (Oct. 30, 1939), John Joe Martin in *They Went by Bus* (Dec. 4, 1939), Kevin McMorna in *The Spanish Soldier* (Jan. 29, 1940), and *William John Mawhinney* (Mar. 23, 1940); appeared as Streeter in *Thunder Rock* (St. Martin's, London, Feb. 5, 1941); performed in his own play, *Tareis an Aifrinn (After Mass)* (Gate, Dublin, Jan. 11, 1942); played Louis Dubedat in *The Doctor's Dilemma* (Haymarket, London, Mar. 4, 1942); Dewis in *The Whiteheaded Boy* (Abbey, Dublin, Aug. 1942); *An Apple a Day* (Abbey, Sept. 7, 1942); John in *The Barrell Organ* (Gaiety, Nov. 1942); at the Abbey, appeared in *Faustus Kelly* (Jan. 25, 1943), played the O'Cuddy in *The O'Cuddy* (Mar. 8, 1943), Michael in *The Old Road* (1943), appeared in *Poor Man's Miracle* (Dec. 27, 1943), played Francis in *The Wise Have Not Spoken* (Feb. 7, 1944), appeared in *The New Regime* (Mar. 6, 1944), played Seuman in *The End House* (Aug. 28, 1944), appeared in *Rossa* (Mar. 31, 1945), and played Dawson in *Tenants at Will* (Sept. 24, 1945).

In 1944, he went into management at the Gaiety Th., forming his own company, Cyril Cusack Productions. In association with Shelah Richards, he appeared as Romeo in *Romeo and Juliet* (Gaiety, 1944). His first appearance with his own company was as Tom in *The Last of Summer* (Gaiety, July 16, 1945); subsequently appeared at the Gaiety, as Sid Hunt in *Hell Bent for Heaven* (July 23, 1945), Dick Dudgeon in *The Devil's Disciple* (Mar. 10, 1947), and Louis Dubedat in *The Doctor's Dilemma* (Mar. 24, 1947); played Nosy in *Pommy* (People's Palace, London, May 8, 1950); with his own company, portrayed Christopher Mahon in *The Playboy of the Western World* (Gaiety, July 20, 1953), and Bluntschli in *Arms and the Man,* which was produced with *Hello, Out There!* (Gaiety, July 27, 1953); toured Ireland with *The Playboy of the Western World,* and, at the request of the government, presented and repeated his role in this play at the first International Theatre des Nations season in Paris (Th. Sarah Bernhardt, June 1954).

At the Gaiety Th. (Dublin), he appeared as Bluntschli in *Arms and the Man* (July 27, 1953), Codger in *The Bishop's Bonfire* (Feb. 28, 1955), Do-the-Right in *The Golden Cuckoo* (June 25, 1956), in a double-bill played Androcles in *Androcles and the Lion* and the Man in *The Rising of the Moon* (July 2, 1956), and the title role in *Hamlet* (Oct. 28, 1957); played Roger Casement in *Casement* (Th. Royal, Waterford, Ireland, Mar. 3, 1958), which he repeated (Gaiety, Dublin, Mar. 10, 1958); Liverpool Shakespeare Th., England, Mar. 31, 1958); Seumas O'Beirne in *Goodwill Ambassador* (Olympia, Dublin, Mar. 2, 1959), in which he also appeared in the US (see above); Krapp in *Krapp's Last Tape,* and Bluntschli in *Arms and the Man* (Empire, Belfast, June 3, 1960; Queen's, Dublin, June 20, 1960), which he repeated at the International Th. des Nations (Th. Sarah Bernhardt, Paris, 1960), and at theatre festivals (1960) in Rotterdam, Amsterdam, The Hague, Utrecht, and Antwerp; toured Ireland as Doolin in *The Voices of Doolin* (1960), which he repeated at the Theatre Festival (Gaiety, Dublin, Sept. 26, 1960); at the Dublin Festival of 1961, presented his own play, *The Temptation of Mr. O,* in which he played the title role (Gaiety, Sept. 19, 1961); appeared as Mobius in *The Physicists* (Aldwych, London, Jan. 9, 1963); at the Royal Shakespeare Memorial Th., Cassius in *Julius Caesar* (Stratford-upon-Avon, season commencing Apr. 9, 1963); and the Teacher in *Andorra* (English Natl. Th., London, 1964).

Mr. Cusack played Conn in the Abbey Th. Co. production of *The Shaughraum* (Dublin, Ireland, Jan. 1967), which he repeated in London, England, during the World Theatre Season (Aldwych, May 1968); appeared at the Dublin (Ireland) Festival as Gaev in *The Cherry Orchard* (Oct. 1968); was Fox Melarkey in *Crystal and Fox* (Gaiety, Dublin, Nov. 1968); and toured with the Abbey Th. (1969–70) in the title role of *Hadrian VII.* He also played Menenius in *Coriolanus* (John F. Kennedy Th., Honolulu, Hawaii, Nov. 1970); Antonio in *The Tempest* (Old Vic, London, England, Mar. 5, 1974); and the Masked Man in *Spring Awakening* (Old Vic, May 28, 1974).

Films. Mr. Cusack played Young O'Brien in *Knocknagow or the Homes of Tipperary,* probably the first Irish film produced (Tipperary, 1916); Driver in *Odd Man Out* (U, 1947); appeared in *Esther Waters* (Pinewood, 1947); *The Blue Lagoon* (U, 1949); *The Small Back Room* (Snader, 1952); *All Over the Town* (U, 1949); *Once a Jolly Swagman* (1949); *The Elusive Pimpernel* (1950); *Gone to Earth* (1950); *Soldiers Three* (MGM, 1951); *The Secret of Convict Lake* (20th-Fox, 1951); *The Blue Veil* (RKO, 1951); *The Man on the Road* (1954); *The Man Who Never Was* (20th-Fox, 1954); *Gideon's Day* (Col., 1955); *Jacqueline* (Rank, 1957); *The Spanish Gardener* (Rank, 1957); *Ill Met by Moonlight* (Rank, 1953); *The Rising of the Moon* (WB, 1957); *Passage Home* (Group Film); *March Hare* (1956); *Floods of Fear* (U, 1959); *Shake Hands with the Devil* (UA, 1959); *A Terrible Beauty* (UA, 1959); *The Night Fighters* (UA, 1960); *The Waltz of the Toreadors* (Continental, 1962); *I Thank a Fool* (MGM, 1962); *80,000 Suspects* (Bath, 1962); and *Saadia* (MGM, 1963).

His other films include *Where the Spies Are* (MGM, 1965); *The Spy Who Came in from the Cold* (Par., 1965); *I Was Happy Here* (Rank, 1966); *Fahrenheit 451* (U, 1966); *Time Lost and Time Remembered* (Continental-Rank, 1966); *The Taming of the Shrew* (Col., 1967); *Harold and Maude* (Par., 1971); *Sacco and Vanzetti* (UMC, 1971); and *The Day of the Jackal* (U, 1973).

Television and Radio. Mr. Cusack was on radio in a series of characters from Charles Dickens (Radio-Eireann); played Pip in *Great Expectations* (BBC, London); was in *The Dark Tower* (BBC, 1946); *Frederic General* (BBC); *The Dead* (BBC); *The Wild Goose* (BBC); and *Troilus and Cressida* (Third Network, London, 1965).

On television, he appeared in *The Shadow of the Glen* (BBC, 1938); *Ship Day* (Elstree, 1948); *Highland Fling* (Elstree, 1948); *The Sensible Man* (Elstree, 1949); *Oedipus Complex* (BBC, 1953); *The Moon and Sixpence* (ABC, US, 1957); *What Every Woman Knows* (ABC, 1959); *The Enchanted* (ABC, 1959); and *The Power and the Glory* (ABC, 1959); *The Dummy* (ABC, 1962); *The Chairs* (Granada, London, 1962); *Don Juan in Hell* (Granada, 1962); *The Lotus Eater* (Granada, 1962); *The Wedding Dress* (Granada, 1963); *Krapp's Last Tape* (BBC, 1963); *Tryptych,* which included *Purgatory* (1963); *In the Train* (1963); Michael McInerney in *The Workhouse Ward* (T.E., 1963); Thomas à Becket in *Murder in the Cathedral;* (BBC Festival, Mar. 25, 1964); the Father in *Six Characters in Search of an Author* (BBC Festival, June 3, 1964); and Petley in *The Big Toe* (Drama '64, ITV, Sept. 20, 1964; and the Prosecuting Counsel in *Johnny Nobody* (Medallion, 1965).

Published Works. A selection of Mr. Cusack's poetry in Gaelic and English has been published in book form, as well as in *The Commonweal,* NY *Times,* and *Transatlantic Review.*

Discography. Mr. Cusack recorded readings from the works of Samuel Beckett, issued as *Beckett: Molloy, Malone Dies,* and *The Unnameable* (Caedmon, 1964).

Awards. He received the International Critics Award for his performances at the Th. des Nations, Paris (1960); the English Tatler Radio Critics Award for his performance in *The Dark Tower* (1954); Sylvania Television Citation for his performance in *The Moon and Sixpence* (1959); and the Irish Television Critics' Award as best actor (1963).

Recreation. Collector of objets d'art of theatrical interest; and rare books and posters of Irish theatrical interest.

CUSHMAN, NANCY. Actress. b. Apr. 26, 1913, Brooklyn, N.Y., to Earl L. and Louise (Radford) Cushman. Father, educator, museum curator; mother, kindergarten teacher. Grad. Packer Collegiate Inst., 1931; Rollins Coll., A.B. 1935. Married Aug. 28, 1949, to Duncan McMartin Baldwin, actor (dec. July 12, 1952). Served USO, WW II. Member of AEA; AFTRA; SAG; Kappa Kappa Gamma; Phi Beta (NY bd. of dir., other offices); Sheldon Museum, Middlebury, Vt. (hon. mbr., bd. of trustees); Town Hall Club (bd. of dir.). Address: (home) 130 W. 57th St., New York, NY 10019, tel. (212) CI 6-1610; (bus.) Artists Service, 170 W. 74th St., New York, NY 10023, tel. (212) SU 7-5400.

Pre-Theatre. Public relations work, business management.

Theatre. Miss Cushman made her stage debut as Lady Anne Pettigrew in *Berkeley Square* (Annie Russell Th., Rollins Coll., Winter Pk., Fla., 1932); her professional debut as Lucy Weston in a stock production of *Kind Lady* (Peterboro, N.H., July 1, 1936); her Bway debut as the Maid and understudy to Jessamine Newcomb as Countess Fillipe in *White Man* (Natl., Oct. 17, 1936); was understudy to Valerie Cossart as Maggie in *Storm Over Patsy* (Guild, Mar. 8, 1937); played in stock at New London, N.H. (Summers 1937–39); appeared as a Tavern Wench in *Gloriana* (Little, N.Y.C., Nov. 25, 1938); in stock (Miami Beach Th., Fla., Winter 1939–40; Cohasset Summer Th., Mass., Aug. 1940).

She was featured as Lucille Colburn in *Janie* (Henry Miller's Th., N.Y.C., Sept. 10, 1942), and on the national tour (opened Colonial, Boston, Mass., Jan. 1944; closed, Yakima, Wash., Nov. 1944); appeared in a USO-touring production of *Junior Miss* (PTO, 1945); performed in stock (Brattleboro, Vt., Summers 1946–49); understudied June Walker as Linda Loman and appeared as Miss Forsythe in a national touring production of *Death of a Salesman* (opened Cass, Detroit, Mich., Sept. 1949); played Linda Loman in stock productions of *Death of a Salesman* (Albany, N.Y., May 1951; Brattleboro, Vt., July 1951); appeared as the Woman in a touring production of *Death of a Salesman* (opened Klein Aud., Bridgeport, Conn., Sept. 8, 1951; closed KRNT Th., Richmond, Va., Jan. 5, 1952); and appeared as Ruth in *Blithe Spirit* (Playhouse-in-the-Park, Philadelphia, Pa., Sept. 1952).

Miss Cushman appeared as Grace Tendel in *Be Your Age* (48 St. Th., N.Y.C., Jan. 14, 1953); played in stock (Elitch Gardens, Denver, Colo., Summer 1953; Lakewood Th., Skowhegan, Me., Summer 1954); appeared in an industrial show on the West Coast (1954); was standby for Mildred Dunnock in *Cat on a Hot Tin Roof* (Morosco, N.Y.C., Mar. 24, 1955); appeared in stock touring productions as Peg Costello in *The Desk Set* (Summer 1957); and as Mrs. Benjamin Duke in the national touring company of *The Happiest Millionaire* (opened Dupont Th., Wilmington, Del., Oct. 2, 1957); closed Tower Th., Atlanta, Ga., May 17, 1958); was a standby for Bibi Osterwald as Madame Elizabeth in *Look Homeward, Angel* (Ethel Barrymore Th., N.Y.C., Nov. 28, 1957); played Letty Gaxton in *The Man in the Dog Suit* (Coronet, Oct. 30, 1958); succeeded Helen Waters as Mrs. Botticelli in *J. B.* (ANTA, Dec. 11, 1958); appeared as Rachel Krupp in *A Mighty Man Is He* (Cort, Jan. 6, 1960); Sara Delano Roosevelt in *Sunrise at Campobello* (Music Circus, Lambertville, N.J.; Cape Playhouse, Dennis, Mass.; Lakewood Th., Skowhegan, Me.; Colonie Summer Th., Latham, N.Y.; Playhouse-in-the-Park, Philadelphia, Pa., Summer 1960); and as Mme. Elizabeth Madame *Look Homeward, Angel* (Pocono Playhouse, Pa., Summer 1960).

She originated Mrs. Barker in *The American Dream* (York, N.Y.C., Jan. 24, 1961); played Monica Breedlove in *The Bad Seed* (Ann Arbor Drama Festival, Mich., Summer 1961); Rose Lovejoy in *Destry Rides Again* (Music Circus, Lambertville, N.J., Summer 1961); Charlotte Orr in a national tour of *Critic's Choice* (opened Municipal Aud., Lafayette, La., Dec. 1, 1961; closed Mansfield, Ohio, Mar. 29, 1962), and repeated the same role in two stock productions (Detroit, Mich.; Highland Pk., Ill., Summer 1962; and Lakewood Th., Skowhegan, Me.; Cape Playhouse, Dennis, Mass., Summer 1962).

She was featured as Mrs. Eggleston in *Little Me* (Lunt-Fontanne, N.Y.C., Nov. 17, 1962); Miss Addy in *Janus* (Lakewood Th., Skowhegan, Me.; Cape Playhouse, Dennis, Mass., Aug. 1963); was standby for Tallulah Bankhead as Mrs. Goforth and for Ruth Ford as the Witch of Capri in *The Milk Train Doesn't Stop Here Anymore* (Brooks Atkinson Th., N.Y.C., Jan. 1, 1964); played Mrs. Barker in the revival of *The American Dream* (Cherry Lane, Apr. 6, 1964); was featured as Mrs. Allerton in *Skyscraper* (Lunt-Fontanne Th., Nov. 13, 1965); played Granny Maude in *Forty Carats* (Palm Beach, Coconut Grove, and Fort Lauderdale, Fla., and Atlanta, Ga., Winter 1969–70; on tour, Nov. 9, 1970, Apr. 6, 1971, and Summer 1971; Meadow Brook Th., Rochester, Mich., 1972); the Mother in *Come Blow Your Horn* (Meadow Brook Th., Rochester, Mich., 1972); again played Mrs. Barker in *American Dream* (John Drew Th., East Hampton, N.Y., Summer 1972); was featured as Lady Wilde in *Dear Oscar* (Playhouse, N.Y.C., Nov. 16, 1972), toured as Mme. Arcati in *Blithe Spirit* (Summer 1973); and appeared in *For the Use of the Hall* (Trinity Square Repertory Th., Providence, R.I., Dec. 1973).

Films. Miss Cushman appeared in *Requiem for a Heavyweight* (Col., 1962) and *The Swimmer* (Col., 1968).

Television. She appeared in The Web (CBS, 1952) and has made occasional appearances on some daytime shows.

Recreation. Collects Early American glass, antiques, and 19th-century etchings and lithographs.

D

Da COSTA, MORTON. Director, actor, producer. b. Morton Tecosky, March 7, 1914, Philadelphia, Pa., to Samuel and Rose (Hulnick) Tecosky. Father, antique dealer. Grad. Germantown H.S., Philadelphia, 1932; Temple Univ., B.S. (education) 1936. Member of DGA; AEA; SSD&C; Theta Alpha Phi.

Theatre. Mr. Da Costa made his stage debut at the Jay Cooke Junior High School (Philadelphia, Pa., 1928); subsequently appeared at Temple Univ., where he acted, directed, and designed scenery and costumes; was president of the Templayers and assistant to the drama director; and after graduation, taught acting at the University's Sch. of the Theatre (Summer 1932).

He made his professional debut as an actor touring with the Clare Tree Major Children's Th.; as a co-founder of the Civic Repertory Th. (Dayton, Ohio); he produced about 60 plays (1937); and was a partner, actor, and director with the Port Players Summer Th. (Port Washington, Wis., 1938–45). Mr. Da Costa made his Bway debut as the Broadcast Official in *The Skin of Our Teeth* (Plymouth, Nov. 18, 1942); played Gen. William F. Smith in *War President* (Shubert, Apr. 24, 1944); played several roles in *Stovepipe Hat* (opened Shubert, Boston, Mass., May 23, 1944); Winthrop Sears, Jr., in the pre-Bway tryout of *Tangled Web* (opened Playhouse, Wilmington, Del., Oct. 13, 1944; closed Ford's Th., Baltimore, Md., Oct. 28, 1944); Mr. Flynn in *It's a Gift* (Playhouse, N.Y.C., Mar. 12, 1945); operated his own summer theatre (Cragsmoor, N.Y., 1945–46); and played Osric in Maurice Evans' production of *Hamlet* (Columbus Circle Th., N.Y.C., Dec. 13, 1945).

He was stage manager of *The Linden Tree* (Music Box, Mar. 2, 1948); directed *The Alchemist* (NY City Ctr., May 6, 1948); as Maurice Evans' assistant, organized the national touring company of *Man and Superman* (c. Sept. 1948); at NY City Ctr., played Henry Straker in *Man and Superman* (May 16,

1949), staged *She Stoops to Conquer* (Dec. 28, 1949), *Captain Brassbound's Conversion* (Dec. 27, 1950), *Dream Girl* (May 9, 1951), and *The Wild Duck* (Dec. 26, 1951); and directed *Dream Girl* (Quirino Th., Rome, It.). He directed *Dark Legend* (President, N.Y.C., Mar. 24, 1952); *The Grey-Eyed People* (Martin Beck Th., Dec. 17, 1952); the national touring company of *Sabrina Fair;* directed productions of the St. Louis (Mo.) Municipal Opera (1952–53), and wrote the book and the lyrics for their production of *Rip Van Winkle* (July 13, 1953).

He directed *Plain and Fancy* (Mark Hellinger Th., N.Y.C., Jan. 27, 1955; Drury Lane, London, Jan. 25, 1956); *No Time for Sergeants* (Alvin, N.Y.C., Oct. 20, 1955); *Auntie Mame* (Broadhurst, Oct. 31, 1956); *The Music Man* (Majestic, Dec. 19, 1957); *Saratoga,* which he also dramatized (Winter Garden, Dec. 7, 1959); *The Wall* (Billy Rose Th., Oct. 11, 1960); the NY World's Fair production of *To Broadway with Love* (Texas Pavilion, Apr. 22, 1964); *Diplomatic Relations* (Royal Poinciana Playhouse, Palm Beach, Fla., Feb. 1, 1965; and Coconut Grove Playhouse, Miami, Fla., Feb. 9, 1965); the stock tryout of William Inge's *Family Things, Etc.* (Falmouth, Mass., Playhouse, July 12, 1965; and Westport Conn., Country Playhouse, July 19, 1965); a stock tryout touring production of *The Coffee Lover* (Summer 1966); was succeeded during the Boston run (opened Colonial Th., Jan. 17, 1967) as director of *Sherry!* (Alvin, N.Y.C., Mar. 28, 1967); collaborated on the book and directed the musical, *Maggie Flynn* (ANTA, Oct. 23, 1968); and directed *Show Me Where the Good Times Are* (Edison, Mar. 5, 1970); *The Women* (46 Street Th., Apr. 25, 1973); and *A Musical Jubilee* (St. James Th., Nov. 13, 1975).

Films. He directed *Auntie Mame* (WB, 1958); produced and directed *The Music Man* (WB, 1962); and *Island of Love* (WB, 1963).

Radio. He produced and directed a 26-week dramatic series, entitled Great Days in Dayton, for the Dayton (Ohio) Power and Light Co. (1941).

Awards. His production of *The Music Man* (1962) was cited by *Film Daily,* received the Golden Globe Award as the best produced and directed film of the year, and he won the California Federation of Women's Clubs Annual Producer Award. He received an honorary L.H.D. degree from Temple Univ. (1959).

Recreation. Photography, interior decorating.

DAILEY, IRENE. Actress, teacher. b. Sept. 12, 1930, New York City, to Daniel and Helen (Ryan) Dailey. Father, hotel manager. Grad. Mother Cabrini H.S., N.Y.C. Studied acting with Lee Strasberg, N.Y.C., 1951–52; Robert Lewis, N.Y.C., 1952–53; Uta Hagen, N.Y.C., 1953–61; Mira Rostova, Anthony Mannino, Jane White; speech with Arthur Lessac; dance with Anna Sokolow; voice with William Horne, Nancy Howard. Relative in theatre: brother, Dan Dailey, actor, singer, dancer. Address: 151 E. 19th St., New York, NY 10003, tel. (212) OR 7-4633.

Pre-Theatre. Designer, maker, and seller of lampshades.

Theatre. Miss Dailey made her debut in summer productions of *Out of the Frying Pan* and *Room Service* (Red Barn Th., Locust Valley, N.Y., June 1941).

She made her N.Y.C. debut as "Shotput" in *Nine Girls* (Longacre, Jan. 13, 1943); played Caroline in the pre-Bway tryout of *Laughing Water,* which closed out of town (opened Bridgeport Aud., Conn., Sept. 1944; closed Shubert, Boston, Mass., Nov. 1944); and appeared in summer productions at the Red Barn Th., (Nuangola, Pa., 1944).

She played Angie in *Truckline Cafe* (Belasco, N.Y.C., Feb. 27, 1946); Shirley in *Idiot's Delight* (NY City Ctr., May 23, 1951); toured New England theatres in *Skylark* (1952); appeared as Mrs. Shin in *The Good Woman of Setzuan* (Phoenix, N.Y.C., Dec. 18, 1956); Adele Farnum in *Miss Lonelyhearts* (Music Box, Oct. 3, 1957); Irene in the ELT production of *Idiot's Delight* (Feb. 1957); and Eloise in *Uncle Wiggly in Connecticut* (HB Studio, Mar. 1959).

She made her London debut as Jasmine Adair in *Tomorrow with Pictures* (Lyric, Hammersmith, June 1, 1960); in the US, toured as Valeria in the pre-Bway tryout of *Daughter of Silence* (Erlanger, Philadelphia, Pa., Oct. 1961); played Abbie in *Desire Under the Elms* (McCarter Th., Princeton, N.J., Oct. 1961); and at the Playhouse-in-the-Park, Philadelphia, appeared as Clara in *Winterskill* (July 1962), Hannah Jelkes in *The Night of the Iguana* (July 1963), and Pamela Pew-Pickett in *Tchin-Tchin* (Aug. 1963).

She played the Señora in *Andorra* (Biltmore, N.Y.C., Feb. 9, 1963); co-starred with her brother, Dan Dailey, in *Tchin-Tchin* (Sombrero Playhouse, Phoenix, Ariz., Feb. 25, 1964); and played Nettie Cleary in *The Subject Was Roses* (Royale, N.Y.C., May 25, 1964).

She appeared in a program of two one-act plays, *Rooms:* as Miss Quincey in *Better Luck Next Time* and as Mrs. Henry in *A Walk in Dark Places* (Cherry Lane Th., Jan. 27, 1966); replaced (Feb. 27, 1968) Eileen Heckart in the roles of Harriet, Edith, and Muriel in *You Know I Can't Hear You When the Water's Running* (Ambassador, Mar. 13, 1968); took the title role in *Mother Courage* (North Carolina School of the Arts, 1969); was Rachel in *Buying Out* (world premiere, Studio Arena Th., Buffalo, N.Y., Nov. 4, 1971); played Beatrice in *The Effect of Gamma Rays on Man-in-the-Moon Marigolds* (Ivanhoe Th., Chicago, 1971); was Eliza Gant in *Look Homeward, Angel* (Ravinia Festival, Hyde Park, Ill., 1971); played the role of Bananas in *The House of Blue Leaves* (Ivanhoe Th., Chicago, 1972); was Joanne in *Company* (Forum Th., Chicago, 1972); Arkadina in *The Seagull* (McCarter Th., Princeton, N.J., 1973); and Mary Tyrone in *Long Day's Journey into Night* (Loeb Th., Purdue Univ., Ind., 1973).

Films. Miss Dailey has been in *Daring Game* (Par., 1968); *No Way to Treat a Lady* (Par., 1968); *Five Easy Pieces* (Col., 1970); and she was co-starred as Ma Grissom in *The Grissom Gang* (Cinerama, 1971).

Television. She made her debut as one of the dancing sisters in *A Farmer's Hotel* (Robert Montgomery Presents, NBC, 1951); and has appeared on The Defenders (CBS), The Naked City (ABC), Twilight Zone (CBS), Sam Benedict (NBC), Dr. Kildare (NBC), Eleventh Hour (NBC); as a guest star in *Heap Logs and Let the Blaze Laugh* (Ben Casey, ABC, 1964); in *Home* (PBS, 1969) and *The Sand Castle* (PBS, 1970); as Pamela Stewart in *Edge of Night* (CBS); in *Jig Saw* (ABC Movie of the Week); and as Liz Mathews in *Another World* (NBC).

Other Activities. In 1961, Miss Dailey founded the School of the Actor's Company in N.Y.C., where she has taught acting techniques and has been artistic director. She has taught also at other schools around the country, including North Carolina School of the Arts; Princeton, Purdue, Northwestern, and Roosevelt Universities; and the Univ. of Chicago.

Discography. Miss Dailey has recorded *The Subject Was Roses* (Col.), and *Of Poetry and Power* and *The Wick and the Tallow* (Folkways).

Awards. Miss Dailey won the Vernon Rice Award in 1966 for her performance in *Rooms;* the Sarah Siddons Award as leading actress in Chicago for her performance in *The Effect of Gamma Rays on Man-in-the-Moon Marigolds;* and was nominated for Joseph Jefferson awards for best actress of the year for her performances in *Marigolds,* as Eliza Gant in *Look Homeward, Angel,* as Bananas in *The House of Blue Leaves,* and as Joanne in *Company.* She was nominated as best actress by the NY Drama Critics for her performance as Arkadina in *The Seagull* and was nominated for an Emmy award for her performance in Edge of Night in 1969–70.

Recreation. Reading, charcoal sketching, water colors, swimming, tennis, chess, bicycle riding, ice-skating and figure skating.

DALE, GROVER. Choreographer, director, singer, dancer. b. Grover Robert Aitken, July 22, 1936, Harrisburg, Pa., to Ronal and Emma Bertha (Cox) Aitken. Father, restaurateur and gambler. Attended Tech. H.S., McKeesport, Pa., 1949–53; studied acting with Mary Tarcai, 1961–64, voice with David Craig, 1963–64. Member of AEA; SAG; AFTRA.

Pre-Theatre. Operated a dancing school in McKeesport, Pa.

Theatre. Mr. Dale made his debut as a dancer in the chorus of a summer stock production of *Call Me Madam* (Pittsburgh Civic Light Opera, June 15, 1953); followed by the Drum Major in the pre-Bway tryout of *The Amazing Adele* (opened Shubert Th., Philadelphia, Pa., Dec. 26, 1955; closed Shubert, Boston, Mass., Jan. 21, 1956).

He made his Bway debut as a dancer in *L'il Abner* (St. James, Nov. 15, 1956); played Snowboy in *West Side Story* (Winter Garden, Sept. 26, 1957); was assistant choreographer to Jerome Robbins in *Ballets U.S.A.* (Alvin, Mar. 8, 1958); played Andrew and understudied Tony Perkins in the role of Gideon Briggs in *Greenwillow* (Alvin, Mar. 8, 1960); toured Israel, France, Germany and Italy as Snowboy in *West Side Story* (Dec. 1960–May 1961); appeared as Barneby Slade in *Sail Away* (Broadhurst, N.Y.C., Oct. 3, 1961; Savoy, London, England, June 20, 1962); and Mr. MacKintosh in the N.Y.C. production of *Too Much Johnson* (Phoenix, Jan. 15, 1964).

He played Pearce in *Half a Sixpence* (Broadhurst, Apr. 15, 1965); choreographed *Billy* (Billy Rose Th., Mar. 22, 1969); did choreography for *Steambath* (Truck and Warehouse Th., June 30, 1970); staged *Pinkville* (Berkshire Th. Festival, Stockbridge, Mass., Summer 1970); helped stage the double bill *Acrobats* and *Line* (Th. de Lys, Feb. 15, 1971); directed and did choreography for *Jump Crow* (Lenox Arts Ctr., N.Y.C., July 1972); was co-choreographer for *Seesaw* (Uris Th., Mar. 18, 1973); choreographer for *Molly* (Alvin, Nov. 1, 1973); supervised choreography for *Rachael Lily Rosenbloom and Don't You Ever Forget It* (previews: Broadhurst, Nov. 26–Dec. 1, 1973); and was director of and choreographer for *The Magic Show* (Cort, May 28, 1974).

Films. Mr. Dale appeared in *The Unsinkable Molly Brown* (MGM, 1964) and *Les Demoiselles de Rochefort* (Comacio, 1967), and he produced and directed *Douglas, James and Joe,* shown at the 1968 NY Film Festival.

Television. He danced on the Jackie Gleason Show (CBS, 1954); Martha Raye Show (NBC, Sept. 18, 1964); The Gershwin Years (CBS, Sept. 1960); appeared on Look Up and Live (CBS, Dec. 1965); and he has also been on the Perry Como Show (NBC). Ed Sullivan Show (CBS), Milton Berle Show (NBC) and Sid Caesar Show (NBC).

Awards. For his choreography for *Billy,* Mr. Dale received the 1969 Drama Desk Award as best choreographer and was nominated for an Antoinette Perry (Tony) Award.

Recreation. Riding, swimming, painting.

DALES, JOHN L. Lawyer, theatre executive. b. John Leighton Dales, Feb. 24, 1907, Santa Monica, Calif., to John Bertram and Leah (Johnson) Dales. Father, businessman. Grad. Los Angeles (Calif.) H.S., 1925; Stanford Univ., A.B. 1929; LL.B. 1932. Married May 29, 1936, to Freda Elizabeth Clubb; two sons. Member of SAG; AAAA. Address: (home) 1555 Club View Dr., Los Angeles, CA 90052, tel. CR 6-1343; (bus.) c/o Screen Actors Guild, 7750 Sunset Blvd., Los Angeles, CA 90052, tel. (213) 876-3030.

From 1943 until his retirement in 1973, Mr. Dales was national executive director of the Screen Actors Guild and from 1961 to 1973 vice-president of Associated Actors and Artistes of America. He has also served on the board of directors of the Hollywood (Calif.) Museum.

DALEY, GUILBERT A. Educator. b. Guilbert Alfred Daley, Dec. 31, 1923, Washington, D.C., to Charles Walter and Mary (Gilbert) Daley. Grad. Paul Lawrence Dunbar H.S., Washington, D.C. 1942; attended Howard Univ., 1942–44; grad. Catholic Univ. of America, A.B. (speech and drama) 1949, M.A. 1952; attended American Univ., Summer 1953; Cornell Univ., Summers 1957–59;

studied playwriting with John W. Parker at Univ. of North Carolina, summers, 1960, 1963, and in 1968, working under John Parker and Thomas Patterson, completed all requirements for the licentiate in dramatic arts. Married Aug. 22, 1953, to Thelma Thomas. Served USAAF, 1944–46; rank, Cpl. Member of ATA; SAA; AAUP; Maryland State Teachers Assn. (exec. secy., 1953–62); Intercollegiate Drama Assn. (exec. secy., 1954–57; pres., 1957–to date); Phi Beta Sigma (Eastern Region dir. of educ., 1964; vice-regional dir., 1970–73; regional dir., 1973–to date). Address: (home) 4417 Elderon Ave., Baltimore, MD 21216, tel. (301) 542-0176; (bus.) Coppin State College, 2500 W. North Ave., Baltimore, MD 21216, tel. (301) 383-3155.

Mr. Daley is a member of the faculty at Coppin State College, where he is a coordinator for the Dept. of Speech, Theatre, and Television, and since 1962 he has been director of drama and assistant professor of drama, speech, and English. From 1953 to 1962, he was instructor of drama, speech, and English at Shaw Univ. Mr. Daley is also director of the Coppin Players at the college and serves frequently as judge and critic teacher for high school drama festivals. Mr. Daley's one-act play, *Kiss the Book*, was produced by the Carolina Playmakers (Univ. of North Carolina, Summer 1960), and published in *The Carolina Quarterly* (Dec. 1960). Mr. Daley's play *So Help You God* was produced by the Carolina Playmakers at Univ. of North Carolina in summer of 1960.

Other Activities. In 1964, Mr. Daley was elected Coppin representative to the Greater Baltimore Arts Council, which sponsors an annual fine arts festival in Charles Plaza, Baltimore. Mr. Daley was treasurer (1966–68) of the Council and president (1968–70).

Awards. Mr. Daley received the Carolina Playmakers Scholarship Award for Playwriting at the Univ. of North Carolina (Summer 1960).

Recreation. Bowling, swimming.

DALLAS, MEREDITH. Educator, actor, director. b. Meredith Eugene Dallas, Dec. 3, 1916, Detroit, Mich., to William and Ethel Dallas. Father, factory foreman. Grad. Grosse Pointe H.S., Mich., 1935; Albion Coll., B.A. 1939; Western Reserve Univ., M.A. 1948; three-year graduate program, Gestalt Institute of Cleveland, 1973–75; Ph.D. program, Union Graduate School, 1973–75; theatre study in Japan and Greece (1966–67) on Great Lakes College Assoc. fellowship. Married Oct. 26, 1940, to Willa Louise Winter; one son, three daughters. Member of AEA; AFTRA. Address: (home) 110 E. Whiteman St., Yellow Springs, OH 45387, tel. (513) 767-7549; (bus.) Antioch Area Theatre, Antioch College, Yellow Springs, OH 45387, tel. (513) 767-7251.

He was a founder and director of the Antioch Shakespeare Festival (1952–53; 1955); played (Summer 1952) a Citizen of Angiers in *King John*, directed and played the title role in *Richard II*, played Hotspur in *Henry IV, Part 1*, Snare and Silence in *Henry IV, Part 2*, directed and played Exeter in *Henry V*, played Warwick in *Henry VI*, Buckingham in *Richard III*, and directed and played Cranmer in *Henry VIII;* directed (Summer 1953) *Coriolanus* and *Pericles*, appeared as the Poet in *Timon of Athens*, Aaron the Moor in *Titus Andronicus*, Marc Antony in *Julius Caesar*, Marc Antony in *Antony and Cleopatra;* played (Summer 1955) the Host in *Merry Wives of Windsor*, directed *As You Like It*, played Malvolio in *Twelfth Night*, Macduff in *Macbeth*, and directed *Cymbeline*.

He served as artistic director of the Antioch Amphitheatre (1961–62); was appointed director in 1963; and was artistic director for "Shakespeare at Antioch" program (Summer 1964).

Mr. Dallas performed at the Cain Park Playhouse (Cleveland, Ohio, 1947); was actor-director with the Shaw Festival (Martha's Vineyard, Mass., Summer 1951) and Springfield (Ohio) Civic Theatre (Sept. 1953; Feb. 1954); performed at the Hyde Park (N.Y.) Playhouse (Summer 1954); Cincinnati Symphony Orchestra, Caliban in the American premiere of Sibelius' score for *The Tempest* (Ohio, Dec. 1955); appeared with Group 20 (Wellesley, Mass., Summer 1956); was director at the Trotwood (Ohio) Circle Theatre (1957–58; 1960); and was guest director of *The Play's the Thing* (Long Wharf Th., New Haven, Conn., 1968).

Mr. Dallas appeared as Malvolio in the NY Shakespeare Festival production of *Twelfth Night* (Belvedere Lake Th., N.Y.C., Aug. 6, 1958); Sergeant Winchell in *Family Reunion* (Phoenix, Oct. 20, 1958); the Governor's Cousin in *The Power and the Glory* (Phoenix, Dec. 10, 1958), Gibbet in *The Beaux' Stratagem* (Phoenix, Feb. 24, 1959); and Caliban in *The Tempest* (350th Anniversary Th., Bermuda, Summer 1959).

Recreation. Painting.

DALRYMPLE, JEAN. Producer, writer, publicist. b. Sept. 2, 1910, Morristown, N.J., to George Hull and Elizabeth Van Kirk (Collins) Dalrymple. Father, concert manager. Educated privately. Married Mar. 30, 1932, to Ward Morehouse (marr. dis. Aug. 4, 1937); married Nov. 1, 1951, to Maj. Gen. Philip de Witt Ginder, US Army, retired (dec. 1968). Member of AEA; AGMA; Dramatists Guild; ATPAM; NY World's Fair of 1964–65 (bd. of dir., Consultant for the Performing Arts); Amer. Natl. Th. and Acad. (bd. member, treas.; exec. dir., publicity dir., 1969–70); Natl. Council on the Arts (music advisory panel); North Carolina School of the Arts (adv. bd.); Museum of the City of NY (Friends of the Theatre and Music Collection); Silver Spring Country Club (Ridgefield, Conn.); Woman Pays Club (N.Y.C.); Soldiers', Sailors' and Airmens' Club (N.Y.C. board of dir.); Professional Childrens Sch.; John Golden Fund; John F. Kennedy Memorial Cultural Center (charter mbr. of the natl. advisory council); Office of Cultural Affairs (N.Y.C., advisory committee). Address: 150 W. 55th St., New York, NY 10019, tel. (212) 246-7820.

Theatre. Miss Dalrymple wrote and performed in comedy sketches for the Keith-Orpheum vaudeville circuit (1929). She was associated (1929–33) with John Golden as general understudy, casting director, play doctor, and press representative; had her own office as publicist and concert manager (1937–44); was personal manager of concert and theatre personalities (1937–44); and was original publicity director for the Amer. Theatre Wing (1940).

She handled the publicity for *Mr. and Mrs. North* (Belasco Th., N.Y.C., Jan. 12, 1941); *One Touch of Venus* (Imperial, Oct. 7, 1943); *Voice of the Turtle* (Morosco, Dec. 8, 1943); *Anna Lucasta* (Mansfield, Aug. 30, 1944); and for many years, headed the public relations for the Ballet Russe de Monte Carlo, and the Lewisohn Stadium Concerts. She produced, with Marc Connelly, *Hope for the Best* (Fulton, Feb. 7, 1945); produced *Brighten the Corner* (Lyceum, Dec. 12, 1945); *Burlesque* (Belasco, Dec. 25, 1946); and *Red Gloves* (Mansfield, Dec. 4, 1948). She was in charge of public relations for the US productions of *Oklahoma!* and *Medea* and other American attractions sent by the State Dept. to the Berlin (Germany) Arts Festival (1951); produced the *ANTA Album* (Ziegfeld, N.Y.C. Spring 1951); and presented summer circuit productions of *The Second Man, Harvey, Voice of the Turtle, A Play for Mary*, and *The Petrified Forest* (Summers 1950–52).

Miss Dalrymple has been associated with the NY City Ctr. of Music and Drama since its inception in 1943, as director of public relations and a member of the board of directors. She became director of the NY City Ctr. Th. Co. (1953), and was in charge of production of four plays with Jose Ferrer (NY City Ctr.): *Cyrano de Bergerac* (Nov. 11, 1953), *The Shrike* (Nov. 25, 1953), *Richard III* (Dec. 9, 1953), and *Charley's Aunt* (Dec. 22, 1953). At NY City Ctr., she served as producer and press representative for *What Every Woman Knows* (Dec. 22, 1954), *The Fourposter* (Jan. 5, 1955), *The Time of Your Life* (Jan. 19, 1955), *The Wisteria Trees* (Feb. 2, 1955), the Brattle Shakespeare Players production of *Othello* (Sept. 7, 1955), and *Henry IV, Part 1* (Sept. 21, 1955).

She wrote, with Charles Robinson, *The Feathered Fauna* (Margo Jones Th., Dallas, Tex., Jan. 31, 1955; Elitch Gardens, Denver, Colo., 1957); produced, with Rita Allen, a Spanish-language production of *The Teahouse of the August Moon (La Casa de Té de la Luna de Agosto)* (Teatro Insurgentes, Mexico City, Apr. 10, 1955), which toured Latin America for the State Dept. (1956).

At NY City Ctr. she was producer and was press representative for Orson Welles' production of *King Lear*, by arrangement with Martin Gabel and Henry M. Margolis (Jan. 12, 1956); a program of pantomime by Marcel Marceau (Feb. 1, 1956), *A Streetcar Named Desire* (Feb. 15, 1956), *The Teahouse of the August Moon* (Nov. 8, 1956), *The Glass Menagerie* (Nov. 21, 1956), and *Mister Roberts* (Dec. 5, 1956).

Miss Dalrymple became director of the NY City Ctr. Light Opera Co. in 1957 and produced *The Beggars' Opera* (Mar. 13, 1957), *Brigadoon* (Mar. 27, 1957; moved Adelphi, Apr. 9, 1957), *The Merry Widow* Apr. 10, 1957), *South Pacific* (Apr. 24, 1957), and *The Pajama Game* (May 15, 1957); was producer and press representative for *Carousel* (Sept. 11, 1957); for an evening of pantomime by Marcel Marceau, by arrangement with Ronald A. Wilford Associates, Inc., and Jean de Rigault (Jan. 21, 1958); and for *Annie Get Your Gun* (Feb. 19, 1958), *Wonderful Town* (Mar. 5, 1958), and *Oklahoma!* (Mar. 19, 1958). She wrote *The Quiet Room* (Wyndham's, London, Mar. 30, 1958); which was produced also in Austria and Australia. She was coordinator of the performing arts for the US at the Brussels (Belgium) World's Fair (1958), arranging for programs of opera, musical comedy, orchestral concerts, ballets, and drama. Among these were the world premiere of Menotti's opera *Maria Golovin;* NY City Ctr. productions of the opera *Susannah*, the musicals *Carousel* and *Wonderful Town*, and the play *The Time of Your Life*, directed by Miss Dalrymple.

For the NY City Ctr. Light Opera Co., she produced *The Most Happy Fella* (Feb. 10, 1959), *Say Darling* (Feb. 25, 1959), and *Lute Song* (Mar. 12, 1959).

As director of the Hudson Celebration Theatre-in-the-Park, which performed in New York City parks, she produced *Guys and Dolls* (July 21, 1959), *Carmen Jones* (Aug. 17, 1959), and *Can-Can* (Aug. 25, 1959), AndréEglevsky's Petit Ballet, an operetta evening with Jan Kiepura and Marta Eggerth, duo-piano recital with José and Amparo Iturbi, the Ballet Russe de Monte Carlo and the World Dance Festival. At NY City Ctr., she presented with Jerry Hoffman, the Piccolo Teatro de Milano in *The Servant of Two Masters* (Feb. 23, 1960); for the Light Opera Co., produced *Finian's Rainbow* (Apr. 27, 1960), *The King and I* (May 11, 1960), *Show Boat* (Apr. 12, 1961), *South Pacific* (Apr. 26, 1961), *Porgy and Bess* (May 17, 1961), *Pal Joey* (May 31, 1961), *Can-Can* (May 16, 1962), *Brigadoon* (May 30, 1962), *Fiorello!* (June 3, 1962), *Brigadoon* (Jan. 30, 1963), *Wonderful Town* (Feb. 13, 1963), *Oklahoma!* (Feb. 27, 1963; return engagement May 15, 1963), *Pal Joey* (May 29, 1963), and *The King and I* (June 10, 1963. She also presented excerpts from *Brigadoon* (White House, Washington, D.C. Mar. 27, 1963).

At NY City Ctr. she produced and was publicist for City Ctr. Light Opera presentations of *West Side Story* (Apr. 8, 1964), *Porgy and Bess* (May 6, 1964), *My Fair Lady* (May 20, 1964), a special Christmas production of *Brigadoon* (Dec. 23, 1964), *Guys and Dolls* (Apr. 27, 1965), *Kiss Me, Kate* (May 12, 1965), *South Pacific* (June 2, 1965), *The Music Man* (June 18, 1965), and a special Christmas production of *Oklahoma!* (Dec. 15, 1965). Also at NY City Ctr., she produced and was publicist for a Frank Loesser festival: *How To Succeed in Business without Really Trying* (Apr. 20, 1966), *The Most Happy Fella* (May 11, 1966), *Where's Charley?* (May 25, 1966), and *Guys and Dolls* (June 8, 1966), which was later presented at the White House, Washington, D.C. (Mar. 18, 1967), and on a USO tour of the Far East; at NY City Ctr. produced and was publicist for the American Playwrights Series: *The Country Girl* (Sept. 27, 1966), *The Rose Tattoo* (Oct. 20, 1966); transferred to the Billy Rose Th., Nov. 9, 1966), and *Elizabeth the Queen* (Nov. 3, 1966); and at the White House presented *Moments from Great American Musicals* (Sept. 14, 1966).

At NY City Ctr., she produced and was publicist for the special Christmas presentation of *Carousel* (Dec. 15, 1966); for *Finian's Rainbow* (Apr. 5, 1967), *The Sound of Music* (Apr. 25, 1967), and *Wonderful Town* (May 17, 1967); produced and was publicist for the second American Playwrights Series: *Life with Father* (Oct. 19, 1967) and *The Tenth Man* (Nov. 8, 1967); and for a special Christmas production of *Brigadoon* (Dec. 12, 1967).

Miss Dalrymple also produced, directed, and was publicist for *Beyond Desire* (Th. Four, Oct. 11, 1967); produced excerpts from *Brigadoon* for Gov. and Mrs. Nelson Rockefeller (Governor's Mansion, Albany, N.Y., 1967); and produced excerpts from *Fiorello!* for the 1968 Governors' Conference dinner (White House, Washington, D.C., Feb. 29, 1968). The 1968 City Ctr. Light Opera musicals at NY City Ctr. were *The King and I* (May 23, 1968) and *My Fair Lady* (June 13, 1968), and the 25th anniversary Christmas musical was *Carnival* (Dec. 12, 1968). In 1969, Miss Dalrymple produced *Salute to Alan Jay Lerner* for the American Acad. of Dramatic Arts and presented *American Musical Highlights* for Gov. and Mrs. Nelson Rockefeller (Governor's Mansion, Albany, N.Y.). She also co-produced, with Cheryl Crawford, *The Web and the Rock* (Th. de Lys, Mar. 19, 1972); presented excerpts from *No, No, Nanette* with Irving Caesar for Gov. and Mrs. Rockefeller (Governor's Mansion, Albany, N.Y., 1972); produced the Agnes de Mille Heritage Dance Th. (1972–73–74); co-produced, with Leonard Schlosburg, *Naomi Court* (Manhattan Th. Club, May 29, 1974); presented Agnes de Mille's *Conversations About the Dance* (1974–75); and was publicist for the return engagement of *Brief Lives* (Booth Th., Oct. 16, 1974).

Television. As a producer-director of the WNTA Play of the Week series, Miss Dalrymple produced *The Cherry Orchard* and *Crime of Passion* (both 1959). She also produced *Reunion in Vienna* (Producer's Showcase, NBC). In Mar. 1960, she was appointed executive producer for Paramount's Intl. Telemeter Co. (Pay TV), and presented for them Menotti's opera *The Consul*, the Fourth St. Th. production of *Hedda Gabler*, also *A Country Scandal*, *The Second City Revue*, and the first live transmission (Apr. 6, 1961) of a Bway show, *Show Girl* (Eugene O'Neill Th.).

Other Activities. As a delegate to the Seventh National Conference, US National Conference, US National Commission for UNESCO (Denver, Colo., 1959), she was the principal speaker on the theatre in Latin America and Mexico.

Published Works. Miss Dalrymple's books include her autobiography, *September Child* (1963); *Careers and Opportunities in the Theatre* (1969); *Jean Dalrymple's Pinafore Farm Cookbook* (1971); with Fay Lavan, *The Folklore and Facts of Natural Nutrition* (1973); and *From the Last Row* (1975), an account of her years at the NY City Ctr. of Music and Drama. She has also written numerous articles for the *Reader's Digest*. .

Awards. For her participation in the Brussels (Belgium) World's Fair, Miss Dalrymple was decorated by the Belgium government as Knight, Order of the Crown. The musical program of the US performing arts, which she coordinated, won the Gold Medal as best presentation at the Brussels World's Fair. She received an honorary D.F.A. from Wheaton (Ill.) Coll. (1959); numerous citations (from Mayor Robert Wagner of N.Y.C.; and the Spirit of Achievement Award from the Albert Einstein Coll. of Medicine, Yeshiva Univ.; the annual "Brava" of the NY Newspaper Women's Club; and the Col. Jacob Ruppert Award for her NY City Ctr. productions. In addition, the Outer Circle critics have cited the NY City Ctr. Light Opera Co. three times.

Recreation. Golf, gardening, cooking.

DALY, JAMES. Actor. b. James Firman Daly, Oct. 23, 1918, to Percifer Charles and Dorothy (Hogan) Daly (Mullen). Father, fuel merchant; mother, CIA employee. Grad. Lincoln H.S., Wisconsin Rapids, Wis., 1936; attended Univ. of Wisconsin (Music) 1933; State Univ. of Iowa (Drama) 1935–36; Carroll Coll., 1937–38; grad. Cornell Coll., B.A. 1941. Married Feb. 20, 1942, to Hope Newell, actress; one son, three daughters. Served US Army, Infantry, 6 mos.; rank, pvt.; USAAF, 2 mos., rank, Cadet; USN 4 1/2 yrs.; rank, Ensign. Member of AEA: AFTRA: SAG.

Theatre. Mr. Daly's first Bway engagement was as understudy to Gary Merrill in the role of Paul Verrall in *Born Yesterday* (Lyceum, Feb. 4, 1946); subsequently appeared as Hobe Kelvin in *virginia Reel* (Princess, Apr. 3, 1947); played a season of stock with the Port Players (Oconomowoc, Wis., Summer 1948); toured as Hector Malone, Jr., in *Man and Superman* (Fall 1948–Spring 1949; and City Ctr., May 16, 1949); played again with the Port Players (Summer 1949); understudied Maurice Evans as Dick Dudgeon in *The Devil's Disciple* (Royale, N.Y.C., Feb. 31, 1950); played Bill Walker in the ELT production of *Major Barbara* (Lenox Hill Playhouse, 1950); and again played a season of stock with the Port Players (Summer 1950).

He appeared as Talbot and Maintopman in *Billy Budd* (Biltmore, N.Y.C., Feb. 10, 1951); Harry in *Mary Rose* (ANTA Th., May 4, 1951); played a season of stock at the Lakewood Th. (Skowhegan, Me., Summer 1951); portrayed Robert de Baudricourt and a Soldier in Warwick's Army in *Saint Joan* (Cort, N.Y.C., Oct. 4, 1951); Rocco Aiello in *Dark Legend* (President, Mar. 24, 1952); Gratiano in *The Merchant of Venice* (NY City Ctr., Mar. 4, 1953); played a season of stock at Bucks County Playhouse (New Hope, Pa., Summer 1954); Jean the Valet, in *Miss Julie* (Phoenix, N.Y.C., Feb. 21, 1956); Tom Wingfield in *The Glass Menagerie* (NY City Ctr., Nov. 21, 1956); and toured in the Theatre Guild production of *Back to Methuselah* (1957).

Mr. Daly appeared as Mr. Walbeck in the world première of Thornton Wilder's one-act play, *Bernice*, which was part of the ANTA-sponsored presentation at the opening of the Congresshalle Th. (Berlin, Germany, Sept. 20, 1957); played Robert Adams in the pre-Bway tryout of *This Is Goggle* (opened McCarter Th., Princeton, N.J., Jan. 23, 1958; closed Shubert Th., Washington, D.C., Feb. 1, 1958); returned to Bway as Manuel in *Handful of Fire* (Martin Beck Th., N.Y.C., Oct. 1, 1958); succeeded (Mar. 12, 1959) Pat Hingle in the title role in *J. B.* (ANTA Th., Dec. 11, 1958); played Ralph Bates in *Period of Adjustment* (Helen Hayes Th., Nov. 10, 1960); appeared in stock at the Bucks County Playhouse (Summer 1962–63); played Warren Curtis in *The Advocate* (ANTA Th., Oct. 14, 1963); and eight Presidents in *The White House* (Henry Miller's Th., May 19, 1964; and tour, Summer 1964).

Mr. Daly subsequently played George in *Who's Afraid of Virginia Woolf?* (Bucks Co. Playhouse, New Hope, Pa., May 31, 1965); King Arthur in *Camelot* (Chastain Amphitheatre, Atlanta, Ga., July 19, 1965); James Tyrone, Jr., in *A Moon for the Misbegotten* (Studio Arena Th., Buffalo, N.Y., Oct. 7, 1965); Murray Burns in *A Thousand Clowns* (Atlanta, Ga., Community Playhouse, Feb. 1, 1966); and appeared in The Center Th. Group production of *The Trial of the Catonsville Nine* (Mark Taper Forum, Los Angeles, 1970–71 season).

Films. Mr. Daly has appeared in *The Court-Martial of Billy Mitchell* (WB, 1955); *The Young Stranger* (RKO, 1957); *I Aim at the Stars* (Col., 1960); *Planet of the Apes* (20th-Fox, 1968); *The Five Man Army* (MGM, 1970); *The Resurrection of Zachery Wheeler* (Vidtronics, 1971); and *Wild in the Sky* (AI, 1972), later retitled *Black Jack* (1973).

Television and Radio. On radio, Mr. Daly was host on Monitor (NBC). He first appeared on television on Parents-Please (Dumont, July 1947); subsequently appeared in over five hundred roles on all major networks, including the series, Foreign Intrigue (1953–54).

His most recent appearances include Great Adventure (CBS); Breaking Point (ABC); the Loretta Young Show (NBC); *A Splendid Misery* (CBS); Hallmark Hall of Fame (NBC); The Today Show (NBC); Dr. Kildare (NBC); Twilight Zone (Ind.); Twelve O'Clock High (ABC); The F.B.I. (ABC); The Fugitive (ABC); *An Enemy of the People* (NET); The Invaders (ABC); Felony Squad (ABC); Combat! (ABC); The Virginian (NBC); Gunsmoke (CBS); Mission: Impossible (CBS); Judd for the Defense (ABC); Run for Your Life (NBC); CBS Playhouse; The World of Disney (NBC); Star Trek (NBC); and *University Medical Center* (CBS), the pilot film for his series, Medical Center (CBS).

Awards. He received the *Theatre World* Award for his performance as Bill Walker in the ELT production of *Major Barbara* (1951); and an honorary (D.F.A.) degree from Cornell Coll. (1956).

Recreation. Swimming, gardening, dog breeding, sheep raising.

DAMON, STUART. Actor, singer. b. Stuart Michael Zonis, Feb. 5, 1937, Brooklyn, N.Y., to Marvin L. and Eva (Sherer) Zonis. Father, manufacturer. Grad. Adelphi Acad., Brooklyn, 1954; Brandeis Univ., B.A. (psychology) 1958. Studied acting with David Pressman and Charles Conrad at the Neighborhood Playhouse Sch. of the Theatre, N.Y.C., Summer 1958; with Uta Hagen, N.Y.C., one year; with Frank Corsaro, N.Y.C., one year; singing with Maude Tweedy, N.Y.C., three years; dance with Luigi, N.Y.C., two years; and ballet with Don Farnsworth, one year. Married Mar. 12, 1961, to Deirdre Ann Ottewill, actress, singer, dancer; one daughter.

Theatre. Mr. Damon first appeared on stage as the Cowardly Lion in an amateur production of *The Wizard of Oz* (Camp Kenmiere Th., Danbury, Conn., Aug. 1948). His first professional appearance was as a singer in the chorus and as the State Trooper in *Plain and Fancy* (Lambertville Music Circus, N.Y., July 1957); followed by Tony in *The Boy Friend* (Cape Playhouse, Dennis, Mass., July 1958); and the title role of *Li'l Abner* (Summer tour, 1959).

He made his Bway debut as a singer in the chorus of *First Impressions* (Alvin, Mar. 19, 1969), in which he also understudied Farley Granger as Fitzwilliam Darcy and Donald Madden as Charles Bingley. He joined the resident company at the Theatre-by-the Sea, Matunuck, R.I., (Summer 1960), where he played the Ghost in *The Enchanted*, Dominic in *Venus Observed*, George in *Twentieth Century*, the Gardener in *Monique*, and Ambrose in *The Matchmaker*.

In N.Y.C., he appeared in the revue *From A to Z* (Plymouth, Apr. 20, 1960); played Frangipane in *Irma La Douce* (Plymouth, Sept. 29, 1960), and appeared as Nestor LeFripe in the Las Vegas, Nev., production (Riviera Hotel, Sept. 1961).

He appeared as Curt in the N.Y.C. production of *Entertain a Ghost* (Actors Playhouse, Apr. 9, 1962); John Shand in *Maggie* (Summer tour, May 1962); Joey in *The Most Happy Fella* (Summer tour, July 1962); in New York, played Antipholus of Syracuse in *The Boys from Syracuse* (Th. Four, Apr. 16, 1963); Leadville Johnny Brown in *The Unsinkable Molly Brown* (Summer tour, June 1963); Conrad Birdie in *Bye Bye Birdie* (Melodyland Th., Berkeley, Calif., Sept. 1963); and both Ed Farrish and Y.M. 2 in the pre-Bway tryout of *Cool Off!* (opened Forrest, Philadelphia, Pa., Mar. 31, 1964; closed there Apr. 4, 1964).

Mr. Damon played Joe Hardy in *Damn Yankees* (Packard Music Hall, Warren, Ohio, June 30, 1964); Sir Lancelot in *Camelot* (Paper Mill Playhouse, Millburn, N.J., Nov. 3, 1965); Eddie Yaeger in *Do I Hear a Waltz?* (46 St. Th., N.Y.C., Mar. 18, 1965); Jack Conner in *Charlie Girl* (Adelphi, London, Dec. 15, 1965); Harry Weiss in *Houdini, Man of Magic* (Piccadilly, London, Nov. 15, 1966); the title role in *Macbeth* (Marlowe, Canterbury, England, 1970); and King Charles in *Nell* (Richmond, London, Apr. 1970).

Television. Mr. Damon made his television debut on Look Up and Live (CBS, Jan. 1960); subsequently appeared on The Bell Telephone Hour (NBC, Feb. 1960); P.M. East (WNEW, Feb. 1961); Naked City (ABC, Feb. 1962); and Talent Scouts (CBS, July 1962); in England, appeared in *A Really Good Jazz Piano* (Associated Rediffusion, 1964); played the Prince in *Cinderella* (CBS, 1965); was a guest on the Memory Lane series (Ind., 1965–66); The Today Show (NBC, 1965–66); and appeared on The Champions (ATV, England).

Awards. He received the *Theatre World* Award for his performance as Antipholus of Syracuse in *The Boys from Syracuse* (1963).

DANA, LEORA. Actress. b. Leora Shepherd Dana, Apr. 1, 1923, New York City, to William Shepherd and Alberta (Webster) Dana. Grad. Lenox H.S., N.Y.C., 1940; secretarial certificate from Katherine Gibbs Sch., N.Y.C., 1942; grad. Barnard Coll., B.A. 1946; RADA, London, England, diploma (silver medal for acting) 1948. Studied acting with Charlotte Perry, four years; Perry-Mansfield Sch. of the Th., Steamboat Springs, Colo. Married June 29, 1952, to Kurt Kasznar (marr. dis. May 1958). Member of AFTRA; SAG; AEA; Zonta Club. Address: (home) 11 E. 63rd St., New York, NY 10021, tel. (212) TE 2-9767; (bus.) Gloria Safier, 667 Madison Ave., New York, NY 10022, tel. (212) TE 8-4868.

Theatre. Miss Dana made her debut in London as June Farrell in *The Chiltern Hundreds* (Vaudeville Th., Aug. 27, 1947) and her first N.Y.C. appearance as Irma in *The Madwoman of Chaillot* (Belasco, Dec. 27, 1948); subsequently played Maman in *The Happy Time* (Plymouth, Jan. 24, 1950); Nancy Gray in *Point of No Return* (Alvin, Dec. 13, 1951), in which she toured (opened Ford, Baltimore, Md., Nov. 24, 1952; closed Biltmore, Los Angeles, Calif., May 24, 1953); appeared as Sabrina in *Sabrina Fair* (National, Nov. 11, 1953); played Portia in *Julius Caesar* (ASTA, Stratford, Conn., July 12, 1955); played Frances Lucas in the pre-Bway tryout of *A Quiet Place* (opened Shubert, New Haven, Conn., Nov. 23, 1955; closed National, Washington, D.C., Dec. 31, 1955); appeared in 10 stock productions (Elitch Gardens, Denver, Colo., June 6–Aug. 1957).

Miss Dana played Alice Russell in *The Best Man* (Morosco, N.Y.C., Mar. 31, 1960), in which she toured (opened Hanna, Cleveland, Ohio, Sept. 18, 1961; closed Forrest, Philadelphia, Pa., Feb. 3, 1962); played Blackie in the world premiere of *The Milk Train Doesn't Stop Here Anymore* (Festival of Two Worlds, Teatro Nuovo, Spoleto, Italy, Summer 1962); played at the Univ. of Utah, Eliza Gant in *Look Homeward, Angel* (Mar. 1963) and Claire Zackenassian in *The Visit* (Oct.–Nov. 1963), which she also played at the Olney (Md). Th. (July, 1964).

She played Emily Bach-Nielsen in *Beekman Place* (Morosco, N.Y.C., Oct. 7, 1964); for the National Repertory Th. of Eva Le Gallienne, she played Gabrielle in *The Madwoman of Chaillot,* Lucy in *The Rivals,* and Andromache in *The Trojan Women* (tour, Nov. 1965–Mar. 1966); she played Lucia in *The Long Christmas Dinner* (Cherry Lane Th., N.Y.C., Sept. 6, 1966); with the John Fernald Company, appeared in *John Gabriel Borkman* (Meadow Brooke Th., Rochester, Mich., 1967); appeared in *Collision Course* (Cafe au Go-Go, N.Y.C., Mar. 1968); played Ann in *The Bird of Dawning Singeth All Night Long* (American Place Th., Dec. 1968); Dr. Anna Balcar in *The Increased Difficulty of Concentration* (Forum, Lincoln Ctr., Dec. 4, 1969); appeared in *Tobacco Road* (Actor's Theatre, Louisville, Ky., 1969–70; and Playhouse-in-the-Park, Cincinnati, Ohio, 1970–71); for the ANTA Matinee Series, she played Meg in *A Place without Mornings* (Th. de Lys, N.Y.C., Jan. 10–11, 1972); played Elizabeth Edwards in *The Last of Mrs. Lincoln* (ANTA Th., Dec. 12, 1972); and appeared in a revival of *The Women* (46 St. Th., Apr. 25, 1973).

Films. Miss Dana made her film debut as the Wife in *3:10 to Yuma* (Col., 1957); subsequently played the Mother in *Kings Go Forth* (UA, 1958); Agnes in *Some Came Running* (MGM, 1958); the Minister's Wife in *Pollyana* (Buena Vista, 1960); and appeared in *Gathering of Eagles* (U, 1963) *The Norman Vincent Peale Story* (Col., 1963); and Mrs. Renfrew in *The Group* (UA, 1966).

Television. She has performed in *The Legacy* (Alfred Hitchcock Presents, CBS, 1956); *The Barretts of Wimpole Street* (The Passing Parade, 1956); *Sauce for the Goose* (US Steel Hour, CBS, 1956); *Eye of Truth* (Suspicion, NBC, 1958); and *Rip Van Winkle* (The Shirley Temple Show, 1958).

She has also appeared on the Philco Television Playhouse (NBC, 1952, 1954); The Web (CBS, 1954); Justice (NBC, 1954); Kraft Television Th. (NBC, 1954, 1956–58); Armstrong Circle Th. (NBC, 1954, 1956); Robert Montgomery Presents (NBC, 1954); Studio One (CBS, 1955–56); Star Tonight (ABC, 1956); Alfred Hitchcock Presents (CBS, 1957); Climax! (CBS, 1957); Schlitz Playhouse (CBS, 1957); US Steel Hour (CBS, 1948, 1962); Alcoa Hour (NBC, 1958); The Verdict Is Yours (CBS, 1958–59); Playhouse 90 (CBS, 1959); Brighter Day (CBS, 1961); The Defenders (CBS, 1961); Ben Casey (ABC, 1962); Stoney Burke (ABC, 1962); The Lieutenant (NBC, 1964); Bus Stop (Ind., 1964); The Third Man (Ind., 1964); Star Th. (Ind., 1964); The Doctors and The Nurses (CBS, 1965); For the People (CBS, 1965); Slattery's People (CBS, 1965); Ben Casey (ABC, 1966); and Alfred Hitchcock Presents (Ind., 1966).

Awards. She received the Derwent Award for her performance as Irma in *The Madwoman of Chaillot* (1949) and the Twelfth Night Award for her performance as Maman in *The Happy Time* (1951).

Recreation. Dancing, painting, studying Greek.

DANEEL, SYLVIA. Actress. b. Sylvia Jadviga Lakomska, June 20, 1931, Warsaw, Poland, to Jan and Wanda (Andrzejowska) Lakomska. Father, industrialist. Grad. Mrs. J. Tyminska's Lycée, Warsaw, 1945; attended RADA, London, Eng., 1947–48; grad. Ohio Univ., B.F.A., 1950; State Univ. of Iowa, M.A., 1951; Studied acting with Ivo Gall, Warsaw, 2 1/2 years; Lee Strasberg, N.Y.C., two years; dance with Wanda Yerzowska, Warsaw, three years; Martha Graham, N.Y.C., two years; voice with David Craig, two years. Married June 9, 1950, to Tad Danielewski (marr. dis. May 1964); one son. Relative in theatre: grandfather, Feliks Andrejowski, known as Feliks Andrieni, opera singer. Member of AEA; SAG; AFTRA.

Theatre. Miss Daneel made her debut in British and Polish Army productions, touring Germany and England (1946–48); and her N.Y.C. debut as Cypriana in *Angelic Doctor* (Blackfriars Th., Feb. 2, 1952); followed by Nina in *The Girl on the Via Flaminia* (Circle in the Square, Feb. 9, 1954; moved to 48 St. Th., Apr. 1, 1954); Cassei in *A Burst of Summer* (Bucks County Playhouse, New Hope, Pa., July 12, 1954); and Guri in the pre-Bway tour of *Tonight in Samarkand* (1954).

She played Estelle Novick in *The Tunnel of Love* (Royale, Feb. 13, 1957); Junior Captain Marfa Zlotochienko in *Romanoff and Juliet* (Plymouth, Oct. 10, 1957); Mrs. Elinor Ashley in *A Desert Incident* (John Golden Th., Mar. 24, 1959); and Agnes in *The Fourposter* (Charles St. Playhouse, Boston, Mass., July 1959).

Films. Miss Daneel appeared as Anna in *Seven Women from Hell* (20th-Fox, 1961).

Television. She has appeared on Armstrong Circle Th. (NBC); I Remember Mama (CBS); Danger (CBS); Kraft Television Th. (NBC); Robert Montgomery Presents (NBC); Omnibus (ABC, 1956–57; NBC, 1958–61); Doorway to Danger (NBC); Suspense (CBS); the Eddie Fisher Show (NBC); Studio One (CBS); the Kate Smith Show (NBC); the All Night Show (ABC); Dr. Kildare (NBC); and Target, the Corruptors (ABC).

Awards. She received the *Theatre World* Award for her performance as Estelle Novick in *Tunnel of Love* (1957).

Recreation. Swimming, tennis, skiing, sailing, reading, writing.

DANIEL, T. Mime, director. b. T. Daniel Heagstedt, Aug. 23, 1945, Evergreen Park, Ill., to Theodore C. and Thelma L. Heagstedt. Father, executive personnel searcher; mother, artist. Grad. Calumet H.S., Chicago, 1963; majored in speech and theatre at Illinois State Univ. at Normal, B.S. 1967, and did further study there for M.A. in theatre. Studied mime with Marcel Marceau at École International de Mime, Paris, France. Member of AFTRA; ATA; NATAS; International Mimes and Pantomimists. Address: (home) 313A Ridge Rd., Wilmette, IL 60091, tel. (312) 251-1471; (bus.) 2326 Greenwood, Wilmette, IL 60091, tel. (312) 251-1471.

Pre-Theatre. Magician and ventriloquist (1963–67); circus clown and performer (1963–69); designer, director, and actor in college theatre.

Theatre. Mr. Daniel made his professional debut in his own mime production *A World of Mime* (Academy Playhouse, Wilmette, Ill., Jan. 17, 1971). He subsequently toured with this production in eastern and midwestern US, Canada, Puerto Rico (1972), made a second midwestern tour and his first western tour (1973), and a third midwestern tour and second eastern tour (1974). He presented his show *The Magic of Mime* at the Ravinia (Ill.) Festival (Aug. 10, 1974) and made his concert debut with the Fort Wayne (Ind.) Chamber Orchestra in Oct. 1974.

Awards. Mr. Daniel won the International Platform Association Preview Award in 1972.

Recreation. Fencing, reading.

DANIELS, DANNY. Choreographer, director, dancer. b. Oct. 25, 1924, Albany, N.Y., to Daniel and Mary (Bucci) Giagni. Attended Hollywood (Calif.) H.S. Married Nov. 29, 1947, to Berenice Grant; two sons, one daughter.

Theatre. Mr. Daniels made his N.Y.C. debut as Junior and understudied Hal Leroy in *Best Foot Forward* (Ethel Barrymore Th., Oct. 1, 1941); subsequently played Champ Watson in *Billion Dollar Baby* (Alvin, Dec. 21, 1945); Dick McGann in *Street Scene* (Adelphi, Jan. 9, 1947); appeared in the revue, *Make Mine Manhattan* (Broadhurst, Jan. 15, 1948); and succeeded (May 22, 1950) Harold Lang as Bill Calhoun in *Kiss Me, Kate* (New Century, Dec. 30, 1948).

He was a dance soloist with Morton Gould's *Concerto for Tap Dancer and Orchestra* (Eastman Th., Rochester, N.Y., Nov. 16, 1952), in which he toured the US and Europe; and toured with Agnes de Mille's Dance Th. (Sept. 1953–Jan. 1954).

He was choreographer for *Shoestring '57* (Barbizon-Plaza Th., Nov. 5, 1956); *All American* (Winter Garden, Mar. 19, 1962); *Best Foot Forward,* which he also directed (Stage 73, Apr. 2, 1963); directed dances and musical numbers for *High Spirits* (Alvin, Apr. 7, 1964); choreographed and, with Joshua Logan, staged the musical numbers for *Hot September* (opened Shubert Th., Boston, Mass., Sept. 14, 1965); closed there Oct. 9, 1965); staged the dances for *Ciao, Rudy* (Sistine Th., Rome, It., Jan. 7, 1966); staged the dances and production numbers for a revival of *Annie Get Your Gun* (NY State Th., N.Y.C., May 31, 1966; Broadway Th., Sept. 21, 1966); and the dances and musical numbers for *Walking Happy* (Lunt-Fontanne Th., Nov. 26, 1966); and directed and choreographed *Love Match* (pre-Bway, opened Palace West, Phoenix, Ariz., Nov. 3, 1968); closed Ahmanson Th., Los Angeles, Calif., Jan. 4, 1969).

Films. He played a Dancing Newsboy in *Star Maker* (Par., 1939).

Television. Mr. Daniels choreographed the Martha Raye Show (NBC, 1955–56); Ray Bolger Show (1956–57); Patrice Munsel Show (1957–58); Voice of Firestone (CBS, 1958–59); Steve Allen Show (NBC, 1957–59); The Fabulous Fifties (CBS, Jan. 1960); Bing Crosby Special (ABC, 1960); Danny Kaye Show (Nov. 6, 1961); three Arthur Godfrey specials (1963–64); the Perry Como Show specials (NBC, 1964–65; 1965–66; 1966–67); and staged the dances and production numbers for the *Annie Get Your Gun* revival adapted for television (NBC, Mar. 19, 1967).

DANIELS, DAVID. Singer, actor. b. David Mitchell Daniels, Apr. 10, 1927, Evanston, Ill., to Thomas L. and Frances H. Daniels. Father, businessman. Grad. Tucson (Ariz.) H.S., 1945; attended Yale Univ., 1945–47; grad. Curtis Institute of Music, diploma 1950. Studied voice with Marion Freschl, Philadelphia, Pa., 1946–51; Lehman Byck,

N.Y.C., 1951–64; drama with Osna Palmer, 1957–60. Member of AEA; SAG; AGMA.

Theatre. Mr. Daniels made his debut in *And For Yale* (Yale Univ., New Haven, Conn., 1946); subsequently sang in a pop concert (Auditorium, St. Paul, Minn., 1948); and with the St. Paul (Minn.) Civic Opera (1948–52), sang the Man in *The Telephone,* Ramfis in *Aïda,* Mephistopheles in *Faust,* and Colline in *La Bohème.*

He was a soloist with the Philadelphia Orchestra, singing the Marquis in *La Traviata* and the Commissioner in *Madama Butterfly* (Acad. of Music, Philadelphia, Pa., 1949); appeared as Kenneth Gibson in *Call Me Madam* (opened Natl., Washington, D.C., May 5, 1952; closed Shubert, Chicago, Apr. 18, 1953); repeated the role (Kansas City, Mo.; Pittsburgh, Pa., June 1953); appeared as soloist with the Minneapolis Symphony Orchestra (Mar. 8, 1954); appeared in *Panama Hattie* (Louisville, Ky., July 1954); and made his N.Y.C. debut as Peter Reber in *Plain and Fancy* (Mark Hellinger Th., Jan. 27, 1955).

Mr. Daniels appeared in *Wish You Were Here* (Kansas City, Mo., Aug. 1956); played Tommy in *Brigadoon* (Music Th., Rye, N.Y., July 1957); Joe Hardy in *Damn Yankees* (Louisville, Ky., July 1957); Young Strauss in *The Great Waltz* (St. Paul Civic Opera, Minn., Oct. 1957); Tony in *The Boy Friend* (Royal Poinciana Playhouse, Palm Beach, Fla., Apr. 1958); Sid in *The Pajama Game* (Louisville, Ky., July 1958); Tony in *The Boy Friend* (Atlanta, Ga., Aug. 1958); Joe Hardy in *Damn Yankees* (Salt Lake City, Utah, Oct. 1958); appeared with the Minneapolis Symphony Orchestra (Nov. 5, 1958); played Dick in *Pound in Your Pocket* (Royal Poinciana Playhouse, Palm Beach, Fla., Mar. 1959); sang four baritone roles in *The Tales of Hoffman* (Civic Th., New Orleans, La., Apr. 1959); portrayed Jeff in *The Bells Are Ringing* and Tommy in *Brigadoon* (Buffalo, N.Y., Aug. 1959); and Jeff in *The Bells Are Ringing* (Toronto, Canada, Sept. 1959).

He played Jimmy Winters in *Oh, Kay!* (E. 74th St. Th., N.Y.C., Apr. 16, 1960); toured as Freddy in *Royal Enclosure* (June–Aug. 1960); toured as Jack in *Where's Charley?* (June–July 1961); played Mark Livingston in *The Banker's Daughter* (Jan Hus House, N.Y.C., Jan. 22, 1962); and toured as Paul in *Carnival!* (opened Bushnell Aud., Hartford, Conn., Oct. 18, 1962; closed Shubert, Boston, Mass., May 11, 1963).

He was Sir Percy Blakeney in *Pimpernel!* (Gramercy Arts Th., Jan. 7, 1964); played Arthur in *Camelot* and David in *Milk and Honey* (North Shore Music Th., Beverly, Mass., July–Aug. 1964); the title role in *Anatol* (Milwaukee Repertory Th., Milwaukee, Wis., Apr. 1966); repeated his performance as Arthur in *Camelot* (South Shore Music Circus, Cohasset, Mass., July 25, 1966); at the Albuquerque (N.M.) Little Th. played Fred Graham and Petruchio in *Kiss Me, Kate* (1966) and Dr. Mark Bruckner in *On a Clear Day You Can See Forever* (Apr. 28, 1967); and replaced (Mar. 4–Nov. 10, 1969) Eric James as Michael in *The Boys in the Band* (Theatre Four, Apr. 15, 1968).

Television. Mr. Daniels played the Man in *The Telephone* (NBC) and Lance Patterson in the daytime serial, From These Roots (NBC, 1959–60).

Awards. He received the Donaldson Award and the *Theatre World* Award for his performance as Peter Reber in *Plain and Fancy* (1955).

Recreation. Art collecting, music, theatre, books, tennis, swimming.

DANIELS, MARC. Director. b. about 1912, Pittsburgh, Pa. Served in US Army, 1941–46; executive officer and general manager of *This Is the Army* troupe; later in combat.

Theatre. Mr. Daniels directed the revue *Phoenix '55* (Phoenix, N.Y.C., Apr. 23, 1955); *Linda Stone Is Brutal* (Bucks County Playhouse, New Hope, Pa., May 18, 1964); and *The Girl in the Freudian Slip* (Booth Th., N.Y.C., May 18, 1967).

Television. Mr. Daniels has directed episodes of Ford Th.; I Love Lucy; Dr. Kildare, Ben Casey; Man from U.N.C.L.E.; Gunsmoke; Star Trek; and other programs.

Awards. Mr. Daniels has received the *Variety* Showmanship Award and the Director of the Year Award from the Radio and Television Editors of America.

DANIELS, WILLIAM. Actor. b. William David Daniels, Mar. 31, 1927, Brooklyn, N.Y., to David and Irene Daniels. Father, builder. Grad. Lodge Private Tutoring, N.Y.C., 1945; Northwestern Univ., B.S.S., 1950. Studied acting and directing with Lee Strasberg at Actors' Studio, N.Y.C., three years. Married June 30, 1951, to Bonnie Bartlett, actress. Served US Army, ETO, 1945–47; rank, S/Sgt. Member of AEA; SAG; AFTRA.

Theatre. Mr. Daniels first appeared in N.Y.C., succeeding (Oct. 1943) Michael Dreyfuss as John and Clarence in *Life with Father* (Empire Th., Nov. 8, 1939); subsequently billed as Bill Daniels, appeared in *Richard II* (NY City Ctr., Jan. 24, 1951); played Sub-Lt. Granger, R.N., in *Seagulls Over Sorrento* (John Golden Th., Sept. 11, 1952); appeared in the pre-Bway tryout of *The Man Who Corrupted Hadleyburg* (Forrest, Philadelphia, Pa., Spring 1953); and in stock, appeared in *The Man Who Had All the Luck* and *Ladies in Retirement* (John Drew Th., East Hampton, L.I., N.Y., Summer 1954).

He played Brick in the national tour of *Cat on a Hot Tin Roof* (opened Richmond, Va., Oct. 24, 1957; closed Geary, San Francisco, Calif., May 17, 1958); billed as William Daniels, appeared as Jimmy Porter in *Look Back in Anger* (41 St. Th., Nov. 11, 1958); succeeded (Sept. 1958) George Segal as Don Parritt in *The Iceman Cometh* (Circle in the Square, May 8, 1956); played Cooper in *The Legend of Lizzie* (54 St. Th., Feb. 9, 1959); and Peter in *The Zoo Story* (Provincetown Playhouse, Jan. 14, 1960).

Mr. Daniels toured South America (1961), appearing in *The Zoo Story, Suddenly Last Summer,* and *I Am a Camera;* played Albert Amundsen in *A Thousand Clowns* (Eugene O'Neill Th., N.Y.C., Apr. 5, 1962); and Dr. Evans in *Dear Me, the Sky Is Falling* (Music Box, Mar. 2, 1963); Dale Harding in *One Flew Over the Cuckoo's Nest* (Cort, Nov. 13, 1963); Warren Smith in *On a Clear Day You Can See Forever* (Mark Hellinger Th., Oct. 17, 1965); Joseph in *Daphne in Cottage D* (Longacre, Oct. 15, 1967); John Adams in *1776* (46 St. Th., Mar. 16, 1969); and he replaced (Feb. 25, 1974) Len Cariou as Fredrik Egerman in *A Little Night Music* (Shubert Th., Feb. 25, 1973).

Films. He appeared in *Ladybug, Ladybug* (UA, 1963); *A Thousand Clowns* (UA, 1965); *Two for the Road* (20th-Fox, 1967); and *The Graduate* (Embassy, 1967).

Television. Mr. Daniels appeared on The Somerset Maugham Th. (ABC, 1952); Profiles in Courage (NBC, 1965); played the title role on Captain Nice (NBC, 1967); and has appeared on other programs, including The Nurses (CBS); East Side/West Side (CBS); The Defenders (CBS); For the People (CBS); and Naked City (ABC).

Awards. He received the Clarence Derwent Award and the *Village Voice* Off-Bway (Obie) Award for his performance as Peter in *The Zoo Story* (1960); and the Argentina Drama Critics Award for the best performance by a foreign actor for Peter in *The Zoo Story* (1962).

Recreation. Chess.

DARDEN, SEVERN. Actor. b. New Orleans, La. Educ. Mexico City (Mexico) Coll.; Univ. of Chicago.

Theatre. Mr. Darden began his acting career at the Barter Th., Abingdon, Va., where his roles included Joseph in *My Three Angels* (June 14, 1954), an M.P. in *Mr. Roberts* (June 21, 1954), Corporal Shultz in *Stalag 17* (July 5, 1954), and Henry Cabot Lodge in *The Hall of Mirrors* (Aug. 13, 1956). At the American Shakespeare Festival, Stratford, Conn., he played Voltemand in *Hamlet* (June 19, 1958), Snug in *A Midsummer Night's Dream* (June 20, 1958), an Officer in *The Winter's Tale* (July 20, 1958), Peter in *Romeo and Juliet* (June 12, 1959), again played Snug in *A Midsummer Night's Dream* (June 20, 1959), was Nym in *The Merry Wives of Windsor* (July 8, 1959), and a French Lord in *All's Well That Ends Well* (July 29, 1959).

He was Foma Fomitch in *Friend of the Family* (Crystal Palace, St. Louis, Mo., Dec. 8, 1958); made his first N.Y.C. appearance in *From the Second City* (Royale, Sept. 27, 1961); and was also in the revues *Seacoast of Bohemia* (Second City at Square East, Jan. 20, 1962) and *My Friend Art Is Dead* (Second City, Chicago, June 20, 1962). He played Jonathan Kobitz In *P.S. 193* (Writers' Stage, N.Y.C., Oct. 30, 1962); and at Second City at Square East appeared in *To the Water Tower* (Apr. 4, 1963) and *Open Season at Second City* (Jan. 22, 1964).

He was Birgasse in *A Murderer Among Us* (Morosco, Mar. 25, 1964); played in *A View from Under the Bridge* (Second City at Square East, Aug. 4, 1964); toured in *From the Second City* (opened Fisher Th., Detroit, Mich., Feb. 16, 1965); was Harry in *Leda Had a Little Swan* (previews: Cort, N.Y.C., Mar. 29–Apr. 10, 1968); and played Sam Adams and Robinson in *The American Revolution, Part I* (Ford's Th., Washington, D.C., June 1, 1973).

Films. Mr. Darden's films include *Goldstein* (Altura, 1965); *Dead Heat on a Merry-Go-Round* (Col., 1967); *The President's Analyst* (Par., 1967); *Luv* (Col., 1968); *They Shoot Horses, Don't They?* (Cinerama, 1969); *Fearless Frank* (Amer. Intl., 1969); *P.J.* (U, 1969); *Model Shop* (Col., 1970); *The Mad Room* (Col., 1970); *Justine* (20th-Fox, 1970) *The Last Movie* (U, 1971); *Pussycat, Pussycat, I Love You* (UA, 1971); *Vanishing Point* (20th-Fox, 1971); *The Hired Hand* (U, 1971); *Werewolves on Wheels* (Fanfare, 1971); *Cisco Pike* (Col., 1971); *Conquest of the Planet of the Apes* (20th-Fox, 1972); *Who Fears the Devil* (Two's Company, 1972); *Battle for the Planet of the Apes* (20th-Fox, 1973); *The War Between Men and Women* (Natl. Gen., 1973); *Every Little Crook and Nanny* (MGM, 1973); *Play It as It Lays* (U, 1973); and *The Day of the Dolphin* (Avco-Embassy, 1974).

Television. Mr. Darden appeared on pay television in *Second City Revue* (July 6, 1961).

Night Clubs. Mr. Darden appeared as a monologist at Gate of Horn (Chicago, Ill., Oct. 1959) and performed at Second City (Chicago) in the following revues: *The Second City Revue* (Dec. 1959), *Too Many Hats* (Feb. 1960), *The Third Program* (July 1960), and *Seacoast of Bohemia* (Nov. 1960). He peformed also in a Second City presentation in Los Angeles, Calif. (Ivar Th., June 7, 1961).

DARLING, JEAN. Singer, actress. b. Dorothy Jean LeVake, Aug. 23, 1925, Santa Monica, Calif., to Rollin P. and Dorothy Hamilton (Darling) LeVake. Father, civil engineer; mother, actress. Grad. Miss Long's Professional Children's Sch., Hollywood, Calif., 1938. Studied singing with William Herman, N.Y.C., three years; with Clementi Di Machi, N.Y.C., five years. Married June 14, 1954, to Reuben Bochert Bowen, known professionally as Kajar the Magician; one son. Relative in theatre: grandfather, Frank C. Hamilton, producer. Member of AEA; AFTRA; SAG; AGVA. Address: 245 E. 72nd St., New York, NY 10021, tel. (212) UN 1-2520.

Theatre. Miss Darling began her professional career as a "free-lance baby" in Hollywood films. As the "leading lady" of Hal Roach's *Our Gang* comedies, she toured, three months each year, major vaudeville theatres (1928–33); and appeared as a single act in vaudeville (1934–35).

She played Bertha in *The Father,* Margaret in *Dear Brutus,* and Josephine in *The Valiant* (El Capitan, Biltmore, Los Angeles, Calif., 1936–38); and made her first N.Y.C. appearance in *Count Me In* (Ethel Barrymore Th., Oct. 8, 1942); toured the US in the USO camp show *Marianne* (1943); toured Italy and North Africa with the USO (1944); and played Carrie Pipperidge in *Carousel* (Majestic, N.Y.C., Apr. 19, 1945).

Miss Darling has appeared in industrial shows and films for such concerns as US Steel, Philco, Servel, and Sylvania. She toured Alaska for the Hollywood Coordinating Committee (1952); and has made personal appearances as a singer in South America, South Africa and the West Indies.

Films. Miss Darling appeared as a child in *Babes in Toyland* (MGM, 1934); and in *Jane Eyre* (Mono, 1934).

Television and Radio. As a child she performed on such Hollywood radio shows as Bobby Benson (1934–35); Hall of Fame (1934–35); the Bing Crosby Show (1934–35); Tom Sawyer (1935); Lanny Ross Show (1935, and 1949–50); H Bar O (WOR, 1949–50); Hilltop House (CBS, 1952–54).

She has appeared on the television programs, the Jean Darling Show (1949–50); Mystery Th. (1951–53); Fireside Th. (1951–52); Hawkins Falls (1952); the Robert Alda Show (1954); Jean Darling, the Singing Knitwitch (KHJ, Hollywood, 1951); American Inventory (NBC, 1955); and Jack Paar Show (NBC, 1960).

Recreation. Painting, knitting.

DARLINGTON, W. A. Drama critic, playwright, author. b. William Aubrey Darlington, Feb. 20, 1890, Tauton, Somerset, England, to Thomas and Annie Edith (Bainbridge) Darlington. Father, school inspector. Grad. Shrewsbury Sch., England, 1909; Cambridge Univ., scholarship in classics, honors in classics and English literature, 1912, M.A. 1922. Married Oct. 3, 1918, to Marjorie Sheppard (dec. Oct. 5, 1973); two daughters. Served in the Northumberland Fusiliers, later in Military Intelligence, British Army (1915–18); rank, Capt. Member of Critics' Circle (pres., 1930; vice-pres. twice; mbr. of council; chmn., drama section); League of Dramatists; Authors' Society; Inst. of Journalists; Garrick Club; Dramatists Club (vice-pres., 1963–64). Address: (home) Monksdown, Bishopstone, Sussex, England; (bus.) c/o Daily Telegraph, Fleet St., London EC 4, England.

Pre-Theatre. Schoolmaster (1913–14); contributor to *Punch* (1916); and on editorial staff of Odhams, Ltd., London (1919).

Theatre. In 1919, Mr. Darlington became editor of *The World*, London, and was chief drama critic for *The Daily Telegraph* (1920–68); and head of the drama department (1925–68). Following his retirement from the drama posts, he continued on the *Daily Telegraph's* editorial staff as theatre columnist and contributor of obituary notices and book reviews. He was also drama correspondent for the NY *Times* (1939–60).

Mr. Darlington first wrote for the stage a dramatization of his own novel, *Alf's Button* (Prince's Th., Dec. 24, 1924; revived New, Oxford, 1925); subsequently wrote *Carpet Slippers* (Embassy, 1930); adapted from the Dutch of Jan Fabricius *A Knight Passed By* (Ambassadors', 1931); adapted *The Streets of London* (Ambassadors', 1932); wrote *Marcia Gets Her Own Back* (Aldwych, 1938); and wrote *The Key of the House* (Hereford, England, 1947).

Films. The silent film, *Alf's Button* (1st Natl., 1922), as well as a 1929 talkie version, was also derived from his novel.

Published Works. He has written *Alf's Button* (1919); *Through the Fourth Wall* (1922); *Literature in the Theatre* (1925); *Sheridan* (1933); *J. M. Barrie* (1938); his autobiography, *I Do What I Like* (1947); *The Actor and His Audience* (1949); *The World of Gilbert and Sullivan* (1950); *6001 Nights* (1960); and *Laurence Olivier* (1968).

Recreation. Formerly games of various kinds; now reading and conversation.

DARVAS, LILI. Actress. b. Apr. 10, 1902, Budapest, Hungary, to Alexander and Berta (Freiberger) Darvas. Immigrated to US 1938, became citizen 1944. Father, physician. Married June 1926, to Ferenc Molnar, (1922–26); (dec. 1952). Member of AEA; AFTRA; SAG. (1926–38);. Address: 240 E. 79th St., New York, NY 10021, tel. (212) BU 8-3953.

Theatre. Miss Darvas made her stage debut in Budapest, Hungary, playing Juliet in *Romeo and Juliet* (1922); subsequently appeared there in both classical and modern plays (1922–26); joined Max Reinhardt's repertory theatre, appearing in Vienna, Aust., and Berlin, Ger. (1926–38); and at the Salzburg (Aust.) Festivals (Summers 1926–29).

With Reinhardt's company she appeared, in German-language productions, as Titania in *A Midsummer Night's Dream* (Century, N.Y.C., Nov. 17, 1927); Faith in *Jedermann* (Everyman) (Century, Dec. 7, 1927); Lucille in *Danton's Tod* (Danton's Death) (Century, Dec. 20, 1927); and Beatrice in *Servant of Two Masters* (Cosmopolitan, Jan. 9, 1928).

Miss Darvas appeared in *The Criminals* at Irwin Piscator's theatre (New Sch. for Social Research, N.Y.C., 1941); as Peter Gray in *Soldier's Wife* (John Golden Th., Oct. 4, 1944); Gertrude, Queen of Denmark in Maurice Evans' production of *Hamlet* (Columbus Circle Th., Dec. 13, 1945); Rosa Rucken in *Bravo* (Lyceum, Nov. 11, 1948); Marie Regnier in *Hidden River* (Playhouse, Jan. 23, 1957); Madame St. Pé in a tour of *The Waltz of the Toreadors* (opened McCarter Th., Princeton, N.J., Sept. 26, 1957; Coronet, N.Y.C., Mar. 4, 1958); played Coco in *Chéri* (Morosco, Oct. 12, 1959); Amalie Freud in *A Far Country* (Music Box, Apr. 4, 1961); Nina Kocei in *First Love* (Morosco, Dec. 25, 1961); and Mrs. Jenny Stern in *My Mother, My Father and Me* (Plymouth, Mar. 23, 1963).

She appeared in Budapest in 1965 in *Olympia* and played Madame Neilsen in *Les Blancs* (Longacre, N.Y.C., Nov. 15, 1970).

Films. Miss Darvas appeared in Germany in the title role of *Marie Baskirchev* (1936); and, in the US, in *Meet Me in Las Vegas* (MGM, 1956). In 1970, in Budapest, she made the film *Love*, distributed in the US in 1972–73.

Television. Since 1950, Miss Darvas has appeared in over 100 productions on the major networks. She played the title role in the N.E.T. Opera Theatre production of *Rachel La Cubana* (PBS, 1973).

da SILVA, HOWARD. Actor, director, producer. b. May 4, 1909, Cleveland, Ohio, to Benjamin and Bertha (Sen) Silverblatt. Father, dress cutter. Attended Carnegie Inst. of Tech., 1928. Married 1950 to Marjorie Nelson (marr. dis. 1960); married June 30, 1961, to Nancy Nutter, actress; two sons; two daughters. Member of AEA; AFTRA; SAG. Address: Croton-on-Hudson, NY.

Pre-Theatre. Steel worker.

Theatre. Mr. da Silva made his theatrical debut, with Eva Le Gallienne's Civic Repertory Co., appearing at the Civic Repertory Th., in NYC (1929–33) as a Slave in *The Would-Be Gentleman* (Sept. 21, 1929); and Apothecary in *Romeo and Juliet* (Apr. 21, 1929); Scaevola in *The Green Cockatoo* (Oct. 9, 1930); an Orderly in *The Three Sisters* (Oct. 9, 1930); Schumann in *Siegfried* (Oct. 20, 1930); Ostrich and Cookson in *Peter Pan* (Nov. 15, 1930); Hodges in *Alison's House* (Dec. 1, 1930); Second Coastguard in *The Good Hope* (Dec. 17, 1930); a Guest in *Camille* (Jan. 26, 1931); Mufti in *The Would-Be Gentleman* (Mar. 12, 1931); Senator Lewis in *Inheritors* (Mar. 28, 1931); a Stationmaster in *The Cherry Orchard* (May 4, 1931); Wolf Biefeld in *Liliom* (Oct. 26, 1932); Ferapont in *The Three Sisters* (Nov. 1, 1932); a Countryman in *Cradle Song* (Nov. 9, 1932); Dr. Samuel Johnson in the Prologue of *Dear Jane* (Nov. 14, 1932); the Cook and the White Knight in *Alice in Wonderland* (Dec. 12, 1932); repeated his role of the Stationmaster in *The Cherry Orchard* (New Amsterdam, N.Y.C., Mar. 6, 1933); toured the US with the US Civic Repertory Th. as Thorvald in *A Doll's House*, Brack in *Hedda Gabler*, and Halvard Solness in *The Master Builder* (1933–34).

With the Brattle Repertory Co. (Cambridge, Mass.), he played Astrov in *Uncle Vanya*, the Artist in *When We Dead Awaken*, Don Victorio in *Fortunato* (Brattle Hall Th., 1933–34); for the Theatre Union, appeared as Sepp Kriz in *Sailors of Cattaro* (Civic Rep. Th., N.Y.C., Dec. 16, 1934) and Hansy McCulloh in *Black Pit* (Civic Repertory Th., Mar. 20, 1935).

Mr. da Silva appeared in *Rain from Heaven*, *Between Two Worlds*, *The Master Builder* (Cleveland Playhouse, Ohio, 1935); directed *Waiting for Lefty* and *Inheritors* (People's Th., Cleveland, 1935); and taught and directed productions at Stage Arts Laboratory (1935).

Under the name of Howard Solness, which he used for one production only, he played Foreman in *Ten Million Ghosts* (St. James, N.Y.C., Oct. 23, 1936); appeared as Lewis in the Group Th. production of *Golden Boy* (Belasco, Nov. 4, 1937); Larry Foreman in the Federal Th. (WPA) production of *The Cradle Will Rock* (Venice Th., Dec. 1937), and repeated the role in the Mercury Th. production Windsor, Jan. 3, 1938); played the Old Man in the Group Th. production of *Casey Jones* (Fulton, Feb. 19, 1938); Jack Armstrong in *Abe Lincoln in Illinois* (Plymouth, Oct. 15, 1938); Speed in *Summer Night* (St. James, Nov. 2, 1939); the Sightseeing Guide in *Two on an Island* (Broadhurst, Jan. 22, 1940); Jud Fry in *Oklahoma!* (St. James, Mar. 31, 1943); Ross Dixon in the pre-Bway tryout of *Shootin' Star* (opened Shubert, New Haven, Conn., Apr. 4, 1946; closed Shubert Boston, Mass., Apr. 27, 1946); and directed *The Cradle Will Rock* (Mansfield, N.Y.C., Dec. 26, 1947).

At the Actor's Lab (Hollywood, Calif., 1948–49), Mr. da Silva appeared in *Monday's Heroes*, and *The Banker's Daughter* and directed *Proud Accent*; played Friend Ed in *Burning Bright* (Broadhurst, NY Co., Oct. 18, 1950); directed and appeared in concert readings from the works of Mark Twain, Anton Chekhov, and Sholom Aleichem for the Actor's Concert Th. (1951–52).

Mr. da Silva produced, with Arnold Perl, directed, and performed in *The World of Sholom Aleichem* (Barbizon-Plaza, Sept. 12, 1953), and on tour in Chicago, Ill., and Los Angeles, Calif.; directed *Sandhog* (Phoenix, N.Y.C., Nov. 23, 1954), which was produced by T. Edward Hambleton and Norris Houghton by special arrangement with Rachel Productions (Howard da Silva and Arnold Perl).

In stock, Mr. da Silva played Doc in *Mister Roberts* (Warwick Musical Th., R.I.; Oakdale Musical Th., Wallingford, Conn., Summer 1954); produced, directed, and performed, at the Crystal Lake (N.Y.) Th., *The Prodigious Snob*, *The Silver Tassie*, *The Cherry Orchard*, *The Caucasian Chalk Circle*, *The World of Sholom Aleichem*, *A Phoenix Too Frequent* and *The Gamblers* (Summer 1955).

Mr. da Silva appeared as The Fixer, Lt. Charles in *The Adding Machine* (Phoenix, N.Y.C., Feb. 9, 1956); Neel Fedoseitch Mamaev in *Diary of a Scoundrel* (Phoenix, Nov. 4, 1956); and in the title role in *Volpone* (Rooftop, Jan. 7, 1957); at the Bucks County Playhouse (New Hope, Pa.), directed and acted in *The World of Sholom Aleichem*, *Anastasia*, *Tea and Sympathy* and *The Lesser Comores* (Summer 1956); staged *Tevya and His Daughters* (Carnegie Hall Playhouse, N.Y.C., Sept. 16, 1957), which he also produced as a member of Banner Productions; and appeared as Horn, the Prosecuting Attorney, in *Compulsion* (Ambassador, Oct. 24, 1957); at the Valley Playhouse Th., Chagrin Falls, Ohio, produced, directed and performed in *Nature's Way*, *Compulsion*, *Holiday for Lovers*, *The Little Foxes*, *Visit to a Small Planet* and *Three Men on a Horse* (Summer 1958). Mr. da Silva played Ben in *Fiorello!* (Broadhurst, N.Y.C., Nov. 23, 1959); directed *The Cradle Will Rock* (NY City Ctr., Feb. 11, 1960); *Purlie Victorious* (Cort, Sept. 28, 1961); appeared as Ottaker in *Romulus* (Music Box, Jan. 10, 1962); directed *Fiorello!* in stock (Paper Mill Playhouse, Millburn, N.J., Summer 1962); and played Calchas in the pre-Bway tryout of *La Belle* (opened Shubert, Philadelphia, Pa., Aug. 13, 1962; closed there Aug. 25, 1962).

Mr. da Silva played Max Hartman in *In the Counting House* (Biltmore, N.Y.C., Dec. 13, 1962); Paul Hirsch in *Dear Me, the Sky Is Falling* (Music Box, Mar. 2, 1963); directed *Cages* (York Playhouse, June 13, 1963); *The Advocate* (ANTA, Oct. 14, 1963); *Thistle in My Bed* (Gramercy Arts, Nov. 19, 1963); and for the NY Shakespeare Festival, appeared as Claudius in *Hamlet* (Delacorte Th., June 17, 1964); played the Archbishop in *The Unknown Soldier and His Wife* (Vivian Beaumont Th., N.Y.C., July 6, 1967); and Benjamin Franklin in *1776* (46 St. Th., Mar. 16, 1969) which he performed at the White House by special invitation of President Richard M. Nixon; and was guest artist with the Syracuse (N.Y.) Repertory Theatre (Oct.

1972–May 1973).

Films. Mr. da Silva made his debut in *Once in a Blue Moon* (Par., 1936); subsequently played Jack Armstrong in *Abe Lincoln in Illinois* (RKO, 1940); appeared in *I'm Still Alive* (RKO, 1940); *The Sea Wolf* (WB, 1941); *Blues in the Night* (WB, 1941); *Navy Blues* (WB, 1941); *Bad Men of Missouri* (WB, 1941); *Strange Alibi* (WB, 1941); *Sergeant York* (WB, 1941); *Nine Lives Are Not Enough* (WB, 1941); *Wild Bill Hickok Rides Again* (WB, 1941); *Steel Against the Sky* (WB, 1941); *Juke Girl* (WB, 1942); *Bullet Scars* (WB, 1942); *Keeper of the Flame* (MGM, 1942); *Reunion* (MGM, 1942); *Omaha Trail* (MGM, 1942); *Tonight We Raid Calais* (20th-Fox, 1942); *Five Were Chosen* (Independent, 1942); *The Lost Weekend* (Par., 1945); *Two Years Before the Mast* (Par., 1946); *Blue Dahlia* (Par., 1946); *Blaze of Noon* (Par., 1947); *Unconquered* (Par., 1947); *They Live by Night* (RKO, 1948); *The Great Gatsby* (Par., 1949); *Border Incident* (MGM, 1949); *Three Husbands* (UA, 1950); *Wyoming Mail* (U, 1950); *Tripoli* (Par., 1950); *The Underworld Story* (UA, 1950); *Fourteen Hours* (20th-Fox, 1951); *Slaughter Trail* (RKO, 1951); *M* (Col., 1951); *David and Lisa* (Continental, 1962); *The Outrage* (MGM, 1964); and *Nevada Smith* (Par., 1966).

Television and Radio. On radio, Mr. da Silva directed the Great Classics series for the Federal Th. (WPA) project (WHN, WEVD, 1936); and performed in the plays of Arch Oboler and Norman Corwin (CBS, 1940).

On television, he appeared in *My Heart's in the Highlands* (Silver Theatre, NBC, 1950); co-directed and acted in *The Walter Fortune Story (NBC, 1950); appeared on Blue Hotel* (CBC, Toronto, Canada, 1961), and *Man on Back* (CBC, 1962); played Claudius in *Hamlet* (CBS); and Mr. Peachum in *The Beggar's Opera* (NET); made guest appearances on The Defenders (CBS, 1963); The Nurses (CBS, 1963); East Side/West Side (CBS, 1963); Outer Limits (ABC); For the People (CBS); Ben Casey (ABC); The Man from U.N.C.L.E. (NBC); The Loner (CBS); and The Fugitive (ABC); narrated *A Heritage of Freedom* (Look Up and Live, CBS); and was interviewed on Camera Three (CBS).

Awards. Mr. da Silva was nominated for Academy (Oscar) Awards for his performances in *The Lost Weekend* (1945) and *Two Years Before the Mast* (1946); and by the British Academy of Motion Picture Arts and Sciences for his performance in David and Lisa (1962).

DAUPHIN, CLAUDE.

Actor, director, writer. b. Claude Maria Eugent LeGrand, Aug. 19, 1904, Corbeil, Seine et Oise, France, to Franc and Marie Madeleine (Dauphin) LeGrand. Father, writer (pen name Franc Nohain); mother, painter. Grad. Lycée Henri IV, Paris, France; La Sorbonne, Paris, Bachelier; École National Supérieure des Beaux Arts, Paris. Married 1934 to Rosine Darieun, actress (marr. dis. 1953); married 1953 to Maria Mauban, actress (marr. dis. 1955); one son; married May 21, 1955, to Norma Eberhardt, actress. Relative in theatre: brother, Jean Nohain, writer and television actor. Served as liason officer in the Free French Army, 1939–45, rank, Lt.; received the Croix de Guerre, Medal of De Gaulle, La Légion d'Honneur. Member of AEA; SAG; AFTRA.

Theatre. Mr. Dauphin first appeared in N.Y.C. as Cradeau in *No Exit* (Biltmore Th., Nov. 26, 1946); subsequently as Papa in *The Happy Time* (Plymouth, Jan. 24, 1950); Denny in *Janus* (Plymouth, Nov. 25, 1955); directed *The Best House in Naples* (Lyceum, Oct. 26, 1956); played the Voice in *The Infernal Machine* (Phoenix, Feb. 3, 1958); Panise in a tour of *Fanny* (July–Sept. 1957); the title role of *Clerambard* (Rooftop Th., N.Y.C., Nov. 7, 1957); General St. Pé in a tour of *The Waltz of the Toreadors* (July–Sept. 1958); Bernard Laroque in *The Deadly Game* (Longacre, N.Y.C., Feb. 2, 1960); Paul Delville in a tour of *The Marriage-Go-Round* (July–Sept. 1961); Frank Brisset in *Giants, Sons of Giants* (Alvin, N.Y.C., Jan. 6, 1962); and played Pierre Lannes in *L'amante anglaise* (Barbizon-Plaza, Apr. 14, 1971).

Mr. Dauphin was set designer for the *Comédie Française* (1923–31). He made his acting debut in Paris in *Le Messenger* (Th. Gymanse, 1933); subsequently appeared at the Th. Gymanse in *Une femme libre* (1934), *L'espoir* (1935), *Le coeur* (1936), *Le voyage* (1937), and *Le cap des tempêtes* (1938). He also appeared in Paris in *Adam* (1938–39) and *Une grande fille toute simple* (1945). From 1945 to 1950, he was director of the Claude Dauphin Th. Co. in Paris and appeared in *Le bal des pompiers* (1946); *L'amour vient en jouant* (1947); *L'homard à l'américaine* (1948); *La soif* (Ambassadeurs, 1949); *Mister Roberts* (Ambassadeurs, 1951); *Souviens toi mon amour* (Th. Henri V, 1954); *La folie* (1959).

In London, he appeared as André de Gascogne in *From the French* (Strand, Sept. 16, 1959).

In Paris, he played in *Adorable Julia* (Th. Sarah Bernhardt, Apr. 1962); *Hedda Gabler* (Th. Montparnasse, 1963); *Mon Faust* (1964); was the Father in a revival of *Les séquestrés d'Altona* (Th. de l'Athénée, Sept. 1965); was in *La bouteille à l'encre* (1966); played Tobias in *A Delicate Balance* (Th. de France, 1967); Pierre Lannes in *L'amante anglaise* (Th. National Populaire, Création à la Salle Gémier, Dec. 16, 1968); was in *The Price* (1969); played Willy Loman in *Death of a Salesman* (1970); appeared in Pirandello's *Naked* (1971); played Shylock in *The Merchant of Venice* (1972); and was Morell in *Candida* (1973).

Films. Mr. Dauphin made his film debut in *Paris Soleil* (France, 1931); followed by *La fortune* (1931); *Mondanités* (1931); *Faubourg Montmartre* (1931); *Tout s'arrange* (1931); *Aux urnes, citoyens* (1932); *Un homme heureux* (1932); *Une jeune fille et un million* (1932); *Pas besoin d'argent* (1933); *L'Abbé Constantin* (1933); *Clair de lune* (1933); *Les surprises du sleeping* (1934); *La fille du regiment* (1934); *Dédé* (1934); *D'amour et d'eau fraîche* (1934); *Le billet de mille* (1935); *Nous ne sommes plus des enfants* (1935); *Retour au paradis* (1935); *La route heureuse* (1935); *Voyage imprévu* (1936); *Conflit* (1936); *Entre des artistes* (1937); *Cavalcade* (1938); *Le monde tremblera* (1939); *La révolte des vivants* (1939); *Battements de coeur* (1939); *Les petits riens* (1940); *L'étrange Suzy* (1941); *Les deux timides* (1941); *Les hommes sans peur* (1941); *Une femme disparaît* (1941); *Promesse à l'inconnue* (1941); *Felicie Nanteuil* (1942); *La belle aventure* (1942); *Salut à la France* (1944); *Cyrano de Bergerac* (1945); *Dorothée cherche l'amour* (1945); *La femme coupée en morceaux* (1945); *Nous ne sommes pas mariés* (1945); *Tombe du ciel* (1946); *Rendezvous à Paris* (1946); *L'éventail* (1947); *Parade du rire* (1947); *Jean de la lune* (1947); *La petite chocolatière* (1947); *Plaisir* (1947); *Croisière pour l'inconnu* (1948); *Route sans issue* (1948); *L'inconnue d'un soir* (1948); *L'impeccable Henri* (1948); *Le bal des pompiers* (1948); *Ainsi finit la nuit* (1948); *Les innocents à Paris* (1951); *Casque d'or* (1953); *Les mauvaises rencontres* (1954); *Mon coquin de père* (1959); *Pourquoi viens-tu si tard?* (1960); *Le diable et les dix commandments* (1962); *Les mystifiés* (1963); and *La bonne soupe* (1963).

His US and British films include *English Without Tears* (Rank, 1943); *Deported* (U, 1950); *Les innocents à Paris* (1951); *April in Paris* (WB, 1952); *Little Boy Lost* (Par., 1953); *Murder in the Rue Morgue* (WB, 1954); *The Quiet American* (UA, 1958); *The Full Treatment* (Val Guest, 1960); *Tiara Tahiti* (Val Guest, 1962); *The Visit* (1963); *Two for the Road* (20th-Fox, 1967); *Hard Contract* (20th-Fox, 1969); *The Madwoman of Chaillot* (WB, 1969); and *Rosebud* (UA, 1975).

Television. Mr. Dauphin appeared on American television in *Shadow of a Man* (Summer Studio One, CBS, July 1953); *The Moment of the Rose* (Video Th., CBS, Nov. 1953); *The Apollo of Bellac* (Omnibus, CBS, Mar. 1954); on Schlitz Playhouse of Stars (CBS) in *Something Wonderful* (Apr. 1954) and *How the Brigadier Won His Medals* (July 1954); on Studio One (CBS) in *Cardinal Mindszenty* (May 1954) and *Sail with the Tide* (Jan. 1955). He appeared on the Paris Precinct series (ABC, 1955); in *Meeting at Mayerling* (Front Row Center, CBS, Sept. 1955); in *The Problem in Cell Thirteen* (Mystery Th., NBC, Aug. 1962); on Naked City (NBC, 1963); and in *France: The Faces of Love* (World Th., NET, Oct. 1964).

DAVENPORT, MILLIA.

Costume designer, writer. b. Mar. 30, 1895, Cambridge, Mass., to Charles B. and Gertrude C. Davenport. Father, director of Station for Experimental Evolution. Grad. Huntington (N.Y.) H.S., 1913; attended Barnard Coll., 1913–15; Teachers Coll. (N.Y.C.), 1915–16. Studied at Cours Désir, Paris, Fr., 1910–11; N.Y. School of Fine and Applied Arts, N.Y.C., 1917–18. Married 1922 to Walter L. Fleisher (marr. dis.); married 1938 to Edward E. Harkavy, physician. Member of United Scenic Artists, Local 829. Address: (home) 445 Buena Vista Rd., New City, NY 10956, tel. (914) NE 4-2205; (bus.) 48 W. 11th St., New York, NY 10011, tel. (212) GR 5-4288.

Theatre. Miss Davenport designed sets and costumes for the Wits and Fingers Studio, N.Y.C. (1918–20); subsequently designed costumes for productions at the Provincetown Playhouse and the Greenwich Village Th. (1924–27), including *Patience* (Provincetown Playhouse, Dec. 29, 1924) and *Love for Love* (Greenwich Village Th., Mar. 31, 1925); and designed costumes for *The Good Hope* (Civic Repertory Th., Oct. 28, 1927); *Shoemaker's Holiday* (Mercury, Jan. 1, 1938); *Heartbreak House* (Mercury, Apr. 29, 1938); *Five Kings* (Colonial, Boston, Feb. 27, 1939); *Love for Love* (Hudson, June 3, 1940); and *Journey to Jerusalem* Natl., Oct. 5, 1940).

Published Works. Miss Davenport is the author of *The Book of Costume* (1948).

Recreation. Gardening, cooking, travel.

DAVENPORT, PEMBROKE.

Musical director, composer, lyricist, arranger. b. Pembroke Mortimer Davenport, July 3, 1911, Dallas, Tex., to Frank Dawson and Margaret Grace (Wilson) Davenport. Father, railroad yardmaster, musician, actor; mother, school teacher, pianist. Grad. Forrest Ave. H.S., Dallas, 1928; attended Southern Methodist Univ., 1928–29. Studied piano with father; conducting and composition with Tibor Serly, N.Y.C., 1943–45. Married Dec. 9, 1930, to Evelyn Woodward (marr. dis. 1956); two daughters; married May 3, 1957, to Sylvia Jurciukonis; one son. Relative in the theatre: son-in-law, Lloyd Richards, director. Member of AFM, Local 802; ASCAP; AGAC; ALA.

Theatre. Mr. Davenport first performed in Dallas, Tex., as piano soloist with the Palace Th. Symphony Orchestra (1929); subsequently composed two editions of *Showstring Follies* (Little Th., Dallas, 1931–32); and approximately 50 productions for Radio City Music Hall (N.Y.C., 1934–37).

He joined (Jan. 1945), as musical director, *The Seven Lively Arts* (Ziegfeld, Dec. 7, 1944); was musical director for Billy Rose's *Concert Varieties* (Zeigfeld, June 1, 1945); *Carib Song* (Adelphi, Sept. 27, 1945); joined (July 1946), as musical director, *The Red Mill* (46 St. Th., Oct. 16, 1945); was musical director for the pre-Bway tryout of *Shootin' Star* which closed out of town (opened Shubert, New Haven, Conn., Apr. 4, 1946; closed Shubert, Boston, Mass., Apr. 27, 1946); was vocal director for *Sweethearts* (Shubert, N.Y.C., Jan. 21, 1947); *Look Ma, I'm Dancin'* (Adelphi, Jan. 29, 1948); musical supervisor for *Sally* (Martin Beck Th., May 6, 1948); musical director of *Kiss Me, Kate* (New Century, Dec. 30, 1948); and *Out of This World* (New Century, Dec. 21, 1950).

He was musical director for *Three Wishes for Jamie* (Los Angeles-San Francisco, Calif., Civic Light Opera Assn., Summer 1952); *Hazel Flagg* (Mark Hellinger Th., N.Y.C., Feb. 11, 1953); the pre-Bway tour of *Can-Can* (Spring 1953); was guest conductor of the Los Angeles Philharmonic (Hollywood Bowl, Calif., Aug. 1953); and was musical director for *Arabian Nights* (Marine Th., Jones Beach, N.Y., Summers 1954–55).

He took over (Sept. 1955) as musical director of *Fanny* (Majestic, N.Y.C., Nov. 4, 1954); also its tour (opened Shubert, Boston, Mass., Dec. 25, 1956; closed Hanna, Cleveland, Ohio, May 25, 1957); and became (Sept. 1959) musical director of *La Plume de ma Tante* (Royale, N.Y.C., Nov. 11, 1958).

Mr. Davenport composed music for *Doctor Willy Nilly* (Barbizon-Plaza Th., June 4, 1959); incidental music for *The Long Dream* (Ambassador, Feb. 17, 1960); was musical director for *The King and I* (NY City Ctr., May 11, 1960); *Hit the Deck* (Marine Th., Jones Beach, Summer 1960); and *Paradise Island* (Marine Th., Jones Beach, Summer 1961). He was vocal arranger and musical director for *13 Daughters* (54 St. Th., N.Y.C., Mar. 2, 1961); *Kean* (Bway Th., Nov. 2, 1961); musical director for the pre-Bway tryout of *La Belle*, which closed out of town (opened Shubert, Philadelphia, Pa., Aug. 13, 1962; closed there, Aug. 25, 1962); a concert engagement by Eddie Fisher (Winter Garden, N.Y.C., Oct. 2, 1962); *Pal Joey* (NY City Ctr., May 29, 1963); the Civic Light Opera Assn. production of *Zenda* (opened Curran, San Francisco, Aug. 9, 1963; closed Pasadena Civic Aud., Calif., Nov. 22, 1963); took over as musical director during the run of *Foxy* (Ziegfeld, N.Y.C., Feb. 16, 1964); and joined (June 1964) as musical director, *110 in the Shade* (Broadhurst, Oct. 24, 1963; and national tour, 1964–65).

He was musical director and vocal arranger for *I Had a Ball* (Martin Beck Th., N.Y.C., Dec. 15, 1964); musical director and orchestra conductor for the revival of *Kiss Me, Kate* (N.Y. City Ctr., May 12, 1965); musical director for the revival of *Oklahoma!* (N.Y. City Ctr., Dec. 15, 1965); the revival of *Where's Charley?* (N.Y. City Ctr., May 25, 1966); *Funny Girl* (Coconut Grove Playhouse, Miami, Fla., Mar. 14, 1967; Parker Playhouse, Fort Lauderdale, Fla., Apr. 3, 1967); and *On a Clear Day You Can See Forever* (Parker Playhouse, Fort Lauderdale, Fla., Apr. 10, 1967; Coconut Grove Playhouse, Miami, Fla., Apr. 18, 1967).

Awards. Mr. Davenport was nominated for the Antoinette Perry (Tony) Awards for his musical direction of *13 Daughters* (1961) and *Kean* (1961).

DAVID, CLIFFORD. Actor. b. June 30, 1933, Toledo, Ohio, to Farris and Lillian (Abdow) David. Grad. Woodward H.S., Toledo, 1948; attended Toledo Univ., 1948. Studied at Mannes Music Sch., 1951; Actors' Studio, N.Y.C. (member 1959–to date). Member of AEA; SAG; AFTRA.

Theatre. Mr. David made his professional debut as the Captain in *Volpone* (Mutual Th., Boston, Mass., June 1959); his N.Y.C. debut as Scipio in *Caligula* (54th St. Th., Feb. 16, 1960); and played the title role in *Epitaph for George Dillon* (Dodge, Princeton, N.J., June 30, 1961).

He appeared as Hank in *Wildcat* (Alvin, N.Y.C., Dec. 16, 1961); Pasquale in *The Aspern Papers* (Playhouse, Feb. 7, 1962); Antipholus in *Boys from Syracuse* (Th. Four, Apr. 16, 1963); Wango in *The Umbrella* (Festival of Two Worlds, Caio Melliso Th., Spoleto, It., June 1962); was Laertes in *Hamlet* (Delacorte Th., N.Y.C., June 16, 1964; Playhouse-in-the-Park, Philadelphia, Pa., July 13–18, 1964); Dauber and Professor Trixie in *The Cradle Will Rock* (Th. Four, N.Y.C., Nov. 11, 1964); Edward Moncrief in *On a Clear Day You Can See Forever* (Mark Hellinger Th., Oct. 17, 1965); Brother Locke in *A Joyful Noise* (Mark Hellinger Th., Dec. 15, 1966); appeared in *Camino Real* (Mark Taper Forum, Los Angeles, Calif., Aug. 21, 1968); was Edward Rutledge in *1776* (46 St. Th., N.Y.C., Mar. 16, 1969); Lord Byron in *Camino Real* (Vivian Beaumont Th., Jan. 8, 1970); and Aegisthus in *Agamemnon* (McCarter Th., Princeton, N.J., Oct. 26, 1972).

Films. Mr. David was in *Invitation to a Gunfighter* (UA, 1964) and *The Party's Over* (Allied Artists, 1966).

Television. Mr. David played Manuel in *The Bridge of San Luis Rey* (Dupont Show, CBS, Jan. 1959); Walter in *Quiet Place* (Kraft Television Th., Feb. 1959); Laertes in *Hamlet* (CBS, June 17, 1964); and was in *Night of Fire* (Decoy, CBS, Dec. 6, 1964).

Recreation. Painting, piano.

DAVID, HAL. Lyricist. b. May 25, 1921, Brooklyn, N.Y. Married 1947 to Anne Rauchmann; two sons. Member ASCAP. Address: Elm Drive, East Hills, Roslyn, NY 11576.

Much of Mr. David's work as lyricist has been done in collaboration with the composer Burt Bacharach, whose entry in this volume supplements the following account.

Theatre. Mr. David wrote the lyrics for *Promises, Promises* (Sam. S. Shubert Th., Dec. 1, 1968) and *Brainchild* (opened Forrest Th., Philadelphia, Pa., Mar. 25, 1974; closed there Apr. 6, 1974).

Films. Mr. David wrote lyrics for songs in *Lost Horizon* (Col., 1973) and a number of other films.

Published Works. Mr. David wrote lyrics for "The Four Winds and the Seven Seas" (1949). He and Burt Bacharach began collaborating in 1957 with the songs "Magic Moments" and "The Story of My Life." Many of Mr. David's lyrics are included in *What the World Needs Now and Other Love Lyrics* (1968) and *The Bacharach-David Song Book* (1970).

Awards. *Promises, Promises* was nominated (1969) for an Antoinette Perry (Tony) Award as best musical. Mr. David and Burt Bacharach shared an Academy (Oscar) Award for "Raindrops Keep Fallin' on My Head," named (1970) as best song in a motion picture.

DAVID, MACK. Composer, lyricist, author. b. July 4, 1912, New York City. Grad. Cornell Univ.; attended St. John's Univ. Law Sch. Member of ASCAP.

Theatre. Mr. David wrote *Rain, Rain Go Away*. He wrote some of the lyrics for the revues *Gilbert Becaud on Broadway* (Longacre, N.Y.C., Oct. 31, 1966) and *Gilbert Becaud Sings Love* (Cort, Oct. 6, 1968) and, with Leonard Adelson, wrote lyrics for *Molly* (Alvin Th., Nov. 1, 1973).

Films. Mr. David contributed material to *Cinderella* (RKO, 1949); *At War with the Army* (Par., 1950); *Sailor Beware* (Par., 1951); *Alice in Wonderland* (RKO, 1951); *Jumping Jacks* (Par., 1952); *Glory Alley* (MGM, 1952); *The Hanging Tree* (WB, 1959); *Walk on the Wild Side* (Col., 1962); *It's a Mad, Mad, Mad, Mad World* (UA, 1963); *Hush. . .Hush, Sweet Charlotte* (20th-Fox, 1965); *Cat Ballou* (Col., 1965); *Hawaii* (UA, 1966); and *The Way West* (UA, 1967).

Published Works. Mr. David's songs include: "Bibbidi Bobbidi Boo," "So This Is Love," "I Don't Care If the Sun Don't Shine," "Candy," "Sunflower," "Chi-Baba, Chi-Baba," "Lili Marlene," "Take Me," "Spellbound," and "The Same Time, the Same Place, Tomorrow Night.".

DAVID, THAYER. Actor. b. Mar. 4, 1927, Medford, Mass. Grad. Harvard Univ., 1948.

Theatre. Mr. David, a founding member (1948) of the Brattle Th., Cambridge, Mass., first appeared on Bway as Sir Tunbelly Clumsey in the Brattle production of *The Relapse* (Morosco, Nov. 22, 1950). His subsequent roles included Grumio in *The Taming of the Shrew* (NY City Ctr., Apr. 25, 1951); Petulant in *The Way of the World* (Cherry Lane, Oct. 2, 1954); the Duke of Cornwall in *King Lear* (NY City Ctr., Jan. 12, 1956); Gollup in *Mister Johnson* (Martin Beck Th., Mar. 29, 1956); and the Inquisitor in *Saint Joan* (Phoenix, Apr. 11, 1956).

He played Dr. Wilhelm Steidl in *Protective Custody* (Ambassador, Dec. 28, 1956); the title role in *Oscar Wilde* (41 St. Th., Apr. 25, 1957); Tiberius in *The Golden Six* (York Playhouse, Oct. 25, 1958); joined the cast of *A Man for All Seasons* after it had opened (ANTA Th., Nov. 22, 1961); was the Pubkeeper in *Andorra* (Biltmore, Feb. 9, 1963); and joined the cast of *Baker Street* after the opening (Broadway Th., Feb. 16, 1965). He also played Miguel Estete in *The Royal Hunt of the Sun* (ANTA Th., Oct. 26, 1965); appeared with the National Rep. Th. (Belasco Th.) as Sorin in *The Seagull* (Apr. 5, 1964), Danforth in *The Crucible* (Apr. 6, 1964), and Messerschnann in *Ring Round the Moon* (on tour); and was Henning in *Those That Play the Clowns* (ANTA Th., Nov. 24, 1966).

Mr. David was Rusty Trawler in *Breakfast at Tiffany's* (previews: closed Majestic, Dec. 14, 1966); appeared in *The Sorrows of Frederick* (Mark Taper Forum, Los Angeles, Calif., June 23, 1967); *The Bench* (Gramercy Arts, Mar. 4, 1968); played Serebryakov in *Uncle Vanya* (Roundabout Th., Jan. 24, 1971); Sir Dymock Blackburn in *The Jockey Club Stakes* (Cort, Jan. 24, 1973); and was in *The Dogs of Pavlov* (Cubiculo, May 2, 1974).

Films. Mr. David's films include *A Time to Love and a Time to Die* (UA, 1958); *Journey to the Center of the Earth* (20th-Fox, 1959); *The Story of Ruth* (20th-Fox, 1962); *Little Big Man* (Natl. Gen., 1970); *House of Dark Shadows* (1970); *Mother's Day* (1973); and *Save the Tiger* (1973).

Television. Mr. David was on the daytime series Dark Shadows for three years; has appeared on Wild, Wild West (CBS); Trials of O'Brien (CBS); and Eternal Light (NBC); and was in *Lamp at Midnight* (Hallmark Hall of Fame, NBC, Apr. 27, 1966) and *The Crucible* (Drama Special, CBS, May 4, 1967).

DAVIDSON, GORDON. Director. b. about 1934, Brooklyn, N.Y., to Jo and Alice Davidson. Father, college professor. Educ. Cornell Univ.; Western Reserve Univ., M.A. Married; one son, one daughter.

Theatre. In 1958, Mr. Davidson began his work in the theatre as an apprentice stage manager at the American Shakespeare Festival, Stratford, Conn. In N.Y.C., he was a co-producer of *Borak* (Martinique, Dec. 13, 1960); production stage manager for Phoenix Theatre productions of *Next Time I'll Sing to You* (Phoenix, Nov. 27, 1963) and *Too Much Johnson* (Phoenix, Jan. 15, 1964); and he was stage manager for one season of the Martha Graham Dance Co.

He was managing director (1964–66) of the Theater Group, Univ. of California, Los Angeles, where he staged *The Deputy* (Schoenberg Hall, Aug. 13, 1965) and *Candide* (Schoenberg Hall, July 12, 1966). In 1966, he became artistic director of the Mark Taper Forum, Los Angeles (Calif.) Music Ctr., where plays he staged included *The Devils* (Apr. 14, 1967), *Who's Happy Now?* (Nov. 3, 1967), *In the Matter of J. Robert Oppenheimer* (May 24, 1968), which later opened in N.Y.C. (Vivian Beaumont Th., Mar. 6, 1969), *Murderous Angels* (Feb. 5, 1970), *Rosebloom* (Nov. 5, 1970), *Trial of the Catonsville Nine* (June 17, 1971), which later moved to N.Y.C. (Good Shepherd-Faith Ch., Feb. 7, 1971; Lyceum Th., May 31, 1971); *Henry IV, Part 1* (Oct. 26, 1972), *Hamlet* (Mar. 14, 1974), *Savages* (Aug. 15, 1974), and *And Where She Stops Nobody Knows* (Apr. 2, 1976).

In addition, Mr. Davidson, with Edward Parone, established the New Theatre for Now Workshop at the Mark Taper Forum for staging new and experimental plays; and Mr. Davidson staged Leonard Bernstein's *Mass* (premiere, Kennedy Ctr., Washington, D.C., Sept. 8, 1971; Mark Taper Forum, Jan. 4, 1973). In 1973, Mr. Davidson was named a consultant for the repertory theatre of the Denver (Colo.) Ctr. of the Performing Arts.

Awards. The New Theatre for Now, directed by Mr. Davidson, and Edward Parone, received (1970) a Margo Jones Award. Mr. Davidson also received a *Village Voice* Off-Bway (Obie) Award (1971) for distinguished direction for *The Trial of the Catonsville Nine*, as well as an Antoinette Perry (Tony) Award nomination (1972) for the same, and a Los Angeles Drama Critics Circle Award (1975) for direction of *Savages*. .

DAVIDSON, RICHARD. Lawyer. b. Richard Ralph Davidson, May 27, 1918, Los Angeles, Calif., to Milton Lincoln and Marion (Lamont) Davidson. Father, manufacturer. Grad. Groton Sch., Mass. (cum laude) 1937, Harvard Univ., A.B. 1941; attended Univ. of Michigan (Horace H. Rackham Grad. School of Arts and Sciences), 1946–47; Grad. New York Univ. School of Law, LLB. 1957. Married Apr. 11, 1947, to Elizabeth Kellermann; two sons, one daughter. Served USNR, 1941–46; rank, Lt. Comdr.; awarded Legion of Merit (US); Croix de Guerre with Gold Star (France); six battle stars. Member of Assn. of the Bar of N.Y.C.; Hasty Pudding Institute of 1770 (Harvard); Spee Club (Harvard); Harvard Club of N.Y.C.; the Coffee House Club; The Century Assn. Address: (home) 165 E. 94th St., New York, NY

10028, tel. (212) LE 4-1106; (bus.) c/o Paul, Weiss, Rifkind, Wharton and Garrison, 345 Park Ave., New York, NY 10022.

Theatre. Mr. Davidson has been a director and secretary of the New Dramatists, Inc. (1961–to date) and of Theatre Development Fund, Inc. (1967–68). He is also assistant secretary of Theatre Incorporated (Phoenix Th., 1960–to date); assistant secretary of the Inst. for Advanced Studies in the Theatre Arts (IASTA, 1959–to date); assistant secretary of Ballet Theatre Foundation, Inc. (American Ballet Theatre, 1960–62); and an officer or director of various other corporations engaged in entertainment activities.

With David Lowe, he produced *The Enchanted* (Lyceum Th., N.Y.C., Jan. 18, 1950).

Films. Mr. Davidson was employed by United World Films, Inc. (Universal Pictures Co.), producing and selling television shows (1947–49). He produced and sold television shows for the Souvaine Co. and participated in the motion picture distribution activities of Souvaine Selective Pictures Corp. (1950–53); and was eastern representative of Western Lithograph Co. (1953–54).

Other Activities. Since receiving his law degree in 1957, he has practiced law largely in the entertainment and publishing fields, first as an associate and then as a partner of Paul, Weiss, Rifkind, Wharton and Garrison.

Recreation. Swimming, sailing, fishing, birdwatching, chess.

DAVIS, ARIEL RUAL. Inventor of theatrical lighting equipment. b. Feb. 14, 1912, Provo, Utah, to Rual D. and Mary (Kitchen) Davis. Father, millwright. Grad. Provo H.S., 1931; Brigham Young Univ., B.S. (physics) 1936. Married Mar. 27, 1941, to Dorothy Jean Harding; two sons. Served USN, 1943–45; rank, Chief Electrician's Mate. Member of Illuminating Engineering Soc.; Natl. Comm. on Stage Lighting; International Solar Engineering Society; Society of Manufacturing Engineers; ATA. Address: (home) 3476 Fleetwood Dr., Salt Lake City, UT 84109, tel. (801) 277-4140; (bus.) Rural Industries, Inc., P.O. Box 9099, Salt Lake City, UT 84109, tel. (801) 272-4225.

Mr. Davis has developed over sixty patents in the field of theatre lighting control. Since 1947 he has been president of his own organizations: Ariel Davis Mfg. Co. (1947–64) and now Rual Industries, manufacturers of ARIEL DAVIS(tm) patch panels, switchboards, and stage lighting equipment. He was a consultant on stage lighting technique at Brigham Young Univ. with T. Earl Pardoe (1932–40); with Lowell Lees at the Univ. of Utah (1947–64); and with Harold Hansen (1957–64).

Awards. Mr. Davis received a certificate of recognition from the Utah Engineering Council for developments and service in stage lighting and dimmer controls (1961). Brigham Young University presented him with the Franklin S. Harris Fine Arts Award (1970) for his unique contribution in one or more of the fields of art, music, drama, or speech.

Recreation. Fishing, inventing, cooking.

DAVIS, BETTE. Actress. b. Ruth Elizabeth Davis, Apr. 5, 1908, Lowell, Mass., to Harlow Morrell and Ruth Elizabeth (Favor) Davis. Father, patent attorney. Attended public school, N.Y.C., Newton (Mass.) H.S., East Orange, N.J.; grad. Cushing Acad. Studied dance with Roshanara, at Mariarden, Peterborough, N.H., Summer c. 1924; at the John Murray Anderson Sch. of the Th. (scholarship), N.Y.C., studied with Martha Graham (dance), Michael Mordkin, Robert Bell, George Currie and John Murray Anderson; also studied with Robert Milton. Married Aug. 18, 1932, to Harmon O. Nelson, Jr., band leader (marr. dis. 1937); married Dec. 31, 1941, to Arthur Farnsworth (dec. 1943); married 1944 to William Grant Sherry, artist (marr. dis. 1950); one daughter; married July 28, 1950, to Gary Merrill, actor, (marr. dis. 1960); one son, one daughter. During WW II co-founded the Hollywood Canteen. Member of SAG; AEA; AFTRA; AMPAS (pres., 1941). Address: Westport, CT 06880.

Theatre. Miss Davis appeared in a student production of *The Famous Mrs. Fair* (John Murray Anderson Sch. of the Th., N.Y.C.); subsequently made her professional debut in a small role in a stock production of *Broadway* (Lyceum Th., Rochester, N.Y., one week); was a resident ingenue for a season in Rochester (Temple Th.); in summer stock, was an usher at the Cape Playhouse, (Dennis, Mass.), but was cast at the ingenue lead in the final production of the season, *Mr. Pim Passes By,* and returned the following two seasons as company ingenue.

She made her N.Y.C. debut in the role of Floy Jennings in *The Earth Between* (Provincetown Playhouse, Mar. 5, 1929), subsequently toured as Hedvig in *The Wild Duck* (1929); appeared as Elaine Bumpstead in *Broken Dishes* (Ritz, Nov. 5, 1929); Bam in *Solid South* (Lyceum, Oct. 14, 1930).

She appeared in the revue *Two's Company* (Alvin, Dec. 15, 1952); toured the US with Gary Merrill in a stage reading of *The World of Carl Sandburg* (1959–60) and, with Leif Erikson, performed in the program on Bway (Henry Miller Th., Sept. 14, 1960); played Maxine Faulk in *The Night of the Iguana* (Royale, Dec. 28, 1961); and played the title role in the pre-Bway tryout of *Miss Moffat* (opened Shubert Th., Philadelphia, Pa., Oct. 7, 1974; closed there Oct. 18, 1974).

Films. Miss Davis made her debut as Laura in *Bad Sister* (U, 1931); followed by Margaret in *Seed* (U, 1931); Janet in *Waterloo Bridge* (U, 1931); the Girl Friend in *Way Back Home* (RKO, 1932); Peggy in *The Menace* (Col., 1932); Peggy in *Hell's House* (Capital, 1932); Grace in *The Man Who Played God* (WB, 1932); Dallas O'Hare in *So Big* (WB, 1932); Malbro in *The Rich Are Always with Us* (1st Natl., 1932); Kay in *The Dark Horse* (1st Natl., 1932); Madge in *Cabin in the Cotton* (1st Natl., 1932); Ruth in *Three on a Match* (1st Natl., 1932); Fay in *20,000 Years in Sing Sing* (1st Natl., 1933); Alabama in *Parachute Jumper* (WB, 1933); Jenny in *The Working Man* (WB, 1933); Helen Bauer in *Ex-Lady* (WB, 1933); Norma in *Bureau of Missing Persons* (1st Natl., 1933); Lynn in *Fashions of 1934* (1st Natl., 1934); Norma in *The Big Shakedown* (WB-1st Natl., 1934); Joan in *Jimmy the Gent* (WB, 1934); Arlene in *Fog Over Frisco* (1st Natl., 1934); and Mildred in *Of Human Bondage* (RKO, 1934).

She was Patricia Berkeley in *Housewife* (WB, 1934); Marie Roark in *Bordertown* (WB, 1935); Miriam Brady in *Girl from 10th Avenue* (1st Natl., 1935); Ellen Garfield in *Front Page Woman* (WB, 1935); Julie Gardner in *Special Agent* (WB, 1935); Joyce Heath in *Dangerous* (WB, 1935); Gabrielle Maple in *The Petrified Forest* (WB, 1936); Daisy Appleby in *The Golden Arrow* (WB-1st Natl., 1936); Valerie Purvis in *Satan Met a Lady* (WB, 1936); Mary in *Marked Woman* (WB, 1937); Fluff in *Kid Galahad* (WB, 1937); Joyce Arden in *It's Love I'm After* (WB, 1937); Mary Donnell in *That Certain Woman* (WB, 1937); Julie in *Jezebel* (WB, 1938); Louise Elliott in *The Sisters* (WB, 1938); Judith Traherne in *Dark Victory* (WB, 1939); Carlotta in *Juraez* (WB, 1939); Charlotte Lovell in *The Old Maid* (WB, 1939); Queen Elizabeth in *The Private Lives of Elizabeth and Essex* (WB, 1939); Henriette Desportes in *All This and Heaven Too* (WB, 1940); Leslie Crosbie in *The Letter* (WB, 1940); Maggie Peterson in *The Great Lie* (WB, 1941); Joan Winfield in *The Bride Came C.O.D.* (WB, 1941); Regina Hubbard Giddens in *The Little Foxes* (RKO, 1941); Maggie Cutler in *The Man Who Came to Dinner* (WB, 1941); Stanley Timberlake in *In This Our Life* (WB, 1942); Charlotte Vale in *Now, Voyager* (WB, 1942); Sara Muller in *Watch on the Rhine* (WB, 1943); and she sang "They're Either Too Old or Too Young" in *Thank Your Lucky Stars* (WB, 1943).

She played Katherine Marlow in *Old Acquaintance* (WB, 1943); Fanny Trellis in *Mr. Skeffington* (WB, 1944); a Hollywood Canteen Hostess in *Hollywood Canteen* (WB, 1944); Miss Moffat in *The Corn Is Green* (WB, 1945); both Kate and Patricia Bosworth in *A Stolen Life* (WB, 1946); Christine Radcliffe in *Deception* (WB, 1946); Susan Grieve in *Winter Meeting* (WB, 1948); Linda Gilman in *June Bride* (WB, 1948); Rosa Moline in *Beyond the Forest* (WB, 1949); Margo Channing in *All About Eve* (20th-Fox, 1950); Joyce Ramsey in *Payment on Demand* (RKO, 1951); Janet Frobisher in *Another Man's Poison* (UA, 1952); a Bedridden Cripple in *Phone Call from a Stranger* (20th-Fox, 1952); Margaret Elliott in *The Star* (20th-Fox, 1953); Queen Elizabeth in *The Virgin Queen* (20th-Fox, 1955); Alice Hall in *Storm Center* (Col., 1956); Aggie Hurley in *The Catered Affair* (MGM, 1956); Catherine the Great in *John Paul Jones* (WB, 1959); the Countess in *The Scapegoat* (MGM, 1959); Apple Annie in *Pocketful of Miracles* (UA, 1961); Jane Hudson in *What Ever Happened to Baby Jane?* (WB, 1962); both Edith Phillips and Margaret de Lorca in *Dead Ringer* (WB, 1964); Dino's Mother in *The Empty Canvas* (Embassy, 1964); and Mrs. Gerald Hayden in *Where Love Has Gone* (Par., 1964).

Among her later films are *The Night of the Iguana* (MGM, 1964); *Hush . . Hush, Sweet Charlotte* (20th-Fox, 1965); *The Nanny* (20th-Fox, 1965); *The Anniversary* (20th-Fox, 1968); *Connecting Rooms* (London Screen, 1969); and *Bunny O'Hare* (Amer. Inter., 1971).

Television and Radio. On radio, Miss Davis has performed on the Th. Guild of the Air, Lux Radio Th., Texaco Star Th., and the Screen Actors' Guild Th.

Television programs on which she appeared include *The Cold Touch* (GE Th., CBS, 1958); *Out There—Darkness* (Alfred Hitchcock Th., CBS, 1959); Wagon Train (NBC, 1959, 1961); Perry Mason (CBS, 1963); Gunsmoke (CBS, 1966); *The Movie Crazy Years* (NET Playhouse, PBS, Feb. 1971); *Madame Sin* (ABC, 1972); The Tonight Show (NBC, 1972); *The Judge and Jake Wyler* (NBC, 1972); *Hello Mother, Goodbye* (NBC, 1973); and the Dick Cavett Show (ABC, 1974). She was co-host, with George Segal, on *Warner Brothers' Movies—A Fifty Year Salute* (NBC, Dec. 1973).

Concerts. Miss Davis appeared in person and on film in the presentation *Legendary Ladies of the Movies* (Town Hall, N.Y.C., Feb. 1973); Symphony Hall, Boston, Mass., 1974; Denver, Colo., Mar. 1974; Acad. of Music, Philadelphia, Pa., Apr. 1974), in which she also toured Australia and New Zealand (Concert Hall, Sydney Opera House, Mar. 1975) and the United Kingdom, where the program was billed as *Miss Bette Davis on Stage and Screen* (opened Fairfield Halls, Croyden, England, Oct. 1975).

Published Works. With Sanford Doty, she wrote her autobiography, *The Lonely Life* (1960), and she wrote commentary for Whitney Stine's *Mother Goddam* (1974).

Awards. Miss Davis received Academy (Oscar) Awards for her performances as Joyce Heath in *Dangerous* (1935) and as Julie in *Jezebel* (1938). In the "best actress" category, she has been nominated for her roles in *Dark Victory* (1939), *The Letter* (1940), *The Little Foxes* (1941), *Now, Voyager* (1942), *Mr. Skeffington* (1944), *All About Eve* (1951), *The Star* (1953), *What Ever Happened to Baby Jane?* (1962). As an actress who began her career in summer stock, Miss Davis received (1970) the Council of Stock Theatres' Straw Hat Award for achievement. In 1974, she received the Cecil B. De Mille Award for outstanding contributions to the entertainment field.

DAVIS, BUSTER. Vocal arranger, vocal director, composer, musical director. b. Carl Estes Davis, Jr., July 4, 1920, Johnstown, Pa. Grad. Mercersburg (Pa.) Acad., 1937; Princeton Univ., B.A. 1941. Studied conducting with Tibor Searly N.Y.C. Member of AFM, Local 820. Address: 152 W. 58th St., New York, NY 10019, tel. (212) 757-2113.

Theatre. Mr. Davis made his debut as the musical director of a USO production of *Anything Goes* (ETO, 1944–45); subsequently played Jerry Evans in *Burlesque* (Greenwich Playhouse, Conn., July 1946); was vocal director for *Barefoot Boy with Cheek* (Martin Beck Th., N.Y.C., Apr. 3, 1947); *High Button Shoes* (Century, Oct. 9, 1947); *Look, Ma, I'm Dancin'* (Adelphi, Jan. 29, 1948); assistant to Jerome Robbins, production director, for *That's the*

Ticket (opened Shubert, Philadelphia, Pa., Sept. 24, 1948; closed there Oct. 2, 1948); vocal director for *Heaven on Earth* (Century, Sept. 16, 1948); vocal arranger for *As the Girls Go* (Winter Garden, Nov. 13, 1948); vocal director for *Gentlemen Prefer Blondes* (Ziegfeld, Dec. 8, 1949); vocal arranger and vocal director for *Make a Wish* (Winter Garden, Apr. 18, 1951); and *Top Banana* (Winter Garden, Nov. 1, 1951).

He was vocal director for *Hazel Flagg* (Mark Hellinger Th., Feb. 11, 1953); musical and vocal director for *John Murray Anderson's Almanac* (Imperial, Dec. 10, 1953); *Phoenix '55* (Phoenix, Apr. 23, 1955); *Bells Are Ringing* (Shubert, Nov. 29, 1956); musical and vocal director for annual industrials *NAMSB Shows* (1957–64); vocal director for *Say, Darling* (ANTA, Apr. 3, 1958); *First Impressions* (Alvin, Mar. 19, 1959); *Do Re Mi* (St. James, Dec. 26, 1960); *Subways Are for Sleeping* (St. James, Dec. 27, 1961); musical and vocal director for *A Tribute to Oscar Hammerstein* (46 St. Th., 1962); and producer, with Arthur Whitelaw, Joan D'Inecco and Lawrence Baker, Jr., of *Best Foot Forward*, for which he was also musical and vocal director (Stage 73, Apr. 2, 1963).

Mr. Davis was vocal arranger and vocal director of *Funny Girl* (Winter Garden, Mar. 26, 1964); *Fade Out—Fade In* (Mark Hellinger Th., May 26, 1964); vocal arranger for *Something More!* (Eugene O'Neill Th., Nov. 10, 1964); *Fade Out—Fade In* (re-opened Mark Hellinger Th., Feb. 15, 1965); *Half a Sixpence* (Broadhurst, Apr. 25, 1965); wrote some of the songs for *People Is the Thing That the World Is Fullest Of* (Bil Baird Th., Feb. 20, 1967); was musical director and vocal arranger for *Hallelujah, Baby!* (Martin Beck Th., Apr. 26, 1967); *Darling of the Day* (George Abbott Th., Jan. 27, 1968); *Look to the Lilies* (Lunt-Fontanne Th., Mar. 29, 1970); *No, No, Nanette* (46 St. Th., Jan. 19, 1971); vocal arranger, with Hugh Martin, for *Lorelei* (Palace Th., Jan. 27, 1974); and musical director and vocal arranger for *Doctor Jazz* (Winter Garden, Mar. 19, 1975); and for *Rodgers & Hart* (Helen Hayes Th., May 13, 1975).

Films. He arranged the dances for *A Star Is Born* (WB, 1954).

Television. Mr. Davis made his television debut as a pianist and singer in Campus Corner (CBS, 1949); subsequently was vocal arranger and vocal director for *Hans Brinker* (Hallmark Hall of Fame, NBC, 1954); Standard Oil Jubilee (NBC, 1955); *Ruggles of Red Gap* (Producers Showcase, NBC, 1956); *Give My Regards to Broadway* (Producers Showcase, NBC, 1956); *Strawberry Blonde* (Producers Showcase, NBC, 1956; Texaco's Swing Into Spring (NBC, 1957); three Chevrolet Specials (NBC, 1957); Showstoppers (Chrysler, CBS, 1958); Art Carney's revue, Small World (CBS, 1958); *Salute to Ethel Barrymore* (Texaco Star Th., NBC, 1959); *Holiday, U.S.A.* (Texaco Star Th., NBC, 1959); the Garry Moore Show (CBS, 1959); Art Carney, V.I.P. (CBS, 1959); two Art Carney revues (CBS, 1960); Opening Night (General Foods Special, CBS, 1962); and the Bell Telephone Hour (NBC, 1961–64), for which, with Marshall Barer, he wrote the song "From the Barns of Maine to the Tents of California.".

Night Clubs. Mr. Davis has performed as a singer and pianist at Spivy's Roof (N.Y.C., 1943); and was musical director for Judy Garland's night club act at the Town and Country (Bklyn., N.Y., 1960).

Awards. Mr. Davis received the NATAS (Emmy) Award for vocal direction and orchestration of the Art Carney, V.I.P. Special (1960).

Recreation. Reading literary criticism.

DAVIS, DONALD. Actor, director, producer. b. Donald George Davis, Feb. 26, 1928, Newmarket, Ontario, Canada, to E. J. Davis, Jr., and Dorothy (Chilcott) Davis. Father, manufacturer. Grad. Newmarket Public Sch., Ontario, 1941; St. Andrew's Coll., Aurora, Ontario, 1946; Univ. of Toronto, B.A. 1950. Relatives in theatre: brother, Murray Davis, actor, producer; sister, Barbara Chilcotte, actress. Member of AEA (Canadian Advisory Committee, 1956–59; councilor, 1965–69); ACTRA; AFTRA; SAG.

Theatre. Mr. Davis made his stage debut as Sir Toby Belch in Josephine Barrington's Juveniles' production of *Twelfth Night* (Hart House Th., Toronto, Canada, Dec. 1, 1937); his professional debut as Henry Bevan in *The Barretts of Wimpole Street* (Woodstock Playhouse, N.Y., Summer 1947); and was a member of the chorus in the Dublin Gate Th. production of *The Old Lady Says No* (Royal Alexandra, Toronto, Canada, Autumn 1947).

In 1948, he founded and produced with his brother, Murray Davis, the Straw Hat Players, a summer stock company which toured the Muskaka Lake resort area in Ontario. With the company (1948–55), he played such roles as Papa in *Papa Is All*, Crocker-Harris in *The Browning Version*, Mr. Winslow in *The Winslow Boy*, and Sir Henry Harcourt Reilly in *The Cocktail Party*, and directed *Laura* and *French without Tears*.

He also co-produced two trans-Canadian tours of *The Drunkard* and a revue, *There Goes Yesterday* (1949–50); appeared in a comedy role in *The Wind and the Rain*, which toured southern Ontario (1950); played the title role in *Noah* and Claudius in *Hamlet* for the Canadian Repertory Th. (Ottowa, Canada, 1951).

He appeared in Great Britain (1950–53) with the Glasgow (Scotland) Citizens Th., the Bristol (England) Old Vic, and the Wilson Barrett Co. as Baptista in *The Taming of The Shrew*, in *The River Line*, Bassanio in *The Merchant of Venice*, and Joseph Surface in *The School for Scandal*.

In 1954, Mr. Davis founded and produced with his brother, Murray Davis, The Crest Th., Toronto, Ontario, a repertory company that presented 76 productions (1954–59), with Donald Davis appearing as Thomas A. Becket in *Murder in the Cathedral*, Malvolio in *Twelfth Night*, Creon in *Antigone*, Vershinin in *The Three Sisters*, in *Haste to the Wedding*, Jack the Skinner in *Jig for the Gypsy*, Mr. Stuart in *Hunting Stuart*, Angus McBane in *The Glass Cage*. He also directed *Bright Sun at Midnight* and *The Crest Revue*.

From 1954–56, as a member of the Stratford (Ontario) Shakespearean Festival Co., Mr. Davis succeeded James Mason as Angelo in *Measure for Measure*, appeared as Tiresias in *Oedipus Rex*, Marc Antony in *Julius Caesar*, Westmoreland in *Henry V*, and Pistol in *The Merry Wives of Windsor;* appeared with this company in the 1956 Edinburgh Festival, repeating his roles in *Oedipus Rex* and *Henry V*. He made his Bway debut as Agydas in the Stratford Shakespearean Festival production of *Tamburlaine the Great* (Winter Garden, Jan. 19, 1956).

He made his London debut, co-producing the Crest Th. production of *The Glass Cage*, in which he also played Angus McBane (Piccadilly, Apr. 26, 1957); and later toured Cambridge, Bournemouth, and Blackpool, England, and Edinburgh, Scotland.

Mr. Davis was the Narrator for the Stravinsky opera, *Oedipus Rex* (NY City Ctr., Sept. 24, 1959); appeared as Krapp in *Krapp's Last Tape* (Provincetown Playhouse, US premiere, Jan. 14, 1960); with the American Shakespeare Festival, played Orsino in *Twelfth Night* (Stratford, Conn., June 8, 1960), and Domitius Enobarbus in *Antony and Cleopatra* (July 31, 1960); appeared in *Roar Like a Dove* (Royal Poinciana Playhouse, Palm Beach, Fla., Feb. 1961); repeated the role of Krapp in *Krapp's Last Tape* (Arena Th., Washington, D.C., Apr. 1961); appeared with the American Shakespeare Festival, Stratford, Conn., playing Jaques in *As You Like It* (June 15, 1961), Duncan in *Macbeth* (June 16, 1961), and Achilles in *Troilus and Cressida* (July 23, 1961); played Gustav in *Creditors* (Mermaid, N.Y.C., Jan. 25, 1962), and with the Theatre Group Univ. of Calif. at Los Angeles, June, 1962); directed *Toy for the Clowns* for Richard Barr's Th. '62 Playwright Series (Cherry Lane, N.Y.C., Dec. 11, 1961); *Deathwatch* for Richard Barr's Festival of the Absurd (Cherry Lane, Feb. 25, 1962); and played the title role in *Becket* (Goodman Memorial Th., Chicago, Ill., Oct. 1962).

Mr. Davis played Sam 40 in *Photo Finish* (Brooks Atkinson Th., N.Y.C., Feb. 12, 1963); succeeded (July 10, 1963) Sheppard Strudwick as George in the matinee company of *Who's Afraid of Virginia Woolf?* (Billy Rose Th., Oct. 13, 1962) and succeeded (Jan. 13, 1964) Arthur Hill in the same role in the evening company. He played the title role in *Macbeth* (IASTA, N.Y.C., Apr. 26, 1964); Henry Macy in *The Ballad of the Sad Cafe* (Goodman Memorial Th., Chicago, Ill., Jan. 8, 1965); performed in *An Evening's Frost* (Mendelssohn Th., Ann Arbor, Mich., Feb. 8, 1965); and repeated his performance as George in *Who's Afraid of Virginia Woolf?* (Manitoba Th. Ctr., Winnipeg, Canada, Apr. 7, 1965).

He was Thomas Jefferson in *Brother to Dragons* (American Place Th., N.Y.C., June 2, 1965); David Bliss in *Hay Fever* (Bucks County Playhouse, New Hope, Pa., June 14, 1965); appeared again in *An Evening's Frost* (Th. de Lys, N.Y.C., Oct. 11, 1965); played the title role in *Agamemnon* and Apollo in *The Eumenides* in the Ypsilanti (Mich.) Greek Th. presentation of *The Oresteia* (June 28, 1966) and at the same theatre was Hoopoe in *The Birds* (June 29, 1966). He played Lord Essex in a revival of *Elizabeth the Queen* (NY City Ctr., Nov. 3, 1966); directed *The Imaginary Invalid* (Studio Arena Th., Buffalo, N.Y., Nov. 2, 1967); at the Springfield (Mass.) Th. Co. was Archie Rice in *The Entertainer* (Feb. 8, 1968) and James Tyrone in *Long Day's Journey into Night* (Apr. 4, 1968); and at the Studio Arena Th., Buffalo, N.Y., played Father in *The Death of Bessie Smith* and Daddy in *The American Dream* (Sept. 10, 1968), Peter in *The Zoo Story* and Krapp in *Krapp's Last Tape* (Sept. 17, 1968), repeating the latter two in N.Y.C. (Billy Rose Th., Oct. 9, 1968); and he played Henry II in *The Lion in Winter* (Studio Arena Th., Buffalo, N.Y., Oct. 31, 1968).

At the Stratford (Ontario) Festival, Mr. Davis appeared as Orgon in *Tartuffe* (Avon Th., Stratford, July 3, 1969); in *The Merchant of Venice* (Festival Th., Stratford, June 8, 1970); and as Judge Brack in *Hedda Gabler* (Festival Th., June 10, 1970). He also appeared in *The Sorrows of Frederick* (Mainstage, Vancouver, B.C., Canada, Nov. 12, 1971); directed *The Royal Family* (Shaw Festival, Niagara-on-the-Lake, Ontario, 1972); played Ezra Mannon in a revival of *Mourning Becomes Electra* (Circle in the Square/Joseph E. Levine Th., N.Y.C., Nov. 15, 1972); the title role in *Lear* (Yale Repertory Th., New Haven, Conn., Apr. 13, 1973); and was in *The Dybbuk* (Manitoba Th. Ctr., Main Stage, Winnipeg, Canada, Jan. 11, 1974).

Films. Mr. Davis played Tiresias in *Oedipus the King* (MPD, 1957) and Anthony Byrd in *Joy in the Morning* (MGM, 1965).

Television and Radio. From 1946–59, Mr. Davis appeared in Canada on such CBC radio programs as The Stage Series, CBC Wednesday Night, Buckingham Th., Ford Th., and CBC Schools Program.

On CBC-TV, he played on such programs as CBC Folio, CBC Festival, and General Motors Th., portraying Sir Henry Watton in *The Picture of Dorian Gray*, Young Marlow in a musical version of *She Stoops to Conquer* called *Gay Deceivers*, Alcibiades in *Socrates*, and Raleigh in *Elizabeth the Queen*. He made his London television debut as an FBI Agent in *I Made News* (BBC-TV, 1951); subsequently played in many other BBC-TV and radio programs, especially those involving American characters.

In the US, he appeared as Hector in *Tiger at the Gates* (Play of the Week, WNTA, Feb. 1960); King Henry in *Henry IV, Part 1* (Play of the Week, WNTA, Sept. 1960); in *Sound of Murder* (Play of the Week, WNTA, Feb. 1961); Socrates in *The Trial and Death of Socrates* (Robert Herridge Th., CBS, 1961); on The Defenders (CBS, 1962, 1963, 1965); The Nurses (CBS, 1962); as Abraham Lincoln in *A Season of War* (CBS Chronicle, 1963); on The Doctors and the Nurses (CBS, 1964); Look Up and Live (CBS, 1966); Mission: Impossible (CBS, 1966); The Eternal Light (NBC); The Catholic Hour (NBC); Camera Three (CBS); Lamp Unto My Feet (CBS); and Directions (ABC).

Awards. Mr. Davis received a *Village Voice*

Off-Bway (Obie) award in 1960 for his performance as Krapp in *Krapp's Last Tape.* .

Recreation. Eating, drinking, rusticating.

DAVIS, FITZROY. Actor, director, singer, writer, lecturer, critic, artist. b. Feb. 27, 1912, Evanston, Ill., to Frank Parker and Edith Amanda (Kelly) Davis. Father, patent lawyer. Grad. Phillips Exeter Acad., 1929; Williams Coll., A.B. (Phi Beta Kappa) 1933; Teachers Coll., Columbia Univ., M.A. 1961. Studied singing with Carolyn Lewis Reilly (1938–47), Helen Foots Calhoun (1956–58), Mina Haker (1959); acting with Lee Strasberg (1939–41), Wendell Phillips (1944–45); drawing and painting at the Evanston (Ill.) Acad. of Fine Arts and the Art Inst. of Chicago. Member of AEA (Credit Comm. of Credit Union, 1963–to date); AFTRA; ALA; ANTA; AETA; IASTA; Midland Authors of Chicago (secy., 1952–54). Address: 143 W. 74th St., New York, NY 10023, tel. (212) TR 3-6874.

Theatre. Mr. Davis first appeared on the stage as the Son in a school production of *Rip Van Winkle* (Miller Sch., Evanston, Ill., 1917). At Williams Coll. Little Th. (Williamstown, Mass., 1929–33), he played Butters in *A Thread of Scarlet;* Henry Apjohn in *How He Lied to Her Husband;* was assistant director of *Judge Lynch* and *The Jewel Merchants;* designed the sets for *The Anniversary;* played Adrian in *The Stepmother;* directed *The Twelve Pound Look, Half an Hour, The Coach to Heaven* and *The Liar;* and directed and played Suds in *The Potboiler.*

He made his professional debut as a walk-on in Romeo and Juliet (Grand Opera House, Chicago, Ill., Nov. 25, 1935); played a walk-on in Orson Welles' touring production of *Julius Caesar* (Erlanger, Chicago, Ill., Mar. 7, 1938); Wayne Fenton in *Skidding* (Red Barn, Westboro, Mass., June 1938); was assistant stage manager and played the Second Officer on the N.Y.C. Subway Circuit tour of *Idiot's Delight* (July 1936); appeared as a walk-on in *Good Hunting* (Hudson, N.Y.C., Nov. 21, 1938); was assistant stage manager for the Lunt-Fontanne repertory tour in *The Seagull, Amphitryon 38,* and *Idiot's Delight,* the latter in which he also played Rossi (Jan.–Apr. 1939).

Mr. Davis played Washington Irving in *Little Old New York* (Threshold Players, Glencoe, Ill., Feb. 29, 1941); Cyril Beverly in *Bird in Hand* (Drama Club, Winnetka, Ill., Apr. 22, 1941); Tommy Turner in *The Male Animal* (Deer Lark Th., Orwigsburg, Pa., June 23, 1941); and Otho in *It's a Wise Child,* Dr. Sterling in *The Ghost Train,* Tony Fox-Collier in *Spring Meeting,* and Tommy Turner in *The Male Animal* (Mountain Th., Braddocks Hts., Md., July–Aug. 1941).

He portrayed Sebastian Sanger in an ELT production of *Escape Me Never* (NY Public Library, 125th St. branch, N.Y.C., May 25, 1945); Alessandro in *The Firebrand* and Jerry Seymour in *Claudia* (Hunterdon Hills Playhouse, Jutland, N.J., July 1945); for ELT, directed, with Lee Furman, and played Trofimov in *The Cherry Orchard* (NY Public Library, 179th St. branch, N.Y.C., May 11, 1946), and produced, directed, and also played Judge Brack in *Hedda Gabler* (NY Public Library, Hudson Park branch, N.Y.C., May 27, 1947); played Carleton Fitzgerald in *Light Up the Sky* (Woman's Club, Evanston, Ill., Nov. 1950); directed *Come Back, Little Sheba* (Drama Club, Winnetka, Ill., Nov. 1950); produced a dramatic reading of Sartre's *The Devil and God* (Drama Club, River Forest, Ill., May 12, 1952); at the Wilmette (Ill.) Little Th. directed *Ring 'Round the Moon* (May 1953), and played Manningham in *Angel Street* (Feb. 1954).

Mr. Davis played Frank Elgin in *The Country Girl* (Star, Minneapolis, Minn., Apr. 20, 1955); Rev. Giles Aldus in *Saint's Day* (White Barn, Westport, Conn., Sept. 21, 1956); Owen Turner in *Light Up the Sky* (Fred Miller Memorial Th., Milwaukee, Wis., Dec. 2, 1957); Capt. Vere in *Billy Budd* (Goodman Memorial Th., Chicago, Ill., Oct. 31, 1958); the title role in *King Lear* (Teachers Coll. Drama Workshop, N.Y.C., Dec. 7, 1960); Vernyhora in *The Wedding* (IASTA, N.Y.C., Apr. 12, 1962); and King Peter in *Leonce and Lena* (IASTA, N.Y.C., May 28, 1962).

He has performed in song recitals at the Mina Hager Studio (N.Y.C., Apr. 13, 1960; May 20, 1962); and presented his one-man show, *An Actor Sings* (Judson Hall, Mar. 31, 1963; Mar. 1, 1964).

Films. Mr. Davis wrote dialogue (without credit) for *Song of Russia* (MGM, 1943), and dialogue (with credit) for *The Heat's On* (Col., 1943). From 1949–55, he appeared in a number of shorts produced by *Encyclopaedia Britannica* and Coronet Films (Chicago).

Television. He made his television debut as emcee of the series Adam vs. Eve, and appeared in his own 15-minute interview program, Backstage with Fitzroy Davis (WBKB, Chicago, Sept. 1946–Mar. 1947). He also appeared in *Split Level* (Studio One, CBS, Oct. 31, 1955), and *Oliver Twist* (Dupont Show of the Month, NBC, Dec. 4, 1959).

Other Activities. Mr. Davis was New York theatre critic for the Evanston (Ill.) *Daily News-Index* (1938–41) and *Townsfolk* magazine (Chicago, Ill., 1941–42); has lectured at the Drama Dept. of Northwestern Univ. School of Speech (1941); appeared in lecture tours (1944–46); was book reviewer on stage, screen, and television for the Chicago Sunday *Tribune* book section (1949–55); taught public speaking, voice, diction, and acting at St. John's Univ. (1961–62); and lectured at Williams Coll. (1962).

He is a professional painter and has had four one-man exhibits of his water-colors (1936, 1940, 1941, 1944).

Published Works. Mr. Davis wrote *Quicksilver,* a novel about people in the theatre (1942); contributed short stories to *Williams Quarterly;* articles to *The Christian Science Monitor, Theatre Arts* magazine; New York *Times* Sunday drama section, New York *Herald Tribune* Sunday drama section, *Players* magazine, *Williams Alumni Review, The Stage* (London), *Playbill, Vision,* and *The New Yorker.*

Awards. Mr. Davis received several literary prizes at Phillips Exeter Acad. (1929) and Williams Coll. (1933).

Recreation. Swimming, stamp collecting, extensive traveling in Europe.

DAVIS, JED H. Educator, director. b. Jed Horace Davis, Jr., July 31, 1921, Stillwater, Minn., to Jed H. and Meda Margarita (Culver) Davis. Father, accountant. Grad. Stillwater, Minn., 1939; attended Univ. of Minnesota, 1939–41; Utah State Agriculture Coll., 1942–43; grad. Univ. of Minnesota, B.A. 1947; M.A. 1949; Ph.D. 1958. Married Aug. 4, 1945, to Betty Jane Crosby; two sons, one daughter. Served US Army, 1942–46. Member of AETA (director of Contact Placement Service, 1959–61; bd. of dir., 1959–61, 1963–65; Time and Place Committee, 1961–63; Standing Committee on Appointments and Research, 1962–64; exec. committee, 1963–65; chmn., nominating committee, 1964; 2nd vice-pres., 1970; 1st vice-pres., 1971). AETA became ATA in 1972 with Mr. Davis as first president; he became a fellow of ATA in 1972 and is chairman, Commission on International Relations, 1973–75.

Mr. Davis belonged also to the Children's Th. Conf. of AETA (chmn., local arrangements committee, 1953–54; chmn., Region 6 Program Committee, 1960–61; chmn., Book Room, 1956–58; chmn., nominating committee, 1959; chmn., Research Committee, 1956–61; governing board, 1955–58; 1961–66; chmn., Time and Place Committee, 1961–63; chmn., regional council, 1961–63; chmn., membership, 1961–63; asst. dir., 1961–63; dir., 1963–65); Secondary School Th. Conference of AETA; American Community Th. Assn. of AETA; Children's Th. Foundation (bd. of trustees, treas.); National Theatre Conference (NTC), 1967–to date; American Assn. of Univ. Professors; Natl. Collegiate Players; Phi Gamma Delta. Address: (home) 2602 Louisiana, Lawrence, KS 66044, tel. (913) VI 3-8684; (bus.) Dept. of Speech and Drama, Univ. of Kansas, Lawrence, KS 66044, tel. (913) UN 4-3534.

Since 1965, Mr. Davis has been professor of speech and drama at the Univ. of Kansas, where he became a member of the faculty in 1960 (assist. prof., 1960–62; assoc. prof., 1962–65). He became director of the Univ. of Kansas Th. in 1967, having served in the summer of 1963 as acting director, and he has served as lighting designer and director for student productions. Previously, he was instructor of speech and drama (1947–50), and assistant professor of speech and drama (1950–53) at Macalester Coll., where he also designed scenery and lighting, and directed student productions; was assistant professor of speech at Michigan State Univ. (1953–60), where he was also lighting and scenic designer for student productions; and at the Univ. of Kansas, he was manager-director of the theatre division of the Midwestern Music and Art Camp (1962–64).

In stock, he designed scenery and lighting at Old Log Th. (Excelsior, Minn., Summer 1948), for productions including *The Glass Menagerie, January Thaw, State of the Union, Petticoat Fever, George Washington Slept Here, Warrior's Husband, Milky Way, Front Page, Skylark, Double Door,* and *The Time of Your Life,* playing small roles in the latter two.

Television. Mr. Davis lectured on children's theatre for the Nebraska Educational Television Council for Higher Education in 1969.

Published Works. Mr. Davis is the author, with Mary Jane Larson Watkins, of *Children's Theatre: Play Production for the Child Audience* (1960); and has contributed articles on children's theatre to *Players* Magazine (1958), *Children's Theatre and Creative Dramatics* (1961), and *Educational Theatre Journal* (1961), *The Speech Teacher* (1962), *Modern Drama* (1963–67), *Theatre News* (1969), and *Encyclopedia Americana* (1973). He compiled and edited *A Directory of Children's Theatres in the United States* (1968).

Recreation. Carpentry, swimming.

DAVIS, LUTHER. Producer, playwright. b. Luther Berryhill Davis, Aug. 29, 1916, New York City, to Charles Thomas and Henriette (Roesler) Davis. Father, manufacturer. Grad. Culver Military Acad., Ind., 1934; Yale Univ., B.A. 1938. Studied under Walter Prichard Eaton, Yale Univ. Married Nov. 3, 1943, to Dorothy de Milhau (marr. dis. July 1960); two daughters. Served USAAF, 1942–45; rank, Maj., awarded Air Medal. Member of Dramatists Guild; SWG. Address: Luther Davis Productions, Inc., 190 N. Canon Dr., Beverly Hills, CA 90210, tel. (213) 273-0463.

Theatre. Mr. Davis' first play, *Lucky Dip,* was produced at Culver Military Academy (1934); and his first Bway play was *Kiss Them for Me* (Belasco, Mar. 20, 1945), an adaptation of Frederic Wakeman's novel *Shore Leave.* Mr. Davis was librettist, with Charles Lederer, of the musical adaptation of *Kismet* (Ziegfeld, Dec. 3, 1953); Stoll, London, Apr. 20, 1955).

Films. He wrote the screenplays for *The Hucksters* (MGM, 1947); *B. F.'s Daughter* (MGM, 1948); *Black Hand* (MGM, 1950); *A Lion Is in the Streets* (WB, 1953); *A Gift of Love* (20th-Fox, 1958); *Holiday for Lovers* (20th-Fox, 1959); *Wonders of Aladdin* (Joseph Levine, 1959); *Lady in a Cage* (Luther Davis Productions, Inc., 1963), which he also produced for Par.; and *Across 110th Street* (UA, 1973).

Television. Mr. Davis' first television assignment was writer for the Schlitz Playhouse of Stars series (CBS, 1953); subsequently wrote for Ford Startime (NBC, 1960); the Bus Stop series (ABC, 1961); wrote and produced for the Kraft Suspense Th. (NBC, 1963–64); wrote teleplays for ABC movies-of-the-week *Daughter of the Mind* (1971) and *The Old Man Who Cried Wolf* (1972); wrote pilots for Run for Your Life series, Double Life of Henry Phyfe series, Silent Force series; produced *The People Trap,* a television special for ABC Stage '67.

Awards. *Kismet* received an Antoinette Perry (Tony) Award (1954). Mr. Davis also received the Mystery Writers of America award (Edgar) and Writers Guild awards.

DAVIS, OSSIE. Actor, director, producer, playwright. b. Dec. 18, 1917, Cogdell, Ga., to Kince Charles and Laura (Cooper) Davis. Father, railway construction engineer. Grad. Center H.S., Waycross, Ga.; attended Howard Univ., 1935–38. Married Dec. 9, 1948, to Ruby Dee (née Ruby Ann Wallace), actress; one son, two daughters. Served US Army, 1942–45, surgical technician. Member of AEA; SAG; AFTRA; CORE. Address: 44 Cortlandt Ave., New Rochelle, NY 10801, tel. (914) BE 5-6867.

Pre-Theatre. Shipping clerk.

Theatre. Mr. Davis made his debut as a member of Rose McClendon's Players, appearing in *Joy Exceeding Glory* (Harlem, N.Y.C., 1941) and other plays. While serving in the US Army, he wrote and directed *Goldbrickers of 1944* (Liberia, Africa).

He made his Bway debut in the title role of *Jeb* (Martin Beck Th., N.Y.C., Feb. 21, 1946); subsequently played Rudolf in the national tour of *Anna Lucasta* (1947); John Hay in *The Washington Years* (Amer. Negro Th. Playhouse, N.Y.C., Mar. 11, 1948); played Trem in *The Leading Lady* (National N.Y.C., Oct. 18, 1948); Stewart in *The Smile of the World* (Lyceum, Jan. 12, 1949); Lonnie Thompson in *Stevedore* (Equity Library Th., Feb. 1949); Jacques in *The Wisteria Trees* (Martin Beck Th., Mar. 29, 1950); Jo in *The Royal Family* (NY City Ctr., Jan. 10, 1951); Gabriel in *The Green Pastures* (Bway Th., Mar. 15, 1951); Al in *Remains To Be Seen* (Morosco, Oct. 3, 1951); wrote *Alice in Wonder* (Elks Community Th., Sept. 15, 1952); played Dr. Joseph Clay in *Touchstone* (Music Box, Feb. 3, 1953); succeeded Elwood Thompson as a Lieutenant in *No Time for Sergeants* (Alvin, Oct. 20, 1955); played Jacques in *The Wisteria Trees* (NY City Ctr., Feb. 2, 1955); and Cicero in *Jamaica* (Imperial, Oct. 31, 1957). He succeeded (Aug. 31, 1959) Sidney Poitier in the role of Walter Lee Younger in *A Raisin in the Sun* (Ethel Barrymore Th., Mar. 11, 1959; and on tour).

Mr. Davis wrote *Purlie Victorious*, in which he played the title role (Cort, Sept. 28, 1961); was producer, with Bernard Waltzer and Page Productions, of *Ballad for Bimshire*, in which he played Sir Radio (Mayfair, Oct. 15, 1963); for the Ira Aldridge Society, wrote *Curtain Call, Mr. Aldridge, Sir.* (Henry Hudson Hotel, May 26, 1963).

Mr. Davis toured with his wife, Ruby Dee, in *A Treasury of Negro World Writing* (1964); directed and appeared with Ruby Dee in *The Talking Skull* (White Barn Th., Westport, Conn., Aug. 1, 1965); played Johannes in *The Zulu and the Zayda* (Cort, N.Y.C., Nov. 10, 1965); and, with Philip Rose and Peter Udell, wrote the book for the musical *Purlie*, (Broadway Th., Mar. 15, 1970), based on his play, *Purlie Victorious*.

Films. Mr. Davis made his debut in *No Way Out* (20th-Fox, 1950); appeared in *Fourteen Hours* (20th-Fox, 1951); *The Joe Louis Story* (UA, 1953); *The Cardinal* (Col., 1963); as Rev. Purlie in *Gone Are the Days* (Hammer Bros., 1963), for which he wrote the screenplay (based on his play, *Purlie Victorious*); appeared in *Shock Treatment* (20th-Fox, 1964); *The Hill* (MGM, 1965); *A Man Called Adam* (Embassy, 1966); *The Scalphunters* (UA, 1968); *Sam Whiskey* (UA, 1969); *Slaves* (Cont., 1969); directed and co-wrote, with Arnold Perl, *Cotton Comes to Harlem* (UA, 1970); spoke the eulogy and appeared in *Malcolm X* (WB, 1972); directed *Black Girl* (Cinerama, 1972); directed *Kongi's Harvest* (Tam Communications, 1973); directed *Gordon's War* (20th-Fox, 1973); and appeared in *Let's Do It Again* (WB, 1975).

Television. Mr. Davis has appeared in *The Green Pastures* (Showtime, USA, Ind., Apr. 7, 1951); in the title role of *Emperor Jones* (Kraft Television Th., NBC, Feb. 24, 1955); in *Seven Times Monday* (Play of the Week, WNTA, Oct. 31, 1960); appeared frequently on The Defenders series (CBS); on The Sheriff (ABC); Night Gallery (NBC); The Name of the Game (NBC); NYPD (ABC); The Outsider (NBC); Run For Your Life (NBC); Look Up and Live (CBS); Slattery's People (CBS); Great Adventure (CBS); Doctors/Nurses (CBS); Eternal Light (NBC); gave readings, with Ruby Dee, on The Creative Person series (Educ., Apr. 20, 1965); was host of The Negro People series (Educ., 1965–66, 1966–67), and wrote the episode, *Slavery* (Oct. 26, 1965), in which he also appeared; appeared in *Tell It on the Mountain* (CBS Special, Dec. 24, 1965); The Fugitive (ABC); 12 O'Clock High (ABC); Car 54, Where Are You? (CBS); *Teacher, Teacher* (Hallmark Hall of Fame, NBC, Feb. 5, 1969); Bonanza (NBC); and various talk shows.

Mr. Davis hosted, with his wife, The Ossie Davis and Ruby Dee Story Hour (Natl. Black Network, 1974, 1975); wrote, directed and appeared in *Today is Ours* (CBS, Feb. 23, 1974); and has written scripts for the East Side/West Side series (*School Teacher*, CBS, 1963) and The Eleventh Hour series (NBC).

Other Activities. Mr. Davis is a frequent contributor of stories, essays and articles to *Freedomways* Magazine; *New Writing by American Negroes; Harlem, USA:* and other periodicals.

Discography. His recorded work includes *The Poetry of Langston Hughes* (Caedmon, 1969) and Mr. Hughes' *Simple Stories* (Caedmon).

Awards. Mr. Davis was nominated for a NATAS (Emmy) Award for his role in *Teacher, Teacher* (1969).

He received the First Mississippi Freedom Democratic Party Citation (1965); The Frederick Douglass Award of the NY Urban League for "distinguished leadership toward equal opportunity" (May 7, 1970); and the Paul Robeson Citation of AEA for "outstanding creative contributions both in the performing arts and in society at large" (June 6, 1975).

DAVIS, SAMMY, JR.

DAVIS, SAMMY, JR. Actor, singer, dancer. b. Dec. 12, 1925, New York City, to Sammy and Elvina (Sanchez) Davis. Parents, entertainers. Studied dancing with Bill Robinson. Married 1958 to Loray White (marr. dis. 1959); married Nov. 13, 1960, to May Britt, actress (marr. dis. 1967); two sons, one daughter; May 11, 1970, to Altovise Gore. Served US Army Special Services, 1943–45; rank, Pvt. Relatives in theatre: father, Sammy Davis, Sr., entertainer; uncle, Will Mastin, entertainer. Member of AEA; SAG; AGVA; AFTRA; Negro Actors Guild; The Friars; Urban League; NAACP.

Theatre. Mr. Davis made his stage debut at one as a surprise walk-on in his parents' vaudeville act (Columbus, Ohio, 1928); his professional debut at three as a member of the Mastin Company vaudeville act (Orpheum Circuit, 1930); performed with his uncle and father (Will Mastin Trio, 1930–45, which became "Will Mastin Trio starring Sammy Davis, Jr.," 1946).

With the US Army Special Services, he wrote, produced and directed camp shows; played Charlie Welch in *Mr. Wonderful* (Bway Th., N.Y.C., Mar. 22, 1956); and Joe Wellington in *Golden Boy* (Majestic, Oct. 20, 1964; Palladium, London, England, Apr. 23, 1968); appeared in his one-man show *Sammy* (Uris Th., N.Y.C., Apr. 23, 1974); and in concert for the benefit of the Harlem-Dowling Children's Service, N.Y.C. (Carnegie Hall, July 7, 1976).

Films. Mr. Davis made his film debut in *Rufus Jones for President* (1928); subsequently appeared in *Anna Lucasta* (UA, 1958); *Porgy and Bess* (Col., 1959); *Sergeants 3* (UA, 1959); *Pepe* (Col., 1960); *Ocean's Eleven* (WB, 1960); *Johnny Cool* (UA, 1963); *Convicts Four* (Allied, 1963); *Threepenny Opera* (Embassy, 1964); *Robin and the Seven Hoods* (RKO, 1964); *A Man Called Adam* (Embassy, 1966); *Salt and Pepper* (UA, 1968; *Sweet Charity* (U, 1969); *One More Time* (UA, 1970); and *Save the Children* (Par., 1973).

Television. Mr. Davis appeared on GE Th. (CBS) in *Auf Wiedersehen* (Oct. 1958) and *Memory in White* (Jan. 1961); Lawman (ABC, 1961); Frontier Circus (CBS, 1962); Hennessey (CBS, 1962); *The Legend* (Dick Powell Th., NBC, 1962); Ben Casey (ABC, 1963); Patty Duke Show (ABC, 1965); Wild, Wild West (CBS, 1966); I Dream of Jeannie (NBC, 1967); Mod Squad (ABC, 1969, 1970); Name of the Game (NBC, 1970); *The Trackers* (ABC, 1971); *GE Presents Sammy* (NBC, Nov. 1973); and on his own talk and variety series, Sammy & Company (NBC, Apr. 1975).

Night Clubs. Mr. Davis appeared with the Will Mastin Trio at El Rancho (Las Vegas, Nev., 1953). Other night clubs where he entertained include Bill Miller's Riviera (Fort Lee, N.J., 1949); Ciro's (Hollywood, Calif., 1956); Copacabana (N.Y.C.); Eden Rock Hotel (Miami, Fla.); Sands Hotel (Las Vegas, Nev.); Deauville Hotel (Miami, Fla.); the Latin Casino (Camden, N.J.) Grosvenor House (London, England, July 1974); Nanuet (N.J.) Theatre Go-Round (Nov. 1974); and Cafe Cristal, Diplomat Hotel (Hollywood, Fla., Feb. 1975).

Published Works. Mr. Davis wrote his autobiography, *Yes I Can* (1965).

Discography. Among Mr. Davis's recordings are *Hey There* (Decca); *What Kind of Fool Am I?* (Decca); *As Long as She Needs Me* (Decca); *Belts Best of Broadway* (Reprise); *At Town Hall* (Decca); *Porgy and Bess* (Decca); *Mr. Entertainment* (Decca); *Shelter of Your Arms* (Reprise); *The Sounds of '66* (Reprise, 1967); and *Sammy Davis, Jr., at the Cocoanut Grove* (Reprise, 1968).

Awards. In 1974, Mr. Davis received a special citation from the National Academy of Television Arts and Sciences for his contributions to television entertainment.

Recreation. Collecting guns of the Old West, horseback riding, studying history of the Old West.

DAWN, HAZEL. Actress. b. Hazel Dawn Tout, Mar. 23, 1894, Ogden City, Utah, to Edwin R. and Sara Elizabeth (Emmett) Tout. Father, contractor, builder. Grad. H.S., London, England; studied violin with Thomas Morris, at Royal Coll. of Music, London, 1910; singing with Nellie Rowe. Married Sept. 26, 1927, to Edward Gruelle; one son, one daughter. Relatives in theatre: sister, Margaret Romaine, singer; sister, Nannie Tout, singer; sister, Eleanor Dawn, actress. Member of AEA; AFTRA. Address: (home) 15 Stuyvesant Oval, New York, NY 10019, tel. (212) OR 7-6018; (bus.) J. Walter Thompson, 420 Lexington Ave., New York, NY 10017, tel. (212) MU 6-7000.

Theatre. Miss Dawn made her theatrical debut in *Dear Little Denmark* (Prince of Wales Th., London, England, Sept. 1, 1909); subsequently appeared in *The Dollar Princess* (Daly's, Sept. 25, 1909); *Balkan Princess* (Prince of Wales Th., 1910); made her N.Y.C. debut in *Pink Lady* (New Amsterdam, Mar. 13, 1911), appeared in the London production (Globe, Apr. 11, 1912), and toured the US (1913); appeared in *Little Cafe* (New Amsterdam, N.Y.C., Nov. 10, 1913); *The Debutante* (Knickerbocker, Dec. 7, 1914); *Century Girl* (Century Opera House, Nov. 6, 1916); played Mable in *Up in Mable's Room* (Eltinge, Jan. 15, 1919); Gertie Darling in *Getting Gertie's Garter* (Republic, Aug. 1, 1921); Gloria Graham in *The Demi-Virgin* (Times Sq., Oct. 18, 1921), and on tour (1922); and played a season of stock in Buffalo, N.Y. (1923), and Washington, D.C. (1925).

She has appeared in the revues *Nifties* (Fulton, N.Y.C., Sept. 25, 1923); *Keep Cool* (Morosco, May 22, 1924); *Ziegfeld Follies* (tour, 1926); *Great Temptations* (Winter Garden, N.Y.C., May 18, 1926); and as Mabel Fenton in *Wonder Boy* (Alvin, Oct. 23, 1931).

Films. Miss Dawn first appeared before the camera in *One of Our Girls* (Famous Players, 1914) and soon followed this with performances in other Famous Players films: *Niobe, The Sales Lady, My Lady Incog, Under Cover, Feud Girl, Heart of Jennifer, Clarissa,* and *Devotion.* She appeared also in *The Lone Wolf* (Selznick Pictures, 1917).

Television. She appeared on Armstrong Circle Th. (CBS, 1947) and Hollywood Screen Test (CBS, 1947).

Recreation. Painting, reading, walking.

DAWSON, MARK. Actor, singer. b. Mark Dawson, Jr., Mar. 23, 1920, Philadelphia, Pa., to Mark and Elsie (Nice) Dawson. Father, salesman. Grad. Upper Darby (Pa.) H.S., 1936; Philadelphia Conservatory of Music, degree in music, 1939. Studied voice with Clyde Dengler, seven years; Douglas Stanley, six years. Married May 17, 1941, to Constance McGann (marr. dis. Dec. 29, 1948); married Jan. 17, 1949, to Aleen Buchanan. Served WW II, USMCR, 1943; Fleet Marine Force H.Q., seventeen months; rank Cpl. Member of AEA; SAG; AFTRA; AGVA; The Lambs (chmn., Jr. Admissions Comm., 1950–57).

Theatre. Mr. Dawson made his debut as vocal soloist with the Philadelphia Orchestra (Philadelphia Acad. of Music, Dec. 1939); subsequently played Ajax in *By Jupiter* (Shubert, N.Y.C., June 9, 1942); Buddy McGraw in the pre-Bway tryout of *Dancing in the Streets* (opened Shubert, Boston, Mass., Mar. 23, 1943; closed there 1943); Prince Franz in *Sweethearts* (Shubert, N.Y.C., Jan. 21, 1947); Oggle in *High Button Shoes* (Century, Oct. 9, 1947); Vince in *Great To Be Alive* (Winter Garden, Mar. 23, 1950); Bob in *Me and Juliet* (Majestic, Apr. 28, 1953); Lt. Bill in *Ankles Aweigh* (Mark Hellinger Th., Apr. 18, 1955); Larry in *New Girl in Town* (46 St. Th., May 14, 1957); Floyd in *Fiorello!* (Broadhurst, Nov. 23, 1959); Mr. Enright in the pre-Bway tryout of *Matter of Position* (opened Walnut, Philadelphia, Pa., Sept. 29, 1962; closed there Oct. 13, 1962); George in *Riot Act* (Lyceum, N.Y.C., Mar. 7, 1963); and succeeded (May 31, 1972) Simon Oakland as Phil in *Celia* on the program *Twigs* (Broadhurst, Nov. 14, 1971).

Television. Mr. Dawson has appeared on Martin Kane (NBC, 1951); Omnibus (CBS); The Nurses (CBS); and Witness (CBS).

Night Clubs. Mr. Dawson was emcee and soloist in his own night club act (Hotel Mt. Royale, Normandie Roof, Montreal, Canada, 1941).

Awards. He won the Federation of Pennsylvania Women's Club Award (1937), and the *Theatre World* Award (1948).

Recreation. Sailing, collecting contemporary paintings, restoring old homes, gardening, bird-watching.

DAYKARHANOVA, TAMARA. Actress, teacher of acting. b. Jan. 14, 1892, Moscow, Russia, to Christopher and Agnes Daykarhanov. Father, Physician. Grad. Moscow Univ., B.A. Studied with Dantchenko; privately with Stanislavsky; and at Moscow Art Th. Sch. Married Apr. 1919, to Sergius A. Vassiliev, civil and aeronautical engineer (dec. Mar. 11, 1962). Member of AEA; AFTRA; SAG; Cosmopolitan Club (N.Y.C.). Address: 155 W. Hudson Ave., Englewood, NJ 07631.

Theatre. In 1935, Mme. Daykarhanova founded the Tamara Daykarhanova Sch. for the Stage in N.Y.C., of which she is the director. She also headed the Drama Dept. at Finch Junior Coll.; and was professor in the Drama Dept. of Barnard Coll.

Mme. Daykarhanova was formerly a member of the Moscow Art Th.

She made her N.Y.C. debut as Maria Josefa in *The House of Bernarda Alba* (ANTA Th., Jan. 7, 1951); followed by the role of Granny in *The Emperor's Clothes* (Ethel Barrymore Th., Feb. 9, 1953); and appeared in *Bullfight* (Th. de Lys, Jan. 1954).

She has also appeared in summer productions, including the role of the Dowager Empress in *Anastasia.*

Films. Miss Daykarhanova played Mrs. Cliadakis in *Andy* (U, 1965); and the Mother-in-Law in *A Dream of Kings* (Natl. Gen., 1969).

Awards. The Tamara Daykarhanova Company, with a training program for young actors, has been founded and named for her by a group of former students.

Recreation. Gardening, cooking, writing.

De BANZIE, BRENDA. Actress. b. Manchester, England to Edward Thomas and Dorothy (Lancaster) de Banzie. Father, musician. Educated privately and at St. Paul's Sch., Manchester. Studied as a child at Lawrence Tiller Sch. of Dancing, 1928; voice with Frank Mullins, 1933. Married to Rupert Marsh. Member of British AEA; SAG. Address: The Pent House, Norton House, Rottingdean, Sussex, England.

Theatre. Miss de Banzie first appeared with repertory groups in Manchester, Bradford, Birmingham, and Nottingham, subsequently toured as Sally in *The Two Mrs. Carrolls,* Olivia in *Night Must Fall,* and Ann in *Man and Superman* (1936); appeared in repertory in Harrogate (1939–40); and toured in the revue *1066 and All That* (1941).

She made her London debut as Mme. La Duchesse de Vilandelle in *Du Barry Was a Lady* (His Majesty's Th., Oct. 22, 1942); toured as Mabel in *Three Men on a Horse* (1943); played Diane in *The Quaker Girl* (Stoll, Feb. 8, 1945); Beattie and the Young Woman in *A Grim Fairy Tale* (Embassy, July 30, 1946); Jessie Dill in *Venus Observed* (St. James's, Jan. 18, 1950); the Mother in *Point of Departure* (Lyric, Hammersmith, Nov. 1, 1950); Freda Jefferies in *Murder Mistaken* (Ambassadors', Nov. 4, 1952); and Theresa in *Hippo Dancing* (Olympia, Dublin, Ireland, Feb. 1954).

She first appeared in N.Y.C. as Annabelle Logan in *Speaking of a Murder* (Royale, Dec. 19, 1956); subsequently played Phoebe Rice in *The Entertainer* (Royal Court, London, Apr. 10, 1957; Royale N.Y.C., Feb 12, 1958).

Films. Miss de Banzie appeared in *A Song To Remember* (Col., 1945); as Mrs. Rogers in *Long Dark Hall* (Brit. Lion, 1951); Mrs. Collins in *A Day to Remember* (Gaumont, 1953); Maggie in *Hobson's Choice* (UA, 1954); in *The Purple Plain* (UA, 1955); as Stella Bentley in *As Long As They're Happy* (Gaumont, 1955); Ruby in *A Kid For Two Farthings* (Ind., 1955); Mme. Ballu in *House of Secrets* (Rank, 1956; released in the US as *Triple Deception*); in *The Man Who Knew Too Much* (Par., 1956); *Doctor at Sea* (Rep., 1956); *Too Many Crooks* (Lopert, 1959; as Aggie in *Room 43* (Brit. Lion, 1959; released in the US as *Passport to Shame);* Nellie Lumsden in *The Thirty-Nine Steps* (Rank, 1959); Phoebe Rice in *The Entertainer* (Continental, 1960); in *Come September* (U, 1961); as Nell Palmer in *Flame in the Streets* (Rank, 1961); Mrs. Cartwright in *The Mark* (20th-Fox, 1961); Gladys Pudney in *A Pair of Briefs* (Rank, 1962); in *The Pink Panther* (UA, 1964); and as Mrs. Innes-Hook in *Pretty Polly* (Rank, 1967).

Television and Radio. She appeared in *Edward My Son* (BBC); *Ladies of the Corridor* (Granada); *Don Quixote Go Home* (ATV); and in several continuing series: Out of the Unknown (BBC), Ten Commandments (Yorkshire TV), Somerset Maugham series (BBC), Creative Impulse (BBC), and Love Story (ATV). She appeared also in a number of plays for BBC radio.

Discography. Miss de Banzie read the part of Mrs. Hardcastle on the recording of *She Stoops to Conquer.* .

Awards. She received the Clarence Derwent Award for her performance as Freda Jefferies in *Murder Mistaken* (1953); the Academy (Oscar) Award nomination for her performance as Maggie in *Hobson's Choice* (1954); the *Evening Standard* Drama Award as best actress of the year for her performance as Phoebe Rice in *The Entertainer* (1958).

DEBUSKEY, MERLE. Press representative. b. Basil Merle Debuskey, Mar. 2, 1923, Baltimore, Md., to Robert M. and Freda B. (Blaustein) Debuskey. Father, insurance broker. Grad. City Coll. H.S., Baltimore, 1940; attended Univ. of Virginia, 1940–43; grad. Johns Hopkins Univ., B.A. (English lit.) 1947; received a certificate of excellency in public relations from the New Sch. for Social Research, 1948. Married July 20, 1958, to Christine Karner, dancer. Served USN, PTO, 1941–46, awarded five combat stars, citation for valor; rank, Lt. Member of ATPAM (chairman, NY Press Agents chapter, 1956–63; vice-pres. 1964–67; pres., 1967–to date). Address: (home) 411 West End Ave., New York, NY tel. (212) 724-9588; (bus.) 300 W. 55 St., New York, NY tel. (212) 247-6634.

Pre-Theatre. Sports reporter, worked on bottling line at whiskey distillery, office cleaner, catcher on paper box cutting press.

Theatre. Mr. Debuskey joined a cooperative theatre company, The Interplayers, which presented four plays at the Provincetown Playhouse (N.Y.C., Summer 1948); and was a member of the group which disassociated itself from The Interplayers to form Off-Broadway, Inc., presenting *Yes Is for a Very Young Man* (Cherry Lane Th., N.Y.C., June 6, 1949), *The Bourgeois Gentleman* (Cherry Lane, Aug. 1949), and *The Silver Whistle* (Carnegie Hall Playhouse, Oct. 1949).

He was apprentice press representative for *Regina* (46 St. Th., Oct. 31, 1949); served as an apprentice press representative three seasons, and became a member of ATPAM (Jan. 1950).

During 1950 to 1952, he was press representative for Theatre-by-the-Sea (Matunuck, R.I.).

In 1951, he was press representative for *The Rose Tattoo, Flahooley, Buy Me a Blue Ribbon,* and *Paint Your Wagon;* in 1952, *One Bright Day,* and *Shuffle Along;* in 1953, *The World of Sholom Aleichem, The Crucible,* and the tour of *A Certain Joy;* in 1954, *Abie's Irish Rose, Mrs. Patterson, Anastasia, The Trouble-makers,* and *The Saint of Bleecker Street;* in 1955, *Plain and Fancy, A View from the Bridge, The Diary of Anne Frank,* and *Inherit the Wind;* in 1957, the tour of *Maiden Voyage,* for *Tevya and His Daughters, Look Homeward, Angel,* and the NY Shakespeare Festival production of *As You Like It;* in 1958, for the NY Shakespeare Festival productions of *Richard III* and *Othello,* for *The Trial of Dmitri Karamazov, Cloud 7, Chapparral,* and *Curtains Up.*

In 1959, he was press representative for A Raisin in the Sun, Mistress and Maidens, the NY Shakespeare Festival production of *Julius Caesar,* for *Summer of the 17th Doll,* and *Marching Song* in 1960, *Semi-Detached,* the tour of *One for the Dame,* the NY Shakespeare Festival productions of *Henry V, Measure for Measure,* and *The Taming of the Shrew,* for *The Wall,* and *The Good Soup;* in 1961, *How To Succeed in Business without Really Trying,* and its national tour (1963), for *Come Blow Your Horn,* and *There Is a Play Tonight;* in 1962, *Little Me,* the double-bill of *The Portrait of the Artist as Young Man* and *The Barroom Monks,* the NY Shakespeare Festival productions of *King Lear, The Tempest* and *The Merchant of Venice,* and for *The Pinter Plays;* in 1963, the cabaret show, *To the Water Tower,* for *Nobody Loves an Albatross, Antony and Cleopatra, On an Open-Roof, The Heroine, The Riot Act, Semi-Detached, Twelfth Night,* and *Mr. Simian.*

In 1964, he was press representative for Abraham Cochrane, Cafe Crown, A Midsummer Night's Dream, Traveller without Luggage, The Sign in Sidney Brustein's Window, The Owl and the Pussycat, A View from Under the Bridge, The Puppet Theatre of Don Cristobal, and *The Shoemaker's Prodigious Wife;* in 1965, for *Peterpat, And Things That Go Bump in the Night, Cambridge Circus, The Decline and Fall of the Entire World as Seen Through the Eyes of Cole Porter revisited,* for the NY Shakespeare Festival Mobile Th. productions of *Henry V, The Taming of the Shrew,* and *Romeo and Juliet;* for *The Royal Hunt of the Sun, The Zulu and the Zayda,* and *The White Devil.*

In 1966, he was press representative for Nathan Weinstein, Mystic, Connecticut, for *Phèdre, 6 from La Mama, The Butterfly Dream,* the NY Shakespeare Festival Mobile Th. production of *Macbeth,* for *The Investigation, Walking Happy,* and *Eh?;* in 1967, for NY Shakespeare Festival productions of *The Comedy of Errors, King John,* and *Titus Andronicus* and for the NY Shakespeare Festival Mobile Th. production of *Volpone,* for *The Ninety-Day Mistress, Drums in the Night, Hallelujah, Baby!, What Do You Really Know About Your Husband?, A Midsummer Night's Dream,* and *Iphigenia in Aulis.*

In 1968, he was press representative for Lovers and Other Strangers, The Goodbye People, NY Shakespeare Festival productions of *Henry IV, Part I* and *Henry IV, Part 2,* for *Before You Go, Portrait of a Queen,* and for the NY Shakespeare Festival (Public Th.) production of *Hair;* in 1969, he was press representative for *Does a Tiger Wear a Necktie?, Come Summer, Trumpets of the Lord,* the NY Shakespeare Festival (Public Th.) production *Invitation to a Beheading,* for *Little Murders, Philosophy in the Boudoir, Love Is a Time of Day, No Place To Be Somebody, From the Second City,* for the NY Shakespeare Festival (Public Th.) production *Sambo,* and for *Seven Days of Mourning.*

In 1970, he was press representative for *Purlie*, for the NY Shakespeare Festival *Peer Gynt, The White House Murder Case*, for *Billy Noname, Chicago 70*, for NY Shakespeare Festival productions of *The Chronicles of King Henry VI, Part 1, The Chronicles of King Henry VI, Part 2*, and *Richard III*, for a NY Shakespeare Festival Mobile Th. revival of *Sambo*, and for the NY Shakespeare Festival (Public Th.) production *The Happiness Cage;* in 1971, for *No, No, Nanette, The House of Blue Leaves, Jesus Christ Superstar, Ain't Supposed To Die a Natural Death*, for *Unlikely Heroes: Three Philip Roth Stories, Two Gentlemen of Verona, Dance wi' Me, The Last Analysis, Sticks and Bones*, and *Iphigenia*.

In 1972, he was press representative for That Championship Season, Mourning Becomes Electra, Joan, NY Shakespeare Festival productions of *Hamlet, Ti-Jean and His Brothers*, and *Much Ado about Nothing*, for *Andrew, His First Step*, and *The Corner*, for *Coney Island Cycle*, and for *Wedding Band;* in 1973, for *Here Are Ladies, Purlie, Uncle Vanya, The Waltz of the Toreadors*, for NY Shakespeare Festival (Lincoln Ctr.) productions of *In the Boom Boom Room, Troilus and Cressida*, and *The Au Pair Man*, for *The Good Doctor*, for NY Shakespeare Festival productions of *As You Like It, King Lear*, and *Two Gentlemen of Verona*, and for NY Shakespeare Festival (Public Th.) productions of *Lotta, More Than You Deserve*, and *Barbary Shore*.

In 1974, he was press representative for NY Shakespeare Festival (Lincoln Ctr.) productions of The Tempest, What the Wine-Sellers Buy, The Dance of Death, and *Short Eyes*, for *Thieves*, for NY Shakespeare Festival (Public Th.) productions *Les Femmes Noires* and *The Killdeer*, and for *Scapino, The National Health*, The NY Shakespeare Festival (Lincoln Ctr.) production *Mert & Phil*, for the pre-Bway tryout of *Miss Moffat*, for NY Shakespeare Festival productions of *Pericles, Prince of Tyre* and *The Merry Wives of Windsor*, for NY Shakespeare Festival (Public Th.) productions *Where Do We Go from Here?, The Last Days of British Honduras*, and *In the Boom Boom Room*, and for the NY Shakespeare Festival (Lincoln Ctr.) production of *Richard III*.

In 1975, he was press representative for NY Shakespeare Festival (Lincoln Ctr.) productions of Black Picture Show, A Doll's House, and *Little Black Sheep*, for *Shenandoah*, for the double bill *Hughie* and *Duet*, for NY Shakespeare Festival (Public Th.) productions of *Kid Champion, Fishing*, and *A Chorus Line*, and for the NY Shakespeare Festival (Lincoln Ctr.) revival of *A Midsummer Night's Dream* and production of *The Taking of Miss Janie.* .

Films. Mr. Debuskey was press representative for *Rome II O'Clock* (TFC, 1953); *Justice Is Done* (BST, 1953); *We Are All Murderers* Kingsley, 1957); *The Crucible* (Kingsley, 1958); *Orders To Kill* (UMP, 1958); *Spartacus* (U, 1960); *A Midsummer Night's Dream* (Showcorporation, 1962); and the Russian film process, Kinopanorama.

Recreation. Tennis, sketching, writing.

DEE, RUBY. Actress, writer. b. Ruby Ann Wallace, Oct. 27, Cleveland, Ohio, to Marshall Edward and Emma (Benson) Wallace. Father, cook, waiter; mother, teacher. Grad. Hunter H.S., N.Y.C.; Hunter Coll., B.A. Studied acting at American Negro Theatre Sch., 1941–44; Morris Carnovsky, 1958–60; Actors Workshop; Paul Mann; Lloyd Richards. Studied voice with Mr. Duke; Prof. Jarahal. Married Dec. 9, 1948, to Ossie Davis; one son, two daughters. Member of AEA; SAG; AFTRA; NAACP; CORE; Negro American Labor Council; Hunter Alumnae Assn. of Artists for Freedom; Student Non-Violent Coordinating Comm.; Southern Christian Leadership Conference; The Ladies Auxiliary to Brotherhood of Sleeping Car Porters (honorary).

Theatre. Miss Dee's first stage appearances in N.Y.C. were in American Negro Theatre productions (all at Library Th.) of *Natural Man* (May 7, 1941), *Starlight* (June 3, 1942), and *Three's a Family* (Nov. 18, 1943). She was understudy to Wini Johnson as Ruth in Howard Rigsby and Dorothy Heyward's *South Pacific* (Cort, Dec. 29, 1943); played Ruth in American Negro Theatre's *Walk Hard* (Library Th., Nov. 30, 1944); was Libby in *Jeb* (Martin Beck Th., Feb. 21, 1946); took over (June 1946) the title role in *Anna Lucasta* (Mansfield Th., Aug. 30, 1944) and toured in the part; played Marcy in *A Long Way from Home* (Maxine Elliott's Th., N.Y.C., Feb. 8, 1948); Evelyn in *Smile of the World* (Lyceum, Jan. 12, 1949); a Defending Angel in *Bontche Schweig* on the program *The World of Sholom Aleichem* (Barbizon-Plaza, May 1, 1953); Ruth Younger in *A Raisin in the Sun* (Ethel Barrymore Th., Mar. 11, 1959); and Lutiebelle Gussie Mae Jenkins in *Purlie Victorious* (Cort, Sept. 28, 1961).

At the American Shakespeare Festival, Stratford, Conn., she alternated with Patricia Hamilton as Katherina in *The Taming of the Shrew* (June 22, 1965) and played Cordelia in *King Lear* (June 23, 1965). She was in *The Talking Skull* (White Barn Th., Westport, Conn., Aug. 1, 1965); at the Ypsilanti (Mich.) Greek Theatre played Cassandra in *Agamemnon* (June 28, 1966) and Iris in *The Birds* (June 29, 1966); was Julia Augustine in *Wedding Band* (Lydia Mendelssohn Th., Ann Arbor, Mich., Dec. 7, 1966); Lena in *Boesman and Lena* (Circle in the Square, N.Y.C., June 22, 1970); repeated her performance as Julia Augustine in *The Wedding Band* (Public Th., Oct. 26, 1972); and was Gertrude to Sam Waterston's *Hamlet* (Delacorte Th., June 1975).

In addition to her performances in plays, Miss Dee has presented programs of readings on tour of the US with her husband.

Films. Miss Dee made her motion picture debut in *The Jackie Robinson Story* (Eagle-Lion, 1950). She was also in *No Way Out* (20th-Fox, 1950); *The Tall Target* (MGM, 1951); *Go, Man, Go!* (UA, 1954); *Edge of the City* (MGM, 1957); *St. Louis Blues* (Par., 1958); *Take a Giant Step* (UA, 1959); *Virgin Island* (Countryman Films, 1960); *A Raisin in the Sun* (Col., 1961); *The Balcony* (Continental, 1963); *Gone Are the Days* (Trans-Lux, 1963), re-released as *Purlie Victorious* (1964); *The Incident* (20th-Fox, 1967); and *Up Tight* (Par., 1968), for which she also collaborated on the script.

Television and Radio. Miss Dee was on the radio in the 1940s and later was on the program This Is Norah Drake (CBS, 1955).

Television programs on which she appeared include *Actor's Choice* (Camera Three, CBS, Oct. 1960); *Seven Times Monday* (Play of the Week, WNTA, Oct. 21, 1960); *Black Monday* (Play of the Week, WNTA, Jan. 1961); The Fugitive (ABC, 1963); *Go Down Moses* (The Great Adventure, CBS, 1963); *Express Stop to Lenox Ave.* (The Nurses, CBS, 1963); *No Hiding Place* (East Side/West Side, CBS, 1964); The Eternal Light (NBC, 1964); *Shakespeare in Love and War* (Repertory Th., Ind., 1965); The Defenders (CBS, 1965); *Slavery* (History of the Negro People, NET, 1965); *Neighbors* (Armchair Th., ABC-TV, Manchester, England, 1966): Peyton Place (ABC, 1968); *Deadlock* (NBC, 1969); *The Sheriff* (ABC, 1971); *To Be Young, Gifted and Black* (NET Playhouse, PBS, 1972); *The Ossie Davis and Ruby Dee Story Hour* (National Black Network, 1974–75); and Police Woman (NBC, 1975).

Night Clubs. With Mr. Davis, Miss Dee appeared in songs and readings at the Village Vanguard, N.Y.C. (July 1964).

Other Activities. Miss Dee has contributed her talents to benefits for civil rights workers and served on various civil rights committees.

Published Works. Miss Davis wrote *Child Glow and Other Poems* (1973). She participated with other black performers in a discussion published as *Voices of the Black Theatre* (1975).

Discography. With Ossie Davis, Miss Dee has recorded *The Poetry of Langston Hughes* (Caedmon).

Awards. Miss Dee and her husband received the Frederick Douglass Award of the Urban League in 1970, and in 1975 they were the recipients of Actors Equity's Paul Robeson Citation for their "outstanding creative contributions in the performing arts and in society at large." Operation PUSH gave Miss Dee its Martin Luther King, Jr., Award in 1972. For her performance in *Boesman and Lena*, Miss Dee received *Village Voice* off-Bway (Obie) and Drama Desk awards in 1971, and for her performance in *The Wedding Band* she received a Drama Desk Award in 1973.

Recreation. Painting, music, sewing.

DEEMS, MICKEY. Actor, comedian, writer. b. Marvin Damaszek, Apr. 22, 1925, Englewood, N.J., to Alfred H. and Goldie (Michaelson) Damaszek. Father, plumbing supplier. Attended Metropolitan Vocational H.S., N.Y.C., 1939–42. Married 1948 to Bonnie Abrams (marr. dis. 1951); married Oct. 16, 1960, to Gertrude Black, private secy. Served WW II, US Army, ETO; rank, Sgt.; awarded five Battle Stars; Purple Heart, with two clusters; Bronze Star. Member of AEA; AFTRA; SAG; AGVA; Canadian Writers Guild.

Pre-Theatre. Musician, dance band arranger.

Theatre. Mr. Deems first performed as a comedian in the Henry Street Settlement Amateur Contest (1936); his first professional engagement was as social director, comedian, and writer for variety shows (Grand View Hotel, Fallsburg, N.Y., 1941); and at Tamiment, Pa. (Summer 1949).

He made his Bway debut in *Alive and Kicking* (Winter Garden Th., Jan. 17, 1950); and appeared in vaudeville (1951–56) at the Radio City Music Hall, Palace, Paramount, and Roxy Theatres (N.Y.C.); performed as a comedian and served as a writer in *Kaleidoscope* (Provincetown Playhouse, June 13, 1957); played Signalman Taylor in *Golden Fleecing* (Henry Miller's Th., Oct. 15, 1959); and appeared in *Vintage '60* (Brooks Atkinson Th., Sept. 12, 1960).

In stock, he appeared as Boris in *Can-Can*, a Gangster in *Kiss Me, Kate*, Panisse in *Fanny*, and Appelgate in *Damn Yankees* (North Shore Music Th., Beverly, Mass., Summer 1959); and Silas in *Naughty Marietta*, the Sheriff in *Bloomer Girl*, and Captain St. James in *Oh, Captain* at the same theatre (Summer 1960).

He appeared as Gogo in *Waiting for Godot* (Charles Th., Boston, Mass., Dec. 1960); Moon in *Anything Goes* (Orpheum, N.Y.C., May 15, 1962); and was understudy to Sid Caesar and appeared as Pinchley, Jr., the Defense Lawyer, German Officer, Production assistant, and Yulnick in *Little Me* (Lunt-Fontanne, Nov. 17, 1962).

He played several roles in *Little Me* (Packard Music Hall, Warren, Ohio, Aug. 25, 1964); replaced Eddie Foy, Jr., during rehearsals, as Mazocha, the Maitre d'Hotel, and Willis in *Royal Flush* (pre-Bway tour, Jan. 1965); played Pseudolus in *A Funny Thing Happened on the Way to the Forum* (North Shore Music Th., Beverly, Mass., July 5 and Aug. 2, 1965; South Shore Music Circus, Cohasset, Mass., July 12, 1965); and Dr. Grimwig in *Oliver* (tour, Summer 1973).

Films. Mr. Deems wrote and directed *Bock Boom* (APS, 1961); appeared in *Diary of a Bachelor* (AI, 1964); *Hold On!* (MGM, 1966); *The Busy Body* (AI, 1967); *The St. Valentine's Day Massacre* (20th-Fox, 1967); *Who's Minding the Mint?* (Col., 1967); and *With Six You Get Eggroll* (Natl. Gen., 1968).

Television. Mr. Deems has appeared on the Ed Sullivan Show (CBS); The Phil Silvers Show (CBS); appeared on and was comedy director for Car 54, Where Are You? (ABC); appeared on The Patty Duke Show (ABC); the series Mister Roberts (NBC); Hero (NBC); was a guest on Hollywood Palace (ABC); and, with Joey Faye, appeared on Mack and Myer (Trans-Lux Corp.).

Night Clubs. Mr. Deems has appeared at the Manhattan Club (Troy, N.Y.); Number One Fifth Ave. (N.Y.C.); the Blue Angel (N.Y.C.); Bon Soir (N.Y.C.); the Copacabana (N.Y.C.); the Flamingo (Las Vegas); and the Fremont (Las Vegas).

Recreation. Ham radio, amateur motion pictures, writing science fiction short stories.

DEERING, OLIVE. Actress. b. Olive Korn, Bronx, N.Y. Father, dental surgeon. Grad. Professional Children's Sch. Relative in theatre: brother, Alfred Ryder, actor, director. Married to Leo Penn, actor (marr. dis.). Member of Actors Studio; AEA; SAG.

Theatre. Miss Deering made her Bway debut in *Girls in Uniform* (Booth, N.Y.C., Dec. 30, 1932); appeared in *Growing Pains* (Ambassador, Nov. 23, 1933); played Dot in *Searching for the Sun* (58 St. Th., Feb. 1936); Iphigenia in *Daughters of Atreus* (Oct. 15, 1936); Queen Isabella in *King Richard II* (St. James, Feb. 5, 1937); appeared in *Medicine Show* (New Yorker, Apr. 5, 1940); played Julie Talent in *They Walk Alone* (John Golden Th., Mar. 12, 1941); appeared in *Nathan the Wise* (New Sch. of Social Research, Mar. 11, 1942; moved to Belasco, Apr. 4, 1942); played Regina Gordon in *Councellor-at-Law* (Royale, Nov. 24, 1942); appeared in *Winged Victory* (44 St. Th., Nov. 20, 1942); played Francey in *Skydrift* (Belasco, Nov. 13, 1945); Mollie Malloy in *The Front Page* (Royale, Sept. 4, 1946); Rosa Perozzi in *Dark Legend* (President, Mar. 24, 1952); The Queen in *The Eagle Has Two Heads* (Actors Playhouse, Dec. 4, 1956); the title role in a staged reading of *Antigone* (Cooper Union, Feb. 10, 1956); Cassandra in *The Trojan Women* (Th. Marquee, Mar. 18, 1957); for the American Shakespeare Festival (Stratford, Conn.), Bianca in *Othello* (June 22, 1957); The Contessa Anne Louise de Sanctis in *The Devil's Advocate* (Billy Rose Th., N.Y.C., Mar. 9, 1961); Eve Adamanski in *Marathon '33* (ANTA, Dec. 22, 1963); a Woman of Canterbury in the Amer. Shakespeare Fest. production of *Murder in the Cathedral* (Stratford, Conn., June 19, 1966); and, as a guest artist at Brandeis Univ. (Waltham, Mass.) played Madame Arkadin in *The Sea Gull* (Spingold Th., Nov. 10, 1966).

She appeared in *Tiny Alice* (Th. Company of Boston, Jan. 3, 1967); played Emma in *The Ceremony of Innocence* American Place Th., N.Y.C., Dec. 14, 1967); appeared in *The Royal Family* (Center Stage, Baltimore, May 22, 1968); and *Tiny Alice* (Nutmeg Playhouse, Storrs, Conn., Summer 1968); played Irma in *The Balcony* (Nutmeg Playhouse, Storrs, Conn., July 23, 1968); appeared in *After the Fall* (Manitoba, Canada, Th. Ctr., Apr. 13, 1970); played Charlotte Shade in *The Sun and the Moon* (Manitoba Th. Ctr., world premiere, Feb. 7, 1972); Eleanor in *Winter Chicken* (Manhattan Th. Club, N.Y.C., May 16, 1974); and appeared in a double-bill of *This Property Is Condemned* and *Portrait of a Madonna* with the collective title of *Two by Tennessee* (Manhattan Th. Club, N.Y.C., June 6, 1974).

Films. Miss Deering has appeared in *Samson and Delilah* (Par., 1949); *Caged* (WB, 1950); *The Ten Commandments* (Par., 1956); and *Shock Treatment* (20th-Fox, 1964).

Television and Radio. Miss Deering was heard on Myrt and Marge (CBS); Against the Storm; the Goldbergs; and Before Breakfast.

Her numerous television appearances include Studio One (CBS); Kraft Mystery Th.; Seven Lively Arts (CBS); and Armstrong Circle Th. (CBS).

DE FORE, DON. Actor, producer, author. b. Aug. 25, 1916, Cedar Rapids, Iowa, to Joseph E. and Albia (Nezerka) De Fore. Father, locomotive engineer. Grad. Washington H.S., Cedar Rapids, Iowa; attended Univ. of Iowa. Studied acting at Pasadena Community Playhouse Sch. of the Th. (scholarship) 1934–37. Married Feb. 14, 1942, to Marion Holms, singer; two sons, three daughters. Served US Army. Member of NATAS (pres., 1954–56); AEA; SAG; AFTRA. Address: 2496 Mandeville Canyon Rd., Los Angeles, CA 90049.

Theatre. Mr. De Fore first appeared on stage in church plays in Cedar Rapids, Iowa. He made his professional debut as Rennie in *Where Do We Go From Here?* (New Hampshire Playhouse, Hollywood, Calif., 1930's) and repeated the role on Bway (Vanderbilt, Nov. 15, 1938). In 1939, at the NY World's Fair, he was one of the principals in the pageant *Railroads on Parade.* He then played Hunky in *Steel* (Provincetown Playhouse, N.Y.C., Dec. 19, 1939); Wally Myers in *The Male Animal* (Cort, Jan. 9, 1940), and on tour; Mike O'Connor in the pre-Bway tryout of *Judy O'Connor* (opened Shubert, New Haven, Conn., Mar. 21, 1946; closed Copely, Boston, Mass., Mar. 30, 1946); in *Claudia* (La Jolla, Calif., Summer Th., 1950); appeared in the title role in the pre-Bway tryout of *Mike McCauley* (opened Lobero, Santa Barbara, Calif., Jan. 26, 1951; closed Harris Th., Chicago, Ill., Feb. 17, 1951); was Clark Redfield and a Mexican in a revival of *Dream Girl* (NY City Ctr., May 9, 1951); was in *Susan Slept Here* (New England, Summer 1964); in *Never Too Late* (Pheasant Run Playhouse, St. Charles, Ill., 1965); in *Generation* (San Diego, Calif., Pheasant Run, St. Charles, Ill., 1967); in *Any Wednesday* (Dallas, Tex., 1969); in *Never Too Late* (Jacksonville, Fla., 1970); in a revival of *Light Up the Sky* (1971); toured the Midwest for twenty weeks in *Any Wednesday* (1972); and toured Florida and Texas for twenty-four weeks in *The Subject Was Roses* (1973–74).

Films. Mr. De Fore made his debut in *Kid Galahad* (WB, 1937); subsequently appeared in *Submarine D-1* (WB, 1937); *We Go Fast* (20th-Fox, 1941); *The Male Animal* (WB, 1942); *A Girl in Every Port* (RKO, 1942); *City Without Men* (Col. 1943); *The Human Comedy* (MGM, 1943); *A Guy Named Joe* (MGM, 1943); *Thirty Seconds Over Tokyo* (MGM, 1944); *The Affairs of Susan* (Par., 1945); *You Came Along* (Par., 1945); *The Stork Club* (Par., 1945); *Without Reservations* (RKO, 1946); *Ramrod* (UA, 1947); *It Happened on Fifth Avenue* (Allied, 1947); *Romance on the High Seas* (WB, 1948); *One Sunday Afternoon* (WB, 1948); *My Friend Irma* (Par., 1949); *Too Late for Tears* (UA, 1949); *Southside 1-1000* (Allied, 1950); *Dark City* (Par., 1950); *The Guy Who Came Back* (20th-Fox, 1951); *No Room for the Groom* (U, 1952); *She's Working Her Way Through College* (WB, 1952); *Jumping Jacks* (Par., 1952); *Susan Slept Here* (RKO, 1954); *Battle Hymn* (U, 1956); *A Time to Love and a Time to Die* (U, 1958); and *Facts of Life* (UA, 1960).

Television. Mr. De Fore appeared on Lux Video Th. (NBC); Philco Television Playhouse (NBC); and Goodyear Playhouse (NBC). He played Thorney in the series Ozzie and Harriet (ABC); and George in the series Hazel (NBC). He appeared in the pilot series Home Team (1960); was guest star in *A Punt, a Pass, and a Prayer* (Hallmark Th., 1968); on My Three Sons (1968); on Mod Squad (ABC, 1969); was mystery guest on What's My Line (CBS, 1969); guest star on All-American College Show (1969); guest star on Mannix (CBS, 1970); and was guest star in *Men of Shiloh* (U, 1970).

Other Activities. Mr. De Fore opened "Don De Fore's Silver Banjo Restaurant" at Disneyland, Calif., in 1957. In 1966, he made a three-week solo visit to American troops in Vietnam, and in 1969 he was a delegate to the Moscow Film Festival. He was appointed in 1970 to a fifteen-member advisory committee in California on rehabilitation.

Published Works. Mr. De Fore wrote *With All My Love, Penny* (1965).

Awards. In 1967, Mr. De Fore was named first honorary mayor of Brentwood, Calif.

De HARTOG, JAN. Playwright. b. Apr. 22, 1914, Haarlem, Holland, to Arnold Hendrik and Lucretia (Meyjes) de Hartog. Father and mother, educators. Attended Amsterdam Naval Coll., 1930–31. Married Sept. 1960 to Marjorie Mein. Served, WW II, Netherlands Merchant Marine as correspondent; awarded Netherlands Cross of Merit; Knight in the Order of Orange Nassau; Officer of the Academy (France). Member of Dramatists Guild; Société des Auteurs (France). Address: c/o English Dept., Univ. of Houston, Houston, TX 77004, tel. CA 4-1681, ext. 625.

Pre-Theatre. Sailor.

Theatre. Mr. de Hartog wrote *The End of the Liberty* (Amsterdam Municipal Th., Holl., May 1939); followed by *Skipper Next to God,* in which he played Joris Kuiper, Captain (Embassy, London, Eng., Nov. 27, 1945); *This Time Tomorrow* (Guild, N.Y.C., Nov. 3, 1947); *Skipper Next to God* (Maxine Elliott's Th., Jan. 4, 1948); and *The Fourposter* (Ethel Barrymore Th., Oct. 24, 1951).

Films. He wrote the screenplays for *Somewhere in Holland* (Filmex, 1939); *Skipper Next to God* (Cooperative du Cinéma Français, 1949); *The Fourposter* (Col., 1952); *The Key* (Col., 1958); *The Spiral Road* (U, 1962); and *Lisa* (20th-Fox, 1962).

Published Works. He wrote *Holland's Glory* (1940); *The Lost Sea* (1951); *The Distant Shore* (1952); *The Little Ark* (1954); *A Sailor's Life* (1956); *The Spiral Road* (1957); *The Inspector* (1960); *Waters of the New World* (1961); *The Artist* (1963); *The Hospital* (1964); *The Captain* (1965); *The Children* (1968); and *The Peaceable Kingdom* (1972).

Awards. Mr. de Hartog received the Antoinette Perry (Tony) Award for *The Fourposter* (1951).

DeKOVEN, ROGER. Actor. b. Roger Bennett DeKoven, Oct. 22, 1907, Chicago, Ill., to Bernard and Clara (Turner) DeKoven. Father, physician. Grad. John Marshall H.S., Chicago, 1922; attended Univ. of Cincinnati, 1922–26; grad. Univ. of Chicago, Ph.B. 1930; graduate studies at Northwestern Univ., 1930, and Columbia Univ., 1931. Studied at Theatre Guild Sch., 1926–27. Married June 6, 1927, to Mona Meltz; one son, one daughter. Member of AEA; SAG; AFTRA. Address: (home) 360 Central Park West, New York, NY 10025, tel. (212) RI 9-4789; (bus.) tel. (212) SU 7-5400.

Theatre. Mr. DeKoven first appeared on the stage as a Soldier in the Stuart Walker (stock) Co. production of *A Woman Disputed* (Cincinnati, Ohio, May 1926); and first appeared in N.Y.C. as a walk-on in *Juarez and Maximillian* (Guild, Oct. 11, 1926); subsequently appeared in the chorus of *The Pirates of Penzance* (Plymouth, Dec. 6, 1926); in the chorus of *Ruddigore* (Cosmopolitan, May 20, 1927); Jacob in *Jacob's Dream* (Neighborhood Playhouse, Oct. 1927); was stage manager and general understudy for *Spring Song* (Nora Bayes Th., Dec. 21, 1927); and was stage manager, played Anson, and succeeded (Mar. 1928) Gordon James as Robert Wheeler in *The Mystery Man* (Nora Bayes Th., Jan. 26, 1928).

He was stage manager and general understudy for *That Ferguson Family* (Little, Dec. 22, 1928); played George's Secretary in *Once in a Lifetime* (Music Box, Sept. 24, 1930) and on tour; appeared as John P. Tedesco in *Counsellor-at-Law* (Harris, Chicago, Ill., Oct. 1930); and appeared in stock productions with the White Roe Players (Livingston Manor, N.Y., Summers 1933–34).

He appeared as the First Knight in the Federal Theatre (WPA) Project production of *Murder in the Cathedral* (Manhattan Th., N.Y.C., Mar. 20, 1936); the Fanatic in *The Eternal Road* (Manhattan Opera House, Jan. 7, 1937); Edmund in *King Lear* (New School Th., Nov. 1939); Albert Anastasia in *Brooklyn, U.S.A.* (Forrest, Dec. 21, 1941); Admiral Marcel Vespery (Darlan) in *The Assasins* (Natl., Oct. 17, 1945); Jeffson (Georges de Tremoille) in *Joan of Lorraine* (Alvin, Nov. 18, 1946); Eddie Fuselli in *Golden Boy* (Detroit, Mich., Aug. 1947); Rabbi Samuels in *Abie's Irish Rose* (Holiday, N.Y.C., Nov. 18, 1954); Vershinin in *The Three Sisters* (Fourth St. Th., Feb. 25, 1955); and the Promoter in *The Lark* (Longacre, Nov. 17, 1955).

Mr. DeKoven played Dr. Montalti in *The Hidden River* (Playhouse, Jan. 23, 1957); Ferdinand Feldscher in *Compulsion* (Ambassador, Oct. 24, 1957); Mr. Fairbrother in *The Making of Moo* (Rita Allen Th., June 11, 1958); Mostachi in the pre-Bway tryout *The Gay Felons* (opened Playhouse, Wilmington, Del., Feb. 12, 1959; closed Ford's, Baltimore, Md., Mar. 14, 1959); followed (Feb. 1960) Sandor Szabo as Vershinin in *The Three Sisters* (Fourth St. Th., Sept. 21, 1959); appeared as the Doctor in *The Miracle Worker* (Playhouse, Oct. 19, 1959); and the Milkman in *The Fighting Cock* (ANTA, Dec. 8, 1959).

During the 1961–62 season, he appeared with the Actor's Workshop (San Francisco, Calif.) as King Henry in *Henry IV, Part 1,* Vershinin in *The Three Sisters,* Friedman in *Friedman and Son,* and the Archbishop in *Becket;* succeeded (May 27, 1963) Alexander Scourby as Gorotchenko in *Tovarich* (Bway Th., N.Y.C., Mar. 18, 1963); appeared as the Actor in *Arturo Ui* (Lunt-Fontanne, Nov. 11, 1963); and Florenz Ziegfeld, Jr., in *Funny Girl* (Winter Garden, Mar. 26, 1964).

He toured as Paul Hirsch with the national company of *Dear Me, the Sky Is Falling* (Aug. 15, 1964–May 29, 1965; Feb. 20–Mar. 6, 1966; June 20–Aug. 21, 1966); played Gustave Kummer in *The Deadly Game* (Provincetown Playhouse, N.Y.C., Feb. 13, 1966); H. Goldblatt in *Walking to Waldheim* (Forum Th., Nov. 10, 1967); the Archbishop of Rheims in *Saint Joan* (Vivian Beaumont Th., Jan. 4, 1968); King Priam in *Tiger at the Gates* (Vivian Beaumont Th., Feb. 29, 1968); Jodelet in *Cyrano de Bergerac* (Vivian Beaumont Th., Apr. 25, 1968); and appeared at the Bucks County Playhouse, New Hope, Pa. (June 7–Aug. 30, 1969), where he played Solomon in *The Price.* He was Mr. Glas in *Slow Dance on the Killing Ground* (Center Stage, Baltimore, Md., Sept. 30, 1969); played in *Steal the Old Man's Bundle* (Fortune Th., N.Y.C., May 15, 1970); was Professor Mannheim in *The Nephew* (Studio Arena, Buffalo, N.Y., Mar. 24, 1971); repeated his role in *Slow Dance on the Killing Ground* (Playhouse in the Park, Cincinnati, Ohio, May 1, 1971); played the Judge in *The Trial of the Catonsville Nine* (Center Stage, Baltimore, Md., Oct. 5, 1971); appeared as the Priest in *The Rose Tattoo* and as Freeman in *The Tavern* (Repertory Th., New Orleans, La., Mar. 5–Apr. 23, 1972); played the Magistrate in *The Ecstasy of Rita Joe* (American premier, Washington Theater Club, May 2, 1973); and was Dr. Carl Heller in *All Is Bright* (Greater Middletown Arts Council, Middletown, N.Y., Nov. 12–Dec. 2, 1973).

Films. Mr. DeKoven appeared in *Up Front* (U, 1951) and as Serge in *Seizure* (1974).

Television and Radio. Mr. DeKoven has appeared on radio as Prof. Allen in Against the Storm; as the Narrator of The Eternal Light, Famous Jury Trials, Gangbusters, and the Phillip Morris Playhouse.

He has appeared on television as Dr. Mendes in Edge of Night (CBS), Ben Casey (ABC), The Detectives (NBC), and on such dramatic series as Camera Three (CBS), Studio One (CBS), Alfred Hitchcock Presents (CBS), Colgate Th. (NBC), and the Somerset Maugham Th. (ABC).

DELANEY, SHELAGH. Playwright. b. 1939, Salford, Lancashire, Eng. Address: c/o Kurt Hellmer, 52 Vanderbilt Ave., New York, NY 10017, tel. (212) MH 6-2222.

Theatre. Miss Delaney wrote *A Taste of Honey,* produced in London (Theatre Workshop, Royal Stratford, May 27, 1958 and Jan. 21, 1959; Wyndham's, Feb. 10, 1959), in N.Y.C. (Lyceum, Oct. 4, 1960), and on the national tour (opened Natl. Th., Washington, D.C., Sept. 11, 1961; closed Blackstone Th., Chicago, Ill., Apr. 7, 1962).

She wrote *The Lion in Love* (Belgrade Th., Conventry, Eng., Sept. 5, 1960; moved Royal Court, London, Dec. 29, 1960); and in N.Y.C. (One Sheridan Sq., Apr. 25, 1963).

Films. Miss Delaney wrote, with Tony Richardson, the screenplay for *A Taste of Honey* (Continental, 1962), and she wrote the screenplay for *Charlie Bubbles* (Regional Films, 1968).

Published Works. Miss Delaney wrote *A Taste of Honey* (1959) and *The Lion in Love* (1961). She has contributed articles to the NY *Times* Magazine (May 28, 1961) and *Cosmopolitan* (Nov. 1962). Excerpts from her book, *Sweetly Sings the Donkey* (1963), have been published in *The Saturday Evening Post* and *Evergreen Review.*

Awards. *A Taste of Honey* won the N.Y. Drama Critics' Circle Award (1961).

de LAPPE, GEMZE. Dancer, actress, choreographer. b. Gemze Mary de Lappe, Feb. 28, 1922, Portsmouth, Va., to Birch W. and Maureen (McDonough) de Lappe. Father, actor, manager, mechanical draftsman, teacher; mother, actress, musician. Attended Peabody Conservatory of Music, Baltimore, Md., 1927–29; Pitt St. Music Sch. of the Henry St. Settlement, N.Y.C., 1931–35; grad. H.S. of Music and Art, N.Y.C. 1939; attended Hunter Coll., 1939–40. Studied at Ballet Arts Sch., Carnegie Hall, N.Y.C., with Irma Duncan, Michel and Vitale Fokine, Yeichi Nimura, Ed Caton, and V. Nemtchinova, 1930–63; Paul Mann Actors Workshop, N.Y.C., 1958, 1962. Married 1959 to John Carisi, composer, arranger; two sons. Member of AEA; AGMA; AFTRA; SAG.

Theatre. Miss de Lappe made her stage debut as a ballet dancer in repertory productions of *Prince Igor, Les Sylphides,* and *Scheherazade* (Lewisohn Stadium, N.Y.C.; Marine Th., Jones Beach, L.I., N.Y.; 1931–36); subsequently played the Child with Pigtails in *Oklahoma!* (Erlanger Th., Chicago, Ill., 1943), and toured in it; and played Laury in the ballet sequence of the national tour of this production (1945).

She made her N.Y.C. debut succeeding (1946) Dania Krupska as Ellen in *Oklahoma!* (St. James, Mar. 31, 1943), played this role in the London production (Drury Lane, Apr. 30, 1947), and staged the dances and production numbers for the Australian tour (1949).

She played Lizzie Borden in the Ballet Th. production of *Fall River Legend* (Metropolitan Opera House, N.Y.C., Apr. 22, 1948); King Simon of Legree in *The Small House of Uncle Thomas* ballet sequence in *The King and I* (St. James, Mar. 29, 1951); Yvonne in *Paint Your Wagon* (Shubert, Nov. 12, 1951); and at the Metropolitan Opera House, the Mother and Wife in *The Harvest According;* appeared in *Three Virgins and the Devil* (1953); *The Judgement of Paris; Billy the Kid* (1953); *Los Capricorns,* and toured Europe in these productions (1953–54).

She appeared in a national tour of the *Agnes De Mille Dance Theatre* (1954); was the solo dancer in *Phoenix '55* (Phoenix, N.Y.C., Apr. 23, 1955); played Laury in the dream ballet sequence of *Oklahoma!* (France, Italy, 1955); and played Louise in *Carousel* (NY City Ctr., Sept. 11, 1957; Amer. Pavillion, Brussels World's Fair, Belg. 1958).

In summer stock, she danced in *Call Me Madam* (St. Louis Municipal Opera, Mo.); played the Ingenue in *The Doctor in Spite of Himself* (Westport Country Playhouse, Conn.); played Molly in *Juno* (Winter Garden, N.Y.C., Mar. 9, 1959); Yvonne in *Paint Your Wagon* (1960); and directed *Oklahoma!* (Rainbow, Winnipeg, Canada, 1962).

Miss de Lappe played Maggie Anderson in *Brigadoon* (NY City Ctr., May 30, 1962; command performance, White House, Washington, D.C., 1963); and was choreographer for *Carousel* (Curran, San Francisco, Calif.; Philharmonic Aud., Los Angeles, Calif., 1963); and repeated her role as Maggie Anderson in *Brigadoon* (NY City Ctr., N.Y.C., Dec. 23, 1964). She was choreographic assistant for *Carousel* (NY State Th., Aug. 10, 1965); restaged *Oklahoma!* (NY City Ctr., Dec. 15, 1965); choreographed *The Birds* (Ypsilanti Greek Th., Ypsilanti, Mich., June 29, 1966); restaged Agnes de Mille' Dances for *Carousel* (NY City Ctr., N.Y.C., Dec. 15, 1966); and restaged *Brigadoon* (NY City Ctr., Dec. 13, 1967).

Films. She played King Simon of Legree in *The King and I* (20th-Fox, 1956); and choreographed *Justine* (20th-Fox, 1969).

Television. Miss de Lappe was a dance soloist on Omnibus (NBC, 1956).

Awards. She received the Donaldson Award (1952) for her performance as Yvonne in *Paint Your Wagon.* .

Recreation. Piano, choral singing, swimming, bicycling, studying French and Italian.

DELARUE, ALLISON. Balletomane, writer. b. Windsor, N.J. Grad. Peddie School, 1924; Princeton Univ., B.A. 1928, M.A. 1929; studied at Oxford Univ., England, and l'Abbaye de Pontigny, France. Member of TLA; ASTR; English Speaking Union; the Princeton Club of N.Y.C. Address: Allison House, Windsor, NJ 08561.

Mr. Delarue was a staff member, Cooper Union's Museum for the Decorative Arts, N.Y.C., 1938–47, and McCarter Th., Princeton Univ., 1951–72. He is the author of *The Chevalier Henry Wikoff: Impresario, 1840* (1968) and many articles that have appeared in dance periodicals. He is preparing a book on Fanny Elssler.

de LAVALLADE, CARMEN. Dancer, actress, choreographer, teacher. b. Carmen Paula de Lavallade, Mar. 6, 1931, Los Angeles, Calif., to Leo Paul and Grace de Lavallade. Father, bricklayer, postman. Grad. Thomas Jefferson H.S., Los Angeles, Calif., 1949; attended Los Angeles City Coll., 1950–52; studied dance with Lester Horton; acting with Stella Adler; singing with Carlo Menotti. Married June 26, 1955, to Geoffrey Holder, dancer; one son. Member of AEA; AGMA; AFTRA; SAG.

Theatre. Miss de Lavallade made her stage debut dancing the role of Salome with the Lester Horton Dance Th. (Dane Th., Los Angeles, Calif., Oct. 1950); subsequently appeared with the company as Yerma and Salome in concert (YMHA, N.Y.C., 1952). She worked with the Lester Horton dance co. until 1954, when she made her Bway debut as Carmen in *House of Flowers* (Alvin, Dec. 30, 1954). Since 1955 she has performed many times and with various companies at the YMHA in N.Y.C., and has made repeated appearances at the Jacob's Pillow Dance Festival in Lee, Mass.

She appeared as dance soloist in *Aida* and *Samson and Dalila* (Metropolitan Opera House, N.Y.C., 1956); was soloist with the John Butler dance co. at the Festival of Two Worlds (Spoleto, Italy, 1958, 1959); danced in the pre-Bway tryout of *"Impulse!"* (opened O'Keefe Center, Toronto, Canada, Mar. 20, 1961; closed there Mar. 25, 1961); danced the roles of Cocaine Lil and the Comet in *Ballet Ballads* (E. 74 St. Th., N.Y.C., Jan. 3, 1961); was assistant artistic director of the de Lavallade-Ailey American dance co. on a cultural tour of South East Asia, sponsored by the US State Dept. (1962); was with the NY City Opera (1962–65); was soloist with the Donald McKayle dance co. at Lincoln Center (Philharmonic Hall, N.Y.C., 1963); played Iram and Rami in *Hot Spot* (Majestic, Apr. 19, 1963); and appeared as Naomi in the Chanukkah Festival (Madison Square Garden, 1963).

In 1964, she appeared with the Donald McKayle dance co. as the Girl in *Reflections in the Park,* and she danced with Geoffrey Holder in Josephine Baker's N.Y.C. engagement (Henry Miller's Th.). In 1965, she again danced at the Festival of Two Worlds (Spoleto, Italy, and was a guest artist with American Ballet Th. for its 25th anniversary season (State Th.), creating the chief role in Agnes de Mille's *The Four Marys* (Mar. 23, 1965) and dancing the role of the wife in a revival of Miss de Mille's *Tally-Ho* under the new title *The Frail Quarry* (Apr. 2, 1965).

Since 1969, Miss de Lavallade has appeared in many productions of the Yale Rep. Th. (New Haven, Conn.), including *Metamorphoses* (Nov. 27, 1969) and *Crimes and Crimes* (Jan. 8, 1970). She played the Specter in Molière's *Don Juan* (May 15, 1970); directed and appeared in Yale Rep's Children's Th. *Red Shoes* (Apr. 19, 1970); was in *Story Theatre* (Oct. 8, 1970), *The Revenger's Tragedy* (Nov. 19, 1970), and *Macbeth* (Feb. 18, 1971). She played Maia in *When We Dead Awaken* (Oct. 14, 1971); did choreography for *The Big House* (Oct. 21, 1971); played Anna II in *The 7 Deadly Sins* (Jan. 20, 1972); appeared in *Life Is a Dream* (Feb. 17, 1972); choreographed and played Naamah in *The Mirror* (Jan. 19, 1973); was in *Baal* (Feb. 16, 1973); played Lady Macbett in *Macbett* (Mar. 16, 1973); Fontanelle in Lear (Apr. 13, 1973); and Ariel in *The Tempest* (Oct. 5, 1973).

She was in *Watergate Classics* (Nov. 16, 1973) and *An Evening with Dead Essex* (Mar. 8, 1974); played the Handmaiden and Innkeeper's Wife in *The Frogs* (May 20, 1974); Lena in *Victory* (Nov. 14, 1974); Titania in *A Midsummer Night's Dream,* for which she also did choreography (May 9, 1975; repeated in the next season, Oct. 2, 1975); appeared again as the Specter in *Don Juan* (Oct. 30, 1975); played Angela in *General Gorgeous* (Feb. 26, 1976); and Helen in *Troilus and Cressida* (Apr. 1, 1976).

Films. She made her debut as soloist with Jack Cole in *Lydia Bailey* (20th-Fox, 1952); followed by the role of a Handmaiden in *Demetrius and the Gladiators* (20th-Fox, 1954); was soloist in *Carmen Jones* (20th-Fox, 1954); and played Kitty in *Odds Against*

Tomorrow (UA, 1959).

Television. She danced in flight on the Bob Herridge Th. (CBS, 1956); appeared as Madame Zaj in *A Drum Is a Woman* (CBS, 1956); as the lead dancer in *Amahl and the Night Visitors* (NBC); appeared with the John Butler dance company or Look Up and Live (CBS, 1959); again with the John Butler company on Lamp Unto My Feet (CBS); and appeared as Bess in the ballet sequence in *The Gershwin Years* (CBS, 1961).

Night Clubs. Miss de Lavallade made her first night-club appearance as soloist with the Lester Horton dance company (Ciro's, Hollywood, Calif., 1953); appeared with the Geoffrey Holder dance company (Cocoanut Grove, 1958); and in the Pearl Bailey Show (Flamingo Hotel, Las Vegas, 1961).

Other Activities. Miss de Lavallade teaches on the faculty of the Yale School of Drama (New Haven, Conn.).

Recreation. The home.

De LIAGRE, ALFRED, JR. Producer, director. b. Oct. 6, 1904, Passaic, N.J., to Alfred and Frida (Unger) de Liagre. Father, business executive. Grad. Riverdale Country Sch., N.Y.C., 1922; Yale Univ., 1926. Married July 25, 1945, to Mary Howard; one son, one daughter. Relative in theatre: brother-in-law, Brian Aherne, actor. Member of League of New York Theatres (bd. of dir., 1940–to date); American Theatre Wing (bd. of dir., 1951–to date); ANTA (bd. of dir., 1962); Natl. Book Committee (bd. of dir., 1958); American Shakespeare Th., Stratford, Conn. (trustee); School of Drama, Yale Univ. Council (chmn.); Actors Fund of America (vice-pres.); Plumstead Playhouse (dir.); Century Assn.; River Club; Maidstone Club (East Hampton, N.Y.). Address: (home) 322 E. 57th St., New York, NY 10022, tel. (212) PL 9-3572; (bus.) 245 W. 52 St., New York, NY 10019, tel. (212) PL 7-4133.

Pre-Theatre. Banking, aviation.

Theatre. Mr. de Liagre was stage manager of *Twelfth Night* (Maxine Elliott's Th., N.Y.C., Oct. 15, 1930); directed and produced, with Richard Aldrich, *Three Cornered Moon* (Cort, Mar. 16, 1933) and *By Your Leave* (Morosco, Jan. 24, 1934); produced, with Richard Aldrich, *Pure in Heart* (Longacre Th., Mar. 20, 1934); directed and produced, with Richard Aldrich, *Petticoat Fever* (Ritz, Mar. 4, 1935) and *Fresh Fields* (Empire, Feb. 10, 1936).

He produced and directed *Yes, My Darling Daughter* (Playhouse, Feb. 9, 1937; *St. James's* London, June 3, 1937); *I Am My Youth* (Playhouse, N.Y.C., Mar. 7, 1938); *Mr. and Mrs. North* (Belasco, Jan. 12, 1941); *The Walrus and the Carpenter* (Cort, Nov. 8, 1941); and *Ask My Friend Sandy* (Biltmore, Feb. 4, 1943). In 1943 also he was co-producer and director of *Hello Out There* (Lobero Th., Santa Barbara, Calif.).

Mr. de Liagre produced *The Voice of the Turtle* (Morosco, Dec. 8, 1943; Piccadilly, London, July 9, 1947); *The Mermaids Singing* (Empire, N.Y.C., Nov. 28, 1945); *The Druid Circle* (Morosco, Oct. 22, 1947); produced and directed *The Madwoman of Chaillot* (Belasco, Dec. 27, 1948; St. James's, London, Feb. 15, 1951); *Second Threshold* (Morosco, N.Y.C., Jan. 2, 1951). He directed for the Central City (Col.) Opera Assn. *Amelia Goes to the Ball* and *The Lovely Galatea* (Aug. 1951). He produced, with John C. Wilson, *The Deep Blue Sea* (Morosco, Nov. 5, 1952); directed and produced, with Roger L. Stevens and Henry Sherek, *Escapade* (48 St. Th., Nov. 18, 1953); presented, with the Phoenix Th., *The Golden Apple* (Alvin, Apr. 20, 1954); produced *Janus* (Plymouth, Nov. 24, 1955; Aldwych, London, Apr. 24, 1957); and produced and directed *Nature's Way* (Coronet, N.Y.C., Oct. 16, 1957). He produced *The Girls in 509* (Belasco, Oct. 15, 1958); *J. B.* (ANTA, Dec. 11, 1958); produced, with Roger L. Stevens, in association with Laurence Olivier, *The Tumbler* (Helen Hayes Th., Feb. 24, 1960); produced *Kwamina* (54 St. Th., Oct. 23, 1961); produced, with Joseph E. Levine, *Photo Finish* (Brooks Atkinson Th., Feb. 12, 1963); and produced *The Irregular Verb to Love* (Ethel Barrymore Th., Sept. 18, 1963).

He produced, with Martha Scott (Plumstead Playhouse), a revival of *Our Town* (ANTA, Nov. 27, 1969) and a revival of *Time of Your Life* (John F. Kennedy Center, Washington, D.C., Dec. 14, 1972).

Films. Mr. de Liagre directed *Springtime for Henry* (20th-Fox, 1934); and produced the motion picture version of *The Voice of the Turtle* (WB, 1947).

Awards. *The Madwoman of Chaillot,* which he produced and directed, received the NY Drama Critics Circle Award (1949); and Mr. de Liagre made Chevalier in the French Legion of Honor (1949). *The Golden Apple,* which he co-produced in 1954, received the "Best Musical" award of the NY Drama Critics, and *J. B.,* produced by Mr. de Liagre in 1958, received the Tony Award and the Pulitzer Prize.

Recreation. Talking about the theatre.

DELL, GABRIEL. Actor. b. Gabriel del Vecchio, Oct. 4, 1919, Barbados, B.W.I. Father, ship's doctor. Married Viola Essen, dancer (marr. dis. May 14, 1953); one son; married Allyson Daniell; one son. Professional training, Actors Studio; mime with Etienne Decroux. Served in Merchant Marines during World War II.

Theatre. Mr. Dell made his stage debut as a Chinese boy in *The Good Earth* (Guild Th., N.Y.C., Oct. 17, 1932). He played T. B. in *Dead End* (Belasco Th., Oct. 28, 1935) and then appeared in a number of motion pictures (see *Films* below).

He was Spud in *Ankles Aweigh* (Mark Hellinger Th., N.Y.C., Apr. 18, 1955); Boris Adzinidzinadze in a revival of *Can-Can* (Theatre-in-the-Park, Aug. 25, 1959); Emanu in *The Automobile Graveyard* (41 St. Th., Nov. 13, 1961); played the title role in *Fortuna* (Maidman Th., Jan. 3, 1962); Leon V. Kaufenman in *Man Out Loud, Girl Quiet* and Martin Hacoen Medina in *The Spanish Armada* (both Cricket Th., Apr. 3, 1962); again played Boris Adzinidzinadze in a revival of *Can-Can* (NY City Ctr., May 16, 1962); was Chick Clark in a revival of *Wonderful Town* (NY City Ctr., Feb. 13, 1963); Ali Hakim in a revival of *Oklahoma!* (NY City Ctr., Feb. 27, 1963); and was Al Marciano in *Marathon '33* (ANTA Th., Dec. 22, 1963).

He played Comptroller Schub in *Anyone Can Whistle* (Majestic, Apr. 4, 1964); played the parts of Mr. Pinchley, Val Du Val, Fred Poitrine, Otto Schnitzler, Prince Cherney, and Noble, Junior in *Little Me* (Melody Top Th., Chicago, Ill., Summer 1964); Sidney Brustein in *The Sign in Sidney Brustein's Window* (Longacre, Oct. 15, 1964) and toured (1965) in the part; replaced (Aug. 24, 1965) Alan Arkin as Harry Berlin in *Luv* (Booth Th., Nov. 11, 1964); was Chico in *The Rogues' Trial* (Actors Studio, N.Y.C., May 25, 1966); and toured as Tom Gordon in a tryout of *The Coffee Lover* (Summer 1966).

He appeared as Andrew Prale in *Chocolates* (Gramercy Arts Th., N.Y.C., Apr. 10, 1967); Phil Caponetti in *Something Different* (Cort, Nov. 28, 1967); the Contestant in *Adaptation* (Greenwich Mews Th., Feb. 10, 1969), which he repeated in Los Angeles, Calif. (Mark Taper Forum, Oct. 23, 1969); was Paul Martino in *Fun City* (Morosco, N.Y.C., Jan. 2, 1972); replaced (June 25, 1973) Hector Elizondo as Mel Edison in *The Prisoner of Second Avenue* (Eugene O'Neill Th., Nov. 11, 1971); was Remo Weinberger in *Where Do We Go from Here?* (Public: Estelle R. Newman Th., Oct. 5, 1974); and Fred Santora in *Lamppost Reunion* (Little Th., Oct. 16, 1975).

Films. Mr. Dell repeated his performance as T. B. in the motion picture of *Dead End* (UA, 1937), and this was followed by *Angels with Dirty Faces* (WB, 1938); *Crime School* (1st Natl., 1938); *They Made Me a Criminal* (WB, 1939); *Hit the Road* (U, 1941); *Mr. Muggs Steps Out* (Monogram, 1943); *Keep 'Em Slugging* (U, 1943); *Bowery Champs* (Monogram, 1944); *Block Busters* (Monogram, 1944); *Follow the Leader* (Monogram, 1944); *Bowery Buckaroos* (Monogram, 1947); *Hard Boiled Mahoney* (Monogram, 1947); *Angels in Disguise* (Monogram, 1949); *300-Year Weekend* (Cinerama, 1971); and *Who Is Harry Kellerman?* (Natl. Gen., 1971).

Television. Mr. Dell appeared on Broadway Open House; the Steve Allen Show (NBC); Naked City (ABC, 1963); Ben Casey (ABC, 1965); Mannix (CBS, 1967); Then Came Bronson (NBC, 1969); I Dream of Jeannie (Ind.); The Governor and J. J. (CBS, 1969); Name of the Game (NBC, 1971); McCloud (NBC, 1971); Banyon (NBC, 1972); and The Corner Bar (ABC, 1972).

De LUCE, VIRGINIA. Actress, singer, dancer. b. Virginia de Luce Wilson, Mar. 25, 1921, San Francisco, Calif., to George Arthur and Hallie Virginia (Wells) Wilson. Father, engineer, inventor; mother, painter. Grad. Newton H.S., Newtonville, Mass., 1938. Studied dancing at Polly Godfrey Dance Sch., Auburndale, Mass., 1935–36; Lula Mae Drake's Sch. of the Dance, Ogdensburg, N.Y. 1934; Chester Hale Ballet Sch., N.Y.C., 1939; acting at Bishop-Lee Sch. of the Theatre, Boston, 1939; voice with Mrs. Edithe Magee, N.Y.C., 1952. Married Nov. 8, 1947, to Andrew Carl Extrom (marr. dis. 1948); married June 8, 1950, to George Arthur Miller (marr. dis. 1951); married Nov. 5, 1953, to Rick Riccardo, Jr. (marr. dis. 1955). Served U.S.C.G. Women's Aux. 1943–44; rank, Seaman 1/c. Member of AEA; SAG; AFTRA; AGVA; Aux. Policewomen (N.Y.C.), Natl. Rifle Assn. Address: P. O. Box 482, Canoga Park, CA 91305.

Theatre. Miss de Luce made her debut at the age of four at a dance recital (Repertory Th., Boston, Mass., May 1925).

She performed at the NY World's Fair (June 1939); played Rusty in *Bonanza* (Boston Univ., Mar. 1950); and at the Tributary Th. (Boston), appeared as the Serpent Goddess in *The Emperor Jones* (Mar. 1951) and Betty in *The Beggar's Opera* (May 1951).

She made her N.Y.C. debut in *New Faces of 1952* (Royale, May 16, 1952), also touring in it (opened Shubert, Boston, Apr. 6, 1953; closed Great Northern, Chicago, Ill., Oct. 1953); played Kate in *Kiss Me, Kate* (Th. No. 3, Manhattan, Topeka, Ft. Riley, and Kansas City Aud., Kan., Mar. 5, 1954); and appeared in a vaudeville show (Palace, N.Y.C., 1955).

She played Gladys in *Pal Joey* (Music Th., Chicago, Aug. 6, 1956); Anna in *The Sacrifice* (Twelfth Night Club, N.Y.C., Mar. 30, 1957); appeared in the revue *New Faces* (Cocoanut Grove Playhouse, Miami, Fla., Apr. 29, 1957); played Rita Marlowe in *Will Success Spoil Rock Hunter?* (Southern Tier Playhouse, Binghampton, N.Y., Aug. 26, 1957); Florence Google in *Who Was That Lady I Saw You With?* (Martin Beck Th., N.Y.C., Mar. 3, 1958); appeared in the revue *Chic* (Orpheum, N.Y.C., May 19, 1959); played Lillian Russell in *Come Away with Me, Lucille* (Museum of the City of New York, Oct. 1959); and succeeded (Oct. 1959) Joyce Jamison in *The Billy Barnes Revue* (York, June 9, 1959; moved to John Golden Th., Sept. 8, 1959; to Carnegie Hall Playhouse, Oct. 20, 1959).

Films. Miss de Luce has appeared in 20th Century-Fox films *Life Begins at 8:30* (1942); *Crash Dive* (1943); *Hello, Frisco, Hello* (1943); *The Immortal Sergeant* (1943); *Jitterbugs* (1943); *The Meanest Man in the World* (1943); *The Gang's All Here* (1943); *Heaven Can Wait* (1943); *Irish Eyes Are Smiling* (1944); *Wilson* (1944); *Something for the Boys* (1944); *Diamond Horseshoe* (1945); *The Dolly Sisters* (1945); and *New Faces* (1954). She has also appeared in *Take It Big* (Par., 1944), and *Cover Girl* (Col., 1944).

Television. She has appeared on the Barry Wood Show (Dumont, 1948); the Arthur Godfrey Show (CBS, 1948); her own program, By Request, which she also wrote (WBKB, Chicago, 1956); You Sometimes Get Rich (NBC, 1956); Sergeant Bilko (NBC, 1956–57); Make Up Your Mind (WNTA, 1958); the Jack Paar Show (NBC, 1959–60); Armstrong Circle Th. (NBC, 1960); *New Faces* (Play of the Week, ANTA, 1960); Midnight Zone (CBS, 1960); Car 54, Where Are You? (NBC, 1961); and the Paul Winchell Show (ABC, 1961).

Night Clubs. Miss de Luce has performed at Leon and Eddie's (N.Y.C., 1939); Mayfair (Boston, 1939); The Pirate's Den (Hollywood, 1940);

Copacabana (N.Y.C., 1942); Roosevelt Hotel (New Orleans, La., 1942); Trocadero (Hollywood, 1943); DiMaggio's Yacht Club (San Francisco, 1945); Copacabana Palace (Rio de Janeiro, Braz., 1946); Three Caballeros (Poughkeepsie, N.Y., 1948); Cocoanut Grove (Hollywood, 1944); I.B.E.W., Local 1031 (Chicago, 1953); Iroquois Gardens (Louisville, Ky., 1955); Nobadeer (Nantucket, R.I., 1949); Blue Angel (N.Y.C., 1955); and One Fifth Avenue (N.Y.C., 1955).

Also, the Bowery Supper Club (Detroit, Mich., 1957); House of Vienna (N.Y.C., 1960); Commodore Supper Club (Windsor, Ontario, Canada, 1960); Le Cabaret (Toronto, Canada, 1960); Ritz-Carleton Hotel (Montreal, Canada, 1961); Camelot (N.Y.C., 1961); and Biltmore Bowl (Los Angeles, Calif., 1963).

Awards. She received the *Theatre World* Award for her performance in *New Faces of 1952.*.

Recreation. Knitting, motorcycling, swimming, water-skiing, aquaplaning, skating, horseback riding, designing, sewing.

de MILLE, AGNES. Choreographer, director, writer. b. Agnes George de Mille, New York City, to William Churchill and Anna (George) de Mille. Father, playwright, director, teacher. Grad. UCLA, B.A. (cum laude). Studied dancing under Theodore Kosloff, Marie Rambert, Tamara Karsavina, Antony Tudor, Lydia Sokolova, Edward Caton, Margaret Craske, Nina Stroganova, Arnold Dolmetsch. Married June 14, 1943, to Walter Foy Prude, concert manager; one son. Relatives in theatre: grandfather, Henry C. de Mille, playwright; grandmother, Beatrice de Mille, play-broker; uncle, Cecil B. de Mille, film director; adopted cousin, Katherine de Mille, actress. Member of AFTRA; AGMA (charter member); SSD&C (3rd pres.); Kappa Alpha Theta; Trustee of Henry George Sch. of Social Science.

Theatre. Miss de Mille made her debut in her own dance compositions (1928), and appeared in them in the US, England, France and Denmark (1928–41); made her Bway debut as Columbine in Mozart's *La Finta Giardiniera,* produced by The Intimate Opera Co. (Mayfair Th., Jan. 17, 1927); was choreographer and dancer in *The Black Crook* (Lyric, Hoboken, N.J., Mar. 11, 1929); and was choreographer for *Nymph Errant* (Adelphia, London, Oct. 6, 1933) and *Tonight at 8:30* (Phoenix, Jan. 9, 1936).

She arranged the mime for the Players' Scene in Leslie Howard's production of *Hamlet* (Imperial, N.Y.C., Nov. 10, 1936); danced in Antony Tudor's ballet *Dark Elegies* (world premiere, Duchess, London, Feb. 19, 1937); was choreographer for *Hooray for What!* (Winter Garden, N.Y.C., Dec. 1, 1937); and created the role of Venus in Mr. Tudor's *Judgment of Paris* (world premiere, Westminster Th., London, June 15, 1938).

Miss de Mille created her first ballet, *Black Ritual,* for Ballet Th. (world premiere, Center Th., N.Y.C., Jan. 22, 1940); for Ballet Th., choreographed *Three Virgins and a Devil* in which she also danced (world premiere, Majestic, Feb. 12, 1941); created the ballet *Drums Sound in Hackensack* for Ballets Jooss (world premiere, Maxine Elliott's Th., Sept. 1941); and choreographed the ballet *Rodeo* for the Ballet Russe de Monte Carlo, and also danced in it (world premiere, Metropolitan Opera House, Oct. 16, 1942).

She choreographed *Oklahoma!* (St. James, Mar. 31, 1943); *One Touch of Venus* (Imperial, Oct. 7, 1943); for Ballet Th., created the ballet *Tally-Ho* (world premiere, Philharmonic Aud., Los Angeles, Calif., Feb. 25, 1944); choreographed *Bloomer Girl* (Shubert, N.Y.C., Oct. 5, 1944); *Carousel* (Majestic, Apr. 19, 1945); and *Brigadoon* (Ziegfeld, Mar. 13, 1947); and directed and choreographed *Allegro* (Majestic, Oct. 10, 1947).

Miss de Mille created the ballet *Fall River Legend* for Ballet Th. (world premiere, Metropolitan Opera House, Apr. 22, 1948); staged *The Rape of Lucretia* (Ziegfeld, Dec. 29, 1948); choreographed *Gentlemen Prefer Blondes* (Ziegfeld, Dec. 8, 1949); directed *Out of This World* (New Century, Dec. 21, 1950); choreographed *Paint Your Wagon* (Shubert, Nov. 12, 1951); and created the ballet *The Harvest According* for Ballet Th. (world premiere, Metropolitan Opera House, Oct. 1, 1952); formed the Agnes de Mille Dance Th. (1953), which toured the US (1953–54); choreographed *The Girl in Pink Tights* (Mark Hellinger Th., N.Y.C., Mar. 5, 1954); created the ballet *The Rib of Eve* for Ballet Th. (world premiere, Metropolitan Opera House, Apr. 1956); choreographed *Goldilocks* (Lunt-Fontanne, Oct. 11, 1958); *Juno* (Winter Garden, Mar. 9, 1959); *Kwamina* (54 St. Th., Oct. 23, 1961); staged (Mar. 9, 1962) for Royal Winnipeg (Manitoba, Canada) Ballet, her ballet *The Bitter Weird* (created in 1953 as *Ballad* and first performed by the Agnes de Mille Dance Th.); and choreographed *110 in the Shade* (Broadhurst, N.Y.C., Oct. 24, 1963). During 1973–75, she directed the Agnes de Mille Heritage Dance Theatre. In 1976, she choreographed the ballet *Texas Fourth.*

She staged dances and musical numbers for a revival of *Brigadoon* (NY City Ctr., Dec. 23, 1964); created for the American Ballet Th. (known before 1957 as Ballet Th.) the ballets *The Wind in the Mountains* (State Th., N.Y.C., Mar. 17, 1965) and *The Four Marys* (State Th., Mar. 23, 1965); for the Royal Winnipeg Ballet, *The Rehearsal,* in which she also appeared (Hunter Coll., Oct. 26, 1965); did choreography for a tour of *Where's Charley?* (1966); created for the Harkness Ballet *The Golden Age* (Broadway Th., N.Y.C., Nov. 8, 1967); directed *Come Summer* (Lunt-Fontanne Th., Mar. 18, 1969); and choreographed for American Ballet Th. *A Rose for Miss Emily* (NY City Ctr., Dec. 30, 1970). In 1973, with the aid of Rockefeller Foundation and National Endowment for the Arts grants and private donations, Miss de Mille founded the Agnes de Mille Heritage Dance Th. at the North Carolina School of the Arts, Winston-Salem, N.C., for the purpose of studying and keeping alive traditional American dances; first performances by the group were at Reynolds Aud., Winston-Salem, Apr. 26–29, 1973.

Films. Miss de Mille choreographed *Romeo and Juliet* (MGM, 1936); *London Town* (Rank, 1945); and *Oklahoma!* (Magna, 1955).

Television. For the program Omnibus (NBC), she was choreographer and appeared in *Balletic Style* and *The Art of Ballet* (1956), *The Art of Choreography* (1956); choreographed *Bloomer Girl* (1956); and was choreographer, writer, and appeared in *Lizzie Borden,* which included her ballet "Fall River Legend" (1957). She choreographed *Gold Rush* (Seven Lively Arts, CBS, 1958); *Cherry Tree Carol* (Bell Telephone Hour, NBC, 1959); restaged her ballet *The Bitter Weird* (CBC, Canada, 1964); and was narrator for the Bolshoi Ballet programs (1965). Her ballet *Rodeo* was presented on NET in 1974.

Published Works. Miss de Mille has written articles for *Vogue, The Atlantic Monthly, Good Housekeeping, McCall's, Esquire* and the NY *Times;* the books *Dance to the Piper* (1952); *And Promenade Home* (1958); *To a Young Dancer* (1962); *The Book of the Dance* (1963); *Lizzie Borden, A Dance of Death* (1968); *Russian Journals* (1970); and *Speak to Me, Dance with Me* (1973).

Awards. In Feb. 1965, President Lyndon B. Johnson appointed Miss de Mille as one of the first members of the National Council on the Arts. She received Donaldson awards for dance direction for *One Touch of Venus* (1944), *Carousel* (1945), and *Brigadoon* (1947); was named best choreographer in the *Variety* NY Drama Critics Poll for *Carousel* (1945) and *Brigadoon* (1947); received Antoinette Perry (Tony) awards for *Brigadoon* and *Kwamina* (1962); an ANTA Award for "outstanding contribution to the art of the living theatre" (1962); and the Capezio Dance Award in 1966. She was named woman of the year by the Press Women's Assn. (1946); received the *Dance* Magazine Award (1957); the Alumni Medal, Univ. of California (1953); the Spirit of Achievement Award from Albert Einstein Coll. of Medicine, Yeshiva Univ. (1958); and the honorary degree of Litt.D. from Mills (1952), Russell Sage (1953), Smith (1954), Western (1955) and Hood (1959) colleges; Northwestern Univ. and Goucher Coll. (both 1960); Univ. of California and Clarke Univ. (both 1962); College (1971) & Marshall Coll. (1966); Western Michigan Univ. (1967); and Nasson College (1971) and D.F.A. degrees from Dartmouth College (1974) and Duke University (1975). She was awarded New York City's Handel Medallion in 1976.

DENHAM, REGINALD. Director, playwright, actor. b. Jan. 10, 1894, London, England, to Harry Barton and Emily Constance (Chapman) Denham. Father, government civil servant; mother, music teacher. Attended the City of London Sch. (1904–1911); studied music and singing with Cairns James at the Guildhall Sch. of Music, London (1913). Married 1920 to Moyna MacGill, actress (marr. dis. 1925); one daughter; married 1926 to Lilian Oldland, actress, playwright (marr. dis. 1946); one daughter; married Mar. 26, 1947, to Mary Orr, actress, playwright. Served Royal Irish Rifles and as staff officer in Tank Corps Cadet Battalion, 1916–1919. Member of SSD&C (exec. board since founding); Dramatists Guild; ALA; WGA, East; Oxford Univ. Dramatic Society (honorary life member). Address: 100 W. 57th St., New York, NY 10019, tel. (212) CI 7-1094.

Theatre. Mr. Denham made his debut as a walk-on in *Joseph and His Brethren* (His Majesty's Th., London, Sept. 2, 1913); subsequently was a member of the Benson Shakespearean (touring) Repertory Co. (1914–1916); played Hawkins in *Abraham Lincoln* (Lyric, Hammersmith, London, Feb. 19, 1919); Paris in *Romeo and Juliet* (Lyric, Apr. 12, 1919); appeared in *The Cinderella Man* (Queen's, June 12, 1919); played Salanio in *The Merchant of Venice* (Duke of York's, 1920); Mishka in *The Government Inspector* (Duke of York's, Apr. 13, 1920); Lt. Graham in *French Leave* (Globe, July 15, 1920); Sidney in *Right to Strike* (Garrick, Sept. 28, 1920); Count Pietro in *The Pilgram of Eternity* (Duke of York's, Nov. 12, 1921); and Trotter in *Fanny's First Play* (Everyman, Feb. 6, 1922).

His first assignment as director in London was *If Four Walls Told* (Comedy, Mar. 12, 1922); subsequently directed the Repertory Players in *The Smiths of Surbiton* (New, Nov. 19, 1922); *Biters Bitten* (Strand, June 11, 1922); and *Colman* (1922); staged *Trespasses* (Ambassadors', Apr. 16, 1923); *The Man Who Ate the Popomack* (Savoy, June 12, 1923); and directed the Oxford Univ. Players in *Heartbreak House, The Rivals, The Master Builder, No Trifling With Love, The Land of Heart's Desire, She Stoops to Conquer, Monna Vanna, La Locandiera,* and *The Importance of Being Earnest* (1923–24).

He played Charles Blazy in, and directed, *Fata Morgana* (Ambassadors', Sept. 15, 1924); directed *No Man's Land* (St. Martin's, Dec. 2, 1924); *Pollyanna* (St. James's, Dec. 18, 1924); *The Colonnade* for the Stage Society (Aldwych, Apr. 5, 1925); *The Czarina* ("Q,"June 22, 1925); *The Moon and Sixpence* (New, Sept. 24, 1925); for the Oxford Univ. Dramatic Society, staged *Peer Gynt* (1925) and *The Tempest* (1927); staged *For None Can Tell* ("Q," June 7, 1926); *A Man Unknown* (Comedy, June 17, 1926); *Confession* (Court, July 18, 1926); *After Dark* (Garrick, Sept. 20, 1926); *The Village* ("Q," Apr. 11, 1927); *Wild-Cat Hetty* (Savoy, June 20, 1927); *Compromising Daphne* (Prince's, Sept. 28, 1927); *Sylvia* (Vaudeville, Dec. 14, 1927); *Lord Babs* (Vaudeville, Jan. 26, 1928); *The Man Who Changed His Name* (Apollo, Mar. 14, 1928); *For Better, For Worse* (Arts Th. Club, May 5, 1928); *The House of Women* ("Q," Sept. 3, 1928); co-directed *Such Men Are Dangerous* (Duke of York's, Sept. 19, 1928); directed a revival of *For None Can Tell,* retitled *To What Red Hell* (Wyndham's, 1928); *Rope* (Strand, Mar. 3, 1929); *The Misdoings of Charley Peace* (Ambassadors', Sept. 12, 1929); and *Jew Suss* (Duke of York's, Sept. 19, 1929).

Mr. Denham directed the N.Y.C. company of *Rope's End* (US title for *Rope*) in London prior to their Bway opening (Th. Masque, Sept. 19, 1929); directed *Tunnel Trench* (Duchess, London, Nov. 1929); *Suspense* (Duke of York's, Apr. 8, 1930); *The Last Chapter* (New, May 27, 1930); the N.Y.C. productions of *Joseph Suss* (US title for *Jew Suss*) (Erlanger's, Jan. 30, 1930) and *Suspense* (Fulton, Aug. 12, 1930); staged *Cold Blood* (Duke of York's, London, Oct. 5, 1932); and *Wellington* (Southport, 1933).

He directed *The Last Straw*, which he wrote with Edward Percy (Comedy, Sept. 29, 1937); wrote with Mr. Percy and staged *Green Holly* ("Q," May 30, 1938), retitled *Give Me Yesterday*, directed by Mr. Denham and Owen Nares (Comedy, Aug. 10, 1938); staged *The Distant Hand*, written with Mr. Percy ("Q," May 8, 1939); *Ladies in Retirement*, written with Mr. Percy (St. James's, Dec. 12, 1939); and wrote and directed *First Night* (Richmond, Jan. 29, 1940).

Mr. Denham staged *Ladies in Retirement* (Henry Miller's Th., N.Y.C., Mar. 26, 1940); *Suspect*, which he wrote with Mr. Percy (Playhouse, Apr. 6, 1940); *Jupiter Laughs* (Biltmore, Sept. 9, 1940); directed the pre-Bway tryout of *Play With Fire* (closed Civic Th., Cincinnati, Ohio); *Guest in the House* (Plymouth, N.Y.C., Jan. 14, 1942); *Yesterday's Magic* (Guild, Apr. 14, 1942); *Malice Domestic*, which he wrote with Edward Percy ("Q," London, 1942); *The Two Mrs. Carrolls* (Booth, N.Y.C., Aug. 3, 1943); *Wallflower*, which he wrote with his wife, Mary Orr (Cort, Jan. 26, 1944); *Dark Hammock*, written with Mary Orr (Forrest, Dec. 11, 1944); *Round Trip*, written with Mary Orr (Biltmore, May 29, 1945); *A Joy Forever* (Biltmore, Jan. 7, 1946); *Obsession* (Plymouth, Oct. 1, 1946); *Temper the Wind* (Playhouse, Dec. 27, 1946); wrote, with Edward Percy, *Dog's Delight* ("Q," London, Apr. 2, 1946).

He directed *Portrait in Black* (Booth, N.Y.C., May 14, 1947); wrote, with Mary Orr, *The Coral Snake* ("Q," London, Sept. 2, 1947); directed *Duet for Two Hands* (Booth, N.Y.C., Oct. 7, 1947); *The Man They Acquitted*, which he wrote with Mr. Percy (Wimbledon, London, Oct. 17, 1949); staged the summer-stock tryout of *The Devil Also Dreams* (opened Somerset Summer Th., Mass., July 26, 1950; closed Syracuse, N.Y., 1950); wrote, with Mary Orr, *The Platinum Set* (Saville, London, Mar. 30, 1950); and directed *Grammercy Ghost* (Morosco, N.Y.C., Apr. 26, 1951). Mr. Denham directed *Dial 'M' for Murder* (Plymouth, Oct. 29, 1952); wrote, with Mary Orr, *Sweet Peril* (St. James's, London, Dec. 3, 1952); directed *Be Your Age*, which he wrote with Mary Orr (48 St. Th., N.Y.C., Jan. 14, 1953); *A Date with April* (Royale, Apr. 15, 1953); *Sherlock Holmes* (New Century, Oct. 30, 1953); and *The Bad Seed* (46 St. Th., Dec. 8, 1954); wrote, with Conrad Sutton Smith, *A Dash of Bitters* (Stockbridge, Mass.; Margo Jones Th., Dallas, Tex., 1955); directed *Janus* (Plymouth, N.Y.C., Nov. 24, 1955); *Hide and Seek* (Ethel Barrymore Th., Apr. 2, 1957); *A Mighty Man Is He* (Cort, Jan. 6, 1960); *A Stranger in the Tea* (Edinburgh, Scot., Apr. 1960); *Once for the Asking* (Booth, N.Y.C., Nov. 20, 1963); and *Oh Mama! No, Papa!* (Pasadena Playhouse, Calif., Sept. 1963), which he adapted from the Spanish work of Alfonso Paso. He directed *Hostile Witness* (Music Box Th., N.Y.C., Feb. 17, 1966); directed and wrote, with Mary Orr, *Minor Murder* (Savoy, London, 1967); and directed *You Never Can Tell* (Washington Univ., St. Louis, Mo., 1969).

Films. Mr. Denham directed *The Village Squire* (Col., 1934); *The Crimson Circle* (Du World, 1936); *Death of a Broadcast* (FIA, 1941); and the Italian film *Fast and Sexy* (Col., 1960).

Television. He has written over 100 television scripts with Mary Orr, including 16 scripts for Suspense (CBS), others for Schlitz Playhouse of the Air (CBS), Colgate Playhouse (NBC), Boris Karloff Th., Ellery Queen, and Mr. and Mrs. North. He also appeared on television in Australia and New Zealand in 1964.

Published Works. His published works include the autobiography, *Stars in My Hair* (1958); his adaptations of Alfonso Paso's plays: *Oh Mama! No, Papa!*, *Recipe for a Crime* and *Blue Heaven* (1951); *The Wisdom of Eve*, with Mary Orr (1964); and *Footlights and Feathers* (1966).

Awards. Mr. Denham received the British Empire Shakespeare Society Gold Medal (1912).

Recreation. Music, ornithology.

DENKER, HENRY. Playwright, director, producer. b. Nov. 25, 1912, New York City, to Max and Jennie (Geller) Denker. Father, furrier. Grad. Morris H.S., Bronx, N.Y., 1930; New York Univ., Law Qualifying Certificate, 1931; LL.B. 1934. Married Dec. 5, 1942, to Edith Heckman. Served WW II, OWI. Member of Dramatists Guild; ALA; WGA; NY State Bar Assn. Address: 241 Central Park West, New York, NY 10024, tel. (212) TR 3-5821.

Pre-Theatre. Lawyer.

Theatre. Mr. Denker wrote with Ralph Berkey, *Time Limit!* (Booth Th., N.Y.C., Jan. 24, 1956); wrote and directed *Olive Ogilvie* (Aldwych, London, England, Mar. 13, 1957); wrote *A Far Country* (Music Box, N.Y.C., Apr. 4, 1961); *Venus at Large* (Morosco, Apr. 12, 1962); and *A Case of Libel* (Longacre, Oct. 10, 1963).

He wrote (based on Ugo Betti's *The Burnt Flower Bed*) *So Much of Earth, So Much of Heaven* (Westport Country Playhouse, Conn., Aug. 30, 1965); wrote *The Name of the Game* (Parker Playhouse, Fort Lauderdale, Fla., Feb. 13, 1967); *What Did We Do Wrong?* (Helen Hayes Th., N.Y.C., Oct. 22, 1967); and *The Headhunters* (Bucks County Playhouse, New Hope, Pa., Aug. 1971; Eisenhower Th., Washington, D.C., May 1, 1974). He has also written the plays *A Sound of Distant Thunder* and *About William*.

Films. Mr. Denker wrote the screenplays for *Time Limit!* (UA, 1957); *The Hook* (MGM, 1963); and *Twilight of Honor* (MGM, 1963). The screenplay for *The Greatest Story Ever Told* (UA, 1965) was based partly on his writings.

Television and Radio. For radio, he wrote *Laughter for the Leader* and *Me? I Drive a Hack* (both for the Columbia Workshop, CBS, 1940, 1941). He was a writer for the Radio Reader's Digest (CBS, 1943–47), The Ethel Barrymore Show, and The Cavalcade of America; and was writer, director and producer of The Greatest Story Ever Told series (ABC, 1947–57).

He has appeared on television on the Christopher Program (ABC); and has written *Material Witness* (Kraft Television Th., NBC, Feb. 19, 1958); *Give Us Barabbas* (Hallmark Hall of Fame, NBC, Mar. 1961); adapted his play, *A Case of Libel* (ABC, Feb. 11, 1968); written *The Choice* (NBC, Mar. 30, 1969); and written *Judgment: The Court Martial of Lt. William Calley* (ABC, Jan. 12, 1975).

Published Works. Mr. Denker has written the novels *I'll be Right Home, Ma; My Son, The Lawyer; Salome, Princess of Galilee; That First Easter; The Director* (Richard W. Baron, N.Y.C., 1970); *The Kingmaker* (1972); and *A Place for the Mighty*.

Awards. As author-director-producer of The Greatest Story Ever Told series on radio, Mr. Denker received the Peabody Award, The Christopher Award, and *Variety* Showmanship Award, and the Brotherhood Award from the Natl. Conference of Christians and Jews.

Recreation. Tennis, walking, theatre-going.

DENMARK, L. KIRK. Educator, director, translator. b. Louis Kirk Denmark, May 17, 1916, Laddonia, Mo., to William Lee and Lillith (Kirk) Denmark. Father, businessman. Grad. Springfield (Mo.) H.S., 1934; Southwest Missouri State Univ., B.A. 1938; Yale Univ., M.A. 1940; Univ. of Wisconsin, Ph.M. 1942. Studied mime and improvisation at Education Par Le Jeu Dramatique, Paris, France, 1953–54; dance with Jacqueline Robinson, Paris, 1953–54; special observer at Comédie Française, 1953–54. Private study with Margaret Webster, 1966–71. Served USN, 1942–46, PTO; rank, Lt. Member of ATA; ANTA (bd. of dir., 1965–68); AEA; USITT. Address: (home) 803 Park Ave., Beloit, WI 53511, tel. 362-7141; (bus.) Beloit College, Box 187, Beloit, WI 53511, tel. 365-3391, ext. 232.

Mr. Denmark founded and was chairman of the Dept. of Theatre Arts at Beloit College (1946–70), where he was assistant professor (1946–49), associate professor (1949–55), professor (1955–73); emeritus professor and visiting theatre artist (1973–to date). He has directed 305 productions at Beloit (1946–to date) for Beloit College Players, which operates during the academic year with college actors, and the Court Theatre, which operated in the summer with professional actors (founded and directed from 1951 through 20th anniversary season in 1971).

Mr. Denmark founded the Springfield (Mo.) Little Th. where he made his debut as director of *The Importance of Being Earnest* (June 1934); subsequently was guest director for the Univ. of Wisconsin Players (Winter 1941–42; Summer 1946), directed productions for the Madison (Wis.) Theatre Guild; Springfield (Mo.) Little Theatre; Rockford (Ill.) Little Theatre; and the Association of Junior Leagues.

Among his Molière translations that have been produced are *The Miser* (Milwaukee Repertory Th., 1967; Syracuse Repertory Th., 1968); *Tartuffe* (Alley Th., Houston, Tex., 1969); and *Les Femmes Savantes*, which he also directed as visiting theatre artist at Hamline Univ. Th. (1972). His translations of Molière have been produced also by colleges and universities in Va., Mont., Tex., Mo., Ill., Neb., Fla., Ore., Minn., N.D., Ohio, and Md. He directed at the New American Th., Rockford, Ill. (1973); Equity Library Theatre showcase, Chicago, Ill. (1973); was guest director and visiting professor at the Univ. of Miami, Fla. (1973); and, for the fortieth anniversary of the Springfield (Mo.) Little Th., directed *The Man Who Came to Dinner* (1974).

Recreation. Writing, bicycling, dancing.

DENNIS, SANDY. Actress. b. Sandra Dale Dennis, Apr. 27, 1937, Hastings, Nebr., to Jack and Yvonne Dennis. Father, postal clerk; mother, secretary. Attended Nebr. Wesleyan Univ.; Univ. of Nebraska. Studied acting with Herbert Berghof at the H B Studio, N.Y.C. Member of Actors Studio. Married June 1965 to Gerry Mulligan, musician. Address: Weston, CT 06880.

Theatre. Miss Dennis made her professional debut as Hilde in *The Lady From the Sea* (Tempo Th., N.y.C., Dec. 12, 1956); played Elma Duckworth in a stock production of *Bus Stop* (Royal Poinciana Playhouse, Palm Beach, Fla., Jan. 1957); was understudy for the roles of Flirt Conroy and Reenie Flood in *The Dark at the Top of the Stairs* (Music Box, N.Y.C., Dec. 5, 1957) and played Reenie Flood in the national tour (opened Playhouse, Wilmington, Del., Jan. 21, 1959); played Mordeen in a revival of *Burning Bright* (Th. East, N.Y.C., Oct. 16, 1959); Nancy in the pre-Bway tryout of *Motel* (opened Wilbur, Boston, Jan. 6, 1960; closed there Jan. 16, 1960); Sister Gabrielle in a revival of *Port Royal* (Grace Protestant Episcopal Church, N.Y.C., Apr. 25, 1960); and made her Bway debut as Millicent Bishop in *Face of a Hero* (Eugene O'Neill Th., Oct. 20, 1960).

She played Ann Howard in *The Complaisant Lover* (Ethel Barrymore Th., Nov. 1, 1961); Sandra Markowitz in *A Thousand Clowns* (Eugene O'Neill Th., Apr. 5, 1962); Ellen Gordon in *Any Wednesday* (Music Box, Feb. 18, 1964); made her London debut as Irina in the Actors Studio production of *The Three Sisters* (World Th. season, Aldwych, May 12, 1965); played the title role in *Daphne in Cottage D* (Longacre, N.Y.C., Oct. 15, 1967); Cherie in *Bus Stop* (Ivanhoe, Chicago, Aug. 11, 1970); Teresa Phillips in *How the Other Half Loves* (Royale, N.Y.C., Mar. 29, 1971); Catherine Reardon in a stock tour of *And Miss Reardon Drinks a Little* (Summer 1971); succeeded (Fall 1971) Julie Harris as Anna Reardon in the national tour of *And Miss Reardon Drinks a Little* (closed Civic Th., Chicago, Mar. 12, 1972) and played that role in a stock tour (Summer 1972); played Hannah Heywood in *Let Me Hear You Smile* (Biltmore, N.Y.C., Jan. 16, 1973); Blanche DuBois in *A Streetcar Named Desire* (Ivanhoe, Chicago, Aug. 1973); Eva in *Absurd Person Singular* (Music Box, N.Y.C., Oct. 8, 1974); which she left to play Maggie in a stock tour of *Cat on a Hot Tin Roof* (Summer 1975), returning to the role on Nov. 12, 1975.

Films. Miss Dennis made her debut in a small role in *Splendor in the Grass* (WB, 1961); played Honey in *Who's Afraid of Virginia Woolf?* (WB, 1966); Irina in the Actors Studio production of *The Three Sisters* (not released commercially, but shown on television; cf. below); appeared in *Up the Down Staircase* (WB, 1967); *The Fox* (Claridge/WB;1968); *Sweet November* (WB, 1968); *Thank You All Very Much* (Col., 1969); *That Cold Day in the Park* (Commonwealth United, 1969); and *The Out-of-Towners* (Par., 1970).

Television. She has appeard on Naked City (ABC, Sept. 26, 1962); Mr. Broadway (CBS); Arrest and Trial (ABC); The Fugitive (ABC); as Irina in *The Three Sisters* (WOR, Jan. 19, 1968); Celia Pope in *A Hatful of Rain* (ABC, Mar. 3, 1968); and in the telefilm *Something Evil* (CBS, Jan. 21, 1972).

Awards. For her performance in *A Thousand Clowns,* she shared, with Barbra Streisand, the *Variety* NY Drama Critics Poll Award (1962), and won the Antoinette Perry (Tony) Award as Best Supporting Actress (1963); for *Any Wednesday,* won the Antoinette Perry (Tony) Award as Best Actress (1964) and the *Variety* NY Drama Critics Poll (1964); for her performance as Catherine Reardon in *And Miss Reardon Drinks a Little,* she won the Strawhat Award as best actress for the summer theatre Season (1971).

She won the Academy (Oscar) Award as best supporting actress for *Who's Afraid of Virginia Woolf?* (1967); and the Moscow Film Fest. Best Actress Award for *Up the Down Staircase* (1967).

DENTON, CRAHAN. Actor. b. Seattle, Wash. Attended Univ. of California. Studied acting at the Neighborhood Playhouse Sch. of the Th., N.Y.C. Member of AEA; AFTRA. Address: 777 Hollywood Blvd., Hollywood, CA 90046.

Theatre. Mr. Denton made his N.Y.C. debut as Gage in *Key Largo* (Ethel Barrymore Th., Nov. 27, 1939); in stock, appeared in *Something About a Soldier* (Bucks County Playhouse, New Hope, Pa., Summer 1940); played one of the Two in *Liberty Jones* (Shubert, N.Y.C., Feb. 5, 1941); Capt. William Smith in *The Story of Mary Surratt* (Henry Miller's Th., Feb. 8, 1947); Mikel Geistner in the New Dramatists' production *KG* (The Palm Garden, N.Y.C., Mar. 19, 1952); T/Sgt. Tolliver in *The Fragile Fox* (Belasco, Oct. 12, 1954); Virgil in *Bus Stop* (Music Box, Mar. 2, 1955); Jake Torrence in *Orpheus Descending* (Martin Beck Th., Mar. 21, 1957); Will Henderson in *Winesburg, Ohio* (Natl., Feb. 5, 1958); and L. D. Royal in *The Buffalo Skinner* (Th. Marquee, Feb. 19, 1959).

Television. Mr. Denton has played in *The Egg and I;* appeared on Big Story (NBC); Robert Montgomery Presents (NBC); The Web (CBS); played in *Mr. Lincoln;* and appeared on Omnibus (CBS).

DERR, RICHARD. Actor. b. Richard LeMar Derr, Norristown, Pa., to Walter and Martha (Kulp) Derr. Father, civil engineer. Grad. Norristown H.S. Served US Army Air Transport Command, 1942–45; rank, Navigator. Member of AEA; SAG; AFTRA. Address: 8965 Cynthia St., Los Angeles, CA 90069, tel. (213) OL 2-7011.

Theatre. Mr. Derr first appeared at the Hedgerow Th. (Moylan, Pa., 1938–40); subsequently played John in a touring production of *John Loves Mary* (Harris, Chicago, Ill., Apr. 1948); made his Bway debut as Lt. Henderson in *The Traitor* (48th St. Th., Mar. 31, 1949); subsequently played Dr. Harriman in *The Closing Door* (Empire, Dec. 12, 1949); Tegeus-Chromis in *A Phoenix Too Frequent* (Fulton, Apr. 26, 1950); and Clark Redfield in a tour of *Dream Girl* (Summer 1951).

He appeared as Raymond Brinton in *Grand Tour* (Martin Beck Th., N.Y.C., Dec. 10, 1951); Max Halliday in *Dial 'M' for Murder* (Plymouth, Oct. 29, 1952); Dan King in *Plain and Fancy* (Mark Hellinger Th., Jan. 27, 1955), which he repeated for his London debut (Drury Lane, Jan. 25, 1956).

He appeared as Mark in *Maybe Tuesday* (Playhouse, N.Y.C., Jan. 29, 1958); appeared as Brick in a tour of *Cat on a Hot Tin Roof* (Summer 1958); in the title role of a tour of *Mister Roberts* (Summer 1959); and as Tucker Grogan in *Invitation to a March* (Music Box, N.Y.C., Oct. 29, 1960).

Films. Mr. Derr made his screen debut in *Man at Large* (20th-Fox, 1941); subsequently appeared in *Commandos Strike at Dawn* (Col., 1942); *The Secret Heart* (MGM, 1946); *The Bride Goes Wild* (MGM, 1948); *Luxury Liner* (MGM, 1948); *Joan of Arc* (RKO, 1948); *Guilty of Treason* (Eagle Lion, 1949); *Something To Live For* (Par., 1950); *When Worlds Collide* (Par., 1950); and *Terror Is a Man* (Valiant, 1959).

Television. Among the many television programs on which Mr. Derr has appeared are The F.B.I. (ABC), Marcus Welby, M.D. (ABC), Barnaby Jones, and as the doctor on the "Movie of the Week" *Morning After.*

Other Activities. Mr. Derr is a realtor member of the Beverly Hills (Calif.) Realty Board.

Awards. He received a *Theatre World* Award for his performance as Lt. Henderson in *The Traitor* (1949).

DE SANTIS, JOE. Actor, teacher, sculptor. b. Joseph V. De Santis, New York City, June 15, 1909, to Pasquale and Maria (Paoli) De Santis. Father, tailor. Educ. P.S. 95 and Stuyvesant H.S., all in New York City and City Coll. of New York. Professional training Leonardo da Vinci Art School, N.Y.; Beaux Arts Institute of Design; apprenticed to Onorio Ruotolo, 1927–29. Married Oct. 19, 1935, to Miriam Moss, actress (marr. dis.); one son; May 23, 1949, to Margaret Draper, actress (marr. dis.); one son; Nov. 23, 1959, to Wanda June Slye. Member of AEA; SAG; AFTRA (Los Angeles local bd.; natl. bd.; convention delegate, 1969–to date); ANTA (bd. of dir., Los Angeles chap.); The Masquers (Los Angeles Jesterate); The Players, New York. Address: (home) Box 327, Etiwanda, CA 91739, tel. (714) 899-1353; (bus.) c/o AFTRA, 1717 N. Highland Ave., Hollywood, CA 90028, tel. (213) 461-8111.

Theatre. Mr. De Santis made his stage debut as Giulio Bernini in *Scampolo* (Casa Italiana, Columbia Univ., N.Y.C., May 11, 1929); his first professional appearance as Mr. Tevenson in *GI' Incoscienti* (Brooklyn Acad. of Music, Sept. 7, 1931); and his first appearance on Bway as Leone in *Sirena* (Waldorf Th., Sept. 21, 1931). He played Abner in *Saul* (Willis Th., Jan. 14, 1932); appeared with the Walter Hampden Repertory Co. as Cuigy in *Cyrano de Bergerac* (Albany, N.Y., Sept. 1932; New Amsterdam Th., N.Y.C., Dec. 22, 1932) and on US tour with the company (Spring 1933) as Giotti in *Caponsacchi* and Francisco in *Hamlet;* was the Doctor in *It Happened* (Columbia Univ., N.Y.C., July 1933); Marquis de Priego in *Ruy Blas* (pre-Bway: opened, Colonial, Pittsfield, Mass., Oct. 9, 1933; closed, Ford Th., Baltimore, Md. Oct. 1933). In 1934, as a member of La Compagnia del Teatro d'Arte, playing Italian repertory, he was Beauchamp in *The Count of Monte Cristo* (Longacre, N.Y.C., Jan. 21), Dr. Servou in *Il Padrone delle Ferriere* (Longacre, Mar. 18), Borniche in *Il Colonello Bridau* (Longacre, Apr. 15), Brabantio in *Othello* (Playhouse, May 6), Giovanni Ansperti in *Romanticismo* (Longacre, May 14), Generico in *Fantasma* (Fleisher Aud., Philadelphia, Pa., May 29), Chenildieu in *Les Miserables* (Longacre, N.Y.C., Sept. 23), Basco in the second part of *Les Miserables* (Longacre, Sept. 23), St. Gaudens in *Camille* (Longacre, Oct. 21). In 1935, he toured as Brutus in *Julius Caesar,* appearing in CCC camps, prisons, and settlement houses with the C.W.A.-E.R.B. Th., a forerunner of the WPA theatre.

He played Dr. Antommarchi in *St. Helena* (Lyceum, Oct. 6, 1936); was in *Il Peccato d'un Angelo* (Lazzara's Music Hall, Jan. 17, 1937); played Caifas in *La Passione* (Teatro Cine-Roma, Mar. 21, 1937); Joe in *Bangtails* (pre-Bway: Atlantic City, N.J., Sept. 2, 1940); the Soothsayer in *Journey to Jerusalem* (National Th., N.Y.C., Oct. 10, 1940); Luigi in *Walk into My Parlour* (pre-Bway: Glen Rock, N.J., Aug. 18, 1941); Ricci in *Keep Covered* (pre-Bway: Baltimore, Md., Sept. 8, 1941); and repeated his performance as Luigi in *Walk into My Parlour* (Forrest Th., N.Y.C., Nov. 19, 1941).

He replaced (Aug. 3, 1942) Bruce Gordon as Officer Klein in *Arsenic and Old Lace* (Fulton Th., Jan. 10, 1941); played Moy in *Men in Shadow* (Morosco, Mar. 10, 1943); the Arabian Bread Seller in *Storm Operation* (Belasco Th., Jan. 11, 1944); the Young Italian Waiter in *The Searching Wind* (Fulton Th., Apr. 12, 1944); Diamond Louie in *Front Page* (Royale, Sept. 4, 1946); replaced (Apr. 1, 1952) Joseph Wiseman as Eddie Fuselli in *Golden Boy* (ANTA Playhouse, Mar. 12, 1952); played the title role in *Liliom* (Brattle Th., Cambridge, Mass., June 24, 1952); Carminelli in *In Any Language* (Cort, N.Y.C., Oct. 7, 1952); and Herbie Milton in *A Certain Joy* (pre-Bway: opened, Playhouse, Wilmington, Del., Feb. 12, 1953; closed, Locust, Philadelphia, Pa., Feb. 21, 1953).

He appeared also as Renato in *The Time of the Cuckoo* (Clinton Playhouse, Clinton, Conn., July 23, 1954); as Gus in *Strictly Dishonorable* (Somerset Th., Somerset, Mass., July 31, 1954); off-Bway replaced (Nov. 19, 1954) Bert Freed as Sam Gordon in *A Stone for Danny Fisher* (downtown National, Oct. 21, 1954); was Bronislau Partos in *The Highest Tree* (Longacre, Nov. 4, 1959); the Police Chief in *The Balcony* (Civic Playhouse, Los Angeles, Calif., Sept. 1961); Prof. Emilio Galuzzi in *Daughter of Silence* (Music Box, N.Y.C., Nov. 30, 1961); and Brabantio in *Othello* (Mark Taper Forum, Los Angeles, Calif., Apr. 8, 1971).

Films. Mr. De Santis made his motion picture debut in the part of Gregory in *Slattery's Hurricane* (20th-Fox, 1949). Subsequent films in which he played include *Man With a Cloak* (MGM, 1951); *The Last Hunt* (MGM, 1956); *Full of Life* (Col., 1957); *Case Against Brooklyn* (Col., 1958); *I Want to Live!* (UA, 1958); *Buchanan Rides Alone* (Col., 1958); *Cry Tough* (UA, 1959); *The George Raft Story* (Allied Artists, 1961); *And Now Miguel* (U, 1966); *An American Dream* (WB, 1966); *The Professionals* (Col. 1966); *Madame X* (U, 1966); *The Venetian Affair* (MGM, 1967); *Chubasco* (WB-7 Arts, 1968); *The Brotherhood* (Kirk Douglas, 1968); *Blue* (Par., 1968); and *Little Cigars* (Amer. Internat., 1973).

Television and Radio. Mr. De Santis has appeared on several thousand radio and television programs since his debut on Italian-speaking radio in 1931; his first radio appearance in English was on Pepper Young's Family (WEAF, Mar. 1940), and he was a regular on such serials as They Live in Brooklyn (WMCA), The Goldbergs (CBS), Kitty Foyle (CBS), Light of the World (NBC), Stand by for Adventure (NBC), The Clock (ABC), Dick Tracy (ABC), Tennessee Jed (ABC), The Sparrow and the Hawk (CBS), Brighter Day (CBS), The Greatest Story Ever Told (NBC), and Eternal Light (NBC). He was narrator on Norman Corwin's *This Is War* (all networks, 1942) and *On a Note of Triumph* (CBS, May 1945); broadcast in Spanish during World War II on shortwave programs to Latin America; and was featured on the US Army's So Proudly We Hail (1949–51). On television, Mr. De Santis made his debut on *See! Hear!* (NBC, Mar. 27, 1940) and has since played more than 300 roles on programs carried by all the major networks, beginning with live appearances during the 1950s on such programs as Danger (CBS), Th. Guild of the Air (NBC), Playhouse 90 (CBS), Studio One (CBS), and Robert Montgomery Presents (NBC). He was a regular on the Red Buttons Show, the Martha Raye Show (NBC), Colgate Comedy Hour (NBC), Texaco Star Th. (NBC), and Caesar's Hour (NBC). He played Lotito in The Untouchables and the Father in *Golden Windows* (both ABC) and Morelli in *Don't Grow Old* (East Side/West Side, CBS). Other shows on which he has appeared include 77 Sunset Strip (ABC), Bonanza (NBC), Desilu Playhouse (NBC), Gunsmoke (CBS), Rawhide (CBS), Perry Mason (CBS), Dr. Kildare (NBC), Sam Benedict (NBC), The Virginian (NBC), The Name of the Game (NBC), Cheyenne (ABC), Mission: Impossible (CBS), Route 66 (CBS), Naked City (ABC), General Electric Theatre (CBS), Ben Casey (ABC), Wagon Train (NBC), Hawaii Five-O (CBS), and the New Dick Van Dyke Show (CBS).

Other Activities. Mr. De Santis had his own

sculpture studio from 1936 to 1940. He taught sculpture at the Henry Street Settlement, the Educational Alliance, and the YMHA at 92nd St. and Lexington Ave., all in N.Y.C. His sculpture has been exhibited at the Robinson and Feragil Galleries, the 1939 World's Fair, and in a group show at the A. C. A. Gallery (June 1940). His portrait of Walter Hampden as Cyrano is in the Walter Hampden Memorial Library. Mr. De Santis also conducted an actors workshop for ANTA (1964–68) and taught dialects for the American Theatre Wing.

Published Works. Mr. De Santis's articles on art have been published in *Progresso Italo-American;* his columm "Remember Radio" appeared in *The Studio Magazine.*.

Recreation. Flying, photography, gardening, gourmet cooking, directed plays at the Masquers, and sculpting in wood and stone.

DETTMER, ROGER. Theatre critic, music critic. b. Roger Christian Dettmer, Aug. 2, 1927, Cincinnati, Ohio, to Christian H. and Cornelia (Van Schouwen) Dettmer. Father, commercial artist; mother, ceramic designer and manufacturer. Grad. Western Hills H.S., Cincinnati, 1945; attended Univ. of Cincinnati, 1945–47; Columbia Univ., 1947; grad. Univ. of Mich., B.A. (Phi Beta Kappa) 1950. Member of AFTRA; American Theatre Critics Assn.; Interamerican Music Critics Assn.; Music Critics' Assn. (charter member, 1953; vice-pres., 1957); Phi Kappa Psi. Address: (home) 415 W. Aldine Ave., Chicago, IL 60657; (bus.) The *Chicago Tribune*, 435 N. Michigan Ave., Chicago, IL 60611, tel. (312) 222-4282.

In Sept. 1974, Mr. Dettmer became theatre critic of the *Chicago Tribune.* From 1953 to 1974, he was theatre-music critic of *Chicago Today* (formerly Chicago *American*), and he has been Chicago correspondent for *Opera* magazine (London) since 1961. Previously, he was assistant manager of the Cincinnati Symphony Orchestra (1950–51); and music writer for the NY *Herald Tribune* (1951–53).

Television and Radio. He was commentator on his own radio program, Roger Dettmer's Byline Review (WGN, Chicago, 1961–64).

For television, he was moderator on Symphony Quiz (WSAI, Cincinnati, 1950–51); and commentator on his own television program, Roger Dettmer Reviews (WTTW, Chicago, 1961–62).

Recreation. Astrology, performer coaching, traveling, cataloguing book and record library, cooking.

DeVINE, LAWRENCE. Drama critic. b. Joseph Lawrence DeVine, Sept. 21, 1935, New York City, to John Justine and Hazel (Tippet) DeVine. Father, film advertising executive. Grad. Monroe (Mich.) Catholic Central H.S., 1953; att. Georgetown Univ., 1953–54; grad. Medill Sch. of Journalism, Northwestern Univ., B.S. 1957. Married to Jane Christian; one son, one daughter (marr. dis. Apr. 8, 1968); marr. July 26, 1968, to Lucy Memory Williamson. Served U.S. Army, 1958–62, U.S. Counter Intelligence Corps, Special Agent, Russian language specialist, Western Europe. Member of Amer. Theatre Critics Assn.; Outer Critics Circle. Address: (home) 1050 Van Dyke, Detroit, MI 48214, tel. (313) 499-0348; (bus.) The Detroit *Free Press*, Detroit, MI 48231, tel. (313) 222-6517.

Mr. DeVine is drama critic for The Detroit *Free Press* (1968–to date). Previously, he was entertainment editor and drama critic for the Los Angeles *Herald-Examiner* (1967–68), and drama critic (1965–67) of the Miami *Herald,* where he formerly served as an architectural writer and arts columnist (1962–65).

Other Activities. He is associate director of the Critics Institute of the Eugene O'Neill Memorial Theater Center (Waterford, Conn.); a former Critic Fellow at the O'Neill Institute (1971); and has lectured in drama criticism at the Univ. of Detroit.

Published Works. Mr. DeVine has contributed articles to *New York* Magazine, and The Los Angeles *Times,* and is a syndicated contributor on the Knight Newspapers wire service.

DE VRIES, PETER. Playwright, editor, novelist. b. Feb. 27, 1910, Chicago, Ill., to Joost and Henrietta (Eldersveld) De Vries. Grad. Calvin Coll., B.A. 1931. Married Oct. 16, 1943, to Katinka Loeser; three sons, one daughter. Address: (home) Cross Highway, Westport, CT 06880; (bus.) c/o *The New Yorker*, 25 W. 43rd St., New York, NY 10036.

Theatre. Mr.De Vries was author, with Joseph Fields, of *The Tunnel of Love,* based on his novel of the same title (Royale, N.Y.C., Feb. 13, 1957; Her Majesty's Th., London, Dec. 3, 1957); and his novel *Reuben, Reuben* was dramatized by Herman Shumlin as *Spofford* (ANTA Th., N.Y.C., Dec. 14, 1967).

Films. Motion pictures made from Mr. De Vries's books include *The Tunnel of Love* (MGM, 1958); *How Do I Love Thee?* (ABC, 1970), based on *Let Me Count the Ways*; and *Pete 'n' Tillie* (1973), based on *Witch's Milk.*

Other Activities. He was editor of a community newspaper in Chicago, Ill. (1931–32); subsequently associate editor (1938–41) and co-editor (1942–44) of *Poetry* magazine; and a member of the editorial staff of *The New Yorker* (July 1944–to date). He is a member of the National Institute of Arts and Letters.

Published Works. Mr. De Vries is the author of *No, But I Saw the Movie* (1952); *The Tunnel of Love* (1954); *Comfort Me with Apples* (1956); *The Mackerel Plaza* (1958); *The Tents of Wickedness* (1959); *Through the Fields of Clover* (1961); *The Blood of the Lamb* (1961); *Reuben, Reuben* (1964); *Let Me Count the Ways* (1965); *The Vale of Laughter* (1967); *The Cat's Pajamas and Witch's Milk* (1968); *Mrs. Wallop* (1970); *Into Your Tent I'll Creep* (1971); *Without a Stitch in Time* (1972); and *Forever Panting* (1973).

DEWELL, MICHAEL. Producer. b. Mar. 21, 1931, West Haven, Conn., to Mansfield H. and Rolly (Dwy) Dewell. Father, engineer. Grad. Hopkins Grammar (prep.) Sch., New Haven, Conn., 1948; Yale Univ., B.A., 1952; RADA, 1954; studied acting with Uta Hagen, N.Y.C., 1954–56. Served US Army, Special Services, 1956–58. Member of ANTA (dir. of NY chap., 1961–64).

Theatre. Mr. Dewell participated in undergraduate drama activites at Yale University's Berkeley College (1949–52); later, at the Royal Academy of Dramatic Arts (London), he appeared in the Restoration comedy, *The Housewives' Confederacy,* which was presented at a Command Performance before Queen Elizabeth (Oct. 1953).

Returning to the US, he appeared in a touring company of *Kiss and Tell* (1954); and directed the revival of *The Heiress* (Carnegie Hall Th., N.Y.C., Sept. 21, 1954); was an assistant to the producers and stage manager for *Dragon's Mouth* (Cherry Lane Th., Nov. 16, 1955), and for *Dandy Dick* (Cherry Lane Th., Jan. 10, 1956).

He founded, with Frances Ann Dougherty, the National Phoenix Th., and produced a touring company of *Mary Stuart* (opened Sacramento H.S., Calif., Oct. 2, 1959; closed National, Washington, D.C., May 7, 1960); produced the national tour company of *Once Upon a Mattress* (opened Veterans' Memorial Aud., Providence, R.I., Oct. 21, 1960; closed Natl., Washington, D.C., May 27, 1961).

Mr. Dewell and Mrs. Dougherty organized The American Festival at the Boston Arts Center (Summer 1961), presenting the American premiere of Benjamin Britten's, *The Turn of the Screw* (July 4–15), also *The American Dance Festival* (July 16–30); and a new musical version of *Anatol* (Aug. 1–20).

Also with Mrs. Dougherty, Mr. Dewell organized the National Repertory Theatre, presenting *Mary Stuart* and *Elizabeth the Queen* (opened Academy of Music, Northampton, Mass., Oct. 19, 1961; closed Rochester Aud., Rochester, N.Y., Apr. 14, 1962); presented *Ring 'Round the Moon, The Crucible,* and *The Seagull* (1963), which toured cross-country. The latter two were presented in N.Y.C. (Belasco, Apr. 5–6, 1964).

In 1967, National Repertory Theatre revivals, produced by Mr. Dewell and Mrs. Dougherty with American National Theatre and Academy (all at ANTA Th., N.Y.C.), were *The Imaginary Invalid* (May 1), *A Touch of the Poet* (May 2), and *Tonight at 8:30* (May 3); in 1968, the National Repertory Theatre moved into the restored Ford's Th., Washington, D.C.), where Mr. Dewell presented *John Brown's Body* (Feb. 12), *The Comedy of Errors* (Feb. 26), and *She Stoops to Conquer* (Mar. 26).

Television and Radio. At Yale, Mr. Dewell produced and directed Radio Workshop (WYBC). During his military service, he was associated with the Television Division of the Dept. of Defense. He has produced 200 color programs for WRAMC-TV and produced *Mary Stuart* (Play of the Week, WNTA, 1960).

Awards. Mr. Dewell received two Outer Circle awards for *Mary Stuart* (1960, 1962).

Recreation. Sailing, restoring antiques.

DEWHURST, COLLEEN. Actress. b. Montreal, Canada. Attended Downer Coll. for Young Ladies, Milwaukee, Wis. Studied for the stage at AADA, 1947; acting with Harold Clurman and Joseph Anthony, N.Y.C. Married 1947 to James Vickery, actor (marr. dis. 1959); married 1960 to George C. Scott, actor, director (marr. dis. July 1965); two sons; remarried July 1967 to Mr. Scott (marr. dis. Feb. 2, 1972). Address: South Salem, NY 10590.

Theatre. Miss Dewhurst made her first professional appearance while a student at the Amer. Acad. of Dramatic Art, as Julia Cavendish in *The Royal Family* (Carnegie Lyceum, N.Y.C., Oct. 15, 1946); made her Bway debut as a Neighbor in *Desire Under the Elms* (ANTA, Jan. 16, 1952); and subsequently played a Turkish Concubine and a Virgin of Memphis in *Tamburlaine the Great* (Winter Garden, Jan. 19, 1956).

At the NY Shakespeare Festival, she appeared as Tamora in *Titus Andronicus* (East Side Amphitheatre, Aug. 1956); Kate in *The Taming of the Shrew* (Emmanuel Presbyterian Church, Nov. 1956); played the title role in *Camille* (Cherry Lane, Sept. 9, 1956); the Queen in *The Eagle Has Two Heads* (Actors Playhouse, Dec. 13, 1956); appeared as Penelope in the pre-Bway tour of *Maiden Voyage* (opened Forrest, Philadelphia, Pa., Feb. 28, 1957; closed there Mar. 9, 1957); at the NY Shakespeare Festival, played Lady Macbeth in *Macbeth* (Belvedere Lake Th., Aug. 1957).

She played Mrs. Squeamish in *The Country Wife* (Adelphi, Nov. 27, 1957); Laetitia in *Children of Darkness* (Circle in the Square, Feb. 28, 1958); appeared at The Festival of Two Worlds (Spoleto, Italy) as Josie Hogan in *A Moon for the Misbegotten* (Summer 1958); played Cleopatra for the NY Shakespeare Festival production of *Antony and Cleopatra* (Heckscher, Jan. 1959); appeared as Caesonia in *Caligula* (54 St. Th., Feb. 16, 1960); Mary Follet in *All the Way Home* (Belasco, Nov. 30, 1960); Phoebe Flaherty in *Great Day in the Morning* (Henry Miller's Th., Mar. 28, 1962); Abbie Putnam in *Desire Under the Elms* (Circle in the Square, Jan. 8, 1963); repeated the role of Cleopatra in the NY Shakespeare Festival production of *Antony and Cleopatra* (Delacorte, June 20, 1963); and appeared as Miss Amelia Evans in *The Ballad of the Sad Café* (Martin Beck Th., Oct. 30, 1963).

She toured as Martha in *Who's Afraid of Virginia Woolf?* (Summer 1965); appeared at the Studio Arena Th., Buffalo, N.Y., in a repeat of her performance as Josie Hogan in *A Moon for the Misbegotten* (Oct. 7, 1965) and as Regina Giddens in *The Little Foxes* (Mar. 24, 1966); toured as Eleanor in *The Lion in Winter* (Summer 1966); appeared as Sara in *More Stately Mansions* (Broadhurst, N.Y.C., Oct. 31, 1967); played Hester in *Hello and Goodbye* (Sheridan Square Playhouse, Sept. 18, 1969); Shen Teh in *The Good Woman of Setzuan* (Vivian Beaumont Th., Nov. 5, 1970); The Mistress in *All Over* (Martin Beck Th., Mar. 27, 1971); appeared at the NY Shakespeare Festival as Gertrude in *Hamlet* (Delacorte Th., July 19–Aug. 5 1972); was Christine Mannon in *Mourning Becomes Electra* (Circle in the Square/Joseph E. Levine Th., Nov. 15, 1972); again appeared as Josie Hogan in *A Moon for the Misbegot-*

ten (Chicago, Summer 1973; Morosco, N.Y.C., Dec. 29, 1973; Ahmanson Th., Los Angeles, Calif., Nov. 26, 1974); and played Margaret in *Artichoke* (Long Wharf Th., New Haven, Conn., Oct. 17, 1975).

Films. Miss Dewhurst's motion pictures include *The Nun's Story* (WB, 1959); *Man on a String* (Col., 1960); *A Fine Madness* (WB, 1966); *The Last Run* (1971); *The Cowboys* (WB, 1972); and *McQ* (WB, 1974).

Television. Miss Dewhurst appeared in *Medea* (Play of the Week, WNTA, 1959); *Burning Bright* (Play of the Week, WNTA, 1959); *I, Don Quixote* (CBS, 1959); *No Exit* (Play of the Week, WNTA, Feb 1961); *Focus* (WNBC, 1962); *Antony and Cleopatra* (CBS, 1963); *In What America?* (World Th., ABC, 1964); *My Mother's House* (Showcase, WNTA, 1967); *The Crucible* (CBS, 1967); *The Price* (Hallmark Hall of Fame, NBC, 1971); *THe Hand of Cormac Joyce* (Hallmark Hall of Fame, NBC, 1972); and *The Story of Jacob and Joseph* (ABC, 1974). She was also in episodes of various series, including East Side/West Side (CBS, 1964); Dr. Kildare (NBC, 1965); The Virginian (NBC, 1965); Alfred Hitchcock (NBC, 1965); Ben Casey (ABC, 1965); The F.B.I. (ABC, 1966); and Big Valley (ABC, 1966).

Awards. Miss Dewhurst won *The Village Voice* Off-Bway (Obie) Award for her performances as the Queen in *The Eagle Has Two Heads* and Kate in *The Taming of the Shrew* (1957) and as Abbie Putnam in *Desire Under the Elms* (1963); and the *Theatre World* (1958) Award for her performance as Laetitia in *Children of Darkness.* She received the Lola D'Annunzio Award and an Antoinette Perry (Tony) Award (1961) for her role as Mary Follet in *All the Way Home;* and was nominated for the Antoinette Perry (Tony) Award (1962) for her performance as Phoebe Flaherty in *Great Day in the Morning.* She was awarded the Sylvania Award (1960) for her performance in *I, Don Quixote;* was nominated for NATAS (Emmy) Award (1962) for her performance as Gertrude Hart in *Focus;* received Drama Desk awards for her performances as Hester in *Hello and Goodbye* (1970) and The Mistress in *All Over* (1971); and for her performance as Josie Hogan in *A Moon for the Misbegotten* received an Antoinette Perry (Tony) Award (1974), another Drama Desk Award, and the Los Angeles (Calif.) Drama Critics Circle Award. In 1972, Lawrence Univ. conferred upon her the honorary degree of D.F.A.

DE WITT, FAY. Comedienne, actress, singer, dialetician. b. Fay Blossom De Witt, Dec. 4, 1935, N.Y., to Albert and Kate (Grebiner) De Witt. Attended New York Univ. (pre-law) 1952–53. Married May 30, 1960, to George Wagner, production stage manager; one son, one daughter; (marr. dis. June 1964). Member of SAG; AFTRA; AEA; AGVA.

Theatre. Miss De Witt first appeared on the stage as Mary in *The Children's Hour* (Pasadena Playhouse, Calif., 1947); and appeared in stock productions at Tamiment, Pa. (Summer 1950).

She made her N.Y.C. debut in the revue, *Pardon Our French* (Bway Th., Oct. 5, 1950); and played Griselda in *Flahooley* (Broadhurst, May 14, 1951).

At the Green Mansions Th., Warrensburg, N.Y., she played Marie in *Come Back, Little Sheba* and Frances Black in *Light Up the Sky* (Summer 1952); later appeared as Meg in *Brigadoon* (Valley Forge Music Fair, Devon, Pa., Summer 1955); Sharon in *Finian's Rainbow* and Annie Oakley in *Annie Get Your Gun* (Vanguard Playhouse, Detroit, Mich.; Karamu Th., Cleveland, Ohio, Summer 1956); appeared in the revue *Shoestring '57* (Barbizon-Plaza, Th., N.Y.C., Nov. 5, 1956); in *The Best of Shoestring* (Casa Manana Th., Ft. Worth, Tex., 1957); as Mme. Nunez in *Roberta* (Music Th., Ohio, Summer 1958); and Ella in *Bells Are Ringing* (Pinebrook, N.J., Summer 1959).

She appeared in the revue *Vintage '60* (Ivar, Los Angeles, Mar. 1960; Brooks Atkinson Th., N.Y.C., Sept. 12, 1960); played Dorothy in *Gentlemen Prefer Blondes* (Meadowbrook Dinner Th., Cedar Grove, N.J., Summer 1961); Cleo in *The Most Happy Fella* (South Shore Music Circus, Cohasset, Mass., 1961); Ado Annie Carnes in a revival of *Oklahoma!* (NY City Ctr., May 15, 1963); the title role in *The Unsinkable Molly Brown* (Lambertville Music Circus, N.J., June 1963); Clotilde in *New Moon* (Cape Cod Melody Top, Hyannis, Mass., July 1963); and replaced Marilyn Maxwell as Ella in *Bells Are Ringing* (Westbury Music Fair, N.Y., Aug. 1963); and Karen Morrow in *The Boys from Syracuse* (Th. Four, N.Y.C., Apr. 15, 1963).

Films. Miss De Witt has appeared in *You're the One* (Par., 1941); *The Patsy* (Par., 1964); *I'll Take Sweden* (UA, 1965); *The Shakiest Gun in the West* (U, 1968); *How To Frame a Figg* (U, 1971); and *The New York Experience* (Trans-Lux, 1973).

Television. She has appeared on Ted Mack's Amateur Hour (CBS), GE Th. (CBS), the Milton Berle Show (NBC, 1952); Stop the Music (1951); the George Jessel Show (NBC), the Frankie Laine Show (1955); The Colgate Comedy Hour (NBC, 1956); Dave Garroway's Today Show (NBC), Lamp Unto My Feet (CBS, 1962); the Jack Paar Show (NBC, 1957–58); the Steve Allen Show (NBC, 1957); Car 54, Where Are You? (NBC, 1962); Ninety Bristol Court (1963); the morning series, Panarama Pacific (Hollywood, CBS, 1964); The Nut House (CBS); Many Happy Returns (CBS); McHale's Navy (ABC); The Jack Benny Show (CBS); Tammy (ABC); and That Girl (ABC).

Night Clubs. She has performed at the Sheraton Biltmore Hotel (Providence, R.I., 1950–51); Le Ruban Bleu (N.Y.C., 1950); Statler Hotel (Cleveland, Ohio, 1952); The Monte Carlo (Pittsburgh, Pa., 1952); Mission Th. Bar (Calif., 1952); in *The George White Show* at the Versailles (N.Y.C., 1953); at El Rancho Vegas (Las Vegas, Nev., 1954); Ciro's (Hollywood, Calif., Jan. 1955); Latin Casino (Philadelphia, Pa., 1955); Sans Souci (Miami Beach, Fla., 1955); Thunderbird Hotel (Las Vegas, 1956); One Fifth Avenue (N.Y.C., 1956); Alpine Village (Cleveland, Ohio, 1956); Mr. Kelly's (Chicago, Ill., 1956–57, 1962); Blue Angel (N.Y.C., 1957, 1959, 1960, 1962); El Morocco (Montreal, Can., 1957); Ritz-Carlton (Montreal, Canada, 1958); The Largo (Los Angeles, Calif., 1958); The Hacienda (Las Vegas, Nev., 1958); The Living Room (N.Y.C. 1958); The Astor Cabaret (London, Eng., 1959), and the Carillon Hotel (Miami Beach, 1959).

She has appeared in her satirical act at the Blue Angel (N.Y.C., 1963); Bon Soir (N.Y.C., 1963); The Embers (Indianapolis, Ind., 1963); The Colony (Omaha, Neb., 1963); Eddie's (Kansas City, Mo., 1963); Mr. Kelly's (Chicago, 1963); and sang at the Hilton and Queen Elizabeth Hotels (Montreal, 1963).

Discography. Miss De Witt's records include *Through Sick and Sin* (Epic); *Drums Around the World* (Columbia); and the cast albums of *Oklahoma!* (Epic), *Flahooley* (Capitol), and *Show Boat* (Columbia).

Recreation. Chess, children, horseback riding, poker, friends.

DEWS, PETER. Director, actor. b. Sept. 26, 1929, Wakefield, Yorkshire, England, to John and Edna (Bloomfield) Dews. Father, railway clerk. Educated at Queen Elizabeth Grammar School, Wakefield; grad. University College, Oxford. Married Dec. 1960 to Ann Christine Rhodes. Member of British Actors' Equity; Association of Cinema and Television Technicians; SSD&C. Address: (home) 39 Elm Park Gardens, London S.W. 10, England tel. 352-9323; (bus.) c/o Dalzell Associates, 14 Clifford St., London W.1, England tel. 499-3811.

Pre-Theatre. Mr. Dews was a schoolmaster from 1951 to 1954.

Theatre. Mr. Dews's first experience with theatre was as a performer in an ELT production of *King Lear* (Sept. 1950). The first production directed by Mr. Dews was *Crime Passionel* (Civic Playhouse, Bradford, England, July 1952), and the first production he directed professionally was *Henry V* (Magdalen Grove, Oxford, June 1957). This was followed by his direction of *Picnic* (Belgrade Th., Coventry, England, Apr. 14, 1958); *The Disciplines of War* (Edinburgh Festival, Fringe, Scotland, Sept. 2, 1958); *The Cheats of Scapin* (Lyric Opera House, Hammersmith, London, England, Mar. 3, 1959). For the touring stage, his first work was direction of *Macbeth* for the British Council, Malta (Oct. 1961). He played Cardinal Wolsey in *A Man for All Seasons* (Playhouse Th., Nottingham, Nov. 4, 1961); directed *Henry IV, Part I* and *Henry IV, Part 2* (Oxford Playhouse, Mar. 14, 1962); and *Richard II* (Ludlow Castle, Shropshire, June 20, 1963).

He worked in America at the Ravinia Festival, Chicago, Ill., where he directed productions of *Henry V; Twelfth Night;* and *Hamlet* (Aug.–Sept. 1964), then returning to Great Britain, where he directed *The Apple Cart* (Arts Th., Cambridge, England, May 29, 1965) and *Galileo* (Royal Lyceum Th., Edinburgh, Scotland, Oct. 28, 1965). From June 1966 to June 1972, he was artistic director of Birmingham (England) Repertory Theatre, where he directed twenty-six plays, including *A Crack in the Ice; 1066 and All That; Hadrian VII; As You Like It; The Circle; Peer Gynt; Hamlet; Quick, Quick Slow; Oedipus Rex;* and *First Impressions.* During the same period, he directed *As You Like It* (Vaudeville Th., London, June 1967), followed by *Hadrian VII* (Mermaid and Haymarket Theatres, London, Apr. 14, 1968). The first play he directed for the Bway stage was *Hadrian VII* (Helen Hayes Th., Jan. 8, 1969), and this was followed by work at the Chichester Festival Theatre, England, where Mr. Dews directed *Antony and Cleopatra* (June 8, 1969); *Vivat! Vivat Regina!!* (Apr. 10, 1970), later transferred to Piccadilly Th., London; and *The Alchemist,* in which he also played Face (June 20, 1970). He returned to the US, where he directed *The Caretaker* (Ravinia Festival, Chicago, Ill., Aug. 12, 1970) and *Vivat! Vivat Regina!!* (Broadhurst, N.Y.C., Feb. 17, 1972). In England, he directed *Crown Matrimonial* (Theatre Royal, Haymarket, London, Oct. 28, 1972); *The Director of the Opera* (Chichester Festival, May 16, 1973); and *Twelfth Night* (Birmingham Repertory, June 10, 1973); in N.Y.C., *Crown Matrimonial* (Helen Hayes Th., Oct. 8, 1973); and back in London, *The Waltz of the Toreadors* (Theatre Royal, Haymarket, Feb. 14, 1974). His first directing at the Stratford (Ontario, Can.) Festival was *King John* (Festival Th., Aug. 1974).

Television and Radio. Mr. Dews was a BBC radio drama producer from 1954 to 1958. The first play he directed for television was *Pitfall* (BBC, Birmingham, England, Sept. 1956). He subsequently directed for television *A Man for All Seasons* (BBC, Birmingham, Jan. 1, 1957); *Henry V* (BBC, London, Dec. 30, 1957); a serialization of *Hilda Lessways* (BBC, Birmingham, May–June 1959); *The Case of Private Hamp* (BBC, Birmingham, Nov. 11, 1959); the series *An Age of Kings* (BBC, London, Apr.–Nov. 1960); *The Alchemist* (BBC, Birmingham, May 12, 1961); *The Cruel Necessity* (BBC, London, Aug. 4, 1962); *The Spread of the Eagle* (BBC, London, Jan.–Apr. 1963); and *The Stretch* (BBC, London, Feb. 16, 1973).

Awards. For his direction of the television series *An Age of Kings,* Mr. Dews received the British Television Directors Guild Award, and he received an Antoinette Perry (Tony) Award for his direction of *Hadrian VII* (1969).

Recreation. Acting and music.

DEXTER, JOHN. Director. b. 1925, Derby, England. Served British Army, WW II.

Theatre. Mr. Dexter began his career as a radio and television actor (BBC).

For the English Stage Co. (Royal Court, London), he staged workshop productions of *Yes–and After,* and *Each in His Own Wilderness* (1957); subsequently directed *Chicken Soup with Barley* (1958); *Roots, The Kitchen, Last Day in Dreamland,* and *A Glimpse of the Sea* (1959); and *Chicken Soup with Barley, This Year Next Year, I'm Talking about Jerusalem,* and *Toys in the Attic* (1960). From 1963–74, he was associate director of The National Th. Co. (Old Vic, London), where he directed *The Kitchen, South,* and *The Keep* (1961); *My Place, The Keep, England, Our England,* co-directed *Chips with Everything,* directed *The Blood of the Bambergs,* a double bill of *The Sponge Room* and *Squat Betty, Jackie the Jumper, Half a Sixpence,* and *Saint Joan,* which was also presented at the Chichester and Edinburgh festivals (1962); *Hobson's Choice, Othello,* co-directed *Royal Hunt of the Sun,* which was repeated at the Chichester Festival (1964); co-directed *Armstrong's Last Goodnight* (also Chichester Fest.), directed *Black Comedy* (also Chichester Fest.), *A Bond Honoured,* and *The Storm* (1966); *Wise Child* (1967); *The Old Ones* (Aug. 8, 1972); *The Misanthrope* (Feb. 22, 1973); *Equus* (July 26, 1973); *In Praise of Love* (Sept. 27, 1973); *The Party* (Dec. 20, 1973); and *Pygmalion* (Albery Th., May 16, 1974).

He made his American directorial debut with *Chips with Everything* (Plymouth, N.Y.C., Oct. 1, 1963); subsequently staged *Do I Hear a Waltz?* (46 St. Th., Mar. 18, 1965); *The Royal Hunt of the Sun* (ANTA, Oct. 26, 1965); *Black Comedy* and *White Lies* (Ethel Barrymore Th., Feb. 12, 1967); *The Unknown Soldier and His Wife* (Vivian Beaumont Th., Nov. 12, 1967); for the American Shakespeare Fest. (Stratford, Conn.) *Hamlet* (June 18, 1969); *Equus* (Plymouth, N.Y.C., Oct. 24, 1974); *In Praise of Love* (Morosco, Dec. 10, 1974); and *The Misanthrope* (St. James Th., Mar. 12, 1975).

Mr. Dexter made his opera debut with the Royal Opera Co. production of *Benvenuto Cellini* (Covent Garden, London, Nov. 1966); and Hamburg (Germany) Opera (1967), staged *House of the Dead, Billy Budd,* and *Il Ballo in Maschera.* In Feb. 1974, he was named production supervisor of the Metropolitan Opera Co. (N.Y.C.), where he has directed new productions of *I Vespri Siciliani; Aida;* and *La Gioconda.*

Films. He has directed the Lawrence Olivier *Othello* (Eagle/WB, 1966); *The Virgin Soldiers* (Col. 1968); *Sidelong Glances of a Pigeon Kicker* (Butcher, 1970); and *I Want What I Want* (Cinerama, 1972).

Television. In England, he directed *Twelfth Night* (ATV).

Awards. He received the London Drama Critics Prize (1962) for *Chips with Everything;* was named *Best Plays* Best Director (1974–75) for *Equus* and *The Misanthrope;* and received the Antoinette Perry (Tony), and Drama Desk awards (1974–75) for *Equus.*.

DHERY, ROBERT. Actor, director, playwright. b. Robert Fourrey, Apr. 27, 1921, Héry, Yonne, France to Leon and Madeleine Fourrey. Father, miller. Attended Conservatoire National, Paris, 1939–42. Married 1943 to Colette Brosset; one daughter. Member of AEA.

Theatre. Mr. Dhéry conceived, wrote, staged, and appeared in *La plume de ma tante* (Garrick Th., London, Nov. 3, 1955; Royale, N.Y.C., Nov. 11, 1958); and wrote the book for and directed *La grosse valise* (54 St. Th., N.Y.C., Dec. 14, 1965).

He made his stage debut with the Marcel Herraud and Jean Marchat repertory company at the "Rideau de Paris" (Th. des Mathurins, Paris, 1938–40); subsequently appeared in *Mon royaume est sur la terre* (1941); and *Sylvie et le Fantome* (Anicet, 1942). Mr. Dhéry wrote, directed, and performed in the following revues in Paris: *Les Branquignols* (Th. La Bruyère, 1948); *Dugudu* (Th. La Bruyère, 1951); *Ah, les belles bacchantes!* (Th. Daunou, 1953); *Jupon vole* (Th. des Variétés, 1954); *Voulez-vous jouer avec moi* (Rascasse, 1955); *Pommes à l'anglaise* (Th. de Paris, 1957); and *La grosse valse* (Th. des Variétés, 1962).

Mr. Dhéry played Zozo in *Machin Chouette* (*Mr. Nobody*) (Th. Antoine, Paris, Oct. 7, 1964); Charley (originally Felix) in a French production of *The Odd Couple* (Paris, 1966); and was in a French production of *Three Men on a Horse* (Paris, 1968).

Films. Mr. Dhéry appeared in *Les adventures des Pieds Nickeles* (1947) and *Bertrand coeur de lion* (1951). He directed, wrote, and appeared in *La Belle Americaine* (Cont., 1961); *Allez France!* (Prodis, 1964); appeared in *La communale* (Gaumont, 1965); wrote, with Pierre Tchernia, directed, and appeared in *The Counterfeit Constable* (Seven Arts, 1966); and wrote, directed, and appeared in *Vos gueles, les mouettes* (*Shut Up, Seagulls!*) (UA, 1974).

DICKINSON, GENEVIEVE. Educator, director. b. Genevieve Gertrude Giesen, Feb. 12, 1909, Roanoke, Va., to Conrad Giesen and Lillian (Mann) Giesen. Father, auditor and sales manager; mother, artist. Grad. New Castle (Va.) H.S., 1924; Radford Teachers Coll., B.S. (summa cum laude) 1929; Va. Polytechnic Inst., M.S. 1951; graduate study, Univ. of Virginia, 1946, 1959, 1962. Married Mar. 25, 1933, to Robert Nelson Dickinson; (dec. Nov. 14, 1947); one daughter, Jeanne Friedman, TV actress. Member of Virginia Speech and Drama Assn. (past pres.); Virginia Educ. Assn.; NEA; AETA; Speech Assn. of the Eastern States; Showtimers, Roanoke, Va. (charter member); Dramatic Actor's Guild for radio (WDBJ, Roanoke, Va.); Natl. Thespian Dramatic Society (Va. state dir.); ANTA (council, 1950–51); Barter Th. (bd. of dir.); Alpha Delta Kappa (state publicity dir.); Tau Kappa Alpha; Pi Gamma Mu. Address: (home) 2903 Clarendon Ave., Roanoke, VA 24012, tel. (703) EM 6-1775; (bus.) c/o Jefferson H.S., Roanoke, VA 24012.

Mrs. Dickinson was head of the Dept. of Speech and Drama, William Fleming High School, Roanoke, Va., from 1941 to 1972. She retired in the latter year, but in 1974 returned to fulltime teaching when she joined the faculty at Jefferson H.S. in Roanoke. As a teacher and director of dramatics, she has coached students individually and in groups to compete in oratory and dramatics on state, regional, and national levels. At William Fleming H.S., she directed and produced such plays as *Jane Eyre* (1952), *Smilin' Through* (1943); *Winterset* (1944), *Pride and Prejudice* (1945), *Arsenic and Old Lace* (1952), *The Man Who Came to Dinner* (1954), *See How They Run* (1956), *Dark of the Moon* (1958), *Dear Ruth, The Diary of Anne Frank* (1962), *The Happy Time,* and *Caesar and Cleopatra* (1963). Later productions directed by Mrs. Dickinson, for civic and high-school theatre, include *Teahouse of the August Moon* (1969), *Blithe Spirit* (1970), *The Curious Savage* (1971), *Li'l Abner* (1972), and *The Rope Dancers* (1973).

At the Roanoke (Va.) Civic Th., she played Eugenie in *Barriers* (Nov. 1932), directed *Dear Brutus* (1934), directed *The Rivals* (1935), played in *Guest in the House* (1939), and in *Street Scene* (1941). She was founder and director of the summer stock group, the Showtimers, staging such productions as *The Late George Apley* (1951), *Winterset* (1952), *The Happy Time* (1953), *Rain* (1957), *Inherit the Wind* (1958), and *The Diary of Anne Frank;* played Mrs. Danvers in *Rebecca* (1954), Mrs. Duke in *The Happiest Millionaire* (1955), and Constance in *The Madwoman of Chaillot* (1956). Mrs. Dickinson also researched, wrote, produced, and directed *A Mighty Fortress,* a pageant in twelve scenes, with sixty-five actors, for the centenary of St. Mark's Lutheran Church, Roanoke, in Oct. 1969.

Awards. Mrs. Dickinson received the Freedom Foundation classroom Teacher's Medal at Valley Forge, Pa. (1960); received a special citation from the American Legion for work done with youth in speech (eight of her students became public speaking champions in the National American Legion Oratorial Contest). In 1968, she was chosen "Mother of the Year in Arts and Sciences" of Roanoke City and Roanoke Valley, and in 1973 Radford College awarded her a citation and plaque as "Outstanding Alumna of Radford College."

While she was head of the Dept. of Speech and Drama, the Fleming High School Thespian School won a prize and citation for its production of *Dark of the Moon* in the National Thespian Dramatic Society Contest (Purdue Univ., Ind., 1958). The Dramatic Dept. of Fleming H.S. has earned the highest prize in the State of Virginia Annual One-Act Play Festival at the Univ. of Virginia since 1941.

Recreation. Horseback riding, gardening, writing and adapting plays.

DICKSON, DOROTHY. Actress, dancer. b. July 26, 1900, Kansas City, Mo., to William Bradford and Clara (Barrett) Dickson. Father, journalist. Attended Chicago Latin Sch. 1912–15. Married June 15, 1916, to Carl Hyson, dancer; one daughter, Dorothy Hyson, actress. During WW II, toured N. Africa to entertain His Majesty's forces, May 1943–Sept. 1945; operated Stage Door Canteen, London, 1944–46. Relative in theatre: son-in-law, Anthony Quayle, actor. Member of British AEA. Address: 42 Eaton Sq., London, S.W.1, England tel. 01-235-6801.

Theatre. Miss Dickson made her debut in *Oh, Boy* (Princess Th., N.Y.C., Feb. 20, 1917); subsequently appeared in the *Ziegfeld Follies* (New Amsterdam, June 12, 1917); as Betty in *Girl o' Mine* (Bijou, Jan. 28, 1918); Dorothy Manners in *Rock-a-Bye Baby* (Astor, May 22, 1918); Carlotta in *The Royal Vagabond* (Cohan & Harris Th., Feb. 17, 1919); and Lady Gwendolyn Spencer-Hill in *Lassie* (Nora Bayes Th., Apr. 6, 1920).

Miss Dickson appeared in London in the title role in *Sally* (Winter Garden, Sept. 10, 1921); as Marilynn Morgan in *The Cabaret Girl* (Winter Garden, Sept. 19, 1922); Carol Stuart in *The Beauty Prize* (Winter Garden, Sept. 5, 1923); the title role in *Patricia* (His Majesty's, Oct. 31, 1924); joined the cast (Oct. 1925) of *Charlot's Revue* (Prince of Wales's, Sept. 23, 1924); played the title role in *Peter Pan* (Shaftesbury, Dec. 17, 1925); Cora-Ann Milton in *The Ringer* (Wyndham's, May 1, 1926); Tip-Toes Kaye in *Tip-Toes* (Winter Garden, Aug. 31, 1926); the title role in *Peter Pan* (Adelphi, Dec. 22, 1926); the title role in *Peggy-Ann* (Daly's, July 27, 1927); and Nita Clive in *The Man Who Changed His Name* (Apollo, Mar. 20, 1928).

She appeared in the revue, *Charivaria* (Hippodrome, Golders Green, Apr. 16, 1929; retitled *Coo-Ee,* moved Vaudeville, London); played Sue O'-Keefe in *Hold Everything* (Palace, July 1929); Liane in *Wonder Bar* (Savoy, Dec. 5, 1930); the title role in a pantomine, *Dick Whittington* (Garrick, Dec. 1931); Princess Potomska in *Casanova* (Coliseum, May 24, 1932); Pearl Sunshine in *The Sunshine Sisters* (Queen's, Nov. 8, 1933); Sylvia Ashwin in *The Private Road* (Comedy, May 31, 1934).

She appeared in the revue *Stop Press* (Adelphi, Feb. 21, 1935); in the revue, *Spread It Abroad* (Saville, Apr. 1, 1936); Peggy and Penelope Lee in *Careless Rapture* (Drury Lane, Sept. 11, 1936); Honey Wortle in *Crest of the Wave* (Drury Lane, Sept. 1, 1937); Princess Katharine in *Henry V* (Drury Lane, Sept. 16, 1938); Marguerite Blakeney in *The Scarlet Pimpernel* (Embassy, Dec. 24, 1938); Felicity Waring in *Second Helping* (Streatham Hill, Dec. 4, 1939); appeared in the revues, *Diversion* (Wyndham's, Oct. 28, 1940), *Diversion No. 2* (Wyndham's, Jan. 2, 1941), and *Fine and Dandy* (Saville, Apr. 30, 1942); played Helen of Troy in *Crisis in Heaven* (Lyric, May 1946); and Lady Grayston in *Our Betters* (Playhouse, Oct. 3, 1946).

Miss Dickson also appeared as guest star in three charity revues, *Yesterday and Today* (Drury Lane, Nov. 6, 1950), *Fashion Through 200 Years* (Wyndham's, Dec. 5, 1950), and *Merely Players* (Drury Lane, Feb. 4, 1951); played Gertie Garter in *Ten Nights in the Green Room* (July 19, 1951); appeared in *Salute to Ivor Novello,* (Coliseum, Oct. 7, 1951); played Helen Conrad in *Red Letter Day* (Garrick, Feb. 21, 1952); appeared in *Olympic Variety Show* (Victoria Palace, Mar. 24, 1952); portrayed Stella Bentley in *As Long as They're Happy* (Garrick, July 8, 1953); appeared in two revues, *Night of 100 Stars* (London Palladium, June 24, 1954) and *Cavalcade of 1906* (Saville, Nov. 25, 1956).

Films. Miss Dickson made her debut in *Money Mad or Paying the Piper* (Par., 1921); subsequently appeared in *Danny Boy* (Butcher's, 1934); *Channel Crossing* (Gaumont, 1934); *La Route Est Belle* (Beautiful Road) (1935); and played Mrs. Stanhope in *Sword of Honour* (Butcher's, 1939).

Television and Radio. On radio, Miss Dickson played the title role in *Sally* (BBC, Aug. 1940). She did *Stage Door Canteen* reminiscences on Today (BBC, May 21, 1968), was on the Woman's Hour (BBC, 1970), *The Life and Times of Ivor Novello* (BBC, Oct. 1973), and *Scrapbook for 1935* (BBC, Mar. 13, 1973). She made her television debut as Cora-Ann Milton in *The Ringer* (BBC, Aug. 1946), and subsequently repeated her role of Stella Bentley in excerpts from *As Long as They're Happy* (BBC, Oct. 5, 1953); played herself in her life story, *Spice of Life* (BBC, June 20, 1954); appeared as Daisy Sable in *Buy Me Blue Ribbons* (BBC-Associated Rediffusion, July 19, 1956); in *Beauty, Grace and Charm* (BBC, May 1959); played herself on *The Ivor Novello Story* (BBC, Jan. 1964); was on *News at Ten* (Feb. 10, 1969); *Late Night Line-Up* (Feb. 11, 1969); and *This Is Noel Coward* (BBC, Mar. 2, 1973).

In the US, she has appeared on *What's My Line* (CBS, 1951) and *This Is Your Life* (NBC, 1956).

Night Clubs. In 1919, she and her husband, Carl Hyson, owned the Palais Royal night club, N.Y.C., where they presented Paul Whiteman and his orchestra in its initial engagement. She and her husband also appeared at the Century Th. Roof (Oct. 1918); and at the Palace Th. (Keith Circuit, Mar. 1920).

Recreation. Painting, skiing, tennis.

DIENER, JOAN. Actress, singer. b. Feb. 24, 1934, Cleveland, Ohio. Attended Sarah Lawrence Coll. Married to Albert Marre; one son, one daughter. Member of AEA; AFTRA; SAG; AGVA.

Theatre. Miss Diener made her N.Y.C. debut in the revue, *Small Wonder* (Coronet Th., Sept. 15, 1948); followed by Deedy Barton in *Season in the Sun* (Cort, Sept. 28, 1950); Kate in a stock production of *Kiss Me Kate* (Sacramento Music Circus, Calif., Summer 1952); Lalume in *Kismet* (Ziegfeld, N.Y.C., Dec. 3, 1953; Stoll, London, Apr. 20, 1955); appeared in the pre-Bway tryout of *The Ziegfeld Follies* (opened Shubert, Boston, Mass., Apr. 16, 1956; closed Shubert, Philadelphia, Pa., May 12, 1956); played Isola Parelli in the pre-Bway tryout of *At the Grand* (opened Philharmonic Aud., Los Angeles, Calif., July 7, 1958; closed Curran, San Francisco, Calif., Sept. 13, 1958); appeared at the Palladium (London, 1959); sang soprano operatic roles (Germany, Italy, 1959–60); at the Cambridge (Mass.) Drama Festival, sang in the opera, *La Belle Helene* (July–Aug. 1960) and in a revised musical comedy version, entitled *La Belle* (Summer 1962); played Frenchy in *Destry Rides Again* (North Shore Th., Beverly, Mass., Summer 1961); and Helen in the pre-Bway tryout of *La Belle* (opened Shubert, Philadelphia, Pa., Aug. 13, 1962; closed there Aug. 25, 1962).

Miss Diener was the original Aldonza in *Man of La Mancha* (Goodspeed Opera House, East Haddam, Conn., June 24, 1965; ANTA-Washington Square Th., N.Y.C., Nov. 22, 1965; Ahmanson, Los Angeles, 1967; and Piccadilly Th., London, 1968); Cloyne in a musical version of *Purple Dust* (Goodspeed Opera House, July 22, 1965); Kathleen Stanton in *Cry for Us All* (Broadhurst, N.Y.C., Apr. 8, 1970); repeated the role of Aldonza in a revival of *Man of La Mancha* (Vivian Beaumont Th., June 22, 1972); and played Penelope in *Odessy,* which was retitled *Home Sweet Homer* (Palace, Jan. 4, 1976).

Television. Miss Diener has appeared in *54th Street Revue* (CBS, 1951–52); *Androcles and the Lion* (Omnibus, CBS, 1956); and on The Today Show (NBC): The Ed Sullivan Show (CBS): and the Johnny Carson Show (NBC).

Night Clubs. She performed at the Blue Angel (N.Y.C., 1950).

Awards. Miss Diener received the *Theatre World* Award for her performance as Lalume in *Kismet* (1954).

DIERLAM, ROBERT J. Educator, director. b. Robert Jackson Dierlam, Feb. 1, 1917, San Francisco, Calif., to Robert Jackson and Mabelle (Ashton) Dierlam. Father, machinist. Grad. Mobridge (S.D.) H.S., 1934; attended Univ. of Colorado, 1934–37; grad. State Univ. of Iowa, B.A. 1938; Univ. of Colorado, M.A. 1939; attended Univ. of Idaho, Summer 1941; Univ. of Colorado, Summer 1942; grad. Cornell Univ., Ph.D. 1948. Studied with Isabelle Halliburton, Sheridan Square Th., N.Y.C. 1960, William Ball, New Sch. for Social Research, 1963. Married Aug. 22, 1945, to Maxine Thompson; one daughter. Member of ASTRA; MLA; Th. Library Assn.; AETA (publications committee, 1960–63; pres., NY region, 1961–62); Theta Xi; St. David's Society of NY. Address: Dept. of Drama and Theatre, Queens College, Flushing, NY 11367.

Since 1970, Mr. Dierlam has been professor of drama and theatre and, since 1959, director of the Queens Coll. Th. (instructor in communication arts and sciences, 1952–57; assistant professor, 1957–61; associate professor, 1961–70). He has also taught and directed at Illinois Wesleyan Univ. (1943–44); Univ. of Colorado (1944–46); Univ. of Florida (1948–50); and Stanford Univ. (1950; 1957–59).

Mr. Dierlam acted with the Federal Th. (WPA) Project (Denver, Colo., 1939), appearing in *Autumn Crocus, The Milky Way,* and *Criminal at Large.* With the Tent Players (Moscow, Idaho, 1941), he appeared in *What a Life!, I Killed the Count* and *The Fireman;* and played Falstaff in *Henry IV Part 1,* (Univ. of Colorado, Summer 1946).

Published Works. His translation of Goethe's *Gotz von Berlichingen* was included in *Ten Major Tragedies* (1969).

Awards. Mr. Dierlam received a Natl. Th. Conference Fellowship (1946–47), and was a Fulbright Research Scholar in Vienna, Austria (1951–52).

Recreation. Gardening, politics, swimming.

DIERS, HANK. Educator. b. Hermann Henry Diers, Sept. 23, 1931, Dubuque, Iowa, to H. H. and E. (Langholz) Diers. Father, Lutheran minister. Attended East H.S., Waterloo, Iowa, 1946–48; grad. Rantoul (Ill.) H.S., 1949; Wartburg Coll., B.A. 1953; attended Univ. of Dubuque, 1949–50, 1953–54; Loras Coll., 1953–54; and Univ. of Illinois, 1956–60, M.A. 1957, Ph.D. 1964. Married, Sept. 5, 1953, to Doris E. Blumreich; two sons, two daughters. Served US Army, 1954–56; PIO specialist. Member of ANTA; ATA; SSA; SAA; SETC (exec. sec., treas., 1962–to date); Florida Theatre Conf. (vice-pres.); Florida Arts Council (1966–67); Cultural Executives Council of Miami (1973); Alumni Assn. of Wartburg Coll. (bd. of dirs., 1968–74); Northwestern Cultural Arts Center (advisory bd., 1974); Florida Discipline Task Force (1974); Alpha Psi Omega (pres.); Alpha Phi Gamma (vice-pres.). Address: (home) 5705 Southwest 107 Place, Miami, FL 33143, tel. (305) 271-3781; (bus.) Ring Theatre, Univ. of Miami, Coral Gables, FL 33124, tel. (305) 284-6439.

Dr. Diers is professor of drama (1969–to date) and chairman of the Drama Dept. (1967–to date) of the Univ. of Miami (Coral Gables, Fla.), having formerly served there as assistant professor (1960–65) and associate professor (1965–69).

Theatre. Dr. Diers has been managing, and later, executive producer of the Southern Shakespeare Repertory Th. (1961–67); executive director-producer at the Summer Festival Th. (1968–to date); and executive producer of the Omni Theatre Festival (Miami, Fla., 1974–75). He is director of the Univ. of Miami London Theatre Institute, which he heads each summer at the Univ. of London (England). In 1973, he was named director of University Theatres.

As a student, he acted in and directed university and community productions. At the Ring Th., Univ. of Miami (Fla.), he has directed *The Great God Brown* (1960); *Rashomon* (1961); *A Streetcar Named Desire* (1962); *Androcles and the Lion* (1962); *Darkness at Noon* (1963); *She Stoops to Conquer* (1963); *Death of a Salesman* (1964); *Little Mary Sunshine* (1964); *Biederman and the Firebugs* (1965); *The Devil's General* (1965); *Once Upon a Mattress* (1966); *Arsenic and Old Lace* (1966); *Philadelphia, Here I Come* (1967); *The Devils* (1968); *The Education of H*Y*M*A*N K*A*P*L*A*N* (1969); *Black Comedy* (1969); *Doctor! Doctor!,* which he wrote (1970); *Jacques Brel Is Alive and Well and Living in Paris* (1972); *Cabaret,* starring Kurt Kasner and Mercedes McCambridge (1973); *The Gingerbread Lady,* starring Gretchen Wyler (1973); and *South Pacific* (1974). Dr. Diers' script, *The Three Hundred and Seventh Defense of Hermann Goering,* was produced by the Ring Theatre (1971).

As managing director of the Southern Shakespeare Rep. Th., he directed *Richard III* (1961); *The Taming of the Shrew* (1961); *Hamlet* (1962, and 1968); *The Merry Wives of Windsor* (1964), *The Merchant of Venice* (1965), *A Midsummer Night's Dream* (1966); and *Twelfth Night* (1967).

At the Coconut Grove Playhouse (Miami, Fla.), Dr. Diers directed *The Royal Hunt of the Sun* (1968); and *Fiddler on the Roof* (1972).

He directed *The Apple Tree* (Parker Playhouse, Fort Lauderdale, Fla., 1969); *The Star Spangled Girl* (Port St. Lucie (Fla.) Star Th., 1970); *The Gorilla* (Port St. Lucie (Fla.) Star Th., 1971); *The Boyfriend* (Springer Opera House, Columbus Ga., 1971); *The Death of the Bishop of Brindisi* (Univ. Sch. of Music, Coral Gables, Fla., 1971); *The Boy Friend* (Parker Playhouse, Fort Lauderdale, Fla.; and American Coll. Th. Fest., Eisenhower Th., Kennedy Center, Washington, D.C., 1972); *Jacques Brel Is Alive and Well and Living in Paris* (Univ. of North Carolina, Greensboro, N.C., 1972; and American Coll. Th. Fest., Eisenhower Th., Kennedy Ctr., Washington, D.C., 1973); *The Sound of Music* (Parker Playhouse, Fort Lauderdale, Fla., 1974); *Cabaret* (Gusman Philharmonic Hall, Miami, Fla., 1974); *The Gingerbread Lady* (Tuscaloosa, Ala., 1974); *Dames at Sea* (Daytona (Fla.) Little Th., 1974); *Jacques Brel Is Alive and Well and Living in Paris* (Fort Lauderdale (Fla.) Dinner Th., 1974); *South Pacific* (North Miami Beach (Fla.) Festival and Roney Plaza, Miami Beach, Fla., 1974); *Cabaret* (Roney Plaza, Miami Beach, Fla., 1974); and *Dames at Sea* (Hyatt House, Miami Beach, Fla., 1974).

Other Activities. Dr. Diers was a member of the faculty senate, serving on the calendar, administrative, sabbatical, and bicentennial committees at the Univ. of Miami. He is a member of the board of trustees of Third Century Bicentennial Corp. (1973–76).

Published Works. He has contributed articles to *One Magazine,* a publication of the Lutheran Church.

Awards. He placed first in the Drake Creative Awards (1947); and received a Speech Award, Univ. of Dubuque (1950); Outstanding Actor Award, Wartburg Coll. (1951); and Outstanding Contribution to Drama Award, Wartburg Coll. (1952). He received an SETC citation (1963); was an award winner in the Kodak International Color Competition for the 1964 World's Fair; received the Miami Herald's Angel Award as best director (1966) and best producer (1967); and received a citation from the Univ. of Miami (1971) for his production of *Fiddler on the Roof.* His productions of *The Boy Friend* (1972) and *Jacques Brel Is Alive and Well and Living in Paris* (1973) won the American Coll. Th. Festival competition and received the Friends of Theatre Award for two consecutive final presentations at Kennedy Center. His production of *The Gingerbread Lady* won at the regional level of the same competition.

Recreation. Boating, sailing, photography.

DIESEL, LEOTA. Editor, drama critic. b. St. Louis, Mo., to Louis C. and Mathilde (Merod) Diesel. Grad. Washington Univ. B.A.; New York Univ., M.A. Married to Charles H. Ashton (dec.). Member of Drama Desk (secy., 1959–61); Margo Jones Award Nominating Comm. Address: New York, NY.

Miss Diesel was associate editor and managing editor of *Theatre Arts* magazine (1956–63), and contributing editor (1951–53). She has also been drama critic for *The Villager,* N.Y.C. (1961–70); editor of *Theatre Today* (1968–69); and free-lance writer on theatre for magazines.

DIETRICH, DANIEL P. Producer, actor. b. Daniel Peter Dietrich, Jan. 16, 1944, Columbus, Ohio, to Edward Jacob and Gertrude Marie (Altop) Dietrich. Father, dairy owner. Educated at Johnstown (Ohio) Monroe High School; grad. Miami Univ., Oxford, Ohio, B.S. (speech/theatre). He received professional training at AADA. Address: (home) 120 Thompson St., New York, NY 10012, tel. (212) 966-7105; (bus.) WPA Theatre, 333 Bowery, New York, NY 10003, tel. (212) 473-9345.

Theatre. Mr. Dietrich began his stage career at Miami Univ. Theatre, where he appeared as Roland Maule in *Present Laughter* (Fall 1966); Ichneuman Fly in *The Insect Comedy* (Winter 1966); the Messenger in *Hippolytus* (Spring 1966); Mr. Shu Fu in *The Good Woman of Setzuan* (Winter 1967); Benedict in *Much Ado About Nothing* (Spring 1967); Rev. Shannon in *The Night of the Iguana* (Winter 1968); Howard Bevans in *Picnic* (Spring 1968); Rev. Hale in *The Crucible* (Fall 1969); and Serjeant Musgrave in *Serjeant Musgrave's Dance* (Spring 1969). He made his summer stock debut at the Miami Univ. Summer Theatre as Willi Eisenring in *The Firebugs* (Village Playhouse, Summer 1968). In Jan. 1970, he played the title role in a children's theatre production of *Johnny Appleseed* (Provincetown Playhouse, N.Y.C.), and in May 1970 he played Senex in a dinner theatre production of *A Funny Thing Happened on the Way to the Forum* (Club Bene, N.J.).

Mr. Dietrich became co-producer of the WPA (Workshop of the Players' Art) Theatre in 1971 and he made his Off-Off-Bway debut the same year as Jip in a WPA production of *A Man's a Man* (Jan. 1971). He has since appeared in other WPA presentations: as Richard Kluger in *The Corrupters* (May 1971); the Mayor in *The Enchanted* (Oct. 1971); Phil Greenblath in *Placebo* (Nov. 1971); Perchihin in *Petty Bourgeois* (Mar. 1972); the Clown in *Charlatans* (May 1972); Harold Scuderi in *The Red Pumps* (Dec. 1972); Mr. Box in *Cox and Box* (Mar. 1973); and Emil in *Oli's Icecream Suit* (Apr. 1974).

Awards. The Workshop of the Players' Art received a special citation (1972–73) from the *Village Voice* Off-Bway (Obie) Award judges for "continued diversity and imagination.".

Recreation. Golf, swimming, and bartending.

DIETRICH, JOHN E. Educator. b. John Erb Dietrich, Nov. 13, 1913, Spokane, Wash., to John Hassler and Louise Ernestine (Erb) Dietrich. Father, clergyman. Grad. Univ. of Wisconsin, B.A. (Speech) 1937; M.A. 1941; Ph.D. 1945. Married Apr. 13, 1949, to Lois Gernhardt; one son, one daughter. Member of ATA (served on committees, 1948–55; exec. comm., 1955–58); Central States Speech Assn. (pres., 1953); SAA (2nd vice-pres., 1957; 1st vice-pres., 1958; pres., 1959; on committees, 1960–to date); Amer. Council on Education (delegate, 1957–59); White House Conference on Children and Youth (delegate, 1960); ANTA (dir., 1960–68). Address: (home) 6150 Birch Row Drive, East Lansing, MI 48823, tel. (517) 351-3573; (bus.) c/o Office of the Provost, Michigan State University, East Lansing, MI 48823, tel. (517) 353-1670.

Mr. Dietrich has been asst. provost for academic analysis and planning, Michigan State Univ., since 1970. Previously he was (1964–69) asst. provost, dir. Educational Development Program, and dir. Instructional Development Service at the university. From 1959 to 1964, he was chmn., Dept. of Speech, Michigan State. He has held academic positions at Purdue Univ. (instructor, 1937–41). Univ. of Wisconsin (lecturer, 1942–45; assistant professor, 1945–47; associate professor, 1947–52; professor, 1952–55); Ohio State Univ. (professor of speech, director of theatre, 1955–59).

At Purdue Univ., Mr. Dietrich was director of the Lafayette Little Th. Assn., and director of WBAA radio players (1937–41); at the Univ. of Wisconsin, he was associate theatre director, directing approximately 20 productions (1942–54), in charge of the television curriculum and training (1952–54), and WHA-TV director of productions (1954).

Published Works. He wrote *Play Direction* (1953); and, with Keith Brooks, *Practical Speaking for the Technical Man* (1958). He has also written articles that appeared in *College & University Business* and the first chapter in the book *Conceptual Frontiers in Speech-Communication*, a report of the New Orleans Conference on Research and Instructional Development, SCA.

DIETZ, HOWARD. Lyricist, playwright. b. Sept. 8, 1896, New York City. Grad. Townsend Harris H.S., N.Y.C., 1913; Sch. of Journalism, Columbia Univ., 1917. Married to Tanis Guinness Montagu (marr. dis.); one daughter; married July 31, 1951, to Lucinda Ballard. Served USN, 1917–19. Member of ASCAP (bd. of dir., 1959–64); AEA; AGVA; AFTRA; Authors and Composers Illustrators' League; Dramatists Guild. Address: 1 Lincoln Plaza, New York, NY 10023.

Theatre. Mr. Dietz wrote the lyrics for *Dear Sir* (Times Square Th., N.Y.C., Sept. 23, 1924); and collaborated with Morrie Ryskind on the book and lyrics for *Merry-Go-Round* (Klaw, May 31, 1927).

Forming his association with composer, Arthur Schwartz, he contributed lyrics and sketches to *The Little Show* (Music Box, Apr. 30, 1929); lyrics to *Grand Street Follies of 1929* (Booth, May 1, 1929); collaborated with Mr. Schwartz on *Here Comes the Bride* (Piccadilly, London, Feb. 20, 1930), *Second Little Show* (Royale, N.Y.C., Sept. 2, 1930), and *Three's A Crowd* (Selwyn, Oct. 15, 1930); contributed lyrics to *Garrick Gaieties* (Guild, Oct. 16, 1930); wrote lyrics, and with George S. Kaufman, the book for *The Band Wagon* (New Amsterdam, June 3, 1931); and collaborated on the lyrics and sketches for *Flying Colors*, which he produced and directed (Imperial, Sept. 15, 1932).

Mr. Dietz wrote the book and lyrics for *Revenge with Music* (New Amsterdam, Nov. 28, 1934); lyrics and sketches for *At Home Abroad* (Winter Garden, Sept. 19, 1935); *Follow the Sun* (Adelphi, London, Feb. 4, 1936); contributed lyrics to *The Show Is On* (Winter Garden, N.Y.C., Dec. 25, 1936); wrote the book with Mr. Schwartz, and lyrics for *Between the Devil* (Imperial, Dec. 22, 1937); was lyricist with Al Dubin for *Keep Off the Grass* (Broadhurst, May 23, 1940); wrote lyrics for the pre-Bway tryout of *Dancing in the Streets* (Shubert, Boston, Mass., 1943); and *Jackpot* (Alvin, Jan. 13, 1944).

He was lyricist, sketch writer, and producer of the Coast Guard revue *Tars and Spars* (1943–44); with Rouben Mamoulian, adapted Somerset Maugham's *Rain*, into the musical, *Sadie Thompson* (Alvin, Nov. 16, 1944); and wrote the lyrics for *Inside U.S.A.* (Century, Apr. 30, 1948). For the Metropolitan Opera Assn. (N.Y.C.), he prepared the English adaptations of *Die Fledermaus* (Dec. 20, 1950); and *La Bohème* (Dec. 27, 1952); subsequently contributed lyrics to *Ziegfeld Follies* (Winter Garden, Mar. 1, 1957); wrote the lyrics for *The Gay Life* (Shubert, Nov. 18, 1961); and *Jennie* (Majestic, Oct. 17, 1963).

Films. Mr. Dietz was director of promotion at MGM (1924–57), and vice-president (1940–57). He was lyricist, co-scenarist, and co-producer of *Hollywood Party* (MGM, 1934); lyricist for *Under Your Spell* (20th-Fox, 1936) and *The Band Wagon* (MGM, 1953); and he wrote lyrics for the title song for *That's Entertainment!* (MGM, 1974).

Television and Radio. He was lyricist for the radio program The Gibson Family (1934). He has written lyrics for the television production *Surprise for Santa* (CBS, 1948); and *A Bell for Adano* (CBS, 1956).

Other Activities. Editor of *Navy Life* (1917–18); publicity director for the US Treasury Dept. (1940–41). He was appointed by the film industry to be industry representative at the US Senate investigation of the film industry in 1941 and, on behalf of the industry, to furnish entertainment to and welcome the delegates to the first United Nations meeting, San Francisco, Calif., 1945.

Published Works. Mr. Dietz's autobiography, *Dancing in the Dark*, was published in 1974. His poetry has been published in magazines and newspapers, including the NY *Sun*, the NY *Times* and *Saturday Review*. He has also written introductions to books on bridge by Goren, Jacoby, and others.

Recreation. Golf, spectator sports, painting, bridge.

DIFFEN, RAY. Costume designer, costumier. b. Raymond Jack Diffen, Feb. 28, 1922, Brighton, Sussex, England, to George William and Esther Dorothy (Cooper) Diffen. Father, naval officer; mother, dressmaker. Attended Varndean Sch., Brighton, England, 1933–39. Served RAF, instructor in wireless telegraphy, 1941–47; rank, Cpl. Member of United Scenic Artists, Local 829; Theatrical Costume Union, Local 38; ILGWU. Address: c/o Ray Diffen Stage Clothes, 121 W. 17th, New York, NY 10011, tel. (212) 675-2634.

Theatre. Mr. Diffen is head of Ray Diffen Stage Clothes, N.Y.C., and as such was in charge of costume execution for *Waltz of the Toreadors* (1957); *Orpheus Descending* (1957); *The Dark at the Top of the Stairs* (1957); *The World of Suzie Wong* (1958); *Destry Rides Again* (1959); *Much Ado About Nothing* (1959); *Fiorello!* (1959); *Five Finger Exercise* (1959); *Caligula* (1960); *Camelot* (1960); *Dear Liar* (1960); *The Happiest Girl in the World* (1961); *Kean* (1961); *First Love* (1961); *No Strings* (1962); *The Aspern Papers* (1962); *I Can Get It for You Wholesale* (1962); *Bravo Giovanni* (1962); *Mr. President* (1962); *The Milk Train Doesn't Stop Here Any More* (1963); *Strange Interlude* (1963); *Jeannie* (1963); *Here's Love* (1963); *The Girl Who Came to Supper* (1963); *Funny Girl* (1964); and the NY Shakespeare Festival (1962–64).

He designed costumes for *Under the Yum Yum Tree* (Henry Miller's Th., Nov. 16, 1960); *The Fun Couple* (Lyceum, Oct. 26, 1962); *Andorra* (Biltmore, Feb. 9, 1963); *The Three Sisters* (Morosco, June 22, 1964); the American Shakespeare Festival production of *Hamlet* (Stratford, Conn., July 2, 1964); and, with Theoni Aldredge, costumes for the NY Shakespeare Festival *Coriolanus* (Delacorte Th., July 7, 1965).

He was costume supervisor for *The Right Honourable Gentleman* (Billy Rose Th., Oct. 19, 1965); *The Royal Hunt of the Sun* (ANTA Th., Oct. 26, 1965); designed costumes for a revival of *Dinner at Eight* (Alvin Th., Sept. 27, 1966); was costume supervisor for *Rosencrantz and Guildenstern Are Dead* (Alvin Th., Oct. 16, 1967); designed costumes for the American Shakespeare Festival production of *Richard II* (Stratford, Conn., June 22, 1968); costumes for the pre-Bway tryout of *Love Match* (opened Palace West Th., Phoenix, Ariz., Nov. 3, 1968; closed Ahmanson Th., Los Angeles, Calif., Jan. 4, 1969); was costume supervisor for *Coco* (Mark Hellinger Th., N.Y.C., Dec. 18, 1969); for *Jesus Christ Superstar* (Mark Hellinger Th., Oct. 12, 1971); for *Emperor Henry IV* (Ethel Barrymore Th., Mar. 28, 1973); for a revival of *The Women* (46 St. Th., Apr. 25, 1973); designed costumes for *Noel Coward in Two Keys* (Ethel Barrymore Th., Feb. 28, 1974); and, with Howard Bay, designed costumes for *Odyssey* (Opera House, John F. Kennedy Ctr., Washington, D.C.), which opened in N.Y.C. as *Home Sweet Homer* (Palace, Jan. 4, 1976).

He was in charge of costume execution for various repertory productions at the Shakespeare Memorial Th. (Stratford-upon-Avon, England, 1948–51); for the Old Vic Th. (London, 1949–50); was costume executor for productions at the Stratford (Ontario) Shakespeare Festival (1953–opening season-to 1959) and for productions at the Tyrone Guthrie Th., Minneapolis, Minn. (1963–65).

Films. Mr. Diffen was in charge of costume execution for *The Cardinal* (UA, 1963).

DILLMAN, BRADFORD. Actor. b. April 14, 1930, San Francisco, Calif., to Dean and Josephine Dillman. Father, investment broker. Attended Hotchkiss Prep. Sch., Lakeville, Conn., 1944–47; Yale Univ., B.A., 1951; studied with Lee Strasberg at Actors' Studio (1955–to date); John Lehne (1962–to date). Married June, 1956, to Frieda Harding (marr. dis. Apr. 4, 1962); one son, one daughter; married Apr. 20, 1963, to Suzy Parker, actress, model; one daughter, two sons. Served USMC, 1951–53, rank, 1st Lt. Member of AEA; AFTRA; SAG; The Players. Address: c/o Contemporary-Korman Artists Ltd., 132 Lasky Dr., Beverly Hills, CA 90212.

Theatre. Mr. Dillman first appeared on stage as an

Angel in a school Christmas play (San Francisco, Dec., 1935).

He made his professional debut as Richard in *The Scarecrow* (Th. de Lys, N.Y.C., June 1953); appeared in stock as Freddie in *Pygmalion*, Marchbanks in *Candida*, and Hadrian in *You Touched Me* (Sharon Playhouse, Conn., Summer 1953); was an understudy in *End as a Man* (Th. de Lys, N.Y.C., Sept. 15, 1953); at the Sharon (Conn.) Playhouse (Summer 1954); appeared as Pierre in *The Madwoman of Chaillot*, Happy in *Death of a Salesman*, a Young Teacher in *The Browning Version*, and Danny in *Night Must Fall;* was an extra in *Inherit the Wind* (National, Apr. 21, 1955); at the Sharon (Conn.) Playhouse (Summer 1955), played Morgan in *The Corn Is Green*, Octavius in *The Barretts of Wimpole Street*, the twins, Frederic and Hugo, in *Ring 'Round the Moon*, and the Radical in *Counsellor-at-Law;* and *Black Chiffon* (Univ. of Michigan, Ann Arbor, 1955).

Mr. Dillman played Kip Ames in *Third Person* (President, N.Y.C., Dec. 29, 1955); Jimmy in *The Rainmaker* (Sharon Playhouse, Conn., Summer 1956); Edmund Tyrone in *Long Day's Journey into Night* (Helen Hayes Th., N.Y.C., Nov. 7, 1956), which he repeated at the Theatre of Nations Festival (Th. Sarah Bernhardt, Paris, France, July 1957); and appeared as Gil Stanford in *The Fun Couple* (Lyceum, N.Y.C., Oct. 26, 1962).

Films. Mr. Dillman appeared in *A Certain Smile* (20th-Fox, 1958); *In Love and War* (20th-Fox, 1958); *Compulsion* (20th-Fox, 1959); *Crack in the Mirror* (20th-Fox, 1960); *Circle of Deception* (20th-Fox, 1961); *Sanctuary* (20th-Fox, 1961); *Francis of Assisi* (20th-Fox, 1961); *A Rage To Live* (UA, 1965); *Jigsaw* (Beverly Pictures, 1968); *Sgt. Ryker* (U, 1968); *Mastermind* (Malcolm Stuart Prod., 1969); *The Bridge at Remagen* (UA, 1969); *Suppose They Gave a War and Nobody Came* (Cinerama, 1970); *Brother John* (Col., 1971); *The Mephisto Waltz* (20th-Fox, 1971); *Escape from the Planet of the Apes* (20th-Fox, 1971); *The Resurrection of Zachary Wheeler* (Gold Key Entertainment, 1971); *The Iceman Cometh* (Amer. Film Th., 1973); *Chosen Survivors* (Col., 1974); *99 and 44/100% Dead* (20th-Fox, 1974); *Gold* (Allied Artists, 1974); and *Bug* (Par., 1975).

Television. Mr. Dillman made his debut as an extra on Kraft Television Th. (NBC, Dec. 1953); from 1953–56, appeared in some 35 productions; since 1962, has appeared on the Eleventh Hour (NBC, 1962); Naked City (ABC, 1963); *To Catch a Butterfly* (Alfred Hitchcock Th., CBS, Feb. 1, 1963); *Chain Reaction* (Alcoa Premiere, ABC, Feb. 21, 1963); The Virginian (NBC, 1963); Espionage (NBC, 1963); The Greatest Show on Earth (ABC, 1963); *The Case Against Paul Ryker* (Kraft Suspense Th., NBC, Oct. 10, 17, 1963); Wagon Train (NBC, 1963); Dr. Kildare (NBC, 1964, 1966); The Nurses (CBS, 1964); Ben Casey (ABC, 1964); Profiles in Courage (NBC, 1965); 12 O'Clock High (ABC, 1966); Bob Hope Chrysler Th. (NBC, 1966, 1967); The F.B.I. (ABC, 1966, 1967, 1968, 1970, 1971); The Man from U.N.C.L.E. (NBC, 1967); Judd for the Defense (ABC, 1968); Mission: Impossible (CBS, 1968, 1972); Fear No Evil (NBC, Mar. 3, 1969); Marcus Welby, M.D. (ABC, 1969); *Longstreet* (ABC, 1971); *Five Desperate Women* (ABC, 1971); Bonanza (NBC, 1971); Night Gallery (NBC, 1971); *The Eyes of Charles Sand* (ABC, 1972); *The Delphi Bureau* (ABC, 1972); Columbo (NBC, 1972); and *Moon of the Wolf* (ABC, 1972).

Awards. He received the *Theatre World* Award for his performance as Edmund Tyrone in *Long Day's Journey into Night* (1957); and the Cannes Film Festival Award for his performance as Artie Straus in *Compulsion* (1959).

Recreation. Golf, literature.

DILLON, MELINDA. Actress. b. Melinda Ruth Dillon, Oct. 13, 1939, Hope, Ark., to W.S. and E. Norine (Barnett) Dillon. Father, Colonel, US Army. Grad. Hyde Park H.S., Chicago, 1958; attended Goodman Theatre Sch., 1958–61. Studied acting with Lee Strasberg, N.Y.C., 1962–64. Married Sept. 30, 1963, to Richard Libertini, actor; one son. Member of AEA; SAG.

Theatre. While still a student, Miss Dillon was an understudy for *The Second City* (Chicago, 1958–61), and then joined the company as ingenue-vocalist (Summer 1961).

At the Arena Stage (Washington, D.C., Oct. 1961–June 1962), she appeared as Grusche in *The Caucasian Chalk Circle;* Caroline in *What Shall We Tell Caroline?* Sonja in *Uncle Vanya;* Blanaid in *The Moon in the Yellow River;* Irma in *The Madwoman of Chaillot;* Felice in *The Burning of the Lepers;* and Kitty in *The Time of Your Life.*

She was understudy to Barbara Harris in the role of Rosalie in *Oh Dad, Poor Dad, Mama's Hung You in the Closet and I'm Feelin' So Sad* (Phoenix, N.Y.C., Feb. 26, 1962); appeared as Honey in the original cast of *Who's Afraid of Virginia Woolf?* (Billy Rose Th., Oct. 13, 1962); appeared in *Conerico Was Here To Stay* (Playwrights Unit, Village South Th., Mar. 8, 1964); was Dorothy in *The Shock of Recognition*, Jill in *The Footsteps of Doves*, and Clarice in *I'll Be Home for Christmas*, all on the program billed as *You Know I Can't Hear You When the Water's Running* (Ambassador, Mar. 13, 1967); was Lilly Seltzer in *A Way of Life* (previews, ANTA Th., Jan. 18–Feb. 1, 1969); appeared in *Marat/Sade* (Arena Stage, Washington, D.C., Mar. 25, 1969); in *A Round with Ring* (ANTA Matinee Th., Th. de Lys, N.Y.C., Oct. 27, 1969); and played various roles in *Paul Sills' Story Theater* (Center Th. Group, Mark Taper Forum, Los Angeles, Calif., June 18, 1970; Ambassador, N.Y.C., Apr. 22, 1971).

Films. Miss Dillon appeared in *Strangers Came to Die* (Germany, 1964) and *The April Fools* (Natl. Gen., 1969).

Television. She has performed on The Defenders (CBS, July 1963); and played Stacy in *The Poet and the Politician* (East Side/West Side, CBS, Nov. 1963).

Awards. For her performance as Honey in *Who's Afraid of Virginia Woolf?*, Miss Dillon was nominated for the Antoinette Perry (Tony) Award (1963); won the *Variety* NY Drama Critics Poll (1963); and received the *Theatre World* Award (1963).

Recreation. Singing, playing the banjo, studying acting, reading, watching old films, rearranging apartment.

DILWORTH, GORDON. Actor, singer. b. Gordon Lincoln Dilworth, May 29, 1913, Brooklyn, N.Y., to Albert Clark and Elizabeth Taylor (Gilchrist) Dilworth. Father, comptroller; mother, singer. Grad. Huntington (N.Y.) H.S., 1931; attended Miami Univ., Ohio, 1932–33; Juilliard Sch. of Music, 1933–41. Studied voice with Henry Jacobi (1944–50); Ivan Velskanoff (1951–54); Sidney Osborne (1954–64). Married Oct. 8, 1961, to Patricia King, singer, dancer. Member of AEA (council, 1957–64); SAG; AFTRA.

Theatre. Mr. Dilworth first appeared in N.Y.C. as an understudy to Alfred Drake in the role of Marshall Blackstone in *Babes in Arms* (Shubert, Apr. 14, 1937); subsequently played Emil in *Sunny River* (St. James, Dec. 14, 1941); Gypsy in *The Fair at Sorochinsk* and Thomsky in *Queen of Spades*, two operas staged by the New Opera Co. (44 St. Th., 1942); Agamemnon in *Helen Goes to Troy* (Alvin, Apr. 24, 1944); and toured in concerts throughout the South and Midwest (1943, 1945).

At the NY City Ctr., he appeared as General Bardini in *The Merry Widow* (Oct. 7, 1944) and later toured in it (1944–45); as Silvio in *Pagliacci* (Sept. 28, 1945); George Germont in *La Traviata* (Sept. 30, 1945); and Barinkay in *The Gypsy Baron* (Oct. 6, 1945). He played Gabriel Von Eisenstein in a USO touring production of *Rosalinda* (PTO, 1945–46); the Red Shadow in a stock production of *The Desert Song* (Royal Alexandra Th., Toronto, Canada, Aug. 12, 1946); and appeared with the Pittsburgh, Pa., Light Opera Co. as Capt. Paul in *Desert Song*, Aramis in *The Three Musketeers*, Dr. Frank in *Rosalinda*, Capt. Duval in *The New Moon*, Francis X. Gilhooley in *Of Thee I Sing*, Capt. Banner in *Rosalie* and the Widow Piper in *Babes in Toyland* (1947–48).

He appeared as Reuben Sloan and Raymond Janney in *Paint Your Wagon* (Shubert, Nov. 12, 1951), which he repeated on tour (opened Hartman, Columbus, Ohio, Oct. 2, 1952; closed Blackstone, Chicago, Ill., Jan. 31, 1953); as Merlin in *A Connecticut Yankee*, Baron Popoff in *The Merry Widow* (Skaneateles, N.Y.); and as Porthos in *The Three Musketeers* and Sergeant Malone in *Rose-Marie* (Louisville, Ky., Summer 1953); Sharkey in *Sandhog* (Phoenix, N.Y.C., Nov. 29, 1954); the Selsey Man, Harry, and Lord Boxington, and later succeeded (Dec. 1961) Ronald Radd as Alfred P. Doolittle in *My Fair Lady* (Mark Hellinger Th., Mar. 15, 1956); played Shamus in *The Unsinkable Molly Brown* (St. Louis Municipal Opera, Forest Park Th., Summer 1963); repeated his role in a stock tour of *My Fair Lady* (St. Louis, Mo.; Dallas, Tex.; Pittsburgh, Pa., Summer 1964); played Mr. Rearson in *Flora, the Red Menace* (Alvin Th., N.Y.C., May 11, 1965); Samuel Welles in *On a Clear Day You Can See Forever* (Mark Hellinger Th., Oct. 17, 1965); and Tubby Wadlow in *Walking Happy* (Lunt-Fontanne Th., Nov. 26, 1966).

Awards. Mr. Dilworth was nominated for an Antoinette Perry (Tony) Award as best supporting actor in a musical (1966–67) for his performance in *Walking Happy.*

DISHY, BOB. Actor. b. Brooklyn, N.Y. Grad. Syracuse Univ., 1955. Address: 20 E. 9th St., New York, NY 10003, tel. (212) 260-8160.

Theatre. Mr. Dishy began his career in summer stock in New York and Pennsylvania. He was Rocky in *Damn Yankees*, joining the cast of that production after it had opened (46 St. Th., N.Y.C., May 5, 1955); appeared in the revues *Chic* (Orpheum, May 18, 1959); *Dig We Must* (John Drew Th., East Hampton, N.Y., Summer 1960); *Medium Rare* (Happy Medium Th., Chicago, Ill., June 29, 1960); *When the Owl Screams* (Square East, N.Y.C., Sept. 12, 1963); and *The Wrecking Ball*, which he also directed (Square East, Apr. 15, 1964).

Mr. Dishy appeared as Theophile in a revival of *Can-Can* (NY City Ctr., May 16, 1962); was Comrade Harry Toukarian in *Flora, the Red Menace* (Alvin, May 11, 1965); Sapiens in a revival of *By Jupiter* (Th. Four, Jan. 19, 1967); the Inventor in *The Unknown Soldier and His Wife* (Vivian Beaumont Th., July 6, 1967); and Sheldon "Bud" Nemerov in *Something Different* (Cort, Nov. 28, 1967). He also played Arthur Korman in *The Goodbye People* (Ethel Barrymore Th., Dec. 3, 1968); Alex Krieger in *A Way of Life* (previews: ANTA Th., Jan. 18–Feb. 1 1969); Adam in *The Creation of the World and Other Business* (Sam S. Shubert Th., Nov. 30, 1972); and Arnold Brody in *An American Millionaire* (Circle in the Square/Joseph E. Levine Th., Apr. 20, 1974).

Films. Mr. Dishy appeared in *The Tiger Makes Out* (Col., 1967).

Television. Mr. Dishy has appeared on That Was the Week That Was.

Discography. Mr. Dishy may be heard on the original cast recording of *Flora, the Red Menace* (RCA, 1965).

DISTLER, P. ANTONIE. Educator, actor, director. b. Paul Antonie Distler, May 5, 1937, Easton, Pa., to Theodore A. and Martha Alice Distler. Father, educator. Grad. Lancaster (Pa.) Country Day School; Mercersburg (Pa.) Academy; Williams College, B.A. (cum laude; Phi Beta Kappa) 1959; Tulane Univ., M.A. (theatre) 1961; Ph.D. (theatre) 1963. Professional training Giles Playfair, Monroe Lippman. Married Apr. 16, 1966, to Anne Goette; two sons; one daughter. Member of AEA; ATA (vice-pres. for administration, 1974–75); UCTA (pres., 1972–73); Virginia Theatre Conference (pres., 1970–72); SETC (chmn., publications comm., 1973); SCA. Address: (home) 2500 Shadow Lake Rd., Blacksburg, VA 24060, tel. (703) 552-8964; (bus.) Performing Arts, Virginia Polytechnic Institute and State Univ., Blacksburg, VA 24061, tel. (703) 951-5335.

In 1972, Mr. Distler became professor of theatre at Virginia Polytechnic Institute and State Univ., Blacksburg, Va. Since 1970, he has also been chairman of the Dept. of Performing Arts and Communications at the same institution. He was associate professor of theatre there from 1967 to 1972 and coordinator, Fine Arts Program, from 1968 to 1970. From 1963 to 1967, he was assistant professor of theatre at Tulane Univ.

Theatre. Mr. Distler made his first appearance on the stage as Whitney in *Life with Father* (Green Room Th., Franklin and Marshall Coll., Nov. 1948). He first played in summer stock as Snobby Price in *Major Barbara* (Cross Rights Stage, Falmouth, Mass., June 1957). He appeared on the professional stage for three years at the Ephrata Star Playhouse in Pennsylvania, where he made his debut as Cates in *Inherit the Wind* (July 1958).

Other Activities. Mr. Distler was managing editor of the *Tulane Drama Review* (later *The Drama Review*) in 1962–63. He served (1972–74) on the Drama Review Committee, Virginia Commission of the Arts and Humanities.

Published Works. *CLIO* and *Educational Theatre Journal* have published articles by Mr. Distler.

Awards. Mr. Distler received a grant from the National Endowment for the Humanities to develop a television script based on early American plays. He received the Gilbert Gabriel Award in theatre from Williams College in 1959.

Recreation. Tennis, woodworking.

DIXON, JEAN. Actress. b. Marie Jacques, July 14, 1894, Waterbury, Conn., to Eugene Leslie and Annie Louise (Ames) Jacques. Father, theatre owner; mother, actress. Attended St. Margaret's Sch., Waterbury, Conn.; received Brevet Supérieur from the Institut de Jeunes Filles, Neuilly-sur-Seine, France, 1913. Studied acting with Sarah Bernhardt in Paris (1912–14). Married Jan. 3, 1936, to Edward S. Ely. Member of AEA; AFTRA; SAG. Address: (home) 812 Fifth Ave., New York, NY 10021; (bus.) c/o AEA, 226 W. 47th St., New York, NY 10036, tel. (212) PL 7-1710.

Theatre. Miss Dixon made her stage debut as Figurante in *La Samaritaine* (Th. Sarah Bernhardt, Paris, France), appearing with Sarah Bernhardt.

She made her N.Y.C. debut as the Maid in *Golden Days* (Gaiety Th., Nov. 1, 1921); succeeded Norma Mitchell as the Stenographer in *To the Ladies* (Liberty, Feb. 20, 1922); appeared with various stock companies in Dayton (Ohio), Columbus (Ohio), and Minneapolis (Minn.); played Mary Maddern in *Wooden Kimono* (Martin Beck Th., N.Y.C., Dec. 27, 1926); Constance Peyton in *Behold, the Bridegroom* (Cort, Dec. 26, 1927); Olga Metz in *Anna* (Lyceum, May 15, 1928); Susan Perry in *Heavy Traffic* (Empire, Sept. 5, 1928); Rose Cady in *Back Here* (Klaw, Nov. 26, 1928); Lucille in *June Moon* (Broadhurst, Oct. 9, 1929); May Daniels in *Once in a Lifetime* (Music Box Th., Sept. 24, 1930); Frieda Chatfield in *Dangerous Corner* (Empire, Oct. 27, 1932); Olga in *Heat Lighting* (Booth, Sept. 15, 1933); and Kate Hastings in *Bright Star* (Empire, Oct. 15, 1935).

She appeared as Annabelle Fuller in *George Washington Slept Here* (Lyceum, Oct. 18, 1940); Mrs. Fentriss in *The Deep Mrs. Sykes* (Booth, March 19, 1945); Sister Monica in *The Velvet Glove* (Booth, Dec. 26, 1949); An Older Woman in *To Be Continued* (Booth, April 23, 1952); and Mrs. Lovejoy in *The Square Root of Wonderful* (National, Oct. 30, 1957); succeeded (Feb. 1958) Evelyn Varden as Muriel Chadwick in *Roar Like a Dove* (Phoenix, London, Sept. 26, 1957); and played Frances Greeley Hastings in *The Gang's All Here* (Ambassador, N.Y.C., Oct. 1, 1959).

Films. Miss Dixon has appeared in *Sadie McKee* (MGM, 1934); *Mr. Dynamite* (UI, 1934), *She Married Her Boss* (Col. 1935); *My Man Godfrey* (UI, 1936); *The Magnificent Brute* (UI, 1936); *Swing High, Swing Low* (Par., 1937); and *Holiday* (Col., 1938).

Television. Miss Dixon appeared in the *The Velvet Glove* (Television Play of the Week) and had roles in several other television productions.

DODDS, WILLIAM. Stage manager. b. Bullington, Iowa, to Horace and Florence Dodds. Father, farmer. Grad. Danville (Iowa) H.S., 1939; Cornell Coll., B.A. 1943. Member of AEA. Address: 711 Amsterdam Ave., New York, NY 10025, tel. (212) 866-6611.

Theatre. Mr. Dodds was stage manager for the Valley Players (Holyoke, Mass., Summers 1948–51); assistant stage manager for the N.Y.C. production of *Cock-a-Doodle-Do* (ANTA Experimental Th., Feb. 26, 1949); stage manager for *The Cenci* (Walt Whitman Sch. Th., Feb. 2, 1950); *Major Barbara* (DeWitt Clinton Community Ctr., Bronx, N.Y., Dec. 7, 1950); and for the John Drew Theatre (East Hampton, L.I., N.Y., Summers 1953–54).

He was assistant stage manager for *Carousel* (NY City Ctr., June 15, 1954); assistant stage manager for *King of Hearts* (National, Oct. 17, 1954); stage manager for *Anastasia* (Lyceum, Mar. 7, 1955), and for the touring production (opened Ford's, Baltimore, Md., Sept. 26, 1955); *Teach Me How To Cry* (Th. de Lys, N.Y.C., Apr. 5, 1955); and Lakewood Th. (Showhegan, Me., Summers 1955–59).

Mr. Dodds was assistant stage manager for *Holiday for Lovers* (Longacre, N.Y.C., Feb. 14, 1957); *Miss Lonelyhearts* (Music Box Th., Oct. 3, 1957); *Conversation Piece* (Barbizon-Plaza, Nov. 18, 1957); stage manager for *Fun and Magic* (John Golden Th., Dec. 27, 1957); and assistant stage manager for the touring production of *A Visit to a Small Planet* (opened Playhouse, Wilmington, Del., Feb. 5, 1958; closed Geary, San Francisco, Calif., June 28, 1958).

He was stage manager for the industrial show tours of Chevrolet (Aug. 1958; Aug. 1959; July 1963); Colgate-Palmolive (Dec. 1958); RCA Service Co. (Jan. 1959); and *Sports Illustrated* Design Awards (May 1959).

He was assistant stage manager for *Look After Lulu* (Henry Miller's Th., Mar. 3, 1959); stage manager for *Five Finger Exercise* (Music Box Th., Dec. 2, 1959), and for the touring production (opened Walnut Street Th., Philadelphia, Pa., Oct. 3, 1960; closed Hartman, Columbus, Ohio, Apr. 22, 1961); stage manager for *Write Me a Murder* (Belasco, Oct. 26, 1961); *Little Me* (Lunt-Fontanne Th., Nov. 17, 1962); *Dylan* (Plymouth, Jan. 18, 1964); *Ben Franklin in Paris* (Lunt-Fontanne Th., Oct. 27, 1964); *Pickwick* (46 St. Th., Oct. 4, 1965); *Happily Never After* (Eugene O'Neill Th., Mar. 10, 1966); *The Star-Spangled Girl* (Plymouth, Dec. 21, 1966); *Henry, Sweet Henry* (Palace, Oct. 23, 1967); *Here's Where I Belong* (Billy Rose Th., Mar. 3, 1968); *The Great White Hope* (Alvin Th., Oct. 3, 1968); *The Engagement Baby* (Helen Hayes Th., May 21, 1970); *Dance of Death* (Ritz Th., Apr. 20, 1971); *No, No, Nanette* (46 St. Th., July 5, 1971); *Night Watch* (Morosco, Feb. 28, 1972); *Via Galactica* (Uris Th., Nov. 28, 1972); *Smith* (Eden Th., May 19, 1973); and *Full Circle* (ANTA Th., Nov. 7, 1973). All theatres are in New York City.

Mr. Dodds was also stage manager for additional industrial shows, as follows: Ford (Aug. 1966 and Jan. 1973); Lincoln Mercury (Aug. 1970 and Aug. 1972); and Goodyear (Feb. 1971).

DODGE, SHIRLEE. Choreographer, director, teacher. b. Prairie Du Sac, Wis., to Thane E. and Lisle (Sisson) Dodge. Father, businessman. Grad. West H.S., Madison, Wis., 1934; attended Univ. of Wisconsin (Madison), 1935–37; studied with Margaret H'Doubler; summer school, Sigtuna, Sweden, 1937; Mary Wigman Central Institute, Dresden, Germany, 1937–39 (honor graduate); Salzburg (Austria) Festival Course, 1937; Hanya Holm Studio, N.Y.C., one year. Studied relaxation and breathing with Hildegard Elsberg. Address: (home) 2280 Hanover St., Palo Alto, CA 94306, tel. (415) 427-2295; (bus.) c/o Drama Dept., Stanford Univ., Stanford, CA 94305.

Miss Dodge joined the Drama Dept., Stanford Univ., as associate professor, choreographer, and movement director in 1969. She had been associate professor of dance-drama, Univ. of Texas (Austin), since 1954. She was instructor of dance, Northwestern Univ. (Summer 1945); and choreographer and teacher in drama, Suffolk (N.Y.) Community College (Summer 1974).

She choreographed and danced in student productions at the Univ. of Texas (Austin) beginning in 1943, and from 1945 to 1969 she choreographed all Shakespearean productions presented by the drama dept. at the university. In 1956, she choreographed and directed at the university the world premiere of Heine's *Mephistola.* At Stanford, she did choreography for the operas *Don Giovanni* and *Rusulka.*

Miss Dodge was choreographer and movement director at Ashland (Ore.) Shakespeare Festival (Summers 1963–69) and choreographer at the Pacific Performing Arts Festival (1970). She has appeared as solo artist in many of her works; has lectured and given lecture demonstrations on movement and dance in relation to theatre before major theatre groups and organizations; concertized extensively; and has choreographed for television.

The Perry-Mansfield Dance & Drama School presents the Shirlee Dodge (scholarship) Award.

Published Works. Her article, "Mary Wigman," appeared in *Dance Observer* (Mar. 1951).

Awards. Miss Dodge was invited by the West German Science and Art Society to attend the celebration in West Berlin honoring Mary Wigman on her eightieth birthday.

Recreation. Travel, reading, drawing.

DODSON, OWEN. Educator, director, playwright, poet. b. Owen Vincent Dodson, Nov. 28, 1914, Brooklyn, N.Y., to Nathaniel and Sarah Elizabeth (Goode) Dodson. Father, journalist. Grad. Thomas Jefferson H.S., Bklyn., 1932; Bates Coll., B.A. (Phi Beta Kappa); Yale Univ., M.F.A. 1939. Served USN, 1942–43; rank Seaman 1/C. Member of AETA; ANTA; NTC. Address: 350 West 51st St., New York, NY 10019, tel. (212) 541-5374.

From 1960 to 1969, Mr. Dodson was professor of drama and chairman of the Dept. of Drama, College of Fine Arts, Howard Univ., where he had taught since 1947. In 1970–71, he was a consultant to the Community Th., Harlem School of the Arts, N.Y.C.

He directed drama at Atlanta (Ga.) Univ. and Spelman Coll. (1938–42); at Hampton Institute (Summer-Fall 1942); at Lincoln Univ., Miss.; at Howard, where, among other productions, he directed *Hamlet* with Earle Hyman; the Theatre Lobby, Washington, D.C.; Inner City Th., Los Angeles; and Univ. of California (Santa Barbara). Mr. Dodson also conducted seminars in theatre and playwriting, lectured, and gave poetry readings of his own work at such institutions as the Univ. of California (Santa Barbara); Iowa Univ.; Vassar Coll., City Coll. of New York, Kenyon Coll., Cornell Univ., Ferris State Coll., Ohio Wesleyan, York Univ., the Univ. of Chicago, Prairie View Coll., Dartmouth Coll., and Coolidge Auditorium, Library of Congress, Washington, D.C. He was also at one time poet in residence at the Univ. of Arizona.

Theatre. Mr. Dodson's play *Amistad* was commissioned by Talladega (Ala.) Coll. and was performed there in 1939; his *Garden of Time* was performed at Yale Univ. in the same year; and during World War II, Mr. Dodson's pageant *New World A-Coming* was presented at Madison Sq. Garden, N.Y.C. Mr. Dodson was a charter member of the Negro Playwrights Co. and directed a N.Y.C. production of *Garden of Time* (135th St. Library Th., Mar. 7, 1945), staged by the American Negro Theatre. He also directed the Howard Players in *Mamba's Daughters,* which, under US State Dept. auspices, toured Norway, Denmark, Sweden, and Germany (Aug.–Nov. 1949) and in Countee Cullen's *Medea in Africa,* adapted from Euripides, which toured New England colleges (Apr. 1963).

Musical works for which Mr. Dodson wrote words include the operas *'Till Victory Is Won,* commemorating Howard University's centennial, and *The Christmas Miracle* (both performed at Howard Univ.) and the song cycle *The Confession Stone,* sung by Maureen Forrester (Carnegie Hall, N.Y.C., Feb. 3, 1968). Mr. Dodson's poems were included in *A Hand Is on the Gate,* a program of black American poetry and folk music (Longacre, N.Y.C., Sept. 21,

1966), and the D.C. Black Repertory Co. presented *Owen's Song*, a tribute to Mr. Dodson, containing excerpts from his poetry and based on his play *Bayou Legend* (Last Colony Th., Washington, D.C., Oct. 24, 1974).

Radio. Mr. Dodson's *Dorie Miller*, set to music by Emanuel Rosenberg, was performed by Lawrence Tibbett and the Lyn Murray Chorus (CBS, Dec. 7, 1944).

Other Activities. Mr. Dodson was executive secretary, Committee for Mass Education in Race Relations, American Film Ctr., N.Y.C., and artistic consultant, Harlem School of the Arts Community Th., N.Y.C.

Published Works. Mr. Dodson's published poetry includes the collection *Powerful Long Ladder* (1946), *The Confession Stone* (1970), and *Cages* (1973). He wrote the novels *Boy at the Window* (1951; reprinted as *When Trees Were Green*, 1973) and *A Bent House* (1973). Among his short stories are "Come Home Early, Chile," "Baptism," "Lodge Sisters at a Funeral," and the prize-winning "The Summer Fire," all of which have been reprinted in anthologies. Among his short plays are *Everybody Join Hands*, published in *Theatre Arts*, and *The Third Fourth of July*, written with Countee Cullen (also published in *Theatre Arts*). Mr. Dodson has also published essays and book reviews in such periodicals as *World Theatre, The Washingtonian, Theatre Arts, Negro Digest, The New Republic*, and *The Washington Times-Herald*.

Discography. James Earle Jones and the Negro Ensemble Co. recorded *The Dream Awake* (Spoken Arts).

Awards. Mr. Dodson has received a General Education Board Fellowship (1938, 1939), a Rosenwald Fellowship (1944), a Guggenheim Fellowship (1953) for creative writing, and a Rockefeller grant (1968). He was awarded an honorary Litt.D. from Bates Coll. (1967).

He won the Maxwell Anderson Verse Play Contest at Stanford Univ. for his play, *Garden of Time* (1940); and received the second prize in a contest sponsored by the *Paris Review* for his short story, "The Summer Fire" (1955).

Recreation. Collecting paintings, swimming.

DOLL, BILL. Press representative. b. Dec. 28, 1910, Grafton, W.Va., to Edgar and Seva Doll. Grad. West Virginia Univ., A.B. Married 1950 to Caren Marsh, actress; two sons. Served USAAF, 1943–44; rank, Staff Sgt. Member of ATPAM; Bway Assn. (bd. of dir.); NY Athletic Club; Beta Theta Pi. 150 W. 52nd St., New York, NY 10019.

Pre-Theatre. Newspaperman in Grafton, W. Va., and on the NY *Herald Tribune* (1933–35).

Theatre. Mr. Doll began as a press representative for the Ivoryton (Conn.) Playhouse (1935–40); and *Three Men on a Horse* (1936); subsequently formed his own company called Bill Doll and Co., The National Press Representatives, of which he was president (1936). With Bernard Hart and Joseph M. Hyman, he represented Cicelia Loftus in *Impersonations and Impressions* (1937), the Yale Puppeteers in *It's a Small World* (1938), and Elsie Janis and her 1939 revue (1939). He served for twenty years as executive vice president and publicity director for Michael Todd. At the World's Fair (1939–40), he publicized Mr. Todd's *Hot Mikado, Gay New Orleans, Dancing Campus*, and *Streets of Paris*. In 1941, he represented Mr. Todd's Theatre Cafe (Chicago, Ill.), and *Star and Garter;* and in 1942, *Something for the Boys*. Also, he represented the Lambertville Music Circus (N.J., 1942–48) and Bucks County Playhouse (New Hope, Pa. 1942).

He served as press representative for the Army Air Force production of *Winged Victory* (1943). He publicized the Algonquin Hotel (1945–54); in 1945, *Hamlet;* in 1946, *The Would-Be Gentleman, January Thaw*, and the NY City Ctr. production of *Hamlet;* in 1947, the NY City Ctr. production of *Up in Central Park*, also *The Heiress, Dear Judas, Caribbean Festival*, and *Angel in the Wings;* in 1948, *Skipper Next to God, The Rats of Norway, Hold It!, Hope's the Thing, Ballet Ballads, Seeds in the Wind, Heaven on Earth, As the Girls Go, Light Up the Sky, Diamond Lil*, and for the NY City Ctr., *Rip Van Winkle* in 1949, Ken Murray's *Blackouts;* in 1951, *Top Banana*, the national tours for Spike Jones City Slickers (1951–56), and the annual Oldsmobile Announcement show (Bway and on tour, 1951–64); in 1952, *Buttrio Square, A Night in Venice, New Faces of 1952*, and *The Climate of Eden;* in 1953, *Sherlock Holmes, Touchstone, Room Service*, and world tour of *Porgy and Bess*.

In 1954, he represented *Hayride, Abie's Irish Rose, Mrs. Patterson, The Saint of Bleecker Street, The Troublemakers*, and *Anastasia;* in 1955, *Plain and Fancy, A Day by the Sea, Carmen Amaya and Her Company*, and *The Threepenny Opera;* in 1956, *Waiting for Godot, Wake Up, Darling, New Faces of '56, Shoestring '57*, the pre-Bway tryout of *Strip for Action, Show Boat* (Jones Beach, L.I., N.Y.), and George Hamid's Steel Pier and the Diving Horse (Atlantic City, N.J., 1956–64); in 1957, *Waiting for Godot, The Potting Shed, A Moon for the Misbegotten, Mask and Gown, Rumple, Compulsion*, Mike Todd's Madison Square Garden Party, the Judy Garland show, and a double-bill of Jean Giraudoux's plays called *The Virtuous Island* and *The Apollo of Bellac;* in 1958, the tour of *Mask and Gown;* in 1959, *The Billy Barnes Revue;* in 1960, *Vintage '60, A Taste of Honey*, and *Do Re Mi;* in 1961, *The Happiest Girl in the World, The Magnificent Hugo, A Curious Evening with Gypsy Rose Lee, Mandingo, The Billy Barnes People*, and the national tour of *Holiday on Ice* (1961–62); in 1962, *The Egg, All American, The Difficult Woman*, and *Eddie Fisher* at the Winter Garden; in 1963, Jack Benny, the Vincent Price Art Collection, the first national tour of the Moscow Circus, The Hague Philharmonic Orchestra, NDR Symphony of Hamburg, Koutev Bulgarian Dance Co., and *Marathon '33* (1963–64); in 1964, *Laterna Magika*, the Ice Capades, *A Girl Could Get Lucky*, the Bayanihan Philippine Dancers, Zizi Jeanmaire, *The Deputy*, the national tour of the Lipizzaner horses from Vienna, and the Dupont World of Chemistry Show, the Pavilion of Spain (NY World's Fair).

Mr. Doll has also been director of public relations for the Ringling Bros., Barnum and Bailey Circus.

Films. He has publicized the film version of *Winged Victory* (20th-Fox, 1944); *Around the World in 80 Days* (UA, 1956); *Hercules* (WB, 1959); *La Dolce Vita* (Astor, 1961); *Long Day's Journey Into Night* (Emb., 1962); and *Mondo Cane* (TFC, 1963). In addition, Mr. Doll has publicized the James E. Strates Shows (1965–70); the Repertory Theatre of Lincoln Center (1967); *Applause*, with Lauren Bacall (1970); Benjamin Franklin (1970); *Brendan Behan* (1971); *El Haj Malik* (1971); Inner City (1971); Disney On Parade (national tour, 1971–73); *The Dirtiest Show in Town* (1972); Circus America (1973); Vinie Burrows (1973); *Seesaw* (1973); Bunraku Puppets of Japan (1973); The Kathakali Dancers of India (1973); the Polish Mime Theatre (1973); Peter Pan Arena Productions (tour, 1973); The Platters (1974); Puf-n-Stuf (1973–74); *The World of Magic and Occult* (1974); and the Ukrainian Festival on Ice (national tour, 1974).

Television and Radio. He has made more than 625 appearances on radio and television.

Published Works. Mr. Doll has written more than 40 feature articles on the theatre for the NY *Times*.

DONAT, PETER. Actor. b. Pierre Collingwood Donat, Jan. 20, 1928, Kentville, Nova Scotia, Canada, to Philip E. and Marie (Bardet) Donat. Father, landscape gardener. Grad. Kings County Acad., Kentville, 1946; Acadia Univ., Wolfville, Nova Scotia, B.A., B.Sc. 1950; attended Yale Univ. School of Drama 1950–51. Studied singing with Homer G. Mowe, N.Y.C., 1950–53; acting with Curt Conway, N.Y.C., 1954–55; voice with Iris Warren, Stratford, Ont., 1961. Married Sept. 8, 1956, to Michael Learned, actress; three sons. Relative in theatre: uncle, Robert Donat, actor. Member of AEA; ACTRA; AFTRA; SAG.

Theatre. Mr. Donat made his first stage appearance as Prince Charming in a school production of *Cinderella* (Kings County Acad., May 1940); his first professional appearance on tour with the Nova Scotia Players (July-Aug. 1950), in the roles of Oswald in *Ghosts* and Manningham in *Angel Street;* subsequently, at the Provincetown (Mass.) Playhouse (June–Aug. 1951) played Valentine in *You Never Can Tell*, Byron in *An Innocent in Time*, Randall in *Heartbreak House*, Faukland in *The Rivals*, and the Doctor in *The Straw*.

He joined the Margo Jones Th. (Dallas, Tex.) to play Lysander in *A Midsummer Night's Dream* (Oct.–Dec. 1951); The Pastor in *The Father* (Jan.–May 1952); and the Poet in *A Gift for Cathy*. At the Pocono Playhouse Mountainhome, Pa., appeared as Tony in *You Can't Take It with You* and Gaston in *Gigi* (July 1952); appeared in *Dangerous Corner* (Falmouth Playhouse, Mass., Sept. 1952); played Peter Crewe in the national touring company of *Jane* (opened New Parsons Th., Hartford, Conn., Oct. 2, 1952; closed Royal Alexandra, Toronto, Canada, Nov. 15, 1952); Arthur Fenwick in a scene from *The Girl I Left Behind Me* in the program *Highlights of the Empire* (Empire Th., N.Y.C., May 24, 1953); Dr. Nicholas Agi in a stock tour of *The Swan* (Pocono Playhouse, Pa.; Falmouth Playhouse, Mass., July 1953); Paul in the national touring company of *My Three Angels* (1953); Metellus Cimber in *Julius Caesar* (American Shakespeare Festival, Stratford, Conn., July 12, 1955); Amphitryon in *A God Slept Here* (Provincetown Playhouse, N.Y.C., Feb. 19, 1957); Prince Leopold in *The Gentleman* Belasco, Apr. 25, 1957); and appeared in *Le Bourgeois Gentilhomme* and *Edward II* (Wellesley, Mass., June, 1957).

Mr. Donat played Dorilant in *The Country Wife* (Adelphi, N.Y.C., Nov. 27, 1957); in *The Entertainer* (Royale, Feb. 12, 1958); at the Stratford Shakespearean Festival (Ontario, Canada) appeared as Florizel in *The Winter's Tale* and Sir Richard Vernon in *Henry IV, Part 1* (Summer 1958); played the President's Son in *The Goodwill Ambassador* (Olympia, Dublin, Ireland Mar. 1959); Tusenbach in *The Three Sisters* (4th St. Th., N.Y.C., Sept. 21, 1959); returned to the Stratford Shakespearean Festival to play Demetrius in *A Midsummer Night's Dream* and Chatillon in *King John* (Summer 1960), Longaville in *Love's Labour's Lost* and the Earl of Surrey in *Henry VIII* (Summer 1961).

He appeared as Morris Townsend in *The Heiress* (Crest Th., Toronto, Canada, 1961); at the Stratford Shakespearean Festival (Ontario, Canada), played Christian in *Cyrano de Bergerac*, Hortensio in *The Taming of the Shrew*, and Ferdinand in *The Tempest* (Summer 1962), and Troilus in *Troilus and Cressida*, Christian in *Cyrano de Bergerac*, and Antipholus of Syracuse in *The Comedy of Errors* (Summer 1963); played Oliver in *The Chinese Prime Minister* (Royale, N.Y.C., Jan. 2, 1964); and Frank O'Keefe in the world premiere of *Return to the Mountain* (Royal Alexandra, Toronto, Can., June 12, 1964).

Mr. Donat appeared again at the Stratford Shakespearean Festival (Festival Th.) as Pistol in *Falstaff*, originally *Henry IV, Part 2* (June 15, 1965) and Cassius in *Julius Caesar* (June 16, 1965). At American Conservatory Th. (ACT), San Francisco, Calif., he was in *An Evening's Frost* (Feb. 17, 1968), *Under Milk Wood* (May 26–Aug. 18, 1968), *Deedle, Deedle Dumpling, My Son God* (June 16–29, 1968), *Staircase* (Jan. 2–May 18, 1969), *The Architect and the Emperor of Assyria* (Mar. 26, 1969), *Hadrian VII* (May 12, 1970; Nov. 18, 1970), *The Importance of Being Earnest* (Mar. 7, 1970), *Six Characters in Search of an Author* (Mar. 17, 1970), *The Merchant of Venice* (Nov. 14, 1970), *An Enemy of the People* (Mar. 2, 1971), and he was George Mason in *The Selling of the President* (Mar. 30, 1971).

He played Pontagnac in *There's One in Every Marriage* (Stratford Shakespearean Festival, Ontario, Canada, Avon Th., Aug. 6, 1971; Royale, N.Y.C., Jan. 3, 1972); was Caesar in *Caesar and Cleopatra* (ACT, Oct. 30, 1971); was in *The Way of the World* (Long Wharf Th., New Haven, Conn., Feb. 18, 1972); and, again at ACT in San Francisco, was in *Sleuth* (Apr. 4, 1972), played the title role in *Cyrano de Bergerac* (Oct. 28, 1972), was Torvald Helmer in *A Doll's House* (Jan. 9, 1973), was in *The Crucible* (Apr. 3, 1973), and *The Cherry Orchard* (Mar. 19,

1974); and in England, he appeared in *A Touch of Spring* (London, 1975), called *Avanti!* in the US.

Television. Mr. Donat made his debut as Playboy in *There Once Was a Diamond Ring* (Robert Montgomery Presents, NBC, Feb. 1953); followed by Stephen Markley in the serial The Brighter Day (CBS, radio and TV, Nov. 1955); and Bert Stanton in the serial As the World Turns (CBS, 1959). In Toronto, he appeared as Tusenbach in *The Three Sisters* (CBS, Oct. 1960); Hjalmar in *The Wild Duck;* the Painter in *The Doctor's Dilemma;* and the Scoundrel in *The Diary of a Scoundrel* (CBS, Oct. 1962). He played the title role in scenes from *Hamlet* (Look Up and Live, CBS, 1964); was in *Heartbreak House* (NET, 1966); in *Enemies* Th. in America, PBS, 1974); and *Cyrano de Bergerac* (Theatre in America, PBS, 1974).

He adapted Jane Austen's *Emma* (Kraft Television Th., NBC, Feb. 1953).

Awards. Mr. Donat received the *Theatre World* Award for his performance as Prince Leopold in *The First Gentleman* (1957).

Recreation. Tennis, photography, swimming, writing.

DONNELLY, RUTH. Actress. b. May 17, 1896, Trenton, N.J., to Harry A. and Elizabeth (Weart) Donnelly. Father, newspaper editor, music critic and columnist. Attended Cadwalader Sch., Trenton, N.J. Married June 27, 1932, to Basic W. de Guichard (dec. May 29, 1958). Member of AEA; SAG; AFTRA.

Theatre. Miss Donnelly made her professional debut in the chorus of a touring production of *The Quaker Girl* (1913); subsequently appeared in a comedy role in a touring company of *Maggie Pepper* (1913); and toured in *Under Cover* (1913).

She made her Bway debut as a Telephone Operator in *A Scrap of Paper* (Criterion Th., May 11, 1914); subsequently appeared in George M. Cohan's productions (1914–17); as a Switchboard Operator in the musical, *Going Up* (Liberty, Dec. 25, 1917); performed in *A Prince There Was* (George M. Cohan Th., Dec. 24, 1918); as Ethel Nutt in *As You Were* (Central, Jan. 27, 1920); Kitty Crockett in *The Meanest Man in the World* (Hudson, Oct. 12, 1920); Aggie in *Madeline and the Movies* (Gaiety, Mar. 6, 1922); and later as Isabel Flynn in *The Riot Act* (Cort, Mar. 7, 1963; Wilbur Th., Boston, Mass., Feb. 13, 1968). She was standby for Pert Kelton as Delia Bresnahan in *I Was Dancing* (Lyceum, N.Y.C., Nov. 8, 1964).

Films. Miss Donnelly first appeared in *Transatlantic* (20th-Fox, 1931); followed by *Blessed Event* (WB, 1932); *Hard To Handle* (WB, 1933); *You Belong to Me* (Par., 1934); *Mr. Deeds Goes to Town* (Col., 1936); *A Slight Case of Murder* (WB, 1938); *Mr. Smith Goes to Washington* (Col., 1939); *The Spoilers* (U, 1942); *Thank Your Lucky Stars* (WB, 1943); *This Is the Army* (WB, 1943); *The Bells of St. Mary's* (RKO, 1945); *Cinderella Jones* (WB, 1946); *In Old Sacramento* (Rep., 1946); *The Ghost Goes Wild* (RKO, 1947); *Fighting Father Dunne* (RKO, 1948); *The Snake Pit* (20th-Fox, 1948); *I'd Climb the Highest Mountain* (20th-Fox, 1951); *The Wild Blue Yonder* (Rep., 1951); *The Secret of Convict Lake* (20th-Fox, 1951); *A Lawless Street* (Col., 1955); and *Autumn Leaves* (Col., 1956).

Television. Miss Donnelly has appeared on Robert Montgomery Presents (NBC); East Side/West Side (CBS, 1964); 90 Bristol Court (NBC, 1964); The Doctors and the Nurses (CBS, 1965); *Are Trees People?*, as Mother O'Brien on the Crossroads series; in Mayor of the Town; Take Me Out to the Ball Game; Dear Phoebe.

Awards. Miss Donnelly received a gold medal from AEA for her 50 years in the theatre (1963); and a gold medal from Photoplay for her performance in *The Bells of St. Mary's* (1945).

Recreation. Writing, portrait painting, lyric writing.

DONOHUE, JACK. Director, choreographer, dancer. b. John Francis Donohue, Nov. 3, 1912, New York City, to John and Ellen (Ling) Donohue. Father, horse dealer. Attended Regis H.S., N.Y.C.; St. Anne's Military Acad. Married to Tutta Rolf (marr. dis.); one daughter. Member of DGA; Screen Producers Guild; TV Directors Guild (pres., 1957–58); Yacht Club of Monaco; Cabrillo Beach Yacht Club; South Coast Corinthian Yacht Club; Club de Yates (Acapulco); Club des Esquies (Acapulco). Address: (home) 13900 Panay Way, R. 204, Marina del Ray, CA 90291; (bus.) 1800 Century Park East, Suite 504, Los Angeles, CA 90067, tel. (213) CR 7-3000.

Pre-Theatre. Brokerage clerk, construction iron worker.

Theatre. Mr. Donohue first performed as a dancer in *Ziegfeld Follies* (New Amsterdam, N.Y.C., Aug. 16, 1927); subsequently danced in *Good News* (46 St. Th., Sept. 6, 1927); in a vaudeville show (Palm Gardenia Th., Sept. 10, 1927); *Follow Through* (46 St. Th., Jan. 9, 1929); *America's Sweetheart* (Broadhurst, Feb. 10, 1931); *Shoot the Works* (George M. Cohan Th., July 21, 1931); and *Free for All* (Manhattan, Sept. 8, 1931).

He was dance director of *Smiling Faces* (Shubert, Aug. 1932); *Music in the Air* (Alvin, Nov. 8, 1932); *Shady Lady* (Shubert, July 5, 1933); *Ball at the Savoy* (Drury Lane, London, Sept. 8, 1933); *Please* (Savoy, Nov. 16, 1933); *Mr. Whittington* (Hippodrome, Feb. 1, 1934); was dance director and played Tim Regan in *Here's Howe* (Saville, Feb. 22, 1934); appeared as Konstantine Morrosine in *On Your Toes* (Palace, Feb. 5, 1937; moved to Coliseum, Apr. 19, 1937); Steve in *The Bowery Touch* (Strand, Nov. 21, 1937); Val in *Wild Oats* (Prince's, Apr. 13, 1938); and Jimmy Gay in *Sitting Pretty* (Prince's, Aug. 17, 1939).

Mr. Donohue directed and appeared in 12 stock productions at the St. Louis (Mo.) Municipal Opera (Summer 1940–41); appeared in *Higher and Higher* (Shubert, N.Y.C., Aug. 5, 1940); appeared in a revue (Chat Noir Th., Oslo, Norway, 1940); a revue, *Vita Plostrot* (Folkan Th., Stockholm, Sweden, 1940); played Mike in *Panama Hattie* (46 St. Th., N.Y.C., Oct. 30, 1941); served as dance director of *Seven Lively Arts* (Ziegfeld, Oct. 7, 1944); and *Are You with It?* (Century, Nov. 10, 1945).

He directed *Top Banana* (Winter Garden, Nov. 1, 1951); staged the musical numbers in *Of Thee I Sing* (Ziegfeld, May 5, 1952); directed *Jollyana* (Curran, San Francisco, Calif., Aug. 1952); directed and choreographed *Mr. Wonderful* (Bway Th., N.Y.C., Mar. 22, 1956); and directed *Rumple* (Alvin, Nov. 6, 1957); and *Oliver!* (Dorothy Chandler Pavilion, Los Angeles, 1973).

Films. Mr. Donohue was dance director for Shirley Temple in *Curly Top* (20th-Fox, 1925); *George White's Scandals* (20th-Fox, 1934); *Bathing Beauty* (MGM, 1934); *Music in the Air* (20th-Fox, 1934); for Shirley Temple in the following films: *Our Little Girl* (20th-Fox, 1935); *The Littlest Rebel* (20th-Fox, 1935); *Little Colonel* (20th-Fox, 1935); and *Captain January* (20th-Fox, 1936).

He was dance director for *Lottery Lover* (20th-Fox, 1935); *Professional Soldier* (20th-Fox, 1935); *Life Begins at 40* (20th-Fox, 1935); *Thanks a Million* (20th-Fox, 1935); appeared in *Smiling Along* (20th-Fox, 1939); was dance director for *Louisiana Purchase* (Par., 1941); *You're in the Army Now* (WB, 1941); *Star Spangled Rhythm* (Par., 1941); *The Fleet's In* (Par., 1942); *The Powers Girl* (UA, 1942); *Girl Crazy* (MGM, 1943); *Best Foot Forward* (MGM, 1943); *Anchors Aweigh* (MGM, 1945); *Easy To Wed* (MGM, 1946); *It Happened in Brooklyn* (MGM, 1947); *On an Island with You* (MGM, 1948); *Duchess of Idaho* (MGM, 1950); and directed Red Skelton in *The Yellow Cab Man* (MGM, 1950), and in *Watch the Birdie* (MGM, 1950).

He was dance director for *Calamity Jane* (WB, 1953); directed *Lucky Me* (WB, 1954); *Babes in Toyland* (Buena Vista, 1961), *Marriage on the Rocks* (WB, 1968); and *Assault on a Queen* (Par., 1969).

Television. Mr. Donohue directed and produced eighty-one segments of the Frank Sinatra Show (CBS, NBC); twenty-seven segments of the Dean Martin Show (NBC); forty-seven segments of the Red Skelton Show (CBS); ten segments of the Colgate Comedy Hour (NBC); one hundred forty-eight segments of the New Lucy Show (CBS, 1963–73); fifty-two segments of The Jim Nabors Hour (CBS, 1969–71); and fourteen segments of The Odd Couple (ABC, 1971–74).

He was producer-director of the Cyd Charisse Special (NBC, 1961); four Dinah Shore European specials (NBC, 1961); four segments of Margie (ABC, 1961); and two segments of Follow the Sun (ABC, 1961).

He was producer-director of the Stan Freberg Special (ABC, 1962); March of Dimes Hour Special (1962); and of "specials" for Dick Van Dyke, Don Knotts, Lucille Ball, Andy Griffith, and Jim Nabors (CBS, 1963–to date).

Recreation. Sailing, horseback riding, water skiing.

DONTCHOS, PATRICIA ANN. Educator, director. b. Mar. 11, 1946, Lincoln, Neb., to Richard H. and Dorothy I. Becker. Father, general manager, *Ak-Sar-Ben;* mother, housewife. Grad. Univ. of Nebraska, B.S., 1967; M.A., 1969. Married Sept. 9, 1970, to Leo E. Dontchos; one son. Member of ATA; SETC; Pi Lambda Theta. Address: (home) 118 College Park Dr., Apt. 7, Barbourville, KY 40906, tel. (606) 546-6148; (bus.) Drama Dept., Union College, Barbourville, KY 40906, tel. (606) 546-4151.

Mrs. Dontchos is assistant professor of speech and drama, Union College, Barbourville, Ky.

Theatre. Her first theatrical experience was acquired at the Univ. of Nebraska Laboratory Th., Lincoln, Neb., where she made her first appearance as an actress, playing the role of Natasha in *Three Sisters,* and directed her first play, *The Tiger.* At the Laboratory Th. she subsequently appeared as Dora in *The Octoroon* (Mar. 1966). Since then she has directed the following: *Curse You, Jack Dalton* (Town Hall Players, Ralston, Neb., July 1966); *The Imaginary Invalid* (Long Branch, N.J., High School, Nov. 1968); *An Italian Straw Hat* (Univ. of Nebraska Laboratory Th., Feb. 1969); and *The Gardenia* (Apr. 1969), which she also wrote. Since 1969 she has directed the following plays at Union College, Barbourville, Ky: *Finian's Rainbow* (Nov. 1969); *The Taming of the Shrew* (Mar. 1970); *Guys and Dolls* (Nov. 1970); *Rhinoceros* (Mar. 1971); *How to Succeed in Business Without Really Trying* (Nov. 1971); *The Miser* (Jan. 1972); *The Rainmaker* (Jan. 1972); *Romeo and Juliet* (Mar. 1972); *You're a Good Man Charlie Brown* (Oct. 1972); *Burdz!,* an original musical adapted by Mrs. Dontchos from Aristophanes' *The Birds* (Jan. 1973); *All My Sons* (Mar. 1973); *Once Upon a Mattress* (Oct. 1973); *The Effect of Gamma Rays on Man-in-the-Moon Marigolds* (Jan. 1974); and *Arms and the Man* (Apr. 1974).

In addition to her work in college theatre, Mrs. Dontchos appeared in summer stock as Renee in *Gypsy* (Lakes Region Playhouse, Laconia, N.H.).

Recreation. Cooking, reading, music.

DOOLEY, RAE. Actress, comedienne, dancer. b. Rachel Rice Dooley, Glasgow, Scotland, to Robert and Mary (Doherty) Dooley. Father, theatrical manager, circus clown. Married 1914 to Eddie Dowling, actor, director, producer, playwright; one son, one daughter. Relatives in theatre: brothers John, William, and Gordon Dooley, actors, dancers. Member of AEA. Address: (home) Harris Ave., R.D. 1, Lincoln, RI 02865; (bus.) c/o The Lambs Club, 130 W. 44th St., New York, NY 10036, tel. (212) JU 2-1515.

Theatre. Miss Dooley made her debut in vaudeville with Tim McMahan's *Watermellon Girls;* subsequently appeared in *Hitchy Koo* (Cohan and Harris Th., N.Y.C., June 7, 1917); and became a headliner at the Palace Th. (N.Y.C.).

She appeared in six editions of *The Ziegfeld Follies* (1919–21, 1924–26), creating the character of Baby Snooks; played Evie Dallas in *The Bunch and Judy* (Globe, Nov. 20, 1922); performed in *The Nifties of 1923* (Fulton, Sept. 25, 1923); and in two editions of

Earl Carroll's Vanities (c. 1928).

She made her first appearance with her husband, Eddie Dowling, in *Sidewalks of New York* (Knickerbocker, Oct. 3, 1927); appeared with him in vaudeville (1931–32); performed with him in his production of *Thumbs Up!* (St. James, Dec. 27, 1934); and played Josey in *Home Life of a Buffalo*, one of a triple bill produced by Mr. Dowling, entitled *Hope's the Thing* (Playhouse, May 11, 1948).

Recreation. Theatre.

DOOLITTLE, JAMES. Theatre executive, producer. b. James Arnold Doolittle, July 8, 1914, Salt Lake City, Utah, to Thomas A. and Margaret Doolittle. Father, mining engineer. Grad. Manual Arts H.S., Los Angeles, Calif., 1931; attended Los Angeles City Coll., 1932–33; grad. Univ. of Southern California. A.B. 1937. Married Nov. 30, 1954, to Leonora Nony, actress, singer (dec. 1965). Member of Wilshire (Los Angeles) Country Club; Sigma Chi. Address: (home) 365 Trousdale Place, Beverly Hills, CA 90210, tel. (213) 273-2612; (bus.) 2700 N. Vermont Ave., Los Angeles, CA 90027, tel. (213) 666-6000.

Pre-Theatre. Investments manager.

Theatre. Mr. Doolittle initially produced *A Song Without Words* (Philharmonic Aud., Los. Angeles; Curran, San Francisco, Calif., 1945); subsequently became general director of the Hollywood Bowl Opera Assn. (1949–50), where he produced *La Traviata* (1949), *Faust* (1950), and *The Vagabond King* (1950). He produced *Strange Bedfellows* (Las Palmas, Los Angeles, 1949); *The Medium* and *The Telephone* (El Capitan, Los Angeles; Curran, San Francisco, 1950); and *Light Up the Sky* (Las Palmas, 1950).

Since 1953, Mr. Doolittle has been general director of the Greek Theatre Assn., Los Angeles, where he has produced *Madame Butterfly* (1953, 1963); *La Boheme* (1953); the ballet performances of Alicia Markova (1953, 1954); NY City Ballet (1954 and ten later seasons); *Carmen* (1954); *The Mikado* (1954); *Wonderful Town* (1955); *The Student Prince* (1956); *The Red Mill* (1956); *La Traviata* (1957); *Coppelia* (1957, 1959); *La Perichole* (1958); and *Giselle* (1958).

In 1959, Mr. Doolittle, in association with the late Lou Lurie, purchased the Biltmore Theatre, Los Angeles. Among the plays presented there until the theatre was sold in 1964 were *The Visit* (1959), *Sunrise at Campobello* and *The Pleasure of His Company* (both 1960), *Gypsy* (1961), *The Unsinkable Molly Brown* (1962), *The Hollow Crown* (1963), and *Who's Afraid of Virginia Woolf?* (1964).

Other presentations arranged by Mr. Doolittle include the Royal Danish Ballet (Greek Th.; Opera House, San Francisco, 1960); the Grand Kabuki (Greek Th.; Opera House, San Francisco; NY City Ctr., June 2, 1960); the Greek Tragedy Th. and its productions of *Electra, The Choephori,* and *The Eumenides* (Greek Th.; Opera House, Chicago, Ill.; NY City Ctr., Sept. 1961); the Comédie Française and its production of *Le bourgeois gentilhomme* (Greek Th.; Opera House, San Francisco, 1962); and Tyrone Guthrie's royal gala performance of the Stratford Festival Production of *H.M.S. Pinafore* (Greek Th.; Opera House, San Francisco, 1962). In N.Y.C., Mr. Doolittle produced, with Oliver Smith and Charles Lowe, the revue *Show Girl* (Eugene O'Neill Th., N.Y.C., Jan 12, 1961).

In 1964, the Greek Theatre Assn. purchased the Huntington Hartford Theatre, Los Angeles, where Mr. Doolittle has produced or presented over a hundred shows to date, starting with Sir Tyrone Guthrie's production of *H.M.S. Pinafore* and continuing with such plays as *Incident at Vichy* (1965), *The Madwoman of Chaillot,* and *The Tiger* and *The Typist* (both 1966), *A Delicate Balance,* Sir John Gielgud in *The Ages of Man,* and *The Show-Off* (all 1967), *The Latent Heterosexual* (1968), Nicol Williamson's *Hamlet* (1969), *Our Town* and *Private Lives* (both 1970), *And Miss Reardon Drinks a Little* (1971), *The Time of Your Life* and *The Country Girl* (both 1972), and *I Do! I Do!* (1973).

Awards. Mr. Doolittle has received awards for cultural contributions from the city and the county of Los Angeles, as well as from the State of California.

Recreation. Golf, coin collecting.

DORFMAN, NAT. Press representative, playwright. b. Nov. 18, 1895, New York City. Married to Belle Bloomfield; one son, Irvin, press representative; one daughter. Member of ATPAM. Dorfman Associates, 1501 Broadway, New York, NY 10036, tel. (212) LO 3-0858.

Theatre. Mr. Dorfman wrote the plays, *Take My Tip* (48 St. Th., Apr. 11, 1932) and *Errant Lady* (Fulton, Sept. 17, 1934). He has also contributed sketch material to Lew Leslie's *Rhapsody in Black* (Sam H. Harris Th., May 4, 1931); *The International Revue* (Majestic, Feb. 5, 1930); and *Blackbirds of 1933* (Apollo, Dec. 2, 1933).

Mr. Dorfman's first assignment as a press representative was for *Meet the Wife* (Klaw, Nov. 26, 1923). He has since represented more than 300 Bway productions, among which were *The Show-Off* (1924), *The Chariot Revue* (1925), *Manhattan Mary* (1927), *This Year of Grace* (1928), *Wake Up and Dream* (1929), *Flying High* (1930), and *DuBarry Was a Lady* (1939).

In 1940, Mr. Dorfman was press representative for *Louisiana Purchase, Panama Hattie,* and *My Sister Eileen;* in 1941, *Junior Miss;* in 1944, *The Late George Apley, The Day Will Come,* and *Slightly Scandalous.*

In 1945, he represented *The Next Half Hour* and *The Firebrand of Florence;* in 1946, *Born Yesterday, A Flag Is Born, Park Avenue,* and *Years Ago;* in 1947, *Little A* and *Dark Memory;* and in 1948, *Inside U.S.A., Town House,* and *Bravo!*

In 1951, *Two on the Aisle, Love and Let Love,* and *Lo and Behold!;* in 1952, *An Evening with Beatrice Lillie, The Millionairess, The Mikado, The Pirates of Penzance, H.M.S. Pinafore, Iolanthe, Fancy Meeting You Again, The Long Watch,* and *Of Thee I Sing;* in 1953, *The Solid Gold Cadillac, The Love of Four Colonels,* and *The Bat;* in 1954, *Home Is the Hero, Hit the Trail,* and *Anniversary Waltz,* and on tour; in 1955, *The Heavenly Twins,* and the pre-Bway tour of *Top Man;* in 1956, *Uncle Willie, Time Limit! Someone Waiting, Affair of Honor,* and *Everybody Loves Me;* in 1957, *Tunnel of Love* and *Fair Game;* in 1958, *International Soirée, Back to Methuselah, Les Ballets de Paris,* and *Sunrise at Campobello;* and in 1959, *Third Best Sport, The Highest Tree, A Majority of One, Requiem for a Nun,* and *God and Kate Murphy.*

In 1960, Mr. Dorfman was press representative for *The Unsinkable Molly Brown, Love and Libel,* and *Answered the Flute;* in 1961, *The Mikado, The Pirates of Penzance, The Gondoliers,* and *H.M.S. Pinafore;* in 1962, *Seidman and Son, Something About a Soldier,* and *Night Life;* and in 1963, *Dear Me, the Sky Is Falling, A Case of Libel, Tambourines To Glory, Jack Benny, Once for the Asking,* and *Love and Kisses;* in 1964, *The Child Buyer, Conversations in the Dark,* and *One by One;* in 1965, *Kelly, All in Good Time,* and the NY City Ctr. Gilbert and Sullivan Co.; in 1965, *All Women Are One,* and *A Very Rich Woman;* in 1966, *The Wayward Stork,* and *Dinner at Eight;* in 1967, *More Stately Mansions,* the NY City Ctr. presentations of the Vienna Burgtheater and Gilbert and Sullivan Repertory, and *Jonah!.*

Mr. Dorfman has been press representative for producers Arch and Edgar Selwyn, George White, Florenz Ziegfeld, Crosby Gaige, Max Gorden, A. H. Woods, Lew Leslie, and Buddy Sylva. He has represented the Theatre Guild, Dore Schary, Joel Schenker, Albert Lewis, Elliot Martin, and the N.Y. Opera Co.

Associated with Mr. Dorfman in the public relations firm of Dorfman Associates is Irvin Dorfman, his son.

Published Works. While at Columbia Univ., he covered campus activities for *New York American,* a newspaper for which he subsequently became a staff reporter. While on its news staff, he wrote a humor column for King Features which appeared nationwide in newspapers for about ten years. During this time he also wrote humorous articles for such publications as *Life, Judge, New Yorker, Vanity Fair, Saturday Evening Post* and *Collier's.*

He also worked for the New York *World-Telegram* and has written for the New York *Herald,* the New York *Tribune* (before the amalgamation of both papers), and for the New York *Times.*

For several years he published and edited a theatre magazine entitled *Stage Pictorial.*.

DORLAG, ARTHUR H. Educator, director. b. Arthur Henry Dorlag, Sept. 6, 1922, St. Louis, Mo., to Arthur Paul and Sophie Caroline Dorlag. Father, meat-cutter. Grad. Brentwood (Mo.) H.S., 1940; Southeast Mo., State Coll., B.S. (education) 1946; Univ. of Wisconsin, M.S. (speech) 1947, Ph.D. 1953. Married April 10, 1947, to Betty Lou Helgerson; one son, one daughter. Served USAF, 1942–45; rank, 1st Lt.; USAFR; rank, Maj. Member of ATA (chmn., Audio-Visual Aids Project, 1958–60). Address: (home) 2201 Jim Lee Road, Tallahassee, FL 32301, tel. (904) 877-4529; (bus.) School of Theatre, Florida State University, Tallahassee, FL 32306, tel. (904) 599-4295.

Since 1958, Mr. Dorlag has been associate professor of speech and director of the theatre at the Florida State Univ. He has held academic positions at Southeast Missouri State Coll. (assistant professor, 1947; associate professor, 1953; professor, 1957), and the Univ. of Wisconsin (visiting lecturer, 1957–58); and has directed student productions at these three schools.

In 1960, Mr. Dorlag founded the Asolo Th. Comedy Festival (Sarasota, Fla.), and was the general director for three seasons, as well as directing and acting there.

Published Works. Mr. Dorlag wrote, with John Irvine, *The Stage Works of Charles MacArthur* (1974).

Awards. Mr. Dorlag received a research grant from the Florida State Univ. Graduate Research Council for study of the impact of avant-garde drama on theatre aesthetics (1963).

Recreation. Gardening, carpentry.

DORN, DOLORES. Actress. b. Dolores Dorn-Heft, Mar. 3, 1935, Chicago, Ill., to Edward and Alice (Eagmin) Dorn-Heft. Father, thoroughbred owner and breeder, mother, office manager. Grad. Calumet H.S., Chicago, 1950; Goodman Sch. of the Theatre, B.F.A., 1953. Studied acting with Uta Hagen, N.Y.C., 1955; Actors Studio, N.Y.C. (member since 1957). Married May 14, 1956, to Franchot Tone, actor (marr. dis. Jan. 1959); married to Ben Piazza, actor. Member of AEA; SAG; AFTRA; AGVA.

Theatre. Miss Dorn made her debut in repertory productions with the Schaffner Players, appearing as the ingenue lead in nine plays, on a tour of the mid-west (June–Sept. 1952); billed as Dolores Dorn-Heft, she played Myra Hagerman in *Oh, Men! Oh, Women!* (Clinton Playhouse, Conn., June 1955); and appeared in *A Mighty Man Is He* (Falmouth Playhouse, Mass., July 1955; Theatre-by-the-Sea, Matunuck, R.I., Aug. 1955).

She made her N.Y.C. debut succeeding Signe Hasso as Elena in *Uncle Vanya* (Fourth St. Th., Jan. 31, 1956); played Janice in *Hide and Seek* (Ethel Barrymore Th., Apr. 2, 1957); appeared in the pre-Bway tryouts of *Starward Ark* (opened National, Washington, D.C., Jan. 1959); and *The Midnight Sun* (opened Taft, New Haven, Conn., Nov. 1959); succeeded Joyce Van Patten (June 1960) as Mary Magdalene in *Between Two Thieves* (York, N.Y.C., Feb. 11, 1960); understudied Georgann Johnson as Angela Ballantine in *Critic's Choice* (Ethel Barrymore Th., Dec. 14, 1960), succeeded Miss Johnson in this role (Jan. 1961); and played the Lady in *To Damascus* (Th. East, Feb. 14, 1961).

Billed as Dolores Dorn, she played Mother Clara in *Someone from Assisi* (the third play of *Plays for Bleecker Street,* Circle in the Square, Jan. 11, 1962); succeeded Patricia Roe (Feb. 1963) as Stella in *The Collection* (the second half of *The Pinter Plays,* Cherry Lane, Nov. 26, 1962); and appeared as the Woman in *Khaki Blue* (the second half of *Lime Green/Khaki Blue,* Provincetown Playhouse, Mar. 26, 1969).

Films. Miss Dorn has appeared in *The Bounty Hunter* (WB, 1954); *Phantom of the Rue Morgue* (WB, 1954); *His Kingdom for a Woman* (Elstree, England, 1954); *Uncle Vanya* (Col., 1958); *Underworld, USA* (Col., 1961); and *13 West Street* (Col., 1962).

Television. She made her debut in *Paris Precinct* (1963); followed by the Charles Ruggles Show (NBC, 1955); Suspicion (NBC, 1958); *Strawberry Blonde* (NBC, 1959); *Target: The Corruptors* (Dick Powell's Zane Grey Th. (CBS, 1962); The Untouchables (ABC, 1962, 1964); US Steel Hour (CBS, 1963); and Run for Your Life (NBC, 1965).

Awards. She received the San Francisco International Film Festival Award for her performance as Elena in *Uncle Vanya* (1957).

Recreation. Sculpting, water skiing.

DOUGHERTY, FRANCES ANN.

Producer. b. Frances Ann Cannon, Nov. 21, Concord, N.C., to Martin L. and Ohla (Brown) Cannon. Father, textile manufacturer. Grad. Ethel Walker, Simsbury, Conn., 1936; Sarah Lawrence Coll., 1938. Married Apr. 27, 1940, to John Hersey, writer (marr. dis. 1958); three sons, one daughter; married Feb. 23, 1963 to Frazer Dougherty, industrial designer. She is a trustee of Sarah Lawrence College (1970–to date) and East Hampton (N.Y.) Guild Hall (1970–to date); a director of the Theatre Development Fund (1970–to date); and is a member of the theatre committee, John Drew Th.; East Hampton, N.Y. (1970–to date); Theatre, Inc. (bd. mem., 1960–64); Natl. Repertory Th. Foundation (pres., 1960–to date); River Club (N.Y.C.); Devon Yacht Club (East Hampton, N.Y.). Address: 35 Beekman Place, New York, NY 10022, tel. (212) PL 5-3997.

Theatre. Mrs. Dougherty produced a cross-country tour of *Mary Stuart* (opened Geary Th., San Francisco, Calif., Sept. 1959; closed May 1960); the national tour of *Once Upon a Mattress* (opened Veterans Memorial Aud., Providence, R.I., Oct. 21, 1960; closed Natl., Washington, D.C., May 27, 1961); and *The Turn of the Screw, Anatol,* and *Elizabeth the Queen* (Boston, Mass., Summer 1961).

With Michael Dewell, she formed the National Repertory Th. (NRT, 1961), which, with Eva Le Gallienne playing the title roles, toured cross-country with *Elizabeth the Queen* and *Mary Stuart* (opened Acad. of Music, Northampton, Mass., Oct. 19, 1961; closed Aud., Rochester, N.Y., Apr. 14, 1962); again with Miss Le Gallienne heading the company, NRT toured with *The Seagull, Ring Round the Moon,* and *The Crucible* (opened Aycock Aud., Greensboro. N.C., Oct. 5, 1963; closed Aud., Dallas, Tex., Mar. 29, 1964); in N.Y.C., NRT presented *The Seagull* (Belasco, Apr. 5, 1964) and *The Crucible* (Belasco, Apr. 6, 1964), in repertory; then in touring repertory, *Hedda Gabler, Liliom,* and *She Stoops to Conquer* (opened Aycock Aud., Greensboro, N.C., Oct. 9, 1964). For the 1965–66 season, NRT's presentations were *The Madwoman of Chaillot, The Rivals,* and *The Trojan Women.* The 1966–67 season included *The Imaginary Invalid* (ANTA, N.Y.C., May 1, 1967); *A Touch of the Poet* (ANTA, May 2, 1967); and *Tonight at 8:30* (ANTA, May 3, 1967). NRT's 1967–68 repertory included *The Comedy of Errors; She Stoops to Conquer;* and *John Brown's Body;* the last of which reopened Ford's Theatre, Washington, D.C. (Feb. 12, 1968), for the first theatrical season since Lincoln's assassination.

Awards. Mrs. Dougherty received the Outer Circle Award (1959) for the best touring production, *Mary Stuart.* The National Repertory Theatre received a special Antoinette (Tony) Award (1964).

Recreation. Art collecting, sailing, cooking.

DOUGLAS, KIRK.

Actor, film producer. b. Issur Danielovitch, Dec. 9, 1920, Amsterdam, N.Y., to Harry and Bryna (Sanglel) Danielovitch Demsky. Father, businessman. Grad. Wilbur Lynch H.S., Amsterdam, N.Y., 1937; St. Lawrence Univ., B.A. 1940; attended AADA (scholarship) 1941. Married 1943, to Diana Dill, actress (marr. dis. 1950); two sons; married May 29, 1954, to Anne Buydens; two sons. Served WW II, USN, PTO; rank, Lt. (jg). Member of AEA; SAG; AFTRA; UN Assn. (dir., Los Angeles, Calif., chapter); Natl. Student Fed. of Amer.; Heart Comm. of the Motion Picture Industry; The Friars; Hon. Soc. of Kixioc; Delta Kappa Alpha (natl. honorary film fraternity). Address: c/o Bryna Productions, 141 El Camino, Beverly Hills, CA 90212.

Theatre. Mr. Douglas made his N.Y.C. debut as a Western Union Boy under the pseudonym of George Spelvin, Jr., in *Spring Again* (Henry Miller's Th., Nov. 10, 1941); subsequently appeared as an orderly in *The Three Sisters* (Ethel Barrymore Th., Dec. 21, 1942); succeeded (1944) Richard Widmark as Lt. Lenny Archer in *Kiss and Tell* (Biltmore, Mar. 17, 1943); succeeded (1945) Mr. Widmark as Ray Mackenzie in *Trio* (Belasco, Dec. 29, 1944); played Steve in *Alice in Arms* (National, Jan. 31, 1945); a Soldier in *The Wind Is Ninety* (Booth, June 21, 1945); in stock, he appeared as Detective McLeod in *Detective Story* (Sombrero Playhouse, Phoenix, Ariz., June 23, 1951); played Randle F. McMurphy in *One Flew Over the Cuckoo's Nest* (Cort, N.Y.C., Nov. 13, 1963).

Films. Mr. Douglas made his film debut in *The Strange Love of Martha Ivers* (Par., 1946); subsequently appeared in *Out of the Past* (RKO, 1946); *I Walk Alone* (Par., 1947); *Mourning Becomes Electra* (RKO, 1947); *The Walls of Jerico* (20th-Fox, 1948); *My Dear Secretary* (20th-Fox, 1948); *A Letter to Three Wives* (20th-Fox, 1948); *Champion* (UA, 1948); *Young Man with a Horn* (WB, 1950); *The Glass Menagerie* (WB, 1950); *The Big Carnival* (Par., 1951); *Along the Great Divide* (RKO, 1951); *Detective Story* (Par., 1951); *The Big Trees* (WB, 1952); *The Big Sky* (RKO, 1952); *The Bad and the Beautiful* (MGM, 1952); *The Story of Three Loves* (MGM, 1953); *The Juggler* (Col., 1953); *Act of Love* (UA, 1953); *Ulysses* (Par., 1954); *20,000 Leagues Under the Sea* (Disney, 1954); *The Racers* (20th-Fox, 1954); *Man without a Star* (UI, 1955); *The Indian Fighter,* which he also produced (UA, 1955); *Lust for Life* (MGM, 1955); *Gunfight at the O.K. Corral* (Par., 1956); and *Top Secret Affair* (WB, 1956).

He produced and appeared in *Paths of Glory* (UA, 1957); *The Vikings* (UA, 1957); appeared in *Last Train from Gun Hill* (Par., 1958); *The Devil's Disciple* (UA, 1958); *Strangers When We Meet* (Col., 1958); produced and performed in *Spartacus* (UI, 1959); *The Last Sunset* (UI, 1960); appeared in *Town without Pity* (UA, 1961); produced and appeared in *Lonely Are the Brave* (UI, 1961); performed in *Two Weeks in Another Town* (MGM, 1962); *The Hook* (MGM, 1962); *For Love or Money* (UI, 1962); produced and appeared in *The List of Adrian Messenger* (UI, 1962); and *Seven Days in May* (1963).

He appeared in *In Harm's Way* (Par., 1965); *Cast a Giant Shadow* (UA, 1966); *Heroes of Telemark* (Col., 1966); *The War Wagon* (U, 1967); *The Way West* (U, 1967); *A Lovely Way To Die* (U, 1968); *The Brotherhood* (Par., 1968); *The Arrangement* (WB, 1969); *There Was a Crooked Man* (WB, 1970); *A Gunfight* (Par., 1971), which he also produced; *The Light at the Edge of the World* (National Gen., 1971); *Summertree* (Col., 1971), which he also produced; *Scalawag* (Par., 1973), which he also directed; and *Hearts and Minds* (WB, 1974).

Mr. Douglas has been president of his own independent film company, Bryna Productions, since 1955.

Television. Mr. Douglas appeared on the GM 50th anniversary show (NBC, 1957); This Is Your LIfe (NBC, 1958); Steve Allen Show (NBC, 1958, 1964); Person to Person (CBS, 1960); Jack Paar Show (NBC, 1960); Best of Paar (NBC, 1960); Tonight Show (NBC, 1962, 1963); and Here's Hollywood (NBC, 1962); and he was narrator for *The Legend of Silent Night* (ABC, 1968).

Awards. Mr. Douglas received Laurel awards from the Motion Picture Exhibitors (1951, 1952, 1956, 1960, 1962); the Distinguished Contribution Award from the American Labor Council; the Foreign Press Golden Globe Award for his performance in *Lust for Life* (1956); a special award of merit from the George Washington Carver Memorial Fund (1957); the Golden Scissors Award (1958); and the Cecil B. DeMille Award (1967 for contributions in the entertainment field. St. Lawrence Univ. awarded him an honorary D.F.A. degree (1958).

Recreation. Art collecting, golf, tennis, swimming.

DOUGLAS, LARRY.

Actor, singer. b. Feb. 17, 1914, Philadelphia, Pa. Father, butcher. Grad. Erasmus H.S., Brooklyn, N.Y.; attended Brooklyn Coll. Married to Onna White, choreographer; one daughter. Member of AEA.

Theatre. Mr. Douglas made his N.Y.C. debut in *Jumbo* (Hippodrome Th., Nov. 16, 1935); subsequently appeared in *Frederika* (Imperial, Feb. 4, 1937); *Three Waltzes* (Majestic, Dec. 25, 1937); *Panama Hattie* (46 St. Th., Oct. 30, 1940); and *Star and Garter* (Music Box, June 24, 1942).

He played Sgt. Willie Klink in *What's Up* (National, Nov. 11, 1943); Paul and Pablo in *The Duchess Misbehaves* (Adelphi, Feb. 13, 1946); "Sarge" Donton in *Hold It!* (National, May 5, 1948); joined as Jack Chesney, *Where's Charley?* (St. James, Oct. 11, 1948); succeeded Dick Smart (Apr. 1949) in the revue *All for Love* (Mark Hellinger Th., Jan. 22, 1949); and followed Georges Guetary for two weeks (Apr. 1950) in the role of Franz in *Arms and the Girl* (46 St. Th., Feb. 2, 1950).

Mr. Douglas played Lun Tha in *The King and I* (St. James, Mar. 29, 1951); Sid Sorokin in the national company of *Pajama Game* (opened Shubert, New Haven, Conn., Jan. 29, 1955; closed Civic, New Orleans, La., Feb. 16, 1957), which he repeated at the NY City Ctr., (May 15, 1957); was understudy to Robert Preston in the role of Harold Hill in *The Music Man* (Majestic, Dec. 19, 1957); toured in *Bells Are Ringing* (Summer 1959); and, played District Attorney Thomas Mara in *Here's Love* (Shubert, N.Y.C., Oct. 3, 1963).

He was Phil Arkin in *Milk and Honey* (Storrowton Music Fair, West Springfield, Mass., Aug. 24, 1964); Judge Aristide Forestier in *Can-Can* (Starlight Musicals, Indianapolis, Ind., July 19, 1965); Achillas in *Her First Roman* (Lunt-Fontanne Th., N.Y.C., Oct. 20, 1968); Edward Duryea Dowling in *Jimmy* (Winter Garden, Oct. 23, 1969); and toured as Mr. Kirkeby in *Promises, Promises* (1970–71).

Television and Radio. He performed on the radio program, Romance (CBS, 1944) and on television appeared on The Defenders (CBS, Jan. 1965).

Night Clubs. Mr. Douglas appeared in An Evening with Jerome Kern (Cotillion Room, Hotel Pierre, N.Y.C., May 26, 1959); and he was at the Chateau Laurier Hotel, Ottawa, Canada (Dec. 1964).

DOUGLAS, MELVIN.

Actor, director, producer. b. Melvyn E. Hesselberg, Apr. 5, 1901, Macon, Ga., to Edouard and Lena G. Hesselberg. Father, musician. Studied in France, Austria, and Germany. Married Apr. 5, 1931, to Helen Gahagan, Congresswoman, actress; one son, one daughter. Served US Army, Med. Corps, 1917–18; staff and administrative, CBI, 1942–45; rank, Maj. Member of AEA; SAG; AFTRA.

Pre-Theatre. Drugstore worker, field hand, writer, newspaper reporter.

Theatre. Mr. Douglas made his professional debut as Bassanio in a repertory production of *The Merchant of Venice;* made his N.Y.C. debut as Ace Wilfong in *A Free Soul* (Playhouse Th., Jan. 12, 1928); subsequently played Sergeant "Terry" O'Brien in *Back Here* (Klaw, Nov. 26, 1928); Boyd Butler in *Now-a-Days* (Forrest, Aug. 5, 1928); Henry C. Martin in *Recapture* (Eltinge, Jan. 29, 1930); the Unknown Gentleman in *Tonight or Never* (Belasco, Nov. 18, 1930); and Sheridan Warren in *No More Ladies* (Booth, Jan. 23, 1934). He directed *Moor Born* (Playhouse, Apr. 3, 1934; staged *Within the Gates* (National, Oct. 22, 1934) and *Mother Lode,* in which he played Carey Reid (Cort, Dec. 22, 1934); appeared as Pat Dantry in *De Luxe* (Booth, Mar. 5, 1935); and Erik in *Tapestry in Gray* (Shubert, Dec. 27, 1935).

He produced, with Herman Levin, the revue *Call Me Mister* (National, Apr. 18, 1946); played Tommy Thurston in *Two Blind Mice* (Cort, Mar. 2, 1949); and Wally Williams in *The Bird Cage* (Coronet, Feb. 22, 1950). He directed *Glad Tidings* in which he appeared as Steve Whitney (Lyceum, Oct. 11, 1951); and played Howard Carol in *Time Out for Ginger* (Lyceum, Nov. 26, 1952); also on tour in the US and Austria (opened Shubert, New Haven, Conn., Oct. 1, 1953). He succeeded (Sept. 17, 1955) Paul Muni as Henry Drummond in *Inherit the Wind* (National, N.Y.C., Apr. 21, 1955), also on tour (opened Blackstone, Chicago, Ill., Feb. 8, 1956; closed Ford's Th., Baltimore, Md., Jan. 19, 1957); appeared as Zeus in the pre-Bway tour of *Maiden Voyage* (opened Forrest, Philadelphia, Pa., Feb. 28, 1957); closed there Mar. 9, 1957); General St. Pe in the touring production of *Waltz of the Toreadors* (opened McCarter Th., Princeton, N.J., Sept. 26, 1956), which played in N.Y.C. (Coronet, Mar. 9, 1958); "Captain" Jack Boyle in the musical *Juno* (Winter Garden, Mar. 9, 1959); Griffith P. Hastings in *The Gang's All Here* (Ambassador, Oct. 1, 1959); William Russell in *The Best Man* (Morosco, Mar. 31, 1960), which he also played on its national tour (opened Hanna, Cleveland, Ohio, Sept. 18, 1961; closed Forrest, Philadelphia, Pa., Feb. 3, 1962); the title role in *Spofford* (ANTA Th., N.Y.C., Dec. 14, 1967); and the male lead in *The First Monday in October* (Cleveland Playhouse, Cleveland, Ohio, Nov. 1975).

Films. He made his debut in *Tonight or Never* (UA, 1931); and subsequently appeared in over forty films, some of which were *As You Desire Me* (MGM, 1932); *Counsellor-at-Law* (U, 1933); *Annie Oakley* (RKO, 1935); *Theodora Goes Wild* (Col., 1936); *The Gorgeous Hussy* (MGM, 1936); *Arsene Lupin Returns* (MGM, 1938); *The Shining Hour* (MGM, 1938); *Ninotchka* (MGM, 1939); *He Stayed for Breakfast* (Col., 1940); *They All Kissed the Bride* (Col., 1940); *That Uncertain Feeling* (UA, 1941); *A Woman's Face* (MGM, 1941); *Three Hearts for Julia* (MGM, 1943); *Sea of Grass* (MGM, 1947); *The Guilt of Janet Ames* (Col., 1947); *Mr. Blandings Builds His Dream House* (RKO, 1948); *My Forbidden Past* (RKO, 1951); *On the Loose* (RKO, 1951); *Billy Budd* (Allied, 1962); *Hud* (Par., 1963); *The Big Parade of Comedy* (MGM, 1964); *The Americanization of Emily* (MGM, 1964); *Rapture* (20th-Fox, 1965); *Hotel* (WB, 1967); *I Never Sang for My Father* (Col., 1970); *One Is a Lonely Number* (MGM, 1972); and *The Candidate* (WB, 1972).

Television. Mr. Douglas appeared in the title role in *The Plot To Kill Stalin* (Playhouse 90, CBS, 1960); and as Mark Twain on the American Heritage Series (NBC). He was in *Once Upon a Tractor* (UN Drama, ABC, Sept. 1965); *Inherit the Wind* (Hallmark Hall of Fame, NBC, Nov. 1965); *Lamp at Midnight* (Hallmark Hall of Fame, NBC, Apr. 1966); *The Crucible* (Drama Special, CBS, May 1967); *Do Not Go Gentle into That Good Night* (CBS, Oct. 1967); *Hunters Are for Killing* (CBS, Mar. 1970); *Death Takes a Holiday* (ABC, Oct. 1971); and appeared on Ben Casey (ABC, 1966); The Fugitive (ABC, 1966); On Stage (NBC, 1967); and Ghost Story (NBC, 1972).

Awards. He received an Antoinette Perry (Tony) Award (1960) for his performance as William Russell in *The Best Man;* the *Look* Television Award (1960) for his performance in the title role in *The Plot To Kill Stalin;* and an Academy (Oscar) Award (1963) for his role as best supporting actor in *Hud.*.

DOUGLAS, ROBERT. Actor, director, producer. b. Robert Douglas Finlayson, Nov. 9, 1910, Bletchley, Bucks, England, to Robert Barnett and Marcia Emily (Bird) Finlayson. Father, Army officer. Attended Bickley Hall, Kent, England, 1918–22. Studied at RADA, London, 1917. Married May 21, 1935, to Dorothy Hyson, actress (marr. dis. 1943); married Aug. 23, 1946, to Sue Weldon (née Hopkinson); one daughter, one son. Served Fleet Air Army, 1939–45. Member of AEA; AFTRA; SAG; Stage Golfing Society; Intl. Sportman's Club.

Theatre. Mr. Douglas made his first stage appearance as Bertie Lennox in *The Best People* (Royal, Bournemouth, July 28, 1927); toured as Tommy Brown in *Crime* (Aug.–Dec. 1927); made his London debut as Godfrey Marvin and the Usher in *Many Waters* (Ambassadors', July 18, 1928); played Peter in *Mrs. Moonlight* (Kingsway, Dec. 5, 1928); Sir Charles Neville in *Black St. Anthony* (Strand, Apr. 7, 1929); Kit Pumphrey in *A Bill of Divorcement* (St. Martin's, July 9, 1929); and Billy in *Barbara's Wedding* (Apollo, Aug. 14, 1929).

He made his N.Y.C. debut as Godfrey in *Many Waters* (Maxine Elliott's Th., Sept. 25, 1929); played Harry Graham in *The Last Enemy* (Fortune, London, Jan. 15, 1930); Pettigrew in *Suspense* (Duke of York's, Apr. 8, 1930); Dickie Wetherby in *Badger's Green* (Prince of Wales's, June 12, 1930); Harry Graham in *The Last Enemy* (Shubert, N.Y.C., Oct. 30, 1930); Ralph in *After All* (Criterion, London, Feb. 2, 1931); William Brown in *The Arch-Duchess* (Phoenix, Mar. 29, 1931); Adam Fenwick-Symes in *Vile Bodies* (Arts, Oct. 8, 1931); Roderick Dean in *Brief Moment* (Belasco, N.Y.C., Nov. 9, 1931); Adam in *Vile Bodies* (Vaudeville, London, Apr. 15, 1932); Charles Tritton in *As It Was in the Beginning* (Arts, June 10, 1932); Colin Derwent in *Ten Minute Alibi* (Embassy, Jan. 2, 1933); produced, with Ronald Adam, *Ten Minute Alibi* (Haymarket, Feb. 8, 1933); appeared as Simon More in *These Two* (Arts, Feb. 5, 1933); George Ferguson in *Men in White* (Lyric, June 28, 1934); Karl Ritter in *Overture 1920* (Phoenix, Oct. 21, 1934); Loreto Santos in *Inside the Room* (Queen's, Dec. 22, 1934); succeeded Laurence Olivier as Tony Cavendish in *Theatre Royal* (Lyric, Jan. 6, 1935); and played Hugh Collimore in *Most of the Game* (Cort, N.Y.C., Oct. 1, 1935).

Mr. Douglas appeared as Jim Wilding in *No Exit* (St. Martin's, London, Feb. 1936); Charles the First in *Stubble Before Swords* (Globe, Mar. 20, 1936); Henry Abbott in *Kind Lady* (Lyric, June 11, 1936); Peter Thurloe in *Official Secret* (New, Sept., 1938); Dr. Deval in *Night Arrival* (Globe, Dec. 16, 1938); Maurice in *The Springtime of Others* (Gate, May 4, 1939); Raymond Clive in *He Lived in Two Worlds* (Wimbledon, May 1946); Richard in *But for the Grace of God* (St. James's, Sept. 3, 1946); and directed *The Ponder Heart* (Music Box, N.Y.C., Feb. 16, 1956); and *Affair of Honor* (Ethel Barrymore Th., Apr. 6, 1956). Mr. Douglas directed and produced, with Richard W. Krakeur and David Wayne, *The Loud Red Patrick* (Ambassador, Oct. 3, 1956); directed *Uncle Willie* (John Golden Th., Dec. 20, 1956); and the pre-Bway tryout of *One Foot in the Door,* (opened Locust, Philadelphia, Pa., Nov. 6, 1957; closed Shubert, Boston, Mass., Nov. 23, 1957).

Films. He made his first appearance in *Many Waters* (B.I.P., 1931, subsequently appeared in *P.C. Josser* (B.I.P., 1931); *The Blarney Stone* (1933); *Death Drives Through* (1936); *Our Fighting Navy* (1937); *The Challenge* (Film Alliance of the US, 1939); *The Lion Has Wings* (UA, 1940); *Over the Moon* (UA, 1940); *The Chinese Bungalow* (1940); *The End of the River* (U, 1948); *The Decision of Christopher Blake* (WB, 1948); *Adventures of Don Juan* (WB, 1948); *Homicide* (WB, 1949); *The Fountainhead* (WB, 1949); *The Lady Takes a Sailor* (WB, 1949); *Spy Hunt* (U, 1950); *Buccaneer's Girl* (U, 1950); *Barricade* (WB, 1950); *Flame and the Arrow* (WB, 1950); *This Side of the Law* (WB, 1950); *Mystery Submarine* (U, 1950); *Kim* (MGM, 1950); *Thunder on the Hill* (U, 1951); *Target Unknown* (U, 1951); *At Sword's Point* (RKO, 1952); *Ivanhoe* (MGM, 1952); *The Prisoner of Zenda* (MGM, 1952); *The Desert Rats* (20th-Fox, 1953); *Flight to Tangier* (Par., 1953); *Fair Wind to Java* (Rep., 1953); *Saskatchewan* (U, 1954); *King Richard and the Crusaders* (WB, 1954); *The Scarlet Coat* (MGM, 1955); *Good Morning, Miss Dove* (20th-Fox, 1955); *The Virgin Queen* (20th-Fox, 1955); and *Helen of Troy* (WB, 1955).

Television. Mr. Douglas has appeared in *The Barretts of Wimpole Street* (Hallmark Hall of Fame, NBC); *The Browning Version* (Apr. 1959); *Impromptu Murder,* and *Arthur* (Alfred Hitchcock Presents, CBS); *The Vigilantes* (Panic); *Night of Decision* (Alcoa, NBC); *Swamp Fox* (Walt Disney Show, ABC); on GE Th. (CBS), Adventures in Paradise (ABC), The Asphalt Jungle, Maverick and 77 Sunset Strip.

He has directed two segments of The Roaring 20's; three segments of Maverick (ABC); 12 segments of 77 Sunset Strip (ABC); nine segments of Surfside 6; four segments of Hawaiian Eye; a pilot film, *Solitaire* (Warner Bros.); and the first segment of Fair Exchange (Desilu); directed and produced *The Long Silence* (Alfred Hitchcock Presents, CBS, 1963), *Final Hour* (The Virginian, NBC, 1964), ten segments for Alfred Hitchcock Presents (CBS, 1963–64); and the Court Martial series (1964).

Recreation. Riding, shooting, fencing, golf, swimming, music.

DOUGLASS, STEPHEN. Actor, director, singer. b. Oct. 27, 1921, Mt. Vernon, Ohio. Married June 21, 1942, to Edith Reis, teacher; two sons, two daughters. Served WW II, USAAF; rank, 1st Lt. Member of AEA; AFTRA; AGVA.

Theatre. Mr. Douglass made his debut as a singer in the chorus of a stock production of *Naughty Marietta* (Paper Mill Playhouse, Millburn, N.J., June 1942); subsequently, for the Paper Mill Playhouse appeared in *Mlle. Modiste* (June 1942); *Sweethearts* (July 1942); *The Red Mill* (July 1942); and *The Pirates of Penzance* (Aug. 1942). He portrayed the Ski Instructor in the pre-Bway tryout of *Love in the Snow* (Bushnell Memorial, Hartford, Conn., Mar. 15, 1946); succeeded (Apr. 2, 1947) Henry Michel as Billy Bigelow in the Bway production of *Carousel* (Majestic, Apr. 19, 1945; and toured in the role, May 1947–Mar. 5, 1949); and appeared again at the Paper Mill Playhouse (Millburn, N.J.) in the role of Schani in *The Great Waltz* (July 1949) and Jeff in *Bloomer Girl* (Oct. 1949).

He was the standby for Georges Guetary in the role of Franz in *Arms and the Girl* (46 St. Th., N.Y.C., Feb. 2, 1950); appeared as Billy Bigelow in *Carousel* (Drury Lane, London, June 7, 1950); Paul Dumont in *Make a Wish* (Winter Garden, N.Y.C., Apr. 18, 1951); and again as Billy Bigelow in a tour of *Carousel* (1952). He later played the role of Bumerli in *The Chocolate Soldier* (Cape Cod Melody Top, Hyannis, Mass., Aug. 1952); and toured again in 1952–53 in *Carousel.*

At the Miami (Fla.) Music Circus, he played John Kent in *Roberta* (Feb. 1953); Captain Tarnitz in *The Student Prince* (Feb. 1953); Oggle in *High Button Shoes* (Mar. 1953); Von Schmidt in *Blossom Time* (Mar. 1953); and Dr. Falke in *Die Fledermaus* (Mar. 1953). and toured role, May 1949); and appeared again N.J.) in the role of

He played Tommy in *Brigadoon* (State Fair Music Hall, Dallas, Tex., June 1953); Gaylord Ravenal in *Show Boat* (Lambertville Music Circus, N.J., Aug. 1953); John Matthews in *Up in Central Park* (South Shore Music Circus, Cohasset, Mass., Aug. 1953); Billy Bigelow in *Carousel* (Carter Barron Th., Washington, D.C., Sept. 1953); Ulysses in *The Golden Apple* (Phoenix, N.Y.C., Mar. 11, 1954); Billy Bigelow in *Carousel* (Oakdale Musical Th., Wallingford, Conn., Sept. 1954); Woody in *Finian's Rainbow* (Oakdale Musical Th., Sept. 1954); succeeded John Raitt (Nov. 15, 1954) as Sid Sorokin in *The Pajama Game* (St. James, N.Y.C., May 13, 1954); played Joe Hardy in *Damn Yankees* (46 St. Th., May 5, 1955); and Nelson Crandal in *Rumple* (Alvin, Nov. 6, 1957).

He played Billy Bigelow in *Carousel* (Palm Beach Musicarnival, Fla., Jan., 1958); Grieg in *Song of Norway* (Jones Beach Marine Th., L.I., June 1958); Gaylord Ravenal in *Show Boat* (Oakdale Musical Th., Wallingford, Conn., Sept. 1958); Grieg in *Song of Norway* (St. Louis Municipal Opera, Mo., June 1959); Jim in *Rio Rita* (St. Louis Municipal Opera, July 1959); the title role in *Li'l Abner* (St. Louis Municipal Opera, July 1959; Warren Aud., Ohio, Aug. 1959); Sid Sorokin in *The Pajama Game* (Carousel Th., Framingham, Mass., Aug. 1959); and Jeff in *Bells Are Ringing* (Carousel Th., Sept. 1959).

Mr. Douglass made his opera debut as Olin Blitch in *Susannah* (Acad. of Music, Philadelphia, Pa., Feb. 1960; Auditorium, Washington, D.C., Feb. 1960);

played Joe Hardy in *Damn Yankees* (Palm Beach Musicarnival, Fla., Mar. 1960); and Red Shadow in *The Desert Song* (St. Louis Municipal Opera, Mo., July 1960); Billy Bigelow in *Carousel* (South Shore Music Circus, Cohasset, Mass., July 1960); Jim Kenyon in *Rose Marie* (Civic Light Opera Co., Pittsburgh, Pa., Aug. 1960); and succeeded John Raitt (St. Louis, Mo., Dec. 23, 1960) as Destry in *Destry Rides Again* (Riviera, Las Vegas, Nev., July 31, 1960).

He played Grieg in *Song of Norway* (State Fair Music Hall, Dallas, Tex., June 1961); Emile de Becque in *South Pacific* (Carter Barron Th., Washington, D.C., Aug. 1961); Joe Hardy in *Damn Yankees* (Carousel Th., Framingham, Mass., Aug. 1961); succeeded Peter Palmer (June 6, 1962) as Tommy in *Brigadoon* (NY City Ctr., May 30, 1962); played Sid Sorokin in *The Pajama Game* (St. Louis Municipal Opera, Mo., July 1962); Frank Butler in *Annie Get Your Gun* (Carter Barron Th., Washington, D.C., July 1962); Grieg in *Song of Norway* (Civic Light Opera Co., Pittsburgh, Pa., Aug. 1962); and played Billy Bigelow in and directed *Carousel* (Playhouse-on-the-Mall, Paramus, N.J., Oct. 1962).

He played Emile de Becque in *South Pacific* (Thunderbird Hotel, Las Vegas, Nev., Dec. 1962); directed and played Fred Graham in *Kiss Me, Kate* (Playhouse-on-the-Mall, Paramus, N.J., Feb. 1963); played Johnny Brown in *The Unsinkable Molly Brown* (St. Paul, Minn., Aud., Apr. 1963); Billy Bigelow in *Carousel* (Lyric Th., Baltimore, Md., May 1963); Paul in *Carnival!* (St. Louis Municipal Opera, Mo., June 1963; Starlight Th., Kansas City, Mo., July 1963); File in *110 in the Shade* (Broadhurst, N.Y.C., Oct. 24, 1963), in which he also toured (Aug. 1964–May 1965); Gaylord Ravenal in *Show Boat* (Starlight Musicals, Indianapolis, Ind., Aug. 9, 1965; NY State Th., N.Y.C., July 19, 1966); played Benvenuto Cellini in a revival of *The Firebrand* (Master Th., N.Y.C., Dec. 10, 1965); Bill Starbuck in *110 in the Shade* (Palace Th., London, England, Feb. 8, 1967); and El Gallo in *The Fantasticks* (Ford's Th., Washington, D.C., 1970).

Television and Radio. Mr. Douglass performed on Rogers and Hammerstein Night (1949); appeared on the Kyle MacDonnell Show (WNBT, 1949); as MacHeath in *The Beggar's Opera* (CBS Workshop, 1952); John Talbot in *The Mercer Girls* (WNBT, 1953); the Woolworth Hour (CBS, 1956); and appeared as a soloist on The Voice of Firestone (ABC, 1959).

Night Clubs. He performed as a member of the quartet in *Venus on the Half Shell* (Diamond Horseshoe, N.Y.C., 1946).

Recreation. Swimming, fishing, sailing.

DOWD, M'EL. Actress. b. Feb. 2, Chicago, Ill., to John J. and Catherine (O'Connor) Dowd. Father, jack-of-all-trades; mother, office manager. Attended Boone (Iowa) H.S. Studied at the Goodman Th., Chicago, 1953–55; with Wynn Handman, N.Y.C., 1959. Married July 1, 1962, to Henri G. Eudes, maître d'hôtel; one son. Member of AEA; SAG; AFTRA.

Theatre. Miss Dowd has appeared with the Shakespearewrights Co. as Lady Macbeth in *Macbeth* (Jan Hus House, N.Y.C., Oct. 19, 1955); Titania in *A Midsummer Night's Dream* (Jan Hus House, Jan. 13, 1956); Lady Capulet in *Romeo and Juliet* (Jan Hus House, Feb. 23, 1956); and as Portia in *Julius Caesar* (Shakespearewrights Th., Oct. 23, 1957); subsequently played Lilith in *Back to Methuselah* (Ambassabor Th., Mar. 26, 1958), in which she later toured; Katarina of Aragon in *Royal Gambit* (Sullivan St. Playhouse, Mar. 4, 1959); was standby for Geraldine Page in *Sweet Bird of Youth* (Martin Beck Th., Mar. 10, 1959); appeared as Morgan Le Fay in *Camelot* (Majestic, Dec. 3, 1960); Agrippina in *The Emperor* (Maidman, Apr. 16, 1963); and Anita Corcoran in *A Case of Libel* (Longacre, Oct. 10, 1963).

Miss Dowd played Hesione Hushabye in *Heartbreak House* (Arena Stage, Washington, D.C., Feb. 11, 1965); Hattie in a tour of *Not Even in Spring* (Summer 1965); Mrs. Emilia Pattison in *The Right Honourable Gentleman* (Billy Rose Th., N.Y.C., Oct. 19, 1965); Mrs. Pelham in *The Right Honourable Gentleman* (Huntington Hartford Th., Los Angeles, Mar. 13, 1967); Elsa Schraeder in *The Sound of Music* (NY City Ctr., N.Y.C. Apr. 26, 1967); Woman in *The Unknown Soldier and His Wife* (Vivian Beaumont Th., July 6, 1967); Louise in *Everything in the Garden* (Plymouth, Nov. 29, 1967); Andromache in *Tiger at the Gates* (Vivian Beaumont Th., Feb. 29, 1968); was understudy to Angela Lansbury as Aurelia in *Dear World* (Mark Hellinger Th., Feb. 6, 1969); played Amelia in *Mercy Street* (American Place Th. at St. Clement's, Oct. 27, 1969); Maude Bodley in *Not Now, Darling* (Brooks Atkinson Th., Oct. 29, 1970); Norma in *A Gun Play* (Cherry Lane Th., Oct. 24, 1971); and Amelia Newsome in *Ambassador* (Lunt-Fontanne Th., Nov. 19, 1972).

Films. Miss Dowd made her film debut as Miss O'Connor in *The Wrong Man* (WB, 1957); played Mrs. Flint in *This Could Be the Night* (MGM, 1957); Rita in *Man on Fire* (MGM, 1957); and appeared in *Three Hundred Year Weekend* (Cinerama, 1971).

Television. She has appeared on Flipper (NBC); The Trial Begins (NBC); The Modern World of Shakespeare (NBC); and Education Exchange (NBC).

DOWNING, ROBERT. Stage manager, actor, director, playwright. b. Guy Robert Downing, Apr. 26, 1914, Sioux City, Iowa, to Clark Elmer and Alice Mae (Tonkinson) Downing. Father, salesman. Grad. Washington H.S., Cedar Rapids, Iowa, 1932. Studied acting with Catharine Hunt, Cedar Rapids, Iowa, 1927–31; with B. Iden Payne at the Univ. of Iowa as member of an all-state high school training program, 1931. Served USO, 1943–45. Member of AEA; AFTRA; Dramatists Guild; SAG; SSD&C; WGA, East; The Players (secy., 1960–to date). Denver Post, Denver, CO 80201, tel. (303) 297-1010; c/o The Players, 16 Gramercy Park, New York, NY 10003, tel. (212) Gramercy 5-6116.

Theatre. Mr. Downing played a small role in B. Iden Payne's production of *Richard II* and Lush in Eugene C. Davis' production of *Captain Applejack* (Univ. of Iowa, Summer 1931); subsequently, with Community Players (Cedar Rapids, Iowa), he played Bud in *Sun-Up* (Dec. 2, 1931); and the Suisse in Dumas' *A Marriage of Convenience* (May 5, 1932); joined Robert Leefers' Players, a commonwealth circle stock company playing small communities near Cedar Rapids, appearing in juvenile roles in *Crooks for a Month, Mystery of the 3rd Gable, Leave It to Dad, Remote Control, House Across the Way, It's the Truth That Hurts,* and *June Time* (May–July 1933); and wrote the one-act play, *Pen in Hand,* which won a playwriting competition conducted by Cedar Rapids churches and was later performed by an amateur cast (1933); played Larry in *The Hottentot* (Ethel Salisbury Hanley Players, Muscatine, Iowa, Aug. 1933); Pops in *The Patsy* (Milo L. Green Players, Corning, Iowa, Sept. 7, 1933); appeared with Robert Leefers Players in *Nancy Gets a Break* (Sept. 17, 1933) and *The Crash* (Sept. 24, 1933); joined Hill & Dale Players, a commonwealth circle stock company playing in communities near Cedar Rapids, appearing in juvenile roles in *Toby and the Balloon Girl, Applesauce,* and *Wanted, a Wife* (Oct.–Nov. 1933); played Chambers in *This One Man* (Community Players, Cedar Rapids, Feb. 1, 1934); the title role in a modern-dress production of *Hamlet* (Community Players, Cedar Rapids, Feb. 27, 1934); appeared with the Boyd B. Trousdale stock company in *Springtime in the Rockies, Penny Arcade, My Friend from Arkansas, Broken Dishes, Tires and Tubes,* and *The Shooting of Dan McGrew* (President, Des Moines, Iowa, Mar. 11–27, 1934); with Hill & Dale Players, toured in *Toby and the Hipnotist, The Awakening,* and played Phineas, St. Clare and a Negro slave in *Uncle Tom's Cabin,* and appeared in *The Little Red Book* (Apr. 24–May 12, 1934; played Pa in *Applesauce* and Judge Hardy in *Skidding* (Milo L. Green Players, Corning, Iowa, June 22–July 11, 1934); and wrote the one-act play, *The Seventh Candle* (Cedar Rapids Woman's Club, Iowa, 1934).

Mr Downing joined the Dixiana Showboat in Chicago, Ill., moored at Diversey Parkway Bridge, playing leading man roles in the melodramas *No Mother to Guide Her* (Aug. 8, 1934); *The Convict's Daughter* (Sept. 10, 1934); *The Fatal Wedding* (Oct. 7, 1934); *Nellie, the Beautiful Cloak Model* (Nov. 12, 1934); *A Little Outcast* (Dec. 13, 1934); *Bertha, the Sewing Machine Girl* (Jan. 27, 1935); Jesse James in *The James Boys in Missouri* (Jan. 28, 1935); *Her First False Step* (Mar. 4, 1935); *Human Hearts* (Apr. 2, 1935); *Forgiven at the Altar* (Apr. 30, 1935); *While the City Sleeps* (May 29, 1935); and *Only a Shop Girl* (July 15, 1935).

He toured as Pontius Pilate in the Great European Passion Play (Calif., Ore., Idaho, Wash.; Sept. 9–Dec. 12, 1935; Sept. 28–Oct. 1, 1936); was emcee of the 12th Annual Los Angeles (Calif.) Food Show (Ambassador Hotel, Nov. 8–15, 1936); played Tristan in *The Vagabond King* (Del Mar Club, Santa Monica, Calif., Nov. 28, 1937); wrote *The Inner Office,* which was presented by the Hollywood (Calif.) H.S. Adult Evening Educational Group as a result of winning its 13th annual one-act playwriting contest (July 4, 1937); joined Al Jackson's tent show stock company (Madison, Wis., May 25–July 5, 1938), played roles in *Broken Dishes, In the Wrong Bed, Yes, My Darling Daughter, The Ghost Train, Petticoat Fever,* and *Goodbye Again;* was assigned (Oct. 31, 1938) as an actor with Federal Th. (WPA) Project, played Dr. Randall in *The Copperhead* (Blackstone, Chicago, Ill., Dec. 26, 1938); toured with the Lunts in *The Seagull, Amphitryon 38,* and as an Italian officer in *Idiot's Delight* (Jan. 10–Apr. 28, 1939); played Harry Easter in the Federal Th. production of *Street Scene* (Great Northern, Chicago, Ill., June 20, 1939); appeared in the melodrama, *Clouds and Sunshine* (Cocoanut Grove Night Club, Chicago, July 7, 1939); performed with an industrial show for Packard Motor Co. (Masonic Temple, Detroit, Mich., Aug. 8, 1939); and was a member of the Federal Writers' (WPA) Project (Chicago, Ill., Aug. 28–Sept. 13, 1939).

Mr. Downing toured with the Lunts as Gregory in *The Taming of the Shrew* (opened Natl., Washington, D.C., Sept. 18, 1939), the tour ending in N.Y.C. (Alvin, Feb. 5, 1940); played the Photographer and was assistant stage manager for *There Shall Be No Night* (Alvin, Apr. 29, 1940), during which time he was also secretary to the Lunts and editor of the weekly backstage newspaper, *The Luntanne Tattler,* now on file in the Harvard Theatre Collection and the NY Public Library Theatre Collection. During 1940, he wrote, with Kermit Love, the play *Yankee Doodle Comes to Town,* which went into rehearsal in N.Y.C., but did not open. He directed *Morning's at Seven* (Community Players, Cedar Rapids, Iowa, Apr. 14, 1941); *The Male Animal* (Community Players, Cedar Rapids, May 19, 1941); wrote, with George Greenberg, *Under Canvas* (Cornel Coll. Summer Th., Mt. Vernon, Iowa, July 17, 1941); appeared in *Tonight We Dance, The Man from Cairo, Lady in Waiting, Margin for Error, The Gingham Girl, Out of the Frying Pan, East Lynne, Windy Hill,* and *My Dear Children* (Bandbox Summer Th., Suffield, Conn., June 24–Aug. 31, 1941); was stage manager for USO-Camp Shows' production of *Junior Miss* (Nov. 25, 1942–May 17, 1943), assuming the role of J. B. (Dec. 1, 1942); assistant stage manager for the touring company of *My Sister Eileen* (opened Shubert, New Haven, Conn., Dec. 25, 1942; closed Her Majesty's, Montreal, Canada, Apr. 26, 1943); was assistant stage manager, later state manager, for *Those Endearing Young Charms* (Booth, N.Y.C., Aug. 2, 1943); played the State Trooper and was assistant stage manager of *The Naked Genius* (Plymouth, Oct. 21, 1943); was assistant stage manager for *Mexican Hayride* (Winter Garden, Jan. 28, 1944); and *Catherine Was Great* (Shubert, Aug. 2, 1944) which subsequently toured (opened Maryland Th., Baltimore, Md., Jan. 15, 1945); stage manager, company manager, and played Dr. Bradley in the USO-Camp Shows' overseas company of *The Man Who Came to Dinner* (Feb. 1, 1945–June 12, 1945); was production stage manager for Maurice Evans' G.I. version of *Hamlet* (Columbus Circle Th., N.Y.C., Dec. 15, 1945), during which time he also taught a course in stage management at the Amer. Th. Wing, N.Y.C.; was production stage manager for the pre-Bway tour of *Heartsong* (opened Shubert, New Haven, Conn., Feb. 27, 1947; closed Walnut St. Th., Philadelphia, Pa., Mar. 29, 1947); production stage manager for *A Streetcar Named Desire* (Ethel Barrymore Th., N.Y.C., Dec. 3, 1947); leaving the company two summers to direct at Bar Harbor (Me.) Playhouse (Summers 1948–49), also touring with the company (opened Locust, Philadelphia, Pa., Dec. 26, 1949) which closed in N.Y.C. (NY City Ctr., Mar. 18, 1950); directed a N.Y.C. Subway Circuit summer tour of *A Streetcar Named Desire* (opened Flatbush Th., Brooklyn, June 20, 1950); was advance director for a summer touring company of *Knickerbocker Holiday* (July 1950); directed at Penthouse Theatres-in-the-Round (Atlanta, Ga., and Jacksonville, Fla., Sept.–Dec. 1950); and appeared as Mr. Wilson in the pre-Bway tryout of *The Man That Corrupted Hadleyburg* (opened Erlanger, Philadelphia, Pa., Apr. 21, 1951; closed there Apr. 28, 1951).

He was production stage manager for the musical *Seventeen* (Broadhurst, N.Y.C., June 21, 1951); stage manager for *Seagulls OVer Sorrento* (John Golden Th., Sept. 2, 1952); wrote *Around We Go* (The Playhouse, Houston, Tex., Apr. 8, 1953); was stage manager for *Lullaby* (Lyceum, N.Y.C., Feb. 3, 1954); directed *My 3 Angels* (Bucks County Playhouse, New Hope, Pa., June 21, 1954); played Doc in *Mister Roberts* (Marblehead Summer Th., Mass., July 5, 1954); was stage manager for *The Tender Trap* (Longacre, N.Y.C., Oct. 13, 1954); directed a touring company of *The Tender Trap* (opened McCarter Th., Princeton, N.J., Jan. 21, 1955); was stage manager for *Cat on a Hot Tin Roof* (Morosco, Mar. 24, 1955), for which he was later temporarily understudy to Burl Ives in the role of Big Daddy (Nov. 28–Dec. 10, 1955); directed *The Tender Trap* (Bucks County Playhouse, New Hope, Pa., Aug. 15, 1955); directed a West Coast touring production of *The Tender Trap* (opened Carthay Circle Th., Los Angeles, Calif., Sept. 13, 1955); wrote and edited the material for Helen Hayes' "Command Performance," celebrating her 50th year in the theatre (Amer. Th. Wing, Waldorf-Astoria Hotel, N.Y.C., Dec. 30, 1955); played the policeman and was assistant director to Ezra Stone for *Wake Up, Darling* (Ethel Barrymore Th., May 2, 1956); production stage manager for *Happy Hunting* (Majestic, Dec. 6, 1956); played the role of the Stage Manager and was production stage manager for *Say, Darling* (ANTA, Apr. 3, 1958); was production stage manager for *J. B.* (ANTA, Dec. 11, 1959); *Cheri* (Morosco, Oct. 12, 1959), in which his pet cat, Ginger, appeared in the role of Fanchette; *The Long Dream* (Ambassador, Feb. 17, 1960); and for *Camelot* (Majestic, Dec. 3, 1960). In 1961, his play *The Limbo Kid* was chosen "play of the year" by the Southeastern Th. Conference (STC), and was presented several times during the course of the year by such groups as the Raleigh (N.C.) Little Th. and the Univ. of Alabama Th., and was presented the following year at Museum Th. (Richmond, Va., Feb. 28, 1962) and at the Univ. of Denver (Colo., July 26, 1962).

He was production stage manager for *Natural Affection* (Booth, N.Y.C., Jan. 31, 1963); was appointed (July 29, 1963), with Frederick de Wilde, production stage manager for the Repertory Th. of Lincoln Center, functioning in that capacity for *After the Fall* (Jan. 23, 1964), *Marco Millions* (Feb. 20, 1964), *But for Whom Charlie* (Mar. 12, 1964), *The Changeling* (Oct. 29, 1964), *Incident at Vichy* (Dec. 3, 1964) and *Tartuffe* (Jan. 14, 1965), all at ANTA-Washington St. Th., N.Y.C.

Films. Mr. Downing was screen-tested at Universal Studios (Universal City, Calif.) in a scene from *Private Lives* under the direction of Norbert Brodine (Feb. 11, 1936). He was an extra in *15 Maiden Lane* (20th-Fox, 1936); *Larceny on the Air* (Rep., 1937); *Join the Marines* (Rep., 1937); *Navy Blues* (Rep., 1937); *Idol of the Crowds* (U, 1937); *Every Day's a Holiday* (Par., 1937); played a Mongol palace guard in *Adventures of Marco Polo* (UA, 1938); appeared in *Romance of the Limberlost* (Mono., 1938); *St. Benny the Dip* (UA, 1951); played Father Vincent in *On the Waterfront* (Col., 1954); and the Hotel Executive in *Splendor in the Grass* (WB, 1961).

Television and Radio. Mr. Downing made his radio debut in the play, *Career* (KWCR, Cedar Rapids, Iowa, Oct. 15, 1933); subsequently performed in *Haunted House* (WMT, Waterloo, Iowa, Nov. 28, 1933); *Sideshow Doyle* (KWCR, Cedar Rapids, Dec. 10, 1933); *Conquest* (KWCR, Cedar Rapids, Jan. 14, 1934); was guest artist on Rudy Vallee's variety show; performed in *The Drunkard* (NBC, Chicago, Ill., Aug. 10, 1935); wrote, directed and performed in the melodrama *Her Fatal Hour* (KFAC, Los Angeles, Calif., Mar. 14, 1936); performed on We, the People (NBC, N.Y.C., Dec. 20, 1936); played David Kenyon in the series Foreign Legion (KEHE, Los Angeles, Calif., Jan. 5–6, 1937); made a number of broadcasts of the series Modern Girl's Romance (KEHE, Los Angeles, Jan.–July, 1937); performed on the US Post Office broadcast (KEHE, Los Angeles, Apr. 7, 1937); in CBS' Shakespeare Cycle (KNX, Hollywood, Calif.) in *Julius Caesar* (July 26, 1937), *The Taming of the Shrew* (Aug. 2, 1937), *King Lear* (Aug. 9, 1937), *As You Like It* (Aug. 16, 1937), and *Henry IV* (Aug. 23, 1937); played Don McAllister on the initial broadcast of the series *Big Town* (CBS, KNX, Hollywood, Calif., Nov. 2, 1937); performed in Curtain Calls series (KFWB, Los Angeles, Nov. 7, 1937); Let's Go Hollywood (KFWB, Los Angeles, Nov. 19, 1937); Lady of Millions (Hollywood, Dec. 15, 1937; Jan. 5, 1938); Headlines on Parade (KNX, Hollywood, Feb. 8, 1938); Strange As It Seems (Hollywood, Feb. 28, 1938); Sunnyside (Hollywood, Mar. 23, 1938); wrote and performed in the sketch *Antidote* (KFVD, Los Angeles, May 6, 1938); *13 O'Clock* (KFVD, Los Angeles, May 10, 1938), in which Mr. Downing's mother also performed; appeared on National Barn Dance Show (WLS-NBC, Chicago, Ill., July 23, 1939); wrote and acted in the play *Lola Montez* (WIND, Chicago, Aug. 20, 1939); wrote series for pilot record transcription, *Lutefisk Ole* (WIND, Chicago, 1939); wrote *Bus Lady's Holiday* (WOR-Mutual, N.Y.C., 1940); and *The Limbo Kid* (NBC, Oct. 5, 1940).

Mr. Downing made his television debut on Fred Allen's show (NBC, Jan. 6, 1952); acted in a sketch with Harpo Marx on Ezio Pinza's show (NBC, Feb. 1, 1952); appeared on Ellery Queen series (ABC, Feb. 1952); Martha Raye's show (NBC, 1952); Colgate Comedy Hour (NBC, June 1, 1952; May 31, 1953); Paul Winchell's show (NBC, June 23, 1952); Assignment Manhunt series (NBC, Aug. 2, 1952); All-Star Revue series (NBC, Nov. 1, 1952; Oct. 3, 1953); appeared as George T. Claridge in nine episodes of Captain Video series (Dumont, Nov. 25–Dec. 5, 1952); on Dark of Night series (WABD-TV, Feb. 6 and Apr. 17, 1953); John Jupiter series (WABD-TV, May 16, 1953); returned to Claridge role in Captain Video series (Dumont, June 1–19, 1953); appeared on Rocky King series (Dumont, July 26, 1953); appeared as a space-ship Captain on Captain Video series (Apr. 13, 15, 1954); in the pilot film for the series, Love That Guy (CBS, Apr. 16, 23, 1954); *Woman with a Past* (CBS, July 1, 1954); Joe and Mabel series (CBS, Nov., 17–22, 1955) *One Way West* (Kraft Television Th., NBC, Aug. 1, 1956); researched and wrote for the Ed Wynn spectacular Texaco Command Appearance (NBC, Sept. 19, 1957); wrote sections of the Ethel Barrymore spectacular Texaco Command Appearance (NBC, Nov. 23, 1957); appeared as emcee and contributed material to *Backstage Broadway*, which was presented on the You Asked For It series (ABC, Mar. 1, 1959); wrote *The Limbo Kid* (CBS, Television Workshop, Feb. 7, 1960); appeared on American Heritage series (NBC, Apr. 10, 1960); played Bertie (Edward VII) in *Victoria Regina* (Hallmark Hall of Fame (NBC, Aug. 1, 1961); and a Member of Parliament on *Mr. Disraeli* (Hallmark Hall of Fame, NBC, Mar. 16–21, 1963).

Other Activities. In 1961, the Univ. of Texas purchased Mr. Downing's theatre collection, amassed during the previous 25 years, which contains approximately 10,000 books, numerous stage and screen photographs, blueprints, costume designs, theatrical correspondence, prompt scripts, autograph material, prints, posters, memorabilia and ephemera. Known as The Robert Downing Theatre Collection, it is on permanent exhibition at the Hoblitzelle Fine Arts Library at the Univ. of Texas.

In 1966, Mr. Downing traveled, largely under US State Dept. sponsorship, from Tokyo, Japan, to Amsterdam, The Netherlands, speaking on American theatre. Later the same year, he gave several lectures in West Germany as a guest of the West German government. He was regional theatre director for ANTA, N.Y.C., in 1967, and from 1967 to 1970 he directed the Denver (Col.) *Post* Opera Foundation's al fresco summer musicals. In 1968–69, he was administrative director for the first season of the Krannert Center for the Performing Arts, Univ. of Illinois, Urbana, Ill., and in 1969 he became drama aditor of the Denver *Post.*.

Published Works. In addition to editing school newspapers and magazines, Mr. Downing contributed articles to the Cedar Rapids (Iowa) *Gazette*, verse and essays to the Des Moines *Register* and articles to *The Christian Science Monitor* (1925–32). He is author of a prize-winning short story, "The Rustic" (Scholastic Magazine, 1932); the one-act plays, *Jimmy Six* and *Sticks and Stones* (Plays magazine, 1953); has contributed articles on theatre to NY *Times* Book Reviews; NY *Times* Sunday theatre section; NY *Herald Tribune* Sunday theatre section; *Films in Review; Photoplay, Screenland, Movie Mirror*, and other fan magazines; *Grolier Encyclopedia; Teatro Spettacolo* encyclopedia; *oxford Companion to the Theatre;* and *Theatre Arts* magazine, including the cat story, *Minnie and Mr. Clark*, which was subsequently published in *Cats* Magazine and anthologized in *Of Cats and Men* (1957) and *The Passionate Playgoer* (1958). Minnie was the house cat at the Winter Garden Th., who "adopted" the late comedian, Bobby Clark.

Mr. Downing is one of the editors of The Players' *Bulletin* (1959–to date); and, since the early 1950's using the byline "Rodo," has contributed book reviews of performing arts books to the Literati Dept. of *Variety*, the weekly theatrical trade journal.

Awards. Mr. Downing received first prize ($2,000) in the Dr. Christian Radio Writing Contest for his play, *Old Hundred*, which was subsequently performed by Jean Hersholt and cast (CBS, 1952).

Recreation. Book-collecting.

DRAKE, ALFRED. Actor, director, singer, writer. b. Oct. 7, 1914, New York City, to John M. and Elena Teresa (Maggiolo) Capurro. Grad. Boys' H.S., Bklyn., N.Y., 1931; Brooklyn Coll., B.A. 1935. Studied singing with Clytie Mundy, 1932–41. Married 1940 to Alma Rowena Tollefsen (marr. dis. Feb. 1944); married Mar. 10, 1944, to Esther Harvey Brown; two daughters. Member of AEA; AFTRA; SAG; AGVA; The Players (pres.). Address: c/o Elias A. Jacobs, 4 West 56th St., New York, NY 10019, tel. (212) 582-1222.

Theatre. Mr. Drake made his N.Y.C. debut at the Adelphi Th., in the choruses of five Lodewick Vroom productions of Gilbert & Sullivan: *The Mikado* (July 15, 1935), *The Pirates of Penzance* (July 22, 1935), *Yeoman of the Guard* (July 29, 1935), *The Gondoliers*, and *Trial by Jury*. He sang the role of Pan in Bach's *Phoebus and Pan* and Rocco in *Fidelio* for the Steel Pier Opera Co. (Atlantic City, N.J., 1935); was a member of the singing ensemble and understudied William Gaxton in the role of Leopold, the Head Waiter, in *White Horse Inn* (Center, N.Y.C., Oct. 1, 1936); played Marshall Blackstone and the High Priest in *Babes in Arms* (Shubert, Apr. 14, 1937), with which he later toured (Dec. 1937–Feb. 1938); as Albert Porter in *The Two Bouquets* (Windsor, N.Y.C., May 31, 1938); in the revue, *One for the Money* (Booth, Feb. 4, 1939); *The Straw Hat Revue* (Ambassador, Sept. 29, 1939); and *Two for the Show* (Booth, Feb. 8, 1940).

He played a season of stock at the Clinton (Conn.) Playhouse (Summer 1940) playing Adolfino in *After the Ball*, appearing in *Her Master's Voice*, and playing Professor Baer in *Little Women* (Summer 1942); Norman Reese in *Out of the Frying Pan*

(Windsor, N.Y.C., Feb. 11, 1941); in stock at the Marblehead (Mass.) Playhouse, appearing in *Mr. and Mrs. North, The Gorilla, Dear Brutus,* and *The Yellow Jacket;* and played Rufus in *Rufus and His Wife* at the Suffern (N.Y.) Playhouse Summer 1941). He appeared as Orlando in *As You Like It* (Mansfield, N.Y.C., Oct. 20, 1941); and Robert in *Yesterday's Magic* (Guild, Apr. 14, 1942).

Mr. Drake played Curly in *Oklahoma!* (St. James, N.Y.C., Mar. 31, 1943); Barnaby Goodchild in *Sing Out Sweet Land* (Intl., Dec. 27, 1944); the Beggar and Macheath in *Beggar's Holiday* (Bway Th., Dec. 26, 1946); for the Salt Lake City (Utah) centennial; appeared in *The Promised Valley* (1947); played in *The Pursuit of Happiness* (Westport Country Playhouse, Conn., Summer 1947); appeared as Larry Foreman in *The Cradle Will Rock* (Mansfield, N.Y.C., Dec. 26, 1947); Alexander Soren in *Joy to the World* (Plymouth, Mar. 18, 1948); in stock, directed and played the Man in *The Man with a Load of Mischief* (Marblehead Playhouse, Mass., Summer 1948); and appeared as Fred Graham and Petruchio in *Kiss Me, Kate* (Century, N.Y.C., Dec. 30, 1948).

Mr. Drake wrote the book, with Edward Eager, and directed the musical, *The Liar* (Broadhurst, May 18, 1950); staged the production of *Courtin' Time* (Natl., June 14, 1951); directed the pre-Bway tryout of *Salt of the Earth* (opened Shubert, New Haven, Conn., Mar. 13, 1952; closed Wilbur, Boston, Mass., Mar. 22, 1952); subsequently in the Summer of 1952, played Laudisi in *Right You Are, If You Think You Are* (Westport Country Playhouse, (Conn.), and John Tanner in *Man and Superman* (Playhouse-in-the-Park, Philadelphia, Pa.). Mr. Drake adapted, with Edward Eager, and played David Petri in *The Gambler* (Lyceum, N.Y.C., Oct. 13, 1952); succeeded (Mar. 1953) Yul Brynner as the King in *The King and I* (St. James, Mar. 29, 1951); played Hajj in *Kismet* (Ziegfeld, N.Y.C., Dec. 3, 1953; Stoll, London, Apr. 20, 1955).

With the American Shakespeare Festival (Stratford, Conn.), Mr. Drake appeared as Iago in *Othello* (June 22, 1957), and as Benedick in *Much Ado About Nothing* (Aug. 3, 1957); and played He in *He Who Gets Slapped* (Westport Country Playhouse, Conn., Summer 1957). He directed *Love Me Little* (Helen Hayes Th., N.Y.C., Apr. 15, 1958); adapted, with Edward Eager, and directed *Dr. Willy Nilly* (Barbizon-Plaza, 1959); directed the pre-Bway tryout of *Lock Up Your Daughters!* (opened Shubert, New Haven, Conn., Apr. 27, 1960; closed Shubert, Boston, Mass., May 7, 1960); appeared as Edmund Kean in *Kean* (Bway Th., Nov. 2, 1961); directed the pre-Bway tryout of *The Advocate* (Bucks County Playhouse, New Hope, Pa., Summer 1962); and appeared with the California Civic Light Opera Co. as Hajj in *Kismet* (Curran, San Francisco Civic Aud., Los Angeles, 1962).

He played the title role in *Lorenzo* (Plymouth, N.Y.C., Feb. 14, 1963); and a dual role in the pre-Bway tryout of *Zenda* (opened Curran, San Francisco, Calif., Aug. 5, 1963; closed Civic Aud., Los Angeles, Calif., 1963). Mr. Drake did the English translation of *Rugantino* (Mark Hellinger Th., N.Y.C., Feb. 6, 1964); and appeared as Claudius in *Hamlet* (Lunt-Fontanne, Apr. 13, 1964). He repeated his performance as Hajj for the Music Theatre of Lincoln Center (NY State Th., June 22, 1965), played Soren Brandes in *Those That Play the Clowns* (ANTA, Nov. 24, 1966); was Aristobulo in *Song of the Grasshopper* (ANTA, Sept. 28, 1967); and appeared as Honoré in *Gigi* (San Francisco, Los Angeles, Detroit, St. Louis, Toronto, and Uris Th., N.Y.C., 1973). He staged *The Royal Rape of Ruari Macagarunde* (Richmond, Va., Feb. 1973).

Films. He appeared in *Tars and Spars* (Col., 1946).

Television. Mr. Drake's many appearances include the title role in *The Adventures of Marco Polo* (NBC, Apr. 14, 1956); *Kiss Me, Kate* (Hallmark Hall of Fame, NBC, Nov. 20, 1958); Jack Point in *Yeoman of the Guard* (Hallmark Hall of Fame, NBC); Mosca in *Volpone* (Play of the Week WNTA); *Music from Shubert Alley; Key Largo* (Alcoa Hour, NBC); the Max Liebman Oldsmobile Special (NBC); the Woolworth Hour Special; the International Harvester Fiftieth Anniversary Special; Simon in *Counsellor-at-Law* (Alcoa Hour, NBC); *Athens—Where the Theatre Began;* Omnibus (NBC); and the Pulitzer Prize Playhouse (ABC).

He has appeared on English television in *Showtime* (BBC); and *Othello* (BBC).

Night Clubs. He appeared at the Persian Room (Hotel Plaza, N.Y.C., 1940).

Published Works. He wrote *Anyone Can Win at Gin Rummy and Canasta* (1950). In collaboration with Edward Eager, he has written the plays, *The Burglar's Opera* and *76;* and with Edward Eager, the adaptation of *La Belle Helene.*

Discography. Mr. Drake has recorded *Oklahoma!* (Decca); *Sing Out Sweet Land* (Decca); *Roberta; Brigadoon* (Vic.); *Down in the Valley; The Vagabond King* (Decca); *Kiss Me, Kate* (Cap.); *Kismet* (Col.); *Kean* (Col.); *Marco Polo; Carousel* (Command); *Songs of Leonard Bernstein;* and *The Rubyat.*

Awards. Mr. Drake won the *Variety* NY Drama Critics Poll (1943) for his performance as Curly in *Oklahoma!;* the Donaldson Award (1949) for his performance as Fred Graham and Petruchio in *Kiss Me, Kate;* and, in 1954, for his performance as Hajj in *Kismet,* won the *Variety* NY Drama Critics' Poll, the Donaldson Award, and the Antoinette Perry (Tony) Award.

Recreation. Reading, fencing, music, and bridge.

DRAPER, ANNE. Actress. b. Marcia Anne Draper, Sept. 1, 1938, New York City, to Raimund Sanders and Marcia (Sucker) Draper. Grad. Foxcroft H.S., Middleburg, Va., 1957. Studied dance at the Amer. Ballet Centre, three years; acting at the ASFTA Training Program, one year; and with Fanny Bradshaw, two years. Relatives in theatre: aunt, Ruth Draper, monologist; uncle, Paul Draper, dancer. Member of AEA; AFTRA; SAG.

Theatre. Miss Draper made her debut as a cast replacement in *Between Two Thieves* (York Th., N.Y.C., Feb. 11, 1960); followed by the First Fairy in the NY Shakespeare Festival production of *A Midsummer Night's Dream* (Wollman Rink, July 31, 1961); and her Bway debut as Mrs. Allen, Nursing Mother, Miss Pieroni and understudy to Marian Seldes as Susan Loring in *A Gift of Time* (Ethel Barrymore Th., Feb. 22, 1962).

She appeared as Jo in a stock production of *A Taste of Honey* (Williamstown Th., Mass., Aug. 1962); was at the American Shakespeare Festival, Stratford, Conn. (Summer 1963) as Alice in *Henry V* (May 31), Cordelia in *King Lear* (June 4), Luce in *The Comedy of Errors* (June 5), and Charmian in *Caesar and Cleopatra* (July 23); appeared in the opera *Jeanne d'Arc au bûcher* (NY City Ctr., Oct. 3, 1963); and returned to the American Shakespeare Festival, Stratford, Conn. (Summer 1964), where she played the Duchess of York in *Richard III* (May 30) and Hero in *Much Ado About Nothing* (June 3).

Miss Draper was Aricie in IASTA's production of *Phèdre* (Greenwich Mews, N.Y.C., Feb. 10, 1966); Julia in IASTA's *The Duchess of Malfi* (IASTA, Apr. 6, 1966); and a Girl in IASTA's *The Butterfly Dream* (Greenwich Mews, May 19, 1966). She was in *Carricknabauna* (Greenwich Mews, Mar. 30, 1967); *Posterity for Sale* (American Place Th., St. Clement's Ch., May 17, 1967); repeated her performance as Luce in *The Comedy of Errors* (Ford's Th., Washington, D.C., Feb. 26, 1968) and at the Great Lakes Shakespeare Festival, Lakewood, Ohio (Aug. 26, 1970), where she also appeared in *The Merchant of Venice* (July 10, 1970), *R.U.R.* (July 15, 1970), and in *Julius Caesar* (July 29, 1970).

DRAPER, PAUL. Dancer, educator. b. Paul Nathaniel Saltonstall Draper, Oct. 25, 1913, Florence, Italy, to Paul and Muriel (Sanders) Draper. Father, singer; mother, writer, lecturer. Grad. Loomis Sch., Windsor, Conn., 1930; attended Polytechnic Inst. of Brooklyn, 1931–32. Studied at Sch. of American Ballet, N.Y.C., 1935; with Laurent Novikoff, Chicago, Ill., 1942. Married July 1, 1941, to Heidi Vosseler, dancer; three daughters. Relatives in theatre: aunt, Ruth Draper, monologist; niece, Anne Draper, actress. Member of AEA; AGVA; SAG. Address: 530 West End Ave., New York, NY 10024.

Pre-Theatre. Writer, advertising man, journalist, music critic, dance instructor, soda jerk.

Theatre. Mr. Draper toured the English provinces as a dancer in the revue *Sensations of 1931* (Autumn 1932); danced in the revue, *Thumbs Up* (St. James, N.Y.C., Dec. 27, 1934); appeared with his aunt in a program entitled *Ruth and Paul Draper* (Booth, Dec. 26, 1940); and in *Fun to Be Free* (Madison Square Garden, Oct. 5, 1941).

With Larry Adler, the harmonica virtuoso, Mr. Draper danced in annual concert tours of the US, giving concerts in New York at both Town Hall and the 92nd Street YMHA (1941–48); appeared at the Roxy Th., Radio City Music Hall, and Loew's State (1940–48); with Larry Adler, appeared in six Christmas season concerts at the NY City Ctr. (1941–47); toured Central America for Cultural Relations (1942); with the USO, to the Arctic Circle, the Caribbean and the Pacific during World War II; and toured Israel with Larry Adler (1951).

Mr. Draper danced again in a program entitled *Ruth and Paul Draper* (Bijou, N.Y.C., Dec. 26, 1954); in Part II of a three-part program entitled *All in One* (Playhouse, Apr. 19, 1955); appeared in *Three for All* (Carnegie Recital Hall, Aug. 2, 1956); toured again (1960–62), appearing at the Berlin (Ger.) Festival (1961); and danced in the Connecticut Coll. Dance Festival (New London, Summers 1962; 1963; 1964; 1965; 1966; 1967; he was on the faculty during the last three years). He appeared in the Dance Festival (Delacorte Th., Central Park, N.Y.C., July 1, 1963); and toured in solo concert (1964). He performed as soloist with the Carnegie-Mellon Kiltie Band in Morton Gould's "Tap Dance Concerto" (Carnegie Hall, N.Y.C., Apr. 1973), and he has lectured and given demonstrations at numerous colleges and universities and dance conventions.

Films. Mr. Draper has appeared in *Colleen* (WB, 1936) and *The Time of Your Life* (UA, 1948).

Television. He has danced on Toast of the Town (CBS, 1950) and Camera Three (CBS, 1962).

Night Clubs. Mr. Draper has performed at the Hotel Pierre (N.Y.C., 1937); the Persian Room, Hotel Plaza (N.Y.C., 1937; 1938; 1939; 1940; 1948); the Café de Paris (London, 1938, 1939); the Cocoanut Grove (Los Angeles, Calif., 1939); the Versailles (N.Y.C., 1939, 1940, 1941); the Waldorf-Astoria Hotel (N.Y.C., 1940, 1941, 1942); the Copacabana (Rio de Janeiro, Braz., 1941, 1944); the Casino de Paris (France, 1952); and the Village Gate (N.Y.C., 1963).

Other Activities. Mr. Draper was associate editor of *Dance* Magazine (1955–64); professor at the Juilliard Sch. of Music and Dance, where he taught rhythm (1962–64); and since 1963 has been teaching rhythm to actors at the HB (Herbert Berghof) Studios. He has been visiting Andrew Mellon professor at Carnegie-Mellon University (1967–68, 1968–74) and is currently Andrew Mellon professor of drama at Carnegie-Mellon, where he is teaching dance and movement to drama students.

Published Works. He has written an article on tap dancing for the Encyclopeadia Britannica (1962).

Awards. He has received the All-Dance Convention D.E.A.; and the Boston Society D.M.A.

Recreation. Cycling, photography, all sports.

DRAPER, STEPHEN. Talent representative. b. Jan. 8, 1906, to Frederick E. and Katherine (Stubbs) Draper. Father, lawyer. Grad. Lansingburgh H.S., Troy, 1924; attended Hamilton Coll., 1924–25. Member of AEA. Address: (home) 100 W. 57th St., New York, NY 10019; (bus.) 37 W. 57th St., New York, NY 10019.

Since 1964, Mr. Draper has headed the Stephen Draper (talent) Agency. Prior to that time, Mr. Draper was a partner in the Lee-Draper (talent) Agency (1946–64), and was associated with M.C.A. (1944–46).

He made his debut as an actor in the revue, *Bare Facts of 1926* (Triangle Th., N.Y.C., July 16, 1926); subsequently appeared as the Lieutenant in *Rapid Transit* (Provincetown Playhouse, Apr. 7, 1927); played 40 weeks of stock in Lindley Cook's stock co. (Rockville Center, N.Y., 1927–28); appeared as Rufe Cagle in *Sun Up,* a one-act play presented in vaudeville (Palace, N.Y.C., Sept. 1928); and in the full-length play *Sun Up* presented here (Princess, 1929); and abroad (Theatre des Mathurins, Paris, June-Aug. 1929; Little Th., London, Aug.–Oct. 1929); and in stock (Paterson, Union City, Jersey City, and Westwood, N.J.; Patchogue and Bay Shore, N.Y., 1930–31).

Recreation. Painting, languages.

DRESSLER, ERIC. Actor. b. Eric Alfred Dressler, Oct. 27, 1896, New York City, to Charles and Carlotta (Mauer) Dressler. Father, precision instrument manufacturer. Grad. Berkely-Irving Prep Sch., N.Y.C., 1915. Married Nov. 3, 1917, to Elizabeth Cronau, painter (marr. dis. July 1942); one son; married Sept. 8, 1942, to Patricia Calvert, actress. Member of AEA (council mbr., 1936–46); AFTRA (local and natl. boards, 1938–48).

Theatre. Mr. Dressler made his debut in a vaudeville sketch with Ruth Gates and Co. (Loew's Circuit, Nov. 1916); appeared in vaudeville with Mattie Choate and Co. (Apr. 1917); toured in *Charley's Aunt* (Sept. 1918–May 1919); played seasons of stock (Paterson, N.J., May 1919; New Haven, Conn., Sept. 1919, Sept. 1920; Scranton, Pa., May and Summer 1920; Albany, N.Y., May 1921).

He made his Bway debut joining (Oct. 1922) the cast of *The Ever Green Lady* (Punch and Judy, Oct. 11, 1922); played Bradley Ingals in *The Goose Hangs High* (Bijou, Jan. 29, 1924), and toured in the role, leaving the show in Chicago (Ill.), to play Henry "Babe" Harrison in *Out of Step* (Hudson, N.Y.C., Jan. 29, 1925); played Bradley Ingals in *The Goose Hangs High* (Boston, Mass., June 1925); Alan Dana, Jr., in *Young Blood* (Ritz, N.Y.C., Nov. 24, 1925); Alan Davis in *The Adorable Liar* (49 St. Th., Aug. 20, 1926); Cameron McDonald in *Trelawney of the Wells* (New Amsterdam, Jan. 31, 1927); Eddie Kane in *Excess Baggage* (Ritz, Dec. 26, 1927); Ed in *Exceeding Small* (Comedy, Oct. 22, 1928); Clement Corbin in *Before You're 25* (Maxine Elliott's Th., Apr. 16, 1929); Michael in *Cross Roads* (Morosco, Nov. 11, 1929); Mike Kelly in *Nigger Rich (The Big Shot)* (Royale, Sept. 20, 1929); Angel in *Penny Arcade* (Fulton, Mar. 19, 1930); a Herald from Sparta in *Lysistrata* (44 St. Th., June 5, 1930); Ronnie Van Horn in *Paging Danger* (Booth, Feb. 26, 1931); Peter Barret in *Adam's Wife* (Ritz, Dec. 28, 1931); succeeded (Feb. 1932) Henry Hull as Hubert Burnet in *The Bride the Sun Shines On* (Fulton, Dec. 26, 1931); appeared at the Westchester Playhouse (Mt. Kisco, N.Y., June 1932); and the Lakewood Th. (Skowhegan, Me., Apr. 1933).

Mr. Dressler played Ham Farnsworth in *All Good Americans* (Henry Miller's Th., N.Y.C., Dec. 5, 1933); Francis Battle in *The Joyous Season* (Belasco, Jan. 29, 1934); Bill Adams in *Are You Decent?* (Ambassador, Apr. 19, 1934); performed at a season at the Berkshire Playhouse (Stockbridge, Mass., June 1934); played Bob in *Good-bye Please* (Ritz, N.Y.C., Oct. 24, 1934); Scotty in *Creeping Fire* (Vanderbilt, Jan. 16, 1935); Alec Winstone in *The Dominant Sex* (Cort, Apr. 1, 1935); and Abram in *Squaring the Circle* (49 St. Th., Oct. 3, 1935).

He toured in *Boy Meets Girl* (opened Harris, Chicago, Ill., Jan. 1936); played Larry Haney in the tryout of *Punches and Judy* (Jackson Heights, N.Y., Oct. 1936); Francis Monfavet in *Little Dark Horse* (Westport Country Playhouse, Conn., July 1941); and Andrey Prozorov in *The Three Sisters* (Ethel Barrymore Th., N.Y.C., Dec. 21, 1942).

Television and Radio. Mr. Dressler performed on radio (1936–60); on television, appeared on The First Hundred Years (CBS); Golden Windows (ABC); The Edge of Night (CBS); and Search for Tomorrow (CBS).

DREXLER, ROSALYN. Playwright. b. Rosalyn Selma Bronznick, Nov. 25, 1926, Bronx, N.Y.C., to George B. and Hilda (Sherman) Bronznick. Father, pharmacist. Married 1946 to Sherman Drexler; one daughter, one son. Member of The New Dramatists; NY Theater Strategy; Dramatists Guild; P.E.N.; Actors Studio.

Pre-Theatre. Lady wrestler, masseuse, playground director, waitress, sculptress.

Theatre. Mrs. Drexler wrote *Home Movies* (Judson Memorial Church, N.Y.C., Mar. 19, 1964; moved to Provincetown Playhouse, May 11, 1964, and presented there on a double bill with *Softly, and Consider the Nearness,* written by Mrs. Drexler, with music by Al Carmines); *The Investigation* (Theatre Co. of Boston, Boston, Mass., Apr. 28, 1966); *Hot Buttered Roll* (Milwaukee Repertory Th., Milwaukee, Wis., Oct. 25, 1966); and *The Line of Least Existence* (Judson Memorial Ch., N.Y.C., Mar. 15, 1968). Her one-act play *Skywriting* was part of the bill of eleven one-act plays presented as *Collision Course* (Cafe Au Go-Go, May 8, 1968; moved to Actors Playhouse, June 4, 1968); and she also wrote *The Bed Was Full* (The Moving Co. at 46 Great Jones St., N.Y.C., Oct. 6, 1972); and *She Who Was He* (N.Y.C., 1973).

Night Clubs. Mrs. Drexler has appeared as a night club singer and sang in the revue *The Peaches* (Judson Garden, N.Y.C., Sept. 1973).

Other Activities. Mrs. Drexler's paintings have been exhibited at the Kornblee Gallery, N.Y.C.

Published Works. Mrs. Drexler wrote the novels *I Am the Beautiful Stranger* (1965); *One or Another* (1970); *To Smithereens* (1972); and *The Cosmopolitan Girl* (1975); and she has published short stories.

Awards. Mrs. Drexler's short story "Dear" won the *Paris Review* Fiction Prize (1966). She received a *Village Voice* off-Bway (Obie) Award (1965) for *Home Movies;* two Rockefeller Foundation grants (1965); and a Guggenheim Fellowship (1970).

DRIVAS, ROBERT. Actor. b. Robert Chris Drivas, Oct. 7, Chicago, Ill., to James and Harriet (Cunningham-Wright) Drivas. Attended Coral Gables (Fla.) H.S.; grad. Lake View H.S., Chicago, Ill.; attended Univ. of Chicago. Member of AEA; AFTRA; SAG.

Theatre. Mr. Drivas made his stage debut in stock as Danny in *Night Must Fall* (Coral Gables, Fla., 1957); subsequently appeared as Tom, Junior in the tryout of *Sweet Bird of Youth* (Actors Studio M, Miami, Fla., 1957); Tom Lee in *Tea and Sympathy* (Coconut Grove Playhouse, Miami, Fla., 1957); and at Highland Park Playhouse (Chicago, Ill., 1957), in *The Lady's Not for Burning; Death of a Salesman; Thieves Carnival;* and Rodolfo in *A View from the Bridge.*

He made his N.Y.C., debut as Rameses in *The Firstborn* (Coronet Th., Apr. 30, 1958); followed by Jacko in *One More River* (Ambassador, Mar. 18, 1960); Stefan Mazur in *The Wall* (Billy Rose Th., Oct. 11, 1960); Benny Rogers in *Diff'rent* (Mermaid, Oct. 17, 1961); Frankie in *Mrs. Dally Has a Lover* (Cherry Lane, Oct. 1, 1962); Giorgio in *Lorenzo* (Plymouth, Feb. 14, 1963); Andrew Rankin in *The Irregular Verb To Love* (Ethel Barrymore Th., Sept. 18, 1963); Sigfrid in *And Things That Go Bump in the Night* (Royale, Apr. 26, 1965); the Young Man in *Sweet Eros* (Gramercy Arts Th., Nov. 21, 1968); and Tommy Flowers in *Where Has Tommy Flowers Gone?* (Yale Rep. Th., New Haven, Conn., Jan. 7, 1971; Eastside Playhouse, N.Y.C., Oct. 7, 1971).

He directed *Bad Habits* (NY Th. Strategy, 1973; Astor Place Th., N.Y.C., Feb. 4, 1974; transferred to Booth Th., May 5, 1974); was Michael in *A Breeze from the Gulf* (Eastside Playhouse, Oct. 15, 1973); directed *The Ritz* (Longacre, Jan. 20, 1975), in which he also replaced (May 12–25, 1975) F. Murray Abraham as Chris; and he directed *Legend* (Ethel Barrymore Th., May 13, 1976).

Television. Mr. Drivas has appeared on Armstrong Circle Th. (NBC, 1958, 1959); US Steel Hour (CBS); The Defenders (CBS); East Side/West Side (CBS); Naked City (ABC); Route 66 (CBS); Young Dr. Malone; Camera Three (CBS); Look Up and Live (CBS); and The Eternal Light (NBC). He was in *The Irregular Verb To Love* (non-network, 1965); episodes of The F.B.I. (ABC, 1966, 1967, 1968, 1970, 1972); Felony Squad (ABC, 1966, 1967); Bonanza (NBC, 1968); and Hawaii Five-O (CBS, 1972); and he appeared as Gonorrhea in *VD Blues* (PBS, Oct. 9, 1972).

Awards. Mr. Drivas received the *Theatre World* Award (1963) and, for his direction of *Bad Habits,* a *Village Voice* Off-Bway (Obie) Award (1974) for distinguished direction.

DRIVER, TOM F. Critic, educator. b. Tom Faw Driver, May 31, 1925, Johnson City, Tenn., to Leslie R. and Sarah (Broyles) Driver. Father, banker. Grad. Bristol (Tenn.) H.S., 1943; Duke Univ., B.A. (Phi Beta Kappa) 1950; Union Theological Seminary, B.D. 1954; attended the Shakespeare Inst., Stratford-on-Avon, 1954; grad. Columbia Univ., Ph.D. 1957. Married June 7, 1952, to Anne Barstow, teacher; two daughters, one son. Served US Army, ETO, 1943–46; rank, Cpl. Member of Natl. Society for Religion in Higher Education; Foundation for Arts, Religion, and Culture; American Academy of Religion; Phi Kappa Phi; Omicron Delta Kappa. Address: (home) 606 W. 122nd St., New York, NY 10027, tel. (212) 662-8209; (bus.) 3041 Broadway, New York, NY 10027, tel. (212) MO 2-7100.

Mr. Driver, an ordained minister of the Methodist Church, is the Paul J. Tillich Professor of Theology and Culture at Union Theological Seminary.

There he directed the first American performance of D. H. Lawrence's *David* (Mar. 25, 1958) and the first N.Y.C. performance of *The Cup of Trembling* (Apr. 30, 1959) by Elizabeth Berryhill.

Mr. Driver was the leader of a traveling seminar on "The Theatre in Europe" (1960). He has been visiting professor of Religion at Barnard College and Fordham University, and visiting professor of drama at Columbia University. He lectures widely and has appeared on numerous television programs. His oratorio, *The Invisible Fire,* was produced on the air with the CBS Symphony Orchestra.

Published Works. He wrote *The Sense of History in Greek and Shakespearean Drama* (1960); the introduction to *Oedipus the King* (1961); *History of the Modern Theater* (1970); was editor, with Robert Pack, of *Poems of Belief and Doubt: An Anthology of Modern Religious Verse* (1964); and has contributed articles and reviews to the New York *Times, The Shakespeare Quarterly, The Christian Century, The Nation, The New Republic, The Reporter, Christianity and Crisis, Religion and Life, Tulane Drama Review, The Christian Scholar, Union Seminary Quarterly Review* and *Motive magazine.*

He was drama critic for station WBAI-FM (N.Y.C., 1960–61).

Awards. Mr. Driver was awarded a Kent Fellowship (1953) and a Guggenheim Fellowship (1962), and received an honorary D.Litt. degree from Denison University in 1970.

Recreation. Skiing, photography.

DRULIE, SYLVIA. Producer, theatrical investment executive. b. Jan. 28, 1928, Belmont, Mass., to Elias Anthony and Ethel (Ratsey) Drulie. Father, retailer. Grad. Tufts Coll., A.B. (magna cum laude) 1948. Married Mar. 7, 1959, to John W. Mazzola, Managing Director of the Lincoln Center for the Performing Arts; two daughters. Comm. member of WNET Channel 13; member of Misquamicut Golf Club (R.I.); Watch Hill Yacht Club (R.I.). Address: 12 Beekman Pl., New York, NY 10022, tel. (212) PL 5-5117.

Pre-Theatre. Charitable and political work.

Theatre. Miss Drulie was production assistant for the pre-Bway tryout of *Reuben Reuben* (opened Shubert Th., Boston, Mass., Oct. 10, 1955; closed there Oct. 22, 1955); *Mr. Johnson* (Martin Beck Th., N.Y.C., Mar. 29, 1956); the pre-Bway tryout of *Build with One Hand* (opened Shubert, New Haven, Conn., Nov. 7, 1956; closed Ford's Baltimore, Md., Nov. 27, 1956); and for *The Sin of Pat Muldoon* (Cort, N.Y.C., Mar. 13, 1957).

She was associate producer of *Livin' the Life* (Phoenix, N.Y.C., Apr. 27, 1957); *West Side Story* (Winter Garden, Sept. 26, 1957); *Music Man* (Majestic, Dec. 19, 1957); *Oh, Captain!* (Alvin, Feb. 4, 1958); Wild West Show and Rodeo (Brussels World's Fair, Belg., 1958); and *The Gang's All Here* (Ambassador, N.Y.C., Oct. 1, 1959).

With Bowden, Barr & Bullock, Miss Drulie produced a tour of *Auntie Mame* (American Shakespeare Th., Stratford, Conn., Apr. 19, 1958; N.Y. City Ctr., Aug. 11, 1958).

Recreation. Raising children.

DRYE, JOHN W., JR. Lawyer. b. John Wilson Drye, Jr., May 28, 1900, Van Alstyne, Tex., to John Wilson and Elizabeth (Cave) Drye. Attended Valparaiso Univ., 1917–18; Univ. of Michigan, 1918; grad. Washington and Lee Univ., LL.B. 1920. Married Oct. 26, 1926, to Loraine Caldwell; one son, one daughter. Served US Army, 1918. Member of American Bar Assn.; NY State Bar Assn.; N.Y.C. Bar Assn.; Sigma Chi; Phi Delta Phi; Knickerbocker Club; Racquet & Tennis Club; Nassau Country Club; Burlington Country Club. Address: (home) 940 Park Ave., New York, NY 10028, tel. (212) BU 8-6024; (bus.) 350 Park Ave., New York, NY 10022, tel. (212) PL 2-5800.

Mr. Drye is a director emeritus of the Lincoln Center for the Performing Arts, Inc., and a director of the Metropolitan Opera; former chairman of the board, and now director of Juilliard School of Music; and president and trustee of the Juilliard Musical Foundation.

Other Activities. He is a partner in the law firm of Kelley, Drye, Newhall, Maginnes & Warren (N.Y.C.).

Awards. Mr. Drye received an honorary LL.D. from Washington and Lee University (1956).

DUBEY, MATT. Lyricist. b. Matthew David Dubinsky, Jan. 20, 1928, Philadelphia, Pa., to Joseph and Dora (Davidson) Dubinsky. Father, paper merchant. Attended Germantown H.S., Philadelphia, 1942–45; grad. Milford (Conn.) Prep. Sch., 1946; Univ. of Miami, B.B.A. 1950. Married 1970 to Jan Anderson. Member of ASCAP, AGAC Council; Dramatists Guild; writing staff at Frank Music; Mason, Phi Epsilon Pi. Address: (home) 25 Central Park West, New York, NY 10023, tel. (212) CI 6-7214; (bus.) 2601 Parkway, Philadelphia, PA tel. (215) PO 9-4550.

Theatre. Mr. Dubey was first a lyricist for songs in the revue, *New Faces of '56* (Ethel Barrymore Th., N.Y.C., July 4, 1956); subsequently wrote the lyrics for *Happy Hunting* (Majestic, Dec. 6, 1956); the lyrics and book, with Felice Bauer, for the pre-Bway tryout of *We Take the Town* (opened Shubert, New Haven, Conn., Feb. 19, 1962; closed Shubert, Philadelphia, Pa., Mar. 17, 1962); the music, lyrics, and book, with Dean Fuller and Tony Hendra, for *Smith* (Eden Th., N.Y.C., May 19, 1973).

Television. Mr. Dubey wrote the lyrics for "The Song of the Sewer" (Jackie Gleason Show, CBS, 1954) and "Spooks" (Arthur Godfrey Show, CBS, 1955).

Night Clubs. He wrote the lyrics for *After Hours,* a night club revue which played in East-coast clubs. (Jan. 1952); for the revue, *Phil Moore and His Flock* (La Vie en Rose, N.Y.C. Sept. 1953); for the production numbers at the Copacabana (N.Y.C., Jan. 1953), and at the Sands Hotel, (Las Vegas, Nev., 1955). He has also written special material for Lena Horne and Pearl Bailey.

Recreation. Words.

DUCLOW, GERALDINE. Theatre librarian. b. Geraldine Anne Hodzima, Sept. 20, 1946, Chicago, Ill., to Steve, Jr., and Irene (Halat) Hodzima. Father, sales representative. Grad. Madonna H.S., Chicago, 1963; DePaul Univ., B.A. (magna cum laude) 1967; Rosary Coll., River Forest, Ill., M.L.S. 1968. Married July 11, 1969, to Donald F. Duclow. Member of Penn. Library Assn.; Theatre Library Assn.; Philadelphia Drama Guild (research staff, 1972–to date). Address: (home) 257 S. 16th St., Philadelphia, PA 19103, tel. (215) KI 5-5293; (bus.) Free Library of Philadelphia, Logan Circle, Philadelphia, PA 19103, tel. (215) MU 6-5427.

Prior to her assignment as librarian-in-charge (1972–to date) of the Theatre Collection of the Free Library of Philadelphia, Mrs. Duclow served as reference librarian for the Literature Dept. of that institution (1969–71), and for the Chicago Public Library (1968–69).

Recreation. Art, needlework, horticulture.

DUERR, EDWIN. Director, educator, writer. b. Feb. 21, 1906, Las Vegas, N.M., to Frank H. and Celia (Connell) Duerr. Father, railroad foreman. Grad. Oakland (Calif.) H.S., 1922; Univ. of California at Berkeley, A.B. 1926; Cornell Univ., M.A. 1931. Address: 10906 Cord Ave., Downey, CA 90241, tel. (213) TO 2-4931.

Mr. Duerr was instructor of English, public speaking and theatre, Univ. of Nevada (1926–30); director of Little Th., Univ. of California at Berkeley (1931–40); assistant professor of theatre, Western Reserve Univ. (1940–43); guest lecturer on playwriting (Carnegie Tech, 1943); and associate professor and professor of Theatre, California State Univ. at Fullerton (1964–74). He is now retired.

Television and Radio. Mr. Duerr was director and producer of radio and television programs for the advertising agencies Young & Rubicam, Inc. (1943–52) and Dancer, Fitzgerald, Sample, Inc. (1952–55); and producer and director of the radio shows The Aldrich Family (seven years); Second Mrs. Burton; Valiant Lady; Young Dr. Malone; Mystery Theatre; and Silver Theatre.

Published Works. Mr. Duerr wrote *Radio and Television Acting* (1950); *The Length and Depth of Acting* (1962); has contributed articles to *Theatre Arts* Magazine and *Quarterly Journal of Speech;* written plays, including *Return to Laughter; Doctor for a Dumb Wife;* an adaptation of *The Tower Beyond Tragedy* by Robinson Jeffers; and translated Molière's *Tartuffe* and Giraudoux's *Intermezzo.*.

DUERRENMATT, FRIEDRICH. Playwright, novelist. b. Jan. 5, 1921, Konolfingen, Switzerland, to Reinhold and Hulda (Zimmermann) Dürrenmatt. Father, clergyman. Educated in Gymnasium, Bern; Univ. of Bern; Univ. of Zurich (art, philosophy). Married 1946 to Lotti Geissler, actress; three children. Address: c/o Kurt Hellmer, 52 Vanderbilt Ave., New York, NY 10017.

Pre-Theatre. Painter.

Theatre. Mr. Duerrenmatt's first play produced in N.Y.C. was *Fools Are Passing Through,* adapted by Maximilian Slater (Jan Hus House, Apr. 2, 1958); followed by *The Visit,* adapted by Maurice Valency (Lunt-Fontanne, May 5, 1958); and *The Deadly Game,* adapted by James Yaffe from Mr. Duerrenmatt's novel *Traps* (Longacre, Feb. 2, 1960). Other American premieres of Mr. Duerrenmatt's work include *The Marriage of Mr. Mississippi,* adapted from the same play as *Fools Are Passing Through* (Actor's Workshop, Marine Th., San Francisco, Calif., May 14, 1960); *Romulus,* adapted by Gore Vidal (Music Box, N.Y.C., Jan. 10, 1962); *An Angel Comes to Babylon,* translated by George White, at the Univ. of California at Berkeley (William Randolph Hearst Greek Th., Sept. 27, 1962); *The Physicists* (Martin Beck Th., N.Y.C., Oct. 13, 1964); and *Play Strindberg* (Forum, Lincoln Ctr., N.Y.C., June 3, 1971).

Mr. Duerrenmatt's first play produced professionally was *Es steht geschrieben* (Schauspielhaus, Zurich, Switzerland, Apr. 19, 1947); followed by *Der Blinde* (Basel, Jan. 10, 1948); *Romulus der Grosse* (Gottingen, Germany, Oct. 1948); *Die Ehe des Herrn Mississippi* (Munich, Germany, Mar. 26, 1952) and, translated and adapted by Eric Peters and Robert Schnorr as *The Marriage of Mr. Mississippi* (Arts, London, England, Sept. 30, 1959); *Nachtliches Gesprach mit einem verachteten Menschen* (Kammerspiele, Munich, Germany, July 1952) and translated by Robert David MacDonald as *Conversation at Night with a Despised Man* (Watford Civic Trust, the Palace, Watford, England, July 19, 1966); and *Ein engel kommt nach Babylon* (Kammerspiele, Munich, Germany, Dec. 22, 1953).

Mr. Duerrenmatt's *Der besuch der altendame* (Scauspielhaus, Zurich, Switzerland, Jan. 29, 1956), presented as *The Visit* in N.Y.C. (see above) and in London (Royalty, June 23, 1960), was followed by *Frank V* (Schauspielhaus, Mar. 19, 1959); *Die Physiker* (Schauspielhaus, Feb. 21, 1962), presented as *The Physicists* in an adaptation by James Kirkup in London (Aldwych, Jan. 9, 1963) and in N.Y.C. (see above); *Herkules und der Stall des Augias* (Schauspielhaus, Mar. 20, 1963), translated by Alexander Gross into English as *Hercules and the Augean Stables* (Quester's Th., Ealing, England, Mar. 19, 1966); and *Der Meteor* (Schauspielhaus, Jan. 20, 1966), translated by James Kirkup into English as *The Meteor* and presented in London (Aldwych, July 28, 1966). Later plays are *Die Wiedertaufer,* a revised version of *Es steht geschrieben* (Schauspielhaus, Mar. 16, 1967); *König Johan* (Stadttheater, Basel, 1968); *Play Strindberg* (Stadttheater, Feb. 9, 1969), later presented in N.Y.C. (see above); *Titus Andronicus* (Schauspielhaus, Dusseldorf, Germany, 1970); *Porträt eines Planeten* (Dusseldorf, 1970); and *Der Mitmacher* (Zurich, Switzerland, 1973).

Films. Mr. Duerrenmatt's novel *The Pledge* was made into the film *It Happened in Broad Daylight* (Continental, 1960), and his play *The Visit* into a film of the same title (20th-Fox, 1964). *Grieche sucht Griechin* has also been filmed.

Television and Radio. Mr. Duerrenmatt wrote several plays for radio, including *Der Doppelgänger* (1946), *Der Prozess um des Esels Schatten* (1951), *Stranitzky und der Nationalheld* (1952), *Nächtliches Gesprach* (1952), *Das Unternehmen der Wega* (1954), *Herkules und der Stall des Augias* (1954), later done for the stage, *Abendstunde im Spätherbst* (1956), and *Die Panne* (1956).

Die Ehe des Herrn Mississippi was presented on television as was a dramatization of Mr. Duerrenmatt's novel, *The Judge and His Hangman* (Studio One, CBS, 1956) and an adaptation of *The Deadly Game* (Suspicion, NBC, Dec. 1957). Mr. Duerrenmatt appeared on *Author at Work* (Goodyear Th., NBC, 1960).

Published Works. Mr. Duerrenmatt's novels include *The Judge and His Hangman,* translated into English by Therese Pol (1955) from the German, entitled *Der Richter undsein Henker,* edited by William Gillis and John J. Newmaier (1961); *The Pledge* translated into English by Richard and Clara Winston (1959); *Traps,* translated by Richard and Clara Winston (1960); and *The Quarry,* translated into English by Eva H. Morreale (1962).

His other writings include *Gerechtigkeit und Recht; Friedrich Schiller; Der Sturz; Theaterprobleme* (1955); *Grieche sucht Griechin* (1961); and *Theatre-Schriften und Reden I, II* (1966).

Awards. For *Die Panne,* Mr. Duerrenmatt received the Prize of the War Blind in 1956 and the literature prize of the *Tribune de Lausanne* in 1958. In 1958, he also received the Prix d'Italia for *Abendstunde im Spätherbst;* in 1959, he was awarded the NY Critics Prize, the Schiller Prize of the city of Mannheim, Germany, and a citation from the city of Bern, Switzerland, for *The Pledge;* and in 1960, he received the prize of the Swiss Schiller Foundation.

DUKAKIS, OLYMPIA. Actress. Grad. Boston Univ. Married to Louis Zorich, actor. Member of AEA; SAG; AFTRA.

Theatre. Miss Dukakis is a founding member of the Charles St. Playhouse (Boston, Mass.), and there gained her earliest professional theatre experience. She appeared in summer stock (Williamstown, Mass.); played Madelena in *The Breaking Wall* (St. Mark's Playhouse, N.Y.C., Jan. 25, 1960); toured with the Phoenix Co. (1960); appeared in *The New Tenant* (Royal Playhouse, N.Y.C., Mar. 9, 1960); with the Second City Co.; appeared in *The Opening of a Window* (Th. Marquee, Sept. 25, 1961); played Widow Leocadia Begbick in *A Man's a Man* (Masque, Sept. 19, 1962); Mary Tyrone in *Long Day's Journey into Night* (McCarter Th., Princeton, N.J., Oct. 1962); Henriette in *Crime and Crime*

(Cricket, N.Y.C., Dec. 16, 1963); played Anne Dowling and understudied Nancy Wickwire in *Abraham Cochrane* (Belasco, Feb. 17, 1964); appeared in *Six Characters in Search of an Author* (Charles St. Playhouse, Boston, Mar. 11, 1964); for the NY Shakespeare Fest., played Chrysothemis in *Electra* (Delacorte, N.Y.C., Aug. 11, 1964); appeared in *The Rose Tattoo* (Studio Arena, Buffalo, Nov. 18, 1965); for the Charles St. Playhouse (Boston) played Madama Irma in *The Balcony* (Nov. 3, 1966), Gertrude in *Hamlet* (Dec. 15, 1966), and the title role in *Mother Courage and Her Children* (Jan. 26, 1967); for the N.Y. Shakespeare Fest., played Tamora in *Titus Andronicus* (Delacorte, N.Y.C., Aug. 2, 1967); Mrs. Bethnal-Green, the Mother, Stepney Green, and Debden in *Father Uxbridge Wants to Marry* (American Place Th. at St. Clement's, Oct. 28, 1967); Helena in *The Memorandum* (Public, Mar. 23, 1968); Ingrid in *Peer Gynt* (Delacorte, July 8, 1969); Goya in *Baba Goya* (Amer. Place Th., May 9, 1973) which was retitled *Nourish the Beast* and reopened (Cherry Lane Th., Oct. 3, 1973); and Ilse in *Who's Who in Hell* (Lunt-Fontanne, Dec. 9, 1974).

Films. She made her film debut in *Twice a Man* (Markopolous, 1964); and appeared in *John and Mary* (20th-Fox, 1969); and *Made for Each Other* (20th-Fox, 1971).

Television. Miss Dukakis' credits include the Ed Sullivan Show (CBS); The Nurses; Dr. Kildare; CBS Workshop; and Wayne and Shuster.

Awards. Miss Dukakis received the Off-Bway (Obie) Award (1963) for her performance in *A Man's a Man.*

DUKE, PATTY. Actress. b. Anna Marie Patty Duke, Dec. 14, 1946, New York, N.Y., to John and Frances (McMahon) Duke. Father, taxi driver; mother, secretary. Grad. Quintanos Sch. for Young Professionals, 1964; coached by John Ross. Married Nov. 25, 1965, to Harry Falk, Jr., television director (marr. dis., 1970); married June 25, 1970, to Mike Tell, concert promoter (marr. dis. 1971); married to Joseph Stitch (marr. dis.); married to John Astin, actor. Member of AEA; AFTRA; SAG; Muscular Dystrophy Assn. (past jr. chairman).

Theatre. Miss Duke made her stage debut at eight; her Bway debut as Helen Keller in *The Miracle Worker* (Playhouse, Oct. 19, 1959); and played Deirdre Striden in *Isle of Children* (Cort, Mar. 16, 1962).

Films. Miss Duke has appeared in *The Goddess* (Col., 1958); subsequently appeared in *Happy Anniversary* (UA, 1959); *The Miracle Worker* (UA, 1962); played the title role of Billie Carol in *Billie* (UA, 1965); did the voice of Thumbelina in *The Daydreamer* (Embassy, 1966); and appeared in *Valley of the Dolls* (20th-Fox, 1967); and *Me, Natalie* (Natl. Gen., 1969).

Television. Miss Duke has appeared in *The Power and the Glory; Meet Me in St. Louis; The Prince and the Pauper; Wuthering Heights; The Swiss Family Robinson;* on the Dupont-Show-of-the-Month (CBS); Armstrong Circle Th. (NBC); Studio One (CBS); Ben Casey (ABC); Wide Country; US Steel Hour (CBS); and her own series, the Patty Duke Show (ABC).

Her subsequent appearances include The Jimmy Dean Show (ABC); The World of Entertainment (ABC); Wonderama (Ind.); The Ernie Ford Show (ABC); Shindig (ABC); Wide Country (Ind.); Ben Casey (ABC); The Perry Como Show (NBC); The Mike Douglas Show (ABC); The Virginian (NBC); *My Sweet Charlie* (MCA-TV); and *You'll Like My Mother* (MCA-TV).

Awards. Miss Duke received the Academy (Oscar) Award for her portrayal of Helen Keller in *The Miracle Worker* (1962); and the Golden Globe Award from the Hollywood Foreign Press Assn. for her performance in *The Miracle Worker* (1963).

Recreation. Horseback riding, skin diving, swimming, boating.

DUKE, ROBERT. Actor. b. Robert Wilkinson Duke, June 22, 1917, Washington, D.C., to Casco Godey and Lois Gwendolyn Duke. Father, in automobile business. Grad. Central H.S., Washington, D.C., 1935; attended American Univ., 1935–1936. Studied with Elizabeth B. Grimball at NY Sch. of the Theatre, 1936–38; with Frieda Richard and with Harold Kreutzberg, at the Mozarteum, Salzburg, Austria, certificate 1937. Member of AEA; AFTRA; SAG; ALA. Address: 233 Mclain St., Bedford Hills, NY 10507, tel. (914) 666-2501.

Pre-Theatre. Teacher; manager of a bookshop.

Theatre. Mr. Duke made his stage debut in *The Romancers* (Central H.S. Drama Club, Washington, D.C., 1932); his first professional appearance as Thad Jennings in a stock production of *Pursuit of Happiness* (Woodstock Playhouse, N.Y., 1938); was stage manager for *No Answer* (Nora Bayes Th., N.Y.C., 1939); appeared in *Blessed Are the Debonair* (Barbizon Plaza Hotel, 1939); and with John Carradine's Shakespearean Repertory Co., playing Laertes in *Hamlet,* Gratiano in *The Merchant of Venice* and Iago in *Othello* (West Coast tour included Geary Th., San Francisco, Calif., 1942–43).

He played Prince Rashid in *My Indian Family* (Stanford Univ., Palo Alto, Calif., 1944); a Brother in a tour of *The Barretts of Wimpole Street* (1946); Florizel in *The Winter's Tale* (Cort, N.Y.C., Jan. 15, 1946); Dolabella in *Antony and Cleopatra* (Martin Beck Th., Nov. 26, 1947); the Earl of Northumberland in *Anne of the Thousand Days* (Shubert, Dec. 8, 1948); Paris in *Romeo and Juliet* (Broadhurst, Mar. 10, 1951); and James in *Gertie* (Plymouth, Jan. 30, 1952).

He played Paul D'Argenson in *Sabrina Fair* (National, Nov. 11, 1953); succeeded (May 1955) Hurd Hatfield as Prince Paul in *Anastasia* (Lyceum, Dec. 9, 1954), and played the role in the national tour (opened Ford's Th., Baltimore, Md., Sept. 26, 1955); played the Reverend Alfred Brand in *Eugenia* (Ambassador, N.Y.C., Jan. 30, 1957); Andrew McNeil in *Miss Isobel* (Royale, Dec. 26, 1957); was standby for Noel Willman as the Husband in *Rashomon* (Music Box, Jan. 27, 1959); was standby for Laurence Olivier as Henry II in *Becket* (St. James, Oct. 5, 1960); played the Young Man in *The Madwoman of Chaillot* and the Assistant in *Once More, With Feeling* (Palm Beach Th., Fla., 1960).

Films. Mr. Duke appeared in *An Angel Comes to Brooklyn* (Rep., 1945), and in *Le Traque* (Joinville, 1950).

Television. In 1930 Mr. Duke performed in a television experiment, appearing in a scene from *High Tor* that was transmitted from a studio in the Grand Central building, N.Y.C., for a distance of two blocks. He later appeared as the Husband in *Flowers From a Stranger* (Studio One, CBS, 1949); and from 1952 to 1961, appeared on Studio One (CBS); Omnibus (CBS); Westinghouse Th. (CBS); and Robert Montgomery Presents (NBC).

DULLEA, KEIR. Actor. b. May 30, 1936, Cleveland, Ohio, to Robert and Margaret (Ruttain) Dullea. Father, bookshop owner. Attended Rutgers Univ.; San Francisco State Coll. Professional training at Neighborhood Playhouse, N.Y.C. (Sanford Meisner, Martha Graham). Married 1960 Margo Bennett, actress (marr. dis.); married 1969 to Susan Lessane. Address: c/o Bresler, Wolff, Cota, and Livingston, 190 N. Canon Dr., Beverly Hills, CA 90210.

Theatre. Mr. Dullea began his acting career in the mid-1950s with five years of summer stock, during which he had parts in about fifty plays. He made his N.Y.C. debut as Timmie Redwin in the off-Bway *Season of Choice* (Barbizon-Plaza Th., N.Y.C., Apr. 13, 1959); played Nick, the young Ernest Hemingway, in *A Short Happy Life* (opened Moore Th., Seattle, Wash., Sept. 12, 1961; closed Huntington Hartford Th., Hollywood, Calif., Oct. 23, 1961); made his Bway debut as Dr. Jim Tennyson in *Dr. Cook's Garden* (Belasco Th., N.Y.C., Sept. 25, 1967); toured Eastern summer theatres in *The Star-Spangled Girl* (Summer 1968); played Don Baker in *Butterflies Are Free* (Booth Th., N.Y.C., Oct. 21, 1969); was Brick in a revival of *Cat on a Hot Tin Roof* (Amer. Shakespeare Th., Stratford, Conn., July 10, 1974; ANTA Th., N.Y.C., Sept. 24, 1974); and Jimmy in *P.S. Your Cat Is Dead* (world premiere: Studio Arena, Buffalo, N.Y., Mar. 6, 1975; Golden Th., N.Y.C., Apr. 7, 1975).

Films. Mr. Dullea's films include *The Hoodlum Priest* (UA, 1961); *David and Lisa* (Continental, 1962); *The Thin Red Line* (Allied Artists, 1964); *Mail Order Bride* (MGM, 1964); *Bunny Lake Is Missing* (Col., 1965); *Madame X* (U, 1966); *The Fox* (WB-7 Arts, 1967); *2001: A Space Odyssey* (MGM, 1968); *De Sade* (Amer. Internatl., 1969); and *Paperback Hero* (Rumson Films, 1975).

Television. Programs on which Mr. Dullea has appeared include a pilot for Route 66 (CBS) and episodes of Naked City (ABC); Bonanza (NBC); Channing (ABC); and 12 O'Clock High (ABC). He had roles in US Steel Hour (CBS) productions, including *The Big Splash* (Feb. 8, 1961); *The Golden Thirty* (Aug. 9, 1961); *Far From the Shade Tree* (Jan. 1962); and *The Young Avengers* (Jan. 9, 1963); and on Alcoa Premiere (ABC), including *People Need People* (Oct. 10, 1961); *Tiger* (Mar. 20, 1962); *Ordeal in Darkness* (Nov. 15, 1962); and *The Broken Year* (Apr. 4, 1964).

He also was in *Mrs. Miniver* (CBS, Jan. 7, 1960); *Give Us Barabbas* (Hallmark Hall of Fame, NBC, Mar. 26, 1961); *All Summer Long* (Play of the Week, Ind., May 1, 1961); *Pale Horse, Pale Rider* (CBC, 1963); *Black Water Gold* (ABC Movie of the Week, Jan. 1970); and *Montserrat* (Hollywood Television Th., PBS, Mar. 2, 1971).

Awards. Mr. Dullea received the best actor award at the 1962 San Francisco Film Festival for his performance in *David and Lisa,* and in 1970 he received the "Star of the Season" Award from the March of Dimes Committee for his performance in *Butterflies Are Free.*

Du MAURIER, DAPHNE. Writer, playwright. b. May 13, 1907. London, England, to Sir Gerald and Muriel (Beaumont) du Maurier. Father, actor; mother, actress. Privately educated in Hampstead and London; in Meudon and Paris, France. Married July 19, 1932, to Sir Frederick Arthur Montague Browning (dec. 1965); one son, two daughters. Member of the Council of the Society of Authors; Royal Society of Literature (Fellow). Address: (home) Kilmarth, Par., Cornwall, England tel. PAR 2766; (bus.) Curtis Brown, Ltd., 1 Craven Hill, London, W.2, England.

Theatre. Miss du Maurier's stage adaptation of her novel, *Rebecca,* was produced in London (Queen's Th., Apr. 5, 1940), and in N.Y.C. (Ethel Barrymore Th., Jan. 18, 1945); followed by her plays *The Years Between* (Wyndham's, London, Jan. 10, 1945); and *September Tide* (Aldwych, Dec. 15, 1948).

Published Works. Miss du Maurier wrote *The Loving Spirit* (1931); *I'll Never Be Young Again* (1932); *The Progress of Julius* (1933); a biography of her father, *Gerald: A Portrait* (1934); *Jamaica Inn* (1936); a history of her family, *The Du Mauriers* (1937); *Rebecca* (1938); *Happy Christmas* (1940); *Frenchman's Creek* (1941); *Come Wind, Come Weather* (1941); *Hungry Hill* (1943); *The King's General* (1946); *The Parasites* (1949); *The Young George du Maurier: Letters 1860–67* (1951); *My Cousin Rachel* (1952); collections of short stories, *Kiss Me Again, Stranger* (1952) and *The Apple Tree* (1952); *Mary Anne* (1954); *The Scapegoat* (1957); *The Breaking Point* (1958); *The Infernal World of Branwell Bronte* (1961); with Arthur T. Quiller Couch, *Castle Dor* (1962); *The Glass-Blowers* (1963); *The Flight of the Falcon,* (1965); *Vanishing Cornwall* (1967); *The House on the Strand* (1969); *Not After Midnight* (1970); and *Rule Britannia* (1972).

Awards. Miss du Maurier received the National Book Award for her novel *Rebecca* (1938). She is a Fellow of the Royal Society of Literature and was made a Dame of the British Empire (D.B.E.) in 1969.

Recreation. Walking, swimming.

DUNCAN, ANGUS. Theatre executive. b. Oct. 1, 1912, to Augustin and Margherita (Sargent) Duncan. Father, actor and director; mother, actress. Attended Dalton Sch. and H.S., N.Y.C., 1923–27, and Trinity H.S., N.Y.C., 1927–30. Studied acting with father. Married June 13, 1942, to Dorothy A. Borner; one son, one daughter. Served US Army, 1943–45, ETO. Member of The Players.

From 1952 until his retirement in 1972, Mr. Duncan was the executive secretary of Actors' Equity Association (AEA). Before joining the Equity staff he was an actor and stage manager (1932–41).

He has been vice-president of the Associated Actors and Artistes of America (AAAA); a member of Theatre Authority, Inc.; American Th. Wing; a member of the NY State Council of the Arts; and board and executive committee member of the American National Theatre and Academy (ANTA).

DUNCAN, TODD. Singer, actor. b. Robert Todd Duncan, Feb. 12, 1903, Danville, Ky., to John C. and Lettie (Cooper) Duncan. Father, mechanic; mother, piano teacher. Grad. Butler Univ., A.B. 1925; Columbia Univ., M.A. 1930; Valparaiso Univ., D.H.L. 1950; Central State Coll., Ph.D. Mus. 1957; Howard Univ., Ph.D. Mus. 1958. Married 1934 to Gladys Jackson; one son. Member of Alpha Phi Alpha.

Pre-Theatre. Assistant professor of music at Howard Univ., Washington, D.C.

Theatre. Mr. Duncan made his debut as Alfio in *Cavalleria Rusticana* (Mecca Temple, N.Y.C., 1934); then played Porgy in *Porgy and Bess* (Alvin Th., Oct. 10, 1935); and toured California in the same role (1937); played Bosambo in *The Sun Never Sets* (Drury Lane, London, England, June 19, 1939); the Lawd's General in *Cabin in the Sky* (Martin Beck Th., N.Y.C., Oct. 25, 1940); and twice repeated his performance as Porgy in *Porgy and Bess* (Majestic, Jan. 22, 1942; 44 St. Th., Sept. 13, 1943).

Mr. Duncan appeared in the roles of Tonio in *Pagliacci* and Escamillo in *Carmen* (NY City Ctr., Sept. 1945); and played Stephan Kumalo in *Lost in the Stars* (Music Box, Oct. 30, 1949).

Mr. Duncan made more than 1,500 concert appearances under Columbia Artists management including tours of Europe, South America, the US, and Australia, between 1944 and his retirement, which followed his singing in 1965 at the Pres. Lyndon B. Johnson inaugural concert.

Films. He appeared in *Syncopation* (RKO, 1942) and played Joe in *Unchained* (WB, 1955).

Awards. For his performance as Stephen Kumalo in *Lost in the Stars,* Mr. Duncan received the Donaldson Award (1950); and shared the NY Drama Critics Award (1950) with Georges Guetary.

DUNHAM, KATHERINE. Dancer, producer, choreographer, writer. b. Chicago, Ill., to Albert Millard and Annette (Poindexter) Dunham. Father, choral singer. Grad. Joliette (Ill.) Township H.S.; Univ. of Chicago, Ph.B.; attended Northwestern Univ., 1935. Married July 10, 1941, to John Thomas Pratt, theatrical designer; one daughter. Member of AGMA (bd. of gov.); AGVA; AFRA; AEA; Negro Actors Guild; Sigma Epsilon; The Royal Society of Anthropology (London); ASCP. Address: Dunham School, 440–442 W. 42nd St., New York, NY 10036, tel. (212) LO 5-8870.

Pre-Theatre. Research student of social anthropology.

Theatre. Miss Dunham first appeared as a dancer with the Chicago (Ill.) Opera Co. (1933–36); subsequently danced at the Chicago World's Fair (1934); and in the ballet, *L'Ag'ya,* for the Federal Th. (WPA) project (Great Northern Th., Chicago, Ill., 1938); became supervisor of the City Theatre Writer's Project on Cultural Studies (1939); and dance director of the Labor Stage (N.Y.C., 1939–40).

She made her debut as Georgia Brown in *Cabin in the Sky* (Martin Beck Th., Oct. 25, 1940); toured the US with her own company in *Tropical Revue* (1943–44); was guest artist with San Francisco (Calif.) Symphony Orchestra (1943) and the Los Angeles (Calif.) Symphony Orchestra (1955); co-staged, and was choreographer of *Carib Song,* in which she also appeared (Adelphi, N.Y.C., Sept. 27, 1945); choreographed the pre-Bway tryout of *Windy City* (opened Shubert, New Haven, Conn., Apr. 18, 1946; closed Great Northern, Chicago, Ill., June 6, 1946); and performed in her own production, *Bal Negre* (Belasco, N.Y.C., Nov. 7, 1946).

In 1947, Miss Dunham and her troupe began appearing internationally and since then have filled engagements all over the world. In 1948, she appeared in her own productions, *Bal Negre* and *New Tropical Revue* (Prince of Wales's, London, England, June–Nov. 1948; Paris, France, Nov. 1948–Jan. 1949).

Miss Dunham provided choreography for operatic productions (Colon Opera, Buenos Aires, Argentina, 1950; Santiago de Chile Opera, 1950); toured Australia (1957) and made a world tour (1957–62); presented her new production *Bamboche* (Huntington Hartford Th., Los Angeles, Calif., Aug. 20, 1962; 54 St. Th., N.Y.C., Oct. 22, 1962); choreographed a new production of *Aida* (Metropolitan Opera House, 1962).

Films. She has appeared in *Carnival of Rhythm* (1941); *Star Spangled Rhythm* (Par., 1942); *Stormy Weather* (20th-Fox, 1943); *Casbah* (U, 1948); and *Mambo* (Par., 1955). She choreographed dances for *Pardon My Sarong* (U, 1942).

Television. Miss Dunham has written scripts which have been produced in Mexico, Australia, France, England, and Italy.

Other Activities. Miss Dunham founded (1943) and was president of the Katherine Dunham Sch. of Cultural Arts, N.Y.C. She served as a US State Dept. adviser on the 1st World Festival of Negro Arts (Dakar, Senegal, 1966); was artistic and technical adviser to the president of Senegal (1966–67); and artist-in-residence at Southern Illinois Univ. (1967).

Published Works. She wrote *Journey to Accompong* (1949); *Dances of Haiti* (1949, 1959), *Touch of Innocence* (1959, 1960); and has contributed short stories and articles to *Esquire, Mademoiselle, Show, Ellery Queen Mystery Magazine, Dance Magazine, Réalités, Travel,* and *Anthropology of American Negro.*

Awards. Miss Dunham is a Chevalier (1950) and Commander (1962) of the Haitian Legion of Honor and Merit and holds an honorary membership in the Women Scientists Fraternity (1939).

Recreation. Steam baths, horseback, riding, cooking, painting (her work has been shown in Sydney, Australia; Milan, Italy; London, England).

DUNN, RALPH. Actor. b. Ralph Alexander Dunn, May 23, 1900, Titusville, Pa., to Ralph Alexander and Anne (Lowry) Dunn. Father, veterinarian; mother, actress. Grad. Colonial Beach (Va.) H.S., 1917. Married July 6, 1945, to Miriam Ruth Lickert, harpist; two sons. Member of AEA (member of nominating committee, 1957–59); SAG; AFTRA; The Lambs.

Theatre. Mr. Dunn made his stage debut with J. A. Coburn's Minstrels (1917); subsequently appeared as a member of the vaudeville teams of Doyle and Dunn and Kemper and Dunn (1920–35); toured in *The Student Prince, Blossom Time* and *My Maryland;* made his Bway debut succeeding Arthur Vinton as Babe, the Photographer, in *Chicago* (Music Box, Dec. 30, 1926); played Jack Stewart in *The Seventh Heart* (Mayfair, May 2, 1927); Captain Hoster in *An Enemy of the People* (Broadhurst, Dec. 28, 1950); Michael O'Neill in *The Moon is Blue* (Henry Miller's Th., Mar. 8, 1951); Gregory Wagner in *Room Service* (Playhouse, Apr. 6, 1953); Hasler in *The Pajama Game* (St. James, May 13, 1954); Mr. Mergenthaler in *Make a Million* (Playhouse, Oct. 23, 1958); Pert Hawkins in *Happy Town* (54 St. Th., Oct. 7, 1959); and Lt. Schmidt in *Tenderloin* (46 St. Th., Oct. 17, 1960).

Mr. Dunn played Bedrock in *Foxy* (Palace Grande, Dawson City, Canada, May 1962); Kolodny in *Apollo and Miss Agnes* (State Fair Music Hall, Dallas, Tex., July 1963); and Martin Hollingshead in *Once for the Asking* (Booth, N.Y.C., Nov. 20, 1963).

Films. Mr. Dunn has appeared in *Laura* (20th-Fox, 1944); *The Hairy Ape* (UA, 1944); *Dark Mountain* (Par., 1944); *Love, Honor and Goodbye* (Rep., 1945); *Within These Walls* (20th-Fox, 1945); *Dick Tracy* (RKO, 1945); *The Jade Mask* (Mono., 1945); *Nobody Lives Forever* (WB, 1946); *Singing Guns* (Rep., 1950); *The Great Plane Robbery* (UA, 1950); *Crowded Paradise* (Tudor, 1956); *The Pajama Game* (WB, 1957); *From the Terrace* (20th-Fox, 1960); and *Murder, Inc.* (20th-Fox, 1960).

Television. He has appeared on television on the Kitty Foyle series (NBC, 1958); and *Arsenic and Old Lace* (Hallmark Hall of Fame, NBC, 1962).

Recreation. Fishing, golf, pool.

DUNNING, PHILIP HART. Playwright, producer, stage director. b. Dec. 11, 1891, Meriden, Conn., to John Michael and Mary (Hart) Dunn. Father, electro-chemist. Married Apr. 26, 1919, to Frances Elizabeth Fox, writer; one daughter. Served in USNR, 1917–19, entertainment director aboard *U.S.S. George Washington,* 1918–1919; rank, Chief Boatswain's Mate. Relatives in theatre: brother, Caesar Dunn, playwright; daughter, Virginia Dunning (Maloney), television director. Member of Dramatists Guild (council, 1929–55); AEA; Actors Fund of America; American Legion; Dutch Treat Club; American Arbitration Assn. (member, panel of arbitrators, 1933–64); Authors League of America Representative to Theatre Authority, Inc. (1964). Address: (home) 22 Little Fox Lane, Westport, CT 06880, tel. (203) CA 7-3558; (bus.) c/o Dramatists Guild, 6 E. 39th St., New York, NY 10016, tel. (212) MU 9-4950.

Theatre. Mr. Dunning was assistant stage manager for and appeared as a Footman in *Pomander Walk* (Wallack's Th., N.Y.C., Dec. 20, 1910); subsequently was stage manager for the touring company of *Bought and Paid For* (1911–1912); was a partner and manager for a motion picture theatre in E. Hartford, Conn. (1912); and an actor and stage manager for the Poli Stock Circuit (Hartford, Conn.; Washington, D.C., Summers 1912–15).

He played in and was stage manager for *Life* (Manhattan Opera House, N.Y.C., Oct. 24, 1914); was stage manager and appeared as Waterman in *Ruggles of Red Gap* (Fulton, Dec. 25, 1915); was stage manager for *The Girl from Brazil* (44 St. Th., Aug. 30, 1916); appeared in *Object Matrimony* (Cohan and Harris Th., Oct. 25, 1916); was stage manager for *Love O' Mike* (Shubert, Jan. 15, 1917); during his service in the Navy, appeared in, and collaborated on the book, with Robert Cohen and William Israel, for *Biff! Bang!* and was stage manager (Century, May 30, 1918).

Mr. Dunning wrote and produced a vaudeville act, "Everysailor," which played the circuits (1919–1920); appeared as Stetson and was stage manager for *The Dancer* (Harris, N.Y.C., Sept. 29, 1919); played Tabers in *The Wonderful Thing* (Playhouse, Feb. 17, 1920); was stage manager for *Guest of Honor* (Broadhurst, Sept. 20, 1920); appeared as John Winford and was stage manager for *Beware of Dogs* (Broadhurst, Oct. 3, 1921); was stage manager for *Whispering Wires* (49 St. Th., Oct. 7, 1922); appeared as Mr. Dysant and was stage manager for *For All of Us* (49 St. Th., Oct. 7, 1923); and was stage manager for *Sunny* (New Amsterdam, Sept. 22, 1925).

With George Abbott, he wrote and directed *Broadway* (Broadhurst, Sept. 16, 1926); with Charlton Andrews, wrote *Get Me in the Movies* (Earl Carroll Th., May 21, 1928); wrote *Night Hostess* (Martin Beck Th., Sept. 12, 1928); wrote and directed *Sweet Land of Liberty* (Knickerbocker, Sept. 23, 1929); and produced *Those We Love* (John Golden Th., Feb. 19, 1930).

With George Abbott, he wrote, produced, and directed *Lilly Turner* (Morosco, Sept. 19, 1932); with Mr. Abbott, produced *Twentieth Century* (Broadhurst, Dec. 29, 1932); *Heat Lightning* (Booth, Sept. 15, 1933); *The Drums Begin* (Shubert, Nov. 24, 1933); *Kill That Story* (Booth, Aug. 29, 1934), written in collaboration with Harry Madden; wrote, with Joseph Schrank, and produced, with Laurence Schwab, *Page Miss Glory* (Mansfield, Nov. 27, 1934); produced *Remember the Day*, which he wrote with Philo Higley (Natl., Sept. 25, 1935); and produced and directed *Schoolhouse on the Lot* (Ritz, Mar. 22, 1938).

Films. Mr. Dunning was author or co-author of screenplays for *Show Folks* (Pathé, 1928); *Broadway* (U, 1929); *Woman Racket* (MGM, 1930); *Lilly Turner* (1st Natl., 1933); *Page Miss Glory* (WB, 1935); *Remember the Day* (20th-Fox, 1941); *Easy Come, Easy Go* (Par., 1947); and *Flamingo Road* (WB, 1949).

Other Activities. Mr. Dunning was editor of the *Dramatists Bulletin*, a monthly publication for members of the Dramatists Guild (1960–63).

Published Works. He has written the play, *Sequel to a Verdict* (1963).

Recreation. Enjoys painting, collecting theatrical mementos, growing Blue Spruce trees.

DUNNOCK, MILDRED. Actress, director. b. Mildred Dorothy Dunnock, Jan. 25, Baltimore, Md., to Walter and Florence (Saynook) Dunnock. Father; textile merchant. Grad., Western H.S., Baltimore; Goucher Coll. A.B.; Columbia Univ., M.A. Studied acting with Maria Ouspenskaya, Tamara Daykarhanova, Lee Strasberg, Robert Lewis, Elia Kazan. Member Actors' Studio, 1949–to date. Married Aug. 21, 1933, to Keith M. Urmy; one daughter. Member of SAG; AEA (council mbr.) AFTRA.

Pre-Theatre. Teacher.

Theatre. Miss Dunnock first appeared in N.Y.C. as Miss Pinty in *Life Begins* (Selwyn, Mar. 28, 1932); subsequently played in productions at the Westchester County Playhouse (Mt. Kisco, N.Y., Summer 1932); where she later returned for several seasons of stock (Summers 1934–38); appeared as a Woman of the Congregation in *The Eternal Road* (Manhattan Opera House, N.Y.C., Jan. 7, 1937); Agnes Riddle in *The Hill Between* (Little, Mar. 11, 1938); and toured in *Herod and Mariamne* (1938).

She played Miss Ronberry in *The Corn Is Green* (National, Nov. 26, 1940); appeared in a pre-Bway tryout of *Madam, Will You Walk* (1941); as Miss Giddon in *The Cat Screams* (Martin Beck Th., N.Y.C., June 16, 1942); Queen Margaret in *Richard III* (Forrest, Mar. 24, 1943); India Hamilton in *Only the Heart* (Bijou, Apr. 4, 1944); Rose and Flora in *Foolish Notion* (Martin Beck Th., Mar. 13, 1945); Madame Tsai in *Lute Song* (Plymouth, Feb. 6, 1946); Lavinia Hubbard in *Another Part of the Forest* (Fulton, Nov. 20, 1946); Etta Hallam in *The Hallams* (Booth, Mar. 4, 1948); and Williams in *The Leading Lady* (National, Oct. 18, 1948).

Miss Dunnock appeared as Linda Loman in *Death of a Salesman* (Morosco, Feb. 10, 1949); Mrs. Bayard Goodale in *Pride's Crossing* (Biltmore, Nov. 20, 1950); Aase in *Peer Gynt* (ANTA, Jan. 28, 1951); Gina in *The Wild Duck* (NY City Ctr., Dec. 26, 1951); Mrs. Constable in *In the Summer House* (Playhouse, Dec. 29, 1953); Big Mama in *Cat on a Hot Tin Roof* (Morosco, Mar. 24, 1955); Susan Shepherd in *Child of Fortune* (Royale, Nov. 13, 1956); and Hera in the pre-Bway tryout of *Maiden Voyage* (opened Forrest, Philadelphia, Pa., Feb. 28, 1957; closed there Mar. 9, 1957).

With the American Shakespeare Festival (Stratford, Conn.), she played Constance in *King John* (June 26, 1956); subsequently appeared in *Pictures in the Hallway* (Phoenix, N.Y.C., Dec. 26, 1959); played Mistress Phoebe Ricketts in *The Crystal Heart* (East 74 St. Th., Feb. 15, 1960); Gertrude Povis in *Farewell, Farewell Eugene* (Helen Hayes Th., Sept. 27, 1960); the title role in *Elizabeth the Queen* (Univ. of Utah, Salt Lake City, Jan. 1961); Mary Tyrone in *Long Day's Journey into Night* (Th. du Nouveau Monde, Montreal, Canada, Mar. 1961); and Mrs. Perpetua in *The Cantilevered Terrace* (41 St. Th., N.Y.C., Jan. 17, 1962).

At the Festival of the Two Worlds (Spoleto, Italy), she played Vera Ridgeway Condotti in *The Milk Train Doesn't Stop Here Anymore* (Teatro Nuovo, world premiere July 10, 1962), which she repeated in N.Y.C. (Morosco, Jan. 16, 1962); Hecuba in *The Trojan Women* (Spoleto, Italy, July 16, 1963; and Circle in the Square, N.Y.C., Dec. 23, 1963); and played Madame Renaud in *Traveller without Luggage* (ANTA, Sept. 17, 1964).

Miss Dunnock directed *Graduation* (Th. de Lys, N.Y.C., Jan. 5, 1965); played Lucy Lewis in *Brother to Dragons* (Amer. Place Th., June 2, 1965); Oenone in the IASTA production of *Phedre* (IASTA, Oct. 31, 1965; Greenwich Mews, Feb. 10, 1966; and the American Embassy, London, June 15, 1966); Mary Tyrone in *Long Day's Journey Into Night* (Long Wharf Th., New Haven, Conn., May 6, 1966); Amanda in *The Glass Menagerie* (Oakland, Calif., National Repertory Th., Dec. 1966); recited the poems for the modern ballet *Chansons de Bilitis* (Caramoor Festival, N.Y., July 1, 1967); played Mrs. Edna Nichols in *Willie Doesn't Live Here Anymore* (ANTA matinee series, Th. de Lys, Feb. 6, 1967); and Hecuba in *The Trojan Women* (Circle in the Square, Dec. 23, 1967); appeared with the Long Wharf Th. (New Haven, Conn., 1967–68, 1968–69, 1969–70); and the Yale Repertory Th., (New Haven, Conn., 1967–69, 1969–70); played Sido in *Colette* (Ellen Stewart Th., N.Y.C., May 6, 1970); with the Repertory Th. of Lincoln Center, played Beth in *Landscape*, on a double bill with *Silence* (Forum, Apr. 2, 1970); Clair Laines in *A Place Without Doors* (Stairway Th., N.Y.C., Dec. 22, 1970; Long Wharf Th., New Haven, Conn., 1970–71 season; and Goodman Th., Chicago, 1971–72 season); and appeared with the Long Wharf Th. (New Haven, Conn., 1972–73 season).

Films. Miss Dunnock made her film debut as Miss Ronberry in *The Corn Is Green* (WB, 1945); subsequently appeared in *Kiss of Death* (20th-Fox, 1947); *Death of a Salesman* (Col., 1951); *I Want You* (RKO, 1951); *The Girl in White* (MGM, 1952); *Viva Zapata!* (20th-Fox, 1952); *The Jazz Singer* (WB, 1953); *The Trouble with Harry* (Par., 1955); *Baby Doll* (WB, 1956); *Love Me Tender* (20th-Fox, 1956); *Peyton Place* (20th-Fox, 1957); *The Story on Page One* (20th-Fox, 1959); *The Nun's Story* (WB, 1959); *Butterfield 8* (MGM, 1960); *Something Wild* (UA, 1961); *Sweet Bird of Youth* (MGM, 1962); *Youngbloode Hawke* (20th-Fox, 1964); *Behold a Pale Horse* (Col., 1964); *Seven Women* (MGM, 1966); and *Whatever Happened to Aunt Alice?* (Cinerama, 1969).

Television. Miss Dunnock has appeared on the Kraft Television Playhouse (NBC), The Defenders (CBS), Studio One (CBS), Alfred Hitchcock Presents (CBS), Camera 3 (CBS), Robert Herridge Th. (CBS); The Reporter (CBS); Alfred Hitchcock (Ind.); *Death of a Salesman* (CBS); Experiment in Television (NBC); The F.B.I. (ABC); and Ghost Story (NBC).

DUQUETTE, TONY. Artist, decorator, designer. b. Anthony Michael Duquette, June 11, 1918, Los Angeles, Calif., to Frank F. and Elsa (Fuhrer) Duquette. Father, businessman; mother, musician. Attended Chouinard Art Inst. Served US Army, 1942–46. Married Feb. 15, 1949, to Elizabeth Johnstone, artist. Member of AID. Address: 824 N. Robertson Blvd., Los Angeles, CA 90069, tel. (213) CR 4-6736.

Pre-Theatre. Commercial designer, owner of art gallery.

Theatre. Mr. Duquette designed the costumes, with Adrian, for *Camelot* (Majestic Th., Dec. 3, 1960); subsequently was production designer for *Jederman* (Salzburg Festival, Austria, Aug. 1, 1961); designed the costumes and sets for *Der Rosenkavalier* (San Francisco Opera, Calif.); was artistic director for the Los Angeles Light Opera Company production of *Kismet* (Philharmonic Aud., 1962).

For the San Francisco Ballet Co., he designed costumes and sets for *Beauty and the Beast* (May 23, 1959); *Danse Concertante* (Oct. 13, 1959); *Lady of Shalot, Caprice, Sinfonia, Danse Brilliant* (1960); *Fantasma* (Apr. 16, 1963); was production designer for *Jest of Cards* (Apr. 17, 1962); and provided the sets and costumes for the ballet *The Magic Flute* (Shrine Auditorium, May 6, 1963).

Films. Mr. Duquette designed sets, costumes and sculptures for the ballet sequences in *Yolanda and the Thief* (MGM, 1945); designed special properties for *Ziegfeld Follies* (MGM, 1946); sets and costumes for *Lovely to Look At* (MGM, 1952); costumes for *Kismet* (MGM, 1955); sets for the ballet sequences in *Can-Can* (20th-Fox, 1960); and designed and executed sculptures and costumes for *The Four Horsemen of the Apocalypse* (MGM, 1962).

Other Activities. Mr. Duquette designed and executed the main stage curtain for the Los Angeles Music Center; has had a series of one-man showings of his paintings and designs for furniture and jewelry (Mitch Liesen Studio, Los Angeles, Calif., Apr. 7, 1947; Musée de Louvre, Pavillion de Marsan, Paris, France, Jan. 1951; De Young Museum, San Francisco, Calif., Sept. 11, 1951; Santa Barbara, Calif. Museum, Dec. 16, 1952; Los Angeles, Calif. County Museum, May 6, 1952; Phoenix, Ariz. Art Museum, Jan. 14, 1960; and Los Angeles Municipal Art Gallery, Barnsdall Park, 1971).

He also exhibited sets and costumes at the California Palace of the Legion of Honor (San Francisco, Sept. 29, 1952); sketches of costumes and sets of *Beauty and the Beast* are in the permanent collection.

Awards. Mr. Duquette won the Antoinette Perry (Tony) Award for his costumes for *Camelot* (1961).

DURAND, CHARLES. Stage manager, actor, director. b. Charles E. Springmeyer, Jr., Apr. 27, 1912, Brooklyn, N.Y., to Charles E. and Sarah Springmeyer. Father, high school principal. Grad. Franklin K. Lane H.S., N.Y.C., 1929; Columbia Univ., A.B. 1933. Studied at the Amer. Theatre Wing, N.Y.C. (1946–47). Married Sept. 10, 1948, to Virginia Mattis, actress; one daughter. Served US Army, 1940–45; rank, T/4. Member of AEA; AFTRA; AGMA; AGVA; Phi Kappa Psi. Address: 310 W. 72nd St., New York, NY 10023, tel. (212) TR 4-4323.

Theatre. Mr. Durand made his first stage appearance in a junior high school production of *The Romancers* (1927); his Bway debut as Malinov in *Judgment Day* (Belasco, Sept. 12, 1934); performed throughout the US in variety shows (1937–39); while serving in the armed forces, was stage manager for *OK-USA*, which toured European theatres (1945).

He played the State Trooper in the pre-Bway tryout of *Barnaby and Mr. O'Malley* (opened Playhouse, Wilmington, Del., Sept. 6, 1946; closed Ford's, Baltimore, Md., Sept. 14, 1946); was stage manager for *The Wanhope Building* (Princess, Feb. 9, 1947); stage manager and appeared in stock productions at the Barter Theatre (Abingdon, Va., 1947–48); was stage manager, and played Nick, in the touring production of *Make Mine Manhattan* (Earle Th., Philadelphia, Pa., Oct. 1949); and appeared in stock at the Peterborough (N.H.) Playhouse (Summer 1950).

He was stage manager for *Season in the Sun* (Cort, N.Y.C., Sept. 28, 1950), which he directed in stock (Roosevelt Playhouse, Miami Beach, Fla., Aug. 1951); was stage manager for *Out West of Eighth* (Ethel Barrymore Th., Sept. 20, 1951); appeared in productions at Martha's Vineyard, Mass. (Summer 1952); was stage manager for *The Seven Year Itch* (Fulton, Nov. 20, 1952), *The Wayward Saint* (Cort, Feb. 17, 1955), *The Righteous Are Bold* (Holiday, Dec. 22, 1955), and *Affair of Honor* (Ethel Barrymore Th., Apr. 6, 1956).

Mr. Durand directed a stock production of *Side by Side* (Peterborough Playhouse, N.H., June 1956); directed productions at the Southbury (Conn.) Playhouse (July 1956); was stage manager for *Speaking of Murder* (Royale, Dec. 19, 1956); directed *A Roomful of Roses* and *A Member of the Wedding* (West Orange, N.J., Mar. 1957); played the School Principal in *The Happy Time* and Mr. Beebe in *The Silver Whistle* (Kennebunkport Playhouse, Me., June 1957).

He was production stage manager for the pre-Bway tryout of *The Carefree Heart* (opened Cass Th., Detroit, Mich., Sept. 30, 1957; closed Hanna, Cleveland, Ohio, Oct. 26, 1957); stage manager for

Jane Eyre (Belasco, May 1, 1958); *Howie* (46 St. Th., Sept. 17, 1958); joined (Mar. 1959) as stage manager for the national tour of *The Warm Peninsula* (opened Playhouse, Wilmington, Del., Oct. 29, 1958; closed Rochester Aud., N.Y., May 9, 1959); and played the Internal Revenue Agent in *Time for Elizabeth* (Sacandaga Spa, Saratoga Springs, N.Y.; Edgewater Beach Hotel, Chicago, Ill., July 1959).

He served as stage manager for *Golden Fleecing* (Henry Miller's Th., N.Y.C., Oct. 15, 1959); *The Cool World* (46 St. Th., Feb. 22, 1960); and for the pre-Bway tryout of *One for the Dame* (opened Ford's, Baltimore, Md., Mar. 24, 1960; closed Colonial, Boston, Mass., Apr. 2, 1960); directed *Golden Fleecing* (Lakewood Th., Skowhegan, Me., June 1960); appeared in stock at the Theatre by the Sea (Mantunuck, R.I., July 1960); was stage manager for *Send Me No Flowers* (Brooks Atkinson Th., N.Y.C., Dec. 5, 1960); played the Adm. in *Roman Candle* and was associate director for *Roar Like a Dove* (Royal Poinciana Playhouse, Palm Beach, Fla., Feb. 1961).

Mr. Durand played Jim Dougherty in *The Pleasure of His Company* (Hunterdon Hills Playhouse, Clifton, N.J., June 1961), also at this theatre he directed *Under the Yum-Yum Tree* (July 1961) and *Harvey* (Aug. 1961); was stage manager for the Polish dance group, *Mazowsze* (Philadelphia Acad. of Music, Pa., Sept. 1961); was production stage manager (Nov. 1961–Dec. 1962) for the national tour of *My Fair Lady* (opened Rochester Aud., Mar. 18, 1957); and production stage manager for the national tour of *How to Succeed in Business Without Really Trying* (opened Hanna, Cleveland, Ohio, Feb. 4, 1963).

Mr. Durand was production stage manager for *Cactus Flower* (Royale, N.Y.C., Dec. 8, 1965); advance director for the stock tour of *The Odd Couple* (Summer 1968); and production stage manager for the national tour of *The Apple Tree* (1968–69). He played the Producer in *You Know I Can't Hear You When the Water's Running* and the Butler in *There's a Girl in My Soup* (Corning Summer Th., Corning, N.Y., 1969); and was production stage manager for *The Price* (Paper Mill Playhouse, Millburn, N.J., Dec. 1969); for the national tour of *The Last of the Red Hot Lovers* (opened National Th., Washington, D.C., Sept. 28, 1970); and (Nov. 1971–Aug. 1972) for the national tour of *1776* (opened Curran Th., San Francisco, Apr. 23, 1970); for the second national touring company of *No, No, Nanette* (opened Music Hall, Dallas, Tex., Oct. 6, 1972; closed Garden State Arts Center, Holmdel, N.J., Aug. 4, 1973); and for the national tour of *That Championship Season* (opened Royal Alexandra Th., Toronto, Ontario, Oct. 1, 1973).

Recreation. Swimming, ice skating, amateur musician, trumpet.

DURANTE, JIMMY. Comedian, actor, singer. b. James Francis Durante, Feb. 10, 1893, New York City, to Bartholomeo and Rosea (Millino) Durante. Father, barber. Attended public schools in N.Y.C., 1900–10. Married 1921 to Jeanne Olson, singer (dec. 1943); married Dec. 14, 1960, to Margie Little, actress, model; one daughter. Member of AEA; SAG; AGVA; AFTRA; ASCAP.

Pre-Theatre. Newsboy, errand boy, dishwasher, photoengraver.

Theatre. Mr. Durante was first a pianist in Diamond Tony's Saloon (Coney Island, N.Y., 1910); later made his Bway debut in the revue, *Show Girl* (Ziegfeld, July 2, 1929); played Jimmie Deegan in *The New Yorkers*, also composed two songs for this show, "The Hot Patata" and "Money, Wood and Data" (Bway Th., Dec. 8, 1930); appeared in the revue *Strike Me Pink* (Majestic, Mar. 4, 1933); played Claudius B. Bowers in *Jumbo* (Hippodrome, Nov. 16, 1935); toured England with a comedy routine (1936); played "Policy" Pinkle in *Red, Hot and Blue!* (Alvin, N.Y.C., Oct. 29, 1936); Bill in *Stars in Your Eyes* (Majestic, Feb. 9, 1939); appeared in the revue *Keep Off the Grass* (Broadhurst, May 23, 1940); and as a singer-comedian at the Palladium (London, May 5, 1952); and performed in his own show at the Melodyland Th. (Anaheim, Calif., Apr. 20–25, 1965).

Films. Mr. Durante made his debut in *Roadhouse Nights* (Par., 1930); subsequently appeared in *New Adventures of Get Rich Quick Wallingford* (MGM, 1931); *Cuban Love Song* (MGM, 1931); *Speak Easily* (MGM, 1932); *The Passionate Plumber* (MGM, 1933); *What! No Beer?* (MGM, 1933); *George White's Scandals* (20th-Fox, 1934); *Palooka* (UA, 1934); *Student Tour* (MGM, 1934); *Land without Music*, also released as *Forbidden Music* and *That's My Boy* (1938); *Start Cheering* (Col., 1938); *Sally, Irene, and Mary* (20th-Fox, 1938); *You're in the Army Now* (WB, 1941); *The Man Who Came to Dinner* (WB, 1941); *This Time for Keeps* (MGM, 1942); *Her Cardboard Lover* (MGM, 1944); *Music for Millions* (MGM, 1944); *Two Girls and a Sailor* (MGM, 1944); *The Ziegfeld Follies* (MGM, 1946); *Two Sisters from Boston* (MGM, 1946); *It Happened in Brooklyn* (MGM, 1947); *On an Island with You* (MGM, 1948); *The Great Rupert* Eagle-Lion, 1950); *The Milkman* (U, 1950); *Billy Rose's Jumbo* (MGM, 1962); and *It's a Mad, Mad, Mad, Mad World* (UA, 1963). Material from some of Mr. Durante's earlier MGM films was included in *Big Parade of Comedy* (MGM, 1964).

Television and Radio. Mr. Durante was star of the Rexall (radio) Show (NBC, 1944–50).

He premiered his own television show, The All-Star Revue (1950); appeared as host and performer on the Texaco Star Th. (NBC); Colgate Comedy Hour (NBC); *Give My Regards to Broadway* (NBC); *Boy Meets Girl* (NBC); the Jimmy Durante Show (NBC); Summer Playhouse (CBS); the Ed Sullivan Show (CBS); the Danny Thomas special (CBS); *These Are Americans* (ABC); *Jimmy Durante Meets the Lively Arts* (ABC); *The Wonderful World of Burlesque* (NBC); the Lucille Ball Show (CBS); Star Salute (Ind.); the Bob Hope Show (NBC); played Humpty-Dumpty in *Alice Through the Looking Glass* (NBC); and appeared on Hollywood Palace (ABC); The Ice Capades special (NBC); the Smothers Brothers Show (CBS); the Danny Thomas Show (NBC); Make Room for Daddy (CBS); the Lennon Sisters Show (ABC); *Jimmy Durante Presents the Lennon Sisters* (ABC); and the Sonny and Cher Show (CBS).

Night Clubs. Mr. Durante opened Club Durante (N.Y.C., 1923) with Eddie Jackson and Lou Clayton as partners (the latter credited with coining Durante's famous nickname, "Schnozzola"), the three men later forming a comedy team, Clayton, Jackson and Durante. In addition, he has performed at Club Alamo (N.Y.C., 1961); Silver Slipper (1920); Les Ambassadeurs (1928); The Rendevous (1929); Copacabana (1948, 1949, 1956, 1957, 1959, 1965); Palumbo's (Philadelphia, 1959–64); Desert Inn (Las Vegas); Blinstrubs (Boston); Latin Casino (Camden, N.J.); Chez Paree (New Orleans); The Palmer House (Chicago); The Nugget (Sparks, Nev., 1965, 1966, 1967); Deauville Hotel (Miami Beach, 1966, 1967); Americana Hotel (San Juan, P.R., 1966); Shoreham Hotel (Washington, D.C., 1966); Hartman Th. (Columbus, Ohio, 1966); The Desert Inn (Las Vegas, 1967); Sahara-Tahoe (Lake Tahoe, Nev. 1967).

Other Activities. In 1966, Mr. Durante served as the national chairman of the Society for Crippled Children and Adults.

Published Works. He is the author of *Schnozzla Durante's Song Book*. .

Awards. He was voted Best TV Performer in the *Motion Picture Daily's* 3rd Annual Television Poll (1951); received a Citation of Merit from the City of New York, presented by Mayor Wagner (1956); the George Foster Peabody Award (1951); Humanitarian Award (1969); and the Silver Lady Award (1974).

DURNING, CHARLES. Actor. b. Feb. 28, 1923, Highland Falls, N.Y. Educ. Columbia Univ., NY Univ. First marriage dissolved; three children; married 1974 to Mary Ann Amelio. Served in US Army, WW II. Member AEA; SAG; AFTRA.

Theatre. Mr. Durning made his professional debut as a member of the national company of *The Andersonville Trial* in 1960. Since 1962, he has appeared in many productions of the NY Shakespeare Festival. His roles included Lucilius in *Julius Caesar* (Heckscher Th., N.Y.C., Feb. 19, 1962; Stephano in *The Tempest* (Delacorte Th., July 16, 1962); First Servant to Cornwall in *King Lear* (Delacorte Th., Aug. 13, 1962); the Porter and Seyton in *Macbeth* (Heckscher Th., Nov. 5, 1962); the Clown in *Antony and Cleopatra* (Delacorte Th., June 13, 1963); Corin in *As You Like It* (Delacorte Th., July 11, 1963); the Clown in *The Winter's Tale* (Delacorte Th., Aug. 8, 1963); Feste in *Twelfth Night* (Heckscher Th., Oct. 7, 1963); and a Purser and a Cuban in *Too Much Johnson* (Phoenix, Jan. 15, 1964).

He appeared also as Paul Rudd in *The Child Buyer* (Garrick Th., Dec. 21, 1964); Pistol in *King Henry V* (Delacorte Mobile Th., June 26, 1965); Grumio in *The Taming of the Shrew* (Delacorte Mobile Th., June 27, 1965); Pincer in *Drat! The Cat!* (Martin Beck Th., Oct. 10, 1965); Dean Stewart and Maurice in *Pousse-Café* (46 St. Th., Mar. 18, 1966); Point and the Discussion Leader in *The World of Gunther Grass* (Pocket Th., Apr. 26, 1966); Lavatch in *All's Well That Ends Well* (Delacorte, June 15, 1966); Pompey in *Measure for Measure* (Delacorte, July 12, 1966); and the 1st Murderer in *Richard III* (Delacorte, Aug. 9, 1966).

At the Pittsburgh (Pa.) Playhouse he was in *A Man's a Man* (Nov. 13, 1966), *The Entertainer* (Dec. 16, 1966), and *The Three Sisters* (Mar. 10, 1967). He played Dromio of Ephesus in *The Comedy of Errors* (Delacorte Th., N.Y.C., June 7, 1967); James Gurney in *King John* (Delacorte, July 29, 1967); and the Narrator in *Titus Andronicus* (Delacorte, Aug. 2, 1967); was Louis Bonnard in *The Happy Time* (Ahmanson Th., Los Angeles, Calif., 1967; Broadway Th., Jan. 18, 1968); Daddy in *Huui, Huui* (Public Th., Nov. 24, 1968); Rodion in *Invitation to a Beheading* (Public, Mar. 8, 1969); Feste in *Twelfth Night* (Delacorte, Aug. 6, 1969); and Ned Buntline in *Indians* (Brooks Atkinson Th., Oct. 13, 1969).

Mr. Durning was Douglas in *Lemon Sky* (world premiere: Studio Arena Th., Buffalo, N.Y., Mar. 26, 1970; Playhouse, N.Y.C., May 17, 1970); the Mayor of London in *Chronicles of King Henry VI, Part 1* (Delacorte, June 23, 1970); Cade in *Chronicles of King Henry VI, Part 2* (Delacorte, June 24, 1970); the Orderly in *The Happiness Cage* (Public Th., Oct. 4, 1970); George Sikowski in *That Championship Season* (Public Th., May 2, 1972; moved to Booth Th., Sept. 14, 1972); the 1st Gravedigger in *Hamlet* (Delacorte, June 20, 1972); Harold in *The Boom Boom Room* (Vivian Beaumont Th., Nov. 8, 1973); and Eugene Hartigan in *The Au Pair Man* (Vivian Beaumont Th., Dec. 27, 1973).

Films. Mr. Durning's films include *Dealing* (WB, 1972); *Sisters* (Amer. Inter., 1973); *The Sting* (U, 1973); and *Dog Day Afternoon* (WB, 1975).

Television. Mr. Durning's television appearances have been on High Chaparral (ABC); East Side/West Side (CBS); The Defenders (CBS); N.Y.P.D. (Ind.); Madigan (NBC); All in the Family (CBS); and other series. He was co-star of *Queen of the Sawdust Ballroom* (CBS, 1975).

Awards. Mr. Durning received a Drama Desk Award (1972) for his outstanding performance in *That Championship Season* and was a *Variety* poll winner (1972) with the rest of the cast of the same play for ensemble playing.

DUSSAULT, NANCY. Singer, actress. b. Nancy Elizabeth Dussault, June 30, 1938, Pensacola, Fla., to Capt. G.A. and Sara I. (Seitz) Dussault. Father, Naval officer. Grad. Washington-Lee H.S., Arlington, Va., 1953; Northwestern Univ., B.Mus. (Phi Beta) 1957. Studied with Mary Lidgerwood, N.Y.C., one yr.; Keith Davis, N.Y.C., three yrs.; Lotte Lehmann. Married Oct. 4, 1958, to James D. Travis. Member of AEA; AFTRA; SAG; AGMA; AGVA; Delta Delta Delta (former vice-pres.). Address: 420 E. 55th St., New York, NY 10022, tel. (212) PL 2-3879.

Theatre. Miss Dussault made her stage debut as Fiona in a high school production of *Brigadoon* (1953); made her professional debut as a Nurse in *South Pacific* and appeared in *Guys and Dolls, Lady in the Dark, Kismet, The Golden Apple,* and *Pal Joey* (Highland Park Music Th., Ill., Summers 1955–56). She appeared as Dulcie and later as Mazie in a summer-theatre tour of *The Boy Friend* (opened Pinebrook Th., N.J., June 1958).

In N.Y.C., she appeared in the revue, 1968; Diversions (Downtown, Nov. 7, 1958); sang the role of Jeanne in *Street Scene* (NY City Ctr., Apr. 2, 1959); played Judy in *Dr. Willy Nilly* (Barbizon-Plaza, June 4, 1959); appeared as Pitti-Sing in *The Mikado* (NY City Ctr., Oct. 1, 1959); Sister Mister in *The Cradle Will Rock* (NY City Ctr., Feb. 11, 1960); and Bobbie in *No For An Answer* (Circle in the Square, Apr. 1960). She appeared as Hilaret in the pre-Bway tryout of *Lock Up Your Daughters!* (opened Shubert, New Haven, Apr. 27, 1960; closed Shubert, Boston, May 7, 1960); Tilda Mullen in *Do Re Mi* (St. James, N.Y.C., Dec. 26, 1960); succeeded (Sept. 15, 1962) Marthà Wright in the role of Maria in *The Sound of Music* (Lunt-Fontanne Th., Nov. 16, 1959); played Miss Agnes in *Apollo and Miss Agnes* (State Music Fair, Dallas, Tex., 1963); and Beatrice in the American premiere of the Berlioz opera, *Beatrice et Benedict* (Washington, D.C., June 1964).

Miss Dussault played Marie in *The Sound of Music* (Pittsburgh Civic Light Opera and St. Louis Municipal Opera, July 1964); appeared in *What Makes Sammy Run* (Valley Music Th., July 1964); played Emily in *Bajour* (Shubert, N.Y.C., Nov. 23, 1964); appeared in *Phoebe* (Bucks County, Pa., Playhouse, Aug. 1965), a musical version of J. M. Barrie's *Quality Street;* played Carrie in *Carousel* (NY City Ctr., Dec. 15, 1966); Sharon in *Finian's Rainbow* (NY City Ctr., Apr. 5, 1967); Marie in *Fiorello* (Feb. 29, 1968) for a special White House performance for the nation's governors; in summer stock, played Nellie in *South Pacific* (Dallas, Tex., July 1967); and Ann in *Half-a-Sixpence* (Kenley circuit, July–Aug. 1967); repeated the role of Nellie in *South Pacific* (Jones Beach, N.Y., Th., Summer 1969); for the Goodspeed Opera House (East Haddam, Conn., Summer 1968) appeared in *After You, Mr. Hyde,* played The Girl in *On Time,* and the title role in *Peter Pan;* played Daisy in *On a Clear Day You Can See Forever* (St. Paul, Minn., Civic Opera, Mar. 26, 1968; and Kansas City, Mo., Starlite Th., July 1970). Off-Bway, she played The First Lady in *Whispers on the Wind* (Th. de Lys, N.Y.C., Spring 1970); and Rose in *Trelawny of the Wells* (Public Th., N.Y.C., Oct. 1970).

She played Elaine in *The Last of the Red Hot Lovers* (North Shore Music Th., Beverly, Mass., Aug. 1972); and The Wife in a revival of *Detective Story* (pre-Bway tour, Feb.–Mar. 1973); appeared in *6 Rms Riv Vu* (Playhouse-on-the-Mall, Paramus, N.J., Nov. 1973); was a principal player in a touring production of *The Gershwin Years* (Summer 1973); again played Nellie in *South Pacific* (Sacramento, Calif., 1974); and played the title role in *Irene* (Paper Mill Playhouse, Millburn, N.J.), May–June 1975).

In addition, Miss Dussault has appeared in special performances including: *Broadway Answers Selma* (Majestic, N.Y.C., Apr. 4, 1965); *ASCAP Salute* (Oct. 15, 1967); *Magic of Cole Porter* (Music Th., Lincoln Ctr., N.Y.C., Nov. 20, 1967); *Music of Vincent Youmens, Harold Arlen, Noel Coward* (Philharmonic Hall, N.Y.C., Nov. 17, 1968); *Music of Kurt Weil* (Philharmonic Hall, N.Y.C., Nov. 9, 1969); *Heyday of Rodgers and Hart* (Philharmonic Hall, N.Y.C., Nov. 16, 1969); *Salute to Rudolph Friml* (Shubert, N.Y.C., Dec. 6, 1969); *Hammerstein Salute* (Philharmonic Hall, N.Y.C., Nov. 12, 1972); *Revue of Revues* (Avery Fisher Hall, N.Y.C., Nov. 11, 1973); and a *Salute to Jule Styne* (Palace, N.Y.C., May 19, 1974).

Television. Miss Dussault made her debut on the Ed Sullivan Show (CBS, Jan. 1, 1961); subsequently appeared on the Tonight Show (NBC, 1962), Calendar (CBS, 1962), and Garry Moore Show (CBS, 1963).

She appeared on The Bell Telephone Hour (Season of 1965–66); played Polly in *The Beggar's Opera* (WNET, 1967); and was a regular on the New Dick Van Dyke Show (1971–73). She has appeared on the Dinah Shore, Burt Reynolds, Lily Tomlin, and Alan King "Specials", and has been a guest on Love, American Style (ABC), the Tonight Show (NBC), the Merv Griffin Show (Metro Media Syndication), the Mike Douglas Show (CBS), Barney Miller (ABC), $10,000 Pyramid (ABC), The Match Game (CBS), Beat the Clock, What's My Line, and To Tell the Truth. Miss Dussault made a pilot for a proposed program, The Nancy Dussault Show (CBS, 1973).

Night Clubs. She appeared in the revue, *Four Below Strike Back* (Upstairs at the Downstairs, N.Y.C., Jan. 3, 1960); performed at the Blue Angel (N.Y.C., July 1960); and at Plaza 9 (N.Y.C., 1966).

Awards. In college, Miss Dussault was chosen by the Chicago Symphony to appear in two Young People's Concerts and received the Young Artists Award.

She received the *Theatre World* Award and was nominated for the Antoinette Perry (Tony) Award for her performance as Tilda Mullen in *Do Re Mi* (1960); received the Kit Kat Club Award for Best Actress presented at the Artists-Models Ball for her performance as Maria in *Sound of Music;* the Applause Award, presented at Northwestern Univ. for her contribution to the Arts (1963); and was nominated for the Antoinette Perry (Tony) Award for her performance in *Bajour,* 1965.

Recreation. Reading, music.

d'USSEAU, ARNAUD. Playwright. b. Apr. 18, 1916, Los Angeles, Calif., to Arnaud and Ottola (Nesmith) d'Usseau. Father, film producer, director, scenarist, story editor; mother, actress. Grad. Beverly Hills H.S. Married to Susan Wells, artist (dec. June 12, 1973). Relative in theatre: brother, Loring d'Usseau, television producer. Served US Army Signal Corp; rank, Sgt. Member of Dramatists Guild (former council mbr.); ALA.

Pre-Theatre. Journalism, book clerk, set dresser.

Theatre. Mr. d'Usseau wrote, with James Gow, *Tomorrow the World* (Ethel Barrymore Th., N.Y.C., April 14, 1943); *Deep Are the Roots* (Fulton, Sept. 26, 1945); and *Legend of Sarah* (Fulton, Oct. 11, 1950). He also wrote, with Dorothy Parker, *Ladies of the Corridor* (Longacre, Oct. 21, 1953). These plays have been produced all over the world.

Films. He has written film scripts for several Hollywood studios.

Awards. He has received the Newspaper Guild Page One Award for his co-authorship of *Tomorrow the World.*

DVONCH, FREDERICK. Conductor, musical director. b. July 18, 1914, to Rudolph and Victoria (Olach) Dvonch. Grad. Chicago Musical Coll., B.M.; N.Y. Coll. of Music, Artists Diploma and Doctor of Music Degree (1943); Juilliard Grad. Sch., double fellowship (violin and conductor); studied violin with Hans Lets and Leopold Auer (scholarship), conducting with Albert Stouessel and Alfred Wallenstein.

Theatre. Mr. Dvonch was musical director for a touring production of *Show Boat* (1947); a touring production of *Carousel* (NY City Ctr., Jan. 25, 1949); conducted *Arms and the Girl* (46 St. Th., Feb. 2, 1950); *Carousel* (Drury Lane, London, June 7, 1950); *The King and I* (St. James, N.Y.C., Mar. 29, 1951; Drury Lane, London, Oct. 8, 1953); *Plain and Fancy* (Mark Hellinger Th., N.Y.C., Jan. 27, 1955); musical director at NY City Ctr. for *Guys and Dolls* (Apr. 20, 1955); *South Pacific* (May 4, 1955); *Finian's Rainbow* (May 18, 1955); *The King and I* (Apr. 18, 1956); *Kiss Me Kate* (May 9, 1956); *South Pacific* (Apr. 24, 1957); *The Pajama Game* (May 15, 1957).

Mr. Dvonch was musical director of *Rumple* (Alvin, Nov. 6, 1957); *Annie Get Your Gun* (NY City Ctr., Feb. 19, 1958); *Oklahoma!* (NY City Ctr., Mar. 1958); *First Impressions* (Alvin, Mar. 19, 1959); *The Sound of Music* (Lunt-Fontanne, Nov. 16, 1959); and *Do I Hear a Waltz?* (46th St. Th., Mar. 18, 1965).

Radio. Mr. Dvonch was conductor of the Dvonch Sinfonietta (WNYC, 1940); conductor for the Federal Symphony (WNYC); assistant conductor to Alfred Wallenstein (Mutual, 1943–46); conductor for Music for Worship (Mutual, 1945); and Steel Horizons (Mutual, 1945–46).

Other Activities. Mr. Dvonch has conducted the American Czechoslovak Orchestral Society (1941–46); the Chautauqua Symphony Orchestra (1943); the Sperry Symphony Orchestra (1944); the Juilliard Symphony Orchestra (1945); was concert master of the Natl. Symphony Orchestra (1946); conductor of Radio City Music Hall Symphony Orchestra (1950–51); conductor of the Lewisohn Stadium Symphony Orchestra (Summers 1952–53); the Carnegie Hall Concerts (1953); the Masonic Symphony (Philharmonic Hall, 1964); and has appeared as violin soloist in recitals and with orchestras.

Discography. Mr. Dvonch was musical conductor for the original cast recordings of *Arms and the Girl; The King and I; First Impressions; The Sound of Music;* and *Do I Hear a Waltz?.*

Awards. Mr. Dvonch received the $1000 violin prize and the gold medals at Chicago Musical College (1925–28); and Paganini Scholarship (1926); Lyon and Healy Violin Prize (1928); the Ditson Award (1928); the MacDowell Young Artist Prize (1935); the Juilliard Foundation Fellowships in violin and conducting (1933); and the Antoinette Perry (Tony) Award for his work as musical director and conductor (1960).

DYCKE, MARJORIE L. Educator. b. Marjorie Louise Platt, Mar. 1916, New York City, to Simon M. and Alma Louis (Broaker) Platt. Father, attorney. Grad. Morris H.S., N.Y.C., 1933; Hunter Coll., A.B. 1936; Teachers Coll., Columbia Univ., A.M. 1938; New York Univ., Ph.D. 1948; certificate in paralegal studies, N.Y.U. Law School, 1973; attended Yale Univ. Sch. of Drama, Summer 1942. Studied acting at Tamara Daykarhanova Sch. for the Stage, 1945. Married Nov. 9, 1935, to Harold Dycke (marr. dis. 1944); married Nov. 6, 1954, to Nicholas Ferrigno. Relative in theatre: grandmother, Julia Anderson, actress. Member of ANTA (bd. of dir.; exec. comm.); AETA (vice-pres., 1960; 1st vice-pres., 1961; pres. 1962); N.Y.C. Speech Assn., Panel on Dramatic Art, US Natl. Comm. of UNESCO; Pi Lambda Theta; Phi Beta Kappa.

From Sept. 1948, until her retirement in Oct. 1972, Dr. Dycke was the first chairman of the drama department of the High School of Performing Arts, N.Y.C.

She was consultant for the Governor's Sch., Winston-Salem, N.C., which is an experiment in education in the performing and fine arts (1963); and has also written articles on theatre in education for professional magazines, and spoken at meetings of professional organizations as well as at the University of Michigan and the University of Delaware.

Dr. Dycke taught speech and drama classes in N.Y.C. high schools (1937–46); and courses in speech correction, oral interpretation, and public speaking at New York Univ. (1945–48), at Hunter Coll. (1946–48), at Teachers Coll., Columbia Univ. (1972), and at York Coll., City Univ. of New York (1972–to date), where she is adj. asst. prof.

Other Activities. Dr. Dycke served as chairman of the successful Ad Hoc Committee to Save the Research Library of the Performing Arts at Lincoln Center (1972), which had been threatened with closing as an economy measure by the NY Public Library.

Recreation. Gardening, travel, civic affairs.

DYE, LYLE, JR. Administrator, director. b. Aug. 29, 1930, Champaign, Ill., to Lyle Cecil and Kathryn Vera (Younglove) Dye. Father, salesman. Grad. Niles Township H.S., Skokie, Ill., 1948; Drake Univ., B.F.A. (magna cum laude) 1955; Yale Univ. Sch. of Drama, M.F.A., 1958. Married Nov. 18, 1951, to Carol Finch (dec. 1962). Served with USAF (1951–54) as cryptographer. Member of

SSD&C; AEA; Alpha Tau Omega; Omicron Delta Kappa; Theta Alpha Phi.

Mr. Dye was assistant head, Drama Dept., Packer Collegiate Institute, Brooklyn, N.Y. (1958–59), where he taught English, speech, and drama, and directed productions; publicity assistant of the Yale Sch. of Drama (1956–58); and administrative assistant, Drake Univ. (1954).

Theatre. He first performed as an actor in walk-on parts (Chicago Railroad Fair, Ill., Summers 1948–50); first speaking part was as Wild Brother Orson in a university production of *The Christmas Carol* (Drake Univ., Nov. 1948); was co-founder and director of the Nagoya (Japan) Th. Guild, at the air force base there (Sept. 1952); director of the Ross (Calif.) Valley Players (1953); of the Carousel Th., Milburn, Conn. (1955); and of the Stillman and Timothy-Dwight Dramats, Yale Univ. (1956–58).

He was stage manager at the Eastern Slope Playhouse (North Conway, N.H., Summer 1956); resident director there (Summer 1957); director at the Barter Th. (Abingdon, Va.), where he staged *The Crucible, Tea and Sympathy, Jada, Visit to a Small Planet,* and *No Time for Sergeants* (Summer 1958); and was a stage manager of *Talent '59* (Broadhurst, N.Y.C., May 8, 1959).

Mr. Dye was managing director of ELT (Equity Library Th., N.Y.C.), where he chose scripts and directors, and advised on casting for the 41 works produced (1959–62); was supervisor of ELT for Children, whose productions were presented in N.Y.C. and on tour in the eastern US and in Can.; appeared in two of their productions, *Nicollo and Nicollette* and *The Stone Tower* (Delacorte Th., N.Y.C., Summers 1961, 1962); and was script consultant for the Drama Dept. of Brandt and Brandt, literary agency (N.Y.C., 1958–62).

Mr. Dye was executive coordinator of The Theatre Group, Univ. Extension, Univ. of California at Los Angeles (UCLA), after The Theatre Group opened in 1959, continuing in that post until Sept. 1964, when he resigned. He then joined the staff of the Greek Theatre Assn., Los Angeles, and became manager of the Huntington Hartford Th., Hollywood. On Nov. 22, 1965, Mr. Dye was appointed executive director, Performing Arts Council, which operated the Los Angeles Music Ctr., where The Theatre Group became the resident theatre; and in 1967, he was a supervisor of the Plays in Progress series staged by Actors Studio West and the UCLA Committee on Fine Arts. He directed *Praise Caesar* and *Bury the Dead* (Minor Latham Playhouse, Barnard Coll., N.Y.C., Feb. 16, 1971).

Television and Radio. He was educational director of KDPS radio station (Des Moines, Iowa, 1954–55).

Awards. He received a Danforth Fellowship (1955–58); and a Ford Foundation Administrative Grant (1962–63).

Recreation. Swimming, collecting theatre books.

DYER, CHARLES. Playwright, actor, director, novelist. b. 1928, Shrewsbury, Shropshire, England, to James Sydney and Florence (Stretton) Dyer. Attended Queen Elizabeth's Sch., Barnet, Hertfordshire, Eng. Married 1960 to Fiona Jean Thomson, actress; three sons. Served with British Royal Air Force, ETO, PTO, 1942–46, rank, Flying Officer. Member of British AEA. Address: "Old Wob," Austenwood Common Gerrards Cross, Buckinghamshire, England tel. Gerrards Cross 83913.

Theatre. Mr. Dyer's first play to be produced on Bway was *Rattle of a Simple Man* (Booth, Apr. 17, 1963).

In 1938, he was a call-boy at the Hippodrome Theatre (Manchester, Eng.); later played Lord Harpenden in *While the Sun Shines* (New Th., Crewe, Eng., 1947); and "Duke" in *Worm's Eye View* (Whitehall, London, Mar. 5, 1947).

Under the pseudonym C. Raymond Dyer, he wrote the plays *Clubs Are Sometimes Trumps* (Hippodrome, Wednesbury, Staffordshire, Apr. 12, 1948), *Who on Earth* ("Q" Th., London, July 24, 1951), and *Turtle in the Soup* (Intimate, London, Dec. 14, 1953).

As Charles Dyer, he wrote *The Jovial Parasite* (Intimate, Dec. 6, 1954); billed as Raymond Dyer, played the Hotel Manager in *Room for Two* (Prince of Wales's, Mar. 7, 1955); succeeded Basil Lord (Feb. 10, 1958) as Flash Harry in *Dry Rot* (Whitehall, Aug. 31, 1954); and appeared in *Painted Sparrows* (Opera House, Cork, Ireland, Summer 1956).

He is the author of *Wanted—One Body,* which toured the British Isles (1956–58); *Time, Murderer, Please,* which toured the British Isles (1957–58); and *Poison in Jest,* which he also staged and played on tour of the British Isles (1958–59). He wrote *Prelude to Fury* (Intimate, Nov. 23, 1959); *Red Cabbages and Kings,* which was produced in stock (King's, Southsea, Summer 1960); *Rattle of a Simple Man* (Garrick, Sept. 19, 1962) and in N.Y.C. (see above); *Staircase* (Aldwych, London, 1966; Biltmore, N.Y.C., Jan. 10, 1968); and *Mother Adam* (Arts, London, 1972; Mr. Dyer directed this, as well as the Royal Shakespeare Theatre's 1973 production at Stratford-upon-Avon and the 1972 productions at the Piccolo Th., Rotterdam, and the Brakke Gronde Th., Amsterdam). Mr. Dyer's later works include *Hot Godly Wind* (1973), an educational play for universities, and *A Loving Allelujah* (1974).

Films. Mr. Dyer appeared in *Loneliness of the Long Distance Runner* (Continental, 1962); and wrote the screenplay and appeared as "Chalky" in *Rattle of a Simple Man* (Elstree, 1964).

Television. He directed the television adaptation of his play, *Wanted—One Body* (BBC, 1958).

Published Works. Mr. Dyer has written the novels *Rattle of a Simple Man* (1964), *Staircase* (1969), *Charlie Always Told Harry Almost Everything* (1969), and *Unter Der Treppe* (1970).

Recreation. Living.

DYNE, MICHAEL. Playwright. b. London, England. Educated in France and Switzerland.

Theatre. Mr. Dyne is the author of *The Right Honourable Gentleman* (Billy Rose Th., N.Y.C., Oct. 19, 1965). His other plays include *A Garden in the Sea* (US tour, 1962); and *Mr. Hennessy's Pocket.*

Television. Since 1949, Mr. Dyne has written over one hundred television plays including *A Man for Oona* (CBS); *Victory* (NBC); *The Master of the Rose;* and dramatizations of such classics as *Treasure Island* (CBS).

Awards. He won the Christopher Award for *The Master of the Rose.*

DYSART, RICHARD A. Actor. b. Richard Allan Dysart, about 1929, Augusta, Me. Grad. Emerson Coll., Boston, Mass. Member AEA; AFTRA; SAG.

Theatre. Mr. Dysart made his N.Y.C. debut in *The Iceman Cometh* (Circle in the Square, May 8, 1956), joining the cast after the play had opened. He was the English Voice in *The Quare Fellow* (Circle in the Square, Nov. 22, 1958); the Stage Manager in *Our Town* (Circle in the Square, Mar. 23, 1959); Barney Evans in *Epitaph for George Dillon* (Actors' Playhouse, Dec. 28, 1960); the Prison Guard in *The Seven at Dawn* (Actors Playhouse, Apr. 7, 1961); the Father in *Six Characters in Search of an Author* (Martinique, Mar. 7, 1963); appeared in *The Madwoman of Chaillot* (Fred Miller Th., Milwaukee, Wis., Oct. 30, 1963); was The Common Man in a revival of *A Man for All Seasons* (NY City Ctr., Jan. 27, 1964); Willy Loman in *Death of a Salesman* (Hartford Stage Co., Hartford, Conn., Nov. 20, 1964); and Uncle Fred in *All in Good Time* (Royale Th., N.Y.C., Feb. 18, 1965).

In 1965 he was a founding member of the American Conservatory Th., Pittsburgh, Pa., going with the organization to San Francisco, where he appeared in such productions as *The Torch-Bearers* (Feb. 1966); *Six Characters in Search of an Author* (1966); *Death of a Salesman* (1966); *Under Milk Wood* (1966); and was director of *The Zoo* on ACT's program *Albee Acts* (Nov. 14, 1967).

Mr. Dysart also played Horace Giddens in a revival of *The Little Foxes* (Vivian Beaumont Th., Oct. 26, 1967; reopened Ethel Barrymore, Dec. 19, 1967), and toured (beginning Mar. 1968) as Benjamin Hubbard in the same play. He appeared on a Joe Orton double-bill, *Crimes of Passion* (Astor Place Th., Oct. 26, 1969); was Pierre Lannes in *A Place without Doors* (Long Wharf Th., New Haven, Conn., Nov. 20, 1970; Stairway Th., N.Y.C., Dec. 22, 1970); and played the Coach in *That Championship Season* (Public, May 2, 1972; moved to Booth Th., Sept. 14, 1972).

Films. Mr. Dysart appeared in *The Hospital* (UA, 1971).

Television. Mr. Dysart has appeared on All in the Family (CBS); Camera Three (CBS); DuPont Show of the Month (NBC); Armstrong Circle Th. (NBC); Look Up and Live (CBS); and was in *Harriet* (NET).

Awards. Mr. Dysart received a Drama Desk Award (1972) for his outstanding performance in *That Championship Season* and was a *Variety* poll winner (1972), for ensemble playing, with the rest of the cast of the same play.

Recreation. Movies, trout fishing.

E

EAKER, IRA. Publisher. b. Jan. 14, 1922, New York City, to Samuel and Hannah (Connor) Eaker. Father, trucking business. Grad. James Monroe H.S., N.Y.C., 1939; City Coll. of New York, 1948. Married Nov. 24, 1946, to Lee Eisenberg; one son, one daughter. Served US Army, 1943–46, ETO, received four commendations. Member of Knights of Pythias, Clearview Lodge #811. Address: (home) 15-72 216 Bayside, Queens, NY tel. (212) 225-1991; (bus.) 165 W. 46th St., New York, NY 10036, tel. (212) LT 1-1080.

Pre-Theatre. Advertising sales writer.

Theatre. Mr. Eaker is publisher and advertising director of *Back Stage,* a weekly theatrical newspaper that he founded in 1960. Previously he was advertising director of *Show Business* (1948–60).

Recreation. Softball, golf.

EARNFRED, THOMAS. Press representative. b. Thomas Sheldon Earnfred, Oct. 1894, Chicago, Ill., to John Frederick and Delia (Gartland) Earnfred. Father, bricklayer. Attended Lowell H.S., San Francisco, Calif., and Gallagher Marsh Business College; San Francisco Law Sch.; Univ. of California extension (San Francisco). Married Sept. 26, 1946, to Jeannete Donnelly. Served WW I, USN; rank, Seaman 2/C. Member of ATPAM; Actors Fund of America; Olympic Club (San Francisco). Address: 2040 Franklin St., San Francisco, CA 94109.

Pre-Theatre. Newspaper boy for San Francisco *Examiner* and San Francisco *Bulletin,* salesman, and various other jobs.

Theatre. From 1922 to 1973, Mr. Earnfred was head of the press department of Lurie Co., Theatrical Enterprises, owner and operator of the Curran Th., San Francisco, Calif., where he previously (1922–52) was ticket seller and head of press activities for Homer Curran, original owner of the theatre.

Recreation. Track.

EASTON, RICHARD. Actor. b. John Richard Easton, Mar. 22, 1933, Montreal, Canada, to Leonard Idell and Mary Louise (Withington) Easton. Father, civil engineer. Grad. Mount Royal H.S., Montreal, 1950. Studied for the stage with the Children's Th., Montreal, 1948–49; Montreal Repertory Th., 1949–50; Gwyneta Thurburn, three years, London; Central Sch. of Speech and Drama, London, 1953–54. Studied with Eleanor Stuart, one year, Montreal. Member of AEA.

Theatre. Mr. Easton made his first stage appearance as Wally in *Our Town* (Brae Manor Playhouse, Canada, 1948); played Hortensio in *The Taming of the Shrew* (Ottawa, Canada, 1950); and during the 1952–53 season, he appeared with the Canadian

Repertory Th. in Ottawa.

He made his London debut as Edward Kinnerton in *Both Ends Meet* (Apollo, June 9, 1954); followed by the roles of Edgar in *King Lear* and Claudio in *Much Ado About Nothing* on tour in Europe, repeating both roles in London (Palace, July 21, 1955); appeared in *Antony and Cleopatra, An Italian Straw Hat,* and *The Three Sisters* (Crest, Toronto, Canada, 1956); played Scroop in *Henry V* and Slender in *The Merry Wives of Windsor* (Stratford, Ontario, and Edinburgh, Scotland, Festivals, 1956).

He made his N.Y.C. debut with the American Shakespeare Festival (ASFTA) at the Phoenix Th. as Claudio in *Measure for Measure* (Jan. 22, 1957), Lucentio in *The Taming of the Shrew* (Feb 20, 1957), and Delio in *The Dutchess of Malfi* (Mar. 19, 1957); with ASTFA (Stratford, Conn.), he played Roderigo in *Othello* (June 22, 1957) and Claudio in *Much Ado About Nothing* (Aug. 3, 1957); played Harcourt in *The Country Wife* (Adelphi, N.Y.C., Nov. 27, 1957); Cain in *Back to Methuselah* (Ambassador, Mar. 26, 1958); and Timothy in the revue *Salad Days* (Barbizon-Plaza, Nov. 10, 1958).

With ASFTA (Stratford, Conn.), he appeared as Puck in *A Midsummer Night's Dream* and Florizel in *The Winter's Tale;* Romeo in *Romeo and Juliet* (June 12, 1959), and repeated the role of Puck in *A Midsummer Night's Dream* (June 20, 1959).

He toured with the Assn. of Producing Artists (APA), playing the title role in *Anatol,* Octavius Robinson in *Man and Superman,* Constantine Trepleff in *The Seagull* (City Hall Th., Hamilton, Bermuda, May 1960; Bucks County Playhouse, New Hope, Pa., Theatre-by-the-Sea, Matunuck, R.I., and John Drew Th., East Hampton, N.Y., Aug. 1960); played Joseph Surface in *School for Scandal* (Haymarket, London, England, 1962), a role which he repeated in New York (Majestic, Jan. 24, 1963) and on a US tour; played Nick in *Who's Afraid of Virginia Woolf?* (Piccadilly, London, Feb. 6, 1964); Barry in *Comfort Me with Apples* (Globe, Sept. 14, 1965); Fagin in *Oliver!* (Opera House, Manchester, Nov. 1965), in which he also toured; and played Marlow in *She Stoops to Conquer,* the Bishop in *The Balcony,* and the title role in *Richard III* (all Oxford Playhouse, Feb. 1967), later touring in these.

In the US, he again appeared with APA, both at the Univ. of Michigan, Ann Arbor, and in N.Y.C. as a Policeman in *Pantagleize* (Ann Arbor, Sept. 19, 1967; Lyceum, N.Y.C., Nov. 30, 1967; and Sept. 3, 1968); King Berenger in *Exit the King* (Ann Arbor, Oct. 10, 1967; Lyceum, Jan. 9, 1968); Trofimov in *The Cherry Orchard* (Lyceum, Mar. 19, 1968); Alceste in *The Misanthrope* (Ann Arbor, Sept. 17, 1968; Lyceum, Oct. 9, 1968); Claudius in *Hamlet* (Ann Arbor, Oct. 1, 1968; Lyceum, Mar. 3, 1969); a Messenger in *Cock-a-Doodle Dandy* (Ann Arbor, Oct. 15, 1968; Jan. 20, 1969); and in the title role of *Macbeth* (Ann Arbor, Sept. 16, 1969). He directed and was Brutus in *Julius Caesar* (Old Globe Th., San Diego, Calif., Summer 1969); and played James Bonham in *Murderous Angels* (Mark Taper Forum, Los Angeles, Calif., Feb. 5, 1970; Playhouse, N.Y.C., Dec. 20, 1971).

Awards. Mr. Easton received the *Theatre World* Award (1958) for his performance as Mr. Harcourt in *The Country Wife.* .

Recreation. Music.

EBB, FRED.

Lyricist. b. Apr. 8, 1932, New York City. Educ. NY Univ.; Columbia Univ.

Theatre. Mr. Ebb contributed material to the revues *From A to Z* (Plymouth, N.Y.C., Apr. 20, 1960) and *Put It in Writing* (Th. de Lys, May 13, 1963); wrote the book and lyrics for *Morning Sun* (Phoenix, Oct. 6, 1963); lyrics for *Flora, the Red Menace* (Alvin Th., May 11, 1965); *Cabaret* (Broadhurst, Nov. 20, 1966); adapted a revival of *By Jupiter* (Th. Four, Jan. 19, 1967); wrote lyrics for *The Happy Time* (Broadway Th., Jan. 18, 1968); *Zorba* (Imperial, Nov. 17, 1968); for *70, Girls, 70,* for which, with Norman L. Martin, he also wrote the book (Broadhurst, Apr. 15, 1971); and, with John Kander, wrote original material for *Liza* (Winter Garden, Jan. 6–26, 1974).

Television. Mr. Ebb wrote sketches for That Was the Week That Was (NBC, 1963–64) and lyrics for the Carroll O'Connor special *Three for the Girls* (CBS, Sept. 1973).

Night Clubs. Mr. Ebb has written material for nightclub appearances of such performers as Liza Minnelli, Chita Rivera, Juliette Prowse, Kaye Ballard, Carol Channing, and Tommy Sands.

Published Works. Among the songs for which Mr. Ebb wrote lyrics, in addition to those for productions named above, are "My Coloring Book" and "I Don't Care Much.".

Awards. With John Kander, Mr. Ebb received an Antoinette Perry (Tony) Award (1967) for *Cabaret* and Tony nominations for The Happy Time (1967) and, with the composer, book author, and producer, for *Zorba* (1969).

EBERHART, RICHARD.

Poet, educator, playwright. b. Apr. 5, 1904, Austin, Minn., to Alpha La Rue and Lena (Lowenstein) Eberhart. Grad. Dartmouth Coll., B.A. 1926; St. John's Coll., Cambridge Univ., 1929; M.A. 1933; Harvard Graduate Sch. of Arts and Sciences, 1932–33. Married Aug. 29, 1941, to Helen Elizabeth Butcher; one son, one daughter. Served USNR, 1942–46; rank, Lt. Cmdr. Member of Natl. Inst. of Arts and Letters; Nat. Acad. of Arts and Sciences; The Century Club, N.Y.C.; Buck Harbor Yacht club, South Brooksville, Me.; Alpha Delta Phi; Yaddo Corp., Saratoga Springs, N.Y. Address: 5 Webster Terrace, Hanover, NH 03755.

Since 1956, Mr. Eberhart has been professor of English and poet in residence at Dartmouth Coll. Previously, he was poet in residence, professor, or lecturer at Princeton Univ. (1955–56), Wheaton Coll. (1954–55), Univ. of Connecticut (1953–54), and Univ. of Washington (1952–53); and Master in English at St. Mark's Sch. (Southborough, Mass., 1933–41).

Mr. Eberhart delivered the Elliston lectures at the Univ. of Cincinnati (1961). He was the first president of the Poet's Theatre, Inc. (Cambridge, Mass.), which he founded, with Lyon Phelps, in 1950. The first production of that theatre was Mr. Eberhart's play, *The Apparition* (Jan. 1951). He has written *The Visionary Farms* (Fogg Museum, Cambridge, Mass., May 21, 1952); the Playhouse, Seattle, Wash., May 1953; the Inst. of Contemporary Arts, Washington, D.C., Oct. 10, 1957; Univ. of Cincinnati, Ohio, Mar. 16–18, 1961); a twin bill, *The Mad Musician* and *Devils and Angels* (Poet's Th., Cambridge, May 30, 1962; Philomatheaum Society, Univ. of Pennsylvania, Apr. 6, 1962); *Preamble II* (Washington and Lee Univ., Nov. 27, 1962); and adopted Lope de Vega's *Justice Without Revenge,* titled *The Bride from Mantua* (Hopkins Ctr., Dartmouth Coll., May 5–9, 1964).

Other Activities. Mr. Eberhart served as Consultant in Poetry at the Library of Congress (1959–61); on the Advisory Committee on the Arts (National Cultural Center, Washington, D.C., 1959); and was appointed honorary Consultant on American letters by the Library of Congress (1963–to date). He read at the London Poetry International in 1973.

Published Works. He is the author of *A Bravery of Earth* (1930); *Reading the Spirit* (1936); *Song and Idea* (1940); *Selected Poems* (1951); *Undercliff: Poems 1946–53* (1953); *Great Praises* (1957); *Collected Poems, 1930–60* (1960); *Collected Verse Plays* (1962); *The Quarry: New Poems* (1964); *Shifts of Being* (1968); and *Fields of Grace* (1972). He has written articles for periodicals including the New York *Times* Book Review.

Awards. Mr. Eberhart has received the Harriet Monroe Memorial Prize (1950); the Shelley Memorial Prize (1951); the Harriet Monroe Memorial Award (Univ. of Chicago, 1955); a grant from National Inst. of Arts and Letters (1955); with John Hall Wheelock, the Bollingen Prize from the Yale Univ. Library (1962); the Pulitzer Prize (1966); and Academy of American Poets Award (1969).

He received honorary Litt.D. degrees from Dartmouth Coll. (1954), Skidmore (1966), Wooster (1969), and Colgate (1974). In 1972, he became honorary president, the Poetry Society of America.

Recreation. Swimming, flying seven-foot kites, cruising the Maine Coast.

EBERT, JOYCE.

Actress. b. Joyce Anne Womack, June 26, 1933, Munhall, Pa., to John Leib and Bertha Louise (Freidel) Womack. Father, engineer. Grad. Munhall (Pa.) H.S., 1951; Carnegie Inst. of Tech., B.A. 1955. Studied acting with Uta Hagen, N.Y.C., 1956; Lee Strasberg, N.Y.C., 1962–64. Married Nov. 10, 1956, to Michael Ebert, actor (marr. dis.); married to Arvin Brown, director. Member of AEA; AFTRA; SAG.

Theatre. Mrs. Ebert made her professional debut in *White Sheep of The Family* (Pittsburgh Playhouse, Pa., Jan. 1953); subsequently at Carnegie Inst. of Tech., appeared as Nina in *The Seagull,* Julia in *The Rivals,* and Miranda in *The Tempest* (1952–55); at the Oregon Shakespeare Festival, played Portia in *The Merchant of Venice,* Ophelia in *Hamlet,* Bianca in *The Taming of the Shrew* (Ashland, Summer 1953–54); and Madge in *Picnic* (Mountain Playhouse, Jennerstown, Pa., Summer 1955).

Mrs. Ebert made her N.Y.C. debut as Julie in the ELT production of *Liliom* (Lenox Hill Playhouse, Feb. 8, 1956); appeared as Alithea Pinchwife in *The Country Wife* (Renata, June 26, 1957); Emmanuele in *Asmodée* (Th. 74, Mar. 25, 1958); Flora in *Sign of Winter* (Th. 74, May 7, 1958); with the Group 20 Players (Wellesley, Mass., 1958) as Maria in *The School for Scandal;* Clara Eynsford-Hill in *Pygmalion;* and Jessica in *The Merchant of Venice;* with the Shakespearewrights, appeared as Condelia in *King Lear* (Players Th., N.Y.C., Jan. 2, 1959); and succeeded (Mar. 3, 1959) Rosina Fernhoff, as Gertrude in *Fashion* (Royal Playhouse, Jan. 20, 1959).

She appeared at the San Diego (Calif.) Shakespeare Festival as Juliet in *Romeo and Juliet;* the Princess of France in *Love's Labour's Lost* and Lady Mortimer in *Henry IV, Part 1* (Old Globe Th., Summer 1959); played Camille in *No Trifling with Love* (St. Mark's Playhouse, N.Y.C., Nov. 9, 1959); Margie in *The Iceman Cometh* and Isabella in *Ring 'Round the Moon* (Arena Stage, Washington, D.C., 1960); Miranda in *The Tempest* (Amer. Shakespeare Festival, Stratford, Conn., June 3, 1960); and with the APA, Annie in *Anatol* (McCarter Th., Princeton, N.J., Sept. 20, 1960).

She played Ophelia in *Hamlet* (Phoenix, N.Y.C., Mar. 16, 1961); in stock (Williamstown Th., Mass.), Gwendolyn in *Becket* (1961). Annie Sullivan in *The Miracle Worker,* Nina in *The Seagull* and Lady Larkin in *Once Upon a Mattress* (Summer 1962).

In a double-bill, she played Rosie Probert, Gossamer Beynon, Polly Garter, Mrs. Cherry Owen, and Bessie Bighead in *Under Milk Wood* and Twelve O'-Clock in *Pullman Car Hiawatha* (Circle in the Square, N.Y.C., Dec. 3, 1962). At the Williamstown (Mass.) Th., appeared as Ann in *Man and Superman,* Elizabeth in *A Far Country,* Miss Fellows in *The Night of the Iguana,* Varya in *The Cherry Orchard,* and Mrs. Booth in *Mr. Booth* (Summer 1963); and played Pegeen Mike in *The Playboy of the Western World* (McCarter Th., Princeton, N.J., 1963).

She succeeded (Nov. 30, 1963) Jacqueline Brookes as the Stepdaughter in *Six Characters in Search of an Author* (Martinique, N.Y.C., Mar. 7, 1963); played Andromache in *The Trojan Women* (Circle in the Square, Dec. 23, 1963); Mariane in *Tartuffe* (Rep. Th. of Lincoln Ctr., ANTA Washington Sq. Th., Jan. 11, 1965); repeated her performance as Andromache in a return engagement of *The Trojan Women* (Circle in the Square, Sept. 3, 1965); was in Long Wharf Th. (New Haven, Conn.) productions of *Misalliance* (Jan. 13, 1967) and *Mother Courage and Her Children* (Feb. 17, 1967); played Sister Jeanne in *The Devils* (Center Th. Group, Mark Taper Forum, Los Angeles, Calif., Apr. 14, 1967); and the title role in *Saint Joan* (Williamstown Th., Mass., Aug. 8–12, 1967).

She appeared in other productions at Long Wharf Th., including *The Glass Menagerie* (Oct. 20, 1967), *The Rehearsal* (Nov. 17, 1967), *The Playboy of the Western World* (Dec. 15, 1967), *Room Service* (Jan. 12, 1968), *A Doctor in Spite of Himself* (Mar. 8, 1968), *Tiny Alice* (Apr. 5, 1968), *The Lion in Winter* (Oct. 18, 1968), *Epitaph for George Dillon* (Dec. 13,

1968), *America Hurrah* (Jan. 10, 1969), *Under Milk Wood* (Apr. 4, 1969), *Ghosts* (May 2, 1969), *Tango* (Nov. 14, 1969), *Country People* (Jan. 9, 1970), *Black Comedy* (Feb. 6, 1970), *A Day in the Death of Joe Egg* (Mar. 6, 1970), and *Spoon River Anthology* (Apr. 3, 1970).

Also in *The Skin of Our Teeth* (Oct. 23, 1970), *Yegor Bulichov* (Dec. 18, 1970), *She Stoops to Conquer* (Jan. 15, 1971), and she was the Wife in *Solitaire* and Barbara in *Double Solitaire* (Feb. 12, 1971; John Golden Th., N.Y.C., Sept. 30, 1971). She appeared also in *Heartbreak House* (Apr. 9, 1971), *The Price* (May 7, 1971, *A Streetcar Named Desire* (Dec. 17, 1971), *Hamlet* (Jan. 21, 1972), *The Way of the World* (Feb. 18, 1972), and in *The Country Woman* on a program billed as *Troika: An Evening of Russian Comedy* (Mar. 17, 1972).

Also in *The Lady's Not for Burning* (Oct. 14, 1972), *Juno and the Paycock* (Mar. 2, 1973), as Ursula in *Forget-Me-Not-Lane* (Apr. 6, 1973), was in *Dance of Death* and *Miss Julie* (May 11, 1973), played Mrs. Holroyd in *The Widowing of Mrs. Holroyd* (Nov. 16, 1973), was in *The Seagull* (Mar. 1, 1974), was Matron in *The National Health* (Apr. 5, 1974; Circle in the Square, N.Y.C., Oct. 10, 1974); Ruth Ferrara in *You're Too Tall, But Come Back in Two Weeks* (Feb. 28, 1975), Clara in *The Show-Off* (Nov. 21, 1975), Maggie Wylie in *What Every Women Knows* (Dec. 1975), Bertha Dorset in *The House of Mirth* (Apr. 9, 1976), and Maisie Madigan in *Daarlin' Juno* (May 19, 1976).

Television. Mrs. Ebert made her debut on Frontiers of Faith (NBC, 1956); followed by a reading of *A Shropshire Lad* (Camera 3, CBS); played Mary in *A Dickens Chronicle* (CBS, 1963); appeared on Kraft Television Th. (NBC); Suspense (CBS); The Big Valley (ABC, 1967); and as Mrs. Holroyd in *The Widowing of Mrs. Holroyd* (PBS, May 1974).

Awards. She received the Atlas Award from the San Diego Shakespeare Festival for her performance as Juliet in *Romeo and Juliet* (1959); the Clarence Derwent Award and *The Village Voice* Off-Bway (Obie) Award (1964) for her performance as Andromache in *The Trojan Women.*

ECKART, JEAN. Designer, producer. b. Jean Levy, Aug. 18, 1921, Chicago, Ill., to Herbert and Catharyn (Rubel) Levy. Father, stock broker. Grad. New Trier Township H.S., Winnetka, Ill., 1939; Sophie Newcomb Coll., B.F.A., 1943; Yale Univ., M.F.A. (stage design) 1949. Married Aug. 28, 1943, to William Eckart, stage designer; one son, one daughter. Served as civilian with the Military Intelligence Div., War Dept., 1944–45. Member of United Scenic Artists (recording secy., 1956–57). Address: 14 St. Luke's Pl., New York, NY 10014, tel. CH 3-7765.

Theatre. Mrs. Eckart has worked in collaboration with her husband throughout her career in the theatre.

They designed scenery and lighting for *Glad Tidings* (Lyceum, Oct. 11, 1951); the sets and lighting for *To Dorothy a Son* (John Golden Th., Nov. 19, 1951); *Gertie* (Plymouth, Jan. 30, 1952); and *Oh, Men! Oh, Women!* (Henry Miller's Th., Dec. 17, 1953); scenery, costumes and lighting for *Maya,* scenery and lighting for *The Scarecrow, The School for Scandal,* and *The Little Clay Cart* (Th. de Lys, Summer, 1953); and scenery and lighting for *Dead Pigeon* (Vanderbilt, Dec. 23, 1953); scenery for *The Golden Apple* (Phoenix, Mar. 11, 1954; moved to Alvin, Apr. 20, 1954); sets and lighting for *Wedding Breakfast* (46th St. Th., Nov. 20, 1954); and *Portrait of a Lady* (ANTA, Dec. 21, 1954); scenery, costumes, and lighting for *Damn Yankees* (46th St. Th., May 5, 1955); the pre-Bway tryout of *Reuben Reuben* (opened Shubert, Oct. 10, 1955; closed there Oct. 22, 1955); *Mister Johnson* (Martin Beck Th., N.Y.C., Mar. 29, 1956); scenery and lighting for *Li'l Abner* (St. James, Nov. 15, 1956); and for the NBC-TV Opera touring productions of *Madame Butterfly* and *The Marriage of Figaro* (1956).

They designed the sets for *Livin' the Life* (Phoenix, N.Y.C., Apr. 27, 1957); sets and lighting for *The Soft Touch,* that closed in rehearsal (1957); for *Copper and Brass* (Martin Beck Th., Oct. 17, 1957); *The Body Beautiful* (Bway Th., Jan. 23, 1958); scenery and costumes for *Once Upon a Mattress* (Phoenix, May 11, 1959; moved to Alvin, Nov. 25, 1959), which they also produced, with T. Edward Hambleton and Norris Houghtin; scenery, costumes and lighting for *Fiorello!* (Broadhurst, Nov. 23, 1959); scenery and lighting for *Viva Madison Avenue!* (Longacre, Apr. 6, 1960); *The Happiest Girl in the World* (Martin Beck Th., Apr. 3, 1961); *Let It Ride* (Eugene O'Neill Th., Oct. 12, 1961); and *Take Her, She's Mine* (Biltmore, Dec. 21, 1961); scenery for *Oh Dad, Poor Dad, Mamma's Hung You in the Closet and I'm Feelin' So Sad* (Phoenix, Feb. 26, 1962); scenery and lighting for *Never Too Late* (Playhouse, Nov. 27, 1962); *She Loves Me* (Eugene O'Neill Th., Apr. 23, 1963); scenery for *Here's Love* (Shubert, Oct. 10, 1963); *Anyone Can Whistle* (Majestic, Apr. 4, 1964); and scenery and lighting for *Fade Out—Fade In* (Mark Hellinger, May 26, 1964).

The Eckarts also did scenery and lighting for *A Sign of Affection* (opened Shubert Th., New Haven, Conn., Mar. 10, 1965; closed Walnut St. Th., Philadelphia, Pa., Apr. 10, 1965); settings for *Flora, the Red Menace* (Alvin, N.Y.C., May 11, 1965); settings and lighting for *The Zulu and the Zayda* (Cort, Nov. 10, 1965); *The Well-Dressed Liar* (Royal Poinciana Playhouse, Palm Beach, Fla., Mar. 7, 1966; Coconut Grove Playhouse, Miami, Fla., May 31, 1966); settings for *Mame* (Winter Garden, N.Y.C., May 24, 1966); and scenery and lighting for *Agatha Sue I love you* (Henry Miller's Th., Dec. 14, 1966).

They were artistic supervisors for the Young People's Repertory Th., which presented (both at Sheridan Square Playhouse) *When Did You Last See My Mother?* (Jan. 4, 1967) and *Antigone* (Jan. 13, 1967); designed settings for *Hallelujah, Baby!* (Martin Beck Th., Apr. 26, 1967); *A Midsummer Night's Dream* (American Shakespeare Festival, Stratford, Conn., June 17, 1967); *The Education of H*Y*M*A*N K*A*P*L*A*N* (Alvin, N.Y.C., Apr. 4, 1968); the pre-Bway tryout of *A Mother's Kisses* (opened Shubert Th., New Haven, Conn., Sept. 23, 1968; closed Morris A. Mechanic Th., Baltimore, Md., Oct. 19, 1968); and *Maggie Flynn* (ANTA Th., N.Y.C., Oct. 23, 1968).

They designed scenery for *The Fig Leaves Are Falling* (Broadhurst, Jan. 2, 1969); *A Way of Life* (previews only: ANTA Th., Jan. 18–Feb. 1, 1969); *Norman, Is That You?* (Lyceum, Feb. 19, 1970); and *Sensations* (Theatre Four, Oct. 25, 1970).

Other Activities. In collaboration with her husband, Mrs. Eckart has designed industrial productions, including the Martex show (1948); the *Glamour* Magazine Fashion Show (1950–57); the Dupont-Borden Show for the N.Y. World's Fair (1964); together, they designed the Rossin House, Helmville, Mont. (1952).

Awards. She and her husband received the Donaldson Award for their set designs in *The Golden Apple* (1954).

ECKART, WILLIAM JOSEPH. Designer, producer. b. Oct. 21, 1920, New Iberia, La., to William Joseph and Annette Cecile (Brown) Eckart. Father, salesman. Grad. New Iberia H.S., 1936; attended Univ. of Southwestern Louisiana, 1936–38; Tulane Univ., B.S. (architecture) 1942; Yale Univ., M.F.A. (stage design) 1949. Married Aug. 28, 1943, to Jean Levy, known as Jean Eckart, stage designer; one son, one daughter. Served WW II, US Army, translator, 1942–46. Member of United Scenic Artists.

Theatre. All Mr. Eckart's theatre work has been done in collaboration with his wife, Jean Eckart.

They designed the sets and lighting for *Glad Tidings* (Lyceum, Oct. 11, 1951); *To Dorothy a Son* (John Golden Th., N.Y.C., Nov. 19, 1951); *Gertie* (Plymouth, Jan. 30, 1952); and *Oh, Men! Oh, Women!* (Henry Miller's Th., Dec. 17, 1953); scenery, costumes, and lighting for *Maya,* scenery and lighting for *The Scarecrow, The School for Scandal,* and *The Little Clay Cart* (Th. de Lys, N.Y.C., Summer 1953); scenery and lighting for *Dead Pidgeon* (Vanderbilt, Dec. 23, 1953); *The Golden Apple* (Phoenix, Mar. 11, 1954; moved to Alvin, Apr. 24, 1954); sets and lighting for *Wedding Breakfast* (46 St. Th., Nov. 20, 1954); *Portrait of a Lady* (ANTA, Dec. 21, 1954); the scenery, costumes, and lighting for *Damn Yankees* (46 St. Th., May 5, 1955); the pre-Bway tryout of *Reuben Reuben* (opened Shubert, Boston, Mass., Oct. 10, 1955; closed there Oct. 22, 1955); *Mister Johnson* (Martin Beck Th., N.Y.C., Mar. 29, 1956); scenery and lighting for *Li'l Abner* (St. James, Nov. 15, 1956); and for the NBC-TV Opera touring productions (1956) of *Madama Butterfly* and *The Marriage of Figaro.* They designed sets for *Livin' the Life* (Phoenix, N.Y.C., Apr. 27, 1957); scenery and lighting for *Copper and Brass* (Martin Beck Th., Oct. 17, 1957); and the scenery and lighting for *The Body Beautiful* (Bway Th., Jan. 23, 1958).

They designed the scenery and costumes for *Once Upon a Mattress* (Phoenix, May 11, 1959), which they also co-produced; scenery, costumes, and lighting for *Fiorello!* (Broadhurst, Nov. 23, 1959); scenery and lighting for *Viva Madison Avenue!* (Longacre, Apr. 6, 1960); *The Happiest Girl in the World* (Martin Beck Th., Apr. 3, 1961); *Let It Ride* (Eugene O'Neill Th., Oct. 12, 1961); *Take Her, She's Mine* (Biltmore, Dec. 21, 1961); the scenery for *O Dad, Poor Dad, Mama's Hung You in the Closet and I'm Feelin' So Sad* (Phoenix, Feb. 26, 1962); scenery and lighting for *Never Too Late* (Playhouse, Nov. 27, 1962); *She Loves Me* (Eugene O'Neill Th., Apr. 23, 1963); and the scenery for *Here's Love* (Shubert, Oct. 10, 1963).

They designed scenery for *Anyone Can Whistle* (Majestic, Apr. 4, 1964); scenery and lighting for *Fade Out—Fade In* (Mark Hellinger Th., May 26, 1964); *A Sign of Affection* (opened: Shubert Th., New Haven, Conn., Mar. 10, 1965; closed: Walnut St. Th., Philadelphia, Pa., Apr. 10, 1965); settings for *Flora, the Red Menace* (Alvin, N.Y.C., May 11, 1965); settings and lighting for *The Zulu and the Zayda* (Cort, Nov. 10, 1965); *The Well-Dressed Liar* (Royal Poinciana Playhouse, Palm Beach, Fla., Mar. 7, 1966; Coconut Grove Playhouse, Miami, Fla., May 31, 1966); settings for *Mame* (Winter Garden, N.Y.C., May 24, 1966); and scenery and lighting for *Agatha Sue I love you* (Henry Miller's Th., Dec. 14, 1966).

They were artistic supervisors for the Young People's Repertory Th., which presented (both at Sheridan Square Playhouse) *When Did You Last See My Mother?* (Jan. 4, 1967) and *Antigone* (Jan. 13, 1967); designed settings for *Hallelujah, Baby!* (Martin Beck Th., Apr. 26, 1967); *A Midsummer Night's Dream* (American Shakespeare Festival, Stratford, Conn., June 17, 1967); *The Education of H*Y*M*A*N K*A*P*L*A*N* (Alvin, N.Y.C., Apr. 4, 1968); the pre-Bway tryout of *A Mother's Kisses* (opened Shubert Th., New Haven, Conn., Sept. 23, 1968; closed Morris A. Mechanic Th., Baltimore, Md., Oct. 19, 1968); and *Maggie Flynn* (ANTA Th., N.Y.C., Oct. 23, 1968).

They designed scenery for *The Fig Leaves Are Falling* (Broadhurst, Jan. 2, 1969); *A Way of Life* (previews only: ANTA Th., Jan. 18–Feb. 1, 1969); *Norman, Is That You?* (Lyceum, Feb. 19, 1970); and *Sensations* (Th. Four, Oct. 25, 1970).

Films. Mr. Eckart designed the costumes for *The Pajama Game* (WB, 1957); and was production designer for *Damn Yankees* (WB, 1958).

Television. He was associated with the NBC-TV scenic design staff in 1943, and later, with his wife, he was a member of the scenic design staff of CBS-TV (1950–51). His designs have been seen on the Ford Foundation's series, *Excursions* (NBC, 1953–54); Rodgers and Hammerstein's *Cinderella* (CBS, 1957); and Bell Telephone's *Adventure in Music* (NBC, 1959).

Other Activities. He has designed for industrial productions, including the *Glamour* Magazine Fashion Show (1950–57); Oldsmobile Show (1955); the Martex Show (1957); and the Dupont-Borden Show for the 1964 World's Fair (N.Y.C.). He designed the Rossin House, Helmville, Mont. (1952).

Awards. Mr. Eckart and his wife received the Donaldson Award (1954) for *The Golden Apple.*

ECKERT, GEORGE. Stage manager, director. b. George Arthur Eckert, Jr., Feb. 23, 1927, Philadelphia, Pa., to George Arthur and Alice Catherine (Watson) Eckert. Father, Capt., Medical Corps. USN. Grad. Rogers H.S., Newport, R.I., 1944; Brown Univ., A.B. 1950. Studied at Sch. of Radio Technique, N.Y.C., 1952. Grad. US Army Command and General Staff College, Ft. Leavenworth, Kans., 1972. Married Nov. 9, 1956, to Bonnie Jean Douglas, concert violinist (marr. dis. 1965). Served US Army, 1944–46, rank, T/4; US Army Reserve, 1946–to date; on active duty, 1972, rank, Lt. Col. Student (see above) and director, Combined Services Task Force, Office of the Chief of Information, Dept. of the Army, Washington, D.C. Member of SSD&C; AEA; AGMA; AFTRA; AGVA; The Lambs; Actors Fund (life member); NATAS; Army and Navy Club (Washington, D.C.). c/o The Lambs, 130 W. 44th St., New York, NY 10036.

Theatre. Mr. Eckert first appeared on stage as an emcee and stage manager for a US Army Special Services show at Camp Croft, S.C. (June 1945); made his first professional appearance in a stock production of *The Petrified Forest* (Casino Th., Newport, R.I., July, 1947); played Bruce, and was stage manager for *Come Back Little Sheba* (Red Barn Th., Westboro, Mass., May, 1953); was stage manager at the Savoy Th., Asbury Park, N.J. (Summer 1953), for *The Moon Is Blue* (June), *The Member of the Wedding* (June), *Bell, Book and Candle* (July), *Mister Roberts* in which he played the Shore Patrol Officer (July), *The Second Man* (July), and *The Country Girl* (Aug. 1953).

At the Paper Mill Playhouse, Millburn, N.J., he was production stage manager for *The Merry Widow* (Sept. 1953), *Brigadoon* (Oct. 1953), *Call Me Madam* (Nov. 1953), and *Paint Your Wagon* (Jan. 1954); stage managed a Johnson & Johnson industrial show (Plaza Hotel, N.Y.C., Feb. 1954); continued at the Paper Mill Playhouse (1954) as production stage manager for *Oklahoma!* (Apr.), *Carmen* (May), *The Great Waltz* (June), *The Vagabond King* (July), *Mister Roberts* (Sept.), *Sabrina Fair* (Oct.), *My 3 Angels* (Oct.), *Goodbye, My Fancy* in which he also played the Phone Man (Nov.), *Stalag 17* (Nov.), and *Time Out for Ginger* (Jan., 1955).

Mr. Eckert toured as production stage manager and played the Voice of Competition in a Coca-Cola industrial show (Feb. 1955); at the Paper Mill Playhouse (1955), was production stage manager for *South Pacific* (Apr.), *Guys and Dolls* (June), *Billie Burke Summer Tour* (July), and *King of Hearts* (Aug.); played the Salesman and was stage manager for a Coca-Cola industrial tour (Aug. 1955); production stage manager for the national tour of *Damn Yankees* (opened Shubert, New Haven, Conn., Jan. 21, 1956; closed Royal Alexandria, Toronto, Can., May 18, 1957); and production stage manager for the Coca-Cola NAMA Convention (Conrad Hilton Hotel, Chicago, Ill., Dec. 1956).

At the Starlight Musicals, Indianapolis, Ind. (1957), he directed *The Pajama Game* (June), *The Desert Song* (July), *Wonderful Town* (July), *Gentlemen Prefer Blondes* (July), *Carousel* (July), *Rosalie* (Aug.), and *Damn Yankees* (Aug.); toured as the production stage manager of *The Chevrolet Show* (Aug. 1957); produced and directed a touring company of *Damn Yankees* (Melbourne, Brisbane, and Sydney, Australia, opened Feb. 1958); and was stage manager for the touring *Esso Standard Oil Show* (Apr. 1958); and the *Columbia Phonograph Show* (May 1958); again at the Starlight Musicals (1958), he directed *Oklahoma!* (June), *Plain and Fancy* (July), *Hit the Deck* (July), *Rosalinda* (July), *Bloomer Girl* (July), *Naughty Marietta* (Aug.), and *Can-Can* (Aug.).

He took over (Aug. 1958) as stage manager for the pre-Bway tryout of *At the Grand* (opened Philharmonic Aud., Los Angeles, Calif., July 7, 1958; closed Curran, San Francisco, Calif., Sept. 13, 1958); was production stage manager for the tour of *Ballets: U.S.A.* (Oct. 1958); succeeded (Feb. 1959) Ruth Mitchell as production stage manager for *West Side Story* (Winter Garden, Sept. 26, 1957), and toured with it (opened Erlanger, Chicago, Ill., Oct. 8, 1959); directed *Damn Yankees* (San Bernardino Aud., Calif., Feb. 1960); was production manager for *Destry Rides Again* (Imperial, Apr. 23, 1959), and toured with it (opened Riviera, Las Vegas, July 31, 1960); stage manager for a Chrysler industrial tour (Oct. 1960); directed *Wonderful Town* (Phoenix East H.S., Ariz., Mar. 1961); and was general stage manager for *The Bartered Bride* (Shrine Aud., Los Angeles, Calif., Mar. 1961).

At the Circle Arts Th. (San Diego, Calif., 1961), he played Lt. Shrank and directed *West Side Story* (June 21); directed *Pal Joey* (June); and *The New Moon* (July).

He was production stage manager for *Guys and Dolls* (Philharmonic Aud., Los Angeles, Aug. 1961); general stage manager for *Cinderella* (Shrine Aud., Los Angeles, Feb. 1962); production stage manager for *Song of Norway* (Philharmonic Aud., Los Angeles, Apr. 1962); *Kismet* (Curran, San Francisco, Aug. 1962); *The Burroughs Corporation Show* (Hotel Riviera, Palm Springs, Calif., Feb. 1963); *Carousel* (Curran Th., San Francisco, Apr. 1963); and directed the industrials *The Ford 1964 New Car Announcement Show* (Aug. 1963), *The Falstaff Brewing Corporation Show* (Hotel Jung, New Orleans, La., Feb. 1964), and *The Marathon Oil Company Show* (Veterans Aud., Columbus, Ohio, March 1964).

He directed *Damn Yankees* (Valley Music Th., Los Angeles, July 1964); was replacement first assistant stage manager for the touring *Here's Love* (Curran Th., San Francisco, Oct.–Dec. 1964); production stage manager for *Pickwick* (pre-Bway engagement, Curran Th., San Francisco, Apr. 19, 1965); directed *Paint Your Wagon* (Valley Music Th., Los Angeles, July 1965); and was production supervisor for *The Proctor & Gamble Year-End Sales Show* (Netherlands Plaza Hotel, Cincinnati, Ohio, Nov.–Dec. 1965) and field company director, *Chevrolet New Car Announcement* shows (1965–67). He directed *Take Her, She's Mine* (Valley Music Th., Los Angeles, July 1966); was production stage manager for *The Tiger* and *The Typist* (Huntington Hartford Th., Los Angeles, 1966); and directed *The International Paper Company Industrial Show* (Sheraton-Huntington Hotel, Pasadena, Calif., Dec. 1969). He was also production stage manager of *Our Town* (Huntington Hartford Th., Los Angeles, 1970); director-choreographer for four companies of industrial shows for Humble Oil Company (first company opened Sheraton-Lincoln Hotel, Houston, Tex., Dec. 15, 1970); production stage manager for *Plaza Suite* (Huntington Hartford Th., Los Angeles, 1971); for Henry Fonda's one-man show (Lobero Th., Santa Barbara, Calif., Mar. 1971); production supervisor of *Ford New Car Announcement* shows on tour (1971–72); and production stage manager for *Clarence Darrow* (Helen Hayes Th., N.Y.C., Mar. 26, 1974).

Films. Mr. Eckert assisted the director, Gene Kelly, on *A Guide for the Married Man* (20th-Fox, 1967). Other films on which he worked are *Hello, Dolly!* (20th-Fox, 1968) and *The Cheyenne Social Club* (MGM, 1969).

Television. Mr. Eckert was dialogue director for the Hawkins series (MGM, Jan.–Nov. 1973).

Recreation. Swimming, traveling by freighter.

EDWARDS, A. C. Educator, publisher. b. Aubrey Carroll Edwards, Aug. 25, 1909, Davenport, Okla., to Rila D. and Mae (Brown) Edwards. Father, geologist. Grad. State Univ. of Iowa, Ph.D. 1941. Married Mar. 23, 1940, to Virginia Busse. Served USAAF, 1942–45; rank, Capt. Member of AAUP. Address: (home) Rural, Route 4, Lawrence, KS 66044, tel. (913) VI 3-2643; (bus.) Dept. of English, Univ. of Kansas, Lawrence, KS 66044.

Mr. Edwards is professor of English at the Univ. of Kansas (1947–to date); and is founder (May 1958), former publisher, and editor of *Modern Drama*, a quarterly journal devoted to the study of drama since Ibsen. Mr. Edwards taught at the State Univ. of Iowa (1938), Oklahoma State Univ. (1941–42), and the Univ. of Illinois (1946).

Recreation. Billiards, gardening, woodworking.

EDWARDS, BEN. Scenery, costume, and lighting designer, producer. b. George Benjamin Edwards, July 5, 1916, Union Springs, Ala., to William Thomas and Sarah (McLaurine) Edwards. Father, businessman, planter. Grad. H.S., Union Springs, 1934; attended Feagin Sch. of Dramatic Arts, N.Y.C., 1934–36; Kane Sch. of Art, N.Y.C., 1935–36. Married Sept. 21, 1963, to Jane Greenwood, costume designer. Served with US Army, 1942–46; rank, Lt. Member of League of N.Y. theatres; United Scenic Artists; The Players (art committee, 1962–63). Address: 321 W. 19th St., New York, NY 10011, tel. (212) WA 9-2931.

Theatre. Mr. Edwards first worked professionally at the Barter Th. (Abingdon, Va., 1935–39), designing sets and lighting for such productions as *Mrs. Moonlight, Pursuit of Happiness, Smilin' Through, Beyond the Hills,* and *The Silver Cord;* he designed sets and costumes for the NY State Federal Th. (WPA) Project productions of *Diff'rent, Pygmalion, Coriolanus, and Captain Jinks of the Horse Marines* (Maxine Elliott's Th., N.Y.C., Jan. 25–Feb. 12, 1938); designed sets for *Another Sun* (Natl., Feb. 23, 1940); sets for *Medea* (Natl., Oct. 20, 1947; NY City Ctr., May 2, 1949); sets for *Sundown Beach* (Belasco, Sept. 7, 1948); created, with William De Forest, sets for *Diamond Lil* (Coronet, Feb. 5, 1949); designed sets and costumes for Margaret Webster's Shakespeare Company's touring productions of *The Taming of the Shrew* and *Julius Caesar* (opened Woodstock Playhouse, N.Y., 1949).

He designed costumes for *The Bird Cage* (Coronet, N.Y.C., Feb. 22, 1950); costumes for *Legend of Sarah* (Fulton, Oct. 11, 1950); at the NY City Ctr., designed sets for *Captain Brassbound's Conversion* (Dec. 27, 1950), *The Royal Family* (Jan. 10, 1951), *King Richard II* (Jan. 24, 1951), and *The Taming of the Shrew* (Apr. 25, 1951); designed costumes for *Desire Under the Elms* (ANTA, Jan. 16, 1952); sets and costumes for *Sunday Breakfast* (Coronet, May 28, 1952); sets and lighting for *The Time of the Cuckoo* (Empire, Oct. 15, 1952); costumes for *The Emperor's Clothes* (Ethel Barrymore Th., Feb. 9, 1953); sets, lighting, and costumes for *The Remarkable Mr. Pennypacker* (Coronet, Dec. 30, 1953); sets and lighting for *Lullaby* (Lyceum, Feb. 3, 1954); sets for *Sing Me No Lullaby* (Phoenix, Oct. 14, 1954); sets, lighting, and costumes for *The Traveling Lady* (Playhouse, Oct. 27, 1954); and sets and costumes for *Anastasia* (Lyceum, Dec. 29, 1954).

Mr. Edwards designed sets and lighting for *Tonight in Samarkand* (Morosco, Feb. 16, 1955); settings for *The Honeys* (Longacre, Apr. 28, 1955); sets and lighting for *Someone Waiting* (John Golden Th., Feb. 14, 1956); sets and lighting for *The Ponder Heart* (Music Box, Feb. 16, 1956); sets, lighting, and costumes for *The Waltz of the Toreadors* (Coronet, Jan. 17, 1957); sets for *The Dark at the Top of the Stairs* (Music Box, Dec. 5, 1957); sets and lighting for *Jane Eyre* (Belasco, May 1, 1958); sets, costumes, and lighting for *A Touch of the Poet* (Helen Hayes Th., Oct. 2, 1958); sets for *The Disenchanted* (Coronet, Dec. 3, 1958); and sets and lighting for *God and Kate Murphy* (54 St. Th., Feb. 26, 1959).

He created sets and lighting for *Heartbreak House* (Billy Rose Th., Oct. 18, 1959); lighting for Gielgud's *Ages of Man* (46 St. Th., Dec. 28, 1959); sets and lighting for *Face of a Hero* (Eugene O'Neill Th., Oct. 20, 1960); *Midgie Purvis* (Martin Beck Th., Feb. 1, 1961); *Big Fish, Little Fish,* which he also produced with Lewis Allen (ANTA, Mar. 15, 1961); *Purlie Victorious* (Cort., Sept. 28, 1961); *A Shot in the Dark* (Booth, Oct. 18, 1961); *The Aspern Papers* (Playhouse, Feb. 7, 1962); *Harold,* which he also produced, with Wigwam Productions, Inc. (Cort, Nov. 29, 1963); sets for *The Ballad of the Sad Cafe,* which he also produced, with Lewis Allen (Martin Beck Th., Oct. 30, 1963); and sets for Richard Burton's *Hamlet* (Lunt-Fontanne, Apr. 9, 1964).

He designed costumes for the Rep. Th. of Lincoln Center production of *The Changeling* (ANTA-Washington Sq. Th., Oct. 29, 1964); sets and lighting for *The Family Way* (Lyceum, Jan. 13, 1965); sets and lighting for *A Race of Hairy Men!* (Henry Miller's Th., Apr. 29, 1965), which he co-produced with Elaine Perry; sets for the summer tryout of William Inge's *Family Things* (Falmouth Playhouse, Mass., July 12, 1965; Westport Country Playhouse, Conn., July 19, 1965); with George Jenkins, was production supervisor of *The Royal Hunt of the Sun* (ANTA, N.Y.C., Oct. 26, 1965); designed sets and lighting for *Nathan Weinstein, Mystic, Connecticut* (Brooks Atkinson Th., Feb. 25, 1966); sets and lighting for *Where's Daddy?* (Billy Rose Th., Mar. 2, 1966); sets and lighting for *How's The World Treating You?* (Music Box, Oct. 24, 1966); sets and lighting for the pre-Bway tryout of *What Do You Really Know About Your Husband?* (opened Shubert, New Haven, Mar. 9, 1967; closed there Mar. 11, 1967); sets for *More Stately Mansions* (Broadhurst, N.Y.C., Oct. 31, 1967); designed, with Jean Rosenthal, sets and lighting for *The Freaking Out of Stephanie Blake* (Eugene O'Neill Th., started previews Oct. 30, 1967; closed before official opening, Nov. 1, 1967); for the Minnesota Th. Co., designed *Twelfth Night* and *The Master Builder* (Tyrone Guthrie Th., Minneapolis, June, 1968); designed sets and lighting for *The Mother Lover* (Booth, N.Y.C., Feb. 1, 1969); designed sets for the Studio Arena Th. (Buffalo, N.Y., 1969–70); designed sets for *Purlie* (Broadway Th., N.Y.C., Mar. 15, 1970; and on tour, opened Shubert, Philadelphia, Nov. 20, 1971); designed sets and lighting for *Hay Fever* (Helen Hayes Th., N.Y.C., Nov. 9, 1970); sets and lighting for *Look Away* (Playhouse, Jan. 7, 1973); sets and lighting for *Finishing Touches* (Plymouth, Feb. 8, 1973); set and lighting for *A Moon for the Misbegotten* (Morosco, Dec. 29, 1973); and set and lighting for *The Headhunters* (Eisenhower Th., Washington, D.C., May 1, 1974).

Films. Mr. Edwards was the art director for the films *Jennifer on My Mind* (UA, 1971); and *Last of the Red Hot Lovers* (Par., 1972). He was the designer for *Class of '44* (WB, 1973).

Television. Mr. Edwards has designed the sets for the Ed Wynn Show (NBC, 1952), and Armstrong Circle Theatre (CBS, 1955).

Awards. In a tie with Cecil Beaton for *Saratoga*, Mr. Edwards won the *Variety* Drama Critics' Poll (1960) for his set designs for *Heartbreak House*.

Recreation. Book collecting, hunting, fishing.

EGAN, JENNY. Actress, director, designer, teacher, writer. b. Ann Jacobson McGonigle, New York City. Father, marketing consultant and inventor; mother, nursery school teacher. Educ. H.S. of Music and Art, N.Y.C.; grad. Grinnell Coll., B.A.; attended Sorbonne, Paris, Fr.; grad. NY Univ., M.A.; Ph.D. Professional training at the Neighborhood Playhouse with Sanford Meisner; Stella Adler School of the Theatre. Married 1950 to William A. McGonigle, systems analyst. Member of AEA; SAG; AFTRA. Address: (home) 179 Sullivan St., New York, NY 10012, tel. (212) AL 4-8169; (bus.) The Four Winds Th., Inc., 37 W. 10th St., New York, NY 10011, tel. (212) 260-3939; Ser: 787-5400.

Theatre. Miss Egan's first theatre experience was with a Parisian medieval repertory company, Les Thophiliens, touring France (1948–49). She made her Bway debut as Mary Warren in *The Crucible* (Martin Beck Th., N.Y.C., Jan. 22, 1953); appeared off-Bway in *Illusion;* played Mary, Queen of Scots in Schiller's *Mary Stuart* (Guild Hall Aud., N.Y.C., Apr. 1956); was in *The Chairs* (Phoenix, Jan. 15, 1958); played Mrs. Smith in *The Bald Soprano* and Jacqueline in *Jack* (both Sullivan St. Playhouse, June 3, 1958); numerous parts in *Under Milk Wood* (Circle in the Square, Mar. 28, 1961); Grandma in *The American Dream* (Cherry Lane, Dec. 10, 1961); directed *The Ancient Love Story of Lao Litang* (IASTA, May 25–27, 1962); was Mrs. Peterson in *The Ballad of the Sad Café* (Martin Beck Th., Oct. 30, 1963); was standby for Anne Bancroft as Sister Jeanne in *The Devils* (Bway Th., Dec. 16, 1965); played the Old Lady in *Box-Mao-Box* (world premiere: Studio Arena, Buffalo, N.Y., Mar. 6, 1968); and Mamma in *The Cuban Thing* (Henry Miller's Th., N.Y.C., Sept. 24, 1968).

In 1957, Miss Egan founded the Four Winds Theatre, Inc., a nonprofit organization, of which she is artistic director. Four Winds has pioneered in presentation of documentary drama in museums, historic sites, and similar locations in the US and abroad. With the cooperation of Thomas Hoving, Metropolitan Mus. of Art, N.Y.C., Four Winds staged Ionesco's *Maid to Marry* and presented *The Garland of Months*, a program of medieval readings, at the museum (June 5–12, 1967).

For Phoenix Th., Miss Egan was assistant to Stuart Vaughan for *The Great God Brown* (Coronet, N.Y.C., Oct. 6, 1959) and *Pictures in the Hallway* (Dec. 28, 1959); and she was assistant to Jean Gascon for *Lysistrata* (Phoenix Th., June 5, 1958; Nov. 24, 1959).

In addition, Miss Egan has been an assistant director, and consultant, NY Shakespeare Festival and Phoenix Th.; resident director, New Dramatists; and organizer and director of the First Phoenix Educational Th.

Films. Miss Egan's screen credits include *Pollyanna* (Buena Vista, 1960) and *They Might Be Giants* (U, 1971). She has been supervising production of Four Winds documentary films on American history for the bicentennial. Some of this work is being done in association with the US National Park Service and several American universities.

Television. Miss Egan played Sis on Mister Peepers (NBC) and was Miss Hollub on Love of Life (CBS), appearing on both of these in the early 1950s. Other television programs on which she has played included Kraft Th. (NBC); Robert Montgomery Show (NBC); Camera Three (CBS); Goodyear Playhouse (NBC); and Philco Playhouse (NBC).

Other Activities. Miss Egan established her own teaching studio, the Jenny Egan Drama Workshop, N.Y.C., in 1964. She has also taught at NY Univ., where she organized a dance-drama workshop; Graduate School of Arts and Science, Columbia Univ. (assoc. prof.); and at such theatrical schools as Stella Adler, HB Studio, and Circle in the Square School.

Discography. Miss Egan is featured on *A Man's a Man* (Spoken Arts, 1962).

Awards. Miss Egan received the Clarence Derwent Award for the best nonfeatured performance on Bway (1953 season) for her role in *The Crucible*. She has received the Grinnell College Alumni Award as a distinguished alumna and a Ford Foundation grant as a young director.

Recreation. Designing houses, fencing.

EGGERTH, MARTA. Singer, actress. b. Apr. 17, 1919, Budapest, Hungary, to Paul and Tilly (Herezegh) Eggerth. Father, banker; mother, singer. Educated privately. Married 1937 to Jan Kiepura, singer (dec. Aug. 15, 1966); two sons. Member of AEA. Address: (home) Park Drive North, Rye, NY 10580, tel. (914) WO 7-5012; (bus.) 17 E. 96th St., New York, NY 10028, tel. (212) EN 9-8959.

Theatre. Miss Eggerth first appeared on the stage at age nine as a Doll in a French musical, *Maniquin* (Budapest, 1928); and subsequently appeared in *The Violet of Montmartre* (Vienna, 1931).

She made her N.Y.C. debut as Minnie Sorenson in *Higher and Higher* (Shubert, Apr. 4, 1940); played Sonia Sadoya in *The Merry Widow* (Majestic, Aug. 4, 1943), with her husband, Jan Kiepura, playing Prince Danilio. They have since repeated these roles over 1,000 times, in five languages in the US and Europe. She has also played Marisha in *Polonaise* (Alvin, Oct. 1945).

Films. Miss Eggerth has made many films, in seven languages, which include *Unfinished Symphony* (CB, 1935); *Casta Diva* (CIL, 1937); *Blond Carmen* (German, 1939); *La Vie de Bohème* (Cinecitta, Rome, 1949); *Valse Brilliante* (1952); *The Land of Smiles* (Berolina, 1959); and *Spring in Berlin* (Berolina, 1960).

Television. She has made television appearances throughout Europe.

Night Clubs. Miss Eggerth appeared with her son Jan Kiepura, Jr., in a medley from *The Merry Widow* (The Bushes, Park Royal Hotel, N.Y.C., Spring 1976).

EICHELBAUM, STANLEY. Critic. b. Oct. 5, 1926, New York City, to Samuel and Rebecca (Rosen) Eichelbaum. Father, businessman. Grad. Morris H.S., N.Y.C., 1943, City Coll. of New York, B.A. (Phi Beta Kappa) 1947; Columbia Univ., M.A. 1948; Univ. of Paris (de la Sorbonne), Diplome d'Etudes 1949. Attended Art Students League, N.Y.C., 1950–52. Member of San Francisco-Oakland Newspaper Guild. Address: (home) 333 Green St., San Francisco, CA 94133, tel. (415) 434-2840; (bus.) c/o *The Examiner*, 110 Fifth St., San Francisco, CA 94119, tel. (415) 781-2424.

Since 1960, Mr. Eichelbaum has been drama editor, and theatre and film critic, for the San Francisco *Examiner*. Previously he was a researcher and reporter for *The New Yorker* (1949–58); joined the San Francisco *Examiner* as Sunday feature writer and editor (1958), and became assistant Sunday editor (1959). Since 1970, he has been a part-time instructor in a critic's workshop (writing course for film and theatre reviewing), at the Univ. of California, San Francisco Ext.

Published Works. He has contributed articles to *The New Yorker, Theatre Arts, Show Business Illustrated, Playbill,* the *Christian Science Monitor, San Francisco,* and *Hollywood Reporter.*

Recreation. Reading, painting (has exhibited).

ELCAR, DANA. Actor. b. Ibson Dana Elcar, Oct. 10, 1927, Ferndale, Mich., to James Aage and Hedwig (Anderberg) Elcar. Father, butcher, carpenter. Grad., Baldwin H.S., Birmingham, Mich., 1946; attended Univ. of Michigan, 1948–51. Studied with Sanford Meisner at the Neighborhood Playhouse Sch. of the Th., N.Y.C. (Summers 1949–50); and Paul Sills at the Second City Workshop, N.Y.C. Married July 1948 to Katherine Frances Mead (marr. dis. May 1950); married Dec. 29, 1953, to Peggy Romano, actress; one daughter, Nora Elcar, actress. Served with USN, weatherman, 1946–48. Member of AEA; AFTRA; SAG.

Pre-Theatre. Carpenter, taxicab driver.

Theatre. Mr. Elcar, as a member of the Arts Theatre Club (Ann Arbor Mich.), produced, acted, or directed such plays as *Othello, The Master Builder, Man Is Man, Little Eyolf,* and *Rocket to the Moon* (1951–54).

He first appeared in N.Y.C. as general understudy for *Oh, Men! Oh, Women!* (Henry Miller's Th., Dec. 17, 1953); subsequently played in *Which Way Is Home?* (Th. de Lys, 1954); toured as an understudy in the national company of *Oh, Men! Oh, Women!* (opened Cass, Detroit, Mich., Nov. 15, 1954; closed Chicago, Ill., Mar. 1955); played Potts in *The Honeys* (Longacre, N.Y.C., Apr. 28, 1955); Grant Cobbler in a stock production of *Oh, Men! Oh, Women!* (Westport Country Playhouse, Conn.; Ivoryton Playhouse, Conn.; Falmouth Playhouse, Mass.; Summer 1955); Commander in the pre-Bway tryout of *Strip for Action* (opened Shubert, New Haven, Conn., Mar. 17, 1956; closed Nixon, Pittsburgh, Pa., Apr. 14, 1956); the Policeman and McFadden in *Good as Gold* (Belasco, N.Y.C., Mar. 7, 1957); King Edward IV in *Richard III* (Heckscher Th., Nov. 25, 1957); and Roo Webber in *Summer of the Seventeenth Doll* (Arena Stage, Washington, D.C., May–June 1958; Players, N.Y.C., Oct. 13, 1959).

He played the Chief of Police in *The Power and the Glory* (Phoenix, N.Y.C., Dec. 10, 1958); Dr. Gibbs in *Our Town* (Circle in the Square, Mar. 23, 1959); Big Daddy in a stock production of *Cat on a Hot Tin Roof* (Fort Lee, N.J., Summer 1959); Father Gagnon in *Semi-Detached* (Martin Beck Th., Mar. 10, 1960); Seumas Shield in *The Shadow of a Gunman* (Olney Summer Th., Md., Summer 1960); Christy, Mahon, Aymon, and Dr. Henchy in *Drums Under the Windows* (Cherry Lane, N.Y.C., Oct. 13, 1960); and Rev. Eli Jenkens, Lord Cut Glass, Jack Black, Sinbad Sailors, and Mr. Pritchard in *Under Milk Wood* (Circle in the Square, Mar. 29, 1961).

Mr. Elcar portrayed Ferrovius in *Androcles and the Lion* (Phoenix, Nov. 21, 1961); the Father in *Childhood*, one of a triple-bill entitled *Plays for Bleecker Street* (Circle in the Square, Jan. 11, 1962); John in a stock production of *Rhinoceros* (Olney Summer Th., Md., Summer 1962); Ben in *The Dumbwaiter*, one of two plays produced under the title *The Pinter Plays* (Cherry Lane, Nov. 26, 1962); Kermontov in a stock production of *A Sound of Distant Thunder* (Playhouse-on-the-Mall, Paramus, N.J., Summer 1963); *When the Owl Screams* (Second City at Square East, N.Y.C., Nov. 26, 1963); and was the stand-by for Alec Guinness in the title role of *Dylan* (Plymouth, Jan. 18, 1964).

He played Pertuiset in *A Murderer Among Us* (Morosco, Mar. 25, 1964); the title role in *Galileo* (Arena Stage, Washington, D.C., Oct. 29, 1964); directed *The Collection* (Arena Stage, 1964); was understudy for Jack Dodson and Jason Robards in *Hughie* (Royale, N.Y.C., Dec. 22, 1964); appeared in *Project Immortality* (Arena Stage, Washington, D.C., Jan. 6, 1966); played Price in *Eh?* (Circle in the Square, N.Y.C., Oct. 16, 1966); appeared in the American premiere of *Crystal and Fox* (Center Th. Group, Mark Taper Forum, Los Angeles, Calif., Apr. 9, 1970); was in *Who Wants to Be the Lone Ranger?* (New Th. for Now Workshop, Mark Taper Forum, Los Angeles, Calif., 1971); *That Championship Season* (American Conservatory Th., San Francisco, Calif., Feb. 20, 1973); *Inherit the Wind* (Arena Stage, Washington, D.C., Nov. 1, 1973); and *The Cherry Orchard* (American Conservatory Th., San Francisco, Calif., Mar. 19, 1974).

Films. He has appeared in *The Fool Killer* (Landau, 1963); *Fail-Safe* (Col., 1964).

Television. He has appeared on The Big Story (NBC, 1957); *Our Town* (1960); *Burning Bright* (WNTA, Newark, N.J., 1960); *The Sacco-Vanzetti Story* (Sunday Showcase, NBC, June 1960); Naked City (ABC, 1961–63); The Catholic Hour (NBC, 1962); The Defenders (CBS, 1962–63); *Big Deal at Laredo* (Dupont Show of the Month, NBC, 1963); East Side/West Side (CBS, 1963); *The Patriots* (Hallmark Hall of Fame, NBC, 1963); The Nurses (CBS); in the daytime serial Dark Shadows; and in *The Crucible* (CBS, May 4, 1967).

Recreation. Bicycle riding, swimming, music, running, reading, flying, museums, art galleries, and Chinese restaurants.

ELDER, ELDON. Setting and lighting designer, costume designer, educator, theatre designer. b. Mar. 17, 1924, Atchison, Kan., to Clifford Philips and Signe (Larsen) Elder. Father, physician. Grad. Kansas State Teachers Coll., B.S. 1944; attended Univ. of Denver, 1947; grad. Yale Univ. Sch. of Drama, M.F.A. 1950. Served USNR 1944–46. Member of United Scenic Artists. Address: 27 W. 67th St., New York, NY 10023, tel. (212) TR 7-2858.

Theatre. Mr. Elder designed his first professional settings and lighting for *The Father* and *Erdgeist* (Provincetown Playhouse, N.Y.C., 1949); taught a course in stagecraft at CCNY (Spring 1950–51) and designed for the City Coll. Th. Workshop, productions of *Measure for Measure* (Mar. 3–5, 1950) and *Everyman* (Mar. 9–11, 1951); at the WEstport (Conn.) Country Playhouse designed settings and lighting for the premieres of *Angel in the Pawnshop, The Life of the Party, Within a Glass Bell, My Fiddle's Got Three Strings,* and *The Long Days* (Summer 1950).

His first N.Y.C. assignment was designing settings and lighting for *The Long Days* (Empire, Apr. 20, 1951); followed by the NY City Ctr. productions of *Dream Girl* (May 9, 1951), and *Idiot's Delight* (May 23, 1951); *Giants in the Earth* (Columbia Univ. Opera Workshop, 1951); at the Westport (Conn.) Country Playhouse for *Candida*, and the premieres of *Love Revisited, Island Fling,* and *Kin Hubbard* (Summer 1951); and for *Legend of Lovers* (Plymouth, N.Y.C., Dec. 26, 1951).

Mr. Elder was supervising designer for *Venus Observed* (Century, Feb. 13, 1952); designed sets and lights for *Hook 'n Ladder* (Royale, Apr. 29, 1952); *Time Out for Ginger* (Lyceum, Nov. 26, 1952); *The Grey-Eyed People* (Martin Beck Th., Dec. 17, 1952); and the following productions at the St. Louis (Mo.) Municipal Opera: *Up in Central Park, Bloomer Girl, Cyrano de Bergerac, Rio Rita, Blossom Time, Rip Van Winkle, No, No Nanette, One Touch of Venus, Carmen, Bitter Sweet,* and *Kiss Me, Kate* (Summer 1953).

He designed settings and lighting for *Take a Giant Step* (Lyceum, N.Y.C., Sept. 24, 1953); *The Girl in Pink Tights* (Mark Hellinger Th., Mar. 5, 1954); and at the St. Louis Municipal Opera for *Call Me Madam, Song of Norway, The New Moon, Roberta, The Mikado, Gentlemen Prefer Blondes, The Three Musketeers, Panama Hattie, Where's Charley?, The Red Mill,* and *Oklahoma!* (Summer, 1954).

Also, for *All in One*, a double bill composed of *Trouble in Tahiti* and *27 Wagons Full of Cotton* (Playhouse, N.Y.C., Apr. 19, 1955); *Phoenix '55* (Phoenix, Apr. 23, 1955); *The Merry Widow, Brigadoon,* and *Wonderful Town* (St. Louis Municipal Opera, (Summer 1955); *The Young and Beautiful* (Longacre, N.Y.C., Oct. 1, 1955); *Heavenly Twins* (Booth, Nov. 4, 1955); *Fallen Angels* (Playhouse, Jan. 17, 1956); and *Shinbone Alley* (Bway Th., Apr. 13, 1957).

He designed the settings and costumes for the NY Shakespeare Festival's productions of *Othello* and *Twelfth Night* (Belvedere Lake Th., Summer 1958); costumes, settings, and lighting for *Lulu* (Fourth St. Th., Sept. 29, 1958); settings and costumes for the NY Shakespeare Festival's productions (Belvedere Lake Th.) of *Julius Caesar* (Aug. 3, 1959); *Henry V* (June 29, 1960); *The Taming of the Shrew* (Aug. 18, 1960); and settings for *Measure for Measure* (July 24, 1960). He designed the costumes, settings, and lighting for *Drums Under the Window* (Cherry Lane, Oct. 13, 1960); sets for the opera, *Esther* (premiere Hunter Coll. Playhouse, Apr. 27, 1961); sets and costumes for the Santa Fe (N.M.) Opera association's productions of *Der Rosenkavalier* and *The Ballad of Baby Doe* (Summer 1961). He designed the new stage and the settings for the NY Shakespeare Festival's productions (Wollman Memorial Rink Th.) of *Much Ado About Nothing* (July 5, 1961), *A Midsummer Night's Dream* (Aug. 28, 1961); and *Richard II* (Aug. 28, 1961).

He designed the settings for the premiere of the opera *Rehearsal Call* (Juilliard Sch. of Music, Feb. 15, 1962); for the Amer. Shakespeare Fest., Stratford, Conn., he designed the new stage (1962), and sets for *Richard II,* (June 16, 1962), and *Henry IV, Part 1* (June 17, 1962); designed the settings and lighting for *The Affair* (Henry Miller's Th. N.Y.C., Sept. 26, 1962); *The Fun Couple* (Lyceum, Oct. 26, 1962) for which he was also assoc. producer; *Morning Sun* (Phoenix, Sept. 6, 1963); and was supervising designer of the settings and lighting for *Rugantino* (Mark Hellinger Th., Feb. 6, 1964).

Mr. Elder designed *I Knock at the Door* (Th. de Lys, Nov. 25, 1964); *Pictures in the Hallway* (Th. de Lys, Dec. 16, 1964); scenery and lighting for *The Child Buyer* (Garrick, Dec. 21, 1964); the stage for the NY Shakespeare Fest. at the Delacorte Th. in Central Park, N.Y.C. (Summer 1965); scenery and lighting for *Madame Mousse* (Westport Country Playhouse, Conn., Aug. 16, 1965); *The World of Ray Bradbury* (Orpheum, N.Y.C., Oct. 8, 1965); scenery for *Mating Dance* (Eugene O'Neill Th., Nov. 3, 1965); designed the festival stage for the Ypsilanti (Mich.) Greek Th., the scenery for their production of *The Oresteia* (June 28, 1966), and scenery and costumes for *The Birds* (June 29, 1966); scenery ahd lighting for *A Whitman Portrait* (Gramercy Arts Th., N.Y.C., Oct. 11, 1966); costumes and lighting for *The Entertainer* (Pittsburgh Playhouse, Hamlet St. Th., Dec. 16, 1966); scenery and lighting for *Of Love Remembered* (ANTA Th., N.Y.C., Feb. 18, 1967); designed *Amazing Grace* (Ann Arbor, Mich., 1967); lighting for *The Megilla of Itzik Manger* (Golden, N.Y.C., Oct. 9, 1968); scenery for *Spiro Who?* (Gate Th., May 18, 1969); and *The Drexler Plays* (Open Space, London, 1970).

He designed *Will Rogers' USA*, which toured (open Ford's Th., Washington, D.C., Sept. 16, 1970; closed Music Center, Los Angeles, Jan. 2, 1971; also toured 1971–72) and subsequently played N.Y.C. (Helen Hayes Th., May 6, 1974); designed *A Cry of Players* (1970–71 season) and *Trial of the Catonsville Nine* (1971–72 season) for Center Stage Co., Baltimore, Md.; scenery and projections for *Pygmalion* (Queens Playhouse, N.Y., Oct. 25, 1972); scenery for *A Family and a Fortune,* and *The Seagull* (1973–74 season), and *Hamlet* (Oct. 1974), for the Seattle (Wash.) Rep. Th.; and designed *Blasts and Bravos: An Evening with H. L. Mencken* (Cherry Lane, N.Y.C., Jan. 16, 1975).

Other Activities. Since 1956, Mr. Elder has been professor of stage design at Brooklyn Coll. He was visiting critic in stage design at Yale Univ. (1954); and stage and lighting consultant for Temple Emanu-el Aud. (1963).

Published Works. He wrote *Modern American Scene Design*, which was published in manuscript form (USIS, 1959).

Awards. He received a Ford Foundation Grant to design with Edward Durrell Stone a 2,000-seat open-air festival theatre (1961); and a Guggenheim Foundation Grant for a study of classical theatres (1963).

ELDER, LONNE III. Playwright, actor. b. Dec. 26, 1933, Americus, Ga. Attended N.J. State Teachers Coll.; Yale Sch. of Drama. Studied acting with Mary Welch. Served US Army. Married Feb. 14, 1969, to Judyann Jonsson, actress; two sons. Member of Harlem Writers Guild; New Dramatists Committee.

Pre-Theatre. Dock worker, waiter, professional gambler.

Theatre. Mr. Elder worked with Brett Warren's Actors' Mobile Th. (late 1950s); made his Bway debut as Bobo in *A Raisin in the Sun* (Ethel Barrymore Th., N.Y.C., Mar. 11, 1959; and national tour); and, with the Negro Ensemble Co., played Clem in *Day of Absence* (St. Mark's Playhouse, N.Y.C., Nov. 15, 1965).

Mr. Elder's thesis drama, *Charades on East 4th Street*, was commissioned by the N.Y.C. Mobilization for Youth and was presented at Expo '67 (Montreal, Canada, 1967). He made his professional debut as a playwright with *Ceremonies in Dark Old Men* (St. Mark's Playhouse, N.Y.C., Feb. 4, 1969; reopened Pocket, Apr. 28, 1969).

From 1967–69, he served as coordinator of the NEC Playwrights-Directors Unit.

Films. Mr. Elder wrote the screenplays for *Sounder* (20th-Fox, 1973); and *Melinda* (MGM, 1973). With Robert Hooks, he founded Bannaker Productions, a film company.

Television. He has written material for Camera Three, N.Y.P.D., and McCloud; and wrote the teleplays for *The Terrible Veil* and *Ceremonies in Dark Old Men*.

Awards. Mr. Elder has been recipient of the John Hay Whitney Fellowship (1965–66); the ABC Television Writing Fellowship (1965–66); the John Golden Fellowship (1966–67); the Joseph E. Levine Fellowship in Filmmaking (1966–67); the Stanley Drama Award (1965); the ANTA Award (1967); the Outer Circle and Drama Desk awards (1968–69); and the Stella Holt Memorial Playwrights Award (1969).

ELDRIDGE, FLORENCE. Actress. b. Sept. 5, 1901, Brooklyn, N.Y., to James and Clara Eugenie McKechnie. Attended Girls' H.S., Brooklyn. Married May 30, 1927, to Fredric March, actor: one son, one daughter. Member of AEA; SAG. Address: Box 25940, Los Angeles, CA 90025.

Theatre. Miss Eldridge first appeared in N.Y.C. as a member of the chorus of *Rock-a-Bye Baby* (Ashton Th., June 1917); subsequently played the ingenue in a national tour of *Seven Days Love,* Dolly McKibble in *Pretty Soft* (Morosco, May 15, 1919); Margaret Nichols in a Th. Guild production of *Ambush* (Garrick, Oct. 10, 1921); Annabelle West in *The Cat and the Canary* (National, Feb. 7, 1922); the Stepdaughter in *Six Characters in Search of an Author* (Princess, Oct. 30, 1922; 44 St. Th., Feb. 16, 1924); Nadine Morand in *The Love Habit* (Bijou, Mar. 14, 1923); Una Lowery in *The Dancers* (Broadhurst, Oct. 17, 1923); Evelyn Gardner in *Cheaper to Marry* (49 St.

Th., Apr. 15, 1924); the Girl in *Bewitched* (National, Oct. 1, 1924); Louise in *Young Blood* (Ritz, Nov. 24, 1924); Daisy Fay in the prologue and Daisy Buchanan in the play, *The Great Gatsby* (Ambassador, Feb. 2, 1926); Marion Taylor in *A Proud Woman* (Maxine Elliott's Th., Nov. 14, 1926); and Alice Reynolds in *Off-Key* (Belmont, Feb. 8, 1927).

During 1927–28, she toured with her husband, Frederic March, in the Th. Guild's productions of *Arms and the Man, Mr. Pim Passes By, The Silver Cord*, and *The Guardsman;* played Alexa in *An Affair of State* (Broadhurst, N.Y.C., Nov. 19, 1930); and Julie Rodman in *Days to Come* (Vanderbilt, Dec. 15, 1936).

Miss Eldridge played Prue in *Yr. Obedient Husband*, in which her husband also appeared (Broadhurst, Jan. 10, 1938); Irma Gunther in *The American Way* (Center, Jan. 21, 1939); Carlotta Thatcher in *Hope for a Harvest* (Guild, Nov. 26, 1941); Mrs. Antrobus in *The Skin of Our Teeth* (Plymouth, Nov. 18, 1942); Annie Jones in *Years Ago* (Mansfield, Dec. 3, 1946); Miss Leonora Graves in *Now I Lay Me Down to Sleep* (Broadhurst, Mar. 1950); Mrs. Stockmann in Arthur Miller's adaptation of Ibsen's *An Enemy of the People* (Broadhurst, Dec. 28, 1950); Rose Griggs in *The Autumn Garden* (Coronet, Mar. 7, 1951); and Mary Cavan Tyrone in *Long Day's Journey into Night* (Helen Hayes Th., Nov. 7, 1956; Sarah Bernhardt Th., Paris, Fr., July 1957).

Films. Miss Eldridge made her debut appearing with her husband in *Studio Murder Mystery* (Par., 1929); subsequently appeared with him in *Les Miserables* (UA, 1935); *Mary of Scotland* (RKO, 1936); *Another Part of the Forest* (U, 1948); *Act of Murder* (MGM, 1948); *Christopher Columbus* (U, 1949); and *Inherit the Wind* (UA, 1960).

Awards. Miss Eldridge won the *Variety* NY Drama Critics Poll for her performance as Mary Cavan Tyrone in *Long Day's Journey into Night* (1957). She also received an honorary Doctor of Humanities from Elmira Coll. and was created a fellow of Timothy Dwight Arts and Letters (May 1964).

ELKIN, SAUL. Educator, actor, director, producer. b. Apr. 8, 1932, to Harry and Mamie Elkin. Grad. Christopher Columbus H.S., N.Y.C.; Columbia Univ., B.A. 1953, M.F.A. 1963; Carnegie-Mellon Univ., Ph.D. 1969. Professional training with Herbert Berghof (acting), Jose Quintero (directing), Ann Hathaway Dodge (jazz piano), and Samuel Morgenstern (composition). Married Sept. 6, 1958, to Sandra A. Elkin; two sons. Served in US Army, 1953–55. Member of AEA; ATA; AAUP. Address: (home) 85 Oakbrook Dr., Williamsville, NY 14221, tel. (716) 688-4910; (bus.) Dept. of Theatre, State Univ. of NY at Buffalo, Buffalo, NY 14214, tel. (716) 831-2045.

In 1968, Mr. Elkin became associate professor of theatre, director of undergraduate studies (theatre), and associate director of the Center for Theatre Research at the State Univ. of NY (Buffalo). He had been (1958–68) chairman of the Dept. of Theatre, Castleton State College, Castleton, Vermont.

As a child, Mr. Elkin was an acting member (1941–49) of the resident company of the Yiddish Art Theatre, N.Y.C., with whom he appeared in a variety of roles. After leaving the Yiddish group, he played Yossel in *Treasure Hunters* (Barbizon-Plaza, N.Y.C., Sept. 1950), and he made his Off-Bway debut as the Narrator, the Stage Manager, and the Husband in *Floydada to Matador* (Amato Th., Dec. 1955). The following year he made his summer stock debut playing Willy Loman in *Death of a Salesman* (Green Mountain Th., Poultney, Vt., July 1956). Other roles he played at Poultney included, in 1956, Tom in *The Glass Menagerie*, Uncle Louis in *The Happy Time*, McKeever in *The Solid Gold Cadillac*, Glenn Griffin in *The Desperate Hours*, the Father in *Tea and Sympathy*. In 1957 he appeared at Poultney as Col. Purdy in *The Teahouse of the August Moon*, Noah in *Flowering Peach*, the Waiter in *Time Remembered*, Patsy in *Three Men on a Horse*, and Daniel Webster in *The Devil and Daniel Webster*, and he directed *The Streets of New York* and *Dial "M" for Murder*.

In the 1958 season, Mr. Elkin played Otto Frank in The Diary of Anne Frank, the Sergeant in *No Time for Sergeants*, Teddy in *Arsenic and Old Lace*, the Rainmaker in *The Rainmaker*, and Goober in *Cat on a Hot Tin Roof*. In 1959, at the Weston Playhouse, Weston, Vt., Mr. Elkin directed *The Best Man* and played the Butler in *The Chinese Prime Minister*, and in 1960, also at Weston, he appeared as the Neighbor in *Send Me No Flowers*. Mr. Elkin was also at Weston in the summer of 1967, directing *A Delicate Balance* and appearing as the Father in *The Subject Was Roses*.

Since 1958 Mr. Elkin has directed numerous university theatre productions including The Physician in Spite of Himself; Much Ado About Nothing; Pictures in the Hallway; Androcles and the Lion; Hamlet; The Trojan Women; Rhinoceros; The Bald Soprano; The Lesson; Stop the World, I Want to Get Off; Ring Around the Moon; The Streets of New York; Under Milkwood; A Thurber Carnival; U.S.A.; Arsenic and Old Lace; The Skin of Our Teeth; The Private Ear and *The Public Eye; Fumed Oak; Red Peppers; Born Yesterday; Gaslight; The Enchanted; Murder in the Cathedral; An Evening with Dorothy Parker; The Crucible; The Visit; America Hurrah; The Show-Off; J.B.; The Serpent; A Man's a Man; The Good Woman of Setzuan; Ergo; Pantagleize; Calm Down, Mother; The Great American Desert;* and *Mystery Play* (van Itallie).

Other Activities. Mr. Elkin was editor and feature writer (1965–66) for *The Resorter*, a weekly magazine published in Vermont.

Awards. Mr. Elkin received (1953) Columbia University's Gold Crown Award as outstanding actor; was named (1955, 1956, 1957) outstanding actor in Vermont summer theatres by the Rutland (Vt.) *Herald;* and in 1968 he received a National Defense Fellowship for doctoral studies.

Recreation. Mr. Elkin is a sculptor and painter who has exhibited in New England regional art shows, and he plays jazz piano.

ELLERBE, HARRY. Actor, director. b. Harry La Coste Ellerbe, Jan. 13, Columbia, S.C., to Alexander W. and Marie Louise (de Treville) Ellerbe. Father, publisher. Grad. Georgia Inst. of Tech., Atlanta, (architecture). Member of AEA; SAG; AFTRA; The Masquers; Sigma Phi Epsilon. Address: 1896 Wyclif Rd., N.W., Atlanta, GA 30309.

Theatre. Mr. Ellerbe made his stage debut with the Stuart Walker Co. (Opera House, Cincinnati, Ohio, 1927); his N.Y.C. debut as Philip in *Philip Goes Forth* (Biltmore Th., Jan. 12, 1931); played Godfrey Black in *Man on Stilts* (Plymouth, Sept. 9, 1931); Al in the pre-Bway tryout of *The Tadpole* (opened Parsons, Hartford, Conn., Dec. 7, 1931); Henry Frost in *The Man Hopes* (Broadhurst, N.Y.C., Dec. 1, 1932); Jerry Powers in *Her Tin Soldier* (Playhouse, Apr. 6, 1933); Richard Westervail in *Thoroughbred* (Vanderbilt, Nov. 6, 1933); and Val in *Strange Orchestra* (Playhouse, Nov. 28, 1933).

He played Jonathan Crale in *Merrilly We Roll Along* (Belasco, Los Angeles, Calif., 1935); Oswald in *Ghosts* (Empire, N.Y.C., Dec. 12, 1935); Tesman in *Hedda Gabler* (Longacre, Nov. 16, 1936); toured as Oswald in *Ghosts* and Tesman in *Hedda Gabler;* succeeded Stephen Haggard as Finch in *Whiteoaks* (Hudson, June 6, 1938), and played the role on tour; toured as Mr. Prior in *Outward Bound* (opened Locust St. Th., Philadelphia, Pa., Oct. 9, 1939); played Rev. David Thatcher in *Feathers in a Gale* (Music Box Th., N.Y.C., Dec. 21, 1943); succeeded (May 11, 1944) Alexander Kirkland as Willis Reynolds in *Junior Miss* (Lyceum, Nov. 18, 1941); and appeared as Donald Sturdevant in *Sleep, My Pretty One* (Playhouse, Nov. 2, 1944).

Mr. Ellerbe directed the West Coast touring company of *The Hasty Heart* (Geary Th., San Francisco, Calif., Aug. 19, 1956); *Accidentally Yours* (J.C. Aud., Sacramento, Calif., Mar. 15, 1947); *For Love or Money* (Henry Miller's Th., N.Y.C., Nov. 4, 1947); directed and appeared as Harland Vye in *Oh, Mr. Meadowbrook!* (John Golden Th., Dec. 26, 1948); played Edward Chamberlayne in the national company of *The Cocktail Party* (opened Curran Th., San Francisco, Calif., Oct. 15, 1951); directed *The Pink Elephant* (Playhouse, N.Y.C., Apr. 22, 1953); played the Man in Shirt-Sleeves in *The Desk Set* (Broadhurst, Oct. 24, 1955), and directed the national company (opened Carthay Circle Th., Los Angeles, Calif., July 16, 1956; closed Harris, Chicago, Ill., May 11, 1957); directed *Black-Eyed Susan* (Music Box, Hollywood, Calif., Aug. 7, 1962); and *Tunnel of Love* (Alcazar, San Francisco, Calif., Oct. 7, 1957).

Films. Mr. Ellerbe made his film debut in *Murder on a Honeymoon* (RKO, 1935); subsequently played Edward in *So Red the Rose* (Par., 1935); played the Man in Shirt-Sleeves in *Desk Set* (20th-Fox, 1957); appeared in *Mardi Gras* (20th-Fox, 1935); *The Young Lions* (20th-Fox, 1958); *The Man Who Understood Women* (20th-Fox, 1959); *House of Usher* (Amer. Intl., 1960); and *Haunted Palace* (Amer. Intl., 1963).

Mr. Ellerbe spent the years 1964–73 working exclusively in regional theatre. He performed at Alliance Th., Atlanta, Ga.; at Meadow Brook Th., Rochester, Mich., where he was in such productions as *Ah, Wilderness!* (May 7, 1960), *The Matchmaker* (Oct. 14, 1971), and *Heartbreak House* (Dec. 9, 1971); in the Oakland Univ. Professional Theatre Program, Detroit, Mich., where he was in *The Skin of Our Teeth* (Nov. 25, 1970); and at Stage/West, Springfield, Mass., where he was in *Ten Little Indians* (Dec. 8, 1972). He was actor-in-residence at the Univ. of New Mexico during the Southwestern Theatre Conference (Oct. 1974) and played Hummel in *The Ghost Sonata*.

ELLIOTT, DENHOLM. Actor. b. Denholm Mitchell Elliott, May 31, 1922, London, England, to Myles and Nina Mitchell Elliott. Attended Malvern (Eng.) Coll., 1936–39; RADA, London, 1939. Married Mar. 1, 1954, to Virginia McKenna (marr. dis. 1957); married June 15, 1962, to Susan Robinson. Served RAF, Bomber Command, 1939–45; rank, Warrant Officer. Member of AEA; AFTRA; SAG. Address: (home) 75 Albert St., London N.W.1, England; (bus.) c/o I.F.A., 11 Hanover St., London W.1, England.

Theatre. Mr. Elliott made his debut in England as Arden Renselaw in an Amersham Repertory Co. production of *The Drunkard* (1945); subsequently played Grimmett in *The Guinea Pig* (Criterion, London, 1946); Junius in *Buoyant Billions* (Prince's, Oct. 10, 1949); and Edgar in *Venus Observed* (St. James's Th., Jan. 18, 1950).

He made his N.Y.C. debut as the twins, Hugo and Frederic, in *Ring Round the Moon* (Martin Beck Th., Nov. 23, 1950); played Julian in *Green Bay Tree* (John Golden Th., Feb. 1, 1951); Pvt. Peter Able in *A Sleep of Prisoners* (St. Thomas's Church, London, May 1951); Kip Ames in *Third Person* (Criterion, Jan. 3, 1952); Colby Simkins in *The Confidential Clerk* (Lyric, Sept. 16, 1953); and Kilroy in *Camino Real* (Phoenix, Apr. 8, 1957).

He played Fernand Ravinel in *Monique* (John Golden Th., N.Y.C., Oct. 22, 1957); at the Shakespeare Memorial Th. (Stratford-upon-Avon, Eng.), played Valentine in *Two Gentlemen of Verona* (Apr. 5, 1960); Bassanio in *Merchant of Venice* (Apr. 12, 1960); and Troilus in *Troilus and Cressida* (July 22, 1960); appeared as the Hon. Clive Rodingham in *Write Me a Murder* (Belasco, N.Y.C., Oct. 26, 1961); toured the US with the Natl. Repertory Co. as Patrice in *Ring Round the Moon*, Trigorin in *The Seagull*, and Hale in *The Crucible*, also playing the latter two roles at the end of the tour in N.Y.C. (Belasco, Apr. 1964). He was in *Come As You Are* (Albery, London, 1970); played Leo in a revival of *Design for Living* (Los Angeles Music Center, 1971); Judge Brack in *Hedda Gabler* (Royal Court Th., London, 1972); and Dick in *Chez Nous* (Globe, London, 1974).

Films. Mr. Elliott has appeared in *Breaking the Sound Barrier* (UA, 1951); *The Cruel Sea* (U, 1952); *They Who Dare* (Ealing, 1953); *The Holly and the Ivy* (PMK, 1954); *Pacific Destiny* (Brit. Lion, 1956); *Scent of Mystery* (MTJ, 1960); *Station 6 Sahara* (Brit. Lion, 1962); *Nothing But the Best* (Elstree, 1963);

King Rat (Col., 1965); *Alfie* (Par., 1966); *The Night They Raided Minsky's* (UA, 1968); *The Sea Gull* (WB-7 Arts, 1968); *Too Late the Hero* (Cinerama, 1970); *Percy* (MGM, 1971); *A Doll's House* (Par., 1973); *The Apprenticeship of Duddy Kravitz* (Par., 1974); and *Percy's Progress* (MGM, 1974).

Television. He has appeared in *The Lark* (Hallmark Hall of Fame, NBC, Feb. 10, 1957); *Wuthering Heights* (Dupont Show of the Month, NBC, 1958); *A Tale of Two Cities* (Dupont Show of the Month, NBC, Mar. 1958); *The Moon and Sixpence* (NBC, Oct. 30, 1959); *Vanity Fair* (CBS, Jan. 12, 1961); *Invincible Mr. Disraeli* (Hallmark Hall of Fame, NBC, Apr. 4, 1963); Sextet Series (BBC 2); and *Endless* (BBC 1 and ITV).

Awards. Mr. Elliott received the Clarence Derwent Award for his performance as Edgar in *Venus Observed* (1950); and the Donaldson Award for his performance as Hugo and Frederic in *Ring Round the Moon* (1950).

Recreation. Swimming, skiing, playing the piano.

ELLIOTT, DON. Musician, composer, singer, arranger. b. Donald Lester Helfman, Oct. 21, 1926, Somerville, N.J., to Al and Nettie Helfman. Father, musician. Grad. Sommerville H.S., 1944; Juilliard Sch. of Music, 1945; attended Univ. of Miami, 1947–48; New York Univ., 1948–49. Studied with Claude E. (Gus) Schappelle, Somerville, N.J., 1939–44. Married Nov. 17, 1960, to Doris Wiss, actress; one son, one daughter. Served USAAF as musician, 1945–47; rank, Sgt. Member of AFM, Local 802; AEA; AFTRA; SAG. Address: (home) Willow Rd., Weston, CT 06880; (bus.) 80 W. 40th St., New York, NY 10024, tel. (212) 524-9677; 15 Bridge Rd., Weston, CT 06880, tel. (203) 226-4200.

Theatre. Mr. Elliott composed the music and performed with his combo in *A Thurber Carnival* (ANTA, N.Y.C., Feb. 24, 1960); composed music for Jerome Chodorov's *Has Anyone Seen Kelly* (tour, 1962); and composed the music and performed with his own orchestra in *The Beast in Me* (Plymouth, N.Y.C., May 16, 1963).

Television. He appeared as an actor-musician on *Look Up and Live* (CBS, 1954); subsequently appeared as performer and conductor on the Jackie Gleason Show (CBS, 1955); Omnibus (NBC, 1955); the Steve Allen Show (NBC, 1955–57); the Today Show (NBC, 1956, 1961, 1962–63); the Home Show (NBC, 1957); American Musical Th. (CBS, 1961); and Music on a Summer Night (ABC, 1961). He scored a television special based on James Thurber's *The Greatest Man in the World* (1964) and did music for *Summer Is Forever* (CBS, 1969), *Neither Are They Enemies* (Hallmark Hall of Fame, NBC, 1970), and *A Memory of Two Mondays* (PBS, 1971). Mr. Elliott has also done music for over 2,000 radio and television commercials.

Awards. Mr. Elliott has received *Downbeat* awards (1953–60), Clio's, Gold Record and BMI Best Record awards, and numerous other broadcasting and communication awards.

Recreation. Electronic experimenting, multitracking his voices.

ELLIOTT, PATRICIA. Actress. b. July 21, 1942, Gunnison, Colo. Grad. Univ. of Colorado. Professional training London Acad. of Dramatic Art.

Theatre. At the Cleveland (Ohio) Playhouse, she was Doreen in *The Private Ear* (Oct 28, 1964), played the title role in *Major Barbara* (Jan. 13, 1965), appeared in *A Midsummer Night's Dream* (Mar. 10, 1965), *Uncle Vanya* (Nov. 24, 1965), was Kate in *Never Too Late* (Dec. 10, 1965), and appeared in *Dylan* (Jan. 19, 1966). She appeared with the Minnesota Th. Co. (Tyrone Guthrie Th.) as Jenney in *The Dance of Death* (June 1, 1966) and as Rosalind in *As You Like It* (June 2, 1966); played Lady Macbeth in *Macbeth* (Front St. Th., Memphis, Tenn., Jan. 19, 1967); and returned to the Minnesota Th. Co., where she appeared (Tyrone Guthrie Th.) in *Thieves' Carnival* (June 2, 1967) and *The House of Atreus* (July 21, 1967) and in *She Stoops to Conquer* (Crawford Livingston Th., Dec. 28, 1967).

Miss Elliott made her first appearance in N.Y.C. as Regan in *King Lear* (Vivian Beaumont Th., Nov. 7, 1968); was at the American Shakespeare Festival, Stratford, Conn., as Beatrice in *Much Ado About Nothing* (June 18, 1969) and Alice in *Henry V* (June 19); repeated the latter in N.Y.C. (ANTA Th., Nov. 10, 1969); and was the Young Woman of the Chorus in *The Persians* (St. George's Ch., N.Y.C., Apr. 15, 1970). She was Mrs. Kristine Linde in *A Doll's House* (Playhouse Th., N.Y.C., Jan. 13, 1971) and Mrs. Elvsted in *Hedda Gabler* (Playhouse Th., Feb. 17 1971) and understudy for Claire Bloom as Nora in the former and in the title role of the latter; played at the Olney (Md.) Th. as Gittel Mosca in *Two for the Seesaw* (July 13, 1971) and Ruth in *The Homecoming* (Aug. 3, 1971); and repeated her performance as Mrs. Linde in *A Doll's House* (Eisenhower Th., John F. Kennedy Ctr., Washington, D.C., Oct. 16, 1971).

She was Frances in *In Case of Accident* (Eastside Playhouse, Mar. 27, 1972); Alice in *The Water Hen* (Chelsea Th. Ctr., Brooklyn Acad. of Music, Brooklyn, N.Y., May 9, 1972); Countess Charlotte Malcolm in *A Little Night Music* (Sam S. Shubert Th., Feb. 25, 1973); and Senora Crochetta and Jenny Diver in *Polly* (Chelsea Th. Ctr., Brooklyn, N.Y., Apr. 29, 1975).

Television. Miss Elliott appeared in the film *The Man Without a Country* (ABC, 1973).

Awards. For her performance in *A Little Night Music*, Miss Elliott received an Antoinette Perry (Tony) Award (1973) as best supporting actress in a musical and a Drama Desk Award (1973) for her outstanding performance.

ELLIOTT, STEPHEN. Actor. Professional training at Neighborhood Playhouse, N.Y.C. (Sanford Meisner). Served WW II, Merchant Marine. Member of AEA; AFTRA; SAG.

Theatre. Mr. Elliott began his professional career touring as Duke Mantee in *The Petrified Forest* and made his Bway debut as the Boatswain in *The Tempest* (Alvin, Mar. 19, 1945), which was followed by appearances as Mickey in *Walk Hard* (Chanin Aud., Mar. 27, 1946); Handler in *The Wonderful Journey* (Coronet, Dec. 25, 1946); Col. Martin in *Command Decision* (Fulton Th., Oct. 1, 1947); Dr. Kramer in *The Shrike* (Cort, Jan. 15, 1952); and replacing Murvyn Vie as Adam Banner in *Rise by Sin* (pre-Bway, opened Shubert Th., New Haven, Conn., Nov. 6, 1952; closed Shubert Th., Washington, D.C., Nov. 15, 1952).

He was the Second Workman and Philip O'Dempsey in *Purple Dust* (Cherry Lane Th., Dec. 27, 1956); Muff Potter in *Livin' the Life* (Phoenix, Apr. 27, 1957); was standby for Jason Robards, Jr., as Manley Halliday in *The Disenchanted* (Coronet, Dec. 3, 1958); and replaced Jack Klugman as Herbie in *Gypsy* (Broadway Th., May 21, 1959). He played Admiral Trenton in *Roman Candle* (Cort, Feb. 3, 1960); appeared in *Drums Under the Window* (Cherry Lane, Oct. 13, 1960); replaced Walter Chiari as Anatol in *The Gay Life* (Sam S. Shubert Th., Nov. 18, 1961); was an understudy for *Photo Finish* (Brooks Atkinson Th., Feb. 12, 1963); played in *The Irregular Verb to Love* (Ethel Barrymore Th., Sept. 18, 1963); was Georges Renaud in *Traveller Without Luggage* (ANTA Th., Sept. 17, 1964); and was in *I Knock on the Door* (Th. de Lys, Nov. 25, 1964) and *Pictures in the Hallway* (Th. de Lys, Jan. 18, 1965).

In the late 1960s, Mr. Elliott appeared at regional theatres in productions of *After the Fall*, *The Sound of Music*, and *The Fantasticks*, and he played leading roles at Bucks County Playhouse (Mountainhome, Pa.) and the Manitoba (Canada) Th. Ctr. (Summers 1967 and 1968). In N.Y.C., he was M. Coulmier in a revival of *Marat/Sade* (Majestic Th., Jan. 3, 1967); Owen Glendower in *Henry IV, Part 1* (Delacorte Th., June 11, 1968); the Lord Chief Justice in *Henry IV, Part 2* (Delacorte Th., June 18, 1968); the Earl of Gloucester in *King Lear* (Vivian Beaumont Th., Nov. 7, 1968); and Sir Thomas in *A Cry of Players* (Vivian Beaumont Th., Nov. 14, 1968). He appeared also as John Lansdale in *In the Matter of J. Robert Oppenheimer* (Vivian Beaumont Th., Mar. 6, 1969); the Magistrate in *The Miser* (Vivian Beaumont Th., May 8, 1969); Sir Toby Belch in *Twelfth Night* (Delacorte Th., Aug. 6, 1969); Michael Carney, Senior, in *A Whistle in the Dark* (Mercury Th., Oct. 8, 1969); Old Mahon in *The Playboy of the Western World* (Vivian Beaumont Th., Jan. 7, 1971); Dr. Stockman in *An Enemy of the People* (Vivian Beaumont Th., Mar. 11, 1971); and God in *The Creation of the World and Other Business* (Shubert Th., Nov. 30, 1972).

Films. Mr. Elliott appeared in *Crossroads* (MGM, 1942); *Three Hours To Kill* (Col., 1954); and other films.

Television. Programs on which Mr. Elliott has appeared include Mystery Playhouse; Silver Th.; Hands of Murder; Big Story; The Girls; Martin Kane; Actors Studio; Captain Video; Inside Detective; and A World Apart (ABC).

Awards. Mr. Elliott was nominated for a Tony for his portrayal of M. Coulmier in *Marat/Sade* (1967).

ELLIOTT, SUMNER LOCKE. Playwright, novelist, former actor. b. Oct. 17, 1917, Sydney, Australia, to Henry Logan and Helena Sumner (Locke) Elliott. Father, journalist; mother, novelist. Educated in Sydney, Cranbrook Sch., 1925–29; Neutral Bay High, 1930–33. Came to US, 1948; naturalized, 1955. Served Australian Army, 1942–46; rank, Staff Sgt. Member of Dramatists Guild; ALA; WGA, East. Address: 230 E. 61st St., New York, NY 10021.

Theatre. Mr. Elliott first worked in the theatre (1934) in Australia as an actor with the Sydney Independent Th. Repertory Co., appearing in such roles as Dick McGann in *Street Scene* (Savoy Th., Feb. 1937), Morgan Evans in *The Corn Is Green* (May 1940), Constantin in *The Seagull* (Independent Th., Jan. 1941), Leo in *The Little Foxes* (Oct. 1946); and appeared in the revue *Sweetest and Lowest* (Minerva Th., Nov. 1946). He first wrote *Rusty Bugles*, produced in Australia by Doris Fitton (Independent Th., Oct. 27, 1948). At first banned as obscene, it reopened (Oct. 31, 1948) and ran for three years, establishing a record for an indigenous theatre work.

Mr. Elliott first wrote for Bway, *Buy Me Blue Ribbons* (Empire Th., Oct. 17, 1951); and contributed sketches to the revue *John Murray Anderson's Almanac* (Imperial, Dec. 10, 1953).

Television and Radio. Before coming to the US, Mr. Elliott wrote and performed on radio in Australia (1935–40). He wrote for US television, *Wish on the Moon* (Philco Television Playhouse, NBC, 1953); *Friday the 13th* (Philco Television Playhouse, NBC, 1954); *Beloved Stranger* (Philco Television Playhouse, NBC, 1955); *You and Me and the Gatepost* (Playwrights 56, NBC, 1955); *The King and Mrs. Candle* (Producers Showcase, NBC, 1955); *Keyhole* (Playwrights 56, NBC, 1956); *Mrs. Gilling and the Skyscraper* (Alcoa, NBC, 1957); and *The Gray Nurse Said Nothing* (Playhouse 90, CBS, 1959).

Published Works. He is the author of the novels *Careful, He Might Hear You* (1963), *Edens Lost* (1969), and *Man Who Got Away* (1972).

ELLIS, ANITA. Singer, actress. b. Anita Kert, Apr. 12, 1926, Montreal, Canada, to Harry and Lilian (Pearson) Kert. Father, businessman, athlete; mother, amateur singer. Grad. Hollywood (Calif.) H.S., 1942; attended Coll. of Music, Cincinnati, Ohio, 1942–43; Univ. of California, Los Angeles, 1946–48; studied acting with Sanford Meisner, Neighborhood Playhouse Sch. of the Theatre, N.Y.C.; with John Howell, Sonya Blinder and C. Gagliardi, N.Y.C.; singing with Glenn Raikes, Mort Werner and Leo Wolfe, Los Angeles, Calif., and Mme. Kruze, Cincinnati, Ohio. Married Jan. 23, 1943, to Col. Frank W. Ellis, SAC (marr. dis. 1946); married July 31, 1960, to Dr. Mortimer F. Shapiro, neurologist, psychiatrist. During WW II, Red Cross nurse's aide, Los Angeles, Calif.; made record albums for Armed Forces Radio; cited by President Roosevelt. Relatives in theatre: brother, Larry Kert, singer, actor, dancer; cousin, Ted Allen, writer. Member of AEA; AFTRA; AGVA; SAG;

Sigma Alpha Iota. Address: 130 East End Ave., New York, NY 10028, tel. (212) 879-3982.

Theatre. Miss Ellis played Lucy in Marc Blitzstein's adaptation of *The Threepenny Opera* (Brandeis Univ. Music Festival, US premiere, Waltham, Mass., June 14, 1952); was standby for Betty Paul in the title role of *Maggie* (National, Feb. 18, 1953); for Pat Suzuki as Linda Low and Arabella Hong as Helen Chao, and played a Night Club Singer in *Flower Drum Song* (St. James, Dec. 1, 1958), and played Linda and then Helen while Miss Suzuki and Miss Hong were on vacation. She was a participant in the Marc Blitzstein Memorial Concert (Philharmonic Hall, Apr. 19, 1964).

Films. Miss Ellis dubbed the singing voice for Rita Hayworth in *Gilda* (Col., 1946), *Down to Earth* (Col., 1947), *Loves of Carmen* (Col., 1947) and *Shanghai Lady* (Col., 1948); for Vera Ellen in *Three Little Words* (MGM, 1950) and *Belle of New York* (MGM, 1952); and for Jeanne Crain in *Gentlemen Marry Brunettes* (UA, 1955); appeared in *The Joe Louis Story* (UA, 1953); sang the title song in *Pull My Daisy* ("G" String Prod., 1960); and appeared in *O.K. End Here* (1963).

Television and Radio. On radio, Miss Ellis sang on Scamby Amby and Moon River shows (WLW, Cincinnati, Ohio, 1942); on her own show, Songs Overseas (CBS); and the Edgar Bergen Show (NBC, 1943); Hallmark Hall of Fame (NBC, 1943); the Jack Carson Show (CBS, 1944); and the Borden's Show (CBS, 1944); her own show, Anita Ellis Sings (Mutual, N.Y.C., 1945); the Red Skelton Show (NBC, Hollywood, 1946–48) and on the Andy Russell-Anita Ellis Show (ABC, N.Y.C., 1949).

Miss Ellis made her television debut as singer-actress in experimental telecasting (NBC, 1950); appeared on the Eddie Albert Afternoon Show (CBS, 1953); Penthouse Party (1958); the Jack Paar Show (NBC, 1959); Dave Garroway's Today Show (NBC, 1959–60); and Camera Three (CBS, 1963).

Night Clubs. Miss Ellis sang at La Vie en Rose (N.Y.C., 1953); Blue Angel (N.Y.C., 1953–57); Village Vanguard (N.Y.C., 1954, 1956); Colony Club (London, 1955); Bon Soir (N.Y.C., 1956); and Havana Riviera (Havana, Cuba, 1957).

Awards. Miss Ellis won a graduation beauty poll at Hollywood (Calif.) H.S.; was named Azalea Queen (Mobile, Ala., 1945); Thanksgiving Day Queen (UCLA, 1948); and won the *Playboy Jazz* Poll (1960).

Recreation. Skiing, sailing, walking, swimming, skin diving, gardening, gourmet cooking, reading, collecting first editions of music and poetry, painting, sculpture, traveling, fighting all prejudice.

ELLIS, MARY. Actress, singer. b. Mary Elsas, June 15, New York City, to H. and Caroline (Reinhardt) Elsas. Father, businessman; mother, pianist. Educated privately. Studied art, N.Y.C., 1916–18; music and dance with Alys Bentley, 1913–19, voice with Frieda Ashforth, N.Y.C., 1915–19; Maestro Tanara, N.Y.C., 1918–19; acting with Maria Ouspenskaya, N.Y.C., 1923–25. Married 1929, to Basil Sydney (marr. dis. 1935); married July 7, 1938, to Jack Muir Stewart Roberts (dec. Mar. 6, 1950). Member of AEA; SAG; AFTRA. Address: c/o Chase Manhattan Bank, 1 Mount St., London, W.1, England.

Theatre. Miss Ellis made her singing debut in the world premiere of *Suor Angelica* (Metropolitan Opera, N.Y.C., Dec. 14, 1918); and also at the Metropolitan Opera, sang Mytil in *The Bluebird* (1919); in *Louise* (1921); *La Reine Fiammette, Gianni Schicchi* and *L'Elisir d'amore;* made her drama debut in stock at the Murat Th. (Indianapolis, Ind., 1921); her Bway debut as Nerissa in *The Merchant of Venice* (Lyceum, Dec. 21, 1922); played the Dancer from Milan in *Casanova* (Empire, Sept. 26, 1923); Brigid Shannahan and Ophelia O'Tandy in *The Merry Wives of Gotham* (Henry Miller's Th., Jan. 16, 1924); the title role in *Rose Marie* (Imperial, Sept. 2, 1924); Leah in *The Dybbuk* (Neighborhood Th., Dec. 15, 1925); Rosario in *The Romantic Young Lady* (Neighborhood, May 4, 1926); Sonia Martinova in *The Humble* (Greenwich Village Th., N.Y.C., Oct. 13, 1926); Anna in *The Crown Prince* (Forrest, Mar. 23, 1927); Katherine Minola in *The Taming of the Shrew* (Garrick, Oct. 25, 1927); and Baroness Spangenburg in *12,000* (Garrick, Mar. 12, 1928).

Miss Ellis appeared at the Newport Casino (R.I., 1928); played Jennifer in *Meet the Prince* (Lyceum, N.Y.C., Feb. 25, 1929); the title role in the Player's Club production of *Becky Sharpe* (Knickerbocker, June 3, 1929); Laetitia in *Children of Darkness* (Biltmore, Jan. 7, 1930); repeated her role in the London production, retitled *Knave and Quean* (Ambassadors', Oct. 1, 1930); and played Nina Leeds in *Strange Interlude* (Lyric, London, Feb. 3, 1931).

She appeared in *Cherries Are Ripe* (Natl., Washington, D.C., Sept. 21, 1931); as Teri in *Jewel Robbery* (Booth, N.Y.C., Jan. 13, 1932); Claire Furber in *Queer Cattle* (Haymarket, London, May 1932); Sybil Livingstone in *Double Harness* (Haymarket, Jan. 12, 1933); Frieda Hatzfeld in *Music in the Air* (His Majesty's, May 19, 1933); the title role in *Josephine* (His Majesty's, Sept. 25, 1934); Militza Hajos in the operetta, *Glamorous Night* (Drury Lane, May 2, 1935); Tina Gerling in *Farewell Performance* (Lyric, Sept. 10, 1936); Laurita Bingham in *The Innocent Party* (St. James's, Jan. 27, 1938); Maria Ziegler in the operetta, *The Dancing Years* (Drury Lane, Mar. 23, 1939); and Marie Foret in *Arc de Triomphe* (Phoenix, Nov. 9, 1943).

She joined the Old Vic Co. (1944), and at the Liverpool Playhouse, appeared as Ella Rentheim in *John Gabriel Borkman,* Linda Valaine in *Point Valaine,* and Lady Teazle in *The School for Scandal.*

Mill Ellis played Maria Fitzherbert in *The Gay Pavilion* (Piccadilly, London, May 15, 1945); Miss Susie in *The Rocking Horse* ("Q," Sept. 24, 1946); Mrs. Dane in *Mrs. Dane's Defence* ("Q," Nov. 19, 1946); Harriet Beecher Stowe in *Hattie Stowe* (Embassy, Feb. 11, 1947); Linda Valaine in *Point Valaine* (Embassy, Sept. 3, 1947); Millie Crocker-Harris in *The Browning Version* and Edna Selby in *A Harlequinade* (Phoenix, Sept. 8, 1948); Caroline Moore in *If This Be Error* (Lyric, Hammersmith, May 24, 1950), and on tour (1949) and the title role in *Celestina* (Embassy, Jan. 9, 1951).

Miss Ellis played Volumnia in *Coriolanus* (Royal Memorial Shakespeare Co., Stratford-on-Avon, 1952); Mrs. Erlynne in *After the Ball,* an adaptation of *Lady Windermere's Fan* (Globe, London, June 10, 1954); Christine Mannon in *Mourning Becomes Electra* (Arts, June 9, 1955); Edie (Mother) Dennis in *Dark Halo* (Arts, Apr. 14, 1959); Eliza Gant in *Look Homeward, Angel* (Phoenix, Apr. 3, 1962), and on tour; and she appeared at the Yvonne Arnaud Th., Guildford, as Mrs. Phelps in *The Silver Cord* (Nov. 1968) and Mrs. Warren in *Mrs. Warren's Profession* (Feb. 1970).

Films. Miss Ellis made her film debut in *Bella Donna* (Olympia, 1935); subsequently appeared in *Paris in Spring* (Par., 1935); *All the King's Horses* (Par., 1935); *Fatal Lady* (Par., 1936); *Glamorous Night* (Rep., 1937); and *Gulliver's Travels* (Col., 1959).

Television and Radio. Miss Ellis appeared on television in The Treasure Hunters (NBC, May 1956); and for BBC, in *Great Catherine, The Distaff Side, The Voice of the Turtle, The Indifferent Shepherd* and *Read to Hilda Brown.*

Recreation. Painting, interior decorating, cooking, skiing, mountain climbing.

ELLIS, MICHAEL. Producer. b. Mayer Ellis Abrahamson, Oct. 25, 1917, Philadelphia, Pa., to Alexander and Mollie (Fein) Abrahamson. Attended Wyoming Seminary, Kingston, Pa., 1930–35; Univ. of Grenoble, France, certificate, Summer 1937; Sorbonne, Paris, certificate, 1937–38; grad. Dartmouth Coll., B.A. 1939; Drew Univ., M.A. (in English) 1973. Served as criminal investigator for USAAF Intelligence, 1942–46. Married Mar. 22, 1953, to Neva Patterson, actress (marr. dis. Mar. 22, 1956); married May 10, 1958, to Mary Elizabeth Wadsworth; two sons, one daughter. Member of AEA; League of N.Y. Theatres; COST. Address: 6393 N. Ocean Blvd., Delray Beach, FL 33444.

Theatre. Mr. Ellis first appeared on the professional stage in a stock production of *Flight to the West* (Yardley, Pa., Sept. 1941); subsequently played a Future Brazilian Admiral in the national tour of *My Sister Eileen* (opened Shubert, New Haven, Conn., Dec. 25, 1941); appeared as Silvio in *The Duchess of Malfi* (Ethel Barrymore Th., N.Y.C., Oct. 15, 1946); and was stage manager for *Finian's Rainbow* (46 St. Th., Jan. 10, 1947).

He produced, with James Russo, *The Last Dance* (Belasco, Jan. 27, 1948); presented, with Gilbert Miller and James Russo, *The Play's the Thing* (Booth, Apr. 28, 1949); produced, with James Russo and Alexander H. Cohen, *Jennie Kissed Me* (Hudson, Dec. 23, 1948); was stage manager for *Magnolia Alley* (Mansfield, Apr. 18, 1949), and *Alive and Kicking* (Winter Garden, Jan. 17, 1950); produced, with James Russo, *Courtin' Time* (Natl., June 13, 1951); was stage manager for *Diamond Lil* (Bway Th., Oct. 15, 1951); and produced, with James Russo, *Two's Company* (Alvin, Dec. 15, 1952).

From 1954 through 1964, he was managing director of Bucks County Playhouse, New Hope, Pa., where he produced approximately five new productions each season, ten shows in twenty weeks, beginning the last Saturday in April. Among the approximately forty-five new plays he produced which later opened in N.Y.C., were *The Champagne Complex, Mask and Gown, Never Too Late, Come Blow Your Horn, The Beauty Part, The Advocate, Barefoot in the Park,* and *Absence of a Cello.*

Mr. Ellis was stage manager for *The Body Beautiful* (Bway Th., Jan. 23, 1958); produced, with William Hammerstein, *Come Blow Your Horn* (Brooks Atkinson Th., Feb. 2, 1961); presented, with Edmund Anderson, *The Beauty Part* (Music Box Th., Dec. 26, 1962); produced, with William Hammerstein, *The Advocate* (ANTA, Oct. 14, 1963); with Jeff Britton, *Absence of a Cello* (Sept. 21, 1964); *The Paisley Convertible* (Feb. 11, 1967); with James McKenzie and Frank Hale, *The Girl in the Freudian Slip* (May 11, 1967); and, with Elliott Martin, *Angela* (Music Box Th., Oct. 30, 1969). His off-Bway productions include the double bill *Sweet Eros* and *Witness* (Gramercy Arts, Nov. 21, 1968); *Ceremonies in Dark Old Men* (Pocket Th., Apr. 28, 1969); and, with Samuel Bronstein, *Who's Happy Now?* (Village South, Nov. 17, 1969).

Mr. Ellis became managing director of the Parker Playhouse, Fort Lauderdale, Fla., season of 1973–74.

Awards. Mr. Ellis received the Margo Jones Award (1963) for his contribution in presenting new dramatic works.

Recreation. Reading, piano, cigars.

ELSOM, ISOBEL. Actress. b. Isabella Reed, Mar. 16, 1896, Cambridge, England, to Joseph and Elizabeth Mary Reed. Grad. Howard Coll., Bedford, England. Married Jan. 16, 1925, to Maurice Elvey (marr. dis. 1939); married Apr. 21, 1940, to Carl Harbord (dec. Oct. 18, 1958). Member of AEA; AFTRA; SAG.

Theatre. Miss Elsom made her debut in London in *The Quaker Girl* (Adelphi Th., Dec. 16, 1911); subsequently played Tommy in *The Dancing Mistress* (Adelphi, Oct. 19, 1912); Violet Vesey in *The Girl from Utah* (Adelphi, Oct. 18, 1913); Dora Manners in *The Girl from Utah* (King's, Glasgow, Scot., Jan. 1914); Doris in *After the Girl* (Gaiety, London, Feb. 7, 1914); Lady Mary Winthrope in *England Expects* (London Opera House, Sept. 1914); succeeded (Oct. 1914) Gladys Cooper in six roles in *My Lady's Dress* (Royalty, Apr. 23, 1914); appeared as the Hon. Muriel Pym in *Milestones* (Royalty, Oct. 31, 1914); Mollie Preston in *The Man Who Stayed at Home* (Royalty, Dec. 10, 1914); appeared in *The Constant Lover* (Palace, June 29, 1915); toured as Josie Richards in *Broadway Jones* and as She in *A Bridal Suite* (Fall 1915).

She played Beatrice Abbott in *The Riddle* (New, London, June 1916); succeeded (Oct. 1916) Winifred Barnes as Mary, Princess of Valeria, in *The Happy Day* (Daly's, May 13, 1916); played Angela in *The Catch of the Season* (Prince's, Feb. 17, 1917); toured in *Broadway Jones* (1917); played Wendy in

Peter Pan (New, London, Dec. 24, 1917); Sheila in *The Freaks* (New, Feb. 14, 1918); Delia in *Belinda* (New, Apr. 8, 1918); toured as Sheila in *Sleeping Partners;* and played Evelyn Bird in *Adam and Eve* (Opera House, Blackpool, Eng., Sept. 1919).

She succeeded (Nov. 1920) Margaret Bannerman as Marcelle in *A Night Out* (Winter Garden, London, Sept. 18, 1920); played Mabel Essington in *Up in Mabel's Room* (Playhouse, Apr. 1921); toured variety theatres in *The Surprise;* played Minnie in *Sweet Lavender* (Ambassadors', London, Dec. 14, 1922); Lalage Sturdee in *The Outsider* (St. James's, May 31, 1923); Lucilla in *The Green Goddess* (St. James's, Sept. 6, 1923); Jessie Weston in *Peter Weston* (Comedy, June 1924); Sally Street in *The Man in the Next Room* (Ambassadors', July 1924); Joanne de Beaudricourt in *The Wandering Jew* (New, Nov. 26, 1924); Jill in a pantomime, *Mother Goose* (Hippodrome, Dec. 1924); Penthilsea in *The Tyrant* (New, Mar. 18, 1925); Antje in *My Lady's Dress* (Adelphi, May 11, 1925); Lady Cristilinda in *Cristilinda* (Garrick, Oct. 1925); and Estelle in *Ashes* (Prince of Wales's, Mar. 1926).

Miss Elsom made her N.Y.C. debut as Julia Price in *The Ghost Train* (Eltinge, Aug. 25, 1926); followed by Anne Lancaster in *The Mulberry Bush* (Republic, Oct. 26, 1927); Elaine Osborne in *People Don't Do Such Things* (48 St. Th., Nov. 23, 1927); Mary in *Sisters* (Klaw, Dec. 24, 1927); Mrs. Jones in *The Silver Box* (Morosco, Jan. 17, 1928); Myra Spaulding in *The Behavior of Mrs. Crane* (Erlanger's, Mar. 20, 1928); and Lalage Sturdee in *The Outsider* (Ambassador, Apr. 9, 1928).

She played Baroness Osterman in *Such Men Are Dangerous* (Duke of York's, London, Sept. 19, 1928); appeared in stock at Elitch Gardens, Denver, Colo. (1929); played Marie Anne in *The Command to Love* (Daly's, London, Jan. 1930); Lalage Sturdee in *The Outsider* (Apollo, Oct. 3, 1930); Anna in *Karl and Anna* (Piccadilly, Dec. 1930); Faith Mallery in *Frailities* (Phoenix, Jan. 1931); toured in *The Outsider* (Apr. 1931); and appeared as Lesley Dean in *Blue Skies Beyond* (Vaudeville, Sept. 1931).

She succeeded (Nov. 1931) Fay Compton as Fanny Grey in *Autumn Crocus* (Lyric, Apr. 6, 1931); toured as Kitty Fane in *The Painted Veil* (Oct. 1932); made her Australian debut as Bridget Drake in *When Ladies Meet* (King's, Melbourne, June 1933), where she also played Amanda Prynne in *Private Lives.*

She played Lady Carr in *Precipice* (Savoy, London, June 1934); the Lady in *My Lady Wears a White Cockade* (Embassy, July 1934); Lady Moira Tremearne in *Romantic Ladies* ("Q", Sept. 1934); Helen Norton in *Living Dangerously* (Strand, June 7, 1934); appeared in 20 repertory productions (Prince of Wales's, Cardiff, Wales, May 1935), and played Princess Lichnowsky in *Muted Strings* (Daly's, London, Nov. 1936).

She appeared as Moll Flanders in *American Landscape* (Cort, N.Y.C., Dec. 3, 1938); Leonora Fiske in *Ladies in Retirement* (Henry Miller's Th., Mar. 26, 1940); Carlotta Garcia in *The Flowers of Virtue* (Royale, Feb. 5, 1942); Auntie B. in *Hand in Glove* (Playhouse, Dec. 4, 1944); Mrs. Alving in *Ghosts* (El Patio, Los Angeles, Calif., Spring 1949); Mrs. Goose in *The Innocents* (Playhouse, N.Y.C., Feb. 1, 1950); Florence in *The Curious Savage* (Martin Beck Th., Oct. 24, 1950); Lady Capulet in *Romeo and Juliet* (Broadhurst, Mar. 10, 1951); and Mrs. Harmston in *The Climate of Eden* (Martin Beck Th., Nov. 6, 1952); Lady Terriford in *The Burning Glass* (Longacre, Mar. 4, 1954); Margo Johnson in *Hide and Seek* (Ethel Barrymore Th., Apr. 2, 1957); Caroline, Princess of Wales, in *The First Gentleman* (Belasco, Apr. 25, 1957); Mrs. Julia Stoddard in *The Man in the Dog Suit* (Salt Creek Playhouse, Hinsdale, Ill., June 1957); and Miss Manchester in *Come to the Dance* (Coconut Grove Playhouse, Miami, Fla., Dec. 1959).

Films. Miss Elsom appeared in *Love Is a Many-Splendored Thing* (20th-Fox, 1955); *Over-Exposed* (Col., 1956); *Rock-a-Bye Baby* (Par., 1958); *The Miracle* (WB, 1959); *The Bellboy* (Par., 1960); *The Second Time Around* (20th-Fox, 1961); *Who's Minding the Store?* (Par., 1963); *My Fair Lady* (WB, 1964); and *The Pleasure Seekers* (20th-Fox, 1965).

Television. She appeared in *The Turn of the Screw* (Playhouse 90, CBS); on Somerset Maugham Th. (ABC); Robert Montgomery Presents (NBC); Climax! (CBS); Studio One (CBS); Alfred Hitchcock Presents (CBS); The Roaring 20's (ABC); 77 Sunset Strip (ABC); Checkmate (NBC); Hawaiian Eye (ABC); Dr. Kildare (NBC); Follow the Sun (ABC); Route 66 (CBS); Moment of Fear (NBC); the Loretta Young Show (NBC); My Three Sons (ABC); and Bourbon St. Beat (ABC).

ELSON, CHARLES. Stage designer, educator. b. Sept. 5, 1909, Chicago, Ill., to Jacob and Rebecca Elson; father, teacher. Educ. Univ. of Illinois; grad. Univ. of Chicago, Ph. B.; Yale Drama School, M.F.A. Married Aug. 1938 to Dorothy E. Elson, actress (stage name, Diana Rivers); one daughter. Relatives in theatre: wife; sister, Elizabeth Elson Cohen; daughter, Alexandra Elson. Member of United Scenic Artists (chmn., exec. comm., 1953–54); ITI. Address: Faraway Farm, 1 Faraway Lane, Armonk, NY 10504, tel. (914) 273-3692.

Mr. Elson became professor emeritus, Hunter College of the City Univ. of New York (CUNY) in Feb. 1974. Since 1948, he had been professor of theatre at Hunter, where he designed forty-eight productions and since 1967 he has participated in the doctoral program in theatre of CUNY. His earlier educational posts had been instructor, Univ. of Iowa, and art director there of the university theatre (1935–36), where he designed ten productions, and associate professor, Univ. of Oklahoma, and art director of the university theatre (1937–43), where he designed forty productions. In addition, he was visiting critic of stage lighting, School of Drama, Yale Univ.

Theatre. Mr. Elson made his theatrical debut as the Dormouse in a production of *Alice in Wonderland* (Hull House Th., Chicago, Ill., Feb. 1915). From June to September 1934, he was art director, Chase Barn Playhouse, Whitefield, N.H., where he designed ten productions, the first being *The Ticket of Leave Man* (July 1934). He was West Coast lighting supervisor and art director for Los Angeles, Federal Theatre (1936–37), for which he designed settings and lighting for thirty-two productions. His first settings for the professional stage were those for a Federal Theatre production of *The House of Connelly* (Mayan Th., Los Angeles, Cal., Mar. 1937). He was art director, Ogunquit (Me.) Playhouse (1939, 1940, 1941–45), where he did designs for forty-four productions.

Mr. Elson's first NYC play was an off-Bway production of *As You Like It* (President, July 3, 1945), for which he designed settings. He was then lighting designer and design assistant to Donald Oenslager for *Pygmalion* (Ethel Barrymore Th., Dec. 26, 1945); *Born Yesterday* (Lyceum, Feb. 4, 1946); *Three to Make Ready* (Adelphi, Mar. 7, 1946); *On Whitman Avenue* (Cort, May 8, 1946); and for the operas *Abduction from the Seraglio* and *La Traviata* (both Central City Opera House, Central City, Colo., July 1946).

He made his debut as a production designer with *Hidden Horizon* (Plymouth, N.Y.C., Sept. 19, 1946); was lighting designer and design assistant to Mr. Oenslager for *Loco* (Biltmore, Oct. 16, 1946); designed the production for *Cordelia* (Shubert Th., New Haven, Conn., July 1946); was lighting designer and design assistant for *The Temporary Mrs. Smith* (Playhouse, Wilmington, Del., Sept. 1946); lighting designer and design assistant to Mr. Oenslager for *Present Laughter* (Plymouth, N.Y.C., Oct. 29, 1946); *Park Avenue* (Shubert Th., Nov. 4, 1946); and *The Fatal Weakness* (Royale, Nov. 19, 1946). He was lighting designer and design assistant for *Years Ago* (Mansfield Th., Dec. 3, 1946); *Land's End* (Playhouse, Dec. 11, 1946); and the opera *Abduction from the Seraglio,* assisting Mr. Oenslager (Metropolitan Opera House, Nov. 29, 1946). He was lighting designer and design assistant for *Lovely Me,* assisting Mr. Oenslager (Adelphi, Dec. 25, 1946); *Washington Square* (Shubert Th., New Haven, Conn., Jan. 1947); designed the production for *A Dangerous Woman* (Erie, Schenectady, N.Y., Jan. 1947); was lighting designer and design assistant for *The Greatest of These* (Shubert Th., Detroit, Mich., Feb. 1947); *The Eagle Has Two Heads,* assisting Mr. Oenslager (Plymouth, N.Y.C., Mar. 19, 1947); designed the production for *Virginia Sampler* (NY City Ctr., Mar. 1947); was lighting designer and design assistant to Mr. Oenslager for *Portrait in Black* (Booth Th., May 14, 1947); and the operas *Fidelio* and *Martha* (both Central City Opera, Central City, Colo., July 1947).

Mr. Elson also designed productions for *Duet for Two Hands* (Booth Th., N.Y.C., Oct. 7, 1947); *The First Mrs. Fraser* (Shubert Th., Nov. 5, 1947); *Power without Glory* (Booth Th., Jan. 13, 1948); *Kathleen* (Biltmore, Feb. 3, 1948); *The Cup of Trembling* (Music Box, Apr. 20, 1948); *Private Lives* (Plymouth, Oct. 4, 1948); *Present Laughter* (Walnut St. Th., Philadelphia, Pa., Nov. 1948); and the opera *Albert Herring* (Tanglewood, Mass., July 1949). He designed lighting for *Regina* (46 St. Th., Oct. 31, 1949); the Katherine Dunham Ballet (Broadway Th., Mar. 1950); *The Lady's Not for Burning,* also technical director (Royale, Nov. 8, 1950); *Out of This World,* also technical director (New Century, Dec. 21, 1950); and designed the production for the opera *The Flying Dutchman* (Metropolitan Opera House, Nov. 1950). He designed lighting for *An Enemy of the People* (Broadhurst, Dec. 28, 1950); *The Rose Tattoo* (Martin Beck Th., Feb. 3, 1951); *Kiss Me, Kate,* also technical director (Coliseum, London, England, Mar. 8, 1951); designed the production for *Borscht Capades* (Royale, N.Y.C., Sept. 1951); designed lighting and was technical director for *Music in the Air* (Ziegfeld Th., Oct. 8, 1951); designed the production *Nina* (Royale, Dec. 5, 1951); designed lighting for *Collector's Item* (Booth Th., Feb. 8, 1952); and designed the production for the opera *La Clemenza di Tito* (Tanglewood, Mass., July 1952).

He designed productions for *The Deep Blue Sea* (Morosco, N.Y.C., Nov. 5, 1952) and for the opera *Lohengrin* (Metropolitan Opera House, Nov. 1952); designed lighting for *The Little Hut* (Coronet, Oct. 7, 1953); designed productions for the opera *Don Giovanni* (Metropolitan Opera House, Dec. 1953); for *His and Hers* (48 St. Th., Jan. 7, 1954); and for the opera *Norma* (Metropolitan Opera House, Mar. 1954); was setting supervisor for *Quadrille* (Coronet, Nov. 3, 1954); and designed productions for *Champagne Complex* (Cort, Apr. 12, 1955); and *The Lovers* (Martin Beck Th., May 10, 1956). He designed lighting for *Compulsion* (Ambassador, Oct. 24, 1957); *Blue Denim* (Playhouse, Feb. 27, 1958); supervised the settings for the opera *Madame Butterfly* (Metropolitan Opera House, Feb. 1958); designed lighting for *Maria Golovin* (Martin Beck Th., Nov. 5, 1958); *La Plume de Ma Tante* (Royale, Nov. 11, 1958); *First Impressions* (Alvin Th., Mar. 19, 1959); and *Wildcat* (Alvin Th., Dec. 16, 1960).

For the American Shakespeare Festival, Stratford, Conn., Mr. Elson designed lighting for *Troilus and Cressida* (July 23, 1961), *Henry IV* (June 17, 1962), *Richard II* (June 16, 1962), and *Shakespeare Revisited* (July 17, 1962). He designed lighting for *Program for Two Players* (Fisher Th., Detroit, Mich., Oct. 1962); *The Perfect Setup* (Cort, N.Y.C., Oct. 24, 1962); *Photo Finish* (Brooks Atkinson Th., Feb. 12, 1963); the Hebrew National Theatre (Billy Rose Th., Mar. 1967); and the opera *Dialogues of the Carmelites* (City Center Opera, NY State Th., Feb. 1968).

Films. Mr. Elson was assistant art director for *A Star Is Born* (WB, 1954).

Other Activities. From July 1943 to Sept. 1945, Mr. Elson was a design engineer, US Navy Training Aids Center. He was a theatre consultant to India (1959–60, 1969–70); on the National Theatre Selection Committee, Fulbright Awards (1957); on the board of directors of the India Council, Asia Society (1963–68); and a member of the Young Artists Committee, Theatre Division, Institute of International Education.

Published Works. Mr. Elson was the American editor for *Stage Design Throughout the World Since*

1935 (1956) and for *Stage Design Throughout the World: 1950–1960* (1963). He wrote the article "American Training of Designers" for the ITI Design 70 Exhibition Book (1974).

Awards. Mr. Elson was made a fellow of the International Institute of Arts and Letters, Zurich, Switzerland, in 1960.

Recreation. Mr. Elson considers his community service activities as recreation. From 1951 to 1969 as art director, North Castle (N.Y.) Players, Armonk, he designed fourteen productions. He was president (1957–59) of the North Castle (N.Y.) Citizens Council, and he has been active in the Friends of the North Castle Public Library as a member of the board of directors (1954–to date) and president (1961–66). He has served also as a trustee of the library (1972–to date).

ELSTON, ROBERT. Actor. b. Robert Gornel Finkelstein, May 29, 1934, New York City, to Jack and Gladys Bell (Thomasson) Finkelstein. Father, restaurateur; mother, secretary. Grad. Stuyvesant H.S., N.Y.C., 1949; grad. City Coll. of New York, B.A. 1953; attended Univ. of Paris (de la Sorbonne), 1955–56; Hunter Coll., 1956–58; New York Univ. Studied acting at HB Studio, N.Y.C.; with Curt Conway at Th. West, Los Angeles, Calif.; mime with Etienne Decroux; voice with Keith Davis. Served US Army, 1953–55; rank, Cpl. Relative in theatre: aunt, Georgia Southern, burlesque performer. Member of AEA; SAG; AFTRA, Th. West. Address: (home) 24 W. 68th St., New York, NY 10023, tel. (212) TR 7-3189; tel. PL 7-6300; (bus.) c/o Richard Bauman, 156 W. 44th St., New York, NY 10036, tel. (212) PL 7-0098.

Theatre. Mr. Elston's first professional appearance was in stock at the Pocono Playhouse (Mountainhome, Pa.) where he appeared in *Gramercy Ghost, The Petrified Forest,* and *They Knew What They Wanted* (Summer 1952); subsequently appeared in *Ah, Wilderness!* and *Legend of Lovers* (Circle in the Square, Philadelphia, Pa., 1953); and toured with the Stanley Woolf Players in *The Moon Is Blue* and *Be Your Age* (Summer 1953).

He made his N.Y.C. debut as Archie in *Summer and Smoke* (Studio Th., New Sch. for Social Research, Apr. 1956); and at the Robin Hood Th. (Arden, Del.) played Brewsie in *Brewsie and Willie,* Finch in *Home of the Brave,* and Jim in *The Rainmaker* (Summer 1956).

He played Armand in *Camille* (Cherry Lane, N.Y.C., Sept. 1956); was general understudy for *The Genius and the Goddess* (Henry Miller's Th., Dec. 10, 1957); played Sherman in *Maybe Tuesday* (Playhouse, Jan. 29, 1958); Rosalio in *The Purification* (Arena Th., Washington, D.C., Nov. 1958); Ray Blent in *Tall Story* (Belasco, N.Y.C., Jan. 29, 1959); Valentine in *Twelfth Night* (Cambridge Shakespeare Festival, Mass., June 1959); Jason Eldridge in *The Golden Fleecing* (Henry Miller's Th., N.Y.C., Oct. 15, 1959); toured as Robert in the national company of *The World of Suzie Wong* (opened National, Washington, D.C., Jan. 4, 1960); played John in the pre-Bway tryout of *Memo* (opened Shubert, New Haven, Conn., Feb. 27, 1963; closed Wilbur, Boston, Mass., Mar. 9, 1963); and appeared in 19 roles in *Spoon River Anthology* (Univ. of California at Los Angeles, May 1, 1963; Booth, N.Y.C., Sept. 29, 1963).

Mr. Elston played Jerome Pendleton in *Undercover Man* (Actors Playhouse, N.Y.C., June 2, 1966; and White Barn Th., Westport, Conn., July 31, 1966); Jim in *An Albino Kind of Love* and The Patient in *Conditioned Reflex* (White Barn Th., Aug. 14, 1966); repeated his role in *Conditioned Reflex* (Th. de Lys, N.Y.C., Jan. 9, 1967), which was a part of *A Program of New American Plays;* he conceived and directed *The Harold Arlen Songbook* (Stage 73, Feb. 28, 1967); which he co-produced with Ray Ramirez; appeared in a touring production of *You Know I Can't Hear You When the Water's Running* (1967–68); played Robert Dudley in *Vivat! Vivat Regina!* (Broadhurst, N.Y.C., Jan. 20, 1972); appeared in *Spoon River Anthology* (Stage 73, Apr. 3, 1973); and *Father's Day* (Ivanhoe Th., Chicago, 1973–74); and directed *Romeo and Juliet* (The Venture '74, Beverly, Mass., Spring 1974).

Television. He made his debut in the title role of *Gerard Manley Hopkins* (Camera Three, CBS, 1960); and has appeared on US Steel Hour (CBS, 1960, 1961); Hennessey (CBS, 1961); the Lloyd Bridges Show (1962); *The Year Joan Crawford Won the Oscar* (Saints and Sinners, 1962).

He played Capt. Hastings in *Company X,* which he also adapted (CBS Workshop, 1963); and Lt. Ditser in a pilot television film, The Lieutenant (NBC, 1963); *The Poetry of Norman Rosten* (Camera Three, CBS); and as guest on The Steve Allen Show (Ind.).

ELY, LYN. Producer. b. Caroline Page Ely, New York City, to G. Page and Caro (Weir) Ely. Father, insurance executive; mother, artist. Grad. Mary C. Wheeler Sch., Providence, R.I., 1939; attended Wheaton Coll., 1940. Graduate of AADA, N.Y.C., 1941–42. Member of AEA; Cosmopolitan Club. Address: (home) 2 Beekman Place, New York, NY 10022, tel. (212) PL 9-1616; (bus.) Old Lyme, CT 06371, tel. (203) 434-2480.

Theatre. Since 1955, Miss Ely has been producer of Theatre in Education, Inc., a touring organization in which professional actors perform scenes from Shakespeare's works at secondary schools in Connecticut, North Carolina, Delaware, New Jersey, and New York.

She appeared in stock productions at the Ivoryton (Conn.) Playhouse, and the Newport (R.I.) Casino Th. (Summers 1945–48); from 1948 to 1952, she was managing director of ELT (Equity Library Th.), helping to establish the Equity Community Th. for which she was executive director (1950–53); and was a field representative for stock theatres for AEA (Summer 1951).

With Norman Kean, she produced *The Worlds of Shakespeare* (Carnegie Recital Hall, N.Y.C., Dec. 3, 1963).

Awards. Miss Ely received a Fulbright Scholarship to study government subsidy to the theatre (1954); plus the Intl. Th. Inst. of UNESCO Award to study French theatre (1954–55); an award of achievement from the Amer. Shakespeare Th. and Acad. (1958); the American Assn. of School Administrators Centennial Award for "outstanding contribution to education"; and the New England Theater Conference Award.

Recreation. Studying Italian and French, piano, ice skating, and fly fishing.

EMERY, KATHERINE. Actress. b. 1908, Birmingham, Ala., to James A. Emery, civil engineer. Grad. Sweetbriar Coll. Member of AEA.

Theatre. Miss Emery made her debut with the University Players (West Falmouth, Mass., 1930); and appeared with the Surry Players (Bar Harbor, Me., 1931). She made her Bway debut as Mrs. Klopp in *Carry Nation* (Biltmore, Oct. 29, 1932); appeared in *Double Door, The Trial of Mary Dugan,* and *Dangerous Corner* (Surry Players, Suffern, N.Y., Summer 1934); played Kay Crosby in *Strangers at Home* (Longacre, N.Y.C., Sept. 14, 1934); Karen Wright in *The Children's Hour* (Maxine Elliott's Th., Nov. 20, 1934); with the Surry Players appeared in *The Nuremberg Egg* and *Candida* (Summer 1937); played Rosalind in *As You Like It* (Ritz, N.Y.C., Oct. 30, 1937) and Kate Grant in *Roosty* (Lyceum, Feb. 14, 1938).

She appeared in *Hedda Gabler, Liliom, The Distaff Side,* and *The Good Hope* (Surry Players, Me., Summer 1938); played the Wife in *Everywhere I Roam* (National, N.Y.C., Dec. 29, 1938); Irina in *Three Sisters* (Longacre, Oct. 15, 1939); appeared in *Something About a Soldier* (Bucks County Playhouse, New Hope, Pa., Sept. 1940); *Yankee Pine* (Bard, Avondale-on-Hudson, N.Y., Oct. 1941); played Smitty in *Proof Through the Night* (Morosco, N.Y.C., Dec. 25, 1942), and Varya in *The Cherry Orchard* (National, Jan. 25, 1944).

EMHARDT, ROBERT. Actor, director. b. Indianapolis, Ind., to Christian J. and Julia Emhardt. Father, lawyer, jurist; mother, teacher. Grad. Manual H.S., Indianapolis; attended DePauw Univ.; grad. Butler Coll., A.B. Studied at RADA, London, England. Married to Silvia Sideli, actress; one son, three daughters. Relative in theatre: father-in-law, Silvio Sideli, opera and concert singer. Member of AEA; SAG; AFTRA.

Theatre. Mr. Emhardt made his debut in the J. B. Priestley Repertoire (Westminster Th., London, 1938–39); subsequently appeared in stock (Suffern, N.Y., 1940), in the pre-Bway tour of *Battle of Angels* (1940); made his N.Y.C. debut as Estaban in *The Pirate* (Martin Beck Th., Nov. 25, 1942); played Calvin Stowe in *Harriet* (NY City Ctr., Sept. 27, 1944), and toured in it.

He directed and appeared in productions for the Valley Players (Holyoke, Mass., 1944–46); played Jacob Engstrand in *Ghosts* (Cort, N.Y.C., Feb. 24, 1948); Hannibal in *The Curious Savage* (Martin Beck Th., Oct. 24, 1950); Dr. Brubaker in *The Seven Year Itch* (Fulton, Nov. 20, 1952); Mr. Harper in *Janus* (Plymouth, Nov. 24, 1955); Congressman Jason in *Good as Gold* (Belasco, Mar. 7, 1957); Winthrop Allen and Francis X. Nella in *The Girls in 509* (Belasco, Oct. 15, 1958), in which he toured (opened Hanna, Cleveland, Ohio, Jan. 26, 1959; closed Nixon, Pittsburgh, Pa., May 9, 1959); and he was The Ex in *What Else Have You Got in the Closet?* (Pasadena Playhouse, Calif., Jan. 1968).

Films. Mr. Emhardt appeared in *The Big Knife* (UA, 1955); *The Intruder* (ASB, 1955); *3:10 to Yuma* (Col., 1957); *The Badlanders* (MGM, 1958); *Wake Me When It's Over* (20th-Fox, 1960); *Underworld U.S.A.* (Col., 1961); *Kid Galahad* (UA, 1962); *The Group* (UA, 1966); and *Where Were You When the Lights Went Out?* (MGM, 1968).

Television. Mr. Emhardt made his television debut in London in *Marco Millions* (BBC, Dec. 1938); and in the US, appeared on over 500 programs, including Suspense (CBS), Danger (CBS), The Web (CBS), Alfred Hitchcock Presents (CBS), Playhouse 90 (CBS), and The Eleventh Hour (NBC).

Recreation. Golf, tennis, gardening.

EMMES, DAVID. Artistic director, director, educator. b. David Michael Emmes, Jan. 26, 1939, Glendale, Calif., to Gerard L. Edwards and Alice R. Emmes. Father, film technician. Grad. California State Univ., B.A., 1961; M.A., 1962; Univ. of Southern California, Ph.D., 1973. Married March 26, 1959, to Leslie Carr; one son, three daughters. Member of ATA; Southern Calif. Educational Th. Assn.; Calif. Th. Council; Newport (Calif.) Harbor Foundation (trustee and pres., 1973–74). Address: (home) 16871 Sea Witch Lane, Huntington Beach, CA 92649; (bus.) 1827 Newport Blvd., Costa Mesa, CA 92627, tel. (714) 646-0364.

Mr. Emmes is professor of theatre arts (1972–to date) at Long Beach City Coll.; having previously served there as instructor (1962–69); and chairman of the Creative Arts Division (1964–70). He has also lectured at the Univ. of Southern Calif. (1970–71).

Theatre. The first production directed by Mr. Emmes was *The Malcontent* (California State Univ., San Francisco, 1961). With Martin Benson, he is co-founder and artistic director (1964–to date) of the South Coast Repertory Co. (Orange Co., Calif.), a professional resident theatre. Mr. Emmes has directed more than eighty productions for this company, including *Waiting for Godot,* his first work for the professional stage (1965); *Othello* (Oct. 12, 1965; *Candida* (Jan. 16, 1966); *Let's Get a Divorce* (Oct. 18, 1966); *Red Magic* (June 20, 1967); *Arms and the Man* (Nov. 17, 1967); *Macbeth* (Mar. 20, 1968); *The Homecoming* (Sept. 27, 1968); *Room Service* (Apr. 25, 1969); *Joe Egg* (Jan. 9, 1970); *Saved* (June 5, 1970); *Tommy* (Sept. 24, 1971); *Uncle Vanya* (Mar. 31, 1972); *Happy Birthday Wanda June* (July 17, 1972); *Tango* (Nov. 23, 1972); *Play Strindberg* (Jan. 7, 1973); *The Tempest* (Apr. 20, 1973); *The Would-Be Gentleman* (Nov. 21, 1973); and *The Philanthropist* (Apr. 24, 1974). He has designed South

Coast Repertory productions of *We Bombed in New Haven* (Sept. 5, 1969) and *One Flew Over the Cuckoo's Nest* (Apr. 10, 1970), and acted in *The Boys in the Band* (Sept. 11, 1970); *The Ginger Man* (May 22, 1971); and *The White House Murder Case.* (Jan. 7, 1972). Mr. Emmes has also directed a production of the opera, *The Gypsy Baron* (Long Beach, Calif., City College).

Films. Mr. Emmes directed *Prunetime* (SCR Productions, May, 1972).

Other Activities. Mr. Emmes contributed to the work of the Council of Arts of Coastal Orange County Calif. (1965–70).

Recreation. Sailing, walking, and reading.

ENGEL, LEHMAN. Composer, conductor, author, lecturer. b. Aaron Lehman Engel, Sept. 14, 1910, Jackson, Miss., to Ellis and Julliette (Lehman) Engel. Father, salesman. Grad. Central H.S., 1926; attended Univ. of Cincinnati, 1926–29; Juilliard Sch. of Music Grad. Sch., 1930–33. Studied composition with Roger Sessions, N.Y.C., 1935. Served USN, 1942–46; rank, Lt. Member of AFM; BMI; Composers and Lyricists Guild of America, Inc.; NARAS; NY Board of Education (adv. comm.); N.Y.H.S. of Performing Arts (adv. board); Theatre and Music Collection, Museum of the City of New York (dir.). Address: 350 E. 54th St., New York, NY 10022, tel. (212) PL 3-3295.

Theatre. Mr. Engel's first composition was *Pierrot of the Minute,* an opera which he conducted at the Coll. of Music (Cincinnati, Ohio, 1929). He was muscial director of *Der Jasager* (Grand St. Playhouse, N.Y.C., Apr. 1933); conducted *It's a Strange House* (AW Studio, Putney, Vt., Aug. 1934); composed incidental music for *Within the Gates* (Natl., N.Y.C., Oct. 22, 1934); a tryout of *The Birds* (Greek Amphitheatre, Bar Harbor, Me., Summer 1935); and *Murder in the Cathedral* (Manhattan Th., N.Y.C., Mar. 20, 1936). In 1936, he founded the Madrigal Singers, who performed in concert through 1939. He composed music for *The Emperor's New Clothes* (Adelphi, N.Y.C., June 2, 1936); conducted *Johnny Johnson* (44 St. Th., Nov. 19, 1936); and *The Second Hurricane* (Grand St. Th., Apr. 21, 1937); composed music for *A Hero Is Born* (Adelphi, Oct. 1, 1937); and *Robin Landing* (46 St. Th., Nov. 18, 1937).

He was musical director for the dress rehearsal of *The Cradle Will Rock* (Maxine Elliott's Th., 1937), which was prevented from a regular run at that time by the government. He wrote incidental music for *The Shoemaker's Holiday* (Mercury, Jan. 1, 1938); *Madame Capet* (Cort, Oct. 25, 1938); Maurice Evans' *Hamlet* (St. James, Oct. 25, 1938); *Everywhere I Roam* (Natl., Dec. 29, 1938); *Family Portrait* (Morosco, Mar. 8, 1939); *The Time of Your Life* (Booth, Oct. 25, 1939); and *Thunder Rock* (Mansfield, Nov. 14, 1939). He conducted *Shadow Play* (Paper Mill Playhouse, Millburn, N.J., Summer 1939); composed *Trial of a Judge* for the Federal Th. (WPA) Project's "Test Th." (Ritz, 1939); wrote incidental music for *Heavenly Express* (Natl., Apr. 18, 1940); was musical director for the pre-Bway tryout of *The Little Dog Laughed* (opened Garden Pier, Atlantic City, N.J., Aug. 14, 1940; closed Shubert, Boston, Mass., Aug. 20, 1940); and for Experimental Th., Inc., he composed *The Trojan Women* (Cort, N.Y.C., 1941).

He staged and conducted *The Beggar's Opera* (Carnegie Inst. of Tech., Mar. 11, 1941; Bucks Co. Playhouse, New Hope, Pa., Sept. 1941); composed incidental music for Maurice Evans' *Macbeth* (Natl., N.Y.C., Nov. 11, 1941); staged and conducted his own opera, *The Chaplet,* for the Museum of Modern Art, N.Y.C. (Coffee Concert, Dec. 10, 1941); and wrote music for *A Kiss for Cinderella* (Music Box Th., Mar. 10, 1942).

Mr. Engel was musical director for *Call Me Mister* (Natl., Apr. 18, 1946); composed music for *Henry VII* (Intl., Nov. 6, 1946); arranged the music for *John Gabriel Borkman* (Intl., Nov. 12, 1946); and *Yellow Jack* (Intl., Feb. 27, 1947); selected and arranged Bach's music for *Dear Judas* (Mansfield, Oct. 5, 1947); was musical advisor for *A Streetcar Named Desire* (Ethel Barrymore Th., Dec. 3, 1947); and musical director for the pre-Bway tryout of *Bonanza Bound* (opened Shubert, Philadelphia, Pa., Dec. 26, 1947; closed there, Jan. 3, 1948).

He arranged music for *Me and Molly* (Belasco, N.Y.C., Feb. 26, 1948); provided the calliope music for *Temporary Island* (Maxine Elliott's Th., Mar. 14, 1948); arranged music for the Margaret Webster Shakespeare Co. tours of *Hamlet* and *Macbeth* (opened Buffalo, N.Y., Sept. 28, 1948); was musical director of the pre-Bway tryout of *That's the Ticket* (opened Shubert, Philadelphia, Pa., Sept. 24, 1948; closed there, Oct. 2, 1948); and composed incidental music for *Anne of a Thousand Days* (Shubert, N.Y.C., Dec. 8, 1948).

Mr. Engel arranged the music for the ELT production of *Uniform of Flesh* (Lenox Hill Playhouse, Jan. 29, 1949); was musical director of the Dallas (Tex.) State Fair Musicals during the summer (1949–1952); wrote incidental music for the pre-Bway tryout of *Signor Chicago* (opened Shubert, New Haven, Conn., Oct. 1949; closed Locust St. Th., Philadelphia, Pa., Nov. 7, 1949); was musical director for *Alive and Kicking* (Winter Garden, N.Y.C., Jan. 17, 1950); *The Consul* (Ethel Barrymore Th., Mar. 15, 1950); wrote incidental music for *The Wisteria Trees* (Martin Beck Th., Mar. 29, 1950); conducted *The Liar* (Broadhurst, May 18, 1950); and *Bless You All* (Mark Hellinger Th., Dec. 14, 1950); and wrote incidental music for Uta Hagen's *Saint Joan* (Cort, Oct. 4, 1951).

He was musical director and vocal arranger for the pre-Bway tryout of *A Month of Sundays* (opened Shubert, Boston, Mass., Dec. 25, 1951; closed Forrest, Philadelphia, Pa., Jan. 26, 1952); returned to N.Y.C., to conduct Gilbert and Sullivan's *The Mikado, H.M.S. Pinafore, The Trial, The Pirates of Penzance,* and *Iolanthe,* in repertory (Mark Hellinger Th., Oct. 20, 1952); and *Wonderful Town,* for which he was also vocal arranger (Winter Garden, Feb. 25, 1953). He composed the music for *The Golden Ladder* (Karamu, Cleveland, Ohio, May 28, 1953); *The Strong Are Lonely* (Broadhurst, N.Y.C., Sept. 29, 1953); was musical director for *Fanny* (Majestic, Nov. 4, 1954); wrote incidental music for *Middle of the Night* (ANTA, Feb. 8, 1956); and *The Ponder Heart* (Music Box Th., Feb. 16, 1956); and conducted *Shangri-La* (Winter Garden, June 13, 1957); *Li'l Abner* (St. James, Nov. 15, 1956); his own opera, *The Soldier* (Carnegie Hall, Nov. 25, 1956); *The Consul* (Theatre-in-the-Park, N.Y.C., Sept. 3, 1957); and *Jamaica* (Imperial, Oct. 31, 1957).

Mr. Engel composed incidental music for *Measure for Measure* (Old Vic, London, Eng., Nov. 19, 1957); was musical director of *Wonderful Town* (NY City Ctr., Mar. 5, 1958); arranged music for *Jane Eyre* (Belasco, May 1, 1958); conducted *Gentlemen Prefer Blondes, Guys and Dolls, The Most Happy Fella,* and *Oklahoma!* (State Fair Musicals, Dallas, Tex., Summer 1958); wrote incidental music for the American Shakespeare Festival and Academy production of *Julius Caesar* (Stratford, Conn., June 12, 1958); conducted *Goldilocks* (Lunt-Fontanne, N.Y.C., Oct. 11, 1958); *Destry* (Imperial, Apr. 23, 1959); and *Take Me Along* (Shubert, Oct. 22, 1959); wrote music for the pre-Bway tryout of *Juniper and the Pagans* (opened Colonial, Boston, Mass., Dec. 10, 1959; closed Forrest, Philadelphia, Pa., Dec. 26, 1959); conducted the NY City Opera Co. revival of *The Cradle Will Rock* (NY City Ctr., Winter 1960); wrote music for *There Was A Little Girl* (Cort, Feb. 29, 1960); and was musical director for *Do Re Mi* (St. James, Dec. 26, 1960).

He conducted *West Side Story, Guys and Dolls, Oklahoma!,* and *Carousel* (San Juan, P.R., Drama Festival, summer 1961) and composed incidental music for *The Aspern Papers* (Playhouse, Feb. 7, 1962). He conducted *I Can Get It for You Wholesale* (Shubert, N.Y.C., Mar. 22, 1962); *Wonderful Town* (NY City Ctr., Feb. 13, 1963); *The Beast in Me* (Plymouth, May 16, 1963); *What Makes Sammy Run?* (54 St. Th., Feb. 27, 1964); *Bajour* (Shubert, Nov. 23, 1964); *La Grosse Valise* (54 St. Th., Dec. 14, 1965); *Porgy and Bess* (Turkish State Opera, 1969); *Scarlett* (Tokyo, 1970); *The Consul* (Temple Univ. Festival, 1971); and *Lost in the Stars* (Kennedy Center, Washington, D.C., 1972).

Films. Mr. Engel composed and conducted the music for *Roogies Bump* (Rep., 1954); *Honduras* (Willard); *Strategic Attack* (RKO Pathé); *National Defense* (RKO Pathé); *Berlin Powder Keg* (RKO Pathé); *Strange Victory* (Target); *The Hedgerow Story* for the US State Dept., as well as USN films during WW II. He recorded four childrens' films (Rome, 1965) and *Imperiale* (Greek-American Film, 1969).

Television and Radio. Mr. Engel's radio performances include Hear It Now (CBS); American Portrait (CBS); Brahm's *Requiem* (NBC); Columbia Workshop; This Is War (all networks); Texaco Star Th. (ABC); Michael and Kitty; Texaco Gene Autry Show (CBS); Texaco (CBS); *The Beggar's Opera* (CBS); and appearances with his Madrigal Singers (NBC, CBS, WOR, WMCA, WEVD). His compositions, *The Creation* (CBS), *The Chaplet* (CBS), and *Second Hurricane* (CBS), have been performed on radio.

On television, he has appeared on Ed Sullivan's Toast of the Town (CBS, Oct. 1955); *The Mikado* (Ford Foundation, CBS); *The Soul of the Great Bell* (NBC); and *The Beggar's Opera* (Columbia Workshop). He composed and conducted the music for *The Taming of the Shrew* (Hallmark Hall of Fame, NBC, Mar. 18, 1956); *Macbeth* (Hallmark Hall of Fame, NBC); Texaco's Command Appearance (NBC, Sept. 19, 1957); *Twelfth Night* (Hallmark Hall of Fame, NBC, Dec. 15, 1957); *Wonderful Town* (CBS, Nov. 30, 1958); and *The Tempest* (Hallmark Hall of Fame, NBC, May 1960). He was musical director for *Miss Teenage America* (CBS, 1972, 1973).

Other Activities. Mr. Engel was director of the music department of the American Musical and Dramatic Th. Acad., N.Y.C. (1962–66), and director of workshops for composers and lyricists sponsored by Broadcast Music, Inc. in New York City, Los Angeles, and Toronto. He was guest conductor for the Boston Pops (1969), the Pittsburgh Symphony (1972), and producer-conductor for revivals of *The Student Prince* and *Desert Song* (two companies) in Philadelphia, Baltimore, Washington, Chicago, Indianapolis, Dallas, and N.Y.C. (Summer 1973). He has lectured at colleges and clubs throughout the US. He is president of Arrow Music Press, Inc.

Published Works. Mr. Engel wrote *Renaissance to Baroque* (1931), *Music for the Classical Tragedy* (1953), *Musical Shows: Planning and Producing* (1957), *The American Musical Theater* (1967), *Words With Music* (1972), *Getting Started in the Theater* (1973), and *This Bright Day* (1974), his autobiography. Other works he has published are *Folk Songs, Poor Wayfaring Stranger,* and another collection of arranged *Folk Songs.* He has contributed articles to the NY *Times,* NY *Herald Tribune, Theatre Arts* Magazine, *Woman's Home Companion,* Chicago *Tribune, Musical America, Musical Leader, Modern Musical, Dance Observer,* and the Dallas *Morning News.*

Discography. Mr. Engel's recordings include *Bayou Ballads* (Decca); *Bing Crosby* (Decca); *The Madrigal Singers* (Col.); *Macbeth* (Vic.); *Bach* (Gamut); *The Selfish Giant* (Decca); *Barry Wood* (Brunswick); *The Shoemaker and the Elves* (Col.); *The Pied Piper of Hamlin* (Col.); *Roustabout Songs* (Decca); *Our Common Hertiage* (Decca); *The Prettiest Song in the World* (Vic.); *Rodgers & Hart* (Vic.); *Cranky Old House* (Col.); *The Happiest Birthday* (Col.); *Bonanza Bound* (Vic.); *Kiss Me Kate* (Vic.); *Mary Martin Sings for You* (Col.); *This Is My Beloved* (Atlantic); *Ezio Pinza* (Col.); *The Consul* (Decca); *Anything Goes* (Col.); *Band Wagon* (Col); *Babes in Arms* (Col.); *Girl Crazy* (Col.); *Pal Joey* (Col.); *Conversation Piece* (Col.); *Porgy and Bess* (Col.); *Christmas Carols* (Col.); *Madrigals* (Col.); *The Faithful Shepherd* (Col.); *The Merry Widow* (Col.); *The Student Prince* (Col.); *On Your Toes* (Col.); *Roberta* (Col.); *Oklahoma!* (Col.); *The Desert Song* (Col.); *Bittersweet* (Col.); *Oh, Kay!* (Col.); *Show Boat* (Vic.); *Fanny* (Vic.); *Carousel* (Vic.); *Li'l Abner* (Vic.); and *Song of Norway* (Decca).

Also, *Wonderful Town* (Col.); *Curtain Going Up* (Col.); *Ballets from Broadway* (Vic.); *Goldilocks* (Col.); *Rose Marie* (Vic.); *Presenting Peter Palmer* (Vic.); *The Chocolate Soldier* (Vic.); *Brigadoon* (Col.); *The Desert Song* (Vic.); *Favorites in Hi Fi* (Vic.); *Jamaica* (Vic.); *I Can Get It for You Wholesale* (Col.); *Do Re Mi* (Vic.); *Take Me Along* (Vic.); *Lady in the Dark* (Col.); eighteen operettas for the *Reader's Digest* series (Vic.); four recordings for *Life* magazine's American History series (Capitol); Medieval Christmas Carols for the *Life* series (Capitol); *What Makes Sammy Run?; and The King and I* (Col., 1964).

Awards. Mr. Engel received the honorary D.Mus. degree from Boguslawski College of Music, Chicago (1944) and the Univ. of Cincinnati (1971) and the doctor of humane letters degree from Millsaps College, Jackson, Miss. (1971). He received also special citations from the Hartford (Conn.) Conservatory of Music in 1971 and the Jackson (Miss.) Chamber of Commerce in 1973. He has received Antoinette Perry (Tony) Awards for his musical direction of *The Consul* (1950), *Wonderful Town* (1953) and the Gilbert and Sullivan Repertory (1953).

ENTERS, ANGNA. Mime, painter, director, writer. b. Apr. 28, 1907, New York City, to Edward W. and Henriette Enters. Educated privately; also attended Center for Advanced Studies, Wesleyan Univ. (Fellow 1962–63). Married July 1936 to Louis Kalonyme (dec. Dec. 1961). Member of AEA. Address: (home) 35 W. 57th St., New York, NY 10019; (bus.) c/o Audrey Wood, 555 Madison Ave., New York, NY 10022.

Theatre. Miss Enters made her debut in a program of dance-mime, *Compositions in Dance Form*, for which she also designed the sets and costumes (Greenwich Village Th., N.Y.C., Mar. 1924); later retitled her concerts, *The Theatre of Angna Enters*.

Since 1928, she has made annual tours of the US and Canada; performed 20 N.Y.C. seasons in such solo pieces as *Queen of Heaven, Boy Cardinal, American Ballet—1914–1916*, and *Oh, the Pain of It*, all for which she was dancer, choreographer, scenery and costume designer, and musical arranger; and appeared in *Pagan Greece* (Metropolitan Museum of Art, 1943), a mime in which she played all 14 roles, and for which she designed costumes and sets, and composed the music.

She wrote the plays, *Love Possessed Juana* (Houston Little Th., Oct. 15, 1947); designed the settings and costumes for *Yerma*, which she also directed (Univ. of Denver Th., Colo., July 1958; Cornell Coll. Th., N.Y., Aug. 1958); designed the settings and costumes for *The Madwoman of Chaillot*, which she also directed (Dallas Th. Ctr., Tex., Jan. 1962); and directed *Moon Over Kylenemo* (92 Th., Wesleyan Univ., Middletown, Conn., Jan. 20, 1963).

She taught classes in mime-for-actors at Baylor Univ. (Waco, Tex., 1961–62); and weekly seminars for advanced students in mime-for-actors, Wesleyan Univ. (1962–63).

Television. Miss Enters performed on a special program (BBC, London, 1952).

Other Activities. Since her first painting exhibition (Mar. 1933), Miss Enters has had numerous exhibitions throughout the US and in London. Her stage and costume drawings and paintings were shown at the Naples International Theatre Exhibition (Oct. 1963).

Published Works. She is the author of *First Person Plural* (1937); *Love Possessed Juana* (1939); *Silly Girl* (1945); *Among the Daughters* (1958); *Artist's Life* (1959); and *On Mime* (1966).

Awards. Miss Enters received a Guggenheim Fellowship (1934–35), and has been an Artist in Residence at the Dallas (Tex.) Theatre Ctr. (Baylor Univ., 1961–64).

ENTERS, WARREN. Director. b. Warren Louis Enters, May 26, 1927, Milwaukee, Wis., to Louis and Elfriede Enters. Father, manager furniture stores. Grad. Shorewood H.S.; Univ. of Wisconsin, B.A. 1950; attended Dartmouth Coll., 1943; Columbia Univ., 1944–Th., Served USN, 1943–46; rank, Lt. Relative in theatre: cousin, Angna Enters, dance mime, painter. Member of AEA. directed,. Address: (home) 47 W. 68th St., New York, NY 10023; Blind Buck Hollow Road, Salem, NY 12865; (bus.) c/o International Famous Agency, Inc., Brigit Aschenberg, 1301 Avenue of the Americas, New York, NY 10019, tel. (212) 556-5600.

Theatre. Mr. Enters first entered the theatre as actor and stage manager with his Port Players (Oconomowoc, Wis., Summer 1951). He made his N.Y.C. debut as producer, with Proscenium Productions, at the Cherry Lane Theatre, and director of *The Way of the World* (Oct. 2, 1954); *Thieves' Carnival* (Feb. 1, 1955); *The Dragon's Mouth* (Nov. 16, 1955); and *Dandy Dick* (Jan. 10, 1956); directed with playwright Joseph Kramm, the pre-Bway tryout of *Build with One Hand* (opened Shubert, New Haven, Conn., Nov. 7, 1956; closed Ford's, Baltimore, Md., Nov. 27, 1956).

At the Crest Th. (Toronto, Can.), he staged *The Italian Straw Hat* (1956) and *Ah, Wilderness!* (1957); directed the touring package show of *Brigadoon* (Summer 1957) and supervised the revisions on *The Marriner Method* for Maurice Evans Productions (1957). At the Boston (Mass.) Summer Th., he directed *The Potting Shed, The Madwoman of Chaillot* (Summer 1957), and again staged *Thieves' Carnival;* directed the pre-Bway production of *The Saturday Night Kid* (opened Westport Country Playhouse, Conn., Sept. 9, 1957); off-Bway, directed *A Palm Tree in a Rose Garden* (Cricket Th., N.Y.C., Nov. 26, 1957); and staged *Colombe* (Arena Stage, Washington, D.C., 1958).

Mr. Enters directed *The Warm Peninsula* (Helen Hayes Th., N.Y.C., Oct. 20, 1959); *The Madwoman of Chaillot* (Royal Poinciana Playhouse, Palm Beach, Fla., Winter 1960); several productions of *The Marriage-Go-Round* (Bucks County Playhouse, New Hope, Pa., Summer 1960; Paper Mill Playhouse, Millburn, N.J., Fall 1960; Sombrero Playhouse, Phoenix, Ariz., Winter 1961); the Natl. Phoenix Th. production of *Anatole;* and served as ballet supervisor for their Boston Dance Festival (Boston, Mass., July 1961). He staged the national company of *Advise and Consent* (opened Shubert, Cincinnati, Ohio, Oct. 2, 1961; closed American Th., St. Louis, Mo., May 5, 1962); and directed *Misalliance* (Arena Stage, Washington, D.C., Feb. 1962).

For the American Shakespeare Festival (Stratford, Conn.), he directed Maurice Evans and Helen Hayes in *Shakespeare Revisited: A Program for Two Players* (June 12–Sept. 16, 1962), and its subsequent cross-country tour (opened Fisher, Detroit, Mich., Oct. 15, 1962; closed Playhouse, Wilmington, Del., Mar. 9, 1963); he directed *The Emperor* (Maidman Playhouse, N.Y.C., Apr. 16, 1963); and the pre-Bway tryout of *The Revelation* (Univ. of Wisconsin, July, 1963); and, with Patrick Dennis, wrote *Good Good Friends* (1964).

In 1967, Mr. Enters became associate director, Studio Arena Theatre, Buffalo, N.Y., and in 1968 associate professor, State Univ. of N.Y. (Buffalo). As guest director, Goodman School of the Theatre, Chicago, Ill., he directed *All the Way Home; Caesar and Cleopatra* (Jan. 12, 1968); and *A Flea in Her Ear* (May 3, 1968). At the Studio Arena in Buffalo, plays he has directed include *The Nephew* (Mar. 24, 1967); *Barefoot in the Park* (June 8, 1967); *A Delicate Balance* (Feb. 8, 1968); *Blithe Spirit* (Dec. 5, 1968); *The Killing of Sister George* (Jan. 8, 1969); *The Homecoming* (Feb. 6, 1969); *The School for Wives* (Apr. 8, 1969); *Tiny Alice* (Nov. 6, 1969); *Don't Drink the Water* (Dec. 11, 1969); *The Only Game in Town* (Jan. 15, 1970); *Uncle Vanya* (Feb. 19, 1970); *Lemon Sky* (world premiere, Mar. 26, 1970); *Scenes from American Life* (Oct. 27, 1970); *The Price* (Dec. 3, 1970); *L.A. Under Siege* (world premiere, Dec. 29, 1970); *The Effect of Gamma Rays on Man-in-the-Moon Marigolds* (Mar. 4, 1971); *Buying Out* (world premiere, Nov. 4, 1971); *Romeo and Juliet* (Mar. 2, 1972); *The Taming of the Shrew* (Mar. 1, 1973); *Child's Play* (Apr. 5, 1973); *Flint* (Jan. 31, 1974); and *The Miser* (Spring 1974).

Mr. Enters also directed productions of *Lemon Sky* in Chicago and N.Y.C. (Playhouse, May 17, 1970); summer tours of *Motive* (1971) and *Under Papa's Picture* (1972); and *The Miracle Worker* (Meadow Brook Th., Rochester, Mich., Jan. 4, 1973).

Television. Mr. Enters directed two Play-of-the-Week productions (WNTA); *Thieves' Carnival* (1959), and *The Enchanted* (1960).

Awards. He received an Antoinette Perry (Tony) Award for his off-Bway productions at the Cherry Lane Th.; the Vernon Rice Memorial Award (1954–55 season); and a citation from French Cultural Attaché for the first successful production of Anouilh in the US.

Recreation. Collecting antiques, books, theatrical memorabilia, travel.

EPHRON, HENRY. Playwright. b. May 26, 1912, New York City, to Isaac and Gussie (Weinstein) Ephron. Father, retailer. Grad. Evander Childs H.S., Bronx, N.Y., 1929; attended Cornell Univ., 1929–32. Married July 31, 1934, to Phoebe Wolkind, known as Phoebe Ephron, playwright (dec. Oct. 13, 1971); four daughters. Member of Dramatists Guild; WGA West; Menninger Foundation; Beverly Hills Tennis Club.

Pre-Theatre. Magazine work, retail carpet business.

Theatre. Mr. Ephron and his wife wrote *Three's a Family;* (Longacre Th., N.Y.C., May 5, 1943) *Take Her, She's Mine* (Biltmore, Dec. 21, 1961); *Everybody Out, the Castle Is Sinking* (pre-Bway, opened Colonial, Boston, Mass., Dec. 26, 1964; closed there Jan. 9, 1965); and *My Daughter, Your Son* (Booth Th., N.Y.C., May 13, 1969).

Films. With his wife, he wrote the screenplays for *Look for the Silver Lining* (WB, 1949); *The Jackpot* (20th-Fox, 1950); *On the Riviera* (20th-Fox, 1951); *Daddy Long Legs* (20th-Fox, 1955); *Carousel*, which he also produced (20th-Fox, 1955), *The Desk Set*, which he also produced (20th-Fox, 1957), and *Captain Newman, M.D.* (UI, 1963).

Other Activities. With the songwriter Johnny Mercer, Mr. Ephron formed a Broadway producing firm, Vulnerable Productions, in 1971.

Awards. Mr. Ephron and his wife received the *Holiday* Magazine Award for *The Jackpot* (1949).

Recreation. Tennis, bridge.

EPSTEIN, ALVIN. Actor, director, teacher of mime, mime. b. May 14, 1925, New York City, to Harry and Goldie Epstein. Father, physician. Attended Walden Sch.; Dewitt Clinton H.S., N.Y.C.; H.S. of Music and Art, N.Y.C., 1942; attended Queens Coll., 1943; Biarritz (France) Amer. Univ., 1945. Studied dance with Martha Graham, 1946–47; at Paris (France) Conservatoire, 1947–51; Etienne Decroux Sch. of Mime, Paris, 1947–51; acting with Sanford Meisner, N. 1951–52; Actors' Studio (observer, 1955–57). Served US Army, Coast and Field Artillery, ETO 1943–46. Relative in theatre: brother, Mark Epstein, director, teacher of mime. Member of AEA; AFTRA. Address: (home) 129 Good Hill Rd., Oxford, CT 06483, tel. (203) 888-0658; (bus.) c/o Peter Witt Assoc., 37 W. 57th St., New York, NY 10019, tel. (212) PL 9-7966.

Mr. Epstein has been a teacher of acting and directing, Yale School of Drama, since 1968. He is associate director of the Yale Repertory Th. and a fellow of Trumbull Coll., Yale Univ., New Haven, Conn.

Theatre. Mr. Epstein appeared in a Biarritz Amer. Univ. production of *Richard III*, which toured US Army bases in Europe (1945); made his N.Y.C. debut as Wint Selby in an ELT production of *Ah, Wilderness!*, for which he designed and executed the sets (Lenox Hill Playhouse, 1947); toured Israel with Etienne Decroux's French Mime Th. Co. (1950), and Paris (1951).

He toured the U.S. as Sganarel in a summer-production of *The Doctor in Spite of Himself* (1951); and was a resident member of the Habima Th. (Tel Aviv, Isr.), where he played Arthur Jarvis in *Lost in the Stars*, Victor Karenin in *The Living Corpse*, the Messiah in *The Golem,* Tony in *The Mother,* Donalbain in *Macbeth,* the Snake in *Legend of Three and Four,* Willy Keith in *The Caine Mutiny Court-Martial,* Count Carlo Di Nolli in Pirandello's *Henry IV,* and the Fool in *King Lear* (1953–55).

He appeared with Marcel Marceau (Phoenix, N.Y.C., Sept. 20, 1955; moved to Ethel Barrymore Th., Oct. 4, 1955), also touring in it; played the Fool in Orson Welles' production of *King Lear* (NY City Ctr., Jan. 12, 1956); was assistant director for the double bill of *Miss Julie* and *The Stronger* (Phoenix, Feb. 21, 1956); played Lucky in *Waiting for Godot* (John Golden Th., Apr. 19, 1956); Puck in *A Midsummer Night's Dream* (Empire State Music Festival, Ellenville, N.Y., July 1956); Satan in *Adam* (White Barn Th., Conn., July 8, 1956); O'Killigain in *Purple Dust* (Cherry Lane, N.Y.C., Dec. 27, 1956); the Devil in *L'Histoire du Soldat* (Kaufmann Concert Hall, May 25, 1957); Johnny Casside in *Pictures in the Hallway* (Ravinia Festival Th., Ill., June 17, 1957); the Ragpicker in *The Madwoman of Chaillot* (Boston Summer Th., Mass., Aug. 5, 1957); the Spy in *Romanoff and Juliet* (Shubert Th., Boston, Mass., Sept. 9, 1957).

Mr. Epstein played Octave in *Clerambard* (Rooftop, N.Y.C., Nov. 7, 1957); Clov in *Endgame* (Cherry Lane, Jan. 28, 1958); Clausius in *The Golden Six* (York, Oct. 26, 1958); the Narrator in the N.Y. Pro Musica Production of *The Play of Daniel* (Chapel of the Intercession, Dec. 26, 1959; Jan. 5, 1959; St. George's Church, Dec. 26, 1961); and Feste in a summer production of *Twelfth Night* (Cambridge Drama Festival, Mass., July 1959).

He appeared in the revue, *From A to Z* (Plymouth, N.Y.C., Apr. 20, 1960); directed an experimental group established through a grant from the Ford Foundation, N.Y.C. (1961–62); played Luc Delbert in *No Strings* (54 St. Th., Mar. 15, 1962); the Sergeant in *Dynamite Tonight* (Actors' Studio, Dec. 1963); Constable Kentinov, Alexander Lomov, and Trotsky in *The Passion of Josef D* (Ethel Barrymore Th., Feb. 11, 1964); appeared in *Brecht on Brecht* (Playhouse-in-the-Park, Philadelphia, Pa., June 1964); played the title role in Pirandello's *Henry IV* (Fred Miller Th., Milwaukee, Wis., July 1964; Harper, Chicago, Oct. 29, 1964); Bob McKellaway in *Mary, Mary* (Bucks County Playhouse, New Hope, Pa., May 17, 1965); various parts in *Postmark Zero* (Brooks Atkinson Th., N.Y.C., Nov. 1, 1965); and Berenger in *The Pedestrian in the Air* (Goodman Memorial Th., Chicago, Ill., Jan. 7, 1966).

In 1966, Mr. Epstein was one of the founders of the Berkshire Theatre Festival, Stockbridge, Mass., where he appeared (June, July) as Mr. Antrobus in *The Skin of Our Teeth* and Shylock in *The Merchant of Venice.* He repeated his performance as the Sergeant in *Dynamite Tonight* (Yale Repertory Th., New Haven, Conn., Dec. 9, 1966), also in N.Y.C. (Martinique Th., Mar. 15, 1967); was Henry Thoreau in *At This Hour* (Nassau Community College Th., N.Y., May 9, 1967); Theseus and Oberon in *A Midsummer Night's Dream* (Th. de Lys, N.Y.C., June 29, 1967); and Arthur Landau in *The Latent Heterosexual* (Huntington Hartford Th., Hollywood, Calif., May 2, 1968).

In Sept. 1968, Mr. Epstein joined Yale Repertory Theatre, New Haven, Conn., and he appeared there during the 1968–69 season as William Clark Brackman in *God Bless* (Oct. 10, 1968); as various characters in *Story Theatre—Grimms' Fairy Tales* (Jan. 23, 1969); as Dionysus in *The Bacchae* (Mar. 6, 1969); and in the title role in *Greatshot* (May 8, 1969). In the 1969–70 season at Yale Rep. Th., he directed *The Rivals* (Oct. 16, 1969); appeared as various characters in *Ovid's Metamorphoses (Story Theatre)* (Nov. 27, 1969); as Maurice in *Crimes and Crimes* (Jan. 8, 1970); as Khlestakov in *The Government Inspector* (Feb. 19, 1970); and in the title role of *Don Juan* (May 15, 1970). During the summer of 1970, he repeated his appearance in *Ovid's Metamorphoses* (John Drew Th., Easthampton, N.Y., July 1970). He appeared as the Questioner in *A Place Without Doors* (American premiere, Long Wharf Th., New Haven, Conn., Nov. 20, 1970), which was repeated in N.Y.C. (Stairway Th., Dec. 22, 1970). For the 1970–71 season of Yale Rep. Th., he appeared in *Story Theatre* (Oct. 8, 1970), playing the title role in *Gimpel the Fool* and various characters in *Olympian Games* (Oct. 8, 1970); played the title role in *Woyzeck* (Apr. 1, 1971); and directed *The Seven Deadly Sins* (May 13, 1971). He repeated his role in *A Place Without Doors* on a national tour (Sept.–Dec. 1971), and for the 1971–72 season of Yale Rep. Th., he directed *Caligula* (Nov. 25, 1971) and a revival of *The Seven Deadly Sins* (Jan. 20, 1972) and appeared as Pietro in *I Married You for the Fun of It* (American premiere, Feb. 17, 1972) and as Dr. Nakamura in *Happy End* (American premiere, Apr. 6, 1972). He became acting artistic director, Yale Rep. Th., for the 1972–73 season and directed *The Bourgeois Gentleman* (Oct. 6, 1972); *In the Clap Shack* (world premiere, Dec. 15, 1972); and, with William Peters and John McAndrew, *Macbett* (American premiere, Mar. 16, 1973). He appeared in the title role of the last and as Warrington and the Judge in *Lear* (American premiere, Apr. 13, 1973). He became associate artistic director of Yale Rep. Th., for the 1973–74 season, and he directed, with Moni Yakim, and appeared as Prospero in *The Tempest* (Oct. 12, 1973); appeared as various characters in *Watergate Classics* (Nov. 24, 1973); directed *The Rise and Fall of the City of Mahagonny* (Feb. 1974); and was Aeakos in *The Frogs* (May 20, 1974). In addition, he directed *Colette* (Berkshire Th. Festival, July 30, 1974). During the 1974–75 Yale Rep. Th. season, Mr. Epstein appeared as Kirilov in *The Possessed* (American premiere, Oct. 9, 1974).

Television. Mr. Epstein made his debut in *The Ballad of Yermo Red* (Studio One, CBS, 1956); subsequently played the Son in *Therese Raquin* (Play of the Week, WNTA), Lucky in *Waiting for Godot* (Play of the Week, WNTA), Noah in *Prayers from the Ark* (Look Up and Live, CBS), appeared in *Terezin Requiem* (CBS), on Lamp Unto My Feet (CBS), The Eternal Light (CBS), Omnibus (NBC), the Ed Sullivan Show (CBS), Ellery Queen (NBC), Accent (CBS), the Pontiac Show (NBC), Mr. Broadway (CBS), and in the television presentation of *Story Theatre—Grimm's Fairy Tales* (PBS).

Concerts. Mr. Epstein presented a program of songs, *The World of Kurt Weill* (Ravinia Festival, Chicago, Ill., Aug. 7, 1967), which has been repeated on several occasions (Ravinia, July 8, 1968; Yale Cabaret, New Haven, Conn., Spring 1968; Berkshire Theatre Festival, July 1970; John Drew Th., Easthampton, N.Y., Aug. 13, 1973; and Williamstown Th., Williamstown, Mass., Aug. 1973 and Aug. 1974). He has also presented another program of Kurt Weill songs, *Whores, Wars, and Tin Pan Alley* (The Bitter End, N.Y.C., June 16, 1969), which has been repeated (Macloren Playhouse, Los Angeles, Calif., Aug. 10, 1970; Washington Theatre Club, Washington, D.C., June 9, 1971).

Other Activities. Mr. Epstein conducted mime classes at the Chamber Th. School (Tel Aviv, Israel, 1952–53); Neighborhood Playhouse School of the Th. (1957–58); Circle in the Square School of the Th. (1961); and Barnard Coll. Summer Th., N.Y.C. He was a fellow at the Salzburg (Austria) American Seminar on the American theatre (Summer 1972).

Awards. He was nominated for the *Variety* NY Drama Critics Poll for his performance as Lucky in *Waiting for Godot* (1956). He received a Ford Foundation Grant (1960); a Brandeis Univ. Creative Arts Award (1966); and a *Village Voice* off-Bway (Obie) Award for his distinguished performance as the Sergeant in *Dynamite Tonite* (1966–67).

Recreation. Playing the piano and harpsichord.

EPSTEIN, JULIUS. Playwright, producer. b. Aug. 22, 1909, New York City, to Henry and Sarah (Kronenberg) Epstein. Father, proprietor of a livery stable. Attended Penn State Coll. Married Apr. 30, 1936, to Frances Sage, actress (marr. dis. 1945); married Oct. 1, 1949, to Ann Lazlo. Relative in theatre: brother, Philip G. Epstein, playwright. Member of Dramatists Guild; SWG.

Pre-Theatre. Advertising.

Theatre. With his brother Philip G. Epstein, Mr. Epstein wrote *And Stars Remain* (Guild Th., N.Y.C., Oct. 12, 1936); *Rufus and His Wife* (County Th., Suffern, N.Y., Sept. 1, 1941); *Chicken Every Sunday* (Henry Miller Th., N.Y.C., Apr. 5, 1944); the pre-Bway tryout of *That's the Ticket* (opened Shubert, Philadelphia, Pa., Sept. 24, 1948; closed there Oct. 2, 1948). Alone, Mr. Epstein wrote *But Seriously. . .* (Henry Miller's Th., N.Y.C., Feb. 27, 1969).

Films. Again with Philip G. Epstein, he wrote the screenplays for *In Caliente* (1st Natl., 1935); *Little Big Shot* (WB, 1935); *Stars Over Broadway* (WB, 1935); *Four Daughters* (WB, 1938); *Daughters Courageous* (WB, 1939); *Saturday's Children* (WB, 1940); *No Time for Comedy* (WB, 1940); *The Bride Came C.O.D.* (WB, 1941); *The Strawberry Blonde* (WB, 1941); *The Man Who Came to Dinner* (WB, 1941); *The Male Animal* (WB, 1942); *Casablanca* (WB, 1942); *Mr. Skeffington* (WB, 1944), which he also co-produced; *Arsenic and Old Lace* (WB, 1944); and *Romance on the High Seas* (WB, 1948).

He wrote the scenario for *Chicken Every Sunday* (20th-Fox, 1948); and the screenplays of *My Foolish Heart* (RKO, 1949), *Take Care of My Little Girl* (20th-Fox, 1951), *Forever Female* (Par., 1953), *The Last Time I Saw Paris* (MGM, 1954), *Young at Heart* (WB, 1954), *The Tender Trap* (MGM, 1955); wrote, with Louis Peterson, the screenplay for and co-produced *Take a Giant Step* (UA, 1959); and *Light in the Piazza* (MGM, 1962).

Awards. Mr. Epstein received an Academy (Oscar) Award (1943), with Philip G. Epstein and Howard Kock, for the screenplay of *Casablanca;* and won a Screen Writers Guild Laurel Award (1955); and an Intercollegiate Boxing Championship (1929).

ERDMAN, JEAN. Choreographer, director, dancer, teacher. b. Feb. 20, Honolulu, Hawaii, to John Pinney and Marion (Dillingham) Erdman. Father, minister; mother, singer. Grad. Miss Hall's, Pittsfield, Mass., 1934; Sarah Lawrence Coll., 1938. Professional training with Martha Graham; Amer. School of Ballet; José Hernandez. Married May 5, 1938, to Joseph Cambell, professor, author. Address: 136 Waverly Place, New York, NY 10014, tel. (212) 929-3956.

Theatre. Miss Erdman was a dancer with the Martha Graham Dance Company (1938–43), with whom she first appeared onstage in N.Y.C.; she danced leading roles in such Graham works as *Every Soul Is a Circus, Punch and the Judy,* and *Letter to the World.* Miss Erdman's *The Transformation of Medusa* was premiered in 1942 (Bennington Summer Festival, Bennington, Vt.), and two years later she founded the Jean Erdman Dance Company. Works created by Miss Erdman for her group and the later (1960) Jean Erdman Theatre of the Dance include *Daughters of the Lonesome Isle* (1945); *Ophelia* (1946); *The Perilous Chapel* (1949); *Changingwoman* (1951); *Otherman—Or the Beginning of a New Nation* (1954); *Fearful Symmetry* (1957); *Duet for Flute and Dancer* (1956); *Harlequinade* (1957); *Four Portraits from Duke Ellington's Shakespeare Album* (1958); *Now and Zen—Remembering* (1959); *Twenty Poems of e. e. Cummings* (1960); *Ensembles* (1969); Voracious (1969); *Safari* (1969); and *The Castle* (1970).

Miss Erdman choreographed a Vassar Coll. production of *The Flies* (1947); composed choreography for a production of *The Enchanted* (Lyceum, N.Y.C., Jan. 18, 1950); wrote, directed and choreographed *The Coach with the Six Insides,* in which she also danced the role of Anna Livia Plurabelle (Village South Th., Nov. 26, 1962), which toured Europe and Japan, and which was revived in N.Y.C. (E. 74 St. Th., May 11, 1967). She composed choreography for *Yerma* (Vivian Beaumont Th., Dec. 8, 1966); directed *The Municipal Water System Is Not Trustworthy* (Sullivan St. Th., 1967); did the choreography for the NY Shakespeare Festival's *The Two Gentlemen of Verona* (Delacorte Th., July 22, 1971; St. James Th., Dec. 1, 1971), revived for Mobile Th. (July–Aug. 1973); and was choreographer and director of *Moon Mysteries,* in which she also appeared as the Queen (Th. at St. Clement's, Nov. 26, 1972). Miss Erdman has also been artistic director of the Theater of the Open Eye, which produced *Fire and*

Ice (Lib. of Congress, Washington, D.C., Mar. 1973; Matinee Series Th. de Lys, N.Y.C., Nov. 1974), repeated on a program with two later works, *Primordial Voices* and *The Women of Trachis* (Th. at St. Clement's, May 13, 1975).

Other Activities. Miss Erdman established her own dance school in N.Y.C. in 1948, and she was head of the dance dept. at Teachers Coll., Columbia Univ. (1949–51); at the Univ. of Colorado, where she was also artist in residence (Summers 1949–55); and chairman of the dance dept. and associate professor at Bard Coll. (1954–57). She was a guest professor at Sarah Lawrence Coll. (1954) and has also taught at the Univ. of British Columbia, Univ. of California (Los Angeles), and the Univ. of Hawaii. In 1966, she established a dance theatre program at NY Univ. School of the Arts.

Published Works. Miss Erdman's articles on dance and theatre have appeared in several periodicals.

Awards. In 1963, *The Coach with Six Insides* brought Miss Erdman a special citation of the *Village Voice* off-Bway (Obie) Award committee for outstanding achievement in off-Bway theatre, and it also received a Vernon Rice Award as best overall production; for her choreography of *The Two Gentlemen of Verona,* she received a Drama Desk Award (1972) and an Antoinette Perry (Tony) Award nomination.

ERICSON, JOHN. Actor. b. Sept. 25, 1926, (?), Dusseldorf, Germany, to Carl F. and Ellen (Wilson) Meibes. Father, president of Flavarol Co. Grad. Newton H.S., Elmhurst, N.Y., 1946; attended AADA, N.Y.C., 1947–49. Studied acting with Michael Chekhov (one year); Sanford Meisner, Los Angeles, Calif. (one year). Married Oct. 12, 1953, to Milly Coury, singer; one son, one daughter. Served WW II, rank, Pvt. Member of AEA; SAG; AFTRA. Address: c/o EBM, 340 N. Camden Dr., Beverly Hills, CA.

Pre-Theatre. Machinist.

Theatre. Mr. Ericson made his stage debut with the Gateway Th. (Gatlinsburg, Tenn., Summers 1949, 1950) in roles which included Allen Conway in *Time and the Conways,* Simon in *Hay Fever,* Bud Norton in *Personal Appearance,* Joe Ferguson in *The Male Animal,* Jerry Seymour in *Claudia,* Danny in *Night Must Fall,* Stephen in *Murder Without Crime,* and Dr. Christian in *The Astonished Heart;* was a member of the Barter Th. crew (Abingdon, Va., Jan.–Mar. 1951); and made his Bway debut as Sefton in *Stalag 17* (48 St. Th., May 8, 1951), which he repeated on tour (opened Biltmore, Los Angeles, Calif., June 26, 1952); closed National, Washington, D.C., May 16, 1953).

In stock, he played the title role in *Mister Roberts* (Grist Mill Playhouse, Andover, N.J., Summer 1959), and Stanley Kowalski in *A Streetcar Named Desire* (Kenley Players, Warren, Ohio, Summer 1961).

Films. Mr. Ericson made his debut in *Teresa* (MGM, 1951), followed by *Rhapsody* (MGM, 1954); *Green Fire* (MGM, 1954); *The Student Prince* (MGM, 1954); *Bad Day at Black Rock* (MGM, 1954); *Return of Jack Slade* (Allied, 1955); *Cruel Tower* (Allied, 1956); *Forty Guns* (20th-Fox, 1957); *Oregon Passage* (Allied, 1957); *Day of the Bad Man* (U, 1958); *Pretty Boy Floyd* (Continental, 1960); *Under Ten Flags* (Par., 1960); *I, Semiramis* APO—Globe, 1962); *Slave Queen of Babylon* (Italian; Amer. Inter., 1962); *Seven Faces of Dr. Lao* (MGM, 1964); *Siete de Pancho Villa* (Spanish; 1967); *Odio per Odio (Hate for Hate)* (Italian; 1967); *The Destructors* (Feature Film Corp. of Amer., 1968); *Bamboo Saucer* (World Entertainment, 1968); *The Money Jungle* (Commonwealth, 1968); *Operation Atlantis* (Italian; 1968); and *Bedknobs and Broomsticks* (Buena Vista, 1971).

Television. He made his debut on *Saturday's Children* (CBS, Oct. 2, 1950), and has appeared on Star Stage (NBC); Cavalcade Th. (ABC); on Schlitz Playhouse (CBS) in *The Letter* (Nov. 23, 1956) and *The Enchanted* (Jan. 25, 1957); on The Millionaire (CBS); Restless Gun (NBC); David Niven Th. (NBC); Philco Television Playhouse (NBC); Kraft Th. (NBC); Climax! (CBS); Playhouse 90 (CBS); Loretta Young Show (NBC); GE Th. (CBS); Campbell's Playhouse (CBS); Chevron Hall of Stars (CBS); Four Star Th. (ABC); Dupont Th. (ABC); The Shirley Temple Story Book (NBC); Wagon Train (NBC); Rawhide (CBS); Bonanza (NBC); US Steel Hour (CBS); Adventures in Paradise (ABC); Zane Grey Th. (CBS); Route 66 (CBS); Target: Corruptors (ABC); Dick Powell Th. (NBC); Burke's Law (ABC); Suspense (CBS); Trailmaster (ABC); The Fugitive (ABC); Profiles in Courage (NBC); Desilu Playhouse (NBC); Vacation Playhouse (CBS); played Sam Bolt in the Honey West series (ABC, premiere Sept. 17, 1965); appeared on The Invaders (ABC); Bob Hope Chrysler Th. (NBC); The F.B.I. (ABC); Gunsmoke (CBS); Ironside (NBC); Marcus Welby, M.D. (ABC); The Men from Shiloh (NBC); Medical Center (CBS); Longstreet (ABC); in *The Bounty Man* (ABC telefilm, Oct. 31, 1972); etc.

Awards. Mr. Ericson received the Laurel Award (1954) for his performance in the film *Bad Day at Black Rock.*.

ERNST, EARLE. Educator, director. b. Dec. 15, 1911, Mifflintown, Pa., to David K. and Esther (Smith) Ernst. Grad. Gettysburg Coll., A.B. 1933; Cornell Univ., M.A. 1938; Ph.D. 1940. Served US Army, FETO, 1944–47; rank, 1st Lt. Member of AETA; Phi Kappa Phi. Address: (home) 3368 Huelani Dr., Honolulu, HI 96822; (bus.) c/o Dept. of Drama and Theatre, John Fitzgerald Kennedy Th., Univ. of Hawaii, Honolulu, Hawaii.

Theatre. At the Univ. of Hawaii, he directed his translation of *The Defeated,* the first post-war Japanese play to be performed outside of Japan (Jan. 1948); *The House of Sugawara,* the first complete Kabuki play presented in English (Mar. 1951); and *Benton and Thief,* a Kabuki play presented in English (Mar. 1953).

Published Works. He wrote *The Kabuki Theatre* (1956); and *Three Japanese Plays from the Traditional Theatre* (1959). He also contributed articles to *Journal of Asian Studies, Educational Theatre Journal, Hudson Review,* and the *Encyclopedia Britannica.*.

ERSKINE, HOWARD. Producer, actor, director. b. Howard Weir Erskine, June 29, 1926, Bronxville, N.Y., to Howard Major and Agnes (Weir) Erskine. Father, public utilities financier. Grad. The Taft Sch., 1945; Williams Coll., B.A. 1949. Married Mar. 3, 1955, to Lou Prentis, actress; one daughter. Served WW II, USN, PTO; rank, QM–2. Member of AEA; SAG; AFTRA; Chi Psi. Address: Cushman Rd., R.D. 2, Patterson, NY 12563.

Mr. Erskine joined Ticketron, June 1, 1970, and is currently Eastern Regional Manager.

Theatre. Mr. Erskine made his stage debut at the Berkshire Playhouse (Stockbridge, Mass., Summer, 1949); subsequently returned there (Summers 1950–51); appeared at Bermudiana Th. (Hamilton, Bermuda, Summer, 1950); Atterbury Playhouse (Albany, N.Y., Winter 1949; Summer 1952).

He was associate producer of *Late Love* (National Th., N.Y.C., Oct. 13, 1953); co-produced, with Joseph Hayes, *The Desperate Hours* (Ethel Barrymore Th., Feb. 10, 1955), which he also produced and directed in London (Hippodrome, Apr. 19, 1955) and on a West Coast tour (opened Alcazar, San Francisco, Calif., 1956). He produced and directed, with Joseph Hayes, *The Happiest Millionaire* (Lyceum, N.Y.C., Nov. 20, 1956), which toured with Mr. Erskine as sole director (opened Dupont, Wilmington, Del., Oct. 2, 1957; closed Tower, Atlanta, Ga., May 17, 1958); produced, with Joseph Hayes and David J. Cogan, the pre-Bway tryout of *The Midnight Sun* (opened Shubert, New Haven, Conn., Nov. 4, 1959; closed Wilbur, Boston, Mass., Nov. 28, 1959); produced with Roger L. Stevens and Joseph Hayes, and succeeded Ben Hayes (Mar. 4, 1963) in the role of Quentin Armstone in *Calculated Risk* (Ambassador, Oct. 31, 1962); directed two stock tours of *Calculated Risk* (Summer 1963); produced with George W. George, Frank Granat, Edward Specter Productions, and Peter S. Katz, *Any Wednesday* (Music Box, Feb. 18, 1964); directed various productions of *Any Wednesday* (Royal Poinciana Playhouse, Palm Beach, Fla., Feb. 22, 1965; Coconut Grove Playhouse, Miami, Fla., Mar. 2, 1965; summer tour, 1966); directed *Minor Miracle* (Henry Miller's Th., N.Y.C., Oct. 7, 1965), which he produced with Zev Bufman; and appeared as Victor Prynne in *Private Lives* (Th. de Lys, May 19, 1968).

Films. Mr. Erskine appeared in *Seminole* (U. 1953).

Television. He produced the Rendezvous series (CBS, 1959) and a pilot film, *Portofino* (1961). He has also performed on all major network programs.

Awards. Messrs. Erskine and Hayes received the Antoinette Perry (Tony) Award (1955) for their production of *The Desperate Hours.*.

Recreation. Skiing, tennis, sailing, hunting.

ESSLIN, MARTIN (JULIUS). Writer. b. June 8, 1918, Budapest, Hungary, to Paul and Charlotte (Schiffer) Pereszlenyi. Father, journalist. Attended Univ. of Vienna, Aust., 1936–38; grad. Max Reinhardt Seminar, Vienna, 1938. Married 1947, to Renate Gerstenberg; one daughter. Chmn., Commission for a British Theatre Institute (1973–to date); member, Arts Council of Gr. Brit. (on drama panel). Address: 64 Loudoun Rd., London N.W. 8, England tel. 01-722-4243; Ballader's Plat, Winchelsea, Sussex, England tel. Winchelsea 392.

Mr. Esslin joined the BBC in 1940; was a producer and script writer (1941–55); became assistant head of the European Productions Dept. (1955); assistant head of Drama (Sound) in 1961; and has been head of that division since 1963.

He has in addition been dramaturg for the Royal Shakespeare Th.; advisory editor of *The Tulane Drama Review* (later *The Drama Review*); and visiting professor of theatre, Florida State Univ. and at the Univ. of California.

Mr. Esslin has been head of drama (sound) for the BBC in London, Advisory dramaturg to the Royal Shakespeare Th., and advisory editor of *The Tulane Drama Review.*

Published Works. Mr. Esslin wrote *Brecht—The Man and His Work* (1961; rev. 1971); *The Theatre of the Absurd* (1962); *Harold Pinter* (1967); *Genius of the German Theatre* (1968); *Reflections, Essays on Modern Theatre* (1969; published in England as *Brief Chronicles,* in 1970); *The Peopled Wound* (1970; rev. ed. *Pinter, A Study of His Plays,* 1973); and he edited *Beckett: A Collection of Critical Essays* (1965) and *The New Theatre of Europe* (1970). He has also written essays on theatre and reviews that have appeared in numerous periodicals.

Awards. Mr. Esslin was made a member of the Order of the British Empire (1972).

EUNSON, DALE. Playwright. b. John Dale Eunson, Aug. 15, 1904, Neillsville, Wis., to Robert and Isla Eunson. Father, logger, farmer, livery stable keeper, sheriff. Grad. Fergus County H.S., Lewistown, Mont., 1921; attended Univ. of Southern California, 1922–23. Married Sept. 18, 1931, to Katherine Albert, writer (dec. 1970); one daughter; married Berenice Tolins Dratler. Member of WGA, West. Address: 16645 Merivale Lane, Pacific Palisades, CA 90272, tel. (213) 454-5047.

Pre-Theatre. Fiction editor of *Cosmopolitan* magazine, publicity at MGM, and secretary to Rupert Hughes.

Theatre. Mr. Eunson wrote, with Hagar Wilde, *Guest in the House* (Plymouth Th., N.Y.C., Feb. 24, 1942); wrote *Public Relations* (Mansfield, Apr. 6, 1944); and with his wife, Katherine Albert, *Loco* (Ethel Barrymore Th., Oct. 16, 1946).

Films. With Katherine Eunson, he wrote the screenplays for *The Star* (20th-Fox, 1953); *Sabre Jet* (UA, 1953); *All Mine to Give* (U, 1957); *On the Loose* (RKO, 1951); *Young Mother* (Rep., 1958); and *Gidget Goes to Rome* (Col., 1963).

Television. In collaboration with Katherine Eunson, he wrote *The Day They Gave Babies Away* (Climax!, CBS, 1952) and hundreds of others. Alone he has written for *The Waltons* (CBS), *Love Story, Apple's Way* (CBS), and *Dirty Sally* (CBS).

Published Works. Mr. Eunson is author of *The Day They Gave Babies Away, Homestead, Up on the Rim,* and dozens of short stories appearing, since 1931, in popular magazines.

Recreation. Piano, cooking, travel, and good friends.

EVANS, MARY JANE. Educator. b. Mary Jane Larson, Apr. 7, 1923, Superior, Wis., to Lionel H. and Hazel (Newland) Larson. Father, retail merchandiser; mother, teacher. Grad. Lincoln H.S., Manitowoc, Wis., 1940; Ely Jr. Coll., A.A. 1942; Northwestern Univ., B.S. (Speech) 1944; attended Western Reserve Univ., 1944–45; Wisconsin State Coll., 1952; Michigan State Univ., M.A. (Theatre) 1955; Univ. of Minnesota, 1958–60. Married July 6, 1946, to Harrison Wills Watkins, Jr. (marr. dis. Mar. 20, 1952); married Dec. 25, 1961, to Robley D. Evans; one son. Member of ATA (dir., 1972–75; exec. comm., 1972–74); CTA (formerly CTC; secy. region 9, 1956–57; chmn. region 9, 1957–59; secy. and mbr. natl. gov. bd., 1958–62; chmn. region 2, 1962–64; administrative asst. to the natl. dir., 1964–66); Zeta Phi Eta; California Educational Theatre Assn.; Theta Alpha Phi (honorary). Address: (home) 16801 Lassen St., Sepulveda, CA 91343, tel. (213) 360-4249; (bus.) Dept. of Theatre, California State Univ., Northridge, CA 91324, tel. (213) 885-3086.

Mrs. Evans became an assistant professor in 1959, an associate professor in 1964, and full professor in 1970 in the Dept. of Theatre, where she is in charge of the courses in drama with and for children, at California State Univ., Northridge. She is also director of the productions performed at the university theatre for children and was acting department head, 1964–66. She was consultant to the Drama/Theatre Framework Comm., California Department of Education, 1969–72.

She directed special projects in drama with handicapped children at Sunbeam Sch. for Crippled Children (Cleveland, Ohio, 1944–46); was a staff member of the children's theatre, Cain Park Th. (Cleveland Heights, Ohio, Summers 1944–45); was a member of the board of Whittier (Calif.) Community Th. (1949–51); and director of the Junior Civic Th. (Kalamazoo, Mich., 1953–54).

Mrs. Evans was associate with Michigan State Univ., first as a graduate assistant directing children's theatre productions with child casts (1954–55), then as a faculty member (1955), and as associate director of the Children's Th. and director of productions from the Michigan State Univ. Touring Children's Th. (1955–59).

Published Works. Mary Jane Larson Watkins wrote, with Jed H. Davis, *Children's Theatre; Play Production for the Child Audience* (1960).

EVANS, MAURICE. Actor, producer. b. Maurice Herbert Evans, June 3, 1901, Dorchester, England, to Alfred Herbert and Laura Eliza (Turner) Evans. Father, analytical chemist. Attended Grocers' Company Sch., London, Eng. Served with US Army, in charge of Army Entertainment Section, Central Pacific Area. 1942–45; rank, Major; awarded Legion of Merit. Member of AEA (1st vice-pres., council member); AFTRA; SAG; Actors Fund of Amer. (trustee); League of NY Theatres (governor); The Players. Address: c/o Lloyd V. Almirall, 1 Chase Manhattan Plaza, New York, NY 10005, tel. (212) 944-4800.

Pre-Theatre. Music publisher.

Theatre. Mr. Evans made his professional debut as Orestes in *The Oresteia* (Festival Th., Cambridge, Eng., Nov. 26, 1926); first appeared on the London Stage as P. C. Andrews in *The One-Eyed Herring* (Wyndham's Aug. 25, 1927); subsequently, played Stephani in *Listeners* (Wyndham's, Feb. 9, 1928); Sir Blayden Coote in *The Stranger in the House* (Wyndham's, Apr. 4, 1928); Jean in *The Man They Buried* (Ambassadors', June 6, 1928); Hector Frome and Edward Clements in *Justice* (Wyndham's, July 4, 1928); Borring and Graviter in *Loyalties* (Wyndham's, Aug. 9, 1928); Wyn Hayward in *Diversion* (Little, Oct. 1, 1928); 2nd Lt. Raleigh in *Journey's End* (Apollo, Dec. 9, 1928); the Young Frenchman in *The Man I Killed* (Savoy, Apr. 7, 1930); the Sailor in *The Queen Bee* (Savoy, Sept. 23, 1930); succeeded (Oct. 1930) to the role of Professor Agi in *The Swan* (St. James's, June 30, 1930); played Owen Llewellyn in *To See Ourselves* (Ambassadors', Dec. 11, 1930); Marius in *Sea Fever* (New, June 30, 1931); Eric Masters in *Those Naughty Nineties* (Criterion, Aug. 27, 1931); and toured England as Ralph in *After All* (1931).

He played Nigel Chelmsford in *Avalanche* (Arts, London, Jan. 27, 1932); Jean Jaques in *The Heart Line* (Lyric, Apr. 5, 1932); Peter in *Will You Love Me Always?* (Globe, Sept. 20, 1932); the Rev. Peter Penlee in *Playground* (Royalty, Nov. 1932); Guy Daunt in *Cecilia* (Arts, Mar. 15, 1933); Dick in *The Soldier and the Gentlewoman* (Vaudeville, Apr. 19, 1933); Arnold White in *Other People's Lives* (Wyndham's, July 11, 1933); Aristide in *Ball at the Savoy* (Drury Lane, Sept. 8, 1933); and Edward Voysey in *The Voysey Inheritance* (Sadler's Wells, May 3, 1934).

In Sept. 1934, Mr. Evans joined the Old Vic Co., appearing at the Sadler's Wells Th. as Octavius Caesar in *Antony and Cleopatra* (Sept. 17, 1934), in the title role in *Richard II* (Oct. 15, 1934), Benedick in *Much Ado About Nothing,* the Dauphin in *Saint Joan* (Nov. 26, 1934), Petruchio in *The Taming of the Shrew* (Jan. 1, 1935), Iago in *Othello* (Jan. 21, 1935), the title role in *Hippolytus* (Feb. 11, 1935), Adolphus Cusins in *Major Barbara* (Mar. 4, 1935), Silence in *Henry IV, Part 2* (Mar. 25, 1935), and the title role of *Hamlet* (Apr. 29, 1935).

Mr. Evans first appeared on Bway as Romeo in *Romeo and Juliet* (Martin Beck Th., Dec. 23, 1935); followed by the Dauphin in *Saint Joan* (Martin Beck Th., Mar. 9, 1936); Napoleon in *St. Helena* (Lyceum, Oct. 6, 1936); the title role in *Richard II* (St. James, Feb. 5, 1937), in which he later toured; Falstaff in *Henry IV, Part 1* (Forrest, Philadelphia, Pa., Nov. 1937); the title role in *Hamlet,* which he produced in association with Joseph Verner Reed and Boris Said (St. James, N.Y.C., Oct. 12, 1938); produced and played Falstaff in *Henry IV, Part 1* (St. James, Jan. 30, 1939); produced and appeared in the title role in *Hamlet* (44 St. Th., Dec. 4, 1939); produced and played the title role in *Richard II* (St. James, Apr. 1, 1940); played Malvolio in *Twelfth Night* (St. James, Nov. 19, 1940), and on tour the following year; produced in association with John Haggott, and appeared in the title role in *Macbeth* (Natl., N.Y.C., Nov. 11, 1941), and on tour (1942).

Mr. Evans made an abbreviated adaptation of *Hamlet,* known as the GI version of *Hamlet,* in which he appeared in the title role, while in the armed forces, on tour, and twice in N.Y.C. (Columbus Circle Th., Dec. 13, 1945; NY City Ctr., June 4, 1946).

He staged and played John Tanner in *Man and Superman* (Alvin, Oct. 8, 1947), establishing record N.Y. run for any play of G. B. Shaw — 293 performances; subsequently toured Sept. 29, 1948–May 14, 1949; produced *The Linden Tree* (Music Box, N.Y.C., Mar. 2, 1948); produced a program of two one-act plays in which he appeared as Arthur Crocker-Harris in *The Browning Version* and Arthur Gosport in *Harlequinade* (Coronet, Oct. 12, 1949); played Dick Dudgeon in *The Devil's Disciple* (NY City Ctr., Jan 24, 1951); Hjalmar Akdal in *The Wild Duck* (NY City Ctr., Dec. 26, 1951); and Tony Wendice in *Dial 'M' for Murder* (Plymouth, Oct. 29, 1952).

In association with George Schaefer, Mr. Evans produced *The Teahouse of the August Moon* (Martin Beck Th., Oct. 15, 1953), and the subsequent tour (opened Colonial, Boston, Mass., Apr. 2, 1956; closed Natl. Washington, D.C., July 7, 1956); in association with Emmett Rogers, he produced *No Time for Sergeants* (Alvin, N.Y.C., Oct. 20, 1955; Her Majesty's, London, Aug. 23, 1956), and two subsequent tours (opened State Fair Aud., Dallas, Tex., June 11, 1956; reopened Erlanger, Chicago, Ill., Sept. 13, 1956; closed Senior H.S. Aud. Appleton, Wis., May 19, 1958; and opened Joffa Mosque, Altoona, Pa., Sept. 23, 1957; closed Natl. Washington, D.C., May 3, 1958). He played King Magnus in *The Apple Cart* (Plymouth, N.Y.C. Oct. 18, 1956), subsequently touring in the role (opened Natl. Washington, D.C., Mar. 4, 1957; closed Huntington Hartford Th., Los Angeles, Calif., June 29, 1957); produced, with Robert L. Joseph, and played Capt. Shotover in *Heartbreak House* (Billy Rose Th., N.Y.C., Oct. 18, 1959); portrayed Rev. Brock in *Tenderloin* (46 St. Th. Oct. 17, 1960); "H. J." in *The Aspern Papers* (Playhouse, Feb. 7, 1962); played opposite Helen Hayes in a program of readings from the plays of William Shakespeare entitled *A Program for Two Players* (American Shakespeare Festival, Stratford, Conn., July 10, 1962), followed by a cross-country tour (opened Fisher, Detroit, Mich., Oct. 15, 1962; closed Playhouse, Wilmington, Del., Mar. 9, 1963); appeared in Washington, D.C., with the National Symphony Orchestra, as narrator in *The Plague* (Apr. 1973); and at the John F. Kennedy Center for the Performing Arts on Sept. 24–30, 1973, in *Festival of Shakespeare Dance and Drama.*

Films. In addition to his British films, prior to his coming to the United States in 1935, Mr. Evans has appeared in *Kind Lady* (MGM, 1951); as Caesar in *Androcles and the Lion* (RKO, 1952); Sir Arthur Sullivan in *Gilbert and Sullivan* (UA, 1953); Macbeth in *Macbeth* (Compass, 1960), and in *War Lord* (U, 1965); *Jack of Diamonds* (MGM, 1967); *Planet of the Apes* (20th-Fox, 1968); *Rosemary's Baby* (Par., 1968); *Thin Air* (Tigon, 1968); *Planet of the Apes Revisited* (20th-Fox, 1969).

Television. Mr. Evans appeared on the Hallmark Hall of Fame (NBC) in *Hamlet* (1953), *Richard II* (1954), *Macbeth* (1954), *Man and Superman* (1956), *Twelfth Night* (1957), *Dial 'M' for Murder* (1958), *The Tempest* (1960), and a rebroadcast of *Macbeth* in a special color film version (1960). For the same series he produced *Alice in Wonderland* (1955), *Dream Girl* (1955), *The Corn Is Green* (1956), *The Good Fairy* (1956), *The Cradle Song* (1956), *The Devil's Disciple,* in which he also appeared (Nov. 20, 1955), and *The Taming of the Shrew,* in which he played Petruchio (1956). Subsequent to 1963, Mr. Evans appeared in a large number of television series including numerous episodes in Bewitched (ABC).

Awards. In 1950, he received a special Antoinette Perry (Tony) citation for his direction of the drama season at the NY City Ctr., of which he was artistic supervisor (1949–51). He has received honorary doctorates from the Univ. of Hawaii, Lafayette Coll., and Brandeis Univ.; has received the Drama League Medal (1937) and the Christopher Award (1953, 1956); for his television production of *The Taming of the Shrew* he was given a special award by the American Shakespeare Festival Theatre and Academy (1956); received the NATAS (Emmy) Award for his performance in *Macbeth* (1961); the Salmagundi Award (1962); and the Veteran's Administrative Voluntary Service Certificate (1961).

Recreation. Golf.

EVANS, MICHAEL. Actor. b. John Michael Evans, July 27, 1926, Sittingbourne, Kent, England, to Alfred John and Marie Rose (Galbraith) Evans. Father, author; mother, musician. Attended Winchester (England) Coll., 1939–43. Studied acting at the Old Vic Sch., London, England. Married 1948, to Patricia Wedgewood; two sons. Member of AEA; SAG; AFTRA.

Theatre. Mr. Evans first appeared with the Worthing Repertory Co. (Mar. 1946); subsequently made his London debut succeeding (Comedy Th., Jan. 22, 1948) John Blythe as Harry Simpkinson in *Mountain Air* ("Q," Apr. 22, 1947); and joined (Piccadilly, Nov. 1948) the cast of *Off the Record* (Apollo, June 3, 1947).

His first Bway role was Patrice Bombelles in *Ring 'Round the Moon* (Martin Beck Th., Nov. 22, 1950); followed by Gaston Lachaille in *Gigi* (Fulton, Nov. 24, 1951); toured as Brian Aherne's successor in the role of Henry Higgins in *My Fair Lady* (opened Rochester Aud., N.Y., Mar. 18, 1957; closed Winnipeg, Canada); succeeded (Jan. 1963) to the role of Dirk Winston in *Mary, Mary* (Helen Hayes, Th.,

Mar. 8, 1961); and repeated the role on tour (opened Ford's Th., Baltimore, Md., Dec. 30, 1962); played Henry Higgins in a touring production of *My Fair Lady* (Summer 1964); and Charles Condomine in *High Spirits* (State Fair Music Hall, Dallas, Tex., June 7, 1965).

Films. Mr. Evans played Claud Paisley in *Bye Bye Birdie* (Col., 1962); and appeared in *The Spy With My Face* (MGM, 1966); *The Plainsman* (U, 1966); *Riot on Sunset Strip* (AI, 1967); *The Love-Ins* (Col., 1967); and *The Thousand Plane Raid* (UA, 1969).

Television. His appearances include The Newly Wed Game (ABC); Laredo (NBC); and Rat Patrol (ABC).

Recreation. Golf, swimming, deep sea fishing, sports cars.

EVANS, RAY. Composer, lyricist. b. Raymond B. Evans, Feb. 4, 1915, Salamanca, N.Y., to Philip and Frances Evans. Father, scrap dealer. Grad. Salamanca H.S., 1931; Univ. of Pennsylvania, Wharton Sch., B.S. (economics) 1936. Married Apr. 19, 1947, to Wyn Ritchie. Member of ASCAP; Composers and Lyricists Guild of Amer.; Dramatists Guild; Beta Sigma Rho; Beta Gamma Sigma. Address: 1255 Angelo Dr., Beverly Hills, CA 90210.

Pre-Theatre. Office work, business trainee.

Theatre. Mr. Evans made his debut as a songwriter with the Bway production of *Hellzapoppin'* (Winter Garden, 1941); subsequently wrote his first full score for *I Love Lydia* (Players Ring, Hollywood, Calif., Dec. 1950); composed the score for *Oh Captain!* (Alvin, N.Y.C., Feb. 4, 1958) and *Let It Ride* (Eugene O'Neill Th., Oct. 12, 1961); songs for *Six of One* (Adelphi, London, Eng., Sept. 26, 1963); and, with Jay Livingston, did music and lyrics for *The Odyssey of Runyon Jones* (world premiere, Valley Music Th., Los Angeles, Calif., Dec. 16, 1972).

Films. In collaboration with Jay Livingston, he wrote songs for the following films (all released by Paramount unless otherwise specified): *Stork Club* (1945); *Monsieur Beaucaire* (1946); *To Each His Own* (1946); *Imperfect Lady* (1947); *My Favorite Brunette* (1947); and, in collaboration with Mr. Livingston and Victor Young, for *Golden Earrings* (1947). With Mr. Livingston, he composed the songs for *The Paleface* (1948); *My Own True Love* (1948); *Dream Girl* (1948); *Isn't It Romantic* (1948); *Whispering Smith* (1948); *Sorrowful Jones* (1949); *Streets of Laredo* (1949); *The Great Lover* (1949); *The Heiress* (1949); *Song of Surrender* (1949); *My Friend Irma* (1949); *Sunset Boulevard*, in which he also acted (1950); *Fancy Pants* (1950); *Captain Carey, U.S.A.* (1950); and with Victor Young and Mr. Livingston, for *Samson and Delilah* (1950).

Mr. Evans, with Jay Livingston, wrote the songs for *Lemon Drop Kid* (1951); *Here Comes the Groom* (1951); *Ace in the Hole* (1951); *My Favorite Spy* (1951); *Aaron Slick from Punkin' Crick* (1951); and with Franz Waxman and Mr. Livingston, for *A Place in the Sun* (1951). With Jay Livingston, he composed songs for *My Friend Irma Goes West* (1950); *Crosswinds* (1951); *Mating Season* (1951); *That's My Boy* (1951); *Rhubarb* (1951); *Somebody Loves Me* (1952); *What Price Glory* (20th-Fox, 1952); *Son of Paleface* (1952); *Anything Can Happen* (1952); *Off Limits* (1953); *Thunder in the East* (1953); *The Stars Are Singing* (1953); *Houdini* (1953); *Those Redheads from Seattle* (1953); *Here Come the Girls* (1953); *Red Garters* (1954); *Casanova's Big Night* (1954); *Three Ring Circus* (1954); *Lucy Gallant* (1955); *The Second Greatest Sex* (U, 1955); *Scarlet Hour* (1956); *The Man Who Knew Too Much* (1956); *Loves of Omar Khayam* (1957); *Istanbul* (U, 1957); *Magic Touch* (1957); *James Dean Story* (WB, 1957); *The Big Beat* (U, 1958); *Another Time, Another Place* (1958); *Tammy and the Bachelor* (U, 1957); *Once Upon a Horse* (U, 1958); *Saddle the Wind* (MGM, 1958); *Houseboat* (1958); *This Happy Feeling* (U, 1958); *Vertigo* (1958); and with Jimmy McHugh and Mr. Livingston, for *A Private Affair* (20th-Fox, 1959). With Mr. Livingston, he wrote songs for *Blue Angel* (20th-Fox, 1959); *Take a Giant Step* (UA, 1959); *All Hands on Deck* (20th-Fox, 1961), and *Two Little Bears* (20th-Fox, 1961); with Henry Mancini and Jay Livingston, for *Dear Heart* (WB, 1965); and with Max Steiner and Mr. Livingston, for *Youngblood Hawke* (WB, 1964).

Mr. Evans also wrote the lyrics to Maurice Jarre's theme for the movie *Is Paris Burning?* (Par., 1966); did songs for *This Property Is Condemned* and *The Night of the Grizzly* (both Par., 1966); and composed the title song for the film *Love Is Forever* (1973).

Television. Mr. Evans wrote songs for Satins and Spurs (NBC, 1954); No Man Can Tame Me (CBS, 1959); and, with Henry Mancini and Jay Livingston, for Peter Gunn (NBC, 1961). He wrote the themes for Bonanza (NBC, 1959); Mister Ed (CBS, 1960); and To Rome with Love (1971).

Night Clubs. He has written special material for Betty Hutton's acts (1952); songs for Dinah Shore's act (1955); and songs written for the opening of the New Frontier Hotel Production Show (Las Vegas, Nev., 1955). He again wrote material for Betty Hutton (1956, 1957); and for Mitzi Gaynor's act (1961, 1963, 1964); and for the Cyd Charisse and Tony Martin Revue (1963).

Awards. He won, with Jay Livingston, the Academy (Oscar) Award for the songs, "Buttons and Bows" (1948); "Mona Lisa" (1951); and "Que Sera, Sera" (Whatever Will Be, Will Be) (1957).

With Mr. Livingston, he was nominated for the Academy (Oscar) Award for the title song of *Tammy* (1958); for the song, "Almost in Your Arms," from *Houseboat* (1959); and, with Jay Livingston and Henry Mancini, for the song "Dear Heart," from the 1965 film of the same name. He was also nominated for the Academy of Recording Arts and Sciences Award for the same song. In 1973, Mr. Evans was elected to the Songwriters Hall of Fame.

Recreation. Tennis, softball, music, reading.

EVANS, WILBUR. Singer, actor, director, coach. b. Aug. 5, 1908, Philadelphia, Pa., to Walter P. and Emma V. Evans. Father, engineer. Grad. West Philadelphia (Pa.) H.S., 1929; Curtis Inst. of Music, B. Mus. 1931. Studied voice with Emilio de Gogorza, 1929–33; Richard Hageman, two years; Dino Gorgioli, London, six years; Sidney Dietch, N.Y.C. Married July 3, 1963, to Eleanor Kramer; two daughters. Served USMCR, 1936–41; rank, Capt. Member of AEA; AFTRA; AGVA; Orpheus Club (Philadelphia); University Glee Club (N.Y.C.).

Theatre. Mr. Evans made his debut as a soloist with oratorio societies and symphonic orchestras (1927); appeared in musical theatre and stock productions in the US and Can., sang Kurvenal in *Tristan und Isolde* (Philadelphia Acad. of Music, Pa., Oct. 1933); made his N.Y.C. debut as Prince Danilo in *The Merry Widow* (Carnegie Hall, July 15, 1942); played Robert Misson in *The New Moon* (Carnegie Hall, Aug. 18, 1942); David Winthrop in *Mexican Hayride* (Winter Garden, Jan. 28, 1944); Baron Bobinet in *La vie parisienne* (NY City Ctr., Jan. 12, 1945); John Matthews in *Up in Central Park* (Century, Jan. 27, 1945); appeared in stock as Cesar in *Fanny* and Bumerli in *The Chocolate Soldier* (St. Louis Municipal Opera, Mo.; Los Angeles, Calif.; San Francisco, Calif., 1950); played Emile de Becque in *South Pacific* (Drury Lane, London, Nov. 7, 1951); Dennis Emery in *By the Beautiful Sea* (Majestic, N.Y.C., Apr. 8, 1954); Macheath in *The Beggar's Opera* (Philadelphia, Pa., 1958); Dommayer in *The Great Waltz* (Music Ctr., Los Angeles, Calif., July 27, 1965); and the Innkeeper in the national touring company of *Man of La Mancha* (opened Shubert Th., New Haven, Conn., Sept. 24, 1966).

Films. He appeared in *Her First Romance* (Mono., 1940); and *Man with a Million* (UA, 1953).

Television and Radio. Mr. Evans performed on radio on the Atwater Kent Sunday Evening Concerts (NBC, 1927–31); the Original Show Boat Hour (NBC, 1933); the Rudy Vallee Show (NBC, 1934); Philco Hall of Fame (NBC, 1944); Coca Cola Showtime (CBS, 1941); and Musical Comedy Cavalcade (WFIL, Philadelphia, Pa., 1960–62).

On television, he appeared on The Verdict is Yours (CBS, 1959–60); Sunday Night at the Palladium (ATV, London, 1961); and he directed the musical comedy wing of WFIL Theatre Workshop (WFIL-TV, Philadelphia, Pa., 1962–to date).

Night Clubs. Mr. Evans has performed at the Thunderbird Hotel (Las Vegas, Nev., 1955); the Cotillion Room (Hotel Pierre, N.Y.C.); and the Queen Elizabeth Hotel (Montreal, Can., 1963).

Awards. Mr. Evans won first prize in the Atwater Kent Auditions of the Air (1927).

Recreation. Chess, tennis.

EVERETT, TIM. Actor, director, choreographer, dancer. b. Thomas Arthur Everett, Feb. 14, 1938, Helena, Mont., to Thomas Grover and Sally Evelyn (Wright) Everett. Father, salesman; mother, ballroom dancing instructor. Grad. Professional Children's Sch., N.Y.C. (Doris Duke Scholarship); attended Neighborhood Playhouse Sch. of the Th. Studied acting with Lee Strasberg, N.Y.C.; Sanford Meisner, N.Y.C.; dancing with Hanya Holm, Charles Weidman, Martha Graham, Richard Thomas, Peter Gennaro, Jack Stanley, Matt Mattox; speech with Elizabeth Dixon, Alice Hermes; singing with James Gregory, Sandy Campbell; vocal production with John Wallowich. Relatives in theatre: sisters, Sherrye Everett, actress; and Tanya Everett, actress, dancer. Member of AEA; SAG; AFTRA; AGVA; BDL; SSD&C.

Theatre. Mr. Everett made his N.Y.C. debut as a dancer in *On Your Toes* (46 St. Th., Oct. 11, 1954); subsequently danced in *Damn Yankees* (46 St. Th., May 5, 1955); played Blazer in the pre-Bway tryout of *Reuben Reuben* (opened Shubert, Boston, Mass., Oct. 10, 1955; closed there Oct. 22, 1955); Tom Sawyer in *Livin' the Life* (Phoenix, N.Y.C., Apr. 27, 1957); Sammy Goldenbaum in *The Dark at the Top of the Stairs* (Music Box, Dec. 5, 1957); and Tobey in *The Cold Wind and the Warm* (Morosco, Dec. 8, 1958); repeated his performance as Tom in *Tom Sawyer* (St. Louis Municipal Opera, July 1959) and played Huck in the same play (Butler Field, Columbia Univ., N.Y.C., Aug. 1959); directed *Not Enough Rope* (May 1963); played Abe O'Brien and assisted June Havoc and Lee Strasberg in directing *Marathon 33* (ANTA Th., Dec. 22, 1963); directed and choreographed *Days of the Dancing* (Westport Country Playhouse, Westport, Conn., June 23, 1964); played Joey in *Pal Joey* (Hyannis, Mass., July 1964); appeared in the Marc Blitzstein Memorial (Philharmonic Hall, Lincoln Ctr., N.Y.C., 1964); directed *The Ripening Seed* (Actors Studio, Jan. 1967); created and directed *The Ski Bum* (Actors Studio, June 1968; June 1969); co-directed *The Honest-to-God Schnozzola* (Apr. 21, 1969); directed *And I Met a Man* (Lincoln Square Cabaret Th., N.Y.C., Apr. 10, 1970); and he choreographed *Die Dreigroschenoper (The Threepenny Opera)* (Bayerisches Staatsschauspiel Residenz Th., Munich, Germany, May 16, 1974). Mr. Everett has also staged and choreographed industrial shows for Simmons, General Motors, the Bell System, and the National Knitwear Show.

Films. Mr. Everett has appeared in *Key to the Future* (General Motors industrial film, 1956); *The Music Man* (WB, 1962); *Les Apartments des Filles* (France, 1964); he appeared in, directed, and choreographed New York sequences of *Gendarme á New York* (France, 1968); and he was in the film *Timmy Everett at Actors Studio* (France, 1968).

Television. Mr. Everett appeared in *Glory in the Flower* (Omnibus, CBS, 1953); danced in five Max Liebman Spectaculars (NBC, 1954); the Steve Allen Show (NBC, 1955); performed in *Day Before Atlanta* (Playhouse 90, CBS, 1958); The Funmaker (1958); The Committee Man (1958); Look Up and Live (1958); The Outlaws (1959); *John Brown's Raid* (NBC, Oct. 25, 1960); Emanuel (Dec. 1960); Ben Casey (NBC, 1963); and Night Life (1965).

Other Activities. Mr. Everett teaches and directs in his own acting workshop; is on the faculty of Dance Educators of America; and teaches jazz dance at Salvador Juarez School of Ballet, N.Y.C. He taught for the Dance Congress (1957, 1958,

1959); for Dance Masters of America (1960–73); taught jazz dance at the June Taylor School of Dance and the NY school of Ballet. Mr. Everett also taught acting and dance at Antioch Coll. (1970; 1971); the Univ. of Texas (1972); Queens Coll. (1973); and at universities and colleges of Kentucky. He created a jazz ballet at Western Kentucky Univ. (Oct. 1974), the Univ. of Boston, and Emerson Coll., Boston, Mass. (Nov. 1974).

Awards. For his performance in *The Dark at the Top of the Stairs,* he received a *Theatre World* Award (1958); he was nominated for a NY Drama Critics Award for best supporting actor for his performance in *The Cold Wind and the Warm* (1958); and the film *Timmy Everett at Actors Studio* won a special award at the Cannes Film Festival (1968).

Recreation. Music, travel, rock collecting, coin collecting, politics.

EVERHART, REX. Actor. b. June 13, 1920, Watseka, Ill., to Arthur M. and Jeanette (Dodson) Everhart. Father, physician. Grad. Western Military Acad., Alton, Ill., 1938; attended Univ. of Missouri, 1938–39; grad. Pasadena Playhouse Sch. of Theatre, B.T.A., 1941; New York Univ., B.S., 1949, M.A. 1950. Studied acting with Paul Mann, N.Y.C., 1952; Martin Ritt, N.Y.C., 1955; Curt Conway, N.Y.C., 1957). Married Feb. 11, 1944, to Jill Reardon, designer (marr. dis. 1952); married Jan. 23, 1957, to Mary Dell Roberts, actress (marr. dis. 1962); married Dec. 22, 1962, to Claire Richard, actress; one daughter. Served USN, 1942–47; rank, Lt. Member of AEA; AFTRA; SAG; Aircraft Owners and Pilots Assn.; Speech Assn. of Amer.; F&AM. Address: 42 N. Compo Rd., Westport, CT 06880, tel. (212) PL 7-6300.

Theatre. Mr. Everhart made his stage debut, playing an Indian Chief's Son in an outdoor pageant, *History of Iroquois County* (Watsega, Ill., May 1929); acted with the Santa Monica (Calif.) Players (1939–41); and at the Pasadena (Calif.) Playhouse; played George Bodell in *Out of the Frying Pan* (1941); the Drunken Rowdy in *One Sunday Afternoon* (1941); Ten Pin in *Knickerbocker Holiday* (1942); and the Son in *Because She Loved Him So* (1942).

He appeared in and directed productions at the New York Univ. Th. (1947–50); was a resident member of Sara Stamm's Th. (Newport, R.I., 1950–52); appeared in productions at the Margo Jones Th. (Dallas, Tex., Oct. 1952–June 1953). For the inaugural season of the American Shakespeare Festival (Stratford, Conn.), he appeared as the Cobbler in *Julius Caesar* (July 12, 1955), as Stephano in *The Tempest* (Aug. 1, 1955); and as Dogberry in the student production of *Much Ado About Nothing* (Aug. 1955).

He played Colonel and Lt. Able in *No Time for Sergeants* (Alvin, N.Y.C., Oct. 20, 1955), succeeded (Jan. 1957) Myron McCormick as Sgt. King in the same play, and toured in this role (opened Joffa Mosque, Altoona, Pa., Sept. 23, 1957; closed National, Washington, D.C., May 3, 1958); played Collins in *Tall Story* (Belasco, N.Y.C., Jan. 29, 1959); Schatzie in a tour of *Say, Darling* (Summer 1959); and Casca in a NY Shakespeare Festival production of *Julius Caesar* (Delacorte, Aug. 1959).

He appeared as Mr. Perisson in *Moonbirds* (Cort, Oct. 9, 1959); as the Drunk in *Lysistrata* (Phoenix Th., Nov. 24, 1959), in *Pictures in the Hallway* (Dec. 26, 1959), played Aslak and Herr Von Eberkopf in *Peer Gynt* (Jan. 12, 1960), Bardolph in *Henry IV, Part 1* (Mar. 1, 1960) and in *Henry IV, Part 2* (Apr. 18, 1960).

He played Luther Billis in a tour of *South Pacific* (Summer 1960); Joe Kovac in *Tenderloin* (46 St. Th., N.Y.C., Oct. 17, 1960); Bardolph in the American Shakespeare Festival (Stratford, Conn.) production of *Henry IV, Part 1* (June 17, 1962); the Policeman in the pre-Bway tryout of *A Matter of Position* (opened Walnut, Philadelphia, Pa., Sept. 29, 1962; closed there Oct. 13, 1962; and at the American Shakespeare Festival, played Dromio in *The Comedy of Errors* (June 11, 1963), Michael Williams in *Henry V* (June 12, 1963), and the Sentinel in *Caesar and Cleopatra* (July 30, 1963).

Mr. Everhart played the Colonel and was standby for Eddie Mayehoff in the role of John T. Kodiak in *A Rainy Day in Newark* (Belasco, N.Y.C., Oct. 22, 1963); at the American Shakespeare Festival (Stratford, Conn.), played Dogberry in *Much Ado About Nothing* (June 9, 1964), the First Gravedigger in *Hamlet* (July 2, 1964), Brutus in *Coriolanus* (June 16, 1965), and Grumio in *The Taming of the Shrew* (June 22, 1965). He played Stanley in *Skyscraper* (Lunt-Fontanne Th., N.Y.C., Nov. 13, 1965); Murray in *The Odd Couple* (Queens Th., London, England, Sept. 1966); Walter P. Bradbury in *How Now, Dow Jones* (Lunt-Fontanne Th., Dec. 7, 1967); and at the American Shakespeare Festival (Stratford, Conn.) he played Charles in *As You Like It* (May 1968), the Editor in *Androcles and the Lion* (June 1968), and Constable Dull in *Love's Labour's Lost* (July 1968). He replaced Howard Da Silva for one month as Benjamin Franklin in *1776* (Mar. 16, 1969) and toured with the national company in the same part (San Francisco, Calif., Apr. 23, 1970 –Capitol Th., Boston Mass., July 1972).

At the American Shakespeare Festival (Stratford, Conn.), he played Casca in *Julius Caesar* (Apr. 1973), Pompey in *Measure for Measure* (May 1973), Sir Jasper Fidget in *The Country Wife* (June 1973), and the Porter in *Macbeth* (July 1973); he repeated his *Macbeth* and *Measure for Measure* roles at the Kennedy Center, Washington, D.C. (Sept.–Oct. 1973); and appeared as Lt. McGloin in *The Iceman Cometh* (Circle in the Square–Joseph E. Levine Th., N.Y.C., Nov. 1973).

Films. Mr. Everhart appears as Deputy Chief Inspector Gilson in *The Seven-Ups* (1973) and as Patrick Scully in *The Blue Hotel* (1974).

Television. He made his first appearance in an experimental program (Par. Studios, 1939); appeared on Rod Brown (CBS, 1950); Lux Video Th. (CBS, 1951); Studio One (CBS, 1955, 56, 58, 59, 60); played Tony Lumpkin in *She Stoops To Conquer* (Omnibus, CBS, 1955); appeared on the daytime serial Valiant Lady (CBS, 1956); on Armstrong Circle Th. (NBC, 1957, 58, 60); played Tommy in *The Hasty Heart* (Dupont Show of the Month, NBC, 1958); La Baron in *The Sacco-Vanzetti Story* (Sunday Showcase, NBC, 1960); The Defenders (CBS, 1961); the Perry Como Show (CBS, 1961); played George in *Windfall* (Dupont Show-of-the-Month, NBC 1962); and appeared on Naked City (CBS, 1962); and GE Theatre (CBS, 1962). He also appeared in the daytime serials Love of Life (CBS), Search for Tomorrow (CBS), Another World (NBC), and Somerset (NBC); and played MacNulty (Mac) in the series *Feeling Good,* a Children's Television Workshop production (PBS, Nov. 20, 1974).

Night Clubs. He played Joe Kovac in *Tenderloin* at the Dunes Hotel (Las Vegas, Nev., 1961).

Recreation. Photography, flying, cooking.

EWELL, TOM. Actor. b. Yewell Tompkins, Apr. 29, 1909, Owensboro, Ky., to Samuel William and Martine (Yewell) Tompkins. Father, playboy. Attended Univ. of Wisconsin, 1927–31. Married Mar. 18, 1946, to Judith Ann Abbott, director, producer, actress (marr. dis. 1946); married Apr. 29, 1948, to Marjorie Gwynne Sanborn, advertising copywriter; one son. Served WW II, USN; rank, Lt. (jg). Member of AEA; SAG; AFTRA; The Players; Phi Eta Sigma; Sigma Phi Epsilon; Rho Epsilon Delta. Address: c/o Smith-Stevens Representation Ltd., 1650 Broadway, New York, NY 10019.

Pre-Theatre. Salesman, odd jobs.

Theatre. Mr. Ewell made his stage debut as Mike in the Al Jackson Players' production of *The Spider* (Park Th., Madison, Wis., Feb. 18, 1928); subsequently appeared as Chester in *Aren't We All* (Park Th., Madison, Wis., 1931); and played there for two seasons, appearing in more than fifty productions.

He made his N.Y.C. debut as Red in *They Shall Not Die* (Royale, Feb. 21, 1934); appeared as a Novice and Member of the Choir in *The First Legion* (46 St. Th., Oct. 1, 1934); Denver in *Geraniums in My Window* (Longacre, Oct. 26, 1934); was stage manager and played the Waiter in *De Luxe* (Booth, Mar. 5, 1935); Young Frank Martin and Small Hardy in *Let Freedom Ring* (Broadhurst, Nov. 6, 1935); Dennis Eady in *Ethan Frome* (Natl., Jan. 21, 1936); succeeded (Forrest, May 1936) Lamar King as Captain Tim in *Tobacco Road* (Masque, Dec. 1933); played Larry Westcott in *Stage Door* (Music Box Th., Oct. 22, 1936); Dan in a touring production of *Brother Rat* (1936–37); Cornelius Hackl in *The Merchant of Yonkers* (Guild, N.Y.C., Dec. 28, 1938); Simon in *Family Portrait* (Morosco, Mar. 8, 1939); Gage in a touring production of *Key Largo* (Philadelphia, Pa., Jan. 2, 1940); Brother Galusha in *Suzanna and the Elders* (Morosco, N.Y.C., Oct. 29, 1940); Dick Brown in *Liberty Jones* (Shubert, Feb. 5, 1941); and Daniel Marshall in *Sunny River* (St. James, Dec. 4, 1941).

He appeared as Elkins in the pre-Bway tryout of *Of All People* (opened Town Hall, Toledo, Ohio, Nov. 29, 1945; closed Ford's Th., Baltimore, Md., Dec. 22, 1945); Huckleberry Haines in a Civic Light Opera revival of *Roberta* (Philharmonic Auditorium, Los Angeles, Calif.; Curran, San Francisco, Calif., 1946); Glen Stover in *Apple of His Eye* (Biltmore, N.Y.C., Feb. 5, 1946); Fred Taylor in *John Loves Mary* (Booth, Feb. 4, 1947); appeared in the revue *Small Wonder* (Coronet, Sept. 15, 1948); in stock, played Tommy Turner in *The Male Animal* (Summer 1949); the title role in *Kin Hunter* (Westport Country Playhouse, Conn., Sept. 3, 1951); Fred Taylor in *John Loves Mary* and Elwood P. Dowd in *Harvey* (Bahama Playhouse, Nassau, Winter 1951); Kenneth Bixby in *Goodbye Again* (Bahama Playhouse, Nassau, Jan. 1952); Richard Sherman in *The Seven Year Itch* (Fulton, N.Y.C., Nov. 20, 1952); in stock, Vladimir in *Waiting for Godot* (Coconut Grove Playhouse, Miami Beach, Fla., Jan. 3, 1956); Augie Poole in *The Tunnel of Love* (Royale, N.Y.C., Feb. 13, 1957); Leon Rollo in *Patate* (Henry Miller's Th., Oct. 28, 1958); Elliott Nash in *The Gazebo* (Central City, Colo., Aug. 1959); in the revue *A Thurber Carnival* (ANTA, N.Y.C., Feb. 26, 1960); and played Frank Michaelson in the national touring company of *Take Her, She's Mine* (opened Walnut St. Th., Philadelphia, Pa., Dec. 10, 1962).

He appeared in *The Thurber Carnival* in London (Savoy, Feb. 1964); toured the US, visiting ninety cities, in a one-man show of eighty years of American humor, *We've Had Some Fun* (1965–66); toured as Father in a revival of *Life with Father* (1967); toured in *The Impossible Years* (Oct. 2–Dec. 16, 1967; Feb. 13–Mar. 30, 1968); toured in *The Apple Tree* (1969); replaced (June 29, 1971) David Byrd as Vladimir (Didi) in a revival of *Waiting for Godot* (Sheridan Square Playhouse, N.Y.C., Feb. 3, 1971); played in London in *You Know I Can't Hear You When the Water's Running* (New, 1968); played in the Philadelphia Drama Guild revival of *Juno and the Paycock* (Walnut St. Th., 1973); and toured in *What Did We Do Wrong?* (1974).

Films. Mr. Ewell made his film debut in *Kansas Kid* (Rep., 1939); subsequently appeared in *They Knew What They Wanted* (RKO, 1940); a series of travel shorts (Par., 1948–49); *Adam's Rib* (MGM, 1949); *A Life of Her Own* (MGM, 1950); *Mr. Music* (Par., 1950); *American Guerilla in the Philippines* (20th-Fox, 1950); *Finders Keepers* (U, 1951); *Up Front* (U, 1951); *Lost in Alaska* (U, 1952); *Willie and Joe Back at the Front* (U, 1953); *The Seven Year Itch* (20th-Fox, 1955); *The Lieutenant Wore Skirts* (20th-Fox, 1956); *The Girl Can't Help It* (20th-Fox, 1956); *The Great American Pastime* (MGM, 1956); *How To Rob a Bank* (20th-Fox, 1957); *Tender Is the Night* (20th-Fox, 1962); *State Fair* (20th-Fox, 1962); *Suppose They Gave a War* (WB, 1964); *To Find a Man* (Col., 1970); *They Only Kill Their Masters* (1972); and *The Great Gatsby* (Par., 1973).

Television and Radio. Mr. Ewell appeared on radio in *The March of Time* (NBC, 1935); and *Ellery Queen* (NBC, 1936). On television, he appeared in *Daisy, Daisy* (Playwrights '56, NBC, Nov. 22, 1955); Alfred Hitchcock Show (CBS, Dec. 4, 1955); the Perry Como Show (NBC, 1956); *The Square Egghead* (US Steel Hour, CBS, Mar. 11, 1959); the series The Tom Ewell Show (CBS, Sept. 27, 1960); and as narrator of *The Fourposter* (Golden Showcase,

CBS, Jan. 13, 1962).

Awards. He won the *Variety* NY Drama Critics' Poll, the Clarence Derwent Award, and the Donaldson Award, for his performance as Fred Taylor in *John Loves Mary* (1947); the Donaldson Award and the Antoinette Perry (Tony) Award for his performance as Richard Sherman in *The Seven Year Itch* (1953).

Recreation. Golf, farming.

F

FABRAY, NANETTE. Actress, singer. b. Ruby Bernadette Nanette Theresa Fabares, Oct. 27, San Diego, Calif., to Raoul Bernard and Lillian (McGovern) Fabares. Father, railroad engineer. Grad. Hollywood (Calif.) H.S.; attended Los Angeles (Calif.) City Coll. Studied acting at the Max Reinhardt Dramatic Workshop. Hollywood, two yrs.; voice, dance with Ernest Belcher, Hollywood: Juilliard Sch. of Music, N.Y.C. Married Oct. 26, 1947, to David Tebet, press representative (marr. dis. July 21, 1951); married Apr. 24, 1957 to Ronald MacDougall, writer, producer, director (dec. Dec. 10, 1973); one son. Member of AEA; SAG; AFTRA; AGVA; Zeta Phi Eta. Address: Pacific Palisades, CA 90272.

Theatre. Miss Fabray began in vaudeville at age three (Paramount Th., Los Angeles, Calif.; and appeared on the Keith vaudeville circuit as Baby Nanette with the Franchon and Marco Unit. After winning a two-year scholarship, she appeared in productions at the Max Reinhardt Sch. of the Th., playing Sister Beatrice in *The Miracle*, the Daughter in *Six Characters in Search of an Author*, and Smeraldina in *Servant with Two Masters*. (Hollywood, Calif., 1939).

Miss Fabray made her N.Y.C. debut in the revue *Meet the People* (Mansfield, Dec. 25, 1940); played Jean Blanchard in *Let's Face It* (Imperial, Oct. 29, 1941); succeeded (Feb. 1943) Constance Moore as Antiope in *By Jupiter* (Shubert, June 3, 1942); played Jean in *My Dear Public* (46 St. Th., Sept. 9, 1943); Sally Madison in *Jackpot* (Alvin, Jan. 13, 1944); succeeded Celeste Holm as Evelina in *Bloomer Girl* (Shubert, Oct. 5, 1944); played Sara Longstreet in *High Button Shoes* (Century, Oct. 9, 1947); Susan Cooper in *Love Life* (46 St. Th., Oct. 7, 1948); Jo Kirkland in *Arms and the Girl* (46 St. Th., Feb. 2, 1950); Janette in *Make a Wish* (Winter Garden, Apr. 18, 1951); Nell Henderson in *Mr. President* (St. James, Oct. 21, 1962); Roberta Bartlett in *No Hard Feelings* (Martin Beck Th., Apr. 8, 1973). Miss Fabray has also appeared in stock productions of *Applause*, (Sacramento Music Circus, Calif., 1973; Long Beach Civic Light Opera, Calif., 1974) and *Plaza Suite* (Pellman Theatre, Milwaukee, Wis., 1973; Carousel Th., Ravenna, Ohio, 1974).

Films. Miss Fabray appeared in *The Monroe Doctrine* (WB, 1939); *The Private Lives of Elizabeth and Essex* (WB, 1939); *A Child Is Born* (WB, 1940); *The Band Wagon* (MGM, 1953); *Fame is the Name of the Game* (U, 1964); *Jigsaw* (U, 1967); *The Happy Ending* (UA, 1969); *Cockeyed Cowboys* (U, 1969); and *Magic Carpet* (U, 1970).

Television and Radio. On radio, she performed on the Showboat Hour, the Charlie Chan series (1936); and the Stars Salute (WNEW, Oct. 27, 1963).

On television she has appeared on Your Show of Shows (NBC, Oct. 7, 1950; Jan. 27, 1951); was a regular performer on Caesar's Hour (NBC, 1954–56); played in *High Button Shoes* (NBC, Nov. 24, 1956); *The Family Nobody Wanted* (CBS, Dec. 20, 1956); *The Original Miss Chase* (Alcoa Hour, NBC, Mar. 17, 1957); *A Man's Game* (Kaiser Aluminum Hour, NBC, Apr. 23, 1957); appeared on the Dinah Shore Chevy Show (NBC, Oct. 20, 1957; Dec. 8, 1957); the Shower of Stars (CBS, Apr. 1958); Laramie (NBC, 1959); the Perry Como Show (NBC, Mar. 21, 1959); Startime (NBC, Jan. 12, 1960; May 31, 1960); the Bell Telephone Hour (NBC, Feb. 12, 1960; Oct. 22, 1963); the Nanette Fabray Show (NBC, Jan. 7, 1961); and the Perry Como Show (NBC, Nov. 16, 1963).

She was a guest star with the Smothers Bros.; Andy Williams; Bob Hope; Dinah Shore; Dean Martin; Jerry Lewis; Carol Burnett; Jack Benny; Hollywood Squares; Joey Bishop, Mike Douglas (CBS); on the Tonight Show; Laugh-In; Hollywood Palace; What's It All About, World?; Love, American Style (ABC); *George M* (CBS, 1970); Magic Carpet; *Alice Through the Looking Glass*, (NBC, 1971); David Frost; Password (ABC); This Is Your Life; and Mary Tyler Moore (CBS).

Night Clubs. Miss Fabray has played in engagements at the Cafe Pierre (N.Y.C., May 1941); and the Sands (Las Vegas, Nev., Mar. 1953).

Other Activities. Miss Fabray has been a board member of the President's Commission on Employment of the Handicapped; was campaign chairman of the Hope for Hearing Foundation, UCLA; on the board of trustees of the Ear Research Institute. She was chairman of the National Advisory Commission on the Education of the Deaf; a trustee of the National Theatre of the Deaf; vice-president of the National Association of Hearing and Speech Agencies; regional campaign chairman of the National Association for Mental Health; of the National Easter Seal Society; and the National Heart Fund. She has also been a trustee of the Eugene O'Neill Foundation and is a board member of the California Museum Foundation.

Awards. For her performance as Sara Longstreet in *High Button Shoes*, Miss Fabray received two Donaldson Awards (1948); the Antoinette Perry (Tony) Award for her performance as Susan Cooper in *Love Life* (1949); the NATAS (Emmy) Award as best comedienne of the year (1955; 1956); a NATAS (Emmy) Award as best supporting performer, for her work on Caesar's Hour (1955); and was voted best dressed actress by the Fashion Acad. (1950).

Miss Fabray received honorary degrees from Gallaudet College (D.H.L. 1970) and Western Maryland College (D.F.A. 1972). She was named woman of the year (1955) by the Radio and Television Editors of America; received the Hollywood Women's Press Club Award (1960); the Achievement Award, Women's Division, Albert Einstein College of Medicine, Yeshiva Univ. (1963); the Eleanor Roosevelt Humanitarian Award (1964); was honorary mayor of Pacific Palisades, Calif. (1967–68); was named woman of the year by the Philadelphia Club of Advertising Women (1968), by the Jewish War Veterans, Women's Division (1969), and by Phi Kappa Zeta of Gallaudet College (1969); received the Human Relations Award of B'nai B'rith (1969); the President's Distinguished Service Award (1970); and the first annual Cogswell Award of Gallaudet College (1970).

Recreation. Rock collecting, boating, fishing.

FAGAN, JOAN. Singer, actress. b. Joan Gertrude Fagan, Aug. 12, 1934, Kansas City, Mo., to Thomas F. and Hester Leah (Jeffries) Fagan. Father, accountant. Grad. Northeast H.S., 1952; attended Central Mo. State Coll., 1952–53; Kansas City Conservatory of Music, 1954; Univ. of Kansas City, 1954; State Univ. of Iowa, 1954–56. Studied acting at the HB (Herbert Berghof) Studio, N.Y.C., 1956–58; singing with Reba Jury, N.Y.C., six years; Jack Lee, N.Y.C., two years. Married Dec. 9, 1962, to David B. Marshall, producer, director; two sons, one daughter. Member of AEA; AFTRA; SAG; AGMA. Address: 300 Central Park W., New York, NY 10024, tel. (212) 362-7709.

Pre-Theatre. Waitress, salesgirl, office worker.

Theatre. Miss Fagan made her debut as Fanchon and a chorus member in *Naughty Marietta* (Starlight Th., Kansas City, Mo., June 1955); and sang in the ensemble for two seasons (Summers 1955–56); played Meg in *Damn Yankees* Leila in *Panama Hattie*, Elizabeth in *Paint Your Wagon* (Summer 1957); and toured as soloist with the Mastersingers for Columbia Concerts (Oct.–Dec. 1957). She made her N.Y.C. debut in the ensemble of *Wonderful Town* (NY City Ctr., Mar. 5, 1958); followed by *The Creation* (Robert Shaw Chorale, Carnegie Hall, Apr. 1958); appeared at the Music Circle (Detroit, Mich., Summer 1958), as Evalina in *Bloomer Girl*, Anna in *The King and I*, and Cleo in *The Most Happy Fella;* and at the Musical Tent (Flint, Mich.), as Huguette in *The Vagabond King*, the title role in *Fanny*, and Jennie in *Me and Juliet*.

She was in the ensemble of *Redhead* (46 St. Th., N.Y.C., Feb. 5, 1959); joined (Apr. 30, 1959) the company as Lucy Brown during the run of *The Threepenny Opera* (Th. de Lys, Sept. 20, 1955); succeeded (Oct. 1959) Pamela Austin as singer in *La plume de ma tante* (Royale, Nov. 11, 1958); in stock, played Dorothy in *Gentlemen Prefer Blondes* (Casa Manaña, Ft. Worth, Tex., June 1960); and Melba in *Pal Joey* (Melody Tent, Buffalo, N.Y., July, 1960).

Miss Fagan played Ellen Roe in *Donnybrook!* (46 St. Th., N.Y.C., May 18, 1961); Sharon in *Finian's Rainbow* (Meadow Brook Dinner Th., Cedar Grove, N.J., Summer 1961); Nellie Forbush in *South Pacific* (Musicarnival, Cleveland, Ohio, Summer 1961); Marianne in *New Moon* and Fiona in *Brigadoon* (Cape Cod Melody Tent, Hyannis, Mass., Summer 1962); was standby for and replaced (Apr. 23, 1964) Inga Swenson as Lizzie in *110 in the Shade* (Broadhurst, N.Y.C., Oct. 24, 1963).

Television. Miss Fagan has appeared on the Ed Sullivan Show (CBS, June, 1961); and CBS Repertoire Workshop (July 1964).

FAIN, SAMMY. Composer. b. June 17, 1902, New York City, to Abraham and Mania (Glass) Feinberg. Father, reverend and cantor. Married June 18, 1941, to Sally Fox (marr. dis. 1949); one son. Relatives in theatre: brother, Harry Fain, violinist; son, Franklin J. Fain, theatrical enterprises; cousins, Willie and Eugene Howard, comedians. Member of ASCAP; American Guild of Authors and Composers; Dramatists Guild; Composers & Lyricists Guild of America, Inc.; AFTRA; the Masonic Order. Address: 1640 San Ysidro Dr, Beverly Hills, CA 90201, tel. (213) CR 5-8607.

Theatre. Mr. Fain began as a staff pianist and composer for Jack Mills, the music publisher; appeared in vaudeville in an act with Artie Dunn, *"Fain and Dunn"* (1928–32); made his Bway debut as composer of the music for *Everybody's Welcome* (Shubert, Oct. 13, 1931); wrote additional songs, with Irving Kahal, for *Right This Way* (46 St. Th., Jan. 4, 1938); subsequently wrote the music for *Hellzapoppin* (46 St. Th., Sept. 22, 1938); *George White's Scandals* (Alvin, Aug. 28, 1939); *Boys and Girls Together* (Broadhurst, Oct. 1, 1940); and wrote the songs for *Sons o' Fun* (Winter Garden, Dec. 1, 1941). He wrote the music for *Toplitzky of Notre Dame* (Century, Dec. 26, 1946); *Flahooley* (Broadhurst, May 14, 1951); *Ankles Aweigh* (Mark Hellinger Th., Apr. 18, 1955); wrote some music for *Catch a Star!* (Plymouth, Sept. 6, 1955); contributed music to *Ziegfeld Follies* (Winter Garden, Mar. 1, 1957); wrote the music for *Christine* (46 St. Th., Apr. 28, 1960); and composed the score for *Around the World in 80 Days* (St. Louis Municipal Opera, 1962; Marine Th., Jones Beach, L.I., N.Y., Summer 1963, 1964).

Films. Mr. Fain has composed theme songs and scores for *Young Man of Manhattan* (Par., 1930); *The Big Pond* (Par., 1930); *College Coach* (WB, 1933); *Footlight Parade* (WB, 1933); *Harold Teen* (WB, 1934); and *Sweet Music* (WB, 1935); *Goin' to Town* (Par., 1935); *New Faces of 1937* (RKO, 1937); *Vogues of 1938* (UA); *Weekend at the Waldorf* (MGM, 1944); *Anchors Aweigh* (MGM, 1945); *George White's Scandals* (RKO, 1945); *Two Sisters from Boston* (MGM, 1946); *Three Daring Daughters* (MGM, 1947); *The Milkman* (U, 1950); *Call Me Mister* (20th-Fox, 1951); *Alice in Wonderland* (RKO, 1951); *Peter Pan* (RKO, 1953); *Calamity Jane* (WB, 1953); *The Jazz Singer* (WB, 1953); *Three Sailors and a Girl* (WB, 1953); and *Lucky Me* (WB, 1954).

He wrote the music for the title song for *Love Is a Many-Splendored Thing,* for which Paul Francis Webster wrote the lyrics (20th-Fox, 1955); the music for *Hollywood or Bust* (Par., 1956); *April Love* (20th-Fox, 1957); *Gift of Love* (20th-Fox, 1957); *Marjorie Morningstar* (WB, 1958); *A Certain Smile* (20th-Fox, 1958); *Mardi Gras* (20th-Fox, 1958); *Imitation of Life* (Univ., 1959); the theme song for *Tender is the Night* (20th-Fox, 1962); the score for *The Incredible Mr. Limpet* (WB, 1963); *Joy in the Morning* (MGM, 1964); and *The Stepmother* (Magic Eye, 1972).

Television. He composed the score for Desilu Productions' television spectacular, *A Diamond for Carla* (CBS, 1960).

Awards. He received an Academy (Oscar) Award for his song "Secret Love" in the film *Calamity Jane* (1953); with Paul Francis Webster who wrote the lyrics, an Academy (Oscar) Award for his music for *Love Is a Many-Splendored Thing* (1955); received Academy (Oscar) Award nominations for his songs "That Old Feeling," "April Love," "A Certain Smile," "A Very Precious Love," "Tender Is the Night," and "Strange Are The Ways of Love." He received a Diploma Di Benenerenza, Hall of Artists (Nice, Fr., 1956); the Augosto Messinese Gold Award (Messina, Italy, 1956); Laurel awards for *A Very Precious Love* and *A Certain Smile* (1959); was made an honorary Kentucky colonel (1961); became a member of the Songwriters Hall of Fame (1972); and received the ASCAP Country Music Award (Nashville, Tenn., 1974).

FALK, PETER. Actor. b. Peter Michael Falk, Sept. 16, 1927, New York City, to Michael and Madeline (Hauser) Falk. Father, merchant; mother, merchant, accountant, buyer. Grad. Ossining (N.Y.) H.S., 1945; attended Hamilton Coll., 1946–48; grad. New Sch. for Social Research, N.Y.C., B.A. 1951; Maxwell Sch. of Syracuse Univ., M.P.A. 1953. Studied acting with Eva Le Gallienne, White Barn Th., Westport, Conn., 1955; Sanford Meisner, Meisner Workshop, N.Y.C. 1957. Served Merchant Marine, cook, 1945–46. Married Apr. 17, 1960, to Alyce Mayo. Member of AEA; SAG; AFTRA.

Pre-Theatre. Efficiency expert for the Budget Bureau, State of Connecticut, Hartford.

Theatre. Mr. Falk made his N.Y.C. debut as Sagnarele in *Don Juan* (Fourth St. Th., Jan. 1956); followed by the role of De Flores in the Norris Hoghton production of *The Changeling* (Barnard Coll., Feb. 1956); Rocky the Bartender in *The Iceman Cometh* (Circle in the Square, May 8, 1956); the Soldier in *Saint Joan* (Phoenix, Sept. 11, 1956); Mamaev's Servant in *Diary of a Scoundrel* (Phoenix, Nov. 5, 1956); Matthew Skipps in *The Lady's Not for Burning* (Carnegie Hall Playhouse, Feb. 21, 1957); followed Mike Kellin as the First Workman in *Purple Dust* (Cherry Lane, Apr. 1957); appeared as Crispin in *Bonds of Interest* (Sheridan Sq. Playhouse, May 6, 1958); the Police Chief in *Comic Strip* (Barbizon-Plaza Th., May 14, 1958); Stalin in *The Passion of Josef D.* (Ethel Barrymore Th., Feb. 11, 1964); and Mel Edison in *The Prisoner of Second Avenue* (Eugene O'Neill Th., Nov. 11, 1971).

Films. He made his film debut as Abe Reles in *Murder, Inc.* (20th-Fox, 1960); subsequently appeared as Joy Boy in *Pocketful of Miracles* (UA, 1961); the Chief of Police in *The Balcony* (Continental, 1962); the Cabbie in *It's a Mad, Mad, Mad, Mad World* (UA, 1963); the Medical Captain in *Italiano Bravo-Gente* (Galatea/Soviet Union, 1963); Guy Gisborne in *Robin and the 7 Hoods* (WB, 1964); and appeared in *The Great Race* (WB, 1965); *Penelope* (MGM-Euterpe, 1966); *Luv* (Col. 1967); *Anzio* (Col., 1967); *Castle Keep* (Col., 1969); *Husbands* (Col., 1970); *Machine Gun McCain* (Col., 1970); and *A Woman Under the Influence* (Faces Intl., 1974).

Television. Mr. Falk played Menderes in *The Sacco-Venzetti Case* (NBC, May 1960); and appeared in *Cold Turkey* (The Law and Mr. Jones, ABC, 1961); and played Aristedes Fresco in *The Price of Tomatoes* (Dick Powell Th., NBC, 1962).

He subsequently appeared on Bob Hope Presents (NBC); DuPont Th. (NBC); Stump the Stars (Ind.); Wagon Train (ABC); Ben Casey (ABC); the Danny Kaye Show (CBS); played the title role on The Trials of O'Brien (CBS); appeared on Naked City (Ind.); Brigadoon (ABC); Twilight Zone (ABC); This Proud Land (ABC); Password (CBS); The Young Set (ABC); The Untouchables (Ind.); Sports Spectacular (CBS); Hollywood Showcase (Ind.); Alfred Hitchcock Presents (Ind.); Dateline: Hollywood (ABC); Dream Girl (ABC); *A Hatful of Rain* (ABC); The Name of the Game (NBC); *A Step Out of Line* (CBS); *Ransom for a Dead Man* (NBC); and his own series, Columbo (NBC Mystery Th.).

Awards. Mr. Falk was nominated for an NATAS (Emmy) Award (1961) for his performance in an episode on *The Law and Mr. Jones;* was nominated for Academy (Oscar) awards for his performance as Abe Reles in *Murder, Inc.* (1961), and for his role as Joy Boy in *Pocketful of Miracles* (1962); and has received the NATAS (Emmy) Award for his performances as Aristedes Fresco in *The Price of Tomatoes;* (Dick Powell Th., NBC, 1962). and the title role in *Columbo.*

Recreation. Reading, golf, chess, billiards.

FALK, RICHARD. Press representative, producer. b. Richard Robert Falk, Dec. 24, 1912, Newark, N.J., to Alexander Clemente and Sophie (Huber) Falk. Relative in theatre: brother-in-law, Mordecai Lawner, teacher and director at the Neighborhood Playhouse Sch. of the Th. Grad. New York Univ., B.A. 1933; attended Columbia Univ., 1934–35; New Sch. for Social Research, 1936. Married Nov. 11, 1944, to Corinne Sherwood Lawner; two daughters Member of ATPAM; Publicist's Guild. 220 W. 42nd St., New York, NY 11036, tel. (212) 244-5797, ext. 98.

Theatre. Mr. Falk was in the chorus of *America's Sweetheart* (Broadhurst, N.Y.C., Feb. 10, 1931); in the Shubert production of *The Student Prince* (Erlanger, Los Angeles, Calif., 1937); and produced *Jim Dandy* (Music Hall, Newark, N.J., 1942).

As a press representative, Mr. Falk worked on *Sons o' Fun* (1941); joined the Lee and J. J. Shubert Enterprises (1943) and worked on *Ziegfeld Follies* (1943). *Blossom Time* (1943), *Ten Little Indians* (1944), *Song of Norway* (1944), *Laffing Room Only* (1944), *Call Me Mister* (1946); was press representative for *The Medium* and *The Telephone* (1947); and worked on *Along Fifth Avenue* (1948).

He founded his own company, Richard R. Falk, Associates, with offices in N.Y.C. (1948) and was press representative for a stock production of *Oklahoma!* (Paper Mill Playhouse, Millburn, N.J., 1949); a US tour of *The Sonja Henie Ice Follies* (1952–54); for *Almost Crazy* (1955); *Simply Heavenly* (1957); associate press representative for *Rape of the Belt* (1960); press representative for *The Happiest Girl in the World* (1961); *Let It Ride* (1961); *Feast of Panthers* (1961); associate press representative for *Sing, Muse* (1961); *A Chekhov Sketchbook* (1962); *Rosmersholm* (1962), *Alcestis Comes Back* (1962); represented Barbra Streisand in *I Can Get It for You Wholesale* (1962); was press representative for a stock production of *The Voice of the Turtle* (Maplewood, N.J., Summer 1962); and was associate press representative for a Jones Beach (N.Y.) production of *Paradise Island* (1962).

He was press representative for *Utopia* (1963); *The Brig* (1963); *Five Queens* (1963); *In the Summer House* (1963); The Carnegie Hall appearances of Norman Mailer and the Dave Brubeck Quartet (1963); the Ellenville (N.Y.) Music Festival (1963); the Motorola Show on tour (1963); a national tour of *Pajama Tops* (1964); the Jayne Mansfield show, *Rabbit Habit* (1965); *Those Wonderful Days of Burlesque* on tour (1965); and, in N.Y., *Swim Low, Little Goldfish* (1965); toured as press representative with *The Owl and the Pussycat* (1966); represented Dana Andrews in *The Odd Couple* (1967); and Noel Harrison in *Joe Egg* (1968); was press representative for tours of *Come Blow Your Horn* (1969); *You're a Good Man, Charlie Brown* (1969); and *Fiddler on the Roof* (1970); was press representative for *The Boy Friend* (1970); and, in N.Y., for *Jacques Brel Is Alive and Well and Living in Paris* (1970); associate press representative for *The House of Blue Leaves* (1971); and press representative of *The Big Show of 1928* (tour, 1972); *Don't Play Us Cheap* (1972); *I Love Thee Freely* (1973); *The Faggot* (1973); *The Foursome* (1973); *Moonchildren* (1974); *Naomi Court* (1974); and *How To Get Rid of It* (1974).

Awards. He received a US Treasury Dept. Citation for selling over one million dollars in War Bonds (1944); a Case Study Citation from *Public Relations News* (1950–51); a US Dept. of Commerce Citation (1951); *Show Business* Best Ballyhooist Award (1954–55–56); and a Beaux Arts Award as a theatrical press agent (1962).

Recreation. Commercial pilot and ground instructor.

FALKENHAIN, PATRICIA. Actress. b. Patricia Jean Falkenhain, Dec. 3, 1926, Atlanta, Ga., to Frederick G. and Emma Seay (Haley) Falkenhain. Father, personnel at Western Electric. Grad. Scotch Plains H.S., N.J., 1944; attended Carnegie Inst. of Technology, Pittsburgh, 1944–46; New York Univ. 1946–48, Married Apr. 29, 1950, to Robert Gerringer actor. Member AEA; AFTRA; Kappa Alpha Theta. Address: 26 Horatio St., New York, NY 10014, tel. (212) WA 9-3241.

Theatre. Miss Falkenhain's first stage appearance in a Carnegie Tech production of *All's Well That Ends Well* (1944), was followed by her performance as Mrs. Tancred in *Juno and the Paycock* (Cherry Lane, July 1946); Alice Deartn in *Dear Brutus* (Cherry Lane, 1946); Jimima Cooney in *Shadow and Substance* (Cherry Lane, 1946); Lisa in *In a Garden* (Jan Hus House, Sept. 7, 1948); in summer stock, as Valerie in *Obsession* (Women's Club Th., Waterbury, Conn., June 24, 1949); off-Bway in the title role of *Hedda Gabler* (Hotel Sutton Th., Oct. 4, 1950); in stock as Pamela in *Separate Rooms,* Mrs. Midget in *Outward Bound,* Lady Isabel in *East Lynne,* and Lady Martin in *Miranda* (Monson Th., Mass., Summer 1950).

She played Blanche in *A Streetcar Named Desire* (Kingsbridge Veterans Hospital, Bronx, N.Y.C., Sept. 1952); Dynamene in *Phoenix Too Frequent* (Kingsbridge Veterans Hospital, Oct. 1952); toured in the industrial show *Carrier* (Air Conditioning) *Caravan* (Jan.–Feb., 1953); portrayed Zeilah in the Passion play, *His Mother's Promise* (St. Boniface Church, Paterson, N.J., Mar. 21, 1953); played in stock as Conjur Woman in *Dark of the Moon,* Mary Hilliard in *Here Today,* Miss Skillon in *See How They Run,* Emmie in *Gently Does It,* Elvira in *Blithe Spirit,* Lady Bracknell in *The Importance of Being Earnest,* Sadie Thompson in *Rain,* Nita Tavermeyer in *For Love or Money,* Harriet in *The Two Mrs. Carrolls,* Carol Arden in *Personal Appearance,* and Mrs. Morgan in *Ten Nights in a Barroom* (Canal Fulton Summer Th., Ohio, June–Sept. 1954); appeared as Paula Wharton in *Over 21,* Mrs. Eynsford Hill in *Pygmalion,* Amanda in *Private Lives,* Kate in *The Taming of the Shrew,* and Nellie Bly in *Frankie and Johnnie* (Canal Fulton Summer Th., Ohio, June–Sept., 1955).

Miss Falkenhain followed Jeanne Jerems as the 3rd Witch in *Macbeth* (Jan Hus House, N.Y.C., Oct. 1955); appeared as Lady Montague in *Romeo and Juliet* (Jan Hus House, Jan. 1956); in stock, played the title role in *Nina,* Mildred Turner in *Oh, Men! Oh, Women!,* Emmie in *You Touched Me,* Baroness Von Rischenheim in *By Candlelight,* Camilla in *Buy Me Blue Ribbons,* Miss Logan in *The Solid Gold Cadillac,* Lizzie in *The Rainmaker,* Helen Sherman in *The Seven Year Itch,* Laura Reynolds in *Tea and Sympathy,* Anna in *Anastasia,* and Olive in *The Voice of the Turtle* (Canal Fulton Summer Th., Ohio, June–Sept. 1956).

She played Alcestis in *Capacity for Wings* (Royal Playhouse, N.Y.C., Jan. 13, 1957); appeared at the NY Shakespeare Festival (Belvedere Lake) as the Nurse in *Romeo and Juliet* (June 1957), Lucetta in *Two Gentlemen of Verona* (July 1957), the First Witch in *Macbeth* (August 1957); was Mme. DuPont-Fredaine in the national tour of *The Waltz of the Toreadors* (opened McCarter, Princeton, N.J., Sept. 26, 1957) and during its rerun engagement (Coronet Th., N.Y.C., Mar. 4, 1958); returned to the NY Shakespeare Festival (Belvedere Lake) to play Bianca in *Othello* (July 2, 1958); was the Spinster in *The Power and the Glory* (Phoenix, Dec. 10, 1958); Dorinda in *The Beaux' Stratagem* (Phoenix, Feb. 24, 1959); Mrs. George Collins in *Getting Married* and the Woman in *Buoyant Billions* (Provincetown Playhouse, May 26, 1959).

She played Lampito in *Lysistrata* (Phoenix, Nov. 24, 1959); the Woman in Green in *Peer Gynt* (Phoenix, Jan. 12, 1960); Doll Tearsheet in *Henry IV, Part 2* (Phoenix, Apr. 18, 1960); Mrs. Hardcastle in *She Stoops to Conquer* (Phoenix, Nov. 1, 1960); Rosie Redmond in *The Plough and the Stars* (Phoenix, Dec. 6, 1960); Queen Gertrude in *Hamlet* (Phoenix, Mar. 16 1961); the Princess in the stock production of *Sweet Bird of Youth* (Canal Fulton Summer Th., Ohio, July 18, 1961); Gertrude in *Hamlet* and Magaera in *Androcles and the Lion* in the Phoenix Th. touring production for the NY Council for the Arts (NY State, Sept. 1961); Magaera in *Androcles and the Lion* (Phoenix, N.Y.C., Nov. 21, 1961); the Cloaked Lady in *Dark Lady of the Sonnets* (Phoenix, Dec. 14, 1961); Miss Prism in *The Importance of Being Earnest*, Nurse in *Medea*, and Catherine in *Arms and the Man* (Antioch Area Th., Yellow Springs, Ohio, July–Sept. 1962); Lady Cynthia in *The Saving Grace* (Writer's Stage, N.Y.C., April 18, 1963); and Albertine in *Toys in the Attic* (Canal Fulton Summer Th., Ohio, June 1963).

Miss Falkenhain played Gertrude in *Hamlet* (Antioch Amphitheatre, Yellow Springs, Ohio, Sept. 2, 1964); Louise in *After the Fall* (Huntington Hartford Th., Los Angeles, Calif., Mar. 16, 1965); appeared at Center Stage (Baltimore, Md.) in *Ardele* (Jan. 6, 1966), as Tamora in *Titus Andronicus* (Feb. 9, 1967), and as Hester Bellboys in *A Penny for a Song* (Apr. 20, 1967); and appeared with American Conservatory Th. (San Francisco, Calif.) alternating with Barbara Colby as Mrs. Patrick Campbell in *Dear Liar* (Geary Th., Nov. 3, 1967) and in *A Delicate Balance* (Marines' Memorial Th., Jan. 29, 1969).

Awards. She received the *Village Voice* Off-Bway (Obie) Award for her roles as The Woman in Green in *Peer Gynt* and Doll Tearsheet in *Henry IV, Part 2* (1960).

Recreation. Cooking, collecting antiques.

FALLON, RICHARD. Educator, director. b. Richard Gordon Fallon, Sept. 17, 1923, New York City, to Perlie P. and Margaret E. (Julia) Fallon. Father, lawyer. Grad. White Plains (N.Y.) H.S., 1940; attended Brown Univ., 1940–41; grad. Columbia Univ., B.A., M.A., 1951; Old Vic Theatre Sch., London, Eng. (Cert. of Excellence) 1943–44. Studied with Peter Copley, London, 1944–45; Gertrude Lawrence, 1946; Florence Reed, 1947; Joseph Wood Krutch, 1946–49; Mark Van Doren, 1948; Milton Smith, 1946–51. Married 1946, to Suzanne Bowkett; one son, one daughter. Served US Army, Special Services, ETO, 1942–45. Member of ANTA (Florida state rep., International Theatre Month, 1960–64); ATA; URTA (pres., 1974–75); National Theatre Conference (bd. mbr.); SAA; SETC; Florida Speech Assn. (vice-pres., 1958–59); Florida Arts Council (vice-pres., 1964; bd. member, 1968); Florida League of the Arts (pres., 1973–74); State (Fla.) Theatre Board; Florida Theatre Conference (pres., 1959–62); Florida Fine Arts Congress; AAUP (local chapter pres., 1963); Eddie Dowling Univ. Theatre Foundation (co-founder, vice-pres., 1961–to date); Beta Theta Pi; The Lambs. Address: (home) 2302 Delgado Dr., Tallahassee, FL 32304; (bus.) Florida State Univ., Tallahassee, FL 32306.

In 1973, Mr. Fallon became dean of the School of Theatre, The Florida State Univ., Tallahassee, Fla., where he had joined the faculty in 1957 as an assistant professor in the Speech Dept., later becoming director of the theatre division of that department and then professor of theatre (1968). He was chairman of the Theatre Dept. from 1969 to 1973, at which time the department was organized as the School of Theatre with Mr. Fallon as dean.

Mr. Fallon began his academic career as professor of theatre and chairman, Dept. of Speech and Theatre, Hartwick Coll., Oneonta, N.Y. (1946–50) and was then professor of theatre and chairman of the Theatre Dept., Maryland State Univ., Towson, Md. (1950–54).

Theatre. While serving in the US Army, Mr. Fallon managed (1943–45) an ETO Army post theatre, the Scala, in London, England, where he directed plays and supervised USO tours playing in London. He appeared on the stage in N.Y.C. as Jim in the Equity Library production of *The World We Make* (May 1946); was executive director, Little Theatre of Jacksonville, Fla. (1955–57); and at Florida State directed American premieres of *Assignment in Judea* (1960), *Last Days of Lincoln* (1962), *The Long Night* (1962), and *Trog* (1963). He has been (1960–to date) executive director of the Asolo State Th., Sarasota, Fla., which he founded in 1960; the theatre has been the home of a year-round Equity repertory company since 1966.

Films. Mr. Fallon was featured in *The True Glory* (Col., 1945) and appeared as General Bradford in *Naked in the Sun* (Allied, 1957).

Radio. Mr. Fallon performed on Living (NBC, 1948); Front Page Farrell (CBS, 1948); and Chaplain Jim (Mutual, 1948). He appeared also on such radio programs as Young Doctor Malone; Mr. District Attorney (NBC); and Jack Armstrong (CBS).

Other Activities. In 1972, Mr. Fallon established the Charles MacArthur Playwriting Award at the Florida State Univ. School of Theatre; premieres of the winning plays are given each year. In 1973, Mr. Fallon founded the privately endowed Charles MacArthur Center for Development of American Theatre, also at Florida State Univ. in Tallahassee, Fla.

Awards. Mr. Fallon received from the National Conference of Christians and Jews a special award for producing and directing *Last Days of Lincoln* (1962); and two certificates of recognition for outstanding contributions to Florida State Univ. for two premieres given in 1961–62. He received the E. Harris Harbison Award for gifted teaching (1970); was nominated by the president of the Florida State Univ. for inclusion in the publication *Outstanding Educators of America* (1972); and honored as Florida State Univ. alumni professor of the year (1971).

Recreation. Bowling, tennis, writing.

FALLS, GREGORY A. Educator, director, actor. b. Gregory Alexander Falls, Apr. 4, 1922, Russellville, Ark., to Marvin Brown and Chole Ethel (Corson) Falls. Father, railroad clerk. Grad. Fort Smith (Ark.) H.S., 1939; Park Coll., B.A. 1943; Northwestern Univ., M.A. 1949, Ph.D. 1953. Studied Institut des Hautes Etudes Cinématographiques, Paris, France, 1942–43; Central Sch. of Drama, Lincoln, England, 1949–50. Married 1953 to Jean Burch, actress; two sons, two daughters. Served US Army Infantry, ETO, 1942–46. Member of AEA; AGMA; WATA (pres., 1967–68); NTC (vice-pres., 1970–71; pres., 1972–73; board, 1974–to date); AETA (exec. bd., 1964–66); ACAE (board, 1972–to date). He is a consultant to the US Office of Education and the Washington State Arts Commission. Address: (home) The Highlands, Seattle, WA 98177, tel. (206) EM 4-7421; (bus.) c/o School of Drama, Univ. of Washington, Seattle, WA 98177, tel. (206) 543-5140; ACT Theatre, 709 First Ave. West, Seattle, WA 98119, tel. (206) 285-3220.

Mr. Falls is professor of drama and chairman of the Drama Arts Group, School of Drama, Univ. of Washington. From 1961 to 1972, he was executive director of the School of Drama, and he was (1952–61) director of drama at the Univ. of Vermont.

In stock, he directed the Mad Anthony Players (Trail Playhouse, Toledo, Ohio, Summers 1952–54); subsequently, at the Stowe (Vt.) Playhouse, appeared as Bernie Dodd in *The Country Girl* and Tommy Turner in *The Male Animal* (Summer 1957), and as Starbuck in *The Rainmaker* (Summer 1958).

He served as director-producer for the Champlain (Vt.) Shakespeare Festival (July–Aug. 1959–62); and directed the premiere performance of the opera, *The Dybbuk* (Seattle Center Playhouse, Jan. 1963).

He founded A Contemporary Theatre (ACT) in Seattle in 1965 and has served as artistic director since, directing over twenty-five productions, including the premiere production of N. Richard Nash's *Echoes*, and the American premiere of Slowomir Mrozek's *Striptease*.

Awards. Mr. Falls received a Fulbright Scholarship to study drama in England (1950); as founder of the Champlain Shakespeare Festival, received the Regional Award by the New England Theatre Conference of the National Theatre Conference. He was made an honorary member of Phi Beta Kappa in 1971 and received the American College Theatre Festival award of excellence in 1973.

FARLEY, MORGAN. Actor, director. b. Francis Morgan Farley, Oct. 3, 1898, Mamaroneck, N.Y., to John Treacy and Marie T. (Morgan) Farley. Father, builder. Attended H.S. of Commerce, N.Y.C. Served US Army, WW II; rank, 2nd Lt. Member of AEA; SAG; Radio Artists of America.

Theatre. Mr. Farley made his debut touring eastern and midwestern states with Stuart Walker's stock company, playing minor roles and serving as assistant stage manager (Winter 1916); also for this company, he played Joe Bullit in the tryout of *Seventeen* (Murat Th., Indianapolis, Ind., 1917), and made his N.Y.C. debut in it (Booth, Jan. 22, 1918); was stage manager for *A Night in Avignon*, *Stinky*, *The Laughter of the Gods*, *The Golden Doom*, *King Argimenes*, *The Gods of the Mountain*, *The Very Naked Boy*, *The Tents of the Arabs*, and *The Book of Job*, also playing minor roles in *The Laughter of the Gods*, *King Argimenes*, *The Gods of the Mountain*, and *The Very Naked Boy* (Punch and Judy Th., N.Y.C., Jan. 15, 1919–Mar. 22, 1919; Murat, Indianapolis, Summer 1919).

He played the Pink Youth in *A Young Man's Fancy* (Playhouse, N.Y.C., Oct. 15, 1919); Tim Simpkins in *The Charm School* (Bijou, Aug. 2, 1920); Charles Deburau in *Deburau* (Belasco, Dec. 23, 1920); Michel Alexis in *The Grand Duke* (Lyceum, Nov. 1, 1921); Arthur Bixby in the pre-Bway tryout of *Nobody's Fool*, which closed out of town (1922); Bobby in *Mary the 3rd* (39 St. Th., Feb. 5, 1923); Tommy in *Home Fires* (39 St. Th., Aug. 20, 1923); Anthony Wescott in *The Wild Wescotts* (Frazee, Dec. 24, 1923); George in *Fata Morgana* (Garrick, Mar. 3, 1924); Paolo in special matinee performances of *Paolo and Francesca* (Booth, Dec. 2, 1924); Arthur Griswold in *Tangletoes* (39 St. Th., Feb. 17, 1925); Eugene Marchbanks in Peggy Wood's *Candida* (Comedy, Nov. 9, 1925); Lawrence Sanbury in *The Unchastened Woman* (Princess, Feb. 15, 1926); Benjamin in *Easter One Day Before* (Princess, Mar. 18, 1926); Clyde Griffiths in *An American Tragedy* (Longacre, Oct. 11, 1926); and made his London debut as Jimmy Dugan in *The Trial of Mary Dugan* (Queen's, Nov. 1927).

At the Civic Repertory Th., N.Y.C., he succeeded Donald Cameron as Romeo in *Romeo and Juliet* (Oct. 6, 1930); played Berend in *The Good Hope* (Dec. 17, 1930); and Armand Duval in Eva Le Gallienne's *Camille* (Jan. 26, 1931); he played Lansing French in *The Passing Present* (Ethel Barrymore Th., Dec. 7, 1931); toured as George in *Fata Morgana* (1932); toured California in Henry Duffy's productions of *Grounds for Divorce* and *The Marquise* (1933); toured in *Wind and the Rain* (Winter 1934); appeared in *The Ten Minute Alibi* (New London, Conn., Summer 1934); played the juvenile lead in the tryout of *Waltz in Fire* (1934); Raskolnikoff in *Crime and Punishment* (Biltmore, N.Y.C., Jan. 22, 1935); Osric in John Gielgud's *Hamlet* (Empire, Oct. 8, 1936); Alexander Mill in Katherine Cornell's *Candida* (Empire, Mar. 19, 1937); and toured with the Mercury Th. as Cassius in *Julius Caesar* and Randall Utterword in *Heartbreak House* (1937–38), also succeeding (May 1938) John Hoysradt as Randall Utterword in *Heartbreak House* (Mercury, N.Y.C., Apr. 29, 1938); and played Herault De Sechelles in *Danton's Death* (Mercury, Nov. 2, 1938).

He served as manager-director of the Siasconset Casino Th. and Yacht Club (Nantucket, Mass., Summers 1938–40); played Scrubby in *Outward Bound* (Playhouse, N.Y.C., Dec. 22, 1938); and toured as Baron Max von Alvenstor in *Margin for Error* (1940).

Films. Mr. Farley appeared in *Love Doctor* (Par., 1929); *Greene Murder Case* (Par., 1929); and *The Mighty* (Par., 1930); *Gentleman's Agreement* (20th-Fox, 1947); *Goodbye, My Fancy* (WB, 1951); *The Wild North* (MGM, 1952); *High Noon* (UA, 1952); *Remains To Be Seen* (MGM, 1953); *Jivaro* (Par., 1954); *The Winner's Circle* (Janus, 1957); and others.

Recreation. Art, in all forms.

FARQUHAR, ROBROY. Director, actor, theatre administrator. b. Feb. 11, 1916, Liverpool, England. Attended Marlborough Coll., England, and Baltimore City Coll. Married Sept. 1948 to Leona Fraki; one son, one daughter. Served US Army, 1943–46, Infantry and Special Services; rank, T/5. Member of AEA; ANTA; SETC (professional th. chmn., 1962–64); North Carolina Travel Council; Henderson County Mutual Concert Assn. (pres., 1961–62); North Carolina Theatre Conference. Address: P.O. Box 248, Flat Rock, NC 28731, tel. (704) 692-2281.

Theatre. Mr. Farquhar first appeared with a stock company in Baltimore, Md., in *The Shanghai Gesture, Madame X,* and *Clarence* (1935).

He founded the Vagabond Players in N.Y.C., presenting the following plays: *The Prince of Liars, The Devil Passes, The Three Cornered Moon, Love in a Mist,* and *Blind Alley* (Fifth Ave. Th., 1938; Cherry Lane, 1939); followed by an engagement at the Springs Hotel (Bedford, Pa., 1939).

With Mr. Farquhar as manager, the company took up residence at Flat Rock, N.C., in the Old Mill Playhouse where they performed until the beginning of WW II, and played through 1951 at Lake Summit Playhouse (Tuxedo, N.C.) with a sixteen-week winter season in 1950 at the Pinellas Playhouse (Pinellas International Airport, Fla.). In 1952, the Players returned to their present location (Flat Rock, N.C.) in their own theatre, the Flat Rock Playhouse.

Mr. Farquhar organized the Flat Rock Vagabond School of the Drama in 1952. The Vagabond Players toured ten Southern states, playing 32 weeks of engagements (1953–55), presenting *See How They Run, The Curtain Rises,* and *Jenny Kissed Me,* among others. In June 1961, the Vagabond Players were officially designated by the North Carolina General Assembly, "the State Theatre of North Carolina." The Vagabond Touring Theatre has presented *The World of Carl Sandburg* in North Carolina high schools (1964–71), *North Carolina's Paul Green* (1972–73) and, in North Carolina elementary schools, *Sacramento Fifty Miles* (1974).

World premieres presented at Flat Rock Playhouse include: *The Crocodile Smile* by Lawrence and Lee (1970); *Opal Is a Diamond* (1971); *Macbeth Did It* (1972); and *Opal's Baby* (1973), all by John Patrick.

Mr. Farquhar also organized and directed the Hendersonville (N.C.) Community Theatre (1948–52) and the Brevard (N.C.) Little Theatre (1951–66).

Awards. With Ernest Frankel, he wrote *Harp for Tomorrow,* which received the annual playwriting awards from the Univ. of Utah and the Univ. of Nebraska. He received the Kiwanis International Distinguished Service Award in 1965.

FARRELL, MARY. Actress, director. b. Mary Magdalen Farrell, July 21, Cumberland, Md., to John J. and Mary Frances (Brough) Farrell. Father, lawyer. Attended Washington Acad., Cumberland, 1908–16; Actors Lab, Hollywood, Calif., 1943; Uta Hagen Studio, N.Y.C., 1961; New York Univ., 1962. Married Oct. 6, 1938, to Harry L. Young, actor, director. Member of AEA; AFTRA; SAG.

Pre-Theatre. Member of the St. Louis (Mo.) Junior Symphony Orchestra.

Theatre. Miss Farrell made her stage debut as a dancer in the Ziegfeld production of *Louie the 14th* (Cosmopolitan Th., N.Y.C., Mar. 3, 1925), in which she toured; subsequently appeared in *No Foolin'* (Globe, N.Y.C., June 24, 1926); danced in *Show Boat* (Ziegfeld, Dec. 27, 1927); toured in *Kid Boots* for one year (1928); staged the dances for *Kid Boots* (Drury Lane, London, Nov. 10, 1928); studied with Max Reinhardt and worked at the Salzburg (Austria) Festival, appearing there in *Everyman* (1934); directed productions at the Brattleboro (Vt.) Summer Th. (1938–41); performed and directed at the Temple of Music and Art in Tucson and Phoenix, Ariz., (1941–42); appeared in productions at the Playhouse (Albany, N.Y., 1947–52).

She played Miss Wingate in the national touring company of *The Shrike* (opened Shubert, New Haven, Conn., Oct. 15, 1952; closed Erlanger, Chicago, Ill., Mar. 21, 1953); played Kate Keller in *All My Sons* (Arena Stage, Washington, D.C., 1954); at the Olney (Md.) Theatre (1954), appeared as Linda Loman in *Death of a Salesman,* Capulet in *Ring Round the Moon,* Mrs. Clandon in *You Never Can Tell,* and Miss Tacher in *Oh, Men! Oh, Women!*

Miss Farrell was understudy to Enid Markey in the title role in *Mrs. Patterson* (National, N.Y.C., Dec. 1, 1954); played Mrs. Bodkin in *The Ponder Heart* (Music Box, Feb. 16, 1956); Mrs. Gallup in *The Loud Red Patrick* (Ambassador, Oct. 3, 1956); Sister Temple in *Orpheus Descending* (Martin Beck Th., Mar. 21, 1957); Mrs. Clatt in *Look Homeward, Angel* (Ethel Barrymore Th., Nov. 28, 1957); succeeded Margaretta Warwick as Emma Leech in *Summer of the 17th Doll* (Players, Oct. 13, 1959); played Rhoda Grant in *Face of a Hero* (Eugene O'-Neill Th., Oct. 20, 1960); Mrs. Durkee in *Midgie Purvis* (Martin Beck Th., Feb. 1, 1960); Melinda in *The Days and Nights of BeeBee Fenstermaker* (Sheridan Square Playhouse, Sept. 16, 1962), and was understudy to Margaret Hamilton, Thelma Ritter, and Doris Rich in *UTBU* (Helen Hayes Th., Jan. 4, 1966).

Television. From 1956–63, Miss Farrell appeared on Camera Three (CBS) Armstrong Circle Th. (CBS); Studio One (CBS); and Love of Life (CBS).

Night Clubs. She appeared as a dancer and singer at the Savoy Hotel (London, 1928); and at Clubs in France, Germany, and Belgium.

FASSETT, JAY. Actor. b. Jacob Sloat Fassett, Jr., Nov. 13, 1889, Elmira, N.Y., to Jacob Sloat and Jennie (Crocker) Fassett. Father, attorney, financier, statesman; mother, philanthropist. Grad. Westminster Sch., Simsbury, Conn., 1908; Cornell Univ., B.A. 1912; graduate work at Harvard Univ., 1915–16. Married June 29, 1912, to Dorothy Chandler (marr. dis. 1939); two sons, one daughter; married June 19, 1939, to Helen Murdoch. Served WW I, US Army, Intelligence; rank, 2nd Lt. Member of The Players; AEA (council); Kappa Alpha Assn.

Pre-Theatre. Banking, publishing.

Theatre. Mr. Fassett was assistant stage manager and made his N.Y.C. debut as Jakov in *Sonya* (48 St. Th., Aug. 15, 1921); translated *Malvaloca,* a play by the Brothers Quintero, produced by the Equity Players (48 St. Th., Oct. 2, 1922); played in stock at McCauley's Th. (Louisville, Ky., 1922); played Johnson in *Rita Coventry* (Bijou, N.Y.C., Feb. 19, 1923); a Light Horseman in *Cyrano de Bergerac* (National, Nov. 1, 1923), and Montfleury in the touring company; succeeded (Feb. 1925) Paul Harvey as Oliver Winslow in *The Youngest* (Gaiety, N.Y.C., Dec. 22, 1924); played Belvawney in *Engaged* (52 St. Th., June 18, 1925); Armin in *One Glorious Hour* (Selwyn, Apr. 14, 1927); Happy in *The White Eagle* (Casino, Dec. 26, 1927); a German Student in *Becky Sharp* (Knickerbocker, June 3, 1929); Charles Lingard in *As Husbands Go* John Golden Th., Mar. 5, 1931); Leander "Bunny" Nolan in *Biography* (Guild, Dec. 12, 1932); Alfred Rouff in *Cross Ruff* (Masque, Feb. 19, 1935); and Horace Kincaid in *Russet Mantle* (Masque, Jan. 16, 1936).

He played M. Dupont in *Tovarich* (Plymouth, Oct. 15, 1936); Dr. Gibbs in *Our Town* (Henry Miller's Th., Feb. 4, 1938); Henry Cristof in *Delicate Story* (Henry Miller's Th., Dec. 4, 1940); John Field in *Dark Eyes* (Belasco, Jan. 14, 1943); Waldo Brewster in *Loco* (Biltmore, Oct. 16, 1946); and Maj. Gen. R. G. Kane in *Command Decision* (Fulton, Oct. 1, 1947).

Films. Mr. Fassett appeared in *My Sin* (Par., 1931) and *The Cheat* (Par., 1931).

Published Works. Mr. Fassett translated from Spanish to English, *The Great Galeoto* (1914), a play by José Echegarey; *Malvaloca* (1916), a play by the Brothers Quintero; *The City of the Discreet* (1917), a novel by Pio Baroja; *The Three Cornered Hat* (1918), a novel by Alarcon; and *Three Plays of the Argentine* (1920).

FAULKNER, SELDON. Educator. b. Mar. 23, 1929, St. Louis, Mo., to John Delmer and Mamie Ellen (Hughes) Faulkner. Father, prison guard. Grad. Central H.S., St. Louis, 1946; Shurtleff Coll., B.A. 1953; St. Louis Univ., M.A. 1954; State Univ. of Iowa, Ph.D. 1957. Married Aug. 9, 1952, to Dona Leah Clark; one son, one daughter. Served US Army, ETO, PTO, 1946–51; rank, PFC. Member of ANTA; AETA (Coll. Curriculum Comm., Project in Musical Th.); Purple Mask Society, State Univ. of Iowa; State Univ. of Iowa (bd. of gov., 1956). Address: University Theatre, Univ. of Colorado, Boulder, CO 80302, tel. (303) 443-2211.

Mr. Faulkner was appointed acting director (1963) of the Univ. Theatre of the Univ. of Colorado, where he previously served as assistant professor of speech and drama (1959). He has directed numerous student productions, including *Bells Are Ringing,* in which he played Inspector Barnes, and which toured the Far East (1961) under the sponsorship of the U.S.O. and AETA. Previously he taught at St. Louis Univ. (1957–59), where he directed four university productions.

Published Works. He is the author of "The Octoroon War," *Educational Theatre Journal* (Nov. 1963); "Set for a Thousand Plays," *Dramatics Magazine,* (1964); and "The Great Train Scene Robbery," *Quarterly Journal of Speech* (1964).

Awards. Mr. Faulkner received a Graduate Drama Award from St. Louis Univ. (1954).

Recreation. Golf, photography.

FAYE, JOEY. Actor. b. Joseph Anthony Palladino, July 12, 1910, New York City, to Anthony and Maria (Noto) Palladino. Father, barber; mother, forelady, dress factory. Grad. Textile H.S., N.Y.C. Married Mar. 4, 1949, to Eileen Jenkins, actress (marr. dis. 1958); married Dec. 26, 1963, to Virginia Carr, actress (dec. July 15, 1972); married Dec. 20, 1973, to Judith Karlin, actress. Relatives in theatre: brother, Vini Faye, actor; sister, Bertha Falacara. Member of AEA; SAG; AGVA; AFTRA; BAA. Address: 325 W. 45th St., New York, NY 10036, tel. (212) CI 6-0430.

Theatre. Mr. Faye made his debut in vaudeville (Poli's Th., New Haven, Conn.); appeared in Billy Minsky's burlesque show (Republic Th., N.Y.C., 1931), and other burlesque productions (1931–38).

He joined the national company of *Room Service* (1938); appeared in the revue *Sing Out the News* (Music Box, N.Y.C., Sept. 24, 1938); took over the role of Banjo in the national company of *The Man Who Came to Dinner* (1939–40); appeared in *Streets of Paris* (NY World's Fair, Summer 1939); played in second company in N.Y.C. and toured in national company of *Meet the People* (Mansfield Th., Dec. 25, 1940); played himself in *Strip for Action* (Natl., N.Y.C., Sept. 30, 1942); Burleigh Sullivan in *The Milky Way* (Windsor, June 9, 1943); and J. Carlyle Benson in *Boy Meets Girl* (Windsor, June 22, 1943); and during WW II appeared in USO productions in hospitals in the US and Europe.

Mr. Faye played a Citizen and Youssouf in *Allah Be Praised* (Adelphi, Apr. 20, 1944), Woonsocket and Goya in *The Duchess Misbehaves* (Adelphi, Feb. 13, 1946); Ruby in the pre-Bway tryout of *Windy City* (opened Shubert, New Haven, Conn., Apr. 18,

1946; closed Great Northern, Chicago, Ill., June 6, 1946); appeared in the revue *Tidbits of 1946* (Barbizon-Plaza Th., N.Y.C., May 20, 1946; moved Plymouth, July 8, 1946); played Max in the pre-Bway tryout of *Three Indelicate Ladies* (opened Shubert, New Haven, Apr. 10, 1947; closed Wilbur, Boston, Mass., Apr. 19, 1947); Mr. Pontdue in *High Button Shoes* (Shubert, Dec. 22, 1947); appeared in the vaudeville company of *Meet the People;* played Pinky in *Top Banana* (Winter Garden, N.Y.C., Nov. 1, 1951), and toured in it (opened Shubert, Philadelphia, Pa., Oct. 6, 1952; closed Biltmore, Los Angeles, Calif., June 27, 1953).

He played the Professor in the pre-Bway tryout of *The Amazing Adele* (opened Shubert, Philadelphia, Dec. 26, 1955; closed Shubert, Boston, Jan. 21, 1956); Danny in the pre-Bway tryout of *Strip for Action* (opened Shubert, New Haven, Mar. 17, 1956; closed Nixon, Pittsburgh, Pa., Apr. 14, 1956); appeared in stock productions in California, including Gogo in *Waiting for Godot* (1959) also playing this role in the Library of Congress Th. (Washington, D.C.); and played Bernie Buchsbaum in *Little Me* (Lunt-Fontanne Th., N.Y.C., Nov. 17, 1962).

He succeeded Irving Jacobson as Sancho in *Man of La Mancha* (ANTA Washington Square Th., Nov. 22, 1965); was in the New Theatre Workshop presentation of *The Hermit's Cock* (Eastside Playhouse, 1969); was in *70, Girls, 70* (Broadhurst, Apr. 15, 1971); and succeeded (June 29, 1971) Oliver Clark as Estragon in *Waiting for Godot* (Sheridan Square Playhouse, Feb. 3, 1971).

Films. Mr. Faye appeared in *Top Banana* (UA, 1954); *The Tender Trap* (MGM, 1955); *Ten North Frederick* (20th-Fox, 1958); *North to Alaska* (20th-Fox, 1960); *That Touch of Mink* (U, 1962); *Penelope* (MGM, 1966); *What's So Bad About Feeling Good?* (U, 1968); *No Way to Treat a Lady* (Par., 1968); *The Grissom Gang* (Cinerama, 1971); and *The War Between Men and Women* (Natl. Gen., 1972).

Television and Radio. He performed on the radio program, The Rookies (WOR, 1941); the Arrow Shirt Show with Phil Silvers; the Kate Smith Show (NBC); the Fred Allen Show and the Dumont Show.

He appeared on experimental television programs for NBC and Dumont (1937–39); the Kate Smith Show (NBC); the Shirley Temple Storybook (NBC); the Ed Sullivan Show (CBS); the Milton Berle Show (NBC); and on his own show, the 54th St. Revue (CBS). Mr. Faye appeared in 200 fifteen-minute segments of *Mack and Myer for Hire* (Trans-Lux Co. and WPIX), and he has been featured on numerous other television programs, both situation comedy and drama. In the former category are included his appearances in twelve segments of Dobie Gillis, three segments of Father Knows Best, five segments of Make Room for Daddy, and on Maude (CBS, 1973); in the latter are included his appearances on Climax (CBS), Playhouse 90 (CBS), Inner Sanctum, The Jazz Singer, and others. He was featured five times on the Jerry Lewis Show (1971), four times on the Dean Martin Show (1972) and made many appearances on talk shows, including two on the Johnny Carson Tonight Show (NBC). He was a regular member of the cast of Candid Camera (CBS) for two and a half years. Mr. Faye has also made numerous television commercials.

Night Clubs. Mr. Faye appeared in *George White's Scandals* at the Riviera and Dunes Hotels (Las Vegas, Nev.) and has made five other appearances in Las Vegas, including one at Circus Circus (1971). He has appeared also in night clubs throughout the US.

Other Activities. Comedy writer of "Floogle Street" sketch and sixty-three other well-known comedy sketches. He is the author, director, and producer of a lecture on comedy, "The Anatomy of Humor," which he has toured around the country, appearing in such theatres as the Coconut Grove Th., Miami, Fla., and the Shubert Th., New Haven, Conn.

Awards. He received the West Coast Critics Award for his performance as Gogo in *Waiting for Godot* (1959).

FEARNLEY, JOHN. Director. b. Johannes Schiott, Apr. 8, 1914, Westport, Conn., to Johannes and Kitta (Knudsen) Schiott. Father, executive. Grad. the Hill Sch., Pottstown, Pa., 1932; attended Asheville (N.C.) Sch., attended Yale Univ.; RADA, London, England. Served WW II, AFS; rank, Lt. Relative in theatre: uncle, David Knudsen, actor. Member of AEA; SSD&C; The Players; Pequot Yacht Club; Cedar Point Yacht Club. Address: 6 Woodhill Rd., Green Farms, CT 06436, tel. (203) 259-8228.

Theatre. Mr. Fearnley made his N.Y.C. debut in the chorus of the revue *Thumbs Up* (St. James Th., Dec. 27, 1934); subsequently was stage manager and appeared in *Tovarich* (Plymouth, Oct. 15, 1936); performed in *Oscar Wilde* (Fulton, Oct. 10, 1938); and as First Man Tourist in *Key Largo* (Ethel Barrymore Th., Nov. 27, 1939); was technical director of the Westport (Conn.) Country Playhouse (1941); production assistant for the Theatre Guild (1941–42); stage manager for *Lifeline* (Belasco, N.Y.C., Nov. 30, 1942); and *Harriet* (Henry Miller's Th., Mar. 3, 1943).

Mr. Fearnley became casting director and production assistant for Richard Rodgers and Oscar Hammerstein (1945), working on *Carousel* (Majestic, Apr. 19, 1945); *Annie Get Your Gun* (Imperial, May 16, 1946); *Allegro* (Majestic, Oct. 10, 1947); *Happy Birthday* (Broadhurst, Oct. 31, 1946); *John Loves Mary* (Booth, Feb. 4, 1947); *South Pacific* (Majestic, Apr. 7, 1949); *Burning Bright* (Broadhurst, Sept. 18, 1950); *The King and I* (St. James, Mar. 29, 1951); and *Pipe Dream* (Shubert, Nov. 30, 1955).

He directed the NY City Ctr. productions of *Oklahoma!* (Mar. 19, 1958; Feb. 27, 1963; May 25, 1963); *Carousel* (Sept. 11, 1957); *South Pacific* (Apr. 24, 1957; Apr. 26, 1961); *The King and I* (Apr. 18, 1956; May 11, 1960); and *Brigadoon* (May 30, 1962; Jan. 30, 1963); the Brussels (Belgium) World's Fair production of *Carousel* (1958); Australian production of *The Music Man* (Melbourne, 1959); *Eddie Fisher at the Winter Garden* (N.Y.C., 1962); was co-director and co-adapter, with James Hammerstein, of *South Pacific* (Thunderbird Hotel, Las Vegas, Nev., 1962); and directed Jones Beach (Wantagh, N.Y.) Th. productions: *Sound of Music* (1970–71), *The King and I* (1972), *Carousel* (1973) and *Fiddler on the Roof* (1974).

Films. Mr. Fearnley was production aide for the film version of *Oklahoma!* (Magna, 1955).

Awards. He was nominated for an Antoinette Perry (Tony) Award for directing *Brigadoon* (1963).

FEDER, ABE. Lighting and scenic designer, producer. b. June 27, 1909, Milwaukee, Wis., to Benjamin and Sane (Byfield) Feder. Father, restaurateur. Grad. West Div. H.S., Milwaukee, 1926; attended Carnegie Inst. of Tech., 1926–29. Married Mar. 23, 1952, to Ciel Grossman, interior decorator; one daughter. Served WW II, USAAF; rank, S/Sgt. Member of United Scenic Artists; US Institute of Theatre Technology; International Assoc. of Lighting Designers (1st pres.); Illuminating Engineering Society; Architectural League of NY; US Expert Committee on Lighting Education in Architecture; The Lambs. Address: 15 W. 38th St., New York, NY 10018, tel. (212) OX 5-3240.

Mr. Feder heads his own firm, Lighting by Feder.

Theatre. Mr. Feder designed the lighting for *Trick for Trick* (Sam Harris Th., N.Y.C., Feb. 18, 1932); *One Sunday Afternoon* (Little, Feb. 15, 1933; the opera *Four Saints in Three Acts* (44 St. Th., Feb. 20, 1934); *Calling All Stars* (Hollywood Th., Dec. 13, 1934); and *Ghosts* (Empire, Dec. 12, 1935).

For the Federal Theatre (WPA) Project, he designed the lighting for *Walk Together Chillun* (Lafayette Th., Feb. 2, 1936); *Conjur Man Dies* (Lafayette, Mar. 11, 1936); *Triple-A Ploughed Under* (Biltmore, Mar. 14, 1936); *Macbeth* (Lafayette, Apr. 9, 1936); *Turpentine* (Lafayette, June 26, 1936); *Injunction Granted* (Biltmore, July 24, 1936); and *Horse Eats Hat* (Maxine Elliott's Th., Sept. 22, 1936). He designed lighting for *Hedda Gabler* (Longacre, Nov. 16, 1936); and returned to Federal Th. to design lighting for *Dr. Faustus* (Maxine Elliott's Th., Jan. 8, 1937); *Native Ground* (Al Jolson Th., Mar. 23, 1937); and *How Long Brethren* (Nora Bayes Th., May 6, 1937). He designed lighting for *I'd Rather Be Right* (Alvin, Dec. 2, 1937); and again returned to Federal Th., designing lighting for *One-Third of a Nation* (Adelphi, Jan. 17, 1938); *Prologue to Glory* (Maxine Elliott's Th., Mar. 17, 1938); lighting productions for the Living Newspaper, including the opera *The Cradle Will Rock* (Al Jolson's Th., May 1938) and the ballet *Immediate Comment* (Adelphi, 1938); and designing lighting for the plays *The Big Blow* (Maxine Elliott's Th., Oct. 1, 1938) and *Androcles and the Lion* (Lafayette, Dec. 16, 1938).

He designed lighting for the tour of Ballet Caravan (1938); for the play *Here Come the Clowns* (Booth Th., N.Y.C., Dec. 7, 1938); for the revue *Sing for Your Supper* (Adelphi, Apr. 24, 1939); *A Passenger to Bali* (Ethel Barrymore Th., Mar. 14, 1940); *Hold on to Your Hats* (Shubert, Sept. 11, 1940); *Johnny Belinda* (Belasco Th., Sept. 18, 1940); served as coordinator of production and lighting designer for the first season of the Ballet Th., including *Great American Goof, Peter and the Wolf,* and *Giselle* (Jan.–Feb. 1941); designed the lighting for *Angel Street* (John Golden Th., Dec. 5, 1941); *Autumn Hill* (Booth, Apr. 13, 1942); *The Walking Gentleman* (Belasco, May 7, 1942); *The Skin of Our Teeth* (Plymouth, Nov. 18, 1942); the USAAF production of *Winged Victory* (44 St. Th., Nov. 20, 1943); *The Gioconda Smile* (Lyceum, Oct. 7, 1950); *The Tower Beyond Tragedy* (ANTA, Nov. 26, 1950); *Out of This World* (New Century, Dec. 21, 1950); *A Sleep of Prisoners* (St. James Church, Oct. 10, 1951); *Dear Barbarians* (Royale, Feb. 2, 1952); *Three Wishes for Jamie* (Mark Hellinger Th., Mar. 21, 1952); *Thunderland* (Biltmore Estate, Asheville, N.C., July, 1952); and the Sonja Henie Ice Revue (Santa Barbara, Calif., Aug. 1952).

Also, *The Immoralist* (Royale, N.Y.C., Feb. 8, 1953); *A Pin to See the Peep Show* (Playhouse, Sept. 17, 1953); *The Boy Friend* (Royale, Sept. 30, 1953); *What Every Woman Knows* (NY City Ctr., Dec. 22, 1954); *The Flowering Peach* (Belasco, Dec. 29, 1954); *The Wisteria Trees* (NY City Ctr., Feb. 2, 1955); *Inherit the Wind* (Natl. Apr. 21, 1955); *Seventh Heaven* (ANTA, May 26, 1955); and the Salute to France production of *Skin of Our Teeth* (Sarah Bernhardt Th., Paris, June 28, 1955), which was also presented in N.Y.C. (ANTA, Aug. 17, 1955); *The Young and the Beautiful* (Longacre, Oct. 1, 1955); *My Fair Lady* (Mark Hellinger Th., Mar. 15, 1956); *A Clearing in the Woods* (Belasco Th., Jan. 1, 1957); *Visit to a Small Planet* (Booth Th., Feb. 7, 1957); *Orpheus Descending* (Martin Beck Th., Mar. 21, 1957); *Time Remembered* (Morosco, Nov. 12, 1957); *At the Grand* (Los Angeles Civic Light Opera, July, 1958); *Goldilocks* (Lunt-Fontanne Th., N.Y.C. Oct. 11, 1958); and *The Cold Wind and the Warm* (Morosco, Dec. 8, 1958).

He also designed the sets and lighting for *Play with Me* (York Playhouse, Apr. 30, 1959); the sets for *Carmen Jones* (Theatre-in-the-Park, Aug. 17, 1959); *April in Paris* (Theatre-in-the-Park, 1959); *Guys and Dolls* (Theatre-in-the-Park, July 21, 1959); *Can-Can* (Theatre-in-the-Park, Aug. 25, 1959); Ballet Russe de Monte Carlo (Theatre-in-the-Park, 1959); *A Loss of Roses* (Eugene O'Neill Th., Nov. 28, 1959); *Greenwillow* (Alvin, Mar. 8, 1960); *Camelot* (Majestic, Dec. 3, 1960); *Tiger, Tiger Burning Bright* (Booth, Dec. 24, 1962); sets and lighting for *Once for the Asking* (Booth, Nov. 20, 1963); space stage setting and lighting for *Blues for Mr. Charlie* (ANTA, Apr. 14, 1964); lighting for *My Fair Lady* (NY City Ctr., May 20, 1964); *The Three Sisters* (Morosco, June 6, 1964); *On a Clear Day You Can See Forever* (Mark Hellinger Th., Oct. 17, 1965); *Country Girl* (NY City Ctr., Sept. 29, 1966); the sets and lighting for *Elizabeth the Queen* (NY City Ctr., Nov. 3, 1966); *Beyond Desire* (Th. Four, Oct. 10, 1967); and lighting for *The King and I* (NY City Ctr., May 23, 1968); *My Fair Lady* (NY City Ctr., June 13, 1968); *Carnival* (NY City Ctr., Dec. 12, 1968); and *Scratch* (St. James, May 6, 1971).

Films. Mr. Feder assisted in the lighting of *Winged Victory* (20th-Fox, 1944).

Other Activities. Mr. Feder was a US delegate to the International Th. Institute (UNESCO, Paris, France, 1950); did exterior and interior lighting designs, including stage lighting, and was stage consultant on rigging, draperies, and equipment for the Amphitheatre, Asheville, N.C. (1953); with Edward Durrell Stone, designed the outdoor Theatre-in-the-Park, Central Park, N.Y.C. (1959); presented a detailed study and critique for all exterior lighting at the NY World's Fair (1963); did interior and exterior lighting designs for La Grande Salle, Montreal (Quebec) Cultural Center (1963); and did exterior and interior lighting designs and served as stage consultant for the Univ. of Illinois Assembly Dome, Urbana, Ill. (1963); San Francisco (Calif.) Civic Center Aud. (1964); the Tulsa (Okla.) Civic Ctr., (1964); Expo Th. and the Garden of Stars, both at Montreal (Quebec) World's Fair (1966); the Springer Opera House, Columbus, Ga. (1972); and the Minskoff Th., N.Y.C. (1973). Mr. Feder also designed lighting for all the stages and the interior and exterior of the John F. Kennedy Center for the Performing Arts, Washington, D.C.

Mr. Feder has conducted workshop seminars on Lighting for drama and architectural students at the following universities. These productions, produced and directed solely by him, are entitled "Dialogue with Light": Carnegie-Mellon Univ., Pittsburgh, Pa. (1966); Univ., of Utah, Salt Lake City, Utah (1968); Univ., of Colorado, Boulder, Colo. (1968); and Springer Opera House, Columbus, Ga. (1971). He has also lectured and conducted other workshops on lighting for the Cornell Univ.; Univ. of Southern California; Univ. of Colorado; Univ. of Utah; Carnegie-Mellon Univ.; Massachusetts Institute of Technology; and Univ. of Michigan.

Published Works. He wrote a chapter on lighting in John Gassner's book *Producing the Play,* and has contributed articles to *AIA Journal, Progressive Architecture, Illuminating Engineer, American City, Interior Design, Designer, Contract,* and others.

Recreation. More lighting and miles of BX cable.

FEIFFER, JULES. Cartoonist, playwright, novelist. b. Jules Ralph Feiffer, Jan 26, 1929, New York City, to David and Rhoda (Davis) Feiffer. Father, salesman; mother, fashion stylist. Grad. P.S. 77 and James Monroe High School (Bronx), N.Y.C. Professional training at Art Students League and Pratt Institute (Brooklyn), N.Y.C. Member of Dramatists Guild; Dramatists Guild Council; PEN Club; Authors League of America; Writers Guild of America, East. Address: c/o Publishers-Hall Syndicate, 30 E. 42nd St., New York, NY 10017.

Mr. Feiffer is creator of the cartoon "Feiffer," syndicated to approximately 100 newspapers in the US and abroad.

Theatre. *Crawling Around* was the first play of Mr. Feiffer's to be staged (Poets' Th., Cambridge, Mass., 1961), and *The Explainers* was his first play to be professionally staged (Playwrights at the Second City, Chicago, Ill., 1961). *The World of Jules Feiffer* (Hunterdon Hills Playhouse, N.J., 1962) was his first play in summer stock. Later plays, with places and times of presentation, include: *The Apple Tree,* of which Part III, "Passionella," is based on a story by Mr. Feiffer (Sam S. Shubert Th., N.Y.C., Oct. 18, 1966); *Little Murders* (Broadhurst, Apr. 25, 1967); *God Bless* (Yale School of Drama, New Haven, Conn., 1968); and *The White House Murder Case* (Circle in the Square, N.Y.C., 1968). Mr. Feiffer's *Little Murders* was his first work on the London Stage (Aldwych, 1967) and his first Off-Bway presentation (Circle in the Square, 1969).

Films. Films of Mr. Feiffer's work include *Little Murders* (20th-Fox, 1971) and *Carnal Knowledge* (Avco Embassy, 1971). He also created the animated cartoon *Munro* (Rembrandt Films, 1963).

Television. The first work by Mr. Feiffer on television was *Crawling Arnold* (CBC, Toronto, Canada, 1962). He was the writer of the "Silverlips" scene for the documentary *V.D. Blue* (PBS, 1972).

Published Works. Mr. Feiffer has published collections of cartoons: *Sick Sick Sick* (1958); *Passionella* (1959); *The Explainers* (1960); *Boy, Girl, Boy, Girl* (1961); *Hold Me!* (1962); *Feiffer's Album* (1963); *The Unexpurgated Memoirs of Bernard Mergenweiler* (1964); *The Great Comic Book Heroes* (1965); *Feiffer on Civil Rights* (1966); *Feiffer's Marriage Manual* (1968); *Pictures at a Prosecution* (1970); and *Feiffer on Nixon* (1974). He is also author of the novel *Harry the Rat with Women* (1963).

Awards. Mr. Feiffer was awarded the George Polk Memorial Award in journalism (1961); received an Academy (Oscar) Award for his cartoon *Munro* (1961); the Off-Bway (Obie) and Outer Circle Critics awards (1969) for *Little Murders;* and the Outer Circle Award (1970) for *The White House Murder Case.*

FEIGAY, PAUL. Producer. b. Paul Anton Feigay, Mar. 13, 1920, New York City, to Bernard and Anne (Dvorak) Feigay. Father, real estate. Grad. Yale University Sch. of Drama, 1939. Member of AEA; NATAS. Address: (home) 405 E. 54th St., New York, NY 10022, tel. (212) PL 8-0970; (bus.) 119 W. 57th St., New York, NY 10019, tel. (212) LT 1-9450.

Theatre. Mr. Feigay was co-producer and stage manager of the New Opera Company, N.Y.C., 1940–43), whose repertoire included *Macbeth; Cosi Fan Tutti; Pique Dame; The Fair of Sorotchinsk;* and *La Vie Parisienne* (44 St. Th., 1941; Bway Th., 1942); produced, with Oliver Smith, *On the Town* (Adelphi, Dec. 28, 1944) and *Billion Dollar Baby* (Alvin, Dec. 21, 1945); with Mr. Smith and Herbert Kenwith, in association with David Cummings, produced *Me and Molly* (Belasco, Feb. 26, 1948); presented a touring stock production of *Rain* (Summer 1952); with Dick Button and Nino Tallon, by arrangement with the Vancouver (British Columbia) Intl. Festival, produced *Do You Know the Milky Way?* (Billy Rose Th., N.Y.C., Oct 16, 1961); and Dick Button's Ice-Travaganza at the NY World's Fair (1964).

Television. Mr. Feigay was associate producer of *Omnibus* (NBC, 1952–57); produced the Standard Oil 75th Anniversary Show (NBC, 1959); a George M. Cohan spectacular, *Mr. Broadway* (NBC, 1959); *Hans Brinker or the Silver Skates* (NBC, 1960); with Dick Button, *All-Star Skating Tribute* (CBS, 1961); *World Skating Championships* (ABC, 1962); *World Gymnastic Championships* (CBS, 1962); *Rainbow of Stars* (NBC, 1962); *Washington International Horse Show* (CBS, 1962); *World Figure Skating Championships* (CBS, 1963); *National Figure Skating Championships* (NBC, 1963); *Modern Pentathlon Championships* (CBS, 1963).

Recreation. Gardening, swimming, collecting theatre art.

FEIST, GENE. Director, producer, playwright. b. Jan. 16, 1930, to Henry and Hattie (Fishbein) Feist. Father, automobile mechanic; mother, beautician. Grad. Carnegie-Mellon Univ., B.F.A.; New York Univ., M.A.; further graduate study at Columbia Univ. and Hunter College. Professional training with Lee Strasberg, Amer. Th. Wing, N.Y.C.; Actors Studio, N.Y.C. Married 1957 to Kathe Schneider (professional name, Elizabeth Owens), actress; two daughters. Served US Air Force four years as military correspondent; rank, Corporal. Member SSD&C; NY State United Teachers, Inc. Address: (home) 351 W. 24th St., New York, NY 10011, tel. (212) 989-5967; (bus.) Roundabout Theatre, 307 W. 26th St., New York, NY 10001, tel. (212) 924-7161.

Theatre. Mr. Feist began his work in theatre as general manager of the Sharon (Conn.) Playhouse in 1957. From 1958 to 1960, he was producer and director, New Theatre Nashville, Nashville, Tenn., where he produced and directed: (in 1958–59) *The Matchmaker; Cat on a Hot Tin Roof; Separate Tables; Children of Darkness; The Crucible; Relative Strangers* (also adapted by Mr. Feist); *The Boy Friend;* and *A Clearing in the Woods;* (in 1959–60) *Say, Darling; Look Back in Anger; Does Poppy Live Here?; La Boheme; As You Like It; Orpheus Descending; Brigadoon; Fallen Angels; No Time for Sergeants;* and *Stock and Trade.*

From 1961 to 1963, Mr. Feist was a member of Molly Kazan's Playwrights Unit, as well as Lee Strasberg's Directors Unit, at the Actors Studio, N.Y.C.; he was a director for Theatre '62 in 1961–62 and directed *Picnic on the Battlefield,* one of Theatre '62's revivals in the series *Theatre of the Absurd* (Cherry Lane Th., N.Y.C., Feb. 11, 1962). From 1963–64, he was drama critic for the *Chelsea Clinton News* of N.Y.C., and from 1963 to 1965 he directed for community and regional theatres in the US and Canada.

Mr. Feist founded the Roundabout Theatre Company in N.Y.C. in 1965 and has been producing director of this Off-Bway group since that time. In 1966–67, the first season of operations, Mr. Feist directed Roundabout Th. productions of *The Father; The Miser; Pelléas and Mélisande;* and *Pins and Needles.* In the 1967–68 season, he directed *Waiting for Lefty; The Bond; King Lear;* and *The Importance of Being Earnest,* and in the 1968–69 season, he directed *Journey's End; King Lear; Candida;* and *Dance of Death.* In 1969–70, Roundabout Th. productions were *Trumpets and Drums; Macbeth; Oedipus;* and *Lady from Maxim's,* which he also adapted; Mr. Feist produced all of these and directed all but *Macbeth.* For 1970–71, he produced and directed Roundabout Theatre's *Hamlet* (Oct. 18, 1970); *Uncle Vanya* (Jan. 24, 1971), which he also adapted; *Chas. Abbott & Son* (Mar. 12, 1971); and *She Stoops to Conquer* (May 30, 1971); and produced *Tug of War* (Dec. 23, 1970). Mr. Feist directed Roundabout's 1971–72 productions of *The Master Builder* (Oct. 17, 1971); *The Taming of the Shrew* (Jan. 30, 1972); *Misalliance* (Mar. 28, 1972); and *Conditions of Agreement.* For the 1972–73 season, Roundabout productions were *Right You Are* (Sept. 12, 1972); *American Gothics* (Nov. 10, 1972); *Anton Chekhov's Garden Party* (Nov. 22, 1972); *The Play's the Thing* (Jan. 9, 1973); and *Ghosts* (May 27, 1973). Mr. Feist directed all but *American Gothics* and *Anton Chekhov's Garden Party;* he adapted *Ghosts,* in addition to producing and directing it. Productions for 1973–74 were *The Father* (Oct. 16, 1973); *The Seagull* (Jan. 23, 1974); *The Circle* (Apr. 17, 1974); and *The Burnt Flowerbed* (July 2, 1974), with Mr. Feist directing all but the last. The 1974–75 season of repertory opened with *All My Sons* (Sept. 10, 1974).

Other Activities. In order to subsidize his early activities in the theatre, Mr. Feist has been a sociological researcher for Columbia Univ., a social worker for the city of New York for five years, and he has taught on the secondary school and college level for ten years.

Recreation. Mr. Feist collects plants and theatrical journals, biographies, and diaries.

FELSENFELD, HERB. Theatre administrator, actor, director, educator, stage manager. b. Herbert E. Felsenfeld, July 10, 1940, Chicago, Ill., to Joseph Nathan and Ida (Stein) Felsenfeld. Father, shoe salesman; mother, switchboard operator. Grad. Austin High School, Chicago, 1950; Goodman School of Drama, Chicago, B.F.A. 1963; M.F.A. 1965. Professional training: acting with Charles McGaw, Bella Itkin, Joseph Slowik, and Eugenie Leontovich; voice with Arthur Lessac and Sue Ann Park; gestalt therapy and bioenergetics with Richard Olney, Milwaukee, Wis. Married July 20, 1969, to Rosella Lee Stern; one daughter. Member of AEA; ATA; ACTF (chmn., Midwest Region, 1973–76); Wisconsin Theatre Assn. (bd. of dir., 1972–to date); Wisconsin Community Theatre Assn. (founding member and vice-pres., 1972–to date); International Amateur Theatre Assn.; Amer. Fed. of Teachers, Local 79. Address: (home) 2728 N. Prospect Ave., Milwaukee, WI 53211, tel. (414) 332-8433; (bus.) Dept. of Theatre Arts, School of Fine Arts, Univ. of Wisconsin-Milwaukee, Milwaukee, WI 53201, tel. (414) 963-4947.

In 1971, Mr. Felsenfeld became assistant professor and chairman of the Dept. of Theatre Arts, Univ. of Wisconsin-Milwaukee. Previously (1970–71) he had been a lecturer in theatre arts there.

Theatre. Mr. Felsenfeld began his work in the theatre as an actor with the Hayward Summer Th.,

Hayward, Wis., where he appeared as Joey in *Lullaby* (June 18, 1962) and as Augie Poole in *The Tunnel of Love* (July 2, 1962). In the summer of 1963, he was at Hawkhill Playhouse, Hartland, Wis., where he played the Fire Chief in *The Bald Soprano* (June 28); Daddy in *The American Dream* (July 2); Rakitin in *A Month in the Country* (July 15); and Eisenring in *The Firebugs* (Aug. 1). He played John in *The Black Hills Passion Play* and managed its Midwestern tour (Sept. 1963).

He became occupied with additional aspects of theatrical work when he joined the San Francisco (Calif.) Actor's Workshop and was a technician for *The Caucasian Chalk Circle* (Jan. 3, 1964); property master for *The Defense of Taipei* (Mar. 4, 1964); and production stage manager for *The Chalk Garden* (Apr. 10, 1964). He returned to Hawkhill Playhouse in the summer of 1964 and was production stage manager for *The Browning Version* and *I Rise in Flames Cried the Phoenix* (both June 18) and directed the original play festival (July 5). He was production stage manager for *Sponono* (Hull House Parkway Th., Chicago, Ill., Mar. 1, 1965) and in the summer of 1965, he was at the Comedy Arts Th., Saratoga Springs, N.Y., as production stage manager for *The Importance of Being Earnest* (June 15); stage manager for *The Madwoman of Chaillot*, in which he also appeared as Dr. Jadin (July 1); played various parts in *Only When I Laugh* (July 12); and was production stage manager for *She Stoops to Conquer* (Aug. 1). He was also production stage manager for the Edward Villella-Patricia McBride dance appearances (Harper Th., Chicago, Ill., Oct. 6, 1965).

At the Charles Playhouse Musical Th. for Children and high school touring project, Boston, Mass., Mr. Felsenfeld was production stage manager of *The Emperor's New Clothes* (Sept. 29, 1965); the tour of the Living Stage (Oct. 10, 1965); *Peter and the Wolf* (Dec. 15, 1965); and *The Rose and the Ring* (Feb. 1, 1966). He was director and co-adapter of *Alice in Wonderland* (Mar. 31, 1966); director and adapter of *Robin Hood* (Sept. 28, 1967); director of the Living Stage tour (Oct. 4, 1967); and stage manager for *The Dutchman* (Nov. 15, 1967). At the Pittsburgh (Pa.) Playhouse, he was production stage manager for *Rashomon* (Feb. 4, 1968); stage manager for *Henry IV, Part 1* (Feb. 15, 1968); and production stage manager for *Three Men on a Horse* (Mar. 5, 1968); *Galileo* (Apr. 14, 1968); and for *The Misanthrope* (Goodman Professional Th. Co., Chicago, Ill., Aug. 1, 1968). At the Univ. of Wisconsin-Milwaukee, Mr. Felsenfeld directed *The Tavern* (1971), *Sergeant Musgrave's Dance* (1972), *All That Fall* (1972), *The Reunion of Sam* (1973), and *Women Beware Women* (1974).

Television. Mr. Felsenfeld directed a television adaptation of *A Comedy of Errors* (WTTW, 1963).

Other Activities. Mr. Felsenfeld was director of Children's Theatre programming, Bernard Horwich Center, Chicago, Ill. (Summers, 1966, 1967, 1968); cultural arts director, Milwaukee Jewish Community Center (1968–70); and has been project director, Milwaukee Youth Theatre Project, Milwaukee Youth Foundation (Summer 1973–to date).

Published Works. Mr. Felsenfeld wrote the article "For Childhood's Bright and Eager Eyes" (Boston *Globe*, 1966); was drama critic for *Intermission Magazine* (1966–67); and has been editor since 1971 of the Wisconsin theatre journal *The Offstage Voice.*

Awards. Mr. Felsenfeld was awarded an undergraduate teaching improvement grant by the Univ. of Wisconsin in 1972 for the purpose of developing a system for the use of video tape to train students in acting, directing, and design.

Recreation. Reading, swimming, jogging, nature hikes.

FERGUSSON, FRANCIS. Educator, writer, drama critic, literary critic. b. Francis de Liesseline Fergusson, Feb. 21, 1904, Albuquerque, N.M., to Harvey Butler and Clara May (Huning) Fergusson. Father, attorney. Grad. Ethical Culture H.S., N.Y.C., 1921; attended Harvard Univ., 1921–23; grad. Oxford Univ., England, B.A. (Rhodes Scholar) 1926. Studied at American Laboratory Th., N.Y.C., 1926–30. Married Jan. 16, 1931, to Marion Crowne, actress, educator (dec. Aug. 11, 1959); one son, one daughter; married July 1962 to Peggy Watts Kaiser, painter, educator. Member of Authors Guild; P.E.N. Address: (home) P.O. Box 143, Kingston, NJ 08528, tel. (609) WA 1-8136; (bus.) c/o Princeton Univ., Princeton, NJ 08540.

He was professor of comparative literature at Rutgers Univ. (1953–69); drama critic for *The Bookman Magazine* (1930–32); member of the editorial board of *Comparative Literature;* lecturer and executive secretary at the New Sch. for Social Research (1932–34); professor of drama and humanities at Bennington (Vt.) Coll. (1934–47); visiting professor of English at Indiana Univ. (1952–53); and general editor of the Laurel Shakespeare series (1957–to date).

Published Works. Mr. Fergusson translated Sophocles' *Electra;* wrote *Idea of a Theater: A Study of Ten Plays* (1949); *Plays of Molière: A Critical Introduction* (1950); *Dante's Drama of the Mind* (1953); *Human Image in Dramatic Literature* (1957); *Poems 1926–61* (1962); *Dante* (1965); *Shakespeare: The Pattern in His Carpet* (1970); and critical essays.

Awards. Mr. Fergusson received the Literature Award from the National Inst. of Arts and Letters (1953); and the Christian Gauss Award (1953) for *Dante's Drama of the Mind.* He became a member of the National Institute of Arts and Letters in 1962.

FERRER, JOSÉ. Actor, director, producer. b. José Vicente Ferrer, Jan. 8, 1912, Santurce, Puerto Rico, to Rafael and Maria Providencia (Cintron) Ferrer. Father, lawyer. Grad. Princeton Univ., B.A. 1933. Married Dec. 8, 1938, to Uta Hagen, actress (marr. dis. 1948); one daughter; married June 9, 1948, to Phyllis Hill, actress (marr. dis. 1953); married July 13, 1953, to Rosemary Clooney, singer; three sons, two daughters. Member of AEA; SAG; AFTRA; AGMA; AFM; DGA; ALA; Princeton Club; The Players.

Theatre. Mr. Ferrer made his first professional appearance playing in a showboat melodrama, "The Periwinkle," which played one-night stands on Long Island Sound (Summer 1934); and was assistant stage manager and appeared in walk-on parts at the Suffern (N.Y.) Country Playhouse (Summer 1935).

He made his Bway debut as the Second Policeman in *A Slight Case of Murder* (48 St. Th., Sept. 11, 1935); performed at the Country Playhouse (Suffern, N.Y., Summer 1935); appeared as the Lippincott in *Spring Dance* (Empire, N.Y.C., Aug. 25, 1936); Dan Crawford in *Brother Rat* (Biltmore, Dec. 16, 1936); and Frederick L. Parsons in *In Clover* (Vanderbilt, Oct. 13, 1937).

His first directorial assignment was Princeton University's Triangle Club's annual production, *Fol-de-Roi* (Princeton, N.J., 1937), which also toured. He appeared as Vergez in *How To Get Tough About It* (Martin Beck Th., N.Y.C., Feb. 8, 1938); Billy Gashade in *Missouri Legend* (Empire, Sept. 19, 1938); Saint Julian in *Mamba's Daughters* (Empire, Jan. 3, 1939); Victor d'Alcale in *Key Largo* (Ethel Barrymore Th., Nov. 27, 1939); and as Lord Fancourt Babberley in *Charley's Aunt* (Cort, Oct. 17, 1940); and produced and directed the pre-Bway tryout of *The Admiral Had a Wife,* in which he appeared as the Admiral. This comedy was scheduled to open in N.Y.C., Dec. 7, 1941, but was cancelled because it dealt with Pearl Harbor.

With Frank Mandel, he directed *Vickie,* in which he appeared as George Roberts (Plymouth, Sept. 22, 1942); succeeded (Feb. 1943) Danny Kaye as Jerry Walker in *Let's Face It* (Imperial, Aug. 17, 1942); appeared as Iago in Paul Robeson's *Othello* (Shubert, Oct. 19, 1943), and toured with it (1943–44); produced and directed *Strange Fruit* (Royale, Nov. 29, 1945); toured as Sandor Turai in *The Play's the Thing;* appeared in the title role in *Cyrano de Bergerac* (Alvin, N.Y.C., Oct. 8, 1946); and toured as Kenneth Bixby in *Goodbye Again* and Leo in *Design for Living* (Summer 1947).

He was general director of the NY City Theatre Co. at the NY City Ctr., where he appeared in the title role in *Volpone,* which he adapted with Richard Whorf and Richard Barr (Jan. 8, 1948); played Mr. Manningham in *Angel Street* (Jan. 22, 1948); in a program of one-act works by Chekhov, entitled *Four One-Act Comedies,* directed *A Tragedian in Spite of Himself,* played Gregory Smirnov in *The Bear,* appeared in the solo role of Ivan Nyukhin in *On the Harmfulness of Tobacco,* and directed *The Wedding* (Feb. 5, 1948). Also at the NY City Ctr., he appeared as Jeremy in *The Alchemist* (May 6, 1948); directed the four one-act plays which comprise *S.S. Glencairn* (May 20, 1948), appearing as Fat Joe in *The Long Voyage Home;* and directed and played Felix and the Yellow Commander in *The Insect Comedy* (June 5, 1948).

Mr. Ferrer appeared as Oliver Erwenter in *The Silver Whistle* (Biltmore, Nov. 24, 1948); directed and appeared as Oscar Jaffe in *Twentieth Century* (ANTA, Dec. 24, 1950), directed and produced *Stalag 17* (48 St. Th., May 8, 1951); directed *The Fourposter* (Ethel Barrymore Th., Oct. 24, 1951); produced, directed, and appeared as Jim Downs in *The Shrike* (Cort, Jan. 15, 1952); produced and directed *The Chase* (Playhouse, Apr. 15, 1952); and directed *My Third Angels* (Morosco, May 11, 1953).

At NY City Ctr., he played his original role in and directed, with Joseph Kramm, *The Shrike* (Nov. 25, 1953); played the title role in *Richard III* (Dec. 9, 1953), Lord Fancourt Babberley in *Charley's Aunt,* which he also directed (Dec. 22, 1953); directed and played his original role in *Cyrano de Bergerac* (Dec. 11, 1953); and directed *The Fourposter* (NY City Ctr., Jan. 1, 1955). He was co-author, with Al Morgan, of the book for *Oh, Captain,* which he also directed (Alvin, Feb. 4, 1958); produced, directed, and appeared in the title role in *Edwin Booth* (46 St. Th., Nov. 24, 1958); and directed *The Andersonville Trial* (Henry Miller's Th., Dec. 29, 1959).

He made his operatic debut in the title role in *Gianni Schicchi* (Sante Fe Opera Co., N.M., 1960): sang the same role at the Brooklyn (N.Y.) Academy of Music (1960); sang Amonasro in *Aïda* (Beverly Hills Opera Co., Calif., 1961); and appeared as the Prince Regent in *The Girl Who Came to Supper* (Bway, N.Y.C., Dec. 8, 1963). Mr. Ferrer played Pseudolus in *A Funny Thing Happened on the Way to the Forum* (Coconut Grove Playhouse, Miami, Fla., Jan. 12, 1965; and Tappan Zee Playhouse, Nyack, N.Y., Sept. 6, 1965); appeared as Dr. Coppelius in the ballet *Coppelia* (Academy Royale Th., Palm Beach, Fla., Apr. 1–3, 1965); played multiple leading roles in *Little Me* (Mineola Playhouse, N.Y., Apr. 22, 1965); Phineas Fogg in *Around the World in 80 Days* (tour, Summer 1965); the title role in *Oedipus Rex* (Salt Lake City, Utah, Feb. 1966); replaced (May 28–June 12, 1966) Richard Kiley in the role of Miguel de Cervantes (Don Quixote) in *Man of La Mancha* (ANTA Washington Square, N.Y.C., Nov. 22, 1965); which he subsequently toured (national company, 1966–67); played Quentin in *After the Fall* (Coconut Grove Playhouse, Miami, Fla., Feb. 1, 1966); and succeeded (Apr. 11, 1967) John Cullum in the role of Don Quixote in the N.Y.C. Company of *Man of La Mancha* (ANTA Washington Square, N.Y.C., Nov. 22, 1965).

Films. Mr. Ferrer appeared in *Joan of Arc* (RKO, 1948); *Whirlpool* (1949); *Crisis* (MGM, 1950); *Cyrano de Bergerac* (UA, 1950); *Anything Can Happen* (Par., 1952); *Moulin Rouge* (UA, 1952); *Miss Sadie Thompson* (Col., 1953); *The Caine Mutiny* (Col., 1945); *Deep in My Heart* (MGM, 1954); *The Shrike,* which he also directed (U, 1955); *The Cockleshell Heroes* (Col., 1956); *The Great Man,* which he also directed (U, 1956); *The High Cost of Loving* (MGM, 1958) and *I Accuse!* (MGM, 1958); directed *Return to Peyton Place* (20th-Fox, 1961), and *State Fair* (20th-Fox, 1962); and *Lawrence of Arabia* (Col., 1962); *Nine Hours to Rama* (20th-Fox, 1963); *Delay at Marienborn* (1963); played Cyrano in *Cyrano et D'Artagnan* (Cocinor, 1964); Herod Antipas in *The Greatest Story Ever Told* (UA, 1965); Rieber in *Ship of Fools* (Col., 1965); Mr. Marlowe in *Enter Laughing* (Col., 1967); and Hassam Bey in *The Young Rebel*

(Commonwealth, 1969).

Television. Mr. Ferrer appeared in the title role in *Cyrano de Bergerac* (Philco Television Hour, NBC, 1949); subsequently played in *What Makes Sammy Run?* (Philco Television Hour, NBC, 1959); and a repeat performance in *Cyrano de Bergerac* (Producer's Showcase, NBC, 1953). He has appeared on many dramatic series and has been a guest on all major talk shows and variety hours, has appeared in many special television productions, including *Kismet* (ABC); *A Case of Libel* (ABC) and *Gideon* (Hallmark Hall of Fame, NBC); and has narrated such television specials as *The Last Giant* (NBC) and *The Island Called Ellis* (NBC). His made-for-television movies include *The Aquarians* (NBC); and *The Cable Car Mystery* (CBS).

Awards. Mr. Ferrer received Donaldson awards for his performance in *Othello* (1944), and for his direction of and performance in *The Shrike* (1952); actor-of-the-year citation from George Jean Nathan (1945–50–51–52); Antoinette Perry (Tony) awards for his performance in *Cyrano de Bergerac* (1947), and for his direction of *Stalag 17, The Shrike,* and *The Fourposter,* and for his performance in *The Shrike* (1952); the American Academy of Arts and Letters Gold Medal for speech (1949); Motion Picture Academy (Oscar) Award for his performance in *Cyrano de Bergerac* (1950); New York Fencers Club Special Award of Merit; Linguaphone Inst. Annual Award for diction in films (1950); the Philadelphia section, Natl. Council of Jewish Women Award for his contribution to American culture (1952); *Variety* NY Drama Critics Poll for directing and acting (1952); Page One Award for dramatic art by the NY Newspaper Guild (1952); and the Federation of Motion Picture and Stage Actors of Cuba Annual Award for acting (1952).

Mr. Ferrer received the following honorary degrees: an M.A. from Princeton Univ. (1947); Doctor of Humanities from Univ. of Puerto Rico (1949); and a doctorate from Bradley Univ.

Recreation. Fencing, tennis, horseback riding, chess, painting, piano.

FERRER, MEL. Actor, director, producer. b. Melchor Gaston Ferrer, Elberon, N.J., Aug. 25, 1917, to Dr. Jose Maria and Marie Irene (O'Donohue) Ferrer. Grad. Canterbury Prep. Sch., 1935; attended Princeton Univ. 1935–37. Married Oct. 23, 1937, to Frances Pilchard (marr. dis.); one son, one daughter; married to Barbara C. Tripp (marr. dis.); one son, one daughter; re-married to Frances Pilchard (marr. dis.); married Sept. 25, 1954, to Audrey Hepburn, actress (marr. dis.); one son. Member of AEA; SAG.

Pre-Theatre. Writer, editor.

Theatre. Mr. Ferrer made his Bway debut as a dancer in *You Never Know* (Winter Garden Th., Oct. 2, 1938); and subsequently appeared in *Everywhere I Roam* (Natl., Dec. 29, 1938); played Peter Santard in *Kind Lady* (Playhouse, Sept. 3, 1940); a Reporter in *Cue for Passion* (Royale, Dec. 19, 1940); and Tracy Deen in *Strange Fruit* (Royale, Nov. 29, 1945); directed *Cyrano de Bergerac* (Alvin, Oct. 8, 1946); directed the pre-Bway tryout of *Heartsong* (opened Shubert, New Haven, Conn., Feb. 27, 1947; closed Walnut St. Th., Philadelphia, Pa., Mar. 29, 1947); directed and produced, with Charles R. Meeker, Jr., the pre-Bway tryout of *Strike a Match* (opened, American Th., St. Louis, Mo.; closed, Memphis, Tenn., Jan. 27, 1953); and played Ritter Hans in *Ondine* (46 St. Th., N.Y.C. Feb. 18, 1954).

Television. Mr. Ferrer was producer-director for NBC radio (1943–45) where he directed Land of the Free. The Hit Parade and the Hildegarde program: and has directed several segments of The Farmer's Daughter television series (ABC, 1963).

He has appeared on Lux Video Th. (CBS, 1953); Omnibus (CBS); Producers Showcase (NBC) Zane Grey Th. (CBS); Bob Hope Chrysler Th. (NBC); and Search (NBC).

Published Works. He wrote the children's book *Tito's Hat* (1940).

FERRIS, BARBARA. Actress. b. Barbara Gillian Ferris, 1943, London, England. Father, publican. Married 1962 to John Quested, film producer. Member of British AEA. Address: c/o Richard Hatton, Ltd., 17a Curzon St., London W1, England.

Theatre. Miss Ferris began her career as a dancer at age fifteen. Her first major appearance was as Nellie in *Sparrows Can't Sing* (Th. Royal, Stratford, England, Aug. 1960; Wyndhams Th., London, Mar. 29, 1961). She played Cinderella in *The Merry Roosters Panto* (Wyndham's Th., Dec. 17, 1963); Jess and Prunella Flack in *A Kayf Up West* (Stratford, East, Mar. 10, 1964); First Girl in *Carving a Statue* (Th. Royal, London, Sept. 17, 1964); and appeared in *Honey, I'm Home* (Leatherhead, England, Nov. 24, 1964). At the Royal Court Th., London, she played Pam in *Saved* (Nov. 3, 1965), Moll in *A Chaste Maid in Cheapside* (Jan. 13, 1966); and Nancy in *The Knack* (Feb. 17, 1966); subsequently played Marion in *There's a Girl in My Soup* (Globe, June 15, 1966), a role in which she also made her American debut (Music Box, N.Y.C., Oct. 18, 1967); Ann in *Slag* (Royal Court, London, May 1970); Jill Tanner in *Butterflies Are Free* (Apollo, Nov. 4, 1970); Begonia Brown in *Geneva* (Mermaid, Nov. 8, 1971); appeared in *Hedda Gabler* (London, 1972–73 season); played Marie-Louise Durham in *The Constant Wife* (Albery, Sept. 19, 1973); and Leslie in *Alphabetical Order* (Hampstead Th. Club, Mar. 11, 1975; May Fair Th., Apr. 8, 1975).

Films. Miss Ferris has appeared in *Sparrows Can't Sing* (Janus, 1963); *Term of Trial* (WB, 1963); *Children of the Damned* (MGM, 1964); *Having a Wild Weekend* (WB, 1965); *The Girl Getters* (AI, 1966); *Interlude* (Col., 1968); and *A Nice Girl Like Me* (Avco Embassy, 1969).

FEUER, CY. Producer, director. b. Jan. 15, 1911, New York City, to Herman and Ann (Abrams) Feuer. Father, theatrical general manager. Attended Juilliard Sch. of Music, 1928–32. Married January 20, 1945, to Posy Greenberg; two sons. Served USAAF, 1942–45; rank, Capt. Member of AFM, Locals 802 and 47. Address: 505 Park Ave., New York, NY 10022, tel. (212) PL 9-4004.

Pre-Theatre. Trumpet player in pit orchestras at movie theatres, band musician.

Theatre. Mr. Feuer produced, with Ernest Martin, the musicals, *Where's Charley?* (St. James, N.Y.C., Oct. 11, 1948); *Guys and Dolls* (46 St. Th., Nov. 24, 1950); *Can-Can* (Shubert, May 7, 1953); *The Boy Friend* (Royale, Sept. 30, 1954); *Silk Stockings,* which he also directed (Imperial, Feb. 24, 1955); *Whoop-Up,* which he directed and co-authored (Shubert, Dec. 22, 1958); *How To Succeed in Business without Really Trying* (46 St. Th., Oct. 14, 1961); *Little Me,* which he directed, with Bob Fosse (Lunt-Fontanne, Nov. 17, 1962); *Skyscraper,* which he directed (Lunt-Fontanne, Nov. 13, 1965); *Walking Happy,* which he directed (Lunt-Fontanne, Nov. 26, 1966); and *The Goodbye People* (Ethel Barrymore Th., Dec. 3, 1968).

Messrs. Feuer and Martin purchased the Lunt-Fontanne Th. (July 1964) and sold it to Max and Stanley Stahl (Mar. 1965).

In Sept. 1975, Messrs. Feuer and Martin were named to succeed Edwin Lester as managing directors of the Los Angeles and San Francisco Civic Light Opera (beginning with the 1976 season).

Films. Mr. Feuer was head of the music dept. (and a musical dir. and composer) for Republic Pictures (1938–42, 1945–47).

He produced, with Mr. Martin, *Cabaret* (AA, 1972).

Awards. Mr. Feuer received NY Drama Critics' Circle awards and Antoinette Perry (Tony) awards for *Guys and Dolls* (1951) and *How To Succeed in Business without Really Trying* (1962).

FICHANDLER, ZELDA. Producer, director. b. Zelda Diamond, Sept. 18, 1924, Boston, Mass., to Harry and Ida (Epstein) Diamond. Father, scientist, engineer and inventor for whom the Harry Diamond Laboratories of the US Army were named. Grad. Woodrow Wilson H.S., Washington, D.C., 1941; Cornell Univ. (Russian language and literature) B.A. (Phi Beta Kappa) 1945; George Washington Univ., M.A. (dramatic arts) 1950. Honorary degree Doctor of Humane Letters, Hood Coll., 1962. Married Feb. 17, 1946, to Thomas C. Fichandler, executive director, Arena Stage; two sons. Member of Theatre Communication Group (member exec. comm.); Amer. Council of Learned Societies. Address: (home) 3120 Newark St., N.W., Washington, DC tel. EM 2-5528; (bus.) Arena Stage, 6th and M Sts., S.W., Washington, DC 20024, tel. (202) 347-0931.

Pre-Theatre. Research analyst, military intelligence, Russian division.

Theatre. Mrs. Fichandler founded (in 1950, with Edward Mangum) the Arena Stage, a professional resident theatre in Washington, D.C. As producing director of the Arena Stage, she has presented more than 200 productions (see Arena Stage elsewhere for complete list), of which she directed the following: *The Firebrand* (Oct. 2, 1950); *The Playboy of the Western World* (Jan. 3, 1951); *The Adding Machine* (Feb. 5, 1951); *The Inspector General* (Mar. 20, 1951); *Twelfth Night* (June 5, 1951; Dec. 26, 1951); *The Importance of Being Earnest* (July 25, 1951; May 27, 1952); *Tonight at 8:30* (Nov. 5, 1952); *The Country Wife* (Feb. 17, 1953); *Boy Meets Girl* (June 23, 1953); *A Phoenix Too Frequent, The Happy Journey,* and *The Bad Angel,* a triple bill (Sept. 1, 1953); *Charley's Aunt* (Dec. 9, 1953); *Blithe Spirit* (Mar. 30, 1954); *Room Service* (June 15, 1954); *Golden Boy* (Nov. 24, 1954); *The World of Sholom Aleichem* (Feb. 15, 1955); *The Mousetrap* (May 17, 1955); *Dream Girl* (Feb. 19, 1957); *Witness for the Prosecution* (May 7, 1957); *Answered the Flute* (Nov. 19, 1957); *The Drowning Version* and *Apollo,* a double bill (Feb. 11, 1958); *Romeo and Juliet* (Mar. 11, 1958); *The Hollow* (Dec. 16, 1958); *The Lady's Not for Burning* (Apr. 7, 1959); *Six Characters in Search of an Author* (Jan. 10, 1961); *Silent Night, Lonely Night* (Feb. 7, 1961); *Once in a Lifetime* (Oct. 23, 1962); *Twelve Angry Men* (Jan. 15, 1963); *The Devils* (Oct. 30, 1963); *Enrico IV* (Apr. 22, 1963); *The Skin of Our Teeth* (Dec. 2, 1965); *The Three Sisters* (Feb. 10, 1966); *The Iceman Cometh* (1967–68 season); *Six Characters in Search of an Author* (1968–69 season); *Edith Stein* (1969–70 season); *The Night Thoreau Spent in Jail* (1970–71 season); and *The Ascent of Mount Fuji* (June 1975).

The Arena Stage has occupied three homes since its founding; the first, a 247-seat theatre, opened with *She Stoops to Conquer* (Aug. 16, 1950) and closed with the Amer. premiere of *The Mousetrap* (May 17, 1955); the second, a 500-seat theatre, opened 16 months later with the expanded version of *A View from the Bridge* (Nov. 7, 1956); closed with *Man and Superman* (May 2, 1961); and in the Fall of 1961, Arena Stage became located in its permanent new home in Washington's Southwest, opening with *The Caucasian Chalk Circle* (Oct. 31, 1961). A second auditorium, the Kreeger Th., was added to the structure and opened with *The Ruling Class* (Jan. 15, 1971).

The Arena Stage received the Margo Jones Award (1971).

FICKETT, MARY. Actress. b. May 23, Bronxville, N.Y., to Homer and Mary (Stewart) Fickett. Father, radio director. Grad. Riverdale (N.Y.) Country Day Sch. for Girls, 1945; attended Wheaton Coll., 1945–46. Studied acting at Neighborhood Playhouse Sch. of the Th., N.Y.C., 1946–48. Married Oct. 26, 1958, to James Congdon, actor. Relatives in theatre: sister-in-law, Melisande Congdon, singer. Member of AEA; AFTRA; SAG. Address: (home) 43 Fifth Ave., New York, NY 10003, tel. Chelsea 3-2592; (bus.) c/o Frank Cooper Associates, 680 Fifth Ave., New York, NY 10019, tel. Plaza 7-1100.

Theatre. Miss Fickett first performed as an apprentice at the Cape Playhouse (Dennis, Mass., 1946); subsequently made her N.Y.C. debut in *The Old Lady Says No* (Mansfield, Feb. 17, 1948); played Katie in *I Know My Love* (Shubert, Nov. 2, 1949) and Sissie in the tour of the same play; played Maman in the national company of *The Happy Time* (opened Cass, Detroit, Mich., Oct. 22, 1951; closed Blackstone, Chicago, Ill., Jan. 1, 1952); succeeded to the role of Laura in *Tea and Sympathy* (Ethel Barrymore Th., N.Y.C., Sept. 30, 1953); played Eleanor Roosevelt in *Sunrise at Campobello* (Cort, Jan. 30, 1958); and Carol Pringle in *Love and Kisses* (Music Box, Dec. 18, 1963).

Films. She appeared in *Man on Fire* (MGM, 1957); and *Kathy O'* (U, 1958).

Television and Radio. She has performed on such radio programs as Music for Fun, Let's Pretend, and Theatre Guild of the Air.

She made her first television appearance (1953); later appeared on the daytime serial Portia Faces Life (1954); and was the hostess of Calendar (CBS, 1961–63).

Awards. She received the *Theatre World* Award (1954) for her performance as Laura in *Tea and Sympathy*..

FIEDLER, JOHN. Actor. b. John Donald Fiedler, Feb. 3, 1925, Plateville, Wis., to Donald and Margaret Fiedler. Father, salesman. Grad. Shorewood H.S., Milwaukee, Wis., 1943; Neighborhood Playhouse Sch. of the Th., N.Y.C., 1947; studied with Sanford Meisner and at Robert Lewis Workshop, N.Y.C. Served USN, 1945–46; rank, Yeoman 3/C. Member of AEA; SAG; AFTRA. 1310 N. Sweetzer St., Los Angeles, CA 90069, tel. (213) CR 5-6724.

Theatre. With the Experimental Theatre (under the auspices of ANTA), Mr. Fiedler played "a Student" in *Danny Larkin* (Lenox Hill Playhouse, N.Y.C., May 8, 1948), and Paw in *Cock-a-Doodle Doo* (Lenox Hill Playhouse, Feb. 26, 1949); he performed in a USO cross-country tour of *The Milky Way* (May–Oct., 1949); and on tour as Alfred in *The Happy Time* (Cass, Detroit, Mich.; Blackstone, Chicago, 1950).

He played Medvedenko in *The Seagull* (Phoenix, N.Y.C., May 11, 1954); Johnny Colton Smith in *Sing Me No Lullaby* (Phoenix, Oct. 14, 1954); Cy Milton in *One Eye Closed* (Bijou, Nov. 24, 1954); Squeak in a revival of *Billy Budd* (Masquers, May 2, 1955); Buckley in *The Terrible Swift Sword* (Phoenix, Nov. 15, 1955); Bill Pfeiffer in *Howie* (46 St. Th., Sept. 17, 1958); Mr. Karl Linder in *A Raisin in the Sun* (Ethel Barrymore Th., Mar. 11, 1959); Lew in *Harold* (Cort, Nov. 29, 1962); Vinnie in *The Odd Couple* (Plymouth, Mar. 10, 1965); Prof. Willard in a revival of *Our Town* (ANTA Th., Nov. 27, 1969); and Father Jerome in *The Mind with the Dirty Man* (Center Th. Group, Mark Taper Forum, Los Angeles, July 12, 1972).

Films. Mr. Fiedler has appeared in *Twelve Angry Men* (UA, 1957); *Stage Struck* (Buena Vista, 1958); *That Kind of Woman* (Par., 1959); *A Raisin in the Sun* (Col., 1961); *That Touch of Mink* (U, 1962); *The World of Henry Orient* (UA, 1964); *Kiss Me Stupid* (Lopert, 1964); *Girl Happy* (MGM, 1965); *A Fine Madness* (WB, 1966); *Fitzwilly* (UA, 1967); *The Ballad of Josie* (U, 1968); as Vinnie in *The Odd Couple* (Par., 1968); in *Rascal* (Buena Vista, 1969); *True Grit* (Par., 1969); *The Great Bank Robbery* (WB, 1969); *Suppose They Gave a War and Nobody Came?* (Cinerama, 1970); *Making It* (20th-Fox, 1971); *Skyjacked* (MGM, 1972); and *The Deathmaster* (Amer. Intl., 1972).

Television. He is a frequent performer on television, having made more than 400 appearances on such shows as Dr. Kildare (NBC), Bonanza (NBC), Alfred Hitchcock Show (CBS), The Fugitive (ABC), Chrysler Th. (CBS), The Farmer's Daughter (ABC), Checkmate (NBC), Adventures in Paradise (ABC), Kraft Television Th. (NBC), Studio One, and US Steel Hour (CBS).

Recreation. Bridge, travel.

FIELD, CRYSTAL. Artistic director, director, actress. b. Crystal Libby Field, Dec. 10, to Fred and Fanny (Stoll) Field. Father, poet, teacher; mother, physician. Educ. P.S. 69 and 93; High School of Music and Art; Juilliard School; and Hunter Coll., all in N.Y.C. Professional training with Martha Graham, Charles Weidman, and José Limón (dance); Paul Mann, Morris Carnovsky, Amer. Shakespeare Acad. (acting); Fredericka Schmitz-Svevo (voice). Married Jan. 27, 1963, to George Bartenieff, actor; one son. Member of AEA; SAG; IASTA; AFTRA. Address: (home) 190 Riverside Dr., New York, NY 10024, tel. (212) EN 2-8911; (bus.) 113 Jane St., New York, NY 10014, tel. (212) 691-2220.

Theatre. Miss Field and her husband, George Bartenieff (q.v.), are artistic directors of Theater for the New City, which they founded in 1970 in association with Lawrence Kornfeld and Theo Barnes.

She made her stage debut in 1939 as the Grandmother in a production of *Puss in Boots;* apppeared off-Bway as the First Fury in *The Flies* (1947); made her summer stock debut at Mount Kisco (N.Y.) Playhouse in 1958 in *A Hatful of Rain* and *Three Men on a Horse:* was in *When I Was a Child* (41st St. Th., N.Y.C., Dec. 8, 1960); and appeared with the Repertory Th. of Lincoln Ctr. (ANTA Washington Sq. Th.) as the Secretary in *After the Fall* (Jan. 23, 1964), Donata in *Marco Millions* (Feb. 20, 1964), and the Scullery Maid in *The Changeling* (Oct. 29, 1964). She was in *Promenade* and *Devices* (Judson Poets' Th., Apr. 8, 1965); played Alice in *Istanboul* (Judson Poets' Th., Sept. 12, 1965); was in *The Madonna in the Orchard* (Cafe La Mama, Nov. 24, 1965); was in *Play I, Play II, Play III* (Judson Poets' Th., Dec. 16, 1965); and in the Playwrights Unit production *Saltflowers* (1965). As a member of the Theater of the Living Arts, Philadelphia, Pa., she was in *Room Service* (Nov. 1, 1966), played Nuala in *Beclch* (Dec. 20, 1966), was in *The Time of Your Life* (Feb. 7, 1967), and in *U.S.A.* (Mar. 28, 1967). She played Ibalya in *The Line of Least Existence* (Judson Poets' Th., N.Y.C., Mar. 15, 1968), and she was Alberta in *Molly's Dream* (Boston Univ. Writers Conference, Tanglewood, Mass., July 23, 1968), repeating her performance in a revised version of the play (New Dramatists' Workshop, N.Y.C., Dec. 5, 1968).

She was Mamma Too Tight in a staged reading of *Goin' a Buffalo* (American Place Th., N.Y.C., June 6–7, 1968); toured in *Room Service* (Mineola, N.Y.; Bucks County Playhouse, New Hope, Pa., 1968) and as Apple in Judson Poets' *In Circles* (July 1969). Her activities with the Theater for the New City since 1970 include direction of *The Celebration: Jooz/Guns/Movies/The Abyss* (Feb. 11, 1972), *Under Cover Cop* and *The Sky Salesman* (Sept. 9, 1972), *The Thing Itself* (Nov. 30, 1972), *Morning to Midnight* (May 24, 1973), *Ten Best Martyrs of the Year* (Nov. 1, 1973), *The Children's Army Is Late* (Mar. 8, 1974).

She directed *Ra-d-io (Wisdom): Sophia, Part One* (Dec. 5, 1974), in which she also played Sophia; *Charley Chestnut Rides the I.R.T.* (Apr. 10, 1975); and street plays presented free by Theater for the New City throughout the boroughs of N.Y.C. each summer, including *Mama Liberty's Bicentennial Party* (Aug.–Sept. 1975), which, with George Bartenieff and members of the Theater for the New City company, she wrote and in which she played Mama Liberty; and *Undercover Cop* (Sept. 1975).

Films. Miss Field played Hazel in *Splendor in the Grass* (WB, 1961).

Television. Miss Field appeared as the Nursemaid in For the People (CBS).

Recreation. Sailing, tennis, driving a car.

FIELD, LEONARD S. Producer, director. b. July 10, 1908, St. Paul, Minn. Father, motion picture theatre operator. Grad. Univ. of Minnesota H.S., 1926; Univ. of Minnesota, B.A. 1930. Studied violin with A. Pepinsky, Minneapolis, Minn., ten years, Joseph Achron, N.Y.C., one year; voice with A. Killeen, Minneapolis, two years Married Aug. 4, 1942, to Ruth Dietrich, actress (mar. dis. 1955); two daughters; married June 9, 1959, to Virginia Clayburgh, painter. Served US Army Signal Corps, 1943–45; rank, PFC. Member of ATPAM. Address: (home) 1100 Park Ave., New York, NY 10028, tel. (212) AT 9-4717; (bus.) 1697 Broadway, New York, NY 10019, tel. (212) 582-1577; 95 Eaton Square, London S.W.1, England tel. 01-235-2810.

Theatre. Mr. Field made his stage debut at the Shubert Th. (Minneapolis, Minn., 1932) where he was stage manager; subsequently played Willie and served as the stage manager for the Boston Co. tour of *Three Men on a Horse* (1935).

He was assistant director for *Symphony* (Cort. N.Y.C., Apr. 25, 1935); assistant director for the London production of *My Kingdom for a Cow* (Savoy, June 4, 1936); produced, with Leo Peters and Robert Weenolsen, *Lend Me Your Ears* (Mansfield, N.Y.C., Oct. 5, 1936); produced, with Jerome Mayer, *Good Hunting* (Hudson, Nov. 21, 1938); was general manager for *Angel Street* (John Golden Th., Dec. 5, 1941); for the Rosalind Russell tour of *Bell, Book and Candle* (opened Playhouse, Wilmington, Del., Dec. 21, 1951; closed Locust St. Th., Philadelphia, Pa., Mar. 14, 1953); for *Porgy and Bess* (Ziegfeld, Mar. 10, 1953), its subsequent US tour and its European tour (opened Rome, Italy, June 6, 1955).

He was company manager for *The Ponder Heart* (Music Box, Feb. 16, 1956); *Orpheus Descending* (Martin Beck Th., Mar. 21, 1957); produced *The Hostage* (Cort, Sept. 20, 1950), and its tour (opened O'Keefe Centre, Toronto, Can., Jan. 30, 1961; closed Geary, San Francisco, Calif., May 13, 1961); produced, with Oscar Lewenstein, *Luv* (New Arts, London, May 9, 1963); produced, with Michael White, *Hogan's Goat* (Dublin Festival, 1966); *3 Bags Full* (Henry Miller's Th., N.Y.C., Mar. 6, 1966); with Haila Stoddard and Mark Wright, *The Birthday Party* (Booth Th., Oct. 3, 1967); *The Au Pair Man* (Duchess Th., London, 1968); with N. Lawrence Golden and Sullivan Productions, *Little Boxes* (New, N.Y.C., Dec. 3, 1969); co-produced, with H. M. Tennet, Ltd., *Suzanna Andler* (Aldwych, London, 1973).

Radio. Mr. Field directed and performed on radio programs for the Mid West Studio, Minneapolis (1934).

Awards. His production of *The Hostage* was voted the best play by the Philadelphia, Pa., drama critics (1961).

Recreation. Art collecting, music.

FIELD, RON. Director, choreographer. b. Ronald Field, 1932(?), Washington Heights, Queens, N.Y. Grad. H.S. of Performing Arts, N.Y.C., 1951.

Theatre. Mr. Field began his career as a child (billed as Ronnie Field), appearing in the ensemble of *Lady in the Dark* (Alvin, N.Y.C., Jan. 23, 1941); at age 8; appeared in *Seventeen* (Broadhurst, June 21, 1951); was a replacement in the ensemble of *Kismet* (opened Ziegfeld, N.Y.C., Dec. 3, 1953) and appeared in the natl. tour (opened Shubert, New Haven, Apr. 25, 1955); and played Marcel and Pepe in the natl. tour of *The Boy Friend* (opened Shubert, New Haven, Nov. 28, 1955; closed Shubert, Philadelphia Jan. 5, 1957).

He choreographed *Anything Goes* (revived Orpheum, N.Y.C., May 15, 1962); *Nowhere To Go But Up* (Winter Garden, Nov. 10, 1962); at the St. Louis Municipal Opera (Summers, 1963–64); *Cafe Crown* (Martin Beck Th., N.Y.C., Apr. 17, 1964); *Show Boat* (revived State Th., Lincoln Ctr., July 19, 1966); *Cabaret* (Broadhurst, Nov. 20, 1966; first national tour, opened Shubert, New Haven, Dec. 23, 1967; second national tour, opened State Fair Music Hall, Dallas, Tex., Aug. 19, 1969; London company, opened Palace, Feb. 28, 1968); and *Zorba* (Imperial, N.Y.C., Nov. 17, 1968; first national tour, opened Philadelphia, Dec. 1969; second national tour, opened Bushnell Aud., Hartford, Conn., Sept. 11, 1970).

He directed and choreographed *Applause* (Palace, N.Y.C., Mar. 30, 1970; first national tour, opened Royal Alexandra Th., Toronto, Canada, Nov. 29, 1971; second national tour, Masonic Aud., Scranton, Pa., Sept. 22, 1972; and the London company, opened Her Majesty's, Nov. 16, 1972); directed and choreographed a revival of *On the Town* (Imperial, N.Y.C., Oct. 31, 1971); and directed and choreographed a tour of *Mack and Mabel* (Parker Playhouse, Ft. Lauderdale, Fla.; Miami Beach Th., Fla., Jan.–Feb., 1976).

For the NYC Opera, he choreographed the US premiere of *Ashmedai* (State Th., Lincoln Ctr., Apr. 1, 1976).

Television. As a dancer, he performed on more than 300 television shows in the 1950's. He has devised choreography for many shows including *Rodgers and Hart Revisited* (Stage 2, CBS); *Jerome Kern and the Princess* (Stage 2, CBS); Hollywood Palace (ABC); the Dean Martin Summer Show (CBS, 1967); the Ed Sullivan Show (CBS, 1967–68); Angela Lansbury's "Thoroughly Modern Millie" number for the Academy Award Show (ABC, Spring 1968); the *Bell Telephone Jubilee* (NBC, Mar. 26, 1976); *Pinocchio* (NBC, Mar. 27, 1976); etc.

Night Clubs. Mr. Field has staged club acts for Liza Minelli, Chita Rivera, Ann-Margret, Carol Lawrence, Gwen Verdon, Shari Lewis, etc.; and has staged shows at the Latin Quarter (N.Y.C., 1962); Carillon Hotel (Miami Beach, Fla.); Casino de Paris (Paris); Casino du Liban (Beirut, Lebanon, 1967); etc.

Awards. For *Cabaret*, Mr. Field received (1967) an Antoinette Perry (Tony) Award for choreography; and for *Applause*, he received (1970) Tony Awards for direction and for choreography, and Drama Desk Awards for direction and choreography.

FIELD, SYLVIA. Actress. b. Harriet Louisa Johnson, Feb. 14, 1901, Allston, Mass., to Eugene Malcolm and Ednah (Bishop) Johnson. Father, lawyer. Attended Arlington (Mass.) H.S., 1915–16. Married May 31, 1924, to Robert J. Frowhlich (marr. dis. June 1929); married Dec. 1930 to Harold Moffet (dec. Nov. 6, 1938); one daughter, Sally Moffet, actress; married Mar. 16, 1941, to Ernest Truex, actor. Member of AEA; AFTRA; SAG. Address: 3140 Reche Rd., Fallbrook, CA tel. 728-8677.

Theatre. Miss Field made her N.Y.C. debut as Joy and the Veiled Figure in *The Betrothal* (Shubert Th., Nov. 18, 1918); subsequently played Azalea in *Thunder* (Criterion, Sept. 22, 1919); toured in *Turn to the Right* (1919–20); played a season of stock (Hamilton, Ontario, Canada, Summer 1920); appeared with the Jessie Bonstelle Company (Detroit, Mich., Summer 1921); succeeded Leah Peck as Annabelle West in *The Cat and the Canary* (National, N.Y.C., Feb. 7, 1922), and played the part on tour (1922–23).

She played the title role in *Connie Goes Home* (49 St. Th., Sept. 6, 1923); Clare in *Cock o' the Roost* (Liberty, Oct. 13, 1923); Delight in *Mrs. Partridge Presents* (Belmont, Jan. 5, 1925); Jane in *The Butter and Egg Man* (Longacre, Sept. 23, 1925); the Gypsy in *The Little Spitfire* (Cort, Aug. 16, 1926); and Billie Moore in *Broadway* (Broadhurst, Sept. 16, 1926); appeared in stock in Baltimore, Md. (June 1927); played Melodie in *Behold This Dreamer* (Cort, N.Y.C., Oct. 31, 1927); Gwen in *The Royal Family* (Selwyn, Dec. 28, 1927); Princess Kukachin in *Marco Millions* (Liberty, Mar. 10, 1930); Columbo the Dove in *Volpone* (Liberty, Mar. 10, 1930), and toured in these two roles for the Theatre Guild; toured as Sulla in *R.U.R.* (Spring 1950); played Bee in *The Up and Up* (Biltmore, N.Y.C., Sept. 8, 1930); Jennifer Lee in *The Queen at Home* (Times Square Th., Dec. 29, 1930); Sally in *Give Me Yesterday* (Charles Hopkins Th., Mar. 4, 1931); Doris Sabin in *Just To Remind You* (Broadhurst, Sept. 7, 1931); Elizabeth Betts in *Caught Wet* (John Golden Th., Nov. 4, 1931); Jennie Adams in *Adam's Wife* (Ritz, Dec. 28, 1931); Mamie Kimmel in *Hilda Cassidy* (Martin Beck Th., May 4, 1933); Marie in the Players Club revival of *Uncle Tom's Cabin* (Alvin, May 29, 1933); Clara in *Birthright* (49 St. Th., Nov. 21, 1933); Sylvia Jillson in *Sing and Whistle* (Fulton, Feb. 10, 1934); Fanny Grey in *Autumn Crocus* (Shubert, Minneapolis, Minn., Nov. 1934); Sylvia Sheldon in *The Distant Shore* (Morosco, N.Y.C., Feb. 21, 1935); Leonora in *There's Always Juliet* (New Rochelle, N.Y., July 1935); appeared in *All This While* (Berkshire Playhouse, Stockbridge, Mass., July 1935); as Judy Linden in *The Shining Hour* (Newport Th., R.I., Aug. 1935); Lou in *Achilles Had a Heel* (44 St. Th., N.Y.C., Oct. 13, 1935); Lucy Hough in *Stick-in-the-Mud* (48 St. Th., Nov. 27, 1935); Fern Davidson in *I Want a Policeman* (Lyceum, Jan. 14, 1936); Jean Hammond in *Pre-Honeymoon* (Lyceum, April 30, 1936); and appeared in *The Bishop Misbehaves*, *Liliom*, and *Two Orphans* (Matunick, R.I., Summer 1936).

Miss Field played Pansy Washington in *Man* (National, N.Y.C., Oct. 17, 1936); Mrs. Robert Levy de Coudray in *Matrimony Pfd.* (Playhouse, Nov. 12, 1936); Una Perkins in *Something for Nothing* (Windsor, Dec. 9, 1937); appeared in *Susan and God*, and *Biography* (Littlewood Th., Showhegan, Maine, Summer 1939); played Florence in *Popsy* (Playhouse, N.Y.C., Feb. 10, 1941); Jennifer Griggs in *But Not Goodbye* (48 St. Th., Apr. 11, 1944); was standby for Dorothy Gish as Mrs. Holmes in *The Magnificent Yankee* (Royale, Jan. 22, 1946), and played the part in the national touring company (1946–47); played Sophie MacDonald in *Oh, Mr. Meadowbrook* (John Golden Th., N.Y.C., Dec. 26, 1948); appeared in *George Washington Slept Here*, and *Ah, Wilderness!* (Bucks County Playhouse, New Hope, Pa., Summer 1950).

Television. She has appeared on Search for Tomorrow (CBS); Philco Television Playhouse (NBC); Kraft Television Th. (NBC); Studio One (CBS); played Mrs. Wilson on the Dennis the Menace series (CBS); appeared on Mr. Peepers (NBC); Make Way for Tomorrow (Lux Video Th., CBS); and in *A Woman of Fifty* (Somerset Maugham Th.).

Recreation. Fishing, golf, raising avocados.

FINKLEHOFFE, FRED F. Producer, playwright, screenwriter. b. Feb. 16, 1911, Springfield, Mass., to Barney and Anni Finklehoffe. Father, merchant. Attended Augusta Military Acad., Ga.; grad. Virginia Military Inst., B.A. 1932; Yale Law Sch., L.L.B. 1935. Married Sept. 23, 1942, to Ella Logan, singer, (marr. dis. Nov. 23, 1954); married Feb. 1956 to Carolyn Jo Phillips, fashion consultant.

Theatre. Mr. Finklehoffe, with John Monks, Jr., wrote the play, *Brother Rat* (Dec. 16, 1936). With Mr. Monks and Sid Silvers, he wrote the book for the musical *Hi Ya, Gentlemen* (opened Horace Bushnell Memorial Hall, Hartford, Conn., Nov. 29, 1940).

He produced *Show Time* (Broadhurst, N.Y.C., Sept. 16, 1942); produced, with Paul Small, a West Coast production of *Big Time* (Curran, San Francisco, Calif., Mar. 1, 1943), which later toured; produced, with Mr. Small, *Laugh Time* (Shubert, N.Y.C., Sept. 8, 1943).

He presented the Jed Harris production of *The Heiress* (Biltmore, Sept. 29, 1947); was production assistant to Mr. Harris for *Red Gloves* (Mansfield, Dec. 4, 1948), and *The Traitor* (48 St. Th., Apr. 4, 1949).

He produced, with Richard W. Krakeur, *Affairs of State* (Royale, Sept. 25, 1950); wrote, with Leo Luberman, produced with Richard W. Krakeur, and directed the pre-Bway tryout of *Mike McCanley* (opened Geary, San Francisco, Calif., Jan. 29, 1951); co-produced a summer tryout production of *The Sun Looks Down* (Valley Playhouse, Holyoke, Mass., Sept. 8, 1952); produced, with Howard Hoyt and Reginald Hammerstein, and directed the musical *Ankles Aweigh* (Mark Hellinger Th., N.Y.C., Apr. 18, 1955); produced, with Mark Marvin and Gabriel Katzka, *Hide and Seek* (Ethel Barrymore Th., Apr. 2, 1957); and, with Lester Braunstein, produced the pre-Bway tryout of *Everybody Out, the Castle Is Sinking* (opened Colonial, Boston, Dec. 26, 1964; closed there Jan. 9, 1965).

Films. Messrs. Finklehoffe and Monk's play was adapted for a film, *Brother Rat* (WB, 1938); subsequently a sequel was made, entitled *Brother Rat and a Baby* (WB, 1940).

Mr. Finklehoffe was co-author of the screenplays for *Strike Up the Band* (MGM, 1940); *Babes on Broadway* (MGM, 1941); *For Me and My Gal* (MGM, 1942); *Meet Me in St. Louis* (MGM, 1944); wrote the screenplay for *Mr. Ace* (UA, 1946); was co-author of the screenplay and co-produced *The Egg and I* (U, 1947); wrote the screenplay for *Words and Music* (MGM, 1948); *At War With the Army* (Par., 1950); and was co-author of the screenplay for *The Stooge* (Par., 1952).

Television. Mr. Finklehoffe wrote *Which Are the Nuts, Which Are the Bolts?* (Richard Boone Show, NBC, 1964).

FINNEY, ALBERT. Actor, director. b. May 9, 1936, Salford, Lancashire, Eng., to Albert and Alice (Hobson) Finney. Father, bookmaker. Attended Salford Grammar Sch. Studied acting at RADA, London, Eng. Married 1957, to Jane Wenham, actress (marr. dis. 1961), one son; married Aug. 7, 1970, to Anouk Aimée, actress. Member of British AEA; SAG; AEA. Address: c/o Memorial Enterprises, Ltd., Sackville House, 40 Picadilly, London W.1, England.

Theatre. Mr. Finney made his stage debut while a student at Salford, playing the title role in *The Emperor Jones.* During 1956–58, he was a member of the Birmingham Repertory Co. and played Decius Brutus in *Julius Caesar*, the title roles in *Hamlet*, *Henry V*, and *Macbeth*, Francis Archer in *The Beaux' Stratagem*, Face in *The Alchemist*, and Malcolm in *The Lizard on the Rock*; appeared as Soya Marshall in *The Party* (New Th., London, May 28, 1958); with the Royal Shakespeare Th. Co. (Memorial Th., Stratford-upon-Avon); played Cassion in *Othello* (Apr. 7, 1959); Lysander in *A Midsummer Night's Dream* (June 2, 1959); First Roman Citizen in *Coriolanus* (July 7, 1959) in which he understudied Sir Laurence Olivier in the title role of Caius Marius Coriolanus and played it in one performance; and Edgar in *King Lear* (Aug. 18, 1959).

He played Ted in *The Lily White Boys* (Royal Court, Jan. 27, 1960); Billy Fisher in *Billy Liar* (Cambridge, Sept. 13, 1960); the title role in *Luther* (Th. Sarah Bernhardt, Paris, Fr., July 1961, Royal Court, London, July 27, 1961); Feste in *Twelfth Night* (Royal Court, Feb. 18, 1962); the title role in *Henry IV* (Citizens, Glasgow, Scot., Mar. 1963); directed his first production, *The Birthday Party* (Citizens, Apr. 8, 1963); and made his N.Y.C. debut, repeating the title role in *Luther* (St. James, Sept. 25, 1963).

He played Don Pedro in the National Theatre Co. production of *Much Ado About Nothing* (Old Vic, London, Feb. 16, 1965); was John Armstrong of Gilnockie in *Armstrong's Last Goodnight* (Festival Th., Chichester, July 6, 1965), which he restaged for a London production (Old Vic, Oct. 12, 1965); appeared as Jean in *Miss Julie* and Harold Gorringe in *Black Comedy* (Festival Th., Chichester, July 27, 1965; Old Vic, London, Mar. 8, 1966); and, through his Memorial Enterprises, presented *Spring and Port Wine* (Apollo, Jan. 3, 1966). He played the dual role of Victor Emmanuel Chandebise and Poche in *A Flea in Her Ear* (Old Vic, Feb. 8, 1966); was Bri in *Joe Egg* (Brooks Atkinson Th., N.Y.C, Feb. 1, 1968); Mr. Elliott in *Alpha Beta* (Royal Court Th., London, Jan. 30, 1972); Krapp in *Krapp's Last Tape* (Royal Court, Jan. 16, 1973); directed *The Freedom of the City* (Royal Court, Mar. 4, 1973); was O'Halloran in *Cromwell* (Royal Court, Aug. 15, 1973); and Phil in *Chez Nous* (Globe, Feb. 6, 1974).

Films. Mr. Finney made his debut in *The Entertainer* (Continental, 1960); subsequently appeared in *Saturday Night and Sunday Morning* (Continental, 1960); *The Victors* (Col., 1963); the title role in *Tom Jones* (Woodfall, 1963); in *Night Must Fall* (MGM, 1964); *Two for the Road* (20th-Fox, 1967); *Charlie Bubbles* (Regional Films, 1968); *Scrooge* (Natl. Gen., 1970); *Gumshoe* (Col., 1972); *Bleak Moments* (British Film Inst., 1973); and *Murder on the Orient Express* (Par. 1974).

Television. Among the productions in which he has appeared since his debut (Jan. 1956) are *View Friendship and Marriage*, *The Claverdon Road Job*, and *The Miser.*

Discography. Mr. Finney recorded *Romeo and Juliet* (Shakespeare Society, 1965).

Awards. For his portrayal of Martin Luther in *Luther*, he was named "best actor of the season" (Th. des Nations, Paris, 1961). For his performance in *Saturday Night and Sunday Morning*, he received the Varsity

Club most promising newcomer award (1961). He was nominated for the Academy (Oscar) Award (1964) for his performance in the title role in *Tom Jones.*

Recreation. Judo, golf, dancing, guitar.

FISHBEIN, FRIEDA. Author' representative. b. Mar. 7, 1895, Bucharest, Rumania, to Osias and Amelia Fishbein. Father, merchant. Educated in Europe and New Orleans, La. Member, American Arbitration Association. Address: 353 West 57th St., New York, NY 10019, tel. (212) CI 7-4398.

FISHER, JULES. Lighting designer. b. Jules Edward Fisher, Nov. 12, 1937, Norristown, Pa., to Abraham and Anne (Davidson) Fisher. Father, retailer. Grad. Norristown H.S., 1955; attended Pennsylvania State Univ., 1955–56; grad. Carnegie Inst. of Tech., B.F.A., 1960. Member of AEA; USITT; ANTA. Address: 267 E. 10th St., New York, NY 10009, tel. (212) CA 8-3153.

Theatre. Mr. Fisher's first assignment was as a lighting designer for a high school production of *January Thaw* (Mar. 1954); subsequently was assistant stage manager and carpenter at the Valley Forge Music Fair (Devon, Pa., Summer 1955), and was an assistant to the electrician in three productions during their pre-Bway tryouts in Philadelphia, Pa.; *The Most Happy Fella, The Ziegfeld Follies,* and *Mr. Wonderful* (all at the Shubert Th., 1956). He also designed the lighting for *Death of a Salesman, The Girl on the Via Flaminia* (Circle in the City Th., Philadelphia, Mar. 1956), and *End as a Man* (Circle in the City Th., Philadelphia, Apr. 1956).

At the Valley Forge Music Fair (Devon, Pa.), he was assistant stage manager (Summer 1956), and stage manager for *The Boy Friend* (Summer 1957); lighting designer and stage manager for *Fanny* (Camden County Music Fair, Summer 1957); lighting designer at the Playhouse-in-the-Park (Philadelphia, Summer 1958); for *Hatful of Rain* (YMHA, Pittsburgh, Pa., Winter 1958); and at the Mountain Th. (Braddock Heights, Md., Summer 1959). He was lighting designer for *All the King's Men* (74 St. Th., N.Y.C., Oct. 15, 1959); *Parade* (Players, Jan. 20, 1960); and *Tobacco Road* (Cricket, May 10, 1960); and lighting designer and stage manager for a tour of *West Side Story* (Summer 1960).

Mr. Fisher was lighting designer for *Here Come the Clowns* (Actors Playhouse, N.Y.C., Sept. 19, 1960); *Greenwich Village, USA* (One Sheridan Square, Sept. 28, 1960); *Marcus in the High Grass* (Greenwich Mews, Nov. 21, 1960); *Ballet Ballads* (74 St. Th., Jan. 3, 1961); *Donogoo* (Greenwich Mews, Jan. 18, 1961); *Cicero* (St. Mark's Playhouse, Feb. 8, 1961); *Tiger Rag* (Cherry Lane, Feb. 16, 1961); and was lighting designer for the musical productions at the Casa Manaña Th. (Fort Worth, Tex., Summer 1961).

He was lighting designer for *Go Show Me a Dragon* (Maidman, N.Y.C., Oct. 27, 1961); *All in Love* (Martinique, Nov. 10, 1961); *Red Roses for Me* (Greenwich Mews, Nov. 27, 1961); the *Hava Kohav* dance program (Kaufmann Concert Hall, YMHA, Nov. 1961); *Moon on a Rainbow Shawl* (E. 11 St. Th., Jan. 15, 1962); *The Banker's Daughter* (Jan Hus House, Jan. 22, 1962); *The Creditors* (Mermaid, Jan. 25, 1962); *Fly, Blackbird* (Mayfair, Feb. 5, 1962); *The Book of Job* (Christ Ch. Methodist, Feb. 9, 1962); *The Golden Apple* (York, Feb. 12, 1962); *This Side of Paradise* (Sheridan Square Playhouse, Feb. 21, 1962); *Nathan the Wise* (78 St. Th., Mar. 22, 1962); *Porgy and Bess* (NY City Ctr., Apr. 2, 1962); and *Half Past Wednesday* (Orpheum, Apr. 6, 1962).

Mr. Fisher was lighting designer for the Casa Manaña Th. (Ft. Worth, Tex., Summer 1962); and for the San Diego (Calif.) Shakespeare Festival (Old Globe Th., Summer 1962); designed the lighting for *O, Say Can You See!* (Provincetown Playhouse, N.Y.C., Oct. 8, 1962); *Riverwind* (Actors Playhouse, Dec. 12, 1962); *The Establishment* (Strollers Th. Club, Jan. 19, 1963); *The Love Nest* (Writers Stage, Jan. 25, 1963); and lighting designer for *An Evening with Maurice Chevalier* (Ziegfeld, Jan. 28, 1963). He was lighting designer for *Six Characters in Search of an Author* (Martinique, Mar. 7, 1963); lighting consultant for *Enter Laughing* (Henry Miller's Th., Mar. 13, 1963); lighting designer for *Best Foot Forward* (Stage 73, Apr. 2, 1963); *The Dragon* (Phoenix, Apr. 9, 1963); and for touring productions of *The Mikado* and *H.M.S. Pinafore* (opened Forrest Th., Philadelphia, Pa., Apr. 15, 1963). He was lighting consultant for *Wonderworld* (NY World's Fair, Apr. 22, 1963); and lighting designer for *A Midsummer Night's Dream* (NY City Ctr., Apr. 25, 1963); and *Don Giovanni* (NY City Ctr., Oct. 25, 1963).

Mr. Fisher designed the lighting for musicals at summer theatres and for the Pittsburgh (Pa.) Civic Light Opera (Summer 1963). During 1962–63, he was lighting designer for the Paper Mill Playhouse (Millburn, N.J.) and the Mineola Playhouse, Long Island, N.Y.); lighting designer for *Spoon River Anthology* (Booth Th., Sept. 29, 1963); lighting consultant for *Chips with Everything* (Plymouth, Oct. 1, 1963); and for *A Rainy Day in Newark* (Belasco, Oct. 22, 1963); lighting designer for *Telemachus Clay* (Writers Stage, Nov. 15, 1963); *The Ginger Man* (Orpheum, Nov. 21, 1963); *Ole! Ole!* (Little Fox, Dec. 14, 1963); and *The Trojan Women* (Circle in the Square, Dec. 23, 1963). He was lighting designer for *Anyone Can Whistle* (Majestic, Apr. 4, 1964); *High Spirits* (Alvin, Apr. 7, 1964); *The White House* (Henry Miller's Th., Apr. 19, 1964); *Wonderful World* (NY World's Fair, Apr. 1964); *The Subject Was Roses* (Royale, May 25, 1964); and *South Pacific* (O'Keefe Ctr., Toronto, Canada, July 6, 1964).

Mr. Fisher also designed lighting for *A Girl Could Get Lucky* (Cort, N.Y.C., Sept. 20, 1964); *Doctor Faustus* (Phoenix, Oct. 5, 1964); the NY City Opera's *Natalia Petrovna* (NY City Ctr., Oct. 8, 1964); *Gogo Loves You* (Th. de Lys, Oct. 9, 1964); *The Sign in Sidney Brustein's Window* (Longacre, Oct. 15, 1964); *P.S. I Love You* (Henry Miller's Th., Nov. 19, 1964); and he was technical consultant for *I Had a Ball* (Martin Beck Th., Dec. 15, 1964). He did the lighting for *Royal Flush* (pre-Bway opened Shubert Th., New Haven, Conn., Dec. 31, 1964; closed Shubert Th., Philadelphia, Pa., Jan. 23, 1965); for Pres. Lyndon B. Johnson's "Salute to Congress" (1965); for *Do I Hear a Waltz?* (46 St. Th., N.Y.C., Mar. 18, 1965); *The Decline and Fall of the Entire World as Seen Through the Eyes of Cole Porter Revisited* (Square East, Mar. 30, 1965); *Half a Sixpence* (Broadhurst, Apr. 25, 1965); *And Things That Go Bump in the Night* (Royale, Apr. 26, 1965); *Square in the Eye* (Th. de Lys, May 19, 1965); *Leonard Bernstein's Theatre Songs* (Th. de Lys, June 28, 1965); *Pickwick* (46 St. Th., Oct. 4, 1965); *The Devils* (Broadway Th., Nov. 16, 1965); *The White Devil* (Circle in the Square, Dec. 6, 1965); *The Yearling* (Alvin Th., Dec. 10, 1965); *New Cole Porter Review* (Square East, Dec. 22, 1965); *Monopoly* (Stage 73, Mar. 5, 1966); *Serjeant Musgrave's Dance* (Th. de Lys., Mar. 8, 1966); *Hooray! It's a Glorious Day. . . and all that* (Th. Four, Mar. 9, 1966); *The Office* (previews, Henry Miller's Th., Apr. 20–30, 1966); *Jeux* (NY City Ballet, State Th., Apr. 28, 1966); *The Kitchen* (81 St. Th., June 13, 1966); *A Hand Is on the Gate* (Longacre, Sept. 21, 1966); *Eh?* (Circle in the Square, Oct. 16, 1966); *Macbeth* (Arena Stage, Washington, D.C., Oct. 25, 1966); *The Threepenny Opera* (Billy Rose Th., N.Y.C., Oct. 27, 1966); and *Hail Scrawdyke!* (Booth Th., Nov. 28, 1966).

Mr. Fisher also did lighting for *Black Comedy* (Ethel Barrymore Th., Feb. 12, 1967); *You're a Good Man Charlie Brown* (Th. 80–St. Mark's, Mar. 7, 1967); *The Natural Look* (Longacre, Mar. 11, 1967); *You Know I Can't Hear You When the Water's Running* (Ambassador, Mar. 13, 1967); *Illya Darling* (Mark Hellinger Th., Apr. 11, 1967); *Little Murders* (Broadhurst, Apr. 25, 1967); a revival of *South Pacific* (NY State Th., June 12, 1967); *The Unknown Soldier and His Wife* (Vivian Beaumont Th., July 12, 1967); *A Minor Adjustment* (Brooks Atkinson Th., Oct. 6, 1967); *Scuba Duba* (New, Oct. 10, 1967); *The Trial of Lee Harvey Oswald* (ANTA, Nov. 5, 1967); *Iphigenia in Aulis* (Circle in the Square, Nov. 21, 1967); and *Before You Go* (Henry Miller's Th., Jan. 11, 1968). He did lighting for *The Grand Music Hall of Israel* (Palace, Feb. 6, 1968); *Here's Where I Belong* (Billy Rose Th., Mar. 3, 1968); *Kongi's Harvest* (St. Mark's Playhouse, Apr. 14, 1968); *Hair* (Biltmore, Apr. 29, 1968); *The Only Game in Town* (Broadhurst, May 20, 1968); *A Moon for the Misbegotten* (Circle in the Square, June 12, 1968); *The Happy Hypocrite* (Bouwerie Lane, Sept. 5, 1968); *The Cuban Thing* (Henry Miller's Th., Sept. 24, 1968); *The Man in the Glass Booth* (Royale, Sept. 26, 1968); and *Love Match* (previews: Palace West, Phoenix, Ariz., Nov. 3, 1968; Ahmanson Th., Los Angeles, Calif., Nov. 19, 1968–Jan. 4, 1969).

He did the lighting for Laura Nyro's concerts (1969–70); for *Canterbury Tales* (Eugene O'Neill Th., Feb. 3, 1969); *But, Seriously. . .* (Henry Miller's Th., Feb. 27, 1969); *The Watering Place* (Music Box, Mar. 12, 1969); *Someone's Comin' Hungry* (Pocket Th., Mar. 31, 1969); the Robert F. Kennedy Th. for Children production of *Peter and the Wolf* (NY City Ctr., Mar. 31, 1969); *Trumpets of the Lord* (Brooks Atkinson Th., Apr. 29, 1969); *Promenade* (Promenade Th., June 4, 1969); *Butterflies Are Free* (Booth Th., Oct. 21, 1969); and for the premiere season (1969–70) of the American Ballet Co., Elliot Feld director (Brooklyn Acad. of Music, Oct. 21–Nov. 1, 1969; Mar. 31–Apr. 12, 1970).

Other productions for which Mr. Fisher did lighting include *Sheep on the Runway* (Helen Hayes Th., Jan. 31, 1970); *Gantry* (George Abbott Th., Feb. 14, 1970); *Minnie's Boys* (Imperial, Mar. 26, 1970); *Dear Janet Rosenberg, Dear Mr. Kooning* (Gramercy Arts, Apr. 5, 1970); *Inquest* (Music Box, Apr. 23, 1970); *The Engagement Baby* (Helen Hayes Th., May 21, 1970); *Steam Bath* (Truck and Warehouse, June 30, 1970); and *Home* (Morosco, Nov. 17, 1970). Also *Soon* (Ritz, Jan. 12, 1971); Judith Anderson's *Hamlet* (Carnegie Hall, Jan. 14, 1971); *No, No, Nanette* (46 St. Th., Jan. 19, 1971); *Lolita, My Love* (pre-Bway, opened Shubert Th., Philadelphia, Pa., Feb. 15, 1971; closed Shubert Th., Boston, Mass., Mar. 27, 1971); *Lenny,* for which he was also co-producer (Brooks Atkinson Th., May 26, 1971); and a revival of *You're a Good Man Charlie Brown* (John Golden Th., June 1, 1971).

Mr. Fisher designed lighting for *Jesus Christ Superstar* (Mark Hellinger Th., Oct. 2, 1971); *Fun City* (Morosco, Feb. 2, 1972); *Pippin* (Imperial, Oct. 23, 1972); *Lysistrata* (Brooks Atkinson Th., Nov. 13, 1972); *Mourning Becomes Electra* (Circle in the Square/Joseph E. Levine Th., Nov. 15, 1972); *The Trials of Oz* (Anderson Th., Dec. 19, 1972); and *Joseph and the Amazing Technicolor Dreamcoat* (Albery, London, England, Feb. 16, 1973). Also *Seesaw* (Uris Th., N.Y.C., Mar. 18, 1973); *Uncle Vanya* (Circle in the Square, June 4, 1973); *Molly* (Alvin Th., Nov. 1, 1973); *Full Circle* (ANTA, Nov. 7, 1973); *Rachael Lily Rosenbloom and Don't You Ever Forget It* (previews, Broadhurst, Nov. 26–Dec. 1, 1973); *The Iceman Cometh* (Circle in the Square–Joseph E. Levine Th., Dec. 13, 1973); and he supervised the rock concert tour *Tommy* (1973).

Mr. Fisher did lighting for Liza Minelli's one-woman show, *Liza* (Winter Garden, N.Y.C., Jan. 6, 1974); for *Ulysses in Nighttown* (Winter Garden, Mar. 10, 1974); *Thieves* (Broadhurst, Apr. 7, 1974); *Billy* (Theatre Royal, Drury Lane, London, England, May 1, 1974); *Sgt. Pepper's Lonely Hearts Club Band on the Road* (Beacon, Nov. 17, 1974); was supervisor of and did the lighting for the David Bowie concert tour (1974); did the lighting for *Man on the Moon* (Little, Jan. 29, 1975); *Chicago* (46 St. Th., June 3, 1975); and supervised and did lighting for the Rolling Stones world tour (1975).

Films. Mr. Fisher has made five short experimental films.

Night Clubs. Mr. Fisher did lighting for *Hallelujah Hollywood* (MGM Grand Hotel, Las Vegas, Nev., Jan. 1974) and *Revue* (Le Scala, Barcelona, Spain, 1974).

Other Activities. He has been lighting designer for industrial shows including the Presbyterian Bi-Centennial Pageant (Syria Mosque, Pittsburgh, Pa., 1958); Cole of California Fashion Show (Savoy Hilton Hotel, N.Y.C., 1960); and the Bell Telephone Show (Commodore Hotel, N.Y.C., 1961).

Mr. Fisher has also been lighting consultant for architects and for many other projects, including Music Fairs, Inc.; the Miracle at Pentecost diorama, Dallas, Tex.; the IBM Presentation Ctr., Washington, D.C.; the School of Education Auditorium, NY Univ.; Harkness Th., N.Y.C.; the Minneapolis (Minn.) Orchestra Hall; and the St. Louis (Mo.) Art Museum. Theatres for which he has been consultant include Univ. of California at Santa Cruz; California Institute of the Arts, Valencia, Calif.; Circle in the Square Th., N.Y.C.; Deauville Star Th., Miami, Fla.; the Oberlin (Ohio) Inter-Arts Ctr.; Modular Th., San Angelo, Tex.; Laboratory Th., NY Univ.; Studio Th., Brooklyn Acad. of Music, N.Y.C.; Interama Amphitheater, Miami Lakes, Fla.; and Denver (Colo.) Symphony Hall, for which he was also lighting consultant.

Awards. Mr. Fisher received Antoinette Perry (Tony) awards for best lighting for *Pippin* (1973) and for *Ulysses in Nighttown* (1974), and he was a nominee for a Tony in 1972 for *Jesus Christ Superstar.* He also received special honors from the Joseph Maharam Foundation for his lighting for *Pippin.*

Recreation. Magic, music/film study and 16mm film making, inventing (i.e., remote control spotlight, etc.).

FISHER, LOLA. Actress, singer. b. Mar. 17, Yonkers, N.Y., to Charles Douglas and Lucile (Rockewell) Fisher. Father, salesman, designer; mother, nursery school owner. Attended New York Univ., 1945–46; Fordham Univ., Summers 1947–48; Alviene Sch., 1947; studied acting with Wyn Handman, Uta Hagen, Jane White, Curt Conway; voice with Sue Seton, thirteen years. Relative in theatre: aunt, Lola Fisher, actress. Member of AEA; AGA; AFTRA.

Pre-Theatre. Office worker, waitress, hat checker, camera girl.

Theatre. Miss Fisher made her first stage appearances in *Romantic Young Ladies* and *The Taming of the Shrew* (Rivington St. Playhouse, N.Y.C., 1948). She was a chorus member and understudied Nola Fairbanks in the revue, *A Night in Venice* (Jones Beach Marine Th., N.Y., Summer 1952) and was a member of the Radio City Music Hall chorus (1952–53).

She made her Bway debut as a member of the chorus in *My Darlin' Aida* (Winter Garden, Oct. 27, 1952); subsequently was a member of the chorus and was understudy in *By the Beautiful Sea* (Majestic, Apr. 8, 1954); She was a resident actress with the Pittsburgh (Pa.) Civic Light Opera Co. (Summer 1954); toured in an industrial show for the Frigidaire Co. (1955); was in the chorus and was understudy to Julie Andrews as Eliza Doolittle in *My Fair Lady* (Mark Hellinger Th., 15, 1956), succeeded Miss Andrews (Aug. 1956) and appeared in the role 116 times on Bway, repeating it for three weeks with the national touring company in the Midwest.

She played the Wife in a stock tour of *Oh, Captain!* (Valley Forge, Pa., Camden, N.J., 1959); Eliza Doolittle for nine weeks in the Russian touring company of *My Fair Lady* (Moscow, Leningrad, Kiev, 1960); Thea in *Fiorello!* (NY City Ctr., June 13, 1962), and repeated the role in Kansas City (Summer 1962); Sarah Brown in *Guys and Dolls* (Washington, D.C., Summer 1962; Dunes Hotel, Las Vegas, Nev., 1963); Eliza Doolittle in *My Fair Lady* (Municipal Opera, St. Louis, Mo., June 1964; Post Opera, Denver, Colo., July 1964); was in *Oh, What a Lovely War!* (Schoenberg Aud., UCLA, Los Angeles, Calif., Jan. 19, 1966); and in *Love and William Shakespeare* (Beverly Hills Playhouse, Calif., 1966).

Television and Radio. She has appeared on various radio shows, including the Woolworth Hour (CBS), Bandstand (NBC), and the Robert Q. Lewis Show (CBS).

She made her television debut on the Ted Mack Show (1951); from 1956–62, appeared as a guest singer on Tonight (NBC), Today (NBC), Tex and Jinx (NBC), Walter Winchell Show (NBC), and Arlene Francis Show (NBC). She has made guest appearances on both British radio and television (BBC, 1961).

Night Clubs. Miss Fisher made her night club debut in a girl trio, "The Mello Belles" (1949); subsequently, was a singer with the Sammy Kaye Band and also a member of the touring Kaydets (1951); performed a single act at the Society, Satire, and Bristol clubs (England, 1961); appeared in a hotel tour (So. Africa, Rhodesia, Kenya, 1961); and played at the Queen Elizabeth Hotel (Montreal, Can., 1962) and at the Hotel Astor (N.Y.C., 1962).

Recreation. Piano playing, swimming, tennis, drawing.

FISHER, NELLE. Dancer, director, choreographer. b. Ethelwyn Nellie Fisher, Dec. 10, 1914, Berkeley, Calif., to Clarence Earl and Mary Alma (Van Nuys) Fisher. Grad. Lincoln H.S., Seattle, Wash., 1932. Studied dance, music, and drama at the Cornish Sch., Seattle, Wash., with Caird Leslie, 1928–30; Lore Deja, 1931–33; Welland Lathrop, 1933–35; at the Neighborhood Playhouse Sch. of the Th., N.Y.C., 1936–38; with Martha Graham, N.Y.C., four years; Agnes de Mille, N.Y.C.; Louis Horst, four years; N.Y.C. Married Nov. 20, 1941, to George Hall, actor, writer (marr. dis. Apr. 6, 1951). Relative in theatre: sister Dorothy, dance director, Fisher Ballet Ctr., Seattle, Wash. Member of AGMA; AFTRA; AEA; AGVA; SAG, Cornish Sch. Alumni Assn.

Theatre. Miss Fisher first danced on stage in Port Townsend, Wash. as the Spirit of New Year (Jan. 1, 1925); later danced in concert with the Martha Graham Co. (N.Y.C., 1939–40); danced and choreographed *Daughter of Caprice* (Dock St. Th., Charleston, S.C., Feb. 4, 1941); was a dancer with the Radio City Music Hall Ballet Co. (N.Y.C., 1941–43); and choreographed and danced in *Six Dancers* (Kaufmann Aud., YMHA, Jan. 18, 1942).

She was a dancer, dance captain, and understudy to Sono Osato, premier danseuse in *One Touch of Venus* (Imperial, N.Y.C., Oct. 7, 1943); was an assistant for Agnes de Mille's ballet *Tally Ho!;* played a High School Girl in *On the Town* (Adelphi, Dec. 28, 1944); Sally in the pre-Bway tryout of *Shootin' Star* (opened Shubert, New Haven, Conn., Apr. 4, 1946; closed Shubert, Boston, Mass., Apr. 27, 1946); danced at the Tamiment (Pa.) Playhouse (June–Aug. 1946); and at the Utah Centennial in *The Promised Valley* (July 1947); appeared in the revue *Make Mine Manhattan* (Broadhurst, N.Y.C., Jan. 15, 1948); and danced again at the Tamiment (Pa.) Playhouse (June–Aug. 1949).

Miss Fisher choreographed *Razzle Dazzle* (Arena, N.Y.C., Feb. 19, 1951); at the Pittsburgh, (Pa.) Light Opera Co., danced in *High Button Shoes* and *One Touch of Venus* (July 1, 1952); at the St. Louis (Mo.) Municipal Opera, appeared as Emmy Lou in *Louisiana Purchase* (July 6, 1953) and played in *One Touch of Venus* (Aug. 3, 1953); played a Local Girl in *The Golden Apple* (Phoenix, N.Y.C., Mar. 11, 1954); was understudy (June 1954) for Joan Holloway as Claudine in *Can-Can* (Shubert, May 7, 1953); choreographed the national tour of *A Victor Herbert Festival* (Dec. 1954); danced in *On the Town* (Fox Valley Playhouse, Ill., July 1955); danced and choreographed at the Brandywine Music Box (Chester, Pa., June–Aug. 1956); choreographed an industrial show for the Reynolds Aluminum Co. (Waldorf-Astoria, N.Y.C., Nov. 26, 1956); and played Claudine in *Can-Can* (Buffalo Melody Fair, N.Y., June 1957).

She was choreographer-soloist for *The Best of Burlesque* (Carnegie Hall Playhouse, N.Y.C., Sept. 27, 1957); created *The Littlest Circus* (Carnegie Hall Playhouse, Oct. 12, 1957); toured as Polly in *He Who Gets Slapped* (Westport Country Playhouse, Conn., June 30, 1958); and as a dancer in *The Littlest Circus* (June 1958). She was choreographer at the Cincinnati (Ohio) Summer Opera Co. (June 1959); directed *Guys and Dolls* (Red Barn Th., Huntington, N.Y., Aug. 4, 1959); *Has Anyone Seen My Profit?* (Blackstone, Hotel, Chicago, Ill., Oct. 1959); her own production of *The Littlest Circus* (John Golden Th., N.Y.C., Dec. 26, 1959); choreographed and staged the musical numbers in *The Russell Patterson Sketchbook* (Maidman, Feb. 6, 1960); and was choreographer at the Cincinnati Opera Co. (Summers 1960–61).

Miss Fisher was director-soloist for a return engagement of *The Littlest Circus* (74 St. Th., N.Y.C., Jan. 1962); choreographed *The Golden Apple* (York, Feb. 12, 1962); toured with *The Littlest Circus* (Mar.–May 1962), including Toronto, Canada (O'-Keefe Ctr., Apr. 1962) and the Seattle World's Fair (May 1962); choreographed for the Cincinnati Opera Co. (June–July 1962); directed the Volkswagon Gala Convention (Waldorf-Astoria and Pierre hotels, N.Y.C., Oct. 1962); at the Vancouver (Canada) Intl. Festival, was choreographer for the operas, *Macbeth* and *The Merry Wives of Windsor,* the musical, *Floradora,* and the musical version of *Peter Pan* (May 1963); choreographed *Pocahontas* (Alhambra, Glasgow, Scotland, Oct. 9, 1963), later produced in London (Lyric, Nov. 15, 1963); directed the Woolknit Assn. fashion show (Rainbow Room, N.Y.C., June 4, 1964); her own show, *The Littlest Circus,* was produced (Oriental, Portland, Ore., July 12, 1964; Vancouver Festival, Queen Elizabeth Playhouse, July 20, 1964); and she created dances for a production of *Guys and Dolls* (Front St. Th., Memphis, Tenn., Feb. 17, 1966).

Films. She danced in *Up in Central Park* (U, 1948).

Television. Miss Fisher appeared on Variety Showcase (CBS, Nov. 30, 1946); American Song (NBC, 1948–49); Your Show of Shows (NBC, 1950–52); All Star Revue (NBC, Sept. 1952); the Kate Smith Show (NBC, Dec. 1952); and the Colgate Comedy Hour (NBC, Nov. 1952). She was a dancer and choreographed the series Melody Tour (ABC, July 1954); was a specialty dancer on Entertainment (ABC, Apr. 25, 1955); made appearances on the Home Show (NBC, Apr. 1956); Captain Kangaroo (CBS, Jan. 21, 1956); danced on The Arthur Murray Dance Party (CBS, Sept. 20, 1956); appeared on the Today Show (NBC, Feb. 8, 1959); directed and danced in *The Littlest Circus* (CBS, Nov. 14, 1963); and was dance consultant for George Rose Entertainers (CBS, 1964).

Night Clubs. Her first night club engagement was with Ron Fletcher in *Vanity Fair* (Vanity Fair Club, N.Y.C., Oct. 1946); subsequently choreographed the touring production *Cross Country* (opened The Latin Quarter, Boston, Mass., Nov. 1949); with Jerry Ross, appeared in *Dance Ballads* (Shoreham Hotel, Washington, D.C., 1950); with Jerry Ross, performed in *Dance Ballads* (Empire Room, Waldorf-Astoria, N.Y.C., Jan. 1951; Hotel Pierre, N.Y.C., May 6, 1952); danced at the Thunderbird Hotel (Las Vegas, Nev., Aug. 1952); Chase Hotel (St. Louis, Mo., Jan. 1953); and the Sans Souci Hotel (Montreal, Canada, Apr. 7, 1953).

Other Activities. Miss Fisher's concert appearances include the Young People's Concerts (Woolsey Hall, New Haven, Conn., Feb. 1956); the Hartford (Conn.) Young People's Symphony (Bushnell Aud., Feb. 27, 1956; Jan. 1951); Jacob's Pillow (Lee, Mass., Aug. 21, 1959); *The Littlest Circus* (Los Angeles Music Festival, Aug. 1961); Young People's Symphony with the Nelle Fisher Ballet (Detroit, Mich., Nov. 1961); the Hart Woodwind Quintet (Port Huron, Mich., Dec. 1961); the Baltimore (Md.) Symphony (Dec. 28, 1963); and at Tufts Univ. with her own ballet company (Medford, Mass., Mar. 13, 1964).

Awards. Miss Fisher was nominated for the Donaldson Award (1948) for *Make Mine Manhattan;* received a plaque from the US Army for the "All Army Entertainment Contest" (1957).

Recreation. Swimming, composing music, collecting small primitive musical instruments.

FITCH, JOSEPH. Educator, director. b. Joseph Clay Fitch, June 16, 1921, Springfield, Tenn., to Joseph Elwood and Annie (Dortch) Fitch. Father, lumberman. Grad. Springville, Tenn., H.S., 1938; Murray State Coll., B.S. 1942, M.A. 1946; Yale Univ., M.F.A. 1949; studied at Amer. Theatre Wing, N.Y.C., 1951. Married Sept. 10, 1948, to Jane Jones; two sons, one daughter. Served USMC, 1942–46, 1952–54; rank, Maj. Member of Kappa Delta Pi; Alpha Psi Omega; Lambda Chi Alpha; ANTA; SAA; Masons; Elks; Natl. Exchange Club;

Northwest Drama Conference; Rocky Mt. Theatre Conference (bd. of dir., 1957–58; vice-pres., 1958–59; pres., 1959–60); AETA (chairman, guidance and counselling projects, 1956–58; Theatre Arch. Consultant, 1958–to date; bd. of dir., 1963–65); Frontier Th. Research Center (assoc., 1961–to date). Address: (home) 1119 W. Curtiss, Bozeman, MT 59715, tel. (406) 586-9644; (bus.) Theatre Arts Dept., Montana State Univ., Bozeman, MT 59715, tel. (406) 994-3901.

He toured, as a child, with a repertory company throughout the Midwest and South (Fitch and Provo Tent Shows, 1933–38); in stock played character roles in *The Lawyer, Silver Cord, Tobias and the Angel*, and *Payment Deferred* (Univ. Th. Company, Lenox and Pittsfield, Mass., Summer 1947); and was managing director of the Loft Th. (Bozeman, Montana, 1962–to date), a community theatre playing a four-play season.

He was assistant editor of *Dramatics* (1956–61), is assistant editor of *Directory of American College Theatre* (1958–to date), and has done research and writing on the theatre and literature of East and Southwest Asia.

Recreation. Music, anthropology, fishing.

FITZGERALD, GERALDINE. Actress, director, singer, writer. b. Nov. 24, 1914, Dublin, Ireland, to Edward and Edith Fitzgerald. Father, attorney. Attended Dublin Art Sch., 1928. Married Nov. 1936 to Edward Lindsay Hogg, writer (marr. dis. 1946); one son; married Sept. 1946 to Stuart Scheftel, business executive; one daughter. Relatives in theatre: aunt, Shelah Richards, actress, director, producer; uncle, Denis Johnston, writer, educator. Member of AEA; AFTRA; SAG.

Pre-Theatre. Painter.

Theatre. Miss Fitzgerald first appeared on the stage in productions at the Gate Th. (Dublin, Ireland, 1932).

She made her Bway debut in the role of Ellie Dunn in *Heartbreak House* (Mercury Th., Apr. 29, 1938); subsequently appeared as Rebecca in *Sons and Soldiers* (Morosco, May 4, 1943); Tanis Talbot in the pre-Bway tryout of *Portrait in Black* (opened Shubert, New Haven, Conn., Dec. 27, 1945; closed Nixon, Pittsburgh, Pa., Jan. 12, 1946); played Jennifer Dubedat in *The Doctor's Dilemma* (Phoenix, N.Y.C., Jan. 11, 1955); Goneril in *King Lear* (NY City Ctr., Jan. 12, 1956); Ann Richards in *Hide and Seek* (Ethel Barrymore Th., Apr. 2, 1957); Gertrude in the American Shakespeare Festival production of *Hamlet* (Stratford, Conn., June 19, 1958); and The Queen in *The Cave Dwellers* (Greenwich Mews Th., N.Y.C., Oct. 15, 1961).

She was the 3rd Woman in *Pigeons* (New Playwrights Series II, Cherry Lane Th., May 3, 1965); in *Ah, Wilderness!* (Ford's Th., Washington, D.C., 1969); played Mary Tyrone in *Long Day's Journey into Night* (Promenade Th., N.Y.C., Apr. 21, 1971); wrote, with Brother Jonathan, and appeared in *Everyman and Roach* (Ethical Culture Soc., N.Y.C., Oct. 4, 1971); was in *Juno and the Paycock* (Hartke Th., Catholic Univ., Washington, D.C., Jan 7, 1972); wrote and directed, with Brother Jonathan, *Everyman at La Mama* (La Mama E.T.C., N.Y.C., Sept. 7, 1972); played Amy in *Forget-Me-Not Lane* (Long Wharf Th., New Haven, Conn., Apr. 6, 1973); the Grandmother in *The Widowing of Mrs. Holroyd* (Long Wharf Th., Nov. 16, 1973); and Essie Miller in *Ah, Wilderness!* (Long Wharf Th., New Haven, Conn., Dec. 20, 1974).

Films. Miss Fitzgerald's screen appearances include *The Turn of the Tide* (Rank, 1934); *The Mill on the Floss* (Standard, 1939); *Wuthering Heights* (UA, 1939); *Dark Victory* (WB, 1939); *A Child Is Born* WB, 1940); *Til We Meet Again* (WB, 1940); *Shining Victory* (WB, 1941); *Flight from Destiny* (WB, 1941); *The Gay Sisters* (WB, 1942); *Watch on the Rhine* (WB, 1943); *Ladies Courageous* (U, 1944); *Wilson* (20th-Fox, 1944); *The Strange Affair of Uncle Harry* (U, 1945); *Nobody Lives Forever* (WB, 1946); *O.S.S.* (Par., 1946); *Three Strangers* (WB, 1946); *So Evil My Love* (Par. 1948); *The Obsessed* (UA, 1951); *Ten North Frederick* (20th-Fox, 1958); *The Fiercest Heart* (20th-Fox, 1961); and *The Pawnbroker* (Landau, 1964).

Television. Miss Fitzgerald has appeared on many television programs, including *The Marble Faun* (Th. Hour, CBS, Oct. 1950); *To Walk the Night* (Robert Montgomery Presents, NBC, Oct. 1951); *The Daughter* (Schlitz Playhouse of Stars, CBS, Feb. 1952); *The Lawn Party* (Goodyear Playhouse, NBC, May 1954); *The Barretts of Wimpole Street* (CBS, June 1955); *Dodsworth* (Producers Showcase, NBC, Apr. 1956); *The Moon and Sixpence* (NBC, Oct. 1959); Naked City (ABC, Sept. 1961); The Nurses (CBS, Feb. 1964); The Defenders (CBS, Dec. 1964); and *The Best of Everything* (ABC, 1970). Her performance in the Long Wharf Th. production of *The Widowing of Mrs. Holroyd* was seen on Th. in America (PBS, 1974).

Concerts. Miss Fitzgerald appeared in concert readings (NY Cultural Ctr., N.Y.C., May 17, 1975); on the Countee Cullen Great Storyteller Series (Afro-American Total Th., Jan. 1975); and in the programs "An Evening of Street Songs and Clown Songs," with Andy Thomas Anselmo (Th. for the New City, May 17, 1975) and "Geraldine Fitzgerald Singing Songs of the Streets" (Circle in the Square, Mar. 7 and 14, 1976).

Awards. The Vernon Rice Award (1971) was given to the cast and director of *Long Day's Journey into Night* in which Miss Fitzgerald appeared as Mary Tyrone, and she was named in the *Variety* NY drama critics poll (1971) as best actress in a leading role off-Bway for the same performance.

Recreation. Painting.

FLAMM, DONALD. Producer. b. Dec. 11, 1899, Pittsburgh, Pa., to Louis and Elizabeth (Jason) Flamm. Father, traveling salesman. Grad. Commercial H.S., Brooklyn, N.Y., 1917. Attended New York Univ., exten. courses, 1917–18. Served OWI (1942–43); rank, Liaison Officer. Member of Catholic Actors Guild; charter member of the Jewish Theatrical Guild; Cinema Lodge; The Friars; Rockefeller Luncheon Club; Le Club; Club El Morocco; United Hunt Club; the Alpine (N.J.) Country Club; and, in London, Annabel's and The White Elephant. Address: (home) Closter, NJ 07624; (bus.) 25 Central Park West, New York, NY 10023.

Theatre. Mr. Flamm was assistant general press representative for the Shuberts (1918–20); with Peter Daubeny, produced *The Late Edwina Black* (Ambassadors' Th., London, Eng., June 1949), later retitled *Edwina Black* (Booth, N.Y.C., Nov. 21, 1950); and, with Donald Wolin, produced *The Brass Ring* (Lyceum, Apr. 10, 1952).

With Donald Wolin and Harold Schiff, he operated the Theatre-by-the-sea, Matunuck, R.I. (1953–57); with Oscar Lewenstein, Tony Richardson, and John Osborne, he operates the London producing firm of Oscar Lewenstein Plays, Ltd. The company has produced, in London, *Billy Liar* (Cambridge Th., Sept. 1960); in association with the English Stage Company, *Luther* (Phoenix, July, 1961); *My Place* (Comedy, Feb. 1962); *To Play with a Tiger* (Comedy, March 22, 1962); with Donald Albery, *Fiorello!* (Piccadilly, Oct. 1962); *All Things Bright and Beautiful* (Phoenix, Dec. 3, 1962); *Baal* (Phoenix, Feb. 10, 1963); in association with Donmar Productions, Ltd., and L.O.P., Ltd., *Semi-Detached* (Saville, Nov. 19, 1963); in association with Tennents and the English Stage Company, *The Seagull* (Queen's Th., Mar. 12, 1964. Mr. Flamm also produced, with Michael Myerberg, *What Did We Do Wrong?* (Helen Hayes Th., N.Y.C., Oct. 22, 1967); and, with Hillard Elkins, the touring *Golden Boy* (Auditorium Th., Chicago, Ill., Apr. 23, 1968; London Palladium, England, June 4, 1968). He co-produced *Spitting Image*, with Oscar Lewenstein in London (Duke of York's Th., Oct. 24, 1968) and with Zev Bufman in N.Y.C. (Th. de Lys, Mar. 2, 1969); and he co-produced, with Oscar Lewenstein, *The Giveaway* (Garrick Th., London, Apr. 8, 1969).

Television and Radio. Since 1960, Mr. Flamm has owned radio stations WMMM and WDJF-FM Westport, Conn.

He owned and was managing director of radio stations WMCA, N.Y.C. (1925–40), and WPCH, N.Y.C. (1927–32); operated Intercity Network with stations from Boston, Mass., to Washington, D.C. (1929–41); was the first broadcaster regularly to review Bway and London theatre openings on his intercity network (1925–27); and was co-owner of WPAT, Paterson, N.J. (1942–47).

Other Activities. Investments; real estate; former owner-operator Aldecress Country Club, Alpine, N.J.; co-owner of the La Salle Hotel, Washington, D.C.

Published Works. Mr. Flamm was publisher of *New York Amusements*, a weekly theatrical magazine (1920–29).

Recreation. Travel, theatre, hiking, winter sports.

FLANDERS, ED. Actor. b. 1934, Minneapolis, Minn. Married Ellen Geer, actress (marr. dis.); one son. Member of AEA; SAG; AFTRA.

Theatre. Mr. Flanders made his acting debut in Mr. Roberts (Globe San Diego); subsequently appeared with the San Diego National Shakespeare Festival (Old Globe Th.), playing Nick Bottom in *A Midsummer Night's Dream* (June 18, 1963); Autolycus in *The Winter's Tale* (June 26, 1963), and the Soothsayer in *Antony and Cleopatra* (July 26, 1963). With the Tyrone Guthrie Th. (Minneapolis, Minn.) he played Fluellen in *Henry V* (May 12, 1964); The Gentleman Caller in *The Glass Menagerie* (June 1, 1964); Petulant in *The Way of the World* (May 11, 1965); Yasha in *The Cherry Orchard* (June 15, 1965); and Jacques in *The Miser* (Sept. 7, 1965); and appeared in *As You Like It* (June 2, 1966), *The Doctor's Dilemma* (Sept. 6, 1966), and *S.S. Glencairn* (Sept. 7, 1966).

He made his Bway debut as Goldberg in *The Birthday Party* (Booth, N.Y.C., Oct. 3, 1967); with the Center Th. Group (Mark Taper Forum, Los Angeles) appeared in *The Devils* (Apr. 14, 1967); *Welcome to Serenity Farms* (Nov. 11, 1968); *The Adventures of the Black Girl in Her Search for God* (Mar. 20, 1969), and *Chemin de Fer* (June 5, 1969); played Father Daniel Berrigan in *The Trial of the Catonsville Nine* (APA/Phoenix at Good Shepherd Faith Church, N.Y.C., Feb. 7, 1971); repeated that role with the Center Th. Group (Mark Taper Forum, Los Angeles, June 17, 1971); with the Amer. Conservatory Theatre (San Francisco), appeared in *The Tavern, House of Blue Leaves* (Oct. 31, 1972), and *That Championship Season* (Feb. 20, 1973); and played Phil Hogan in *A Moon for the Misbegotten* (Kennedy Ctr., Washington, D.C., Dec. 4, 1973; and Morosco, N.Y.C., Dec. 29, 1973).

He has also appeared with the Manitoba Th. Centre (Winnipeg, Canada), and The Milwaukee (Wisc.) Repertory Company.

Films. He made his film debut in *The Grasshopper* (Natl. Gen., 1970); and played Father Daniel Berrigan in *The Trial of the Catonsville Nine* (Cinema 5, 1972).

Television. Mr. Flanders has made numerous appearances on Hawaii Five-O (CBS); and on Indict and Convict (ABC. 1974).

Awards. For his performance in *A Moon for the Misbegotten*, Mr. Flanders received the Antoinette Perry (Tony), and the Drama Desk awards (1973–74).

FLATT, ERNEST O. Choreographer, director, producer. b. Ernest Orville Flatt, Oct. 30, 1918, Denver, Colo., to Ernest Scorrow and Della May Flatt. Father, carpenter. Grad. Englewood (Col.) High School. Served US Army, 1941–45. Member of SSD&C; AEA; AFTRA; SAG; Directors Guild. Address: 1240 N. Wetherly Dr., Los Angeles, CA 90069, tel. (213) 271-1426.

Theatre. Mr. Flatt's first work for the stage was as a dancer with the national company of *Oklahoma!* (Biltmore Th., Los Angeles, 1947), and his first work for Bway was the choreography for *Fade Out—Fade In* (Mark Hellinger Th., May 26, 1964). Later N.Y.C. productions choreographed by Mr. Flatt include *It's a Bird! It's a Plane! It's Superman!* (Alvin Th., Mar. 29, 1966) and *Lorelei* (Palace, Jan.

27, 1973).

Television. Mr. Flatt was choreographer for Your Hit Parade (NBC, 1955–57); the Garry Moore Show (CBS, 1958–62); and the Carol Burnett Show (CBS, 1968–74). He was producer of the Jimmy Dean Show (CBS, July 1970). In addition, Mr. Flatt has been choreographer for a number of specials, including *Kiss Me, Kate* (NBC, 1960); *Julie and Carol at Carnegie Hall,* also associate producer (CBS, June 11, 1961); *Carol and Co.,* also director (CBS, Feb. 1963); *Calamity Jane,* also director (CBS, 1964); *Annie Get Your Gun* (NBC, 1967); *Damn Yankees* (NBC, 1968); and *Julie and Carol at Lincoln Center* (CBS, July 1, 1971).

Night Clubs. Mr. Flatt has done night club acts for such performers as Mitzi Gaynor, Juliet Prowse, Dorothy Collins, and Bobby Vinton.

Awards. Mr. Flatt received the Christopher Award for the Garry Moore Show; the Golden Rose and NATAS (Emmy) awards for *Julie and Carol at Carnegie Hall;* and the Emmy Award (1970) for the Carol Burnett Show.

Recreation. Avocado cultivation.

FLEMYNG, ROBERT. Actor, director. b. Benjamin Arthur Flemyng, Jan. 3, 1912, Liverpool, England, to George Gilbert and Rowena Eleanor (Jacques) Flemyng. Father, physician. Grad. Haileybury Coll., Hertford, Eng. 1930. Married Nov. 25, 1939, to Carmen Marta Sugars; one daughter. Served British Army, ETO and Middle East, 1939–45; rank, Lt. Col. (ret.); awarded Military Cross (1941), Officer of the Order of the British Empire (1945). Member of British AEA (council, 1960–to date), AEA, Garrick Club (London). Address: (home) L. Northbourne Rd., London, S.W. 4, England tel. (Ol) 622-1028; (bus.) International Famous Artistes, 11/12 Hanover St., London, W.I., England tel. (Ol) 629-8080.

Theatre. As a student at Haileybury Coll., Mr. Flemyng first appeared on the stage as Philip the Bastard in *King John* (1928); made his professional debut as Kenneth Raglan in *Rope* (County Th., Truro, England, June 2, 1931).

He made his London debut as a walk-on in *The Anatomist* (Westminster, Oct. 7, 1931); toured England in *After All* (1932); was an understudy in *Dangerous Corner* (Lyric, London, May 1932); appeared in 36 productions of the Liverpool Repertory Co. (Playhouse, 1932–35); played Edward in *Worse Things Happen at Sea* (St. James's, London, Mar. 26, 1935); Dickie in *Accent on Youth* (Globe, Sept. 3, 1935); Tom Willets in *Tread Softly* (Daly's Nov. 7, 1935); Bill Harvey in *Wisdom Teeth* (Savoy, Mar. 18, 1936); Lord Lynyates in *When the Bough Breaks* (Arts, June 7, 1936); Kit in *French without Tears* (Criterion, Nov. 6, 1936); and Jones in *Banana Ridge* (Strand, Apr. 27, 1938).

He made his Bway debut as Tony in *Spring Meeting* (Morosco, Dec. 8, 1938); subsequently appeared as Makepiece Lovell in *No Time for Comedy* (Ethel Barrymore Th., Apr. 17, 1939); appeared as the Earl of Harpendon in *While the Sun Shines* (Th. de Marigny, Paris, France, Oct. 1945); as Nigel Loraine in *The Guinea Pig* (Criterion, London, Feb. 19, 1946); as Algernon in *The Importance of Being Earnest* (Royale, N.Y.C., Mar. 3, 1947); and as Ben in *Love for Love* (Royale, May 26, 1947); and directed *The Little Dry Thorn* (Lyric, Hammersmith, London, Nov. 11, 1947).

He appeared as Rowlie Bateson in *People Like Us* (Wyndham's, July 6, 1948); Philotas in *Adventure Story* (St. James's, Mar. 17, 1949) and on tour (1949); Alan Howard in *French without Tears* (Vaudeville, July 15, 1949); and as Edward Chamberlayne in *The Cocktail Party* (Lyceum, Edinburgh, Scotland, Aug. 22, 1949; Henry Miller's Th., N.Y.C., Jan. 21, 1950).

Mr. Flemyng played Mark in *Who Is Sylvia?* (Criterion, London, Oct. 24, 1950); Sam Hartley in *Indian Summer* (Criterion, Dec. 12, 1951); Philip in *The Little Hut* and Toni Rigi in *To Dorothy, a Son* (Her Majesty's, Johannesburg, South Africa, Mar. 1952); succeeded (July 1952) Robert Morley as Philip in *The Little Hut* (Lyric, London, Aug. 23, 1950); toured the US (1952–53) in *The Constant Wife;* played David Slater in *The Moon Is Blue* (Duke of York's, London, July 7, 1953); and Rupert Forster in *Marching Song* (St. Martin's, Apr. 8, 1954).

He appeared as Gilbert Osmond in *Portrait of a Lady* (ANTA, N.Y.C., Dec. 21, 1954); played Anthony Henderson in *Bell, Book and Candle* (Streatham Hill, London, Dec., 1956) and on tour; James Callifer in *The Potting Shed* (Bijou, N.Y.C., Jan. 29, 1957); Powell in *Beth* (Apollo, London, Mar. 20, 1958); toured England in *Dear Delinquent* (June 1958); appeared as Kevin in *80 in the Shade* (Globe, London, Jan. 8, 1959); Colin in *A Sparrow Falls* (St. Martin's, Feb. 10, 1960); and as Hugo Cavanati in *The Last Joke* (Phoenix, Sept. 28, 1960).

Mr. Flemyng also played the role of Dr. Sloper in *The Heiress* (Ashcroft, Croyden, 1964); toured Australia as Anthony Wilcox in *Difference of Opinion* (1965); toured the United Kingdom as Arthur Winslow in *The Winslow Boy* (1965); appeared in the US as Harcourt Reilly in *The Cocktail Party* (Goodman Memorial Th., Chicago, 1965); toured the United Kingdom as Gary Essendine in *Present Laughter* (1966); played Richard Halton in *On Approval* (St. Martin's, London, 1966); Gregory Butler in *Happy Family* (St. Martin's, 1966); Col. Melketh in *Black Comedy* (Lyric, 1966); and directed *Doll's House* (Thorndike Th., Leatherhead, Surrey, 1968). He appeared as Shylock in *The Merchant of Venice* (Newcastle, 1969); Sir Colenso Ridgeon in *The Doctor's Dilemma* (Shaw Festival, Niagara, Ontario, Canada, 1969); toured the United Kingdom as Basham in *On the Rocks* (1969); appeared as Her Husband in *How He Lied to Her Husband* and General Mitchener in *Press Cuttings,* part of the bill *Three* (Fortune, London, 1970); played Arthur du Gros in *My Darling Daisy* (Lyric, 1970); toured the United Kingdom as Maitland in *The Chalk Garden* (1970); played Morrell in *Candida* (Bromley, 1971); George in *Harlequinade* (Haymarket, 1972); toured the United Kingdom as Sir Max Crawford-Jones in *Death on Demand* (1972) and as Andrew Wyke in *Sleuth* (1973); and appeared in South Africa as Sebastian in *In Praise of Love* (1974).

Films. Since his debut in *Head Over Heels* (Gaumont, 1937); he has played Nigel Lorraine in *The Guinea Pig* (MGM, 1949); appeared in *The Conspirators* (MGM, 1950); *The Blue Lamp* Eagle-Lion, 1950); *Blackmailed* (Bell, 1951); *The Man Who Never Was* (20th-Fox, 1956); *Cast a Dark Shadow* (Elstree, 1955); *Funny Face* (Par., 1957); *Let's Be Happy* (Allied, 1957); *Windom's Way* (Rank, 1958); *A Touch of Larceny* (Par., 1960); *Blind Date* (Beaconsfield, 1959); *Mystery Submarine* (Shepperton, 1962); *Raptus* (Rome, 1962); *The King's Breakfast* (Shepperton, 1962); *The Spy with a Cold Nose* (Embassy, 1966); *The Deadly Affair* (Col., 1967); *The Quiller Memorandum* (20th-Fox, 1967); *Vampire Blood* (1967); *Oh, What a Lovely War!* (Par., 1969); *The Battle of Britain* (UA, 1969); *The Body Stealers* (Tigon, 1969); *The Firechasers* (Rank, 1970); *Young Winston* (Col., 1972); *The Darwin Adventure* (20th-Fox, 1972); and *Travels with My Aunt* (MGM, 1972).

Television. He made his debut in By Candlelight (BBC, 1949); subsequently appeared as Warwick in *St. Joan* (Omnibus, NBC, 1955); in *Sting of Bees* (Elgin Hour, ABC, 1955); *Reunion in Vienna* (NBC, 1955); *Holiday for Simon* (BBC, 1955); *Blackwings* (Alcoa Hour, NBC, 1955); *Adventure in Diamond* (Alcoa Hour, NBC); on Playhouse 90 (CBS, 1957); the Alfred Hitchcock Hour (CBS, 1957); in *Woman in White* (Dow Hour, NBC, 1960); *The Dachet Diamonds,* a Somerset Maugham series (ABC, 1961); the Family Solicitor series (Granada, London, 1961); *Zero One* (BBC, 1962); Probation Officer (ATV, 1962); *This Is the End* (Coventry Cathedral, 1962); Man of the World (ATV, 1962); as Bruce in the Compact series (BBC, 1963–64); on The Living Room (BBC, 1964); Hawks and Doves (Rediffusion, 1966); *A Day by the Sea* (BBC, 1966); *The Maide Man* (Thames TV, 1967); The Straum Family (ATV, 1971); Flat 51 (BBC, 1971); Major Lavender (ATV, 1972); McCleod's Wedding Day (Scottish TV, 1972); *Public Eye* (London Weekend, 1972); Miss Nightingale (Southern TV, 1973); Edward VII (ATV, 1974); and Spy Trap (BBC, 1974).

Awards. For his performance as Edward Chamberlayne in *The Cocktail Party,* he won *Variety* NY Drama Critics Poll (1950).

Recreation. Riding, gymnastics.

FLETCHER, ALLEN. Director, educator. b. Allen Dinsmoor Fletcher, July 19, 1922, San Francisco, Calif., to Allen and Jessica (Dinsmoor) Fletcher. Father, US Army officer. Grad. New Mexico Milit. Inst., Roswell, N.M., 1942; Stanford Univ., B.A. 1947, M.A. 1950; attended Yale Univ. Sch. of Drama, 1951–52; Bristol Old Vic Th. Sch. and LAMDA, London, England, (Fulbright study grant), 1957–58. Married Dec. 20, 1953, to Anne Lawder; one son, one daughter. Served US Army, ETO, 1942–46; rank, Lt. Member of AEA; AGMA; APA. Address: (home) 680 West End Ave., New York, NY 10025, tel. (212) RI 9-0033; (bus.) c/o Amer. Conservatory Th., 450 Geary St., San Francisco, CA 94102, tel. (415) 771-3880.

Theatre. Mr. Fletcher made his stage debut as an actor, playing Henry Gow in *Fumed Oak* (Stanford Univ. Little Th., Calif., July 1946). He taught speech and directed at Purdue Univ. (1948–50); and was associate professor at Carnegie Inst. of Tech. (1952–59), teaching acting and directing.

Mr. Fletcher first directed professionally at the Oregon Shakespeare Festival, Ashland, Ore., including *King John* (Aug. 1948); *Othello* (Aug. 1949); *The Taming of the Shrew* (Aug. 1949); *Henry IV, Part I* (July 1950); *Julius Caesar* (July 1952); *Coriolanus* (July 1953); *Merry Wives of Windsor* (July 1954); *Love's Labour's Lost* (July 1956); and *Richard III* (July 1956). For the Antioch Area Shakespeare Festival Theatres (Toledo and Yellow Springs, Ohio), Mr. Fletcher directed *Henry VIII* (Aug. 1957).

For the San Diego Shakespeare Festival, Old Globe Th., San Diego, Calif., he staged productions of *Hamlet* (July 1955); *King Lear* (July 1957); *Much Ado About Nothing* (July 1958); *Romeo and Juliet* (July 1959); *Love's Labour's Lost* (July 1959); re-staged *Hamlet* (July 1960); *As You Like It* (Sept. 1960); *Merchant of Venice* (July 1961); *Richard III* (July 1961); *Othello* (July 1962); *Antony and Cleopatra* (July 26, 1963); *Measure For Measure* (July 14, 1964); and *Two Gentlemen of Verona* (July 14, 1966).

For the Assn. of Producing Artists (APA), he directed *Man and Superman* (premiere, Municipal Th., Hamilton, Bermuda, May 1960); *The Importance of Being Earnest* (premiere, McCarter, Princeton, N.J., Nov. 10, 1960); *As You Like It* (premiere, McCarter, Princeton, N.J., Mar. 4, 1961); and *Twelfth Night* (premiere, Boston Arts Festival, Boston Common, Mass., June 1961).

In New York, Mr. Fletcher directed for the NY City Opera (NY City Ctr.), he directed *Rigolette* (Oct. 30, 1960), *Aida* (Oct. 1961), the world premiere of the opera *The Crucible* (Oct. 26, 1961), the world premiere of *The Golem* (Mar. 13, 1962), *The Turn of the Screw* (Mar. 14, 1962), the world premiere of *The Passion of Jonathan Wade* (Oct. 11, 1962), *Jeanne d'Arc au Bûcher* (Oct. 3, 1963), and *Carmen* (Oct. 4, 1964); and for the City Ctr. Gilbert and Sullivan Co. (NY City Ctr.), he directed *H.M.S. Pinafore* (Jan. 1961), *Yeoman of the Guard* (Mar. 18, 1964), restaged *H.M.S. Pinafore* (Mar. 20, 1964), directed *The Pirates of Penzance* (Apr. 25, 1968), and re-staged *H.M.S. Pinafore* (Apr. 27, 1968) and *Yeoman of the Guard* (May 8, 1968).

For the San Francisco Opera (Calif.) Co., he staged *Romeo and Juliet* and *Martha* (War Memorial Opera House, May 1961); directed the program entitled *Mr. Gilbert, Mr. Sullivan and Mr. Green* (Playhouse-in-the-Park, Philadelphia, Pa., Aug. 1961); at the Fred Miller Th. (Milwaukee, Wis.), he directed *The Matchmaker* (Dec. 26, 1961) and the play, *The Crucible* (Feb. 27, 1962).

Mr. Fletcher taught classical and operatic acting at the Circle in the Square Th. Sch., N.Y.C., (1961–62) and directing at Brooklyn College (1962).

In June, 1962, he began his association with the American Shakespeare Festival Theatre and Academy, Stratford, Conn. He was head of the company's training program (Fall 1962–Summer 1965); artistic director (1965 season); and directed the following productions: *Richard II* (June 14, 1962); *King Lear* (June 7, 1963); *Richard III* (June 17, 1964); *Much Ado About Nothing* (June 18, 1964); *Coriolanus* (June 19, 1965); *Romeo and Juliet* (June 20, 1965); and *King Lear* (June 23, 1965).

He became (July 1, 1966) artistic director of the Seattle Rep. Th. (Center Playhouse, Seattle, Wash.; cf. for complete list of plays produced), and directed for them *Blithe Spirit* (Dec. 14, 1966); *The Crucible, The Hostage, Tartuffe,* and *The Night of the Iguana* (1966–67 season); *Henry IV, Part 1, You Can't Take it with You, The Threepenny Opera,* and *The Death of Bessie Smith* (1967–68 season); and *Our Town, A Midsummer Night's Dream, Serjeant Musgrave's Dance, A View from the Bridge,* and *Mourning Becomes Electra* (1968–69 season); before he resigned his post at the end of the 1969–70 season.

Mr. Fletcher founded (1970) The Actors' Company (Univ. of Michigan Professional Th., Ann Arbor, Mich.), for which he directed *In the Matter of J. Robert Oppenheimer;* co-directed *Little Murders;* and produced *Summertree* (all in 1970).

For the American Conservatory Theatre (ACT, San Francisco), he directed *Death of a Salesman* (1965); *Uncle Vanya* (1966); *Arsenic and Old Lace* (1967); *The Crucible* (1968); *The Hostage* (1969); and *Hadrian VII* (1970). He became Conservatory Dir. of ACT (1970 to date), and has since directed for them *A Doll's House,* which he also translated, and *That Championship Season* (1972–73 season); *The Miser* and *Hot l Baltimore* (1973–74 season); *The Pillars of the Community,* adapted and translated by him from Henrik Ibsen's *The Pillars of Society* (1974–75 season); *The Ruling Class* (Mar. 18, 1975); *Desire Under the Elms* (Oct. 21, 1975); and *Antony and Cleopatra; Paradise Lost; The Latent Heterosexual;* and *An Enemy of the People.* .

Awards. In 1959, Mr. Fletcher was awarded a Ford Foundation grant to Directors in the Professional Theatre, for study and experimentation.

FLETCHER, BRAMWELL. Actor, director. b. Feb. 20, 1906, Bradford, Yorkshire, England, to Benjamin and Jane (Scott) Fletcher. Attended Creditor Grammar Sch., England. Studied drama with Margaret Carrington, N.Y.C. (1935–38). Married Feb. 14, 1935, to Helen Chandler (marr. dis.); married July 30, 1942, to Diana Barrymore (marr. dis.); married Apr. 12, 1950, to Susan Robinson (marr. dis.); married Sept. 26, 1970, to Lael Tucker Wertenbaker; two sons, one daughter. Served WW II, US Army, rank, Pvt. Member of ASA; SAG; AFTRA. Address: R.F.D., Marlborough, NH 03455.

Theatre. Mr. Fletcher made his first stage appearance at the Shakespeare Memorial Theatre (Stratford-upon-Avon, England) as Florizel in *The Winter's Tale* (May, 1927); made his London debut as Prince Yashvil in *Paul I* (Court, Oct. 4, 1927); subsequently played Oscar Nordholm in *Sauce for the Gander* (Lyric, Dec. 1928); Martin in *Thunder on the Left* (Arts, July 26, 1928); Harold Marquess in *The Chinese Bungalow* (Duke of York's Th., Jan. 9, 1929); and Jimmie Chard in *The Devil in the Cheese* (Comedy, June 4, 1929).

He appeared in N.Y.C. as Kent Heathcote in *Scotland Yard* (Sam H. Harris Th., Sept. 27, 1929); played Ray Fanshawe in *Red Planet* (Cort, Dec. 17, 1932); Colin Derwent in *Ten Minute Alibi* (Ethel Barrymore Th., Nov. 17, 1933) and on tour (1933–34); Simon More in *These Two* (Henry Miller's Th., N.Y.C., May 7, 1934); The Dreamer in *Within the Gates* (National, Oct. 22, 1934); Dick Shale in *The Dominant Sex* (Cort, Apr. 1, 1935); Hsieh Ping-Kuei in *Lady Precious Stream* (Booth, Jan. 27, 1936); and Rodney Bevan in *Boy Meets Girl* (Shaftesbury, London, Eng., May 27, 1936).

He toured the US in *To-Night at 8:30* (Jan. 1937–Mar. 19, 1938); appeared as Arnold Champion-Cheney in *The Circle* (Playhouse, N.Y.C., Apr. 12, 1938); played the dual roles of Ruy Blas and Don Caesar in *Ruy Blas* (Central City Opera House, Central City, Colo.); Mr. Prior in *Outward Bound* (Playhouse, N.Y.C., Dec. 22, 1938): Baron von Alvenstor in *Margin for Error* (Plymouth, Nov. 3, 1939); followed by a season of stock at the Ogunquit (Me.) Playhouse (Summer 1940).

On Bway he played Jacob Wait in *Eight O'Clock Tuesday* (Henry Miller's Th., Jan. 6, 1941); Louis Dubedat in *The Doctor's Dilemma* (Shubert, Mar. 11, 1941); Capt. Sutton in *Storm Operation* (Belasco, Jan. 11, 1944); Maxim de Winter in *Rebecca* on a coast-to-coast tour before opening on Bway (Ethel Barrymore Th., Jan. 18, 1945); toured as Sgt. Rough in *Angel Street* (June–Aug. 1945); appeared as the Newspaper Reporter in the pre-Bway tryout of *The Greatest of These* (opened Shubert-Lafayette, Detroit, Mich., Feb. 18, 1947; closed Selwyn, Chicago, Ill., Mar. 15, 1947); toured as Lord Darlington in *Lady Windermere's Fan* (1947); appeared as Richard Brinsley Sheridan in *The Lady Maria* (Cape Playhouse, Dennis, Mass., Summer 1947); toured as President Merrill in *Goodbye, My Fancy* (Selwyn, Chicago, Nov. 1949); played George, Duke of Bristol, in *The Day After Tomorrow* (Booth, N.Y.C., Oct. 26, 1950); Collins in *Getting Married* (ANTA, May 7, 1951); Mr. Burgess in *Candida* (National Apr. 22, 1952); Alick Wylie in *Maggie* (National, Feb. 18, 1953); and Lord Summerhays in *Misalliance* (Ethel Barrymore Th., Mar. 6, 1953). He played David Slater in a national touring company of *The Moon Is Blue* (1954); the Psychiatrist in *The Cocktail Party* and the Duke in *Venus Observed* (Olney, Md., Th., Summer 1954); Gavin Leon Andrée in *The Wisteria Trees* (NY City Ctr., Feb. 2, 1955); Marechal Francois de Sevres in *The Little Glass Clock* (John Golden Th., Mar. 26, 1956); Clement of Metz in *The Lovers* (Martin Beck Th., May 10, 1956); and Aeneas Posket in *Posket's Family Skeleton* (Westport Country Playhouse, Conn., Aug. 1956).

He was stand-by for Rex Harrison in the role of Henry Higgins in *My Fair Lady* (Mark Hellinger Th., N.Y.C., Mar. 15, 1956) and played the part more than 200 times; appeared as Mephisto in *Faust* (Goodman Th., Chicago, Oct. 1961); Ulric Brendel in *Rosmersholm* (4th St. Th., Apr. 11, 1962); and Gaev in *The Cherry Orchard* at the same theatre (Nov. 14, 1962). Mr. Fletcher presented a one-man show called *Parnassus '63* (ANTA, Dec. 19, 1962); later changed the title to *Love, Laughter and Baseball,* and toured US universities and colleges with it (1963–64), including a N.Y.C. performance (New Sch. of Social Research, Mar. 6, 1964); appeared in another one-man show, *The Bernard Shaw Story,* which Mr. Fletcher compiled and arranged and first performed at Pfeiffer Coll., Misenheimer, N.C., Sept. 24, 1964, subsequently touring it intermittently for three years under the auspices of Sol Hurok; at the Washington Th. Club (Washington, D.C.), directed *The Deadly Game* (Mar. 2, 1965) and *A Touch of the Poet* (Mar. 30, 1965); played Andrew Undershaft in *Major Barbara* (Westport Country Playhouse, Conn., May 1965); Sir Ormsby-Gore and Dr. York in *A Step Away from War* (American Place Th., N.Y.C., June 21, 1965); and played the title role in *The Miser* (Goodman Th., Chicago, Oct. 20, 1967). He collaborated with Lael Tucker Wertenbaker on the Educational Th. project, *Operation Gadfly,* a play for colleges, under the auspices of the Natl. Endowment for the Humanities (1970).

Films. Mr. Fletcher made his debut in England in *Chick* (Br. Lion, 1928); and has appeared in *To What Red Hell* (Br. Lion, 1928); *So This Is London* (20th-Fox, 1930); *Raffles* (UA, 1930); *Inside the Lines* (RKO, 1930); *Svengali* (WB, 1931); *The Millionaire* (WB, 1931); *Men of the Sky* (First Natl., 1931); *The Daughter of the Dragon* (Par., 1931); *The Secret Witness* (Col., 1931); *Once a Lady* (Par., 1931); *The Mummy* (U, 1932); *A Bill of Divorcement* (RKO, 1932); *The Face on the Barroom Floor* (Invincible, 1932); *Only Yesterday* (U, 1933); *The Right to Romance* (RKO, 1933); *The Monkey's Paw* (RKO, 1933); *The Scarlet Pimpernel* (UA, 1935); *Random Harvest* (MGM, 1942); *White Cargo* (MGM, 1942); *The Undying Monster* (20th-Fox, 1942); *The Immortal Sergeant* (20th-Fox, 1943); and *Line Engaged.*

Television. Mr. Fletcher's appearances include more than 200 leading roles in major network dramatic shows.

Other Activities. He is a portrait painter, and lectures on the Humanities and the Arts.

Recreation. Writing, his three children.

FLETCHER, ROBERT. Costume and set designer, producer. b. Robert Fletcher Wyckoff, Aug. 29, 1923, Cedar Rapids, Iowa, to Harry and Mary Fletcher (Keahey) Wyckoff. Father, actor, known as Leon Ames. Grad. Abraham Lincoln H.S., Council Bluffs, Iowa, 1941; attended Harvard Univ., 1941–42, 1946–48; attended Univ. of Iowa, 1943–44. Served WW II, USAAF 1942–43, bombardier. Member of United Scenic Artists; Costume Designers Assn. (pres. 1954); Signet Society, Cambridge, Mass. Address: 388 Third Ave., New York, NY 10016, tel. (212) LE 2-0386.

Theatre. Mr. Fletcher was first engaged in the theatre as director and designer for *Night Must Fall* (Little Th., Council Bluffs, Iowa, 1938).

He played a Swiss Guard in *Embezzled Heaven* (National, N.Y.C., Oct. 31, 1944); Salarino in *Dream Girl* (Coronet, Dec. 14, 1945); and Young Fashion in *The Relapse* (Morosco, Nov. 22, 1950).

As a member of the board of directors of the Brattle Th. (Cambridge, Mass., 1947–52), he designed costumes for 87 productions; and for the New England Opera Co., he designed sets for *Carmen, La Bohème,* and *Pique Dame.*

He designed costumes for *The Little Blue Light* (ANTA, N.Y.C., Apr. 29, 1951); costumes for the N.Y.C. Ballet production of *La gloire* (NY City Ctr., 1952); for the NY City Ctr., created costumes for *Love's Labour's Lost* (Feb. 4, 1953) and *Misalliance* (Feb. 18, 1953); designed the revue *Walk Tall,* which closed during its pre-Bway tour (1954); scenery and costumes at Camp Tamiment, Pa. (1954); at the NY City Ctr., created costumes for *Othello* (Sept. 7, 1955) and *Henry IV, Part 1* (Sept. 21, 1955); designed costumes and sets for *Il ballo dalla* and *Ingrate* (Chicago Lyric Opera, Ill., 1955); and for the American Shakespeare Fest., (Stratford, Conn.) costumes for *Julius Caesar* (July 12, 1955) and *The Tempest* (Aug. 1, 1955).

He designed costumes for *King Lear* (NY City Ctr., Jan. 12, 1956); scenery and costumes for *The Abduction from the Seraglio* (Connecticut Mozart Festival, 1956); costumes for *Saint Joan* (Phoenix, N.Y.C., Sept. 11, 1956); at the NY City Ctr., designed costumes for *The Beggar's Opera* (Mar. 13, 1957) and costumes for the ballet *The Unicorn, the Gorgon and the Manticore* (1957); designed scenery and costumes for *Don Carlo* (Chicago Lyric Opera, Ill., 1957); and sets and costumes for the Pro Musica production of *The Play of Daniel* (The Cloisters, N.Y.C., Jan. 2, 1958).

He designed *Voyage to the Moon* (Boston Opera Co., Mass., 1958); sets and costumes for *L' Assassinio Nella Cathedrale* (Empire State Music Festival, N.Y.C., 1958); costumes for *The Firstborn* (Coronet, N.Y.C., Mar. 30, 1958); sets and costumes for *Taboo Revue* (Showplace, 1959); sets for *The Geranium Hat* (Orpheum, Mar. 17, 1959); sets and costumes for *Ole!* (Greenwich Mews, Mar. 18, 1959); *The Rake's Progress* (Washington Opera Society, 1959); and *Cosi fan Tutte* (Washington Opera Society and NY City Ctr., 1959); costumes for *Thais* and *La Gioconda* (Chicago Lyric Opera, Inc., 1959); scenery and costumes for the American Shakespeare Fest. production of *The Tempest* (Stratford, Conn., June 19, 1960); scenery and costumes for *Helen of Troy* (Cambridge Drama Festival, Mass., 1960); scenery and costumes for *Farewell, Farewell, Eugene* (Helen Hayes Th., N.Y.C., Sept. 27, 1960); and costumes and lighting for the industrial show, *G.M. Motorama* (1960).

Mr. Fletcher created costumes for *A Family Affair* (Billy Rose Th., N.Y.C., Jan. 27, 1961); *The Happiest Girl in the World* (Martin Beck Th., Apr. 3, 1961); *How To Succeed in Business without Really Trying* (46 St. Th., Oct. 14, 1961), and the tour (1963); designed the production of *Dear Liar* (Th. Marquee, N.Y.C., Mar. 17, 1962); costumes for *A Pair of Pairs,* four plays presented in repertory (Vandam, Mar. 24, 1962); *Half-Past Wednesday* (Orpheum, Apr. 6, 1962); *The Moon Besieged* (Lyceum, May 5, 1962); *Nowhere To Go But Up* (Winter Garden, Oct. 10,

1962); and *Little Me* (Lunt-Fontanne, Nov. 11, 1962); designed scenery and costumes for *Best Foot Forward* (Stage 73, Apr. 2, 1963); and sets and costumes for *A Midsummer Night's Dream* (NY City Ctr., Spring 1963) and for *Don Giovanni* (NY City Ctr., Fall 1963).

He designed the Robert Joffrey touring production of the ballet *Palace* (1963); costumes for *Foxy* (Ziegfeld, N.Y.C., Feb. 13, 1964); and produced with Lester Osterman and Richard Horner, *High Spirits*, for which he also designed costumes and settings (Alvin, Apr. 7, 1964).

He designed the costumes for the English production of *Little Me* (Cambridge Th., London, Nov. 18, 1964); produced, with Richard Horner, *The Queen and the Rebels* (Th. Four, N.Y.C., Feb. 25, 1965); designed the scenery for the ballet *Vaudeville* (premiere Harkness Ballet, Opera Comique, Paris, France, Mar. 1965); costumes for the pre-Bway tryout of *The Coffee Lover* (US, summer stock, 1966); *Walking Happy* (Lunt-Fontanne, Nov. 26, 1966); *A Midsummer Night's Dream* (American Shakespeare Fest., Stratford, Conn., June 17, 1967); sets and costumes for L'Histoire du Soldat (Spoleto Fest., Italy, Summer 1967); designed for the Center Th. Group (Los Angeles, 1967–68 season); designed sets and costumes for *Hadrian VII* (Helen Hayes Th., N.Y.C., Jan. 8, 1969; and for the national tour, opened Stratford Fest., Ontario, Canada, Aug. 5, 1969; closed Fisher, Detroit, US, May 30, 1970); sets for *The Madwoman of Chaillot* (Sokol Th., Sokol Hall, Mar. 22, 1970); supervised the costumes for *Borstal Boy* (Lyceum, Mar. 31, 1970); designed the costumes for *Cry for Us All* (Broadhurst, Apr. 8, 1970); sets and lighting for a national tour of *Dear Love* (opened Alley, Houston, Tex., Sept. 17, 1970; closed Shubert, New Haven, Jan. 16, 1971); and designed the costumes for a revival of *Johnny Johnson* (Edison, N.Y.C., Apr. 11, 1971), which he produced with Timothy Gray, in association with Midge La Guardia.

Mr. Fletcher joined the American Conservatory Th. (San Francisco) in 1969, and has designed sets and costumes for them in each of their seasons.

Films. Mr. Fletcher designed the costumes for *The Ballad of Cable Hogue* (WB, 1970).

Television. As staff designer for NBC-TV (1954–1960), Mr. Fletcher designed the NBC Opera Co. productions of *Sister Angelica, Tosca, Rigoletto,* and *The Dialogues of the Carmelites;* the closed circuit opening of the Ziegfeld Th. (N.Y.C.); the General Motors Anniversary Show; Festival of Music; Festival of Magic; *The Great Sebastians; Ruggles of Red Gap; Washington Square;* the Stanley series; *Cinderella; Romeo and Juliet;* the Jack Paar Show; Jimmy Rodgers Show; Alcoa Presents, Chevy Show; Mr. Wizard; the Standard Oil Show; Eydie Gormé-Steve Lawrence; Accent on Love; Dave King Show; and Mary Martin; designed scenery and costumes for *Music from Shubert Alley;* and in 1963 was art director for the Perry Como Show.

Other Activities. Mr. Fletcher has served as a member of the examination committee of the Costumers Union.

Recreation. Painting, book collecting.

FLICKER, THEODORE. Director, actor, producer, playwright. b. Theodore Jonas Flicker, June 6, 1930, Freehold, N.J., to Sidney and Ray (Lopatin) Flicker. Father, executive. Grad. Admiral Farragut Acad., Pine Beach, N.J., 1948; attended Bard Coll., 1948–50; grad. RADA, diploma 1952. Served US Army, 1952–54. Member of WGA (bd. of dirs.); DGA SAG; and Academy of Motion Picture Arts and Sciences (exec. bd., writers branch). Address: Beverly Hills, CA 90210.

Theatre. Mr. Flicker made his N.Y.C. debut as Philip Judah in *Once Around the Block* (Cherry Lane Th., Oct. 1955); and subsequently was author and director of *The Nervous Set* (Henry Miller's Th., May 12, 1959).

One of the pioneers in improvisational theatre, Mr. Flicker produced, with David Shepherd, *The Compass* (Compass, Chicago, Ill., Jan. 1956); produced, directed, and performed in *The Compass Players* (Crystal Palace, St. Louis, Mo., Apr. 1957); produced, directed and played in *The Premise* (Premise Th., N.Y.C., Nov. 22, 1960; Nash's Barn, Westport, Conn., June 1961; Shoreham Hotel, Washington, D.C., Jan. 1962); also directed and performed in the same play in London (Comedy, July 26, 1962); and produced and directed *The Living Premise* (Premise, N.Y.C., June 13, 1963).

In cabaret theatre, Mr. Flicker produced, directed and played in *Waiting for Godot* (Crystal Palace, St. Louis, Mo., Feb. 1958); produced, directed and wrote the revue, *Whaddya Want* (Gourmet Room, Park Plaza Hotel, St. Louis, July 1958); at the New Crystal Palace (St. Louis); produced, directed, and played in *Loves Success* (Nov. 1958), *Friend of the Family* (Dec. 1958), *Endgame* (Jan. 1959), and *Clerambard* (Feb. 1959).

Films. Mr. Flicker wrote, produced (with Robert Gaffny), directed, and performed in *The Troublemaker* (Janus 1964); wrote the screenplay for *Spinout* (MGM, 1966); wrote and directed *The President's Analyst* (Par., 1967); and wrote and directed *Three in the Cellar* (1970).

Awards. For *The Premise,* he received the Vernon Rice Award (1961) and *The Village Voice* Off-Bway (Obie) Award (1961). He received W.G.A. nominations for best original comedy screenplay for *The President's Analyst* (1967); and best original musical screenplay for *Spinout* (1966).

FOCH, NINA. Actress, director, educator. b. Nina Consuelo Maud Fock, Apr. 20, 1924, Leyden, Netherlands, to Dirk and Consuelo (Flowerton) Fock. Father, conductor; mother, actress. Grad. Lincoln Sch., N.Y.C., 1940; attended Columbia Univ.; Parsons Art Sch.; AADA. Studied acting with Stella Adler, Lee Strasberg, Harold Clurman. Married 1954 to James Lipton (marr. dis. 1958); married 1959 to Dennis Brite (marr. dis. 1963); one son. Member of AEA; AFTRA; SAG; ATAS; AMPAS; Actors' Fund of America.

Theatre. Miss Foch made her first appearance on the stage touring in *Western Union, Please* (1941); first appeared in N.Y.C. as Mary McKinley in *John Loves Mary* (Booth Th., Feb. 4, 1947); toured as Lizzie McKaye in *The Respectful Prostitute* (1949); played Olivia in *Twelfth Night* (Empire, N.Y.C., Oct. 3, 1949); appeared in *Congressional Baby* (Albany, Mar. 1950); played Dynamene in *A Phoenix Too Frequent* (Fulton, N.Y.C., Apr. 26, 1950); appeared in stock productions of *The Philadelphia Story* and *Light Up the Sky* (Summer 1950); and played Cordelia in *King Lear* (National, N.Y.C., Dec. 25, 1950).

At the American Shakespeare Festival Th. (Stratford, Conn.) she played Isabella in *Measure for Measure* (June 27, 1956) and Katharine in *The Taming of the Shrew* (Aug 5, 1956); in N.Y.C., repeated these two roles (Phoenix, Jan. 22, 1957; Feb. 20, 1957); and played Jane in *A Second String* (Eugene O'Neill Th., Apr. 13, 1960).

Miss Foch played Frances in *Windows* and Frieda in *I Rise in Flame, Cried the Phoenix* in *An Evening of Williams, Pinter and Schisgal* (Schoenberg Hall Auditorium, UCLA, Los Angeles, Calif. June 4, 1965); directed *Ways and Means,* on a Noel Coward triple bill with *Fumed Oak,* and *Still Life,* entitled *Tonight at 8:30* (ANTA, May 3, 1967); and with the Seattle (Wash.) Repertory Th., appeared in *All Over* (1972–73 season), and *The Seagull* (1973–74 season).

Films. Miss Foch made her film debut in *Nine Girls* (Col., 1944); followed by *Escape in the Fog* (Col., 1945); *A Song To Remember* (Col., 1945); *My Name Is Julia Ross* (Col., 1945); *An American in Paris* (MGM, 1952); *Scaramouche* (MGM, 1952); *Sombrero* (MGM, 1953); *Fast Company* (MGM, 1953); *Executive Suite* (MGM, 1954); *Four Guns to the Border* (U, 1954); *Illegal* (WB, 1955); *You're Never Too Young* (Par. 1955); *The Ten Commandments* (Par., 1956); *Three Brave Men* (20th-Fox, 1957); *Cash McCall* (WB, 1959); *Spartacus* (U, 1960) and *Such Good Friends* (Par. 1971).

Television. She has appeared frequently on all major networks since 1947, including such shows as Playhouse 90 (CBS), Studio One (CBS), Route 66 (CBS), Naked City (ABC); Kraft Suspense Th. (NBC); The Steve Allen Show (Ind.); Bus Stop (Ind.); Arrest and Trial (ABC); Burke's Law (ABC); The Trailmaster (ABC); *Special for Women* (ABC); Mr. Broadway (CBS); Dr. Kildare (NBC); Outer Limits (Ind.); and various talk shows.

Other Activities. Miss Foch was appointed visiting drama professor at the Univ. of Southern California Sch. of the Performing Arts (Summer 1966).

Awards. She was nominated for an Academy (Oscar) Award (1955) for her performance as the Secretary in *Executive Suite.* .

Recreation. Painting, cooking, "my son.".

FOLEY, PAUL A. Stage manager, actor, director. b. Paul Arthur Foley, May 11, 1902, Kellerton, Iowa, to Dennis Benedict and Amy (Ambrosier) Foley. Father, farmer. Grad. Garner (Iowa) H.S., 1922; State Univ. of Iowa, B.A. (Phi Beta Kappa) 1926. Married Sept. 2, 1931, to Betty Amiard (marr. dis. May 1945); married June 22, 1946, to Willadell Allen, educator; one son, two daughters. Member of AEA. Address: River Rd., Box 78, Cape Neddick, ME 03902, tel. (207) 363-3372.

Theatre. Mr. Foley made his first stage appearance as Tom Burton in *Her Temporary Husband* (Chautauqua Circuit, Summer 1926); subsequently, at the Cleveland (Ohio) Play House, played Rufe Cagle in *Sunup* (Sept. 1, 1926), and various other parts (1926–May 30, 1929); toured as James Ponsonby Makeshyfte in *The Servant in the House* (Chautauqua Circuit, June 16–Aug. 28, 1929); was a play-reader for Kenneth Macgowan (Mar. 2–May 18, 1930); played Jimmy Gilley in *Bought and Paid For* (Chautauqua Circuit, June 18–Aug. 30, 1930); was director of dramatics at Knox Coll. (Sept. 1930–June 1935); and directed and acted in stock at the Theatre in the Woods (Boothbay Harbor, Me., 1931–35).

Mr. Foley made his first N.Y.C. appearance as a Waiter in *Triumph* and also served as stage manager (Fulton, Oct. 14, 1935); subsequently played Johnson and was stage manager for a tour of *Personal Appearance* (Oct. 1935–May 1936); taught at Knox Coll. (Sept. 1936–June 1938); played the Photographer, and was stage manager for *Kiss the Boys Goodbye* (Henry Miller's Th., N.Y.C., Sept. 28, 1938); in stock, was resident director-actor at the Mountain Th. (Braddock Heights, Md., Summer 1939); and played Burns and was stage manager for *Lady in Waiting* (Martin Beck Th., N.Y.C., Mar. 27, 1940).

He served as stage manager for *Out from Under* (Biltmore, Apr. 4, 1940); and *Jupiter Laughs* (Biltmore, Sept 9, 1940); was stage manager, assistant director and played Burns in the tour of *Lady in Waiting* (Nov. 1940–May 1941); directed the Experimental Theatre production of *Steps Leading Up* (Cort, N.Y.C., 1941); was resident director at the Mountain Playhouse (Jennerstown, Pa., June 19, 1941–Sept. 6, 1941); stage manager for Maurice Evans production of *Macbeth* (National, N.Y.C. Nov. 11, 1941), and toured with it (Mar. 9–June 5, 1942); stage manager for *Janie* (Henry Miller's Th., N.Y.C., Sept. 10, 1942), and toured with it (May 1943–May 1945); directed *A Boy Who Lived Twice* (Biltmore, N.Y.C., Sept. 11, 1945); succeeded (Oct. 9, 1945) Bradford Hatton as stage manager and assistant director for *Harvey* (48 St. Th., Nov. 1, 1944), and for its tour (1949); was stage manager for *Love Me Long* (48 St. Th., N.Y.C., Nov. 7, 1949); and for *Mr. Barry's Etchings* (48 St. Th., Jan. 31, 1950).

Mr. Foley directed *Harvey* (Honolulu Community Th., Hawaii, Apr.–May 1950), for an Australian tour (May–June 1950), and for the N.Y.C. Subway Circuit (July–Aug. 1950); was production stage manager for *Hilda Crane* (Coronet, N.Y.C., Nov. 1, 1950); and *Little Blue Light* (ANTA, Apr. 29, 1951); producer-director at the Cragsmoor (N.Y.) Th. (June–Sept. 1951); stage manager for the tour of *The Rose Tattoo* (opened His Majesty's, Montreal, Canada, Oct. 29, 1951; closed Curran, San Francisco, Calif., Apr. 5, 1952); succeeded (June 1, 1952) William Weaver as stage manager for *The Fourposter* (Ethel Barrymore Th., N.Y.C., Oct. 24,

1951), and for the national tour (opened Civic Aud., Pasadena, Calif., July 25, 1952; closed National, Washington, D.C., May 30, 1953); was associate director for *Macbeth* at the Bermuda Festival (Fort St. Catherine, June–July 1953); directed the N.Y.C. Subway Circuit production of *The Fourposter* (July–Aug. 1953).

He was production stage manager for *Madam, Will You Walk* (Phoenix, N.Y.C., Dec. 1, 1953); directed a West Coast tour of *Harvey* (opened Santa Barbara, Calif., Dec. 27, 1953); a tour of *The Fourposter* (Mar.–Apr. 1954); and a summer production of *The Show-Off* (May–Aug. 1954); was stage manager for a tour of *Face to Face* (Sept. 1954); also for *The Fourposter* (NY City Ctr., Jan. 5, 1955); *The Honeys* Longacre, Apr. 28, 1955); *A Day by the Sea* (ANTA, Sept. 26, 1955); the pre-Bway tryout of *A Quiet Place* (opened Shubert, New Haven, Conn., Nov. 23, 1955); closed National, Washington, D.C., Dec. 31, 1955); and a West Coast tour of *Anastasia* (1956); succeeded (Sept. 10, 1956) E.W. Swackhammer, as stage manager for *Cat on a Hot Tin Roof* (Morosco, N.Y.C., Mar. 24, 1955), and for the national tour (opened National, Washington, D.C., Nov. 26, 1956; closed Erlanger, Chicago, Ill., June 1, 1957); was advance director for the summer production of *The Man in a Dog Suit* (June–Aug. 1957); stage manager for the return engagement of *The Waltz of the Toreadors* (Coronet, N.Y.C., Mar. 4, 1958); advance director for the try-out of *Triple Play* (June–Aug. 1958); stage manager for *The Man in a Dog Suit* (Coronet, N.Y.C., Oct. 30, 1958); and for *Triple Play* (Playhouse, Apr. 15, 1959).

He was stage manager-director at the Ogunquit (Me.) Playhouse (July–Aug. 1959); stage manager for the national Phoenix tour of *Mary Stuart* (Oct. 1959–May 1960); stage manager for the national tour of *Once Upon a Mattress* (opened Erlanger, Chicago, Ill., Sept. 1, 1960; closed Colonial, Boston, Mass., Mar. 18, 1961); was stage manager for the National Repertory Theatre's tour of *Elizabeth the Queen* and *Mary Stuart* (opened Acad. of Music, Northampton, Mass., Oct. 19, 1961; closed Rochester, N.Y., Apr. 14, 1962); production stage manager for *Calculated Risk* (Ambassador, N.Y.C., Sept. 1962–May 1963); and succeeded (May 14, 1963) Frederic De Wilde as production stage manager of *A Man for All Seasons* (ANTA, Nov. 22, 1961), and for the tour (opened Greek Th., Hollywood, Calif., July 18, 1963; closed Blackstone, Chicago, Ill., May 30, 1964).

He was production stage manager for *The Physicists* (Martin Beck Th., N.Y.C., Oct. 13, 1964); *Mrs. Dally* (John Golden Th., Sept. 22, 1965); *Hostile Witness* (Music Box Th., Feb. 17, 1966–July 2, 1966) and for US tour (Sept. 6, 1966–Apr. 1967) and director of the Australian production (Sydney and Melbourne, Apr.–May 1967); production stage manager for *By George* (Lyceum, N.Y.C., Oct. 12, 1967); for tour of *Hadrian VII* (July 1, 1969–May 30, 1970); for tour of *Sleuth* (Sept. 1971–Jan. 1973) and for N.Y.C. company (June 25–Oct. 1973); for the Washington, D.C., engagement of *The Headhunters* (Eisenhower Th., John F. Kennedy Ctr., Mar. 17–June 1, 1974); for *Everyman* (Clarence Brown Th., Knoxville, Tenn., and tour; Oct. 5–Dec. 14, 1974); and for the tour of *Noel Coward in Two Keys* (Feb. 10–Aug. 2, 1975).

Recreation. Farming, remodeling old houses.

FONDA, HENRY. Actor. b. Henry Jaynes Fonda, May 16, 1905, Grand Island, Nebr., to William Brace and Herberta (Jaynes) Fonda. Father, businessman. Grad. Omaha (Neb.) Central H.S., 1923; attended Univ. of Minnesota, 1924–25. Married Dec. 25, 1931, to Margaret Sullavan, actress (marr. dis. 1933); married Sept. 16, 1936, to Frances Brokaw (dec. 1950), one son, one daughter; married Dec. 27, 1950, to Susan Blanchard, (marr. dis. 1956), one daughter; married Mar. 9, 1957, to Afdera Franchetti (marr. dis. 1962); married Dec. 3, 1965, to Shirlee Mae Adams. Served USN, 1942–46 (Bronze Star; Presidential Citation); rank Lt. Relatives in theatre: daughter, Jane Fonda, actress; son, Peter Fonda, actor. Member of AEA; SAG; AFTRA. Address: (home) 151 E. 74th St., New York, NY 10021; (bus.) c/o C. H. Renthal, 1501 Broadway, New York, NY 10036, tel. CH 4-6575.

Theatre. Mr. Fonda first appeared on stage as Ricky in *You and I* (Omaha Community Playhouse, Nebr., Sept. 1925); subsequently played Chris Miller in *The Barker* (Cape Playhouse, Dennis, Mass., July 1928); appeared in the University Players' productions of *Is Zat So?* and *The Thirteenth Chair* (Falmouth, Mass., Summer, 1928); played in stock productions of the National Junior Th. (Washington, Jan.–May 1929) as Sir Andrew Aguecheek in *Twelfth Night,* the Policeman in *A Kiss for Cinderella,* in *A Midsummer Night's Dream, Master Skylark,* and *The Prince and the Pauper;* and with the University Players, appeared in *The Devil and the Cheese, Outward Bound, The Bad Man, The Firebrand, Juno and the Paycock, The Straw Hat, The Watched Pot, Thunder on the Left* and *The Masque of Venice* (Summer 1929).

He made his Bway debut as a walk-on in *The Game of Love and Death* (Guild Th., Nov. 25, 1929); subsequently reappeared with the University Players in *Paris Bound, Ghost Train, Coquette, Silent House, The Royal Family, Mr. Pim Passes By, A Kiss for Cinderella, In the Next Room* and as Merton in *Merton of the Movies* (Summer 1930); at the National Junior Th. (Washington, D.C., 1930–31), directed and played the Cowardly Lion in *The Wizard of Oz,* and appeared in *Penrod and Sam, Little Women, Tom Sawyer, Little Minister,* and *Treasure Island;* with the University Players he directed *Hell Bent 'Fer Heaven* and appeared in *Holiday, Her Cardboard Lover, The Watched Pot, The Czarina, The Bad Man, Wooden Kimono, The Last Warning, The Constant Nymph,* and *Crime* (Summer 1931); remained with the company to appear in their Winter productions (Baltimore, Md., 1931–32) of *Devil in the Cheese, Mr. Pim Passes By, The Silent House, The Constant Nymph, Mary Rose, The Second Man, The Last Mile, It's a Wise Child, The Trial of Mary Dugan, Murray Hill,* and *The Dark Hours.*

He designed sets for stock productions of *Murray Hill* and *Michael and Mary* (Surrey Playhouse, Me., Summer 1932); played Eustace in *I Loved You Wednesday* (Harris Th., Oct. 11, 1932); Laurie in a stock production of *Little Women* (East Orange, N.J., 1933); played a Gentleman and was understudy to Fred Keating in *Forsaking All Others* (Times Sq. Th., Mar. 1, 1933); was scenic designer at the Westchester Playhouse (Mt. Kisco, N.Y.), for *Journey's End* and *Candida,* and appeared as the Iceman in *It's a Wise Child,* as Max Christman in *Pursuit of Happiness* (Summer 1933); played in *New Faces* (Fulton Th., N.Y.C., Mar. 15, 1933); appeared in *The Swan, Coquette,* and *Up Pops the Devil* (Westchester Playhouse, Mt. Kisco, N.Y., Summer 1934); played Dan Harrow in *The Farmer Takes a Wife* (46 St. Th., N.Y.C., Oct. 30, 1934); and appeared in *The Virginian* (Westchester Playhouse, Mt. Kisco, N.Y.; Westport Country Playhouse, Conn., Aug. 1935); and Hayden Chase in *Blow Ye Winds* (47 St. Th., N.Y.C., Sept. 23, 1937).

Mr. Fonda played Lt. Roberts in *Mister Roberts* (Alvin, Feb. 18, 1948), and on tour (1951); Charles Gray in *Point of No Return* (Alvin, N.Y.C., Dec. 13, 1951); and on tour (opened Ford's Th., Baltimore, Md., Nov. 24, 1952; closed Biltmore, Los Angeles, Calif., May 23, 1953); Lt. Barney Greenwald in *Caine Mutiny Court-Martial* (Plymouth, N.Y.C., Jan. 20, 1954); the Actor in *The Country Girl* (Omaha Civic Ctr., Nebr., June, 1955); Tommy Turner in *The Male Animal* (Cape Playhouse, Dennis, Mass.; Falmouth Playhouse, Mass., Aug. 1956); appeared as Jerry Ryan in *Two for the Seesaw* (Booth, N.Y.C., Jan. 16, 1958); John in *Silent Night, Lonely Night* (Morosco, Dec. 3, 1959); Parker Ballantine in *Critic's Choice* (Ethel Barrymore Th., Dec. 14, 1960); Charles Christian Wertenbaker in *A Gift of Time* (Ethel Barrymore Th., Feb. 22, 1962); Jim Bolton in *Generation* (Morosco, Oct. 6, 1965); the Stage Manager in *Our Town* (ANTA, Nov. 27, 1969); toured in the one-man show *Fathers Against Sons Against Fathers* (1970); directed *The Caine Mutiny Court-Martial* (Ahmanson Th., Los Angeles, Calif., Nov. 30, 1971); toured (1971–72) as Joe in *The Time of Your Life;* toured (1972) in *The Trial of A. Lincoln;* and toured in another one-man show, *Clarence Darrow,* appearing in the part in N.Y.C. (Helen Hayes Th., Mar. 26, 1974; Minskoff Th., Mar. 3, 1975), then touring the US and England, where he appeared in London (Summer 1975).

Films. Mr. Fonda made his film debut as Dan Harrow in *The Farmer Takes a Wife* (20th-Fox, 1935); subsequently appeared in *Way Down East* (20th-Fox, 1935); *I Dream Too Much* (RKO, 1935); *The Trail of the Lonesome Pine* (Par., 1936); *The Moon's Our Home* (Par., 1936); *Spendthrift* (Par., 1936); *Wings of the Morning* (20th-Fox, 1937); *You Only Live Once* (UA, 1937); *Slim* (WB, 1937); *That Certain Woman* (WB, 1937); *I Met My Love Again* (UA, 1938); *Jezebel* (WB, 1938); *Blockade* (UA, 1938); *Spawn of the North* (Par., 1938); *The Mad Miss Manton* (RKO, 1938); *Jesse James* (20th-Fox, 1939); *Let Us Live* (Col., 1939); *The Story of Alexander Graham Bell* (20th-Fox, 1939); *Young Mr. Lincoln* (20th-Fox, 1939); *Drums Along the Mohawk* (20th-Fox, 1939); *The Grapes of Wrath* (20th-Fox, 1940); *Lillian Russell* (20th-Fox, 1940); *The Return of Frank James* (20th-Fox, 1940); *Chad Hanna* (20th-Fox, 1940); *The Lady Eve* (Par., 1941); *Wild Geese Calling* (20th-Fox, 1941); *You Belong to Me* (Col., 1941); *The Male Animal* (WB, 1942); *Rings on Her Fingers* (20th-Fox, 1942); *The Magnificent Dope* (20th-Fox, 1942); *Tales of Manhattan* (20th-Fox, 1942); *The Big Street* (RKO, 1942); *The Immortal Sergeant* (20th-Fox, 1943); *The Ox Bow Incident* (20th-Fox, 1943); *My Darling Clementine* (20th-Fox, 1946); *The Long Night* (RKO, 1947); *The Fugitive* (RKO, 1947); *Daisy Kenyon* (20th-Fox, 1947); *A Miracle Can Happen* (UA, 1947); *Fort Apache* (RKO, 1948); *Mister Roberts* (WB, 1955); *War and Peace* (Par., 1956); *The Wrong Man* (WB, 1957); *12 Angry Men* (UA, 1957); *The Tin Star* (Par., 1957); *Stage Struck* (RKO, 1958); *Warlock* (20th-Fox, 1959); *The Man Who Understood Women* (20th-Fox, 1959); *How the West Was Won* (MGM, 1962); *Advise and Consent* (Col., 1962); *The Longest Day* (20th-Fox, 1962); *Spencer's Mountain* (WB, 1962); *Fail Safe* (Col., 1963); *The Best Man* (UA, 1964); *Sex and the Single Girl* (WB, 1964); *The Rounders* (MGM, 1964); *The Battle of the Bulge* (WB, 1965); *The Dirty Game* (Amer. Internatl., 1966); *A Big Hand for the Little Lady* (WB, 1966); *Welcome to Hard Times* (MGM, 1967); *Firecreek* (WB, 1968); *Yours, Mine, and Ours* (UA, 1968); *Madigan* (U, 1968); *The Boston Strangler* (20th-Fox, 1968); *Once Upon a Time in the West* (Par., 1969); *Too Late the Hero* (Cinerama, 1970); *There Was a Crooked Man* (WB, 1970); *Cheyenne Social Club* (Natl. Gen., 1970); *Sometimes a Great Notion* (U, 1971); *The Serpent* (Avco Embassy, 1973); *Ash Wednesday* (Par., 1973); *My Name Is Nobody* (U, 1974); and *The Last Days of Mussolini* (Par., 1974).

Television. Mr. Fonda has appeared on the series The Deputy (NBC, 1959–60) and The Smith Family (ABC, 1971–72); in the television film *Stranger on the Run* (1967); and in such specials as *John Steinbeck's America and Americans* (CBS, 1967); *Travels with Charley* (NBC, Mar. 17, 1968); *The Red Pony* (NBC, Mar. 18, 1973); and *The Henry Fonda Special.*

Awards. In addition to his military decorations (see above), Mr. Fonda received an Antoinette Perry (Tony) Award (1948) and the Barter Theatre Award (1949), both for his performance in *Mr. Roberts;* a special Straw Hat achievement award (1971) for distinction in the performing arts; and a Drama Desk Award (1974) for his outstanding performance as Clarence Darrow. He received the honorary degree of L.H.D. from Ursinus College, Collegeville, Pa., and Lincoln Sq. Academy, N.Y.C., awarded him an honorary diploma for his aid to young people in the theatre.

Recreation. Painting.

FONDA, JANE. Actress. b. Jane Seymour Fonda, Dec. 21, 1937, New York City, to Henry and Frances (Seymour) Fonda. Father, actor. Attended Emma Willard Sch., Troy, N.Y., 1952–56; Vassar Coll., 1956–58. Studied acting at the Actors' Studio (member 1960–to date), and with Andrea Voutsinas. Married Aug. 14, 1965, to Roger Vadim, film producer and director (marr. dis. 1973); one child; married Jan. 20, 1973, to Tom Hayden. Relatives in theatre: father, Henry Fonda, actor; brother, Peter Fonda, actor. Member of AEA; SAG; AFTRA.

Pre-Theatre. Photographer's model.

Theatre. Miss Fonda first appeared on stage as Nancy Stoddard in *The Country Girl* (Community House, Omaha, Neb. 1954); subsequently appeared in stock as Patricia Stanley in *The Male Animal* (Cape Playhouse, Dennis, Mass., Aug. 19, 1956; Falmouth Playhouse, Mass., Aug. 27, 1956); Patty O'Neill in *The Moon Is Blue* (North Jersey Playhouse, Fort Lee, N.J., June, 1959); and Jacky Durrant in the tryout of *No Concern of Mine* (Westport Country Playhouse, Conn., July 11, 1960).

She made her N.Y.C. debut as Toni Newton in *There Was a Little Girl* (Cort Th., Feb. 29, 1960); subsequently appeared as Norma Brown in *Invitation to a March* (Music Box, Oct. 29, 1960); Tish Stanford in *The Fun Couple* (Lyceum, Oct. 26, 1962); and Madeline Arnold in *Strange Interlude* (Hudson, Mar. 11, 1963).

Films. Miss Fonda made her screen debut in *Tall Story* (WB, 1960); subsequently appeared in *A Walk on the Wild Side* (Col., 1962); *The Chapman Report* (WB, 1962); *Period of Adjustment* (MGM, 1962); *In the Cool of the Day* (MGM, 1963); *Sunday in New York* (MGM, 1964); *The Love Cage* (MGM, 1964); *La Ronde* (Paris Films, 1964); *Joy House* (MGM, 1964); *Les Felins* (MGM, 1964); *Cat Ballou* (Col., 1965); *Circle of Love* (Read-Sterling, 1965); *The Chase* (Col., 1966); *La Curee* (Cocinor, 1966); *Any Wednesday* (WB, 1966); *The Game Is Over* (RFI, 1966); *Hurry Sundown* (Par., 1967); *Barefoot in the Park* (Par., 1967); *Barbarella* (Par., 1968); *Spirits of the Dead* (AI, 1969); *They Shoot Horses, Don't They?* (Cinerama, 1969); *Klute* (WB, 1971); *"FTA"* (AI, 1972); *Steelyard Blues* (WB, 1973); and *A Doll's House* (Par., 1973).

Television. Miss Fonda's appearances include *A String of Beads* (NBC); Girl Talk (ABC); *People and Other Animals* (Ind.); The Living Camera (Ind.); and the Merv Griffin (Ind.) and the Tonight (NBC) shows.

Awards. She won the *Variety* NY Drama Critics Poll for her performance as Toni Newton in *There Was a Little Girl;* the Laurel Award from the Motion Picture Exhibitors of America for *Tall Story* (1960); and an Academy (Oscar) Award (1971) for her performance in *Klute.*

Recreation. Swimming, painting, music.

FONTANNE, LYNN.

Actress. b. Lillie Louise Fontanne, Dec. 6, Essex County, England, to Jules Pierre Antoine and Frances Ellen (Thornley) Fontanne. Father, brass type founder. Studied acting with Ellen Terry, 1903. Married to Alfred Lunt, May 26, 1922. Member of AEA. Address: Genesee Depot, WI 53127.

Theatre. Miss Fontanne first appeared in a touring production of *Alice Sit-By-The-Fire* (1905); and made her London stage debut in the pantomine, *Cinderella* (Drury Lane Th., Dec. 26, 1905); toured as Rose in *Lady Frederick* (1909); in London, appeared in *Where Children Rule* (Garrick, Dec. 11, 1909), and as Lady Mulberry in *Billy's Bargain* (Garrick, June 23, 1910). She first appeared in N.Y.C. as Harriet Budgeon in *Mr. Preedy and the Countess* (39 St. Th., Nov. 7, 1910); then in London as Gwendolen in *The Young Lady of Seventeen* (Criterion, Feb. 22, 1911); and Mrs. Gerrard in *A Storm in a Tea Shop* (Vaudeville, Sept. 9, 1911); toured as Gertrude Rhead in *Milestones* (1912–13); played Liza and Mrs. Collison in *My Lady's Dress* (Royalty, London, Apr. 23, 1914); Gertrude Rhead in *Milestones* (Royalty, Oct. 31, 1914); the Nurse in *Searchlights* (Savoy, Feb. 11, 1915); the title role in *The Terrorist* (Playhouse, May 30, 1915); Ada Pilbeam in *How to Get On* (Victoria Palace, July 12, 1915); appeared in *The Starlight Express* (Kingsway, Dec. 29, 1915); played Winifred in *The Wooing of Eve* (Rochester, N.Y., Mar. 1916); Olive Hood in *The Harp of Life* (Globe, N.Y.C., Nov. 27, 1916); "Princess" Lizzie in *Out There* (Globe, Mar. 27, 1917); Winifred in *The Wooing of Eve* (Liberty, Nov. 9, 1917); Miss Perkins in *Happiness* (Criterion, Dec. 31, 1917); succeeded (May 20, 1918) Laura Hope Crews as Mrs. Rockingham in *A Pair of Petticoats* (44 St. Roof Th., Mar. 18, 1918; moved to Bijou, Apr. 22, 1918); and played Mrs. Glendenning in *Someone in the House* (Knickerbocker, Sept. 9, 1918). She met her husband, Alfred Lunt, while appearing in a Washington, D.C., production of *A Young Man's Fancy* (June 16, 1919); then played Anna in *Chris* (Nixon's Apollo Th., Atlantic City, N.J., Mar. 8, 1920; Broad St. Th., Philadelphia, Mar. 15, 1920); Zephyr in *One Night in Rome* (Garrick, London, May 3, 1920); and Dulcinea in *Dulcy* (English Theatre, Indianapolis, Ind., Feb. 13, 1921; Cort, Chicago, Ill., Feb. 1921; Frazee, N.Y.C., Aug. 13, 1921).

Miss Fontanne played Lady Castlemaine in *Sweet Nell of Old Drury* (48 St. Th., N.Y.C., May 18, 1923); Ann Jordan in *In Love with Love* (Ritz, Aug. 6, 1923); the Actress in *The Guardsman* (Garrick, Oct. 13, 1924); Raina in *Arms and the Man* (Guild, Sept. 14, 1925); Stanja in *The Goat Song* (Guild, Jan. 25, 1926); Laura Pasquale in *At Mrs. Beam's* (Guild, Apr. 26, 1926); Eliza Doolittle in *Pygmalion,* with Alfred Lunt as Higgins (Guild, Nov. 15, 1926); Agrafena in *The Brothers Karamazov* (Guild, Jan. 3, 1927); Mrs. Frayne in *The Second Man* (Guild, Apr. 11, 1927); Jennifer Dubedat in *The Doctor's Dilemma* (Guild, Nov. 21, 1927); Nina Leeds in *Strange Interlude* (John Golden Th., Jan. 30, 1928); Ilsa Von Ilsen in *Caprice* (Guild, Dec. 31, 1928; St. James's, London, Eng., June 4, 1929); Ann Carr in *Meteor* (Guild, N.Y.C., Dec. 23, 1929); Queen Elizabeth in *Elizabeth the Queen* (Guild, Nov. 3, 1930); Elena in *Reunion in Vienna* (Martin Beck Th., Nov. 16, 1931); produced with Alfred Lunt and Noel Coward, and played Gilda in *Design for Living* (Ethel Barrymore Th., Jan. 24, 1933); repeated the role of Elena in *Reunion in Vienna* (lyric, London, Jan. 3, 1934); played Linda Valaine in *Point Valaine* (Ethel Barrymore Th., N.Y.C., Jan. 16, 1935); Katherine in *The Taming of the Shrew* (Guild, Sept. 30, 1935); Irene in *Idiot's Delight* (Shubert, Mar. 24, 1936); Alkmena in *Amphitryon 38* (Shubert, Nov. 1, 1937); and Irina in *The Seagull* (Shubert, Mar. 28, 1938).

In London she repeated Alkmena in *Amphitryon 38* (Lyric, May 17, 1938); toured the US in *The Seagull, Idiot's Delight,* and *Amphitryon 38* (1938–39); toured coast-to-coast (beginning Washington, D.C., Oct. 2, 1939) as Katherine in *The Taming of the Shrew* (Alvin Th., N.Y.C., Feb. 5, 1940); played Miranda Valkonen in *There Shall Be No Night* (Alvin, Apr. 29, 1940); toured in *There Shall Be No Night* (1940–41 and Fall 1941); was Manuela in *The Pirate* (Martin Beck Th., Nov. 25, 1942); repeated her performance as Miranda in *There Shall Be No Night* (Aldwych, London, Dec. 15, 1943); played Olivia Brown in *Love in Idleness* (Lyric, London, Dec. 20, 1944); toured military bases in Europe (1945); played Olivia Brown in *Love in Idleness,* retitled *O Mistress Mine* (Empire, N.Y.C., Jan. 23, 1946); toured in *O Mistress Mine* (1947–48); toured (beginning Feb. 22, 1949) as Emily Chanler in *I Know My Love* (opened Shubert Th., N.Y.C., Nov. 2, 1949); toured again in same role (1950–51); appeared as the Marchioness of Heronden in *Quadrille* (Phoenix, London, Sept. 12, 1952; Coronet, N.Y.C., Nov. 3, 1954); as Essie Sebastian in *The Great Sebastians* (ANTA, Jan. 4, 1956); toured in *The Great Sebastians* (1956–57); toured England (beginning Dec. 24, 1957) as Claire Zachanassian in a tryout of *Time and Again,* which was retitled *The Visit* when she re-created the role (Lunt-Fontanne Th., N.Y.C., May 5, 1958); toured the US as Claire (1959–60, ending at NY City Ctr., Mar. 8, 1960); played Claire in London (Royalty Th., June 23, 1960).

Films. She appeared as Rose Bauman in *Second Youth* (1924); Mrs. Edwin Macaulay, Jr., in *The Man Who Found Himself* (1925); the Actress in *The Guardsman* (MGM, 1931); and as herself (with Alfred Lunt) in *Stage Door Canteen* (UA, 1943).

Television. Miss Fontanne appeared as Essie in *The Great Sebastians* (Producer's Showcase, NBC, Apr. 1, 1957); Mrs. Dowery in *The Old Lady Shows Her Medals* (US Steel Hour, NBC, June 12, 1963); in *Athens— Where the Theatre Began* (CBS, Sept. 11, 1963); played Fanny Holmes in *The Magnificent Yankee* (with Alfred Lunt) (Hallmark Hall of Fame, NBC, Jan. 28, 1965; repeated Feb. 3, 1966); the Dowager Empress in *Anastasia* (Hallmark Hall of Fame, NBC, Mar. 17, 1967); and appeared with Alfred Lunt and Noel Coward on the Dick Cavett Show (ABC, Feb. 10, 1970; repeated June 1, 1970).

Awards. She has received honorary degrees from Dartmouth Coll., New York Univ., Beloit Coll., Carroll Coll., and the Univ. of Wisconsin; and a special medal for diction from the American Academy of Arts and Letters.

On Feb. 17, 1958, the Globe Th. was renamed in honor of Miss Fontanne and her husband, the Lunt-Fontanne Th.

Miss Fontanne and Mr. Lunt received, jointly, the President's Medal of Freedom (announced, July 4, 1964). Yale Univ. conferred the honorary degree of L.H.D. on Miss Fontanne, June 15, 1964.

FOOTE, HORTON.

Playwright. b. A. Horton Foote, Wharton, Tex., to A. H. and Hallie (Brooks) Foote. Grad. Wharton H.S.; attended Pasadena Playhouse; Daykarhanova Sch. of Theatre. Married Lillian Vallish; two sons, two daughters. Member of Dramatists Guild; WGA.

Theatre. Mr. Foote wrote *Texas Town* (Provincetown Playhouse, N.Y.C., Dec. 1942); *Only the Heart* (Bijou Th., Apr. 4, 1944); *Celebration* (Maxine Elliott's Th., Apr. 11, 1948), a one-act play of a triple-bill; *The Chase* (Playhouse, Apr. 15, 1952; Bamberger Th., Hamburg, Germany, 1961); and *The Trip to Bountiful* (Henry Miller's Th., N.Y.C., Nov. 3, 1953; Arts, London, July 4, 1956), also Amsterdam, Dublin, Liverpool and Brighton; and *The Traveling Lady* (Playhouse, N.Y.C., Oct. 27, 1954). He also wrote *The Dancers* (Fiesta Hall, Los Angeles, Calif., Oct. 28, 1963) and the book for the musical *Gone with the Wind* (world premiere, London, England, 1971; American premiere, Dorothy Chandler Pavilion, Los Angeles, Calif., Aug. 28, 1973).

Films. Mr. Foote wrote the screenplays for *Storm Fear* (UA, 1956); *To Kill a Mockingbird* (U, 1962); *Baby, the Rain Must Fall* (Col., 1965), which was based on his 1954 play *The Traveling Lady; The Stalking Moon* (1969); and *Tomorrow* (Filmgroup, 1972).

Television. Mr. Foote is the author of *Only the Heart* (Kraft Television Th., NBC, 1947; repeated 1951); *Ludie Brooks* (CBS, 1951; NBC, 1955); *The Travelers* (NBC, Mar. 1952); *The Old Beginning* (NBC, Nov. 1952); *The Trip to Bountiful* (NBC, Mar. 1953); *Young Lady of Property* (NBC, Apr. 1953); *The Oil Well* (NBC, May 1953); *Rocking Chair* (NBC, June 1953); *Expectant Relations* (NBC, June 1953); *Death of the Old Man* (NBC, July 1953); *Tears of My Sister* (NBC, Aug. 1953); *John Turner Davis* (NBC, Nov. 1953); *The Midnight Caller* (NBC, Dec. 1953); *The Dancers* (NBC, Mar. 1954); *The Shadow of Willie Greer* (NBC, May 1954); *The Roads to Home* (ABC, Apr. 1955); *Flight* (NBC, Feb. 1956); *Drugstore; Sunday Noon* (ABC, Dec. 1956); *Member of the Family* (CBS, Mar. 1957); *Traveling Lady* (CBS, Apr. 1957); *The Old Man* (CBS, Nov. 1959); *Tomorrow* (CBS, Mar. 1960); *The Shape of the River* (CBS, May 1960); *Nights of the Storm (Roots in a Parched Ground)* (CBS, Mar. 1961); *Gambling Heart* (NBC, Feb. 1964); and *Tomorrow* (Playhouse 90, CBS, 1971).

In London, *The Traveling Lady* (BBC, 1958); *The Oil Well* (BBC, 1959); *Young Lady of Property* (ABC, 1960); and *Summer's Pride (Flight)* (BBC, 1961). *The Trip to Bountiful* was presented on television in Holland and Belgium (1957).

On radio, *The Trip to Bountiful* was performed in Canada (CBC, 1957), London (BBC, 1957), Israel and Australia (1957). *The Dancers* was broadcast in London (BBC, 1957).

Published Works. In addition to his published plays, Mr. Foote is the author of *The Chase* (1956), a novel on which the screenplay of the same title was based. His published plays appear separately, in collections and in anthologies.

Awards. Mr. Foote received the Writers Guild of America Screen Award (1962) and the Academy (Oscar) Award (1963) for his screenplay *To Kill a Mockingbird.*

FORBES, BRENDA. Actress. b. Brenda Forbes Taylor, Jan. 14, 1909, London, England, to Ernest John and Mary (Forbes) Taylor. Father, business executive; mother, actress. Grad. St. Helen's Sch., London, 1926. Studied acting at the Old Vic (scholarship) 1927. Married Apr. 5, 1942, to Frederic Voight (dec. 1946); married June 17, 1947, to Merrill Shepard, attorney. Relatives in theatre: brother, Ralph Forbes, actor; sister-in-law, Ruth Chatterton, actress. Member of AEA; AFTRA; SAG. Address: 81 East Elm St., Chicago, IL 60611, tel. (312) SU 7-0849.

Theatre. Miss Forbes, while a student at the Old Vic, made her stage debut as a Serving Wench in *The Taming of the Shrew* (Lyric, Hammersmith Th., Sept. 12, 1927); her N.Y.C. debut as Wilson in *The Barretts of Wimpole Street* (Empire, Feb. 9, 1931), and on tour (1932); played Marina in *Lucrece* (Belasco, N.Y.C., Dec. 20, 1932); toured as Prosperine Garnet in *Candida* and Lady Montague in *Romeo and Juliet* (1933–34); repeated the role of Lady Montague in *Romeo and Juliet* (Martin Beck Th., N.Y.C., Dec. 20, 1934), and succeeded (Jan. 14, 1935) Edith Evans as the Nurse. Miss Forbes played Wilson in *The Barretts of Wimpole Street* (Martin Beck Th., Feb. 25, 1935); Beryl Hodgson in *The Flowers of the Forest* (Martin Beck Th., Apr. 8, 1935); Charlotte Lucas in *Pride and Prejudice* (Music Box, Nov. 5, 1935); Jemima Barrett in *Black Limelight* (Mansfield, Nov. 9, 1936); Lisbet Skirving in *Storm Over Patsy* (Guild, Mar. 8, 1937); Mistress Binns in *Yr. Obedient Husband* (Broadhurst, Jan. 10, 1938); Elfrida von Zedlitz-Wetzel in *Save Me the Waltz* (Martin Beck Th., Feb. 28, 1938); Nurse Guiness in *Heartbreak House* (Mercury, Apr. 29, 1938); and performed in the revues, *One for the Money* (Booth, Feb. 4, 1939); and *Two for the Show* (Booth, Feb. 8, 1940).

Miss Forbes appeared as Mrs. Banner in *Yesterday's Magic* (Guild, Apr. 14, 1942); Prosperine Garnett in *Candida* (Shubert, Apr. 27, 1942); Mrs. Lane in *Morning Star* (Morosco, Sept. 14, 1942); Miss Tinkham in *Suds in Your Eye* (Cort, Jan. 12, 1944); Wilson in *The Barretts of Wimpole Street* (USO Camp Shows, ETO, 1944); Ethel Barrymore Th., N.Y.C., Mar. 26, 1945); performed in the revue, *Three to Make Ready* (Adelphi, Mar. 7, 1946); played Isabelle's Mother in *Ring Round the Moon* (Martin Beck Th., Nov. 23, 1950); toured as Millicent Tower in *Jane* (1952); played Lady Harriet Ripley in *Quadrille* (Coronet, N.Y.C., Nov. 3, 1954); Mabel Crosswaithe in *The Reluctant Debutante* (Henry Miller's Th., Oct. 10, 1956), and as Sheila Broadbent on a tour of the West Coast (1957).

Miss Forbes appeared as Mrs. Malaprop in *The Rivals* (Goodman Memorial Th., Chicago, Ill., Apr. 28, 1963); Valerie Clayton in world premiere, *The Camel Bell* (Drury Lane Th., London, Jan. 16, 1963); and for the US State Dept., performed in *Medea* (Th. Sarah Bernhardt, Paris, Fr., June 14, 1955). She directed *The Barretts of Wimpole Street* (Goodman Memorial Th., 1966); played Trilbe Costello in *The Loves of Cass McGuire* (Helen Hayes Th., N.Y.C., Oct. 22, 1966); played Lady Vale in *Darling of the Day* (George Abbott Th., Jan. 27, 1968); narrated *Jeanne d'Arc au bûcher* for the Chicago Symphony Orchestra (1968); played Lady Utterword in *Heartbreak House* (Goodman Memorial Th., May 29, 1970); Lady Bracknell in *The Importance of Being Earnest* (Goodman Th., Oct. 30, 1971); toured as Letty in *The Day After the Fair,* (1973).

Films. Miss Forbes appeared in *Vigil in the Night* (RKO, 1940); *Mrs. Miniver* (MGM, 1942); *This Above All* (20th-Fox, 1942); and *The White Cliffs of Dover* (MGM, 1944).

Television. She has appeared on Studio One (CBS); Producers Showcase (CBS); US Steel Hour (CBS); Kraft Television Th. (NBC); Four Star Playhouse (CBS); and in *Blithe Spirit* (CBS, Jan. 14, 1956); *The Magnificent Yankee* (NBC, Feb. 28, 1965); *Anastasia* (NBC, Mar. 17, 1967); and *La voix humaine* (Ch. 11, Chicago, 1971).

Recreation. Golf, dressmaking, needlepoint.

FORBES, MERIEL. Actress. b. Sept. 13, 1913, London, England, to Frank and Honora (McDermot) Forbes-Robertson. Attended sch., Eastbourne, England; Brussels, Belgium; Paris, France. Married 1944 to Sir Ralph Richardson, actor; one son. Member of AEA.

Theatre. Miss Forbes made her debut touring England with her father's company as Mrs. de Rooley in *The Passing of the Third Floor Back* (1929); appeared in productions with the Dundee Repertory Co. (1931); made her London debut as Simone D'Ostignac in *Porcupine Point* (Gate, Sept. 14, 1931); toured with the Birmingham (England) Repertory Th. Co. in *Musical Chairs;* played Kitty and was an understudy in *Dinner at Eight* (Palace, London, Jan. 6, 1933); played Joan Taylor in *First Episode* ("Q," Sept. 11, 1933); Diana Mauteby in *This Side Idolatry* (Lyric, Oct. 19, 1933); Mary Wallman in *Angel* (Vaudeville, Dec. 7, 1933); Joan Taylor in *First Episode* (Comedy, Jan. 26, 1934); Daisy Dowling in *The Dark Tower* (Shaftesbury, May 10, 1934); Dae Beldon in *. . . and a Woman Passed by* (Duke of York's, Apr. 9, 1935); Stella Hardcastle in *Red Night* (Queen's, Mar. 4, 1936); Princess Xraine in *Rise and Shine* (Drury Lane, May 7, 1936); Daisy in *The Amazing Dr. Clitterhouse* (Haymarket, Aug. 6, 1936); Rén ée la Lune in *I Killed the Count* (Whitehall, Dec. 10, 1937); Julia in *The Rivals* (Old Vic, Dec. 6, 1938); and Crystal Allen in *The Women* (Strand, Apr. 22, 1940).

Miss Forbes played Muriel Eden in the Norman Marshall Company's production of *The Gay Lord Quex* (1943); Milly Smith in *A Soldier for Christmas* (Wyndham's, London, Feb. 3, 1944); Katerine Fantina in *Royal Circle* (Wyndham's, Apr. 27, 1948); Elizabeth Imbrie in *The Philadelphia Story* (Duchess, Dec. 1, 1949); Peggy Dobson in *Home at Seven* (Wyndham's, Mar. 7, 1950); Patricia Smith in *The Millionairess* (New, June 27, 1952); Lydia Truscott in *The White Carnation* (Globe, Mar. 20, 1953); and toured Australia with her husband in *Separate Tables,* and *The Sleeping Prince* (1955).

She made her N.Y.C. debut as Mlle. de Ste. Euverte in *The Waltz of the Toreadors* (Cort, Jan. 17, 1957); played Mamie in *Roseland* (St. Martin's, London, Feb. 12, 1958); succeeded (Oct. 1958) Wendy Hiller as Isobel Cherry in *The Flowering Cherry* (Haymarket, Nov. 21, 1957); played the Duchess of Clausonnes in *Look After Lulu* (Royal Court, London, July 29, 1959); Lady Sneerwell in *The School for Scandal* (Haymarket Th., London, Apr. 15, 1962, and Majestic, N.Y.C., Jan. 24, 1963); Titania in *A Midsummer Night's Dream* (Royal, Brighton, England, Feb. 1964); repeated that role in a tour of South America, Lisbon, Portugal, Paris, and Athens, sponsored by the British Council; and played the lead in *Lloyd George Knew My Father* (Her Majesty's Th., Melbourne, Australia, 1973; and Eisenhower Th., Kennedy Ctr., Washington, D.C., July 2, 1974).

Films. Miss Forbes made her film debut in 1934. More recent appearances include *Home at Seven* (British Lion, 1952) and *Oh, What a Lovely War!* (Par., 1969).

Television. She appeared in the series *Blandings' Castle.*

Recreation. Miss Forbes collects Staffordshire china.

FORD, CONSTANCE. Actress. b. July 1, Bronx, N.Y., to Edwin and Cornelia (Smith) Ford. Grad. St. Barnabas H.S., N.Y.C.; attended Hunter Coll. Married 1946 to Shelley Hull, stage manager (marr. dis. 1955). Member of AEA; SAG; AFTRA.

Pre-Theatre. Conover fashion model.

Theatre. Miss Ford made her professional debut in stock, performing in nine productions at the Ivoryton, Conn., Playhouse (Summer 1946), including Agnes Willing in *The Late George Apley,* Kitty Duval in *The Time of Your Life,* the Maid in *Night Must Fall,* Katrin in *I Remember Mama,* Laura in *The Glass Menagerie,* in *Dear Ruth,* etc.; was understudy to Patricia Neal as Regina in *Another Part of the Forest* (Fulton, N.Y.C., Nov. 20, 1946); toured in the National co. of *John Loves Mary* (opened Harris, Chicago, Feb. 9, 1948), assuming the role of Lily after the opening; and made her Bway debut as Miss Forsythe in *Death of a Salesman* (Morosco, Feb. 10, 1949).

She appeared in *The Kidders* (Brattle Th., Cambridge, Mass., Apr. 1951); played Lorna Moone in a stock tour (Summer 1951); Janna in *See the Jaguar* (Cort, N.Y.C., Dec. 3, 1952); Denia Cameron in *One Eye Closed* (Bijou, Nov. 24, 1954), but did not play the opening night performance; Sharon Kensington in *Career* (Playhouse in the Park, Philadelphia, Aug. 26, 1957); Frankie Jordan in *Say, Darling* (ANTA, N.Y.C., Apr. 3, 1958); Ann Knutsen in *The Golden Fleecing* (Henry Miller's Th., Oct. 15, 1959); Hildy Jones in *Nobody Loves an Albatross* (Lyceum, Dec. 19, 1963); and Valerie Rogers in *UTBU* (Helen Hayes Th., Jan. 4, 1966).

Films. Miss Ford made her debut in *The Last Hunt* (MGM, 1956); subsequently appeared in *The Iron Sheriff* (UA, 1957); *Bailout at 43,000* (UA, 1957); *A Summer Place* (WB, 1959); *Claudelle Inglish* (WB, 1961); *Home from the Hill* (MGM, 1960); *All Fall Down* (MGM, 1962); *Rome Adventure* (WB, 1962); *The Cabinet of Caligari* (20th-Fox, 1962); *House of Women* (WB, 1962); *The Caretakers* (UA, 1963); and *99 44/100% Dead* (20th-Fox, 1974).

Television. Miss Ford plays the role of Ada McGowan on the daytime serial Another World (NBC, fall 1969 to date). She has also performed on Armstrong Circle Th. (NBC, Nov. 6, 1951); as Bonnie in *Burlesque* (Kraft Th., NBC, Jan. 14, 1954); the title role in *Anna Christie* (Pond's Th., ABC, Mar. 3, 1955); in *The Comedian* (Playhouse 90, CBS, Feb. 14, 1957); on The Web (CBS); Philco Playhouse (NBC); Plymouth Playhouse (ABC); Studio One (CBS); Kraft Th. (NBC); Goodyear Playhouse (NBC); Twilight Zone (CBS); Way of the World (NBC); Phil Silvers Show (CBS); Appointment with Adventure (CBS); Climax (CBS); Lux Video Th. (NBC); The Millionaire (CBS); Rawhide (CBS); State Trooper; Surfside 6 (ABC); Bat Masterson (NBC); Zane Grey Th. (CBS); Deputy (NBC); Dakotas (ABC); Father Knows Best (ABC); Alfred Hitchcock Presents (CBS); Perry Mason (CBS); Shane (ABC); Dr. Kildare (NBC); East Side/West Side (CBS); Gunsmoke (CBS); 20th-Fox Hour (CBS); Matinee Th. (NBC); Trackdown (CBS); Have Gun, Will Travel (CBS); The Plainsman (NBC); Thriller (NBC); Wanted Dead or Alive (CBS); The Untouchables (ABC); 87th Precinct (NBC); Naked City (ABC); Target: Corrupters (ABC); Adventures in Paradise (ABC); Frontier Circus (CBS); Sam Benedict (NBC); Temple Houston (NBC); and Rose Peterson on Search for Tomorrow (CBS).

Awards. Miss Ford received a NATAS (Emmy) Award nomination for *Anna Christie* (1955).

FORD, FRANK. Producer, critic. b. Sept. 29, 1916, Philadelphia, Pa., to Benjamin and Bella Ford. Father, merchant. Grad. Simon Gratz H.S., Philadelphia, 1934; Univ. of Pennsylvania, A.B. 1939. Married June 10, 1951, to Dorothy Smallwood; one daughter. Served USAF, 1942–46; rank, Staff Sgt. Member of MATA.

Theatre. With Lee Guber and Shelly Gross, Mr. Ford was a founder, officer, and director of Music Fair Enterprises, Inc., which owns, operates, and produces musicals for summer theatres.

Messrs. Ford, Guber, and Gross produced national bus-and-truck tours; *Li'l Abner* (opened Riviera Hotel, Las Vegas, Nev., Sept. 1, 1958; closed Royal Alexandra, Toronto, Canada, Jan. 3, 1959); *The Pleasure of His Company* (opened Aud., Rochester, N.Y., Sept. 15, 1960; closed Shubert, New Haven, Conn., Mar. 25, 1961); *The Andersonville Trial* (opened Center Th., Norfolk, Va., Sept. 28, 1960; closed Community Ctr., Hershey, Pa., Apr. 15, 1961); *A Thurber Carnival* (opened Center Th., Norfolk, Va., Sept. 22, 1961; closed Music Hall, Kansas

City, Mo., Apr. 28, 1962); and, by arrangement with David Merrick, *Carnival!* (opened Bushnell Aud., Hartford, Conn., Oct. 18, 1962; closed Shubert, Boston, Mass., May 11, 1963).

With Lee Guber and Shelly Gross, he produced *Catch Me if You Can* (Morosco, N.Y.C., Mar. 9, 1965); and *Sherry!* (Alvin, Mar. 28, 1967).

Television and Radio. Mr. Ford worked for 11 years (1946–57) as radio and television producer for Philip Klein Advertising Agency, Philadelphia (Pa.).

In 1966, Mr. Ford discontinued active production association with Music Fair Enterprises, Inc., and joined WCAU (Philadelphia) as a theatre and film critic.

FORD, GEORGE. Manager, author. b. Aug. 28, 1879, Washington, D.C., to Henry Clay and Blanche (Chapman) Ford. Father, theatre manager; treasurer of Ford's Th., Washington, D.C.; mother, actress. Educ. Franklin H.S., Washington, D.C.; Erasmus Hall H.S., Brooklyn, N.Y.; grad. Dartmouth Coll., 1903. Married Aug. 9, 1918, to Helen Ford, actress and singer. Relative in theatre: uncle, John T. Ford, theatre owner and operator. Address: 5147 Oakwood Ave., La Canada, CA 91611.

Theatre. After graduation from college, Mr. Ford became carloader and company manager for Viola Allen's coast-to-coast tours in the US. In 1905, he became a press agent and company manager for such producers as the Shuberts, William A. Brady, John D. Williams, and R. E. Johnson; in 1912, he became a summer stock manager in Troy, Albany, and Schenectady, N.Y.; and Columbus, Ohio. He was company manager and press agent for Lionel Barrymore in *The Copperhead* (Shubert Th., N.Y.C., Feb. 18, 1918). In 1921, he organized the production *George Ford Presents*, starring Fritz Leiber, and during the next four seasons toured this Shakespearean company coast-to-coast twice, as well as opening it in N.Y.C. (Knickerbocker Th., 1924). He was manager for *Love's Comedy* (Hudson Th., N.Y.C., 1922); *Dearest Enemy* (Knickerbocker Th., Sept. 18, 1925); and *Miss Gulliver's Travels* (Hudson, Nov. 25, 1931), of which he was, with Ethel Taylor, co-author.

From 1927, Mr. Ford was manager for Elsie Janis, John Charles Thomas, Beniamino Gigli, and other artists. He was company manager of the Ballets Russes de Monte Carlo for nineteen seasons, of the American Ballet Theatre for two seasons, and assistant manager at the Metropolitan Opera House for the N.Y.C. debut of the Royal Danish Ballet and manager for the tour that followed. He was company manager for Katharine Cornell in *The Three Sisters* (Ethel Barrymore Th., N.Y.C., Dec. 21, 1942); for *Music at Midnight* (1961) and for the Moral Re-Armament show, *Space Is So Startling*. He retired in 1963.

Published Works. Mr. Ford wrote *These Were Actors*, the history of his mother's family—the Chapmans and the Drakes—as stars of the English and the American stage.

Awards. Mr. Ford was a special honorary guest in 1968 at the official dedication ceremonies of the restored Ford's Th. in Washington, D.C., which his father and uncle had owned and operated at the time of Pres. Lincoln's assassination.

FORD, HELEN. Actress, singer. b. Helen Isabel Barnett, June 6, Troy, N.Y., to George and Emma (Barry) Barnett. Father, manufacturer. Educated in public and private schools. Studied piano and singing at Troy Conservatory of Music. Married Aug. 9, 1918, to George Denham Ford, theatrical manager, producer, author. Member of AEA; SAG. Address: 5147 Oakwood Ave., La Canada, CA tel. (213) 790-2517.

Theatre. Miss Ford first performed as a child in stock productions in Troy (N.Y.); subsequently toured as a concert singer; and made her N.Y.C. debut as Annie Wood in a vaudeville sketch with music, *The Heart of Annie Wood* (Palace Th., Nov. 11, 1918).

She played Enid Vaughan, as a replacement, in *Sometime* (Shubert, Oct. 4, 1918); Toinette Fontaine in *Always You* (Central, Jan. 5, 1920); Natalie Blythe in *Sweetheart Shop* (Knickerbocker, Sept. 31, 1920), touring in it for one year; appeared in the pre-Bway tryout of *Little White House* (opened National, Washington, D.C., Dec. 1921; closed Balitmore, Md., Dec. 1921); played Marjorie Leeds in *For Goodness Sake* (Lyric, N.Y.C., Feb. 20, 1922); Mary Thompson in *The Gingham Girl* (Earl Carroll Th., Aug. 28, 1922); Helen McGuffy in *Helen of Troy, N.Y.* (Selwyn, June 19, 1923); Hope Franklin in *No Other Girl* (Morosco, Aug. 13, 1924); and Betsy Burke in her husband's production of *Dearest Enemy* (Knickerbocker, Sept. 18, 1925).

She played the title role in *Peggy-Ann* (Vanderbilt, Dec. 27, 1926); the title role in *Chee-Chee* (Mansfield, Sept. 25, 1928); Patricia Harrington in *The Patsy* (King's Th., Southsea, England, Dec. 10, 1928); appeared at the London Palladium in a program of songs (Apr. 1929); and played Norma Besant in *Coquette* (Apollo, June 6, 1929).

Miss Ford appeared as a singer at the Palace (N.Y.C., Dec. 20, 1929); played Susie Sachs in her husband's production of *A Church Mouse* (Hollis St. Th., Boston, Mass., Apr. 30, 1932); appeared in *The Fair Intruder* (Provincetown Th., Mass., July 1932); played Claire in *The Other One* (Biltmore, N.Y.C., Oct. 3, 1932); Adele in *Champagne, Sec* (Morosco, Oct. 14, 1933); Yum-Yum in a stock production of *The Mikado* (Long Beach, N.Y., Summer 1934); and at the Westport (Conn.) Country Playhouse, appeared in *The Chimes of Normandy* and played Clara Kenny in *So Many Paths* (Summer 1934).

She played Kathie in *The Student Prince* and Barbara Frietche in *My Maryland* (Shubert's Nevin Field, Detroit, Mich., Summer 1934); Patricia Harrington in *The Patsy* (Westchester County Playhouse, Mt. Kisco, N.Y., July 19, 1935); the title role in the opera *Patience* (Westchester County Playhouse, Sept. 2, 1935); appeared in *Fashion* and *Baby Mine* (Mary Young Th., Centerville, Mass., July –Aug. 1936); played Mariette Fleurly in *Mariette* (Berkshire Playhouse, Stockbridge, Mass., June 28, 1937); appeared in *The Patsy* (Majestic, Brooklyn, N.Y., Feb. 21, 1938); as Franzi Wiesner in *Franzi* (Rye Beach, N.H., July 1938); and as Freelove Clark in *Great Lady* (Majestic, N.Y.C., Dec. 1, 1938).

Miss Ford played Nella Vaga in *Tonight or Never* (Brattle Hall, Cambridge, Mass., July 6, 1940); Frances Galligan in *Retreat to Pleasure* (Belasco, N.Y.C., Dec. 17, 1940); and Lucy in *The Rivals* (Shubert, Jan. 14, 1942).

She was senior hostess and mistress of ceremonies at the Stage Door Canteen (1942–44, N.Y.C.); and toured in a USO production of *Over 21* (Southwest Pacific Theatre of War, Sept. 1944–Feb. 1945).

She played Mrs. Fairweather in *The Banker's Daughter* (LAB Th., Los Angeles, Calif., 1950); and Mrs. Gans in *Anniversary Waltz* (La Jolla Playhouse, Calif., July 15, 1954).

Films. She has appeared in *Apartment for Peggy* (20th-Fox, 1948); *The Model and the Marriage Broker* (20th-Fox, 1952); and *Sound Off* (Col., 1952).

Television. She has performed in many revues and musical comedies.

Recreation. Decorating, painting, swimming, gardening.

FORD, PAUL. Actor. b. Paul Ford Weaver, Nov. 2, 1901, Baltimore, Md., to Louis and Effie (Ford) Weaver. Father, businessman. Grad. Germantown H.S., Pa., 1918; attended Dartmouth College 1920–21. Married Dec. 27, 1924, to Nell Campbell; two sons, three daughters. Member of AEA (council 1953–55, 1962–67); SAG; AFTRA; ATAS; The Players. Address: 37 W. 12th St., New York, NY 10011, tel. (212) AL 5-3838.

Pre-Theatre. Proofreader, salesman, writer, night watchman, gas station attendant, caterer, puppeteer.

Theatre. Mr. Ford made his stage debut with the Dartmouth Players as Sir Lucius O'Trigger in *The Rivals* (Dartmouth Coll., Hanover, N.H., 1920); subsequently played the Foreman and Old Peter in *Steel* (Provincetown Playhouse, N.Y.C., Dec. 19, 1939); Sergeant Carey in *Decision* (Belasco, Feb. 2, 1944); Sen. Zachariah Chandler in *The War President* (Shubert, Apr. 24, 1944); Burks in *Lower North* (Belasco, Aug. 25, 1944); Mr. Hardy in *Kiss Them for Me* (Belasco, Mar. 20, 1945); Mr. Sullivan in the pre-Bway tryout of *Mr. Cooper's Left Hand* (opened Wilbur, Boston, Sept. 25, 1945; closed there, Oct. 6, 1945); Ulee Jackson in *Flamingo Road* (Belasco, Mar. 19, 1946); and succeeded (June 1946) Robert Simon as Walter Lund in *On Whitman Ave.* (Cort, May 8, 1946).

He appeared as Harold Penniman in *Another Part of the Forest* (Fulton, Nov. 20, 1946); Pastor Flaten in *As We Forgive Our Debtors* (Princess, Mar. 9, 1947); Arthur Malcolm in *Command Decision* (Fulton, Oct. 1, 1947); Charley in the national tour of *Death of a Salesman* (1949–50); George's Father in *The Brass Ring* (Lyceum, N.Y.C., Apr. 10, 1952); Col. Wainright Purdy III in *The Teahouse of the August Moon* (Martin Beck Th., Oct. 15, 1953); Congressman Fairweather in *Good As Gold* (Belasco, Mar. 7, 1957); and Karl Kellenbach in *Whoop-Up* (Shubert, Dec. 22, 1958).

Mr. Ford succeeded (June 1, 1959) David Burns as Mayor Shinn in *The Music Man* (Majestic, Dec. 19, 1957); appeared in *A Thurber Carnival* (ANTA, Feb. 26, 1960), Harry Lambert in *Cradle and All* (Playhouse, Dennis, Mass., July 1962), subsequently re-titled *Never Too Late* (Playhouse, Nov. 27, 1962); Bascom Barlow in *Three Bags Full* (Henry Miller's Th., Mar. 6, 1966); Farnsworth Parker in *Send Us Your Boy* (Summer tour, 1966); in *You Can't Take it with You* (Summer tour, 1966); Walter Davis in *What Did We Do Wrong?* (Helen Hayes Th., N.Y.C., Oct. 22, 1967); Elwood P. Dowd in *Harvey* (Summer tour, 1968); in *Captain Brassbound's Conversion* (Ahmanson, Los Angeles, Fall 1968); Mr. Carver in *Three Men on a Horse* (Lyceum, N.Y.C., Oct. 16, 1969); succeeded (Jan. 1970) Jules Munshin (who succeeded John McGiver) as the Mayor in *The Front Page* (Ethel Barrymore, Oct. 18, 1969); toured as William H. Gallagher in *Light Up the Sky* (opened Fisher, Detroit, Aug. 17, 1971); and played the Mailman in *Fun City* (Morosco, N.Y.C., Jan. 2, 1972).

Films. Mr. Ford made his film debut as a Police Sergeant in *The House on 92nd Street* (20th-Fox, 1945); subsequently appeared as a Detective in *Naked City* (U, 1948); the Sheriff in *Lust for Gold* (Col., 1949); a Legislator in *All the Kings Men* (Col., 1949); the Judge in *Perfect Strangers*, (WB, 1950); Copeland in *The Kid From Texas* (U, 1950); repeated the role of Col. Purdy in the film adaptation of *The Teahouse of the August Moon* (MGM, 1956); played the Bartender in *The Missouri Traveler* (Buena Vista, 1958); Horace Vandergelder in *The Matchmaker* (Par., 1958); repeated the role of Mayor Shinn in *The Music Man* (WB, 1962); Senator Danta in *Advise and Consent* (Col., 1962); the Judge in *Who's Got the Action* (Par., 1962); Ex-Col. Wilberforce in *It's A Mad, Mad, Mad, Mad, World* (UA, 1963); repeated the role of Harry Lambert in *Never Too Late* (WB, 1965); played Ballinger in *A Big Hand For the Little Lady* (WB, 1966); Fendall Hawkins in *The Russians Are Coming, The Russians Are Coming* (UA, 1966); American General in *The Spy With a Cold Nose* (Embassy, 1966); Mr. Smith in *The Comedians* (MGM, 1967); Scotty's Dad in *Lola* (Amer. Int., 1973); and in *Journey Back to Oz* (Filmation, 1974).

Television. Mr. Ford first appeared on television in 1948, subsequently playing on numerous dramatic and comedy shows, including four seasons as Col. Hall on the Phil Silvers ("Sgt. Bilko") Show (CBS, premiere Sept. 20, 1955; through Spring 1959); in *Bloomer Girl* (Producer's Showcase, NBC, May 28, 1956); *Junior Miss* (Dupont Show of the Month, CBS, Dec. 20, 1957); *The Girls in 509* (Play of the Week, WNTA, Apr. 18, 1960); repeated the role of Col. Purdy in *The Teahouse of the August Moon* (Hallmark Hall of Fame, NBC, 1962); Sam Bailey in the series, *The Baileys of Balboa* (CBS, 1964–65); etc.

Awards. Mr. Ford was nominated for NATAS

(Emmy) Awards for his performance as Col. Hall in the Phil Silvers Show (1956, 1957, 1958); and for his performance as Col. Purdy in *The Teahouse of the August Moon* (1962); received nominations for Antoinette Perry (Tony) Awards for his performances as Col. Purdy in *The Teahouse of the August Moon* (1953) and Harry Lambert in *Never Too Late* (1962).
Recreation. Sculpting, painting, writing, bridge.

FORD, RUTH. Actress, playwright. b. Ruth Elizabeth Ford, Hazelhurst, Miss., to Charles Lloyd and Gertrude (Cato) Ford. Father, in hotel business; mother, painter. Grad. Our Lady of the Lake H.S., San Antonio, Tex.; attended All Saints' Episcopal Jr. Coll.; Mississippi State Coll. for Women; Univ. of Mississippi, B.A.; M.A. (philosophy). Married 1941 to Peter Van Eyck, actor (marr. dis.); one daughter; married July 6, 1952, to Zachary Scott, actor (dec. 1965). Member of AEA; AFTRA; SAG; Chi Omega (pres., coll. chap.). Address: 1 W. 72nd St., New York, NY 10023, tel. (212) TR 3-5452.

Pre-Theatre. Photographer's model.

Theatre. Miss Ford made her stage debut with the Ivoryton (Conn.) Players, as Nanny in *Ways and Means;* Judy in *Idiot's Delight;* the Fourth Athenian Woman in *Lysistrata;* First Lady in *Dead End;* Lois Fisher in *The Children's Hour;* and Mildred in *The Jazz Age* (Summer 1937).

She made her Bway debut as Jane in the Orson Welles' production of *The Shoemaker's Holiday* (Mercury Th., Jan. 1, 1938); played Rosalie in *Danton's Death* (Mercury, Nov. 2, 1938); Mrs. Billings in *Too Much Johnson* (Stoney Creek, Conn., Summer 1939); was resident leading lady at the Green Mansions Th. (Warrensburg, N.Y., Summer 1939), appearing as the Bridesmaid in *Trial by Jury;* the Lady in *The Dark Lady of the Sonnets;* Desdemona in *Othello;* in *Interesting Experiment;* Stella Cartwright in *Ways and Means;* Lady Maureen Gilpin in *Hands Across the Sea;* Mrs. Omar Dobbs in *The Best Dressed Woman in the World;* and Suzy Courtois in *Topaz.*

Miss Ford appeared in *Swingin' the Dream* (NY City Ctr., Nov. 29, 1939); as Irma Szabo in *The Glass Slipper* (Barbizon-Plaza, Oct. 1940); toured as Roxanne in Jose Ferrer's production of *Cyrano de Bergerac* (May 1946); in stock, played Matilda Rockley in *You Touched Me* (Mt. Kisco, July 1946); appeared as Estelle in *No Exit* (Biltmore, N.Y.C., Nov. 26, 1946); in stock, appeared as Maggie in *The Man Who Came to Dinner* (Westport Country Playhouse, Conn., Summer 1947); played Yolan in *This Time Tommorrow* (Ethel Barrymore Th., N.Y.C., Nov. 3, 1947); and in stock, appeared as Laetitia in *Children of Darkness* (Summer 1948).

Miss Ford played Ophelia in *Hamlet* (Kronberg Castle, Elsinore, Denmark, June 1949); was resident leading lady at Elitch Gardens (Denver, Col., Summer 1949), appearing in *The Heiress, The Winslow Boy, Twentieth Century, The Traitor,* and *Clutterbuck;* played Deborah Pomfret in *Clutterbuck* (Biltmore, Dec. 3, 1949); and Martirio in *The House of Bernarda Alba* (ANTA, Jan. 1, 1951).

At the Brattle Th. (Cambridge, Mass.) she appeared as Estelle in *No Exit* (July 1950), the stepdaughter in *Six Characters in Search of an Author* (Oct. 1950), Lady Macbeth in *Macbeth,* Dynamene in *A Phoenix Too Frequent,* in *The Failures* (Summer 1951), and Sally Bowles in *I Am a Camera* (1953); appeared in *The Shewing Up of Blanco Posnet* and *The Apollo of Bellac* (Westport Country Playhouse, Conn., July, 1954); as the Patient in *Too True to Be Good* (Playhouse-in-the-Park, Philadelphia, Pa., July 1954); and Sabina in *The Skin of Our Teeth* (Boston Commons Arts Festival, Mass., 1955).

Miss Ford played Pia in *Island of Goats* (Fulton, N.Y.C., Oct. 4, 1955); in two one-act plays, Mrs. X, an Actress, in *The Stronger;* and Kristin, the Cook, in *Miss Julie* (Phoenix, Feb. 21, 1956); Temple Drake in *Requiem for a Nun,* which she adapted (Royal Court, London, Nov. 26, 1957; John Golden Th., N.Y.C.; Jan. 30, 1959); appeared as the Nun in *The Umbrella* and as Mommy in *The American Dream;* (Festival of Two Worlds, Spoleto, Italy, 1963); and Vera Ridgeway Condotti in the revised version of *The Milk Train Doesn't Stop Here Anymore* (Brooks Atkinson Th., N.Y.C., Jan. 1, 1964).

Miss Ford was Dorothy Cleves in *Any Wednesday* (Palm Beach and Coconut Grove, Fla., 1965); Virginia Varnum in *Lovey* (Cherry Lane Th., N.Y.C., Mar. 25, 1965); Hattie Loomis in *Dinner at Eight* (Alvin Th., Sept. 27, 1966); Judith Hastings in *The Ninety-Day Mistress* (Biltmore, Nov. 6, 1967); and Aunt Adelaide in *Hunger and Thirst* (Berkshire Th. Festival, Stockbridge, Mass., 1969). In 1970, she was in *The Button* during its pre-Bway tour (closed out of town). She played Verena Talbo in *The Grass Harp* (Martin Beck Th., Nov. 2, 1971); Comtesse de Saint-Fond in *Madame de Sade* (Th. de Lys, Oct. 30, 1972); Loraine in *A Breeze from the Gulf* (Eastside Playhouse, Oct. 15, 1973); and Clarissa Halley-Yshot in *The Charlatan* (Mark Taper Forum, Los Angeles, Calif., 1974).

Films. Miss Ford has appeared in *Roaring Frontiers* (Col., 1941); *Gorilla Man* (WB, 1942); *The Man Who Returned to Life* (Col., 1942); *Truck Busters* (WB, 1943); *Adventure in Iraq* (WB, 1943); *Wilson* (20th-Fox, 1944); *The Keys of the Kingdom* (20th-Fox, 1944); *Circumstantial Evidence* (20th-Fox, 1945); *Dragonwyck* (20th-Fox, 1946); as Mrs. George Kaufman in *Act One* (WB, 1963); as Mrs. Gagnon in *The Tree* (Robert Guenette, 1968); and as Carlotta in *Play It As It Lays* (U, 1972).

Awards. Miss Ford received a nomination by the London drama critics as the best actress of the season for her performance as Temple Drake in *Requiem for a Nun* (1957).

Recreation. Reading, talking, music, collecting art.

FORDIN, HUGH G. Producer, editor, author, publisher. b. Hugh Grant Fordin, Dec. 17, 1935, Brooklyn, N.Y., to Leon and Annette (Bernstein) Fordin. Father, leather manufacturer. Grad. James Madison H.S., Brooklyn, 1953; Syracuse Univ., B.S. 1957. Member of League of NY Theatres; Phi Epsilon Pi (natl. secty., 1953–57); Boar's Head (pres., 1955–57). Address: 404 E. 55th St., New York, NY 10022, tel. (212) PL 8-5177; R.D. 1, Box 112, New Hope, PA 18938, tel. (215) 794-8979.

Theatre. Mr. Fordin's first assignment was as an apprentice in summer stock at Seacliff, N.Y. (1954); was a producer at the Northport (N.Y.) Country Playhouse (1955); served as managing director of the Sacandaga (N.Y.) Summer Theatre (1956); and produced touring productions of *Gentlemen Prefer Blondes* and *Anniversary Waltz* (Summer 1957).

He was a casting agent for MCA (N.Y.C., 1959–60); produced a tour of *Critic's Choice* (Summer 1961), produced, with Robert Herrman, the national tour (opened Municipal Aud., Lafayette, La., Dec. 1, 1961; closed Mar. 25, 1962), and produced a bus-and-truck tour of this play (1961–62).

During 1962–63, Mr. Fordin produced stock tours of *Bye Bye Birdie, Fiorello!, The Flower Drum Song, Come Blow Your Horn, Carnival!Finian's Rainbow, Brigadoon, Irma La Douce* and *Under the Yum-Yum Tree.* He was also the associate producer, with Len Bedso and Hal Grossman, of the national tour of *The Boys from Syracuse* (opened Allentown, Pa., Jan. 6, 1964).

Mr. Fordin operated Mount Tom Playhouse, Holyoke, Mass. (1964–65) and was director of casting for David Productions, N.Y.C. (1966–69), being responsible for such presentations as *Hello, Dolly!; How Now, Dow Jones; Rosencrantz and Guildenstern Are Dead;* and *Mata Hari.* He was casting director for Twentieth Century-Fox in 1969 and executive assistant to David Brown, vice-president in charge of creative affairs at Twentieth Century-Fox (1969–70). In the latter capacity, Fordin acquired properties and such complete film packages as *M*A*S*H; Play It Again, Sam;* and *Joanna;* he served also as liaison for Twentieth Century-Fox of Southern Africa in 1970.

Published Works. Mr. Fordin was publisher and editor-in-chief in 1970–71 of *Film-TV Daily* and the *Yearbook of Motion Pictures and Television.* He is author of *Hollywood's Royal Family: The Freed Unit; The New Jerome Kern Song Book;* and *That's Entertainment!*

Awards. Mr. Fordin received a special award of the All-American Press Association in 1970.

FORNES, MARIA. Playwright, director, designer. b. May 14, 1930, Havana, Cuba, to Carlos and Carmen (Collado) Farnes. Father, bureaucrat. Attended Havana public schools. Member of New York Theatre Strategy (pres., 1972); Dramatists' Guild; Authors' League of America; ASCAP. Address: 1 Sheridan Square, New York, NY 10014, tel. (212) YU 9-7216.

Pre-Theatre. Textile designer.

Theatre. Miss Fornes is the author of *Tango Palace,* originally entitled *There ! You Died* (Actors Workshop, San Francisco, Nov. 1963; Festival of Two Worlds, Spoleto, Italy, June 1964; Firehouse Th., Minneapolis, Minn., Jan. 1965; The Genesis, N.Y.C., Jan. 1973; and US Information Service, Calcutta, India, June 1973); *The Successful Life of 3* (Firehouse Th., Minneapolis, Minn., Jan. 1965; Open Th., N.Y.C., Mar. 1965; Judson Church, N.Y.C., May 1967; Little Th., London, England, Mar. 1968; Studio Th., Amsterdam, Holland, Dec. 1968; Traverse Th., Glasgow, Scotland, Dec. 1969; Little Arkus Th., Svalegange, Denmark, Dec. 1970; Odyssey, Los Angeles, Aug. 1971; and The Proposition, Cambridge, Mass., June 1972); *Promenade* (Judson Church, N.Y.C., Apr. 1965; Promenade Th., N.Y.C., June 1969); Kingston Mines, Chicago, Oct. 1972; and Cricket Th., Minneapolis, Jan. 1975); *The Office* (Henry Miller's Th., N.Y.C., Apr. 20, 1966; played seven preview performances, did not open); *A Vietnamese Wedding* (Angry Arts Week, Washington Sq. Church, N.Y.C., Feb. 1967; Moore Coll., Philadelphia, Pa., May 1967; and The Changing Scene, Denver, Colo., Dec. 1968); *The Annunciation* (Judson Church, N.Y.C., May 1967); *Dr. Kheal* (Village Gate, N.Y.C., April, 1968; New Arts Laboratory, London, England, Dec. 1969; Monasch Th., Melbourne, Australia, Dec. 1971; and Th. Genesis, N.Y.C., Feb. 1973); *The Red Burning Light* (Open Th., Zurich, Switzerland, Jan. 1968; and Cafe La Mama E.T.C., N.Y.C., Apr. 1969); *Molly's Dream* (Boston Univ. Tanglewood Workshop, July 1968; and NY Th. Strategy, N.Y.C., June 1973); *The Curse of the Langston House* (Cincinnati, Ohio, Playhouse, Oct. 1972); and *Aurora* (NY Th. Strategy, N.Y.C., June 1973).

She directed all productions of her plays which took place at the Firehouse Th. (Minneapolis, Minn.); Washington Square Church (N.Y.C.); Moore Coll. (Philadelphia, Pa.); Cincinnati (Ohio) Playhouse; Th. Genesis (N.Y.C.); and NY Th. Strategy (N.Y.C.); and directed *The Annunciation* at Judson Church (N.Y.C.).

Awards. Miss Fornes has received grants from the John Hay Whitney Fdtn. (1961–62); the Centro Mexicano de Escritores (1962–63); ODAR, Univ. of Minnesota (1965); Cintas Fdtn. (1967–68); Yale Univ. (1968–69); the Rockefeller Fdtn. (1971–72); CAPS (1972–73); and the John Simon Guggenheim Memorial Fdtn. (1972–73). She is the recipient of the Village Voice Off-Bway (Obie) Award for *A Successful Life of 3* and *Promenade.* .

Recreation. Carpentry, cooking.

FORREST, GEORGE. Lyricist, composer. b. George Forrest Chichester, Jr., July 31, 1915, Bklyn., N.Y., to George Forrest and Isabel (Paine) Chichester. Father, banker and investment counselor. Attended Lake Worth, (Fla.) H.S. and Miami (Fla.) H.S.; grad. Palm Beach (Fla.) H.S., 1931. Studied with Marion Andre, Lake Worth, Fla.; Fannie Greene, N.Y.C. Member of ASCAP; AGAC; Dramatists Guild. Address: 138 Columbia Heights, Brooklyn, NY 11202, tel. (212) UL 8-6011.

Pre-Theatre. Dance orchestra leader and pianist, night-club entertainer, accompanist.

Theatre. Mr. Forrest and Robert Wright, have collaborated for the musical theatre, first composing music and lyrics for *Thank You, Columbus* (Hollywood Playhouse, Calif., Nov. 15, 1940); followed by lyrics for additional music in stock productions of

Naughty Marietta and *Rio Rita* (Curran Th., San Francisco, 1941; Philharmonic Aud., Los Angeles, Calif., 1941); composed for *Fun for the Money* (Hollywood Playhouse, Aug. 1941); and for 11 Camp Tamiment summer revues (Tamiment Playhouse, Stroudsburg, Pa., 1942).

They contributed material to the revue, *Ziegfeld Follies* (Winter Garden, N.Y.C., Apr. 1, 1943); wrote music and lyrics for *Song of Norway*, the score for which was adapted from the music of Edvard Grieg (Imperial, N.Y.C., Aug. 21, 1944; Palace, London, Mar. 7, 1946); composed music and lyrics for the pre-Bway tryout of *Spring in Brazil* (opened Shubert, Boston, Mass., Oct. 1, 1945; closed Great Northern Th., Chicago, Ill., Jan. 12, 1946). They directed and wrote new lyrics for *Gypsy Lady*, the score for which was derived from the Victor Herbert operettas, *The Fortune Teller* and *Serenade* (Century, N.Y.C., Sept. 17, 1946), and the London production, which was retitled *Romany Love* (His Majesty's, Mar. 7, 1947); adapted the music of Hector Villa-Lobos and provided lyrics for *Magdalena* (Ziegfeld, N.Y.C., Sept. 20, 1948); provided lyrics for a revised stock production of *The Great Waltz* (Curran, San Francisco, 1949; Philharmonic Aud., Los Angeles, 1949), and additional lyrics for a second production (Philharmonic Aud., Los Angeles, 1953; Curran, San Francisco, 1953).

Messrs. Forrest and Wright wrote lyrics and did the musical adaptation for *Kismet*, which was based on the melodies of Alexander Borodin (Ziegfeld, N.Y.C., Dec. 3, 1953; Stoll, London, Apr. 20, 1955); wrote the book, music, and lyrics for the pre-Bway tryout of *The Carefree Heart* (opened Cass, Detroit, Mich., Sept. 30, 1957; closed Hanna, Cleveland, Ohio, Oct. 26, 1957); music and lyrics for the pre-Bway tryout of *At the Grand* (opened Philharmonic Aud., Los Angeles, Calif., July 7, 1958; closed Curran, San Francisco, Calif., Sept. 13, 1958); composed for a revised London production of *The Carefree Heart* called *The Love Doctor* (Piccadilly, Oct. 12, 1959); wrote the music and lyrics for *Kean* (Bway Th., N.Y.C., Nov. 2, 1961); provided lyrics and additional musical adaptation for a revival of *The Great Waltz* (Music Ctr., Los Angeles, July 27, 1965); wrote lyrics and music (based on themes of Rachmaninoff) for *Anya* (Ziegfeld, N.Y.C., Nov. 29, 1965); and wrote lyrics and music for a musical version of *Cyrano de Bergerac* (toured Spring and Summer, 1973).

Films. Messrs. Forrest's and Wright's first musical collaboration was for the short feature, *New Shoes* (MGM, 1936). They wrote the lyrics, or lyrics and music, including musical adaptation, for *The Longest Night* (MGM, 1936); *After the Thin Man* (MGM, 1936); *Libeled Lady* (MGM, 1936); *Sinner Take All* (MGM, 1936); *Maytime* (MGM, 1937); *The Firefly* (MGM, 1937); *The Good Old Soak* (MGM, 1937); *London By Night* (MGM, 1937); *Madame "X"* (MGM, 1937); *Mama Steps Out* (MGM, 1937); *Mannequin* (MGM, 1937); *Man of the People* (MGM, 1937); *Navy Blue and Gold* (MGM, 1937); *Parnell* (MGM, 1937); *Saratoga* (MGM, 1937); *Bad Man of Brimstone* (MGM, 1938); *You're Only Young Once* (MGM, 1938); *Boys' Town* (MGM, 1938); *The First Hundred Years* (MGM, 1938); *Lord Jeff* (MGM, 1938); *Marie Antoinette* (MGM, 1938); *Paradise for Three* (MGM, 1938); *Sweethearts* (MGM, 1938); *Three Comrades* (MGM, 1938); *The Toy Wife* (MGM, 1938); *Vacation From Love* (MGM, 1938); the short features, *Happily Buried* (MGM, 1938); *The Magician's Daughter* (MGM, 1938); *Nuts and Bolts* (MGM, 1938); *Our Gang Follies* (MGM, 1938); *Snow Gets in Your Eyes* (MGM, 1938); the full length features, *Broadway Serenade* (MGM, 1939); *The Girl Downstairs* (MGM, 1939); *The Hardys Ride High* (MGM, 1939); *Honolulu* (MGM, 1939); *Let Freedom Ring* (MGM, 1939); *Balalaika* (MGM, 1939); *These Glamor Girls* (MGM, 1939); *The Women* (MGM, 1939); *Florian* (MGM, 1940); *New Moon* (MGM, 1940); *Strange Cargo* (MGM, 1940); *Music in My Heart* (Col., 1940); *Dance, Girl, Dance* (RKO, 1940); *South of Pago-Pago* (UA, 1940); *Kit Carson* (UA, 1940); and *Blondie Goes Latin* (Col., 1941); the short features, *Cubana* (Hal Roach, 1941) and *Fiesta* (Hal Roach, 1941); the full length feature, *I Married an Angel* (MGM, 1942); the film adaptation of *Kismet* (MGM, 1955); and *The Great Waltz* (MGM, 1972). The film, *Song of Norway* (Cinerama, 1970) was suggested by their musical.

Television and Radio. Messrs. Forrest and Wright have composed music and lyrics for the Vicks Radio Hour (NBC, 1936); Maxwell House Good News (NBC, 1937); Tune-Up Time (NBC, 1940); the US Treasury radio show, Treasury Story Parade (world broadcasting transcriptions played on all networks, 1942–43); and 13 revues for the television program Startime Hour (Dumont 1950).

Night Clubs. They have collaborated on the Folies Bergère Revue (Edison Hotel, N.Y.C., 1942–43); Vaughn Monroe's Commodore Hotel Revue, (N.Y.C., 1942–43); four Copacabana revues (N.Y.C., 1942–43); three Colonial Inn revues (Hollywood, Fla., 1945–48); and created night club acts and special material for Jane Froman (1942 through 1956); Celeste Holm (1943); and Anne Jeffreys and Robert Sterling (1952–53).

Awards. Messrs. Forrest and Wright were nominated for an Academy (Oscar) Award (1937) for the song, "Donkey Serenade," from *The Firefly*. They received the Antoinette Perry (Tony) Award (1953) for their music and lyrics in *Kismet*

Recreation. Theatre, concerts, opera, travel.

FORSYTH, JAMES. Playwright, poet, painter. b. James Law Forsyth, Mar. 5, 1913, Glasgow, Scotland, to Richard and Jessie (Law) Forsyth. Father, civil engineer; mother, schoolteacher. Grad. Glasgow (Scot.) H.S., Higher Leaving with Art Distinction 1930; Glasgow Sch. of Art, diploma in drawing and painting 1934. Two sons by first marr. (dis. 1953); married 1955 to Louise Tibble. Served Scots Guards, 1940–46, rank, Capt; Battalion Adjutant; awarded Bronze Cross of the Netherlands, Member of Society of Authors and League of Dramatists' Radio Writers' Association (exec. member, 1965–to date); Theatres Advisory Council (exec. member, 1963–68); Dramatists Guild; Society of Scottish Artists. Address: (home) "Old Place," Ansty, Nr. Haywards Heath, Sussex, England tel. HA 3345; (bus.) London Management, 235/41 Regent St., London W1, England; Stephen Sheppard, 12 E. 41st St., New York, NY 10017.

Theatre. Mr. Forsyth wrote plays while serving as a picture teaching expert with C. K. Ogden on the Basic English Project (1937), subsequently was invited by Laurence Olivier to join the Old Vic Co. as dramatist-in-residence, where he also worked with the Old Vic School and the Young Vic, with Michel Saint-Denis, George Devine, and Glen Byam Shaw (1946); wrote *The Medicine Man* (Embassy Th., London, Feb. 14, 1950); *Heloise* (Duke of York's, Nov. 14, 1951); *The Other Heart* (Old Vic, Apr. 15, 1952); *The Pier* (Bristol Old Vic, May 27, 1958); *Trog* (Belgrade Th., Coventry, Oct. 12, 1959); *Fifteen Strings of Money* (Pitlochry, Scot., Apr. 22, 1961); a new version of *Everyman* (Coventry Cathedral, Eng., Dec. 5, 1962); a new English version of *Brand* ("Questors", London, 1964); *Dear Wormwood* (London, 1965–66); *If My Wings Heal* (Stroud Festival, 1966); and a new English version of *Cyrano* (New Shakespeare Co., London, 1967).

His first play in the US was *Heloise* (Gate,) N.Y.C., Sept. 24, 1958); followed by *Emmanuel* (Gate, Dec. 4, 1960); *Brand* (Boston Univ., Mass., 1961); *Defiant Island*, produced while he was dramatist-in-residence at Howard Univ., (Washington, D.C., 1962); a new version of *Cyrano de Bergerac* (Asolo Th., Sarasota, Fla., 1963); and *Seven Scenes for Yeni* (Boston, Coll., Mass., May, 1963). He was guest director and lecturer at Tufts Univ. (Boston, Mass.), where he directed his *The Other Heart* (July 1963); and was at Florida State Univ. as distinguished-professor-in-residence, where his play *Trog* was produced (Conradi Th., Tallahassee). Later American productions of Mr. Forsyth's work include his version of *Cyrano de Bergerac* (Vivian Beaumont Th., N.Y.C., Apr. 25, 1968) and *Defiant Island* (Black Arts West Th., Seattle, Wash., 1974).

Films. He worked with GPO Film Unit (Grierson and Cavalcanti), writing *The End of the Road* (1937–40); and wrote *Francis of Assisi* (20th-Fox, 1961).

Television and Radio. He adapted (1949–66) his own plays for the BBC (London) including *Emmanuel, The Bronze Horse, The Other Heart, Heloise, Adelaise, For He's a Jolly Good Fellow, The Festive Spirit, Lisel, The Nameless One of Europe, Trog, Brand, Christophe*, and *Every Pebble on the Beach;* wrote *The Pier* (ABC, 1957); *Underground* (ABC, 1958); *Emmanuel* (Play-of-the-Week, WNTA, 1960); *Old Mick Mack* (BBC, 1961); *The English Boy* (BBC, 1969); *Four Triumphant* (ATV, 1968–69); *The Old Man's Mountain* (ATV, 1972); *The Last Journey* (Granada, 1972); and *Rise Above It* (BBC, 1972).

Other Activities. Mr. Forsyth and his wife conduct a theatre workshop and community theatre, known as Forsyth's Barn Theatre, in a medieval barn on his property in Sussex.

Published Works. In addition to many of his theatrical and television plays, Mr. Forsyth has published *Joshua*, libretto of an oratorio (1960) and *The Road to Emmaus* (1972).

Awards. *The Last Journey* was the choice of ITV Companies for the Italia Prize (1972).

Recreation. 16th Century home and garden with medieval barn theatre attached; care of three sheep, two dogs, and thirty white doves.

FORSYTHE, CHARLES. Producer, actor, director. b. Lambros Charles Vocalis, West Palm Beach, Fla., to Charles D. and Helen (Gerakitis) Vocalis. Father, real estate owner. Grad. Boys H.S., Atlanta, Ga., Univ. of Georgia, B.F.A. Studied at Robert Lewis Th. Workshop (N.Y.C.). Served US Army, ETO, code deciphering specialist, script writer for Armed Forces Network; rank, Staff Sgt. Member AEA; AFTRA; AGMA; SSD&C (charter member). Address: (home) 465 W. 57th St., New York, NY 10019, tel. (212) CI 7-3436; (bus.) Forsythe Productions, 1841 Broadway, New York, NY 10023, tel. (212) 489-6544.

Theatre. Mr. Forsythe made his stage debut as Tom in a university production of *The Glass Menagerie* (Univ. of Georgia, Athens, 1947); apprenticed at the Barter Theatre (Abingdon, Va., 1948); his N.Y.C. debut as Marc Antony's Servant in *Julius Caesar* (Arena Th., Edison Hotel, June 20, 1950); at the Arena Th., was stage manager for *The Show-Off* (May 31, 1950) and production stage manager for *The Medium* and *The Telephone* (July 19, 1950); directed *I Pagliacci* and *Down in the Valley* (Atlanta Opera Co., Ga., Nov. 30, 1951); was stage manager at the Penthouse Th. (Atlanta, 1952); joined production staff of Katharine Cornell and Guthrie McClintic (1952); was production stage manager for the Greek Natl. Theatre's productions at the Mark Hellinger Th. (N.Y.C.) of *Electra* (Nov. 19, 1952); and *Oedipus Tyrannus* (Nov. 24, 1952); stage manager for *A Girl Can Tell* (Royal, Oct. 29, 1953); Playhouse-in-the-Park (Philadelphia, Pa., 1953); Astor Th. (Syracuse, N.Y., 1953); the Penthouse Th. (Atlanta, Ga., 1954); was a founder of the Shakespearewrights (N.Y.C.) an organization producing Shakespearean works, appearing as Sebastian in *Twelfth Night*, Lorenzo in *The Merchant of Venice* and Paris in *Romeo and Juliet* (1954–56).

Mr. Forsythe was production stage manager for *A Roomful of Roses* (Playhouse, Oct. 17, 1955); played the English Soldier in the national touring production of *The Lark* (opened Central City Opera House, Colo., Aug. 4, 1956); was co-producer of the American Savoyards' Gilbert & Sullivan season (N.Y.C., 1957); was stage manager for *A Handful of Fire* (Martin Beck Th., N.Y.C., Oct. 1, 1958); *Cheri* (Morosco, Nov. 12, 1959); *Under the Yum-Yum Tree* (Henry Miller's Th., Nov. 16, 1960); directed the same play (Coconut Grove Playhouse, Miami, Fla., 1961; Cape Playhouse, Dennis, Mass., Summer 1961; Ogunquit Playhouse, Me., Summer 1961; and Bucks County Playhouse, New Hope, Pa., Summer 1962).

He was production stage manager for *The Caretaker* (Lyceum, N.Y.C., Oct. 4, 1961); and on tour (opened Sombrero Playhouse, Phoenix, Ariz., Oct.

16, 1962; closed Biltmore, Los Angeles, Calif., Nov. 3, 1962); directed (1962) a tour of *Reclining Figure* (Garden Centre Th., Vineland, Ontario, Lakes Region Playhouse, Laconia, N.H.; Cape Playhouse, Dennis, Mass.; Kennebunkport Playhouse, Me.; Lake Whalom Playhouse, Mass.; and Lakewood Th., Skowhegan, Me.).

Mr. Forsythe was production stage manager for *Andorra* (Biltmore, N.Y.C., Feb. 9, 1963); *Oh Dad, Poor Dad, Mama's Hung You in the Closet and I'm Feelin' So Sad* (Morosco, Aug. 27, 1963), and for the touring production (opened Civic Th., Chicago, Ill., Apr. 2, 1963); the pre-Bway tryout of *The Time of the Barracudas* (opened Curran, San Francisco, Calif., Oct. 21, 1963; closed Huntington Hartford Th., Los Angeles, Calif., Nov. 23, 1963); and directed productions of *Oh, Dad, Poor Dad, Mama's Hung You in the Closet and I'm Feelin' So Sad* (Brown, Louisville, Ky., Feb. 18, 1964; Sombrero Playhouse, Phoenix, Ariz., Mar. 3, 1964); summer stock tour opened Playhouse-in-the-Park, Philadelphia, Pa., closed Ivoryton (Conn.) Playhouse, 1964; Piccadilly Th., London, 1965; and Elitchs' Gardens Th., Denver, Colo., 1964).

For *Beekman Place*, he was production stage manager (Morosco, N.Y.C., Oct. 8, 1964); and director (Summer, 1965, tour, opened Elitchs' Gardens Th., Denver, Colo.; closed Westport (Conn.) Country Playhouse; and Royal Poinciana Playhouse, Palm Beach, Fla., 1965); produced and directed *A Remedy for Winter* (1965 tour, opened Westport, Conn., Country Playhouse; closed Mt. Tom Playhouse, Holyoke, Mass.); produced *Nobody Loves an Albatross* (1965 tour, opened Playhouse-in-the-Park, Philadelphia, Pa.; closed Elitchs' Gardens Th., Denver, Colo.); produced and directed *The Time of the Cuckoo* (Summer 1966 tour, opened Cape Playhouse, Dennis, Mass.; closed Corning, N.Y., Summer Th.); and *The Impossible Years* (Summer 1965 tour, opened Lakewood, Me., Th.; Closed Elitchs' Gardens Th., Denver, Colo.); directed *Generation* (Summer 1967 tour, opened Playhouse-in-the-Park, Philadelphia, Pa.; closed Ogunguit, Me., Playhouse; and national tour, 1967–68); and *The Impossible Years* (Royal Poinciana Playhouse, Palm Beach, Fla., 1967; and national tour, 1967–68).

With Frederick Brisson, he co-produced *The Flip Side* (Booth, N.Y.C., Oct. 10, 1968); was producer-director of *Blithe Spirit* (Summer 1970 tour, opened Elitchs' Gardens Th., Denver, Colo.; closed Ivoryton, Conn., Playhouse); directed *Boeing, Boeing* (Summer 1970 tour, opened Ivoryton, Conn., Playhouse; closed Westport, Conn., Country Playhouse); produced summer (1971) tours of *I Do! I Do!* (opened Playhouse-in-The-Park, Philadelphia, Pa.; closed Central City, Colo., Opera House), *The Pleasure of His Company* (opened Pocono Playhouse, Mountainhome, Pa.; closed Corning, N.Y., Summer Th.), *My Daughter, Your Son* (opened Ogunquit, Me., Playhouse; closed Playhouse-on-the-Mall, Paramus, N.J.), and Plaza Suite (opened Playhouse-on-the-Mall, Paramus, N.J.; closed Ogunquit, Me., Playhouse); directed *Here Today* and *You Know I Can't Hear You When the Water's Running* (Royal Poinciana Playhouse, Palm Beach, Fla., 1971); produced summer (1973) tours of *The Gingerbread Lady* (opened North Shore Music Circus, Beverly, Mass.; closed South Shore Music Circus, Cohasset, Mass.), *Butterflies Are Free* (opened Cape Playhouse, Dennis, Mass., closed Pocono Playhouse, Mountainhome, Pa.), *Next* and *George's Night Out* (opened Gilford, N.H., Playhouse; closed Candlewood Th., New Fairfield, Conn.), *The Irregular Verb To Love* (opened Pellman Th., Milwaukee, Wisc.; closed Gilford, N.H., Playhouse), *A Shot in the Dark* (opened Elitchs' Gardens Th., Denver, Colo.; closed Corning, N.Y., Summer Th.), and *Lovers and Other Strangers* (opened Playhouse-in-the-Park, Philadelphia, Pa.; closed Cherry Country Playhouse, Traverse City, Mich.); directed *The Owl and the Pussycat* (Pellman Th., Milwaukee, Wis., 1973); and *Barefoot in the Park* (Carillon Th., Miami Beach, Fla., 1973); produced summer tours (1974) of *Crown Matrimonial* (opened Playhouse-in-the-Park, Philadelphia, Pa.; closed Tappan Zee Playhouse, Nyack, N.Y.), *A Community of Two* (opened Gilford, N.H., Playhouse; closed Falmouth, Mass., Playhouse), *The Marriage Gambol* (opened Elitchs' Gardens Th., Denver, Colo.; closed Lakewood, Me., Th.), and *Gigi* (opened Town and Country Playhouse, Rochester, N.Y.; closed Playhouse-on-the-Mall, Paramus, N.J.); produced and directed *Arsenic and Old Lace* (Summer 1974 tour, opened Corning, N.Y., Summer Th., closed Town and Country Playhouse, Rochester, N.Y.); and directed *Lovers and Other Strangers* (tour, Chateau de Ville Dinner Theatres, Mass., 1974).

Films. Mr. Forsythe appeared in *Feeling Right* (Canadian Films, 1949). He was associate producer for *Generation* (Avco-Embassy, 1969), and *Mrs. Pollifax—Spy* (Avco-Embassy, 1971).

Television. He has appeared on television as Charles in *The Barretts of Wimpole Street* (Producers Showcase, NBC, 1956), and has appeared on all major television networks.

Other Activities. Mr. Forsythe was associate editor (1956–58) for *Talent, Personalities, Teen Life*, and *Teenage Review*.

Awards. He received Faberge's Straw Hat Award and the first Best Director Award from the Council of Stock Theatres for his production of *Boeing, Boeing* (1971).

FORSYTHE, HENDERSON. Actor, director. b. Sept. 11, 1917, Macon, Mo., to Cecil P. and Kate (Henderson) Forsythe. Father, businessman. Grad. Monroe City, Mo. H.S., 1935; attended Culver-Stockton Coll., 1935–37; grad. State Univ. of Iowa, B.A. 1939, M.F.A. 1940. Married May 26, 1942, to Dorothea M. Carlson; two sons. Served US Army, 1941–46; rank, Capt. Member of AEA; AFTRA; SAG; ANTA. Address: 204 Elm St., Tenafly, NJ 07670, tel. (201) 569-8737.

Theatre. Mr. Forsythe made his first professional stage appearance as Dicky Reynolds in a stock production of *Accent on Youth* (Pt. Chautauqua, N.Y., Aug. 1940); subsequently played Geoffrey Cole in *Vinegar Tree* and Prince Rudolf in *Candle-Light* at the same theatre; at the Cleveland (Ohio) Playhouse, he played the Reporter in *Margin for Error* (Sept. 1940); Spencer Grant in *Here Today* (Oct. 1940); Cupid Holliday in *We Were Here First* (Dec. 1940); Tim Shields in *Tony Draws a Horse* (Jan. 1941); Paul Rambusch in *Middletown Mural* (Feb. 1941); and James in *Family Portrait* (March 1941).

With the Erie (Pa.) Playhouse, he appeared as Rough in *Angel Street* (Sept. 1946); Harry Archer in *Kiss and Tell* (Oct. 1946); Benjamin Griggs in *But Not Goodbye* (Nov. 1946); Ernest Friedman in *Design for Living* (Jan. 1947); Tommy Turner in *The Male Animal* (Feb. 1947); Norman in *Out of the Frying Pan* (March 1947); Dr. A. Shelby in *Blind Alley* (March 1947); in several roles in *My Sister Eileen* (April 1947); and as Horace Giddons in *The Little Foxes* (May 1947).

During the 1947 Summer season, he appeared at the Cain Park Th. (Cleveland Heights, Ohio) as Rev. Jones in *The Barber and the Cow;* Grandpa Vanderhof in *You Can't Take It with You;* Editor Webb in *Our Town;* Clarke Redfield in *Dream Girl;* and in *Sing Out, Sweet Land.* At the Erie (Pa.) Playhouse, played Albert Kummer in *Dear Ruth* (Sept. 1947); Kingsley in *Stage Door* (Oct. 1947); the title role in *Uncle Harry* (Oct. 1947); Dennis Curtin in *Anything Can Happen* (Nov. 1947); Dr. Ferguson in *Men in White* (Jan. 1948); David Bellow in *I Like It Here* (Feb. 1948); Ned Farrar in *Her Master's Voice* (March 1948); George Apley in *The Late George Apley* (Apr. 1948); and John in *John Loves Mary* (May 1948).

In 1948, at the Cain Park Th. (Cleveland, Ohio) he played Tchang in *Lute Song;* the Prime Minister of China in *The Reluctant Virgin;* and Petruchio in *The Taming of the Shrew,* which he also directed.

At the Erie (Pa.) Playhouse, he played Grant Matthews in *State of the Union* which he also directed (Sept. 1948); Dr. Johnson in *I Remember Mama* (Oct. 1948); Prof. Chas. Burnett in *Parlor Story* (Nov. 1948); Kenneth Bixby in *Goodbye Again* (Dec. 1948); Clarke Redfield in *Dream Girl* (Jan. 1949); the Colonel in *Hasty Heart* (Feb. 1949); Petruchio in *The Taming of the Shrew,* which he also directed (March 1949); the Doctor in *Life with Father* (Apr. 1949); Snowflake in *Ruined by Drink* (Apr. 1949); and Bill Paige in *Voice of the Turtle* (May 1949).

He appeared in *Sing Out, Sweet Land* (Penn Playhouse, Meadville, Pa., Summer 1949); at the Erie (Pa.) Playhouse appeared as Gen. K. C. Denis in *Command Decision* (Sept. 1949); the Judge in *Happy Birthday* (Oct. 1949); Lance Corporal in *See How They Run* (Nov. 1949); Uncle Stanley in *George Washington Slept Here* (Dec. 1949); Tommy Thurston in *Two Blind Mice* (Jan. 1950); directed *The Cellar and the Well* (Jan. 1950); played Horatio Channing in *Invitation to a Murder* (Feb. 1950); Stephen Minch in *Star Wagon* (March 1950); Father Moynihan in *Jenny Kissed Me* (April 1950); and the Colonel in *Jacobowsky and the Colonel* (May 1950).

Mr. Forsythe made his Bway debut as Mr. Hubble in *The Cellar and the Well,* which he also directed (ANTA, Dec. 10, 1950); at the Erie (Pa.) Playhouse, played Elwood P. Dowd in *Harvey* (Jan. 1951); Mathew Cromwell in *Strange Bedfellows* (Jan. 1951); Clarke Storey in *The Second Man* (Feb. 1951); Jonah Goodman in *The Gentle People* (Apr. 1951); Macauley-Connor in *The Philadelphia Story* (Apr. 1951); and Tom in *The Glass Menagerie* (May 1951).

At Penn Playhouse (Meadville, Pa.) he played Tommy Turner in *The Male Animal;* Elwood P. Dowd in *Harvey;* and Nat in *Ah, Wilderness!* (Summer 1951); at the Erie (Pa.) Playhouse, he played Ed Devery in *Born Yesterday* (Oct. 1951); Curley in *Green Grow the Lilacs* (Nov. 1951); Capt. Bluntschli in *Arms and the Man* (Dec. 1951); Mr. Adams in *Junior Miss* (Jan. 1952); Jeff in *The Curious Savage* (Feb. 1952); directed *The Women* (Feb. 1952); appeared as Clarence Day in *Life with Mother* (Mar. 1952); Preston Mitchell in *For Love or Money* (Apr. 1952); Creon in *Antigone* (May 1952); directed *Charley's Aunt* (May 1952); played Papa Bonnard in *The Happy Time* (Oct. 1952); Steven Wayne in *First Lady* (Oct. 1952); Henderson in *Gramercy Ghost* (Nov. 1952); Detective McLeod in *Detective Story* (Nov. 1952); Mr. Brown in *Let Us Be Gay* (Dec. 1952); directed *Montserrat* (Dec. 1952); played Derrick in *Rip Van Winkle* (Dec. 1952); appeared as Prof. Pearson in *Velvet Glove* (Jan. 1953); in *The Happiest Days of Your Life* (Jan. 1953); as Clarke Redfield in *Dream Girl* (Feb. 1953); in the title role in *Mister Roberts* (Mar. 1953); as Sam Stover in *Apple of His Eye* (Apr. 1953); as Jason in *Medea* (May 1953; and as Maj. Joppolo in *A Bell for Adano* (May 1953).

Also at the Erie (Pa.) Playhouse, he played David Slater in *The Moon Is Blue* (Oct. 1953); Grandpa Vanderhof in *You Can't Take It with You* (Nov. 1953); Milo Alcott in *Lo and Behold* (Dec. 1953); directed *I Remember Mama* (Dec. 1958); appeared as Sgt. Schultz in *Stalag 17* (Jan. 1954); Father Malachy in *Father Malachy's Miracle* (Feb. 1954); Walter Burns in *Front Page* (March 1954); directed *Be Your Age* (Mar. 1954) and *As You Like It* (Apr. 1954); played Charles Colburn in *Janie* (May 1954); Henderson in *Bell, Book and Candle* (Oct. 1954); Malcolm Bryant in *Point of No Return* (Nov. 1954); appeared as Capt. Ernest Caldwell in *At War with the Army* (Dec. 1954); Howard Carol in *Time Out for Ginger* (Jan. 1955); O'Flingsley in *Shadow and Substance* (Feb. 1955); the Inspector in *Dial "M" for Murder* (Feb. 1955); Linus in *Sabrina Fair* (Mar. 1955); Prof. Charles Burnett in *Mother Was a Statesman* (Apr. 1955); and He in *The Fourposter* (May 1955).

Mr. Forsythe played Friar Lawrence in *Romeo and Juliet* (Shakespearean Workshop Th., N.Y.C., Jan. 1956); Ned Gates in *Miss Lonelyhearts* (Music Box Th., N.Y.C., Oct. 3, 1957); succeeded (June 1956) Conrad Bain as Larry in *The Iceman Cometh* (Circle in the Square, May 8, 1956); succeeded (Dec. 1957) Jason Robards, Jr., as Hickey in the same play; played Peter Stockman in *An Enemy of the People* (Actors Playhouse, Feb. 4, 1949); appeared as Banquo in *Macbeth* (Cambridge Drama Festival, Mass., July 1959); succeeded (May 1960) Donald Davis as Krapp in *Krapp's Last Tape* (Provincetown Playhouse, Jan. 14, 1960); played G. B. Shaw in *A Figleaf in Her Bonnet* (Gramercy Arts, June 14, 1961); and succeeded (May 11, 1962) Lee Richardson as Father Francis in *Someone From Assisi* and Dana Elcar (June 1962) as the Father in *Childhood* in the bill of three one-act plays, entitled *Plays for Bleecker Street* (Circle in the Square, Jan. 11, 1962).

He played Harry in *The Collection*, part of a double bill of one-act plays, entitled *The Pinter Plays* (Cherry Lane, Nov. 26, 1962); Chip Reegan in a tour of *The Indoor Sport* (Summer 1963); succeeded Arthur Hill (Jan. 15, 1964) as George in *Who's Afraid of Virginia Woolf?* (Billy Rose Th., N.Y.C., Oct. 13, 1962); played Bert in *Dark Corners* (Actors Playhouse, May 5, 1964); Edward in *A Slight Ache* (Writers Stage Th., Dec. 9, 1964); Donald Crawford in *The Right Honourable Gentleman* (Billy Rose Th., Oct. 19, 1965); Cox, Miles, and a Doctor in *Malcolm* (Sam S. Shubert Th., Jan. 11, 1966); Harry in *A Delicate Balance* (Martin Beck Th., Sept. 22, 1966); Petey in *The Birthday Party* (Booth Th., Oct. 3, 1967); Tobias in *A Delicate Balance* (Studio Arena Th., Buffalo, N.Y., Feb. 8, 1968); Franklin in *Sunrise at Campobello* (Hyde Park Th., N.Y., Summer 1969); William Chumley in a revival of *Harvey* (ANTA, Feb. 24, 1970); Nelson Longhurst in *The Engagement Baby* (Helen Hayes Th., May 21, 1970); Dr. Freytag in *The Happiness Cage* (NY Shakespeare Festival Public Theater's Estelle R. Newman Th., Oct. 4, 1970); Vladimir (Didi) in *Waiting for Godot* (Sheridan Square Playhouse, Feb. 3, 1971); Harry in *In Case of Accident* (Eastside Playhouse, Mar. 27, 1972); Auditor in *Not I* (Forum Th., Nov. 22, 1972); the Senator in *An Evening With the Poet-Senator* (Playhouse 2, Mar. 21, 1973); and the Priest in *Freedom of the City* (Alvin Th., Feb. 17, 1974).

Television. Mr. Forsythe has appeared on the US Steel Hour (CBS, Oct. 1955); Studio One (CBS); Hallmark Hall of Fame (NBC); Alcoa Hour (NBC); Camera Three (CBS); Frontiers of Faith (NBC); Kaiser Aluminum Hour (NBC); Big Story (NBC); Wide Wide World (NBC); True Story (NBC); Kraft Studio Th. (NBC); Armstrong Circle Th. (CBS); The Investigator (CBS); American Heritage (NBC); Dupont Show-of-the-Month (NBC); The Witness (CBS); Play-of-the-Week (WNTA); CBS News Specials; The Defenders (CBS); Naked City (ABC); Dr. Kildare (NBC); Look Up and Live (CBS); Love of Life (CBS); Hotel Cosmopolitan (CBS); Edge of Night (CBS); From These Roots (NBC); and As the World Turns (CBS).

Recreation. Golf, carpentry, woodwork, and tennis.

FORSYTHE, JOHN. Actor. b. John Lincoln Freund, Jan. 29, 1918, Carney's Point, N.J., to Samuel Jeremiah and Blanche Materson (Blohm) Freund. Father, factory manager. Attended Univ. of N.C. Studied at Actors' Studio (N.Y.C.). Married to Parker McCormick, actress (marr. dis.); one son; married 1943 to Julie Warren, actress; two daughters. Served USAAF, 1942–45. Member of AEA; AFTRA; SAG.

Pre-Theatre. Runner in brokerage house, waiter, elevator operator.

Theatre. Mr. Forsythe first performed as the Captain in Clare Tree Major's Children's Th. production of *Dick Whittington and His Cat* (Major's Children Th., Chappaqua, N.Y., Sept. 1939); subsequently succeeded Edmund Glover as Private Cootes in *Vickie* (Plymouth, N.Y.C., Sept. 22, 1942); played a Coast Guard in *Yankee Point* (Longacre, Nov. 23, 1942); and for the USAAF, Ted Bricker in *Winged Victory* (44 St. Th., Nov. 20, 1943); and toured as Bill Page in *The Voice of the Turtle* (1944).

He appeared in *Woman Bites Dog* (Belasco, N.Y.C., Apr. 17, 1946); succeeded (1947) Arthur Kennedy as Chris Keller in *All My Sons* (Coronet, Jan. 29, 1947); played Bill Renault in *It Takes Two* (Biltmore, Feb. 3, 1947); toured as Lt. Roberts in *Mister Roberts* (1949), succeeded (Oct. 1950) Henry Fonda as Lt. Roberts in the N.Y.C. production (Alvin, Feb. 18, 1948); appeared in stock production of *A Case of Scotch* (Westport Country Playhouse, Conn., Aug. 27, 1951); played Captain Fisby in *The Teahouse of the August Moon* (Martin Beck Th., N.Y.C., Oct. 15, 1953); Detective McLeod in *Detective Story* (Westport Country Playhouse, Conn., June 27, 1955); directed *Mister Roberts* NY City Ctr., Dec. 5, 1956); was Senator MacGruder in *Weekend* (Broadhurst, Mar. 13, 1968); and Lt. Greenwald in *The Caine Mutiny* (Ahmanson Th., Los Angeles, Calif., Nov. 30, 1971).

Films. Mr. Forsythe has appeared in *Destination Tokyo* (WB, 1943); *Northern Pursuit* (WB, 1943); *The Captive City* (UA, 1952); *It Happens Every Thursday* (U, 1953); *Escape from Fort Bravo* (MGM, 1953); *The Trouble with Harry* (Par., 1955); *The Ambassador's Daughter* (UA, 1956); *Everything But the Truth* (U, 1956); *Kitten with a Whip* (U, 1964); *Madam X* (U, 1966); *In Cold Blood* (Col., 1968); *The Happy Ending* (UA, 1969); and *Topaz* (U, 1969).

Television and Radio. He was a radio sports announcer (NBC) and director and performed on the series, Dangerous Corner.

On television, he appeared in *Premonition* (Alfred Hitchcock Presents, CBS, 1955); *Return to Casino* (NBC, 1956); *A Place To Be Alone* (Star Stage, NBC, 1956); and *Stardust No. 2* (Alcoa Hour, NBC, 1956). He appeared in the title role of the series, Bachelor Father (NBC, CBS, ABC, 1957); played in *Shooting for the Moon* (Climax!, CBS, 1958); *Wuthering Heights* (Dupont Show of the Month, CBS, 1958); *The Miss and the Missiles* (CBS, 1959); *The Teahouse of the August Moon* (Hallmark Hall of Fame, NBC, 1962); *The Sweet Taste of Vengeance* and *The Kamchatka Incident* (both Kraft Suspense Th., NBC, 1964); *In Any Language* (Bob Hope Chrysler Th., NBC, 1965); and was a guest on Celebrity Game (CBS, 1964–65) and the Today Show (NBC, 1965–66).

He was Host for the 14th annual International Beauty Pageant (NBC, Aug. 13, 1965); was on the John Forsythe Show (NBC, 1965–66); was a reporter for the Tournament of Roses Parade (CBS and NBC, Jan. 1, 1966); was in *I Saw the Whole Thing* and *Premonition* (both Alfred Hitchcock, Ind., 1966); was on the Merv Griffin Show (Ind., 1966–67); The Face Is Familiar (CBS, 1966–67); Zane Grey (Ind., 1966); Password (CBS, 1966–67); in *The Third Side of the Coin* (Dick Powell Th., Ind., 1966); *The Light Fantastic, or How To Tell Your Past, Present and Maybe Even Your Future Through Social Dancing* (Stage 67, ABC, 1967) *A Choice of Evils* (Run for Your Life (NBC, 1967); *A Bell for Adano* (Hallmark Hall of Fame, NBC, 1967); on It Takes a Thief (ABC, 1968); in *Shadow on the Land* (ABC, 1968); on To Rome with Love (CBS, 1969–71); Columbo (NBC, 1971); Mannix (CBS, 1971); and was host of The World of Survival (ABC, 1972–74).

He has also appeared on Studio One (CBS); Kraft Television Th. (NBC); and the Actors Studio Th. (ABC).

Awards. Mr. Forsythe received the TV Guide Award (1952) as the best television actor of the year.

Recreation. Sailing, sports, music, painting.

FOSSE, BOB. Director, actor, choreographer. b. Robert Louis Fosse, June 23, 1927, Chicago, Ill., to Cyril K. and Sarah (Stanton) Fosse. Father, vaudevillian, salesman. Grad. Amundsen H.S., Chicago, 1945; attended Amer. Theatre Wing, N.Y.C., 1947–48. Married to Gwen Verdon, actress. Served USN, ETO, 1946–47; rank, Spec. (E) 3/C. Member of SSD&C (treas. 1963–64); AEA; SAG; AFTRA. Address: 91 Central Park West, New York, NY 10023.

Theatre. Mr. Fosse first performed at age 14, appearing in nightclubs, vaudeville, and burlesque houses; subsequently appeared in the national tours of *Call Me Mister* (1948) and *Make Mine Manhattan* (1948–49). He made his Bway debut in the revue *Dance Me a Song* (Royale, Jan. 20, 1950); was choreographer for *The Pajama Game* (St. James, May 13, 1954); staged the dances and musical numbers in *Damn Yankees* (46 St. Th., May 5, 1955); with Jerome Robbins, staged the dances and musical numbers in *Bells Are Ringing* (Shubert, Nov. 29, 1956); and staged the dances and musical numbers in *New Girl in Town* (46 St. Th., May 14, 1957).

He was director and choreographer for *Redhead* (46 St. Th., Feb. 5, 1959); played the title role in *Pal Joey* (NY City Ctr., May 31, 1961); staged the musical numbers for *How to Succeed in Business Without Really Trying* (46 St. Th., Oct. 14, 1961); and was choreographer for and, with Cy Feuer, directed *Little Me* (Lunt-Fontanne, Nov. 17, 1962); and again played the title role in *Pal Joey* (NY City Ctr., May 29, 1963).

He directed and choreographed *Pleasures and Palaces* (opened Fisher Th., Detroit, Mich., Mar. 11, 1965; closed there, Apr. 10, 1965); conceived, staged, and choreographed *Sweet Charity* (Palace, N.Y.C., Jan. 29, 1966); directed and choreographed *Pippin* (Imperial, Oct. 23, 1972); directed and choreographed *Liza* (Winter Garden, Jan. 6, 1974); and directed and choreographed *Chicago* (46 St. Th., June 3, 1975), for which he also wrote the book.

Films. Mr. Fosse made his debut in *Give a Girl a Break* (MGM, 1953); subsequently appeared in *The Affairs of Dobie Gillis* (MGM, 1953); *Kiss Me, Kate* (MGM, 1953); choreographed and appeared in *My Sister Eileen* (Col., 1955); choreographed the film adaptations of *The Pajama Game* (WB, 1957) and *Damn Yankees* (WB, 1958); directed and did choreography for the film *Sweet Charity* (U, 1969); directed the film *Cabaret* (Allied Artists, 1972); was in *The Little Prince* (Par., 1974); and directed *Lenny* (UA, 1975).

Television. Mr. Fosse co-produced, directed, and choreographed *Liza with a Z* (NBC, Sept. 10, 1972).

Awards. For his choreography in *The Pajama Game*, Mr. Fosse received the Donaldson Award and an Antoinette Perry (Tony) Award (both 1955). He also received Tony awards for his choreography in *Damn Yankees* (1956), *Redhead* (1959), *Little Me* (1963), *Sweet Charity* (1966), and *Pippin* (1973); the *Dance Magazine* Award (1963) for his contributions as choreographer; and he won the *Saturday Review* Drama Critics Poll for *Little Me*. For *Pippin*, in addition to his Tony as best choreographer, Mr. Fosse received a Tony for best director of a musical in 1973, the same year that he received a NATAS (Emmy) award for *Liza with a Z* and an AMPAS (Oscar) award for directing the film version of *Cabaret*. In 1973, Mr. Fosse was also named by the Drama Desk as an outstanding director and as the outstanding choreographer, both for *Pippin*; he received the Outer Circle Award for his direction of the same show; and he won the best director award for the film *Cabaret* from the British Society of Film and Television Arts.

FOSTER, GLORIA. Actress. b. Chicago, Ill. Attended Illinois State Univ. Professional training at Goodman Th., Chicago (studied under Bella Itkin); Univ. of Chicago Court Th. Married Nov. 2, 1967, to Clarence Williams III, actor. Member of AEA; SAG; AFTRA. Address: c/o Albert L. Shedler, 225 W. 34th St., New York, NY 10001, tel. (212) 564-6656.

Theatre. As a student at the Goodman Th., Miss Foster played the title role in a production of *Medea*, Oparre in *The Wingless Victory*, and Sabina in *The Skin of Our Teeth*; at the Court Th., Univ. of Chicago, she appeared as Jocasta in *Oedipus Rex*, Hecuba in *The Trojan Women*, and Volumnia in *Coriolanus*. In 1961, she was Ruth in *A Raisin in the Sun* (Regent Th., Syracuse, N.Y.), later touring summer stock theatres in the role (1962).

Miss Foster made her N.Y.C. debut off-Bway in *In White America* (Sheridan Square Playhouse, Oct. 31, 1963); played Andromache in *The Trojan Women* (Murray Th., Ravinia, Ill., 1965); the title role in *Medea* (Martinique, N.Y.C., Nov. 28, 1965); participated in the NY Shakespeare Festival *Poetry and Folk Music of American Negroes* (Delacorte Th., Aug. 15, 1966), repeating this when the program was done on Bway as *A Hand Is on the Gate* (Longacre, Sept. 21, 1966). She played the title role in *Yerma* (Vivian Beaumont Th., Dec. 8, 1966); was in *A Dream Play* (Goodman Th., Chicago, Ill., Mar. 31, 1967); played Titania and Hippolyta in *A Midsum-*

mer Night's Dream (Th. de Lys, N.Y.C., June 29, 1967); the title role in *Sister Son/ji* on the program *Black Visions* (Public Th., Apr. 4, 1972); and was Mme. Ranyevska in *The Cherry Orchard* (Public Th., Dec. 7, 1972).

Films. Miss Foster appeared in *The Cool World* (Shirley Clarke, 1963); *Nothing But a Man* (Cinema V, 1963); *The Comedians* (MGM, 1967); *The Angel Levine* (UA, 1970); and *Man and Boy* (Levitt-Pickman Film Corp., 1972).

Television and Radio. Miss Foster was in the radio series The Great Ones (Group W, Westinghouse Broadcasting Co.); appeared on closed circuit television in the NAACP *Freedom Spectacular* (Madison Sq. Garden, N.Y.C., May 14, 1964); was in *In What America?* (Esso World Th.); *Shakespeare's Women* (CBS Repertoire Workshop); and in the special *To All My Friends on Shore* (CBS, 1972).

Awards. At Illinois State, Miss Foster took first place in women's oratory, the State Oratorical Contest, and she was elected the university's first "Sweetheart of the Campus." She received a *Village Voice* off-Bway (Obie) Award and the Drama Desk-Vernon Rice Award (both 1964) for her work in *In White America;* the *Theatre World* Award (1966) as one of the promising personalities of the season; and the Alpha Kappa Alpha Award (1966) for outstanding contribution in the field of the arts.

FOWLER, KEITH. Director, actor, producer. b. Keith Franklin Fowler, Feb. 23, 1939, San Francisco, Calif., to Jack Franklin and Jacklyn Dorothy Lucille Montgomery Hocking Fowler. Grad. San Francisco State, B.A. (magna cum laude); Yale School of Drama, D.F.A. Professional training at the Shakespeare Institute, Stratford-upon-Avon, England; one year as observer with directors unit of Actors Studio. Married June 16, 1962, to Janet Lynne Bell, actress; one son. Member of AEA; ATA; Alpha Psi Omega. Address: (home) 2119 Stuart Ave., Richmond, VA 23221, tel. (804) 359-6851; (bus.) VMT Rep, Boulevard & Grove, Richmond, VA 23221, tel. (804) 770-6333.

Pre-Theatre. From 1964 to 1968, Mr. Fowler was on the faculty at Williams College, Williamstown, Mass., as instructor in drama (1964–66), assistant professor of drama (1966–68), and director of the experimental theatre (1964–68) at the college. In 1969, he became producing director of the Virginia Museum Theatre, Richmond, Va., where he founded the professional repertory company.

Theatre. Mr. Fowler bowed as an actor on the professional stage in the part of the Newsboy in *A Streetcar Named Desire* (Cellar Stage, San Francisco, Calif., 1955). He appeared as the Boy in *The Beautiful People* (Cellar Stage, 1955); as Henry in *The Skin of Our Teeth* (Opera Ring, San Francisco, 1956); and in many other roles in various San Francisco theatres (1956–59). In 1958, he performed at the Oregon Shakespeare Festival as Lorenzo in *The Merchant of Venice* and as Oswald in *King Lear,* and in 1959 he was Bertram in the San Francisco Shakespeare Festival production of *All's Well That Ends Well.* He also played Robespierre in *Danton's Death* (San Francisco State, 1959) and returned in 1960 to the Oregon Shakespeare Festival as Marc Antony in *Julius Caesar.*

He began directing with a production of *Hamlet,* in which he also played the title role (San Francisco State, 1960), and he made his professional directing debut with a presentation of *Mother Courage* (Stratford-on-Avon Hippodrome, England, 1961). In England, he also appeared as the First King in the *Coventry Nativity Play* (1961). Upon returning to the US, he played Lysander in *A Midsummer Night's Dream* (Yale Univ., 1962) and directed five productions for a stock company at Williams Bay, Wis. (1962). His first directing for summer stock was at the Casino Playhouse, Holyoke, Mass., 1963 with productions of *J. B.* and *A Far Country.* In 1964, he played the title role in *Everyman* at Yale Univ., and from 1964 to 1968 he directed nine productions at Williams Coll. In addition, he directed *Oh Dad, Poor Dad . .* (Williamstown Summer Th., 1965); *Macbeth* (Festival Th., El Paso, Tex., 1966); *A Midsummer Night's Dream* (Asolo State Th., Fla., 1968); and played Sir Epicure Mammon in *The Alchemist* (Asolo State Th., Fla., 1968).

Between 1969 and 1974, Mr. Fowler, as producing director at the Virginia Museum Theatre (VMT) in Richmond, Va., directed and produced thirty-two productions for VMT, including *Twelfth Night; Sorrows of Frederick; Macbeth; A Christmas Carol; Marat/Sade; Indians;* and *Homecoming.* He also appeared in VMT productions: as Brutus in *Julius Caesar* (1972); Vanya in *Uncle Vanya* (1973); and as Sir Roger Casement in *Prisoner of the Crown* (American premiere, 1973).

Radio. Mr. Fowler was host/narrator for the program Keith Fowler Presents (WRFK-FM, Richmond, 1973–74).

Discography. The recorded series *Keith Fowler Presents* includes excerpts from twenty authors, including Chaucer, Shakespeare, George Bernard Shaw, and Edgar Allan Poe.

Awards. Mr. Fowler received the Bordon Prize (1957); a Fulbright grant to the Shakespeare Institute in England (1960–61); a Woodrow Wilson Fellowship at Yale (1961–62); and the John Shubert Memorial Scholarship in directing (1963–64).

Recreation. Music, reading, swimming, whiffling.

FOWLIE, WALLACE. Writer, educator. b. Wallace Adams Fowlie, Nov. 8, 1908, Brookline, Mass., to Wallace Bruce and Helen (Adams) Fowlie. Grad. Harvard Univ., B.A. 1930; M.A. 1933; Ph.D. 1936. Address: Dept. of Romance Languages, Duke University, Durham, NC 27706.

Among his translations are Claudel's *Break of Noon* and *Tidings Brought to Mary* (1960); *Classical French Drama* (1962), which includes *The Cid, Phaedra, The Intellectual Ladies, Game of Love and Chance,* and *The Barber of Seville;* and *Journals of Jean Cocteau* (1963).

Mr. Fowlie has contributed articles on the theatre to journals and collections, including *View: Yale French Studies; Commonweal; Sewanee Review; Tulane Drama Review; Ramparts.*

A professor of French at Duke Univ. since 1964, Mr. Fowlie also taught French at Yale Univ. (assist. prof., 1940–45); Univ. of Chicago (assoc. prof., 1946–49); Bennington College (head of dept., 1950–62); and Univ. of Colorado (prof., 1962–64).

Awards. He has twice been the recipient of Guggenheim Fellowships (1948–49; 1961–62).

FOX, FREDERICK. Designer. b. July 10, 1910, New York City, to Charles L. and Esther (Jacobs) Fox. Father, dentist. Grad. Phillips Exeter Acad., 1928; attended Yale Univ., 1930–32; Natl. Acad. of Design, 1933. Married 1933 to Gladys Bain (marr. dis. 1952); one son, one daughter; married Nov. 25, 1954, to Margery Quitzau; two sons. Member of United Scenic Artists, Local 829. Address: (home) 148 E. Linden Ave., Englewood, NJ; (bus.) c/o St. James Theatre Bldg., 246 W. 44th St., New York, NY 10036, tel. (212) LO 3-2095.

Theatre. Mr. Fox's first professional experience as a designer was in summer stock (Ivoryton, Conn., 1933–38).

His initial Bway designing assignment was for *Farewell Summer* (Fulton Th., Mar. 29, 1937); subsequently designed the set for 200 Bway productions, including *There's Always a Breeze* (Windsor, Mar. 2, 1938); *The Man from Cairo* (Broadhurst, May 4, 1938); *The Strangler Fig* (Lyceum, May 6, 1940); *Johnny Belinda* (Belasco, Sept. 18, 1940); *Blind Alley* (Windsor, Oct. 15, 1940); *Brooklyn Biarritz* (Royale, Feb. 27, 1941); *Snookie* (John Golden Th., June 3, 1941); *All Men Are Alike* (Hudson, Oct. 6, 1941); *Junior Miss* (Lyceum, Nov. 18, 1941); *Men in Shadow* (Morosco, Mar. 10, 1942); *Land of Fame* (Belasco, Sept. 21, 1942); *Wine, Women and Song* (Ambassador, Sept. 28, 1942); *Yankee Point* (Longacre, Nov. 23, 1942); *The Doughgirls* (Lyceum, Dec. 30, 1942); *Those Endearing Young Charms* (Booth, June 16, 1943); *The Two Mrs. Carrolls* (Booth, Aug. 3, 1943); *The Snark Was a Boojum* (48 St. Th., Sept. 1, 1943); sets and lighting for *Land of Fame* (Belasco, Sept. 21, 1943), which he also co-produced; sets for *The Naked Genius* (Plymouth, Oct. 21, 1943); and *Lady Behave* (Cort, Nov. 16, 1943).

Mr. Fox also designed the sets for *Ramshackle Inn* (Royale, Jan. 1, 1944); *Decision* (Belasco, Feb. 2, 1944); *Only the Heart* (Bijou, Apr. 4, 1944); *Career Angel* (National, May 23, 1944); *Anna Lucasta* (Mansfield, Aug. 30, 1944); *Dear Ruth* (Henry Miller's Th., Dec. 13, 1944); *Kiss Them for Me* (Belasco, Mar. 20, 1945); *The Wind Is Ninety* (Booth, June 21, 1945); *Marriage Is for Single People* (Cort, Nov. 21, 1945); *Georgia Boy* (Copley, Boston, Mass., Dec. 29, 1945); *Little Brown Jug* (Martin Beck Th., N.Y.C., Mar. 6, 1946); *Shootin' Star* (Shubert, Apr. 4, 1946); and *Mr. Peebles and Mr. Hooker* (Music Box, Oct. 10, 1946).

He served as setting and lighting designer for *John Loves Mary* (Booth, Feb. 4, 1947); designed the sets for *Make Mine Manhattan* (Broadhurst, Jan. 15, 1948); *Light Up the Sky* (Royale, Nov. 18, 1948); *They Knew What They Wanted* (Music Box, Feb. 16, 1949); *Southern Exposure* (Biltmore, Sept. 26, 1949); *Darkness at Noon* (Alvin, Jan. 13, 1951); and *Angels Kiss Me* (National, Apr. 17, 1951).

He designed the sets and the lighting for *Never Say Never* (John Golden Th., Nov. 19, 1951); the sets for *The Climate of Eden* (Martin Beck Th., Nov. 13, 1952); the set and the lighting for *The Seven Year Itch* (Fulton, Nov. 20, 1952); the sets for *Room Service* (Playhouse, Apr. 6, 1953); *King of Hearts* (Lyceum, Apr. 1, 1954); *Anniversary Waltz* (Broadhurst, Apr. 7, 1954); sets and lighting for *Reclining Figure* (Lyceum, Oct. 7, 1954); sets for *Lunatics and Lovers* (Broadhurst, Dec. 13, 1954); the sets and costumes for *Andrea Chénier* (Metropolitan Opera, 1954); the sets for *The Wayward Saint* (Cort, Feb. 17, 1955); *Speaking of Murder* (Royale, Dec. 19, 1956); the sets and costumes for *Tosca* (Metropolitan Opera, 1956); the sets for *The Greatest Man Alive,* which he also produced (Ethel Barrymore Th., May 8, 1957); *Fair Game* (Longacre, Nov. 2, 1957); *Howie* (46 St. Th., Sept. 17, 1958); *Golden Fleecing* (Henry Miller's Th., Oct. 15, 1959); *The Warm Peninsula* (Helen Hayes Th., Oct. 20, 1959); *Simon Boccanegra* (Metropolitan Opera, 1959); *A Mighty Man Is He* (Cort, Jan. 6, 1960); *One for the Dame* (Ford's Th., Baltimore, Md., Mar. 24, 1960); sets and lighting for *The Hostage* (Cort, N.Y.C., Sept. 20, 1960); *Send Me No Flowers* (Brooks Atkinson, Dec. 6, 1960); sets, costumes and lighting for *Julia, Jake and Uncle Joe* (Booth, Jan. 28, 1961); and sets and lighting for *Mandingo* (Lyceum, May 22, 1961); and *From the Second City* (Royale, Sept. 26, 1961). He designed the sets and costumes for *Tosca* (Metropolitan Opera, premiere Mar. 19, 1965), and supervised the decor for *La Grosse Valise* (54 St. Th., Dec. 14, 1965).

During the years 1962–74, Mr. Fox concentrated on airport complex planning.

Television. Mr. Fox has designed sets for The Admiral Hour (NBC, 1949); Your Show of Shows (NBC, 1942–52); and Max Liebman's first color spectaculars (NBC, 1953–55).

Awards. He received the Donaldson Award (1951) for his setting for *Darkness at Noon.*

Recreation. Painting, photography.

FOX, MAXINE. Producer. b. Dec. 26, 1943, Baltimore, Md., to Merral A. and Marian (Marmer) Fox. Father and mother, in advertising. Attended Forest Park H.S. (Baltimore, Md.); Boston Univ. Married June 17, 1973, to Kenneth Waissman (producer). Member of League of N.Y. Theatres (bd. of gov., 1973–74, 1974–75). 1564 Broadway, New York, NY 10036, tel. (212) 246-0005.

Theatre. Maxine Fox began her theatrical career with the Vagabond Players (Baltimore, Md., 1960–61). She served her professional apprenticeship at the Painters Mill Music Fair (Owings Mills, Md., Summer 1962); and made her Bway debut as production assistant with *Funny Girl* (Winter Garden, 1964). She produced *Fortune in Men's Eyes,* directed by Sal Mineo (Stage 73, N.Y.C., Oct. 22, 1969); and *Grease* (Royale, N.Y.C., Feb. 14, 1972).

With her husband, she subsequently co-produced the London production of *Grease* (New London Th., June 1973); as well as *And Miss Reardon Drinks a Little* (Morosco Th., N.Y.C., 1971); and produced *Over Here!* (Shubert Th., N.Y.C., Mar. 6, 1974).

Awards. She was nominated for an Antoinette Perry (Tony) Award for Producer, Best Musical, for *Grease* (1971–72) and for *Over Here!* (1973–74).

FOY, EDDIE JR. Actor, comedian, singer, dancer. b. Edwin Fitzgerald Foy, Jr., Feb. 4, 1910, New Rochelle, N.Y., to Edwin Fitzgerald and Madeleine (Morando) Foy. Father known as Eddie Foy, performer; mother, ballerina. Educated privately. Married June 5, 1933, to Anne Marie McKenney (dec. Feb. 1952); one son. Relatives in theatre: brothers, Brynie, Charlie, Dick, and Irving Foy, performers; sisters, Mary, and Madeleine Foy, performers. Member of AEA; SAG; AFTRA.

Theatre. Mr. Foy appeared in vaudeville at age five with his brothers and sisters as the Seven Little Foys (New Rochelle, N.Y., 1915), and toured the major vaudeville circuits (1915–29).

He made his Bway debut in the revue, *Show Girl* (Ziegfeld, July 2, 1929); subsequently played Corporal Jack Sterling in *Ripples* (New Amsterdam, Feb. 11, 1930); Gilbert Stone in *Smiles* (Ziegfeld, Nov. 18, 1930); Alexander Sheridan in *The Cat and the Fiddle* (Globe, Oct. 15, 1931); appeared in the revue, *At Home Abroad* (Winter Garden, Sept. 19, 1935) and *All the King's Horses* (London, Eng., 1935).

Mr. Foy played Bubbles Wilson in *Orchids Preferred* (Imperial, N.Y.C., May 11, 1937); during World War II, he traveled overseas with the Victory Committee entertaining the allied troops (1942–44); played Kid Conner in *The Red Mill* (Ziegfeld, N.Y.C., Oct. 16, 1945); toured in *High Button Shoes* (1947); played Hines in *The Pajama Game* (St. James, N.Y.C., May 13, 1954); the title role in *Rumple* (Alvin, Nov. 6, 1957); appeared in a stock production of *Show Boat* (Civic Light Opera, Los Angeles, Calif., 1960); played Mikeen Flynn in *Donnybrook!* (46 St. Th., N.Y.C., May 18, 1961); Hines in *The Pajama Game* (Town and Country Playhouse, East Rochester, N.Y., Aug. 8, 1966); and played Frank in *Show Boat* (Curran, San Francisco, Summer 1967).

Films. Mr. Foy has appeared in *Present Arms* (RKO, 1932); *Yankee Doodle Dandy* (WB, 1939); played in 10 short subjects for Columbia Pictures (1940); appeared in *Wilson* (20th-Fox, 1944); *And the Angels Sing* (Par., 1944); *Lucky Me* (WB, 1954); *The Pajama Game* (WB, 1957); *Bells Are Ringing* (MGM, 1960); and *Thirty is a Dangerous Age, Cynthia* (Col., 1968).

Television. Mr. Foy has appeared on Fair Exchange (CBS); *No Man Can Tame Me* (CBS); the Dinah Shore Show; The Danny Kaye Show (CBS); played Eddie Foy, Sr., in *The Seven Little Foys* (Bob Hope Presents, NBC); appeared on Burke's Law (ABC); My Living Doll (CBS); Glynis (CBS); *Olympus 7-0000* (Stage 67, ABC); *Sun City Scandals '72* (CBS); the Mike Douglas Show (ABC); the Dean Martin Show (NBC); and My Three Sons (CBS).

Recreation. Baseball, football, prize fights.

FRANCE, RACHEL. Designer, educator. b. Rachel Anne Mehr France, May 21, 1936, New York City. Grad. High School of Music and Art, N.Y.C., 1953; Vassar College, B.A. (drama and art history) 1957; Yale School of Drama, M.F.A. (design) 1967; did post-graduate study in dramatic theory and criticism, Carnegie-Mellon Univ., 1971–72. Married 1969 to Richard Xavier France, playwright; two daughters. Member of AEA; United Scenic Artists. Address: (home) 18 Oak St., Geneseo, NY 14454, tel. (716) 243-0749; (bus.) Dept. of Dramatic Arts, State Univ. of N.Y., Geneseo, NY 14454, tel. (716) 245-5441.

Mrs. France became assistant professor of dramatic arts, SUNY (Geneseo, N.Y.), in 1973.

Theatre. Mrs. France's first work in theatre was as costume designer, Cecilwood Th., Fishkill, N.Y., in 1957 and 1958. She was assistant to the designer for *Blood Wedding* (Actors' Playhouse, N.Y.C., 1958) and *Camino Real* (Circle in the Square, N.Y.C., 1959) and in charge of wardrobe for *Our Town* (Circle in the Square, 1959). She was costume designer for the Tamiment Summer Theatre (1959) and costumer for productions of *Noontide* (Th. Marquee, N.Y.C., June 1, 1961) and *One Way Pendulum* (E. 74 St. Th., Sept. 18, 1961). She was set and costume designer for the Washington Th. Club (1962); costume designer for *King of the Whole Damn World!* (Jan Hus House, N.Y.C., Apr. 14, 1962); set and costume designer for Playhouse-in-the-Park, Cincinnati, Ohio (1963); and assistant to the designer for *Dynamite Tonight* (York Playhouse, Mar. 15, 1964). In 1973, she was set designer for a production of *Amahl and the Night Visitors* by the Albuquerque (N.M.) Symphony.

Television. Mrs. France worked on *Mister Roger's Neighborhood* (PBS, 1972).

Awards. Mrs. France received a Patrons Fellowship in Drama (1971–72) and a NY State Council on the Arts Guest Lectorship Grant (May 1972).

Recreation. Reading, painting, collecting old furniture.

FRANCE, RICHARD. Actor, director, choreographer, singer, dancer. b. Richard Gene Schweizer, Jan 6, 1930, Chicago, Ill., to Eugene and Suzanne (France) Schweizer. Father, singer; mother, singer, voice teacher. Grad. YMCA H.S., Chicago, 1948. Studied dance with John Petri, Chicago, Ill., (1945–48); Antony Tudor, N.Y.C. (1951–53); acting with Paul Mann (1952–56); voice with mother, Suzanne France (1957–63). Married Oct. 25, 1958, to Ellen Ray, choreographer, dancer. Member of AEA; SAG; AFTRA.

Theatre. Mr. France first performed at age eight as Hansel in *Hansel and Gretel* (Bway Hollywood Dept. Store, Chicago, Ill., 1938); made his first professional dance appearance in *Aida* with the Chicago Civic Opera Ballet (Chicago Opera House, Ill., 1946); subsequently performed as the Indian Ceremonial dancer in the national tour of *Annie Get Your Gun* (1948); and as the Defense Attorney in the *Tiger Lily* ballet in the national tour of *Inside U.S.A.* (1949).

He made his Bway debut as Lester in *Seventeen* (Broadhurst, June 21, 1951); followed by Lenny in *Wish You Were Here* (Imperial, June 25, 1952), choreographed the London production (Casino, Oct. 10, 1953), and the national tour (opened Shubert, Chicago, Ill., Dec. 8, 1953); succeeded (Mar. 1953) Harold Lang in the title role in *Pal Joey* (Broadhurst, N.Y.C., Jan. 3, 1952); played Mickey in *By the Beautiful Sea* (Majestic, Apr. 8, 1954); and again succeeded (May 19, 1954) Harold Lang in the London production of *Pal Joey* (Prince's, Mar. 31, 1954).

Mr. France played Mickey in a stock production of *By the Beautiful Sea* (Lambertville Music Circus, N.J., Summer 1954); again played the title role in *Pal Joey* (Stamford Playhouse, Conn., Apr. 12, 1955); at the NY City Ctr., appeared as Bill Calhoun in *Kiss Me, Kate* (May 9, 1956), as 1st Helper and dancer in the "Steam Heat" number in *The Pajama Game* (May 15, 1957), and as Tommy Keller in *Annie Get Your Gun* (Feb. 19, 1958); in summer stock, played Huck Finn in *Tom Sawyer* (Kansas City Starlight Th., Mo., Summer 1958) and Og in *Finian's Rainbow* (St. Paul Civic Opera, Minn., Summer 1958).

He was the musical ensemble director at the Kansas City (Mo.) Starlight Th. (Summer 1959) for such productions as *Oklahoma!, Bells Are Ringing, New Moon,* and *Say, Darling;* appeared in the revue, *The Girls Against the Boys* (Alvin, N.Y.C., Nov. 2, 1959); at the NY City Ctr., played Frank in *Show Boat* (Apr. 12, 1961) and Neil in *Fiorello!* (June 13, 1962); appeared as Lt. Cable in *South Pacific* (Musicarnival Th., Palm Beach, Fla., 1962); Conrad Birdie in *Bye Bye Birdie* (Casa Mañana Th., Ft. Worth, Tex., Summer 1962); Will Parker in *Oklahoma!* (NY City Ctr., Feb. 27, 1963); and Riff in *West Side Story* and Marco in *Carnival!* (Casa Mañana Th., Ft. Worth, Tex., Summer 1963).

Mr. France played Tracy Clark in *What Makes Sammy Run?* (54 St. Th., N.Y.C., Feb. 27, 1964), and was understudy to Steve Lawrence in the title role, replacing Mr. Lawrence the week of Jan. 4, 1965; played Will Parker in *Oklahoma!* (NY City Ctr., Dec. 15, 1965); directed *The Boy Friend* (Equity Library Th., Feb. 4, 1966); was resident director at the Casa Mañana Th. (Ft. Worth, Tex., Summer 1966), and there directed *How To Succeed in Business without Really Trying* (May 23, 1966), *Showboat* (June 6, 1966), *Guys and Dolls* (June 20, 1966), *Li'l Abner* (July 4, 1966), *What Makes Sammy Run?* (July 18, 1966), in which he played Sammy Glick, *Flower Drum Song* (Aug. 1, 1966), *Once Upon a Mattress* (Aug. 15, 1966), and *West Side Story* (Aug. 29, 1966), in which he played Riff.

At the Kansas Circle Th. (Kansas City, Mo.), he directed *Harvey* (Feb. 1, 1967) and directed and choreographed *Pal Joey* (Mar. 29, 1967); and at the NY City Ctr., he played Chick Clark in *Wonderful Town* (May 17, 1967), and Marco the Magnificent in *Carnival* (Dec. 12, 1968).

By Presidential request, Mr. France played Will Parker in a 35-minute digest of *Oklahoma!* at the White House (July 27, 1964).

Television. Mr. France has appeared on the Show of Shows (NBC, 1951); The Web (CBS, 1952); Ed Sullivan Show (CBS, 1952); Colgate Comedy Hour (NBC, 1952); Arthur Godfrey Show (CBS, 1960); and Shari Lewis Show (CBS, 1963).

He has been choreographer for the Bell Telephone Hour (NBC), Marineland Circus (NBC), and for the United Fund Spectacular (NBC).

Night Clubs. Mr. France appeared as a dancer in the Whiffenpoof Revue (Blackhawk Restaurant, Chicago, Ill., 1949); formed his own act, *Doran and France,* which played at the Blackhawk and Chez Paree (Chicago, Ill., 1949–50).

Recreation. Oil painting.

FRANCINE, ANNE. Actress, singer. b. Anne Hollingshead Francine, Aug. 8, 1917, Atlantic City, N.J., to Albert Phillip and Emilie (Ehret) Francine. Grad. Chatham (Va.) Hall, 1935. Studied singing with Robert Fram, twelve years; Burt Knepp, one year; Norman Fields; dance with Valerie Bettis. Member of AEA; SAG; AFTRA; AGVA; Episcopal Actors Guild.

Theatre. Miss Francine first performed as Eileen Ellers in *Too Many Girls* (Wilson Th., Detroit, Mich., 1940); subsequently toured Boston, Mass. and Montreal, Quebec Canada, as Ethel Brander in *Rose Marie* (1941); played Rena Leslie in *George Washington Slept Here* (Bucks County Playhouse, New Hope, Pa., 1944); and appeared in *Sugar 'n Spice* (Copley Th., Boston, Mass., 1944).

She played Liz Courtney in the pre-Bway tryout of *Dinner for Three* (1945); toured as Martha Ladd in *Without Love* (1945); played Judith Canfield in *Stage Door* (Stamford, Conn., 1945); and made her N.Y.C. debut as Reena Rowe in *Marriage Is for Single People* (Cort, Nov. 21, 1945).

She toured as Irene Livingston in *Light Up the Sky* (Summer 1950); Kate in an ELT production of *The Taming of the Shrew* (1950); the Grand Duchess Olga Katrina in an ELT production of *You Can't Take It with You* (Lenox Hill Playhouse, N.Y., 1950); toured as Irene Burroughs in *Susan and God* (1951); and played Mrs. George in an ELT production of *Getting Married* (Lenox Hill Playhouse, N.Y., 1951).

Miss Francine toured New England as Dorothy Shaw in *Gentlemen Prefer Blondes* (1953); appeared in *Hay Fever* and as Janet Archer in *Kiss and Tell* (Palm Beach Th., Fla., 1953); Flora Busch in *By the Beautiful Sea* (Majestic, N.Y.C., Apr. 8, 1954); Madeline in *The Wayward Kiss* (Bucks County Playhouse, New Hope, Pa., 1955); and Colonel Yerka Bradacova in *The Great Sebastians* (ANTA, N.Y.C., Jan. 4, 1956), and on tour (opened Shubert, Detroit, Mich., Oct. 8, 1956).

She appeared as Queen Elizabeth in *The Dark Lady of the Sonnets* (Berkshire Festival, Stockbridge, Mass., 1956); Marian Hunt in *Made in Heaven* (Berkshire Playhouse, Stockbridge, Mass., 1956);

and at the Robin Hood Th. (Wilmington, Del.), played Mrs. St. Maugham in *The Chalk Garden* (1956) and Romaine in *Witness for the Prosecution* (1957).

She played Lily Schaeffer in a tour of *Time for Elizabeth* (Summer 1957); at the Corning (N.Y.) Summer Th. (1958), appeared as Miss Casewell in *The Mousetrap* and Mrs. Benjamin Gulle in *The Happiest Millionaire;* played Sister Tornera in *Cradle Song* (Berkshire Playhouse, 1958); and toured as Cornelia Scott in *Something Unspoken* and Sister Felicity in *Suddenly Last Summer,* both of which were presented on a double-bill as *Garden District* (opened Warren Th., Atlantic City, N.J., Mar. 11, 1959).

She played Pamela Barry in *Separate Rooms* (Fulton Th., Lancaster, Pa., 1959); appeared in the revue *Quick Changes* (Chicago, Ill., 1959); as Ninotchka in *Silk Stockings* (Starlight Musicals, Indianapolis, Ind., 1959); Rayna in *Guitar* (Jan Hus House, N.Y.C., Nov. 10, 1959); Octavia Brooks in *Innocent as Hell* (Lyric, Hammersmith, London, June 29, 1960); and Mrs. Hurstpierpoint in *Valmouth* (York, N.Y.C., Oct. 6, 1960).

She succeeded to a role in *Tenderloin* (46 St. Th., N.Y.C., Oct. 17, 1960); at the John Drew Th. (East Hampton, L.I., N.Y.), played Theresa in *Walk Alone Together* (1961), and appeared in *Critics' Choice* (1962); played the Contessa in *If Five Years Pass* (Th. 73, N.Y.C., May 10, 1962); Susan B. Anthony in *Asylum* (Th. de Lys, 1962); the Fortune Teller in *The Skin of Our Teeth* (Brandeis Univ., Mass., 1963); and Maria in *Twelfth Night* (Playhouse-in-the-Park, Cincinnati, Ohio, 1963). She also appeared in *Diary of a Scoundrel* (Milwaukee Rep. Th., Nov. 18, 1965); *Mother Courage* (Milwaukee Rep. Th., Jan. 13, 1966); *The Flies* (Association of Performing Artists, Ann Arbor, Mich., Oct. 25, 1966); played Olga in *You Can't Take It with You* (APA Rep. Co., Lyceum, N.Y.C., Feb. 10, 1967); replaced Beatrice Arthur (July 10, 1967, and Sept. 23, 1968) as Vera Charles in *Mame* (Winter Garden Th., May 24, 1966); replaced Vicki Cummings (May 30, 1968) in the national tour of *Mame;* appeared in *Are You Now or Have You Ever Been* (Th. of Riverside Church, N.Y.C., Nov. 27, 1973); played Mrs. Sprode in *Miss Moffat* (pre-Bway tryout, Shubert, Philadelphia, Oct. 7, 1974); and appeared in *The Importance of Being Earnest* (Syracuse, N.Y., Stage, Jan. 17, 1975).

Films. Miss Francine has appeared in *Juliet of the Spirits* (Rizzoli, 1965); *Stand Up and Be Counted* (Col., 1972); and *Savages* (Angelika, 1972).

Television. She appeared in *The Great Sebastians* (Producers Showcase, NBC, 1957).

Night Clubs. Miss Francine has performed at the Coq Rouge (1938–40); Persian Room (Plaza Hotel), N.Y.C., (1940); Club Cuba (1940); Cafe Pierre (1941); Versailles (N.Y.C., 1941); Le Petit Palais (1941); Embassy Club (1941–43); Copacabana (N.Y.C., 1942); Queen Mary (1942); Armendo's, (1943–45); Les Ambassadeurs (Paris, 1947); Monseigneur's (Paris, 1947); Ciro's (Paris, 1947); La Martinique (Paris, 1947); The Ritz (Montreal, 1949–51); British Colonial (Nassau, B.W.I., 1952); The Black Patch (St. Thomas, V.I., 1961); Upstairs at the Duplex (N.Y.C., 1962); and the Blue Angel (N.Y.C., 1963).

FRANCIOSA, ANTHONY. Actor. b. Anthony Papaleo, Oct. 25, 1928, New York City, to Anthony and Jean (Franciosa) Papaleo. Father, construction worker. Attended Benjamin Franklin H.S., N.Y.C.; studied acting at Dramatic Workshop of New School for Social Research, N.Y.C.; Actors Studio; and with Joseph Geiger, N.Y.C. Married 1952 to Beatrice Bakalyar, actress (marr. dis. Apr. 19, 1957); married May 4, 1957, to Shelley Winters, actress (marr. dis. Nov. 18, 1960); married Dec. 31, 1961, to Judy Balaban Kantor (marr. dis.); married to Rita Thiel, model. Member of AEA; SAG; AFTRA.

Pre-Theatre. Waiter.

Theatre. Mr. Franciosa appeared as Ferdinand in *Yes Is for a Very Young Man* (Cherry Lane, N.Y.C., June 6, 1949); the Second Orderly in *End As a Man* (Th. de Lys, Sept. 15, 1953) then played Starkson when this play moved (Vanderbilt, Oct. 14, 1953), and later succeeded William Smithers as Marquale.

He appeared as Ralph in *Wedding Breakfast* (48 St. Th., Nov. 20, 1954); Michael Gardiner in *Wedding Breakfast* (Boston Summer Th., Mass., Aug. 22, 1955); and Polo Pope in *A Hatful of Rain* (Lyceum, N.Y.C., Nov. 9, 1955).

Films. Mr. Franciosa made his debut in *A Face in the Crowd* (WB, 1957); subsequently appeared in *This Could Be the Night* (MGM, 1957); *Wild Is the Wind* (Par., 1957); *A Hatful of Rain* (20th-Fox, 1957); *The Long, Hot Summer* (20th-Fox, 1958); *The Naked Maja* (UA, 1959); *Career* (Par., 1959); *The Story on Page One* (20th-Fox, 1959); *Go Naked in the World* (MGM, 1961); *Period of Adjustment* (MGM, 1962); *Senelita* (Col.); *Rio Conchos* (20th-Fox, 1964); *The Pleasure Seekers* (20th-Fox, 1964); *A Man Could Get Killed* (U, 1966); *Assault on a Queen* (Par., 1966); *The Swinger* (Par., 1966); *Fathom* (20th-Fox, 1967); *The Sweet Ride* (20th-Fox, 1968); *In Enemy Country* (U, 1967); *A Man Called Gannon* (U, 1969); *Across 110th Street* (UA, 1972); and *The Drowning Pool* (WB, 1975).

Television. He has appeared on Studio One (CBS); Kraft Televison Th. (NBC); Philco Television Playhouse (NBC); *The Cradle Song* (Hallmark Hall of Fame, NBC, May 6, 1956); *County Fair Time* (Goodyear Playhouse, July 15, 1956); The Steve Allen Show (Ind., 1964–65); Bob Hope Presents (NBC, 1964); Arrest and Trial (ABC, 1964, 1965); The Breaking Point (ABC, 1964); *The World of Entertainment* (ABC, 1964); Valentine's Day (ABC, 1964–65); Dick Powell Theatre (Ind., 1965); *Fame Is the Name of the Game* (NBC, 1966), a made-for-television movie which led to the series The Name of the Game (NBC, 1968–70); The Virginians (NBC, 1970); The Men from Shiloh (NBC, 1970); *The Deadly Hunt* (CBS, 1971); *Earth II* (ABC, 1971); and his own series, Matt Helm (ABC, 1975).

Awards. Mr. Franciosa received the *Theatre World* Award (1956) for his performance as Polo Pope in *A Hatful of Rain;* and the Count Volpe di Misurata Cup at the Venice Film Festival (1957) for his performance in the film *A Hatful of Rain.*.

FRANCIS, ARLENE. Actress. b. Arlene Francis Kazanjian, Oct. 20, Boston, Mass., to Aram and Leah (Davis) Kazanjian. Father, photographer. Attended Coll. of Mt. St. Vincent; Finch Coll., Th. Guild Dramatic Sch., N.Y.C. Married May 14, 1946, to Martin Gabel, actor, producer, director; one son. Member of AEA; SAG; AFTRA.

Theatre. Miss Francis appeared in the Federal Th. (WPA) project's production of *Horse Eats Hat* (Maxine Elliott's Th., N.Y.C., Sept. 21, 1936); subsequently played Princess Tamara in *The Women* (Ethel Barrymore Th., Dec. 26, 1936); Sylvia Jordan in *Angel Island* (Natl., Oct. 30, 1937); Elena in *All That Glitters* (Biltmore, Jan. 19, 1938); Marion in *Danton's Death* (Mercury, Nov. 2, 1938); Judy Morton in *Michael Drops In* (John Golden Th., Dec. 27, 1938); Catherine Daly in *Young Couple Wanted* (Maxine Elliott's Th., Jan. 24, 1940); Miriam in *Journey to Jerusalem* (National, Oct. 5, 1940); Doris in *The Walking Gentleman* (Belasco, May 7, 1942); Natalia Chodorov in *The Doughgirls* (Lyceum, Dec. 30, 1942); Cora Overton in *The Overtons* (Booth, Feb. 6, 1945); Jacqueline Carlier in *The French Touch* (Cort, Dec. 8, 1945); Sheila Vane in *The Cup of Trembling* (Music Box, Apr. 20, 1948); Madeleine Benoit-Benoit in *My Name Is Aquilon* (Lyceum, Feb. 9, 1949); Carolyn Hopewell in *Metropole* (Lyceum, Dec. 6, 1949); Judith in *Little Blue Light* (ANTA, Apr. 29, 1951); Constance Warburton in *Late Love* (National, Oct. 13, 1953) in stock, appeared in *The Road to Rome* (Montclair, N.J., Summer 1955); played Dolly Fabian in *Once More, With Feeling* (National, Oct. 21, 1958), and on tour; in stock, appeared in *Amphitryon 38* (Summer, Winter 1960); and in *Old Acquaintance* (Summers, Winters 1961–62); succeeded (March 1963) Margaret Leighton as Pamela Pew-Pickett in *Tchin-Tchin* (Plymouth, Oct. 25, 1962); and in stock, appeared in *Janus* (Summer, Winter 1963). She played Pamela Piper in *Beekman Place* (Morosco, Oct. 7, 1964); Evalyn in *Mrs. Dally* (John Golden Th., Sept. 22, 1965); Carlotta Vance in a revival of *Dinner at Eight* (Alvin Th., Sept. 27, 1966); replaced (Jan. 24, 1974) Agnes Moorehead as Aunt Alicia in *Gigi* (Uris Th., Nov. 13, 1973); and was Miriam Croydon in *Don't Call Back* (Helen Hayes Th., Mar. 18, 1975).

Miss Francis has also appeared in stock in *Kind Sir* (Playhouse-on-the-Mall, Paramus, N.J.; Mineola Playhouse, L.I., N.Y.; Yonkers Playhouse, N.Y.; Westport Country Playhouse, Conn.; Ivoryton Playhouse, Conn.; Elitch Gardens, Denver, Colo., 1964); and in *Pal Joey, The Time of the Cuckoo, Who Killed Santa Claus?,* and *The Lion in Winter.*.

Films. Miss Frances appeared in *One, Two, Three* (UA, 1961) and *The Thrill of It All* (U, 1963).

Television and Radio. Miss Francis has appeared on radio on What's My Name? (CBS); Blind Date (1940); Arlene Francis Show (WOR); Monitor (Home Show); and New Ideas on Decorating (syndicated show). On television, she has appeared on What's My Line (CBS, 1950–to date); was hostess on Home (NBC, 1953–57); appeared on the television versions of Blind Date and The Arlene Francis Show; and replaced at various times Dave Garroway, Jack Paar, and Bill Cullen on their shows (all NBC).

Other Activities. Miss Francis is on the national advisory council of the Univ. of Utah, and she is on the boards of directors of Bonwit Teller, Ritz Associates, and the Atrium Club.

Published Works. Miss Francis wrote *That Certain Something* (1960) and is the author of a cookbook.

Discography. She recorded *Bible Stories for Children* (MGM Lion, 1960).

Awards. Miss Francis received the honorary degree of L.H.D. from American International Coll. (1965) and Keuka Coll. (1966) and was elected to the US Hall of Fame (1967).

FRANK, MARY K. Theatre executive, producer. b. Mary Salome Knabenshue, July 10, 1911, Cleveland, Ohio, to F. G. and Maud (Hill) Knabenshue. Father, colonel, US Army. Attended Balboa (Canal Zone) H.S. 1923–25; Miss Baird's Sch., Orange, N.J., 1926–27; RADA, 1936; Columbia Univ. 1948; Theatre Business Sch.; Weems Sch. of Navigation, Annapolis, Md. 1940–41. Married July 28, 1933, to R. J. Jondreau, USN (dec. 1944); married July 14, 1945, to William K. Frank, engineer; one daughter. Served WW II, instructor of navigation to Army and Navy personnel in Washington, D.C. Member of League of NY Theatres; New Dramatists Comm., Inc. (pres., 1960–to date). Address: New Dramatists Comm., Inc., 424 W. 44th St., New York, NY 10036, tel. (212) PL 7-6960.

Pre-Theatre. Newspaper reporter; free-lance writer; dress designer; insurance saleswoman.

Theatre. Mrs. Frank produced, with The Playwrights Company, *Tea and Sympathy* (Ethel Barrymore Th., N.Y.C., Sept. 30, 1953), which subsequently toured (opened St. James, Asbury Pk., N.Y., Nov. 5, 1954; closed Auditorium, Schenectady, N.Y., May 5, 1956); produced *Too Late the Phalarope* (Belasco, N.Y.C., Oct. 11, 1956); *One More River* (Ambassador, Mar. 18, 1960); and *Sponono* (Cort, Apr. 2, 1964).

Recreation. Breeding Skye Terriers, gardening.

FRANK, T. DAVID. Producer, director, teacher. b. Timothy David Frank, Aug. 28, 1944, Belfast, Northern Ireland, to A. D. and Jessica Frank. Father, air vice marshal. Educated Midhurst Grammar School, England; professional training at Rose Bouford College of Speech and Drama, London, England. Married June 15, 1968, to Barbara M. Arnold, actress. Address: (home) 844 Ravensridge, St. Louis, MO 63119, tel. (314) 962-5666; (bus.) 130 Edgar Rd., St. Louis, MO 63119, tel. (314) 968-0500.

Pre-Theatre. Part-time drama teacher at Garrison Forest School for three years.

Theatre. Mr. Frank has been active in regional theatre since Jan. 1967, when he joined Center Stage, Baltimore, Md., as house manager. Subsequently, he was an actor and voice coach (Oct. 1967), director of Center Stage's touring program (Sept. 1968), and the company's general manager (June 1969). In August 1972, he became managing director for the Loretto-Hilton Th., St. Louis, Mo., where he produced ten plays during the next two years. He was director of the theatre's *Henry V* (Feb. 1974).

FRANKEL, GENE. Director, acting teacher. b. Dec. 23, 1923, New York City, to Barnet and Anna (Tellerman) Frankel. Attended NY Univ. Married to Pat Carter; one son, one daughter. Address: Media Center for the Performing Artist, 342 E. 63rd St., New York, NY 10021, tel. (212) 421-1666.

Mr. Frankel began his directing career at the Green Mansions Th. (Warrenburg, N.Y., Summer 1947) where productions included *27 Wagons Full of Cotton;* made his NYC debut with N.Y. People's Drama Th., directing the off-Bway production of *They Shall Not Die* (June 7, 1949) and *Nat Turner* (Dec. 6, 1950); at the Resident Th. (Kansas City, Summers 1950–53), directed *All My Sons, Stalag 17, My Heart's in the Highlands, The Country Girl,* and *A Streetcar Named Desire;* directed, and with Sidney Bernstein, in association with Ronnie Lee, produced *Volpone* (Rooftop Th., N.Y.C., Jan. 7, 1957; directed *Richard II* (McCarter, Princeton, N.J., 1958; produced, with Al Sperhuto and Richard Kart, and directed *An Enemy of the People* (Actors Playhouse, N.Y.C., Feb. 4, 1959); directed *Machinal* (Gate, Apr. 7, 1960); *Once There Was a Russian* (Music Box, Feb. 18, 1961); *The Blacks* (St. Mark's Playhouse, May 4, 1961); *Brecht* (Th. de Lys, Jan. 3, 1962; revived Sheridan Sq. Playhouse, July 9, 1963); *The Firebugs* (Maidman Playhouse, Feb. 11, 1963); *Enrico IV* (Harper, Chicago, 1964); and for the Berkshire Th. Festival (Stockbridge, Mass.) directed *Waiting for Godot* (1965) and *A Cry of Players* (1966).

He directed *The Niggerlovers* (Orpheum, N.Y.C., Oct. 1, 1967); the Repertory Th. of Lincoln Ctr. production of *A Cry of Players* (Vivian Beaumont Th., Nov. 14, 1968); for the Edinburgh (Scotland) Th. Festival, and subsequent tour, directed *The Emperor Jones* (1968); *A Dream Play* (Queen's Coll., 1968); *To Be Young, Gifted, and Black* (Cherry Lane Th., N.Y.C., Jan. 2, 1967); *Indians* (American premiere, Arena Stage, Washington, D.C., May 6, 1969, and Brooks Atkinson Th., N.Y.C., Oct. 13, 1969); *The Engagement Baby* (Helen Hayes Th., May 21, 1970); *Pueblo* (world premiere, Arena Stage, Washington, D.C., Feb. 26, 1971); *A Gun Play* (Cherry Lane Th., N.Y.C., Oct. 24, 1971); *Lost in the Stars* (Imperial, Apr. 18, 1972); *The Lincoln Mask* (Plymouth, Oct. 30, 1972); *Othello* (Actors Studio, Feb. 8, 1973); and *The Night That Made America Famous* (Ethel Barrymore Th., Feb. 26, 1975).

He directed a European tour of *The Blacks* (1964) which included Germany and Italy; and, under the auspices of the US Dept. of Stage, Yugoslavian productions of *Oh Dad, Poor Dad, Mama's Hung You in the Closet and I'm Feeling So Sad* (1965) and *Luv* (1966).

Mr. Frankel continues to teach acting, and is the founder (1974), executive director and producer of the Media Center for the Performing Artist, an outgrowth of his workshop and teaching programs begun in 1956.

Films. Mr. Frankel directed for Laurel Films.

Television. He has directed *Volpone* for the Play of the Week (NET); *Moment of Fear* (NBC); and *To Be Young, Gifted and Black* (NET).

Other Activities. Mr. Frankel has been a visiting professor at Boston Univ., Queen's Coll., Columbia Univ., and the Univ. of Wisconsin; and has lectured at N.Y. Univ.; and has taught classes at the Amer. Theatre Wing and the Dramatic Workshop.

Awards. Mr. Frankel received the *Village Voice* Off-Bway (Obie) Award for his direction of *Volpone* (1967); and of *Machinal* (1960) which also received the Vernon Rice Award. He was the recipient of the first Lola D'Annunzio Award for Outstanding Achievement, and of a Ford Foundation grant.

FRANKEN, ROSE. Playwright, director. b. Dec. 28, 1898, Gainesville, Tex. Attended Ethical Culture Sch., N.Y.C. Married Sept. 1, 1915 to Dr. S.W.A. Franken, physician (dec. 1932); three sons; married Apr. 27, 1937, to William Brown Meloney, V. Address: 605 Park Ave., New York, NY 10021.

Theatre. Miss Franken wrote *Another Language* (Booth Th., N.Y.C., Apr. 25, 1932), which toured, played a return engagement in N.Y.C. (Waldorf, May 8, 1933), and was produced in London (Lyric, Dec. 1, 1932). She wrote and directed the following: *Claudia* (Booth, Feb. 12, 1941; toured US; and played a return engagement in N.Y.C. at the St. James, May 24, 1942); *Outrageous Fortune* (48 St. Th., Nov. 3, 1943), which also played in England and Australia; *Doctors Disagree* (Bijou, N.Y.C., Dec. 28, 1943); *Soldier's Wife* (John Golden Th., Oct. 4, 1944); and *The Hallams* (Booth, Mar. 4, 1948).

Films. Miss Franken wrote screenplays for *Beloved Enemy* (UA, 1936); *The Secret Heart* (MGM, 1946); and *Claudia and David* (20th-Fox, 1946). Her play, *Another Language,* was adapted (MGM, 1933), as was *Claudia* (20th-Fox, 1943).

Published Works. Miss Franken wrote the novels *Pattern* (1925); *Of Great Riches* (1937); *The Quiet Heart* (1954); *Rendezvous* (1954); *Intimate Story* (1955); her autobiography, *When All Is Said and Done* (1963); and *You're Well Out of a Hospital* (1966). Her *Claudia* novels were published in an omnibus edition, *The Complete Book of Claudia, The Early Years: Claudia, Claudia and David, Another Claudia* (1964).

FREEDMAN, GERALD. Director, writer. b. Gerald Alan Freedman, June 25, 1927, Lorain, Ohio, to Barnie B. and Fannie (Sepsenwal) Freedman. Grad. Northwestern Univ., B.S., M.A. (summa cum laude). Professional training with Alvina Krause, Emmy Joseph (voice); Actors Studio; Cleveland Institute of Art. Member of SSD&C; SDG; AGMA; Dramatists Guild. Address: (home) 150 W. 87th St., New York, NY 10024, tel. (212) 724-0786; (bus.) c/o Coleman-Rosenberg, 667 Madison Ave., New York, NY 10021, tel. (212) TE 8-0734.

Theatre. Mr. Freedman was assistant director of *Bells Are Ringing* (Sam S. Shubert Th., N.Y.C., Nov. 29, 1956; also London, 1957); and *West Side Story* (Winter Garden, N.Y.C., Sept. 26, 1957; also London, 1957; Paris, France; Israel). He directed the first revival of *On the Town* (Carnegie Hall Playhouse, N.Y.C., Jan. 15, 1959); was assistant director of *Gypsy* (Broadway Th., May 21, 1959); directed *The Taming of the Shrew* (NY Shakespeare Festival, Belvedere Lake, Aug. 18, 1960); directed and composed music for the double-bill *Rosemary* and *The Alligators* (York Playhouse, Nov. 15, 1960); and directed *The Gay Life* (Sam S. Shubert Th., Nov. 18, 1961).

He directed *The Tempest* (NY Shakespeare Festival, Delacorte Th., July 16, 1962); *Oh Dad, Poor Dad, Mama's Hung You in the Closet and I'm Feelin' So Sad* for national tour (opened Civic Th., Chicago, Ill., Apr. 2, 1963; closed Sept. 4, 1964); *As You Like It* (NY Shakespeare Festival, Delacorte Th., N.Y.C., July 11, 1963); a revival of *West Side Story* (NY City Ctr., Apr. 8, 1964); *Electra* (NY Shakespeare Festival, Delacorte Th., Aug. 11, 1964); *The Day the Whores Came Out To Play Tennis* (The Players Th., Mar. 15, 1965); *Love's Labour's Lost* (NY Shakespeare Festival, Delacorte Th., June 9, 1965); and *A Time for Singing,* for which he also wrote, with John Morris, the book and lyrics (Broadway Th., May 21, 1966).

Also *Richard III* (NY Shakespeare Festival, Delacorte Th., Aug. 9, 1966); *The Barber of Seville* (NY City Opera, 1966); and, for the NY Shakespeare Festival, *The Comedy of Errors* (Delacorte Th., June 7, 1967); *Titus Andronicus* (Delacorte Th., Aug. 2, 1967); *Hair* (premiere, Public Th., Oct. 29, 1967); *Ergo* (Public Th., Mar. 3, 1968); *Henry IV, Part 1* (Delacorte Th., June 11, 1968); *Henry IV, Part 2* (Delacorte Th., June 18, 1968); and he wrote the lyrics for *Take One Step* (NY Shakespeare Festival, Mobile Th., June 24, 1968). He directed *King Lear* (Lincoln Ctr. Rep., Vivian Beaumont Th., Nov. 7, 1968); and, for the NY Shakespeare Festival, *Cities in Bezique* (Public Th., Jan. 4, 1969); *Invitation to a Beheading* (Public Th., Mar. 8, 1969); *Peer Gynt* (Delacorte Th., July 8, 1969); *Sambo* (Public Th., Dec. 12, 1969); and *Black Electra* (Aug. 5, 1969).

He directed *Colette* (Ellen Stewart Th., May 6, 1970); *Timon of Athens* (NY Shakespeare Festival, Delacorte Th., June 25, 1971); *The Incomparable Max* (Royale, Oct. 19, 1971); *Beatrix Cenci* (world premiere, Opera Society of Washington, Opera House, Kennedy Ctr., Washington, D.C., Sept. 10, 1971); *The Wedding of Iphigenia* (NY Shakespeare Festival, Public Th., N.Y.C. Dec. 16, 1971); *L'Orfeo* (San Francisco Opera, San Francisco, Calif., 1972); *Hamlet* (NY Shakespeare Festival, Delacorte Th., June 20, 1972); *The School for Scandal* (City Ctr. Acting Co., Good Shepherd-Faith Ch., Sept. 27, 1972); *The Creation of the World and Other Business* (Sam S. Shubert Th., Nov. 30, 1972); Bach's *St. Matthew Passion* (San Francisco Opera, San Francisco, Calif., 1973); *The Coronation of Poppaea* (NY City Opera, Caramoor Festival, Katonah, N.Y., July 8 and 14, 1972; State Th., N.Y.C., Mar. 8, 1973); *The Au Pair Man* (Vivian Beaumont Th., N.Y.C., Dec. 27, 1973); *Beatrix Cenci* (NY City Opera, State Th., Mar. 14, 1973); *Love's Labour's Lost* (City Ctr. Acting Co., 1974); *An American Millionaire* (Circle in the Square-Joseph E. Levine Th., Apr. 20, 1974); *Idomeneo* (Opera House, Kennedy Ctr., Washington, D.C., May 23, 1974); *Ariadne* (American Opera Soc., N.Y.C., 1974); *Die Fledermaus* (NY City Opera, State Th., Sept. 18, 1974); and *Idomeneo* (NY City Opera, State Th., Mar. 16, 1975).

Mr. Freedman has also done industrial shows for Ford, Pontiac, Buick, Cadillac, Volkswagen, and the Milliken Breakfast Show.

Television. Productions directed by Mr. Freedman include the *Anne Bancroft Special* (CBS, Feb. 18, 1970); *Antigone;* Dupont Show of the Month (NBC); Robert Montgomery Presents (NBC); Ford Th. (NBC); Blondie; Celebrity Playhouse; and Oldsmobile Music Th.

Other Activities. Mr. Freedman has taught at Yale Univ. and the Juilliard School of Drama, and he has lectured at Northwestern, Louisiana State, and Southern Methodist universities, the Univ. of Southwest Texas, and Occidental College.

Published Works. Mr. Freedman wrote prefaces and commentaries for editions of *Love's Labour's Lost* (1968) and *Titus Andronicus* (1970).

Awards. Mr. Freedman has been awarded gold and silver medallions by the American College Theatre Festival for raising university theatre standards; he received a *Village Voice* off-Bway (Obie) Award in 1960 as best director for *The Taming of the Shrew;* and the *Jersey Journal* named him best director in 1968.

Recreation. Mr. Freedman has sung as a cantor since 1960, and he enjoys painting.

FREEMAN, AL JR. Actor. b. Mar. 21, 1934, San Antonio, Tex., to Albert Cornelius and Lottie Brisette (Coleman) Freeman. Father, jazz pianist. Attended Los Angeles City Coll., 1951, 1954–57; studied acting with Jeff Corey, Harold Clifton, and Frank Silvera (Los Angeles). Married Jan. 8, 1960, to Sevara E. Clemon. Served USAF, 1951–54. Member of AEA; SAG; AFTRA.

Theatre. Mr. Freeman played many roles with the Ebony Showcase (Los Angeles, 1955–59). He made his Bway debut as Rex (Fishbelly) Tucker in *The Long Dream* (Ambassador, N.Y.C., Feb. 17, 1960); played Silky Satin in the pre-Bway tryout of *Kicks and Co.* (opened Arie Crown Th., Chicago, Oct. 11, 1961; closed there, Oct. 14, 1961); toured in *A Raisin in the Sun* (Summer 1962); played Dan Morris in *Tiger Tiger Burning Bright* (Booth, N.Y.C., Dec. 22, 1962); appeared in the revue, *The Living Premise* (Premise Th., June 6, 1963); played Rev. Ridgley Washington in *Trumpets of the Lord* (Astor Place

Playhouse, Dec. 21, 1963); Richard Henry in *Blues for Mr. Charlie* (ANTA Th., Apr. 23, 1964) and at the World Th. Season in London (Aldwych, May 3, 1965); John in *Conversation at Midnight* (Billy Rose Th., N.Y.C., Nov. 12, 1964); Walker Vessels in *The Slave* (St. Marks Playhouse, Dec. 16, 1964), presented on a double-bill with *The Toilet;* succeeded Robert Hooks as Clay in *Dutchman* (Cherry Lane Th., Mar. 24, 1964), after playing the role in Los Angeles; played Diomedes in *Troilus and Cressida* (NY Shakespeare Fest., Delacorte Th., Aug. 4, 1965); and succeeded (Sept. 6, 1965) Louis Gossett as Eddie Satin in *Golden Boy* (Majestic, Oct. 20, 1964).

For the NY Shakespeare Fest. (Delacorte Th.), he played Charles Dumaine in *All's Well That Ends Well* (June 15, 1966) and Lucio in *Measure for Measure* (July 12, 1966); Kilroy in *Camino Real* (Playhouse in the Park, Cincinnati, Ohio July 18, 1968); Stanley Pollack in *The Dozens* (Booth, N.Y.C., Mar. 13, 1969); Homer Smith in *Look to the Lilies* (Lunt-Fontanne Th., Mar. 29, 1970); Paul Robeson in the premiere of *Are You Now or Have You Ever Been* (Yale Rep. Th., New Haven, Conn., Nov. 10, 1972); the Messenger in *Medea* (Circle in the Square/Joseph E. Levine Th., N.Y.C., Jan. 17, 1973); Scag and other roles in *The Great Macdaddy* (Negro Ensemble Th., St. Marks Playhouse, Feb. 12, 1974); in *Sweet Talk* (NY Shakespeare Fest., Other Stage, Nov. 3, 1974); and in *Tis Pity She's a Whore* (McCarter Th., Princeton, N.J., Nov. 14, 1974).

Films. Mr. Freeman appeared in *Torpedo Run* (MGM, 1958); *This Rebel Breed* (WB, 1960); *Sniper Ridge* (20th-Fox, 1961); *Mr. Pulver and the Captain* (WB); *No Man Walks Alone; Black Like Me* (Cont., 1964); *The Troublemaker* (Janus, 1964); played Clay in *Dutchman* (Cont., 1966); appeared in *The Detective* (20th-Fox, 1968); *Finian's Rainbow* (WB, 1968); *Castle Keep* (Col., 1969); *The Lost Man* (U, 1969); the title role in *My Sweet Charlie* (U, 1970); produced, directed and starred in the film version of *Slave*, entitled *A Fable* (MFR, 1971); and co-narrated a documentary, *Thermidor* (Altura, 1971).

Television. He has appeared on GE Th. (CBS); Suspicion (NBC); The Millionaire (CBS); Adventures in Paradise (ABC); Bourbon Street Beat (ABC); Day in Court; The Defenders (CBS); Slattery's People (CBS); The FBI (ABC); Judd for the Defense (ABC); the title role in *My Sweet Charlie* (NBC telefilm, Jan. 20, 1970); on Mod Squad (ABC); *To Be Young, Gifted and Black* (NET Playhouse, Jan. 22, 1972); was a regular on the Hot l Baltimore series (ABC, premiere Jan. 24, 1975); and has played Ed Hall on the daytime series, One Life to Live (ABC, to date).

Awards. He was nominated for a NATAS (Emmy) Award (1970) for *My Sweet Charlie.*.

FREEMAN, CHARLES K. Critic, director. b. July 11, 1900, Birkenhead, England, to Bernard and Rebecca (Goodman) Freeman. Father, manufacturer. Grad. Malden (Mass.) H.S. Married 1942, to Letty Cooper (dec.); one daughter. Member of the Outer Circle (pres., 1968–to date); AEA; SSD&C; Dramatists Guild. Address: 18 Overlook Rd., Ossining, NY 10562.

Theatre. Since 1954, Mr. Freeman has been drama critic for the Westchester-Rockland County (N.Y.) Group of ten daily newspapers, and he is currently theatre critic-columnist, Tri-State Suburban Group Newspapers. Mr. Freeman directed *Girls in Uniform* (Blackstone, Chicago, Ill., 1934); *Merry-Go-Round* (Selwyn, 1935); *Sixteen* (Blackstone, 1935); with the Federal Th. (WPA) Project, directed *The Life and Death of an American* (Maxine Elliott's Th., N.Y.C., May 19, 1939); was a supervisor for the Federal Dance (WPA) Project; staged a production of *Hellzapoppin* (1942); was a member of the War Writers Board (WW II); and dramatized *See Here Private Hargrove* for the USO Camp Shows.

He directed *Song of Norway* (Imperial, N.Y.C., Aug. 21, 1944); adapted with Gerald Savory, *Hand in Glove*, based on Mr. Savory's novel *Hughie Roddis* (Playhouse, Dec. 4, 1944), and produced in England; staged the touring production of *Song of Norway* (Summer 1944); *The Great Waltz* (Summer 1945); directed *I Like It Here* (John Golden Th., N.Y.C., Mar. 22, 1946); the pre-Bway tryout of *Wet Saturday* (closed Boston, Mass., 1947); for the American Negro Th., directed *The Washington Years* (ANTA, N.Y.C., March 11, 1948); directed 20 weeks of stock (Montclair Th., N.J., Summer 1948); directed the revival of *Diamond Lil* (Coronet, N.Y.C., Feb. 5, 1949). At the Sombrero Playhouse (Phoenix, Ariz., Winter 1955), he directed *Oh, Men! Oh, Women!, Dial 'M' for Murder, Stalag 17, My 3 Angels, The Caine Mutiny Court Martial,* and *Picnic;* was resident director of the Amer. Th. Wing Studio Co. (Cape Playhouse, Dennis, Mass., Summer 1958), and directed *Arms and the Man.*

He adapted the film *Calamity Jane* for the musical stage; it was produced during the summer of 1964 and later presented in London and on the Continent.

Films. Mr. Freeman was dialogue director for *Three Smart Girls* (U, 1937); and a writer-director for MGM (1942–43).

Television and Radio. He has written for the Cavalcade of America series. For television, he directed *Burlesque* and *Nothing But the Truth* (Independent). His musical adaptation of *Calamity Jane* was a Carol Burnett TV spectacular.

Other Activities. Mr. Freeman has written articles for the New York *Times;* an article on Soviet television for *Variety;* an article on the Beveridge Report (1939); and has been director of the musical theatre division of the Amer. Th. Wing (1954–64). He made a survey of the Irish theatre during the summer of 1971, and during the summer of 1972 he reported for *Variety* on theatre and films at the "Festival Avignon-Jean Vilar" (France). He was a critic-panelist at the International Theatre Symposiums; Max Reinhardt Archive, SUNY (Binghamton) and the Reinhardt Centennial Symposium, also at Binghamton, N.Y., in 1973.

Recreation. Theatre, travel.

FREEMAN, STAN. Composer, conductor, pianist. b. April 3, Waterbury, Conn., to Nathan and Augusta Freeman. Father, restaurateur. Educ. Hartt School of Music, Hartford, Conn. Studied piano with Moshe Paranov and Harold Bauer; composition with Paul Creston and Vittorio Giannini. Served US Air Force, 1943–46. Member of AFM; AFTRA. Address: 306 E. 81st St., New York, NY 10028, tel. (212) 988-6634.

Theatre. Mr. Freeman wrote the music and lyrics for *I Had a Ball* (Martin Beck Th., N.Y.C., Dec. 15, 1964) and for *Lively Ladies, Kind Gentlemen* (Majestic, Dec. 28, 1970). He was orchestra conductor for *Marlene Dietrich* (Mark Hellinger Th., Oct. 3, 1968).

Radio. Mr. Freeman was host of the Stan Freeman Show (NBC, 1968).

Night Clubs. From 1950 to 1965, Mr. Freeman performed at such night clubs as the Blue Angel (N.Y.C.); the Colony (London); and the Fontainebleau (Miami Beach, Fla.) as pianist and comedian.

Concerts. Since 1950, Mr. Freeman has given piano concerts throughout the US and appeared as soloist with such orchestras as the Buffalo, Denver, Memphis, Toledo, and National symphonies.

Discography. Mr. Freeman's music has been recorded by such performers as Sara Vaughan, Sammy Davis, Jr., Louis Armstrong, Peggy Lee, Bobby Darin, and Buddy Hackett.

Awards. Mr. Freeman received the MacDowell Club Award (1942) as the best young American pianist.

Recreation. Antiques, collecting rare 78 rpm recordings of old film, stage, and theatre personalities.

FREITAG, DOROTHEA. Composer, musical director, arranger, pianist. b. Dorothea Hackett Freitag, Baltimore, Md., to William F. and Belle (Hackett) Freitag. Father, musician; mother, dancer. Grad. Eastern H.S., Baltimore, 1930; awarded scholarship to attend Curtis Institute, 1930–33; Peabody Conservatory, teacher's certificate, 1934; Ecole Normale, Paris, France, 1934–36. Studied piano with Alexander Sklarevski, Baltimore, and with Isabelle Vengerna; composition with Nadia Boulanger, Baltimore and Santa Barbara, Calif., two years, Bohuslav Martinu, N.Y.C., one Year; orchestration with Mario Castelnuovo-Tedesco, Beverly Hills, Calif., one year. Married Mar. 16, 1931, to Charles Yukl, musician (marr. dis. 1943); two sons. Member of ASMA; AFM; ASCAP. Address: 333 E. 30th St., New York, NY 10016.

Theatre. Miss Freitag was first a duo pianist in a recital with George Bauer (Town Hall, N.Y.C., 1946).

She first composed the ballet music for the tryout of *Windy City* (opened Shubert, New Haven, Conn., Apr. 18, 1946; closed Great Northern, Chicago, June 6, 1946); was pianist and vocal arranger for *Lend an Ear* (Natl., N.Y.C., Dec. 16, 1948); composed the music for "Veracruzana" and "Jazz in Five Movements" in the Katherine Dunham dance revue (Bway Th., Apr. 19, 1950); and was pianist for *Courtin' Time* (Natl., June 14, 1951).

She was arranger of the dance music, and pianist for *High Time* (Somerset Playhouse, Mass., Apr. 1953; Grist Hill Playhouse, Andover, N.J., Aug. 1953); pianist for *Phoenix '55* (Phoenix, N.Y.C., Apr. 23, 1955); musical director and pianist for *Annie Get Your Gun* (Capri Th., Long Beach, N.Y., June 1956); composed the music, was musical arranger, and played her own piano composition in *Autobiography*, a program of dances (Booth, N.Y.C., Oct. 2, 1956); and was musical director, arranger, and pianist for *Shoestring '57* (Barbizon-Plaza, N.Y.C., Nov. 5, 1956).

She was musical director and pianist for *Out of This World* (Bucks County Playhouse, New Hope, Pa., May 1957) and *The Wizard of Oz* (Mill Playhouse, Hammonton, N.J., June 1957); musical director, arranger, and pianist for *Mask and Gown* (John Golden Th., N.Y.C., Sept. 10, 1957), and for the touring production (opened Curran, San Francisco, Calif., July 1, 1958; closed Great Northern, Chicago, Ill., Oct. 4, 1958); musical director and pianist for *The King and I* (Corning Summer Th., N.Y., July 1959); and musical director, arranger, and pianist for *Oh Kay!* (E. 74 St. Th., N.Y.C., Apr. 16, 1960).

She composed the dance music and additional arrangements for the pre-Bway tryout of *Kicks and Co.* (opened Arie Crown Th., Chicago, Ill., Oct. 11, 1961; closed there Oct. 14, 1961); for her ballet *District Storyville* (Kaufmann Aud., YM-YWHA, N.Y.C., May 1962; Hunter Coll., Sept. 1962; Delacorte Th., Sept. 1963; Brooklyn Academy of Music, Oct. 1963); composed additional dance music for *Tovarich* (Bway Th., Mar. 18, 1963); wrote dance music for *Golden Boy* (Majestic, Oct. 20, 1964); for *Zorba* (Imperial, Nov. 17, 1968); for *Dear World* (Mark Hellinger Th., Feb. 6, 1969); wrote dance music and played Lorraine in *70, Girls, 70* (Broadhurst, Apr. 15, 1971); wrote incidental arrangements for *Raisin* (46 St. Th., Oct. 18, 1973).

Television. Miss Freitag's ballet *District Storyville* was performed in Ottawa, Canada (BBC, 1962), and Miss Freitag did the dance arrangements for the Leslie Uggams series (CBS).

Night Clubs. She was arranger for *Medium Rare* (Happy Medium, Chicago, Ill., June 29, 1960); arranger, conductor, and pianist for Eartha Kitt (Persian Room, Plaza Hotel, May 1961, Copacabana, June 1961, N.Y.C.; Sao Paolo, Brazil, 1961); and was musical director, arranger, and pianist for *No Shoestrings* (Upstairs at the Downstairs, N.Y.C., June 1962).

Awards. At age fourteen, Miss Freitag won a Steinway in a national piano contest. The Peabody Conservatory, Baltimore, Md., gave her an award (1968) for distinguished service in the field of music, and she has received annual awards from ASCAP.

Recreation. Books, writing, cooking.

FREY, LEONARD. actor. b. Sept. 4, 1938, Brooklyn, N.Y. Father, wholesale grocer. Studied painting at Cooper Union Sch., N.Y.C., 1958–59 (Dramatics Club, vice-pres.); grad. Neighborhood

Playhouse Sch. of the Th., N.Y.C. (1961). Member of AEA; SAG; AFTRA.

Theatre. Mr. Frey played the Man in *The Apollo of Bellac* (Cooper Union Sch., N.Y.C., Dec. 18, 1958); made his professional debut as a replacement in the role of Yellow Feather in *Little Mary Sunshine* (opened Players, Nov. 18, 1959); played a variety of roles in *The Coach with the Six Insides* (Village South Th., Nov. 26, 1962; and on tour at the Spoleto, Italy, Fest.; Dublin, Ireland, Th. Fest.; Th. des Nations, Paris; Honolulu; and Tokyo); the Funnyhouse Man in *Funnyhouse of a Negro* (East End Th., Jan. 14, 1964); and Mendel, the Rabbi's son, in *Fiddler on the Roof* (Imperial, Sept. 22, 1964), later succeeding to the role of Perchik, then Motel, the tailor (Aug. 1965).

He was a member of Jerome Robbins' American Theatre Laboratory (1966–68); played Sapiens in *By Jupiter* (Goodspeed Opera House, E. Haddam, Conn., June 1967); Harold in *The Boys in the Band* (Th. Four, N.Y.C., Apr. 14, 1968; Wyndham's, London, Feb. 11, 1969; Huntington Hartford Th., Los Angeles, Apr. 15, 1969); Harry in *The Time of Your Life* (Vivian Beaumont Th., N.Y.C., Nov. 6, 1969); Neil McRae in *Beggar on Horseback* (Vivian Beaumont Th., May 14, 1970); Claire Quilty in the pre-Bway tryout of *Lolita, My Love* (opened Shubert, Philadelphia, Feb. 16, 1971; closed there, Feb. 27, 1971; re-opened after revisions, Shubert, Boston, Mar. 23, 1971; closed there, Mar. 27, 1971); Don in *People Are Living There* (Forum, Lincoln Ctr., N.Y.C., Nov. 18, 1971); and Sir Andrew Aguecheek in *Twelfth Night* (Vivian Beaumont Th., Mar. 2, 1972).

At the Yale Rep. Th. (New Haven, Conn.), Mr. Frey played Mr. Jourdain in *The Bourgeois Gentleman* (Oct. 6, 1972), Dr. Murray Zeller in Ronald Ribman's *A Break in the Skin* (Oct. 13, 1972), and Lionel Stander in Eric Bentley's *Are You Now or Have You Ever Been* (Nov. 10, 1972); at the Stratford (Ontario, Canada) Shakespearean Fest., played in Gogol's *The Marriage Brokers* (Avon Th., Aug. 3, 1973); played Ulysses in *Troilus and Cressida* (NY Shakespeare Fest., Newhouse Th., Nov. 10, 1973); Barnet in *The National Health* (Circle in the Square/-Joseph E. Levine Th., Oct. 10, 1974); and in the revue *Oh Coward!* (Playhouse in the Park, Cincinnati, Ohio, June 5, 1975).

Films. Mr. Frey appeared as "a celebrant" in *Finnegan's Wake* (Brandon, 1966); played Harold in *The Boys in the Band* (Natl. Gen., 1970); Guiles in *Tell Me That You Love Me, Junie Moon* (Par., 1970); the psychiatrist in *The Magic Christian* (Commonwealth, 1970); and Motel, the tailor, in *Fiddler on the Roof* (UA, 1971).

Television. He has appeared on Hallmark Hall of Fame (NBC, Spring 1970); on Mission: Impossible (CBS); and the Mary Tyler Moore Show (CBS).

Awards. Mr. Frey received (1963) a Vernon Rice Award for *The Coach with the Six Insides* and was nominated (1975) for an Antoinette Perry (Tony) Award as best supporting actor for his performance in *The National Health.* He was nominated (1972) for an Academy (Oscar) Award as best supporting actor for *Fiddler on the Roof.*.

FRIEBUS, FLORIDA. Actress, playwright. b. Oct. 10, 1909, Auburndale, Mass., to Theodore and Beatrice (Mosier) Friebus. Father, actor. Attended Dana Hall, Wellesley, Mass., 1922–25; Pine Manor, Wellesley, Mass., 1925–26; Th. Guild Sch., N.Y.C., 1926–27. Married Aug. 21, 1934, to Richard Waring, actor (marr. dis. 1952); one daughter. Member of AEA (council mbr., 1949–1965; various committees, including anti-blacklist (chmn.); ELT (chmn.); contract and negotiating; asst. editor, *Equity* Magazine, 1950–52); AFTRA (bd. of dir., N.Y.C. and natl., 1952); Dramatists Guild; SAG.

Theatre. Miss Friebus made her N.Y.C. debut as Kitty Reilly, an Usher, in *Triple Crossed* (Morosco, May 5, 1927); succeeded (Nov. 7, 1927) Helen Chandler as Thora in *The Ivory Door* (Charles Hopkins Th., Oct. 18, 1927); in stock, appeared as Alexandra in *The Swan;* Ann in *Outward Bound;* Dinah in *Mr. Pim Passes By;* Kitty in *The Buffoon;* and Melisande in *The Romantic Age,* (Berkshire Playhouse, Stockbridge, Mass., Summer 1928); played Hilda Wangel in the Actor's Th. production of *The Lady from the Sea* (Bijou, N.Y.C., Mar. 18, 1929); understudied Bette Davis as Hedwig in the touring production of *The Wild Duck* (opened Walnut St. Th., Philadelphia, Pa., Apr. 1929); succeeded Alfred Ryder as Curly in *Peter Pan* (Broad St. Th., Philadelphia, Pa., Apr.–May 1929).

Miss Friebus joined the Civic Repertory Th. (N.Y.C., Fall 1929) and played Sister Sagrario in *The Cradle Song* (Sept. 17, 1929); Lucille Jourdain in *The Would-Be Gentleman* (Sept. 1929), Caroline Bourrat de Vermaud in *Mademoiselle Bourrat* (Oct. 7, 1929), Doris in *Inheritors* (Oct. 26, 1929), Sasha in *The Living Corpse* (Dec. 6, 1929), Frieda Foldal in *John Gabriel Borkman* (Mar. 28, 1930), was a dancer in *Romeo and Juliet* (Apr. 21, 1930), played Blanca in *Lady from Alfaqueque* (Oct. 9, 1930), a Village Girl in *The Women Have Their Way* (Nov. 18, 1930), Leslie in *Alison's House* (Dec. 1, 1930), a walk-on in *The Cherry Orchard* (May 4, 1931), Louise in *Liliom* (Oct. 26, 1932), Anais in *Camille* (Oct. 27, 1932), and the Cheshire Cat in *Alice in Wonderland,* which she dramatized with Eva Le Gallienne (Dec. 12, 1932).

She played Sidney in *A Bill of Divorcement* and Ann in *The Queen's Husband* (Berkshire Playhouse, Stockbridge, Mass., Summer 1933); Nichette in *Camille* (Shubert, N.Y.C., Dec. 4, 1935); Angela in *The Women Have Their Way* (Shubert, Dec. 7, 1935); succeeded Ethel Barrymore Colt as Fanny Ellsler in Miss Le Gallienne's touring production of *L'Aiglon;* succeeded (Jan. 22, 1936) Helen Chandler as Jane Bennett in *Pride and Prejudice* (Music Box, N.Y.C., Nov. 5, 1935); played Maggie in *The Primrose Path* (Biltmore, Jan. 4, 1938); Edith Chester in the pre-Bway tryout of *Bill Come Back* (opened Trenton, N.J.; closed New Haven, Conn., 1945); was stand-by for Ruth Hussey as Mary Matthews in *State of the Union* (Hudson, N.Y.C., Nov. 14, 1945); and Miss Friebus' and Miss Le Gallienne's adaptation of *Alice in Wonderland,* was revived (International, Apr. 5, 1947).

She played Miss Pettigrew in *Church Street* (New Stages, Feb. 9, 1948); Lucie in *The Victors* (New Stages, Dec. 26, 1948); succeeded Polly Rowles as standby for Shirley Booth as Lola in *Come Back, Little Sheba* (Booth, Feb. 15, 1950); played Minerva Pinney in *Legend of Sarah* (Berkshire Playhouse, Stockbridge, Mass., July 9, 1951); played Helen McCarthy in *Collector's Item* (Booth, N.Y.C., Feb. 8, 1952); Lily Sears in *Tea and Sympathy* (Ethel Barrymore Th., Sept. 30, 1953); was narrator for a Sunday performance of *The Boy with a Cart* (Bway Tabernacle Church, Apr. 4, 1954); wrote the one-act play *Dora Sees Through It,* which was sponsored by AEA (Building Trades Council Aud., Los Angeles, Calif., Oct. 2, 1958); played Jessie Bartley in *Blue Denim* (Players Ring Th., Hollywood, Calif., Dec. 29, 1958); wrote the one-act play, *Dora Looks at Civil Rights,* which was produced for the Amalgamated Laundry Workers and sponsored by AEA (Hilton Hotel, N.Y.C., Dec. 14, 1963); and played Celia Pilgrim in *Absence of a Cello* (Royal Poinciana Playhouse, Palm Beach, Fla., Mar. 1, 1965) and on tour (opened Clewes Hall, Indianapolis, Ind., Jan. 4, 1966; closed Huntington Hartford Th., Los Angeles, June 4, 1966).

Films. Miss Friebus dubbed in the voice of Isle for *Maedchen in Uniform* (KAC, 1932).

Television and Radio. She has made many appearances on both radio and television shows. Her radio work includes the serials David Harum, Just Plain Bill, Stella Dallas, and Ma Perkins; as well as Ford Th.; Roses and Drums; Snow Village Sketches; Texaco Star Th.; and Th. Guild of the Air.

Her television script for *Alice in Wonderland* was produced by Hallmark Hall of Fame (NBC, Oct. 23, 1955). She played Winifred Gillis, Dobie's mother, on the Dobie Gillis series (CBS, 1959–1963); and has appeared on Kraft Th. (NBC); Philco Playhouse (NBC); Playhouse 90 (CBS); My Mother, the Car (NBC); Perry Mason (CBS); Ben Casey (ABC); This Is the Answer (ABC); This Is the Life (ABC); *The Love Nest* (CBS pilot film, Mar. 14, 1975); and others.

Awards. Miss Friebus received the John Golden Award for her essay on "Why the United States Needs the United Nations," which was presented on Human Rights Day (Dec. 10, 1954); was nominated for a local NATAS (Emmy) Award in Los Angeles, Calif. (1961); and received an award from NAFBRAT for the regional children's program, Look and Listen (Spring 1962).

Recreation. Driving, swimming, walking, and gardening.

FRIED, MARTIN. Director, actor, stage manager. Married Brenda Vaccaro, actress (marr. dis.). Member of AEA; SSDC; Actors Studio.

Theatre. Mr. Fried began his career as an actor (1952–60) making his Bway debut as The Newsboy and assistant stage manager in *Winesburg, Ohio* (May 5, 1958). He subsequently stage managed the national company of *The Dark at the Top of the Stairs* (opened Playhouse, Wilmington, Del., Jan. 21, 1959; closed Pabst, Milwaukee, May 16, 1959); stage managed the pre-Bway tryout of *The Pink Jungle* (opened Alcazar; San Francisco, Oct. 14, 1959; closed Shubert, Boston, Dec. 12, 1959); played Mike and was assistant stage manager for *The Best Man* (Morosco, N.Y.C., Mar. 31, 1960; and national tour); and directed a national tour of *The Best Man* (opened Shakespeare Festival Th., Stratford, Conn., Jan. 7, 1962; closed Hartman, Columbus, Ohio, Apr. 28, 1962). He stage managed *The Affair* (Henry Miller's Th., N.Y.C., Sept. 20, 1962); and *The Lady of the Camellias* (Winter Garden, Mar. 20, 1963); was production stage manager for the Actors Studio productions of *Marathon '33* (ANTA, Dec. 22, 1963), and *The Three Sisters* (Morosco, June 22, 1964); and directed scenes for the Actors Studio playwrights unit (1964).

Mr. Fried made his N.Y.C. directing debut with *The Coop* (Actors Playhouse, Mar. 1, 1966); followed by *Fragments* (Berkshire Festival, Stockbridge, Mass., Summer 1966); *The Country Girl* (NY City Ctr., N.Y.C., Sept. 29, 1966); *The Natural Look* (Longacre, Mar. 11, 1967); and *Daphne in Cottage D* (Music Box, Oct. 15, 1967). At the American Place Th. (St. Clement's Church), he directed *The Cannibals* (Oct. 7, 1968); *The Bird of Dawning Singeth All Night Long* (Dec. 12, 1968) on a triple-bill with *The Acquisition* and *The Young Master Dante; Papp* (May 5, 1969); *Duet for Solo Voice,* on a double-bill entitled *Two Times One* (Apr. 5, 1970) that included *The Last Straw; Pinkville* (Mar. 17, 1971); *Fingernails Blue as Flowers* (Amer. Place Th., Dec. 22, 1971) on a double-bill with *Lake of the Woods;* and *Bread* (Jan. 28, 1974).

Mr. Fried has also directed productions of *The Silent Partner* (Actors Studio, May 11, 1972); *Twelve Angry Men* (Queens, N.Y., Playhouse, Dec. 3, 1972); and a double-bill of *Hughie* and *Duet* (John Golden Th., N.Y.C., Feb. 11, 1975).

Films. He was assistant director for *Career* (Par., 1959).

FRIEDERICH, W. J. Educator, writer, director. b. Apr. 6, 1916, Summerfield, Ill., to Edwin P. and Emilie (Blum) Friederich. Grad. Community H.S., Mascoutah, Ill., 1934; McKendree Coll., B.A. 1938; Univ. of Illinois, M.A. 1940; attended New York Univ., 1940–41; and Northwestern Univ., Summer 1943. Married June 12, 1940, to Betty Phillips, teacher; one son, one daughter. Member of SCA (formerly SAA, exec. council, 1954–57); ATA; Ohio Coll. Teachers of Speech; Alpha Psi Omega; Pi Kappa Delta; Phi Kappa Phi. Address: (home) 501 Foster Lane, Marietta, OH 45750, tel. (614) FR 4-7046; (bus.) Marietta College, Marietta, OH 45750, tel. (614) FR 3-4643. Since 1946, Mr. Friederich has been a professor in charge of the drama dept., and Director of Theatre at Marietta Coll. Previously, he held academic positions at the Univ. of Illinois (instructor, 1941–43); Dakota Wesleyan Univ. (assistant professor and Director of Theatre, 1943–45); Carroll Coll. (assistant professor and Director of Theatre, 1945–46); was a visiting professor at Lehigh Univ. (Summer 1941); and at the Univ. of New Brunswick, Canada (Summer 1955).

Mr. Friederich has directed and designed over 100 productions in university theatre.

Published Works. His books include *Scenery Design for Amateur Stage* (1950); *Teaching Speech in High Schools* (1953); *The High School Drama Course* (1957); and he wrote "Teaching Delivery Techniques in Oral Interpretation" in *Oral Interpretation and the Teaching of Literature* (1969). He was book review editor for *Dramatics* Magazine (1952–62).

Awards. He won the Playwriting competition at the National Folk Drama Festival (1937).

Recreation. Bridge, refinishing antique furniture, reading.

FRIEDMAN, PHIL. Production stage manager. b. Philburn Friedman, Oct. 31, 1921, Tacoma, Wash., to Harry and Dorothy Friedman. Father, jeweler. Grad. Tacoma H.S., 1939; studied acting with Ruth Radford Herman, nine years. Served US Army, ETO, 1941–45; rank, Warrant Officer (jg); Bronze Star. Member of AEA. Address: 347 E. 53rd St., New York, NY 10022, tel. (212) PL 1-3781.

Theatre. Mr. Friedman was assistant stage manager and stage manager for the Los Angeles and San Francisco Civic Light Opera Assn. (1946–53). In N.Y.C., he was production stage manager for *Kismet* (Ziegfeld, Dec. 3, 1953); the national tour of *The Boy Friend* (opened Shubert, New Haven, Conn., Nov. 28, 1955; closed Shubert, Philadelphia, Pa., Jan. 5, 1957); and the national tour of *Auntie Mame* (opened Hanna, Cleveland, Ohio, Oct. 20, 1957; closed Erlanger, Chicago, Ill., Jan. 17, 1959).

He was also production stage manager for *Whoop-Up* (Shubert, N.Y.C., Dec. 22, 1958); *First Impressions* (Alvin, Mar. 19, 1959); *The Conquering Hero* (ANTA, Jan. 16, 1961); *How to Succeed in Business Without Really Trying* (46 St. Th., Oct. 14, 1961); *Little Me* (Lunt-Fontanne, Nov. 17, 1962); *Skyscraper* (Lunt-Fontanne Th., Nov. 13, 1965); *Walking Happy* (Lunt-Fontanne Th., Nov. 26, 1966); *Darling of the Day* (George Abbott Th., Jan. 27, 1968); *Come Summer* (Lunt-Fontanne Th., 1969); *Lovely Ladies, Kind Gentlemen* (Majestic, Dec. 28, 1970); and *Pippin* (Imperial, Oct. 23, 1972).

Television. Mr. Friedman was production stage manager for the television special *Liza With a 'Z'* (Lyceum, June 1972).

FRIEDMAN, SAMUEL. Press representative. b. Samuel Joseph Friedman, Jan. 9, 1912, New York City, to Abraham and Flora (Stern) Friedman. Father, manufacturer. Grad. Evander Childs Sch., N.Y.C., 1929; attended Columbia Univ., 1929–31. Married Apr. 25, to Florence Taussig, one daughter. Member of ATPAM (bd. of dir.); IATSE; Publicists. Local 872. Address: (home) 38 W. 9th St., New York, NY 10011, tel. (212) GR 3-6075; (bus.) 38 W. 9th St., New York, NY 10011, tel. (212) GR 3-6075.

Theatre. Mr. Friedman's first assignment was in the Shubert press dept., publicizing a series of operattas, *Hooray for What!* (1937); *Bachelor Born* (1938); *You Never Know* (1938); and *Hellzapoppin* (1938).

He was advance press representative for the tour of *What a Life* (1939); at the NY World's Fair (1939), press representative for the Cuban Village, the Arctic Girl and Doughnuts; handled the advance publicity for the tour of *Pal Joey* (1941); served as press representative for *The Duke of Darkness* (1944); *Trio* (1944); *Home of the Brave* (1945); *Finian's Rainbow* (1947); *The Last Dance* (1948); *The Play's the Thing* (1948); *Lend an Ear* (1948); *Jenny Kissed Me* (1948); *At War with the Army* (1949); *The Biggest Thief in Town* (1949); *Season in the Sun* (1950); *Courtin' Time* (1951); *Lace on Her Petticoat* (1951); *To Dorothy a Son* (1951); *Two's Company* (1951); and *Springtime for Henry* (1952).

Mr. Friedman was publicity director at the Oakdale Musical Th. (Wallingford, Conn., 1954–61); press representative at the Phoenix Th., N.Y.C., for *The Golden Apple* (1954), *The Seagull* (1954), *Sing Me No Lullaby* (1954), and *The Doctor's Dilemma* (1955); press representative for *The Threepenny Opera* (1955), *The Potting Shed* (1957), *A Moon for the Misbegotten* (1957), *The Cave Dwellers* (1957), and *Rumple* (1957).

He was press representative at the Marine Th. (Jones Beach, N.Y.) for *Show Boat* (1957), and *Song of Norway* (1958); in N.Y.C. for *Mask and Gown, Romanoff and Juliet, Compulsion,* and *Miss Isobel* (1957); *Take Me Along* (1959). He took over as producer of two shows he publicized—*The Billy Barnes Revue* (1959) and Gertrude Stein's *In Circles.* He was press representative for the tour of *The Hostage* (1961); *Pajama Tops* (1963); *In White America* (1963); *Fair Game for Lovers* (1964); at the NY World's Fair (1964), for the Texas Pavillion and the musical revue, *To Broadway with Love;* the pre-Bway tour of *Golden Boy* (opened Shubert, Philadelphia, Pa., June 25, 1964); the 1965–66 tour of *The Subject Was Roses; That Summer—That Fall* (1967); *The Only Game in Town* (1968); and, as publicity director for Hillard Elkins, he publicized *Oh! Calcutta!* (1969); *The Rothschilds* (1970); *An Evening with Richard Nixon* (1972); Claire Bloom's *A Doll's House* (1971) and *Hedda Gabler* (1971). After returning from a nationwide tour ahead of *Man of La Mancha,* he was publicity director for *The Me Nobody Knows* (1970); *Brother Gorski* (1973); and *The Lemmings.*

Films. Mr. Friedman publicized *Pinocchio* (RKO, 1940); *Moulin Rouge* (UA, 1952); *My Son John* (Par., 1952); *The Ten Commandments* (Par., 1956); *The Bridge on the River Kwai* (Col., 1957); and *West Side Story* (UA, 1961). In 1961, he became national publicity director for United Artists; he served one year before returning to the legitimate theatre.

Night Clubs. He was press representative for the Roseland Ballroom (N.Y.C., 13 years), Billy Rose's Diamond Horseshoe (N.Y.C., 1946), and he handled El Chicho and The Hurricane.

Recreation. Poker.

FRIEL, BRIAN. Playwright, short story writer. b. Jan. 9, 1929, Omagh, County Tyrone, Ireland, to Patrick and Christina (MacLoone) Friel. Father, teacher. Educ. St. Columb's College, Derry; St. Patrick's College, Maynooth; and St. Joseph's Training College, Belfast. Married 1954 to Anne Morrison; five children. Address: Muff Lifford County Donegal, Ireland tel. Muff 30.

Pre-Theatre. Mr. Friel was a school teacher from 1950 to 1960 and thereafter concentrated on his writing.

Theatre. Mr. Friel's first plays were both produced in Belfast: *The Francophile* (1950) and *The Doubtful Paradise* (1960). These were followed by *The Enemy Within* (Abbey Th., Dublin, 1962) and *The Blind Mice* (Eblana Th., Dublin, 1963). *Philadelphia, Here I Come!* (Gaiety Th., Dublin Th. Festival, Sept. 28, 1964) was Mr. Friel's first play to be produced in America (Helen Hayes Th., N.Y.C., Feb. 16, 1966). Later works include *The Loves of Cass McGuire* (world premier, Helen Hayes Th., Oct. 6, 1966); *Lovers* (Gate Th., Dublin, July 1967; Vivian Beaumont Th., N.Y.C., July 25, 1968); *Crystal & Fox* (Gate Th., Dublin, Nov. 1968; American premier, Mark Taper Forum, Los Angeles, Calif., Apr. 9, 1970; McAlpin Rooftop, N.Y.C., Apr. 23, 1973); *The Mundy Scheme* (Olympia, Dublin, June 10, 1969; Royale, N.Y.C., Dec. 11, 1969); *The Gentle Island* (Olympia, Dublin, Nov. 30, 1971); and *The Freedom of the City* (Abbey Th., Dublin, 1973).

Published Works. Mr. Friel's short stories have been published in *The New Yorker* magazine, and two collections have been issued: *The Saucer of Larks* (1962) and *The Gold in the Sea* (1966).

Awards. Mr. Friel was awarded the Macaulay Fellowship by the Irish Arts Council in 1965, and he received the honorary degree of D.Litt. from Rosary College, Chicago, Ill., in 1974. *Philadelphia, Here I Come!* was nominated for an Antoinette Perry (Tony) Award for best play in 1966, and Mr. Friel was named in the *Variety* poll of the NY drama critics as most promising new Bway playwright for the same work.

FRIERSON, MONTE L. Theatre manager, producer. b. Monte Lew Frierson, Feb. 15, 1930, Tulsa, Okla., to Ambrose Montgomery and Frances Veronica (Knigge) Frierson. Father, oil producer. Grad. Bristow (Okla.) H.S., 1948; Univ. of Oklahoma, B.B.A. 1953. Served US Army, 1953–55; rank, 1st Lt. Address: 401 W. 6th Ave., Bristow, OK 74010, tel. (918) 367-5309.

Mr. Frierson was the general manager of the McCarter Th. of Princeton Univ. (1963–64).

He was manager of the Celebrity Concert Series at the Univ. of Oklahoma (1952–53); East Coast manager of various groups and individuals (1956–65); served as director of public relations and assistant to the executive producer of the Theatre Guild, N.Y.C. (1956); was assistant treasurer of the American Shakespeare Festival (Stratford, Conn., Summer 1956); assistant to Helen Menken at the American Theatre Wing (N.Y.C., 1957–58); treasurer of St. John Terrell's Music Circus, Lambertville, N.J. (1958–59; 1962–63); producer of *The Buffalo Skinner* (Th. Marquee, N.Y.C., Feb. 19, 1959); treasurer of the North Shore Music Th. (Beverly, Mass., Summer 1960); general manager of the Peninsula Players (Fish Creek, Wis., Summer 1961); press representative of the Westport Country Playhouse (Spring 1962); produced the National Ballet (Acad. of Music, Philadelphia, Pa., Jan. 31, 1963); was general manager of the Carousel Th., Framingham, Mass. (1964–67); manager of the Boston (Mass.) *Herald Traveler* Repertory of Classical Drama (1967); manager of the Bridgeport (Conn.) Festival Th. (Summer 1968); partner of Durgom & Frierson Management, N.Y.C. (1968–69); director of public relations of the New Jersey Shakespeare Festival, Cape May, N.J. (Summer 1970); and production manager of the Oklahoma City (Okla.) Symphony Orchestra (1972).

Recreation. Music, reading, swimming.

FRINGS, KETTI. Playwright, novelist. b. Katherine Hartley, Columbus, Ohio, to Guy Herbert and Pauline (Sparks) Hartley. Father, salesman. Attended Lake Sch., Milwaukee, Wis.; Principia Coll. Married 1938, to Kurt Frings, agent; one son, one daughter. Member of SWG; Dramatists Guild; League of NY Theatres.

Theatre. Mrs. Frings wrote *Mr. Sycamore* (Guild, N.Y.C., Nov. 13, 1942); *Look Homeward, Angel,* based on the novel by Thomas Wolfe (Ethel Barrymore Th., Nov. 28, 1957); and *The Long Dream,* which was produced by Cheryl Crawford and Joel Schenker, in association with Mrs. Frings' firm, October Productions, Inc. (Ambassador, Feb. 17, 1960). She wrote, with Roger O. Hirson, the book for *Walking Happy* (Lunt-Fontanne Th., Nov. 26, 1966).

Films. Mrs. Frings wrote the screenplays for *Guest in the House* (UA, 1944); *Come Back, Little Sheba* (Par., 1952); *About Mrs. Leslie* (Par., 1954); *Fox-Fire* (U, 1955); and *The Shrike* (U, 1955).

Television. Mrs. Fring's adaptation of *Look Homeward, Angel* was televised (CBS, Feb. 25, 1972).

Published Works. She is the author of two novels; *Hold Back the Dawn* (1942) and *God's Front Porch* (1945); has contributed short stories and serials to *The Saturday Evening Post, Good Housekeeping, Collier's,* and *McCall's* magazines; and, in 1950, was a feature writer for United Press.

Awards. In 1958 for her play, *Look Homeward, Angel,* she received the Pulitzer Prize in Drama and the NY Drama Critics' Circle Award; was voted "Woman of the Year" by the Los Angeles *Times* (1958); received the Martha Kinney Cooper Ohiana Library Assn. Ohiana Award (1958); and received the Distinguished Achievement Award from Theta Sigma Phi, the national fraternity for women in journalism. In 1962, her works, manuscripts, and papers were donated to the Univ. of Wisconsin for the Ketti Frings Collection.

FRISCH, MAX. Playwright, journalist, writer. b. May 15, 1911, Zurich, Switzerland, to B. Franz and Lina (Wildermuth) Frisch. Father, architect. Grad. Gymnasium, Zurich; Univ. of Zurich, (degree in philology); and Eidgenossische Technische Hochschule, Zurich (diploma in architecture). Married 1942 to Gertrud Constanze von Meyenburg. Member of P.E.N. Club.

Theatre. U.S. productions of Mr. Frisch's plays include *A House in Berlin,* produced by the Erwin Piscator Dramatic Workshop (N.Y.C., Dec. 1952); *The Chinese Wall* (Univ. Playhouse, Univ. of Washington, Seattle, Feb. 7, 1958; Schoenberg Hall, Los Angeles, Calif., July 31, 1962); *Andorra* (Biltmore, N.Y.C., Feb. 9, 1963); *The Firebugs* (Maidman, Feb. 11, 1963); and *A Public Prosecutor Is Sick of It All* (Kreeger Th., Arena Stage, Washington, D.C., Feb. 1, 1973). He also wrote *Count Oederland* (Victoria Rooms, Univ. of Bristol, England, Feb. 21, 1963); *Edge of Reason* (Th. Royal, Stratford, Sept. 18, 1964); and *Biography* (Zurich, Switz., 1968).

Published Works. In addition to his works that have been published in German, Mr. Frisch wrote *Phillip Hotz's Fury, Leaves from a Knapsack, Santa Cruz,* and *Sketchbook* (1974); and the novels, *The Difficult One* (1943), *I'm Not Stiller* (1958), *Homo Faber, A Report* (1959), and *A Wilderness of Mirrors* (1966).

Awards. Mr. Frisch received a Rockefeller Foundation Grant, 1951–52, for study in the US and in Mexico; the Schleussner-Schueller Prize (1955); the Hessian Radio Wilhelm-Raabe Prize (Braunschweig); he is an honorary member of the Seiss Schiller Foundation, received the George Buchner-Charles Veillon Literature Prize (Zurich, Switzerland, 1958); and is a member of the German Acad. of Languages and Poetry (Darnstadt, Germany, 1954).

FROSCH, AARON R. Lawyer. b. July 9, 1924, New York City. Grad. James Madison H.S., Brooklyn, 1940; Brooklyn Coll., B.A. 1944; Brooklyn Law Sch., LL.B. 1947. Married; three daughters. Member of Assn. of the Bar of the City of NY; NY County Lawyers Assn.; Amer. Bar Assn.; US Comm. for the UN (bd. mbr., 1963–64); William Hale Harkness Foundation, Inc. (bd. mbr., vice-pres., gen. counsel 1961–64); Rebekah Harkness Foundation (bd. mbr., vice-pres., gen. counsel 1961–64); Gallery of Modern Art (trustee, 1963–64); NY Shakespeare Festival (trustee, 1963–to date). Address: (home) 300 Central Park West, New York, NY 10024; (bus.) 445 Park Ave., New York, NY 10022, tel. (212) PL 8-0801.

Mr. Frosch has been president of Marilyn Monroe Productions, Inc. (1962–64) and vice-president of Elizabeth Taylor Productions, Inc. (1963–64); provides legal counsel to British and American stage and film actors producers, directors, and other related persons and companies; and is a specialist in theatre, film, tax, and family law.

FRY, CHRISTOPHER. Playwright, actor, director, translator. b. Christopher Fry Harris, Dec. 18, 1907, Bristol, England, to Charles John and Emma Marguerite Fry (Hammond) Harris. Father, church lay reader. Educated Bedford Modern Sch., Bedford, England, 1918–1926. Married Dec. 3, 1936, to Phyllis Marjorie Hart, journalist; one son. Served with the Pioneer Corps, 1940–44. Member of Dramatists Guild; Fellow at the Royal Society of Literature. Address: 37 Blomfield Rd., London, W.9, England.

Pre-Theatre. Preparatory Sch. teacher.

Theatre. Mr. Fry first performed a season with a Bath repertory co. in Eng. (1927); subsequently was a director of a repertory company at Tunbridge Wells (1932–35); and directed a musical *How-do, Princess.*

He wrote *The Boy with a Cart,* produced in 1937; a pageant, *The Tower* (Tewkesbury Festival, July 18, 1939); and was producer-director at the Oxford Repertory Players (1940; 1944–46).

Mr. Fry directed, at the Arts Th., London, *The Circle of Chalk* (Aug. 9, 1945) and *The School for Scandal* (Sept. 21, 1945). He wrote *A Phoenix Too Frequent* (Mercury, Apr. 25, 1946); *The Lady's Not for Burning* (Arts, Mar. 10, 1948); *The Firstborn* (Edinburgh Festival, Scotland, Aug. 1948); *Thor, with Angels* (Canterbury Festival, England, 1948; Lyric, Hammersmith, London, Sept. 27, 1951); *Venus Observed* (St. James's Th., Jan. 18, 1960); and translated and adapted Jean Anouilh's *L'Invitation au château* as *Ring Round the Moon* (Globe, Jan. 26, 1950). He wrote *A Sleep of Prisoners* (St. Thomas's Ch., May 1951); *The Dark Is Light Enough* (Aldwych, Apr. 30, 1954); translated Anouilh's *The Lark* (Lyric, Hammersmith, London, May 11, 1955); Jean Giraudoux's *Tiger at the Gates* (Apollo, June 2, 1955); wrote *Curtmantle* (Stadsschouwburg, Tilburg, Holland; Edinburgh Festival, Scotland, Sept. 4, 1962; Aldwych, London, England, Oct. 6, 1962); and translated Giraudoux's *Judith* (Her Majesty's, London, June 20, 1962); adapted in verse *Peer Gynt* (1970); and wrote *A Yard of Sun* (Nottingham Playhouse, July 11, 1970; Old Vic, London, Aug. 10, 1970).

American productions of Mr. Fry's work include *A Phoenix Too Frequent* (Radcliffe Coll., Cambridge, Mass., Apr. 7, 1948; Fulton Th., N.Y.C., Apr. 26, 1950); *The Lady's Not for Burning* (Royale, Nov. 8, 1950); *Ring Round the Moon* (Martin Beck Th., Nov. 23, 1950); *Thor, with Angels* (Catholic Univ. Th., Washington, D.C., Dec. 1, 1950); *A Sleep of Prisoners* (St. James Ch., N.Y.C., Oct. 16, 1951); *Venus Observed* (Century, Feb. 13, 1952); *The Boy with a Cart* (Seamen's Ch. Inst., June 23, 1953); *The Dark Is Light Enough* (ANTA Th., Feb. 23, 1955); *Tiger at the Gates* (Plymouth, Oct. 3, 1955); *The Firstborn* (Coronet, Mar. 30, 1958); and his translation and adaptation of Jean Giraudoux's *Pour Lucrèce* as *Duel of Angels* (Helen Hayes Th., Apr. 19, 1960); and *A Yard of Sun* (Cleveland Playhouse, Ohio, Oct. 13, 1972).

Films. Mr. Fry was a screenwriter for *A Queen Is Crowned* (U, 1953); *The Beggar's Opera* (WB, 1953); *Ben Hur* (MGM, 1959); *Barabbas* (Dino de Laurenti's Productions, 1962); and *The Bible* (20th-Fox, 1966).

Television. Television productions of Mr. Fry's work include *The Lady's Not for Burning* (Omnibus, NBC, 1958); *Tiger at the Gates* (Play of the Week, WNTA); and *A Sleep of Prisoners* (NET, Jan. 8, 1965). Mr. Fry wrote for television the four-part series *The Brontes of Haworth* (Yorkshire TV, England, 1973).

Published Works. In addition to his plays, Mr. Fry's lecture to the Critic's Circle was published under the title *An Experience of Critics* (1953).

Awards. Mr. Fry received an award (1948); from the Shaw Prize Fund for *The Lady's Not For Burning;* The Foyle Prize for Poetry (1950); Royal Society of Literature, Heinemann Prize (1962); and The Queen's Gold Medal for Poetry (1962).

FRYER, ROBERT. Producer. b. Nov. 18, 1920, Washington, D.C., to S. Harold and Ruth (Reade) Fryer. Father, department store manager. Grad. Western Reserve Univ., B.A. 1946. Served US Army, 1942–46; rank Capt. Member of League of NY Theatres (bd. of gov. 1957–62); Episcopal Actors Guild (vice-pres.). Address: (home) 12 Beekman Place, New York, NY 10022, tel. (212) EL 5-1181; 8800 Thrasher Ave., Los Angeles, CA 90069; (bus.) 15 E. 48th St., New York, NY 10017, tel. (212) 593-2277.

From 1971 to date, Mr. Fryer has been managing director of the Center Th. Group's Ahmanson Th. (135 N. Grand Ave., Los Angeles).

Theatre. Mr. Fryer was assistant to the producer for the Old Vic season (Century, N.Y.C., Oct. 23, 1946); and was managing director for the Cape Playhouse (Dennis, Mass., Summer 1947); and the Ogunquit (Me.) Playhouse (Summer 1948).

He produced with George Abbott, *A Tree Grows in Brooklyn* (Alvin Th., N.Y.C., Apr. 19, 1951); produced *Wonderful Town* (Winter Garden, Feb. 25, 1953); *By the Beautiful Sea* (Majestic, Apr. 8, 1954); and *Saratoga* (Winter Garden, Dec. 7, 1959); produced with Lawrence Carr, *Desk Set* (Broadhurst, Oct. 24, 1955), *Shangri-La* (Winter Garden, June 13, 1956), *Auntie Mame* (Broadhurst, Oct. 31, 1956), *Redhead* (46 St. Th., Feb. 5, 1958), *There Was a Little Girl* (Cort, Feb. 29, 1960), *Advise and Consent* (Cort, Nov. 17, 1961), and its tour (opened Shubert, Cincinnati, Ohio, Oct. 2, 1961; closed American, St. Louis, Mo., May 5, 1962); with Lawrence Carr and the Theatre Guild, *A Passage to India* (Ambassador, N.Y.C., Jan. 31, 1962), and *Hot Spot* (Majestic, Apr. 19, 1963); produced, with Lawrence Carr, Joseph and Sylvia Harris and John Herman, *A Dream of Swallows* (Jan Hus Playhouse, Apr. 14, 1964), and *Roar Like a Dove* (Booth, May 21, 1964); produced, with Lawrence Carr, and Joseph and Sylvia Harris, *Sweet Charity* (Palace, Jan. 29, 1966), and *Mame* (Winter Garden, May 24, 1966); and produced, with James Cresson, *Chicago* (46 St. Th., June 3, 1975).

Films. With his partner James Cresson, Mr. Fryer produced *The Boston Strangler* (20th-Fox, 1968); *The Prime of Miss Jean Brodie* (20th-Fox, 1969); *Myra Breckinridge* (20th-Fox, 1970); *Travels with My Aunt* (MGM, 1972); *Mame* (WB, 1974); and *The Abdication* (WB, 1974).

Television. Mr. Fryer was asst. producer for Studio One (CBS, 1949–51); and casting director for 30 CBS programs (1951–53). He produced *Wonderful Town* (CBS, Nov. 30, 1958) and *Great Expectations* (1974).

Published Works. Mr. Fryer wrote *Professional Theater Management in New York City* (1947).

Awards. He received the Antoinette Perry (Tony) Award (1958) for his production of *Redhead.*.

FUCHS, LEO. Actor. b. Abraham Leon Springer Fuchs, May 15, 1911. Lwow, Poland, to Jacob and Rosa (Summer) Fuchs. Father, actor; mother, actress. Educated in public schools in Lwow. Studied violin at Lwow Conservatory. Married 1936, to Muriel Gruber (marr. dis. 1942); married Nov. 9, 1943, to Rebecca Richman, actress; one son. Member of AEA; AFTRA; SAG; AGVA; ASCAP; City of Hope.

Theatre. Mr. Fuchs first appeared on stage as a child actor at the Gimpel Th. (Lwow, Poland, 1916), where he subsequently appeared in plays by Shakespeare, Grilpztzer, Ansky and Tolstoy (1916–27).

He toured Europe in musical comedies (1927–28); appeared in the revues, *Fuchs Dances, Fuchs Sings,* and *Fuchs Goes to the Races* (Qui Rio Quo, Warsaw, Pol., 1928); and toured Poland in one-man shows (1934–35).

He first appeared in the US in a Yiddish Th. production of *Lucky Boy* (Second Ave. Th., N.Y.C., Oct. 1935); subsequently appeared in Maurice Schwartz' production of *Salvation* (59 St. Th., Oct. 1936); *Man of Tomorrow* (National Oct. 1938); *Galician Cowboy* (Parkway Th., N.Y.C., Sept. 1943); Alexandria, London, Mar. 1948); appeared in American and Yiddish plays (1946–50); and in his own production of *Laugh and Be Happy* (Public Th., N.Y.C., Sept. 1951–Jan. 1952).

He appeared in stock in *Girl Crazy* (St. Louis Municipal Opera, Mo.; Pittsburgh Light Opera Co., Pa., 1952); *The Fifth Season* (Sombrero Playhouse, Phoenix, Ariz.; Palm Springs Playhouse, Calif., 1958); *Uncle Willie* (Band Box, Hollywood, Calif., 1959); was "resident star" at the Anderson Yiddish Th. (N.Y.C.), where he appeared in productions of *Bei Mir Bist du Schoen* and *Cowboy in Israel* (1961–63) and directed, wrote special material for, and was David Kayser in *The Poor Millionaire* (Oct. 22, 1966). He toured as Herr Schultz in the national company of *Cabaret* (opened Shubert Th., New Haven, Conn., Dec. 26, 1967); was in a one-man show, *A Time to Laugh* (Carnegie Hall, N.Y.C., Apr. 11, 1970); played Hirsch in a revival of *The Great Waltz* (Drury Lane, London, England, July 9, 1970); was in *The Laugh Maker* (Eden, N.Y.C., Oct. 19, 1971); and directed and played Shumel Zanvel in *Here Comes the Groom* (Mayfair Th., Oct. 8, 1973).

Films. Mr. Fuchs was in *The Story of Ruth* (20th-Fox, 1961).

Television. He has appeared on the Ed Sullivan Show (CBS); December Bride (Oct. 1956); *The Damon Runyon Story* (Climax!, CBS, 1957); *The Gentleman from 7th Avenue* (Playhouse 90, CBS, 1959); Ann Sothern Show (1960); Danny Thomas Show

(CBS, 1960); and on Wagon Train (NBC, 1963).

Night Clubs. He performed at the Tic Toc (Montreal, Canada, 1943).

Awards. He received the Torch of Hope Award for his charitable work in behalf of the City of Hope (Los Angeles, Calif., 1962).

FUCHS, THEODORE. Consulting engineer, educator. b. Jan. 28, 1904, Brooklyn, N.Y., to Theodore and Clara (Heller) Fuchs. Father, manufacturer. Grad. Polytechnic Inst. of Bklyn., B.S. 1923; Northwestern Univ., M.A. 1937. Married Aug. 18, 1934, to Elinor Rice, educator. Member of ATA; ANTA; USITT; SMPTE; Illuminating Engineering Soc.; NTC: AAUP. Address: 1426 Chicago Ave., Evanston, IL 60201, tel. (312) 864-6233. Mr. Fuchs became professor emeritus of dramatic production at Northwestern Univ. in 1972. He had been assistant professor (1934–39), associate professor (1939–47), chairman of the theatre department and director of the theatre (1939–51), and professor (1947–72).

He has been a registered professional engineer in the State of Illinois since 1946; has been editor and consultant for the Drama League of America (1924–28); stage lighting specialist for General Electric Co. (1923–26); production manager for the Goodman Th., Chicago (1932–33); and since 1926, has conducted a private practice as a consulting engineer specializing in the design of auditoriums, stages, theatres, and associated facilities. As of 1974, he had been associated professionally with 265 theatre planning projects, most of them for educational institutions and community theatres.

Published Works. Mr. Fuchs wrote *Stage Lighting* (1929; rev. 1964) and *Lighting Equipment for the Small Stage* (1939). He has contributed articles to such magazines as *Theatre Arts, Drama* Magazine, *Players* Magazine, *Journal of the Illuminating Engineering Society,* and *Educational Theatre Journal.*

Awards. Mr. Fuchs received the Alpha Theta Phi Award (1960) for leadership in educational theatre, a special award (1967) of the New England Theatre Conference, and the ATA Award of Merit (1970).

FUGARD, ATHOL. Playwright, actor, director. b. June 11, 1932, Middleburg, Cape Province, South Africa. Educated Port Elizabeth Technical Coll.; Cape Town Univ., 1950–53. Married 1955 to Sheila Meiring; one daughter. Address: c/o William Morris Agency, 1350 Ave. of the Americas, New York, NY 10019.

Pre-Theatre. Seaman, journalist.

Theatre. Mr. Fugard began his career in theatre as a stage manager, and, since 1959, has been an actor, director and playwright. In 1965, he became director of The Serpent Players (Port Elizabeth, So. Africa); and, in 1972, was one of the founders of an experimental theatre, The Space (Cape Town, So. Africa).

He is the author of *No-Good Friday* (Cape Town, 1956); *Nongogo* (Cape Town, 1957); *The Blood Knot* (Johannesburg, 1960; London, 1961; and Cricket, N.Y.C., Mar. 2, 1964); *Hello and Goodbye* (Johannesburg, 1965; and Sheridan Square Playhouse, N.Y.C., Sept. 18, 1965); *People Are Living There* (Glasgow, Scotland, 1968; Cape Town, 1969; and Th. de Lys, N.Y.C., Nov. 11, 1968, and Forum, Nov. 18, 1971); *Boesman and Lena* (Cape Town, 1969; and Circle in the Square, N.Y.C., June 22, 1970); *Statements After an Arrest Under the Immorality Act* (Cape Town, 1972); and, with John Kani and Winston Ntshona, co-author of *Sizwe Banzi Is Dead* (Nov. 13, 1974), and *The Island* (Nov. 24, 1974), presented in repertory (Edison, N.Y.C.).

Mr. Fugard directed and acted in the South African productions of most of his plays, In addition, he directed *The Trials of Brother Jero* (Hampstead Th. Club, London, June 28, 1966); and the London productions of *The Blood Knot,* in which he also appeared (Hampstead Th. Club, June 30, 1966); and *Boesman and Lena* (London, 1971).

Television. He is the author of *Mille Miglia* (England, 1968); and acted in the televised version of *The Blood Knot* (England).

Awards. Mr. Fugard received the 1970 Village Voice Off-Bway (Obie) Award for distinguished foreign play for *Boesman and Lena.*.

FULFORD, DAVID. Director, actor, producer. b. Charles David Fulford, Aug. 31, 1925, Newport News, Va., to Charles and Carrie Chestine (Groom) Fulford. Father, minister. Grad. Barberton, Ohio H.S., 1943; attended Bucknell Univ., 1943–45; Yale Univ. Sch. of Drama, 1949–50; Carnegie Inst. of Tech., 1950–51. Served WW II, Korean War, US Navy; rank, Lt. (jg). Member of AEA; SSD&C. Address: 60 W. 45th St., New York, NY 10017, tel. (212) MU 2-1570.

Theatre. Mr. Fulford made his debut as Jack Spratt in an elementary school Christmas pageant (Dec. 1934); his professional debut as Amphitryon in a stock production of *Amphitryon 38* (Hilltop Th., Lutherville, Md., July 1947); in stock, performed and was a designer at Beacon, N.Y. (1947); appeared in the chorus of the N.Y.C. production of *Dear Judas* (Mansfield, Oct. 5, 1947); and performed in stock at Rochester, N.Y. (Summer 1948).

Mr. Fulford appeared in, and directed, stock productions at the Dorset (Vt.) Playhouse (Summer 1949–50, 1952); played in *Verily I Do* (Originals Only, May 1953); appeared with the Group 20 Players, Wellesley, Mass. (1953); performed and directed at the Palm Beach (Fla.) Playhouse (1953); directed and co-produced with William Dempsey *Fashion* (Royal Playhouse, Jan. 20, 1959); *The Moon in the Yellow River* (East End Th., Feb. 8, 1961); a stock production of *Fashion* (Fred Miller Th., Milwaukee, Wis., 1962); producer, with William Dempsey (until 1966), at the Canal Fulton (Ohio) Summer Arena (1954–to date). Fulford produced, with William Dempsey, and directed an Off-Bway presentation of *Colombe* (Garrick Th., Feb. 23, 1965). In April 1973, he opened the year-round, 500-seat dinner theatre The Carousel, Ravenna, Ohio.

Films. Mr. Fulford appeared in *Saadia* (Marrakesh, Morocco, 1953).

Awards. He received the Vernon Rice Award for *Fashion* (1959).

FULLER, DEAN. Composer, playwright. b. Walter Dean Fuller, Jr., Dec. 12, 1922, Woodbury, N.J., to Walter Dean and Sara (Kane) Fuller. Father, publisher. Attended Park Lodge Sch., Pav. Fr., 1931–33; grad. Episcopal Acad., Overbrook, Pa., 1941; Yale Univ., B.A. 1947. Studied music with Frederick Schlieder, Philadelphia, Pa. 1938–41; with Quincy Porter, New Haven, Conn. 1945–47. Married Jan. 3, 1955, to Beverly Bozeman, dancer, actress; one daughter. Served with Amer. Field Service, Ambulance Corps, British 8th Army and French 1st Army, 1943–45; rank, Lt.; awarded British Army's "Italy" Star (1944), and French Army's Croix de Guerre (1944). Member of Dramatists Guild; ASCAP; AGAC; Eastern L.I. Sound Station of the Midget Ocean Racing Club (MORC) (Rear Commodore, 1963; Fleet Capt., 1964).

Theatre. Mr. Fuller composed the score for *Hand in Hand* (Clinton Playhouse, Conn.; Olney Th., Md.; Cape May Playhouse, N.J., Summer 1948); subsequently was musical director for *On the Town* (Chatham, N.Y., Summer 1949); contributed songs to the revue *Dance Me a Song* (Royale, N.Y.C., Jan. 20, 1950); was musical director for the New England Summer Th. production of *Connecticut Yankee* (1951); composed, arranged, and played the incidental music for *The Grand Tour* (Martin Beck Th., N.Y.C., Dec. 10, 1951); was musical director of the touring company of *On Your Toes* (Summer 1952); and arranged the music for the national tour of *A Tree Grows in Brooklyn* (opened Klein Aud., Bridgeport, Conn., Oct. 10, 1952; closed Shubert, Chicago, Ill., Nov. 29, 1952).

He wrote the music for *Walk Tall* (Houston Playhouse, Tex., 1952); composed the dance arrangements for *Maggie* (National, N.Y.C., Feb. 18, 1953); was staff composer for musical productions at the Tamiment Playhouse (Pa., Summers 1954–57); wrote the music for *Once Over Lightly* (Barbizon Playhouse, N.Y.C., 1955); contributed music to *New Faces of '56* (Ethel Barrymore Th., June 14, 1956) and to *Ziegfeld Follies* (Winter Garden, Mar. 1, 1957); wrote, with Jay Thompson and Marshall Barer, the book for *Once Upon a Mattress* (Phoenix, May 11, 1959; moved Alvin, Nov. 25, 1959), which toured twice nationally (opened Erlanger, Sept. 1, 1960; closed Colonial, Mar. 18, 1961; opened Veteran' Memorial Aud., Providence, R.I., Oct. 21, 1960; closed National, Washington, D.C., May 27, 1961); and as musical director for the National Repertory Th., composed and arranged the score for *Ring Round the Moon* (1963–64); wrote music for National Repertory Th. revivals (at ANTA Th., N.Y.C.) of *The Imaginary Invalid* (May 1, 1967), *A Touch of the Poet* (May 2, 1967), and *Tonight at 8:30* (May 3, 1967); and he wrote the book, with Tony Hendra and Matt Dubey, and the music and lyrics, with Matt Dubey, for *Smith* (Eden Th., May 19, 1973), for which he also did the choral arrangements.

Television. *Once Upon a Mattress* was produced on television (CBS, June 3, 1964).

Night Clubs. Mr. Fuller has been arranger-accompaniest for Mary McCarty (Spivy's Roof; Village Vanguard, N.Y.C., 1948), and musical director and arranger for Tallulah Bankhead (Sands Hotel, Las Vegas, Nev., 1953).

Recreation. Sailing and sailboat racing.

FULLER, FRANCES. Executive, actress. b. Frances Leonore Fuller, Oct. 4, 1907, Charleston, S.C., to Wallace Watt and Leonore (Byrnes) Fuller. Father, electrical engineer; mother, federal government exec. Grad. Acad. of the Sacred Heart, Manhattanville, N.Y., 1925; attended AADA, N.Y.C., 1926–28. Married Mar. 30, 1929, to Worthington C. Miner, producer-director; one son, two daughters. Member of AEA; SAG; AFTRA; ALA; BMI; Author's League. Address: (home) 145 W. 58th St., New York, NY 10019; (bus.) AADA, 120 Madison Ave., New York, NY 10016, tel. (212) MU 6-9244.

Pre-Theatre. Part-time typist, doctor's assistant.

Theatre. Miss Fuller first appeared on the Stage as Lady Patricia Vere de Vere in a children's play, *Racketty-Packetty House* (Dec. 23, 1912); she appeared as Portia, at age 12, in a school production of *The Merchant of Venice* (Washington, D.C., 1919).

She made her Bway debut as Peggy Grant in *The Front Page* (Times Square Th., Aug. 14, 1928); subsequently appeared as Jane Geddis in *Cafe* (Ritz, Aug. 28, 1930); Jenny Townsend in *Five Star Final* (Cort, Dec. 30, 1930); Daisy Sage in *The Animal Kingdom* (Broadhurst, Jan. 12, 1932); Victoria Meredith in *I Love You Wednesday* (Harris, Oct. 11, 1932); Queena Farrar in *Her Master's Voice* (Plymouth, Oct. 23, 1933); Kaye Hamilton in *Stage Door* (Music Box, Oct. 22, 1936); Lollie in *Excursion* (Vanderbilt, Apr. 9, 1937); and Mrs. Green in *Home Is the Hero* (Booth, Sept. 22, 1954); was standby for Helen Hayes and Betty Field in *A Touch of the Poet* (Helen Hayes Th., Oct. 2, 1958); and appeared as Nanine in *Lady of the Camellias* (Winter Garden, Mar. 20, 1963).

Films. Miss Fuller appeared in *One Sunday Afternoon* (Par., 1933); *Elmer and Elsie* (Par., 1934); as Mrs. Stanford White in *The Girl in the Red Velvet Swing* (20th-Fox, 1955); appeared in *They Might Be Giants* (U, 1970); and *Homebodies* (Cinema, 1973).

Television. Her credits include Studio One (CBS); Play of the Week (NTA); US Steel Hour (CBS); Suspense Th. (CBS); Kraft Television Th. (NBC); Lamp Unto My Feet (CBS); Today (NBC); and she appeared as Aunt Carrie on the series Love of Life (CBS, 1966–69).

Other Activities. Miss Fuller has been affiliated with the Amer. Academy of Dramatic Art as president and director, 1954–65; director, 1964–74; co-chairman of the board, 1974–to date.

FULLER, JOHN G. Author, columnist, playwright, documentary film producer. b. John Grant Fuller, Jr., Nov. 30, 1913, Philadelphia, Pa., to John Grant and Alice (Carey) Jenkins Fuller. Father, dentist. Attended Friends Central Sch.,

Philadelphia, Pa.; grad. Franklin and Marshall Acad., Lancaster, Pa., 1932; Lafayette Coll., A.B. 1936. Studied drama with Paul Morrison. Married Nov. 1938 to Marion Hedrick (marr. dis. 1960); two sons; married Feb. 1962 to Nora Wheatley; one son (marr. dis. 1971). Member of WGA, East; Dramatists Guild; Authors League; Directors Guild of America, Inc.; Delta Kappa Epsilon. Address: (home) 72 River Rd., Weston, CT 06880, tel. (203) CA 7-6848; (bus.) c/o International Famous Agency, 1301 Avenue of the Americas, New York, NY 10019.

Pre-Theatre. Advertising, book publishing.

Theatre. Mr. Fuller wrote *The Pink Elephant* (Playhouse Th., Apr. 22, 1953) and *Love Me Little* (Helen Hayes Th., Apr. 15, 1958). He also has written industrial shows for such corporations as A.T.&T. and Chrysler Motors.

Films. He wrote, directed and produced for the US Information Agency such documentaries as *Labor of Love; The Making of a Champion; The Handyman; Miracle in the Desert; State Visit; Basketball: New Big Game in Africa,* and many others, including films on drug abuse and problem drinking for educational use. He has also made numerous industrial films for AT&T, *U.S. News and World Report,* Chrysler Corp., and the US Army Signal Corps.

Television. Mr. Fuller was writer-director for *Fire Rescue* (Dupont Show of the Week, NBC, Sept. 1963); several programs for Twentieth Century (CBS, 1957–58); several programs for 1-2-3-GO! (NBC, 1961–62); two shows for Conquest (CBS, 1957); and 13 films for Dateline: U.N. (Syndicated, 1958). He was staff writer for the Garry Moore Show (CBS, 1958–59) and I've Got a Secret (CBS, 1956–57); staff writer and film director for 300 programs for the Home Show (NBC, 1953–56); wrote 13 programs for Candid Camera (CBS, 1961); and was creator and editor of 130 programs of Road to Reality (ABC, 1959–60). He has also written for Armstrong Circle Th. (NBC, 1950–51) and Colgate Th. (NBC, 1950). In addition, Mr. Fuller produced two of the annual Emmy Award shows; the Great American Dream Machine (NET, 1971); and the documentary *Countdown to 2001* (ABC, 1973).

Other Activities. Mr. Fuller wrote the column "Trade Winds" in *Saturday Review* on alternate weeks (1957–67).

Published Works. He is the author of *The Gentleman Conspirators* (1962); *The Money Changers* (1962); *Incident at Exeter* (1966); *The Interrupted Journey* (1967); *Games for Insomniacs* (1967); *The Day of St. Anthony's Fire* (1968); *The Great Soul Trial* (1969); *200,000,000 Guinea Pigs* (1972); *Fever! The Hunt for a New Killer Virus* (1974); and *Arigo: Surgeon of the Rusty Knife* (1974).

Awards. Mr. Fuller was honored by the following organizations for his television series on group psychoanalysis in action, Road to Reality: The National Association for the Improvement of Mental Health (1960); The National Association of Women's Clubs (1960); and The National Association of Social Workers (1960). Mr. Fuller received an Emmy Award for *Great American Dream Machine.*

FUNKE, LEWIS. Drama editor, author. b. Lewis Bernard Funke, Jan. 25, 1912, Bronx, N.Y., to Joseph and Rose (Keimowitz) Funke. Father, construction worker. Grad. James Monroe H.S., Bronx, 1928; New York Univ., B.A. 1932. Married July 5, 1938, to Blanche Bier, teacher; one son, one daughter. Address: 61 Alta Dr., Mt. Vernon, NY 11152.

From 1944 until his retirement in 1973, Mr. Funke was drama editor of the NY *Times* (free-lance contributor to the sports dept., 1928–36; staff sports writer, 1936–44), and he was also assistant cultural news editor (1970–73). As drama editor, Mr. Funke contributed a weekly column of theatre news to the Sunday edition, entitled "News of the Rialto."

He was editor, with John E. Booth, of *Actors Talk About Acting* (1961); collaborated with Mr. Gordon on *Max Gordon Presents* (1963); wrote *A Gift of Joy* with Helen Hayes (1965), and *The Curtain Rises; The Story of Ossie Davis* (1971); and edited *Playwrights Talk About Playwriting* (1974). He has contributed articles to national magazines, including *Saturday Evening Post, Coronet, Pageant,* and *Reader's Digest.* He is currently (1974) arts columnist for *The Money Manager.*

Mr. Funke lectured and taught nonfiction writing and marketing at the City Coll. of New York (1950–52). He is an adjunct lecturer at Queens (N.Y.) Coll., Visiting Distinguished Professor at Florida State Univ., and public relations director, Eugene O'Neill Memorial Theater Center, Waterford, Conn.

Recreation. Gardening, golf.

G

GABEL, MARTIN. Producer, actor. b. Philadelphia, Pa., to I. H. and Rebecca Gabel. Father, jeweler. Attended Allentown Prep. Sch., Pa.; Lehigh Univ.; student at AADA, N.Y.C. Married May 14, 1946, to Arlene Francis, actress; one son. Served WW II, US Army. Member of AEA; AFTRA; SAG; League of NY Theatres.

Theatre. Mr. Gabel played Hunk in *Dead End* (Belasco, N.Y.C., Oct. 28, 1935); subsequently played Cassius in the Orson Welles' production of *Julius Caesar* (Mercury, Nov. 11, 1937), and *Danton's Death* (Mercury, Nov. 2, 1938); with Carly Wharton, he produced *Medicine Show* (Apr. 12, 1940), and *Cafe Crown* (Cort, Jan. 23, 1942); with Carly Wharton, in association with Alfred Bloomingdale, he produced and directed *The Assassin* (Natl., Oct. 17, 1945); with Peter Viertel, he produced and directed *The Survivors* (Jan. 1, 1948); played the Earl of Kent in Louis Calhern's *King Lear* (Natl., Dec. 25, 1950); Jonas Astorg in *The Reclining Figure,* which he also produced, with Henry M. Margolis, in association with Peter Cusick (Lyceum, Oct. 7, 1954); played Irving LaSalle in *Will Success Spoil Rock Hunter?* (Belasco, Oct. 13, 1955); for the NY City Ctr. Th. Co., by arrangement with Mr. Gabel, and Henry M. Margolis, produced Orson Welles' *King Lear* (NY City Ctr., Jan. 12, 1956); with Henry M. Margolis, he produced *The Hidden River* (Playhouse, Jan. 23, 1957); and played Stephen A. Douglas in *The Rivalry* (Bijou, Feb. 7, 1959).

He produced, with Henry M. Margolis, *Once More, With Feeling* (National, Oct. 21, 1958); played Basil Smythe in *Big Fish, Little Fish* (ANTA, Mar. 15, 1961); Melvin Peabody in *Children from Their Games* (Morosco, N.Y.C., Apr. 11, 1963); Professor Moriarity in *Baker Street* (Broadway Th., N.Y.C., Feb. 16, 1965); Henry in *The Lion in Winter* (tour, 1966); Joseph Mayflower in *Sheep on the Runway* (Helen Hayes Th., N.Y.C., Jan. 31, 1970); and Mark Walters in *Praise of Love* (Morosco, N.Y.C., Dec. 10, 1974).

Television and Radio. Mr. Gabel narrated Norman Corwin's radio play, *On a Note of Triumph* (CBS, 1945). On television, he appeared as Ulysses in *Tiger at the Gates* (Play of the Week, WNTA, 1961); narrated *Vincent Van Gogh, A Self Portrait* (NBC, 1962); narrated *The Making of the President* (1964); and, with his wife, Arlene Francis, made numerous appearances on *What's My Line?* (CBS).

Awards. He received the Antoinette Perry (Tony) Award and the *Variety* NY Drama Critics Poll for his performance as Basil Smythe in *Big Fish, Little Fish* (1961).

GABLE, JUNE. Actress. b. June 5, 1945, New York City. Grad. Carnegie-Mellon Inst. Tech. Drama Sch. Member of AEA; SAG; AFTRA.

Theatre. Miss Gable was a replacement in *MacBird!* (opened Village Gate, N.Y.C., Feb. 22, 1967); replaced (May 7, 1968) Alice Whitfield in the revue *Jacques Brel is Alive and Well and Living in Paris* (Village Gate, Jan. 22, 1968), and appeared in the premieres of the show in London (Duchess Th., July 9, 1968) and Los Angeles (June 10, 1969); appeared in the Chorus of Women in *Mod Donna* (NY Shakespeare Fest., Public Th., May 3, 1970); played Gloria in *In Three Zones* (Charles Playhouse, Boston, Oct. 1970), Penny in *A Day in the Life of Just About Everyone* (Bijou, N.Y.C., Mar. 9, 1971); Alicia in *Lady Audley's Secret* (Goodman Mem. Th., Chicago, May 24, 1971); Shorty in *Wanted* (Cherry Lane Th., N.Y.C., Jan. 19, 1972); played Alicia again in *Lady Audley's Secret* (Washington, D.C., Th. Club, May 25, 1972; and in N.Y.C., Eastside Playhouse, Oct. 3, 1972); succeeded (Oct. 24, 1972) June Helmers as Lucy Lockit in *The Beggar's Opera* (revived Chelsea Th. Ctr. Brooklyn, N.Y., Acad., Mar. 21, 1972; moved McAlpin Roof Th., May 30, 1972); was standby for Virginia Vestoff in the revue *Nash at Nine* (Helen Hayes Th., May 17, 1973); played Lois Lane in *Kiss Me Kate* (Playhouse in the Park, Cincinnati, O., June 21, 1973); the Old Lady in the revised version of *Candide* (Chelsea Th., Brooklyn Acad., Dec. 11, 1973; Bway Th., Mar. 5, 1974); Adriana in *The Comedy of Errors* (NY Shakespeare Fest., Delacorte Th., Summer 1975); and succeeded (OCt. 27, 1975) Rita Moreno as Googie Gomez in *The Ritz* (Longacre, Jan. 20, 1975).

Television. Miss Gable has appeared on *It's All in Your Head;* and Camera Three (CBS).

Awards. Miss Gable was nominated (1974) for an Antoinette Perry (Tony) Award as best supporting actress in a musical for her performance in *Candide.*

GAFFNEY, FLOYD. Educator, director, choreographer, dancer. b. June 11, 1930, Cleveland, Ohio, to George E. and Bertha Gaffney. Grad. Adelphi Univ., Garden City, N.Y., B.A. 1959 and M.A. 1962; Carnegie-Mellon Univ., Pittsburgh, Pa., Ph.D. 1966. Professional training with Murray Lewis (1949), Katherine Dunham's School of Afro-Cuban Dance (1949–50), Alwin Nikolais (1950–51), Doris Humphrey (1950), Hanya Holm (choreography, 1951), Harry Bernstein, Bunty Kelly (Adelphi, 1956–59). Married Aug. 1959 to Yvonne Gaffney; two sons; two daughters. Served in US Navy, Special Service (1951–56). Member of AAUP; ATA (bd. mbr., 1973–74; chmn., Black Theatre Program, 1973–74); ASTR; Dance Teachers of America; Phi Lambda Rho. Address: (home) 12889 Indian Trail Rd., Poway, CA 92064, tel. (714) 478-5586; (bus.) Drama Dept., Univ. of California at San Diego, La Jolla, CA 92037, tel. (714) 453-2000, ext. 2809.

Dr. Gaffney was appointed associate professor of drama, instructor of dance, and chairman of the Black Cultural Arts Sequence, Univ. of California, San Diego (UCSD) in 1971. Previously, he had been a teaching assistant in dance, Adelphi Univ. (1959–61); instructor of dance and stage movement, Jerome School of Dancing, Williston Park, N.Y. (1960–62); instructor of dance at Adelphi and teacher of dance and drama, Waltann School of Creative Arts, Brooklyn, N.Y. (1961); graduate assistant in speech at Clark College, Atlanta, Ga. (1962–63); guest artist, American Conservatory Th., Pittsburgh, Pa. (1965); and guest dance instructor, Univ. of Pittsburgh (Summer 1966). From 1966 to 1969, he was assistant professor of theatre, Ohio Univ., Athens, Ohio, where he assisted in designing the Black Studies Institute, and from 1969 to 1971 he was associate professor of drama, Univ. of California at Santa Barbara (UCSB) and co-chairman, Black Studies Dept. In addition, Dr. Gaffney served as director of fine arts, Project Upward Bound, Florida A&M Univ., Tallahassee, Fla. (Summer 1968) and guest instructor, US International Univ., San Diego, Cal. (Spring 1973).

Theatre. Dr. Gaffney made his stage debut as Morgan Evans in *The Corn Is Green* (Gilpin Players, Karamu House, Cleveland, Ohio, Feb. 1949). He made his professional debut playing various roles in *In White America* (American Conservatory Th., Pittsburgh, Pa., Oct. 1965). Since then he has directed, at Ohio Univ., *Black Showcase* (1966); *The World of Carl Sandburg* (1967); choreographed *Irma La Douce* (1968); directed *The Hand Is on the Gate* (1969); and choreographed *The Would-Be Gentleman* (1970). At UCSB, he directed *Black Showcase*

'70 (1970); choreographed *Afro-Cuban Ritual* (1970); and directed *Ceremonies in Dark Old Men* (1971); and at UCSD he directed *Blood Knot* (1971); and *Clara's Ole Man* and *Day of Absence* (both 1972). He also directed *The Me Nobody Knows* (Southeast Performing Arts Consortium, 1972); *Christopher Sly* (Univ. Extension, Opera Workshop, 1972); another production of *Ceremonies in Dark Old Men* (Old Globe Th., San Diego, Fall 1973); played M. Loyal in *Tartuffe* (UCSD, 1974); and directed *No Place To Be Somebody* (UCSD, 1974).

Films. Dr. Gaffney was in an educational dance film, *White Madonna* (May 1955), with Ruth St. Denis.

Television. Dr. Gaffney appeared on the Harry Belafonte Special as a dancer (NBC, Apr. 1962).

Other Activities. Dr. Gaffney appeared as a dancer in *The Black Widow* (Civic Opera Association, Cleveland, Ohio, Spring 1948); choreographed and staged his modern dance debut (Severance Hall, Cleveland, May 1949); and was a member of the Pearl Primus African Dance Company, N.Y.C. (1950–51). He appeared as a dancer in a production of *Carmen Jones* (Fall 1951) and with the Walter Nick Dance Company (Kaufmann Auditorium, YMHA, N.Y.C., Apr. 1962).

Published Works. Dr. Gaffney wrote the chapter on Imamu Amiri Baraka (LeRoi Jones) in *Nine Black Writers on Communication* (1973), and his articles and book reviews have appeared in such publications as *Negro Digest; Educational Theatre Journal; Players* Magazine; *Secondary School Theatre; The Drama Review;* and *Black World.*

Awards. Dr. Gaffney was awarded several fellowships, assistanceships, and grants when a student. He has received faculty senate grants from UCSB (1970) and UCSD (1971–73) and a Ford Foundation grant (1970). He was a US Information Service cultural exchange professor to Brazil (Summer 1972); on the National Humanities faculty (1974–75); and he held a Univ. of California Creative Arts Institute grant (1974).

Recreation. Swimming, fishing, boating, restoring and refinishing antique furniture, amateur horticulture.

GAHAGAN, HELEN. Actress, singer, congresswoman. b. Helen Mary Gahagan, Nov. 25, 1900, Boonton, N.J., to Walter Hamer and Lillian Rose (Mussen) Gahagan. Father, contractor. Attended Berkeley Sch. for Girls, Brooklyn, N.Y.; Capen Sch. for Girls, Northampton, Mass.; Barnard Coll., NYC. Married Apr. 5, 1931, to Melvyn Douglas, actor; one son, one daughter. Member of AEA; SAG; Natl. Council of Negro Women (life member); Amer.-Christian Palestine Committee (natl. officer).

Theatre. Miss Gahagan first performed in *Shoot!* (Macdowall Gallery, N.Y.C., June 14, 1922); made her Bway acting debut as Sybil Herrington in *Manhattan* (Playhouse, Aug. 15, 1922); subsequently played Anne Baldwin in *Dreams for Sale* (Playhouse, Sept. 13, 1922); Paula in *Fashions for Men* (National, Dec. 5, 1922); Jean Trowbridge in *Chains* (Playhouse, Sept. 19, 1923); the title role in *Leah Kleschna* (Lyric, Apr. 21, 1924); Jeanne in *Beyond* (Provincetown Playhouse, Jan. 26, 1925); Krista in *The Sapphire Ring* (Selwyn, Apr. 15, 1925); Lady Caroline Dexter in *The Enchanted April* (Morosco, Aug. 24, 1925); Laura Simmons in *Young Woodley* (Belmont, Nov. 2, 1925); Rose in *Trelawney of the Wells* (New Amsterdam, Jan. 31, 1927); and Comtesse Zicka in *Diplomacy* (Erlanger, May 28, 1928); toured Europe as an opera singer (1928–30), appearing in *La Tosca* (Prague, Czechoslovakia, 1929).

She made her Bway singing debut as the Prima Donna in *Tonight or Never* (Belasco, Nov. 18, 1930), and also toured in it; played Shirley in *The Cat and the Fiddle* (Los Angeles Civic Light Opera, Calif., 1932); Emily Brontë in *Moor Born* (Playhouse, N.Y.C., Apr. 3, 1934); toured as Mary Stuart in *Mary, Queen of Scotland* (1934); appeared as Hannah Hawkins in *Mother Lode* (Cort, N.Y.C., Dec. 22, 1934); Cynthia Hope in *And Stars Remain* (Guild, Oct. 12, 1936); sang on concert tours (1937); and at the Salzburg (Austria) Festival (1937).

Miss Gahagan played Lucy Chase Wayne in *First lady* (NY City Ctr., May 28, 1952); appeared in *One Plus One* (Brooklyn Acad. of Music, Oct. 6, 1955); and performed in concerts and poetry readings (1952–62).

Films. She appeared in the title role of *She* (RKO, 1935).

Television. Miss Gahagan was a reader on the *An Essay on Death* special (NET, Nov. 20, 1964).

Other Activities. She was elected to the US House of Representatives (Dem., Calif., 1944, 1946, 1948); appointed US alternate delegate to General Assembly of the United Nations by President Harry S Truman (1946); appointed by President Lyndon B. Johnson as his Personal Representative, with the rank of Special Ambassador, to head the US Delegation at the Inaugural Ceremonies of President William V.S. Tubman of Liberia (Jan. 1964); is a member of the Jane Addams Peace Assn., Inc., was a member of the delegation to the Soviet-American Women's Conference (Moscow, USSR, April 1964).

Published Works. She wrote *Eleanor Roosevelt We Remember* (1963).

Awards. Miss Gahagan was honored by *Ms.* magazine with a luncheon (Oct. 3, 1973).

GAIGE, TRUMAN. Actor. b. Stanley Ruhland, New York City, to Sidney and Pauline (Loewenstein) Ruhland. Father, musician; mother, educator. Member of AEA; SAG. Address: 230 Central Park So., New York, NY 10019, tel. (212) CI 5-7274.

Theatre. Mr. Gaige, billed as Stanley Ruhland, made his N.Y.C. debut as Gerald Saunders in *Appearances* (Hudson Th., Apr. 1, 1928); then, billed as Truman Gaige, played the Third Flunkey in *A Wonderful Night* (Majestic, Oct. 31, 1929); Mr. Proutie in *Bitter Sweet* (44 St. Th., May 7, 1934); a Footman in *Music Hath Charms* (Majestic, Dec. 29, 1934); a Conductor in *Three Waltzes* (Majestic, Dec. 25, 1937); and succeeded (Nov. 13, 1944) Sig Arno as Count Peppi Le Loup in *Song of Norway,* later taking over Philip White's role as Father Nordraak and Walter Kingsford's role as Father Grieg in this production (Imperial, Aug. 21, 1944).

For the Los Angeles (Calif.) Civic Light Opera Assn., he appeared in *Louisiana Purchase* (1947) and *Carousel* (1953); played Jawan in *Kismet* (Ziegfeld, N.Y.C., Dec. 3, 1953); Germain in *Time Remembered* (Morosco, Nov. 12, 1957); Rodolpho in the pre-Bway tryout of *At the Grand* (opened Philharmonic Aud., Los Angeles, July 7, 1958; closed Curran, San Francisco, Calif., Sept. 13, 1958); M. Begué in *Saratoga* (Winter Garden, N.Y.C., Dec. 7, 1959); Kogan in *The Wall* (Billy Rose Th., Oct. 11, 1960); toured as Alper in the national company of *The Tenth Man* (opened Natl., Washington, D.C., Sept. 25, 1961; closed Blackston, Chicago, Ill., May 26, 1962); and the Doctor in the pre-Bway tryout of *Zenda* (opened Curran, San Francisco, Aug. 16, 1963; closed Pasadena Civic Aud., Calif., Nov. 16, 1963).

He played Jawan again in a revival of *Kismet* (NY State Th., Lincoln Ctr., N.Y.C., June 22, 1965) and toured in the production; was Duclos and the Concierge in *Dumas and Son* (Los Angeles Civic Light Opera, Summer 1967); Cardinal Berstein in *Hadrian VII* (Helen Hayes Th., N.Y.C., Jan. 8, 1969); played Stephen Hopkins in the national co. of *1776* (opened San Francisco, Cal., Apr. 23, 1970) and in the N.Y.C. production during final six months of run (closed Majestic, Feb. 13, 1972); and played Manuel in the Los Angeles & San Francisco Civic Light Opera production *Gigi* (opened San Francisco, Cal., 1973; Uris Th., N.Y.C., Nov. 13, 1973).

Recreation. Bridge.

GALLAGHER, HELEN. Actress, singer, dancer, vocal coach. b. 1926, Brooklyn, N.Y. Studied at Amer. Ballet Sch. Married Oct. 14, 1956, to Frank Wise. Member of AEA; AFTRA; AGVA.

Theatre. Miss Gallagher made her N.Y.C. debut taking over Billie Worth's role in the revue *The Seven Lively Arts* (Ziegfeld Th., Dec. 7, 1947); subsequently appeared in the chorus of *Mr. Strauss Goes to Boston* (Century, Sept. 6, 1945); as a Flapper in *Billion Dollar Baby* (Alvin, Dec. 21, 1945); in the chorus of *Brigadoon* (Ziegfeld, Mar. 13, 1947); as Nancy, the maid in *High Button Shoes* (Century, Oct. 9, 1947); and in the revue, *Touch and Go* (Broadhurst, N.Y.C., Oct. 13, 1949; Prince of Wales', London, May 19, 1950).

She played Poupette in *Make a Wish* (Winter Garden, N.Y.C., Apr. 18, 1951); Gladys Bumps in *Pal Joey* (Broadhurst, Jan. 2, 1952); the title role in *Hazel Flagg* (Mark Hellinger Th., Feb. 11, 1953); Annie Oakley in *Annie Get Your Gun* (Oakdale Musical Th., Wallingford, Conn., July 3, 1954), Miss Adelaide in *Guys and Dolls* (NY City Ctr., Apr. 20, 1955); Sharon McLonergan in *Finian's Rainbow* (NY City Ctr., May 18, 1955); succeeded (June 6, 1955) Carol Haney as Gladys in *The Pajama Game* (St. James, May 13, 1954); toured as Cherie in *Bus Stop* (July 15, 1956); played Meg Brockie in *Brigadoon* (NY City Ctr., Mar. 27, 1957); Kitty O'Hara in *Portofino* (Adelphi, Feb. 21, 1958); Ado Annie in *Oklahoma!* (NY City Ctr., Mar. 19, 1958; St Louis Municipal Opera, Mo., Summer 1958); and also at the St. Louis Municipal Opera, played Miss Adelaide in *Guys and Dolls* (Summer 1958). She played Small Servant in *Pound in Your Pocket* (Palm Beach Playhouse, Fla., Mar. 1959).

Miss Gallagher played Gladys in *The Pajama Game* (St. Paul Civic Opera, Minn., Jan. 1964); Lola in *Damn Yankees* (Municipal Opera, St. Louis, July 27, 1964); Nellie Forbush in *South Pacific* (summer tour, 1965); played Nickie and was standby for Gwen Verdon (as Charity) in *Sweet Charity* (Palace, N.Y.C., Jan. 29, 1966), playing the role (July 11, 1966) during Miss Verdon's vacation and succeeding her (June 1967) during the N.Y.C. run; played Nickie in the tour of *Sweet Charity* (opened Shubert, Boston, Sept. 11, 1967; closed O'Keefe, Toronto, Canada, Jan. 20, 1968); succeeded (May 1968) Jane Connell as Gooch in *Mame* (Winter Garden, N.Y.C., May 24, 1966); played Bessie Legg in *Cry For Us All* (Broadhurst, Apr. 8, 1970); Lucille Early in *No, No, Nanette* (46 St. Th., Jan. 19, 1971); appeared in the revue, *The Gershwin Years* (Summer tour, 1973); and played Roz Duncan in *Hothouse* (Chelsea Th., Brooklyn Academy of Music, Oct. 23, 1974).

Films. Miss Gallagher appeared in *Strangers When We Meet* (Col., 1960).

Television. She has appeared in *Shangri-La* (Hallmark Hall of Fame, NBC, Oct. 24, 1960); on the Colgate Comedy Hour (NBC); the Ed Sullivan Show (CBS); the Kraft Television Th. (NBC); the Today Show (NBC); and other programs. She played the continuing role of Maeve Ryan in the serial Ryan's Hope (ABC, premiere Summer 1975).

Night Clubs. Miss Gallagher has performed at the Thunderbird (Las Vegas, Nev., 1951); Mocambo (Hollywood, Calif., 1951); Plaza Hotel (N.Y.C., May 27, 1954); in the revue *Too Good for the Average Man* (Camelot, N.Y.C., 1960); at Reno Sweeney (N.Y.C., 1974); and Brothers and Sisters (N.Y.C., 1974).

Awards. Miss Gallagher received the Antoinette Perry (Tony) Award for *Pal Joey* (1952), as best supporting actress in a musical, and for *No, No, Nanette* (1971), as best actress in a musical.

GALLAWAY, MARIAN. Educator, writer, director. b. Marian Hesse, Mar. 1, 1903, Savannah, Ga., to Herman W. and Mattie (Wilfert) Hesse. Father, physician. Grad. Savannah H.S., 1921; attended Goucher Coll., 1921–24; grad. Univ. of Michigan, A.B. 1925, M.A. 1929; State Univ. of Iowa, Ph.D. 1941. Married 1924 to William Francis Gallaway (marr. dis. 1935; dec. Dec. 1944). Member of Authors' Guild; AETA; Southeastern Th. Conference (vice-pres., 1966; pres., 1967; and past chmn. of New Play Project); Alabama Th. Conference. Address: (home) 29 Woodridge, Tuscaloosa, AL 35401, tel. (205) 752-2486; (bus.) c/o Univ. of Alabama, Tuscaloosa, AL 35401, tel. (205) 752-7441.

Miss Gallaway is professor emeritus of speech and has been director of the Univ. Theatre at the Univ. of Alabama since 1948. Previously, she was director of the Cedar Rapids (Iowa) Community Plays (1935); assistant professor at Arizona State College (1942–44), assistant professor at Eastern Illinois State Coll. (1944–46), assistant professor at the State University of Iowa (1946–48), and associate director of the Black Hills (S.D.) Playhouse (Summer 1948).

Published Works. She is the author of *Constructing a Play* (1950) and *Director in the Theatre* (1962).

She has also written *An Explanatory Study of the Effect of the Medium on the Manuscripts of Plays (Southern Speech Journal,* Vol. XXIV, No. 2, Winter 1958). This article was the result of a research grant given to Miss Gallaway to study the evolution of plays in N.Y.C. rehearsals.

She has two works in progress: *Acting: A Test for the Performer* and *Man and the Theatre.*

Awards. She received the Distinguished Career Award and the Suzanne David Award for contributions to the Southeastern Th. Conference; and the Amoco Award for Service to Nat. Coll. Th. Festival.

Recreation. Reading, theatregoing, people, travel.

GAM, RITA. Actress. b. Rita Eleanore Mackay, Apr. 2, 1928, Pittsburgh, Pa., to Milton and Belle Mackay. Step-father, Ben Gam, manufacturer. Grad. Fieldston H.S., Riverdale, N.Y., 1945; attended Columbia Univ., 1945–46. Studied Actors Studio (member, 1960–to date). Married Dec. 1948 to Sidney Lumet, director (marr. dis. 1956); married Mar. 23, 1956, to Thomas Guinzburg (marr. dis. 1964). Relative in theatre; brother, Alex Gam, director. Member of AEA; SAG; AFTRA.

Theatre. Miss Gam first appeared on the N.Y.C. stage in Equity Library productions of *A New Way to Pay Old Debts* (Nov. 1945) and *The Hasty Heart* (Apr. 1946). She succeeded Allan Frank as David the King in *A Flag is Born* (Alvin, Sept. 5, 1946); was in Equity Library's *Abe Lincoln in Illinois* (Dec. 1946); played Bunny in *A Temporary Island* (Maxine Elliott's Th., Mar. 21, 1948); appeared in Equity Library's *Men in White* (May 1948); and played Clythia in *The Insect Comedy* (NY City Ctr., June 3, 1948). Miss Gam also appeared at the Straight Wharf Th., Nantucket, Mass., as Jo in *Little Women,* Dorcas Burnell in *Salem Trade,* in *Mooney's Kid Don't Cry,* and *The Long Goodbye.*

She played Gloria and was understudy to Doe Avedon as Drucilla Eldridge in *The Young and the Fair* (Morosco, Nov. 22, 1948); understudied Julie Harris as Felisa in *Montserrat* (46th St. Th., Oct. 29, 1949); and played Bellisa in *Don Perlinplinet and Bellisa,* and Carla in *The Sky Is Red* (Actor's Workshop, 1951).

In stock, she played Kate in *The Taming of the Shrew* (Straight Wharf Th., Nantucket, Mass., Summer 1951); the title role in *Laura* (Hunterdon Hills Playhouse, Hunterdon Hills, N.J., Summer 1951); Polly in *Court Olympus* (Westport County Playhouse, Conn., Summer 1956); and Bille Dawn in *Born Yesterday* (North Jersey Playhouse, Fort Lee, N.J., Summer 1960).

Miss Gam toured with the New York Repertory Th. in South America and Mexico, as Sally Bowles in *I Am a Camera* and Katherine in *Suddenly Last Summer* (1962). With the Minnesota Theatre Co. (Tyrone Guthrie Th., Minneapolis) she played Elise in *The Miser* (May 8, 1963) and Masha in *The Three Sisters* (June 18, 1963). She was in stock productions of *Bell, Book, and Candle* (Atlanta, Ga., and Moorstown, N.J., 1964); and *Will Success Spoil Rock Hunter?* (Paramus, N.J., 1964); was Cleopatra in *Antony and Cleopatra* (Front Street Th., Memphis, Tenn., Apr. 4, 1966); Clare in *There's a Girl in My Soup* (Music Box, N.Y.C., Oct. 18, 1967); Marguerite Gautier in *Camino Real* (Seattle Repertory Th., Seattle, Wash., Nov. 22, 1972); and Miss Hatch in a revival of *Detective Story* (pre-Bway: Paramus Playhouse, N.J., Feb. 18, 1973–Shubert Th., Philadelphia, Pa., Mar. 24, 1973).

Films. Miss Gam made her debut in a film without dialogue, entitled *The Thief* (UA, 1952); subsequently appeared in *Saadia* (MGM, 1953); *Night People* (Fox, 1954); *Magic Fire* (Rep. 1956); *Mohawk* (20th-Fox, 1956); *Attila* (1958); *Sierra Baron* (20th-Fox, 1958); *Costa Azura* (Mevolli, 1958); *King of Kings* (MGM, 1961); *Hannibal* (WB, 1961); *No Exit* (Zen, 1962); *Klute* (WB, 1971); and *Such Good Friends* (Par., 1971).

Television. Miss Gam was in *Appearance and Reality* (Somerset Maugham Th., NBC, 1951); appeared on Danger (CBS, June 26, 1951); Suspense (CBS); Lux Television Th. (CBS); *Dark of the Moon* (Cameo Th., NBC, Jan. 1952); *The Bridge of San Luis Rey* (Dupont Show of the Month, CBS, Jan. 21, 1958); played Yelna in *Uncle Vanya* (CBC, 1964); appeared on the Jackie Gleason Show (CBS); A Family Affair (NBC, 1966); McMillan and Wife (CBS); and Mannix (NBC).

Other Activities. While appearing at the Tyrone Guthrie Th., Minneapolis, Minn., Miss Gam lectured at the college in Minneapolis.

Published Works. Miss Gam wrote *The Beautiful Woman* (1969).

Awards. For her performance as Estelle in *No Exit,* Miss Gam received the Silver Bear (Berlin Film Festival, 1963).

Recreation. Photography, skiing, tennis, cooking, yoga, caring for children in hospitals, ice skating.

GARD, ROBERT E. Educator, writer, director. b. Robert Edward Gard, July 3, 1910, Iola, Kan., to Samuel Arnold and Louisa Maria Gard. Father, attorney. Grad. Iola H.S., 1928; Univ. of Kansas, B.A., 1934; Cornell Univ., M.A. 1938. Married June 7, 1939, to Maryo Kimball; two daughters. Member of AETA; NTC (trustee, 1959–62); Appraisal of the American Theatre Comm. (chmn., 1962–64); Pi Kappa Alpha; Wisconsin Arts Council (pres.). Address: (home) 3507 Sunset Dr., Madison, WI 53703, tel. (608) CE 3-0267; (bus.) Univ. of Wisconsin, Madison, WI 53703, tel. (608) 262-1361.

Since 1967 Mr. Gard has been regional writer-in-residence, Univ. of Wisconsin, and director (1945–to date) of the Wisconsin Idea Theatre at the university, where he has taught since 1945 (assistant professor 1945–48; associate professor 1948–55; professor 1955–to date). He directed the NY State playwriting project (1938–43), and the Alberta Folklore and Local History project (1943–45); and taught at the Banff Sch. of Fine Arts (1943–45). Mr. Gard was a Rockefeller Foundation Fellow (1938–43); and a Fulbright Research scholar at the Univ. of Helsinki (1959–60).

In 1961, he was a US State Dept. specialist in drama, and served as a US delegate to the World Theatre Conference in Vienna.

Published Works. Mr. Gard wrote *Wisconsin Is My Doorstep* (1948); *Grassroots Theatre: a search for regional arts in America* (1955); with Gertrude Burley, wrote *Community Theatre* (1959); wrote *Playwright in Finnish Theatre* (1960); with L. D. Sorden, edited *Wisconsin Lore* (1962); and, with Marston Balch, wrote *Theatre in America* (1968). His other books include *Wiconsin Lore; This Is Wisconsin; University, Madison U.S.A.; Wisconsin Sketches; A Woman of Little Importance;* and the *Wild Goose Marsh.* He wrote for children, *Johnny Chinook* (1945); edited James W. Schultz's *My Life as an Indian* (1957); *Midnight: Rodeo Champion* (1951); *Scotty's Mare* (1957); *Run to Kansas* (1958); *The Big One* (1959); and *Devil Red* (1963).

He was a field editor for Duell, Sloan and Pearce, publishers in N.Y.C. during 1958–60.

Awards. Mr. Gard was awarded a citation from the Univ. of Kansas Alumni, Dept. of Speech, 1958; a medal from the Univ. of Helsinki, 1963; and a gold medal from the Finnish National Th., 1961, for work with Finnish playwrights and for organizing a new drama dept. at the Univ. of Helsinki. He was also awarded the Wisconsin Local History Award; a citation from the Wisconsin Academy of Sciences, Arts, and Letters; and has held many foundation grants, including the first major grant made by the National Endowment for the Arts in behalf of the arts in smaller communities.

GARDE, BETTY. Actress. b. Katharine Elizabeth Garde, Sept. 19, 1905, Philadelphia, Pa., to Charles Pierie and Katharine (Cropper) Garde. Father, newspaper editor. Attended West Philadelphia (Pa.) H.S., 1918–22. Married Sept. 20, 1943, to Frank Lennon, stage electrician, sound engineer. Member of AEA; AFTRA; SAG. Address: 1555 East 19th St., Brooklyn, NY tel. (212) 998-1737.

Theatre. Miss Garde made her professional debut in stock productions with the Mae Desmond Players (Philadelphia, Pa., Summer 1922); and appeared as Harriet Underwood in the touring production of *The Nervous Wreck* (1924).

She made her N.Y.C. debut as Alma Borden in *Easy Come, Easy Go* (George M. Cohan Th., Oct. 26, 1925); subsequently appeared as Julia Winters in a touring production of *The Poor Nut* (1926); and appeared with the (William H.) Wright Players (Flint, Mich.; Jackson, Mich.; 1927–30).

She played Gloria Hall in *The Social Register* (Fulton, N.Y.C., Nov. 9, 1931); Millie in *The Best People* (Waldorf, Mar. 15, 1933); Emma Wallace in *The Primrose Path* (Biltmore, Jan. 4, 1939); Madame Muscat in *Liliom* (Westport, Conn., Summer 1941); and Aunt Eller in *Oklahoma!* (St. James, N.Y.C., Mar. 31, 1943). She toured in USO productions overseas, playing, among other roles, Gertrude Lennox in *Meet the Wife* (July 1945–Feb. 1946); played Sarah Rock in the pre-Bway tryout of *A Little Evil* (opened Playhouse Th., Wilmington, Del., Feb. 8, 1952; closed Plymouth Th., Boston, Mass., Feb. 16, 1952); Frosine in *The Miser* (Downtown Natl. Th., Mar. 24, 1955); in *Three Rings For Michelle* (Avenue Th., Toronto, Canada, Nov. 15, 1956); appeared as Aunt Eller in *Oklahoma!* (NY City Ctr., Mar. 19, 1958; Feb. 27, 1963); Mrs. Gordon in *Agatha Sue I love you* (Henry Miller's Th., Dec. 14, 1966); and Dante in *Stephen D* (E. 74 St. Th., Sept. 24, 1967).

Films. Miss Garde has appeared in *The Lady Lies* (Par., 1929); *Queen High* (Par., 1930); *Secrets of a Secretary* (Par., 1931); *Girl Habit* (Par., 1931); *Damaged Love* (Sono Art-World Wide, 1931); *Call Northside 777* (20th-Fox, 1948); *Caged* (WB, 1950); *The Prince Who Was a Thief* (U, 1951); *One Desire* (U, 1955); and *The Wonderful World of the Brothers Grimm* (MGM, 1962).

Television and Radio. Miss Garde has performed on radio on the Lux Radio Th. (CBS, 1933–57); Phillip Morris Playhouse (CBS); Cavalcade of America (NBC); Orson Welles' Mercury Th. (CBS); Columbia Workshop (CBS); Great Plays (NBC); the Kate Smith Hour (CBS); Theatre Five (ABC); and played Belle Jones on the serial Lorenzo Jones (NBC-Red); Mother Connie on My Son and I (CBS); and for four years, the title role in Mrs. Wiggs of the Cabbage Patch (NBC-Red).

On television, she has appeared on US Steel Hour (CBS); Suspense (CBS); Dupont Show of the Month (CBS); Look Up and Live (CBS); The Twilight Zone (CBS); The Outlaws (NBC); Route 66 (CBS); Adventures in Paradise (ABC); Checkmate (NBC); The Untouchables (ABC); The Real Mccoys (CBS); One Step Beyond (Ind.); and Ben Casey (ABC).

Recreation. Cooking, dachshunds, bridge, swimming.

GARDENIA, VINCENT. Actor. b. Vincenzio Scognamiglio, Jan. 7, 1923, Naples, Italy, to Gennaro and Elisa (Ausiello) Scognamiglio. Father, actor. Studied acting with Harold Clurman, 1954. Served US Army, 1942–44; rank, Pvt. Member AEA; AFTRA; SAG.

Theatre. Mr. Gardenia made his first stage appearance at age five as the Shoeshine Boy in an Italian production of *Shoe Shine* (Fifth Ave. Th., N.Y.C., 1928); made his first professional appearances at the Hampton (N.H.) Playhouse, as Stanley in *A Streetcar Named Desire,* Joseph in *My Three Angels,* and Stosh in *Stalag 17* (Summer 1954); subsequently played Johnson in *Mister Roberts;* (Sea Cliff Playhouse, N.Y., Summer 1955); and *Burlesque* (Clinton Th., N.J., Summer 1955); appeared as Hugo in *In April Once* (Bway Congregational Church, N.Y.C., Mar. 13, 1955); Piggy in *The Man with the Golden Arm* (Cherry Lane, May 21, 1956); Corvino in *Vol-*

pone (Rooftop, Jan. 7, 1957); in stock, General St. Pé in *The Waltz of the Toreadors* (Webster, Mass., 1957); and Fyodor in *The Brothers Karamazov* (Gate, N.Y.C., Dec. 6, 1957).

Mr. Gardenia played the First Blind Man in *The Visit* (Lunt-Fontanne Th., May 5, 1958); Jim Nightingale in *The Cold Wind and the Warm* (Morosco, Dec. 18, 1958); and succeeded Jack Bittner (Apr. 7, 1959) as the Deputy in *Rashomon* (Music Box Th., Jan. 27, 1959). He appeared as Mitrich in *The Power of Darkness* (York Playhouse, Sept. 29, 1959); the Chairman in *Only in America* (Cort, Nov. 19, 1959); George H. Jones in *Machinal* (Gate, Apr. 7, 1960); Pavel Menkes in *The Wall* (Billy Rose Th., Oct. 11, 1960); and the Warden in *Gallows Humor* (Gramercy Arts, Apr. 18, 1961). He played Panisse in a stock production of *Fanny* (Lambertville Music Circus, N.J., July 10, 1961); Sergeant Manzoni in *Daughter of Silence* (Music Box Th., N.Y.C., Nov. 30, 1961); the Warden in Parts 1 and 2 of *Gallows Humor,* which was part of a quadruple bill entitled, *Theatre of the Absurd* (Cherry Lane, Feb. 11, 1962); and played Popoff in *The Chocolate Soldier* (Lambertville Music Circus, N.J., July 12, 1962).

He appeared as Wilenski in *Seidman and Son* (Belasco, N.Y.C., Oct. 15, 1962); Mr. Jones in *The Lunatic View* (Th. de Lys, Nov. 27, 1962); as Willy Loman in *Death of a Salesman* (Moorstown, N.Y., 1964); as Edmund Tyrone in *Long Day's Journey into Night* (Moorstown, N.Y., 1965); Carol Newquist in the revival of *Little Murders* (Circle in the Square, Jan. 5, 1969); in *A View from the Bridge* (Charles Playhouse, Boston, Mass., Feb. 15, 1968); as Charles Ferris in *The Son Who Hunted Tigers in Jakarta* and as Nick Esposito in *The Burial of Esposito,* two of the three one-act plays presented as *Passing Through from Exotic Places* (Sheridan Square Playhouse, Dec. 7, 1969); as Marty Mendelsohn in *Dr. Fish,* one of two one-act plays billed as *The Chinese and Dr. Fish* (Ethel Barrymore Th., Mar. 10, 1970); as the Father in *The Carpenters* (American Place Th., Dec. 21, 1970); and as Harry Edison in *The Prisoner of Second Avenue* (Eugene O'Neill Th., Nov. 11, 1971).

Films. Mr. Gardenia has appeared in *Cop Hater* (UA, 1958); *Murder, Inc.* (20th-Fox, 1960); *Mad Dog Call* (Col., 1961); *The Hustler* (20th-Fox, 1961); *A View from the Bridge* (Continental, 1962); *Jemmy* (Cinerama, 1970); *Where's Poppa?* (UA, 1970); *Cold Turkey* (UA, 1971); *Hickey & Boggs* (UA, 1972); as the American Colonel in *Re: Lucky Luciano* (Titanus, 1973); as Dutch Schnell in *Bang the Drum Slowly* (Par., 1973); and as Detective Ochoa in *Death Wish* (Par., 1974).

Television. He has played Mr. Petri on The Untouchables (ABC, 1961); Mr. Beckerman in *Ride in Terror* (1963); Frank Lorenzo in *All in the Family* (CBS, 1973–74); and appeared on numerous other television programs.

Awards. Mr. Gardenia received *The Village Voice* Off-Bway (Obie) Awards for his performances as George H. Jones in *Machinal* (1959) and as Ferris and Esposito in *Passing Through from Exotic Places* (1970); for his performance in *The Prisoner of Second Avenue,* he won an Antoinette Perry (Tony) Award (1972) as best supporting actor; and for his performance as Dutch Schnell in *Bang the Drum Slowly,* he was nominated for an Academy Award (Oscar), and received the NY Young Film Critics Award.

GARDNER, HERB. Playwright. b. 1934, Brooklyn, N.Y. Grad. H.S. of Performing Arts, N.Y.C., 1952; attended Carnegie Inst. of Tech.; Antioch Coll., Ohio. Married April 1957 to Rita Gardner, actress, singer (marr. dis.). Member of Dramatists Guild; ALA.

Theatre. Mr. Gardner wrote the play, *A Thousand Clowns* (Eugene O'Neill Th., N.Y.C., Apr. 5, 1962); wrote and directed *The Goodbye People* (Cort, Dec. 3, 1968); and wrote *Thieves* (Broadhurst, Apr. 7, 1974).

Films. Mr. Gardner wrote the screenplay (based on his play) for *A Thousand Clowns* (UA, 1965); he wrote (based on his short story) and co-produced, *Who is Harry Kellerman and Why Is He Saying Those Terrible Things About Me?* (Natl. Gen., 1971).

Television. He was one of the writers of the Anne Bancroft special, *Annie, The Women in the Life of a Man* (CBS, 1969–70 season).

Other Activities. Cartoonist (creator of "The Nebbish").

Published Works. He wrote the novel *A Piece of the Action* (1958).

Awards. For his screenplay for *A Thousand Clowns,* Mr. Gardner received a Screen Writers Guild Award, and two Academy (Oscar) Award nominations (for Best Picture and Best Screenplay, 1965). He received a NATAS (Emmy) Award as one of the writers of *Annie, The Women in the Life of a Man* (1970).

GARDNER, RITA. Actress, singer. b. Oct. 23, Brooklyn, N.Y. Attended H.S. of the Performing Arts, N.Y.C.; Brooklyn Coll. (two years). Studied acting at HB Studio, N.Y.C. (two years). Married April 1957 to Herb Gardner, playwright (marr. dis.). Member of AEA; SAG; AFTRA.

Theatre. Miss Gardner first worked professionally at the Gateway Playhouse, Somers Point, N.J., in *Wonderful Town, Pal Joey, Hit the Deck, Finian's Rainbow* and *Time Out for Ginger.* In N.Y.C., she appeared off-off Bway in *By Hex* (Tempo Th.); *Aria da Capo* and *Faraway Princess* (Tapestry Th.); and in the revue *Nightcap* (Showplace, 1959). She created the role of the Girl in *The Fantasticks* (Sullivan St. Playhouse, May 3, 1960); played Sally Nathan in *A Family Affair* (Billy Rose Th., Jan. 27, 1962); Linda English in *Pal Joey* (NY City Ctr., May 29, 1963); appeared in *Oh, Lady, Lady* (Goodspeed Opera House, East Haddam, Conn., July 1963); and played Elsie in *The Yeoman of the Guard* (Stratford Festival, Ontario, Canada, July 3, 1964).

She played Sister Mister in a revival of *The Cradle Will Rock* (Th. Four, Nov. 8, 1964); succeeded Susan Watson (as Janine Nicolet) in *Ben Franklin in Paris* (Lunt-Fontanne, Oct. 27, 1964); played Minnie Symperson in *Engaged, or, Cheviot's Choice* (Goodspeed Opera House, East Haddam, Conn., July 18, 1966); the title role in *The Unsinkable Molly Brown* (Coconut Grove Playhouse, Fall 1967); appeared intermittently (1968–71) in *Jacques Brel Is Alive and Well and Living in Paris* (Village Gate Th., N.Y.C., Jan. 22, 1968); appeared in *To Be Young, Gifted and Black* (Cherry Lane, Jan. 2, 1969); was standby for the role of Elaine Navazio in *Last of the Red Hot Lovers* (Eugene O'Neill Th., Dec. 28, 1969); was standby for Constance Towers as Kitty Fremont (and played the role in the Washington, D.C., tryout during Miss Tower's illness) in *Ari* (Mark Hellinger Th., Jan. 15, 1971); played Billie Malone in the pre-Bway tryout of *Keep Off the Grass* (opened Mechanic, Baltimore, Apr. 3, 1972; closed Hanna, Cleveland, Apr. 22, 1972); and has appeared in productions of *1776* and *The Prisoner of Second Avenue.*

Films. Miss Gardner sang the title song for *A Thousand Clowns* (UA, 1965).

Television. Miss Gardner was an Arthur Godfrey Talent Scouts winner (CBS), and has appeared on the Johnny Andrews Show; the Jinx Falkenberg Show; the Jack Paar Show (NBC); Armstrong Circle Th. (NBC); the Mike Wallace Show; the Merv Griffin Show (NBC); The Nurses (CBS); The Doctors (CBS); Lamp Unto My Feet (CBS); and the Today Show (NBC).

Night Clubs. She has performed at La Maisonette (St. Regis Hotel, N.Y.C., 1968) and was a singer with Ray Eberle's Band.

Other Activities. Since 1963, Miss Gardner has been an instructor of musical comedy technique at the H B Studio (N.Y.C.).

GARFEIN, JACK. Director. b. Jacob Garfein, July 2, 1930, Mukacevo, Czechoslovakia, to Herman and Blanka (Spiegel) Garfein. Father, businessman. Attended New Sch. for Social Research, 1947–49; Amer. Th. Wing, N.Y.C., 1950. Studied with Lee Strasberg, N.Y.C., two years; Erwin Piscator, N.Y.C., two years; Actors Studio (mbr., 1954–to date). Married Apr. 5, 1955, to Carroll Baker, actress (marr. dis.); one son, one daughter. WW II survivor of 11 concentration camps; liberated at Auschwitz, Poland, by the British forces, Apr. 16, 1945. Member of AEA; DGA; SSD&C.

Theatre. Mr. Garfein played Moritz in *The Burning Bush,* presented by the Dramatic Workshop (President Th., NYC, 1948); directed *End as a Man* (Th. de Lys, Sept. 15, 1953; moved Vanderbilt, Oct. 14, 1953); *Girls of Summer* (Longacre, Nov. 19, 1956); *The Sin of Pat Muldoon* (Cort, Mar. 13, 1957); *Shadow of a Gunman* (Bijou, Nov. 20, 1958); and a stock production of *Arms and the Man* (Lakeside, Chicago, Ill., and Long Branch, N.J.).

Mr. Garfein has been West Coast director of Actors Studio and, with Lyle Dye, Jr., supervisor of the series Plays in Progress, sponsored by Actors Studio West and the UCLA Committee on Fine Arts. He directed *Anna Christie* (Huntington Hartford Th., Los Angeles, Calif., 1965); *Don't Go Gentle* (Schonberg Hall, UCLA, Feb. 21, 1967); and *How Tall Is Toscanini?* (Schonberg Hall, 1968).

Films. Mr. Garfein directed *The Strange One* (Col., 1957); and *Something Wild* (UA, 1961), for which he wrote the screenplay.

Television. He directed a dramatic segment for the Kate Smith Show (NBC, 1952); and wrote *A Man Dies* (The Web, CBS).

Awards. Mr. Garfein received the Show Business Award for his direction of *End as a Man* (1954–55).

Recreation. Swimming, chess, reading.

GARRETT, BETTY. Actress, singer. b. May 23, 1920, St. Joseph, Mo., to Curtis and Octavia Garrett. Father, salesman. Attended Annie Wright Seminary, Tacoma, Wash. Studied at Neighborhood Playhouse Sch. of the Th., N.Y.C., 1936; singing with Madame Lazzeri; night club routines with Bob Fram; dance with Martha Graham, N.Y.C. Married Sept. 8, 1944, to Larry Parks, actor; (dec. Apr. 13, 1975); two sons. Member of AEA; SAG; AFTRA.

Pre-Theatre. Saleslady, elevator operator.

Theatre. Miss Garrett played the off-stage voice and understudied Mary Wickes as Christine in *Danton's Death* (Mercury, N.Y.C., Nov. 22, 1938); appeared in *Railroads on Parade* (NY World's Fair, 1939); *You Can't Sleep Here* (Barbizon-Plaza Th., Apr. 26, 1940); played Martha in *This Proud Pilgrimage* (June 1940); appeared in *Musical Revue* (Pauline Edwards, N.Y.C., Nov. 1940); and *A Piece of Our Mind* (Mail Studios, N.Y.C., Dec. 1940).

She joined the cast of the revue *All in Fun* (Majestic, Dec. 27, 1940); appeared on *Of V We Sing* (Concert Th., Feb. 14, 1942); *Let Freedom Sing* (Longacre, Oct. 5, 1942); played Mary-Frances and understudied Ethel Merman as Blossom Hart in *Something for the Boys* (Alvin, Jan. 7, 1943); appeared as Sgt. Maguire in *Jackpot* (Alvin, Jan. 13, 1944); appeared in the revues *Laffing Room Only* (Winter Garden, Dec. 23, 1944), and *Call Me Mister* (National, Apr. 18, 1946).

She appeared in vaudeville at the Stage (Cleveland, Ohio, July 21, 1949); London Palladium (1950); Glasgow, Scotland (1950); and the Casino (Toronto, Canada, May 9, 1952).

She played Marion Maxwell in the pre-Bway tryout of *The Anonymous Lover* (opened Worcester Playhouse, Mass., July 8, 1952); substituted for Judy Holliday for two weeks (Aug. 26, 1957) as Ella Peterson in *Bells Are Ringing* Shubert, Nov. 29, 1956); played Clara in *Beg, Borrow or Steal* (Martin Beck Th., Feb. 10, 1960); and played various roles in *Spoon River Anthology* (Booth, Sept. 29, 1963).

She was Penny Moore in *A Girl Could Get Lucky* (Paper Mill Playhouse, Millburn, N.J., Aug. 10, 1964; Cort, N.Y.C., Sept. 10, 1964); toured (1965) as Gloria in *The Tiger* and Sylvia in *The Typists;* played Mary in *Who's Happy Now?* (Center Th. Group, Mark Taper Forum, Los Angeles, Calif., Nov. 3, 1967); toured (1968–71) as Karen Nash, Muriel Tate, and Norma Hubley in *Plaza Suite;* replaced Kim Hunter as Catherine Reardon in *And Miss Reardon Drinks a Little* on tour (1972); again appeared in *Spoon River* (Th. West, Los Angeles, Calif., May 19, 1972); and appeared in *Betty Garrett and Other Songs* (Los Angeles, 1974–75).

Films. Miss Garrett has appeared in *The Big City* (MGM, 1948); *Words and Music* (MGM, 1948); *Take Me Out to the Ball Game* (MGM, 1949); *On the Town* (MGM, 1949); *The Skipper Surprised His Wife* (MGM, 1950); *My Sister Eileen* (Col., 1955); *Shadow on the Window* (Col., 1957); and *The Missing Witness.*

Television. Miss Garrett was in *A Smattering of Bliss* (Ford Th., Nov. 17, 1955); *The Penlands and the Poodle* (Ford Th., ABC, Jan. 23, 1957); on Spotlight Playhouse (CBS, 1957); Fugitive (ABC, 1964, 1965); Girl Talk (ABC, Ind., 1964–65); and on All in the Family (CBS, 1973–to date).

Night Clubs. She has performed at the Village Vanguard (N.Y.C., 1942); La Martinique, (N.Y.C.) Glover Club (Hollywood, Calif.), Drake Hotel (Chicago, Ill.), and the Latin Quarter (Boston, Mass.).

Awards. Miss Garrett received the Donaldson Award for her performance in *Call Me Mister* (1945); the Star of Tomorrow Award (1949); and the Los Angeles Drama Critics Circle Award (1975) for her performance in *Betty Garrett and Other Songs.*

Recreation. Cats, dogs.

GARTEN, H. F. Author, educator. b. Hugo F. Koenigsgarten, Apr. 13, 1904, Brünn, Austria, to Fritz and Elizabeth (Brück) Koenigsgarten. Father, industrialist. Grad. Bismarck Gymnasium, Berlin, Ger., 1923; Heidelberg Univ., D. Phil. 1930; New Coll., Oxford Univ., D. Phil. 1944. Married Mar. 8, 1952, to Anne Smith, teacher. Address: 10 Priory Mansions, Drayton Gardens, London S.W. 10, England.

From 1928 to 1933, Mr. Garten was a free-lance writer in Berlin, and from 1933 to 1938 he wrote sketches for a cabaret in Vienna. He taught (1947–65) at Westminster School, London, and lectured (1965–73) at the Univ. of Surrey, England.

Theatre. Mr. Garten is the author of two operatic librettos, both with music by Mark Lothar, entitled *Tyll* (1928) and *Lord Spleen* (1930), which have been performed in Dresden, Berlin, Hamburg, Prague, Moscow, and elsewhere. He has directed amateur productions of *Everyman* (New Coll., Oxford, 1940); *The Clouds* (New Coll., Oxford, 1941); *The Post Office* (New Coll., Oxford, 1943); *The Knight of the Burning Pestle* (New Coll., Oxford, 1944); *The Critic* (St. Edward's Sch., Oxford, 1945); *Everyman* (Westminster Sch., 1948); and *Noye's Fludde* (Westminster Abbey, 1963).

Published Works. Mr. Garten's published works in German included *Tyll* (1928); *Lord Spleen* (1930); *Georg Kaiser*, a monograph (1928); *Rosinchen* (1932); and *Mareile will Theater spielen* (1935); two plays for children. His English works include *Gerhart Hauptmann* (1954) and *Modern German Drama* (1959). He has translated two plays by Georg Kaiser: *The Raft of Medusa* (1951), which was produced at 92 Th. (Middleton, Conn., 1959); and *The Protagonist (Tulane Drama Review*, 1961). He has edited three volumes of German plays for educational theatre: *Der Hauptmann von Köpenick* by Carl Zuckmayer (1961); *Romulus der Grosse* by Friedrich Dürrenmatt (1962); and *Andorra* by Max Frisch (1964); and was a contributor to *German Men of Letters* (Vol. I, 1961; Vol. II, 1962).

Mr. Garten contributes to the *Times Literary Supplement* (London), *Drama* (London), and *German Life and Letters* (Oxford).

GARVIN, LAWRENCE W. Playwright, editor, administrator. b. July 20, 1945, Buenos Aires, Argentina, to Lester and Barbara (Nash) Garvin. Father, bank executive. Attended Kenyon College, Gambier, Ohio; grad. City College of N.Y., B.A. 1970. Received training at Hatch-Billops Studio, Inc., N.Y.C. Address: (home) 443 E. 6th Street, New York, NY 10009, tel. (212) 228-5090; (bus.) c/o Hatch-Billops Studio, Inc., 736 Broadway, New York, NY 10003, tel. (212) 673-1509.

Theatre. Mr. Garvin wrote, with James V. Hatch and Aida Morales, *Conspiracy* (Washington Square Methodist Church, N.Y.C., May 1970); with James V. Hatch, *If I Do Not Die* (Hatch-Billops Studio, May 1971); and with James V. Hatch, *Safe At Last* (New Village Th., Feb. 16, 1973).

Other Activities. Mr. Garvin was administrative director for research for the Hatch-Billops Collection, N.Y.C. (1970–74) and became the executive director of Off-Center Space, N.Y.C., in 1974. He became theatre editor of *Afro U.S.A.* in 1974.

GATES, LARRY. Actor. b. Lawrence Wheaton Gates, Sept. 24, 1915, St. Paul, Minn., to Lloyd R. and Marion (Wheaton) Gates. Father, advertising counselor. Grad. Central H.S., St. Paul Minn., 1933; attended Univ. of Minnesota, 1933–37. Studied acting with Joseph Kramm and Edward J. Bromberg at Amer. Th. Wing, N.Y.C., 1948–49. Married Aug. 2, 1959, to Tania Wilkof (dec. Sept. 28, 1961); married Apr. 11, 1963, to Judith Seaton. Served WW II, US Army, Corps of Engineers 1941–46, rank, Mjr.; awarded Bronze Star, three battle stars. Member of AEA (council member, 1952–63); AFTRA; SAG; The Players; Amer. Tree Farm Assoc.; Amer. Forestry Assoc. Address: (home) Old River Rd., West Cornwall, CT 06753, tel. (203) OR 2-6568; (bus.) c/o Barna Ostertag, 501 Fifth Ave., New York, NY 10017, tel. (212) OX 7-6339.

Pre-Theatre. Speech instructor, Univ. of Minnesota.

Theatre. Mr. Gates made his stage debut as Tranio in *The Taming of the Shrew* (Univ. of Minnesota, Oct. 1933); and his professional debut as Prof. Willard in *Our Town* (Barter Th., Abingdon, Va., July 1939).

He first appeared on Bway in the roles of Gabriel and the Pope in *Speak of the Devil* (Nora Bayes Th., Oct. 13, 1939); was understudy to Arthur Kennedy in the touring production of *Madam, Will You Walk?* (Nov. 1939); understudy and walk-on in *Twelfth Night* (St. James, Nov. 19, 1940); appeared as a walk-on in *The Respectful Prostitute* (Harris, Chicago, Ill., May 1949) presented on a double bill with *Hope Is a Thing with Feathers,* in which he played Sweeney.

Mr. Gates played Sidney Redlitch in *Bell, Book and Candle* (Ethel Barrymore Th., N.Y.C., Nov. 14, 1950); Christopher Sly in *The Taming of the Shrew* (NY City Ctr., Apr. 25, 1951); portrayed, with the Margaret Webster Shakespeare Co., Casca in the national tour of *Julius Caesar* (1950–51); Capt. Bluntschli in *Arms and the Man* (Playhouse-in-the-Park, Philadelphia, Pa., 1953); played Col. Wesley Brientenspiegel in *The Love of Four Colonels* (Shubert, N.Y.C., Jan. 15, 1953); Capt. McLean in *The Teahouse of the August Moon* (Martin Beck Th., Oct. 15, 1953); Clay Dixon in *Sing Me No Lullaby* (Phoenix, Oct. 14, 1954); and the Storyman in *The Carefree Tree* (Phoenix, Oct. 11, 1955).

He appeared as Logan Harvey in the pre-Bway tryout of *Build with One Hand* (opened Shubert, New Haven, Conn., Nov. 7, 1956; closed Ford's, Baltimore, Md., Nov. 27, 1956); at the American Shakespeare Festival (Stratford, Conn.) played Brabantio in *Othello* (June 22, 1957), the Duke of Venice in *The Merchant of Venice* (July 10, 1957), and Dogberry in *Much Ado About Nothing* (Aug. 7, 1957), and on tour (Dec. 30, 1957–Mar. 1, 1958); returned to Stratford as Tom Snout in *A Midsummer Night's Dream* (June 20, 1958); at Stratford (1959), appeared as Lord Montague in *Romeo and Juliet* (June 12), Falstaff in *Merry Wives of Windsor* (July 8), and the King of France in *All's Well That Ends Well* (Aug. 1).

Mr. Gates played John Devereaux in *The Highest Tree* (Longacre, N.Y.C., Nov. 4, 1959); the Director in *Six Characters in Search of an Author* (Univ. of California at Los Angeles Th. Group, 1959); William Jennings Bryan in *Inherit the Wind* (Playhouse-in-the-Park, Philadelphia, Pa., 1961); succeeded (Blackstone, Chicago, Ill., Feb. 18, 1963) Hiram Sherman as Oscar Nelson in the national company of *Mary, Mary* (opened Sacramento H.S. Aud., Calif., May 31, 1962; closed Blackstone, Chicago, Ill., June 15, 1963); and played Boyd Bandix in *A Case of Libel* (Longacre, N.Y.C., Oct. 10, 1963).

Mr. Gates appeared as Merton in *Conversation at Midnight* (Billy Rose Th., Nov. 12, 1964); as Orgon in *Tartuffe* (ANTA Th., Jan. 14, 1965); Undershaft in *Major Barbara* (Canadian Shaw Festival, 1967); the Father in *Carving a Statue* (Gramercy Arts, Apr. 30, 1968); and he played Max in *The Homecoming* and Shylock in *The Merchant of Venice* (Center Stage, Baltimore, Md., 1968–69). He appeared as Benjamin in *The Little Foxes* (Ivanhoe Th., Chicago, Ill., 1969); as Nat Miller in *Ah, Wilderness!* (Ford's Th., Washington, D.C., 1969); as Marcus Hubbard in *Another Part of the Forest* (Ivanhoe Th., 1971); and portrayed Capt. Boyle in *Juno and the Paycock;* Vladimir in *Waiting for Godot;* Orgon in *Tartuffe;* and Sir Oliver Surface in *The School for Scandal* (Guthrie Th., Minneapolis, Minn. 1973–74).

Films. Mr. Gates has appeared as the Psychiatrist in *The Body Snatchers* (Allied, 1956); in *Has Anybody Seen My Gal?* (UI, 1952); *Glory Alley* (MGM, 1952); as Capt. Parsons in *Above and Beyond* (MGM, 1952); in *Francis Cover the Big Town* (UI, 1953); Prof. French in *Some Came Running* (MGM, 1958); the Doctor in *Cat on a Hot Tin Roof* (MGM, 1958); Louis Rosen in *The Hoodlum Priest* (UA, 1961); in *The Young Savages* (UA, 1961); *Underworld, USA* (Col., 1961); *Ada* (MGM, 1961); and *The Spiral Road* (U, 1962).

Mr. Gates was seen as Jameson in *The Sand Pebbles* (20th-Fox, 1965); the Orchid Grower in *In the Heat of the Night* (UA, 1967); played Clum in *Hour of the Gun* (UA, 1968); the Mayor in *Death of a Gunfighter* (U, 1968); the Airport Commissioner in *Airport* (U, 1969); Judge Harlan in *Re: Lucky Luciano* (Titanus, 1973); and Bernard Baruch in *Funny Lady* (Col., 1974).

Television. He has performed on Playhouse 90 (CBS); Frontiers of Faith (NBC); Armstrong Circle Th. (CBS); Hallmark Hall of Fame (NBC, 1953–62); The Americans (NBC); The Untouchables (ABC); Twilight Zone (CBS); The Law and Mr. Jones (ABC); *Cain's Hundred* (NBC), Then Came Bronson (NBC); The Ceremony of Innocence (NET); The Guiding Light (CBS); Banyon (NBC); Owen Marshall (NBC); *The Pueblo* (ABC, 1973); and *The Missiles of October* (ABC).

Awards. He received the Barter Theatre Young Actor Award from Laurette Taylor (May 1939), and was nominated for an Antoinette Perry (Tony) Award for his performance as Boyd Bendix in *A Case of Libel* (1964).

Recreation. Tree farming.

GATESON, MARJORIE. Actress. b. Marjorie Augusta Gateson, Jan. 17, 1891, Brooklyn, N.Y., to Daniel and Augusta Virginia (Smith) Gateson. Father, contractor; mother, speech teacher. Attended Packer Collegiate Inst., Bklyn., 1909. Bklyn. Conservatory of Music, 1909. Served in USO during and after WW II. Member of AEA (council, 1947–58); SAG; AFTRA (natl. board, 1952); Episcopal Actors' Guild (board of dir.); Catholic Actors' Guild; Actors' Fund of Amer. (life member).

Theatre. Miss Gateson made her Bway debut in the chorus of the musical comedy *Dove of Peace* (Bway Th., Nov. 4, 1912); subsequently performed in the chorus of *American Maid* (Bway Th., Mar. 3, 1913); appeared in the chorus and was understudy to Peggy Wood in *Mlle. Modiste* (Globe, May 26, 1913).

She appeared in a small role and as understudy to Hazel Dawn, Grace Leigh, and Alma Francis in *The Little Cafe,* performing in each of their roles on three consecutive nights (New Amsterdam, Nov. 10, 1913); played a small role and was understudy to Georgie O'Ramey in the revue *Around the Map* (New Amsterdam, Nov. 1, 1915); appeared as Amy in *Her Soldier Boy* (Astor, Dec. 6, 1916); Marilyn Miller's sister in *Fancy Free* (Astor, Apr. 11, 1918); Lulu in *Little Simplicity* (Astor, Nov. 4, 1918); appeared in the revue *Shubert Gaieties 1919* (44 St. Th., July 17, 1919), during which time she was active in the AEA strike; played Amy Shirley in *Little Miss Charity* (Belmont, Sept. 2, 1920); Fleurette in *The Rose Girl* (Ambassador, Feb. 11, 1921); Countess

Irma in *The Love Letter* (Globe, Oct. 4, 1921); and Enid Crawford in *Lady Butterfly* (Globe, Jan. 22, 1923).

Miss Gateson made her debut as a dramatic actress in the role of Nina Buckmaster in *Strange Bedfellows* (Henry Miller's Th., June 16, 1924); subsequently appeared as Gaby Cordier in *Man in Evening Clothes* (Henry Miller's Th., Dec. 5, 1924); Ida in *The Blond Sinner* (Cort, July 14, 1926); the Hon. Gwendolyn Fairfax in the musical *Oh, Ernest!* (Royale, May 9, 1927); Kate Du Plessis in *Hidden* (Lyceum, Oct. 4, 1927); and Madame Estelle in *The Great Necker* (Ambassador, Mar. 6, 1928).

For the Actors' Fund, she appeared as Hermia in an all-star production of *A Midsummer Night's Dream* (Lyceum Th., Forest Hills Stad., 1928); played Mrs. Eleanor Banning in *As Good as New* (Times Sq. Th., Nov. 3, 1930); succeeded (1930) Mary Servoss as Anna Maurrant in *Street Scene* (Playhouse, Jan. 10, 1929); and later toured Italy and the Azores as Janet Archer in a USO production of *Kiss and Tell* (seven months, 1945). On her return to the US, she incorporated a USO speakers' tour with the West Coast Co. production of *Dear Ruth*, in which she played Mrs. Edith Wilkins (1945); appeared as Dame Lucy in *Sweethearts* (Shubert, Jan. 26, 1947); Parthy Ann in *Show Boat* (NY City Ctr., May 5, 1954); at the St. Louis (Mo.) Municipal Opera, played Maggie in *Lady in the Dark* (1958) and the Queen in *Rosalie*. .

Films. Miss Gateson made her film debut in *The Beloved Bachelor* (Par., 1931); subsequently appeared in many pictures, including *The False Madonna* (Par., 1932); *Street of Women* (WB, 1932); *King's Vacation* (WB, 1933); *Your Uncle Dudley* (20th-Fox, 1935); *Private Number* (20th-Fox, 1936); *Milky Way* (Par., 1936); *Turn of the Moon* (Par., 1937); *First Lady* (WB, 1937); *Vogues of 1938* (UA, 1937); *Stable Mates* (MGM, 1938); *Geronimo* (Par., 1939); *Ever Since Venus* (Col., 1944); *Seven Days Ashore* (RKO, 1944); and *Passage West* (par., 1951).

Television and Radio. On the radio, Miss Gateson played Mrs. Barbour in the series, One Man's Family (NBC, 1949–52). On television, she has been Grace Tyrell in the series, The Secret Storm (CBS); and she has appeared on the US Steel Hour (CBS); Sgt. Bilko (CBS); True Story (NBC); and Girl Talk (ABC).

GAVER, JACK. Drama editor, critic. b. Claude H. Gaver, Tolono, Ill., to Hayden and Drusilla P. Gaver. Grad. Hartford City (Ind.) H.S., 1924; attended Univ. of Illinois, 1926–29. Married 1945 to Jessyca Russell, writer; one daughter. Member of NY Drama Critics' Circle; The Players. Address: (home) 7 Peter Cooper Rd., New York, NY 10010; (bus.) c/o United Press International, 220 E. 42nd St., New York, NY 10017, tel. (212) MU 2-0400. Since 1931, Mr. Gaver has been drama editor and critic for the United Press International.

Published Works. Mr. Gaver wrote, with Dave Stanley, *There's Laughter in the Air* (1945); is the author of *Curtain Calls* (1949) and *Season In, Season Out* (1966). He edited *Critics' Choice* (1954), a series of plays selected by the NY Drama Critics' Circle during its first twenty years. The anthology includes a history of the Circle written by Mr. Gaver.

GAYE, FREDA. Editor, actress, museum curator. b. Dec. 27, 1907, Hunmanby, Yorkshire, England, to Wilfrid and Harriet Jane (Pickard) Gaye. Father, civil engineer; mother, spinster. Attended Putney H.S. and Margaret Morris Sch., London, Eng. Studied speech with Herbert Scott, 1935–37. Collateral descendant of John Gay, playwright. Address: 17 Tryon St., Chelsea, London S.W.3 3LG, England.

Miss Gaye was editor of *Who's Who in the Theatre* (1958–70), and was curator of the British Theatre Museum Assn. (1963–64). She has also contributed to the *Dictionary of National Biography*, the *Oxford Companion to the Theatre* (1974), and other reference works.

Theatre. She made her debut in London as a dancer in *The Tempest* (Aldwych Th., Feb. 1, 1921); followed by the role of Miss Lucy in *Brer Rabbit* (Everyman, Dec. 1926); Henrietta in *The Barretts of Wimpole Street* (Birmingham Repertory Th., Eng., Dec. 1931), appearing in productions with this company until June 1932; played Rose Belcher in *Evensong* (Queen's London, June 30, 1932; Selwyn, N.Y.C., Jan. 31, 1933); Bell Brown in *Gallows Glorious* (Shaftesbury, London, May 1933); toured in Shakespearean roles with H.V. Neilson's company (1934–35); played Poppy Straight in *Limelight* (Birmingham Rep. Th., 1936); Fay Beaudine in *London After Dark* (Apollo, London, Apr. 7, 1937); toured as Lady Ursula in *The Zeal of Thy House* (1938–39); appeared in repertory with Matthew Forsyth's Co. (De la Warr Pavillion, Bexhill, 1939–40); and toured Wales and Durham mining areas in Old Vic productions, appearing in *Macbeth, Medea*, and *King John* (1940–43).

She played the Nurse in *Medea* (New, London, July 16, 1941); toured in *Fire at Callart*, and *Punch and Judy* for Ann Casson's Curtain Th. Co. (Scotland and Orkney Is., 1943–44); played Nancy Steele in *Sense and Sensibility* (Embassy, London, Aug. 15, 1946); Agatha in *The Family Reunion* (Mercury, Oct. 31, 1946); Dr. Jean Linden in *The Linden Tree* (Duchess, Aug. 15, 1947); toured West Germany as Ellen Creed in *Ladies in Retirement* (1949); played the Nurse Secretary and took over the role of Lavinia Chamberlayne in *The Cocktail Party* (New, London, May 3, 1950); played Gertrude Timms in *Up the Garden Path* (New Boltons, May 28, 1952); Lady Melbourne in *Caro William* (Embassy, Oct. 22, 1952); toured as Pitt in *Liberty Bill* (Feb. 1954); as guest artist, appeared as Marie Anne in *The Ermine* (Playhouse, Nottingham, Sept. 1955); and for the Bristol Old Vic Co., played Elizabeth Hector-Crammles in *The Strangers* (Th. Royal, June 1957).

Television and Radio. Miss Gaye has performed on radio and television, and was co-author of the radio play *Judith* (BBC, 1936).

Recreation. Travel.

GAYNES, GEORGE. Actor, singer. b. George Jongejans, May 3, 1917, Helsinki, Finland, to Gerritt and Iya, Lady Abdy Jongejans. Father, businessman; mother, artist. Grad. College Classique Cantonal, Lausanne, Switzerland, 1937; attended Milan (It.) Sch. of Music, 1938–39; studied acting with Lee Strasberg, N.Y.C., 1953–58; John Daggett Howell, 1960–to date. Married Dec. 20, 1953, to Allyn Ann McLerie, actress; one son, one daughter. Served as C.P.O., Royal Netherlands Navy, 1943–45; rank, Sub-Lt.; Royal British Navy, 1945–46. Relative in theatre: uncle, Gregory Gay, actor. Member of AGMA; AEA; AFTRA; SAG; Actors' Studio (1960–to date). Address: c/o Rifkin David Agency, 9615 Brighton Way, Beverly Hills, CA 90210, tel. (213) 276-3136.

Theatre. Mr. Gaynes first appeared on the stage in an amateur production of *Malade Imaginaire* (Maison du Peuple, Lausanne, Switzerland, 1935).

Billed as George Jongejons, his first professional appearances were in the operas *Pulcinella* and *The Wizard* (Teatro della Triennale, Milan, Italy, 1940). He appeared in a concert (Salle du Conservatoire, Paris, France, 1947); was first and second basso at the Opera House (Mulhouse, France, 1947–48); first basso at the Opera House (Strasbourg, 1948–49); and since 1949, has appeared as a basso with the New York City opera, in roles including Leporello in *Don Giovanni*, Dandini in *Cenerentola*, Figaro in *The Marriage of Figaro* and in Gilbert and Sullivan operettas.

He played Mr. Kofner in *The Consul* (Ethel Barrymore Th., Mar. 15, 1950); Jupiter in *Out of This World* (New Century, Dec. 21, 1951). Under the professional name, George Gaynes, which he used thereafter, he appeared as Baker in *Wonderful Town* (Winter Garden, N.Y.C., Feb. 25, 1953); and King David in *Absalom* (Artists Th., May 1956). He played Jeff Moss in *Bells Are Ringing* (Coliseum, London, Nov. 14, 1957); Erno Gero in *Shadow of Heroes* (York Playhouse, Dec. 5, 1961); and in the ANTA matinee production of *Brecht on Brecht*, (Th. de Lys, Nov. 14, 1961).

He played a Buyer in *The Lady of the Camellias* (Winter Garden, Mar. 20, 1963); the Prisoner in *Dynamite Tonight* (York, Mar. 15, 1964); Don Pedro in the Berlioz opera *Beatrice and Benedict* (US premiere, Washington, D.C., June 3, 1964); and Henry Higgins in a tour of *My Fair Lady* (Summer 1964); replaced Don Porter in *Any Wednesday* (Music Box, N.Y.C., 1965); appeared in *Jacobowsky and the Colonel* (tour, 1967); played The Father in *Of Love Remembered* (ANTA, N.Y.C., Feb. 18, 1967); appeared in *God Bless* (Yale Drama Sch., New Haven, Conn., Oct. 10, 1968); played Henry Higgins in *My Fair Lady* (Honolulu, 1968); appeared in *Metamorphoses* (Mark Taper Forum, Los Angeles, 1972); played Michael Jardeen in *A Community of Two* (tour, opened Dupont Th., Wilmington, Del., Dec. 31, 1973); and appeared in *Wonderful Town* in San Francisco and Los Angeles in 1975.

Films. Mr. Gaynes has appeared in *P.T. 109* (WB, 1962); *The Group* (UA, 1966); and *The Way We Were* (Col., 1973).

Television. Mr. Gaynes has played the Dancing Master in *The Would-Be Gentleman* (CBS, 1955); and has appeared on The Defenders (CBS); Armstrong Th. (NBC), US Steel Hour (CBS), Alfred Hitchcock (CBS), Accent (CBS), Hallmark Hall of Fame (NBC), East Side/West Side (CBS, 1963), Bonanza (NBC), Colombo (NBC), The Law (NBC), $6,000,000 Man (ABC), Woman of the Year (CBS), Mannix (CBS), and Mission Impossible (CBS).

Recreation. Scuba diving, fencing, riding.

GAZZARA, BEN. Actor. b. Biagio Anthony Gazzara, Aug. 28, 1930, New York City, to Antonio and Angela (Cusumano) Gazzara. Father, artisan. Grad. St. Simon Stock H.S., N.Y.C., 1947; attended City Coll. of New York, 1947–49. Studied acting at Erwin Piscator's Dramatic Workshop, 1949–51; Actors Studio (mbr. since 1951). Married June 7, 1952, to Louise Erickson (marr. dis. Mar. 1956); married Nov. 26, 1959, to Janice Rule, actress; two daughters. Member of AEA; AFTRA; SAG.

Theatre. Mr. Gazzara made his first professional appearance touring as Micah in *Jezebel's Husband* (Cape May Playhouse, N.J.; Pocono Playhouse, Mountainhome, Pa., Summer 1952); and subsequently appeared in *A Day of Grace* (Westport Country Playhouse, Conn., Summer 1953).

He made his N.Y.C. debut as Jocko de Paris in *End as a Man* (Th. de Lys, Sept. 15, 1953; moved to Vanderbilt, Oct. 14, 1953); subsequently appeared as Brick in *Cat on a Hot Tin Roof* (Morosco, Mar. 24, 1955); Johnny Pope in *Hatful of Rain* (Lyceum, Nov. 9, 1955), and succeeded Mark Richman (Mar. 1957) in the same role of the national tour (opened Selwyn, Chicago, Ill., Oct. 15, 1956; closed Plymouth, Boston, Mass., May 4, 1957); played Joy in *The Night Circus* (John Golden Th., N.Y.C., Dec. 2, 1958); George Dillon in tour of *Epitaph for George Dillon* (Summer 1959); Jerry Ryan in a stock production of *Two for the Seesaw* (Coconut Grove Playhouse, Miami, Florida, Jan. 1960); Edmund Darrell in the Actors' Studio production of *Strange Interlude* (Hudson, N.Y.C., March 11, 1963); Gaston in *Traveller without Luggage* (ANTA, Sept. 17, 1964); and played the title role in *Hughie* (Booth, Oct. 14, 1974).

Films. Mr. Gazzara first appeared as Jocko de Paris in *The Strange One* (Col., 1957); subsequently played in *Anatomy of a Murder* (Col., 1959); *The Passionate Thief* (Titanus, 1960); *The Young Doctors* (UA, 1961); *The Captive City* (Maxima, 1962); *Convicts Four* (Allied, 1962); *A Rage To Live* (UA, 1965); *Conquered City* (AI, 1966); made a guest appearance in *If It's Tuesday, This Must be Belgium* (UA, 1969); appeared in *Husbands* (Col., 1970); was a narrator for *Thermidor* (Altura, 1971); and appeared in *The Neptune Factor* (20th-Fox, 1973).

Television. Mr. Gazzara's appearances include Danger (CBS); The Web (CBS); Kraft Television Th. (NBC); Armstrong Circle Th. (CBS); DuPont Show of the Month (NBC); and Playhouse 90 (CBS); Arrest and Trial (ABC); Kraft Suspense Th.

(NBC); *Carol for Another Christmas* (ABC); Run for Your Life (NBC); The Today Show (NBC); The Mike Douglas Show (ABC); *When Michael Calls* (ABC); *Fireball Foreward* (ABC); *The Family Rico* (CBS); Pursuit (ABC); and *QB VII* (ABC).

Awards. For his performance as Jocko de Paris in *End as a Man*, Mr. Gazzara received the *Theatre World* Award (1954) and the *Variety* NY Drama Critics Poll (1954).

Recreation. Tennis, swimming, riding, music, reading.

GAZZO, MICHAEL V. Playwright, actor, director. b. Michael Vincente Gazzo, Apr. 5, 1923, Hillside, N.J., to Michael Basile and Elvira (Lungo) Gazzo. Father, bartender. Educated Thomas Jefferson H.S., Elizabeth, N.J. Studied at Dramatic Workshop, New Sch. for Social Research, N.Y.C., diploma 1949; Actors Studio, N.Y.C. (member since 1952). Address: 447 W. 44th St., New York, NY 10036, tel. (212) CI 6-3484.

Pre-Theatre. Machinist.

Theatre. Mr. Gazzo wrote *A Hatful of Rain* (Lyceum Th., N.Y.C., Nov. 9, 1955); and *Night Circus* (John Golden Th., Dec. 2, 1958). While a student at the Dramatic Workshop, he played Tripe Face in *The Aristocrats* (President, 1946). At the Great Neck Playhouse, N.Y., he directed *Androcles and the Lion*, played Dr. Einstein in *Arsenic and Old Lace*, and was associate director for *Alfred* (Summer 1946).

At the Dramatic Workshop, he directed *The Imbecile* and *The Cause of It All* and helped Erwin Piscator prepare *The Trial* and *The Aristocrat* for presentation. He acted in Dramatic Workshop productions at the President Th. and the Rooftop Th. (1946–49), playing Ben Hubbard in *The Little Foxes*, Shields in *The Shadow of a Gunman*, Captain Boyle in *Juno and the Paycock*, the Uncle in *The Trial*, and he appeared in *The Sheepwell*. During the same period, his play *My Name Ain't Abe* was produced by the Dramatic Workshop.

Mr. Gazzo was associate director, with Alexis Solomas, of the On Stage's production of *The Dog Beneath the Skin*, in which he played the role of Destructive Desmond (Cherry Lane, July 21, 1947). For the Interplayers, he directed *Within the Gates* (Provincetown Playhouse); was producer-director of Off-Bway Inc., directing Kim Stanley in *Yes Is for a Very Young Man* (June 6, 1949). He played the Beggar in an ELT production of Odet's *Night Music* (ANTA Playhouse, Apr. 8, 1951); and A. Ratt in *Camino Real* (Natl., Mar. 19, 1953). The Actors Studio presented Mr. Gazzo's plays *And All That Jazz* and *Like They Did the Buffalo* (1967).

Films. Mr. Gazzo appeared in *On the Waterfront* (Col. 1954); *The Gun* (Col.); *The Gang That Couldn't Shoot Straight; Crazy Joe;* and played Frankie (Five Angels) Pentangelli in *The Godfather II* (Par., 1974). He wrote the screenplays for *A Hatful of Rain* (20th-Fox, 1957); *King Creole* (Par., 1958); and *The World of Johnny Cool* (UA, 1964).

Television. He made his debut as a Russian Officer on Philco Television Playhouse (NBC, 1950), and has appeared on dramatic programs (1950–53).

Other Activities. Mr. Gazzo began teaching acting privately in 1950, in addition to teaching classes in theatre at Studio Six, the Actors Cine Lab, and the Dramatic Workshop of the New Sch. for Social Research (1950–62). He taught acting at the American Academy of Dramatic Arts, and he moderated a playwriting unit at the Actors Studio.

Awards. For his play, *A Hatful of Rain*, he tied with Paddy Chayefsky as Promising Playwright of 1955–56 in the *Variety* Drama Critics' poll. The film, *A Hatful of Rain*, which he adapted from his play, was included in the *Film Daily* Filmdom's Famous Five as one of the best screenplays of the year (1957). He received a Rockefeller Foundation grant to produce his play *The Death of the Kitchen Table in Our Fair City* (1966).

Recreation. Painting, photography, films, sculpting.

GEAR, LUELLA. Actress. b. Luella Gardner Van Nort Gear, Sept. 5, 1899, New York City, to James Bruce and Luella (Glosser) Gear. Father, hardware dealer, contractor; mother, school teacher, writer, lawyer. Attended Hunter Coll. Teachers' Training Grammar Sch., N.Y.C., 1909–13; Wadleigh H.S., N.Y.C., 1913; Pensionatte Delstanch, Brussels, Belgium, 1914; Castle Sch., Tarrytown, N.Y., 1915; Finch Sch., N.Y.C., 1916. Married Sept. 5, 1919, to Byron Chandler (marr. dis. 1925); married Sept. 28, 1927, to G. Maurice Heckscher, financier (marr. dis. 1933); married Apr. 9, 1938, to Frederick W.A. Engel, textiles (marr. dis. 1941). Member of AEA; AFTRA; SAG. Address: 305 E. 72nd St., New York, NY 10021, tel. (212) LE 5-3629.

Theatre. Miss Gear made her N.Y.C. debut as Luella in *Love O' Mike* (Shubert Th., Jan. 17, 1917); subsequently appeared as Eleanor Montgomery in *The Gold Diggers* (Lyceum, Sept. 30, 1919); Amelia Annesley in *A Bachelor's Night* (Park, Oct. 17, 1921); Margery Hammond in *Elsie* (Vanderbilt, Apr. 2, 1923); Mary Delafield in *Poppy* (Apollo, Sept. 3, 1923; Gaiety Th., London, Eng., Sept. 4, 1924); Florence Cole in *Queen High* (Ambassador, N.Y.C., Sept. 8, 1926); and in the revue, *The Optimists* (Century Th. Roof, Jan. 1928); Ethel Billings in *Ups-a-Daisy* (Shubert, Oct. 8, 1929); Hortense in *Gay Divorce* (Ethel Barrymore Th., Nov. 29, 1932); in the revue, *Life Begins at 8:40* (Winter Garden, Aug. 27, 1934); Peggy Portersfield in *On Your Toes* (Imperial, Apr. 11, 1936); Pamela Pennington in *Love in My Fashion* (Ritz, Dec. 3, 1937); in the revue, *Streets of Paris* (Broadhurst, June 19, 1939); in the revue, *Crazy With the Heat* (44 St. Th., Jan. 14, 1941); Vera Trenton in *Pie in the Sky* (Playhouse, Dec. 22, 1941); in the musical, *Count Me In* (Ethel Barrymore Th., Oct. 8, 1942); and in a USO production of *Three's a Family* (PTO, 1943).

she played Martha Blair in *That Old Devil* (Playhouse, June 5, 1944); Octavia Fotheringham in *My Romance* (Shubert, Oct. 19, 1948); Silvie Martineau in *To Be Continued* (Booth, Apr. 23, 1952); Julia Ward McKinlock in *Sabrina Fair* (Natl., Nov. 11, 1953); and Audrey Pender in *Four Winds* (Cort, Sept. 25, 1957).

Miss Gear has appeared in stock as Muriel Chadwick in *Roar Like a Dove* (Westport Country Playhouse, Conn., July 1960); Mrs. Barto in *Warm Heart, Cold Feet* (Falmouth Playhouse, Mass., Aug. 24, 1964); Nancy Driscoll in *The Well Dressed Liar* (Royal Poinciana Playhouse, Palm Beach, Fla., Mar. 7, 1966); Laura in *The Vinegar Tree;* and in *The Happiest Millionaire; Elizabeth Steps Out; George Washington Slept Here; Yes, My Darling Daughter;* and *Goldfish Bowl.*

Films. Miss Gear made her debut in *Adam and Eva* (Par., 1923); and has appeared in *Carefree* (RKO, 1938); *The Perfect Marriage* (Par., 1946); *Jigsaw* (UA, 1949); and *Phffft* (Col., 1954).

Television and Radio. On radio, she performed on the Greatest Story Ever Told, and Ford Theatre. On television, she has appeared on Studio One (CBS); Kraft Television Th. (NBC); Play of the Week (NTA); Plain Clothesman (Dumont); The Defenders (CBS); The Trap (CBS); Sure as Fate (CBS); Broadway Television Th. (Ind.); The Web (CBS); The Elgin Hour (ABC); Producers Showcase (NBC); *Juno and the Paycock* (Play of the Week, ABC, Feb. 1, 1960); and was a regular on the series, Joe and Mabel (CBS, premiere Sept. 20, 1955, to 1956).

Recreation. Golf, riding, boating.

GEER, ELLEN. Actress. b. Ellen Ware Geer, Aug. 29, 1941, New York City, to Will and Herta Geer. Father, actor; mother, balladeer. Grad. C.P.S. H.S., N.Y.C., 1959. Studied acting at ASFTA, N.Y.C., and Stratford, Conn., 1959–60. Married Jan. 29, 1963, to Edward Flanders, actor (marr. dis. 1968); one son. Relatives in theatre: sisters, Kate Geer and Melora Marshall, actresses; brother, Thad Geer, actor; brother-in-law, Larry Lindville, actor. Member of AEA; AFTRA; SAG. Address: 2418 Entrada Rd., Topanga, CA 90290, tel. (213) 455-2178.

Theatre. Miss Geer made her debut as an angel in *The Green Pastures*, which was produced in her father's theatre (Topanga Canyon, Calif., Summer 1953), and also appeared there in *This Property Is Condemned* (1954).

At the Putnam County Playhouse (Mahopac, N.Y.), she was a chorus girl in *Gentlemen Prefer Blondes, Pal Joey*, and *Paint Your Wagon* (Summer 1955).

At the Robin Hood Th. (Arden, Del.), she played Gretta in *Witness for the Prosecution* and Emily in *Hello Out There* (Summer 1956); at the Phonecia (N.Y.) Playhouse, she played Ermengarde in *The Matchmaker* and Laurey in *Green Grow the Lilacs* (Summer 1957), and at the Players Th. (Sarasota, Fla.), she appeared as a chorus girl in *Lady in the Dark*, Bridget in *Roomful of Roses*, Celestinet in *Can-Can* and appeared in *Night Must Fall* (Winter, 1957).

She made her N.Y.C. debut as Alice in *Alice in Wonderland* (Cricket, Winter 1959), and played Agnes in an ELT production of *The Beautiful People* (Lenox Hill Playhouse, Dec. 11, 1959).

With the Amer. Shakespeare Festival and Academy (Stratford, Conn.), she toured as the 1st Fairy in *A Midsummer Night's Dream* and Dorcas in *The Winter's Tale* (1960); at the Robin Hood Th., she played the Girl in *The Cave Dwellers* and Laura in *The Glass Menagerie* (Summer 1961); for the APA (Assn. of Producing Artists) at the Fred Miller Th. (Milwaukee, Wis.), she played Nina in *The Seagull* (Oct. 19, 1961); Sally in *The Tavern* (Nov. 3, 1961); Maria in *The School for Scandal* (Nov. 17, 1961); and Gertrude in *Fashion* (Dec. 1, 1961).

At the Fred Miller Th., she played Minnie Fay in *The Matchmaker* and the Prompter in *Six Characters in Search of an Author* (1962); at the Old Globe Th. (San Diego, Calif.), she played Bianca in *The Taming of the Shrew*, Desdemona in *Othello*, and Lady Percy in *Henry IV, Part 2* (Summer 1962); with the APA at the Trueblood Aud. (Ann Arbor, Mich.), she appeared as Jessica in *The Merchant of Venice* (Feb. 20, 1963); and the Queen in *Richard II* (Feb. 27, 1963).

At the Tyrone Guthrie Th. (Minneapolis, Minn.), she played Ophelia in *Hamlet* (May 7, 1963); Mariane in *The Miser* (May 8, 1963); Irina in *The Three Sisters* (June 18, 1963); the title role in *Saint Joan* (May 12, 1964); Laura in *The Glass Menagerie* (June 1, 1964); Lady Anne in *Richard III* (May 10, 1965); Mrs. Fainall in *The Way of the World* (May 11, 1965); Dunyasha in *The Cherry Orchard* (June 15, 1965); Mariane in *The Miser* (Sept. 7, 1965); Gladys in *The Skin of Our Teeth* (May 31, 1966); and Rosalind in *As You Like It* (June 2, 1966).

At the American Conservatory Th., San Francisco, Calif., she played Nina in *The Seagull* (1967); Viola in *Twelfth Night* (Oct. 31, 1967); Miss MyFanwy Price in *Under Milk Wood* (Nov. 21, 1967); Elaine in *Arsenic and Old Lace* (1968); Emily in *Our Town* (Jan. 25, 1968); Julia in *A Delicate Balance* (Mar. 23, 1968); and Masha in *Long Live Life* (1968). She appeared at the Old Globe Shakespeare Festival, San Diego, Calif., as Hero in *Much Ado About Nothing* (June 9, 1970); the Queen in *Richard II* (June 12, 1970); and Imogen in *Cymbeline* (July 9, 1970). She played Estelle in *Father's Day* (Mark Taper Forum, Los Angeles, Calif., Oct. 14, 1973); and at Theatricum Botanicum, Topanga, Calif., her father's theatre, she played Rosalind in *As You Like It* and Hermione/Perdita in *The Winter's Tale* (both 1973); directed *Romeo and Juliet* (1973); played Titania in *A Midsummer Night's Dream* (1974); and Viola/Sebastian in *Twelfth Night* (1975).

Films. Miss Geer was in *Petulia* (WB, 1968); *The Reivers* (Natl. Gen., 1969); *Kotch* (Cinerama, 1971); *Harold and Maude* (Par., 1971); *Abraham and Isaac* (1972); *Silence* (Cinema Financial, 1974); and *Memory of Us*, for which she also wrote the screenplay (Cinema Financial, 1974).

Television. Miss Geer played the Daughter in *The Wooden Dish* (Play of the Week, WNTA, 1961); appeared on My Friend Tony (NBC, Jan. 1969); the Jimmy Stewart Show (NBC, 1971); The Waltons

(CBS, 1972); *The New Land* (ABC, 1974); and Archer (NBC, Jan.–Mar. 1975).

GEER, WILL. Actor, director. b. Will Aughe Geer, Mar. 9, 1902. Frankfort, Ind., to Roy and Kate (Aughe) Geer. Father, postal service worker; mother, teacher. Attended Frankfort H.S., 1916–1919; grad. Waller H.S., Chicago, 1918; Univ. of Chicago, Ph.B., 1924; attended Columbia Univ., 1924; Oxford Univ., England, 1924. Married Oct. 12, 1936, to Herta Ware, actress; (marr. dis.; dec.); one son, two daughters, Kate and Ellen, actresses; sons-in-law, Larry Linville and Ed Flanders, actors. Member of AEA; SAG; AFTRA. Address: Topanga Blvd., Topanga, CA; 1384 Elm St., Stratford, CT 06497, tel. (203) 375-9764.

Theatre. Mr. Geer made his first stage appearance in a Waller H.S. (Chicago) production of *You Never Can Tell*, in which he played Crampton (Nov. 1918). His first professional engagements were with the Sothern-Marlowe Shakespearean Repertory Co. as a walk-on in *Hamlet, Romeo and Juliet*, and *Much Ado About Nothing* (Studebaker, Chicago, Ill., Dec. 1920); and he subsequently appeared with the Coleman Co. as Polonius in *Hamlet* (Jan. 1922) and Bottom in *A Midsummer Night's Dream* (Apr. 1922). He played in stock engagements, including the part of the Warden in *Peter Ibbetson* with the Stuart Walker Stock Co. (Murat, Indianapolis, Ind., June 1921); with the Elwin Strong Co., played in tent shows in Nebraska, in Toby shows, in showboat productions along the Ohio and Mississippi rivers, and portrayed Simon Legree in *Uncle Tom's Cabin* (Triangle Th., Greenwich Village Th., Punch and Judy Th., N.Y.C., Dec. 1924); was a supernumerary in *The Call of Life* (Comedy, Oct. 9, 1925); appeared with the Henry Jewitt Stock Co. (Boston, Mass.) in *The Rivals* and *Rip Van Winkle* (1925). He was with the Goodman Th. Co. (Chicago, Ill., 1926); rejoined the Stuart Walker Stock Co. (Grand Masonic Temple, Cincinnati, Ohio, 1927); and appeared in Shakespearean productions at the Garden (outdoor) Th. (St. Louis, Mo., Summer 1927).

Mr. Geer played Pistol in Mrs. Fiske's production of *The Merry Wives of Windsor* (Knickerbocker, N.Y.C., Mar. 19, 1928); and with her touring company, played Dobbin in *Becky Sharpe* and the Prosecutor in *Ladies of the Jury* (until 1930). He played in stock at the Ivoryton (Conn.) Playhouse (Summer 1930); portrayed Elam in the pre-Bway tryout of *Eldorado* (closed Shubert, New Haven, Conn., Aug. 1930); Engstrand in a production of *Ghosts* (Orange Grove, Los Angeles, Calif., Oct. 8, 1933); Bob Brierly in *The Ticket of Leave Man* (Tony Pastor's Th., Los Angeles, Mar. 10, 1934). He helped to found the New Theatre Group at the Musart Playhouse (Los Angeles, 1934–35), playing Lem in *Stevedore* (Aug. 29, 1934) and appearing in the double-bill *Waiting for Lefty* and *Till the Day I Die* (Hollywood Playhouse, Calif., May 22, 1935).

He appeared as John Kirkland in *Let Freedom Ring* (Broadhurst, N.Y.C., Nov. 6–30, 1935; reopened Civic Rep. Th., Dec. 17, 1935). At the same theatre, under the auspices of the New Theatre League, appeared as Brother Simpkins in *Unto Such Glory*, in a program of one-act plays (Sunday, Jan. 12, 1936); under the auspices of the Theatre of Action, appeared as a Soldier in *Snickering Horses* (Civic Repertory Th., Jan. 1936); and under the auspices of the Actors' Repertory Co., played the Reporter in *Bury the Dead* and directed the curtain-raiser, *Over Here* (Civic Repertory Th., May 14, 1936); and repeated his role as the Reporter in *Bury the Dead* and played Poppy in the curtain raiser, *Prelude*, which replaced *Over Here* when the productions were moved to the Ethel Barrymore Th. (Apr. 18, 1936). He again played the Reporter in *Bury the Dead*, a Soldier in *Snickering Horses*, and Brother Simpkins in *Unto Such Glory*, and appeared in *Private Hicks* and *Let Freedom Ring*, touring New England under the auspices of the Textile Union (May 1936).

Mr. Geer appeared as Farley Sprinkle in *200 Were Chosen* (48 St. Th., N.Y.C., Nov. 20, 1936); Mr. Mooney in *A House in the Country* (Vanderbilt, Jan. 11, 1937); Slim in *Of Mice and Men* (Music Box, Jan. 24, 1937); and Dan Raldny in *Steel* (Labor Stage, Feb. 14, 1937). For the Federal Th. (WPA) Project (N.Y.C.), he appeared as Brother Simpkins in *Unto Such Glory* (Ritz, May 7, 1937) in a series of matinees. With the Mercury Th., he appeared as Mister Mister in *The Cradle Will Rock* (Venice, June 16, 1937); produced and appeared in the revue *Americana*, which toured by bus (N.J., Del., Summer 1937); appeared in matinee performances as the Boss in *Jig* and as an Officer in *Freedom of the Press* (Belasco, N.Y.C., Dec. 12, 1937) for the Newspaper Guild. He repeated his role of Mister Mister in *The Cradle Will Rock* (Windsor, Jan. 3, 1938); appeared as Simon Dye in *Journeymen* (Fulton, Jan. 29, 1938); and performed in the revue, *Sing Out the News* (Music Box, Sept. 24, 1938).

He succeeded (Forrest, Dec. 11, 1939) James Barton as Jeeter Lester in *Tobacco Road* (Masque, Dec. 4, 1933); appeared as Lockhart in *The More the Merrier* (Cort, Sept. 15, 1941); Doc Blossom in *Johnny on the Spot* (Plymouth, Jan. 8, 1942); in stock, played Justice Holmes in *The Magnificent Yankee* (Matunuck, R.I., Summer 1942); Lincoln in *Abe Lincoln in Illinois* (Keith Th., Providence, R.I., 1942); played a comedy role in *My Maryland* (Shubert, Boston, Mass., 1942); appeared as Uncle Yancy Sylvaine in *The Moon Vine* (Morosco, N.Y.C., Feb. 11, 1943); with the Boston Symphony Orchestra, appeared as Lincoln in *A Portrait of Lincoln* (Carnegie Hall, Apr. 25, 1943); for the CIO, performed in a "bandwagon" tour (Boston, Mass.; St. Louis, Mo.; Chicago, Ill.; Sept. 1943), appearing in sketches impersonating Herbert Hoover, Westbrook Pegler, and Thomas Dewey; appeared as Rufus in the pre-Bway tryout of *Champagne for Everybody* (opened National, Washington, D.C., Sept. 4, 1944; closed Walnut St. Th., Philadelphia, Pa., Sept. 16, 1944); Ernest Hopkins in *Sophie* (Playhouse, N.Y.C., Dec. 25, 1944); and Jim Loveridge in the pre-Bway tryout of *Merely Coincidental* (opened Wilbur, Boston, Mass., May 11, 1945; closed there May 19, 1945).

Mr. Geer played Doc Watterson in *Flamingo Road* (Belasco, N.Y.C., Mar. 19, 1946); Ed Tilden in *On Whitman Avenue* (Cort, May 8, 1946); Mister Mister in *The Cradle Will Rock* (Mansfield, Dec. 26, 1947); Sweeney in the Six O'Clock Th. Studio production of *Hope Is the Thing with Feathers* (Maxine Elliott's Th., Apr. 11, 1948); repeated the same role in the ANTA production of the same play (Playhouse, May 11, 1948); and appeared as the Captain in *Thunder Rock* (Circle Th., Hollywood, Calif., 1950). He played the role of Sicinius in *Coriolanus* (Phoenix, Jan. 19, 1954); Shamrayev in *The Seagull* (Phoenix, May 11, 1954); performed in the Jack London Show (Royal Playhouse, 1954); the Mark Twain Show (Fourth St. Th., 1954); the Whitman Show (1954); and played Bowman Witherspoon in *The Wisteria Trees* (NY City Ctr., Feb. 2, 1955).

He appeared as Uncle Garvey in *The Vamp* (Winter Garden, Nov. 10, 1955); Dorris R. Gladney in *The Ponder Heart* (Music Box, Feb. 16, 1956); succeeded (Nov. 1956) Floyd Buckley as Pa Stockdale in *No Time for Sergeants* (Alvin, Oct. 20, 1955); toured as Stuyvesant in *Knickerbocker Holiday* (Summer 1956); joined the American Shakespeare Festival (Stratford, Conn.) as Antonio in *Much Ado About Nothing* (Aug. 3, 1957); played Francisco and First Gravedigger in *Hamlet* (June 19, 1958); Snout in *A Midsummer Night's Dream* (June 20, 1958); and the Old Shepherd in *A Winter's Tale* (July 20, 1958).

He played Michael Marthraum in *Cock-a-Doodle Dandy* (Carnegie Hall Playhouse, N.Y.C., Nov. 21, 1958); Adam Trueman in *Fashion* (Royal Playhouse, Jan. 20, 1959); at the American Shakespeare Festival (Stratford, Conn.), appeared as Shallow in *The Merry Wives of Windsor* (July 8, 1959), Lord Lafeu in *All's Well That Ends Well* (July 29, 1959), a Sea Captain in *Twelfth Night* (June 8, 1960), Agrippe in *Antony and Cleopatra* (July 31, 1960); toured as Snout in *A Midsummer Night's Dream* (1960); played the Banished Duke in *As You Like It* (June 27, 1961), Siward in *Macbeth* (June 28, 1961), Priam in *Troilus and Cressida* (July 23, 1961).

For the APA, he appeared as Vandergelder in *The Matchmaker*, Adam Trueman in *Fashion*, and Sir Peter Teazle in *The School for Scandal* (Folksbiene Playhouse, N.Y.C., Mar. 17, 1962); at the Univ. of Michigan Professional Th. (Ann Arbor), played Sir Peter Teazle in *The School for Scandal* (Oct. 3, 1962), Walt Whitman in *We Comrades Three* (Oct. 10, 1962), and Sir Timothy Bellboys in *A Penny for a Song* (Oct. 31, 1962).

With the American Shakespeare Festival (Stratford, Conn.), he played the Earl of Northumberland in *Richard II* and the Earl of Northumberland in *Henry IV, Part 2* (June 12–Sept. 16, 1962); for the APA at the Univ. of Michigan Professional Th. (Ann Arbor), he appeared as Robin Starveling in *A Midsummer Night's Dream* (Feb. 1963), Old Gobbo and Tubal in *The Merchant of Venice* (Feb. 20, 1963), and John of Gaunt in *Richard II* (Feb. 27, 1963). He repeated his role as Robin Starveling in *A Midsummer Night's Dream* at the Boston (Mass.) Arts Festival (July 8, 1963); played H. C. Curry in *110 in the Shade* (Broadhurst, N.Y.C., Oct. 24, 1963); Mister Mister in *The Cradle Will Rock*, which was part of a memorial to the author, Marc Blitzstein (Philharmonic Hall, Lincoln Ctr., Apr. 19, 1964); and toured with *110 in the Shade*, and *Mark Twain Meets Walt Whitman* (1964–65).

He was in *An Evening's Frost* (Mendelssohn Th., Ann Arbor, Mich., Feb. 10, 1965; Th. de Lys, N.Y.C., Oct. 11, 1965); at the San Diego (Calif.) National Shakespeare Festival (Old Globe Th.), played Sir John Falstaff in *The Merry Wives of Windsor* (June 15, 1965), Cominius in *Coriolanus* (July 13, 1965), Friar Lawrence in *Romeo and Juliet* (June 14, 1966), and Prospero in *The Tempest* (June 22, 1966); and he conceived and appeared in *Will Geer's Americana* (Th. de Lys, N.Y.C., Jan. 18, 1966). He repeated his performance as Walt Whitman in *We Comrades Three* (APA-Phoenix Repertory, Univ. of Michigan, Ann Arbor, Oct. 18, 1966; Lyceum, N.Y.C., Dec. 20, 1966); alternated as Sir Peter in *The School for Scandal* (APA Repertory, Lyceum, Nov. 21, 1966) and as the Governor in *Right You Are* (Nov. 22, 1966); repeated his performance in *An Evening's Frost* (Amer. Conservatory Th., Marines' Mem'l. Th., San Francisco, Calif., Feb. 17, 1968); was The Voice in *Horseman, Pass By* (Fortune, N.Y.C., Jan. 15, 1969); played the title role in *Scratch* (St. James Th., May 6, 1971); and again appeared in *Will Geer's Americana* (Barter Th., Abingdon, Va., May 13, 1973).

Films. He appeared in *Misleading Lady* (Par., 1930); a U.S. Film Service documentary, *Fight for Life* (1940); also *Lust for Gold* (Col., 1949); *Intruder in the Dust* (MGM, 1949); *Winchester 73* (U, 1950); *Broken Arrow* (20th-Fox, 1950); *Advise and Consent* (Col., 1962); *Seconds* (Par., 1966); *In Cold Blood* (Col., 1966); *The Reivers* (Natl. Gen., 1969); *Jeremiah Johnson* (WB, 1972); *Napoleon and Samantha* (Buena Vista, 1972); *Executive Action* (Natl. Gen., 1973); *Memory of Us* (Cinema Financial of America, 1974); and *Silence* (Cinema Financial of America, 1974).

Television. Mr. Geer has appeared on such programs as Bonanza (CBS); Gunsmoke (CBS); Mission: Impossible (CBS); Hawaii Five-O (CBS); Young Rebels (NBC); East Side/West Side (CBS); and Trials of O'Brien (CBS). He was narrator of *Journey to China* (Camera Three, CBS, Nov. 7, 1965); read selections from Robert Frost and Walt Whitman on Camera Three (CBS, Jan. 2, 1966); played Giles in *The Crucible* (Drama Special, CBS, May 4, 1967); Candy in *Of Mice and Men* (ABC, Jan. 31, 1968); was in *The Brotherhood of the Bell* (CBS, Sept. 17, 1970); and created the role of Grandpa in The Waltons (CBS, 1972–to date).

Other Activities. In Feb. 1933, Mr. Geer began operating the Folksay Th., N.Y.C., which gave weekend performances of American ballads and folklore. He has also established the Theatricum Botanicum near his Topanga Canyon, Calif., home, where productions of Shakespeare are presented and displays of Elizabethan gardens have been created by Mr. Geer.

Discography. Mr. Geer is narrator on *Woody's Story* (Folkways 1973).

Awards. Mr. Geer was a recipient (shared with the Establishment Th. Co.) of the $500 Lola D'Annunzio Award in 1966 for "his continued contribution to off-Broadway theatre over the years and for his portrayal of Robert Frost in *An Evening's Frost.*".

Recreation. Plant breeding, medieval and Shakespearean gardens.

GELB, ARTHUR. Editor, writer, critic. b. Feb. 3, 1924, New York City, to Daniel and Fannie (Gehrig) Gelb. Grad. DeWitt Clinton H.S., 1940; grad. New York Univ., B.A. 1946. Married June 2, 1946, to Barbara Stone; two sons. Address: New York Times, 229 W. 43rd St., New York, NY 10036, tel. (212) LA 4-1000. Since Oct. 1, 1967, Mr. Gelb has been metropolitan editor of the NY *Times*, where he had been general assignment reporter and critic (1954–63), chief cultural reporter and assistant director of cultural news (1962–63), and assistant metropolitan editor (1963–67).

Published Works. Mr. Gelb, with his wife Barbara Gelb, wrote *O'Neill* (1962).

GELB, BARBARA. Writer. Grad. Swarthmore Coll., 1946. Married June 2, 1946, to Arthur Gelb, NY *Times* assistant managing editor; two sons.

Mrs. Gelb, with her husband, is the author of *O'Neill*, (1962), a biography of Eugene O'Neill.

Other Activities. She is the author of *So Short a Time; A Biography of John Reed and Louise Bryant* (1973); with her husband, wrote Salvatore B. Cutolo's autobiographical account, *Bellevue Is My Home* (1973); and wrote *On the Tracks of Murder* (1975).

GELB, JAMES. Stage manager, director. Member of AEA.

Theatre. Mr. Gelb was stage manager for *Prologue to Glory* (Maxine Elliott's Th., N.Y.C., Mar. 17, 1938); *Close Quarters* (John Golden Th., Mar. 6, 1939); a season of stock (Cedarhurst, N.Y., Summer 1939); assistant stage manager for *One Touch of Venus* (Imperial, N.Y.C., Oct. 7, 1943); stage manager for *Trio* (Belasco, Dec. 29, 1944); *Dunnigan's Daughter* (John Golden Th., Dec. 26, 1945); *Finian's Rainbow* (46 St. Th., Jan. 10, 1947), and directed its London production (Palace, Oct. 21, 1947).

He was stage manager for *The Biggest Thief in Town* (Mansfield, N.Y.C., Mar. 30, 1949); *The Bird Cage* (Coronet, Feb. 22, 1950); *Courtin' Time* (National, June 13, 1951); *Lace on Her Petticoat* (Booth, Sept. 4, 1951); *Desire Under the Elms* (ANTA, Jan. 16, 1952); *Golden Boy* (ANTA, Mar. 12, 1952); *Sunday Breakfast* (Coronet, May 28, 1952); and directed a N.Y.C. subway circuit tour of *The Time of the Cuckoo* (opened Jamaica Th., N.Y., June 30, 1953).

Mr. Gelb was stage manager for *The Ladies of the Corridor* (Longacre, Oct. 21, 1953); *Mademoiselle Colombe* (Longacre, Jan. 6, 1954); *The Traveling Lady* (Playhouse, Oct. 27, 1954); *Festival* (Longacre, Jan. 18, 1955); *Once Upon a Tailor* (Cort, May 23, 1955); *Tiger at the Gates* (Plymouth, Oct. 3, 1955); *Henry V* and *Saint Joan* (Sander's Hall, Harvard Univ., Mass., Summer 1956); *The Sleeping Prince* (Coronet, N.Y.C., Nov. 1, 1956); *Orpheus Descending* (Martin Beck Th., Mar. 21, 1957); *Fanny* (Philharmonic Aud., Los Angeles, Calif., Summer 1957); *Goldilocks* (Lunt-Fontanne Th., N.Y.C., Oct. 11, 1958); *The Cold Wind and the Warm* (Morosco, Dec. 8, 1958); *Flowering Cherry* (Lyceum, Oct. 21, 1959); the pre-Bway tryout of *Sweet Love Remember'd* (opened Shubert, New Haven, Conn., Dec. 28, 1959; closed there Dec. 31, 1959); *Invitation to a March* (Music Box, N.Y.C., Oct. 29, 1960); *Mandingo* (Lyceum, May 22, 1961); *Milk and Honey* (Martin Beck Th., Oct. 10, 1961); *Too True To Be Good* (54 St. Th., Mar. 12, 1963); *A Rainy Day in Newark* (Belasco, Oct. 22, 1963); and *Anyone Can Whistle* (Majestic, Apr. 4, 1964).

Mr. Gelb was production stage manager for *A Girl Could Get Lucky* (Cort, N.Y.C., Sept. 20, 1964); *The Amen Corner* (Ethel Barrymore Th., Apr. 15, 1965); *The Impossible Years* (Playhouse, Oct. 13, 1965); the pre-Bway tryout of *Chu Chem* (opened New Locust, Philadelphia, Nov. 15, 1966; closed there Nov. 19, 1966); *Hallelujah, Baby!* (Martin Beck Th., N.Y.C., Apr. 26, 1967); *Portrait of a Queen* (Henry Miller's Th., Feb. 28, 1968); *Cry for Us All* (Broadhurst, Apr. 8, 1970); the revival of *Man of La Mancha* (Vivian Beaumont Th., June 22, 1972); and production co-ordinator for the pre-Bway tryout of *Halloween* (Bucks County Playhouse, New Hope, Pa., opened Sept. 20, 1972; closed there Oct. 1, 1972); and production stage manager for *Irene* (Minskoff, Mar. 13, 1973).

GELBART, LARRY S. Writer. b. Larry Simon Gelbart, Feb. 25, 1923, Chicago, Ill., to Harry and Frieda Gelbart. Father, barber. Attended John Marshall H.S., Chicago, Ill.; Fairfax H.S., Los Angeles, Calif. Married Nov. 25, 1956, to Pat Marshall, actress-singer; three sons, two daughters. Served US Army, 1946–47. Member of WGA; Dramatists Guild; ASCAP. Address: Ghent, NY 12075, tel. (518) Chatham 8-7014.

Theatre. Mr. Gelbart wrote the book for the musical, *The Conquering Hero* (ANTA Th., N.Y.C., Jan. 16, 1961); and with Burt Shevelove, wrote the libretto for *A Funny Thing Happened on the Way to the Forum* (Alvin, May 8, 1962).

Films. He wrote the screenplay for *The Notorious Landlady* (Col., 1962); the story for *The Thrill of It All* (U, 1963); the screenplay, with Burt Shevelove, for *The Wrong Box* (Col., 1966); with Norman Panama and Peter Barnes, for *Not with My Wife, You Don't* (WB, 1966); and the book by him and Burt Shevelove was the basis for the screenplay for *A Funny Thing Happened on the Way to the Forum* (UA, 1966).

Television and Radio. For radio in Hollywood, Mr. Gelbart wrote scripts for the Fanny Brice Show (CBS, May 1946); and Duffy's Tavern (NBC, Sept. 1946); wrote the Command Performance series (Armed Forces Radio Service, 1946–47); wrote for the Joan Davis Show (CBS, 1949); Jack Paar Show (CBS, 1949); and the Bob Hope Show (NBC, Sept. 1949–52).

In N.Y.C., he began writing for television with the Red Buttons Show (CBS, Sept. 1952); was a member of the CBS writing staff (Sept. 1953–54); from 1954–62, wrote for the Patrice Munsel Show (ABC), the Sid Caesar Show (NBC, Sept. 1955–57), the Pat Boone Show (ABC), four programs for Art Carney Specials (CBS, Apr. 1962); the Sid Caesar special (CBS, Apr. 5, 1967); the Marty Feldman Show (ABC, 1971); and for M*A*S*H (CBS, 1972).

Awards. Mr. Gelbart received both a NATAS (Emmy) Award and a Sylvania Award for writing the Art Carney Specials (1958); the Antoinette Perry (Tony) Award, with Burt Shevelove, for *A Funny Thing Happened on the Way to the Forum* (1963).

Recreation. "Raising and enjoying my five children.".

GELBER, JACK. Playwright. b. Jack Allen Gelber, Apr. 12, 1932, Chicago, Ill., to Harold and Molly (Singer) Gelber. Father, tinsmith. Grad. Univ. of Illinois, B.S. (journalism) 1953. Married Dec. 22, 1957, to Carol Westenberg; one son, one daughter. Address: (home) 697 West End Ave., New York, NY 10025, tel. (212) AC 2-6076; (bus.) c/o Ronald Konecky, One Dag Hammarskjold Plaza, New York, NY 10017, tel. (212) 754-1452.

Theatre. Mr. Gelber is the author of *The Connection* (Living Th., N.Y.C. July 15, 1959); *The Apple* (Living Th., Dec. 7, 1961); *Square in the Eye* (Th. de Lys, May 19, 1965). He then directed *The Kitchen* (New, May 9, 1966) and *Indians* (world premiere, London, England, July 4, 1968). He wrote and directed *The Cuban Thing* (Henry Miller's Th., N.Y.C., Sept. 24, 1968); directed *Kool Aid* (Forum, Nov. 3, 1971); wrote *Sleep* (American Place Th., Feb. 10, 1972); directed *The Chickencoop Chinamen* (May 27, 1972) and *The Kid* (Nov. 2, 1972), both at American Place Theatre; wrote and adapted from Norman Mailer's novel and directed *Barbary Shore* (Public Th., Jan. 13, 1974).

Films. He wrote the screenplay for *The Connection* (FAW, 1962).

Other Activities. At Columbia Univ., Mr. Gelber was an associate professor in the Graduate Th. Dept. (1967–72), and since 1972 he has been an associate professor at Brooklyn College.

Published Works. Mr. Gelber wrote the novel *On Ice* (1974).

Awards. Mr. Gelber received *The Village Voice* Off-Bway (Obie) Award for *The Connection* (1959–60); won the *Variety* NY Drama Critics' Poll, (1959–60); received the Vernon Rice Award (1959–60); Guggenheim fellowships (1963–64 and 1966–67); was a Rockefeller playwright-in-residence (1972); received the Obie as best director for his work on *The Kid* (1972–1973); and was a National Endowment Fellow (1974) and a CBS Fellow at Yale (1974).

GENET, JEAN. Playwright, novelist, poet. b. Dec. 19, 1910, Paris, France, to Gabrielle Genet. Sent to reform school for stealing (1920). Condemned to life imprisonment (1948), after 10 convictions for theft in France; granted a pardon by President Auriol as a result of the efforts of France's leading men of letters. Address: c/o Grove Press, 64 University Place, New York, NY 10003.

Theatre. Mr. Genet's *The Maids (Les bonnes)*, his second play, was the first to be staged, in a production of Louis Jouvet (Athénée, Paris, France, Apr. 19, 1947). This was followed by a French production in England (Institute of Contemporary Arts, Mercury Th., London, Oct. 29, 1952) and one in English (New Lindsey Th. Club, June 5, 1956); the US premiere was in N.Y.C. (Tempo Playhouse, May 6, 1955). M. Genet's first play, *Deathwatch (Haute surveillance)*, written in 1944–45, was produced in Paris by the author (Th. des Mathurins, Feb. 24, 1949); this was followed by productions in N.Y.C. (Th. East, Oct. 9, 1958) and London (Arts, June 25, 1961).

M. Genet's *The Balcony (Le balcon)* received its world premiere in a private London performance (Arts Theatre Club, Apr. 22, 1957), was performed in N.Y.C. (Circle in the Square, Mar. 3, 1960), and in Paris, France, directed by Peter Brook (Th. du Gymnase, May 18, 1960).

His *The Blacks (Les nègres)* was written in 1957, first performed in Paris under the direction of Roger Blin by a group of Negro actors, Les Griots (Th. de Lutèce, Oct. 28, 1959), and produced in N.Y.C. (St. Mark's Playhouse, May 4, 1961).

His *The Screens (Les paravents)* was published in 1961 and part of it was premiered in West Berlin, Germany (Schlosspark Th., May 19, 1961). The first twelve of its seventeen scenes were staged by Peter Brook and Charles Marowitz with members of the Royal Shakespeare Co. Experimental Th. Group (Donmar Rehearsal Rooms, London, May 4, 1964); the first performance of the complete play was in Swedish (Alléteatern, Stockholm, Sweden, Summer 1964). This was followed by a French production (Odéon–Th. de France, Paris, Apr. 16, 1966), and the first production in English of the complete play was in N.Y.C. (Chelsea Th. Ctr. of Brooklyn Acad. of Music, Nov. 30, 1971).

Films. Motion pictures of M. Genet's plays include *the Balcony* (Cont., 1963) and an independently filmed version of *Deathwatch*, shown at the 1965 San Francisco (Calif.) Film Festival. He wrote the screenplay for *Mademoiselle* (Lopert-Woodfall, 1966).

Published Works. Bernard Frechtman translated all of M. Genet's plays into English, and they have been published in the US: *Deathwatch* and *The Maids* (both 1954); *The Balcony* (1958); *The Blacks* (1960); and *The Screens* (1962).

M. Genet's other works include poems and five novels; all but one of the novels were translated into English by Mr. Frechtman: *Notre-Dame des fleurs* (1944), translated as *Our Lady of the Flowers* (1949; pub. in US, 1963); *Miracle de la rose* (1946), translated as *Miracle of the Rose* (pub. in US, 1965); *Pompes funèbres* (1947), translated as *Funeral Rites* (pub. in US, 1969); *Querelle de Brest* (1947), translated into English by Anselm Hollo as *Querelle* (pub. in US, 1974); and *Journal du voleur* (1949), published in the US as *The Thief's Journal* (1964) as translated by Mr. Frechtman. M. Genet's novels

and his poems are collected in the French editions, *Oeuvres complètes*, vol. 2 (1951) and vol. 3 (1953).
Awards. M. Genet received *The Village Voice* off-Bway (Obie) Award for *The Balcony* (1960) and *The Blacks* (1962).

GENN, LEO. Actor. b. Aug. 9, 1905, London, England, to Willy and Ray (Asserson) Genn. Father, merchant. Grad. City of London Sch., 1924; Cambridge Univ., B.A. 1927. Married May 1933, to Marguerite van Praag. Served British Army, 1938–45; awarded Croix de Guerre; rank, Lt. Col. Member of AEA; SAG; AFTRA; Garrick Club; Savage Club; Stage Golfing Society; The Travellers (Paris).

Theatre. Mr. Genn made his American debut as Commander Henry Carr in *The Flashing Stream* (Biltmore, Apr. 10, 1939); followed by Benjamin Hubbard in *Another Part of the Forest* (Fulton, Nov. 20, 1946); General Sir William Howe in *Small War on Murray Hill* (Ethel Barrymore Th., Jan. 3, 1957); Monsignor Blaise Meredith in *The Devil's Advocate* (Billy Rose Th., Mar. 9, 1961); Chester Witten in *Fair Game for Lovers* (Cort, Feb. 10, 1964); Thomas Lockwood in *The Only Game in Town* (Broadhurst, May 20, 1968); Caesar in *Caesar and Cleopatra* (University Th., State Coll., Pa., Feb. 22, 1968); and the title role in *Dr. Faustus* (Pioneer Th., Salt Lake City, Utah, Oct. 1969).

He made his London debut as Peter in *A Marriage Has Been Disarranged* (Royalty, Dec. 9, 1930); subsequently played Mr. Ackroyd in *No. 17* (Royalty, Dec. 26, 1930); Rudolf Menelli in *Money, Money!* (Royalty, Feb. 24, 1931); Clement in *Tiger Cats* (Royalty, May 27, 1931); Thomas in *Judas* (Royalty, June 23, 1931); Patrick in *Champion North* (Royalty, Nov. 27, 1931); Buckie's Daddy in *Buckie's Bears* (Royalty, Dec. 26, 1931; Garrick, Dec. 19, 1932); Neville Hammond in *While Parents Sleep* (Royalty, Jan. 19, 1932); Singh in *Beggars in Hell* (Garrick, Apr. 17, 1933); Nurdo in *Ballerina* (Gaiety, Oct. 10, 1933); and Wedderburn in *Clive of India* (Wyndham's, Jan. 25, 1934).

With the Old Vic Co., he appeared as Sextus Pompeius and Eros in *Antony and Cleopatra* (Sept. 17, 1934); Duke of Norfolk, Scroop, and Exton in *Richard II* (Oct. 15, 1934); Don John in *Much Ado About Nothing* (Nov. 5, 1934); Dunois in *Saint Joan* (Nov. 26, 1934); Cassio in *Othello* (Jan. 21, 1935) Tranio in *The Taming of the Shrew* (Jan. 1, 1935); Bill Walker in *Major Barbara* (Mar. 4, 1935); the Archbishop of York in *Henry IV, Part II* (Mar. 25, 1935); Horatio in *Hamlet* (Apr. 29, 1935); various roles in *Peer Gynt* (Sept. 23, 1935); Brutus in *Julius Caesar* (Oct. 22, 1935); Macduff in *Macbeth* (Dec. 3, 1935); Joseph Surface in *The School for Scandal* (Dec. 20, 1935); Tyrrel in *Richard III* (Jan. 14, 1936); and General Montholon in *St. Helena* (Feb. 4, 1936; Daly's, Mar. 19, 1936).

Also, Dr. Cardin in *The Children's Hour* (Gate, Nov. 12, 1936); Orsino in *Twelfth Night* (Old Vic, Feb. 23, 1937); Duke of Burgundy in *Henry V* (Old Vic, Apr. 6, 1937); Horatio in an Old Vic production of *Hamlet* (Elsinore Castle, Helsingor, Den., June, 1937); Commander Henry Carr in *The Flashing Stream* (Lyric, London, Sept. 1, 1938); Paul Nathan in *Juggernaut* (Saville, June 28, 1939); the Prince of Wales in *The Jersey Lily* (Gate, Apr. 10, 1940); King David in *Jonathan* (Aldwych, July 29, 1948); Nicholas Cunningham in *The Seventh Veil* (Prince's, Mar. 14, 1951); Duke of Buckingham in *Henry VIII* (Old Vic, May 6, 1953); John Brunton in *The Bombshell* (Westminster, May 11, 1954); Jean Monnerie in *The Hidden River* (Cambridge, Apr. 13, 1959); Juror No. 8 in *Twelve Angry Men*, which he produced with Rero Productions, Ltd., in association with Kenneth Wagg (Queens Th., July 9, 1964); and was Major Liconda in a revival of The Sacred Flame (Duke of York's, Feb. 2, 1967).

Films. Mr. Genn made his debut in *Jump for Glory* (Criterion, 1937); followed by *The Rat* (RKO, 1938); *Drums* (UA, 1938); *Kate Plus Ten* (Wainwright, 1938); *Contraband* (London Films, 1940); was narrator for *Desert Victory* (20th-Fox, 1943); appeared in *The Way Ahead* (20th-Fox, 1945); *Henry V* (UA, 1946); *Caesar and Cleopatra* (UA, 1946); *Green for Danger* (Eagle Lion, 1947); *Mourning Becomes Electra* (RKO, 1947); *The Velvet Touch* (RKO, 1948); *The Snake Pit* (20th-Fox, 1948); *The Wooden Horse* (London Films, 1949); *The Miniver Story* (MGM, 1950); *Quo Vadis* (MGM, 1951); *Plymouth Adventure* (MGM, 1952); *Affair in Monte Carlo* (Allied, 1953); was narrator for *Elizabeth Is Queen* (1953); appeared in *The Paratrooper* (Col., 1954); *The Green Scarf* (Associated Artists, 1955); *Moby Dick* (WB, 1956); *Chantage* (Blackmail, French, 1956); *Beyond Mombasa* (Col., 1957); *Steel Bayonet* (UA, 1958); *Lady Chatterley's Lover* (Kingsley, 1959); *Too Hot To Handle* (MGM, 1959); *No Time To Die* (Col., 1959); *The Longest Day* (20th-Fox, 1962); *55 Days at Peking* (Bronston, 1963); *Circus of Fear* (Allied Artists, 1966); *Ten Little Indians* (7 Arts, 1966); *Connecting Rooms* (London Screen, 1969); *Night of the Blood Monster* (Amer. Inter., 1972); *A Lizard in a Woman's Skin* (Amer. Inter., 1973); and *Escape to Nowhere* (Peppercorn-Wormser, 1974).

Television and Radio. In London, Mr. Genn narrated the radio programs for the coronations of George VI (1937) and Elizabeth II (1953). In the US, he played King Herod in *Salome* (Omnibus, CBS, Dec. 18, 1955); appeared on Your Show of Shows (NBC, 1952); in *Mrs. Miniver* (NBC, 1960); on The Defenders (CBS); in *The Colossus* (Apr. 1963); in *Days of Gavin Heath* on The Defenders (CBS, Dec. 1963); *The Fifth Passenger* (Bob Hope Chrysler Th., Aug. 1963); *Saint Joan* (Hallmark Hall of Fame, NBC, Dec. 1967); *Strange Report* (NBC, 1971); and Persuaders (ABC, 1972).

Other Activities. Mr. Genn has been a member of the Court of Governors, Mermaid Th., London; the Council of Arts Educational Trust, London; and on the Council of the Yvonne Arnaud Memorial Th., Guildford, England. He was visiting professor of drama, Univ. of Utah (1965); and Distinguished Visiting Professor of Theatre Arts, Penn. State Univ. (State Coll., Pa., 1968).

Awards. He received an Academy (Oscar) Award for his performance as Gaius Petronius in *Quo Vadis* (1951).

Recreation. Farming, golf, law.

GENNARO, PETER. Producer, choreographer, dancer. b. Metairie, La., to Charles and Conchetta Gennaro. Father, tavern owner. Grad. Metairie H.S.; studied at the Amer. Theatre Wing, N.Y.C., 1949. Married Jan. 24, 1948, to Jean Kinsella; one son, one daughter. Served US Army, 1944; rank, Staff Sgt. Member of AFTRA, SSD&C. Address: 228 Alpine Drive, Paramus, NJ 07652.

Pre-Theatre. Operated father's tavern.

Theatre. Mr. Gennaro made his debut as a dancer with the San Carlo Opera Co. (Chicago Opera House, Ill., 1948).

He made his N.Y.C. debut in the revue, *Make Mine Manhattan* (Broadhurst, Jan. 15, 1948); subsequently danced in *Kiss Me, Kate* (Century, Dec. 30, 1948); *Arms and the Girl* (46 St. Th., Feb. 2, 1950); *Guys and Dolls* (46 St. Th., Nov. 24, 1950); *By the Beautiful Sea* (Majestic, Apr. 8, 1954); and he played the Worker, and danced the "Steam Heat" number in *The Pajama Game* (St. James, May 13, 1954).

Mr. Gennaro was choreographer for the musical, *Seventh Heaven*, adapted from the play of the same title (ANTA, May 26, 1955); and played Carl in *Bells Are Ringing* (Shubert, Nov. 29, 1956). With director Jerome Robbins, he choreographed *West Side Story* (Winter Garden, Sept. 26, 1957). Mr. Gennaro was the choreographer for *Fiorello!* (Broadhurst, Nov. 23, 1959); *The Unsinkable Molly Brown* (Winter Garden, Nov. 3, 1960); and *Mr. President* (St. James, Oct. 20, 1962).

He staged the musical numbers for *Bajour* (Sam S. Shubert Th., Nov. 23, 1964); *Jimmy* (Winter Garden, Oct. 23, 1969); and the revival of *Irene* (Minskoff Th., Mar. 13, 1973). He has been producer/choreographer at Radio City Music Hall, N.Y.C. (Sept. 1971–to date).

Films. Mr. Gennaro was the choreographer for the film version of *The Unsinkable Molly Brown* (MGM, 1964).

Television. He has been dancer or choreographer for the Ed Sullivan Show (CBS); the Judy Garland Show (CBS); the Andy Williams Show (NBC); the Red Skelton Show (CBS); the Bell Telephone Hour (NBC); the Perry Como Show (NBC); and the Tonight Show (NBC). He was a guest on the Robert Goulet special (CBS, Nov. 19, 1964); choreographed *The Andy Griffith, Don Knotts, Jim Nabors Special* (CBS, Oct. 7, 1965); appeared on Hollywood Palace (ABC, 1965–66); the *Words and Music by Cole Porter* special (NBC, Nov. 25, 1965); choreographed *Brigadoon* (ABC, Oct. 15, 1966); appeared in *Rodgers and Hart Today* (Stage 67, ABC, Mar. 2, 1967); and choreographed the *Zero Hour* special (ABC, May 1, 1967).

Awards. Mr. Gennaro twice received the DEA (Dance Educators of America) Dance Award for his contribution to dance (1957, 1961); received a *Dance* magazine award (1964); and was nominated for an Antoinette Perry (Tony) Award as best choreographer for *Irene*. .

Recreation. Swimming, painting, teaching.

GEOLY, ANDREW. Theatrical costumer. b. Aug. 5, 1907, to Charles and Constance (Ciofalo) Geoly. Father, president of Eaves Costume Co.; mother, officer in same company. Married June 5, 1927, to Mildred Snyder; two sons, one daughter. Member of The Lambs; The Friars; AETA; Catholic Th. Guild; Jewish Th. Guild; Pine Holly Country Club. Eaves Costume Co., 151 W. 46th St., New York, NY 10036, tel. (212) PL 7-3730.

Mr. Geoly began in 1925 as an errand boy in his father's firm, the Eaves Costume Company, which has supplied costumes since 1870. Subsequently, he became shopper, stockboy, salesman, workroom supervisor, and finally president of the firm (1959).

Eaves Costume Company established the Eaves Award in 1958, which it granted annually until 1962, for outstanding educational theatre work. The selection was made by AETA in two categories: Senior, for a university or college theatre, and Junior, for a secondary-school official or organization. The prizes were $1000 in the senior division and $500 in the junior.

Recreation. Golf, collecting costume books.

GERARD, ROLF. Set designer, costume designer. b. c.1910, Berlin, Germany. Educated in Switzerland and Germany.

Theatre. In 1936, Mr. Gerard went to England, where he designed productions of *Figaro* (Royal Opera House, Covent Garden), and *Cosi fan Tutti* (Edinburgh Festival); and various ballets for the Sadlers Wells Company, as well as numerous plays and reviews for other companies.

On Bway, he made his American debut as designer of sets and costumes for *That Lady* (Martin Beck Th., N.Y.C., Nov. 22, 1949); followed by *Caesar and Cleopatra* (National, Dec. 21, 1949); the sets for the pre-Bway tryout of *Captain Carvallo* (Erlanger, Buffalo, N.Y., Dec. 6, 1950); and for *An Evening with Beatrice Lillie* (Booth, N.Y.C., Oct. 2, 1952); sets and costumes for *The Love of Four Colonels* (Sam S. Shubert Th., Jan. 15, 1953); *The Strong Are Lonely* (Broadhurst, Sept. 29, 1953); *The Fighting Cock* (ANTA, Dec. 8, 1959); and *Irma La Douce* (Plymouth, Sept. 29, 1960); and sets for *Tovarich* (Broadway Th., Mar. 18, 1963).

For the Metropolitan Opera Co. (N.Y.C., 1949–69), Mr. Gerard designed the settings and costumes for productions of *Don Carlos, Die Fledermaus, Aida, Cosi fan Tutti, Carmen, La Bohème, Faust, Tannhauser, Arabella, The Tales of Hoffman, Der Rosenkavalier, Pagliacci, Cavalleria Rusticana, The Gypsy Baron, Les Sylphides, Romeo et Juliette* and *Orfeo et Euridice*, and costumes for *La Traviata*. .

Other Activities. Mr. Gerard is a painter and sculptor. He has been exhibited at various galleries including Wildenstein's (N.Y.C., 1961), and a retrospective entitled *Twenty Years at the Met* was shown at the Wright-Hepburn-Webster Gallery (N.Y.C., 1969).

GERBER, ELLA. Director, actress, playwright, acting coach. b. Aug. 25, 1916, New York City, to Isadore and Esther (Treisman) Gerber. Father, linguist; mother, seamstress. Attended Columbia Univ., 1942–43; Univ. of Birmingham Shakespeare Inst., Stratford-upon-Avon, Eng., 1955; New York Univ. (Television and Film Workshop), 1962. Studied acting in N.Y.C. (1934–38) with Lee Strasberg, Sanford Meisner, Morris Carnovsky, Louis Leverett, Mary Virginia Farmer, Benno Schneider, Margaret Barker; acting with Michael Chekhov, N.Y.C., 1942; Amer. Theatre Wing, N.Y.C., 1948–49; Robert Lewis Th. Workshop, N.Y.C., 1960–61; Actors' Studio, N.Y.C. (mbr., directors unit, 1960–62). Married May 29, 1943, to Sam Kasakoff, actor, photographer. Served as civilian actress-technician with US Army Special Services, 1945–47. Member of AEA; AFTRA; SSD&C. Address: 329 E. 58th St., New York, NY 10022, tel. (212) 688-2356.

Theatre. Miss Gerber made her debut with the Knickerbocker Players and the Playmart Productions (N.Y.C., 1933–34); subsequently appeared in stock productions with the Lippitt Players (Cumberland Hill, R.I., Summer 1936); played in the revue, *Pins and Needles* (Labor Stage Th., N.Y.C., June 18, 1938; moved Windsor, 1939), and toured cross-country in it (June 1940–May 1941); appeared in *Theatre Brief*, which was comprised of scenes from the plays, *Idiot's Delight, Private Lives, Winterset, Our Town*, and *Michael and Mary* (Barbizon-Plaza, Nov. 1941), and toured in it; danced in *Lunch Hour Follies*, which the American Th. Wing presented in war plants on the East Coast (1942); and directed war plant productions on the West Coast (1943).

She directed productions in community centers (Los Angeles, Calif., 1943); a summer production of *Blind Alley* (Th. Vanguard, Hollywood, Calif., Aug. 1945); for the US Army Special Services, appeared as Laura in *The Glass Menagerie* (Univ. of Hawaii, Feb. 18, 1946); directed and appeared in *My Sister Eileen, Room Service*, and *Goodbye Again* (Ernie Pyle Th., Tokyo, Japan, Mar. 1946), also touring theatres in Japan (Apr. 1946) and Korea (Feb. 1947).

Miss Gerber directed *Lucy* (Coronet, Hollywood, Calif., Sept. 1948); the ELT production of *Dark of the Moon* (Lenox Hill Playhouse, N.Y.C., Feb. 14, 1949); productions at the Fairhaven (Mass.) Summer Th. (June 1949); *Design for a Stained-Glass Window* (Mansfield, N.Y.C., Jan. 23, 1950); the ELT production of *Primrose Path* (Lenox Hill Playhouse, Apr. 7, 1950); *Home Coming* (Th. 108, Mar. 1950); summer productions at the Watkins Glen (N.Y.) Th. and the Bradford (Pa.) Th. (1950); *Summer and Smoke* and *My Sister Eileen* (Le Petit Théâtre du Vieux Carré, New Orleans, La., Sept. 1950); *Dark of the Moon;* (Youngstown Playhouse, Ohio, Mar. 7, 1951); and *The Glass Menagerie* (Corning Summer Th., N.Y., Oct. 10, 1951).

She directed the ELT double-bill of *All God's Chillun Got Wings* and *O Distant Land* (Lenox Hill Playhouse, N.Y.C., Mar. 26, 1952); was dramatic coach and assistant to the director, Robert Breen, for *Porgy and Bess* (Ziegfeld, Mar. 10, 1953), also on world tour (June 1952–June 1955); directed productions at the Lakewood Summer Playhouse (Barnsville, Pa., 1956); productions at the Peabody Summer Th. (Daytona Beach, Fla., 1957); *Porgy and Bess* (Civic Light Opera Co., Pittsburgh, Pa., June 1958), and a summer tour of it; the ELT productions of *Dial 'M' for Murder* (Lenox Hill Playhouse, N.Y.C., Jan. 29, 1958), and *Flight into Egypt* (Lenox Hill Playhouse, Apr. 17, 1958); productions at the Oakdale Music Th. (Wallingford, Conn.) and the Warwick (R.I.) Music Th. (Summer 1959); appeared as Emily in *Inside Emily Payne* (Erie Playhouse, Pa., Oct. 1959); directed *Look Homeward, Angel* (Youngstown Playhouse, Pa., Oct. 14, 1960); *Dark of the Moon* (Acorn Civic Th., Miami Beach, Fla., Nov. 1960), and productions (Summer 1960) at the Oakdale Music Th. (Wallingford, Conn.), Warwick (R.I.) Music Th.; Northland Playhouse (Detroit, Mich.); Dixie Plaza Music Th. (Toronto, Ontario, Canada); Colonie Music Th. (Latham, N.Y.); and the Kenley Playhouse (Warren, Ohio).

Miss Gerber directed *Blue Island* (New Dramatists' Studio, N.Y.C., Mar. 1960); *The Tiger Rag* (Cherry Lane, N.Y.C., Feb. 16, 1961); *Dark of the Moon* (Th. Servi, Rome, Italy, June 1961); *Skylark* (Drury Lane, Chicago, Ill., Oct. 1961); *Come Blow Your Horn* (Coconut Grove Playhouse, Miami, Fla., Jan. 1962); productions at the Gladiators Arena Th. (North Totowa, N.J., Dec. 1962; July–Aug. 1963); a tour of *Gypsy* (Camden County Music Fair, Haddenfield, N.J.; Valley Forge Music Fair, Pa.; Westbury Music Fair, L.I., N.Y.; Painters Mill Th., Md.; Storrowtown Music Fair, Springfield, Mass., Summer 1962); played the Madame in *The Laundry* (Gate, N.Y.C., Feb. 13, 1963); directed *Kiss Me, Kate* (Oakdale Music Th., Wallingford, Conn., July 1963); *Come Blow Your Horn* (Youngstown Playhouse, Ohio, Oct. 31, 1963); *See How They Run* (Youngstown Playhouse, Feb. 13, 1964) *The Unsinkable Molly Brown* (Theatre Inc., Houston, Tex., Mar. 18, 1964); *Milk and Honey* and *Guys and Dolls* (Coconut Grove Playhouse, Miami, Fla., Spring, 1964); and *Porgy and Bess* (St. Louis Municipal Opera, Mo.; Starlight Th., Kansas City, Mo.; Aug. 1964).

Miss Gerber was artistic director of the Youngstown (Ohio) Playhouse during 1964–65.

In 1965, Miss Gerber directed additional productions of *Porgy and Bess*, one for the New Zealand Opera Co., which played at the Pan-Pacific Arts Festival (Christ Church, 1965) and toured North and South islands, and others that played in N.Y.C. (NY City Ctr. Opera), Canada, Wisconsin, Massachusetts, Connecticut, New Jersey, Pennsylvania, Maryland and Florida. She directed *Gypsy* (Coconut Grove Playhouse, Fla., 1965) and in Ohio directed *Wonderful Town, Miracle Worker, Desperate Hours*, and *A Thousand Clowns* (all 1965). In 1966, she directed a summer theatre-in-the-round tour of *Camelot* (New Jersey, Pennsylvania, and Maryland); *Clearing in the Woods* (Amer. Acad. of Dramatic Arts of NY); and additional productions of *Porgy and Bess:* one in Israel (Habimah Th., Tel Aviv) and tour; one in the US (Butler Univ., Indianapolis) and US and Canadian tour; and another New Zealand production, this time with an all-Maori cast, that toured New Zealand and Australia, appearing also at the Adelaide Arts Festival.

In 1967 she directed *Gypsy* for a summer theatre tour and *Little Foxes* (Amer. Acad. of Dramatic Arts), and in 1968 she directed *Carousel* in South Africa (Johannesburg Operatic Society) and excerpts from *The Consul, The Telephone*, and *Porgy and Bess* (London Opera Centre, London, England). She directed an Equity Th. production of *Lost in the Stars* (Master Th., N.Y.C., Mar. 22, 1968); *Holy Hang-Up* (Spencer Memorial Ch., N.Y.C., 1968); and *Peer Gynt* (Amer. Musical and Dramatic Acad., N.Y.C., 1968).

In 1969, Miss Gerber directed *The Miser* for Th. Nashville (Vanderbilt Univ., Nashville, Tenn.); *Hallelujah Train* for a college and university tour; productions of *Muzeeka, Private Ear, Used Car for Sale, The Boor, Marriage Proposal*, and *The Man with the Flower in His Mouth*, all for Arts/Six, a Title 3 educational theatre project, for schools in Brookline, Waltham, and Belmont, Mass.; and she directed *You Can't Take It with You* (Youngstown Playhouse, Ohio). In 1970, she directed more plays for Arts/Six: *The Lesson, Lunchtime Concert, This Property Is Condemned, The Animal*, and *Loveliest Afternoon of the Year*, which were presented in Lexington, Watertown, and Newton, Mass., schools. She also directed in 1970 the tricentennial celebration production of *Porgy and Bess* for Charleston, S.C.

In 1971, she directed *School for Wives* and *Summertree* (Wayside Th., Middletown, Va.), and in 1972 she directed *The Madwoman of Chaillot* (Duke Univ., Durham, N.C.) and two additional productions of *Porgy and Bess*, for the Memphis (Tenn.) Opera Co. at Memphis Univ. and in Fort Worth, Tex. (Casa Manana Th.). In 1973, she directed *The Flying Doctor, Marriage Proposal, The Lovers*, and *The Chinamen*, all for the South Carolina Open Road Ensemble of Columbia, S.C., making an educational theatre tour throughout South Carolina. She also directed in 1973 *Love and Conflict*, a series of classic scenes for a Th. in Education tour in North Carolina, New Jersey, Connecticut, and New York. Recent productions of *Porgy and Bess* directed by Miss Gerber include those at the Teatre Nacional de San Carlos of Lisbon, Portugal (1973); the Los Angeles Civic Light Opera Co. (Ahmanson Th., May 21, 1974); and Th. of the Stars, Atlanta, Ga. (Aug. 1974).

Films. She directed an industrial film, *Fashion Over the Shoe*, for US Rubber Co. (1949); and appeared in *Barabbas* (Col., 1962).

Television. She has appeared on numerous interview programs in the US, relating to her directorial efforts. With Howard Richardson, she wrote *Aftermath of a Conviction* (True Story, NBC, 1960).

Other Activities. Miss Gerber has been on the faculty, Amer. Acad. of Dramatic Arts (AADA), N.Y.C., since 1966 and on the faculty, Amer. Musical and Dramatic Acad., N.Y.C., since 1967. She conducted acting classes and directed at private schools, summer camps, settlement houses, and community theatres (1935–43); was dramatic director for community center, Los Angeles, Calif. (1943–45); operated the Studio of the Th. (1947–48); was on the AADA faculty (1957–59); conducted an acting and directing seminar for the Acorn Civic Th., Miami Beach, Fla. (1962); conducted acting classes for the Canadian Drama Guild, Canadian Drama Studio, Montreal, Que. (1963) and for the Youngstown (Ohio) Playhouse (1963–64); was on the guest faculty, London Opera Centre, London, England (1968); taught acting for the Arts/Six educational theatre project (1969–72); and was a guest lecturer, Hamline Univ., St. Paul, Minn. (1972) and at Stage Studio, Washington, D.C. (1973).

Awards. Miss Gerber received resident fellowships from MacDowell Colony, Peterborough, N.H., in 1966 and 1967.

Recreation. Sculpting, travelling in foreign countries and theatre-going.

GEROLD, ARTHUR. Costumer, director, producer, general manager. b. Arthur William Gerold, Aug. 23, 1923, West New York, N.J., to Arthur and Jeanette (Bloodgood) Gerold. Father, dry cleaner. Grad. Weehawken (N.J.) H.S., 1940; Rutgers Univ., B.S. 1947; Columbia Univ., M.A. 1948. Married Feb. 23, 1952, to Marilyn Day, singer, actress; one son, two daughters. Served WWII, USN, PTO; rank, Lt. Address: (home) RD 1, New Hope, PA 18938; (bus.) Brooks-Van Horn Costume Company, 117 W. 17th St., New York, NY 10011, tel. (212) 989-8000.

Since 1962, Mr. Gerold has been president of Brooks-Van Horn Costume Company, at which time the two companies merged. Since 1956, he had been associated with Van Horn & Son Theatrical Costumers as sales manager and vice-president.

Mr. Gerold produced a season of stock at the Red Barn Th. (Westboro, Mass., Summer 1950); was general manager at the Miami (Fla.) Music Circus (Winter 1950); and was assistant director at the Music Circus (Lambertville, N.J., Summer 1951). From 1951–56, he was general manager of the Music Circus of America, which operates musical theatres-in-the-round (Lambertville and Neptune, N.J.; Miami and St. Petersburg, Fla.; and Dallas, Tex.) and provided technical assistance in the operation of music circuses (Sacramento, Calif.; Hyannis and Cohasset, Mass.).

In 1973, Mr. Gerold joined the board of directors, Bucks County Playhouse, New Hope, Pa. He was appointed also to the advisory board of the Pennsylvania Council of the Arts for Theatre.

Other Activities. In 1965, Mr. Gerold was one of the founders of the New Hope Pro Musica Society, and he remains a board member. In 1974, he opened Bucks Country Vineyards and Winery, the first large-scale winery operation in Bucks County, and established the Bucks County Wine Museum.

Recreation. Tennis, swimming.

GERRINGER, ROBERT. Actor. b. Robert Joseph Geiringer, May 12, 1926, New York City, to Arthur Joseph and Mary (Moran) Geiringer. Father, surgeon. Grad. Xavier H.S., N.Y.C., 1944; Fordham Coll., B.F.A. (cum laude) 1948; attended the Pasadena Playhouse Coll. of Theatre Arts, Summer 1947. Married Apr. 29, 1950, to Patricia Falkenhain, actress. Member of AEA; AFTRA; SAG; Fordham Alumni Assn.; The Players. Address: 26 Horatio St., New York, NY 10014.

Pre-Theatre. Taught speech and rhetoric at Fordham College.

Theatre. Mr. Gerringer made his first appearance on the stage as Buckingham in a university production of *Richard III* (Fordham Univ. Th., 1946); subsequently appeared as Adrian in *In a Garden* (Jan Hus House, N.Y.C., Sept. 7, 1948); as Maurice in a stock production of *Obsession* (Women's Club, Waterbury, Conn., June 24, 1949); and as the Rev. Brontë in *Moor-born* (Hotel Sutton Th., N.Y.C., Oct. 4, 1950). In stock, he played Jim in *Separate Rooms*, Mr. Prior in *Outward Bound*, Archibald in *East Lynne* and Sir Paul Martin in *Miranda* (Monson Th., Mass., Summer 1950). He appeared as a Mexican in *A Streetcar Named Desire* (Kingsbridge Veterans' Hospital, N.Y.C., Feb. 1952); as Don Juan in *Don Juan in Hell* (Kingsbridge Veterans' Hospital, Sept. 1952); as Caiphas in *His Mother's Promise* (St. Boniface Church, Paterson, N.J., Mar., 21, 1953); and as the Lieutenant in *The Man of Destiny* (Kingsbridge Veterans' Hospital, Oct. 1953).

Mr. Gerringer performed in stock at the Canal Fulton (Obie) Th. as Preacher Hagler in *Dark of the Moon*, Stanley Dale in *Here Today*, the Bishop in *See How They Run*, Philip Mortimer in *Gently Does It*, Charles in *Blithe Spirit*, John Worthing in *The Importance of Being Earnest*, the Rev. Davidson in *Rain*, Geoffrey in *The Two Mrs. Carrolls*, Gene Tuttle in *Personal Appearance*, and Joe Morcan in *Ten Nights in a Bar-Room* (June–Sept. 1954).

He appeared as the Town Crier in *Thieves' Carnival* (Cherry Lane, N.Y.C., Feb. 1, 1955); with the American Shakespeare Festival (Stratford, Conn.) as Ligarius, Lepidus, and Casca in *Julius Caesar* (July 12, 1955), and the Captain in *The Tempest* (Aug. 1, 1955); with the Shakespearewrights as Seyton in *Macbeth* (Jan Hus House, N.Y.C., Oct. 19, 1955); succeeded Lester Rawlins as Friar Laurence in *Romeo and Juliet* (Jan Hus House, Feb. 23, 1956); appeared in *I Knock at the Door* (YMHA, Mar. 18, 1956), and *Pictures in the Hallway* (YMHA, May 27, 1956). He returned to the Canal Fulton (Ohio) Th. to play Gerard Dupuis in *Nina*, Alan Coles in *Oh, Men! Oh, Women!*, Cornelius Rockley in *You Touched Me*, Josef in *By Candlelight*, McKeever in *The Solid Gold Cadillac*, Starbuck in *The Rainmaker*, Richard Sherman in *The Seven Year Itch*, Bill Reynolds in *Tea and Sympathy*, and Bounine in *Anastasia* (June–Sept., 1956).

He made his Bway debut in the multiple roles of Uncle Tom, the Jewish Vendor, the Minister, and the Old Man with Cancer of the Tongue, in a concert reading of *Pictures in the Hallway* (Playhouse, Sept. 16, 1956); subsequently played the Third Workman in *Purple Dust* (Cherry Lane, Dec. 27, 1956); with the NY Shakespeare Festival, played the Duke in *The Two Gentlemen of Verona* (Belvedere Lake Th., July 1957); and Banquo in *Macbeth* (Belvedere Lake Th., Aug. 15, 1957); Father Ambrose in *The Waltz of the Toreadors* (Coronet, Mar. 4, 1958); appeared in an ANTA matinee series production of *Guests of the Nation* (Th. de Lys, May 28, 1958); and with the NY Shakespeare Festival as Iago in *Othello* (Belvedere Lake Th., July 1958).

Mr. Gerringer portrayed John Wilkes Booth in *Edwin Booth* (La Jolla Playhouse, La Jolla, Calif., Sept. 1958); Downing in *The Family Reunion* (Phoenix, N.Y.C., Oct. 20, 1958); the Lieutenant in *The Power and the Glory* (Phoenix, Dec. 10, 1958); and Boniface in *The Beaux' Stratagem* (Phoenix, Feb. 24, 1959); toured summer theatres as the Gentleman Caller in *The Glass Menagerie* (July–Aug. 1959); Jasper Culver in *The Andersonville Trial* (Henry Miller's Th., N.Y.C., Dec. 29, 1959); performed in *U.S.A.* (John Drew Th., East Hampton, L.I., N.Y., Summer 1960; Palm Beach Playhouse, Fla., Dec. 1960); played the First Narrator in *Under Milk Wood* (Circle in the Square, N.Y.C., Mar. 29, 1961); and Driscoll in *The Long Voyage Home* (Mermaid, Oct. 17, 1961).

He appeared as Benedict in *Much Ado About Nothing* and the Rev. Chasuble in *The Importance of Being Earnest* (Antioch Th., Yellow Springs, Ohio, Summer 1962); performed in a reading of *Tristram* (YMHA, N.Y.C., Oct. 28, 1962); and played Petruchio in the Phoenix Th. production of *The Taming of the Shrew* (Anderson Th., Mar. 6, 1963).

From Sept. 1967 through the fall of 1969, Mr. Gerringer was a member of the American Conservatory Theatre (ACT), San Francisco, where he played for varying lengths of time in the repertory: Orgon in *Tartuffe*, the Stage Manager in *Our Town*, Francis Nurse in *The Crucible*, Tobias in *A Delicate Balance*, Pat in *The Hostage*, and the Poche / Chandel double role in *A Flea in Her Ear*. He returned to NYC in the ACT production of the last (ANTA Th., Oct. 3, 1969).

In the summer of 1970, he was in the NY Shakespeare Festival's *Wars of the Roses*, appearing as Lord Humphrey in *The Chronicles of King Henry VI, Part 1* (June 23) and *Part 2* (June 24) and as Buckingham in *Richard III* (June 25). In 1971, Mr. Gerringer appeared at the Playhouse Th., N.Y.C., as Krogstad in *A Doll's House* (Jan. 13) and Judge Brack in *Hedda Gabler* (Feb. 17), and he toured in *A Doll's House* (Royal Alexandra Th., Toronto, Canada, Sept. 13, 1971; Eisenhower Th., John F. Kennedy Center, Washington, D.C., Oct. 18, 1971). He played the Paycock in *Juno and the Paycock* (Catholic Univ., Washington, D.C., Winter 1972); Harry in *A Delicate Balance* (Playhouse in the Park, Cincinnati, Ohio, Feb. 1, 1973); James Tyrone in *Long Day's Journey into Night* (Playhouse in the Park, Mar. 1, 1973); and Fergus Crampton in *You Never Can Tell* and George Antrobus in *The Skin of Our Teeth* (both Arlington Park Th., Ill., Arlington Heights, Ill., Summer 1973).

Films. Mr. Gerringer has appeared in *Requiem for a Heavyweight* (Col., 1962); *Black Like Me* (Walter Reade, 1964); *Lovely Way to Die* (U, 1968); *The Way We Were* (Col., 1973); and *The Exorcist* (WB, 1973).

Television. He made his television debut as Mercutio in *Romeo and Juliet* (NBC, 1949), subsequently appeared on Suspense (CBS); Danger (CBS); played Skips in *The Lady's Not for Burning* (Omnibus, NBC); performed on *Men in White* Dupont, NBC, 1961); *The 91st Day* (NET, 1964); *The Last Hangman* (Dupont, NBC, 1964); on the series Love of Life (CBS, 1960–64); The Nurses (CBS, 1962–63); The Defenders (CBS, 1964); The Doctors (NBC); Search for Tomorrow; A Time for Us; A Brighter Day; and others. He was in *Ceremony of Innocence* (NET Playhouse, PBS, Oct. 29, 1970).

Other Activities. Mr. Gerringer has taught at the Harvard Univ. summer theatre festival (Summers 1972–74) and appeared there as Vandergelder in *The Matchmaker;* Mangan in *Heartbreak House;* Lord Augustus Lorton in *Lady Windermere's Fan;* and Lapinet in *Cher Antoine.*

Awards. Mr. Gerringer received a *Village Voice* (Obie) Award for his performance in *Guests of the Nation* (1958).

Recreation. Chess, water-color painting, gun collecting, the NY Mets, cabinet work and wood-restoring.

GERSHWIN, IRA. Lyricist. b. Dec. 6, 1896, New York City, to Morris and Rose (Bruskin) Gershwin. Father, restaurant owner. Grad. Townsend Harris H.S., N.Y.C., 1913; attended Coll. of the City of N.Y., 1914–16. Married Sept. 14, 1926, to Leonore Stunsky. Relative in theatre: brother, George Gershwin (dec. July 11, 1937), composer. Member of ASCAP; Dramatists Guild. Address: 1021 N. Roxbury Dr., Beverly Hills, CA 90210.

Theatre. Mr. Gershwin, under the pseudonym of Arthur Francis, contributed lyrics to the pre-Bway tryout of *A Dangerous Maid* (opened Atlantic City, N.J., Mar. 21, 1921; closed Pittsburgh, Pa., May 1921); subsequently wrote lyrics for *Two Little Girls in Blue* (George M. Cohan Th., N.Y.C., May 3, 1921; *Be Yourself* (Sam H. Harris Th., Sept. 3, 1924); and billed as Ira Gershwin, the name he used thereafter, wrote lyrics, with Desmond Carter, for *Primrose* (Winter Garden, London, Sept. 11, 1924).

He wrote lyrics for *Lady, Be Good* (Liberty, N.Y.C., Dec. 1, 1924); wrote lyrics, with B. G. DeSylva, for *Tell Me More* (Gaiety, Apr. 13, 1925); wrote lyrics for *Tip-Toes* (Liberty, Dec. 28, 1925); for the pre-Bway tryout of *Strike Up the Band* (opened, Philadelphia, Pa., Sept. 5, 1927); *Oh, Kay!* (Imperial, N.Y.C., Nov. 8, 1926); *Funny Face* (Alvin, Nov. 22, 1927); wrote, with P. G. Wodehouse, lyrics for *Rosalie* (New Amsterdam, Jan. 10, 1928); and with Douglas Furber, the lyrics for *That's a Good Girl* (Hippodrome, London, June 5, 1928).

He wrote the lyrics for *Treasure Girl* (Alvin, N.Y.C., Nov. 8, 1928); wrote, with Gus Kahn, the lyrics for *Show Girl* (Ziegfeld, July 2, 1929); wrote the lyrics for a revised version of *Strike Up the Band* (Time Square Th., Jan. 14, 1930); for *Girl Crazy* (Alvin, Oct. 14, 1930); *Of Thee I Sing* (Music Box, Dec. 26, 1931); *Pardon My English* (Majestic, Jan. 20, 1933); *Let 'Em Eat Cake* (Imperial, Oct. 21, 1933); wrote the lyrics, with E. Y. Harburg, for *Life Begins at 8:40* (Winter Garden, Aug. 27, 1934); and, with DuBose Heyward, the book and lyrics for *Porgy and Bess* (Alvin, Oct. 10, 1935), from *Porgy* by DuBose and Dorothy Heyward. He wrote the lyrics for *Ziegfeld Follies* (Winter Garden, Jan. 30, 1936); *Lady in the Dark* (Alvin, Jan. 23, 1941); *The Firebrand of Florence* (Alvin Th., Mar. 22, 1945); *Park Avenue* (Shubert Th., Nov. 4, 1946); and lyrics for songs used in *The Harold Arlen Songbook* (Stage 73, Feb. 28, 1967); in the revue *Do It Again!* (Promenade Th., Feb. 18, 1971); and in the revue *Berlin to Broadway With Kurt Weill* (Th. de Lys, Oct. 1, 1972).

Films. Mr. Gershwin wrote the lyrics for *Delicious* (20th-Fox, 1931); *Shall We Dance?* (RKO, 1937); *A Damsel in Distress* (RKO, 1937); *The Goldwyn Follies* (Goldwyn-UA, 1938); *North Star* (RKO, 1943); *Cover Girl* (Col., 1944); *Where Do We Go From Here?* (20th-Fox, 1947); *The Shocking Miss Pilgrim* (1947); *The Barkleys of Broadway* (MGM, 1949); *An American in Paris* (MGM, 1951); *Give a Girl a Break* (MGM, 1953); *A Star is Born* (Transcona-WB, 1954); *The Country Girl* (Par., 1954); *Kiss Me, Stupid!* (Lopert, 1964); and the film *When the Boys Meet the Girls* (MGM, 1965) was based on the musical *Girl Crazy*, for which Mr. Gershwin wrote the lyrics.

Published Works. Mr. Gershwin wrote *Lyrics on Several Occasions* (1959), and has written articles for magazines, including *The Saturday Review.*

Awards. *Of Thee I Sing*, for which Mr. Gershwin wrote the lyrics, received the Pulitzer Prize (1932); he was awarded the Townsend Harris Medal (City College of N.Y., 1952; the Univ. of Maryland awarded him an honorary D.F.A. (1966); and he received the James K. Hackett Award (1972).

Recreation. Books, billiards, cigars, collecting light verse.

GERSTAD, JOHN. Producer, actor, director, playwright. b. John Leif Gjerstad, Sept. 3, 1924, Boston, Mass., to Leif Augustus and Adelaide (Johannesen) Gjerstad. Father, journalist, insurance salesman; mother, exec. secy., Norwegian Consulate, Boston. Attended Boston Latin Sch., 1936–42; Harvard Univ., 1942–43. Married June 4, 1945, to Annabel Lee Nugent; one son, two daughters. Relative in theatre: father-in-law, Elliott Nugent, actor, director, playwright. Member of AEA (life member; council member); SSD&C (charter member); AFTRA; SAG; Dramatists Guild; League of NY Theatres; The Players; American Inst. of Science and Engineering. Address: 345 E. 57th St., New York, NY 10022, tel. (212) MU 8-0490, (212) MU 8-0593.

Theatre. Mr. Gerstad's first assignment in a theatrical production was in Boston Latin Sch., where he produced and directed a twin bill of *Box and Cox* and *Rainshine* (Washington Irving H.S., Roslindale, Mass., Apr. 1939); subsequently made his professional debut as Alexander in *The Spider* (Cambridge Summer Th., Mass., July 1940).

He wrote *Sun at Midnight* (New England Repertory Co., Boston, Mass., 1952); made his Bway debut as a Citizen, Brabanito's Servant, a Messenger, understudy, and assistant stage manager in Paul Robeson's *Othello* (Shubert, N.Y.C., Oct. 19, 1943); adapted for ELT Ibsen's *The Wild Duck* (1944) and *Ghosts* (1945); appeared as Hank Gudger in *Dark of the Moon* (46 St. Th., Mar. 14, 1945); in a USO touring production of *Three's a Family* (It., 1945); as John Roberts in *By Appointment Only* (Lyric, Bridgeport, Conn., Jan. 1946); with James Lee, wrote *The Monday Man* (Falmouth Playhouse, Mass.; Martha's Vineyard Playhouse, Mass., 1947); and was understudy in *Joy to the World* (Plymouth, N.Y.C., Mar. 18, 1948).

With James Lee, Mr. Gerstad wrote *The French Have a Word for It* (Ridgefield Th., Conn., Summer 1948); with Robert Scott, wrote *When the Bough Breaks* (Abbe Workshop, N.Y.C., Mar. 1950); appeared in *Not for Children* (Coronet, Feb. 13, 1951); played Michael Barnes in *The Male Animal* (NY City Ctr., Apr. 30, 1952); with Norman Brooks, wrote *The Fig Leaf* (Spa Summer Th., Saratoga Springs, N.Y., July 8, 1952), and on pre-Bway tour (opened Empress Playhouse, St. Louis, Mo., Sept. 30, 1952; closed Selwyn, Chicago, Ill., Oct. 18, 1952); staged *The Seven Year Itch* (Fulton, N.Y.C., Nov. 20, 1952; Aldwych, London, May 14, 1953); directed *The Champagne Complex* and *The Automobile Man* (Bucks County Playhouse, New Hope, Pa., Summer 1954); staged *The Wayward Saint* (Cort, N.Y.C., Feb. 17, 1955); *Debut* (Holiday, Feb. 22, 1956); a touring production of *The Male Animal* (1956); and *Double in Hearts* (John Golden Th., N.Y.C., Oct. 16, 1956).

In association with Frederick Fox and Elliott Nugent, Mr. Gerstad produced *The Greatest Man Alive* (Ethel Barrymore Th., May 8, 1957); produced, with the Playwrights Co. and James M. Slevin, and directed *Howie* (46 St. Th., Sept. 17, 1958); with Henry Sherek, TIP (Theatrical Interests Plan, Inc.), of which Mr. Gerstad was a founder, officer and director, produced *Odd Man In* (opened Playhouse, Wilmington, Del., Oct. 1, 1959; closed, Memorial Aud., Burlington, Iowa, Mar. 5, 1960); TIP also presented the national touring production of *Look Homeward, Angel* (opened Playhouse, Wilmington, Del., Oct. 21, 1959); in association with the Theatre Guild Productions, Inc., and Joel Schenker, Mr. Gerstad produced *The Captains and the Kings* (Playhouse, N.Y.C., Jan. 2, 1962); played multiple roles in the tryout of *The Beauty Part* (Bucks County Playhouse, New Hope, Pa., Summer 1962); in *The Trial of Lee Harvey Oswald* (ANTA, Nov. 5, 1967); played Labe in *Come Summer* (Lunt-Fontanne Th., 1969); Cord Elam in a revival of *Oklahoma!* (NY State Th., June 23, 1969); Reverend Sickles in *The Penny Wars* (Royale, Oct. 15, 1969); was a newspaperman in *All Over* (Martin Beck Th., Mar. 28, 1971); directed *All the Girls Came Out to Play* (Cort. Apr. 20, 1972).

Films. Mr. Gerstad was dialogue director and associate director of *Lost Boundaries* (FC, 1949) and has appeared in *The Cop Hater* (UA, 1958); *Up the Down Staircase* (WB, 1967); *Star!* (20th-Fox, 1968); *No Way to Treat a Lady* (Par., 1968); *The Swimmer* (Col., 1968); *Lovely Way to Die* (U, 1968); *What's So Bad About Feeling Good?* (U, 1968); *Generation* (Avco Embassy, 1969); *B.S., I Love You* (20th-Fox, 1971); and *Lady Liberty* (UA, 1972).

Television. He has written scripts for Lights Out and The Clock (both NBC, 1950–51), for which programs he was also associate producer and story editor; with Norman Brooks, wrote the jazz musical *O, Didn't He Ramble?* (CBS-TV Workshop, 1951); with George Schaefer, adapted the book for *One Touch of Venus* (Hallmark Hall of Fame, NBC, 1953); directed *Best Foot Forward* (NBC, 1954); played Homer Van Meter in *A Year to Kill* (The Dillinger Story, NBC, 1960); Lemuel in *Give Us Barabbas!* (Hallmark Hall of Fame, NBC, 1961); produced and directed the Shari Lewis Show (NBC, 1963); and appeared in *Damn Yankees* (NBC, 1967). He had running parts on The Nurses; As the World Turns; and Edge of Night (all CBS) and was in the following Hallmark Hall of Fame (NBC) productions: *Galileo; The Florence Nightingale Story; Little Moon of Alban; The Patriots; The Admirable Crichton; St. Joan;* and *Barefoot in Athens.*.

Recreation. Bridge, bicycling, scuba-diving and logging flight hours to qualify for pilots licence.

GERSTEN, BERNARD. Producer, director, stage manager. b. Jan. 30, 1923, Newark, N.J., to Jacob Israel and Henrietta (Henig) Gersten. Father, garment worker. Grad. West Side H.S., Newark, N.J., 1940; attended Rutgers Univ., 1040–42. Married Apr. 21, 1968 to Cora Cahan, dancer. Served US Army, 1942–45; technical director of Maurice Evans' Special Services Unit, Hawaii, two years; Infantry, one year. Relative in theatre: brother, Leon Gersten, stage manager (Mineola, L.I., N.Y.). Member of AEA; AGMA. Address: (home) 56 Seventh Ave., New York, NY 10014, tel. (212) OR 5-5817; (bus.) NY Shakespeare Festival, 425 Lafayette St., New York, NY 10003, tel. (212) 677-1750.

Mr. Gersten is Assoc. Prod. of the NY Shakespeare Fest. (1960 to date; see NY Shakespeare Fest. for list of plays produced).

Theatre. Mr. Gersten made his debut at age 7 in a grammar school play (Bruce St. Elementary Sch., Newark, N.J., 1930); for Maurice Evans' *G.I. Hamlet,* was asst. stage manager in N.Y.C. (International Th., Dec. 13, 1945), and stage manager on tour (Sept. 1946–May 1947).

Mr. Gersten was producer at Hunterdon Hills Playhouse (Jutland, N.J., 1947), where he also played Jake in *Papa Is All;* was stage manager for *Kathleen* (Mansfield, N.Y.C., Feb. 3, 1948); technical director of Actors' Laboratory (Hollywood, Calif., Mar.–Nov. 1948); production manager for New Stages, Inc. (N.Y.C., Nov. 1948–May 1949); production stage manager for *Anna Christie* (NY City Ctr., Jan. 9, 1950); *All You Need Is One Good Break* (Mansfield, Feb. 9, 1950); and a touring company of *The Guardsman* (opened Erlanger, Buffalo, N.Y., Jan. 1950). He produced three O'Casey plays (Yugoslav Hall, N.Y.C., Spring 1951); was production stage manager for *Tovarich* (NY City Ctr., May 14, 1952); the pre-Bway tryout of *A Certain Joy* (opened Playhouse, Wilmington, Del., Feb. 12, 1953; closed Locust St. Th., Philadelphia, Pa., Feb. 21, 1953); general manager and lighting designer for *The World of Sholom Aleichem* (Barbizon-Plaza, N.Y.C., May 1, 1953); production stage manager for *Sandhog* (Phoenix, Nov. 23, 1954); *Guys and Dolls* (NY City Ctr., Apr. 20, 1955); *South Pacific* (NY City Ctr., May 4, 1955); *Finian's Rainbow* (NY City Ctr., May 18, 1955); and *Mr. Wonderful* (Bway Th., Mar. 22, 1956).

He was general stage manager for the Dallas (Tex.) Civic Opera production of *L'Italiana in Algeria* (Nov. 1958); production stage manager for *Edwin Booth* (46 St. Th., N.Y.C., May 24, 1958); *Legend of Lizzie* (54 St. Th., Feb. 9, 1959); *Roman Candle* (Cort, Feb. 3, 1960); the pre-Bway tryout of *Laurette* (opened Shubert, New Haven, Conn., Sept. 26, 1960; closed there, Oct. 1, 1960); *Do Re Mi* (St. James, N.Y.C., Dec. 26, 1960), which he directed, with Max Bygraves, in London (Prince of Wales's, Oct. 12, 1961); directed *No for an Answer* (Circle in the Square, N.Y.C., Apr. 19, 1960); and was production stage manager of *Arturo Ui* (Lunt-Fontanne, Nov. 11, 1963).

He was executive stage manager for the American Shakespeare Festival (Stratford, Conn.) productions of *Othello, The Merchant of Venice,* and *Much Ado About Nothing* (Summer 1957); *Hamlet, A Midsummer Night's Dream,* and *The Winter's Tale* (Summer 1958); *Romeo and Juliet, The Merry Wives of Windsor, All's Well That Ends Well,* and *A Midsummer Night's Dream* (Summer 1959); and toured as executive stage manager with *Much Ado About Nothing* (opened Locust St. Th., Philadelphia, Pa., Dec. 27, 1957; closed Shubert, Boston, Mass., Mar. 15, 1958).

He conceived and co-directed the children's productions, *Potluck!* (July 7, 1966) and *Lallapalooza* (June 29, 1967) which toured N.Y.C. in the NY Shakespeare Festival's Mobile Th.

Television. Mr. Gersten was production supervisor for NBC-TV (1951); production manager of *Showtime USA* (ABC, 1951): associate producer of *The Merchant of Venice* (CBS, 1962); *Antony and Cleopatra* (CBS, 1963); and *Hamlet* (CBS, 1964).

Other Activities. Mr. Gersten was a member of the faculty of the Th. Arts Div. of Columbia Univ. (1967–69).

Awards. He received (Aug. 22, 1972) the Bronze Medallion of the City of NY.

Recreation. Abstract collage artist.

GERSTMAN, FELIX G. Impresario, producer. b. Vienna, Austria, to Hermann and Marye (Schueller) Gerstman. Father, merchant. Grad. Univ. of Vienna, Fine Arts. Served WW I, Austrian Army, rank, Lt.; Pioneer Corps of England, 1940. Member of Intl. Assn of Concert Managers; AFM.

Mr. Gerstman died January 11, 1967, New York City, at the age of 68 years.

Theatre. Mr. Gerstman was business manager for *Yours Is My Heart* (Shubert Th., Sept. 5, 1946).

Since 1940, has presented the "Players from Abroad" in German-language productions, including *Faust* (Barbizon-Plaza Th., N.Y.C., Oct. 1947) and *The Master Builder* (Barbizon-Plaza Th., Jan. 1948); produced a concert version of *The Threepenny Opera* (Town Hall, 1953); *The World of Carl Sandburg* (Brooklyn Acad. of Music, N.Y. 1959); with Gert von Gontard and Deutsches Th., Inc., produced the German revue, *Between Whiskey and Vodka* (Barbizon-Plaza Th., Oct. 3, 1961); presented the Hamburg Schauspielhaus in *Faust, Part I* (NY City Ctr., Feb. 7, 1961); the Duesseldorf Schauspielhaus in a program including *Nathan the Wise* and *Before Sundown* (Fashion Inst. of Tech., Mar. 6, 1962); a German-language production of *Dear Liar* (Barbizon-Plaza Th., May 3, 1963); with James A. Doolittle, produced *Wiener Blut* (Vienna Life) (Lunt-Fontanne Th., Sept. 18, 1964); and the Schiller Th. of West Berlin at the New York State Th. in *Don Carlos* (Nov. 24, 1964), and *Der Hauptmann von Koepenick* (The Captain from Koepenick) (Dec. 1, 1964); produced Lotte Lenya's concert at Carnegie Hall (Jan. 1965); in association with Sid Bernstein, presented *The All-Star Israeli Show* (Carnegie Hall, Apr. 10, 1965); was one of the producers of the Bavarian State Theater, Munich, productions of Wozzeck (NY City Ctr., Apr. 5, 1966) and *Die Ratten* (NY City Ctr., Apr. 12, 1966); and of the Die Brucke Theatre Ensemble, which presented *Nathan Der Weise, Burger Schippel* and *Kennen Sie Die Milchstrasse* (Barbizon-Plaza, Dec. 8, 1966).

Other Activities. Owner of a papermill (1930 to date).

Awards. He received the Verdienstkreuze (Service Cross) from Germany for promoting cultural exchange (1961); and the Goldene Ehrenzeichen (Golden Medal of Honor) from Austria for promoting cultural exchange (1962).

GESEK, TADEUSZ. Educator, scenic designer. b. Thaddeus Joseph Gesek, Mar. 14, 1925, Salem, Mass., to Frank Stefan and Antonina (Lech) Gesek. Educated at Salem (Mass.) H.S.; School of the Museum of Fine Arts (Boston, Mass.), 1951; Tufts Univ., B.S. 1951; Yale Univ., M.F.A. 1959. Studied at Yale School of Drama with Donald Oenslager. Served USMCR (1943–45); on duty in South Pacific. Married Aug 11, 1962, to Mary Elizabeth Meeker; one daughter, one son. Member of United Scenic Artists of America (N.Y.C.), Local 829, parent member. Address: (home) 110 Overocker Rd., Poughkeepsie, NY 12603, tel. (914) 454-3863; (bus.) Vassar College, Poughkeepsie, NY 12601, tel. (914) 452-7000.

Pre-Theatre. Assistant headmaster at a private school.

Theatre. Mr. Gesek is an associate professor at Vassar Coll. (1965–to date); and scenic designer for the Vassar Experimental Theatre, and the Power House Theatre.

He has been scenic designer for eight-production seasons of the Arena Th. (Tufts Coll., 1950–53; 1956–57); for the Experimental Th. (Vassar Coll., 1959–to date), including productions of *Arms and the Man, S.R.O., The Madwoman of Chaillot, The Cherry Orchard, A Doll's House, The Matchmaker, Tiger at the Gates, Crimes and Crimes, The Skin of Our Teeth, Pericles, Everyman, Uncle Vanya, The Italian Straw Hat, The Would-Be Gentleman,* and *Lady Precious Stream.*

He has designed summer stock productions for the Marblehead (Mass.) Playhouse; Beaupre Music and Arts Center (1954–55); Chase Barn Playhouse (1957); Summer of Musicals, Ill. (1958); Mt. Kisco (N.Y.) Summer Th. (1964); Dartmouth Repertory Th., where *As You Like It, Rhinoceros,* and *The Beaux' Stratagem* played in repertory; and the Santa Fe (N.M.) Theatre Co., where productions included *The Rose Tattoo, Barefoot in the Park, Luv, A View from the Bridge, The Subject Was Roses,* and *Born Yesterday.*

In New York, he designed settings for the double bill *Come Out, Carlo!,* and *In the Penal Colony* (41 St. Th., N.Y.C., May 3, 1962); *Bohikee Creek* (Stage '73, N.Y.C., Apr. 28, 1966); and *Javelin* (Actors' Playhouse, N.Y.C., Nov. 9, 1966).

His opera and ballet designs include settings for *The Dialogue of the Carmelites* (Newburgh, N.Y., 1963); *L'Elisir d'Amore* (Boston Opera Group, 1964); *The Barber of Seville* (Wappingers Falls, N.Y., H.S. Auditorium, 1967); *The Rites of Spring* (Poughkeepsie, N.Y., H.S. Auditorium, 1971); and *Faust* (Dutchess Community Coll., N.Y., 1975).

Other Activities. Mr. Gesek has been represented in exhibitions in Guadalcanal and Guam (1944–45); São Paulo, Brazil (1957); the Boston Museum of Fine Arts (1959; 1963); Three Arts Gallery (Poughkeepsie, N.Y., 1964; 1966; 1968); Vassar Coll. Art Gallery (1967); the Colorado Coll. exhibit, "Contemporary Crafts of the Americas" (1975); and in a traveling exhibition arranged by AETA and ANTA (1959–63).

He also holds copyrights and patents dealing with artistic innovations in scenic design.

Awards. Mr. Gesek was awarded the Clarissa Bartlett scholarship (1960–63) of the School of the (Boston) Museum of Fine Arts and received a grant (1969–70) from the Zelosky Fund of the Kosciuszko Foundation. In 1965–66, he held a faculty fellowship from Vassar to study and observe theatre in Europe, concentrating on Polish theatre.

Recreation. Music, painting, sculpting, golf.

GEVA, TAMARA. Dancer, actress, director, choreographer. b. Tamara Gevergeva, Leningrad, Russia. Attended Russian Academic (formerly Imperial) Ballet Sch., Leningrad. Married to George Balanchine, choreographer (marr. dis.); married to Kapa Davidoff, businessman (marr. dis.); married to John Emery, actor (marr. dis.). Member of AEA; SAG.

Theatre. Miss Geva first appeared with Diaghilev's Ballet Russe de Monte Carlo in Europe. She made her N.Y.C. debut in Balieff's *Chauve-Souris* (Cosmopolitan Th., Oct. 10, 1927); subsequently played Yolanda in *Whoopee* (New Amsterdam, Dec. 4, 1928); appeared in the revues, *Three's a Crowd* (Selwyn, Oct. 15, 1930), and *Flying Colors* (Imperial, Sept. 15, 1932); played Lania in *Divine Drudge* (Royale, Oct. 26, 1933), and Mimi in *The Red Cat* (Broadhurst, Sept. 19, 1934); danced in *Errante,* the first performance of Balanchine's American Ballet (Adelphi, Mar. 1935); played Vera Barnova and danced the roles of Princesse Zenobia and the Strip-Tease Girl in *On Your Toes* (Imperial, Apr. 11, 1936); appeared as Irene in *Idiot's Delight* (Apollo, London, Eng., Mar. 22, 1938); Helen of Troy in the Experimental Theatre production of *The Trojan Women* (N.Y.C., 1941).

She succeeded (May 1943) Eugenie Leontovich as Natasha Rapakovitch in *Dark Eyes* (Belasco, Jan. 14, 1943); played Leonie Cobb in *Peepshow* (Fulton, Feb. 3, 1944); Lilly Garland in *Twentieth Century* (El Patio Playhouse, Los Angeles, Calif., Fall 1946); directed *No Exit,* in which she also played Inez (Coronet, Los Angeles, Aug. 1947); portrayed Zilla in *Pride's Crossing* (Biltmore, Nov. 20, 1950); Lina in *Misalliance* (NY City Ctr., Feb. 18, 1953, moved to The Ethel Barrymore Th. for the rest of the season); directed an ELT production of *Lysistrata* (Lenox Hill Playhouse, Dec. 12, 1956); and adapted, with Haila Stoddard, *Come Play with Me* (York, Apr. 1959); appeared as the Prostitute in Ugo Betti's *The Queen and the Rebels* (Th. Four, N.Y.C., Mar. 1965).

Films. Miss Geva made her debut in *Their Big Moment* (RKO, 1934); subsequently appeared in *Manhattan Merry-Go-Round* (Rep., 1937); *Orchestra Wives* (20th-Fox, 1942); and *Night Plane from Chung-king* (Par., 1943). She choreographed the film, *The Specter of the Rose* (Rep., 1946).

Published Works. Miss Geva wrote a novelized autobiography entitled *Split Seconds* (Harper & Row, 1973).

Awards. She received an award from *Musical Courier* magazine for best choreography for *The Specter of the Rose* (1946).

GHOSTLEY, ALICE. Actress, singer. b. Alice Margaret Ghostley, Aug. 14, Eve, Mo., to Harry F. and Edna M. (Rooney) Ghostley. Father, railroad telegrapher. Attended Henryetta (Okla.) H.S.; Univ. of Oklahoma. Studied singing with Eleanor McLellan, N.Y.C., twelve years. Married Oct. 6, 1951, to Felice Orlandi, actor. Member of AEA; AGMA; SAG; AFTRA; AGVA.

Pre-Theatre. Secretary, usherette, cashier, detective.

Theatre. Miss Ghostley made her debut as Flo in an ELT production of *Good News* (Walton Community Ctr., Bronx, N.Y., Nov. 1950); and her N.Y.C. debut in *New Faces of 1952* (Royale Th., May 16, 1952), also touring in it (1953).

She played Sheela Cavanaugh in *Sandhog* (Phoenix, Nov. 23, 1954); Dinah in the opera, *Trouble in Tahiti,* part of a triple-bill entitled *All in One* (Playhouse, Apr. 19, 1955); Alice in a stock production of *A Palm Tree in a Rose Garden* (Pocono Playhouse, Mountainhome, Pa., Summer 1956); Miss Brinklow in *Shangri-La* (Winter Garden, N.Y.C., June 13, 1956); her voice was heard on recordings in *A Box of Watercolors* (Bway Chapel Players, Bway Congregational Church, Feb. 17, 1957); played Aunt Polly in *Livin' the Life* (Phoenix, Apr. 27, 1957); Lois in *Maybe Tuesday* (Playhouse, Jan. 29, 1958); and Lady Jane in *Rose Marie* (Dallas Summer Musicals, Tex., 1958).

Miss Ghostley played eleven roles in *A Thurber Carnival* (ANTA, Feb. 26, 1960); Lily in a summer theatre tour of *Take Me Along* (1961); Octavia Weatherwax, Grace Fingerhead, and Kitty Entrail in *The Beauty Part* (Music Box, N.Y.C., Dec. 26, 1962); Belle Boyd, the Dowager, a Southern Lady, and the Nurse in a NY City Opera Co. production of *Gentlemen, Be Seated* (NY City Ctr., Oct. 10, 1963); Mavis Paradus Bryson in *The Sign in Sidney Brustein's Window* (Longacre, Oct. 15, 1964); and appeared in the pre-Bway tryout of *Love Is A Ball!* (opened Civic Auditorium, San Jose, Calif., Sept. 27, 1965, closed Civic Auditorium, Ft. Worth, Tex., Oct. 25, 1965).

Films. Miss Ghostley made her debut in *New Faces* (20th-Fox, 1954); subsequently appeared as Aunt Stephanie in *To Kill a Mockingbird* (U, 1962); the Housekeeper in *My Six Loves* (Par., 1963); Mrs. Packard in *The Flim-Flam Man* (20th-Fox, 1967); Mrs. Singleman in *The Graduate* (Embassy, 1967); The Housekeeper in *With Six You Get Eggroll* (Natl. Gen., 1968); Hattie in *Viva Max!* (Commonwealth United, 1969); and Sister Lite in *Ace Eli and Rodger of the Skies* (20th-Fox, 1973).

Television. She has appeared on *The Show-off* (Best of Broadway, CBS), on Art Carney specials, the Tom Ewell Show (CBS), Car 54, Where Are You? (NBC), played one of the Stepsisters in Rodgers and Hammerstein's *Cinderella* (CBS, Mar. 1957); Maria in *Twelfth Night* (Hallmark Hall of Fame, NBC), Miss Brinklow in *Shangri-La* (Hallmark Hall of Fame, NBC), appeared in *Talk, Talk, Talk* (Stage 2, CBS), performed her own material on the Dinah Shore Show (NBC), and played Agnes in *Agnes and Arthur* (Jackie Gleason's American Scene Magazine, CBS, 1963–64).

Miss Ghostley's subsequent appearances include Valentine's Day (ABC); The Johnny Carson Show (NBC); The Trials of O'Brien (CBS); The Tom Ewell Show (Ind.); Bewitched (ABC); Please Don't Eat the Daisies (NBC); Get Smart (NBC); Girl Talk (ABC); Captain Nice (NBC); and The Paul Lynde Show (NBC).

Night Clubs. Miss Ghostley made her nightclub debut at the Fireside Inn, N.Y.C. (1950); and has appeared at the Bon Soir, The Blue Angel, Downstairs at the Upstairs; and Plaza 9.

Awards. For her performance in *The Sign in Sidney Brustein's Window,* Miss Ghostley won the Antoinette Perry (Tony) Award and first place in the Annual Variety N.Y. Drama Critics Poll (1965).

GIBSON, WILLIAM. Playwright, novelist. b. Nov. 13, 1914, New York City, to George and Florence (Dore) Gibson. Father, clerk. Grad. Townsend Harris Hall, N.Y.C., 1930; attended City Coll. of N.Y., 1930–32. Married Sept. 6, 1940, to Margaret Brenman, psychologist; two sons. Member of Dramatists Guild, P.E.N. Address: (home) Stockbridge, MA 01262; (bus.) c/o Leah Salisbury, 234 W. 44th St., New York, NY 10036.

Theatre. Mr. Gibson wrote and appeared in *I Lay in Zion* (Topeka Civic Th., Kan., Easter 1943); and wrote *A Cry of Players* (Topeka Civic Th., Feb. 1948); *Two for the Seesaw* (Booth Th., N.Y.C., Jan. 16, 1958), which toured cross-country (opened Ford's Th., Baltimore, Oct. 6, 1958) and again (opened Center, Norfolk, Va., Sept. 28, 1959; closed Veterans Memorial Aud., Providence, R.I., Feb. 13, 1960), and was produced in London (Haymarket, Dec. 17, 1958); *The Miracle Worker* (Playhouse, Oct. 19, 1959), which subsequently toured (opened Playhouse, Wilmington, Del., Apr. 12, 1961; closed Veterans Memorial Aud., Providence, R.I., Mar. 31, 1962); *Dinny and the Witches* (Cherry Lane, N.Y.C., Dec. 9, 1959; wrote, with Clifford Odets, the musical version of *Golden Boy* (Majestic, Oct. 20, 1964); wrote *A Cry of Players* (Berkshire Theatre Festival Stockbridge, Mass., July 24, 1968; revision, Lincoln Center, N.Y.C., Nov. 14, 1968); wrote *American Primitive* (Ford's Th., Washington, D.C., Jan. 1971; premiered as *John and Abigail* at Berkshire Th. Festival, Stockbridge, Mass., July 24, 1969); and wrote *The Body and the Wheel* (Pierce Chapel, Lenox, Mass., Apr. 5, 1974).

Television. Mr. Gibson originally wrote *The Miracle Worker* for television (CBS, 1957).

Published Works. Mr. Gibson's published works include the one-act play, *I Lay in Zion* (1947); a collection of poems, *Winter Crook* (1948); a novel, *The Cobweb* (1954); the television version of *The Miracle Worker* (1957); *Two for the Seesaw* (1959); *The Seesaw Log,* a chronicle of the Bway production of *Two for the Seesaw* (1959); the stage adaptation of *The Miracle Worker* (1960); *Dinny and the Witches* (1960); *A Mass for the Dead,* a family chronicle with poems, (1968); and *A Season in Heaven* (1974).

GIELGUD, SIR JOHN. Actor, director, producer. b. Arthur John Gielgud, Apr. 14, 1904, London, England, to Frank and Kate Terry (Lewis) Gielgud. Father, stockbroker. Attended Westminster Sch., London, 1917; Lady Benson's Sch., London, 1921; RADA, 1922. Relatives in theatre: brother, Val Gielgud, producer; second cousin, Hazel Terry, actress; second cousin, Edward Gordon Craig, stage designer; aunt, Mabel Terry Lewis, actress; grandmother, Kate Terry, actress; great aunts, Ellen Terry, Marion Terry, actresses; great uncle, Fred Terry, actor. Member of AEA.

Theatre. Sir John Gielgud first appeared on stage as the Herald in *Henry V* (Old Vic, London, Nov. 7, 1921); subsequently performed in *King Lear, Wat Tyler* and *Peer Gynt;* toured (1922) as stage-manager and understudy for *The Wheel;* played Felix in *The Insect Play* (Regent Th., London, May 5, 1923); the Aide-de-Camp in *Robert E. Lee* (Regent, June 20, 1923); Charles Wykeham in *Charley's Aunt* (Comedy, Dec. 18, 1923); appeared with J. B. Fagan's repertory company (Oxford Playhouse, Jan.–Feb. 1924); played Romeo in *Romeo and Juliet* (Regent, May 22, 1924); rejoined (Oct. 1924) Fagan's repertory company at the Oxford Playhouse; portrayed Castalio in *The Orphan* (Aldwych, London, May 10, 1925); and succeeded (May 1925) Noel Coward as Nicky Lancaster in *The Vortex* (Royalty, Dec. 16, 1924).

He played Peter Trophimoff in *The Cherry Orchard* (Lyric, Hammersmith, May 25, 1925); Konstantin Treplev in *The Seagull* (Little, Oct. 19, 1925); Sir John Harington in *Gloriana* (Little, Dec. 8, 1925); Robert in *L'Ecole des cocottes* (Prince's, Dec. 1925); Ferdinand in *The Tempest* (Savoy, Jan. 7, 1926); Baron Tusenbach in *The Three Sisters* (Barnes, Feb. 16, 1926); George Stibelev in *Katerina* (Barnes, Mar. 30, 1926); succeeded Noel Coward (Oct. 1926) as Lewis Dodd in *The Constant Nymph* (New, Sept. 14, 1926); and played Dion Anthony in *The Great God Brown* (Strand, June 19, 1927).

He made his first N.Y.C. appearance as the Grand Duke Alexander in *The Patriot* (Majestic, Jan. 19, 1928); returned to London to play Oswald in *Ghosts* (Wyndham's, Mar. 27, 1928); Dr. Gerald Marlowe in *Holding Out the Apple* (Globe, June 16, 1928); Capt. Allenby in *The Skull* (Shaftesbury, Aug. 6, 1928); Felipe Rivas in *The Lady from Alfaqueque* and Alberto in *Fortunato* (Court, Oct. 22, 1928); John Marstin in *Out of the Sea* (Strand, Nov. 23, 1928); Fedor in *Red Dust* (Little, Feb. 28, 1929); succeeded Leslie Banks (Apr. 1929) as Henry Tremayne in *The Lady with a Lamp* (Garrick, Jan. 24, 1929); and played Trotsky (Bronstein) in *Red Sunday* (Arts, June 27, 1929).

With the Old Vic Co., he appeared as Romeo in *Romeo and Juliet* (Sept. 14, 1929), Antonio in *The Merchant of Venice* (Oct. 7, 1929), Cleante in *The Imaginary Invalid, Richard II* (Nov. 18, 1929), Oberon in *A Midsummer Night's Dream* (Dec. 9, 1929), Mark Antony in *Julius Caesar* (Jan. 20, 1930), Orlando in *As You Like It* (Feb. 10, 1930), the Emperor in *Androcles and the Lion* (Feb. 24, 1930), *Macbeth* (Mar. 17, 1930), and the title role in *Hamlet* (Apr. 28, 1930), which he repeated (Queen's, May 28, 1930). He played John Worthing in *The Importance of Being Earnest* (Lyric, Hammersmith, July 7, 1930); with the Old Vic, portrayed Hotspur in *Henry IV, Part I* (Sept. 13, 1930), Prospero in *The Tempest* (Oct. 6, 1930), Lord Trinket in *The Jealous Wife* (Oct. 27, 1930), and Antony in *Antony and Cleopatra* (Nov. 24, 1930).

He appeared with the Old Vic Co. as Malvolio in *Twelfth Night* (Sadler's Wells Th., Jan. 6, 1931); as Sergius Saranoff in *Arms and the Man* (Old Vic Th., Feb. 16, 1931), Benedick in *Much Ado About Nothing* (Old Vic Th., Mar. 16, 1931), and in the title role of *King Lear* (Old Vic Th., Apr. 13, 1931); played Inigo Jollifant in *The Good Companions* (His Majesty's. May 14, 1931); Joseph Schindler in *Musical Chair* (Arts, Nov. 15, 1931); Richard II in *Richard of Bordeaux* (Arts, June 26, 1932), and in a return engagement which he also directed (New, Feb. 2, 1933).

He directed *Strange Orchestra* (St. Martin's, Sept. 27, 1932), and *Sheppey* (Wyndham's, Sept. 14, 1933); directed and produced, with Richard Clowes, *Spring 1600* (Shaftesbury, Jan. 31, 1934); directed *Queen of Scots* (New, June 8, 1934); and played Roger Maitland in *The Maitlands* (Wyndham's, July 4, 1934); staged *Hamlet*, in which he also appeared in the title role (New, Nov. 14, 1934); directed *The Old Ladies* (New, Apr. 3, 1935); played the title role in *Noah* (New, July 2, 1935); directed *Romeo and Juliet*, in which he also portrayed Mercutio and later alternated with Laurence Olivier as Romeo (Nov. 1935). He played Boris Trigorin in *The Seagull* (New, May 20, 1936); the title role in *Hamlet* (Empire, N.Y.C., Oct. 8, 1936); Mason in *He Was Born Gay*, which he also directed, with Emlyn Williams (Queen's, London, May 26, 1937).

As manager of the Queen's Th. (Sept. 1937–May 1938), he appeared there in the title role in *Richard II*, which he also directed (Sept. 6, 1937), and as Joseph Surface in *The School for Scandal* (Nov. 25, 1937), Col. Vershinin in *The Three Sisters* (Jan. 28, 1938), and Shylock in *The Merchant of Venice*, which he also directed (Apr. 21, 1938); directed *Spring Meeting* (Ambassadors', May 31, 1938); played Nicholas Randolph in *Dear Octopus* (Queen's, Sept. 14, 1938); John Worthing in *The Importance of Being Earnest*, which he also directed (Globe, Jan. 31, 1939); directed *Scandal in Assyria* (Globe, Apr. 30, 1939); produced *Rhondda Roundabout* (Globe, May 31, 1939); played the title role in *Hamlet* (Lyceum, June 28, 1939; and in Denmark, Kronborg Castle, Elsinor).

He repeated his role as Worthing in *The Importance of Being Earnest* (Globe, London, Aug. 16, 1939), toured in the role and played it in London (Globe, Dec. 26, 1939); directed *The Beggars' Opera* (Haymarket, Mar. 5, 1940), and temporarily replaced (Mar. and Apr.) Michael Redgrave in the role of Macheath; played the title role in *King Lear* (Old Vic, Apr. 15, 1940); Prospero in *The Tempest* (May 29, 1940); appeared in benefit performances of *Fumed Oak, Hands Across the Sea*, and *Swan Song* (Globe, 1940), and toured military bases in these productions; directed *Dear Brutus*, in which he also played Will Dearth (Globe, London, Jan. 20, 1941); directed *Ducks and Drakes* (Apollo, Nov. 26, 1941); directed *Macbeth*, and played the title role (Piccadilly, July 8, 1942); and appeared as John Worthing in *The Importance of Being Earnest* (Phoenix, Oct. 14, 1942).

He toured Army camps in Gibraltar with Beatrice Lillie and Edith Evans in a revue (Dec. 1942); temporarily replaced (Jan. 1943) Peter Glenville as Louis Dubedat in *The Doctor's Dilemma* (Haymarket, Mar. 4, 1942); played Valentine in *Love for Love*, which he also directed (Phoenix, Apr. 8, 1943); staged *Landslide* (Westminster, Oct. 5, 1943); *The Cradle Song* (Apollo, Jan. 27, 1944); *Crisis in Heaven* (Lyric, May 10, 1944); and *The Last of Summer* (Phoenix, June 7, 1944). He appeard in repertory productions at the Haymarket, playing Champion-Cheney in *The Circle* (Oct. 11, 1944), Valentine in *Love for Love* (Oct. 12, 1944), the title role in *Hamlet* (Oct. 13, 1944), Oberon in *A Midsummer Night's Dream* (Jan. 25, 1945), and Ferdinand in *The Duchess of Malfi* (Apr. 18, 1945); and also directed *Lady Windermere's Fan* (Aug. 21, 1945).

He toured India, Burma, and Far East troop stations (1945–46) as Hamlet and as Charles Condamine in *Blithe Spirit;* toured England as Raskolnikoff in *Crime and Punishment*, and repeated this role in London (New, June 18, 1946); toured Canada and the US as John Worthing in *The Importance of Being Earnest* and Valentine in *Love for Love*, appearing in N.Y.C. in *The Importance of Being Earnest* (Royale, Mar. 3, 1947), and as Valentine in *Love for Love* (Royale, May 26, 1947); played Jason in *Medea*, which he also directed (National, Oct. 20, 1947); and Raskolnikoff in *Crime and Punishment* (National, Dec. 22, 1947).

He directed *The Glass Menagerie* (Haymarket, London, July 28, 1948); *Medea* (Globe, Sept. 29, 1948); played Eustace Jackson in *The Return of the Prodigal* (Globe, Nov. 24, 1948); directed *The Heiress* (Haymarket, Feb. 1, 1949); played Thomas Mendip in *The Lady's Not for Burning*, which he also directed, (Globe, May 11, 1949); directed *Much Ado About Nothing*, and also played Benedick (Stratford-upon-Avon, May 1949), *Treasure Hunt* (Apollo, Sept. 14, 1949); and the double bill, *Shall We Join the Ladies?* and *The Boy with a Cart* (Lyric, Hammersmith, Jan. 19, 1950). At the Shakespeare Memorial Th. (Stratford-upon-Avon), he played Angelo in *Measure for Measure* (Mar. 9, 1950), Cassius in *Julius Caesar* (May 2, 1950), and the title role in *King Lear* (July 18, 1950), which, with Anthony Quayle, he directed.

He played Thomas Mendip in *The Lady's Not for Burning* (Royale, N.Y.C., Nov. 8, 1950); Leontes in *The Winter's Tale* (Phoenix, London, June 27, 1951); directed *Indian Summer* (Criterion, Dec. 12, 1951); directed *Much Ado About Nothing* and also played Benedick (Phoenix, Jan. 11, 1952); directed *Macbeth* for the Shakespeare Memorial Th. (Stratford-upon-Avon, June 10, 1952); directed *Richard II* (Lyric, Hammersmith, London, Dec. 24, 1952); *The Way of the World*, in which he also played Mirabel (Lyric, Hammersmith, Feb. 19, 1953); and appeared as Jaffeir in *Venice Preserv'd* (Lyric, Hammersmith, May 15, 1953).

He toured Rhodesia in the title role in *Richard II* (July 1953); appeared as Julian Anson in *A Day by the Sea*, which he also directed (Haymarket, London, Nov. 26, 1953); directed *Charley's Aunt* (New, Feb. 10, 1954), his own adaptation of *The Cherry Orchard* (Lyric, Hammersmith, May 21, 1954), and *Twelfth Night* for the Shakespeare Memorial Th. (Stratford-upon-Avon, Apr. 12, 1955); toured Europe and the English provinces with the Shakespeare Memorial Th., playing Benedick in *Much Ado About Nothing*, which he directed, and also appearing in the title role in *King Lear*, and repeating the roles of Benedick (Palace, London, July 21, 1955) and King Lear (Palace, July 26, 1955); directed *The Chalk Garden* (Haymarket, Apr. 11, 1956); played Sebastian in and directed, with Noel Coward, *Nude with Violin* (Globe, Nov. 7, 1956).

He directed his first opera, *The Trojans* (Covent Garden, June 6, 1957); played Prospero in *The Tempest* (Shakespeare Memorial Th., Stratford-upon-Avon, Aug. 13, 1957; Drury Lane, London, Dec. 5, 1957); James Callifer in *The Potting Shed* (Globe, Feb. 5, 1958); directed *Variations on a Theme* (Globe, May 8, 1958); appeared as Cardinal Wolsey in *Henry VIII* (Old Vic, May 13, 1958), and toured France, Holland, and Belgium in the role.

He directed *Five Finger Exercise* (Comedy, London, July 17, 1958); toured Canada and the US in *The Ages of Man*, a solo recital which was then presented in N.Y.C. (46 St. Th., Dec. 18, 1958); he toured in *The Ages of Man* (Venice and Spoleto, Italy, 1959); staged *The Complaisant Lover* (Globe, London, June 18, 1959); appeared in *The Ages of Man* (Queen's, July 8, 1959); directd *Much Ado About Nothing* and also played Benedick (Cambridge Drama Festival, Boston, Mass., Aug. 1959; Lunt-Fontanne, N.Y.C., Sept. 17, 1959); staged *Five Finger Exercise* (Music Box, Dec. 2, 1959); and appeared in *The Ages of Man* (Haymarket, London, Apr. 13, 1960), in which he also toured Trieste, Milan, Bologna, and Rome, Italy (1960). He appeared as Prince Ferdinand Cavanati in *The Last Joke* (Phoenix, N.Y.C., Sept. 28, 1960); directed Benjamin Britten's opera, *A Midsummer Night's Dream* (Covent Garden, London, Feb. 3, 1961).

He staged *Big Fish, Little Fish* (ANTA, N.Y.C., Mar. 15, 1961); played the title role in *Othello* (Stratford-upon-Avon, England, Oct. 10, 1961); Gaev in *The Cherry Orchard* (Stratford-on-Avon, 1961) and repeated the role in London (Aldwych, 1961–62); toured Israel in *The Ages of Man* (1962), followed by tours of Australia and New Zealand (Oct. 1963–Jan. 1964), and tours of Gothenberg, Copenhagen, Stockholm, Helsinki, Warsaw, Moscow, and Leningrad (May 1964).

He directed *The School for Scandal* (Haymarket, London, Apr. 5, 1962) and replaced (Oct. 1962) John Neville as Joseph Surface in the same production before opening in N.Y.C. (Majestic, Jan. 24, 1963); appeared in a return engagement of *The Ages of Man* (Lyceum, Apr. 14, 1963); played Julius Caesar in *The Ides of March* (Haymarket, London, Aug. 8, 1963); appeared on a program of readings, *Homage to Shakespeare* (Philharmonic Hall, N.Y.C., Mar. 15, 1964); directed Richard Burton's *Hamlet*, a production in which his own recorded voice was The Ghost (Lunt-Fontanne Th., Apr. 9, 1964); played Julian in *Tiny Alice* (Billy Rose Th., Dec. 29, 1964), and during the run of that play appeared for a single performance in *The Ages of Man* at the White House, Washington, D.C. (Mar. 29, 1965).

He played Nikolai Ivanov and adapted and directed *Ivanov* (Yvonne Arnaud Th., Guildford, England, Aug. 30, 1965; Phoenix, London, Sept. 30, 1965; Sam S. Shubert Th., N.Y.C., May 3, 1966); performed in *Men and Women of Shakespeare* (Hunter Coll., Jan. 22, 1967); and *Ages of Man* in California (Huntington Hartford Th., Los Angeles, Jan. 30, 1967).

He played Orgon in *Tartuffe* (Old Vic, London, Nov. 21, 1967); directed *Halfway Up the Tree* (Queen's Th., Nov. 23, 1967); played the title role in *Oedipus* (Old Vic, Mar. 19, 1968); directed the opera *Don Giovanni* (Coliseum, Aug. 1968); played the Headmaster in *Forty Years On* (Apollo, Oct. 31, 1968); and was Gideon in *The Battle of Shrivings* (Lyric, Feb. 5, 1970). He also played Harry in *Home* (Royal Court, June 17, 1970; Morosco, N.Y.C., Nov. 1, 1970); directed *Private Lives* (Queen's Th., London, Sept. 21, 1972; on US-Canadian tour, 1974–75; 46 St. Th., N.Y.C., Feb. 6, 1975); directed *The Constant Wife* (Albery, London, Sept. 19, 1973; on tour in US, 1974–75; Shubert Th., N.Y.C., Apr. 14, 1975); played William Shakespeare in *Bingo* (Royal Court, London, Oct. 5, 1974); and was Spooner in *No Man's Land* (Old Vic, Apr. 23, 1975).

Films. Sir John Gielgud appeared in *Insult* (1932); *The Good Companions* (20th-Fox, 1933); *The Secret Agent* (Gaumont, 1936); as Disraeli in *The Prime Minister* (WB, 1941); Cassius in *Julius Caesar* (MGM, 1953); the Duke of Clarence in *Richard III* (Lopert, 1956); Warwick in *Saint Joan* (UA, 1957); the Valet in *Around the World in 80 Days* (UA, 1956); and Louis, King of France, in *Becket* (Par., 1963).

His other films include *The Loved One* (MGM, 1965); *Chimes at Midnight,* also known as *Falstaff* (Peppercorn-Wormser-Saltzman, 1967); *Sebastian* (Par., 1968); *The Charge of the Light Brigade* (UA, 1968); *The Shoes of the Fisherman* (MGM, 1968); *Oh! What a Lovely War* (Par., 1969); *Eagle in a Cage* (1969); and *Julius Caesar* (Commonwealth United, 1969).

Television. He made his television debut in London in *A Day by the Sea* (ITV, Mar., 1959) and first appeared on US television in *The Browning Version* (CBS, Apr. 23, 1959). He was also on television in *The Rehearsal* (London, Jan. 1963); *The Professors and the Professionals* (U.S.A.—Th., NET, 1966); *The Ages of Man* special (CBS, Jan. 23, and 30, 1966); *The Love Song of Barney Kempinski* (Stage 67, ABC, July 1966); *Alice in Wonderland* (BBC, Aug. 1966); a John Gielgud special consisting of selected readings (BBC, London, Oct. 2, and 9, 1966); a repeat of his appearance in the title role of *Ivanov,* which, with John Bowen, he adapted for television (CBS, May 30, 1967); *From Chekhov with Love* (BBC, June 14, 1967); *St. Joan* (BBC, Feb. 1968); *In Good King Charles's Golden Days* (BBC, Apr. 1969); *Conversation at Night* (BBC, Apr. 1969); *Hassan* (BBC, Apr. 1970); *Hamlet* (Hallmark Hall of Fame, NBC, Nov. 17, 1970); and *Home* (PBS, Nov. 29, 1971).

Published Works. Sir John's books include his autobiography, *Early Stages* (1939); *Stage Directions* (1964); *Distinguished Company* (1973); and his adaptations of *The Cherry Orchard* and *Ivanov* (1966).

Awards. Sir John's knighthood was announced on the Coronation Honours List of June 2, 1953. He is also a chevalier of the French Legion of Honor and received honorary degrees from St. Andrews' Univ., Scotland (LL.D., 1950), Oxford Univ. (D. Litt., 1953), and Brandeis Univ. (LL.D., 1965). He received a special Antoinette Perry (Tony) Award in 1959 for *The Ages of Man;* a Tony (1961) for his direction of *Big Fish, Little Fish;* was named in the *Variety* poll of London critics as best male performer (1968–69) for *Forty Years On;* and for his performance in *Home,* he received a Drama Desk Award (1971) and a Tony nomination as best actor.

Recreation. Music, painting, attending films.

GIERASCH, STEFAN. Actor. b. Feb. 5, 1926, New York City. Member of AEA; SAG; Actors Studio (1953–to date).

Theatre. Mr. Gierasch made his NY debut as assistant stage manager and understudy in the part of Dexter in *Kiss and Tell* (Biltmore, Mar. 17, 1943), which he performed occasionally. He subsequently appeared as a replacement in *Get Away Old Man* (Cort, Nov. 24, 1943); played the Third Legionnaire in *Snafu* (Hudson, Oct. 25, 1944); replaced Douglas Jones as the Newsboy in *Billion Dollar Baby* (Alvin, Dec. 21, 1945); played a Soldier in *Montserratt* (Fulton, Oct. 29, 1949); Marty in *Night Music* (ANTA Th., Apr. 8, 1951); Valentin in *Maya* (Th. de Lys, June 9, 1953); Micah in *The Scarecrow* (Th. de Lys, June 16, 1953); Sanathanaka in *The Little Clay Cart* (Th. de Lys, June 30, 1953); the Drunk in *Mardi Gras* (pre-Bway tryout, opened Locust, Philadelphia, Jan. 13, 1954; closed there Jan. 23, 1954); Smith in *The Threepenny Opera* (Th. de Lys, Sept. 20, 1955); Matvai in *A Month in the Country* (Phoenix Th., Apr. 13, 1956); Postmaster in *Purple Dust* (Cherry Lane Th., Dec. 27, 1956); Max Steiner in *Compulsion* (Ambassador, Oct. 24, 1957); the Guard in *Deathwatch* (Th. East, Oct. 9, 1958); Tommy Owens in *The Shadow of a Gunman* (Bijou, Nov. 19, 1958); Herr Zeller in *The Sound of Music* (Lunt-Fontanne Th., Nov. 16, 1959); Patch Keegan in *Little Moon of Alban* (Longacre, Dec. 1, 1960); Jimmy Beales in *Roots* (Mayfair, Mar. 6, 1961); Leon Hallet in *Isle of Children* (Cort, Mar. 16, 1962); replaced John Becher (May 28, 1963) as Guss in *The Collection,* on a double-bill with *The Dumbwaiter* (Cherry Lane Th., Nov. 26, 1962); played Kenneth O'Keefe in *The Ginger Man* (Orpheum, Nov. 21, 1963); Jacobson in *The Deputy* (Brooks Atkinson Th., Feb. 26, 1964); at the Milwaukee Repertory Th., appeared in *The Tempest* (Jan. 27, 1965); *Under Milk Wood* (Feb. 17, 1965); *Pantagleize* (Mar. 10, 1965), *Mother Courage* (Jan. 13, 1966), *Henry IV, Part 1* (Feb. 24, 1966), *The Glass Menagerie* (Mar. 17, 1966), *Saint Joan* (Oct. 28, 1965), and *The Time of Your Life* (Dec. 9, 1965); at Trinity Sq. Playhouse (Providence, R.I.), appeared in *Saint Joan* (Oct. 11, 1966), and *Ah, Wilderness!* (Jan. 17, 1967); played Pierre in the APA production of *War and Peace* (Lyceum, N.Y.C., Mar. 21, 1967); appeared in *Enrico IV* (Studio Arena, Buffalo, Jan. 11, 1968); at the American Shakespeare Fest. Th. (Stratford, Conn.), appeared in *As You Like It* (June 23, 1968) and *Love's Labour's Lost* (June 26, 1968); played Phil Hogan in *A Moon for the Misbegotten* (tour, May 12, 1969); Zelo Shimanksy in *Seven Days of Mourning* (Circle in the Square, Dec. 16, 1969); Perowne in *AC/DC* (Brooklyn Academy of Music, Feb. 23, 1971); appeared in *Hamlet* (Long Wharf Th., New Haven, Conn., Jan. 21, 1972); *Owners* (Mercer-Shaw Th., N.Y.C., May 14, 1973); played Moke in *Nellie Toole & Co.* (Th. Four, Sept. 24, 1973); Harry Hope in *The Iceman Cometh* (Circle in the Square/-Joseph E. Levine Th., Dec. 13, 1973); and Candy in *Of Mice and Men* (Brooks Atkinson Th., Dec. 18, 1974).

Films. Mr. Gierasch has appeared in *The Young Don't Cry* (Col., 1957); *Stage Struck* (BV, 1957); *The Hustler* (20th-Fox, 1961); *The Traveling Executioner* (MGM, 1970); *What's Up, Doc?* (WB, 1972); *The New Centurians* (Col., 1972); *Jeremiah Johnson* (WB, 1972); *High Plains Drifter* (U, 1973); and *Claudine* (20th-Fox, 1974).

GIGLIO, A. GINO. Manager-producer. b. July 16, Elizabeth, N.J., to A.S.V. and Rose (Marinello) Giglio. Father, physician. Grad. New Utrecht H.S., Brooklyn, N.Y., 1949; Yale Univ., B.A. 1953; NY Sch. of Radio and Television, certificate, 1955; attended Columbia Univ. Drama Sch., 1955–56; Yale Univ. Sch. of Drama, 1958. Married May 26, 1961, to Rita Nolan (marr. dis. Sept, 29, 1967); two daughters. Served US Army, personnel psychologist, 1953–55; rank, Cpl. Member of AEA; ATPAM (membership comm., 1962–64; bd. of gov., 1962–to date; agent, 1971–72); SSD&C (founding mem.; negotiating comm. for SSD&C for 1st and 2nd League of NY Theatres contracts); Yale Alumni Assn.; Boys Club of NY Alumni Assn.; The Yale Club of NYC. Address: c/o SSD&C, 1619 Broadway, New York, NY 10036, tel. (212) 246-5118.

Theatre. Mr. Giglio served as assistant to the producers of *The Threepenny Opera* (Th. de Lys, N.Y.C., Sept. 20, 1955); production assistant for *The Beautiful Changes* (President, Mar. 1956); stage manager and publicity director at the Poultney (Vt.) Playhouse (Summer 1956). He was assistant to the producers of *The Potting Shed* (Bijou, N.Y.C., Jan. 29, 1957); resident manager of the Valley Forge Music Fair (Devon, Pa., Summer 1957); publicity assistant for the Theatre Guild productions of *Tunnel of Love* (Royale, N.Y.C., Feb. 13, 1957); *Sunrise at Campobello* (Cort, Jan. 30, 1958); and others; director at the Hilltop Th. (Owings Mills, Md., Summer 1958); directed *The Redemptor* (Cricket, N.Y.C., May 1959); and was resident manager of the Neptune (N.J.) Music Circus (Summer 1959).

He served as treasurer for *Time of Vengeance* (York Playhouse, N.Y.C., Dec. 10, 1959); for *Between Two Thieves* (York Playhouse, Feb. 11, 1960); succeeded (Feb. 1961) the late Manny Davis as company manager for *A Taste of Honey* (Lyceum, Oct. 4, 1960), and the national tour (opened Natl., Washington, D.C., Sept. 11, 1961; closed Blackstone, Chicago, Ill., Apr. 7, 1962); was company manager for *Ross* (Eugene O'Neill Th., N.Y.C., Dec. 26, 1961); *I Can Get it for You Wholesale* (Shubert, Mar. 22, 1962); *An Evening With Belafonte* (Civic Aud., Pittsburgh, Pa., Aug. 1962); management consultant for the Little Th. (N.Y.C., Oct. 1962); company manager for *Les Poupées de Paris* ("The Dolls of Paris") (York Playhouse, Dec. 11, 1962); general manager for *The Threepenny Opera* (Civic Th., Chicago, Ill., Apr. 1963); the Dorchester Music Hall (Dolton, Ill., May–Sept. 1963); and *Semi-Detached* (Music Box, N.Y.C., Oct. 7, 1963); company manager for *Arturo Ui* (Lunt-Fontanne, Nov. 11, 1963); *Man and Boy* (Brooks Atkinson Th., Nov. 12, 1963); *Rugantino* (Lunt-Fontanne, Feb. 6, 1964); and *To Broadway With Love* (Texas Pavilion, NY World's Fair, Apr. 20, 1964). Mr. Giglio was first general manager of Theatre of the Living Arts, Philadelphia's (Pa.) first regional theatre (1964–to August 1965). He was company manager (Sept. 1965–June 26, 1971) for *Man of La Mancha* (ANTA Washington Sq., Nov. 22, 1965); general manager of *Tea Party* and *The Basement* (Eastside Playhouse, Oct. 15, 1968); and he directed *The Reason Why* and *Fame* (New Theatre Workshop, Dec. 1969). He became house manager, Minskoff Th., N.Y.C., on Dec. 4, 1972.

Films. He was assistant director for *Shadows* (Lion Intl., 1961). He produced *The Reason Why* in 1970.

Other Activities. He was copywriter for MCA-TV (Sept. 1955–Mar. 1956); and assistant to the director of public relations for the Council of the Living Theatre (League of NY Theatres; Oct. 1959–Aug. 1961).

Recreation. Swimming; winning US government patents.

GILBERT, LOU. Actor. b. Louis Gitlitz, Aug. 1, 1909, Sycamore, Ill., to Morris and Rose (Chosid) Gitlitz. Father, iron construction worker. Grad. Central H.S., Cleveland, Ohio, 1926. Studied at Actors Studio (member since 1948). Married May 5, 1951, to Martha Lou Hawkins; one son, one daughter. Member of AEA; SAG; AFTRA; Jewish Orphan Home Alumni.

Pre-Theatre. Buying and reclaiming old photographic and X-ray films.

Theatre. Mr. Gilbert first performed on a stage as George Washington in *Life of Washington* (Jewish Orphans Home, Cleveland, Ohio, 1916); subsequently played Lapo in *The Jest* (Cleveland Play House, Ohio, 1924); appeared in *Fashion* (1929); played Hind-End of the Horse in *White Wings;* the Third Murderer in *Macbeth;* an Office Worker in *The Adding Machine;* Augustus Fogg in *Fashion;* and performed in *The Green Cockatoo* (1928).

At the Jewish Peoples Inst. (Cleveland, Ohio), he served as stage manager for *The Royal Family* (1929); played Dobchinsky in *The Inspector General* (1929); Blanguet in *Bird in Hand* (1930); Tanchum in *The Golem* (1931); and appeared in the Jewish Peoples Inst. production of *The Tenth Man* (Palace Th., Chicago, Ill., May 1931).

He played Fremont in *Precedent* (Goodman Th., Chicago, Apr. 1933); Morry Norton in *Fortune Heights* (Women's Club Th., Chicago, Mar. 1935); Harry Fayett in *Waiting for Lefty* (Civic Th., Chicago, May 1935); Kucher in *The Young Go First* (Chicago Repertory Hall, Apr. 1936); the Chain Gang Captain in *Hymn to the Rising Sun,* and Harry Fayett in *Waiting for Lefty* (Chicago Community Centers, June 1936); and Pop in *Black Pit* (Moose Hall, Chicago, Nov. 1936).

At the Repertory Group Hall, Chicago, he played Pvt. Webster in *Bury the Dead* (Nov. 1937); John L. Lewis in *One Third of a Nation* (Feb. 1938); and Harry in *The Cradle Will Rock* (Oct. 1939); appeared as Matt Mathews in *A Time to Remember* (Hull

House, Northwestern Univ., Evanston, Ill., Feb. 1940); Jedidiah Peck in *The Man of Monticello* (Chicago Repertory Group Th., May 1941); Inspector Slannery in a stock production of *Thunder Rock* (Cedarhurst Th., N.Y., Jan. 1944); the Man in the Audience in *That They May Win* (Henry Hudson Hotel, N.Y.C., Apr. 1944); and played Burle Sullivan in *The Milky Way* and Binion in *Room Service* (Lyric, Allentown, Pa., July 1944).

He made his Bway debut as the Second Italian Soldier in *Common Ground* (Fulton Th., N.Y.C., Apr. 25, 1945); served as assistant stage manager and played Ziggie in *Beggars Are Coming to Town* (Coronet, Oct. 27, 1945); appeared as the Man with a Pail in *Truckline Cafe* (Belasco, Feb. 27, 1946); Luigi in *Dream Girl* (Harris, Chicago, Aug. 1946); and was assistant stage manager for *The Whole World Over* (Biltmore, N.Y.C., Mar. 27, 1947).

He played Notorio in *Volpone* (NY City Ctr., Jan. 8, 1948); Charlie in *Hope Is a Thing with Feathers* (Maxine Elliott's Th., Apr. 11, 1948); was assistant stage manager and played the Old Man in *Sundown Beach* (Belasco, Sept. 7, 1948); Joe Feinson in *Detective Story* (Hudson, Mar. 23, 1949); and Moish in a pre-Bway tryout of *My Fiddle's Got Three Strings* (Westport Country Playhouse, Conn., Aug. 1950).

Mr. Gilbert appeared as the Town Drunkard in Arthur Miller's adaptation of *An Enemy of the People* (Broadhurst, N.Y.C., Dec. 28, 1950); a supernumerary in *Anna Christie* (NY City Ctr., Jan. 9, 1952); Dr. Maurice Ritz in the pre-Bway tour of *The Grass Harp* (Colonial, Boston, Mass., Mar. 1952); Dan Harkavy in *The Victim* (President, N.Y.C., May 2, 1962); Simon Cabot in *Desire Under the Elms* (Cecilwood Th., Fishkill, N.Y., July 1952); and E. T. Ganning in *First Lady* (Cecilwood Th., Aug. 1952).

He played Sam in *Whistler's Grandmother* (President, N.Y.C., Dec. 11, 1952); the Man in the Window in the pre-Bway tryout of *The Frogs of Spring* (Falmouth Th., Mass., July 1953); the Super in *His and Hers* (48 St. Th., Jan. 7, 1954); Mannheim in *The Front Page* (Playhouse-in-the-Park, Philadelphia, Pa., July 1954); and at the Westport (Conn.) Country Playhouse (July 1954), appeared as Mr. Cracheton in *The Apollo of Bellac* and performed in *The Shewing Up of Blanco Posnet.*

Mr. Gilbert appeared in stock as the Doctor in *The Dragon Slayer* (Theatre-by-th-Sea, Matunuck, R.I., Aug. 1958); Dr. Chumley in *Harvey* (Easton, Pa., June 1959); a Russian Commissar in *Silk Stockings* (Clio-Musical Tent, Mich., July 1959); the Woodcutter in *Roshomon* (Music Tent, Highland Park, Ill., Aug. 1959); Augusto in *Time of Vengence* (York Playhouse, N.Y.C., Dec. 10, 1959); and at the Tapia Th., San Juan (P.R.) Drama Festival, played Dr. Einstein in *Arsenic and Old Lace* (Dec. 1959–Jan. 1960); Mackenzie in *The Pleasure of His Company* (Feb. 1960); and Eddie Brock in *Born Yesterday* (Mar. 1960).

He appeared as Ellis in *Between Two Thieves* (Cleveland Play House, Ohio, Nov. 1960); Doc in tours of *West Side Story* (Summers 1960, 1961); the Judge, the Uncle, and Barbedart in *The Egg* (Cort, N.Y.C., Jan. 8, 1962); at the NY Shakespeare Festival, played Gonzalo in *The Tempest* (Delacort, July 1962); and the French Doctor in *King Lear* (Delacorte, Aug. 1962); played Harry Stein in *In the Counting House* (Biltmore, N.Y.C., Dec. 13, 1962); Mac Davies in *The Caretaker* (Second City, Chicago, Ill., Feb. 1963); and appeared in *Come Blow Your Horn* and as the Spaniard in *Journey to Bahia* (Berkshire Playhouse, Stockbridge, Mass., 1964).

He played Sender in *The Dybbuk* (Fourth St. Th., N.Y.C., Oct. 26, 1954); Mr. Cohen in *Abie's Irish Rose* (Holiday, Nov. 18, 1954); Felix Ducatel in a Subway Circuit tour of *My Three Angels* (N.Y.C., Dec. 1954); Kugelman in *Highway Robbery* (President, Nov. 1955); Pablo Gonzales in *A Streetcar Named Desire* (Royal Poinciana Playhouse, Palm Beach, Fla., Jan.–Feb. 1956; NY City Ctr., Feb. 15, 1956); Mr. Shaaf in *A Month in the Country* (Phoenix, N.Y.C., Apr 3, 1956); and at the Casino Th. (Newport, R.I.), appeared as Dr. Brubaker in *The Seven Year Itch* (June 1956); and Max Pincus in *The Fifth Season* (July 1956).

He played Pilsudski in *Good as Gold* (Belasco, N.Y.C., Mar. 7, 1957); Dr. Tehebutykin in *The Three Sisters* (Arena Th., Edison Hotel, Apr. 1957); succeeded (May 1957) Jack Gilford as Dr. Dussel in *The Diary of Anne Frank* (Cort, Oct. 5, 1955), and toured in it (opened Huntington Hartford Th., Hollywood, Calif., July 29, 1957; closed National, Washington, D.C., July 14, 1958).

Mr. Gilbert played Ottoman in *Sing To Me Through Open Windows,* and Old Gayve in *The Day the Whores Came Out To Play Tennis* (Players, N.Y.C., Mar. 14, 1965); Benny Grassman in *Big Man* (Cherry Lane Th., May 19, 1966); Servino in *The Rogues' Trial* (Actors Studio, May 25, 1966), which was a studio project developed in the Actors Unit; the Shell Shocked Soldier in *Dynamite Tonite* Martinique, Mar. 14, 1967); understudied Menasha Skulnik in the title role in the pre-Bway tryout of *Chu Chem* (opened New Locust, Philadelphia, Nov. 14, 1966; closed there Nov. 19, 1966): played Hardrader in *The Happy Haven* (Columbia Univ. Summer Rep. Th., N.Y.C., Aug. 1, 1967); Goldie in *The Great White Hope* (Arena Stage, Washington, D.C., 1967–68 season; and Alvin, N.Y.C., Oct. 3, 1968); with the Repertory Co. of Lincoln Center, Wong in *The Good Woman of Setzuan* (Vivian Beaumont Th., Nov. 4, 1970); played Arab in *The Time of Your Life* (opened Kennedy Ctr., Washington, D.C., Jan. 12, 1972; closed Huntington Hartford Th., Los Angeles, Apr. 8, 1972); appeared with the company at Arena Stage (Washington, D.C., 1971–72 season); played Chemuel, Angel of Mercy in *The Creation of the World and Other Business* (Shubert, N.Y.C., Nov. 30, 1972); Antonio in *Much Ado About Nothing* (NY Shakespeare Fest., Summer, 1972); the Old Man in *Baba Goya* (American Place Th., May 21, 1973); the Old Man in *Nourish the Beast* (Cherry Lane Th., Oct. 3, 1973); Mr. Greenburg in *A Community of Two* (tour, opened Dupont Th., Wilmington, Del., Dec. 31, 1973); and Adam in *As You Like It* (NY Shakespeare Fest., Delacorte Th., N.Y.C., Summer 1973).

Films. Mr. Gilbert made his debut as Pablo Gomez in *Viva Zapata!* (20th-Fox, 1952); subsequently appeared in *Middle of the Night* (Col., 1959); as Elijah—The Prophet in *Goldstein,* which was exhibited at the Cannes (France) Film Festival (May 1964); Obidiah, the junk peddler in *Across the River,* shown at the Venice (Italy) Film Festival (Aug. 1964); Requiem for a Heavyweight (Col., 1962); *Goldstein* (Altura, 1965); *Petulia* (WB-Seven Arts, 1968); *The Great White Hope* (20th-Fox, 1970); *Fearless Frank* (AI, 1970); and *Jennifer on My Mind* (UA, 1971).

Television. He played Norby in *What Makes Sammy Run?* (Philco Television Playhouse, NBC, 1949); the Bum in the Park in *The Great Association* (ABC, 1951); and the Townsman on the opening segment of the Herb Shriner Show (NBC, 1951). His subsequent appearances include The Defenders (CBS); Trials of O'Brien (CBS); Hawk (ABC); *An Enemy of the People* (NET); Hallmark Hall of Fame (NBC); and The Eternal Light (NBC).

Awards. Mr. Gilbert received the Clarence Derwent Award for his performance as Charlie in *Hope Is a Thing with Feathers* (1948–49); the American Newspaper Guild Award and the Page One Award for his performance as Joe Feinson in *Detective Story* (1949).

Recreation. Family.

GILBERT, WILLIE. Playwright. b. William Gilbert Gomberg, Feb. 24, 1916, Cleveland, Ohio, to Louis and Jessie (Pollock) Gomberg. Father, grocer. Grad. Glenville H.S., 1934; Ohio State Univ., B.S. Ed., 1938. Married Oct. 25, 1957, to Jane Hutchinson; two daughters. Served US Army, 1942; rank T/Sgt. Member of Dramatists Guild; WGA; ASCAP. Address: (home) 225 E. 70th St., New York, NY 10021, tel. (212) UN 1-6156; (bus.) tel. (212) 687-1295.

Pre-Theatre. Wrote comedy-variety shows and dramatic shows for television (1950–61).

Theatre. Mr. Gilbert wrote, with Jack Weinstock and Abe Burrows, the book for *How to Succeed in Business Without Really Trying* (46 St. Th., Oct. 14, 1961); and, with Jack Weinstock, the book for *Hot Spot* (Majestic, Apr. 19, 1963), and the play, *Catch Me If You Can* (Morosco, Mar. 9, 1965).

Films. Mr. Gilbert wrote, with Jack Weinstock, the screenplay for *Santa Claus Conquers the Martians* (Embassy, 1964).

Awards. *How to Succeed in Business Without Really Trying* received the Pulitzer Prize (1962); Antoinette Perry (Tony) Award (1962); and the NY Drama Critics Circle Award (1962).

Recreation. Painting.

GILDER, ROSAMOND. Writer, editor, lecturer. b. Janet Rosamond de Kay Gilder, Marion, Mass., to Richard Watson and Helena (de Kay) Gilder. Father, poet, editor of *Century* Magazine; mother, painter. Attended Brearley Sch., N.Y.C. Member of ANTA (secy., 1946–50; board, vice-pres., 1946–68); NTC (editorial secy., 1932–36); New York Drama Critics' Circle (secy., 1946–50; hon. member, 1950–to date); Natl. Commission for UNESCO (chmn., panel on dramatic art, 1948–54); Cosmopolitan Club (pres., 1930). Address: (home) 24 Gramercy Park, New York, NY 10003; (bus.) c/o International Theatre Institute of the US, 245 W. 52nd St., New York, NY 10019, tel. (212) PL 7-4133.

Since 1948, Miss Gilder has been director of the US Center of Intl. Theatre Institute (ITI), of which she was a founder and vice-pres. (1947–62), and pres. (1963–to date); has been chairman of the US delegations to ITI Congresses (1947–73).

She was on the editorial committee of *World Theatre,* for which she wrote quarterly reports about the theatre in the US; was an associate editor, drama critic, and editor of *Theatre Arts Monthly* (1925–48); and has contributed articles on the theatre to magazines. She was director of the Bureau of Research and Publications of the Federal Theatre (WPA) Project, N.Y.C. (1935–36).

She was an instructor in English at Barnard Coll. (1949–55), and has lectured on the theatre in the US, Europe, India, and Japan.

Published Works. Miss Gilder compiled and edited *Letters of Richard Watson Gilder* (1916); translated and helped write *My Life* by Emma Calve (1922); compiled *A Theatre Library,* a bibliography of 100 books relating to the theatre (1932); and, with George Freedley, compiled *Theatre Collections in Libraries and Museums* (1936); wrote *John Gielgud's Hamlet* (1937); was an editor of *Theatre Arts Anthology* (1950); and wrote *Enter the Actress* (1960).

Awards. In recognition of her achievements in the cause of American and world theatre, she received the Medaille de Reconnaisance Française and was made Officier de l'Ordre des Arts et des Lettres in 1965. Her American awards include a "Tony" in 1948, AETA Award in 1961, Kelcey Allen Award in 1963, ANTA Award in 1965, and USITT Award in 1967. She received a Guggenheim Fellowship (1950); a Fulbright Fellowship (1955–56); and a US American Specialists Grant (1961; 1963).

GILES, PAUL KIRK. Union executive, former actor. b. Dec. 23, 1895, Lancaster, Pa., to Joseph L. and Laura (Eshleman) Gyles. Grad. Franklin & Marshall Acad., Lancaster, 1922; Franklin & Marshall Coll., Lancaster, 1926. Married June 23, 1923, to Mary Randolph (marr. dis. Jan. 1944); married July 22, 1944, to Mary Ashby Acree; two daughters. Served USN, 1917–19, North Sea Mine Force; USO, 1945. Member of AEA; AFTRA; The Lambs; Episcopal Actors Guild (vice-pres.); St. Cecile Masonic Lodge 586; Little Church Around the Corner, N.Y.C. (vestryman). Address: (home) 4801 42nd St., Sunnyside, NY 11104, tel. (212) ST 4-4183; (bus.) The Bedside Network, Dir. Hospital Services, 353 W. 57th St., New York, NY 10019, tel. (212) 757-8657.

Pre-Theatre. Broker.

Theatre. Mr. Giles was president of the NY branch of the Screen Actor's Guild (1951–53), and has been assistant executive secretary (1953–64).

He made his first appearance as an actor, with the Crane-Burkley Stock Co. (Lancaster, Pa., 1923); performed in five plays with the Playlikers (Univ. of

North Carolina, Durham, 1931); played Gibbett in *Beaux' Strategem* (Columbia Univ., N.Y.C., 1937); appeared in stock at Harvey's Lake Th. (Wilkes Barre, Pa., Summers 1937–38); and in the variety musical, *American Jubilee* (NY World's Fair, 1940).

Mr. Giles toured as Uncle Willis in the national company of *Junior Miss* (opened Locust Th., Philadelphia, Pa., Nov. 1942), in which he subsequently toured for the USO (Western Pacific, 1945); and performed with a resident company at Lowell, Mass. (Summer 1944). He made his Bway debut as the Sgt. in *Pillar to Post* (Playhouse, Dec. 19, 1943); subsequently appeared as a Furniture Mover in the pre-Bway tryout of *Champagne for Everybody* (opened Natl., Washington, D.C., Sept. 4, 1944; closed Walnut St. Th., Philadelphia, Pa., Sept. 16, 1944); Mr. Snyder in the pre-Bway tryout of *Horses Are Like That* (Shubert-Lafayette, Detroit, Mich., Oct. 24, 1944; closed there Nov. 4, 1944); was stage manager and played a small role in *Kiss Them for Me* (Belasco, N.Y.C., Mar. 20, 1945); appeared with a resident company at Mt. Gretna (Pa.) Playhouse (Summer 1946); played the Barber in the national tour of *Born Yesterday* (opened Erlanger, Chicago, Ill., Jan. 1947), and succeeded (Feb. 1950) Gerald Cornell as the assistant manager in the N.Y.C. production of the same play (Lyceum, Feb. 4, 1946); and appeared as Reed Armstrong in *The Small Hours* (Natl., Feb. 15, 1951).

Films. Mr. Giles appeared as the hotel clerk in *Barefoot in the Park* (Par., 1966).

Television. Mr. Giles appeared on Studio One (CBS); Kraft Television Th. (NBC); Dark Shadows; As the World Turns (CBS); and Love Is a Many Splendored Thing.

Radio. Mr. Giles was regularly heard on The Lone Ranger; Green Hornet; Call of the Yukon; Gangbusters; March of Time; and Cavalcade of America.

Other Activities. Mr. Giles contributed sketches and illustrations to *Equity Magazine* (1946–52).

Recreation. Water-color paintings, crayon sketches.

GILFORD, JACK. Actor. b. Jacob Gellman, July 25, New York City, to Aaron and Sophie Gellman. Father, furrier. Attended Commercial H.S., Brooklyn, N.Y. Married Apr. 6, 1949, to Madeline Lee, actress. Relatives in theatre: son, Joseph E. Gilford, film maker; sister-in-law, Thelma Lee, comedienne; sister-in-law, Fran Lee, actress. Member of AEA; AFTRA; AGVA; SAG; AGMA.

Pre-Theatre. Textile business.

Theatre. Mr. Gilford began his career as a comedian in an amateur night show (Bronx Opera House, N.Y., Mar. 1934); subsequently appeared as a comedian in the *Leavitt and Lockwood Revue* (Shamokin, Pa.; Nanticoke, Pa., Apr. 1934); and in amateur night presentations in N.Y.C. and vicinity (Summers 1934–35); and toured eastern cities as a vaudeville comedian with the Mildred Harris Chaplin Revue (Dec. 1934).

He appeared as a comedian in the *Milton Berle Revue* (Chicago Th., Ill., Dec. 1935; RKO Palace, Chicago, Sept. 1937; RKO, Boston, Mass., Mar. 1938; Loew's State, N.Y.C., Oct. 1938); in a stage show (Roxy Th., N.Y.C., Oct. 1936); toured eastern theatres in vaudeville (Winter 1936); toured US and Canada in the *Ina Ray Hutton Revue* (Fall 1937; Winter 1937–38); appeared in a vaudeville show (State Th., Hartford, Conn., Sept. 1938); in a comedy act with Elsie Janis (Music Box Th., N.Y.C., 1939); appeared as a comedian in *Meet the People* (Hollywood Playhouse, Calif., Mar. 1940), toured in it (1941) and appeared in it in N.Y.C. (Mansfield, Dec. 25, 1940).

He appeared as a comedian in a vaudeville show (Chicago Th., June 1941); toured the Midwest in Paul Whiteman's stage show (July 1941); appeared in Jimmy Dorsey's stage show (Paramount Th., N.Y.C., Sept. 1941); as a comedian in a stage show (Olympia Th., Miami, Fla., Oct. 1941); played Barney Snediker in *They Should Have Stood in Bed* (Mansfield, N.Y.C., Feb. 13, 1942); appeared as a comedian in *Count Me In* (Ethel Barrymore Th., Oct. 8, 1942); *Meet the People* (Assistance League Th., Hollywood, Calif., July 1943); and toured with the USO as emcee and comedian in a variety show (US Army Camps and Hospitals, Mid-Pacific Theatre of Operations, Feb. 1945).

He appeared as emcee and comedian at Loew's theatres in Cleveland (Ohio) and St. Louis (Mo., July 1949); as a comedian in *Alive and Kicking* (Winter Garden, Jan. 17, 1950); in a stage show (Palace, Mar. 1950); as Sol Margolis in *The Live Wire* (Playhouse, Aug. 17, 1950); and Frosch in the opera *Die Fledermaus* (Metropolitan Opera House, N.Y.C., Dec. 1950), on tour (1951–52); and again at the Metropolitan (1958–59, 1962–63, 1963–64, 1966–67).

He appeared as Bontche Schweig in *The World of Shalom Aleichem* (Barbizon-Plaza, May 1, 1953); Alexander Gross in *Passion of Gross* (Th. de Lys, Jan. 22, 1955); as a comedian in *Once Over Lightly* (Barbizon-Plaza, Mar. 15, 1955); Mr. Dussel in *The Diary of Anne Frank* (Cort, Oct. 5, 1955); the Second Soldier in *Romanoff and Juliet* (Plymouth, Oct. 10, 1957); Dr. Ullman in *Drink to Me Only* (54 St. Th., Oct. 8, 1958); and Yacob Von Putziboum in *Look After Lulu* (Henry Miller's Th., Mar. 3, 1959).

He played King Sextimus in *Once Upon a Mattress* (Phoenix, May 11, 1959); toured as a comedian in the Oldsmobile Show (Aug. 1959); played Mr. Zitorsky in *The Tenth Man* (Booth, Nov. 5, 1959); appeared in comedy roles in stock productions of *The Desert Song, Can-Can,* and *Cinderella* (South Shore Music Circus, Cohasset, Mass.; St. Louis Municipal Opera, Mo.; Aug. 1961); played Goddard Quagmeyer in *The Beauty Part* (Bucks County Playhouse, New Hope, Pa., Sept. 1961); the Sergeant in *The Policemen* (Phoenix, N.Y.C., Dec. 10, 1961); Hysterium in *A Funny Thing Happened on the Way to the Forum* (Alvin, May 8, 1962); Herr Schultz in *Cabaret* (Broadhurst, Nov. 20, 1966); Erwin Trowbridge in *Three Men on a Horse* (Lyceum, Oct. 16, 1969); Jimmy Smith in *No, No, Nanette* (46th St. Th., Jan. 19, 1971); replaced (Oct. 1973) Jack Albertson as Willie Clark in *The Sunshine Boys* (Broadhurst, Dec. 20, 1972).

Films. Mr. Gilford has appeared in *Hey, Rookie* (Col., 1944); *Reckless Age* (U, 1944); and *Main Street to Broadway* (MGM, 1953); *The Daydreamer* (Avco Embassy, 1965); *A Funny Thing Happened on the Way to the Forum* (UA, 1965); *Mr. Budwing* (MGM, 1966); *Enter Laughing* (Col., 1966); *Who's Minding the Mint?* (Col., 1967); *The Incident* (20th-Fox, 1967); *Catch-22* (Par., 1969); *They Might Be Giants* (U, 1969); and *Save the Tiger* (Par., 1972).

Television and Radio. He performed on the radio program, the Philip Morris Show (NBC, 1947).

Mr. Gilford has appeared on television as Mr. Arrow on the Arrow Show (NBC, 1948); on the Garry Moore Show (CBS, 1950); the Milton Berle Show (NBC, 1951); the Jack Carson Show (NBC, 1951); the Frank Sinatra Show (CBS, 1951); *The World of Shalom Aleichem* (Play of the Week, WNTA, 1960); *Cowboy and the Tiger* (ABC, 1963); *Once Upon a Mattress* (CBS, 1964); The Defenders (CBS, 1964); Car 54, Where Are You? (NBC, 1964); the Allan Sherman Special (NBC, 1965); The Lucy Show (CBS, 1968); The Ghost and Mrs. Muir (1968); Get Smart (CBS, 1969); The Governor and J. J. (CBS, 1969); David Frost Revue (1971, 1972); Carol Burnett Show (CBS, 1972); *Once Upon a Mattress* (CBS, 1972); *Of Thee I Sing* (CBS, 1972); and *Hotel 90* (CBS, 1973).

Night Clubs. He has performed at the Chez Paree (Chicago, Ill., 1936); Paradise Restaurant (N.Y.C., 1936); in hotel revues at Camp Copake (N.Y., 1937, 1938); Cafe Society Downtown (N.Y.C., 1938, 1948); Roosevelt Hotel (New Orleans, La., 1939); Cafe Society Uptown (N.Y.C., 1941, 1946); Green Mansions (N.Y., 1946, 1948); Rio Bomba (Chicago, Ill., 1947); the Chanticleer (Baltimore, Md., 1947); Chase Hotel (St. Louis, Mo., 1947); Cafe Society Downtown (N.Y.C., 1953); and the hungry i (San Francisco, Calif., 1957).

GILKEY, STANLEY. Producer. b. Aug. 17, 1900, Wilmington, Del., to Samuel D. and Jean (Neal) Gilkey. Grad. Harvard Univ., B.S. 1922.

Theatre. Mr. Gilkey was general manager for the Katharine Cornell-Guthrie McClintic productions (1928–62).

With Gertrude Macy and Robert F. Cutler, he produced the revue, *One for the Money* (Booth, N.Y.C., Feb. 8, 1940); with Barbara Payne, *The Deep Mrs. Sykes* (Booth, Mar. 19, 1945), and *Three to Make Ready* (Adelphi, Mar. 7, 1946); with Michael Grace and Harry Rigby, *John Murray Anderson's Almanac* (Imperial, Dec. 10, 1953); with Guthrie McClintic, *A Roomful of Roses* (Playhouse, Oct. 17, 1955); and with the Producers Th., *The Day the Money Stopped* (Belasco, Feb. 20, 1958).

For the Rothschild Foundation, he presented Martha Graham and her dance company (1960–62); managed the Robert Shaw Chorale on its tour of Berlin, Ger., and Moscow, USSR (1962); and with Robert Whitehead, produced *Foxy* (Palace Grand Th., Dawson City, Yukon, Alas., July 2, 1962).

Mr. Gilkey was general manager of the Repertory Theatre of Lincoln Center (ANTA Washington Sq. Th., N.Y.C.), which presented *The Changeling* (Oct. 29, 1964), *Incident at Vichy* (Dec. 3, 1964), and *Tartuffe* (Jan. 14, 1965), at which time he became acting administrator of the Repertory Theatre. The company moved to the Lincoln Center for the Performing Arts (Vivian Beaumont Th.), where he continued as general manager for their productions of *Danton's Death* (Oct. 21, 1965); *The Country Wife* (Dec. 9, 1965); *The Condemned of Altona* (Feb. 3, 1966); *The Caucasian Chalk Circle* (Mar. 24, 1966); *The Alchemist* (Oct. 13, 1966); *Yerma* (Dec. 8, 1966); *The East Wind* (Feb. 9, 1967); and *Galileo* (Apr. 13, 1967).

GILL, BRENDAN. Critic, playwright, writer. b. Oct. 4, 1914, Hartford, Conn., to Michael Henry and Elizabeth (Duffy) Gill. Father, physician, Grad. Kingswood Sch., 1932; Yale Univ., B.A. 1936. Married 1936, to Anne Barnard; two sons, five daughters. Member of ALA; Century Club; The Coffee House; Elizabethan Club; Fine Arts Federation of New York (bd. of dir.); Municipal Art Soc. (chmn. of bd.); Landmarks Conservancy of NY (chmn. of bd.); Institute for Art and Urban Resources (chmn. of bd.); Film Soc. of Lincoln Ctr., N.Y.C. (vice-pres.); Irish-Georgian Soc. (bd. of dir.). Address: (home) 1 Howe Pl., Bronxville, NY 10708, tel. (914) 337-1462; (bus.) 25 W. 43rd St., New York, NY 10036, tel. (212) OX 5-1414.

Theatre. Mr. Gill wrote, with Maxwell Anderson, *The Day the Money Stopped,* based on his book of the same title (Belasco Th., Feb. 20, 1958); wrote the book for the pre-Bway tryout of the musical *La Belle* (opened Shubert, Philadelphia, Pa., Aug. 13, 1962; closed there Aug. 25, 1962); and, with Richard Dufallo, the book for the music theatre piece *Meeting Mr. Ives* (San Francisco Opera, Feb. 1976).

Other Activities. Mr. Gill became the *New Yorker* magazine's Bway theatre critic in 1968. He was (1961–67) film critic, and he has been a contributor to the magazine since 1936.

Published Works. He is the author of the novels *The Trouble of One House* (1950) and *The Day the Money Stopped* (1958); *Ways of Loving* (1974), a book of fiction; the biographies *Cole* (1971), with Robert Kimball; *Tallulah* (1972); and, with Jerome Zerbe, *Happy Times* (1973); and *Here at the New Yorker* (1975), the story of the magazine's first fifty years. He also edited and wrote a biographical introduction for *States of Grace,* eight plays by Philip Barry.

Awards. For his novel *The Trouble of One House,* he received a Special Citation from the National Book Award (1951), and a grant from the Institute of Arts and Letters (1951).

GILLETTE, ANITA. Actress, singer. b. Anita Lee Luebben, Aug. 16, 1936, Baltimore, Md., to John Alfred and Juanita Luebben. Father, machinist; mother, secretary. Grad. Kenwood H.S., Baltimore, 1954; studied voice with Bob Kobin, three years; with Frank Bibb, Peabody Conservatory, three years; acting with Lee Strasberg, N.Y.C., and Robert Lewis. Married Oct. 13, 1957, to Dr. Ronald Gillette, physiologist (marr. dis.); two sons. Member of AEA; SAG; AFTRA. Address: c/o Robert M. Rehbock & Associates, Inc., 207 East 62nd St., New York, NY 10021.

Theatre. Miss Gillette first appeared in stock at the North Shore Music Th. (Beverly, Mass., Summer 1957–58), where she sang in the chorus of *Oklahoma!* and in such musicals as *Roberta;* subsequently appeared as Susan in *Desert* (Paper Mill Playhouse, Milburn, N.J., Sept. 1958); Contrary Mary in *Babes in Toyland* (St. Louis Municipal Opera, July 15, 1959); and Linda in *Pal Joey* (Paper Mill Playhouse, Sept. 1959).

She made her N.Y.C. debut as a chorus member and as understudy to Merle Letowt in the role of June in *Gypsy* (Bway Th., May 21, 1959); appeared in the revue *Russell Patterson's Sketchbook* (Maidman Playhouse, Feb. 6, 1960); was in the chorus and understudied Anna Maria Alberghetti as Lili in *Carnival!* (Imperial, Apr. 13, 1961), replacing her for 9 performances (Aug. 9, 1961), also played the part for two weeks as guest star (Dec. 1961); and appeared as Gusti in *The Gay Life,* a role eliminated from the script during pre-Bway tour (1961).

She appeared in an industrial revue for RCA (Edgewater Hotel, Chicago, Ill., Oct. 1961); played Susan in *All American* (Winter Garden, N.Y.C., Mar. 19, 1962); Leslie in *Mr. President* (St. James, Oct. 20, 1962); Sarah Brown in *Guys and Dolls* (O'-Keefe Center, Toronto, Can., June 5, 1962); and the title role in *Pocahontas* (Lyric, London, Eng., Nov. 14, 1963).

Miss Gillette returned to N.Y.C. to play Angela in *Kelly* (Broadhurst, Feb. 6, 1965) and Sarah in *Guys and Dolls* (NY City Ctr., April 28, 1965). She went to Los Angeles to play Resi in *The Great Waltz* (Music Center, July 1965); returned to N.Y.C. as Susan in *Don't Drink the Water* (Morosco, Nov. 17, 1966); replaced (May 1968) Jill Haworth as Sally Bowles in *Cabaret* (Broadhurst, Nov. 20, 1966) and opened as Betty Compton in *Jimmy* (Winter Garden, Oct. 23, 1969). She played Tina in *Knickerbocker Holiday* (San Francisco and Los Angeles Light Opera, May 1971) and Nellie Forbush in *South Pacific* (Pittsburgh Light Opera Company, Summer 1974).

Films. She appeared in an industrial film for Dupont Industries (1961).

Television. Miss Gillette made her television debut on the Ed Sullivan Show (CBS, Apr. 12, 1963); subsequently appeared on Mike Wallace's PM East (WNEW, 1961–1962); and on Jack Paar's Tonight Show (NBC, Summer 1961).

Miss Gillette was featured in a number of specials including *Pinocchio* (CBS, 1969) and *George M!* (CBS, 1970) and was in two series, Me and the Chimp (CBS, 1971–72) and Bob & Carol & Ted & Alice (ABC, 1973). She is seen regularly on game shows such as What's My Line?; (CBS); Password (ABC); $10,000 Pyramid (ABC); Celebrity Sweepstakes (NBC); Beat the Clock (local); and Match Game 74 (CBS). She has also appeared frequently on the Tonight Show (NBC); Merv Griffin Show (local); Mike Douglas Show (CBS); and Love American Style (ABC); and was featured in a special *Married Is Better* (NBC, 1974).

Awards. Miss Gillette received the *Theatre World* Award for her performance in *Russell Patterson's Sketchbook* (1960).

Recreation. Cooking, watching horse races.

GILLETTE, A. S. Educator, scenic designer. b. Arnold Simpson Gillette, June 6, 1904, Phoenixville, Pa., to James Walter and Georgia (Simpson) Gillette. Father, electrical engineer. Grad. Fergus County H.S., Lewistown, Mont., 1923; Univ. of Montana, B.A. 1928; Yale Univ., M.F.A. 1931. Married June 9, 1932, to Josephine Jay; one son, one daughter. Member of NTC (bd. of trustees, 1957; chmn., nominating comm., 1960–63); ATA (counselor to legislative body, 1957–58; chmn., time and place comm., 1960; 2nd vice-pres., 1961; 1st vice-pres. and program chmn., 1962; pres., 1963). Address: (home) 4 Rowland Ct., Iowa City, IA 52240, tel. (319) 337-4819; (bus.) c/o University Theatre, State Univ. of Iowa, Iowa City, IA 52240, tel. (319) 338-0511.

Mr. Gillette was director of the University Theatre of the State Univ. of Iowa from 1956 to 1971, when he retired, and a full professor from 1949 to 1971. He taught courses in scenic design and technical production. Mr. Gillette worked in educational theater at the same university from 1931 until his retirement. He designed or supervised the designs (excluding the productions of 1935–36) of 390 shows.

Published Works. Mr. Gillette is the author of *Stage Scenery: Its Construction and Rigging* (1960; 2nd ed., 1973) and *An Introduction to Scenic Design* (1967).

Awards. He received a Rockefeller Traveling Grant to study scenic design in Europe (1935–36), was appointed a fellow of ATA (1967) and received the ATA award of merit (1969), the distinguished service award of the Univ. of Montana (1969), and an award of merit from the US Institute of Theatre Technology (1973).

Recreation. Fishing, golf.

GILLETTE, RUTH. Singer, actress. b. Ruth Eleanor Gillette, Aug. 16, 1907, Chicago, Ill., to J. Walter and Goldena (Oswald) Gillette. Father, construction engineer. Grad. Nicholas Senn H.S., Chicago; attended Northwestern Univ. Studied at American Conservatory of Music, Chicago, two years; singing with Vitorio Trevisan of the Chicago Opera, two years, and Estelle Liebling, N.Y.C. Married Dec. 31, 1926, to Rowland Robbins (marr. dis. 1933); one son; married Aug. 13, 1937, to Stuart Hacker (marr. dis. 1941); married Feb. 28, 1946, to Harry Archer (dec. 1960). Relative in theatre: cousin, William Gillette, actor. Member of AEA (councillor, 1957–to date); SAG; AFTRA. Address: 148 E. 48th St., New York, NY 10017, tel. (212) PL 5-3000.

Theatre. Miss Gillette first sang in Loew's State motion picture houses (Los Angeles, Calif., 1924), and at the Capitol Th., (N.Y.C., 1924).

She subsequently appeared in the revue *Gay Paree* (Shubert, Aug. 18, 1925); in *Passions of 1926,* originally titled *The Merry World* (Imperial, June 8, 1926); sang Nedda in *Pagliacci* (Philharmonic Aud., Los Angeles, Calif., Fall 1935); appeared in *The Fortune Teller* (St. Louis Municipal Opera Th., Mo., Summer 1949); toured as Aunt Eller in *Oklahoma!* (1950); played Nettie in *Carousel* (1953); Dolly Tate in *Annie Get Your Gun* (Detroit Civic Opera, Mich., 1954); Dolly in *Bloomer Girl* (St. Louis Municipal Opera Th., Mo., Summer 1951); the title role in *Roberta* and Mrs. Kramer in *One Touch of Venus* (Pittsburgh Light Opera, Pa., 1952); succeeded (Apr. 1955) Marguerite Shaw as Mabel in *The Pajama Game* (St. James, May 13, 1954), and repeated the role in a touring production (Feb.–Apr. 1957); played Mrs. Chandler in *The Gazebo* (Lyceum, N.Y.C., Dec. 12, 1958); and appeared in *70, Girls, 70* (Broadhurst, Apr. 15, 1971).

She appeared in industrial shows: Quaker Oats (1961); Oldsmobile (ANTA, N.Y.C., 1961; Mark Hellinger Th., 1963), and its touring productions (1961, 1963).

Films. Miss Gillette performed in *The Great Ziegfeld* (MGM, 1936); *San Francisco* (MGM, 1936); *In Old Chicago* (20th-Fox, 1938); *Hello, Frisco, Hello* (20th-Fox, 1943); *Everybody Does It* (20th-Fox, 1949); *In a Lonely Place* (Col., 1950); *Nob Hill* (20th-Fox, 1954).

Television. She has appeared on Campbell Theatre (NBC, 1947); Your Hit Parade (NBC, 1955–56); the Sid Caesar Show (NBC); The Nurses (CBS, 1962); Dennis the Menace (CBS, 1963); McHale's Navy (ABC, 1963); The Real McCoys (NBC, 1963); and in *The Powder Room* (Repertoire Th., CBS, 1963).

Night Clubs. Miss Gillette has performed at Chez Paree (Chicago, Ill., 1932); and played Mabel in *The Pajama Game* at the Riviera and the Dunes hotels (Las Vegas, Nev., 1957).

Recreation. Golf, horsebacking riding, poker, knitting, sewing.

GILLMORE, MARGALO. Actress. b. May 31, 1897, London, England, to Frank and Laura (MacGillivray) Gillmore. Father, one of AEA founders and first president, and actor; mother, actress. Attended high school, N.Y.C. Studied for the theatre at AADA, 1917. Married Nov. 9, 1935, to Robert F. Ross, director, actor (dec. Feb. 23, 1954). Member of AEA; SAG.

Theatre. Miss Gillmore made her stage debut as Laurel Masterman in *The Scrap of Paper* (Apollo, Atlantic City, N.J., Sept. 1917; Criterion, N.Y.C., Sept. 17, 1917); subsequently appeared as the Daughter in *April* (Punch and Judy, Apr. 6, 1918); Elsie Harris in *Her Honor, the Mayor* (Fulton, May 20, 1918); Etta Silver in *Up from Nowhere* (Comedy, Sept. 8, 1919); Sylvia Fair in *The Famous Mrs. Fair* (Henry Miller's Th., Dec. 22, 1919); Eileen Carmody in *The Straw* (Greenwich Village Th., Nov. 19, 1921); Rose Lane in *Alias Jimmy Valentine* (Gaiety, Dec. 8, 1921); Consuelo in *He Who Gets Slapped* (Garrick, Jan. 9, 1922); Melisande in *The Romantic Age* (Comedy, Nov. 14, 1922); Celia in *As You Like It* (44 St. Th., Apr. 23, 1923); succeeded (June 1923) Lotus Robb as Judith Anderson in *The Devil's Disciple* (Garrick, Apr. 23, 1923); played Aline de Kercadiou in *Scaramouche* (Morosco, Oct. 24, 1923); Ann in *Outward Bound* (Ritz, Jan. 7, 1924); Mrs. Elvsted in *Hedda Gabler,* performed in special matinees by the Equity Players (48 St. Th., May 16, 1924); Claire Marsh in *The Far Cry* (Cort, Sept. 30, 1924); Anne Kingsley in *The Habitual Husband* (48 St. Th., Dec. 24, 1924); and Venice Pollen in *The Green Hat* (Broadhurst, Sept. 15, 1925).

For the Th. Guild, she appeared as Mrs. Asta Allmers in special matinees of *Little Eyolf* (Guild, Feb. 2, 1926), Princess Agnes Salm in *Juarez and Maximilian* (Guild, Oct. 11, 1926), Jenny in *Ned McCobb's Daughter* (John Golden Th., Nov. 29, 1926), Hester in *The Silver Cord* (Guild, Dec. 20, 1926), Monica Grey in *The Second Man* (Guild, Apr. 11, 1927), Princess Kukachin in *Marco Millions* (Guild, Jan. 9, 1928), Colomba in *Volpone* (Guild, Apr. 9, 1928), and Sesaly Blaine in *Man's Estate* (Biltmore, Apr. 1, 1929).

She played Helen Pettigrew in *Berkeley Square* (Lyceum, Nov. 4, 1929); Mademoiselle Henriette in *The Little Father of the Wilderness,* which was on the same bill with the Players' Club production of *Milestones* (Empire, June 2, 1930); and succeeded (May 1931) Margaret Barker in the role of Henrietta Moulton-Barrett in *The Barretts of Wimpole Street* (Empire, Feb. 9, 1931).

In stock, Miss Gillmore appeared in *Forsaking All Others, Counselor-at-Law,* and *By Candle Light* (Elitch Gardens, Denver, Colo., June–Aug. 1933); played Jessica Wells in *The Dark Tower* (Morosco, N.Y.C., Nov. 25, 1933); Mariella Linden in the pre-Bway tryout of *The Shining Hour* (closed Ford's Th., Baltimore, Md., Apr. 1934), and succeeded (June 1934) Helen Hayes as Mary Stuart in the Theatre Guild production of *Mary of Scotland* (Guild, N.Y.C., Nov. 27, 1933).

She appeared, in stock, as Marion Froude in *Biography* (Falmouth Playhouse, Mass., July 1934); Mary Philipse in the Theatre Guild production of *Valley Forge* (Guild, N.Y.C., Dec. 10, 1934); played Henrietta Moulton-Barrett in *The Barretts of Wimpole Street* (Martin Beck Th., Feb. 25, 1935); and Mercia Huntbach in *Flowers of the Forest* (Martin Beck Th., Apr. 8, 1935); appeared at the Ann Arbor (Mich.) Drama Festival in *The Compromisers, Remember the Day, The Distaff Side,* and *The Night of January 16* (Summer 1936); played Mary Haines in *The Women* (Ethel Barrymore Th., N.Y.C., Dec. 26, 1936); Amanda Smith in *No Time for Comedy* (Ethel Barrymore Th., Apr. 17, 1939); in stock, played Milady in *The Three Musketeers* (Forest Park, St. Louis, Mo., July 1941); replaced (Aug. 1941) Dorothy Stickney, during her vacation, as Vinnie Day in *Life with Father* (Empire, N.Y.C., Nov. 8, 1939), and succeeded Lillian Gish in the same role on tour (1942–43); and appeared as Madeleine Harris in

Outrageous Fortune (48 St. Th., N.Y.C., Nov. 3, 1943).

Miss Gillmore appeared as Leslie Crosbie in *The Letter*(Royal Alexandra, Toronto, Ontario, Canada, June 1944); played Arabel Moulton-Barrett in an overseas tour of *The Barretts of Wimpole Street* (ETO, Aug. 4, 1944–Feb. 8, 1945); succeeded (Jan. 1946) Kay Johnson as Kay Thorndyke in *State of the Union* (Hudson, N.Y.C., Nov. 14, 1945); made her London debut as Kate Keller in *All My Sons* (Lyric, Hammersmith, May 11, 1948; Globe, June 16, 1948); played Anna Miller in *Kind Sir* (Alvin, N.Y.C., Nov. 4, 1953); Mrs. Darling in *Peter Pan* (Winter Garden, Oct. 20, 1954); Monica Breedlove in *The Bad Seed* (Aldwych, London, Apr. 14, 1955); succeeded (Jan. 1954) Dennie Moore as Mrs. Van Daan in *The Diary of Anne Frank* (Cort, N.Y.C., Oct. 5, 1955); succeeded (July 1958) Jean Dixon as Muriel Chadwick in *Roar Like a Dove* (Phoenix, London, Sept. 26, 1957); and played Mrs. Van Mier in *Sail Away* (Broadhurst, N.Y.C., Oct. 3, 1961).

Films. Miss Gillmore appeared in *Perfect Strangers* (WB, 1950); *The Happy Years* (MGM, 1950); *Behave Yourself* (RKO, 1951); *High Society* (MGM, 1956); and *Gaby* (MGM, 1956).

Television and Radio. She performed on such radio programs as *The First Waltz* (NBC, Nov. 1937); *Beyond the Horizon* (NBC, July 1938); and the Magic Key program (NBC, Jan. 1939).

On television, she appeared in *Old Witch, Old Witch* (Lux Video Th., NBC, Sept. 5, 1957); and *The Girls in 509* (Play of the Week, WNTA, Apr. 18, 1960).

Published Works. Miss Gillmore wrote *The B.O.W.S. (The Barretts of Wimpole Street)* (1945), in collaboration with Patricia Collinge, and an autobiography, *Four Flights Up* (1964).

GILMORE, VIRGINIA. Actress. b. Virginia Sherman Poole, July 26, 1919, El Monte, Calif., to Albion Winchester and Lady May (Adams) Poole. Father, aviator. Grad. San Mateo (Calif.) H.S., 1937; attended Univ. of California; grad. Univ. of Vienna (Cytology) 1955. Married 1944 to Yul Brynner, actor (marr. dis. 1960); one son. Member of AEA; SAG; AFTRA.

Theatre. Miss Gilmore first appeared as Curley's Wife in a pre-Bway tryout of *Of Mice and Men* (John Steinbeck's Th., Monterey, Calif., 1937); performed in stock productions at the Curran and Geary theatres (San Francisco, Calif., 1937–39).

She made her N.Y.C. debut as Helen in *Those Endearing Young Charms* (Booth, June 16, 1943); subsequently appeared as Sally in *The World's Full of Girls* (Royale, Dec. 7, 1943); Ruth Wilkinson in *Dear Ruth* (Henry Miller's Th., Dec. 13, 1944); Ferne Rainer in the pre-Bway tryout of *Dunnigan's Daughter;* Anne in *Truckline Cafe* (Belasco, Feb. 27, 1946); Alice Hart in *The Grey-Eyed People* (Martin Beck Th., Dec. 17, 1952); Ivy London in *Critic's Choice* (Ethel Barrymore Th., Dec. 14, 1960); and the Princess in a stock production of *Sweet Bird of Youth* (Playhouse-on-the-Mall, Paramus, N.J., Summer 1962).

Films. Miss Gilmore made her film debut in *Winter Carnival* (UA, 1939); subsequently appeared in other pictures, including *Manhattan Heartbeat* (20th-Fox, 1940); *Jennie* (20th-Fox, 1940); *The Westerner* (UA, 1940); *Laddie* (RKO, 1940); *Swamp Water* (20th-Fox, 1941); *Tall, Dark and Handsome* (20th-Fox, 1941); *Western Union* (20th-Fox, 1941); *Berlin Correspondent* (20th-Fox, 1942); *The Pride of the Yankees* (RKO, 1942); *Chetniks* (20th-Fox, 1943); *Wonder Man* (RKO, 1945); and *Walk East on Beacon* (Col., 1952).

Television. Miss Gilmore has appeared on Philco Television Playhouse (NBC), Kraft Television Th. (NBC), and Studio One (CBS).

Other Activities. Miss Gilmore is a qualified cytologist.

GILROY, FRANK D. Playwright. b. Oct. 13, 1925, New York City. Grad. De Witt Clinton H.S.; Dartmouth Coll., B.A. (magna cum laude) 1950; attended Yale Univ. Drama Sch., 1950–51. Served US Army, 1943–46. Married 1954, to Ruth Dorothy Gaydos; three sons. Member of Dramatists Guild (mbr. of the council; pres., 1969–71). Address: c/o Random House, Inc., 457 Madison Ave., New York, NY 10022.

Theatre. Mr. Gilroy is the author of *Who'll Save the Plowboy?* (Phoenix, N.Y.C., Jan. 9, 1962); *The Subject Was Roses* (Royale, May 25, 1964); *That Summer, That Fall* (Helen Hayes Th., Mar. 16, 1967); *The Only Game in Town* (Broadhurst, May 23, 1968); and an evening of four one-acts entitled *Present Tense* (Sheridan Sq. Playhouse, July 18, 1972), including *Come Next Tuesday, Twas Brillig, So Please Be Kind,* and the title piece.

Films. He co-authored the screenplay for *The Fastest Gun Alive* (MGM, 1956); *The Gallant Hours* (UA, 1961); adapted *The Subject Was Roses* for the screen (MGM, 1968); wrote the screenplay for *The Only Game in Town* (20th-Fox, 1970); and wrote the screen adaptation and directed *Desperate Characters* (ITC and TDJ, 1971).

Television. Mr. Gilroy wrote *A Matter of Pride* (1957), an adaptation of John Landon's short story *The Blue Serge Suit; Far Rockaway* (1965); wrote the screen adaptation and directed *Gibbsville* (NBC, 1975), based upon stories by John O'Hara; and wrote television plays for US Steel Hour (ABC); Omnibus (CBS); Kraft Th. (NBC); Studio One (CBS); Lux Video Th. (NBC); and Playhouse 90 (CBS).

Published Works. He is the author of a novel, *Private* (Harcourt Brace, 1970); and, with his wife, Ruth D. Gilroy, wrote *Little Ego* (Simon and Schuster, 1970).

Awards. Mr. Gilroy won The Village Voice Off-Bway (Obie) Award (1961–62) for *Who'll Save the Plowboy?;* The Pulitzer Prize for Best American Play, The NY Drama Critics Circle Award, and the Antoinette Perry (Tony) Award (1965) for *The Subject Was Roses;* and the Berlin Film Festival Silver Bear (1971) for *Desperate Characters.*

In 1966, he received an honorary degree of Dr. of Letters from Dartmouth Coll.

GINGOLD, HERMIONE. Actress. b. Hermione Ferdinanda Gingold, Dec. 9, 1899, London, England, to James and Kate (Walter) Gingold. Father, stock broker. Educated privately. Attended Rosina Filippi Sch. of the Th., London. Married to Michael Josef, publisher (marr. dis.); two sons; one of whom is director and founder, Th. in the Round, Studio Theatre, Ltd., Scarborough, Eng.; married to Eric Maschwitz, O.B.E., program director, BBC (marr. dis.). Member of AEA; SAG; AFTRA; ALA. Address: (home) 405 E. 54th St., New York, NY 10022, tel. (212) PL 5-4326; (bus.) International Famous Artists c/o Milton Goldman, 1301 Ave. of the Americas, New York, NY 10019, tel. (212) 956-5800.

Theatre. Miss Gingold made her US debut in the revue *It's About Time* (Brattle Th., Cambridge, Mass., Mar. 1951); followed by her N.Y.C. debut in *John Murray Anderson's Almanac* (Imperial, Dec. 10, 1953); appeared as Jane Banbury in a West Coast tour of *Fallen Angels* (1956); the Grand Duchess in a West Coast tour of *The Sleeping Prince* (opened Huntington Hartford Th., Los Angeles, Calif., Nov. 22, 1956; closed Geary, San Francisco, Calif., Jan. 12, 1957); Mrs. Bennett in *First Impressions* (Alvin, N.Y.C., Mar. 19, 1959); appeared in the revue *From A to Z* (Plymouth, Apr. 20, 1960); played Julia in winter and summer stock tours of *Abracadabra* (1961–63); succeeded (1962) Molly Picon as Clara Weiss in *Milk and Honey* (Martin Beck Th., N.Y.C., Oct. 10, 1961); succeeded (1963) Jo Van Fleet as Madame Rosepettle in *Oh, Dad, Poor Dad, Mamma's Hung You in the Closet and I'm Feelin' So Sad* (Phoenix, N.Y.C., Feb. 26, 1962), and repeated the role on tour (opened Civic, Chicago, Ill., Apr. 2, 1963), played in N.Y.C. during the tour (Morosco, Aug. 27, 1963), and resumed the tour (closed Sept. 4, 1964). She played Madame Armfeldt in *A Little Night Music* (Shubert Th., Feb. 25, 1973).

Miss Gingold made her stage debut in London as Cardinal Wolsey in a kindergarten production of *Henry VIII,* and made her professional debut as the Herald in *Pinkie and the Fairies* (His Majesty's, Dec. 19, 1908). She subsequently played the Child in *In the Name of the Czar;* appeared in *Where the Rainbow Ends;* played the Page in *The Merry Wives of Windsor* (His Majesty's, June 21, 1909); Cassandra in *Troilus and Cressida;* appeared in *The Marriage Market* (Daly's, May 17, 1913); played Jessica in *The Merchant of Venice* (Old Vic, Apr. 1914); Liza in *If* (Ambassadors', May 30, 1921); the Old Woman in *The Dippers* (Criterion, Aug. 22, 1922); appeared in *Little Lord Fauntleroy* (Gate, Jan. 7, 1931); played the Second Daughter in *From Morn to Midnight* (Gate, May 3, 1932); appeared in *One More River* (Gate); appeared as Lily Malone in *Hotel Universe* (Gate); in *This World of Ours* (Gate, Dec. 1935); *Maya* (Gate); and the revue, *Spread It Abroad* (Saville, Apr. 1, 1936); played May in *Laura Garrett* (Arts, Sept. 1936); and the Leading Lady in *In Theatre Street* (Mercury, Apr. 1937).

She appeared in the revues, *The Gate Revue* (Gate, Dec. 19, 1938); *Swinging the Gate* (Ambassadors', May 22, 1940), *Rise Above It* (Comedy, June 5, 1941); *Sky High* (Phoenix, June 4, 1942); *Sweet and Low* (Ambassadors', June 10, 1943), *Sweeter and Lower* (Ambassadors', Feb. 17, 1944), and *Sweetest and Lowest* (Ambassadors', May 9, 1946); was author with Charles Hickman of *Slings and Arrows* (Comedy, Nov. 17, 1948); and appeared on a double bill as Mrs. Rocket in *Fumed Oak* and as Jane Banbury in *Fallen Angels* (Ambassadors', Nov. 29, 1949).

Films. Miss Gingold appeared in the English films, *Mary Goes to Town; Somebody at the Door; Cosh Boy; Pickwick Papers* (Kingsley, 1954); and *The Adventures of Sadie* (20th-Fox, 1955). In the US she appeared in *Around the World in 80 Days* (UA, 1956); *Gigi* (MGM, 1958); *Bell, Book and Candle* (Col., 1958); *The Naked Edge* (UA, 1961); *The Music Man* (WB, 1962); *Gay Purree* (WB, 1962); *I'd Rather Be Rich* (U, 1964); and *Harvey Middleman, Fireman* (UA, 1964).

Television. She has appeared on the Steve Allen Show (NBC); One Minute Please; the Ed Sullivan Show (CBS); Ford Omnibus (CBS); Truth or Consequences; the Today Show (NBC); Person to Person (CBS); Jack Paar Show (NBC); Alfred Hitchcock Presents (CBS); Jack Benny Show (CBS); Play Your Hunch; Joe Franklin (NBC); George Gobel Show; This Is Your Life (CBS); Victor Borge Show (CBS); I've Got a Secret (CBS); Merv Griffin Show (NBC); What's My Line? (CBS); Garry Moore Show (CBS); Arthur Murray Show (CBS); Talent Scouts (NBC); Art Carney Special (CBS); Ernie Ford Show (NBC); Girl Talk (ABC); *Assassination in Theran;* Academy (Oscar) Award presentations (CBS); Antoinette Perry (Tony) Award presentations (CBS); Matinee Th. (NBC); and the Oscar Levant Show.

Night Clubs. Miss Gingold has performed at the Cafe de Paris (London, 1953; 1954).

Published Works. Miss Gingold wrote her autobiography, *The World Is Square* (1945); and *Sirens Should Be Seen and Not Heard* (1963).

Discography. Miss Gingold has recorded *La Gingold* (Dolphin); and *Façade* (Decca).

GINSBURY, NORMAN. Playwright. b. Nov. 8, 1902, London, England, to J. S. and Rachel Cecily (Schulberg) Ginsbury. Grad. Univ. of London, B.S. (honors) 1921. Married Aug. 21, 1945, to Dorothy A. Jennings, opera singer. Served with RAF, 1940–44; rank F/Lt. Member of ASCAP; British Drama League (exec. committee, 1961); Dramatists Guild; Radio Writers Assn. Address: Barum Lodge, 25 Prideaux Rd., Eastbourne, Sussex, England tel. Eastbourne 29603.

Pre-Theatre. Analytical chemist, free-lance journalist.

Theatre. Mr. Ginsbury's first play produced in the US was *The Happy Man* (White Barn Th., Westport, Conn., July 23, 1950); followed by *The First Gentleman* (Belasco, N.Y.C., Apr. 25, 1957); and his translation and adaptation of Ibsen's *Peer Gynt* (Phoenix,

Jan. 12, 1960).

His first play to be produced in London was *Viceroy Sarah* (Arts, May 27, 1934; revived Whitehall, Feb. 12, 1935); subsequently translated and adapted Ibsen's *Ghosts* for the Old Vic Festival (Buxton, Eng., Aug. 31, 1937), subsequently produced in London (Vaudeville, Nov. 8, 1937); wrote *Walk in the Sun* ("Q" Th., Jan. 23, 1939); and translated and adapted Ibsen's *An Enemy of the People* (Old Vic, Feb. 21, 1939). His *Viceroy Sarah* was produced at the Old Vic Festival (Buxton, Aug. 29, 1939); wrote, with Winifred Holtby, *Take Back Your Freedom* (Neighbourhood, London, Aug. 20, 1940); his adaptation of *Ghosts* was revived (Duke of York's, June 25, 1943). His translation and adaptation of Ibsen's *Peer Gynt* was first produced by the Old Vic Co. (New, Aug. 31, 1944).

He wrote *The First Gentleman* (New, July 18, 1945); adapted Dostoevsky's *The Gambler* (Embassy, Nov. 7, 1945); adapted Ibsen's *A Doll's House* (Winter Garden, Jan. 17, 1946); wrote *The Happy Man* (New, June 27, 1948); and wrote, with Maurice Moiseiwitsch, *My Dear Isabella* (Th. Royal, Stratford-upon-Avon, Feb. 21, 1949); *School for Rivals*, presented by the Old Vic Co. at the Bath Festival (Th. Royal, May 23, 1949); *The Happy Man* was staged in the US (see above); wrote *The First Comers* for the Festival of Britain, (Crane Th., Liverpool, July 25, 1951).

Mr. Ginsbury's *The First Gentleman* was presented in the US (see above); his adaptation of *Ghosts* was revived (Old Vic, London, Nov. 12, 1958); his adaptation of Ibsen's *Peer Gynt* was produced in the US (see above); he translated and adapted Ibsen's *Rosmersholm* (Playhouse, Sheffield, Eng., Feb. 29, 1960), *The Pillars of Society* (Vanbrugh, London, June 21, 1961), and *John Gabriel Borkman* (Mermaid, Feb. 16, 1961). He translated and adapted August Strindberg's *The Dance of Death* (Tyrone Guthrie Th., Minneapolis, Minn., June 2, 1966); and he wrote *The Forefathers* to celebrate the 250th anniversary of the sailing of the Pilgrims to America (Athenaeum, Plymouth, Eng., May 11, 1970).

Films. Mr. Ginsbury wrote the screen adaptation of his *The First Gentleman* (Col., 1947); and collaborated on the film script for *The Magic Bow* (U, 1947).

Television. He translated Ibsen's *An Enemy of the People* (BBC, London, Nov. 3, 1950); adapted his own plays, *Viceroy Sarah* (Assoc. Radifussion, Mar. 22, 1956), and *The Gambler* (BBC, Aug. 9, 1956); translated Ibsen's *Ghosts* (ABC, US, Sept. 22, 1957); translated Ibsen's *The Master Builder* (ABC, Jan. 19, 1958); translated and adapted, with Jacques Sarch, Dumas' *The Lady of the Camellias* (ABC, Feb. 16, 1958); wrote *The Fabulous Money-Maker* (ABC, Mar. 1, 1959); adapted his own play, *The First Gentleman* (Old Vic TV Th., London, Aug. 9, 1956); wrote, with Halstead Welles, *The Silk Petticoat*, based on a story by Joseph Shearing (May 17, 1961); and adapted, with John Hastings, *I Saw the Whole Thing*, from a story by Henry Cecil (July 18, 1961). Mr. Ginsbury adapted also for television his *Peer Gynt* translation (BBC, Aug. 22, 1973).

Radio. He has adapted many of his plays for radio and has also written radio dramas including *Man in the Next Carriage* (July 14, 1956); *The Recording Angel* (Aug. 7, 1954); *The Queen's Confidante* (Mar. 29, 1954); and with Jacques Sarch, *Madame Sans-Gene, The Story of Tosca, Poison for the King*, and *The Patriots*, adaptations of works by Sardou. He has also written for radio *Where There's a Will* (Mar. 8, 1961); *The Plantation* (June 23, 1962); *Le Petit Café*, in collaboration with Jacques Sarch, and adapted from Tristan Bernard (July 28, 1962); *The Old Lags' League*, adapted from a work by W. Pett Ridge (Sept. 28, 1962); and *Beltraffio*, adapted from Henry James (Aug. 28, 1963). He adapted Sarah Orne Jewett's *The Only Rose* (Aug. 11, 1964) and wrote *The Voyage To Guiana* (Sept. 18, 1965).

GISH, LILLIAN. Actress. b. Oct. 14, 1899, Springfield, Ohio, to James Lee and Mary (Robinson) Gish. Father, salesman; mother, actress. Self-educated. Relative in theatre: sister, Dorothy Gish, actress. Member of AEA; SAG; AFTRA. Address: 430 E. 57th St., New York, NY 10022.

Theatre. Miss Gish made her stage debut at five in a melodrama, *In Convict Stripes* (Rising Sun, Ohio, 1904); toured cross country (1905–12) with her mother and sister in *Her First False Step, At Duty's Call, Volunteer Organist, The Child Wife*, and *Little Red School House;* made her N.Y.C. debut as Marjanie in *A Good Little Devil* (Republic, Jan. 8, 1913); Helena in *Uncle Vanya* (Booth, N.Y.C., Sept. 22, 1930); and Marguerite Gautier in *Camille* (Central City, Colo., July 1932).

She played Effie Holden in *Nine Pine Street* (Longacre, N.Y.C., Apr. 27, 1933); Christina Farley in *The Joyous Season* (Belasco, Jan. 29, 1934); the Young Whore in *Within the Gates* (Natl., Oct. 22, 1934); Charlotte Lovell in *The Old Maid* (Kings' Th., Glasgow, Scot., Mar. 1936); Ophelia in John Gielgud's production of *Hamlet* (Empire, N.Y.C., Oct. 8, 1936); Martha Mich in *The Star Wagon* (Empire, Sept. 29, 1937); and Grace Fenning in *Dear Octopus* (Broadhurst, Jan. 11, 1939).

She appeared as Vinnie in *Life with Father* on tour (1940–41); Jane Gwilt in *Mr. Sycamore* (Guild, N.Y.C., Nov. 13, 1942); the Marquise Eloise in *The Marquis* and Leonora in *The Legend of Leonora* in stock (Summer 1947); Katerina Ivanna in *Crime and Punishment* (Natl., N.Y., Dec. 22, 1947); Ethel in *The Curious Savage* (Martin Beck Th., Oct. 24, 1950); toured in the title role of *Miss Mabel* (1950–51); played Mrs. Carrie Watts in *The Trip to Bountiful* (Henry Miller's Th., N.Y.C., Nov. 3, 1953); Miss Madrigal in stock productions of *The Chalk Garden* (Westport Country Playhouse, Conn.; John Drew Th., East Hampton, L.I., N.Y., Aug. 1956); and appeared in the one-act plays *Portrait of a Madonna* and *The Wreck of the 5:25* (Congress Hall, Berlin, Ger., 1957). Miss Gish played Catherine Lynch in *All the Way Home* (Belasco, N.Y.C., Oct. 30, 1960); succeeded Gladys Cooper as Mrs. Moore in *A Passage to India* (Ambassador, Jan. 31, 1962); played Mrs. Mopply in *Too Good to Be True* (54 St. Th., Mar. 12, 1963); the Nurse in *Romeo and Juliet* (American Shakespeare Festival, Stratford, Conn., June 20, 1965); the Dowager Empress in *Anya* (Ziegfeld Th., Nov. 29, 1965); Margaret Garrison in *I Never Sang for My Father* (Longacre, Jan. 25, 1968); and Marina, the nurse in *Uncle Vanya* (Circle in the Square–Joseph E. Levine Th., June 4, 1973).

Films. Miss Gish appeared in silent films in *The Unseen Enemy* (Biog., 1912); *Life's Pathway* (Biog., 1913); *The Mothering Heart* (Biog., 1913); *Home Sweet Home* (Mutual, 1914); *Birth of a Nation* (UA, 1915); *The Battle of the Sexes* (Griffith, 1916); *Intolerance* (Griffith, 1916); *Diane of the Follies* (Gateway, 1917); *Hearts of the World* (Comstock-World, 1917); *Souls Triumphant* (Fine-Arts Triangle, 1917); *The Great Love* (Griffith, 1918); *True Heart Susie* (Artcraft, 1918) *Broken Blossoms* (Griffith), *The Greatest Thing* (Griffith, 1919); *The Greatest Question* (1st Natl. 1920); *Way Down East* (UA, 1920); *Orphans of the Storm* (UA, 1922); *The White Sister* (MGM, 1924); *Romola* (MGM, 1924); *The Scarlet Letter* (MGM, 1925); *La Bohème* (MGM, 1926); *Annie Laurie* (MGM, 1927); *The Enemy* (MGM, 1928); and *Wind* (MGM, 1928).

She made her sound film debut in *One Romantic Night* (UA, 1930); subsequently appeared in *His Double Life* (Par., 1933); *Miss Susie Slagle's* (Par., 1945); *Duel in the Sun* (Selznick, 1946); *Portrait of Jenny* (Selznick, 1948); *The Night of the Hunter* (UA, 1955); *The Cobweb* (MGM, 1955); *Orders to Kill* (Lynx Film, 1958); *The Unforgiven* (UA, 1960); *Follow Me, Boys!* (Buena Vista, 1966); *Warning Shot* (Par., 1967); and *The Comedians* (MGM, 1967.).

Television. Miss Gish appeared on television in *Birth of the Movies; The Late Christopher Bean* (Philco Television Playhouse, NBC); *The Trip to Bountiful; Ladies in Retirement; Mrs. Bibb; The Day Lincoln Was Shot; Grandma Moses* (CBS, 1952); The Defenders (CBS, 1962–64); Alfred Hitchcock Presents (CBS, 1963); Mr. Novak (NBC, 1963); Breaking Point (ABC, 1963); *Arsenic and Old Lace* (ABC, 1968); and *The Movies* (ABC, 1974).

Published Works. Miss Gish wrote *The Movies, Mr. Griffith, and Me* (1969) and *Dorothy and Lillian Gish* (1973).

Awards. Miss Gish has received the honorary degrees of doctor of art from Rollins College and doctor of humanities from Mount Holyoke. In 1971, the Academy of Motion Picture Arts and Sciences awarded her an honorary Oscar, and in 1973 she received the Handel Medallion from the City of New York.

GLENVILLE, PETER. Director, actor, producer, playwright. b. Oct. 28, 1913, London, England, to Shaun and Dorothy (Ward) Glenville. Grad. Stonyhurst Coll., 1921; attended Oxford Univ., Christ Church, 1932. Pres., Oxford Univ. Dramatic Society. Address: c/o Aaron Frosch, 445 Park Ave., New York, NY 10022.

Theatre. Mr. Glenville first performed on the stage with the Oxford Univ. Dramatic Society, playing the title role in *Edward II* (1932); Pandulph in *King John* (1932); Puck in *A Midsummer Night's Dream* (1933); the title role in *Richard III* (1933); and *Hamlet* (1934); subsequently made his professional debut as Dr. Agi in *The Swan* (Manchester Repertory Co., Eng., Sept. 10, 1934); also for the Manchester Repertory Company, he played Toni Perelli in *On the Spot* (1934); Jack Maitland in *The Maitlands* (1934); and Eugene Marchbanks in *Candida* (1934).

He appeared in the title role in *Rossetti* (Arts Th., London, Eng., May 1935); as Orsino in *Twelfth Night* (Open Air Th., June 18, 1935); Octavius Robinson in *Man and Superman* (Cambridge, Aug. 12, 1935); performed in *The Hangman* (Duke of York's Th., Oct. 1935); played Tony Cavendish in *The Royal Family* (Playhouse, Oxford, Dec. 1935); and at the Shakespeare Memorial Th. (Stratford-on-Avon, 1936), portrayed Romeo in *Romeo and Juliet*, Petruchio in *The Taming of the Shrew*, Marc Antony in *Julius Caesar*, and Feste in *Twelfth Night*.

Mr. Glenville played a variety of roles at the Theatre Royal (Margate, 1937); Lucentio in *The Taming of the Shrew* (Old Vic, London, Mar. 28, 1939); Tony Howard in *Behind the Schemes* (Shaftesbury Th., Jan. 8, 1940); Charlie Stubbs in *Down Our Street* (Tavistock Little Th., Jan. 30, 1940); Oedipus in *The Infernal Machine* (Arts, Sept. 5, 1940); Bertram in *All's Well That Ends Well* (Vaudeville, Oct, 3, 1940); and Prince Hal in *Henry IV, Part 1* (Vaudeville, Oct. 23, 1940).

He played Robert in *The Light of Heart* (Globe, June 4, 1941); succeeded Cyril Cusack as Louis Dubedat in *The Doctor's Dilemma* (Haymarket, Mar. 4, 1942); directed the Old Vic Co. at the Liverpool Playhouse (Aug. 1944) in *John Gabriel Borkman* (Aug. 1944); *Point Valaine* (Oct. 1944); *The School for Scandal* (Dec. 1942); adapted and directed *Lisa* (Sept. 1944); appeared as Face in *The Alchemist* (Jan. 1945); and in the title role in *Hamlet* (Feb. 1945).

He succeeded John Mills (Sept. 1945) as Stephen Case in *Duet for Two Hands* (Lyric, June 27, 1945); directed *The Time of Your Life* (Lyric, Hammersmith, Feb. 14, 1946); played John Wilkes Booth in *The Assassin* (Lyric, Hammersmith, Oct. 15, 1946); directed *Point Valaine* (Embassy, Sept. 3, 1947); *Major Barbara* (Arts, Mar. 30, 1948); *The Gioconda Smile* (New, June 3, 1948); *Crime Passionnel* (Lyric, Hammersmith, June 17, 1948); the double bill, *The Browning Version* and *A Harlequinade* (Phoenix, Sept. 8, 1948); *The Return of the Prodigal* (Globe, Nov. 24, 1948); *Adventure Story* (St. James's, Mar. 17, 1949); *The Power of Darkness* (Lyric, Apr. 28, 1949); also directed the double bill, *The Browning Version* and *A Harlequinade* (Coronet, N.Y.C., Oct. 12, 1949); *The Innocents* (Playhouse, Feb. 1, 1950); *The Curious Savage* (Martin Beck Th., Oct. 24, 1950); and *Romeo and Juliet* (Broadhurst, Mar. 10, 1951).

Mr. Glenville directed *Summer and Smoke* (Lyric, Hammersmith, London, Nov. 22, 1951); *Under the Sycamore Tree* (Aldwych, Apr. 23, 1952); *Letter from Paris* (Strand, Oct. 10, 1952); *The Living Room* (Wyndham's, Apr. 16, 1953); produced, with Tennents Ltd., and directed *The Prisoner* (Globe, Apr. 14, 1954); *Separate Tables* (St. James's, Sept. 22, 1954; Music Box, N.Y.C., Oct. 25, 1956); and *Island of Goats* (Fulton, Oct. 4, 1955).

In association with Tennents, Ltd., he directed his adaptation of *Hotel Paradiso* (Winter Garden, London, May 2, 1956; Streatham Hill, July 15, 1957); co-produced and directed its N.Y.C. production (Henry Miller's Th., N.Y.C., Apr. 11, 1957); produced, with David Susskind, and directed *Rashomon* (Music Box, Jan. 27, 1959); directed *Take Me Along* (Shubert, Oct. 23, 1959); *Silent Night, Lonely Night* (Morosco, Dec. 3, 1959); *Becket* (St. James, Oct. 5, 1960); *Tchin-Tchin* (Plymouth, Oct. 25, 1962); *Tovarich* (Bway, Mar. 18, 1963); *Dylan* (Plymouth, Jan. 18, 1964); *Everything in the Garden* (Plymouth, Nov. 29, 1967); *A Patriot For Me* (Imperial, Oct. 5, 1969); *A Bequest to the Nation* (Haymarket, London, Sept. 23, 1970); and *Out Cry* (Lyceum, N.Y.C., Mar. 1, 1973).

Films. Mr. Glenville directed *The Prisoner* (Col., 1955); *Me and the Colonel* (Col., 1958); *Summer and Smoke* (Par., 1961); wrote and directed *Term of Trial* (WB, 1962); directed *Becket* (Par., 1964); wrote, directed, and produced *Hotel Paradiso* (MGM, 1966); and directed and produced *The Comedians* (MGM, 1967).

Recreation. History, music, travel.

GLOVER, WILLIAM. Drama critic. b. William Harper Glover, Jr., May 6, 1911, New York City, to William H. and Lily P. (Freir) Glover. Father, telegraph company executive. Grad. Rutgers Univ., Litt. B. 1932. Married Oct. 26, 1936, to Isobel M. Cole (marr. dis. 1973). Served with US Maritime Service; rank, Lt. (jg), 1943–45. Member of NY Drama Critics Circle (pres., 1967–68); The Drama Desk, Overseas Press Club; New York Press Club; The Players; Sigma Delta Chi; Phi Beta Kappa. Address: (home) 4 E. 88th St., New York, NY 10028, tel. (212) LE 4-5382; (bus.) c/o The Associated Press, 50 Rockefeller Plaza, New York, NY 10020, tel. (212) 262-4079.

He served as city editor with the Asbury Park (N.J.) *Press* from 1936–1939, at which time he joined the Associated Press as a writer.

In 1953, after several years of diverse writing assignments, Mr. Glover began to specialize in topics involving the entertainment world. He was appointed the drama critic of the Associated Press in 1960. Mr. Glover's articles, which appear in various periodicals, cover motion pictures as well as theatrical subjects of the US, Canada, and Europe.

GOETZ, RUTH. Playwright. b. Ruth Goodman, Jan. 11, 1912, Philadelphia, Pa., to Philip and Lily (Cartun) Goodman. Father, theatrical producer. Attended Miss Marshall's Classes for Young Ladies, N.Y.C. Married Oct. 11, 1932, to Augustus Goetz, playwright (dec. 1957); one daughter. Member of Dramatists Guild (council); ALA (council). Address: 530 East 72nd St., New York, NY 10021, tel. (212) RE 4-0750.

Pre-Theatre. Costume and scenic designer; translator; publishing field.

Theatre. Mrs. Goetz wrote, with her husband, the pre-Bway tryout *Franklin Street* (Natl. Th., Washington, D.C., Sept. 1940); *One Man Show* (Ethel Barrymore Th., N.Y.C., Feb. 8, 1945); *The Heiress* (Biltmore, Sept. 29, 1947); *The Immoralist*, based on André Gide's novel of the same name, (Royale, Feb. 8, 1954; Bouwerie Lane Th., Nov. 7, 1963); and *The Hidden River* (Playhouse Th., Jan. 23, 1957).

She wrote *Sweet Love Remembered*, (opened Shubert, New Haven, Conn., Dec. 28, 1959; closed there Dec. 31, 1959, because of the death of Margaret Sullivan); *Madly in Love*, an adaptation of *L'Amour fou* by André Roussin (summer theatre tryout, 1964); and with Bart Howard, adapted *Play on Love*, from the French of Francoise Dorin (St. Martin's Th., London, Jan. 14, 1970).

Films. Mrs. Goetz wrote, with her husband, the screen adaptation of their play, *The Heiress* (Par., 1949); *Carrie* (Par., 1952); *Rhapsody* (MGM, 1954); *Trapeze* (UA, 1956), and *Stagestruck* (Buena Vista, 1958).

Television. Her play, *The Heiress* was presented as a television special (Jan. 1961).

Awards. Mrs. Goetz received an Academy (Oscar) Award for the filmed version of *The Heiress*.

Recreation. Living.

GOFF, LEWIN. Educator. b. Lewin Alkire Goff, Oct. 21, 1919, Oklahoma City, Okla., to Strauder Allan and Euva (May) Goff. Father, engineer. Grad. Classen H.S., Oklahoma City, 1937; Central State Coll., Edmond, Okla., 1937–38; Oklahoma Univ., B.A. 1941, M.F.A. (fellowship) 1946; Western Reserve Univ., Ph.D. 1948. Studied with Rupel Jones, Oklahoma Univ.; Barclay Leathem, Western Reserve Univ. Married Sept. 9, 1941, to Jean Ann Erikson; one son, one daughter. Served USAAF, 1942–45; rank, Capt. Member of NTC (treas., 1959–60); AETA (bd. of dir., 1960; regional chmn., 1960; 2nd vice-pres., 1965; 1st vice-pres., 1968; pres., 1969); delegate to International Theatre Institute Congress in Vienna (1961); International Theatre Institute (chmn., Permanent Committee on training for the professional stage); delegate and chairman of International Theatre Institute Congress (1963–69); chairman of AETA/USO Overseas Touring Committee (1970–71); and chairman, American College Theatre Festival Central Committee (1971–72); Lamda Chi Alpha. Address: University Theatre, University of Kansas, Lawrence, KS 66044.

Mr. Goff has been director of University Theatre (Univ. of Iowa) since 1973. He was director of University Theatre (Univ. of Wisconsin, 1972–73); chairman, Dept. of Drama (Univ. of Texas, 1968–72); director of Theatre Programs (Cornell Univ., 1967); director of University Theatre (Univ. of Kansas, 1955–61); assistant professor (Michigan State Univ., 1954); and assistant professor (Univ. of Iowa, 1948–54). Since 1948, he has directed approximately 50 student productions of plays and operas.

Television. Mr. Goff has directed about 40 dramatic programs on television (WOI-TV, Ames, Iowa, 1953–54).

Published Works. He has contributed articles to the *Educational Theatre Journal* ("The Popular-priced Actors", 1950; "The Owen Davis-Al Woods Melodrama Factory, " 1956); three speeches published in *L'Enseignement de L'Art Dramatique* ("The American University Theatre," "The American University Theatre Curriculum," and "The University Theatre's Relationship with Other Departments," Brussels, 1964); *Kultura U.S.A.* (Amerykanski Theatre Uniwersytecki," 1963); *Stiri Cultuale Din, SUA* ("Teatrul Universitar American," Lagatia Americana, Bucuresti, Numarul 3, 1963); *Theatre* ("Report of the Belgian Symposium," April 1963); *Pameitnik Teatralny* ("Amerykanski Theatre Uniwersytecki," ROK XIV, 1965); and *Cultural Affairs and Foreign Relations* ("Theatre's Role in Cultural Relations Among Nations," April 1964).

Awards. Mr. Goff received a Ford Foundation, director-observer grant (1960); a Fulbright research grant for theatre research at the Univ. of Vienna (1962–63); and was made a Fellow of the American Theatre Association (1971).

Recreation. All spectator sports, fishing.

GOFORTH, FRANCES. Actress, playwright. b. Frances Annabel Goforth, Galesburg, N.D., to R. D. and Florence (Morrow) Goforth. Grad. King's Mountain (N.C.) H.S., 1936; Brevard Jr. Col., 1938; Univ. of North Carolina; A.B. 1940. Studied drama with Frederick H. Koch, 1938–40; Harry Davis, 1938–40; and Samuel Seldon, 1938–40. Member of AEA; ALA; Carolina Playmakers; Société des Auteurs et Compositeurs Dramatiques (Paris, France). Address: Benjamin Franklin Hotel, 222 W. 77th St., New York, NY 10024, tel. (212) EN 2-1100.

Pre-Theatre. Junior high school teacher; assistant city clerk.

Theatre. Miss Goforth made her professional acting debut in stock with the Town Players, North Leeds, Me. (Summer 1941); subsequently appeared in the pre-Bway tour of *Dark of the Moon* (Brattle Hall, Cambridge, Mass., Summer 1944); played Miss Metcalf in the Bway production of the same play (46 St. Th., Mar. 14, 1945), also toured in the national company (opened Ford's Th., Baltimore, Md., Dec. 31, 1945, and appeared in its revival Carnegie Hall Playhouse, N.Y.C., Feb. 26, 1958).

She collaborated with Howard Richardson in writing *Catch on the Wing*, which was produced in stock (New Milford Playhouse, Conn., July 10, 1947); and *Widow's Walk* (Barter Th., Abingdon, Va., Aug. 3, 1948); and subsequently played Deedy Sparks in *Sodom, Tennessee* (Hayloft Th., Allentown, Pa., July 12, 1950).

She wrote, with Howard Richardson, *The Cat in the Cage* (Hayloft Th., Allentown, Pa., Summer 1951), which was presented as *Chat dans la cage* (Th. Noctambule, Paris, Fr., Nov. 9, 1952), and which received a pre-Bway tryout (opened Quarter Deck Th., Hotel Morton, Atlantic City, N.J., July 3, 1952). She collaborated with Mr. Richardson on an adaptation of *God's Little Acre* (Hayloft Th., Allentown, Pa., July 4, 1961); and on *Set for Life* (Hayloft, 1962).

Films. Miss Goforth and Mr. Richardson wrote four documentary films concerning educational problems in public schools (NEA, 1947).

Television. She played Miss Metcaff in *Dark of the Moon* (Cameo Playhouse, NBC, 1952); and she wrote, with Howard Richardson, *Ark of Safety* (Goodyear Playhouse, NBC, 1956).

GOLDEN, EDWARD J. JR. Director, actor, educator. b. Edward Joseph Golden, Jr., Mar. 11, 1934, Boston, Mass., to Edward J. and Marie L. (Hohman) Golden. Father, English master. Grad. Boston Latin Sch., 1951; Harvard Univ., B.A. 1955; Boston Univ., M.F.A. 1956. Studied acting with Peter Kass, Allan Leavitt, and David Pressman at Boston Univ. and Actors Workshop, Boston, Mass., two years. Served US Army, Counter Intelligence Corps, 1957–59. Member of AEA; ANTA; Harvard Club of Maryland.

Theatre. Mr. Golden founded and was producing director of Center Stage, Baltimore, Md., where during the 1963–64 season he directed *La ronde; You Touched Me; Zoo Story; The Maids; Arms and the Man; Beyond the Horizon; The Mousetrap; Amphitryon 38; The Chairs* and *The Lesson; Light Up the Sky; Summer of the Seventeenth Doll; The Importance of Being Earnest; Silent Night, Lonely Night; Portrait of a Madonna; The Respectful Prostitute; U.S.A.;* and *Anna Christie.* During the 1964–65 season he directed *The Country Wife; A Touch of the Poet; The Physicists;* and *The Lady's Not for Burning.* In June 1965, he was appointed director of University Th., Johns Hopkins Univ., and left Center Stage, where he was succeeded by William Bishnell and Douglas Seale.

Mr. Golden made his theatrical debut playing the Prince in *Snow White and the Seven Dwarfs* (Boston Tributary Th., Mass., Jan. 1947). His first professional appearance was as Lucius in *Julius Caesar* (Brattle Th., Cambridge, Mass., July 1950). In stock, he performed at the Orleans Arena Th., Orleans, Mass. (Summers 1951–52); with Group 20, Wellesley, Mass. (1955); at the Provincetown (Mass.) Playhouse (1957–59); and directed thirteen productions for the Baltimore Jewish Community Center (1959–62).

Other Activities. Mr. Golden also conducts private classes for actors in Baltimore.

Recreation. Swimming, reading, music appreciation, attending opera, ballet, woodworking.

GOLDEN, JOSEPH. Arts administrator, playwright. b. Oct. 13, 1928, Winthrop, Mass., to William and Mary (Walker) Golden. Father, garment cutter. Grad. Revere (Mass.) H.S., 1946; Tufts Univ., A.B. 1951; Indiana Univ., M.A. 1952; Univ. of Illinois, Ph.D. 1954. Married June 9, 1951, to Fay Ann Inman, children's theatre director; two sons. Served US Army, Quartermaster Corps, 1946–47; rank, Cpl.; director of Camp Lee, Va., Theatre Guild. Member of ATA; SAA; Speech Assn. of Eastern States; CTC; Theta Alpha Phi; NCP; IAAM. Address: (home) 214 Cambridge St., Syracuse, NY 13210, tel. (315) 472-7129; (bus.) Cultural Resources Council, 113 E. Onandaga St., Syracuse,

NY 13202, tel. (315) 471-1761.

Mr. Golden is executive director (1966–to date) of the Cultural Resources Council of Syracuse and Onandaga County, Inc.; and managing director (1974–to date) of the Civic Center of Onandaga County (N.Y.). He was an associate professor of drama at Syracuse Univ. (1963–66); and has held other academic positions at the Univ. of Illinois (teaching assistant, 1951–52, publicity assistant, 1952–54); Elmira Coll. (associate professor of speech and theatre arts, chairman of the dept., and acting chairman of the Div. of Fine Arts, 1954–58); and Cornell Univ. (assistant professor of speech and drama, director of studio theatre, 1958–63).

Mr. Golden was the director of the Hopewell (Va.) Community Th. (1946–47); Tufts Summer Arena Th. (1952); Illini Student Guild (Univ. of Illinois, 1953); the director and co-founder of the Magic Circle Th. for Children (Tufts Univ., 1953, 1957); an actor with Group 20 (Wellesley, Mass., Summer 1953); and organizer and producer of the Southern Tier Children's Th., a touring repertory company (1954–58).

Mr. Golden has written plays for the stage and television, chiefly for children's theatre; his plays have been produced by approximately 30 community, university, and children's theatres. He was the author, designer, and co-director of "How To Grow a Musical," a State Dept. sponsored show on the history of the American musical presented by the Cornell Univ. Th. (Central and South America, Summer 1962). Three of his short plays, *Garden Shady, Spinner Boy,* and *The Exhibit* were given off-Bway trial performances (Sheridan Sq. Playhouse, Apr. 1964); and he is the author of *Brave* (ANTA, N.Y.C., April 1969).

Television and Radio. He appeared as announcer, writer, and actor for Casper-Gordon Studios (Boston); and on local radio stations WLYN (Lynn, Mass.), WILL (Urbana, Ill.), WENY (Elmira, N.Y.), and WTTS-TV (Bloomington, Ind.); wrote the "Introduction and Guide" for *A Salute to the American Theatre,* produced by CBS-TV and distributed on film (1960). His one-act drama, *River Deep,* was produced by CBS-TV on its Repertoire Workshop series (Jan., Feb. 1964).

He co-produced and hosted "Arts Forum" (WCNY-TV, Syracuse, N.Y., 1967–71); was host of "Arts Comment" (WHEN-TV, Syracuse, N.Y., 1972); wrote *Human Tapestry,* six thirty-minute television shows for the N.Y. State Dept. of Mental Health (1968); and, under an NEH grant, wrote *The Promise and the Problem,* a six-part television series based upon the preamble to the Constitution (WHEN-TV, 1973–74).

Published Works. His one-act play, *The Exhibit,* appeared in a literary periodical, *Syracuse 10* (Fall 1963), and his fantasy, *Johnny Moonbeam and the Silver Arrow,* was published by Children's Theatre Press. This work was selected to represent the US at the International and Overseas Children's Theatre Conference (London, Eng., May 1964). *The Butterfly That Blushed,* a musical fantasy, was published by the Pioneer Press. *Spinner Boy,* a fable for concert staging, was published by *The New York State Community Theatre Journal* (June 1963). He has contributed articles on theatre subjects to several periodicals, including *Players* Magazine, *New Theatre* Magazine, *Theatre Arts, Today's Speech,* and *Television Quarterly.*.

Awards. He received five First Prize awards (1962–64) in national playwriting competitions for his adult and children's plays.

GOLDINA, MIRIAM.

Actress, director, drama coach, translator. b. Mar. 28, 1898, Volgagrad, Russia, to Joseph and Batia (Brudno) Goldin. Father, merchant. Attended drama school, Charkov, Russia, 1914–17; Univ. of Leningrad, 1917–21; drama school, Moscow, 1922–24. Studied with Eugene Vakhtangov and Constantin Stanislavsky in Moscow (1922); Habimah Th., Moscow (1922). Married 1924 to Nahum Zemach, actor, founder of the Moscow Habimah Th. (dec. 1939); one son. Member of AEA AFTRA; SAG. Address: 243 West End Ave., New York, NY 10024, tel. (212) 877-0848.

Theatre. Miss Goldina toured the US with the Habimah Th. in *Jacob's Dream, The Eternal Jew,* and *The Dybbuk* (in Hebrew), later touring with the company in Europe (1928–29).

She made her Bway debut as the Scarlet Woman in *Within the Gates* (Natl., Oct. 22, 1934); subsequently played Ipolita in *Nowhere Bound* (Imperial, Jan. 22, 1935); directed the Malin Studios productions of the one-act plays, *At Liberty* and *The Boor* (1942), *The Informer* (1944), *The Twelve Pound Look* (1946), and *The Dear Departed* (1946).

She played Anna in *Heart of a City* (Henry Miller's Th., Feb. 12, 1942); Marguerita in *A Bell for Adano* (Cort, Dec 6, 1944); directed an ELT production of *A Doll's House* (1946); at the Greenwich Mews Th., N.Y.C., and at Noroton Heights, Conn., directed *Joan of Lorraine, Nine Pine Street, The Romantic Young Lady* and *A Doll's House* (1947); appeared as Leah in *The Dybbuk* (Pasadena Playhouse, Calif., 1948); Rita in *Diamond Lil* (Coronet, N.Y.C., Feb. 5, 1949); directd *Angel Street* (Bryn Mawr Coll. Summer Th., Pa., 1949); *The Chalked Circle* (1953); and *The Jewish Wife* and *Mooney's Kid Don't Cry* (Circle-in-the-Square Workshop, N.Y.C., 1954).

Miss Goldina played Signora Frola in *Right You Are If You Think You Are* (Carl Fisher Hall, N.Y.C., 1957); directed *The Courageous One* (Greenwich Mews, 1958), which she adapted from Gorky's *Meschane;* directed *A Doll's House* (Greenwich Mews, 1958); played Isabel in *The Highest Tree* Longacre, Nov. 4, 1959); appeared as da Bruja in *Bullfight* (Coronet, Hollywood, Calif., Nov. 1961); and played Doña Patricia in *Crossroads* (Puerto Rican Traveling Th., N.Y.C., Aug. 5, 1969).

Television. Miss Goldina made her debut in *The Desert Shall Rejoice* (CBS, Dec. 18, 1946); subsequently appeared in Philco Television Playhouse (NBC, 1957); Robert Montgomery Presents (NBC); Studio One (CBS); Big Story (NBC); Alcoa-Goodyear (NBC); The Detectives (NBC); The Untouchables (ABC); Perry Mason (CBS, 1965); and Arrest and Trial (Ind., 1965).

Other Activities. She was director for the Bryn Mawr Coll. Acting Lab. (Summers 1948–49).

Published Works. Miss Goldina translated Gurchakov's book, *The Director's Lessons of Stanislavsky,* published under the title *Stanislavsky Directs* (1954); and adapted Gorky's *Meschane (The Courageous One)* (1958).

Recreation. Skating, piano.

GOLDMAN, JAMES.

Playwright, lyricist, author. b. James A. Goldman, June 30, 1927, Chicago, Ill., to M. Clarence and Marion (Weil) Goldman. Father, businessman. Grad. Highland Park H.S., Ill., 1944; Univ. of Chicago, Ph.B. 1947; M.A. 1950; attended Columbia Univ., 1952. Married Mar. 5, 1962, to Marie McKeon; two children. Relative in theatre: brother, William Goldman, playwright, novelist. Served US Army, 1952–54; rank, PFC. Member of Dramatists Guild.

Theatre. Mr. Goldman wrote *They Might Be Giants* (Theatre Royal, Stratford, Eng., June 28, 1961); with his brother, William Goldman, *Blood, Sweat and Stanley Poole* (Morosco Th., N.Y.C., Oct. 5, 1961); wrote the lyrics and, with William Goldman, the book for the musical *A Family Affair* (Billy Rose Th., Jan. 27, 1962); wrote *The Lion in Winter* (Ambassador Th., Mar. 3, 1966); and the book for *Follies* (Winter Garden, Apr. 4, 1971).

Films. Mr. Goldman wrote the screenplays for *The Lion in Winter* (Levine-Embassy, 1968); *Nicholas and Alexandra* (Col., 1971) and *They Might Be Giants* (U, 1971).

Published Works. Mr. Goldman wrote the novels *Waldorf* (1965) and *The Man from Greek and Roman* (1974).

Awards. Mr. Goldman received (1968) a NATAS (Oscar) Award for his screenplay for *The Lion in Winter* and was nominated (1972) for an Antoinette Perry (Tony) Award for writing the best book for a musical—for *Follies.*

Recreation. Croquet, tennis, music, reading.

GOLDMAN, WILLIAM.

Playwright, novelist. b. William W. Goldman, Aug. 12, 1931, Chicago, Ill., to Maurice Clarence and Marion (Weil) Goldman. Father, businessman. Grad. Highland Park (Ill.) H.S., 1948; Oberlin Coll., B.A. 1952; Columbia Univ., M.A. 1956. Married Apr. 15, 1961, to Ilene Jones; one daughter. Relative in theatre: brother, James Goldman, playwright, lyricist. Served US Army, 1952–54; rank, Cpl. Member of ALA; Dramatists Guild.

Theatre. Mr. Goldman was author with James Goldman of *Blood, Sweat and Stanley Poole* (Morosco Th., Oct. 5, 1961); and, with James Goldman and John Kander, of the book for the musical, *A Family Affair* (Billy Rose Th., Jan. 27, 1962).

Films. The screenplays for *Soldier in the Rain* (Allied Artists, 1963) and *No Way to Treat a Lady* (Par., 1968) were based on Mr. Goldman's novels of the same titles. He wrote the screenplay for *Harper* (WB, 1966), based on Ross MacDonald's *The Moving Target;* for *Butch Cassidy and the Sundance Kid* (20th-Fox, 1969); *The Stepford Wives* (Col., 1975), based on a novel by Ira Levin; *The Great Waldo Pepper* (U, 1975), based on a story by George Roy Hill; *The Marathon Man* (Par., 1976), based on his own novel of the same name; and for *All the President's Men* (WB, 1976), based on Robert Woodward and Carl Bernstein's book of the same name.

Published Works. Mr. Goldman wrote the novels, *The Temple of Gold* (1957), *Your Turn to Curtsy, My Turn to Bow* (1958), *Soldier in the Rain* (1960), *No Way to Treat a Lady* (1964), *Boys and Girls Together* (1964), *The Thing of It Is. . .* (1967), *Father's Day* (1971), *The Princess Bride* (1973), and *The Marathon Man* (1974). His *The Season* (1969) is an account of a Bway theatre season.

Recreation. Movies, mystery novels, tennis, figuring out baseball statistics.

GOLDSBY, ROBERT.

Educator, director. b. Robert Weddington Goldsby, Dec. 11, 1926, Brooklyn, N.Y., to Robert Echols and Winifred (Wailes) Goldsby. Father, lawyer and mortgage banker. Grad. Columbia H.S., Maplewood, N.J., 1945; Columbia Coll., B.A., 1950; Yale Univ., M.F.A., 1953. Attended Univ. of Manila, 1946–47; Univ. of Paris, 1948–49; Columbia Univ. Grad. Faculties, 1955–57; Actors' Studio, an observer, 1960–61. Married Sept. 27, 1953, to Angela Paton, actress; two sons, one daughter. Served with US Army, Philippine Is., 1946–47; rank, Cpl. Member of AETA; AEA. Address: (home) 2639 Piedmont Ave., Berkeley, CA 94704, tel. (415) TH 8-7909; (bus.) Dept. of Dramatic Arts, Univ. of California at Berkeley, Berkeley, CA 94720, tel. (415) 845-6000.

Since 1957, he has directed productions for the university theatre and, since 1958, he has been a guest director at the Actor's Workshop in San Francisco.

He first appeared on stage as Charley in a US Army Special Service production of *Three Men on a Horse* (Philippine Is., 1946); subsequently played in stock at the Norwich (Conn.) Summer Th. (1951); the Chase Barn Playhouse (Whitefield, N.H., Summers 1952–53); and the Showcase Th. (Evanston, Ill., Winter 1953).

He was director and production stage manager at the Cragsmoor (N.Y.) Summer Th. (1956), and directed an ELT production of *Autumn Garden* (Lenox Hill Playhouse, N.Y.C., Spring 1956). At the Actor's Workshop in San Francisco, he staged *The Busy Martyr* (Sept. 10, 1959) and *Becket* (Dec. 23, 1961). With his wife and Jean Renoir, he translated Renoir's play, *Carola* (world premiere, Univ. of California, Berkeley, 1961).

During 1966–68, Mr. Goldsby was conservatory director, actor, and stage director for the American Conservatory Th.

Other Activities. Mr. Goldsby was a consultant for the Columbia Univ. Art Center (1962).

Published Works. With his wife, Mr. Goldsby translated *Let's Get a Divorce,* published in the anthology, *Let's Get a Divorce and Other Plays* (1958).

GOLONKA, ARLENE. Actress. b. Arlene Leanore Golonka, Jan. 23, 1936, Chicago, Ill., to Edward and Eleanor (Wrobleski) Rejba. Father, owns Garden Ctr. Grad. Tuley H.S., 1953; Goodman Memorial Th. and Sch. of Drama, 1956. Studied acting with Uta Hagen, one year; Curt Conway, one year; Lonnie Chapman, one year; Lee Strasberg, four years; Paul Sills, one year; singing with Michael Longo, two years; dancing with Luigi Lewis, five years. Married Nov. 17, 1962, to Michael Longo, jazz pianist, (marr. dis.); married Feb. 14, 1969, to Larry Delaney, press manager. Relative in theatre: sister, Zorine Morton, actress. Member of AEA; SAG; AFTRA.

Theatre. Miss Golonka first appeared on the stage in the title role in *Cinderella* in a Chicago settlement house production (Wicker Park, 1948); later appeared in the chorus of *The Mikado* (Blackstone Th., Chicago, 1953); and at the Salt Creek Playhouse, (Hinsdale, Ill. 1955–57), played Mazie in *Burlesque,* appeared in *Detective Story,* and *Separate Tables;* and appeared in *Will Success Spoil Rock Hunter?* (Eagle River, Wisc. 1957).

She made her N.Y.C. debut as Nellie Milwaukee in *Night Circus* (John Golden Th., Dec. 2, 1958); followed by Belle in *Take Me Along* (Shubert, Oct. 22, 1959); and Peggy Evans in *Come Blow Your Horn* (Brooks Atkinson Th., Feb. 22, 1961).

She appeared as Fainting Fanny in *Oh Lady, Lady* (Goodspeed Opera House, East Haddam, Conn., 1963); Ado Annie in *Oklahoma!* (Cape Cod Melody Top, Hyannis, Mass., 1963); played Candy Starr in *One Flew Over the Cuckoo's Nest* (Cort, N.Y.C., Nov. 13, 1963); Fran in *Ready When You Are, C. B.* (Brooks Atkinson Th., Dec. 7, 1964); Avril in a musical version of *Purple Dust* (Goodspeed Opera House, East Haddam, Conn., July 22, 1965); and Mrs. Maggie Stevens in *The Wayward Stork* (46th St. Th., N.Y.C., Jan. 19, 1966).

Films. She made her debut in *Love with a Proper Stranger* (Par., 1963); followed by roles in *Diary of a Bachelor* (Amer. Intl., 1964); *Harvey Middleman, Fireman* (Col., 1965); *Penelope* (MGM, 1966); *The Busy Body* (Par., 1967); *Welcome to Hard Times* (MGM, 1967); and *Hang 'Em High* (UA, 1968).

Television. Miss Golonka played the continuing role of Millie on the Mayberry, R.F.D., series (CBS, premiere Sept. 23, 1968), as well as appearing on the US Steel Hour (CBS); Garry Moore Show (CBS); Charley Weaver Show; Kitty Foyle series; Naked City (ABC); The Defenders (CBS); Car 54, Where Are You? (NBC); The Nurses (CBS); Andy Griffith Show (CBS); Vacation Playhouse (CBS); That Girl (ABC); *The Love Song of Barney Kempinski* (Stage 67, ABC, Sept. 14, 1966); Girl Talk (ABC); and The Today Show (NBC).

Discography. Miss Golonka is heard on the comedy album *You Don't Have To Be Jewish* (1965).

GOODHART, WILLIAM. Playwright. b. New Haven, Conn. Attended Yale Univ.; Grad. Yale Drama Sch. 1949. Served US Army, WW II. Three daughters.

Theatre. Mr. Goodhart is the author of *Generation* (Morosco, N.Y.C., Oct. 6, 1965).

Films. He wrote the screenplay for *The Moviegoer.*.

GOODMAN, DODY. Actress. b. Dolores Goodman, Oct. 28, Columbus, Ohio, to Dexter and Leona Goodman. Grad. North H.S., Columbus, Ohio, 1940. Studied dancing at the Jorg Fasting School, Columbus; Sch. of American Ballet, and Metropolitan Opera Ballet Sch., N.Y.C., 1939–43.

Theatre. Miss Goodman made her stage debut as a dancer with the corps de ballet at Radio City Music Hall (N.Y.C., 1940); her Bway debut as a dancer in *High Button Shoes* (Century, Oct. 9, 1947); was in the chorus of *Miss Liberty* (Imperial, July 15, 1949); *Call Me Madam* (Imperial, Oct. 2, 1950); played Violet in *Wonderful Town* (Winter Garden, Feb. 25, 1953); and appeared in the revues, *Shoestring Revue* (President, Feb. 28, 1955); *Shoestring '57* (Barbizon-Plaza, Nov. 5, 1956); and *Parade* (Players, Jan. 20, 1960).

She toured as Winifred in *Once Upon a Mattress* (opened Erlanger, Chicago, Ill., Sept. 1, 1960; closed Colonial, Boston, Mass., Mar. 18, 1961); played Dora in *Fiorello!* (NY City Ctr., June 13, 1962); Elizabeth Lamb in *A Rainy Day in Newark* (Belasco, Oct. 22, 1963); the First Woman in *A Thurber Carnival* (Bucks County Playhouse, New Hope, Pa., June 28, 1965); appeared in *Ben Bagley's Cole Porter Revue* (Square East, N.Y.C., Dec. 22, 1965); played Sally Ellis in *My Daughter, Your Son* (Booth, May 13, 1969); Jenny in *The Front Page* (Ethel Barrymore Th., Oct. 18, 1969); Dolly Gallagher in *The Matchmaker* (Mummers Th., Oklahoma City, 1971–72 season); and Mrs. Ella Spofford in *Lorelei* (Palace, N.Y.C., Jan. 27, 1974).

Films. Miss Goodman made her screen debut in *Bedtime Story* (UI, 1964).

Television. Miss Goodman has appeared on the Sid Caesar Show (CBS, 1956); the Martha Raye Show (NBC, 1956); the Sergeant Bilko Show (CBS, 1956); the Ray Bolger Show (1957); the Jack Paar Show (NBC, 1957–64); Girl Talk (ABC); The Merv Griffin Show (Ind.); and Mary Hartman, Mary Hartman (Ind.).

Published Works. Miss Goodman wrote *Women, Women, Women!* (1966).

GOODMAN, RANDOLPH. Educator, playwright. b. May 1908, New York City, to Philip S. and Bertha (Kahn) Goodman. Father, insurance broker. Grad. DeWitt Clinton H.S., N.Y.C., 1927; New York Univ., B.S. 1931; Yale Univ. Sch. of Drama (Rockefeller Grant and Geo. Pierce Baker Scholarships), M.F.A. 1946; London (Eng.) Univ. (Inst. for Intl. Educ. fellowship), Certificate in Drama, 1950; Columbia Univ., Ph.D. 1951. Member of ASTR; IASTA (chmn., playwrights' and directors' comm., 1963–64); ANTA; Classical Club of NY. Address: (home) 176 E. 77th St., New York, NY 10021, tel. (212) 734-1999; (bus.) Brooklyn Coll., Brooklyn, NY 11210, tel. (212) 780-5194.

Since 1968, Mr. Goodman has been professor of English at Brooklyn Coll., where, previously, he had been temporary instructor (1946–50), instructor (1950–58), assistant professor (1958–61), and associate professor (1961–68). He also taught playwriting, and Greek and Roman drama, at the New Sch. for Social Research (evenings, 1950–55); and was adjunct assoc. prof. in the Grad. Sch. of the Arts, Columbia Univ. (1967–69).

He wrote *Gidion* (Yale Univ., New Haven, Conn., Dec. 19, 1945); with Walter Carroll, *A Long Way from Home,* based on Gorky's *The Lower Depths* (Maxine Elliott's Th., N.Y.C., Feb. 8, 1948); wrote *I, Walt Whitman* (Whitman Hall, Brooklyn Coll., N.Y., Jan. 13, 1955); and *Johnny Merripranks,* a children's play presented in public schools in N.Y.C. and throughout the US under the auspices of the Junior Leagues of America, Inc. (1962). His translation of Ingmar Bergman's *The Apes Shall Inherit the Earth* was performed at the Two Worlds Festival, Spoleto, Italy (1965), at Colorado State Coll. (1965), at Columbia Univ. (1969), and on WOR-TV (1966). He wrote a musical version of *Johnny Merripranks,* which was presented in summer theatres (1971).

Television and Radio. Mr. Goodman spoke on Walt Whitman (Book Festival, WNYC, 1955), and on the program, The Enjoyment of Poetry (WEVD, Dec. 29, 1963). For television, he wrote two programs which were seen on Brooklyn Coll. closed-circuit and on Channel 31, WNYC: *Robert Browning's Dramatic Monologues* (1965) and *Folk Songs in America* (1966). He discussed *The Seagull* by Anton Chekhov (Th. Interviews, WNYC-TV, 1968).

Other Activities. He was a reporter on the NY *Post* and NY *Evening Journal,* and a radio writer (1935–38). At Brooklyn Coll., he served on the Shakespeare Scholarship Comm. (1968–74) and on the Honors and Awards Comm. (1972–74). He presented a paper on Tennessee Williams' *Slapstick Tragedy* at the AETA convention (Miami Beach, Fla., Aug. 1966).

Published Works. Mr. Goodman was assistant editor of the American drama section of the *Enciclopedia dello Spettacolo* (Rome, Italy, 1954–59), for which he wrote sixty-five articles, and he wrote twenty-five articles on American theatre for *Collier's Encyclopedia* (1956–61). He compiled a chronological table of Sean O'Casey's plays, *Selected Plays of Sean O'Casey* (1954), and a bibliography dealing with Arena Theatre for ANTA (1957), and, with Leif Sjoberg, he translated two Swedish one-act plays: *The Apes Shall Inherit the Earth* by Werner Aspenström and *Wood-Painting* by Ingmar Bergman (*Tulane Drama Review,* Winter 1961). He wrote an introduction to *The Merchant of Venice* (1966) and is the author of the books *Drama on Stage* (1961) and *From Script to Stage: Eight Modern Plays* (1971).

Recreation. Traveling, reading, theatregoing.

GOODNER, CAROL. Actress. b. Carol Marie Goodner, May 30, 1904, New York City, to Frank William and Marie Elizabeth (Miller) Goodner. Father, photographer, actor; mother, dancer, actress. Grad. P.S. 69, N.Y.C.; attended Hunter H.S and Julia Richman H.S. Married May 14, 1940, to Thomas Marshall, Jr., real estate manager (marr. dis. 1943); married Jan. 30, 1949, to Frederic Hunter, actor (marr. dis. July 1963). Member of AEA; SAG; AFTRA.

Theatre. Miss Goodner made her stage debut at age four as a Dutch Girl in a touring company of *The Red Mill* (1908); subsequently toured with her mother for five years in vaudeville; appeared in *The Music Box Revue* (Music Box, N.Y.C., Sept. 22, 1923); and later appeared as Catherine Rogers in *The Great Gatsby* (Ambassador, Feb. 2, 1926).

She made her London debut as Jane Weston in *The Butter and Egg Man* (Garrick, Aug. 30, 1927); appeared as Miss Baxter in *Skin Deep* (Criterion, May 1928); succeeded Ursula Jeans as Miss Carruthers in *Passing Brompton Road* (Criterion, July 10, 1928); played Olie Warrington in *The Black Ace* (Globe, May 1929); and Margaret Fielding in *Yesterday's Harvest (Apollo, Sept. 1929).*

She played Elsie Fraser in The First Mrs. Fraser (Playhouse, N.Y.C., Dec. 28, 1929); Miss Taylor in *Late Night Final (Five Star Final)* (Phoenix, London, June 25, 1931); Irene Baumer in *Musical Chairs* (Arts, Nov. 15, 1931); Miss Critchlow in *Cloudy with Showers* (St. Martin's, Apr. 1932); Kitty Packard in *Dinner at Eight* (Palace, Jan. 6, 1933); Catherine in *The Sowers* (Arts, May 1933); and Princess Ganivre in *Finished Abroad* (Fulham, Oct. 1933).

She appeared as Sarah Glassman in *Success Story* (Fulham, Jan. 1934); Anne Darrow in *Double Door* (Globe, Mar. 21, 1934); Jane in *Secret Orchard* (Arts, Apr. 1934); Helen Norton in *Living Dangerously* (Strand, June 7, 1934); Margaret of Clare in *Rose and Glove* (Westminster, Sept. 1934); Anna Penn in *Anthony and Anna* (Fulham, Nov. 12, 1934); Hippolita in *'Tis Pity She's a Whore* (Arts, Dec. 30, 1934); Delia Freyne in a two-month tour of *Further Outlook* (Oct. 1935); Mrs. Darling in *Peter Pan* (Palladium, Dec. 26, 1935); toured as Delia Lovell in *The Old Maid* (Mar. 1936); played Lady Pakenham in *Heroes Don't Care* (St. Martin's, June, 10, 1936); Sophy Raffety in *He Was Born Gay* (Queen's, May 1937); Ada Isaacs Menken in *The Great Romancer* (New, June 1937); the title role in *Gertie Maude* (St. Martin's, Aug. 1937); Jane in *Punch and Judy* (Vaudeville, Oct. 1937); Masha in *The Three Sisters* (Queen's, Jan. 28, 1938); Jennifer in *The Doctor's Dilemma* (Richmond, June 1938); Dorothy Houghton in *Official Secret* (New, Sept. 1938); and Bess Stanforth in *They Walk Alone* ("Q," Nov. 21, 1938).

Miss Goodner played Lorraine Sheldon in *The Man Who Came to Dinner* (Music Box, N.Y.C., 1939); Bess Stanforth in *They Walk Alone* (John Golden Th., Mar. 12, 1941); Aunt Gen in *The Wookey* (Plymouth, Sept. 10, 1941); Ruth in *Blithe Spirit* (Chicago, Ill., 1942); succeeded Eve Arden as Maggie Watson in the reopening of *Let's Face It!* (Imperial, N.Y.C., Aug. 17, 1942); played Mrs. Parrish in *The Family* (Windsor, Mar. 30, 1943); Lennie Lorrimer in *Lovers and Friends* (Plymouth, Nov. 29, 1943); appeared in a USO touring production of *Junior Miss* (ETO, Nov. 1944–July 1945); played Alice Langdon in *Deep Are the Roots* (Fulton,

N.Y.C., Sept. 26, 1945); and Margaret Stevenson in *How I Wonder* (Hudson, Sept. 30, 1947).

She spent a season at the Dallas (Tex.) Community Th. (1947–48), appearing in the title role of *Hedda Gabler* and in other plays; toured with the Margaret Webster Shakespeare Co. as Lady Macbeth in *Macbeth* and Gertrude in *Hamlet* (opened Buffalo, N.Y., Sept. 28, 1948; closed Philadelphia, Pa., Apr. 26, 1949); succeeded (Sept. 1950) Eileen Peel as Lavinia Chamberlayne in *The Cocktail Party* (Henry Miller's Th., N.Y.C., Jan. 21, 1950); played Constance Tuckerman in *The Autumn Garden* (Coronet, Mar. 7, 1951); Margaret Westman in *The Brass Ring* (Lyceum, Apr. 10, 1952); in stock, played Mildred Watson Drake in *Old Acquaintance* (1952); appeared as a Visitor in *Horses in Midstream* (Royale, N.Y.C., Apr. 2, 1953); Mrs. Dennis in *The Living Room* (Henry Miller's Th., Nov. 17, 1954); and Alice More in *A Man for All Seasons* (ANTA, Nov. 22, 1961).

Films. Miss Goodner appeared in *The Ringer* (1st Division, 1932), *Just Smith* (Gaumont, 1934); *The Dominant Sex* (1937); *The Frog* (20th-Fox, 1939); *La Vie Parisienne* and *Heidelberg*.

Television and Radio. On radio, she played in the serial Wendy Warren and the News (CBS, 1950). On television, she appeared in Where There's a Will (NBC, Mar. 2, 1947).

Recreation. Cooking.

GOODRICH, FRANCES. Playwright. b. Belleville, New Jersey, to Henry W. and Madeleine (Lloyd) Goodrich. Grad. Passaic Collegiate H.S., Passaic, N.J., 1908; Vassar College, B.A. 1912; Sch. of Social Work, N.Y.C., 1912–13. Married May 3, 1917, to Robert Ames, actor (marr. dis. 1923); married Nov. 23, 1927, to Henrik Willem Van Loon, writer, (marr. dis. 1930); married Feb. 7, 1931, to Albert Hackett, writer. Member of Dramatists Guild; SWG (secy., 1936, member of board 1936–39); Vassar Club; Cosmopolitan Club. Address: 88 Central Park West, New York, NY 10023, tel. (212) 724-9389.

Theatre. Miss Goodrich made her stage debut with a stock company (Northampton Municipal Th., Mass., 1913–16); and her Bway debut, succeeding (Apr. 1917) Alice Lindahl in the part of Cora Falkner in *Come Out of the Kitchen* (Cohan Th., Oct. 23, 1916); appeared as Lady Gay Hawthorne in *Queen Victoria* (48 St. Th., Nov. 15, 1923); succeeded Juliette Crosby as Clara in *The Show-Off* (Playhouse, Feb. 5, 1924); appeared as June Lawler in *A Good, Bad Woman* (Playhouse, June 22, 1925); succeeded Merle Madden as Madame De Charriere in a touring company of *In the Next Room* (1924–25); followed (Sept. 1928) Jean Dixon as Susan Perry in *Heavy Traffic* (Empire, Sept. 5, 1928); played Rita Rydell in *Excess Baggage* (Ritz, N.Y.C., Dec. 26, 1927); and appeared in stock (Elitch Gardens, Denver, Colo., Summer 1927; Lakewood Th., Skowhegan, Me., Summers 1928–29).

With Albert Hackett, she wrote *Up Pops the Devil*, their first produced play on Bway (Masque, N.Y.C., Sept. 1, 1930); *Bridal Wise* (Cort, May 30, 1932); *The Great Big Doorstep* (Morosco, Nov. 26, 1942); the dramatization of *The Diary of Anne Frank* (Cort, Oct. 5, 1955).

Films. With Mr. Hackett, Miss Goodrich wrote the screenplays for *The Secret of Madame Blanche* (MGM, 1933) *Penthouse*, (MGM, 1933); *Hide-Out* (MGM, 1934); *The Thin Man* (MGM, 1934); *Ah, Wilderness!* (MGM, 1935); *Naughty Marietta* (MGM, 1935); *Rose Marie* (MGM, 1936); *After the Thin Man* (MGM, 1936); *The Firefly* (MGM, 1937); *Another Thin Man* (MGM, 1939); *Lady in the Dark* (Par., 1944); *The Hitler Gang* (Par., 1944); *The Virginian* (Par. 1946); *It's A Wonderful Life* (RKO, 1946); *Easter Parade* (MGM, 1948); *The Pirate* (MGM, 1948); *In the Good Old Summertime* (MGM, 1949); *Father of the Bride* (MGM, 1950); *Too Young To Kiss* (MGM, 1951); *Father's Little Dividend* (MGM, 1951); *Give a Girl a Break* (MGM, 1953); *Seven Brides for Seven Brothers* (MGM, 1954); *The Long, Long Trailer* (MGM, 1954); *Gaby* (MGM, 1956); *A Certain Smile* (20th-Fox, 1958); *The Diary of Anne Frank* (20th-Fox, 1959); and *Five Finger Exercise* (Col., 1962).

Awards. For the play *The Diary of Anne Frank*, Miss Goodrich and Mr. Hackett received the Pulitzer Prize, the NY Drama Critics Circle Award, the Antoinette Perry (Tony) Award (1956); and for the film, they received the Screen Writers Guild Award, and a nomination for the Academy (Oscar) Award. The following screenplays received the Screen Writers Guild Award and were nominated for Academy (Oscar) Awards: *The Thin Man; Ah, Wilderness!; Easter Parade; Father of the Bride* (which also received a Christopher Award); and *Seven Brides for Seven Brothers*. Miss Goodrich also received the Screen Writers Guild Award for Achievement and the Laurel Award (both 1956).

GORDON, BRUCE. Actor. b. 1916, Fitchburg, Mass. Attended Geiger Sch. of Dramatics. Served WW II, USN. Member of AEA; SAG; AFTRA.

Pre-Theatre. Merchant Seaman.

Theatre. Mr. Gordon made his Bway debut as a walk-on in *The Eternal Road* (Manhattan Opera House, Jan. 7, 1937); subsequently joined the company of *Naughty Naught '00* (American Music Hall, Jan. 23, 1937); played Bowery B'hoy in *The Fireman's Flame* (American Music Hall, Oct. 9, 1937); and a Cowhand in *The Girl from Wyoming* (American Music Hall, Oct. 29, 1938); toured as Herbert Z. Harner in *Kiss the Boys Goodbye* (1939); played Officer Klein in *Arsenic and Old Lace* (Fulton, N.Y.C., Jan. 10, 1941); toured as Marcellus in Maurice Evans' GI *Hamlet* (1946); appeared as Ventidius in *Antony and Cleopatra* (Martin Beck Th., N.Y.C., Nov. 26, 1947); played Aegeus in the national tour of *Medea* (opened Lobero, Santa Barbara, Calif., Aug. 1948), and in its return engagement (NY City Ctr., May 2, 1949); toured in *That Lady* (opened Harris, Chicago, Jan. 30, 1950); succeeded Kent Smith as Yancy Loper in *The Wisteria Trees* (Martin Beck Th., Mar. 29, 1950); and at the NY City Ctr., played Sidi El Assif in *Captain Brassbound's Conversion* (Dec. 27, 1950), and Thomas Mowbray in *King Richard II* (Jan. 24, 1951).

He appeared as Dulac in *Legend of Lovers* (Plymouth, Dec. 26, 1951); Sonny Bannerman in *The Pink Elephant* (Playhouse, Apr. 22, 1953); La Hire in *The Lark* (Longacre, Nov. 17, 1955); Antinous in the pre-Bway tryout of *Maiden Voyage* (opened Forrest Th., Philadelphia, Pa., Feb. 28, 1957; closed there March 9, 1957); Anthony Baiello in *Nowhere To Go But Up* (Winter Garden, N.Y.C., Nov. 10, 1962); Thomas Cromwell in the national tour of *A Man for All Seasons* (opened Greek Th., Los Angeles, Calif., July 22, 1963), which played a N.Y.C. engagement (NY City Ctr., Jan. 27, 1964), and resumed its tour (closed Blackstone, Chicago, Ill., May 30, 1964); and Maximiliano Orton in *Diamond Orchid* (Henry Miller's Th., Feb. 10, 1965).

Films. Mr. Gordon made his debut in *Love Happy* (UA, 1949); subsequently appeared in *The Buccaneer* (Par., 1958); *Hannibal* (WB, 1960); *The Tower of London* (UA, 1962); *Rider on a Dead Horse* (Allied, 1962); *Slow Run* (Film-Makers, 1968); and *Hello Down There* (Par., 1969).

Television. Since 1949, Mr. Gordon has appeared on some five hundred television programs, including *The Lark* (Hallmark Hall of Fame, NBC, Feb. 10, 1957); *Bernadette of Lourdes* (Look Up and Live, CBS, Aug. 11, 1957); and The Untouchables (ABC).

Recreation. Fishing, hunting, dog breeding.

GORDON, MAX. Producer. b. Mechel Salpeter, June 28, 1892, New York City, to Herschel and Doba Salpeter. Father, tailor. Grad. P.S. 171, N.Y.C., 1907; attended Townsend Harris H.S. Married Mildred Bartlett, actress, May 23, 1921. Relative in theatre; brother, Cliff Gordon, comedian. Served WW I, US Army, Pvt. Member of The Lambs; The Players; City Athletic Club.

Theatre. Mr. Gordon made his debut in vaudeville as a publicist (advance man) for the touring Behman Show (1910); and for his brother, Cliff Gordon, in *The Passing Parade* (1911); and became a booking agent in partnership with Al Lewis for vaudeville acts, including one-act plays, such as Eugene O'Neill's *In the Zone*.

In association with Sam H. Harris, Messrs. Lewis and Gordon produced in N.Y.C., *Welcome Stranger* (Cohen and Harris Th., Sept. 13, 1920); *Six-Cylinder Love* (Sam H. Harris Th., Aug. 25, 1921); *Rain* (Maxine Elliott's Th., Nov. 7, 1922); *Secrets* (Fulton, Dec. 25, 1922); *The Nervous Wreck* (Sam H. Harris Th., Oct. 9, 1923); *The Family Upstairs* (Gaiety, Aug. 17, 1925); *The Jazz Singer* (Fulton, Sept. 14, 1925); and *Easy Come, Easy Go* (George M. Cohan Th., Oct. 26, 1925).

Mr. Gordon produced his first independent Bway production, *Three's a Crowd* (Selwyn, Oct. 15, 1930), which later toured; followed by *The Band Wagon* (New Amsterdam, N.Y.C., June 3, 1931); *The Cat and the Fiddle* (Globe, Oct. 15, 1931); *Flying Colors* (Imperial, Sept. 15, 1932); *Her Master's Voice* (Plymouth, Oct. 23, 1933); *Roberta* (New Ambassador, Nov. 18, 1933); *The Shining Hour* (Booth, Feb. 13, 1934); *Dodsworth* (Shubert, Feb. 24, 1934); *The Great Waltz* (Center, Sept. 22, 1934); *Spring Song* (Morosco, Oct. 1, 1934); and *The Farmer Takes a Wife* (46th St. Th., Oct. 30, 1934).

With Sam H. Harris, he co-produced *Jubilee* (Imperial, Oct. 12, 1935); presented *Pride and Prejudice* (Music Box, Nov. 5, 1935); *Ethan Frome* (Natl., Jan. 21, 1936); *St. Helena* (Lyceum, Oct. 6, 1936); *The Women* (Ethel Barrymore Th., Dec. 26, 1936); *Othello* (New Amsterdam, Jan. 6, 1937); in association with Sam Harris, produced *Save Me the Waltz* (Martin Beck Th., Feb. 28, 1938); and, independently, *Spring Thaw* (Martin Beck Th., Mar. 21, 1938).

In association with Guthrie McClintic, Mr. Gordon produced *Missouri Legend* (Empire, Sept. 19, 1938); in association with George S. Kaufman and Moss Hart, produced *Sing Out the News* (Music Box Th., Sept. 24, 1938); produced, with Sam H. Harris, *The American Way* (Center, Jan. 21, 1939); and produced *Very Warm for May* (Alvin, Nov. 17, 1939); *My Sister Eileen* (Biltmore, Dec. 26, 1940); *The Land Is Bright* (Music Box, Oct. 28, 1941); *Junior Miss* (Lyceum, Nov. 18, 1941); *Sunny River* (St. James, Dec. 4, 1941); *The Doughgirls* (Lyceum, Dec. 30, 1942); *Men in Shadow* (Morosco, Mar. 10, 1943); *Those Endearing Young Charms* (Booth, June 16, 1943), *Over 21* (Music Box, Jan. 3, 1944), *Where the Sun Shines* (Lyceum, Sept. 19, 1944); *The Late George Apley* (Lyceum, Nov. 23, 1944); and *The Firebrand of Florence* (Alvin, Mar. 22, 1945).

In association with Meyer Davis, Mr. Gordon produced *Hollywood Pinafore* (Alvin, May 31, 1945); presented *The Next Half Hour* (Empire, Oct. 24, 1945); *Born Yesterday* (Lyceum, Feb. 4, 1946); *Park Avenue* (Shubert, Nov. 4, 1946); *Years Ago* (Mansfield, Dec. 3, 1946); *Town House* (Natl., Sept. 23, 1948); *Bravo!* (Lyceum, Nov. 11, 1948); *Metropole* (Lyceum, Dec. 6, 1949); *The Small Hours* (Natl., Feb. 15, 1951); *The Solid Gold Cadillac* (Belasco, Nov. 5, 1953); and the pre-Bway tryout of *Everybody Loves Me* (opened McCarter, Princeton, N.J., Nov. 8, 1956; closed Locust St. Th., Philadelphia, Pa., Nov. 24, 1956).

Films. Mr. Gordon's first film assignment was as assistant to the Marx Brothers in *Monkey Business* (Par., 1931), and *Horse Feathers* (Par., 1932); subsequently was producer of *Abe Lincoln in Illinois* (RKO, 1940), and the screen version of *Year's Ago*, entitled *The Actress* (MGM, 1953).

Television. Mr. Gordon became production adviser to NBC (1939); and produced the Frank Sinatra Show (CBS, premiere Oct. 9, 1951).

Published Works. Mr. Gordon wrote, with Lewis Funke, his autobiography, *Max Gordon Presents* (1963).

GORDON, MICHAEL. Director, actor. b. Sept. 6, 1909, Baltimore, Md., to Paul and Eva (Kunen) Gordon. Father, manufacturer; mother, pianist. Grad. Baltimore (Md.) City Coll. H.S., 1925; Johns Hopkins Univ., B.A. 1929; Yale Univ., M.F.A. 1932. Studied at Yale Univ. Sch. of Drama with George Pierce Baker (1929–32); with the

Group Theatre (1935–40). Married Oct. 2, 1937, to Elizabeth Cane; one son, two daughters. Member of DGA; AEA (1932–40). Address: 259 N. Layton Dr., Los Angeles, CA 90052, tel. (213) GR 6-2024.

Mr. Gordon became a member of the theatre arts faculty, Univ. of California at Los Angeles, in 1971 and has been professor-in-residence since 1973.

Theatre. Mr. Gordon made his first acting appearance in the title role of *The Dictator* (Johns Hopkins Univ., Dec. 1927); his first professional appearance in a supernumerary role in the opera, *Boris Gudanov* (Lyric Th., Baltimore, Md., Apr. 1928); and subsequently played Henry in *Springtime for Henry* (Camp Walden, Lake George, N.Y., May 1932).

His first N.Y.C. appearance was in the chorus of *Walk a Little Faster* (St. James, Dec. 7, 1932), for which he was also second assistant stage manager; subsequently appeared in *The Exiles* (New Sch. for Social Research, July 1933); and at the Civic Repertory Th., played in and was stage manager for *Peace on Earth* (Nov. 29, 1933), served as assistant director and played Charley Freeman in *Stevedore* (Apr. 18, 1934); and was director for *Sailors of Cattaro* (Dec. 10, 1934) and *Black Pit* (Mar. 20, 1935).

He was stage manager for the Group Theatre productions of *Weep for the Virgins* (46 St. Th., Nov. 30, 1935); *The Case of Clyde Griffiths* (Ethel Barrymore Th., Mar. 13, 1936); *Johnny Johnson* (44 St. Th., Nov. 19, 1936); and *Golden Boy* (Belasco, Nov. 4, 1937).

Mr. Gordon was lighting designer for *Casey Jones* (Fulton, Feb. 19, 1938); was stage manager and played Mickey in *Golden Boy* (St. James's, London, June 21, 1938); was lighting designer for *Rocket to the Moon* (Belasco, N.Y.C., Nov. 24, 1938), *Gentle People* (Belasco, Jan. 5, 1939), and *My Heart's in the Highlands* (Guild, Apr. 13, 1939); directed *In a Yiddische Grocery* (2nd Ave. Th., Oct. 1939); and was lighting designer for *Thunder Rock* (Mansfield, Nov. 14, 1939), *Night Music* (Broadhurst, Feb. 22, 1940), and *Heavenly Express* (Natl., Apr. 18, 1940).

He directed *Storm Operation* (Belasco, Jan. 11, 1944); *Sophie* (Playhouse, Dec. 25, 1944); a summer-theatre production of *The Gods Sit Back* (Provincetown, Mass., June 1945); *Home of the Brave* (Belasco, N.Y.C., Dec. 27, 1945); and the touring production of *Laura* (opened Playhouse, Wilmington, Del., Apr. 19, 1946).

Mr. Gordon also directed *Anna Christie* (NY City Ctr., Jan. 9, 1952); *One Bright Day* (Royale, Mar. 19, 1952); *The Male Animal* (NY City Ctr., Apr. 30, 1952); *See the Jaguar* (Cort, Dec. 3, 1952); *Maggie* (Natl., Feb. 18, 1953); *His and Hers* (48 St. Th., Jan. 7, 1954); *The Magic and the Loss* (Booth, Apr. 9, 1954); *The Tender Trap* (Longacre, Oct. 13, 1954); *Champagne Complex* (Cort, Apr. 12, 1955); *Deadfall* (Holiday, Oct. 27, 1955); and *The Lovers* (Martin Beck Th., May 10, 1956).

Films. From Sept. 1940–Mar. 1942, Mr. Gordon was dialogue director for Columbia films, including *Here Comes Mr. Jordon* (1941), *Bedtime Story* (1941), and many others.

Also, he directed *Boston Blackie Goes to Hollywood* (Col., 1942); *Underground Agent* (Col., 1942); *One Dangerous Night* (Col., 1943); *Crime Doctor* (Col., 1943); *Another Part of the Forest* (U, 1947); *The Web* (U, 1947); *An Act of Murder* (U, 1948); *The Lady Gambles* (U, 1949); *Woman in Hiding* (U, 1949); *Cyrano de Bergerac* (UA, 1950); *I Can Get It for You Wholesale* (20th-Fox, 1951); *The Secret of Convict Lake* (20th-Fox, 1951); *Pillow Talk* (U, 1959); *Portrait in Black* (U, 1960); *Boys Night Out* (MGM, 1961); *For Love or Money* (U, 1962); *Move Over, Darling* (20th-Fox, 1963); *The Smashmaster Caper* (20th-Fox, 1964); *A Very Special Favor* (U, 1965); *Texas Across the River* (U, 1966); and *The Impossible Years* (MGM, 1968).

Television. Mr. Gordon directed several segments for the series, Decoy (Syndicated, Jan. 1958); episodes for *Room 222* (1971); *Anna and the King* (1972); and *Banyon* (1972).

Recreation. Golf, chess, playing recorder.

GORDON, RUTH. Actress, playwright. b. Ruth Gordon Jones, Oct. 30, 1896, Wollaston, Mass., to Clinton and Annie Tapley (Ziegler) Jones. Father, factory foreman. Grad. Quincy (Mass.) H.S., 1914; attended AADA, N.Y.C., 1914–15. Studied singing with Keith Davis (1962–to date). Married Dec. 1927 to Gregory Kelly, actor; married 1942 to Garson Kanin, playwright, director; one son. Member of AEA; ALA; Dramatists Guild.

Theatre. Miss Gordon made her debut as Nibs in *Peter Pan* (Empire Th., Dec. 21, 1915); subsequently appeared in *The Little Minister* (Empire, Jan. 11, 1916); toured in *Fair and Warmer* (1916); played Lola Pratt in *Seventeen* (Booth, Jan. 22, 1918), and on tour (1918–19); appeared in the pre-Bway tour of *Piccadilly Jim* (1919–20); and portrayed Cora Wheeler in *Clarence* (Blackstone, Chicago, Ill. 1920), in which she also toured.

She played Grace in *The First Year* (Little, N.Y.C., Oct. 20, 1920, and on tour; appeared in *Bristol Glass* (Blackstone, Chicago 1923); as Winsora Tweedles in *Tweedles* (Frazee, N.Y.C., Aug. 13, 1923); played in *The Phantom Ship* (1925); portrayed Katherine Everitt in *Mrs. Partridge Presents* (Belmont, Jan. 5, 1925); appeared in *Collision* (Rochester, N.Y., 1925); as Eva Hutton in *The Fall of Eve* (Booth, Aug. 31, 1925); in the title role of *Holding Helen* (1925); as Bobby in *Saturday's Children* (Booth, Jan. 26, 1927), and on tour; played in *King's X* (1928); the title role in *Serena Blandish* (Morosco, Jan. 23, 1929); Lily Malone in *Hotel Universe* (Martin Beck Th., Apr. 14, 1930); Ilona Sobri in *The Violet* (Henry Miller's Th., Sept. 29, 1930); Susie Sachs in *A Church Mouse* (Playhouse, Oct. 12, 1931); Trixie Ingram in *The Wiser They Are* (Plymouth, Apr. 6, 1931); Mary Hilliard in *Here Today* (Ethel Barrymore Th., Sept. 6, 1932), later appeared in the same role in Boston, Mass. and Chicago, Ill.; portrayed Elizabeth Rimplegar in *Three-Cornered Moon* (Cort, Mar. 16, 1933); Lucy Wells in *They Shall Not Die* (Royal, Feb. 21, 1934); Harriet Marshall in *A Sleeping Clergyman* (Guild, Oct. 8, 1934).

Miss Gordon appeared in Boston and Chicago in *Here Today* (1935); as Epiphania in a stock production of *The Millionairess* (Berkshire Playhouse, Stockbridge, Mass., 1935); appeared in *Captain Brassbound's Conversion* (White Plains, N.Y., 1935); and as Mattie Silver in *Ethan Frome* (Natl., Jan. 21, 1936).

She made her London debut as Mrs. Pinchwife in *The Country Wife* (Old Vic, Oct. 6, 1936); repeated the role on Bway (Henry Miller's Th., Dec. 1, 1936); and played Nora Helmer in *A Doll's House* (Morosco, Dec. 27, 1937).

She appeared as Linda in the pre-Bway tryout of *The Birds Stopped Singing* (1939); and in the tryout of *Portrait of a Lady* (1911); played Iris Ryan in *The Strings, My Lord, Are False* (Royale, N.Y.C., May 19, 1942); Natasha in *The Three Sisters* (Ethel Barrymore Th., Dec. 21, 1942); wrote and appeared as Paula Wharton in *Over 21* (Music Box, Jan 3, 1944); wrote *The Leading Lady* and played Gay Marriott in it (Natl., Oct. 18, 1948); wrote *Years Ago* (Mansfield, Dec. 3, 1946); produced, with Garson Kanin, Victor Samrock, and William Fields, *How I Wonder* (Hudson, Sept. 30, 1947); played Sara Boulting in *The Smile of the World* (Lyceum, Jan. 12, 1949).

She toured stock theatres in the title role in *The Amazing Adele*, and played Natalia in *A Month in the Country* (Westport Country Playhouse, Conn., Summer 1949); appeared as Mrs. Levi in *The Matchmaker* (Haymarket, London, Nov. 4, 1954; Edinburgh Festival, Scot., 1954; Berlin Festival, Ger., 1954); repeated the role on Bway (Royale, Dec. 5, 1955), and on tour (opened Shubert, Detroit, Mich., June 30, 1957); portrayed Marie-Paule in *The Good Soup* (Plymouth, N.Y.C., Mar. 2, 1960); the Countess in *A Time to Laugh* (Piccadilly, London, 1962); and Rona Halpern in *My Mother, My Father and Me* (Plymouth, N.Y.C., Mar. 23, 1963).

Adapted from the French play by Phillippe Heriat, Miss Gordon wrote *A Very Rich Woman* (Belasco, N.Y.C., Sept. 30, 1965), in which she played Mrs. Lord; and played the title role in *The Loves of Cass McGuire* (Helen Hayes Th., Oct. 6, 1966).

Films. Miss Gordon made her debut as Mary Todd in *Abe Lincoln in Illinois* (RKO, 1940); subsequently appeared as Mrs. Ehrlich in *Dr. Ehrlich's Magic Ballet* (WB, 1940); *Two-Faced Woman* (1941); *Edge of Darkness* (WB, 1943); and *Action in the North Atlantic* (WB, 1943). She also collaborated on the screen plays of *A Double Life* (U, 1948); *Adam's Rib* (MGM, 1949); *The Marrying Kind* (Col., 1952); *Pat and Mike* (MGM, 1952); and *The Actress* (MGM, 1953).

After a twenty-three year absence from motion pictures, Miss Gordon appeared in *The Loved One* (MGM, 1965), but her role was edited out before its release. She played The Dealer in *Inside Daisy Clover* (WB, 1965); Stella Barnard in *Lord Love a Duck* (UA, 1966); Minnie Castavet in *Rosemary's Baby* (Par., 1968); Mrs. Dunnock in *What Ever Happened to Aunt Alice?* (Cinerama, 1969); Mrs. Hocheiser in *Where's Poppa?* (UA, 1970); and Maude in *Harold and Maude* (Par., 1971).

Television. She has played Mommy in *The American Dream* (1963); Mme. Arcati in *Blithe Spirit* (NBC); and Carlton's mother on *Rhoda* (CBS, 1975).

Published Works. Miss Gordon is the author of *Myself Among Others* (1971); and has contributed articles to *Readers Digest; Forum; Atlantic Monthly; McCall's; Ladies Home Journal; Vogue;* and the New York *Times.*

Awards. Miss Gordon received the Academy Award for Best Supporting Actress (1968) for her performance in *Rosemary's Baby.*.

GORDONE, CHARLES. Playwright, actor, director. b. Oct. 12, 1925, Cleveland, Ohio. Grad. Elkhart (Ind.) H.S., Los Angeles State Coll., B.A. 1952. Served US Air Force; Special Services (1944–45). Married to Jeanne Warner; one daughter. Address: c/o Bobbs Merrill Co., Inc., 4300 W. 62nd St., Indianapolis, IN 46268.

Pre-Theatre. Janitor, bus-boy, private detective, waiter.

Theatre. Mr. Gordone is the author of *No Place To Be Somebody* (NY Shakespeare Festival/Other Stage/Public Th., N.Y.C., May 4, 1969; ANTA, Dec. 30, 1969; and Promenade, Jan. 20, 1970); which was subsequently revived in a production directed by Mr. Gordone (Morosco, Sept. 9, 1971). He also wrote, directed, and appeared in his one-man show, *Gordone Is a Muthah* (Carnegie Recital Hall, May 8, 1970).

Mr. Gordone played Logan in *The Climate of Eden* (Martin Beck Th., Nov. 6, 1952); appeared in *Mrs. Patterson* (1957); played the Valet in the Negro Ensemble Co.'s production of *The Blacks* (St. Mark's Playhouse, May 4, 1961); directed *Detective Story* (Equity Library Th., 1961); replaced Harold Scott (Nov. 12, 1967) as Jero in *The Trials of Brother Jero* (Greenwich Mews Th., Nov. 9, 1967); and replaced Walter Jones (Jan. 1970) as Sweets Crane in the ANTA engagement of *No Place To Be Somebody.*

In addition, he founded his own theatre, Vantage (Queens, N.Y., 1950's) where he directed and acted in productions of *Tobacco Road, Detective Story, Hell-Bent fer Heaven, Faust, Of Mice and Men,* and *Fortunato.*.

Films. He was associate producer for *Nothing But a Man* (Cinerama, 1964); and did the voices for Preacher and Brother Fox in the animated film *Coonskin* (Bryanston Pictures, 1975).

Television. Mr. Gordone played Logan in *The Climate of Eden* (Play of the Week, NET, 1961).

Other Activities. Mr. Gordone has toured extensively as a folk and calypso singer. With Godfrey Cambridge, he founded (1962) The Committee for the Employment of Negroes. He is currently engaged (1975–to date) in a prison inmate rehabilitation program called Cell Block Theatre.

Published Works. A critical study entitled "Yes, I Am a Black Playwright, But. . ." appeared in the NY *Times* (Jan. 25, 1970).

Awards. For *No Place To Be Somebody,* Mr. Gordone received the Drama Desk Award (1967–69) for Most Promising Playwright, a Kahn Performing Arts grant (1969), and the Pulitzer Prize (1969–70).

GORELIK, MORDECAI. Scenic Designer, director, playwright, educator. b. Aug. 25, 1899, Shchedrin, Minsk, Russia, to Morris and Bertha (Dirskin) Gorelik. Grad. Boys H.S., Bklyn., N.Y., 1917; Pratt Inst., 1920. Studied for the theatre with Robert Edmond Jones, Norman Bel Geddes, and Serge Soudeikine. Married 1935 to Frances Strauss; one son, one daughter; married 1972 to Loraine Kabler. Served Student Army Corps, 1917. Member of United Scenic Artists, Local 829; ATA; SAA. Address: 19532 Sandcastle Lane, Huntington Beach, CA 92647, tel. (714) 536-3312; (summer) Seaview, Fire Island, NY 11782, tel. (516) 583-5996.

Mr. Gorelik has been emeritus professor, Southern Illinois Univ., since 1972. He was research professor in theatre at the university from 1960 to 1972 and was previously instructor-designer for the School of the Theatre, N.Y.C. (1921–22); and was on the faculty of the American Academy of Dramatic Arts (1926–32), the Drama Workshop of the New School for Social Research (1940–41), Biarritz (Fr.) American Univ. (1945–46), Univ. of Toledo (1956), Univ. of Miami (1958), New York Univ. (1956), Bard Univ. (1959), and Brigham Young Univ. (1961).

Theatre. Mr. Gorelik was a scene painter and stage technician for productions at the Provincetown Playhouse, N.Y.C. (1920–21). He designed the Elizabeth Grimball-Hedgerow Th. production of *King Hunger* (Players Club, Philadelphia, Pa., Dec. 6, 1924); the Theatre Guild's production of *Processional* (Garrick, N.Y.C., Jan. 12, 1925); *The Last Love* (Schildkraut Th., Bronx, N.Y., Jan. 22, 1926); *Nirvana* (Greenwich Village Th., Mar. 3, 1926); *The Moon Is a Gong* (Cherry Lane Th., Mar. 12, 1926); *Loudspeaker* (52 St. Th., Mar. 2, 1927); *The Final Balance* (Provincetown Playhouse, Oct. 30, 1928); and *God, Man and the Devil* (Yiddish Art Th., N.Y.C., Dec. 21, 1928); and *Uncle Moses* (Yiddish Art Th., N.Y.C., Nov. 1930).

He designed *1931–* (Mansfield, Dec. 10, 1931); *Success Story* (Maxine Elliott's Th., Nov. 26, 1932); *Big Night* (Maxine Elliott's Th., Jan. 17, 1933); *Little Ol' Boy* (Playhouse, Apr. 24, 1933); *Men in White* (Broadhurst, Sept. 26, 1933); *All Good Americans* (Henry Miller's Th., Dec. 5, 1933); *Gentlewoman* (Cort, Mar. 1934); *Sailors of Cattaro* (Civic Repertory Th., Dec. 10, 1934); *Mother* (Civic Repertory Th., Nov. 19, 1935); *The Young Go First* (Park Th., May 28, 1935); *Golden Boy* (Belasco, Nov. 4, 1937); *Tortilla Flat* (Henry Miller's Th., Jan. 12, 1938); *Casey Jones* (Fulton, Feb. 19, 1938); *Thunder Rock* (Mansfield Th., Nov. 14, 1938); *Rocket to the Moon* (Belasco Th., Nov. 24, 1938); *The Quiet City* (Belasco Th., Apr. 16, 1939); *Night Music* (Broadhurst, Feb. 22, 1940); and *Walk Into My Parlor* (Sayville, N.Y., Aug. 12, 1941).

Mr. Gorelik designed *Volpone* (Actors Laboratory Th., Los Angeles, June 1, 1944; Rooftop, N.Y.C., Jan. 7, 1957); directed and designed *Doctor Knock* (Biarritz American Univ., Fr., 1945); designed *All My Sons* (Coronet, N.Y.C., Jan 29, 1947); directed and designed his own play, *Paul Thompson Forever* (Actors Laboratory Th., 1947); designed *Desire Under the Elms* (ANTA, N.Y.C., Jan. 16, 1952); directed and designed *Danger—Men Working* (Circle Workshop, Los Angeles, 1952); designed a tour of *Saint Joan* (opened Playhouse, Wilmington, Del., Sept. 16, 1954; closed Hartman, Columbus, Ohio, Nov. 1954); and *The Flowering Peach* (Belasco, N.Y.C., Dec. 28, 1954).

He designed *A Hatful of Rain* (Lyceum, Nov. 9, 1955); was American scenic supervisor for the visiting productions of the Comédie Française and Old Vic Co. (1956); directed and designed *Born Yesterday* (Univ. of Toledo, Ohio, 1956); designed *The Sin of Pat Muldoon* (Cort, N.Y.C., Mar. 3, 1957); *Guests of the Nation* (Theatre Marquee, June 26, 1958); and *A Distant Bell* (Eugene O'Neill Th., Jan. 13, 1960).

He directed and designed *The Dybbuk* (Brigham Young Univ., Utah, 1961; San José State College, Calif., 1965); at Southern Illinois Univ., he directed and designed *The Annotated Hamlet,* which he also adapted (1961), *The House of Bernarda Alba* (1962); *Marseilles* (1962), and *The Good Woman of Setzuan* (1964); at California State Univ., he translated, directed, and designed *The Firebugs* (1964); and he directed and designed his own play, *Rainbow Terrace* (1966).

Films. Mr. Gorelik was production designer for *Days of Glory* (RKO, 1944); *Our Street* (Rep., 1944); *None But the Lonely Heart* (RKO, 1944); *Salt to the Devil* (Eagle-Lion, 1949); and the French film, *L'Ennemi publique no. 1 (Most Wanted Man)* (Cité Films, 1954).

Other Activities. He was consultant in theatre for the US military government in Germany (1949). He wrote radio adaptations of American plays for the US Office of War Information (1944). He has been an advocate of the epic theatre of Bertolt Brecht and Erwin Piscator since 1935.

Published Works. He wrote *New Theatres for Old* (1940). He has also contributed articles to *Theatre Arts* Magazine, *N.Y. Times, Drama Survey, Encyclopaedia Britannica, Encyclopedia Americana,* and *Collier's Encyclopedia.* He is also translator of *The Firebugs,* by Max Frisch.

Awards. He received a John Simon Guggenheim Memorial Foundation Fellowship (1936–37) and a Rockefeller Foundation Grant (1949–51), both for study of European theatre, and a Fulbright Grant for study of Australian theatre (1967).

GORMAN, CLIFF. Actor. b. Oct. 13, 1936, New York City. Grad. High School of Music and Art, N.Y.C., 1954; attended Univ. of New Mexico, 1954–55; UCLA, 1955–56; grad. New York Univ., B.S. (education) 1958. Professional training, Wynn Handman, coach, N.Y.C., 1963–64; Jerome Robbins, American Theatre Laboratory, 1965–66. Married May 1963 to Gayle Stevens. Member of AEA; AFTRA; SAG; Honor Legion, N.Y.C., Police Dept.; life member, Friends of George Spelvin. Address: c/o Becker and London, 15 Columbus Circle, New York, NY 10023, tel. (212) JU 2-8800.

Theatre. Mr. Gorman made his stage debut as Peter Boyle in the Off-Bway production *Hogan's Goat* (American Place Th., Nov. 11, 1965). He later appeared as Arnulf in *Ergo* (NY Shakespeare Festival Public Th., Mar. 3, 1968); as Emory in *The Boys in the Band* (Theatre Four, Apr. 14, 1968); and in his Bway debut as Lenny Bruce in *Lenny* (Brooks Atkinson Th., May 26, 1971).

Films. Mr. Gorman played Toto in *Justine* (20th-Fox, 1970); recreated the role of Emory in the motion picture version of *The Boys in the Band* (Natl. Genl., 1970); and was Tom in *Cops and Robbers* (UA, 1973).

Television. Mr. Gorman has appeared on Hawk; N.Y.P.D.; Dan August; *Paradise Lost* (NET); *Class of "63"* (Metromedia); Police Story (NBC); and on English television in *Trial of the Chicago Seven* (BBC).

Awards. Mr. Gorman received the *Village Voice* Off-Bway (Obie) Award (1968) for distinguished performance for Emory in *The Boys in the Band,* and for his performance as Lenny Bruce he received the Antoinette Perry (Tony) Award (1972) for best actor in a dramatic play, the Drama Desk Award (1971), and the *Show Business* magazine award (1971). In 1971 also, he received the LaGuardia Memorial Award for cultural achievement.

GORNEY, JAY. Composer, director, producer, writer, educator. b. Dec. 12, 1896, Bialystok, Russia, to Jacob and Frieda (Perlstein) Gornetzky. Father, mechanical engineer. Grad. Cass Tech. H.S., Detroit, Mich., 1913; Univ. of Michigan, A.B., 1917; LL.B. 1919. Studied harmony, counterpoint, and orchestration with Earl V. Moore, 1914–17. Married Jan. 27, 1943, to Sondra Karyl, public relations manager for Institute of International Education; one son; one daughter, Karen Gorney, actress; one son from previous marriage. Served WW I, USN, bandleader, Great Lakes Training Center. Member of ASCAP (advisory bd.); AGAC (vice-pres., 1960–63). Address: 905 West End Ave., New York, NY 10025, tel. (212) UN 5-3205.

Theatre. Mr. Gorney wrote the songs for *The Dancing Girl* (Winter Garden, N.Y.C., Jan. 24, 1923); with Herbert Stothardt, composed the music for the revue *Vogues of 1924* (Shubert, Mar. 27, 1924); contributed one of the songs to *The Greenwich Village Follies of 1924* (Shubert, Sept. 16, 1924); wrote the music to Owen Murphy's lyrics for *Top Hole* (Fulton, Sept. 1, 1924); with Mr. Murphy, wrote additional lyrics and music for *Artists and Models of 1924* (Astor, Oct. 15, 1924); contributed a song to *Sweetheart Time* (Imperial, Jan. 19, 1926); and with Henry Souvaine, wrote the score for *Merry-Go-Round* (Klaw, May 31, 1927).

Mr. Gorney contributed songs to *Earl Carroll's Sketch Book* (Earl Carroll Th., July 1, 1929); *Earl Carroll's Vanities* (New Amsterdam, July 1, 1930); *Ziegfeld Follies* (Ziegfeld, July 31, 1931); *Shoot the Works* (George M. Cohan Th., July 31, 1931); *Americana* (Shubert, Oct. 5, 1932); composed the score for and co-produced the revue *Meet the People,* which was first presented in Hollywood (Assistance League Playhouse, Dec. 24, 1939); then on Bway (Mansfield, Dec. 25, 1940); toured the US for two seasons, and then was presented in new editions in Hollywood (1943, 1944). He composed the score for *Heaven on Earth* (New Century, N.Y.C., Sept. 16, 1948); wrote the music for the revue *Touch and Go* (Broadhurst, Oct. 13, 1949; Prince of Wales's, London, May 19, 1950); and adapted the music of Offenbach to provide the score for *The Happiest Girl in The World* (Martin Beck Th., N.Y.C., Apr. 3, 1961).

Films. Mr. Gorney was composer and musical advisor for Paramount Studios (N.Y.C., 1929–30); was a member of their editorial board (1931); and a producer for Columbia Pictures (1942–43). He has written music for *The Battle of the Sexes* (UA, 1928); *Glorifying the American Girl* (Par., 1929); *Roadhouse Nights* (Par., 1930); *Moonlight and Pretzels* (U, 1933); *Jimmy and Sallie* (20th-Fox, 1933); *Stand Up and Cheer* (20th-Fox, 1934); *Romance in the Rain* (U, 1934); *Marie Galante* (20th-Fox, 1934); *The Heat's On* (Col., 1943); *Hey, Rookie!* (Col., 1944); and *The Gay Senorita* (Col., 1945), which he also produced.

Television and Radio. During WW II, Mr. Gorney wrote songs and sketches for radio programs sponsored by the Hollywood Writers Mobilization Committee. Since 1952, he has produced, written, and composed music for CBS television spectaculars. In 1961, he wrote music for the series, Frontiers of Faith (NBC-TV).

Other Activities. In 1948, Mr. Gorney and his wife founded the Music Play Department of the Dramatic Workshop of the New School for Social Research, N.Y.C., and were chairmen for three years, producing five student musicals. In 1952, they joined the faculty of the American Theatre Wing professional training program, where they produced the original student musical *On the Wing* (1954).

Published Works. Mr. Gorney collaborated with Henry Myers on two children's musical fantasies, *The Georgrafoof* (1959); and *Kris Kringle Rides Again* (1959). Among his 300 published songs are: "What Wouldn't I Do for That Man" (1929); "Brother, Can You Spare a Dime?" (1932); "You're My Thrill" (1933); "Ah, But Is It Love" (1933); "Baby, Take a Bow" (1934); "I Found a Dream" (1934); "In Chichicastenango" (1940); "The Stars Remain" (1940); "A Fellow and a Girl" (1940); "Let's Steal a Tune from Offenbach" (1940); "The Happiest Girl in the World" (1961); and "Five Minutes of Spring" (1961).

Awards. Mr. Gorney received a special Antoinette Perry (Tony) Award for ten years of outstanding teaching in musical theatre (1962).

GOSSETT, LOUIS. Actor. b. Louis Gossett, Jr., May 27, 1936, Brooklyn, N.Y., to Louis Gossett, Sr., and Helen (Wray) Gossett. Father, head of mail dept. of Brooklyn Union Gas Co. Grad. Lincoln H.S., Brooklyn, 1954; New York Univ., B.A. 1959. Studied acting with Frank Silvera, one year; Nola Chilton, one year; Eli Rill, two years; Lloyd Richards, one year. Member of AEA; SAG; AFTRA; AGVA; Negro Actors Guild; AFM, Local

802; Alpha Phi Alpha.

Theatre. Mr. Gossett made his Bway debut as Spencer Scott in *Take a Giant Step* (Lyceum, Sept. 24, 1953); followed by Kenny in *The Desk Set* (Broadhurst, Sept. 24, 1955); and succeeded (Jan. 1957) Bill Gunn as Spencer Scott in *Take a Giant Step* (Jan Hus House, Sept. 25, 1956).

Mr. Gossett played Absalom Kumalo in *Lost in the Stars* (NY City Ctr., 1957); George Murchison in *A Raisin in the Sun* (Ethel Barrymore Th., Mar. 11, 1959); Edgar Alas Newport News and subsequently Archibald Wellington and Deodatus Village in *The Blacks* (St. Marks Playhouse, Mar. 4, 1961); and Big-Eyed Buddy Lomax in *Tambourines to Glory* (Little Th., Nov. 2, 1963).

He succeeded (Jan. 1964) Clayton Corbin as the Prophet in *Telemachus Clay* (Writers Stage Th., Nov. 15, 1963); succeeded (June 9, 1964) James Earl Jones as Zachariak Pieterson in *The Blood Knot* (Cricket Th., Mar. 2, 1964); played Frank in *Golden Boy* (Majestic, Oct. 20, 1964); Paulus in *The Zulu and the Zayda* (Cort, Nov. 10, 1965); Charles Roberts in *My Sweet Charlie* (Longacre, Dec. 6, 1966); Willie Nurse in *Carry Me Back to Morningside Heights* (John Golden Th., Feb. 27, 1968); Patrice Lumumba in *Murderous Angels* (Mark Taper Forum, Los Angeles, Feb. 5, 1970); again played Lumumba in the Bway production of that play (The Playhouse Th., N.Y.C., Dec. 20, 1971); and appeared as Henderson Josephs in *The Charlatan* (Mark Taper Forum, Los Angeles, May 23, 1974).

Films. Mr. Gossett played George Murchison in the film version of *A Raisin in the Sun* (Col., 1961); and has since appeared in *The Landlord* (UA, 1970); *The Bushbaby* (MGM, 1970); *Skin Game* (WB, 1971); *The Laughing Policeman* (20th-Fox, 1973); and *The White Dawn* (Par., 1974).

Television. He has appeared on The Big Story (NBC, 1954); Philco Television Playhouse (NBC, 1954); in *The Day They Shot Lincoln* (CBS, 1955); on The Nurses (CBS, 1962); The Defenders (CBS, 1964); the Best of Broadway (ABC, 1964); the Ed Sullivan Show (CBS, 1964); The Young Rebels (ABC); *Big Fish, Little Fish* (NET); Mod Squad; The Invaders; Cowboy in Africa; Daktari; Black Bart; and *Fuzz Brothers* (ABC).

Night Clubs. During the 1960's, Mr. Gossett sang in N.Y.C. at the Bitter End, Folk City, the Gaslight Club, the Black Pussy Cat, and Cafe Id.

Recreation. Basketball, record collecting.

GOTTFRIED, MARTIN. Drama critic. b. Oct. 9, 1933, New York City, to Isidore and Rae (Weitz) Gottfried. Father, book dealer. Grad. Stuyvesant H.S., N.Y.C., 1951; Columbia Univ., B.A. (English) 1955; attended Columbia Law Sch., 1955–57. Married July 1, 1961, to Judith M. Houchins, pianist; one daughter. Served US Army Military Intelligence Corps, overseas, 2 yrs. Member of N.Y. Drama Critics Circle; Drama Desk; Kelcey Allen Award Committee (N.Y.C.); Columbia Alumni Assn. (N.Y.C.). Address: c/o New York Post, 210 South St., New York, NY tel. (212) 349-5000.

In Sept. 1974, Mr. Gottfried became drama critic for the NY *Post.* Previously, he had been drama critic for *Women's Wear Daily,* a music critic for *The Village Voice* and an editor at Fairchild Publications.

Published Works. Mr. Gottfried wrote *A Theater Divided* (1968).

Awards. He received first prize in the Fairchild News Reporting Competition, N.Y.C., 1961), and he was winner of the George Jean Nathan Award in 1968 for his book, *A Theater Divided.*

GOTTLIEB, MORTON. Producer, general manager, company manager. b. Morton Edgar Gottlieb, May 2, 1921, Bklyn., N.Y., to Joseph W. and Hilda (Newman) Gottlieb. Father, lawyer. Grad. Erasmus H.S., Bklyn., 1937; Yale Univ., B.A. 1941. Member of ATPAM; League of NY Theatres. Address: (home) 26 W. 9th St., New York, NY 10011, tel. (212) AL 4-4717; (bus.) 1564 Bway., New York, NY 10036, tel. (212) 245-3420.

Theatre. Mr. Gottlieb first performed as a singer in a charity show, *Go Home and Tell Your Mother* (Brooklyn Acad. of Music, Jan. 1928); and made his first professional appearance as a walk-on in *Liberty Jones* (Shubert Th., New Haven, Conn., Jan. 1941).

He was assistant press representative for the Theatre Incorporated presentation of *Pygmalion* (Ethel Barrymore Th., N.Y.C., Dec. 26, 1945); press representative at the Cape Playhouse (Dennis, Mass., Summer 1946); assistant business manager (Sept. 1946) for *Dream Girl* (Coronet, N.Y.C., Dec. 14, 1945); and for *Joan of Lorraine* (Alvin, Nov. 18, 1946); and general manager at the Cape Playhouse (Dennis, Mass., Summer 1947).

He was company manager for the pre-Bway tryout of *The Big People* (opened Lyric, Bridgeport, Conn., Sept. 20, 1947; closed Locust St. Th., Philadelphia, Pa., Sept. 27, 1947); *Eastward in Eden* (Royale, N.Y.C., Nov. 18, 1947); and at the New Stages Th., was business manager for *Lamp at Midnight* (Dec. 21, 1947), *The Respectful Prostitute* (Feb. 9, 1948), and *To Tell the Truth* (Apr. 18, 1948).

He was general manager at the Cape Playhouse (Dennis, Mass., Summer 1948); for *Edward, My Son* (Martin Beck Th., N.Y.C., Sept. 30, 1948), manager to Robert Morley during its Australian production (Theatre Royal, Sydney, Sept. 1949; Comedy Th., Melbourne, Dec. 1949); and general manager for *An Enemy of the People* (Broadhurst, N.Y.C., Dec. 28, 1950). In Mar. 1951, he became general manager of Henry Miller's Th., N.Y.C., for Gilbert Miller; and was general manager for Mr. Miller's productions of *Gigi* (Fulton, Nov. 24, 1951), *Caesar and Cleopatra* (Ziegfeld, Dec. 19, 1951), *Antony and Cleopatra* (Ziegfeld, Dec. 20, 1951) and *Horses in Midstream* (Royale, Apr. 2, 1953).

Mr. Gottlieb produced a tour of *Arms and the Man* (1953); produced, with Albert Selden, *His and Hers* (48 St. Th., Jan. 7, 1954); with Laurence Olivier, *Waiting for Gillian* (St. James's London, Apr. 2, 1954); produced the pre-Bway tryouts of *The Stronger Sex* (Hyde Park Th., N.Y., July 1954), *The Last Tycoon* (Woodstock Playhouse, N.Y., Aug. 1954), and *The Facts of Life* (Bucks County Playhouse, New Hope, Pa., Aug. 1954).

He was company manager of *The Traveling Lady* (Playhouse, N.Y.C., Oct. 27, 1954); succeeded (Jan. 1955) Ben Rosenberg as company manager of *Tea and Sympathy* (Ethel Barrymore Th., Sept. 30, 1953); co-produced a stock tour of *A Palm Tree in a Rose Garden* (July–Aug. 1955); *The Better Mousetrap* (Bucks County Playhouse, New Hope, Pa., July 1955); produced, with Albert Selden, the pre-Bway tryout of *The Amazing Adele* (opened Shubert, Philadelphia, Pa., Dec. 26, 1955; closed Shubert, Boston, Mass., Jan. 21, 1956); and for the American Shakespeare Festival, was general manager for *King John* (Stratford, Conn., June 26, 1956); *Measure for Measure* (June 27, 1956); *The Taming of the Shrew* (Aug. 5, 1956); *Othello* (June 23, 1957); *The Merchant of Venice* (July 10, 1957); and *Much Ado About Nothing* (Aug. 7, 1957).

He was company manager for *The Sleeping Prince* (Coronet, N.Y.C., Nov. 1, 1956); *The Rope Dancers* (Cort, Nov. 20, 1957); *Handful of Fire* (Martin Beck Th., Oct. 1, 1959); *The Gazebo* (Lyceum, Dec. 12, 1958); *Look After Lulu* (Henry Miller's Th., Mar. 3, 1959); and at the Cambridge (Mass.) Drama Festival was general manager for *Twelfth Night, Macbeth,* and *Much Ado About Nothing* (July–Aug. 1959).

He produced *A Adventure* (Tappan Zee Playhouse, Nyack, N.Y.; Bristol Playhouse, Pa., July–Aug. 1959); was company manager for *Cheri* (Morosco, N.Y.C., Oct. 12, 1959); *Five Finger Exercise* (Music Box, Dec. 2, 1959); the tour of *Duel of Angels* (opened Huntington Hartford Th., Los Angeles, Calif., July 12, 1960; closed Natl., Washington, D.C., Oct. 15, 1960); *Under the Yum-Yum Tree* (Henry Miller's Th., N.Y.C., Nov. 16, 1960); and *The Best Man* (Morosco, Mar. 31, 1961); and produced, with Henry Guettel, a tour of *The Best Man* (opened American Shakespeare Festival Th., Stratford, Conn., Jan. 7, 1962; closed Hartman, Columbus, Ohio, Apr. 28, 1962).

He was general manager for *Sail Away* (Broadhurst, N.Y.C., Oct. 3, 1961); *The Affair* (Henry Miller's Th., Sept. 20, 1962); *The Hollow Crown* (Henry Miller's Th., Jan. 29, 1963); produced *Enter Laughing* (Henry Miller's Th., Mar. 13, 1963); produced, with Helen Bonfils, *Chips With Everything* (Plymouth, Oct. 1, 1963); with Miss Bonfils and Gilbert Miller, *The White House* (Henry Miller's Th., May 19, 1964); with Miss Bonfils, *P.S. I Love You* (Henry Miller's Th., Nov. 19, 1964); with Miss Bonfils, *The Killing of Sister George* (Belasco Th., Oct. 5, 1966); with Miss Bonfils, *Come Live With Me* (Billy Rose Th., Jan. 26, 1967); with Miss Bonfils and Peter Bridge, *The Promise* (Henry Miller's Th., Nov. 14, 1967); with Miss Bonfils, *Lovers* (Vivian Beaumont Th., July 25, 1968); with Miss Bonfils, *We Bombed In New Haven* (Ambassador Th., Oct. 16, 1968); with Miss Bonfils, *The Mundy Scheme* (Royale Th., Dec. 11, 1969); and, with Miss Bonfils and Michael White, *Sleuth* (Music Box, Nov. 12, 1970).

Films. Mr. Gottlieb was a reader in the story dept. of Columbia Pictures (1941). He produced the film *Sleuth* (20th-Fox, 1972).

Other Activities. He was drama critic for the N.J. *Bayonne Facts* (1942); and headed the Actors' Studio Benefit Committee, which raised the funds to buy the Actors' Studio building in N.Y.C. Mr. Gottlieb has also written articles for *Harper's Bazaar, New York* Magazine, and *The Travel Agent.* He lectures on the theatre for universities and colleges (including Yale, Wesleyan, Queens, and Connecticut College).

Recreation. Watching old movies.

GOULD, MORTON. Composer, conductor. b. Dec. 10, 1913, Richmond Hill, L.I., N.Y., to James and Frances (Arkin) Gould. Attended Inst. of Musical Arts, 1921. Studied piano with Abby Whiteside, 1926; composition and theory with Dr. Vincent Jones of New York Univ., 1926. Member of ASCAP (pres. board dir.); Natl. Assn. of Composers and Conductors; American Symphony Orchestra League (bd. mbr.); National Endowment for the Arts (music panel). Address: 609 Fifth Ave., New York, NY 10017.

Theatre. Mr. Gould's first work, *Just Six,* a waltz for piano, was published when he was six. Following a period of concert, vaudeville, and theatre appearances as solo and duo pianist, he was engaged, at the age of 17, as staff arranger by the Radio City Music Hall, and subsequently was on the staff of NBC.

Mr. Gould composed the music for the ballet *Interplay* (Metropolitan Opera House, Oct. 17, 1945), and conducted the world premiere; wrote the score for *Billion Dollar Baby* (Alvin, Dec. 21, 1945); was commissioned by the Ballet Theatre to write the music for *Fall River Legend* (Metropolitan Opera House, Apr. 22, 1948), which he also conducted; wrote the score for the musical adaptation of *The Pursuit of Happiness,* called *Arms and the Girl!* (46 St. Th., Feb. 2, 1950).

Other works commissioned for specific occasions are *Symphony for Band,* which he conducted at the West Point (N.Y.) Sesquicentennial Celebration (1952); *Inventions for Four Pianos, Brass and Percussion,* for the Steinway Centennary (1953); the *St. Lawrence Suite,* for the Power Authority of the State of New York and Hydro-Electric Power Commission of Ontario, Canada (1958); and *Dialogues for Piano and String Orchestras* and *Rhythm Gallery,* for the Little Orchestra Society, N.Y.C. (1958).

Mr. Gould has appeared as guest conductor and soloist with major symphony orchestras in programs of his own works, including the N.Y. Philharmonic, with whom he performed his *Dialogues* (Jan. 12–15, 1961), and conducted a week of *Promenade Concerts* (June 1963). He wrote the music for the ballet *Clarinade* (NY State Th., Lincoln Center, Apr. 29, 1964), which was performed by the NY City Ballet Co., and the A.T.&T. Ride (Bell Telephone Exhibit, NY World's Fair, 1964).

His compositions have been performed and recorded by conductors such as Arturo Toscanini, Dmitri Mitropoulos, Pierre Monteux, Leopold Stokowski, Arthur Rodzinski, Vladimir Golschmann, and Fritz Reiner.

Films. Mr. Gould wrote the music for and appeared in *Delightfully Dangerous* (UA, 1945); and wrote the scores for *Cinerama Holiday* (SW, 1955); and *Windjammer* (DRH, 1958).

Television and Radio. During 1934, Mr. Gould conducted and arranged a weekly series of orchestral programs (WOR-Mutual, N.Y.C.), and a series of programs featuring his own orchestral settings of popular music and original works (CBS). His *Lincoln Legend* was premiered by the NBC Symphony Orchestra under the direction of Arturo Toscanini (NBC, 1942). He was commissioned to write *Declaration* by WRC-NBC, for the National Symphony Orchestra, which was first performed at the Inaugural Concert (Constitution Hall, Washington, D.C., Jan. 20, 1957).

He was commissioned to write the scores for the television productions of *The Secret of Freedom* (NBC, 1960); *The Turn of the Century* (The 20th Century, CBS, 1960); *Verdun* (The 20th Century, CBS, 1963); and a documentary series of twenty-six installments on World War I (CBS).

Published Works. Mr. Gould's compositions include: Piano Concerto (1936); four *American Symphonettes* (1938); *Foster Gallery* (1940); *Spirituals for Orchestra* (1941); *Latin-American Symphonette* (1941); *A Lincoln Legend* (1942); *Fanfare for Freedom* (1943); *Interplay for Piano and Orchestra* (1943); Symphony No. 1 (1943); *Cowboy Rhapsody* (1943); Symphony No. 2 (1944); Concerto for Orchestra (1945); *Harvest* (1945); *Ballad for Band* (1946); *Minstrel Show* (1946); *Holiday Music* (1947); Symphony No. 3 (1947); *Philharmonic Waltzes* (1948); *Fall River Legend* (1948); *Serenade of Carols* (1949); *Tap Dance Concerto* (1952); *Symphony for Band* (1952); Dance Variations (1953); *Inventions* (1953); *Showpiece for Orchestra* (1954); *Jekyll and Hyde Variations* (1957). *Venice for Two Orchestras* (1967); *Columbia* (1967); Viraldi Gallery (1968); *Troubador Music;* and *Soundings.*

Discography. Mr. Gould is an RCA-Victor Red Seal recording artist.

GOULET, ROBERT. Actor, singer. b. Robert Gerard Goulet, Nov. 26, 1933, Lawrence, Mass., to Joseph and Jeanette (Gauthier) Goulet. Father, laborer, Grad. St. Joseph's H.S., Edmonton, Alberta, Canada, 1951; Royal Conservatory of Music, Toronto, Ont., Canada, 1952–54. Studied singing with Joseph Furst and Dr. Ernesto Vinci. Married 1956 to Louise Longmore (marr. dis. Mar. 12, 1963); one daughter; married Aug. 12, 1963, to Carol Lawrence, actress; two sons. Member of AEA; AFTRA; SAG.

Theatre. Mr. Goulet made his concert debut in Handel's oratorio, *The Messiah* (Edmonton, Alberta, Canada, 1951). He appeared in *Thunder Rock* and *Visit to a Small Planet* (Crest, Toronto, Ont.); at the Stratford (Ont., Canada) Shakespeare Festival played Captain MacHeath in *The Beggar's Opera* (Avon Th., Summer 1958); appeared in *South Pacific,* as Woody in *Finian's Rainbow,* and played in *Gentlemen Prefer Blondes* (Theatre-Under-the-Stars, Vancouver, B.C., Canada).

In the US, he appeared in summer stock in *Pajama Game;* as Jeff in *Bells Are Ringing* (Packard Music Hall, Warren, Ohio, Summer 1959).

Mr. Goulet made his N.Y.C. debut as Lancelot in *Camelot* (Majestic Th., Dec. 3, 1960); appeared in a revue (Dallas, Tex., Summer 1963); toured in *Carousel* (Summer 1965); played Jacques Bonnard in *The Happy Time* (Broadway Th., N.Y.C., Jan. 18, 1968); toured in *I Do, I Do* (Summer 1970); and appeared in *The Robert Goulet Show* (Musicarnival, Cleveland, Ohio, July 1971).

Films. Mr. Goulet's voice was heard in *Gay Purr-ee* (WB, 1962), and he appeared in *His and Hers* (MGM, 1964); *The Richest Girl in Town* (MGM, 1964); *Honeymoon Hotel* (MGM, 1964); *I'd Rather Be Rich* (U, 1964); *I Deal in Danger* (20th-Fox, 1966); and *Underground* (UA, 1970).

Television and Radio. Mr. Goulet was a radio disc jockey (CKCA, Edmonton, Canada, 1951); and on television, has played in *Little Women* (CBC, Canada, 1955); *Spring Thaw* (CBS); appeared on Showtime (CBC). His US television debut, on the Ed Sullivan Show (CBS, Jan. 8, 1961), was followed by additional appearances on that program and on other programs, such as the Garry Moore Show (CBS); Danny Thomas Show (CBS, 1961); Bell Telephone Hour (CBS, 1962); and the shows of Jack Paar (NBC), Red Skelton (NBC), Patty Duke (ABC), Jack Benny (CBS), Dean Martin (NBC), Judy Garland (NBC), and Bob Hope (NBC). He had his own show, the Robert Goulet Show); was on The Lucy Show (CBS, 1963–67); Kraft Suspense Th. (NBC, 1965); Blue Light (ABC, 1966); and Here's Lucy (CBS, 1968–72); and he appeared on such specials as *The Enchanted Nutcracker* (ABC, Dec. 1961); *The Broadway of Lerner and Loewe* (NBC, Feb. 1962); *Rainbow of Stars* (NBC, Apr. 1962); *Robert Goulet Hour* (CBS, Nov. 1964); *Brigadoon* (ABC, Oct. 1966); *Carousel* (ABC, May 1967); *Kiss Me, Kate* (ABC, Mar. 1968); *Robert Goulet Show Starring Robert Goulet* (ABC, Apr. 1970); and *Monsanto Night Presents Robert Goulet and Carol Lawrence* (NBC, Nov. 1973).

Night Clubs. Mr. Goulet made his N.Y.C. supper club debut at the Persian Room (Plaza Hotel, Nov. 6, 1962) and later appeared there again (Nov. 1964; Oct. 1971). Other clubs at which he appeared include the Shoreham Hotel (Washington, D.C., 1962); Empire Room (Waldorf Astoria, N.Y.C., 1969; June 1973); Frontier Hotel (Las Vegas, Nev., Oct. 1969); Cafe Cristal (Hotel Diplomat, Miami Beach, Fla., Feb. 1970); Sands Hotel (Las Vegas, Nev., Apr. 1975); Nanuet (N.Y.) Star Th. (Apr. 1975); Coconut Grove (Los Angeles, Calif.); Fairmont Hotel (San Francisco, Calif.); and the Sahara Hotel (Las Vegas, Nev.).

Discography. Mr. Goulet's recordings include "What Kind of Fool Am I?" (Col.); *The Lamp Is Low* (Col. 1961); the original cast album of *Camelot* (Col.); and the albums *Annie Get Your Gun* (Col.) and *Robert Goulet on Tour* (Col.).

Awards. Mr. Goulet received an Antoinette Perry (Tony) Award as best male musical star (1967–68) for his performance in *The Happy Time.*

Recreation. Body building and music.

GRACE, CAROL. Actress. b. Carol Wellington-Smythe Marcus, 1923. Attended Dalton Sch., N.Y.C.; Natl. Park Seminary, Md. Married Feb. 20, 1943, to William Saroyan, writer (marr. dis. Nov. 16, 1949); one son, one daughter; married Aug. 21, 1959, to Walter Matthau, actor; one son. Member of AEA; SAG.

Theatre. Miss Grace made her first stage appearance in *Jim Dandy* (Princeton, N.J.). She made her N.Y.C. debut as Lois in *Across the Board on Tomorrow Morning* (Belasco Th., Aug. 17, 1942); subsequently played a Secretary in *Will Success Spoil Rock Hunter?* (Belasco, Oct. 13, 1955); Mary L. in *The Time of Your Life* (NY City Ctr., Jan. 19, 1955); was standby for Anne Baxter as Mollie Lovejoy in *The Square Root of Wonderful* (National, Oct. 30, 1957); played Myra in *The Cold Wind and the Warm* (Morosco, Dec. 8, 1958); and Vera in *Once There Was a Russian* (Music Box, Feb. 18, 1961).

Films. She made her debut in *Votre Devoué* and has appeared in *Stage Struck* (Buena Vista, 1958) and *Gangster Story* (Ind., 1960).

Published Works. Miss Grace wrote the novel *The Secret in the Daisy.*.

GRACIE, SALLY. Actress. b. Sarah Ellen Gracie, Little Rock, Ark., to John Price and Helen Marie (Heinz) Gracie. Father, cotton planter. Attended Little Rock (Ark.) H.S.; Mt. St. Mary's Acad., Little Rock, Ark.; Little Rock Jr. Coll. Studied acting with Sanford Meisner at the Neighborhood Playhouse Sch. of the Th., and Martin Ritt, Curt Conway. Married Oct. 28, 1952, to Rod Steiger, actor (marr. dis. Feb. 1959); married July 3, 1959, to Charles Kebbe; one son. Member of AEA; AFTRA; SAG. Address: 38 E. 85th St., New York, NY 10028, tel. (212) TR 9-3833.

Theatre. Miss Gracie made her N.Y.C. debut as Helen Palmer in *At War with the Army* (Booth, Mar. 8, 1948); subsequently played the Woman in *Dinosaur Wharf* (Natl., Nov. 8, 1951); Julia Wilson in *Goodbye Again* (Helen Hayes Th., Apr. 24, 1956); Rummie Mitchums in *Major Barbara* (Martin Beck Th., Oct. 30, 1956); Arlene in *Fair Game* (Longacre, Nov. 2, 1957); appeared in a pre-Bway theatre tour of *Third Best Sport* (Summer 1958); played Betty Stone in *Venus at Large* (Morosco, N.Y.C., Apr. 12, 1962); Aphrodite in *Helen* (Bouwerie Lane Th., Dec. 10, 1964); the Woman in *The Bicycle* (Playwright's Workshop, Nov. 14, 1967); and Miss Dugan in *Naomi Court* (Stage 73, May 29, 1974).

She made summer theatre appearances at the Barter Th. (Abingdon, Va.); Bucks County Playhouse (New Hope, Pa.); Playhouse-in-the-Park (Philadelphia, Pa.); Clinton (Conn.) Playhouse; Ogunquit (Me.) Playhouse; Pocono Playhouse (Mountainhome, Pa.); Spa Music Th. (Saratoga, N.Y.); and Cecil Wood Th. (Fishkill, N.Y.).

Films. She appeared in *Patterns* (UA, 1956); *The Fugitive Kind* (UA, 1960); *The Rain People* (1968); and *The Swimmer* (Col., 1968).

Television. Miss Gracie appeared on The Guiding Light (CBS, 1957–58); Purex Special for Women (1961); Naked City (ABC); The Untouchables (ABC, 1962); The Defenders (CBS, 1962); Studio One (CBS); Robert Montgomery Presents (NBC); Philco Television Playhouse (NBC); Danger (CBS); Kraft Television Th. (NBC); Route 66 (CBS, 1962); Ben Casey (ABC, 1963); and Madigan (CBS, 1970). She has played Martha Allen in The Doctors (NBC) since 1968.

GRAHAM, IRVIN. Composer, lyricist, writer. b. Irvin Abraham, Sept. 18, 1909, Philadelphia, Pa., to Henry and Rose (Glickstein) Abraham. Father, jeweller. Grad. West Philadelphia, Pa., H.S., 1927; attended Zeckwer-Hahn Musical Acad., 1928; studied with Norman Lloyd, 1944. Married Sept. 6, 1942, to Lillian Goldstein, secretary. Member of ACA; Dramatists Guild; ASCAP; WGA; AGVA; SAG; Composer's Guild; American Guild of Authors and Composers. Address: 360 E. 55th St., New York, NY 10022, tel. (212) EL 5-2467.

Theatre. Mr. Graham contributed songs, including "You Better Go Now," to the revues, *New Faces of 1936* (Vanderbilt Th., N.Y.C., May 19, 1936); *Who's Who* (Hudson, Mar. 1, 1938); *All in Fun* (Majestic, Dec. 27, 1940); wrote his first score for *Crazy with the Heat* (44 St. Th., Jan. 14, 1941); and a song in the revue, *New Faces of '56* (Ethel Barrymore Th., June 14, 1956).

Films. Mr. Graham wrote the original story for the film *The Whale Who Wanted to Sing at the Met* (Disney, 1948).

Television and Radio. Mr. Graham wrote musical material and scripts for the Fred Waring radio show (NBC, 1948), and, on television, for Imogene Coca and guest stars on Your Show of Shows (NBC, 1951); Don Ameche's Holiday Hotel (ABC, 1951); the Colgate Comedy Hour (NBC, 1954); the Jane Froman Show (CBS, 1952–55); wrote a Ford Special (NBC, 1960); the score, lyrics, and book for a Chevrolet Special (NBC, 1961); and musical material for the Garry Moore Show (CBS, 1959). He has appeared in Edge of Night and made some television commercials.

Night Clubs. Mr. Graham composed the music and lyrics for the first revue written for a supper club, *All About Love,* by George Axelrod and Max Wilk (Versailles, N.Y.C., 1952); and has written supper club acts for Patrice Munsel, Marguerite Piazza, Eddie Albert and Margo, Jane Froman, Jane Morgan, Constance Bennett, Imogene Coca, and Mimi Benzell.

Awards. Mr. Graham received the Christopher Award for the song "I Believe" and was composer in residence at the MacDowell Colony (Peterborough, N.H., Apr.–May 1964) to work on the score and lyrics for a new musical, *A Man of Pleasure.*

Recreation. Reading, drawing, walking.

GRAHAM, KENNETH L. Educator. b. Apr. 25, 1915, Coffeyville, Kan., to Ethan L. and Maud Graham. Father, businessman. Grad. Field Kindley H.S., Coffeyville, 1932; Coffeyville Jr. Coll., 1934; State Univ. of Iowa, B.A. 1937; Northwestern Univ., M.A. 1939; attended Univ. of Minnesota, 1937–42; grad. Univ. of Utah, Ph.D. 1947. Married Dec. 15, 1945, to Barbara L. Fowler (dec. July 1969); one son, one daughter. Served USNR, as instructor in antisubmarine warfare and personnel director, Admiral's Staff, 1942–46; rank, Lt. Member of ATA (pres., 1964; 1st vice-pres., 1963; 2nd vice-pres., 1962; bd. of dir., 1955–64; exec. secy.-treas., 1956–58; dir. of CTC, 1952–53); ANTA (exec. bd., 1959–61); American Playwrights Theatre (bd. of trustees, 1963–to date); Univ. Resident Theatre Assoc. (bd. of dir., 1970–72); American College Theatre Festival (central comm., 1962–69); Minnesota Assn. of Teachers of Speech (pres., 1950–52); NCP; Beta Theta Pi. Address: (home) 2007 W. 49th St., Minneapolis, MN 55409, tel. (612) WA 6-8681; (bus.) Univ. of Minnesota, 110 Rarig Center, Minneapolis, MN 55455.

Mr. Graham became chairman of the Theatre Arts Dept. and director of the University Th., both at the Univ. of Minnesota, in 1971. From 1963 to 1971, he was chairman of the Dept. of Speech, Communication, and Theatre Arts. He has been a member of the faculty at the Univ. of Minnesota since 1939 and was associate director of the University Th. from 1947 to 1971.

Mr. Graham taught speech and dramatics in Watertown, S.D., 1936–37; and at North Kansas City H.S., Kansas City, Mo., 1937–38.

He directed the School of the Theatre, Cain Park Community Th., Cleveland Heights, Ohio (Summers 1941–42; 1946–47).

Theatre. Major productions directed by Mr. Graham at the Univ. of Minnesota include *And People All Around; Annie Get Your Gun; Anything Goes; The Bluebird; But Not Goodbye; The Copperhead; Caste; Captain Brassbound's Conversion; Doctor in Spite of Himself; The Fantasticks; Gammer Gurton's Needle; The Happy Time; Harvey; Hedda Gabler; Idiot's Delight; The Inheritance; Julius Caesar; King Richard III; King Henry IV, Part 1; Knickerbocker Holiday; Marco Millions; Major Barbara; Misalliance; Mr. Roberts; The Night Thoreau Spent in Jail; Pal Joey; On Borrowed Time; Romeo and Juliet; School for Wives; The Summer People* (American premiere); *Tall Story; Teahouse of the August Moon; Twelfth Night; Two for the Seesaw; Venus Observed; The Young Idea; The Zoo Story;* and *The American Dream.*

At the Univ. of Minnesota Young People's Theatre and Peppermint Tent, which he has supervised since 1940, Mr. Graham has directed: *Arthur and the Magic Sword; Caddie Woodlawn; The Emperor's New Clothes* (also designed sets and props); *Heidi; Huckleberry Finn; King Midas and the Golden Touch; Seven Little Rebels; Tom Sawyer;* and *You're a Good Man, Charlie Brown.*

In addition to his work as a director, Mr. Graham has acted a number of parts in productions at other institutions, including Charles Condamine in *Blithe Spirit* (Norfolk Community Th., Norfolk, Va.); Arnwood in *Bird in Hand* (Univ. of Iowa); Nicholas Tandolph in *Dear Octopus* (Minneapolis Women's Club); Baseurdin in *Divorcon* (Cain Park Th., Cleveland); Sir Walter Raleigh in *Elizabeth the Queen* (Univ. of Iowa); the male lead in the musical *Guess Again* (Northwestern Univ.); Peter Stuyvesant in *Knickerbocker Holiday* (Univ. of Minnesota); Washington Irving in *Knickerbocker Holiday* (Cain Park Th., Cleveland); Shem in *Noah* (Univ. of Iowa); Malcolm in *Macbeth* (Cain Park Th., Cleveland); Bert in *Mary Poppins* (Northwestern Univ.); Leader of the Chorus in *Oedipus* (Northwestern Univ.); Mr. Darling in *Peter Pan* (Northwestern Univ.); Walter Franz in *The Price* (Honolulu Community Th.); Col. Pickering in *Pygmalion* (Theatre-in-the-Round, Minneapolis); Frederick Granton in *The Queen's Husband* (Coffeyville Jr. College, Coffeyville, Kans.); Romeo in *Romeo and Juliet* (Univ. of Minnesota); Rims O'Neil in *Saturday's Children* (Coffeyville Jr. College, Coffeyville, Kans.); Grant Mathews in *State of the Union* (Univ. of Utah, Salt Lake City); the title role in the musical *Stephen Foster* (Cain Park Th., Cleveland, Ohio); Feste in *Twelfth Night* (Northwestern Univ., Evanston, Ill.); the Judge and other roles in *Under the Gaslight* (Univ. of Iowa); and the Hessian Captain in *Valley Forge* (Univ. of Iowa).

Other Activities. Mr. Graham held a Ford Foundation director observership, New Dramatists' Committee, N.Y. (1960); was a delegate to a US Office of Education conference on creative behavior in the arts, Univ. of California at Los Angeles (1963); has served as chairman of the McKnight and Bush Foundation graduate theatre fellowship program (1963–to date); was critic judge, US Army, Europe, for a tournament of plays (June 1964); director of a US Office of Education developmental conference on relationships between educational and professional theatre (1966); and served as an Office of Education research consultant in the Arts and Humanities Branch (1966–68).

Awards. Mr. Graham received the Univ. of Utah's W. McFarlane Fellowship (1946–47) and received the American College Theatre Festival award of excellence (1973).

Recreation. Fishing.

GRAHAM, RONNY. Actor, director, composer, lyricist, writer, singer. b. Aug. 26, 1919, Philadelphia, Pa., to Steve and Florence (Sweeney) Graham. Parents, vaudevillians. Attended Germantown H.S., Philadelphia. Married 1947, to Jean Spitzbarth (marr. dis. 1950), one child; married Mar. 4, 1951, to Ellen Hanley, singer, actress (marr. dis. Dec. 4, 1963), two children; married 1965 to Sigyn Lund, two children. Served USAAF, 1942–45; rank, Sgt. Member of AEA; AGVA; AFTRA; SAG; AFM.

Theatre. Mr. Graham appeared in the revue, *It's About Time* (Brattle Th., Cambridge, Mass., Mar. 21, 1951); made his Bway debut in *New Faces of 1952,* to which he contributed music, lyrics, and sketches (Royale, May 16, 1952; and on US tour); subsequently played Charlie Reader in *The Tender Trap* (Longacre, N.Y.C., Oct. 13, 1954); wrote music, lyrics, and with Sidney Carroll, the continuity, for *Mask and Gown* (Golden, Sept. 10, 1957); played Mr. Applegate in *Damn Yankees* (Camden, N.J.; Philadelphia, Pa., Summer 1960); contributed material to *Let it Ride!* (Eugene O'Neill Th., Oct. 12, 1961); wrote the lyrics for *Bravo, Giovanni!* (Broadhurst, May 19, 1962); contributed to the revue, *The Cats' Pajamas* (Sheridan Sq. Playhouse, May 31, 1962); and at the NY World's Fair, directed and performed in *America, Be Seated* (Louisiana Pavilion, May 15, 1964).

He appeared as Monte Checkovitch in *Something More* (Eugene O'Neill Th., Nov. 10, 1964); contributed to the revue, *Wet Paint* (Renata, Apr. 12, 1965); directed *Mating Dance* (Eugene O'Neill Th., Nov. 3, 1965); acted in a tour of *Luv* (Summer 1967); contributed lyrics, music and sketches to *New Faces of 1968* (Booth, May 2, 1968); directed a tour of *Here Lies Jeremy Troy* (Summer 1968), and the subsequent pre-Bway tryout of the revised version, *Jeremy Troy* (opened Forrest, Philadelphia, Feb. 24, 1969; closed National, Washington, D.C., Mar. 22, 1969); directed *Grin and Bare It!* and *Postcards* (Belasco, N.Y.C., Mar. 16, 1970; directed *A Place for Polly* (Ethel Barrymore Th., Apr. 17, 1970); was guest artist with the Seattle Rep. Th. (Season 1971–72) and the St. Louis Rep. Th. (Season 1971–72); and appeared in *That Championship Season* (Seattle Rep. Th., Season 1973–74).

Films. Mr. Graham made his screen debut in *New Faces* (20th-Fox, 1954), for which he wrote the screenplay; and appeared in *Dirty Little Billy* (Col., 1972).

Television. He has appeared on Toast of the Town (CBS); the Phil Silvers Show (CBS); the Colgate Comedy Hour (NBC); *Highlights of New Faces* (Play of the Week, NTA, Nov. 28, 1960); the Johnny Carson Show (NBC); Steve Allen Show (CBS); Omnibus (CBS); etc.; and wrote for the New Bill Cosby Show (CBS).

Night Clubs. Mr. Graham has performed in N.Y.C. at the Ruban Bleu, the Blue Angel, the Plaza 9 (Plaza Hotel), and the Brothers and Sisters (1975); and at Punchinello's East (Chicago, 1969). At the Upstairs at the Downstairs (N.Y.C.) he wrote and performed in the revues, *Take Five* (Oct. 1957) and *Graham Crackers* (Feb. 18, 1963); and directed *Money* (July 12, 1963) and *Free Fall* (Mar. 20, 1969).

Awards. For his performance in *New Faces of 1952,* Mr. Graham received the Donaldson Award (1952–53) and the Theatre World Award (1952–53). He was nominated for the Antoinette Perry (Tony) Award for his lyrics for *Bravo, Giovanni!* (1962–63).

Recreation. Mountain climbing, swimming, playing jazz piano, chess, collecting rare scores and libretti.

GRAHN, MARY. Theatre librarian. b. 1901, Easton, Pa., to Ernest and Fredericka (Zwirner) Grahn. Father, clergyman. Grad. New York State Coll. for Teachers, B.A. 1921; Radcliffe, M.A. 1923; attended Yale Univ. Sch. of Drama, 1927–28; Columbia Library Sch., 1947. Member of Theatre Library Assn. Address: 420 Whitney Ave., New Haven, CT 06511.

Miss Grahn was librarian at the School of Drama, Yale Univ., from 1947 to 1967.

GRANGER, FARLEY. Actor. b. Farley Earle Granger II, July 1, 1925, San Jose, Calif., to Farley Earle and Eva (Hopkins) Granger. Attended Hollywood H.S. Studied acting with Sanford Meisner, Stella Adler, Lee Strasberg. Served USN, 1944–46, Special Services, Maurice Evans' unit, Hawaii; rank, Maj. Member of AEA; SAG; AFTRA; AMPAS.

Theatre. Mr. Granger first appeared on stage at age five as the Elf in a school Christmas pageant (San Jose, Calif., Dec. 1930). He made his professional stage debut as John in *John Loves Mary* (Theatre-by-the-Sea, Matunuck, R.I., July 1955) and on tour of other summer theatres.

He first appeared in N.Y.C. as the Actorman in *The Carefree Tree* (Phoenix, Th., Oct. 11, 1955); subsequently played Fitzwilliam Darcy in *First Impressions* (Alvin, Mar. 19, 1959); Jack Williams in *The Warm Peninsula* (Helen Hayes Th., Oct. 20, 1959); the King in *The King and I* (NY City Ctr., May 11, 1960); Jeff Douglas in *Brigadoon* (NY City Ctr., May 30, 1961); and Brig. Anderson in the national tour of *Advise and Consent* (opened Shubert, Cincinnati, Ohio, Oct. 2, 1961; closed American Th., St. Louis, Mo., May 5, 1962); toured with the National Repertory Th. (1963–64), as Konstantin in *The Seagull,* Frederic and Hugo in *Ring Round the Moon,* and John Proctor in *The Crucible,* and repeated his roles in *The Seagull* (Belasco, N.Y.C., Apr. 5, 1964), and *The Crucible* (Belasco, Apr. 6, 1964); and again toured with the National Repertory Th. (1964–65), as Lovborg in *Hedda Gabler,* Marlow in *She Stoops To Conquer,* and the title role in *Liliom.* He replaced (Aug. 18, 1965) George Grizzard as the Son in a revival of *The Glass Menagerie* (Brooks Atkinson Th., May 4, 1965).

Films. Mr. Granger made his debut, at age 17, in *The North Star* (RKO, 1943); subsequently appeared in *The Purple Heart* (20th-Fox, 1944); *They Live By Night* (RKO, 1948); *Rope* (WB, 1948); *Enchantment* (RKO, 1948); *Edge of Doom* (RKO, 1950); *Our Very Own* (RKO, 1950); *Strangers on a Train* (WB, 1951); *I Want You* (RKO, 1951); *Behave Yourself* (RKO, 1951); *O'Henry's Full House* (20th-Fox, 1952); *Hans Christian Andersen* (HOB, 1952); *The Story of Three Loves* (MGM, 1953); *Small Town Girl* (MGM, 1953); *The Naked Street* (UA, 1955); *The Girl in the Red Velvet Swing* (20th-Fox, 1955); *Senso* (Lux, Rome, Italy, 1956); *A Man Called Noon* (Natl. Gen., 1973); and *Arnold* (Cinerama, 1973).

Television. Mr. Granger made his television debut in *Splendid with Swords* (Schlitz Playhouse of Stars, CBS, June 1955). He also appeared on US Steel Hour (CBS) in *Incident in an Alley* (Nov. 1955), *The Bottle Imp* (Mar. 1957), *The Hidden River* (July 1958), and *The Wound Within* (Sept. 1958); in *Caesar and Cleopatra* (Producers Showcase, NBC, Mar. 1956); on Robert Montgomery Presents (NBC) in *Pistolero* (Apr. 1956) and *The Clay Pigeon* (Jan. 1957); on Playhouse 90 (CBS) in *Seidman and Son* (Oct. 1956) and *The Clouded Image* (Nov. 1957); on Kraft Th. (NBC) in *Circle of Fear* (Aug. 1957), *Man* *in a Trance* (Oct. 1957), and *Come to Me* (Dec. 1957); on Dupont Show of the Month (CBS) in *Beyond This Place* (Nov. 1957), *Arrowsmith* (Jan. 1960), and *The Prisoner of Zenda* (Jan. 1961); on Bob Hope Chrysler Th. (NBC) in *Nightmare* (Sept. 1966) and *Blind Man's Bluff* (Feb. 1967). He was in *The Inn of the Flying Dragon* (Great Mysteries, NBC, Oct. 1960); *Born a Giant* (Our American Heritage, NBC, Dec. 1960); *The Heiress* (Family Classics, CBS, Feb. 1961); and the special *Laura* (ABC, Jan. 1968). Mr. Granger also appeared on episodes of Climax (CBS, 1956); Wagon Train (NBC, Nov. 1957); Ironside (NBC, 1967); Name of the Game (NBC, 1968); Hawaii Five-O (CBS, 1969); Medical Center (CBS, 1969); and the daytime serial One Life to Live (ABC, 1976).

Recreation. Sailing, skiing, tennis, collecting modern paintings.

GRANT, LEE. Actress. b. Lyova Haskell Rosenthal, New York City, to A. W. and Witia (Haskell) Rosenthal. Father, educator, realtor; mother, teacher. Grad. P.S. 193, N.Y.C.; attended Art Students League, N.Y.C.; H.S. of Music and Art, N.Y.C.; grad. George Washington H.S., N.Y.C.; attended Juilliard Sch. of Music; studied acting at the Neighborhood Playhouse Sch. of the Th. (scholarship) with Sanford Meisner; ballet at Metropolitan Opera Ballet Sch.; Actors Studio (member 1949–to date). Married to Arnold Manoff, novelist, playwright (marr. dis.); one daughter; married 1965 (?) to Joe Feury; one daughter. Member of AEA; AFTRA; SAG.

Theatre. Miss Grant made her stage debut as Hoo-Chee in the opera *L'Oracolo* (Metropolitan Opera House, N.Y.C., Jan. 20, 1933); her professional debut at Camp Tamiment (Pa., Summer 1946) and at the Green Mansions Th. (Warrensburg, N.Y., Summer 1947) in works that included *Liliom* and *This Property is Condemned.*

She made her Bway debut succeeding (June 21, 1948) Lois Hall as Mildred in *Joy to the World* (Plymouth, Mar. 18, 1948); appeared as the Shoplifter in *Detective Story* (Hudson, Mar. 23, 1949); Diane in *All You Need Is One Good Break* (Mansfield, Feb. 9, 1950); Raina Petkoff in *Arms and the Man* (Arena, Oct. 19, 1950); Daisy Durole in *Lo and Behold!* (Booth, Dec. 12, 1951); at the Mt. Kisco (N.Y.) Playhouse, played Sally in *I Am a Camera* (Summer, 1952), Amy in *They Knew What They Wanted* (Summer 1953), and the title role in *Gigi* (Summer 1954); played Stella in *Wedding Breakfast* (48 St. Th., Nov. 20, 1954); at Mt. Kisco (N.Y.) Playhouse, played Eliza in *Pygmalion* (Summer 1956) and Lizzie in *The Rainmaker* (Summer 1957).

Miss Grant appeared as Mrs. Rogers in *A Hole in the Head* (Plymouth, N.Y.C., Feb. 27, 1957); replaced (June 29, 1959) Anne Bancroft as Gittel Mosca in *Two for the Seesaw* (Booth, Jan. 16, 1958); played Rose Collins in *The Captains and the Kings* (Playhouse, Jan. 2, 1962); appeared in touring productions of *The Tender Trap* (1962) and as Ninotchka in *Silk Stockings* (1963); played Solange in *The Maids* (One Sheridan Square, N.Y.C., Nov. 14, 1963); and at the NY Shakespeare Festival, appeared in the title role in *Electra* (Delacorte Th., Aug. 11, 1964).

Miss Grant played the title role in *St. Joan* (Moorestown, N.J., Th., June 28, 1966); directed *The Adventures of Jack and Max* (Actors Studio West, Los Angeles 1967–68 season); played the three woman's roles in *Plaza Suite* (Geary, San Francisco, Sept. 16, 1968; Huntington Hartford Th., Los Angeles, Oct. 15, 1968); Edna Edison in *The Prisoner of Second Avenue* (Eugene O'Neill Th., N.Y.C., Nov. 11, 1971); and Regina in a West coast production of *The Little Foxes* (1975).

Films. Miss Grant appeard as the Shoplifter in *Detective Story* (Par., 1951); in *Storm Fear* (UA, 1955); *Middle of the Night* (Col., 1959); *An Affair of the Skin* (Zenith, 1963); *Pie in the Sky* (Ind., 1963); *The Balcony* (Continental, 1963); *Terror in the City* (Allied, 1966); *Divorce American Style* (Col., 1967); *Buena Sera, Mrs. Campbell* (UA, 1968); *The Big Bounce* (WB, 1969); *Marooned* (Col., 1969); *There Was a Crooked Man* (WB, 1970); *The Landlord* (UA, 1970); *Plaza Suite* (Par., 1971); *Portnoy's Complaint* (WB, 1972); *The Internecine Project* (Allied, 1974); and *Shampoo* (Col., 1975).

Television. Her numerous appearances include *Screwball* (The Play's the Thing, CBS, Apr. 28, 1950); Comedy Th. (CBS); Danger (CBS); Bway TV Th. (Ind.); ABC Album; Summer Th. (CBS); Philco Playhouse (NBC); Pond's Th. (ABC); Alcoa Hour (NBC); Playwrights '56 (NBC); *Mooney's Kid Don't Cry* (Kraft Th., NBC, Apr. 16, 1958); Martirio in *The House of Bernarda Alba* (Play of the Week, WNTA, Jan. 6, 1960); *Saturday's Children* (CBS, Feb. 25, 1962); the Avenging Angel in *The World of Sholem Aleichem* (Play of the Week, WNTA, June 5, 1962); East Side/West Side (CBS); Lizzie in *The Respectful Prostitute* (BBC, London, Jan. 1964); The Defenders (CBS); The Nurses (CBS); The Fugitive (ABC); Ben Casey (ABC); Brenner (CBS); Slattery's People (CBS); Doctors/Nurses (CBS); For the People (CBS); played Steela Chernak on the Peyton Place series (ABC, from July 1965); appeared in *The Love Song of Barney Kempinski* (ABC Stage 67, Sept. 14, 1966); *The People Trap* (ABC Stage 67, Nov. 9, 1966); Big Valley (ABC); Bob Hope Th. (NBC); Ironside (NBC); Judd for the Defense (ABC); Mission: Impossible (CBS); Medical Center (CBS); Name of the Game (NBC); Mod Squad (ABC); *Night Slaves* (ABC telefilm, Sept. 29, 1970); *The Neon Ceiling* (NBC telefilm, Feb. 8, 1971); *Ransom for a Dead Man* (NBC telefilm, Mar. 1, 1971); Men at Law (CBS); *Lt. Schuster's Wife* (ABC, telefilm, Oct. 11, 1972); co-authored, co-directed, and appeared in *The Shape of Things* (CBS, Oct. 19, 1973); directed Oliver Hailey's *For the Use of the Hall* (Hollywood TV Th., KCET, PBS, 1975), and played the title role in her own series, Fay (NBC, premiere Sept. 1975).

Other Activities. Miss Grant has exhibited her paintings at the Proscenium Gallery (N.Y.C., 1963).

Awards. She won the NY Drama Critics Circle Award (1949) for her performance in *Detective Story;* the *Village Voice* Off-Bway (Obie) Award (1964) for *The Maids;* for the film, *Detective Story,* received the Cannes Film Fest. Best Actress Award and was nominated for an Academy (Oscar) Award (1952) as best supporting actress; for *The Landlord,* was nominated (1971) for an Oscar as best supporting actress; and for *Shampoo,* won (1976) the Oscar as best supporting actress. She won the NATAS (Emmy) Award as best supporting actress (1966) for her role as Stella Chernak on Peyton Place, and as best actress (1971) for *The Neon Ceiling.*

GRAY, CHARLES D. Actor, playwright. b. Donald Marshall Gray, Aug. 29, 1928, Bournemouth, England, to Donald and Maude (Marshall) Gray. Father, surveyor. Member of AEA; British AEA. Address: London Management Ltd., 235-41 Regent St., London, W.1, England.

Theatre. Mr. Gray made his Bway debut with the Old Vic Co., at the Winter Garden Th. appearing as Henry Bolingbroke in *Richard II* (Oct. 23, 1956), the Chorus and Escalus in *Romeo and Juliet* (Oct. 24, 1956), Lennox in *Macbeth* (Oct. 29, 1956), and Achilles in *Troilus and Cressida* (Dec. 26, 1956), all of which he repeated on a US tour, including Washington, D.C., Boston, Mass., Philadelphia, Pa., and Chicago, Ill. Billed as Oliver Gray, he played the Prince of Wales in *Kean* (Bway Th., N.Y.C., Nov. 2, 1961); billed as Charles D. Gray, played Maxime in *Poor Bitos* (Cort, Nov. 11, 1964); and Sir Charles Dilke in *The Right Honourable Gentleman* (Billy Rose Th., Oct. 19, 1965).

In London, he played Charles, the Wrestler, in *As You Like It* (Open Air Th., Regents Park, May 29, 1952); the Roman Captain and Jupiter in *Cymbeline* (Open Air, July 1952); Demiwulf in *Boy With a Cart* (Open Air, July 29, 1952); understudied the title role in *Comus* (Open Air, July 29, 1952); toured England as Ross in the Arts Council production of *Macbeth* (Sept.–Nov. 1952); joined the Shakespeare Memorial Th., Stratford-upon-Avon, to play walk-on roles in *The Merchant of Venice* (Mar. 17, 1953), *Richard III* (Mar. 24, 1953), *Antony and Cleopatra* (Apr. 28, 1953), and *King Lear* (July 14, 1953), and then toured in *Antony and Cleopatra* (1954).

With the Old Vic in London he played the Lord Marshall in *Richard II* (Jan. 18, 1955), Duke Frederick in *As You Like It* (Mar. 1, 1955), Hastings in *Henry IV, Part 1* (Apr. 27, 1955), the Vinter in *Henry IV, Part 2* (Apr. 28, 1955), the Lord in *The Taming of the Shrew* (May 23, 1955); Marullus in *Julius Caesar* (Sept. 7, 1955), Polyxenes in *The Winter's Tale* (Nov. 1, 1955), the Duke of Burgundy and the Constable of France in *Henry V* (Dec. 13, 1955), Lodovico in *Othello* (Feb. 21, 1956), Achilles in *Troilus and Cressida* (Apr. 3, 1956), Macduff in *Macbeth* (May 23, 1956), the Chorus and Escalus in *Romeo and Juliet* (June 12, 1956), and Henry Bolingbroke in *Richard II* (July 3, 1956).

After the US tour, he played Captain Cyril Mavors in *Expresso Bongo* (Saville, London, Apr. 23, 1958); Bernard Acton in *Everything in the Garden* (Duke of York's, May 16, 1962); Sir Epicure Mammon in *The Alchemist* (Old Vic, Nov. 28, 1962); Maxime in *Poor Bitos* (Arts, Nov. 11, 1963; moved to Duke of York's, Jan. 6, 1964); appeared in the revue *Hang Down Your Head and Die* (Comedy Th., Mar. 19, 1964); and played Braham in *The Philanthropist* (Royal Court, Aug. 3, 1970). Mr. Gray also wrote the one-act play *The Old Soldier* (1971) and *The Pot Plant* (1972).

Films. Mr. Gray appeared in *The Entertainer* (Continental, 1960); *The Man in the Moon* (Trans-Lux, 1961); *The Shabby Tiger* (Dearden/Relph, 1964); *Night of the Generals* (Col., 1967); and *You Only Live Twice* (UA, 1967).

Television. He appeared in *Romeo and Juliet* (NBC, US, 1957); *Small Backroom* (BBC, London, Mar. 1959); *The Big Client* (ABC, US, May 1959); *No Hiding Place* (AR, London, Dec. 1959); *The First Gentleman* (Southern TV, 1960); *Tiger at the Gates* (Granada TV, 1961); *Sanatorium* (Somerset Maugham Hour, AR, 1961); *The Ant and the Grasshopper* (Somerset Maugham Hour, AR, 1961); *You Can't Escape* (BBC, 1961); *Any Other Business* (ATV Tennants, 1961); *Design for Murder* (BBC, 1961); *Voices from the Past* (BBC, 1962); *The Tycoons* (ABC, US, 1962); *A Matter of Principle* (ATV Tennants, London, 1962); *Private and Personal* (BBC, July 1963); *The Perfect Friday* (ATV, Aug. 1963); *Tea Party* (BBC, Mar. 1965); and *Anastasia* (Hallmark Hall of Fame, NBC, Mar. 1967).

Awards. Mr. Gray received the Clarence Derwent Award for his performance as Maxime in *Poor Bitos* (1964).

GRAY, DOLORES. Actress, singer. b. June 7, 1930, Chicago, Ill., to Harry and Barbara Marguerite Gray. Attended St. Agnes Sch., Los Angeles, Calif.; St. Marys Sch., Hollywood, Calif.; Hollywood (Calif.) Professional Childrens Sch. Studied at RADA (1948–49). Relatives in theatre: brother, Richard Gray, producer. Member of SAG; AFTRA; AEA; AGVA.

Theatre. Miss Gray first performed on Bway in the revue, *Seven Lively Arts* (Ziegfeld Th., Dec. 7, 1944); subsequently played Bunny La Fleur in *Are You With It?* (Century, Nov. 10, 1945); Diana Janeway in the pre-Bway tryout of *Sweet Bye and Bye* (opened Shubert, New Haven, Conn., Oct. 10, 1946; closed Erlanger, Philadelphia, Pa., Nov. 5, 1946); made her London debut as Annie in *Annie Get Your Gun* (Coliseum, June 7, 1947); and played Nell Gwynne in a command performance of excerpts from *Good King Charles's Golden Days* (Drury Lane, Oct. 1948); appeared in the revue, *Two on the Aisle* (Mark Hellinger Th., N.Y.C., July 19, 1951); played Eliza Doolittle in *Pygmalion* (Westport Country Playhouse, Conn., Summer 1952); Cornelia in *Carnival in Flanders* (Century, N.Y.C., Sept. 8, 1953); Pistache in *Can-Can* (Municipal Opera, St. Louis, Mo., Summer 1957; Municipal Auditorium, Dayton, Ohio, Summer 1957); Ninotchka in *Silk Stockings,* Pistache in *Can-Can* (Pittsburgh Civic Opera, Pa., Summer 1957); Liza Elliott in *Lady in the Dark* and Ninotchka in *Silk Stockings* (Municipal Opera, St. Louis, Summer 1958).

She appeared at the London Palladium (1958); toured the continent; played Frenchy in *Destry Rides Again* (Imperial, N.Y.C., Apr. 23, 1959); Pistache in *Can-Can* (Municipal Opera, St. Louis, Summer 1961); Frenchy in *Destry Rides Again* (Municipal Auditorium, Dayton, Ohio, Summer 1961); Babe in *The Pajama Game*, Annie in *Annie Get Your Gun* (Municipal Opera, St. Louis, Summer 1962); Pistache in *Can-Can* (Th. Under the Stars, Atlanta, Ga., Summer 1962); Molly in *The Unsinkable Molly Brown* (Municipal Opera, St. Louis, Summer 1963); Wildcat Jackson in *Wildcat* (Owens Auditorium, Charlotte, N.C., Summer 1963); Molly in *The Unsinkable Molly Brown* (Pittsburgh Light Opera, Pa., Summer 1963); Lorraine Sheldon in *Sherry!* (Alvin Th., N.Y.C., Mar. 27, 1967); and Rose in *Gypsy* (Piccadilly Th., London, 1973).

Films. Miss Gray has appeared in *It's Always Fair Weather* (MGM, 1954); *Kismet* (MGM, 1955); *The Opposite Sex* (MGM, 1956); and *Designing Woman* (MGM, 1957).

Television and Radio. She first performed on radio as a singer, on the Rudy Vallee Show (1940). Her television credits include the Milton Berle Show (1955); the Buick Circus Hour (1952–53); *Salute to Cole Porter* (CBS, 1957); Steve Allen Show (NBC, 1959); a Sid Caesar Special (CBS, 1959); the Perry Como Show (NBC 1957–58–59); the Ed Sullivan Show (CBS sixteen times); the US Steel Hour (CBS); the Bell Telephone Hour (NBC 1960–61–62); the Tonight Show (NBC, 1961); Firestone Theatre (1962); Mike Douglas Show (CBS, 1960–61–62–63, 1966); *The Good Old Days* (Leeds Television, England, Mar. 1974); and *Sunday Night at the Palladium* (Leeds Television, Apr. 1974).

Night Clubs. She first appeared in night clubs in *Cabaret* at the Copacabana (N.Y.C., June 1944); subsequently appeared in Las Vegas, Nev., in London; and, in Paris (1952–58); at the Empire Room, Waldorf-Astoria, N.Y.C. (1962); the Cork Club, Houston, Tex. (1962); the Talk of Town, London (1963); and the Tivoli Gardens, Copenhagen, Denmark (1964).

Awards. Miss Gray received the Antoinette Perry (Tony) Award, for her performance as Cornelia in *Carnival in Flanders*; and the Film Exhibitors Laurel Medallion (1956) for her performance in *The Opposite Sex*. .

Recreation. "Work, work, work." She is an owner-breeder of thoroughbred race horses at Oakridge Farm, Calif.

GRAY, SIMON. Playwright, educator. b. Simon J Gray, Oct. 21, 1936, Hayling Island, Great Britain, to James Davidson and Barbara Mary Cecilia Gray. Father, pathologist. Educated at Westminster School; Dalhousie Univ., Nova Scotia, Can.; Univ. of Clermont-Ferrand, France; Trinity College, Cambridge, England. Married 1966 to Beryl Mary Kevern; one son. Member of Dramatists Guild of America; Societé des Auteurs, France.

Theatre. Mr. Gray has written *Wise Child* (Wyndham's, London, 1967); *Dutch Uncle* (Aldwych, Mar. 26, 1968); *The Idiot*, adapted from Dostoevsky's novel (National, 1970); and *Butley* (Critereon, July 14, 1971; Morosco, N.Y.C., Oct. 31, 1972).

Films. A motion picture has been done of *Butley* (Amer. Film Th., 1974).

Television. Among Mr. Gray's plays written for television are the following, all originally produced as the Wednesday Play (BBC): *Death of a Teddy Bear* (Feb. 15, 1967); *Spoiled* (Aug. 28, 1968); and *Sleeping Dog* (1968). His other television plays include *Pig in a Poke* (L.W.T., 1968) and *Man in a Sidecar* (BBC, 1971).

Other Activities. Mr. Gray has lectured on English literature at Queen Mary's College, London Univ.

Published Works. Mr. Gray has published four novels: *Little Portia; Simple People; Colmaine;* and *A Comeback for Stark*.

Awards. Mr. Gray won the Writers Guild best play award for *Death of a Teddy Bear*.

Recreation. Squash and cricket.

GRAY, TIMOTHY. Writer, performer, director, composer, lyricist. b. John Baker Gray, Sept. 5, Chicago, Ill., to Daniel M. and Mary (Baker) Gray. Father, designer (golf clubs). Attended Kelvyn Park H.S., Chicago, 1941–43. Studied drama with Maurice Tei Dunn, N.Y.C.; voice with Keith Davis, N.Y.C. Member of Dramatists Guild; ASCAP; AGAC; AEA; AGVA; SAG; AFTRA; British AEA.

Theatre. Mr. Gray made his stage debut as the Street Singer in a school production of *The Fortune Teller* (Lloyd Grammar Sch. Aud., 1937); subsequently toured US Army bases for USO with a vocal act (1948); made his Bway debut in a vocal group in *Heaven on Earth* (New Century Th., Sept. 16, 1948); sang in vocal groups in *As the Girls Go* (Winter Garden, Nov. 13, 1948); *Gentlemen Prefer Blondes* (Ziegfeld, Dec. 8, 1949); in stock, played Bud in *Best Foot Forward* (Falmouth Playhouse, Mass., 1949); and sang "Mamie Is Mimi" in *Gentlemen Prefer Blondes* (Greek Th., Los Angeles, Calif., 1950).

With Hugh Martin, Mr. Gray wrote the score for *Love from Judy* (Saville, London, Sept. 25, 1952); contributed material to the revue *Airs on a Shoestring*, and appeared in it (Royal Court, Apr. 22, 1953); and, with Jerry De Bono and Dolores Claman, wrote the revue *From Here and There* (Royal Court, June 29, 1955).

Mr. Gray appeared in the pre-Bway tryout of *Ziegfeld Follies* (opened Shubert, Boston, Mass., Apr. 16, 1956; closed Shubert, Philadelphia, Pa., May 12, 1956); contributed material to the revue *Welcome, Darlings*, in which he toured (Summer 1956); directed *Cast of Characters* (Downtown, N.Y.C., June 1959); played Sprog in *Scapa* (Adelphi, London, March 9, 1962); and, with Hugh Martin, wrote the music, lyrics, and book for *High Spirits* (Alvin, N.Y.C., Apr. 7, 1964).

He produced, with Robert Fletcher and Midge La Guardia, a revival of *Johny Johnson* (Edison Th., Apr. 11, 1971); directed and, with Hugh Martin, wrote music, lyrics, and sketches for the revue *They Don't Make 'Em Like That Anymore* (Plaza 9 Music Hall, June 8, 1972); and, with Hugh Martin, did vocal arrangements and musical supervision for a revival of *Good News* (St. James Th., Dec. 23, 1974).

Films. Mr. Gray made his film debut as a Cadet in *West Point Story* (WB, 1950); subsequently appeared in *In the Cool of Day* (MGM, 1962); and *The Victors* (Col., 1963).

Television. Mr. Gray made his debut as a member of the Lyn Duddy Quintet on the Lanny Ross Television Show (NBC, 1948); subsequently appeared in and wrote material for the Washington Square series, (NBC, 1957); appeared on the Steve Allen Show (NBC, 1957) and the Tonight Show (NBC, 1957); wrote material for and appeared on the Patrice Munsel Show (ABC, 1958); was vocal director and arranger for the Milton Berle Special (NBC, 1960); vocal co-director for the Revlon Revue (CBS, Jan.–June 1960); made his British debut in a guest appearance on the Joan Regan Show (ITV, 1961); was singer-dancer in Sunday Night at the London Palladium (ITV, May, 1962); and played Ronnie Miles in *The Hatchet* (BBC, June 1962).

Night Clubs. Mr. Gray made his debut as a soloist at the Longwood Cafe (Chicago, Ill., 1943); subsequently performed in night clubs in Chicago, on the Kemp Circuit in the South and the Levy Circuit in the Northwest (1943–47); wrote, directed, and co-produced *Timothy Gray's Taboo Revue* (The Showplace, N.Y.C., 1959); and wrote material for the Edie Adams night club act (1960–63).

GRAYSON, RICHARD. Company manager, actor, director, stage manager. b. Richard Andrew Rosenblatt, May 2, 1925, San Francisco, Calif., to Martin S. and Margaret (Cohn) Rosenblatt. Father, business executive. Grad. Lowell H.S., San Francisco, 1942; attended Stanford Univ., 1942–43. Served USN, 1943–44; rank, seaman 2/C. Member of ATPAM; AEA; AFTRA; SAG; AGVA. Address: 1132 First Ave., New York, NY 10021, tel. (212) TE 8-1889.

Theatre. Mr. Grayson made his stage debut as the Cheshire Cat and Humpty-Dumpty in *Alice in Wonderland* in a children's community theatre production (San Francisco, Calif., 1932); subsequently was stage manager for the opera, *The Devil and Daniel Webster* (Veteran's Aud., San Francisco, Calif., Winter 1942).

He was assistant stage manager for *Catherine Was Great* (Shubert, N.Y.C., Aug. 2, 1944); stage manager for *Sleep, My Pretty One* (Playhouse, Nov. 2, 1944); assistant to the director for *Signature* (Forrest, Feb. 14, 1945); at the Provincetown Playhouse, played Hertibise in *Orphée* and he was business manager (July–Aug. 1945); was assistant stage manager for *The Ryan Girl* (Plymouth, Sept. 24, 1945), played the role of Victor Sellers on tour (opened Shubert, Philadelphia, Pa., 1945; closed Blackstone, Chicago, Ill., 1945).

With Therese Hayden, he produced the ELT production of *Live Life Again* and *This Property Is Condemned* (1945–46); played the juvenile in *The Shining Hour* (Nov. 26, 1946); was stage manager for *The Royal Family* (John Drew Th., East Hampton, L.I., N.Y., July 1946); and business manager for the Hilltop Summer Th. (Lutherville, Md., July–Sept. 1947).

Mr. Grayson was assistant stage manager for ANTA's Experimental Th. production of *Ballet Ballads* (Maxine Elliott's Th., May 9, 1948); for a tour of Lynn Rigg's *All the Way Home* (Aug. 1948); succeeded (two weeks after opening) Guy Thomajan as assistant stage manager and in the role of Loutec in *Red Gloves* (Mansfield, Dec. 4, 1948), and subsequently became stage manager; was stage manager at Town Hall Th. (Fairhaven, Mass., July–Sept. 1949), performing in two shows, *Yes, My Darling Daughter* and *The Barker;* appeared in *The Barker* (Lake Hopatcong, N.J., Aug. 1949) and *Yes, My Darling Daughter* (Bucks County Playhouse, New Hope, Pa., Sept. 1949); was assistant stage manager and played the Tutor in *Cry of the Peacock* (Mansfield, N.Y.C., Nov. 4, 1950); was stage manager for *The Live Wire* (Playhouse, Aug. 17, 1950); and produced, with Jerome Moross and Bruce Savan, *Ballet Ballads* (Century, Hollywood, Calif., Nov. 10, 1950).

Until 1951, Mr. Grayson used the professional name, Richard A. Martin, thereafter, Richard Grayson.

Mr. Grayson was advance stage manager for the American Shakespeare Festival Th. touring production of *An Evening with Will Shakespeare* (major Eastern cities, Winter 1953); was associated with Lawrence Langner (June 1953–Nov. 1955), with assignments encompassing all of Mr. Langner's theatrical activities, including the Th. Guild, Westport (Conn.) Country Playhouse, and the television program US Steel Hour; and was executive coordinator for the American Shakespeare Festival (Stratford, Conn.) 1954 through its first season (1955).

Mr. Grayson was assistant stage manager and understudy to Louis Jourdan as Michel in *The Immoralist* (Royale, N.Y.C., Feb. 8, 1954); joined as assistant stage manager (Dec. 1955) for *No Time for Sergeants* (Alvin, Oct. 20, 1955); was general production manager for Maurice Evans Productions, Inc. (Dec. 1955–Feb. 1957); stage manager for *The Apple Cart* (Plymouth, Oct. 18, 1956) and on tour (opened Forrest, Philadelphia, Pa., Feb. 4, 1957; closed Huntington Hartford Th., Los Angeles, Calif., June 1957); stage manager for a tour of *The Reluctant Debutante* (opened Alcazar, San Francisco, Calif., July 1957; closed Huntington Hartford Th., Los Angeles, Calif., Oct. 1957), in which he played the role of David Hoylake-Johnston for three performances in San Francisco.

He was apprentice company manager for *The Body Beautiful* (Bway Th., N.Y.C., Jan. 23, 1957; Playhouse-in-the-Park, Philadelphia, Pa., Summer 1958); and apprentice house manager at the New Locust Th. (Philadelphia, Pa., Fall 1958). For community theatres, he directed *The Royal Family* (Cheltenham Playhouse, Pa., Winter 1959) and *The Desperate Hours* (Flagg Court Playhouse, Brooklyn, N.Y., Spring 1959).

Mr. Grayson was general manager for *Heartbreak House* (Billy Rose Th., N.Y.C., Oct. 18, 1959); *Little Mary Sunshine* (Orpheum, Nov. 18, 1959); succeeded (Aug. 1960) Vince McKnight as company manager of *Take Me Along* (Shubert, Oct. 22, 1959); succeeded (Sept. 1960–Feb. 1961) Vince McKnight as company manager of *Gypsy* (Bway Th., May 21, 1959), and joined (Boston, Mass., Apr. 24, 1961) the national tour as company manager (opened Rochester Aud., N.Y., Mar. 29, 1961; closed American, St. Louis, Mo., Dec. 9, 1961); succeeded (Nov. 1960) Ben Boyar as company manager of *La Plume de Ma Tante* (Royale, N.Y.C., Nov. 11, 1958), and on tour (Riviera Hotel, Las Vegas, Nev., Dec. 22, 1960); was company manager for *Carnival!* (Imperial, N.Y.C., Apr. 13, 1961); and joined (Civic Opera House, Chicago, Ill.) a second tour of *Gypsy* as company manager (opened Shubert, Detroit, Mich., Sept. 14, 1961; closed Hanna, Cleveland, Ohio, Jan. 20, 1962).

As company manager, he joined (McVikers, Chicago, Ill., Feb. 1962) the tour of *Do Re Mi* (opened O'Keefe Ctr., Toronto, Canada, Jan. 16, 1962; closed Fisher, Detroit, Mich., Mar. 19, 1962); joined (Montreal, Canada, May 2, 1962) as company manager, the national tour of *Irma La Douce* (opened Colonial, Boston, Mass., Jan. 4, 1962; closed Denver, Colo., Sept. 1962); was company manager (Sept.–Nov. 1962) for *Anything Goes* (Orpheum, N.Y.C., May 15, 1962); *Tovarich* (Bway Th., Mar. 18, 1963); and for a tour of *The Sound of Music* (opened Vancouver, Canada, Dec. 1963; closed Minneapolis, Minn., Mar. 1964); was general manager for *Roar Like a Dove* (Booth, N.Y.C., May 21, 1964); and at the NY World's Fair, was stage manager for the Dupont Pavilion (June 30, 1964).

He was general manager for the bus-and-truck *Oliver!* (July 1964–Spring 1965) and for the bus-and-truck *Camelot* (Fall 1964); company manager for the revival of *The Glass Menagerie* (Brooks Atkinson Th., N.Y.C., May 4, 1965); company manager for the tour of the revival of *Kismet* (Aug.–Nov. 1965); company manager for *Mame* (Jan. 1966–Winter 1970); for *The Fig Leaves Are Falling* (Nov. 1968–Jan. 1969); associate general manager, Alvin Ailey American Dance Theatre (Jan. 1969–May 1971); and company manager for the off-Bway *Boys in the Band* (Spring 1970). He was co-general manager of *Bob and Ray—The Two and Only* (John Golden Th., Sept. 24, 1970); of *Gandhi* (Playhouse Th., Oct. 20, 1970); of *Sensations* (Th. Four, Oct. 25, 1970); and *Kiss Now* (Martinique, Apr. 20, 1971). He was general manager, Joffrey City Center Ballet (Dec. 1970–Nov. 1971); company manager of the touring company of *Hair* (Venus company) (Nov. 21, 1971–Dec. 10, 1972); and company manager for the tour of *Disney on Parade* (Small World Unit I) (Dec. 12, 1972–Aug. 26, 1973; Performing Arts Centre, San Antonio, Tex., Jan. 3, 1973). He played the role of John Cleves in *Any Wednesday* (Curtain-Up Dinner Th., Baldwin, Mo., Sept. 18–Oct. 14, 1973); and was company manager, Alvin Ailey City Center Dance Th. (NY State Th., N.Y.C., Aug. 12–25, 1974).

Films. Mr. Grayson appeared in *Down Among the Sheltering Palms* (20th-Fox, 1951); *Chain of Circumstance* (Col., 1951); *Flat Top* (Mono., 1952); *Thunderbirds* (Rep., 1952); *Bonzo Goes to College* (U, 1952); *Eight Iron Men* (Col., 1952); *Lili* (MGM, 1952); and *Above and Beyond* (MGM, 1952).

Television and Radio. On radio Mr. Grayson played John Royal in *Quiet Wedding* (Th. Guild of the Air, NBC, May 3, 1953). He has appeared on television as a Quartermaster in *Battleship Bismark* (Studio One, CBS, Oct. 24, 1949); as Cotton Candy Operator in *The Barker* (Ford Th., CBS, Jan. 13, 1950); Jimmy in *Fable of Honest Harry* (Armstrong Circle Th., NBC, Nov. 25, 1952); and Thompson in *Dial "M" for Murder* (Hallmark Hall of Fame, NBC, Apr. 1958).

Other Activities. Mr. Grayson was co-owner of La Bottega, Ltd., manufacturers of men's toiletries (1963–70). He directed employee training shows at Bloomingdale's, N.Y.C., Christmas 1961, 1962 and 1963. Since Nov. 5, 1973, he has been an executive at Bloomingdale's.

GREBANIER, BERNARD.

GREBANIER, BERNARD. Writer, educator, director. b. Mar. 8, 1903, New York City, to Benjamin and Otillie (von Storenberg) Grebanier. Father, accountant. Grad. Evander Childs H.S., N.Y.C., 1920; City Coll. of New York, B.A. 1926; New York Univ., M.A. 1930, Ph.D. 1935. Married Sept. 22, 1925, to Frances Winwar (marr. dis. 1942). Member of P.E.N.; The Players; Composers, Authors, and Artists of America (1st natl. vice-pres., 1973–to date). Address: 215 W. 88th St., New York, NY 10024.

From 1930 to 1963, Mr. Grebanier was professor of drama at Brooklyn Coll. He retired as professor emeritus (Feb. 1963) to devote his time to writing and travel.

Theatre. He directed *Othello* (Cherry Lane Th., May 1951); and his own adaptation of *Phaedra* (President, May 1955), which was produced by the Piscator Dramatic Workshop. At Brooklyn Coll. he staged *Phaedra* (May 1951); *The Merchant of Venice* (Jan. 1956); *King Lear* (Dec. 1956); and his version of *Oedipus the King* (Oct. 1960).

Published Works. Mr. Grebanier wrote *Fauns, Satyrs, and a Few Sages* (1945); *Mirrors of the Fire* (1946); *English Literature* (two vols., 1948); *The Other Love* (1957); prepared an acting version of Racine's *Phaedra* (1958); adapted Molière's *The Misanthrope* (1959); wrote *The Heart of Hamlet* (1960); *Playwriting* (1961); *The Truth About Shylock* (1962); *Thornton Wilder* (1964); *The Great Shakespeare Forgery* (1965); *Armenian Miniatures* (1967); *The Uninhibited Byron* (1970); *Edwin Arlington Robinson* (1970); *Pegasus of the Seventies* (1973); and *Players Hide* (1974). In the *Barron's Simplified Approach* series, he did volumes on Chaucer (1964); Milton (1965); Molière (1966); Rousseau (1967); and Shakespeare's *Henry IV, Part 1* (1967) and *Richard II* (1968). He wrote with Seymour Reiter, *College Writing and Reading* (1959) and *Introduction to Imaginative Literature* (1960). He was chief contributing author of *English Literature and Its Background* (1949), and *European Literature* (1952).

Awards. Mr. Grebanier was elected (1947) to membership in the Poetry Society of America and has been president of the NY chapter (1972–to date).

Recreation. Collecting ancient vases, intaglios, and paintings; playing piano.

GREEN, ADOLPH. Playwright, performer, lyricist. b. Dec. 2, Bronx, N.Y., to Daniel and Helen Green. Grad. DeWitt Clinton H.S, N.Y.C. Married Jan. 31, 1960 to Phyllis Newman, actress, singer; one son, one daughter. Member of AEA; AGVA; ASCAP; AFTRA; WGA, East; WGA, West; Dramatists Guild; SWG.

Theatre. Mr. Green first wrote, with Betty Comden, the book and lyrics for *On the Town*, in which he also played Ozzie (Adelphia, N.Y.C., Dec. 28, 1944). He collaborated with Miss Comden on all future works.

They wrote the book and lyrics for *Billion Dollar Baby* (Alvin, Dec. 21, 1945); sketches and lyrics for *Two on the Aisle* (Mark Hellinger Th., July 19, 1951); lyrics for *Wonderful Town* (Winter Garden, Feb. 25, 1953); and *Peter Pan* (Winter Garden, Oct. 20, 1954); book and lyrics for *Bells Are Ringing* (Shubert, Nov. 29, 1956); and lyrics for the songs in *Say, Darling* (ANTA, Apr. 3, 1958).

Mr. Green appeared as Leonardo da Vinci in the pre-Bway tryout of *Bonanza Bound* (opened Shubert, Philadelphia, Dec. 26, 1947; closed there Jan. 3, 1948); appeared with Miss Comden in the revue *A Party*, consisting of songs and sketches from their works (Cherry Lane, N.Y.C., Mon. nights, Nov. 10, Nov. 17, 1958), later expanded to *A Party With Betty Comden and Adolph Green*, in which they again performed (Golden, Dec. 23, 1958; reopened Apr. 16, 1959); they wrote the lyrics for *Do Re Mi* (St. James, Dec. 26, 1960); the book and lyrics for *Subways Are for Sleeping* (St. James, Dec. 27, 1961); and participated in the Marc Blitzstein Memorial Concert (Philharmonic Hall, Lincoln Ctr., Apr. 19, 1964).

They wrote the book and lyrics for *Fade Out—Fade In* (Mark Hellinger Th., May 26, 1964); lyrics for *Hallelujah, Baby!* (Martin Beck Th., Apr. 26, 1967); the book for *Applause* (Palace, Mar. 30, 1970); and new lyrics for *Lorelei* (National Th., Washington, D.C., May 15, 1973; Palace, N.Y.C., Jan. 27, 1974).

Films. Mr. Green wrote with Miss Comden the screenplays for *Good News* (MGM, 1947) and *The Barkleys of Broadway* (MGM, 1949); screenplay and lyrics for *On the Town* (MGM, 1949); lyrics for *Take Me Out to the Ball Game* (MGM, 1949); screenplay and lyrics for *Singin' in the Rain* (MGM, 1952), *The Band Wagon* (MGM, 1955), and *It's Always Fair Weather* (MGM, 1955); screenplay for *Auntie Mame* (WB, 1958); screenplay and lyrics for *Bells Are Ringing* (MGM, 1960) and *What a Way To Go* (20th-Fox, 1964).

Night Clubs. Mr. Green was a member of The Revuers (two others were Betty Comden and Judy Holliday), a group which wrote and performed their own material at the Village Vanguard (N.Y.C., 1939), and later at the Rainbow Room and the Blue Angel (1940–44).

Concerts. Mr. Green and Miss Comden appeared together in the series *Lyrics and Lyricists* (YM-YWHA, N.Y.C., Jan. 1971).

Awards. With Miss Comden, Mr. Green received the Donaldson Award for the lyrics of *Wonderful Town* (1953); Screenwriters branch of WGA awards for *On the Town* (1949), *Singin' in the Rain* (1952) and *It's Always Fair Weather* (1955); and the *Village Voice* Off-Bway (Obie) Award for *A Party with Betty Comden and Adolph Green* (1959). *Applause* received an Antoinette Perry (Tony) Award (1970) as best musical.

GREEN, CAROLYN. Playwright. b. New York City. Attended the Brearley Sch., N.Y.C.; Vassar Coll. Member of Dramatists Guild. Address: Dalton, PA.

Theatre. Miss Green wrote *Janus* (Plymouth Th., N.Y.C., Nov. 24, 1955); and *A Sign of Affection* (pre-Bway tryout, opened Shubert, New Haven, Mar. 10, 1965; closed Walnut St. Th., Philadelphia, Apr. 10, 1965).

GREEN, JOHN H. Educator. b. John Hurlbut Green, May 20, 1915, Meeker, Okla., to James Taylor and Zaidee (Morgan) Green. Father, carpenter. Grad. Shawnee (Okla.) H.S., 1933; Oklahoma Central State Coll., B.A. 1937; attended Northwestern Univ., Summers, 1938–39, M.A. 1941; Univ. of Denver, Ph.D. 1954. Married June 10, 1939, to Anna Gene Hathcock; one son, one daughter. Served in USNR, PTO 1943–46; rank Lt. (sq). Member of AETA. Address: Dept. of Theatre Arts, California State University, Long Beach, CA 90801.

Mr. Green has also held other academic positions in educational theatre, including instructor and director of drama, Oklahoma Central State Coll. (1938–40); graduate assistant in stage lighting, Northwestern University Th. (1940–41); instructor and technical director, Wilson City Coll. (1941–43); and technical director, Oklahoma State Univ. (1946–55).

Recreation. Woodworking, model building.

GREEN, PAUL. Playwright, educator. b. Paul Eliot Green, Mar. 17, 1894, Lillington, N.C., to William A. and Betty Lorine (Byrd) Green. Father, farmer. Grad. Buie's Creek Acad., N.C., 1914; Univ. of North Carolina, B.A. 1921; attended Cornell Univ. 1922–1923. Married July 6, 1922, to Elizabeth Lay; one son, three daughters. Served in US Army, 105th Engineers, 30th Div., AEF; 45th Royal Engineers of the British Army, 1918–19; rank, Sgt. Maj. and 2d Lt. Member of Dramatists Guild; ALA; ASCAP; ANTA (bd. of dir., 1959–61); Natl. Inst. of Arts and Letters; NTC (pres., 1940–42); Natl. Folk Festival (pres., 1934–45); UNESCO (genl. conference, Paris, 1951; member, US Natl. Commission, 1950–52). Address: Old Lystra Rd., Chapel Hill, NC 27514, tel. (919) 942-3858.

Theatre. Mr. Green's first play presented in New York was the one-act work, *The No 'Count Boy* staged by the Little Th. of Dallas, Tex. (Belasco Th., May 6, 1925), which won first prize in the third annual Little Th. Tournament; his first full-length work produced in N.Y.C., was *In Abraham's Bosom* (Provincetown Playhouse, Dec. 30, 1926; moved Garrick, Feb. 14, 1927; reopened Provincetown, May 8, 1927); followed by his play, *The Field God* (Greenwich Village Th., Apr. 21, 1927).

His play, *The House of Connelly* was the initial production staged by the Group Th. (Martin Beck Th., Sept. 28, 1931); followed by his play, *Roll Sweet Chariot,* originally titled *Potter's Field,* (Cort, Oct. 2, 1934); and two of his one-act works, *Hymn to the Rising Sun* and *Unto Such Glory,* presented on a bill with two other one-act plays by the Theatre Union at a Sunday performance (Civic Rep Th., Jan. 12, 1936).

His play, *Johnny Johnson,* was produced (44th St. Th., Nov. 19, 1936 and Edison Th., N.Y.C., April 11, 1971). *Hymn to the Rising Sun* and *Unto Such Glory* were presented by the Federal Th. (WPA) Project (Ritz, May 6, 1937); and his first symphonic drama, *The Lost Colony,* an historic outdoor play was produced at the Waterside Amphitheatre (Roanoke Island, N.C., 1937), where it has been staged every year thereafter, except for four years during WW II. His second symphonic drama, *The Highland Call,* was produced at Fayetteville, N.C. (Summers 1939–40).

He adapted *Native Son* with Richard Wright, from the latter's novel (St. James, N.Y.C., Mar. 24, 1941; Majestic, Oct. 23, 1942); *The Common Glory,* another symphonic drama, was produced at the Matoaka Lake Amphitheatre (Williamsburg, Va., Summer 1947), and repeated annually; his symphonic drama, *Faith of Our Fathers,* was produced at the Carter Barron Amphitheatre (Washington, D.C., Summers 1950–51); he adapted *Peer Gynt* (ANTA, N.Y.C., Jan. 28, 1951); adapted in English the libretto of *Carmen,* staged at the Central City Opera Festival (Central City, Colo., Summer 1954); a program of three one-act works, entitled *Salvation on a String,* consisting of *The No 'Count Boy, Chair Endowed,* and *Supper for the Dead,* was staged in N.Y.C. (Th. de Lys, July 6, 1954; and he wrote *Sing All a Green Willow,* the Carolina Playmakers fiftieth anniversary play (1969).

Other symphonic dramas he has written are *Wilderness Road,* presented at the Indian Fort Amphitheatre (Berea, Ky., Summers 1955–56–57–58 and reopened 1972 for annual production.); *The Founders,* staged at the Cove Amphitheatre (Williamsburg, Va., Summers 1957–58–64); *The Confederacy* at the Robert E. Lee Amphitheatre (Virginia Beach, Va., Summers 1959–60); *The Stephen Foster Story* at the J. Dan Talbott Amphitheatre (Bardstown, Ky., 1959, annually in summer-long production); *Cross and Sword,* St. Augustine Amphitheatre (St. Augustine, Fla., 1965, and annually in summer-long production); *Texas,* Pioneer Amphitheatre (Palo Duro Canyon, Texas, 1966 and annually in summer-long production); *Trumpet in the Land,* Tuscarawas Valley Amphitheatre (New Philadelphia, Ohio, 1970 and annually in summer-long production); *Drumbeats in Georgia,* Jekyll Island Amphitheatre, (Jekyll Island, Georgia, 1973 and annually in summer-long production).

Films. Screenplays and film adaptations Mr. Green has written or collaborated on include *Cabin in the Cotton* (1st Natl., 1932); *Dr. Bull* (20th-Fox, 1933); *Voltaire* (WB, 1933); *State Fair* (20th-Fox, 1933); *David Harum* (20th-Fox, 1934); and many others.

Other Activities. Mr. Green was professor of dramatic art at the Univ. of North Carolina (1939–44) and assistant professor and associate professor of philosophy at the University (1923–39); has lectured in Asia on the American theatre on a grant from the Rockefeller Foundation (1951); and was the editor of the magazine, *The Reviewer* (1925).

Published Works. Volumes of his one-act plays include *The Lord's Will and Other Carolina Plays* (1925); *Lonesome Road, Six Plays for the Negro Theatre* (1926); and *In the Valley and Other Carolina Plays* (1928). One-act plays published individually include *Fixin's,* written with Erma Green (1934); *White Dresses* (1935); *The Southern Cross* (1938); and *The Sheltering Plaid* (1965). Mr. Green's volumes of long and short plays include *Out of the South, the Life of a People in Dramatic Form* (1939); and *Five Plays of the South* (1936). His full-length plays published individually include *The Field God* and *In Abraham's Bosom* (1927); *Shroud My Body Down* (1935); *Roll Sweet Chariot* (1935); *The Enchanted Maze* (1939); *Johnny Johnson* (1937); and *The Honeycomb,* a play with masks and music (1972).

Mr. Green's published plays for radio include *A Start in Life* in the volume, *The Free Company Presents* (1941); and *Wings for to Fly, Three Plays of Negro Life,* containing *The Thirsting Heart, Lay This Body Down,* and *Fine Wagon* (1959).

Mr. Green's fiction includes *Wide Fields* (1928); *The Laughing Pioneer,* novel (1932); *This Body the Earth,* novel (1935); *Salvation on a String,* a collection of short stories (1946); *Dog on the Sun,* short stories (1949); *Words and Ways,* short stories and sketches (1968); and *Home to My Valley,* stories and sketches (1970).

His volumes of essays include *The Hawthorn Tree* (1943); *Forever Growing* (1945); *Dramatic Heritage* (1953); *Drama and the Weather, Some Notes and Papers on Life and the Theatre* (1958); and *Plough and Furrow* (1963).

He has contributed articles and stories to magazines including *Theatre Arts, Dramatists Guild Bulletin,* the *NY Times* Magazine, the *Atlantic,* and *Esquire.*

Awards. Mr. Green received the Pulitzer Prize (1927) for his play, *In Abraham's Bosom;* a Kenan Philosophy Fellowship for graduate study at Cornell Univ. (1921–23); the Belasco Cup (1925) for his play, *The No 'Count Boy;* first prize for his play, *Supper for the Dead,* in a one-act play contest at Le Petit Théâtre du Vieux Carré (New Orleans, La., 1926); a Guggenheim Fellowship (1928–30); the Claire M. Senie Drama Study Award (1937) for *Johnny Johnson;* the Sir Walter Raleigh Award for Literary Achievement (1952); the Freedoms Foundation George Washington Medals for *Faith of Our Fathers* (1951), *Wilderness Road* (1956, and *Texas* (1966); a Paul Green Year was proclaimed by SETC (South Eastern Th. Conference), with productions of his works by member organizations (1956–57); North Carolina Achievement Award (1964); the Theta Alpha Phi (Natl. Theatre Honors Frat.) Medallion of Honor (1965); and Distinguished Alumnus Award, Univ. of N.C. (1973).

He has received the honorary degree of Litt.D. from Western Reserve Univ. (1941), Davidson Coll. (1948), the Univ. of North Carolina (1956), Berea Coll. (1957), the Univ. of Louisville (1957), and Campbell College (1969).

Recreation. Farming and music.

GREEN, STANLEY. Writer. b. May 29, 1923, New York City, to Rudy and Frances (Kuschner) Green. Grad. Union Coll., B.A., 1943; Univ. of Nebraska, ASTP 1944. Married Aug. 8, 1954, to Catherine Hunt; two children. Served WW II, US Army, Signal Corps; rank, T/5. Address: 169 State St., Brooklyn, NY 11201, tel. (212) UL 2-4767.

Mr. Green was vice-president, Lynn Farnol Group, Inc., public relations consultants (1963–66).

Theatre. Mr. Green wrote *Salute to American Musical Theatre* (1967), which, under sponsorship of the Manhattan School of Music, was presented at the Waldorf-Astoria, N.Y.C., and the White House, Washington, D.C.; he wrote the script *The Music of Kurt Weill,* presented under sponsorship of the Foundation for International Child Care at Philharmonic Hall, N.Y.C. (1969); and he was music adviser, *Revue of Revues,* sponsored by AADA and presented at Avery Fisher Hall (formerly Philharmonic Hall) in 1973.

Radio. From 1961 to 1965, Mr. Green conducted the program, The World of Musical Comedy (WBAI-FM).

Other Activities. He lectured at the Brooklyn Academy of Music (1961–62); at Gould House (New York Univ.) Ardsley-on-Hudson, N.Y. (1963); and at the New England Theatre Conference (1970).

Published Works. He wrote *The World of Musical Comedy* (1960, rev. 1974); *The Rodgers and Hammerstein Story* (1963); *Ring Bells! Sing Songs!* (1971); *Starring Fred Astaire* (1973); and contributed articles to *Saturday Review,* New York *Times, Musical America, Variety, Atlantic Monthly, Encyclopedia Year Book, Encyclopedia International;* and was contributing editor of *HiFi/Stereo Review* (1957–63).

Discography. Mr. Green was co-producer of the album *Starring Fred Astaire* (1973).

GREEN, WILLIAM. Theatre historian, educator, theatrical administrator. b. July 10, 1926, New York City, to Louis and Hanna (Bernstein) Green. Father, musician. Grad. Newton H.S., 1944; Queens Coll., B.A. 1949; Columbia Univ., M.A. 1950, Ph.D. 1959. Studied dramatic literature and theatre at Columbia with Oscar J. Campbell, Joseph Wood Krutch, Maurice Valency, Mark Van Doren, Alfred Harbage, Margaret Bieber, Milton Smith, Edward Kook, and Forrest Haring; at Queens Coll. with John Gastner and Robert H. Ball. Married Aug. 14, 1960, to Marguerite Joan Mayer; one son, one daughter. Served US Navy, 1944–46. Member of Theatre Library Assn.; Amer. Society for Theatre Research (corresponding sect. for the US, 1970–to date; US delegate to the Univ. Commission, 1973–to date); Modern Language Assn.; Renaissance Society of Amer.; Malone Society; Coll. English Assn.; AFM, Local 802; Professional Staff Congress. Address: (home) 50-10 199th St., Fresh Meadows, NY 11365, tel. (212) 225-4083; (bus.) Queens College, Flushing, NY 11367, tel. (212) 520-7238.

Since 1957, Dr. Green has been affiliated with the English Dept. of Queens Coll. of CUNY. He is a professor of English, and a consultant of the NY State Education Dept. College Proficiency Examination Program in Shakespeare (1964–to date). Previously, he was a lecturer in the English Dept. at Upsala Coll. (1953–56).

Theatre. Dr. Green appeared as a walk-on in *The City Madame* (Brander Matthews Th., Columbia Univ., Fall 1950); was lighting director for the Woodstock (N.Y.) Playhouse (Summer 1951); a technician for *Lady in the Dark* (ELT, N.Y.C., 1952); a play reader for the ANTA Th. (1952 Play Series); production assistant for a touring production of *An Evening with Will Shakespeare* (Amer. Shakespeare Festival, 1953); business manager for the Salt Creek Summer Th. (Hensdale, Ill., 1953); and stage manager for the Entertainment Division of the General Electric Co (Henderson Harbor, N.Y., 1956).

Other Activities. From 1944–71, Dr. Green was a free-lance musician, playing clarinet.

Published Works. In addition to many articles on theatre, he has written *Shakespeare's Merry Wives of Windsor* (1962); edited *The Merry Wives of Windsor* (1965); with John Gassner, wrote *Elizabethan Drama* (1967); and contributed to *A Style Manual for College Students* (1973).

Awards. He was the recipient of a scholarship in Elizabethan and Shakespearean Drama to the Univ. of Birmingham Post-Graduate Summer School, Stratford-upon-Avon (1950); and of a research fellowship in the Dept. of English, Univ. of Manchester (England, 1956–57).

Recreation. Music, photography, philately.

GREENBERG, EDWARD M. Producer, actor, director, teacher, writer. b. July 22, 1924, Brooklyn, N.Y., to Herman M. and Bess (Levy) Greenberg. Father, salesman. Attended Townsend Harris H.S., N.Y.C.; City College of N.Y.; Univ. of Wisconsin, M.A. 1948; New York Univ. He trained for the theatre with Erwin Piscator at the Dramatic Workshop of the New School (N.Y.C.), 1946; and with Lee Strasberg at The American Theatre Wing (N.Y.C.), 1949. Married Apr. 29, 1957, to Sara Dillon, singer-actress; one daughter, one son. Served in US Army Signal Corps, 1941–46. Member of AEA; The Players. Address: (home) 161 E. 79th St., New York, NY 10021, tel. (212) 737-7515; (bus.) Queens College, Flushing, NY 11367, tel. (212) 520-7573.

Theatre. Mr. Greenberg is associate professor of drama and theatre, Queens College, City Univ. of N.Y. (1971–to date). He has been theatre design consultant for arena theatres in Anaheim, Calif. (1966), Phoenix, Ariz. (1969), and Rockland County (N.Y.) Community Coll. (1973), among others. He was founder and head of the Musical Th. Workshop (1963–70) of the Los Angeles–San Francisco Civic Light Opera Assns.

Mr. Greenberg made his debut as a resident actor at the Univ. Playhouse (Hyannis, Mass., Summer 1948); he subsequently worked there as an actor and stage manager (Summer 1950); acted with the Falmouth (Mass.) Playhouse (Summer 1951); stage managed at Hyannis (Mass.) and Cohasset (Mass.) Music Circuses (Summers 1951–52); and directed various musicals at Hyannis, Mass., Cohasset, Mass., Fox Valley, Ill., Jacksonville, Fla., Miami, Fla., Oakdale, Conn., Warwick, R.I., Milwaukee, Wisc., Bucks County, Pa. (Summers 1953–56). He directed ten musical productions for the St. Louis (Mo.) Municipal Opera (Summers 1957–59); directed *Billy Budd* (Equity Library Th., N.Y.C., 1957); *Hit the Deck* (Jones Beach, N.Y., Marine Th., Summer 1960); *Carousel, The Merry Widow, Guys and Dolls, Show Boat, Kismet,* and *Song of Norway* (Los Angeles–San Francisco Civic Light Opera Assns., March 1961–Oct. 1963); and *Guys and Dolls* (Desert Inn, Las Vegas, Dec. 1962–Sept. 1963). For the inaugural productions at the Richard Rodgers' Music Th. of Lincoln Center (N.Y.C., Nov. 1963–Oct. 1965), he was director and production supervisor of *The King and I, The Merry Widow, Carousel,* and *Kismet;* associate producer and resident director of *Musical Theatre Cavalcade, The Student Prince, My Fair Lady,* and *Rosalinda* (Los Angeles–San Francisco Civic Light Opera Assns., Dec. 1965–Dec. 1970); directed *Many Happy Returns* (Desert Inn, Las Vegas, Jan.–May 1969); and *The Merry Widow* (Dallas Civic Opera, Dec. 1969); produced and directed *The Sounds of Children* (The White House Conference on Children, Washington, D.C., Dec. 1970); and is executive producer of the St. Louis Municipal Opera (Jan. 1971–to date).

Television. Mr. Greenberg directed the Bob Hope special, *Roberta,* (NBC, 1959).

Published Works. Mr. Greenberg formerly reviewed for the theatrical trade paper, *Show Business;* is the B'way reviewer for *The Amer. Musical Th. Newsletter;* has written articles for *Amer. Educational Th. Journal* and other periodicals; and has re-written for current leasing *The Merry Widow* and *The Student Prince.*

GREENE, GRAHAM. Writer, playwright. b. Oct. 2, 1904, Berkhamsted, England, to Charles Henry and Marion (Raymond) Greene. Attended Berkhamsted Sch.; Balliol Coll., Oxford Univ. Married 1927 to Vivien Dayrell-Browning; one son, one daughter. Served in British Foreign Office, 1941–44. Address: 9 Bow St., London W.C.2, England.

Theatre. Mr. Greene's first play to be presented in the US was his dramatization of his novel, *The Heart of the Matter,* in association with Basil Dean, which was tried out in Boston, Mass. (1950). He also wrote *The Living Room* (Wyndham's, London, Apr. 16, 1953; Henry Miller's Th., N.Y.C., Nov. 17, 1954); *The Potting Shed* (Bijou, N.Y.C., Jan. 29, 1957; Globe, London, Feb. 5, 1958); adapted with Dennis Cannan and Pierre Bost his own novel, *The Power and the Glory* (Phoenix Theatre, London, Apr. 5, 1956; Phoenix, N.Y.C., Dec. 12, 1958); wrote *The Complaisant Lover* (Globe, London, June 18, 1959; Ethel Barrymore Th., N.Y.C., Nov. 1, 1961); and wrote *Carving a Statue* (Haymarket, London, Sept. 17, 1964).

Films. Mr. Greene wrote the screenplay, *The Fallen Idol* (Selznick, 1949), adapted from his short story, *The Basement Room;* the original script for *The Third Man* (Selznick, 1949); the screenplay of *Brighton Rock* (Boulting Brothers, 1947), issued as *Young Scarface* (Mayer-Kingsley, 1951); and the screenplays *Our Man in Havana* (Col., 1960) and *The Comedians* (MGM, 1967), both based on his novels of the same titles.

Television. His play, *The Power and the Glory,* was produced on NBC (Mar. 1961) and CBS (Oct. 1961).

Other Activities. Mr. Greene was literary editor of *The Spectator* (1940–41); a director of Spottiswoode, Ltd. (1944–48); was correspondent in Indo-China for the London *Sunday Times* and *Le Figaro* (1951–54); and a director of Bodley Head (1958–68).

Published Works. He wrote *Babbling April* (1925); *The Man Within* (1929); *The Name of Action* (1930); *Rumour at Nightfall* (1931); *Stamboul Train* (1932); *England Made Me* (1935), reprinted as *Shipwrecked* (1935); *Journey Without Maps* (1936); *This Gun for Hire* (1936); *Brighton Rock* (1939); *The Lawless Roads* (1939); *The Confidential Agent* (1939); *The Power and the Glory* (1940); *British Dramatists* (1942); *The Ministry of Fear* (1943); *Nineteen Stories* (1947); *The Little Train* for children (1947); *The Heart of the Matter* (1948) *The Third Man* (1950); *The Little Fire Engine* for children (1950); *The End of the Affair* (1951); *The Lost Childhood and Other Essays* (1951); *The Little Horse Bus* for children (1952); *The Little Steamroller* for children (1953); *Essais Catholiques* (1953); *Twenty-one Stories* (1954); *Loser Take All* (1955); *The Quiet American* (1955); *Our Man in Havana* (1958); *A Burnt-Out Case* (1961); *In Search of a Character; Two African Journals* (1961); *A Sense of Reality* (1963); *The Comedians* (1966); *May We Borrow Your Husband and Other Comedies of the Sexual Life,* short stories (1967); *Collected Essays* (1969); *Travels with My Aunt* (1969); *A Sort of Life* (1971); *The Pleasure Dome,* collected film criticism (1972); and *The Honorary Consul* (1973).

He edited *The Old School* (1934); and compiled *The Best of Saki* (1961).

Awards. Mr. Greene received the Hawthornden Prize (1940) and the Catholic Literary Award (1952); an Hon. Litt.D. from Cambridge Univ. (1962) and an Hon. D.Litt. from Edinburgh Univ. (1967); was made honorary fellow of Balliol College, Oxford Univ. (1963); and was created a Companion of Honor in 1966. He was awarded the Shakespeare Prize at Hamburg in 1968 and the Thomas More Medal in 1973.

GREENE, HERBERT. Producer, conductor, composer, arranger. b. June 16, 1921, New York City, to David and Eva (Walzer) Greene. Father, tailor. Grad. Abraham Lincoln H.S., Brooklyn, N.Y., 1939; attended Juilliard Sch. of Music, 1940; Brooklyn Coll., 1941. Married Mar. 27, 1944, to Lucy Grossman (marr. dis. Aug. 11, 1960); one son, one daughter; married Aug. 13, 1960, to Norma Geist. Member of AFM, Local 802. Address: 853 Hanley Ave., Los Angeles, CA 90049, tel. (213) GR 2-1169.

Theatre. Mr. Greene made his N.Y.C. stage debut as the 3rd Workman, a Musician, a Waiter, and a Conductor in *On the Town* (Adelphi Th., Dec. 28, 1944) and succeeded (Apr. 26, 1945) Max Goberman as musical director; succeeded (Summer 1946) Max Goberman as the musical director of *Billion Dollar Baby* (Alvin, Dec. 21, 1945); did the vocal arrangements for *Small Wonder* (Coronet, Sept. 15, 1948); did vocal arrangements and was conductor for *Two on the Aisle* (Mark Hellinger Th., July 19, 1951); did the vocal arrangements and was musical director for *Silk Stockings* (Imperial, Feb. 24, 1955); was orchestra and choral director for *The Most Happy Fella* (Imperial, May 3, 1956); and did the vocal arrangements and was vocal director for *Bells Are Ringing* (Shubert, Nov. 29, 1956).

Mr. Greene produced, with Kermit Bloomgarden and in association with Frank Productions Inc., *The Music Man,* for which he also did the vocal arrangements and was musical director (Majestic, Dec. 19, 1957); did the vocal arrangements and was musical director for *The Unsinkable Molly Brown* (Winter Garden, Nov. 3, 1960), and *The Gay Life* (Shubert, Nov. 18, 1961); was producer, with Kermit Bloomgarden, in association with Steven H. Scheuer, for *Nowhere To Go But Up,* for which he was also musical director and vocal arranger (Winter Garden, Nov. 10, 1962); and was the musical director and vocal arranger for *Anyone Can Whistle* (Majestic, Apr. 4, 1964); and vocal arranger for a revival of *The Music Man* (NY City Ctr., June 16, 1965).

Television. Mr. Greene did the vocal arrangements for GE College Bowl (NBC, 1951).

Other Activities. He was assistant professor of music at Brooklyn Coll. (1948).

Awards. Mr. Greene received the Antoinette Perry (Tony) Award for Best Musical Direction for *The Music Man* (1958).

Recreation. Study of antiquity.

GREENE, MILTON. Musical director, composer, arranger, pianist. b. Milton Louis Greene, New York City. Grad. James Madison H.S., Brooklyn, N.Y.; attended Long Island Univ.; grad. New York Univ., B.S. M.A. Studied orchestration with Philip James, N.Y.C.; piano with Modena Scovill, N.Y.C.; conducting with Warren Erb at New York Univ.; with Myron Levite, N.Y.C. Married 1943, to Beulah Goldenberg; two sons. Member of AFM; ASCAP; Sinfonia.

Theatre. Mr. Greene was a night club pianist and arranger; from 1948–60, he was musical director and arranger for a series of revues in an experimental theatre project at the Tamiment (Pa.) Summer Th.; was pianist for *The Pajama Game* (St. James Th., N.Y.C., May 13, 1954); musical director and vocal arranger for the revue, *Catch a Star!* (Plymouth, Sept. 6, 1955); served as composer, vocal arranger and musical director for the revue, *Joyride* (Huntington Hartford Th., Hollywood, Calif., Jan. 1956); was pianist for *Bells Are Ringing* (Shubert, N.Y.C., Nov. 29, 1956); musical director and vocal arranger for *The Body Beautiful* (Bway Th., Jan. 23, 1958); musical director and pianist for the revue, *A Party with Betty Comden and Adolph Green* (John Golden Th., Dec. 23, 1958); musical director and vocal arranger for *From A to Z* (Plymouth, Apr. 20, 1960); orchestra conductor (Aug. 1960–Oct. 1961) for *Fiorello!* (Broadhurst, Nov. 23, 1959); and musical director and vocal arranger for *Fiddler on the Roof* (Imperial, Sept. 22, 1964); and *The Rothschilds* (Lunt-Fontanne Th., Oct. 19, 1970).

Television and Radio. Mr. Greene served as musical director for his own radio program, the Milton Greene Show (WMCA).

For television, he was musical director for the Bert Parks Show (CBS, NBC); was staff musical director for the Alan Dale Show; and the Jim McKay Show (CBS); and conducted the CBS Orchestra on the Musical Theatre series (CBS, 1964).

Recreation. Golf, tennis, travel.

GREENWOOD, CHARLOTTE. Actress. b. Frances Charlotte Greenwood, June 25, 1893, Philadelphia, Pa., to Frank and Anna Bell Jaquet (Higgins) Greenwood. Attended public schools, Boston, Mass., and Norfolk, Va. Married Dec. 22, 1924, to Martin Broones. Member of AEA; SAG. Address: 806 N. Rodeo Dr., Beverly Hills, CA.

Theatre. Miss Greenwood made her debut as a chorus girl in *The White Cat* (New Amsterdam Th., N.Y.C., Nov. 2, 1905); subsequently appeared as Lola in *The Rogers Brothers in Panama* (Bway Th., Sept. 1907); performed in *Nearly a Hero* (Casino, Feb. 1908); played vaudeville in Chicago and cross country on various circuits (1909–11); appeared as Fanny Silly in *The Passing Show of 1912* (Winter Garden, N.Y.C., July 22, 1912); Sidonie in *The Man with Three Wives* (Weber and Fields' Th., Jan. 23, 1913); appeared in the revue *The Passing Show of 1913* (Winter Garden, July 24, 1913); toured as the Queen in *The Tik-Tok Man of Oz* (St. Louis, Mo., and Los Angeles, Calif., (1913–14); played Letitia Proudfoot in *Pretty Mrs. Smith* (Casino, N.Y.C., Sept. 21, 1914); appeared in the revue *Town Topics* (Century, Sept. 1915); played Letty Robins in *So*

Long, Letty (Shubert, Oct. 23, 1916); Letty in *Linger Longer Letty* (Fulton, Nov. 20, 1919); Letty in *Let 'Er Go, Letty,* touring the US and Canada (1921); the title role in *Letty Pepper* (Vanderbilt, N.Y.C., Apr. 10, 1922); appeared in *The Music Box Revue* (Music Box, Oct. 23, 1922); *Hassard Short's Ritz Revue* (Ritz, Sept. 17, 1924); and *Rufus Le Maire's Affairs* (Majestic, Mar. 28, 1927); toured the vaudeville circuits with her act called "Her Morning Bath" (Keith-Albee, Orpheum, 1928–29); played Alice Hinedale in *Mebbe* (Chicago, Ill., Apr., 1930); performed in *She Couldn't Say No, She Knew What She Wanted,* and *Parlor, Bedroom and Bath* (El Capitan Th., Hollywood, Calif., 1930); and in *The Alarm Clock* (Alcazar, San Francisco, Calif., Apr. 1932).

She made her London debut in *Wild Violets* (Drury Lane, Oct. 31, 1932); played Abbie in *The Late Christopher Bean* (El Capitan, Hollywood, Calif., Oct. 1933); appeared in the musical *Three Sisters* (Drury Lane, London, Apr. 1934); played Isabel Ferris in *Gay Deceivers* (Gaiety, May 23, 1935); performed in *Leaning on Letty* (San Francisco, Calif., Dec. 1935), in which she toured the US (1936–38) and Australia (May 1939); also in Australia, appeared in *She Couldn't Say No*— toured in it in the US (1942–43); toured as Mama in *I Remember Mama* (opened Colonial, Boston, Mass., 1947; closed 1948); and appeared as Juno in *Out of This World* (New Century, N.Y.C., Dec. 21, 1950).

Films. Miss Greenwood made her debut in *Jane* (Par., 1915); subsequently appeared in *The Man in Possession* (20th-Fox, 1931); *Young People* (20th-Fox, 1940); *Down Argentine Way* (20th-Fox, 1940); *Moon Over Miami* (20th-Fox, 1941); *Springtime in the Rockies* (20th-Fox, 1942); *The Gang's All Here* (20th-Fox, 1943); *Home in Indiana* (20th-Fox, 1944); *Peggy* (U, 1950); *Dangerous When Wet* (MGM, 1953); *Oklahoma* (Magna, 1955); *Glory* (RKO, 1956); and *The Sound of Laughter* (Union, 1964).

Television and Radio. The Charlotte Greenwood Show was a regular radio feature (1944–46). Miss Greenwood's television appearances include Best of the Post (ABC).

Published Works. A volume of her reminiscences, entitled *Just for Kicks,* was published in 1947.

GREENWOOD, JANE.

Costume designer. b. Apr. 30, 1934, Liverpool, England, to John Richard and Florence Sarah Mary (Humphries) Greenwood. Attended Merchant Taylor's Girls Sch., Liverpool. Married to Ben Edward, set designer; two daughters.

Theatre. Miss Greenwood made her costume designing debut with the Oxford Rep. production of Pirandello's *Henry IV* (Playhouse, Oxford, England, 1958); debuted in London with *The Hamlet of Stepney Green* (Lyric, Hammersmith, July 15, 1958); as an associate of Ray Diffin, assisted in the designs for *The Importance of Being Earnest* (Madison Ave. Playhouse, N.Y.C., Feb. 25, 1963); subsequently designed the costumes for *The Ballad of the Sad Café* (Martin Beck Th., Oct. 30, 1963); *Hamlet* (Lunt-Fontanne, Apr. 9, 1964); *Incident at Vichy* (ANTA, Washington Sq. Th., Dec. 3, 1964); *Tartuffe* (ANTA, Washington Square Th., Jan. 14, 1965); supervised Loudon Sainthill's designs for *Half a Sixpence* (Broadhurst, Apr. 25, 1965); designed the costumes for *A Race of Hairy Men* (Henry Miller's Th., Apr. 29, 1965); *Tartuffe* (Amer. Conservatory Th., ACT, Pittsburgh, July 15, 1965); *Nathan Weinstein, Mystic, Connecticut* (Brooks Atkinson Th., N.Y.C., Feb. 25, 1966); *Where's Daddy?* (Billy Rose Th., Mar. 2, 1966); for the American Shakespeare Festival (ASF), Stratford, Conn., *Murder in the Cathedral* (June 19, 1966), and *Twelfth Night* (June 21, 1966); supervised the costumes for *The Killing of Sister George* (Belasco, N.Y.C., Oct. 5, 1966); designed the costumes for *How's the World Treating You?* (Music Box, Oct. 24, 1966); *What Do You Really Know About Your Husband?* (pre-Bway, opened Shubert Th., New Haven, Mar. 9, 1967; closed there Mar. 11, 1967); for the National Rep. Th. (Ford's Th., Washington, D.C.), *The Comedy of Errors* (Feb. 26, 1968), and, with Alvin Colt, *She Stoops to Conquer* (Mar. 26, 1968); designed the costumes for *More Stately Mansions* (Broadhurst, N.Y.C., Oct. 31, 1967); *The Prime of Miss Jean Brodie* (Helen Hayes Th., Jan. 16, 1968); *The Seven Descents of Myrtle* (Ethel Barrymore Th., Mar. 27, 1968); *I'm Solomon* (Mark Hellinger Th., Apr. 23, 1968); for ASF (Stratford, Conn.) *Androcles and the Lion* (June 25, 1968), and *Love's Labour's Lost* (June 26, 1968); *The Mother Lover* (Booth, N.Y.C., Feb. 1, 1969); *The Wrong Way Light Bulb* (John Golden Th., Mar. 4, 1969); for ASF (Stratford, Conn.), *Much Ado About Nothing* (June 18, 1969, matinee), *Hamlet* (June 18, 1969), and *Three Sisters* (July 23, 1969); the double-bill *Episode in the LIfe of an Author* and *The Orchestra* (Studio Arena, Buffalo, N.Y., Sept. 16, 1969); *The Penny Wars* (Royale, N.Y.C., Oct. 15, 1969); *Crimes of Passion* (Astor Place Th., Oct. 26, 1969); *Angela* (Music Box, Oct. 30, 1969); and *Sheep on the Runway* (Helen Hayes Th., Jan. 31, 1970).

For the American Shakespeare Fest. (Stratford, Conn.), she designed the costumes for *All's Well that Ends Well* (June 16, 1970), *The Devil's Disciple* (June 19, 1970), and *Othello* (June 17, 1970; transferred to ANTA Th., N.Y.C., Sept. 14, 1970); *Gandhi* (Playhouse Th., N.Y.C., Oct. 20, 1970); *Hay Fever* (Helen Hayes Th., Nov. 9, 1970); *Les Blancs* (Longacre, Nov. 15, 1970); *The House of Blue Leaves* (Truck and Warehouse Th., Feb. 10, 1971); *70, Girls, 70* (Broadhurst, Apr. 15, 1971); for the ASF (Stratford, Conn.), *The Merry Wives of Windsor* (June 12, 1971), *The Tempest* (June 12, 1971), and *Mourning Becomes Electra* (June 16, 1971); *Wise Child* (Helen Hayes Th., N.Y.C., Jan. 27, 1972); *That's Entertainment* (Edison, Apr. 14, 1972); for the ASF (Stratford, Conn.) *Julius Caesar* (June 22, 1972), *Anthony and Cleopatra* (June 23, 1972), and *Major Barbara* (June 27, 1972); *Look Away* (Playhouse, N.Y.C., Jan. 7, 1973); *Finishing Touches* (Plymouth, Feb. 8, 1973); for the ASF (Stratford, Conn.), *The Country Wife* (June 1, 1973), *Measure for Measure* (June 2, 1973), and *Macbeth* (July 2, 1973); at the Eisenhower Th., John F. Kennedy Center (Washington, D.C.), *The Head Hunters* (world premiere, 1973–74 season), *The Prodigal Daughter* (world premiere, Nov. 1, 1973, and *A Moon for the Misbegotten* (Dec. 4, 1973; Morosco, N.Y.C., Dec. 29, 1973); *Getting Married* (Hartford, Stage Co., Nov. 9, 1973); *Finishing Touches* (Ahmanson Th., Los Angeles, Dec. 4, 1973); for the ASF (Stratford, Conn.) *Twelfth Night* (June 15, 1974), *Romeo and Juliet* (June 16, 1974), and *Cat on a Hot Tin Roof* (July 10, 1974; ANTA Th., N.Y.C., Sept. 24, 1974); *Beyond the Horizon* (McCarter Th., Princton, N.J., Oct. 10, 1974); *Same Time, Next Year* (Brooks Atkinson Th., N.Y.C., Mar. 13, 1975); for the ASF (Stratford, Conn.), *King Lear* (June 14, 1975), and *A Winter's Tale* (July 22, 1975); *A Long Day's Journey into Night* (Brooklyn Acad. of Music, N.Y.C., Jan. 28, 1976); *A Matter of Gravity* (Broadhurst, Feb. 3, 1976); *Who's Afraid of Virginia Woolf?* (Music Box, Apr. 1, 1976); and *California Suite* (Ahmanson, Los Angeles, Apr. 23, 1976; Eugene O'Neill Th., N.Y.C., June 10, 1976).

She has designed the costumes for Metropolitan Opera Forum productions of *Four Saints in Three Acts, Phedre, Dido and Aeneas,* and, for the main stage, *Adriana auf Naxon; La Favorita* (San Francisco Opera Co.); *Night Creatures* (Alvin Ailey Dance Co.); and for the NY City Opera Co.; and the Guthrie Th. (Minneapolis, Minn.).

Television. Miss Greenwood has costumed *Moon for the Misbegotten; Look Homeward, Angel* (CBS); *The House without a Christmas Tree* (NBC); *The Thanksgiving Treasure* (NBC); and *A Touch of the Poet* (NET).

Other Activities. Miss Greenwood has taught costume design at the Lester Polakov Th. Studio (N.Y.C.); and lectures at the Juilliard School's Dept. of Drama (N.Y.C.).

Awards. For her designs for *Tartuffe* (1965) she received the Maharam and *Saturday Review* awards; received *Best Plays* citation (1967–69) as best costumer for her designs for *More Stately Mansions* and *The Prime of Miss Jean Brodie;* an Antoinette Perry (Tony) nomination (1967–68) for *More Stately Mansions;* the *Variety* Poll of NY Drama Critics nomination (1967–68) for *More Stately Mansions* and *The Prime of Miss Jean Brodie;* and an Antoinette Perry (Tony) nomination (1970–71) for *Hay Fever* and *Les Blancs.*

GREENWOOD, JOAN.

Actress. b. Mar. 4, 1921, Chelsea, London, England, to Sydney Earnshaw and Ida (Waller) Greenwood. Father, artist. Attended St. Catherine's, Bramley, Surrey; RADA. Married May 16, 1960, to André Morell, actor; one son. Member of British AEA.

Theatre. Miss Greenwood appeared as Lucasta Angel in *The Confidential Clerk* (Morosco Th., N.Y.C., Feb. 11, 1954).

She made her debut on the London stage as Louisa in *The Robust Invalid* (Apollo, Nov. 15, 1938); subsequently played Timpson in *Little Ladyship* (Strand, Feb. 1939); Little Mary in *The Women* (Strand, Apr. 23, 1940); Pamela Brent in *Dr. Brent's Household* (Richmond, May 27, 1940); Wendy in *Peter Pan* (Adelphi, Dec. 24, 1941); Henriette in *Damaged Goods* (Whitehall, May 6, 1943); succeeded Deborah Kerr as Ellie Dunn in *Heartbreak House* (Cambridge, Mar. 18, 1943); and Ophelia in *Hamlet,* on tour with Donald Moffit's Co. (1944).

She appeared as Lady Teazle in *School for Scandal,* Cleopatra in *Antony and Cleopatra,* and Nora in *A Doll's House* (Oxford Playhouse, Feb.–Nov. 1945); Bertha in *Frenzy* (St. Martin's, London, Apr. 1948); Sabina Pennant in *Young Wive's Tale* (Savoy, July 7, 1949); the title role in *Peter Pan* (Scala, Dec. 21, 1951); Noel Thorne in *The Uninvited Guest* (St. James, May 27, 1953); a Visitor in *The Moon and the Chimney* (Lyceum, Edinburgh, Scotland, Jan. 1955); Gillian Holroyd in *Bell, Book, and Candle* (Phoenix, London, Oct. 5, 1954); Mrs. Mallett in *Card of Identity* (Royal Court, June 26, 1956); the title role in *Lysistrata* (Royal Court, Dec. 27, 1957); Hattie in *The Grass Is Greener* (St. Martin's, Dec. 2, 1958); the title role in *Hedda Gabler* (Oxford Playhouse, Feb. 1960); Hedda in *The Irregular Verb To Love* (Criterion, London, Mar., 1961); played in *The Broken Heart* and Ilyena in *Uncle Vanya* (Chicester Festival Th., June 1952); and the title role in *Hedda Gabler* (St. Martin's, London, Feb. 12, 1964).

She played Olga Sergeyevna Ilyinska in *Oblomov* (New Lyric, Hammersmith, Oct. 6, 1964), repeating that role in the revised *Son of Oblomov* (Comedy, Dec. 2, 1964); was Valentina Ponti in *Those That Play the Clowns* (ANTA Th., N.Y.C., Nov. 24, 1966); Julia Sterroll in a revival of *Fallen Angels* (Vaudeville Th., London, Apr. 4, 1967); played the title role in a revival of *Candida* (Richmond Th., Richmond, England, 1968); Mrs. Rogers in *The Au Pair Man* (Duchess, London, Apr. 23, 1969); Lady Kitty in a revival of *The Circle* (New, Bromley, 1970); and Miss Madrigal in *The Chalk Garden* (Yvonne Arnaud, Guilford, Nov. 1970).

Films. Miss Greenwood made her debut in *My Wife's Family* (Powers, 1932); followed by appearances in *Kind Hearts and Coronets* (Elstree, 1950); *The Man in the White Suit* (U, 1952); *The Importance of Being Earnest* (U, 1952); *The Detective* (Col., 1954); *Moon Fleet* (MGM, 1955); *Stage Struck* (Buena Vista, 1958); *Mysterious Island* (Col., 1961); *Tom Jones* (UA, 1963); and *The Moon-Spinners* (Buena Vista, 1964).

Television. Miss Greenwood appeared in *The King and Mrs. Candle* (Philco Playhouse, NBC, 1954); was Violet Robinson in *Man and Superman* (Hallmark Hall of Fame, NBC, 1956); was on *Muses with Milligan* (BBC, London, England, 1964); in *The Reluctant Debutante* (ITV, 1966); *The Paper Chase* (Secret Agent, CBS, 1966); and played Aunt Frances in *The Moon-Spinners* (Walt Disney's World, NBC, 1966).

GREER, EDWARD G.

Director, acting teacher and coach drama critic. b. Edward Gabriel Greenberg, Apr. 10, 1920, Cambridge, Mass., to Louis H. and Mollie (Eisenman) Greenberg. Grad. Harvard Coll., B.A.; Yale Drama School. Served in US Army during WW II. Member of AEA; SSD&C; Actors Studio (Directors' Unit, 1960–65). Address: 175 W. 12th St., New York, NY 10011, tel. (212)

OR 5-5443.

Mr. Greer became assistant curator, Theatre Dept., Museum of Modern Art, N.Y.C., in 1944 and assistant professor in the Drama Dept., Syracuse (N.Y.) Univ. in 1974. He has also been an instructor in classic acting style, American Theatre Wing, and at English summer theatre school under the sponsorship of the Univ. of Washington; an instructor and director of the dramatic reading series, New School for Social Research, N.Y.C. (1954–56); and has lectured at Vassar Coll. and the Hammond Museum, North Salem, N.Y.

Theatre. Mr. Greer worked as a stage manager with the Chautauqua (N.Y.) Opera Co. (1944); directed *Music at Night* (U.S. premiere: Nat. Th. Conf. Tryout Studio, N.Y.C., Oct. 1948); summer stock at Martha's Vineyard, Mass., and Sayville, N.Y.; was director at the Hampton (N.H.) Playhouse (Summers 1949, 1950); directed *Murder in the Cathedral* (Equity Library Th., N.Y.C., 1950); *The Little Clay Cart* (Th. de Lys, June 30, 1953); *Dr. Faustus* (Equity Library Th., 1953); and directed a series of readings at the New School for Social Research, N.Y.C., which included such works as *Elektra* and *The Tempest* (both 1954) and *The Importance of Being Earnest.* He directed *Waters of the Moon* (Chanin Th., 1956); *All That Fall* (Carnegie Th., 1957); Christopher Marlowe's *Edward II* (ANTA Matinee Series, Th. de Lys); and, as director at Actors Playhouse, Boston, Mass. (Autumn–Winter 1962), directed *Gallows Humour* and *American Blues.*

He also directed *The Beaux Stratagem* (Equity Library Th., N.Y.C., Mar. 25, 1966); *She Stoops to Conquer* (Cubiculo Th., Mar. 1971); *A Flea in Her Ear* (Guignol Th., Univ. of Kentucky, Lexington, Ky., Apr. 1971); and he was English narrator for the appearances at NY City Ctr. of the Obraztsov Russian Puppet Th. (1963), the Moscow Art Th. (1965), and the Comédie Française (1966, 1970).

Other Activities. Mr. Greer is a theatre advisor, NY State Council on the Arts.

Published Works. Mr. Greer has been a contributor to the British theatre magazine *Drama* and has contributed the entry on NY theatre to the *Annual Register of World Events,* both since 1974.

Discography. Mr. Greer recorded *Language for Daily Use* and albums of poetry readings (Harcourt, Brace, 1965).

Awards. Mr. Greer was a Fulbright Fellow in England (1950–51), where he studied acting style from the Elizabethan period through the 18th century and was an assistant director at the Old Vic, London, and with companies in Bristol, Stratford-upon-Avon, Birmingham, Nottingham, and Liverpool.

Recreation. Theatre going, music, dance, collecting antique painting, sculpture, porcelain, and silver.

GREGORY, ANDRE.

Director, producer. Studied acting with Lee Strasberg. Member of Actors Studio, directors unit; Writers Stage Co. (founding mbr., 1961).

Mr. Gregory is artistic director (1970–to date) of The Manhattan Project, an experimental performing group based in N.Y.C., for whom he has directed *Alice in Wonderland* (The Extension, Oct. 8, 1970); *Endgame* (NY Univ., Feb. 2, 1973); *Our Late Night* (The Manhattan Proj. Th., Mar. 6, 1974); and *The Sea Gull* (Public/Martinson Hall, Apr. 29, 1975). The productions have been performed subsequently at various theatres in the NYC area.

Prior to his association with The Manhattan Project, Mr. Gregory was a stage manager at NY City Ctr. and the Phoenix Th., and manager of the American Th. at the Brussels World's Fair (1958). He subsequently co-produced *Deirdre of the Sorrows* (Gate, N.Y.C., 1959); with Sidney Bernstein and George Edgar, co-produced *The Blacks* (St. Mark's Playhouse, May 4, 1961); directed *P.S. 193* (Writers Stage, Oct. 30, 1962); and, as associate artistic director of the Seattle (Wash.) Repertory Th., directed *The Firebugs* (Nov. 14, 1963).

As artistic director of Th. of the Living Arts (Philadelphia, 1965–67), he staged productions of *Galileo* (Jan. 6, 1965); *Endgame* (May 26, 1965); *Uncle Vanya* (Feb. 8, 1966); *Beclech* (Dec. 20, 1966); and *Poor Bitos* (Feb. 8, 1966). On Bway, he directed *Leda Had a Little Swan* (closed after final preview, Cort Th., N.Y.C., Apr. 10, 1968).

Awards. Mr. Gregory received the *Village Voice* Off-Bway (Obie) Award special citation (1969–70), and the Drama Desk Award (1970–71) for *Alice in Wonderland.*.

GREGORY, JAMES.

Actor. b. Dec. 23, 1911, Bronx, N.Y., to James G. and Axemia T. (Ekdahl) Gregory. Father, railroad engineer. Grad. New Rochelle (N.Y.) H.S., 1930. Married May 25, 1944, to Anne C. Miltner. Served USN and USMC, 1942–45; PTO. Member of AEA; SAG; AFTRA; Society for the Preservation and Encouragement of Barber Shop Quartet Singing in America, Inc. Address: Screen Actors' Guild, 7750 W. Sunset Blvd., Los Angeles, CA 90046.

Pre-Theatre. Real estate, businessman, salesman, private secretary.

Theatre. Mr. Gregory made his first professional appearance in stock (Deer Lake, Pa., Summers 1936–37); at the Playhouse (Millbrook, N.Y., 1938); and the Mountain Th. (Braddock Hts., Md., 1939). His first N.Y.C. appearance was as Jerry in *Key Largo* (Ethel Barrymore Th., Nov. 27, 1939); subsequently played Festus in *Journey to Jerusalem* (Natl., Oct. 5, 1940); Officer Hanan in *Glamour Preferred* (Booth, Nov. 15, 1940); in stock at the Bucks County Playhouse (New Hope, Pa., Summer 1941); Dillan in *In Time To Come* (Mansfield, N.Y.C. Dec. 28, 1941); Frank in *Autumn Hill* (Booth, Apr. 13, 1942); a Policeman in *Dream Girl* (Coronet, Dec. 14, 1945); succeeded Karl Malden as George Deever in *All My Sons* (Coronet, Jan. 29, 1947); succeeded Arthur Kennedy as Biff in *Death of a Salesman* (Morosco, Feb. 10, 1949); appeared in stock at the Ivy Tower Th. (Spring Lake, N.J., Summers 1950–51); as Charlie in *Dinosaur Wharf* (Natl., N.Y.C., Nov. 8, 1951); Glenway Trent in *Collector's Item* (Booth, Feb. 8, 1952); Lt. Monahan in *Dead Pigeon* (Vanderbilt, Dec. 23, 1953); Lt. Col. Clyde Bartlett in *Fragile Fox* (Belasco, Sept. 12, 1954); and Jesse Bard in *The Desperate Hours* (Ethel Barrymore Th., Feb. 10, 1955).

Films. Mr. Gregory first performed in *Naked City* (U, 1948); subsequently appeared in *The Frogman* (20th-Fox, 1951); *The Scarlet Hour* (Par., 1956); the Investigator in *Nightfall* (Col., 1956); *Gun Glory* (MGM, 1957); *The Big Caper* (U, 1957); the Detective in *The Young Stranger* (RKO, 1957); the Lt. Comm. in *Underwater Warrior* (MGM, 1958); the Priest in *Hey Boy, Hey Girl* (Col., 1959); a Columnist in *Two Weeks in Another Town* (MGM, 1962); Senator Iselin in *The Manchurian Candidate* (UA, 1962); Comdr. Ritchie in *PT-109* (WB, 1962); Col. Pyser in *Captain Newman, M.D.* (UI, 1963); Norris Bixby in *Twilight of Honor* (MGM, 1963); Gen. Quait in *A Distant Trumpet* (WB, 1964); and the Admiral in *Quick, Before it Melts!* (MGM, 1964). He appeared also in four *Matt Helm* features; *X-15; Shootout; Beneath the Planet of the Apes* (20th-Fox); *The Million Dollar Duck* (Disney Prod.); *The Sons of Katie Elder* (Par., 1965); and *The Secret War of Harry Frigg* (U, 1968).

Television and Radio. On radio, Mr. Gregory played the Captain of Detectives for one year on 21st Precinct (CBS, 1955).

On television, he has appeared on major programs since 1948, including US Steel Hour (CBS); Studio One (CBS); Climax! (CBS); Kraft Television Th. (NBC); Goodyear Playhouse (NBC); Philco Television Playhouse (NBC); Suspense (CBS); Barney Riditsky in The Lawless Years (NBC, 1959–61); Danger (CBS); The Web (CBS); Alfred Hitchcock Presents (CBS); The Virginian (NBC); Wagon Train (NBC); Twilight Zone (CBS); Rawhide (CBS); Eleventh Hour (NBC); Sam Benedict (NBC); Ben Casey (ABC); Breaking Point (ABC); The Dick Powell Th. (NBC); The Defenders (CBS); Crime Syndicated (NBC); Police Story (ABC); Robert Montgomery Presents (NBC); You Are There (CBS); Alcoa Hour (NBC); Lamp Unto My Feet (CBS); The Billy Rose Show (ABC); Bonanza (NBC); Gunsmoke (CBS); Ironside (NBC); The F.B.I. (ABC); Police Story (NBC); McCloud; Columbo; Paul Lynde; Love, American Style; Big Valley; and Rawhide.

Recreation. Golf, barber shop quartet singing.

GREGORY, PAUL.

Producer, actor, talent representative. b. Jason Gregory Lenhart, Aug. 28, 1920, Waukee, Iowa, to James Clifford and Esther May (Taylor) Lenhart. Married 1966 to Janet Gaynor, actress. Father, farmer. Attended Drake Univ.

Pre-Theatre. Soda jerk.

Theatre. Mr. Gregory produced a tour of the Gilbert & Sullivan troupe (1945); Dennis Morgan and the Hollywood Presbyterian Church Choir (1946); served as head of the concert division of MCA (1947–48); and produced the tour of Charles Laughton readings (1948). He presented the First Drama Quartet in a concert reading of *Don Juan in Hell,* which played one performance at Carnegie Hall (N.Y.C., Oct. 22, 1951), and on Bway (New Century Th., Nov. 29, 1951; reopened Plymouth, Mar. 30, 1952), and toured. His next production was *John Brown's Body,* (Century, N.Y.C., Feb. 14, 1953), and on tour; followed by *The Caine Mutiny Court-Martial* (Plymouth, N.Y.C., Jan. 20, 1953), and on tour. He produced the touring *Elsa Lancaster's Private Music Hall* (1953). He produced the revue *3 for Tonight* (Plymouth, N.Y.C., Apr. 6, 1955), which later toured.

He produced *Foolin' Ourselves* (opened Santa Barbara, Calif., Jan. 4, 1957; closed Fresno, Calif., Jan. 20, 1957); with George Boroff, he presented *The Rivalry* (Orpheum, Seattle, Wash., Sept. 24, 1957); produced *The Marriage-Go-Round* (Plymouth, N.Y.C., Oct. 29, 1958), and on tour; and the pre-Bway tryout of *The Pink Jungle* (opened Alcazar, San Francisco, Calif., Oct. 14, 1959; closed Shubert, Boston, Mass., Dec. 12, 1959). His production of *The Captains and the Kings* was presented by Theatre Guild Productions, Inc., and Joel Schenker (Playhouse, N.Y.C., Jan. 2, 1962); with Amy Lynn, he produced *Lord Pengo* (Royale, Nov. 19, 1962) he produced the pre-Bway tryout of *Prescription: Murder* (opened Curran, San Francisco, Calif., Jan. 15, 1962; closed Shubert, Boston, Mass., May 26, 1962); and produced, in association with American Conservatory Theater, Judith Anderson in *Hamlet* (Carnegie Hall, N.Y.C., Jan. 14, 1971).

Films. Mr. Gregory appeared in *Sing a Jingle* (U, 1944), distributed *Hobson's Choice* (UA, 1954); with Charles Laughton, produced *The Night of the Hunter* (UA, 1955); and produced *The Naked and the Dead* (WB, 1958).

Television and Radio. He had his own radio program at age fourteen, entitled *The Carrier Salesman's Parade* (Des Moines, Iowa, KSO, 1934).

For television, he produced *The Caine Mutiny Court-Martial* (Ford Star Jubilee, CBS, Nov. 1955); *The Day Lincoln was Shot* (CBS, Feb. 11, 1956); and *Crescendo* (Dupont Show of the Month, CBS, Sept. 29, 1957).

Awards. His production of *Don Juan in Hell* received a special citation from the NY Drama Critics' Circle (1952); and his production of *The Caine Mutiny Court-Martial* received (1954) the Outer Circle Award. He was awarded the Alumni Distinguished Service Award from Drake Univ. (1959); and is an honorary member of Theta Alpha Phi.

GRENFELL, JOYCE.

Actress, lyricist, writer. b. Joyce Irene Phipps, Feb. 10, 1910, London, England, to Paul and Nora (Langhorne) Phipps. Father, architect. Married Dec. 12, 1929, to Reginald Pascoe Grenfell, chartered accountant, company director. Entertained troops in hospital wards and isolated units throughout northern Africa, Near and Middle East, 1943–45. Relatives in theatre: brother, Thomas Phipps, playwright; cousin, Nicholas Phipps, writer, actor. Member of AFTRA; AEA; Performing Rights Society; Society of Women Writers and Journalists (past pres.). Address: c/o Christopher Mann Ltd., 140 Park Lane, London, S.W,1, England tel. May 8444.

Pre-Theatre. Journalist, poetess.

Theatre. Miss Grenfell made her London debut performing her own monologues in *The Little Revue* (Little, Apr. 21, 1939); subsequently performed in the revues *Diversion* (Wyndham's, Oct. 28, 1940); *Diversion No. 2* (Wyndham's, Jan. 2, 1941); and joined (Aug. 1942) the revue *Light and Shade* (Ambassadors', July 29, 1942).

She performed in *Sigh No More* (Piccadilly, Aug. 22, 1945); *Tuppence Coloured* (Lyric, Hammersmith, Sept. 4, 1947); *Penny Plain* (St. Martin's, June 28, 1951); wrote and appeared in *Joyce Grenfell Requests the Pleasure . . .* (Fortune, June 2, 1954), and repeated her performance in N.Y.C. (Bijou, Oct. 10, 1955); and toured the US and Canada in *Joyce Grenfell Bids You Good Evening,* which she also wrote (1956).

She presented a series of monologues and songs, *Joyce Grenfell* (Lyric, Hammersmith, London, Oct. 8, 1957), which she repeated in N.Y.C. (Lyceum, Apr. 7, 1958) and on tour of the US and Canada (1958–60).

She performed in *Joyce Grenfell Bids You Good Evening* (Phillip St. Th., Sydney, Australia, July –Oct. 1959); again toured the US and Canada in *Joyce Grenfell* (Apr. 1960) and played a return engagement at the Haymarket (London, 1962); toured the principal cities of Australia in *An Evening with Joyce Grenfell* (Aug.–Oct. 1963); and has continued to tour, performing her one-woman shows, playing in Australia, New Zealand, Singapore, and Hong Kong (1963–64); Canada and Switzerland (1964); in London (Queen's, Mar. 23, 1965); Australia (1966); Great Britain (1965, 1967, 1968, 1970); etc.

Many of Miss Grenfell's lyrics have been set to music by Richard Addinsell.

Films. She has appeared in *The Lamp Still Burns* (Two Cities, 1943); *The Demi-Paradise* (Two Cities, 1943); *While the Sun Shines* (Assoc. Brit., 1947); *A Run for Your Money* (Ealing, 1949); *Stage Fright* (WB, 1950); *The Happiest Days of Your Life* (Brit. Lion, 1950); *The Magic Box* (Brit. Lion, 1951); *Laughter in Paradise* (Assoc. Brit., 1951); *The Galloping Major* (Ind. Film Dist., 1951); *The Pickwick Papers* (Renown, 1952); *Genevieve* (U, 1954); *The Belles of St. Trinian's* (Brit. Lion, 1954); *Man With a Million* (UA, 1954); *Blue Murder at St. Trinian's* (Cont., 1958); *Happy is the Bride* (Kossler, 1959); *The Pure Hell of St. Trinian's* (Brit. Lion, 1960); *The Old Dark House* (Col., 1963); *The Americanization of Emily* (MGM, 1964); and *The Yellow Rolls-Royce* (MGM, 1965).

Television and Radio. Miss Grenfell has frequently performed monologues on BBC radio (1939–to date); for television, wrote (with Stephen Potter) the How series (1946–63); appeared on the team of We Beg To Differ (1949); and in the US, has appeared on the Ed Sullivan Show (CBS, 1955–56); and on Fest. of the Performing Arts (1963).

Other Activities. She was a member of the Pilkington Committee (1960–62), which made a survey of radio and television broadcasting in the British Isles.

Awards. She received the Order of the British Empire (O.B.E.) in 1946, in recognition of her services for the armed forces during WW II.

Recreation. Tennis, bird watching, music, sewing, sketching.

GREY, JOEL. Actor. b. Apr. 11, 1932, Cleveland, Ohio, to Mr. and Mrs. Mickey Katz. Father, comedian. Attended Cleveland (Ohio) Playhouse, Neighborhood Playhouse, N.Y.C. Married to Jo Wilder; two children.

Theatre. As a child, Mr. Grey traveled with his father as a stand-up comic, and song and dance man, appearing in New York in *Borscht Capades* (Royale, Sept. 17, 1951). He made his off-Bway debut in *The Littlest Revue* (Phoenix, May 22, 1956); subsequently succeeded Warren Berlinger as Buddy Baker in *Come Blow Your Horn* (opened Brooks Atkinson Th., Feb. 22, 1961); played Little Chap in the national company of *Stop the World-I Want to Get Off* (opened Pabst, Milwaukee, Wis., Mar. 25, 1963; closed Forrest, Philadelphia, Apr. 18, 1964); during vacation, replaced Tommy Steele in the role of Arthur Kipps in *Half a Sixpence* (Broadhurst, N.Y.C., Apr. 25, 1965); appeared in *Harry, Noon and Night* (American Place Th., Mar. 12, 1965); played the Master of Ceremonies in *Cabaret* (Broadhurst, Nov. 20, 1966); George M. Cohan in *George M!* (Palace, Apr. 10, 1967; and national tour, opened Curran, San Francisco, May 8, 1969); and the Dauphin of France in *Goodtime Charley* (Palace, Mar. 3, 1975).

Films. He recreated the role of the Master of Ceremonies in *Cabaret* (AA, 1972); and played Franklin Willis in *Man on a Swing* (Par., 1974).

Television. Mr. Grey played George M. Cohan in the televised version of the Bway musical *George M!* (1970). Other appearances include the Dean Martin Show (NBC); Lawman (Ind.); Vacation Playhouse (CBS); the Tonight Show (NBC); the Mike Douglas Show (ABC); the Today Show (NBC); Password (CBS); What's My Line? (CBS); Our Place (CBS); and The Carol Burnett Show (CBS).

Awards. For his performance in *Cabaret,* Mr. Grey received the Antoinette Perry (Tony) Award (1967), first place in the NY Drama Critics Poll (1967), and, for the film version, the Academy Award for best supporting actor (1973).

GRIBBLE, HARRY WAGSTAFF. Playwright, actor, director, producer. b. Harry Wagstaff Graham Gribble, Mar. 27, 1896, Sevenoaks, Kent, England, to Theodore Graham and Mary Amelia (Soltau) Gribble. Father, construction engineer. Attended Clarence Sch., Weston Super Mare, England, Emmanuel Coll., Cambridge, 1910–12. Served with A.E.F., 1917–18.

Theatre. Mr. Gribble first appeared on the stage professionally in *Ann* (Coronet, London); later, with the Benson Players, he toured England; with H. B. and Laurence Irving, he appeared at Stratford-upon-Avon; and toured with a company in South Africa.

He was stage manager for Mrs. Patrick Campbell's production of *Pygmalion* (Park, N.Y.C., Oct. 12, 1914), which also toured the U.S. He succeeded Arthur Chesney as Sam Tomlin in *Quinneys* (Maxine Elliott's Th., N.Y.C., Oct. 18, 1915), and on tour (opened Auditorium, Baltimore, Md., Apr. 24, 1916). In the service, he directed an army musical, *You Know Me, Al* (Lexington, N.Y.C., Apr. 11, 1918); wrote, with William A. Halloran, the book and lyrics for *Let's Beat It* (Century, Mar. 24, 1919); wrote *The Outrageous Mrs. Palmer* (39 St. Th., Oct. 12, 1920); wrote and directed *The Temperamentalists* (Neighborhood Club, Bklyn., June 30, 1921), which was produced under the title, *March Hares* (Bijou, N.Y.C., Aug. 11, 1921); and wrote and directed *Shoot!* (Macdowall Gallery, June 14, 1922).

With M. Francis Weldon (choreographer), he directed the revue *Artists and Models,* to which he also contributed sketches (Shubert, Aug. 20, 1923); He wrote, with Harold Atteridge, *The Courtesan;* and the revue *Topics of 1923* (Broadhurst, Nov. 20, 1923).

Mr. Gribble played Eumenes, a Poet in *Tyrants* (Cherry Lane, Mar. 4, 1924); wrote the revue *Artists and Models of 1924* (Astor, Oct. 15, 1924); adapted, with Wilton Lackaye, the farce *Oh Mama,* from the French original of Louis Verneuil (Playhouse, Aug. 19, 1925); compiled and directed *Cherry Pie* (Cherry Lane, Apr. 14, 1926); directed *Loud Speaker* (52 St. Th., Mar. 2, 1927); wrote, with Wallace A. Manheimer, *Mister Romeo* (Wallack's, Sept. 5, 1927); his play, *March Hares,* was revived (Little, Apr. 2, 1928); wrote and directed *Revolt* (Vanderbilt, Oct. 31, 1928); co-produced and directed *After Dark* (Rialto, Hoboken, N.J., Dec. 1928); and directed *The Black Crook* (Lyric, Hoboken, N.J., 1929).

He directed *Houseparty* (Knickerbocker, N.Y.C., Sept. 9, 1929); *City Haul* (Hudson, Dec. 30, 1929); adapted, from three seventeenth and eighteenth century plays, *The Royal Virgin,* which he also directed (Booth, Mar. 17, 1930); directed *The Last Enemy* (Shubert, Oct. 30, 1930); adapted, from the German original, the book for the musical, *Meet My Sister* (Shubert, Dec. 30, 1930); directed *The Silent Witness* (Morosco, Mar. 23, 1931); *Old Man Murphy,* which he also wrote, with Patrick Kearney (Royale, May 18, 1931), and the return engagement (Hudson, Sept. 14, 1931); directed *Cynara* (Morosco, Nov. 2, 1931); *Trick for Trick,* which he wrote with Vivian Crosby and Shirley Warde (Sam H. Harris Th., Feb. 18, 1932); directed and adapted the second version of the pre-Bway tryout of *A Trip to Pressburg* (opened Chestnut St. Opera House, Philadelphia, Pa., Mar. 6, 1933; closed Locust St. Th., Philadelphia, 1933); and directed *No More Ladies* (Booth, Jan. 23, 1934), and its return engagement (Morosco, Sept. 3, 1934).

Mr. Gribble wrote and directed *The Perfumed Lady* (Ambassador, Mar. 12, 1934); directed *Living Dangerously* (Morosco, Jan. 12, 1935); *The Simpleton of the Unexpected Isles* (Guild, Feb. 18, 1935); staged the summer tryout of *If This Be Treason* (Westport Country Playhouse, Conn., Summer 1935), and the Bway production (Music Box, Sept. 23, 1935); *The Taming of the Shrew* (Guild, Sept. 30, 1935); *There's Wisdom in Women* (Cort, Oct. 30, 1935); *Mainly for Lovers* (48 St. Th., Feb. 21, 1936); and in stock, *Fanny's First Play* (Westport Country Playhouse, Conn., Summer 1936).

He directed *The Golden Journey* (Booth, Sept. 15, 1936); *Aged 26* (Lyceum, Dec. 21, 1936); *There's Always a Breeze* (Windsor, Mar. 2, 1938); *The Man from Cairo* (Broadhurst, May 4, 1938); the pre-Bway tryout of *Angela is 22* (opened Columbus, Ohio, 1939); in stock appeared in and directed *Easy Virtue* (Summer 1939); directed *Billy Draws a Horse* (Playhouse, N.Y.C., Dec. 21, 1939); managed the Ted Shawn Dance Co. (Philadelphia, Pa., Jan. 1940); and directed a special production of *The Taming of the Shrew* (Alvin, N.Y.C., Feb. 5, 1940).

He produced and directed *Johnny Belinda* (Belasco, Sept. 18, 1940); directed *All Men Are Alike* (Hudson, Oct. 6, 1941); wrote and directed *Almost Faithful* (Clinton Playhouse, Conn., Aug. 22, 1942); and, with Frank W. Delmar, wrote and directed *Twelve Midnight* (Scarsdale, N.Y., 1942); directed, for the American Negro Th., *Anna Lucasta* (135 St. Library Th., N.Y.C., June 8, 1944), on Bway (Mansfield, Aug. 30, 1944), in Chicago (Civic Th., Sept. 1945), and again on Bway (National, Sept. 22, 1947).

He wrote, directed, and co-produced the pre-Bway tour of *A Lady Passing Fair* (opened Lyric Th., Bridgeport, Conn., Jan. 3, 1947; closed Newark Opera House, N.J., Jan. 11, 1947); wrote with James Proctor, *Ride the Right Bus* (Harlem, N.Y.C., 1952); and appeared in *The Thorntons* (Provincetown Playhouse, Feb. 14, 1956).

Films. Mr. Gribble first appeared in *Nellie's Ride* (1913). He wrote the screen play for *A Bill of Divorcement* (RKO, 1932) and *Silent Witness* (Fox, 1932); was co-director of *Madame Racketeer* (Par., 1932); and was a screen writer for *Trick for Treat* (Fox, 1933), *Our Betters* (RKO, 1933), and *Nana* (UA, 1934).

GRIFFIES, ETHEL. Actress. b. Apr. 26, 1878, Sheffield, Yorkshire, England, to Samuel Rupert and Lillie (Roberts) Woods. Father, actor; mother, actress. Attended George Green Coll. Married Dec. 1899 to Walter Beaumont (dec. 1910); married June 1914 to Edward Cooper (dec. 1956). Member of British AEA; SAG; AFTRA. Address: 19 Craven Hill, London, W.2. 3EN, England.

Theatre. Miss Griffies made her stage debut as a child, appearing as Willie Carlyle in *East Lynne* (Whitehaven, Eng., Feb. 1881); subsequently toured England in *Love and Honour;* made her London debut as Alice in *Uncles and Aunts* (Great Queen St. Th., Nov. 4, 1901); toured as Zelie in *The Orchard,* Saavedra in *The School Girl,* and the Colonel's wife in *Lady Madcap* (1903–06); toured with Alan Wilkie's Shakespearean Repertory Co. (1911); played Viola in *Twelfth Night* (Queen's Th., Manchester, Eng., 1912); toured as Sophia Fulgarney in *The Gay Lord Quex* (1912); with the Manchester Repertory Co., played in *The Last of the DeMullins* and *Mrs. Dane's Defense* (Gaiety Th., Manchester,

1913); toured as Paula in *The Second Mrs. Tanqueray* (Aug. 1913–Dec. 1914); played Miss Parker in *Postal Orders* (Haymarket, London, 1916); during WW I, entertained the troops, appearing in plays and skits; played Emilia in *Othello* (Scala, London, Nov. 17, 1919); Lady Marden in *Mr. Pim Passes By* (New, Jan. 5, 1920); Mrs. Mendham in *The Wonderful Visit* (St. Martin's, Feb. 10, 1921); Virginia Grayling in *Trespasses* (Ambassadors', Apr. 16, 1923); Lady Highkno *Our Ostriches* (Court, Nov. 14, 1923); and Alice Derring in *Havoc* (Haymarket, London, Jan. 16, 1924).

Miss Griffies first appeared in the US as Alice Derring in *Havoc* (Maxine Elliott's Th., N.Y.C., Sept. 1, 1924); subsequently played Adela Heythrop in *Old English* (Ritz, Dec. 23, 1924); Sarah Britt in a touring company of *Loose Ends* (1925–26); Mrs. Bewley in *Mariners* (Plymouth, N.Y.C., Mar. 28, 1927); succeeded (May 1927) Elizabeth Risdon as Mrs. Higgins in *Pygmalion* (Guild, Nov. 15, 1926); played Mrs. Barme in *Interference* (Empire, Oct. 18, 1927), and during the run of this play, appeared as Charlotte in special matinees of *The Cherry Orchard* (Bijou, Mar. 5, 1928); portrayed Volumnia Dedlock in *Lady Dedlock* (Ambassadors', Dec. 31, 1928); Miss Brady in *The Criminal Code* (Natl., Oct. 2, 1929); and Frau Lucher in *Reunion in Vienna* (Curran Th., San Francisco, Calif., 1932–33).

She portrayed Mrs. Branson in *Night Must Fall* (Cambridge, London, July 9, 1936); Dona Mercedes in a touring company of *Matador* (Mar.–May, 1937); with the Shakespeare Memorial Th. (Stratford-upon-Avon, 1938), played the Nurse in *Romeo and Juliet*, the Abbess in *The Comedy of Errors*, and Lady Macduff in *Macbeth;* toured the US as Mrs. Danvers in *Rebecca* (Aug. 1945–Jan. 1946); played Mrs. White in *The Druid Circle* (Morosco, N.Y.C., Oct. 22, 1947); Mrs. Hallam in *The Hallams* (Booth, Mar. 4, 1948); Mrs. Gilson in *The Leading Lady* (Natl., Oct. 18, 1948); Mathilde Heiss in *The Shop at Sly Corner* (Booth, Jan. 18, 1949); the Countess in *Miss Liberty* (Imperial, July 15, 1949); Clementine Pinney in *Legend of Sarah* (Fulton, Oct. 11, 1950); Fanny Cavendish in *The Royal Family* (NY City Ctr., Jan. 10, 1951), and also at the Ann Arbor (Mich.) Drama Festival (Lydia Mendelssohn Th., Summer 1951); played Mrs. Mary Ellis in *The Autumn Garden* (Coronet, N.Y.C., Mar. 7, 1951); played Flora Van Huysen in a tour of *The Matchmaker* (Shubert, Detroit, Mich., Feb. 4, 1957); an Old Lady in *Who's Your Father?* (Cambridge, Dec. 16, 1958); Florence Boothroyd in *Billy Liar* (Cambridge, Sept. 13, 1960); and Dr. Elizabeth Wolley in *Write Me a Murder* (Belasco, N.Y.C., Oct. 26, 1961), a role that she repeated at the Ogunquit (Me.) Playhouse (July 2, 1962). She again played the role of Florence Boothroyd in an Off-Bway production of *Billy Liar* (Gate, Mar. 17, 1965); was Mae in *A Very Rich Woman* (Belasco Th., Sept. 30, 1965); Avdotya Nazarovna in *Ivanov* (Sam S. Shubert Th., May 3, 1966); and the Countess in *The Natural Look* (Longacre, Mar. 11, 1967).

Films. Miss Griffies appeared in silent films in England during the 1920's; in the US, played Adela Heythrop in *Old English* (WB, 1930); appeared in *The Millionaire* (WB, 1931); *Chances* (1st Natl., 1931); *Stepdaughters* (Par., 1931); *Road to Singapore* (WB, 1931); *Waterloo Bridge* (U, 1931); *Once a Lady* (Par., 1931); *Manhattan Parade* (WB, 1932); *Union Depot* (1st Natl., 1932); *Lovers Courageous* (MGM, 1932); *Impatient Maiden* (U, 1932); *Are You Listening?* (MGM, 1932); *Devil's Lottery* (20th-Fox, 1932); *Westward Passage* (RKO, 1932); *Love Me Tonight* (Par., 1932); *Payment Deferred* (MGM, 1932); *Ladies of the Evening* (Par., 1932); *One Forgotten* (Par., 1932); *Tonight Is Ours* (Par., 1933); *Midnight Club* (Par., 1933); *The Good Companions* (20th-Fox, 1933); *Looking Forward* (MGM, 1933); *Doctor Bull* (20th-Fox, 1933); *Torch Singer* (Par., 1933); *Bombshell* (MGM, 1933); *White Woman* (Par., 1933); *Horse Play* (U, 1933); *Alice in Wonderland* (Par., 1933); *Olsen's Big Moment* (20th-Fox, 1934); *Fog* (Col., 1934); *Four Frightened People* (Par. 1934); *House of Rothschild* (UA, 1935); *Bulldog Drummond Strikes Back* (UA, 1934); *Sadie McKee* (MGM, 1934); *Call It Luck* (20th-Fox, 1934); *Jane Eyre* (Mono., 1934); *Of Human Bondage* (RKO, 1934); *We Live Again* (UA, 1934); *Painted Veil* (MGM, 1934); *Edwin Drood* (U, 1934); *Enchanted April* (RKO, 1935); *Vanessa, Her Love Story* (MGM, 1935); *Hold 'Em Yale* (Par., 1935); *Werewolf of London* (U, 1935); *Anna Karenina* (MGM, 1935); and *The Return of Peter Grimm* (RKO, 1935).

Also *Twice Branded* (Twickenham, 1935) *Guilty Malody* (Shepherds Bush, 1935); *Mr. Davies* (Shepherds Bush, 1935); *Not So Dusty* (Twickenham, 1935); *Kathleen Mavourneen* (Garden City, 1935); *Man of Many Faces* (Elstree, 1935); *A Yank at Oxford* (MGM, 1938); *Missouri* (Par., 1939); *The Star Maker* (Par., 1939); *We Are Not Alone* (WB, 1939); *Vigil in the Night* (RKO, 1940); *Over the Moon* (UA, 1940); *Irene* (RKO, 1940); *Waterloo Bridge* (MGM, 1940); *Anne of Windy Poplars* (RKO, 1940); *Stranger on the Third Floor* (RKO, 1940); *Dead Men Tell* (20th-Fox, 1941); *Wings of Destiny* (1st Natl., 1941); *Billy the Kid* (MGM, 1941); *A Yank in the RAF* (20th-Fox, 1941); *Man at Large* (20th-Fox, 1941); *Great Guns* (20th-Fox, 1941); *How Green Was My Valley* (20th-Fox, 1941); *The Postman Didn't Ring* (20th-Fox, 1942); *Castle in the Desert* (20th-Fox, 1942); *Son of Fury* (20th-Fox, 1942); *Right to the Heart* (20th-Fox, 1942); *Mrs. Wiggs of the Cabbage Patch* (Par., 1942); *Between Us Girls* (U, 1942); *Changing Years* (RKO, 1942); *First Comes Courage* (Col., 1943); *Tomorrow* (Gen. Ser., 1943); *Holy Matrimony* (20th-Fox, 1943); *Jane Eyre* (20th-Fox, 1944); *The White Cliffs of Dover* (MGM, 1944); *Canterville Ghost* (MGM, 1944); *Keys to the Kingdom* (20th-Fox, 1944); *Music for Millions* (MGM, 1944); *Horn Blows at Midnight* (WB, 1945); *Thrill of a Romance* (MGM, 1945); *Molly and Me* (20th-Fox, 1945); *The Strange Affair of Uncle Harry* (U, 1945); *Devotion* (WB, 1946); *Forever Amber* (20th-Fox, 1947); *Home Stretch* (20th-Fox, 1947); *Millie's Daughter* (Col., 1947); *Brasher Doubloon* (20th-Fox, 1947); *Billy Liar* (Shepperton, Eng., 1962); *The Birds* (U, 1963); *Bed of Roses* (U, 1965); and *Bus Riley Comes to Town* (U, 1965).

Television. Miss Griffies appeared as Mrs. Bramson in *Night Must Fall* (BBC, London, July 1936); and the Grandmother in *Don't Shake the Family Tree* (Theatre Guild, US, 1963). From 1965 to 1967, she appeared as a guest on many Merv Griffin television shorts (Little Th., N.Y.C.).

Recreation. Reading, sewing, painting.

GRIFFITH, HUGH. Actor. b. Hugh Emrys Griffith, May 30, 1912, Marian Glas, Anglesey, North Wales, Great Britain, to William and Mary (Williams) Griffith. Father, Dir. of Education, Anglesey. Attended Llangefni Grammar Sch., 1922–39; RADA (Leverhulme Scholarship; Bancroft Gold Medal). Married 1947 to Adelgunde Margaret Beatrice Von Dechend. Served 1st Battillion, Royal Welsh Fusiliers, British Army (CBI) 1940–46. Member of British AEA; AFTRA; SAG. Stage Golfing Soc., Garrick Club. Address: London International, 11-12 Hanover St., Park St., London W.1, England.

Pre-Theatre. Banking.

Theatre. Mr. Griffith made his U.S. debut as The Father in *Legend of Lovers* (English title, *Point of Departure*) (Plymouth, Dec. 26, 1951); and appeared as W.O. Gant in *Look Homeward, Angel* (Ethel Barrymore Th., Nov. 28, 1957).

He made his stage debut in London as Jimmy Farrell in *The Playboy of the Western World* (Mercury, Jan. 27, 1939); subsequently played Rev. Dan Price in *Rhonda Roundabout* (Globe, May 31, 1939); Shawn Keogh in *The Playboy of the Western World* (Duchess, Oct. 24, 1939); Marullus Poplius, Lina, and Lepidus in a modern dress version of *Julius Caesar* (Embassy, Nov. 1939); and toured in *The Millionairess* (1940), prior to its London opening.

He joined (1946) the Memorial Theatre Company at Stratford-upon-Avon (Eng.), playing Trinculo in *The Tempest*, Holofernes in *Love's Labour's Lost;* the King of France in *Henry V;* Touchstone in *As You Like It*, the First Witch in *Macbeth;* and Mephistopheles in *Dr. Faustus;* appeared as old Wilmot in *Fatal Curiosity* (Arts, London, Dec. 5, 1946); Cardinal Monticelso in *The White Devil* (Duchess, Mar. 6, 1947); the Senator in *The Respectable Prostitute* (Lyric Hammersmith, July 17, 1947); Rev. John Williams in *A Comedy of Good and Evil* (Arts, Feb. 11, 1948); Old Mahon in *The Playboy of the Western World* (Mercury, Apr. 1948); and Nicia in Macciavelli's *Mandragola* (Mercury, Jan. 24, 1949); at the Swansea Festival, played the title role in *King Lear* (Grand, Oct. 1949); toured as Thomas Cranmer in *The White Falcon* and Ulric Brendel in *Rosmersholm* (Jan. 1950); played The Father in *Point of Departure* (Lyric-Hammersmith, London, Nov. 1, 1950); and at Stratford-upon-Avon (1951); played Glendower in *Henry IV, Part I;* John of Gaunt in *Richard II;* and Caliban in *The Tempest.*

He played Andrew Deeson in *Escapade* (St. James's, London, Jan. 20, 1953); Belmann in *The Dark Is Light Enough* (Aldwych, Apr. 30, 1954); General St. Pe in *The Waltz of the Toreadors* (Arts, Feb. 24, 1956); Count Cenci in *The Cenci* (Old Vic, Apr. 24, 1959); Azdak in *The Caucasian Chalk Circle* (Aldwych, Mar. 29, 1962); the Teacher in *Andorra* (Biltmore, N.Y.C., Feb. 9, 1963); and Sir John Falstaff in *Henry IV, Part I & II* (Royal Shakespeare Th., Stratford-upon-Avon).

Films. Since his debut in *Neutral Port* (Shepheard Bush, 1939), Mr. Griffith has appeared in *The Three Weird Sisters* (BN, 1947); *The First Gentleman* (Col., 1948); *London Belongs to Me* (GFD, 1948); *So Evil of Dolwyn* (1949); *Kind Hearts and Coronets* (Eagle Lion, 1950); *Dr. Morellte* (1949); *Gone To Earth* (1950), released in US as *The Wild Heart* (RKO, 1952); *A Run for Your Money* (U, 1948); *The Galloping Major* (SUV, 1951); *Laughter in Paradise* (ABC, 1950); *The Titfield Thunderbolt* (U, 1952); *The Beggar's Opera* (WB, 1953); *The Sleeping Tiger* (Astor, 1954); *Passage Home* (Elstree, 1955); *Good Companions* (ABC, 1958); *Lucky Jim* (Kingsley Intl., 1958); *Ben Hur* (MGM, 1959); *The Story on Page One* (20th-Fox, 1959); *Exodus* (UA, 1962); *The Day They Robbed the Bank of England* (MGM, 1960); *The Counterfeit Traitor* (Par., 1962); *The Inspection* (MGM, 1962); *Mutiny on the Bounty* (MGM, 1962); *Term of Trial* (WB, 1963); *The Bargee* (ABC, 1963); *Tom Jones* (Lopert, 1963); *Hide and Seek* (U, 1964); *The Amorous Adventures of Moll Flanders* (Par., 1965); *How to Steal a Million* (20th-Fox, 1966); *Oh Dad, Poor Dad . .* (Par., 1967); *The Sailor from Gibralter* (Lopert, 1967); *Dr. Dolittle* (20th-Fox, 1967); *The Chastity Belt* (WB, 1968); *The Fixer* (MGM, 1968); *Oliver* (Col., 1968); *On My Way to the Crusades I Met a Girl Wha . .* (WB, 1969); *Start the Revolution without Me* (WB, 1970); *The Abominable Dr. Phibes* (Amer. Internatl., 1971); and *Dr. Phibes Rides Again* (Amer., Internatl., 1972).

Television. He made his debut in England (BBC, 1938); in the US, appeared in *Ah, Sweet Mystery of Mrs. Murphy* (Omnibus, NBC, Mar. 1, 1959); played General St. Pé in *The Waltz of the Toreadors* (Play of the Week, WNTA, Nov. 16, 1959); performed in *The Citadel* (General Mills, ABC, Feb. 19, 1960); *Treasure Island* (DuPont Show of the Month, CBS, Mar. 5, 1960; *The Poppy Is Also a Flower* (ABC, Apr. 22, 1966); and *Dare I Weep, Dare I Mourn* (Stage 67, ABC, Sept. 21, 1967).

Awards. Mr. Griffith received the Clarence Derwent Award (1951) for his performance as The Father in *Point of Departure* (*Legend of Lovers*); an Academy (Oscar) Award for best supporting actor and the National Board of Review Award for his performance in *Ben Hur* (1959); and was nominated for an Academy (Oscar) Award (1964) as best supporting actor for his performance as Squire Western in *Tom Jones.* The Univ. of Wales awarded him an honorary D.Litt.

Recreation. Writing in Welsh and English, painting, and small farming.

GRIMES, TAMMY. Actress. b. Jan. 30, 1934, Lynn, Mass. Father, hotel manager. Grad. Beaver Country Day Sch., Boston, Mass.; attended Stephens Jr. Coll.; The Neighborhood Playhouse Sch. of the Th. Married 1956, to Christopher Plummer, actor (marr. dis.); one daughter. Relative in theatre: brother, Nichols Grimes, actor. Member of AEA; AFTRA.

Theatre. Miss Grimes made her N.Y.C. debut as a two-week replacement for Kim Stanley in the role of Cherie in *Bus Stop* (Music Box Th., Mar. 2, 1955); followed by the title role in the pre-Bway tryout of *The Amazing Adele* (opened Shubert, Philadelphia, Pa., Dec. 26, 1955; closed Shubert, Boston, Mass., Jan. 21, 1956).

She appeared in *The Littlest Revue* (Phoenix, N.Y.C., May 22, 1956); toured as Agnes Sorel in *The Lark* (opened Central City Opera House, Colo., Aug. 4, 1956); played the Flounder in *Clerambard* (Rooftop, N.Y.C., Nov. 7, 1957); Mopsa in *The Winter's Tale* and Mistress Quickly in *Henry IV, Part 1* (Stratford Shakespearean Festival Co., Ont., Can., June 1958); Lulu in *Look After Lulu* (Henry Miller's Th., N.Y.C., Mar. 3, 1959); Moll in *The Cradle Will Rock* (NY City Ctr., Feb. 11, 1960); Molly Tobin in *The Unsinkable Molly Brown* (Winter Garden, Nov. 3, 1960), and on tour (opened Bushnell Memorial Aud., Hartford, Conn., Feb. 13, 1962); Cyrenne in *Rattle of a Simple Man* (Booth, N.Y.C., Apr. 17, 1963); and Elivira in *High Spirits* (Alvin, Apr. 7, 1964).

Miss Grimes played Cyrenne in *Rattle of a Simple Man* (Coconut Grove Playhouse, Miami, Fla., May 18, 1965; Huntington Hartford Th., Los Angeles, Calif., May 25, 1965); Doreen in *The Private Ear* and Belinda in *The Public Eye* on tour (Summer 1965); Sharon McLonergan in *Finian's Rainbow* (Hyatt Music Th., Burlingame, Calif., July 27, 1965); Ruth Arnold in *The Warm Peninsula* (Royal Poinciana Playhouse, Palm Beach, Fla., Feb. 28, 1966); at the request of Pres. and Mrs. Lyndon B. Johnson, entertained at the White House (Washington, D.C., Jan. 26, 1966); appeared in Ben Bagley's *The Decline and Fall of the Entire World As Seen Through the Eyes of Cole Porter* (Huntington Hartford Th., Apr. 17, 1967); played Fran Walker in *The Only Game in Town* (Broadhurst, N.Y.C., May 23, 1968); Amanda Prynne in *Private Lives* (Billy Rose Th., Dec. 4, 1969); with the Philadelphia Drama Guild appeared in *The Imaginary Invalid* (1971–72) and played Katherine in *The Taming of the Shrew* (1973–74); and appeared in *A Musical Jubilee* (St. James Th., N.Y.C., Nov. 13, 1975).

Films. Miss Grimes played Miss Sparrow in *Three Bites of the Apple* (MGM, 1967); and appeared in *Play It as It Lays* (U, 1972).

Television. Miss Grimes appeared in *Forty-five Minutes from Broadway* (Omnibus, CBS); *archy and mehitable* (The Play of the Week, WNTA); *Four for Tonight; Holly Sings; The Datchet Diamonds; The Fourposter;* and performed on the Ed Sullivan Show (CBS), Andy Williams Show (NBC), The Virginians (NBC), The Garry Moore Show (CBS); Celebrity Game (CBS); Mr. Broadway (CBS); To Tell the Truth (CBS); Trials of O'Brien (CBS); The Dan Martin Show (NBC); The Danny Kaye Show (CBS); Hollywood Palace; played Tammy Ward on The Tammy Grimes Show (ABC): and appeared on the Gypsy Rose Lee Show (ABC); Dateline: Hollywood (ABC); Tarzan (NBC); The Las Vegas Show (Ind.); The Pat Boone Show (NBC); The Smothers Brothers Show (CBS); Everybody's Talking (ABC); The Outcasts (ABC); *The Other Man* (NBC); and Love, American Style (ABC).

Night Clubs. She appeared at the Downstairs-at-the-Upstairs (N.Y.C.) and Caesar's Palace (Las Vegas).

Discography. Miss Grimes has recorded *Tammy Grimes* (Col.), and *The Unmistakable Tammy Grimes* (Col.).

Awards. For her performance in *The Unsinkable Molly Brown,* Miss Grimes received The Antoinette Perry (Tony) Award (1960), the *Variety* Drama Critics (1961) and the Comaedia Matinee Club (1961) awards; and, for *Private Lives,* the Antoinette Perry (Tony) Award (1970).

GRINER, BARBARA. Producer, theatre owner. b. Barbara Helen Bankoff, Mar. 27, 1934, New York City, to Sydney and Jessie Bankoff. Father, inspector with N.Y.C. Dept. of Welfare. Grad. Abraham Lincoln H.S., Brooklyn, N.Y., 1951; Brooklyn Coll., B.A. 1955; Columbia Univ., M.F.A. 1956. Married Sept. 1, 1954, to Norman Griner, photographer, designer. Relative in theatre: Cousin, Jane Friedlander, producer. Member of League of Off-Bway Theatres (membership comm.); Natl. Speech and Hearing Assn.; Natl. Educational Th. Assn. Address: (home) 312 W. 76th St., New York, NY 10023, tel. (212) TR 7-2299; (bus.) 35 W. 53rd St., New York, NY 10019, tel. (212) LT 1-3410.

Theatre. Miss Griner served as production assistant for *Look Back in Anger* (Lyceum, N.Y.C., Oct. 1, 1957); was associated with Chelsea Productions in the production of *Look Back in Anger* (41 St. Th., Nov. 11, 1958); was a general manager for *Mark Twain Tonight!* (41 St. Th., Apr. 6, 1959); associate producer of *The Deadly Game* (Longacre, Feb. 2, 1960); and, in association with Morton Segal and Gene Andrewski, produced *Valmouth* (York, Oct. 6, 1960). In 1961, she presented with Eleanor Horn a series of plays under the title *The Summer Comedy Festival* (41 St. Th.): *The Voice of the Turtle* (June 27), *Susan Slept Here* (July 11), *The Little Hut* (July 25), *The Moon is Blue* (Aug. 8), and *The Tender Trap* (Aug. 25).

She served as general manager for the *Automobile Graveyard* (41 St. Th., Nov. 13, 1961), and *Poppa Is Home* (Gate, Dec. 1961); in association with Michael P. Santangelo and Eric Franke, produced *Black Nativity* (41 St. Th., Dec. 11, 1961), and later presentations of the work at the Festival of Two Worlds (Spoleto, It., June 21, 1962), in London (Criterion, Aug. 14, 1962), on tour in England and Europe, a return engagement in N.Y.C. (Philharmonic Hall, Lincoln Center), and again in Europe.

Miss Griner has been the owner of the 41 St. Th., N.Y.C.

Television. She produced *Black Nativity* (Westinghouse Th., CBS, July 19, 1962).

Awards. *Black Nativity* received the Silver Dove Award for the best television show (1962), and, in London, the Critics Award for Best Musical (1963).

GRIZZARD, GEORGE. Actor. b. George Cooper Grizzard, Jr., Apr. 1, 1928, Roanoke Rapids, N.C., to George Cooper and Mary Winifred (Albritton) Grizzard. Father, accountant. Grad. Woodrow Wilson H.S., Washington, D.C., 1945; Univ. of North Carolina, B.A. 1949. Studied acting with Sanford Meisner and Phillip Burton. Member of AEA; SAG; AFTRA. Address: New Preston, CT 06777.

Pre-Theatre. Advertising account executive.

Theatre. Mr. Grizzard made his first stage appearance as a Miner in *The Corn Is Green* (June 1945), and Raymond Pringle in *Kiss and Tell* (Aug. 1945) at the Crossroads Th. (Bailey's Crossroads, Va.).

From Jan. 1952–June 1954, he was a member of the resident company at the Arena Stage (Washington, D.C.), he played Sam Bean in *The Delectable Judge* (Oct. 1950); Biondello in *The Taming of the Shrew* (Nov. 1950); the White Rabbit in *Alice in Wonderland* (Dec. 1950); Rowley in *The School for Scandal* (Jan. 1952); Harry in *Three Men on a Horse* (Feb. 1952); Witch Boy in *Dark of the Moon* (Apr. 1952); Yank in *The Hasty Heart* (June 1952); Eben in *Desire Under the Elms* (Oct. 1952); and Don in *All Summer Long* (Jan. 13, 1952). He appeared in stock (Hyde Park Playhouse, N.Y., Summer 1954).

He was understudy to John Kerr in the role of Don in *All Summer Long* (Coronet Th., N.Y.C., Sept. 23, 1954); subsequently appeared as Hank Griffin in *The Desperate Hours* (Ethel Barrymore Th., Feb. 10, 1955); Angier Duke in *The Happiest Millionaire* (Lyceum, Nov. 20, 1956), which he played for the natl. tour (opened Playhouse, Wilmington, Del., Oct. 2, 1957; closed Tower, Atlanta, Ga., May 17, 1958); Shep Stearns in *The Disenchanted* (Coronet, Dec. 3, 1958); and, in stock, he played Claudio in *Much Ado About Nothing* (Th. on the Green, Wellesley, Mass., June 1959).

He appeared as Harold Rutland, Jr., in *Face of a Hero* (Eugene O'Neill Th., N.Y.C., Oct. 20, 1960); Ronnie Johnson in *Big Fish, Little Fish* (ANTA, Mar. 15, 1961).

With the Association of Producing Artists in repertory at the Folksbiene Th., N.Y.C., he played the Vagabond in *The Tavern* (Apr. 4, 1962), and Joseph Surface in *The School for Scandal* (Mar. 17, 1962). He appeared as Nick in *Who's Afraid of Virginia Woolf?* (Billy Rose Th., Oct. 13, 1962).

At the Tyrone Guthrie Th. (Minneapolis, Minn.), he appeared in the title role in *Hamlet* (May 7, 1963); as the Clerk in *The Miser* (May 8, 1963); as Captain Solyony in *Three Sisters* (June 18, 1963); in the title role in *Henry V* (May 11, 1964); Dauphin in *St. Joan* (May 12, 1964); and as Mosca in *Volpone* (June 29, 1964).

He played the role of Tom in a revival of *The Glass Menagerie* (Brooks Atkinson Th., N.Y.C., May 4, 1965); was Alceste in *The Misanthrope* (Univ. of Chicago, Feb. 1966); took the title role in *Stephen D* (Olney, Md., Aug. 1966); and in *Cyrano de Bergerac* (Studio Arena, Buffalo, N.Y., Oct. 6, 1966). He played Jack Barnstable in *The Shock of Recognition,* the Salesman in *The Footsteps of Doves,* and Herbert in *I'm Herbert,* all given under the title *You Know I Can't Hear You When the Water's Running* (Ambassador, Mar. 13, 1967); appeared in the musical revue *Noel Coward's Sweet Potato* (Ethel Barrymore Th., Sept. 29, 1968); and was Vincent in *The Gingham Dog* (Golden Th., Apr. 23, 1969). He appeared as Julius Rosenberg in *Inquest* (Music Box Th., Apr. 23, 1970); Bernie Dodd in a revival of *The Country Girl* (Billy Rose Th., Mar. 15, 1972); Lucifer in *The Creation of the World and Other Business* (Shubert Th., Nov. 30, 1972); and Edward VIII in *Crown Matrimonial* (Helen Hayes Th., Oct. 2, 1973).

Films. Mr. Grizzard played Lex Porter in *From the Terrace* (20th-Fox, 1960); Senator Van Ackerman in *Advise and Consent* (Col., 1962); and was in *Warning Shot* (Par., 1967); and *Happy Birthday, Wanda June* (Col., 1971).

Television. Mr. Grizzard made his first appearance as the piano player in Casey, Crime Photographer (CBS, 1951); and, since 1956, has appeared on dramatic shows on major networks.

Awards. He won the *Variety* Drama Critics Poll for his role as Hank Griffin in *Desperate Hours* (1955); the *Theatre World* Award for his role as Angier Duke in *The Happiest Millionaire* (1956); received nominations for the Antoinette Perry (Tony) Award for his role as Shep Stearns in *The Disenchanted* (1958); and Ronnie Johnson in *Big Fish, Little Fish* (1960); and received the Kit Kat Award for his performance as Nick in *Who's Afraid of Virginia Woolf?* (1962).

GRODIN, CHARLES. Actor, director, playwright, screenwriter. b. Apr. 21, 1935, Pittsburgh, Pa., to Ted and Lana Grodin. Grad. Peabody H.S., Pittsburgh, Pa., 1953; attended Univ. of Miami, 1953; grad. Pittsburgh Playhouse Sch., 1956; and studied acting with Lee Strasberg (three years) and Uta Hagen (three years), N.Y.C. Married to Julia — (marr. dis.); one daughter. Member of AEA; SAG; AFTRA.

Theatre. Mr. Grodin made his Bway debut as Robert Pickett in *Tchin-Tchin* (Plymouth, N.Y.C., Oct. 25, 1962); played Perry Littlewood in *Absence of a Cello* (Ambassador, Sept. 21, 1964); wrote the book (with Maurice Teitelbaum) and lyrics (with Ethel Bieber and Mr. Teitelbaum) for, and directed *Hooray! It's a Glorious Day. . .And All That* (Th. Four, May 9, 1966); directed *Lovers and Other Strangers* (Brooks Atkinson Th., Sept. 18, 1968); produced, with Richard Scanga, and directed *Thieves* (Broadhurst, Apr. 7, 1974); and played George in *Same Time, Next Year* (Brooks Atkinson Th., Mar. 13, 1975).

Mr. Grodin wrote *One of the All Time Greats,* which had a stock tryout (Tappan Zee Playhouse, Nyack, N.Y., May 1972).

Films. He played Dr. Hill, the young obstetrician, in *Rosemary's Baby* (Par., 1968); Aardvark in *Catch-22* (Par., 1970); the title role in *The Heartbreak Kid* (20th-Fox, 1972); and Chesser in *11 Harrowhouse* (20th-Fox, 1974), which he adapted from the novel of the same name.

Television. Mr. Grodin has appeared on The Defenders (CBS); Camera Three (CBS); Armstrong Circle Th. (NBC); The Nurses (CBS); My True Story; Love of Life (CBS); *Black Monday* (Play of the Week, WNTA, Jan. 16, 1961); Trials of O'Brien (CBS); and *Autumn Garden* (Sunday Showcase, May 1966). He directed the Simon and Garfunkel special *Songs of America* (Nov. 30, 1969), and the Marlo Thomas special *Acts of Love and Other Comedies* (ABC, Mar. 16, 1973); and briefly wrote and directed the Candid Camera show.

Awards. He won (1975) an Outer Critics Circle Award for *Same Time, Next Year;* and won (1973) a Golden Globe Award for his role in the film *The Heartbreak Kid.*.

GROSBARD, ULU. Director, producer. b. Israel ("Ulu") Grosbard, Jan. 9, 1929, Antwerp, Belgium, to Morris and Rose (Tennenbaum) Grosbard. Father, diamond dealer. Emigrated to US in 1948; became naturalized citizen, 1954. Grad. Univ. of Chicago, B.A. 1950; M.A. 1952; attended Yale Univ. Sch. of Drama, 1952-53. Studied with Lee Strasberg, Actors Studio, N.Y.C. (mem. of Directors Unit, 1961–to date). Married Feb. 24, 1965, to Rose Gregorio, actress. Served US Army Intelligence, 1953–55; rank, Pfc. Member of SSD&C; DGA; Dramatists Guild.

Pre-Theatre. Diamond cutter, language teacher.

Theatre. During the summers of 1957, 1958, Mr. Grosbard directed at the Gateway Th. (Bellport, L.I., N.Y.). With Judith Marechal, he produced *The Days and Nights of Beebee Fenstermaker* (Sheridan Sq. Playhouse, N.Y.C., Sept. 17, 1962), which he also directed.

Mr. Grosbard's first Bway assignment was to direct *The Subject Was Roses* (Royale, May 25, 1964); subsequently he directed and was one of the producers of the revised version of *A View From the Bridge* (Sheridan Sq. Playhouse, Jan. 28, 1965); directed the national touring production of *The Subject Was Roses* (opened Huntington Hartford Th., Los Angeles, Sept. 13, 1965; closed Forrest, Philadelphia, June 25, 1966); was co-author and director of the English language version of *The Investigation* (Ambassador, N.Y.C., Oct. 4, 1966); directed *That Summer- That Fall* (Helen Hayes Th., Mar. 16, 1967); directed *The Price* (Morosco, Feb. 7, 1968).

Films. Mr. Grosbard was assistant director for NY locations on *Splendor in the Grass* (WB, 1961); *West Side Story,* (UA, 1961); *The Hustler* (20th-Fox, 1961); and *The Miracle Worker* (UA, 1962); and unit manager for *The Pawnbroker* (AA-Landau, 1965).

He directed *The Subject Was Roses* (MGM, 1968); and directed and co-produced *Who is Harry Kellerman and Why is He Saying All Those Terrible Things About Me?* (Nat. Gen., 1971).

Television. Mr. Grosbard was production manager for the series, Deadline (1959-60); directed the *Far Rockaway* segment of the *Lincoln Center- New York City* special (Educ., Sept. 24, 1965); and adapted and co-directed *The Investigation* (NBC, Apr. 14, 1967).

Awards. For his direction of *A View From the Bridge,* he received a *Village Voice* Off-Bway (Obie) Award, a Vernon Rice Award, and a Drama Desk Award (1965).

Recreation. Swimming, chess.

GROSS, JESSE. Executive, theater reporter. b. Joshua Gross, June 27, 1929, Brooklyn, N.Y., to Isaac and Sophie (Kass) Gross. Grad. Erasmus Hall H.S., Brooklyn, 1947. Married Apr. 27, 1962, to Elissa Baer, *Variety* subscription manager, (marr. dis.); married May 1, 1969, to Elena Lanin. Served US Army, Military Govt., ETO, 1951–52; rank, Cpl. American Theatre Society, 226 W. 47th St., New York, NY 10036, tel. (212) 765-2950.

Mr. Gross serves as Administrator to the Amer. Th. Society, where he began as associate manager in 1965. Until his resignation (Sept. 27, 1965) from the staff of *Variety,* he was a theatre reviewer-reporter covering off-Bway (from 1949), and Bway (from 1953), having joined that publication as a part-time copy boy (1946).

GROSS, SHELLY. Producer, theatre executive. b. Sheldon H. Gross, May 20, 1921, Philadelphia, Pa., to Samuel and Anna R. Gross. Father, physician; mother, teacher. Grad. Central H.S., Philadelphia, 1938; Univ. of Pennsylvania, A.B. (Phi Beta Kappa) 1942; Northwestern Univ., M.S.J. 1947. Married May 1, 1946, to Joan Seidel; three sons. Served USN, 1942–46; rank, Lt. Member of MATA (bd. of dir., 1962–63); YMHA, Philadelphia (bd. of dir., 1962–to date); Sigma Delta Chi.

Theatre. In 1955, with Frank Ford and Lee Guber, Mr. Gross founded Music Fair Enterprises, Inc., of which he is president, which owns, operates, and produces musicals and artists-in-concert for seven summer theatres including Valley Forge Music Fair (Devon, Pa., 1955–to date); Westbury (L.I., N.Y.) Music Fair (1956–to date); Camden County Music Fair (Haddonfield, N.J., 1957–to date); Storrowton Music Fair (West Springfield, Mass., 1959–to date); Painters Mill Music Fair (Owings Mills, Md., 1960–to date); Shady Grove Music Fair (Gaithersburg, Md., 1962–to date); and the John B. Kelly Playhouse-in-the-Park (Philadelphia, Pa., 1964–to date).

Messrs. Guber, Ford and Gross co-produced national bus and truck tours of *Li'l Abner* (opened Riviera Hotel, Las Vegas, Sept. 1, 1958; closed Royal Alexandra, Toronto, Canada, Jan. 3, 1959); *The Pleasure of His Company* (opened Rochester, N.Y., Aud., Sept. 15, 1960; closed Shubert, New Haven, Mar. 25, 1961); *The Andersonville Trial* (opened Center Th., Norfolk, Va., Sept. 28, 1960; closed Community Ctr., Hershey, Pa., Apr. 15, 1961); *A Thurber Carnival* (opened Center Th., Norfolk, Va., Sept. 22, 1961; closed Music Hall, Kansas City, Mo., Apr. 28, 1962); and, by arrangement with David Merrick, *Carnival!* (opened Bushnell Aud., Hartford, Conn., Oct. 18, 1962; closed Shubert, Boston, May 11, 1963).

On Bway, Messrs. Guber, Ford and Gross co-produced *Catch Me If You Can* (Morosco, Mar. 9, 1965); and *Sherry!* (Alvin, Mar. 28, 1967). With Mr. Guber, Mr. Gross subsequently produced, by arrangement with Bruno Coquatrix, *The Grand Music Hall of Israel* (Palace, Feb. 6, 1968); the national tour of *Mame* (opened Bushnell, Hartford, Conn., Sept. 25, 1969; closed Fisher, Detroit, May 13, 1970); *Inquest* (Music Box, N.Y.C., Apr. 23, 1970); and the pre-Bway tour of *Lorelei* (opened Civic Ctr. Music Hall, Oklahoma City, Feb. 26, 1973), which was revised and retitled *Lorelei, or "Gentlemen Still Prefer Blondes"* (Palace, N.Y.C., Jan. 27, 1974). With Joseph Harris, Messrs. Guber and Gross produced *Charles Aznavour on Broadway* (Minskoff, Oct. 15, 1974); and *Tony Bennett and Lena Horne Sing* (Minskoff, Oct. 30, 1974).

In a management-programming arrangement with NY City Ctr. (1976), Messrs. Guber and Gross, under the aegis of Music Fair Concerts, Inc., have presented *The Monty Python Show* (Apr. 12, 1976) and the Pennsylvania Ballet (June 15, 1976); with other limited-engagement presentations to include the revue *A Man and a Woman,* starring Isaac Hayes and Dionne Warwick, the Newport Jazz Festival and *Peter Pan.*.

Other Activities. Under the Music Fair Enterprises banner, Messrs. Guber and Gross operate the Amer. Wax Museum in Independence Hall (Philadelphia) and have had their own advertising agency. In 1971, they obtained the franchise for the closed-circuit telecast of the Joe Frazier-Muhammed Ali heavyweight championship fight for showing in their summer theatres.

GROSSVOGEL, DAVID. Educator, writer, editor. b. July 19, 1925, San Francisco, Calif. Grad. Univ. of California at Berkeley, B.A. 1949; Columbia Univ., M.A. 1951; Ph.D. 1954. Married Apr. 4, 1953, to Anita Vidossoni (marr. dis. 1973); one son, one daughter. Served USAAF, 1943–46. Address: Cornell Univ., Ithaca, NY 14850, tel. (607) 275-4264.

Mr. Grossvogel joined the faculty of Columbia Univ. in 1952, Harvard Univ. in 1956, and, in 1960, Cornell Univ., where he is Goldwin Smith Professor of Comparative Literature and Romance Studies. He is the founder and editor of *Diacritics: A Journal of Contemporary Criticism* (1971–to date).

Published Works. He is author of *The Self-Conscious Stage in Modern French Drama* (1958); reprinted in paperback as *Twentieth Century French Drama* (1961); *Jean Anouilh: Antigone* (1961), *Four Playwrights and a Postscript: Brecht, Ionesco, Beckett, Genet* (1962); *The Graves of Academe* (1963); *Limits of the Novel* (1968); and *Divided We Stand* (1970).

GROVER, STANLEY. Actor, singer. b. Stanley Grover Nienstedt, Mar. 28, 1926, Woodstock, Ill., to Harry B. and Maude (Grover) Nienstedt. Father, insurance broker. Grad. Woodstock Community H.S., 1944; Univ. of Missouri, A.B. 1949; attended Roosevelt Univ., 1949–50. Studied with John Daggett Howell, Chicago and N.Y.C., 1949. Married Apr. 7, 1956, to Linda Glavey, govt. secy. (marr. dis. Feb. 28, 1974); two sons, one daughter. Served USNR, PTO, June 1944–June 1945; NROTC, Univ. of Missouri, Sept. 1945–June 1946. Member of AEA; SAG; AFTRA; AGVA; Phi Mu Alpha Sinfonia (natl. hon. music fraternity). Address: 325 Central Park West, New York, NY 10025, tel. (212) MO 3-9046.

Pre-Theatre. NBC page boy at Chicago Studios (Summer 1943); vocational counsellor; farm laborer; furniture factory worker.

Theatre. Mr. Grover sang in college productions; and played in stock (Shady Lane Playhouse, Marengo, Ill., Summer 1949). He made his N.Y.C. debut in the chorus of *Seventeen* (Broadhurst, June 21, 1951); played Fred and was an understudy in *Wish You Were Here* (Imperial, June 25, 1952); succeeded Robert Whitlow as Lt. Cable in the first national tour of *South Pacific* (opened Shubert, Chicago, Ill., Nov. 14, 1950); in stock played Woody in *Finian's Rainbow* (Starlight Th., Kansas City, Mo., 1955); in 1956, Caliph in *Kismet* (Valley Forge Music Fair, Devon, Pa.), Peter in *Plain and Fancy* (Lambertville Music Circus, N.J.); Chick in *Wish You Were Here* (Chicago Melody Top, Ill.; Camden County Fair, N.J.); understudied the title role in *Candide* (Martin Beck Th., N.Y.C., Dec. 1, 1956); played the Singer in *Time Remembered* (Morosco, Nov. 12, 1957); in stock, appeared as Marius in *Fanny* (South Shore Music Circus, Cohasset, Mass., 1958); in 1959, Tommy in *Brigadoon* (Chautauqua, N.Y.), and Curly in *Oklahoma!* (San Juan, P.R.), Fred in *Wish You Were Here* (North Shore Music Th., Beverly, Mass.; and Albany, N.Y.), Peter in *Plain and Fancy* (Meadowbrook Dinner Th., Cedar Grove, N.J.); in 1960, Caliph in *Kismet* (Meadowbrook Dinner Th.), and toured as Jack in *Where's Charley?*

He appeared as Willoughby in *13 Daughters* (54 St. Th., N.Y.C., Mar. 2, 1961); Lt. Cable in *South Pacific* (NY City Ctr., Apr. 26, 1961); appeared in *Tribute to Oscar Hammerstein* (46 St. Th.); in stock, played Chick in *Wish You Were Here* (Cape Cod Melody Tent, Hyannis, Mass., 1961); Carver in *Let It Ride* (Eugene O'Neill Th., N.Y.C., Oct. 12, 1961); in stock, toured as Tommy in *Brigadoon* (Summer 1962); played Lt. Cable in *South Pacific* (Anaheim, Calif., July 1962); played Charley Wayne in *Mr. President* (St. James, N.Y.C., Oct. 20, 1962); in stock, in 1963, played Red Shadow in *Desert Song* (Cape Cod Melody Tent, Hyannis, Mass.), and Tony in *West Side Story* (Casa Mañana, Fort Worth, Tex.); played Woody in *Finian's Rainbow* (Casa Mañana, Fort Worth, Tex., Summer 1964); Tommy in *Brigadoon* (Tenthouse Th., Highland Park, Ill., Summer 1965); Tony in *West Side Story* (Beverly, Cohasset, and Hyannis, Mass., Summer 1965); Spofford in *Gentlemen Prefer Blondes* and Sid in *Pajama Game* (on the music fair circuit—Baltimore, Md.; Washington, D.C.; Westbury, N.Y.; Camden, N.J.; Valley Forge, Pa.; West Springfield, Mass.—Summer 1966); Woody in a revival of *Finian's Rainbow* (NY City Ctr., Apr. 5, 1967); Oscar in *Sweet Charity* and Eddie in *Do I Hear a Waltz?* (Warren, Columbus, and Dayton, Ohio, Summer 1967); Luntha in *The King and I* (NY City Ctr., May 23, 1968); Dr. Taylor in *Allegro* (Goodspeed Opera House, East Haddam, Conn., July 1968); Michael in *I Do! I Do!* (Woodstock Playhouse, Woodstock,

N.Y., Summer 1969); replaced (Mar. 29, 1971) Charles Braswell as Larry in *Company* (Alvin Th., N.Y.C., Apr. 26, 1970); and played Paul in a revival of *Desert Song* (pre-Bway tour; Kennedy Ctr., Washington, D.C.; Uris Th., N.Y.C., 1973).

Television. Mr. Grover was a radio commentator from the ship the S.S. Liberté (1952); on television, he was a winning contestant on Arthur Godfrey's Talent Scouts (CBS, 1950); appeared on the Mike Wallace Show (ABC, 1952); was a winner on the talent show, Chance (1955–56); appeared on the Libby Show (San Juan, P.R., 1955, 1956); Music for a Summer Night (ABC, 1959); and The Good Years (CBS Special, 1961). He was on That Was the Week That Was (NBC, 1964); played Dr. Kevin Reid on Edge of Night (CBS, 1971); Lt. Bernie Green on Love Is a Many Splendored Thing (CBS); Mark Mercer on *Somerset* (NBC, 1974); and has appeared on various other daytime television serials.

Night Clubs. His first single act was at the Missouri Athletic Club (1948); was a singer and emcee at Chez Paree (Chicago, Ill., 1950–51); emcee for a variety show for President Truman (Washington, D.C., 1952); appeared at such hotels as the Caribe Hilton (San Juan, P.R., 1955–56); Number 1 Fifth Ave. (N.Y.C., 1955, 1956, 1959), and the Queen Elizabeth Hotel (Montreal, Quebec, Canada, 1959).

Discography. Mr. Grover's recordings include the *Reader's Digest*-RCA albums *Treasury of Great Operettas* (N.Y.C., 1962) and *All-Time Broadway Hit Parade* (London, Eng., Oct. 1965).

Recreation. Swimming, water skiing, maps and geography, traveling, his children.

GRUNDMAN, CLARE. Composer, arranger. b. Clare Ewing Grundman, May 11, 1913, Cleveland, Ohio, to Fred William and Leah (Grace) Grundman. Father, draftsman. Grad. Shaw H.S. East Cleveland, Ohio, 1930; Ohio State Univ., B.S. in Ed. 1934, M.A. in Mus. 1939. Studied composition with Paul Hindemith, Tanglewood, Mass. (Summer 1941). Served US Coast Guard Chief Musician, 1942–45. Member of AFM, Local 802; ASCAP; Phi Mu Alpha; Kappa Kappa Psi. Address: Route 2, Box 346, South Salem, NY 10590, tel. (914) SO 3-3485.

Pre-Theatre. Mr. Grundman was an instructor in orchestration, woodwinds, and bands, and was a member of the Music Dept. faculty, Ohio State Univ. (1937–41). Music teacher.

Theatre. Mr. Grundman orchestrated the music for *Lend an Ear* (Natl., N.Y.C., Dec. 16, 1948), and was conductor for the tour (1949–50); *Two's Company* (Alvin, Dec. 15, 1952); orchestrated, with Ralph Burns, *Phoenix '55* (Phoenix, Apr. 23, 1955); orchestrated *Joyce Grenfell Requests the Pleasure. . .* (Bijou, Oct. 10, 1955); the *Hollywood Ice Revue* (Tour, 1955); *Copper and Brass* (Martin Beck Th., N.Y.C., Oct. 17, 1957); Jerome Robbin's *Ballets, U.S.A.* (ANTA, Oct. 8, 1961); and *Show Girl* (Eugene O'Neill Th., Jan. 12, 1961). He did some orchestrations for *Drat! The Cat!* (Martin Beck Th., Oct. 10, 1965); *Coco* (Mark Hellinger Th., Dec. 18, 1969); and *Mass* (world premiere, John F. Kennedy Center, Washington, D.C., Sept. 8, 1971).

Films. He composed original music and orchestrated for *Sportscopes* and *This is America* (RKO Pathé News, 1946–51).

Television and Radio. Mr. Grundman was arranger and composer for various radio programs originating from N.Y.C., including Helen Hayes Th. (CBS, 1941–42); Treasury Salutes programs (NBC, 1945); Sound-Off (NBC, 1946); The Clock (NBC, 1946–47); Treasury Agent (ABC, 1948–49); Candid Microphone (ABC, 1950–51); and Mr. and Mrs. North (CBS, 1950).

For television, he did arrangements for the Ford 50th Anniversary Show (CBS, 1953); Caesar's Hour (NBC, 1954–57); 45 Minutes from Broadway (NBC, 1959); and the Telephone Hour (NBC, 1960).

Night Clubs. Mr. Grundman arranged the music for *The Roaring 20's Revue* (N.Y.C., 1950).

Published Works. Mr. Grundman has composed "American Folk Rhapsody 1" (1948); "Suite for Symphonic Band" (Little March, second movement, 1949); "A Walking Tune" (1949); "March Processional" (1950); "Bagatelle" (1950); "The Blue-Tail Fly" (1951); "The Green Domino" (1951); "Fantasy on American Sailing Songs" (1952); "American Scene" (1952); "Westchester Overture" (1952); "Two Sketches" (1953); "Midnight Beguine" (1953); "Three Songs for Christmas" (1953); "Kentucky 1800" (1955); "Black Knight" (1956); "Music for a Carnival" (1957); "Little Suite for Band" (1957); "American Folk Rhapsody 2" (1959); "Quiet Christmas" (1959); "Pipe Dream" (1960); "Caprice for Clarinets" (1961); "Blue and Gray" (1961); "Hebrides Suite" (1962); "Harlequin" (1962); "Hay-up Hoe-down" (1963); "Señor, Señor" (1963); "Chessboard Suite" (1964); "Spirit of '76" (1964); "Diversian" (1964); "A Medieval Story"(1966); "Three Carols for Christmas" (1965); "Burlesque for Band" (1966); "English Suite" (1968); "Little English Suite" (1968); "Western Dance" (1968); "Dance and Interlude" (1968); "Three Sketches for Winds" (1968); "A Welsh Rhapsody" (1968); "Japanese Rhapsody" (1969); "Three Noels" (1969); "American Folk Rhapsody 3" (1970); "Irish Rhapsody" (1971); "March: Winds" (1971); "Festive Piece" (1972); "Puppets" (1971); "A Classical Overture" (1972); "Concertante" (1973); and "Zoo Illogical" (1974).

Recreation. Golf, bridge, chess.

GUARE, JOHN. Playwright. b. Feb. 5, 1938, New York City, to Eddie and Mrs. (Grady) Guare. Attended St. Joan of Arc Elem. Sch., Jackson Heights, N.Y.; St. John's Prep. Sch., Brooklyn, N.Y.; grad. Georgetown Univ., A.B. 1960; Yale Univ. Sch. of Drama, M.F.A. 1963. Member of Dramatists Guild (council). Address: 105 Bank St., New York, NY 10014, tel. (212) 242-5841.

Theatre. Mr. Guare wrote *Did You Write My Name in the Snow?* (Yale Univ., New Haven, Conn., 1962); *To Wally Pantoni, We Leave a Credenza* (New Dramatists Comm. Workshop, N.Y.C., 1964); the one-act plays *The Loveliest Afternoon of the Year* and *Something I'll Tell You Tuesday* (Caffe Cino, Oct. 1966); the one-act play *Muzeeka*, first produced in Los Angeles (Mark Taper Forum, Fall 1967), and later, with Sam Shepard's one-act play, *Red Cross* (Provincetown Playhouse, N.Y.C., Apr. 28, 1968), and in London, with Geoffrey Bush's *The Fun War* (Open Space, Feb. 23, 1969); wrote the one-act plays *Cop-Out* and *Home Fires* (Cort, N.Y.C., Apr. 7, 1969), and *A Day for Surprises* (Basement Th., London, Oct. 18, 1971, on a double-bill with Arrabal's *Impossible Loves).*

He wrote and created the music and lyrics for *The House of Blue Leaves* (Truck and Warehouse Th., N.Y.C., Feb. 10, 1971); wrote the lyrics and, with Mel Shapiro, the libretto (based on Shakespeare's play) for the musical *Two Gentlemen of Verona* (NY Shakespeare Fest., Delacorte Th., July 22, 1971; moved to St. James, Dec. 1, 1971; revived NY Shakespeare Fest. Mobile Th., July 31, 1973; Phoenix, London, Apr. 26, 1973); wrote *Marco Polo Sings a Solo* (Cyrus Pierce Th., Nantucket, Mass., Aug. 1973); for the Natl. Th. of the Deaf, wrote a second act introduction to *Optimism, or The Adventures of Candide* (premiere, Eugene O'Neill Foundation Th., Waterford, Conn., Sept. 1973); and wrote *Rich and Famous* (NY Shakespeare Fest., Newman Th., N.Y.C., Feb. 19, 1976).

In 1966, Mr. Guare was invited to become a member of the Eugene O'Neill Mem. Th. Playwrights' Conference, where *The House of Blue Leaves* (1966), *Muzeeka* (1967), and *Cop-Out* (1968) had their first readings.

Films. He wrote, with Milos Forman, Jean-Claude Carriere, and John Klein, the screenplay for *Taking Off* (U, 1971).

Television. Mr. Guare wrote *Kissing Sweet*, one of ten short plays about pollution, together entitled *Foul!* (NY Television Th., WNET, Nov. 25, 1969).

Awards. For *Muzeeka*, Mr. Guare received (1968) a *Village Voice* Off-Bway (Obie) Award; for *Cop-Out*, he won (1969) the *Variety* Poll of NY Drama Critics Award as most promising playwright; for *The House of Blue Leaves*, he won (1971) an Obie for best play, the NY Drama Critics Circle Award for best American play, and an Outer Critics Circle Award; and for *Two Gentlemen of Verona*, he won (1972) Antoinette Perry (Tony) awards for best musical and best book for a musical, the NY Drama Critics Circle Award for best musical, Drama Desk awards for both lyrics and book, and the *Variety* Poll of NY Drama Critics Award as best lyricist.

GUBER, LEE. Producer, theatre executive. b. Leon M. Guber, Nov. 20, 1920, Philadelphia, Pa., to Jack and Elizabeth (Goldberg) Guber. Father, motel operator, realtor. Grad. Central H.S., Philadelphia, 1938; Temple Univ., B.S. 1942, M.A. 1949; attended Univ. of Michigan, 1953; Univ. of Pennsylvania, 1952–55. Studied directing at the Amer. Theatre Wing, N.Y.C., 1957; film production at the New Sch. for Social Research, N.Y.C., 1962. Served WW II, US Army, PTO; rank, 1st Lt.; awarded Battle Star. Married Dec. 8, 1963, to Barbara Walters, television reporter and newscaster (marr. dis. Mar. 23, 1976); one daughter. Member of League of N.Y. Theatres; MATA.

Pre-Theatre. Night club owner, research assistant.

Theatre. In 1955, with Frank Ford and Shelly Gross, Mr. Guber founded Music Fair Enterprises, Inc., of which he is vice-president, which owns, operates and produces musicals and artists-in-concert for seven summer theatres including Valley Forge Music Fair (Devon, Pa., 1955–to date); Westbury (L.I., N.Y.) Music Fair (1956–to date); Camden County Music Fair (Haddonfield, N.J., 1957–to date); Storrowton Music Fair (West Springfield, Mass., 1959–to date); Painters Mill Music Fair (Owings Mills, Md., 1960–to date); Shady Grove Music Fair (Gaithersburg, Md., 1962–to date); and the John B. Kelly Playhouse-in-the-Park (Philadelphia, Pa., 1964–to date).

Messrs. Guber, Ford and Gross co-produced national bus and truck tours of *Li'l Abner* (opened Riviera Hotel, Las Vegas, Sept. 1, 1958; closed Royal Alexandra, Toronto, Canada, Jan. 3, 1959); *The Pleasure of His Company* (opened Rochester, N.Y., Aud., Sept. 15, 1960; closed Shubert, New Haven, Mar. 25, 1961); *The Andersonville Trial* (opened Center Th., Norfolk, Va., Sept. 28, 1960; closed Community Ctr., Hershey, Pa., Apr. 15, 1961); *A Thurber Carnival* (opened Center Th., Norfolk, Va., Sept. 22, 1961; closed Music Hall, Kansas City, Mo., Apr. 28, 1962); and, by arrangement with David Merrick, *Carnival!* (opened Bushnell Aud., Hartford, Conn., Oct. 18, 1962; closed Shubert, Boston, May 11, 1963).

On Bway, Messrs. Guber, Ford and Gross co-produced *Catch Me If You Can* (Morosco, Mar. 9, 1965); and *Sherry!* (Alvin, Mar. 28, 1967). With Mr. Gross, Mr. Guber subsequently produced, by arrangement with Bruno Coquatrix, *The Grand Music Hall of Israel* (Palace, Feb. 6, 1968); the national tour of *Mame* (opened Bushnell, Hartford, Conn., Sept. 25, 1969; closed Fisher, Detroit, May 13, 1970); *Inquest* (Music Box, N.Y.C., Apr. 23, 1970); and the pre-Bway tour of *Lorelei* (opened Civic Ctr. Music Hall, Oklahoma City, Feb. 26, 1973), which was revised and retitled *Lorelei or "Gentlemen Still Prefer Blondes"* (Palace, N.Y.C., Jan. 27, 1974). With Joseph Harris, Messrs. Guber and Gross produced *Charles Aznavour on Broadway* (Minskoff, Oct. 15, 1974); and *Tony Bennett and Lena Horne Sing* (Minskoff, Oct. 30, 1974).

In a management-programming arrangement with NY City Ctr. (1976), Messrs. Guber and Gross, under the aegis of Music Fair Concerts, Inc., have presented *The Monty Python Show* (Apr. 12, 1976) and the Pennsylvania Ballet (June 15, 1976); with other limited-engagement presentations to include the revue *A Man and a Woman*, starring Isaac Hayes and Dionne Warwick, the Newport Jazz Festival and *Peter Pan.*.

Other Activities. Under the Music Fair Enterprises banner, Messrs. Guber and Gross operate the Amer. Wax Museum in Independence Hall (Philadelphia) and have had their own advertising agency. In 1971, they obtained the franchise for the closed-circuit telecast of the Joe Frazier-Muhammed Ali heavyweight championship fight for showing in their summer theatres.

GUEST, JEAN H. Theatre executive. b. Genia P. Hindes, Mar. 1, 1921, New York City, to Dr. Albert George and Frieda Muldavin (Sadvoronsky) Hindes. Grad. H.S. in New York City; attended New York Univ., 1939–41; New School for Social Research, N.Y.C.; New Theatre Sch.; Paul Mann Theatre Workshop. Married Dec. 29, 1945, to the Hon. Peter Haden Guest, British Official, United Nations; two sons; one daughter. During WW II, she worked for the Office of Scientific Research and Development (Cornell Medical Sch.). Member of ANTA. Address: 40 E. 9th St., New York, NY 10003, tel. (212) 677-6163; 198 Old Stone Highway, Easthampton, NY 11937, tel. (516) 324-4954.

Since 1974 Mrs. Guest has been an assoc. director of Theatre Communications Group.

She was theatre party administrator for the Playwrights Co. (1954–56); free-lance script reader for United Artists Film Corp. (1956–57); casting director for Frederick Brisson Prods. (1957–58); director of the National Theatre Service Dept. of ANTA (1958–67); and vice-president of Wender & Associates, theatrical agents (1968–74).

GUETTEL, HENRY. Producer. b. Henry Arthur Guettel, Jan. 8, 1928, Kansas City, Mo., to Arthur A. and Sylva H. (Hershfield) Guettel. Father, merchant. Grad. Pembroke Country Day Sch., Kansas City, 1944; attended Univ. of Pennsylvania, 1944–47; Univ. of Kansas City, 1947–48. Studied at the Actors' Lab., Hollywood, Summer 1948. Married June 5, 1948, to Miriam Broud (marr. dis. May 1952); one daughter; married Oct. 4, 1957, to Ann L. Noyes, producer (marr. dis. Sept. 1961); married Oct. 14, 1961, to Mary Rodgers, composer; one son. Served US Army, 1954–56; rank, PFC. Member of AEA; League of NY Theatres. Address: 115 Central Park West, New York, NY 10023, tel. (212) 724-9704.

Theatre. Mr. Guettel was first an actor at the Cape Playhouse (Dennis, Mass., Summer, 1947); subsequently joined (Sept. 1949) as assistant stage manager and appeared in *Goodbye, My Fancy* (Morosco Th., Nov. 17, 1948); was assistant stage manager and actor at the Cape Playhouse (Summer 1949); was stage manager, created stage effects, and appeared as Aristide and the Third Indian in *Now I Lay Me Down to Sleep* (Broadhurst, N.Y.C., Mar. 2, 1950); was stage manager at the Falmouth (Mass.) Playhouse (Summer 1952); general manager of the Royal Winnipeg Ballet for its US and Canadian tours (1953); and was general manager at the Sacramento (Calif.) Music Circus (Summer 1956) and at the Sombrero Playhouse (Phoenix, Ariz., 1957).

He produced, with Morton Gottlieb, a bus and truck tour of *The Best Man* (opened American Shakespeare Festival Th., Stratford, Conn., Jan. 7, 1962; closed Hartman Th., Columbus, Ohio, Apr. 28, 1962); was associate producer of the Roger L. Stevens production of *Romulus* (Music Box, Jan. 10, 1962); produced, by arrangement with the Bway producers, the second national tour of *The Sound of Music* (opened Community Th., Hershey, Pa., Sept. 17, 1962; closed Orpheum, Minneapolis, Minn., Mar. 22, 1964); produced a tour of *Take Her, She's Mine* (Summer 1963); produced, with Arthur Cantor, the second national tour of *Camelot* (opened Masonic Temple, Scranton, Pa., Oct. 3, 1963), a bus-and-truck touring production of *Camelot* (opened O'Keefe Ctr., Toronto, Ontario, Canada, Aug. 3, 1964; closed Rochester, N.Y., Dec. 19, 1964), and the second national tour of *Oliver!* (Community Th., Hershey, Pa., Sept. 30, 1964). At Lincoln Ctr. (N.Y.C.) Music Th., he was general manager for production of *Kismet* (June 22, 1965), *Carousel* (Aug. 10, 1965), *Annie Get Your Gun* (May 31, 1966; transferred to Broadway Th., Sept. 21, 1966), and *Show Boat* (July 19, 1966); he resigned his Lincoln Ctr. post Jan. 4, 1967, and he produced *The Magic of Cole Porter* (NY State Th., Nov. 20, 1967).

Films. He produced and directed films for the Armed Forces Public Information Office (1954–56).

Television and Radio. Mr. Guettel was an actor on radio (1948–49) and performed on *Mr. Ace and Jane* (CBS); and was radio television co-producer of The Chamber Music Society of Lower Basin Street (NBC, ABC, June 1950).

On television, he appeared on Danger (CBS, 1952); Suspense (CBS, 1952); Philco Television Playhouse (NBC, 1952); was assistant producer of *March On* (US Army and combined forces, National Distrib., 1955); and was assistant to the producer of Matinee Th. (NBC, Oct. 1956).

Recreation. Music, bridge, tennis, sailing, collecting and repairing antique clocks.

GUINNESS, SIR ALEC. Actor, director. b. Apr. 2, 1914, London, England, to Andrew and Agnes (Cuffe) Geddes. Attended Pembroke Lodge, Southbourne, Hampshire, 1922–27; Rodborough, Eastbourne, Sussex, 1927–32. Studied at Fay Compton Studio of Dramatic Art (scholarship), London (1934); with Martita Hunt (1934). Married June 20, 1938, to Merula Salaman, actress; one son. Served WW II, Royal Navy; rank, Lt. Member of British AEA; SAG; Atheneum (London), Garrick Club.

Pre-Theatre. Advertising copywriter (18 months).

Theatre. Sir Alec made his first stage appearance in a non-speaking role in the London production of *Libel!* (Playhouse, Apr. 2, 1934); subsequently appeared in *Queer Cargo* (Piccadilly, Aug. 14, 1934); and at the New Theatre he appeared as Osric and the Third Player in *Hamlet* (Nov. 14, 1934), the Wolf in *Noah* (July 2, 1935), Sampson and the Apothecary in *Romeo and Juliet* (Oct. 17, 1935), and the Workman and, later, Yakov in *The Seagull* (May 20, 1936).

In 1936, he became a member of the Old Vic Co., and during the 1936–37 season, played Boyet in *Love's Labour's Lost* (Sept. 14, 1936), Le Beau and William in *As You Like It* (Nov. 10, 1936), Old Thorney in *The Witch of Edmonton* (Dec. 8, 1936), Reynaldo and Osric in *Hamlet* (Jan. 5, 1937), Sir Andrew Aguecheek in *Twelfth Night* (Feb. 23, 1937), and Exeter in *Henry V* (Apr. 6, 1937), toured in *Hamlet*, playing Osric, Reynaldo and the Player Queen (Kronborg Castle, Elsinore, Denmark, June 1937).

Sir Alec became a member of the John Gielgud Co., and during the 1937–38 season at the Queen's Th. he played Aumerle and the Groom in *Richard III* (Sept. 6, 1937), Snake in *The School for Scandal* (Nov. 25, 1937), Fedotik in *The Three Sisters* (Jan. 28, 1938), and Lorenzo in *The Merchant of Venice* (Apr. 21, 1938).

He returned to the Old Vic Co. for the 1938–39 season, playing Arthur Gower in *Trelawny of the Wells* (Sept. 20, 1938), the title role in a modern dress production of *Hamlet* (Oct. 11, 1938), Bob Acres in *The Rivals* (Dec. 6, 1938); toured Europe and Egypt, repeating his roles of Hamlet and Bob Acres, and also playing the Chorus in *Henry V* and Emile Flordon in *Libel!* (Jan.–Apr. 1939). He returned to the Old Vic. Th. (London) to play Michael Ransom in *The Ascent of F.6* (June 27, 1939).

He played Romeo in the Scottish Th. Festival's production of *Romeo and Juliet* (Perth, Scotland, July 1939); he adapted Dickens' *Great Expectations* and played Herbert Pockett (Rudolf Steiner Hall, London, Dec. 7, 1939); played Richard Meilhac in *Cousin Muriel* (Globe, Mar. 7, 1940); Ferdinand in *The Tempest* (Old Vic Th., May 29, 1940); and toured as Charleston in *Thunder Rock* (Glasgow, Scotland; Nottingham, England; and bombed out in Bristol, England, 1940).

While serving as a Lieutenant in the Royal Navy, he was granted permission to play Lt. Teddy Graham in the N.Y.C. production of *Flare Path* (Henry Miller's Th., Dec. 23, 1942), for three weeks; and after his discharge, he returned to the London stage playing Mitya Karamazov in his own adaptation of Dostoevsky's *The Brothers Karamazov* (Lyric, Hammersmith, London, June 4, 1946).

Sir Alec appeared as Garcin in *Vicious Circle* (Arts, July 1946); rejoined the Old Vic Co., and, at the New Th., appeared as the Fool in *King Lear* (Sept. 24, 1946); Eric Birling in *An Inspector Calls* (Oct. 1, 1946); Compte de Guiche in Brian Hooker's translation of *Cyrano de Bergerac* (Oct. 24, 1946); Abel Drugger in *The Alchemist* (Jan. 14, 1947); the title role in *Richard II* (Nov. 18, 1947); the Dauphin in *Saint Joan* (Dec. 3, 1947); Hlestakov in D. J. Campbell's adaptation of *The Government Inspector* (Feb. 3, 1948); and Menenius Agrippa in *Coriolanus* (Mar. 31, 1948).

He directed *Twelfth Night* for the Old Vic Co. (New, Sept. 19, 1948); subsequently played Dr. James Y. Simpson in *The Human Touch* (Savoy, Feb. 11, 1949); the Unidentified Guest in *The Cocktail Party* (Lyceum, Edinburgh, Scotland, Aug. 1949; Henry Miller's Th., N.Y.C., Jan. 21, 1950); directed and played the title role in *Hamlet* (New, London, May 17, 1951); played the Scientist in *Under the Sycamore Tree* (Aldwych, Apr. 23, 1952); and at the Stratford Shakespearean Festival of Canada, he played the title role in *Richard III* and appeared as the King in *All's Well That Ends Well* (Ontario, Canada, Summer 1953).

Sir Alec appeared in the title role in *The Prisoner* (Globe, London, Apr. 14, 1954); Boniface in *Hotel Paradiso* (Winter Garden, May 2, 1956); the title role in *Ross* (Haymarket, May 12, 1960); Berenger the First in *Exit the King* (Edinburgh, Scotland, Fest.; subsequently at the Royal Court, London, Sept. 12, 1963); and appeared in the title role of *Dylan* (Plymouth, N.Y.C., Jan. 18, 1964).

He played Von Berg in *Incident at Vichy* (Phoenix, London, Jan. 26, 1966); the title role in *Macbeth* (Royal Court, Oct. 20, 1966); "Mrs. Artminster" in *Wise Child* (Wyndham's, Oct. 10, 1967); directed and played The Unidentified Guest (Sir Harcourt-Reilly) in *The Cocktail Party* (Chicester Fest., May 28, 1968; subsequently at Wyndham's, London, Nov. 6, 1968); John in *Time Out of Mind* (Arnaud Th., Guildford, July 14, 1970); the Father in *A Voyage Round My Father* (Haymarket, London, Aug. 4, 1971); and Arthur Wicksteed in *Habeas Corpus* (Lyric, May 10, 1973).

Films. He made his first motion picture appearance in *Great Expectations* (U, 1947); and has since appeared in *Kind Hearts and Coronets* (Eagle Lion, 1950); *Last Holiday* (Stratford, 1950); *A Run for Your Money* (U, 1950); *The Mudlark* (20th-Fox, 1950); *Oliver Twist* (UA, 1951); *The Lavender Hill Mob* (U, 1951); *The Promoter* (U, 1952); *The Man in the White Suit* (U, 1952); *The Captain's Paradise* (UA, 1953); *The Malta Story* (UA, 1954); *The Detective* (Col., 1954); *The Prisoner* (Col., 1955); *To Paris with Love* (Cont. Pics., 1955); *The Ladykillers* (Cont., 1956); *The Swan* (MGM, 1956); *The Bridge on the River Kwai* (Col., 1957); *All at Sea* (MGM, 1958); played Gulley Jimson in *The Horse's Mouth* (UA, 1958); appeared in *The Scapegoat* (MGM, 1959); *Tunes of Glory* (Lopert, 1960); *Our Man in Havana* (Col., 1960); *A Majority of One* (WB, 1961); *Lawrence of Arabia* (Col., 1962); *Damn the Defiant* (Col., 1962); *The Fall of the Roman Empire* (Par., 1964); *Situation Hopeless—But Not Serious* (Par., 1965); *Dr. Zhivago* (MGM, 1965); *Hotel Paradiso* (MGM, 1966); *The Quiller Memorandum* (Rank, 1966); *The Comedians* (MGM, 1967); *Cromwell* (Col., 1970); *Scrooge* (Natl. Gen., 1970); *Hitler: The Last Ten Days* (Par., 1972); and *Brother Sun, Sister Moon* (Par., 1973).

Television. Sir Alec made his first appearance on US television in *The Wicked Scheme of Jebal Deeks* (Ford Startime, NBC, Nov. 10, 1959), and played a scene from *Dylan* (Ed Sullivan Show, CBS, June 7, 1964).

His British television appearances include being host for a documentary, *The Actor* (ABC, Mar. 15, 1968); playing Malvolio in *Twelfth Night* (1969); appearing in *Solo* (1970); in *The Gift of Friendship* (1974); and as Caesar in *Caesar and Cleopatra* (1975).

Awards. He was nominated for an Academy (Oscar) Award for his performance in *The Lavender Hill Mob* (1951); received the Academy (Oscar) Award, the Golden Globe Award, and the British Film Acad. Award for his performance as Colonel Nicholson in *The Bridge on the River Kwai* (1957); voted Best Actor by the Venice Film Festival for his performance as Gulley Jimson in *The Horse's Mouth* (1958); was nominated for the Academy (Oscar) Award for his screen adaptation of *The Horse's Mouth* (1958); tied (with Rex Harrison) for the London *Evening Standard* Award for his performance in *Ross* (1960); and won the Antoinette Perry (Tony) Award for his performance as *Dylan* (1964).

A Commander of the British Empire (C.B.E.) was conferred upon him in the Birthday Honours of 1955; he was created a Knight Bachelor by Queen Elizabeth at the New Year Honours of Jan. 1, 1959; and received the honorary degree of D.F.A. from Boston Coll. (1962).

GURNEY, DENNIS. Actor, director. b. Dennis Alexander Jacks, Feb. 25, 1897, London, Eng., to Frederick William and Beatrice Mary (Cooper) Jacks. Father, stock broker; mother, actress. Grad. St. Anne's, Red Hill, Surrey, Eng., 1913. Served Royal Naval Reserve, 1915–18; rank, Midshipman. Relative in theatre: stepfather, Edmund Gurney, actor. Member of AEA; AFTRA.

Pre-Theatre. Sailor, film exhibitor, farmer.

Theatre. Mr. Gurney made his N.Y.C. debut as a walk-on in *If Winter Comes* (Gaiety, Apr. 2, 1923); played Arthur Wells and understudied Leslie Howard as the Hon. Willie Tatham in *Aren't We All* (Gaiety, May 21, 1923); played Private Jones in *Havoc* (Maxine Elliott's Th., Sept. 1, 1924); Mr. Gourlay in *Shall We Join the Ladies?* which was presented with *Isabel* (Empire, Jan. 13, 1925); Reginald Ridgeley in *Aloma of the South Seas* (Lyric, Apr. 20, 1926); for the American Grand Guignol Players at the Grove Street Playhouse, N.Y.C., appeared as Mark in *Cocktail Impromptu,* Clement in *The Last Torture,* and the Delivery Agent in *Maid of all Work,* which was on a double bill with *The Claw* (Jan. 12, 1927), the Man in *The House of Rest,* Dick in *Butterflies,* Alf Barnes in *We're All in the Gutter,* the Gaoler in *A Minuet,* and the Figure in *The Maker of Images,* which was presented with *The Florentine Tragedy, Napoleon's Barber,* and *Casualties* (Feb. 1, 1927).

He played George Hunter and was stage manager for *Bless You, Sister* (Forrest, Dec. 26, 1927); Pretty Pietro in *The Grey Fox* (Playhouse, Oct. 22, 1928); Arthur St. John Wilberforle, Lord Somerset, in *The Prince of Pilsen* (Al Jolson's Th., Jan. 13, 1930); Josef in *An Affair of State* (Broadhurst, Nov. 19, 1930); Augustus Raby in *The Anatomist* (Bijou, Oct. 24, 1932); Montague in *Hotel Alimony* (Royale, Jan. 29, 1934); succeeded (June 1934) Royal C. Stout as Edwards in *Aren't You Decent?* (Ambassador, Apr. 19, 1934); played Quartermaster Swan in *The Distant Shore* (Morosco, Feb. 21, 1935); Corporal Thompson in *Good Hunting* (Hudson, Nov. 21, 1938); joined the cast of *Kismet* (Ziegfeld, Dec. 3, 1953), and toured in it (1955).

Mr. Gurney acted and directed in stock productions (1927–53), and directed 43 productions for the Blackfriar's Th. (N.Y.C., 1927–53).

Recreation. Reading, bridge.

GUSS, LOUIS. Actor. b. Jan. 4, 1918, New York City, to Shiman and Anna (Rienstein) Guss. Grad. James Monroe H.S., Bronx, N.Y. Studied acting with Erwin Piscator, Dramatic Workshop of the New School, two years; Stella Adler, one year; Morris Carnovsky, one year; Paul Mann, one year. Served WW II US Army, rank, Pvt. Member of AEA; AFTRA; SAG; AFM, local No. 802.

Pre-Theatre. Trumpeter and musician.

Theatre. Mr. Guss appeared as Bologinini in *The Girl on the Via Flaminia* (Circle in the Square, N.Y.C., Feb. 9, 1954; moved to 48th St. Th., Apr. 1, 1954); as Papa Briguet in *He Who Gets Slapped* (Actors Playhouse, Jan. 20, 1956); the Husband in *Mandragola* (Pantomime Th.); Scwiefka in *The Man with the Golden Arm* (Cherry Lane, May 21, 1956); understudied the parts of Hugo Kalmer, Piet Wetjoen, and Rocky Pioggi in *The Iceman Cometh* (Circle in the Square, May 18, 1956); played the Innkeeper in *Bonds of Interest* (Sheridan Sq. Playhouse, May 6, 1958); and Luigi Bardini in the tour of *Once More, With Feeling* (Summer 1958).

He appeared as Matias in *Handful of Fire* (Martin Beck Th., N.Y.C., Oct. 1, 1958); Padre Manuel in *And the Wind Blows* (St. Mark's Playhouse, Apr. 28, 1959); Manuel in the pre-Bway tryout of *Juniper and the Pagans* (opened Colonial Th., Boston, Mass., Dec. 10, 1959; closed Forrest Th., Philadelphia, Pa., Dec. 26, 1959); Luis in *One More River* (Ambassador, N.Y.C., Mar. 18, 1960); Sancho Panza and A. Ratt in *Camino Real* (St. Mark's Playhouse, May 16, 1960); Baron Razumni in *Once There Was a Russian* (Music Box, Feb. 18, 1961); and Jake Latta in *The Night of the Iguana* (Royale Th., Dec. 28, 1961).

Mr. Guss played Guy Tabarie in a tour of *The Vagabond King* (June–July 1962); Pitkin W. Bridgework in a tour of *On the Town* (July–Aug. 1962); the Sergeant and the Peasantman in *Mother Courage and Her Children* (Martin Beck Th., N.Y.C., Mar. 28, 1963); Buroff in a tour of *Silk Stockings* (June 1963); played Guy Tabarie in a stock production of *The Vagabond King* (Melody Top, Hillside, Ill., Aug. 1963); Ted Ragg in *Arturo Ui* (Lunt-Fontanne, Nov. 11, 1963); and Commendatore Agazzi in *Right You Are, If You Think You Are* (Fred Miller Th., Milwaukee, Wis., Feb. 3, 1964).

He was the Bartender in *Days of the Dancing* (Westport Country Playhouse, Westport, Conn., June 22, 1964; Paper Mill Playhouse, Millburn, N.J., June 30, 1964); Portero in *Diamond Orchid* (Henry Miller's Th., N.Y.C., Feb. 10, 1965); Comrade Galka in *Flora, the Red Menace* (Alvin Th., May 11, 1965); Gottlieb Biedermann in *The Firebugs* (Studio Arena Th., Buffalo, N.Y., Jan. 6, 1966); and toured as Moishe in *Send Us Your Boy* (Summer 1966). He played Murray in *The Odd Couple* (Coconut Grove Playhouse, Miami, Fla., Dec. 27, 1966; Community Playhouse, Atlanta, Ga., Jan. 31, 1967; Parker Playhouse, Fort Lauderdale, Fla., Feb. 6, 1967; Harrah's, Reno, Nev., Aug. 1967; Sombrero Playhouse, Phoenix, Ariz., Feb. 20, 1968); was Vincent in *But, Seriously . .* (Henry Miller's Th., N.Y.C., Feb. 27, 1969); Patel in *Gandhi* (Playhouse, Oct. 20, 1970); and the Cadi in *Captain Brassbound's Conversion* (Ethel Barrymore Th., Apr. 17, 1971).

Films. Mr. Guss appeared in *Middle of the Night* (Col., 1961); *Run Across the River* (SPC, 1961); *Love With the Proper Stranger* (Par., 1963); and *Ready for the People* (WB, 1964).

Television. Mr. Guss has appeared on Naked City (ABC); Route 66 (CBS); The Defenders (CBS); Dupont Show of the Month (NBC); East Side/West Side (CBS); The Nurses (CBS); *A Tale of Two Cities* (Dupont, NBC); *The Thirteen Clocks; For Whom the Bell Tolls* (Playhouse 90, CBS); and *The Moon and Sixpence* (NBC).

Recreation. Swimming, listening to music.

GUSTAFSON, CAROL. Actress. b. Elsie Carol Gustafson, Dec. 25, 1925, New York City, to Herman and Ida Christina (Johanson) Gustafson. Father, hairdresser; mother, hairdresser. Grad. Julia Richman H.S., N.Y.C., 1940; attended Theodora Irvine, 1942–43. Studied acting with Erwin Piscator at the Dramatic Workshop, New Sch. for Social Research, 1947–49; with Boris Tumarin, Joseph Anthony, and Peter Frye at the Amer. Th. Wing, 1948–49; with Felix Brentano at Columbia Univ.; voice with Larry Davidson, 1964. Married Sept. 23, 1949, to Larry M. Ward, actor, writer (marr. dis. Aug. 22, 1962); one son, one daughter. Member of AEA; AFTRA; SAG. Address: 603 W. 111th St., New York, NY 10025, tel. (212) MO 6-3398.

Pre-Theatre. Model, salesgirl.

Theatre. Miss Gustafson made her professional debut as Electra in *The Flies* (President Th., N.Y.C., Apr. 17, 1947); subsequently appeared as Giovanna in the touring production of *The Time of the Cuckoo* (opened Opera House, Central City, Colo., Aug. 1, 1953); Duchess de la Tremouille in the pre-Bway tryout of *Saint Joan,* with Jean Arthur (opened National Th., Washington, D.C., Sept. 20, 1954; closed Hartman Th., Columbus, Ohio, Nov. 6, 1954); Olga Sergeyevna in *The Three Sisters* (4th St. Th., Feb. 25, 1955); a Handmaiden in the pre-Bway tryout of *Maiden Voyage* (opened Forrest Th., Philadelphia, Pa., Feb. 28, 1957; closed there Mar. 9, 1957); made her Bway debut succeeding Beryl Measor as Miss Cooper in *Separate Tables* (Music Box, Oct. 25, 1956), in which she also understudied Geraldine Page as Anne Shankland and Miss Railton-Bell.

Miss Gustafson played the offstage voice of Miss Kitchell in *Maybe Tuesday* (Playhouse, Jan. 29, 1958); Viola in the NY Shakespeare Festival production of *Twelfth Night* (Belvedere Lake Th., Aug. 1958); understudied the role of Mrs. Gower Stevens in *Requiem for a Nun* (John Golden Th., Jan. 30, 1959); played Olga Sergeyevna in *The Three Sisters* (4th St. Th., Sept. 1959); replaced Dran Seitz for nine performances as Gwendolyn in *Becket* (St. James, Oct. 5, 1960); understudied the roles of M/Sgt. Florence Denzil and Mrs. Bucci in *Blood, Sweat and Stanley Poole* (Morosco, Oct. 5, 1961); played Portia in *The Merchant of Venice* (Gate, Feb. 2, 1962); Amelia Earhart in *Asylum* (scheduled to open Th. de Lys, Mar. 11, 1963), which closed after four preview performances; understudied Hermione Gingold as Madame Rosepettle in the touring production of *Oh Dad, Poor Dad, Mama's Hung You in the Closet and I'm Feelin' So Sad* (opened Civic Th., Chicago, Ill., Apr. 2, 1963), and for the return engagement (Morosco, N.Y.C., Aug. 27, 1963); played Katherine Anne Porter in *Dylan* (Plymouth, Jan. 18, 1964); at Hyde Park Playhouse, N.Y., appeared in *Anastasia, Anna Christie, Bell, Book and Candle, Picnic* and *Affairs of State* (Summer 1954).

Miss Gustafson understudied Monica Evans as Cicely Pigeon in *The Odd Couple* (Plymouth, Mar. 10, 1965); toured (1968–69) in the Minnesota Theatre Co. productions of *Arturo Ui* and *The House of Atreus;* appeared at Arena Stage, Washington, D.C., as the Prioress in *Edith Stein* (Oct. 23, 1969), the Russian duchess in *You Can't Take It With You* (Dec. 4, 1969), Madame Ranevskaya in *The Cherry Orchard* (Jan. 15, 1970); was standby to Sada Thompson for the seven-month national tour of *Twigs,* assuming the role herself at the Falmouth (Mass.) Playhouse (Aug. 1973); played the title role in *The House of Bernarda Alba* (Pennsylvania State Univ., May 1974); and was Bessie in *Awake and Sing* (Harvard Univ. Summer School, July 1974).

Films. Miss Gustafson appeared in the films *The Group* (UA, 1966); *Bye, Bye Braverman* (WB, 1968); *Going Home;* and *Such Good Friends.*

Television. Miss Gustafson has appeared on US Steel Hour (CBS); Dupont Show of the Week (CBS); Armstrong Circle Th. (CBS); and the Phil Silvers Show (CBS). She has also done commercials for such products as FAB and Lucky Whip.

Recreation. Tennis, dance, writing.

GWYNNE, FRED. Actor. b. July 10, 1926, New York City. Father, stockbroker. Grad. Groton, Conn., Prep. Sch., 1944; attended Phoenix Sch. of Design, N.Y.C.; grad. Harvard Coll., B.A. 1951. Married to Jean Reynard; four children. Served USN, WW II. Member of AEA; SAG; AFTRA.

Theatre. With the Brattle Th. (Cambridge, Mass.), Mr. Gwynne played Bottom in *A Midsummer Night's Dream* and Silence in *Henry IV, Part II* (1951), and in *The Imaginary Invalid* and *Androcles and the Lion;* made his Bway debut as Stinker in *Mrs. McThing* (Morosco, N.Y.C., Feb. 20, 1952); played Dull in *Love's Labour's Lost* (NY City Ctr., Feb. 4, 1953); and Luther Raubel in *The Frogs of Spring* (Broadhurst, Oct. 20, 1953).

He played Polyte-le-Mou in *Irma La Douce* (Plymouth, Sept. 29, 1960); Marvin Shellhammer in *Here's Love* (Shubert, Oct. 3, 1963); Abraham Lincoln in *The Lincoln Mask* (Plymouth, Oct. 30, 1972); the Inspector in *The Enchanted* (Eisenhower Th., Washington, D.C., Mar. 3, 1973); Maj. Michael Dillon in *More Than You Deserve* (NY Shakespeare Fest., Newman Th., Nov. 21, 1973); and at the Amer. Shakespeare Th. (Stratford, Conn.), played Sir Toby Belch in *Twelfth Night* (June 15, 1974), Big

Daddy in *Cat on a Hot Tin Roof* (July 10, 1974; transferred to ANTA Th., N.Y.C., Sept. 24, 1974; and at the Eisenhower Th., Washington, D.C., Feb. 12, 1975), the Stage Manager in *Our Town* (June 14, 1975), and Autolycus in *The Winter's Tale* (July 30, 1975).

Films. He appeared in a bit part in *On the Waterfront* (Col., 1954), and played Herman Munster in *Munster, Go Home* (U, 1966).

Television. Mr. Gwynne played Francis Muldoon on the series Car 54, Where Are You? (NBC, premiere Sept. 17, 1961) for two seasons; and Herman Munster on the series The Munsters (CBS, premiere Sept. 24, 1964) for two seasons. He has also appeared on the Phil Silvers Show (CBS); Studio One (CBS); Suspicion (NBC); Kraft Th. (NBC); on the Dupont Show of the Month (CBS); in *Harvey* (Sept. 22, 1958) and *The Hasty Heart* (Dec. 18, 1958); in *The Old Foolishness* (Play of the Week, WNTA, Mar. 6, 1961); on US Steel Hour (CBS); in Ionesco's *The Lesson* (NY TV Th., WNDT, Oct. 17, 1966); Thornton Wilder's *Infancy* (NET Playhouse, WNET, Dec. 15, 1967); a pilot film, *Guess What I Did Today?* (NBC, Sept. 10, 1968); as Jonathan Brewster in *Arsenic and Old Lace* (ABC, Apr. 2, 1969); in *The Littlest Angel* (Hallmark Hall of Fame, NBC, Dec. 6, 1969); Clifford Odets' *Paradise Lost* (NET Playhouse, WNET, Feb. 25, 1971); *The Police* (Hollywood TV Th., KCET, Oct. 14, 1971); *Dames at Sea* (NBC, Nov. 15, 1971); and *Harvey* (Hallmark Hall of Fame, NBC, Mar. 22, 1972).

Other Activities. From 1955 to 1960, Mr. Gwynne was a copywriter for the J. Walter Thompson advertising agency, N.Y.C.

Published Works. Mr. Gwynne has written and illustrated *What's a Nude?*, and the children's books, *Best in Show; The Battle of the Frogs and Mice* (1962); *The Story of Ick; The King Who Rained;* and *God's First World* (1970).

H

HAAS, DOLLY. Actress. b. Dorothy Clara Louise Haas, Apr. 29, 1910, Hamburg, Ger., to Charles Oswald and Margarethe (Hansen) Haas. Father, publisher. Attended Lyceum of Dr. Lowenberg, Hamburg, 1917–27. Married Sept. 9, 1943, to Albert Hirschfeld, caricaturist; one daughter. Member of AEA; AFTRA. Address: 122 E. 95th St., New York, NY 10028, tel. (212) LE 4-6172.

Theatre. Miss Haas made her debut in the US as Hai-Tang in *The Circle of Chalk* (New Sch. for Social Research, NYC, Mar. 1941); also at the New Sch. for Social Research, appeared in *Winter Soldiers*, and *War and Peace* (1942).

She made her debut in Germany in *The Mikado* (Grosses Schauspielhaus, Berlin, 1927); subsequently in *The Nelson Revue* at the Katakombe Cabaret (Berlin, 1928); at the Kabarett Der Komiker (Berlin, 1929); in the operetta, *Waltz Dream* (Deutsches Th., Munich, 1929); in *Wie Werde Ich Reich und Gluecklich* (Reinhardt Th., Die Komoedie, Berlin, 1930); in *Scampolo* (Kuenstler Th., Berlin, 1934), and also toured Europe in it.

She made her N.Y.C. debut in *Doctors Disagree* (Bijou, Dec. 28, 1943); succeeded (June 3, 1946) Mary Martin as Tchao-Ou-Niang in *Lute Song* (Plymouth, Feb. 6, 1946), also touring in it (closed Natl., Washington, D.C., June 1947); played Sonia in *Crime and Punishment* (Natl., N.Y.C., Dec. 22, 1947); took over Viveca Lindfors' role as Anna in *Anastasia* (Lyceum, Dec. 29, 1954), and toured in it (opened Ford's, Baltimore, Md., Sept. 26, 1955; closed Blackstone, Chicago, Ill., Feb. 7, 1956).

She succeeded (Sept. 1956) Lotte Lenya as Jenny in *The Threepenny Opera* (Th. de Lys, N.Y.C., Sept. 20, 1955), and remained in the role until Mar. 1957; played Tchao-Ou-Niang in *Lute Song* (NY City Ctr., Mar. 12, 1959); and joined the cast of *Brecht on Brecht* (Th. de Lys, Jan. 3, 1962).

Films. Miss Haas made her debut in Dolly *Mach Karriere* (UFA, Ger., 1931); followed by *Liebes Commando* (Superfilm, 1932); *Der Ball* (UFA, 1932); *Scampolo* (Kit, 1935); *Broken Blossoms* (IML, 1937); and *I Confess* (WB, 1953).

Awards. Miss Haas was honored by the 25th Berlin (Ger.) International Film Festival (June 1975).

HACKETT, ALBERT. Playwright, actor. b. Albert Maurice Hackett, Feb. 16, 1900, New York City, to Maurice and Florence (Spreen) Hackett. Mother, actress. Relatives in theatre: sister, Janette Hackett, producer-dancer; brother, Raymond Hackett, actor (dec.). Tutored privately; attended Professional Children's Sch., N.Y.C., 1914–16. Married February 7, 1931, to Frances Goodrich, playwright. Member of Dramatists Guild; WGA, West; The Players. Address: 88 Central Park West, New York, NY 10023, tel. (212) SC 4-9389.

Theatre. Mr. Hackett made his N.Y.C. stage debut as a little girl in *Lottie, the Poor Saleslady* (1906); appeared in vaudeville, joining the cast of a sketch, "Children of France" (Loew's Circuit, N.Y.; Southern State, 1917); toured with Maude Adams in *Peter Pan* (1918); and succeeded Morgan Farley as Tim Simpkins on tour in *The Charm School* (1920–21).

He played Jerry in *Up the Ladder* (Playhouse, N.Y.C., Mar. 6, 1922); Chester Underwood in *The Nervous Wreck* (Sam H. Harris Th., Oct. 9, 1923); succeeded (Apr. 1927) Douglas Montgomery as Tommy Brown in *Crime* (Eltinge, Feb. 22, 1927); and played Chester Underwood in the musical *Whoopee*, based on the play *The Nervous Wreck* (New Amsterdam, Dec. 4, 1928).

With Frances Goodrich, he wrote *Up Pops the Devil* (Masque, Sept. 1, 1930), in which he played the role of Biney; with Miss Goodrich, wrote *Bridal Wise* (Cort, May 30, 1932); he played Mr. North in *Mr. and Mrs. North* (Belasco, Jan. 12, 1941); and with Miss Goodrich, wrote *The Great Big Doorstep* (Morosco, Nov. 26, 1942); and *The Diary of Anne Frank* (Cort, Oct. 5, 1955).

Films. He appeared in *Come Out of the Kitchen* (Par., 1919); *Anne of Green Gables* (Realart, 1919); and *Molly O* (20th-Fox, 1921).

With Miss Goodrich, he wrote screenplays for *The Secret of Madame Blanche* (MGM, 1933); *Penthouse* (MGM, 1933); *Hide-Out* (MGM, 1934); *The Thin Man* (MGM, 1934); *Naughty Marietta* (MGM, 1935); *Ah, Wilderness!* (MGM, 1935); *Rose Marie* (MGM, 1936); *After the Thin Man* (MGM, 1936); and *The Firefly* (MGM, 1937). The Hacketts also wrote *Another Thin Man* (MGM, 1939); *Lady in the Dark* (Par., 1944); *The Hitler Gang* (Par., 1944); *The Virginian* (Par., 1946); *It's a Wonderful Life* (RKO, 1946); *Easter Parade* (MGM, 1948); *The Pirate* (MGM, 1948); *In the Good Old Summertime* (MGM, 1949); *Father of the Bride* (MGM, 1950); *Too Young to Kiss* (MGM, 1951); *Father's Little Dividend* (MGM, 1951); *Give a Girl a Break* (MGM, 1953); *Seven Brides for Seven Brothers* (MGM, 1954); *The Long, Long Trailer* (MGM, 1954); *Gaby* (MGM, 1956); *A Certain Smile* (20th-Fox, 1958); *The Diary of Anne Frank* (20th-Fox, 1959); and *Five Finger Exercise* (Col., 1962).

Awards. Mr. Hackett and his wife received the Screen Writers Guild Award for *The Thin Man; Ah, Wilderness!; Easter Parade; Father of the Bride* and for *Seven Brides for Seven Brothers;* won the Pulitzer Prize for Drama, the NY Drama Critics Circle Award, and the Antoinette Perry (Tony) Award for *The Diary of Anne Frank* (1956); and received the Laurel Award (1956).

Recreation. Gardening, polishing shoes, scraping furniture.

HACKETT, JOAN. Actress. b. Joan Ann Hackett, Mar. 1, New York City, to John and Mary (Esposito) Hackett. Father, postal clerk; mother, pepper-packer. Grad. St. Jean Baptiste Sch., N.Y.C., 1952. Studied with Mary Welch, 1958; Lee Strasberg, 1958–63. Married Jan. 3, 1966, to Richard Mulligan, actor (marr. dis. 1973). Member of AFTRA; AEA; SAG.

Pre-Theatre. Model, candy-butcher, cartoonist.

Theatre. Miss Hackett made her N.Y.C. debut in *A Clearing in the Woods* (Sheridan Square Playhouse, Feb. 12, 1959); in stock, appeared in *The Play's the Thing* (Princeton Univ. Playhouse, N.J., June 1959); was understudy for Hero in *Much Ado About Nothing* (Lunt-Fontanne, N.Y.C., Sept. 17, 1959); and played Marguerite in a pre-Bway tryout of *Laurette* (opened Shubert, New Haven, Conn., Sept. 26, 1960). She appeared as Chris in *Call Me By My Rightful Name* (One Sheridan Square, Jan. 31, 1961); appeared in stock productions of *Two Queens of Love and Beauty* (Bucks County Playhouse, New Hope, Pa., July 1961), and *Journey to the Day* (Westport Country Playhouse, Conn., Aug. 1961). She appeared in a pre-Bway stock production of *She Didn't Say Yes* (Summer 1963); was Pat in *Peterpat* (Longacre, N.Y.C., Jan. 6, 1965); the Young Woman in *Park* (Center Stage, Baltimore, Md., Feb. 25, 1970; John Golden Th., N.Y.C., Apr. 22, 1970); and Elaine Wheeler in *Night Watch* (Morosco, Feb. 28, 1972).

Films. Miss Hackett's films include *The Group* (UA, 1966); *Will Penny* (Par., 1968); *Support Your Local Sheriff* (UA, 1969); *Assignment to Kill* (WB-Seven Arts, 1969); *The Rivals* (Avco-Embassy, 1972); *The Last of Sheila* (WB, 1973); *The Terminal Man* (WB, 1974); and *Mackintosh and T. J.* (Penland, 1975).

Television. Miss Hackett made her debut on Ellery Queen (NBC, Feb. 1959); subsequently had running roles in Young Doctor Malone (NBC, 1959–60) and The Defenders (NBC, 1961–62). She appeared in Diagnosis Unknown (CBS, 1960); the Armstrong Circle Th. (CBS, Dec. 1960); the Alfred Hitchcock Show (NBC, Apr. 1961); Twilight Zone (CBS, Oct. 1961); The New Breed (ABC, Oct. 1961); Ben Casey (ABC, Oct. 1961; Dec. 1964); Westinghouse Special (NBC, Nov. 1961); Gunsmoke (CBS, Dec. 1961); Dr. Kildare (NBC, Jan. 1962); *Rebecca* (NBC, Mar. 1962); Alcoa Premiere (ABC, May, Dec. 1962); Combat (ABC, July 1962); The Nurses (NBC, Dec. 1962); Empire (NBC, May 1963); *Pale Horse, Pale Rider* (CBC, Apr. 1963); Great Adventure (CBS, Dec. 1963); Channing (NBC, Jan. 1964); *Echo of Evil* (Bob Hope Chrysler Th., NBC, June 1964); Bonanza (NBC, Dec. 1964; Jan. 1972); *The Highest Fall of All* (Bob Hope Chrysler Th., NBC, Dec. 1965); Danny Thomas Show (NBC, Oct. 1967); Judd for the Defense (ABC, Dec. 1967); Name of the Game (NBC, Sept. 1968); *The Young Country* (ABC, Mar. 1970); *How Awful About Allan* (ABC, Sept. 1970); *The Other Man* (NBC, Oct. 1970); Love, American Style (ABC, Feb. 1971); John Dos Passos' *USA* (Hollywood Television Th., PBS, May 1971); *Five Desperate Women* (ABC, Sept. 1971); and Mission: Impossible (CBS, Jan. 1972.

Night Clubs. Miss Hackett's night club appearances include a singing engagement at Reno Sweeney (N.Y.C., Oct. 1974).

Other Activities. In 1972, Miss Hackett served as spokesman for a group of 62 theatrical performers urging Mayor John V. Lindsay of N.Y.C. to move against crime and vice in the Times Square area of Manhattan.

Awards. For her performance as Chris in *Call Me By My Rightful Name*, she received *The Village Voice* Off-Bway (Obie) Award (1961), the *Theatre World* Award (1961), and the Vernon Rice Award (1961); and she received an NATAS (Emmy) Award nomination for her performance on Ben Casey (1962).

HAGEN, UTA. Actress, teacher of acting. b. Uta Thyra Hagen, June 12, 1919, Gottingen, Germany, to Oskar F. L. and Thyra (Leisner) Hagen. Father, educator; mother, opera singer. Grad. Wisconsin H.S., Madison, 1936; attended Univ. of Wisconsin, 1937. Studied at RADA, London, England, 1936–37. Married Dec. 8, 1938, to Jose Ferrer, actor, director (marr. dis. June 1948); one daughter; married Jan. 25, 1951, to Herbert Berghof, actor, director, teacher. Member of AEA; AFTRA. Address: (home) 27 Washington Square North, New York, NY 10011; (bus.) c/o HB Studio, 120 Bank St., New York, NY 10014.

Theatre. Miss Hagen made her debut as Sorrel in

Hay Fever (Bascom Hall, Univ. of Wisconsin, July 1935).

She played Ophelia in *Hamlet*, which was directed by Eva Le Gallienne (Cape Playhouse, Dennis, Mass., Aug. 1937); and made her N.Y.C. debut as Nina in *The Seagull* (Shubert, Mar. 28, 1938).

She appeared as Louka in *Arms and the Man* and the Ingenue in *Mr. Pim Passes By* (Ridgefield Summer Th., Conn., July 1938); Suzanna in *Suzanna and the Elders* (Westport Country Playhouse, Conn.; Mt. Kisco Playhouse, N.Y., Aug. 1938); and toured as Nina in the national company of *The Seagull* (Oct. 1938–Jan. 1939).

She played Edith in *The Happiest Days* (Vanderbilt, N.Y.C., Apr. 11, 1939); a Chinese Girl in *Flight into China* and a Nurse in *Men in White* (Paper Mill Playhouse, Millburn, N.J., Aug. 1939); Alegre d'Alcala in *Key Largo* (Ethel Barrymore Th., N.Y.C., Nov. 27, 1939); the Secretary in *Topaze* (Mt. Kisco Playhouse, July 1940); Ella in *Charley's Aunt* (Ann Arbor Drama Festival, Mich., May 1941), also touring the N.Y.C. subway circuit in it (June 1941); and played Ellen Turner in *The Male Animal* and the Woman in *The Guardsman* (Suffern County Playhouse, N.Y., July–Aug. 1941).

Also the Wife in the pre-Bway tryout of *The Admiral Had a Wife* (opened Playhouse, Wilmington, Del., Nov. 1941; closed National, Washington, D.C., Dec. 1941); toured as Desdemona in the Theatre Guild's production of *Othello* (July–Aug. 1942), played the title role in *Vicki* (Plymouth, N.Y.C., Sept. 22, 1942); Desdemona in Paul Robeson's *Othello* (Shubert, Oct. 19, 1943), also touring in it (Sept. 1944), and returned to N.Y.C. in it (NY City Ctr., May 22, 1945).

She played Olga Vorontsov in *The Whole World Over* (Biltmore, Mar. 27, 1947); Mrs. Manningham in *Angel Street* (Yardley Th., Pa., July 1947); toured as the leading lady in *Dark Eyes* (July–Aug. 1947), and at the Barbizon-Plaza Th., (N.Y.C.), appeared in two German language productions: as Gretchen in *Faust* (Oct. 1947), and Hilda in *The Master Builder* (Jan. 1948).

She played Mrs. Manningham in *Angel Street* (NY City Ctr., Jan. 22, 1948); succeeded (June 1948) Jessica Tandy as Blanche DuBois in *A Streetcar Named Desire* (Ethel Barrymore Th., Dec. 3, 1947), also touring in it (Sept. 1948–June 1949), repeated the role in N.Y.C. (Ethel Barrymore Th., June 1949–Feb. 1950), on tour (Feb. 1950), and returned to N.Y.C. in it (NY City Ctr., May 23, 1950).

Miss Hagen played Georgie in *The Country Girl* (Lyceum, Nov. 10, 1950); the title role in *Saint Joan* (Cort, Oct. 4, 1951); Tatiana in *Tovarich* (NY City Ctr., May 14, 1952), also toured in it (June–Aug. 1952); toured in a summer production of *The Play's the Thing* (July–Aug. 1952); played Hannah King in *In Any Language* (Cort, N.Y.C., Oct. 8, 1952); toured as Jennet Jourdemayne in *The Lady's Not for Burning* and Georgie in *The Country Girl* (June–Aug. 1953); played Grace Wilson in *The Magic and the Loss* (Booth, N.Y.C., Apr. 9, 1954); toured summer theatres in the title role of *Cyprienne* (June–Aug. 1954); played Lavinia in *Michael and Lavinia* (Th. by the Sea, Matunuck, R.I., Sept. 1954); Jennet Jourdemayne in *The Lady's Not for Burning* (Nassau, Bahamas, Feb. 1955); and played all the female roles in *The Affairs of Anatol* (Ann Arbor Drama Festival, Mich., May 1955; Edgewater Beach Hotel, Chicago, Ill., July 1955).

She played Agata in *Island of Goats* (Fulton, N.Y.C., Oct. 4, 1955); Natalia Petrovna in *A Month in the Country* (Phoenix, Apr. 3, 1956); Shen Te in *The Good Woman of Setzuan* (Phoenix, Dec. 18, 1956); Argia in *The Queen and the Rebels* (Bucks County Playhouse, New Hope, Pa., Aug. 1959); Angelique in the American premiere of *Port Royal* (Grace Church, N.Y.C., May 1960); Leah in *Sodom and Gomorrah* (Vancouver Intl. Festival, Canada, Aug. 1961); Martha in the evening company of *Who's Afraid of Virginia Woolf?* (Billy Rose Th., N.Y.C., Oct. 13, 1962), and also played this role in London (Piccadilly, Feb. 6, 1964).

Films. Miss Hagen made her motion picture debut as Ada in *The Other* (20th-Fox, 1972).

Television. Miss Hagen has appeared as Natalia Petrovna in *A Month in the Country* (Play of the Week, WNTA, 1956); Maude in *Out of Dust* (Playhouse 90, CBS, 1959), and others.

Other Activities. Since Sept. 1947, she has taught acting at the HB (Herbert Berghof) Studio, which her husband owns.

Published Works. Miss Hagen is the author of *Respect for Acting* (1973).

Awards. She received the Donaldson Award, Antoinette Perry (Tony) Award, and the NY Drama Critics *Variety* Poll for her performance as Georgie in *The Country Girl* (1951); the Antoinette Perry (Tony) Award, NY Drama Critics *Variety* Poll, and the Outer Circle Award for her performance as Martha in *Who's Afraid of Virginia Woolf?* (1963), for which she also was voted Best Female Performance by the London critics (1964).

Recreation. Cooking, knitting, handicrafts.

HAGUE, ALBERT. Composer. b. Oct. 13, 1920, Berlin, Ger., to Dr. Harry and Mimi (Marcuse) Hague. Studied piano and composition with Arthur Perleberg, Berlin, Ger., 1935–37, and with Dante Alderight, Santa Cecilia Acad., Rome, It., 1939; grad. Coll. of Music, Univ. of Cincinnati, B.M., composition, 1939–42. Married Sept. 24, 1951, to Renee Orin, actress. Served USAAF, 1942–45; rank, Sgt. Member of ASCAP; Dramatists Guild. Address: 115 Central Park West, New York, NY 10023.

Theatre. Mr. Hague composed the music for *Reluctant Lady*, with book and lyrics by Maurice Valency (Cain Park Th., Cleveland, Ohio, July–Aug. 1947). A song from the show "One is a Lonely Number," was included in the revue *Dance Me a Song* (Royale N.Y.C., Jan. 20, 1950). He composed most of the incidental music for *The Madwoman of Chaillot* (Belasco, Dec. 27, 1948); wrote incidental music for *All Summer Long* (Coronet, Sept. 23, 1954); music for *Plain and Fancy* (Mark Hellinger Th., Jan. 27, 1955); music for *Redhead* (46th St. Th., Feb. 5, 1958); for *Cafe Crown* (Martin Beck Th., Apr. 17, 1964); and for *The Fig Leaves Are Falling* (Broadhurst, Jan. 2, 1969).

Films. He was composer for the background music for the short subject, *Coney Island, U.S.A.*, and he composed music for the film *The Funniest Man in the World* (1969).

Television. He was composer for *The Mercer Girls* (Hallmark Hall of Fame, NBC, 1953) and for *How the Grinch Stole Christmas* (1966).

Published Works. Mr. Hague's first published song was "Wait for Me, Darling" (1954). Two of his songs were included in Carl Sandburg's anthology, *New American Songbag* (1950). He devised the piano arrangements for the *Burl Ives Song Book* (1953).

Awards. *Coney Island, U.S.A.*, for which Mr. Hague composed the background score, won first prizes at the Edinburgh and Venice Film festivals (1951). He received an Antoinette Perry (Tony) Award for his music in *Redhead* (1959).

HAIGH, KENNETH. Actor. b. Mexboro, Yorkshire, England, to William and Margaret (Glynn) Haigh. Father, coal miner. Attended Central School of Speech and Dramatic Art, London. Member of British AEA; AEA; SAG; AFTRA.

Theatre. Mr. Haigh made his stage debut as Cassio in *Othello* (Drogheda, Ireland, 1952), as a member of Anew McMaster's Shakepearean Company, subsequently playing various roles and touring with the company until 1955. He made his first London appearance as Geoffrey Baines in *Dear Liz* (New Lindsay, Sept. 2, 1954); and appeared during the Shakespearean season at the Open Air Th. (Regent's Park).

In 1956 he was engaged by the English Stage Co., and in repertory at the Royal Court Th., London, played Peter in *The Mulberry Bush* (Apr. 2, 1956), Jimmy Porter in *Look Back in Anger* (May 8, 1956), and Beaufort in *Card of Identity* (June 26, 1956).

He made his N.Y.C., debut as Jimmy Porter in *Look Back in Anger* (Lyceum, Oct. 1, 1957; and on national tour); subsequently played the title role in *Caligula* (54 St. Th., Feb. 16, 1960); Jerry in *The Zoo Story* (Arts, London, Aug. 25, 1960); Franz and the S. S. Man in *Altona* (Royal Court, Apr. 19, 1961; transferred to Saville, June 5, 1961); joined the Royal Shakespeare Co. to play Friend in *Playing with Fire*, and James in *The Collection*, presented on a double-bill (Aldwych, June 18, 1962); and Marcus Antonius in *Julius Ceasar* (Stratford-on-Avon, Apr. 9, 1963); again played the title role in *Caligula* (Phoenix, London, Apr. 6, 1964); played Patrick Casey in *Maggie May* (Adelphi, Sept. 22, 1964); and the Burglar in *Too True To Be Good* (Edinburgh Festival, Scotland, Sept. 6, 1965; Strand, London, Sept. 22, 1965). At the Yale Sch. of Drama (New Haven, Conn.), he played Prometheus in *Prometheus Bound* (May 7, 1967); directed *Tis Pity She's a Whore* (Oct. 20, 1967), and played the title role in *Enrico IV* (Feb. 7, 1968); subsequently played Gov. Endecott in *Endecott and the Red Cross* (American Place Th. at St. Clement's Church, N.Y.C., Apr. 18, 1967); succeeded Paul Scofield (New, London, Dec. 9, 1967) as Laurie in *The Hotel in Amsterdam* (opened Royal Court, July 3, 1968); and appeared in *The Revenger's Tragedy* (Yale Repertory Th., New Haven, Conn., Jan. 7, 1971); repeated the role of Prometheus in *Prometheus Bound* (London, 1971); wrote and appeared in *Schreiber's Nervous Illness* (London, 1972–73 season); and appeared in *Marching Song* (Greenwich Th., London, 1974–75 season).

Films. He made his debut as Tony in *My Teenage Daughter* (1956); subsequently played Brother Martin in *Saint Joan* (U, 1957); Tony in *High Flight* (Col., 1958); Brutus in *Cleopatra* (20th-Fox, 1963); and Pvt. Tommy Atkins in *Weekend in Zuydcoote* (Paris Film Prods.); and appeared in *A Hard Day's Night* (UA, 1964); *Weekend at Dunkirk* (20th-Fox, 1965); *The Deadly Affair* (Co., 1967); *A Lovely Way To Die* (U, 1968); and *Eagle in a Cage* (NG, 1972).

Television. Mr. Haigh has appeared in *Golden Boy* (BBC, London, 1954); *Boswell and Johnson* (NBC, 1957); *Project Immortality* (CBS, 1959); *Bellingham* (Studio One, CBS, 1968); *Ten Little Indians* (NBC, 1959); *Misalliance* (CBS, 1959); *Beyond the Horizon* (Granada, London, 1960); *A Walk in the Desert* (BBC, London, 1960); *The Zoo Story* (Granada, London, 1960); *The Ways of Love* (ABC, 1961); *Captain Brassbound's Conversion* (BBC, London, 1962); *The Full Chatter* (BBC, London, 1963); Twilight Zone (Ind.); played David Douglas Home in a segment of the Sunday Night series (BBC, London, 1966); MacHealth in *The Beggar's Opera* (NET, 1967); and appeared in the series Men at the Top (Thames-TV, London, 1972).

Other Activities. Mr. Haigh has been an honorary professor at Yale Drama School (New Haven, Conn.).

HAILEY, MARIAN. Actress. b. Portland, Oregon. Grad. Univ. of Washington, B.F.A. 1961. Member of AEA; SAG; AFTRA.

Theatre. Miss Hailey made her stage debut while in college; subsequently, at the Oregon Shakespeare Fest. (Ashland), appeared as Valeria in *Coriolanus* and the Courtesan in *The Comedy of Errors* (Summer 1962); played Mistress Quickley in *The Merry Wives of Windsor*, Juliet in *Romeo and Juliet*, and Jacquenetta in *Love's Labour's Lost* (Oregon Shakespeare Fest., July 24–Sept. 7, 1973); the Horse Girl in *The Balcony* and Grace in *Telegraph Hill* (San Francisco Actor's Workshop, 1963–64); made her off-Bway debut as Robin Austin in *Under the Yum-Yum Tree* (Mayfair Th., N.Y.C., May 28, 1964); played Sybil in *Private Lives* (San Francisco Actors Workshop, 1965); made her unexpected Bway debut as an emergency replacement (June 18, 1965) for three performances during Barbara Cook's illness in the leading role in *Any Wednesday* (Music Box, Feb. 18, 1964); subsequently played Kelly Lewis in *The Mating Dance* (Eugene O'Neill Th., Nov. 3, 1965); appeared in a double-bill of *The Rope* and *A Week from Today* (ANTA Matinee Series, Th. de Lys, Nov. 23, 1965); played Alicia Hopper in *The*

Best Laid Plans (Brooks Atkinson Th., Mar. 25, 1966); Diana in *All's Well That Ends Well* (Delacorte, June 15, 1966); on a triple-bill entitled *An Evening with Thornton Wilder,* which included *The Happy Journey to Trenton and Camden,* played Leonora in *The Long Christmas Dinner,* and Marie-Sidonie Cressaux in *Queens of France* (Cherry Lane, Sept. 6, 1966); for the American Shakespeare Fest. (Stratford, Conn.), played Ismene in *Antigone* (June 18, 1967), and Nerissa in *The Merchant of Venice* (June 20, 1967); played Florence Brady in *Keep It in the Family* (Plymouth, N.Y.C., Sept. 27, 1967); Celia in *As You Like It* (ASF, Stratford, Conn., June 23, 1968); Myrtle Mae Simmons in *Harvey* (Univ. of Michigan (Ann Arbor) Professional Th. Program, Feb. 2, 1970; ANTA Th., N.Y.C., Feb. 24, 1970); Betsy Kress in *The Castro Complex* (Stairway Th., Nov. 18, 1970); replaced Beth Howland (May 13, 1971) as Amy in *Company* (Alvin, Apr. 26, 1970); and played Peggy (Mrs. John Day) in *The Women* (46 St. Th., Apr. 25, 1973).

Films. Miss Hailey has appeared in *Jenny* (Cinerama, 1970); and *Lovers and Other Strangers* (Cinerama, 1970).

Television. Her appearances include Trials of O'-Brian; Search for Tomorrow (CBS); Hey, Landlord; and *Read Me a Happy Ending* (CBS).

Other Activities. Miss Hailey is creative director of Actors Counciling Service, Inc.

HAILEY, OLIVER. Playwright. b. Oliver D. Hailey, Jr., July 7, 1932, Pampa, Tex., to Oliver D., Sr., and Hallie May (Thomas) Hailey. Father, butcher, mother, teacher. Attended Borger, Tex., public schools; grad. Univ. of Texas, B.A. 1954; Yale Univ., M.A. 1962. Married June 25, 1960, to Elizabeth Ann Forsythe; two daughters. Address: 11747 Canton Place, Studio City, CA 91604, tel. (213) 763-7827.

Pre-Theatre. Feature reporter for the Dallas (Tex.) *Morning News,* 1957–59.

Theatre. Mr. Hailey's first produced play was *Hey You, Light Man!* (Yale Univ., New Haven, Conn., Jan. 10, 1962); it was also his first work to be professionally produced (Theatre-by-the-Sea, Matunuck, R.I., July 1962) and his first off-Bway production (Mayfair, Feb. 26, 1963). Other works include *A Comedy for Orphans* (Yale Univ., Oct. 1962); *Home by Hollywood* (Mitchell College, New London, Conn., May 15, 1964); *Animal* and *Picture,* his first off-off-Bway productions (Caffe Cino, June 1965); *First One Asleep, Whistle* (Belasco Th., Feb. 26, 1966), his first Bway production; *Who's Happy Now?* (Village South Th., Nov. 17, 1969); *Crisscross* (Evergreen Stage, Los Angeles, Calif., Mar. 6, 1970); *Continental Divide* (Washington Th. Club, Washington, D.C., May 6, 1970); *Orphan* (Evergreen Stage, Los Angeles, June 17, 1970); *Father's Day* (Golden Th., N.Y.C., Mar. 6, 1971); and *For the Use of the Hall* (Trinity Square Repertory Co., Providence, R.I., Jan. 2, 1974).

Television. Mr. Hailey wrote "Panic" on Bracken's World (NBC, Oct. 1969) and was story editor for McMillan & Wife (NBC, 1972–74).

Awards. Mr. Hailey received the Phyllis S. Anderson Fellowship in playwriting for 1961 and 1962; won the Vernon Rice Award and a Drama Desk award for *Hey You, Light Man!* (1963); and received the certificate of merit of the Los Angeles Drama Critics Circle for *Father's Day* (1973).

HAINES, WILLIAM WISTER. Playwright, novelist. b. Sept. 1908, Des Moines, Iowa, to Diedrich Jansen and Ella (Wister) Haines. Father, engineer. Attended Culver (Ind.) Military Acad., 1922–23; grad. Roosevelt H.S., Des Moines, 1926; Univ. of Pennsylvania, B.S. 1931. Married Sept. 1934 to Frances Tuckerman; one son, one daughter. Served USAAF, 1942–45; rank, Lt. Col. Member of ALA; Dramatists Guild; WGA, West; Western Writers of Amer.

Theatre. Mr. Haines wrote *Command Decision,* (Cleveland Playhouse, Ohio, Nov. 1946; Fulton, N.Y.C., Oct. 1, 1948).

Films. He wrote the screenplay for *Alibi Ike* (WB, 1935); *Man of Iron* (WB, 1935); was co-author of the screenplay for *Black Legion* (WB, 1936); *Mr. Dodd Takes the Air* (WB, 1937); wrote the screenplay for *Slim,* which was based on his novel of the same title (WB, 1937); and was co-author of the screenplay for *The Texans* (Par., 1938); and for *Beyond Glory* (Par., 1948). *Command Decision,* was made into a motion picture of the same title (MGM, 1949).

He was co-author of the screenplay for *The Racket* (RKO, 1951); *One Minute to Zero* (RKO, 1952); wrote the story for *The Eternal Sea* (Rep., 1954); was co-author of the screenplay for *Wings of Eagles* (MGM, 1956); and *Torpedo Run* (MGM, 1958).

Published Works. Mr. Haines has written *Slim* (1934); *High Tension* (1938); *Command Decision* (adapted from his play, 1947); *The Honorable Rocky Slade* (1957); *The Winter War* (1961); *Target* (1964); and *The Image* (1968).

He has also written stories and articles for magazines.

Recreation. Shotgunning, carpentry.

HALL, ADELAIDE. Actress, singer. b. Adelaide Louise Hall, Oct. 20, 1910, Brooklyn, N.Y., to William and Elizabeth (Gearard) Hall. Father, music teacher. Married May 26, 1929, to Bert Hicks, artists' manager (dec. Nov. 4, 1963). Relative in theatre: cousin, Ronnie Chapman, singer. Member AEA; AFTRA. Address: 118 W. 111th St., New York, NY 10026, tel. (212) MO 3-4360.

Theatre. Miss Hall made her N.Y.C. debut as Adalade in *Runnin' Wild* (Colonial, Oct. 29, 1923); subsequently played in *Blackbirds of 1928* (Liberty, May 9, 1928); Betty Lou Johnson in *Brown Buddies* (Liberty, Oct. 7, 1930); appeared as Fitema in *The Sun Never Sets* (Drury Lane, London, June 9, 1938); toured during WW II with ENSA in Germany; played Hattie in the London production of *Kiss Me, Kate* (Coliseum, Mar. 8, 1951); Butterfly in *Love from Judy* (Saville, Sept. 25, 1952); Geneva in *Someone to Talk To* (Duchess, July 18, 1956); and Grandma Obeah in *Jamaica* (Imperial, N.Y.C., Oct. 31, 1957).

Films. Miss Hall has appeared in *The Thief of Bagdad* (UA, 1940); and *Night and the City* (20th-Fox, 1950).

Television. She appeared in the first TV show in Paris, entitled Paris Soir.

Night Clubs. Miss Hall has performed in the US and Europe including the Alhambra, Les Ambassadeurs, the Lido and the Moulin Rouge (Paris, 1934–38); the Cotton Club and the Savoy (N.Y.C., 1937); and the Savoy (London, 1938). She had her own club The Big Apple (Paris); and opened her own club, the New Florida Club (London, 1939).

Recreation. Painting, sewing, guitar.

HALL, ADRIAN. Director. b. Dec. 3, 1928, Van, Tex., to Lennie and Mattie (Murphee) Hall. Father, farmer. Grad. Van H.S., 1944; Texas State Teachers Coll., B.S. 1948; Pasadena (Calif.) Playhouse, B.T.A. 1951. Studied with Al McCleery at CBS Directors Workshop, N.Y.C., 1960–61; Lee Strasberg in Directors Unit of Actors Studio, N.Y.C., 1961–63. Served US Army, Special Services, ETO, 1951–53; rank, Cpl. Member of AEA; Directors Guild of America, Inc. Address: Trinity Square Repertory Company, 201 Washington St., Providence, RI 02903.

Theatre. Mr. Hall directed summer productions at the Playhouse Th. and the Alley Th. (Houston, Tex., 1953–54).

For the ELT (Lenox Hill Playhouse, N.Y.C.), he directed *Another Part of the Forest* (Nov. 14, 1956), and *The Time of Your Life* (1957).

He directed summer productions at the Phoenicia (N.Y.) Playhouse (1957–60); an ELT production of *The Trip to Bountiful* (Th. East, N.Y.C., Feb. 26, 1959); *Orpheus Descending* (Gramercy Arts, Oct. 5, 1959); *The Mousetrap* (Maidman Playhouse, Nov. 5, 1960); and *Donogoo* (Greenwich Mews, Jan. 18, 1961).

Also, summer productions at the Civic Aud. (Charlotte, N.C., 1961); the national tour of *Toys in the Attic* (opened Playhouse, Wilmington, Del., Sept. 27, 1961); *Red Roses for Me* (Greenwich Mews, N.Y.C., Nov. 27, 1961); *Riverwind* (Actors Playhouse, Dec. 12, 1962); and productions for the Repertory Players (Omaha, Neb., Feb. 1963).

He directed a revised production of *The Milk Train Doesn't Stop Here Anymore* (Barter Th., Abingdon, Va., Sept. 1963); and *The Hostage* (Fred Miller Th., Milwaukee, Wis., Jan. 1964).

In 1965, Mr. Hall became director of the Trinity Square Repertory Co., founded the preceding year in Providence, R.I. From his first season through the summer of 1974, Mr. Hall directed fifty-four productions for the company, of which the following were world premieres: *All to Hell Laughing* (1965); *The Eternal Husband* (1966); *The Grass Harp,* a musical (1967); *Year of the Locust* (1968); *Wilson in the Promised Land* (1969); *Lovecraft's Follies* (1969); *Son of Man and the Family* (1970); *The Good and Bad Times of Cady Francis McCullum and Friends* (1971); *Feasting with Panthers* (1973); and *Aimée* (1974). He was co-author, with Timothy Taylor, of *Son of Man and the Family* and, with Richard Cumming, of *Feasting with Panthers,* and he directed the television production of the latter (PBS, Mar. 27, 1974).

In 1968, Trinity Square Repertory Co. became the first American regional theatre to perform at the Edinburgh (Scotland) International Festival. Other appearances outside Providence include ANTA Th., N.Y.C. (1972); Cincinnati (Ohio) Playhouse and Sombrero Playhouse, Phoenix, Ariz. (both 1973); and Walnut St. (Philadelphia) Th. and Wilbur Th., Boston (both Summer 1974).

Awards. Mr. Hall received a Ford Foundation Grant to study regional theatre in Hawaii (1964). In 1969, he received the Margo Jones Award for outstanding work toward continuing production of new playwrights, and in 1972, Brown Univ. awarded him an honorary D.F.A. degree and Rhode Island College gave him the John Fitzgerald Kennedy Award for outstanding service to the community.

HALL, GRAYSON. Actress. b. Shirley Grossman, Philadelphia, Pa. Attended Temple Univ., Cornell Univ. Married 1956 to Sam Hall, writer; one son. Member of AEA; SAG; AFTRA.

Theatre. Billed as Shirley Grayson, she played Ann Whitefield in *Man and Superman* (Equity Library Th., Lenox Hill Playhouse, N.Y.C., Feb. 20, 1953); the Actress in *La Ronde* (Circle in the Square, June 27, 1955); and the Second Woman in *Six Characters in Search of an Author* (Phoenix, Dec. 11, 1955). Billed as Grayson Hall, she played the Penitent in *The Balcony* (Circle in the Square, Mar. 3, 1960), later succeeding Nancy Marchand as Madame Irma; played a season of stock at the Hedgerow, Pa., Th. (Summer 1961); Agata in *The Buskers* (Cricket, N.Y.C., Oct. 30, 1961); Myra Blake in *Subways Are for Sleeping* (St. James, Dec. 27, 1961); Crystal Seekfest in *The Love Nest* (Writers' Stage, Jan. 25, 1963); Connie Cerelli in *Shout from the Rooftops* (Renata, Oct. 28, 1964); Fru Gerdes in *Those That Play the Clowns* (ANTA, Nov. 24, 1966); Madge in *The Last Analysis* (revived, Circle in the Square, June 23, 1971); Melba in *Friends* and Stephanie de Milo in *Relations,* presented on a double-bill (Provincetown Playhouse, Oct. 14, 1971); Warda in *The Screens* (Chelsea Th., Brooklyn Acad., Nov. 30, 1971); Mrs. Fugleman in *The Secrets of the Citizens Correction Committee* (St. Clements Church, Oct. 17, 1973); Louise in *The Sea* (Manhattan Th. Club, Mar. 12, 1975); Comtesse de la Briere in *What Every Woman Knows* (Roundabout, May 28, 1975); and the 1st Interpreter in *The Leaf People* (Booth, Oct. 20, 1975).

Films. Miss Hall played in *Satan in High Heels* (Cosmic, 1962); Judith Fellows, the school teacher, in *Night of the Iguana* (MGM, 1964); in *That Darn Cat* (Buena Vista, 1965); *Adam at 6 A.M.* (Natl. Gen., 1970); *End of the Road* (Allied, 1970); and played Dr. Julia Hoffman in *House of Dark Shadows* (MGM, 1970) and Carlotta Drake in *Night of Dark Shadows* (MGM, 1971).

Television. She played Dr. Julia Hoffman and other characters in the daytime serial Dark Shadows (ABC, 1966–71). Her other appearances include Chrysler Th. (NBC); The Man from UNCLE (NBC); The Girl from UNCLE (NBC); Night Gallery (NBC); *The Two Lives of Sean Doolittle* (ABC Mystery Movie, 1975); and other programs.

Awards. She received (1965) an Academy (Oscar) Award nomination as best supporting actress for her performance in *Night of the Iguana.*

HALL, PETER. Director. b. Peter Reginald Frederick Hall, Nov. 22, 1930, Bury St. Edmunds, England, to Reginald Edward Arthur and Grace (Pamment) Hall. Father, stationmaster. Attended Perse Sch., Cambridge, Eng.; grad. St. Catharine's Coll., Cambridge Univ., B.A. (honors) 1953, M.A. 1958. Married 1956 to Leslie Caron, actress (marr. dis. 1965); one son, one daughter; married 1965 to Jacqueline Taylor; one son, one daughter. Served Natl. Service RAF Education Corps. Member of Arts Council. Address: (home) The Wall House, Mongewell Park, Wallingford, Berks, England; (bus.) The National Theatre, The Archway, 10a, Aquinas St., London, S.E.1, England.

Theatre. On Nov. 1, 1973, Mr. Hall succeeded Lord Olivier as director of England's National Th. From 1960 to 1968, he had been managing director of the Royal Shakespeare Co. (RSC)—known until 1961 as the Shakespeare Memorial Th.—at Stratford-upon-Avon. Mr. Hall created the RSC as a permanent ensemble and opened its London home, the Aldwych Th., in 1960. Following his resignation as managing director of the RSC in 1968, he became a consultant.

The first production he directed in N.Y.C. was *The Rope Dancers* (Cort, Nov. 20, 1957); subsequently, members of his Royal Shakespeare Company appeared in *The Hollow Crown,* a royal revue (Henry Miller's Th., Jan. 29, 1963), in *King Lear* (NY State Th., May 18, 1964), *The Comedy of Errors* (NY State Th., May 20, 1964); *The Homecoming* (Music Box, Jan. 5, 1967); *Old Times* (Billy Rose Th., Nov. 16, 1971); and *Via Galactica* (Uris Th., Nov. 28, 1972).

In England, Mr. Hall directed student productions at Cambridge, including *Uncle Vanya, Saint's Day, Love's Labour's Lost* and Pirandello's *Henry IV* for the Amateur Dramatic Club, the Marlowe Society, and the University Actors; his first professional directing was for *The Letter* (Th. Royal, Windsor, 1953); he directed modern and classical plays at the Oxford Playhouse and Worthing Repertory (1954–55).

He was assistant director of the Arts Th. (London, Jan. 1954), where he staged *Blood Wedding* (Mar. 3, 1954); *The Immoralist* (Nov. 3, 1954); became director of the Arts Th. (1955); and staged *The Lesson* (premiere, Mar. 9, 1955); *South* (Mar. 30, 1955); *Mourning Becomes Electra* (June 9, 1955); *Waiting for Godot* (English language premiere, Aug. 3, 1955); *The Burnt Flower-Bed* (Sept. 9, 1955); *Listen to the Wind* (Dec. 16, 1955); and *The Waltz of the Toreadors,* (premiere, Feb. 24, 1956).

He directed *Summertime* (Apollo, Nov. 9, 1955) and *Gigi* (New, May 23, 1956); *Love's Labour's Lost* (Stratford-upon-Avon, July 3, 1956); and a touring production of *The Gates of Summer* (Eng., Aug.–Sept. 1956).

Mr. Hall founded (1957) the Intl. Playwrights' Th. and became its artistic director, staging its first presentation, *Camino Real* (Phoenix, London, Apr. 8, 1957); staged his first opera, *The Moon and Sixpence* (Sadler's Wells, world premiere, May, 1957); directed *Cymbeline* (Shakespeare Memorial Th., Stratford-upon-Avon, July 2, 1957); *Cat on a Hot Tin Roof* (Comedy, London, Jan. 30, 1958); *Twelfth Night* (Shakespeare Memorial Th., Stratford-upon-Avon, Apr. 22, 1958); *Brouhaha* (Aldwych, London, Aug. 27, 1958); *Shadow of Heroes* (Piccadilly, Oct. 7, 1958); *Madame de . . .* and *Traveller without Luggage* (Arts, Jan. 29, 1959); at the Shakespeare Memorial Th. (Stratford-upon-Avon), *A Midsummer Night's Dream* (June 2, 1959), and *Coriolanus* (July 7, 1959); and *The Wrong Side of the Park* (Cambridge, London, Feb. 3, 1960).

As managing director of the Shakespeare Memorial Th., he staged *The Two Gentlemen of Verona* (Stratford-upon-Avon, Apr. 5, 1960); *Twelfth Night* (Stratford-upon-Avon, May 17, 1960); with John Barton, *Troilus and Cressida* (Stratford-upon-Avon, Aug. 30, 1960); and *Twelfth Night* (Aldwych, London, Dec. 19, 1960).

Mr. Hall directed *Ondine* (Aldwych, Jan. 12, 1961); *Becket* (Aldwych, July 11, 1961); *Romeo and Juliet* (Stratford-upon-Avon, Aug. 15, 1961); *A Midsummer Night's Dream* (Stratford-upon-Avon, Apr. 17, 1962); *The Collection* (Aldwych, London, June 18, 1962); *Troilus and Cressida* (Aldwych, Oct. 15, 1962); and *The Wars of the Roses* (edited version, presented in *Henry VI, Parts 1, 2,* and *3* and *Richard III* (Stratford-upon-Avon, July 17, and Aug. 20, 1963; Aldwych, London, Jan. 11, 1964).

As part of the 1964 celebration for the 400th anniversary of Shakespeare's birth, the Royal Shakespeare Company appeared in *King Lear* and *The Comedy of Errors* (Berlin, Prague, Budapest, Belgrade, Bucharest, Warsaw, Helsinki, Leningrad, Moscow, Washington, Boston, Philadelphia and New York (see above).

For the Royal Shakespeare Co., Mr. Hall staged *Richard II* (Stratford-upon-Avon, Apr. 15, 1964); *Henry IV, Part 1* and *Henry IV, Part 2* (Stratford-upon-Avon, Apr. 16, 1964), *Henry V* (Stratford-upon-Avon, June 3, 1964) and repeated *The War of the Roses* (Summer 1964), completing a seven-play history cycle, never before attempted.

He also directed *The Homecoming* (Aldwych, London, June 3, 1965); produced the opera *Moses and Aaron* (Royal Opera House, Covent Garden, London, June 28, 1965); directed *Hamlet* (Stratford-upon-Avon, Aug. 19, 1965); *The Government Inspector* (Aldwych, Jan. 1966); produced *The Magic Flute* (Covent Garden, July 5, 1966); directed *A Delicate Balance* (Aldwych, Jan. 14, 1969); *Landscape* and *Silence* (Aldwych, July 2, 1969); *The Battle of Shrivings* (Lyric, London, Feb. 5, 1970); produced the operas *La Calisto* (Glyndebourne, 1970), *The Knot Garden* (Royal Opera House, Covent Garden, London, 1970), and *Eugene Onegin* (Royal Opera House, 1971); directed *Old Times* (Aldwych, 1971); produced *Tristan und Isolde* (Royal Opera House, Covent Garden, London, 1971); directed *All Over* (Aldwych, London, 1972); produced the opera *Il Ritorno d'Ulisse* (Glyndebourne, 1972); directed *Alte Zeiten,* an Austrian production of *Old Times* (Burgtheater, Vienna, 1972); produced the opera *The Marriage of Figaro* (Glyndebourne, 1973); directed *The Tempest* (Old Vic Th., London, Mar. 5, 1974); and *No Man's Land* (Old Vic Th., Apr. 1975).

Films. Mr. Hall directed *Work Is a Four Letter Word* (Rank, 1968); *A Midsummer Night's Dream* (Eagle, 1969); *Three Into Two Won't Go* (U, 1969); *Perfect Friday* (Chevron, 1970); *The Homecoming* (American Film Th., 1973); and *Akenfield* (1974).

Television. Mr. Hall's *Wars of the Roses* was filmed for television (BBC, 1965), and his *Midsummer Night's Dream* was shown in the US (CBS, Feb. 9, 1969).

Other Activities. Mr. Hall is associate professor of drama, Warwick Univ.

Awards. The Order of Commander of the British Empire (C.B.E.) was conferred upon him (Oct. 30, 1963). He was made an honorary fellow at St. Catharine's Coll., Cambridge Univ. (1964); a chevalier de l'ordre des Arts et des Lettres (1965); and he received honorary doctorates from the universities of York (1966), Reading (1973), and Liverpool (1974) and the Shakespeare Prize of Hamburg (Germany) Univ. (1967). Mr. Hall also received London Theatre Critics awards as best director for *The Wars of the Roses* in 1963 and for *The Homecoming* and *Hamlet* in 1965; was awarded an Antoinette Perry (Tony) Award as best director for *The Homecoming* (1966); *A Midsummer Night's Dream* (CBS, 1969); received a nomination for a NATAS (Emmy) Award as best dramatic program; and Mr. Hall was nominated for a Tony for best direction (1972) for *Old Times.* .

Recreation. Music.

HALPERN, MARTIN. Playwright, actor, educator, critic-scholar, poet, literary critic. b. Oct. 3, 1929, New York City, to Louis and Edith (Eisinger) Halpern. Father, furrier. Attended DeWitt Clinton H.S.; Champlain Coll.; Univ. of Rochester, B.A. 1950, M.A. 1953; Harvard Univ., Ph.D. 1959. Married 1959 to Nancy M. Homer; one son, one daughter. Served US Army Signal Corp, 1951–53. Member of ATA. Address: (home) 14 Waban St., Natick, MA 01760, tel. (617) 655-4796; (bus.) Theater Arts Dept., Brandeis Univ., Waltham, MA 02154, tel. (617) 647-2574.

Mr. Halpern is associate professor of playwrighting and dramatic literature, and chairman of the Theatre Arts Dept. and a former assistant professor, at Brandeis Univ. (1965–to date). He was assistant professor at the Univ. of Massachusetts at Amherst (1964–65); instructor, then assistant professor at the Univ. of California at Berkeley (1959–64); and teaching fellow at Harvard Univ. (1954–56, 1957–59).

Theatre. He is the author of *Mrs. Middleman's Descent* (The Poets Th., Cambridge, Mass., 1958; and the Univ. of Calif. Dramatic Arts Dept., 1961); and *Reservations* (staged reading, San Francisco Playhouse, 1962; Judson Th., N.Y.C., 1962; Image Th., Cambridge, Mass., 1965; Univ. of Mass. Spring Arts Festival, 1965). His play, *The Mentor,* was a finalist in the ANTA competition for the Robert H. Bishop Award in Playwrighting, 1966; and was rewritten under the title *Visitations* (staged reading, the Berkshire Th. Festival Winter Series, 1973). He has written *Tameem* (Laurie Th., Brandeis Univ., 1966; and Calif. Olympiad of the Arts, 1968); *The Messiah* (Spingold Th., Brandeis Univ., 1970); *The Damned Thing* (Area Players, Milford, N.H., for the N.H. Th. Festival, 1972); *The Lower Drawer* (staged reading, Berkshire Th. Festival Winter Series, 1971; staged reading, the New Poets Th., 1968); and *Siege of Syracuse* (Laurie Th., Brandeis Univ., 1971).

Mr. Halpern has acted and directed with the Poets' Th., the Provincetown Playhouse, the Canal Zone Repertory Th., the El Panama Circle Th., and the Brandeis Univ. Theater Arts Dept. He produced and directed the staged oratorio *Let Us Arise and Sing,* commemorating the twentieth anniversary of the founding of the State of Israel (Boston Symphony Hall, May 1968).

Radio. *The Damned Thing* was produced by the Corp. for Public Broadcasting (1971), and has been widely broadcast here and abroad.

Published Works. He is the author of *Two Sides of an Island and Other Poems* (Univ. of N.C. Press, 1963); and *William Vaughn Moody* (Twayne Publishers, 1964). His poems and literary articles have appeared in numerous publications including *Literary Review, Quarterly Review of Literature, Publications of the Modern Language Association, Massachusetts Review, Atlantic Brief Lives,* and the Boston *Herald-Traveler* Supplement.

Awards. He was the recipient of a Fulbright Scholarship (1956–57); and a Howard Foundation Fellowship in creative writing (1962–63). His play, *Tameem,* was a Special Award winner in the Calif. Olympiad of the Arts (1968); and the radio play, *The Damned Thing,* received a Bronze Medal in international competition sponsored by the Corp. for Public Broadcasting and Radio Nederland (1971).

Recreation. Music, "serious amateur performer on the flute," tennis, reading.

HALSTEAD, WILLIAM P. Educator. b. William Perdue Halstead, Feb. 10, 1906, Terre Haute, Ind., to William L. and Jessie (Perdue) Halstead. Father, newspaper executive. Grad. Indiana Univ., A.B. 1927; attended Northwestern Univ., Summer 1928; grad. Univ. of Michigan, Ph.D. 1935. Married June 17, 1952, to Claribel Buford Baird, educator. Served US Army, 1942–46; Chief of Education Dept., Army Information Sch.; rank, Capt.; Army commendation ribbon with an oak leaf cluster. Member of AAUP; ATA (exec. secy., 1947–49; vice-pres., 1951; pres., 1953); ANTA (bd. of dir., 1953–62); Phi Kappa Phi; Sigma Delta Chi; Theta Alpha Phi. Address: (home) 2409 Vinewood Blvd.,

Ann Arbor, MI 48104, tel. (313) NO 8-8087; (bus.) 1502 Frieze Building, Speech Dept., Univ. of Michigan, Ann Arbor, MI 48104, tel. (313) 763-3019.

Mr. Halstead has taught at the Univ. of Michigan since 1934, becoming full professor in 1952, and chairman of the Theatre Committee, Dept. of Speech, in 1956. He formerly taught and directed plays at Sacramento Jr. College from 1929–31.

He has directed and/or acted in more than 50 plays, musicals, and operas in university theatre.

Published Works. He is the author of *Stage Management for the Amateur Theatre and an Index to the Published Works on Stagecraft* (1937); *Principles of Theatre Arts*, written in collaboration with H. Darkes Albright and Lee Mitchell (1955); "History of National Educational Organizations Connected with Theatre," written with Clara Behringer, published in *History of Speech Education in America* (1954). He has contributed articles to *Educational Theatre Journal* and *Quarterly Journal of Speech*. .

Recreation. Gardening, travel in Europe, and keeping a clipping file on theatre.

HAMAR, CLIFFORD E. Educator, director. b. Clifford Eugene Hamar, Jan. 17, 1914, Portland, Ore., to Clyde C. and Blanche Ethel (Green) Hamar. Father, farmer, transporation worker. Grad. Lincoln H.S., Portland, Ore., 1932; Whitman Coll., (Phi Beta Kappa) B.A. 1937; attended Univ. of Washington, Summer 1937; Stanford Univ., M.A. (speech and drama) 1941, Ph.D. (theatre and drama) 1951; attended Yale Univ., 1946–47; Danforth Fellow, Univ. of California at Berkeley, Summer 1961. Married June 20, 1941, to Jean Sturtevant, vocational counselor for Oregon State Employment Service; one son, two daughters. Served US Army, 1941–45; rank, Capt. Member of AETA (chmn., Bibliography Comm., 1951–53); SAA; ASTR; Tau Kappa Epsilon; Tau Kappa Alpha (hon.); Alpha Psi Omega (hon.). Address: (home) 0236 S.W. Palatine Hill Rd., Portland, OR 97219, tel. (503) CH 6-1361; (bus.) c/o Lewis and Clark Coll., 0615 S.W. Palatine Hill Rd., Portland, OR 97219, tel. (503) 244-6161.

Since 1962, Mr. Hamar has been professor of speech arts, director of international programs, and assistant Dean of Faculty at Lewis and Clark Coll., Portland, Ore. Between 1953–62, he was associate professor and professor of drama there as well as director of the college theatre.

Previously he had been an instructor in English and journalism at Walla Walla (Wash.) H.S. (1937–39); instructor of English, speech and drama, and director of dramatics at Ventura (Calif.) Junior H.S. (1939–41). During WW II, he served in the Middle East as Program Director of the Armed Forces Radio Station, Teheran, Iran (1942–43); as chief of Army News Service Persian Gulf Command, Teheran (1942–43).

He has been business and stage manager for the University Th. Company in productions at Lennox and Pittsfield, Mass. (Summer 1947); acting instructor of speech, Stanford University (1948–49); assistant prof. of speech and director of forensics at Kenyon Coll., Gambier, Ohio (1949–51); and assistant prof. of speech and drama and director of the theatre at Eastern New Mexico Univ. (1951–53).

Mr. Hamar has also served as a member of the Fine Arts advisory comm. to the mayor, Portland, Ore. (1958–62); and president of the board of trustees of the Portland Civic Th. (1957–58).

Recreation. Clipping collection devoted to visual arts and theatre history.

HAMBLETON, T. EDWARD. Producer. b. Thomas Edward Hambleton, Feb. 12, 1911, Towson, Md., to T. Edward and Adelaide Rose (McAlpin) Hambleton. Father, banker. Attended Gilman Sch., Baltimore, Md., 1920–25; St. Pauls Sch., Concord, N.H., 1925–30; grad. Yale Coll. B.A. 1934; Yale Univ. Sch. of Drama, 1935. Married 1936, to Caroline Hoysradt (dec. 1947); three daughters; married Feb. 19, 1949, to Mary Merrell Hopkins; two sons, one daughter. Served USNR, Air Combat Intelligence; rank, Lt. Comdr. Member of League of N.Y. Theatres (gov., 1953–59); Popular Awards Panel of ASCAP; Council of Living Th.; dir., Farrar, Straus & Giroux; dir., Peale Museum (Baltimore); Players Club; Century Assn. Address: 530 E. 86th St., New York, NY 10028, tel. (212) RE 4-5263.

Theatre. Mr. Hambleton is managing director of the Phoenix Theatre in N.Y.C., which he founded in partnership with Norris Houghton in Dec. 1953; the Phoenix merged with the Association of Producing Artists (APA) in 1964, to become the APA-Phoenix (a project of Theatre, Inc., of which Mr. Hambleton is vice-president); and reverted to the name Phoenix (Spring 1969) when APA was dissolved. The Phoenix has produced over 70 plays (for complete list, see Phoenix Th. in the Theatre Biographies section).

Mr. Hambleton was manager of the Theatre-by-the-Sea (Matunuck, R.I., Summers 1935–37); producer of *Robin Landing*(46 St. Th., N.Y.C., Nov. 18, 1937); *I Know What I Like* (Hudson, Nov. 24, 1939); and *The First Crocus*(Longacre, Jan. 2, 1942).

For the Experimental Theatre, Inc., sponsored by ANTA, he produced *The Great Campaign* (Princess, Mar. 30, 1947); *Galileo* (Maxine Elliott's Th., Dec. 7, 1947); *Temporary Island* (Maxine Elliott's Th., Mar. 14, 1948); and *Ballet Ballads* (Maxine Elliott's Th., May 9, 1948); which he then co-produced with Alfred R. Stern when it moved (Music Box, May 18, 1948).

Mr. Hambleton produced *Pride's Crossing* (Biltmore, Nov. 20, 1950); presented, with Norris Houghton, *The Power and the Glory* (Phoenix, Dec. 10, 1958); and produced, with Norris Houghton, William and Jean Eckart, *Once Upon a Mattress* (Phoenix, May 11, 1959; moved Alvin, Nov. 25, 1959).

He was director of Lumadrama, Inc., for which he produced the light-and-sound spectacle, *The American Bell* (Independence Hall, Philadelphia, Pa., Summers 1962–63).

Television. For Media Productions, which he formed with John Houseman, Howard Teichmann, and Alfred R. Stern, he produced TV films, including two documentaries for the US State Dept., and two recording series of the American Entertainment Industry, for broadcast on French radio, also for the US State Dept. (1948–51).

HAMILTON, MARGARET. Actress. b. Margaret Brainard Hamilton, Sept. 12, 1902, Cleveland, Ohio, to Walter J. and Jennie (Adams) Hamilton. Father, attorney. Grad. Hathaway-Brown H.S., Cleveland, 1921; attended Wheelock Kindergarten Training Sch., Boston, 1921–23. Studied voice with Miss Grace Probert, Cleveland (1917–21); at the Cleveland Play House (1927–30); studied acting and pantomine with Mme. Marie Ouspenskaya, N.Y.C., Joseph Moon, N.Y.C. (1932–33), and makeup with Mme. Daykarhanova, N.Y.C. (1933–34). Married June 13, 1931, to Paul Boynton Meserve (marr. dis. 1938); one son. Relative in theatre: niece, Sylvia Dick, dancer. Member of AEA (council, 1954–64); SAG; AFTRA; Los Angeles Junior League. Address: 34 Gramercy Park, New York, NY 10003, tel. (212) SP 7-7047.

Pre-Theatre. Nursery-school and kindergarten teacher.

Theatre. Miss Hamilton made her first N.Y.C. appearance as Helen Hallam in *Another Language* (Booth Th., Apr. 25, 1932); subsequently appeared as Hattie in *The Dark Tower* (Morosco, Nov. 25, 1933); Lucy Gurget in *The Farmer Takes a Wife* (46 St. Th., Oct. 30, 1934); played in stock at the Lakewood Th. (Skowhegan, Me., Summer 1941), in *Major Barbara, Kind Lady, Lady-in-Waiting, Old Acquaintance* and *Ladies in Retirement.*

She appeared as Gertrude in *Outrageous Fortune* (48 St. Th., N.Y.C., Nov. 3, 1943); as the Aunt in *On Borrowed Time* (Patio Th., Los Angeles, Calif., 1946); as Gwennie in *The Men We Marry* (Mansfield, N.Y.C., Jan. 16, 1948); appeared in *Three's a Family* (Tent Th., San Francisco Valley, Calif.); *Little Boy Blue* (Los Angeles, Summer 1950); as Mrs. Hammer in *Silver Whistle,* and Mrs. Fisher in *The Showoff* (Berkshire Playhouse, Stockbridge, Mass., Summer 1951); as Lucy Bascombe in *Fancy Meeting You Again* (Royale, N.Y.C., Jan. 14, 1952); Mrs. Zero in *The Adding Machine*(Phoenix, Feb. 9, 1946); Parthy Ann in *Show Boat* (State Fair Music Hall, Dallas, Tex., Summer 1956); and as Madame Kleopatra Mamaeva in *Diary of a Scoundrel* (Phoenix, N.Y.C., Nov. 5, 1956).

She played in the St. Louis (Mo.) Municipal Opera as Parthy Ann in *Show Boat* and the Wicked Witch in *The Wizard of Oz*(Summer 1957); appeared as Bessie in *Goldilocks*(Lunt-Fontanne Th., N.Y.C., Oct. 11, 1958); as Dolly Tate in *Annie Get Your Gun* (N.Y. City Ctr., Feb. 19, 1958); Mrs. Dudgeon in *The Devil's Disciple* (Playhouse-in-the-Park, Philadelphia, Pa.; Pocono Playhouse, Mountainhome, Pa., Summer 1958); as Mme. Dilly in *On the Town* and Sue in *Bells are Ringing* (Outdoor Th., Atlanta, Ga., Summer 1959); Cissy in *A Tree Grows in Brooklyn* Grand Th., Sullivan, Ill., 1960); and Dolly in *Bloomer Girl* (Grand Th., 1961); as the Witch in *The Wizard of Oz* (Casa Manaña, Ft. Worth, Tex.; Starlight Th., Indianapolis, Ind., and Brunswick Playhouse, Me., 1961); as Sabrina in *Old Acquaintance* (Royal Poinciana Playhouse, Palm Beach, Fla.; Sombrero Th., Phoenix, Ariz., 1962); as Grandma in *The American Dream* (Civic Th., Los Angeles, Calif., Mar. 1962); the Wicked Witch in *The Wizard of Oz* and Aunt Eller in *Oklahoma!*(St. Louis Municipal Opera, Mo., Summer 1962). She played Clara in *Save Me a Place at Forest Lawn* (Pocket Th., N.Y.C., May 8, 1963); Louise in *The Strangers* (Westport Country Playhouse, Conn., Nov. 1963); Clara in *Hay Fever* (June 14, 1965) and Miss Western in *Tom Jones* (July 26, 1965) at the Bucks County Playhouse, New Hope, Pa.; Mme. Pernelle in *Tartuffe* (Cleveland Playhouse, Ohio, Oct. 6, 1965); Connie Tufford in *UTBU* (Helen Hayes Th., N.Y.C., Jan. 4, 1966); the Mother in *Lullaby* (Little Th., Sullivan, Ill., May 20, 1966); Parthy Ann in *Show Boat* (NY State Th., N.Y.C., July 19, 1966); Madame Arcati in *Blithe Spirit* (Seattle, Wash., Repertory Th., Dec. 14, 1966; also, Cleveland Playhouse, Ohio, Jan. 25, 1967); Mrs. Malaprop in *The Rivals* (Seattle, Wash., Repertory Th., 1967–68 season); Dorinda Pratt in *Come Summer* (Lunt-Fontanne, N.Y.C., Mar. 18, 1969); Aunt Eller in *Oklahoma* (NY State Th., June 23, 1969); Mrs. Soames in *Our Town* (ANTA, Nov. 27, 1969); Madame Arcati in *Blithe Spirit* (Alley Th., Houston, Tex., Spring 1970); Mrs. Dudgeon in *The Devil's Disciple* (American Shakespeare Fest., Stratford, Conn., Summer 1970); in the premiere of *The Nephew* (Studio Arena Th., Buffalo, N.Y., 1970–71 season); Madame Desmermortes in *Ring Round the Moon* (Seattle, Wash., Repertory Th., Fall 1971); succeeded Ruth McDevitt as Stella Livingston in a tour of *Light Up the Sky* (Fall 1971); and played Madame Armfeldt in the national tour of *A Little Night Music* (opened Forrest, Philadelphia, Pa., Feb. 26, 1974).

Miss Hamilton was a co-founder (in Apr. 1969, with Rosetta Lenoire, Mara Kim, and Greta Gruenen) of AMAS, a repertory theatre and school, currently based at St. Paul's/St. Andrew's Church, 263 W. 86th St., N.Y.C. She was a vice-president (1969–73) and is on the board of directors.

Films. Miss Hamilton has appeared in *Another Language* (MGM, 1933); *Broadway Bill* (Col., 1934); *Hat, Coat and Glove* (RKO, 1934); *There's Always Tomorrow* (U, 1934); *The Farmer Takes a Wife* (Fox, 1935); *Way Down East* (Fox, 1935); *People Will Talk* (Par., 1935); *The Witness Chair* (RKO, 1936); *These Three* (MGM, 1936); *Chatterbox* (RKO, 1936); *Good Old Soak* (U, 1936); *The Moon's Our Home* (Par., 1936); *You Only Live Once* (UA, 1937); *Nothing Sacred* (UA, 1937); *When's Your Birthday?* (RKO, 1937); *Mountain Justice* (WB, 1937); *Laughing at Trouble* (20th-Fox, 1937); *I'll Take Romance* (Col., 1937); *Saratoga* (MGM, 1937); *Stablemates* (MGM, 1938); *A Slight Case of Murder* (WB, 1938); *The Adventures of Tom Sawyer* (New Trends, 1938); *Four's a Crowd* (WB, 1938); *Mother Carey's Chickens* (RKO, 1938); *Breaking the Ice* (RKO, 1938); *The Wizard of Oz* (MGM, 1939); *Babes in Arms* (MGM, 1939); *Angels Wash Their Faces* (WB, 1939); *Main Street Lawyer* (Rep., 1939); *My Little Chickadee* (U, 1940);

I'm Nobody's Sweetheart Now (U, 1940); *The Villain Still Pursued Her* (RKO, 1940); *Babes on Broadway* (MGM, 1941); *Play Girl* (RKO, 1941); *The Invisible Woman* (U, 1941); *The Gay Vagabond* (Rep., 1941); *Twin Beds* (UA, 1942); *Once Upon a Thursday* (MGM, 1942); *Meet the Stewarts* (Col., 1942); *Journey for Margaret* (MGM, 1942); *The Ox-Bow Incident* (20th-Fox, 1942); *Johnny Come Lately* (UA, 1943); *Guest in the House* (UA, 1944); *George White's Scandals* (RKO, 1945); *Faithful in My Fashion* (MGM, 1946); *Janie Gets Married* (WB, 1946); *Mad Wednesday* (UA, 1947); *Driftwood* (Rep., 1947); *Dishonored Lady* (UA, 1947); *State of the Union* (MGM, 1948); *Bungalow 13* (20th-Fox, 1948; *Texas, Brooklyn and Heaven* (UA, 1948); *The Beautiful Blonde from Bashful Bend* (20th-Fox, 1949); *The Sun Comes Up* (MGM, 1949); *The Red Pony* (Rep., 1949); *Riding High* (Par., 1950); *Wabash Avenue* (20th-Fox, 1950); *The Great Plane Robbery* (UA, 1950); *People Will Talk* (20th-Fox, 1951); *Thirteen Ghosts* (Col., 1960); *the Daydreamer* (Embassy, 1966); *Rosie* (U, 1967); *Angel in My Pocket* (U, 1968); *Brewster McCloud* (MGM, 1970); and *The Anderson Tapes* (Col., 1971).

Television. Miss Hamilton has appeared on *The Egg and I* (1952); A Date with Judy (ABC, 1953); in *The Man Who Came to Dinner* (Best of Broadway, CBS, Oct. 13, 1954); *The Guardsman* (Best of Broadway, CBS, Mar. 2, 1955); *The Devil's Disciple* (Hallmark Hall of Fame, NBC, Nov. 20, 1955); *The Trial of Lizzie Borden* (Omnibus, ABC, Mar. 24, 1957); *On Borrowed Time* (Hallmark Hall of Fame, NBC, Nov. 17, 1957); *Once Upon a Christmas Time* (NBC, Dec. 9, 1959); *The Silver Whistle* (Playhouse 90, CBS, Dec. 24, 1959); *The Bat* (Great Mysteries, NBC, Mar. 31, 1960); *The Night Strangler* (ABC, Jan. 16, 1973); and on numerous other dramatic and comedy shows, including the Paul Winchell Show; Ethel and Albert (ABC, 1957–58); the Phil Silvers Show (CBS); Ichabod and Me (CBS); Studio One (CBS); Ghostbreaker (NBC); and others.

HAMILTON, MURRAY. Actor. b. Washington, D.C. Member of AEA; SAG; AFTRA.

Theatre. Mr. Hamilton made his N.Y.C. debut as a Mill Hand in *Strange Fruit* (Royale Th., Nov. 29, 1945); subsequently played the Shore Patrol Officer in *Mister Roberts* (Alvin, Feb. 18, 1948); succeeded David Wayne as Ensign Pulver in that play, and toured in the role. He toured as Donald Gresham in *The Moon Is Blue* (opened Cass, Detroit, Mich., Apr. 19, 1951); and played Gary Mortimer in the pre-Bway tryout of *Modern Primitive* (opened New Parsons, Hartford, Conn., Dec. 26, 1951; closed there Dec. 29, 1951); played Bubber Reeves in *The Chase* (Playhouse, N.Y.C., Apr. 15, 1952); Robert E. Lee Prewitt in *Stockade* (President, Feb. 4, 1954); Sefton in a stock production of *Stalag 17* (Summer 1954); appeared in *A Burst of Summer* (Bucks County Playhouse, New Hope, Pa.); played Dion Kapakos in *Critics' Choice* (Ethel Barrymore Th., N.Y.C,, Dec. 14, 1960); and Jerry Hubley in *The Heroine* (Lyceum, Feb. 19, 1936).

He played (Sept. 23, 1964–June 1964) Bob McKellaway in *Mary, Mary* (Helen Hayes Th., Mar. 8, 1964), having replaced Biff McGuire in that part; was Otis Clifton in *Absence of a Cello* (Ambassador, Sept. 21, 1964); Dr. Herbert Garland in *The Man with the Perfect Wife* (Royal Poinciana Playhouse, Palm Beach, Fla., Mar. 22, 1965; Coconut Grove Playhouse, Miami, Fla., Mar. 30, 1965); and Billy Boylan in *Forty Carats* (Morosco, N.Y.C., Dec. 26, 1968).

Films. Mr. Hamilton made his debut in *Bright Victory* (U, 1951); subsequently appeared in *Whistle at Eaton Falls* (Col., 1951); *The Girl He Left Behind* (WB, 1956); *Toward the Unknown* (WB, 1956); *The Spirit of St. Louis* (WB, 1957); *Jeanne Eagels* (Col., 1957); *Too Much, Too Soon* (WB, 1958); *No Time For Sergeants* (WB, 1958); *Darby's Rangers* (WB, 1958); *The F.B.I. Story* (WB, 1959); *Anatomy of a Murder* (Col., 1959); *Tall Story* (WB, 1960); *Seconds* (Par., 1966); and *An American Dream* (WB, 1966).

Television. Mr. Hamilton has appeared on many programs, including the Loretta Young Show (NBC, 1964); Kraft Suspense Th. (NBC, 1964); The Untouchables (Ind., 1964, 1965); The Defenders (CBS, 1964, 1965, 1967); Slattery's People (CBS, 1965); Twilight Zone (Ind., 1965); Eleventh Hour (Ind., 1965); *Inherit the Wind* (Hallmark Hall of Fame, NBC, Nov. 18, 1965); Route 66 (Ind., 1965, 1966); The Trials of O'Brien (CBS, 1965, 1966); Dr. Kildare (NBC, 1966); Hawk (ABC, 1966); The F.B.I. (ABC, 1966); The Man Who Never Was (ABC, 1966–67); The Invaders (ABC, 1967); Playhouse 90 (CBS); and Gunsmoke (CBS).

HAMILTON, NANCY. Writer, actress, producer, playwright, lyricist. b. July 27, 1908, Sewickley, Pa., to Charles Lee and Margaret Miller (Marshall) Hamilton. Father, merchant. Grad. Miss Dickinson's Sch., Sewickley, 1925; attended Univ. of Paris (de la Sorbonne), 1925–26; grad. Smith Coll., B.A. 1930. Member of Dramatists Guild (on council, 1943); Amer. Th. Wing; ASCAP. Address: 328 E. 51st St., New York, NY 10022, tel. (212) PL 8-0743.

Pre-Theatre. Saleswoman, amateur critic for RKO.

Theatre. Miss Hamilton made her first stage appearance as Rosalind in *As You Like It* (Outdoor Private Theatricals, Sewickley, Spring 1918).

At the Student's Building of Smith Coll., she played Nanki-Poo in *The Mikado,* which she also produced and directed (Spring 1928), and appeared in the musical revue, *And So On,* which she directed, produced, and wrote (Spring 1930).

She made her N.Y.C. debut, succeeding (Mar. 19, 1932) Thelma Harbuick as the Runner in *The Warrior's Husband,* in which she also understudied Katharine Hepburn as Antiope (Morosco, Mar. 11, 1932); appeared in *At Mrs. Beam's* (Milbrook Summer Th., N.Y. 1933); contributed material to, and appeared in the revue, *New Faces,* for which she also directed her own sketches and songs (Fulton, N.Y.C., Mar. 15, 1934); played Miss Bingley in *Pride and Prejudice* (Music Box, Nov. 5, 1935); Nancy in *The Women* (Forrest, Philadelphia, Pa., Fall 1936); wrote the sketches and lyrics and appeared in the revue, *One for the Money* (Booth, N.Y.C., Feb. 8, 1939), and also appeared in it in Chicago, Ill. (Harris, June–July, 1939).

She wrote the sketches and lyrics for *Two for the Show* (Booth, N.Y.C., Feb. 8, 1940); contributed material to, and appeared in the USO production of *Kit Cornell's Jamboree* (Martha's Vineyard H.S., Mass., Aug. 8, 1942); wrote special material for Luella Gear in *Count Me In* (Ethel Barrymore Th., N.Y.C., Oct. 8, 1942); wrote the Army play, *The Man Who Wouldn't Be King* (Special Playwrights for G.I.'s, 1942–43); wrote for USO hospital shows 1942–45); was assistant manager and understudy in *The Barretts of Wimpole Street* (ETO, Aug. 4, 1944–Feb. 8, 1945); contributed material to Bea Lillie's revue, *Sigh No More* (Picadilly, London, Aug. 22, 1945); and wrote the sketches and lyrics for the revue *Three to Make Ready* (Adelphi, N.Y.C., Mar. 7, 1946).

She wrote special songs for Cyril Ritchard in a West Coast tour of *Peter Pan* (Summer 1954); and served as "Chef" for the *Dear Liar* Cornell-Aherne Land Cruising Tour (1959–60).

Films. Miss Hamilton wrote with Rosemary Casey, James Snute, and Frederick Loewe, the screen play for *Fools for Scandal* (WB, 1938); adapted *DuBarry Was a Lady* (MGM, 1943); was on the writing staff for *Women at War* (Office of War Information, 1943); was co-author and producer of *Helen Keller in Her Story* (de Rochemont Film Assoc., 1954), and wrote and produced the film, *This Is Our Island* for the tri-centenial of Martha's Vineyard, Mass. (Ross-Gaffney Films, 1971).

Radio. She performed on March of Time (CBS, 1932); wrote scripts for the Beatrice Lillie Show (CBS, 1935–36); wrote and performed in the sketch, "The Story of the Opera" (Duffy's Tavern, CBS, 1939); performed her song, "I Hate the Spring" (Duffy's Tavern, CBS, 1939); and wrote scripts for Billie Burke's *Fashions in Rations* (CBS, 1943–44).

Night Clubs. She contributed lyrics for Beatrice Lillie's appearance at the Mon Paris (London, 1934); wrote special material for Elsa Maxwell at the Versailles (N.Y.C., 1936); Brenda Forbes at the Blue Angel and Ruban Bleu (N.Y.C., 1941); Kitty Carlisle at the Rainbow Room (N.Y.C., 1942–43); Ray Bolger, Kaye Ballard, Gene Kelly, and others.

Published Works. She has contributed verse and articles to *Redbook* and *Stage* magazines.

Awards. Miss Hamilton received a civilian citation from the US Army for hospital shows and the ETO tour of *The Barretts of Wimpole Street* (1944–45).

For *Helen Keller in Her Story,* she received the Academy (Oscar) Award for Best Full-Length Documentary Film, and the Golden Reel Award for one of the ten best documentary films released in 16 mm. (1956), the Brussels (Belgium) World's Fair Film Festival Award (1958), the Venice (Italy) Film Festival Award and the Edinburgh (Scotland) Award; also, the ASCAP Special Award (1961).

Recreation. "Collecting inania, and occasionally my thoughts.".

HAMILTON, NEIL. Actor. b. James Neil Hamilton, Sept. 9, 1899, Lynn, Mass., to Alexander and Elizabeth (O'Neill) Hamilton. Father, metal polisher. Attended H.S. in Athol, Mass. 1912–14. Married Nov. 27, 1922, to Elsa Whitmer. Member of SAG; AFTRA; AEA (life member).

Pre-Theatre. Worked in hardware store.

Theatre. Mr. Hamilton made his debut in a touring production of *The Better 'ole* (1919); subsequently toured as Jack Torrence in *The "Ruined" Lady* (1920); and toured in *An Artist's Wife* (1921). He appeared with the Toledo (Ohio) Stock Co. (1921) and with the Sponer Stock Co. (Brooklyn, N.Y., 1922). Mr. Hamilton made his N.Y.C. debut as Henry Burton in *Many Happy Returns* (Playhouse Th., Jan. 5, 1945); followed by Ozzie Sykes in *The Deep Mrs. Sykes* (Booth, Mar. 19, 1945); General Thare in the pre-Bway tryout of *Crescendo* (opened Bushnell Memorial Th., Hartford, Conn., Jan. 18, 1946; closed Shubert, Philadelphia, Pa., Feb. 16, 1946); Grant Matthews in the national company of *State of the Union* (1946–47), and played this role for two weeks in N.Y.C. (Hudson, June 1947).

He played Dr. Alan Lambert in *The Men We Marry* (Mansfield, Jan. 16, 1948); Claude Franklin in *To Be Continued* (Booth, Apr. 23, 1952); Graham Colby in *Late Love* (National, Oct. 13, 1953); and Edward L. McKeever in the national company of *The Solid Gold Cadillac* (1955).

Films. Mr. Hamilton made his debut as an extra in *Claw* (Select, 1918); subsequently appeared in 300 films, including *The White Rose* (UA, 1923); *America* (UA, 1924); *Beau Geste* (Par., 1926); *Dawn Patrol* (WB, 1928); *the Sin of Madelon Claudet* (MGM, 1931); *Here Comes the Groom* (Par., 1934); *The Daring Young Man* (20th-Fox, 1935); *The Keeper of the Bees* (Col., 1947); *The Little Shepherd of Kingdom Come* (20th-Fox, 1961); and *The Patsy* (1964).

Television. Mr. Hamilton was emcee on Hollywood Screen Test (ABC, 1948–53) and appeared on Perry Mason (CBS, 1963–64); Outer Limits (ABC, 1964); *The Anne Hutchinson Story* (Profiles in Courage, NBC, Jan. 21, 1965); *In Darkness Waiting* (Kraft Suspense Th., NBC, Jan. 1965); Mister Ed (CBS, 1965); Cara Williams Show (CBS, 1965); Hawk (NBC, 1966); and Here's Debbie (NBC, 1969).

HAMMERSTEIN, JAMES. Producer, director, stage manager. b. James Blanchard Hammerstein, Mar. 23, 1931, New York City, to Oscar Hammerstein II and Dorothy (Blanchard) Hammerstein. Father, lyricist and librettist. Grad. George Sch., Newton, Pa., 1948: attended Univ. of North Carolina, 1948–50. Married June 7, 1954, to Barbara Regis (marr. dis. Aug. 1960); one son; married Jan. 20, 1962 to Millette Alexander (marr. dis. Mar. 1972); one son, one daughter; married Apr. 1972 to Geraldine Sherman. Relative in theatre: brother, William Hammerstein, producer. Member of AEA; League of NY Theatres; SSD&C. Address: 100 Prince St., New York, NY 10012, tel. (212) 431-9187.

Theatre. Mr. Hammerstein joined (Sept. 1950) the company as a replacement extra in *Mister Roberts*

(Alvin, N.Y.C., Feb. 18, 1948); subsequently was assistant stage manager for *Music in the Air* (Ziegfeld, Oct. 8, 1951); joined (May 1952) as assistant stage manager for *The Fourposter* (Ethel Barrymore Th., Oct. 24, 1951); was stage manager for *Maggie* (National, Feb. 18, 1953); succeeded (Mar. 1953) Beau Tilden as assistant stage manager for *South Pacific* (Majestic, Apr. 7, 1959); *Me and Juliet* (Majestic, May 28, 1953); production stage manager for *On Your Toes* (46 St. Th., Oct. 11, 1954); *Damn Yankees* (46 St. Th., May 5, 1955; Riviera, Las Vegas, Nev., Oct. 1957). The London production of *Damn Yankees* (Coliseum, Mar. 28, 1957) was directed by Mr. Hammerstein.

With Barbara Wolferman, he produced *Blue Denim* (Playhouse, N.Y.C., Feb. 27, 1958); staged *Damn Yankees* in stock (Music Fair, Camden, N.J., May 1958); was production stage manager for *Flower Drum Song* (St. James, N.Y.C., Dec. 1, 1958); in stock, directed *Show Boat* (Pinebrook Tent, Pinebrook, N.J., June 1959); with Stanley Prager, produced *Carmen Jones* (Theatre-in-the-Park, N.Y.C., Aug. 17, 1959); directed *Flower Drum Song* (Thunderbird, Las Vegas, Nev., Dec. 1961; Westchester Dinner Th. Playhouse, Yonkers, N.Y., May 1961); joined (June 1961) as stage manager for *Come Blow Your Horn* (Brooks Atkinson Th., N.Y.C., Feb. 22, 1961); and in stock, staged *The King and I* (Oakdale Musical Th., Wallingford, Conn., Aug. 1961).

Also, he directed *Come Blow Your Horn* (Poinciana Playhouse, Palm Beach, Fla., Jan. 1962; Paper Mill Playhouse, Millburn, N.J., Mar. 1962); staged *Flower Drum Song* (Mineola Playhouse, L.I., N.Y., Apr. 1962); *The Tender Trap* (Camden Music Fair, N.J., Aug. 1962); *Harvey* (Bucks County Playhouse, New Hope, Pa., Sept. 1962); and at the Mineola (L.I., N.Y.) Playhouse, *Come Blow Your Horn* (Oct. 1962) and *South Pacific* (Nov. 1962), both of which he repeated the following summer at the Warwick (R.I.) Musical Th. (July 1963); with John Fearnley, directed *South Pacific* (Thunderbird, Las Vegas, Nev., Dec. 1962); and staged *The King of Hearts* (Bucks County Playhouse, New Hope, Pa., Sept. 1963).

Mr. Hammerstein also directed *Absence of a Cello* (Ambassador, N.Y.C., Sept. 21, 1964); a revival of *South Pacific* (NY City Ctr., June 2, 1965); *The King and I* (Tel Aviv, Israel, 1966); *The Paisley Convertible* (Henry Miller's Th., N.Y.C., Feb. 11, 1967); the double bill *The Indian Wants the Bronx* and *It's Called the Sugar Plum* (Astor Place Th., Jan. 17, 1968); *State Fair* (St. Louis Municipal Opera, 1968); the double bill *Tea Party* and *The Basement* (Eastside Playhouse, N.Y.C., Oct. 15, 1968); the touring company of *Canterbury Tales* (Dec. 1969–May 1970); directed the London production of *The Tea Party* and *The Basement* (Duchess Th., 1970); co-produced and directed *Line* (Th. de Lys, N.Y.C., Feb. 15, 1971); directed *Wise Child* (Helen Hayes Th., Jan. 27, 1972); *Butley* (Morosco, Oct. 31, 1972) and road tour (1973); directed *Alfred the Great* (world premiere, Eugene O'Neill Th. Ctr., Waterford, Conn., Aug. 4, 1972; also Pittsburgh Playhouse, 1973; Trinity Square Rep. Co., Providence, R.I., Nov. 28, 1973); and directed a revival of *The Beauty Part* (American Place Th., N.Y.C., Nov. 5, 1974).

Mr. Hammerstein has been director in residence at the Playwrights Conference, Eugene O'Neill Th. Ctr., New London, Conn. (Summers 1967, 1969–72, 1974), and he has directed at various summer theatres productions of such musicals as *Camelot, South Pacific, Carousel, The Pajama Game, Guys and Dolls, My Fair Lady, How To Succeed in Business without Really Trying, The Music Man,* and *The Unsinkable Molly Brown.*

Recreation. Piano, tennis, skin diving.

HANDMAN, WYNN. Director, acting teacher. Grad. City Coll. of New York, B.A.; Columbia Univ., M.A.; The Neighborhood Playhouse Sch. of the Th., 1948. Served USCGR, 1943–46; rank, Lt. (jg). Member of AEA; SSD&C. Address: The American Place Theatre, 111 W. 46th St., New York, NY 10036.

Theatre. Since 1963, Mr. Handman has been director of the American Place Theatre in New York City, which develops and produces new plays by American writers. Previously, he taught acting and directed at the Neighborhood Playhouse Sch. of the Th. (1950–55); formed the Wynn Handman Studio, where he has conducted classes in acting (1955–to date).

HANLEY, WILLIAM. Playwright. b. William Gerald Hanley, Jr., Oct. 22, 1931, Lorain, Ohio, to William Gerald and Anne (Rodgers) Hanley. Father, house painter. Grad. Bayside (N.Y.) H.S., 1949; attended Cornell Univ., 1950–51; AADA, 1954–55. Married 1956, to Shelley Post (marr. dis. 1961); married Feb. 19, 1962, to Pat Stanley, actress; one daughter. Relative in theatre: sister, Ellen Hanley, actress. Served US Army, infantry, 1952–54; rank, 2nd Lt. Member of Dramatists Guild. Address: 470 West End Ave., New York, NY 10024, tel. (212) TR 4-5986.

Theatre. Mr. Hanley is the author of the one-act plays, *Whisper into My Good Ear* and *Mrs. Dally Has a Lover* (Cherry Lane, Oct. 1, 1962); the pre-Bway tryout of *Conversations in the Dark* (opened Walnut St. Th., Philadelphia, Pa., Dec. 23, 1963; closed there Jan. 4, 1964); *Slow Dance on the Killing Ground* (Plymouth, N.Y.C., Nov. 30, 1964; revived Sheridan Square Playhouse, May 13, 1970); and *Today Is Independence Day,* presented with *Mrs. Dally Has a Lover* as *Mrs. Dally* (John Golden Th., Sept. 22, 1965). *Whisper into My Good Ear* was later presented in England (Hampstead Th. Club, London, Apr. 3, 1966).

Films. Mr. Hanley wrote the screenplay for *The Gypsy Moths* (MGM, 1969).

Television. *Whisper Into My Good Ear* was presented on NY Television Th. (WNET, Nov. 29, 1965). He wrote *Flesh and Blood* (NBC, Feb. 1968).

Published Works. Mr. Hanley wrote a novel, *Blue Dreams* (Delacorte Press, N.Y.C., 1971).

Awards. For *Whisper into My Good Ear* and *Mrs. Dally Has a Lover,* he received the Vernon Rice Award (1963); for *Slow Dance on the Killing Ground,* he won the Annual *Variety* NY Drama Critics' Poll (Most Promising Playwright, 1964–65) and an Outer Circle Award (1965) as "an outstanding new playwright.".

HANSEN, HAROLD I. Educator. b. Mar. 10, 1914, Logan, Utah, to Hans D. and Nelsine (Hartman) Hansen. Grad. Logan H.S., 1933; Utah State Univ., B.S. 1937; State Univ. of Iowa, M.A. 1940, Ph.D. 1949. Studied theatre with Ruth Moench Bell, Logan, 1928–32; Maria Ouspenskaya, N.Y.C., 1937; Fred McConnell, Cleveland, Ohio, 1946. Married July 16, 1940, to Betty M. Kotter; four daughters. Member of Western Speech Assn. (drama comm., 1961–62); AETA (touring exhibits member, 1960–to date; overseas touring, 1962); Natl. Univ. Th. Festival (chmn. Region IV, 1963); NTC (bd. of trustees, 1963); Rocky Mountain Th. Conference (co-founder, 1952; pres., 1953–54; program chmn., 1955); Natl. USO Board; Brit. Society for Th. Research (honorary); NCP; Theta Alpha Phi (faculty advisor, 1962–to date; regional dir., 1954–to date; natl. pres., 1968–70); ATA-USO Overseas Touring Committee (chmn., 1957–74); USO Campus Shows (natl. chmn., 1974– ; Playwriting Awards, ATA University Festival (chmn., Region IV, 1974–. Address: (home) 440 E. 2875 North, Provo, UT tel. (801) FR 4-0942; (bus.) Dept. of Dramatic Arts, Brigham Young Univ., Provo, UT tel. (801) FR 4-1211.

Mr. Hansen was chairman of the Speech and Dramatic Arts Dept., Brigham Young Univ. (1952–68). He has produced and directed over seventy-five plays at the Brigham Young Univ. Th., including a production of *Blithe Spirit* which toured the US and the Far East (1961), and *The Man Who Came to Dinner* (1964), and USO tours of *Bye Bye Birdie* (1968), *Hello Dolly!* (1970), *Christmas in the Orient* (1971), and *Fiddler on the Roof* (1974).

Mr. Hansen also held academic positions at Michigan State Univ. (assist. prof., 1947); Utah State Univ. (assist. prof., 1948; assoc. prof., 1950; prof., 1951).

Theatre. He toured with the Progression Players (Idaho, Utah, 1935); played character roles with the Tent Players (Utah, Idaho, Nevada, 1936–37); adapted and directed the annual outdoor religious pageant of the Church of the Latter Day Saints, *America's Witness for Christ* (Hill Cumorah, Palmyra, N.Y., Summers 1937–to date); was a staff actor at the Cleveland (Ohio) Playhouse (1942–43); co-manager and company owner of Ledges Playhouse (Grand Ledge, Mich., 1957–to date); and was director-observer of the N.Y.C. production of *Gideon* (Plymouth, Nov. 9, 1961).

HAPGOOD, ELIZABETH REYNOLDS. Translator. b. Elizabeth Kempley Reynolds, Jan. 29, 1894, New York City, to Edwin Lewis Reynolds and Margaret Tay (Hewson) Reynolds. Father, Naval Officer. Grad. Ely Sch., Greenwich, Conn., 1910; attended Bryn Mawr Coll., 1910–11; Univ. of Paris, France, Diploma of Russian Studies, School of Living Oriental Languages, 1913. Married Dec. 13, 1916, to Norman Hapgood, editor, author (dec. Apr. 29, 1937); two sons, one daughter. Member of the Cosmopolitan Club, N.Y.C.

Theatre. Mrs. Hapgood's translation from Russian of George Shdanoff's adaptation of Dostoyevsky's *The Possessed* was produced on Bway (Lyceum, Oct. 24, 1939); and her translation from Russian of Eugene Schwarz's *The Dragon* was staged at the Phoenix Th. (Apr. 9, 1963).

Other Activities. Mrs. Hapgood was a lecturer at Columbia University (1915); founded the Russian Dept. at Dartmouth Coll. (1918–19); and taught Russian at Hunter Coll. (1943).

Published Works. Mrs. Hapgood translated from Russian Constantin Stanislavsky's *An Actor Prepares* (1936), *Building a Character* (1949), *Stanislavski's Legacy* (1958), *Creating a Role* (1961) and *An Actor's Handbook* (1963).

She translated *Home from the Sea, Robert Louis Stevenson in Samoa* by Richard A. Bermann (1939); *Second Wind,* autobiography by Carl Zuckmayer (1940); *The Angel with the Trumpet* by Ernest Lothar (1944); *One Page Missing* by Hans Jaray (1948); *Tolstoy, A Life of My Father* by Alexandra Tolstoy (1953); *Sons of the Sun* by Marcel F. Homet (1963); and *On the Trail of the Sun Gods* by Marcel F. Homet (1964).

HARBAGE, ALFRED. Educator, writer. b. Alfred Bennett Harbage, July 18, 1901, Philadelphia, Pa., to John Albert and Elizabeth (Young) Harbage. Father, grocer. Grad. Univ. of Pennsylvania, A.B. (Phi Beta Kappa) 1924; M.A. 1926; Ph.D. 1929. Married Sept. 7, 1926, to Eliza Price Finnesey; two sons, two daughters. Member of MLA; Shakespeare Assn. of America (advisory comm.); Yale Elizabethan Club; Tudor and Stuart Club (Johns Hopkins); American Academy of Arts and Sciences; American Philosophicol Society; and Signet Club (Harvard). Address: 52 Grant Ave., Cherry Hill, NJ 08034; (summer) 8626 Sunset Ave., Stone Harbor, NJ 08247.

Dr. Harbage was Henry B. and Anne M. Cabot professor of English literature at Harvard Univ. from 1952 to 1970, when he became Cabot Professor Emeritus of Harvard; he now writes and edits books. Previously, he taught at the Univ. of Pennsylvania (1925–47) and Columbia Univ. (1947–52).

Published Works. Dr. Harbage has written *Cavalier Drama* (1936; rev. 1964); *Annals of English Drama, 975–1700* (1940; new ed. 1963); *Shakespeare's Audience* (1941; new ed. 1961); *As They Liked It* (1947; new ed. 1961); *Theatre for Shakespeare* (1955); *William Shakespeare: A Reader's Guide* (1962); *Conceptions of Shakespeare* (1966); *Shakespeare's Songs* (1970); and *Shakespeare Without Words* (1972). In 1956, Dr. Harbage became general editor of *The Pelican Shakespeare,* completed in 38 vols. in 1967 and issued revised in one volume in 1969.

Awards. He received honorary Litt.D. degrees from the Univ. of Pennsylvania (1954) and from Bowdoin Coll. (1972); a Shakespeare Assn. of N.Y.

Award (1953); an ASFTA Book Award (1955); a Macmillan Book Award (1952); and the Harvard Faculty Prize (1966).

Recreation. Water sports, photography, gardening.

HARBURG, E. Y. ("Yip"). Lyricist, playwright. b. Edgar Y. Harburg, Apr. 8, 1898, New York City, to Lewis and Mary (Ricing) Harburg. Father, garment worker. Grad. Townsend Harris H.S., N.Y.C., 1914; Coll. of the City of NY, B.S. 1918. Married 1923 to Alice Richmond (marr. dis. 1929); one son, one daughter; married Jan. 6, 1943, to Edelaine Roden. Member of ASCAP; Dramatists Guild; ALA. Address: 262 Central Park West, New York, NY 10024, tel. (212) SU 7-6996.

Pre-Theatre. Newspaper writer; proprietor of electrical appliance company; wrote light verse for newspapers and magazines.

Theatre. Mr. Harburg contributed lyrics to eight songs in *Earl Carroll's Sketchbook* (Earl Carroll's Th., July 1929); wrote lyrics for *The Garrick Gaieties* (3rd Edition, Guild, June 4, 1930); Earl Carroll's *Vanities* (8th Edition, New Amsterdam, July 1, 1930); *Shoot the Works* (George M. Cohan Th., July 21, 1931); *Ballyhoo of 1932* (44 St. Th., Sept. 6, 1932); and *Americana* (3rd Edition, Shubert, Oct. 5, 1932).

He was lyricist of *Walk a Little Faster* (St. James, Dec. 7, 1932); *Ziegfeld Follies* (Winter Garden, Jan. 4, 1934); *Life Begins at 8:40* (Winter Garden, Aug. 27, 1934); *Hooray for What!* (Winter Garden, Dec. 1, 1937); *Hold on to Your Hats*, (Shubert, Sept. 11, 1940); and *Bloomer Girl* (Shubert, Oct. 5, 1944).

He was lyricist and author with Fred Saidy of *Finian's Rainbow* (46 St. Th., Jan. 10, 1947); *Flahooley* (Broadhurst, May 14, 1951); *Jamaica* (Imperial, Oct. 31, 1957); was lyricist and author with Mr. Saidy and Henry Myers of *The Happiest Girl in the World* (Martin Beck Th., Apr. 3, 1961); with Sue Lawless and Russell Baker wrote *Spread Eagle* (Washington Th. Club, Washington, D.C., May 19, 1966); wrote lyrics for *Darling of the Day* (George Abbott Th., N.Y.C., Jan 27, 1968); for Bil and Cora Baird Marionettes' *The Wizard of Oz* (Bil Baird Th., Nov. 27, 1968); for *A New Musical Entertainment* (Center Theatre Group, Mark Taper Forum, Los Angeles, Calif., June 17, 1971); and lyrics for *I Got a Song*, for which he also wrote the book with Fred Saidy (pre-Bway; opened Studio Arena, Buffalo, N.Y., Sept. 26, 1974; closed there Oct. 20, 1974).

Films. Mr. Harburg wrote lyrics for *The Sap from Syracuse* (Par., 1930); *Queen High* (Par., 1930); *Moonlight and Pretzels* (U, 1933); *Leave it to Lester* (Par., 1933); *The Count of Monte Cristo* (U, 1934); *Take a Chance* (Par., 1933); *The Singing Kid* (1st Natl., 1936); *Gold Diggers of 1937* (1st Natl., 1936); *Andy Hardy Gets Spring Fever* (MGM, 1937); *The Wizard of Oz* (MGM, 1939); *A Day at the Circus* (MGM, 1939); *Babes on Broadway* (MGM, 1941); *Ship Ahoy* (MGM, 1942); *Cairo* (MGM, 1942); *Rio Rita* (MGM, 1942); *Song of Russia* (MGM, 1943); *Cabin in the Sky* (MGM, 1943); *Meet the People* (MGM, 1944); *Hollywood Canteen* (WB, 1944); *Can't Help Singing* (U, 1944); *Kismet* (MGM, 1944); *Centennial Summer* (20th-Fox, 1946); *Stage Struck* (Mono., 1946); *California* (Par., 1946); and *Gay Purr-ee* (WB, 1962).

Concerts. Mr. Harburg appeared in the YM-YWHA (N.Y.C.) series *Lyrics and Lyricists* (Jan. 1972) and *The Librettists* (Dec. 1974).

Published Works. Mr. Harburg has written the following songs: "Over the Rainbow," "Happiness Is a Thing Called Jo," "Brother Can You Spare a Dime?," "April in Paris," "It's Only a Paper Moon," "What Is There To Say?," "Suddenly," "I'm Yours," "Isn't It Heavenly?," "You're a Builder Upper," "Ah, But Is It Love?," "More and More," "Evelina," "Right as the Rain," "Old Devil Moon," "On That Great Day Comin' Mañana," "How Are Things in Glocca Morra?," and "We're Off to See the Wizard." He also wrote the book *Rhymes for the Irreverent* (1966).

Awards. Mr. Harburg received the Academy (Oscar) Award for his lyrics in "Over the Rainbow" in *The Wizard of Oz* (1939); the Academy (Oscar) Award (1943) for "Happiness Is a Thing Called Jo;" the Henderson Award for his book and lyrics in *Finian's Rainbow* (1947–48); and the Townsend Harris Award from the City Coll. of New York as an alumnus (1950). Mr. Harburg was honored with a "salute" to his mini-musical called *Something Sort of Grandish* (All Souls Players, All Souls Fellowship Hall, N.Y.C., Jan. 22–26, 1976).

Recreation. Golf, tennis, swimming, traveling.

HARDING, ANN. Actress. b. Dorothy Walton Gatley, Aug. 7, 1902, Fort Sam Houston, San Antonio, Tex., to George Grant and Bessie Walton (Crabbe) Gatley. Father, army officer. Grad. East Orange (N.J.) H.S., 1919. Studied acting with Jasper Deeter, 1922. Married 1926 to Harry C. Bannister, actor (marr. dis. 1932; dec. 1960); one daughter; married Jan. 17, 1937, to Werner Janssen, conductor (marr. dis. 1963). Member of AEA; AFTRA; SAG (founder, 1st vice-pres.); The Cosmopolitan Club; Y.W.C.A. (Natl. Headquarters Committee).

Pre-Theatre. Home reader for Famous-Players-Lasky Corp.

Theatre. Miss Harding made her stage debut with the Provincetown Players, N.Y.C., as Madeline Morton in *Inheritors* (Provincetown Playhouse, Mar. 21, 1921); appeared with the Jessie Bonstelle Stock Co. (Buffalo, N.Y., June, 1921); made her Bway debut as Phyllis Weston in *Like a King!* (39 St. Th., Oct. 3, 1921); with the Jessie Bonstelle Stock Co., played the title role in *Peter Pan*, and appeared in *The Bird of Paradise* and *The Man Who Came Back* (June 1922); played Letitia Tevis in *Tarnish* (Belmont, Oct. 1, 1923); Sue Wynne in *The Horse Thief* (Chicago, 1923), which came to N.Y.C. as *Thoroughbreds* (Vanderbilt, Sept. 8, 1924); at the Hedgerow Th., Moylan, Pa., appeared in the title role of *Candida*, as Hilda in *The Master Builder*, Lina in *Misalliance*, and Lady Cecily in *Captain Brassbound's Conversion;* and played Venice Pollen in *The Green Hat* (Chicago, Ill., Apr. 12, 1925).

She appeared as Marie Millais in *Stolen Fruit* (Eltinge, N.Y.C., Oct. 7, 1925); Bianca in special matinees of *The Taming of the Shrew* (Klaw, Dec. 18, 1925); Anna Schweiger in *Schweiger* (Mansfield, Mar. 23, 1926); Marie-Ange in *A Woman Disputed* (Forrest, Sept. 28, 1926); Mary Dugan in *The Trial of Mary Dugan* (National, Sept. 19, 1927), and in Chicago (1928); and toured as Nina Leeds in *Strange Interlude* (Mar. 1929).

Miss Harding made her London debut in the title role of *Candida* (Globe, Feb. 10, 1937) (G.B.S. attended rehearsals); touring in the role in the US (1938); toured as Ann Murray in *Yes, My Darling Daughter* (Summer 1949); succeeded (Oct. 1949) Ruth Hussey as Agatha Reed in *Goodbye, My Fancy* (Martin Beck Th., N.Y.C., Nov. 17, 1948), and appeared in the role in Chicago (Harris, Dec. 26, 1949).

She succeeded (May 1958) Hortense Alden in the double-bill *Garden District*, appearing as Grace Lancaster in *Something Unspoken* and as Mrs. Venable in *Suddenly Last Summer* (York Playhouse, Jan. 7, 1958); toured as the Mother in *September Tide* (Summer 1958); Mrs. Amelia Dampler in *Two Queens of Love and Beauty* (Bucks County Playhouse, New Hope, Pa., July 1961); Rena Seeger in *General Seeger* (Lyceum, N.Y.C., Feb. 28, 1962); Charlotte Banderol in the pre-Bway tryout of *Banderol* (opened Forrest, Philadelphia, Sept. 17, 1962; closed there Sept. 22, 1962); toured as Miss Moffatt in *The Corn Is Green* (West Coast, Summer 1963); Amanda in *The Glass Menagerie* (West Coast, 1963); played Mrs. Devere in *The Moments of Love* (Westport, Conn., Country Playhouse, Oct. 29 1963); and played Myra Holliday in *Abraham Cochrane* (Belasco, N.Y.C., Feb. 17, 1964).

Films. Miss Harding made her film debut in *Paris Bound* (Pathé, 1929); subsequently appeared in *Condemned* (UA, 1929); *War and Women* (1929); *Her Private Affair* (Pathé, 1929); *Holiday* (Pathé, 1930); *Girl of the Golden West* (1st Natl., 1930); *East Lynne* (20th-Fox, 1931); *Devotion* (Pathé, 1931); *Prestige* (RKO, 1932); *The Conquerors* (RKO, 1932); *Westward Passage* (RKO, 1932); *The Animal Kingdom* (RKO, 1932); *Double Harness* (RKO, 1933); *Right to Romance* (RKO, 1933); *When Ladies Meet* (MGM, 1933); *Gallant Lady* (UA, 1933); *The Life of Vergie Winters* (RKO, 1934); *The Fountain* (RKO, 1934); *Enchanted April* (RKO, 1935); *Peter Ibbetson* (Par., 1935); *Biography of a Bachelor Girl* (MGM, 1935); *The Flame Within* (Par., 1935); *The Lady Consents* (RKO, 1936); *The Witness Chair* (RKO, 1936); *Love from a Stranger* (UA, 1937); *Stella Dallas* (UA, 1937); *Eyes in the Night* (MGM, 1942); *The Male Animal* (WB, 1942); *Mission to Moscow* (WB, 1943); *The North Star* (RKO, 1943); *Nine Girls* (Col., 1944); *Janie* (WB, 1944); *Those Endearing Young Charms* (RKO, 1945); *Janie Gets Married* (WB, 1946); *It Happened on Fifth Avenue* (Allied, 1947); *Christmas Eve* (UA, 1947); *the Magnificent Yankee* (MGM, 1950); *Two Weeks with Love* (MGM, 1950); *The Unknown Man* (MGM, 1951); *The Man in the Grey Flannel Suit* (20th-Fox, 1956); *I've Lived Before* (U, 1956); and *Strange Intruder* (Allied, 1956).

Television. She has appeared on Pulitzer Prize Playhouse (ABC, 1952); Hollywood Opening Night (NBC); Ford Th. (NBC); Schlitz Playhouse (CBS); Danger (CBS); Video Th. (CBS); Stage 7 (CBS); Armstrong Circle Th. (CBS); Lux Video Th. (NBC); Damon Runyon Th. (CBS); GE Th. (CBS); Crossroads (ABC); Matinee Th. (NBC); in *The Late George Apley* (20th-Fox Hour, CBS, Nov. 16, 1955); on Climax (CBS); Front Row Center (CBS); The Defenders (CBS); Playwrights '56 (NBC); Dupont Th. (ABC); Kraft Th. (NBC); the June Allyson Show (CBS); Our American Heritage (NBC); in *Morning's at Seven* (Play of the Week, WNTA, Apr. 25, 1960); on Westinghouse Presents (CBS); as Mrs. Callifer in *The Potting Shed* (Play of the Week, WNTA, Jan. 9, 1961); on Alfred Hitchcock Presents (CBS); Burke's Law (ABC); Dr. Kildare (NBC); Ben Casey (ABC); and Eleventh Hour (NBC).

Other Activities. Miss Harding was guest instructor in techniques of acting at the Sch. of Speech and Drama, Eastern New Mexico Univ. (June 3–July 31, 1964).

Recreation. Reading mostly and my stereophonic recordings of classical music.

HARDY, JOSEPH. Actor. b. Joseph Francis John Hoare, Aug. 10, 1918, Arlington, Mass., to James Joseph and Nora (Curtin) Hoare. Father, blacksmith. Educ. Arlington public schools; Leland Powers School of Theatre. Married Aug. 17, 1966, to Lynne Emery, actress (stage name, Lynne Hardy). Member of AEA; AFTRA; SAG; Actors' Fund of America; Actors Studio; the Lambs (honorary member of Sons of the Desert). Address: Radio City Station, P.O. Box 238, N.Y.C., NY 10019.

Theatre. Mr. Hardy first appeared on stage as a member of casts in high school productions in Arlington and Everett, Mass., in 1938. He began appearing in summer stock as Dr. Jennings in *Margin for Error* (Boston Stock Co., Malden, Mass., June 23, 1941) and made his professional debut as George Kittridge in *The Philadelphia Story* (Lake Whalom Th., Fitchburg, Mass., June 30, 1942) following with his appearance there as Mr. Purkiss in *Theatre* (July 7, 1942). He made his Bway debut as a robot in a revival of *R.U.R.* (Ethel Barrymore Th., Dec. 3, 1942) and appeared at the Cedarhurst (N.Y.) Playhouse in 1943 as Kurt Muller in *Watch on the Rhine* (Aug. 3), George Simon in *Counsellor at Law* (Aug. 11), and Richard Winthrop in *The Ghost Train* (Dec. 24). In 1944, he appeared there as Theseus in *The Warrior's Husband* (Jan. 1) and played at the Queensboro Th., Elmhurst, N.Y., as Uncle Willis in *Junior Miss* (May 16), Boris Kolenkhov in *You Can't Take It With You* (May 23), Lt. Rooney in *Arsenic and Old Lace* (July 11), the Butler in *Let Us Be Gay* (Sept. 26), and Joe Franklin in *Three's a Family* (Oct. 10). He starred in the title role of *Dracula* (Casino Park Playhouse Tent, Virginia Beach, Va., July 31, 1944).

Mr. Hardy appeared as the Shipmaster in *The Tempest* (Shubert Th., Philadelphia, Pa., Dec. 26, 1944), traveled to Boston with the production, and opened in it in N.Y.C. (Alvin Th., Jan. 25, 1945). During the summer of 1945, he played at the Grove Th., Nuangola, Pa., as Jim Blackman in *Chicken Every Sunday* (July 16), Col. Tadeusz Sterbinsky in *Jacobowsky and the Colonel* (Aug. 13), and Lt. Andrew Crewson in *Kiss Them for Me* (Aug. 20). He played Antonio in *The Tempest* (Shubert Th., New Haven, Conn., Sept. 13, 1945) and toured with the production; appeared in ELT productions of *The Lawyer* and *The Hasty Heart* (both N.Y.C., Apr. 1946); and in the summer of 1946 appeared at the Music Hall, Clinton, N.J., as Sergeant Rough in *Angel Street* (June 3), Nifty Miller in *The Barker* (June 8), and Major William Cardew in *Too Many Husbands* (Sept. 2). He played Jimmy Murphy in *The Front Page* (Civic Th., Chicago, Ill., Feb. 14, 1947); and in the summer of 1947 played at the Olney (Md.) Th. as Clark Redfield in *Dream Girl* (May 30), Grey Meredith in *A Bill of Divorcement* (June 24), Tallant in *The Late Christopher Bean* (July 15), Horace Giddens in *The Little Foxes* (July 22), Gene Tuttle in *Personal Appearance* (Aug. 5), and Digger in *The Hasty Heart* (Aug. 12). He returned to the Music Hall, Clinton, N.J., as Gabby Sloan in *The Milky Way* (Aug. 25, 1947) and Kenneth Bixby in *Goodbye Again* (Sept. 1, 1947); played Osric in *Hamlet* (Litchfield Summer Th., Conn., Sept. 9, 1947); and Albert von Eckhardt in *Caprice* (Plaza Th., Reading, Pa., Dec. 1, 1947). In the summer of 1948 he played at Town Hall, Cohasset, Mass., as Clark Redfield in *Dream Girl* (July 5), Benjamin Hubbard in *Another Part of the Forest* (July 12), George Deever in *All My Sons* (Aug. 2), State Trooper Brendle in *Papa Is All* (Aug. 9), in several parts in *Seven Keys to Baldpate* (Aug. 16), and Charlie Dawes in *Art and Mrs. Bottle* (Aug. 23). He was David Bellow in *I Like It Here* (Music Hall, Clinton, N.J., Sept. 6, 1948) and, at the Crest Th., Long Beach, N.Y. (Summer 1949), the Trumpeter in *Amphitryon 38* (July 11), Detective Britten in *Native Son* (Aug. 1), and Lane in *The Importance of Being Earnest* (Sept. 5). He appeared as Jimmy Murphy in *The Front Page* (Astor Th., East Hartford, Conn., Oct. 24, 1949); Fred Clark in *The Respectful Prostitute* (Selwyn Th., N.Y.C., Dec. 23, 1949); Detective Tom Gallagher in *Detective Story* (Hudson Th., Apr. 24, 1950); the Motorcycle Officer in *The Small Hours* (National, Feb. 15, 1951); and substituted for Matt Briggs as Ed Keller in *The Male Animal* (Music Box Th., May 17, 1952).

Mr. Hardy played the role of Reed in *Stalag 17* (Bucks County Playhouse, New Hope, Pa., Aug. 9, 1954; Stamford Playhouse, Conn., Mar. 16, 1955) and appeared at Olney (Md.) Th. in Summer 1955 as Grant Cobbler in *Oh Men, Oh Women* (July 12) and as Tom in *The Time of Your Life* (Aug. 23). He was Chief Johnson in a revival of Mr. Roberts (NY City Ctr., Dec. 5, 1956); Robert Kensington in *Career* (Actor's Playhouse, May 17, 1957); Franklin D. Roosevelt in *Sunrise at Campobello* (Gateway Playhouse, Bellport, N.Y., Aug. 2, 1960); Father in *Life With Father* (Nutmeg Playhouse, Storrs, Conn., July 17, 1962); Herbert Sebastian in *A Perfect Frenzy* (Bucks County Playhouse, New Hope, Pa., June 29, 1964); Sergeant Tinley in *The Plough and the Stars* (Charles Playhouse, Boston, Mass., Mar. 10, 1965); Mayor Crane in *Never Too Late* (Country Dinner Th., Dallas, Tex., Sept. 3, 1969; Beef 'n Boards Dinner Th., Ky., July 4, 1970); Mr. Jones in *Mutilations* (Th. Genesis, N.Y.C., May 12, 1972); and Father Christmas in *The Masque of St. George and the Dragon* (Actor's Studio, Dec. 23, 1972).

Films. Mr. Hardy first appeared in motion pictures as a soldier in *Stage Door Canteen* (UA, 1943), and since then he has had parts in many other films, including *Never Too Late* (WB, 1966); *Reflections in a Golden Eye* (WB, 1967); *Star!* (20th-Fox, 1967); *Where Were You When the Lights Went Out?* (MGM, 1968); *No Way to Treat a Lady* (Par., 1968); *The Night They Raided Minsky's* (UA, 1968); *The Godfather* (1972); *Shamus* (1972); *Cops and Robbers* (1972); and *For Pete's Sake* (1974).

Television and Radio. Mr. Hardy began performing on radio on the Souls of Steel series presented by the Leland Powers Players in Boston, Mass., over station WHDH (1939–40). He subsequently was on such coast-to-coast network programs as Major Bowes' Original Radio Amateur Hour (CBS, 1942, 1943) and the Arthur Godfrey Talent Scouts (CBS, 1947) in a mimicry act.

He made his television debut doing his night club act of imitations (Dumont, Oct. 25, 1944). His many television performances since then include appearances in *The Raven* (Pulitzer Prize Playhouse, WJZ-TV, Nov. 10, 1950); Martin Kane, Private Eye (WNBT, May 3, 1951); *Just for the Record* (The Clock, WNBT, Nov. 28, 1951); *The Town* (Pulitzer Prize Playhouse, WJZ-TV, Jan. 16, 1952); *Letter from a Soldier (pilot for The Doctor, May 1952); Time Bomb* (Philco Playhouse, WNBT, Oct. 3, 1954); Love of Life (CBS, 1955, 1956); The Secret Storm (CBS, 1954–55–56–57); *The Constitution* (Omnibus, CBS, Feb. 19, 1956); *The Man Who Could Not Say No* (Kraft Television Th., NBC, Feb. 13, 1957); *There Shall Be No Night* (Hallmark Hall of Fame, NBC, Mar. 15, 1957); The Edge of Night (CBS, 1957); *Fire and Ice* (Kraft Television Th., NBC, Apr. 1957); *The Invincible Mr. Disraeli* (Hallmark Hall of Fame, NBC, Mar. 20, 1963); and Woody Allen Political Special (NET, Dec. 7, 1971).

Night Clubs. Mr. Hardy has presented his mimicry act in a wide variety of night spots, beginning at the Paradise Cafe, Boston, Mass., Oct. 1, 1938, and including the Coronet Club, Philadelphia, Pa. (Nov. 20, 1945) and La Martinique, N.Y.C. (Nov. 27, 1945).

Other Activities. Mr. Hardy has had parts in a variety of Actors Studio projects in N.Y.C. and was made a permanent observer at Actors Studio because of his participation. He has also appeared in showcase presentations of the New Dramatists, N.Y.C., and the Performing Arts Library, Lincoln Center, N.Y.C.

Recreation. Mr. Hardy's hobbies include the recording of sound tracks of old motion pictures and playing them back and writing short stories for his own entertainment.

HARLEY, MARGOT. Producing director, school administrator, actress, dancer. b. Margot Isadora Holdstein, Nov. 21, 1935, to Walter Myron and Sophie (Bick) Holdstein. Educ. Dalton School, N.Y.C., 1939–53; Sarah Lawrence College, 1953–57. Professional training at London Academy of Music and Dramatic Art, 1960–61; Uta Hagen; Doris Humphrey; Hanya Holm; American School of Ballet, Bessie Schonberg. Address: (home) 225 E. 74th St., New York, NY 10021, tel. (212) 628-6373; (bus.) City Center Acting Co., 130 W. 56th St., New York, NY 10019, tel. (212) 489-8548.

Theatre. Miss Harley became producing director of the City Center Acting Company, N.Y.C., when it was formed in 1972. She began her career in the theatre as a dancer with the Doris Humphrey Repertory Dance Company, making her first appearance as a sister in *Shakers* (Connecticut College Summer Dance Festival, New London, Conn., Aug. 1955). She remained with the Doris Humphrey company until 1957, appearing as the Black Dove in *Dawn in New York*, the Beautiful Stranger in *The Race of Life*, and in *Life of the Bee* and *Descent into Dream*. She was choreographer of *A Hole Is to Dig*, her first work to be presented on the stage (Kaufmann Concert Hall, YMHA, N.Y.C., Apr. 1957). In 1959–60, she was a member of the Helen Tamiris Company.

She made her theatrical debut in summer stock as Nancy in *High Button Shoes* (Detroit Melody Circus, June 1956) and her off-Bway debut as Fay in *The Boy Friend* (Cherry Lane Th., N.Y.C., Oct. 1958), followed by appearances as Charity in *The Crystal Heart* (E. 74th St. Th., Feb. 15, 1960) and Alice in *Ernest in Love* (Gramercy Arts Th., May 4, 1960). She made her Bway debut as a dancer in *Milk and Honey* (Martin Beck, Th., N.Y.C., Oct. 10, 1961, with which she went on tour (Jan. 1963).

Miss Harley became administrator of the Drama Division, Juilliard School, N.Y.C., in 1969, and the actor training program there led to formation of the City Center Acting Company in 1972, with Miss Harley as producing director. The company opened its first professional season at the Saratoga Performing Arts Center, Saratoga Springs, N.Y., in July 1972 with *The School for Scandal, Women Beware Women, The Hostage, U.S.A.*, and *Scapin* and, with the addition of *The Lower Depths* to the repertoire, followed with a N.Y.C. season (Good Shepherd-Faith Church, Sept.–Oct. 1972) and tour (Oct. 1972–Apr. 1973). The company's second season, again beginning at Saratoga (Summer 1973), continuing in N.Y.C. (Billy Rose Th., Fall 1973), and ending with a tour (Sept. 1973–May 1974), included *The Three Sisters, The Beggar's Opera, Measure for Measure*, and *Next Time I'll Sing to You*. In July 1974, the company presented *Love's Labour's Lost*, Edward II, and *Play/Orchestra* at Saratoga.

Other Activities. Miss Harley was associate producer, KQED, San Francisco, Cal. (1965–67) and executive director, Friends of Channel 13, N.Y.C. (1967–69).

Awards. Miss Harley received a Fulbright scholarship for drama to the London Academy of Music and Drama in 1960. The City Center Acting Company received a special citation from the *Village Voice* Off-Bway (Obie) Award committee for its inaugural classical repertory season.

HARMON, CHARLOTTE. Editor, producer. b. Charlotte Josephine Buchwald, May 26, New York City, to Ephraim and Jennie (Heyman) Buchwald. Grad. Wadleigh H.S., N.Y.C.; attended Columbia Univ. (drama and writing). Married June 27, 1938, to Lewis Harmon, press representative; one daughter, Jill Harmon, actress. Member of AEA. Address: (home) 205 W. 57th St., New York, NY 10019, tel. (212) CI 7-0354; (bus.) c/o *Backstage*, 165 W. 46th St., New York, NY 10036, tel. (212) 581-1080.

Since 1961, Mrs. Harmon has been legitimate stage editor of *Backstage*.

She was producer-director of Chapel Playhouse (Guilford, Conn., Summers 1946–50), where three plays she wrote were produced: *Sex Is Out* (1946), *Strawberries in January* (1947), and *You Have To Be Crazy* (1949); and was producer-director of the Clinton Playhouse (Clinton, Conn., Summers 1951–58), where her play *That Foolish Age* was staged.

She was a radio commentator and wrote dramatic programs for WMCA and WNEW (N.Y.C.), and WNHC (New Haven, Conn., 1938–39, 1950–55).

Published Works. Mrs. Harmon has written articles for magazines including *Theatre Arts* and the NY *Times Magazine;* and the books, *Broadway in a Barn*, with Rosemary Taylor (1957); *How To Break into the Theatre* (1961); and *How To Make Money Selling at Antique Shows and Flea Markets* (1974).

Recreation. Handiwork, art, designing, and making jewelry.

HARMON, LEWIS. Press representative, producer, company manager. b. Feb. 14, 1911, Newark, N.J., to Charles and Amelia (Yokel) Harmon. Father, textile executive; pres. of Chas. Harmon & Co. Attended George Washington H.S., N.Y.C. Married June 27, 1938, to Charlotte Buchwald, writer, editor, producer; one daughter, Jill, actress. Member of ATPAM (chmn. of Press Agents Chapter, 1955–56); Players Club. Address: (home) 205 W. 57th St., New York, NY 10019, tel. (212) CI 7-0354; (bus.) 229 W. 42nd St., New York, NY 10036, tel. (212) CH 4-1482.

Theatre. Mr. Harmon was assistant press representative for Florenz Ziegfeld (1927–28), and was associated with *Rio Rita* (1927), *Show Boat* (1927), *Sunny* (1928), and *The Three Musketeers* (1928).

He worked for Alex Yokel as company manager for *Three Men on a Horse* (Playhouse, N.Y.C., Jan. 20, 1935); was assistant company manager and assistant casting director for *Bury the Dead* (Ethel Barrymore Th., Apr. 18, 1936); company manager, casting director, and playreader for *Love from a Stranger* (Fulton, Sept. 29, 1936); and *Young Mr. Disraeli* (Fulton, Nov. 10, 1937).

He was press representative for the Stony Creek (Conn.) Playhouse (1938); Chapel (Conn.) Playhouse (1939); Clinton (Conn.) Playhouse (1940); Chapel Playhouse, Guilford, Conn. (1941); and for the national and Canadian tour of *Pygmalion* and *Treat Her Gently* (Jan.–May 1941).

As associate press representative, Mr. Harmon worked with the Th. Guild on *The Time of Your Life* (1940); and was associated with the productions of Lee and J. J. Shubert (1940–41). For Michael Todd, he was associate press representative for *Star and Garter* (1942); and *Something for the Boys* (Alvin, Jan. 7, 1943).

Mr. Harmon was press representative for *Mexican Hayride, Pick-up Girl, Catherine was Great* (1944); and *The Bees and the Flowers* (1946).

He produced with his wife, Charlotte Harmon, at the Chapel Playhouse, Guilford, Conn. (Summers 1946–50).

In N.Y.C., he publicized *If the Shoe Fits* (1946); *All My Sons, Bathsheba, Tenting Tonight* (1947); *My Last Dance, Joy to the World, The Play's the Thing, Lend an Ear, The Ivy Green, Jenny Kissed Me* (1948); *Forward the Heart, The Happiest Years* (1949); *The Devil's Disciple, Bless You All* (1950); *The Constant Wife, The Wild Duck* (1951); *Anna Christie, Come of Age,* and *The Brass Ring* (1952). He co-produced with his wife at the Clinton (Conn.) Playhouse (Summers 1951–58).

He was press representative for the national tour of *Death of a Salesman* (1951–52); the Natl. Th. of Greece (1952); the N.Y.C. productions of *The Teahouse of the August Moon, Madame Will You Walk, John Murray Anderson's Almanac* (1953); *Coriolanus, One Eye Closed* (1954); *Southwest Corner, No Time for Sergeants, A Roomful of Roses* (1955); *Purple Dust* (1956); *I Knock at the Door, Look Back in Anger* (1957); *The Entertainer, Blue Denim, The Crucible, A Party with Comden and Green* (1958); *Sweet Bird of Youth, The Warm Peninsula, Fiorello!* (1959); *West Side Story, Ernest in Love, Tenderloin* (1960); *Donnybrook!, A Call on Kuprin, Write Me a Murder, Take Her, She's Mine* (1961); *The Aspern Papers, Black Monday, A Funny Thing Happened on the Way to the Forum* (1962); *She Loves Me* (1963); *The Burning, Worlds of Shakespeare, Diary of a Madman, Awakening of Spring, Place for Chance,* (1963); American Shakespeare Festival (1963–64); and *Fiddler On the Roof* (1964–72).

He was press representative for *Diamond Orchid, A Race of Hairy Men, Shout from the Rooftops, On the Necessity of Being Polygamous* (1965); *Generation, The Right Honourable Gentleman,* the national company of *Fiddler on the Roof* (1966); *A Joyful Noise, To Bury a Cousin* (1967); *Loot, New Faces of '68,* Th. Institute of Childe (Barbizon-Plaza) Plaza) (1968); *Red, White and Maddox,* Lincoln Center Festival with Companie de Théâtre de la Cité de Villeurbanne and Belgrade's Atelje 212 (Vivian Beaumont and Forum Ths.) in *The Three Musketeers, George Dandin,* and *Tartuffe; The Progress of Bora, The Tailor, Ubu Roi, Who's Afraid of Virginia Woolf?, Victor, or The Children Take Over* (1969); *Harvey* (ANTA), *Arena Conta Zumbi, The Brownstone Urge, I Dreamt I Dwelt in Bloomingdale's, Dark of the Moon, Not Now, Darling, The School for Wives, Three by Ferlinghetti, The Trial of the Catonsville Nine, The Homecoming* (Bijou, 1970); *Murderous Angels, Divorce of Judy and Jane, One for the Money* (1971); City Center Acting Company's *School for Scandal, USA, The Hostage, Women Beware Women, Lower Depths, Next Time I'll Sing to You* (1972); *Children of the Wind, A Streetcar Named Desire* (St. James Th.), City Center Acting Company's *The Three Sisters, The Beggar's Opera, Measure for Measure, Scapin* (1973). He was press representative for Equity Library Th. (1970–74) and for CSC Repertory Company's 1973–74 season at Abbey Th.

Films. Mr. Harmon was press representative for Warner Bros. (1929–33); and participated in the Vitaphone Campaign for the early "talkies" (N.Y.C., 1929–33).

Recreation. Mountain climbing, hiking, bicycling, reading, photography.

HARNICK, JAY. Director, producer. b. Jay Malcolm Harnick, June 8, 1928, Chicago, Ill., to Harry and Esther (Kanter) Harnick. Father, dentist. Grad. Carl Schurz H.S., Chicago, 1945; Univ. of Ill., B.A. 1949. Studied dramatics with Stella Adler, Uta Hagen, Harold Clurman, N.Y.C., voice with Eva Brown and Reba Jury, N.Y.C. Served in U.S Army, 1951–52; rank, Pvt. Relative in theatre: brother, Sheldon Harnick, lyricist. Member of AEA; AFTRA; Phi Epsilon Pi. Address: (home) 465 West End Ave., New York, NY tel. (212) SU 7-8497; (bus.) 123 W. 3rd St., New York, NY 10036, tel. (212) 575-8549.

Theatre. Mr. Harnick made his stage debut in Sept. 1949 as successor to Enzo Stuarti in the roles of The Butler and Secret Service Man in *As the Girls Go* (Winter Garden Th., N.Y.C., Nov. 13, 1948); and appeared in the revue *Alive and Kicking* (Winter Garden, Jan. 17, 1950); joined (Mar. 1950) the chorus of *Gentlemen Prefer Blondes* (Ziegfeld, Dec. 8, 1949), playing a Deck Steward during the musical's Chicago run (Palace, Sept. 1951).

He appeared in the chorus of *Of Thee I Sing* (Ziegfeld, May 5, 1952); was a resident player at the Nutmeg Playhouse (Brookfield Center, Conn., Summer 1953); toured as Henry in a stock production of *Gentlemen Prefer Blondes* (Summer 1953); and appeared in the chorus of *John Murray Anderson's Almanac* (Imperial, N.Y.C., Dec. 10, 1953); toured as Antipholus of Ephesus in a stock production of *The Boys from Syracuse* (Summer 1954); subsequently performed in the revue *Phoenix '55* (Andover, N.J., 1955); appeared in the pre-Bway tryout of *Ziegfeld Follies* (Shubert, Boston, Mass., April 16, 1956; closed Shubert, Philadelphia, Pa., May 12, 1956); was advance director for a touring production of *Welcome, Darlings* (Summer 1956); and stage manager of *Purple Dust* (Cherry Lane, N.Y.C., Dec. 27, 1956).

Mr. Harnick directed six musical productions at the Flint (Mich.) and Detroit (Mich.) Music Tents (Summers 1957–58); and conducted and directed two musicals for the Lansing (Mich.) Light Opera Co. (Jan. 1958); staged the ELT production of *On the Town* (Lenox Hill Playhouse, Feb. 3, 1959); was production manager for a series of industrial shows (Apr. 1959); directed seven musicals at the Palm Beach (Fla.) Music Carnival (Feb. 1960); and also directed seven musicals at the Melody Top (Chicago, Ill., Summer 1960).

He directed the children's show *Young Abe Lincoln* (Eugene O'Neill Th., N.Y.C., Apr. 25, 1961; York, May 8, 1961), and later on tour (Dec. 1961), directed six musicals at the Melody Top (Chicago, Summers 1961–62); *Can-Can,* for Theatre Inc. of Houston, Tex. (Oct. 1962); directed and co-produced a tour of the *Preludes To Greatness* series, including *Young Abe Lincoln* (Dec. 1961), *Young Tom Edison* (Nov. 1962), and *Young Tom Jefferson* (Apr. 1963); and directed seven musicals and one drama at the Chicago and the Milwaukee (Wis.) Melody Top theatres (Summer 1963).

He was a production stage manager for the Rep. Th. of Lincoln Ctr., N.Y.C. (1964–65); directed *Anatol* (Milwaukee Rep. Th., Wis., Mar. 31, 1965); and produced, with Gene Persson, Orin Lehman, and Cora Gray Carr, *The Sudden and Accidental Re-education of Horse Johnson* (Belasco Th., Dec. 18, 1968).

Awards. He received a Teaching Fellowship at Univ. of Michigan extension (1949).

HARNICK, SHELDON. Lyricist, composer. b. Sheldon Mayer Harnick, Apr. 30, 1924, Chicago, Ill., to Harry Michael and Esther (Kanter) Harnick. Father, dentist. Grad. Carl Schurz H.S., Chicago, 1942; Northwestern Univ., B. Mus. 1950. Studied at Boguslawski Music Sch., Chicago, 1940–42; Lewis Institute, Chicago, 1942–43; violin with David Glass. Chicago, eight years; Michael Wilkomirski, Chicago, two years; harmony and counterpoint with Simon Stein, Chicago, two years. Married 1950 to Mary Boatner, actress (marr. dis. 1957); married 1962 to Elaine May, actress, writer (marr. dis. 1963); married to Margery Gray, actress. Served US Army Signal Corps, 1943–46; rank, T/4. Relatives in theatre: brother, Jay Harnick, director, producer; cousin, Theodore Bikel, singer, actor; uncle, Milton Kanter, actor, producer; aunt, Anne Kanter, singer. Member of BMI; Dramatists Guild. Address: (home) 365 West End Ave., New York, NY 10023, tel. (212) TR 3-7162; (bus.) c/o David J. Cogan, 350 Fifth Ave., New York, NY 10001, tel. (212) LW 4-9191.

Pre-Theatre. Violinist with dance orchestra.

Theatre. Mr. Harnick contributed music and lyrics to a Northwestern Univ. show (Evanston, Ill., Apr. 1947); subsequently wrote the lyrics and music for a song in *New Faces of 1952* (Royale, N.Y.C., May 16, 1952); lyrics and music for a song in *Two's Company* (Alvin, Dec. 15, 1952); with Ray Golden, wrote a song in *High Time* (Grist Mill Playhouse, Andover, N.J., Aug. 1953); wrote lyrics and music for a song in *John Murray Anderson's Almanac* (Imperial, N.Y.C., Dec. 10, 1953); was lyricist for *Horation* (Margo Jones Th., Dallas, Tex., Mar. 8, 1954); contributed several songs to *Shoestring Revue* (President, Feb. 28, 1955); and wrote additional lyrics for the pre-Bway tryout of *The Amazing Adele* (opened Shubert, Philadelphia, Pa., Dec. 26, 1955; closed Shubert, Boston, Mass., Jan. 21, 1956).

Mr. Harnick contributed music and lyrics for the song "Shape of Things," in *The Littlest Revue* (Phoenix, N.Y.C., May 22, 1956); additional lyrics for *Shangri-La* (Winter Garden, June 13, 1956); lyrics for a song in *Shoestring '57* (Barbizon-Plaza, Nov. 5, 1956); contributed two song lyrics to *Kaleidoscope* (Provincetown Playhouse, June 13, 1957); was lyricist for *The Body Beautiful* (Bway Th., Jan. 23, 1958); wrote additional lyrics for *Portofino* (Adelphi, Feb. 21, 1958); was lyricist for *Fiorello!* (Broadhurst, Nov. 23, 1959); contributed two lyrics to *Vintage '60* (Brooks Atkinson Th., Sept. 12, 1960); was lyricist for *Tenderloin* (46 St. Th., Oct. 17, 1960); *Smiling the Boy Fell Dead* (Cherry Lane, Apr. 10, 1961); wrote lyrics for the title song of *Never Too Late* (Playhouse, Nov. 27, 1962); was lyricist for *The Man in the Moon* (Biltmore, Apr. 11, 1963); *She Loves Me* (Eugene O'Neill Th., Apr. 23, 1963); and *Fiddler on the Roof* (Imperial, Sept. 22, 1964).

He created, with Jerry Bock, an act for Mayor John V. Lindsay of N.Y.C. to perform at the Inner Circle show of the NY Political Writers (NY Hilton, Mar. 1966); wrote the book, with Jerry Bock, and lyrics for *The Apple Tree* (Sam S. Shubert Th., Oct. 18, 1966); lyrics for *The Rothschilds* (Lunt-Fontanne Th., Oct. 19, 1970); for Bil Baird Marionettes productions (all at Bil Baird Th.) was assistant on *Peter and the Wolf* (Dec. 18, 1971) and wrote lyrics for *Pinocchio* (Dec. 15, 1973) and *Alice in Wonderland* (Mar. 1, 1975); and he wrote lyrics for *Rex* (Lunt-Fontanne Th., Apr. 25, 1976).

Films. Mr. Harnick contributed a song to *New Faces of 1952* (20th-Fox, 1954).

Television. He wrote the opening number for Cavalcade of Stars and was assistant to lyricist, Ogden Nash, for Art Carney Meets Peter and the Wolf (ABC, 1958).

Night Clubs. He contributed a song to *Take Five* at Julius Monk's Downstairs Room (N.Y.C., 1957); and wrote several songs for *Medium Rare* (Happy Medium, Chicago, Ill., 1960).

Awards. Mr. Harnick won the Pulitzer Prize, Antoinette Perry (Tony) Award, NY Drama Critics Circle Award, BMI Citation of Achievement Award and the *Variety* NY Drama Critics Poll for *Fiorello!* (1960); the *Variety* NY Drama Critics Poll and the *Saturday Review of Literature* Poll for *She Loves Me* (1963); and the NARAS (Grammy) Award for the Best Show Album of 1963 for *She Loves Me;* and he received Tony nominations (1967) for the book and for the lyrics for *The Apple Tree* and (1971) for *The Rothschilds.*

Recreation. Chess, swimming, symphonic music, art, ping-pong.

HARRINGTON, DONAL. Educator. b. Donal Francis Harrington, Dec. 29, 1905, Butte, Mont., to Denis and Hannah (Harrington) Harrington. Father, miner. Grad. Butte Central H.S., 1923; Univ. of Montana, B.A. 1928; Columbia Univ.,

M.A. 1933. Address: (home) 307-4141 Brooklyn Ave., N.E., Seattle, WA 98105, tel. (206) 633-0570; (bus.) School of Drama, Univ. of Washington, Seattle, WA 98105, tel. (206) 543-5140.

From 1952 to 1973, when he became professor emeritus, Mr. Harrington was professor of drama at the Univ. of Washington. He served on the faculty there as instructor and director (1938–43), assistant professor (1943–47), and associate professor (1947–52). He also held academic positions and directed student productions at New York Univ. (dramatic coach, 1931), and at the Univ. of Montana (instructor and dir., 1936–38). In 1947, he was visiting professor, Univ. of Southern California. He has directed a total of 142 student productions at the Univ. of Washington.

Recreation. Travel, photography.

HARRIS, BARBARA. Actress, director. b. Evanston, Ill., to Oscar and Natalie (Densmoor) Harris. Father, restauranteur; mother, piano teacher. Attended high school in Chicago. Studied improvisational theatre with Paul Sills. Member of AEA; SAG; AFTRA; AGVA.

Theatre. Miss Harris made her stage debut with the Playwrights (repertory) Th. Club (Chicago, Ill., 1959); subsequently performed with the *Second City* improvisational group (Chicago, 1960), and appeared in *From the Second City* (Royale, N.Y.C., Sept. 26, 1961); played Rosalie in *Oh, Dad, Poor Dad, Mamma's Hung You in the Closet and I'm Feelin' So Sad* (Phoenix, Feb. 26, 1962); appeared with the Second City group in *Seacoast of Bohemia* and *Alarums and Excursions* (Second City at Square East, May 29, 1962); Yvette Pottier and a Girl Singer in *Mother Courage and Her Children* (Martin Beck Th., Mar. 28, 1963); appeared in *When the Owl Screams* (Second City at Square East, Sept. 12, 1963); and *Open Season at Second City* (Square East, Jan. 22, 1964); and Tlimpattia in the Actors' Studio Th. production of *Dynamite Tonight* (York, Mar. 15, 1964).

Miss Harris played Daisy Gamble and Melinda in *On a Clear Day You Can See Forever* (Mark Hellinger Th., N.Y.C., Oct. 17, 1965); Eve in *The Diary of Adam and Eve*, Princess Barbara in *The Lady or the Tiger?* and Ella and Passionella in *Passionella*, the three parts of *The Apple Tree* (Shubert, Oct. 18, 1966); directed *The Penny Wars* (Royale, Oct. 15, 1969); and played Jenny in *The Rise and Fall of the City of Mahagonny* (Anderson, Apr. 28, 1970).

Films. Miss Harris played Sandra Markowitz in *A Thousand Clowns* (UA, 1965); Rosalie in *Oh Dad, Poor Dad, Mama's Hung You in the Closet and I'm Feelin' So Sad* (Par., 1967); Muriel Tate in *Plaza Suite* (Par., 1971); Allison in *Who Is Harry Kellerman and Why Is He Saying Those Terrible Things About Me?* (Natl. Gen., 1971); Terry Kozlenko in *The War Between Men and Women* (Natl. Gen., 1972); Kathy in *Mixed Company* (UA, 1974); and Albuquerque in *Nashville* (Par., 1975).

Television. Miss Harris' appearances include The Doctors/The Nurses (CBS); The Defenders (CBS); the The Bell Telephone Hour (NBC).

Awards. Miss Harris received the *Theatre World* Award and the *Village Voice* Off-Bway (Obie) Award for her performance as Rosalie in *Oh Dad, Poor Dad, Mamma's Hung You in the Closet and I'm Feelin' So Sad* (1962); the *Cue* Magazine Entertainer of the Year Award (1966); and the Antoinette Perry (Tony) Award (1967) for her performance in *The Apple Tree.*

HARRIS, FRED ORIN. Educator. b. Frederick Orin Harris, Jan. 24, 1901, Sumpter, Ore., to Orin and Mary Ellen (Murphy) Harris. Father, engineer. Grad. Washington H.S., Portland, Ore., 1918; Univ. of Washington, B.F.A. 1924; New York Univ., M.F.A. 1939. Studied acting with Maria Ouspenskaya, N.Y.C., and Hollywood, three years; Margaret McLean, N.Y.C. and Hollywood, two years; Alexander Koiransky, N.Y.C. and Hollywood, two years. Married July 26, 1931, to Mary Caroline Blaisdell. Address: Univ. of California at Berkeley, Berkeley, CA 94720.

Mr. Harris was on the faculty, Dept. of Dramatic Art, Univ. of California at Berkeley, from 1941 until his retirement in 1968, as lecturer (1941–44), associate professor (1945–51), and as professor (1951–68). He was chairman of the department (1944–60) and an assistant dean in the College of Letters and Science (1964–68). He served also as chairman of the academic planning committee for the Zellerbach Auditorium and Playhouse on the Berkeley campus (1957–68).

Noteworthy play presentations with student actors directed by Mr. Harris on the Berkeley campus included: in the Greek Theatre, the Oresteian trilogy (1946 and 1958) and *Lazarus Laughed;* in Wheeler Auditorium, the uncut editions of *King Lear* (1947), *Antony and Cleopatra* (1948) and *Hamlet* (1950).

Prior to going to Berkeley, Mr. Harris taught and directed at several places. He was an instructor in design at the Univ. of Oregon (1929–31). He directed, with Mary C. B. Harris, the Little Theater in Padua Hills, Claremont, Calif. (1931–33) and, also with Mrs. Harris, the Portland (Ore.) Civic Theater (1933–35). He was an instructor in design at the Univ. of Iowa (Summer 1936) and directed the Peterborough (N.H.) Players (1937–39). In 1939–40, he served on the staff of the Ouspenskaya Studio of Acting, Hollywood, Calif., and in 1940–41 directed the Student Theatre, Univ. of California at Berkeley.

HARRIS, JED. Producer, director. b. Feb. 25, 1900, Vienna, Austria, to Meyer W. and Esther (Shurtz) Horowitz. Attended Yale Univ., 1917–20. Married to Anita Green (marr. dis. 1928); married to Louise Platt (marr. dis. 1944); one daughter.

Pre-Theatre. Theatrical reporter, editor, press agent.

Theatre. Mr. Harris produced *Weak Sisters* (Booth Th., Oct. 13, 1925); *Love 'Em and Leave 'Em* (Harris, Feb. 3, 1926); *Broadway* (Broadhurst, Sept. 16, 1928); *Spread Eagle* (Martin Beck Th., Apr. 4, 1927); *Coquette* Maxine Elliott's Th., Nov. 8, 1927); *The Royal Family* (Selwyn, Dec. 28, 1927); *The Front Page* (Times Square Th., Apr. 14, 1928); and *Serena Blandish* (Morosco, Jan. 23, 1929).

He has directed *Uncle Vanya* (Cort, Apr. 15, 1930); *Mr. Gilhooley* (Broadhurst, Sept. 30, 1930); *Inspector General* (Hudson, Dec. 23, 1930); *The Wiser They Are* (Plymouth, Apr. 6, 1931); and *Wonder Boy* (Alvin, Oct. 23, 1931).

Mr. Harris also produced *The Fatal Alibi* (Booth, Feb. 8, 1932); and produced and directed *The Green Bay Tree* (Cort, Oct. 20, 1933); *The Lake* (Martin Beck Th., Dec. 26, 1933); *Life's Too Short* (Broadhurst, Sept. 20, 1935); *Spring Dance* (Empire, Aug. 25, 1936); *A Doll's House* (Morosco, Dec. 27, 1937); *Our Town* (Henry Miller's Th., Feb. 4, 1938); *Dark Eyes* (Belasco, Jan. 14, 1943); and *The World's Full of Girls* (Royale, Dec. 6, 1943). He produced and staged, with Wesley McKee, *Our Town* (NY City Ctr., Jan. 10, 1944); produced and directed *One-Man Show* (Ethel Barrymore Th., Feb. 8, 1945); produced, in association with Walter Huston, and directed *Apple of His Eye* (Biltmore, Feb. 5, 1946); produced and directed *Loco* (Biltmore, Oct. 16, 1946); directed *The Heiress* (Biltmore, Sept. 29, 1947), and *Red Gloves* (Mansfield, Dec. 4, 1948); produced and directed *The Traitor* (48 St. Th., Apr. 4, 1949); directed *The Crucible* (Martin Beck Th., Jan. 22, 1953); produced and directed *Child of Fortune* (Royale, Nov. 13, 1956) and the opera *Wings of the Dove* (NY City Ctr., 1956); and replaced (after opening) Henry Ephron as director of *Everybody Out, the Castle Is Sinking* (closed during pre-Bway tryout; opened Colonial, Boston, Mass., Dec. 26, 1964; closed there Jan. 9, 1965).

Films. He produced with Arthur Carter, and also wrote *Operation Mad Ball* (Col., 1957).

Published Works. His autobiography, *Watchman, What of the Night*, was published in 1962.

HARRIS, JULIE. Actress. b. Julia Ann Harris, Dec. 2, 1925, Grosse Pointe Park, Mich., to William Pickett and Elsie (Smith) Harris. Father, investment banker; mother, trained nurse. Grad. Grosse Pointe Country Day Sch., 1941; attended Miss Mary C. Wheeler's Sch., Providence, R.I., 1942; studied acting at Miss Hewitt's Classes, N.Y.C.; at the Perry-Mansfield Sch. of the Dance and Theatre, Steamboat Springs, Colo., Summers 1941–43; attended Yale Univ. Sch. of Drama, 1944–45. Married Aug. 16, 1946 to Jay I. Julien (marr. dis. July 1954); married Oct. 21, 1954, to Manning Gurian; one son. Member of AEA; AGVA; SAG; Actor's Studio. Address: c/o Actor's Equity Assn..

Theatre. Miss Harris made her stage debut at age 14 in a Grosse Pointe Country Day Sch. production of *The Hunchback of Notre Dame.* She first appeared on Bway as Atlanta in *It's a Gift* (Playhouse, Mar. 12, 1945); subsequently appeared as a walk-on in the Old Vic company's productions of *Henry IV, Part 2* (Century, May 13, 1946) and *Oedipus* (Century, May 20, 1946); played Nelly in *The Playboy of the Western World* (Booth, Oct. 26, 1946); the White Rabbit in *Alice in Wonderland* (Intl., Apr. 5, 1947); and Arianne in a pre-Bway tryout of *We Love a Lassie* (opened Shubert, Boston, Mass., Aug. 25, 1947; closed National, Washington, D.C., Sept. 6, 1947).

She played one of the Weird Sisters in Michael Redgrave's production of *Macbeth* (National, N.Y.C., Mar. 31, 1948); Ida Mae in the Actors Studio production of *Sundown Beach* (Belasco, Sept. 8, 1948); Nancy Gear in *The Young and Fair* (Fulton, Nov. 22, 1948); Angel Tuttle in *Magnolia Alley* (Mansfield, Apr. 18, 1949); Felisa in *Montserrat* (Fulton, Oct. 29, 1949); Frankie Addams in *The Member of the Wedding* (Empire, Jan. 5, 1950); Sally Bowles in *I Am a Camera* (Empire, Nov. 28, 1951), and on tour (opened Cass, Detroit, Mich., Sept. 1, 1952; closed Her Majesty's, Montreal, Canada, May 2, 1953); the title role in *Mademoiselle Colombe* (Longacre, N.Y.C., Jan. 6, 1954); Joan in *The Lark* (Longacre, Nov. 17, 1955), and on tour (opened Central City Opera House, Colo., Aug. 4, 1956; closed National, Washington, D.C., Dec. 22, 1956); and Mrs. Margery Pinchwife in *The Country Wife* (Adelphi, N.Y.C., Nov. 27, 1957).

Miss Harris appeared as Ruth Arnold in *The Warm Peninsula* (Helen Hayes Th., Oct. 20, 1959); Brigid Mary Mangan in *Little Moon of Alban* (Longacre, Dec. 1, 1960); at the Stratford Shakespeare Festival of Canada (Summer 1960), played Juliet in *Romeo and Juliet* and Blanche of Spain in *King John;* subsequently played Josefa Lantenay in *A Shot in the Dark* (Booth, N.Y.C., Oct. 18, 1961); and June in *Marathon '33* (ANTA, Dec. 22, 1963).

Miss Harris played Ophelia in *Hamlet* (Delacorte Th., June 16, 1964; Playhouse in the Park, Philadelphia, Pa., July 13, 1964); Annie in *Ready When You Are, C. B.!* (Brooks Atkinson Th., N.Y.C., Dec. 7, 1964); Teresa in *The Hostage* (Bucks County Playhouse, New Hope, Pa., May 1, 1965); Georgina in *Skyscraper* (Lunt-Fontanne Th., N.Y.C., Nov. 13, 1965); Blanche Dubois in *A Streetcar Named Desire* (Falmouth Playhouse, Falmouth, Mass., June 22, 1967); Ann Stanley in *Forty Carats* (Morosco, N.Y.C., Dec. 26, 1968); and was in the cast of a revival of *The Women* (Rep. Th. of New Orleans, La., May 15, 1970). She was Anna Reardon in *And Miss Reardon Drinks a Little* (Morosco, N.Y.C., Feb. 25, 1971) and on tour (1971–72); Claire in Voices (Ethel Barrymore Th., Apr. 3, 1972); Mrs. Lincoln in *The Last of Mrs. Lincoln* (ANTA Th., Dec. 12, 1972); Mrs. Rogers in *The Au Pair Man* (Vivian Beaumont Th., Dec. 27, 1973); and Lydia Cruttwell in *In Praise of Love* (Morosco, Dec. 10, 1974).

Films. Miss Harris recreated her stage roles in the film versions of *The Member of the Wedding* (Col., 1952) and *I Am a Camera* (Distributors Corp., 1955); and appeared as Abra in *East of Eden* (WB, 1955); *The Truth About Women* (Continental, 1958); *The Poacher's Daughter* (Showcorporation, 1960); *Requiem for a Heavyweight* (Col., 1962); and *The Haunting* (MGM, 1963); *The Moving Target* (WB,

1966); *Harper* (WB, 1966); *You're a Big Boy Now* (WB-7 Arts, 1967); *Reflections in a Golden Eye* (WB-7 Arts, 1967); *The Split* (MGM, 1968); *The People Next Door* (Avco Embassy, 1970); *The Hiding Place* (World Wide, 1974).

Television and Radio. Miss Harris appeared on the Hallmark Hall of Fame (NBC) in *Wind from the South* (1955), *The Good Fairy* (1955, 1956), *The Lark* (1956, 1957), in *Little Moon of Alban* (1958, 1964), *Johnny Belinda* (1958, 1959), *A Doll's House* (1959, 1960), *Victoria Regina* (1961, 1962), *Pygmalion* (1962, 1963), *Ethan Frome, The Heiress,* as Florence Nightingale in *The Holy Terror* (Apr. 18, 1965), and in the title role of *Anastasia* (Mar. 17, 1967). She appeared also as Ophelia in *Hamlet* (CBS, June 17, 1964); in *The Robrioz Ring* (Kraft Suspense Th., NBC, Sept. 24, 1964); at various times on Girl Talk (ABC, 1964–65–66–67); on Rawhide (CBS, 1965); *Laredo (NBC, 1965); the Today Show (NBC, 1965–66); the Bell Telephone Hour (NBC, 1966); Bob Hope Presents (NBC, 1966); Tarzan (NBC, Mar. 10 and 17, 1967); was in the telecast of the inaugural evening at the restored Ford's Th., Washington, D.C. (CBS, Jan. 30, 1968); The Big Valley (ABC, 1968); appeared on the Dick Cavett Show (ABC, 100 1969); and in How Awful About Allan* (ABC, 1970). Miss Harris also played on the radio in *The Queen of Darkness* (WOR Mystery Th., June 11, 1975).

Published Works. Miss Harris wrote *Julie Harris Talks to Young Actors* (1972).

Discography. Miss Harris is on a recording of *The Hostage* (Columbia Records, 1965); on Asia Society Readings (1967); and *Heroes, Gods and Monsters of the Greek Myths* (Spoken Arts, 1968).

Awards. Miss Harris received the *Theatre World* Award (1949); the Donaldson Award for her performances as Frankie Addams in *The Member of the Wedding* (1950); the Donaldson Award and the *Variety* NY Drama Critics Poll for her performance as Sally Bowles in *I Am a Camera* (1952); the Sylvania (TV) Award for her performance in *Wind from the South* (1955); and NATAS (Emmy) awards for her performances as Brigid Mary Mangan in *Little Moon of Alban* (1959) and in the title role of *Victoria Regina* (1962).

She received an Antoinette Perry (Tony) Award nomination (1966) for best female musical star for her performance in *Skyscraper* and a Tony award (1969) for best actress for her performance in *Forty Carats.* For her performance in the title role of *The Last of Mrs. Lincoln* she received the Outer Circle Award, the Drama Desk Award, and a Tony award, all in 1973, and she was nominated (1974) for a Tony for her performance in *The Au Pair Man.*

HARRIS, ROSEMARY. Actress. b. Rosemary Ann Harris, Sept. 19, Ashby, Suffolk, England, to Stafford Berkley and Enid Maud Francis (Campion) Harris. Father, in Royal Air Force. Educated in England and India. Studied acting at RADA, London, 1952; with Mary Duff, 1952–to date. Married Dec. 4, 1959, to Ellis Rabb, director, actor (marr. dis. May 1967). Married Oct. 21, 1967, to John Ehle, writer; one daughter. Member of AEA; AFTRA; SAG. Address: (home) 125 Westview Drive N., Winston Salem, NC 27104; (bus.) c/o William Morris Agency, 1350 Ave. of Americas, New York, NY 10019.

Theatre. Miss Harris made her first appearance on a stage as Mrs. Otherly in *Abraham Lincoln* (Westwing Sch., Penzance, England, 1946). In 1949, she joined the Phoenix Players of the Bogner Regis (England) Repertory Co., playing 32 roles in weekly stock (Apr. 1949–Jan. 1950); appeared in 40 roles with the Falcon Players Co. (Bedford, England, Jan. 1950–Jan. 1951); appeared in stock with Winwood Productions (Margate and Eastbourne, England, Jan.–May 1951); and in 17 plays with the Penzance Repertory Co. (June–Aug. 1951).

She understudied Gillian Lutyens as Sally, and Yvette Wyatt as Peggy in *The Gay Dog* (Piccadilly Th., London, June 11, 1952); made her N.Y.C. debut as Mabel in *The Climate of Eden* (Martin Beck Th., Nov. 13, 1952); played the Girl in *The Seven Year Itch* (Aldwych, London, May 14, 1953); toured as Lucasta Angel in *The Confidential Clerk* (Brighton, England; Edinburgh, Scotland; Dublin, Ireland; Paris, France, Intl. Festival, 1954).

For the Bristol Old Vic Co., she played Elizabeth Proctor in *The Crucible,* Beatrice in *Much Ado About Nothing,* Hermione in *The Winter's Tale,* Portia in *The Merchant of Venice,* and Isabel in *The Enchanted* (Nov. 1954–Apr. 1955); with the London Old Vic Co., played Calpurnia in *Julius Caesar* (Sept. 7, 1955); Dorcas in *The Winter's Tale* (Nov. 1, 1955); Desdemona in *Othello* (Feb. 21, 1956); Cressida in *Troilus and Cressida* (Apr. 3, 1956); and repeated her role in *Troilus and Cressida* in N.Y.C. (Winter Garden, Dec. 26, 1956), also touring in it; appeared as Hilde in *Interlock* (ANTA, N.Y.C., Feb. 6, 1958); Jere Halliday in *The Disenchanted* (Coronet, Dec. 3, 1958); with the Group 20 Players (Wellesley, Mass.), played Eliza Doolittle in *Pygmalion* (July 1958), Beatrice in *Much Ado About Nothing* (June 1959), Anne Whitefield in *Man and Superman* (July 1959), and the title role in *Peter Pan* (Aug. 1959); and played Lennie in *The Tumbler* (Helen Hayes Th., N.Y.C., Feb. 24, 1960).

Miss Harris is a charter member of the Association of Producing Artists (APA), of which her first husband, Ellis Rabb, was artistic director. She has appeared in the following APA productions: at City Hall Th. (Hamilton, Bermuda) as Gabrielle in *Anatole* (May 12, 1960), Anne Whitefield in *Man and Superman* (May 18, 1960), Nina in *The Seagull* (May 31, 1960), and Bianca in *The Taming of the Shrew* (July 4, 1960); at the McCarter Th. (Princeton, N.J.), as Cecily in *The Importance of Being Earnest* (Nov. 10, 1960), Titania in *A Midsummer Night's Dream* (Feb. 9, 1961), Viola in *Twelfth Night* (Feb. 23, 1961), and Phoebe in *As You Like It* (Mar. 5, 1961); during the summer of 1961, at the Boston (Mass.) Arts Festival; Highfield Th. (Falmouth, Mass.); Bucks Co. Playhouse (New Hope, Pa.); John Drew Th. (East Hampton, L.I.); and Olney (Md.) Th., she played Viola in *Twelfth Night,* Mme. Arcadina in *The Seagull,* Lady Teazle in *The School for Scandal,* and Virginia in *The Tavern* (June 21–Sept. 3); at the Fred Miller Th. (Milwaukee, Wis., Oct. 19, 1961), she repeated these roles, adding Seraphina in *Fashion;* at the Folksbiene Playhouse (N.Y.C.), she appeared as Lady Teazle in *The School for Scandal* (Mar. 17, 1962), Nina in *The Seagull* (Mar. 21, 1962), and Virginia in *The Tavern* (Apr. 4, 1962).

For the inaugural season at the Chichester (England) Festival Th., Miss Harris appeared as Penthea in *The Broken Heart* and Constantia I in *The Chances* (Summer 1962). Later that Season she rejoined the APA at the Univ. of Michigan (Lydia Mendelssohn Th.), playing Lady Teazle in *The School for Scandal* (Oct. 2, 1962), the Girl in *We, Comrades Three* (Oct. 10, 1962), Virginia in *The Tavern* (Oct. 17, 1962), and Regina in *Ghosts* (Oct. 24, 1962); at the Trueblood Aud., she played Titania in *A Midsummer Night's Dream* (Feb. 13, 1963), Portia in *The Merchant of Venice* (Feb. 20, 1963), and the Duchess of Gloucester in *Richard II* (Feb. 27, 1963).

At the Chichester Festival Th., Miss Harris played Yelena in *Uncle Vanya* (Mar. 1963); then appeared with the Natl. Th. Co. in its first London season as Ophelia in *Hamlet* (Oct. 1963); again as Yelena in *Uncle Vanya* (Nov. 1963); and Woman One in *Play* (Apr. 1964).

In Sept. 1964 she rejoined the APA at the Univ. of Michigan and later at the 74th St. Th. (N.Y.C.) playing the title role in *Judith;* Violet in *Man and Superman,* and Natasha in *War and Peace.* When APA joined with the Phoenix Th. to become APA-Phoenix at the Lyceum Th. (N.Y.C.) in 1965, she played Alice in *You Can't Take It with You;* Lady Teazle in *The School for Scandal;* Gina in *The Wild Duck;* Señora Ponza in *Right You Are* and Natasha in *War and Peace.* She played Eleanor in *The Lion in Winter* (Ambassador Th., Mar. 3, 1966); Lady Teazle in *The School for Scandal* (Huntington Hartford Th., Los Angeles, Calif., 1966); appeared in *Plaza Suite* (Lyric Th., London, England, 1969); played Irene in *Idiot's Delight* (Ahmanson Th., Los Angeles, Calif., Mar. 17, 1970); and Anna in *Old Times* (Billy Rose Th., N.Y.C., Nov. 16, 1971; Kennedy Center, Washington, D.C., 1972; and Shubert Th., Philadelphia, Pa., 1972). She joined the Lincoln Center Repertory Company for the 1973 season playing Portia in *The Merchant of Venice* and Blanche du Bois in *A Streetcar Named Desire.* .

Films. Miss Harris made her debut as Mrs. Fitzherbert in *Beau Brummell* (MGM, 1954); and appeared as Lilly in *The Shiralee* (Ealing, 1956); and Gabrielle in *Flea in Her Ear* (20th-Fox, 1970).

Television. In England, Miss Harris' first appearance was as Tassy in *Cradle of Willow* (BBC, 1951) and played Desdemona in *Othello* (BBC, 1955). In the US, she played Edith in *The Prince and the Pauper* (Dupont Show of the Month, CBS, 1957); appeared in *I Killed the Count, The Glass Eye,* and *Lord Arthur Savilles Crime* (Alfred Hitchcock Presents, CBS, 1957); played Viola in *Twelfth Night* (Hallmark Hall of Fame, NBC, 1957); Lucy Manette in *A Tale of Two Cities* (Dupont Show of the Month, CBS, Mar. 1958); The Wife in *Dial 'M' for Murder* (Hallmark Hall of Fame, NBC, Mar. 1958); and Cathy in *Wuthering Heights* (Dupont Show of the Month, CBS, Apr. 1958); and Mrs. Dickens in *A Dickens Chronicle* (CBS, 1962). In Canada, she has appeared as Dynamane in *A Phoenix Too Frequent* (Folio, CBC, Apr. 1958), and as Norah in *The Land of Promise* (CBC, Aug. 1959). She also played Antigone and Myra at the Th. of Dionysus (Athens, Greece) for the program *Athens, Where the Theatre Began* (CBS, 1963).

Miss Harris appeared in *Moment of Truth* (Omnibus); as Mary MacDowell in *Profiles in Courage;* as Miss Isabel in *The Enchanted* (NET); as The Voice in *Eh Joe?* (CBS); and *N.Y.: Portrait of a City.* She played Elvira in *Blithe Spirit* (Hallmark Hall of Fame, NBC, 1966); Charlotte Marshall in *Dear Friends* (CBS Playhouse, 1967); *13 Stars for Channel 13* (PBS, 1967); Yelena in *Uncle Vanya* (NET Playhouse, PBS, 1967); and George Sand in *Notorious Woman* (BBC, 1974).

Awards. Miss Harris received the Bancroft Gold Medal and the H. M. Tennent Contract Prize from RADA (1952); the *Theatre World* Award for her performance as Mabel in *The Climate of Eden* (1953); was nominated for a NATAS (Emmy) Award for her television performance as Cathy in *Wuthering Heights* (1958); and received a *Village Voice* Off-Bway (Obie) Award for her performances during the APA repertory season at the Folksbiene Playhouse (1962); and a *Village Voice* Off-Bway (Obie) for her performances during the APA repertory season at the 74th St. Th. (1965); an Antoinette Perry (Tony) Award for Eleanor in *The Lion in Winter* (1966); the Delia Austrian Drama League of New York Award for Gina in *The Wild Duck* (1967); won the Anglo-American Whitbread Award (1965, 1966, and 1967); the London Evening Standard Award for *Plaza Suite* (Lyric Th., London, England, 1969); the Outer Circle Critics Award (1972), the Drama Desk Award (1972), and was nominated for an Antoinette Perry (Tony) Award for Anna in *Old Times* (1972); the Drama Desk Award for Portia in *The Merchant of Venice* and Blanche in *A Streetcar Named Desire* (Lincoln Center Repertory Co., 1973); and was given an honorary doctorate from Smith College (Mass.).

HARRISON, REX. Actor. b. Rex Carey Harrison, Mar. 5, 1908, Huyton, England, to William Reginald and Edith Mary (Carey) Harrison. Father, stock exchange. Attended Birkdale Prep. Sch., Sheffield; Liverpool Coll. Married June 1934 to Noel Marjorie Collette Thomas (marr. dis. 1943), one son; married Dec. 1943, to Lilli Peiser, known as Lilli Palmer, actress (marr. dis. 1957), one son; married Aug. 1957, to Kay Kendall, actress (dec. 1959); married Mar. 21, 1962, to Rachel Roberts, actress (marr. dis.); married 1971 to Elizabeth Harris (marr. dis.). Served Royal Air Force, 1940–44; rank, Flight Lt. Member of AEA; SAG; Garrick Club; Green Room Club; The Players. Address: (home) Villa San Genesio, Portofino, Italy; (bus.) c/o Ashley Famous Agency, Inc., 9255 Sunset Blvd., Los Angeles, CA 90029.

Theatre. Mr Harrison first appeared on stage with

the Liverpool Repertory Th. Co. as the Husband in *Thirty Minutes in a Street* (Sept. 1924), appeared with this company (1924–27); and toured England in *Charley's Aunt, Potiphar's Wife, Alibi, The Chinese Bungalow,* and *A Cup of Kindness* (1927–30).

He made his London debut as the Hon. Fred Thrippleton in *Getting George Married* (Everyman Th., Nov. 26, 1930); followed by Rankin in *The Ninth Man* (Prince of Wales's, Feb. 1931); appeared with the Cardiff (Wales) Repertory Co. (May–Sept. 1931); toured as Ralph in *After All* (Oct.–Dec. 1931); and in *Other Men's Wives* and *For the Love of Mike* (Jan.–Oct. 1932).

He understudied Herbert Marshall in *Another Language* (Lyric, Dec. 1, 1932); toured in *Road House* and *Mother of Pearl* (Feb.–Oct. 1933); played Peter Featherstone in *No Way Back* (Whitehall, London, May 1934); John Murdoch in *Our Mutual Father* (Piccadilly, Nov. 1934); Anthony Fair in *Anthony and Anna* (Fulham, Nov. 12, 1934); Paul Galloway in *Man of Yesterday* (St. Martin's, Feb. 19, 1935); Mark Kurt in *Short Story* (Queen's, Nov. 1935), and Rodney Walters in *Charity Begins* Aldwych, Jan. 1936).

He made his N.Y.C. debut as Tubbs Barrow in *Sweet Aloes* (Booth, Mar. 2, 1936); played Tom Gregory in *Heroes Don't Care* (St. Martin's, London, June 10, 1936); the Hon. Alan Howard in *French without Tears* (Criterion, Nov. 6 1936); Leo in *Design for Living* (Haymarket, Jan. 25, 1939); Gaylord Easterbrook in *No Time for Comedy* (Haymarket, Mar. 27, 1941); Henry VIII in *Anne of the Thousand Days* (Shubert, N.Y.C., Dec. 8, 1948); the Unidentified Guest in *The Cocktail Party* (New, London, May 3, 1950); Shepherd Henderson in *Bell, Book and Candle* (Ethel Barrymore Th., N.Y.C., Nov. 14, 1950); the Duke of Alter in *Venus Observed* (Century, Feb. 13, 1952); The Man and the Wicked Fairy in *The Love of Four Colonels,* which he also directed (Shubert, Jan. 15, 1953); Shepherd Henderson in *Bell, Book and Candle,* which he also directed (Phoenix, London, Oct. 5, 1954), and directed *Nina* (Haymarket, July 27, 1955).

He played Henry Higgins in *My Fair Lady* (Mark Hellinger Th., N.Y.C., Mar. 15, 1956; Drury Lane, Apr. 30 1958); directed *The Bright One* (Winter Garden, London, Dec. 10, 1958); played the General in *The Fighting Cock* (ANTA, N.Y.C, Dec. 8, 1959); the title role in *Platonov* (Royal Court, London, Oct. 13, 1960); appeared in *August for the People* at the Edinburgh (Scotland) Festival and in London (Royal Court, Aug. 1961); played the male lead in *The Lionel Touch* (London, 1969); the title role in *Emperor Henry IV* (Ethel Barrymore Th., N.Y.C., Mar. 28, 1973); also in the same play presented as *Henry IV* (Her Majesty's Th., London, Eng., Jan. 1974); and played Sebastian Cruttwell in *In Praise of Love* (Morosco, N.Y.C., Dec. 10, 1974).

Films. Mr. Harrison has appeared in *The Constant Husband* (MGM, 1936); *Storm in a Teacup* (UA, 1937); *Men Are Not Gods* (UA, 1937); *The Citadel* (MGM, 1938); *Over the Moon* (UA, 1938); *Ten Days in Paris* (1938); *School for Husbands* (Hoffberg, 1939); *Sidewalks of London* (Par., 1940); *Night Train* (20th-Fox, 1940); *Escape* (MGM, 1940); *Major Barbara* (UA, 1941); *Blithe Spirit* (UA, 1945); *Anna and the King of Siam* (20th-Fox, 1946); *Notorious Gentleman* (U, 1946); *The Ghost and Mrs. Muir* (20th-Fox, 1947); *The Foxes of Harrow* (20th-Fox, 1947); *Unfaithfully Yours* (20th-Fox, 1948); *Once a Thief* (UA, 1950); *The Long Dark Hall* (Elstree, 1951); *The Fourposter* (Col., 1952); *King Richard and the Crusaders* (WB, 1954); *The Reluctant Debutante* (MGM, 1958); *Midnight Lace* (UA, 1960); *The Happy Thieves* (UA, 1962); *Cleopatra* (20th-Fox, 1963); *My Fair Lady* (WB, 1964); *The Yellow Rolls-Royce* (MGM, 1965); *The Agony and the Ecstasy* (20th-Fox, 1965); *The Honey Pot* (UA, 1967); *Dr. Doolittle* (20th-Fox, 1967); and *A Flea in Her Ear* (1968).

Television. Mr. Harrison has appeared in *Man in Possession* (US Steel Hour, ABC, 1951); on Crescendo (CBS, 1957); The Fabulous Fifties (CBS, Jan. 31, 1960); was Professor Higgins in an excerpt from *My Fair Lady* (ATV, England, Jan. 31, 1965); and appeared as a guest on the Today Show (NBC, 1964–65); the Ed Sullivan Show (CBS, 1965–66); and Hollywood Backstage (Ind., 1967–68).

Published Works. Mr. Harrison wrote *Rex: An Autobiography* (1975).

Awards. Mr. Harrison received the Order of Merit of the Italian Republic (1967). He received the Antoinette Perry (Tony) Awards for his performances as Henry VIII in *Anne of the Thousand Days* (1949), and Henry Higgins in *My Fair Lady* (1957); the London *Evening Standard* Award for his performance in the title role of *Platonov* (1961); was nominated for an Academy (Oscar) Award for his performance as Julius Caesar in *Cleopatra* (1964); for his performance as Henry Higgins in the film version of *My Fair Lady* received the Academy Award as best actor, the NY Film Critics Award, the Hollywood Foreign Press Assn. Golden Globe Award (all 1964), the talent trophy of the Film Critics' Circle of the Foreign Language Press of NY, and the David of Donatello Award (both 1965); and received a special Tony Award (1969).

Recreation. Golf, tennis, reading.

HARRON, DONALD.

Actor. b. Donald Hugh Harron, Sept. 19, 1924, Toronto, Canada, to Lionel W. and Delsia A. Harron. Father, civil engineer. Grad. Univ. of Toronto B.A. (with honors) 1948. Studied acting with Sanford Meisner 1956–57. Married 1949 to Gloria Fisher (marr. dis. 1959); two daughters; married 1959 to Virginia Leith. Served RCAF, Pilot Officer, 1943–45. Member of AEA; SAG; AFTRA; ACTRA.

Theatre. Mr. Harron first performed on stage in a school production of *Uncle Tom's Cabin* (Toronto, Canada, 1935); and made his professional debut as the Playboy in *The Playboy of the Western World* (Museum Th., Toronto, Canada, 1946); subsequently succeeded (Aldwych, London, 1950) John Forrest in the role of the Young Collector in *A Streetcar Named Desire;* appeared as Peter Gay in *The Seventh Veil* (Prince's, Mar. 14, 1951); and as Captain Smith in *Poor Judas* (Arts, July 18, 1951). He made his N.Y.C. debut as Peter Able in *A Sleep of Prisoners* (St. James Episcopal Church, 1951); and appeared in *Dangerous Corner* (Olney Playhouse, Md.; Westport Country Playhouse, Conn.).

With the Bristol (England) Old Vic Co., Mr. Harron played in *Antony and Cleopatra* and in *A Comedy of Errors* (Sept. 1953); with the Stratford (Ontario, Canada) Shakespeare Festival, appeared as Bertram in *All's Well That Ends Well* (1953); Lucio in *Measure for Measure,* and Tranio in *The Taming of the Shrew* (1954), and as Bassanio in *The Merchant of Venice* and Octavius Caesar in *Julius Caesar* (1955).

Me made his Bway debut as Willie O'Reilly in *Home Is the Hero* (Booth, Sept. 22, 1954); subsequently played Jakob in *The Dark Is Light Enough* (ANTA, Feb. 23, 1955); and Charles Stratton in *Separate Tables* (Music Box, Oct. 25, 1956).

At the American Shakespeare Festival (Stratford, Conn.), he played Claudio in *Measure for Measure* and Lucentio in *The Taming of the Shrew* (Summer 1956); and Bassanio in *The Merchant of Venice* and Verges in *Much Ado About Nothing* (Summer, 1957).

Subsequently, he succeeded (Hanna Th., Cleveland, Ohio, Dec. 1958), Kenneth Haigh in the role of Jimmy Porter in a national tour of *Look Back in Anger* (opened Ford's Th., Baltimore, Md., Sept. 22, 1958; closed Geary, San Francisco, Calif., May 9, 1959); played Arthur Landau in *The Tenth Man* (Booth, N.Y.C., Nov. 5, 1959); at the Amer. Shakespeare Festival, appeared as Banquo in *Macbeth,* Orlando in *As You Like It,* and Thersites in *Troilus and Cressida* (Stratford, Conn., Summer 1961).

He played Bradford in *Everybody Loves Opal* (Longacre, N.Y.C., Oct. 11, 1961); the Hon. David Rodingham in *Write Me a Murder* (O'Hare Inn Th., Chicago, Ill., June 1962); Cornelius Hackl in *The Matchmaker* (Robin Hood Th., Wilmington, Del., July 1962); and Edmund in *King Lear* (NY Shakespeare Festival, Delacorte Th., Aug. 1962); Bob McKellaway in *Mary, Mary* (Queen's Th., London, Feb. 1963); and repeated the role of Edmund in The Theatre Group production of *King Lear* (Los Angeles, Summer 1964). He adapted for the stage, and co-authored the lyrics for the musical version of *Anne of Green Gables* (NY City Ctr., Dec. 21, 1971).

Films. He has appeared in *The Spy with My Face* (MGM, 1966); *I Deal in Danger* (20th-Fox, 1966); and *The Hospital* (UA, 1971).

Television. Mr. Harron's appearances include One Step Beyond (Ind.); Dr. Kildare (NBC); Outer Limits (ABC); Profiles in Courage (NBC); Voyage (ABC); Desilu Playhouse (NBC); The Man from U.N.C.L.E. (NBC); Mr. Novak (NBC); Twelve O'-Clock High (ABC); Esso Repertory Theatre (Ind.); The Defenders (CBS); Repertoire Workshop (CBS); On Stage (Ind.); The Fugitive (ABC); The F.B.I. (ABC); Amos Burke (ABC); Blue Light (ABC); Armchair Th. (ABC); Time Tunnel (ABC); Mission: Impossible (CBS); Walt Disney's World (NBC); and Please Don't Eat the Daisies (NBC). In addition, he co-authored and appeared in *Operation Chicken* (CBC-TV, Toronto); and *Sh! It's the News* (Global-TV); and wrote the teleplay for *The Yahi Bahi Society* (CBC-TV).

Other Activities. Mr. Harron adapted, *The Broken Jug,* which was based on a play by Heinrich von Kleist (Stratford Festival Co. of Canada, Phoenix Th., N.Y.C., Apr. 1, 1958).

Awards. Mr. Harron is a recipient of a Canada Council Award (1967).

Recreation. Football, swimming.

HART, M. BLAIR.

Educator, director. b. Milton Blair Hart, Sept. 27, 1907, Delevan, Minn., to William W. and Lizzie A. (Blair) Hart. Father, farmer; mother, teacher. Grad. Delevan H.S., 1925; Macalester Coll., B.A. 1932; State Univ. of Iowa, M.A., 1936; Univ. of Denver, Ed.D. 1951. Married Sept. 4, 1946, to Opal G. Munger. Served USAAF, 1941–45; rank, Tech. Sgt. Member of Arkansas Speech Assn. (pres., 1939; exec. secy., 1955–63); ATA; SAA (legislative council, 1962–64); SPA; SWTC; NCP (2nd vice-pres., 1958–63, pres., 1964–70); Arkansas State Council of Arts and Humanities (1967–to date); Univ. of Arkansas American Revolution Bicentennial (chmn., 1973–to date). Address: (home) 1674 W. Maple, Fayetteville, AR 72701, tel. (501) HI 2-8716; (bus.) c/o Dept. of Speech and Dramatic Art, Univ. of Arkansas, Fayetteville, AR 72701, tel. (501) 575-2954.

From 1953 to 1968, Mr. Hart was chairman of the Dept. of Speech and Dramatic Art at the Univ. of Arkansas, where he joined the faculty in 1936 (instructor, 1936–40; assist. prof., 1946–50; assoc. prof., 1950–55; prof., 1955–to date).

He has also held academic positions at Macalester Coll. (1933–35); Emmetsburg Junior Coll. (1941); and Henderson State Teachers Coll. (1946).

Awards. Mr. Hart received the Univ. of Arkansas Distinguished Teaching Award in 1971.

HARTIG, MICHAEL FRANK.

Talent representative, acting teacher. b. Aug. 11, 1936, Brooklyn, N.Y., to Herman Nathan and Rhoda (Stryker) Hartig. Grad. Abraham Lincoln H.S., Brooklyn, N.Y., 1953; Brooklyn Coll., B.A. 1958. Married July 9, 1974, to J. Gurman. Member of TARA. Address: (home) 238 E. 74th St., New York, NY 10021; (bus.) 850 Seventh Ave., New York, NY 10019, tel. (212) 489-8484.

In Sept. 1961, Mr. Hartig established his own talent agency in N.Y.C. He was a talent representative at General Artists Corp. (Jan.–June 1961); Willard Alexander, Inc. (1959–60); and with Deborah Coleman (1958).

He was company manager at the Capri Th. (Atlantic Beach, N.Y., Summer 1954), where he produced *Finian's Rainbow* (Summer 1958).

He began teaching professional acting classes July, 1972.

Recreation. Swimming, dancing.

HARTKE, REV. GILBERT O.P.

Educator. b. Gilbert Francis Hartke, Jan. 16, 1907, Chicago, Ill., to Emil A. and Lillian (Ward) Hartke. Father, pharmacist. Grad. Loyola Acad., Chicago, 1925; Providence Coll., A.B. 1929; ordained as Dominican priest, 1939; grad. Catholic Univ. of Amer.,

M.A. (English) 1938; attended Northwestern Univ., 1941–42. Member of Order of Preachers (O.P.) (1929); ANTA (bd. of dir.); AETA (pres., 1955; bd. mbr.); NCTC (pres.); SAA; Advisory Comm. for the Natl. Cultural Ctr.; US Fine Arts Commission (drama rep.); National Council on the Arts; American College Theatre Festival; UNESCO (Natl. Commission of Arts & Sciences); Natl. Commission of USO (1959–60); Fulbright Comm.; Natl. Assn. of Arts & Letters (bd. mbr.); Ford's Theatre Society (pres. emeritus); Washington D.C., Theatre Club; District of Columbia Commission on the Arts; Variety Club of Washington, D.C. (Chaplain); Natl. Alumni of Catholic Univ. (Chaplain); AAUP. Address: (home) Dominican House of Studies, 487 Michigan Ave., N.E., Washington, DC 20017, tel. (202) LA 9-5300; (bus.) Dept. of Speech & Drama, The Catholic Univ. of Amer., Washington, DC 20017, tel. (202) 635-5350. Fr. Hartke has been head of the Dept. of Speech and Drama at Catholic Univ. of America, which he founded in 1937.

In 1949, he was the founder of the Univ. Players at Catholic Univ. of Amer., which operates in two categories: the Natl. Players, a touring repertory company; and an Equity summer theatre company at Olney Th. (Olney, Md.). Father Hartke is president and chairman of the board of trustees of the Univ. Players.

During his association with the Univ. Players, he has directed dramas and original musicals: he directed *The Little World of Don Camillo,* which he adapted from the novel by Giovanni Guareschi (Mar. 1957), and Helen Hayes in *Good Morning, Miss Dove* (Jan. 23, 1964).

In addition to his activities in educational theatre, Father Hartke is a lecturer and speaker and a theatrical director in the Washington, D.C., community.

He was one of the founders of the Chicago (Ill.) Loyola Community Th. (1927).

Films. During WW II, he appeared in *Army Chaplain* (RKO, 1942), and in a series of short subjects on *This Is America* (RKO Pathé).

Awards. He has received an honorary LL.D. from the Univ. of Notre Dame (1951); an honorary Litt.D. from Susquehanna Univ. (1974); an honorary degree from Caldwell (N.J.) College; awards from the Amer. Th. Wing, the Washington Board of Trade, The U.S. Dept. of Defense, NCTC, and the Jewish Home for the Aged. Fr. Hartke has also received the George M. Cohan Award and Variety's "Heart of Gold." In 1965, the Benemerenti Medal was conferred upon him by Pope Paul VI, and in May 1972, he was named man of the year in education by the American Univ. chapter of Phi Delta Kappa fraternity.

HARTLEY, NEIL.

Producer, production supervisor. b. Neil Clingman Hartley, July 14, 1919, Blowing Rock, N.C., to Granville L. and Pearl (Story) Hartley. Mother, teacher. Attended Mars Hill Coll.; grad. Appalachian State Teachers Coll., B.S. 1939; attended Univ. of North Carolina, 1940; Yale Univ., M.F.A. 1949. Served WW II, USNR; rank, Lt. Member of AEA. Address: (home) 295 Central Park West, New York, NY 10024; (bus.) American Woodfall Film Co., New York, NY.

Theatre. Mr. Hartley's first stage assignment in N.Y.C., was production stage manager of *Pal Joey* (Broadhurst, Jan. 2, 1952); subsequently was production stage manager for *Hazel Flagg* (Mark Hellinger Th., Feb. 11, 1953); directed *Pal Joey* (Princess, London, Mar. 31, 1954); was production stage manager for *Hit the Trail* (Mark Hellinger Th., N.Y.C., Dec. 2, 1954); *Ankles Aweigh* (Mark Hellinger Th., Apr. 18, 1955); *The Vamp* (Winter Garden, Nov. 10, 1955); and *Middle of the Night* (ANTA, Feb. 8, 1956).

He joined David Merrick's staff (1957) and was production supervisor and sometime casting director for *Jamaica* (Imperial, Oct. 31, 1957); *The Entertainer* (Royale, Feb. 12, 1958); *The World of Suzie Wong* (Broadhurst, Oct. 14, 1958); *La Plume de Ma Tante* (Royale, Nov. 11, 1958); *Destry Rides Again* (Imperial, Apr. 23, 1959); *Gypsy* (Bway Th., May 21, 1959); *Take Me Along* (Shubert, Oct. 22, 1957); *The Good Soup* (Plymouth, Mar. 2, 1960); *Irma La Douce* (Plymouth, Sept. 29, 1960); *Becket* (St. James, Oct. 5, 1960); *Do Re Mi* (St. James, Dec. 26, 1960); *Carnival!* (Imperial, Apr. 13, 1961); *Subways Are for Sleeping* (Shubert, Feb. 22, 1962); *Stop the World, I Want to Get Off* (Shubert, Oct. 3, 1962); *Oliver!* (Imperial, Jan. 6, 1963); *Luther* (St. James, Sept. 25, 1963); *The Rehearsal* (Royale, Sept. 23, 1963); *110 in the Shade* (Broadhurst, Oct. 24, 1963); *Arturo Ui* (Lunt-Fontanne, Nov. 11, 1963); and *One Flew Over the Cuckoo's Nest* (Cort, Nov. 13, 1963); associate producer of *The Milk Train Doesn't Stop Here Anymore* (Brooks Atkinson Th., Jan. 1, 1964); and production supervisor of *Foxy* (Ziegfeld, Feb. 16, 1964); and *Hello Dolly!* (St. James, Jan. 16, 1964).

Films. As head of Tony Richardson's American-Woodfall Co. (June 1964–to date), Mr. Hartley was associate producer of *The Loved One* (MGM, 1965); with Oscar Lewenstein, co-produced *The Sailor from Gibraltar* (Lopert, 1967); produced *The Charge of the Light Brigade* (UA, 1968); the Nicol Williamson *Hamlet* (Col. 1969); and *Ned Kelly* (UA, 1970); and was executive producer for *A Delicate Balance* (Amer. Film Th., 1973).

HARTNOLL, PHYLLIS.

Theatre historian, writer, lecturer. b. Phyllis May Hartnoll, Sept. 22, 1906, London, England, to Herbert Nicholas and Hetty Kate (Roberts) Hartnoll. Father, Lt. and Quartermaster, R.E., British Army (d. 1916); mother, headmistress. Grad. St. Katherine's Sch., Wantage, Eng., 1923; attended Univ. of Lyon, France; Univ. of Algiers, Algieria, Licencié ès Lettres 1926; St. Hugh's Coll., Oxford, England, M.A. 1929. Address: Hill Crest, Ware Lane, Lyme Regis, England.

Theatre. Miss Hartnoll's first play, *Peter Peppercorn, Physician,* was staged by The Taverners, a nonprofessional group (1938); subsequently she wrote *Day Before Dawn* (Studio of the London Little Th., Ontario, Canada, 1948); adapted *The Lady of the Camellias* (Northampton Repertory Th., England, 1955); and translated Hjalmar Bergman's *The Swedenhjelms* as *The Family Affair* (Birmingham Repertory Th., England, July 1960); televised ITV, Nov. 1960).

Other Activities. Miss Hartnoll joined the editorial staff of the English publishing firm Macmillan's in 1934. She was a founder of the Society for Th. Research (committee mbr., 1948–62; vice-chairman, 1952–58); a lecturer in the history of theatre at RADA, London (1952–55); corresponding member of La Société d'Histoire du Théâtre, Paris; Institut für Theatre Wissenschaft, Vienna; founder-member of the International Federation for Th. Research and editor of its journal, *Theatre Research/Recherches Théâtrales* (1958–61); lecturer on theatre for the City of London; gave seven lectures as visiting scholar at Richmond, Va. (1958); and lectured in N.Y.C., Princeton, N.J., Dallas and Austin, Tex., and Purdue and Lafayette, Ind. (1958).

Published Works. Miss Hartnoll is the editor of *The Oxford Companion to the Theatre* (1951; rev. 1957, 1965; 3d ed. 1967); published three volumes of poems; a novel, *The Grecian Enchanted* (1952); a translation of Fernando de Rojas' *La Celestina* (1959); compiled an illustrated supplement for Dent's *Everyman Dictionary of Shakespeare Quotations* (1964); prepared a volume of essays, *Shakespeare in Music,* that includes a catalogue of musical works based on Shakespeare (1964); wrote *A Concise History of the Theatre* (1968); and has written articles for *Theatre Arts* magazine and *Theatre Newsletter* and dramatic criticism for the London *Times*. .

Awards. Miss Hartnoll received the Newdigate Prize for English Verse (Oxford, England, 1929); was the first woman to receive the Oxford Prize for a poem on a sacred subject (1947); received the Poetry Society's Gold Medal for the Speaking of Verse (London, 1963); and received a second Newdigate Prize in 1965.

Recreation. Music, embroidery, toy theatres, cats.

HARTZOG, TOM.

Producer. b. Thomas Shelton Hartzog, July 17, 1937, Selma, Ala., to Levy Shelton and Kathryn (Welch) Hartzog. Father, fast foods executive. Educ. East High School, Memphis, Tenn.; Univ. of Colorado (1955–57); grad. Memphis State Univ., BBA, 1960. Married Apr. 10, 1965, to Joye Ann Bradford; one daughter. Served USAF Reserve, 1960–64. Member of Variety Clubs International; Delta Sigma Pi. Address: (home) 5232 Keatswood Cove, Memphis, TN 38117, tel. (901) 525-1746; (bus.) 2115 Sterick Bldg., Memphis, TN 38103, tel. (901) 525-5574.

Theatre. Mr. Hertzog presented country music shows and rock shows (1960–74) and has been an investor in N.Y.C. (off-Bway) and Los Angeles, Calif. theatrical productions. At his Off-Broadway Th., San Diego, Calif., he produced, with his partner, Don Wortman, *Gypsy* (Mar. 28, 1973); *Under Papa's Picture* (May 1, 1973); *Lenny* (June 7, 1973); *Blithe Spirit* (July 5, 1973); *Pal Joey* (Aug. 2, 1973); *The Boys in the Band* (Aug. 30, 1973); *The Prisoner of Second Avenue* (Oct. 4, 1973); *Status Quo Vadis* (Nov. 14, 1973); *The Decline and Fall of the Entire World as Seen Through the Eyes of Cole Porter* (Dec. 27, 1973); *Lenny* (Jan. 23, 1974); *Irma La Douce* (Mar. 6, 1974); *Father's Day* (Apr. 3, 1974); *Bimbo's Cosmic Circus* (May 1, 1974); *Bus Stop* (May 29, 1974); *Sweet Charity* (June 27, 1974); and *Dames at Sea* (Aug. 1, 1974). In addition to their Off-Broadway Th. productions, Mr. Hertzog and Mr. Wortman produced *Lenny* in Chicago, Ill. (11 St. Th., May 23, 1974).

Radio. Mr. Hertzog was owner and operator of station WLIQ, Mobile, Ala., from 1960 to 1965.

Other Activities. Mr. Hertzog founded Hawkeye Security Systems.

Published Works. Mr. Hertzog has published *Jeanette MacDonald: A Pictorial Treasury* (1974).

Awards. Mr. Hertzog's production of *Lenny* in Chicago received nominations for four Joseph Jefferson awards.

Recreation. Mr. Hertzog collects movie costumes, primarily from MGM films. His collections have been displayed at the Memphis (Tenn.) Museum, Meridian (Miss.) Little Th., Mid-South Fair, and Metropolitan Museum of Art, N.Y.C. (Nov. 1974–Mar. 1975). Mr. Hertzog also collects full-length MGM films.

HARVEY, HELEN.

Literary representative, producer. b. Helen Brandebury Harvey, Aug. 18, 1916, Huntington, W.Va., to Thomas William and Helen (Brandebury) Harvey. Father, lawyer. Grad. Columbus (Ohio) Sch. for Girls, 1933; attended Bryn Mawr Coll., 1934–36; grad. Ohio State Univ., A.B. 1938. Married July 3, 1947, to Howard Linkoff (marr. dis.); two sons, one daughter. Member of AEA; Amer. Arbitration Assn; Society of Author Representatives. Address: (home) 430 E. 86th St., New York, NY 10028, tel. (212) TR 9-5579; (bus.) Helen Harvey Associates Inc., 110 W. 57th St., New York, NY 10019, tel. (212) 581-5610.

Miss Harvey was head of the drama dept., William Morris Agency (1951–67) and drama agent at International Famous Agency (1968–69). In 1969, she formed her own agency, Helen Harvey Associates, Inc.

Theatre. *The Natural Look* (Longacre, Mar. 11, 1967) was Miss Harvey's production.

HASSO, SIGNE.

Actress, composer, lyricist, writer. b. Signe Eleonora Cecilia Larsson, Aug. 15, 1918, Stockholm, Sweden, to Kefas and Helfrid (Lindström) Larsson. Father, businessman; mother, artist, writer, painter. Educated in private schools in Stockholm. Grad. Royal Dramatic Acad., Stockholm, 1931. Married Oct. 12, 1936, to Harry Hasso, scientist (marr. dis. 1941); one son (dec. Jan. 1957). Member of AEA; SAG; AFTRA; STIM (Scandinavian Musician's Union). Address: (home) 215 W. 90th St., Apt. 7F, New York City, NY 10024, tel. (212) TR 3-5745; (bus.) Lionel Larner Ltd., 850 7th Ave., New York City, NY 10019, tel. (212) 246-3105.

Theatre. Miss Hasso made her debut as Louisan in a Royal Dramatic Th. production of *Le Malade Imaginaire* (1928); and later played Manuela in *Maids in Uniform* (Blanche Th., Stockholm, 1934).

For the Royal Dramatic Th. company, she appeared in plays by Strindberg, Ibsen, Shakespeare, Schiller, Eugene O'Neill, and Maxwell Anderson, playing such roles as Mary, Queen of Scots, in *Mary Stuart*, Nora in *A Doll's House*, and Hilda Wangel in *The Master Builder*.

Miss Hasso made her N.Y.C. debut as Judith in *Golden Wings* (Cort, Dec. 8, 1941); subsequently played Rebecca West in an Ibsen Festival production of *Rosmersholm* (St. Martin's, London, Aug. 22, 1950); Elizabeth Grahm in *Edwina Black* (Booth, N.Y.C., Nov. 21, 1950); Maud Abbott in *Glad Tidings* (Lyceum, Oct. 11, 1951); and toured summer theatres in *Love from a Stranger*. She played Elena Andreevna in *Uncle Vanya* (Fourth St. Th., N.Y.C., Jan. 31, 1956); Orinthia in *The Apple Cart* (Plymouth, Oct. 18, 1956), in which she also toured; Stella in *The Key of the Door* (Lyric, Hammersmith, London, May 27, 1958), also touring in England and Scotland in it; appeared in *The Final Moment* (Lilla, Stockholm, Jan. 1959); and toured the US with the National Repertory Co. in the title role of Schiller's *Mary Stuart* (opened H.S. Aud., Sacramento, Calif., Oct. 2, 1959; closed National Th., Washington, D.C., May 7, 1960); she repeated her role in *The Final Moment* (Stockholm, 1961); played Annie Sullivan in *The Miracle Worker* (Parsons Coll. Fine Arts Festival, July 23–27, 1963); was Rina Givros in *The Tender Heel* (Curran Th., San Francisco, Calif., Sept. 30–Oct. 3, 1963); appeared in *The Mountain Giants* (Upsala and Stockholm, Swed., 1964); toured the US again (1964–65) with the National Repertory Co. in *Liliom* and in the title role of *Hedda Gabler;* played Miss Alice in *Tiny Alice* (Los Angeles, 1965–66; Kansas Circle Th., Kansas City, Apr. 26, 1967); and played Fraulein Schneider in *Cabaret*, first as vacation replacement for Lotte Lenya in the N.Y.C. production and then on national tour (opened: Shubert Th., New Haven, Conn., Dec. 23, 1967).

Films. Miss Hasso appeared in films in Sweden prior to 1940. In the U.S., she has appeared in *Assignment in Brittany* (MGM, 1943); *Heaven Can Wait* (20th-Fox, 1943); *The Seventh Cross* (MGM, 1944); *The Story of Dr. Wassell* (Par., 1944); *Dangerous Partners* (MGM, 1945); *Johnny Angel* (RKO, 1945); *The House on 92nd Street* (20th-Fox, 1945); *Strange Alibi* (20th-Fox, 1946); *Where There's Life* (Par., 1947); *A Double Life* (U, 1948); *To the Ends of the Earth* (Col., 1948); *Crisis* (MGM, 1950); *True and False* (Helene Davis, 1955); and *A Reflection of Fear* (Col., 1973).

Television. She has made television specials in Sweden; in the US appeared in *Camille* (Kraft Th., NBC, Dec. 1954); *Reunion in Vienna* (Playhouse 90, CBS, Apr. 4, 1955); *The Diamond as Big as the Ritz* (Kraft Th., NBC, Sept. 1955); *Mary Stuart* (Play of the Week, PBS, May 23, 1960); played Herda Sarclet in *Duet for Two Hands* (Play of the Week, PBS, Oct. 24, 1960); appeared on Checkmate (CBS, 1962); Route 66 (CBS, 1962); in *The Contenders* (Alcoa Premiere, ABC, Dec. 1962); on Bonanza (NBC, 1963); Outer Limits (ABC, 1964); The Girl from U.N.C.L.E. (NBC, 1967); in *QB VII* (ABC, 1974); and on Streets of San Francisco (ABC, 1974).

Night Clubs. She wrote and performed in a one-woman show of her own songs at the Berns Club (Stockholm, 1958–59).

Other Activities. Miss Hasso has written songs, short stories, and articles, and has published two collections of poetry, one in Swedish and one in English.

Discography. Miss Hasso recorded poetry and songs for Telestar in Sweden. She wrote the lyrics for the album *Scandinavian Folk Songs—Sung and Swung* (Philips Records, 1965).

Awards. In 1972, the King of Sweden awarded Miss Hasso the Royal Order of Vasa with the rank of Knight First Class. She has also received the Anders de Wahl Award for her performance as Manuela in *Maids in Uniform* (1934); the first Swedish "Oscar" award presented to a woman for her performance in *Carriere* (1937); and the Gösta Ekman Scandinavian Award for Theatre (1938).

Recreation. "Life in general but seriously more than just hobby-medicine.".

HATCH, JAMES V.

HATCH, JAMES V. Playwright, educator. b. Oct. 25, 1928, Oelwein, Iowa, to Mac K. and Eunice (Smith) Hatch. Father, boilermaker. Grad. Oelwein H.S., 1946; Iowa State Teachers Coll., B.A. 1949; State Univ. of Iowa, M.A. 1955, Ph.D. 1958. Married Aug. 12, 1949, to Evelyn Marcussen (marr. dis. Nov. 1, 1963); one son, one daughter; married Camille Billops, artist. Address: Dept. of English, City College of New York, 138th St. & Convent Ave., New York, NY 10031.

Mr. Hatch has been associate professor, Dept. of English, City College of New York (CCNY) since 1965 and associate professor of theatre, Davis Performing Arts Center, also at CCNY, since 1972. Previously, he taught English, speech, and drama in Iowa high schools (1949–55) and in North Chicago, Ill. (1955–56); was a graduate teaching assistant in playwriting, State Univ. of Iowa (1956–58); assistant professor of theatre arts, Univ. of California (1958–62); and teacher of scenario writing, High Cinema Institute and Television Institute, Cairo, United Arab Republic (1962–65).

At CCNY, Mr. Hatch also served as a member of the English faculty's auxiliary appointments committee (1970–72) and of the Theatre Planning Committee for the Davis Performing Arts Center (1971–72). He was consultant, Institute of Dramatic Arts, Univ. of California at Santa Barbara (Summer 1967); the Saturday Academy, N.Y. City Bd. of Education (1969); a lecturer in creative writing, Chautauqua (N.Y.) Institute (Summers 1969, 1970); a consultant to the Institute in Dramatic Arts, Winston-Salem (N.C.) State Univ. (Summer 1970); to the Afro-American Institute, Columbia Univ. (Summer 1970); and a visiting professor, Dept. of Drama, N.Y. Univ. (Summer 1973).

Theatre. Mr. Hatch's plays, widely performed in professional and educational theatres throughout the US, include *Dagzil* (State Univ. of Iowa, July 1956); *Tallest Baby* (Univ. of California at Los Angeles, Dec. 1958); *Fly Blackbird* (Th. Vanguard, Sept. 1960; Mayfair, N.Y.C., Feb. 5, 1962); *Liar, Liar* (ANTA Children's Th., Los Angeles, Nov. 1962); *Easter Song* (Margo Jones Th., Dallas, Tex., Nov. 1968); *Conspiracy* (Washington Sq. Methodist Ch., N.Y.C., May 1970); *If It Do Not Die* (Last Chance Th., N.Y.C., May 1971); *Safe at Last*, with Larry Garvin (New Village Th., N.Y.C., Feb. 16, 1973).

Films. He has written films for the State Univ. of Iowa (1956–58); *This Is Worth Remembering* (Herbert Hoover Foundation, 1957), *Autumn* (State Univ. of Iowa, 1960); *Three Days of Suez* (CoProductions, 1964); a documentary for the US Information Agency, *Paper Pulp from Sugar Cane* (1965); the documentary *Denmark 43* for the Jewish Council of Los Angeles (1972); and, for the Oelwein (Iowa) Centennial Committee, the documentary *Oelwein Centennial* (1973).

Television. He was a staff writer for the State Univ. of Iowa's TV Division (1957); wrote *The Sole Survivor* (OZ Television Productions, Hollywood, Calif., 1960); and *Modern Arabic Women* (General Film Organization, U.A.R., 1963).

Other Activities. Mr. Hatch founded in 1968 and has since been a director of Hatch/Billops Studio Th., N.Y.C., and in 1972 he founded Educational Workshop, Inc., N.Y.C., of which he is vice-president. In addition, he was administrator (1963–64) for Fulbright summer orientation workshops for Egyptians traveling to the US; a consultant to the John D. Rockefeller III Foundation in the Arts (1969) and to Drama Brook Specialists, N.Y.C. (1970–72); and he was project director (1973) for a collection of oral histories of Afro-American artists under a National Endowment for the Humanities grant.

Published Works. Mr. Hatch's books include, with I. Ibn Ismael, *Poems for Niggers and Crackers* (1965); *The Black Image on the American Stage, 1770–1970* (1970); with Victoria Sullivan, *Plays By and About Women* (1973); *and Black Theatre U.S.A., 1847–1974* (1974). He has written numerous articles, which have appeared in such periodicals as *American Cultural Review, Theatre, College English, The Nation, The Drama Review*, and *The Village Voice*.

Awards. He received the Thomas Wood Stevens Award from Stanford Univ. for *Easter Song* (1958), the George Washington Honor Medal Award (Freedom Foundation) for *This Is Worth Remembering* (1958); honorable mention at the San Francisco (Calif.) Film Festival and an Amsterdam Intl. Film Festival Award for *Autumn* (1960), *The Village Voice* Off-Bway (Obie) Award for *Fly Blackbird* (1962); the Unity Award for promotion of race relations, Better Race Relations Bureau, Hollywood, Calif.; and for *Denmark 43* he received the gold medal at the Atlanta Film Festival (1972) and the Golden Eagle Cine Award (1972) as co-writer.

HATFIELD, HURD

HATFIELD, HURD. Actor. b. William Rukard Hurd Hatfield, Dec. 7, 1920, New York City, to William Henry and Adele Steele (McGuire) Hatfield. Attended Morristown Prep. Sch., Lincoln Sch., Bard Coll. Studied acting at Chekhov Th. Studio, Devonshire, England, Member of AEA; SAG; AFTRA; Faculty Club of Columbia Univ.; The Players.

Theatre. Mr. Hatfield made his debut in Devonshire, England, playing the Baron in scenes from *The Lower Depths* (Chekhov Th. Studio, Spring 1939) and toured eastern and southern US as Sir Andrew Aguecheek in *Twelfth Night*, Caleb Plummer in *Cricket on the Hearth*, and Gloucester in *King Lear*.

He made his N.Y.C. debut as Kirilov in The Possessed (Lyceum, Oct. 24, 1939); followed by the Religious Man in *The Strings, My Lord, Are False* (Royale, May 19, 1942); appeared in three West Coast premieres;—as the son in *The Skin of Our Teeth*, the Witch Boy in *Dark of the Moon*, and the Senator's Son in *The Respectful Prostitute* (Coronet, Hollywood, Calif.); and played Richard Halton in the pre-Bway tryout of *On Approval* (opened Shubert, New Haven, Conn., May 13, 1948; closed Chicago, Ill., 1948). He played John Forster in *The Ivy Green* (Lyceum, N.Y.C., Apr. 5, 1949); Dominic in *Venus Observed* (Century, Feb. 13, 1952); Sir Nathaniel in *Love's Labour's Lost* (NY City Ctr., Feb. 4, 1953); Lord Byron and Don Quixote in *Camino Real* (National, Mar. 19, 1953); Domingo Salamanca in *Bullfight* (Th. de Lys, Jan. 1954); and Prince Paul in *Anastasia* (Lyceum, Dec. 29, 1954).

During the inaugural season of the Amer. Shakespeare Festival Th. and Acad. (Stratford, Conn.), he played the title role in *Julius Caesar* (July 12, 1955) and Gonzolo in *The Tempest* (Aug. 1, 1955); appeared as Father Grigoris in *The Lovers* (Martin Beck Th., N.Y.C., May 10, 1956); narrated the NY City Opera Company's production of *L'Histoire du Soldat* (NY City Ctr., Oct. 16, 1956); played the Cardinal in *The Duchess of Malfi* (Phoenix, Mar. 19, 1957); and Grandiet in the US premiere of *The Devils* (Arena Stage, Washington, D.C., Oct. 30, 1963); appeared in *Marat/Sade* (Center Stage, Baltimore, Md., Oct. 23, 1970); was Dr. Austin Sloper in *Washington Square* (Washington Th. Club, Washington, D.C., Mar. 22, 1972); Jones in *Victory* (Yale Repertory Th., New Haven, Conn., Nov. 14, 1974); and appeared in *A Doll's House* (Seattle Repertory Th., Seattle, Wash., Feb. 5, 1975).

Films. Mr. Hatfield has appeared in *Dragon Seed* (MGM, 1944); *The Picture of Dorian Gray* (MGM, 1945); *Diary of a Chambermaid* (UA, 1946); *The Unsuspected* (WB, 1947); *The Checkered Coat* (20th-Fox, 1948); *Joan of Arc* (RKO, 1948); *Destination Murder* (RKO, 1950); *Tarzan and the Slave Girl* (RKO, 1950); *The Beginning of the End* (MGM, 1957); *The Left-Handed Gun* (WB, 1958); *King of Kings* (MGM, 1961); *El Cid* (AA, 1961); *Mickey One* (Col., 1965); *The Double-Barrelled Detective Story* (Ind., 1965); and *Von Richtofen and Brown* (UA, 1971).

Television. Mr. Hatfield appeared in *The Rivals*

and *The Importance of Being Earnest* (Masterpiece Playhouse, NBC, 1950); *Mademoiselle Fifi* (Story Th., NET, 1950); *The Nativity Play* (Studio One, CBS, 1952); *Greed* (Summer Studio One, CBS, 1953); *Seventh Heaven* and *The Hasty Heart* (Broadway Television Th., NET, 1953); The Hunchback of Notre Dame (Robert Montgomery Presents, NBC, 1954); *The King's Bounty* (Kraft Th., NBC, 1955); Climax (CBS, 1956; 1958); *The Last Man* (Playhouse 90, CBS, 1958); in Dupont Show of the Month (CBS) productions of *The Prince and the Pauper* (1957), *The Count of Monte Cristo* (1958), and *I, Don Quixote* (1959); in *Don Juan in Hell* (Play of the Week, NET, 1960); *One Day in the Life of Ivan Denisovich* (Bob Hope Chrysler Th., NBC, 1963); on Hallmark Hall of Fame (NBC) in *The Invincible Mr. Disraeli* and *A Cry of Angels* (both 1963) and *Lamp at Midnight* (1965); in *Ten Blocks on the Camino Real* (NET Playhouse, 1966); The FBI (ABC, 1972); and Search (NBC, 1972).

Discography. He has recorded *Hearing Poetry, I and II, The Picture of Dorian Grey, The Tempest,* and *Romeo and Juliet.*

Awards. Hatfield was nominated for a NATAS (Emmy) Award for his performance as Rothschild in *Disraeli* (1963).

HAUSMAN, HOWARD L. Talent representative. b. Nov. 8, 1914, New York City, to Jack Hausman and Tillie (Hoffman) Hausman. Grad. New York Univ., B.S., 1934; Harvard Law Sch., LL.B. 1937. Married May 10, 1940, to Marie; two sons. Member of ARA (1st vice-pres. and dir.); TARA (exec. secy.); Society of Authors' Representatives (vice-pres. in charge of Dramatic Branch). Address: (home) Croton-on-Hudson, NY 10520; (bus.) William Morris Agency Inc., 1350 Avenue of the Americas, New York, NY 10019, tel. (212) JU 6-5100.

Mr. Hausman is secretary and vice-president of the William Morris Agency, talent represntatives, where he has been a member of the firm since 1950. He was vice-president, director of personnel relations, and staff attorney for CBS (1938–1950).

HAVOC, JUNE. Actress, director, playwright. b. Nov. 8, 1916, to John Olaf and Rose (Thompson) Hovick. Father, newspaperman. Relative in theatre: sister, Gypsy Rose Lee, performer. Member of AEA; SAG; AGVA; SSD&C; Dramatists Guild; Actors' Studio (member of actor, director and playwright unit). Address: Newtown Turnpike, Weston, CT 06880.

Theatre. Miss Havoc made her debut at the age of two in vaudeville, subsequently toured the Orpheum Circuit as "Baby June and Company" (1924–28); and appeared in musicals at the St. Louis (Mo.) Municipal Opera (Summer 1936).

She made her N.Y.C. debut as Rozsa in *Forbidden Melody* (New Amsterdam Th., Nov. 2, 1936); played Crystal Allen in *The Women* (Aud., Chicago, Ill., 1938); appeared at the Starlight Th. (Pawling, N.Y.) in *Yes, My Darling Daughter, Tonight at 8:30, Mary's Other Husband,* and *Spooks* (Summer 1938); played Gladys in *Pal Joey* (Ethel Barrymore Th., N.Y.C., Dec. 25, 1940); Montana in *Mexican Hayride* (Winter Garden, Jan. 28, 1944); the title role in *Sadie Thompson,* a musical adaptation of Somerset Maugham's *Rain* (Alvin, Nov. 16, 1944); Venetia Ryan in *The Ryan Girl* (Plymouth, Sept. 24, 1945); Ferne Rainier in *Dunnigan's Daughter* (Golden, Dec. 26, 1945); and succeeded (1946) Haila Stoddard as Georgina Allerton in *Dream Girl* (Coronet, Dec. 14, 1945).

At the Westport (Conn.) Country Playhouse, Miss Havoc played the title role in *Anna Christie,* and Amy in *They Knew What They Wanted* (Summers 1946, 1948, 1949). She succeeded (June, 1950) Celeste Holm as Irene Elliott in *Affairs of State* (Royale, Sept. 25, 1960); played Rose in the pre-Bway tryout of *One Foot in the Door* (opened Locust St. Th., Philadelphia, Pa., Nov. 6, 1957; closed Shubert, Boston, Mass., Nov. 23, 1957); Queen Jocasta in *The Infernal Machine* (Phoenix, Feb. 3, 1958); and Titania in an Amer. Shakespeare Festival production of *A Midsummer Night's Dream* (Stratford, Conn., June 20, 1958).

She played Mistress Sullen in *The Beaux' Stratagem* (Phoenix, N.Y.C., Feb. 24, 1959); Joanne de Lynn in *The Warm Peninsula* (Helen Hayes Th., Oct. 20, 1959); and Sabina in the State Dept. sponsored tour of *The Skin of Our Teeth* (Europe-Latin America, 1960–61).

Miss Havoc wrote and directed *Marathon '33* (ANTA, N.Y.C., Dec. 22, 1963); played Millicent Jordan in Sir Tyrone Guthrie's revival of *Dinner at Eight* (Alvin Th., Sept. 27, 1966); and Mrs. Malaprop in *The Rivals* (New Repertory Th., New Orleans, Apr. 6, 1967); and directed and starred in a touring production of *A Delicate Balance* (1967).

As artistic director of the New Repertory Theatre (New Orleans, La.), she staged and appeared as Jenny in *The Threepenny Opera;* directed *Luv; The Women; A Streetcar Named Desire;* and *The Fantasticks;* directed and played Sabina in *The Skin of Our Teeth;* directed *As You Like It;* and wrote and directed *Love Regatta.*

She directed and starred in touring productions (1972) of *The Effect of Gamma Rays on Man-in-the-Moon Marigolds;* and *The Gingerbread Lady;* appeared as Fanny Brads in the premiere production of her play *I, Said the Fly* (Tyrone Guthrie Th., Minneapolis, Minn. Sept. 20, 1973); and starred in *Twigs* (Chicago, 1975). Her musical, *Oh Glorious Tintinnabulation,* received a workshop production at the Actors Studio (N.Y.C., May 23, 1974).

Films. Miss Havoc made her screen debut as a child, in Hal Roach comedies (1918–24); subsequently appeared in *Four Jacks and a Jill* (RKO, 1941); *Powder Town* (RKO, 1942); *My Sister Eileen* (Col., 1942); *Sing Your Worries Away* (RKO, 1943); *Hello, Frisco, Hello* (20th-Fox, 1943); *No Time for Love* (Par., 1934); *Sweet and Low Down* (20th-Fox, 1944); *Brewster's Millions* (UA, 1945); *Intrigue* (UA, 1947); *Gentlemen's Agreement* (20th-Fox, 1947); *Iron Curtain* (20th-Fox, 1948); *When My Baby Smiles at Me* (20th-Fox, 1948); *Red, Hot and Blue* (Par., 1949); *Chicago Deadline* (Par., 1949); *Once a Thief* (UA, 1950); *Follow the Sun* (20th-Fox, 1951); and *Lady Possessed* (Rep., 1952).

Television and Radio. She has performed on 300 radio programs, including adaptations of *Golden Boy, They Knew What They Wanted, Anna Christie,* and *Daisy Mayme.*

She made her television debut on Kraft Television Th. (NBC, 1949); appeared on Studio One (CBS); Celanese Playhouse (NBC); played the title role in *Anna Christie* (NBC, 1952); appeared on her own show, *Willy* (CBS, 1952–54); in *Theatre* (BBC, London, England, 1955); on her own talk show, *More Havoc,* and as a guest on other talk shows; and made guest star appearances on Walt Disney's *The Boy Who Stole the Elephant* (NBC), and *MacMillan and Wife* (NBC); and starred in *Nightside* (ABC, 1973), a television pilot film.

Night Clubs. She has performed at the Cafe de Paree (London), and hotels in Las Vegas, Nev. (1958–64).

Published Works. Miss Havoc wrote *Early Havoc,* her autobiography (1959); and has contributed articles to *Esquire,* and *Horizon* magazines.

Awards. She received an award in South America as Best Foreign Actress (1961); was nominated for the Antoinette Perry (Tony) Award as best director for *Marathon '33* (1963); and was nominated for the Jefferson Award (Chicago, Ill.) as best guest actress for *Twigs* (1975).

Recreation. Home.

HAWES, DAVID S. Educator, director. b. David Stewart Hawes, June 17, 1910, Skowhegan, Me., to William Holbrook and Eldena Josephine (Smith) Hawes. Father, lawyer. Grad. Skowhegan H.S., 1928; Dartmouth Coll., B.A. 1934; Cornell Univ., M.A. 1940; Stanford Univ., Ph.D. 1954. Married June 16, 1951, to Betty Davies; two sons, two daughters. Served USAAF, Intelligence, 1942–46; rank, Capt. Member of ATA (bd. of dir., 1960–63); Speech Assn. of Amer.; AAUP; CTC; Zeta Psi. Address: (home) R.R. #3, Box 126, Bloomington, IN 47401, tel. (812) 339-6364; (bus.) c/o Dept. of Theatre and Drama, Indiana Univ., Bloomington, IN 47401.

Mr. Hawes, an associate professor of theatre and drama at Indiana Univ., has been a staff director since 1955. Previously, he was instructor at the Univ. of Illinois (1954–55); instructor, director at the Univ. of California at Berkeley (1952–54); acting assistant professor, director at Stanford Univ. (1950–52); executive officer, director at American Army Univ. (Biarritz, France, 1945–46); instructor, director at Montana State Coll. (1940–42); and head of the English Dept., director of dramatics at the Skowhegan (Me.) H.S. (1934–40). At these schools, dating from his first year at the Skowhegan H.S., he has directed more than fifty productions. Works he directed included his original variety show, *Sidewalks of New York* (Montana State Coll., 1942), the opera *The Devil and Daniel Webster* (Stanford Univ., 1950), *Twelfth Night, The Would-Be Invalid, The Cherry Orchard,* and his dramatic adaptation of Ruskin's *The King of the Golden River,* a three-act play for children (Indiana Univ., 1960).

He also acted in educational theatre, in parts that included Bob Acres in a production of *The Rivals* that had both professional and university actors in the cast (Stanford Univ., 1948); Calisthenes in an original work, *The Omen* (Fine Arts Festival, Univ. of Illinois, 1954); Lopahin in *The Cherry Orchard* (1961), and Captain Shotover in *Heartbreak House* (1965) both presented at Indiana Univ. Since 1965, he has been writing and presenting a series of illustrated talks and one-man shows based on the life, times, and laughter of American humorists and the comic characters they created.

Other Activities. He was news editor for the *Educational Theatre Journal* (1957–60). Mr. Hawes is particularly interested in teaching development of dramatic literature, oral interpretation of literature, and theatre for children.

Published Works. Mr. Hawes has contributed articles to the *Educational Theatre Journal, Quarterly Journal of Speech,* and *Midcontinent American Studies Journal.* .

Recreation. Camping, fishing, oil-painting, reading, gardening.

HAYDEN, TERESE. Director, actress, producer. b. Feb. 25, Nashville, Tenn. Grad. West End H.S., Nashville, 1939; attended Vanderbilt Univ., 1940. Studied acting at AADA, N.Y.C., 1940–41; member of Actors Studio, N.Y.C. Married 1954 to William E. Clow (marr. dis.). Member of AEA; AFTRA. Address: 205 W. 54th St., New York, NY 10019, tel. (212) CI 7-7735.

Theatre. Miss Hayden made her debut in summer productions at the Roadside Th. (Washington, D.C., 1941); and toured as an understudy in *Angel Street* (1942). During 1943–44, she organized productions for military hospitals and canteens; in 1944, she was one of the organizers of the ELT (Equity Library Theatre) and participated in its presentations as actress, director, and producer including: *Measure for Measure* (1944–45); *One Man Show* (1945–46); *Live Life Again* (1945–46); *Jason* (1945–46); *Fanny's First Play* (1947–48); *The Millionairess* (1948–49); and *Candida,* in which she played the title role (Master Institute Th., Dec. 7, 1963).

She was assistant to producer-director, José Ferrer, for *Strange Fruit* (Royale, Nov. 29, 1945); and was resident director at the Crest Th., Long Beach, N.Y. (Summer 1946). She took over Timothy Lynne Kearse's roles of Assistant Stage Manager and Aurore in *Joan of Lorraine* (Alvin, N.Y.C., Nov. 18, 1946); was an understudy in *Red Gloves* (Mansfield, Dec. 4, 1948); and toured as an understudy in *A Streetcar Named Desire,* for which she was also assistant stage manager (1949).

At the Fulton Th., N.Y.C., she produced, with Sam Wanamaker, *Parisienne* (July 24, 1950); *Lady from the Sea* (Aug. 7, 1950), and *Borned in Texas* (Aug. 21, 1950). She was resident director at the Ivy Tower Playhouse, Spring Lake, N.J. (Summers 1951; 1956); directed and produced *Dinosaur Wharf* (Natl., N.Y.C., Nov. 8, 1951); and produced at the Th. de Lys (June–Sept. 1953) *Maya, The Scarecrow,*

The School for Scandal (which she also directed), and *The Little Clay Cart.*

From 1953 to 1963, she was a production associate to Herman Shumlin. She was an understudy in *Wedding Breakfast* (48 St. Th., Nov. 20, 1954); assistant director for *Inherit the Wind* (National Th., Apr. 21, 1955); and for *Bicycle Ride to Nevada* (Cort, Sept. 24, 1963). At the Princeton (N.J.) University Th., she directed, with Karl Light, a season of summer productions.

With Ira J. Bilowit and Elaine Aiken, she produced *The Secret Concubine,* which she also directed (Carnegie Hall Playhouse, N.Y.C., Mar. 21, 1960); directed *Our Town* and *Charley's Aunt* (Cherry Lane, 1962); produced and directed *Five Evenings* (Village South Playhouse, May 9, 1963); directed *The Plebeians Rehearse the Uprising* (Actors' Studio, 1968); and produced and directed *Owners* (Mercer-Shaw Th., May 15, 1973).

Films. Miss Hayden produced and directed the films *This Property Is Condemned* (Par., 1966) *and Hello Out There.*

Television. She was programmer for Vanity Fair (CBS, 1952); and assistant programmer for the Aldrich Family (NBC, 1953).

Other Activities. She was the original editor and publisher of the casting directory, *Players' Guide* (1944).

HAYDON, JULIE. Actress. b. Donella Lightfoot Donaldson, June 10, 1910, Oak Park, Ill., to Orren Madison and Ella Marguerite (Horton) Donaldson. Father, editor, publisher, founder of weekly news magazines; mother, musician, editorial assistant, music critic. Attended Gordon Sch. for Girls, Hollywood, Calif. Married June 19, 1955, to George Jean Nathan, drama critic, editor (dec. April 8, 1958). Relative in theatre: grandmother, Ella Lightfoot, actress. Member of AEA; AFTRA; SAG.

Pre-Theatre. Sketched for a Hollywood costumer.

Theatre. Miss Haydon first performed as the Maid in a West Coast production of *Mrs. Bumpstead-Leigh* (Los Angeles, Santa Barbara, and San Francisco, Calif., 1929); subsequently played Ophelia in a benefit matinee of *Hamlet* (Hollywood Playhouse, Calif., 1931); the Lady in Spectacles in *Autumn Crocus* (El Capitan, Hollywood; Alcazar Th., San Francisco, 1934); and Titania in *A Midsummer Night's Dream* (Hollywood Bowl Sept. 17, 1934).

She made her Bway debut as Hope Blake in *Bright Star* (Empire, Oct. 15, 1935); appeared in *A Family Affair* (Cape Playhouse, Dennis, Mass., Summer 1937); and *The Queen Was in the Parlour* (Cohasset Playhouse, Mass., Summer 1937); played Brigid in *Shadow and Substance* (John Golden Th., N.Y.C., Jan. 26, 1938), and on tour; appeared in *Springtime for Henry,* the production which opened the inaugural season of the Bucks County Playhouse (New Hope, Pa., July 1, 1939), and at the same theatre, Maggie in *What Every Woman Knows* (Summer 1939); Kitty Duval in *The Time of Your Life* (Booth, N.Y.C., Oct. 25, 1939; Guild, Sept. 23, 1940), and on tour (1940–41); and, at the Cape May (N.J.) Playhouse, appeared in *Shadow and Substance, Invitation to a Voyage, The Showoff, Sweeney in the Trees, Cradle Song,* and *Smilin' Through* (Summer 1941); played Patricia Carleon in *Magic,* presented on a double-bill with *Hello, Out There,* in which she played Ethel (Belasco, N.Y.C., Sept. 29, 1942).

She appeared as Patsy Jefferson in a six-month tour of *The Patriots* (1942) and played in the N.Y.C. production (NY City Ctr., Dec. 20, 1943); Laura in the world premiere of *The Glass Menagerie* (Civic, Chicago, Ill., Dec. 26, 1944; Playhouse, N.Y.C., Mar. 31, 1945); Cicely in *Miracle in the Mountains* (Playhouse, Apr. 25, 1947); Libeth Arbarbanel in *Our Lan'* (Royale, Sept. 27, 1947); Stella in the pre-Bway tryout of *Springboard to Nowhere* (Selwyn, Chicago, Ill., Oct. 1950); succeeded Marsha Hunt in the role of Celia Coplestone in the national touring company of *The Cocktail Party* (opened Curran, San Francisco, Calif., Oct. 15, 1951); and Catherine in the pre-Bway tryout of *The Intruder* (opened Locust St. Th., Philadelphia, Pa., Dec. 4, 1952; closed Northampton, Mass., Jan. 12, 1953).

Miss Haydon appeared as Masha in *Uncle Vanya,* Nastya in *The Lower Depths,* Masha in *The Seagull,* in *Major Barbara, Man and Superman, Joan of Lorraine, The Barretts of Wimpole Street, Serena Blandish, Birds Without Wings, Guest in the House, Uncle Harry, Nine Pine Street, Little Women, Peg O' My Heart, Mrs. Moonlight, The Enchanted, A Streetcar Named Desire, There's Always Juliet, Happy Birthday, The Silver Whistle,* and *Angel Street.* She appeared in *Shadow and Substance* (St. Mary's Coll., Notre Dame, South Bend, Ind.); *Mrs. McThing* (St. Teresa's Coll., Minn.); *Twelfth Night* (Millikin Univ., Decatur, Ill.); *The Great Debate* (Pasadena Playhouse, Calif., Dec. 1961); and in a pre-Bway tryout of *Mr. Broadway* (John Drew Th., East Hampton, L.I., N.Y., Summer 1962).

She toured universities in three programs of readings from the works of George Jean Nathan; *Encore for George Jean Nathan, Realm of a Critic,* and *Profiles of a Critic.*

She was in *Never, Never Ask His Name* (Univ. Th., Florida State Univ., Tallahassee, Fla., Mar. 24–28, 1965); played Amanda Wingfield in *The Glass Menagerie* (Troy State Coll., Troy, Ala., Apr. 1966); joined (Aug. 1966) the resident company at Theatre Atlanta (Ga.), from which she took a leave of absence (Spring 1967) to make an acting-lecture tour of southern colleges; and she again played Amanda Wingfield in *The Glass Menagerie* (Globe of the Great Southwest Th., Odessa, Tex., 1972).

Films. Following her motion picture debut in *The Great Meadow* (MGM, 1931), she appeared in two Tom Keene Westerns (RKO, 1932); as a bridge expert in a short subject (RKO, 1932); in *The Conquerors* (RKO, 1932); was Fay Wray's scream in *King Kong* (RKO, 1933); played a farm girl in *From Dawn 'til Dawn* (Ind., 1933); appeared in *Golden Harvest* (Par., 1933); as Gora Moore in *The Scoundrel* (Par., 1935); in *A Son Comes Home* (Par., 1936); *The Longest Night* (MGM, 1936); and as the elder sister in *Andy Hardy Gets Spring Fever* (MGM, 1939).

HAYES, BILL. Actor, singer. b. William Foster Hayes, June 5, 1925, Harvey, Ill., to William F. and Betty (Mitchell) Hayes. Father, sales manager. Grad. Thornton Township H.S., Harvey, Ill., 1942; DePauw Univ., B.A. 1947; Northwestern Univ., M.Mus. 1949. Studied singing in N.Y.C. with David Alexander, two years, and John Lowell, several years; acting with Robert Lewis, N.Y.C., one year. Married Feb. 1, 1947, to Mary Hobbs (marr. dis. 1970); two sons, three daughters. Served USN 1943–45; rank, Aviation Cadet. Member of AEA; AFTRA; SAG; AGVA.

Pre-Theatre. Western Union messenger, haberdashery clerk, cafeteria cashier, railroad crew dispatcher.

Theatre. Mr. Hayes made his debut at age nine as Wobin Wed-Bweast in a grammar school presentation of *Frolics* (Whittier Sch., Harvey, Ill., May 1934); subsequently made his professional debut in the chorus of *Carousel* (Shubert Th., Chicago, Ill., July 1947); sang Giuseppe in *La Traviata* (Shubert, Chicago, Apr. 1948); toured as a singer in *Funzapoppin* (Chicago Stadium, Ill.; Indianapolis Coliseum, Ind.; Madison Square Garden, N.Y.C., 1949); sang in *Grandstand Gaieties* (Canadian Natl. Exhibition, Toronto, Ontario, Canada, Aug. 1949); *Laffzapoppin* (Strand, N.Y.C., Nov. 1949); at Music in the Round (Chicago Fair, Ill.) he was Nanki-Poo in *The Mikado* (June 1950), Wintergreen in *Of Thee I Sing* (June 1950), Prince Danilo in *The Merry Widow* (July 1950), and Gaby in *On the Town* (July 1950). He appeared in a variety show (Chicago Th., Chicago, Ill., June 1951); played Karl Reder in *Music in the Air* (St. Louis Municipal Opera, Mo., June 1951); Horace in *Miss Liberty* (St. Louis Municipal Opera, Mo., July 1951); appeared in a variety show at the Roxy Th. (N.Y.C., Apr. 1952); and played Johnny in *A Tree Grows In Brooklyn* (State Fair Music Hall, Dallas, Tex., June 1952).

Mr. Hayes made his Bway debut as Larry in *Me and Juliet* (Majestic, May 28, 1953), and repeated the role (Shubert, Chicago, Ill., Apr.–May 1954); played Gaby in *On the Town* (Music Th., Highland Park, Ill., July 1954); appeared in a variety show (Olympia Th., Miami Beach, Fla., Sept. 1954); another variety show (Chicago Th., Chicago, Ill., Mar. 1955); played Lt. Cable in *South Pacific* (Music Th., Highland Park, Ill., June 1955); Mercury in *Out of This World* (Music Th., Aug. 1956); toured as Johnny in the *Oldsmobile Dealer Show* (1956, 1957); appeared in a pop concert with the Cincinnati (Ohio) Symphony Orchestra (Music Hall, Mar. 1957); played Marius in *Fanny* (State Fair Music Hall, Dallas, Tex., July 1957); the Witch Boy in *Dark of the Moon* (Canal Fulton Summer Th., Ohio, July 1957); Duke in *Happy Hunting* (Starlight Th., Kansas City, Mo., July 1958); and for Oldsmobile, he toured as Johnny in *Good News* (Sept. 1958).

He gave a concert tour (Nov.–Dec. 1958); appeared in concert at the Music Hall, St. Louis, Mo. (Apr. 1959); played Curly in *Oklahoma!* (Starlight Th., Kansas City, Mo., June 1959); toured for Oldsmobile as Johnny in *Girl Crazy* (Aug. 1959); and played Con Blarney in *Friend of the Corpse* (The Lambs, N.Y.C., May 1960).

Mr. Hayes appeared as Billy in *Anything Goes* (St. Louis Municipal Opera, Mo., June 1960); Karl Franz in *The Student Prince* (Starlight Th., Kansas City, Mo., July 1960); David in *Who Was That Lady I Saw You With?* (Canal Fulton Summer Th., Ohio, Aug. 1960); Charley in *Where's Charley?* (Town and Country Musicals, Rochester and Syracuse, N.Y., Aug. 1960); toured as Albert in *Bye Bye Birdie* (opened Curran, San Francisco, Calif., Apr. 24, 1961; closed Orpheum, Minneapolis, Minn., Mar. 17, 1962); played Ben in the pre-Bway tour of *Foxy* (Palace Grand Th., Dawson City, Yukon Territory, Canada, 1962); Romeo in *Romeo and Juliet* (Millikin Univ., Decatur, Ill., Nov. 1962); appeared in a pop concert at the Masonic Temple (Peoria, Ill., May 1963); played Mike in *Sunday in New York* (Gateway Playhouse, Bellport, N.Y., June 1963); Curly in *Oklahoma!* (Charlotte Summer Th., N.C., June 1963); toured as Billy in *Anything Goes* (June 1963); played Curly in *Green Grow the Lilacs* (Parsons Coll., Fairfield, Iowa, Sept. 1963); toured as Prince Karl Franz in *The Student Prince* (Summer 1965); toured as Lancelot in *Camelot* (Summer 1966); played Tommy in a revival of *Brigadoon* (NY Cty Ctr., N.Y.C., Dec. 13, 1967); and toured in a bus-and-truck production of *On a Clear Day You Can See Forever* (Dec. 1967–May 1968).

Films. Mr. Hayes played Lance in *Stop! You're Killing Me* (WB, 1952); appeared (1955–62) in the Columbia Pictures musical travelogues *Wonders of Manhattan, Wonders of New Orleans, Wonders of Washington, Wonders of Puerto Rico, Wonders of Chicago, Wonders of Ontario, Wonders of Dallas,* and *Wonders of Arkansas;* played Frank Fermoyle in *The Cardinal* (Col., 1963).

Television and Radio. Mr. Hayes performed on Songs You Remember (WSJD, Chicago, Ill., 1948); The Woolworth Hour (CBS, 1955); Bandstand (NBC, 1956); and was host on Monitor (NBC, 1962).

On television he appeared in the Homer Herk series (MGM, Chicago, 1949); *Fire-Ball* (NBC, 1949); Fun for All (NBC, 1949); Your Show of Shows (NBC, 1950); the Bob Hope Show (NBC, 1950); This Is Show Business (CBS, 1951); played Ira in *The Nothin' Kid* (Armstrong Circle Th., NBC, 1952); appeared on the Ed Sullivan Show (CBS, 1953); the Arthur Murray Party (NBC, 1953); the Kate Smith Show (NBC, 1953); Rodgers and Hammerstein Cavalcade (NBC, CBS, ABC, 1954); Home Show (NBC, 1954); the Imogene Coca Show (NBC, 1954); Max Liebman Presents (NBC, 1955); the Perry Como Show (NBC, 1955); the Milton Berle Show (NBC, 1955); Caesar Presents (NBC, 1955); Masquerade Party (ABC, 1955); Bandstand Revue (ABC, 1956); Panorama (NBC, 1956); the Paul Winchell Show (NBC, 1956); the Ernie Kovacs Show (NBC, 1956); Rocket Revue (ABC, 1956); the Robert Q. Lewis Show (NBC, 1957); the Will Rogers Show (CBS, 1957); Hold That Note (NBC, 1957); the Jo Stafford Show (CBS 1957); played Fairfax in *The Yeoman of the Guard* (Hallmark Hall of Fame, NBC, 1957); sang on Baseball Spectacular (Olds Special, NBC, 1957); and appeared on The Big Record (CBS, 1957).

Mr. Hayes played Bill Calhoun in *Kiss Me, Kate* (Hallmark Hall of Fame, NBC, 1958); John in *Little Women* (Schaefer Pen Th., CBS, 1958); Spike in *A Family Alliance* (US Steel Hour, CBS, 1958); and appeared in *The Killer in Decoy* (1958); performed on the Patti Page Show (ABC, 1958); the Jack Paar Show (NBC, 1959); The Voice of Firestone (ABC, 1959); the Bing Crosby Show (ABC, 1959); Television Music Th. (ABC, 1960); the Bell Telephone Hour (NBC, 1960); played Larry on My True Story (NBC, 1961); sang on Music of the Thirties (NBC, 1961); the Shari Lewis Show (NBC, 1961); and Great Music from Chicago (1962); played The Minstrel in *Once Upon a Mattress* (CBS, June 3, 1964); and appeared in Cade's County (CBS, 1972); and Days of Our Lives (NBC, 1972–74).

Night Clubs. Mr. Hayes has performed at the Blue Angel (N.Y.C., 1950); Beverly Hills Country Club (Newport, Ky., 1954); Saxony Hotel (Miami Beach, Fla., 1954); Casa Seville (Franklin Sq., N.Y., 1954); Casino Royal (Washington, D.C., 1955); Boulevard, L.I., N.Y., 1955); Chaudiere (Ottawa, Ontario, Canada, 1955); Detroit (Mich.) Athletic Club (1958).

Also, the St. Regis Hotel (N.Y.C., 1959); Drake Hotel (Chicago, Ill., 1962); the Queen Elizabeth Hotel (Montreal, Quebec, Canada, 1963); Eddys' (Kansas City, Mo., 1963); Chateau (Cleveland, Ohio, 1963); Maramor (Columbus, Ohio, 1964); Celebrity Room (Palm Beach, Fla., 1964); and Cabana (Dallas, Tex., 1964).

Discography. He recorded *The Real Davy Crockett* (1955); *The Best of Disney* (1957); *Jimmy Crack Corn* (1958); and *Songs of Faith and Inspiration* (1958).

Awards. Mr. Hayes won the *Photography* Magazine Contest of Stars (1953); received a gold record for his recording of *The Ballad of Davy Crockett*, which sold over 1,000,000 copies, and which was cited by *Variety* (1955).

Recreation. Writing.

HAYES, HELEN. Actress. b. Helen Hayes Brown, Oct. 10, 1900, Washington, D.C., to Francis Van Arnum and Catherine Estelle (Hayes) Brown. Father, salesman for wholesale butcher company. Grad. Acad. of the Sacred Heart Convent, Washington, D.C., 1917. Married Charles G. MacArthur, Aug. 17, 1928, playwright, (dec. Apr. 21, 1956); one son, James Gordon MacArthur, actor; one daughter, (dec. 1949). Member of AEA; SAG; AFTRA; ANTA (pres.); Am. Th. Wing (pres. emerita, 1949; mbr. of bd., 1964); March of Dimes (natl. chairman of Women's Div.); American Girl Scouts (mbr. of bd., 1948–55). Since 1975, Miss Hayes has been second vice-president of the Actor's Fund.

Theatre. Miss Hayes first appeared on stage in Washington, D.C., as Prince Charles in the Columbia Players' production of *A Royal Family* (National Th., 1905); where she subsequently performed in *Little Lord Fauntleroy; The Prince Chap;* and in a dual role in *The Prince and the Pauper* (1908).

She made her N.Y.C. debut as The Little Mime in *Old Dutch* (Herald Square Th., Nov. 22, 1909); played Psyche Finnegan in *The Summer Widowers* (Bway Th., June 4, 1910); and Fannie Hicks in *The Never Homes* (Bway Th., Oct. 5, 1911).

After further summer appearances with the Columbia Players (1913–16), she played "Little" Simone in *The Prodigal Husband* (Empire, N.Y.C. Sept. 7, 1914); Pollyanna Whittier in *Pollyanna* (tour, 1917–18); Margaret Schofield in *Penrod* (Globe, N.Y.C., Sept. 2, 1918); Margaret in *Dear Brutus* (Empire, Dec. 23, 1918); Dorothy Fessenden in *On the Hiring Line* (National, Washington, D.C., June 1919); Cora Wheeler in *Clarence* (Hudson, N.Y.C., Sept. 20, 1919); the title role in *Bab* (Park, Oct. 18, 1920); Seeby Olds in *The Wren* (Gaiety, Oct. 10, 1921); Mary Anne in *Golden Days* (Gaiety, Nov. 1, 1921); and Elsie Beebe in *To the Ladies* (Liberty, Feb. 20, 1922; on tour, 1922–24).

Miss Hayes appeared as Mary Sundale in *We Moderns* (Gaiety, N.Y.C., Mar. 11, 1924); Constance Neville in *She Stoops To Conquer* (Empire, June 9, 1924); Catherine Westcourt in *Dancing Mothers* (Booth, Aug. 11, 1924); Dinah Partlett in *Quarantine* (Henry Miller's Th., Dec. 16, 1924); Cleopatra in *Caesar and Cleopatra* (Guild, Apr. 13, 1925); Georgia Bissell in *Young Blood* (Ritz, Nov. 24, 1925); Maggie Wylie in *What Every Woman Knows* (Bijou, Apr. 13, 1926); Norma Besant in *Coquette* (Maxine Elliott's Th., Nov. 8, 1927; on tour, 1928–29); Nellie Fitzpatrick in *Mr. Gilhooley* (Broadhurst, N.Y.C., Sept. 30, 1930); Peggy Chalfont in *Petticoat Influence* (Empire, Dec. 15, 1930); Lu in *The Good Fairy* (Henry Miller's Th., Nov. 24, 1931); Mary Stuart in *Mary of Scotland* (Alvin, Nov. 27, 1933; on tour, 1934).

She appeared in a revival of *Caesar and Cleopatra* (County Th., Suffern, N.Y., Aug. 21–31, 1935); played Queen Victoria in *Victoria Regina* (Broadhurst, N.Y.C., Dec. 26, 1935); and, while in Chicago during the tour of *Victoria Regina* (1937–38), played Portia in three matinee performances of *The Merchant of Venice* (Shubert, Jan. 1938).

After appearing at the Suffern (N.Y.) Country Playhouse as Maggie Wylie in *What Every Woman Knows* (Sept. 1938), she again played Queen Victoria in *Victoria Regina* (Martin Beck Th., N.Y.C., Oct. 3, 1938); Miss Scott in *Ladies and Gentlemen* (Martin Beck Th., Oct. 17, 1939); Viola in *Twelfth Night* (St. James, Nov. 19, 1940); Madeline Guest in *Candle in the Wind* (Shubert, Oct. 22, 1941); and Harriet Beecher Stowe in *Harriet* (Henry Miller's Th., Mar. 3, 1943; on tour, 1944–45).

She appeared as Mrs. Grey in *Alice-Sit-by-the-Fire* (Bucks County Playhouse, New Hope, Pa., July 1946); Addie in *Happy Birthday* (Broadhurst, N.Y.C., Oct. 31, 1946); Amanda in *The Glass Menagerie* (Haymarket, London, July 28, 1948); and Mrs. Burnett in *Good Housekeeping* (Olney Th., Md.; and Falmouth Playhouse, Mass., Summer 1949).

Miss Hayes played Lucy Andree Ransdell in *The Wisteria Trees* (Martin Beck Th., N.Y.C., Mar. 29, 1950); produced *Mary Rose* (ANTA, May 4, 1951); appeared as Mrs. Howard V. Larue II in *Mrs. McThing* (ANTA, Feb. 20, 1952); in a Helen Hayes Festival in her original roles in *What Every Woman Knows, The Wisteria Trees,* and *Mary of Scotland* (Falmouth Playhouse, Mass., Summer 1954); as Maggie Wylie in *What Every Woman Knows* (NY City Ctr., Dec. 22, 1954); and repeated her role in *The Wisteria Trees* (NY City Ctr., Feb. 2, 1955).

She appeared as Mrs. Antrobus in *The Skin of Our Teeth* (Th. Sarah Bernhardt Paris, June 1955; and ANTA, N.Y.C. Aug. 17, 1955); played Amanda in *The Glass Menagerie* (NY City Ctr., Nov. 21, 1956); played the Duchess of Pont-au-Bronc in *Time Remembered* (Morosco, Nov. 12, 1957); Nora Melody in *A Touch of the Poet* (Helen Hayes Th., Oct. 2, 1958); and Lulu Spencer in *A Adventure* (Tappan Zee Playhouse, Nyack, N.Y., July 1959). She performed in *The Cherry Orchard* (Royal Poinciana Playhouse, Palm Beach, Fla., Jan. 25, 1960); and played Mrs. St. Maugham in *The Chalk Garden* (Tappan Zee Playhouse, Nyack, N.Y., Aug. 8, 1960); and toured 28 countries in Europe and South America (1960–61) as Mrs. Antrobas in *The Skin of Our Teeth* and as Amanda in *The Glass Menagerie.* This tour was sponsored by the US Dept. of State.

At the American Shakespeare Festival (Stratford, Conn., July 17, 1962), she appeared with Maurice Evans in a program of readings and songs entitled *Shakespeare Revisited,* and toured with the production (1962–63). Miss Hayes appeared in *The White House* (Henry Miller's Th., N.Y.C., May 19, 1964; on tour, Summer 1964). With Jack Manning, she produced the Helen Hayes Repertory Co. which presented *Lovers, Villains and Fools,* scenes from Shakespeare narrated by Miss Hayes; and *The Circle,* in which she played Lady Catherine Champion-Cheney (tour, Spring 1966). As a member of the APA/Phoenix Repertory Co. (Lyceum Th., N.Y.C.), she played Mrs. Candor in *The School for Scandal* (Nov. 21, 1966); Signora Frola in *Right You Are If You Think You Are* (Nov. 22, 1966); the Mother in *We, Comrades Three* (Dec. 20, 1966); and Mrs. Fisher in *The Show-Off* (Dec. 5, 1967; reopened Sept. 13, 1968; and tour, opened Shubert, Boston, Sept. 30, 1968). She subsequently appeared as Mrs. Grant in *The Front Page* (Ethel Barrymore Th., N.Y.C., Oct. 18, 1969); and Veta Louise Simmons in *Harvey* (ANTA, Feb. 24, 1970).

Films. Miss Hayes made her film debut in *Jean and the Calico Doll* (Vitagraph 1910); has appeared in *The Sin of Madelon Claudet* (MGM, 1931); *Arrowsmith* (UA, 1931); *A Farewell to Arms* (Par., 1932); *Son-Daughter* (MGM, 1932); *The White Sister* (MGM, 1933); *Another Language* (MGM, 1933); *Night Flight* (MGM, 1933); *What Every Woman Knows* (MGM, 1934); *Vanessa, Her Love Story* (MGM, 1935); *Stage Door Canteen* (UA, 1943); *My Son John* (Par., 1952); *Main Street to Broadway* (MGM, 1953); *Anastasia* (20th-Fox, 1956); and several vignettes including *Third Man on the Mountain* (Buena Vista, 1959). She subsequently appeared in *Airport* (U, 1970); *Herbie Rides Again* (Buena Vista, 1974); *Helen Hayes: Portrait of an American Actress* (Phoenix, 1974); and *One of Our Dinosaurs Is Missing* (Buena Vista, 1975).

Television and Radio. Miss Hayes first appeared on radio in 1930 in a series of fifteen-minute talks; played on New Penny (1935); the Bambi programs (1936); produced and acted for the Helen Hayes Th. (CBS, Sept. 1940–Dec. 1941); began a recruiting program for nurses in the Army and Navy in 1945; appeared on the Elastic Th. (CBS, 1948–49); Stage Door Canteen; in a series of readings on Weekday (NBC, 1956); and narrated a radio play for young people (CBS, May 1956).

On television, she appeared on *Dear Brutus* (Omnibus, CBS, Jan. 8, 1956); *Springtime USA* (ABC, Mar. 19, 1956); as Mother Seraphim in *One Rose for Christmas* (US Steel Hour, CBS, Dec. 17, 1958); as Essie Miller in *Ah, Wilderness!* (Hallmark Hall of Fame, NBC, Apr. 28, 1959); as Mme. Ranevskaya in *The Cherry Orchard* (Play of the Week, WNTA, Dec. 28, 1959); as Mother Hildebrand in *The Velvet Glove* (Play of the Week, WNTA, Oct. 17, 1960); in *Woman: The Lonely Years* (CBS, 1960); as Sister Theresa in *Four Women in Black* (Playhouse 90, CBS, Aug. 22, 1961); on the Ed Sullivan Show (CBS, Nov. 20, 1955); narrated the documentary *Precious Cargo* (NBC, 1964); was a guest on the June Havoc Show (Ind., 1964–65); the Today Show (CBS, 1965–66); Education Exchange (ABC, 1965–66, 1966–67); and Girl Talk (ABC, 1966–67); was hostess narrator for *Or Do We Still Live?* (NET, 1967); narrated *Yankee Don't Go Home* (CBS, 1967); appeared on the Tarzan series (NBC, 1967); and in *Arsenic and Old Lace* (ABC, 1969); *The Front Page* (Ind., 1970); *Do Not Fold, Spindle or Mutilate* (ABC, 1971); Here's Lucy (CBS, 1972); played Veta Louise Simmons in *Harvey* (Hallmark Hall of Fame, NBC, 1972); appeared on a segment of Ghost Story (NBC, 1972); and, with Mildred Natwick, co-starred in the pilot film (NBC, 1972) and subsequent series of *The Snoop Sisters* (NBC, 1973).

Published Works. Miss Hayes, with Mary Kennedy, wrote *Star on Her Forehead* (1949); and, with Lewis Funke, *A Gift of Joy* (1965).

Awards. For her performance in *The Sin of Madelon Claudet,* Miss Hayes received an Academy (Oscar) Award (1931); the Drama League of NY Delia Austrian Medal (1936) for her performance as Queen Victoria in *Victoria Regina;* the Antoinette Perry (Tony) Award (1947) for her performance as Addie in *Happy Birthday;* the Best Radio Actress Award (1940) for the Helen Hayes Th.; a NATAS (Emmy) Award (1952); and the Academy Award for best supporting actress (1970) for her performance in *Airport.*

She has received an honorary Doctor of Fine Arts degree from Princeton Univ. (1956); and other honorary degrees from Hamilton Coll.; Smith Coll.; Columbia Univ.; Brown Univ.; Carnegie Inst. of Tech.; Elmira Coll.; Denver Univ.; Brandeis Univ.; New York Univ.; and St. Mary's Coll. She has received the Medal of the City of New York; and the Medal of Arts, Finland.

HAYES, JOSEPH. Playwright, director, producer, novelist. b. Joseph Arnold Hayes, Aug. 2, 1918, Indianapolis, Ind., to Harold J. and Pearl M. (Arnold) Hayes. Father, furniture dealer. Grad. Arsenal Tech. H.S., Indianapolis, 1936; Indiana Univ., B.A. 1941. Married Feb. 5, 1938, to Marrijane Johnston; three sons. Member of Dramatists Guild; WGA, West; League of NY Theatres; SSD&C; The Players. Address: 1168 Westway Dr., Sarasota, FL 33577; Obtuse Hill, Brookfield Center, CT 06805.

Pre-Theatre. Editorial staff, Samuel French, Inc.

Theatre. Mr. Hayes wrote *Leaf and Bough* (Cort Th., N.Y.C., Jan. 21, 1949); subsequently wrote and, with Howard Erskine, produced *The Desperate Hours* (Ethel Barrymore Th., Feb. 10, 1955); directed and, with Mr. Erskine, produced *The Happiest Millionaire* (Lyceum, Nov. 20, 1956); wrote *The Midnight Sun*, a pre-Bway tryout which he produced with Mr. Erskine and David J. Cogan (opened Shubert, New Haven, Conn., Nov. 4, 1959; closed Wilbur, Boston, Mass., Nov. 28, 1959). His play, *Calculated Risk* (Ambassador, N.Y.C., Oct. 31, 1962), was produced by Mr. Hayes, Mr. Erskine, and Roger L. Stevens in association with Lyn Austin and by arrangement with Peter Bridge.

Mr. Hayes wrote, with his wife, nineteen comedies, which were published and released for amateur and stock production (1941–53).

Films. Mr. Hayes wrote the screen adaptation *The Desperate Hours* (Par., 1955); and the scripts for *The Young Doctors* (UA, 1961); *Bon Voyage* (Buena Vista, 1962); and, with his wife, *Summer in Copenhagen* (1974).

Published Works. Mr. Hayes wrote *The Desperate Hours* (1954); *The Hours After Midnight* (1958); *Bon Voyage*, with his wife, (1956); *Don't Go Away Mad* (1964); *The Third Day* (1965); *The Deep End* (1967); *Like Any Other Fugitive* (1971); and *The Long Dark Night* (1974).

Awards. For *The Desperate Hours*, Mr. Hayes received two (as author and producer with Howard Erskine) Antoinette Perry (Tony) Awards (1955) and the Edgar Allen Poe Award (1955) for best suspense screenplay. He received the Distinguished Alumni Award of Indiana Univ. in 1970 and the honorary degree of Doctor of Humane Letters, also from Indiana Univ. in 1972.

Recreation. Softball, tennis, travel.

HAYES, PETER LIND. Actor. b. Joseph Conrad Lind, June 25, 1915, San Francisco, Calif., to Joseph Conrad and Grace Dolores (Hayes) Lind. Father, railroad man and then singer; mother, actress. Attended parochial schools in Cairo, Ill., 1921–32. Married Dec. 19, 1940, to Mary Healy, actress; one son, one daughter. Served USAAF, PTO, 1942–46; awarded Bronze Star, two battle stars; rank, T/Sgt. Member of AEA; AFTRA; SAG; NY Athletic Club, Pelham (N.Y.) Country Club.

Theatre. Mr. Hayes made his professional debut in vaudeville (Palace Th., N.Y.C., 1932); performed with his mother, Grace Hayes (1932–42); played O'Brien in *Winged Victory* (44 St. Th., N.Y.C., Nov. 1943); James Aloysius McCarthy in *Heaven on Earth* (New Century, Sept. 16, 1948); David Wilson in *Who Was That Lady I Saw You With?* (Martin Beck Th., Mar. 3, 1958); and replaced (Nov. 4, 1968) Art Carney as Andy Tracey in *Lovers* (Vivian Beaumont Th., July 25, 1968).

Films. Mr. Hayes made his debut in *Outside of Paradise* (Rep., 1938); followed by *Million Dollar Legs* (Par., 1939); *These Glamour Girls* (MGM, 1939); *Seventeen* (Par., 1940); *Dancing on a Dime* (Par., 1941); *Playmates* (RKO, 1941); *Seven Days Leave* (RKO, 1942); *Winged Victory* (20th-Fox, 1944); *The Senator Was Indiscreet* (U, 1947); *The 5000 Fingers of Dr. T.* (Col., 1953); and *Once You Kiss a Stranger* (WB, 1969).

Television and Radio. He performed on his own radio program, The Peter Lind Hayes Show (CBS, 1954–57); with his wife on The Peter and Mary Show (CBS, 1958); and Peter Lind Hayes and Mary Healy (WOR, 1963).

For television, he has appeared on Inside U.S.A. (CBS, 1949); The Stork Club (CBS, 1954); the Peter Lind Hayes Show (ABC, 1958); Peter Loves Mary (NBC, 1960); and with Robert J. Crean, wrote *Come to Me* (Kraft Television Th., NBC, 1957). He was also in *One Sunday Afternoon* (Lux Video Th., NBC, Jan. 1957); *Miracle on 34th Street* (NBC, Nov. 1959); episodes of Outer Limits (ABC, 1964); and made several appearances on the Ed Sullivan Show (CBS) between 1946 and 1964.

Night Clubs. He has performed with his wife in supper clubs in the US (1946–to date).

Published Works. Mr. Hayes, with his wife, wrote *Twenty-five Minutes from Broadway* (1961); with Robert Allen, the song, "Come to Me"; with Frank Loesser, "Why Do They Call a Private a Private?"; with Nacio Herb Brown, "Cool Alaska Rock and Roll"; and wrote the lyrics and music for "When You Used to Dance with Me.".

Recreation. "Golf addict—8 handicap.".

HAYS, DAVID. Designer. b. David Arthur Hays, June 2, 1930, New York City, to Mortimer and Sarah (Reich) Hays. Father, attorney. Grad. Woodmere (N.Y.) Acad., 1948; Harvard Coll., A.B. (magna cum laude) 1952. Fulbright Scholarships, Old Vic, 1952–53; Yale Univ. Sch. of Drama, 1953–54; grad. Boston Univ., M.F.A. 1955. Married Dec. 28, 1954, to Leonore Landau; one son, one daughter. Member of United Scenic Artists, Local 829; Société Nautique de Casablanca; White's Point Yacht; US Inst. Th. Tech. (edit. bd.); Phi Beta Kappa. 1860 Broadway, New York, NY 10023, tel. (212) 246-2277; 118 E. 64th St., New York, NY 10021, tel. (212) PL 3-7893.

Theatre. Mr. Hays first worked in the theatre in Cambridge (Mass.), as assistant and designer at the Brattle Th. (1949–52); was subsequently assistant to designers at the Old Vic (1952–53); was designer at the Green Mansions (N.Y.) Summer Th. (1954); for the opera department at the Tanglewood (Mass.) Festival (Summer 1955). His first N.Y.C. assignment was as designer of the sets and lighting for *The Cradle Song* (Circle in the Square, Dec. 1, 1955).

Mr. Hays subsequently designed the sets and lighting for *The Innkeepers* (John Golden Th., Feb. 2, 1956); and for *The Iceman Cometh* (Circle in the Square, May 8, 1956); and sets for *Long Day's Journey into Night* (Helen Hayes Th., Nov. 7, 1956).

For the NY City Ballet (NY City Ctr.), he designed sets and costumes for *The Masquers* (Jan. 29, 1957); and sets for *Pastorale* (Feb. 14, 1957); designed the production of *Career* (Seventh Ave. S. Th., Apr. 30, 1957); the sets for the ballet *Stars and Stripes* (NY City Ctr., Jan. 18, 1958); the sets, lighting, and costumes for *Endgame* (Cherry Lane, Jan. 28, 1958); and for *Children of Darkness* (Circle in the Square, Feb. 28, 1958); and at the American Shakespeare Festival (Stratford, Conn.), the sets for *Hamlet* (June 19, 1958) and *A Midsummer Night's Dream* (June 20, 1958).

He was design and lighting consultant for *Salad Days* (Barbizon-Plaza, N.Y.C., Nov. 10, 1958); and designed the sets, lighting, and costumes for *The Quare Fellow* (Circle in the Square, Nov. 22, 1958); the sets for *The Night Circus* (John Golden Th., Dec. 2, 1958); and *The Rivalry* (Bijou, Feb. 7, 1959); at the Metropolitan Opera (N.Y.C.), was associate designer of *Wozzeck* (Mar. 5, 1959); designed the sets and lighting for *Triple Play* (Playhouse, Apr. 15, 1959); for the opera *The Triumph of St. Joan* (NY City Ctr., Apr. 16, 1959); for the ballet *Gagako* (Imperial Household of Dancers of Japan, NY City Ctr., May 26, 1959); for *The Tenth Man* (Booth, Nov. 5, 1959); and for the ballet, *Native Dancers* (NY City Ctr., Jan. 15, 1959).

He designed sets and lighting for the NY City Ballet production of *Episodes* (NY City Ctr., May 14, 1959); and for the American Shakespeare Festival (Stratford, Conn.), was set designer for *Romeo and Juliet* (June 12, 1959). At the Cambridge (Mass.) Drama Festival, he designed sets and lighting for *Macbeth* (1959); was set and lighting designer of *Our Town* (Circle in the Square, N.Y.C., Mar. 23, 1959); *Roman Candle* (Cort, Feb. 3, 1960); the ballets *Panamerica* (NY City Ctr., Jan. 20, 1960); and *The Cradle Will Rock* (NY City Ctr., Feb. 11, 1960).

He was lighting designer for the ballet, *Theme and Variations* (NY City Ctr., Feb. 6, 1960); designed sets and lighting for *The Balcony* (Circle in the Square, Mar. 3, 1960); and was sent to Japan as technical supervisor of the Kabuki Theatre's NY City Ballet Co. (1960); at the NY City Ctr., designed *Donizetti Variations* (Nov. 16, 1960); and *Liebeslieder Waltzer* (Nov. 22, 1960); designed sets and lighting for *All the Way Home* (Belasco, Nov. 30, 1960); and *Love and Libel* (Martin Beck Th., Dec. 7, 1960); and again for the NY City Ballet Co., designed lighting and sets for *Creation of the World, Ebony Concerto, Les Biches*, and *Ragtime* (NY City Ctr., Dec. 8, 1960).

Mr. Hayes designed lighting for *Smiling the Boy Fell Dead* (Cherry Lane, Apr. 19, 1961); sets and lighting for *Look: We've Come Through* (Hudson, Oct. 25, 1961); *Gideon* (Plymouth, Nov. 9, 1961); and *Sunday in New York* (Cort, Nov. 29, 1961); lighting for the ballets, *Valse and Variations, Raymonda Variations* (NY City Ctr., Dec. 7, 1961); and *A Midsummer Night's Dream* (NY City Ctr., Jan. 17, 1962); sets and lighting for *A Family Affair* (Billy Rose Th., Jan. 27, 1962); *No Strings* (54 St. Th., Mar. 15, 1962); and the pre-Bway tryout of *A Matter of Position* (opened Walnut St. Th., Philadelphia, Pa., Sept. 29, 1962; closed there Oct. 13, 1962); for *In the Counting House* (Biltmore, N.Y.C., Dec. 13, 1962); *Lorenzo* (Plymouth, Feb. 14, 1963); *Desire Under the Elms* (Circle in the Square, Jan. 8, 1963); *Strange Interlude* (Hudson, Mar. 11, 1963); and, at the NY City Ctr., for the ballets, *Bugaku* (Mar. 20, 1963); *Arcade* (Mar. 28, 1963); *The Chase* (Sept. 18, 1963); and lighting for *Fantasia* (Sept. 24, 1963).

He designed sets and lighting for *Next Time I'll Sing to You* (Phoenix, Nov. 27, 1963); lighting for the ballet, *Quatour* (NY City Ctr., Jan. 16, 1964); sets and lighting for *Marco Millions* (ANTA-Washington Square Th., Feb. 20, 1964); *A Murderer Among US* (Morosco, Mar. 25, 1964); lighting for *Baby Want a Kiss* (Little, Apr. 13, 1964); and for the ballet, *Clarinade* (NY City Ctr., Apr. 29, 1964); and scenery for the ballet, *Irish Fantasy* (NY City Ctr., 1964).

Mr. Hays designed the scenery and lighting for *The Last Analysis* (Belasco, Oct. 1, 1964); *The Changeling* (ANTA-Washington Square Th., Oct. 29, 1964); *Hughie* (Royale, Dec. 22, 1964; Huntington Hartford Th., Los Angeles, Feb. 22, 1965); *Peterpat* (Longacre, N.Y.C., Jan. 6, 1965); the scenery for *Tartuffe* (ANTA-Washington Square Th., Jan. 14, 1965); scenery and lighting for *Diamond Orchid* (Henry Miller's Th., Feb. 10, 1965); was assoc. designer for *Wozzeck* (Metropolitan Opera, Feb. 19, 1965) and designed the Metropolitan Opera National Co. touring productions of *Susannah* (1965) and *La Boheme* (1966); designed scenery and lighting for *Matty and the Moron and Madonna* (Orpheum, Mar. 29, 1965); *Mrs. Dally* (John Golden Th., Sept. 22, 1965); *Drat! The Cat!* (Martin Beck Th., Oct. 10, 1965); *UTBU* (Helen Hayes Th., Jan. 4, 1966); the scenery for *Murder in the Cathedral* (American Shakespeare Fest., Stratford, Conn., June 19, 1966) and *Divertimento No. 15* (NY City Ballet, NY City Ctr., 1966); scenery and lighting for *Dinner at Eight* (Alvin, Sept. 27, 1966); *We Have Always Lived in the Castle* (Ethel Barrymore Th., Oct. 19, 1966); *Dr. Cook's Garden* (Belasco, Sept. 25, 1967); *The Tenth Man* (NY City Ctr., Nov. 8, 1967); and the scenery for the Rep. Th. of Lincoln Center productions (Vivian Beaumont Th.) of *Yerma* (Dec. 8, 1966); *Saint Joan* (Jan. 4, 1968); *Tiger at the Gates* (Feb. 29, 1968); *Cyrano de Bergerac* (Apr. 5, 1968); *A Cry of Players* (Nov. 14, 1968); and *The Miser* (May 8, 1969).

He designed the scenery and lighting for *The Goodbye People* (Ethel Barrymore Th., Dec. 3, 1968); the scenery for *Two by Two* (Imperial, Nov. 10, 1970); *The Gingerbread Lady* (Plymouth, Dec. 13, 1970); and the scenery for the musical version of *Gone with the Wind* (Chandler Pavillion, Los Angeles, Aug. 28, 1973; Curran, San Francisco, Nov. 24, 1973), previously presented in Japan as *Scarlett* (Tokyo, 1970).

Mr. Hays was a co-founder (mbr., bd. of trustees and vice-pres.) of The Eugene O'Neill Mem. Th. Foundation (Waterford, Conn.; N.Y.C. offices at 1860 Broadway, New York, N.Y. 10023), from 1965 to date.

He is the producing director of the national Th. of the Deaf, which he founded in 1967. The company, which is based at the Eugene O'Neill Mem. Th. Ctr., Waterford, Conn., has made seventeen national tours and five European tours. For the company, Mr. Hays has designed the sets for *Blueprints, Gianni Schicci,* and *Tale of Kasane* (N.Y.C. appearance at Longacre Th., Feb. 24, 1969); directed *On the Harmfulness of Tobacco* (Longacre, Mar. 9, 1969); directed and designed the set for *Songs from Milkwood* (ANTA, Jan. 12, 1970); and designed the set for *The Dybbuk* and *Priscilla, Princess of Power* (Brooklyn Academy of Music, Apr. 7, 1975).

Other Activities. Mr. Hays was instructor in stage design at New York Univ. (1961–62); at the Circle in the Sq. (1962); and at Boston Univ. (1963). He was lighting designer for Tony Bennett (Carnegie Hall, N.Y.C., 1962); and Diahann Carroll (Philharmonic Hall, N.Y.C., 1962); and, with John Johansen, architect and designer of the Mummers Theatre (Oklahoma City, Okla., 1963).

Awards. He received a Ford Foundation grant for the project, "Eight Theatres: Ideal Concepts" (1959–61). He received the *Village Voice* Off-Bway (Obie) awards for his designs of *The Quare Fellow* (1959); and *The Balcony* (1960); and won the *Variety* NY Drama Critics' Poll for his settings for *No Strings.* He received the New England Th. Conf. annual award (1967).

Recreation. Sailing. In his cutter "Rose of York," he set a record of 34 days for small boat passage from Africa to New York (1963).

HEALY, MARY. Actress, singer. b. Apr. 14, 1918, New Orleans, La., to John Joseph and Viola (Armbuster) Healy. Married Dec. 19, 1940, to Peter Lind Hayes, actor; one son, one daughter. Member of AEA; SAG; AFTRA; Pelham (N.Y.) Country Club.

Theatre. Miss Healy made her N.Y.C. debut in the revue *Count Me In* (Ethel Barrymore Th., Oct. 8, 1942); subsequently appeared as Geegee in *Common Ground* (Fulton, Apr. 25, 1945); Mrs. Aouda in *Around the World in Eighty Days* (Adelphi, May 31, 1946); and Ann Williams in *Who Was That Lady I Saw You With?* (Martin Beck Th., Mar. 3, 1958).

Films. Miss Healy appeared in *Second Fiddle* (20th-Fox, 1939); *20,000 Men a Year* (20th-Fox, 1939); *Stardust* (20th-Fox, 1940); and *The 5,000 Fingers of Dr. T* (Col., 1953).

Television and Radio. She appeared on her husband's radio programs, Peter Lind Hayes Show (CBS, 1954–57); The Peter and Mary Show (CBS, 1958); and Peter Lind Hayes and Mary Healy (WOR, 1963).

On television, she appeared in *Inside U.S.A.* (CBS, 1949); *One Sunday Afternoon* (Lux Video Th., NBC, Jan. 1957); Peter Lind Hayes Show (ABC, 1958); *Miracle on 34th St.* (NBC, Nov. 1959); and Peter Loves Mary (NBC, 1960).

Night Clubs. Miss Healy and her husband have performed in supper clubs in the US (1946–to date).

Published Works. With her husband, she wrote *Twenty-five Minutes from Broadway* (1961).

Recreation. Golf, tennis.

HEATH, GORDON. Actor, singer. b. Seifield Gordon Heath, Sept. 20, 1918, New York City, to Cyril G. and Harriet Heath. Father, social worker. Grad. H.S. of Commerce, N.Y.C.; attended CCNY. Member of AEA. Address: 247 W. 63rd St., New York, NY 10023, tel. (212) 799-9299.

Pre-Theatre. Commercial artist, radio announcer, and script writer.

Theatre. Mr. Heath appeared as "a Native" in the drama *South Pacific* (Cort, N.Y.C., Dec. 29, 1943); as Absyrtus in *Garden of Time* (American Negro Th., 135 St. Library Th., Mar. 7, 1945); Brett Charles in *Deep Are the Roots* (Fulton, Sept. 26, 1945; Wyndham's, London, July 8, 1947); the Troll King in *Peer Gynt* (ELT, N.Y.C., Mar. 1947); the title role in *Hamlet* (Hampton Inst., 1947); General McClellan in *The Washington Years* (American Negro Th., Mar. 11, 1948); and Death in *Death Takes a Holiday* (YMHA, 1948).

In England, he toured for the Arts Council in the title role of *Othello* (Aug. 1951); performed in the revue *Cranks* (New Watergate, London, Dec. 19, 1955); and played the title role in *The Expatriate* (Croydon, 1961). Moving to Paris, he played "the Negro" in *La Respectueuse* (Gymnase, 1962); Cal in *Petits Renards* (*Little Foxes;* Th. Sarah Bernhardt, Dec. 1963); returned to England to play John Kirby in *The Man on the Stairs* (New Lyric, Hammersmith, London, June 17, 1964); appeared in *In White America* (New Arts Th. Club, Nov. 16, 1964), which he subsequently appeared in and directed in Paris (Paris Workshop Group, Amer. Church, Feb. 8, 1965); appeared in *After the Fall* (Paris, Feb. 1, 1966); in a French language version of James Saunders's *The Neighbours* (Th. Lutece, Fall, 1966); in *The Connection* (Paris, 1968–69 season); and again in *The Neighbours* (Paris, 1968–69 season).

Returning to the US, Mr. Heath played the title role in *Oedipus* (Roundabout, N.Y.C., Feb. 15, 1970); wrote the music and lyrics, and directed *The Lady from Maxim's* (Roundabout, May 3, 1970), from a play by Feydeau; and returned to Paris to appear in *Dos Passos' USA* (Amer. Cultural Ctr., 1971–72 season) and Jack Good's *Othello Story* (1972–73 season).

Films. Mr. Heath has appeared in *Les Héros sont fatigués* (French; 1955); *Passionate Summer* (English; Pinewood, 1958); *Sapphire* (Pinewood, 1959); *Les lâches vivent d'espoir* (French; 1961); *Mon oncle du Texas* (French; 1962); *Lost Command* (Col., 1966); *The Madwoman of Chaillot* (WB, 1967); and *Staircase* (20th-Fox, 1969).

Television. He played the title role in *Emperor Jones* (London, BBC, 1953); appeared in *Troubled Air* (BBC, 1953); *Halcyon Days* (BBC, 1954); *The Concert* (BBC, 1954); the title role in *Othello* (BBC, 1955); in *For the Defense* (BBC, 1956); and in *Cry, the Beloved Country* (BBC, 1958).

Night Clubs. Mr. Heath established his own club, L'Abbaye, in Paris, in which he has performed since 1949 with his partner, Lee Payant.

Recreation. Wood-engraving, playing the violin and guitar, singing.

HEATHERTON, RAY. Actor, singer. b. Raymond Joseph Heatherton, June 1, 1910, Jersey City, N.J., to John J. and Daisy (Johannah) Heatherton. Grad. Hempstead (N.Y.) H.S., 1929. Studied voice with Paul Reimers, N.Y.C., five years; Pasquale Amato, one year; voice and music with Father Finn, Paulist Choristers, four years. Married Thanksgiving, 1941, to Davenie Watson; one son, one daughter, Joey Heatherton, actress. Served USMC, PTO, 1943–45; rank, 1st Lt. Member of AEA; SAG; AFTRA (natl. vice-pres., 1961–62; local vice-pres., 1964–to date; natl. treas., 1964–to date).

Theatre. Mr. Heatherton made his Bway debut in the revue, *The Garrick Gaieties* (Guild Th., June 4, 1930); subsequently played Val La Mar in *Babes in Arms* (Shubert, Apr. 14, 1937); appeared in *The Desert Song* (Earle Th., Washington, D.C., 1946; Philadelphia, Pa., 1947); in a national tour of *The Chocolate Soldier* (opened St. Paul Municipal Opera, Mo.; closed Virginia Beach, Va., 1948); *Little Jesse James* (Clinton, Conn., 1939); in burlesque (1949); acted in stock productions of *Anniversary Waltz* (Sea Cliff, N.Y., Summer 1960); and *The Captain's Paradise* (Red Barn, Northport, L.I., N.Y., 1962).

Television. Mr. Heatherton appeared in the title role of the series *The Merry Mailman* (WOR, WPIX, 1950–61); on Luncheon at Sardi's (1953–57); Celebrity Table (1960–61; The Clay Cole Show (1965–66); was host of New York Talent Search (1965–66); and appeared with his daughter on *Joey and Dad* (CBS, June 1975).

Night Clubs. He performed with his own orchestra at the Rainbow Room (N.Y.C., 1939); and the Biltmore Hotel (N.Y.C., 1940–43, 1948).

Recreation. Horses and boating.

HECHT, PAUL. Actor. b. Aug. 16, 1941, London, England. Attended McGill Univ.; grad. National Th. Sch. of Canada, 1963. Married to Ingeberg Uta; one daughter.

Theatre. Mr. Hecht appeared in *Look After Lu Lu* (Equity Library Th., N.Y.C., Apr. 2, 1965); made his off-Bway debut as A Pugnacious Collier in *Sergeant Musgrave's Dance* (Th. de Lys, Mar. 8, 1966); played John Ken O'Dunc and Wayne of Morse in *Macbird!* (Village Gate, Feb. 22, 1967); made his Bway debut as the Player in *Rosencrantz and Guildenstern Are Dead* (Alvin, Oct. 16, 1967); played John Dickinson in *1776* (46 St. Th., Mar. 16, 1969); Nathan Rothschild in *The Rothschilds* (Lunt-Fontanne Th., Oct. 19, 1970); appeared in the title role in *Cyrano de Bergerac* (Tyrone Guthrie Th., Minneapolis, Minn., Summer 1971); appeared in *The Ride Across Lake Constance* (Forum, N.Y.C., Jan. 13, 1972); with the American Shakespeare Festival (Stratford, Conn., Summer 1972), played Marcus Antonius in *Julius Caesar* and in *Antony and Cleopatra;* with The New Phoenix Repertory Co., played Mr. Brown in *The Great God Brown* (Dec. 10, 1972), and the title role in *Don Juan* (Lyceum, N.Y.C., Dec. 11, 1972); and played Baron Tito Belcredi in *Emperor Henry IV* (Ethel Barrymore Th., Mar. 28, 1973).

HECKART, EILEEN. Actress. b. Anna Eileen Heckart, March 29, 1919, Columbus, Ohio, to John W. and Esther Stark (Purcell) Heckart. Father, general contractor. Grad. Berky H.S., Columbus; Ohio State Univ. B.A. 1942. Married June 26, 1943, to John H. Yankee, insurance broker; five sons. Appeared with USO during WW II. Member of AEA: AFTRA: SAG; Phi Beta (pledge pres., 1938; rush chmn., 1940; pres., 1941). Address: (home) 135 Comstock Hill Rd., New Canaan, CT 06840, tel. (203) 966-3860; (bus.) c/o International Famous Artists, 1301 Ave. of Americas, New York, NY 10019.

Theatre. Miss Heckart made her debut with Blackfriar's Guild in *Tinker's Dam* (Blackfriars' Th., Dec. 1943); her Bway debut as an understudy and as assistant stage manager for *The Voice of the Turtle* (Morosco, Dec. 8, 1943); subsequently appeared in *Our Town* (NY City Ctr., Jan. 10, 1944); toured in *Jamie* (1944); and performed with the Shorewood Players (Milwaukee, Wis., 1944–45).

She was an understudy in *Brighten the Corner* (Lyceum, N.Y.C., Dec. 12, 1945); played a season of stock in Boston and Cambridge (Mass., 1946); toured in *Windy Hill* (1947); and in *Made In Heaven* (Summer 1947); played Elaine in a stock production of *Waltz Me Around Again* (Brighton Th., Bklyn, N.Y., Sept. 14, 1948); and toured in *Blind Alley* (1948).

She was an understudy in *They Knew What They Wanted* (Music Box, N.Y.C., Feb. 16, 1949); appeared in the pre-Bway tryout of *The Stars Weep* (closed Boston, Mass. 1949); succeeded Jean Hagan in the role of Eva McKeon in *The Traitor* (48th St. Th., N.Y.C., Mar. 31, 1949); played Nell Bromley in *Hilda Crane* (Coronet, Nov. 1, 1950); Valerie McGuire in *In Any Language* (Cort, Oct. 7, 1952); Rosemary Sidney in *Picnic* (Music Box, Feb. 19, 1953); Mrs. Daigle in *The Bad Seed* (46th St. Th., Dec. 8, 1954); Agnes in *A Memory of Two Mondays;* Beatrice in *A View from the Bridge* (Coronet, Sept. 29, 1955); and Lottie Lacey in *The Dark at the Top of the Stairs* (Music Box, Dec. 5, 1957).

She appeared in an ANTA production of *Before Breakfast* (Congress Hall, Germany, 1958; Th. de Lys, N.Y.C., 1959); played Deedee Grogan in *Invitation to a March* (Music Box, N.Y.C., Oct. 29, 1960); in stock, performed in *The Shemansky Affair* (Masillon, Ohio, 1960), and in *Mother Courage* (Univ. of California at Los Angeles, 1960); played the title role in *Everybody Loves Opal* (Longacre, N.Y.C., Oct. 11, 1961); Melba in *Pal Joey* (NY City Ctr., May 31, 1961); Tilly Siegal in *A Family Affair* (Billy Rose Th., Jan. 27, 1962); and Sweetie in *Too*

True to Be Good (54 St. Th., Mar. 12, 1963); Ruby in *And Things That Go Bump in the Night* (Royale, Apr. 26, 1965); succeeded (Sept. 20, 1965); Mildred Natwick as Mrs. Banks in *Barefoot in the Park* (Biltmore, Oct. 23, 1963); played Harriet, Edith, and Muriel in *You Know I Can't Hear You When the Water's Running* (Ambassador, Mar. 13, 1967); and Mrs. Haber in *The Mother Lover* (Booth Th., Feb. 1, 1969).

She was Mrs. Baker in *Butterflies Are Free* (Booth Th., Oct. 21, 1969), also in the English company (London, Nov. 4, 1970); played Beatrice in the national company of *The Effect of Gamma Rays on Man-in-the-Moon Marigolds* (Boston, Mass., Apr. 20, 1971); and The Woman in *Veronica's Room* (Music Box, Oct. 25, 1973).

Films. Miss Heckart appeared in *Miracle in the Rain* (WB, 1956); *Somebody Up There Likes Me* (MGM, 1956); *Bad Seed* (WB, 1956); *Bus Stop* (20th-Fox, 1956); *Hot Spell* (Par., 1958); and *Heller in Pink Tights* (Par., 1960); *My Six Loves* (Par., 1963); *Up the Down Staircase* (WB, 1967); *No Way To Treat a Lady* (Par., 1968); and *Butterflies Are Free* (Col., 1972).

Television. Miss Heckart first appeared on television in 1947 and since has been on many programs, including The New Breed (ABC, 1964); The Fugitive (ABC, 1964); Eleventh Hour (NBC, 1964); The Doctors and the Nurses (CBS, 1965); Naked City (ABC, 1965); Gunsmoke (CBS, 1965); The F.B.I. (ABC, 1965); Girl Talk (ABC, 1965–66, 1966–67). She was Clara in *Save Me a Place at Forest Lawn* (NY Television Th., NET, Mar. 7, 1966); appeared on Ben Casey (ABC, 1966); Felony Squad (ABC, 1966); repeated her stage role in *The Effect of Gamma Rays on Man-in-the-Moon Marigolds* (NY Television Th., NET, Oct. 3, 1966); was on The Defenders (CBS, 1967); and appeared in Secrets (CBS Playhouse, May 15, 1968).

Awards. Miss Heckart's awards include an Outer Circle Award (1953) and the Sylvania TV Award (1954). She received the Donaldson Award (1955) for her performance in *The Bad Seed;* was nominated for an Academy (Oscar) Award in 1956; received the *Variety* NY Drama Critics Award in 1958 for best supporting actress for her performance in *The Dark at the Top of the Stairs;* a NATAS (Emmy) Award for her performance in *Save Me a Place at Forest Lawn;* was nominated for an Antoinette Perry (Tony) Award in 1970 for her performance in *Butterflies Are Free;* received the Strawhat Award (1972) for her summer theatre appearances in *Remember Me;* and received an Academy (Oscar) Award (1973) for best supporting actress for her performance in the film of *Butterflies Are Free.*

HEFFERNAN, JOHN. Actor. b. May 30, 1934, New York City. Attended City Coll. of New York; Columbia Univ.; grad. Boston Univ., B.F.A. Member of AEA; SAG; AFTRA.

Theatre. Mr. Heffernan was co-founder of the Charles St. Playhouse (Boston, Mass.), where he played Judge Cool in *The Grass Harp,* appeared in *Blood Wedding, No Exit,* played Eddie Carbone in *A View from the Bridge,* appeared in *The Iceman Cometh, Hotel Paradiso, Shadow of a Gunman,* and *The Crucible.*

He made his N.Y.C. debut as Arthur Olden in *The Judge* (Masque, May 13, 1958); subsequently played Ledpidus in the NY Shakespeare Festival production of *Julius Caesar* (Aug. 3, 1959); and the Older Draftsman in *The Great God Brown* (Coronet, Oct. 6, 1959).

At the Phoenix Th., he played Lykon in *Lysistrata* (Nov. 24, 1959); Her Father in *Peer Gynt* (Jan. 12, 1960); several roles in *Henry IV, Part 1* (Mar. 1, 1960); and Robert Shallow and a Drawer in *Henry IV, Part 2* (Apr. 18, 1960).

For the NY Shakespeare Festival, he played the Tailor and the Pedant in *The Taming of the Shrew* (Aug. 18, 1960); and at the Phoenix Th., appeared as Tony Lumpkin in *She Stoops To Conquer* (Nov. 1, 1960), Young Covey in *The Plough and the Stars* (Dec. 6, 1960), Jacob McCloskey in *The Octoroon* (Jan. 27, 1961), Polonius in Donald Madden's *Hamlet* (Mar. 16, 1961), and Androcles in *Androcles and the Lion* (Nov. 21, 1961).

He played Galy Gay in *A Man's a Man* (Masque, Sept. 19, 1962); at the Univ. of Illinois Festival of Contemporary Arts, played in *The Man with the Oboe* (Mar. 6, 1963); the Old Shepherd in the NY Shakespeare Festival production of *The Winter's Tale* (Aug. 8, 1963); Weinard in *Luther* (St. James, Sept. 25, 1963), and succeeded (Jan. 24, 1963) Albert Finney in the title role of this production, and also on tour.

Mr. Heffernan appeared at the Edgartown Summer Th. and the Cambridge (Mass.) Summer Festival.

Mr Heffernan played Subtle in *The Alchemist* (Gate Th., N.Y.C., Sept. 14, 1964); Butler in *Tiny Alice* (Billy Rose Th., Dec. 29, 1964); The Common Man in *A Man for All Seasons* (Mill Run Playhouse, Niles, Ill., July 2, 1965; and Coconut Grove Playhouse, Miami, Apr. 12, 1966); appeared in *Postmark Zero* (Brooks Atkinson Th., N.Y.C., Nov. 1, 1965); played Kermit in *Malcolm* (Sam S. Shubert Th., Jan. 11, 1966); Martin Ruiz in the West Coast production of *The Royal Hunt of the Sun* (Greek Th., Los Angeles, Calif., June 30, 1966); appeared in a tour of *Beyond the Fringe* (Summer 1966); played Captain Bluntschli in *Arms and the Man* (Sheridan Square Playhouse, N.Y.C., June 22, 1967); and, with the Repertory Co. of Lincoln Center, played the Inquisitor in *Saint Joan* (Vivian Beaumont, Jan. 4, 1968). He played the Chorus Leader in *Final Solution* (Felt Forum, Mar. 11, 1968); Jan Ballos in the NY Shakespeare Festival production of *The Memorandum* (Anspacher, Apr. 23, 1968); John Rocky Park in *Woman Is My Idea* (Belasco, Sept. 25, 1968); on a triple-bill, played Tillich in *Morning,* Kerry in *Noon,* and Robin Breast Western in *Night* (Henry Miller's Th., Nov. 28, 1968); with the NY Shakespeare Festival, Cincinnatus the Prisoner in *Invitation to a Beheading* (Public, Mar. 8, 1969); and Solveig's Father, Priest, and Button Moulder in *Peer Gynt* (Delacorte, July 15, 1969); Ol' Cap'n in *Purlie* (Broadway Th., Mar. 15, 1970); Seamus Shields in *The Shadow of a Gunman* (Sheridan Square Playhouse, Feb. 29, 1972); appeared in *Dear Liar* (Syracuse (N.Y.) Rep. Th. Apr. 27, 1973); on a double-bill entitled *Bad Habits* (Astor Place Th., N.Y.C., Feb. 4, 1974; closed Apr. 28, 1974; opened Booth, May 5, 1974); took over (June 1974) the roles of Jason Pepper, M.D., in *Ravenswood,* and Hugh Gumbs in *Dunelawn* and appeared in *The Sea* (Manhattan Th. Club, Mar. 16, 1975).

Films. He has appeared in *The Time of the Heathen.*

Television. Mr. Heffernan's appearances include Camera Three (CBS); The Inheritance (NBC); Look Up and Live (CBS); The Catholic Hour (NBC); Lamp Unto My Feet (CBS); Directions '66 (ABC); Hawk (ABC): NY Television Th. (NET); and Experiment in TV (NBC).

Awards. For his performance in *Tiny Alice,* Mr. Heffernan tied for first place in the Annual Variety New York Drama Critics Poll (best performance by an actor in a supporting role, 1964–65).

HEFFNER, HUBERT. Educator, writer. b. Hubert Crouse Heffner, Feb. 22, 1901, Maiden, N.C., to Sylvanus Lafayette and Lily (Crouse) Heffner. Father, manufacturer. Grad. South Fork Institute, Maiden, N.C., 1917; Univ. of North Carolina, A.B. (honors) 1921, M.A. 1922. Married Apr. 8, 1922, to Ruth Penny; one son. Served US Army, 1943–46, TI&E, 1944–46; rank, Capt. Member of MLA; SAA (admin. council, 1960–63); AETA (pres., 1949); NTC; ANTA (bd. of dir., 1949–51); British Soc. for Th. Research; ASTR; Amer. Studies Assn.; Western Coll. Assn. (exec. comm.; chmn., research comm., 1949–52); Fulbright Awards (reviewing comm., 1952–61, chmn., 1958–61). Address: (home) 1301 Hunter Ave., Bloomington, IN 47401, tel. (812) ED 2-0434; (bus.) Dept. of Speech & Theatre, Indiana Univ., Bloomington, IN 47401, tel. (812) 332-0211, ext. 337-6389.

Since 1955, Mr. Heffner has been a professor of dramatic literature at Indiana Univ., becoming Distinguished Service Professor in 1961. He was Carnegie visiting professor at the Univ. of Hawaii (1959); Univ. of Denver (Summer 1962); and Univ. of Minnesota (Summer 1963).

Mr. Heffner was instructor in English and director of dramatics at the Univ. of Wyoming, 1922–23, and at the Univ. of Arizona, 1923–26; assistant professor of English, Univ. of North Carolina, and associate director and manager of the Carolina Playmakers, 1926–30; at Northwestern Univ., professor of dramatic literature from 1930, and Chairman, Th. Division, 1938; Intl. Research Fellow, Huntington Library (1935–36); professor of drama at Stanford Univ. (Summer 1937), and at Univ. of California at Berkeley (Summer 1939); professor of dramatic literature and executive head of the Dept. of Speech and Drama, Stanford Univ. (1939).

During WW II, he served as chief of the Fine Arts Division, and head of the Theatre and Radio Arts branch, Biarritz American Univ. (1945–46); assimilated rank, Col.

He returned to Stanford Univ. in 1946; taught theatre courses at Cornell Univ. (Summer 1948), and at Univ. of Colorado (Summers 1950; 1965). In 1968–69, he was Berg Professor of English, New York Univ., and in 1973, he was visiting professor of drama, Tufts Univ.

Published Works. Mr. Heffner wrote "Dod Gast Ye Both" in *Carolina Folk Plays,* first series (1922); *A Guide for the Director of Amateur Plays* (1926); wrote, with Samuel Selden and Hunton D. Sellman, *Modern Theatre Practice* (1935); *The Nature of Drama* (1959). He edited, with Isaac Goldberg, "Davey Crockett and Other Plays" for *America's Lost Plays* (1940).

Awards. In 1950–51, he was a Rockefeller Grant Research Fellow (England, France); and visiting professor in dramatic literature at Univ. of Bristol, England (Fulbright Lectureship, 1954–55). He was awarded honorary degrees of doctor of humane letters, Illinois Wesleyan Univ. (May 31, 1964) and Litt.D., Univ. of North Carolina (1969).

HEFLIN, FRANCES. Actress. b. Mary Frances Heflin, Sept. 20, 1922, Oklahoma City, Okla., to Emmett Evan and Fanny (Shippey) Heflin, Sr. Father, dentist. Grad. Classen H.S., Oklahoma City. Married Dec. 29, 1945, to Sol Kaplan; one son, two daughters. Relative in theatre: brother, Van Heflin, actor. Member of AEA (council, 1945–47); AFTRA; SAG. Address: 441 West End Ave., New York, NY 10024, tel. (212) EN 2-5430.

Theatre. Miss Heflin made her N.Y.C. debut as understudy to three ingenues in *Charley's Aunt* (Cort Th., Oct. 17, 1940); subsequently appeared in the pre-Bway tryout of *Punch and Julia* (1941); played Bickey in *The Walrus and the Carpenter* (Cort, Nov. 8, 1941); Jean in *All in Favor* (Henry Miller's Th., Jan. 20, 1942); Gladys Antrobus in *The Skin of Our Teeth* (Plymouth, Nov. 18, 1942); Adele in *The World's Full of Girls* (Royale, Dec. 6, 1943); Florrie in *Sheppey* (Playhouse, Apr. 18, 1944); Christine, and succeeded (June 1945) Joan Tetzel as Katrin in *I Remember Mama* (Music Box, Oct. 19, 1944).

Miss Heflin played Miranda in *The Tempest* (Alvin, Jan. 25, 1945); Virginia in *Galileo* (Coronet, Hollywood, Calif., 1946); Laura in *The Glass Menagerie* (Haymarket, London, Eng., July 28, 1948); and toured stock theatres in *The Hasty Heart* (Summer 1954); and in *The Rainmaker* (Summer 1955).

She appeared as Stella in *A Streetcar Named Desire* (NY City Ctr., Feb. 5, 1956); temporarily replaced Teresa Wright as the Mother, and Eileen Heckart as Lottie Lacy in *The Dark at the Top of the Stairs* (Music Box, Dec. 5, 1957); Tamara in *Five Evenings* (Village South Th., May 9, 1963); and the wife in *The Physicists* (Martin Beck Th., Oct. 14, 1964).

Films. She appeared in *The Molly Maguires* (Par., 1968).

Television and Radio. In addition to performances in both media, Miss Heflin has appeared for five years as Mona Kane on the daytime television drama *All My Children* (ABC).

HEINEMANN, EDA. Actress. b. Eda Gertrude Heinemann, Nov. 10, 1880, Yokohama, Japan, to Paul and Ina (Fischer) Heinemann. Father, importer of raw silk and tea. Grad. Botsford Sch., Staten Island, N.Y., 1898; Smith Coll., B.L. 1902. Studied modern drama at Columbia Univ., 1913; Molière and German drama at Univ. of Wisconsin, 1917. Married Apr. 5, 1926, to Charles Kuhn, artist. Member of AEA (life member); AFTRA; Actors Fund; SAG; Smith Coll. Club of NY. Address: 355 E. 86th St., New York, NY 10028, tel. (212) SA 2-5220.

Theatre. Miss Heinemann appeared as a walk-on in the N.Y.C. production of *The Sorceress* (New Amsterdam Th., Oct. 10, 1904); and played the Keeper of the Slaves in Mrs. Patrick Campbell's *Electra* (Garden, Feb. 11, 1908).

She appeared in *Pie* (Provincetown Playhouse 1920); as Miss Streeter in *Love 'Em and Leave 'Em* (Sam H. Harris Th., Feb. 23, 1926); Mary Sunshine in *Chicago* (Music Box Th., Dec. 30, 1926); Ada Pickle in *The Commodore Marries* (Plymouth, Sept. 4, 1929); Mrs. Bumpstead in *Broken Dishes* (Ritz, Nov. 5, 1929); Lizaveta Bogdanovna in *A Month in the Country* (Guild, Mar. 3, 1930); Edith in *Autumn Crocus* (Morosco, Nov. 19, 1932); Lily in *Ah, Wilderness!* (Guild, Oct. 2, 1933); Zuella McBee in *Miss Quis* (Henry Miller's Th., Apr. 7, 1937); Madame Bovary, Sr., in *Madame Bovary* (Broadhurst, Nov. 16, 1937); Mrs. Thrush in *An International Incident* (Ethel Barrymore Th., Apr. 2, 1940); a Prospective Tenant in *My Sister Eileen* (Biltmore, Dec. 26, 1940); and Anise in *Watch on the Rhine* (Martin Beck Th., Apr. 1, 1941).

She appeared in summer productions at Elitch Gardens (Denver, Colo., 1945); played Amanda Merkle in *Woman Bites Dog* (Belasco, N.Y.C., Apr. 17, 1946); Mrs. Shackleford in *Goodbye, My Fancy* (Morosco, Nov. 17, 1948); Dr. Didier in *Make a Wish* (Winter Garden, Apr. 18, 1951); Mrs. Potter in *The Potting Shed* (Bijou, Jan 29, 1957); Mae in *Silent Night, Lonely Night* (Morosco, Dec. 3, 1959); Mrs. Elder in *Giants, Sons of Giants* (Alvin, Jan. 6, 1962); and Mrs. Kauffman in *My Mother, My Father and Me* (Plymouth, Mar. 23, 1963).

Miss Heinemann retired in 1963 from active participation in the theatre.

Television. Miss Heinemann appeared on Armstrong Circle Th. (NBC), You Are There (CBS), Robert Montgomery Presents (NBC), Celanese Th. (ABC), Valiant Lady (CBS), and Edge of Night (CBS).

Other Activities. She taught drama at Wellesley Coll. and Lake Erie Coll.

Recreation. Vacationing in Connecticut.

HELLER, CLAIRE. Producer. b. Claire Anne Heller, Aug. 25, 1929, San Francisco, Calif., to Walter and Claire (Strauss) Heller. Grad. Lowell H.S., 1946; attended Univ. of California at Berkeley, 1946–49. Married July 13, 1955, to William Smithers, actor (marr. dis. Feb. 1960); Dec. 31, 1965, to Thomas Orme, actor. Member of National Board of Film Preview. Address: 300 Central Park West, New York, NY 10024, tel. (212) LY 5-7366.

Theatre. Miss Heller produced *End As a Man* (opened Th. de Lys, N.Y.C., Sept. 15, 1953; moved Vanderbilt Th., Oct. 14, 1953).

HELLER, JOSEPH. Writer. b. May 1, 1923, Brooklyn, N.Y. Grad. New York Univ., B.A., 1948; Columbia, M.A., 1949; attended Oxford Univ. (Fulbright scholar), 1949–50. Served USAAF, WW II. Married Sept. 3, 1945, to Shirley Held; two children. Address: Alfred A. Knopf, Inc., 501 Madison Ave., New York, NY 10022.

Theatre. Mr. Heller wrote *We Bombed in New Haven* (Ambassador, Oct. 16, 1968); and an adaptation of his novel *Catch-22* (unproduced to date).

Films. His novel, *Catch-22,* was made into a film (Par., 1970).

Other Activities. Mr. Heller was on the staff of *Time* Magazine (1952–56); and *Look* Magazine (1956–58); and served as promotion manager for *McCall's* Magazine (1958–61).

Published Works. Mr. Heller is the author of *Catch-22* (1961); *Something Happened* (1974); and an adaptation, in play form, of *Catch-22* (1971).

HELLMAN, LILLIAN. Playwright, author. b. June 20, 1907, New Orleans, La., to Max and Julia (Newhouse) Hellman. Attended New York Univ., 1923–24; Columbia Univ., 1924; Tufts Coll., M.A., 1941. Married Dec. 31, 1925, to Arthur Kober, writer (marr. dis. 1930). Member of Dramatists Guild (on council); SWG; AFTRA; Amer. Acad. of Arts and Letters; Acad. of Arts and Sciences (fellow). Address: 630 Park Ave., New York, NY 10021.

Pre-Theatre. Book reviewer, manuscript reader for publisher.

Theatre. Miss Hellman's first produced N.Y.C. play was *The Children's Hour* (Maxine Elliott's Th., Nov. 20, 1934); followed by *Days to Come* (Vanderbilt, Dec. 15, 1936); *The Little Foxes* (National, Feb. 15, 1939); *Watch on the Rhine* (Martin Beck Th., Apr. 1, 1941); *The Searching Wind* (Fulton, Apr. 12, 1944); and *Another Part of the Forest* (Fulton, Nov. 20, 1946).

She dramatized Roble's novel *Montserrat* (Fulton, Oct. 29, 1949); wrote *The Autumn Garden* (Coronet, Mar. 7, 1951); adapted Jean Anouilh's *The Lark* (Longacre, Nov. 17, 1955); and the book for musical version of Voltaire's *Candide* (Martin Beck Th., Dec. 1, 1956). She wrote *Toys in the Attic* (Hudson, Feb. 25, 1960); *My Mother, My Father and Me,* based on Burt Blechman's novel *How Much* (Plymouth, Mar. 23, 1963); and some of the lyrics for *Leonard Bernstein's Theatre Songs* (Th. de Lys, June 28, 1965).

Films. Miss Hellman wrote the screenplays for *The Dark Angel* (UA, 1935); *These Three* (UA, 1936); *Dead End* (UA, 1937); *The Little Foxes* (RKO, 1941); *The North Star* (RKO, 1943); *The Searching Wind* (Par., 1946); and *The Chase* (Col., 1966).

Television. Miss Hellman appeared as a guest on *Is the Theater Worth Saving?* (Open End, Ind., June 7, 1974) and was on the Pinter Puzzle special (NET, Apr. 9, 1967).

Other Activities. Miss Hellman was appointed distinguished professor of Romance languages, City Univ. of NY (Hunter) in 1972.

Published Works. She edited *The Letters of Anton Chekhov* (1955) and *The Big Knockover* (1966); and she wrote the autobiographical *An Unfinished Woman* (1969) and *Pentimento* (1973).

Awards. Miss Hellman received the NY Critics Circle Award for *Watch on the Rhine* (1941); *Toys in the Attic* (1960); an award from Brandeis Univ., 1961; honorary L.L.D., from Wheaton Coll. (1961); Douglass (Rutgers) Coll. (1963); Brandeis Univ. (1965); and Yale Univ. (1974); a Gold Medal from the Acad. of Arts and Letters for distinguished achievement in the theatre (1964); the Natl. Book Award (1969) for *An Unfinished Woman;* and the "Woman of the Year" award of the NY Univ. Alumnae Club (1973).

HELLMER, KURT. Literary representative. b. Dec. 26, 1909, Frankfurt am Main, Ger., to Arthur and Maria Hellmer. Address: 52 Vanderbilt Ave., New York, NY 10017, tel. (212) MU 6-2222.

Since 1952, Mr. Hellmer has been a literary representative, representing playwrights and other writers in the US and Europe. He was also editor of the German-language paper, *Aufbau* (N.Y.C., 1939–52); and stage director and translator in German and Austrian, (1930–38).

HELM, FRANCES. Actress. b. Mary Frances Helm, Oct. 14, Panama City, Fla., to Thomas W. and Grace (Spencer) Helm. Attended John Marshall H.S., Richmond, Va.; Richmond Professional Inst.; Columbia Univ. Studied acting with Sanford Meisner, N.Y.C., 1951–53. Married Jan. 3, 1948, to Brian Keith, actor (marr. dis. Jan. 1955); married April 5, 1963, to Walter C. Wallace; one daughter. Member of AEA; AFTRA; SAG.

Theatre. Miss Helm's first appearance on stage was as Elsa Karling in a Richmond (Va.) Professional Institute production of *The Curtain Rises;* in winter stock in Reading, Pa., she played Henrietta in *The Barretts of Wimpole Street,* Ruth in *Dear Ruth,* the title role in *Claudia,* and appeared in *John Loves Mary* and *All My Sons* (1948).

She played Gwen in *The Royal Family* (Casino Playhouse, Newport, R.I., 1951); toured summer theatres as Amy in *The Show-Off* (1954); at the British Colonial Playhouse, Nassau, she appeared in *Pygmalion,* played the title role in *Gigi,* Alison in *The Lady's Not for Burning,* Celia in *The Cocktail Party,* Laura in *The Glass Menagerie,* and Pat in *The White Sheep of the Family* (Winter, 1954).

She made her N.Y.C. debut succeeding (Sept. 1956) Bethel Leslie as Rachel Brown in *Inherit the Wind* (National, Apr. 21, 1955); played A Visitor in *The Deadly Game* (Longacre, Feb. 2, 1960); toured cross-country as Laura James in *Look Homeward, Angel* (1960); played Angela in *Critics Choice* (Hollywood, May–July 1962; Brown Th., Louisville, Ky., Feb. 1963); and Janet in *Pets* (Provincetown Playhouse, N.Y.C., May 14, 1969); the title play of a triple-bill including *Baby With a Knife* and *Silver Grey Toy Poodle.*

Films. Miss Helm has appeared in *Revolt at Fort Laramie* (UA, 1957); and *The Ugly American* (U, 1963).

Television. She played Linda on the daytime serial Valiant Lady (CBS, 1954–55). She has appeared on Kraft Television Th. (NBC), Philco Television Playhouse (NBC), Goodyear Th. (NBC), Armstrong Circle Th. (NBC), Matinee Th. (NBC), Gunsmoke (CBS), 77 Sunset Strip (ABC), Hazel (NBC), Perry Mason (CBS), The Deputy (NBC), The New Breed (ABC), and on the daytime serial Edge of Night (CBS).

Recreation. Horseback riding, piano playing, bicycling, skiing.

HELMORE, TOM. Actor. b. Thomas Helmore, Jan. 4, London, England, to Ernest and Marion (Pulver) Helmore. Attended Tonbridge Sch., Kent, Eng. Married 1931 to Evelyn Hope (marr. dis. 1944); married June 2, 1945, to Mary Drayton; one daughter. Served WW II, British Air Transport Command. Became US citizen in 1946. Member of AEA; SAG; AFTRA.

Theatre. Mr. Helmore made his stage debut touring as Cyril in *Loose Ends* (England, 1926); appeared as Hooper in *Official Secret* (Streatham Hill Th., Aug. 22, 1938; moved to New Th., Sept. 27, 1938); made his US debut in a pre-Bway tryout of *The Birds Stop Singing* (opened Princeton, N.J., Jan. 21, 1939; closed Chestnut St. Th., Philadelphia); N.Y.C. debut succeeding (Aug. 28, 1939) Robert Flemyng as Makepeace Lovell in *No Time For Comedy* (Ethel Barrymore Th., Apr. 17, 1939); subsequently played Gerald Barker in *The Day Before Spring* (National, Nov. 22, 1945); Valentine in *You Never Can Tell* (Martin Beck Th., Mar. 16, 1948); Julian Pugh in *Clutterbuck* (Biltmore, Dec. 3, 1949); Adam Harwick in *The Legend of Sarah* (Fulton, Oct. 11, 1950).

He played Dr. Jeffreys in *The High Ground* (48 St. Th., Feb. 20, 1951); Dr. Fred Stevens in *Love and Let Love* (Plymouth, Oct. 19, 1951); played in stock productions of *The Philanderer, Pygmalion, Sailor's Delight* and *Debut* (1953); played Martin Carew in *The Winner* (Playhouse, Feb. 17, 1954); Gordon Cameron in *One Eye Closed* (Bijou, Nov. 24, 1954); succeeded John Williams as Belman in *The Dark Is Light Enough* (ANTA, Feb. 23, 1955); played in stock productions of *The Constant Wife* (Playhouse in the Park, Philadelphia, June 13, 1955) and *The Champagne Complex* (Summer 1955); played Wyn Spaulding in *Debut* (Holiday, Feb. 22, 1956); was standby for Rex Harrison as Henry Higgins in *My Fair Lady* (Mark Hellinger Th., Mar. 15, 1956); and toured as Dirk Winston in *Mary, Mary* (opened Sacramento H.S. Aud., Calif., May 31, 1962).

He played Henry Higgins in *My Fair Lady* (summer tour, 1964); Paul Delville in *The Marriage-Go-Round* (summer tour, 1965); David Michaels in his wife's play, *The Playroom* (Brooks Atkinson Th., N.Y.C., Dec. 5, 1965); toured again as Dirk Winston in *Mary, Mary* (Summer 1966); and played

Lord Jamison in the revival of *House of Flowers* (Th. de Lys, N.Y.C., Jan. 28, 1968). Other stock appearances include *This Happy Breed,* and *Petticoat Fever.*

Films. Mr. Helmore made his debut in *Tip Toes* (Par., 1927); and subsequently appeared in *White Cargo* (British Intl., 1930); *Three Daring Daughters* (MGM, 1948); *Scene of the Crime* (MGM, 1949); *Malaya* (MGM, 1949); *Shadow on the Wall* (MGM, 1950); *Trouble Along the Way* (WB, 1953); *Let's Do It Again* (Col., 1953); *Lucy Gallant* (Par., 1955); *The Tender Trap* (MGM, 1955); *Designing Woman* (MGM, 1957); *This Could Be the Night* (MGM, 1957); *Vertigo* (Par., 1959); *Count Your Blessings* (MGM, 1959); *The Man in the Net* (UA, 1959); *The Time Machine* (MGM, 1960); *Advise and Consent* (MGM, 1962); and *Flipper's New Adventure* (MGM, 1964).

Television. He has appeared on GE Th. (CBS); Alfred Hitchcock Presents (CBS); the Loretta Young Show (NBC); Schlitz Playhouse (CBS); Alcoa Hour (NBC); Markham; Have Gun, Will Travel (ABC); Moment of Fear (NBC); Dr. Kildare (NBC); Thriller (Ind.); Star Th. (Ind.); the Gale Storm Show (ABC); and Beacon Hill (CBS).

Published Works. He is the author of the novel, *Affair at Quala* (1964).

Awards. Mr. Helmore received the Donaldson Award for his performance as Gerald Barker in *The Day Before Spring* (1946).

Recreation. Sailing.

HELPMANN, ROBERT. Choreographer, actor, director, dancer. b. Robert Murray Helpman, Apr. 9, 1909, Mount Gambier, Southern Australia, to James Murray and Mary (Gardiner) Helpman. Attended Prince Alfred's Coll., Adelaide, Australia; studied under Laurent Novikov, Australia. Member of British AEA.

Theatre. Mr. Helpmann first appeared on the stage in Australia as a dancer in *The Ugly Duckling* (Th. Royal, Adelaide, 1923); subsequently danced in *Frasquita* (His Majesty's, Sydney, Apr. 1927); and in a number of musicals in Australia, including *Tip Toes* and *Queen High* (1927), *This Year of Grace* (1929), and *The New Moon, The Merry Widow* and *Katinka* (1930). As an actor, he appeared in *The Barretts of Wimpole Street* (Criterion, Sydney, Apr. 1932); and made his London debut as an actor, in *I Hate Men* (Gate, Feb. 28, 1933).

In 1933, he entered the Sadler's Wells Ballet Sch., dancing in the company's corps de ballet, and soon rose to soloist. From 1933–50, he was leading dancer and mime with the company, touring Europe, America, and Canada and has been a guest artist with many other companies, including at Oslo, Norway (Jan. 1950), and La Scala, Milan, Italy (Apr. 1950). As an actor, he played Duval in *Precipice* (Savoy, London, June 5, 1934); and appeared with the Old Vic as Oberon in *A Midsummer Night's Dream* (Dec. 24, 1937); played Felix, Mr. Cricket and Chief of Yellow Ants in *The Insect Play* (Playhouse, Apr. 27, 1938); and with the Old Vic played Gremio, the Tailor, and Nicholas in *The Taming of the Shrew* (Mar. 28, 1939). He became one of the principal choreographers for the Sadler's Wells Ballet (now the Royal Ballet) and created the ballet, *Hamlet* (premiere, New, London, May 19, 1942), in which he danced the title role; portrayed the title role in *Hamlet* in the Old Vic production (New, Feb. 12, 1944); choreographed and danced in the ballet, *Miracle in the Gorbals,* for Sadler's Wells (premiere, Prince's Th., Oct. 26, 1944); and created and danced in the ballet, *Adam Zero* (premiere, Covent Garden Opera House, Apr. 1946).

He appeared as Oberon in *The Fairy Queen* (Covent Garden, Dec. 12, 1946); the Shakespeare Memorial Th., played the title role in *Hamlet,* the title role in *King John,* and appeared as Shylock in *The Merchant of Venice* (Stratford-upon-Avon, Apr. 1948); played Mercury in the opera, *The Olympians* (Covent Garden, Sept. 1949); directed *Madame Butterfly* for the Royal Opera (Covent Garden, Jan. 6, 1950); and directed, with Michael Benthall, *Golden City* (Adelphi, June 15, 1950).

With Sir Laurence Olivier, Mr. Helpmann played Apollodorus in *Caesar and Cleopatra* (St. James's, London, May 10, 1951; Ziegfeld, N.Y.C., Dec. 19, 1951); and Octavius Caesar in *Antony and Cleopatra* (St. James's, London, May 11, 1951; Ziegfeld, N.Y.C., Dec. 20, 1951); and played the Doctor in *The Millionairess* (New, London, June 27, 1952; Shubert, N.Y.C., Oct. 17, 1952). He directed *The Wedding Ring* (Opera House, Manchester, England, Aug. 1952); *Murder in the Cathedral* (Old Vic, London, Mar. 31, 1953); *The Tempest* (Old Vic, Apr. 13, 1954); and *After the Ball* (Globe, June 10, 1954).

At the Edinburgh (Scotland) Festival (1954), for the Old Vic, he choreographed and played Oberon in *A Midsummer Night's Dream* (which subsequently played at the Metropolitan Opera, N.Y.C., Sept. 21, 1954, and toured the US and Canada), and choreographed and played the Devil in *A Soldier's Tale;* he directed *As You Like It* (Old Vic, London, Mar. 1, 1955); toured Australia with the Old Vic, playing Shylock in *The Merchant of Venice,* Petruchio in *The Taming of the Shrew,* and Angelo in *Measure for Measure* (1955); directed *Romeo and Juliet* (Old Vic, London, June 12, 1956; Winter Garden, N.Y.C., Oct. 24, 1956); with the Old Vic (Dec. 1956–May 1957), played Shylock in *The Merchant of Venice,* Launce in *The Two Gentlemen of Verona,* Saturnius in *Titus Andronicus,* Dr. Pinch in *The Comedy of Errors,* the title role in *Richard III,* and directed *Antony and Cleopatra;* and he played Georges de Valera in *Nekrassov* (Edinburgh Fest., Aug. 1957; Royal Court, London, Sept. 17, 1957).

Mr. Helpmann succeeded (Nov. 1957) John Gielgud as Sebastien in *Nude with Violin* (Globe, Nov. 7, 1956); danced with the Royal Ballet (1958) in *The Rake's Progress, Hamlet, Coppelia, Miracle in the Gorbals* and *Petrushka;* toured Australia in *Nude with Violin* (1958–59); directed *The Marriage-Go-Round* (Piccadilly, London, Oct. 29, 1959); and directed *Aladdin* (Coliseum, Dec. 17, 1959).

He directed *Duel of Angels* (Helen Hayes Th., N.Y.C., Apr. 19, 1960); a tour of *Finian's Rainbow* (1961); for the Old Vic world tour (opening in Australia, 1961), directed *Twelfth Night, Duel of Angels* and *The Lady of the Camellias;* he choreographed *Elektra* and devised a new production of *Swan Lake* at the Royal Opera House (London, 1963); directed *Camelot* (Drury Lane, Aug. 19, 1964); and created the ballet, *The Display,* for the Australian Ballet (Mar. 1964), of which he became co-director (with Dame Peggy van Praagh) in 1965, and solo director in 1974.

Mr. Helpmann directed *La Contessa* (Royal, Newcastle, England, Apr. 7, 1965, and on tour); with the Royal Ballet, narrated *Wedding Bouquet (revived Metropolitan Opera House, N.Y.C., May 9, 1965);* for the Australian Ballet, choreographed *Yugen* (Th. Royal, Sydney, Australia, May 2, 1965); Covent Garden, London, Oct. 1, 1965); and has also choreographed the ballets of *Cinderella, Comus, The Birds,* and *Sun Music* (1968).

He appeared for the Australian Ballet Co. as Don Quixote and Dr. Coppelius (1969–70); was director of the Adelaide (Austria) Fest. of Arts (1970); for three years (1971–73) directed a Christmas production of *Peter Pan* (Coliseum, London); and wrote the book, with Eaton Magoon, Jr., for the musical *Heathen* (Billy Rose Th., N.Y.C., May 21, 1972).

Films. Mr. Helpmann has appeared in *One of Our Aircraft is Missing* (Brit. Natl./UA, 1942); *Henry V* (UA, 1946); *Caravan* (Eagle-Lion, 1947); *The Red Shoes* (Eagle-Lion, 1948), which he also choreographed; *The Tales of Hoffman* (Lopert, 1951); *The Big Money* (Rank, 1956); *The Iron Petticoat* (MGM, 1956); *55 Days at Peking* (Allied, 1963); choreographed and played the Devil in *The Soldier's Tale* (Brit. Home Enter., 1964); appeared in *The Quiller Memorandum* (20th-Fox, 1966); *Chitty Chitty Bang Bang* (UA, 1968); as the Mad Hatter in *Alice's Adventures in Wonderland* (Amer. Natl., 1972); and directed, with Rudolf Nureyev, and danced the title role in *Don Quixote* (Cont., 1973).

Television. Mr. Helpmann's British appearances include a solo performance in *Box for One* (1953); *An Evening with Robert Helpmann* (1963); *The Ghost Sonata* (1963); and *Catch as Catch Can* (1964).

In the US, Mr. Helpmann has appeared in *Two for Two* (Lux Video Th., CBS, Jan. 5, 1953).

Awards. He received the Scroll of Honor from the King of Norway (1950); was awarded the medal of Lebanese Merit, Order of the Cedars, by Pres. Chamoun (1957); received the Queen Elizabeth II Coronation Award (1960) from the Royal Acad. of Dancing for outstanding service to British ballet; was decorated by King Gustav (Sweden) with the Order of the Knight of the Northern Star.

The order of the Commander of the British Empire (C.B.E.) was conferred upon him in the Queen's Birthday Honours (1964) and he was made Knight of the British Empire in the New Years Honours (1968).

Recreation. Swimming, riding, tennis.

HEMING, VIOLET. Actress. b. Jan. 27, 1895, Leeds, England, to Alfred and Mabel (Allen) Hemming. Attended Malverne House Sch., Southport, Lancashire, England. Married 1920 to Grant Mills (marr. dis.); married 1945 to Bennett Champ Clark, US senator (dec. 1954). Relative in theatre: uncle, Charles Dalton, actor.

Theatre. Miss Heming made her US debut taking over Mildred Morris's role as Wendy in Charles Frohman's children's company of *Peter Pan* (1908); followed by her N.Y.C. debut as Carrie Crewe in *Fluffy-Ruffles* (Criterion Th., Sept. 7, 1908); played Rebecca in *Rebecca of Sunnybrook Farm* (Springfield, Mass., Sept. 16, 1909); toured as Rose Dufard in *Daddy Dufard* (1910), and played the role in N.Y.C. (Hackett, Dec. 6, 1910).

She appeared as Kate Delaney in *The Fox* (Chicago, Ill., Apr. 1911); toured as Laura Moore in *The Deep Purple* (1911–12), Su in *The Unwritten Law* (1912); played Madge Hale in *Honest Jim Blunt* (Hudson, N.Y.C., Sept. 16, 1912); toured as Lady Clarissa Pevensey in George Arliss' *Disraeli* (Fall 1912–Summer 1914); and appeared in a season of productions with the Columbia Stock Co. (Washington, D.C., May–June 1914).

Miss Heming played Ethel Cartwright in *Under Cover* (Cort, N.Y.C., Aug. 26, 1914); Beatrice in *A Modern Girl* (Comedy, Sept. 12, 1914); Lucy Shale in *The Lie* (Sam H. Harris Th., Dec. 24, 1914); Ethel Willoughby in *Under Fire* (Hudson, Aug. 11, 1915); Pamela Cabot in *The Flame* (Lyric, Sept. 4, 1916); Ernestine Waite in *The Love Drive* (Criterion, Oct. 30, 1917); Eloise Farrington in *Losing Eloise* (Harris, Nov. 17, 1917); and toured as Annie in *DeLuxe Annie* (1918).

She played Helene in *Three Faces East* (Cohan and Harris Th., N.Y.C., Aug. 13, 1918), also touring in it (1919–20); the title role in *Sonya* (48 St. Th., N.Y.C., Aug. 15, 1921); Germaine Glandelle in *The Rubicon* (Hudson, Feb. 21, 1922); Lydia Languish in *The Rivals* (Empire, June 5, 1922; 48 St. Th., May 7, 1923); Pamela Carey in *The Lucky One* (Garrick, Nov. 20, 1922); Margaret Sones in *Spring Cleaning* (Eltinge, Nov. 9, 1923), also touring in it (1924); Avonia Bunn in *Trelawny of the Wells* (Knickerbocker, N.Y.C., June 1, 1925); and Lucy Meredith in *Chivalry* (Wallack's, Dec. 15, 1925).

Also, Ginevra in *The Jest* (Plymouth, Feb. 4, 1926); Nina Grant in *Loose Ends* (Ritz, Nov. 1, 1926); toured in a vaudeville act, *The Snob* (1927); played Mrs. Dane in *Mrs. Dane's Defense* (Cosmopolitan, N.Y.C., Feb. 6, 1928); Mary Turner in *Within the Law* (Csomopolitan, Mar. 5, 1928); Anne Marvin in *This Thing Called Love* (Maxine Elliott's Th., Sept. 17, 1928); Brenda Ritchie in *Soldiers and Women* (Ritz, Sept. 2, 1929); and Nancy Whitney in *Ladies All* (Morosco, July 28, 1930); Veronica Vare in *Divorce Me, Dear* (Avon, Oct. 6, 1931); Leonora Perrycoste in *There's Always Juliet* (Ethel Barrymore Th., Oct. 27, 1932); Mrs. Jelliwell in *Springtime for Henry* and Gilda in *Design for Living* (Ann Arbor, Mich., June 1933); played Mariella Linden in the Chicago (Ill.) company of *The Shining Hour* (Selwyn, Apr. 1934); Josie Frampton in *All Rights Reserved* (Ritz, N.Y.C., Nov. 6, 1934); Sabine Brandon in *De Luxe* (Booth, Mar. 5, 1935); Constance Nevins in *Yes, My Darling Daughter* (Playhouse, Feb. 9,

1937), also touring in it (1938); played Marion Bingham in *Summer Night* (St. James, N.Y.C., Nov. 2, 1939); Mrs. Frail in *Love for Love* (Hudson, June 3, 1940); May Flowers in *Beverly Hills* (Fulton, Nov. 7, 1940); Ruth in *Blithe Spirit* (Curran, San Francisco, Calif., 1948); Mrs. Friske in *Dear Barbarians* (Royale, N.Y.C., Feb. 21, 1952); and she was in *The G. B. eSsence of Women* (Th. de Lys, Dec. 8, 1964).

Films. Miss Heming appeared in *Almost Married* (M, 1919) and *The Man Who Played God* (WB, 1932).

Television. She has appeared on The Verdict Is Yours (CBS), From These Roots (NBC), and Target.

Recreation. Yachting, dogs, architecture.

HENDERSON, FLORENCE. Actress, singer. b. Feb. 14, 1934, Dale, Ind., to Joseph and Elizabeth (Elder) Henderson. Attended St. Francis Acad., Owensboro, Ky. Studied singing with Christine Johnson, Owensboro, Ky., 1950; acting at AADA, N.Y.C., 1951–52; with Dolf Swing, N.Y.C., 1954–64; Mary Tarcai, N.Y.C., 1955–59. Married Jan. 9, 1956, to Ira Bernstein, theatrical manager; two sons, two daughters. Relative in theatre: father-in-law, Karl Bernstein, press representative. Member of AEA; AFTRA; AGMA; SAG.

Theatre. Miss Henderson made her Bway debut as the New Girl in *Wish You Were Here* (Imperial, June 25, 1952); toured as Laurey in *Oklahoma!* (opened Hartford, Conn., Aug. 29, 1952); and played this role in N.Y.C. (NY City Ctr., Aug. 31, 1953); and with the Los Angeles Civic Light Opera Association, she played Resi in *The Great Waltz* (Philharmonic Aud., Los Angeles, Calif.; Curran, San Francisco, Calif., Summer 1953).

She played the title role in *Fanny* (Majestic, N.Y.C., Nov. 4, 1954); appeared in Oldsmobile industrial shows (1958–61); toured as Baroness Maria Rainer Von Trapp in *The Sound of Music* (opened Riviera, Detroit, Mich., Feb. 27, 1961); and played Mary Morgan in *The Girl Who Came to Supper* (Bway Th., N.Y.C., Dec. 8, 1963). She performed with Mayor John V. Lindsay of N.Y.C. in *New Faces of 1966*, appeared in the Inner Circle Show of the NY Political Writers (NY Hilton, Mar. 1966); and played Ensign Nellie Forbush in a revival of *South Pacific* (NY State Th., June 12, 1967).

Films. Miss Henderson made her motion picture debut in *Song of Norway* (Cinerama, 1970).

Television. Miss Henderson was an offstage voice on the Ed Sullivan Show (CBS, 1952); sang on the *Rodgers and Hammerstein Anniversary Show* (Mar. 1954); appeared in the US Steel Hour (CBS) productions of *Huck Finn* (1957) and *A Family Alliance* (1958); and subsequently in a production of *Little Women* (CBS, 1958). She was also on the Today Show (NBC, 1959–60); was hostess on Hayes and Henderson (NBC, 1959); co-host of Oldsmobile Th. (NBC, 1959); appeared in *The Gershwin Years* (CBS, 1961); on the Bell Telephone Hour (NBC, 1964); and I Spy (NBC, 1966). She was co-star of The Brady Bunch (ABC, 1969–72); and has appeared on many variety and talk shows, including the Dick Cavett Show (ABC, 1970, 1972); Tom Jones Show (ABC, 1970); Don Knotts Show (NBC, 1970); Ice Capades (NBC, 1970); the Dean Martin Show (NBC); Jack Paar Show (NBC); Jackie Gleason Show (CBS); Jonathan Winters Show (NBC); Tonight Show (NBC); and Hollywood Palace (NBC).

Night Clubs. Miss Henderson has made appearances at many clubs, including the Detroit (Mich.) Athletic Club (1957); as the Maisonette, St. Regis Hotel, with Bill Hayes (N.Y.C., 1958); Fontainebleau Hotel (Miami, Fla.); Empire Room, Waldorf-Astoria Hotel (N.Y.C., Feb. 1967); Caribe Hilton (San Juan, Puerto Rico, Apr. 1968); Century Plaza (Los Angeles, Calif., Apr. 1968); Shamrock Hotel (Houston, Tex., Feb. 1970); Persian Room, Plaza Hotel (N.Y.C., Mar. 1970); and at clubs in Reno and Las Vegas, Nev. (1972).

Awards. Miss Henderson received the Sarah Siddons Award for her performance as Baroness Maria Rainer Von Trapp in *The Sound of Music* (1962).

HENDERSON, LUTHER. Orchestrator, arranger, pianist, composer, musical director. b. Luther Lincoln Henderson, Mar. 15, 1919, to Luther Lincoln Henderson and Florence (Black) Henderson. Father, educator, actor, singer; mother, educator, civic worker. Grad. Evander Childs H.S., N.Y.C., 1935; Juilliard Sch. of Music, B.S. 1942; attended City Coll. of New York, 1935–38; New York Univ., 1946. Studied piano with Sonoma Talley, 1925–38; Shillinger System with Rudolph Schramm. Married June 1941 to Tealene Berry (marr. dis. 1956); two sons; married 1956 to Stephanie Locke, actress, singer; one daughter. Served USNR, 1944–46; rank, PO-3. Member of ASCAP; AFM, Local 802.

Theatre. Mr. Henderson performed in, arranged, and orchestrated the music for the pre-Bway tryout of *Tropical Review* (His Majesty's, Toronto, Canada, 1943); served on the arrangers and orchestrators staff at the USN Sch. of Music, Washington, D.C. (1944–46); was one of the orchestrators for *Beggar's Holiday* (Bway Th., N.Y.C., Dec. 26, 1946); has been associated with the Oldsmobile industrial shows as dance and vocal arranger, orchestrator, composer, and adapter (1955–to date); prepared dance arrangements and special ballet for *The Flower Drum Song* (St. James, Dec. 1, 1958); orchestrations for *Do Re Mi* (St. James, Dec. 26, 1960); dance arrangements and orchestrations for *Bravo Giovanni* (Broadhurst, May 19, 1962); orchestrations for *Hot Spot* (Majestic, Apr. 1963); and dance orchestrations and arrangements for *Funny Girl* (Winter Garden, Mar. 26, 1964).

He arranged dance music for *I Had a Ball* (Martin Beck Th., Dec. 15, 1964); did dance orchestrations for *Hallelujah, Baby!* (Martin Beck Th., Apr. 26, 1967); with Marvin Hamlisch for *Golden Rainbow* (Sam S. Shubert Th., Feb. 4, 1968); orchestrations and choral arrangements, with Garry Sherman, for *Purlie* (Bway Th., Mar. 15, 1970; Billy Rose Th., Dec. 27, 1972); and arranged dance music and composed incidental music for a revival of *No, No Nanette* (46 St. Th., Jan. 19, 1971). He also did orchestrations for *Wild and Wonderful* (Lyceum Th., Dec. 7, 1971); orchestrations and arrangements for *That's Entertainment* (Edison Th., Apr. 14, 1972); arrangements for *F. Jasmine Addams* (Circle in the Square, Oct. 27, 1971); composed and arranged dance and incidental music for a revival of *Good News* (St. James Th., Dec. 23, 1974); arranged dance and incidental music for *Doctor Jazz* (Winter Garden Th., Mar. 19, 1975); and was orchestrator and dance music arranger for *Rodgers & Hart* (Helen Hayes Th., May 13, 1975).

Television. Mr. Henderson was musical director for the *The Helen Morgan Story* (Playhouse 90, CBS, 1957); the *Victor Borge Show* (CBS, 1958, 1961); and the Phil Silvers specials, *Summer in New York* and *Polly and Me* (CBS, 1960); prepared dance arrangements and orchestrations for *Home for the Holidays* (NBC, Nov. 1961); arranged and orchestrated the final segment of *The Broadway of Lerner and Loewe* (NBC, Dec. 1961); created dance and vocal arrangements and orchestrations for the Ed Sullivan Show (CBS); the Garry Moore Show (CBS); the Perry Como Show (NBC); and the Bell Telephone Hour (NBC).

Night Clubs. Mr. Henderson has appeared with Lena Horne, Polly Bergen, Carol Haney, and Anita Ellis as pianist, orchestrator, and conductor; he has orchestrated and arranged music for the night club acts of Teresa Brewer, Nancy Wilson, Carol Lawrence, and Marge and Gower Champion. He has also arranged music for the Duke Ellington Orchestra.

Discography. Mr. Henderson has conducted, or orchestrated and arranged, *Clap Hands, The Greatest Sounds Around, Pop! Goes the Western, The Luther Henderson Sextet*, and popular recordings featuring Eileen Farrell, Polly Bergen, Anna Maria Alberghetti, Teresa Brewer, Carmen McRae, Ed Kenney, Tammy Grimes, and Sandra Church, as well as the original cast recordings of *The Flower Drum Song, Do Re Mi, Theatre Party, Bravo Giovanni*, and *Funny Girl*.

He has also served as arranger, orchestrator and piano soloist for several numbers on The Columbia Album of Richard Rodgers. .

Recreation. Music, chess, walking, crossword puzzles.

HENDERSON, ROBERT MORTON. Librarian, director, designer, educator. b. Jan. 14, 1926, Muskegon, Mich., to James Fournier and Marion (Rann) Henderson. Grad. Mich. State Univ., B.A.; Carnegie-Mellon Univ., M.F.A.; N.Y. Univ., Ph.D. Married Feb. 14, 1953, to Mary Malanga; three sons. Served US Navy 1943–46. Member of Theatre Library Assn. (pres., 1972–to date); Amer. Society for Stanislavsky Research (bd. of dir.); National Choral Council; former member of ATA; Speech Assn. of the Eastern States; Speech Assn. of America; National Society of Interior Designers. Address: (home) 859 Meadow Lane, Franklin Lakes, NJ 07417, tel. (201) 337-7033; (bus.) Library and Museum of the Performing Arts, Lincoln Center, New York, NY 10023, tel. (212) 799-2200.

Mr. Henderson is chief librarian of the General Library and Museum of the Performing Arts at Lincoln Center.

Theatre. Mr. Henderson made his debut as the Mad Hatter in *Alice in Wonderland* (1938); was a theatre manager (Michigan Th., Muskegon, 1941–43; and Skouras Ths., N.Y.C., 1953–54); was designer and technical director for a summer theatre in Richmond, Va. (1948); producer-director at the Manistee (Mich.) Summer Festival (Ramsdell Th., 1951–52); designer and director of the Adelphi College Th. (Garden City, N.Y., 1955–60); and director of the theatre at American Univ. (Washington, D.C., 1960–64) where he presented *Mr. Roberts, The Scarecrow, Cymbeline, Measure for Measure, Henry IV, Part 1, Caligula, The Guardsman*, and *You Never Can Tell*.

Films. He has directed documentary films dealing with the NY Shakespeare Festival (1958); and *The American University* (1963); and, for Lincoln Center, *LMPA* (1965).

Published Works. Mr. Henderson is the author of *D. W. Griffith, The Years at Biograph* (1970); and *D. W. Griffith, His Life and Works* (1972).

HENRITZE, BETTE. Actress. b. May 23, Betsy Layne, Ky. Grad. Univ. of Tennessee; American Acad. of Dramatic Arts.

Theatre. Billed as Bette Howe, she appeared as Mary Delany in *Jenny Kissed Me* (Hudson, N.Y.C., Dec. 23, 1948); subsequently, as Bette Henritze, played several roles in *Pictures in the Hallway* (Playhouse, Sept. 15, 1956); and Cloyne in *Purple Dust* (Cherry Lane Th., Dec. 27, 1956). With the Phoenix Theatre Co., she played a Peasant Woman in *The Power and the Glory* (Dec. 10, 1958); Nikodike in *Lysistrata* (Nov. 24, 1959); Pimple in *She Stoops To Conquer* (Nov. 1, 1960); Bessie Burgess in *The Plow and the Stars* (Dec. 6, 1960); and Mrs. Peyton in *The Octoroon* (Jan. 27, 1961); with the NY Shakespeare Festival (Wollman Mem. Skating Rink), played Margaret in *Much Ado About Nothing* (July 5, 1961), and the Duchess of York in *King Richard III* (Aug. 28, 1961); subsequently appeared as Mrs. Gensup in *Giant, Son of Giants* (Alvin, Jan. 6, 1962); played Mary Todd in *Abe Lincoln in Illinois* (Anderson, Jan. 21, 1963); Cross-Lane Nora in *The Lion in Love* (One Sheridan Square, Apr. 25, 1963); Mrs. Hasty Malone in *The Ballad of the Sad Cafe* (Martin Beck Th., Oct. 30, 1963); Young Lady, Louise, Landlady, and Maja in *Baal* (Martinique, May 6, 1965); and, with the NY Shakespeare Festival (Delacorte), was a replacement in the role of Emilia in *Othello* (opened July 8, 1964; moved to Martinique, Oct. 1964), and played Mariana in *All's Well That Ends Well* (June 15, 1966); and Mariana in *Measure for Measure* (July 12, 1966).

On a bill entitled *Three by Thornton Wilder* (Cherry Lane Th., Sept. 6, 1966) that included *Happy Journey to Trenton and Camden*, Miss Henritze played Ermengarde in *The Long Christmas Dinner*, and Mlle. Pointevin in *Queens of France;* Mrs.

Shortley in *The Displaced Person* (St. CLement's Church, Dec. 29, 1966); Mary Windrod in *The Rimers of Eldritch* (Cherry Lane Th., Feb. 20, 1967); Bea Schmidt in *Dr. Cook's Garden* (Belasco, Sept. 25, 1967); Mrs. Bacon in *Here's Where I Belong* (Billy Rose Th., Mar. 3, 1968); on a triple-bill entitled *Trainer, Dean, Liepolt & Co.* (Amer. Place Th., Dec. 12, 1968) that included *The Bird of Dawning Singeth All Night Long* and *The Young Master Dante,* played Edna in *The Acquisition;* and played Jessie Mason in *Crime of Passion* (Astor Place Th., Oct. 26, 1969). With the NY Shakespeare Festival (Delacorte), she played Margaret Jourdain in *Henry VI, Part I* (June 23, 1970), and the Duchess of York in *Henry VI, Part 2* (June 24, 1970), and in *King Richard III* (June 25, 1970); Anna Ames in *The Happiness Cage* (Estelle Newman Th. at the Public, Oct. 4, 1970); Clarice, Wendy, Fay, and the Woman in *Older People* (Anspacher Th. at the Public, May 14, 1972); Ursula in *Much Ado About Nothing* (Delacorte, Summer 1972; and Winter Garden, Nov. 11, 1972); Trixie in *Lotta, or The Best Thing Evolution's Ever Come Up With* (Anspacher/Public, Nov. 28, 1973); and Margaret in *King Richard III* (Mitzi E. Newhouse Th., Oct. 20, 1974). Miss Henritze also played the Mother in *Over Here!* (Sam S. Shubert Th., Mar. 6, 1974).

HENRY, GEORGE H. Educator, director. b. George Harry Henry, Sept. 20, 1903, Birdsboro, Pa., to Harry and Mary Henry. Father, steel co. exec. Grad. Birdsboro H.S., 1922; Temple Univ., A.B. 1926; Columbia Univ., M.A., Ed.D. 1950. Attended Pennsylvania Museum Sch., 1922–23; Von Sternberg Sch. of Music; Leschetizki School of Music. Married Sept. 2, 1953, to Mabel C. Wright, member, exec. board, ANTA. Member of AETA (mbr., exec. bd., 1961–66); DDA (pres.); DETVA (pres.); State National Council of Teachers of English (pres.); Kappa Delta Phi; Phi Kappa Phi; John Dewey Society; National Society for Study of Education. Address: (home) 99 W. Park Place, Newark, DE 19711, tel. 368-3728; (bus.) College of Education, Univ. of Delaware, Newark, DE 19711.

Since 1972, Mr. Henry has been emeritus professor at the Univ. of Delaware, where he previously had held positions as professor of education (1949–64) and professor of English and education (1964–72). He was director of dramatics at Dover (Del.) H.S. (1929–46); has written articles and lectured on dramatics in education; and holds positions in a number of education theatre associations.

Mr. Henry was co-editor of *Short Stories for Our Times* (1950); and is a former director of WHYY-TV (Newark, Del., 1961).

Recreation. Collecting paintings, playing piano.

HENRY, MARTHA. Actress. b. Feb. 17, 1938, Detroit, Mich. Grad. Carnegie Inst. of Technology.

Theatre. Miss Henry made her stage debut at age fourteen in the title role in *Peter Pan.* She has worked extensively with the Stratford (Ontario) Shakespeare Festival of Canada (1962–to date) appearing there as Miranda in *The Tempest,* and Lady Macbeth in *Macbeth* (Summer 1962); Cressida in *Troilus and Cressida,* Luciana in *The Comedy of Errors,* and Temandra in *Timon of Athens* (Summer 1963); Dorimene in *Le Bourgeois Gentilhomme,* Cordelia in *King Lear,* and Mistress Squeamish in *The Country Wife* (Summer 1964); Lady Percy in *Henry IV,* Parts 1 and 2, and Dunyasha in *The Cherry Orchard* (Summer 1965); Joan La Pucelle in *Henry VI,* and Viola in *Twelfth Night* (Summer 1966); Elmira in *Tartuffe,* Titania in *A Midsummer Night's Dream,* and Milady de Winter in *The Three Musketeers* (Summer 1968); again appeared with this company in *There's One in Every Marriage* (Third Stage, Aug. 6, 1971); and in *Pericles, Prince of Tyre* (July 24, 1973; production repeated June 4, 1974); and *King John* (July 23, 1974).

In addition, Miss Henry appeared in *The Crucible* and in *Look Back in Anger* (Arena Stage, Washington, D.C., Mar. 11, 1967); with the Repertory Co. of Lincoln Center, made her NYC debut as Pegeen Mike in *The Playboy of the Western World* (Vivian Beaumont Th., Jan. 7, 1971); appeared in *Scenes from American Life* (Forum, Mar. 25, 1971); played the title role in *Antigone* (Vivian Beaumont Th., May 13, 1971); Georgina in *Narrow Road to the Deep North* (Vivian Beaumont Th., Jan. 6, 1972); Olivia in *Twelfth Night* (Vivian Beaumont Th., Mar. 2, 1972); and Elizabeth Proctor in *The Crucible* (Vivian Beaumont Th., Apr. 27, 1972).

In London, she played Connie Bell in *Who Killed Santa Claus?* (Piccadilly, Apr. 2, 1970); and, with Manitoba Th. Ctr. (Winnipeg, Canada), played the title role in *Hedda Gabler* (Main Stage, Jan. 8, 1973). She has also appeared at The Pittsburgh (Pa.) Playhouse.

Television. Miss Henry appeared in *A Scent of Flowers* (NET); and played Milady de Winter in *The Three Musketeers* (NET).

Awards. She was the recipient of a *Theatre World* Award (1970–71) for her work with the Repertory Company of Lincoln Center.

HEPBURN, AUDREY. Actress. b. May 4, 1929, Brussels, Belgium, to Joseph Anthony and Baroness Ella (van Heemstra) Hepburn-Rustin. Educated Day Sch., Arnheim, Netherlands; and Conservatory of Music, Arnheim. Studied ballet with Sonia Gaskel, Amsterdam; and Marie Rambert, London. Married Sept. 25, 1954 to Melchor Gaston Ferrer, actor (marr. dis. 1968); one son; married Jan. 18, 1969 to Andrea Dotti, psychiatrist; one son. Member of AEA; SAG; AFTRA.

Theatre. Miss Hepburn's first stage appearance was behind locked doors, giving underground concerts to raise funds for the Dutch resistance during WW II. She made her professional debut in *High Button Shoes* (1948); her Bway debut in the title role in *Gigi* (Fulton Th., Nov. 24, 1951); subsequently appeared in the title role in *Ondine* (46 St. Th., Feb. 18, 1954).

Films. Miss Hepburn has appeared in *Laughter in Paradise* (Stratford, 1951); *The Lavender Hill Mob* (U, 1951); *Secret People* (Lippert, 1952); *Roman Holiday* (Par., 1953); *Young Wives' Tales* (Allied, 1954); *Monte Carlo Baby; Sabrina* (Par., 1954); *War and Peace* (Par., 1956); *Funny Face* (Par., 1957); *Love in the Afternoon* (Allied, 1957); *Green Mansions* (MGM, 1959); *The Nun's Story* (WB, 1959); *The Unforgiven* (UA, 1960); *Breakfast at Tiffany's* (Par., 1961); *The Children's Hour* (UA, 1962); *Charade* (U, 1963); *Paris When It Sizzles* (1963); *My Fair Lady* (WB, 1964); *Two for the Road* (20th-Fox, 1967); *Wait Until Dark* (WB-7 Arts, 1967); and *Robin and Marian* (Col., 1976).

Television. She appeared in *Mayerling* (Producer's Showcase, NBC, 1957).

Awards. For her performance in *Roman Holiday,* Miss Hepburn received an Academy (Oscar) Award (1953). In 1968, she received a special Antoinette Perry (Tony) Award.

HEPBURN, KATHARINE. Actress. b. Katharine Houghton Hepburn, Nov. 8, 1909, Hartford, Conn., to Dr. Thomas Norval and Katharine (Houghton) Hepburn. Father, urologist. Grad. Hartford Sch. for Girls; Bryn Mawr Coll., B.A. 1928. Studied acting with Frances Robinson-Duff; and dancing with Michael Mordkin. Married Dec. 12, 1928, to Ludlow Ogden Smith (marr. dis. May 8, 1934). Relative in theatre: brother, Richard Houghton Hepburn, playwright. Member of AEA; SAG; AFTRA. Address: P.O. Box 17-154, West Hartford, CT 06117.

Theatre. Miss Hepburn made her professional debut in the Edwin Knopf Stock Co. production of *The Czarina* (Baltimore, Md., 1928); and appeared in *The Big Pond* (Great Neck, N.Y.).

She made her N.Y.C. debut as a Hostess in *Night Hostess* (Martin Beck Th., Sept. 12, 1928); played Veronica Sims in *These Days* (Cort, Nov. 12, 1928); understudied Hope Williams as Linda Seton in *Holiday* (Plymouth, Nov. 26, 1928); and played Grazia in a touring production of *Death Takes a Holiday* (1929). She succeeded (April 1930) Hortense Alden as Katia in *A Month in the Country* (Guild Th., N.Y.C., Mar. 17, 1930); played Judy Bottle in *Art and Mrs. Bottle* (Maxine Elliott's Th., Nov. 18, 1930); appeared in stock productions at Ivoryton (Conn., Summer 1931); played Antiope in *The Warrior's Husband* (Morosco, N.Y.C., Mar. 11, 1932); Stella Surrege in *The Lake* (Martin Beck Th., Dec. 26, 1933); toured in the title role of *Jane Eyre* (1937); played Tracy Lord in *The Philadelphia Story* (Shubert, N.Y.C., Mar. 28, 1939); and Jamie Coe Rowan in *Without Love* (St. James, Nov. 10, 1942). She played Rosalind in *As You Like It* (Cort, Jan. 26, 1950), and repeated the role on tour.

She made her London debut as the Lady in *The Millionairess* (New, June 27, 1952), and repeated the role in N.Y.C. (Shubert, Oct. 17, 1952). In 1955, Miss Hepburn toured Australia with the Old Vic Co., appearing as Katharina in *The Taming of the Shrew,* Isabella in *Measure for Measure,* and Portia in *The Merchant of Venice.* At the American Shakespeare Festival (Stratford, Conn.), she repeated the role of Portia in *The Merchant of Venice* (July 10, 1957), played Beatrice in *Much Ado About Nothing* (Aug. 3, 1957), and Viola in *Twelfth Night* and Cleopatra in *Antony and Cleopatra* (June 3–Sept. 11, 1960).

She returned to the N.Y.C. stage in the title role of the musical *Coco* (Mark Hellinger Th., Dec. 18, 1969) and then toured with the show (1971).

Films. Miss Hepburn made her debut as Sydney Fairfield in *A Bill of Divorcement* (RKO, 1932); subsequently appeared in *Christopher Strong* (RKO, 1933); *Little Women* (RKO, 1933); Morning Glory (RKO, 1934); *Spitfire* (RKO, 1934); *The Little Minister* (RKO, 1934); *Alice Adams* (RKO, 1935); *Sylvia Scarlet* (RKO, 1935); *Break of Hearts* (RKO, 1935); *Mary of Scotland* (RKO, 1936); *A Women Rebels* (RKO, 1936); *Quality Street* (RKO, 1937); *Stage Door* (RKO, 1937); *Bringing Up Baby* (RKO, 1938); *Holiday* (Col., 1938); *The Philadelphia Story* (MGM, 1940); *Woman of the Year* (MGM, 1942); *Keeper of the Flame* (MGM, 1942); *Dragon Seed* (MGM, 1944); *Without Love* (MGM, 1945); *Undercurrent* (MGM, 1946); *Song of Love* (MGM, 1947); *The Sea of Grass* (MGM, 1947); *State of the Union* (MGM, 1948); *Adam's Rib* (MGM, 1949); *The African Queen* (UA, 1951); *Pat and Mike* (MGM, 1952); *Summertime* (UA, 1955); *The Iron Petticoat* (MGM, 1956); *The Rainmaker* (Par., 1956); *Desk Set* (20th-Fox, 1957); *Suddenly Last Summer* (Col., 1959); *Long Day's Journey Into Night* (Emb., 1962); *Guess Who's Coming to Dinner* (Col., 1967); *The Lion in Winter* (Emb., 1968); *The Madwoman of Chaillot* (WA, 1968); *The Trojan Women* (Cinerama, 1970); and *A Delicate Balance* (Amer. Film Th., 1972).

Television. Miss Hepburn played the role of the Mother in a television production of *The Glass Menagerie* (Apr. 1973) and was interviewed on the Dick Cavett Show (Sept. 1973).

Awards. For her performance in *Morning Glory,* Miss Hepburn received an Academy (Oscar) Award and the Hollywood Reporter Gold Medal (1933). She was nominated for an Academy (Oscar) Award for her performance in the title role in *Alice Adams;* won the NY Film Critics Award (1940) for *The Philadelphia Story,* for which she was also nominated for an Academy (Oscar) Award. She was also nominated for Academy (Oscar) Awards for her performances in *Woman of the Year, The African Queen, Summertime, The Rainmaker,* and *Suddenly Last Summer,* and she received Academy awards for her performances in *Guess Who's Coming to Dinner* and *The Lion in Winter.*

Miss Hepburn received the award for best actress from the Cannes Film Festival (1962) for her performance as Mrs. Tyrone in *Long Day's Journey Into Night.*

Recreation. Tennis, swimming, riding, golf.

HERBERT, DON. Producer. b. Manuel D. Herbert, Philadelphia, Pa., to Meyer and Frances (Pressman) Herbert. Grad. Central H.S., Philadelphia, 1946; Pennsylvania State Univ., B.A. 1950. Married June 25, 1961, to Roberta Mazer. Served USCG, 1951–54; Journalist 1st Class. Member of League of NY Theatres. Address: (home) 330 E. 33rd St., New York, NY 10016, tel. (212) OR

9-4391; (bus.) c/o Theatre Guild, 27 W. 53rd St., New York, NY 10019, tel. (212) CO 5-6170.

Theatre. Mr. Herbert produced *Oscar Wilde* (41 St. Th., Apr. 16, 1957). The Theatre Guild, in association with Mr. Herbert, produced the subscription tour of *Tunnel of Love* (opened Veteran's War Memorial Aud., Columbus, Ohio, Oct. 4, 1958; closed Coliseum, Evansville, Ind., Dec. 6, 1958); and the Playwrights' Co. and Mr. Herbert presented *The Flowering Cherry* (Lyceum, Oct. 21, 1959). He was an associate producer of *The Tumbler* (Helen Hayes Th., Feb. 24, 1960); *The Best Man* (Morosco, Mar. 31, 1960); *A Passage to India* (Ambassador, Jan. 31, 1962); *Jack Benny on Broadway* (Ziegfeld, Feb. 27, 1963); a summer tour of *The Millionairess* (opened July 8, 1963, closed Aug. 31, 1963); and *Conversations in The Dark* (opened Walnut St. Th., Philadelphia, Dec. 23, 1963, closed there Jan. 4, 1964).

Mr. Herbert was assoc. producer of *The Child Buyer* (Garrick Th., N.Y.C., Dec. 21, 1964); with Russ Kaiser, produced *Sing To Me Through Open Windows* and *The Day the Whores Came Out To Play Tennis*, a double-bill (Players, Mar. 15, 1965); was assoc. producer of *The Royal Hunt of the Sun* (ANTA, Oct. 26, 1965); and co-produced, with the Theatre Guild and Peter Bridge, *Help Stamp Out Marriage* (Booth, Sept. 29, 1966).

HERBERT, JOCELYN. Designer of theatre opera and film sets and costumes. b. Feb. 22, 1927, London, England, to Alan Patrick Herbert and Gwendolen Herbert. Father, writer. Grad. of St. Pauls Girls Sch. (England); attended Slade Design Course; London Th. Studio; Andre L'Hote Sch. (Paris, France); and Leon Underwood-Drawing Sch. Married Nov. 11, 1937, to Anthony Bauch Lousada (marr. dis. 1960); three daughters and one son. Member of ACTT; United Scenic Artists. Address: 45 Pottery Lane, London, W.11, England tel. 727-1104.

Theatre. Miss Herbert first designed for the Royal Court Theatre's (London) production of *The Chairs* (1957), followed by *Purgatory* (1957). She continued to work for the Royal Court Th. designing *The Sport of My Mad Mother, The Lesson, Endgame,* and *Krapp's Last Tape* (1958); *Roots* and *Serjeant Musgrave's Dance* (1959); the *Wesker Trilogy—Chicken Soup with Barley, Roots,* and *I'm Talking About Jerusalem*—and *Trials by Logue* (1960); *The Changling, The Kitchen* and *Luther* (1961); *A Midsummer Night's Dream, Chips with Everything,* and *Happy Days* (1962); *Skyvers* and *Exit the King* (1963). For the Phoenix Th. (England) she did *Baal* (1962).

She began designing for the English Stage Co. at the Queens Th. (London) with *The Seagull* (1964) and *St. Joan of the Stockyards* (1964). She continued to work for the company designing *Inadmissible Evidence* and *A Patriot for Me* (1965); *The Lion and the Jewel* (1966); *Life Price* (1969); *Three Months Gone* (1970); *The Changing Room* (1971); *Endgame, Not I, Savages,* and *Cromwell* (1973); and *Life Class* (1974).

Miss Herbert's designs for the National Th. (Old Vic) include *Othello* (1964); *Mother Courage* (1966); *A Woman Killed with Kindness* and *Tyger* (1971). For the Royal Shakespeare Co., she designed *Richard III* (1961), *Ghosts* and *The Round House* (1966); and *Hamlet* (1969). For the Alberry Th. (London) she designed *Pygmalion* (1974).

She designed for Sadlers Wells the opera *Orpheus and Eurydice* (1966).

Films. Miss Herbert served as color and costumer consultant for *Tom Jones* (Lopert, 1963); production designer for *Isadora* (U, 1969); for *If* (Par., 1969); for *Hamlet* (Col., 1969); *Ned Kelly* (UA, 1970); and *O Lucky Man* (WB, 1973).

HERGET, BOB. Choreographer, director, dancer. b. Robert Eugene Herget, Feb. 27, 1924, Crete, Nebr., to Joseph E. and Helen K. (Smejdir) Herget. Grad. Dorchester (Nebr.) H.S., 1940; attended Doane Coll., 1940–43; Randolph Macon Coll., 1943–44; RADA, London, Eng., 1945–46; New Sch. for Social Research, 1946–47. Studied dance in N.Y.C. with Helen Platova, 1947–50, Charles Weidman, 1946–50, Doris Humphrey, 1946–50, and Gertrude Shurr, 1950–to date. Married Dec. 11, 1945, to Marion Watkins (marr. dis. Apr. 1954). Served WW II, US Army, rank, Cpl. Member of AGMA; AGVA; ASCAP; AGMA; AFTRA; AEA; SSD&C (charter member). Address: 337 W. 70th St., New York, NY 10023, tel. (212) 787-2575.

Theatre. Mr. Herget made his Bway debut as a dancer in *Allegro* (Majestic, Oct. 10, 1947); subsequently danced as a replacement (June 1948) in *High Button Shoes* (Century, Oct. 9, 1947); in *Lend an Ear* (Natl., Dec. 16, 1948); and *Razzle-Dazzle* (Arena Th., Edison Hotel, N.Y.C., Feb. 19, 1951).

He staged the musical numbers for *Mr. Wonderful* (Bway Th., Mar. 22, 1956); in stock, choreographed *Tall Kentuckian* (Iroquois Amphitheatre, Louisville, Ky., Summer 1956); with Alex Romer, staged the dances and musical numbers for *Happy Hunting* (Majestic, N.Y.C., Dec. 6, 1956); directed *The Wizard of Oz, Girl Crazy,* and *Grist for the Mill* (Mill Playhouse, Hammonton, N.J., Summer 1957); choreographed *One for the Road* (Royal Alexandra, Toronto, Can., 1957); staged the 50th anniversary performance of *Schola Cantorum* (Carnegie Hall, N.Y.C., Apr. 27, 1960); choreographed for *Petticoat Fever* (Bucks County Playhouse, New Hope, Pa., Summer 1960); *Take Me Along* (Carousel Th., Framingham, Mass., Summer 1961); and *Guys and Dolls, Carousel,* and *Oklahoma!* (San Juan, P.R., Drama Festival 1961).

Mr. Herget staged the musical numbers for *A Family Affair* (Billy Rose Th., N.Y.C., Jan. 27, 1962); at the Corning (N.Y.) Summer Th., directed *The Music Man, Fiorello!, The Student Prince,* and *Oklahoma!* (Summer 1962); and for the NY State Arts Council, staged the musical numbers for *The Matchmaker* (Summer 1962); was choreographer for *The Boys from Syracuse* (Th. Four, N.Y.C., Apr. 15, 1963); and for the tour of *Top Banana* (Guber-Ford-Gross Circuit, Summer 1963); choreographed *The Boys from Syracuse* (Drury Lane, London, Nov. 13, 1963); choreographed *Straussiana* for the first Promenade concert, with six dancers and full orchestra (Philharmonic Hall, Lincoln Ctr., N.Y.C., 1963); restaged his choreography for the touring company of *The Boys from Syracuse* (opened Lyric, Allentown, Pa., Jan. 10, 1964); directed and staged a touring production of *The Sound of Music* (opened Kennebunkport Playhouse, Me., July 8, 1964); staged the musical numbers for *Something More* (Eugene O'Neill Th., N.Y.C., Nov. 11, 1964); *A Race of Hairy Men* (Henry Miller Th., Apr. 29, 1965); and *Show Me Where the Good Times Are* (Edison Th., Mar. 5, 1970).

In stock and dinner theatres, he has directed *Finnian's Rainbow, Sound of Music* (Municipal Th., Atlanta, Ga.); *Fiorello, Oklahoma, The Music Man, The Student Prince* (Corning Summer Th., Corning, N.Y.); *Funny Girl, Gentlemen Prefer Blondes* (Painter's Mill Music Fair, Baltimore, Md.); *Funny Girl, West Side Story, The Music Man, Butterflies are Free* (Chateau de Ville, Bridgeport, Conn.); and *Half-a-Sixpence* (Shady Grove Music Fair, Washington, D.C.).

He has directed industrial shows for Coca Cola, RCA, Admiral, Buick, Men's Fashion Industry, *Woman's Day* Magazine, Detroit Diesel Allison, Cessna, and Volks Wagen.

Television. Mr. Herget has danced on about 300 shows, and has choreographed for the Steve Allen Show (NBC); Fred Allen Show (NBC); Don Ameche Playhouse (ABC); America Sings (NBC); Red Buttons Show (NBC); Gene Kelly Special (NBC); Victor Borge Special (ABC); Bell Telephone Hour (NBC); Mort Sahl Special (NBC); Caesar's Hour (NBC); Perry Como Show (NBC); Yves Montand Show (ABC); TV Guide Awards Show (NBC); Fred Waring Special (NBC); Goodyear Revue (ABC); Arthur Godfrey Special (CBS); Your Hit Parade (NBC); Jewish Tercentenary (NBC); Patrice Munsel Show (ABC); Arthur Murray Dance Party (CBS); Kyle McDonnell Show (NBC); Nothing But the Best (NBC); Omnibus (CBS); Places Please (CBS); Ed Sullivan Show (CBS); Studio One (CBS); Playhouse of Stars (CBS); Paul Whiteman Show (ABC) and We the People (NBC); *25th Anniversary Tony Awards Show* (ABC); *I'm a Fan* (CBS); *Hard Travelin* (NET); *Rachel la Cubana* (PBS); and *The Dangerous Christmas of Little Red Riding Hood* (NBC).

Night Clubs. He has directed about 22 night Club acts among which were for Teresa Brewer, Dorothy Collins, Edie Adams, Russell Nype, Abbe Lane-Xavier Cugat, Joan Holloway, Jaye P. Morgan, Dorothy Sarnoff, Jane and Audrey Meadows, Enid Mosier and Al Fonsu Marshall, Doretta Morrow, Versailles Revue, Nancy Wilson, Patrice Munsel, Chris and Peter Allen, and Lesley Gore. Mr. Herget directed the opening show for Caesar's Palace, Las Vegas.

HERING, DORIS. Dance critic, editor, arts administrator. b. Doris M. Hering, New York City, to Harry and Anna (Schwenk) Hering. Father, painter. Grad. Jamaica H.S., Queens, N.Y.; Hunter Coll., B.A. (Phi Beta Kappa); Fordham Univ., H.A. Address: (home) 140 W. 79th St., New York, NY 10024; (bus.) National Assn. for Regional Ballet, 1564 Broadway, New York, NY 10036, tel. (212) 575-9540.

Miss Hering is executive director of the National Assn. for Regional Ballet. She is critic-at-large for *Dance Magazine,* and adjunct associate professor of Dance History, New York Univ. (SCE). She serves as consultant to state arts agencies; is a member of the dance panel of the National Endowment for the Arts; and lectures on dance at museums, universities, and arts conferences.

Published Works. She is the author of a book on American Dance for the US Dept. of State, and the official lecture, *Ballet in America,* used by US embassies. She edited the book, *25 Years of American Dance* (1950); is the author of *Wild Grass,* the memoirs of Rudolph Orthwine (1967); and has contributed articles to *Collier's Encyclopedia Annual, Encyclopedia Americana, Musical America Annual, Theatre Arts, World Scope Encyclopedia, Grolier's Encyclopedia Yearbook,* the New York *Times,* Funk and Wagnall's *Encyclopedia,* and *Show Magazine.*

Awards. Miss Hering was awarded honorary membership in Chi Tau Epsilon, a dance honor society.

Recreation. Reading, traveling, and beach combing.

HERLIE, EILEEN. Actress. b. Mar. 8, 1920, Glasgow, Scotland, to Patrick and Isobel (Cowden) O'Herlihy. Attended Shawland's Academy, Glasgow, 1927–39. Married Aug. 12, 1942 to Philip Barrett (marr. dis. 1947); married 1951 to Witold Kuncewics (marr. dis. 1960). Member of AEA; AFTRA; CAG.

Theatre. Miss Herlie made her stage debut with the Scottish National Players in *Sweet Aloes* (Lyric, Glasgow, 1938); appeared with the Rutherglen Repertory Company (1939–40); was understudy to Winifred Shotter in *The Divorce of Lady X* (1941); toured as Lady Isobel in a production of *East Lynne* (1942), produced by Philip Barrett, whom she married during the run; toured as Mrs. de Winter in *Rebecca,* making her London debut in the role (Ambassador's Th., Dec. 26, 1942), also playing it in the revival (Scala, Apr. 26, 1943); played Peg in *Peg o' My Heart* (Scala, May 26, 1943); and toured as Regina in *The Little Foxes* (1944).

Miss Herlie joined the Old Vic Repertory Co. (Liverpool, 1944) and played Mrs. Fanny Wilton in *John Gabriel Borkman;* Varvara in *Lisa;* Paula in *The Second Mrs. Tanqueray;* Lady Sneerwell in *The School for Scandal;* the title role in *Anna Christie;* Queen Gertrude in *Hamlet;* Dol Common in *The Alchemist;* Stella de Gex in *His Excellency the Governor;* and Zinaida in *He Who Gets Slapped.*

She played Andromache in *The Trojan Women* (Lyric, Hammersmith, London, Nov. 5, 1945); Mary in *The Time of Your Life* (Lyric, Hammersmith, Feb. 14, 1946); Alcestis in *The Thracian Horses* (Lyric, Hammersmith, May 8, 1946); the Queen in *The Eagle Has Two Heads* (Lyric, Hammersmith, Sept. 4, 1946; moved to Haymarket, Feb. 11, 1947); the title role in the Edinburgh Festival's production of *Medea* (Aug. 1948), which she repeated

(Globe, London, Sept. 29, 1948); Paula in *The Second Mrs. Tanqueray* (Haymarket, Aug. 29, 1950); Mrs. Marwood in *The Way of the World* (Lyric, Hammersmith, Feb. 19, 1953); Belvidera in *Venice Preserved* (Lyric, Hammersmith, May 15, 1953); Irene Carey in *A Sense of Guilt* (King's, Glasgow, Scot., Nov. 1953); and Mrs. Molloy in *The Matchmaker* (Haymarket, London, Nov. 4, 1954), the role in which she made her N.Y.C. debut (Royale, Dec. 5, 1955). Miss Herlie played Emilia Marty in *The Makropoulos Secret* (Phoenix, Dec. 3, 1957); subsequently appeared with the Canadian Shakespearean Festival as Paulina in *The Winter's Tale*, and Beatrice in *Much Ado About Nothing* (Stratford, Ontario, Canada, Summer 1958); played Ruth Gray in *Epitaph for George Dillon* (John Golden Th., N.Y.C., Nov. 4, 1958); and in its revival (Henry Miller's Th., Jan. 12, 1959); Lily in *Take Me Along* (Shubert, Oct. 22, 1959); Elizabeth Hawkes-Bullock in *All American* (Winter Garden, Mar. 19, 1962); Stella in *Photo Finish* (Brooks Atkinson Th., Feb. 12, 1963); and Queen Gertrude in Richard Burton's *Hamlet* (Lunt-Fontanne Th., Apr. 4, 1964).

She played Mrs. Rossiter (Lila) in *The Right Honorable Gentleman* (Huntington Hartford Th., Los Angeles, Mar. 13, 1967); Lady Fitzbuttress in *Halfway Up the Tree* (Brooks Atkinson Th., N.Y.C., Nov. 7, 1967); Miss Moffatt in *The Corn Is Green* (Ivanhoe Th., Chicago, Apr. 1969); Martha in *Who's Afraid of Virginia Woolf?* (Ivanhoe, Chicago, Oct. 1970); appeared in the premiere of Tennessee Williams' *Out Cry* (Ivanhoe, Chicago, July 8, 1971); as Countess Matilda Spina in *Emperor Henry IV* (Pirandello's *Enrico IV*), which toured before playing N.Y.C. (Ethel Barrymore Th., Mar. 28, 1973); and as Queen Mary in *Crown Matrimonial* (Helen Hayes Th., Oct. 2, 1973), recreating the role for a stock tour (Summer 1974).

Films. Miss Herlie first appeared in *Hungry Hill* (U, 1947); subsequently played Queen Gertrude in *Hamlet* (Rank/U, 1948); and appeared in *The Angel with the Trumpet* (British Lion, 1950); *Gilbert and Sullivan* (UA, 1953); *Isn't Life Wonderful* (Assoc. Brit. Pic. Corp., 1953); *For Better, For Worse* (Assoc. Brit., 1954; released in US as *Cocktails in the Kitchen*); *She Didn't Say No* (Assoc. Brit., 1958); *Freud* (U, 1962); as Queen Gertrude again in a filmed version of Richard Burton's *Hamlet* (Electronovision, 1964); and in *The Seagull* (WB, 1968).

Television. She has played Hesione Hushabye in *Heartbreak House* (WNET, Apr. 24, 1966); Rose Griggs in *The Autumn Garden* (Showcase—Drama, WNET, May 22, 1966); appeared in *Lemonade* (Hollywood Television Th., KCET, Oct. 21, 1971); and in *Portrait: The Woman I Love* (ABC, Dec. 17, 1972).

HERLIHY, JAMES LEO. Playwright, actor, writer. b. Feb. 27, 1927, Detroit, Mich., to William Francis and Grace (Oberer) Herlihy. Father, engineer. Attended John J. Pershing H.S., Detroit, 1942–44; Black Mountain Coll., 1947–48; Yale Univ. Sch. of Drama, 1956–57; studied at Pasadena (Calif.) Playhouse, 1948–50; Playwrights' unit of Actors' Studio, N.Y.C.; (member, 1962–to date). Served USN, 1945–46; rank, Yeoman, 3rd Class. Member of Dramatists Guild; ALA; AEA. Address: (home) 1438 N. Spaulding Ave., Hollywood, CA 90046; (bus.) c/o Arnold Weissberger, 120 E. 56th St., New York, NY 10022, tel. (212) PL 8-0800.

Theatre. Mr. Herlihy wrote *Moon in Capricorn* (Th. de Lys, Oct. 27, 1953); with William Noble, *Blue Denim* (Playhouse, Feb. 27, 1958); and *Crazy October*, which he also directed (opened Shubert, New Haven, Conn., Oct. 8, 1958; closed Geary, San Francisco, Calif., Jan. 3, 1959).

He played Jerry in *The Zoo Story* (Rockport Playhouse, Mass., July 1962; Th. Charles-de-Rochefort, Paris, Fr., June–July 1963; Boston Playhouse, Mass., Aug. 1963); and Aston in *The Caretaker* (Boston Playhouse, Sept. 1963).

Films. Motion pictures of Mr. Herlihy's works include *Blue Denim* (20th-Fox, 1959); *All Fall Down* (MGM, 1962); and *Midnight Cowboy* (UA, 1969). He appeared as Jack Haislip in *In the French Style* (Col., 1962).

Published Works. Mr. Herlihy is the author of *The Sleep of Baby Filbertson and Other Stories* (1959); *All Fall Down* (1960); *Midnight Cowboy* (1965); *A Story That Ends with a Scream* (1967); and *The Season of the Witch* (1971).

HERMAN, JERRY. Composer, lyricist. b. Gerald Herman, July 10, New York City, to Harry and Ruth (Sachs) Herman. Father, children's camp owner; mother, teacher. Grad. Henry Snyder H.S., Jersey City, N.J.; Parson's Sch. of Design, N.Y.C.; Univ. of Miami, A.B. 1961. Served US Army, 1954–55. Member of Dramatists Guild; AFM, Local 802; ASCAP; Zeta Beta Tau (historian); Omicron Delta Kappa (natl.); Iron Arrow (Univ. of Miami's highest honorary); Theta Alpha Phi (natl. drama honorary). Address: 50 W. 10th St., New York, NY 10011.

Theatre. Mr. Herman was composer and lyricist for *I Feel Wonderful* (Th. De Lys, N.Y.C., Oct. 18, 1954); *Nightcap* (Showplace, May 18, 1958); *Parade* (Players, Jan. 20, 1960), and produced on the West Coast (Hollywood Ctr., Calif., 1961; Purple Onion, San Francisco, Calif., 1963); was lyricist of the song, "Best Gold," included in the revue, *From A to Z* (Plymouth, N.Y.C., April 20, 1960); wrote music and lyrics for *Milk and Honey* (Martin Beck Th., Oct. 10, 1961); *Hello, Dolly!* (St. James, Jan. 16, 1964); *Mame* (Winter Garden, May 24, 1966); and *Dear World* (Mark Hellinger Th., Feb. 6, 1969).

Films. Mr. Herman's music and lyrics were used in the motion picture versions of *Hello, Dolly!* (20th-Fox, 1969) and *Mame* (WB, 1974).

Awards. Mr. Herman received the WPAT Gaslight Award for best song of 1961, "Shalom;" was nominated (1962) for an Antoinette Perry (Tony) Award for his score of *Milk and Honey*; and received an Antoinette Perry (Tony) Award and the NY Drama Critics' Circle Award for *Hello, Dolly!* (1964), and a gold record for the *Hello, Dolly!* album (1964); and was nominated (1966) for a Tony Award for his music and lyrics for *Mame*, won the *Variety* poll (1966) for *Mame's* lyrics and was nominated in the *Variety* poll for *Mame's* score. Mr. Herman also received a Grammy Award (1966) for his score for *Mame* and a gold record for the *Mame* album (1966). In 1970, the Univ. of Miami awarded him its order of merit.

HERR, MELVIN. Theatre administrator. b. Melvin Albert Herr, Jan. 19, 1916, Cleveland, Ohio, to Melvin and Marion R. (Reynolds) Herr. Father, accountant; mother, entertainer. Grad. Lansing (Mich.) Central H.S., 1935; attended Michigan State Univ., 1942–43. Married Dec. 21, 1940, to Pauline D. Sleeseman. Member of Lansing Sales and Advertising Club (board member; treas., 1958–59); Community Theatre Assn. of Mich. (life member); Mich. Fine Arts Commission; Lansing Civic Center (commissioner, 1960–64; head of commission, 1963–to date); Lansing Press Club. Address: (home) 115 E. Kilborn, Lansing, MI 48906, tel. (517) 484-3047; (bus.) 308 N. Washington Ave., Lansing, MI 48906, tel. (517) IV 4-9115.

Mr. Herr was one of the founders of the Community Theatre Association of Michigan, where he has served as treasurer (1957–58), president (1958–59), and as editor of the organization's newsletter (1960–61).

Mr. Herr has been active with the Lansing Civic Players for forty years as a performer and administrator, serving as executive director for twenty years and business manager since 1958.

Appointed by Gov. George Romney, Mr. Herr served for three years on the Mich. Council for the Arts.

Awards. He was made an honorary Commander in the Michigan Naval Militia by Gov. George Romney and served a term as Commander in Chief. For two years he served on Gov. Romney's Water Safety and Boating Commission and has received various awards for public service from the City of Lansing. He was appointed a Kentucky Colonel by former Gov. Louis B. Nunn.

Recreation. Sailing, fishing, golf, collecting and restoring antiques.

HERRIDGE, FRANCES. Drama and movie editor, movie and dance critic. b. Frances Elizabeth Herridge, Troy, N.Y., to Frederick T. and Elizabeth (Osgood) Herridge. Grad. Smith Coll., B.A. 1933, attended New York Univ., 1935–37; New Sch. for Social Research, 1937–44. Married 1946 to John Tull Baker, educator (marr. dis. 1956, dec. 1962); one son. Address: (home) 305 W. 28th St., New York, NY 10001; (bus.) c/o New York *Post*, 210 South St., New York, NY 10002, tel. (212) 349-5000.

Since 1954, Miss Herridge has been drama editor and critic for the NY *Post*, and since 1964, movie editor, second-string critic, and dance critic. She joined the newspaper in 1949 as assistant to Max Lerner, then became beauty and children's editor (1950).

HERSCHER, SYLVIA. Artists' and literary representative, general manager, producer. b. Sylvia Kossovsky, Dec. 10, 1913, New York City, to Louis and Anna (Spar) Kossovsky. Grad. Univ. of Arizona, B.A. 1934. Married Nov. 3, 1935, to Seymour Herscher, theatrical manager; one son, one daughter. Address: (home) 175 Riverside Dr., New York, NY 10024, tel. (212) TR 4-4671; (bus.) Edwin H. Morris & Co., 1370 Ave. of the Americas, New York, NY 10019, tel. (212) 582-5656.

Theatre. Mrs. Herscher's first assignment was as production assistant for *Make A Wish* (Winter Garden, Apr. 18, 1951), and subsequently for *Pal Joey* (Broadhurst, Jan. 3, 1952); was general manager for *Hazel Flagg* (Mark Hellinger Th., Feb. 11, 1953); associate producer, with Jule Styne, for *Will Success Spoil Rock Hunter?* (Belasco, Oct. 13, 1955); general manager for *Mr. Wonderful* (Bway Th., Mar. 22, 1956); *Visit to a Small Planet* (Booth, Feb. 7, 1957); *Say, Darling* (ANTA, Mar. 3, 1958); and *First Impressions* (Alvin, Mar. 19, 1959).

From 1960 to 1966, Mrs. Herscher was a writers' and artists' representative with the William Morris Agency and was involved in *Tchin-Tchin* (1962) and *Dylan* (1964), both by Sidney Michaels; *Ben Franklin in Paris* (1964) by Sidney Michaels and Mark Sandrich, Jr.; *Any Wednesday* (1964) by Muriel Resnik; *The Right Honorable Gentleman* (1965) by Michael Dyne; *Take Her, She's Mine* (1964) by Phoebe and Henry Ephron; *Blood Knot* (1964) by Athol Fugard; *Oh What a Lovely War!* (1964) by Ted Allan; *Golden Boy* (1964) by William Gibson, Lee Adams, and Charles Strouse; and *I Had a Ball* (1964) by Stan Freeman and Jack Lawrence.

Mrs. Herscher has been head of the Theatre Dept., Edwin H. Morris Co., music publishers, since 1966. She specializes in matching composers and lyricists with book writers, suggesting and developing properties for the musical stage and the subsequent publication of their scores by Edwin H. Morris Co. In this capacity she has been involved in *Mame* (1966), *Superman* (1966), *How Now, Dow Jones* (1967), *Applause* (1970), *Grease* (1972), *Fashion* (1972), *The Contrast* (1972), *Mack & Mabel* (1974), and *Shenandoah* (1975).

HESSELTINE, STARK. Talent and literary representative. b. Philip Stark Hesseltine, Jr., Aug. 20, 1929, Boston, Mass., to Philip Stark and Anne (Smith) Hesseltine. Father, private school headmaster. Attended Cincinnati (Ohio) Country Day Sch. 1944–46; grad. The Noble and Greenough Sch., Dedham, Mass., 1948; Harvard Univ., B.A. 1952. Member of The Hasty Pudding Club (chairman, Hasty Pudding Theatricals, 1951–52). Address: Hesseltine-Baker Assocs., Ltd., 119 W. 57th St., New York, NY 10019, tel. (212) 489-0966.

Since 1974, Mr. Hesseltine has been a partner of Hesseltine-Baker Associates, Ltd., a theatrical talent agency. Formerly, he was an artists' representative with the Music Corp. of America; head of the theatre department at Creative Management Associates; and a partner in the firm of Hesseltine, Bookman & Seff.

Theatre. Mr. Hesseltine's first assignments were as actor, ticket seller, usher, stage manager, and dresser for guest stars at the Brattle Th. (Cambridge, Mass., 1948–52); subsequently he was house manager at the Cape Playhouse (Dennis, Mass., Summer 1952); general office assistant for Aldrich and Meyers productions (Sept. 1952–May 1953); and producer of the 103rd edition of *The Hasty Pudding Show* (Harvard Univ., Cambridge, Mass., Winter 1953).

He participated in *Mrs. Patterson* (National, N.Y.C., Dec. 1, 1954); was casting director and assistant to the producers at the Phoenix Th. (1954–57), where he conceived, with Nicholas Benton, *Phoenix '55* (Apr. 23, 1955), and served as stage manager for *Six Characters in Search of an Author* (Dec. 11, 1955); a double bill, *Miss Julie* and *The Stronger* (Feb. 21, 1956); *The Littlest Revue* (May 22, 1956); *Saint Joan* (Sept. 11, 1956); and *The Good Woman of Setzuan* (Dec. 18, 1956).

HEWES, HENRY. Drama critic, playwright. b. Apr. 9, 1917, Boston, Mass., to Dr. Henry and Margaret (Warman) Hewes. Father, physician; mother, producer. Attended Dexter Sch., Brookline, Mass.; Noble and Greenough, Dedham, Mass.; Harvard Univ., 1935–39; Carnegie Inst. of Tech., 1940–41; grad. Columbia Univ., B.S. 1949. Married Aug. 21, 1945, to Jane Fowle; three sons. Served USAAF, 1941–45; rank, T/Sgt. Member of ANTA (exec. dir., Greater NY Chapter, 1953–58); Board of Standards and Planning for the Living Th. (exec. secy., 1956–66); Amer. Th. Planning Bd. (exec. secy., 1966–to date); NY Drama Critics Circle (1953–to date); Drama Desk (member, vice-pres., 1969–71; pres., 1971–73); Intl. Assn. of Drama Critics (1951–to date; pres., 1967–to date); Margo Jones Award Comm. (1963–to date; chmn., 1965–to date); Inst. of Outdoor Drama (advisory bd., 1963–to date).

Theatre. Since 1952, Mr. Hewes has been drama editor, and, since 1954, drama critic of the *Saturday Review*. He was previously on the staff of the NY *Times*, progressing from copy boy to newsclerk, news assistant, and staff writer (1949–51).

He adapted *La Belle Adventure* by Robert de Flers, G. A. Caillavet, and M. Etienne Rey, which was produced as *Accounting for Love* (Saville Th., London, England, Dec. 1, 1954; Pittsburgh Playhouse, Pa. Jan. 4, 1956); adapted and directed Tennessee Williams' *Three Players of a Summer Game* (White Barn Th., Conn., July 19, 1955); adapted and, with Siobhan McKenna in the title role, directed an experimental production of *Hamlet* (Th. de Lys, N.Y.C., Jan. 28, 1957), directed *Hughie* (Actors Studio, Nov. 1958), *Our Very Own Hole in the Ground* (La Mama ETC, Oct. 1973), directed and adapted Watergate version of Shakespeare's *Measure for Measure* (Great Lakes Shakespeare Festival, Lakewood, Ohio, Aug. 1, 1974).

Other Activities. Mr. Hewes lectured on theatre at Sarah Lawrence Coll., 1955–56; and on playwriting at Columbia Univ., 1956–57. He participated in the Salzburg Seminar in Amer. Studies (1970), and is associated with the New Sch. for Social Research (1972–to date). He is a recipient of the Amoco gold medallion of excellence for his contribution to the development of college drama (1972).

Published Works. In 1961, Mr. Hewes took over the editorship of the annual *Best Plays Series* begun in 1920 by Burns Mantle, and containing, in addition to supplementary material, the texts of the editor's choice for the ten best plays produced in N.Y.C. during each season, and within his three years as editor revised the book from its original Bway orientation into an annual covering theatres nationally and internationally. He served as editor of *Famous American Plays of the 1940's* (1960), and has contributed articles on the theatre to the *Encyclopaedia Britannica, Information Please Almanac, Grolier Encyclopaedia Yearbook,* and *Theatre Arts Monthly.*

Recreation. Stamp collecting, tennis, football.

HEWETT, CHRISTOPHER. Actor, director. b. Christopher George Hewett, Apr. 5, Worthing, England to Christopher Fitzsimon and Eleanor Joyce (Watts) Hewett. Father, company director; mother, actress, known as Rhoda Cleighton. Attended Beaumont Coll., Old Windsor, England. Studied voice with Tomasini, London. Served RAF WW II, 1938–42. Member of AEA; AFTRA.

Theatre. Mr. Hewett made his theatrical debut at age seven (Th. Royal, Dublin, Ireland); was member of the Oxford Repertory Co., 1940–42); made his London debut as Khadja in *The Merry Widow* (His Majesty's Th., London, Mar. 4, 1943); appeared as the Junior Counsel in *The Rest Is Silence* (Prince of Wales's Th., Apr. 20, 1944); the Hotel Manager in the Millionairess ("Q", May 29, 1944); succeeded (July 1944) Bonar Colleano as a principal in the revue, *Sweeter and Lower* (Ambassadors', Feb. 17, 1944); and appeared in the revue, *Sweetest and Lowest* (Ambassadors', May 9, 1946); and the revue *Slings and Arrows* (Comedy, Nov. 17, 1948). He succeeded (Sept. 1949) Liam Gaffney in the role of Norwood Beverley in *On Monday Next . .* (Comedy, June 1, 1949).

He directed *After the Show* (Watergate, Nov. 7, 1950); appeared in *See You Later* (Watergate, Oct. 3, 1951); toured as Fred Graham in *Kiss Me, Kate* (1952); and directed the revue, *See You Again* (Watergate, London, Feb. 21, 1952). He played Pinky Harris in *Wish You Were Here* (Casino, Oct. 10, 1953); was assistant director of the revue *Cockles and Champagne* (Saville, May 31, 1954).

In N.Y.C., he directed *Shoestring Revue* (President, Feb. 28, 1955); staged the sketches in the revue *Almost Crazy* (Longacre, June 20, 1955); and appeared as the Bystander and Zoltan Karpathy in *My Fair Lady* (Mark Hellinger Th., Mar. 15, 1956). He directed the sketches in the pre-Bway tour of *The Ziegfeld Follies* (opened Shubert, Boston, Apr. 16, 1956; closed Shubert, Philadelphia, May 12, 1956); played the Archangel Raphael in a Phoenix Th. production in *Tobias and the Angel* (Bway Cong. Church, N.Y.C., Oct. 20, 1957); Mr. Collins in *First Impressions* (Alvin, Mar. 19, 1959); staged *From A to Z* (Plymouth, Apr. 20, 1960); and appeared as Uncle Edward in *Roar Like a Dove* (Westport Country Playhouse, Conn., July 1960).

He appeared as Roberts in *The Unsinkable Molly Brown* (Winter Garden, N.Y.C., Nov. 3, 1960), Barnaby in *Kean* (Bway Th., Nov. 2, 1961), and Tom Orbell in *The Affair* (Henry Miller's Th., Sept. 20, 1962); and directed *The Boys from Syracuse* (Th. 4, N.Y.C., Apr. 15, 1963; Drury Lane, London, Nov. 7, 1963).

Mr. Hewett directed *Glad Tidings* (Coconut Grove Playhouse, Miami, June 30, 1964; and Cape Playhouse, Dennis, Mass., July 20, 1964). At the Storrowton Music Fair (West Springfield, Mass.), he directed *I Married an Angel* (July 13, 1964), *My Fair Lady* (July 20, 1964), and *Camelot* (Aug. 17, 1964); subsequently directed *Affairs of State* (Royal Poinciana Playhouse, Palm Beach, Fla., Jan. 25, 1965; and Paper Mill Playhouse, Millburn, N.J., Feb. 2, 1965); *Bell, Book and Candle* (Paper Mill, Mar. 2, 1965); *Gigi* (Royal Poinciana, Mar. 8, 1965; Paper Mill Playhouse, Mar. 16, 1965); *Rattle of a Simple Man* (Coconut Grove, May 18, 1965; and Huntington Hartford Th., Los Angeles, May 25, 1965); touring productions of *Annie Get Your Gun* and *The Marriage-Go-Round* (Summer 1965); directed and staged a touring production of *Lady in the Dark* (Summer 1965); directed *Quality Street* (world premiere Bucks County Playhouse, New Hope, Pa., Aug. 23, 1965); *The Warm Peninsula* (Royal Poinciana Playhouse, Feb. 28, 1966); *Where's Charley?* (NY City Ctr., May 25, 1966); played Sir in *The Roar of the Greasepaint—The Smell of the Crowd* (Coconut Grove Playhouse, June 28, 1966; Paper Mill Playhouse, Aug. 1, 1966); directed touring productions of *Beyond the Fringe* and *Camelot* (Summer 1966); directed and was one of the producers of *By Jupiter* (Th. 4, N.Y.C., Jan. 19, 1967); played Max Detweiler in *The Sound of Music* (NY City Ctr., Apr. 26, 1967); Sir Edward Ramsey in *The King and I* (NY City Ctr., May 20, 1967); Father St. Albans, Prepositor-General of Jesuits in *Hadrian VII* (Helen Hayes Th., Jan. 8, 1969); Kolinsky in *Show Me Where the Good Times Are* (Edison Th., Mar. 5, 1970); Max Detweiler in *The Sound of Music* (Jones Beach Th., L.I., N.Y., July 1, 1970; and July 8, 1971); directed *No Sex Please, We're British* (Ritz Th., N.Y.C., Feb. 10, 1973); played Lord Porteous in *The Circle* (Roundabout Th., Mar. 26, 1974); and Sir Anthony Absolute in *The Rivals* (Roundabout Th., Dec. 3, 1974).

Films. Since his debut in *Love Story,* he has appeared as Mike in *Pool of London* (U, 1951); Inspector Talbot in *The Lavender Hill Mob* (U, 1951); and in *Man with a Million* (UA, 1954).

Television and Radio. Mr. Hewett appeared on radio in England in the revues *Hold Everything* (1950); and as Welbeck Doom on the weekly series Home at Eight (1951–52).

On television he has appeared on *The Merry Widow* (CBS, 1955); the Kraft Television Th. (NBC, 1955); Robert Montgomery Presents (NBC, 1956); and the Ed Sullivan Show (CBS, 1959).

Night Clubs. He has appeared in such London cabarets as Ciro's, 96 Piccadilly, The Orchid Room, The Carousel, Dorchester, the Players' Club Th., the Colony Restaurant, and the Café de Paris.

Recreation. Collecting Staffordshire china, swimming.

HEWITT, ALAN. Actor, director. b. Alan Everett Hewitt, Jan. 21, 1915, New York City to William M. and Hortense (Baum) Hewitt. Father, advertiser-publisher; mother, manufacturer. Grad. Townsend Harris Hall H.S., N.Y.C., 1930; Dartmouth Coll., B.A. 1934. Studied acting with Benno Schneider, 1937; at Amer. Theatre Wing, N.Y.C., 1946–51; voice with Clytie Hine Mundy, 1947–51. Served US Army, 1943–46, rank, Staff Sgt. Relative in theatre: cousin, Don Hewitt, television producer. Member of AFTRA; SAG; AEA (council, 1940–51). Address: 400 E. 52nd St., New York, NY 10022, tel. (212) PL 5-7375.

Theatre. Mr. Hewitt first appeared in a school play, *The Death of Bad Grammar* (1925); made his professional debut as Mose in the South Shore Players' production of *The Pursuit of Happiness* (Cohasset, Mass., July 1934); with whom he performed as Douglas Helder in *Interference,* Tom Crosby in *Song and Dance Man,* Philip in *You Never Can Tell,* Al Diamond in *Minick,* and Lord Clinton in *Mary Tudor* (Summer 1934); toured as the Delivery Boy in *Bring on the Girls* (Oct. 1934) and as the Third Huntsman and Philip in *The Taming of the Shrew* (Apr. 1935); played Dorilant in *The Country Wife,* Sgt. Duval in *Ode to Liberty,* and the Interned Officer in *The Coward* (Westport Country Playhouse, Conn., July 1935).

He made his Bway debut as Lucentio in *The Taming of the Shrew* (Guild, Sept. 30, 1935); appeared as the First Officer in *Idiot's Delight* (Shubert, Mar. 24, 1936); played Jeremy in *Love for Love,* Pat in *Dr. Knock,* Juggins in *Fanny's First Play,* and the Music Master in *The Would-Be Gentleman;* (Westport Country Playhouse, Conn., Summer 1936); appeared as Clayton Herrick in *The Golden Journey* (Booth, N.Y.C., Sept. 15, 1936); Fritzi in *The Masque of Kings* (Shubert, Feb. 8, 1937); at the Mt. Kisco (N.Y.) Playhouse and at the Westport (Conn.) Country Playhouse as Sir James Fenton in *Petticoat Feber,* Mr. Dermott in *At Mrs. Beam's,* Frederick Ogden in *The Virginian,* and Boze Hertzlinger in *The Petrified Forest* (Summer 1937).

He played the Warrior in *Amphitryon 38* (Shubert, N.Y.C., Nov. 1, 1937); Yacov in *The Seagull* (Shubert, Mar. 28, 1938); appeared at the Ann Arbor (Mich.) Dramatic Season as Martin Holme in *The Ghost of Yankee Doodle,* Wolf Beifeld in *Liliom,* Hon. Alan Howard in *French without Tears,* and Clendon Wyatt in *Rain from Heaven* (Lydia Mendelssohn Th., May–June, 1938); played Bill Chapman in *Away from It All* (Rockridge, Carmel, N.Y., June 1938); appeared in stock productions as Wolf Beifeld in *Liliom,* David Kingsley in *Stage Door,* and the Hon. Alan Howard in *French Without Tears* (Suffern, N.Y., July 1938); in Newport, R.I., as Toby Cartwright in *Ways and Means*, Alec Harvey in *Still Life*, Homer Sampson in *Grandpa*, the Hon. Alan Howard in *French Without Tears*, and Corbier in *Cognac* (Casino, Aug. 1938); in Suffern, N.Y., in *One for the Money* (Sept. 1938); and in Maplewood (N.J.) and Albany (N.Y.) as Mago in *The Road to Rome* (Sept. 1938).

Mr. Hewitt played Alex Hewitt in *The American Way* (Center, N.Y.C., Jan. 21, 1939); appeared as Philip Graves in *Here Today* (Berkshire Playhouse, Stockbridge, Mass., July 1939; Westport Country Playhouse, Conn., July 1939); toured as Lucentio in *The Taming of the Shrew* (1939–40); repeated the role (Alvin, N.Y.C., Feb. 5, 1940); and played David F. Windmore in *Love's Old Sweet Song* (Plymouth, May 2, 1940).

He toured (Summer 1940) as Warwick Wilson in *Biography*; Brooks in *The Bat*; Alastair Fitzfassenden in *The Millionairess*; and as Philip Graves in *Here Today*, and again in Boston, Mass. (Copley, Oct. 28, 1940; Selwyn, Chicago, Ill., Dec. 9, 1940). He appeared as Lawrence Vail in *Once in a Lifetime* (Suffern, N.Y., Summer 1941); as Wilfred Marks in *The Walrus and the Carpenter* (Cort, N.Y.C., Nov. 8, 1941); Capt. Loft in *The Moon Is Down* (Martin Beck Th., Apr. 7, 1942); toured as Rudd Kendall in *Old Acquaintance* (July 1942).

Mr. Hewitt appeared in stock (Aug. 1947) as Tony Kenyon in *Skylark*, and as Capt. Jensen in *The Skull Beneath*; played Morgan Kilpatrick in *The Gentleman from Athens* (Mansfield, N.Y.C., Dec. 9, 1947); Howard Wagner in *Death of a Salesman* (Morosco, Feb. 10, 1949); and Pemberton Maxwell in *Call Me Madam* (Imperial, Oct. 12, 1950); Valentine in *You Never Can Tell*, and Lord Allan Frobisher in *Jane* (Stockbridge, Mass., July 1953); Lord Chamberlain and the First Judge in *Ondine* (46 St. Th., N.Y.C., Feb. 18, 1954); Cardinal Richelieu in *The Three Musketeers* (St. Louis Municipal Opera, Mo., July 1954); succeeded (Oct. 1956) Tony Randall as E. K. Hornbeck in *Inherit the Wind* (National, N.Y.C., Apr. 21, 1955).

He staged *Bus Stop* (Stockbridge, Mass., July 1957); and repeated his role in *Inherit the Wind* (Grist Mill Playhouse, Andover, N.J., July 1957), which he also directed; appeared as Angelo in *Measure for Measure* (Library of Congress, Washington, D.C., May 1958); and directed *Who Was That Lady I Saw You With?* (Bucks County Playhouse, New Hope, Pa., June 1959).

Films. Since his debut as Matt Hemsley in *Career* (Par., 1959), he has appeared in *A Private's Affair* (20th-Fox, 1959); *The Absent-Minded Professor* (Buena Vista, 1961); *Bachelor in Paradise* (MGM, 1961); *Follow That Dream* (UA, 1962); as Dr. Gruber in *That Touch of Mink* (U, 1962); in *Days of Wine and Roses* (WB, 1962); *Son of Flubber* (Buena Vista, 1963); *The Misadventures of Merlin Jones* (Buena Vista, 1964); and *How To Murder Your Wife* (UA, 1964); *The Monkey's Uncle* (Buena Vista, 1965); *The Horse in the Grey Flannel Suit* (Buena Vista, 1968); *The Brotherhood* (Par., 1969); *Sweet Charity* (U, 1969); *The Computer Wore Tennis Shoes* (Buena Vista, 1970); *R.P.M.** (Col., 1970); *The Barefoot Executive* (Buena Vista, 1971); and *Now You See Him, Now You Don't* (Buena Vista, 1972).

Television and Radio. His radio appearances include the Th. Guild on the Air (NBC); Cavalacade (NBC); The Greatest Story Ever Told (ABC); Famous Jury Trials (ABC); and Radio Reader's Digest (CBS). He has appeared on such television programs as Alfred Hitchcock Presents (CBS); The Defenders (CBS); Dr. Kildare (NBC); Perry Mason (CBS); US Steel Hour (CBS); and Omnibus (CBS); Bewitched (ABC); Gomer Pyle (CBS); I Dream of Jeannie (Ind.); Lost in Space (Ind.); Love, American Style (ABC); Daktari the Bob Newhart Show (CBS); Slattery's People; Hec Ramsay; Wild, Wild West; Felony Squad; ABC Movie of the Week; NBC World Premiere. He played Lt. Brennan on My Favorite Martian (1964–66); was on the ABC special *Pueblo* (1973); and has done numerous television and radio commercials and "voice-overs" for a variety of products.

Other Activities. Mr. Hewitt has planned and supervised employment surveys for AEA and written annual reports for theatrical seasons since 1961; in 1970, his 1961–68 report was reprinted in *Performing Arts Review* (vol. 1, no. 4).

Recreation. Swimming, timetables and road maps, transportation in general, good music, theatre-going.

HEWITT, BARNARD WOLCOTT.

Educator, writer, director. b. Dec. 23, 1906, North Tonawanda, N.Y., to Charles E. and Ruth (Barnard) Hewitt. Father, newspaper publisher. Grad. North Tonawanda H.S., 1924; Cornell Univ., B.A. (Phi Beta Kappa) 1928, M.A. 1929, Ph.D. 1934. Married Aug. 2, 1932, to Rose S. Lancaster, teacher; one daughter. Member of ATA (pres. 1953); ANTA (bd. of dir., 1953–56); ASTR; British Society for Theatre Research; Theatre Library Assn.; Phi Kappa Phi. Address: (home) 2205 Brett Dr., Champaign, IL 60004, tel. (217) 356-5262; (bus.) 4-122 Krannert Center for the Performing Arts, University of Illinois, Urbana, IL 61801, tel. (217) 333-2371.

Before his retirement (Aug. 1975), Mr. Hewitt was professor of theatre (1948–75), and chairman (1967–75) of the Dept. of Theatre at the Univ. of Illinois, where he has also served as professor of speech (1948–67); and associate director (1948–67) of the University Theatre. He was instructor (1936–38), and assistant professor (1938–48) of English and speech at Brooklyn Coll.; instructor and assistant professor of English and director of the Montana Masquers at Montana State Univ. (1932–36); and instructor of English and director of the theatre at the Univ. of Colorado (1930–31).

Other Activities. He was founding editor of the *Educational Theatre Journal* (1949–51).

Published Works. Mr. Hewitt wrote *The Art and Craft of Play Production* (1940); *Play Production: Theory and Practice* (1952); *Theatre U.S.A., 1668 to 1957* (1959); was general editor for the series of theatre books published by the Univ. of Miami Press for AETA (1958–61); and edited *The Renaissance Stage* (1958); Adolphe Appia's *The Work of Living Art, A Theory of the Theatre*, trans. by H. K. Albright; *Man Is the Measure of All Things*, trans. by Mr. Hewitt (1960); and Adolphe Appia's *Music and the Art of the Theatre* (1962). He has also written articles for the *Tulane Drama Review, Theatre Annual, Educational Theatre Journal, Quarterly Journal of Speech*, and *Theatre Research*. He is the author of *History of the Theatre from 1800 to the Present* (1970).

Awards. Mr. Hewitt was awarded a Guggenheim Fellowship for research (1962–63) in N.Y.C. and London, on the life of Stephen Price, early American theatre manager; the AETA Senior Award for service to The Educational Th. (1962); was named an ATA Charter Fellow (1965); and received the Theta Alpha Phi Medallion of Honor (1973).

HICKEY, WILLIAM.

Actor, director, teacher. b. William Edward Hickey, 1928 (?), Brooklyn, N.Y., to Edward and Nora Hickey. Attended Richmond Hills H.S., N.Y.C. Studied acting with Herbert Berghof and Uta Hagen, N.Y.C., 1950–to date. Member of AEA; SAG; AFTRA. c/o HB Studio, 120 Bank St., New York, NY 10014, tel. (212) OR 5-2370.

Theatre. As a child performer, Mr. Hickey appeared on the variety stage. He played Francisco and performed the Player Prologue in a production of *Hamlet* (NY Rep. Group, Cherry Lane Th., N.Y.C., Dec. 3, 1948); made his Bway debut in three walk-on roles in *Saint Joan* (Cort, Oct. 4, 1951); played the Concierge, and was asst. stage manager for *Tovarich* (NY City Ctr., May 14, 1952), in which he then toured; and toured in *The Play's the Thing* (Summer 1952). He played Jimmy in the pre-Bway tryout of *Mardi Gras* (opened Locust, Philadelphia, Jan. 13, 1954; closed there Jan. 23, 1954); directed a tour of *The Lady's Not for Burning* (1954); played Cash in the pre-Bway tryout of *As I Lay Dying* (1955); the title role in *Amedee* (Tempo Playhouse, N.Y.C., Oct. 31, 1955); Pierrot in *Don Juan, or The Feast with the Statue* (Downtown Th., Jan. 3, 1956); and Chandra in *The Lesser Comores* (Bucks County Playhouse, New Hope, Pa., June 18, 1956).

He played Fats Goldsmith in *Miss Lonelyhearts* (Music Box, N.Y.C., Oct. 3, 1957); Albert in *The Body Beautiful* (Bway, Jan. 23, 1958); for the American Shakespeare Festival (Stratford, Conn.), appeared as the Second Gravedigger in *Hamlet* (June 19, 1958), Flute in *A Midsummer Night's Dream* (June 20, 1958), and the Young Shepherd in *The Winter's Tale* (July 20, 1958); played Bernie Leeds in *Make a Million* (Playhouse, N.Y.C., Oct. 23, 1958); Ozzie on *On the Town* (revived Carnegie Hall Playhouse, Jan. 15, 1959); Scaltivo in *The Queen and the Rebels* (Bucks County Playhouse, New Hope, Pa., Aug. 24, 1959); and Etienne Perisson in *Moonbirds* (Cort, N.Y.C., Oct. 9, 1959).

At the American Shakespeare Festival (Stratford, Conn.), Mr. Hickey played Fabian in *Twelfth Night* (June 8, 1960), Trinculo in *The Tempest* (June 19, 1960), toured for the company as Flute in *A Midsummer Night's Dream* (1960–61) and played Sir Andrew Aguecheek in the Festival's Student Matinee production of *Twelfth Night* (Spring 1961). He directed a stock production of *All You Need Is One Good Break* (Phoenicia Playhouse, N.Y., Summer 1961); appeared as Boats in the musical *The Undercover Lover* (Adelphi Coll. Summer Th. Workshop, Garden City, L.I., N.Y., Aug. 10, 1961); was associate director of *Do You Know the Milky Way?* (Billy Rose Th., N.Y.C., Oct. 16, 1961); played the Neighbor and directed *Not Enough Rope*, part of a triple-bill entitled 3 × 3 (Maidman, Mar. 1, 1962); played Bagdad in *Step on a Crack* (Ethel Barrymore Th., Oct. 17, 1962); and directed *Name of a Soup* (H B Studio, June 8, 1963).

Mr. Hickey directed *Diary of a Madman* (Gramercy Arts, Apr. 16, 1964), and alternated (with Zack Matalon) in the show's only role; was "consultant" to *On the Necessity of Being Polygamous* (Gramercy Arts, Dec. 8, 1964); appeared in the revue *The Decline and Fall of the Entire World as Seen Through the Eyes of Cole Porter Revisited* (Square East, Mar. 3, 1965); played Arnold in the pre-Bway tryout of *This Winter's Hobby* (opened Shubert, New Haven, Mar. 21, 1966; closed Walnut St. Th., Philadelphia, Apr. 9, 1966); Adam, a chemist, in *The Devils* (Mark Taper Forum, Los Angeles, Apr. 14, 1967); at the Amer. Shakespeare Festival (Stratford, Conn.), played the Centurion in *Androcles and the Lion* (June 25, 1968), Costard in *Love's Labour's Lost* (June 26, 1968), the Second Watch in *Much Ado About Nothing* (June 18, 1969), and the Second Gravedigger in *Hamlet* (June 26, 1969); and succeeded (Nov. 1, 1969) Dick Van patten, who succeeded James Coco, as Marion Cheever in *Next* on a double-bill with *Adaptation* (Greenwich Mews Th., N.Y.C., Feb. 10, 1969).

He played Looseleaf Harper in *Happy Birthday, Wanda June* (Th. de Lys, Oct. 7, 1970); Steve in *Small Craft Warnings* (Truck and Warehouse Th., Apr. 2, 1972); Seth Beckwith in *Mourning Becomes Electra* (Circle in the Square/Joseph E. Levine Th., Nov. 15, 1972); "Grandmother Kroner" in *Siamese Connections* (NY Shakespeare Fest., Public Th., Jan. 25, 1973); Pandarus and Calchas in *Troilus and Cressida* (NY Shakespeare Fest., Mitzi E. Newhouse Th., Dec. 2, 1973); and Johnny MacDonald (the Street Man) in *Thieves* (Broadhurst, Apr. 7, 1974).

Films. Mr. Hickey played Apples in *A Hatful of Rain* (20th-Fox, 1957); appeared in *Operation Madball* (Col., 1957); *Invitation to a Gunfighter* (UA, 1964); *The Boston Strangler* (20th-Fox, 1968); *The Producers* (Embassy, 1968); *Little Big Man* (Natl. Gen., 1970); as Looseleaf Harper in *Happy Birthday, Wanda June* (Col., 1971); and in *The Telephone Book* (Rosebud, 1971).

Television. Mr. Hickey has played the Artful Dodger in *Oliver Twist* (Dupont Show of the Month, CBS. Dec. 4, 1959); on Studio One (CBS); Camera Three (CBS); Philco Playhouse (NBC); The Reporter (CBS); The Phil Silvers Show (CBS); Mr. Broadway (CBS); THe Hawk (ABC); as the Menagerie Keeper in the Richard Rodgers musical, *Androcles and the Lion* (NBC, Nov. 15, 1967); and others.

HIGGINS, MICHAEL. Actor, director. b. Michael Patrick Higgins, Jan. 20, 1922, Brooklyn, N.Y., to Michael Peter and Mary Katherine (McGowan) Higgins. Studied for the theatre under the professional training program at the Amer. Th. Wing, 1946–52; singing with Charles Zimnoch, N.Y.C., 1957–59. Married Mar. 2, 1946, to Elizabeth Lee Goodwin; two sons, one daughter. Served US Army, Infantry, 1942–45, received the Purple Heart and Bronze Star Medal; rank, 1st Lt. Member of AEA; AFTRA; SAG. Address: (home) 3 Stuyvesant Oval, New York, NY tel. (212) OR 7-4590; (bus.) c/o Milton Goldman, International Famous Agency, 1301 Ave. of the Americas, New York, NY 10019, tel. (212) 556-5600.

Pre-Theatre. Shipyard carpenter while engaged in first theatre work.

Theatre. Mr. Higgins made his stage debut as Lucentio in *The Taming of the Shrew* (1936) with the Shakespeare Fellowship of America, a repertory company that played schools and parks in the N.Y.C. area, also appearing in *Twelfth Night, Romeo and Juliet, Julius Caesar,* and *A Midsummer Night's Dream* (1936–40); and played the Boy in *Because Their Hearts Were Pure* or *The Secret of the Mine* (Cragsmoor Playhouse, N.Y., Summer 1941).

He made his Bway debut as the Third Guard in *Antigone* (Cort, Feb. 18, 1946); was understudy to Marlon Brando as Eugene Marchbanks in *Candida* (Cort, Apr. 3, 1946); appeared as Tommy Tucker in an ELT production of *The First Year* (Greenwich Mews Th., Apr. 1947); in stock at the Chapel Th. (Great Neck, L.I., N.Y.), as Michael Barnes in *The Male Animal* (June 16, 1947), and as Geoffrey Cole in *The Vinegar Tree* (June 30, 1947); the Second Rebel Soldier in *Our Lan'* (Royale, N.Y.C., Sept. 27, 1947); toured veteran and army hospitals with the American Th. Wing as Burleigh in *The Milky Way* and Bud in *Personal Appearance* (1947); played Bobby in an ELT production of *Fanny's First Play* (Lenox Hill, Feb. 27, 1948); toured veterans and Army hospitals as Jeff Douglas in an American Th. Wing production of *Brigadoon* (Oct. 11, 1948–May 14, 1949); in the same role, toured Europe and Africa for US Army of Occupation (June–July, 1949); appeared as Daniele in *Sky Is Red* (45 Univ. Pl., N.Y.C., Oct. 1949); for ELT's Irish Drama Festival, as Charlie in *Crabbed Youth and Age* and Patrick in *Cathleen Ni Houlihan* (Lenox Hill, Apr. 21, 1950); in stock, as Christie in *The Devil's Disciple* (Westport Country Playhouse, Conn.; Cape Playhouse, Mass., Falmouth Playhouse, Mass., July 3–22, 1950); and Benvolio in *Romeo and Juliet* (Broadhurst, N.Y.C., Mar. 10, 1951).

Mr. Higgins played the title role in *Billy the Kid* (Carnegie Recital Hall, Aug. 20, 1951); Prince Hall in ELT's Scrapbook production of *Henry IV, Part 1* (Lenox Hill, Jan. 1952); toured colleges in a two-character comedy and drama program for ELT (June–July, 1952); played Touchstone in *As You Like It* (Lenox Hill, Dec. 3, 1952); toured women's clubs in the East and Midwest in a two-character dramatic concert program, *Theatre As You Like It* (Jan–Feb., 1953); and portrayed the title role in the ELT production of *Dr. Faustus* (Lenox Hill, N.Y.C., Apr. 15, 1953); appeared with Group 20 (Theatre-on-the-Green, Wellesley, Mass.), as Hortensio in *The Taming of the Shrew* (June 20, 1953), John, the Witch Boy, in *Dark of the Moon* (July 7, 1953), the Captain in *Androcles and the Lion* (July 14, 1953), Silvius in *As You Like It* (July 28, 1953), Captain Absolute in *The Rivals* (Aug. 4, 1953), and Dick Dudgeon in *The Devil's Disciple* (Aug. 11, 1953).

He played Bertrand de Poulengey and the Inquisitor in *Saint Joan* (Univ. of Puerto Rico, Rio Piedras, Jan. 25, 1954), Hortensio in *The Taming of the Shrew* (Feb. 1, 1954), and the Captain in *Androcles and the Lion* (Feb. 5, 1954); at the Theatre-on-the-Green (Wellesley, Mass.) Flute in *A Midsummer Night's Dream* (June 21, 1954), John Proctor in *The Crucible* (June 30, 1954), Sir Charles Marlow in *She Stoops To Conquer* (July 14, 1954), and Bertrand de Poulengey and Peter Cauchon in *Saint Joan* (July 21, 1954).

Mr. Higgins played John Proctor in *The Crucible* (Arena Stage, Washington, D.C., Sept. 8, 1954); Starbuck in *Moby Dick* (Kaufmann Aud., N.Y.C., Feb. 9, 1955); Duke of Brachiano in *The White Devil* (Phoenix Th., Mar. 14, 1955); with Group 20, at the Theatre-on-the-Green (Wellesley, Mass.), Humphrey in *The Lady's Not for Burning* (June 27, 1955), Eben in *Desire Under the Elms* (July 6, 1955), the title role in *Henry IV, Part 1* (July 20, 1955), *Henry IV, Part 2* (July 23, 1955); Ben in *Love for Love* (Aug. 3, 1955), and Orestes in Euripides' *Electra* (Aug. 30, 1955).

He played the Fifth Son in *The Carefree Tree* (Phoenix, N.Y.C., Oct. 11, 1955); Brother Ladvenu in *The Lark* (Longacre, Nov. 17, 1955); with Group 20, appeared as Ninian Edwards in *Abe Lincoln in Illinois* (Boston Arts Festival, Mass., June 16, 1956); and as Eddie Carbone in *A View from the Bridge* (Theatre-on-the-Green, Wellesley, Mass., July 3, 1956); played the title role in *Hamlet* (Antioch Arena Th., Yellow Springs, Ohio; Toledo Amphitheatre, Ohio, Aug. 8–Sept. 9, 1956); Eddie Carbone in *A View from the Bridge* (Arena Stage, Washington, D.C., Nov. 7, 1956); and Elis in *Easter* (Fourth St. Th., Jan. 16, 1957).

With Group 20, at the Theatre-on-the-Green (Wellesley, Mass.), Mr. Higgins played Octavius in *Man and Superman* (July 16, 1957); Christian in *Cyrano de Bergerac* (Aug. 6, 1957), Dick Johnson in *Girl of the Golden West* (Aug. 20, 1957), and Christy in *Playboy of the Western World* (Sept. 3, 1957); Herod in *For the Time Being* (Th. de Lys, N.Y.C., Dec. 17, 1957); John Proctor in *The Crucible* (Martinique, Mar. 11, 1958); Prince Myshkin in *The Idiot* (Master's Inst., Apr. 7, 1958); and Son of Cuchulain in *On Baile's Strand* and the Street Singer in *Death of Cuchulain* (Beekman Tower Hotel Th., Apr. 12, 1959).

He succeeded (Oct. 12, 1959) James Daly in the title role in *J. B.* (ANTA, Dec. 11, 1958); and played the role in the national tour (opened Shubert, New Haven, Conn., Oct. 28, 1959; closed Locust St. Th., Philadelphia, Pa., Mar. 26, 1960); appeared as Hector in *Tiger at the Gates* (Arena Stage, Washington, D.C., Mar. 7, 1961); in stock, as Monsieur Levert in *Dead Letter* (Off Beach Th., Westhampton, L.I., N.Y., Aug. 17, 1961); Capt. Caleb Williams in *Diff'rent* (Mermaid, N.Y.C., Oct. 17, 1961); Olson in *The Long Voyage Home* (Mermaid, Dec. 4, 1961); Dr. Ama in *It's All Yours* (Van Dam, Apr. 26, 1962); Earl of Kent in the NY Shakespeare Festival production of *King Lear* (Delacorte, Aug. 13, 1962); the title role in the NY Shakespeare Festival production of *Macbeth* (Heckscher, Nov. 15, 1962), which subsequently toured schools in N.Y.C., and NY state; and Antony in *Antony and Cleopatra* (Delacorte, N.Y.C., June 20, 1963).

He appeared as Segismund in *Life Is a Dream* (Actor Place Playhouse, Mar. 19, 1964); and for the Boston (Mass.) Arts Festival, Peter Cauchon and Robert de Beaudricourt in *Saint Joan* (June 16, 1964), Eddie Carbone in *A View from the Bridge* (July 20, 1964), and Lord Byron in *Camino Real* (July 27, 1964).

He played Ephraim Cabot in *Desire Under the Elms* (Circle in the Square, tour, Oct. 12, 1964); Amos in *Queen and the Rebels* (Th. Four, Feb. 25, 1965); James Tyrone Sr. in *Long Day's Journey into Night* (Arena Stage, Washington, D.C., Apr. 1965); Jason in *Medea* (Martinique, Nov. 28, 1965); Karl in *Break-Up* (Long Wharf Th., New Haven, Conn., May 6, 1966); David Wylie in *What Every Woman Knows* (Goodspeed Opera House, East Haddam, Conn., Aug. 1966); the title role in *Macbeth,* Inspector Messiter in *The Magistrate,* and John Proctor in *The Crucible* (Arena Stage, Washington, D.C., Oct. 1966–Feb. 1967).

He again assumed the role of Ephraim Cabot in *Desire Under the Elms* (Th. Company of Boston, June 28, 1967); Betencourt in *The Only Game in Town* (pre-Broadway tour, Jan. 1968); Alfred Allmers in *Little Eyolf* (Artists Th. Festival, Long Island, N.Y., July 18, 1968); the title role in *Tom Paine* (Goodman, Mar. 28, 1969); the title role in *Santacqua* (H B Playwrights Foundation, Dec. 12, 1969); the title role in *Uncle Vanya* (Studio Arena, Buffalo, N.Y., Feb. 19, 1970); John Adams in *John and Abigail* (Ford's Washington, D.C., Jan. 18, 1971); James Tyrone Sr. in *Long Day's Journey into Night* (Catholic Univ., Washington, D.C., May 18, 1971; George Washington in *Sally, George and Martha* (Th. de Lys, Dec. 20, 1971).

He was the President in *Conflict of Interest* (Arena Stage, Feb. 9, 1972); Herman in *Wedding Band* (Ivanhoe, Chicago, Ill., May 19, 1972); the Father in *Canadian Gothic* (Manhattan Th. Club, Nov. 1973); Half Cherry in *L'ete* (Cherry Lane, Apr. 1973); replaced George C. Scott as Dr. Astrov in *Uncle Vanya* (Circle in the Square, May 1973); played Larry Slade in *The Iceman Cometh* (Circle in the Square, Dec. 13, 1973); Tom Giordano in *Dear Mr. Giordano* (HB Playwrights Foundation, Mar. 21, 1974); H. R. Haldeman in *Expletive Deleted* (Th. of Riverside Church, June 3, 1974); and Frank Strang in *Equus* (Plymouth, Oct. 24, 1974).

Films. Mr. Higgins appeared in *Edge of Fury* (UA, 1958); as Michael in *The Arrangement* (1969); as Mr. Dennis in *Wanda* (1970); in *Desperate Characters* (1971); *The Conversation* (1974); *The Godfather, Part II* (1974); and *The Stepford Wives* (1974).

Television. Mr. Higgins made his television debut appearance in *A Strange Christmas Dinner* (NBC, Dec. 9, 1945); subsequently played Johnny Roberts in the series One Man's Family (NBC, 1949–50); Hector in *The Iliad* (Omnibus, CBS, Apr. 1955); the Newspaperman in The Secret Storm (CBS, Apr. –July 1959); the Psychiatrist in As the World Turns (CBS, May–Oct. 1960); Ed Lawson in Our Five Daughters (NBC, Jan.–Sept. 1962); in The Patriots (Hallmark Hall of Fame, NBC, 1963); and Herb in The Secret Storm (CBS, Mar.–June 1964); and appeared on CBS-TV Workshop; Pulitzer Prize Th. (ABC); Studio One (CBS); You Are There (CBS); Ethel and Albert (ABC); Camera Three (CBC); US Steel Hour (CBS); Lamp Unto My Feet (CBS); GE Th. (CBS); Playhouse 90 (CBS); The Verdict Is Yours (CBS); Armstrong Circle Th. (NBC); Look Up and Live (CBS); Best of the Post; Alcoa Presents (NBC); the Jackie Gleason Show (CBS); Great Ghost Tales; The Eternal Light; The Defenders (CBS); The Nurses (CBS); Ben Casey (ABC); Outer Limits (ABC); and Gunsmoke (CBS); The Virginian (NBC), Andy Griffith Show and Guiding Light.

Awards. He received *The Village Voice* Off-Bway (Obie) Award for his performance as John Proctor in *The Crucible* (1958), and Best Actor of the Year Award (1970) Buffalo, N.Y., for his playing the title role in *Uncle Vanya..*

HIKEN, GERALD. Actor, director, producer. b. May 23, 1927, Milwaukee, Wis., to Nathan and Marian (Shapiro) Hiken. Father, merchant. Grad. Washington H.S., Milwaukee, 1945; Univ. of Wisconsin, B.A. 1949. Studied acting with Uta Hagen, N.Y.C., 1955–56; Actors' Studio (mbr., 1959–to date). Married Sept. 23, 1961, to Barbara Lerner, make-up artist; one daughter. Relatives in theatre: cousin, Nat Hiken, writer (dec.); cousin, Charlotte Rae, singer, actress. Member of AEA (on council, 1961–67); SAG; AFTRA.

Theatre. Mr. Hiken first appeared on stage as Peter Quince in a junior high school production of *A Midsummer Night's Dream* (Milwaukee, 1943); subsequently produced, directed, and played Richard in *Hay Fever* (Linden Circle, Wis., June, 1949); was assistant director of the Little Th., Houston, Texas, appearing in *Twelfth Night,* and *The Physician in Spite of Himself,* (Winter 1949–50); appeared in productions at Lake Geneva, Wis. (Summer 1950); directed Rice Institute's productions of *Beautiful People,* and *Earnest* (Houston, Texas, 1951); played Eddie Brock in *Born Yesterday* (Erie Playhouse, Pa., Sept. 1951); and appeared in other productions at the Erie Playhouse (Winters 1951–53); Brattle Th., Cambridge, Mass. (Summer 1952); the Port Players, Wis. (Summer 1953); and at the Arena Stage, Washington, D.C. (1953–55).

He made his N.Y.C. debut as Trofimoff in *The Cherry Orchard* (Fourth St. Th., Oct. 18, 1955); played Telegin Ilya Ilyich in *Uncle Vanya* (Fourth St. Th., Jan. 31, 1956), and later (May 1956) played

Vanya in this production; replaced (Spring 1957) Larry Robinson as Don Parritt in *The Iceman Cometh*(Circle in the Square, May 8, 1956); played Blaise in *The Lovers* (Martin Beck Th., May 10, 1956); Semyen Semyonovitch Medvedenko in *The Seagull*(Fourth St. Th., Oct. 22, 1956); Wong in *The Good Woman of Setzuan* (Phoenix, Dec. 18, 1956); succeeded (Feb. 1957) Ellis Rabb as Alceste in *The Misanthrope* (Th. East, Nov. 12, 1956); played the Father in *The Cave Dwellers* (Bijou, Oct. 19, 1957); succeeded (Feb. 1958) Alvin Epstein as Clov in *Endgame*(Cherry Lane, Jan. 28, 1958); appeared as the Supervisor in *The Enchanted* (Renata, Apr. 22, 1958); toured as Moishe in *Sweet and Sour*(Summer 1958); played Hovstad in *An Enemy of the People* (Actors Playhouse, N.Y.C., Feb. 4, 1959); Max the Millionaire in *The Nervous Set* (Henry Miller's Th., May 12, 1959); appeared in *Dig We Must* (John Drew Th., East Hampton, N.Y., Summer 1959); played Andrey Prezeroff in *The Three Sisters* (Fourth St. Th., Sept. 21, 1959); Michepain in *The Fighting Cock*(ANTA, Dec. 8, 1959); and in Princeton, N.J. (Summer 1960), appeared in *Major Barbara*, and played Stockman in *An Enemy of the People.*

Mr. Hiken played Moishe (Morris) Golub in *The 49th Cousin* (Ambassador, N.Y.C., Oct. 27, 1960); the Condemned Man and the Hangman in *Gallows Humor*(Gramercy Arts, Apr. 18, 1961); played Arthur Groomkirby in *One Way Pendulum* (E. 74 St. Th., Sept. 18, 1961); succeeded (Apr. 1962) Douglas Campbell in the title role of *Gideon* (Plymouth, Nov. 9, 1961); was a replacement (Oct. 1962) in *Brecht on Brecht* (Th. de Lys, Jan. 3, 1962); was assistant director of *Mother Courage and Her Children* (Martin Beck Th., Mar. 28, 1963); and played Shortcut in *Foxy* (Ziegfeld, Feb. 16, 1964).

He played Andrei in the Actors Studio production of *The Three Sisters* (Morosco, June 22, 1964), making his London debut in the role with the same company, at the World Th. Season (Aldwych, May 12, 1965); played Stanley in *The Birthday Party* (UCLA Th. Group, Los Angeles, July 26, 1965); became a member of the resident company of the Stanford Univ. Rep. Th. (1965) and Artistic Director of the company and a lecturer in acting at the Univ. (Sept. 1966–June 1968), druing which time he played the title role in *Scapin* (Oct. 27, 1965), Lafeu in *All's Well That Ends Well*(Mar. 31, 1966), Wong in *The Good Woman of Setzuan*(May 11, 1966), Caesar in *Antony and Cleopatra*(Oct. 19, 1966), Gaev in *The Cherry Orchard*(Mar. 1, 1967), Bill Maitland in *Inadmissable Evidence*(Apr. 5, 1967), the Playwright in *Once in a Lifetime*(May 10, 1967), the Author in *The Cavern*(Nov. 29, 1967), Mathern in *Cock-a-Doodle Dandy* (Mar. 6, 1968), Ossip in *The Inspector General*(Apr. 24, 1968), and Sidney in *The Sign in Sidney Brustein's Window* (May, 1968).

In 1968, Mr. Hiken and Paul E. Richards formed The New Theatre (TNT), a two-man repertory theatre featuring their own works. TNT has toured extensively, including a limited run at the Chelsea Th. (Brooklyn Acad. of Music, Mar. 20–Apr. 1, 1973).

Films. He played "Waffles" in the motion picture version of *Uncle Vanya* (Cont., 1958); and has appeared in *The Goddess* (Col., 1958); *Invitation to a Gunfighter* (UA, 1964); *Funnyman* (New Yorker, 1971); *Fuzz*(UA, 1972); *The Candidate*(WB, 1972); and *Company of Killers* (U, 1972).

Television. Mr. Hiken made his debut in the title role of *Uncle Vanya*(Camera 3, CBS, July 1956); and played St. Ignatius on Lamp Unto My Feet (CBS July 1956). Since 1957, he has appeared on Armstrong Circle Theatre (CBS); US Steel Hour (CBS); Car 54, Where Are You? (NBC); The Untouchables (ABC); You'll Never Get Rich (NBC); in *There Shall Be No Night* (Hallmark Hall of Fame, NBC); Studio One (CBS); Eternal Light; Cain's Hundred; The Defenders (CBS); Eleventh Hour (NBC); CBS Workshop; Dupont Show of the Month (NBC); appeared in *The Lady's Not for Burning;* The Farmer's Daughter (ABC); Naked City (ABC); and Occasional Wife (NBC).

Awards. He received the *Village Voice* Off-Bway (Obie) Award, and the Clarence Derwent Award, for his performance in the title role of *Uncle Vanya*(1955–56).

HILL, ANN. Executive. b. Ann Geddes Stahlman, Apr. 15, 1921, to James Geddes and Mildred (Thornton) Stahlman. Father, newspaper publisher. Grad. Ward-Belmont H.S., Nashville, Tenn., 1939; Vanderbilt Univ., B.A. 1943. Married 1947, to George de Roulhac Hill; two sons, two daughters. Served USNR, Waves Communications Officer; rank, Lt. (jg). Member of ATA; Delta Delta Delta; Phi Beta Kappa; Junior League. Address: 201 Lynwood Blvd., Nashville, TN 37205, tel. (615) 269-5169.

Mrs. Hill has served the ATA as president (1975): member of the Awards Committee (1962–63), the Structure Committee (1967–71), the Finance Committee (1969–71; chmn., 1971); and the Executive Committee and board of directors (1969–to date); as vice-president for Administration (1972–73); and as president-elect (1974).

For the Children's Theatre Association of ATA, she has been regional chairman (1957); chairman of the Ways and Means Committee (1959–63); member of the governing board (1960–63); comptroller (1962–66); assistant director (1967–69); and director-president (1969–71). In her work with the South Eastern Theatre Conference, she held the posts of Children's Theatre divisional chairman (1958–59); executive vice-president (1960–61); president (1962–63); and chairman of the New Play Project (1963–64). She was a founder (1968) of the Tennessee Theatre Association, and was vice-president for middle Tennessee. For the Nashville Children's Th., she was president (1956–58); secretary-treasurer (1954–56); and chairman (1954–56) of fund-raising drives. She is a member of the Theatre Advisory Panel of the Tennessee Arts Commission (1968–to date).

Mrs. Hill is a trustee of the Children's Theatre Foundation, and a former member of the board of directors of the Amer. National Theatre and Academy (1963–66). She was an American delegate to the first International Children's Theatre Conference (London, England, May 16–19, 1964); was executive secretary (1967–73) of the US Center for ASSITEJ (International Association of Theatre for Children and Youth); and a US delegate to congresses and festivals in London, Moscow, The Hague, Venice, Montreal, and Albany, N.Y. She was registrar and treasurer for the Fourth Congress of ASSITEJ in Albany (1972), the first such gathering to be held in the Western hemisphere. As executive director, she handled all funds, registrations, and general operations of the Congress.

Published Works. Mrs. Hill was a reporter and drama columnist for the Nashville *Banner* (1964–71), and has had articles published in *Children's Theatre Review; Southern Speech Journal;* and *Southern Theatre.* A compilation of her previously-printed newspaper articles, entitled *European Children's Theatre and the Second Congress of the International Children's Theatre Association,* has been published in book form.

Recreation. Art, music.

HILL, ARTHUR. Actor. b. Arthur Edward Spence Hill, Aug. 1, 1922, Melfort, Saskatchewan, Canada, to Olin D. and Edith (Spence) Hill. Father, lawyer. Grad. King Edward H.S., Vancouver, Canada, 1940; attended Univ. of British Columbia, 1940–47. Married Sept. 1942, to Peggy Hill; one son, one daughter. Served in Royal Canadian Air Force, 1942–45. Member of AEA; AFTRA; SAG; British AEA. Address: 1515 Club View Drive, Los Angeles, CA 90024.

Theatre. Mr. Hill made his stage debut as Finch in *Home of the Brave*(Westminster Th., London, Nov. 1, 1948); subsequently played Tommy Turner in *The Male Animal*(Arts, May 18, 1949); Hector Malone in *Man and Superman* (Prince's, June 2, 1951); Paul in *Country Girl*(St. James's 1952); and Cornelius Hackl in *The Matchmaker*(Haymarket, Nov. 4, 1954); the role in which he made his Bway debut (Royale, Dec. 5, 1955) and in which he later toured (opened Shubert, Detroit, Feb. 4, 1957).

He played Ben Gant in *Look Homeward, Angel* (Ethel Barrymore Th., N.Y.C., Nov. 28, 1957); Bruce Bellingham in *The Gang's All Here*(Ambassador, Oct. 1, 1959); Jay Follet in *All the Way Home* (Belasco, Nov. 30, 1960); George in *Who's Afraid of Virginia Woolf?* (Billy Rose Th., Oct. 13, 1962; Piccadilly, London, Feb. 6, 1964); Bill Deems in *Something More!* (Eugene O'Neill Th., N.Y.C., Nov. 10, 1964); Harold Potter in *The Porcelain Year*(opened Locust St. Th., Philadelphia, Pa., Oct. 11, 1965; closed Shubert Th., New Haven, Conn., Nov. 13, 1965); and Simon Harford in *More Stately Mansions* (Ahmanson Th., Los Angeles, Calif., Sept. 12, 1967; Morosco, N.Y.C., Oct. 31, 1967).

Films. Mr. Hill's films include *The Ugly American* (U, 1963); *Moment to Moment* (U, 1966); *Harper* (WB, 1966); *Petulia* (WB-7 Arts, 1968); *The Chairman*(20th-Fox, 1969); *Rabbit Run*(WB, 1970); *The Andromeda Strain*(U, 1971); and *The Pursuit of Happiness* (Col., 1971).

Television. Mr. Hill appeared on Route 66 (CBS, 1964); Slattery's People (CBS, 1964); The Defenders (CBS, 1964); Reporter (CBS, 1964); Ben Casey (ABC, 1966); The F.B.I. (ABC, 1966); read on the William Carlos Williams segment of the *U.S.A. Poetry*series (NET, Mar. 3, 1966); played Dr. Ed Harriman in *The Closing Door*(Play of the Week, NET, 1966); appeared on Mission: Impossible (CBS, 1966); played Donald Hammond in *The Fatal Mistake*(Bob Hope Chrysler Th., NBC, Nov. 30, 1966); was on Invaders (ABC, 1967); Voyage (ABC, 1967); and on Owen Marshal, Counselor at Law (ABC, 1971).

Awards. He received an Antoinette Perry (Tony) Award for his performance as George in *Who's Afraid of Virginia Woolf?* (1963).

Recreation. Reading, sailing.

HILL, ERROL. Educator, author, actor, director, playwright. b. Errol Gaston Hill, Aug. 5, 1921, Trinidad, West Indies, to Thomas David and Lydia Caroline Hill. Father, accountant; mother, housewife. Educated Ideal H.S., Trinidad; grad. Yale College, B.A.; RADA, graduate diploma; Yale School of Drama, M.F.A.; D.F.A. Married in 1956 to Grace L. I. Hope; three daughters; one son. Relatives in theatre: brother, Sydney Hill, film maker; sister, Jean Sue-Wing, drama officer for government of Trinidad and Tobago. Served 1943–45 as chief clerk, US Engineers, in Trinidad, in lieu of military service. Member of ATA (bd. member); NTC (bd. member); ASTR; AEA; Assoc. for Commonwealth Literature and Language Studies. Address: (home) 3 Haskins Rd., Hanover, NH 03755, tel. (603) 643-4059; (bus.) Dartmouth College, Hanover, NH 03755, tel. (603) 646-2750.

Mr. Hill has been professor of drama, Dartmouth College, since 1969. He began his academic career at the Univ. of the West Indies, Kingston, Jamaica, as a drama tutor (1952–58) and a creative arts tutor (1958–65). From 1965 to 1967, he was a teaching fellow in drama, Univ. of Ibadan, Nigeria, and in 1967–68 associate professor of drama, City Univ. of New York. He joined the Dartmouth faculty as associate professor of drama in 1968–69.

Theatre. Mr. Hill's first acting role was the lead in *A Man in the Street,* produced in Trinidad about 1937; in 1948 he first directed a play, *A Boy Comes Home,* and produced a play, *Brittle and the City Fathers,* both in Trinidad. His professional debut as an actor was as Cliff in *How I Wonder*(Unity Th., London, England, Mar. 1950), and two years later he was stage manager for an Arts Council tour of the provinces in England of *His Excellency* (Feb.–Mar. 1952).

Plays written by Mr. Hill, with dates of first production, are *Oily Portraits*(1948); *Square Peg*(1949); *The Ping Pong*(1953); *Dilemma*(1953); *Broken Melody* (1954); *Wey-Wey* (1957); *Strictly Matrimony* (1959); *Man Better Man* (1960); and *Dance Bongo* (1965). *Man Better Man* was his first play to be produced professionally (St. Mark's Playhouse, N.Y.C., May 1969).

Mr. Hill has performed over forty roles in amateur and professional productions in the West Indies, England, the US, and Nigeria. He has appeared recently in Dartmouth Summer Repertory as Malvolio in *Twelfth Night* (1968) and in the title role of *Othello* (1969). He has directed over a hundred plays and pageants in the countries listed above, among the most recent, all at Dartmouth College, being *Ti Jean and His Brothers* (Hopkins Center Th., 1972); *The Bloodknot* (Bentley Th., 1972); *The Blacks* (Hopkins Center Th., 1973); and *King Lear* (Hopkins Center Th., 1974).

Radio. Mr. Hill wrote the script for and had a role in *The Ping Pong* (BBC, 1950).

Published Works. Mr. Hill has edited (1971–to date) *Bulletin of Black Theatre.* He edited and contributed to *The Artist in West Indian Society: A Symposium* (1964); wrote *The Trinidad Carnival: Mandate for a National Theatre* (1972); and was joint author of *Why Pretend?* (1973).

Awards. Mr. Hill held a British Council Scholarship (1949–51) to attend RADA and a Rockefeller Foundation Fellowship (1958–59) to attend the Yale School of Drama. He received a Theatre Guild Playwriting Fellowship in 1961 to complete his doctoral studies; held a Rockefeller Teaching Fellowship in 1956–57 to teach at Ibadan (Nigeria) Univ.; and received the Humming Bird Gold Medal in 1973 for meritorious service in drama to Trinidad and Tobago.

Recreation. Mr. Hill is a collector of Caribbean folk music.

HILL, GEORGE ROY. Director, writer. b. Dec. 20, 1923, Minneapolis, Minn., to George Roy and Helen Hill. Father, businessman. Grad. Blake Sch., 1939; Yale Univ., B.A. 1943; Trinity Coll., Dublin, Ire., B. Litt. 1949. Married Apr. 7, 1951, to Louisa Horton; two sons, two daughters. Served WW II, USMC, Aviation, Korean War; rank, Maj. Member of DGA; AEA; SAG; WGA. Address: 259 E. 78th St., New York, NY 10021, tel. (212) LE 5-8987.

Theatre. Mr. Hill first appeared in a walk-on role in *The Devil's Disciple* (Gaiety, Dublin, Ire., Jan. 1948). He subsequently played Gustav in *The Creditors* (Cherry Lane, N.Y.C., Oct. 21, 1950); directed *Look Homeward, Angel* (Ethel Barrymore Th., Nov. 11, 1957); *The Gang's All Here* (Ambassador, Oct. 1, 1959); *Greenwillow* (Alvin, Mar. 8, 1960); *Period of Adjustment* (Helen Hayes Th., Nov. 10, 1960); *Moon on a Rainbow Shawl* (East Eleventh St. Th., Jan. 15, 1962); and *Henry, Sweet Henry* (Palace, Oct., 23, 1967).

Films. He directed *Period of Adjustment* (MGM, 1962); *Toys in the Attic* (UA, 1962); *The World of Henry Orient* (UA, 1963); *Hawaii* (UA, 1965); *Thoroughly Modern Millie* (U, 1966); *Butch Cassidy and the Sundance Kid* (20th-Fox, 1969); *Slaughterhouse-Five* (U, 1972); *The Sting* (U, 1973); and *The Great Waldo Pepper* (U, 1974).

Television. He appeared in and wrote *My Brother's Keeper* (Kraft Television Th., NBC, 1953); wrote, produced, and directed *A Night to Remember* (Kraft Television Th., NBC, 1954); *The Helen Morgan Story* (Playhouse 90, CBS, 1954); and *Judgement at Nuremberg* (Playhouse 90, CBS, 1957).

Awards. Mr. Hill was nominated for two NATAS (Emmy) Awards (1954) for his writing and direction of *A Night to Remember;* received the Sylvania Award and the Christopher Award (1954) for his *A Night to Remember;* was nominated for the Emmy Award (1957) for his direction of *The Helen Morgan Story;* and was nominated for the Antoinette Perry (Tony) Award (1957) for his direction of *Look Homeward, Angel.* He was nominated for an Emmy Award for *Child of Our Time* (1958); was nominated for an Academy (Oscar) Award for *Butch Cassidy and the Sundance Kid* (1970), for which he was also nominated by the Directors Guild as best director. The Directors Guild also nominated him as best director for *Slaughterhouse-Five* (1973) and *The Sting* (1974), and he received the 1974 Academy (Oscar) Award as best director for *The Sting.*

Recreation. Flying.

HILL, JOHN-EDWARD. Managing director, producer. b. June 19, 1947, Buffalo, N.Y., to John Vernon and Charlotte Adelle Hill. Father, industrial shop foreman. Grad. Northwestern Univ., B.S. 1970; Yale Sch. of Drama, M.F.A. 1974. Studied at Yale Sch. of Drama with Herman Kramitz, John Hightower, Martin Feinstein, Michael David and Robert Brustein. Relative in theatre; John P. Wolanczyk, scene painter. Address: (home) 52 Clarence St., Brockton, MA 02401, tel. (617) 586-5996; (bus.) Spingold Th., Brandeis University, Waltham, MA 02154, tel. (617) 894-4394.

Theatre. Mr. Hill is general manager of the Spingold Th., Brandeis Univ. (Waltham, Mass., 1974–to date). He was the managing director of Cheektowaga Children's Th. (Buffalo, N.Y., 1965–67); the Camp Kiniya drama program (Milton, Vt., 1969); general manager of the Northwestern Gilbert and Sullivan Guild (Evanston, Ill., 1969–70); treasurer and business manager of the Rooftop Players Visual and Performing Arts Centre, Inc. (Buffalo, N.Y., 1971); associate director and member of the board, Poco Productions, Inc. (New Haven, Conn., 1973); general manager, Stowe Summer Th. (Stowe, Vt., 1972); and assistant managing director, Yale Rep. Th. (New Haven, Conn., 1973–74).

While affiliated with the above enterprises, Mr. Hill often acted, directed and stage managed their productions.

Other Activities. He was a radio personality and news director for WXRL (Buffalo, N.Y., 1971), and holds a first-class FCC license.

Awards. He received fellowships for his administrative work with the Yale Cabaret Th. and Yale Repertory Th.

Recreation. Collecting cylinder records and players, magic lanterns and hand painted slides.

HILL, LUCIENNE. Playwright, translator. b. Lucienne Palmer, London, England, to Arthur and Louise (Moutarde) Palmer. Father, dentist; mother, teacher. Grad. Oxford Univ., B.A. 1943. Married Feb. 1959; one son, two daughters. Served British Army Intelligence Corps, 1943–45. Member of Dramatists Guild, Society of Authors. Address: c/o Jan Van Loewen, 81-3 Shaftsbury Ave., London W.1, England tel. GER-5546.

Theatre. Miss Hill was first an actress in British repertory companies (1945); and appeared with the Birmingham Repertory Th. (1950–51). She translated Jean Anouilh's play, *Ardele* (Birmingham, 1950; moved to London in a new production, Vaudeville, Aug. 30, 1951; Cricket, N.Y.C., Apr. 8, 1958); and M. Anouilh's *Thieves' Carnival* (Birmingham, 1951; Cherry Lane, N.Y.C., Feb. 1, 1955).

She translated M. Anouilh's *The Waltz of the Toreadors* (Arts, London, Feb. 24, 1956; Coronet, N.Y.C., Jan. 17, 1957), which also toured (opened McCarter, Princeton, N.J., Sept. 26, 1957; reopened Coronet, N.Y.C., Mar. 4, 1958); adapted M. Anouilh's *The Fighting Cock* (ANTA, Dec. 8, 1959); Colette's novel, *A Second String* (Eugene O'Neill Th., Apr. 13, 1960); translated Anouilh's *Becket* (St. James, Oct. 5, 1960); translated Françoise Sagan's play, *Castle in Sweden* (Piccadilly, London, 1962); Anouilh's *Poor Bitos* (Duke of York's, 1963); *Traveller without Luggage* (ANTA, N.Y.C., Sept. 18, 1964); *Dear Antoine* (Chichester, England, 1971); *Director of the Opera* (Chichester, England, 1973); and *The Arrest* (Bristol Old Vic, 1974).

Television and Radio. Miss Hill translated Albert Camus' play, *The Just* for radio (BBC Sound, London, 1952).

For television, she adapted Alexander Dumas' *Lady of the Camellias* (BBC, 1964).

Recreation. Gardening.

HILL, MARTHA. Educator. b. East Palestine, Ohio. Grad. Normal Sch. of Phys. Ed., Battle Creek, Mich.; Teachers Coll., Columbia Univ., B.A.; New York Univ., M.A.; Doctor of Humane Letters, Adelphi Univ., June 1965; Doctor of Fine Arts, Mount Holyoke Coll., Nov. 1966; Doctor of Letters, Bennington Coll., June 1969; attended Inst. of Musical Art, N.Y.C. Studied dancing with Kobeloff, Martha Graham, Anna Duncan, Margaret H. Doubler. Married to Thurston J. Davies. Address: c/o Juilliard School of Music, 120 Claremont Ave., New York, NY 10027.

Since 1951, Dr. Hill has been director of the Dance Dept. of Juilliard Sch. of Music. She has held academic positions at Kellogg Sch., Battle Creek, Mich. (dir. of dance); Kansas State Teacher Coll. (dir. of Physical education); Univ. of Oregon (dance instructor); Lincoln Sch. of Teachers Coll.; New York Univ. (dir. of dance, 1930–51); Bennington Sch. of the Dance (dir., 1934–39); and Bennington Sch. of the Arts (dir., 1940–42).

She was founder and co-director (1948) of the Connecticut Coll. Sch. of the Dance and the American Dance Festival.

Dr. Hill is currently a member of the Dance Panel, US Dept. of State, Bur. of Educational Cultural Affairs, Office of Cultural Presentations; a member of Advisory Comm. on the Performing Arts, Sch. of Performing Arts, Bd. of Ed., N.Y.C.; a former member of Natl. Council on the Arts and Govt.; and a former member of Dance Panel of Natl. Council on the Arts (Natl. Foundation on the Arts and the Humanities).

Awards. Dr. Hill received the Amer. Dance Guild Award in June 1974.

HILLARY, ANN. Actress. b. Ann Margaret Francis, Jan. 8, 1931, Jellico, Tenn., to Paul and Sallie B. Francis. Attended Univ. of Kentucky; Northwestern Univ.; grad. AADA, 1949. Studied acting with Isabel Merson and Sanford Meisner, N.Y.C. Married Nov. 10, 1953, to Frederick Knott, playwright; one son. Member of AEA; AFTRA; SAG; AGVA.

Theatre. Miss Hillary made her stage debut as Judy in *Junior Miss* (Fitchburg Playhouse, Mass., 1951); and her N.Y.C. debut as Vicki Holly in *Be Your Age* (48 St. Th., Jan. 14, 1953); followed by Agnes Sorel in *The Lark* (Longacre, Nov. 17, 1955); in the double-bill, *Separate Tables,* played Jean Stratton in *Table Number Seven* and Jean Tanner in *Table by the Window* (Music Box, Oct. 25, 1956); and Barbara Allen in *Dark of the Moon* (Carnegie Hall Playhouse, Feb. 26, 1958).

Television. Miss Hillary made her debut as Henry's Girl on the Aldrich Family (NBC, 1951–52); and has appeared on Broadway TV Th. (1953); The Brighter Day (CBS, 1954–55); Dr. Hudson's Secret Journal (ABC, 1956); The Verdict Is Yours (CBS, 1961); From These Roots (ABC, 1962); Studio One (CBS); and Armstrong Circle Th. (CBS).

Recreation. Swimming.

HILLER, WENDY. Actress. b. Wendy Margaret Hiller, Aug. 15, 1912, Bramhall, Cheshire, England, to Frank Watkin and Marie Elizabeth (Stone) Hiller. Father, mill director. Grad. Winceby House Sch., Bexhill, England. Studied acting at Manchester (Eng.) Repertory Th. Married Feb. 25, 1937, to Ronald Gow, playwright; one son, one daughter. Relative in theatre: cousin, Eric Hiller, artist, scenic designer. Member of British AEA (committee member, 1954); SAG. Address: 9 Stratton Rd., Beaconsfield, England.

Theatre. Miss Hiller made her debut as the Maid in *The Ware Case* (Manchester Rep. Th., Sept. 1930); subsequently toured as a walk-on and understudy in *Evensong* (1932); as Sally Hardcastle in *Love on the Dole* (May 1934); made her London debut in that role (Garrick Th., Jan. 30, 1935) and her N.Y.C. debut (Shubert, Feb. 24, 1936).

At the Malvern (England) Festival, she played the title role in *Saint Joan* and Eliza Doolittle in *Pygmalion* (July 1936); toured as Viola in *Twelfth Night* (Aug. 1943); appeared as Sister Joanna of the Cross in *The Cradle Song* (Apollo, London, Jan. 27, 1944); Princess Charlotte in *The First Gentleman* (New, July 18, 1945); Tess in *Tess of the D'Urbervilles,* Portia in *The Merchant of Venice* (Bristol Old Vic Co., 1946); and played Tess in the London production of *Tess of the D'Urbervilles* (New, Nov. 26, 1946).

She played Catherine Sloper in *The Heiress* (Biltmore, N.Y.C., Sept. 29, 1947); subsequently appeared in the title role of *Ann Veronica* (Piccadilly, London, May 20, 1949); succeeded (Jan. 1950) Peggy Ashcroft as Catherine Sloper in *The Heiress* (Haymarket, Feb. 1, 1949); played Evelyn Daly in *Waters of the Moon* (Haymarket, Apr. 19, 1951) and Margaret Tollemache in *The Night of the Ball* (New, Jan. 12, 1955).

With the Old Vic Co., at the Old Vic Th. (London), she appeared as Portia in *Julius Caesar* (Sept. 7, 1955); Mistress Page in *The Merry Wives of Windsor* (Sept. 27, 1955); Hermione in *The Winter's Tale* (Nov. 1, 1955); Emilia in *Othello* (Feb. 21, 1956); and Helen in *Troilus and Cressida* (Apr. 3, 1956).

Miss Hiller played Josie Hogan in *A Moon for the Misbegotten* (Bijou, N.Y.C., May 2, 1957); succeeded (June 1958) Celia Johnson as Isobel Cherry in *Flowering Cherry* (Haymarket, London, Nov. 21, 1957); played Marie Marescaud in *All in the Family* (Gaiety, Dublin, Ire., June 1959); Isobel Cherry in *Flowering Cherry* (Lyceum, N.Y.C., Oct. 21, 1959); Carrie Berniers in *Toys in the Attic* (Piccadilly, London, Nov. 10, 1960); Tina in *The Aspern Papers* (Playhouse, N.Y.C., Feb. 7, 1962); Susan Shepherd in *The Wings of the Dove* (Lyric, London, Dec. 3, 1963); and Queen Mary in *Crown Matrimonial* (Haymarket, London, Oct. 22, 1972).

Films. Miss Hiller has appeared in *Lancashire Luck* (British Par., 1937); *Pygmalion* (MGM, 1938); *Major Barbara* (UA, 1941); *I Know Where I'm Going* (U, 1947); *Outcast of the Islands* (UA, 1952); *Sailor of the King (20th-Fox, 1953); Something of Value* (MGM, 1957); *How to Murder a Rich Uncle* (Col., 1957); *Separate Tables* (UA, 1958); *Sons and Lovers* (20th-Fox, 1960); *Toys in the Attic* (UA, 1964); *A Man for All Seasons* (Col., 1968); and *Murder on the Orient Express* (Par., 1974).

Awards. Miss Hiller was given an O.B.E. (Order of the British Empire) in 1971. She received the Academy (Oscar) Award (1958) for her performance as Miss Cooper in *Separate Tables.*

HINES, PATRICK. Actor, director. b. Mainer Patrick Hines, Mar. 17, 1930, Burkeville, Tex., to Ruben Mainer and Edice (Miller) Hines. Father, mechanic; mother, teacher. Grad. Univ. of Texas, B.F.A. 1952. Studied acting with B. Iden Payne. Served US Army, Special Services, 424th Army Band, 1954–56; rank, SP3. Member of AEA; AFTRA; SAG. Address: (home) 46 W. 95th St., New York, NY 10025; (bus.) I.C.M., 40 W. 57th St., New York, NY 10019, tel. (212) 556-5600.

Pre-Theatre. Drama and speech teacher.

Theatre. Mr. Hines made his stage debut with the Oregon Shakespeare Festival, Ashland, Oregon (Summers 1952, 1953), playing Alonzo in *The Tempest,* Menenius Agrippa in *Coriolanus,* Gremio in *The Taming of the Shrew,* Tubal in *The Merchant of Venice,* Regnier in *Henry VI, Part 1,* Leonato in *Much Ado About Nothing,* Flavius in *Julius Caesar,* and Gower in *Henry V;* directed community theatre groups in Port Arthur, Beaumont, and El Paso, Texas. With the American Shakespeare Festival, Stratford, Conn., he played Lord Bigot in *King John* (June 26, 1956); Friar Peter in *Measure for Measure* (June 27, 1956); Baptista in *The Taming of the Shrew* (Aug. 5, 1956), Rosencrantz in *Hamlet* (June 19, 1958), Aegeus in *A Midsummer Night's Dream* (June 20, 1958), Antigonus in *A Winter's Tale* (July 20, 1958), Old Capulet in *Romeo and Juliet* (June 12, 1959), Master Page in *The Merry Wives of Windsor* (July 8, 1959), the Duke of Florence in *All's Well That Ends Well* (July 29, 1959), Antigonus in *A Winter's Tale* (Apr. 23, 1960), Gonzalo in *The Tempest* (June 19, 1960); and the Priest in *Twelfth Night* (June 8, 1960). He was assistant director and played Mardian in *Antony and Cleopatra* (July 31, 1960), played Duke Frederick in *As You Like It* (June 15, 1961), was assistant director and played Ross in *Macbeth* (June 16, 1961), and assistant director and appeared as Agamemnon in *Troilus and Cressida* (July 23, 1961); the Earl of Worcester in *Henry IV, Part 1,* Duke of York in *Richard II* (June 12–Sept. 16, 1962); Earl of Gloucester in *King Lear,* Solinus in *The Comedy of Errors,* King Charles VI in *Henry V* and Pothinus in *Caesar and Cleopatra* (May 31–Sept. 15, 1963); played Leonato in *Much Ado About Nothing* (June 9, 1964), Duke of Buckingham in *Richard III* (June 10, 1964), and Polonius in *Hamlet* (July 2, 1964); Menenius Agrippa in *Coriolanus* (June 19, 1965), Friar Laurence in *Romeo and Juliet* (June 20, 1965), Earl of Gloucester in *King Lear* (June 23, 1965); Justice Silence in *Falstaff (Henry IV, Part 2,* June 18, 1966), Baron William de Traci in *Murder in the Cathedral* (June 19, 1966), Sir Toby Belch in *Twelfth Night* (June 21, 1966), and Casca in *Julius Caesar* (June 22, 1966).

For the Seattle Rep. Th. (Seattle, Wash.), he appeared as Pat in *The Hostage,* Danforth in *The Crucible,* the Burgermeister in *The Visit,* Capt. Ahab in *Moby Dick,* and Falstaff in *The Merry Wives of Windsor* (season 1966–67); Mr Kirby in *You Can't Take It With You,* Falstaff in *Henry IV, Part 1,* Sir Lucius O'Trigger in *The Rivals* and Mr. Peachum in *The Threepenny Opera* (Season 1967–68); Bottom in *A Midsummer Night's Dream* and Capt. Boyle in *Juno and the Paycock* (Season 1968–69).

For the Oregon Shakespeare Fest. (Ashland, Ore.), he directed *Hamlet* (July 21, 1968) and played the title role in *Henry VIII* (July 23, 1968); played Prospero in *The Tempest,* and Friar Laurence in *Romeo and Juliet,* which he also directed (Summer 1969).

Mr. Hines has also appeared at the Phoenix Th. in the American Shakespeare Festival productions, as Friar Peter in *Measure for Measure* (Jan. 22, 1957), Baptista in *The Taming of the Shrew* (Feb. 20, 1957), and Pescara in *The Duchess of Malfi* (Mar. 19, 1957).

At the Antioch Th., Yellow Springs, Ohio (Summer 1957), he played Bottom in *A Midsummer Night's Dream,* the title role in *Julius Caesar,* Sir Toby Belch in *Twelfth Night,* and the title role in *Henry VIII;* toured as Leonato in *Much Ado About Nothing* (opened Locust St. Th., Philadelphia, Pa., Dec. 1957); played the Lord Mayor in *The Geranium Hat* (Orpheum, N.Y.C., Mar. 17, 1959); Mr. Brown in the Phoenix production of *The Great God Brown* (Coronet, Oct. 6, 1959); the Magistrate in *Lysistrata* (Phoenix, Nov. 24, 1959); Dr. Begriffenfeldt in *Peer Gynt* (Phoenix, Jan. 12, 1960); the Earl of Worcester in *Henry IV, Part 1* (Phoenix, Mar. 1, 1960); toured as Peter Quince and was assistant director of *A Midsummer Night's Dream* (opened Colonial, Boston, Mass., Sept. 26, 1960; closed National, Washington, D.C., Feb. 25, 1961); played Dr. Callendar in *A Passage to India* (Ambassador, N.Y.C., Jan. 31, 1962); the Boy's Father in *The Fantasticks* (Fred Miller Th., Milwaukee, Wis., Dec. 1, 1962); succeeded (Jan. 15, 1963) Donald Babcock as the Boy's Father in *The Fantasticks* (Sullivan St. Playhouse, N.Y.C., May 3, 1960); and directed *Madwoman of Chaillot* (Fred Miller Th., Milwaukee, Wis., Oct. 31, 1963).

He played Max in *The Homecoming* (Trinity Sq. Th., Providence, R.I., Jan.–Mar. 1969); Simon Laquedeem in the APA production of *The Chronicles of Hell* (Mendelssohn Th., Ann Arbor, Mich., Autumn 1969); the Miller in the national tour of *The Canterbury Tales* (opened Playhouse, Wilmington, Del., Dec. 29, 1969; closed National, Wash., D.C., Apr. 11, 1970); Cardinal Beaufort in *The Wars of the Roses (Henry VI, Parts 1 and 2,* NY Shakespeare Fest., Delacorte Th., N.Y.C., June 23, 1970); John Dickinson in the second national company of *1776* (opened Masonic Aud., Scranton, Pa., Sept. 18, 1970; closed Palace, Albany, N.Y., May 14, 1971) and joined the first national company (Colonial, Boston, July 1971; closed Forrest, Philadelphia, Sept. 1971); played Northumberland in *Richard II* (Ahmanson, Los Angeles, Feb. 1972); the Friar in the pre-Bway engagement of *Pippin* (Opera House, Kennedy Ctr., Wash., D.C., Apr.–May 1972); John Dickinson in *1776* (Summer tour, 1972); Montfleury in *Cyrano* (Palace, N.Y.C., May 13, 1973); Ed Mosher in *The Iceman Cometh* (Circle in the Sq., Joseph E. Levine Th., Dec. 13, 1973); King Edward IV and the Lord Mayor in *Richard III* (Mitzi Newhouse Th., Oct. 4, 1974); the Commandant and the Old Colonel in *Mother Courage* (McCarter Th., Princeton, N.J., Feb. 1975); Red in *The Last Meeting of the Knights of the White Magnolia* (Arena Th., Wash., D.C., Mar. 1975); and directed *The Tavern,* played Sheridan Whiteside in *The Man Who Came to Dinner,* and Ben Franklin in *1776* (Fulton Opera House, Lancaster, Pa., Summer 1975).

Films. Mr. Hines made his debut as Samuel Chase in *1776* (Col., 1972); and appeared in *W.W. and the Dixie Dancekings* (20th-Fox, 1975).

Television. Mr. Hines has portrayed Theodore Roosevelt on Camera Three (CBS, Mar. 1957); Menenius in *Coriolanus* (Esso Rep. Th., Ind., May 12, 1965); and appeared on The Adams Chronicles (WNET, 1976).

HINGLE, PAT. Actor. b. Martin Patterson Hingle, July 19, 1924, Denver, Colo., to Clarence and Marvin Hingle. Father, building contractor; mother, school teacher, musician. Grad. Weslaco (Tex.) H.S., 1941; Univ. of Texas, B.F.A. 1949; studied at Amer. Th. Wing, N.Y.C., 1949–50; Actors Studio (member since 1952); HB (Herbert Berghof) Studios, N.Y.C., 9 mos.; acting with Uta Hagen, N.Y.C., four mos.; voice with Albert Malver, N.Y.C., with Alice Hermes, N.Y.C. Married June 3, 1947, to Alyce Dorsey; one son, two daughters. Served USN, 1941–46, 1951–52; rank, BT 1/c. Member of AEA; AFTRA; SAG.

Pre-Theatre. Waiter.

Theatre. Mr. Hingle made his debut as Lachie in *Johnny Belinda* (Centre Playhouse, Rockville Centre, N.Y., May 1950); appeared there as Fritz in *Claudia,* Lexy in *Candida,* the Prosecutor in *Redemption,* the Gentleman Caller in *The Glass Menagerie,* and Sgt. Rough in *Angel Street* (1950); and played Dowdy in *Mister Roberts* (Cecilwood Th., Fishkill, N.Y., July 1953). He made his Bway debut as Koble in *End As a Man* (Vanderbilt, Sept. 14, 1953); subsequently played Joe in *Festival* (Longacre, Jan. 1, 1955); Gooper in *Cat on a Hot Tin Roof* (Morosco, Mar. 24, 1955); Taggert in *Girls of Summer* (Longacre, Nov. 19, 1956); Rubin Flood in *Dark at the Top of the Stairs* (Music Box, Dec. 5, 1957); the title role in *J.B.* (ANTA, Dec. 11, 1958); and Trapp in *The Deadly Game* (Longacre, Feb. 2, 1960).

At the American Shakespeare Festival and Academy (Stratford, Conn.), he played the title role in *Macbeth* (June 16, 1961), and Hector in *Troilus and Cressida* (July 23, 1961); appeared as Sam in *Strange Interlude* (Hudson, N.Y.C., Mar. 11, 1963); and as Parnell in *Blues for Mr. Charlie* (ANTA, April 23, 1964).

Mr. Hingle played Andy Willard in *A Girl Could Get Lucky* (Cort Th., N.Y.C., Sept. 20, 1964); The Gentleman Caller in *The Glass Menagerie* (Paper Mill Playhouse, Millburn, N.J., Mar. 30, 1965) which was later transferred to Bway (Brooks Atkinson Th., N.Y.C., May 4, 1965); succeeded (Feb. 28, 1966) Jack Klugman in the role of Oscar Madison in *The Odd Couple* (Plymouth, Mar. 10, 1965); played Harry Armstrong in *Johnny No-Trump* (Cort, Oct. 8, 1967); Victor Franz in *The Price* (Morosco, Feb. 7, 1968); Joseph Dobbs in *Child's Play* (Royale, Feb. 17, 1970); and Senator George W. Mason in *The Selling of the President* (Shubert, Mar. 22, 1972).

Films. He made his debut as the Waiter in *On the Waterfront* (Col., 1954); and has since appeared in *The Strange One* (Col., 1957); *No Down Payment* (20th-Fox, 1957); *Splendor in The Grass* (WB, 1961); *The Ugly American* (U, 1962); *All the Way Home* (Par., 1964); played Sam Brewster in *Invitation to a Gunfighter* (UA, 1964); Big Foot in *Nevada Smith* (Par., 1966); Harry Mitchell in *Sol Madrid* (MGM, 1968); Judge Adam Fenton in *Hang 'Em High* (UA, 1968); appeared in *Jigsaw* (U, 1968); played Sam Pendlebury in *Bloody Mama* (AI, 1970); Bingamon in *WUSA* (Par., 1970); Grady in *Norwood* (Par., 1970); Capt. Pearson in *The Carey Treatment* (MGM, 1972); Capt. Stewart in *One Little Indian* (BV, 1973); Eli in *Happy as the Grass Was Green* (Martin, 1973); Lt. Novick in *The Supercops* (MGM, 1974); and appeared in *Deadly Honeymoon* (MGM, 1974).

Television. Mr. Hingle has appeared on Studio One (CBS); Alcoa/Goodyear (NBC); Suspense (CBS); Suspicion (CBS); Play of the Week (WNTA); Danger (CBS); The Phil Silvers Show (NBC); Doctor Kildare (NBC); The Untouchables (ABC); Route 66 (CBS); Kraft Television Th. (NBC); Armstrong Circle Th. (NBC); Eleventh Hour (NBC); Alfred Hitchcock Presents (CBS); Twilight Zone (CBS); The Defenders (CBS); and Lamp Unto My Feet (CBS); The Fugitive (ABC); Look Up and Live (CBS); Kraft Suspense Th. (NBC); Eternal Light (NBC); *Carol for Another Christmas* (ABC); Rawhide (CBS); Daniel Boone (NBC); Eleventh Hour (Ind.); The Andy Griffith Show (CBS); The Loner (CBS); Route 66 (Ind.); Shenandoah (ABC); Play of the Week (NET); narrated *The Victims* (NET); played the Gentleman Caller in *The Glass Menagerie* (CBS); and appeared in Mission Impossible (CBS); Judd for the Defense (ABC); Bob Hope Chrysler Theatre (NBC); The Invaders (ABC); Felony Squad (ABC); High Chaparral (NBC); The Bold Ones (NBC); Bonanza (NBC); *The Ballad of Andy Crocker* (ABC); Lancer (CBS); Medical Center (CBS); *A Clear and Present Danger* (NBC); The Young Lawyers (ABC); Gunsmoke (CBS); *If Tomorrow Comes* (ABC); *All the Way Home* (Hallmark Hall of Fame, NBC); Ironside (NBC); and Owen Marshall (ABC).

Recreation. All sports.

HINKEL, CECIL E. Educator. b. Cecil Ellworth Hinkel, Oct. 26, 1913, Harrisonburg, Va., to Elmer E. and Margaret J. (Rogers) Hinkel. Father, farmer. Grad. Port Republic (Va.) H.S., 1932; Bridgewater (Va.) Coll., B.A. 1936; attended Univ. of Virginia, Charlottesville, Va., Summers 1939, 1941; studied at Catholic Univ. Washington, D.C., with Walter Kerr, Leo Brady, Josephine Callan, and Father Gilbert Hartke, M.F.A. 1947; studied at Ohio State Univ. with Charles McGaw, John H. McDowell, and John E. Dietrich, Ph.D. (theatre) 1959. Married Dec. 22, 1961 to Martha Condra. Served USMC, artillery officer with the Fleet Marine Force, 1942–46; rank, Maj. Member of AAUP; AEA; AETA; Sigma Alpha Epsilon. Address: (home) Univ. of Conn., Box #398, Storrs, CT 06268, tel. (203) 429-1700; (bus.) Dept. of Theatre, Univ. of Connecticut, Storrs, CT 06268, tel. (203) 486-4025.

From 1961 to 1971, Dr. Hinkel was head of the Dept. of Theatre at the Univ. of Connecticut. He was an instructor (1949), became assistant professor (1951), associate professor (1958), and full professor (1963); directed 37 plays at the University and at the Nutmeg Summer Playhouse (Storrs, Conn.), which is operated by the University.

In 1962, the Playhouse became a professional Equity company, with Mr. Hinkel as managing director. He staged *Tea and Sympathy* (June 25, 1957); *The Voice of the Turtle* (July 16, 1957); *The Teahouse of the August Moon* (July 1, 1958); *The Desperate Hours* (June 30, 1959); *Oh, Men! Oh, Women!* (July 26, 1960); *Make a Million* (July 11, 1961); *The Philadelphia Story* (July 10, 1962); *Come Blow Your Horn* (June 25, 1963); *A Shot in the Dark* (June 30, 1964); *Nobody Loves an Albatross* (July 6, 1965); *The Tender Trap* (July 5, 1966); *Luv* (July 4, 1967); *The Impossible Years* (July 2, 1968); *Lovers* (July 1, 1969); and *Black Comedy/White Lies* (June 30, 1970).

He was principal of Mt. Pleasant Elementary Sch. in Elkton (Va., 1936–38); assistant principal and director of theatre of Dayton (Va.) H.S., where he directed over ten plays and taught courses in English, math, and drama (1938–42).

While a masters candidate at Catholic Univ. (1946–47), Mr. Hinkel was a part-time instructor in theatre and technical director for the theatre at Marjorie Webster Junior Coll. (Washington, D.C.). He was instructor in theatre and speech at the Univ. of Tennessee (1947–49), serving as technical director of its theatre (1947–48) and director (1948–49). Joining the staff of the Dept. of Speech and Drama upon its inception at the Univ. of Connecticut in 1949, Dr. Hinkel became the first department head of the Dept. of Theatre when it was created in 1961 as a division of the School of Fine Arts. He retired as department head in 1971 to devote full time to teaching and research, having been granted two sabbatic leaves (1966 and 1974) to study the ruins of the ancient theatres in Greece, Italy, and Asia Minor. He is currently teaching history of theatre and dramatic theory.

Published Works. Mr. Hinkel wrote *The Necessity for a Single Standard in Drama* for the University of Tennessee *News Letter* (1948).

Recreation. Baseball.

HINNANT, BILL. Actor. b. John Fletcher Hinnant, Jr., Aug. 28, 1935, Chincoteague, Va., to John F. and Leonna (Bridges) Hinnant. Father, druggist; mother, teacher. Educ. St. Andrews School, Wilmington, Del. (grad. magna cum laude, 1st in class); grad. Yale Univ., B.A. (drama) 1959. Professional training with Uta Hagen and Harold Clurman (acting); David Craig (musical comedy performing). Relative in theatre, brother, Skip Hinnant, actor. Member of AEA; SAG; AFTRA. Address: 240 W. 89th St., New York, NY 10025, tel. (212) UN 6-0993.

Theatre. Mr. Hinnant made his stage debut as Hansel in a school production of *Hansel and Gretel* (1942). His first professional work was in 1953, touring as Whitney in a revival of *Life with Mother*, starring Billie Burke, and appearing as Enoch Snow, Jr., in a summer stock production of *Carousel* (Ogunquit, Me., Playhouse). He made his N.Y.C. debut as Lt. Cover in *No Time for Sergeants* (Alvin Th., Oct. 20, 1955); appeared in a revival of *The Cradle Will Rock* (NY City Ctr., Feb. 11, 1960); was Lyle, the Giant, in *All Kinds of Giants* (Cricket, Dec. 18, 1961); appeared in the revue *Put It in Writing* (Th. de Lys, May 13, 1963); and replaced Fred Gwynne as Marvin Shellhammer in *Here's Love* (Sam S. Shubert Th., Oct. 3, 1963), later touring with the production.

He created the role of Snoopy in *Your're a Good Man, Charlie Brown* (Th. 80 St. Marks, Mar. 7, 1967); played Boy Jones in *Love Match* (opened Palace West, Phoenix, Ariz., Nov. 3, 1968; closed Ahmanson Th., Los Angeles, Calif., Jan. 4, 1969); was in the revue *The American Hamburger League* (New Th., N.Y.C., Sept. 16, 1969); and played Manuel in *Frank Merriwell, or Honour Challenged* (Longacre, Apr. 24, 1971).

Films. Mr. Hinnant appeared in *Four Boys and a Gun* (UA, 1957) and *A Nice Girl Like Me* (Avco-Embassy, 1971).

Television. Mr. Hinnant's television appearances began with the Sergeant Bilko Show (CBS, 1956). He was the NBC Page on the Perry Como Show; Bruce on Pete and Gladys; was in the Children's Folk Tales series (Masquerade, NET); appeared in a special, *Funny Papers* (CBS); recreated the role of Snoopy on *You're a Good Man, Charlie Brown* (Hallmark Hall of Fame, NBC); was on Jack Paar's *Political Special* (NBC); in *Oliver Twist* (Dupont Show of the Month, NBC); the television revue *On the Brink;* the pilot *Easy Aces;* and appeared at various times on Route 66 (CBS); Naked City (ABC); Camera Three (CBS); Today Show (NBC); Merv Griffin Show (Ind.); Danny Kaye Show (CBS); Shari Lewis Show; Pat Boone Show; Ed Sullivan Show (CBS); Phil Silvers Show (CBS); and To Tell the Truth (CBS).

Night Clubs. Mr. Hinnant appeared in Julius Monk's revues *Pick a Number, Sixteen* (Plaza 9 Room, Plaza Hotel, N.Y.C., Oct. 14, 1965); *Dressed to the Nines* (Upstairs at the Downstairs, N.Y.C.); and *Four Below Strikes Back* (Downstairs at the Upstairs, N.Y.C.).

Discography. Mr. Hinnant is on the original cast album of *You're a Good Man, Charlie Brown* and on the recording of *Dressed to the Nines* (MGM Records).

Awards. Mr. Hinnant received the Vernon Rice-Drama Desk Award (1967) for his playing of Snoopy in *You're a Good Man, Charlie Brown*. .

Recreation. Gardening, music.

HIRSCH, JOHN. Director. b. Jan. 5, 1930, Siofok, Hungary, to Joseph and Illona (Harjath) Hirsch. Grad. Gymnasium, Budapest, Hungary; Univ. of Manitoba, Canada, B.A. 1952.

Pre-Theatre. Office boy, porter, sandwich man, file clerk.

Theatre. Mr. Hirsch is founding artistic director, and artistic consultant of the Manitoba Th. Centre (Winnipeg, Canada, founded 1958), a group formed by the merger of the Winnipeg Little Th., where he worked as production stage manager (1953–57) and Theatre 77, founded by Mr. Hirsch in 1957.

His directing credits include *Peter Pan* (Vancouver International Th.); *Mother Courage* (Th. de Nouveau Monde, Montreal); for the Stratford Canada Shakespeare Festival, productions of *The Cherry Orchard* (July 26, 1965); *Henry VI* (June 7, 1966), *Richard III* (June 12, 1967), *Colours in the Dark* (July 25, 1967), *A Midsummer Night's Dream* (June 12, 1968), *The Three Musketeers* (July 22, 1968), *Hamlet* (June 9, 1969; also presented at the Univ. of Mich., Ann Arbor, Spring 1969), and *The Satyricon* (July 4, 1969). At the Manitoba Th. Ctr., recent productions include *A Man's a Man* (Nov. 2, 1970), *What the Butler Saw* (Oct. 25, 1971), *Guys and Dolls* (Feb. 5, 1973), and *The Dybbuk* (Jan. 11, 1974) which Mr. Hirsch also adapted.

He made his US directorial debut with the Repertory Co. of Lincoln Ctr. (Vivian Beaumont Th., N.Y.C.) production of *Yerma* (Dec. 8, 1966); subsequently staging *Galileo* (Apr. 13, 1967); *Saint Joan* (Jan. 4, 1968); *The Time of Your Life* (Nov. 6, 1969); *Beggar on Horseback* (May 14, 1970); *The Playboy of the Western World* (Jan. 7, 1971); and *Antigone* (May 13, 1971). Other productions directed by Mr. Hirsch include a sketch for the touring company of the National Th. for the Deaf (opened Eugene O'-Neill Mem. Th. Fdtn., Waterford, Conn., Sept. 21, 1967; closed Los Angeles, Apr. 15, 1968); *We Bombed in New Haven* (Ambassador, N.Y.C., Oct. 16, 1968); *Tyger! Tyger! and Other Burnings*, a sketch included in the repertory of the National Th. of the Deaf (Longacre, Mar. 5, 1969); *A Man's a Man* (Guthrie Th. Co., Minneapolis, Aug. 11, 1970); the Chelsea Th. Ctr. production of *AC/DC* (Brooklyn Academy of Music, Feb. 13, 1971); *A Midsummer Night's Dream* (Guthrie Th. Co., Minneapolis, July 7, 1972); and the Center Th. Group production of *The Dybbuk; Between Two Worlds*, for which he did the adaptation and choreography (Mark Taper Forum, Los Angeles, Jan. 30, 1975).

Television. Mr. Hirsch has directed numerous productions on Canadian television including *Fifteen Miles Over Broken Glass* (CBC).

Other Activities. He has served as a theatre advisor for the Canadian Center for the Performing Arts; as vice president of the Canadian Th. Center; and has been on the board of directors of the Royal Winnipeg Ballet, and the Theatre Communications Group.

Awards. Mr. Hirsch received the Outer Critics Circle Award (1966–67) for *Galileo;* and the Off-Bway (Obie) Award for Distinguished Direction (1970–71) for *AC/DC*. In addition, he was named a Leonard Memorial Scholar (1952); received a Poetry Society award (1952); the National Council of Jewish Women Award (1958); the Order of Canada Service Medal (1967); and the honorary degrees of D.Litt. from the Univ. of Manitoba (1966), and L.L.D. from the Univ. of Toronto (1967).

HIRSCHFELD, AL. Artist. b. Albert Hirschfeld, June 21, 1903. St. Louis, Mo., to Isaac and Rebecca (Rothberg) Hirschfeld. Attended Natl. Acad., 1918; Art Students League, 1920; County Council, London, Eng., 1925; Julienne's, Paris, France, 1924. Married July 13, 1927, to Florence Ruth Hobby (marr. dis. 1939); married May 18, 1943, to Dorothy Haas, actress (known as Dolly Hass); one daughter. Address: (home) 122 E. 95th St., New York, NY 10028; (bus.) c/o The New York *Times*, New York, NY 10036.

Since 1925, Mr. Hirschfeld has been theatre caricaturist for the New York *Times* His drawings, which appear in the Sunday edition, have concealed his daughter's name (NINA) in every design since her birth, Oct. 20, 1945. The exact number of NINA's hidden in the drawing is designated by a numeral immediately following Mr. Hirschfeld's signature.

He was Moscow theatre correspondent for the New York *Herald Tribune* (1927); his murals hang in the Fifth Avenue Cinema, and the Manhattan Hotel's Playbill Room (N.Y.C.); and in the Eden Roc Hotel, Miami Beach, Fla., and were on exhibit at the Brussels (Belgium) World's Fair, 1958.

His works hang permanently in the St. Louis (Mo.) Art Museum, Butler Institute of American Art, Fogg Museum, Cleveland (Ohio) Art Museum, New York Public Library, New York City Museum, Whitney Museum of American Art, Metropolitan Museum of Art, Brooklyn Museum, Museum of Modern Art, the Hyde Park Museum, Davenport (Iowa) Museum, and Magnes Museum, Berkeley, California.

Published Works. Mr. Hirschfeld's books include *Manhattan Oases* (1932), *Harlem* (1941), *Show Business Is No Business* (1951), *The American Theatre* (1961), *The World of Hirschfeld* (1972), and, in collaboration with Brooks Atkinson, *The Lively Years* (1973).

Awards. He received an American Specialist grant (1960) from the US State Dept.

HIRSON, ROGER O. Playwright. Grad. Yale Univ.

Theatre. Mr. Hirson wrote *Journey to the Day* (Th. de Lys, N.Y.C., Nov. 11, 1963); with Ketti Fringe, co-authored the book for the musical, *Walking Happy* (Lunt-Fontanne Th., Nov. 26, 1966); wrote *World War 2½* (The News, London Apr. 6, 1967; and Martinique, N.Y.C., Mar. 24, 1969); and the book for *Pippin* (Imperial, Oct. 23, 1972).

Television. He was a major contributor to dramatic programming during the 1950's and 1960's. Mr. Hirson wrote *The First Day* (CBS, 1962); and adaptations of *Ninotchka* and *Vanity Fair* (CBS, 1961); as well as numerous scripts for Playhouse 90 (CBS); Philco Playhouse (NBC); Goodyear Theatre (NBC); Studio One (CBS); Armstrong Circle Theatre (NBC); Westinghouse Television Theatre (CBS); and Sunday Showcase (NBC), among others.

HOBART, ROSE. Actress. b. Rose Kefer, May 1, 1906, New York City, to Paul and Marguerite (Buss) Kefer. Father, cellist; mother, opera singer. Attended N.Y.C. public schools. Married May 13, 1924, to Ben Webster (marr. dis. 1928); married Oct. 9, 1932, to William Grosvenor, Jr. (marr. dis. Feb. 24, 1942); married Oct. 10, 1948, to Barton H. Bosworth; one son. Member of AEA; AFTRA; SAG (board member, 1946–47). Address: 4030 Oakfield Drive, Sherman Oaks, CA 91403, tel. (213) 784-8404.

Theatre. Miss Hobart made her professional debut on the Chautauqua Circuit playing Betsy Grimsby in *Cappy Ricks* (opened Abbeville, La.; closed 18 weeks later, Billings, Mont., 1920); and toured as Louise in *Liliom* (opened Brooklyn, N.Y., Oct. 2, 1922).

She made her Bway debut as the Young Girl in *Lullaby* (Knickerbocker, Sept. 17, 1923); played Gertie in *Out of Step* (Hudson, Jan. 29, 1925); Charmian in *Caesar and Cleopatra* (Guild, Apr. 13, 1925); Miriam Hale in *Lucky Sam McCarver* (Playhouse, Oct. 21, 1925); Frida Foldal in *John Gabriel Borkman* (Booth, Jan. 29, 1926); succeeded (Feb. 1, 1926) Molly Kerr as Bunty Mainwaring in *The Vortex* (Henry Miller's Th., Sept. 26, 1925); appeared as Lady Sybil Lazenby in *What Every Woman Knows* (Bijou, Apr. 13, 1926); with the Civic Repertory Co., played Donina in *Saturday Night* (Oct. 25, 1926) and Irina in *The Three Sisters* (Nov. 8, 1926); appeared as the Lady in the Blue-Fox Fur in *Puppets of Passion* (Masque, Feb. 24, 1927); Frances Sewell in *The Fanatics* (49 St. Th., Nov. 7, 1927); and Muriel Haward in *Diversion* (49 St. Th., Jan. 11, 1928).

She made her London debut as Nona Rolf in *The Comic Artist* (Strand, June 24, 1928); played Consuelo Poole in *Crashing Through* (Republic, N.Y.C., Oct. 29, 1928); Wynne Madison in *Zeppelin* (Natl., Jan. 15, 1929); Marguerite Brace in *A Primer for Lovers* (Longacre, Nov. 18, 1929); Grazia in *Death Takes A Holiday* (Ethel Barrymore Th., Dec. 26, 1929); and Leslie in *Let Us Divorce* (Geary, San Francisco, Calif., Apr. 12, 1932).

She appeared as Cynthia Williams in *I Loved You Wednesday* (Harris, N.Y.C., Oct. 11, 1932); Fraulein von Bernberg in *Girls in Uniform* (Booth, Dec. 30, 1932); Margot Drake in *Our Wife* (Booth, March 2, 1933); and Miss Smith in *Springtime for Henry* (Ann Arbor, Mich., June 1933).

She played Marjorie in *Eight Bells* (Hudson, N.Y.C., Oct. 28, 1933); Anne Hargraves in *The Wind and the Rain* (Ritz, Feb. 1, 1934); Virginia Blaine in *With All My Heart* (Locust Valley, N.Y., July 1935); Lucy Rigby in *The Country Chairman* (Natl., N.Y.C., May 25, 1936); Cynthia Randolph in *Dear Octopus* (Broadhurst, Jan. 11, 1939); Linda in *No Time for Comedy* (Geary, San Francisco, Calif., 1941); and Maggie Cutler in *The Man Who Came to Dinner* (El Capitan, Hollywood, Calif., Sept. 19, 1941).

She played Ellen Turner, with the USO Camp Shows, in *The Male Animal* (Aleutian Islands, 1944–45); Alice Pangdon in *Deep Are the Roots* (Belasco, Los Angeles, Calif., Jan. 12, 1948; Natl., San Francisco, Calif., Feb. 14, 1948); Mother in *Years Ago* (Laguna Playhouse, Laguna Beach, Calif., Aug. 9, 1950); Lavinia Chamberlayne in *The Cocktail Party* (Biltmore, Los Angeles, Calif., Oct. 12, 1952), and on tour; Dolly de Vries in *Theatre* (Sombrero Playhouse, Phoenix, Ariz., Feb. 29, 1954; La Jolla Playhouse, Calif., Mar. 2, 1954); Serena in *Quadrille* (Pasadena Playbox, Calif., Mar. 19, 1958); Madame Clerembard in *Clerembard* (Stage Society, Los Angeles, Calif., Oct. 3, 1958); Charlotte Orr in *Critic's Choice* (Sombrero Playhouse, Phoenix, Ariz., Mar. 12, 1963); and Katherine Senesh in *The Legend of Hannah Senesh* (Princess, Hollywood, Calif., May 2, 1964).

Films. Miss Hobart made her debut in *A Lady Surrenders* (U, 1930) subsequently appeared in *Liliom* (20th-Fox, 1930); *Compromised* (Brit. Intl., 1931); *East of Borneo* (U, 1931); *Chances* (1st Natl., 1931); *Scandal for Sale* (U, 1932); *Dr. Jekyll and Mr. Hyde* (Par., 1932); *Convention Girl* (1st Division, 1935); *Tower of London* (U, 1939); *Wolf of New York* (Rep., 1940); *Susan and God* (MGM, 1940); *A Night at Earl Carroll's* (Par., 1940); *Nothing But the Truth* (Par., 1941); *Ziegfeld Girl* (MGM, 1941); *I'll Sell My Life* (Select, 1941); *Singapore Woman* (WB, 1941); *No Hands on the Clock* (Par., 1941); *Mr. and Mrs. North* (MGM, 1941); *Dr. Gillespie's New Assistant* (MGM, 1942); *Gentleman at Heart* (20th-Fox, 1942); *Who Is Hope Schuyler?* (20th-Fox, 1942); *Prison Girls* (PRC, 1942); *Salute to the Marines* (MGM, 1943); *The Mad Ghoul* (Rep., 1943); *Swingshift Maisie* (MGM, 1943); *Song of the Open Road* (UA, 1944); *Soul of a Monster* (Rep., 1944); *The Cat Creeps* (1944); *Conflict* (WB, 1945); *The Brighton Strangler* (RKO, 1945); *Claudia and David* (20th-Fox, 1946); *Canyon Passage* (U, 1946); *The Farmer's Daughter* (RKO, 1947); *The Trouble with Women* (Par., 1947); *Cass Timberlane* (MGM, 1947); *Mickey* (Eagle Lion, 1948); and *Bride of Vengeance* (Par., 1949).

Television. Miss Hobart played Sister Margaret on the Danny Thomas Show (CBS, 1960); Martha Thomas on Day in Court (1965); and Mary in Peyton Place (1966–68). She appeared also in Gunsmoke (CBS, 1967); The Possessed (1967); Cannon (CBS, 1968); The Breakthrough (1968); The King Is Dead (1970); The Invaders; The FBI; and Dan August.

HOBGOOD, BURNET. Educator, director. b. Burnet McLean Hobgood, June 23, 1922, Lotumbe, D.C.C.M., Leopoldville, Republic of the Congo, to Henry Clay and Tabitha (Alderson) Hobgood. Father and mother, missionaries. Grad. Lafayette Sch., Lexington, Ky., 1940; Transylvania Coll., B.A. 1947; Western Reserve Univ., M.A., M.F.A. 1950; Cornell Univ. (A. M. Drummond Fellowship), Ph.D. 1964. Student of Stark Young, 1956–60. Married June 1, 1947, to Jane Bishop, folk singer, choreographer; two sons, one daughter. Served US Army, 1943–46, Signal Corps, PTO; rank, T/3 Sgt. Member of ATA (formerly AETA; chmn., college curriculum project, 1956–60; admin. vice-pres., 1960–61; dir., 1960–64; 2nd vice-pres., 1968; 1st vice-pres., 1969; pres., 1970; fellow, 1971; chmn., committee on standards in educational theatre); SETC (exec. secy.-treas., 1956–58); Southwest Theatre Conference (pres., 1967); American College Theatre Festival (steering comm., 1968–70; dir. of first ACTF regional selections, 1968, 1969); Texas Educational Theatre Assn.; League of Professional Theatre Training Programs (exec. comm., 1974–to date); Amer. Society for Aesthetics; Southern Speech Assn.; SAA; ANTA; AAUP; Phi Kappa Tau (vice-pres., Theta Chapter, 1946–47); Phi Kappa Phi. Address: (home) 6810 Ellsworth Ave., Dallas, TX 75214; (bus.) Theatre Dept., Southern Methodist Univ., Dallas, TX 75275.

Mr. Hobgood was director-producer for the following outdoor historical dramas: Paul Green's *The Lost Colony* (Manteo, N.C., 1957); Kermit Hunter's *The Golden Prairie* (Decatur, Ill., 1960); Mr. Hunter's *Bound for Kentucky* (Iroquois Amphitheatre, Louisville, Ky., 1961); and Mr. Hunter's *Stars in My Crown* (Murray, Ky., 1963). Previously, he appeared as Squire Sims in *Wilderness Road* (Forest Th., Berea, Ky., 1955–56); Jefferson Davis in *The Confederacy* (Virginia Beach, Va., 1958); and as Amos Bradford in *Chucky Jack* (Gatlinburg, Tenn., 1959).

Mr. Hobgood was assistant professor and acting chairman of the Drama and Speech Dept., Catawba College, from 1950 to 1954. From 1954 to 1958, he was associate professor; from 1954 to 1961, chairman; and from 1958 to 1961, professor. He became chairman, Theatre Dept., Meadows School of the Arts, Southern Methodist Univ., and head of curricula in directing and theatre education in 1965 and professor of theatre and drama at Southern Methodist in 1967. Mr. Hobgood has directed over a hundred productions, including Sophocles' *Oedipus, the King*, which was invited to the National American College Theatre Festival, Washington, D.C., in 1972 and, among new plays, J. F. Bailey's *The Badlands* (1973).

Mr. Hobgood was founding editor of the SETC quarterly, *Southern Theatre* (1956–59); editor and writer for *The Projects Progress Newsletter* (1960); general editor of the AETA *Directory of American College Theatre* (1960); and consulting editor of the 1967 *Directory.* From 1966 to 1968, he edited books in review for *Educational Theatre Journal* and among articles he has had published in *Educational Theatre Journal* are "Theatre in U.S. Higher Education: Emerging Patterns and Problems" (May 1964); "The Concept of Experiential Learning in the Arts" (March 1971); and "Central Conceptions in Stanislavski's System" (May 1973).

Recreation. Writing, study, swimming and biking, travel.

HOBSON, HAROLD. Drama critic. b. Thorpe Hesley, Aug. 4, 1904, Yorkshire, England, to Jacob and Minnie (McKegg) Hobson. Father, insurance superintendent. Grad. Sheffield Grammar Sch., Eng.; Oriel Coll., Oxford Univ., Eng., B.A. 1928, M.A. (Modern History) 1935. Married July 13, 1935, to Gladys Bessie (Elizabeth) Johns; one daughter. Member of Beefsteak Club; M.C.C.; The Critics' Circle (councilor; pres., 1935). Address: (home) 905 Nelson House, Dolphin Sq., London, S.W.1, England tel. Victoria 3800; (bus.) 4/5 Grosvenor Place, London, S.W.1, England. Mr. Hobson has been drama critic with *The Christian Science Monitor* (1933–to date). Also, for *The Sunday Times* (London), he was assistant literary editor (1944), assistant drama critic (1944–49), and became drama critic in 1949. He was also television critic for *The Listener* (1947–51).

Published Works. Mr. Hobson's theatre criticisms have been collected in two volumes: *Theatre* (1948) and *Theatre II* (1950). He is the author of *Verdict at Midnight* (1952), *The Theatre Now* (1953), and *The French Theatre of Today* (1953); and the editor of *The International Theatre Annual* (1956–60).

Awards. Mr. Hobson was created a chevalier, Legion of Honor, France (1960) and a Commander of the Most Excellent Order of the British Empire (1971).

Recreation. Theory of bridge, cricket, reading foreign newspapers.

HOCHHUTH, ROLF. Playwright. b. Apr. 1, 1931, Eschwege, Werra, Germany, to Walter and Ilse (Holzapfel) Hochhuth. Father, shoe manufacturer. Attended Univ. of Marburg; Univ. of Munich; Univ. of Heidelberg. Married to Marianne Heinemann; two children. Address: Basel, Switzerland.

Pre-Theatre. Reader and editor for publishing company.

Theatre. Mr. Hochhuth is the author of *The Deputy* (Brooks Atkinson Th., N.Y.C., Feb. 26, 1964) which was originally presented as *Der Stellvertreter* (Th. Kurfurstendam, Berlin, Feb. 20, 1963), subsequently entitled *The Vicar,* and, in England, *The Representative* (Aldwych, London, Sept. 1963). He wrote *Soldaten* (world premiere, Freie Volksbuhne Th., Berlin, Oct. 9, 1967) which was presented in English translation as *The Soldier* (Royal Alexandria Th., Toronto, Canada, Feb. 28, 1968; and Billy Rose Th., N.Y.C., May 1, 1968).

He has also written *Guerillas* (Stuttgart, Germany, May 1970); *The Midwife* (Munich, Germany, July 1972); and *Lysistrata* (Vienna, Austria, Feb. 1974).

Published Works. His other writings include the novella, *The Berlin Antigone* (1965).

Awards. For *The Deputy,* Mr. Hochhuth received the Gerhardt-Hauptman Prize (Nov. 1962); The West German Young Generation Prize (May 1963); and the Frederic G. Melcher Book Award (May 1965).

HOCKER, DAVID. Producer, talent representative. b. June 27, 1911, Philadelphia, Pa., to Edward and Lucretia F. (Fleming) Hocker. Father, superintendent of American Ice Co. Grad. West Philadelphia H.S., 1928. Address: (home) 40 Park Ave., New York, NY 10016, tel. (212) 686-2555; (bus.) 65 E. 55th St., New York, NY 10022, tel. (212) 751-8450.

Mr. Hocker is in partnership with Chandler Warren in Hocker-Warren Productions. Previously, he was vice-president of MCA Artists, Ltd. (1948–62); president of Concert Theatre, Inc. (1943–48); and vice-president of James A. Davidson Management, Inc. He managed Robin Hood Concerts in Philadelphia (1936–45); the Concert Bureau of the Curtis Institute (1937); and the Philadelphia Orchestra Youth Concerts (1930–36).

Theatre. He packaged *More Stately Mansions,* starring Ingrid Bergman (Ahmanson, L.A., 1967; and Broadhurst, N.Y.C., Oct. 31, 1967); and, with Chandler Warren, produced *My Daughter, Your Son* (Booth, N.Y.C., May 13, 1969).

Television. He produced a series of specials entitled *Jane Goodall and the World of Animal Behavior* (ABC).

Awards. He received the Leopold Stokowski Citation for his work with the Philadelphia Orchestra (1936), having served on the board of Philadelphia Orchestra from 1933–36.

HOCTOR, HARRIET. Dancer, teacher. b. 1907, Hoosick Falls, N.Y., to Timothy and Elizabeth (Kearney) Hoctor. Father, tombstone maker. Studied dance with Louis Chalif (1918–21); Ivan Tarasoff (1921).

Theatre. Miss Hoctor made her Bway debut joining (1921) the cast of *Sally* (New Amsterdam, Dec. 21, 1920); toured in vaudeville (1923); played Henrique and was the premiere danseuse in *Topsy and Eva* (Sam H. Harris Th., N.Y.C., Dec. 23, 1924); appeared in *A La Carte* (Martin Beck Th., Aug. 17, 1927); as the premiere danseuse of the court in *The Three Musketeers* (Lyric, Mar. 13, 1928); in the revue *Show Girl* (Ziegfeld, July 2, 1929); as premiere danseuse in *Simple Simon* (Ziegfeld, Feb. 18, 1930); and in a vaudeville bill (Palace Th., May 1931).

She made her London debut in *Bow Bells* (Hippodrome, Jan. 4, 1932); appeared in *Earl Carroll's Vanities* (Bway Th., N.Y.C., Sept. 27, 1932); performed in vaudeville at Radio City Music Hall (May 1933), Roxy Th. (May 1933), and Loew's State Th. (July 1933); created and staged the ballets and appeared as premiere danseuse in *Hold Your Horses* (Winter Garden, Sept. 25, 1933); appeared in vaudeville at the Paramount (Los Angeles, Calif., Nov. 1934); and in *Ziegfeld Follies* (Winter Garden, N.Y.C., Jan. 30, 1936).

Miss Hoctor formed her own dance company and performed in *Ballet Fantasie* (St. Louis, Mo., Aug. 1936); in vaudeville, performed at the Earle Th. (Philadelphia, Pa.; Washington, D.C., Nov. 1937); at Loew's State (N.Y.C., Oct. 1939); and at the Hippodrome (Baltimore, Md., June 1940).

Films. Miss Hoctor has appeared in *The Great Ziegfeld* (MGM, 1936); and *Shall We Dance?* (RKO, 1937).

Night Clubs. She was a member of *The Casa Mañana Revue for 1937* (Fort Worth, Tex., July 1937).

Awards. She was awarded Medal of Distinction by the Dancing Masters of America (1930).

HODGE, FRANCIS RICHARD. Educator, director. b. Dec. 17, 1915, Geneva, N.Y., to Richard D. and Mabel E. (Clark) Hodge. Father, barber. Grad. Geneva H.S., 1934; Hobart Coll., B.A. 1939; Cornell Univ., M.A. 1940, Ph.D. 1948. Served USAAF, 1942–45; rank, Staff Sgt. Member of ATA; SCA; AFTR; TLA; TETA; Phi Kappa Phi. Address: (home) 1109 Bluebonnet Lane, Austin, TX 78704, tel. (512) 442-8412; (bus.) Dept. of Drama, Univ. of Texas, Austin, TX 78712, tel. (512) 471-5231.

Since 1949, Mr. Hodge has been professor of drama at the Univ. of Texas. He has held academic positions at Carroll Coll. (1940–42); Cornell Univ. (1946–48); State Univ. of Iowa (1948–49); Univ. of Colorado (Summer 1960); Univ. of British Columbia (Summer 1962); and Banff School of Fine Arts (Summers 1961, 1962, 1964–68).

During the thirty years he has been associated with educational theatre, Mr. Hodge has directed approximately seventy-five plays in the United States and Canada including: *The Glass Menagerie; Juno and the Paycock; The Devil's Disciple; Liliom; The Mikado; Morning's at Seven; The Grass Harp; Mother Courage; Fanny's First Play; Man and Superman; Les Prècieuses Ridicules; The Bald Soprano; Gamblers; Six Characters in Search of an Author; The Flowering Peach; The Dark Lady of the Sonnets; The Lark; How He Lied to Her Husband; The Shewing Up of Blanco Posnet; The Beaux' Stratagem; The Good Woman of Setzuan; Midsummer Night's Dream; Saint Joan; Doctor Faustus; The Lady from the Sea; The Winter's Tale; Henry IV, Part 1; Shoemaker's Holiday; Rhinoceros; The Caucasian Chalk Circle; The Red Peppers; The Phoenix Too Frequent; Sparkin'; Ah, Wilderness!; Idiot's Delight; The Crucible;* and *Beyond the Horizon.*

Published Works. Mr. Hodge wrote the chapter entitled "German Drama in America" in *The German Theatre Today* (1964); the introduction to Noah Ludlow's *Dramatic Life as I Found It;* "European Influences on American Theatre, 1700–1969" in *The American Theatre: A Sum of Its Parts;* "The Private Theatre Schools in the Late Nineteenth Century" in *Speech Education in America.* He is the author of *Yankee Theatre: The Image of America on the Stage, 1825–1850* (1964) and *Play Directing* (1971). He was twice associate editor of the *Educational Theatre Journal* (1952–54 and 1963–65) and its editor (1966–68), and the theatre editor of *Quarterly Journal of Speech.* He has contributed articles and book reviews to the above publications, as well as *Theatre Annual, Texas Quarterly, Western Speech Journal, Southern Speech Journal, Theatre Arts,* and *Theatre Survey.* He edited and published *Innovations in Stage and Theatre Design* for ASTR in 1972.

HOFFMAN, JANE. Actress. b. Jane Ruth Hoffman, July 24, Seattle, Wash., to Samuel Lewis and Marguerite (Kirschbaum) Hoffman. Father, salesman. Grad. Garfield H.S., Seattle, 1927; attended Univ. of Washington, 1927–28; grad. Univ. of California, B.A. 1931. Studied acting with Maria Ouspenskaya and Tamara Daykarhanova, N.Y.C., 1934–35; singing with Robert Fram, 1940–50; Actors Studio, N.Y.C. (charter mbr., 1947); acting with Paul Gordon, N.Y.C., 1947. Married July 1936, to James W. McGlone, Jr., businessman (marr. dis. 1945); married Dec. 9, 1945, to William Friedberg, writer (marr. dis. 1950); married Sept. 9, 1950, to Richard McMurray, actor; one son. Member of AEA (negotiating committee, 1950–60; magazine committee, 1957; repertory committee, 1959); AFTRA; SAG; AGVA.

Pre-Theatre. Saleslady, restaurant hostess.

Theatre. Miss Hoffman made her stage debut in an elementary school production of *Charley's Aunt* (1923); her professional debut as a walk-on in *The Poor Nut* (Henry Duff's Stock Co., Seattle, Wash., 1926); and toured in stock as the Secretary in *Personal Appearance* (N.Y., N.J., R.I., July 1936). She made her N.Y.C. debut in the revue, *'Tis of Thee* (Maxine Elliott's Th., Oct. 26, 1940); appeared in a tabloid version of *Crazy With the Heat* (opened Loew's State Th., Apr. 24, 1941; closed Buffalo, N.Y., July 15, 1941); played the Kid and understudied for the roles of Gladys and Reporter in a midwestern tour of *Pal Joey* (Jan.–Mar. 1942); appeared in *The Desert Song* and *The New Moon* (Paper Mill Playhouse, Millburn, N.J., Aug.–Sept. 1942); and understudied Betty Bruce as Betty-Jean in *Something for the Boys* (Alvin, N.Y.C., Jan. 7, 1943).

She played Rose and understudied Paula Laurence as Molly in *One Touch of Venus* (Imperial, Oct. 7, 1943); played Lotus in *Calico Wedding* (National, Mar. 7, 1945); Mrs. James in *Mermaids Singing* (Empire, Nov. 28, 1945); the Sister in *The Constant Wife* (John Drew Th., East Hampton, L.I., N.Y., July 1946); Dagmar in *The Trial of Mary Dugan* (Bucks County Playhouse, New Hope, Pa., May 1947); Marion Froude in *Biography* (Hunterdon Hills Playhouse, N.J., July 1947); Miss Evans in *A Temporary Island* (Maxine Elliott's Th., N.Y.C., Mar. 14, 1948); appeared in *Chicken Every Sunday* and *Twentieth Century* (Olney Playhouse, Md., July 1948); played Mrs Whiting in *Story for Strangers* (Royale, N.Y.C., Sept. 21, 1948); Miss Johnson in *Two Blind Mice* (Cort, Mar. 2, 1949); Liz in *The Philadelphia Story* (McCarter, Princeton, N.J., June 1949); and Stella in *Anna Lucasta* (McCarter, Princeton, N.J., July 1949; Lakewood Th., Barnsville, Pa.; Hartford Actors Th., Conn., Nov. 7, 1949).

Miss Hoffman played Flora in *The Rose Tattoo* (Martin Beck Th., N.Y.C., Feb. 3, 1951); Ada Ryan in *Tin Wedding* (Westport Country Playhouse, Conn., Sept. 1952); Mrs. Putnam and understudied Beatrice Straight as Elizabeth Proctor in *The Crucible* (Martin Beck Th., N.Y.C., Jan. 22, 1953); and at the Cecil Wood Th., appeared in *Affairs of State* and *Life with Father* (Fishkill, N.Y., Aug. 1953).

She understudied Una O'Connor as Janet Mackenzie in *Witness for the Prosecution* (Henry Miller's Th., N.Y.C., Dec. 16, 1954); played Mrs. Yang in *The Good Woman of Setzuan* (Phoenix, Dec. 18, 1956); Amy Underhill in *The Third Best Sport* (Ambassador, Dec. 30, 1958); Mommy in *The Sandbox* (Jazz Gallery, May 15, 1960); the Housewife in *Rhinoceros* (Longacre, Jan. 9, 1961); Mommy in *The American Dream* (York Playhouse, Jan. 24, 1961); Mommy in *The Sandbox,* Mother in *Picnic on the Battlefield,* Mommy in *The American Dream* and Mrs. Peep in *The Killer* in a bill of one-act plays, entitled *Theatre of the Absurd* (Cherry Lane, Feb. 11, 1962).

She appeared in the revue, *The World of Jules Pfeiffer* (Hunterdon Hills Playhouse, N.J., June 1962); played a Peasant Woman and Old Woman in *Mother Courage and Her Children* (Martin Beck Th., N.Y.C., Mar. 28, 1963); Mommy in *The American Dream* (Cherry Lane, May 28, 1963); Emilie Ducotel in *My 3 Angels* (Playhouse-on-the-Mall, Paramus, N.J.); Mrs. Bennington in *Fair Game for Lovers*

(Cort, N.Y.C., Feb. 10, 1964); Mlle. Suisson in *A Murderer Among Us* (Morosco, Mar. 25, 1964); Mommy in *The American Dream* (Cherry Lane, Apr. 21, 1964); and the Nurse in *Medea* (Lib. of Congress, Washington, D.C., May 4–5, 1964). She played Charity Perrin in *The Child Buyer* (Garrick, 1974); Mrs. Antrolius in *The Skin of Our Teeth*, Nerine in *The Scoundrel Scapin*, the Countess in *All's Well That Ends Well*, the Old Woman in *The Chairs*, and Flora in *A Slight Ache* (Stanford Repertory Th., Univ. of Stanford, Calif., 1965–66); the Wife in *Inadmissable Evidence*, the Gossip Columnist in *Once in a Lifetime*, and Mrs. Peachum in *The Beggars Opera* (Stanford Repertory, 1966–67 season).

She was Agnes in *A Delicate Balance* (summer tour, June–Aug. 1967); Mrs. Coffman in *Come Back, Little Sheba* and Stella in *Light Up the Sky* (Mineola Th., Summer 1968); Grandma in *The Corner of the Bed* (Gramercy Arts, Feb. 26, 1969); Mrs. Gershon in *Someone's Comin Hungry* (Pocket, Mar. 31, 1969); Mrs. Croft in *The Killing of Sister George* (Tappanzee Playhouse, Apr. 21, 1969); a member of the revue *The American Hamburger League* (New Th., Sept. 16, 1969); Vlasta Huml in *Increased Difficulty of Concentration* (Forum, Dec. 4, 1969); Mother in *Shaw Memories* (ANTA, Nov. 16, 1970); Tante Frumkah in *The Last Analysis* (Circle in the Square, 1971); and Lady Mount-Temple in *Dear Oscar* (Playhouse, Nov. 16, 1972).

Films. Miss Hoffman made her debut dubbing in the voice of Chemda in *My Father's House* (Kline-Levin, 1947); subsequently played a Social Worker in a film for the Greater NY Fund, Lexington Sch. for the Deaf (1954); a Party Worker in an election film, sponsored by the Ford Foundation, titled *Where Were You?* (1960); Mrs. Hayworth in *Ladybug, Ladybug* (UA, 1964); the interviewer in *Where's Poppa?* (UA, 1971); the Information Operator in *They Might Be Giants* (U, 1971); the Mother in *Up the Sandbox* (Col., 1972).

Television. Miss Hoffman has appeared on Actors Studio (ABC, 1948); Goodyear Television Playhouse (NBC, 1953; 1954); Alcoa Hour (NBC, 1957); Camera Three (CBS, 1958); Big Story (NBC, 1958); Look Up and Live (CBS, 1959); played the Housekeeper in *Waltz of the Toreadors* (Play of the Week, WNTA, 1959); appeared in the serial Edge of Night (CBS, 1960); on Route 66 (CBS, 1961); played Mommy in *The Sandbox* (Fierce, Funny and Far Out, Feb. 27, 1961); appeared on The Defenders (CBS, 1962); Naked City (ABC, 1962); East Side/West Side (CBS, 1963); and Love of Life (1963). Since 1972, she has been playing Mrs. Shannon on Love of Life (CBS). She has appeared on several educational television specials and several commercials.

HOFFMAN, THEODORE. Educator, playwright, critic. b. Theodore Joseph Clegg Hoffman, July 4, 1922, Brooklyn, N.Y., to Theodore Joseph and Ethel Margaret (Clegg) Hoffman. Father, baseball player, clerk. Attended James Madison H.S., Brooklyn, 1937–39; grad. McBurney Sch., N.Y.C., 1940; Columbia Univ., A.B. 1944; M.A. 1953. Married July 4, 1950, to Lynn Baker; three daughters. Member of Theatre Communications Group (chmn., executive comm., 1960–to date); AETA (bd. of dir., 1960–63); Pittsburgh Press Club.

Mr. Hoffman is professor of drama at NY Univ. School of the Arts where he began his association as director of the theatre program (1960). From 1962–64, Mr. Hoffman was visiting professor of drama at Stanford Univ. Previously, he was associate professor (1958–61) and professor (1961–62) of drama and head of the Drama Dept., Coll. of Fine Arts, Carnegie Inst. of Tech.; visiting assistant professor, Univ. of California (1957–58) assistant professor, director of theatre (1953–57) and chairman (1956–57), Div. of Art, Music, Drama, and Dance, Bard Coll.; and has directed university productions at the colleges in which he has taught (1953–to date).

He was a teacher at Professional Children's Sch., N.Y.C., (1952–53); European director, Salzburg Seminar in American Studies, Salzburg, Austria (1948–50); taught part-time for US Armed Forces Troop Education Program (1948–50), teaching American literature, and psychology.

Mr. Hoffman has produced the International Th. Festival in Salzburg, Austria, which included eleven plays performed by European theatre groups (June 1950). He has acted and directed at the East Chop Playhouse (Martha's Vineyard, Mass., Summer 1953) playing the Arab in *Time of Your Life*. He directed *No Exit* (Open Door, N.Y.C., Jan. 1954); and wrote *Rich, But Happy* (Playwrights' Th., Chicago, Ill., Dec. 1954); his translation of *An Italian Straw Hat* was produced in England (Th. Royal, Stratford, Nov. 22, 1955); and he directed and produced a Gridiron show (Pittsburgh Playhouse, Pa., 1960).

Films. From 1946–47, for Loew's Intl. Corp. (N.Y.C.), Mr. Hoffman coordinated translation of main titles into foreign languages; and was publicist for educational 16mm films in foreign countries. He has also written and edited 18 educational movie shorts for MGM (France, 1947–48).

Television and Radio. Mr. Hoffman has appeared on radio as an actor and announcer (WNYC, N.Y., 1943–45). He has been director, producer, and commentator for educational television programs (WQED, Pittsburgh, Pa., 1958–62); and was writer and director of a musical revue, *Tove* (WQED, 1960).

Other Activities. He is a former associate editor of the *Tulane Drama Review;* has lectured on American literature and drama for the US State Dept. in Germany and Austria (1949–50); and has also lectured at such universities as Oxford, Tulane, and Pennsylvania.

He is associate editor of *Alternative Theatre* and served as drama critic for the NY *Herald Tribune*, and the Westinghouse "Group W" Broadcasting Network.

Published Works. He edited and translated (with Eric Bentley) *The Brute and Other Farces by Chekhov* (1958), and has translated plays including *Wozzeck, Celimare*, and *Ruzzante Returns from the Wars*. Mr. Hoffman has contributed articles to publications including *Variety, The Kenyon Review, Partisan Review, Theatre Arts, Educational Theatre Journal*, New York *Times, Tulane Drama Review, The New Republic*, and *Dramatists' Bulletin*.

With Kenneth M. Cameron, Mr. Hoffman is the author of The Theatrical Response (Macmillan, 1969); and Guide to Theatre Study (1974).

Awards. He has received the Columbia Univ. Boar's Head Prize for Poetry (1943) and for Prose (1944); Philolexian Centennial Award for Oratory (1944); Playwrights' Theatre Prize (1954); and has been a Kenyon Review Fellow in Dramatic Criticism (1956).

HOFFMAN, WILLIAM M. Playwright, director, educator, editor. b. Apr. 12, 1939, New York City, to Morton and Johanna (Papiermeister) Hoffman. Father, caterer; mother, jeweler. Grad. Bronx H.S. of Science, N.Y.C.; City College of New York, B.A. (*cum laude*, Phi Beta Kappa; majored in Latin) 1960. Relative in theatre: Wolf Younin, playwright, poet. Member of ASCAP; NY Theatre Strategy (a founder). Address: (home) 199 Prince St., New York, NY 10012; (bus.) c/o Helen Merrill, 337 W. 22nd St., New York, NY 10011, tel. (212) 924-6314.

Theatre. The first play by Mr. Hoffman that was performed was *Thank You, Miss Victoria* (Caffe Cino, N.Y.C., Aug. 17, 1965); it was subsequently presented on the program *6 from La Mama* (Martinique Th., Apr. 12, 1966). Later plays include *Saturday Night at the Movies* (Caffe Cino, 1966); *Good Night, I Love You* (Caffe Cino, 1966); *Spring Play* (La Mama ETC, 1967); *Three Masked Dances* (La Mama ETC, 1967); *Uptight!*, a musical (Old Reliable Th., 1968); "*xxxxx*," also directed by Mr. Hoffman (Old Reliable, Aug. 5, 1969); *Luna*, directed by Mr. Hoffman (Old Reliable, 1970); and *A Quick Nut Bread To Make Your Mouth Water*, also directed by Mr. Hoffman (Old Reliable, 1970).

The presentation of "*xxxxx*" in London (Open Space, 1970) was the first performance of a Hoffman play in England; this work has also been presented in Amsterdam, Antwerp, and in French theatres. Mr. Hoffman also directed *First Death* (Extension Th., N.Y.C., 1972); directed several presentations of his *A Quick Nut Bread to Make Your Mouth Water* (Changing Scene, Denver, Col., 1972; Manhattan Theatre Club, N.Y.C., 1973; La Mama, Hollywood, Calif., 1974); wrote *From Fool to Hanged Man* (Clark Center, N.Y.C., 1972); *The Children's Crusade* (Clark Center, 1972); and *I Love Ya, Ya Big Ape*, which he also directed (Univ. of Massachusetts, Boston, 1973).

Other Activities. Mr. Hoffman is director of The Wolf Company, which he founded; it is a nonprofit organization of writers, actors, and stage technicians devoted to exploring and furthering theatrical experience. He has taught in college and high school. In 1960–61, he was an editorial assistant with Barnes & Noble, publishers, and from 1961 to 1968 he was an assistant editor, associate editor, and drama editor with Hill & Wang. He has been editor of Hill & Wang's *New American Plays* series since 1968. Mr. Hoffman was a lecturer for the Theatre Discussion Series, Eugene O'Neill Foundation; is literary adviser, *Scripts* magazine (1971–to date); and was drama adviser, Cable Arts Foundation (1973); and visiting lecturer in theatre arts, Univ. of Minnesota (1973). He was artist-in-residence, The Changing Scene, Denver, Col., under a grant from the Colorado Council of the Arts, in 1972 and artist-in-residence, Lincoln Center Student Program in 1971–72.

Published Works. Mr. Hoffman wrote the lyrics for the song cycle *The Cloisters*, composed by John Corigliano (1968). He is author also of *Fine Frenzy* (1972), and his poetry appears in *31 New American Poets* (1970). He edited and wrote introductions for *New American Plays*, vols. 2, 3, 4 (1968, 1970, 1971).

Awards. Mr. Hoffman was awarded a MacDowell Fellowship (1971) in playwriting; a P.E.N. playwriting grant (1972); and a Guggenheim Fellowship (1974) in creative writing for the theatre.

Recreation. Table tennis.

HOLBROOK, HAL. Actor, writer. b. Harold Rowe Holbrook, Jr., Feb. 17, 1925, Cleveland, Ohio, to Harold Rowe and Aileen (Davenport) Holbrook. Mother, chorus girl. Grad. Culver Military Acad., 1942; Denison Univ., B.A. 1948. Studied acting at the H.B. (Herbert Berghof) Studio, N.Y.C., 1953; singing with George Griffin, 1956–58. Married Sept. 22, 1945, to Ruby Elaine Johnston (marr. dis.); one son, one daughter. Married Dec. 28, 1966, to Carol Rossen, actress. Relative in theatre: great-uncle, George H. Rowe, actor. Served US Army Corps of Engineers, 1943–46; rank, Pvt. Member of AEA; AFTRA; SAG; Intl. Platform Assn.; Mark Twain Memorial Assn.; Ad Hoc Drama Panel (State Dept. Cultural Exchange Program); The Players; The Lambs.

Theatre. Mr. Holbrook made his first professional appearance with a stock company where he played in *The Man Who Came to Dinner, The Vagabond King*, and *In Time to Come* (Cain Park Th., Cleveland, Ohio, 1942); subsequently spent four seasons in stock, appearing in *Three Men on a Horse, The Male Animal, George Washington Slept Here, Our Town, The Guardsman, The Constant Wife*, and directing *The Winslow Boy* (Denison Univ., Granville, Ohio, 1947–50); teaming with his wife, Ruby Johnston, presented scenes of famous characters from the classics, on tour (Winters 1948–53); and appeared with the Valley Players (Holyoke, Mass., 1951–52).

He first appeared in his original one-man show, *Mark Twain Tonight!* (The Purple Onion, N.Y.C., Feb. 1955; The Upstairs at the Duplex, Oct. 1955–Apr. 1956); performed in a musical version of *The Doctor in Spite of Himself* (Westport Country Playhouse, Conn., Summer 1958); appeared in his *Mark Twain Tonight!* (41 St. Th., N.Y.C., Apr. 6, 1959); toured with *Mark Twain Tonight!* (1963); and auspices of the US State Dept. and ANTA, in the US; throughout Europe; and in Saudi Arabia

(1959–60; 1960–61).

He played the Man in *Do You Know the Milky Way?*(Billy Rose Th., N.Y.C., Oct. 16, 1961); at the American Shakespeare Festival (Stratford, Conn.), he played John of Gaunt, Duke of Lancaster in *Richard II* (June 16, 1962), and Hotspur in *Henry IV, Part 1* (June 17, 1962); toured in *Mark Twain Tonight!* (Fall 1962); played Abraham Lincoln in the Phoenix Th. production of *Abe Lincoln in Illinois* (Anderson, N.Y.C., Jan. 21, 1963); Andrew Mackerel in a tour of *The Mackerel Plaza*(Westport Country Playhouse, Conn.; Westchester County Playhouse, Dobbs Ferry, N.Y.; the Fayetteville Country Playhouse, N.Y.; Brown Th., Louisville, Ky., Summer 1963); toured the US with *Mark Twain Tonight!*(1963); and with the Repertory Th. of Lincoln Center, played the Reverend Harley Barnes in *After the Fall*(ANTA Washington Sq. Th., Jan. 23, 1964), and Marco Polo in *Marco Millions* (ANTA Washington Sq. Th., Feb. 20, 1964); and alternated with Jason Robards, Jr., as Quentin, in *After the Fall* (ANTA Washington Sq. Th., July 4, 1964).

As a member of the Repertory Theatre of Lincoln Center company, Mr. Holbrook played a Major in *Incident at Vichy*(ANTA Washington Sq. Th., Dec. 3, 1964); and M. Loyal and Prologue in *Tartuffe* (Jan. 14, 1965); succeeded (Aug. 18, 1965) Pat Hingle in the role of the Gentleman Caller in *The Glass Menagerie* (Brooks Atkinson Th., N.Y.C., May 4, 1965); returned to Bway in his one-man show, *Mark Twain Tonight!* (Longacre, Mar. 23, 1966); substituted (Apr. 6–July 5, 1967) for Alan Alda in the roles of Adam, Captain Sanjar, and Prince Charming in *The Apple Tree* (Sam S. Shubert Th., Oct. 18, 1966); played Gene Garrison in *I Never Sang for My Father* (Longacre, Jan. 25, 1968); during Jose Ferrer's vacation, played Cervantes and Don Quixote in *Man of La Mancha*(Martin Beck Th., July 1968); played Mr. Winters in *Does a Tiger Wear a Necktie?* (Belasco, Feb. 25, 1969); and Winnebago in *Lake of the Woods* (Amer. Place Th., Dec. 22, 1971).

Films. Mr. Holbrook played Gus LeRoy in *The Group* (UA, 1966); Senator Fergus in *Wild in the Streets* (AI, 1968); David Hoffman in *The People Next Door* (Avco-Embassy, 1970); Cameron in *The Great White Hope*(20th-Fox, 1971); Watkins in *They Only Kill Their Masters* (MGM, 1972); Lt. Briggs in *Magnum Force* (WB, 1973); Joe in *The Girl from Petrovka* (U, 1974); and provided the Elder's Voice in *Jonathan Livingston Seagull* (Par., 1973).

Television and Radio. In the Army, he broadcast on the Special Services radio programs, including the Army Engineer Show (ABC, 1946). On television, he has appeared on Hollywood Screen Test (ABC, 1953); The Brighter Day (CBS, Jan. 4, 1954–July 1959); as Mark Twain on the Tonight Show (NBC, 1956), the Ed Sullivan Show (CBS, 1956), and The Sound of Laughter (NBC, 1958); I Remember Mama (CBS, 1958); played in scenes from *Abe Lincoln in Illinois,* on the Ed Sullivan Show (CBS, 1963), and portrayed Abraham Lincoln in the series Exploring (NBC, 1963).

His aging techniques for the title role in *Mark Twain Tonight!* were featured on a segment of The Frank McGee Report series (NBC, 1966); and he subsequently recreated the role of Twain for television (CBS, 1967).

He played Tom in *The Glass Menagerie* (CBS); appeared in *The Cliff Dwellers* (ABC); on segments of Coronet Blue (CBS); and The F.B.I. (ABC); played the title role in the series Travis Logan, D.A. (CBS); and in *The Senator,* as part of The Bold Ones (NBC); and appeared in *A Clear and Present Danger* (NBC); *Suddenly Single* (ABC); *That Certain Summer* (ABC); and *Pueblo* (ABC).

Awards. For his performance in *Mark Twain Tonight!,* Mr. Holbrook received a Vernon Rice Award (1959); a *Village Voice* (Obie) Award (1959); the Outer Circle Award (1959); a special citation from the NY Drama Critic's Circle (1966), and an Antoinette Perry (Tony) Award (1966). He received the NATAS (Emmy) Award for Best Actor (1970) for his performance in *The Senator*(The Bold Ones, NBC).

Mr Holbrook has received The Torch of Liberty award of the Anti-Defamation League of B'nai B'rith (1972).

Recreation. Swimming, skiing, mountain climbing.

HOLDER, GEOFFREY. Dancer, director, costume designer, choreographer, singer, writer, painter. b. Geoffrey Lamont Holder, Aug. 1, 1930, Port-of-Spain, Trinidad, W.I., to Arthur and Louise (De Frense) Holder. Father, sales rep. Attended Queens Royal Coll., Port-of-Spain, Trinidad, 1948. Married June 26, 1955, to Carmen De Lavallade, dancer; one son. Relative in theatre: brother, Boscoe Holder, choreographer, dancer, painter. Member of AGVA; AFTRA; AGMA; SAG; AEA. Address: 215 W. 92nd, New York, NY 10025, tel. (212) 873-9474.

Pre-Theatre. Worked for the Govt. of Trinidad, Port Services.

Theatre. Mr. Holder first appeared on the stage with his brother's dance company in Trinidad (1942); took charge of the touring company in 1950; subsequently the group performed in Puerto Rico and throughout the Islands (1953); he and his company made their first appearances in the US in 1953 (Castle Hill, Mass.; White Barn Th., Westport, Conn.; the Jacob's Pillow Dance Festival, Lee, Mass.); and reappeared at the latter theatre for five alternate years. With three members of his company, he made his Bway debut in *House of Flowers* (Alvin, Dec. 30, 1954); appeared as solo dancer at the Metropolitan Opera in *Aida* and *La Perichole* (1956–57); was solo dancer in *Show Boat* (Marine Th., Jones Beach, L.I., Summer 1957); appeared with the Geoffrey Holder Dance Company in two concerts each year at the Kaufmann Aud. (YMHA, N.Y.C., 1956–60); played Lucky in *Waiting for Godot* (Ethel Barrymore Th., Jan. 21, 1957); appeared at Theatre Under the Stars (Central Park, N.Y.C., June 1957); Radio City Music Hall (Nov. 1957); and the Festival of Two Worlds (Spoleto, Italy, 1958).

He designed costumes and appeared with the John Butler Dance Theatre (Kaufmann Aud.., YMHA, N.Y.C., 1958); was choreographer for *Brouhaha* (Folkesbiene Playhouse, Apr. 26, 1960); played in Shakespearean works, including *Twelfth Night,* (Cambridge Drama Festival, Mass., July 1960); danced in the Vancouver (B.C.) Festival (Aug. 1960); was solo dancer at the International Festival in Lagos, Nigeria (1962); and appeared with his group at the Harkness Dance Festival N.Y.C. (Delacorte Th., Central Park, Sept., 1963).

He choreographed the Actors Studio production of *Mhil Daiim* (Mar. 1964); danced with Josephine Bakers's Revue (Brooks Atkinson Th., Feb. 4, 1964), and on tour, followed by a return engagement (Henry Miller's Th., Mar. 31, 1964); and at the Jacob's Pillow Dance Festival (Lee, Mass.) did choreography and costumes for *Three Songs for One* and costumes for *The Twelve Gates* (both Ted Shawn Th., Aug. 11–15, 1964). His costumes and choreography were used in various programs of the Rebekah Harkness Foundation Dance Festival (Delacorte Th., N.Y.C., Aug. 30–Sept. 7, 1966); he did the choreography for *I Got a Song* (closed before Bway, Buffalo Studio Arena, Buffalo, N.Y., Sept. 26–Oct. 20, 1974); and he directed and designed costumes for *The Wiz* (Majestic, N.Y.C., Jan. 5, 1975).

Films. Mr. Holder danced in the British film *All Night Long* (Pinewood, 1961).

Television. He first appeared with his dance company in *Stage Your Number* (1953); later in *Aladdin* (CBS, 1958); and *The Bottle Imp* (US Steel Hour, 1958); choreographed productions for Station WELI in Boston, Mass., (1959); choreographed and was solo dancer (CBS, 1962; became drama critic for WNBC-TV (1973).

Night Clubs. Mr. Holder appeared as a dancer and singer at the Cocoanut Grove, Los Angeles, Calif. (Dec. 1957); Hotel Americana in Miami Beach, Fla. (1957); Village Gate, N.Y.C., (1959–60); and the Arpeggio, N.Y.C. (1960).

Other Activities. Mr. Holder has had exhibitions of his paintings at the Barbados Museum (San Juan, Puerto Rico); the Barone Gallery (N.Y.C., 1955–59); theatre portraits in the Gallery of the Brooks Atkinson Th. (N.Y.C., Sept. 1960); the Gropper Gallery (Cambridge, Mass., 1961); the Griffin Gallery (N.Y.C., 1963); and Grinnel Galleries (Detroit, Mich., Mar. 23–Apr. 17, 1964).

Published Works. With Tom Harshman, he wrote five novellas entitled *Black Gods, Green Islands* (1957); he wrote *Geoffrey Holder's Caribbean Cookbook* (1974); and he has contributed articles to the New York *Times Magazine, Show, The Saturday Review,* and *Playbill.*

Discography. He has recorded albums of West Indian songs (Riverside Records) and an album of Song Stories (Mercury).

Awards. He received a Guggenheim Fellowship in painting (1957); the United Caribbean Youth Award (1962); and for *The Wiz* received a Drama Desk Award (1975) for costume design and an Antoinette Perry (Tony) Award (1975) as best director of a musical.

HOLLAND, ANTHONY. Actor. b. James Gardiner Holland, Oct. 17, 1933, Brooklyn, N.Y., to Myron and Edith (Gardiner) Holland. Father, shoe business. Grad. Francis W. Parker H.S., Chicago, Ill.; Univ. of Chicago, B.A., 1955. Studied acting with Lee Strasberg, N.Y.C., 1956–58; Fanny Bradshaw, N.Y.C., 1958. Married Aug. 24, 1954, to Barbara Lust (marr. dis. 1957). Member of AEA; AFTRA; SAG; AGVA. Address: 201 W. 16th St., New York, NY 10011.

Pre-Theatre. Teacher.

Theatre. Mr. Holland made his first stage appearance as General Burgovne in *The Devil's Disciple* (Francis W. Parker H.S., Chicago, Ill.); and made his professional debut as Azdak in *The Caucasian Chalk Circle* (Playwrights Th., Chicago, 1954); subsequently played Lentullus in *Androcles and the Lion* (Studebaker, Chicago, Oct. 1956); Lucky in *Waiting for Godot* (Ann Arbor Drama Festival, Mich., July 1958); Antonio in *Venice Preserved* (Phoenix Th. sideshow, N.Y.C., 1956); appeared as a walk-on in *The Duchess of Malfi* (Phoenix, Mar. 19, 1957); and played Jud Steiner in *Compulsion,* and Apples in *A Hatful of Rain* (Woodstock Summer Th., N.Y., 1957).

He played Prisoner C in *The Quare Fellow* (Circle in the Square, N.Y.C., Nov. 22, 1958); appeared in *Second City* (Second City, Chicago, Ill., 1960–61; Square East, N.Y.C., 1961); left the cast to play Bernie Halpern in *My Mother, My Father and Me* (Plymouth, Mar. 23, 1963); returned to *Second City* and toured with *Second City* (opened Royal Alexandra, Toronto, Can., 1963); appeared in the revue *Dynamite Tonight* (York, N.Y.C., Mar. 15, 1964); and in *The New Tenant* and *Victims of Duty* (Writers Stage, May 24, 1964).

Mr. Holland portrayed various roles with the (Washington, D.C.) Arena Theatre (1966), and with the Yale Repertory Theatre (New Haven, Conn., 1967); appeared in *We Bombed in New Haven* (Ambassador, N.Y.C., Oct. 16, 1968); *The White House Murder Case* (Circle in the Square, N.Y.C., Feb. 18, 1970); *Waiting for Godot* (Sheridan Square Th., N.Y.C., Feb. 3, 1971); directed Terrence McNally's *The Tubs* (Yale Repertory Th., New Haven, Conn., 1973–74 season); and appeared in *Dreyfus in Rehearsal* (Ethel Barrymore Th., N.Y.C., Oct. 17, 1974).

Films. Mr. Holland has appeared in Bye Bye, Braverman (WB-Seven Arts, 1968); Midnight Cowboy (UA, 1969); The Out-of-Towners (Par. 1970); Lovers and Other Strangers (Cinerama, 1970); Klute (WB, 1971); Hammersmith Is Out (Cinerama, 1972); and Hearts of the West (1974).

Television. He has appeared on I Stand Accused (WGN, Chicago, 1954); Camera Three (CBS, 1962); Open End (WNTA, 1962); Doctor Kildare (ABC, 1963); Combat (ABC, 1963); Dupont Show of the Month (NBC, 1963); the Steve Allen Show (Syndicate, 1964); ABC Comedy News (ABC, 1973); M*A*S*H (CBS, 1973); Love, American Style (ABC, 1973); and the Mary Tyler Moore

Show (CBS, 1974).

Awards. Mr. Holland received the Village Voice Off-Bway (Obie) Award, and the NY Critic's Poll Award for best supporting actor for his performance in *The White House Murder Case* (1970).

Recreation. Reading.

HOLLAND, BETTY LOU. Actress. b. Dec. 25, 1931, New York City, to Horace B. and Eleanor (Bosley) Holland. Father, coal executive. Attended Spence H.S., N.Y.C., until age 15, when she entered theatre career and private tutoring. Studied with Wynn Handman, Harold Clurman, Fanny Bradshaw, and Charles Weidman. Married Jan. 28, 1962, to Robert A. Cordier, director; one daughter. Relative in theatre: Bosley Crowther, film critic. Member of AEA; SAG; AFTRA. Address: (home) 1158 Fifth Ave, New York, NY 10029, tel. (212) TE 1-2630; (bus.) c/0 Jane Broder, New York, NY tel. (212) MU 8-0960.

Theatre. Miss Holland made her Bway debut as actress, singer and dancer in the revue *Call Me Mister*(National Th., Apr. 18, 1946; succeeded (Dec. 1, 1947) Betty Anne Nyman as Winnie Tate in *Annie Get Your Gun* (Imperial, May 16, 1946); Carol in *Goodbye, My Fancy*(Morosco, Nov. 17, 1948); Essie in *The Devil's Disciple*(NY City Ctr., Jan. 25, 1950); was understudy to Julie Harris as Frankie Addams in *The Member of the Wedding* (Empire, Jan. 5, 1950), and played the role on tour (opened Cass, Detroit, Mich., Sept. 3, 1951; closed Shubert, New Haven, Conn., May 3, 1952); and succeeded (June 1, 1953) Kim Stanley as Millie in *Picnic*(Music Box, N.Y.C., Feb. 19, 1953).

She played Ruby in *Kilgo Run* (Bucks County Playhouse, Pa., Summer 1954); Leila in *Palm Tree in a Rose Garden* (tour, Summer 1955); the Stepdaughter in *Six Characters in Search of an Author* (Phoenix, N.Y.C., Dec. 1, 1955); Linsie in the pre-Bway tryout of *The Diamond Rattler* (Boston, Mass., May 16, 1960); and Margaret of Anjou in *The White Rose and The Red*(Stage 73, N.Y.C., Mar. 16, 1964).

At the Playhouse in the Park (Cincinnati, Ohio), she played Regina Engstrand in *Ghosts* (Apr. 7, 1965) and on a double-bill, Stella in *The Collection* and Sarah in *The Lover*(Apr. 28, 1965); and played Celia in *The Exhaustion of Our Son's Love* (Cherry Lane Th., N.Y.C., Oct. 18, 1965), which appeared on a double-bill with *Good Day.*

She has given concert readings of the works of Yeats and Gide at the Donnell Library and Irish Institute, N.Y.C.

Films. Miss Holland made her screen debut in *The Goddess*(Col., 1958); and has appeared in *The Man in the Net*(UA, 1959).

Television. Miss Holland made her television debut on Studio One (CBS, 1952); subsequently appeared in *Johnny Belinda* (NBC, 1959); *The Devil and Daniel Webster*(NBC, 1960); and *Decoy*(CBS).

Recreation. Swimming, music, reading, languages.

HOLLAND, R. V. Educator. b. Reginald V. Holland, June 4, 1916, Cadillac, Mich., to Valentine V. and Amelia C. (Schmelling) Holland. Grad. Northwestern Univ., B.S. 1939; Michigan State Univ., M.A. 1948; Cornell Univ., Ph.D. 1951. Married June 14, 1941, to Beryl F. Holland, teacher; two daughters. Served USN, 1941–46; USNR, 1941–62. Member of Texas Speech Assn. (exec. secy., 1958–61); AETA; SAA; SSA; AAUP; SWTC; Alpha Delta Phi. Address: 1421 Kendolph, Denton, TX tel. 382-2244; Dept. of Speech, Communication and Drama, North Texas State Univ., Denton, TX 76203.

Mr. Holland has been active in educational theatre since 1939.

Since 1951, he has been director of speech and drama at North Texas State University. He has held academic positions at Michigan State Univ. (1939–40); Muskegon H.S. (1940–41); Michigan State Univ. (1946–48); and Cornell Univ. (1948–51).

Awards. Mr. Holland received a fellowship from Cornell Univ. (1948); and was chosen as an outstanding member of the faculty at North Texas State Univ. (1960).

HOLLOWAY, STANLEY. Actor, singer. b. Stanley Augustus Holloway, Oct. 1, 1890, London, England, to George and Florence Mary (Bell) Holloway. Attended private school in London. Studied voice with Ferdinando Guarino, Milan, Italy. Married Jan. 2, 1939, to Violet Marion Lane. Served WW I, Connaught Rangers, France. Member of SAG; AEA; AFTRA; British AEA; The Garrick Club; The Green Room Club. Address: (home) Pyefleet, Tamarisk Way, East Preston, Sussex, England; (bus.) 42 Welbeck St., London W1, England; "Nightingales" Penn., Buckinghamshire, England.

Theatre. Mr. Holloway made his N.Y.C. debut as Bottom in *A Midsummer Night's Dream* (Metropolitan Opera House, Sept. 21, 1954); subsequently played Alfred P. Doolittle in *My Fair Lady* (Mark Hellinger Th., Mar. 15, 1956); presented his one-man show, *Laughs and Other Events*(Ethel Barrymore Th., Oct. 10, 1960); and appeared in several roles in the pre-Bway tryout of *Cool Off!* (Forrest Th., Philadelphia, Pa., Mar. 31–Apr. 4, 1964).

Mr. Holloway first appeared on the stage as a boy singer (1905), and made his professional debut in a British Concert Party (1910); subsequently appeared as Captain Wentworth in *Kissing Time*(Winter Garden, London, May 20, 1919); Rene in *A Night Out* (Winter Garden, Sept. 18, 1920); was an original member of the company of *The Co-Optimists* (Royalty, June 27, 1921), and appeared with the group in England and in Paris (Th. Edouard VII, 1926) until it disbanded in 1927; appeared as Bill Smith in *Hit the Deck* (Hippodrome, London, Nov. 3, 1927); Lt. Richard Manners in *Song of the Sea* (His Majesty's, Sept. 6, 1928); appeared in the revue, *Cooee*(Vaudeville, Apr. 1929); *The Co-Optimists* (Vaudeville, July 8, 1929; Hippodrome, Apr. 1930); the revue, *Savoy Follies* (Savoy, July 1932); the revue, *Here We Are Again* (Lyceum, Oct. 1932); appeared as Eustace Titherley in *Three Sisters* (Drury Lane, Apr. 1934).

Mr. Holloway played Abanazar in the pantomine *Aladdin* (Prince of Wales's, Birmingham, Dec. 1934; Leeds, Dec. 1935; Golder's Green, London, Dec. 1936; Edinburgh, Scotland, Dec. 1937; and Manchester, England, Dec. 1938).

He appeared in the revue *All Wave* (Duke of York's, Nov. 1936); the revue, *London Rhapsody* (Palladium, Apr. 1938); toured in *All the Best* (opened June 1938); appeared in the revue, *Up and Doing* (Saville, London, Apr. 17, 1940; May 20, 1941); the revue, *Fine and Dandy* (Saville, Apr. 30, 1942); played Squire Skinflint in *Mother Goose* (Casino, Dec. 20, 1946); and the First Gravedigger in *Hamlet* (New, May 17, 1951).

At the Edinburgh (Scotland) Festival, with the Old Vic Co., he played Bottom in *A Midsummer Night's Dream* (Summer 1954), in which he subsequently toured Canada and the US and in N.Y.C. (see above). Mr. Holloway appeared in 1970 at the Shaw Festival, Niagara on the Lake, Ontario, Canada, as Burgess in *Candida* (Court House Th.); he was in *Siege* (London, 1971); and in 1973 again appeared at the Shaw Festival in Ontario in *You Never Can Tell* (June 1973).

He has made frequent appearances in variety theatres throughout England, performing humorous monologues and songs. The song "Albert and the Lion" is especially identified with Mr. Holloway.

Films. He made his debut in *The Rotters* (Elstree, 1921); his other films include *The Way Ahead* (20th-Fox, 1945); *Brief Encounter* (U, 1946); *This Happy Breed* (U, 1947); *Hamlet* (U, 1948); and *The Lavender Hill Mob* (U, 1951). He repeated his performance as Alfred Doolittle in the motion picture version of *My Fair Lady* (WB, 1964); was in *In Harm's Way* (Par., 1965); *Operation Snafu* (Amer. Intl., 1965); *Ten Little Indians* (7 Arts, 1966); *The Sandwich Man* (Rank, 1966); *Mrs. Brown, You've Got a Lovely Daughter*(British, 1968); *The Private Life of Sherlock Holmes* (1970); and *The Flight of the Doves* (1971).

Television. Mr. Holloway made his debut at the Alexandra Palace (London, 1936). He appeared on the Jo Stafford Special (Ind., Sept. 2, 1964); was Bellomy in *The Fantasticks*(Hallmark Hall of Fame, NBC, Oct. 18, 1964); made guest appearances on the Perry Como Show (NBC, 1964–65), the Bell Telephone Hour (NBC, 1964–66), the Red Skelton Show (CBS, 1965–66), the Dean Martin Show (NBC, 1965–67), the Danny Kaye Show (CBS, 1966–67); was in the series Blandings Castle (1967); played Beach in *Lord Emsworth and the Girl Friend* (World of Wodehouse, BBC-1, Feb. 24, 1967); and was in the television film *Run a Crooked Mile*(1969).

Published Works. Mr. Holloway wrote *Wiv a Little Bit of Luck* (1967).

Awards. Mr. Holloway is a member of the Order of the British Empire; he was nominated for an Academy (Oscar) Award as best supporting actor for his role in the film version of *My Fair Lady* (1964).

Recreation. Golf, crossword puzzles.

HOLLOWAY, STERLING. Actor. b. Cedartown, Ga., to Sterling Price and Rebecca (Boothby) Holloway. Father, cotton broker. Attended Cedartown (Ga.) H.S.; Georgia Military Acad., College Park, Ga.; AADA, 1923. Served US Army, Special Services, US and ETO, 1941; rank, Sgt. Member of AEA; AFTRA; SAG.

Theatre. Mr. Holloway appeared as the Second Phantom in *The Failures*(Garrick, N.Y.C., Nov. 19, 1923); Henry in *Fata Morgana* (Garrick, Mar. 3, 1924); appeared in a West Coast touring company's production of *The Shepherd of the Hills* (Tant, Torrance, Calif., June 1924); in the Th. Guild revue, *The Garrick Gaieties* (Garrick, N.Y.C., June 8, 1925); as Johnny Loring in *Get Me in the Movies* (Earl Carroll Th., May 21, 1928); in another production of *The Garrick Gaieties* (Guild, June 4, 1930), for which he also wrote some of the sketch material; and appeared in a revised version of *The Garrick Gaieties* (Guild, Oct. 16, 1930); and in Christopher Morley's *Shoe String Revue* (Lyric, Hoboken, N.J., Nov. 22, 1929).

While in the Army, Mr. Holloway produced, directed, and appeared in *Hey Rookie* (1942); played the Barber in *The Grass Harp* (Martin Beck Th., N.Y.C., Mar. 27, 1952); in Seattle, Wash., appeared in stock productions of *the Seven Year Itch* (Mar. 12, 1960) and *Send Me No Flowers* (June 10, 1961); and at the Sacramento (Calif.) Music Circus, appeared in *Song of Norway* (Summers 1959–60); *The Wizard of Oz* (Summer 1960); and *Anything Goes* (Summer 1963); as Prologus and Pseudolus in *A Funny Thing Happened on the Way to the Forum* (Aug. 16, 1965); and as Benjamin Kidd in *The Desert Song* (July 25, 1966).

Films. Mr. Holloway has appeared in *Walk in the Sun* (20th-Fox, 1945); *Hell Below* (MGM, 1945); *The Beautiful Blonde from Bashful Bend* (20th-Fox, 1949); *Her Wonderful Lie*(Col., 1950); *Alice in Wonderland* (Par., 1951); has narrated and dubbed in voices for the Walt Disney productions *Bambi* (RKO, 1941); *Dumbo*(RKO, 1942); *Winnie the Pooh* (1964); and *The Jungle Book* (Buena Vista, 1967).

Television. Mr. Holloway was the voice of Amos in *Ben and Me* and narrator for *Peter and the Wolf* (Walt Disney's World, NBC, Nov. 15, 1964); appeared on The Life of Riley (CBS, 1960–64); Baileys of Balboa (CBS, 1964–65); Family Affair (CBS, 1967); and Please Don't Eat the Daisies (NBC, 1967).

Night Clubs. He appeared in an act at Ciro's (N.Y.C., 1926).

Recreation. Collects modern paintings.

HOLLY, ELLEN. Actress. b. Ellen Virginia Holly, Jan. 17, 1931, Queens, N.Y., to William and Grayce (Arnold) Holly. Father, chemical engineer; mother, librarian. Grad. Richmond Hill (N.Y.) H.S., 1948; Hunter Coll., B.A. 1952. Studied acting at Perry-Mansfield Sch. of the Th. (Colo.), and with Charlotte Perry, Barney Brown, Uta Hagen, Mira Rostova, and Eli Rill (N.Y.C.). Member of AEA; SAG; AFTRA; Delta Sigma Theta.

Theatre. Miss Holly first appeared on stage as Electra in a Hunter Coll. production of *Daughters of Atreus* (1953); subsequently appeared as Tatiana in *The Anniversary* and Naida Gisben and Sharon Guilders in *A Switch in Time*, on a double-bill entitled *2 for Fun* (Greenwich Mews Th., May 25, 1955); and at the Davenport (N.Y.C.) Th., played the Slave Girl in *Salome* and Bianca in *A Florentine Tragedy* (1955).

Miss Holly made her Bway debut as Stephanie in *Too Late the Phalarope* (Belasco, Oct. 11, 1956); played the Rich Woman's Daughter in *Tevya and His Daughters* (Carnegie Hall Playhouse, Sept. 16, 1957); Desdemona in *Othello* (Belvedere Lake Th., July 2, 1958); Elizabeth Falk in *Face of a Hero* (Eugene O'Neill Th., Oct. 20, 1960); Rosa in *Moon on a Rainbow Shawl* (E. 11 St. Th., Jan. 15, 1962); Cille Morris in *Tiger, Tiger Burning Bright* (Booth, Dec. 22, 1962); Iras in *Antony and Cleopatra* (NY Shakespeare Fest., Delacorte Th., June 13, 1963); the Duchess of Hapsburg in *Funnyhouse of a Negro* (East End Th., Jan. 14, 1964).

For the NY Shakespeare Fest., Miss Holly played Titania in *A Midsummer Night's Dream* (Mobile Th. tour opened Mt. Morris Park, June 26, 1964; Bd. of Educ. Sch. tour opened Heckscher Th., Oct. 5, 1964; closed Aviation Voc. H.S., Dec. 18, 1964); and played Katharine, Princess of France, in the Mobile Th. tour of *Henry V* (opened June 26, 1965; closed Aug. 21, 1965; school tour opened Oct. 4, 1965; closed Dec. 17, 1965), in repertory was Katharina (Kate) in the Mobile Th. tour of *The Taming of the Shrew* (opened June 27, 1965; closed Aug. 22, 1965). She played "Clara Passmore who is the Virgin Mary who is the Bastard who is the Owl" in *The Owl Answers* (White Barn Th., Westport, Conn., Aug. 29, 1965; Th. de Lys, N.Y.C., Dec. 14, 1965); and for the NY Shakespeare Fest., played Lady Macbeth in the Mobile Th. tour of *Macbeth* (opened Chelsea Park, June 25, 1966; closed Aug. 20, 1966); appeared in *An Evening of Negro Poetry and Folk Music* (Delacorte, Aug. 15, 1966), which was subsequently produced on Bway as *A Hand Is on the Gate* (Longacre, Sept. 21, 1966); and played Lady Macbeth again in the school tour of *Macbeth* (opened Oct. 10, 1966; closed Dec. 16, 1966).

With the National Repertory Theatre, Miss Holly toured (opened Aycock Aud., Univ. of N.C., Greensboro, N.C., Oct. 16, 1967; closed Civic, Chicago, Dec. 16, 1967; and Ford's Th., Wash., D.C., opened Feb. 12, 1968; closed May 18, 1968) in several roles in *John Brown's Body* and as the Courtesan in *The Comedy of Errors;* at the Cincinnati (Ohio) Playhouse, appeared as Marguerite Gautier in *Camino Real* (July 18, 1968) and in *Crime on Goat Island* (Aug. 8, 1968); for the NY Shakespeare Fest., played Varya in *The Cherry Orchard* (Anspacher Th., Dec. 7, 1972) and Regan in *King Lear* (Delacorte, July 26, 1973); and played Hippolita in *'Tis Pity She's a Whore* (McCarter Th., Princeton, N.J., Nov. 14, 1974; and Goodman Th., Chicago, Jan. 3, 1975).

Films. Miss Holly appeared in *Take a Giant Step* (UA, 1959) and *Cops and Robbers* (UA, 1973).

Television. Miss Holly played Tituba in a dramatization of the Salem witch trials (Odyssey, CBS, 1957); and has appeared on the Big Story (NBC); Confidential File (WPIX); The Nurses (CBS); The Defenders (CBS); Sam Benedict (ABC); Look Up and Live (CBS); Dr. Kildare (NBC); played Sally Travers on the daytime series Love of Life (CBS); and Carla Benari Hall on One Life to Live (ABC, 1968–to date).

Other Activities. Writing.

HOLLYWOOD, DANIEL. Literary representative, producer. b. Daniel Lawrence Hollywood, July 15, Eight Frankfield Villa, County Cork, Ireland, to Patrick Lawrence and Ellen (Sullivan) Hollywood. Married Sept. 24, 1960, to Ginger Edwards; two daughters. Relative in theatre: uncle, Jimmy Hollywood, originator of the Radio Rogues. Address: (home) 1710 Camino Palmero, Hollywood, CA 90046; (bus.) Diamond Artists Ltd., 8400 Sunset Blvd., Hollywood, CA 90069.

Theatre. Mr. Hollywood has served as literary representative for *The Seven Year Itch; Fever for Life; Tevya and His Daughters; Time of Storm;* and *The World of Sholom Aleichem.* With Elliot Martin, he produced *Cradle and All* (Lakewood Th., Skowhegan, Me., 1959), which was later retitled *Never Too Late;* produced, with William Darrid and Eleanor Saidenberg, *The Andersonville Trial* (Henry Miller's Th., N.Y.C., Dec. 29, 1959); produced, with Elliot Martin, *Never Too Late* (Playhouse, Nov. 27, 1962); produced, with Elliot Martin, Bernard Delfont, and Fredrick Granville, the London production of *Never Too Late* (Prince of Wales Th., Sept. 24, 1963); and wrote and produced *All the Girls Came Out to Play* (Cort, N.Y.C., April 1972).

Films. Mr. Hollywood was George Axelrod's literary representative for *Phfft* (Col., 1954) and *The Seven Year Itch* (20th-Fox, (1955); and represented the authors of *The Last Frontier* (Col., 1955); *The Young Strangers* (U, 1957); *Island in the Sun* (20th-Fox, 1957); *The Black Orchid* (Par., 1959); *Angel Baby* (Allied, 1961); *Question 7* (de Rochemont, 1961); *John Knox* (de Rochemont, 1962); and *The War Lover* (Col., 1962).

HOLM, CELESTE. Actress, singer. b. Apr. 29, 1919, New York City, to Theodor and Jean (Parke) Holm. Father, insurance adjustor; mother, artist. Grad. Francis W. Parker H.S., Chicago, Ill., 1934. Studied drama at Univ. of Chicago, 1932–34 (while attending high school); with Benno Schneider, N.Y.C. (1938–41); music and voice with Clytie Hine Mundy, N.Y.C. (1940–45); playwrighting at Univ. of California at Los Angeles (1948); music and voice with Alberto Sciarretti, N.Y.C. (1959–63). Entertained US troops in Europe in USO productions, 1945; Military Air Command productions, 1949. Relative in theatre: aunt, Hinda Hand, actress. Member of AEA; SAG; AFTRA; AGVA; IATSE (hon. member). Address: c/o Gerald Siegal, 1650 Broadway, New York, NY 10019, tel. (212) 541-5460.

Theatre. Miss Holm made her debut as Roberta Van Renssalaer, in *Night of January 16* (Orwigsburg Summer Th., Deer Lake, Pa., June 1936); understudied the role of Ophelia in the national tour of Leslie Howard's *Hamlet* (Dec. 1936–Apr. 1937); and toured as Crystal Allen in *The Women* (Oct. 1937–Mar. 1938). She made her N.Y.C. debut as Mary L. in *The Time of Your Life* (Booth, Oct. 25, 1939); played Maria in *Another Sun* (Natl., Feb. 23, 1940); the Governor's Daughter in *The Return of the Vagabond* (Natl., May 17, 1940); appeared in productions at the Ivoryton (Conn.) Playhouse (Summer 1940); played Marcia Godden in *Eight O'Clock Tuesday* (Henry Miller's Th., N.Y.C., Jan. 6, 1941); Lady Keith-Odlyn in *My Fair Ladies* (Hudson, Mar. 23, 1941); Frances Ballard in *Love in Our Time* (Westport Country Playhouse, Conn., Aug. 4, 1941); Rena Clift in *U.S. 90* (Paper Mill Playhouse, Millburn, N.J., Aug. 18, 1941); and toured as Ellen Turner in *The Male Animal* (1941).

Miss Holm played Emma in *Papa Is All* (Guild, N.Y.C., Jan. 6, 1942); Fifi Oritanski in *All the Comforts of Home* (Longacre, May 25, 1942); Calla Longstreet in *The Damask Cheek* (Playhouse, Oct. 22, 1942); Ado Annie in *Oklahoma!* (St. James, Mar. 31, 1943); Evelina in *Bloomer Girl* (Shubert, Oct. 5, 1944); Kate Hardcastle in *She Stoops to Conquer* (NY City Ctr., Dec. 8, 1949); Irene Elliott in *Affairs of State* (Royale, Sept. 25, 1950); the title role in *Anna Christie* (NY City Ctr., Jan. 9, 1952); temporarily succeeded Gertrude Lawrence (July 1952) as Anna in *The King and I* (St. James, Mar. 29, 1951); played Maggie Palmer in *His and Hers* (48 St. Th., Jan. 7, 1954); Mlle. Suzette in *Sudden Spring* (Detroit Melody Circus, Mich., Aug. 1956); toured as Eve and Lillith in *Back to Methuselah* (1957); played Mrs. Price in *Interlock* (ANTA, N.Y.C., Feb. 6, 1958); Helen Sayre in *Third Best Sport* (Ambassador, Dec. 30, 1958); appeared in summer productions at the Spa Th. (Saratoga, N.Y., 1959); toured summer theatres in the revue, *What a Day* (July 1959), and as Kate Sedgwick in *Royal Enclosure* (June 1960).

She appeared as Camilla Jablonski in *Invitation to a March* (Music Box, N.Y.C., Oct. 29, 1960); Natalia Petrovna in *A Month in the Country* (Maidman Playhouse, May 28, 1963); Angela in a tryout of *Madly in Love* (Playhouse in the Park, Philadelphia, Pa., Aug. 1963); Hannah Jelkes in *Night of the Iguana* (Brown Th., Louisville, Ky., Apr. 1964); and Irene in *Affairs of State*, which she also directed (La Jolla Playhouse, Calif.; Lobero Th., Santa Barbara, Calif., June 1964). In 1963, 1964, and 1965, she made a nationwide tour with the *Theatre in Concert* program, and she was sent abroad with the production during the summer of 1966 by the US State Dept.

In 1968–69, she starred in the national company of *Mame.* She starred in *Candida* (Great Lakes Shakespeare Festival, 1970); toured as the Mother in *Butterflies Are Free* (1972); toured in the Americanized version of *The Irregular Verb To Love* (1973); and toured in *Finishing Touches* (1974).

Films. Miss Holm made her debut in *Three Little Girls in Blue* (20th-Fox, 1946); followed by *Carnival in Costa Rica* (20th-Fox, 1947); *Gentlemen's Agreement* (20th-Fox, 1948); *Road House* (20th-Fox, 1948); *The Snake Pit* (20th-Fox, 1949); *Chicken Every Sunday* (20th-Fox, 1949); *Come to the Stable* (20th-Fox 1949); *Everybody Does It* (20th-Fox, 1949); *Champagne for Caesar* (U, 1950); *All About Eve* (20th-Fox, 1950); *The Tender Trap* (MGM, 1955), *High Society* (MGM, 1956); *Bachelor Flat* (20th-Fox, 1961); *Doctor, You've Got To Be Kidding!* (MGM, 1967); and she played Aunt Polly in *Tom Sawyer* (UA, 1973).

Television and Radio. She had her own radio program, People at the United Nations (NBC). She made her television debut on the Chevrolet Show (CBS, 1949); and has appeared in *Honestly Celeste* (CBS, 1954); *Jack and the Beanstalk* (Producers Showcase, NBC, 1956); *The Wedding Present* (Schlitz Playhouse, CBS, 1957); *The Princess Back Home* (Goodyear Playhouse, NBC, 1957); *The Yeoman of the Guard* (Hallmark Hall of Fame, NBC, 1957); *A Clearing in the Woods* (Play of the Week, ANTA, 1960); on Who Pays (NBC), the Perry Como Show (NBC), the Ed Sullivan Show (CBS), Doctor Kildare (NBC), Eleventh Hour (NBC), and others. She was the Fairy Godmother in *Cinderella* (1965); appeared on Name of the Game (NBC); played Abby in the series Nancy (NBC, 1970); guest starred on Medical Center; and was in *The Underground Man* (1974) and *Streets of San Francisco* (ABC Movie-of-the-Week, 1974).

Night Clubs. She has performed at La Vie Parisienne (N.Y.C., 1943); the Persian Room, Hotel Plaza (N.Y.C., 1944, 1951, 1953, 1954, 1958, 1959); the Empire Room, Palmer House (Chicago, Ill., 1953); the Cotillion Room, Pierre Hotel (N.Y.C., 1957); Ritz Carlton (Montreal, Can., 1958); The Tropicana (Las Vegas, Nev., 1958 and 1959); La Vie en Rose (N.Y.C., 1958 and 1959); and others.

Other Activities. Miss Holm has been a member of the governing board of the World Federation of Mental Health, and she is on the governing board of the National Association for Mental Health (chmn., 1969–70, 1970–71). She is also a member of UNICEF.

Awards. Miss Holm received the Academy (Oscar) Award for her performance in *Gentlemen's Agreement* (1947); and was nominated for Academy (Oscar) Awards for her performances in *Come to the Stable* (1949) and *All About Eve* (1950); received the Brotherhood Award of the National Conference of Christians and Jews (1952); the Performer of the Year Award from the Variety Clubs of America (1966, 1973); and the Sarah Siddons Award for her performance in the national company of Mame (1969).

Recreation. Sewing, knitting, cooking, tennis, badminton.

HOLM, HANYA. Choreographer, director, dancer, teacher. b. Johanna Eckert, Worm-am-Rhine, Germany, to Valentin and Marie (Moerschel) Eckert. Father, wine merchant; mother, inventor. Grad. Englische Fraulein Convent, Mainz, Germany, 1911; attended Hoch Conservatory, Frankfurt, Germany, 1913–15; Dalcroze Inst.,

Frankfurt and Hellerau, certificate, 1916; Wigman School of the Dance, Dresden, Germany, dance diploma 1923. Married Aug. 1918 to Reinhold Martin Kuntze, painter and sculptor (marr. dis. 1921); one son, Klaus Holm, stage designer and lighting specialist. Member of SSD&C (bd. of gov., 1959; 2nd vice-pres., 1959–60); ANTA (dance advisory panel, 1962–to date); American Arbitration Assn. (natl. panel of arbitrators, 1958–to date); Fellow of Intl. Inst. of Arts and Letters (Kreuzlingen, Switzerland, 1961–to date). 1233 Sixth Ave., New York, NY 10019, tel. (212) PL 7-0289.

Theatre. Miss Holm appeared in one of the first productions of Max Reinhardt's *The Miracle* (Frankfurt, Germany); joined (1923) the Mary Wigman dance company and performed with it in Europe (1923–28); directed summer productions (Ommen, Netherlands, 1927–28); danced in Stravinsky's *L'Histoire du soldat* (State Playhouse, Dresden, Germany, 1927); and was associate director, with Mary Wigman, of *Totenmal*, in which she danced (Munich, Germany, 1930).

She made her American concert debut with her own dance company (Denver, Colo., 1936); made three transcontinental tours; gave annual performances in N.Y.C. (1936–44); appeared with her group (Colorado Springs, Colo., Summers 1941–to date); made her Bway debut as choreographer of *The Eccentricities of Davey Crockett* from *Ballet Ballads* (Maxine Elliott's Th., May 9, 1948); choreographed *The Insect Comedy* (NY City Ctr., June 3, 1948); *E = mc*(Brander Matthews Hall, June 15, 1948); choreographed and staged the musical numbers of *Kiss Me, Kate* (Century, Dec. 30, 1948); did the incidental choreography for *Blood Wedding* (New Stages, Feb. 6, 1949); choreographed and staged the musical numbers for *The Liar* (Broadhurst, May 18, 1950); *Out of This World* (Century, Dec. 21, 1950); *Kiss Me, Kate* (Coliseum, London, Mar. 8, 1951); *My Darlin' Aida* (Winter Garden, N.Y.C., Oct. 27, 1952); choreographed *The Golden Apple* (Phoenix, Mar. 11, 1954); and choreographed and staged the musical numbers for the pre-Bway tryout of *Reuben Reuben* (opened Shubert, Boston, Mass., Oct. 10, 1955; closed there Oct. 22, 1955).

Miss Holm choreographed and staged the musical numbers for *My Fair Lady* (Mark Hellinger Th., N.Y.C., Mar. 15, 1956); directed and choreographed the opera, *The Ballad of Baby Doe* (Central City Opera House, Colo., world premiere, July 7, 1956); choreographed and staged the musical numbers of *Where's Charley?* (Palace, London, Feb. 20, 1958); *My Fair Lady* (Drury Lane, Apr. 30, 1958); directed and choreographed the opera *Orpheus and Eurydice* at the Vancouver (B.C.) Festival (Queen Elizabeth Th., July 18, 1959); choreographed and staged the musical numbers for *Christine* (46 St. Th., Apr. 28, 1960); *Camelot* (Majestic, Dec. 3, 1960); choreographed and directed the opera Orpheus and Eurydice (O'Keefe Ctr., Toronto, Canada, May 26, 1962); and revised the production of *Camelot* for a bus-and-truck tour (opened, Masonic Temple, Scranton, Pa., Oct. 3, 1963).

She staged the musical numbers and choreographed the NY City Ctr. Light Opera Co. revivals of *My Fair Lady* (NY City Ctr., May 20, 1964) and *Kiss Me Kate* (NY City Ctr., May 12, 1965); choreographed and staged musical numbers for *Anya* (Ziegfeld Th., Nov. 29, 1965); and for another NY City Ctr. Light Opera Co. revival of *My Fair Lady* (NY City Ctr., June 13, 1968).

Films. Miss Holm was choreographer for *The Vagabond King* (Par., 1955).

Television and Radio. On radio, she has been heard in many interviews and talks in the US, Canada, and Europe. On television, she performed with her own dance company in a modern dance production, "Metropolitan Daily" (NBC, 1939); appeared on Garroway's Wide, Wide World (NBC, Jan. 6, 1957); was narrator and assistant script writer for "The Dance and the Drama" (CBC, Toronto, Canada, Feb. 13, 1957); choreographer for "Pinocchio" (NBC, Oct. 13, 1957); participated in *Tactic* for the American Cancer Society campaign (NBC, Feb. 10, 1959); was a judge on the Arthur Murray Show (Feb. 14, 1960); appeared on the Ed Sullivan Show Lerner-Loewe Tribute (CBS, Mar. 19, 1961); and choreographed a dance scene for "Dinner with the President" (CBS, Jan. 31, 1963).

Other Activities. Miss Holm has been director of her own school in N.Y.C.; the director of the dance department of the Musical and Dramatic Th. Academy (N.Y.C.); director of summer dance sessions at Colorado Coll. (1961–to date) and has performed, lectured, and taught in US colleges and universities.

Published Works. Miss Holm wrote the articles "Pioneer of the Dance" *(The American Dancer)* (1933); "Mary Wigman" *(Dance Observer)* (1935); "Dance on the Campus; Athletics or Art? *(Dance)* (1937); "Who Is Mary Wigman?" *(Dance Magazine)* (1956); the book, *Dance* (1941); articles for the World Book Encyclopedia (1946); "The Wigman I Know" and "Dance in the Making" in *The Dance Has Many Faces* (1951).

Awards. Miss Holm received a NY *Times* Award for her dance composition, *Trend* (1937); a *Dance* Magazine award for her group choreography *Tragic Exodus* (1939); represented Women in Art at the centennial celebration at Duke Univ. (1939); won the *Variety* NY Drama Critics Poll for her choreography for *Kiss Me, Kate* (1949); an Antoinette Perry (Tony) Award nomination for her choreography for *My Fair Lady* (1956); Award of Honor from the Federation of Jewish Philanthropies (1958); received an honorary D.F.A. from Colorado Coll. (1960); and an annual award from the Westchester Dance Council (1962).

Recreation. Music, painting, wood carving, handicrafts, chess, gardening.

HOLM, JOHN CECIL. Playwright, actor, director, author. b. Nov. 4, 1904, Philadelphia, Pa., to Charles Hedley and Lucinda (Bair) Holm. Father, electrical contractor. Attended West Philadelphia H.S., 1920–23; grad. Perkiomen Sch., Pennsburg, Pa., 1924; attended Univ. of Pennsylvania, 1924–25. Married July 16, 1932, to Fae Brown Drake, theatrical agent (dec. Jan. 1959); married Feb. 11, 1960, to Dolores Leids Boland, columnist. Member of AEA; AFTRA; SAG; Dramatists Guild; ALA; WGA; The Lambs; The Players (board of dir. 1961–64). Address: 241 E. 75th St., New York, NY 10021, tel. (212) SU 7-5400.

Theatre. Mr. Holm first appeared on the stage in the musical, *Joan of Arkansas* (Forrest Th., Philadelphia, Pa., 1925), a Mask and Wig Club (Univ. of Pennsylvania) production; and first appeared professionally as Dempsey in *The Devil Within* (James G. Carroll Players, Colonial, Pittsfield, Mass., Oct. 3, 1925); subsequently was stage manager and actor with another stock company group, the Lillian Desmond Players (Stone Opera House, Binghamton, N.Y., Feb. 1926); appeared with and was assistant director for the same group (Idora Park, Youngstown, Ohio, June 1926); was stage manager and actor with the Plateau Players (Fairmount Park, Philadelphia, Pa., 1927); played in stock (Gloucester, Mass., Summer 1927); appeared as Roy Lane in a Southern Co. tour of *Broadway* (Sept. 1927); joined the James Carroll Players (Bijou, Bangor, Me., Mar. 1928); played in stock in *Old Heidelberg* and appeared as Roy Lane in *Broadway* (Rialto, Hoboken, N.J., Nov. 1928).

He understudied and replaced for ten performances (1929) Lee Tracy in the part of Hildy Johnson in *The Front Page* (Times Square Th., N.Y.C., Aug. 14, 1928); billed as Cecil Holm, he played Charles Black in *Whirlpool* (Biltmore, Dec. 3, 1929); Thomas Mason in *Penal Law 2010* (Biltmore, Apr. 18, 1930); succeeded (Dec. 12, 1930) Donald McDonald as Doggie in *The Up and Up* (Biltmore, Sept. 8, 1930); played Mac in *Wonder Boy* (Alvin, Oct. 23, 1931); James Knox in *Bloodstream* (Times Square Th., Mar. 30, 1932); appeared with the NY Repertory Co. (Westport Country Playhouse, Conn., June 27, 1932); played Gordon Whitehouse in *Dangerous Corner* (Empire, N.Y.C., Oct. 27, 1932); and Jamie in *Mary of Scotland* (Alvin, Nov. 27, 1933).

Billed as John Cecil Holm, he wrote, with George Abbott, *Three Men on a Horse* (Playhouse, Jan. 30, 1935), and with Mr. Abbott, directed the Chicago (Ill.) Co. (Erlanger, Jan. 4, 1935) and the London (Eng.) production (Wyndham's, Feb. 18, 1936). He wrote the book for *Best Foot Forward* (Ethel Barrymore Th., N.Y.C., Oct. 1, 1941). *Three Men on a Horse* was made into the musical *Banjo Eyes* (Hollywood Th., Dec. 25, 1941). He directed *Three Men on a Horse* (Forrest, Oct. 9, 1942); with Matt Taylor, wrote the book for *Dancing in the Streets* (opened Shubert Th., Boston, Mar. 23, 1943; closed there Apr. 10, 1943); played Carl Greenleaf in the tryout of *Bee in Her Bonnet* (Dock St. Th., Charleston, S.C., Feb. 1945); wrote *Brighten the Corner* (Lyceum, N.Y.C., Dec. 12, 1945); and revised the book for a revival of *Sweethearts* (Shubert, Jan. 21, 1947).

He played Charlie in the pre-Bway tour of his own play, *Gramercy Ghost* (Sail Loft Th., Germantown, N.Y., Aug. 1947), and in the Bway production (Morosco, April 26, 1951); and succeeded (July 1951) John Marley as the Ambulance Driver. He wrote *Golden Harvest* for the 50th Anniversary of the Gaylord Farm Hospital (1953); and was resident actor at the Falmouth (Mass.) Playhouse (Summer 1953).

He appeared in the Univ. of Michigan's Ann Arbor Drama Festival (1954) as the Ticket Seller in *A Trip to Bountiful;* the First Ambulance Driver in his own play, *Gramercy Ghost;* and Putnam in *The Crucible.* He wrote *The Southwest Corner,* adapted from the novel of the same title by Mildred Walker, and directed the pre-Bway tour (Spa Summer Th., Saratoga Springs, N.Y., Aug. 9, 1954), subsequently opened in N.Y.C. (Holiday, Feb. 3, 1955). He played Clyde Miller in tours of *Life with Mother* (Summer 1955), and Metcalf in *The Solid Gold Cadillac* (Summer 1956); directed *Three Men on a Horse* and played Clarence (Cincinnati, Ohio; Fayetteville, N.Y.; and Vineland, Ontario, Can., Summer 1957); was standby for Chester Morris as Major Bartley in *Blue Denim* (Playhouse, N.Y.C., Feb. 27, 1958); played Dr. John Holden in *A Mighty Man Is He* (Cort., Jan. 6, 1960); and Al Smith in a tour of *Sunrise at Campobello* (Summer 1960).

He played Luther Plunkett in *Midgie Purvis* (Martin Beck Th., N.Y.C., Feb. 1, 1961); Jim Daugherty in a tour of *The Pleasure of His Company* (Summer 1961). Another musical version of his play, *Three Men on a Horse,* retitled *Let It Ride,* was produced (Eugene O'Neill Th., N.Y.C., Oct. 12, 1961). He played Chester Kincaid in *Mr. President* (St. James, Oct. 20, 1962); his play *Best Foot Forward* was revived (Stage 73, Apr. 2, 1963); played Ed Hoffman in *Time Out for Ginger* (Cape Playhouse, Dennis, Mass.; Ogunquit Playhouse, Me., 1963); and Arthur Burns in *The Advocate* (ANTA, N.Y.C., Oct. 14, 1963).

He played Sir Francis Beekman in *Gentlemen Prefer Blonds* (Carousel Th., Framingham, Mass., June 20, 1964); at the Casa Manana Th. (Ft. Worth, Tex.), played Sen. Billboard Rawkins in *Finian's Rainbow* (July 27, 1964) and Col. Pickering in *My Fair Lady* (Aug. 24, 1964); Mr. Twilling in *Her Master's Voice* (41 St. Th., N.Y.C., Dec. 26, 1964); Dr. James Kimbrough in *Never Too Late* (Royal Poinciana Playhouse, Palm Beach, Fla., Feb. 15, 1965; Coconut Grove Playhouse, Miami, Fla., Feb. 23, 1965); Mayor Crane in *Never Too Late* (Paper Mill Playhouse, Millburn, N.J., July 20, 1965); was standby for Tom Ewell (as Edward T. Wellspot), Robert H. Harris (as Spiro Olympus) and Heywood Hale Broun (as Michael Wellspot) in *Xmas in Las Vegas* (Ethel Barrymore Th., N.Y.C., Nov. 4, 1965); played Ben Burton and understudied Joseph Boland (as Master Boyle) and Donald Marye (as Canon Mick O'Byrne) in *Philadelphia, Here I Come!* (Helen Hayes Th., Feb. 16, 1966); played Capt. Brackett in *South Pacific* (Jones Beach Marine Th., L.I., N.Y., June 27, 1968); Mr. Latham in *Forty Carats* (Morosco, Dec. 26, 1968); the conductor in *Twentieth Century* (Coconut Grove Playhouse, Miami, Fla; Parker Playhouse, Ft. Lauderdale, Fla., Feb. 1971); and understudied Richard Woods (as Chumley) and Edgar Meyer (as Gaffney) in a tour of *Harvey* (opened Opera House, Central City, Colo., July 31,

1971; closed Studebaker, Chicago, Nov. 20, 1971).

Films. Mr. Holm first appeared in *Here Comes the Groom* (Par., 1929); he was a screenwriter for 20th-Fox (1940); his unproduced play, *Blonde Inspiration* was adapted for film (MGM, 1941), as were his plays, *Three Men on a Horse*(WB, 1936) and *Best Foot Forward*(MGM, 1943); he played Aaron Caldwell in *It Happened to Jane* (Col., 1959).

Television. He has appeared as the Bartender in *Three Men on a Horse*(Prudential Family Playhouse, Nov. 21, 1950); adapted his own play, *The Southwest Corner*(Kraft Television Th., NBC); supervised the production of his play, *Gramercy Ghost* (Kraft Television Th., NBC, 1955); his play, *Three Men on a Horse* was presented on Playhouse 90 (CBS, 1956); he played Metesky in *The Mad Bomber* (Big Story, ABC, 1957); the Sheriff in *Johnny Belinda* (Hallmark Hall of Fame, NBC, 1958); and appeared on Directions '65 (ABC); The Trials of O'Brien (CBS); Look Up and Live (CBS); etc.

Published Works. Mr. Holm wrote his autobiography, *Sunday Best* (1942); *Quiet Facing the Park*, which was included In *Best One-Act Plays of 1943;* and *McGarrity and the Pigeons* (1947); and has had articles and stories published in *The Saturday Evening Post, Woman's Day,* and *College Humor.*.

Recreation. Collecting antiques and first editions.

HOLM, KLAUS. Scenic and lighting designer, theatre consultant. b. Klaus Kuntze, June 27, 1920, Dresden, Germany, to Martin and Hanya (Holm) Kuntze. Father, sculptor, painter; mother, Hanya Holm, dancer, choreographer. Grad. Cherry Lawn Sch., Darien, Conn., 1939; New York Univ., B.S. 1948; Yale Univ. Sch. of Drama, M.F.A. 1951. Married Aug. 23, 1958, to Heidi Buettel; two daughters. Served USN, 1943–46; rank, AM 3/C. Member of United Scenic Artists.

Pre-Theatre. Draftsman.

Theatre. Mr. Holm's first assignment was designing sets and lights for a college production of *The Insect Comedy* (Colorado Coll., Colorado Springs, Aug. 1947); subsequently appeared as an Ant in the same play at the NY City Ctr., June 2, 1948); designed the lighting for stock productions (Town Hall Th., Fairhaven, Mass., Summer 1949); designed sets and lighting (New London Players, N.H., 1950–51); and lighting for the National Th. of Greece (Mark Hellinger Th., N.Y.C., 1952).

He was lighting designer for *The Girl on the Via Flaminia* (Circle in the Sq., Feb. 9, 1954); at the Phoenix Th., for *The Golden Apple* (Mar. 11, 1954), *The Seagull* (May 11, 1954), and *Sing Me No Lullaby* (Oct. 14, 1954); assistant lighting designer for *Wedding Breakfast* (48 St. Th., Nov. 20, 1954); *Portrait of a Lady* (ANTA, Dec. 21, 1954); designed both sets and lighting for *The Doctor's Dilemma* (Phoenix, Jan. 11, 1955); and lighting for *Phoenix '55* (Phoenix, Apr. 23, 1955).

Mr. Holm designed the lighting for *La Ronde* (Circle in the Square, June 27, 1955); *The Carefree Tree* (Phoenix, Oct. 11, 1955); was assistant set and lighting designer for the pre-Bway tryout of *A Quiet Place* (opened Shubert, New Haven, Conn., Nov. 23, 1955; closed National, Washington, D.C., Dec. 31, 1955); at the Phoenix Th. (N.Y.C.), designed sets and lighting for *Six Characters in Search of an Author* (Dec. 11, 1955); *Miss Julie* and *The Stronger* (Feb. 21, 1956); *A Month in the Country* (Apr. 3, 1956); *The Littlest Revue* (May 22, 1956); and *Saint Joan* (Sept. 11, 1956).

He was assistant set and lighting designer for *Major Barbara* (Martin Beck Th., Oct. 30, 1956); assistant set designer for *The Sleeping Prince* (Coronet, Nov. 1, 1956); at the Phoenix Th., designed sets and lighting for *The Diary of a Scoundrel* (Nov. 5, 1956), lighting for *The Good Woman of Setzuan* (Dec. 18, 1956), and *Livin' the Life* (Apr. 27, 1957); was stage and lighting consultant for the US Theatre (Brussels World's Fair, Belgium, 1958); for the NY City Opera Co., designed the lighting for *The Ballad of Baby Doe* (NY City Ctr., Apr. 3, 1958); designed the lighting for *The Power and the Glory* (Phoenix, Dec. 10, 1958); *Orpheus and Eurydice* (Queen Elizabeth Th., Vancouver, B.C., Canada, July 1959); the Montreal (Canada) Cultural Ctr. (1959); *Semi-Detached* (Martin Beck Th., N.Y.C., Mar. 10, 1960); *The King and I* (NY City Ctr., May 11, 1960); was stage and lighting consultant for the Goodspeed Opera House (East Haddam, Conn., 1960); and the Broadmoor Intl. Ctr., (Cold Springs, Colo., 1960); and for the NY City Opera Co., designed the lighting for the NY City Opera Co. productions of *The Prisoner* and *Orfeo* (NY City Ctr., Sept. 29, 1960).

He designed the lighting for *Advise and Consent* (Cort, Nov. 17, 1960); *Once There Was a Russian* (Music Box, Feb. 18, 1961); *Donnybrook!* (46 St. Th., May 18, 1961); the NY City Opera Co.'s *Wings of the Dove* (NY City Ctr., Nov. 21, 1961); *Something About a Soldier* (Ambassador, Jan. 4, 1962); *The Magic Flute* (Queen Elizabeth Th., Vancouver, B.C., Canada, July 1962); *Caesar and Cleopatra* (Queen Elizabeth Playhouse, Vancouver, Aug. 1962); *Moby Dick* (Ethel Barrymore Th., N.Y.C., Nov. 28, 1962); *The Heroine* (Lyceum, Feb. 19, 1963); for the pre-Bway tryout of *Zenda* (opened Curran, San Francisco, Calif., Aug. 5, 1963; closed Philharmonic Aud., Los Angeles, Calif., Nov. 1963); *The Private Ear and the Public Eye* (Morosco, N.Y.C., Oct. 9, 1963); *Too Much Johnson* (Phoenix, Jan. 15, 1964).

At the Opera House (Central City, Colo.), Mr. Holm designed the lighting for *Madame Butterfly* (June 27, 1964) and the world premiere production of *The Lady from Colorado* (July 3, 1964). He was design supervisor for *Oh, What a Lovely War!* (Broadhurst Th., N.Y.C., Sept. 30, 1964); associate to Donald Oenslager for *One by One* (Belasco, Dec. 1, 1964); assistant to William and Jean Eckart for *Flora, the Red Menace* (Alvin, May 11, 1965); assistant to Rouben Ter-Arutunian for *The Devils* (Bway Th., Nov. 16, 1965); lighting and design supervisor for *Wait a Minim!* (John Golden Th., Mar. 7, 1966; tour opened Mechanic Th., Baltimore, July 19, 1967; closed Colonial, Boston, May 25, 1968); and associate designer for *The Wrong Way Light Bulb* (John Golden Th., N.Y.C., Mar. 4, 1969); was stage and lighting consultant for NY State Th., Lincoln Philharmonic Hall, Lincoln Ctr. (1961–62); Ctr. for the Performing Arts (1962–62); Wilkes Coll. (Wilkes-Barre, Pa., 1963–64); Spingold Th. (Brandeis Univ., Mass., 1964); and the NY St. Pavilion and the General Cigar Co., NY World's Fair (1964).

Television. Mr. Holm was assistant set designer for the Kate Smith Show (NBC, 1951).

Awards. Mr. Holm shared with Alvin Colt *The Village Voice* off-Bway (Obie) Award for design and lighting (1956).

Recreation. Photography.

HOLTZ, LOU. Performer. b. Apr. 11, 1898, San Francisco, Calif., to Asher and Olga (Levine) Holtz. Attended Lowell H.S., San Francisco, 1910. Married 1937 to Phyllis Gillma (marr. dis. 1946); married Sept. 19, 1962, to Gloria Warfield; two sons. Entertained troops in USO productions during World War II. Member of AEA; AFTRA; SAG; AGVA; The Friars; Hillcrest Country Club. Address: 1272 Hillgreen Dr., Los Angeles, CA 90035, tel. (213) CR 6-3393.

Theatre. Mr. Holtz made his N.Y.C. debut as a member of the Elsie Janis Trio (Palace, 1914); subsequently joined (July 1919) the cast of *George White's Scandals* (Liberty, June 2, 1919); appeared in the following two editions of this revue (Globe, June 7, 1920; Liberty, July 11, 1921); played Monty Sipkin in *Tell Me More* (Astor, Apr. 13, 1925); took over for Lester Allen in *La Maire's Affairs* (Shubert, 1927); appeared as Sam Katz in *Manhattan Mary* (Apollo, Sept. 26, 1927); Pinkie Pincus in *You Said It,* which he also produced (46 St. Th., Jan. 19, 1931); appeared in a vaudeville show that established a record run of three months at the Palace Th. (1931); and produced and starred in *Lou Holtz Vauderevue* (Hollywood Th., 1932) and in the revue *Calling All Stars* (Hollywood Th., Dec. 13, 1934).

He made his London (England) debut in *Transatlantic Rhythm* (Adelphi, Oct. 1, 1936); appeared in *Laughter over London* (Victoria Palace, Mar. 15, 1937); in the revue, *Priorities of 1942* (46 St. Th., N.Y.C., Mar. 12, 1942); performed at the Capital Th. (N.Y.C.), establishing a record run there for a stage show of eight weeks (1943); appeared in the revue *Star Time* (Majestic, Sept. 12, 1944); and gave a concert at Carnegie Hall in N.Y.C. (1945).

Television and Radio. Mr. Holtz performed on his own radio program, the Lou Holtz Show (CBS, 1942); appeared for twenty-two consecutive weeks on the Rudy Vallee Show (NBC) and performed for twelve weeks on the Bing Crosby Show (NBC) and for eight weeks on the Fanny Brice Show. On television he has appeared on the Jack Paar Show (NBC); the Ed Sullivan Show (CBS); and the Johnny Carson (NBC) and Merv Griffin shows.

Night Clubs. Mr. Holtz has appeared in night clubs in Las Vegas, Nev., as well as in many other cities throughout the US.

Recreation. Stock market, walking, baseball.

HOME, WILLIAM DOUGLAS. Playwright, actor. b. June 3, 1912, Edinburgh, Scotland, to the 13th Earl of Home and Lilian (Lambton) Home. Father, peer of the realm. Attended Eton Coll., 1927–32; grad. New Coll., Oxford Univ., B.A. 1935. Studied for the theatre at RADA, 1935–37. Married July 26, 1951, to Rachel Brand; one son, three daughters. Served WW II, British Army, 1940–44. Member of British AEA; SWG; League of Dramatists; Society of Authors; Travellers Club; Dramatists Club.

Theatre. Productions in the US of Mr. Home's plays include *Yes, M'Lord* (Booth, N.Y.C., Oct. 4, 1949), which had been previously produced in London as *The Chiltern Hundreds; The Reluctant Debutante* (Henry Miller's Th., Oct. 10, 1956); *The Jockey Club Stakes* (Cort, Jan. 24, 1973); and *Lloyd George Knew My Father* (John F. Kennedy Ctr., Washington, D.C., July 2, 1974); all had been previously produced in England (see below).

Mr. Home made his acting debut with the Brighton (England) Repertory Th. in 1937; wrote *Great Possessions* (Duke of York's Th., London, 1937); played Brian Morellian in *Bonnet Over the Windmill* (New, London, Sept. 8, 1937); and Johnny Greystoke in *Plan for a Hostess* (St. Martin's, Mar. 10, 1938).

The following plays of his have been produced in London: *Passing By* ("Q," Apr. 29, 1940); *Now Barabbas* (Boltons, Feb. 11, 1947); *The Chiltern Hundreds* (Vaudeville, Aug. 26, 1947), in which he played Lord Pym for two weeks (July, 1948); *Ambassador Extraordinary* (Aldwych, 1948); *The Thistle and Rose* (Boltons, 1949); *Master of Arts* (Strand, 1949); a new production of *The Thistle and Rose* (Vaudeville, 1951); *Caro William* (Embassy, Oct. 22, 1952); *The Bad Samaritan* (Criterion, June 24, 1953); *The Manor of Northstead* (Duchess, Apr. 28, 1954); *The Reluctant Debutante* (Cambridge, May 24, 1955), in which he played Jimmy Broadbent for three weeks (Oct. 1955); *The Iron Duchess* (Cambridge, Mar. 14, 1957); *Aunt Edwina* (Fortune, Nov. 3, 1959); *The Bad Soldier Smith* (Westminster, 1961); *The Cigarette Girl* (Duke of York's Th., 1962); *The Drawing Room Tragedy,* in Salisbury (Salisbury Th., 1963); and *The Reluctant Peer* (Duchess, London, Jan. 15, 1964).

He also wrote *The Home Secretary* and *Lady J P 2,* which were presented under the collective title *Two Accounts Rendered* (Comedy Th., London, Sept. 15, 1964); *Betzi* (Salisbury Playhouse, Salisbury, Mar. 23, 1965); *A Friend Indeed* (Cambridge Th., London, Apr. 27, 1966); *The Queen's Highland Servant* (Savoy, May 2, 1968); *The Secretary Bird* (Savoy, Oct. 20, 1968); *The Jockey Club Stakes* (Vaudeville Th., Sept. 30, 1970); *The Douglas Cause* (Duke of York's Th., Nov. 10, 1971); *Lloyd George Knew My Father* (Savoy, July 4, 1972); *At the End of the Day* (Savoy, Oct. 3, 1973); *The Dame of Sark* (Wyndham's, Oct. 1974); and *The Bank Manager* (1975).

Films. Mr. Home wrote the screen adaptations of *Now Barabbas* (De Grunwald, 1949); *The Chiltern Hundreds* (Rank, 1949); *The Colditz Story* (Rep., 1957); and *The Reluctant Debutante* (MGM, 1958).

Published Works. He wrote his autobiography, *Half-Term Report* (1952).
Recreation. Golf, racing.

HOMOLKA, OSCAR. Actor, director. b. Aug. 12, 1903, Vienna, Austria, to Heinrich and Anna (Handl) Homolka. Attended Royal Acad. Married May 27, 1949, to Joan Tetzel, actress. Member of AEA; SAG; AFTRA.
Theatre. Mr. Homolka made his stage debut in the title role in *Richard III* at the Raimund Th., Vienna, where he appeared for several seasons in repertory; played Mortimer in Brecht's *Edward II* (Kammerspiele, Munich, Germany), which he also directed, with the playwright. He appeared in the title role of *Baal* (Deutsches Th., Berlin); and, with Max Reinhardt's Co., appeared as Ferdinand de Levis in *Loyalties,* Hulin in *Bonaparte,* Sir Colenso Ridgeon in *The Doctor's Dilemma,* played in *King Lear, A Midsummer Night's Dream, Troilus and Cressida, The Ringer, The Squeaker,* Juarez in *Juarez and Maximilian,* Mephistopheles in *Faust,* and Captain Jack Boyle in *Juno and the Paycock.* Mr. Homolka produced, directed, and played Professor Henry Higgins in *Pygmalion* (Lessing Th., Berlin, 1932); followed by his English-language debut as Dr. Mesmer in *Mesmer* (King's Th., Glasgow, Scotland, May 6, 1935); appeared as Gustave Bergmann in *Close Quarters* (Embassy Th., London, June 25, 1935); and Dr. Galen Marshall in *Power and Glory* (Savoy, London, April 1938).

Mr. Homolka made his N.Y.C. debut as James Grantham in *Grey Farm* (Hudson, May 3, 1940); played Captain Jonsen in *The Innocent Voyage* (Belasco, Nov. 15, 1942); Uncle Chris in *I Remember Mama* (Music Box, Oct. 19, 1944); Edgar in *The Last Dance* (Belasco, Jan. 27, 1948); and Zoltan Lazko in *Bravo* (Lyceum, Nov. 11, 1948). He played the Judge in *The Broken Jug* (Burg Th., Salsburg Festival, Austria, 1950); appeared in *Le Diable et le bon Dieu* (Zurich, Switzerland, 1951); played Solness in *The Master Builder,* which he also directed with the assistance of Ire Girker (Phoenix, N.Y.C., Mar. 1, 1955); and played the Wigmaker in *Rashomon* (Music Box, Jan. 27, 1959).
Films. Mr. Homolka made his debut in films produced by UFA Studios (Berlin); his first English-language film was *Rhodes* (Gaumont-British, 1936); and his Hollywood debut was in *Ebb Tide* (Par., 1937). Subsequently he appeared in *Mission to Moscow* (WB, 1943); *The Shop at Sly Corner* (1946); as Uncle Chris in *I Remember Mama* (RKO, 1948); *War and Peace* (Par., 1956); *A Farewell to Arms* (20th-Fox, 1957); *Tempest* (Par., 1959); and *The Long Ships* (Warwick, 1964).
Television. Mr. Homolka appeared in *Love Song* (Television Hour, ABC, 1954); *Darkness at Noon* (Producers Showcase, NBC, 1955); in *The Master Builder* and *You Touched Me* (both Matinee Th., NBC, 1957); in *The Plot To Kill Stalin* and *Heart of Darkness* (both Playhouse 90, CBS, 1958); *Arrowsmith* (Dupont Show of the Month, CBS, 1960); *Assassination Plot at Teheran* (ABC, 1960); *Victory* (NBC, 1960); *Rashomon* (Play of the Week, NET, 1960); Burke's Law (ABC, 1964); Hazel (NBC, 1964); and *Dr. Jekyll and Mr. Hyde* (ABC, 1968).

HONIG, EDWIN. Educator, translator, poet, literary critic. b. Sept. 3, 1919, Brooklyn, N.Y., to Abraham and Jane (Freundlich) Honig. Father, salesman. Grad. Abraham Lincoln H.S., Brooklyn, 1935; Univ. of Wisconsin, B.A. (Spanish and English) 1941, M.A. (English) 1947; attended Columbia Univ., Summers 1936, 1946; Univ. of Michigan, Summer 1942; British Council Sch., Eng., 1945; Univ. of Edinburgh, Scot., 1946; Brown Univ., M.A. (ad eundem) 1958. Married Apr. 1, 1940, to Charlotte Gilchrist, pyschologist (dec. 1963); married Dec. 15, 1963, to Margot Stevenson Dennes. Served US Army Signal Corps, 1943–46; ETO; rank, T/5. Member of MLA. Address: (home) 32 Fort Ave., Cranston, RI 02912, tel. (401) 781-8169; (bus.) Brown Univ., Providence, RI 02912, tel. (401) UN 1-2900.

Mr. Honig became professor of English at Brown Univ. in 1960. He joined the faculty as associate professor in 1957 and has also been professor of comparative literature (1961) and chairman of the Dept. of English (1967–68). In 1964–65, he was visiting professor of English, Univ. of California at Davis. Before going to Brown, Mr. Honig was at Harvard Univ. as instructor of English, 1949–52; Briggs-Copeland assistant professor of English, 1952–57. He has been an instructor of English at Purdue Univ. (1942–43); New York Univ. and Illinois Inst. of Tech. (1946–47); Univ. of New Mexico (1947–48); and a lecturer at Claremont Coll. (Summer 1949).

Mr. Honig was employed by the Federal Writers (WPA) Project in Madison, Wis. (1938–39); was poetry editor for the *New Mexico Quarterly,* (1948–52); and studied Spanish classical drama (Spain, 1958–59).

Mr. Honig's verse play *The Widow* was first produced by the Poets' Th., Cambridge, Mass., and later by the Actors' Workshop, San Francisco, Calif. (Mar. 8, 1961). His translation of Cervantes' *The Cave of Salamanca* was produced by the Univ. Students Workshop, Brown Univ., Providence, R.I. (1961), and his translation of Calderón's *The Phantom Lady* was produced by the Institute for Advanced Studies in the Theater Arts, N.Y.C. (Mar. 20, 1965), also in Washington, D.C., and Denver, Col. His translation of Calderón's *Life Is a Dream* was produced (1971–72–73–74) at Brown Univ.; the Univ. of Colorado; and Cornell Univ., and his translations of various Cervantes' *Interludes* were produced in London (1973–74).
Films. He collaborated with Hans Richter on the script *8 × 8* (Hans Richter, 1957).
Radio. Mr. Honig's translation of Calderón's *Life Is a Dream* was given a radio performance in England (BBC, 1971).
Other Activities. Mr. Honig delivered his lecture "Transfiguring Calderón" at Stanford Univ. (Jan. 1974 and as the Faber Lecture at Princeton Univ. (Feb. 27, 1974), and he lectured on "Lorca's Last Work" at Northeastern Univ., Boston, Mass. (Mar. 1974). He has also given other lectures on drama and readings of his own poetry at colleges and universities.
Published Works. Mr. Honig is author of *García Lorca* (1944; rev. ed. 1963) and two books of literary criticism, *Dark Conceit: The Making of Allegory* (1959) and *Calderón: The Seizures of Honor* (1972). His translations include *Calderón: Four Plays,* containing an introduction by Mr. Honig (1961); *Cervantes: Eight Interludes* (1964); Calderón's *Life Is a Dream* (1971); *Fernando Pessoa: Selected Poems* (1972); and *García Lorca: Divan and Other Writings* (1974). Mr. Honig has also published several books of his own poetry: *The Moral Circus* (1955); *Gazebos: 41 Poems* (1960; paperback edition with *The Widow* added, 1962); *Survivals: Selected Poems* (1964); *Spring Journal: Poems* (1968); *Four Springs* (1972); *Shake a Spear with Me, John Berryman* (1974); and *At Sixes* (1974). He has edited the *Mentor Book of Major American Poets* (1962); *The Major Metaphysical Poets,* with Oscar Williams (1968); and *Spenser* (1968). In addition, Mr. Honig is the author of articles on the plays of Calderón and García Lorca that have been published in such periodicals as *Tulane Drama Review* (now *The Drama Review*) and *Kenyon Review.* .
Awards. Mr. Honig received a Guggenheim Fellowship (1948) for studies in allegorical imagination in European literature at Sandoval, N.M.; and for studies in the drama of Calderón de la Barca (1962). He won the *Saturday Review* Annual Poetry Award for his poem "Outer Drive" (1956); and the Golden Rose of the New England Poetry Club, Boston, Mass., for "achievement in poetry" (1961). He was the Phi Beta Kappa Poet at Brown Univ. (1961). He received a grant for poetry and translation from the National Institute of Arts and Letters, N.Y. (May 1966); the Amy Lowell Traveling Fellowship in Poetry (1968); and the Rhode Island Governor's Award for Excellence in the literary arts (1970).

HOOKS, DAVID. Actor, director. b. David Woodall Hooks, Jan. 9, 1920, to Thel and Eva (Hood) Hooks. Father, M.D. Grad. Smithfield (N.C.) H.S. 1937; attended Mars Hill (N.C.) Junior Coll., 1937–39; grad. Univ. of North Carolina, B.A. 1941. M.A. 1947. Served USNR, 1941–46; rank, Lt. Member of AEA; AFTRA; SAG. Address: 210 Forsyth St., New York, NY 10002, tel. (212) 260-2094.
Theatre. Mr. Hooks made his debut as George Washington in grade school (1927); his professional debut in *The Ghost Train* (Hunterdon Hills, N.J., Playhouse, Summer 1941); at the Univ. of North Carolina, played Argaste in *The School for Husbands* and Thomas Diaforus in *The Imaginary Invalid,* which he also directed (Mar. 1946); at the Yellow Springs (Ohio) Area Th., played Kit Carson in *The Time of Your Life,* Oscar in *The Little Foxes,* and Durand in *Joan of Lorraine,* which he also directed for the Univ. of Florida (Summer 1947); Lord Fancourt Babberly in *Charley's Aunt* and Dromio of Syracuse in *The Comedy of Errors* (Summer 1948); Mosca in *Volpone* and Marc Antony in *Julius Caesar* (Winter 1948–49); Master Ford in *The Merry Wives of Windsor,* General Dennis in *Command Decision* and Young Cheney in *The Circle* (Summer 1949); and Dunois in *Saint Joan* (Winter 1949); at the St. Petersburg (Fla.) Th., he played the Father in *Dear Ruth,* which he directed, and the Doctor in *Dracula* (Winter, 1950); appeared with the Margaret Webster touring company as Le Tremouille and the Executioner in *Saint Joan* and a Servant in *The Taming of the Shrew* (Winter 1950); played Jerry in *Peg O' My Heart,* Sidney Black in *Light Up the Sky,* Dr. Merrill in *Goodbye, My Fancy,* Dr. Sloper in *The Heiress,* and Elwood P. Dowd in *Harvey* (Surry Playhouse, Me., Summer 1950).

Mr. Hooks made his Bway debut as understudy and stage manager for *Pride's Crossing* (Biltmore, Nov. 20, 1950); played Hugo in *Present Laughter,* Oliver T. Erwenter in *The Silver Whistle,* Marvin Hudgins in *Dark of the Moon* and Jelliwell in *Springtime for Henry* (Surry Playhouse, Summer 1951); played Sosie in an ELT production of *Amphitryon 38* (Lenox Hill Playhouse, Autumn 1951); with the Touring Players, Inc., played Caliban in *The Tempest,* which he also directed; Mr. Antrobus in *The Skin of Our Teeth;* Brewsie in *Brewsie and Willie* and Captain Howard in *Fashion* (Winter 1952); at the Antioch Shakespeare Festival, played the title role in *Henry V,* and Prince Hal in *Henry IV, Parts 1 and 2* (Antioch Area Th., Summer 1952); Hector in *Troilus and Cressida,* the title role in *Coriolanus,* and Metellus Cimber and Clitus in *Julius Caesar,* which he also directed (Summer 1953).

He played Brewsie in *Brewsie and Willie* (Th. de Lys, Fall 1953); played the Court Clerk and understudied Norman Lloyd as Mr. Dockwiler in *Madam, Will You Walk* (Phoenix, Dec. 1, 1953), a Servant and understudied Robert Ryan in the title role in *Coriolanus* (Phoenix, Jan. 19, 1954), and Theron in *The Golden Apple* (Phoenix, Mar. 11, 1954); at the Antioch Shakespeare Festival, played Christopher Sly in *The Taming of the Shrew,* the First Outlaw and Antonio in *The Two Gentlemen from Verona,* which he also directed; Mercutio in *Romeo and Juliet,* and directed *The Tempest* (Summer 1954); with the Phoenix, Th., played the Night Shift Foreman in *Sandhog* (Nov. 29, 1954), a Waiter in *The Doctor's Dilemma* (Jan. 11, 1955), a Workman in *The Master Builder* (Mar. 14, 1955), and was assistant stage manager for *Phoenix '55* (Apr. 23, 1955).

With the Antioch (Ohio) Shakespeare Festival, he played Pistol in *The Merry Wives of Windsor,* which he also directed, Feste in *Twelfth Night* and a Gaoler in *The Winter's Tale,* which he directed (Summer 1955); in N.Y.C., played Macduff in *Macbeth,* the Banker in *The Lost Love of Don Juan* and Euripides in *The Thesmophoriazusae* (Rooftop Th., Autumn 1955); and played Cooper in the national touring company of *Inherit the Wind* (opened Blackstone, Chicago, Ill., Feb. 8, 1956); returned to the Antioch Shakespeare Festival to direct and play the Second Soldier in *All's Well That Ends Well,* played Antipholus of Ephesus in *The Comedy of Errors,* directed, and played Mercade in *Love's Labour's Lost,* and played Polonius in *Hamlet* (summer 1956).

In stock at Myrtle Beach, S.C., played the Devil in *Will Success Spoil Rock Hunter?* and Abel in *The Desk Set* (Summer 1957); at the Festival of Two Worlds (Spoleto, Italy), played James Tyrone in *A Moon for the Misbegotten* (Summer 1957); for the Festival Theatre Assn. (Toledo, Ohio) played Gonzalo in *The Tempest*, the Salesman in *Ah, Wilderness!*, Uncle Titus in *The Devil's Disciple*, which he also directed, Lord Fancourt Babberly in *Charley's Aunt* and directed *Pictures in the Hallway* (Summer 1957); played the Bandit in *Tobias and the Angel* (Th. '60, N.Y.C., 1958); succeeded Douglas Watson as the Narrator in *Pale Horse, Pale Rider* (Jan Hus House, Dec. 9, 1958); the Count in *Ardele* (Cricket, Apr. 8, 1958); Joseph in *Christmas Oratorio* (Th. de Lys, Dec. 1958); Agrippa in a reading of *Antony and Cleopatra* for the NY Shakespeare Festival (Heckscher Th., Jan., 1959); and Sutter in *Ping Pong* (Seven Arts Center, Apr., 1959).

With the San Diego (Calif.) Shakespeare Festival, played Boyet in *Love's Labour's Lost*, Friar Lawrence in *Romeo and Juliet* and Worcester in *Henry IV, Part 1* (Aug., 1959); played Creon in *Antigone* (74 St. Th., N.Y.C., Sept., 1959); James Tyrone in *A Moon for the Misbegotten* (Charles Playhouse, Boston, Mass., Oct.–Dec. 1959), and the Count in *Children of Darkness* (Charles Playhouse, Feb.–Mar. 1960).

With the APA (Association of Producing Artists), Mr. Hooks played Max in *Anatol*, Dr. Dorn in *The Seagull* and Old Malone in *Man and Superman* (Bermuda Th., Hamilton, Spring 1960), appeared in the same productions at Bucks County Playhouse, New Hope, Pa.; Theatre-by-the-Sea, Matunuck, R.I.; John Drew Th., Easthampton, L.I. (May–Aug. 1960); played James Tyrone in *Long Day's Journey into Night* (Crest Theatre, Toronto, Canada, Sept.–Nov. 1960); with the APA, played Kent in *King Lear*, Quince in *A Midsummer Night's Dream*, Antonio in *Twelfth Night* and the First Grave Digger in *Hamlet* (McCarter Th., Princeton, N.J., Jan.–Mar. 1961); the title role in *Adam, the Creator* (Fred Miller Th. (Milwaukee, Wis.), Apr.–May 1961); and with the Akron (Ohio) Shakespeare Festival, played Flute in *A Midsummer Night's Dream* and Battista in *The Taming of the Shrew* (July 1961).

He appeared in three one-act plays *The Table, Water Under the Bridge*, and *The Squirrel* (White Barn Playhouse, Westport, Conn., Aug. 1961); played Jahleel and Ozni, and was understudy for Frederic March as the Angel in *Gideon* (Plymouth, N.Y.C., Nov. 6, 1961); with the APA, appeared at the Folksbiene Playhouse, N.Y.C., as Sir Oliver Surface in *The School for Scandal* (Mar. 17, 1962); Doctor Dorn in *The Seagull* (Mar. 21, 1962); and Freeman in *The Tavern* (Apr. 4, 1962); and appeared in an ANTA matinee performance of *The Squirrel* (Th. de Lys, Apr. 1962).

Mr. Hooks played Danny in *Janus* (Grist Mill Playhouse, Andover, N.J., July, 1962); with the APA, played Lamprett Bellboys in *A Penny for a Song* (Bucks County Playhouse, New Hope, Pa.; John Drew Th., East Hampton, L.I., N.Y., Aug. 1962); with the APA, played Sir Oliver Surface in *The School for Scandal*, Freeman in *The Tavern*, Engstrand in *Ghosts*, and Lamprett Bellboys in *A Penny for a Song* (Univ. of Michigan, Ann Arbor, Sept.–Dec. 1962); directed a touring production of *A Shot in the Dark* (Poinciana Playhouse, Palm Beach, Fla.; Coconut Grove Playhouse, Miami, Fla.; Mineola, L.I., Playhouse; Paper Mill Playhouse, Millburn, N.J., 1963); at the McCarter Th., played Marc Antony in *Julius Caesar*, the Fencing Master in *Le Bourgeois Gentilhomme*, the Inquisitor in *Galileo* and directed *Fuente Ovejuno* (Princeton, N.J., Jan.–Mar. 1963); at Vassar Coll., played Mr. Antrobus in *The Skin of Our Teeth* (Poughkeepsie, N.Y., Apr., 1963); portrayed Daddy in *The American Dream* and Peter in *The Zoo Story* (Cherry Lane, N.Y.C., May 28, 1963); directed *The Queen and the Rebels* (Antioch Area Th., Yellow Springs, Ohio, Aug. 1963); and played Cust in *Corruption in the Palace of Justice* (Cherry Lane, N.Y.C., Oct. 8, 1963).

At the Playhouse in the Park, Cincinnati, Ohio, Mr. Hooks played Sganarelle in *The Forced Marriage* (May 27, 1964), Berenger in *Rhinoceros* (June 17, 1964), and James Tyrone, Jr., in *A Moon for the Misbegotten*, which he also directed (July 8, 1964). He directed *King Henry IV, Part 1* (Antioch Amphitheatre, Yellow Springs, Ohio, Aug. 19, 1964) and *As You Desire Me* (McCarter Th., Princeton, N.J., Mar. 18, 1965); and returned to the Playhouse in the Park, Cincinnati, where he played Jakob Engstrand in *Ghosts* (Apr. 7, 1965), Harry in *The Collection* (Apr. 28, 1965), and Andrew Undershaft in *Major Barbara* (May 19, 1965), and directed *Summer of the Seventeenth Doll* (June 9, 1965).

He directed *The Taming of the Shrew* (Antioch Amphitheatre, July 1, 1965); returned again to the Playhouse in the Park, where he directed *The Glass Menagerie* (Aug. 11, 1965) and played the Girl's Father in *The Fantasticks* (Sept. 1, 1965). He was Peter Cauchon in *Saint Joan* (Community Playhouse, Atlanta, Ga., Oct. 12, 1965); Creon in *Medea* (Martinique, N.Y.C., Nov. 28, 1965); and, at the Playhouse in the Park, Cincinnati, Ohio, directed *Man and Superman* (Apr. 6, 1966), played Captain Amasa Deland in *Benito Cereno* (Apr. 28, 1966), directed *Charley's Aunt* (June 16, 1966), played Reverend Mort in *Eh!* (July 13, 1966), Mr. Antrobus in *The Skin of Our Teeth* (Aug. 4, 1966), and repeated his role of the Girl's Father in *The Fantasticks* (Aug. 31, 1966).

Mr. Hooks was Judge Cool in the musical version of *The Grass Harp* (Trinity Square Rep. Co., Providence, R.I., Dec. 26, 1966); returned again to the Playhouse in the Park, Cincinnati, where he was in *The Cavern* (June 8, 1967), in *Escurial*, which he also directed (July 6, 1967), *Anatol*, which he also directed (Aug. 31, 1967), and directed *Misalliance* (Apr. 4, 1968), appeared in *The Miser* (June 13, 1968), and directed *Crime on Goat Island* (Apr. 8, 1968). He played Reverend Toomis in *Gantry* (George Abbott Th., Feb. 14, 1970); appeared at the NY Shakespeare Festival (Delacorte Th.) as Warwick in *Henry VI, Parts 1* and *2* (June 23, 24, 1970); was Doc in *Small Craft Warnings* (Truck and Warehouse Th., Apr. 2, 1972); Gorodnov in *The Headhunters* (John F. Kennedy Ctr., Washington, D.C., May 1974); and appeared in *The Amazing Activity of Charley Contrare and the Ninety-Eighth Street Gang* (Circle Rep. Th. Co., Jan. 20, 1974).

Films. Mr. Hooks appeared in *Dark Odyssey* (ERA-KM, 1957).

Television. He made his television debut as Brewsie in *Brewsie and Willie* (Omnibus, NBC, Nov. 7, 1954); appeared on the Perry Como Show (NBC, Dec. 1955); The Defenders (NBC, 1963); The Doctors (1963); Naked City (ABC, 1963); in *A Splendid Misery* (CBS, 1964); and *The Forced Marriage* (Rep. Th., Inc., Mar. 1965).

Other Activities. Mr. Hooks was Professor of Drama at the Univ. of Florida (1947–48) and at Antioch Coll. (1948–49).

Recreation. Reading, swimming, hiking, traveling.

HOOKS, ROBERT. Actor, director, producer. b. Bobby Dean Hooks, Apr. 18, 1937, Washington, D.C., to Edward and Bertha (Ward) Hooks. Grad. West Philadelphia H.S.; attended Temple Univ. Studied acting at Bessie V. Hichs Sch. of the Th., Philadelphia. Married Oct. 6, 1957; two sons. Member of AEA; SAG; AFTRA; Players Club. Address: c/o Chartwell Artist Ltd., 1345 Ave. of the Americas, New York, NY 10019.

Theatre. Billed as Bobby Dean Hooks, he made his professional debut as a replacement in the role of George Murchison in *A Raisin in the Sun*, subsequently touring with that production (national tour, opened Wilbur, Boston, Sept. 12, 1960); succeeded Lincoln Kilpatrick as Deodatus Village in *The Blacks* (St. Mark's Playhouse, N.Y.C., May 4, 1961); played the Boy in *A Taste of Honey* (tour opened National Washington, D.C., Sept. 11, 1962; closed Blackstone, Chicago, Apr. 7, 1962); Dewey Chipley in *Tiger, Tiger Burning Bright* (Booth, N.Y.C., Dec. 22, 1962); played Dennis Thornton in *Ballad for Bimshire* (Mayfair, Oct. 15, 1963); appeared in *Arturo Ui* (Lunt-Fontanne, Nov. 11, 1963); and played the Stage Assistant in *The Milk Train Doesn't Stop Here Anymore* (Brooks Atkinson Th., Jan. 1, 1964).

Billed as Robert Hooks, he played Clay in *Dutchman* on a program entitled *Three at the Cherry Lane* (Cherry Lane Th., N.Y.C., Mar. 24, 1964); repeating that performance on a bill with *The Zoo Story* (Cherry Lane Th., Nov. 24, 1964); played the title role in N.Y. Shakespeare Fest. production of *King Henry V* (Mobile Th., June 6, 1965); produced a bill of one-acts (St. Mark's Playhouse, Nov. 11, 1965), playing Junie in *Happy Ending*, and John in *Day of Absence;* played Razz in *Where's Daddy?* (Billy Rose Th., Mar. 2, 1966); and Clem in *Hallelujah, Baby!* (Martin Beck Th., Apr. 26, 1967); and co-produced *Walk Together Children* (Greenwich Mews Th., Nov. 11, 1968).

From 1963–68, he operated the Group Th. Workshop, a tuition-free training program for young black actors. In 1968, with Douglas Turner Ward (artistic director) and Gerald S. Krone (administrative director), Mr. Hooks co-founded and became executive director of the Negro Ensemble Co. established in permanent quarters off-Bway at the St. Mark's Playhouse (133 Second Ave., N.Y.C.). There, productions have included *Song of the Lusitanian Bogey* (Jan. 2, 1968); *Summer of the Seventeenth Doll* (Feb. 20, 1968); *Kongi's Harvest* (Apr. 14, 1968), in which he played Daoudu; *Daddy Goodness* (June 4, 1968); *God Is a (Guess What?)* (Dec. 17, 1968); *Ceremonies in Dark Old Men* (Feb. 2, 1969); *An Evening of One Acts* (Apr. 1, 1969); which included *Strings, Contribution*, and *Malcochon; Man Better Man; The Reckoning* (Sept. 4, 1969); *The Harangues* (Jan. 13, 1970), in which he played Col; *Brotherhood* and *Day of Absence* (Mar. 17, 1970); *Akokawa* (May 26, 1970); *Ododo* (Nov. 17, 1970); *Perry's Mission* and *Rosalee Pritchett* (Jan. 21, 1971); *The Dream on Monkey Mountain* (Mar. 14, 1971); *Ride a Black Horse* (May 25, 1971); *The Sty of the Blind Pig* (Nov. 23, 1971); *A Ballet Behind the Bridge* (Mar. 15, 1972); *Frederick Douglass . . Through His Own Words* (May 9, 1972); *The River Niger* (St. Mark's Playhouse, Dec. 5, 1972; moved to Brooks Atkinson Th., Mar. 27, 1973; national tour, opened New Locust, Philadelphia, Oct. 16, 1973; closed Shubert, Philadelphia, May 27, 1974); *The Great MacDaddy* (St. Mark's Playhouse, N.Y.C., Feb. 14, 1974); a program entitled *A Season-within-a-Season* (Mar. 19–Apr. 14, 1974) that included *Black Sunlight, Nowhere to Run, Nowhere To Hide, Terraces*, and *Heaven and Hell's Agreement; In the Deepest Part of Sleep* (June 4, 1974); *The First Breeze of Summer* (Mar. 2, 1975); and *A Season-within-a-Season* (Apr. 28–May 28, 1975) including *Liberty Call, Two Plays by Don Evans, Two by Rudy Wallace, Waiting for Mongo*, and *Welcome to Black River*.

Mr. Hooks is one of the founders (1972) and executive director of the D.C. Black Repertory Co. (Washington, D.C.), permanently housed in the last Colony Th. He directed, and played Village in *The Blacks* in the company's guest appearance at Kennedy Ctr. (May 1973).

Films. Mr. Hooks mae his film debut in *Sweet Love . . Bitter* (Film 2 Assoc., 1967); and has appeared in *Hurry Sundown* (Par., 1967); *Last of the Mobile Hot Shots* (WB, 1970); and *Trouble Man* (20th-Fox, 1972). With Lonne Elder III, he founded Bannaker Productions, a film company.

Television. In addition to his series, N.Y.P.D. (ABC), Mr. Hooks' television appearances include Naked City; East Side/West Side; Dupont Show of the Week; Profiles in Courage (NBC); Carter's Army (ABC); and *Vanished*. He co-hosted Like It Is (WABC-TV, N.Y.C.); and co-produced the D.C. Black Repertory Co. production of *Happy Ending* (WTOP-TV, Washington, D.C.).

Other Activities. He was chosen by Leonard Bernstein to narrate Mark Blitzstein's "Airborne Symphony" (Philharmonic Hall, N.Y.C.).

Awards. Mr. Hooks received the *Theatre World* Award (1965–66) for his performances in *King Henry V*, and *Happy Ending* and *Day of Absence*.

HOPKINS, JOHN. Playwright. b. Jan. 27, 1931, London, England. Attended Raynes Park County Grammar Sch.; St. Catherines Coll., Cambridge, B.A. in English. Served in British Armed Forces 1950–51. Married 1954 to Prudence Balchin; married 1970 to Shirley Knight, actress; two children. Address: c/o Hatton and Bradley, Ltd., 17A Curzon St., London W. 1, England.

Theatre. Mr. Hopkins debuted as a playwright with *This Story of Yours* (Royal Court Th., London, Dec. 11, 1968); followed by *Find Your Way Home* (Open Space, May 5, 1970; and Brooks Atkinson Th., N.Y.C., Jan. 2, 1974); *The Greeks and Their Gifts* (Playhouse, London, June 20, 1972); *Economic Necessity* (Haymarket Th., Leicester, England, Nov. 1973); and *Next of Kin* (National Th. at the Old Vic, London, May 2, 1974).

Films. He co-authored the Screenplay for *Thunderball* (UA, 1965) and wrote the scripts for *Virgin Soldiers* (Col., 1970); *The Offence* (UA, 1973), which was based upon his play, *This Story of Yours;* and *Divorce His/Divorce Hers.*.

Television. Mr. Hopkins worked as a studio manager, producer and writer for the BBC (1962–64) and, as a freelance writer, has continued to produce original works for British television. His plays include *Break Up* (1958); *After the Party* (1958); *The Small Back Room* (1959); *Dancers in Mourning* (1959); *A Woman Comes Home* (1961); *A Chance of Thunder* (1961); *By Invitation Only* (1961); *The Second Curtain* (1962); the Z Car series (1962–65); *The Pretty English Girls* (1964); *I Took My Little World Away* (1964); *House Party,* a ballet scenario (1964); *The Make Believe Man* (1965); *Fable* (1965); *Horror of Darkness* (1965); *You Pays Your Money* (1965); *More Than Meets the Eye* (1965); *A Man Like Orpheus* (1965); *Talking to a Stranger* (1966), which included *Anytime You're Ready I'll Sparkle, No Skill or Special Knowledge Is Required, Gladly My Cross-Eyed Bear,* and *The Innocent Must Suffer; Some Place of Darkness* (1966); *A Game-Like Only a Game* (1966); *The Burning Bush* (1967); *The Gambler* (1968); *Beyond the Sunrise* (1969); *The Dolly Scene* (1970); *Some Distant Shadow* (1971); *That Quiet Earth* (1972); *Walk into the Dark* (1972); and *The Greeks and Their Gifts* (1972).

HORNE, GEOFFREY. Actor. b. Aug. 22, 1933, Buenos Aires, Argentina, to George W. and Evelyn (Horton) Horne. Father, merchant. Attended Tutoring Sch. of N.Y. (1950); Stanford Univ. (1950–51); Davis and Elkins Coll., 1951–52; Fresno State Coll., 1952; grad. Univ. of California at Berkeley, B.A. 1954. Studied acting with Lee Strasberg. Actors Studio (mbr. since 1954). Married Feb. 1958 to Nancy Berg, model, actress (marr. dis.); married June 28, 1963, to Collin Wilcox, actress. Member of AEA; AFTRA; SAG.

Pre-Theatre. Dance instructor.

Theatre. Mr. Horne made his N.Y.C. debut as Rob Lawson in *High Named Today* (Th. de Lys, Dec. 10, 1954); subsequently appeared in *Tea and Sympathy* (Hyde Park, N.Y., Summer Th., Aug. 1956); played Dick Vorster in *Too Late the Phalarope* (Belasco, N.Y.C., Oct. 11, 1956); appeared in *Desire Under the Elms* (North Jersey Playhouse, Fort Lee, N.J., Jan. 27, 1959); played Frederic in *Jeannette* (Maidman, Mar. 24, 1960); Dave Mannin in *Under the Yum-Yum Tree* (Coconut Grove Playhouse, Miami, Fla., Summer 1961); Doug in *Call Me by My Rightful Name* (Theatre O, Washington, D.C., 1961), with the Theatre Group; Claudio in *Measure for Measure* (UCLA, Jan. 15, 1962); Gordon in *Strange Interlude* (Hudson, N.Y.C., Mar. 11, 1963); and with the Theatre Group, Constantine in *The Seagull* (UCLA, Jan. 10, 1964).

Films. Mr. Horne has appeared in *The Strange One* (Col., 1957); *The Bridge on the River Kwai* (Col., 1957); *Bonjour Tristesse* (Col., 1958); *Esterina* (Di Laurentis, 1958); *The Tempest* (Par., 1959); *The Corsican Brothers* (Italy, 1961); *Joseph and His Brethren* J. V. Cremonin, 1962); *Three Good Men* (Spain, 1963); and *Two People* (U, 1973).

Television. He has appeared on the Philco Television Playhouse (NBC, 1955); in *Billy Budd* (1955); *The Young and the Beautiful* (Robert Montgomery Presents, NBC, 1955); and *Cradle Song* (Hallmark Hall of Fame, NBC, 1957). He has also appeared on the Twilight Zone (CBS); Studio One (BBS); Great Adventure series; Outer Limits; Route 66 (CBS); Adventures in Paradise (ABC); Alfred Hitchcock Th. (NBC); The Doctors/The Nurses (CBS); The F.B.I. (ABC); The Virginian (NBC); The Road West (NBC); The Green Hornet (ABC); Run for Your Life (NBC); and Ghost Story (NBC).

Recreation. Reading.

HORNE, LENA. Actress, singer. b. June 30, 1917, Brooklyn, N.Y., to Edwin F. and Lena (Calhoun) Horne. Father, clerk; mother, actress. Attended Girls' H.S., N.Y.C., 1933. Married 1937 to Louis J. Jones (dec. 1944); one son (dec. 1971), one daughter; married 1947 to Lennie Hayton, musical director (dec. 1971). Served WW II, U.S.O., Hollywood Victory Committee. Relatives in theatre: daughter, Gail Jones, actress; son-in-law, Sydney Lumet, director. Member of AGVA; AEA; SAG; AFTRA; AGMA; NAACP; Delta Sigma Theta; Natl. Council of Negro Women.

Theatre. Miss Horne made her N.Y.C. debut as a Quadroon Girl in *Dance with Your Gods* (Mansfield, Oct. 6, 1934); gave a concert at Carnegie Hall, billed as Helena Horne (1941); played Savannah in *Jamaica* (Imperial, Oct. 31, 1957); toured in *Nine O'-Clock Revue* (opened O'Keefe Ctr., Toronto, Ontario, Canada, Oct. 16, 1961; closed Shubert, New Haven, Conn., Nov. 18, 1961); and appeared, with Alan King (Westbury Music Fair, Long Island, N.Y., May 1971; Deauville Star Th., Miami Beach, Fla., Feb. 20–25, 1972).

Films. Miss Horne made her debut in *Panama Hattie* (MGM, 1942); and has since appeared in *Cabin in the Sky* (MGM, 1943); *I Dood It* (MGM, 1943); *Swing Fever* (MGM, 1943); *Broadway Rhythm* (MGM, 1944); *As Thousands Cheer* (MGM, 1943); *Stormy Weather* (20th-Fox, 1943); *Two Girls and a Sailor* (MGM, 1944); *Ziegfeld Follies* (MGM, 1946); *Till The Clouds Roll By* (MGM, 1946); *Words and Music* (MGM, 1948); *Meet Me in Las Vegas* (MGM, 1956); and *Death of a Gunfighter* (U, 1969).

Television and Radio. On radio, Miss Horne performed on Strictly from Dixie (NBC, 1941) and The Cats 'n' Jammers Show (MBS, 1941). Her television appearances include the Perry Como Show (NBC, Feb. 21, 1959); the Lena Horne Show (Assoc. Rediffusion, London, England, Dec. 1959); Here's to the Ladies (ABC, Feb. 15, 1960); the Bell Telephone Hour (NBC, Jan. 1964); a non-network special originally recorded in London (WNEW, N.Y.C., Dec. 1965); the special *Lena in Concert* (NBC, Sept. 10, 1969); and, with Harry Belafonte, the special *Harry and Lena* (ABC, Mar. 22, 1970).

Night Clubs. She made her first appearance as a chorine at the Cotton Club (N.Y.C., 1933); subsequently appeared as a singer with Noble Sissle's orchestra in one-night stands, on tour; billed as Helena Horne, she sang at the Cafe Society Downtown (N.Y.C., 1941); in Paris, appeared at Club des Champs Elysées (1947); in London, at the Savoy Hotel (Sept. 21, 1959); in Windsor, Ontario, at the Elmwood (Dec. 7, 1972).

Miss Horne has appeared at all major night clubs in the US, including the Empire Room (Waldorf-Astoria, N.Y.C. 1963).

Concerts. Miss Horne appeared in concert with Tony Bennett (O'Keefe Ctr., Toronto, Ont., Can., Oct. 1974; Minskoff Th., N.Y.C., Oct. 30, 1974). She has performed for numerous benefits, including the Southern Christian Leadership Conference (Municipal Aud., Atlanta, Ga., Aug. 1963) and the Foundation for Internat'l. Child Health (Carnegie Hall, N.Y.C., Oct. 6, 1963).

Published Works. With Richard Schickel, Miss Horne wrote her autobiography, *Lena* (1965).

Discography. Her first recording was *Birth of the Blues* (RCA, 1940); followed by *Moanin' Low* (RCA); *Little Girl Blue* (RCA); *Classics in Blue* (RCA); *Porgy and Bess* (RCA); *The Lady Is a Tramp* (MGM); *Now* (Fox); *A Friend of Yours* (RCA); *Sands* (Victor, 1961); *At the Waldorf* (Victor, 1958); *Like Latin* (Charter, 1963); *Lovely and Alive* (Victor, 1962); *On the Blue Side* (Victor, 1962); *Sings Your Requests* (Charter, 1963); *Till the Clouds Roll By* (MGM, 1946); and *Words and Music* (MGM, 1948).

Recreation. Classical music.

HORNER, HARRY. Director, scenic designer. b. July 24, 1912, Holic, Czechoslovakia, to Felix and Gisela (Kohn) Horner. Father, mechanical engineer. Grad. Univ. of Vienna, Austria, 1934. Studied acting and directing at Max Reinhardt's Theatrical Seminary, Vienna, 1933–35. Married Sept. 1939 to Betty Pfaelzer (dec. Aug. 1951); married Oct. 1952 to Joan; three sons. Served US Army, Air Force Camouflage Unit and Special Services, 1943–45; rank, T/Sgt. Member of SDG; SSD&C; AGMA; Art Directors Guild; United Scenic Artists, Local 829; AMPAS; USITT; ANTA; Intl. Inst. of Arts and Letters. Address: 728 Brooktree Road, Pacific Palisades, CA 90272.

Pre-Theatre. Architect.

Theatre. Mr. Horner made his debut playing the "Fascist" and serving as scenic designer for productions at the Political Cabaret (Vienna, 1932); subsequently played the Pupil in *Faust* and cook in *Everyman,* which were produced by Max Reinhardt at the Salzburg (Austria) Festival (Summer 1933–35); played Bottom in *A Midsummer Night's Dream* and Orlando in *As You Like It,* and directed both productions (Theatre in the Josephstadt, Vienna, 1935–36); and repeated his role in *A Midsummer Night's Dream* (Castle of Glessheim, Summer 1934).

He was scenic designer for *Victoria Regina,* which toured Italy (1935); appeared in and directed the European tours of *Mary Stuart, Six Characters in Search of an Author,* and *Roulette* (1935); was scenic and costume designer for *Wings of a Century* (History of Railroads) (Cleveland Fair, Ohio, Summer 1936); played Smallens in *Iron Men* (Longacre, N.Y.C., Oct. 19, 1936), for which he was also stage manager; appeared in and was assistant to Max Reinhardt and Norman Bel Geddes for the pageant, *The Eternal Road* (Manhattan Opera House, Jan. 7, 1937); assistant to Arturo Toscanini for the production of *The Magic Flute* (Salzburg Festival, Summer 1937); and directed and designed the *Ice Follies of 1937* (Cleveland Fair, Summer 1937).

He designed sets for *All the Living* (Fulton, N.Y.C., Mar. 24, 1938); *Night People* (1938); *Jeremiah* (Guild, Feb. 3, 1939); *Family Portrait* (Morosco, Mar. 8, 1939); *Orfeo* (Metropolitan Opera House, 1939); and *Herod* (1939); sets and costumes for *Railroads on Parade* (NY World's Fair, Summer 1939); sets for *The World We Make* (Guild, Nov. 20, 1939); *Il Trovatore* (Metropolitan Opera House, Nov. 1940); *Lady in the Dark* (Alvin, Jan. 23, 1941); *Let's Face It* (Imperial, Oct. 29, 1941); *Electra* (San Francisco Opera, 1941); *Banjo Eyes* (Hollywood Th., N.Y.C., Dec. 25, 1941); *Lily of the Valley* (Windsor, Jan. 26, 1942); *Heart of a City* (Henry Miller's Th., Feb. 12, 1942); *Fidelis* (San Francisco Opera, 1942); and *Star and Garter* (Music Box Th., N.Y.C., June 24, 1942).

While serving in the US Army, he was set designer for the Air Force musical *Winged Victory* (44 St. Th., Nov. 20, 1943); and wrote and designed *You Bet Your Life,* a Special Services production for training of camouflage units.

He was designer for *Me and Molly* (Belasco, N.Y.C., Feb. 26, 1948); *Joy to the World* (Plymouth, Mar. 18, 1948); *Tovarich* (NY City Ctr., 1952); *Hazel Flagg* (Mark Hellinger Th., Feb. 11, 1953); and designed the following operas at the San Francisco Opera: *Turandot* (1953), *The Portuguese Inn* (1954), and *The Flying Dutchman* (1955).

He designed *The Magic Flute* (Metropolitan Opera House, N.Y.C., 1956); designed and directed *Joan at the Stake* (American premiere, San Francisco Opera, 1956); *The Dialogues of the Carmelites* (American premiere, San Francisco Opera, 1957); Darius Milhaud's *King David* (world premiere, Hollywood Bowl, 1958); *A Midsummer Night's Dream* (Vancouver Music Festivals, Canada, 1961); *The Magic Flute* (Vancouver Music Festivals, 1962; also new production at Metropolitan Opera, N.Y.C., 1963); and *Aida* (Seattle Festival Opera House, Wash., 1963). Mr. Horner also designed Metropolitan Opera productions of Gluck's *Orfeo* and Verdi's *Il Trovatore* and San Francisco Opera productions of *Elektra* and *Fidelio.*

In addition to the operas, Mr. Horner designed productions for the Ahmanson Th., Los Angeles, Calif., of *Idiot's Delight* (1970) and *The Time of the Cuckoo* (1974).

Films. Mr. Horner was production designer and art director for *Our Town* (UA, 1940); *The Little Foxes* (RKO, 1941); *Stage Door Canteen* (UA, 1943); *A Double Life* (U, 1948); *The Heiress* (Par., 1949); *Outrage* (RKO, 1950); *Born Yesterday* (Col., 1950); *He Ran All the Way* (U, 1951); and *Androcles and the Lion* (RKO, 1952). He directed *Beware My Lovely* (RKO, 1952); *Vicki* (20th-Fox, 1953); *New Faces* (20th-Fox, 1954); *A Matter of Life and Death* (20th-Fox, 1954); *The Wild Party* (UA, 1956); and *The Man from Del Rio* (UA, 1956). He was production designer and art director for *Separate Tables* (UA, 1958); *The Wonderful Country* (UA, 1959); and *The Hustler* (20th-Fox, 1961).

In 1964, Mr. Horner formed his own production company, Enterprise Films, in Canada; as president and executive producer, he moved to London, England, where Anglo Enterprise Films produced *Fahrenheit 451* (U, 1966). Returning to the US, Horner designed the production for *They Shoot Horses, Don't They?* (Cinerama, 1969). He also designed *Who Is Harry Kellerman?* (Natl. Gen., 1971); *Lady Sings the Blues* (Par., 1972); and *Up the Sandbox* (Natl. Gen., 1972).

Television. He has directed such programs as Curtain Up (NBC); Omnibus (CBS); Four Star Playhouse (CBS); Gunsmoke (CBS); Schlitz Playhouse (CBS); Dupont Th.; and Shirley Temple's Fairy Tales.

Awards. Mr. Horner received the League of Nations Award for his film scenario based on Beethoven's Ninth Symphony, on the subject of peace (1932); Academy (Oscar) Award nominations for his art direction for *Our Town* (1940), *The Little Foxes* (1941), and *A Double Life* (1948); an Academy Award for his art direction for *The Heiress* (1949); Academy Award nominations for his art direction for *Born Yesterday* (1950) and *Separate Tables* (1958); and Academy Awards for his art direction for *The Hustler* (1961) and *They Shoot Horses, Don't They?* (1969).

Recreation. Painting, book collecting, stamp collecting, swimming, skiing, tennis, mountain climbing.

HORNER, JED.

Director. b. Jedediah Edward Horner, May 10, 1922, Newark, N.J., to Sam and Mae (Meyerson) Horner. Father, grocer. Grad. Arizona State Univ., B.A. 1943; Univ. of California at Los Angeles, M.S. 1945. Married June 10, 1963, to Renata Vaselle, actress. Member of AEA; SSD&C (charter member).

Pre-Theatre. College professor.

Theatre. Mr. Horner was first engaged as director at the Entime Th. (Princeton, N.J., 1953); subsequently directed *Cloud 7* (John Golden Th., Feb. 14, 1958); was resident director for the John B. Kelly Playhouse-in-the-Park (Philadelphia, Pa., Summer 1958); directed *Paptate* (Henry Miller's Th., N.Y.C., Oct. 28, 1958); and the touring English production of *Make a Million* (1959); and a US touring company of *The Andersonville Trial* (1960).

He directed stock productions at the Northland Playhouse (Detroit, Mich., Summer 1961); Tenthouse Th. (Highland Park, Ill., Summer 1962); Vanguard Playhouse (Detroit, Mich., Summer 1962); Ann Arbor (Mich.) Drama Festival (Lydia Mendelssohn Th., Summer 1962); and at the Edgewater Beach Playhouse (Chicago, Ill., Summer 1962); staged the Chrysler-Imperial industrial show (Ziegfeld, N.Y.C., 1963); and was resident director at the Goodspeed Opera House (E. Haddam, Conn., Summer 1964).

Films. Mr. Horner was staff director for industrial films (MPO, 1963).

HORNER, RICHARD.

General manager, producer. b. Richard Hollis Horner, June 29, 1920, Portland, Ore., to Godfrey Richard and Ruby (Weller) Hoerner. Father, plant pathologist. Grad. Corvallis (Oregon) H.S., 1938; attended Oregon State Univ., 1938–40; Univ. of Washington, B.A., 1942. Married Dec. 11. 1959, to Lynne Stuart, actress-singer; two sons, one daughter. Served USN, 1942–46; rank, Lt. Member of AEA; SAG; AFTRA; Assn. of Theatrical Press Agents and Managers (pres., 1963); Delta Upsilon; The Lambs; New York Athletic Club.

Theatre. Mr. Horner made his stage debut as a walk-on in the Oberammergau Passion Play (Corvallis, Ore., 1934); first appeared professionally in a season of stock, playing such roles as John in *John Loves Mary* (Showshop, Canton, Conn., Summer 1946); followed by another season of stock (Summer Th., Nuangola, Pa., Summer 1947); and was business manager for the Playhouse (Windham, N.H., Summer 1948).

He was stage manager for *The Curious Savage* (Martin Beck, N.Y.C., Oct. 24, 1950); the pre-Bway tryout of the Katharine Cornell production of *Captain Carvallo* (opened Buffalo, N.Y., Dec. 1950; closed Cleveland, Ohio, Dec. 1950); *The Constant Wife* (National, N.Y.C., Dec. 8, 1951); and the Cornelia Otis Skinner production, *Paris '90* (Booth, Mar. 4, 1952); was company manager for *I've Got Sixpence* (Ethel Barrymore Th., Dec. 2, 1953); the Martha Graham Dance Company (Alvin, May 17, 1953); a touring production of *Twin Beds* (1953–54); and the touring Agnes de Mille Dance Th. (1953–54).

He was company manager for *The Pajama Game* (St. James, N.Y.C., May 13, 1954); *On Your Toes* (46 St. Th., Oct. 11, 1954); *The Dark is Light Enough* (ANTA, Feb. 23, 1955); and *Damn Yankees* (46 St. Th., May 5, 1955). He produced, with Justin Sturm, *Debut* (Holiday, Feb. 22, 1956); was general manager for *Cranks* (Bijou, Nov. 26, 1956); company manager for *New Girl in Town* (46 St. Th., May 14, 1957); and *West Side Story* (Winter Garden, Sept. 26, 1957); general manager for *Copper and Brass* (Martin Beck Th., Oct. 17, 1957); and *Clerambard* (Rooftop Th., Nov. 7, 1957); and produced, with Justin Sturm, for Brisson, Griffith and Prince in association with Taylor, a touring company of *Damn Yankees* (opened Mosque, Altoona, Pa., Jan. 18, 1958; closed Paramount, Omaha, Nebr., May 10, 1958).

Mr. Horner was general manager for *Blue Denim* (Playhouse, N.Y.C., Feb. 27, 1958); and *The Next President* (Bijou, Apr. 9, 1958); company manager for *Goldilocks* (Lunt-Fontanne Th., Oct. 11, 1958); *Make a Million* (Playhouse, Oct. 23, 1958); and *Redhead* (46 St. Th., Feb. 5, 1959); general manager for *The Geranium Hat* (Orpheum, Mar. 17, 1959); company manager for *Destry Rides Again* (Imperial, Apr. 23, 1959); general manager for *The Nervous Set* (Henry Miller's Th., May 12, 1959); and *Chic* (Orpheum, May 19, 1959); company manager for *Take Me Along* (Shubert, Oct. 22, 1959); and company manager for *Little Mary Sunshine* (Orpheum, Nov. 18, 1959); and *Fiorello!* (Broadhurst, Nov. 23, 1959).

He was general manager for *Russell Patterson's Sketchbook* (Maidman, Feb. 6, 1960); *The Crystal Heart* (East 74 St. Th., Feb. 15, 1960); *The Cool World* (Eugene O'Neill Th., Feb. 22, 1960); *The Jackass* (Barbizon Plaza Th., Mar. 23, 1960); *Farewell, Farewell Eugene* (Helen Hayes Th., Sept. 27, 1960); *Greenwich Village, U.S.A.* (Sheridan Square, Sept. 28, 1960); *Face of a Hero* (Eugene O'Neill Th., Oct. 20, 1960); *Love and Libel* (Martin Beck Th., Dec. 7, 1960); and *The Rules of the Game* (Gramercy Arts, Dec. 19, 1960).

He was company manager for *Rhinoceros* (Longacre, Jan. 9, 1961); general manager for *Show Girl* (Eugene O'Neill Th., Jan. 12, 1961); *The Tattooed Countess* (Barbizon-Plaza, Apr. 3, 1961); *Moby Dick* (Madison Ave. Playhouse, Apr. 10, 1961); *Young Abe Lincoln* (York, May 8, 1961); company manager for *A Call on Kuprin* (Broadhurst, May 25, 1961); general manager for *The Thracian Horses* (Orpheum, Sept. 27, 1961); *Sing Muse* (Van Dam, Dec. 6, 1961); *New Faces of 1962* (Alvin, Feb. 1, 1962); *The Aspern Papers* (Playhouse, Feb. 7, 1962); and *Isle of Children* (Cort, Mar. 16, 1962).

He was general manager for *The Boys from Syracuse* (Th. Four, Apr. 15, 1963); *Something More!* (Eugene O'Neill Th., Nov. 10, 1964); *Fade Out —Fade In* (re-opened Mark Hellinger Th., Feb. 15, 1965); with Robert Fletcher, produced *The Queen and the Rebels* (Th. Four, Feb. 25, 1965); was general manager for *The Office* (Henry Miller's Th., closed Apr. 30, 1966, during previews); *Dinner at Eight* (Alvin, Sept. 27, 1966); *The Flip Side* (Booth, Oct. 10, 1968); *Hadrian VII* (Helen Hayes Th., Jan. 8, 1969); *Norman, Is That You?* (Lyceum, Feb. 19, 1970); and *Borstal Boy* (Lyceum, Mar. 31, 1970).

In 1959, Mr. Horner became Lester Osterman's general manager for the Eugene O'Neill Th., subsequently serving in that position for the 46th St. Th. (1960); and the Alvin Th. (1962). With Mr. Osterman and Robert Fletcher, he produced *High Spirits* (Alvin, Apr. 7, 1964). Under the aegis of Osterman Productions (Lester Osterman, Richard Horner, and Lawrence Kasha), he produced and was general manager for the pre-Bway tryout of *A Mother's Kisses* (opened Shubert, New Haven, Sept. 23, 1968; closed Mechanic, Baltimore, Oct. 19, 1968); was general manager of Osterman Prods. national tour of *Hadrian VII* (opened Stratford (Ontario, Canada) Shakespeare Festival, Aug. 5, 1969; closed Fisher, Detroit, May 30, 1970); with Lester Osterman, in association with Michael Codron, presented *Butley* (Morosco, N.Y.C., Oct. 31, 1972); and *Crown Matrimonial* (Helen Hayes Th., Oct. 2, 1973); with Elliot Martin and Lester Osterman produced *A Moon for the Misbegotten* (Morosco, Dec. 29, 1973); and with Lester Osterman, presented the George Spota Prods. presentation of *James Whitmore in Will Rogers' U.S.A.* (Helen Hayes Th., May 6, 1974).

Recreation. Tennis, golf.

HOROVITZ, ISRAEL.

Playwright. b. Mar. 31, 1939, Wakefield, Mass., to Julius C. and Hazel (Solberg) Horovitz. Father, lawyer; mother, nurse. Attended Wakefield (Mass.) schools; Royal Academy of Dramatic Art, London, 1961–63; City Univ. of N.Y. (Ph.D. program), 1970–to date. Married Dec. 25, 1959, to Doris Keefe (marr. dis., 1972); one daughter, two sons. Member of Dramatists Guild; Societe des Auteurs et Compositeurs Dramatique; PEN; Authors League of America; Screen Writers Guild; Eugene O'Neill Memorial Th. Foundation (charter playwright-member); Actors Studio; New Dramatists Committee. Address: 7 W. 84th St., New York, NY 10024.

Theatre. Mr. Horovitz debuted as a playwright at age seventeen, with *The Comeback* (Emerson Th., Boston, 1958); subsequently wrote *The Death of Bernard the Believer* (1960); *This Play Is About Me* (1961); *The Hanging of Emanuel* (1962); *Hop* (1963); *Skip* and *Jump* (1964), which were produced at Il Cafe Cabaret Th. (South Orange, N.J.); *It's Called the Sugar Plum* and *The Indian Wants the Bronx* (Astor Place Th., N.Y.C., Jan. 17, 1968); *Brownstone* (1967); *Rats,* which was presented with ten other short plays under the title *Collision Course* (Cafe Au Go-Go, N.Y.C., May 8, 1968); *Morning* (Festival of Two Worlds, Spoleto, Italy, July 1968), presented as *Chiaroscuro,* and, as part of a triple-bill including *Noon,* by Terrance McNally and *Night,* by Leonard Melfi (Henry Miller Th., Nov. 28, 1968); *Leader,* and *The Honest-to-God Schnozzola* (Gramercy Arts Th., Apr. 17, 1969); *Acrobats* and *Line* (Th. de Lys, Feb. 15, 1971); *Dr. Hero* (The Actors' Co., Great Neck, N.Y., Apr. 7, 1972; and *The Shade Co.,* N.Y.C., Mar. 22, 1973); *Shooting Gallery* (W.P.A. Th., June 22, 1972); *Our Father's Failing* and *Alfred Dies* (1972); *Alfred the Great* (Pittsburgh, Pa., Playhouse, Mar. 16, 1973); *Spared* (Manhattan Th. Club, N.Y.C., Mar. 21, 1974); and *Turnstile* (Dartmouth Coll., N.H., Aug. 18, 1974; also presented at Cubiculo, N.Y.C., Dec. 18, 1974).

Films. He wrote the screenplays for *Alfredo; McCain!; The Strawberry Statement* (MGM, 1970); and *Believe in Me* (MGM, 1971); and adapted his play, *Acrobats,* for the screen.

Television. Mr. Horovitz is the author of *Play for Trees*(NET, 1971); and *Play for Germs*(NET, 1973); which he also directed.

Published Works. Mr. Horovitz is the author of *Cappella,* a novel; has contributed monthly columns of criticism to *Eye* Magazine (1968–70); and *Le Magazine Litteraire* (Paris, 1971–to date); quarterly articles on fiction and poetry to *The Village Voice* (1969–to date); and various critical pieces to *Craft Horizons* Magazine (1969–71).

Awards. For *It's Called the Sugar Plum* and *The Indian Wants the Bronx,* Mr. Horovitz received the Vernon Rice-Drama Desk Award (1967), *The Village Voice* Off-Bway (Obie) Award (1967); and the *Plays and Players* Best Foreign Play Award (England, 1969). In addition, *The Indian Wants the Bronx* received the French Societe des Auteurs Foreign Play Award (1970). He received the *Showbusiness* Grand Award for best American playwright (1969) for *Rats* and *Morning,* which was also nominated for Best Play (1969–70) by The Bway Theatre Critics. *Leader* and *The Honest-to-God Schnozzola* received the *Village Voice* Off-Bway (Obie) Award for Best Play (1969–70). *The Strawberry Statement* was the winner of the Prix du Jury at the Cannes (France) Film Festival (1970); and *Play for Germs* received the Christopher and NATAS (Emmy) Awards (1973). In addition, he was the recipient of fellowships in playwrighting from the Rockefeller Foundation (1969, 1970), the NY State Council on the Arts (1972), and the National Endowment of the Arts (1974); and the American Academy of Arts and Letters Award in Literature (1972).

HORWITT, ARNOLD B. Lyricist, sketch writer. b. Arnold Bernard Horwitt, July 21, 1918, Richmond, Ind., to Jacob and Min (Zimmermann) Horwitt. Grad. DeWitt Clinton H.S., N.Y.C., 1934; New York Univ., B.A. 1938; Columbia Sch. of Journalism, M.S. 1939. Married 1948 to Joan Bower; one son, two daughters. Served US Army, Special Services, 1944–1946; rank Sgt. Member of WGA, East; Dramatists Guild (council).

Pre-Theatre. Public relations.

Theatre. Mr. Horwitt was first a contributing sketch writer and lyricist for *Pins and Needles*(Labor Hall Th., N.Y.C., Nov. 27, 1937); subsequently wrote lyrics for *Are You with It?* (Century, Nov. 10, 1945); contributed sketches to *Call Me Mister*(Natl., Apr. 18, 1946); wrote sketches and lyrics for *Make Mine Manhattan* (Broadhurst, Jan. 15, 1948); contributed sketches to *Inside U.S.A.* (Century, Apr. 30, 1948) and *Two's Company* (Alvin, Dec. 15, 1952); lyrics for *Plain and Fancy* (Mark Hellinger, Jan. 27, 1955); and sketches and lyrics for *The Girls Against the Boys* (Alvin, Nov. 2, 1959).

Television. He has written comedy and variety shows for NBC, CBS, ABC (1950), television-films for Twentieth-Century Fox-TV, Revue Productions, United Artists-TV, and Screen Gems.

Awards. *Make Mine Manhattan* received the George Jean Nathan Award for best revue of the season (1948).

Recreation. Golf.

HOSKWITH, ARNOLD K. Talent representative, free-lance casting director. b. Mar. 27, 1917, Brooklyn, N.Y., to George M. and Anna (Komow) Hoskwith. Father, salesman; mother, teacher. Grad. Abraham Lincoln H.S., Brooklyn, N.Y., 1933; Columbia Univ., B.A. 1937; Yale Univ. Sch. of Drama, M.F.A. 1941. Member of Yale Drama Alumni Assn. (chmn. Alumni comm., 1953–54). Address: 24 W. 69th St., New York, NY 10023.

Mr. Hoskwith does free-lance casting for films, television, and theatre. He has also been associated with Liebling-Wood Agency, as literary assistant (1942); Samuel Goldwyn Pictures, Inc., as reader and assistant story editor (1942–44); Frederick Bros. Agency, as head of legitimate play and casting departments (1944); Michael Todd Productions, as casting director (1944–45); Myron Selznick—Famous Artists Agency, as head of the casting department (1945–47); Warner Bros. Pictures, Inc., as assistant head of talent and casting departments (1947–59), and as assistant head of the story department (1951–59); Baum-Newborn Agency, as talent representative (1959–60); General Artists Corp., as talent representative (1960–62); Ashley Famous Agency, N.Y.C., as talent representative (1962–65); and Educational Broadcasting Corp., N.Y.C. (Ch. 13 and NET) as casting director (1965–72).

Awards. Mr. Hoskwith received the Columbia University Philolexian Poetry Prize (1936).

Recreation. Travel.

HOSTETLER, PAUL. Educator, actor, singer. b. Paul Smith Hostetler, June 9, 1921, Butte, Mont., to Ivan Paul and Genevieve (Smith) Hostetler. Father, school administrator; mother, teacher. Educ. Miami, Ariz., public schools; grad. Stanford Univ., B.A. 1943; M.A. 1949; Louisiana State Univ., Ph.D. 1964. Professional training at Lessac Institute for Voice and Speech. Served WW II, US Naval Reserve, 1943–46; highest rank, Lieutenant (senior grade). Married 1939 to Patricia Willis (marr. dis.), one daughter; married 1950 to Virginia Sherwood (marr. dis.), two sons; one daughter; married 1971 to Diane Schuldenfrei. Member of AEA; SAG; AFTRA; ATA; NTC; ASTRA; League of Professional Theatre Training Programs, Inc. (secy.-treas., 1972–to date). Address: School of Drama, Univ. of Washington, Seattle, WA 98195, tel. (206) 543-5140.

In 1974, Dr. Hostetler was appointed executive director of the School of Drama at the Univ. of Washington. He had previously been on the faculty of the Dept. of Theatre and Speech, Tulane Univ., where he advanced from instructor to professor (1949–67), was director of theatre (1960–67), and department head (1964–67). From 1967 to 1974, he was professor and chairman of the Dept. of Theatre, Temple Univ.

Theatre. Dr. Hotstetler made his stage debut as a small boy, playing the part of the Gypsy Child in *The Gypsy Rover*(Miami, Ariz., 1925). As a student at Stanford, he appeared as the Acrobat in *Now I Lay Me Down to Sleep*(July 1949), and he made his professional debut as the Doctor and general understudy in a revival of *Life with Father*(Walnut St. Th., Philadelphia, July 1972).

Dr. Hostetler also directed *The Cat and the Canary* (Forestburgh Summer Th., Forestburgh, N.Y., July 1970) and in 1958 participated in productions of the New Orleans Experimental Opera at the Civic Th., where he appeared as the Beggar in *The Beggar's Opera* and the Pasha in *Abduction from the Seraglio.*

Films. Dr. Hostetler made his film debut as Dr. Gaffney in *Panic in the Streets* (20th-Fox, 1950). He appeared also as the Foreman in *New Orleans Uncensored*(Col., 1955); the Skipper in *Bayou*(Col., 1958); the Priest in *A Damned Citizen* (UI, 1958); and Mr. Norris in *Malatesta's Carnival* (Windmill, 1972).

Television. Dr. Hostetler appeared in Route 66 (CBS, 1962), and he played the Husband in *The Corridor* on WCAU-TV, Philadelphia (CBS, 1969).

Published Works. Dr. Gaffney's articles and book reviews have appeared in a variety of periodicals.

Recreation. Reading, travel, swimming, golf, crewel.

HOUGHTON, NORRIS. Producer, designer, educator, writer. b. Charles Norris Houghton, Dec. 26, 1909, Indianapolis, Ind., to Charles D. M. and Grace (Norris) Houghton. Father, lumber dealer. Grad. Shortridge H.S., Indianapolis, 1927; Princeton Univ., B.A. (Phi Beta Kappa) 1931. Served USNR, 1942–45; rank, Lt. Member of United Scenic Artists; SSD&C; ANTA (bd. of dir. 1954–60; 1962–to date), AETA; NTC; AAUP; Century Club; Coffee House Club; Bucks Club (London). Address: (home) 11 E. 9th St., New York, NY 10003, tel. (212) OR 4-7718; 202 Millwood Rd., Chappaqua, NY 10514; (bus.) S.U.N.Y. College, Purchase, NY 10577, tel. (914) 253-5016.

Theatre. Mr. Houghton made his professional debut as stage manager for a Univ. Players summer theatre production of *Paris Bound*(Falmouth, Mass., June 1931). His first N.Y.C. assignment was as set designer for *Carry Nation* (Biltmore Th., Oct. 29, 1932). He was assistant to Robert Edmond Jones, art director of Radio City Theatres, N.Y.C. (Dec. 1932); stage manager of *Both Your Houses* (Royale, Mar. 6, 1933); and set designer for productions at Mt. Desert Playhouse (Bar Harbor, Me., June–Aug. 1933).

He designed the sets for *Spring in Autumn*(Henry Miller's Th., Oct. 24, 1933); was stage manager for *They Shall Not Die* (Royale, Feb. 21, 1934); set designer at the Mt. Desert Playhouse (June–July 1934); stage manager for *Libel*(Henry Miller's Th., N.Y.C., Dec. 20, 1935); set designer for the Suffern (N.Y.) County Playhouse (June–Aug. 1936); and stage manager for *High Tor* (Martin Beck Th., N.Y.C., Jan. 9, 1937).

Mr. Houghton was set designer for *In Clover* (Vanderbilt, Oct. 13, 1937); *Stop-Over* (Lyceum, Jan. 11, 1938); *How To Get Tough About It* (Martin Beck Th., Feb. 8, 1938); *Whiteoaks* (Hudson, Mar. 23, 1938); *Dame Nature* (Booth, Sept. 26, 1938); *Waltz in Goosestep* (Plymouth, Nov. 1, 1938); *Good Hunting* (Hudson, Nov. 21, 1938); and was set designer for 18 musical productions at the St. Louis (Mo.) Municipal Opera (Summers 1939–40).

He directed the London production of Michael Redgrave's *Macbeth* (Aldwych, Dec. 18, 1947; Natl., N.Y.C., Mar. 31, 1948); directed productions at Elitch Gardens (Denver, Colo., June–Aug. 1948); *Uniform of Flesh* for ANTA's Experimental Th. (Lenox Hill Playhouse, N.Y.C., Jan. 29, 1949); again directed at Elitch Gardens (June–Aug. 1949); *Clutterbuck* (Biltmore, N.Y.C., Dec. 3, 1949); and *Billy Budd* (Biltmore, Feb. 10, 1951).

He directed a summer theatre tour (July–Aug. 1951), and a national tour of Olivia de Havilland's *Candida* (opened Amer., St. Louis, Mo., Sept. 1951); and directed *The Tall Kentuckian* (Iroquois Amphitheatre, Louisville, Ky., May 1953).

In Sept. 1953, with T. Edward Hambleton, he founded the Phoenix Th., N.Y.C., and became its co-managing director. The first work presented was *Madam, Will You Walk?* (Dec. 1, 1953). Since then the Phoenix Th. has staged more than fifty works. Mr. Houghton directed *The Seagull* (Phoenix, May 11, 1954); designed the setting for Bway production *The Sleeping Prince* (Coronet, Nov. 1, 1956); *The Makropoulos Secret* (Phoenix, Dec. 3, 1957); *The Family Reunion* (Phoenix, Oct. 20, 1958); *Who'll Save the Plowboy?*(Phoenix, Jan. 9, 1961); for a touring production of *The Matchmaker* in NY State (under auspices of NY State Council on the Arts, opened Poughkeepsie, Oct. 1962); and for *The Dragon* (Phoenix, Apr. 9, 1963). He resigned his managing directorship in 1963, but remained a member of the board of directors and vice-president of the corporation.

Television. Mr. Houghton was producer-director of the CBS Television Workshop (Dec. 1951–May 1952); and lectured weekly on contemporary drama for educational television, N.Y.C., (Oct. 1958–May 1959).

Other Activities. In 1967, Mr. Houghton became professor and dean of the Division of Theatre Arts, State Univ. of New York College at Purchase.

He is a member and president (1973–to date) of the American Council for the Arts in Education. He was professor of drama and director of the Experimental Th. at Vassar Col. (1962–67) and visiting professor and guest director at Harvard Univ. (Loeb Drama Ctr., July–Aug. 1963). Previously, he was adjunct professor of drama at Vassar Coll. (Sept. 1959–June 1960); adjunct professor of drama at Barnard Coll. (1954–58); lecturer in comparative literature at Columbia Univ. (1948–53); and lecturer on drama at Smith Coll. (Feb.–June 1947).

Mr. Houghton lectured on the American Theatre in Europe for the US Dept. of State (Feb.–Mar. 1961).

Published Works. He has written *Moscow Rehearsals* (1936); *Advance from Broadway* (1941); *But Not Forgotten: The Adventure of the University Players* (1951); *Great Russian Short Stories,* which he edited and selected (1958); *Great Russian Plays*, which he edited and selected (1959); *Return Engagement* (1962); *Masterpieces of Continental Drama*, which he edited (1963); and *The Exploding Stage* (1972).

Mr. Houghton has also written articles for *Saturday Review*, *The New Yorker*, *American Scholar*, *Atlantic*, *Stage*, NY *Times* magazine, and *Theatre Arts*, for which he was associate editor (1945–48).

Awards. Mr. Houghton, with T. Edward Hambleton, received a special citation for the accomplishments of the Phoenix Th. from ANTA (1954); he received *The Village Voice* Off-Bway (Obie) Award for his settings for *Who'll Save the Plowboy?* in 1962.

He also received Guggenheim Fellowships (1934, 1935, 1960); an honorary D.F.A. degree from Denison Univ. (1959); and a grant from the Amer. Council of Learned Societies to attend an international conference on Soviet literature at Oxford Univ. He is a fellow of the American Academy of Arts and Sciences.

Recreation. Gardening, cooking, reading, travel.

HOUSEMAN, JOHN. Producer, actor, director, teacher, writer. b. Jacques Haussman, Sept. 22, 1902, Bucharest, Romania, to Georges and May (Davies) Haussmann. Father, grain and commodity exporter. Attended Clifton Coll., Bristol, Eng., 1911–19. Married Dec. 1950 to Joan Courtney; two sons. Served 1941–43 as Chief Overseas Radio Programmer for OWI. Member of SAG; AEA; AGVA; SSD&C; Screen Producers Guild.

Theatre. In 1934, Mr. Houseman directed the opera, *Four Saints In Three Acts*, produced by "The Friends and Enemies of Modern Music" (Athenaeum, Hartford, Conn.), later presented on Bway, in association with Harry Moses (44 St. Th., Feb. 20, 1934). He directed *The Lady from the Sea* (Little, May 1, 1934); *Valley Forge* (Guild, Dec. 10, 1934); *Panic* (Imperial, Mar. 14, 1935); and Leslie Howard's *Hamlet* (Imperial, Nov. 10, 1936).

For the Federal Th. (WPA) Project, he was managing producer of the Negro Th., and the Classical Th. (Project 891) Projects. For the Negro Th. group, he produced (Lafayette Th.). *Walk Together Chillun!* (Feb. 2, 1936); *Conjur Man Dies* (Mar. 11, 1936), *Macbeth* (Apr. 14, 1936), and *Turpentine* (June 26, 1936); and for the Classical Th., *Horse Eats Hat* (Maxine Elliott's Th., Oct. 7, 1936), *Dr. Faustus* (Maxine Elliott's Th., Jan. 8, 1937), and *The Cradle Will Rock* (Venice, July, 1937).

With Orson Welles, he founded the Mercury Th. (N.Y.C.), where he produced *Julius Caesar* (Nov. 11, 1937), *Shoemaker's Holiday* (Jan. 1, 1938), *Heartbreak House* (Apr. 29, 1938); *The Cradle Will Rock* (Windsor, Jan. 3, 1938); *Danton's Death* (Mercury, Nov. 2, 1938); and *Five Kings*.

Mr. Houseman directed the opera *The Devil and Daniel Webster* (Martin Beck Th., May 18, 1939); *Liberty Jones* (Shubert, Feb. 5, 1941); with Orson Welles, produced *Native Son* (St. James, Mar. 24, 1941); directed *Lute Song* (Plymouth, Feb. 6, 1946); *King Lear* (National, Dec. 25, 1950); and *Coriolanus* (Phoenix, Jan. 19, 1954).

As artistic director for the American Shakespeare Festival (Stratford, Conn.) he directed, with Jack Landau, *King John*, *Measure for Measure*, *The Merry Wives of Windsor*, *Much Ado About Nothing*, and *The Winter's Tale*; and directed *Othello*, *Hamlet*, and *All's Well That Ends Well* (1956–59).

From 1959–64, he was artistic director for the Theatre Group of the Univ. of California at Los Angeles Extension, directing *Murder in the Cathedral* (Jan. 1, 1960), *The Three Sisters* (Aug. 3, 1960), *Six Characters in Search of an Author* (Jan. 17, 1961), *The Iceman Cometh* (Aug. 25, 1961), *Antigone* (Oct. 23, 1962), and *The Seagull* (Jan. 10, 1964). He directed the opera, *Otello* (Dallas Opera Co., Tex., 1962 season); for the Theatre Group, directed *King Lear* (Los Angeles, Summer 1964); and, for The American Shakespeare Festival, in collaboration with Pearl Long, directed *Murder in the Cathedral* (Stratford, Conn., June 19, 1966); and *Macbeth* (Summer, 1967). As producing director of A.P.A. (1967–69), he directed *The Chronicles of Hell*; with Ellis Rabb, co-directed *Pantagleize* (Lyceum, N.Y.C., Nov. 30, 1967); was producing-director of *The Criminals* (Sheridan Sq. Playhouse, Feb. 25, 1970); directed a revival of *The Country Girl* (Billy Rose Th., Mar. 15, 1972); and *Clarence Darrow* (Helen Hayes Th., Mar. 26, 1974).

Mr. Houseman was appointed director of the drama division of the Juilliard Sch. of the Performing Arts (1965). For the Juilliard Opera Th., he directed production of *The Mines of Sulphur* (1967); *Antigone* (1969); and *The Losers* (1971). He is the founder and artistic director of The Acting Company (1975), a national repertory theatre originally called The City Center Acting Company (founded in 1972), which grew out of his work at Juilliard.

Films. Mr. Houseman has produced two documentaries, *Tuesday in November* (OWI, 1944); and *Voyage to America*, for the US Pavillion (NY World's Fair, 1964).

He produced *The Unseen* (Par., 1945); *Miss Susie Slagle's* (Par., 1945); *The Blue Dahlia* (Par., 1946); *Letter from an Unknown Woman* (Rampart, 1947); *They Live by Night* (RKO, 1948); and *The Twisting Road* (RKO, 1948). In 1950, he became associated with MGM and subsequently produced *Holiday for Sinners* (1952); *The Bad and the Beautiful* (1952); *Julius Caesar* (1953); *Executive Suite* (1954); *Moonfleet* (1955); *The Cobweb* (1955); *Lust for Life* (1956); *All Fall Down* (1962); and *Two Weeks in Another Town* (1962).

Mr. Houseman played Kingsfield in *The Paper Chase* (20th-Fox, 1973); and appeared in *Rollerball* (UA, 1975); and *Three Days of the Condor* (Par., 1975).

Television and Radio. For radio during 1938–39, he was editor and associate producer of Mercury Theatre on the Air; in 1938–40, wrote for the Helen Hayes Th.; and was director of Studio One and special productions for CBS.

For television, he was executive producer of the Seven Lively Arts (CBS, 1957); producer of Playhouse 90 (CBS, 1958–59); The Great Adventure (CBS, 1963); *The Dancer's World* (CBS, 1969); and *Three by Martha Graham* (CBS, 1969).

Other Activities. He was associate professor of drama (Vassar Coll., 1937–38); lecturer in drama (Barnard Coll., 1949); and regent's lecturer in theatre arts (Univ. of California at Los Angeles, 1960).

Published Works. Mr. Houseman is author, with Jack Landau, of *The Birth of a Theatre* (1958).

He had a weekly column in the NY *Star*, and has written articles for such publications as *Theatre Arts Monthly*, *Vogue*, *Harper's Magazine*, *Hollywood Quarterly*, *Massachusetts Review*, *Playbill*, *Sight and Sound*, and the NY *Times* Drama and Book sections.

Awards. Mr. Houseman received the Academy Award for Best Supporting Actor (1974), for his performance in *The Paper Chase*; and was awarded an honorary Dr. of Arts degree from Temple Univ. (1973).

HOWARD, BART. Composer, lyricist. b. Howard Joseph Gustafson, June 1, 1915, Burlington, Iowa, to Harry and Naomi Gustafson. Attended Burlington H.S.; St. Patrick's Bus. School, 1930. Served US Army, 1941–46; rank, Sgt. Member of Dramatists Guild; ASCAP; AFM. Address: North Salem, NY 10560, tel. (914) 669-5744.

Theatre. Mr. Howard contributed music to the pre-Bway tryout of the revue, *Curtain Going Up* (Forrest Th., Philadelphia, Pa., Feb. 15, 1952; closed there Mar. 1, 1952). He wrote the music and lyrics for the song, "My Love Is a Wanderer" for the revue, *John Murray Anderson's Almanac* (Imperial, N.Y.C., Dec. 10, 1953); contributed songs to the revue, *Fourth Avenue North* (Madison Ave. Playhouse, Sept. 27, 1961); and adapted, with Ruth Goetz, Françoise Dorin's *Comme au Théâtre*, produced in London as *Play on Love* (1969).

Television. He wrote the score for a short Imogene Coca musical (1952), profiled on Amer. Musical Th. (1961), and profiled on the Today Show (NBC, July 1965).

Night Clubs. Mr. Howard was accompanist to Mabel Mercer (1948–1950) and was master of ceremonies and pianist at the Blue Angel (N.Y.C., 1950–59).

Recreation. Cooking, reading Tolstoy.

HOWARD, KEN. Actor, singer. b. Mar. 28, 1944, El Centro, Calif. Grad. Amherst Coll.; Yale Drama Sch. Married 1974 to Louise Sorel.

Theatre. Mr. Howard was an apprentice at the Williamstown (Mass.) Theatre; and, while at Yale, appeared in the world premiere of *We Bombed in New Haven* (Dec. 4, 1967). He made his Bway debut as Bartender Eddie in *Promises, Promises* (Sam S. Shubert Th., N.Y.C., Dec. 1, 1968); subsequently played Thomas Jefferson in *1776* (46 St. Th., Mar. 16, 1969); Paul Reese in *Child's Play* (Royale, Feb. 17, 1970); Jerry in *Seesaw* (Uris, Mar. 18, 1973); Jack Hassler in *Little Black Sheep* (Vivian Beaumont Th., May 7, 1975); and Tom in *The Norman Conquests* (Morosco, Dec. 7, 1975).

Films. Mr. Howard made his film debut in the role of Arthur in *Tell Me That You Love Me, Junie Moon* (Par., 1970).

Television. He was co-star of the series *Adam's Rib* (ABC, 1973); and the central character in the series *Manhunter* (CBS, 1974).

Awards. Mr. Howard received the Theatre World Award (1968–69) for his performance in *1776*; and the Antoinette Perry (Tony) Award for best supporting actor (1969–70) for *Child's Play*.

HOWARD, PETER. Musical director, conductor, composer, coach, music arranger, pianist. b. Howard Peter Weiss, July 29, 1927, Miami, Fla., to Morris and Ann Weiss. Father, grocer. Grad. S.J. Tilden H.S., Brooklyn, N.Y. 1944; Juilliard Sch. of Music, B.S. 1948; Teachers Coll., Columbia Univ., M.S. 1951. Studied with Carl Friedberg, Lonny Epstein, Adi Bernard. Married Apr. 16, 1961, to Margot Howard, artist. Served US Army 1946–47, Special Service; rank, Sgt. Member of AFM, local 802; Lotus Club, (N.Y.C., entertainment comm.). Address: 853 Seventh Ave., New York, NY 10019, tel. (212) JU 6-8266.

Theatre. Mr. Howard gave a solo recital at Town Hall (N.Y.C., 1944), and composed the ballet music for *All for Love* (Mark Hellinger Th., Jan. 22, 1949); subsequently was assistant to the conductor of *Plain and Fancy* (Mark Hellinger Th., Jan. 27, 1955) and *My Fair Lady* (Mark Hellinger Th., Mar. 15, 1956); was musical director for the touring company of *Welcome Darling* (Summer 1956); and conducted a tour of *Babes in Arms*, for which he also composed a new ballet score (1958).

He was musical director for *A Party With Comden and Green* (John Golden Th., N.Y.C., Dec. 23, 1958); was musical director for *On the Town* (Carnegie Hall Playhouse, Jan. 15, 1959); composed incidental music for *Desert Incident* (John Golden Th., Mar. 24, 1959); and was assistant conductor for *The Sound of Music* (Lunt-Fontanne, Nov. 16, 1959); composed dance music for *Carnival!* (Imperial, Apr. 13, 1961); was musical director for *Gypsy* (Riviera Hotel, Las Vegas, Nev., 1961); composed the dance music for *Subways Are for Sleeping* (St. James, N.Y.C., 27, 1961); and dance and incidental music for *I Can Get It for You Wholesale* (Shubert, Mar. 22, 1962). He was assistant conductor for *No Strings* (54 St. Th., Mar. 15, 1962); composed dance music for *Here's Love* (Shubert, Oct. 3, 1963); dance and incidental music for *Hello, Dolly!* (St. James, Jan. 16, 1964), and became its musical director on Apr. 20, 1964.

He composed dance and incidental music for *Roar of the Greasepaint— The Smell of the Crowd* (Sam S. Shubert Th., May 16, 1965); was dance and vocal arranger and music director for *How Now, Dow Jones* (Lunt-Fontanne Th., Dec. 7, 1967); dance and incidental music arranger and music director for *Her First Roman* (Lunt-Fontanne Th., Oct. 20, 1968); dance music arranger and music director for *1776* (46 St. Th., Mar. 16, 1969); dance and incidental music arranger for *La Strada* (Lunt-Fontanne, Dec. 14, 1969); dance music arranger for *Minnie's Boys* (Imperial, Mar. 26, 1970); musical director, dance and vocal arranger for *Millikan* show (1970, 1971, 1972, 1973, 1974); did dance arrangements for *Ari*

(Mark Hellinger Th., Jan. 15, 1971); musical direction and incidental music arrangement for *Prettybelle* (Shubert Th., Boston, Mass., Feb. 1, 1971; closed there, Mar. 6, 1971); for *One for the Money* (Eastside Playhouse, N.Y.C., May 24, 1972); dance and incidental music arrangements for *Tricks* (Alvin, Jan. 8, 1973); and musical arrangements for *In Fashion* (world premiere, Macauley Th., Louisville, Ky., Feb. 22, 1973).

Films. Mr. Howard did the dance music for the films *1776* (Col., 1972) and *Mame* (WB, 1974).

Television. Mr. Howard was a winner of the Arthur Godfrey Talent Scouts competition. He has since been assistant conductor for the television productions of *Pinocchio; Hansel and Gretel; Peter Pan;* the Tammy Grimes-Eddie Albert Special; Stover At Yale (Omnibus, CBS); pianist on Chance of a Lifetime; the Today Show (NBC); and PM East. He was music coordinator for the *Hello, Dolly!* special (NBC); conductor for three Ed Sullivan productions (CBS); and music director and arranger for the *In Fashion* special (NET, 1974).

Night Clubs. He has appeared as pianist at the Hotel Delmonico (N.Y.C., 1949); at the Ritz-Carlton (N.Y.C., 1950); was assistant conductor for *All About Love* at the Versailles (N.Y.C., 1951); and was pianist at Spivy's (Paris, France, 1952).

Other Activities. Mr. Howard has been vocal coach to Lauren Bacall, Nancy Dussault, José Ferrer, Elliot Gould, Betty Grable, Barbara Harris, Rex Harrison, Paula Laurence, Carol Lawrence, Bibi Osterwald, Ginger Rogers, Barbra Streisand, Julie Wilson.

HOWES, SALLY ANN. Actress, singer. b. July 20, St. John's Wood, London, England, to Bobby and Patricia (Malone Clark) Howes. Father, actor; mother, singer, Patricia Malone. Attended Queensboro Coll., Herts, England. Married Jan. 3, 1958 to Richard Adler, composer (marr. dis., 1966); two sons. Member of British AEA; AEA; SAG; AFTRA.

Theatre. Miss Howes made her stage debut in *Caprice* (Alhambra Th., Glasgow, Scotland, 1951); toured the Moss Empire theatres as a vocalist (1951); and appeared in the 1951 Royal Variety Performance. pantomime

She played Jan in *Bet Your Life* (London Hippodrome, Feb. 18, 1952; revised version, June 13, 1952); Jennifer Rumson in *Paint Your Wagon* (Her Majesty's, London, Feb. 11, 1953); Robin Hood in the pantomime *Babes in the Woods* (Golder's Green Hippodrome, Dec. 1954); Margaret in *Romance in Candlelight* (Piccadilly, Sept. 15, 1955); Karolka in *Summer Song* (Prince's, Feb. 16, 1956); and Celia Pope in *A Hatful of Rain* (Prince's, Mar. 7, 1957).

Miss Howes made her N.Y.C. debut succeeding (Feb. 3, 1958) Julie Andrews as Eliza Doolittle in *My Fair Lady* (Mark Hellinger Th., Mar. 15, 1956); subsequently appeared as Eve in *Kwamina* (54 St. Th., Oct. 23, 1961); Fiona MacLaren in *Brigadoon* (NY City Ctr., May 30, 1962; Jan. 30, 1963); Kit Sargent in *What Makes Sammy Run?* (54 St. Th., Feb. 27, 1964); and Anna in *The King and I* (London, 1973–74 season).

Films. Miss Howes' films include *Honeymoon Deferred* (UI, 1940); *Thursday's Child* (Eding, 1942); *Dead of Night* (VI, 1945); *Pink String and Sealing Wax* (Eagle-Lion, 1945); *Nicholas Nickleby* (J. Arthur Rank, 1947); *Anna Karenina* (20th-Fox, 1948); *The Admirable Crichton* (Col., 1957); and *Chitty Chitty Bang Bang* (UA, 1968).

Television. Miss Howes has appeared on the Ed Sullivan Show (CBS, Feb. 9, 1958); as Della Young in *The Gift of the Magi* (CBS, Dec. 9, 1958); on the Perry Como Show (NBC, 1958); the Patti Page Show (1958); Bell Telephone Hour (Oct. 1959, Jan. 1962); the Chevy Show (Dec. 1959); US Steel Hour (CBS, 1960); *The Fifth Column* (CBS, Jan. 1960); Sunday Showcase (NBC, Mar. 1960); *Holiday in Music* (Bell Telephone Hour, NBC, Sept. 30, 1960); as Maeve McHugh in *The Old Foolishness* (Play of the Week, NTA, Mar. 6, 1961); the title role in *Jane Eyre* (CBS, Apr. 27, 1961); the Jack Paar Show (NBC, 1962–64); The Voice of Firestone (ABC, Sept. 1962; Feb. 1963); the Lincoln Center Special (CBS, Sept. 1963); *Brigadoon* (ABC); and was hostess for the *Miss USA* (1965) and *Miss Universe* (1965) pageants.

HRUBY, NORBERT J. College administrator, director, producer, educator, writer. b. Norbert Joseph Hruby, Feb. 4, 1918, Cicero, Ill., to Thomas J. and Marie F. Hruby. Father, real estate broker. Grad. Riverside-Brookfield (Ill.) H.S., 1935; Loyola Univ., Ph.B. 1939, M.A. 1941, Ph.D. 1951; attended Yale Univ. Sch. of Drama, 1946–47; Univ. of Chicago, 1958. Since 1958, attended various workshops and conferences on adult education at the Univ. of Chicago and elsewhere. Married June 19, 1943, to Dolores M. Smith; one son, two daughters. Served with US Army, 1942–46; rank, Capt. Member of National Catholic Educational Assn. (vice-chmn., College Dept., 1973–to date); North Central Assn. of Colleges and Secondary Schools (examiner and consultant, 1972–to date); National Advisory Council on Adult Education (1973–to date); Blue Key and Alpha Sigma Nu; Pi Gamma Mu; Phi Alpha Rho; Beta Pi; Monogram Club; Dean's Key. Address: (home) 245 Briarwood S.E., Grand Rapids, MI 49506, tel. (616) 459-1149; (bus.) Aquinas College, Grand Rapids, MI 49506, tel. (616) 459-8281.

Mr. Hruby has served (1969–to date) as president, Aquinas College, Grand Rapids, Mich. Previously he was at Loyola Univ., as graduate assistant in the English Dept. (1939–41); English instructor (1947–48); assistant dean, College of Commerce (1948–51); assistant professor (1951); director, Public Information Center (1951–55). From 1958 to 1962, he was associate dean, University College, Univ. of Chicago, and from 1962 to 1969 he was vice-president, Mundelein College, Chicago, Ill.

Theatre. Mr. Hruby produced and directed stage productions for the Univ. of Chicago fund-raising campaign: *From Stagg Field to Geneva*, a spectacular on atomic energy (Orchestra Hall, Chicago, Nov. 1955), and *Your University Today*, about present-day university life (Civic Opera House, Chicago, May 1956).

He has also directed several productions for the Court Th. (Univ. of Chicago). These plays include *Dr. Faustus* (Aug. 1957), *The Cenci* (Aug. 1958), and *Francesca da Rimini* (Aug. 1959); adapted *Henry VIII* (Aug. 1960); and directed *Six Characters in Search of an Author* (July 1961).

Mr. Hruby was founder and first executive director of the Assn. of Community Theatres of the Chicago metropolitan area (1961–62). In the summer of 1961, he planned and directed the Midwest Theatre Conference (Univ. of Chicago), with Harold Clurman, Jo Mielziner, Burgess Meredith, Kenneth Burke, and others. He has been a member of the board of directors, Civic Theatre of Grand Rapids, Mich. (1973–to date).

Television and Radio. Mr. Hruby entered educational theatre as a performer, writer, and producer of radio and television discussions, documentaries, and dramatic series for Loyola Univ. on commercial stations in Chicago (WCFL, WBBM, radio; WBBM, WBKB, WNBQ, WGN, television, June 1951–May 1955). He was also Loyola representative to the Chicago Educ. TV Assn. (1952–55). During this time he collaborated with George Probst of the Univ. of Chicago and the late George Jennings of the Chicago Board of Education in planning and establishing the Chicago educational television station, Channel 11 (WTTW). As director of radio and television at the Univ. of Chicago (1955–1958), he wrote, directed, and produced the following radio series: The Sacred Note (1955–to date); Impetus, a discussion of influential books (1958); Voices of Christmas (1956); and Faith of Our Fathers, a religious series (1957). He also created, directed, and produced such television programs as The Complete Spectator, a series on popular culture (1958); I'd Like to Be, a series on career information for adolescents (1957); Atomic Primer, on the history of atomic science, starring Nobel Prize Winner Harold C. Urey, which was syndicated for national distribution (1958).

Other Activities. While serving as director of the Public Information Center, Loyola Univ., Mr. Hruby wrote and published promotional and fund-raising brochures, one of which won a national award, and he was ghost writer for the president of the university. He was also public relations consultant, Forest Preserve, Dist. of Cook County (1958–62), and communications consultant, Amer. Mutual Insurance Alliance (1960); and from 1971 to 1973, president, Grand Rapids Area Council of Churches.

Published Works. Mr. Hruby is author of *Survival Kit for Invisible Colleges* (1973).

Awards. For his radio series, The Sacred Note, he received the Ohio State Regional and National Award for three consecutive years (1956–58); and received the same award for his radio show, Voices of Christmas (1956).

Recreation. Tennis, local politics.

HUBER, GUSTI. Actress. b. July 27, 1914, Vienna, Austria, to Franz and Auguste (Rozsypal) Huber. Attended public school in Vienna until 1929; Academy for Music and Representative Art, Vienna, 1929–30. Married 1938 to Gottfried Koechert, jeweler (marr. dis. 1943); two daughters; married 1946 to Joseph G. Besch, film producer; one son, one daughter. Relative in theatre: daughter, Bibiara Besch, actress. Member of AEA; SAG; AFTRA.

Theatre. Miss Huber made her stage debut in *Everyman* (Deutsches Volkstheatre, Vienna, 1929); played in summer theatre (Bernel, Switzerland, 1930); appeared in plays by Shakespeare, Goethe, Schiller, and Shaw, as well as in American plays and musicals (Schauspielhaus, Zurich, Switzerland, 1930–35); appeared at the Deutsches Volkstheatre (1935–38); Burgtheatre and Akademie Theatre (1940–45).

She made her N.Y. debut as Lili Engle in *Flight into Egypt* (Music Box Th., Mar. 18, 1952); subsequently appeared as Margot Wendice in *Dial 'M' for Murder* (Plymouth, Oct. 29, 1952); Mrs. Frank in *The Diary of Anne Frank* (Cort, Oct. 5, 1955).

Films. She again played Mrs. Frank in the film version of *The Diary of Anne Frank* (20th-Fox, 1959).

Television. Miss Huber has appeared on Playhouse 90 (CBS); Dupont Show of the Month (CBS); Robert Montgomery Presents (NBC); Sam Benedict (NBC); Suspense (CBS); and Danger (CBS).

Recreation. Word games, crossword puzzles, double crostics.

HUGHES, ANNA MAY. Educator. b. Anna May Wilson, Nov. 23, 1918, Mt. Airy, Md., to John L. and Lillian W. (Kemp) Wilson. Father, railroad engineer; mother, bookkeeper. Grad. Brunswick (Md.) H.S., 1935; Hood Coll., B.A. 1939; graduate study at Univ. of Maryland, 1952. Married May 16, 1942, to Clinton K. Hughes. (dec. Dec. 1970); two daughters. Member of ATA (pres., Mid-Atlantic chapter, 1971–72); Maryland Speech and Drama Assn; Natl. Thespian Society. Address: (home) Braddock Hts., MD 21714, tel. (301) 371-7139; (bus.) Governor Thomas Johnson High School, Frederick, MD 21701, tel. (301) 662-9200.

Since 1966, Mrs. Hughes has taught speech and drama, and directed student productions, at Gov. Thomas Johnson H.S. She taught speech and drama at the Frederick (Md.) H.S. (1953–65). Mrs. Hughes was the first president (1960–63) and one of the four co-founders of the Maryland Speech and Drama Association, and since 1958, has been regional director (Md.) for the National Thespian Society. In 1972, she was appointed the theatre representative for Maryland to the National Alliance for the Arts. She is the chairman (1973–to date) for the Committee on Certification of Drama Teachers, a joint project of ATA and the Speech Communications Assn.

Mrs. Hughes has taught in Maryland at the Brunswick H.S. (1940–42); Frederick H.S. (1942–44); Middletown H.S. (1947); and directed student productions at all these schools.

She was publicity manager, prop girl, and box office manager for the Mountain Theatre (Braddock Heights, Md., 1955–58).

In 1973, a $75,000 theatre arts scholarship fund was established in her name by Norman Todd of Frederick, Md. The fund will provide annual scholarships of $2,000, and $1,000 for twenty-five years.

HUGHES, BARNARD. Actor. b. July 16, 1915, Bedford Hills, N.Y. Grad. Our Lady of Good Counsel (N.Y.C.), La Salle Academy (N.Y.C.); attended Manhattan Coll. Served U.S. Army, WW II. Married April 19, 1950, to Helen Stenborg, actress; one son, one daughter. Member of AEA; SAG; AFTRA.

Pre-Theatre. Wall St. runner.

Theatre. Mr. Hughes began his career with the Frank Lee Short touring classical repertory company; made his Bway debut in *The Cat and the Canary* (Majestic, N.Y.C., June 14, 1937); played Joe in *Please, Mrs. Garibaldi* (Belmont Th., N.y.C., Mar. 16, 1939); appeared in the pre-Bway tryout of *Herself, Mrs. Patrick Crowley* (Wilmington, Dela., Nov. 1939); subsequently appeared with The Highland Park (Ill.) Tenthouse Th., The Shelton-Amos Players (Richmond, Va.), the Palm Springs (Calif.) Playhouse, and companies in Surrey, Me., and Middletown, N.Y.; played Martin in *The Ivy Green* (Lyceum, N.Y.C., Apr. 5, 1949); Clancy in *Dinosaur Wharf* (National, Nov. 8, 1951); Captain McLean in a national touring company of *The Teahouse of the August Moon* (opened Hartman, Columbus, Ohio, Dec. 16, 1954); repeating that role in a NYC revival (NY City Ctr., Nov. 18, 1956); with Equity Library Th. (Lennox Hall Playhouse) played Major Jappolo in *A Bell for Adano,* and T. J. in *Home of the Brave;* Lantry in *The Will and the Way* (Th. East, Dec. 2, 1957); played Inspector Norcross, and was standby for Sir Cedric Hardwicke in *A Majority of One* (Sam S. Shubert Th., Feb. 16, 1959); and Senator Tom August in *Advise and Consent* (Cort, Nov. 17, 1960).

He played Peter Mortensgaard in *Rosmersholm* (Fourth St. Th., N.Y.C., Apr. 11, 1962); Nils Korgstad in *A Doll's House* (Th. Four, Feb. 2, 1963); The Governor in *The Advocate* (ANTA, Oct. 14, 1963); Bert Howell in *Nobody Loves an Albatross* (Lyceum, Dec. 19, 1963); Marcellus and The Priest in *Hamlet* (Lunt-Fontanne, Apr. 9, 1964); Fr. Frank Feeley in *I Was Dancing* (Lyceum, Nov. 8, 1964); Fr. Stanislaus Coyne in *Hogan's Goat* (Amer. Place Th. at St. Clement's, Nov. 11, 1965); concurrently was standby for Henry Fonda as Jim Bolton in *Generation* (Morosco, Oct. 6, 1965), appearing several times in that role, and then replacing Mr. Fonda; later replaced Robert Young (Fisher Th., Detroit, Aug. 17, 1966) in the road company of *Generation;* played Senator McFetridge in *How Now, Dow Jones* (Lunt-Fontanne, N.Y.C., Dec. 7, 1967); Judge Belknap in *The Wrong-Way Light Bulb* (John Golden Th., Mar. 4, 1969); Gen. Fitzhugh in *Sheep on the Runway* (Helen Hayes Th., Jan. 31, 1970); appeared in *Line* (Th. de Lys, Feb. 15, 1971); played Fulbert in *Abelard and Heloise* (Brooks Atkinson Th., Mar. 10, 1971); various roles in *Older People* (Public, May 14, 1972); with the NY Shakespeare Festival, played Polonius in *Hamlet* (Delacorte, June 20, 1972); and Dogberry in *Much Ado About Nothing* (Delacorte, Aug. 16, 1972; moved to Winter Garden, Nov. 11, 1972); Alexander Serebryakov in *Uncle Vanya* (Circle in the Square/Joseph E. Levine Th., June 4, 1973); on recording, was the Voice in *Edgar Allen Poe* (Alice Tully Hall, Oct. 28, 1973); and appeared in various roles in *The Good Doctor* (Eugene O'Neill Th., Nov. 27, 1973).

For the NY Shakespeare Festival, he played Falstaff in *The Merry Wives of Windsor* (Delacorte, July 24, 1974), and Gower/Chorus in *Pericles, Prince of Tyre* (Delacorte, July 25, 1974); played Dr. Lionel Morris in *All Over Town* (Booth, Dec. 29, 1974); and, in a revised and re-titled version of *Edgar Allen Poe,* he repeated his performance on recording, as Voice of Newspaper in *Edgar Allan Poe: A Condition of Shadow with Jerry Rockwood* (URGENT Th., Feb. 12, 1975).

Films. He has appeared in *Treehouse; Playgirl* (RKO, 1941); *The Young Doctors* (UA, 1961); *Midnight Cowboy* (UA, 1969); *Cold Turkey* (UA, 1971); *The Pursuit of Happiness* (Col., 1971); *Hospital* (UA, 1971); and *Rage* (WB, 1972), among others.

Television. Mr. Hughes has made hundreds of appearances on network television, including such shows as Robert Montgomery Presents (NBC); *Hawkins Falls, Pop. 6,200* (NBC); Hollywood Screen Test (ABC); The Defenders (CBS); Naked City (ABC); Kraft Th. (NBC); Car 54, Where Are You? (NBC); US Steel Hour (ABC); Armstrong Circle Th. (NBC); The Nurses (CBS); Dupont Show of the Week (CBS); All in the Family (CBS); and *A Memory of Two Mondays* (NET). For several years he played Dr. Bruce Banning on the daytime serial, The Guiding Light (CBS); and he plays the title role in his series, Doc (CBS).

HUGHES, DEL. Production stage manager, actor, director. b. Delbert Charles Hughes, Detroit, Mich., to Albert J. and Lena (Meilstrup) Hughes. Father, shipping clerk and farmer. Attended Vassar H.S., Mich., 1924–25; grad. Northwestern H.S., Detroit, Mich. 1927; attended IBM Service Sch., Endicott, N.Y., 1928; Amer. Theatre Wing, N.Y.C., 1946. Married Sept. 12, 1937, to Julia Johnston, actress; one daughter. Served WW II, US Army, with Special Services; PTO; rank, Sgt. Member of AEA (on Council); AFTRA; SAG; DGA; The Lambs. Address: 30 Norman Ave., Amityville, L.I., NY 11701, tel. (516) AM 4-2234.

Pre-Theatre. Serviceman for IBM.

Theatre. Mr. Hughes made his first stage appearance as Justin Stock in *Oliver, Oliver* (Brattleboro Th., Vt., July 4, 1935); subsequently appeared in the revue *Sunday Nights at Nine* (Barbizon-Plaza, N.Y.C., Nov. 1935); succeeded Warren Douglas as Captain Tim in a touring production of *Tobacco Road* (Louisville, Ky.); and succeeded (Forrest Th., Sept. 17, 1936) Tom Ewell in this role in the N.Y.C. production (Masque, Dec. 4, 1933). He spent a season in stock in Phoenix and Tucson, Ariz. (Jan. 6, 1942–Mar. 1942); was stage manager for *Vickie* in which he played Mr. Hatch (Plymouth, N.Y.C., Sept. 22, 1942); stage manager for *Dark Eyes* (Belasco, Jan. 14, 1943); and understudied Carl Gose, now known as Scott McKay, in the role of Larry Field, and Geza Korvin, now known as Charles Korvin, as Prince Nicolai. He played Bob in *Open House* (Cort, June 3, 1947); the Town Crier and a Villager in *Rip Van Winkle* (NY City Ctr., July 15, 1947); was production stage manager for, and replaced John Randolph as Lt. Jake Goldberg for six weeks, in *Command Decision* (Fulton, Oct. 1, 1947); was production stage manager for *Death of a Salesman* (Morosco, Feb. 10, 1949) and assistant to Elia Kazan, the director, for the London production (Phoenix, July 28, 1949); production stage manager for *Montserrat* (Fulton, Oct. 29, 1949); production supervisor for *The Man* (Fulton, Jan. 19, 1950); and *Legend of Sarah* (Fulton, Oct. 11, 1950); production stage manager for *The Autumn Garden* (Coronet, Mar. 7, 1951); director of the road company of *Death of a Salesman* (opened Klein Aud., Bridgeport, Conn., Sept. 8, 1951; closed KRNT Th., Richmond, Va., Jan. 5, 1952); and production stage manager for *One Bright Day* (Golden, N.Y.C., Mar. 19, 1952).

Mr. Hughes was production stage manager and succeeded (June, 1953) E. G. Marshall as Rev. Hale in *The Crucible* (Martin Beck Th., Jan. 22, 1953); was production supervisor for *The Children's Hour* (Coronet, Dec. 8, 1952) and director for the touring production (Sept. 1953); was production stage manager for *The Confidential Clerk* (Morosco, N.Y.C., Feb. 11, 1954); played Rev. Hale in a stock production of *The Crucible* (Univ. of Michigan, Ann Arbor, May 1954); and was production stage manager for *A Taste of Honey* (Lyceum, N.Y.C., Oct. 4, 1960); *The Complaisant Lover* (Ethel Barrymore Th., Nov. 1, 1961), and was director for a subsequent stock production (Sombrero, Phoenix, Ariz.; Bucks County Playhouse, Pa.; and Westport Country Playhouse, Conn., Summer 1962); production stage manager for *The Perfect Setup* (Cort, Oct. 24, 1962); *Enter Laughing* (Henry Miller's Th., March 13, 1963); *One Flew Over the Cuckoo's Nest* (Cort, Nov. 13, 1963); *Traveller Without Luggage* (ANTA, Sept. 17, 1964); *Peterpat* (Longacre, Jan. 6, 1965); *The Porcelain Year* (pre-Bway: opened Locust St. Th., Philadelphia, Pa., Oct. 11, 1965; closed New Haven, Conn., Nov. 13, 1965); *King Lear* (Brandeis Univ., Waltham, Mass., Feb. 1966); directed *Years Ago* (Indianapolis, Ind., July 1966); was production stage manager for *The Investigation* (Ambassador, Oct. 4, 1966); *That Summer—That Fall* (Helen Hayes Th., Mar. 16, 1967); directed *The Diary of Anne Frank* (Huntington Performing Arts, May 1967); and was production stage manager of *The Trial of Lee Harvey Oswald* (ANTA, Nov. 5, 1967). He was also production stage manager of *The Price* (Morosco, Feb. 7, 1968) and directed the London company (Mar. 4, 1969) and the national company (New Haven, Conn., Sept. 24, 1969).

Films. He played the Television Director in *A Face in the Crowd* (WB, 1957).

Television. He appeared as Larry Knox and was director of *The Brighter Day* (CBS, 1953–59); One Life to Live (ABC, 1969); and All My Children (ABC, 1970–74).

Recreation. Boating, fishing.

HUGHES, ELINOR. Drama and film critic. b. Elinor Lambert Hughes, Mar. 3, 1906, Cambridge, Mass., to Hector James and Elinor (Lambert) Hughes. Father, professor of civil engineering, Harvard Coll. Grad. May Sch., Boston, 1923; Radcliffe Coll., B.A. 1927. Married July 14, 1957, to David Dinkel Jacobus, mech. engineer; two stepsons. Member of Newspaper Guild; Women's City Club of Boston (exec. committee, 1934–37, 1949–55; 3rd vice-pres., 1952–54; 2nd vice-pres., 1954–55); Natl. League of Penwomen; Boston Authors' Club; Soc. for Preservation of New England Antiquities; Trustees of Reservations; Quarter Century Club, Boston Herald-Traveler Corp. Address: 24 Academy Lane, Bellport, L.I., NY 11713.

Since April 1935, Miss Hughes has been drama and film critic for the *Boston Herald,* which she has been associated with since her graduation from Radcliffe.

Published Works. She is the author of *Famous Stars of Filmdom (Men)* (1932); *Famous Stars of Filmdom (Women)* (1932); and *Passing Through to Broadway* (1947). Her review, in blank verse, of the film *Romeo and Juliet* was published in *Best News Stories of 1937–38. Her review of John Gielgud's Hamlet* (written 1936) was published in *"Hamlet"—Enter Critic* (1970).

Recreation. Fishing, golf, reading, bridge.

HUGHES, TOM. Producer. b. Lloyd Thomas Hughes, Jr., Aug. 26, 1932, Dallas, Tex., to Lloyd Thomas, Sr. and Kathryn L. Hughes. Grad. Carrollton (Tex.) H.S., 1948; N. Texas State Univ., B.A. 1951; Michigan State Univ., M.A. 1952. Served US Army, FETO, Intelligence, 1952-55. Member of Blue Key; Pi Kappa Delta; Kappa Delta Pi; Sigma Tau Delta. Music Hall at Fair Park, Dallas, TX 75226, tel. (214) 823-4116.

Theatre. Mr. Hughes was director of the Camp Zama Players, Japan, while in the army. He was assistant producer of the Dallas Summer Musicals, Dallas, Tex. (Summers 1956–60), and subsequently became the producer (1961). He is managing director of Music Hall in Dallas and director of Theatrical Activities, State Fair of Texas, Inc.

Awards. He has received honorary membership in the Lion's and Kiwanis clubs of Dallas, for his contribution to theatre in Dallas; is an honorary member I.A.T.S.E., Local 127; received the Playbill Award for best musical (Dallas, 1961; 1962); R. J. O'Donnell Memorial Award for "Showman of the Year," (Dallas, 1962); Mr. Show Business of 1963, Dallas, Tex., presented by B'nai B'rith Women of Dallas; and the Distinguished Alumnus Award, North Texas State Univ., 1971.

HUGO, LAURENCE. Actor. b. Laurence Victor Hugo, Dec. 22, 1917, Berkeley, Calif., to Mathias and Margaret (O'Toole) Hugo. Father, accountant, teacher; mother, teacher. Grad. Univ. of California, A.B. 1939. Studied Neighborhood Playhouse Sch. of the Th., N.Y.C., 1940–42 with Sanford Meisner; RADA, London, Eng., 1946; Actors Workshop, San Francisco, Calif., 1960–61. Married Oct. 24, 1941, to Carolyn Gary, public relations executive; one son, one daughter. Served US Army, ETO, 1944–46; rank, Cpl. Member of AEA; AFTRA; SAG; The Lambs; The Players. Address: "Glen Dá Lough", Rockfish, VA 22966.

Theatre. Mr.Hugo made his professional debut in stock as Michael Barnes in *The Male Animal* (Sayville Playhouse, N.Y., June 1941); made his N.Y.C. debut as the Guard in *The Distant City* (Longacre Th., Sept. 22, 1941); succeeded (1943) Montgomery Clift as Henry Antrobus in *The Skin of Our Teeth* (Plymouth, Nov. 18, 1942); played Joe Kindle in *I'll Take the High Road* (Ritz, Nov. 9, 1943); Tommy Riggs in *Decision* (Belasco, Feb. 2, 1944); Paul Verrall in *Born Yesterday* (Erlanger, Chicago, Ill., Spring 1947); later joined the N.Y.C. company of the latter play in this role; played Price in *Stalag 17* (48 St. Th., May 8, 1951); appeared in stock productions (Elitch Gardens, Denver, Colo.; Olney Th., Md., Summers 1954–55); played Mack Daniels in *Double in Hearts* (John Golden Th., N.Y.C., Oct. 16, 1956); appeared in *U.S.A.* (Martinique, Oct. 28, 1959); replaced (May 13, 1968) Gig Young as Robert Danvers in *There's a Girl in My Soup* (Music Box Th., Oct. 18, 1967); was Claudius and the Ghost in Judith Anderson's *Hamlet* (Carnegie Hall, Jan. 14, 1971); played in *Life with Father* (Playhouse in the Park: Robert S. Marx Th., Cincinnati, Ohio, Nov. 1, 1971); appeared in *The Price* (Meadow Brook Th., Rochester, Mich., Apr. 27, 1972; Neptune Th., Halifax, N.S., Can., Mar. 9, 1972); in *Camino Real* (Seattle Repertory Th., Seattle, Wash., Nov. 22, 1972); and played Oliver in *The Enclave* (world premiere, Washington Th. Club, Washington, D.C., Feb. 21, 1973).

Films. Mr. Hugo appeared in *Three Hours to Kill* (Col., 1953) and *Deathwatch* (1974).

Television. From 1961 to 1970, he played Mike Karr on The Edge of Night (CBS). He has appeared on Kraft Television Th. (NBC), US Steel Hour (CBS), Studio One (CBS), Philco Television Playhouse (NBC), Goodyear Playhouse (NBC), Armstrong Circle Th. (CBS), Omnibus (NBC), The Web (CBS), Danger (CBS), Dupont Show of the Month (CBS), Hallmark Hall of Fame (NBC), Look Up and Live (CBS), As the World Turns (CBS), and Search for Tomorrow (CBS).

Awards. He received a Ford Foundation grant as artist in residence at the Actor's Workshop, San Francisco, Calif. (1960–61).

Recreation. Bee-keeping.

HULL, HENRY. Actor, playwright. b. Oct. 3, 1890, Louisville, Ky., to William M. and Elinor (Bond) Vaughan. Father, drama critic, Louisville *Courier-Journal.* Attended Coll. of the City of New York, 1904; Cooper Union, 1906–08; Columbia Univ., 1909. Married Nov. 30, 1913, to Juliet van Wyck Fremont; two sons. Member of AEA; SAG; AFTRA.

Pre-Theatre. Mining engineer assayer, mineralogist, and prospector in N. Quebec, Can. (1910–11).

Theatre. Mr. Hull made his N.Y.C. debut as Henry Steele in *Green Stockings* (39 St. Th., Oct. 2, 1911); subsequently appeared as Thorton Brown in *Believe Me, Xantippe* (39 St. Th., Aug. 19, 1913); Henry Potter in *The Man Who Came Back* (Playhouse, Sept. 2, 1916); Napoleon Gibbs in *39 East* (Broadhurst, Mar. 31, 1919); Carey Harper in *When We Are Young* (Broadhurst, Nov. 22, 1920); the Earl of Warwick in *The Trial of Joan of Arc* (Shubert, Apr. 12, 1921); John McFarlane in *Everyday* (Bijou, Nov. 16, 1921); and Paul Jones in *The Cat and the Canary* (National, Feb. 7, 1922).

With Leighton Osmun, he wrote *Manhattan* (Playhouse, Aug. 15, 1922). He played the title role in *Roger Bloomer* (48 St. Th., Mar. 1, 1923); Robert Metcalf in *In Love with Love* (Ritz, Aug. 6, 1923); Tony Mason in *The Other Rose* (Morosco, Dec. 20, 1923); Richard Winslow in *The Youngest* (Gaiety, Dec. 22, 1924); George Randall in *Lulu Belle* (Belasco, Feb. 9, 1926); King Hilary and King Perivale in *The Ivory Door* (Charles Hopkins Th., Oct. 18, 1927); Niccolo Machiavelli in *The Grey Fox* (Playhouse, Oct. 22, 1928); Alexander in *Young Alexander* (Biltmore, Mar. 12, 1929); Morgan Wallace in *Congratulations,* which he wrote (National, Apr. 30, 1929); Philip Haven in *Ladies Leave* (Charles Hopkins Th., Oct. 1, 1929); Charlie Riggs in *Veneer* (Harris, Nov. 12, 1929); Michael in *Michael and Mary* (Charles Hopkins Th., Dec. 13, 1929); and Baron von Gaigern in *Grand Hotel* (National, Nov. 13, 1930); also the Young Man in *The Roof* (Charles Hopkins Th., Oct. 30, 1931); Hubert Burnet in *The Bride the Sun Shines On* (Fulton, Dec. 26, 1931); Darrell Blake in *The Moon in the Yellow River* (Guild, Feb. 29, 1932); Tito Lanni in *Foreign Affairs* (Avon, Apr. 13, 1932); succeeded (May 1932) Leslie Banks as Henry Dewlip in *Springtime for Henry* (Bijou, Dec. 9, 1931), toured in it, returned to N.Y.C. in it (Ambassador, May 1, 1933). He played Jeeter Lester in *Tobacco Road* (Masque, Dec. 4, 1934); Edgar Allen Poe in *Plumes in the Dust* (46 St. Th., Nov. 6, 1936); Crown Prince Rudolph in *Masque of Kings* (Shubert, Feb. 8, 1937). Decius Heiss in the pre-Bway tryout of *The Shop at Sly Corner* (McCarter Th., Princeton, N.J., Nov. 1941); and Sam Whitaker in the pre-Bway tryout of *The Wife Takes the Child* (closed Wilbur, Boston, Dec. 1942).

He appeared in a series of "Grand Guignol" one-act plays presented as *Horror Tonight* (Belasco, Los Angeles, Calif., June 1943); played Henry Burton in the pre-Bway tryout of *Many Happy Returns* (Nov. 1944); Jim Hapgood in *Foolish Notion* (Martin Beck Th., N.Y.C., Mar. 13, 1945); Morris Troup in the pre-Bway tryout of *Georgia Boy* (opened Copley, Boston, Dec. 29, 1945; closed there, Jan. 5, 1946); took over (Oct. 1949) the role of Doc in *Mister Roberts* (Alvin, N.Y.C., Feb. 18, 1948); played Daniel Rock in the pre-Bway tryout of *A Little Evil* (opened Playhouse, Wilmington, Del., Feb. 8, 1952); Shylock in *The Merchant of Venice* and Malvolio in *Twelfth Night* (Shakespearean Festival, Idyllwild, Calif., 1954); and Uncle Charley Hawley in *Happy Town* (54 St. Th., N.Y.C., Oct. 7, 1959).

Films. Mr. Hull made his debut in *The Little Rebel* (1916); later appeared in *Yellow Jack* (MGM, 1938); *Three Comrades* (MGM, 1938); *Boys Town* (MGM, 1938); *The Great Waltz* (MGM, 1938); *Jesse James* (20th-Fox, 1939); *Stanley and Livingstone* (20th-Fox, 1939); *Babes in Arms* (MGM, 1939); *My Son, My Son* (UA, 1940); *High Sierra* (WB, 1941); *Lifeboat* (20th-Fox, 1944); *Objective Burma* (WB, 1945); *Deep Valley* (WB, 1947); *Mourning Becomes Electra* (RKO, 1947); *The Fountainhead* (WB, 1949); *The Great Gatsby* (Par., 1949); *The Return of Jesse James* (Lippert, 1950); *The Last Posse* (Col., 1953); *Inferno* (20th-Fox, 1953); *Thunder Over the Plains* (WB, 1953); *Man with the Gun* (UA, 1955); *The Sheriff of Fractured Jaw* (20th-Fox, 1958); *The Treasure of Lost Canyon* (U, 1958); *Proud Rebel* (Buena Vista, 1958); *The Buccaneer* (Par., 1959); *Master of the World* (AMI, 1961); *The Fool Killer* (Landau, 1965); and *The Chase* (Col., 1966).

Television. Mr. Hull has appeared on Armstrong Circle Th. (NBC, 1951); Video Th., (CBS, 1952); Center Stage (ABC, 1954); You Are There (CBS, 1955); Climax (CBS, 1956); in *Face of a Hero* (Playhouse 90, CBS, 1959); on Wagon Train (NBC, 1959, 1960, 1961); Naked City (ABC, 1959); Bonanza (NBC, 1960); Zane Grey Th. (CBS, 1960); and in *The Wooden Dish* (Play of the Week, NET, 1961); *The Man with the Shine on His Shoes* (Alcoa Premiere, ABC, 1962); and The Travels of Jaimie McPheeters (ABC, 1963).

Recreation. Traveling.

HULL, LORAINE. Educator, actress, director. b. S. Loraine Boos, August 5, Algona, Iowa, to Myron and Vera (Cleal) Boos. Father, wholesale grocer. Grad. Drake Univ., B.F.A.; Univ. of Wisconsin (Madison), M.A. Professional training with Lee Strasberg, N.Y.C., and at Lee Strasberg Th. Institute, Los Angeles, Calif.; H B Studio, N.Y.C. Married Jan. 4, 1949, to John Calkins Hull; one daughter, Dianne Lee Hull, actress; one son, Donald John Hull, songwriter. Member ITA (US delegate, 1971, 1973, 1975); North American Regional Theatre Alliance (fdr., 1971; pres., 1973–74–75); ATA (intl. comn.); ACTA (bd. mbr., 1970–74; newsletter ed., membership chmn., 1970; state, regional play festival judge, 1971–to date); Wisconsin Idea Theatre Conference (pres., 1968–70; vice-pres., 1967; secy., 1965–66; bd. mbr., 1965–70; play dir., 1965–70); Wisconsin Arts Fdtn. and Council (arts comm., 1969–72); Wisconsin Community Theatre Assn. (fdr., 1st pres., 1969, 1970; bd. mbr., 1970–73); Wisconsin Theatre Assn.; Fond du Lac Co. (Wis.) Arts Council (fdr., 1968; pres., 1968–70); Fond du Lac Community Th. (founder, 1958; pres. and dir., 1958–to date). Address: (home) 2308 Takodah Dr., Fond du Lac, WI 54935, tel. (414) 922-3234; (Summer) Lee Strasberg Theatre Institute, 6757 Hollywood Blvd., Los Angeles, CA 90028, tel. (213) 461-4333; (bus.) Ripon College, Ripon, WI 54971, tel. (414) 748-8136.

Mrs. Hull has been assistant professor of drama, Ripon (Wis.) Coll. (1973–to date) and supervisor and a consultant developing new programs at Lee Strasberg Theatre Institute, Hollywood, Calif. (1972–to date). Previously she was a creative dramatics instructor and children's theatre director (1950–55); a secondary school theatre instructor in Iowa and Fond du Lac, Wis. (1956–65); and a theatre specialists and drama coordinator for Fond du Lac public schools (1965–72).

Theatre. Mrs. Hull played various roles in student productions while attending Drake Univ. (1946–49) and later (1958–66) at the Fond du Lac Community Theatre. She was in stock at the Green Ram Summer Th., Baraboo, Wis., where she played Emma in *Roar Like a Dove* (June 1965).

Plays she directed at Fond du Lac Community Theatre are *The Sound of Music* (1965), *The Diary of Anne Frank* (1965), *Carousel* (1966), *Oklahoma!* (1966), *My Fair Lady* (1967), *Camelot* (1968), *Barefoot in the Park* (1969), *Wait Until Dark* (1970), *South Pacific* (1971), and *Fiddler on the Roof* (1973). Her other directorial work in community theatres includes *The Miracle Worker* (Sheboygan, Wis., 1964); *A Majority of One* (Rhinelander, Wis., Summer 1965); *The Dirty Old Man* (Kenosha, Wis., 1967; Omaha, Nebr., 1969); *The Indian Wants the Bronx* (Sheboygan, Wis., 1969); *The Zoo Story* (Waukesha Wis.; Columbus, Ohio; Univ. of Wisconsin, Madison, all 1971; and Omaha Playhouse, Omaha, Neb., Apr. 1972); and *The Cage* (Stevens Point, Wis., and Lincoln, Nebr., 1973).

For the Ripon College Th., Mrs. Hull directed *Butterflies Are Free* (1973); was faculty advisor for *Antigone* (1973); directed *You're a Good Man Charlie Brown* (1974); *A Streetcar Named Desire* (1974); and *The Threepenny Opera* (1975).

Films. Mrs. Hull performed in Kiekhafer Corp. documentaries (1958–62); was on Chicago telefilm (1958–63); and appeared on a Canadian Broadcasting Corp. documentary about Monaco (1973).

Television. Mrs. Hull was an actress and director with KNRT, Des Moines, Iowa (1949). She has also been associated at various times with WBAY, Green Bay, Wis.; KFIZ, Fond du Lac, Wis.; and WISM, Milwaukee, Wis.

Published Works. Mrs. Hull's writings include numerous articles on aspects of community theatre, published in college, state, and national theatre group newsletters.

Awards. Under a Ford Foundation grant, Mrs. Hull was an interne supervisor, Univ. of Wisconsin, Madison (1963–65). She received the Lunt-Fontanne Award for directing the first-place state theatre play winner in Wisconsin in 1964, 1965, 1967, 1969, 1971, and 1973; received the Detroit ATA-ACTA certificate of merit (1969); and was a regional winner in the 1971 and 1973 ACTA National Play festivals.

Recreation. Reading, swimming, traveling, snowmobiling.

HUMPHREY, CAVADA. Actress. b. June 17, Atlantic City, N.J. Grad. Ashley Hall Sch., Charleston, S.C.; Smith Coll., B.A. Married to Jerome Kilty, actor, director, producer, playwright. Member of AEA; AFTRA; SAG. Address: 7 W. 16th St., New York, NY 10011, tel. (212) AL 5-3822.

Theatre. Miss Humphrey first appeared on the stage at the age of four in a ballet solo at the Philadelphia (Pa.) Acad. of Music.

She played Ellen in *Ladies in Retirement* (New London Players, Barn Playhouse, New London, N.H., Summer 1940); made her N.Y.C. debut as Esther in *A Man's House* (Blackfriars Guild, Apr. 1, 1943); subsequently played Naomi Fisher in *The House in Paris* (Fulton, Mar. 20, 1944); understudied Eva Le Gallienne as Mme. Ranevska for a cross-country tour of *The Cherry Orchard* (1944).

As a member of the Amer. Repertory Th., she was assistant stage manager and appeared in their productions at the Intl. Th., N.Y.C. (Nov. 6, 1946–April 5, 1947) as a maid in *What Every Woman Knows*, a Christian in *Androcles and the Lion*, a girl in *Pound on Demand*, and a Lady of the Court in *Henry VIII;* played Madame Sajou in *The Song of Bernadette* (Belasco, Feb. 26, 1946); Miss Swenson in *As the Girls Go* (Winter Garden, Nov. 13, 1948); Mrs. Williamson, and later Mrs. Dudgeon, in *The Devil's Disciple*, (NY City Ctr., Jan. 25, 1950; moved to Royale, Feb. 21, 1950).

With the Brattle Th. (Cambridge, Mass.), Miss Humphrey played the Mother in *Six Characters in Search of an Author*, (Oct. 1951), Olga in *The Three Sisters* (Dec. 1951), Lady Sneerwell in *The School for Scandal* (Feb. 1952), the Third Witch in *Macbeth* (Sept. 1952), Goneril in *King Lear* (Oct. 1952), Anna in *Ivanov* (Nov. 1952), Genevieve in *The Long Christmas Dinner* (Dec. 1952), Lady Mortimer in *Henry IV, Part 1* (July 1954), Margaret in *Much Ado About Nothing* (Aug. 1954), Emilia in *Othello* (Aug. 1954), and Cassandra in *Troilus and Cressida* (Jan. 1955). She played Mme. Zoe in *Moon in Capricorn* (Th. de Lys, N.Y.C., Oct. 27, 1953); and the title role in *The Madwoman of Chaillot* (Evanston Th., Chicago, Ill., 1955).

She has played the following roles in Shakespearean productions at the NY City Ctr.: the Duchess of Gloucester in *King Richard II* (Jan. 24, 1951), a Widow in *The Taming of the Shrew* (Apr. 25, 1951), Maria in *Love's Labour's Lost* (Feb. 4, 1953), understudied Florence Reed as Queen Margaret in *Richard III* (Dec. 9, 1953), and in the Brattle Th. productions, repeated her roles as Emilia in *Othello* (Sept. 7, 1955), and Lady Mortimer in *Henry IV, Part 1* (Sept. 21, 1955).

She appeared as the Actress in *The Guardsman* (Studebaker, Chicago, Ill., Mar. 15, 1957); and the Fortune Teller in *The Skin of Our Teeth* (Boston Arts Festival, Mass., June 18, 1957); with the Group 20 Players (Wellesley, Mass.) she played Mme. Desmortes in *Ring Round the Moon* (July 1956), Violet in *Man and Superman* (Aug. 1957), Wowkle in *The Girl of the Golden West* (Aug. 1957), Lady Teazle in *The School for Scandal* (July 1958), Mrs. Higgins in *Pygmalion* (Aug. 1958), and Blanche DuBois in *A Streetcar Named Desire* (July 1959).

She played Wowkle in *The Girl of the Golden West*, directed by her husband, Jerome Kilty (Phyllis Anderson Th., N.Y.C., Nov. 5, 1957); was standby (Feb.–Apr. 1958) for Helen Hayes as the Duchess Pont-au-Bronc in *Time Remembered* (Morosco, Nov. 12, 1957); and appeared as Madrecita in *Camino Real* (Boston Arts Fest., Summer 1958); and Mrs. Trellington in the pre-Bway tryout of *Listen to the Mockingbird* (opened Colonial, Boston, Dec. 27, 1958; closed Shubert, Washington, D.C., Jan. 29, 1959).

Since 1960, Miss Humphrey has toured in her husband's play *Dear Liar*, playing Mrs. Patrick Campbell to his George Bernard Shaw (Criterion, London, June 14, 1960; Intimate Th., Johannesburg, South Africa, June 21, 1961; Durban and Capetown, South Africa; Th. Marquee, N.Y.C., Mar. 17, 1962; on college campuses in the US, etc.); meanwhile appearing with the Association of Producing Artists (APA) in their season at the Mendelssohn Th., Ann Arbor, Mich., as Lady Sneerwell in *The School for Scandal* (Oct. 3, 1962), the Mother in *We, Comrades Three* (Oct. 10, 1962), and Hester in *Penny for a Song* (1962).

Opposite her husband, she toured South Africa as Martha in *Who's Afraid of Virginia Woolf?* (Oct.–Dec. 1963); played Stella in the English-speaking cast of *Life Is a Dream* (Astor Place Playhouse, N.Y.C., Mar. 19, 1964); Clodia Pulcher in her husband's play, *Ides of March* (Boston Arts Fest., Summer 1964); and again toured South Africa as Martha in *Who's Afraid of Virginia Woolf?* (City Hall, Pt. Elizabeth, Sept. 9, 1964; Sultan Th., Durban, Sept. 16, 1964; Univ. Th., Johannesburg, Sept. 23, 1964).

Miss Humphrey played Madame Alexandra in *Colombe* (Garrick, N.Y.C., Feb. 23, 1965); replaced (Dec. 6, 1965) Claribel Baird as Grand Duchess Olga in *You Can't Take it with You* (Lyceum, Nov. 23, 1965); played Queen Elinor in *King John* (NY Shakespeare Fest., Delacorte Th., July 5, 1967); Lady Fitch, the Doctor and Aunt Mildred in *Leda Had a Little Swan* (Cort, began previews Mar. 29, 1968; closed Apr. 10, 1968, before official opening); Eleanor of Aquitaine in *The Lion in Winter* (Comedy Club, 1969); Proserpine Garnett in *Candida* (Longacre, Apr. 6, 1970); toured as Madame Arcati in *Blithe Spirit* (Summer 1970); Baroness de Simiane in *Madame de Sade* (ANTA Matinee Series, Th. de Lys, Oct. 30, 1972); and played Queen Elizabeth I in the one-woman drama, *Henry's Daughter*, which Miss Humphrey compiled from various sources (Manhattan Th. Club, Stage 73, Feb. 20, 1973; Triangle Th., May 9, 1974; etc.).

Films. Miss Humphrey appeared in *The Naked City* (U, 1948) and as Miss Flannery in *Thoroughly Modern Millie* (U, 1967).

Television. She made her debut on the Somerset Maugham Th. (NBC, 1946); subsequently played Miss Malin Nat Og Dog in the two-part *Deluge at Nordenay* (Camera Three, CBS, May 3, 16, 1964); appeared on Kraft Television Th. (NBC); *Colette by Herself* (Camera Three, CBS); as Mrs. Campbell in *Dear Liar* (WNET, Apr. 16, 1965); *The Prodigal* (NET Playhouse, WNET, May 1969); Dark Shadows (ABC); and *The Adams Chronicles* (WNET).

Awards. She received the Kraft Television Award for outstanding featured performances, and was nominated for the Sarah Siddons Award (Chicago) for her performance in the title role of *The Madwoman of Chaillot* (Chicago, 1955).

Recreation. Study of the Elizabethan period, dress design, fashion.

HUNT, HUGH. Director, playwright, writer, educator. b. Hugh Sydney Hunt, Sept. 25, 1911, Camberley, Surrey, England, to Cecil Edwin and Ethel Helan (Crookshank) Hunt. Father, British Army officer. Grad. Marlborough Coll., Eng., 1929; Univ. of Paris (de la Sorbonne), diploma in French civilization, 1929; Heidelberg Univ., Germany, diploma in German civilization, 1930; Oxford Univ., B.A. 1933; M.A. 1961. Married Nov. 16, 1940, to Janet Mary Gordon; one son; one daughter, Caroline Hunt, actress. Served British Army, Intelligence, ETO, 1939–46; rank, Maj. Member of Arts Council of Gr. Brit. (drama panel), Liverpool Playhouse (trustee), Lancashire Community Council (drama panel), Independent Television Authority. Address: (home) Cae Terfyn, Criccieth, Caerns, North Wales; (bus.) c/o Dept. of Drama, University of Manchester, Manchester, England tel. Ardwick 3333.

Mr. Hunt has been emeritus professor at Manchester Univ. since 1973; he had been professor of drama at the university from 1961 to 1973.

Theatre. Mr. Hunt directed the N.Y.C. productions of *The White Steed* (Cort, Jan. 10, 1939); and *The Living Room* (Henry Miller's Th., Nov. 17, 1954).

He started in the theatre directing, with Giles Playfair, *King John* (Oxford Univ. Dramatic Society, Nov. 1932).

He served as resident director of the Maddermarket Th. (Norwich, Eng.), where he directed *Macbeth, Much Ado About Nothing, Strife, Ralph Roister Doister, On the Rocks*, and *End and Beginning* (1934); was resident director of the Croydon Repertory Th. (1934–35); and directed William Devlin's *King Lear* (Westminster, Oct. 8, 1934).

He was resident director of the Abbey Th. (Dublin, Ire., 1935–38), where he staged *Purgatory, Shadow and Substance, Hassan, Katie Roche, Boyd's Shop, The Playboy of the Western World, Riders to the Sea, The Plough and the Stars, Deirdre*, and *The Moon in the Yellow River.* Also at the Abbey Th., he directed *The Invincibles*, which he wrote with Frank O'Connor (1937); and directed and wrote *In the Train.*

He directed *The Golden Cuckoo* (Duchess, London, Jan. 2, 1940), and *Shadow and Substance* (Duke of York's, May 25, 1943).

For the Bristol Old Vic Co., he directed the London productions of *Tess of the D'Urbervilles* (New, Nov. 26, 1946; Piccadilly, May 20, 1947), *King Lear* (Embassy, May 26, 1947), *Much Ado About Nothing* (Embassy, June 2, 1947), *Hamlet* (St. James's, July 13, 1948); and for the London Old Vic Co., directed *The Cherry Orchard* (New, Nov. 25, 1948).

He was resident director of the London Old Vic Co. (1949–51; 1952–53), directing *Love's Labour's Lost* (New, Oct. 11, 1949), *Captain Brassbound's Conversion* (Old Vic, Apr. 17, 1951), *The Merry Wives of Windsor* (Old Vic, May 31, 1951), *Romeo and Juliet* (Old Vic, Sept. 15, 1952), *The Merchant of Venice* (Old Vic, Jan. 6, 1953), *King Lear* (Old Vic, Feb. 23, 1953), and *Julius Caesar* (Old Vic, Feb. 24, 1953). He directed *The White Countess* (Saville, Mar. 24, 1954).

He was executive director of the Australian Elizabethan Th. Trust Co. in Sydney (1955–60), where he presented *Medea, Hamlet, Murder in the Cathedral, Twelfth Night, Julius Caesar*, and *Summer of the 17th Doll.*

For the Arts Council, Mr. Hunt directed a touring production of *Five Finger Exercise* (Wales, Sept. 1960) and directed *Abelard and Heloise* (Arts, London, Nov. 1960).

He returned to the Abbey Theatre, Dublin, as artistic director in 1968. His productions for the Abbey included *The Shaughraun* (1968), later presented at the World Theatre Season (Aldwych, London); *The Hostage* (1969), later presented in a tour of European capitals; *The Silver Tassie* (1972), later presented in Helsinki and Brussels; and *Three Sisters* (1973).

In addition to his work at the Abbey, Mr. Hunt is vice-chairman of the International Federation for Theatre Research.

Films. He was assistant director for *Men of Tomorrow* (London Films, 1934).

Published Works. He wrote *Old Vic Prefaces* (1954), *The Director in the Theatre* (1954), *The Making of Australian Theatre* (1960), *The Live Theatre* (1961), and *In the Train* (1973) a one-act play adapted from Frank O'Connor's short story.

HUNT, MARSHA. Actress. b. Marcia Virginia Hunt, Oct. 17, 1917, Chicago, Ill., to Earl R. and Minabel M. Hunt. Father, lawyer, insurance company executive, Social Security administrator; mother, voice teacher and coach, accompanist, organist. Relative in theatre: nephew, Allan Hunt, television and film actor. Grad. Horace Mann Sch. for Girls (H.S.), N.Y.C., 1934; attended Theodora Irvine's Studio for the Theatre, N.Y.C., 1934–35; studied with Phyllis Lawton, Paramount Studios, Hollywood, Calif., 1935–37; Nina Mouise, Hollywood, Calif., 1938. Married Nov. 23, 1938, to Jerry Hooper, film director (marr. dis. 1945); married Feb. 10, 1946, to Robert Presnell, Jr., screenwriter, playwright, television writer, novelist; one stepson. Served WW II, Women's Ambulance and Defense Corps; rank, Staff Sgt.; extensive USO work in Hollywood Canteen, and entertained service men in camps and hospitals in US and Canada. Member of SAG (bd. of dir., 1945–46); AEA; AFTRA; British AEA; Australian AEA; San Fernando Valley (Calif.) Youth Foundation (bd., 1955–to date);

Community Relations Conference of Southern Calif. (bd., 1959–to date); US Committee for Refugees (board, 1960–to date); United Nations Assn. (World Refugee chairman, So. Calif. State council, 1960–to date; pres. of San Fernando Valley chapter, 1961–62; Peace Strategy Council, 1961–63; Freedom from Hunger Committee of So. Calif., 1963–to date). Address: Shiffrin-Litto Agency, 315 S. Beverly Dr., Beverly Hills, CA tel. (312) CR 4-7641.

Pre-Theatre. John Powers fashion model, N.Y.C.

Theatre. Miss Hunt made her N.Y.C. debut as Ann in *Joy to the World* (Plymouth Th., Mar. 18, 1948); subsequently appeared in a stock production of the play (Subway Circuit, N.Y.C., 1948); played Ann in *Goodbye Again* (Princeton, N.J.; Marblehead, Mass., 1948); appeared in *The Man with a Load of Mischief* (Cape May, N.J., 1948); played the title role in *Laura* (Hartford, Conn.; Penthouse Th., Atlanta, Ga., Nov. 13, 1950; Redmont Hotel, Birmingham, Ala., Feb. 26, 1951); Judith Anderson in *The Devil's Disciple* (NY City Ctr., Jan. 26, 1950; moved Royale, Feb. 21, 1950); Hannie in *Borned in Texas* (Fulton, Aug. 21, 1950); Minerva Pinney in *Legend of Sarah* (Fulton, Oct. 11, 1950), a role she repeated in stock (Penthouse Th., Atlanta, Ga., 1951).

She appeared as Gilda in *Design for Living* (Hilltop Th. in the Round, Sheraton Belvedere Hotel, Baltimore, Md., Jan. 23, 1951); toured as Celia Coplestone in the national production of *The Cocktail Party* (opened Curran, San Francisco, Calif., Oct. 15, 1951); toured as Jennet in *The Lady's Not for Burning* (La Jolla Playhouse, Calif.; Alcazar, San Francisco, Sept. 1952; Empress Playhouse, St. Louis, Mo., Apr. 1954); played Irene Elliott in *Affairs of State* (La Jolla Playhouse, July 29, 1952); Carthay Circle, Los Angeles; Geary, San Francisco, Oct. 1952–Jan. 1953); Sybil in *Private Lives* (Tenthouse Th., Palm Springs, Calif., 1953); Barbara in *Major Barbara* (Glen Aire Country Club, Los Angeles, Calif., 1953); Alice in *Anniversary Waltz* (Carthay Circle, Los Angeles, Apr. 11, 1955); Susan in *The Little Hot* (Princess, Melbourne, Austl., 1955), and toured in the latter role (La Jolla Playhouse; Carthay Circle, Los Angeles, Calif., 1956).

Miss Hunt appeared as Nancy Fallon in *A Roomful of Roses* (Cincinnati, Ohio, July 30, 1956); Mrs. Stephen Douglas in *The Rivalry* (Beverly Hilton Hotel, Beverly Hills, Calif., 1957); Isolde Poole in *The Tunnel of Love* (Coconut Playhouse, Miami, Fla., Dec. 9, 1957); succeeded (Natl., Jan. 20, 1958) Kaye Lyder as Isolde Poole in *The Tunnel of Love* (Royale, N.Y.C., Feb. 13, 1957); and repeated the role on the national tour (opened Shubert, Detroit, Mich., Feb. 26, 1958; closed there Mar. 15, 1958); played Anna in *The King and I* (Sacramento Music Circus, Calif., July 14, 1958); Content Lowell in *Marriage-Go-Round* (Opera House, Monterey, Calif., Jan. 1961; Circque Playhouse, Seattle, Wash., Feb. 1961; Pasadena Playhouse, Calif., Apr. 28, 1961); Mary Follet in *All the Way Home* (Playhouse-in-the-Park, Philadelphia, Pa., July 10, 1961); Mary Rhodes in *The Complaisant Lover* (Avondale Playhouse, Indianapolis, Ind., July 3, 1962; Lobero Th., Santa Barbara, Calif., July 16, 1962); and Lady Utterwood in *Heartbreak House* (Theatre Group, Schoenberg Hall, Univ. of California at Los Angeles, June 5, 1963); and Meg Tynan in *The Paisley Convertible* (Henry Miller's Th., N.Y.C., Feb. 11, 1967).

Films. Miss Hunt made her debut in *The Virginia Judge* (Par., 1935); subsequently appeared in *Gentle Julia* (20th-Fox, 1936); *Desert Gold* (Par., 1936); *Arizona Raiders* (Par., 1936); *Hollywood Boulevard* (Par., 1936); *College Holiday* (Par., 1936); *Easy to Take* (Par., 1936); *The Accusing Finger* (Par., 1936); *Murder Goes to College* (Par., 1937); *Easy Living* (Par., 1937); *Thunder Trail* (Par., 1937); and *Annapolis Salute* (RKO, 1937).

Also, *Born to the West* (Par., 1938); *Come On Leathernecks* (Rep., 1938); *Long Shot* (Grand Natl., 1938); *Star Reporter* (Mono., 1939); *The Hardys Ride High* (MGM, 1939); *These Glamour Girls* (MGM, 1939); *Joe and Ethel Turp Call on the President* (MGM, 1939); *Winter Carnival* (UA, 1939); *Irene* (RKO, 1940); *Flight Command* (MGM, 1940); *Pride and Prejudice* (MGM, 1940); *Woman in Hiding* (U, 1940); *Ellery Queen, Master Detective* (Col., 1940); *Cheers for Miss Bishop* (UA, 1941); and *The Trial of Mary Dugan* (MGM, 1941).

Also, *The Penalty* (MGM, 1941); *I'll Wait for You* (MGM, 1941); *Blossoms in the Dust* (MGM, 1941); *Unholy Partners* (MGM, 1941); *Panama Hattie* (MGM, 1942); *Joe Smith, American* (MGM, 1942); *The Affairs of Martha* (MGM, 1942); *Seven Sweethearts* (MGM, 1942); *Kid Glove Killer* (MGM, 1942); *Pilot No. 5* (MGM, 1943); *Lost Angel* (MGM, 1943); *Cry Havoc* (MGM, 1943); *The Human Comedy* (MGM, 1943); *Thousands Cheer* (MGM, 1943); *Music for Millions* (MGM, 1944); *None Shall Escape* (Col., 1944); *Bride by Mistake* (RKO, 1944); *The Valley of Decision* (MGM, 1945); *A Letter for Evie* (MGM, 1945); *Smash-up, the Story of a Woman* (U, 1947); *Carnegie Hall* (UA, 1947); *The Inside Story* (Rep., 1948); *Raw Deal* (Eagle Lion, 1948); *Jigsaw* (UA, 1949); *Take One False Step* (U, 1949); *Mary Ryan, Detective* (Col., 1950); *Actors and Sin* (UA, 1952); *The Happy Time* (Col., 1952); *No Place to Hide* (Allied, 1956); *Bombers B-52* (WA, 1957); *Back From the Dead* (20th-Fox, 1957); *Blue Denim* (20th-Fox, 1959); *The Plunderers* (Allied, 1960); *Welcome to the Club* (Col., 1971); *Johnny Got His Gun* (Cinemation, 1971); and *Dracula A.D. 1972* (WB, 1972).

Television and Radio. During WW II, Miss Hunt made radio transcriptions in French for the Office of War Information, as well as radio transcriptions of songs and poetry for the troops overseas.

She made her television debut as Viola in a live production of Shakespeare's *Twelfth Night*, the first coast-to-coast telecast of a Shakespeare play (NBC, 1949). She has appeared on the Philco Television Playhouse (NBC, 1949); Ford Th. (CBS, 1949); Studio One (CBS, 1950); Silver Th. (NBC, 1950); This Is Show Business (CBS, 1950–51); Perry Como Show (NBC, 1951); Ezio Pinza Show (1952); Cosmopolitan Th. (ABC, 1953); Matinee Th. (NBC, 1955); Climax! (CBS, 1957–58); the series Peck's Bad Girl (CBS, 1959); Cain's Hundred (NBC, 1961); The Americans (1961); Sam Benedict (NBC, 1962); Twilight Zone (CBS, 1963); Gunsmoke (CBS, 1963); and The Breaking Point (ABC, 1963).

Also, the GE Th. (CBS), The Defenders (CBS), Ford Th. (CBS), Zane Grey Th. (CBS), The Detectives (NBC), Alfred Hitchcock Presents (CBS), Grand Jury, Laramie, O. Henry Playhouse, Channing, Outer Limits, Profiles in Courage; Run for Your Life (NBC); My Three Sons (CBS); Accidental Family (NBC); The Outsider (NBC); Fear No Evil (NBC); Ironside (NBC); The Young Lawyers (ABC); and Jigsaw (ABC). She has also filmed a series of interviews, A Visit with Marsha Hunt.

From 1951–56, she spoke on the Cerebral Palsy Telethon in Los Angeles, Calif., and was the mistress of ceremonies on the Cerebral Palsy Telethons in San Francisco, Calif.; Indianapolis, Ind.; Denver, Colo.; Fresno, Calif.; Spokane, Wash.; and Phoenix, Ariz. In 1959–60, she produced a television documentary film on the United Nations World Refugee Year called *A Call from the Stars*.

Other Activities. During and after WW II, Miss Hunt sold US Savings Bonds; conducted appeals for money or clothing for The March of Dimes, Easter Seals, Red Cross, as well as the Korean War refugees. In 1959–60, she conducted a weekly drama workshop at the San Fernando Valley (Calif.) Youth Foundation Center; and sponsored the Summer Teen-Age Drama Workshop at San Fernando Valley State Coll. She has produced a UN Day Festival in the San Fernando Valley (Oct., 1960) and has dramatized a US Senate debate on refugee legislation. Since 1960, she has made numerous speeches on world refugees; the UN; UN Specialized Agencies; "Women—Social Conscience of the World" (pub. Y.W.C.A. magazine, May 1963); human relations; civil rights; and equal opportunity. In 1963, she produced a benefit concert for the UN Freedom from Hunger Campaign.

Awards. She has received various plaques and scrolls for humanitarianism from chapters of Hadassah, the Humanists, Mount Holyoke Coll. Alumnae of Southern Calif., Women's International League for Peace and Freedom, and City of Hope. She was given a citation for meritorious service by the US Committee for Refugees (May 25, 1961).

Recreation. "People and Peace.".

HUNT, WILLIAM E. Producer, actor, director. b. William Evans Hunt, Jan. 25, 1923, New York City, to William and Essie P. Hunt. Grad. Poly Prep. Sch., Brooklyn, N.Y., 1939; attended Johns Hopkins Univ., 1939–42; grad. Neighborhood Playhouse Sch. of the Theatre, N.Y.C., 1944. Member of CORST (pres.); AEA; American Newspaper Guild (N.Y. chapter).

Theatre. Mr. Hunt first appeared as Douglas Fairbanks Rosenbloom in a school production of *A Slight Case of Murder* (Johns Hopkins Univ., Baltimore, Md., 1941); his first professional appearance was as a Native in *White Cargo* (Hilltop Th., Baltimore, Md., July 1942); and was a member of the company of the Cedarhurst Playhouse (L.I., N.Y., July–Aug. 1943).

He made his N.Y.C. debut as a walk-on in *I'll Take the High Road* (Ritz Th., Nov. 9, 1943); subsequently appeared as Peter (Stinky) Jastrombowski in *Hickory Stick* Mansfield, May 8, 1944); appeared as Bill Hughes in *Men to the Sea* (National, Oct. 3, 1944); and in the ELT production of *Kiss Them for Me* (1944). He toured for the USO in *What a Life* (Alaska and Aleutian Islands, July–Nov. 1945); and appeared in *Lady Godiva's Horse* (Callboard, Hollywood, Calif., Feb. 1946).

Mr. Hunt directed *Joe McGinnacle* at the Actors' Studio (Hollywood, Calif., Jan. 1946); he produced and directed *The Beautiful People* (Th. East. N.Y.C., 1957); produced *The Will and the Way* (American premiere, Th. East, Jan. 1960); and *Tobias and the Angel* (Th. East, Feb. 1960); produced and directed *Black Monday* (Van Dam Th., Mar. 6, 1962); directed *Say Nothing* (Jan Hus House, Jan. 27, 1965); *Friends* and *Enemies* (Th. East, Sept. 16, 1965); *The Madness of Lady Bright* and *Ludlow Fair* (Th. East, Mar. 22, 1966); *Three Hand Reel* (Renata Th., Nov. 7, 1966); *Lemonade* and *The Autograph Hound* (Jan Hus House, Dec. 13, 1968); *Three by Ferlinghetti* (Jan Hus Th., Sept. 22, 1970); conceived and directed *The Sunshine Train* (Abbey Th., June 15, 1972); directed *Green Julia* (Sheridan Square Playhouse, Nov. 16, 1972); *The Boys Who Came To Leave* (Astor Place Th., June 6, 1973); and *High Time* (Th. for the New City, Oct. 1974).

Mr. Hunt has also operated Tinker's Pond Th. (Woodbury, N.Y.), where he produced his own adaptation of *Roberta* (1963), and he was operator of Crest Pier Th. (Wildwood Crest, N.J., 1947), Sea Cliff (N.Y.) Summer Th. (1948), and Red Barn Th. (Northport, N.Y., 1953–68).

He has operated the following summer theatres, Crest Pier Th. (Wildwood Crest, N.J., 1947); Sea Cliff Summer Th. (Sea Cliff, L.I., N.Y., 1948); Red Barn Th. (Northport, L.I., N.Y., 1953–to date), where he presented *The Will and the Way* and *Black Monday;* and Tinker's Pond Th. (Woodbury, L.I., N.Y., 1963–to date), where he has produced his own adaptation of *Roberta* (1963).

Films. Mr. Hunt appeared in *Margie* (20th-Fox, 1946); *Naked City* (U, 1948); *Beyond Glory* (Par., 1948); and *Sorority Girl* (Amer. Intl., 1957).

Television and Radio. He wrote scripts for the radio programs. Five Minute Mysteries and So Proudly We Hail.

He was associate producer-director for the television program, Doorway to Danger (NBC, 1952), and wrote two of the eight half-hour scripts; and was chief cost estimator and budget controller for all live television production at NBC (1950–52).

Other Activities. Mr. Hunt designed the Th. East (1957), and designed and remodeled Tinker's Pond Th. (1963). He is a feature writer for the Long Island *Daily Press* (Jamaica, N.Y.).

Awards. Mr. Hunt was winner of the John Golden Auditions (1943).

Recreation. Golf, tennis.

HUNTER, FREDERICK J. Educator. b. Frederick James Hunter, May 31, 1916, Denver, Colo., to John L. and Mary (Affolter) Hunter. Father, advertising manager. Grad. Longmont (Colo.) H.S., 1934; attended Los Angeles (Calif.) City Coll., 1935–38; grad. Univ. of California, A.B. 1940; Univ. of North Carolina, M.A. 1942; Stanford Univ., Ph.D. 1954. Married Aug. 15, 1945, to Elberta (Casey) Hunter, actress, artist; three sons. Served USAAF, 1942–46; rank, Capt. Member of ATA; ASTR; SWTC; Tau Sigma Delta. Dept. of Drama, Univ. of Texas, Austin, TX 78712; 4803 Timberline Dr., Austin, TX 78746.

From 1960 to 1971, Dr. Hunter was curator of the Hoblitzelle Th. Arts Library at the Univ. of Texas. Since 1969, he has been Professor of Drama in the Dept. of Drama at the Univ. of Texas at Austin, where he has been a member of the faculty since 1957.

Since entering college teaching in Theatre and Drama in 1946, he has directed fifty-two productions for the stage including: *Right You Are* (1951); *The Sea Gull* (1952); *Juno and the Paycock* (1953); *Death of a Salesman* (1954); *Man and Superman* (1955); *Waltz of the Toreadors* (1958); and *Purple Dust* (1959).

As an actor, he has appeared in at least fifty productions of college theatre and in the professional productions of *Dangerous Corner* (Circle Th., Los Angeles, Calif., 1940); *The Lost Colony* (Manteo, N.C., 1941), and Hume Cronyn's production of *Now I Lay Me Down to Sleep* (Stanford Univ., 1949).

He is the author of *Guide to Theatre Collections in the University of Texas* (1966), *Drama Bibliography: A Guide to Selected Readings* (1971), *A Catalog of the Norman Bel Geddes Theatre Collection* (1973), and *The Power of Dramatic Form* (1974).

Recreation. Woodworking, reading.

HUNTER, KERMIT. Playwright, educator. b. Oct. 3, 1910, Hallsville, W.Va., to O.J. and Lillian (Farley) Hunter. Father, merchant; mother, teacher. Grad. Welch (W.Va.) H.S., 1927; attended Emory & Henry Coll., 1927–28; grad. Ohio State Univ., B.A. 1931; attended Univ. of California, 1949; grad. Univ. of North Carolina, M.A. 1949; Ph.D. 1955; Emory & Henry Coll., D. Litt. 1958. Studied piano and musical theory at Juilliard Sch. of Music, N.Y.C. Served US Army, 1941–45; awarded Legion of Merit; rank, Lt. Col. Married Sept. 6, 1952, to Josephine Christison. Member of AETA; AAUP; MLA; SAMLA; Institute of Outdoor Drama (bd. of administrators). Address: Division of Fine Arts, Southern Methodist Univ., Dallas, TX tel. (214) 366-2666.

Mr. Hunter is dean of the Division of Fine Arts at Southern Methodist Univ. (Dallas, Texas).

He was a graduate assistant in the Dept. of English, Univ. of North Carolina (1947–55); professor in the Dept. of Dramatic Art and Chairman, Division IV (music, drama, fine arts), Hollins Coll. (1956–64); and has conducted student art tours abroad (1958, 1962, 1964).

Mr. Hunter has lectured in the major cities in the Southeast, on such topics as "New Horizons in the American Theatre," "Religious Drama," "The Business of Teaching the English Language," and "Around the Bend in American Education."

He wrote an outdoor historical pageant, *Unto These Hills,* as his Master's thesis, which has been produced annually at Cherokee, N.C. (1950–to date); wrote the outdoor historical dramas, *Forever This Land* (New Salem, Ill., 1951–52); *Horn in the West* (Boone, N.C., 1952–to date); *The Bell and the Plow* (Tucson, Ariz., 1953); *Voice in the Wind* (Ruskin, Fla., 1955); *The Eleventh Hour* (Staunton, Va., 1956); *Chucky Jack* (Gatlinburg, Tenn., 1956–to date); *Thy Kingdom Come* (Roanoke and Salem, Va., 1957–60); *Heart of a City* (Roanoke, Va., 1958); *Dawn of Promise* (Roanoke, Va., 1959); *The Home Road* (Bethania, N.C., 1959); *Mistress of the Inn* (Roanoke, Va., 1959); *Homecoming in Magdala* (Hollins, Va., 1959); *The Golden Crucible* (Pittsburgh, Pa., 1959); *The Third Frontier* (New Bern, N.C., 1960); *The Golden Prairie* (Decatur, Ill., 1960); *The Golden Land* (Dillon, S.C., 1960); *This Burning Hour* (Louisville, Ky., 1960); *Honey in the Rock* (Beckley, W.Va., 1961–to date); *Thunder on the River* (Peoria, Ill., 1961); *Bound for Kentucky* (Louisville, Ky., 1961); *Next Day in the Morning* (Jacksonville, Fla., 1962); *Stars in My Crown* (Murray, Ky., 1963); *In This Mighty Struggle* (Richmond, Va., 1963); *The Trail of Tears* (Tahlequoh, Okla., June 26, 1969); *Walk Toward the Sunset* (Sneedville, Fla., 1970); *Wings of the Morning* (St. Mary's City, Md., July 3, 1975); and *Beyond the Sundown* (Livingston, Tex.). Mr. Hunter wrote *The Inn at Gorgov* (Univ. of No. Carolina, 1955; Gatlinburg, Tenn., 1958; Aurora, Ill., 1959); *The Paper Rose* (Hollins Coll., 1958); and *The Faithful Lightning* (Dallas, Tex., 1961; E. Carolina Coll., 1963).

Other Activities. He is vice-president, Allied Restoration Co., Dallas, Texas.

Published Works. He wrote the article, "University Theatre" in the *Encyclopaedia Britannica;* has written articles for the journals of the Southern Speech Assn.; East Tennessee Historical Society; AETA; and North Carolina Historical Society; and has also contributed articles to the NY *Times;* Nashville *Tennessean;* and St. Louis *Post Dispatch.*.

Awards. Mr. Hunter received the Vandewater Poetry Prize, Ohio State Univ., (1931); Joseph Feldman Award in Playwriting, Univ. of North Carolina (1949); a Rockefeller Foundation Grant in Playwriting (1950); Charles Cannon Cup for Historical Writing (1952); Guggenheim Foundation Grant in Creative Writing (1955); Woodrow Wilson Foundation Citation (1956); and a Federation of Music Clubs Citation (1962).

HUNTER, KIM. Actress. b. Janet Cole, Nov. 12, 1922, Detroit, Mich., to Donald and Grace (Stebbins) Cole. Father, engineer. Grad. Miami Beach (Fla.) Senior H.S., 1940. Studied acting with Charmine Lantaff, Miami Beach, Fla., 1938–40; Actors Studio (member since 1948). Married Feb. 11, 1944, to William A. Baldwin (marr. dis. 1946); one daughter; married Dec. 20, 1951, to Robert Emmett, writer; one son. Member of AEA (council, 1953–59); SAG; AFTRA; AMPAS. Address: 42 Commerce St., New York, NY 10014.

Theatre. Miss Hunter made her first stage appearance in the title role in *Penny Wise* (Miami Woman's Club, Fla., 1939); subsequently played ingenue roles at the Old Mill Playhouse (Flat Rock, N.C., 1940); an Eskimo in *Petticoat Fever,* the Maid in *Angela Is 22,* and the Secretary in *The Night of January 16* (Gant Gaither Th., Miami Beach, Fla., 1940–41); Cecily in *The Importance of Being Earnest* (Th. of the "15," Coral Gables, Fla., 1941); performed in stock, at Th. of the "15," Baltimore, Md.; Old Mill Playhouse, Flat Rock, N.C.; and Th. of the "15," Coral Gables, Fla. (1941–42). She appeared in the title role in *Claudia* (Summer Th., Stamford, N.Y.; Music Hall, Detroit, Mich., 1947); and as Cathy in *Wuthering Heights* (Lake George Playhouse, N.Y., 1947).

She made her N.Y.C. debut as Stella Kowalski in *A Streetcar Named Desire* (Ethel Barrymore Th., Dec. 3, 1947); played Nancy in *Sundown Beach* (Westport Country Playhouse, Conn., Summer 1948); toured as Karen in *Two Blind Mice* (1950); appeared as Luba in *Darkness at Noon* (Alvin, N.Y.C., Jan. 13, 1951); Daisy Sage in *The Animal Kingdom* (Westport Country Playhouse, Conn., Summer 1951); Ruby Hawes in *The Chase* (Playhouse, N.Y.C., April 15, 1952); toured as Amy in *They Knew What They Wanted* (Summer 1952); played Karen Wright in *The Children's Hour,* Bway revival (Coronet Th., N.Y.C., Dec. 18, 1952); Patty O'Neill in *The Moon Is Blue* (Roosevelt Playhouse, Miami Beach, Fla., April, 1954); Sylvia Crews in *The Tender Trap* (Longacre, N.Y.C., Oct. 13, 1954); Dunreath Henry in *King of Hearts* (Bucks County Playhouse, New Hope, Pa., Summer 1955); Laura Creech in *I Hear You Singing* (Spa Summer Th., Saratoga, N.Y., Summer 1955); Nora Parker in *Down Came a Blackbird* (John Drew Th., Easthampton, N.Y., Summer 1955); Celia Pope in *A Hatful of Rain* (Playhouse-in-the-Park, Philadelphia, Pa.; Pocono Playhouse, Mountainhome, Pa., Summer 1957); and Kate Adams in the pre-Bway tryout of *This Is Goggle* (McCarter Th., Princeton, N.J., Jan. 23, 1958; Shubert, Washington, D.C., Feb. 1, 1958).

Miss Hunter played Cora Flood in *The Dark at the Top of the Stairs* (Tapia Th., San Juan, P.R., Jan. 1959; Ann Arbor, Mich., May 24, 1960); Alma Winemiller in *Summer and Smoke* (Coconut Grove Playhouse, Miami, Fla., 1959); Billie Dawn in *Born Yesterday* (Civic Th., Charlotte, N.C., 1960); Jere Halliday in *The Disenchanted* (Tenthouse Th., Highland Park, Ill.; Playhouse-in-the-Park, Philadelphia, Pa.; Coconut Grove Playhouse, Miami, Fla., 1960); in the Summer 1961, appeared with the American Shakespeare Festival (Stratford, Conn.), as Rosalind in *As You Like It* (June 15), the First Witch in *Macbeth* (June 16), and Helen in *Troilus and Cressida* (July 23).

She played Julie Sturrock in *Write Me a Murder* (Belasco, N.Y.C., Oct. 26, 1961); the title role in *Major Barbara* (Univ. of Utah, Feb. 7, 1963); performed scenes from Shakespeare in a program entitled, *Come Woo Me* (Library of Congress, Washington, D.C., April 29, 1963); played Paula in the summer tryout of *Linda Stone Is Brutal* (Bucks County Playhouse, New Hope, Pa.; Olney Playhouse, Md., May–June 1964); played Sally Thomas in *Signpost to Murder* (Paramus, N.J., Nov. 1965); Emily Dickinson in *Come Slowly, Eden* (Nassau Community Coll., Garden City, N.Y., May 3–15, 1966; White Barn Th., Westport, Conn., July 17, 1966; Library of Congress, Wash., D.C., Nov. 28, 29, 1966; ANTA Matinee Series, Th. de Lys, Dec. 5, 6, 1966); Miss Wilson in *Weekend* (Broadhurst Th., N.Y.C., Mar. 13, 1968); Alma Winemiller in *Eccentricities of a Nightingale* and Masha in *The Three Sisters* (L.I. Repertory Festival, Mineola, N.Y., Spring and Summer 1968); Hester in *Hello and Goodbye* (ANTA Matinee Series, Th. de Lys, N.Y.C., Nov. 11 and 12, 1968); the title role in *The Prime of Miss Jean Brodie* Summer tour, 1969); Carrie Bishop in *The Penny Wars* (Royale, N.Y.C., Oct. 15, 1969); Catherine in *And Miss Reardon Drinks a Little* (national tour, Sept. 6–Jan. 15, 1971–72); Amanda Wingfield in *The Glass Menagerie* (Alliance Th., Atlanta, Ga., Feb. 1973); and Mary Haines in *The Women* Bway revival (46 St. Th., N.Y.C., April 25, 1973).

Films. She made her debut in *The Seventh Victim* (RKO, 1943); and has appeared in *Tender Comrade* (RKO, 1943); *When Strangers Marry* (Mono., 1944); *You Came Along* (Par., 1945); *Stairway to Heaven* (U, 1946); *A Canterbury Tale* (Eagle Lion, 1949); *A Streetcar Named Desire* (WB, 1951); *Anything Can Happen* (Par., 1952); *Deadline, U.S.A.* (20th-Fox, 1952); *Storm Center* (Col., 1956); *The Young Stranger* (U, 1957); *Bermuda Affair* (DCA, 1957); *Money, Women and Guns* (U, 1958); *Lilith* (Col., 1964); *Planet of the Apes* (20th-Fox, 1968); *The Swimmer* (Col., 1968); *Beneath the Planet of the Apes* (20th-Fox, 1970); and *Escape from the Planet of the Apes* (20th-Fox, 1971).

Television. She has appeared on Philco Television Th. (NBC); Ford Th. (CBS); Studio One (CBS); Climax! (NBC); Kaiser Aluminum Hour (NBC); GE Th. (CBS); Alcoa Hour (NBC); Goodyear Playhouse (NBC); Lamp Unto My Feet (CBS); the Trial Scene from *Saint Joan* (Omnibus, NBC, 1955); six Playhouse 90 programs (CBS), including *Requiem for a Heavyweight* and *The Comedian; Secret of Freedom* (NBC Special); *Give Us Barabbas* (Hallmark Hall of Fame, NBC, 1961; repeated 1963); Purex Special for Women (NBC); Adventures in Paradise (ABC); The Nurses (CBS); US Steel Hour (CBS); a series of three programs produced by Richard Siemanowski, called Americans, A Portrait in Verses (CBS, Aug. 1962, repeated, 1963); *Russians: Self Impressions* (CBS, Jan. 1963); and *The French—They Are So French* (CBS, Oct. 1963); Breaking Point (ABC, Oct. 1963); Arrest and Trial (ABC, Dec. 1963); That Was the Week That Was (NBC, Jan. 1964); Alfred Hitchcock Presents (CBS, Mar. 1964); the Jackie Gleason Show (CBS, Mar. 1964; second appearance, Oct. 1968); Mr. Broadway (CBS); The Defenders (CBS); Dr. Kildare (NBC); *Lamp at Midnight* (Hallmark Hall of Fame, NBC,

1965); Confidential for Women (ABC); Hawk (ABC); Mannix (CBS); Disney's Wonderful World of Color (NBC, 1968); Bonanza (NBC, 1968); Johnny Carson's Tonight Show (NBC, 1968); *The People Next Door* (CBS Playhouse, 1968); *When This You See Remember Me* (NET, 1970); *Give Us Barabbas* (Hallmark Hall of Fame, third repeat, 1969); *The Prodigal* (NET, 1969); *Dial Hot Line* (ABC Movie, 1970); Eternal Light (NBC, 1970); *No Deposit-No Return* (ABC Special, 1970); David Frost Show (ABC, 1970); The Young Lawyers (ABC, 1970); Bracken's World (NBC, 1970); The New Doctors (NBC, 1970); *The Search of America* (ABC Special, 1971); Mannix (CBS, 1971); The Tonight Show (NBC, 1971); What's My Line (NBC, 1971); Medical Center (CBS, 1971); Gunsmoke (CBS, 1971); Cannon (CBS, 1971); Columbo (NBC, 1971); Night Gallery (NBC, 1972); Owen Marshall (ABC, 1972); Love, American Style (ABC, 1972); Young Dr. Kildare (CBS, 1972); The Evil Touch (ABC, 1973); Mission Impossible (CBS, 1973); *The Magician* (NBC Movie, 1973); Marcus Welby, M.D. (ABC, 1973); Hec Ramsey (NBC, 1973); Griff (ABC, 1973); Police Story (NBC, 1973); *Unwed Father* (ABC Movie, 1974); and Ironside (NBC, 1974).

Awards. For her performance as Stella Kowalski in *A Streetcar Named Desire,* Miss Hunter received a Donaldson Award and won the *Variety* NY Drama Critics' Poll (1948); for her performance in the screen version of the play, she received an Academy (Oscar) Award, a *Look* Award, and the Golden Globe (Foreign Correspondents) Award (1952).

HUNTINGTON, CATHARINE. Actress, director, producer. b. Catharine Sargent Huntington, Dec. 29, 1889, Ashfield, Mass., to George Putnam and Lilly St. Agnan (Barrett) Huntington. Father, clergyman. Grad. Miss Haskell's Sch., Boston, Mass., 1906; Radcliffe Coll., A.B. (cum laude) 1911. Studied at Laboratory Th., N.Y.C., 1924. Radcliffe representative with the Wellesley unit of the YMCA entertaining troops stationed in France, 1918–19; aide for Réconstruction Aisne Devastée, Union des Femmes de France, 1919; factory worker for Red Cross supplies, 1943–44; wood worker's assistant in South Boston Navy Yard, 1944–46. Relatives in theatre: cousin, John Huntington, producer-manager; cousin, Mary Manning (Howe), actress, producer, playwright. Member of NETC; Beacon Hill Garden Club (secy., 1950–54; 1st vice-pres., 1956–58, 2nd vice-pres., 1959–60); Hospital Service (chairman, 1961); New England Poetry Club (associate member, 1963); Committee on Tree Planting and Conservation.

Pre-Theatre. Teacher at Westover School, Middlebury, Conn. (1915–17).

Theatre. Since 1960, Miss Huntington has been president and a member of the board of directors of the Provincetown (Mass.) Playhouse on the Wharf.

She started as an apprentice at the Orleans Summer Th. (Cape Cod, Mass., 1923), and became a member of the board of directors of the Boston Stage Society (Fall 1923), also at The Barn (Boston), played Mrs. Popov in *The Boor* (Nov. 19, 1923), Masha in *The Seagull,* which she also directed (Jan. 1924), Marie Duplessis in *Debureau* (Mar. 24, 1924), Dona Sirena in *Invisible Threads* (May 21, 1924), directed *The Last Night of Don Juan* (Dec. 15, 1924), played the Hostess in *The Unknown Woman,* which she also directed (Feb. 9, 1925), Sarah Jennings and the Duchess of Devonshire in *Marlborough Rides Away to the Wars* (Feb. 26, 1925), Cyclist in *Wedding Breakfast on the Eiffel Tower,* which she also directed (Apr. 13, 1925), Madame des Aubels in *The Revolt of the Angels* (Dec. 4, 1925), directed *Uncle Vanya* (Dec. 13, 1926), and *Buddha's Gardens* (Mar. 18, 1927).

For the Allied Arts Center, she directed *The Lost Disciple* (Fine Arts Th., Boston, Mass., Dec. 11, 1930); joined Mr. Punch's Workshop, a professional puppeteer company (1931–36); and played Mrs. Millington in *Youth's the Season* (Copley Th., Boston, May 14, 1937).

For the New England Repertory Co.'s plays (Huntington Chambers, Boston), she was producer with Virginia Thoms, director of publicity, and appeared as Frau Alden and Mlle. Alaret in *Maedchen in Uniform* (Nov. 19, 1938), and Martine in *The Physician in Spite of Himself* (Feb. 7, 1939), also playing this role at the Samoset Playhouse (Nantucket, Mass., July 25, 1939).

She played Madame Muskat in the New England Repertory Co.'s production of *Liliom* (Huntington Chambers, Boston, May 16, 1939), and Aunt Isabel in *The Inheritors* (Peabody Playhouse, Boston, Mar. 29, 1940).

At the Artists Th. (Provincetown), Miss Huntington played Martine in *The Physician in Spite of Himself* (July 8, 1940), the Lion in *Androcles and the Lion* (July 15, 1940), Lady Utterword in *Heartbreak House* (July 29, 1940), Mrs. Webb in *Our Town* (Aug. 12, 1940), and Madame Muskat in *Liliom* (Aug. 26, 1940).

For the New England Repertory Co. (Joy St. Playhouse, Boston), she repeated her roles as Mrs. Webb in *Our Town* (Oct. 24, 1940), and Martine in *The Physician in Spite of Himself* (Nov. 8, 1940), and directed *The Emperor Jones* (May 19, 1941).

At the Artists Th., she repeated her role as the Lion in *Androcles and the Lion,* played Wilson in *East Lynne,* Clara Hibbert in *The Vortex,* and Mrs. Chamberlain in *Me and Harry* (July 1941); at the Joy St. Playhouse, repeated her role as Mrs. Chamberlain in *Me and Harry,* played Florence Lancaster in *The Vortex,* May Beringer in *The Old Ladies,* and repeated her role as Mrs. Webb in *Our Town* (Nov. 19, 1941–May 20, 1942).

For the New England Repertory Co. (Provincetown Playhouse on the Wharf), she played Lizzie Twohig in *Is Life Worth Living?* (July 7, 1947), Amanda in *The Glass Menagerie* (Aug. 11, 1947), Miss Birdseye in *The Bostonians,* Mrs. Wenham in *The World of Light,* Miss Simpson in *Eastward in Eden* (Summer 1948); Essie Miller in *Ah, Wilderness!* and directed *As You Like It* (Summer 1949), played Marty Owen in *Anna Christie,* Signora Frola in *Right You Are If You Think You Are,* Mrs. Tarleton in *Misalliance,* Baroness Montfacon in *Ladies in Arms,* Louise Maske in *The Snob,* and directed *Much Ado About Nothing* (Summer 1950).

Also, at the Provincetown Playhouse, she appeared as Mrs. Stockmann in *An Enemy of the People* (July 9, 1951), Mrs. Malaprop in *The Rivals* (July 16, 1951), Lady Melbourne in *An Innocent in Time* (Aug. 12, 1951), and the Landlady in *The Chief Thing* (Aug. 27, 1951).

She played Marion in the Poets' Th. production of *Orpheus* (Peabody Playhouse, Boston, Dec. 1951), Mrs. Candour in *The School for Scandal* (Brattle, Cambridge, Mass., Feb. 1952), and Signora Nenni in *Right You Are If You Think You Are* (Brattle, Apr. 12, 1952).

At the Provincetown Playhouse, she appeared as Maud Mockridge in *Dangerous Corner* (July 7, 1952), Lady Britomart in *Major Barbara* (July 21, 1952), Margaret in *First Love* (Aug. 4, 1952), Madame Pace in *Six Characters in Search of an Author* (Aug. 18, 1952), and Mrs. Lamson in *The Tavern* (Aug. 25, 1952).

She played Mrs. Ramsden in *Man and Superman* (Penn Valley Playhouse, Philadelphia, Pa., Feb. 23, 1953), and at the Provincetown (Mass.) Playhouse, appeared as Lady Farwaters in *The Simpleton of the Unexpected Isles* (July 13, 1953), Liz in *Chicago* (Aug. 10, 1953), the Duchess de Sarennes in *Our Betters* (Aug. 24, 1953), Sarah Atkins in *Beyond the Horizon* (July 1, 1954), Charlotta in *The Cherry Orchard* (July 12, 1954), Dingley and Mrs. Van Homrigh in *The Dreaming Dust* (July 19, 1954), Clotilde in *Yes Is for a Very Young Man* (July 26, 1954), and Mrs. Northrop in *When We Are Married* (Aug. 30, 1954).

For the Poets' Th., she repeated her roles as Dingley and Mrs. Van Homrigh in *The Dreaming Dust* (Poets' Th., Cambridge, Mass., Jan. 4, 1955), and at the Provincetown Playhouse, appeared as Mrs. Crosby in *Diff'rent* (July 2, 1955), Agnes in *The Moon in the Yellow River* (July 11, 1955), Mrs. Touchett in *Portrait of a Lady* (July 18, 1955), Marina in *Uncle Vanya* (July 25, 1955), Eugenie in *Ondine* (Aug. 29, 1955), Mrs. St. Maugham in *The Chalk Garden* (July 30, 1956), and Essie Miller in *Ah, Wilderness!* (Aug. 27, 1956).

She played Mrs. Mallow, Alga, and the Nurse in *The Immortal Husband* (Poets' Th., Cambridge, Mass., Nov. 19, 1956), and at the Provincetown Playhouse, appeared in *In the Counting House* (July 15, 1957), played Mrs. Callifer in *The Potting Shed* (Aug. 19, 1957), and Julia Cromwell in *Strange Bedfellows* (Aug. 26, 1957), and played Mrs. Mallet in *Words Upon the Window Pane* (Poets' Th., Cambridge, Nov. 12, 1957).

At the Provincetown Playhouse, Miss Huntington appeared as Amy in *The Family Reunion* (July 21, 1958), Mrs. Railton-Bell in *Separate Tables* (July 28, 1958), Katherine Pommeroy in *The Summer's Treason* (Aug. 11, 1958), Lady Elizabeth Mulhammer in *The Confidential Clerk* (July 7, 1959), Aunt Julia in *Dona Rosita* (July 21, 1959), Lady Markby in *An Ideal Husband* (Aug. 18, 1959), Dolly in *The Grass Harp* (July 11, 1960), Lady Hunstanton in *A Woman of No Importance* (Aug. 15, 1960), Mrs. Crosby in *Diff'rent* (Aug. 22, 1960), Mrs. Greenborough in *Captain Jinks of the Horse Marines* (July 31, 1961), Grandma in *The Sandbox* (Aug. 14, 1961), Lady Saltburn in *Present Laughter* (July 9, 1962), Grandma in *The American Dream* (Aug. 13, 1962), the Mother in *Playing with Fire* (Aug. 19, 1963), and Lady Flinteye in *All at Sea* (Aug. 26, 1963).

At the Provincetown Playhouse Miss Huntington, with Virginia Thoms LePeer and Edward Dodge Thommen, presented *Ah, Wilderness!* (June 29, 1964), *Miss Lonelyhearts* (July 6, 1964), *The Private Ear* and *The Public Eye* (July 13, 1964), *The Night of the Iguana* (July 27, 1964), in which she played Miss Judith Fellowes, *Mr. Arcularis* (Aug. 3, 1964), in which she played Mrs. Merrick (later, Lady In Tweeds), *Village Wooing* and *A Web, a Thread, a String of a Teabag* (Aug. 17, 1964), in which she played Wife, *Lucrece* (Aug. 24, 1964), in which she played the First Citizeness, *The Best Man* (Aug. 31, 1964), *Hughie* and *Sweeney Agonistes* (June 28, 1965), *The Typists* and *The Tiger* (July 4, 1965), *Period of Adjustment* (July 12, 1965), *The Second Man* (July 26, 1965), *The Late Christopher Bean* (Aug. 16, 1965), in which she played Mrs. Haggett, *Light Up the Sky* (Aug. 23, 1965), *The Torch-Bearers* (Aug. 30, 1965), in which she played Mrs. Nelly Fell, *The Moon of the Caribbees* and *Bound East for Cardiff* (July 18, 1966), *A Touch of the Poet* (July 25, 1966), *A Moon for the Misbegotten* (Aug. 1, 1966), *Long Day's Journey into Night* (Aug. 6, 1966), *A Touch of the Poet* (Aug. 15, 1966), *Beyond the Horizon* (Aug. 22, 1966), in which she played Mrs. Atkins, and *Ah, Wilderness!* (Aug. 29, 1966), in which she played Essie.

At the Provincetown Playhouse Miss Huntington has since presented *Bound East for Cardiff, The Great God Brown, The Lover* and *The Collection, Camino Real,* in which she appeared, *White Lies* and *Black Comedy, Rosencrantz and Guildenstern Are Dead,* and *Everything in the Garden* (Summer 1969); *The Tea Party* and *The Basement* (June 26, 1970), *Desire Under the Elms* (July 13, 1970), *A Midsummer Night's Dream* (July 27, 1970), *You Know I Can't Hear You When the Water's Running* (Aug. 10, 1970), *The Balcony* (Aug. 24, 1970), and *Waiting for Godot* (Sept. 1, 1970); *More Stately Mansions* (June 24, 1971), *The Star Spangled Girl* (July 1, 1971), *Colette* (July 15, 1971), *Orpheus Descending* (July 29, 1971), and *Next, Noon* and *Bringing It All Back Home* (Aug. 2, 1971).

In 1972, a fire destroyed much of the theatre, but Miss Huntington announced a season of *Where Has Tommy Flowers Gone?* (July 11, 1972), *A Long Day's Journey into Night* (July 21, 1972), *The Affairs of Anatol* (Aug. 1, 1972), *The Complete Works of Studs Edsel* (world premiere, Aug. 15, 1972), and *Old Times* (Aug. 29, 1972).

In 1973, the Provincetown Playhouse was sold to Adelle Heller.

Awards. Miss Huntington was a recipient of the Rodgers and Hammerstein Award (May 10, 1966); and has been honored by the Alumnae Association of Radcliffe College (June 15, 1968).

Recreation. Gardening.

HURRELL, JOHN D. Educator, writer. b. John Dennis Hurrell, Nov. 8, 1924, London, England, to Frank William and Violet Louise Hurrell. Father, engineer. Attended County Grammar Sch., Sidcup, Kent, England, 1935–41; Birkbeck Coll., Univ. of London, 1946–47; King's Coll., Univ. of London, B.A. (English) 1949; Shakespeare Inst., Stratford-upon-Avon, Ph.D. (English) 1954. Served with British Royal Navy, 1943–46; rank, Seaman. Married Apr. 29, 1949, to Rosamond Isobel Hurrell; one son, one daughter. Member of AETA. Address: (home) 71 Melbourne Ave., S.E., Minneapolis, MN 55414, tel. (612) 332-5687; (bus.) c/o English Dept., Univ. of Minnesota, Minneapolis, MN 55455, tel. (612) 373-2557.

Mr. Hurrell has been chairman of the graduate program in comparative literature at the Univ. of Minnesota (1963–64), where he has taught in the English Dept. since 1957 as assistant professor (1958–61), associate professor (1961), and professor (1961–to date). He was appointed associate dean of the College of Liberal Arts in 1964. He taught English at Egyptian State Univ. (Cairo, 1950–52); State Univ. of Iowa (1954–55); Williams Coll. (1955–56); and Ryerson Inst. (Toronto, Canada, 1956–57).

In 1961, Mr. Hurrell founded the drama periodical, *Drama Survey,* and has subsequently served as editor.

Television. Mr. Hurrell presented a series of twelve programs on repertory theatre (KTCA-TV, 1961).

Published Works. He is the editor of *Two Modern American Tragedies* (1961), an analysis of reviews and criticism of *Death of a Salesman* and *A Streetcar Named Desire.*

He has also contributed articles to drama and literary magazines, such as *Texas Studies in Literature, Educational Theatre Journal, Quarterly Journal of Speech,* and *Twin Citian.*

Awards. Mr. Hurrell received the George Smith Prize of the Univ. of London (1949), awarded to the top-ranking graduate in English.

Recreation. Photography.

HURST, DAVID. Actor, director, teacher. b. Heinrich Theodor Hirsch, May 8, 1926, Berlin, Germany, to Julius and Johanna (Wulkan) Hirsch. Father, journalist, critic; mother, fashion journalist. Attended schools in Berlin, Ger., and Vienna, Aust., 1931–38; Coll. of Art, Belfast, N. Ire., 1940–44. Married Nov. 28, 1949, to June Douglas-Reid (marr. dis. 1957); one daughter; married July 26, 1957, to Barry Ann Wharton; one son, two daughters. Served British Army, 1944–47. Member of AEA; AFTRA; SAG; Actors Studio.

Theatre. He first performed on the stage as Joshua Muller in *Watch on the Rhine,* with the Savoy Players (Belfast, Northern Ireland, May 1944); subsequently appeared in Special Services productions for the British Army, including *Someone at the Door, By Candlelight, Arsenic and Old Lace,* and *The Late Christopher Bean* 1945–47); toured England as the Gangster in *There's Always Tomorrow* Dec. 1947); made his London debut as Winkel in *The Perfect Woman* (Playhouse, Sept. 11, 1948); played the German Officer in *Yes Is for a Very Young Man* (Th. 48, 1949); the Marquis and Sir Lionel's Spirit in *Nuts in May* (Torch Aug. 16, 1949); appeared in a revue, *Sauce Piquante* (Cambridge, Apr. 27, 1950), which he also produced (Watergate, June 27, 1950); Sam Feinschreiber in *Awake and Sing* (Saville, Oct. 24, 1950); toured as Solomon Greenbaum in *Common Property* (Mar. 1951), and in London (Embassy, Apr. 3, 1951); and played various roles in stock (1951).

He played Ebag in *The Great Adventure* (Arts, Dec. 4, 1951); Siegfried Shrager in *The Pink Room* (Lyric, Hammersmith, June 18, 1952); Appopolous in *Wonderful Town* (Prince's, Feb. 4, 1955); the Spy in *Romanoff and Juliet* (Piccadilly, May 17, 1956), and succeeded (Dec. 17, 1956) Peter Ustinov in the role of the General; and directed and appeared in stock productions of *A View from the Bridge, Romanoff and Juliet,* and *Black Coffee* Royal, Portsmouth, Sept. 1957).

Mr. Hurst made his N.Y.C. debut in two Ionesco plays, as Mr. Smith in *The Bald Soprano* and the Father in *Jack* (Sullivan St. Playhouse, June 3, 1958); followed by his role as an Inspector of Police in *Look After Lulu* (Henry Miller's Th., Mar. 3, 1959); Britannus in *Caesar and Cleopatra* (Edgewater Beach Th., Chicago, Ill., June 22, 1959; Northland Th., Detroit, Mich., July 6, 1959; Westport Country Playhouse, Conn., July 13, 1959); the Scoundrel in *Physician for Fools* (Margo Jones Th., Dallas, Tex., Oct. 6, 1959); succeeded (Dec. 1959) Albert Paulson in the role of Andrei in *The Three Sisters* (Fourth St. Th., N.Y.C., Sept. 21, 1959); played the Scientist in *Under the Sycamore Tree* (Cricket, Mar. 7, 1960); O. O. Protopopoff in *Brouhaha* (E. Bway Playhouse, Apr. 26, 1960); and appeared in *Happy Ending* (Bucks County Playhouse, New Hope, Pa., Aug. 1960); played Merlyn in *Camelot* (Majestic, N.Y.C., Dec. 3, 1960); appeared in *The Chairs* and *The Dock Brief* at the Univ. of Wisconsin (Madison, July 25, 1961); and played the Burgomeister in *The Visit* (Playhouse-in-the-Park, Philadelphia, Pa., Aug. 1961).

From Oct. 1961 to June 1962, Mr. Hurst appeared in repertory at the Arena Stage (Washington, D.C.) as Azdak in *The Caucasian Chalk Circle,* the Husband in *What Shall We Tell Caroline?,* the Ragpicker in *The Madwoman of Chaillot.* Tausch in *The Moon in the Yellow River,* Father Gilbert in *The Burning of the Lepers,* the title role in *Uncle Vanya,* and the Arab in *The Time of Your Life.* He played the Logician in *Rhinoceros* (Westport Country Playhouse, Conn., July 1962); joined (Aug. 1962) *Brecht on Brecht* (Th. de Lys, Jan. 3, 1962); appeared as Doc in *The Fun Couple* (Lyceum, Oct. 26, 1962); after which he returned (Jan. 6, 1962) to the production of *Brecht on Brecht.*

He played the title role in *Christopher Columbus* (Goodman, Chicago, Ill., Feb. 15, 1963); Ignaty Ilyitch Shigelsky in *A Month in the Country* (Maidman, N.Y.C., May 28, 1963); toured as the Doctor in *The Millionairess* (July 1963); was the Captain in *Dynamite Tonight* (York Playhouse, N.Y.C., Mar. 15, 1964); and Paedagogus in *Electra* (Delacorte Th., Aug. 11, 1964).

He appeared at the Th. of the Living Arts, Philadelphia, Pa., in the title role of *Galileo* (Jan. 6, 1965) and as Hamm in *Endgame* (May 26, 1965); played the title role in *King Lear* (American Conservatory Th., Pittsburgh, Pa., Sept. 1965); appeared again with the Th. of the Living Arts, repeating his performance in the title role of *Uncle Vanya* (Nov. 16, 1965), was Signor Pasticcio Ritornello, the Earl of Leicester, Lord Burleigh, and the Tower Bridge in *The Critic* (Dec. 28, 1965), Brassac (Tallien) in *Poor Bitos* (Feb. 8, 1966), Bummidge in *The Last Analysis* (May 3, 1966), and Sasha Smirnoff in *Room Service* (Nov. 1, 1966). At the Yale Repertory Th., New Haven, Conn., he played the title role in *Volpone* (Jan. 31, 1967) and Ocean in *Prometheus* (May 10, 1967); he was Count Bodo von Ubelohe-Zabernsee in *The Marriage of Mr. Mississippi* (Center Th. Group, Los Angeles, Calif., Aug. 25, 1967); was Dr. Caius in *The Merry Wives of Windsor* (Delacorte Th., N.Y.C., July 25, 1974); and appeared at the Seattle (Wash.) Repertory Th. in *The Waltz of the Toreadors* (Jan. 8, 1975) and *A Doll's House* (Feb. 5, 1975).

In addition to his acting, Mr. Hurst was also an associate professor at Yale School of Drama, New Haven, Conn. (1966) and director of a training program for young actors at Center Theatre Group, Mark Taper Forum, Los Angeles (1967–68).

Films. Mr. Hurst's films include *The Perfect Woman* (Eagle-Lion, 1950); *Tony Draws a Horse* (Film Assoc., 1951); *The Assassin* (UA, 1953); *So Little Time* MacDonald, 1953); *Shoot First* (UA, 1953); *Always a Bride* (U, 1954); *Mr. Potts Goes to Moscow* (Allied, 1954); *River Beat* (Lippert, 1954); and *As Long as They're Happy* (Rank, 1957).

Television and Radio. He performed on radio and television in England, where he played many roles (1951–57). He made his television debut in the US in *The Abbe of Paris* (Armstrong Circle Th., NBC, 1957); subsequently appeared in *Tiger at the Gates* (1960) and *The Emperor's Clothes* (Play of the Week, WNTA, 1960); *Roughing It* (1960); *Datchet Diamonds* (1960); the Patty Duke Show (ABC, 1965); The Man from U.N.C.L.E. (NBC, 1965); Look Up and Live (CBS, 1965); and in *Anastasia* (Hallmark Hall of Fame, NBC, 1967).

Awards. He received the Clarence Derwent Award (1959) for his performance as an Inspector of Police in *Look After Lulu;* and *The Village Voice* Off-Bway (Obie) Award for Distinguished Performance (1964) for his performance in *A Month in the Country.*

HUSMANN, RON. Actor, singer. b. Ronald Hugh Husmann, June 30, 1937, Rockford, Ill., to B. J. and Emma O. (Ohlhues) Husmann. Father, dry cleaner. Grad. East Rockford H.S., 1955; Northwestern Univ., B.S. 1959. Married Dec. 6, 1959, to Patsy Peterson; one son. Member of AEA; AFTRA; AGVA; SAG; Delta Upsilon; Deru; Norelegamma. Address: c/o A.P.A., 120 W. 57th St., New York, NY 10019, tel. (212) LT 1-8860.

Theatre. Mr. Husmann was first a resident chorus member at the Highland Park (Ill.) Music Th. (Summer 1956); and the Oakdale Music Th. (Wallingford, Conn., Summer 1957).

He made his N.Y.C. debut as the Fourth Card Player and understudy to Bob Holiday as Neil in *Fiorello!* (Broadhurst Th., Nov. 23, 1959); subsequently played Tommy in *Tenderloin* (46 St. Th., Oct. 17, 1960); in stock, played Tommy in *Brigadoon* (Dallas Summer Musicals, State Fair Music Hall, Tex., Summer 1961); Edwin Bricker in *All American* (Winter Garden, N.Y.C., Mar. 19, 1962); Nestor in a stock tour of *Irma La Douce* (Guber-Ford-Gross circuit, Summer 1963); Capt. Fisby in *Lovely Ladies, Kind Gentlemen* (Majestic, Dec. 28, 1970); Hector in *Look Where I'm At* (Theatre Four, Mar. 5, 1971); Gabey in a revival of *On the Town* (Imperial, Oct. 31, 1971); and he succeeded Monte Markham (May 31, 1973) as Donald Marshall in *Irene* (Minskoff Th., Mar. 13, 1973).

Television. Mr. Husmann has appeared on Bell Telephone Hour (NBC, June 16, 1964), and was a regular singer on the Steve Allen Show (Independent, 1963–64). He was in *Once Upon a Mattress* (CBS, 1972).

Awards. For his performance as Tommy in *Tenderloin,* Mr. Husmann received the *Theatre World* Award (1961) and was nominated for an Antoinette Perry (Tony) Award (1961).

Recreation. Gardening, photography.

HUSSEY, RUTH. Actress. b. Oct. 30, Providence, R.I., to George and Julia Hussey. Grad. Classical and Technical H.S.; Brown Univ. (Pembroke Women's College), B. Phil.; attended Univ. of Mich. Married Aug. 9, 1942, to C. Robert Longenecker, television executive; two sons, one daughter. Member of AEA; SAG; AFTRA. Address: 201 N. Carmelina Ave., Los Angeles, CA 90049, tel. (213) GR 2-4656.

Pre-Theatre. Radio fashion commentator, Powers model.

Theatre. Miss Hussey made her professional debut as Kay in the touring company of *Dead End* (1937); made her N.Y.C. debut as Mary Mathews in *State of the Union* (Hudson Th., Nov. 14, 1945); took over Madeleine Carroll's role as Agatha Reed in *Goodbye, My Fancy* (Morosco, Nov. 17, 1948); and played Julie Cavendish in *The Royal Family* (NY City Ctr., Jan. 10, 1951).

In stock, Miss Hussey appeared in *Dream Girl* (Laguna Beach Playhouse Th., Summer 1944); *The Guardsman* (La Jolla Playhouse, Calif., Summer 1944); *The Philadelphia Story* (Sombrero Playhouse, Phoenix, Ariz., Summer 1950); a tour of *The Royal Family* (Michigan Drama Festival, Ann Arbor, Newport Casino, R.I.; Pocono Playhouse, Mountainhome, Pa.; Salt Creek Th., Hinsdale, Ill., Summer 1951); and toured in *Desk Set* (Cape Playhouse, Dennis, Mass.; Pocono Playhouse; Th.-in-the-Park,

Philadelphia, Pa.; Th. by the Sea, R.I., Summer 1958).

Films. Miss Hussey made her debut in *Rich Man Poor Girl* (MGM, 1938); subsequently appeared in *The Philadelphia Story* (MGM, 1940); *Flight Command* (MGM, 1940); *Northwest Passage* (MGM, 1940); *Our Wife* (Col., 1941); *H. M. Pulham, Esq.* (MGM, 1941); *Bedtime Story* (Col., 1941); *The Uninvited* (Par., 1944); *Tender Comrade* (RKO, 1943); *Marine Raiders* (RKO, 1944); *I, Jane Doe* (Rep., 1948); *The Great Gatsby* (Par., 1949); *Louisa* (U, 1950); *Mr. Music* (Par., 1950); *That's My Boy* (Par., 1951); *Stars and Stripes Forever* (20th-Fox, 1952); *The Facts of Life* (UA, 1960).

Television. She has appeared in *The Women* (Producers Showcase, NBC, 1953); *Craig's Wife* (Lux Video Th., NBC, 1954); on Climax! (CBS), GE Th. (CBS), Alfred Hitchcock Presents (CBS), Studio One (CBS), Elgin Playhouse (ABC), Pulitzer Prize Playhouse (ABC), the Nash Airflyte Th., and has made two guests appearances on the Red Skelton Show (CBS). She has also appeared in several Family Th. feature holiday films which are telecast each holiday season in the US and Europe; also appeared in *Marcus Welby, M.D.* (ABC, 1972); *The New Perry Mason* (CBS, 1973); *My Darling Daughter's Anniversary* (ABC, 1973).

Awards. Miss Hussey was nominated for an Academy (Oscar) Award as best supporting actress in *The Philadelphia Story* (1940); and was nominated for a NATAS (Emmy) Award for her performance in *Craig's Wife* (1955).

She received an honorary D.F.A. from Pembroke Coll. (1950).

Recreation. Painting, swimming, horseback riding, music, golf, drawing house plans to actual scale.

HUSTON, PHILIP. Actor, director, writer. b. Philip Pryor Huston, Mar. 14, 1908, Wilmington, Del., to Philip Pryor and Dulcie (Moxham) Huston. Father, manufacturer. Attended Flushing (L.I., N.Y.) H.S., 1922–24; Blair Acad., Blairstown, N.J., 1924–26. Married Oct. 31, 1947, to Diane Gardiner; one daughter. Member of AEA; SAG; AFTRA. Address: (home) 319 W. 75th St., New York, NY 10023, tel. (212) TR 7-6642; (bus.) c/o Actors' Equity Assn., 165 W. 46th St., New York, NY 10036, tel. (212) SU 7-5400.

Theatre. Mr. Huston first appeared on stage in vaudeville as Tome in *The Love Racketeer* (Newark, N.Y., Mar. 1931), in which he later toured (New York, Pennsylvania, Massachusetts, Mar.–Apr. 1931); subsequently appeared in a stock production as Geoffry Cole in *The Vinegar Tree* (Nantucket Playhouse, Mass., July 1931); and made his N.Y.C. debut in *The Unknown Soldier* (Cherry Lane, Oct. 26, 1931); followed by *Fool's Way* (Cherry Lane, Dec. 1931).

From Feb. 8, 1932–June 1, 1933, Mr. Huston appeared in stock productions at the Riviera, N.Y.C., Westchester Th., Mount Vernon, N.Y.; and the Apollo, Atlantic City, N.J., where he played Dolph in *Broadway*, McDermott in *The Royal Family*, Polydorous in *Lysistrata*, and Baron Frank von Ullrich in *A Church Mouse*. He appeared in stock tryouts, playing Stuart Mason in *Tourists Accommodated*, Robert Stairs in *Survival*, and appeared in Lyon Rigg's *Talent* (Cape Playhouse, Dennis, Mass., June–Sept. 1933).

He played the Young Reporter in *Whatever Possessed Her* (Mansfield, N.Y.C., Jan. 25, 1934); Colin West in a stock tryout of *Round Trip*, Mickey Linden in *The Shining Hour*, and the Young Man Living in Freedom in *Autumn Crocus* (Cape Playhouse, Dennis, Mass., June–Sept. 1934); Mickey Linden in *The Shining Hour* and Richard Westover in *Thoroughbred* (Pabst Th., Milwaukee, Wis., Oct.–Nov. 1934); Thomas Armstrong in *Romance* (Blackstone, Chicago, Ill., Nov. 26, 1934); Col. Mortimer Sherwood in *The Pursuit of Happiness*, Rip Van Bret in *Double Door*, Mickey Linden in *The Shining Hour* and Warren Creamer in *The Late Christopher Bean* (The Playhouse, St. Petersburg, Fla., Feb. 12–Apr. 1935); Bill Stanton in *It's a Wise Child*, Rims O'Neill in *Saturday's Children*, and Richard Miller in *Ah, Wilderness!* (Cape Playhouse, Dennis, Mass., June–Sept. 1935); Thomas Armstrong in *Romance* (Cape Playhouse, Dennis, Mass., Aug. 27, 1935); Tim Crabbe in *Fresh Fields*, Duke Mantee in *The Petrified Forest*, and John Heming in *Fly Away Home* (Maryland Th., Baltimore, Oct.–Dec. 1935).

He appeared as Dr. Brooks in a pre-Bway tryout of *Danger, Men Working* (opened Nixon, Pittsburgh, Pa., Feb. 1936; closed Broad St. Th., Philadelphia, Pa., Mar. 1936); Brooke Gibson in *Storm Child* (Copley Th., Boston, Mass., Apr. 8, 1936); in stock, played Com. Peter Gilpin, Toby Cartwright, and Alec Harvey in *Tonight at 8:30*, Duke Mantee in *The Petrified Forest*, Ben Gannett in a stock tryout of *Damn Deborah*, and appeared in a stock tryout of *Marriage Royal* (Cape Playhouse, Dennis, Mass. June–Sept. 1937); again played his roles in *Tonight at 8:30*, appeared as Van in *High Tor*, and Joe in *They Knew What They Wanted* (Auditorium, Baltimore, Apr.–May 1938); Henry Higgins in *Pygmalion*, John Marvin in *Lightnin'*, and Hon. Alan Howard in *French Without Tears* (Cape Playhouse, Dennis, Mass., June–Sept. 1938).

Mr. Huston played Ben Longwood in *The Girl from Wyoming* (American Music Hall, N.Y.C., Oct. 29, 1938); Jack Garfield in *Window Shopping* (Longacre, Dec. 23, 1938); and Frank Plover in *Naughty Naught '00* (American Music Hall, Jan. 24, 1939); appeared in stock as Thomas Armstrong in *Romance*, Lauze de Perret in *Charlotte Corday*, Valere in *School for Husbands*, and Lucentio in *The Taming of the Shrew* (Mohawk Drama Festival, Schenectady, N.Y., June–Sept. 1939); played Private Broughton in *Journey's End* (Empire, N.Y.C., Sept. 18, 1939); and the R.F.D. in *They Knew What They Wanted* (Empire, Oct. 2, 1939); directed and played the title role in a Loyola Coll. production of *Cenodoxus* (Auditorium Th., Baltimore, Feb. 29, 1940); in stock, played Damon Welles in *The Dark Tower*, James Salston in *No More Ladies*, Rev. William Duke in *Outward Bound*, and Robert Adams in *Just Married* (Maine Civic Th., Portland, Spring 1940); and Richard Kurt in *Biography*, Lysander in *A Midsummer Night's Dream*, De Mauprat in *Richelieu*, and John Hay in *Abraham Lincoln* (Mohawk Drama Festival, Schenectady, July–Sept. 1940).

He appeared as Valentine in the Theatre Guild Production of *Twelfth Night* (St. James, N.Y.C., Nov. 19, 1940); Donald Gibson in *Nancy's Private Affair* (Royal Alexandra, Toronto; His Majesty's, Montreal, Canada, June 1941); Jean in *The Lady Has a Heart* (Royal Alexander, Toronto, Canada, His Majesty's Montreal, July 1941); Angus in the Theatre Guild production of *Macbeth* (National, Nov. 11, 1941); Dr. Jack Davidson in *Johnny Belinda* (Empire, Providence, R.I., June 1942); Damon Welles in *The Dark Tower* (Brattle Hall, Cambridge, Mass., July 1942); Dallas Chaytor in *Quiet Wedding* (Brattle Hall, Cambridge, Mass., Aug. 1942); Robert Smith in *Suspect* (Brattle Hall, Cambridge, Mass., Aug. 1942); Lodovico in a stock production of *Othello* (Brattle Hall, Cambridge, Mass., Aug. 1942; McCarter Th., Princeton, N.J., Sept. 1942); toured as Henry Higgins in *Pygmalion* (N.Y.C. Subway Circuit, Sept. 1942); Mortimer Brewster in a USO tour of *Arsenic and Old Lace* (US Army and Navy bases, Oct. 1942–Mar. 1943); played Mike Connors in *The Philadelphia Story* (Bucks County Playhouse, New Hope, Pa.; Bellevue Stratford Hotel, Philadelphia, Pa., June 1943); Paul Carrell in *Without Love* (Bucks County Playhouse, New Hope, Pa.; Bellevue Stratford Hotel, Philadelphia, Pa., June 1943); Leo Mercure in *Design for Living* (Hanna, Cleveland, Ohio, July 1943); Bob Brown in *Let Us Be Gay* (Hanna, Cleveland, July 1943).

He played Lodovico in the Theatre Guild production of *Othello* (Shubert, N.Y.C., Oct. 19, 1943); adapted, and played Macbeth in *The Story of Macbeth* (New Sch. for Social Research, N.Y.C., Apr. 2, 1944); appeared as both Greg and Gregory Orloff in *Catherine Was Great* (Shubert, Aug. 2, 1944); succeeded (Sept. 5, 1944) Warren Ashe as Jeff Connors in *School for Brides* (Royale, Aug. 1, 1944); played Alonso, King of Naples, in *The Tempest* (Alvin, Jan. 25, 1945); Lodovico in *Othello* (NY City Ctr., May 22, 1945); Vic Arnold in *Make Yourself at Home* (Ethel Barrymore Th., Sept. 13, 1945); and both Time and Dion in *A Winter's Tale* (Cort, Jan. 15, 1946). In stock, he appeared as the Captain in *Androcles and the Lion* (Morristown Playhouse, N.J., May 18, 1946); Grant in *State of the Union* (Middletown Playhouse, N.Y., July 1946); directed and played Henry Higgins in *Pygmalion* (Th.-by-the-Sea, Matunuck, R.I., Aug. 1946); portrayed Almady in *The Play's the Thing* (Th.-by-the-Sea, Matunuck, R.I., Aug. 27, 1946; His Majesty's, Montreal, Sept. 3, 1946); wrote, with Elizabeth Goodyear, and played Guy Smith in *Painted Wagon* (White Barn Th., Westport, Conn., July 27, 1947).

Mr. Huston toured as Sebastian Sanger in *Escape Me Never* (Shubert-Lafayette, Detroit, Mich., June 20, 1948; N.Y.C. Subway Circuit; Wilmington, Del.; Philadelphia, Pa.; Toronto and Montreal, Can., until Dec. 1948); Amphitryon in *Amphitryon 38* (Falmouth Playhouse, Mass.; Sea Cliff, L.I., N.Y.; Washington, D.C., June–Sept. 1949); appeared as the Pastor in *The Father* (Cort, N.Y.C., Nov. 16, 1949); and Dr. Walter Lucas in *With a Silk Thread* (Lyceum, Apr. 12, 1950); in stock, directed, and played Paul Verrall in *Born Yesterday*, directed, and played Henry Higgins in *Pygmalion*, directed, and appeared as Matt Cole in *Goodbye, My Fancy*, directed, and played Dr. Lyman Sanderson in *Harvey*, directed, and portrayed Senator Billboard Rawkins in *Finian's Rainbow*, and appeared in the title role in *Hamlet* (Peaks Island, Me., June–Sept. 1950); and played Aegisthus in *The Tower Beyond Tragedy* (ANTA, N.Y.C., Nov. 26, 1950); and Don Gregory in *The Shrike* (Cort, Jan. 15, 1952).

He toured as Senator Nolan in *Biography* (Princeton, N.J.; East Hampton, L.I., N.Y.; Falmouth, Mass.; Olney, Md., July–Sept. 1952); played George Henderson in *Affairs of State*, Bill Page in *Voice of the Turtle*, Mr. Allen in *Dark of the Moon*, Lov Bensey in *Tobacco Road*, Maury in *The Number*, and the title role in *Macbeth* (Providence Playhouse, R.I., Nov. 1952–Feb. 1953), all of which he also directed; and played Christopher Isherwood in *I Am a Camera* (Somerset Playhouse, Mass., Aug. 17, 1953).

He appeared as Le Bret in *Cyrano de Bergerac* (NY City Ctr., Nov. 12, 1953); Don Gregory in *The Shrike* (NY City Ctr., Nov. 26, 1953); Earl Rivers in *Richard III* (NY City Ctr., Dec. 9, 1953); alternated with Robert Preston in the role of George Wilson in *The Magic and the Loss* (Booth, Apr. 9, 1954); appeared in stock as Almady in *The Play's the Thing*, Prince Rudolph in *By Candlelight*, Shepherd Henderson in *Bell, Book and Candle*, and George Henderson in *Affairs of State* (Pickwick Playhouse, Birmingham, Ala., July–Sept. 1954).

Mr. Huston played D'Estivit in the pre-Bway tryout of Jean Arthur's *Saint Joan* (opened National, Washington, D.C., Sept. 20, 1954; closed Hartman, Columbus, Ohio, Nov. 6, 1954); was standby and succeeded (Shubert, N.Y.C., May 21, 1956) Martin Gabel as Irving LaSalle in *Will Success Spoil Rock Hunter?* (Belasco, Oct. 13, 1955); appeared in stock as Homer Wallace in *The Primrose Path* (New Hyde Park Playhouse, N.Y.; Lido, Long Beach, L.I., N.Y.; Memorial Hall, Warren, Ohio, June–July 1957; Robin Hood Th., Arden, Del., July 21, 1957); Gil in *Janus* (Southern Tier Playhouse, Binghampton, N.Y., Aug. 19, 1957); Irving LaSalle in *Will Success Spoil Rock Hunter?* (Southern Tier Playhouse, Binghampton, N.Y., Aug. 26, 1957); H. C. Curry in *The Rainmaker*, Mr. Coade in *Dear Brutus*, Toby Cartwright in *Tonight at 8:30*, and Jacob Friedland in *Nude With Violin* (Elitch Gardens, Denver, Colo., June–Sept. 1958).

He played Abraham in *The Cave at Machpelah* (Living Th., June 30, 1959); Henry Higgins in a tour of *Pygmalion* (University Th., Univ. of Akron, Ohio, Nov. 5, 1959); Barrie Trexel in *Susan and God* (Pocono Playhouse, Mountainhome, Pa.; Northland Playhouse, Detroit, Mich.; Famous Artists Th., Syracuse, N.Y.; Memorial Hall, Warren, Ohio; Cape Playhouse, Dennis, Mass., June–July, 1960); appeared as Edwin Gilroy Purvis in the pre-Bway tour of *Midgie Purvis* (Locust St. Th., Philadelphia, Dec. 27, 1960); Doc Redfield in *Mandingo* (Lyceum,

N.Y.C., May 22, 1961); Experience in *Chalk Marks on the Wall* (Take Three, July 15, 1961); the One-Armed Man, Dr. Ross, the Deck Steward, Miguel Telleria, and a Man in *A Gift of Time* (Ethel Barrymore Th., Feb. 22, 1962); replaced (Nov. 1965) Henderson Forsythe as Mr. Donald Crawford in *The Right Honourable Gentleman* (Billy Rose Th., Oct. 19, 1965); presented a series of dramatic readings (Shakespeare, Edwin Arlington Robinson, Emily Dickinson, Edna St. Vincent Millay, and others) in N.Y.C. (In Boboli, Summer 1966) and on tour.

Films. Mr. Huston has appeared as Clark Jenkins in *The Big Game* (RKO, 1936); Dick Miller in *The Man Who Found Himself* (RKO, 1937); Bennet in *Behind the Headlines* (RKO, 1937); and Joe Gibbons in *Close-Up* (Eagle Lion, 1948).

Television and Radio. Mr. Huston appeared on radio as Robert in *Beyond the Horizon* (Arthur Hopkins Great Play Series, NBC, 1944).

He wrote, with Rodelle Heller, and made his television debut as the Man in *Three Flights Up* (WPIX, Mar. 1948); subsequently appeared as Abraham Lincoln in *The Story of Booth* (Kraft Television Th., NBC); Banquo in *Macbeth* (Kraft Television Th., NBC); Captain Video (Dumont); The Chesterfield Hour (NBC); Colgate Comedy Hour (NBC); *The Road to Rome* on Ed Sullivan's *Salute to Robert Sherwood* (CBS); Armstrong Circle Th. (NBC); the Second Priest in *The Power and the Glory* (CBS, 1959); The Nurses (CBS); Dr. Hemingway in *At the Hemingways* (Camera Three, CBS, Oct. 28, 1963); *The Highest of Prizes* (Naked City, ABC, 1963); and *City Upon a Hill* (Lamp Unto My Feet, CBS, July 7, 1963).

Awards. Mr. Huston received the Ward Morehouse Award (1958) for his portrayal of H. C. Curry in *The Rainmaker.*

Recreation. Swimming, walking, reading, music, theatre.

HUTCHERSON, LEVERN. Actor, singer. b. Paris, Tenn. Attended Henry County Public Sch., Tenn.; Fisk Univ. Studied voice and music with John W. Work, Edward H. Boatner. Member of AEA.

Theatre. Mr. Hutcherson first performed touring the US with the Fisk Jubilee Singers; subsequently sang in concerts; was engaged by Major Bowes to sing at the St. Louis (Mo.) Municipal Opera and toured in the Major Bowes Show.

He appeared as Joe in *Carmen Jones* (NY City Ctr., May 2, 1945), also touring in it; played in *Show Boat* (St. Louis Municipal Opera, Mo.); toured in *Finian's Rainbow* and appeared in a series of concerts presented in theatres and universities.

He played Porgy in *Porgy and Bess* (Ziegfeld, N.Y.C., Mar. 10, 1953), alternated this role with William Warfield in the London (England) production, and in its European tour, appeared in it in the USSR (Moscow Opera House, 1953), and toured Scandinavia, Israel, and the Orient.

He sang with symphonic orchestras; appeared at Carnegie Hall (N.Y.C.); in the opera, *The Circus; played David in the London premiere of the opera, It Happened in Heaven; appeared in productions of On the Town;* and toured South America and the British West Indies in the latter play.

Films. Mr. Hutcherson sang for Sidney Poitier, who played Porgy in the motion picture version of *Porgy and Bess* (Col., 1959).

Night Clubs. He has appeared as a singer at the Last Frontier (Las Vegas, Nev.).

HUTCHINSON, JOSEPHINE. Actress. b. Oct. 12, Seattle, Wash., to Charles James and Leona (Doty) Hutchinson. Father, building contractor; mother, Leona Roberts, actress. Grad. Broadway H.S., Seattle, 1921. Studied acting with Maurice Browne, Ellen Van Volkenburg, and Moroni Olsen, Cornish Sch., Seattle, Summer 1921; studied dance with George Faurot, Seattle, 1915–16; Mary Ann Wells, Seattle, 1919–20. Married Apr. 12, 1924, to Robert Bell, director, coach (marr. dis. July 7, 1930); married Jan. 12, 1935, to James F. Townsend, talent representative. Member of AEA; SAG; AFTRA. c/o Sid Gold-Jack Fields Agency, Suite 1001, 9255 Sunset Blvd., Hollywood, CA 90069, tel. (312) CR 4-7247.

Theatre. Miss Hutchinson made her stage debut as a dancer in *The Little Mermaid* (Metropolitan Th., Seattle, Wash., 1920); and subsequently played Columbine in *Aria da Capo* (Cornish Th., Seattle, Wash., 1921).

She played a bit part and was general understudy for the *Hairy Ape* (Provincetown Playhouse, Mar. 9, 1922; Plymouth, Apr. 1922); played Elsie Tillinger in *Turn to the Right* (Summer tour, 1922); Lyssom in *Crowns* (Provincetown Playhouse, N.Y.C., Nov. 1922); at the Rams Head Playhouse (Washington, D.C., 1923–24), played Graciosa in *The Jewel Merchants,* Cecily Cardew in *The Importance of Being Earnest,* the title role in *Grania,* Phrynette in the pantomime *L'Enfant prodique,* Melisande in *The Romantic Age,* Sue in *Gold,* and Eleanora in *Easter;* and at the Wardman Park Th. (Washington, D.C., 1924–25), played Thérèse de Dorget in *L'Aiglon,* Francesca in *Paolo and Francesca,* Nora in *A Doll's House* and Louisette in the pantomime *The Bird Cage.*

Miss Hutchinson played Louisette in special matinee performances of *The Bird Cage* (52 St. Th., N.Y.C., June 2, 1925); Edie Tuttle in *A Man's Man* (52 St. Th., Oct. 13, 1925); Emily Madden in *The Unchastened Woman* (Princess, Feb. 15, 1926); Bessie Carvil in *One Day More* (Princess, Mar. 18, 1926); Jane Atherton in a summer stock production of *Children of the Moon;* and repeated her role in *The Bird Cage* (Provincetown Playhouse, Cape Cod, Mass., Aug. 1926).

She joined Eva Le Gallienne's Civic Repertory Co. (14 St. Th., N.Y.C.) and succeeded (Nov. 27, 1926) Rose Hobart as Irina in *The Three Sisters* (Oct. 26, 1926); followed (Dec. 1926) Ellida Pierra as Mrs. Fanny Wilton in *John Gabriel Borkman* (Nov. 9, 1926); succeeded (Dec. 1926) Beatrice Terry as Ortensia in *La Locandiera* (Nov. 22, 1926); played Maria in *Twelfth Night* (Dec. 20, 1926); Teresa in *The Cradle Song* (Jan. 24, 1927); Madeline Feievary Morton in *Inheritors* (Mar. 7, 1927); Clementine in *The Good Hope* (Oct. 18, 1927); Othella Lustig in *2 × 2 = 5* (Nov. 28, 1927); Anita Peri in *The First Stone* (Jan. 13, 1928); Olga in *Improvisations in June* (Feb. 26, 1928); Mrs. Elvsted in *Hedda Gabler* (Mar. 26, 1928); Anya in *The Cherry Orchard* (Oct. 15, 1928); Wendy in *Peter Pan* (Nov. 26, 1928); Nina in *The Seagull* (Sept. 16, 1929); the title role in *Mlle. Bourrat* (Oct. 7, 1929); Lisa in *The Living Corpse* (Dec. 6, 1929); Angela in *The Women Have Their Way* (Jan. 27, 1930); A Nurse in *A Sunny Morning* (Apr. 7, 1930); succeeded (Nov. 1930) Margaret Mower as Eva in *Siegfried* (Oct. 20, 1930); Louise in *Alison's House* (Dec. 1, 1930); Nichette in *Camille* (Jan. 26, 1931); and Jane Austen in *Dear Jane* (Nov. 14, 1932). Miss Hutchinson also played Alice in *Alice in Wonderland* (Civic Rep. Th., Dec. 12, 1932), which she repeated on tour of the eastern US (Fall 1933). During a national tour with this company (Spring 1933), she played Nora in *A Doll's House,* Mrs. Elvsted in *Hedda Gabler,* and Kaia in *The Master Builder.*

In stock, she played Mariella in *The Shining Hour* at the Berkshire Playhouse (Stockbridge, Mass., Summer 1936).

Films. Miss Hutchinson made her debut in *Little Princess* (Artcraft, 1917); subsequently appeared in *Happiness Ahead* (1st Natl., 1934); *Oil for the Lamps of China* (WB, 1935); *The Melody Lingers On* (UA, 1935); *The Story of Louis Pasteur* (WB, 1935); *I Married a Doctor* (1st Natl., 1936); *Mountain Justice* (WB, 1937); *The Women Men Marry* (MGM, 1937); *The Crime of Dr. Hallet* (U, 1938); *The Son of Frankenstein* (U, 1939); *Tom Brown's Schooldays* (RKO, 1940); *My Son, My Son* (UA, 1940); *Her First Beau* (Col., 1941); *Somewhere in the Night* (20th-Fox, 1946); *The Tender Years* (20th-Fox, 1947); *Cass Timberlaine* (MGM, 1947); *Adventure in Baltimore* (RKO, 1949); *Love Is Better Than Ever* (MGM, 1951); *Ruby Gentry* (20th-Fox, 1952); *Many Rivers to Cross* (MGM, 1955); *Miracle in the Rain* (WB, 1956); *Gun for a Coward* (U, 1957); *Sing Boy Sing* (20th-Fox, 1958); *Step Down to Terror* (U, 1958); *North by Northwest* (MGM, 1959); *The Adventures of Huckleberry Finn* (MGM, 1960); *Walk Like a Dragon* (Par., 1960); *Traveling Lady* (Col., 1964); *Baby, the Rain Must Fall* (Col. 1965); *Nevada Smith* (Par. 1966); and *Rabbit Run* (WB, 1969).

Television. Miss Hutchinson made her debut as Lyddie in *Wait for George* (Revue, 1955), has appeared on Lux Television Th. (CBS), Perry Mason (CBS), Matinee Th. (NBC), Men of Annapolis (ABC), Wagon Train (NBC), The Deputy (NBC), GE Th. (CBS), Wells Fargo (NBC), The Rifleman (ABC), Dick Powell Th. (NBC), Wirlybirds (CBS), Gunsmoke (CBS), Barbara Stanwyck Show (NBC), Rawhide (CBS), Schlitz Playhouse (CBS), Twilight Zone (CBS), The Real McCoys (ABC), The Law and Mr. Jones (ABC), The New Breed (ABC), Checkmate (CBS), True Story (NBC), Kraft Television Th. (NBC), Arrest and Trial (ABC), Dr. Kildare (NBC), Burke's Law (ABC); The Partridge Family, (ABC); *Shadow Over Elveron* (NBC); Name of the Game (NBC); Then Came Bronson (NBC); The Bold Ones (NBC); Mod Squad (ABC); Mannix (CBS); Longstreet (ABC); *The Homecoming* (CBS); and Sixth Sense (ABC).

Recreation. Gardening.

HUTTO, JACK. Literary representative. b. Jack Riley Hutto, Nov. 30, 1928, Columbia, S.C., to William Riley and Rena (Dell) Hutto. Grad. Columbia (S.C.) H.S., 1945; attended Univ. of South Carolina, 1945–46. Studied acting and directing at YMHA, N.Y.C., 1947–48; playwriting at New Sch. for Social Research, N.Y.C., 1949–50. Address: (home) 30 Fifth Ave., New York, NY 10011, tel. (212) 777-5464; (bus.) Helen Harvey Assoc., 110 W. 57th St., New York, NY 10019, tel. (212) 581-5610.

Mr. Hutto is associated with the literary agent, Helen Harvey (1974–to date). He was an agent with the William Morris Agency (1956–71); and worked on the production of the recorded library for SESAC, a music licensing firm (1951–55).

Mr. Hutto was an apprentice with the Town Th. (Columbia, S.C.), on 14 plays, under Fred Coe, the resident director (1944–45).

Recreation. Record collecting.

HYAMS, BARRY. Press representative, producer, writer, critic. b. Apr. 7, 1911, New York City, to Phineas and Fanny (Gold) Hyams. Father, teacher. Attended Brooklyn Coll., 1930–34. Served USN Chaplain's Div., 1944–45; rank, Sp/3c. Married Jan. 1937 to Ruth Hurok (marr. dis. 1951); one son, one daughter; married May 18, 1955, to Helen Baron, actress; one daughter. Member of ATPAM.

Theatre. Mr. Hyams was editor for the Natl. Play Bureau (1935–37) and press representative and production associate to S. Hurok (1937–50).

He was press representative and associate producer for *Medea* (Natl. Th., N.Y.C., Oct. 20, 1947); general press rep. for Robert Whitehead and Roger Stevens (1951–62), and for the Producers Th. (from 1953), during which time he was associate producer and publicist for *The Member of the Wedding* (Empire, Jan. 5, 1950); press representative for *Saint Joan* (Cort, Oct. 4, 1951); *I Am a Camera* (ANTA, Feb. 20, 1951); *Mrs. McThing* (ANTA, Feb. 20, 1952); *Golden Boy* (ANTA, Mar. 12, 1952); *Four Saints in Three Acts* (ANTA, Apr. 16, 1952); and *Desire Under the Elms* (ANTA, June 16, 1952).

He was associate producer and press representative for *The Time of the Cuckoo* (Empire, Oct. 15, 1952); press representative for *The Emperor's Clothes* (Ethel Barrymore Th., Feb. 9, 1953); *The Remarkable Mr. Pennypacker* (Coronet, Dec. 30, 1953); *Portrait of a Lady* (ANTA, Dec. 21, 1954); *The Flowering Peach* (Belasco, Dec. 28, 1954); *Bus Stop* (Music Box, Mar. 2, 1955); *The Skin of Our Teeth* (ANTA, Aug. 17, 1955); *Tamburlaine the Great* (Winter Garden, Jan. 19, 1956); *Separate Tables* (Music Box, Oct. 25, 1956); *The Waltz of the Toreadors* (Coronet, Jan. 17, 1957); *A Hole in the Head* (Plymouth, Feb. 28, 1957); and *Copper and Brass* (Martin Beck Th., Oct. 17, 1957).

Mr. Hyams produced *Endgame* (Cherry Lane, Jan. 28, 1958); was press representative for *The Day the Money Stopped* (Belasco, Feb. 20, 1958); *The Visit* (Lunt-Fontanne Th., May 5, 1958); produced *Ulysses in Nighttown* (Rooftop, June 5, 1958); was press representative for *A Touch of the Poet* (Helen Hayes Th., Oct. 2, 1958); *Goldilocks* (Lunt-Fontanne Th., Oct. 11, 1958); *The Cold Wind and the Warm* (Morosco, Dec. 8, 1958); *Much Ado About Nothing* (Lunt-Fontanne Th., Sept. 17, 1959); *Moonbirds* (Cort, Oct. 9, 1959); *The Shoemaker and the Peddler* (E. 74 St. Th., Oct. 14, 1960); *Rhinoceros* (Longacre, Jan. 9, 1961); *The Conquering Hero* (ANTA, Jan. 16, 1961); *A Man for All Seasons* (ANTA, Nov. 22, 1961); and produced *The Bald Soprano* (Gate, Sept. 17, 1963).

Mr. Hyams was director of public relations for the Repertory Th. of Lincoln Center (1963–1966); producing consultant to the Berkshire Th. Festival (Stockbridge, Mass., 1966–67); and public relations consultant for the Center Th. Group (Mark Taper Forum, Los Angeles, 1967–69).

Television. Mr. Hyams wrote scripts for the US Steel Hour (CBS, 1961), and other programs.

Other Activities. He has been theatre critic for the *American Examiner* (from 1963), and correspondent for *Teatron* (Haifa, Israel). He has published articles in the NY *Times*, NY *Herald-Tribune*, *Theatre Arts* and *Coronet;* and edited *Theatre: the Annual of the Repertory Theatre of Lincoln Center* (Hill and Wang, vol. 1, 1964; vol. 2, 1965).

HYDE-WHITE, WILFRID. Actor. b. May 12, 1903, Bourton-on-the-Water, Gloucestershire, England, to Rev. William Edward White and Ethel Adelaide (Drought) White. Father, Canon of Gloucester. Attended Harlborough Sch.; RADA, London, Married 1928 to Blanche Hope Aitken, known as Blanche Glynne, actress (marr. dis. 1948; dec. 1954); one son; married 1957 to Ethel Korenman, known as Ethel Drew, actress; one son, one daughter. Served WW II; H.M. Armed Forces. Relative in theatre: uncle, Benjamin Fisher-White, actor. Member of AEA; SAG; AFTRA; Buck's Club, London; The Green Room, London.

Theatre. Mr. Hyde-White made his stage debut as Maitland in *Tons of Money* (Ryde Th., Isle of Wight, Aug. 1922); and made his London debut as the Juror in *Beggar on Horseback* (Queens, May 7, 1925); subsequently appeared as the Courtier in *The Firebrand* (Wyndham's, Feb. 8, 1926); Alphonse in *The Rat* (Prince of Wales's, Feb. 12, 1927); toured as Marks in *The Terror* (1928); appeared as the Advocate-General in *No Other Tiger* (St. James's, London, Dec. 26, 1928); the Police Sgt. in *The Man at Six* (Queen's, Mar. 30, 1929); Salterthwaite in *The Grain of Mustard Seed* (Ambassadors', Oct. 27, 1930); and Mr. Carrington in *The Crime at Blossoms* (Playhouse, May 21, 1931).

He played P.C. Peck in *A Bit of a Test* (Aldwych, Jan. 30, 1933); Marks in *The Terror* (Lyceum, Nov. 11, 1933); the Marquess of Arlesford in *The Aunt of England* (Savoy, Mar. 27, 1935); General Gratz in *Sauce for the Goose* (St. Martin's, Jan. 29, 1936); the Man in *Her Last Adventure* (Ambassadors', Mar. 30, 1936); and Capt. Batty-Jones in *A Lady Reflects* ("Q," Apr. 22, 1940).

He appeared in the revues, *Come Out of Your Shell* (Embassy, May 13, 1940) and *In Town Again* (Criterion, Sept. 6, 1940); in two editions of *Rise Above It* Comedy, June 5, 1941; June 1942); and *Its About Time* (Comedy, June 17, 1942). He played George Prout, R.O.I., in *It Depends What You Mean* (Westminster, Oct. 12, 1944); toured as Kenneth Doble in *Elusive Lady* (opened Apr. 1946); and appeared as Charles Brunel in *My Wives and I* (Strand, London, July 31, 1947).

He made his N.Y.C. debut as Sir Alec Dunne in *Under the Counter* (Shubert, Oct. 3, 1947); subsequently played in *Happy with Either* (St. James's, London, April 22, 1948); was William Tracey in *The Philadelpia Story* (Duchess, Dec. 1, 1949); and performed with Sir Laurence Olivier's Co. as Britannus in *Caesar and Cleopatra* (St. James's, May 10, 1951) and Lepidus in *Antony and Cleopatra* (St. James's, May 11, 1951). He repeated these performances in N.Y.C. at the Ziegfeld Th.; Britannus in *Caesar and Cleopatra* (Dec. 19, 1951) and Lepidus in *Antony and Cleopatra* (Dec. 20, 1951).

He played Philip Russell in *Affairs Of State* (Cambridge, London, Aug. 21, 1952); Henry Poole in *Hippo Dancing* (Golders Green Hippodrome, Mar. 29, 1954); William in *A Kind of Folly* (Duchess, Feb. 15, 1955); Jimmy Broadbent in *The Reluctant Debutante* (Cambridge, London, May 24, 1955; Henry Miller's Th., N.Y.C., Oct. 10, 1956); Antony Drexel Biddle in *The Happiest Millionaire* (Bournemouth, Eng., Sept. 1957); and Andrew Bennett in *Not in the Book* (Criterion, London, Apr. 2, 1958).

He was Sir Ralph Bloomfield-Bonington in *The Doctor's Dilemma* (Haymarket, London, May 23, 1963); Lord Augustus Lorton in *Lady Windermere's Fan* (Phoenix, Oct. 13, 1966); George Triple in *Meeting at Night* (Duke of York's Th., Jan. 1971); replaced (Mar. 1971) Alastair Sim as the Marquis of Candover in *The Jockey Club Stakes* (Vaudeville Th., Sept. 30, 1970; Cort, N.Y.C., Jan. 24, 1973); and was Father Anthony Perfect in *The Prodigal Daughter* (Eisenhower Th., John F. Kennedy Ctr., Washington, D.C., Nov. 1, 1973).

Films. Mr. Hyde-White made his debut in *Rembrandt* (UA, 1936); subsequently appeared in *The Browning Version* (U, 1951); *Man with a Million* (UA, 1954); *Betrayed* (MGM, 1954); *Quentin Durward* (MGM, 1955); *The March Hare; Northwest Frontier; Two-Way Stretch* (Showcorporation, 1961); *Let's Make Love* (Fox, 1960); *On The Double* (Par., 1960); *Ada* (MGM, 1961); *In Search of the Castaways* (Buena Vista, 1962); *My Fair Lady* (WB, 1964); *John Goldfarb, Please Come Home* (20th-Fox, 1964); *You Must Be Joking!* (British Lion, 1965); *Ten Little Indians* (7 Arts, 1965); *Operation Snafu* (Amer. Intl., 1965); *The Sandwich Man* (Rank, 1966); *Bang, Bang, You're Dead!* (Amer. Intl., 1966); *The Liquidator* (MGM, 1966); *Chamber of Horrors* (WB, 1966); and *The Million Eyes of Su-Muru* (Amer. Intl., 1967).

Television. Mr. Hyde-White was in *The Priceless Pocket* (Douglas Fairbanks, Jr., Presents, NBC, 1953); *Mrs. Gilling and the Skyscraper* (Alcoa Hour, NBC, 1957); on the *Lucy in London* special (CBS, 1966); in *The Sunshine Patriot* (NBC, 1969); *Fear No Evil* (NBC, 1969); *Run a Crooked Mile* (ABC, 1969); and *Ritual of Evil* (NBC, 1970). He has also appeared on episodes of Ben Casey (CBS); Twilight Zone (CBS); Route 66 (CBS); Peyton Place (ABC); Mission Impossible (CBS); Daniel Boone (NBC); The Name of the Game (NBC); It Takes a Thief (ABC); and Columbo (NBC).

Recreation. Owns and races horses.

HYMAN, EARLE. Actor. b. George Earle Hyman, Oct. 11, 1926, Rocky Mount, N.C., to Zachariah and Marie (Plummer) Hyman. Father and mother, teachers. Grad. Franklin K. Lane H.S. Brooklyn, N.Y., 1943. Studied acting with Eva Le Gallienne at Amer. Theatre Wing; Robert Lewis; Actors Studio (member 1956–to date). Member of SAG; AFTRA; AEA (council member). Address: 109 Bank St., New York, NY 10014, tel. (212) OR 5-2683.

Theatre. Mr. Hyman first appeared on stage as a Church-Goer in *Run, Little Chillun* (Hudson Th., N.Y.C., Aug. 11, 1943); subsequently played Rudolf in *Anna Lucasta* (Mansfield, Aug. 30, 1944); Everett Du Shayne (Babe) in the pre-Bway tryout of *A Lady Passing Fair* (opened Lyric Th., Bridgeport, Conn., Jan. 3, 1947; closed Newark Opera House, N.J., Jan. 11, 1947); again played Rudolf in *Anna Lucasta* (His Majesty's Th., London, Eng., Oct. 29, 1947); appeared as Turner Thomas in *Sister Oakes* (Lenox Hill Playhouse, Apr. 23, 1949); Logan in *The Climate of Eden* (Martin Beck Th., Nov. 13, 1952); the Prince of Morocco in *The Merchant of Venice* (NY City Ctr., Mar. 4, 1953); the title role in *Othello* (Jan Hus House, Oct. 1953); and the Prince of Morocco in *The Merchant of Venice* (Jan Hus House, Feb. 22, 1955); and appeared at the American Shakespeare Festival (Stratford, Conn.) as a Soothsayer in *Julius Caesar* (July 12, 1955) and the Boatswain in *The Tempest* (Aug. 1, 1955).

He played Lieutenant in *No Time for Sergeants* (Alvin, N.Y.C., Oct. 20, 1955); the title role in *Mr. Johnson* (Martin Beck Th., Mar. 29, 1956); Melun in the American Shakespeare Festival production of *King John* (Stratford, Conn., June 26, 1956); Dunois in Siobhan McKenna's *Saint Joan* (Phoenix, N.Y.C., Sept. 11, 1956); the Voice of the Player King in Siobhan McKenna's *Hamlet* (Th. de Lys, Jan. 28–29, 1957); Vladimir (Didi) in *Waiting for Godot* (Ethel Barrymore Th., Jan. 21, 1957); and Antonio in *The Duchess of Malfi* (Phoenix, Mar. 19, 1957). At the American Shakespeare Festival (Stratford, Conn.) he played the title role of *Othello* (June 22, 1957), and the Prince of Morocco in *The Merchant of Venice* (July 10, 1957); appeared as the Ghost of Laius in *The Infernal Machine* (Phoenix, N.Y.C., Feb. 3, 1958); at the American Shakespeare Festival (Stratford, Conn.), he played Horatio in *Hamlet* (June 19, 1958); Philostrate in *A Midsummer Night's Dream* (June 20, 1958), and Autolicus in *The Winter's Tale* (July 20, 1958).

In London, he portrayed Ephriam in *Moon on a Rainbow Shawl* (Royal Court, Dec. 4, 1958); and Walter Lee Younger in *A Raisin in the Sun* (Adelphi, Aug. 4, 1959); at the American Shakespeare Festival (Stratford, Conn.), appeared as Caliban in *The Tempest* (June 19, 1960), and Alexas in *Antony and Cleopatra* (July 31, 1960); played the title role in the ELT production of *Mister Roberts* (Master Th., N.Y.C., Sept. 28, 1962); the title role in *Othello* (Den Nationale, Bergen, Norway, Mar., 1963); the title role in *Emperor Jones* (Det Norske Teatret, Oslo, Norway; Det Kungliga Dramatiska Teatern, Stockholm, Sweden; and Théâtre Sarah Bernhardt, International Theatre Festival; all 1965); Gayev in *The Cherry Orchard* (Public Th., N.Y.C., Dec. 7, 1972); and the Harlem Politician and Scrapbook Keeper in *House Party* (American Place Th., Oct. 29, 1973).

Films. Mr. Hyman appeared as Doc Johnson in *The Bamboo Prison* (Col., 1954); played Charles, the butler in *The Possession of Joel Delaney* (UA, 1972); and played a detective in *Super Cops* (MGM, 1973).

Television. He played Adam Hezdrel in *Green Pastures* (Hallmark Hall of Fame, NBC, 1957) and Neil Davenport in Edge of Night (CBS, 1969).

Other Activities. He has been teaching a class in the basic principles of acting technique at H. B. (Herbert Berghof) Studios (1961–to date).

Awards. Mr. Hyman received the Canada Lee Foundation Award (1953); the *Theatre World* Award (1956); and the GRY statuette in Oslo, Norway, for the best performance of the year in 1965 for his *Emperor Jones.*

Recreation. Fencing, skiing.

I

INGLIS, WILLIAM H. Educator, actor, director, producer, administrator. b. William Heard Inglis, III, June 7, 1937, to William Heard, Jr. and Ruth Lee (Brown) Inglis. Father, salesman; mother, teacher. Educ. Benjamin Franklin H.S., Rochester, N.Y.; Cornell Univ.; grad. Univ. of Rochester, B.S. 1963; Univ. of Washington, M.A. 1966; Ph.D. 1974. Served in Corps of Engineers, US Army, 1956–58; US Army Reserves, 1958–62. Married June 30, 1962, to Kari Fougner; two sons. Member of ATA (chmn., Student Advisory Comn., 1969); UCTA; CTA; SSTA; Ariz. Speech & Drama Assn.; Ariz. Alliance for Arts Educ. Address: (home) 1808 E. Concorda Dr., Tempe, AZ 85281, tel. (602) 966-9315; (bus.) Dept. of Speech & Theatre, Arizona State Univ., Tempe, AZ 85281, tel. (602) 965-7136.

Mr. Inglis became assistant professor and director of theatre at Arizona State Univ. in 1972. Previously, he had been at the Univ. of Washington as staff assistant to the executive vice-pres. and publicity director, School of Drama (1966–68) and at the American Theatre Assn. (ATA), Washington, D.C., as acting executive director (1969–70) and associate executive director (1970–72).

Theatre. Mr. Inglis made his theatrical debut as the principal in *Best Foot Forward* (Benjamin Franklin H.S., Rochester, N.Y., Mar. 1954). He was an extra in *The Skin of Our Teeth* (Cornell Univ., Nov. 1955); played Happy in *Death of a Salesman* (Rochester Community Th., Dec. 1958); and at the Univ. of Rochester directed *A Midsummer Night's Dream* (Nov. 1961), was the Sergeant in *The Devil Came from Dublin* (Feb. 1962), and directed *Purgatory* and *The Stronger* (both Oct. 1962) and *Judith* (Oct. 1963). At the Univ. of Washington, he directed *The Creditors* (Feb. 1964), played Nestor in *Troilus and Cressida* (Apr. 1964), and directed *Gammer Gurton's Needle* (Nov. 1964). He made his professional acting debut at A Contemporary Theatre, Seattle, Wash., as a Bellboy in *Oh Dad, Poor Dad . .* (July 1965), then playing Burt Dinwitty in *Dark of the Moon* (Aug. 1965). At the Univ. of Washington, he directed *The Prodigal* (Nov. 1965), *A Thurber Carnival* (Feb. 1966), and *An Original Review*, which he also wrote (Mar. 1967). He was general manager for sixty-five performances of *The Lost Colony* (Waterside Amphitheatre, Roanoke Island, N.C., 1972); at Arizona State Univ. directed *See How They Run* (June 7, 1973) and *The Ghost Sonata* (Feb. 7, 1974); and appeared as Lilas Pastia in *Carmen* (San Diego Opera Co., Phoenix, Ariz., Nov. 11–12, 1974).

Radio. Mr. Inglis was host of the program Drama Review (KUOW-FM, Seattle, Wash., 1966–68).

Published Works. Mr. Inglis has written newspaper articles, was an editorial assistant for *Theatre Backstage A to Z* by Warren Lounsbury (Univ. of Washington Press, 1967), was managing editor (1969–70) on *Educational Theatre Journal*, and editor of the monthly *Theatre News* (1969–72).

Awards. Mr. Inglis held a Univ. of Washington assistantship for graduate education, and in 1968–69 he was president, Graduate & Professional Student Senate, Univ. of Washington.

Recreation. Hiking, camping, reading.

INNESS-BROWN, VIRGINIA ROYALL. Executive. b. Virginia Portia Royall, May 4, 1901, Medford, Mass., to John Allen Crosskeys and Agatha Caroline (Freeman) Royall. Father, oil industrialist. Grad. French School, Warrenton, Va.; Warrenton Country School, 1918. Married March 26, 1921, to Hugh Alwyn Inness-Brown; one son, three daughters. Member of IASTA; Natl. Inst. of Soc. Sciences; Mus. of Modern Art; Metropolitan Mus. of Art; Rhode Island Sch. of Design.

Mrs. Inness-Brown was pres. (1952–68) of the Greater NY chapter of ANTA. She was also a director and member of the exec. comm. (1953–68) and vice-pres. (1963); and for ANTA Intl. Cultural Exchange was vice-pres. (1954–63), vice-chmn., coordinator of Intl. Cultural Exchange's Performing Arts Program (1954–55) and a member of the music, drama, and dance advisory panels (1954–63). During her presidency of the Greater New York ANTA, the ANTA Matinee Series was inaugurated in 1956.

Mrs. Inness-Brown was also a special consultant to the Asst. Secy. of State for Educational and Cultural Affairs, US Dept. of State (1962–64); delegate to the 10th ITI Congress (Warsaw, Poland, 1963); member of the Natl. Council on the Arts and Government (1963–71); chmn. of the US committee for the 1st World Festival of Negro Arts (1964–65); chmn., US delegation to the Festival (Dakar, Senegal, 1966); and member of the council, African-American Institute (1966–68).

She was a founding member, dir. (1950–60), and exec. vice-pres. (1961–71) of the American Portuguese Cultural Soc.; a trustee (1954–64) and vice-pres. (1962) of the V. Beaumont Allen Fdtn., N.Y.C.; mbr. of the adv. bd. (1957–64) and a trustee (1960–64), Empire State Music Festival; on the Phoenix Th. (N.Y.C.) council (1959–60); on the adv. bd. (1958–61) and a dir. and bd. mbr. (1961), Festival Fdtn. for the Festival of Two Worlds, N.Y., and Spoleto, Italy; on the adv. bd., Clarion Concerts Soc., Inc., N.Y. (1959) and a dir. (1961); was a founding mbr. and dir. (1960–67), Agnes DeMille Lyric Th. Dance Co., N.Y.; mbr., NY Friends Committee of Robert Coll., Istanbul, Turkey (1960–64); and a mbr., adv. comm. on the arts (1962–69) and trustee (1964–69), Inst. of Intl. Educ., N.Y.C.; and was on the Little Orchestra Soc. (N.Y.C.) council (1966–68).

Other Activities. Mrs. Inness-Brown was a director of the Spence-Chapin Adoption Service, N.Y.C. (1950–64) and a trustee (1955–64), 1st vice-pres. (1957–59), treas. (1959–60), and secy. (1961) of the Professional Children's School, N.Y.C. Mrs. Inness-Brown served on the Natl. Conference of Christians and Jews (NCCJ, 1959–63); was a NCCJ director in Manhattan (1963–68); and was natl. representative of NCCJ to the Conference Group of US national organizations on the UN (1964).

Awards. Mrs. Inness-Brown has been awarded the Medaille de Versailles (Paris, 1955; N.Y., 1956); Freedom Bell (Berlin, 1957); Handel Award, City of New York (1959); Citation for Achievement, Congress Hall (Berlin, 1959); Commander's Cross, Legion of Merit of Federal Republic of Germany (1961); Brotherhood Award, Natl. Conference of Christians and Jews (1962); ANTA Citation (1962); and she was made a commander of the Republic of Senegal's l'Ordre National (1966).

IONESCO, EUGÈNE Playwright. b. Nov. 13, 1912, Slatina, Romania, to Eugène and Thérèse (Icard) Ionesco. Father, lawyer. Attended Univ. of Bucharest, Romania; grad. Univ. of Paris (de la Sorbonne), Licencié ès Lettres. Married June 12, 1936, to Rodica Burileano; one daughter. Address: (home) 14 Rue de Rivoli, Paris 4c, France; (bus.) c/o Editions Gallimard, 5 Rue Sebastien-Bottin, Paris 7e, France; c/o Grove Press, Inc., 64 University Place, New York, NY 10003.

Pre-Theatre. French teacher, literary critic, and worked in publishing.

Theatre. Ionesco, a Romanian playwright, who has written in French, wrote *La cantatrice chauve (The Bald Soprano)* (Th. des Noctambule, Paris, May 11, 1950); subsequently wrote *La Leçon (The Lesson)* (Th. de Poche-Montparnasse, Feb. 20, 1951); *Les chaises (The Chairs)* (Th. Nouveau-Lancy, Apr. 22, 1952); *Victimes du devoir (Victims of Duty)* (Th. Quartier, Feb. 1953); and the short plays, *La jeune fille, A marrier, Le maître, Les grandes chaleurs, Le connaissez-vous, La Nièce-épouse*, and *Le salon d'automobile* (Th. de la Huchette, Sept. 1, 1953).

He wrote *Amédée, ou comment s'en debarrasser*, (premiere, Th. du Babylone, Apr. 14, 1954), which was adapted by Derek Prouse and Dominique Clauyel as *Amédée, or How To Disentangle Yourself* (Tempo Playhouse, N.Y.C., Oct. 31, 1955); *Jacques, ou la soumission* and *Le tableau* (Th. de la Huchette, Paris, Oct. 1955); *The New Tenant (Le nouveau locataire;* premiere, Finland, 1955); *The Lesson* (Tempo Playhouse, French Art Th., N.Y.C., 1955–56); *L'Impromptu de l'Alimat, ou le caméléon du berger* (Studio des Champs-Elysées, Paris, Feb. 1956); *Impromptu pour la Duchesse de Windsor* (private performance, May 1957); and *L'Avenir est dans les oeufs, ou il faut de tout pour faire un monde* (1957).

Other productions of Mr. Ionesco's plays include *The Lesson* and *The Chairs* (Phoenix Th., N.Y.C., Jan. 9, 1958); *The Bald Soprano* and *Jack* (Sullivan St. Playhouse, June 3, 1958); *Rhinoceros* (Th. l'Odéon, Paris, Jan. 25, 1959); *Tuer sans gages* (Th. Récamier, Feb. 27, 1959); *Victims of Duty* (Th. de Lys, N.Y.C., Jan. 19, 1960); *The New Tenant* and *The Lesson* (Royal Playhouse, Mar. 9, 1960); *Tuer sans gages*, translated by Donald Watson as *The Killer* (Seven Arts Th., Mar. 22, 1960); and *Rhinoceros*, translated by Derek Prouse (Royal Court, London, Apr. 28, 1960), and in N.Y.C. (Longacre, Jan. 9, 1961).

Ionesco wrote the scenario for Deryk Mendal's ballet, *Apprendre à marcher* (Th. de l'Etoile, Paris, Apr. 1960). The ANTA Matinee series sponsored the production of his *Improvisation, or The Shepherd's Chameleon* (Th. de Lys, N.Y.C., Nov. 29, 1960). *The Killer* was presented as part of the Theatre of the Absurd repertoire (Cherry Lane, Feb. 11, 1962). *Le maître*, was the basis for the opera, *The Great Man*, presented with the opera, *The Bald Soprano*, based on the play of the same name (Judson Hall, May 28, 1963). Mr. Ionesco wrote the story for the ballet-pantomime, *Le piéton de l'air* (Th. l'Odéon, Paris, 1963; NY City Ctr., Mar. 3, 1964), first presented in Donald Watson's English translation as *The Pedestrian in the Air* (Goodman Memorial Th., Chicago, Ill., Jan. 7, 1966); the play *Le roi se meurt*, which was translated by Donald Watson and presented as *Exit the King* (Royal, Newcastle, England, Aug. 27, 1963; Lyceum, Edinburgh, Scotland, Sept. 2, 1963; Royal Court, London, Sept. 12, 1963; Lyceum, N.Y.C., Jan. 9, 1968); *La soif et la faim* (Paris, 1965); *Délire a deux* (Paris, 1966); *Mêlées et démêlées* (Paris, 1966); *Jeux de massacre* (Paris, 1970); *Macbett* (Th. Rive Gauche, Paris, Feb. 1972); and *Ce formidable bordel* (Th. Moderne, Paris, 1973).

Films. He wrote the narration for the Polish cartoon-film, *Monsieur Tête* (1959); wrote the episode "Anger" for the film *Seven Capital Sins* (Embassy, 1962); and wrote and starred in *La vase* (1972).

Radio. BBC radio's Third Programme sponsored productions of Mr. Ionesco's *Le Tableau*, translated by Donald Watson as *The Picture* (Mar. 11, 1957) and *Rhinoceros* (Nov. 6, 1959).

Published Works. In addition to his plays, Mr. Ionesco wrote *Notes and Counter Notes*, translated by Donald Watson (1964), and a novel, *The Hermit* (1974).

Awards. Ionesco received a grant from the French government (1938) to do research in France on modern French poetry; the film, *Monsieur Tête*, won the Prix de la Critique at the Tours Festival (1959); he was named Chevalier des Arts et Lettres (1961), and he is an Homme des Lettres.

IRELAND, JOHN. Actor, director, writer. b. John Benjamin Ireland, Jan. 30, 1916, Victoria, B.C., Canada, to John Benjamin and Katherine (Ferguson) Ireland. Father, rancher; mother, educator. Attended Commerce H.S., N.Y.C. Studied for the theatre at the Davenport Free Th., N.Y.C. Married 1940 to Elaine Gudman (marr. dis. 1949); two sons; married 1949 to Joanne Dru, actress (marr. dis. 1956); married 1962 to Daphne Myrick. Relatives in theatre: brother, Tommy Noonan, actor, producer; son, John Ireland, Jr., actor. Member of SAG; AEA; SDG; WGA.

Pre-Theatre. Professional swimmer.

Theatre. Mr. Ireland made his debut as an apprentice (Robin Hood Th., Arden, Del., 1939); subsequently apprenticed at Martha's Vineyard (Mass., 1940); made his N.Y.C. debut with the Irish Repertory Players (Cherry Lane Th., 1939); played in stock at Martha's Vineyard (Mass., Summer 1939); toured with a Shakespearean Repertory Co. as Horatio in *Hamlet*, Lorenzo in *The Merchant of Venice*, Macduff in *Macbeth*, and Iago in *Othello* (1940); and played Captain Hook in a Clare Tree Major Children's Th. touring production of *Peter Pan* (cross-country, 1940).

He made his Bway debut as the Sergeant and First Murderer in *Macbeth* (National, Nov. 11, 1941); joined as the Miner in the national tour of *The Moon Is Down* (1942); played the Reporter in *Native Son* (Majestic, N.Y.C., Oct. 23, 1942); Krafft in *Counterattack* (Windsor, Feb. 3, 1943); the First Murderer in *Richard III* (Forrest, Mar. 24, 1943); Gustave Jensen in *A New Life* (Royale, Sept. 15, 1943); Mr. Deane in *Doctors Disagree* (Bijou, Dec. 28, 1943); and Sir Archibald Mackenzie in *A Highland Fling* (Plymouth, Apr. 28, 1944).

Mr. Ireland appeared as Dr. John Buchanan, Jr., in a tour of *Summer and Smoke* (opened La Jolla Playhouse, Calif., 1950); played Buck Carpenter in *Deadfall* (Holiday, N.Y.C., Oct. 27, 1955); and Brutos in *Infidel Caesar* (Music Box, Apr. 27, 1962); toured as Murray Burns in the national company of *A Thousand Clowns* (opened Providence, R.I., Sept. 3, 1963; closed American Th., St. Louis, Mo., Apr. 18, 1964: and appeared in *Macbeth* (Ahmanson Th., Los Angeles, Calif., Jan. 28, 1975).

Films. Mr. Ireland made his debut in *A Walk in the Sun* (20th-Fox, 1945); subsequently appeared in

Wake Up and Dream (20th-Fox, 1946); *My Darling Clementine* (20th-Fox, 1946); *The Gangster* (Allied, 1947); *Red River* (UA, 1948); *Roughshod* (RKO, 1949); *All the King's Men* (Col., 1949); *The Return of Jesse James* (Lippert, 1950); *The Scarf* (UA, 1951); *Vengeance Valley* (MGM, 1951); *Red Mountain* (Par., 1951); *The Basketball Fix* (Realart, 1951); *The Bushwackers* (Realart, 1952); *Hurricane Smith* (Par., 1952); *The 49th Man* (Col., 1953); *Combat Squad* (Col., 1953); *Outlaw Territory,* which he also co-produced and co-directed (Realart, 1953); *The Fast and the Furious,* which he also co-directed (Amer. Intl., 1954); *Southwest Passage* (UA, 1954); *Security Risk* (Allied, 1954); *Steel Cage* (UA, 1954); *Queen Bee* (Col., 1955); *Hell's Horizon* (Col., 1955); *The Good Die Young* (UA, 1955); *Gunfight at OK Corral* (Par., 1957), *Spartacus* (U, 1960); *55 Days at Peking* (Allied, 1963); *Ceremony* (UA, 1963); and *The Fall of the Roman Empire* (Par., 1964).

Other films in which he appeared include *Faces in the Dark* (States Rights, 1964); *I Saw What You Did* (Univ., 1965); *Fort Utah* (Par., 1967); *Once Upon a Time in the West* (Par., 1969); *The Adventurers* (Par., 1970); and *Escape to the Sun* (Cinevision, 1972).

Television. Mr. Ireland appeared on Philco Playhouse (NBC) in *Confession* (Jan. 1951) and *Time Bomb* (Oct. 1954); in several Schlitz Playhouse of Stars productions (CBS, 1952, 1954, 1955, 1956); in *Prologue to Glory* (GE Th., CBS, Feb. 1956); *This Land Is Mine* (Fireside Th., NBC, Apr. 1956); on Playhouse 90 (CBS) in *Without Incident* (June 1957) and *A Sound of Different Drummers* (Oct. 1957); in *Obituary for Mr. 'X'* (Dick Powell Th., NBC, Jan. 1962); *The Matched Pearl* (Alfred Hitchcock Th., NBC, Apr. 1962); and other television dramas.

He appeared also in episodes of such series as Asphalt Jungle (ABC, 1961); Rawhide (CBS, 1962, 1965); Burke's Law (ABC, 1963, 1965); Branded (NBC, 1965, 1966); Gunsmoke (CBS, 1966, 1967); Bonanza (NBC, 1967); Daniel Boone (NBC, 1967); Name of the Game (NBC, 1969); Men from Shiloh (NBC, 1970); Mission: Impossible (CBS, 1972); and others.

Other Activities. Mr. Ireland wrote the lyrics for the song "No Head on My Pillow" (music by singer Julie London).

Awards. Mr. Ireland was nominated for the Academy (Oscar) Award for his performance in *All the King's Men* (1950).

Recreation. Swimming, tennis, writing, reading.

IRVING, GEORGE S. Actor, singer. b. George Irving Shelasky, Nov. 1, 1922, Springfield, Mass., to Abraham and Rebecca (Saks) Shelasky. Father, clothier. Grad. Classical H.S., Springfield, 1940; attended Leland Powers Sch. (Boston Mass.), 1940. Studied voice with Mme. Cora Claiborne, Springfield, Mass., two yrs.; studied voice with Henry Jacobi, N.Y.C., 1946; with Hunter Kimball, N.Y.C., 1947; with Sidney Dietch, N.Y.C., 1947; lieder with Max Rudolph, N.Y.C., 1946; with William Tarrasch, N.Y.C., 1947–48; with Elema Gerhardt, London, 1948; and with Sidney Osborne N.Y.C., 1960. Married Oct. 17, 1948, to Maria Karnilova, actress, dancer; one son, one daughter. Served US Army, 1943–46. PTO; rank, Sgt. Member of AEA; AFTRA; SAG; AGMA.

Theatre. Mr. Irving first performed as the Suitor in a high sch. production of *The Marriage Proposal* (Apr. 1940); made his professional debut as the Stableman in a stock production of *Dark Victory* (Casino, Sandwich, Mass., June 1941); also in stock, played in *Flight to the West* and *The Flying Gerardos* (Rye Beach, N.H., July 1941); sang in the chorus of a touring production of *The Student Prince* (1941); appeared in the chorus and played roles in *Glamorous Night, Sally, Song of the Flame, Girl Crazy, Show Boat,* and *The New Moon* (St. Louis Municipal Opera Co., Mo., June 1942); and in *The Vagabond King, Robin Hood,* and *Babes in Toyland* (Paper Mill Playhouse, Millburn, N.J., Sept. 1942).

He made his Bway debut in the chorus of *Oklahoma!* (St. James, Mar. 31, 1943); appeared in the chorus of *Lady in the Dark* (Bway Th., Feb. 27, 1943); the revue *Call Me Mister* (National, Apr. 18, 1946); sang the role of Ben in the opera *The Telephone* (Aldwych, London, May 1948) and Mr. Gobineau in *The Medium* (Aldwych, May 1948; Th. de la Renaissance, Paris, France, June 1948); appeared in the revue *Along Fifth Avenue* (Broadhurst, N.Y.C., Jan. 13, 1949); as the Senator in the pre-Bway tryout of *That's the Ticket* (opened Shubert, Philadelphia, Pa., Sept. 24, 1948; closed there, Oct. 2, 1948); and Mr. Gage in *Gentlemen Prefer Blondes* (Ziegfeld, N.Y.C., Dec. 8, 1949).

At the State Fair Music Hall (Dallas, Tex., Summer 1952), he played Harry in *A Tree Grows in Brooklyn;* Dr. Engel in *The Student Prince;* and Jigger in *Carousel;* appeared in the revue, *Two's Company* (Alvin, N.Y.C., Dec. 15, 1952); as Dario in *Me and Juliet* (Majestic, May 28, 1953); sang Varlaam in the opera *Boris Godunov* (Her Majesty's, Montreal, Canada, 1953); succeeded (July 6, 1954) Hans Conreid, as Boris in *Can-Can* (Shubert, N.Y.C., May 7, 1953), and also toured in it (opened National, Washington, D.C., June 25, 1955; closed there May 1956).

He appeared as Charlie in *Annie Get Your Gun* (New England Mutual, Boston, Mass., June 24, 1956); Jigger in *Carousel* (New England Mutual, Boston, Mass., July 1, 1956); Mr. Peachum in *The Beggar's Opera* (Sanders Th., Cambridge, Mass., July 25, 1956); and as Dr. Fiefield in *The Remarkable Mr. Pennypacker* (Bucks County Playhouse, New Hope, Pa., Aug. 20, 1956).

Mr. Irving played Larry Hastings in *Bells Are Ringing* (Shubert, N.Y.C., Nov. 29, 1956); Mr. Peachum in *The Beggar's Opera* (NY City Ctr., Mar. 13, 1957); Big Bill in *Shinbone Alley* (Bway Th., Apr. 13, 1957); and at the Starlight Th. (Kansas City, Mo., Summer 1957) appeared as Harbison and understudied Emile de Becque in *South Pacific,* played Boris in *Can-Can,* and performed in *Damn Yankees.*

He played the Chiropractor in *The Soft Touch* (Coconut Grove, Miami, Fla., Jan. 1958); made his debut with the NY City Opera Co., as Ben Hubbard in *Regina* (NY City Ctr., Apr. 17, 1958); subsequently singing with them in *The Good Soldier Schweik, The Love of Three Oranges,* and *The Ballad of Baby Doe;* appeared in stock as Markovich in *Silk Stockings,* the First Gangster in *Kiss Me, Kate,* Orlofsky in *Die Fledermaus,* Panisse in *Fanny,* and Jud in *Oklahoma!* (Rye Music Th., N.Y., Summer 1958); appeared as Boris in *Can-Can* and Jud in *Oklahoma!* (Pittsburgh Light Opera Co., Pa., July, 1958); and in the title role of *Oh Captain!* (Oakdale Musical Th., Wallingford, Conn.; Warwick Musical Th., R.I., Aug. 1958); played Senator Jack S. Phogbound in *Li'l Abner,* Captain Andy in *Show Boat,* Sandor in *Bells Are Ringing,* Pinky in *Wish You Were Here,* and Percival Brown in *The Boy Friend* (Music Tent, Pinebrook, N.J., June 1959); and appeared as Sandor in *Bells Are Ringing* (Carousel Th., Framingham, Mass., Sept. 1959).

He played The Doorman, Alphonse, Raymond, The Tough, and The Other Man in *The Good Soup* (Plymouth, N.Y.C., Mar. 2, 1960); Setmore in the pre-Bway tryout of *Lock Up Your Daughters* (opened Shubert, New Haven, Apr. 27, 1960; closed Shubert, Boston, May 7, 1960); succeeded (May 25, 1960) Bernie West as McGee in *Oh, Kay* (E. 74 St. Th., N.Y.C., Apr. 16, 1960); played Wazir in *Kismet* (Carousel, Framingham, Mass., July 25, (1960); the Inspector in *Irma La Douce* (Plymouth, N.Y.C., Oct. 10, 1960); Metallus in *Romulus* (Music Box, Jan. 10, 1962); Signor Bellardi in *Bravo Giovanni* (Broadhurst, May 19, 1962); Rosenzweig in *Seidman and Son* (Belasco, Oct. 15, 1962); and Charles Davis in *Tovarich* (Bway Th., Mar. 18, 1963).

He directed a production of *Irma La Douce* (Summer tour 1963); played Marolles in *A Murderer Among Us* (Morosco, Mar. 25, 1964); Mr. Smith in *Alfie!* (Morosco, Dec. 17, 1964); the Narrator in *Die Dreigroschenoper (The Threepenny Opera,* NY City Ctr., Mar. 11, 1965); at the Bucks County Playhouse, New Hope, Pa., played Squire Western in *Tom Jones* (July 26, 1965) and Edward L. McKeever in *The Solid Gold Cadillac* (Aug. 9, 1965); played Chernov in *Anya* (Ziegfeld, N.Y.C., Nov. 29, 1965); Mr. Darling and Captain Hook in *Peter Pan* (Coconut Grove Playhouse, Miami, Fla., Mar. 29, 1966; Paper Mill Playhouse, Millburn, N.J., May 11, 1966); the Ballad Singer in *Galileo* (Vivian Beaumont Th., N.Y.C., Apr. 13, 1967); Phillipe Bonnard in *The Happy Time* (Broadway, Jan. 18, 1968); Hannibal Beam in *Up Eden* (Jan Hus Playhouse, Nov. 27, 1968); the Mayor in *Promenade* (Promenade Th., June 4, 1969); the TV repairman and the Real Estate Agent in *Four on a Garden* (Broadhurst, Jan. 30, 1971); the title role in *An Evening with Richard Nixon and. . .* (Shubert, Apr. 30, 1972); Capitano Cockalorum in the pre-Bway tryout of *Comedy* (opened Colonial, Boston, Nov. 6, 1972; closed there, Nov. 18, 1972); Madame Lucy in *Irene* (Minskoff, Mar. 13, 1973); Elbert C. Harland in *Who's Who in Hell* (Lunt-Fontanne, Dec. 9, 1974); and replaced (Spring 1975) Barnard Hughes as Dr. Lionel Morris in *All Over Town* (Booth, Dec. 29, 1974).

Television. Mr. Irving sang on Barry Wood's Variety Show (CBS, 1948); in the operas, *Chicken Little, The Mighty Casey,* and *The Sleeping Beauty* (Omnibus, CBS); and has appeared on Look Up and Live (CBS); Camera Three (CBS); *Rosemary* (NY Television Th., Educ., Feb. 27, 1967); and as Chernov in *Anastasia* (Hallmark Hall of Fame, NBC, Mar. 17, 1967).

Awards. Mr. Irving received an Antoinette Perry (Tony) Award (1973) as "best actor in a supporting role in a musical" for *Irene.*

IRVING, JULES. Director, actor, producer, educator. Grad. New York Univ., B.A. 1947; Stanford Univ., M.A. 1949; Ph.D. Married Dec. 28, 1947, to Priscilla Pointer; one son, two daughters. Served US Army, 1943–46, ETO. Member of Theatre Communications Group (exec. comm., 1960–to date); Organization of Legitimate Theatres (pres.); SSD&C. Address: (home) 160 West End Ave., New York, NY 10023; (bus.) 150 W. 65th St., New York, NY 10023.

Theatre. With Herbert Blau, Mr. Irving founded (1952 the San Francisco Actor's Workshop and was the consulting director until 1965. Also with Mr. Blau, he was joint director of the Repertory Th. of Lincoln Ctr., N.Y.C. (1965–67) and, following Mr. Blau's resignation in 1967, sole director until 1972, when he himself resigned.

At the Actor's Workshop, Mr. Irving directed *Hotel Universe* (Feb. 28, 1952), *I Am a Camera* (May 16, 1952), *Hedda Gabler* (Oct. 10, 1952), and *Blood Wedding* (Dec. 4, 1952). He appeared in *Playboy of the Western World* (Feb. 26, 1953); staged *The Miser* (June 1, 1953), *Lysistrata* (Oct. 23, 1953), and *Death of a Salesman* (Feb. 26, 1954).

Also at the Actor's Workshop, he appeared in *The Crucible* (Dec. 3, 1954), and *Camino Real* (July 10, 1955); subsequently staged *The Girl on the Via Flamina* (Aug. 19, 1955), *The Importance of Being Earnest* (Oct. 14, 1955), *Ticklish Acrobat* (June 22, 1957), *The Potting Shed* (Sept. 27, 1957), and *The Entertainer* (Feb. 6, 1959); appeared in *Three Japanese Noh Plays* (June 4, 1959); staged *The Plaster Bambino* (Sept. 16, 1959), *The Rocks Cried Out* (Nov. 10, 1960), the double bill of *Krapp's Last Tape* and *The Zoo Story* (Feb. 7, 1961), *Misalliance* (May 10, 1961); *Friedman & Son* (Jan. 6, 1962), *Henry IV, Part 1* (Apr. 21, 1962), *The Glass Menagerie* (Nov. 9, 1962), *Telegraph Hill* (Jan. 18, 1963), and *The Caretaker* (Nov. 16, 1963).

In addition to being a director of the Repertory Th. of Lincoln Ctr., Mr. Irving directed the following productions for the company: *The Caucasian Chalk Circle* (Vivian Beaumont Th., Mar. 24, 1966); *The Alchemist* (Vivian Beaumont Th., Oct. 13, 1966); *The Inner Journey* (Forum, Mar. 20, 1969); *The Birthday Party* (Forum, Feb. 5, 1971); the one-act double bill *Landscape* and *Silence* (Forum, Feb. 9, 1971); *An Enemy of the People* (Vivian Beaumont Th., Mar. 11, 1971); *Mary Stuart* (Vivian Beaumont Th., Nov. 11, 1971). Mr. Irving also directed a return engagement of the Lincoln Ctr. Repertory revival of *A Streetcar Named Desire* (St. James Th., Oct. 4, 1973).

Television. Mr. Irving was a guest on *Lincoln Center: The Plan and the Promise* (Community Dialogue, Ind., Apr. 1965); appeared on *Lincoln Center: The*

End of the Beginning (Eye on New York, CBS, May 1965); and *The Next Stage* (Eye on New York, CBS, Oct. 1965).

Other Activities. Mr. Irving has been associate professor at Stanford Univ.; was professor of drama, San Francisco (Calif.) State Coll. (1949–62); lectured at the New School for Social Research, N.Y.C. (1965); and was a chief instructor at Fordham Univ. (1970–71).

Awards. Mr. Irving received the first annual San Francisco State Coll. Presidential Award for Distinguished Service (1965) and the Margo Jones Award (1972).

IRWIN, WILL. Musician, pianist, arranger, composer, musical director. b. William C. K. Irwin, Feb. 3, 1907, San Francisco, Calif., to William C. K. and Bessie May (Allan) Irwin. Father, businessman; mother, singer, actress. Grad. Professional Children's Sch., N.Y.C., 1926. Studied at Louisville (Ky.) Conservatory of Music, 1919; Chicago, (Ill.) Conservatory, 1922; Juilliard Sch. of Music, N.Y.C., 1923–29; piano with James Friskin, 1923–29; composition with A. Madley Richardson 1923–29; Leopold Mannes, 1923–29; George Wedge, 1923–29; Rubin Goldmark, 1923–29. Married Dec. 28, 1946, to Helen Thomas, harpist; one son. Member of ASCAP; AFM, Local 802; ALA; Dramatists Guild; American Radio Relay League. Address: (home) 33 Lakeview Terrace, Staten Island, NY tel. (212) SA 7-5896; (bus.) c/o Radio City Music Hall, 1260 Ave. of Americas, New York, NY 10020, tel. (212) CI 6-4600.

Theatre. Mr. Irwin contributed music for the ballet scenes to *Three's a Crowd* (Selwyn, N.Y.C., Oct. 15, 1930); subsequently contributed to the score of *Hey Nonny Nonny!* (Shubert, June 6, 1932); was pianist for *Of Thee I Sing* (Imperial, May 15, 1933); pianist and musical sec. for *As Thousands Cheer* (Music Box, Sept. 30, 1933); and pianist for *Let 'Em Eat Cake* (Imperial, Oct. 21, 1933).

He contributed to the score of *Fools Rush In* (Playhouse, Dec. 25, 1934); *Earl Carroll's Sketchbook* (Winter Garden, June 4, 1935); *White Horse Inn* (Center, Oct. 1, 1936); *The Show Is On* (Winter Garden, Dec. 25, 1936); and *Sing Out the News* (Music Box, Sept. 24, 1938). He was pianist for *Hooray for What* (Winter Garden, Dec. 1, 1938); *Set to Music* (Music Box, Jan. 18, 1939); and *Streets of Paris* (Broadhurst, June 19, 1939); wrote the ballet music for *Very Warm for May* (Alvin, Nov. 17, 1939), and for *The Third Little Show* (Music Box, June 1, 1941); and was pianist for *Best Foot Forward* (Ethel Barrymore Th., Oct. 1, 1941).

He wrote the music for the ballet scenes of *Sons o' Fun* (Winter Garden, Dec. 1, 1941) and *Star and Garter* (Music Box, June 24, 1942); was pianist and wrote ballet music for *Count Me In* (Ethel Barrymore Th., Oct. 8, 1942); was musical director for *Follow the Girls* (Century, Apr. 8, 1944), *Are You with It?* (Century, Nov. 10, 1945), *What's Up?* (Natl., Nov. 11, 1945), and *If the Shoe Fits* (Century, Dec. 5, 1946); became the musical director of *Oklahoma!* (St. James, 1947), and was with the national touring company (1948–49); was musical director for *Texas Li'l Darlin'* (Mark Hellinger Th., Nov. 25, 1949); orchestrated and composed the musical score and was the musical director for *Angel in the Pawnshop* (Booth, Jan. 18, 1951); and for *The Littlest Revue* (Phoenix, May 22, 1956).

With Louis Bellson, he composed the music for *Portofino* (Adelphi, Feb. 21, 1958); with Paul Crabtree, composed the music and was choral arranger and musical director for the pageant, *The Twenty-Seventh Star* (Cooley Stadium, West Palm Beach, Fla., Mar. 1959). He was musical director of the national touring company of *South Pacific* (1951–53); became the musical director of *The King and I* (St. James, N.Y.C., 1954), and toured with the show (1954–55); was choral and musical director for Anthony Brady Farrell's Summer Th. (Sacandaga, N.Y., 1957, 1958, 1959), and musical director for four Chevrolet industrial shows. Mr Irwin serves as choral dir. (1960–to date), staff composer (1965–to date), and musical dir. (Aug. 1, 1974–to date) at Radio City Music Hall (N.Y.C.).

Radio. Mr. Irwin was pianist for Frank Sinatra's Band Box (CBS); and for Ray Sinatra (CBS).

Discography. He played the piano, composed the music, and was arranger for *Hi-Fi Harp* (1955). He was choral arranger for the album, *Kate Smith at Carnegie Hall* (1964), and vocal arranger and choral director for the album, *Merry Christmas New York from the Radio City Music Hall*, Special Souvenir Edition.

Awards. Mr. Irwin received scholarships to study at the Louisville (Ky.) Conservatory of Music (1919); the Chicago (Ill.) Conservatory (1922); and the Juilliard Sch. of Music (1923).

Recreation. Amateur radio operator (licensed 1922, call letters W2CUQ); and fishing.

ISAACSON, CARL L. Educator. b. June 14, 1920, to Martin and Petra Isaacson, Grad. Comertown (Mont.) H.S., 1939; Montana State Univ. B.A. (honors) 1943; Univ. of Denver, M.A. (radio-television) 1949; Ph.D. (rhetoric and communications) 1954; attended Univ. of Southern California, Summers 1951–52. Married Ruth Stephens; one daughter. Served WW II, US Army, rank, Maj.; received Bronze Star, Purple Heart with oak-leaf cluster. Member of Western Speech Assn.; Alpha Psi Omega; SAA; Pi Kappa Delta; National Assn. for Studies in Communication; Tau Kappa Alpha; Amer. College Public Relations Assn. Address: (home) Rt. 2, Box 56, Bozeman, MT 59715, tel. (406) 586-5612; (bus.) Director of Information, Montana State Univ., Bozeman, MT 59715, tel. (406) 994-2721.

Mr. Isaacson was head, Division of Communication, Idaho State Coll. (1961–63), where he had been a member of the faculty since 1947 (instructor in speech, debate coach, and director of radio, 1947–50; assistant professor, 1950–53; director of forensics and radio, 1950–56; associate professor of speech, 1954–59; head, Dept. of Speech-Drama, 1956–61; professor of speech and drama, 1959–63). Mr. Isaacson has conducted summer courses in communication for the Railroad Labor Inst. (1960–62); the Intl. Assn. of Machinists (1960); the Northwest Machinists Leadership Sch. (1961–62); Basic Law Enforcement Acad. (1954–62); US Army and Idaho Natl. Guard (1948–62); and USAAF (1959–62). He was appointed Director of Information, Montana State Coll. (1963).

Mr. Isaacson was a general contractor (1946–47, and a supervisor in the soil conservation program (1939–41).

Films. He appeared in *Midnight to Dawn* (1961); and while a member of the Army Special Services played Captain Fontaine in *Desert Song* (WB, 1943).

Television and Radio. He was a part-time radio announcer (KGVO, Missoula, Mont., 1941–43), director of radio and television at Idaho State Coll. (FM station, KBGL). For television, he was author with Charles Bilyeu of *Planned* (Tee-vee Studios, Beverly Hills, Calif.).

ITKIN, BELLA. Director, coach. b. Bella Davidovna Itkin, Feb. 17, 1920, Moscow, USSR; to David and Leno Itkin. Father, actor-director with Moscow Art Th. Grad. Lake View H.S., Chicago, Ill., 1938; Goodman Th., B.F.A. 1941, M.F.A. 1942; Western Reserve Univ., Ph.D. 1954. Married July 29, 1969, to Frank John Runrath. Member of ATA; CTC; ANTA; AAUP.

Miss Itkin emigrated to the US in 1932 and became a naturalized citizen in 1942. In 1944, she began teaching and directing at the Goodman Th. in Chicago, where she was head of the Children's Theatre (1959–65) and director and producer (1965–to date). Productions she directed include *The Winter's Tale* (Nov. 26, 1965) and *The Eccentricities of a Nightingale* (Feb. 5, 1967); and, For Children's Th. Co., *Rumpelstiltskin* (Oct. 11, 1969), *A Doctor in Spite of Himself* (Mar. 28, 1970), *Ali Baba and the Magic Cave* (Nov. 21, 1970); *Appleseed* (Jan. 26, 1974), *The Popcorn Man* (June 24, 1974), and *The Prince, the Wolf, and The Firebird* (Oct. 19, 1974).

Miss Itkin has also worked with television programs for Channel 11 and CBS (Chicago); and has directed for summer stock (Lake Zurich, Ill.). In 1960 she taught theatre courses (Kansas Univ.).

Recreation. Music, art.

IVES, ANNE. Actress. b. circa 1892, Providence, R.I. Professional training at Amer. Acad. of Dramatic Arts. Address: 1 W. 72nd St., New York, NY 10023, tel. (212) TR 3-4169.

Theatre. Miss Ives made her debut as Rita Nichols in *The Chorus Lady* (Savoy Th., N.Y.C., Sept. 1, 1906) and had an active theatrical career until World War I, when she went into other work in Washington, D.C. She returned to the stage following her retirement.

She toured as Nannie in *Black Chiffon* (opened Hartman Th., Columbus, Ohio, Oct. 8, 1951; closed Locust St. Th., Philadelphia, Pa., Nov. 3, 1951); replaced (1952) Madeleine King as Miss Marble in *Point of No Return* (Alvin Th., N.Y.C., Dec. 13, 1951) and toured as Esther Gray in the same play (opened Ford's Th., Baltimore, Md., Nov. 24, 1952; closed Biltmore, Los Angeles, Calif., May 23, 1953). She was Rebecca Nurse in *The Crucible* (Martinique, N.Y.C., Mar. 11, 1958); Mrs. Emily Hilburt in *Masquerade* (John Golden Th., Mar. 16, 1959); and was Phoebe in a revival of *Her Master's Voice* (41 St. Th., Dec. 26, 1964).

Miss Ives also played Miss Juliana Tesman in *Hedda Gabler* (Stratford Festival, Stratford, Ontario, Canada, June 10, 1970); the Carpet Dealer's Wife in *The Good Woman of Setzuan* (Vivian Beaumont Th., Nov. 5, 1970); was in *Wipe-Out Games* (Arena Stage, Washington, D.C., Apr. 9, 1971); toured (1971–72) as Nanny in *The Effect of Gamma Rays on Man-in-the-Moon Marigolds*; was standby for Lillian Gish as Marina and Cathleen Nesbitt as Mrs. Voinitsky in *Uncle Vanya* (Circle in the Square/Joseph E. Levine Th., N.Y.C., June 4, 1973); played Old Mrs. Ewbank in *The Contractor* (Chelsea Th. Ctr., Brooklyn, N.Y., Oct. 17, 1973); and the Doctor's Widow and the Fragile Lady in *Ice Age* (Chelsea Th. Ctr., Nov. 18, 1975).

Films. Miss Ives appeared in *The Producers* (Embassy, 1968).

Radio. Miss Ives was on the serial Young Widder Brown.

Awards. She was nominated by the Los Angeles (Calif.) Drama Critics Circle as best supporting actress for her performance in *The Effect of Gamma Rays on Man-in-the-Moon Marigolds*.

IVES, BURL. Actor, singer, writer. b. Burl Icle Ivanhoe Ives, Jun. 14, 1909, Hunt City Township, Jasper County, Ill., to Frank and Cordella Ives. Father, contractor. Grad. Newton (Ill.) H.S.; attended Eastern Ill. State Teachers Coll.; Juilliard Sch. of Music, N.Y.C. Married Dec. 6, 1945, to Helen Peck Ehrlich, concert manager (marr. dis. 1971); one son; married April 7, 1971, to Dorothy Koster. Served in USAAF; rank, Sgt.

Pre-Theatre. After college, Mr. Ives became a vagabond, working at various jobs to earn a living-playing professional football, traveling with a tent show, and singing as a lead for an evangelist's choir. With all of this experience, he acquired a wealth of folk music.

Theatre. He appeared as the Tailor's Apprentice in *The Boys from Syracuse* (Alvin, N.Y.C., Nov. 23, 1938); after his induction into the army, as Pvt. Burl Ives in *This Is the Army* (Bway Th., July 4, 1942), and toured with the show; performed in the musical *Sing Out, Sweet Land!* (Intl., Dec. 27, 1944); played Squire Hardcastle in the NY City Theatre Co. production of *She Stoops to Conquer* (NY City Ctr., Dec. 28, 1949); Ben Rumson in a touring company of *Paint Your Wagon* (opened Hartman, Columbus, Ohio, Oct. 2, 1952; closed Blackstone, Chicago, Ill., Jan. 31, 1953); Captain Andy in *Show Boat* (NY City Ctr., May 5, 1954); Big Daddy in *Cat on a Hot Tin Roof* (Morosco, Mar. 24, 1955); the title role in *Joshua Beene and God* (Dallas Th. Ctr., Tex., Dec. 12, 1961); and Dr. Leonard Cook in *Dr. Cook's Garden* (Belasco, N.Y.C., Sept. 25, 1967).

Films. Mr. Ives has appeared in *Smoky* (20th-Fox, 1946); *Green Grass of Wyoming* (20th-Fox, 1948); *Station West* (RKO, 1948); *So Dear to My Heart* (RKO, 1948); *Sierra* (U, 1950); *East of Eden* (WB, 1955); *The Power and the Prize* (MGM, 1956); *Wind Across the Everglades* (WB, 1958); *Desire Under the Elms* (Par., 1958); *Cat on a Hot Tin Roof* (MGM, 1958); *The Big Country* (UA, 1958); *Day of the Outlaw* (UA, 1959); *Our Man in Havana* (Col., 1960); *Let No Man Write My Epitaph* (Col., 1960); *The Spiral Road* (UA, 1962); *Summer Magic* (BV, 1963); *The Brass Bottle* (U, 1964); *Ensign Pulver* (WB, 1964); did the voice of Father Neptune in *The Daydreamer* (Embassy, 1966); played P. T. Barnum in *Those Fantastic Flying Fools* (AI, 1967); and appeared in *The McMasters* (Chebron, 1971).

Television and Radio. He has performed on radio with his own show *The Wayfaring Stranger.* On television, he has appeared on the Perry Como Show (NBC); the Red Skelton Show (CBS); Person to Person (CBS); Bell Telephone Hour (NBC); Dinah Shore Show (NBC); GE Th. (CBS); the Dick Powell Th. (NBC); the Bell Telephone Hour (NBC); GE Fantasy Hour (NBC); OK Crackerby! (ABC); Walt Disney's World (NBC); the Andy Williams Show (NBC); Zane Grey Th. (CBS); The Name of the Game (NBC); Hallmark Hall of Fame (NBC); Daniel Boone (NBC); Alias Smith and Jones (ABC); Night Gallery (NBC); The Bold Ones (NBC); and *The Man Who Wanted To Live Forever* (ABC).

Published Works. His published works include *The Wayfaring Stranger,* an autobiography (1948); *Sailing on a Very Fine Day* (1954); *Tales of America* (1954); *Burl Ives' Song Book* (1953); *Burl Ives' Sea Songs* (1956); *Burl Ives' Book of Irish Songs* (1958); *America's Musical Heritage-Song in America* (1962); *A Wayfarer's Note Book* (1962); *Albad the Oaf* (1965); and *More Burl Ives' Songs* (1966).

Discography. His recordings include *The Wild Side of Life* (Decca); *Songs For and About Men* (Decca); *Coronation Concert* (Decca); *In the Quiet of the Night* (Decca); *Women—Folk Songs about the Fair Sex* (Decca); *Down to the Sea in Ships* (Decca); *Burl Ives Sings for Fun* (Decca); *Songs of Ireland* (Decca); *Cheers* (Decca); *Captain Burl Ives' Ark* (Decca); *Australian Folk Songs* (Decca); *Christmas Eve with Burl Ives* (Decca); *Old Time Varieties* (Decca); *Songs of the West* (Decca); *The Versatile Burl Ives* (Decca); *Funny Way of Laughin'* (Decca); *Sunshine in My Soul* (Hymns); *Burl* (Decca); *The Best of Burl's for Boys and Girls* (Decca); *Singin' Easy* (Decca); *The Best of Burl* (Decca); *Lonesome Train* (Decca); *True Love* (Decca); *Burl Ives' Animal Folk* (Disneyland); *Burl Ives' Talk Lullabies* (Disneyland); *Great American Poems* (Disneyland); *Burl Ives Presents America's Musical Heritage* (Grolier); *Songs I Sang in Sunday School* (World); *Burl Ives & the Korean Orphan Choir Sing of Faith & Joy* (World); *The Wayfaring Stranger* (Col.); *Return of the Wayfaring Stranger* (Col.); *Burl Ives Sings "Little White Duck"* and *Other Children's Favorites* (Col.); *Ballads* (United Artists); *Burl Ives Sings Irving Berlin* (United Artists); and *Manhattan Troubador* (United Artists).

Awards. Mr. Ives received the Donaldson Award (1945) for his performance in *Sing Out, Sweet Land!* an Academy (Oscar) Award (1958) for his performance in *The Big Country;* and a NARAS (Grammy) Award for his recording *Funny Way of Laughin'* (1962).

IZENOUR, GEORGE. Theatre designer and engineering consultant. b. George Charles Izenour, July 24, 1912, New Brighton, Pa., to Charles S. and Wilhelmina F. Izenour. Father, electrical contractor. Grad. Mansfield H.S., Ohio, 1930; Wittenberg Coll., A.B. 1934, M.A. 1936. Married 1937 to Hildegard H. Izenour; one son. Served as research engineer, Office of Scientific Research & Development, US Government, 1943–46. Member of Amer. Inst. of Electrical and Electronic Engineers; Amer. Assn. for Advancement of Science; NY Acad. of Sciences; Conn. Acad. of Arts and Sciences.

Since 1961, Mr. Izenour has been professor of Theatre Design and Technology at Yale Univ. Sch. of Drama. He founded the research laboratory in technical theatre at Yale Univ. in 1939. Previously, he was director of drama at Wittenberg Coll. (Springfield, Ohio, 1934–36); director of lighting at Federal Th. (WPA) Project (Los Angeles, Calif., 1937–38); technical director at Federal Th. (WPA) Project (San Francisco World's Fair, Calif., 1939).

Mr. Izenour is the inventor of the electronic console for theatre lighting (1947); the synchronous winch system for theatre (1958); the steel accoustical shell (1962); and holds about nineteen patents in related fields.

He has served as a design and engineering consultant for the following theatre projects realized since 1956: Art Center (Univ. of South Florida); Dallas (Tex.) Th. Center; Art Center (Univ. of Bahia, Brazil); Loeb Drama Center (Harvard Univ.); Phillips Andover Academy; Jewish Community Art Center (Hartford, Conn.); Little Carib Th. (Port of Spain, Trinidad); Goucher Coll. Arts Center; Gammage Auditorium (Ariz. State Univ.); Art Center (Univ. of New Mexico); Art Center, Fathers of the Confederation (Charlottetown, Prince Edward Is., Canada); Art Center (Macalester Coll., St. Paul, Minn.); Jesse Jones Hall for Performing Arts (Houston, Tex.); the restoration of the Chicago (Ill.) Auditorium; Municipal Auditorium (Jackson, Miss.); Loretto Hilton Art Center (Webster Coll., Webster Groves, Mo.); Milwaukee (Wis.) Performing Arts Center; Theatre Center (Woman's Coll. of the Univ. of North Carolina); Wichita (Kan.) Cultural Center; Performing Arts Hall (Univ. of Virginia); Manitoba Arts Center (Winnipeg, Canada); Brandon (Manitoba, Canada) Auditorium; Creative Arts Center (West Virginia Univ.); Krannert Center (Univ. of Ill.); Theater of Performing Arts (Ft. Wayne, Ind.); Performing Arts Hall (Civic Center, El Paso, Texas); Edwin Thomas Hall (Akron, Ohio, Univ.); Arts Center (Choate Sch., Wallingford, Conn.); Arts Center (St. Catherine Coll., St. Paul, Minn.); Sala Rios Reyna (Caracas, Venezuela); Arts Center and Longstreet Th. (Univ. of So. Carolina); remodeling of Bushnell Memorial Hall (Hartford, Conn.); Mabee Center (Oral Roberts Univ., Tulsa, Okla.); Speech Arts Building and multiple use coliseum (Washington State Univ., Pullman, Wash.).

Awards. He was a Fellow of the Rockefeller Foundation (1939–43, 1947–48); received a D.F.A. (honorary) from Wittenberg Coll. (1950); a Ford Foundation grant (1960–61); and the Rogers and Hammerstein Prize, (1962), with architect, Hugh Stubbins, for the design of Loeb Drama Center, Harvard Univ. He is the recipient of a Guggenheim Fellowship (1972–73).

Recreation. Working, listening to music, and living on an island.

J

JACKSON, ANNE. Actress. b. Anna June Jackson, Sept. 3, 1926, Allegheny, Pa., to John J. and Stella G. (Murray) Jackson. Father, beautician. Grad. Franklin K. Lane H.S., Brooklyn, N.Y., 1942; attended Neighborhood Playhouse Sch. of the Th., NYC, 1943–44; New Sch. for Social Research, NYC, Summer 1943; Actors' Studio (1948–to date). Studied acting with Herbert Berghof, Sanford Meisner, Lee Strasberg. Married Mar. 1948 to Eli Wallach, actor; one son, two daughters. Member of AEA; AFTRA; SAG. Address: 90 Riverside Dr., New York, NY 10023, tel. (212) TR 4-2225.

Theatre. Miss Jackson made her professional debut as Anya in a touring production of *The Cherry Orchard* (Sept. 1944); subsequently played Alice Stewart, in the pre-Bway tryout of *Signature* (opened Forrest, Philadelphia, Pa., Feb. 14, 1945; closed there Feb. 15, 1945); in stock at the Clinton (N.J.) Playhouse (1945); appeared with Eva Le Gallienne's American Repertory Th. (International Th. N.Y.C.) in *Henry VIII* (Nov. 6, 1946), *What Every Woman Knows* (Nov. 8, 1946), as Frida Foldal in *John Gabriel Borkman* (Nov. 12, 1946), as a Christian in *Androcles and the Lion* (Dec. 19, 1946) and Miss Blake in *Yellow Jack* (Feb. 27, 1947).

Miss Jackson played Judith in *The Last Dance* (Belasco, Jan. 27, 1948); in stock, appeared as Pat in *The Young and Fair* (Falmouth Playhouse, Mass., Summer 1948); Nellie in *Summer and Smoke* (Music Box, N.Y.C., Oct. 6, 1948); Nita in *Magnolia Alley* (Mansfield, Apr. 18, 1949); toured in *The Barretts of Wimpole Street* (West Coast, 1949); played Margaret Anderson in *Love Me Long* (48 St. Th., N.Y.C., Nov. 7, 1949); understudied Jean Arthur in the title role in *Peter Pan* (Imperial, Apr. 24, 1950); appeared as Hilda in *The Lady from the Sea* (Fulton, Aug. 7, 1950); Luka in *Arms and the Man* (Arena, Edison Hotel, Oct. 19, 1950); Coralie Jones in *Never Say Never* (Booth, Nov. 20, 1951); Mildred in *Oh, Men! Oh, Women!* (Henry Miller's Th., Dec. 17, 1953), and on tour (opened Carthay Circle, Los Angeles, Calif., April 1955).

Miss Jackson played the Daughter in *Middle of the Night* (ANTA, Feb. 8, 1956); succeeded Glynis Johns in the title role of *Major Barbara* (Martin Beck Th., Oct. 30, 1956); played Laura in *The Glass Menagerie* (Westport Country Playhouse, Conn.; John Drew Th. East Hampton, L.I., Summer 1959); and gave poetry readings at the John Drew Th. (Summer 1960).

She was Daisy in *Rhinoceros* (Longacre, N.Y.C., Jan. 9, 1961); appeared in *Brecht on Brecht* (Th. de Lys, Jan. 3, 1962); with her husband, Eli Wallach, played in a double-bill of two-character one-act plays, *The Typists and The Tiger* (Orpheum, N.Y.C., Feb. 4, 1963; London, 1964); was the Actress in *The Exercise* (Berkshire Festival, Stockbridge, Mass., Summer 1967; John Golden Th., N.Y.C., Apr. 24, 1968); Ellen Manville in *Luv* (Booth Th., Nov. 11, 1964); Molly Malloy in a revival of *The Front Page* (Ethel Barrymore Th., May 10, 1969); Ethel Rosenberg in *Inquest* (Music Box, Apr. 23, 1970); toured as Mother H, Grandmother H, Doris, and Joan in *Promenade, All!* (Summer 1971), then appearing in N.Y.C. (Alvin Th., Apr. 16, 1972); and starred with her husband in two productions of *The Waltz of the Toreadors* (Philadelphia; Eisenhower Th., Kennedy Center, Washington, D.C., national tour, and in N.Y.C. at Circle in the Square/Joseph E. Levine Th., Sept. 13, 1973.).

Films. Miss Jackson made her film debut in *So Young So Bad* (UA, 1950); subsequently appeared in *The Journey* (MGM, 1959), *Tall Story* (WB, 1960); *The Tiger Makes Out* (Col., 1967); *How To Save a Marriage and Ruin Your Life* (Col., 1968); *The Secret Life of an American Wife* (20th-Fox, 1968); *Zig-Zag* (MGM, 1970); *Lovers and Other Strangers* (Cinerama, 1970); and *Dirty Dingus Magee* (MGM, 1970).

Television. Miss Jackson appeared in *Johny Pickup* (Armstrong Circle Th., NBC, Aug. 28, 1951); *The Vanished Hours* (CBS, May 28, 1952); in several episodes of The Doctor (NBC, 1952–53); in Philco Playhouse's *The Big Deal* (NBC, July 19, 1953) and *Statute of Limitations* (NBC, Feb. 21, 1954); on *The Merry-Go-Round* (Goodyear Playhouse, NBC, Sept. 25, 1955); in *O'Hoolihan and the Leprechaun* (GE Th. CBS, June 3, 1956); with her husband, Eli Wallach, in *Lullaby* (Play of the Week, WNTA, Jan. 18, 1960); in *Cooker in the Sky* (The Untouchables, ABC, Oct. 2, 1962); *Moment of Truth* (The Defenders, CBS, Mar. 21, 1964); *Dear Friends* (CBS Playhouse, Dec. 6, 1967); *The Typists* (Hollywood Television Th., Oct. 10, 1971); on Gunsmoke (CBS, Feb. 21, 1972); Marcus Welby, M.D. (ABC, Mar. 7, 1972); in the NY Shakespeare Festival's *Sticks and Bones* (CBS, 1973); and in *Come into My Parlour* (Anglia, 1974).

Awards. Miss Jackson received the *Village Voice* Off-Bway (Obie) Award for her performance in *The Typists and The Tiger* (1962).

Recreation. Ice skating, bicycling, water colors.

JACKSON, ERNESTINE. Singer, actress. b. Sept. 18, Corpus Christi, Texas. Attended Del Mar (Texas) Coll.; Juilliard Sch. of Music (N.Y.C.); Hunter Coll. Member of AEA.

Theatre. Miss Jackson made her professional debut in the chorus of *Show Boat* (NY State Th., N.Y.C., July 19, 1966); subsequently appeared in *Finian's Rainbow* (NY City Ctr., Apr. 5, 1967); and replaced (Nov. 12, 1967) Emily Yancy in the role of Irene Malloy in *Hello Dolly* (St. James Th., Jan. 16, 1964).

She appeared in the chorus of *Applause* (Palace Th., N.Y.C., Mar. 30, 1970); *Jesus Christ Superstar* (Mark Hellinger Th., Oct. 12, 1971); played Ernestina in *Tricks* (Alvin, Jan. 8, 1973); and Ruth Younger in *Raisin* (Arena Stage, Washington, D.C., May 23, 1973; moved to 46 St. Th., N.Y.C., Oct. 18, 1973).

Awards. Miss Jackson received the Theatre World Award (1974) for her performance in *Raisin*..

JACKSON, NAGLE. Director, actor. b. Paul Nagle Jackson, Apr. 28, 1936, Seattle, Wash., to Paul J. and Gertrude (Dunn) Jackson. Father, English professor. Educ. Portsmouth (R.I.) Priory School; Whitman College, Walla Walla, Wash. Professional training at École du Mime Étienne Decroux, Paris, France; Circle-in-the-Square Directors' Workshop, N.Y.C. Married Sept. 15, 1963, to Sandra Suter; two daughters. Member of AEA. Address: (home) 2918 N. Farwell, Milwaukee, WI 53211, tel. (414) 964-6237; (bus.) Milwaukee Repertory Th., Milwaukee, WI 53202, tel. (414) 273-7121.

Theatre. Mr. Jackson made his stage debut at the Oregon Shakespeare Festival, Ashland, Ore., as Speed in *Two Gentlemen of Verona* (Aug. 1957); he appeared at the Festival again in 1958 and in 1959, when he played Feste in *Twelfth Night* and *The Maske of the New World* (July 28, 1959); the Earl of Salisbury in *King John* (July 29, 1959); Lucio in *Measure for Measure* (July 30, 1959); and Octavious Caesar in *Antony and Cleopatra* (July 31, 1959). He first appeared in N.Y.C. as the Boy in *Measure for Measure* (Shakespeare-in-the-Park, July 25, 1960) and was again at the Oregon Shakespeare Festival (Summer 1961) as the Player King in *Hamlet* (July 25), Bertram in *All's Well That Ends Well* (July 26), the Earl of Westmoreland in *Henry IV, Part I* (July 27), and Face in *The Alchemist* (Aug. 21). He performed in the cabaret revues *Dime a Dozen* (Plaza 9 Room, Hotel Plaza, N.Y.C., Oct. 18, 1962); *Struts and Frets* (Julius Monk's, Chicago, Ill., May 9, 1963); *Baker's Dozen* (Plaza 9 Room, Plaza Hotel, N.Y.C., Jan. 9, 1964); and *Bits and Pieces* (Plaza 9 Room, Oct. 6, 1964); returned to the Oregon Shakespeare Festival (Summer 1965), where he played Benedick in *Much Ado About Nothing* (July 26), Autolycus in *The Winter's Tale* (July 28), and Hume and the Lieutenant in *King Henry VI, Part 2* (July 29), and directed *Volpone* (Aug. 28).

He performed in *The Decline and Fall of the Entire World as Seen Through the Eyes of Cole Porter* (Little Fox, San Francisco, Calif., July 1966); returned to the Oregon Shakespeare Festival (Summer 1966), where he played Demetrius in *A Midsummer Night's Dream* (July 23), directed *Two Gentlemen of Verona* (July 25), and played Lewis XI in *King Henry VI, Part 3* (July 26); repeated his performance in *The Decline and Fall* . . (Huntington Hartford Th., Los Angeles, Calif., Apr. 1967); again went to the Oregon Shakespeare Festival (Summer 1967), where he directed *Pericles* (July 22), played Octavius in *Antony and Cleopatra* (July 23), and Hortensio in *The Taming of the Shrew* (July 24). At the American Conservatory Th., San Francisco, Calif., he did costumes for *Twelfth Night* (May 22, 1968); directed *Little Murders* (Jan. 1, 1969); *In White America* (Jan. 25, 1969); *Room Service* (May 28, 1969); *Little Malcolm and His Struggle Against the Eunuchs* (Apr. 23, 1970). He directed *Richard II* (Oregon Shakespeare Festival, June 29, 1970); *The Tempest* (Shakespeare Festival, Washington, D.C., July 1970); *The Miser* (Seattle Repertory Th., Seattle, Wash., Dec. 9, 1970); *The Misanthrope* (Mummers Th., Oklahoma City, Okla., Jan. 1971); *Blithe Spirit* (Hartford Stage, Hartford, Conn., Apr. 2, 1971); and *The Taming of the Shrew* (Old Globe Th., San Diego, Calif., June 1971).

In Sept. 1971, Mr. Jackson became artistic director, Milwaukee (Wis.) Repertory Th., where he directed *Cat Among the Pigeons* (Oct. 8, 1971); the English *Mystery Plays*, which he also compiled and adapted (Nov. 16, 1971); *Measure for Measure* (Feb. 11, 1972); *Journey of the Fifth Horse* (May 5, 1972); and *Two Gentlemen of Verona* (Oct. 6, 1972), all at the Todd Wehr Th. At the American Conservatory Th., San Francisco, Calif., he directed his compilation of the English *Mystery Plays* (Dec. 5, 1972), and at Milwaukee Repertory Th., he directed *All Together*, of which he was a writer (June 8, 1963); *Prisoner of the Crown* (Oct. 5, 1973); *Our Town* (Jan. 11, 1974); and *The Tragicall Historie of Doctor Faustus* (Mar. 1, 1974), again all at the Todd Wehr Th.; for Milwaukee Repertory Theater's Court Street Th., he directed *An Occasional Piece Suitable to Openings of Theaters*, which he also wrote (Apr. 25, 1974) and *Passing Charlie Greeley* (May 15, 1974); and for Milwaukee Repertory Theater's Young People's Th., he directed *The Diaries of Adam and Eve* (Oct. 23, 1973), presented in schools throughout Wisconsin.

Television. Mr. Jackson appeared as a variety performer on the Jack Paar Show (Oct. 1964).

Night Clubs. Mr. Jackson was a folk singer at Ivar's 5th Avenue, Seattle, Wash. (Nov. 1959).

Other Activities. Mr. Jackson taught acting at the American Conservatory Th., San Francisco, Calif., and the Univ. of Washington, Seattle, Wash.

Awards. Mr. Jackson was awarded a Fulbright Fellowship in 1958 and was named one of America's outstanding young men by the Junior Chamber of Commerce.

JACOBI, LOU. Actor. b. Louis Harold Jacobi, Dec. 28, 1913, Toronto, Canada, to Joseph and Fay Jacobi. Attended Jarvis Collegiate School, Toronto. Married July 15, 1957, to Ruth Ludwin. Member of AEA; SAG; AFTRA. Address: 240 Central Park, S., New York, NY 10019.

Pre-Theatre. Drama director of the Toronto Y.M.H.A. (1940).

Theatre. Mr. Jacobi made his stage debut as the Young Hero in *The Rabbi and the Priest* (Princess Th., Toronto, Can., 1924); his professional debut in the revue, *Spring Thaw* (Museum Th., Toronto, 1949); his London debut as Morris Rosenberg in *Remains to Be Seen* (Her Majesty's, Dec. 16, 1952); was standby for Sam Levene as Nathan Detroit and played Liver Lips Louie in *Guys and Dolls* (Coliseum, May 28, 1953); appeared as Ludlow Lowell in *Pal Joey* (Prince's Mar. 31, 1954); played Father Abraham in "Bontche Schweig," Rabbi David in "A Tale of Chelm" and the Russian Tutor in "The High School," in *The World of Sholom Aleichem* (Embassy, Jan. 11, 1955); and Miller in *Into Thin Air* (Streatham Hill, May 2, 1955).

Mr. Jacobi made his Bway debut as Mr. Van Daan in *The Diary of Anne Frank* (Cort. Oct. 5, 1955), and toured in the role (1957–58); played Schlissel in *The Tenth Man* (Booth, N.Y.C., Nov. 5, 1959); Mr. Baker in *Come Blow Your Horn* (Brooks Atkinson Th., Feb. 22, 1961); Lionel Z. Governor in *Fade Out—Fade In* (Mark Hellinger Th., May 26, 1964; re-opened Feb. 15, 1965); Walter Hollander in *Don't Drink the Water* (Morosco, Nov. 17, 1966); Max Krieger in *A Way of Life* (ANTA, began previews Jan. 18, 1969; closed Feb. 1, 1969, before official opening); Ben Chambers in *Norman, Is That You?* (Lyceum, Feb. 19, 1970); Epstein in "Epstein" and Tzuref in "Eli, the Fanatic" in *Unlikely Heroes* (three plays by Phillip Roth, Plymouth, Oct. 26, 1971); and replaced (Fall 1973) Sam Levene as Al Lewis in *The Sunshine Boys* (Shubert, Dec. 27, 1972), subsequently playing the role on tour (Summer 1974).

Films. Mr. Jacobi made his debut as Blackie Isaacs in the British film *A Kid for 2 Farthings* (Lopert, 1956); subsequently appearing as Mr. Van Daan in *The Diary of Anne Frank* (20th-Fox, 1959); the manager of Franz Liszt in *Song Without End* (Col., 1960); Moustache in *Irma La Douce* (UA, 1963); Papa Leo in *The Last of the Secret Agents?* (Par., 1966); Ducky in *Penelope* (MGM, 1966); the Judge in *Little Murders* (20th-Fox, 1971); and Sam in *Everything You Always Wanted to Know About Sex But Were Afraid to Ask* (UA, 1972).

Television and Radio. In England, he performed on the radio program, Mid-Day Music Hall (BBC, 1953–54); and made his television debut on The Rheingold Theatre (BBC, 1954).

On US television, he has appeared on Douglas Fairbanks, Jr. Presents (NBC); Playhouse 90 (CBS); *Volpone* (Play of the Week, WNTA, 1960); the Milton Berle Show (NBC); The Texan (CBS); The Defenders (CBS); Trials of O'Brien (CBS); Alfred Hitchcock Presents (CBS); The Nurses (CBS); Sam Benedict (NBC); the Tonight Show (NBC); That's Life (ABC); That Girl (ABC); Love, American Style (ABC); Man from U.N.C.L.E. (NBC); Make Room for Granddaddy (ABC); The Judge and Jake Wyler (NBC); and was a regular (Mr. Kapopolis) on the Dean Martin Show (CBS, 1971–73).

Night Clubs. Mr. Jacobi has performed at Ciro's (London, Dec. 1951), and at a command performance at the London Palladium (1952).

JACOBS, MORRIS. General business manager, producer. b. May 29, 1906, New York City, to Abraham and Ella (Buchrard) Jacobs. Father, fruit wholesaler. Attended Eastern District H.S., Brooklyn, two years. Married June 10, 1927, to Beatrice Goldhaber; one son, one daughter. Member of ATPAM, The Lambs.

Theatre. From 1925–41, Mr. Jacobs was associated with Sam H. Harris productions, as assistant manager for *Cradle Snatchers* (Music Box Th., N.Y.C., Sept. 7, 1925); *Easy Come, Easy Go (Biltmore, Oct. 26, 1925); The Cocoanuts* (Lyric, Dec. 8, 1925); *The Donovan Affair* (Fulton, Aug. 30, 1926); *We Americans* (Harris, Oct. 2, 1926); *Chicago* (Music Box, Dec. 30, 1926); *The Spider* (46 St. Th., Feb. 27, 1928); *Animal Crackers* (44 St. Th., Oct. 23, 1928); and *The Big Fight* (Majestic, Sept. 18, 1928).

He was manager for *Congai* (Harris, Nov. 27, 1928); *The Marriage Bed* (Booth, Jan. 7, 1929); *The Amourous Antic* (Masque, Dec. 2, 1929); assistant manager for *Once in a Lifetime* (Music Box, Sept. 24, 1930); manager for *Oh, Promise Me* (Morosco, Nov. 24, 1930); *Just to Remind You* (Broadhurst, Sept. 7, 1931); *Of Thee I Sing* (Music Box, Dec. 26, 1931); general manager for *Here Today* (Ethel Barrymore Th., Sept. 6, 1932); assistant manager for *Dinner at eight* (Music Box, Oct. 22, 1932); manager for *Face the Music* (44 St. Th., Jan. 31, 1933); assistant manager for *June Moon* (Broadhurst, May 15, 1933); *As Thousands Cheer* (Music Box, Sept. 30, 1933); and manager for *Let 'Em Eat Cake* (Imperial, Oct. 21, 1933); assistant manager for *Merrily We Roll Along* (Music Box, Sept. 29, 1934); manager for *Rain* (Music Box, Feb. 12, 1935); general manager for *Jubilee* (Imperial, Oct. 12, 1935); was assistant manager for *First Lady* (Music Box, Nov. 26, 1935); *Stage Door* (Music Box, Oct. 22, 1936); general manager for *Night Must Fall* (Ethel Barrymore Th., Sept. 28, 1936); *I'd Rather Be Right* (Alvin, Nov. 2, 1937); assistant manager for *Of Mice and Men* (Music Box, Nov. 23, 1937); general manager for *The Fabulous Invalid* (Broadhurst, Oct. 8, 1938); *The American Way* (Center, July 17, 1939); *The Man Who Came to Dinner* (Music Box, Oct. 16, 1939); *George Washington Slept Here* (Lyceum, Oct. 18, 1940); and *Lady in the Dark* (Alvin, Jan. 23, 1941).

Mr. Jacobs was general manager for *The Land Is Bright* (Music Box, Oct. 28, 1941); *The Connecticut Yankee* (Martin Beck Th., Nov. 17, 1943); *I Remember Mama* (Music Box, Oct. 19, 1944); *You Can't Take It with You* (NY City Ctr., Mar. 26, 1945); *Annie Get Your Gun* (Imperial, May 16, 1946); *Happy Birthday* (Broadhurst, Oct. 31, 1946); *John Loves Mary* (Booth, Feb. 4, 1947); *South Pacific* (Majestic, Apr. 7, 1949); *The Happy Time* (Plymouth, Jan. 24, 1950); *Burning Bright* (Broadhurst, Oct. 18, 1950); *The King and I* (St. James, Mar. 29, 1951); *Me and Juliet* (Majestic, May 28, 1953); *Pipe Dream* (Shubert, Nov. 30, 1955); *The Flower Drum Song* (St. James, Dec. 1, 1958); and *No Strings* (54 St. Th., Mar. 15, 1962). He produced, with Jerome Whyte, *Avanti!* (Booth Th., Jan. 31, 1968).

He was general manager for the touring companies of *Show Boat* (1943–44) and *Oklahoma!* (1944–45); and business manager of Sam H. Harris' Music Box Th. in N.Y.C. (1937–54).

Recreation. Golf, fishing, photography.

JACOBSON, IRVING. Actor, producer. b. 1905, Cincinnati, Ohio, to Joseph and Elizabeth Jacobson. Father, actor; mother, actress. Attended P.S. 20, N.Y.C. Married 1929, to Mae Schoenfeld, actress; one son. Member of AEA; Hebrew Actors' Union.

Theatre. Since the 1920's, Mr. Jacobson has been associated with the Yiddish Th. in N.Y.C. He appeared in *Abi Gezunt* (1949); produced and appeared in *Mazeltov, Molly* (Second Ave. Th., Sept. 30, 1950); *Don't Worry* (Second Ave. Th., Oct. 13, 1951); *Girl of My Dreams* (Second Ave. Th., Dec. 29, 1952), which he also co-directed; *Wish Me Luck* (Second Ave. Th., Dec. 1954); appeared in *It's a Funny World* (Downtown Natl. Th., Oct. 20, 1956); and produced, with Julius Adler, *Go Fight City Hall,* in which he played Naftula (Mayfair, Nov. 12, 1961).

Mr. Jacobson made his Bway debut as Mr. Foreman in *Enter Laughing* (Henry Miller's Th., Mar. 13, 1963); played Sancho Panza in *Man of La Mancha* (Goodspeed Opera House, East Haddam, Conn., June 24, 1965); the Postmaster in *Purple Dust* (Goodspeed Opera House, July 22, 1965); and played Sancho Panza in the N.Y.C. production of *Man of La Mancha* (ANTA Th., Nov. 22, 1965), which he repeated in a revival (Vivian Beaumont Th., June 22, 1972).

Films. Mr. Jacobson was in *The Art of Love* (U, 1965).

Television. Mr. Jacobson appeared on the U.S. Steel Hour (CBS, 1961) and on Memory Lane (Ind., 1965–66).

JACOBSON, SOL. Press representative. b. Sol A. Jacobson, July 3, 1912, Harrisburg, Pa., to Morris E. and Fanny (Klein) Jacobson. Father, merchant. Grad. William Penn H.S., 1930; attended Dartmouth Coll., 1930–33. Married June 14, 1935, to Barbara Scott, actress (dec. Apr. 9, 1972); two daughters; Jan. 1, 1973, to Barbara S. Sprogull. Served US Army, 1944–45; received Purple Heart, presidential unit citation, (29th Div.); rank, Sgt. Member of ATPAM (bd. of gov., 1956–57; chmn. press agent's chapter, 1963–64); Wilderness Society; Wrightstown, Pa., Friends Meeting; Players Club. Address: (home) 264 Windy Bush Rd., New Hope, PA 18938, tel. (215) 862-5458; (bus.) 229 W. 42nd St., New York, NY 10036, tel. (212) CH 4-1482.

Pre-Theatre. Worked with the American Friends Service Committee.

Theatre. Mr. Jacobson was press representative for Hedgerow Th. (Moylan, Pa., 1933–37); Chase Barn (Whitefield, N.H., 1937); was associated with the Shubert Press Dept. (1937); the George Abbott Press Dept. (1938–39); and Richard Maney (1939–44); was press representative for Bucks County Playhouse (New Hope, Pa., 1939–40); and McCarter Th. (Princeton, N.J., Summer 1943).

He served as press representative for *Three To Make Ready* (1946); in 1947, *Winners and Losers, The Deputy of Paris, The Heiress, Man and Superman, Our Lan', Washington Square,* and *Message for Margaret;* in 1948, *Summer and Smoke;* in 1949, *Man and Superman, The Velvet Glove, The Ivy Green,* and *The Happiest Years;* in 1951, *The Constant Wife,* and *Twilight Walk;* at NY City Ctr. (1951–52), *The Wild Duck, Anna Christie, Come of Age, The Male Animal,* and *To Be Continued;* in 1953, for the National Th. of Greece, *Electra* and *Oedipus Tyrannus;* also in 1953, *Maggie,* and *The Teahouse of the August Moon;* in 1954, *One Eye Closed,* and *Libby Holman's Blues Ballads and Sin-Songs;* in 1955, *Tonight in Samarkand, A Roomful of Roses,* and *No Time for Sergeants;* in 1956, *The Man with the Golden Arm, Purple Dust,* the doublebill of *The Dark Lady of the Sonnets* and *The Admirable Bashville,* and the tour of *Teahouse of the August Moon;* in 1957, *Career,* and *I Knock at the Door;* in 1958, *The Crucible, The Time of the Cuckoo,* the tour of *Warm Peninsula, A Party with Betty Comden and Adolph Green, Cock-a-Doodle Dandy,* the pre-Bway tryout of *A Swim in the Sea, Blue Denim, The Entertainer, Look Back in Anger, Bonds of Interest, Endgame,* and *The Saturday Night Kid.*

In 1959, Mr. Jacobson was press representative for *A Clearing in the Woods, Sweet Bird of Youth, Warm Peninsula, Fiorello! Tall Story,* and *Time of Vengeance;* in 1960, *Earnest in Love, Gay Divorce, Tenderloin, Under the Sycamore Tree,* and *West Side Story;* in 1961, *A Call on Kuprin, Write Me a Murder, Take Her, She's Mine, Elsa Lancaster—Herself, Two for Fun,* and *Donnybrook!;* in 1962, *The Night Is Black Bottles, Black Monday,* the pre-Bway tryout of *Get on Board—the Jazz Train, A Funny Thing Happened on the Way to the Forum,* and *The Aspern Papers;* in 1963, *She Loves Me,* and *A Wilde Evening with Shaw;* was national press representative, American Shakespeare Festival, Stratford, Conn., (1963–72); and was press representative for *Fiddler on the Roof* (1964–72).

In 1965, Mr. Jacobson was press representative for *Diamond Orchid, A Race of Hairy Men, Shout From the Rooftops,* and *On the Necessity of Being Polygamous;* in 1966, *Generation, The Right Honourable Gentleman,* and the national company of *Fiddler on the Roof;* in 1967, *A Joyful Noise,* and *To Bury a Cousin;* in 1968, *Loot, New Faces of 68,* and Theatre Institute of Childe (Barbizon-Plaza); in 1969, *Red, White and Maddox,* Lincoln Center Festival with Companie de Théâtre de la Cité de Villeurbanne and Belgrade's Atelje 212 in Vivian Beaumont and Forum theatres; *The Three Musketeers, George Dandin,* and *Tartuffe;* also in 1969, *The Progress of Bora, The Tailor, Ubu Roi, Who's Afraid of Virginia Woolf?,* and *Victor, or the Children Take Over;* in 1970; *Harvey* at ANTA, *Arena Conta Zumbi, The Brownstone Urge, I Dreamt I Dwelt in Bloomingdale's, Dark of The Moon, Not Now, Darling, The School for Wives, Three by Ferlinghetti, The Trial of the Catonsville Nine,* and *The Homecoming* (Bijou); in 1971, *Murderous Angels, Divorce of Judy and Jane,* and *One for the Money;* in 1972, City Center Acting Company's *School for Scandal, USA, The Hostage, Women Beware Women, Lower Depths, Next Time I'll Sing to You;* in 1973, *Children of the Wind, A Streetcar Named Desire* (St. James Th.), City Center Company's *The Three Sisters, The Beggar's Opera, Measure for Measure, Scapin.* In addition, Mr. Jacobson was press representative for Equity Library Th. (1970–74) and for CSC Repertory Company's 1973–74 season at Abbey Th., N.Y.C.

Recreation. Dogs (Welsh Corgis), gardening, travel, reading.

JAFFE, SAM. Actor. b. Samuel Jaffe, Mar. 8, 1893, New York City, to Bernard and Ada (Steinberg) Jaffe. Grad. City Coll. of New York, B.S.; attended Columbia Univ. (engineering). Married Nov. 15, 1925, to Lillian Taiz, actress (dec. Feb. 28, 1941); married June 7, 1956, to Bettye Ackerman, actress. Served US Army Engineers, 1918; rank, Pvt. Member of AEA (council, 1940–50); SAG; AFTRA. Address: 302 N. Alpine Dr., Beverly Hills, CA 94710.

Theatre. Mr. Jaffe made his N.Y.C. debut as understudy with the Washington Sq. Players for the part of Thaddeus Trask in *The Clod* (Bandbox, 1915), and appeared in the part at a matinee; toured with the Washington Sq. Players (1916); and with the Elsie Herndon Kearns-George Sommes Shakespearean Co. (1917); with the Washington Sq. Players, played the Minister in *Youth* (Comedy, N.Y.C., Feb. 20, 1918), and Rev. Samuel Gardner in *Mrs. Warren's Profession* (Comedy, Mar. 11, 1918); and Kristensen in *Samson and Delilah* (Greenwich Village Th., Nov. 17, 1920).

He made his Bway debut as Leibush in *The Idle Inn* (Plymouth, Dec. 20, 1921); subsequently played Reb Ali in *The God of Vengeance* (Provincetown Playhouse, Dec. 20, 1922); Izzy Goldstein in *The Main Line* (Klaw, Mar. 25, 1924); Eli Iskowvitch in *Izzy* (Broadhurst, Sept. 16, 1924); Lum Crowder in *Ruint* (Provincetown Playhouse, Apr. 7, 1925); Yudelson in *The Jazz Singer* (Fulton, Sept. 14, 1925), toured with it (1926); played Job in Horace M. Kallen's version of the book of Job as a Greek tragedy (1926); played in the return engagement of *The Jazz Singer* (Century, N.Y.C., Apr. 18, 1927); played Kringelein in *Grand Hotel* (Natl., Nov. 13, 1930), and toured with it (1931); appeared as Herschkowitz in *The Bride of Torozko* (Henry Miller's Th., N.Y.C., Sept. 19, 1934); the Adversary in the Max Reinhardt production of *The Eternal Road* (Manhattan Opera House, Jan. 17, 1937); Nils Krogstad in *A Doll's House* (Morosco, Dec. 27, 1937); Shylock in *The Merchant of Venice* (Pennsylvania State College, 1938); Jonah Goodman in *The Gentle People* (Belasco Th., N.Y.C., Jan. 5, 1939); and the title role in *King Lear* (New School of Social Research, 1941).

Mr. Jaffe toured as Rosenbaum in *The King's Maid;* played Hymie in *Cafe Crown* (Cort, N.Y.C., Jan. 23, 1942); played Svoboda in *Thank You, Svoboda* (Mansfield, Mar. 1, 1944); Khan Mirza Siraj-Uddin in the pre-Bway tryout *The Greatest of These* (opened Shubert-Lafayette, Detroit, Mich., Feb. 18, 1947; closed Selwyn, Chicago, Ill., Mar. 15, 1947); Dr. Wouterson in *This Time Tomorrow* (Ethel Barrymore Th., N.Y.C., Nov. 3, 1947); and the title role in Obey's *Noah* (White Barn, Westport, Conn., 1949).

He appeared in the title role of *Tartuffe* (Brattle, Cambridge, Mass., 1950); and repeated the role (Ivar, Hollywood, Calif., 1952). In stock played Paul Virag in his translation of Molnar's *Delilah,* which he retitled *The Blue Danube* (Bucks County Playhouse, New Hope, Pa., Summer 1952); appeared as Gourette in *Mademoiselle Colombe* (Longacre, N.Y.C., Jan. 6, 1954); Peter Sorin in *The Seagull* (Phoenix, May 11, 1954); and the Inquisitor in the pre-Bway tour of *Saint Joan* (opened Natl., Washington, D.C., Sept. 20, 1954; closed Hartman, Columbus, Ohio, Nov. 6, 1954); toured as Cauchon in the national company of *The Lark* (1956); and played Zero in *The Adding Machine* (Phoenix, Feb. 9, 1956); Jonas Astorg in *The Reclining Figure* (Roosevelt Playhouse, Miami, Fla., 1956); Dr. Waldersee in *Idiot's Delight* (Ahmanson Th., Los Angeles, Calif., 1970); Shylock in *The Merchant of Venice* (Dickinson State Coll., Dickinson, N.D., Oct. 1971); and Abel Shaddick in *Storm in Summer* (Off-Broadway Th., San Diego, Cal., 1973).

Films. Mr. Jaffe appeared as Grand Duke Peter in *The Scarlet Empress* (Par., 1934); Lurie in *We Live Again* (UA, 1934); the Grand Lama in *Lost Horizon* (Col., 1937); the title role in *Gunga Din* (RKO, 1939); as himself in *Stage-Door Canteen* (UA, 1943); Mayor Galimard in *13, Rue Madeleine* (20th-Fox, 1946); the Professor in *Gentleman's Agreement* (20th-Fox, 1947); the Laboratory Technician in *Accused* (Par., 1948); Dr. Francis Hunter in *Rope of Sand* (Par., 1949); Dr. Riedenschneider in *The Asphalt Jungle* (MGM, 1950); Mr. Garver in *Under The Gun* (U, 1950); Sam Cooper in *I Can Get It for You Wholesale* (20th-Fox, 1951); Dr. Barnhardt in *The Day the Earth Stood Still* (20th-Fox, 1951); Sam Cooper in Georges Clouzot's French film, *Les Espions* (1957); Henry Hueskin in *The Barbarian and the Geisha* (20th-Fox, 1958); Simonides in *Ben Hur* (MGM, 1959); in a cameo in *A Guide for the Married Man* (20th-Fox, 1967); as Father Joseph in *Guns for San Sebastian* (MGM, 1968); Brother Lilac in *The Great Bank Robbery* (WB, 1969); Old Whateley in *The Dunwich Horror* (Amer. Internat., 1970); the Old Man in *The Telltale Heart* (Amer. Film Inst., 1971); and Bookman in *Bedknobs and Broomsticks* (Walt Disney, 1971).

Television. Mr. Jaffe appeared in *The Dingaling Girl* (Playhouse 90, CBS, Feb. 26, 1959); *Lepke* (Desilu Playhouse, CBS, Nov. 20, 1959); two episodes of Alfred Hitchcock Presents (CBS); The Sound of Trumpets (Playhouse 90, CBS, Feb. 9, 1960); *In the Presence of Mine Enemies* (Playhouse 90, CBS, May 18, 1960); *Legend of Lovers* (Play of the Week, Oct. 10, 1960); *No Sale* (The Law and Mr. Jones, ABC, Dec. 2, 1960); *The Terrible Clockman*

(Shirley Temple Th., NBC, Jan. 29, 1961); The Untouchables (ABC, Feb. 9, 1961); *An Economy of Death* (Naked City, ABC, May 3, 1961); the Robert Herridge Th.; The Westerner; The Defenders (CBS); *Final Judgment* (Cain's Hundred, NBC, Dec. 19, 1961); and he played Dr. Zorba on Ben Casey (ABC, 1961–65). Mr. Jaffe also appeared as Gandhi on Perspective in Greatness; was on Daniel Boone (NBC, Dec. 9, 1965); *Quarantined* (World Premiere, ABC, Feb. 24, 1970); *The Old Man Who Cried Wolf* (Movie of the Week); *Sam Hill* (Movie of the Week, NBC, Feb. 1, 1971); Bonanza (NBC); three episodes of Alias Smith and Jones (ABC, 1971); *Enemies* (Hollywood Television Th., Nov. 11, 1971); Love American Style (ABC, 1972); Owen Marshall, Counsellor at Law (ABC, 1972); the Andy Williams Show; *Next Year in Jerusalem* (CBC); the television special *Saga of Sonora;* the television movie *QB VII;* and the pilots Ghost Story (NBC, 1972), Milk and Honey, and Night Gallery (NBC, Nov. 8, 1969).

Other Activities. Mr. Jaffe was dean of mathematics, Bronx Cultural Institute, N.Y.C., in 1915–16. With George Freedley, he founded the Equity Library Theatre in 1944.

Awards. Mr. Jaffe received the Venice Film Festival International Award for best male performance of the year, the M.W.A. Edgar Allen Poe Award, the Brazilian Award, and an Academy (Oscar) Award nomination for best supporting actor for his performance as Dr. Riedenschneider in *The Asphalt Jungle* (1950). He was nominated for a NATAS (Emmy) Award for his performance as Dr. Zorba on Ben Casey (1961–62) and received the Townsend Harris Medal for notable achievement (1962). Since 1966, he has been represented in the Movieland Wax Museum, Buena Park, Calif. He received the James K. Hackett Medal (1971) and the City College of the City Univ. of New York's 125th anniversary medal (Oct. 20, 1973).

JAMES, CLIFTON. Actor. b. May 29, 1921, Spokane, Wash., to Harry and Grace (Dean) James. Father, journalist; mother, teacher. Grad. Univ. of Oregon, B.A. 1950. Studied at Actors Studio (member, 1956–to date). Married Nov. 1950 to Laurie Harper, writer; two sons, three daughters. Served US Army, Infantry, PTO; rank, Sgt.; awarded Silver Star, Purple Heart. Member of AEA; SAG; AFTRA; The Players; Univ. of Oregon Alumni Club. Address: 95 Buttonwood Dr., Dix Hills, NY 11746.

Theatre. Mr. James made his debut as the First Cop in *The Time of Your Life* (NY City Ctr., Jan. 19, 1955); played Robert Kensington in *Career* (Seventh Ave. S. Playhouse, Apr. 30, 1957); the Wrecking Crew Boss in *The Cave Dwellers* (Bijou, Oct. 19, 1957); the First Roustabout in *J. B.* (ANTA, Dec. 11, 1958); Blick in *The Time of Your Life* (Brussels World's Fair, Belgium, 1958–59); Michaud in the ANTA Matinee Series production of *Sweet Confession,* presented with *I Rise in Flame, Cried the Phoenix* (Th. de Lys, N.Y.C., Apr. 14, 1959); Willie Stark in *All the King's Men* (E. 74 St. Th., Oct. 15, 1959); and Clem in *The Long Dream* (Ambassador, Feb. 17, 1960).

With the American Shakespeare Festival (Stratford, Conn.), he played Antonio in *Twelfth Night* (June 8, 1960), Stephano in *The Tempest* (June 19, 1960), and Pompey in *Antony and Cleopatra* (July 31, 1960); appeared as Ralph Follet in *All the Way Home* (Belasco, N.Y.C., Nov. 30, 1960); Brennan Farrell in *Great Day in the Morning* (Henry Miller's Th., Mar. 28, 1962); Polly Baker in *A Man's a Man* (Masque, Sept. 19, 1962); the Carpenter in *Andorra* (Biltmore, Feb. 9, 1963); Bottom in the NY Shakespeare Festival touring production of *A Midsummer Night's Dream* (June 26–Aug. 29, 1964); U. S. Grant in *The Last Days of Lincoln* (Library of Congress, Washington, D.C., Apr. 12, 1965; Th. de Lys, N.Y.C., Apr. 20, 1965); Lawrence Phelps, the Prosecuting Attorney, in *The Trial of Lee Harvey Oswald* (ANTA Th., Nov. 5, 1967); and the title role in *Felix* (Actors Studio, Feb. 23, 1972).

Films. Mr. James played in *On the Waterfront* (Col., 1954); *The Strange One* (Col., 1957); *David and Lisa* (Continental, 1962); *Experiment in Terror* (Col., 1962); *The Chase* (Col., 1966); *The Happening* (Col., 1967); *The Caper of the Golden Bulls* (Embassy, 1967); *Cool Hand Luke* (WB, 1967); *Will Penney* (Par., 1968); *The Reivers* (Natl. Gen., 1969); *WUSA* (Par., 1970); *. . . Tick . . . Tick . . . Tick* (MGM, 1970); *The Iceman Cometh* (Amer. Film Th., 1972); *The New Centurions* (Col., 1972); *The Laughing Policeman* (20th-Fox, 1973); *Live and Let Die* (UA, 1973); *Bank Shot* (UA, 1974); *The Last Detail* (Col., 1974); *Juggernaut* (UA, 1974); *Buster and Billie* (Col., 1974); *The Man with the Golden Gun* (UA, 1974); and *Rancho DeLuxe* (1974).

Recreation. Golf, bridge, swimming.

JAMES, RICHARD H. Teacher, setting and lighting designer, technical director, administrator. b. Richard Henry James, May 22, 1931, Chicago, Ill., to Richard H. and Winifred (Riley) James. Grad. Northwestern Univ., B.S., M.A. Served in US Army, 1954–56. Married Aug. 29, 1958, to Sarah J. Schmidt (marr. dis. July 30, 1964). Member of ATA; National Assn. of Schools of the Theatre (comptroller, 1973, 1974; bd. of dir., 1971–to date); Rocky Mountain Theatre Conference (bd. of dir., 1974); USITT; Missoula Area Arts Council. Address: (home) 706 Parkview Way, Missoula, MT 59801, tel. (406) 549-4246; (bus.) Dept. of Drama, Univ. of Montana, Missoula, MT 59801, tel. (406) 243-4481.

Mr. James is professor and chairman, Dept. of Drama, Univ. of Montana, Missoula. He joined the Univ. of Montana faculty in 1959 as assistant professor and previously was (1958–59) instructor, Wisconsin State Univ. (Eau Claire).

In 1968–69, he became production manager, designer, and technical director, Montana Repertory Th.; from 1969 to 1972, he was executive director of the theatre; and in 1973, he became chairman of the theatre's executive board. He has worked on over 200 dramatic productions, including the designs for more than a hundred, and has directed and performed in a number of them.

Mr. James has been active as a consultant on theatre design and the equipping of theatres in the Midwest and the northern Rocky Mountain region. He was designer and technical director, Bigfork (Mont.) Summer Playhouse (1960), and he has worked on accreditation for theatre programs of several universities.

Recreation. Gardening.

JAMESON, JOYCE. Actress. b. Joyce Beverly Jameson, Sept. 26, 1932, Chicago, Ill. Grad. Los Angeles (Calif.) H.S.; Univ. of California at Los Angeles, B.A. (theatre arts) 1955. Studied acting with Estelle Harman, Los Angeles, 1955–57. Married Nov. 10, 1951, to Billy Barnes, playwright, composer, lyricist (marr. dis. 1955); one son. Member of AEA; AFTRA; SAG; Zeta Phi Eta (pres., 1952).

Pre-Theatre. Counselor, drama and dance teacher.

Theatre. Miss Jameson made her first stage appearance at age four impersonating Mae West (Palmer House, Chicago, Ill., 1936); at the Univ. of California Th., she appeared as Alice in *Alice in Wonderland,* Belle in *Ah, Wilderness!* and Jackie in *Hay Fever;* played Lily in *Baby Face O'Flynn* (Gallery Th., Los Angeles, Summer 1952); and Lalume in *Kismet* (Sacramento Music Circus, Calif., July 1955).

She appeared in *Billy Barnes Revue* (Las Palmas Th., Los Angeles, Oct. 15, 1958; moved to York Playhouse, N.Y.C., June 9, 1959; moved to John Golden th., Aug. 4, 1959), made her London debut in it (Lyric, Hammersmith, Apr. 4, 1960), toured England and Scotland (May-June 1960), and appeared in it in summer stock (Playhouse-in-the-Park, Philadelphia, Pa., 1962, 1963).

She appeared in *The Billy Barnes People* (Royale, N.Y.C., June 13, 1961; Las Palmas Th., Dec. 1961); played Rose in *The Egg* (John Houseman Th., Univ. of California at Los Angeles, 1961); Olive Ogleby in *Venus at Large* (Morosco, N.Y.C., Apr. 12 1962); appeared in *Billy Barnes, L.A.* (Coronet, Los Angeles, Oct. 10, 1962). *The Best of Billy Barnes* (Coronet, June 1963); *Billy Barnes, Hollywood* (Las Palmas Th., May 26, 1964); and was Miss Adelaide in *Guys and Dolls* (Music Circus, Sacramento, Calif., Aug. 2, 1965; Music Circus, Fresno, Calif., Aug. 16, 1965).

Films. Miss Jameson has appeared in *Gang-Busters* (Visual Drama, 1955); *Crime Against Joe* (UA, 1956); *Tip on a Dead Jockey* (MGM, 1957); *The Apartment* (UA, 1960); *Tales of Terrors* (AI, 1962); *The Balcony* (World, 1963); *Good Neighbor Sam* (Col., 1964); *Comedy of Terrors* (Assoc. Ind. Prod., 1964); and *Boy, Did I Get a Wrong Number!* (UA, 1966).

Television. She has appeared on Matinee Th. (NBC); Playhouse 90 (CBS); Studio One (CBS); Stagecoach West (NBC); Dante (CBS); the Mike Wallace Show (ABC); Science Fiction Th., Checkmate (NBC); *Sound of the 60's* (NBC): the Art Linkletter Show (NBC); Playboy Penthouse; the Dobie Gillis Show (CBS); Stump the Stars; the Jack Paar Show (NBC); First Impressions Twilight Zone (CBS); GE Th. (CBS); Burke's Law (ABC); the Bob Cummings Show (CBS); the Spike Jones Show (CBS, NBC); the Steve Allen Show (NBC, ABC); the Andy Griffith Show (CBS); the Danny Thomas Show (CBS); Perry Mason (CBS); the Phil Silvers Show (CBS); the Danny Kaye Show (CBS); McHale's Navy (ABC); Alfred Hitchcock Presents (CBS); Grindl (NBC); and The Bob Hope Chrysler Th. (NBC).

Also on the Red Skelton Show (CBS); The Munsters (CBS); Trails West (Ind.); The Man from U.N.C.L.E. (NBC); The Girl from U.N.C.L.E. (NBC); Gomer Pyle, USMC (CBS); Dick Van Dyke (CBS); Hollywood Palace (ABC); and Hogan's Heroes (CBS).

Night Clubs. Miss Jameson has performed in *Billy Barnes Revue* (Cabaret Concert, Hollywood, 1956; the hungry i, in San Francisco, Calif., 1957; The Mocambo, Hollywood, 1957; and the Cresendo, Los Angeles, 1958).

JAMPOLIS, NEIL PETER. Lighting, scenic, and costume designer. b. Mar. 14, 1943, Brooklyn, N.Y., to Samuel and Beatrice (Swenken) Jampolis. Grad. Art Institute of Chicago, B.F.A. 1965. Married July 24, 1971, to Maritza Jane Reisman. Member of United Scenic Artists of America.

Theatre. Mr. Jampolis designed the sets for *The Barretts of Wimpole Street* (Goodman Memorial Th., Chicago, Mar. 26, 1965); sets and lights for *Uncle Vanya* (Th. of the Living Arts, Philadelphia, Nov. 16, 1965); designed for the Cincinnati (Ohio) Playhouse-in-the-Park (1965–66); for the Hartford (Conn.) Stage Co., sets for *Poor Bitos* (Oct. 7, 1966), sets and lights for a double-bill of *Endgame* and *Act without Words* (Nov. 11, 1966), and *Three Sisters* (Dec. 16, 1966), and sets for *Under the Gaslight* (Jan. 20, 1967); designed the sets for *The Balcony* (Baltimore Ctr. Stage, Oct. 7, 1967); designed the lighting for *King Lear* (Morris Th., Morristown, N.J., Jan. 27, 1967); *Not a Way of Life* (Sheridan Square Playhouse, N.Y.C., Mar. 22, 1967); *Tea Party* and *The Basement* (Eastside Th., Oct. 15, 1968); *The People vs. Ranchman* (Fortune, Oct. 27, 1968); and *Little Murders* (Circle in the Square, jan. 5, 1969); sets for *War Games* (Fortune, Apr. 17, 1969); sets and lights for *In the Bar of a Tokyo Hotel* (Eastside Playhouse, May 11, 1969); lights for a double-bill of *Arf* and *The Great Airplane Snatch* (Stage 73, May 27, 1969); *Rondelay* (Hudson West Th., Nov. 5, 1969); and *Show Me Where the Good Times Are* (Edison, Mar. 5, 1970); was set supervisor and designed the lights for *Borstal Boy* (Lyceum, Mar. 31, 1970); lights for *Les Blancs* (Longacre, Nov. 15, 1970); sets, lights and costumes for a double-bill of *Acrobats* and *Line* (Th. de Lys, Feb. 15, 1971); and *One Flew Over the Cuckoo's Nest* (Mercer-Hansberry Th., Mar. 23, 1971); sets and lights for *To Live Another Summer, To Pass Another Winter* (Helen Hayes Th., Oct. 21, 1971); and lights for *Wild and Wonderful* (Lyceum, Dec. 7, 1971); and *Wise Child* (Helen Hayes Th., Jan. 27, 1972). He supervised the English settings for *Don't Bother Me, I Can't Cope* (Playhouse Th., Apr. 19, 1972); designed lights and costumes for *Butley* (Morosco, Oct. 31, 1972; and national tour); lighting for *Let Me Hear You Smile* (Biltmore, N.Y.C., Jan. 16, 1973); supervised the lighting of the British production *Warp I: My Battlefield, My Body* (Ambassador, Feb. 14, 1973), and designed the lighting and supervised the British sets for *The Emperor Enrico IV* (Ethel Barrymore Th., Mar. 28, 1973); designed the lights for *Crown Matrimonial* (Helen Hayes Th., Oct. 2, 1973); supervised the sets for the British production, *Brief Lives* (Booth, Oct. 16, 1974); designed the lights for *The Wager* (Eastside Playhouse, Oct. 21, 1974); sets for *Anthony Newley/Henry Mancini* (Uris, Oct. 31, 1974); sets and lights for *One Flew Over the Cuckoo's Nest* (Huntington Hartford Th., Los Angeles, Nov. 1, 1974; and Arlington Park (Ill.) Th., 1973–74 season); lights for *Sherlock Holmes* (Broadhurst, N.Y.C., Nov. 12, 1974); sets for *Johnny Mathis and The Miracles* (Uris, Nov. 31, 1974); and *Raphael in Concert with the Voices of New York* (Imperial, Dec. 19, 1974); and served as scenic consultant for *A Gala Tribute to Joshua Logan* (Imperial, Mar. 9, 1975).

He has designed numerous productions for the Santa Fe (N.M.) Opera; Houston (Tex.) Grand Opera; St. Paul (Minn.) Opera; and the Opera Society of Washington, among others.

Awards. Mr. Jampolis received the Antoinette Perry (Tony) Award (1974–75) for his lighting design for *Sherlock Holmes*.

JANES, KENNETH H. Educator, actor, director, playwright. b. Oct. 14, Glastonbury, Somerset, England, to Harold James and Lily Harriett (Penny) Janes. Grad. Strode Technical Coll., Street, Somerset, England, N.R.D.; came to US in 1956; attended Yale Univ., 1956–57; Univ. of Wisconsin, 1957–58; Union Theological Seminary, 1958. Served British Army, 1940–45; rank, Cpl. Address: (home) 400 W. 119th St., New York, NY 10027, tel. (212) 866-9983; (bus.) c/o Minor Latham Playhouse, Barnard Coll., 606 W. 120th St., New York, NY 10027, tel. (212) UN 5-4000.

Mr. Janes has been associated with Barnard Coll. since Sept. 1961, as a prof. of English, supervisor of the school's drama program, and director of the Minor Latham Playhouse; he has been dir. of the Barnard Coll. Th. Co. since its establishment (Fall 1966).

Theatre. He made his stage debut in community and repertory theatres in the west of England (1952); wrote one-act plays, presented by the Somerset Drama Council, including *Yellow Cornfield, Love on a Matchstick Spent, Shadow of Judas, No Flowers by Request*, and *In the Long Run* (1951–55); at the Glastonbury Festival Th., appeared as Benedick in *Much Ado About Nothing*, wrote and directed *Martyr Abbot* (1952); played Harcourt-Reilly in *The Cocktail Party* (Byre Th., Wells); Morris in *The Heiress* (Knightstone Th., Weston, 1954); Sir Andrew Aguecheek in *Twelfth Night* (Blackwell Playhouse, Bristol, 1955); Felix in *Captain Brassbound's Conversion* (Byre Th., Wells, 1955); and the title role in *The Noble Spaniard* (Byre Th., Wells; Blackwell Playhouse, Bristol; tour, 1955).

Mr. Janes wrote and directed historical pageants in Kent, Ilminster and Glastonbury (1955–56); at Backwell Playhouse (Bristol), played Creon in Anouilh's *Antigone* (1958); the Captain in *Last Candle* (1958); wrote and staged *Gilded House* (1958); *High Tide* (1959); and played in *Double in Mexico* (1960).

He appeared in student productions in the US as Harcourt-Reilly in *The Cocktail Party* (Yale Univ., 1956), Lord Hurn in *Charles XII* (Yale Univ., 1957), and Creon in Anouilh's *Antigone* (Union Theological Seminary, 1958), and he wrote and directed *The Pool* (Univ. of Wis., 1958).

At the Minor Latham Playhouse, Barnard Coll., he has directed *The Hollow Crown* (Oct. 6, 1966); devised, adapted from Shakespeare, and directed *Praise Caesar* (Feb. 16, 1971); directed Sir John Vanbrugh's *The Provoked Wife* (Apr. 10, 1973); adapted, from the John Gay play, and directed, *Polly* (Feb. 26, 1974); devised and directed *The Legends of Glastonbury* (staged at Cathedral Church of St. John the Divine, May 3, 1974); and directed *The Family Reunion* (Minor Latham Playhouse, Oct. 29, 1974), among others.

Other Activities. He was a founder of the Glastonbury Arts Festival and the Glastonbury Arts Club (1952); and was a committee member of the Somerset County Drama Council (England, 1952–55).

Awards. He was awarded a Rockefeller Foundation Fellowship for study and travel in the US (1956–58).

Recreation. Painting, reading, tennis, dancing.

JANIS, CONRAD. Actor, jazz musician. b. Feb. 11, 1928, New York City, to Sidney and Harriet Janis. Father, art dealer, writer; mother, writer. Married May 20, 1948, to Vicki Quarles, model (marr. dis. June 1957); one son, one daughter. Member of AEA; SAG; AFTRA; AFM, Local 802. Address: (home) 72 Perry St., New York, NY 10014, tel. (212) 242-2373; (bus.) c/o Sidney Janis Gallery, 6 W. 57th St., New York, NY 10021, tel. (212) 586-0110.

Theatre. Mr. Janis made his Bway debut as a replacement (Sept. 2, 1942) in the role of Haskell Cummings III in *Junior Miss* (Lyceum Th., Nov. 18, 1941), subsequently toured in this role with the natl. company (opened Harris Th., Sept. 14, 1942); appeared as Floyd Allen in *Dark of the Moon* (46 St. Th., N.Y.C., Mar. 14, 1945); Barney Brennen in *The Next Half Hour* (Empire, Oct. 29, 1945); Charlie in *The Brass Ring* (Lyceum, Apr. 10, 1952); Eddie Davis in *Time Out for Ginger* (Lyceum, Nov. 26, 1952); Waldo in *Remains to Be Seen* (Clinton Th., Conn., July 1952); Cantrell in *The Terrible Swift Sword* (Phoenix, Nov. 15, 1955); appeared in the musical revue *Joy Ride* (Huntington Hartford Th., Hollywood, Jan. 1956); Conrad in *Visit to a Small Planet* (Booth, Feb. 7, 1957); Timothy in *The Velvet Shotgun* (Duchess, London, June 14, 1958); Johnny King in *Make a Million* (Playhouse, N.Y.C., Oct. 23, 1958); Adam in *Sunday in New York* (48 St. Th., Nov. 29, 1961); played Rudy, the Band Leader, and Emcee for the Actors Studio Th. production of *Marathon '33* (ANTA Th., Dec. 22, 1963), for which he and his band, the Tail Gate Five, provided music; Kruger in a revival of *Front Page* (Barrymore Th., 1969–70); and Skouras in *No Hard Feelings* (Mark Hellinger Th., 1973).

Mr. Janis has given concerts with his band, "Conrad Janis and the Tailgaters" at Carnegie Hall and Town Hall, N.Y.C., Yale Univ.; Univ. of Pennsylvania; Univ. of Virginia, etc.

Films. He played Ronald in *Snafu* (Col. 1946); Johnikins in *Margie* (20th-Fox, 1946); and appeared in *The Brasher Dubloon* (20th-Fox, 1947); *That Hagen Girl* (WB, 1947); *Beyond Glory* (Par., 1948); *Airport 1975* (UI, 1974); and *The Happy Hooker* (Independent, 1975).

Television. Mr. Janis has appeared on Suspense (CBS); Kraft Th. (NBC); Studio One (CBS); Gulf Playhouse (NBC); The Untouchables (ABC); The Nurses (NBC); Colgate Comedy Hour (NBC); CBS-TV Workshop (CBS); Actors Studio Th. (CBS); Philco Th. (NBC); with his band, on the Steve Allen Show (NBC); Tonight Show (NBC); Arthur Godfrey Show (CBS); Stork Club Show (NBC); the Home Show (NBC); *Cannon* (CBS); *Banacek* (NBC); and *Virginia Hill*, a made-for-television movie (NBC).

Night Clubs. Mr. Janis has appeared with his band in N.Y.C. at Jimmie Ryans, Central Plaza, Child's Paramount, Basin Street and the Metropole Cafe. He has also played at Beverly Caverns, Hollywood, Calif.; Savoy Club, Boston, Mass.; and Jazz Ltd., Chicago, Ill.

Awards. He received the Silver Theatre TV Award for best supporting performance of 1950; the Theatre World Award (1951–52), for his performance as Charlie in *The Brass Ring;* and was nominated best jazz trombonist, *Playboy* Magazine Jazz Poll (1961–62).

Recreation. Following bullfights throughout Spain and Mexico, baseball, tennis, sports car racing, photography and travel.

JANNEY, BEN. Director, production stage manager. b. Benjamin Bowman Janney, Feb. 12, 1927, Muncie, Ind., to H. Lester and Helen (Bowman) Janney. Father, civil engineer. Grad. Central H.S., Muncie, 1945. Studied at Pasadena (Calif.) Playhouse, 1947–49; student of Shakespeare with John Burrell, N.Y.C., six months. Married June 22, 1969, to Nelle Nugent. Served USN 1945–46. Member of AEA; SSDC. Address: 140 W. 87th St., New York, NY 10024, tel. (212) TR 4-7787.

Theatre. Mr. Janney made his stage debut as the Villain in a stock production of *Gold in the Hills* (Boothbay Playhouse, Me., June 1947); subsequently directed *Love's Labour's Lost* (Pasadena Playhouse, Calif., Oct. 1947), and directed and appeared in 20 productions (Pasadena Playhouse, Oct. 1947–Aug. 1949); was technical advisor for 12 productions at the Indianapolis (Ind.) Civic Th. (Aug. 1949–May 1950); director, actor, and stage manager for six productions each season at the Barn Stage (Nantucket, Mass., 1951–54); and was stage manager for the Hilltop Theatre (Baltimore, Md., Dec. 1953–May 1954).

He was a cast replacement (Jan. 1955) in *Lunatics and Lovers* (Broadhurst, N.Y.C., Dec. 13, 1954); at the American Shakespeare Festival (Stratford, Conn.), he was assistant stage manager and played a Messenger, Dardanius, and the 6th Citizen in *Julius Caesar* (July 12, 1955), was assistant stage manager for *The Tempest* (Aug. 1, 1955), and for *Much Ado About Nothing* (Aug. 1955); and for the pre-Bway tryout of *The Amazing Adele* (opened Shubert, Philadelphia, Pa., Dec. 26, 1955; closed Shubert, Boston, Mass., Jan. 21, 1956).

He played the 2nd Soldier in *Affair of Honor* (Ethel Barrymore Th., N.Y.C., Apr. 6, 1956); and at the American Shakespeare Festival (Stratford, Conn.), he was assistant stage manager for *King John* (June 26, 1956), *Measure for Measure* (June 27, 1956), and *The Taming of the Shrew* (Aug. 5, 1956).

He succeeded (Oct. 12, 1956) Harold Stone as stage manager of *The Matchmaker*, also understudying Arthur Hill as Cornelius Hackl (Bway Th., Dec. 5, 1955), and toured in it (opened Shubert, Boston, Mass., Dec. 25, 1956; closed Hanna, Cleveland, Ohio, May 25, 1957); was stage manager and understudy to Gerald Sarracini as Romanoff in *Romanoff and Juliet* (Plymouth, Oct. 10, 1957), and on tour (opened Royal Alexandra, Toronto, Canada, Sept. 15, 1958; closed Blackstone, Chicago, Ill., Jan. 3, 1959).

He succeeded Neil Hartley as stage manager of *The Entertainer* (Royale, Feb. 12, 1958); was stage manager for *Destry Rides Again* (Imperial, Apr. 23, 1959); directed *Romanoff and Juliet* (Huntington Hartford Th., Hollywood, Calif.; Geary, San Francisco, Calif., June 1959); was stage manager for *The Good Soup* (Plymouth, N.Y.C., Mar. 2, 1960); appeared in the revue *La Plume de Ma Tante* (Royale, July 4, 1960); was production stage manager for *Irma La Douce* (Plymouth, Sept. 29, 1960), and for *Giants, Sons of Giants* (Alvin, Jan. 6, 1962); assistant director for the operas *The Ballad of Baby Doe* and *The Consul* (NY City Ctr., Mar. 22, 1962); advance director for a tour of *Sunday in New York* (July 1962); with the N.Y.C. Opera Co. (Oct. 4, 1962), he was assistant director for *La Boheme, Louise, Wings of the Dove, The Mikado, Madame Butterfly*, and *The Marriage of Figaro;* and was production stage manager for *Photo Finish* (Brooks Atkinson Th., Feb. 12, 1963), *The Irregular Verb to Love* (Ethel Barrymore Th., Sept. 18, 1963), *Sponono* (Cort Th., 1964), *Ben Franklin in Paris* (Lunt-Fontanne Th., 1964), *Boeing-Boeing* (Cort Th., 1965), *And Things That Go Bump in the Night* (Royale, 1965), *Me and Thee* (Golden Th., 1965), *Venus Is* (Billy Rose Th., 1966), *Love in E Flat* (Brooks Atkinson Th., 1967), *The Unknown Soldier and His Wife* (Vivian Beaumont Th., 1967), *After the Rain* (Golden Th., 1967), *Joe Egg* (Brooks Atkinson Th., 1968); *The Flip Side* (Booth Th., 1968), *Hadrian VII* (Helen Hayes Th., 1969), *Gantry* (George Abbott Th., 1970), *Not Now, Darling* (Brooks Atkinson Th., 1970), *American Ballet Th.* (NY City Ctr., 1970), *Promenande, All!* (Alvin Th., 1972), *Dear Oscar* (Playhouse Th., 1972), *Crown*

Matrimonial (Helen Hayes Th., 1973), and *My Fat Friend* (Brooks Atkinson Th., 1974).

Mr. Janney directed touring productions of *Marat/Sade* (1966); *Relatively Speaking* (1970); and *Crown Matrimonial* (1974). He was resident director at the Cherry County (Mich.) Playhouse during the summer of 1974.

Awards. Mr. Janney received the Hale Award from the Pasadena Playhouse (1949).

Recreation. Cello playing, collecting autographed letters of 18th-century theatre personalities.

JANNEY, LEON. Actor. b. Leon Elbert Janney, Apr. 1, 1917, Ogden, Utah, to Nathan Haines and Bernice (Kohn) Janney, Jr. Father, salesman. Grad. Hollywood (Calif.) Professional H.S., 1932; attended Cornell Univ., 1942. Studied with Marshall Stedman, Hollywood, 1925; Michael Chekhov, N.Y.C., 1941. Married Mar. 26, 1936, to Jessica Pepper, showgirl (marr. dis. Aug. 1936); married March 20, 1939, to Wilma Francis Sareussen, actress (marr. dis. Sept. 1942); married Feb. 14, 1945, to Isabel Kroener; one son. Served US Army, 1943–44; rank, Cpl. Member of AEA (council from 1961); SAG (bd. of dir., 1960–to date); AFTRA (pres. of NY local, 1963; local and natl. bd., from 1948); The Lambs; The Players; Actors Fund (life mbr.); NAACP (life mbr.). Address: 1334 Wellington Gate, Teaneck, NJ 07666, tel. (201) TE 6-5738.

Theatre. Mr. Janney made his stage debut in an amateur contest, at age 2-1/2, reciting *Winken, Blinken and Nod* (Pantages, Ogden, Utah, Nov. 1919); toured in vaudeville (1922–30); played the RKO and Loew's circuits (1932–33); and made his legitimate bow in the title role in *Tommy* (Copley Th., Boston, Oct. 1933).

He made his Bway debut as Raymond Clark in *Every Thursday* (Royale, May 10, 1934); appeared as Willie Baxter in a stock production of *Seventeen* (Ivoryton Playhouse, Conn., Summer 1934); Janga in *The Simpleton of the Unexpected Isles* (Guild, N.Y.C., Feb. 18, 1935); performed in the revue *Parade* (Guild, May 20, 1935); played Richard in *Ah, Wilderness!* (Ivoryton Playhouse, Conn., Summer 1935); succeeded (Dec. 1935) Hurst Amyx as Robert Lewis in *Mulatto* (Vanderbilt, N.Y.C., Oct. 24, 1935); played the Boy in *The Bough Breaks* (Little Th., Nov. 19, 1937); toured as Billy Randolph in *Brother Rat* (N.Y.C. Subway Circuit, 1938); played George in *Foreigners* (Belasco, N.Y.C., Dec. 5, 1939); Geoffrey Tracey in *Ghost for Sale* (Daly's, Sept. 29, 1941); Charles Jones in *The Days of Our Youth* (New Sch. Studio Th., Nov. 28, 1941); Francesco Barberini in *Lamp at Midnight* (New Stages, Dec. 21, 1947); Clochet in *The Victors* (New Stages, Dec. 26, 1948); Danny in *Night Must Fall* (Olney, Md., Th., Aug. 1949); the Native Prince in *Island Fling* (Westport Country Playhouse, Conn., Cape Playhouse, Dennis Mass., Summer 1951); Benjamin Backbite in *The School for Scandal Pa., (Th. de Lys, N.Y.C., June 23, 1953); Aubrey in The Show Off* (Playhouse-in-the-Park, Philadelphia, Pa., Summer 1953); and the Magistrate in *Madam, Will You Walk?* (Phoenix, N.Y.C., Dec. 1, 1953).

Mr. Janney played Benson in *Boy Meets Girl* and Bensinger in *The Front Page* (Playhouse-in-the-Park, Philadelphia, Pa., Summer 1954); Ham in *The Flowering Peach* (Belasco, N.Y.C., Dec. 28, 1954); succeeded (Jan. 1956) Frederic Downs as Mr. Peachum in *The Threepenny Opera* (Th. de Lys, Sept. 20, 1955); and succeeded (Apr. 9, 1956) Henry Lascoe as Ivanov in *Silk Stockings* (Imperial, Feb. 24, 1955), and repeated the role with the national touring company (opened Curran, San Francisco, Calif., Apr. 23, 1956).

Mr. Janney played Elbow in *Measure for Measure* (Phoenix, N.Y.C., Jan. 22, 1957); Mr. Sparkish in *The Country Wife* (Renata, June 26, 1957); the Man in *A Shadow of My Enemy* (ANTA, Dec. 11, 1957); Mr. Applegate in a touring company of *Damn Yankees* (opened Mosque, Altoona, Pa., Jan. 18, 1959; closed Paramount, Omaha, Nebr., May 10, 1958); Count Peppi Le Loup in *Song of Norway* and Ivanov in *Silk Stockings* (St. Louis Municipal Opera, Mo.; Columbus, Ohio; Dayton, Ohio, 1958).

He played Lt. Jenkins in *The Gazebo* (Lyceum, N.Y.C., Dec. 12, 1958); Barney in *Summer of the 17th Doll* (Players, Oct. 13, 1959); Captain Queeg in *The Caine Mutiny Court Martial* (Arena Th., Washington, D.C., 1960); Trifonov in *A Call on Kuprin* (Broadhurst, N.Y.C. May 25, 1961); the General in *The Policeman*, performed on a double bill with *Androcles and the Lion* (Phoenix, Nov. 21, 1961); Jack Carr in *Venus at Large* (Morosco, Apr. 12, 1962); Mike Harper in *Nobody Loves an Albatross* (Lyceum, Dec. 19, 1963); Winkleman in *The Last Analysis* (Belasco, Oct. 1, 1964); Augie Masters in *Kelly* (Broadhurst, Feb. 6, 1965); Bureyev in the pre-Bway tryout of *Pleasures and Palaces* (opened Fisher, Detroit, Mich., Mar. 11, 1965; closed there Apr. 10, 1965); and Clarence Dobbins in a revival of *Three Men on a Horse* (Lyceum, N.Y.C., Oct. 16, 1969).

Films. Mr. Janney made his debut as a child, playing bit parts and small roles, including Little Abie in *Abie's Irish Rose* (Par., 1927); in *The Wind* (MGM, 1928); three *Our Gang* comedies (Roach, 1928–29); *Handful of Clouds* and *Sin Flood* (1930). He had a great success in *Courage* (WB, 1930); followed by *Doorway to Hell* (WB, 1930); *Old English* (WB, 1930); *Father's Son* (1st Natl., 1930); *Their Mad Moment* (Fox, 1931); *Penrod and Sam* (1st Natl., 1931); *Police Court* (Mono., 1932); *Fame Street* and *Old Dutch* (1932); *Terror Abroad* (Par., 1933); *Should Ladies Behave?* (MGM, 1933); *Stolen Paradise* (Mono., 1941); *The Last Mile* (UA., 1959); and *Charly* (Cinerama, 1968).

Television and Radio. Mr. Janney made his radio debut performing monologues on the Uncle John program (KHJ, Los Angeles, 1925–27); played the Archduke Otto of Austria on the March of Time (WABC, N.Y.C., 1934); Richard Parker on The Parker Family (NBC, 1939–43); the title role on the Chick Carter series; The No. 1 Son on the Charlie Chan series; and performed on many other radio programs broadcast from N.Y.C. (1944–59).

He made his television debut as Richard on The Parker Family (NBC, 1941); subsequently appeared on US Steel Hour (CBS); Armstrong Circle Th. (NBC); Kraft Th. (NBC); The Defenders (CBS); Eternal Light (NBC); Mr. District Attorney (ABC); Mr. Citizen (ABC); East Side/West Side (CBS); Car 54, Where Are You? (NBC); on the daytime series Edge of Night (CBS), Young Dr. Malone (NBC), From These Roots (NBC), and as Jim Matthews on Another World (NBC); and was host on the Rheingold Rest, for all NY Met baseball games (1962, 1963).

Recreation. Bowling, golf, NY Met fan, astronomy, world history.

JEAKINS, DOROTHY. Costume designer. b. Jan. 11, 1914, San Diego, Calif., to George Tyndall and Sophie-Marie (von Kempf) Jeakins. Father, stockbroker; mother, designer. Grad. Fairfax H.S., Los Angeles, 1931; Otis Art Institute, Los Angeles, 1934. Two sons. Member of Costume Designers Guild. Address: 2926 Torito Road, Santa Barbara, CA 93108, tel. (805) 969-0777.

Theatre. Miss Jeakins' first costume designs for the theatre were for *The Taming of the Shrew* (American Shakespeare Festival, Stratford, Conn., Aug. 5, 1956); her first assignment on Bway was designing the costumes for *Affairs of State* (Royale, Sept. 25, 1950); subsequently Louis Calhern's *King Lear* (National, Dec. 25, 1950); for *Too Late the Phalarope* (Belasco, Oct. 11, 1956); *Major Barbara* (Martin Beck Th., Oct. 30, 1956); *The Taming of the Shrew* (Phoenix, Feb. 20, 1957); *Winesburg, Ohio* (National, Feb. 5, 1958); *The World of Suzie Wong* (Broadhurst, Oct. 14, 1958); *Cue for Passion* (Henry Miller's Th., Nov. 25, 1958); for the Amer. Shakespeare Festival (Stratford, Conn.), *Romeo and Juliet* (June 12, 1959); *The Winter's Tale* (July 20, 1959); and *All's Well That Ends Well* (July 29, 1959).

She designed costumes for a touring production of *Showboat* (Philharmonic Aud., Los Angeles, Calif., Aug. 15, 1960); *A Taste of Honey* (Lyceum, N.Y.C., Oct. 4, 1960); *My Mother, My Father and Me* (Plymouth, Mar. 23, 1963); for a West Coast touring production of *Carousel* opened Curran, San Francisco, Calif., Apr. 22, 1963; closed Pasadena Civil Aud., Calif., Aug. 3, 1963); and the costumes for ten productions and the sets for three productions for the Th. Group at the Univ. of California, Los Angeles, including costumes for *King Lear* (June 5, 1964); *Naked* (June 9, 1965); *Yeats & Company* (Oct. 23, 1965); and *Who's Happy Now?* (Nov. 3, 1967). Work for the Center Theatre Group at the Mark Taper Forum, Los Angeles, includes costumes for *Crystal & Fox* (Apr. 9, 1970); *Othello* (Apr. 8, 1971); and *Juno and the Paycock*. .

Films. Miss Jeakins designed costumes for over fifty films, including *Joan of Arc* (RKO, 1948); *Samson and Delilah* (Par., 1949); *Friendly Persuasion* (Allied, 1956); *South Pacific* (Magna, 1958); *Elmer Gantry* (UA, 1960); *The Music Man* (WB, 1962) *The Night of the Iguana* (MGM, 1964); *The Sound of Music* (20th-Fox, 1964); *Little Big Man* (Natl. Gen., 1970); *Fat City* (Col., 1972); *The Way We Were* (Col., 1973); *The Iceman Cometh* (American Film Th., 1973); and *Young Frankenstein* (20th-Fox, 1974).

Other Activities. Miss Jeakins did the documentary research for *Voyage to America* (US Pavilion, World's Fair, 1964) and was curator of costumes and textiles, Los Angeles County (Calif.) Museum of Art (1967).

Awards. Miss Jeakins received a Guggenheim Foundation Fellowship (1962); shared with Karinska, the Academy (Oscar) Award (1948) for the design of the costumes in *Joan of Arc;* with three other designers, an Academy Award for the design of the costumes in *Samson and Delilah* (1950); and received her third Academy Award for her costumes (black and white) in *The Night of the Iguana.*

Recreation. Cooking, bird-watching, gardening, books.

JEFFORD, BARBARA. Actress. b. Barbara Mary Jefford, July 26, 1930, Plymstock, England, to Percival Francis and Elizabeth Mary Ellen (Laity) Jefford. Father, bank manager. Grad. Weirfield School, Taunton, England, 1946; Eileen Hartly-Hodder Studio, Bristol, England, L.G.S.M. (speech and drama) 1947; RADA, London, 1949. Married Mar. 5, 1953, to Terence Longdon, actor (marr. dis. Mar. 1961); married May 13, 1967, to John Turner, actor. Member of British A.E.A.

Theatre. Miss Jefford made her professional debut in Brighton, England as a walkon in *Our Town* (Dolphin Th., 1949) where she also played the Secretary in *Love in Idleness* and Viola in *Twelfth Night.*

She made her London debut as Bertha in *Frenzy* ("Q", 1949); subsequently appeared with the Dundee (Scotland) Repertory Co. (1949–50) as Lydia Languish in *The Rivals,* Janet Spence in *The Gioconda Smile,* the Queen in *The Three Musketeers,* Beatrice in *Rebecca,* Sheba in *Dandy Dick,* and the Mother in *The Rising Generation.*

At the Shakespeare Memorial Th., (Stratford-on-Avon, England), she played Isabella in *Measure for Measure* (Mar. 9, 1950), and on tour in Germany (1950); Anne Boleyn in *Henry VIII* (Mar. 28, 1950); Hero in *Much Ado About Nothing;* Lady Percy in *Henry IV, Part 1* (Apr. 3, 1951); Calpurnia in *Julius Caesar* (May 2, 1951); Lady Percy in *Henry IV, Part 2* (May 8, 1951); and Juno in *The Tempest* (June 26, 1951).

In London, she played Rose Trelawny in *Trelawney of the Wells* (Lyric, Hammersmith, May 14, 1952); in 1953, toured Australia and New Zealand with the Shakespeare Memorial Company as Desdemona in *Othello,* Rosalind in *As You Like It,* and Lady Percy in *Henry IV, Part 2;* at Stratford-upon-Avon (England), as Desdemona in *Othello* (Mar. 16, 1954); Helena in *A Midsummer Night's Dream* (Mar. 23, 1954); Katherina in *The Taming of the Shrew* (June 1, 1954); and Helen of Troy in *Troilus and Cressida* (July 13, 1954).

She toured New Zealand with the New Zealand Players as Jennet Jourdemayne in *The Lady's Not for Burning* (1954–55); Andromache in *Tiger at the Gates* (Apollo, London, June 2, 1955), and made her first Bway appearance as Andromache in *Tiger at the Gates* (Plymouth, Oct. 3, 1955). At the Old Vic Th.

(London), she played Imogen in *Cymbeline* (Sept. 11, 1956); Beatrice in *Much Ado About Nothing* (Oct. 23, 1956); Portia in *The Merchant of Venice* (Dec. 11, 1956); Julia in *Two Gentlemen of Verona* (Jan. 22, 1957); Lady Anne in *Richard III* (May 29, 1957); Tamora in *Titus Andronicus*, presented on a double-bill with *The Comedy of Errors*, in which she played the Courtesan (Apr. 23, 1957); returned the following season as Queen Margaret in *Henry IV, Part 1* and *Henry IV, Part 2* (Oct. 16, 1957); Isabella in *Measure for Measure* (Nov. 19, 1957); Regan in *King Lear* (Feb. 19, 1958); and Viola in *Twelfth Night* (Apr. 1, 1958).

Miss Jefford repeated her role as Viola in the Old Vic's production of *Twelfth Night* (Bway Th., N.Y.C., Dec. 9, 1958); played Ophelia in *Hamlet* (Bway Th., Dec. 16, 1958); and Beatrice in *The Cenci* (Old Vic, London, Apr. 29, 1959).

For her fourth season with the Old Vic, she played Rosalind in *As You Like It*, Gwendolen Fairfax in *The Importance of Being Earnest*, and the title role in *Saint Joan* (Feb. 9, 1960); toured England and Eastern Europe (Moscow, Leningrad, USSR; and Warsaw, Poland) in the above roles and also as Lady Macbeth in *Macbeth* (Sept. 1960–Mar. 1961); toured Europe (opened Emmen, Holland) in a solo recital, *Heroines of Shakespeare;* at the Old Vic (London), played Viola in *Twelfth Night* (Apr. 18, 1961) and Lavinia in *Mourning Becomes Electra* (Nov. 21, 1961).

In the US with the Old Vic Co., she played Lady Macbeth in *Macbeth* (NY City Ctr., Feb 6, 1962; Feb 20, 1962; national tour, opened Walnut St. Th., Philadelphia, Pa., Mar. 20, 1962); toured in *Saint Joan* in Europe and the Near East (June–Aug. 1962); in England, played Lena in *Misalliance* and Dora in *The Just* at the Oxford Playhouse (Oct.–Dec. 1962), repeated her role as Lena in *Misalliance* (Royal Court, London, Jan. 8, 1963; moved Criterion, Jan. 28, 1963); and appeared as the Stepdaughter in *Six Characters in Search of an Author* (Mayfair, June 1963).

She appeared as Portia in *The Merchant of Venice* and Helena in *A Midsummer Night's Dream* (Royal, Brighton, Feb. 1964), then toured South America (Mar.–Apr. 1964) in both roles and appeared with the company (June 1964) at the Paris (France) Festival; was one of the readers in *A Tribute to T. S. Eliot* (LAMDA Th. Club, London, Feb. 14, 1965); played Nan in *Ride a Cock Horse* (Piccadilly Th., London, June 24, 1965); at the Playhouse, Oxford, played Cleopatra in *Antony and Cleopatra* (Sept. 27, 1965), Lady Cicely in *Captain Brassbound's Conversion* (Nov. 22, 1965), the title role in *Phèdre* (Jan. 10, 1966), Jennet Jourdemayne in *The Lady's Not for Burning*, and Alkmena in *Amphitryon 38;* and at the Nottingham Playhouse repeated her performance as Cleopatra in *Antony and Cleopatra* (Oct. 12, 1966) and was Maggie Harris in *Fill the Stage with Happy Hours* (Nov. 9, 1966).

She was Irma in *The Balcony* (Oxford Playhouse, Feb. 1967; London, July 1967); again played Alkmena in *Amphitryon 38* (premiere production Kenton Th., Henley-on-Thames, Mar. 20, 1967); was Patsy Newquist in *Little Murders* (Aldwych, London, June 21, 1967); was in the recital *The Labours of Love* (Southampton, England, Univ. of Victoria, British Columbia, Canada; West Africa; all 1968); played the Woman in *As You Desire Me* (Yvonne Arnaud Th., Guilford, England, 1968); toured again in *The Labours of Love* (Rome, Italy, and Middle East, both 1968; South America, 1969; India, Pakistan, and Far East, 1969–70), appeared in *The World's a Stage* (Arts, Cambridge, England, Nov. 1970; and played Katherina in *The Taming of the Shrew* and the title role in *Hedda Gabler* (both Bristol Old Vic, 1971).

She toured South America in *The Labours of Love* (1971); appeared in *Two Women of Greece* (Aldeburgh, Eng., 1971); toured Australia in *The Labours of Love* (1972); again played Portia in *The Merchant of Venice* and was Margaret in *Dear Brutus* (both Oxford Playhouse, 1973); and was Mother Marie-Therese Vauzou in *Mistress of Novices* (Piccadilly Th., London, Feb. 15, 1973).

Films. Miss Jefford was Molly Bloom in *Ulysses* (Cont., 1967); and was in *A Midsummer Night's Dream* (Eagle, 1968); *The Shoes of the Fisherman* (MGM, 1968); *To Love a Vampire* (1970); and *Hitler: The Last Ten Days* (Par., 1972).

Television and Radio. On radio, Miss Jefford was in *Measure for Measure* (Third Network, London, Nov. 13, 1964) and played the title role in *Phaedra* (Third Network, Apr. 2, 1965).

On television, her BBC appearances include the title roles of *Rahab* (1948); *Tess of the D'Urbervilles* (1952); and Katherine Howard in *Rose Without a Thorn* (1953). On ATV, she played Therese Raquin in *Guilt* (1959), Marceline in *The Unquiet Spirit* (1960). Elizabeth in *Boule de Suif* (1961), and the title role in *Medea* (1963). She appeared in the US as Ophelia in *Hamlet* (CBS, 1959) and as Kate Hardcastle in *She Stoops To Conquer* (Omnibus, NBC, 1956). She played Kate in an excerpt from *The Taming of the Shrew* (Golden Drama Special, ATV, London, England, Jan. 31, 1965); Ella in *A Little Temptation* (BBC, Mar. 17, 1965); Olive Latimer in *The Edwardians—Olive Latimer's Husband* (ITV, May 17, 1965) was in *Millions of Muzafariyah* (Man in Room 17, Granada, July 9, 1965); was the voice of Mata Hari in *Mata Hari* (BBC, Nov. 25, 1965); and appeared on the serial Canterbury Tales (1969).

Awards. Miss Jefford was made a member of the Order of the British Empire (O.B.E.) in the Queen's Birthday Honours (June 1965).

Recreation. Music, gardening, collecting shells, "swimming in shark-infested waters.".

JEFFREYS, ANNE. Actress, singer. b. Anne Jeffreys Carmichael, Jan. 26, 1928, Goldsboro, N.C., to Mack Curtis and Kate Hurt (Jeffreys) Carmichael. Father, lumber exporter and importer; mother, educator. Grad. Andrews (N.C.) H.S.; attended Anderson Jr. Coll. Studied singing with Mebane Beasley, fifteen years. Married Nov. 21, 1951, to Robert Hart Sterling, actor; three sons. Member of AEA; AFTRA; SAG; AGVA.

Theatre. Miss Jeffreys made her debut with the New York City Opera Co. singing Mimi in *La Boheme* and Cio-Cio in *Madame Butterfly* (Mecca Temple, 1940–41); subsequently appeared in the revue, *Fun for the Money* (Hollywood Playhouse, Calif., 1941); sang in a concert with the NBC Symphony Orchestra (N.Y.C., 1946); appeared as Sara in *Bittersweet* (Greek Th., Los Angeles, Calif., June 1946); and sang the title role in *Tosca* (Brooklyn Acad. of Music, N.Y., Oct. 22, 1946).

She played Rose Maurrant in the musical *Street Scene* (Adelphi, N.Y.C., Jan. 9, 1947); Sonia Sadoya in *The Merry Widow* (Greek Th., Los Angeles, Calif., July, 1947); Mme. Rita Cavallini in the pre-Bway tryout of *My Romance* (opened Shubert, New Haven, Conn., Feb. 12, 1948); Sara in *Bittersweet* (Greek Th., Los Angeles, Calif., July, 1948); Mme. Rita Cavallini in a revised version of *My Romance* (Shubert, N.Y.C., Oct. 19, 1948); the title role of *Tosca* (Philharmonic Aud., Los Angeles, Calif., May 1949); and Lilli Vanessi in the national touring production of *Kiss Me, Kate* (opened Philharmonic Aud., Los Angeles, Calif., Summer 1949), and succeeded (June 1950) Patricia Morison in the Bway production (New Century, Dec. 30, 1948).

Miss Jeffreys played Sara in *Bittersweet* (War Memorial Opera House, San Francisco, Calif., July 1951); Maeve Harrigan in *Three Wishes for Jamie* (Mark Hellinger Th., N.Y.C., Mar. 21, 1952); in stock, Alice in *Anniversary Waltz* (Oakdale Musical Th., Wallingford, Conn.; Warwick Musical Th., R.I., 1957); and, at the same theatres, Ella Peterson in *Bells Are Ringing* (Summer 1958).

She played Frenchy in *Destry Rides Again* (Philharmonic Aud., Los Angeles, Calif.; War Memorial Opera House, San Francisco, Calif., July 1960; St. Louis Municipal Opera Th., Forest Park, Mo., June 1961); Lalume in *Kismet* (Curran, San Francisco, Calif., Aug. 6, 1962); Rosabella in *The Most Happy Fella* (Long Beach Civic Light Opera Assn., San Diego, Calif., Summer 1963); Julie in *Carousel* (Circle Arts, San Diego, Calif.); Ella Peterson in *Bells Are Ringing* (Melodyland, Inc., Berkeley, Calif.); Alice in *Anniversary Waltz* (Melodyland Th., Anaheim, Calif., Jan. 21, 1964); succeeded (Colonial Boston, Mass., Mar. 16, 1964) Kathryn Grayson as Guenevere in the national touring production of *Camelot* (closed San Francisco Opera House, Calif., July 13, 1963) and was Lalume in *Kismet* (State Th., N.Y.C., June 22, 1965).

Films. Miss Jeffreys appeared in *I Married an Angel* (MGM, 1942); *Step Lively* (RKO, 1944); *Nevada* (RKO, 1944); *Sing Your Way Home* (RKO, 1945); *Dillinger* (Cont., 1945); *Zombies on Broadway* (RKO, 1945); *Riffraff* (RKO, 1947); *Trail Street* (RKO, 1947); *Return of the Badmen* (RKO, 1948); and *Boy's Night Out* (MGM, 1962).

Television. She made her debut as a guest on the Milton Berle Show (NBC, 1948); subsequently appeared in two television series, Topper (NBC, 1952–54) and Love That Jill (ABC, 1958); performed on the Ed Sullivan Show (CBS); Lux Video Th. (CBS); Wagon Train (NBC); the Steve Allen Show (NBC); the Perry Como Show (NBC); Dupont Show of the Month (NBC); and productions of *The Merry Widow* (NBC, Apr. 1955); and *Dearest Enemy* (NBC, Nov. 1955).

Other programs on which she appeared include Dr. Kildare (NBC, 1965); Bonanza (NBC, 1966); Wagon Train (NBC, 1967); The Man from U.N.C.L.E. (NBC, 1966); the pilot *Ghostbreaker* (NBC, 1967); Tarzan (NBC, 1967); Bright Promise (NBC, 1971); Love, American Style (ABC, 1972); and Delphi Bureau (ABC, 1972).

Night Clubs. Miss Jeffreys appeared at the Chase Hotel (St. Louis, Mo., Jan. 1952); the Waldorf Astoria Hotel (N.Y.C.); the Sands Hotel (Las Vegas, Nev.); the Hilton and Baker Hotels (Dallas, Tex.); the Fairmont Hotel (San Francisco, Calif.) and the Broadmoor (Colorado Springs, Colo.).

Recreation. Art, painting, music.

JELLICOE, ANN. Playwright, director. b. July 15, 1927, Middlesborough, Yorkshire, England, to John and Andrea Jellicoe. Attended Polam Hall Sch., Darlington, Durham, England; Queen Margaret's Sch., Castle Howard, York, England. Studied for the theatre at The Central Sch. of Speech and Drama, London (1944–47). Married 1950 to C. E. Knight-Clarke (marr. dis. 1961); married 1962 to Roger Mayne; two children.

Theatre. Miss Jellicoe began her theatrical career as an actress, stage manager, and director in the provinces of England (1947–51).

She subsequently founded The Cockpit Th. Club (London, 1951) to experiment with the open-stage concept. While there, she directed *The Confederacy, Rosmersholm* (her own adaptation), *The Frogs, Miss Jluie, Saint's Day, The Comedy of Errors*, and *Olympia.* She returned to The Central Sch. (1954–56) as a lecturer in acting and as director.

She wrote an adaptation of Ibsen's *Rosmersholm* (produced in London, 1952; revised version produced at Chandler Pavilion, San Francisco, 1960); wrote *The Sport of My Mad Mother*, which she co-directed (London, 1968); adapted *The Lady from the Sea* (London, 1961); wrote *The Knack* (Cambridge, 1961; London, 1962; N.Y.C., 1964), the British productions of which she co-directed; and an adaptation of *The Seagull* (London, 1964); adapted the libretto for the opera *Der Freischutz* (London, 1964); wrote *Shelly; or, The Idealist*, which she directed (London, 1965); *The Rising Generation* (London, 1967); *The Giveaway* (Edinburgh, 1968; London, 1969); and *You'll Never Guess* (Unicorn Th., London, 1973).

Films. *The Knack* (Lopert, 1965) was based upon her play.

Published Works. Miss Jellicoe is the author of *Some Unconscious Influences in the Theatre* (Cambridge Univ. Press, 1967).

JELLIFFE, ROWENA WOODHAM. Executive director, the Karamu Foundation. b. Rowena Woodham, Mar. 23, 1892, Albion, Ill., to John Franklin and Minnie (Saxe) Woodham. Father, county clerk. Grad. Southern Collegiate Institute; Oberlin College, A.B. 1914; Univ. of Chicago, M.A. 1915. Studied for the theatre at the John Murray Anderson School of the Theatre and Dance, N.Y.C., 1926, with John Murray Anderson and Robert Milton. Married May 28, 1915, to Russell Wesley Jelliffe, co-founder and co-director of Karamu House, 1915, and Karamu Theatre, 1920; one son. Member of ANTA; AETA; NTC; Natl. Council for the Arts in Education; The National Woman's Party (since 1913); The Ohio Community Theatre Association; Delta Kappa Gamma; Delta Sigma Theta; CTA; ACLU; NAACP; United World Federalists; Cleveland Museum of Art (life member). Address: The Karamu Foundation, 12427 Fairhill Road, Cleveland, OH 44120, tel. (216) 231-3323.

Theatre. In 1920, Mrs. Jelliffe founded the Karamu Theatre, Cleveland, Ohio, where she directed about 100 productions (1920–46); became executive director (1946); directed the Karamu Unit of the Federal Theatre (W.P.A.) Project under Hallie Flannigan (1935–39); retired from active theatre direction, remaining as director emeritus (April 1963). With her husband, she remains director of the Karamu Foundation (1963–to date), concerned with the incorporation of the arts into the general education system.

Awards. Mrs. Jelliffe and her husband jointly received the Eisenman Award (1941); honorary LL.D. degrees from Oberlin College (1944), H.H.D. degrees from Western Reserve University (1951), L.H.D. degrees from Cleveland State University (1967); Centennial citation from Wilson College (1969); were twice named as citizens of the year by the Cleveland Press (1950 and 1959); received the National Conference of Christians and Jews Award (1952); Distinguished Citizens Award (1960); Cleveland City Council Award (1963); Cleveland Women's City Club Art Award (1963); and the National Federation of Settlements Distinguished Service Award (1964); a Ford Foundation grant for the study and promotion of the arts in education (1973).

Recreation. Theatre, music, dance, visual arts.

JENKINS, DAVID. Set designer. Mr. Jenkins designed the sets for *The Importance of Being Earnest* (McCarter Th., Princeton, N.J., Mar. 19, 1971); *The Homecoming* (McCarter Th., Apr. 2, 1971); *Child's Play* (Trinity Square Playhouse, Providence, R.I., Sept. 21, 1971); *The Way of the World* (Long Wharf Th., New Haven, Conn., Feb. 18, 1972); *The Tooth of Crime* (McCarter, Princeton, Nov. 9, 1972); *The Changing Room* (Long Wharf Th., New Haven, Nov. 17, 1972; and Morosco, N.Y.C., Mar. 6, 1973); *Scenes from American Life* (Goodman Memorial Th., Chicago, Nov. 26, 1972); for the McCarter Th., *The Tempest* (Mar. 1, 1973), and *Rosmersholm* (Mar. 29, 1973); *One Flew Over the Cuckoo's Nest* (Kreeger Th., Arena Stage, Washington, D.C., May 2, 1973); *The Freedom of the City* (Goodman Memorial Th., Chicago, Oct. 9, 1973; and Alvin, N.Y.C., Feb. 17, 1974); *The Widowing of Mrs. Holroyd* (Long Wharf Th., New Haven, Nov. 16, 1973); *Tom* (Kreeger Th., Arena Stage, Washington, D.C., Dec. 14, 1973); the double-bill, *In Celebration* and *Relatively Speaking* (Kreeger Th., Arena Stage, May 23, 1974); *The Sea* (Goodman Memorial Th., Chicago, Nov. 14, 1974); *Boccaccio* (Kreeger Th., Arena Stage, Washington, D.C., Nov. 15, 1974); *Mother Courage and Her Children* (McCarter Th., Princeton, N.J., Feb. 13, 1975); *Afore Night Come* (Long Wharf Th., New Haven, Apr. 4, 1975); *Rogers and Hart* (Helen Hayes Th., N.Y.C., May 13, 1975); and *Gorky* (American Place Th., Nov. 16, 1975).

JENKINS, GEORGE. Set and lighting designer. b. George Clarke Jenkins, Baltimore, Md., to Benjamin W. and Jane (Clarke) Jenkins. Father, merchant. Grad. St. Thomas H.S., Scranton, Pa., 1928; studied architecture at the Univ. of Pennsylvania, 1929–31. Married May 7, 1953, to Phyllis Adams; two daughters. Member of Soc. of Motion Picture Art Directors; SDG; United Scenic Artists; ANTA (mbr., board for Standards and Planning for Living Theatre 1953–65).

Pre-Theatre. Interior and industrial designer, (1934–35); assistant to Jo Mielziner, (1937–41); plant engineer, Simmons Aerocessories Co., (1941–43).

Theatre. Mr. Jenkins' first production in N.Y.C., for which he designed the sets and lighting, was *Early to Bed* (Broadhurst, June 17, 1943); subsequently designed settings for *Mexican Hayride* (Winter Garden, Jan. 28, 1944); *I Remember Mama* (Music Box, Oct. 19, 1944); settings and lighting for *Dark of the Moon* (46 St. Th., Mar. 14, 1945); and for *Common Ground* (Fulton, Apr. 25, 1945); setting for *Strange Fruit* (Royale, Nov. 29, 1945); settings and lighting for *Are You with It?* (Century, Nov. 10, 1945); settings for *Lost in the Stars* (Music Box, Oct. 30, 1949); *Bell, Book and Candle* (Ethel Barrymore Th., Nov. 14, 1950); and *Three Wishes for Jamie* (Mark Hellinger Th., Mar. 21, 1952).

He designed the settings and lighting for *Gently Does It* (Playhouse, oct. 28, 1953; settings for *The Immoralist* (Royale, Feb. 8, 1954; settings and lighting for *The Bad Seed* (46 St. Th., Dec. 8, 1954); *Ankles Aweigh* (Mark Hellinger Th., Apr. 18, 1955); *The Desk Set* (Broadhurst, Oct. 24, 1955); *Too Late the Phalarope* (Belasco, Oct. 11, 1956); *The Happiest Millionaire* (Lyceum, Nov. 20, 1956); settings for *The Merry Widow* (NY City Ctr., Apr. 10, 1957); settings and lighting for *Rumble* (Alvin, Nov. 6, 1957); *Two for the See-saw* (Booth, Jan. 16, 1958); *Tall Story* (Belasco, Jan. 29, 1959); *The Miracle Worker* (Playhouse, Oct. 19, 1959); and *One More River* (Ambassador, Mar. 18, 1960). He designed the settings for *Critic's Choice* (Ethel Barrymore Th., Dec. 14, 1960); settings and lighting for *A Thousand Clowns* (Eugene O'Neill Th., Apr. 5, 1962); settings for *Jennie* (Majestic, Oct. 17, 1963); and for the Marine Th. (Jones Beach, L.I., N.Y.), designed settings for *Song of Norway* (1958–59), *Hit The Deck* (1960), *Paradise Island* (1961–62), and *Around the World in Eighty Days* (1963–64).

For the San Francisco (Calif.) Opera Assn., he designed the settings for *La Bohème, Cosi Fan Tutte,* and *Ariadne auf Naxos.*

Mr. Jenkins designed the scenery for *A Thousand Clowns* (Comedy Th., London, June 2, 1964); *Around the World in 80 Days* (Jones Beach Marine Th., N.Y., June 27, 1964); scenery and lighting for the pre-Bway tryout of *Everybody Out, the Castle Is Sinking* (opened Colonial, Boston, Dec. 26, 1964; closed there Jan. 9, 1965); *Catch Me If You Can* (Morosco, N.Y.C., Mar. 9, 1965); *Mardi Gras* (Jones Beach Marine Th., N.Y., June 26, 1965); *Generation* (Morosco, N.Y.C., Oct. 6, 1965; national touring production opened Fisher Th., Detroit, Aug. 8, 1966); with Ben Edwards, was production supervisor of *The Royal Hunt of the Sun* (ANTA, N.Y.C., Oct. 26, 1965); designed the scenery and lighting for *Wait Until Dark* (Ethel Barrymore Th., Feb. 2, 1966; Strand, London, July 27, 1966; and national tour, 1967); designed the sets for *The Student Prince* (San Francisco, 1966); *Mardi Gras* (Jones Beach Marine Th., N.Y., Summer 1966); and *The Only Game in Town* (Jones Beach Marine Th., N.Y., Summer, 1968).

Films. Mr. Jenkins has designed sets for Samuel Goldwyn for *The Best Years of Our Lives* (1946); *The Secret Life of Walter Mitty* (1947); *Bishop's Wife; Enchantment* (1948), *A Song Is Born* (1948); *Roseanna McCoy* (1949); *Monsoon* (UA, 1953); *San Francisco Story* (WB, 1952); *At War with the Army* (Par., 1956); *The Miracle Worker* (UA, 1962); *Mickey One* (Col., 1965); and did the art direction for *Up the Down Staircase* (WB, 1967); *The Pursuit of Happiness* (Col., 1971); *1776* (Col., 1972); *Paper Chase* (20th-Fox, 1973); and *The Parallax View* (Par., 1974).

Television. He was set designer and directed the pilot film of Four Star Playhouse (CBS); designed settings for *Out of the Dark, Revue Prod, New Revue* (CBS), *The Royal Family* (CBS), *Annie Get Your Gun* (NBC), *An Afternoon with Mary Martin* (NBC), and *An Evening with Mary Martin* (NBC).

Other Activities. Mr. Jenkins was theatre consultant for the new Hopkins Ctr. (Dartmouth Univ. 1962); and for the new Marine Stadium (Miami, Fla. 1963).

Awards. He received the Donaldson Award (1945) for his settings for *I Remember Mama.*

Recreation. Photography.

JENS, SALOME. Actress. b. May 8, 1935, Milwaukee, Wis., to Arnold John and Salomea (Szujeuska) Jens. Father, mason contractor. Grad. Bay View H.S., Milwaukee, 1953; attended Univ. of Wisconsin, 1953–54; Northwestern Univ., 1954–55. Studied acting with Herbert Berghof, one year; Actors Studio (member, 1958–to date). Member of AEA; SAG; AFTRA. Address: William Morris Agency, c/o Ed Bondy, 1350 Ave. of Americas, New York, NY 10019, tel. (212) JU 6-5100.

Pre-Theatre. Secretary.

Theatre. Miss Jens made her N.Y.C. debut as Miss Ferguson in *Sixth Finger in a Five Finger Glove* (Longacre Th., Oct. 8, 1956); subsequently appeared in a double-bill, as Mary in *The Bald Soprano* and Roberts in *Jack* (Sullivan St. Playhouse, June 3, 1958); Georgette in *The Disenchanted* (Coronet, Dec. 3, 1958); and as Deirdre in *Deirdre of the Sorrows* (Gate, Oct. 14, 1959).

In stock she played Abbie Putnam in *Desire Under the Elms* and in *Will Success Spoil Rock Hunter?* (Summer 1959); appeared in *U.S.A.* (Martinique, N.Y.C., Oct. 28, 1959); played the Girl in *The Balcony* (Circle in the Square, Mar. 3, 1960); in stock, appeared in *The Lady's Not for Burning,* and *As You Like It* (Toledo, Ohio, 1960).

Miss Jens appeared as Martha Bernays Freud in *A Far Country* (Music Box, N.Y.C., Apr. 4, 1961); in stock, performed in *The Skin of Our Teeth* (Olney Playhouse, Md., 1961); *U.S.A.* (Royal Poinciana Playhouse, Palm Beach, Fla., 1961); *Anna Christie* (Playhouse-in-the-Park, Philadelphia, Pa., 1962); played Lady Macbeth in *Macbeth* (Pittsburgh Playhouse, Pa., 1962); Anna in *Night Life* (Brooks Atkinson Th., N.Y.C., Oct. 23, 1962); succeeded Colleen Dewhurst as Abbie Putnam in *Desire Under the Elms* (Circle in the Square, Jan. 8, 1963); played Lizzie in *The Rainmaker* (Royal Poinciana Playhouse, Palm Beach, Fla., 1963); and for the NY Shakespeare Festival, Hermione in *The Winter's Tale* (Delacorte Th., Aug. 9, 1963).

She became a member of the Repertory Company of Lincoln Center in 1963, and appeared with the company as Louise in *After the Fall* (ANTA-Washington Square Th., Jan. 23, 1964) and Gilian Prosper in *But for Whom Charlie* (ANTA-Washington Square Th., Mar. 12, 1964). She played Josie Hogan in *A Moon for the Misbegotten* (Circle in the Square, June 12, 1968) and toured in the production; played Abigail in *John and Abigail* (Ford's Th., Washington, D.C., 1970); toured summer theatres in *And Miss Reardon Drinks a Little* (1970); appeared in the title role in *Mary Stuart* (Vivian Beaumont Th., N.Y.C., Nov. 11, 1971); played in *The Ride Across Lake Constance* (Forum Th., Jan. 13, 1972); was Cleopatra in *Antony and Cleopatra* (American Shakespeare Festival, Stratford Conn., June 23, 1972); and was Gertrude in *Hamlet* (Mark Taper Forum, Los Angeles, Calif., 1974).

Films. Miss Jens made her debut in *Angel Baby* (Allied, 1961); followed by *Fool Killer* (Landau, 1963); *Seconds* (Par., 1966); *Me Natalie* (Natl. Gen., 1969); and *Cold Sweat* (1973).

Television. She has appeared on Kraft Television Th. (NBC); US Steel Hour (CBS); Naked City (ABC); Stoney Burke (ABC); The Defenders (CBS); The Untouchables (ABC); and Play of the Week (WNTA); Gunsmoke (CBS, 1973); McMillan and Wife (1973); and ABC Mystery Movie of the Week (1974).

Awards. Miss Jens received the Clarence Derwent Award (1960) for her performance in *The Balcony;* the Straw Hat Award for her performance in *Miss Reardon Drinks A Little;* and the Cliff Dwellers Award for Josie in *A Moon for The Misbegotten.* .

Recreation. Piano, modern dance, tennis.

JESSEL, GEORGE. Actor, producer, playwright, composer, lyricist, writer, master of ceremonies. b. George Albert Jessel, Apr. 3, 1898, New York City, to Joseph A. and Charlotte (Schwartz)

Jessel. Father, playwright, writer, master of ceremonies, school for eight months, N.Y.C. Married 1920 to Florence Courtney, singer (marr. dis. 1922); re-married Florence Courtney May 22, 1923 (marr. dis. Oct. 25, 1932); remarried Florence Courtney (marr. dis.); married Apr. 23, 1934, to Norma Talmadge, actress (marr. dis. Aug. 11, 1939); married Apr. 13, 1940, to Lois Andrews, show girl (marr. dis. Aug. 24, 1942); one daughter; married Sept. 1960 to Paula Jacobson; one son. Member of AEA; SAG; AFTRA; AGVA; The Friars (Abbott, 1933); Writers Club; Variety Clubs of America; Natl. Vaudeville Artists (hon. life pres.); Jewish Theatrical Guild (vice-pres., 1941); Hillcrest Country Club.

Theatre. Mr. Jessel made his stage debut at age ten, appearing in vaudeville with Jack Weiner and Walter Winchell as The Imperial Trio (Imperial Th., Harlem, N.Y.C., 1909); subsequently joined the Gus Edwards vaudeville troupe and toured cross-country in Kid Kogaret (1910–14); toured England's variety theatres (1914–17); and toured the US in vaudeville (1917–19).

He appeared in *Gaieties of 1919* (Winter Garden, N.Y.C., 1919); wrote, produced and appeared in *The Troubles of 1920* (Alhambra, Sept. 10, 1920); *The Troubles of 1921* (Palace, Aug. 8, 1921); appeared as a solo act "George Jessel," in which he would pick up a telephone on stage and converse with his mother (Fifth Ave. Th., Jan. 27, 1922); wrote, produced and appeared in *George Jessel's Troubles* (N.Y.C., 1922), which also toured; produced, with Rufus Lemaire, *Helen of Troy*, New York (Selwyn, N.Y.C., June 19, 1923); appeared in *George Jessel and Company* (Palace, May 28, 1924); and played Jack Robin in *The Jazz Singer* (Fulton, Sept. 14, 1925).

He appeared as a solo act, "George Jessel" (Chicago Th., Ill., Mar. 21, 1928); played Eddie Rosen in *The War Song* (National, N.Y.C., Sept. 24, 1928); Joseph in *Even in Egypt* (Werba's Flatbush, Brooklyn, Jan. 13, 1930), which was presented on Bway as *Joseph* (Liberty, Feb. 12, 1930); and produced *The Man's Town* (Ritz, Mar. 10, 1930).

Mr. Jessel appeared in the revue *Sweet and Low* (46 St. Th., Nov. 17, 1930); wrote the music, lyrics, and sketches, designed the costumes and sets and appeared in the pre-Bway tryout of the revue, *Box of Tricks* (New Brighton, Brooklyn, July 13, 1931); appeared in *Cantor-Jessel Show* (Palace, N.Y.C., Nov. 1931); *Bizarrities* (Casino de Paree, 1934); produced the pre-Bway tryout of *Glory for All* (opened Erlanger, Philadelphia, Pa., 1937); and produced *Little Old New York* (NY World's Fair, 1939–40).

He was co-author, with Bert Kalmar and Harry Ruby, of *High Kickers*, in which he played George M. Krause, Sr. (Broadhurst, N.Y.C., Oct. 31, 1941), and repeated his role on tour (opened June 1942; closed Chicago, Ill., Aug. 1942); appeared in *Show Time* (Broadhurst, N.Y.C., Sept. 16, 1942), and toured summer theatres in it (1957); appeared at the Roxy Th., (N.Y.C., May 1946); was the master of ceremonies for the benefit revue, *Red, White and Blue* (Paramount, Oct. 7, 1950); and starred in *That Wonderful World of Vaudeville* (Playhouse on the Mall, Paramus, N.J., Oct. 10, 1975).

Films. Mr. Jessel played with Eddie Cantor and Trudy Shattuck in a two-reeler, *Widow at the Races* (Edison, 1911); subsequently appeared in *Private Izzy Murphy* (WB, 1926); *Sailor Izzy Murphy* (WB, 1927); and appeared in the short subjects for Vitaphone (1927); *George Jessel, Comedy Monologue, Comedy Monologue and Solo, At Peace with the World*, and *Comedy Skit*.

He appeared in *Ginzberg the Great* (WB, 1928); *George Washington Cohen* (Tiffany, 1929); wrote dialogue and played in *Lucky Boy* (Tiffany, 1929); appeared in *Love, Live and Laugh* (Fox, 1929); *Happy Days* (Fox, 1930); and *George Jessel and the Russian Choir* (Vitaphone, 1931).

He produced the two-reelers, *The Broadway Kid* (WB, 1937) and *The Life of Haym Solomon* (WB, 1937); collaborated with Jack Meskill and Ted Shapiro on the songs for *Vivacious Lady* (RKO, 1938); and appeared in short subjects for RKO (1939).

Mr. Jessel produced *The Dolly Sisters* (20th-Fox, 1945); *Do You Love Me?* (20th-Fox, 1946); *Nightmare Alley* (20th-Fox, 1947); *I Wonder Who's Kissing Her Now* (20th-Fox 1947); *When My Baby Smiles At Me* (20th-Fox, 1948); *Dancing in the Dark* (20th-Fox, 1949); *Meet Me After the Show* (20th-Fox, 1951); *Anne of the Indies* (20th-Fox, 1951); *Golden Girl* (20th-Fox, 1951); *Wait 'Till the Sun Shines, Nellie* (20th-Fox, 1952); *Bloodhounds of Broadway* (20th-Fox, 1952); *The I Don't Care Girl* (20th-Fox, 1953); *Tonight We Sing* (20th-Fox, 1953); wrote the screenplay and narrated *Yesterday and Today* (UA, 1953); and appeared in *Can Heironymus Merkin Ever Forget Mercy Humppe and Find True Happiness* (Regional, 1969).

Television and Radio. On radio, Mr. Jessel has performed on The Voice of Columbia Show (CBS, 1934); Thirty Minutes in Hollywood (WOR, 1936–37); with his wife Norma Talmadge, Jessel's Jamboree (NBC, 1938–39); George Jessel's Celebrity Program (NBC, 1940); and the George Jessel Show (KCOP, Hollywood, Calif., 1958).

On television, he appeared as the master of ceremonies on Variety Show (ABC, 1953); as a guest comedian on the Milton Berle Show (NBC, 1956); performed on his own program, George Jessel's Show Business (1958); and has appeared on the Jack Paar Show (NBC, 1960); Bob Hope Show (NBC); Johnny Carson Show (NBC, 1963–64); and Merv Griffin Show (WNEW-TV).

Night Clubs. He has performed at such night clubs as the Versailles (N.Y.C., 1938); Monte Carlo (N.Y.C., 1942); The International (N.Y.C., 1962); The College Inn (Chicago, Ill., 1963); and the Palms Shore Club (Brooklyn, N.Y., 1963).

Other Activities. Known as "The Toast Master General of the United States," Mr. Jessel first made dinner speeches in 1925, campaigning for James J. Walker who was running for mayor of N.Y.C. He appeared frequently at the White House as toastmaster during the Roosevelt, Truman, and Kennedy administrations. He has represented Bonds for Israel and the City of Hope Medical Center (Durante, Calif.). On Apr. 15, 1973, a dinner in Mr. Jessel's honor at the NY Hilton Hotel benefited the USO; and Mr. Jessel received a special award for overseas entertainment he had provided for members of the armed forces during his 19 USO tours to bases in Korea, South Vietnam, and other locations.

Published Works. He wrote an autobiography, *So Help Me* (1943), *Hello Momma* (1946), *This Way, Miss* (1955); *You, Too, Can Make a Speech* (1956); *Jessel, Anyone* (1960); *Elegy in Manhattan* (1961); *Talking to Mother; Halo Over Hollywood* (1964); *Between the Giants and I* (1966); and *The World I LIved In* (1975).

Awards. He was voted Man of the Year (1952) by the Beverly Hills Chapter of B'nai B'rith, and was made honorary member of the USAF.

Recreation. Book collecting.

JEWELL, JAMES. Theatre engineer, consultant, lighting designer, educator. b. James Earl Jewell, July 26, 1929. Los Angeles, Calif., to Earl C. and Frances Estelle Jewell. Father, accountant. Grad. Elk Grove (Calif.) H.S., 1947; Univ. of the Pacific, B.A. 1951; Yale Univ. Sch. of Drama, M.F.A. 1957. Served US Army, 1953-55; rank Spec. 3. Member of Northwest Drama Conference (dir. 1959-61); Regional Theatre Council for Northern California and Nevada (bd. of govs., 1958-60, 1963-65; pres., 1961, 1962); ATA (formerly AETA, chmn., theatre architecture project, 1959-61; dir., 1963-65; administrative vice-pres., 1966-68; secy., 1969-70; finance comm., 1971-73; chmn., finance comm., 1973); ANTA (regional dir., 1963-65, 1966-68); USITT (dir., 1961-63, 1964-66); American Community Th. Assn. (bd. of govs., 1962-64); Illuminating Engineering Society (theatre lighting comm., 1971-74; energy advisory comm., 1973, 1974); SMPTE; Soc. of Architectural Historians; Pacific Coast Electrical Assn.; Theatre Historical Soc.; US Natl. Comm., Internatl. Lighting Comn.; Edison Electric Institute (street and highway lighting comm., 1971, 1972); Bohemian Club. Address: (home) 749 Rhode Island St., San Francisco, CA 94107, tel. (415) AT 2-3135; (bus.) 77 Beale St., San Francisco, CA 94106, tel. (415) SU 1-4211.

Mr. Jewell is a lighting designer and chief illuminating engineer with Pacific Gas and Electric Co., a firm he joined in 1968. From 1957 to 1967, he was head of the Theatre Engineering Division, Holzmueller Corp., San Francisco, Calif., and he was also lecturer in theatre engineering and history, Dept. of Dramatic Art, Univ. of California at Berkeley from 1962 to 1966.

He began his career, designing and serving as technical director for an historical pageant at Murphys, Calif. (Summer 1948); was production manager for the Columbia and Monterey (Calif.) historical pageants (Summer 1949); lighting designer for productions at Green Mansions Th., Warrensberg, N.Y. (Summers 1952, 1956); technical director for productions at Smith Coll. Th., Northampton, Mass. (1952–53); lighting designer for Fred Waring's touring concert, *Festival of Song* (1952); and productions at the Mill Playhouse, Hammonton, N.J. (Summer 1953); and scene designer for the Southwestern Sun Carnival Queen Coronation (El Paso Coliseum, Tex., Dec. 1954).

He served as consultant for the Ft. Bliss (Tex.) Theatre Planning and Construction program (1955); was technical director for *Coriolanus* (Yale Sch. of Drama, New Haven, Conn., 1956); lighting designer for *Unexpected Truth* (Yale Sch. of Drama, 1956); *Sweet Executive* (Alcazar, San Francisco, Dec. 11, 1957); *Let There be Light* (IES National Technical Conference, San Francisco, Sept. 6, 1959); *Rip Van Winkle* (July 1959); *The Soldier and Mr. Lincoln* (July 1960); *The Green Mountain Boys* (July 1963), *The Armada* (July 1974), all produced at the Bohemian Grove, Calif.; lighting designer for *The Birds* (Greek Th., Berkeley, Calif., Sept. 1961); also at the same theatre, *An Angel Comes to Babylon* (Sept. 27, 1962); *Antony and Cleopatra* (Sept. 1963); and *Dr. Faustus* (Summer 1964).

Mr. Jewell served as consultant for the design of the Performing Center for Waring Enterprises, Stroudsburg, Pa. (1953); Station KTVU (Oakland, Calif., 1958); Compton (Calif.) Coll. Television Center (1958); Cerritos Coll. Th. (Norwalk, Calif., 1959); the Coll. of San Mateo (Calif.) Th., (1959); El Camino H.S. (San Bruno, Calif., 1960); City College of San Francisco Little Theatre (1960); Foothill Coll. Th., Los Altos, Calif. (1961); the drama building, Napa Coll. (Calif., 1964); the speech and drama building, San Jose (Cal.) City College; Mira Th., Vallejo, Cal.; and Hertz Hall, Univ. of California at Berkeley.

Other Activities. Among Mr. Jewell's numerous community service activities is his work with the Boy Scouts of America. He was a district commissioner (1959-62, 1965-67); served as vice-chairman (1969-73) and chairman (1973-74) of the Council Activities Comm. and was director of Ceremonies and Shows, 8th National Jamboree—West.

JOHNS, GLYNIS. Actress. b. Oct. 5, 1923, Pretoria, Union of South Africa, to Mervyn and Alys Maude (Steele-Payne) Johns. Father, actor; mother, concert pianist. Attended Clifton H.S. and Hampstead H.S., England, Studied ballet in Bristol (1929–1933), teaching degree. Married to Anthony Forward (marr. dis.); one son; married Feb. 1, 1952, to David Ramsey Foster (marr. dis.); married 1960 to Cecil Peter Henderson (marr. dis. 1961); married Oct. 1, 1964, to Elliott Arnold, author. Member of AEA; SAG; AFTRA.

Theatre. Miss Johns made her N.Y.C. debut in the title role in *Gertie* (Plymouth, Jan. 30, 1952); followed by the title role in *Major Barbara* (Martin Beck Th., Oct. 30, 1956); Jennifer Wren in a stock production of *Plaintiff in a Pretty Hat* (Coconut Grove, Fla., Mar. 1958); Miss Mopply in *Too True To Be Good* (54 St. Th., N.Y.C., Mar. 12, 1963). She played the title role in *The Marquise* (Eisenhower Th., John F. Kennedy Ctr., Washington, D.C., May 29, 1972), in which she also toured the US, Great Britain, and Canada; was Desirée Armfeldt in *A Little Night Music* (Shubert Th., N.Y.C., Feb. 25, 1973); and played the female lead in a revival of *Ring*

'Round the Moon (Ahmanson Th., Los Angeles, Calif., Apr. 1, 1975).

She made her first stage appearance at the age of three weeks, when her parents presented her to an audience. She made her professional debut as the ballerina, Ursula, in *Buckie's Bears* (Garrick Th., London, Eng., Dec. 26, 1935); followed by Hortense Bertrand in *St. Helena* (Old Vic, Feb. 4, 1936); succeeded Mavis Edwards as Mary Tilford in *The Children's Hour* (Gate, Nov. 12, 1936); both the Elf and the Child in *The Melody That Got Lost* (Embassy, Dec. 26, 1936); Sonia Kuman in *Judgment Day* (Embassy, May 19, 1937); Cinderella in *A Kiss for Cinderella* (Phoenix, Dec. 24, 1937); Miranda Bute in *Quiet Wedding* (Richmond, Apr. 5, 1938); Sonia Kuman in *Judgment Day* (Phoenix, Nov. 21, 1939); Miranda Bute in *Quiet Week End* (Wyndham's, July 22, 1941).

She played the title role in *Peter Pan* (Cambridge, Dec. 24, 1943); was Corinne in a touring production of *I'll See You Again* (Oct. 1944); Pam in *Fools Rush In* (Fortune, Sept. 2, 1946); Mary Flemin in *The Way Things Go* (Phoenix, Mar. 2, 1950); Anne of Cleves in *The King's Mare* (Garrick Th., July 20, 1966); and four different roles in four plays billed as *Come As You Are!* (King's Th., Edinburgh, Scotland, Oct. 21, 1969); New, London, Jan. 1970; transferred to Strand, June 1970).

Films. Miss Johns made her debut in *South Riding* (UA, 1938); followed by *Murder in the Family* (20th-Fox); *Prison without Bars* (UA, 1939); *The Fugitive* (U, 1940), released in England as *On the Night of the Fire; The Prime Minister* (WB, 1941); *The Invaders* (Col., 1942), released in England as *49th Parallel; The Adventures of Tartu* (MGM, 1943); *The Halfway House* (AFE, 1945); *Vacation from Marriage* (MGM, 1945); *Frieda* (U, 1948); *An Ideal Husband* (20th-Fox, 1948); the Mermaid in *Miranda* (Eagle-Lion, 1949); *Dear Mr. Prohack* (Pentagon, 1950); *The Great Manhunt* (Col., 1950), shown in England as *State Secret; No Highway in the Sky* (20th-Fox, 1951); *The Promoter* (U, 1952); *Encore* (Par., 1952); *The Sword and the Rose* (RKO, 1953); *Rob Roy, the Highland Rogue* (RKO, 1953); *Personal Affair* (UA, 1954); *The Weak and the Wicked* (Allied, 1954); *Mad About Men* (General Films); *The Beachcomber* (UA, 1955); *Land of Fury* (U, 1955), released in England as *The Seekers; Josephine and Men* (British Lion); *The Court Jester* (Par., 1956); *Loser Takes All* (Distributors, 1957); *All Mine to Give* (U, 1957); *Shake Hands with the Devil* (UA, 1959); *Another Time, Another Place* (Par., 1958); *The Last of the Few* (documentary for the South African government); *The Sundowners* (WB, 1960); *The Spider's Web* (Col.); *The Chapman Report* (WB, 1962); *The Cabinet of Caligari* (20th-Fox, 1962); *Papa's Delicate Condition* (Par., 1963); *Mary Poppins* (Buena Vista, 1964); *Dear Brigitte* (20th-Fox, 1965); *Don't Just Stand There* (U, 1968); *Lock Up Your Daughters* (Col., 1969); and *Vault of Horrors* (Cinerama, 1973).

Television. Miss Johns appeared in *Lily, The Queen of the Movies* (Studio One, CBS, Apr. 1952); *Two for Tea* (Video Th., CBS, Jan. 1953); *The $200 Parlay* (GE Th., CBS, Oct. 1961); *Safari* (Dick Powell Th., NBC, Apr. 1962); *Windfall* (Dupont Show of the Month, NBC, Jan. 1963); and other television dramas. She also was in episodes of such series as Roaring 20s (ABC, 1961); Naked City (ABC, 1961); Burke's Law (ABC, 1964); 12 O'Clock High (ABC, 1964); and Batman (ABC, 1967); and had her own program, Glynis (CBS, 1963–64).

Awards. Miss Johns was nominated for an Academy (Oscar) Award (1961) for her performance in *The Sundowners* and received an Antoinette Perry (Tony) Award (1973) as best actress in a musical for her performance in *A Little Night Music.*

Recreation. Cooking, golf, writing, poetry, books, ballet, and music.

JOHNSON, ALBERT E. Educator, writer, director. b. Sept. 6, 1912, Brooklyn, N.Y., to Oscar Algott and Olga Ida (Olsen) Johnson. Father, accountant. Grad. Freeport (N.Y.) H.S., 1930; Univ. of Virginia (Phi Beta Kappa), B.A. 1934, M.A. 1936; Cornell Univ., Ph.D. 1948. Married Oct. 17, 1943, to Isabelle Dodd, teacher. Member of AETA (bibliography comm., 1954–56); ANTA; SWTC; CTC; SAA (comm. on microfilming source materials in theatre, 1955–61); Southern Speech Assn.; Texas Speech Assn.; Phi Kappa Phi. Address: Dept. of Speech and Drama, Memphis State Univ., Memphis, TN 38152.

Since 1966, Mr. Johnson has been professor of speech and drama at Memphis State Univ. Previously, he was professor of speech and chairman of the dept. at Texas Coll. of Arts and Industries (1955–66), assistant professor of drama (1948–55) and chairman of the Dept. of Drama at the Univ. of Texas (Summers 1952, 1954); assistant professor of drama at the Univ. of Virginia (Summer 1948); graduate assistant in speech at Cornell Univ. (1946–48); teacher of English and drama at Lane H.S., Charlottesville, Va. (1942–46); director of school and community drama at Univ. of Virginia (1939–42); and associated with the Child Training Inst. of New York (1937–38).

He first performed at the Univ. of Virginia, in student productions as a Crewman and a monologist in *At Yale* (1933); Besinger in *The Front Page* (1934); and George Preble in *Post Road* (1935); wrote skits for and appeared in the annual university show, *The Virginia Reel* (1939–42); and later at the University played the title role in *Macbeth* (1944). While teaching at Lane H.S., Charlottesville, Va., he directed *Our Town, The Man Who Came to Dinner, A Midsummer Night's Dream,* and *Ladies in Retirement* (1942–46); at Cornell Univ. played the Father in *Yankee Land,* the Policeman in *A Pound on Demand* (1946), Sid in *Ah, Wilderness!,* and Christopher Wellwyn in *The Pigeon,* and directed *The Second Shepherds' Play* (1947); at the Univ. of Texas, directed *My Sister Eileen, The Enchanted, Misalliance;* and the operas *Gianni Schicchi, Cox and Box, Sunday Excursion, Hind und Zuruch,* and *Street Scene* (1948–55); played Carleton Fitzgerald in *Light Up the Sky* (1951); staged *Mr. Pim Passes By* (1952) and *Dangerous Corner* (Little Th., Austin, Tex., 1953).

At the Texas Coll. of Arts and Industries, he directed *The Taming of the Shrew* (Oct. 1955); *The Ivory Door* (Mar. 1956); *Julius Caesar* (Oct. 1956); *Two Blind Mice* (Mar. 1957); *Hamlet* (Oct. 1957); *Misalliance* (Mar. 1958); *The Merchant of Venice* (Oct. 1958); *Sabrina Fair* (Mar. 1959); *Romeo and Juliet* (Oct. 1959); *Dear Brutus* (Mar. 1960); *Twelfth Night* (Oct. 1960); *Morning's at Seven* (Mar. 1961); and *Othello* (Oct. 1962).

Other Activities. He is honorary consultant to the National Assn. on Standard Medical Vocabulary.

Published Works. Mr. Johnson has contributed articles to *Theatre Arts Monthly, Players Magazine, American Mercury, Educational Theatre Journal, Southern Speech Journal,* and *Quarterly Journal of Speech.*

Recreation. Reading, silent movies, bridge, swimming.

JOHNSON, FLORENCE. Drama and music critic. b. Florence Clara Richter, Nov. 19, 1902, New Haven, Conn., to Louis Raymond and Louise (Rehbein) Richter. Father, tool designer. Attended Hillhouse H.S., 1920; Columbia Sch. of Journalism, 1924; Yale Univ., 1925. Married June 15, 1928, to Henry Ferdinand Johnson, advertising executive; one daughter. Member of West End Club, New Haven (bd. of dir., 1974–76); Westville Garden Club, New Haven (bd. of dir., 1974–76); Outer Circle of Drama Critics (pres., 1958–61; vice-pres., 1961–to date). Address: (home) 72 Roger Rd., New Haven, CT 06515, tel. (203) 387-3250; (bus.) c/o New Haven *Journal-Courier,* , New Haven, CT 06511, tel. (203) 562-3131.

Since 1925, Miss Johnson has been music and drama critic of the New Haven *Journal-Courier.*

Recreation. Golf.

JOHNSON, LAMONT. Director, actor, producer. b. Ernest Lamont Johnson, Jr., Sept. 30, 1922, Stockton, Calif., to Ernest Lamont and Ruth Alice (Fairchild) Johnson. Father, realtor. Grad. Pasadena Jr. Coll., 1942; attended Univ. of California at Los Angeles, 1942–43. Studied acting with Sanford Meisner at the Neighborhood Playhouse Sch. of the Theatre, 1948, and with Lee Strasberg, N.Y.C., 1949–50. Married July 27, 1945, to Toni Merrill, actress; one son, one daughter. Member of AEA; SAG; DGA. Address: 601 Paseo Miramar, Pacific Palisades, CA 90272, tel. (213) 454-9649.

Pre-Theatre. Radio announcer while a college student.

Theatre. Mr. Johnson first performed as Tadeusz in *Manya* (Pasadena Playhouse, Calif., 1939); understudied Zachary Scott in *Those Endearing Young Charms* (Booth, N.Y.C., June 16, 1943); played Peter Santard in a USO tour of *Kind Lady* (ETO, 1945); produced and played in *Yes Is for a Very Young Man* (world premiere, Pasadena Playhouse, Los Angeles, Calif., 1946); played Ainger in *Young Woodley* (Westport Country Playhouse, Conn., Summer 1946); made his Bway debut as a Lord in Michael Redgrave's production of *Macbeth* (National, Mar. 31, 1948); subsequently directed *Yes Is for a Very Young Man* (Cherry Lane Th., June 6, 1949); played Weldon "Pete" Carter in *The Pony Cart* (Th. de Lys, Sept. 14, 1954); directed *The Potting Shed* (La Jolla Playhouse, Calif., Summer 1957); the opera, *The Man in the Moon* (Hollywood Opera Th., Calif., March 1957); directed *The Skin of Our Teeth* and *Edwin Booth* (La Jolla Playhouse, Calif., Summer 1958).

Mr. Johnson was a founder of the Theatre Group, Univ. of California at Los Angeles, in 1959, when he also became a member of the executive committee. For the Theatre Group, he directed, all at Schoenberg Hall, UCLA, *Under Milk Wood* (Aug. 5, 1959), *4 Comedies of Despair,* one-act plays by Albee, Ionesco, Tennessee Williams, and Beckett (Aug. 23, 1960), and *The Egg* (July 31, 1961). He directed the N.Y.C. production of *The Egg* (Cort, Jan. 8, 1962); directed *The Perfect Setup* (Cort, Oct. 24, 1962); and for the Theatre Group, he developed *Spoon River Anthology* (Humanities Bldg. Aud., May 1, 1963), and directed, at Schoenberg Hall, *Peribañez* (Aug. 6, 1963) and *'Tis Pity She's a Whore* (Aug. 7, 1963). Mr. Johnson also directed the Center Theater Group (formerly Theatre Group, UCLA) production of *The Adventures of the Black Girl in Her Search for God* (Mark Taper Forum, Mar. 20, 1969).

For the Los Angeles Concert Opera (Philharmonic Aud., Calif.), he directed *Iphigenia in Tauris* (Jan. 18, 1964) and *Semiramide* (Jan. 29, 1964).

Films. Mr. Johnson appeared as Captain Tink O'-Grady in *Retreat Hell!* (WB, 1952); he directed *A Covenant with Death* (WB, 1967); *The McKenzie Break* (UA, 1970); *A Gunfight* (Par., 1971); *The Groundstar Conspiracy* (U, 1972); *You'll Like My Mother* (U, 1972); and *The Last American Hero* (20th-Fox, 1973).

Television and Radio. From 1941–1954, he performed on radio in The F.B.I. in Peace and War, Columbia Workshop, and Suspense.

He made his television debut as Marullus and Cinna in *Julius Caesar* (Studio One, CBS, 1949); played the title role in *Aesop* (Hallmark Hall of Fame, NBC, 1952); Mike in *Prize Winner* (Philco-Television Playhouse, NBC, 1953–54); directed the Matinee Th. (NBC, 1956–58); Naked City (ABC); Twilight Zone (CBS); Dr. Kildare (NBC); directed and appeared in Profiles in Courage (NBC, 1964); directed the Richard Boone Show (NBC); Alcoa Th. (NBC); The Defenders (CBS); *Losers Weepers* (Experiment in Th., NBC, Feb. 19, 1967); and directed the television films *My Sweet Charlie* (U, 1970), which was later shown in theatres; *That Certain Summer* (ABC, 1972); and *The Execution of Private Slovik* (NBC, 1974).

Awards. Mr. Johnson received the Screen Directors Guild most distinguished directorial achievement in television award for the premiere of Profiles in Courage (1964) and for My Sweet Charlie (1970).

Recreation. Collecting recordings.

JOHNSON, LOUIS. Choreographer, dancer. b. 1930, Statesville, N.C. Studied with Doris Jones and Clara Haywood (Washington, D.C.); Sch. of American Ballet (N.Y.C.); Katherine Dunham.

Theatre. Mr. Johnson made his professional debut with the NY City Ballet in Jerome Robbins' *Ballade* (NY City Ctr., 1952); his Bway debut as a dancer in *Four Saints in Three Acts* (Broadway Th., Apr. 16, 1952); subsequently appeared in *My Darling Aida* (Winter Garden, Oct. 27, 1952); *House of Flowers* (Alvin, Dec. 30, 1954); *Damn Yankees* (46 St. Th., June 5, 1955); *The World's My Oyster* (Actors Playhouse, July 31, 1956); *Kwamina* (54 St. Th., Oct. 23, 1961); and *Hallelujah, Baby!* (Martin Beck Th., Apr. 16, 1967).

Mr. Johnson made his choreographic debut with *Lament*, as part of the NY Ballet Club's Annual Choreographer's Night (1953); participated in *Talent 55*, a showcase for Bway performers; was a resident choreographer for the Westport (Conn.) White Barn Th. (early (1950s); choreographed *Black Nativity* (41 St. Th., N.Y.C., Dec. 11, 1961); was assistant director for *The Believers* (Garrick, May 9, 1966); choreographed the NY Shakespeare Festival's Mobile Th. production of *Electra* (Washington Sq. Park, Aug. 5, 1969); *Purlie* (Broadway Th., Mar. 15, 1970); and its subsequent revival (Billy Rose Th., Dec. 27, 1972); *Les Blancs* (Longacre, Nov. 15, 1970); *Lost in the Stars* (Imperial, Apr. 18, 1972); *Changes* (Washington, D.C., Black Repertory, Dec. 6, 1973), with Mike Malone *Treemonisha* (Palace, N.Y.C., Oct. 21, 1975); and, for the Metropolitan Opera Co., *Aida* (Feb. 6, 1976).

For the Negro Ensemble Co. (St. Mark's Playhouse, N.Y.C.), he has choreographed *The Song of the Lusitanian Bogey* (Jan. 2, 1968); *Kongi's Harvest* (Apr. 15, 1968); *God Is a (Guess What?)* (Dec. 17, 1968); and *A Ballet Behind the Bridge* (Mar. 15, 1972). The Louis Johnson Dance Theatre made its debut (St. Mark's Playhouse, Feb. 17, 1969) under the auspices of the NEC, the outgrowth of a workshop program conducted there by Mr. Johnson.

He has created original works for, among others, the Brooklyn Ballet Co., the Washington (D.C.) Ballet, the Alvin Ailey Dance Theatre, the Robert Joffrey Ballet, the Dance Theatre of Harlem, and Marvin Gordon's *Ballet Concepts*. .

Films. Mr. Johnson danced in *Damn Yankees* (WB, 1958); and was the choreographer for *Cotton Comes to Harlem* (UA, 1970).

Other Activities. Mr. Johnson has worked as a teacher and dancer with Harlem Youth Opportunities Unlimited (Summer 1965); and the Harlem Cultural Council Dancemobile (Summer 1968). He currently teaches at Howard Univ. (Washington, D.C.).

JOHNSON, SUSAN. Singer, actress. b. Marilyn Jeanne Johnson, July 6, 1927, Columbus, Ohio. Attended Ohio State Univ. Married May 11, 1963, to Robert Pastene (marr. dis.). Member of AEA.

Theatre. Miss Johnson made her N.Y.C. debut as a member of the chorus, succeeding Pamela Britton as Meg Brockie in *Brigadoon* (Ziegfeld Th., Mar. 13, 1947), which she repeated on tour, and in a revival (NY City Ctr., May, 1950); toured in *Texas Li'l Darlin'*; played Annie in a stock production of *Annie Get Your Gun* (Stonehenge Th., Ridgefield, Conn., July 15, 1952); appeared as Terry Patterson in *Buttrio Square* (New Century, N.Y.C., Oct. 14, 1952); Jacqueline in the pre-Bway tryout of *The Carefree Heart* (opened Cass, Detroit, Mich., Sept. 30, 1957; closed Hanna, Cleveland, Ohio, Oct. 26, 1957); Cleo in *The Most Happy Fella* (Imperial, N.Y.C., May 3, 1956); Mae in *Oh Captain!* (Alvin, Feb. 4, 1958); Glenda Swenson in *Whoop-Up* (Shubert, Dec. 22, 1958); Kathy Carey in *Donnybrook!* (46 St. Th., May 18, 1961); and Signora Ponza in *Right You Are (If You Think You Are)* (Roundabout Th., Sept. 12, 1972).

Night Clubs. Miss Johnson appeared at the Ruban Bleu, N.Y.C.

Awards. For her performance as Cleo in *The Most Happy Fella*, Miss Johnson received the *Theatre World* Award (1956).

JOHNSTON, DENIS. Playwright, director, educator. b. William Denis Johnston, June 18, 1901, Dublin, Ireland, to William John and Kathleen Johnston. Father, Judge of the Supreme Court of Ireland. Attended St. Andrew's Coll., Dublin, 1908–15, Merchiston Castle Sch., Edinburgh, Scot., 1915–17; Cambridge Univ., Eng. M.A., LL.M., 1919–23; Pugsley Scholar at Harvard Law Sch., 1923–24. Married Dec. 28, 1928, to Shelah Kathleen Richards, actress (marr. dis. 1944); one son, one daughter; married Mar. 26, 1945, to Betty Chancellor, actress; two sons. During WW II, War Correspondent for BBC. Member of the English and Irish Bars, Assn. of Cinema and Allied Technicians (Eng.), AFRA, Royal Irish Yacht Club, Garrick Club. c/o Dept. of Theatre and Speech, Smith Coll., Northampton, MA 01060.

Since 1966, Mr. Johnston has been professor emeritus of theatre and speech, Smith Coll., where he was formerly chairman of the department. From 1950 to 1961, he was professor of English, Mt. Holyoke Coll.

Theatre. He directed a production of *King Lear* for the Dublin (Ireland) Drama League (Abbey Th., Nov. 26, 1928). He wrote *The Old Lady Says "No"!* (Dublin Gate Th., July 3, 1929); *The Moon in the Yellow River* (Abbey, Dublin, Apr. 27, 1931; Th. Guild, Feb. 29, 1932); and *Storm Song* (Gate, Dublin, Jan. 30, 1934). He was on the board of directors of the Dublin Gate Th. (1931–36).

He directed a production of *Ah, Wilderness!* (Westminster, London, Mar. 4, 1936); played An-Lu-Shan in *Armlet of Jade* (Westminster, Apr. 13, 1936). His play, *A Bride for the Unicorn* was produced (Westminster, July 4, 1936); *Blind Man's Buff* his adaptation of a play by Ernst Toller, was produced in Dublin (Abbey, Dec. 26, 1938). He wrote *The Golden Cuckoo* (Gate, Apr. 25, 1938); and *Dreaming Dust* (Gaiety, Mar. 26, 1940).

He directed for a season at the Highfield Playhouse (Cape Cod, Mass., Summer 1950); and at the Provincetown (Mass.) Playhouse (Summer 1952); his play, *The Strange Occurrence on Ireland's Eye* was producer in Dublin (Abbey Th., Aug. 20, 1956); he wrote the libretto for the opera version of *Six Characters in Search of an Author* (NY City Ctr., Apr. 26, 1956); was the literary consultant, and an alternate narrator, for *Ulysses in Nighttown* (Rooftop Th., June 5, 1958).

Films. Mr. Johnston directed the picture *Guests of the Nation;* he appeared in *Riders to the Sea* (Flanagan) and *The Story of Lili Marlene* (Crown Film Unit). He wrote the screenplays for *Ourselves Alone* and *Autumn Fire*.

Television and Radio. Since 1937, he has written and produced radio and television programs for BBC, including *Lillibulero, Death at Newtownstewart, The Parnell Commission*, and four television adaptations of his own plays. He wrote scripts for the Theatre Guild of the Air (NBC, N.Y.C., 1947–50).

Awards. He received an Order of the British Empire (O.B.E.) for services as a correspondent during WW II. Received a Guggenheim Fellowship (1955–56).

JOHNSTON, JUSTINE. Actress, singer. b. Justine Alice Johnston, June 13, Evanston, Ill., to Joseph E. and Alice J. (Schleicher) Johnston. Father, salesman. Grad. Emerson H.S., Gary, Ind.; Univ. of Chicago. Studied acting at the Goodman Memorial Th., Chicago, Ill. Member of AEA (councillor, 1969–to date); AFTRA; SAG. Address: (home) 35-48 75th St., Jackson Heights, NY 11372, tel. (212) 458-1293; (bus.) Talent Exchange, Inc., 250 W. 57th St., New York, NY 10019, tel. (212) JU 6-6300.

Theatre. Miss Johnston played Aunt Penniman in the bus-and-truck tour of *The Heiress* (opened Biloxi, Miss., Sept. 1949); in stock, Cousin Cora in *Life with Mother*, Mrs. Struthers in *Personal Appearance* (Ivoryton Playhouse, Conn., Summer 1953), and Mrs. Watson-Courtneidge in *I Am a Camera* (Monticello Playhouse, N.Y., Summer 1953); made her N.Y.C. debut as the Mother in *The Chair* (Originals Only Th., 1954); and later appeared as Lorene in *The Time of Your Life* (NY City Ctr., Jan. 19, 1955).

Miss Johnston made her Bway debut, succeeding (Mar. 1956) Ruth Gillette as Mabel in *The Pajama Game* (St. James, May 13, 1954); played Miss Rector in the pre-Bway tryout of *A Sudden Spring* (opened Pocono Playhouse, Mountainhome, Pa., June 1956; closed Farmington, Mich., Sept. 1956); and succeeded (Philadelphia, Oct. 1956) Marguerite Shaw as Mabel in the national tour of *The Pajama Game* (opened Shubert, New Haven, Conn., Jan. 29, 1955; closed Civic, New Orleans, La., Feb. 16, 1957); and she repeated the latter role at the Pittsburgh (Pa.) Civic Light Opera, and the Kansas City (Mo.) Starlight Th. (Summer 1957).

She appeared as Mrs. Allen in *Dark of the Moon* (Carnegie Hall Playhouse, N.Y.C., Feb. 26, 1958); in stock, Meg Boyd in *Damn Yankees* (Lakewood Th., Barnesville, Pa., Summer 1958); the Landlady and the Old Lady in a tour of *Show Boat* (music circuses, Neptune, N.J.; Brandywine, Pa.; Lambertville, N.J., Summer 1958); as Mrs. McIlhenny in *The Time of the Cuckoo* (Sheridan Sq. Playhouse, N.Y.C., Oct. 27, 1958); and toured as Mathilda in *The Gazebo* (opened Central City Opera House, Colo., Aug. 1959; closed Geary, San Francisco, Calif., Oct. 1959). With Town and Country Musicals (Syracuse and E. Rochester, N.Y.), she played Aunt Maude in *Redhead* (Summer 1960); at the Kansas City (Mo.) Starlight Th., appeared as Grand Duchess Anastasia in *The Student Prince*, and played Mabel in *The Pajama Game* (Summer 1960).

She played Mrs. Pampinelli in the ELT production of *The Torch Bearers* (Lenox Hill Playhouse, N.Y.C., Dec. 6, 1960); Amanda Gatsby in *Smiling, the Boy Fell Dead* (Cherry Lane, Apr. 19, 1961); toured as Mabel in *The Pajama Game* (Guber-Ford-Gross Circuit, Summer 1961); at the North Shore Music Th. (Beverly, Mass.), appeared in *The Great Waltz*, Aunt Eller in *Oklahoma!*, and Lady Beekman in *Gentlemen Prefer Blondes* (Summer 1961); played Mrs. Jacoby in *A Majority of One* (Barn Th., Augusta, Mich., Summer 1961); and Mrs. Paroo in *The Music Man* (Paper Mill Playhouse, Milburn, N.J., Fall 1961). In Dec. 1961, she appeared in the pre-Bway tryout of *Giants, Sons of Giants*, in the role of Jane, which was eliminated from the play following the Boston engagement.

She succeeded Janice Mars (Players Th., N.Y.C., Apr. 1962) as Ernestine VonLiebedich in *Little Mary Sunshine* (Orphem, Nov. 18, 1959); played Mrs. Paroo in *The Music Man* (Colonie Summer Th., Latham, N.Y., Summer 1962); and Aunt Julia in *Sabrina Fair* (Allenberry Playhouse, Boiling Springs, Pa., Fall 1962); succeeded (1962) Adda Negri as Mrs. Weinstein in *Milk and Honey* (Martin Beck Th., N.Y.C., Oct. 10, 1961); repeated the role on tour (opened Shubert, Philadelphia, Pa., Jan. 29, 1963; closed Biltmore, Los Angeles, Calif., Sept. 7, 1963); played the role of Mrs. Perlman in the same play for engagements at the Paper Mill Playhouse (Millburn, N.J.); Mineola Playhouse (L.I., N.Y., Fall 1963); and toured as Domina in *A Funny Thing Happened on the Way to the Forum* (opened Forrest, Philadelphia, Pa., Dec. 25, 1963; closed Chicago, Ill., Nov. 14, 1964); appeared as the Grand Duchess in *The Student Prince* (St. Louis Municipal Opera, 1965); played stock engagements as Domina in *A Funny Thing* . . at East Rochester, N.Y., and Nyack, N.Y., and as Mrs. Paroo in *The Music Man* (North Tonawanda, N.Y. (all 1965); again played Domina in *A Funny Thing* . . (Atlanta, Ga., 1966); played Miss Jones in *How To Succeed in Business Without Really Trying* (NY City Ctr., Apr. 20, 1966; St. Louis Municipal Opera, 1966); appeared as Mama Krantz in *Blossom Time* (Paper Mill Playhouse, Millburn, N.J., 1966); again played Domina in *A Funny Thing* . . (Wedgewood Dinner Th., Glen Cove, N.Y., 1968); was Mabel in *The Pajama Game* (Kansas City Starlight Th. and Indianapolis Starlight Th. 1968); Mrs. Rosen in *The Man in the Glass Booth* (Parker Playhouse, Fort Lauderdale and Coconut Grove Playhouse, Miami, Fla., 1969); and toured the music fairs circuit as the Grand Duchess in *The Student Prince* (1969) and as Miss Jones in *How To Succeed* . . (1970); played Heidi Schiller in

Follies (Winter Garden, N.Y.C., Apr. 4, 1971); repeated at the St. Louis Municipal Opera and Shubert Th., Century City, Los Angeles, Calif. (1972); substituted for Patsy Kelly as Mrs. O'Dare in *Irene* for six performances (National Th., Washington, D.C., 1973); and was Mrs. Frazini in *Molly* (Alvin Th., N.Y.C., Nov. 1, 1973).

Television. Miss Johnston appeared as Nurse Ginnigan in *Arrowsmith* (Dupont Show of the Month, NBC, 1960) and as the Bakery Clerk in *Sisters* (A.I.P., 1973).

Discography. Miss Johnston sings "One More Kiss" from *Follies* on the album *Sondheim: A Musical Tribute* (WB, 1973).

JOHNSTONE, ANNA HILL. Costume designer. b. Apr. 7, 1913, Greenville, S.C., to Albert S. and Anna W. (Watkins) Johnstone. Father, banker, Presbyterian minister. Grad. St. Catherine's H.S., 1930; Barnard Coll., A.B. 1934. Married May 7, 1937, to Curville J. Robinson, engineer. Member of United Scenic Artists. Address: 2501 Palisades Ave., Bronx, NY 10463, tel. (212) KI 6-4355.

Theatre. Miss Johnstone's first assignments were costume designs for the Columbia Univ. Laboratory Players (1935–36); Clare Tree Major's Children's Th. (1935); and Charles Coburn's Mohawk Drama Festival (Union Coll., Schenectady, N.Y., 1936–37).

She designed costumes for *Temper the Wind* (Playhouse, N.Y.C., Dec. 27, 1946); *For Love or Money* (Henry Miller's Th., Nov. 4, 1947); *Lost in the Stars* (Music Box, Oct. 30. 1949); *The Curious Savage* (Martin Beck Th., Oct. 24, 1950); *The Country Girl* (Lyceum, Nov. 10, 1950); *Bell, Book and Candle* (Ethel Barrymore Th., Nov. 14, 1950); *The Autumn Garden* (Coronet, Mar. 7, 1951); *Flight into Egypt* (Music Box, Mar. 18, 1952); *The Children's Hour* (Coronet, Dec. 18, 1952); *Tea and Sympathy* (Ethel Barrymore Th., Sept. 30, 1953); *All Summer Long* (Coronet, Sept. 23, 1954); *The Tender Trap* (Longacre, Oct. 12, 1954); supervised the costuming for *The Chalk Garden* (Ethel Barrymore Th., Oct. 26, 1955); designed costumes for the pre-Bway tryout of *A Quiet Place* (opened Shubert, New Haven, Conn., Nov. 23, 1955; closed Natl., Washington, D.C., Dec. 31, 1955); *The Hidden River* (Playhouse, N.Y.C., Jan. 23, 1957); *The Sin of Pat Muldoon* (Cort, Mar. 23, 1957); *The Egghead* (Ethel Barrymore Th., Oct. 9, 1957); the pre-Bway tryout of *This Is Goggle* (opened McCarter, Princeton, N.J., Jan. 23, 1958; closed Shubert, Washington, D.C., Feb. 1, 1958); *The Man in the Dog Suit* (Coronet, N.Y.C., Oct. 30, 1958); *Whoop-Up* (Shubert, Dec. 22, 1958); *Sweet Bird of Youth* (Martin Beck Th., Mar. 10, 1959); *Portrait of a Madonna, A Pound on Demand, Bedtime Story,* and a monologue, *Some Comments on the Harmful Effects of Tobacco,* all under the billing, *Triple Play* (Playhouse, Apr. 18, 1959); *One More River* (Ambassador, Mar. 18, 1960); the Lincoln Center Repertory Th. production of *After the Fall* (ANTA Washington Sq., Jan. 23, 1964); and *The Investigation* (Ambassador, N.Y.C., Oct. 4, 1966).

Films. Miss Johnstone designed the costumes for *Portrait of Jennie* (Selznick, 1948); *On the Waterfront* (Col., 1945); *East of Eden* (WB, 1955); *Baby Doll* (WB, 1956); *Edge of the City* (MGM, 1957); *A Face in the Crowd* (WB, 1957); *Odds Against Tommorrow* (UA, 1959); *Wild River* (20th-Fox, 1960); *Splendor in the Grass* (WB, 1961); *David and Lisa* (Continental, 1963); *America America* (WB, 1963); *Ladybug, Ladybug* (UA, 1964); *The Pawnbroker* (Landau, 1964); *Fail Safe* (Col., 1964); *The Group* (UA, 1966); *Bye, Bye Braverman* (WB-Seven Arts, 1968); *The Night They Raided Minsky's* (UA, 1968); *Alice's Restaurant* (UA, 1969); *The Subject Was Roses* (MGM, 1968); *Me, Natalie* (Natl. Gen., 1969); *There Was a Crooked Man* (WB, 1970); *Cotton Comes to Harlem* (UA, 1970); *Who Is Harry Kellerman?* (UA, 1971); *The Godfather* (Par., 1972); *Play It Again, Sam* (Par., 1972); *Come Back, Charleston Blue* (WB, 1972); *The Effect of Gamma Rays on Man-in-the-Moon Marigolds* (20th-Fox, 1973); *Summer Wishes, Winter Dreams* (Col., 1973); *Serpico* (Par., 1973); *The Taking of Pelham One, Two, Three* (UA, 1974); *Gordon's War* (20th-Fox, 1973); *The Stepford Wives* (Col., 1975); *Dog Day Afternoon* (WB, 1975).

Recreation. Tennis, riding.

JONES, AL. Theatre manager, company manager. b. May 31, 1909, Brooklyn, N.Y., to Walter and Nellie (Moore) Jones. Father, attorney; mother, registered nurse. Grad. Erasmus Hall H.S., Brooklyn, 1927. Relative in theatre: aunt, Zara Dolaro, actress. Member of ATPAM (bd. of gov., 1964); AEA; The Lambs (vice-chmn., house comm., 1953; membership comm., 1954; entertainment comm., 1958–62). Address: (home) 45 W. 54th St., New York, NY 10019, tel. (212) CI 6-5575; (bus.) c/o Morosco Theatre, 217 W. 45th St., New York, NY 10036, tel. (212) 246-6230.

Pre-Theatre. Banking.

Theatre. Mr. Jones made his professional debut in *The Saint* (Greenwich) Village Th., N.Y.C., Oct. 11, 1924); joined the cast of *They Knew What They Wanted* (Garrick, Nov. 24, 1924); played Valis in *The Padre* (Ritz, Dec. 27, 1926); was assistant to the producers of *Are You With It?* (Century, Nov. 10, 1945); produced a touring company of *Hand in Hand* (Summer 1948); was stage manager for *A Red Rainbow* (Royale, N.Y.C., Sept. 14, 1953); general manager for *Plain and Fancy* (Mark Hellinger Th., Jan. 27, 1955); manager for Boris Goldowsky and the New England Opera Co. (1956); company manager for *My Fair Lady* (Mark Hellinger Th., N.Y.C., Nov. 15, 1956–60); and general manager of the pre-Bway tryout of the *Ziegfeld Follies* (closed Philadelphia, Pa., 1957).

Mr. Jones was company manager for the touring company of *Damn Yankees* (opened Mosque, Altoona, Pa., Jan. 18, 1958; closed Paramount, Omaha, Neb., May 10, 1958); for *Li'l Abner* (opened Ford's Th., Baltimore, Md., Dec. 1, 1958).

He succeeded Ira Bernstein as company manager of *Gideon* (Plymouth, N.Y.C., Nov. 9, 1961); Richard Horner as general manager of *New Faces of 1962* (Alvin, Feb. 1, 1962); and was company manager for *Right You Are If You Think You Are* (Carl Fischer Hall), *Caligula* (York), the national company of *Sweet Charity* (1967), *The Education of H*y*m*a*n K*a*p*l*a*n* (Alvin Th., Apr. 4, 1968); the first national company of *Fiddler on the Roof* (1968–70); *Norman, Is That You?* (Lyceum, Feb. 19, 1970); *Borstal Boy* (Lyceum, Mar. 31, 1970), and *Follies* (Winter Garden, Summer 1973); house manager, Helen Hayes Th., during the run of *Crown Matrimonial* (1973); and company manager for *Sisters of Mercy* (Th. de Lys, Sept.–Oct. 1973).

Mr. Jones was personal manager for Leo Carillo (1934–60); general manager for James W. Gardiner (1945–67); operated the Th. by the Sea, Matunuck, R.I. (1949–50), where he produced and directed *Pal Joey, Born Yesterday,* and *The Corn Is Green;* was substitute house manager (1956–60) and general manager (1962–64) of the Mark Hellinger Th., N.Y.C. He was manager of the Alvin Th. (1959–67) and became manager of the Morosco Th. in 1970.

Television. He has appeared on the Martin Kane series (NBC, 1953).

Other Activities. Banking and real estate, member of the board of directors of the 45 West 54th St. Corp.

Recreation. Traveling.

JONES, BARRY. Actor, producer, theatre manager. b. Mar. 6, 1893, Guernsey, Channel Islands, England, to William John and Amelia Hammond (Robilliard) Jones. Attended Elizabeth Coll., Guernsey, England. Served with the Royal Guernsey Light Infantry and Royal Irish Fusiliers, Aug. 1914–Feb. 1921; as Special Constable in Royal Navy Volunteer Reserve, 1942–45; RNVR (active mbr., to date). Member of AEA; British AEA; Royal Automobile Club (RAC); United Club (Guernsey).

Pre-Theatre. Worked in shipping office.

Theatre. Mr. Jones first appeared on the stage as a walk-on in *The Knight of the Burning Pestle* (Kingsway Th., Nov. 24, 1920); subsequently, with Sir Frank R. Benson's Shakespearean Company, played the Clerk of the Court in *The Merchant of Venice* (Grand, Leeds, England, Mar. 29, 1921); toured with the latter company (1921–23).

He appeared in stock engagements (1923) in Toronto (Canada), and in Boston (Mass.); made his N.Y.C. debut in the roles of the Fifth Banker and an Officer in *Man and the Masses* (Garrick, Apr. 14, 1924); played Stanley Winton in *The Bully* (Hudson, Dec. 25, 1924); replaced Alan Mowbray as Algernon Sprigge in *The Sport of Kings* (Lyceum, May 4, 1926); appeared as Robert Mainwaring in *The Constant Nymph* (Selwyn, Dec. 9, 1926); and Mago in *The Road to Rome* (Playhouse, Jan. 31, 1927).

With Maurice Colbourne, he formed a theatrical partnership, the Colbourne-Jones Co., which lasted seventeen years, and toured the US and Canada (1928–31), presenting such plays as *You Never Can Tell, John Bull's Other Island, The Philanderer, The Doctor's Dilemma, The Dark Lady of the Sonnets, Fanny's First Play, The Applecart, The Dover Road, The Importance of Being Earnest,* and *The Perfect Alibi* The Colbourne and Jones Co. managed the Ambassadors' Th. (London), their first production being *The Queen's Husband,* in which Mr. Jones played King Eric III; he subsequently played the Man in *Queer Cattle* (Haymarket, May 1932).

The Company toured Canada with *Too True To Be Good* and *The Apple Cart* Sept. 1932); Mr. Jones played Lawrence Brooke in *Women Kind* (Phoenix, London, Sept. 1933); Jacques in *As You Like It* (Phoenix, Sept. 1933). Lawrence Brooke in *Women Kind,* retitled *And Be My Love* (Ritz, N.Y.C., Jan. 18, 1934); and toured the US as Rudolph in *Reunion in Vienna* (1934).

Under H. M. Tennent's management in London, he appeared as Charles Lankaster in *Moonlight Is Silver* (Queen's, Sept. 1934), Anthony Lynton in *Mrs. Nobby Clark* (Comedy, Feb. 1935); King Stefan in *Glamourous Night* (Drury Lane, May 2, 1935); and replaced (Apr. 1936) Ralph Richardson as Emile Delbar in *Promise* (Shaftesbury, Feb. 26, 1936); with his own company, played Charles I in *Charles the King* (Lyric, Oct. 9, 1936); Anthony Thorne in *Lovers' Meeting* (Embassy, June 1937); Dr. Mallaby in *The Switchback* ("Q," Nov. 1937); Stephen Davis in *Mary Goes to See* (Haymarket, Feb. 1938); Lord Bayfield in *Comedienne* (Haymarket, June 16, 1938); and Sir Colenso Ridgeon in *The Doctor's Dilemma* (Westminster, Feb. 17, 1939).

Mr. Jones toured Canada in the title role of *Charles the King* (Oct. 1939); played the Judge in *Geneva* and Tobias in *Tobias and the Angel;* with Gilbert Miller, Colbourne and Jones, produced *Geneva,* in which Mr. Jones played the Judge (Henry Miller's Th., N.Y.C., Jan. 30, 1940); he appeared as Valentine in the Players Club production of *Love for Love* (Hudson, June 3, 1940); toured in *The Curtain Rises, Serena Blandish,* and as Ilan Carve in *The Great Adventure* (1940).

For the British War Charities, he toured with Gertrude Lawrence in *Private Lives* (1941); replaced (June 1941) Colin Keith-Johnston as Dr. Blenkinsopp in *The Doctor's Dilemma* (Shubert, N.Y.C., Mar. 11, 1941), and on tour; played in *Behold We Live* (Dennis, Mass., Aug. 1941); Frederick in *Home and Beauty* (Playhouse, London, Nov. 12, 1942); and with the ENSA, toured in *The Applecart* (Austria, Germany, and Italy, 1945–46).

He appeared as Hopeful in *The Pilgrim's Progress* (Covent Garden, London, July 19, 1948); replaced (Mar. 1949) Eric Portman as Andrew Crocker-Harris in *The Browning Version,* on a double bill with *Harlequinade,* in which he played Arthur Gosport (Phoenix, Sept. 8, 1948); appeared as Howard Jones in *Mrs. Inspector Jones* (Savoy, Nov. 2, 1950); Socrates in *Barefoot in Athens* (Martin Beck Th., N.Y.C., Oct. 31, 1951); Mr. Tarleton in *Misalliance* (NY City Ctr., Feb. 18, 1953); the King in *The Cave Dwellers* (Bijou, Oct. 19, 1957); Mackenzie Savage in *The Pleasure of His Company* (Haymarket, London, Apr. 23, 1959); and he was in *The Tigers Are Coming, O.K.?* (London, 1974).

Films. Since his debut as Bluntschli in *Arms and the*

Man(1931), Mr. Jones has appeared in *Spring Cleaning* (Elstree, 1932); *Number 17* (20th-Fox, 1921); *Seven Days to Noon* (Mayer-Kingsley, 1950); *The Bad Lord Byron* (Intl. Releasing Org., 1951); *The Clouded Yellow* (Col., 1952); *Island Rescue* (U, 1952); *The Plymouth Adventure* (MGM, 1952); *Brigadoon* (MGM, 1954); *Demetrius and the Gladiators* (20th-Fox, 1954); *Prince Valiant* (20th-Fox, 1954); played Aristotle in *Alexander the Great* (UA, 1956); Count Rostov in *War and Peace* (Par., 1956); appeared in *Saint Joan* (UA, 1957); *The Safecracker* (MGM, 1958); *Dancing with Crime; Appointment with Venus;* and *Carolvia Die Rejectre.*

Television. He first appeared in Max and Mrs. Max (BBC, London, 1935); subsequently played Polonius in *Hamlet;* and appeared on Kraft Television Th. (NBC); Lux Video Th. (CBS); Robert Montgomery Presents (NBC); Studio One (CBS); played *The Little Moon of Alban* (Hallmark Hall of Fame, NBC, Mar. 1958); *Time Remembered;* and in England for BBC, *Hamlet,* and *Victoria Regina* (1961–62); in Toronto (Canada), *Something Old, Something New* (1962); on the serials, The Saint (1962–63); and the Third Man; played Julius Caesar in *Spread of the Eagle* (1963); appeared in his own series, Old Martin Chuzzlewit (BBC, London, 1964); and played in *Pilgrim, Why Did You Come?* (CBC, Canada, May 1964).

Recreation. Painting, gardening.

JONES, BROOKS. Producer, director, composer, singer, arranger. b. David Brooks Jones, Oct. 23, 1934, Columbus, Ohio, to Edwin A. and Katharine (McKee) Jones. Father, industrialist. Grad. St. Mark's Sch., Southboro, Mass., 1952; Princeton Univ., B.A. (with honors) 1956. Served US Army, 1957–58. Relative in theatre: sister, Gloria Jones, actress. Member of AEA; AFTRA; AFM, Local 802; National Theatre Conference (1968–74); Princeton Triangle Club (pres., 1956); N.J. Tercentenary Committee (appointee, 1962). Address: 400 W. 57th St., New York, NY 10019, tel. (212) JU 2-4587.

Theatre. Mr. Jones' first assignment was at Princeton Univ., producing, writing, and acting in three annual Triangle Club shows (1954–56); subsequently he wrote, directed, and appeared in *3 Folk Sing* (Actors Playhouse, N.Y.C., June 14, 1956), which toured colleges (opened Oct. 10, 1956); directed and acted in *De Good Book* (Seoul, Korea, 1958); joined the McCarter Th. (Princeton, N.J.), as associate producer (1958), and assisted in the production of *Man and Superman, Right You Are If You Think You Are, The Seagull, The Affairs of Anatol, The Tavern, Scapin, Cat and the Moon, The Lady's Not for Burning, King Lear, Hamlet, As You Like It, A Midsummer Night's Dream* and the operetta, *Cox and Box.*

He was composer-arranger for *Borak* (Martinique, N.Y.C., Dec. 13, 1960); at the McCarter Th. (Princeton, N.J., 1960–62), produced *Saint Joan, Androcles and the Lion, Our Town,* and *Long Christmas Dinner;* with the Playhouse in the Park (Cincinnati, Ohio, 1962), produced *The Hostage, The Devil's Disciple, Enrico IV, Arms and the Man, The Burnt Flower Bed, The Doctor in Spite of Himself, The Forced Marriage, Rhinoceros, A Moon for the Misbegotten;* directed and produced *The Zoo Story, The Fantasticks, Calvary, Act Without Words II, Don Perlimpin, Oh Dad, Poor Dad, Mamma's Hung You in the Closet and I'm Feelin' So Sad* and *The Threepenny Opera;* produced and served as composer-arranger for *The Lady's Not for Burning* and *Twelfth Night.*

From 1963 to 1971, he produced and directed at Cincinnati's Playhouse in the Park *He Who Gets Slapped, Endgame, The Good Woman of Setzuan, Anatol, The Birthday Party, The Collection, The Lover, The Blood Knot, The Balcony, Benito Cereno, Escurial, The Skin of Our Teeth, Muzeeka, The American Dream, Tour, Saint Joan,* and *Three Men and a Monster.* In addition, he produced *Ghosts, Major Barbara, Summer of the Seventeenth Doll, She Stoops to Conquer, The Glass Managerie, Man and Superman, Sodom and Gomorrah, Charley's Aunt, Eh?, Honour and Offer, Comedy of Errors, The Importance of Being Earnest, The Cavern, Uncle Vanya, Misalliance, The Miser, Camino Real, Crime on Goat Island, The Madwoman of Chaillot, Volpone, Dutchman, Lady Audley's Secret, Six Characters in Search of an Author, Come Back, Little Sheba, Ardele, Many Happy Returns,* and *Pygmalion.*

Other than his work in Cincinnati, Mr. Jones directed for Center Stage, Baltimore, Md., *The Birthday Pary* (1966) and *The Balcony* (1967); for PETA-Company, Manila, Philippines, he directed *The Good Woman of Setzuan, Kalbaryo,* and *The Chinese Wall* (all 1972); and for the Long Wharf Theatre, New Haven, Conn., *The Resistible Rise of Arturo Ui* (1974), and he was co-author and director of *Not What He Intended* (1974).

Films. He conceived the idea for the short subject *Genesis I–27,* which he co-directed and for which he wrote the score, and he produced and directed a 30-minute film for television, *Silent Night,* which was shown on WGBH-TV, Boston (Dec. 1972).

Television. He appeared on the Ed Sullivan Show (CBS, 1955); and Hootenanny (ABC, 1963, 1964). He directed Samuel Beckett's *Act without Words II* and William Butler Yeats's *Calvary* (Esso Th. Series, 1966). In 1971–72, he was artist-in-residence, WGBH-TV, Boston, where he created the Fleamarket series, Don't Tell Your Parents, and the Timecheck series. In 1972, he was producer of continuity prototypes for WNET-TV, New York, and director of a pilot for Cancion de la Calle, a bilingual program for KUHT-TV, Houston. He served as a consultant for Cumberland Mountain Media Project (1972–74), and was a development consultant for KCET-TV, Los Angeles, in 1973.

Night Clubs. He has sung at The Caucus Room (Detroit, Mich., 1956); The Back Room (Cleveland, Ohio, 1957); Blue Angel (N.Y.C., 1958, 1963); and at The Bitter End (N.Y.C., 1964).

Other Activities. Mr. Jones was on the board of directors of ANTA (1964), of TCG (Theatre Communications Group) (1966–70), on the Third World Committee, International Theatre Institute (1973–74), and on the advisory board, St. Clement's Theatre, N.Y.C. (1974).

Awards. Mr. Jones won *Cine's* Golden Eagle Award for the film *Genesis I–27.*

JONES, HENRY. Actor. b. Henry Burk Jones, Aug. 1, 1912, Philadelphia, Pa., to John F. X. and Helen (Burk) Jones. Grad. Joseph's Prep., Philadelphia, 1931; St. Joseph's Coll., A.B. 1935. Married Jan. 14, 1942, to Yvonne Bergere, actress (marr. dis. Oct. 1942); married June 1946 to Judy Briggs, fashion model (marr. dis. Mar. 1961); one son, one daughter. Served US Army, 1942–45; rank, Pfc. Member of AEA; AFTRA; SAG; The Players.

Theatre. Mr. Jones first performed on the stage at Notre Dame Acad., Philadelphia, Pa., playing Scrooge in *A Christmas Carol* (Dec. 1926); made his professional debut as Doctor Glenn in *An American Tragedy* (Hedgerow Th., Moylan, Pa., Dec. 1935).

He made his Bway debut as Reynaldo and the Second Gravedigger in Maurice Evans' *Hamlet* (St. James, Oct. 12, 1938); played Justice Silence and Francis in Maurice Evans's *Henry IV, Part 2* (44th St. Th., Jan. 30, 1939); succeeded Curt Conway in the role of Dudley Bostwick (Mar. 15, 1940) in *The Time of Your Life* (Booth, Oct. 25, 1939); played Hubert Carter in *Village Green* (Henry Miller's Th., Sept. 3, 1941); and replaced Richard Quine in the role of Frank Lippincott in *My Sister Eileen* (Biltmore, Oct. 1, 1941).

In the army, he played Mr. Brown in *This Is the Army* (Bway Th., July 4, 1942; continuing with the musical until his separation from the service); subsequently appeared as Sheriff Carson in *January Thaw* (John Golden Th., Feb. 4, 1946); was understudy for Romney Brent, who played the Dauphin in *Joan of Lorraine* (Alvin, Nov. 18, 1946); appeared as Humpty Dumpty and the Mouse in *Alice in Wonderland* (International, Apr. 5, 1947); Walter Smith in *How I Wonder* (Hudson, Sept. 30, 1947); Seamus MacGonigal in *Kathleen* (Mansfield, Feb. 3, 1948); Vince Barber in *Town House* (Natl., Sept. 23, 1948); the Doctor in *They Knew What They Wanted* (Music Box, Feb 16, 1949); Stumm in *Metropole* (Lyceum, Dec. 6, 1949); the Stage Manager in *A Story for a Sunday Evening* (Playhouse, Nov. 17, 1950); Clifford Snell in *The Solid Gold Cadillac* (Belasco, Nov. 5, 1953); Leroy in *The Bad Seed* (46 St. Th., Dec. 8, 1956); Louis McHenry Howe in *Sunrise at Campobello* (Cort, Jan. 30, 1958); and Seab Cooley in *Advise and Consent* (Cort, Nov. 17, 1960).

Films. Mr. Jones made his debut in *This Is the Army* (WB, 1943); subsequently played in *The Lady Says No* (UA, 1951); *Taxi* (20th-Fox, 1953); *The Bad Seed* (WB, 1956); *The Girl He Left Behind* (WB, 1956); *The Girl Can't Help It* (20th-Fox, 1956); *Will Success Spoil Rock Hunter?* (20th-Fox, 1957); *310 to Yuma* (Col., 1957); *Vertigo* (Par., 1958); *Cash McCall* (WB, 1959); *Bramblebush* (WB, 1960); *Angel Baby* (Allied, 1961); and *Never Too Late* (WB, 1965).

Television. Among the many television programs on which he has appeared are Alfred Hitchcock Presents (CBS, 1958–59; NBC, 1965; Ind., 1966); The Investigators (NBC, 1959); Playhouse 90 (CBS, 1959); Alcoa Hour (NBC, 1960); Wagon Train (NBC, 1960); Checkmate (NBC, 1960; Ind., 1964); Frontier Circus (CBS, 1960); Route 66 (CBS, 1960, 1964); Twilight Zone (CBS, 1960; ABC, 1965); The Defenders (CBS, 1961); Adventures in Paradise (ABC, 1961); Dupont Show of the Month (NBC, 1962); The Untouchables (ABC, 1962); The New Breed (ABC, 1962); Thriller (NBC, 1962; Ind., 1964, 1965); The Real McCoys (NBC, 1962); Eleventh Hour (NBC, 1962; Ind., 1964); Channing (ABC, 1964); Kraft Suspense Th. (NBC, 1964); The Man from U.N.C.L.E. (NBC, 1964, 1967); Bonanza (NBC, 1964); and Trailmaster (ABC, 1964–65, 1965–66).

He played Hamilton Fish in *The Ulysses S. Grant Story* (Profiles in Courage, NBC, Mar. 7, 1965); was on Bewitched (ABC, 1966); portrayed Reverend Paris in *The Crucible* (Drama Special, CBS, May 4, 1967); appeared on Gunsmoke (CBS, 1967); Daniel Boone (NBC, 1967); Mod Squad (ABC, 1968); The Name of the Game (NBC, 1969); The Virginian (NBC, 1970); Love Hate Love (ABC, 1971); Night Gallery (NBC, 1972); The Daughters of Joshua Cabe (ABC, 1972); and Adam-12 (NBC, 1972).

Awards. Mr. Jones received the Antoinette Perry (Tony) Award and won the *Variety* NY Drama Critics Poll for his performance as Louis McHenry Howe in *Sunrise at Campobello* (1958).

Recreation. Postal chess, grunion fishing.

JONES, JAMES EARL. Actor. b. Jan. 17, 1931, Tate County, Miss., to Robert Earl and Ruth (Williams) Jones. Father, actor; mother, tailor. Grad. Norman Dickson H.S., Brethren, Mich., 1949; Univ. of Michigan, B.A. 1953; Amer. Theatre Wing, Diploma 1957. Studied acting with Lee Strasberg and Tad Danielewsky, N.Y.C. Served US Army; rank, 1st Lt. Member of AEA; SAG; AFTRA.

Pre-Theatre. Brick mason.

Theatre. Mr. Jones first appeared on stage as a student at the Univ. of Michigan, (1949–50), where he played Brett in *Deep Are the Roots,* Verges in *Much Ado About Nothing,* the King in *The Birds,* and David King in *A Sleep of Prisoners.* He performed in summer stock at the Manistee (Mich.) Summer Th. (1955–59) appearing in *Stalag 17, The Caine Mutiny, Velvet Gloves, The Tender Trap, Arsenic and Old Lace, Desperate Hours,* and played the title role in *Othello.*

His first N.Y.C. assignment was as understudy to Lloyd Richards, as Perry Hall in *The Egghead* (Ethel Barrymore Th., Oct. 9, 1957); followed by the role of Sgt. Blunt in *Wedding in Japan* (Graystone Hotel, 1957); Edward in *Sunrise at Campobello* (Cort, Jan. 30, 1958); Jessie Prince in *The Pretender* (1959); and Gregory in the NY Shakespeare Festival production of *Romeo and Juliet* (Heckscher Th., Dec. 1955), and on tour.

He appeared as Harrison Thurston in *The Cool World* (Eugene O'Neill Th., N.Y.C., Feb. 22, 1960); for the NY Shakespeare Festival, played Williams in *King Henry V* (Belvedere Lake Th., Central Park, June 29, 1960), and Abhorson in *Measure for Measure* (Belvedere Lake Th., July 25, 1960); played

Deodatus Village in *The Blacks* (St. Marks Playhouse, May 4, 1961); rejoined the NY Shakespeare Festival as Oberon in *A Midsummer Night's Dream* (Wollman Rink, Central Park, July 31, 1961), and Lord Marshall in *King Richard II* (Wollman Rink, Aug. 28, 1961); appeared as Roger Clark in *Clandestine on the Morning Line* (Actor's Playhouse, Oct. 30, 1961); Ace in *The Apple* (Living Th., Dec. 7, 1961); Ephraim in *Moon on a Rainbow Shawl* (E. 11 St. Th., Jan. 15, 1962); and Cinna in *Infidel Caesar* (Music Box, Apr. 27, 1962). He appeared with the NY Shakespeare Festival as the Prince of Norocco in *The Merchant of Venice* (Delacorte Th., Central Park, June 13, 1962), and Caliban in *The Tempest* (Delacorte, July 16, 1962); and played Henry in *Toys in the Attic* (Corning Summer Th., N.Y., 1962).

Mr. Jones played Mario Saccone in *P.S. 193* (Writers' Stage, Oct. 30, 1962); succeeded (1963) Ramon Bieri as Macduff for a NY Shakespeare Festival production of *Macbeth* (Heckscher Th., Nov. 15, 1962); played George Gulp in *The Love Nest* (Writers' Stage, Jan. 25, 1963); succeeded Melvin Stewart as Mr. Ash in *The Last Minstrel* (Pocket, May 8, 1963); played the title role in *Othello* (Corning Summer Th., N.Y., 1963); Camillo in the NY Shakespeare Festival production of *The Winter's Tale* (Delacorte, N.Y.C., Aug. 9, 1963); the title role in an ELT production of *Mr. Johnson* (Masters Inst., Oct. 5, 1963); Rudge in *Next Time I'll Sing to You* (Phoenix, Nov. 27, 1963); and Zachariah Pieterson in *Bloodknot* (Cricket, Mar. 2, 1964).

Mr. Jones played the title role in *Othello* (Delacorte Th., N.Y.C., July 14, 1964; Martinique, Oct. 12, 1964); Brutus in *The Emperor Jones* (Boston Public Garden Th., Boston, Aug. 4, 1964); Ekart in *Baal* (Martinique, N.Y.C., May 6, 1965); Junius Brutus in *Coriolanus* (Delacorte, July 7, 1965); Ajax in *Troilus and Cressida* (Delacorte, Aug. 4, 1965); Philippeau in *Danton's Death* (Vivian Beaumont Th., Oct. 21, 1965); Arnie and Bo in *Bohikee Creek* (Stage 73, Apr. 28, 1966); alternated with Michael McGuire in the roles of Macbeth and Macduff in the New York Shakespeare Festival Mobile Theatre touring production of *Macbeth* (opened Chelsea Park, June 25, 1966; closed Aug. 20, 1966); appeared in *An Evening of Negro Poetry and Folk Music* (Delacorte, Aug. 15, 1966) which was subsequently presented on Broadway as *A Hand Is on the Gate* (Longacre, Sept. 21, 1966); played Randall in *The Displaced Person* (American Place Th., Dec. 16, 1966); toured Europe in *The Emperor Jones* (Summer 1967); originated the role of Jack Jefferson in *The Great White Hope* (Arena Stage, Washington, D.C., Dec. 1967; and Alvin, N.Y.C., Oct. 3, 1968); played Boesman in *Boesman and Lena* (Circle in the Square, June 22, 1970); Tshembe Matoseh in *Les Blancs* (Longacre, Nov. 15, 1970); the title role in *Othello* (Mark Taper Forum, Los Angeles, 1971); Claudius in *Hamlet* (Delacorte, N.Y.C., June 20, 1972); Lopahin in *The Cherry Orchard* (Public Th., Jan. 11, 1973); the title role in *King Lear* (Delacorte Th., July 26, 1973); Hickey in *The Iceman Cometh* (Circle in the Square, Dec. 13, 1973); and Lenny in *Of Mice and Men* (Brooks Atkinson Th., Dec. 18, 1974).

Films. He appeared as Lt. Lothar Logg in *Dr. Strangelove* (Col., 1963); appeared in *The Comedians* (MGM, 1967); *The Great White Hope* (20th-Fox, 1970); *The End of the Road* (AA, 1970); *The Man* (Par., 1972); and *Claudine* (20th-Fox, 1974); and was the narrator for *Malcolm X* (WB, 1972).

Television. He played Detective Andrews on the Defenders (CBS, 1962); appeared on the Catholic Hour (CBS, 1962); played Joe in *Who Do You Kill?* (East Side/West Side, CBS, 1963); and performed Camera 3 (CBS, 1963); Look Up and Live (CBS, 1963); Repertoire Workshop (CBS); Dr. Kildare (NBC); The Guiding Light (CBS); Tarzan (NBC); NET Playhouse (NET); and NYPD (ABC).

Awards. Mr. Jones won *The Village Voice* Off-Bway (Obie) awards for his performances in NY Shakespeare Festival productions, and in *Clandestine on the Morning Line, The Apple,* and *Moon on a Rainbow Shawl* (1962). He also received the *Theatre World* Award for his performance as Ephraim in *Moon on a Rainbow Shawl* (1962); the Village Voice Off-Bway (Obie) Award for *Baal* (1965); The Vernon Rice Award (1965) for his performance in *Othello;* and the Antoinette Perry (Tony) Award (1969) for his performance in *The Great White Hope.*

Recreation. Mountain climbing, chess.

JONES, JOHN. Educator, writer, director, designer. b. John Hayford Jones, Apr. 26, 1917, Waukesha, Wis., to Owen L. and Mildred H. Jones. Father, salesman. Grad. Alhambra (Calif.) H.S., 1934; Univ. of California at Los Angeles, B.Ed. (art) 1941, M.A. (art) 1948. Married 1953, to June Beck, educator; one son, one daughter. Member of ATA. Address: (home) 6224 Jumilla Ave., Woodland Hills, CA 91364, tel. (213) 340-7907; (bus.) Univ. of California at Los Angeles, Los Angeles, CA 90024.

Mr. Jones is a professor of design (1967–to date) at the Univ. of California at Los Angeles, where he has been a lecturer (1942–52); assistant professor (1952–58); and associate professor (1958–67).

Theatre. Mr. Jones made his acting debut in California as Mephistopheles in *Doctor Faustus* (UCLA Campus Th., 1940); danced with the Myra Kinch Dancers (Redlands Bowl, UCLA, 1940), and toured until 1942; and designed the costumes for the Billy Barnes Group (Chi-Chi Club, Palm Springs, Calif., 1945).

He has designed sets and costumes for the University Th. and at Royce Hall, was director and costume designer for his drama, *The Pearl* (May 1954); director for his *Montezuma* (Dec. 1956); designer of costumes for his *A Game of Gods* (May 1959); director of *Allegro* (Th. 170, Los Angeles, Calif.); *Griffin and the Minor Canon* (Little Th., Los Angeles, Calif., 1963); and *The Infernal Machine* (Magowan Hall Th., Dec. 1963).

For the Th. Group productions at Schoenberg Hall, UCLA, Mr. Jones was lighting designer for *Under Milk Wood* (1959); set and lighting designer for *Mother Courage* (1959); lighting designer for *The Three Sisters* (1960); and *Four Comedies of Despair* (1960); costume designer for *Peribanez* (1963); and *'Tis a Pity She's a Whore* (1963).

For a joint USO-UCLA tour of the Far East, Mr. Jones directed *45 Minutes from Broadway* (1961); was stage director of the Opera Workshop production of *Don Giovanni* (Schoenberg Hall, 1962); directed and choreographed *Carousel* for a Far East USO tour (Summer 1964); for the USO-UCLA, directed, choreographed, and designed the sets and costumes for *How to Succeed in Business Without Really Trying* for a tour of Germany (1969); and directed *A Funny Thing Happened on the Way to the Forum* for a tour of the Orient (1973).

At UCLA, he directed *The Tempest* (1966); and *Noah and a Flood of Other Stuff* (1966); directed and designed costumes for *Agamemnon* (1967); and directed *Anything Goes* (1968); and *Celebration.* He directed *El Nino Ha Nacido* in Spanish for the UCLA Latin American Center (1966); directed *Annabelle Broom* (Huntington Hartford Th., Los Angeles, 1966); and wrote *Tyger, Tyger,* a mixed-media show based on the life and works of William Blake (staged reading, UCLA, 1970).

Films. Mr. Jones was designer and choreographer for the educational film *The Highwayman* (Kurt Simon, 1956); and was producer and photographer-director for *The Golden Voyage of the Jones Family* (NBC, 1966).

Other Activities. Mr. Jones lectured at the Film Inst. (Cairo, Egypt, 1960–61; 1964–65).

JONES, LEROI. See BARAKA, Imamu Amiri.

JONES, TOM. Playwright, lyricist. b. Feb. 17, 1928, Littlefield, Tex., to W. T. and Jessie (Bellomy) Jones. Father, hatcheryman. Grad. Coleman (Tex.) H.S., 1945; Univ. of Texas, B.F.A. 1949, M.F.A. 1951. Married June 1, 1963, to Elinor Wright. Served US Army, C.I.C., 1951–53. Member of ASCAP; Dramatists Guild.

Theatre. Mr. Jones was writer-lyricist for *Shoestring '57* (Barbizon-Plaza Hotel, N.Y.C., Nov. 5, 1956); *Kaleidoscope* (Provincetown Playhouse, June 13, 1957); wrote the book and lyrics for the one-act musical, *The Fantasticks* (Barnard Summer Th., N.Y.C. 1959), which was expanded to full length (Sullivan St. Playhouse, N.Y.C., May 3, 1960; Apollo, London, 1961).

He adapted the book and wrote the lyrics for the musical version of *Anatol* (City Hall Th., Hamilton, Bermuda, Spring 1960); wrote the lyrics for *110 in the Shade* (Broadhurst, N.Y.C., Oct. 24, 1963); the book and lyrics for *I Do! I Do!* (46 St. Th., Dec. 5, 1966); for *Celebration* (Ambassador, Jan. 22, 1969); and lyrics for *Colette* (Ellen Stewart Th., May 6, 1970).

In 1974, Mr. Jones and his collaborator, the composer Harvey Schmidt, established Portfolio Studio in N.Y.C. as a nonprofit company to experiment with productions of original musical presentations. Portfolio presented *Portfolio Revue* (Dec. 6, 1974); *Philemon* (Jan. 3, 1975; re-opened Apr. 8, 1975); a revival of *Celebration* (Jan. 31, 1975); and *The Bone Room* (Mar. 8, 1975).

Films. Mr. Jones produced, with Harvey Schmidt, *A Texas Romance, 1909* (Janus, 1965).

Television. Mr. Jones wrote the book and lyrics for *New York Scrapbook* (Play of the Week, WNTA, 1961). *The Fantasticks* was televised (Hallmark Hall of Fame, NBC, Oct. 18, 1964).

Night Clubs. He wrote and directed an Act for Tom Poston and Gerry Matthews at Le Reuban Bleu (N.Y.C., Apr. 1954); and he was author-lyricist of the revues, *Four Below* (Downstairs at the Upstairs, N.Y.C., 1956); and *Demi-Dozen* (Upstairs at the Downstairs, N.Y.C., 1958–59); and contributed lyrics to the revue *Pick a Number XV* (Plaza 9 Room, Hotel Plaza, N.Y.C., Oct. 14, 1965).

Discography. Recordings have been made of *The Fantasticks* (MGM Records); *Shoestring '57* (Offbeat); *110 in the Shade* (Victor); and Celebration (Capitol).

Awards. He received the Vernon Rice Award for outstanding contributions to off-Bway theatre, and the Stockholm Critics Award for best new play for *The Fantasticks* (1962). *I Do! I Do!* received an Antoinette Perry (Tony) Award (1967) as best musical play, and Mr. Jones and Harvey Schmidt received Tony nominations for best lyricist and composer, respectively. Messrs. Jones and Schmidt received the Outer Critics' Circle Award (1975) for the outstanding contributions made by Portfolio Studio to the musical theatre.

Recreation. Swimming, croquet, English bowls.

JORY, JON V. Producer, director. b. Jon Victor Jory, June 1, 1938, Pasadena, Cal., to Victor E. and Jean (Inness) Jory. Father, actor; mother, actress. Educ. Univ. of Utah; Yale Drama School, M.A. Served US Army, 1960–61. Married May 27, 1971, to Lee Anne Fahey. Member of AEA; SSD&C; DGA; SAG. Address: (home) 508 Belgravia Court, Louisville, KY 40208; (bus.) 316 Main St, Louisville, KY 40208.

Theatre. Mr. Jory made his stage debut at the age of six as Tiny Tim in *A Christmas Carol* (Pasadena Playhouse, Calif., 1944), and his first appearance on television followed in two years when he appeared in a production of *Macbeth.* His first role on the touring stage was in the second company of *Cat on a Hot Tin Roof* (1954). He made his Bway debut as director of *In Fashion* (Alvin Th., Jan. 8, 1973), a musical that he had written with Jerry Blatt and Lonnie Burstein.

With Harlan Kleiman, Mr. Jory founded the Long Wharf Theatre, New Haven, Conn., in 1965 and was its artistic director until 1967, a period during which he was responsible for productions of *The Trojan Women, The Rivals, Oh, What a Lovely War!, Hay Fever, Uncle Vanya, The Crucible, The Bald Soprano, Under Milk Wood, Thumbelina, The Hostage, Volpone, Little Mary Sunshine, The Plough and the Stars, Room Service, The Night of the Iguana,* and *A Doctor in Spite of Himself.*

Mr. Jory became producing director of Actors Th., Louisville, Ky., in 1969, and through 1974 productions he had staged included *Under Milk Wood, Tartuffe, Hamlet, Tobacco Road, Charley's Aunt,*

Death of a Salesman, Hedda Gabler, A Man for All Seasons, Long Day's Journey into Night, Man of Destiny, The Taming of the Shrew, Macbeth, Major Barbara, Marat/Sade, What the Butler Saw, Volpone, Star-Spangled Girl, A Midsummer Night's Dream, She Stoops, In Fashion, and *Tricks.* The last of these, a musical, was also written by Mr. Jory in collaboration with Jerry Blatt and Lonnie Burstein.

As guest director at other regional playhouses, Mr. Jory has directed *Arms and the Man, Barefoot in the Park,* and *Hay Fever* (all at Stage/West, West Springfield, Mass.); *Look Back in Anger* (Charles Playhouse, Boston, Mass.); *Twelfth Night* and *The Beggar's Opera* (both at McCarter Th., Princeton, N.J.); *Marat/Sade* and *The Man Who Came to Dinner* (both at the Buffalo Studio Arena, Buffalo, N.Y.); *Arms and the Man* (Pittsburgh Playhouse, Pittsburgh, Pa.) and *Tricks* (Arena Stage, Washington, D.C.). In summer theatres, Mr. Jory has directed *In Fashion, Our Town, Black Comedy, Romeo and Juliet, Captain Jinks of the Horse Marines, Merton of the Movies,* and *In Fashion* (all at the Penn State Festival Th., State College, Pa., 1968–71); *Blithe Spirit* and *Who's Afraid of Virginia Woolf?* (Totem Pole Playhouse, Fayetteville, Pa.); *The Adding Machine, Charley's Aunt,* and *Rhinoceros* (Nutmeg Playhouse, Storrs, Conn.); and *Becket, Look Back in Anger, Tender Trap, Cat on a Hot Tin Roof, Present Laughter, The Boy Friend, A Thurber Carnival, The Night of the Iguana* (all at Clinton Playhouse, Clinton, Conn., which was founded by Mr. Jory).

Television. Mr. Jory was author and director of *In Fashion,* presented on television (PBS, 1973).

Other Activities. Mr. Jory has taught at Pennsylvania State Univ., Univ. of Louisville, Univ. of Hawaii, and Indiana Univ. He has lectured on aspects of theatrical work at such meetings as the Mississippi Theatre Conference (1970); First American Theatre Conference (1974); and Southeastern Theatre Congress (1970; 1974).

Awards. Mr. Jory received the Margo Jones Award in 1963–64 and in 1966–67 for producing new plays. He received an honorary doctor of arts and letters degree from the Univ. of Louisville (1973); was voted Kentucky's outstanding young man by the Kentucky Junior Chamber of Commerce (1973); and received Louisville's Fleur de Lis Award.

JORY, VICTOR. Actor, producer. b. Nov. 23, 1903, Dawson City, Alaska, to Edwin and Joanna (Snyder) Jory. Father, rancher. Grad. Pasadena (Calif.) H.S., 1922; attended Fullerton (Calif.) Junior Coll., 1922–23; studied at Pasadena Playhouse, 1920–23. Married Dec. 23, 1928, to Jean Inness, actress; one son, one daughter. Relatives in theatre: son, Jon Jory, actor, writer, producing director; daughter, Jean Jory, actress. Member of AEA; SAG; AFTRA; USO. Masons.

Theatre. Mr. Jory made his debut in stock in companies in Dayton and Columbus (Ohio); Chicago, Ill.; and Denver, Colo. (1929–32); subsequently played Mr. Manningham in *Angel Street* (Chicago, Ill., 1942); made his Bway debut as Geoffrey in *The Two Mrs. Carrolls* (Booth, Aug. 3, 1943); played Dale Williams in *The Perfect Marriage* (Ethel Barrymore Th., Oct. 26, 1944); Lt. Cmdr. William Marshall in the pre-Bway tour of *Bill Comes Back* (opened Aud., Trenton, N.J., Feb. 24, 1925; closed Shubert, New Haven, Conn., Mar. 10, 1945); Laurent in *Therese* (Biltmore, N.Y.C., Oct. 9, 1945); and at the International Th., the title roles in *Henry VIII* (Nov. 6, 1946) and *John Gabriel Borkman* (Nov. 12, 1946); Ferrovius in *Androcles and the Lion* (Dec. 19, 1946; and James Carroll in *Yellow Jack* (Feb. 27, 1947).

He played Jack Rance in a touring production of *The Girl of the Golden West* (1947); Anthony Anderson in *The Devil's Disciple* (NY City Ctr., Jan. 25, 1950); succeeded (June 1951) Richard Whorf as George Crane in *Season in the Sun* (Cort., Sept. 28, 1951), and toured in it (1951–52); played Elyot Chase in a touring production of *Private Lives* (Summer 1952); and Big Daddy in the national touring production of *Cat on a Hot Tin Roof* (opened Richmond, Va., Oct. 24, 1957; closed Geary, San Francisco, Calif., May 17, 1958).

At the Actors Th. of Louisville (Ky.), he played Big Daddy in *Cat on a Hot Tin Roof* (Feb. 5, 1970), Jeeter Lester in *Tobacco Road* (Mar. 5, 1970), the Stage Manager in *Our Town* (Nov. 12, 1970), was in *A Thurber Carnival* (Dec. 10, 1970), directed *My Three Angels* (Mar. 9, 1972), was Willy Loman in *Death of a Salesman* (Apr. 13, 1972), played in *A Man for All Seasons* (Oct. 19, 1972), and directed *You Can't Take It with You* (Nov. 16, 1972).

Films. Mr. Jory has appeared in more than 120 films since his debut in *Sailor's Luck* (20th-Fox, 1933), including *Tom Sawyer* (UA, 1938); *Gone With The Wind* (MGM, 1939); *State Fair* (20th-Fox, 1945); *Loves of Carmen* (Col., 1948); *The Fugitive Kind* (UA, 1960); *The Miracle Worker* (UA, 1962); and *Cheyenne Autumn* (WB, 1964).

Television and Radio. Mr. Jory appeared on more than 150 radio programs, including Dangerously Yours (CBS, 1944) and Vicks Matinee Theatre (CBS, 1945).

On television, he had his own series, Manhunt, and was in *The Second Oldest Profession* (Philco Playhouse, NBC, Mar. 26, 1950); *Angel Street* (Broadway Television Theatre, Ind., May 13, 1952); *Moby Dick* (Hallmark Hall of Fame, NBC, May 16, 1954); *A Connecticut Yankee in King Arthur's Court* (Kraft Th., ABC, July 8, 1954); *Key Largo* (Alcoa Th., NBC, Oct. 14, 1956); *Moment of Decision* (Ford Th., ABC, Apr. 10, 1957); *Johnny Belinda* (Hallmark Hall of Fame, NBC, Oct. 13, 1958); was Andrew Jackson in *The Testing of Sam Houston* (Great Adventure, CBS, Jan. 31, 1964); Charles Carlin in *The Oscar W. Underwood Story* (Profiles in Courage, NBC, Nov. 8, 1964); Peralta in *Who Has Seen the Wind?* (ABC, Feb. 19, 1965); in *That Time in Havana* (Kraft Suspense Th., NBC, Feb. 11, 1965); *Hong Kong with Victor Jory* (Thrill Hunters, Ind., Sept. 23, 1966); and *It's Your World* (ABC, Oct. 2, 1966).

He has also appeared on many other programs, including 87th Precinct (ABC); Suspense (CBS); The Virginian (NBC); Burke's Law (ABC); Farmer's Daughter (ABC); Gunsmoke (CBS); Hazel (CBS); I Spy (NBC); Jesse James (ABC); F Troop (ABC); The Untouchables (ABC); Bonanza (NBC); Dr. Kildare (NBC); Road West (NBC); Green Hornet (ABC); Iron Horse (ABC); The Virginian (NBC); Mannix (CBS); and Banacek (NBC).

JOSEPH, ROBERT L. Producer, playwright. b. Robert Leonard Joseph, March 10, 1924, New York City, to Lazarus and Henrietta Joseph. Father, attorney. Attended Horace Mann H.S., N.Y.C.; Columbia Grammar Prep., N.Y.C.; Syracuse Univ., B.S., M.A. Served US Army; rank, Pfc. Member of League of NY Theatres (vice-pres.); Dramatists Guild; SWG; WGA, East; WGA, West; Zeta Beta Tau.

Theatre. Mr. Joseph adapted and, with Richard W. Krakeur, produced *The Father* (Cort, N.Y.C., Nov. 16, 1949); subsequently produced, with Alexander H. Cohen, Louis Calhern's *King Lear* (National, Dec. 25, 1950); produced *My Darling Aida* (Winter Garden, Oct. 27, 1952); with Jay Julien, *Mademoiselle Colombe* (Longacre, Jan. 6, 1954); presented *Tiger at the Gates* (Apollo, London, June 2, 1955); and on Bway, with the Playwrights Co., in association with Henry M. Margolis (Plymouth, Oct. 3, 1955); with the Producers Th., Charles Laughton's *Major Barbara* (Martin Beck Th., Oct. 30, 1956); produced *Brouhaha* (Aldwych, London, Aug. 27, 1958); and with Maurice Evans, *Heartbreak House* (Billy Rose Th., N.Y.C., Oct. 18, 1959).

He wrote *Face of a Hero* (Eugene O'Neill Th., Oct. 20, 1960) and *Isle of Children* (Cort, Mar. 16, 1962).

Films. Mr. Joseph wrote and produced *The Third Secret* (20th-Fox, 1964) and *End of Summer* (Byanston, 1975).

Television. He has written for all of the major networks and shows, including Playhouse 90 (CBS), for which he originally wrote *Face of a Hero* (1958). GE Th. (CBS), Robert Herridge Th. (CBS), Kraft Suspense Th. (NBC); and Chrysler Th. (NBC).

Awards. He received the Syracuse Univ. Award (1955) for Distinguished Service in the American Theatre.

Recreation. Fishing, horseback riding.

JOURDAN, LOUIS. Actor. b. Louis Gendre, June 19, 1920, Marseilles, France, to Henri and Yvonne (Jourdan) Gendre. Studied with Rene Simon (c.1938). Married to Berthe Frederique; one son; married to Micheline Preale. Member of AEA; SAG; AFTRA.

Theatre. Mr. Jourdan appeared on the Paris stage prior to coming to the US. He made his N.Y.C. debut as Michel in *The Immoralist* (Royale, Feb. 8, 1954); followed by the role of Sourab Kayam in *Tonight in Samarkand* (Morosco, Feb. 16, 1955); played Dr. Mark Bruckner in the pre-Bway run of *On A Clear Day You Can See Forever* (Colonial Th., Boston, opened Sept. 7, 1965; closed Oct. 9, 1965); and appeared in *Private Lives* (Arlington Park Th., Arlington Heights, Ill., June 1972–May 1973).

Films. Mr. Jourdan made his debut in *Le Corsaire* (France, 1940). He continued in French films until 1945, appearing in *Premier rendez-vous L'Arlesienne, Monsieur la souris, Pie de Boheme, La Belle, Felicie nanteuil,* and *Adventure.*

In the US, he has appeared in *The Paradine Case* (Selznick, 1948); *Letter from an Unknown Woman* (U, 1948); *No Minor Vices* (MGM, 1948); *Madame Bovary* (MGM, 1949); *Bird of Paradise* (20th-Fox, 1951); *Anne of the Indies* (20th-Fox, 1951); *The Happy Time* (Col., 1952); *Decameron Nights* (RKO, 1953); *Three Coins in the Fountain* (20th-Fox, 1954); *The Swan* (MGM, 1956); *Julie* (MGM, 1956); *Escapade* (DCA, 1957); *Dangerous Exile* (Rank, 1958); *Gigi* (MGM, 1958); *The Best of Everything* (20th-Fox, 1959); *Streets of Montmartre; Can-Can* (20th-Fox, 1960); *The Story of the Count of Monte Cristo* (WB, 1962); *The VIP's* (MGM, 1963); *Made in Paris* (MGM, 1966); and *Peau D'Espion* (Gaumont, 1967).

Television. Mr. Jourdan played Count Lupo-Pietro in *The Man Who Beat Lupo* (Ford Th., ABC, Feb. 27, 1957); appeared in *Fear No Evil* (NBC); *Run a Crooked Mile* (NBC); *Ritual of Evil* (NBC); and has made numerous appearances on such series as The F.B.I. (ABC); Name of the Game (NBC); Bob Hope Presents (NBC); Greatest Show (ABC); Hollywood Palace (ABC); Kraft Suspense Th. (NBC); What's My Line? (CBS); Showcase (NBC); Jericho (CBS); and The Invaders (ABC).

JOYCE, STEPHEN. Actor. b. Mar. 7, 1933, New York City. Grad. Fordham Univ.

Theatre. Mr. Joyce played Romeo in *Romeo and Juliet* in the NY Shakespeare Festival's second year of production (portable theatre in Central Park, June 1957); made his Bway debut as Henry Appleton in *The Legend of Lizzie* (54 St. Th., Feb. 9, 1959); and, on a bill entitled *Three Plays by John Millington Synge* (Th. East, Mar. 6, 1959), which included *In the Shadow of the Glen,* played Michael Byrne in *The Tinker's Wedding,* and Bartley in *Riders to the Sea.*

With the San Diego National Shakespeare Festival, he played Puck in *A Midsummer Night's Dream* (June 18, 1963); Leontes in *The Winter's Tale* (June 26, 1963), and Enobarbus in *Antony and Cleopatra* (July 27, 1963); subsequently, with the Seattle (Wash.) Repertory Co., played a Fireman in *The Firebugs* (Nov. 4, 1963), Edgar in *King Lear* (Nov. 13, 1963), Richard in *The Lady's Not for Burning* (Jan. 16, 1964), Biff Loman in *Death of a Salesman* (Feb. 12, 1964), Gabor Peter in *Shadows of Heroes* (Apr. 1, 1964), Henry J. Straker in *Man and Superman* (Oct. 15, 1964), and the title role in *Hamlet* (Mar. 13, 1965). He repeated his performance as Edgar in *King Lear* with the Center Th. Group (Ahmanson, Los Angeles, June 5, 1964); appeared in *Saint Joan* (Arena Stage, Washington, D.C., Oct. 10, 1965); and, with the American Shakespeare Festival (Stratford, Conn.), played the title role in *Coriolanus* (June 19, 1965), Edgar in *King Lear* (June 23, 1965); the Archbishop in *Falstaff* (June 18, 1966); the First Tempter in *Murder in the Cathedral* (June 19, 1966); and Marcus Antonius in *Julius Caesar* (June 22,

1966).

Mr. Joyce played Prince in *Those that Play the Clown* (ANTA, N.Y.C., Nov. 24, 1966); John, Lumberjack, Orderly, Waiter, Enrique, Mac Walsey, and Anselmo in the pre-Bway tryout of *The Hemingway Hero* (opened Shubert, New Haven, Feb. 21, 1967; closed Wilbur, Boston, Mar. 4, 1967); Andrea Sarte in the Lincoln Ctr. Repertory Co. production of *Galileo* (Vivian Beaumont Th., N.Y.C., Apr. 13, 1967); Stephen Dedalus in *Stephen D.* (East 74 St. Th., Sept. 24, 1967); again, with the Lincoln Ctr. Repertory Co., played Ladveno in *Saint Joan* (Vivian Beaumont Th., Jan. 4, 1968); the Actor in *The Exercise* (John Golden Th., Apr. 24, 1968); and replaced Paul Ballantyne (Apr. 5, 1971) as Crysalde in *The School for Wives* (Lyceum, Feb. 16, 1971).

With the Yale Repertory Co. (New Haven, Conn.), he appeared in various productions including *Life Is But a Dream* (1971); played Bill Crocker in *Happy End* (Apr. 6, 1972); Paul Holliman in *A Break in the Skin* (Oct. 13, 1972); and Larry Parks in *Are You Now or Have You Ever Been?* (Nov. 10, 1972). In addition, he appeared there in *Baal* (Feb. 16, 1973), played Banco in *Macbett* (Mar. 16, 1973); Prisoner, (M.O.), and Officer in *Lear* (Apr. 13, 1973); and appeared in *Watergate Classics* (Nov. 16, 1973).

At the Olney (Md.) Th., he appeared in the role of Charlie Now in *Da* (Aug. 7, 1973), played Bill Crocker in *Happy End* (June 25, 1974); and Richard Halvey in *Summer* (Aug. 6, 1974).

Films. Mr. Joyce appeared in *Streets of Sinners* (UA, 1957); *Captain Newman, M.D.* (U, 1964); and *The Greatest Story Ever Told* (UA, 1965).

Television. He has appeared on numerous specials and series segments including *Troilus and Cressida;* Camera Three (CBS); Omnibus (CBS); Play of the Week (Ind.); Studio One (CBS); Matinee Theatre (NBC); The Outer Limits (ABC); and The Adams Chronicles (NET).

Awards. Mr. Joyce received a Theatre World Award (1967–68) for his performance in *Stephen D.*

JULIEN, JAY. Producer, attorney. b. Aug. 11, 1919, New York City, to Louis and Sara (Tenen) Julien. Father, attorney. Grad. City Coll. of New York, B.S.S. 1939; Georgetown Univ., LL.B. 1942. Married June 8, 1958, to Ann Weidner; two sons; one daughter. Relative in theatre; brother, Edward Julien, stage manager. Served US, 1942–46; rank, Lt. (j.g.). Member of League of NY Theatres and Producers, Inc. (bd. of gov., 1957–71); Amer. Bar Assn.; Dramatists Guild. Address: 9 E. 41st St., New York, NY 10017, tel. (212) OX 7-9680.

Theatre. Mr. Julien produced, with Robert L. Joseph, *Mademoiselle Colombe* (Longacre Th., N.Y.C., Jan. 6, 1954); produced *A Hatful of Rain* (Lyceum, Nov. 9, 1955), and its subsequent tour (opened Selwyn, Chicago, Ill., Oct. 15, 1956; closed Plymouth, Boston, Mass., May 4, 1957); *The Night Circus* (John Golden Th., N.Y.C., Dec. 2, 1958); in association with Andre Goulston and Eldon Elder, produced *The Fun Couple* (Lyceum, Oct. 26, 1962); was one of the producers of *Cambridge Circus* (Plymouth Th., Oct. 6, 1964; transferred to Square East, Jan. 14, 1965); with Andre goulston, produced *Hostile Witness* (Music Box, Feb. 17, 1966); and with Sidney Eden produced *Hughie/Duet* (Golden Th., Feb. 11, 1975).

Recreation. Fishing, baseball.

K

KAHN, MICHAEL. Artistic and producing director, educator. b. Sept. 9, New York City, to Frederick Joseph and Adele (Gaberman) Kahn. Educ. High School of the Performing Arts, N.Y.C.; Columbia Coll.; Columbia Univ. Professional training with Michael Howard; Actors' Studio. Member of SSD&C. Address: American Shakespeare Theatre, Stratford, CT 06497, tel. (203) 378-7321.

Theatre. Mr. Kahn was executive producer of *P.S. 193* (Writers' Stage, N.Y.C., Oct. 30, 1962), and he directed *The Love Nest* (Writers' Stage, Jan. 25, 1963); *Funnyhouse of a Negro* (East End Th., Jan. 14, 1964); the double bill *The New Tenant* and *Victims of Duty* (Writers' Stage, May 11, 1964); *That 5 A.M. Jazz* (Astor Place Playhouse, Oct. 19, 1964); *Helen* (Bouwerie Lane Th., Dec. 10, 1964); *America Hurrah* (Cafe La Mama, Apr. 28, 1965); *The Owl Answers* (Th. de Lys, Dec. 14, 1965); the triple bill *The Long Christmas Dinner, Queens of France,* and *The Happy Journey to Trenton and Camden* (Cherry Lane Th., Sept. 6, 1966); *Measure for Measure* (NY Shakespeare Festival, Delacorte Th., July 12, 1966); *The Rimers of Eldritch* (Cherry Lane Th., Feb. 20, 1967); *The Cavern* (Playhouse in the Park, Cincinnati, Ohio, June 8, 1967); *The Merchant of Venice* (American Shakespeare Festival, Stratford, Conn., June 20, 1967); *The Freaking Out of Stephanie Blake* (previews: Eugene O'Neill Th., N.Y.C., Oct. 30–Nov. 1, 1967); *Here's Where I Belong* (Billy Rose Th., Mar. 3, 1968); at the American Shakespeare Festival, *Richard II* (June 22, 1968) and *Love's Labour's Lost* (June 26, 1968); *Camino Real* (Playhouse in the Park, Cincinnati, Ohio, July 18, 1968); *The Death of Bessie Smith* (Billy Rose Th., N.Y.C., Oct. 2, 1968); and *Crimes of Passion* (Astor Place Th., Oct. 26, 1969).

In 1969, Mr. Kahn was appointed artistic director, American Shakespeare Festival, Stratford, Conn., where he directed *Henry V* (June 19, 1969), *Three Sisters* (July 23, 1969), *All's Well That Ends Well* (June 16, 1970), *Othello* (June 17, 1970), *The Merry Wives of Windsor* (June 12, 1971), and *Mourning Becomes Electra* (June 16, 1971). He directed *Hough in Blazes* (premiere: Harold Prince Th., Philadelphia, Pa., Oct. 19, 1971); *Tartuffe* (Walnut St. Th., Philadelphia, 1972); at the American Shakespeare Festival, *Julius Caesar* (June 22, 1972) and *Antony and Cleopatra* (June 23, 1972); *Old Times* (Goodman Memorial Th., Chicago, Ill., Oct, 8, 1972); and *Women Beware Women* (City Ctr. Acting Co., Good Shepherd-Faith Church, N.Y.C., Oct. 16, 1972).

Also, at the American Shakespeare Festival, *Measure for Measure* (June 2, 1973) and *Macbeth* (July 6, 1973), both of which were also presented at the Kennedy Center, Washington, D.C. (1973), where Mr. Kahn supervised the staging for *Shakespeare Dance and Drama* (Kennedy Ctr., Opera House, Sept. 25, 1973). At American Shakespeare Festival, Mr. Kahn also directed the Studio Workshop productions of *Friend* (Aug. 2, 1973) and, with Larry Carpenter, *Better Dead Than Sorry* (Aug. 23, 1973); he directed a N.Y.C. production of *Friend* (Th. de Lys, Dec. 3, 1973); *The Tooth of Crime* (Goodman Memorial Th., Chicago, Ill., Jan. 8, 1974); and, at the American Shakespeare Festival, *Romeo and Juliet* (June 17, 1974) and *Cat on a Hot Tin Roof* (July 21, 1974; ANTA Th., N.Y.C., Sept. 24, 1974).

In 1974 he was named producing director of the McCarter Th., Princeton, N.J.

Television. Mr. Kahn directed *The Epic of Buster Friend* (Connecticut Public Television, Hartford, Conn., 1973).

Other Activities. Mr. Kahn is on the Drama Dept. faculty, Juilliard School, N.Y.C.

Awards. Mr. Kahn was nominated for the Vernon Rice Award for his direction of the three Thornton Wilder plays and for the NY Shakespeare Festival *Measure for Measure* in 1966 and for *The Rimers of Eldritch* in 1967; he received the *Saturday Review* Award (1966) as best director of a revival for *Measure for Measure;* and he was nominated for the Jefferson Award for his direction of *The Tooth of Crime* (Goodman Memorial Th., Chicago, 1974).

KAHN, SY M. Educator, lecturer, writer, editor, director. b. 1924, New York City. Grad. George Washington H.S., N.Y.C., 1942; Univ. of Pennsylvania, B.A. (honors) 1948; Univ. of Connecticut, M.A. 1951; Univ. of Wisconsin, Ph.D. 1957. Served in US Army, 1943–45. Member of MLA; AAUP; Central Calif. Philological Assn.; ATA; Theta Alpha Phi; Phi Kappa Phi. Address: c/o Fallon House Theatre, Columbia State Historic Park, Columbia, CA 95310.

Mr. Kahn has been chairman, Dept. of Drama, professor of English and drama, and director of the University Th., Univ. of the Pacific, since 1969. He began his teaching career under fellowships at the Univ. of Connecticut, where he was a half-time instructor in English (1949–51), and the Univ. of Wisconsin, where he was a graduate teaching assistant (1951–55). He was an instructor (1955–57) and then assistant professor (1957–58, 1959–60) of English at Beloit Coll.; assistant professor of English, Univ. of South Florida (1960–63); associate professor of English at Raymond Coll. and the Univ. of the Pacific (dual appointment, 1963–66) and then professor of English at those institutions (1967–68). In 1968–69, he became director of the University Th. and professor of English and drama, Univ. of the Pacific.

Additional academic posts held by Mr. Kahn at various times include the chair of American literature, Univ. of Salonika, Greece, as Fulbright professor (1958–59); associate professor of English, NDEA Summer Institute for Contemporary Critical Methods (Summers 1965, 1968); Fulbright professorship in American literature, Univ. of Warsaw, Poland (1966–67); professor of English, Univ. of California at Berkeley (Summer 1969); and professor of American literature, Univ. of Vienna (1970–71).

Theatre. As chairman of the Univ. of the Pacific Drama Dept., director of the University Th., and executive director of the summer repertory residence theatre—Fallon House Th., Columbia (Calif.) State Historic Park—Mr. Kahn directs five to seven productions each year. Recent plays include: *Henry IV, Part 1; The Balcony; Oh! What a Lovely War; J. B.; Marat/Sade; The Threepenny Opera; Tea and Sympathy; The Dumbwaiter; A Flea in Her Ear; The Deputy;* and *The Boys in the Band.* Mr. Kahn has also toured with the University Drama Dept., performing American plays under US Information Service (USIS) auspices in Germany and Austria (Winters 1972, 1973); and he wrote the one-act *So a Herring Doesn't Whistle* while a fellow at the Salzburg (Austria) seminar in American drama (Summer 1972).

Other Activities. Mr. Kahn lectured during his Fulbright years at many Eastern and Western European universities and in Israel, and the USIS sponsored lecture tours in Europe for him (1971, 1972). Mr. Kahn has also lectured and given poetry readings at American universities since 1965.

Published Works. Mr. Kahn's articles on literary topics have appeared in such publications as *The Student Writer; The Midwest Quarterly;* and *The Journal of Modern Literature.* He has contributed to a series of books on the fiction, poetry, and drama of the 1920s, 1930s, 1940s, and 1950s, issued by Everett Edwards, Inc., and to *Modern American Drama: Essays in Criticism* (1968).

Mr. Kahn has also been an editor of the *Beloit Poetry Journal,* and his own poems have been published in that periodical and in *Epos, Lynx, Bitterroot, Orange Street Poetry Journal, Rongwrong, Florida Education, South and West,* and others. Published collections of his poems include *Our Separate Darkness* (1963); *Triptych* (1964); *A Later Sun* (1966); *The Fight Is With Phantoms* (1966); and *Another Time* (1968).

Awards. In addition to his graduate teaching fellowships and his Fulbrights, Mr. Kahn was a faculty research lecturer, Raymond Coll. (1966), and he held a summer study grant from the Univ. of the Pacific for theatre study in London (Summer 1969). He was named as "Outstanding Educator" by the Univ. of the Pacific (1971). His writing awards include the Univ. of Wisconsin's Gardner Writing Awards in poetry, fiction, and essay (1954–55) and the Univ. of Wisconsin Play Circle Award for verse drama (1955); and Baraboo (Wis.) Th. prize for one-act verse drama (1956); a Crosby Writing Fellowship, Roccasinibalda, Italy (Summers, 1962, 1963); and the Promethean Lamp Prize (1966).

KALEM, THEODORE. Drama critic. b. Theodore Eustace Kalem, Dec. 19, 1919, Malden, Mass., to George Eustace and Urania Sophie Kalem. Father, insurance agent. Grad. Harvard Univ., A.B. (cum laude) 1942. Married Aug. 26, 1953, to Helen Newlin; two sons, one daughter. Served US Army, Infantry, 1942–45; rank, Staff Sgt. Intell. & Operations; awarded Bronze Star. Member of NY Drama Critics Circle (vice-pres., 1963–64; pres., 1964–66). Address: (home) 135 E. 18th St., New York, NY 10003, tel. (212) AL 4-6741; (bus.) *Time* Magazine, 1271 Ave. of the Americas, New York, NY 10019, tel. (212) JU 6-1212.

Mr. Kalem was a book reviewer for the newspaper, *Christian Science Monitor* (1948–50); joined (1951) the staff of *Time* Magazine, as a book reviwer, becoming an assoc. editor; and succeeded (1961) Louis Kronenberger as drama critic of *Time* (to date).

KALFIN, ROBERT. Director, artistic director. b. Robert Zangwill Kalfin, Apr. 22, 1933, New York City, to Alfred A. and Hilda S. Kalfin. Father, realtor; mother, teacher. Educ. H.S. of Music and Art, N.Y.C.; Alfred Univ., B.A. (speech and dramatic production) 1954; Yale Drama School, M.F.A. (directing) 1957; M.A.T.A. theater management course, certificate 1964. Member of SSD&C; Dramatists Guild (dir.); Th. Communications Group. Address: (home) 312 West 20th St., New York, NY 10011; (bus.) Chelsea Th. Ctr., Brooklyn Acad. of Music, 30 Lafayette Ave., Brooklyn, NY 11217, tel. (212) 873-5110.

Theatre. As a student at Alfred Univ. (1951–54) and Yale Drama School (1954–57), Mr. Kalfin worked in all phases of theatre, including direction of and composing music for a production at Alfred of William Saroyan's *Opera, Opera* (Spring 1954) and direction at Yale of *Sunday Costs Five Pesos* (1954–55) and *Five Days* and *Three Parakeets* (both 1955–56).

During his college years, Mr. Kalfin was also on the production staff and a performer at Gateway Th., Bellport, Long Island, N.Y. (Summer 1953); Camden Hills (Me.) Th. (Summer 1954); and Rockland County Playhouse, Blauvelt, N.Y. (Summer 1956). He directed *Season in the Sun* (Theatre-by-the-Sound, New Rochelle Community Th., New Rochelle, N.Y., Summer 1956); and at Saranac Lake (N.Y.) Summer Th. was associate director of *The Seven Year Itch, The Little Hut, Ten Little Indians,* and in addition performed in six other productions (Summer 1957).

His first work in N.Y.C. was as assistant stage manager for an off-Bway production of *Uncle Vanya* (Fourth St. Th., Summer 1956); he was assistant to the producers for the double bill *The Bald Soprano* and *Jack* (Sullivan St. Playhouse, June 3, 1958); a performer with the Equity Library Traveling Children's Theater (Sullivan St. Playhouse, 1958–59); director and co-producer of *The Golem* (St. Marks Playhouse, Feb. 25, 1959); and producer of *An Evening of European Theater* (41 St. Th., 1960).

He was producer's assistant (White Barn Th., Westport, Conn., Summer 1960); adaptor and director of *The Good Soldier Schweik* (The Actors Playhouse, N.Y.C., Summer 1961); a performer in the Peppermint Players' *Pinocchio* (Martinique, 1962); director of *The Solid Gold Cadillac* (A.R.T. Repertory Co., Rockville, Md., Summer 1962); and director of *The Love of Four Colonels; Anniversary Waltz; Witness for the Prosecution; The Male Animal; The Little Hut; Night Must Fall;* and *Private Lives* (all Tanglewood Barn Th., Clemmons, N.C., Summer 1964).

In 1965, Mr. Kalfin founded the Chelsea Theater Ctr. in N.Y.C., and he has been its artistic director since that time. At Chelsea, he directed *Five Days; One of Us Has Been Ignited;* and *The Furthermost Finger of Fillmore* (all 1965–66). In Canada, he directed *The Rainmaker* (Manitoba Th. Ctr., 1966); was director-instructor, Drumheller Drama Seminar, at the invitation of the Province of Alberta (1966); and directed *The Glass Menagerie* (The Citadel Th., Alberta, 1966). He was director of *Puntila and His Hired Man* (Milwaukee Repertory Th., Milwaukee, Wis., Apr. 6, 1967).

Other plays directed by Mr. Kalfin at Chelsea Th. Ctr., include *Christophe* and *My Friend Weissmann Is Back!* (both 1968) and *The Judas Applause* (1969); and he directed the Scandinavian touring production of *The Skin of Our Teeth* (1968). Later productions directed by Mr. Kalfin (all at Chelsea Th. Ctr., which moved to the Brooklyn Academy of Music in 1968) include *Things to Hear, Things to See — An Evening with Huckleberry Finn* and *The Universal Nigger* (both 1970); *Tarot* (Dec. 11, 1970; moved to Circle in the Square, Mar. 4, 1971); *Kaddish* (Feb. 1, 1972; moved to Circle in the Square, Mar. 7, 1972); and *Sunset* (Dec. 5, 1972). He also directed the New Repertory Co. production of *The Lady from the Sea* (Sept. 18, 1973), and, at Chelsea Th. Ctr., *Total Eclipse* (Feb. 23, 1974); *Yentl, the Yeshiva Boy,* which moved to Bway as *Yentl* (Eugene O'Neill Th., Oct. 23, 1975); and *Polly* (May 8, 1975).

Television. Mr. Kalfin was production coordinator for WOR-TV, Ch. 9 (N.Y.C., 1958); associate producer and production assistant for WNTA-TV, Ch. 13 (N.Y.C., 1959–60); and night studio manager at WNTA (Spring 1960).

Other Activities. Mr. Kalfin worked as a theatre consultant on a research project for a cultural center and resident professional theatre in Portland, Me. (1963–64); served (1964–65–66) as associate director, Dept. to Extend the Professional Theater, Actors' Equity Foundation, Inc.; was guest instructor, Drumheller Drama Seminar (advanced acting and directing), Provincial Government of Alberta (1971); guest lecturer, NY State Community Th. Assn. (1971); and guest lecturer, Southeast Th. Conf. (1971).

Awards. In addition to scholarships awarded him by Alfred Univ. (1951–52) and Yale Drama School (1956–57), Mr. Kalfin was awarded a scholarship to the Spoleto (Italy) Festival (Summer 1959), which he declined in order to work on a Bway production of *Mother Courage* (cancelled).

KALICH, JACOB. Director, actor, producer, playwright. b. Nov. 18, 1891, Rymanov, Poland, to Gershon and Miriam Kalich. Father, rabbi. Attended rabbinical schools in Poland, Romania, Hungary, and Austria. Married June 29, 1919, to Molly Picon, actress. Member of Hebrew Actors' Union (pres., 1950); Yiddish Theatrical Alliance (exec. bd.); SAG; AFTRA; Jewish Writers Guild; Hebrew Actors Club. Address: Croton Falls Rd., Mahopac, NY 10541, tel. (914) MA 8-2114.

Theatre. Mr. Kalich has produced, directed, written plays for, and appeared in Yiddish Theatre productions since 1910, both in the US and abroad. He first worked with the Szignitza (repertory) Th. (Bucharest, Rom., 1910), where he remained for two years; subsequently appeared in London in a company managed by Joe Kessler (1912–14); produced and acted in plays with his own company in Winnipeg, Can. (1914); rejoined Joe Kessler's Co. in Chicago, Ill., as director and actor (Empire Th., 1915–1917); directed his own company at the Grand Opera House (Boston, Mass., 1918–20); from 1920–23, directed and acted, with his wife, Molly Picon, in Yiddish repertoire which included *Yankele, Zepke,* and *Molly Dolly* (Lancry Th., Paris, Fr., 1920; Eforie Th., Bucharest, Rom., 1921; Kaminsky Th., Warsaw, Pol., 1922; Stefanie Th., Vienna, Austria, 1923).

In N.Y.C., he directed and appeared in productions at the Second Ave. Th., including Mechel in *Yonkele* (1923); Milton in *Tzipke,* and *Gypsy Girl;* directed at this theatre, *Little Devil, Raizele, Good Luck, Hello Molly* and *Little Mother* (1923–29); at the Molly Picon Th., produced and directed *Girl of Yesterday* (1930) and *Love Thief* (1931); produced and directed *Here Runs the Bride* (Second Ave. Th., 1934); produced *Birdie* (Majestic, Brooklyn, N.Y., 1935); directed, produced, and appeared in his own play, *Oy Is Dus a Leben* ("Oh What a Life") (Molly Picon Th., 1942; and on tour); toured in a Yiddish vaudeville act with his wife (1944); wrote and directed *Abi Gezunt* (1949); directed *Sadie Was a Lady* (1949); *Mazel Tov Molly* (Sept. 25, 1950); *Take It Easy* (1950); appeared in a summer-theatre production of *Make Momma Happy* (Monticello, N.Y., 1953); wrote, directed, and appeared in *Fablonjete Honeymoon* (Palace, Brooklyn, N.Y., 1955); appeared in *The World of Sholom Aleichem* (Lido Beach, N.Y., 1957); and wrote, directed, and appeared in *Kosher Widow* (Phyllis Anderson Th., N.Y.C., 1959), and on tour.

Films. Mr. Kalich appeared in *East and West* (Vienna, 1919) and *Fiddler on the Roof* (UA, 1971); and served as artistic supervisor for the Polish film version of *Mamale* ("Little Mother") (Sphinx, 1939).

Television and Radio. He wrote, directed, and acted on his own radio programs in N.Y.C. (WMCA, 1936–40; WHN, 1940–45; WEVD, 1946–52; WMGM, 1952).

On television, he appeared as Hymie Kaplan in *The Education of Hymie Kaplan* (Studio One, CBS, Sept. 27, 1954); Grandpa in *Littlest Leaguer* (1957); Look Up and Live (CBS); and Car 54, Where Are You? (NBC, 1962).

Other Activities. Mr. Kalich has appeared in concert tours with his wife in the US and abroad (1937; 1941–43; 1945–46; 1947–59); and has also served as his wife's manager in N.Y.C. productions.

Awards. He received a Humanitarian Award from the Yiddish Theatrical Alliance (1958); a Certificate of Esteem from the US Dept. of Defense for his work in entertaining the troops (1951); has honorary membership in the Z.O.A.; and is a Guardian of the State of Israel (1957).

Recreation. Walking, reading, music.

KANDER, JOHN. Composer, arranger, conductor, pianist. b. John Harold Kander, Mar. 18, 1927, Kansas City, Mo., to Harold and Bernice (Aaron) Kander. Father, businessman. Grad. Westport H.S., Kansas City, 1944; Oberlin Coll., B.A. 1951; Columbia Univ., M.A. 1954. Served US Army; US Merchant Marine Cadet Corps. Member of AFM, Local 802; Dramatists Guild.

Theatre. Mr. Kander first worked in the theatre at Oberlin Coll. (1950–51), when he composed *Second Square Opus Two* and *Requiem for Georgie;* subsequently was choral director and conductor for the Warwick (R.I.) Musical Th. (Summers 1955–57); was pianist for the pre-Bway tryout of *The Amazing Adele* (opened Shubert Th., Boston, Mass., Jan. 26, 1956); and for the Florida tour of *An Evening with Bea Lillie;* was conductor for *Conversation Piece* (Barbizon-Plaza Th., N.Y.C., Nov. 18, 1957); arranged the dance music for *Gypsy* (Bway Th., May 21, 1959); and *Irma La Douce* (Plymouth, Sept. 29, 1960); composed the score of *A Family Affair* (Billy Rose Th., Jan. 27, 1962); and the incidental music for *Never Too Late* (Playhouse, Nov. 27, 1962).

He composed the music for *Flora, the Red Menace* (Alvin, May 11, 1965); *Cabaret* (Broadhurst, Nov. 20, 1966); *The Happy Time* (Broadway Th., Jan. 18, 1968); *Zorba* (Imperial, Nov. 17, 1968); and *70, Girls, 70* (Broadhurst, Apr. 15, 1971). He appeared with Fred Ebb in *An Evening with Fred Ebb and John Kander* (YM-YWHA, Kaufmann Concert Hall, N.Y.C., Apr. 8, 1973); with Fred Ebb, he prepared musical material for *Liza* (Winter Garden, Jan. 26, 1974); he wrote music for the revue *The Kander and Ebb Coloring Book* (Octagon, Mar. 25, 1975); and he composed music for *Chicago* (46 St. Th., June 3, 1975).

Published Works. In addition to his theatre works, Mr. Kander's songs (with words by Fred Ebb) include "My Coloring Book" and "I Don't Care Much.".

Awards. Mr. Kander and Fred Ebb won the NY Drama Critics poll and Antoinette Perry (Tony) awards for best composer and best lyricist, respectively, for *Cabaret,* which was also awarded a Tony as best musical play of 1966–67. They received Tony nominations, again for best composer and best lyricist, for *The Happy Time,* which was nominated for a Tony as best musical play of 1967–68; *Zorba* was nominated for a Tony as best musical play of 1968–69; and *Chicago* received Tony nominations in 1975–76 for best musical play, best musical book, and best score.

KANIN, FAY. Playwright, actress. b. Fay Mitchell, New York City, to David and Bessie (Kaiser) Mitchell. Father, dept. store manager. Grad. Elmira (N.Y.) Free Academy, 1933; attended Elmira Coll., 1933–36; grad. Univ. of Southern California, B.A. 1937. Married Apr. 1940, to Michael Kanin, writer, producer, director; one son. Relatives in theatre: brother-in-law, Garson Kanin, director, playwright, actor; sister-in-law, Ruth Gordon, actress, writer. Member of WGA, West (vice-pres., 1974; pres., Screen Branch, 1973); Dramatists Guild; SWG; ACTF (exec. bd., Southern Cal. region); ANTA. Address: 653 Ocean Front, Santa Monica, CA 90402.

Theatre. Mrs. Kanin appeared in stock in Hollywood and in *Petticoat Fever*, presented at the RKO Studios (1948).

She wrote *Goodbye, My Fancy* (Morosco, N.Y.C., Nov. 17, 1948; and later she played the lead in it at the Pasadena Playhouse, Calif.). With her husband, she wrote *His and Hers* (48 St. Th., Jan. 7, 1954); *Rashomon*, based on stories by Ryunosuke Akutagawa (Music Box Th., Jan. 27, 1959); and the book for *The Gay Life* (Shubert, Nov. 18, 1961).

Films. With her husband, she wrote the screenplays for *Sunday Punch* (MGM, 1942); *My Pal Gus* (20th-Fox, 1952); *Rhapsody* (MGM, 1954); *The Opposite Sex* (MGM, 1956); *Teacher's Pet* (Par., 1958); *The Right Approach* (20th-Fox, 1961); and *The Swordsman of Siena* (MGM, 1962).

Television. She wrote *The Source* (Tomorrow Ent., NBC); *Heat of Anger* (CBS, 1972); and *Tell Me Where It Hurts* (CBS, 1974). The latter two were television special movies.

Awards. With her husband, Michael Kanin, Mrs. Kanin was nominated for the Academy (Oscar) Award for best original story and screenplay, and the SWG nomination for best written American comedy, *Teacher's Pet* (1958). She won the Gavel Award of the American Bar Association for *Heat of Anger* in 1973.

KANIN, GARSON. Director, playwright. b. Nov. 24, 1912, Rochester, N.Y., to David and Sadie (Levine) Kanin. Attended James Madison H.S., 1926–27; AADA, 1932–33. Married Dec. 4, 1942, to Ruth Gordon, actress, playwright. Served US Army, ETO, 1941–45; highest rank, captain in OSS (1943). Relatives in theatre: brother, Michael, playwright; sister-in-law, Fay Kanin, playwright; sister, Ruth E. Kanin. Stage, television producer. Member of the Dramatists Guild; SDG; WGA; ASCAP; AFTRA; SSD&C; AMPAS; Actor'Fund; The Players; The Friars; The Lambs; Coffee House Club; Jewish Theatrical Guild. 39 W. 55th St., New York, NY 10019, tel. (212) 586-7850.

Theatre. Mr. Kanin first performed as an actor as Tommy Deal in *Little Ol' Boy* (Playhouse, N.Y.C., Apr. 24, 1933); subsequently played a Young Man in *Spring Song* (Morosco, Oct. 1, 1934); Red in *Ladies' Money* (Ethel Barrymore Th., Nov. 1, 1934); was assistant to director George Abbott and appeared as Al in *Three Men on a Horse* (Playhouse, Jan. 30, 1935); played Izzy Cohen in *The Body Beautiful* (Playhouse, Oct. 31, 1935); was assistant to director George Abbott and played Green in *Boy Meets Girl* (Cort, Nov. 27, 1935); appeared as Vincent Chenevski in *Star Spangled* (John Golden Th., Mar. 10, 1936); was assistant to director George Abbott in *Brother Rat* (Biltmore, Dec. 16, 1936).

Mr. Kanin directed *Hitch Your Wagon* (48 St. Th., Apr. 8, 1937); was assistant to director George Abbott in *Room Service* (Cort, May 19, 1937); directed *Too Many Heroes* (Hudson, Nov. 15, 1937), and *The Rugged Path* (Plymouth, Nov. 10, 1945); wrote and directed *Born Yesterday* (Lyceum, Feb. 4, 1946); directed *Years Ago* (Mansfield, Dec. 3, 1946); *How I Wonder* (Hudson, Sept. 30, 1947); and *The Leading Lady* (National, Oct. 18, 1948); wrote and directed *The Smile of the World* (Lyceum, Jan. 12, 1949); *The Rat Race* (Ethel Barrymore Th., Dec. 22, 1949); and *The Live Wire* (Playhouse, Aug. 17, 1950).

He wrote a new English libretto for, and directed *Fledermaus* (Metropolitan Opera, Dec. 20, 1950); directed *The Diary of Anne Frank* (Cort, Oct. 5, 1955); *Small War on Murray Hill* (Ethel Barrymore Th., March 3, 1957); and *A Hole in the Head* (Plymouth, Feb. 28, 1957); adapted and directed *The Good Soup* (Plymouth, Mar. 2, 1960); wrote the book for, and directed *Do Re Mi* (St. James, Dec. 26, 1960); directed *Sunday in New York* (Cort, Nov. 29, 1961); adapted and directed *A Gift of Time* (Ethel Barrymore Th., Feb. 22, 1962); wrote and directed *Come On Strong* (Morosco, Oct. 4, 1962); directed *Funny Girl* (Winter Garden, Mar. 26, 1964); *A Very Rich Woman* (Belasco Th., Sept. 30, 1964); *I Was Dancing* (Lyceum, Nov. 8, 1964); *We Have Always Lived in the Castle* (Ethel Barrymore Th., Oct. 19, 1966); adapted from his book, directed, and appeared in *Remembering Mr. Maugham* (Kaufmann Concert Hall, YMHA, N.Y.C., Nov. 13, 1966; Mark Taper Forum, Los Angeles, Calif., July 22, 1969); directed a revival of *Idiot's Delight* (Ahmanson Th., Los Angeles, Mar. 17, 1970); and adapted and directed *Dreyfus in Rehearsal* (Ethel Barrymore Th., Oct. 17, 1974).

Films. Mr. Kanin worked for Samuel Goldwyn 1937; directed *A Man to Remember* (RKO, 1938); *Next Time I Marry* (RKO, 1938); *The Great Man Votes* (RKO, 1939); *Bachelor Mother* (RKO, 1939); *My Favorite Wife (RKO, 1940), They Knew What They Wanted* (RKO, 1940); and *Tom, Dick and Harry* (RKO, 1941). During WW II, he directed, with Carol Reed, *The True Glory*, Gen. Eisenhower's official film report of the war in Europe. Kanin also directed for the Office of War Information the documentaries *Ring of Steel* (1942) and *Salute to France* (1946), for the Office of Emergency Manpower *Fellow Americans* (1942), and for the SPARS *Battle Stations* (1944).

With his wife, Ruth Gordon, he wrote the screenplays for *A Double Life* (U, 1948); *Adam's Rib* (MGM, 1949); *Pat and Mike* (MGM, 1952); *The Marrying Kind* (Col., 1952); and *It Should Happen to You* (Col., 1954). Mr. Kanin wrote the screenplay for *The Rat Race* (Par., 1960); wrote and directed *Some Kind of a Nut* and *Where It's At (1969); collaborated on From This Day Forward* and *The More the Merrier;* and wrote original stories for *The Right Approach; High Time* (20th-Fox, 1960); and *The Girl Can't Help It*. .

Television. Mr. Kanin adapted for television and co-directed *Born Yesterday* (Hallmark Hall of Fame, NBC, Oct. 29, 1956). He created, wrote, and directed a pilot for the series *Broadway* (CBS, 1964); *An Eye on Emily; The He-She Chemistry;* and *Something to Sing About*. .

Published Works. Among Mr. Kanin's published works are *Do Re Mi* (1955); *Blow Up a Storm* (1959); *The Rat Race* (1960); *Remembering Mr. Maugham* (1966); *Where It's At* (1969); *Tracy and Hepburn* (1971); *A Thousand Summers* (1973) and *Hollywood* (1974). He also contributed to *Felix Frankfurter: A Tribute* (1964).

Awards. The film, *The True Glory*, which he co-directed, received an Academy (Oscar) Award, a citation from the NY Film Critics' Circle, and was named best film of the year by the National Board of Review (1945).

For his play, *Born Yesterday*, Mr. Kanin shared the Sidney Howard Memorial Award with Arthur Laurents, received Donaldson awards (1946), and the Award of Achievement of the American Academy of Dramatic Arts alumni (1958).

KANIN, MICHAEL. Playwright, director, producer. b. Feb. 1, 1910, Rochester, N.Y., to David and Sadie Kanin. Father, builder. Attended James Madison H.S., Brooklyn, N.Y., 1926–27; Art Students League, N.Y.C., 1928; NY Sch. of Design, 1929. Married Apr. 7, 1940, to Fay Mitchell, playwright (Fay Kanin); one son. Relatives in theatre: brother, Garson Kanin, director, playwright, actor; sister, Ruth Kanin Brown, designer, writer; sister-in-law, Ruth Gordon, actress, writer. Member of Dramatists Guild; WGA, West (bd. member, 1943, 1944; treas., 1944, 1945); SWG (member of exec. bd., 1933–34; treas., 1944–45); AMPAS; ANTA; ACTF. Address: 653 Ocean Front, Santa Monica, CA 90402.

Pre-Theatre. Commercial and scenic artist, musician, entertainer.

Theatre. Mr. Kanin wrote, with Harry Ingram, *We, The Willoughbys*, produced in stock (Berkshire Playhouse, Stockbridge, Mass., Summer 1939).

In association with Aldrich and Meyers, he produced, *Goodbye, My Fancy* (Morosco, N.Y.C., Nov. 17, 1948); with his wife, Fay Kanin, he wrote *His and Hers* (48 St. Th., Jan. 17, 1954); *Rashomon*, based on stories by Ryunosuke Akutagawa (Music Box, Jan. 27, 1959); and the book for *The Gay Life* (Shubert, Nov. 18, 1961). With the Theatre Guild Productions, Inc. and Joel Schenker, he produced *Seidman and Son* (Belasco, Oct. 15, 1962).

Films. Mr. Kanin wrote, with Jo Pagano, the screenplay for *They Made Her a Spy* (RKO, 1939); wrote the screenplay for *Panama Lady* (RKO, 1939), and *Anne of the Windy Poplars* (RKO, 1949); with Fay Kanin, the screenplay for *Sunday Punch* (MGM, 1942); with Ring Lardner, Jr., the screenplay for *Woman of the Year* (MGM, 1942); with Ring Lardner, Jr., and Robert Andrews, the screenplay for *The Cross of Lorraine* (MGM, 1943); wrote the screenplay for *Centennial Summer* (20th-Fox, 1946); *Honeymoon* (RKO, 1947); produced *A Double Life* (U, 1948); wrote and directed *When I Grow Up* (Eagle Lion, 1948); with Fay Kanin, wrote the screenplays for *My Pal Gus* (20th-Fox, 1952); *Rhapsody* (MGM, 1954); *The Opposite Sex* (MGM, 1956); *Teacher's Pet* (Par., 1958); *The Right Approach* (20th-Fox, 1961); *Swordsman of Siena* (MGM, 1962); wrote the screenplay and was associate producer for *The Outrage* (MGM, 1964), and with Ben Starr wrote *How To Commit Marriage* (Cinerama, 1969).

Awards. Mr. Kanin received, with Ring Lardner, Jr., the Academy (Oscar) Award for best original screenplay (1942) for *Woman of the Year;* with his wife, the Academy Award and Writers Guild nominations for best written American comedy (1958), *Teacher's Pet*. He received gold and silver medallions from Amoco for his work in the American College Theatre Festival (1972, 1973); a special citation from the City of Los Angeles for encouraging youth in the theatre (1974); and a certificate of merit from the Los Angeles drama critics for organizing the playwriting awards of the American College Theatre Festival (1974).

Recreation. Painting, sculpture, music, books.

KAPLAN, SOL. Composer, pianist. b. 1919, Philadelphia, Pa., to Harry and Anna Kaplan. Attended Curtis Institute, 1929–39. Married Dec. 29, 1945, to Frances Heflin, actress; one son, two daughters. Served WW II, US Army Signal Corps; rank, Pfc.

Theatre. Mr. Kaplan composed the score for the pre-Bway tryout of *Shootin' Star* (opened Shubert, New Haven, Conn., Apr. 4, 1946; closed Shubert, Boston, Mass., Apr. 27, 1946).

He composed the incidental music for the N.Y.C. production of *Tonight in Samarkand* (Morosco, Feb. 16, 1955); *Once Upon a Tailor* (Cort, May 23, 1955); *The Matchmaker* (Royale, Dec. 5, 1955); *Uncle Willie* (John Golden Th. Dec. 28, 1956); *Dear Liar* (Billy Rose Th., Mar. 17, 1960); *Rape of the Belt* (Martin Beck Th., Nov. 5, 1960); and *Midgie Purvis* (Martin Beck Th., Feb 1, 1961); the score for *The Banker's Daughter* (Jan Hus House, Jan. 22, 1962); and music for *Venus Is* (previews, Billy Rose Th., Apr. 5–9, 1966).

Films. He composed the background music for *The Tell-Tale Heart* (Du World, 1934); *Tales of Manhattan* (20th-Fox, 1942); *Mr. 880* (20th-Fox, 1950); *Titanic* (20th-Fox, 1950); *Niagara* (20th-Fox, 1950); *I Can Get It for You Wholesale* (20th-Fox, 1951); *Seven Wonders of the World* (Stanley Warner, 1956); *Happy Anniversary* (UA, 1959); *The Victors* (Col. 1963); *The Young Lovers* (MGM, 1964); wrote and conducted the score for *The Guns of August* (U, 1964); and wrote music for *The Spy Who Came in from the Cold* (Par., 1965); and *Judith* (Par., 1966).

Television. Mr. Kaplan wrote the score for *My 3 Angels* (1959); *Dear Arthur* (1960); and *The Enchanted Nutcracker* (ABC, Dec. 1961). He appeared on The Art of Film series (NET, 1964, 1965).

Other Activities. He gave piano recitals at Town Hall (Feb. 21, 1939) and Carnegie Hall (Feb. 12, 1940; Mar. 4, 1941).

KARINSKA, BARBARA. Costume maker and designer. b. Varvara Zhmoudsky, Oct. 3, 1886, Kharkov, Ukraine, Russia. Father, merchant. Married (husband dec.); one daughter. Member of United Scenic Artists. Address: (home) 17 E. 63rd St., New York, NY 10021; (bus.) Karinska, 20 W. 53rd St., New York, NY 10019, tel. (212) CI 7-3341.

Pre-Theatre. Karinska was an artist in Moscow, where she also ran a dress shop and taught embroidery. In 1928, she left the USSR and settled in Paris, where she began making costumes for professional entertainers.

Theatre. Mme. Karinska executed costumes for *Too Many Girls* (Imperial, N.Y.C., Oct. 18, 1939); *Call Me Madam* (Imperial, Oct. 12, 1950); *Can-Can* (Shubert, May 7, 1953); *The Girl in the Pink Tights* (Mark Hellinger Th., Mar. 5, 1954); *Silk Stockings* (Imperial, Feb. 24, 1955); *Candide* (Martin Beck Th., Dec. 1, 1956); and *Becket* (St. James, Oct. 5, 1960).

She made costumes based on artists' designs for many ballets or created her own designs and then executed the costumes. Her first ballet costumes were for the Ballet Russe de Monte Carlo productions *Cotillon,* after designs by Christian Bérard (Monte Carlo, Apr. 12, 1932) and *La Concurrence,* after designs by André Derain (Monte Carlo, Apr. 12, 1932). Among the many other ballets for which she created costumes were the Ballet Russe de Monte Carlo's *Bacchanale,* based on suggestions by Salvador Dali (Metropolitan Opera House, N.Y.C., Nov. 9, 1939); Ballet Theatre's *Aurora's Wedding* (Anton Dolin), based on Léon Bakst's designs (Palacio de Bellas Artes, Mexico City, Oct. 23, 1941; 44 St. Th., N.Y.C., Nov. 26, 1941); and Ballet Theatre's *Black Swan Pas de Deux* (Anton Dolin), based on Rouben Ter-Arutunian's designs (Metropolitan Opera House, Oct. 23, 1944). Also Ballet Theatre's *Don Quixote Pas de Deux,* after designs by Esteban Francés (Metropolitan Opera House, Oct. 25, 1944); Les Ballets des Champes-Elysées' *Le Spectre de la Rose,* after designs by Léon Bakst (Paris, 1947); NY City Ballet's *Harlequinade Pas de Deux,* based on designs by Rouben Ter-Arutunian (NY City Ctr., Dec. 1952); the Grand Ballet du Marquis de Cuevas revival of *Petrouchka,* after designs by Alexandre Benois (Paris, season 1952-53); Ballet Russe de Monte Carlo's *Sombreros,* based on William Cecil designs (Carter Barron Amphitheatre, Washington, D.C., June 18, 1956; Metropolitan Opera House, N.Y.C., Apr. 26, 1957); and NY City Ballet's revival of *Firebird,* based on designs by Marc Chagall (State Th., May 28, 1970).

Ballets for which Mme. Karinska both designed and made costumes include (all for NY City Ballet at NY City Ctr. unless otherwise noted): *Bourrée Fantasque,* for which she also did the decor (Dec. 1, 1949); *La Valse* (Feb. 20, 1951); *Capriccio Brillant* (June 7, 1951); *Scotch Symphony,* with David Ffolkes (Nov. 11, 1952); *Metamorphoses* (Nov. 25, 1952); *Harlequinade Pas de Deux* (Dec. 16, 1952); *Concertino* Dec. 30, 1952); *Valse Fantaisie* (Jan. 6, 1953); and *The Nutcracker* (Feb. 2, 1954).

Also *Divertimento No. 15* and *A Musical Joke* (both American Shakespeare Festival Th. by NY City Ballet, May 31, 1956); *Gounod Symphony* (Jan. 8, 1958); *Stars and Stripes* (Jan. 17, 1958); *Waltz-Scherzo* (Sept. 9, 1958); *Pas de Deux (Swan Lake)* (Mar. 29, 1960); and, with Esteban Francés, *Donizetti Variations* (Nov. 16, 1960). Also *Liebeslieder Walzer* (Nov. 22, 1960); American Ballet Theatre's *Grand Pas—Glazounov,* with Tom Lingwood (Music Hall, Cleveland, Ohio, Jan. 28, 1961; Broadway Th., N.Y.C., Apr. 25, 1961); and NY City Ballet's *Valse et Variations,* later *Raymonda Variations* (Dec. 7, 1961); *A Midsummer Night's Dream* (Jan. 17, 1962); *Bugaku* (Mar. 20, 1963); *Tarantella* (Jan. 7, 1964); *Ballet Imperial* (NY State Th., Oct. 15, 1964; also new production Jan. 12, 1973); *Brahms-Schoenberg Quartet* (NY State Th., Apr. 21, 1966); *Jewels* (NY State Th., Apr. 13, 1967); *Who Cares?* (NY State Th., Feb. 5, 1970); and *Scherzo a la Russe* (June 21, 1972).

In addition to her work for theatre and ballet, Mme. Karinska executed costumes for several Metropolitan Opera productions (all at Metropolitan Opera House, N.Y.C.), including: *Don Giovanni,* after designs by Eugene Berman (Oct. 31, 1957); *Turandot,* designs by Cecil Beaton (Dec. 24, 1961); *La Sonnambula,* designs by Rolf Gerard (Feb. 22, 1963); *Otello,* designs by Eugene Berman (Mar. 10, 1963); *Falstaff,* designs by Franco Zeffirelli (Mar. 6, 1964); and *La Traviata,* designs by Cecil Beaton (Sept. 24, 1966). She also did costumes for La Scala (Milan, It.) productions of *Macbeth* and *Turandot.*

Films. Mme. Karinska executed costumes for *Lady in the Dark* (Par., 1944); *Gaslight* (MGM, 1944); *Frenchman's Creek* (Par., 1944); *Kismet* (MGM, 1944); *Kitty* (Par., 1945); and designed the costumes for *Joan of Arc* (RKO, 1948).

Awards. She shared with Dorothy Jeakins, an Academy (Oscar) Award (1948) for the costuming of *Joan of Arc;* and received the Capezio Award (1961).

Recreation. Raising sheep; making blankets, tapestries; crocheting; arranging flowers; collecting antique furniture.

KARL, THEODORE O.H. Educator, director, producer. b. Theodore Oscar Henry Karl, Oct. 27, 1912, Marinette, Wis., to Carl John and Emelie Karl. Father, minister; mother, musician. Grad. St. Peter (Minn.) H.S., 1930; Gustavus Adolphus Coll., A.B. 1934, M.A. 1936; Stanford Univ., 1952; Univ. of Southern California, 1960–63. Married June 20, 1953, to Elizabeth Yount. Served A.M.S., Adjutant Gen. on loan to Special Services, Feb. 1944–July 1946. Member of ANTA; Speech Association of America; AETA; Western Speech Assoc. (activities co-ordinator, 1955–58; 2nd vice-pres., 1958; 1st vice-pres., 1960; pres., 1961). Address: Dept. of Speech, Pacific Lutheran Univ., Tacoma, WA 98447, tel. LE 7-8611, ext. 305.

Since Fall 1948, Mr. Karl has been director of the Dept. of Speech at Pacific Lutheran Univ., where he has directed more than fifty productions, touring pageants and annual drama-music festivals.

Previously, he taught speech at Los Angeles City Coll. (1947–48); was director of public relations for federal agencies in Calif. (1946–47); manager of Industrial Stationery and Printing Co. in Los Angeles (1942); and state supervisor with the National Youth Administration (Minn., 1936).

Recreation. Golf, swimming.

KARNILOVA, MARIA. Dancer, actress. b. Aug. 3, 1920, Hartford, Conn. Studied ballet with Michael Mordkin and Michel Fokine at Metropolitan Opera Sch., 1927–34; with Nenette Charisse and Margaret Craske. Married Oct. 17, 1948, to George S. Irving, actor; one son, one daughter. Member of AEA; AFTRA; SAG; AGMA.

Theatre. Miss Karnilova first appeared as a dancer in the children's corps de ballet of the Metropolitan Opera (1927–34); appeared with the Dandria Opera Co. (Caracas, Venezuela, 1935); was soloist with the Ballet Th. (1939–48); and returned as ballerina to the Metropolitan Opera Co. (1952–53), where she danced in *Manon, La Traviata, Alceste,* and *Die Fledermaus.* She again danced with the Ballet Th. (1955–56, 1959); and danced at the Boston (Mass.) Arts Festival in *America Dances* (July 1962). Her repertoire with the Ballet Th. includes: Helen in *Helen of Troy,* the Cat in *Peter and the Wolf,* the Priggish Virgin in *Three Virgins and a Devil,* Myrtha in *Giselle,* an Officer in *Russian Soldier,* Boulotte in *Bluebeard,* Slavonika and Marushia in *Slavonika,* Juno in *Judgment of Paris,* and the Dance Hall Girl in *Billy the Kid.* Also, she danced the pas de huit in *Capriccioso,* the Lady-in-Waiting in *Goya Pastoral,* Muse in *Romantic Age,* Queen of Hearts in *The Fantastic Toy Shop,* Episode in His Past in *Jardin aux lilas,* the French Ballerina in *Gala Performance,* Chiarina in *Carnival,* and A Lady No Better Than She Should Be in *Tally-Ho.*

Miss Karnilova made her first Bway appearance in the chorus of *Stars in Your Eyes* (Majestic Th., Feb. 9, 1938); danced in *Hollywood Pinafore* (Alvin, May 31, 1945); *Call Me Mister* (National, Apr. 18, 1946); and toured in *High Button Shoes* (May–Sept. 1948).

She was a principal in the revue *Two's Company* (Alvin, Dec. 15, 1952); in stock, was principal dancer in *Cyrano de Bergerac* (St. Louis Municipal Opera, Mo., Summer 1953); *Paint Your Wagon* and *New Moon* (State Fair Music Hall, Dallas, Tex., Summer 1953); and again danced in *Paint Your Wagon* (Paper Mill Playhouse, Millburn, N.J., Fall 1953). At the Cambridge (Mass.) Drama Festival, she played Dolly Trull in *The Beggar's Opera* (1956); and repeated this role at the NY City Ctr. (Mar. 13, 1957). She appeared in the revue *Kaleidoscope* (Provincetown Playhouse, June 13, 1957); and, with Jerome Robbins' *Ballet: U.S.A.,* as the Mad Ballerina in *The Concert* (Alvin, Sept. 4, 1958).

Miss Karnilova played Tessie Tura in *Gypsy* (Bway Th., May 21, 1959); Signora Pandolfi in *Bravo Giovanni* (Broadhurst, May 19, 1962); Mrs. Dolly Gallagher Levi in *The Matchmaker* (Fred Miller's Th., Milwaukee, Wis., Dec. 1962); Therese Kolodney in a summer tryout of *Apollo and Miss Agnes* (State Fair Music Hall, Dallas, Tex., Summer 1963); Golde in *Fiddler on the Roof* (Imperial, N.Y.C., Sept. 22, 1964); Hortense in *Zorba* (Imperial, N.Y.C., Nov. 17, 1968); Mamita in *Gigi* (Uris, N.Y.C., Nov. 13, 1973); and Rose Benjamin in *God's Favorite* (Eugene O'Neill Th., N.Y.C., Dec. 11, 1974).

Films. Miss Karnilova made her debut in *The Unsinkable Molly Brown* (MGM, 1964).

Television. Miss Karnilova has appeared on the Ed Sullivan Show (CBS, 1958); The Fabulous Fifties; The Voice of Firestone (CBS); and Look Up and Live (CBS).

Recreation. Dressmaking, gardening, interior decorating.

KARR, HAROLD. Composer. b. Harold H. Katz, Oct. 31, 1921, Philadelphia, Pa., to Kolman and Sophie S. (Emas) Katz. Father, orchestra leader, dental technician; mother, deputy collector, IRS. Grad. Central H.S., Philadelphia, 1939; Temple Univ., D.D.S. 1944. Studied at Fleisher Symphony Club, Philadelphia, 1937–39; Philadelphia Musical Acad., 1937–41; Leo Ornstein Sch., Philadelphia, 1941–43; piano with David Sokoloff, Philadelphia, six years; harmony composition with William Happach, Philadelphia, four years. Married Sept. 10, 1944, to Jacqueline Weiner; two daughters. Served US Army Medical Corps, US Public Health Service, 1945–46; rank, Lt. (j.g.). Member of ASCAP; Dramatists Guild; AFM, Local 77; Alpha Omega Dental Fraternity; Intl. Anesthesia Society; Intl. Acad. of Orthodontics; Amer. Dental Society; Philadelphia Orthodontic Study Group; Assn. of Military Surgeons; Eastern Dental Society.

Pre-Theatre. Dentist, piano teacher, orchestra leader, vocal coach, commercial recording.

Theatre. Mr. Karr composed music for songs in the revue *New Faces of '56* (Ethel Barrymore Th., N.Y.C., June 14, 1956); and subsequently composed the music for *Happy Hunting* (Majestic, Dec. 6, 1956); and for the pre-Bway tryout of *We Take the Town* (opened Shubert, New Haven, Conn., Feb. 17, 1962; closed Shubert, Philadelphia, Pa., Mar. 17, 1962).

Night Clubs. He composed the music for *After Hours Revue,* which toured cross-country (opened Bay Brook, West Haven, Conn., Mar. 23, 1952); and wrote the score for the Copacabana Club Shows (N.Y.C., 1953–54), which later played at the Sands Hotel (Las Vegas, Nev., 1954).

KARR, PATTI. Singer, actress, dancer. b. Patsy Lou Karkalits, July 10, 1932, St. Paul, Minn., to C. F. and Estelle (Klebold) Karkalits. Father, fruit and vegetable broker. Grad. Paschal H.S., Fort Worth, Tex., 1949; attended Texas Christian Univ.,

1949–50. Studied dancing with Margaret Craske, Anthony Tudor, Frank Wagner, Don Farnworth, Matt Mattox; singing with John Bartis, Henry Rosenblatt, and Rosalie Snyder (1964); acting with Joseph Leon, Ezra Stone, Danny Levin, and Jane White. Member of AEA; AGVA. Address: 336 West End Ave., New York, NY 10023, tel. (212) 362-8246.

Theatre. Miss Karr first performed as a dancer in stock productions at the Summertime Light Opera Co., Houston, Tex., Summer 1950; and subsequently as a dancer in the national tour of *Brigadoon* (1950–51).

As Patti Karkalits, she made her Bway debut as a dancer in *Maggie* (National, Feb. 18, 1953); appeared as a dancer in *Carnival in Flanders* (New Century, Sept. 8, 1953); appeared at Green Mansions (N.Y.), in works which included *The Threepenny Opera* and *Hello Out There* (Summers 1954, 1955, 1956); billed as Patti Karr, performed as a dancer in *Bells Are Ringing* (Shubert, N.Y.C., Nov. 29, 1956); a dancer in *New Girl in Town* (46 St. Th., May 14, 1957); in *The Body Beautiful* (Bway Th., Jan. 23, 1958); appeared as a dancer and understudy in *Redhead* (46 St. Th., Feb. 5, 1959); and in *Once Upon a Mattress* (Phoenix, May 11, 1959).

She was a dancer and understudy to Chita Rivera as Rose Grant in *Bye Bye Birdie* (Martin Beck Th., Apr. 14, 1960); played Essie Whimple in *Redhead* (Paper Mill Playhouse, Millburn, N.J.; Cape Cod Melody Tent, Hyannis, Mass., Summer 1960); appeared as one of the Dance Team and as an Animal Girl in *Do Re Mi* (St. James, N.Y.C., Dec. 26, 1961); in *New Faces of 1962* (Alvin, Feb. 1, 1962); as Rose in a touring production of *Bye Bye Birdie* (1962); and as Lucy McPherson and His Press Representative in *Come on Strong* (Morosco, N.Y.C., Oct. 4, 1962). She repeated the role of Rose in *Bye Bye Birdie* (Sheraton Palace Dinner Th., San Francisco, Calif., Spring 1963); played Rosalie in *Carnival!;* and Ellie in *Show Boat* (Starlight Th., Kansas City, Mo., Summer 1963); and appeared in *To Broadway with Love* (NY World's Fair, Texas Pavilion, Apr. 22, 1964).

She was Gladys in *The Pajama Game* (Music Circus, Sacramento, Calif., July 5, 1965); toured as Rose Alvarez in *Bye Bye Birdie* (Summer 1965); was Dorothy Shaw in a summer tour of *Gentlemen Prefer Blondes;* appeared in the Japanese production of *West Side Story* (Tokyo, Japan); was in the revue *Skits-Oh-Frantics!* (Bert Wheeler Th., N.Y.C., Apr. 2, 1967); played Gwen in *Month of Sundays* (Th. de Lys, Sept. 16, 1968); Desirée in *Up Eden* (Jan Hus Playhouse, Nov. 26, 1968); was understudy for all the female roles in a revival of *A Funny Thing Happened on the Way to the Forum* (Lunt-Fontanne Th., Mar. 30, 1972); played Mrs. Hepplewhite's Mother and Kimberly Langley in *Different Times* (ANTA Th., May 1, 1972); replaced (Oct. 1973) Michele Lee as Gittel Mosco in *Seesaw* (Uris Th., May 18, 1973); and replaced Carmen Alvarez as Helen McFudd in a revival of *Irene* (Minskoff Th., Mar. 13, 1973).

Night Clubs. Miss Karr made her debut as Beatrice in the dance team of "Gomez and Beatrice," at the Monte Carlo Hotel (Miami Beach, Fla.); at the Clover Club (Miami, Fla.); White Hall (Palm Beach, Fla.); Hollywood Beach Hotel and Club (Fla., 1952); and performed as a dancer at the Sheraton Mt. Royal Hotel (Montreal, Can., Jan.–Apr. 1954).

KASE, C. ROBERT. Educator, author. b. Charles Robert Kase, June 27, 1905, Lewistown, Pa., to Charles W. and Hannah L. (Traub) Kase. Father in real estate and insurance. Grad. Lewistown (Pa.) H.S., 1922; Gettysburg Coll., A.B. 1926; New York Univ., M.A. 1930, Ph.D. 1935. Married Aug. 1930 to Elizabeth Baker; one son, one daughter. Served US Army, 1942–45, officer in charge of military, USO, and celebrity shows in Caribbean area; rank, Maj. Member of ANTA (bd. of dir., 1946–69); ATA, formerly AETA (fellow; pres., 1946; chmn., Overseas Touring Com., 1958–60); ACTF (chmn., 1969–71); Delaware Educational Television Assn. pres., 1955); Delaware Inst. of History and Culture (pres., 1958); Delaware Dramatic Assn. (pres., 1936; bd. of dir., 1936–70); Eastern States Theatre Assn. (pres., 1958, 1959; bd. of dir., 1956–66); NTC; SAA; USO (natl. council, 1959–63); AAUP; Phi Beta Kappa; Phi Delta Theta. Address: 606 Vanderbaker Rd., Temple Terrace, FL 33617.

He is past president and a former member of the board of directors (until 1970) of the Chapel St. Players (formerly the Univ. Drama Group). He was director of the E.52 Univ. Th. companies which toured the Far East and Europe for the Defense Department (1958, 1961); was visiting professor of theatre at the Univ. of Minnesota and a director at the Camden Hills (Me.) Summer Theatre (Summer 1946); taught at the Somerville (N.J.) H.S. (1926–27).

Other Activities. In 1945 and 1946 Dr. Kase lectured on theatre in the Southeast and East for the Assn. of Amer. Colleges; made a survey of US theatres (Fall 1952) for ANTA.

Published Works. He wrote *Three Chaucer Studies* (1932); *Children's Theatre Comes of Age* (1956); and wrote and edited *Stories for Creative Acting* (1961).

Awards. In 1972, Mr. Kase received the ATA silver medallion award of excellence.

Recreation. Golf, travel.

KASHA, LAWRENCE N. Producer, director. b. Lawrence Nathan Kasha, Dec. 3, 1933, Brooklyn, N.Y., to Irving and Rose (Katz) Kasha. Parents, beauticians. Grad. James Madison H.S., Brooklyn, 1950; New York Univ., B.A. 1954, M.A. 1955. Studied at Amer. Theatre Wing, N.Y.C., 1957; Fagin Intl. Sch., 1948–49; acting with Harold Clurman, N.Y.C., 1956–57, and with Robert Lewis, N.Y.C., 1957. Served USAFR, 1951–54. Relative in theatre: brother, Alfred Kasha, songwriter. Member of AEA; SSD&C; Kappa Nu.

Theatre. Mr. Kasha's first assignment was as a stage manager of Grove Playhouse (Nuangola, Pa., Summers 1952–53); subsequently was stage manager at the Gateway Playhouse (Somers Point, N.J., Summers 1954–55); production manager for an ELT production of *High Button Shoes* (Lenox Hill Playhouse, N.Y.C., Mar. 2, 1955); and production assistant for *Silk Stockings* (Imperial, Feb. 24, 1955).

He was stage manager for the national tour of *Silk Stockings* (opened Curran, San Francisco, Calif., Apr. 23, 1956); also *Li'l Abner* (St. James, N.Y.C., Nov. 15, 1956), and directed a touring production of it (opened Bushness Aud., Hartford, Conn., Oct. 10, 1958); was stage manager for *Whoop-Up* (Shubert, N.Y.C., Dec. 22, 1958); directed musical productions at the Colonie Summer Th. (Latham, N.Y., 1959); was stage manager of *Happy Town* (54 St. Th., N.Y.C., Oct. 7, 1959); produced the revue, *Parade* (Players Th., Jan. 20, 1960); and directed an industrial production, *the Kleinert Rubber Show* (Hotel Astor, N.Y.C., 1960, 1962).

He directed a stock tour of *Li'l Abner* (Summer 1960); *Silk Stockings* and *High Button Shoes* (Meadowbrook Th., Cedar Grove, N.J., Summer 1960); a tour of *The Male Animal* (Summer 1960); *South Pacific* and *Desert Song* (Brunswick Playhouse, Me., Summer 1960). He was stage manager for *How To Succeed in Business without Really Trying* (46 St. Th., N.Y.C., Oct. 14, 1961); produced and directed *Parade* (Hollywood Centre Th., Calif., July 19, 1961); in summer theatre, produced *Future Perfect* (Cape Playhouse, Dennis, Mass., July 24, 1961); directed *Gentlemen Prefer Blondes* (Meadowbrook Th., Cedar Grove, N.J., Aug. 1961); directed *guys and Dolls* and *The Most Happy Fella* (O'Keefe Centre, Toronto, Canada, Summer 1962); produced and directed the Con Edison Show (Biltmore Hotel, N.Y.C., 1962); and directed *Plain and Fancy* (Westchester Th., Aug. 1962).

He directed *Anything Goes* (Orpheum, N.Y.C., May 15, 1962); with Harold Prince and Philip C. McKenna, produced *She Loves Me* (Eugene O'Neill Th., Apr. 23, 1963); directed productions at the Dallas (Tex.) Summer Musicals (State Fair Music Hall, Summer 1963); and a tryout of *A More Perfect Union* (La Jolla Playhouse, Calif., July 22, 1963); was associate director for *Funny Girl* (Winter Garden, N.Y.C., Mar. 26, 1964); and directed *The Sound of Music* at the San Bernardino (Calif.) Civic Light Opera (Apr. 30, 1964). On May 1, 1964, Mr. Kasha became executive producer of the Seven Arts Associated Corp., legitimate theatre department.

Mr. Kasha directed the bus and truck touring production of *Camelot* (opened State Fair Music Hall, Dallas, Aug. 17, 1964; closed Orpheum, Madison, Wis., Oct. 26, 1966); *Bajour* (Sam S. Shubert Th., N.Y.C., Nov. 23, 1964); and *Funny Girl* (Prince of Wales' Th., London, Apr. 13, 1966). In association with Lester Osterman, he produced a tryout touring production of *The Coffee Lover* (Summer 1966); subsequently directed *Show Boat* (NY State Th., N.Y.C., July 19, 1966); co-produced the pre-Bway tryout of *A Mother's Kisses* (opened Shubert, New Haven, Sept. 23, 1968; closed Mechanic, Baltimore, Oct. 19, 1968); staged the national touring production of *Cactus Flower* (opened Municipal Aud., Norfolk, Va., Sept. 20, 1968); produced *Hadrian VII* (Helen Hayes Th., N.Y.C., Jan. 8, 1969); co-produced *Applause* (Palace, Mar. 30, 1970); directed *Lovely Ladies, Kind Gentlemen* (Majestic, Dec. 28, 1970); with Joseph Kipness, produced *Father's Day* (John Golden Th., Mar. 16, 1971); co-produced *Inner City* (Ethel Barrymore Th., Dec. 19, 1971); *Seesaw* (Uris, Mar. 18, 1973); and *No Hard Feelings* (Martin Beck Th., Apr. 8, 1973).

Awards. Mr. Kasha received the Outer Circle Award for his direction of *Anything Goes* (1962).

KASZNAR, KURT. Actor. b. Kurt S. Kasznar, Aug. 12, 1913, Vienna, Austria, to Ferdinand and Leopoldine Kasznar. Grad. Public School, Vienna; Max Reinhardt Seminar, Vienna. Married Cornelis Whooly (dec.); married Leora Dana (marr. dis.). Served US Army Special Service and Signal Corps, 1945; rank, Cpl. Member of AEA; SAG; AFTRA; Authors League.

Theatre. Mr. Kasznar wrote a one-act play, entitled *First Cousin* that was produced along with four others that won an enlisted man's contest, and were presented on a program sponsored by John Golden, in cooperation with the Special Service Branch Headquarters 2nd Service Command (46 St. Th., N.Y.C., June 14, 1943). He appeared in the road company of *Don Juan in Hell;* subsequently played Dmitri Oumansky in *Joy to the World* (Plymouth, N.Y.C., Mar. 3, 1948); Monk in *Montserrat* (Fulton, Oct. 29, 1949); Uncle Louis in *The Happy Time* (Plymouth, Jan. 24, 1950); Boule in *Seventh Heaven* (ANTA, May 26, 1955); and appeared in the Tyrone Guthrie production of *Six Characters in Search of an Author* (Phoenix, Dec. 11, 1955).

He played Pozzo in *Waiting for Godot* (John Golden Th., Apr. 19, 1956); the Prince of Salestria in *Look After Lulu* (Henry Miller's Th., Mar. 3, 1959); Max Detweiler in *The Sound of Music* (Lunt-Fontanne, Nov. 16, 1959); Victor Velasco in *Barefoot in the Park* (Biltmore, Oct. 23, 1963); and Piccadilly Th., London, Nov. 24, 1965); Macheath in *Die Dreigroschenoper* (NY City Ctr., N.Y.C., Mar. 11, 1965); Orgon in *Tartuffe* (Philadelphia Drama Guild, 1972–73 season); Tevye in *Fiddler on the Roof* (Pittsburgh Playhouse, 1972–73 season); and appeared in *Cyrano de Bergerac* (Ahmanson, Los Angeles, 1973–74 season).

In summer stock, he has appeared in *My Three Angels, Once More with Feeling, The Happy Time, The Little Hut,* and *Arms and the Man.*

Films. Mr. Kasznar appeared in *The Happy Time* (Col., 1942); *Valley of the King* (MGM, 1945); *Lovely to Look At* (MGM, 1952); *Glory Alley* (MGM, 1952); *Talk About a Stranger* (MGM, 1952); *Anything Can Happen* (Par., 1952); *All the Brothers Were Valiant* (MGM, 1953); *Kiss Me, Kate* (MGM, 1953); *Give a Girl a Break* (MGM, 1953); *Sombrero* (MGM, 1953); *Ride Vaquero* (MGM, 1953); *Lili* (MGM, 1953); *The Last Time I Saw Paris* (MGM, 1954); *Jump into Hell* (WB, 1955); *Flame of the Islands* (Rep., 1955); *My Sister Eileen* (Col., 1955); *Anything Goes* (Par., 1956); *The Light Touch* (U, 1956); *Legend of the Lost* (UA, 1957); *A Farewell to Arms* (20th-Fox, 1957); *For the First Time* (MGM, 1959); *The Journey*

(MGM, 1959); and *55 Days at Peking* (Allied, 1963) *Casino Royale* (Col., 1967); *The Perils of Pauline* (U, 1967); *King's Pirate* (U, 1967); and *The Ambushers* (Col., 1967).

Television. His appearances include The Reporter (CBS); Naked City (Ind.); Desilu Playhouse (NBC); The Trials of O'Brien (CBS); The Girl from U.N.C.L.E. (NBC); *Waiting for Godot* (NET); Run for Your Life (NBC); That Girl (ABC); I Spy (NBC); The Man from U.N.C.L.E. (NBC); My Three Sons (CBS); It Takes a Thief (NBC); Land of the Giants (NBC); *Once Upon a Dead Man* (NBC); *The Snoop Sisters* (NBC); and Search (NBC).

KAY, HERSHY. Orchestrator, composer. b. Nov. 19, 1919, Philadelphia, Pa., to Louis H. and Ida (Aisen) Kay. Father, printer. Scholarship student, Curtis Inst. of Music, Philadelphia, 1935–39. Member of AFM; ASCAP. Address: 205 W. 57th St., New York, NY 10019, tel. (212) CI 7-5420.

Theatre. Mr. Kay made his musical debut as a cellist in theatre orchestras while attending school in Philadelphia, Pa. His first N.Y.C. assignment was as arranger for the Brazilian soprano, Elsie Houston (1940); subsequently orchestrated Leonard Bernstein's score for *On the Town* (Adelphi, Dec. 28, 1944); Walter Hendl's incidental music for *Dark of the Moon* (46 St. Th., Mar. 14, 1945); Kurt Weill's score for *A Flag Is Born* (Alvin, Sept. 5, 1946); did arrangements for the Martha Graham Dance Co., his first compositions for dance (1947); orchestrated Leonard Bernstein's music for *Peter Pan* (Imperial, Apr. 24, 1950); and scored the ballet, *The Thief Who Loved a Ghost*, adapted and orchestrated from music by Carl Maria von Weber, for the Ballet Th. (Metropolitan Opera House, Apr. 11, 1951).

He adapted and orchestrated the score for *Cakewalk*, based on music by Louis Moreau Gottschalk, for the N.Y.C. Ballet (NY City Ctr., June 12, 1951); orchestrated *The Golden Apple* (Phoenix, Mar. 11, 1954), music by Jerome Moross; *Sandhog* (Phoenix, Nov. 23, 1954), music by Earl Robinson; arranged and orchestrated the score for *Western Symphony*, based on American folk tunes, for the N.Y.C. Ballet (NY City Ctr., Sept. 7, 1954); orchestrated the pre-Bway tryout of *Reuben Reuben*, music by Marc Blitzstein (opened Shubert, Boston, Mass., Oct. 10, 1955; closed there Oct. 22, 1955); orchestrated Leonard Bernstein's music in *Candide* (Martin Beck Th., N.Y.C., Dec. 1, 1956); Jack Urbont's music in *Livin' the Life* (Phoenix, Apr. 27, 1957); and adapted and orchestrated *Stars and Stripes*, after music of John Philip Sousa, for the N.Y.C. City Ballet (NY City Ctr., Jan. 17, 1958).

Mr. Kay completed the opera, *The Good Soldier Schweik* after the death of its composer, Robert Kurka (NY City Opera, NY City Ctr., world premiere Apr. 23, 1958); orchestrated Marc Blitzstein's music for *Juno* (Winter Garden, Mar. 9, 1959); Mary Rodgers' music for *Once Upon a Mattress* (Phoenix, May 11, 1959); with Robert Russell Bennett, he orchestrated *The Happiest Girl in the World* (Martin Beck Th., Apr. 3, 1961), which they arranged from music by Jacques Offenbach; orchestrated *Milk and Honey* (Martin Beck Th., Oct. 10, 1961), music by Jerry Herman; *110 in the Shade* (Broadhurst, Oct. 24, 1963), music by Tom Jones; and *Tarantella*, a reconstruction and orchestration, based on Louis Moreau Gottschalk's *Grand Tarantelle, Opus 76*, for the N.Y.C. Ballet (NY State Th., Lincoln Ctr., Jan. 7, 1964).

He did the orchestrations for *Kelly* (Broadhurst Th., N.Y.C., Feb. 6, 1965); with Clare Grundman, for *Drat! The Cat!* (Martin Beck Th., Oct. 10, 1965); *I'm Solomon* (Mark Hellinger Th., Apr. 23, 1968); *Coco* (Mark Hellinger Th., Dec. 18, 1969); with Leonard Bernstein, for the revival of *On the Town* (Imperial, Oct. 31, 1971); and for the Chelsea Th. Center's *Candide* (Brooklyn Academy of Music, Dec. 11, 1973; moved to Broadway Th., N.Y.C., Mar. 5, 1974).

Films. Mr. Kay's film orchestrations include *Man With a Gun* (UA, 1955); *King and Four Queens* (UA, 1957); and *South Sea Paradise*, music by Alex North; *Girl of the Night* (WB, 1960), music by Sol Kaplan; and documentary films produced by the US State Dept.

Television. His first assignment was as arranger-orchestrator for the Startime Show (NBC, 1959); subsequently orchestrated the music for The Valiant Years (ABC); wrote the score for the NBC special, *This Nation at War* (1962); orchestrated music for the FDR series (ABC); The Twentieth Century (CBS); and for the Victor Borge spectacular, composed a Concerto for Two Pianos and Two Conductors (1963).

Other Activities. Under a commission by the pianist, Eugene List, Mr. Kay wrote the piano concerto, *Grande Tarantella*, reconstructing and orchestrating a score based on themes by Gottschalk.

Discography. He composed and conducted the original music for *Mother Goose* (Caedmon); conducted *Focus* (Sauter-Getz) (Verve); and arranged and conducted *Bergerettes* for Lily Pons (Columbia).

Recreation. Hunting, fishing, photography, sport cars.

KAYE, DANNY. Actor, comedian, conductor. b. David Daniel Kominski, Jan. 18, 1913, Brooklyn, N.Y., to Jacob and Clara (Nemerovsky) Kominski. Father, tailor. Attended Thomas Jefferson H.S., Brooklyn. Married Jan. 3, 1940, to Sylvia Fine, composer, pianist, writer; one daughter. Member of AEA; SAG; AFTRA; The Lambs; UNICEF (UN Children's Fund).

Pre-Theatre. Insurance clerk.

Theatre. Mr. Kaye appeared in vaudeville as a member of the Three Terpsichoreans (1933); toured the US and Far East in the revue, *La Vie Paris* (1933–34); appeared in *Left of Broadway* (Keynote, N.Y.C., Mar. 12, 1939); and *The Straw Hat Revue* (Ambassador, Sept. 29, 1939).

He played Russell Paxton in *Lady in the Dark* (Alvin, Jan. 23, 1941); appeared in a vaudeville show (Palace, 1941); played Jerry Walker in *Let's Face It* (Imperial, Oct. 29, 1941); performed with the USO in World War II camp shows and war bond drives; toured Vietnam for the USO (1966); and played Noah in *Two by Two* (Imperial, N.Y.C., Nov. 10, 1970).

He performed annually at the Palladium (London, 1948–52); at the Canadian National Exhibition (1950); Curran Th., (San Francisco, Calif., Sept. 7, 1952; Feb. 17, 1959); Palace Th. (N.Y.C., 1953); Shubert Th. (Detroit, Mich., 1955); Greek Th. (Los Angeles, Calif., July 1958); Sidney and Melbourne, Australia (1959); Carousel Th. (Framingham, Mass., July–Aug. 1961); and Ziegfeld Th. (N.Y.C., Apr. 10, 1963).

In addition, Mr. Kaye has made many appearances worldwide to help raise money for UNICEF.

Films. Mr. Kaye made his first appearance in *Up in Arms* (RKO, 1944); subsequently appeared in *Wonder Man* (RKO, 1945); *The Kid from Brooklyn* (RKO, 1946); *The Secret Life of Walter Mitty* (RKO, 1947); *A Song Is Born* (RKO, 1948); *The Inspector General* (WB, 1949); *On the Riviera* (20th-Fox, 1951); *Hans Christian Anderson* (RKO, 1952); *Knock on Wood* (Par. 1954); *White Christmas* (Par., 1954); *The Court Jester* (Par., 1956); *Merry Andrew* (MGM, 1958); *Me and the Colonel* (Col., 1958); *The Five Pennies* (Par., 1959); *On the Double* (Par., 1961); and *The Man from the Diners Club* (Col., 1963).

Television and Radio. Mr. Kaye performed on his radio program, The Danny Kaye Show (CBS, 1945).

On television, he has appeared on See It Now (CBS, 1956); and on his own Danny Kaye specials (CBS, 1960, 1961; NBC, 1962); was emcee for Twelve Star Salute (ABC, 1961); and has appeared on his own weekly show, The Danny Kaye Show (CBS, 1963–64) and on the Lucy Show (CBS, 1964). His voice was heard on the special *The Emperor's New Clothes* (ABC, Feb. 21, 1972), and he was on the opera special *Danny Kaye's Look-In at the Metropolitan Opera* (CBS, Apr. 1975).

Night Clubs. He has performed at the Dorchester Hotel (London, 1938); at summer resorts on the "borscht circuit" (Catskill Mountains, N.Y.) as a "toomler"; Camp Tamiment, Pa. (1939); La Martinique (N.Y.C., 1940); The Desert Inn (Las Vegas, Nev., 1960, 1961); and Harrah's Club (Lake Tahoe, Nev., 1962).

Concerts. Mr. Kaye has served as orchestral conductor for Musicians Fund Benefit programs and has conducted various orchestras for charity, including the Los Angeles (Calif.) Philharmonic (Feb. 3, 1972); Halle Orchestra (Manchester, England, May 23, 1974); Chicago (Ill.) Symphony (June 4, 1974); and Yale Philharmonic Orchestra (Woolsey Hall, Yale Univ., New Haven, Conn., Apr. 24, 1976).

Discography. His recordings include *Danny Kaye Entertains* (1953), *At the Palace, Mommy, Gimme a Drink of Water*, and *Best*.

Awards. Mr. Kaye received the Big Brother of the Year Award (1956); the Lane Bryant Award (1957) for his work with UNICEF; and the Lions International humanitarian award for his work on behalf of impoverished children of the world.

He received the Tony Pastor Memorial Plaque as the outstanding musical star of the season (1940); the Preis der Deutschen Filmkritik as the best foreign actor for his performance in *Me and the Colonel* (1958–59); the Sam S. Shubert Award for outstanding contributions to the American theatre (1970–71); the Gold Baton of the American Symphony Orchestra League (1973); and a NATAS (Emmy) Award (1976) for his special *Danny Kaye's Look-In at the Metropolitan Opera*. .

Recreation. Golf, tennis, baseball, aviation.

KAYE, JOSEPH. Journalist, writer. Married 1947 to Frances Golub. Member of The Drama Desk, Outer Critics Circle (secy., 1950–to date); United Nations Correspondents Assn. Address: 405 E. 54th St., New York, NY 10022, tel. (212) PL 5-1932.

Since 1930, Mr. Kaye has been the New York Correspondent for the Kansas City *Star*, also covering the theatre and musical events. He formerly served as a dance critic for *Dance* Magazine.

Published Works. He is the author of *Victor Herbert*, a biography of the composer (1931), and, with Doris J. Gribetz, of *Jimmie Walker* (1932). He has also published articles on theatre and music.

KAYE, STUBBY. Comedian, singer. b. 1918, New York City. Attended DeWitt Clinton H.S., Bronx, N.Y. Married July 15, 1967, to Angela Bracewell, dancer. Member of AEA; SAG; AFTRA.

Theatre. Mr. Kaye was a singer at Loew's Boulevard Th. (Bronx, N.Y.); and a comedian in vaudeville (1939–42). During World War II, he appeared in USO productions in London and N. Africa.

He made his N.Y.C. debut as Nicely-Nicely Johnson in *Guys and Dolls* (46 St. Th., Nov. 24, 1950); which he repeated in London, England (Coliseum, May 28, 1953) and in Las Vegas, Nev. (1954); played Marryin' Sam in *Li'l Abner* (St. James, N.Y.C., Nov. 11, 1956); Solomon in *Everybody Loves Opal* (Longacre, Oct. 11, 1961); Toby Kester in *Man of Magic* (Piccadilly, London, England, Nov. 16, 1966); toured (Oct. 1971–Mar. 1972) as Barney Cashman in *Last of the Red Hot Lovers*; played Pooch Kearney in a revival of *Good News* (St. James, N.Y.C., Dec. 23, 1974); and replaced (Oct. 1975) Jack Weston as Gaetano Proclo in *The Ritz* (Longacre, Jan. 20, 1975).

Films. Mr. Kaye played Nicely-Nicely Johnson in *Guys and Dolls* (MGM, 1955); appeared in *You Can't Run Away from It* (Col., 1956); *It Happened One Night* (1956); *Li'l Abner* (Par., 1959); *The Cool Mikado* (UA, 1963); *40 Pounds of Trouble* (U, 1963); *Cat Ballou* (Col., 1965); *Sex and the Single Girl* (WB, 1965); and *The Way West* (UA, 1967).

Television and Radio. He was a winning contestant on Major Bowes' Amateur Hour radio program (1939).

For television he appeared on Crescendo (CBS, 1957); Love and Marriage (NBC); and My Sister Eileen (CBS, 1960).

Night Clubs. He was master of ceremonies with

the Freddy Martin Orchestra; and the Charlie Barnett Orchestra.

Awards. Mr. Kaye received an Outer Circle Award for his performance in *Li'l Abner.*.

KAYSER, KATHRYN E. Educator. b. Sept. 13, 1896, Minneapolis, Minn., to Lyman B. and Nellie Amy (Richards) Kayser. Father, railroad agent. Grad. Bronson (Kans.) H.S., 1914; attended Kansas State Coll., 1916–17; grad. Kansas State Teacher's Coll., B.S. 1929, M.S. 1935; attended School of Speech and Drama, London, England, 1933. Member of AETA; ANTA; Rocky Mountain Th. Assn.; CTC (dir., Region IV, 1960–62); Kappa Kappa Gamma. Address: (home) 2085 S. Josephine, Denver, CO 80210, tel. (303) 733-4150; (bus.) Department of Theatre, Univ. of Denver, Denver, CO 80210, tel. (303) 753-2510.

Miss Kayser was associate professor in the Dept. of Theatre in the Sch. of Communication Arts at the Univ. of Denver, where she was a member of the faculty from 1946 until her retirement in 1972.

She is also director of the children's theatre at the university, teaching classes in creative drama, children's theatre, and acting.

She organized the Honolulu Th. for Youth (1960–61); taught creative drama classes at the Univ. of Hawaii (Summers 1955, 1958); and supervised teacher training, and taught classes in speech and drama at Kansas State Teacher's Coll. (1935).

Awards. Miss Kayser received the Marine Corps Civilian Citation for her work as a USO director (1945), the Alumni Award, Kansas State Teachers Coll. (1963), and the Outstanding Faculty Award, Univ. of Denver (1972).

KAZAN, ELIA. Director, actor, producer, writer. b. Sept. 7, 1909, Istanbul, Turkey, to George and Athena (Sismanoglou) Kazan. Father, rug dealer. Grad. New Rochelle (N.Y.) H.S., 1926; Williams Coll., A.B. (Phi Beta Kappa) 1930; Yale Univ. Sch. of Drama, hon. M.F.A. 1932. Studies as an apprentice to the Group Th. under Lee Strasberg and Harold Clurman, 1932–33. Married Dec. 2, 1932, to Molly Day Thatcher, playwright (dec. 1963); two sons, two daughters. Member of SDG; SAG; SSD&C (on board); AEA; Screen Writers Guild; Dramatist Guild; Actors Studio (co-director, 1947–62). Address: 1545 Broadway, New York, NY 10036, tel. (212) CI 6-9760.

Theatre. Mr. Kazan made his Bway debut as Louis in *Chrysalis* (Martin Beck Th., Nov. 15, 1932), for which he was also assistant stage manager; subsequently played the Orderly in and became stage manager of *Men in White* (Broadhurst, Sept. 26, 1933); played Polyzoides and was stage manager in *Gold Eagle Guy* (Morosco, Nov. 28, 1934); played Baum in *Till the Day I Die;* Agate Keller in *Waiting for Lefty,* a double-bill (Longacre, Mar. 26, 1935); with Alfred Saxe, directed *The Young Go First* (Park, May 28, 1935); and played Agate Keller in *Waiting for Lefty* on a double-bill with *Awake and Sing,* for which he was stage manager (Belasco, Sept. 9, 1935).

Mr. Kazan played Kewpie in *Paradise Lost* (Longacre, Dec. 9, 1935); Pvt. Kearns in *Johnny Johnson* (44 St. Th., Nov. 19, 1936); Eddie Fuselli in *Golden Boy* (Belasco, Nov. 4, 1937; on tour, 1938–39); directed *Casey Jones* (Fulton, N.Y.C., Feb. 19, 1938); made his London debut repeating his role in *Golden Boy* (St. James's, June 21, 1938); played Eli Lieber in *The Gentle People* (Belasco, N.Y.C., Jan. 5, 1939); Steve Takis in *Night Music* (Broadhurst, Feb. 22, 1940); the Sparrow in *Liliom* (44 St. Th., Mar. 25, 1940); directed *Thunder Rock* (Mansfield, Nov. 14, 1939); and played Adam Boguris in *Five Alarm Waltz* (Playhouse, Mar. 13, 1941).

Mr. Kazan directed *Cafe Crown* (Cort, Jan. 23, 1942); *The Strings, My Lord, Are False* (Royale, May 19, 1942); *The Skin of Our Teeth* (Plymouth, Nov. 18, 1942); *Harriet* (Henry Miller's Th., Mar. 3, 1943); *One Touch of Venus* (Imperial, Oct. 7, 1943); *Jacobowsky and the Colonel* (Martin Beck Th., Mar. 14, 1944); *Dunnigan's Daughter* (John Golden Th., Dec. 26, 1945); with Harold Clurman, produced *Truckline Cafe* (Belasco, Feb. 27, 1947); staged *Deep Are the Roots* (Fulton, Sept. 26, 1945); *All My Sons* (Coronet, Jan. 29, 1947), which he produced with Harold Clurman and Walter Fried; and directed *A Streetcar Named Desire* (Ethel Barrymore Th., Dec. 3, 1947).

A founding member with Cheryl Crawford and Robert Lewis of the Actors Studio, Mr. Kazan directed its production of *Sundown Beach* (Belasco, Sept. 7, 1948); staged *Love Life* (46 St. Th., Oct. 7, 1948); *Death of a Salesman* (Morosco, Feb. 10, 1949; Phoenix, London, July 28, 1949); *Flight into Egypt* (Music Box, Mar. 18, 1952); *Camino Real* (National, Mar. 19, 1953); *Tea and Sympathy* (Ethel Barrymore Th., Sept. 30, 1953); *Cat on a Hot Tin Roof* (Morosco, Mar. 24, 1955); *The Dark at the Top of the Stairs* (Music Box, Dec. 5, 1957), which he produced with Saint Subber; directed *J. B.* (ANTA, Dec. 11, 1958); and *Sweet Bird of Youth* (Martin Beck Th., Mar. 10, 1959).

With Robert Whitehead, Mr. Kazan has been director of the Repertory Th. of Lincoln Ctr., staging its first production, *After the Fall* (ANTA Washington Sq. Th., Jan. 23, 1964) and *But for Whom Charlie?* (ANTA Washington Sq. Th., Mar. 12, 1964).

Mr. Kazan, with Robert Whitehead, was a co-director of the Repertory Th. of Lincoln Ctr. for the Performing Arts (ANTA Washington Square Th., N.Y.C., 1964–65), for which he directed *After the Fall* (Jan. 23, 1964), *But for Whom Charlie?* (Mar. 12, 1964), and *The Changeling* (Oct. 29, 1964).

Films. Mr. Kazan made his debut as Googie in *City for Conquest* (WB, 1940); played the Clarinetist in *Blues in the Night* (WB, 1941); directed *A Tree Grows in Brooklyn* (20th-Fox, 1945); *Sea of Grass* (MGM, 1947); *Boomerang* (20th-Fox, 1947); *Gentleman's Agreement* (20th-Fox, 1947); *Pinky* (20th-Fox, 1949); *Panic in the Streets* (20th-Fox, 1950); *A Streetcar Named Desire* (WB, 1951); *Viva Zapata!* (20th-Fox, 1952); *Man on a Tightrope* (20th-Fox, 1953); *On the Waterfront* (Col., 1954); *East of Eden* (WB, 1955); *Wild River* (20th-Fox, 1960); formed the film company Newton Productions, directing and producing *Baby Doll* (WB, 1956); *A Face in the Crowd* (WB, 1957); *Splendor in the Grass* (WB, 1961); for Athena Enterprises, he directed and produced *America America* (WB, 1964), which he adapted from his book of the same title; wrote, produced, and directed *The Arrangement* (WB-Seven Arts, 1969); and directed *The Visitors* (UA, 1972).

Radio. Mr. Kazan performed on the Philip Morris Hour, the Kate Smith Hour and the Group Th. radio program.

Published Works. He wrote the autobiographical novel *America America* (1962); articles for magazines including *Theatre Arts* and *Esquire; The Arrangement* (1967); *The Assassins* (1972); and *The Understudy* (1975).

Awards. Mr. Kazan won the *Variety* NY Drama Critics Poll for his direction of *The Skin of Our Teeth* (1943); *All My Sons* (1947) (tied with John Gielgud); *Death of a Salesman* (1949); *Sweet Bird of Youth* (1959); received the Donaldson Award and the Antoinette Perry (Tony) Award as director of *All My Sons* (1947); the Donaldson Award for *A Streetcar Named Desire* (1948); the Antoinette Perry (Tony) and the Donaldson awards for *Death of a Salesman* (1949); the Donaldson Award for *Tea and Sympathy* (1954); *Cat on a Hot Tin Roof* (1955); and the Antoinette Perry (Tony) Award for *J. B.* (1959). He received an Academy (Oscar) Award for his direction of *Gentleman's Agreement* (1947); *On the Waterfront* (1954); an award from the Natl. Board of Review of the Venice Film Festival for *A Streetcar Named Desire* (1951); the honorary degree of D.Litt. from Wesleyan Univ. (1954) and from Carnegie Inst. of Tech. (1962).

Recreation. Tennis.

KEACH, STACY. Actor, director. b. June 2, 1941, Savannah, Ga., to Stacy Keach, Sr., actor, and Mary Cain (Peckham) Keach, actress. Grad. Univ. of Calif. at Berkeley, A.B. 1963; attended Yale Drama Sch. (1963–64); London Academy of Music and Dramatic Arts (1964–65). Member of AEA; SAG.

Theatre. Mr. Keach made his stage debut in an elementary school production of *Rip Van Winkle.* While at the Univ. of Calif. (1959–63) he appeared in *The Antifarce of John and Leporello, To Learn to Love, Galileo, Purple Dust, The Changeling, Bartholomew Fair, Escurrial, A Touch of the Poet,* and *Don Juan;* directed *The American Dream* and *C'est la vie;* and wrote and directed *The 1960 Axe Revue.* He subsequently played Armand in *Camille* (Tufts Arena, 1961); at the Oregon Shakespeare Festival (Ashland, Ore., Summer 1962) played Westmoreland in *Henry IV, Part II;* and Antipholus in *The Comedy of Errors;* and (Summer 1963), Mercutio in *Romeo and Juliet,* Berowne in *Love's Labour's Lost,* and the title role in *Henry V.* He appeared in *The Voyage* (Yale Drama Sch., New Haven, Conn., 1963); made his London directorial debut (LAMDA, 1964) with productions of *Pullman Car Hiawatha, The Stronger,* and *The Maids.*

Mr. Keach made his New York debut as Marcellus and the First Player in the NY Shakespeare Festival's production of *Hamlet* (Delacorte, June 1964); returned to LAMDA (1965) where he appeared in *Julius Caesar,* and *Hughie;* and toured England (1965) in *Playing with Fire.* With the Repertory Co. of Lincoln Center (Vivian Beaumont Th., N.Y.C.) he played Cutler and Turnkey in *Danton's Death* (Oct. 21, 1965), Mr. Horner in *The Country Wife* (Dec. 9, 1965), and several roles in *The Caucasian Chalk Circle* (Mar. 24, 1966); at the Williamstown (Mass.) Summer Th. (1966), appeared in *Annie Get Your Gun, You Can't Take It with You,* and *The Lion in Winter;* and at the Long Wharf Th. (New Haven, Conn., 1966) played Baron Tusenbach in *The Three Sisters,* and the Master of Ceremonies in *Oh, What a Lovely War!*

He made his off-Bway debut in the title role in *MacBird!* (Village Gate, Feb. 22, 1967); played Capt. Starkey in *We Bombed in New Haven* (Yale Repertory Th., New Haven, Conn., Oct. 1967); and, on a double-bill entitled *The Niggerlovers* (Orpheum, N.Y.C., Oct. 1, 1967), played August in *The Demonstration,* and The Man in *Man and Dog.* With the NY Shakespeare Festival (Delacorte Th.) he played Sir John Falstaff in *Henry IV, Part 1* (June 11, 1968) and *Part 2* (June 18, 1968); subsequently played Edmund in *King Lear* (Vivian Beaumont Th., Nov. 7, 1968); with the Yale Repertory Th. (New Haven, Conn. 1968) appeared in *Henry IV, The Three Sisters,* and *Coriolanus;* played Buffalo Bill in *Indians* (Arena Stage, Washington, D.C., Spring 1969); and Brooks Atkinson Th., N.Y.C., Oct. 13, 1969); played the title role in the NY Shakespeare Festival production of *Peer Gynt* (Delacorte, July 15, 1969); in the Berlioz opera based upon *Much Ado About Nothing,* played Benedict in *Beatrice and Benedict* (Los Angeles Music Center, 1970); James Tyrone, Jr., in *Long Day's Journey into Night* (Promenade, N.Y.C., Apr. 21, 1971); played the title role in *Hamlet* (Long Wharf Th., New Haven, Conn., Feb. 13, 1972); repeated that role for the NY Shakespeare Festival (Delacorte, N.Y.C., July 17, 1972); and, for the Center Th. Group, again played *Hamlet* (Mark Taper Forum, Los Angeles, Mar. 14, 1974).

Films. Mr. Keach made his film debut in *The Heart Is a Lonely Hunter* (WB-7 Arts, 1968); subsequently appeared in *Brewster McCloud* (MGM, 1970); *The Traveling Executioner* (MGM, 1970); *End of the Road* (AA, 1970); *Doc* (UA, 1971); *The Life and Times of Judge Roy Bean* (National General, 1972); *Fat City* (Col., 1972); *The New Centurions* (Col., 1972); *Luther* (Amer. Film Th., 1973); and *Conduct Unbecoming* (AA, 1975).

Television. He wrote, directed, and starred in *The Repeater,* a segment of The Great American Dream Machine (NET); for Shakespeare Repertory Theatre (NET), played Banquo in *Macbeth,* Feste in *Twelfth Night,* and Autolycus in *The Winter's Tale;* and appeared in *The Century Next Door* (WCBS); Hollywood Television Theatre (NET); *Orville and Wilbur* (NET); and his own series, Caribe (ABC).

Other Activities. Mr. Keach was associate professor of drama at Yale Univ. (New Haven, Conn., 1967–68).

Published Works. His article "The Take: A

Screen Actor in Search of His Character," appeared in the Sunday NY *Times* Magazine (Aug. 24, 1970).

Discography. He recorded *Earth Day* (Caedmon, 1974).

Awards. Mr. Keach received the Best Actor Award (1963) of the Univ. of California; the Oliver Thorndike acting award (Yale Univ. Drama Sch., 1963–64); a Fulbright Scholarship to LAMDA (1964); the Off-Bway (Obie) and Vernon Rice-Drama Desk awards for both *MacBird!* (1967) and *Long Day's Journey into Night* (1971); and the *Saturday Review* Accolade for best male lead in a comedy (1967) for *MacBird!*.

KEAN, BETTY. Actress, comedienne. b. Betty Wynn Kean, Dec. 15, 1920, Hartford, Conn., to Robert S. and Annette Helen Kean. Father, insurance business. Grad. Hartford (Conn.) H.S. Married Mar. 10, 1956, to Lew Parker, actor; one daughter. Relatives in theatre: sister, Jane Kean, actress, comedienne; brother-in-law, Richard Linkroum, director, producer. Member of AEA; SAG; AFTRA; The Troupers; The Props (Miami, Fla.).

Theatre. Miss Kean first performed as a dancer in the revue, *Crazy with the Heat* (44 St. Th., N.Y.C., Jan. 14, 1941); subsequently appeared as a comedienne and dancer in *Ziegfeld Follies* (Winter Garden, Apr. 1, 1943); and during World War II, performed with the USO at hospitals, canteens, and army bases entertaining the troops.

She appeared in the revue *Call Me Mister* (National, N.Y.C., Apr. 18, 1946); succeeded Nancy Walker in *Along Fifth Avenue* (Broadhurst, Jan. 13, 1949); and played Elsey in *Ankles Aweigh* (Mark Hellinger Th., Apr. 18, 1955).

Films. She has appeared in several Universal films.

Television. She has made nine appearances on the Ed Sullivan Show (CBS); appeared on the Jackie Gleason Show (CBS); Four Star Review (CBS); Naked City (ABC); the Milton Berle Show (NBC); Jack Paar Show (NBC); Johnny Carson Show (NBC); and Steve Allen Show (NBC). She has also performed on several panel shows.

Night Clubs. She has appeared in an act with her sister, Jane Kean, at the Copacabana, Blue Angel, Latin Quarter, and Bon Soir (N.Y.C.); Las Vegas, Nev.; and Miami, Fla.

Awards. Miss Kean and her sister were voted Actress-Troupers of the Year; and received a Royal Plaque at the Palladium (London, England).

Recreation. Television, sleeping.

KEAN, JANE. Actress, singer. b. Jane Dawn Kean, Apr. 10, 1928, Hartford, Conn., to Robert S. and Annette H. Kean. Father, insurance. Relatives in theatre: sister, Betty Kean, comedienne; brother-in-law, Lew Parker, comedian. Attended Julia Richmond H.S., N.Y.C.; Fay Compton Drama Sch., London, England. Studied acting with Sanford Meisner; and singing with Kay Thompson. Married Nov. 17, 1963, to Richard Linkroum, writer and producer. Member of AEA; SAG; AFTRA.

Theatre. Miss Kean made her N.Y.C. debut as Eileen in the musical comedy, *Early to Bed* (Broadhurst Th., June 17, 1943); subsequently appeared in *Call Me Mister* (Natl., Apr. 18, 1946); succeeded Carol Bruce in *Along Fifth Avenue* (Broadhurst, Jan. 13, 1949); played Wynne in *Ankles Aweigh* (Mark Hellinger Th., Apr. 18, 1955); Babe Williams in *The Pajama Game* (NY City Ctr., May 15, 1957); Ellie in *Show Boat* (NY City Ctr., Apr. 12, 1961); and replaced (Majestic Th., 1962) Kaye Ballard as the Incomparable Rosalie in *Carnival!* (Imperial, Apr. 13, 1961).

In stock, Miss Kean appeared in *Born Yesterday* (1948); *Bus Stop* (Capri, Atlantic Beach, N.J., 1960); toured the East Coast in *Burlesque* (1961); the musical *Happy Hunting* (Starlight Th., Kansas City, Mo., 1961); *Kiss Me, Kate* (Starlight, 1961); *Gentlemen Prefer Blondes* (Sacramento Opera Assn., Calif., 1962); and *Anything Goes* (Sacramento Light Opera House, 1963). She appeared in vaudeville shows at the Palladium, London.

Night Clubs. From 1950 to 1958, Miss Kean made several appearances at the Copacabana (N.Y.C.); and the Sands Hotel (Las Vegas, Nev.).

Recreation. Swimming, riding, interior decorating.

KEAN, NORMAN. General manager, producer, theatre owner and operator, stage manager. b. Norman Alan Kean, Oct. 14, 1934, Colorado Springs, Colo., to Barney B. and Flora (Bienstock) Kean. Father, business executive; mother, legal secretary. Grad. Colorado Springs H.S., 1952; attended Univ. of Denver, 1952–54. Married Oct. 12, 1958, to Gwyda DonHowe, actress. Served US Army, Special Services, 1954–55. Member of ATPAM; AEA. Address: (home) 280 Riverside Dr., New York, NY 10025, tel. (212) 749-0861; (bus.) c/o Edison Theatre, 240 W. 47th St., New York, NY 10036, tel. (212) 586-7870.

Theatre. Mr. Kean first appeared in a junior-h.s. production of *A Date with Judy* (Feb. 1946). His first professional assignment was as lighting designer at the Bar Harbor (Me.) Playhouse, where he also played Wint Selby in *Ah, Wilderness!* (Summer 1953); subsequently worked at the Barn Th. (Augusta, Mich.) as actor, stage manager, and designer (Summer 1954); was stage manager for the Theatre in Education Shakespeare touring productions (Conn., Feb.–Apr. 1956); and stage manager at the Straight Wharf Playhouse (Nantucket, Mass., June–Sept. 1956).

He was production stage manager for *Johnny Johnson* (Carnegie Hall Playhouse, N.Y.C., Oct. 21, 1956); technical supervisor of *Androcles and the Lion* (Queens Coll., Dec. 1956); and stage manager for *Orpheus Descending* (Martin Beck Th., Mar. 21, 1957). He was production stage manager at the Grist Mill Playhouse (Andover, N.J., June–Aug. 1957); stage manager for the national touring production of *The Waltz of the Toreadors* (opened McCarter Th., Princeton, N.J., Sept. 26, 1957), which played in N.Y.C. (Coronet, Mar. 4, 1958).

He was founder and, with Harriet Crawford, producer of the Silo Circle Playhouse (Black Mountain, N.C., June–Sept. 1958); director and, with Peter Poor, associate producer at the Straight Wharf Playhouse (Nantucket, Mass., June–Sept. 1958); was stage manager for *A Touch of the Poet* (Helen Hayes Th., N.Y.C., Oct. 2, 1958); produced, with Joseph Brownstone, at the Bristol (Pa.) Star Playhouse (June–Aug. 1959); was production stage manager for the Shakespeare Festival Players tour (Sept.–Dec. 1959); the Theatre in Education, Inc. Shakespeare tour (Conn., Feb.–Apr. 1960); and for *Camino Real* (St. Mark's playhouse, N.Y.C., May 16, 1960).

Mr. Kean was stage manager for the pre-Bway tryout of *Laurette* (opened Shubert, New Haven, Conn., Sept. 26, 1960; closed there Oct. 1, 1960); company manager of the national touring production of *The Pleasure of His Company* (opened Aud., Rochester, N.Y., Sept. 15, 1960; closed Shubert, New Haven, Conn., Mar. 25, 1961); and directed stock productions of *The Importance of Being Earnest* and *Gigi* (Eastern Slope Playhouse, Conway, N.H., June–July 1961).

He was company manager for the Bayanihan Philippine Dance Co., on tour (Aug.–Nov. 1961), and in N.Y.C. (Metropolitan Opera House, Nov. 1961); for *General Seeger* (Lyceum, Feb. 28, 1962); for *Half Past Wednesday* (Orpheum, Apr. 6, 1962); for the Royal Dramatic Th. of Sweden at the Seattle (Wash.) World's Fair (World's Fair Playhouse, Apr. 1962), and in N.Y.C. (Cort, May 14, 1962); company manager for the Bayanihan Philippine Dance at the Seattle World's Fair (World's Fair Opera House, May–June 1962); Phoenix Theatre-NY Council on the Arts touring production of *The Matchmaker* (Aug.–Nov. 1962); *Tiger, Tiger Burning Bright* (Booth, N.Y.C., Dec. 22, 1962); *Candida* (Charles Playhouse, Boston, Mass., Apr. 1963); for *Cages* (York, N.Y.C., June 13, 1963); and with Lyn Ely, he produced *Worlds of Shakespeare* for a college tour (Nov.–Dec. 1963), and in N.Y.C. (Carnegie Recital Hall, Dec. 4, 1963).

In Sept. 1963, Mr. Kean was appointed general manager of the Phoenix Th. (N.Y.C.) and was responsible for the following productions: *Morning Sun* (Oct. 6, 1963), *Next Time I'll Sing to You* (Nov. 27, 1963), *The Brontes* (Dec. 10, 1963), *Too Much Johnson* (Jan. 15, 1964), *The Lower Depths* (Mar. 3, 1964), the APA repertory production of *Right You Are* (Mar. 4, 1964), *The Tavern* (Mar. 5, 1964), *Scapin and Impromptu at Versailles* (Mar. 9, 1964). He was general manager for the Laterna Magika production, from Prague, Czechoslovakia (Carnegie Hall, N.Y.C., Aug. 3, 1964); producer of *The Bernard Shaw Story* (East 74 St. Th., Nov. 1964); and was general manager of the APA Phoenix Broadway production of *You Can't Take It with You* (Lyceum Th., Sept. 1964).

Mr. Kean became the owner (1965–66) of the East 74th St. Playhouse (N.Y.C.), and from April 1965 through April 1969 he was general manager of APA Phoenix Repertory Company and its 21 productions including: *War and Peace, The Wild Duck, The School for Scandal, Right You Are, The Show-Off, The Flies, Cock-a-Doodle Dandy, Pantagleize, Exit the King, The Cocktail Party* and *Hamlet*. He was general manager for *Oh Calcutta!* (Eden Th., N.Y.C., June 17, 1969; San Francisco, Sept. 1969; and Los Angeles, Nov. 1969). He became president of the Edison Th. Corp. (Jan. 1, 1970); designed and built Edison Th. which opened officially on Mar. 12, 1970, with *Show Me Where the Good Times Are*, followed by *Happy Birthday, Wanda June* and *Johnny Johnson*. He was general manager for *Don't Bother Me, I Can't Cope* (Edison Th., June, 1972; Happy Medium Th., Chicago, Sept. 1972–Dec. 1973; Huntington Hartford Th., Los Angeles, Oct. 1972–June 1973; Royal Alexandra Th., Toronto, Canada, June 1973; Geary Th., San Francisco, June–Sept. 1973; Coconut Grove Playhouse, Miami, Fla., May–July 1974; Mechanic Th., Baltimore, Md., Sept.–Oct. 1974; and Peachtree Playhouse, Atlanta, Ga., Dec. 1974). He was general manager with Leonard Soloway of *Sizwe Banzi Is Dead* and *The Island* (Edison Th., Nov. 1974); was general manager for *Orlando Furioso* from Rome, which was presented in an air dome in Bryant Park; and he produced *Hosanna* (Bijou Th., N.Y.C., Oct. 14, 1974).

Mr. Kean is president of Norman Kean Prod. (1965); Edison Enterprises, Inc. (1974); Mister Kelly's, Chicago (1971–73); and Happy Medium Th., Chicago (1971–74).

Films. Mr. Kean was associate producer of *Bayanihan* (Robt. Snyder, Dec. 1961).

KEATHLEY, GEORGE. Director, producer. b. 1925, Miami, Fla. Served US Army, 1943–46.

Theatre. In 1950, Mr. Keathley founded the Studio M Playhouse (Miami, Fla.), where he produced and directed 100 plays (1950–56), including *Sweet Bird of Youth* (world premiere Apr. 1956).

He directed *The Square Root of Wonderful* (National, N.Y.C., Oct. 30, 1957); the State Dept. sponsored overseas tour of *The Glass Menagerie* (1961); and served as artistic director for the Playhouse-in-the-Park (Philadelphia, Pa., 1961–63).

He directed *The Immoralist* (Bouwerie Lane Th., N.Y.C., Nov. 8, 1963); *Madly in Love* (Coconut Grove Playhouse, Miami, Fla., Dec. 26, 1963; *Uncle Vanya* (Trinity Square Playhouse, Providence, R.I., Jan. 6, 1965); *The Glass Menagerie* (Paper Mill Playhouse, Millburn, N.J., Mar. 30, 1965; Brooks Atkinson Th., N.Y.C., May 4, 1965); *Come Back, Little Sheba* (Paper Mill Playhouse, Aug. 16, 1965); *Oh, What a Lovely War!* (Queen Elizabeth Playhouse, Vancouver, B.C., Canada, Oct. 14, 1965); *Rooms* (Cherry Lane, N.Y.C., Jan. 27, 1966); *The Glass Menagerie* (Coconut Grove Playhouse, Miami, Fla., May 17, 1966; Huntington Hartford Th., Los Angeles, Calif., June 13, 1966); *Captain Brassbound's Conversion* (Pasadena Playhouse, Pasadena, Calif., Sept. 28, 1966); and *The Right Honourable Gentleman* (Huntington Hartford Th., Los Angeles, Mar. 13, 1967).

As producer-director at Ivanhoe Th., Chicago, Ill. (1968–75), Mr. Keathley staged *The Impossible Years* (1968); *Affairs of State* (1968); *The Rose Tattoo* (Nov. 1968); *Little Mary Sunshine* (Nov. 1968); *Staircase* (1969); *Sweet Bird of Youth* (1969); *The*

Little Foxes (1969); *The Waltz of the Toreadors* (1969); *The Corn Is Green* (May 1969); *Tchin-Tchin* (Oct. 14, 1969); *The King of Hearts* (Nov. 25, 1969); *The Miracle Worker* (Nov. 1969); *Cat on a Hot Tin Roof* (Jan. 6, 1970); *The Member of the Wedding* (Feb. 17, 1970); *The Time of the Cuckoo* (Mar. 31, 1970); *A Shot in the Dark* (May 14, 1970); *Who's Afraid of Virginia Woolf?* (June 25, 1970); *Bus Stop* (Aug. 6, 1970); and *Summer and Smoke* (Sept. 17, 1970).

Also *The Biggest Thief in Town* (Dec. 8, 1970); *The Effect of Gamma Rays on Man-in-the-Moon Marigolds* (Jan. 21, 1971); *Suddenly Last Summer* and *I Can't Imagine Tomorrow* (Mar. 18, 1971); *Another Part of the Forest* (Apr. 29, 1971); *Journey to the Day* (June 10, 1971); *The Two-Character Play* (July 8, 1971); *Status Quo Vadis* (Aug. 26, 1971); *Out Cry* (Aug. 1971); *The Happy Apple* (Nov. 1971); *The House of Blue Leaves* (Mar. 1972); *Father's Day* (Aug. 1972); *Jacques Brel Is Alive and Well and Living in Paris* (1972); *I Do! I Do!* (1972); *Da* (Jan. 1973), which was directed by Richard Waring; *The Dark at the Top of the Stairs* (Mar. 1973); and *The Last Straw* (Mar. 1975).

In N.Y.C., Mr. Keathley produced, with Jack Lenny, *Status Quo Vadis* (Brooks Atkinson Th., Feb. 18, 1973).

KEEL, HOWARD. Actor, singer. b. Harry Keel, Apr. 13, 1919, Gillespie, Ill. Attended Fallbrook (Calif.) H.S. Married Jan. 3, 1949, to Helen Anderson, dancer (marr. dis. Dec. 1970); one son, two daughters. Married Dec. 21, 1970, to Judy Magamoll; one daughter. Member of SAG (pres., 1960); AFTRA; AGMA; AEA. Suite 504, 1800 Century Park East, Los Angeles, CA 90067.

Theatre. Mr. Keel (billed as Harold Keel) made his debut succeeding to the role of Billy Bigelow in *Carousel* (Majestic Th., Apr. 19, 1945); subsequently, succeeded Harry Stockwell as Curly in *Oklahoma!* (St. James, Mar. 31, 1943; Drury Lane, London, Eng., Apr. 30, 1947); and repeated the role of Billy Bigelow in *Carousel* (NY City Ctr., Sept. 11, 1957); played Clint Maroon in *Saratoga* (Winter Garden, Dec. 7, 1959); succeeded Richard Kiley as David Jordan in *No Strings* (54 St. Th., Mar. 15, 1962); and appeared as Lambert Strether in *Ambassador* (opened in London, 1971; and Lunt-Fontanne, N.Y.C., Nov. 19, 1972).

He has appeared in stock productions of *Carousel, Kismet, Mr. Roberts, Sunrise at Campobello, Kiss Me, Kate, The Rainmaker, South Pacific, The Crossing, Plaza Suite, Man of La Mancha,* and *The Unsinkable Molly Brown.*

Films. Mr. Keel made his debut in *The Small Voice* (London, 1948); subsequently appeared in *Hideout* (Rep., 1949); *Annie Get Your Gun* (MGM, 1950); *Pagan Love Song* (MGM, 1950); *Show Boat* (MGM, 1951); *Three Guys Named Mike* (MGM, 1951); *Callaway Went That-a-Way* (MGM, 1951); *Ride, Vacquero* (MGM, 1953); *Desperate Search* (MGM, 1952); *Fast Company* (MGM, 1953); *Kiss Me, Kate* (MGM, 1953); *Rose Marie* (MGM, 1954); *Seven Brides for Seven Brothers* (MGM, 1954); *Kismet* (MGM, 1955); *Jupiter's Darling* (MGM, 1955); *The Big Fisherman* (Buena Vista, 1959); *Floods of Fear* (U, 1959); *Armoured Command* (Allied, 1961); and *Day of Triffids* (Allied, 1963).

Recreation. Golf.

KEELER, RUBY. Actress, dancer. b. Aug. 25, 1910, Halifax, Nova Scotia, Canada, to Ralph and Elnora (Lahy) Keeler. Married 1928 to Al Jolson, singer (marr. dis. 1939); one son; married Oct. 29, 1941, to John Lowe (dec. 1970); one son, three daughters. Member of AEA; SAG.

Theatre. Miss Keeler made her N.Y.C. debut in the chorus of *The Rise of Rosy O'Reilly* (Liberty Th., Dec. 25, 1923); subsequently played Ruby in *Bye-Bye, Bonnie* (Ritz, Jan. 13, 1927); Mazie Maxwell in *Lucky* (New Amsterdam, Mar. 22, 1927); Ruby in *The Sidewalks of New York* (Knickerbocker, Oct. 3, 1927); appeared in the revue, *Show Girl* (Ziegfeld, July 2, 1929); and played Shirley in *Hold Onto Your Hats* (Grand Opera House, Chicago, Ill., July 15, 1940). She played Gillian in *Bell, Book and Candle* (Ivanhoe Th., Chicago, Ill., Feb. 6, 1968); and was Sue Smith in a revival of *No, No, Nanette* (46 St. Th., N.Y.C., Jan. 19, 1971), later touring music fairs in the role (Oct.–Nov. 1973).

Films. Miss Keeler made her debut in *42nd Street* (WB, 1933); subsequently appeared in *Gold Diggers of 1933* (WB, 1933); *Footlight Parade* (WB, 1933); *Dames* (WB, 1934); *Flirtation Walk* (1st Natl., 1934); *Go into Your Dance* (1st Natl., 1935); *Shipmates Forever* (1st Natl., 1935); *Colleen* (WB, 1936); *Ready, Willing and Able* (WB, 1937); *Mother Carey's Chickens* (RKO, 1938); and *Sweetheart of the Campus* (Col., 1941).

Television. Miss Keeler has appeared on the Jackie Gleason Show (CBS); This Is Your Life (CBS, Nov. 1957); Jerry Lewis Show; and The Greatest Show on Earth (ABC).

Awards. Miss Keeler received the George M. Cohan Award of the Catholic Actors Guild of America (1971) and the woman of the year award of the Harvard Hasty Pudding Club (1972).

Recreation. Golf.

KEEN, GEOFFREY. Actor. b. Aug. 21, 1918, London, England, to Malcolm Keen. Father, actor. Attended Bristol (Eng.) Grammar Sch. Studied at RADA, London, 1935–36. Married to Hazel Terry (marr. dis.); married to Madeleine Howell; one daughter. Served British Army, 1940–44. Member of AEA; SAG; The Green Room Club (London).

Theatre. Mr. Keen made his first appearance on stage as Trip in *The School for Scandal* (Bristol Grammar Sch., May 9, 1932); subsequently as a member of the Old Vic Co., played Florizel in *The Winter's Tale* (Mar. 17, 1936); and Edgar in *King Lear* (Apr. 7, 1936); appeared as David French in *Follow Your Saint* (Queen's, London, Sept. 24, 1936); Danny in *Night Must Fall* (Cambridge, Oct. 1936); Will Hopcyn in *The Ripening Wheat* (Royalty, Feb. 1937); the Hon. Gerald Sinclair in *Great Possessions* ("Q," Feb. 8, 1937); Brian Decker in *Old Music* (St. James's, Aug. 18, 1937); and Bije Warner in *Welcome Stranger* (Saville, Feb. 17, 1938).

He joined the Stratford-upon-Avon Shakespeare Co. (1938); appeared as Israel Hand in *Treasure Island* (Savoy, London, Dec. 26, 1938); at Stratford-upon-Avon (Summer 1939), played Lucentio in *The Taming of the Shrew,* Orlando in *As You Like It,* the Duke of Clarence in *Richard III,* Cassio in *Othello,* Sebastian in *Twelfth Night* and Cominius in *Coriolanus.* While serving with the British Army during WW II, he joined the "Stars and Battle Dress," an entertainment unit, appearing in such plays as *Men in Shadow* and *While the Sun Shines.*

Mr. Keen played Lyngstrand in *The Lady from the Sea* (Arts, London, Mar. 13, 1946); Geoffrey Stewart in *Exercise Bowler* (Arts, Apr. 18, 1946); toured for the British Council (1946–47), appearing in *Hamlet, Othello,* and *Candida;* played Justin Corbel in *Rain on the Just* (Aldwych, London, Aug. 31, 1948); with the Shakespeare Memorial Th. (Stratford-upon-Avon, 1957), played Cassius in *Julius Caesar* (May 28, 1957), and Iachimo in *Cymbeline* (July 2, 1957); appeared in a double-bill, playing George Renaud in *Traveller without Luggage* and the Ambassador in *Madame de . . .* (Arts, London, Jan. 29, 1959); portrayed the Turkish Military Governor in *Ross* (Haymarket, May 12, 1960), and repeated the latter role in N.Y.C. (Eugene O'Neill Th., Dec. 26, 1961); and Sven Johnson in *Man and Boy* (Brooks Atkinson Th., Nov. 13, 1963).

Films. Mr. Keen appeared in *Dr. Syn* (GB, 1937); *Odd Man Out* (U, 1947); *The Third Man* (SRO, 1950); *Treasure Island* (RKO, 1950); *Cry, the Beloved Country* (UA, 1952); *Rob Roy, the Highland Rogue* (RKO, 1953); *Genevieve* (U, 1954); *Doctor in the House* (Rep., 1955); *The Divided Heart* (Rep., 1955); *The Glass Tomb* (Lippert, 1955); *Carrington, V.C.* (Kingsley-Intl., 1955); *Doctor at Sea* (Rep., 1956); *The Angry Silence* (Valiant, 1960); *Sink the Bismarck* (Fox, 1960); *Court Martial* (UA, 1962); *The Mind Benders* (Amer. Intl., 1963); *Drums Along the Nile;* and *Live Now, Pay Later; The Heroes of Telemark* (Rank, 1965); *Dr. Zhivago* (MGM, 1965); and *Born Free* (Col., 1966).

Television. Mr. Keen has appeared on Walt Disney's World (NBC, 1964); Mystery Hour (Ind., 1965); *The Mogul* (BBC, 1965); *The Gaming Book* (BBC, 1965); Secret Agent (CBS, 1966); Court Martial (ABC, 1966); *Words Are Softer Than Oil* (BBC, 1967); and *The Trouble Shooters* (BBC, 1970).

Awards. He received the Bancroft Gold Medal from the Royal Academy of Dramatic Arts (1936).

KEENE, DONALD. Translator, professor of Japanese. b. June 18, 1922, to Joseph Frank and Rena Keene. Grad. Columbia Univ., A.B. 1942; M.A. 1946; Ph.D. 1951; Cambridge Univ., M.A. 1950. Served USN 1942–46. Member of Japan Society; Amer. Academy of Arts and Sciences; Amer. Oriental Society; Phi Beta Kappa. Address: 407 Kent Hall, Columbia Univ., New York, NY 10027.

Since 1955, Mr. Keene has been professor of Japanese at Columbia Univ.

He has translated the Japanese plays, *Hanjo* and *The Lady Akane* (original title: *The Lady Aoi),* which were presented as a double bill (Th. de Lys, N.Y.C., Nov. 15, 1960); *The Damask Drum* and *Sotoba Komachi,* also produced as a double bill (Players Th., Feb. 3, 1961; Inst. for the Advanced Study of Th. Arts, Jan. 1962).

Published Works. Mr. Keene has translated *The Battles of Coxinga* by Chikamatsu Monzaemon (1951); *Five Modern Nō Plays* (1957), and *Madame de Sade* (1967) by Yukio Mishima; *Friends* (1969) by Kobo Abe; *Major Plays of Chikamatsu Monzaemon* (1961); *Essays in Idleness* by Kenko (1967); *ChIshingura* (1971); and the novel, *After the Banquet* by Yukio Mishima (1963).

He is author of *The Japanese Discovery of Europe* (1952); *Japanese Literature, An Introduction for Western Readers* (1953); *Anthology of Japanese Literature* (1955); *Living Japan* (1959); *Bunraku: the Art of the Japanese Puppet Theatre* (1965); *Nō, the Classical Theatre of Japan* (1966); and *Landscapes and Portraits* (1971).

KEIM, BETTY LOU. Actress. b. Elizabeth Louise Keim, Sept. 27, 1938, Malden, Mass., to Buster and Dorothy Keim. Father, choreographer; mother, dancer. Grad. Lodge H.S., N.Y.C., 1956. Married Feb. 18, 1960, to Warren Berlinger, actor; one son, one daughter. Member of AFTRA; AEA; SAG.

Theatre. Miss Keim made her N.Y.C. debut as Laura Dean in *Strange Fruit* (Royale Th., Nov. 29, 1945); subsequently appeared as a Child of the Village in *Rip Van Winkle* (NY City Ctr., July 15, 1947); Polya in *Crime and Punishment* (Natl., Dec. 22, 1947); Dogie Smith in *Texas Li'l Darlin'* (Mark Hellinger Th., Nov. 25, 1949); Jane Moser in the pre-Bway tryout of *Child of the Morning* (opened Bway Th., Springfield, Mass., Nov. 16, 1951; closed Shubert, Boston, Mass., Dec. 1, 1951); the First Pupil in *The Remarkable Mr. Pennypacker* (Coronet, N.Y.C., Dec. 30, 1953) and Bridget MacGowan in *Roomful of Roses* (Playhouse, Oct. 17, 1955).

Films. Miss Keim appeared in *Teenage Rebel* (20th-Fox, 1956); *These Wilder Years* (MGM, 1956); *The Wayward Bus* (20th-Fox, 1957); and *Some Came Running* (MGM, 1958).

Television. She has appeared on Playhouse 90 (CBS), Alcoa Presents (NBC), Riverboat (NBC), and The Deputy (NBC).

Awards. Miss Keim has received the Woman's Clubs of America Award (1956), the *Daily Variety* Award (1956), and the *Motion Picture Daily* Award (1956), all as most promising actress.

KEITH, ROBERT. Actor, director, producer, playwright. b. Robert Keith Richey, Feb. 10, 1898, Fowler, Ind., to James H. and Mary (Dell) Richey. Father, businessman. Married May 1920 to Helena Shipman (marr. dis. June 1926); one son; married May 10, 1930, to Dorothy Tierney. Relative in theatre: son, Brian Keith, actor. Member of AEA (council, 1934–40); SAG (former director, recording secy., 1951–60); AFTRA; The Lambs; Masquers Club (Hollywood).

Theatre. Mr. Keith made his stage debut as Jimmy in a stock production of *Got a Match?* (New Th., St. Charles, Ill., Dec. 25, 1914); and subsequently appeared in repertory and stock companies from coast to coast (1914–21).

He first appeared on Bway as Ralph Armstrong in *The Triumph of X* (Comedy Th., Aug. 14, 1921); toured as Tom in *Three Wise Fools* (Sept. 1921); appeared as John Marvin in *Lightnin'* (Sept. 1922); was a replacement for the part of Recan in *Seventh Heaven* (Booth, N.Y.C., Oct. 30, 1922); played Thomas Bates, Jr., in *New Brooms* (Fulton, Nov. 17, 1924); Dion Anthony in *The Great God Brown* (Greenwich Village Th., Jan. 23, 1926); Dick Cameron in *Gentle Grafters* (Music Box, Oct. 27, 1926); Robert Mayo in *Beyond the Horizon* (Mansfield, Nov. 30, 1926); and Charlie in *Fog* (National, Feb. 7, 1927).

Mr. Keith wrote *The Tightwad* (49 St. Th., Apr. 16, 1927); succeeded (Dec. 10, 1927) Robert Williams as Jimmie Turner in *Jimmie's Women* (Biltmore, Sept. 26, 1927); played in the touring company of *John Ferguson* and *Ned McCobb's Daughter* (1928); wrote *Singapore* (48 St. Th., N.Y.C., Nov. 14, 1932); played John Douglas in *Under Glass* (Ambassador, Oct. 30, 1933); Peter Owens in *Peace on Earth* (Civic Repertory Th., Nov. 29, 1933); Jessie W. Lazear in *Yellow Jack* (Martin Beck Th., Mar. 6, 1934); Jack in *Goodbye Again* (Ritz, Oct. 24, 1934); Dr. Joseph Cardin in *The Children's Hour* (Maxine Elliott's Th., Nov. 20, 1934); Cornelius Prentiss in *Work Is for Horses* (Windsor, Nov. 20, 1937); Pilon in *Tortilla Flat* (Henry Miller's Th., Jan. 12, 1938); Malcolm Eldred in *The Good* (Windsor, Oct. 5, 1938); Reynolds in *Ladies and Gentlemen* (Martin Beck Th., Oct. 17, 1939); the title role in *The Romantic Mr. Dickens* (Playhouse, Dec. 2, 1940); Papa in the touring company of *Papa Is All* (1942); and Henry Archer in *Kiss and Tell* (Biltmore, N.Y.C., Mar. 17, 1943).

Mr. Keith appeared as Dr. Miles Carter in *No Way Out*, which he produced and directed with the author, Owen Davis (Cort, Oct. 30, 1944); played Charles Reddy in *A Place of Our Own* (Royale, Apr. 2, 1945); Colonel Rainsford in the pre-Bway tour of *The Rugged Path* (Sept. 1945); Herbert Gage in *January Thaw* (John Golden Th., Feb. 4, 1946); and Doc in *Mister Roberts* (Alvin, Feb. 18, 1948).

Films. Mr. Keith was a dialogue writer for Universal Pictures and Columbia Pictures (1929–1933); made his debut as an actor as the Father in *My Foolish Heart* (RKO, 1949); and then played Sam in *The Reformer and the Redhead* (MGM, 1950); Clovis in *Branded* (Par., 1950); the Detective in *Woman on the Run* (U, 1950); the Detective in *Eagle of Doom* (Goldwyn, 1950); the Father in *I Want You* (RKO, 1951); Featherstowe in *Girl Across the Street* (1951); the Father in *14 Hours* (20th-Fox, 1951); the Editor in *Here Comes the Groom* (Par., 1951); Sam in *Somebody Loves Me* (Par., 1952); the Father in *Small Town Girl* (MGM, 1953); the Colonel in *Battle Circus* (MGM, 1953); Warden in *Devil's Canyon* (RKO, 1953); the Police Chief in *The Wild One* (Col., 1954); Pal in *Drumbeat* (WB, 1954); the Father in *Young at Heart* (WB, 1954); Father Reilley in *Underwater* (RKO, 1955); Joe in *Love Me or Leave Me* (MGM, 1955); the Father in *Written on the Wind* (U, 1956); the Police Chief in *Ransom* (MGM, 1956); the Colonel in *Between Heaven and Hell* (20th-Fox, 1956); the Colonel in *Men in War* (UA, 1957); the Father in *My Man Godfrey* (U, 1957); the General in *They Came to Cordura* (Col., 1959); the Captain in *Tempest* (Par., 1959); the Editor in *Cimarron* (MGM, 1960); and appeared in *Posse from Hell* (U, 1961); and *Orazzi E Curiazzi* (Tiberia Lux, Italy, 1961).

Television. Mr. Keith's television appearances include the Alfred Hitchcock Th. (CBS, 1961; 1964); The Dick Powell Show (NBC, 1962); Eleventh Hour (NBC, 1963); The Fugitive (ABC, 1963); and Twilight Zone (CBS, 1963).

KEITH-JOHNSTON, COLIN. Actor. b. Oct. 8, 1896, London, England, to Robert and Jessy (Macfie) Keith-Johnston. Attended Felsted Sch., 1911–14. Married 1925 to Mary Cooper (marr. dis.); married 1952 to Rett Cookson. Served WW I in B.E. Force, Infantry and Air Force; awarded the M.C., 1917; WW II, Royal Army, entertainment officer in Middle East, 1942–45; rank, Capt. Member of AEA; British AEA.

Theatre. Mr. Keith-Johnston made his London debut as a walk-on in *The Daughter of Madame Angot* (Drury Lane Th., July 2, 1919); toured in *The Luck of the Navy, Charley's Aunt, Mr. Pim Passes By*, and *Brown Sugar* (1920–21); with the Birmingham Repertory Th. Co. (April 1921), appeared in such roles as Geoffrey Cassilis in *The Cassilis Engagement*, Eugene Marchbanks in *Candida*, Oswald in *Ghosts*, Bob Acres in *The Rivals*, John Rhead in *Milestones*, Rowland in *The Shoemaker's Holiday*, Randall Utterwood in *Heartbreak House*, George Smerdon in *The Farmer's Wife*, and Adam and Pygmalion in *Back to Methuselah*, in which he also appeared in London (Court, Feb. 18, 1924).

He appeared as George Smerdon in *The Farmer's Wife* (Court, Mar. 11, 1924); the title role in *Hamlet* (Kingsway, Aug. 25, 1925); and Donald Farfrae in *The Mayor of Casterbridge* (Barnes, Sept. 8, 1926); Vassili Pestoff in *The Greater Love* (Prince's, Feb. 23, 1927); He in *The Might-Have-Beens* (Prince's, May 22, 1927); and Lord Teylesmore in *The High Road* (Shaftesbury, Sept. 7, 1927); *Back to Methuselah* (Court, May 5, 1928); Landolph in *The Mock Emperor* (Queen's, Jan. 29, 1929); and Capt. Stanhope in *Journey's End* (Arts, May 1929), the role in which he made his N.Y.C. debut (Henry Miller's Th., Mar. 22, 1929).

He played John Ford in a London production of *Jane's Legacy* (Duchess, Dec. 16, 1930); the Young Man in *The Life Machine* (Players, July 15, 1931); Laertes in *Hamlet* (Broadhurst, N.Y.C., Nov. 5, 1931); Theseus in *The Warrior's Husband* (Morosco, Mar. 11, 1932); and Robert Chatfield in *Dangerous Corner* (Empire, Oct. 27, 1923); Anthony Reading in *Angel* (Vaudeville, London, Dec. 7, 1933); Robin O'Neill in *Saturday's Children* (Westminster, Jan. 23, 1934); John Cooper in *Magnolia Street* (Adelphi, Mar. 8, 1934); Clive in *Clive of India* (Wyndham's, June 25, 1934); George West in *Ringmaster* (Shaftesbury, Mar. 11, 1935); and Ham in *Noah* (New, July 2, 1935).

Mr. Keith-Johnston appeared as Mr. Darcy in *Pride and Prejudice* (Music Box, N.Y.C., Nov. 5, 1935); Rev. Mark Ahern in *The First Legion* (Richmond, London, June 7, 1937); John Egerton in *Flood Tide* (Phoenix, Mar. 23, 1938); Otterleigh in *White Secrets* (Fortune, June 10, 1938); Hector in *Troilus and Cressida* (Westminster, Sept. 21, 1938); Maurice Atkins in *Tree of Eden* (Apollo, Oct. 12, 1938); Hovstad in *An Enemy of the People* (Old Vic, Feb. 21, 1939); Hon. Gerald Piper in *The Family Reunion* (Westminster, Mar. 21, 1939); and Marshall in *Only Yesterday* (Playhouse, May 25, 1939).

He again appeared as Capt. Stanhope in *Journey's End* (Empire, N.Y.C., Sept. 18, 1939); played Ken Sutter in *The Woman Brown* (Biltmore, Dec. 8, 1939); Capt. English in *A Passenger to Bali* (Ethel Barrymore Th., Mar. 14, 1940); Dr. Blenkinsop in *The Doctor's Dilemma* (Shubert, Mar. 11, 1941), later succeeding (May 1941) Raymond Massey in the role of Sir Colenso Ridgeon; Bill Randall in *The Strings, My Lord, Are False* (Royale, May 19, 1942); and Peter Launders in *Lifeline* (Belasco, Nov. 30, 1942).

He toured the US as Camillo in *The Winter's Tale* (Sept. 1945), and repeated it in N.Y.C. (Cort, Jan. 15, 1946); appeared as Aubrey Stewart in *The Dancer* (Biltmore, June 5, 1946); Robin Claydon in *The Rats of Norway* (Booth, Apr. 15, 1948); toured as Arthur Winslow in *The Winslow Boy* (Summer 1950); appeared as Father Soames in *Getting Married* (Los Angeles and San Francisco, Calif., June 1950); Gen. Benjamin Griggs in *The Autumn Garden* (Coronet, N.Y.C., Mar. 7, 1951); Laurence Lovell in *Point of No Return* (Alvin, Dec. 13, 1951), and on tour (1952–53); again toured in *The Winslow Boy* (Summer 1955); and played Peter Shirley in *Major Barbara* (Martin Beck Th., Oct. 30, 1956).

KELLIN, MIKE. Actor. b. Myron Kellin, Apr. 26, 1922, Hartford, Conn., to Samuel and Sophie (Botuck) Kellin. Father, businessman. Attended Thomas Snell Weaver H.S., Hartford (1937–39); Bates College (1939–40); Boston Univ. (1940–41); grad. Trinity College, A.B. (philosophy) 1943; attended Randall Sch., Hartford (1946–47); Yale Univ. (1948). Studied acting with Lee Strasberg, Tamara Daykarhanova, Stella Adler, and Sanford Meisner. Married Jan. 27, 1951, to Nina Caiserman (dec. May 6, 1963); one daughter; married Aug. 2, 1966, to Sally Moffet. Served USNR, LCI Squadron, 1943–46; rank, Lt. Cmdr. of LCI squadron. Member of AEA (council, 1962–to date); SAG; AFTRA; The Fortune Society (adv. bd.); Rockland County (N.Y.) legislature's blue ribbon committee on criminal justice; Tau Epsilon Phi; Duces of Hartford; former member, bd. of dir., sponsors of Synanon. Address: International Famous Agency, Inc., 9255 Sunset Blvd., Los Angeles, CA 90067.

Theatre. Mr. Kellin made his stage debut at seven in the title role in *The Little Lost Prince* (Hartford, Conn.); his professional debut as the Elevator Boy in *Junior Miss* (Clinton Playhouse, Conn., Summer, 1946), where he also played the Policeman in *Angel Street*; in stock, played the Sea Captain and a Priest in *Twelfth Night* and Blossom in *The Hasty Heart* (Barter Th., Abingdon, Va., Summer 1947); David in *Claudia*, the Senator in *John Loves Mary* and the title role in *Papa Is All* (Pitchford Playhouse, Conn., Summer 1948).

He made his Bway debut as Staff Sergeant McVay in *At War with the Army* (Booth Th., Mar. 8, 1949) and played it on tour (1950); played Frank in *The Bird Cage* (Coronet, N.Y.C., Feb. 22, 1950); succeeded (Sept. 10, 1951) Robert Strauss as Stosh in *Stalag 17* (48 St., May 8, 1951); played the Sheriff in *Time of Storm* (Greenwich Mews Th., 1952); directed *Widowers Houses* (Greenwich Mews Th., 1952); played the 2nd Rottenbiller Brother in *The Emperor's Clothes* (Ethel Barrymore Th., Feb. 9, 1953); Krupp in *The Time of Your Life* (NY City Ctr., Jan. 19, 1955); Joe Mancinni in *Ankles Aweigh* (Mark Hellinger Th., Apr. 18, 1955); and Hazel in *Pipe Dream* (Shubert, Nov. 30, 1955).

He played Christopher Sly in the American Shakespeare Festival production of *The Taming of the Shrew* (Stratford, Conn., Aug. 5, 1956); General Anton Kroutitsky in *Diary of a Scoundrel* (Phoenix, N.Y.C., Nov. 5, 1956); the 1st Workman in *Purple Dust* (Cherry Lane, Dec. 27, 1956); repeated his role in the Amer. Shakespeare Festival production of *The Taming of the Shrew* (Phoenix, Feb. 20, 1957); played Tevya in *Tevya and His Daughters* (Carnegie Hall Playhouse, Sept. 16, 1957); the title role in *Winkelberg* (Renata, Jan. 4, 1958); and Sean Murphy in *God and Kate Murphy* (54 St. Th., Feb. 26, 1959).

He played Kulygin in the Theatre Group (UCLA) production of *The Three Sisters* (Schoenberg Hall, Los Angeles, Calif., Aug. 3, 1960); Fierro in the pre-Bway tryout of *We Take the Town* (opened Shubert, New Haven, Conn., Feb. 19, 1962; closed Shubert, Philadelphia, Pa., Mar. 17, 1962); Dribble in *Rhinoceros* (Longacre, N.Y.C., Jan. 9, 1961); with the Th. Group (UCLA), Ben Stark, D.D.S., in *Rocket to the Moon* (Schoenberg Hall, Los Angeles, Calif., Aug. 27, 1962); played the Cook in *Mother Courage and Her Children* (Martin Beck Th., N.Y.C., March 28, 1963); and with the Th. Group (UCLA), Earl of Kent in *King Lear* (Schoenberg Hall, Los Angeles, Calif., June 6, 1964); and Ted in *Windows* (world premiere, June 4, 1965). He was Fagin in *Oliver!* (Sacramento, Calif., Light Opera Co., 1966); replaced (Oct. 3, 1966) Pat Hingle as Oscar Madison in *The Odd Couple* (Plymouth, N.Y.C., Mar. 10, 1965); was Caesario Grimaldi in *Tchin-Tchin* (Ivanhoe Th., Chicago, Ill., Nov. 1969); toured in East Coast stock as Tevye in *Fiddler on the Roof* (1971); was in *The Love Suicide at Schofield Barracks* (H B Playwrights' Foundation, N.Y.C., Apr. 1971); directed *The Death and Resurrection of Mr. Roche* (New Dramatists, N.Y.C., 1971); directed *The August Insurrection of Nate Shapiro* (HB Playwrights'

Foundation, 1973); co-directed and appeared in *They Could Be Indians* (H B Playwrights' Foundation, 1973); played George in *Bread* (American Place Th., N.Y.C., Jan. 28, 1974); played the Director and the Inquisitor in *Joan of Lorraine* (Good Shepherd-Faith Presbyterian Church, N.Y.C., May 6, 1974); and was in *Apple Pie* (Other Stage, Public Th., Jan. 19, 1975).

Films. Mr. Kellin made his debut in *So Young, So Bad* (UA, 1949); subsequently appeared as Staff Sergeant McVay in *At War with the Army* (Par., 1950); appeared as Dicer in *Hurricane Smith* (Par., 1952); in *Lonely Hearts* (UA, 1958); *The Mountain Road* (Col., 1960); *The Wackiest Ship in the Army* (Col., 1960); *The Great Imposter* (U, 1960); *Hell Is for Heroes* (Par., 1962); *Invitation to a Gunfighter* (U, 1964); *Banning* (U, 1967); *The Incident* (20th-Fox, 1967); *Riot* (Par., 1969); *The Boston Strangler* (20th-Fox, 1968); *Cover Me, Babe* (20th-Fox, 1970); *The Phynx* (WB, 1970); *The People Next Door* (Avco Embassy, 1970); *Fool's Parade* (Col., 1971); and *Freebie and the Bean* (WB, 1974).

Television. He has appeared on Suspense (CBS); Kraft Television Th. (NBC); Philco Television Playhouse (NBC); Studio One (CBS); Goodyear Playhouse (NBC); The Untouchables (ABC); Omnibus (CBS); The Rifleman (ABC); The Defenders (CBS); Naked City (ABC); Route 66 (CBS); Lost in Space (WNEW-Ind.); and Love, American Style (ABC). He was in *One Day in the Life of Ivan Denisovich* (Bob Hope Chrysler Show, NBC, 1963); a pilot film, *Connection* (ABC, Feb. 27, 1963); starred as Chief Miller in the series The Wackiest Ship in the Army (premier: NBC, Sept. 19, 1965); appeared in the pilots *Munich Project* (ABC, 1972) and *Nightside* (ABC, Apr. 1973); and was in *The 10th Level* (CBS, Playhouse 90, 1975).

Recreation. Composing and playing the piano, the recorder, and guitar.

KELLY, BOB. Wigmaker, make-up artist. b. Hugh Robert Kelly, Oct. 2, 1923, Brooklyn, N.Y., to Hugh Thomas and Mary T. Kelly. Grandfather, wigmaker. Married 1974 to Camille Antoinette DiBello, assistant literary agent with International Famous Agency. Three daughters, one son. Served U.S. Army, 1940–45. Member of IATSE, Local 798. Address: (home) 244 Argyle Rd., Brooklyn, NY 11218; (bus.) 151 W. 46th St., New York, NY 10036.

Theatre. Mr. Kelly was make-up artist for the Metropolitan Opera Co. (N.Y.C., five yrs.), and was wigmaker for *The Girls in 509* (Belasco Th., Oct. 15, 1958); *The Good Soup* (Plymouth, Mar. 2, 1960); *Irma La Douce* (Plymouth, Sept. 29, 1960); *Becket* (St. James, Oct. 5, 1960); *The Rape of The Belt* (Martin Beck Th., Nov. 5, 1960); *A Far Country* (Music Box, Apr. 4, 1961); *Gideon* (Plymouth, Nov. 9, 1961); *A Man for All Seasons* (ANTA, Nov. 22, 1961); *Sunday in New York* (Cort, Nov. 29, 1961); *First Love* (Morosco, Dec. 25, 1961); *The Egg* (Cort, Jan. 8, 1962); *Romulus* (Music Box, Jan. 10, 1962); *A Family Affair* (Billy Rose Th., Jan. 27, 1962); *A Gift of Time* (Ethel Barrymore Th., Feb. 22, 1962); *A Funny Thing Happened on the Way to the Forum* (Alvin, May 8, 1962); *Mr. President* (St. James, Oct. 20, 1962); *Tchin-Tchin* (Plymouth, Oct. 25, 1962); *Nowhere to Go But Up* (Winter Garden, Nov. 10, 1962); *Little Me* (Lunt-Fontanne, Nov. 17, 1962); *The Moon Besieged* (Lyceum, Dec. 5, 1962); *The Milk Train Doesn't Stop Here Anymore* (Morosco, Jan. 16, 1963); *Photo Finish* (Brooks Atkinson Th., Feb. 12, 1963); *Lorenzo* (Plymouth, Feb. 14, 1963); *The Heroine* (Lyceum, Feb. 19, 1963); *Tovarich* (Bway Th., Mar. 18, 1963); *Mother Courage and Her Children* (Martin Beck Th., Mar. 28, 1963); *Sophie* (Winter Garden, Apr. 15, 1963).

He was also wigmaker for the NY City Ctr. production of *Brigadoon*, as well as *Can-Can* (May 16, 1962).

He was wigmaker for *On the Town* (Imperial, Oct. 31, 1971); *Voices* (Ethel Barrymore Th., Apr. 3, 1972); *Pippin* (Imperial, Oct. 23, 1972); *The Lincoln Mask* (Plymouth, Oct. 30, 1972); *Much Ado About Nothing* (Wintergarden, Nov. 11, 1972); *Lysistrata* (Brooks Atkinson Th., Nov. 13, 1972); *Via Galactica* (Uris, Nov. 28, 1972); *Irene* (Minskoff, Mar. 13, 1973); *Lorelei* (Palace, Jan. 27, 1974); *Over Here* (Shubert, Mar. 6, 1974); *Jumpers* (Billy Rose Th., Apr. 22, 1974); *Gypsy* (Wintergarden, Sept. 23, 1974); *Mack and Mabel* (Majestic, Oct. 6, 1974); *Shenandoah* (Alvin, Jan. 7, 1975); *The Ritz* (Longacre, Jan. 20, 1975); and *Good Time Charlie* (Palace, Mar. 3, 1975); and has served as wigmaker to the NY City Opera, the NY Shakespeare Festival, and the touring company of the Houston Grand Opera.

Films. Mr. Kelly was make-up artist for *The Court Martial of Billy Mitchell* (WB, 1955); *Miracle in the Rain* (WB, 1956); *Twelve Angry Men* (UA, 1957); *Street of Sinners* (UA, 1957); *Four Boys and a Gun* (UA, 1957); *The Cop Killers; Little Big Man* (Par., 1970); *The Godfather* (Par., 1972); *The Godfather, Part II* (Par., 1974); *The Great Gatsby* (Par., 1974); *For Pete's Sake* (Col., 1974); *Lenny* (UA, 1974); and *The Happy Hooker* (Cannon, 1975).

Television. In addition to designing makeup for numerous commercials, he has been make-up artist for You Are There (CBS); I Remember Mama (CBS); the Ed Sullivan Show (CBS); I Spy; Man Against Crime; Guy Lombardo series; Sgt. Bilko series; and Joe and Mabel; and for American Parade (CBS), a bi-centennial presentation.

Recreation. Making life masks of famous theatrical actors.

KELLY, GENE. Actor, director, producer, dancer. b. Eugene Curran Kelly, August 23, 1912, Pittsburgh, Pa., to James Patrick and Harriet (Curran) Kelly. Father, salesman. Grad. Peabody H.S., Pittsburgh, 1929; Univ. of Pittsburgh, B.A. 1933. Married, Sept. 22, 1941, to Betsy Blair, actress (marr. dis. 1957); one daughter; married Aug. 6, 1960, to Jeanne Coyne, dancer; one son, one daughter. Served USN (1944–46); rank, Lt. (jg). Relative in theatre: brother, Fred Kelly, actor, director. Member of SAG (vice-pres., 1947); DGA; AFTRA. Address: (home) 725 N. Rodeo Dr., Beverly Hills, CA; (bus.) Curran Film Corp., 315 So. Beverly Dr., Beverly Hills, CA 90210.

Pre-Theatre. Taught dancing school in Pittsburgh and Johnstown, Pa. (1931–37).

Theatre. Mr. Kelly made his N.Y.C. debut as a dancer in *Leave It to Me* (Imperial Th., Nov. 9, 1938); subsequently appeared in the revue *One for the Money* (Booth, Feb. 4, 1939); as Harry in *The Time of Your Life* (Booth, Oct. 25, 1939); Joey Evans in *Pal Joey* (Ethel Barrymore Th., Dec. 25, 1940); was choreographer for *Best Foot Forward* (Ethel Barrymore Th., Oct. 1, 1941); and directed *Flower Drum Song* (St. James, Dec. 1, 1958).

He choreographed a jazz ballet, *Pas des Dieux* (Paris Opera Ballet, Paris, 1960).

Films. Mr. Kelly appeared in *For Me and My Gal* (MGM, 1942); *Pilot No. 5* (MGM, 1943); *Du Barry Was a Lady* (MGM, 1943); *Thousands Cheer* (MGM, 1943); *The Cross of Lorraine* (MGM, 1943); *Cover Girl* (Col., 1944); *Christmas Holiday* (U, 1944); choreographed and appeared in *Anchors Aweigh* (MGM, 1945); appeared in *Ziegfeld Follies* (MGM, 1946); *Living in a Big Way* (MGM, 1947); *The Pirate* (MGM, 1948); *The Three Musketeers* (MGM, 1948); *Words and Music* (MGM, 1948); wrote the original story, appeared in, and choreographed *Take Me Out to the Ball Game* (MGM, 1949); co-directed, choreographed, and appeared in *On the Town* (MGM, 1949); appeared in *Black Hand* (MGM, 1950); *Summer Stock* (MGM, 1950); choreographed and appeared in *An American in Paris* (MGM, 1951); appeared in *It's a Big Country* (MGM, 1951); co-directed, choreographed, and appeared in *Singin' in the Rain* (MGM, 1952); appeared in *The Devil Makes Three* (MGM, 1952); choreographed and appeared in *Brigadoon* (MGM, 1954); appeared in *Crest of the Wave* (MGM, 1954); co-directed, choreographed, and appeared in *It's Always Fair Weather* (MGM, 1955); directed, choreographed, and appeared in *Invitation to the Dance* (MGM, 1956); produced, directed, and appeared in *The Happy Road* (MGM, 1957); appeared in *Les Girls* (MGM, 1957); *Marjorie Morningstar* (WB, 1958); directed *The Tunnel of Love* (MGM, 1958); appeared in *Inherit the Wind* (UA, 1960); directed *Gigot* (20th-Fox, 1961); appeared in *What a Way To Go* (20th-Fox, 1964); directed *A Guide for the Married Man* (20th-Fox, 1966); directed *Hello, Dolly!* (20th-Fox, 1968); directed *The Cheyenne Social Club* (Natl. Gen., 1970); and appeared in *Forty Carats* (Col., 1972).

Television. Mr. Kelly created, choreographed, and danced in *Dancing—A Man's Game* (Omnibus, NBC, 1958), *The Gene Kelly Show* (CBS, 1959), and *The Gene Kelly Show II* (NBC, 1959); appeared on *Hollywood: The Golden Years* (NBC, 1961); *Going My Way* (ABC, 1962); *Person to Person* (Ed Murrow, CBS, 1958); and Hollywood Palace (ABC, 1964); was a special guest star on the Julie Andrews Show (NBC, 1965); was host, star, and choreographer for *New York, New York* (CBS, 1966); director, star, and choreographer for *Jack and the Beanstalk* (NBC, 1967); guest star on the *Peggy Fleming Special;* star of *Children's Letters to God* (NBC, 1969); guest star on *American Sportsman* (ABC, 1970); star of *Wonderful World of Girls* (NBC, 1970); host of The Funny Side (NBC, 1971); guest star on The Changing Scene, Parts I & II (ABC, 1970); special guest star on *Ole Blue Eyes Is Back* (NBC, 1973); host of *Grammy Salutes Oscar* (CBS, 1974); and host of *Entertainment Hall of Fame* (ABC, 1974).

Other Activities. He has lectured on the dance at the Univ. of Southern California, the Univ. of California at Los Angeles, the London Ballet Circle, and the San Francisco Museum of Art.

Awards. Mr. Kelly received Box Office Blue Ribbon Awards for *The Three Musketeers* (1948), *Take Me Out to the Ball Game* (1949), *An American in Paris* (1952), *Brigadoon* (1954), and *Les Girls* (1957); a nomination by the Academy of Motion Picture Arts and Sciences for his performance in *Anchors Aweigh* (1945); the *Look* Magazine Film Achievement Award (1951); an honorary award from the Academy of Motion Picture Arts and Sciences (1952); the *Picturegoer* Magazine Seal of Merit Award for *An American in Paris* (1953); a Diploma of Merit from the tenth international Edinburgh Film Festival and the Golden Bear first prize award at the sixth international Berlin Film Festival for *Invitation to the Dance* (1956); the Hollywood Foreign Press Assn. Award, the Gold Medal from *Parents' Magazine*, and a Certificate of Award from the Southern California Motion Picture Council, Inc., for *The Happy Road* (1957); the *Dance* Magazine Award for *Dancing—A Man's Game* (1959); and was named Chevalier of the Legion of Honor by the French Govt. (1960).

Recreation. Tennis, swimming, volleyball, reading.

KELLY, GRACE. Actress. b. Grace Patricia Kelly, Nov. 12, 1929, Philadelphia, Pa., to John Brendan and Margaret (Majer) Kelly. Father, building contractor. Grad. Stevens Sch., Germantown, Pa., 1947. Studied acting with Sanford Meisner, N.Y.C., 1952; and at AADA, N.Y.C., 1947–49. Married Apr. 19, 1956, to Rainier III, Prince of Monaco; one son, two daughters. Relatives in theatre: uncle, George Kelly, playwright; uncle, Walter Kelly, actor. Member of AEA; SAG; AFTRA; TVA; Red Cross (pres., Monegasque chap.). Address: The Palace, Principality of Monaco.

Theatre. Miss Kelly, first performed with the Old Academy Players (Philadelphia, Pa.), appearing in *Don't Feed the Animals* (1939); made her first professional appearances in *The Torch Bearers* (Bucks County Playhouse, New Hope, Pa., July 1949); and appeared in *The Heiress* (Bucks County Playhouse, 1949).

She made her N.Y.C. debut as the Captain's Daughter in *The Father* (Cort, Nov. 16, 1949); at Elitch Gardens (Denver, Colo.), appeared in *Ring Round the Moon* (1951); *For Love or Money* (1951), *Detective Story, The Cocktail Party*, and *The Man Who Came to Dinner;* performed in *Ring Round the Moon* (Ann Arbor Drama Festival, Mich., 1951); *For Love or Money* (Playhouse-in-the-Park, Philadelphia, 1952); *Accent on Youth* (Bucks County Playhouse, 1952); played the Young Woman in *To Be Continued* (Booth, N.Y.C., Apr. 23, 1952); and appeared in *The Moon Is Blue* (Playhouse-in-the-Park, 1953).

Films. Miss Kelly made her debut in *Fourteen Hours* (20th-Fox, 1951); subsequently appeared in *High Noon* (UA, 1952); *Mogambo* (MGM, 1953); *Dial "M" For Murder* (WB, 1954); *Rear Window* (Par., 1954); *The Bridges at Toko-Ri* (Par., 1954); *The Country Girl* (Par., 1954); *Green Fire* (MGM, 1954); *To Catch a Thief* (Par., 1955); *The Swan* (MGM, 1956); and *High Society* (MGM, 1956).

Television. She made her debut on the Philco Television Playhouse (NBC, 1949); subsequently played on Philco Playhouse (NBC, 1950); appeared in *The Swan* (1950); in *The Play's the Thing; Berkeley Square; Rich Boy* (Philco Television Playhouse, NBC, 1952); performed on Studio One (CBS); Hallmark Hall of Fame (NBC); Somerset Maugham Th. (ABC); Treasury Men in Action (NBC); Lux Video Th. (CBS); Kraft Television Th. (NBC); Robert Montgomery Presents (NBC); Armstrong Circle Th. (NBC); Suspense (CBS); and Danger (CBS).

Awards. Miss Kelly received the NY Film Critics' Award (1954) for her performance in *Rear Window;* the NY Film Critics' Award and the Academy (Oscar) Award for her performance as Georgie in *The Country Girl* (1954).

KELLY, KEVIN. Drama and film critic. b. Kevin St. Clair Kelly, Aug. 5, 1934, to St. Clair and Joan (Sinnott) Kelly. Grad. Boston (Mass.) Univ. (scholarship), A.A., B.A., M.A. 1953. Address: (home) 39 Mount Hope, Norwell, MA 02061, tel. (617) 659-7761; (bus.) c/o The Boston Globe, Morrissey Blvd., Boston, MA 02171, tel. (617) AV 8-8000.

Mr. Kelly is drama and film critic for the *Boston Globe.* He was formerly an editor and writer for a business publication house.

Awards. He received the National Press Assn. Scholarship, 1949, editorial awards from the *Boston Globe* (1946, 1947), and was recently elected to the Boston Univ. Collegium of Distinction.

Recreation. Music, reading, skiing, swimming, gardening.

KELLY, NANCY. Actress. b. Mar. 25, 1921, Lowell, Mass., to John A. and Ann Mary (Walsh) Kelly. Father, theatre ticket broker; mother, model, actress. Attended Immaculate Conception Acad., N.Y.C.; St. Lawrence Acad., L.I., N.Y.; Bentley Sch. for Girls. Married Feb, 19, 1941, to Edmond O'Brien, actor (marr. dis. Feb. 2, 1942); married to Fred Jackman, Jr., cameraman (marr. dis. Jan. 13, 1950); married Nov. 25, 1955, to Warren Caro, producer, Theatre Guild executive; one daughter. Relatives in theatre: brother, Jack Kelly, actor; sister, Carole Elizabeth, known as Karolee Kelly, actress; sister-in-law, May Wynn, actress. Member of AEA; SAG; AFTRA.

Pre-Theatre. Child model.

Theatre. Miss Kelly made her Bway debut as Buteus Maiden in *Give Me Yesterday* (Charles Hopkins Th., Mar. 4, 1931): was understudy in *One Good Year* (Lyceum, Nov. 27, 1935); appeared as Anne Greer in a stock tryout of *So Proudly We Hail* (Red Barn, Locust Valley, N.Y., Aug. 4, 1936); Blossom Trexel in *Susan and God* (Plymouth, N.Y.C., Oct. 7, 1937); Patricia Graham in *Flare Path* (Henry Miller's Th., Dec. 23, 1942); toured as Evelyn Heath in *Guest in the House* (1942); Marion Castle in *The Big Knife* (National, N.Y.C., Feb. 24, 1949); and Emily Crane in *Season in the Sun* (Cort, Sept. 28, 1950).

She played Irene Livingston in *Light Up the Sky* (Las Palmas Th., Hollywood, Calif., 1950); Kate Scott in *Twilight Walk* (Fulton, N.Y.C., Sept. 24, 1951); toured as Georgie Elgin in *The Country Girl* (1953); played Christine Penmark in *The Bad Seed* (46 St. Th., N.Y.C., Dec. 8, 1954), which she repeated on tour (opened Playhouse, Wilmington, Del., Dec. 1, 1955; closed Harris, Chicago, Ill., June 30, 1956); Katy Maartens in *The Genius and the Goddess* (Henry Miller's Th., Dec. 10, 1957); Adele Douglas in *The Rivalry* (Bijou, Feb. 7, 1959); and Barbara Smith in *A Mighty Man Is He* (Cort, Jan. 6, 1960).

Miss Kelly played Jane McLeod in a stock tryout of *A Whiff of Melancholy* (Bucks County Playhouse, New Hope, Pa., Aug. 21, 1961); Myra Brisset in *Giants, Sons of Giants* (Alvin, N.Y.C., Jan. 6, 1962); in the pre-Bway tour, succeeded Rita Hayworth as Ellen in *Step on a Crack* (Cleveland, Ohio, Sept. 1962); replaced (July 8, 1963) Uta Hagen during her vacation as Martha in *Who's Afraid of Virginia Woolf?* (Billy Rose Th., Oct. 13, 1962), subsequently touring in this role (1963–64); and, on a double-bill with *Box,* played the Long-Winded Lady in *Quotations from Chairman Mao Tse-Tung* (Billy Rose Th., Sept. 30, 1968).

Miss Kelly was a member of the Studio Arena Th. Co. (Buffalo, N.Y., 1968–69 season); subsequently played Irene in *Remote Asylum* (Ahmanson, Los Angeles, 1970–71 season); Evy Meara in *The Gingerbread Lady* (tour, opened Huntington Hartford Th., Los Angeles, Oct. 22, 1971; closed Playhouse, Wilmington, Del., May 6, 1972); and appeared in *King Richard III,* Long Wharf Th., New Haven, May 9, 1975).

Films. Miss Kelly made her debut as a child in *The Untamed Lady* (Par., 1926); subsequently appeared in *The Great Gatsby* (Par., 1926); *Mismates* (1st Natl., 1925); *Girl on the Barge* (U, 1929); *Submarine Patrol* (20th-Fox, 1938); *Stanley and Livingston* (20th-Fox, 1939); *Jesse James* (20th-Fox, 1939); *Tail Spin* (20th-Fox, 1939); *Frontier Marshall* (20th-Fox, 1939); *He married His Wife* (20th-Fox, 1940); *Private Affairs* (U, 1940); *Sailors Lady* (20th-Fox, 1940); *Parachute Battalion* (RKO, 1941); *Scotland Yard* (20th-Fox, 1941); *A Very Young Lady* (20th-Fox, 1941); *Fly by Night* (Par., 1942); *Friendly Enemies* (UA, 1942); *To the Shores of Tripoli* (20th-Fox, 1942); *Tornado* (Par., 1943); *Tarzan's Desert Mystery* (RKO, 1943); *Women in Bondage* (Mono., 1943); *Gambler's Choice* (Par., 1944); *Double Exposure* (Par., 1944); *Show Business* (RKO, 1944); *Betrayal from the East* (RKO, 1945); *Song of the Sarong* (U, 1945); *The Woman Who Came Back* (Rep., 1945); *Murder in the Music Hall* (Rep., 1946); *The Bad Seed* (WB, 1956); and *Crowded Paradise* (Tudor, 1956).

Television and Radio. Miss Kelly's radio credits include Forty-Five Minutes from Hollywood; The March of Time (1932–37); *The Wizard of Oz* (WEAF, 1933); *Myrt and Marge* (CBS, 1933); The Shadow (MBS, 1936–37); Gangbusters (WABC, CBS, 1936–37); Aunt Jenny's Real Life Stories (CBS, 1937–38); Court of Human Relations; and True Story.

On television, she has appeared on the Kaiser Aluminum Hour (NBC, July 31, 1956); played Sister Mary Aquinas in *The Pilot* (Studio One, CBS, Nov. 6, 1956); *Murder Is a Witch* (Climax, CBS, Aug. 15, 1957); appeared in *Four O'Clock* (Alfred Hitchcock Presents, CBS, Sept. 30, 1957); Sam Benedict (Ind.); Thriller (Ind.); and Girl Talk (ABC).

Awards. Miss Kelly was named "Star of Tomorrow" by the *Motion Picture Herald* Hall of Fame Poll (1942); received the Antoinette Perry (Tony) Award (1955) for her performance as Christine Penmark in *The Bad Seed;* and was nominated for the Academy (Oscar) Award for her performance in the screen version of *The Bad Seed* (1956). She also received the Sarah Siddons Award (1956) for her performancce in *The Bad Seed,* and a NATAS (Emmy) Award for her role as Sister Mary Aquinas in *The Pilot* (1957); and the Sarah Siddons Society Award for best performancee by an actress in Chicago (1965) in *Who's Afraid of Virginia Woolf?.*

Recreation. Horseback riding, golf, swimming.

KENLEY, JOHN. Producer. b. John Kremchek Zayanskovsky, Feb. 20, 1907, Denver, Colo., to John Kremchek and Anna (Machuga) Zayanskovsky. Parents, saloon and store keepers. Grad. Academy H.S., Erie, Pa., 1922. Served USMC, 1942–47, rank, Lt. (jg). Member of AEA. Address: (home) 6947 Cranbrook Dr., Cleveland, OH 44141, tel. (216) 526-1523; (bus.) c/o Kenley Players, Warren, OH 44483, tel. (216) 394-1577.

Pre-Theatre. Secretary to superintendent of fields, East Ohio Gas Company, Cleveland, Ohio.

Theatre. Mr. Kenley first performed on the vaudeville stage and in night clubs in the Midwest as a specialty dancer (1923); subsequently was understudy, singer, and dancer in a touring company of *Greenwich Village Follies* (1924); made his N.Y.C. debut in the chorus and in a sketch of *Artists and Models of 1925* (Winter Garden, June 24, 1925), with which he later toured (1926–27); and appeared in the chorus of *Hit the Deck* (Belasco, N.Y.C., Apr. 25, 1927). For the next two years, he worked as a dancer and mimic in night clubs and vaudeville across the US; in March, 1930, joined the staff of the Shubert organization, in N.Y.C., as assistant to the production director and casting director; became play reader and a supervisor of dramatic productions, remaining with the Shuberts until 1940; in Feb. 1940, produced and directed, with Jackson Halliday, a touring production of *Worth a Million* (played Boston, Mass.; Toronto, Can.; Baltimore, Md.; Princeton, N.J.).

In June 1940, Mr. Kenley became producer-director of a summer theatre the Kenley Players, in Deer Lake (Pa.); became producer and managing director (1947, 1948); in the summer of 1949, moved to Barnesville (Pa.), where he operated the Kenley Players until 1953; in 1949, organized a touring production of *The Barretts of Wimpole Street* (opened Aud., Hershey, Pa., Oct. 1949; closed Shubert, Washington, D.C., Mar. 1950); in the summer of 1952, opened a second theatre for one season in York, Pa., and in Sept. of the same year produced *Maid in the Ozarks,* which toured the East and Midwest. In the summer of 1955, he moved his summer-theatre operations to Bristol, Pa., where the Kenley Players performed in 1956; in 1957, moved to Dayton, Ohio, and the following summer (1958) to Warren, Ohio; in Sept. 1958, formed a touring company of *Can-Can* (played Cleveland, Ohio; Detroit, Mich.; Erie, Pa.; Buffalo, N.Y.; Dayton, Ohio; and New Haven, Conn.).

Mr. Kenley subsequently opened a second theatre in Columbus, Ohio (1961), and since then has operated two proscenium summer theatres for the Kenley Players under a star policy (Columbus and Warren, Ohio). In 1966, with his acquisition of the Dayton Th., Mr. Kenley began producing for and operating three proscenium summer theatres. The large seating capacity available to Mr. Kenley combined with his low admission policy has contributed to the success of his theatres. In addition to presenting plays in his own theatres, Mr. Kenley produces plays and musicals for theatres in Toledo, Ohio, and Flint, Mich.

Recreation. Swimming, travel, and weight lifting.

KENNEDY, ADRIENNE. Playwright. b. Adrienne Lita Hawkins, Sept. 13, 1931, Pittsburgh, Pa., to Cornell Wallace and Etta (Haugabook) Hawkins. Father, executive secretary for the YMCA; mother, teacher. Graduated Glenville, H.S.; Ohio State Univ., B.S. Studied at the New School; Amer. Th. Wing; Circle in the Square (with Edward Albee). Married 1953 to Joseph Kennedy (marr. dis.), two sons. Member of Actors Studio (1963–65). Ronald Hobbs Agency, 172 W. 79th St., New York, NY 10024, tel. (212) 687-1417.

Theatre. Miss Kennedy wrote *Funnyhouse of a Negro* (Th. 1964, N.Y.C., repeated in London, England at the Royal Court Th., and in Paris, France, 1969); *The Owl Answers* (ANTA Matinee Series, Th. de Lys, N.Y.C., 1965); for Joseph Papp, *Cities in Bezique* (N.Y. Shakespeare Festival, N.Y.C., 1968); *The Lennon Play* (The National, London, England, 1969); *A Rat's Mass* (Cafe La Mama tours of U.S. and European colleges, 1971); *A Lesson in Dead Language* (Th. Genesis, N.Y.C., 1972); *Sun* (Cafe La Mama, N.Y.C., 1973); and *Evening with Dead Essex* (Yale Rep. Co. at The Amer. Place Th., N.Y.C., 1974).

Published Works. *Funnyhouse of A Negro* has been anthologized in *Contemporary Black Drama; Black Drama; Best Short Plays of 1970;* and *The Negro* *in the Theatre. The Owl Answers* appears in *Kintu Drama; A Rat's Mass* in *New Black Playwrights; A Lesson in Dead Language* in *Collision Course; Sun* in *Spontaneous Combustion* and *Scripts;* and *The Lennon Play* in *Best Short Plays of World Theatre.*

Awards. Miss Kennedy has received Rockefeller and Guggenheim grants, and fellowships from Yale Univ. and the National Endowment for the Arts. She received the 1964 Off-Bway (Obie) Award for Best Play for *Funnyhouse of a Negro.*

Recreation. Collecting letters from famous people.

KENNEDY, ARTHUR. Actor. b. John Arthur Kennedy, Feb. 17, 1914, Worcester, Mass., to John T. and Helen (Thompson) Kennedy. Father, dentist. Grad. Worcester (Mass.) Academy; Carnegie Inst. of Technology, B.A. (drama) 1936. Married 1938, to Mary Cheffey, former actress; one son, one daughter. Served USAAF, 1st Motion Picture Unit. Member of AEA; AFTRA; SAG; Phi Kappa Psi. Address: 2840 S. County Rd., Palm Beach, FL 33480.

Theatre. Mr. Kennedy began with the Group Theatre; billed as John Kennedy he made his Bway deput as Bushy in Maurice Evans' *King Richard II* on tour (1937)) and in N.Y.C. (St. James, Sept. 15, 1937); and played Sir Richard Vernon in Maurice Evans' *Henry IV, Part 1* (St. James, Jan. 30, 1939).

Billed as J. Arthur Kennedy, he played Jerry Dorgan in *Life and Death of an American* (Maxine Elliott's Th., May 19, 1939); billed as Arthur Kennedy, Smithers in *International Incident* (Ethel Barrymore Th., Apr. 2, 1940); Chris Keller in *All My Sons* (Coronet, Jan. 29, 1947); Biff in *Death of a Salesman* (Morosco, Feb. 10, 1948); Dave Ricks in *See the Jaguar* (Cort, Dec. 3, 1952); John Proctor in *The Crucible* (Martin Beck Th., Jan. 22, 1953); Lt. Col. William F. Edwards in *Time Limit!* (Booth, Jan. 24, 1956); Patrick Flanagan in *The Loud Red Patrick* (Ambassador, Oct. 3, 1956); and Thomas Becket in the national tour of *Becket* (opened Colonial, Boston, Mass., Mar. 29, 1961), and in N.Y.C. (Hudson, May 8, 1961). He appeared as Walter Franz in *The Price* (Morosco Th., Feb. 1968); and as the Man in *Veronica's Room* (Music Box, Oct. 29, 1973).

Films. Mr. Kennedy made his debut in *City for Conquest* (WB, 1940). He subsequently appeared in *Highway West* (WB, 1941), *High Sierra* (WB, 1941), *Strange Alibi* (WB, 1941), *Knockout* (WB, 1941), *Desperate Journery* (WB, 1942), *Air Force* (WB, 1943), *Devotion* (WB, 1946), *Boomerang* (20th-Fox, 1947), *Cheyenne* (WB, 1947), *The Window* (RKO, 1949), *Chicago Deadline* (Par., 1949), *Champion* (UA, 1949), *The Glass Menagerie* (WB, 1950), *Bright Victory* (U, 1951), *Red Mountain* (Par., 1951), *Rancho Notorious* (RKO, 1952), *The Girl in White* (MGM, 1952), *The Lusty Men* (RKO, 1952), *Bend of the River* (U, 1952), *Rodeo* (Mono., 1952), *The Naked Dawn* (U, 1955), *Crashout* (Filmmakers, 1955), *The Man from Laramie* (Col., 1955), *The Desperate Hours* (Par., 1955), *Trial* (MGM, 1955), *The Rawhide Years* (U, 1956), *Peyton Place* (20th-Fox, 1957), *Elmer Gantry,* (UA, 1960), *Claudelle Inglish* (WB, 1961), *Murder She Said* (MGM, 1962), *Hemingway's Adventures of a Young Man* (20th-Fox, 1962), *Lawrence of Arabia* (Col. 1962), *Il Bravo Gente* (1963), and *Cheyenne Autumn* (1964), and *Fantastic Voyage* (20th-Fox, 1966).

Television. Mr. Kennedy performed on Kraft Suspense Th. (NBC); he played in *Third Commandment* and starred in *Crawlspace* (CBS, 1971).

Awards. Mr. Kennedy received the Antoinette Perry (Tony) Award for his performance as Biff in *Death of a Salesman* (1949); the NY Film Critics Award for his performance in *Bright Victory* (1951); the Foreign Press (Golden Globe) Award for his performance in *Trial* (1955); the Carnegie Inst. of Technology Award of Merit (1959); the *Film Daily* Award, Filmdom's Famous Five, for his performance in *Elmer Gantry* (1960); the Limelight Award for his performance in *Elmer Gantry* (1960).

Recreation. Swimming, tennis, traveling.

KENNEDY, HAROLD J. Director, actor, producer, playwright. Grad. Dartmouth, (Rufus Choate scholar) B.A. 1935; Yale Univ., M.A. 1937.

Theatre. Mr. Kennedy made his Bway debut in a walk-on part in the Mercury Theatre's producton of *Julius Caesar* (Mercury Th., 1937); and appeared in *In Time to Come* (Mansfield Th., Dec. 28, 1941). He wrote and played the role of Tony in *A Goose for the Gander* (Playhouse, N.Y.C., Jan. 23, 1945); wrote *Horace* (McCarter Th., Princeton, N.J., Aug. 1947); directed the first West Coast productions of *Tiger at the Gates* and *Time Limit* (Ivor Th., Hollywood, 1956); wrote and appeared in the pre-Bway tryout of *Good-by Ghost* (Little Th. on the Square, Sullivan, Ill., Dec. 28, 1965); directed and played Bensinger in a revival of *The Front Page* (Ethel Barrymore Th., N.Y.C., May 10, 1969); produced and directed touring packages of *Light Up the Sky,* in which he appeared (opened Camden, N.J. Music Fair, June 20, 1972), and *Sabrina Fair* (opened Tappan Zee Playhouse, July 10, 1972); directed and played Endicott Sims in a pre-Bway tryout of a revival of *Detective Story* (opened Playhouse-on-the-Mall, Paramus, N.J., Feb. 18, 1973; closed Shubert, Philadephia, Mar. 24, 1973); wrote and directed a touring package of *Don't Frighten the Horses* (opened Pocono Playhouse, Mountain Home, Pa., July 1973; closed Candlewood Th., Candlewood Lake, Conn., Aug. 1973); and directed the pre-Bway tryout of *Me Jack, You Jill* (closed during previews, Mar. 14, 1976).

In addition, he served as assistant to John Houseman in the Mercury Th. Co. (1938); and has been producer-director-actor with the Amherst (Mass.) Drama Festival (Summer 1940); a summer stock company in Springfield, Mass. (1941), which became a rotating company including Hartford and New Haven, Conn. (Summer 1942); a summer touring company of *Pygmalion* (1945); the McCarter Th. (Princeton, N.J., Summers 1947–49); the Astor Th. (East Hartford, Conn., Winter 1949–50); the Montclair (N.J.) Th. (Summer 1955); and the Grist Mill Playhouse (Andover, N.J., 1955–60). He has also produced numerous packages wich toured throughout the country, including *Accent on Youth, Treat Her Gently, Bell, Book and Candle,* and *A Man for All Seasons.*

Mr. Kennedy has been a popular theatre lecturer since his early association with the Mercury Theatre.

Films. He has been seen in *Captive City* (UA, 1952); *It Should Happen to You* (Col., 1953); and *Riot in Cell Block Eleven* (AA, 1954).

Television. Mr. Kennedy's appearances include *I Remember Mama* (CBS); *Bachelor Father;* and Dragnet (NBC).

Awards. Mr. Kennedy received the Chicago *Daily News* Critics' Award (1966) for his direction of *A Man for All Seasons.*

KENNEDY, JOHN. Director. b. New York City, to Peter and Elizabeth (McCormick) Kennedy. Father, producer; mother, actress. Married May 7, 1945, to Mary Stevenson, actress; one daughter, Susan Kennedy, actress; step-son, James Stevenson, actor. Served USMC. Member of AEA (councillor, 1941–49; 1st vice-pres., 1949–52; chairman of television authority, 1950).

Theatre. Mr. Kennedy was production stage manager for *Face the Music* (New Amsterdam, N.Y.C., Feb. 17, 1932); subsequently for the national touring company of *Of Thee I Sing* (Sept. 1932); *As Thousands Cheer* (Music Box, N.Y.C., Sept. 30, 1933); *Merrily We Roll Along* (Music Box, Sept. 29, 1934); *Jubilee* (Imperial, Oct. 12, 1935); *Stage Door* (Music Box, Oct. 22, 1936); *Save Me the Waltz* (Martin Beck Th., Feb. 23, 1938); *The Fabulous Invalid* (Broadhurst, Oct. 8, 1938); *The American Way* (Center, Jan. 21, 1939); *Swinging the Dream* (Center, Nov. 29, 1939); and *Lady in the Dark* (Alvin, Jan. 23, 1941).

He directed two seasons of stock with the St. Louis (Mo.) Municipal Opera Co. (Forest Park, June 1942, June 1943), and was named production director (Sept. 15, 1943). In his 24-year association with the company (he resigned as director in Sept. 1967), he directed and produced about 250 musical comedies and operettas.

Mr. Kennedy directed *The First Million* (Ritz, N.Y.C., Apr. 28, 1943); *Artists and Models* (Bway Th., Nov. 5, 1943); *Mexican Hayride* (Winter Garden, Jan. 28, 1944); *Up in Central Park* (Century, Jan. 27, 1945); *The Would-Be Gentleman* (Booth, Jan. 9, 1946); *Sweethearts* (Shubert, Jan. 21, 1947); *Angel in the Wings* (Coronet, Dec. 11, 1947); and *Ziegfeld Follies* (Winter Garden, Mar. 1, 1957).

At the Marine Th. (Jones Beach, L.I., N.Y.), Mr. Kennedy produced and directed *Show Boat* (June 21, 1956, repeated Summer 1957), *Song of Norway* (June 26, 1958), and *Hit the Deck* (June 23, 1960). He directed *Oklahoma!* at the NY State Th. (N.Y.C., June 23, 1969).

Recreation. Theatre.

KENNER, WILLIAM HUGH. Educator, writer. b. William Hugh Kenner, Jan. 7, 1923, Peterborough, Ontario, Canada, to H.R.H. and Mary I. Kenner. Father, high-school principal; mother, teacher. Grad. Peterborough Collegiate Inst., Ontario, Canada, 1941; Univ. of Toronto, B.A. 1945, M.A. 1946; Yale Univ., Ph.D. 1950. Married Aug. 30, 1947, to Mary Josephine Waite (marr. dis.); two sons, three daughters; married 1965; two children. Address: Dept. of English, John Hopkins University, Baltimore, MD 21218.

Since 1973, Mr. Kenner has been professor of English at Johns Hopkins Univ. Previously he was a member of the faculty at the Univ. of California at Santa Barbara (instructor, 1950–51; assistant professor, 1951–56; associate professor, 1956–58; professor, 1958–73; and chairman of the dept., 1956–62); was assistant professor in the English Dept. at Assumption Univ., Windsor, Ontario (1946–48); and a visiting profesor at the Univ. of Michigan (Summer 1956), the Univ. of Chicago (Summer 1962) and the Univ. of Virginia (Fall 1963).

Published Works. Mr. Kenner wrote *Wyndham Lewis* (1954), *Dublin's Joyce* (1956), *Gnomon: Essays in Contemporary Literature* (1958), *The Invisible Poet: T. S. Eliot* (1959), *Art of Poetry* (1959), *Samuel Beckett* (1961), edited *T. S. Eliot: A Collection of Critical Essays* (1962), wrote *Flaubert, Joyce and Beckett: The Stoic Comedians* (1963), and edited *Seventeenth-Century Poetry: The Schools of Donne and Johnson* (1964). He is also the author of *Bucky: A Guided Tour of Buckminster Fuller* (1973).

He has written articles and reviews on contemporary literature for the *Kenyon Review, Hudson Review, Poetry, Shenandoah, National Review, Virginia Quarterly Review, Prairie Schooner,* and *Spectrum.* .

Awards. Mr. Kenner received the John Addison Porter Prize from Yale Univ. (1950); two Guggenheim Fellowships (1957–58; 1963–64); and has been a Fellow of the Royal Society of Literature (1958–to date).

Recreation. Photography, electronics.

KERMOYAN, MICHAEL. Actor, singer. b. Kalem Missak Kermoyan, Nov. 29, 1925, Fresno, Calif., to Missak and Berjuhi Kermoyan. Father, florist; mother, singer. Grad. George Washington H.S., San Francisco; Commerce H.S., San Francisco; attended Stanford Univ.; Univ. of Southern California; Los Angeles (Calif.) Conservatory of Music; in San Francisco, studied with Giulio; Dr. Jan Popper; in Los Angeles, drama with Carl Ebert; voice with Richard Dresdner and with Leon Cepparo. Married Sept. 11, 1955, to Katia Geleznova, dancer; one son. Served WW II, USNAF, PTO; citation for heroism overseas. Member of AEA; AFTRA; SAG; AGMA; AGVA. Address: 817 West End Ave., New York, NY 10025, tel. (212) UN 5-5414.

Theatre. Mr. Kermoyan made his first theatre appearance as Hobson in the opera *Peter Grimes* (San Francisco Opera House, Calif., 1948); with the Stanford Players, he played Mitifio in *L'Arlesienne* (Palo Alto, Calif., 1949); appeared as Filippo Fiorentino in *Street Scene* (Players Ring Th., Hollywood, Calif., 1950); with the Guild Opera (Los

Angeles), sang in the operas including *Ariadne auf Naxos, Albert Herring, Don Pasquale, The Abduction from the Seraglio, Faust, Tales of Hoffmann, The Marriage of Figaro, The Magic Flute, The Consul, The Barber of Seville, Angelique, Schwanda, L'Education Manquée, The Bartered Bride,* and *Dark Waters* (1950–53); and in stock, he appeared as Jigger in *Carousel* (Music Circus, Sacramento, Calif., Summer 1953).

He made his N.Y.C. debut, billed as Kalem Kermoyan, as Mike in *The Girl in the Pink Tights* (Mark Hellinger Th., Mar. 5, 1954); in stock, played Jud in *Oklahoma!* and Porthos in *The Three Musketeers* (Starlight Th., Kansas City, Mo., Summer 1954); and Rudolpho in *Naughty Marietta* (State Fair Music Hall, Dallas, Tex., Summer 1954). Billed as Michael Kermoyan, he appeared as Joe Novak in *Sandhog* (Phoenix, N.Y.C., Nov. 23, 1954); in stock, played Ali Ben Ali in *The Desert Song,* Jigger in *Carousel,* and Apopoulis in *Wonderful Town* (Iroquois Amphitheatre, Louisville, Ky., Summer 1955); with the national touring company replaced Stefan Schnabel as Papa Yoder in *Plain and Fancy* (opened Forrest, Philadelphia, Pa., Mar. 6, 1956; closed Nixon, Pittsburgh, Pa., May 5, 1956); and in stock, appeared as Jacob in *Paint Your Wagon,* Massakroff in *The Chocolate Soldier,* and repeated his roles as Jigger in *Carousel* and Papa Yoder in *Plain and Fancy* (Starlight Th., Kansas City, Mo., Summer 1956).

In the Summer of 1957, he played Eddie Carbone in *A View from the Bridge* and Renato di Rossi in *The Time of the Cuckoo* (Robin Hood Th., Arden, Del.); Papa Yoder in *Plain and Fancy* (St. Louis Municipal Opera, Mo.); the Wazir in *Kismet* (Musicarnival, Cleveland, Ohio); and repeated his roles in *Carousel* and *Plain and Fancy* (Chastain Park, Atlanta, Ga.); in the Summer of 1958, played Jud in *Oklahoma!* (St. Louis Municipal Opera, Mo.), and Injun Joe in *Tom Sawyer* (Starlight Th., Kansas City, Mo., world premiere); played Jiggs Rock Medicine in *Whoop-Up* (Shubert Th., N.Y.C., Dec. 22, 1958); and, in stock, played Bullmoose in *Li'l Abner* and Josephus Gage in *Gentlemen Prefer Blondes* (St. Louis Municipal Opera, Summer 1959).

He appeared as Glenn Richards in *Happy Town* (54 St. Th., N.Y.C., Oct. 7, 1959); in stock, Ali Ben Ali in *The Desert Song* and the Wazir in *Kismet* (St. Louis Municipal Opera, Summer 1960); played George Poppet in *Redhead* and Jud in *Oklahoma!* (Chastain Park, Atlanta, Ga., Summer 1960); Sir Ozanna in *Camelot* (Majestic, N.Y.C., Dec. 3, 1960); and Jupiter in *The Happiest Girl in the World* (Martin Beck Th., Apr. 3, 1961), succeeding to the role of Kenesias; played Mr. Crocker in *Fly Blackbird* (Mayfair, Feb. 5, 1962); succeeded Paul Sparer as Auda Abu Tayi in *Ross* (Eugene O'Neill Th., Dec. 26, 1961); and, for the Metropolitan Opera Sch., sang the role of Don Basilio in *The Barber of Seville* (1962).

In stock, played Jud in *Oklahoma!* (Civic Light Opera Co., Pittsburgh, Pa., The Kenley Players, Columbus, Ohio, Summer 1962); appeared as Nishan Hagopian in *Angels of Anadarko* (York Th., N.Y.C., Oct. 10, 1962); and played Admiral Boris Souqhomine and was Jean Pierre Aumont's standby in the role of Mikail in *Tovarich* (Bway Th., Mar. 18, 1963).

He played the Kralahome and was understudy to Darren McGavin as the King in *The King and I* (NY State Th., N.Y.C., July 6, 1964); Lepescu in *Something More!* (Eugene O'Neill Th., Nov. 10, 1964); Bounine in *Anya* (Ziegfeld, Nov. 29, 1965); Bill Sikes in *Oliver!* (Paper Mill Playhouse, Millburn, N.J., Apr. 12, 1966); Jigger in *Carousel* (NY City Ctr., Dec. 15, 1966); Velan in *The Guide* (Hudson, Mar. 6, 1968); the King in *The King and I* (NY City Ctr., May 20, 1968); toured in the title role of *Zorba* (opened Bushnell Aud., Hartford, Conn., Sept. 11, 1970; closed Memorial Aud., Worcester, Mass., May 18, 1971); played Uncle Chris in the world premiere of the musical version of *I Remember Mama,* entitled *Mama* (Studio Arena Th., Buffalo, N.Y., Jan. 6, 1972); appeared in *King Lear* (North Shore Music Th., Beverly, Mass., Apr. 1973); and played Ali Ben Ali in *The Desert Song* (Summer tour 1973; Uris Th., Sept. 5, 1973).

Films. Mr. Kermoyan appeared in *The Story of Jean Lafitte* (MGM, 1949); and has dubbed voices for various films, including *With a Song in My Heart* (20th-Fox, 1952) and *Lion in the Streets* (WB, 1953).

Television. Mr. Kermoyan has sung in *Salome* (1954) and *War and Peace* (1958), with the NBC Opera; and has appeared in *archy and mehitabel* (Play of the Week, WNTA, 1959); as Mephistopheles in *Terezin Requiem* (CBS); on The Trials of O'Brien (CBS); the Tonight Show (NBC); and in *Macbeth* (Actors' Co., NET, Apr. 18, 1968).

Recreation. Hunting, fishing, cooking.

KERNODLE, GEORGE R. Educator, writer, director. b. George Riley Kernodle, Mar. 17, 1907, Camp Hill, Ala., to J. A. and Annie (Slaughter) Kernodle. Father, farmer; mother, teacher. Grad. St. Lawrence Univ., B.S. 1926; studied drama, Carnegie Inst. of Tech., 1926–28; studied English, Columbia Univ., 1928–29; attended Univ. of Berlin, Ger., Summer 1929; grad. Univ. of Chicago, M.A. (English) 1930; attended Univ. of Chicago, graduate study, 1932–34; grad. Yale Univ., Ph.D. (Drama) 1937. Married 1935, to Portia Baker. Address: (home) 420 Rebecca St., Fayetteville, AR 72701, tel. (501) HI 2-8886; (bus.) Univ. of Arkansas, Division of Fine and Applied Arts, Dept. of Speech and Dramatic Art, Fayetteville, AR 72701.

Since 1952, Mr. Kernodle has been professor of dramatic arts in the Dept. of Speech and Dramatic Arts at the Univ. of Arkansas. Previously, he was associate professor of speech and dramatic arts at the State Univ. of Iowa (1945–50), assistant professor of English and drama at Western Reserve Univ. (1936–45), and associate professor of speech and drama at Univ. of Tulsa (1950–52).

He was a visiting lecturer at the summer sessions of the State Univ. of Iowa (1938, 1945); Univ. of California at Los Angeles (1947); Univ. of Colorado (1951); Michigan State Univ. (1952); Shakespeare Inst. in England and Univ. of Utrecht (1956); San Francisco State Coll. (1959); Univ. of British Columbia (1963); Univ. of Amsterdam, Univ. of Leiden, and Univ. of Birmingham, England (1968); and the World Center for Shakespeare Studies, London (1973).

Mr. Kernodle has directed more than 100 productions since 1930, including *A Midsummer Night's Dream* for the Colorado Shakespearean Festival (July 1959) and *Twelfth Night* for the State Univ. of Iowa (Mar. 1962).

Published Works. Mr. Kernodle is the author of *From Art to Theatre* (1944, 1965); and, with Allardyce Nicoll and John McDowell, of *The Renaissance Stage* (1958), *Invitation to the Theatre* (1967); and *Invitation to the Theatre: Brief Edition* (1971).

He has written articles on theatre for such magazines as *Theatre Research* and *Educational Theatre Journal.*

Awards. Mr. Kernodle received a Sterling Fellowship for theatre research at Yale Univ. and in Europe (1938–39), a Rockefeller Fellowship for study in Europe (Summer 1939), and the Award to Faculty Member for Distinguished Scholarship by Univ. of Arkansas Alumni Assn. (1972).

Recreation. Music, gardening.

KERR, DEBORAH. Actress. b. Deborah Jane Kerr-Trimmer, Sept. 30, 1921, Helnsburgh, Scotland, to Arthur Charles and Colleen Rose (Smale) Kerr-Trimmer. Father, civil engineer. Attended Northumberland House Sch., Clifton-Bristol, England, 1937. Studied acting at Phyllis Smale Sch. of Drama, Clifton-Bristol, 1930–38; dance at the Sadler's Wells Ballet Sch., London, England, (scholarship) 1938–39. Married Nov. 28, 1946, to Anthony Charles Bartley (marr. dis. July 1959); two daughters; married July 23, 1960, to Peter Viertel, screenwriter. Relative in theatre: aunt, Phyllis Smale, actress, drama teacher. Member of AMPAS; SAG; British AEA.

Theatre. Miss Kerr first appeared on the stage as Harlequin in a mime play *Harlequin and Columbine* (Knightstone Pavillion, Weston-Super-Mare, England, 1937). She made her London debut as a member of the corps de ballet in *Prometheus* (Sadler's Wells Th., 1938); subsequently appeared in walk-on and small roles in Shakespearean repertory (Open Air Th., Regents Park, London, England, 1939); as Margaret in *Dear Brutus,* and Patty Moss in *The Two Bouquets* with the Oxford Repertory Th. (Playhouse, Oxford, England, May 1940); and as Ellie Dunn in *Heartbreak House* (Cambridge Th., London, Mar. 18, 1943); and on tour (Manchester, England; Glasgow and Edinburgh, Scotland, 1943); For ENSA, she toured the service camps as Mrs. Manningham in *Angel Street* (Belgium, Holland, France, 1945).

Miss Kerr made her N.Y.C. debut as Laura Reynolds in *Tea and Sympathy* (Ethel Barrymore Th., Sept. 30, 1953), which she repeated on the national tour (opened St. James Th., Asbury Park, N.J., Nov. 5, 1954); was Edith in *The Day After the Fair* (Lyric, London, England, Oct. 4, 1972), which she repeated on tour in the US (opened Auditorium Th., Denver, Colo., Sept. 4, 1973; closed John F. Kennedy Ctr., Washington, D.C., Jan. 20, 1974); and played Nancy in *Seascape* (Sam S. Shubert Th., N.Y.C., Jan. 26, 1975).

Films. Miss Kerr made her debut as a Hatcheck Girl in *Contraband* (Brit. Natl., 1939); subsequently, appeared in *Major Barbara* (U, 1941); *Love on the Dole* (U, 1941); *Penn of Pennsylvania* (Brit. Natl.); *The Day Will Dawn* (Denham); *The Life and Death of Colonel Blimp* (UA, 1945); *Vacation from Marriage* (MGM, 1945); *Black Narcissus* (U, 1947); *The Adventuress* (Eagle-Lion, 1947); *The Hucksters* (MGM, 1947); *If Winter Comes* (MGM, 1947); *Hatter's Castle* (Par., 1948); *Edward, My Son* (MGM, 1949); *King Solomon's Mines* (MGM, 1950); *Please Believe Me* (MGM, 1950); *Quo Vadis* (MGM, 1951); *Prisoner of Zenda* (MGM, 1952); *Young Bess* (MGM, 1953); *Dream Wife* (MGM, 1953); *Julius Caesar* (MGM, 1953); *Thunder in the East* (Par., 1953); *From Here to Eternity* (Col., 1953); *The End of the Affair* (Col., 1955); *Tea and Sympathy* (MGM, 1956); *The King and I* (20th-Fox, 1956); *The Proud and the Profane* (Par., 1956); *Heaven Knows, Mr. Allison* (20th-Fox, 1957); *An Affair to Remember* (20th-Fox, 1957); *Bonjour Tristesse* (Col., 1958); *Separate Tables* (U, 1958); *Count Your Blessings* (MGM, 1959); *Beloved Infidel* (20th-Fox, 1959); *The Journey* (MGM, 1959); and *The Sundowners* (WB, 1959).

Also *The Grass Is Greener* (U, 1960); *The Naked Edge* (UA, 1961); *The Innocents* (20th-Fox, 1961); *The Chalk Garden* (U, 1964); *The Night of the Iguana* (MGM, 1964); *Marriage on the Rocks* (WB, 1965); *Casino Royale* (Col., 1967); *Eye of the Devil* (MGM, 1967); *The Gypsy Moths* (MGM, 1969); and *The Arrangement* (WB, 1969).

Television. On British television, Miss Kerr has appeared in the roles of Moira Shepleigh, Grace Annesly and Miranda Watney in *Three Roads to Rome* (ATV, 1961).

Awards. Miss Kerr received the NY Film Critics Award for her performances in *Black Narcissus,* and *The Adventuress* (1947); in *Heaven Knows, Mr. Allison* (1957); and in *The Sundowners* (1960). She was nominated for the Academy (Oscar) Award for her performances in *Edward, My Son* (1949), *From Here to eternity* 1953), *The King and I* (1956), *Heaven Knows Mr. Allison* (1957), *Separate Tables* (1958), and *The Sundowners* (1960).

For her performance as Laura Reynolds in the N.Y.C. production of *Tea and Sympathy,* she won the NY Publicists Guild Award (1954), the *Variety* NY Drama Critics Poll (1954), the Donaldson Award (1954), and the Sarah Siddons Award (1955).

She also received the Hollywood Foreign Press (Golden Globe) Award for her performances as Anna in *The King and I* (1956), and in *Separate Tables* (1958); *Box Office* Blue Ribbon Award for her performance in *King Solomon's Mines* (1950) and *The King and I* (1956); and was named star of the year by the Theatre Owners of America Award (1958).

Recreation. Needlework, tennis, swimming.

KERR, GEOFFREY. Actor, playwright. b. Jan. 26, 1895, London, England, to Frederick and Lucy Houghton (Dowson) Keen. Father, actor. Attended St. Andrew's Sch., Eastbourne, and Charterhouse, England. Married June 27, 1926, to June Walker, actress (marr. dis. 1943); one son, John Kerr, actor; married Sept. 14, 1943, to Margot Kling. Served WW I, British Army, RFC and RAF; WW II, RASC and Intelligence Corps. Member of AEA; British AEA.

Theatre. Mr. Kerr made his theatre debut in London as Kenneth Lester in *A Cardinal's Romance* (Savoy, June 14, 1913); subsequently played Lord Walter Sark in *People Like Ourselves* (Globe, Oct. 1913); Charley Wyckham in *Charley's Aunt* (Prince of Wales's, Dec. 1913); Pemberton in *The Bull* (Prince of Wales's, June 1914); Tony in *Outcast* (Wyndham's, Sept. 1, 1914); Richard in *Tilly of Bloomsbury* (Apollo, July 10, 1919); and Lord Roftus in *Skittles* (Apollo, July 1921).

Mr. Kerr made his N.Y.C. debut as George in *Just Suppose* (Henry Miller's Th., Nov. 1, 1920); followed by Knox in *East of Suez* (Eltinge, Sept. 21, 1922); Roderick White in *You and I* (Belmont, Feb. 19, 1923); Wicky Faber in *The Changelings* (Henry Miller's Th., Sept. 17, 1923); Ernest Fairleight in *In His Arms* (Fulton, Oct. 13, 1923); Lionel Deport in *The Stork* (Cort, Jan. 26, 1925); and Jean in *First Love* (Booth, Nov. 8, 1926).

He wrote *Don't Play with Fire* (Coliseum, London, 1927); played John Ashley in *The Bachelor Father* (Belasco, N.Y.C., Feb. 28, 1928); George Craft in *London Calling* (Little, Oct. 18, 1930); Joseph Gresham, Jr. in *This Is New York* (Plymouth, Nov. 28, 1930); Dr. Gestzi in *Collision* (Gaiety, Feb. 16, 1932); Jean Servin in *We Are No Children* (Booth, Mar. 31, 1932); Cremone in *Domino* (Playhouse, Aug. 16, 1932); Dwight Houston in a touring production of *There's Always Juliet* (Fall 1932); Shakespeare in *Foolscap*, which he directed (Times Square, Jan. 11, 1933); Leo in *Design for Living* at the Ann Arbor (Univ. of Michigan) Dramatic Festival (Lydia Mendelssohn Th., June 1933); and Stackpoole in *Yellow Jack* (Martin Beck Th., N.Y.C., Mar. 6, 1934).

He wrote *Till the Cows Come Home* (St. Martin's, London, Oct. 27, 1936); with Bert Lee and Clifford Grey, *Oh! You Letty* (Place, 1937); wrote *Black Swans* (Apollo, 1937); *Cottage to Let* (Wyndham's, Apr. 22, 1941); and *The Man in the Street* (St. James's, Oct. 9, 1947).

Mr. Kerr played Frederick Chanler in *I Know My Love* (Shubert, Nov. 2, 1949); wrote *Welcome to Killoon* (Whitehall, London, Sept. 23, 1951); played Dr. John Kingsley in *The Apples of Eve* (Comedy, Oct. 14, 1952); Matthew in *Hunter's Moon* (Winter Garden, Feb. 26, 1958); and Lambert in *The Elder Statesman* at the Edinburgh (Scotland) Festival (Aug. 25, 1958) and in London (Cambridge, Sept. 25, 1958).

Recreation. Photography, magic.

KERR, JEAN. Playwright, author. b. Bridget Jean Collins, July 10, 1923, Scranton, Pa., to Thomas J. and Kitty (O'Neill) Collins. Father, construction superintendent. Grad. Marywood Sem., Scranton, Pa., 1939; Marywood Coll., Scranton, B.A. 1943; Catholic Univ. of Amer., M.A. 1944. Married Aug. 9, 1943, to Walter Kerr, drama critic; five sons, one daughter. Member of the Dramatists Guild (editorial comm. of Dramatists' *Bulletin*, 1964–to date), ALA; ASCAP.

Pre-Theatre. Teacher.

Theatre. Mrs. Kerr first wrote *Jenny Kissed Me* (Hudson Th., N.Y.C., Dec. 23, 1948); with her husband, Walter Kerr, wrote the revue, *Touch and Go* (Broadhurst, N.Y.C., Oct. 13, 1949; Prince of Wales's, London, May 19, 1950); wrote two sketches, "My Cousin Who?" and "Don Brown's Body" for the revue, *John Murray Anderson's Almanac* (Imperial, Dec. 10, 1953); wrote, with Eleanor Brooke, *King of Hearts* (Lyceum, Apr. 1, 1954); with her husband, wrote the book for *Goldilocks* (Lunt-Fontanne, Oct. 11, 1958); wrote *Mary, Mary* (Helen Hayes Th., N.Y.C., Mar. 8, 1961; Queen's, London, Feb. 27, 1963, *Poor Richard* (Helen Hayes Th., Dec. 2, 1964); and *Finishing Touches* (Plymouth, Feb. 8, 1973).

Television. She adapted her book, *Please Don't Eat the Daisies*, for the series of the same name (NBC, 1965–66).

Published Works. Mrs. Kerr wrote the books *Please Don't Eat the Daisies* (1954) *The Snake Has All the Lines* (1960); and *Penny Candy* (1970).

Awards. Mrs. Kerr received an honorary L.H.D. degree from Northwestern Univ. (1962); with her husband, received the Notre Dame Univ. Laetare Medal (1971); and the Campion Award (1971).

KERR, JOHN. Actor. b. John Grinham Kerr, Nov. 15, 1931, New York City, to Geoffrey and June (Walker) Kerr. Father, actor, playwright; mother, actress (known as June Walker). Grad. Phillips Exeter Acad., 1948; Harvard Coll., A.B. (cum laude) 1952; attended Columbia Univ., 1953–55. Married Dec. 28, 1952, to Priscilla Smith; one son, two daughters. Member of AEA; SAG; AFTRA; WGA.

Theatre. Mr. Kerr made his professional debut in a stock production of *O Mistress Mine* (Cape Playhouse, Dennis, Mass., Summer 1948); subsequently appeared in *September Tide* (Cape Playhouse, Summer 1949); and in *Twelfth Night, Billy Budd, A Midsummer Night's Dream*, and *A Sleep of Prisoners* (Brattle Th., Cambridge, Mass., Summers 1949–52).

He made his first appearance in N.Y.C. as Arthur Beaumont in *Bernadine* (Playhouse, Oct. 16, 1952); played Tom in *Tea and Sympathy* (Ethel Barrymore Th., Sept. 30, 1953); Don in *All Summer Long* (Coronet, Sept. 23, 1954); Oedipus in the *The Infernal Machine* (Phoenix, Feb. 3, 1958); Tony Burgess in *Cue for Passion* (Henry Miller's Th., Nov. 25, 1958); and Arthur Landau in *The Tenth Man* (NY City Ctr., Nov. 8, 1967).

In stock, he appeared in *The Hasty Heart* (Fred Miller Th., Milwaukee, Wis., 1960) and *The Teahouse of the August Moon* (Swan, Milwaukee, Wis., 1961); directed *See the Jaguar* (Horseshow Stage, Los Angeles, Calif., 1961); *The Sound of Murder* and *Five Finger Exercise* (La Jolla Playhouse, Calif., 1961).

Films. Mr. Kerr made his debut in *The Cobweb* (MGM, 1955); appeared in *Gaby* (MGM, 1956); *Tea and Sympathy* (MGM, 1956); *The Vintage* (MGM, 1957); *South Pacific* (Magna, 1958); and *The Crowded Sky* (WB, 1960).

Television. He has performed on Lux Video Th., (CBS, 1953); You Are There (CBS, 1953); Danger (CBS, 1953); Suspense (CBS, 1953); The Web (CBS, 1953); Studio One (CBS, 1954); Philco Television Playhouse (NBC, 1954); Hallmark Hall of Fame (NBC, 1955); Elgin Th. (ABC, 1955); Climax (CBS, 1956); Checkmate (NBC, 1962); Rawhide (CBS, 1962); US Steel Hour (CBS, 1962); The Defenders (CBS, 1962); Bus Stop (ABC, 1962); The Virginian (NBC, 1962); Arrest and Trial (ABC, 1963); Twelve O'Clock High (ABC); Profiles in Courage (NBC); Alfred Hitchcock Presents (NBC); The Trailmaster (ABC); The Long Hot Summer (NBC); Peyton Place (ABC); Riverboat (Ind.); Flipper (NBC); High Chaparral (NBC); The F.B.I. (ABC); Name of the Game (NBC); Adam 12 (NBC); The Bold Ones (NBC); The Young Lawyers (ABC); *Yuma* (ABC); Owen Marshall (ABC); and Mod Squad (ABC).

Awards. Mr. Kerr received the *Theatre World* Award, and won the *Variety* NY Drama Critics' Poll for his performance as Arthur Beaumont in *Bernadine* (1953); and received the Donaldson Award and the Antoinette Perry (Tony) Award for his performance as Tom in *Tea and Sympathy* (1954).

KERR, WALTER. Drama critic, writer. b. Walter F. Kerr, July 8, 1913, Evanston, Ill., to Walter Sylvester and Esther M. (Daugherty) Kerr. Father, carpenter, foreman. Grad. St. George H.S., Evanston, Ill., 1931; attended De Pauw Univ., 1931–33; grad. Northwestern Univ., B.S. (Speech) 1937, M.A. 1938. Married Aug. 9, 1943, to Jean Collins, writer; five sons, one daughter. Member of NY Drama Critics Circle (pres., 1955–57); Dramatists Guild; Ala; Newspaper Guild; ASCAP.

Theatre. Mr. Kerr is a drama critic for the New York *Times* (1966–to date). Previously, he has been drama critic with *Commonweal* magazine (1950–52); and the New York *Herald-Tribune* (1951–66).

He first wrote, with Leo Brady and Nancy Hamilton, the revue *Count Me In* (Ethel Barrymore Th., Oct. 8, 1942); subsequently wrote and directed *Sing Out Sweet Land* (Intl., Dec. 27, 1944); with his wife, Jean Kerr, wrote the revue *Touch and Go*, which he also directed (Broadhurst, N.Y.C., Oct. 13, 1949; Prince of Wales's Th., London, May 19, 1950); staged *King of Hearts*, which his wife wrote with Eleanor Broke (Lyceum, N.Y.C., Apr. 1954); with his wife, wrote the book for *Goldilocks*, which he also directed (Lunt-Fontanne, Oct. 11, 1958); and wrote an acting version of *The Birds* (Terrace Th., Univ. of Denver, Colo., July 23, 1964).

Television. Mr. Kerr was host for the Esso Repertory Theatre (1965).

Other Activities. Mr. Kerr was associate professor of drama (1945–49) and instructor of speech and drama (1938–45) at Catholic Univ.

He is drama consultant to Robert Saudek Associates.

Published Works. Mr. Kerr is the author of *How Not To Write a Play* (1955); *Criticism and Censorship* (1957); *Pieces at Eight* (1957); *The Decline of Pleasure* (1962); and *Theatre in Spite of Itself* (1963).

He also wrote the plays, *Stardust* (1946), an adaptation of Moliere's *The Miser* (1942); and a translation of Aristophanes' *The Birds* (1952); *Tragedy and Comedy* (1967); *Thirty Plays Has November* (1969); and *God on the Gymnasium Floor* (1971).

Discography. He has recorded a series of lectures entitled *Walter Kerr's Guide to the Theater* (1972).

Awards. Mr. Kerr received the $4,000 George Jean Nathan Drama Criticism Award (1963).

He received the honorary degrees of L.H.D. from Northwestern Univ. (1962), LL.D. from St. Mary's Notre Dame (1956), and D.Litt. from La Salle Univ. (1956); the Dineen Award of the National Catholic Th. Conf. (1965); with his wife, Jean Kerr, the Laetare Medal (1971) from Notre Dame Univ.; and the Award for Literature from the American Academy of Arts and Letters and the National Institute of Arts and Letters (1972).

KERT, LARRY. Actor, singer, dancer. b. Frederick Lawrence Kert, Dec. 5, 1934, Los Angeles, Calif., to Harry and Lillian (Pearson) Kert. Father, jeweler; mother, actress. Grad. Hollywood (Calif.) H.S.; attended Los Angeles City Coll. Studied acting with Sanford Meisner, N.Y.C., and singing with Keith Davis, N.Y.C. Relatives in theatre: sister, Anita Ellis, singer, actress; sister, Evelyn Kert, folk singer. Served USNR. Member of AEA; AFTRA; SAG.

Theatre. In 1950, Mr. Kert joined "Bill Norvas and the Upstarts," a group of singing and dancing entertainers in Los Angeles, Calif. The group was subsequently featured in a variety show (Roxy Th., N.Y.C., 1950); and in the revue, *Tickets, Please!* (Coronet, Apr. 1950). He joined (1952) the Players Ring Th. group (Hollywood, Calif.), and appeared there in *Look Ma, I'm Dancin'* (1952); and subsequently performed in a stock production of *Walk Tall* (Houston, Tex., June 1953).

He was a member of the chorus and understudy to Carlton Carpenter in the revue *John Murray Anderson's Almanac* (Imperial, Dec. 10, 1953), substituting several times for Harry Belafonte in the same production; appeared in the pre-Bway tryout of the *Ziegfeld Follies* (opened Shubert, Boston, Apr. 16, 1956; closed Shubert, Philadelphia, May 12, 1956); succeeded (Nov. 1956) Bob Kole in the role of the stage manager in *Mr. Wonderful* (Bway Th., N.Y.C., Mar. 22, 1956); played Tony in *West Side Story* (Winter Garden, Sept. 26, 1957), and on tour (opened Erlanger, Chicago, Oct. 18, 1959; closed Shubert, Boston, Apr. 23, 1960); and again (Winter Garden, Apr. 27, 1960).

Mr. Kert appeared in *The Medium* and *The Telephone* (Palm Springs Th. Circus, Calif., Mar., 1961); *West Side Story* (Circle Arts Th., San Diego Calif., June 21, 1961); *Pal Joey* (Lambertville Music Circus, N.J., 1961); and *The Merry Widow* (Westbury Music Fair, L.I., N.Y., Aug. 10, 1961); played Gerry Siegel in *A Family Affair* (Billy Rose Th. N.Y.C., Jan. 27, 1962); succeeded (June 14, 1962) Elliott Gould in the role of Harry Bogen in *I Can Get It for You Wholesale* (Shubert, Mar. 22, 1962), and on tour (opened Rochester, N.Y., Aud., Nov. 1, 1962; closed O'Keefe Ctr., Toronto, Ontario, Canada, Mar. 9, 1963).

He played Tony in *West Side Story* (Stadium Bowl, k of Utah, Salt Lake City, July 8, 1965); Carlos in *Holly Golightly*, which was retitled *Breakfast at Tiffany's*, and closed during previews (Majestic, N.Y.C., closed Dec. 14, 1966); replaced John Cunningham in the role of Clifford Bradshaw in *Cabaret* (Broadhurst, Nov. 20, 1966; moved to Broadway Th., Oct. 7, 1968); played Mario in *La Strada* (Lunt-Fontanne Th., Dec. 14, 1969); succeeded Dean Jones as Robert in *Company* (Alvin, Apr. 26, 1970); played Proteus in *Two Gentlemen of Verona* (tour, Jan.–Oct. 1973); appeared in *Music! Music!* (NY City Ctr., Apr. 11, 1974); and played Joe in the West Coast company of *Sugar* (Los Angeles, Sept. 3, 1974).

Films. As a teenager, he appeared as stunt man, stand-in, and extra in nearly 100 films; and subsequently played Bob Adamic in *Synanon* (Col., 1965).

Television. With "Bill Norvas and the Upstarts," he appeared on the Milton Berle Show (NBC), and the Ed Sullivan Show (CBS). He has also performed on such dramatic series as Private Secretary, Man Behind the Badge, and Checkmate (NBC); and Alfred Hitchcock Presents (CBS): appeared as a regular on the Ray Bolger Show (NBC), and the Kate Smith Show (CBS); played on the Specials, *Romeos And Juliets—A Theme with Variations; The Song and Dance Man;* and *Wild Is Love;* and on *Combat!* (ABC).

Night Clubs. With "Bill Norvas and the Upstarts," he made a nationwide tour of night clubs, which included the Cocoanut Grove (Hollywood), and the Copacabana (N.Y.C.). He was production singer at the Silver Slipper and the Last Frontier (Las Vegas, Nev.) and has also appeared at the Empire Club (Bermuda).

Recreation. Horseback riding, swimming, golf, waterskiing, bowling, photography, pratfalls.

KERZ, LEO. Designer, director, producer. b. Nov. 1, 1912, Berlin, Germany, to Nathan and Nechuma (Spira) Kerz. Father, dress manufacturer. Grad. Friedrich Ebert Oberreal Sch., Berlin, B.A. 1932; attended Acad. of Arts and Science, Berlin, 1933; studied with Bertolt Brecht, Laszlo Moholy-Nagy, Erwin Piscator, 1928–32; with Traugott Mueller, Berlin, 1930–33. Married 1963 to Louise Manning, actress; two sons. Member of United Scenic Artists, League of NY Theatres. Address: 333 E. 69th St., New York, NY 10021, tel. (212) UN 1-0610.

Theatre. Mr. Kerz's first assignment was in Berlin as designer for two studio productions of the Theatre-am-Schiffbauerdamm (1932); subsequently designed settings in Amsterdam, London, and Prague (1935–36); created the Pioneer Theatre in Johannesburg, South Africa, where he designed, produced, and staged *The Threepenny Opera, Miracle at Verdun, Golden Boy, The Cradle Will Rock,* and *The Hairy Ape* (1937–42).

In the US, Mr. Kerz worked as assistant to designers Jo Mielziner, Watson Barratt, and Stewart Chaney (1942); designed sets at the Bucks County Playhouse (New Hope, Pa., 1943–44); his first N.Y.C. assignment was to design two pageants directed by Erwin Piscator, *The Rally of Hope* and *The Golden Doors* (Madison Sq. Garden, 1946); was art director for the Pittsburgh (Pa.) Civic Light Opera Assoc. (1946–47); and assistant to designers George Jenkins and Harry Horner.

His first Bway assignment as designer was *Antony and Cleopatra* (Martin Beck Th., Nov. 26, 1947); followed by *A Long Way from Home* (Maxine Elliot's Th., Feb. 8, 1948); *Bravo* (Lyceum, Nov. 11, 1948); *The Biggest Thief in Town* (Mansfield, Mar. 30, 1949); and *The Gypsies Wore High Hats* (Cape Playhouse, Dennis, Mass., Summer 1952); *The Victim* (President, N.Y.C., May 2, 1952); *The Sacred Flame* (President, Oct. 7, 1952); for the San Francisco (Calif.), Opera Assn., designed the US premiere of *Troilus and Cressida, Macbeth, Aida, Lohengrin,* and *Der Rosenkavalier* (1955); and became art director, designer and lighting director for the company (1956).

Mr. Kerz designed settings for *Parsifal* and *The Magic Flute* (Metropolitan Opera House, N.Y.C., 1956); was designer at the Curtis Inst. of Music (Philadelphia, Pa.), where he was production designer for the opera *Landara* (May 1956); as artistic director, with Erich Leinsdorf, of the NY City Opera Co., at the NY City Ctr., designed and staged *Orpheus in the Underworld* (Sept. 20, 1956); *Susannah* (Sept. 27, 1956) and the US premiere of *The Tempest* (Oct. 11, 1956).

He did the designs and lighting for the Chevrolet Industrial Show (Detroit, Mich., 1957); produced and designed the American premiere of *Clerambard,* which, with Alvin Sapinsley, he adapted into English (Rooftop, Nov. 7, 1957); designed industrial exhibits and conventions; designed the pre-Bway tryout of *Listen to the Mockingbird* (opened Colonial, Boston, Mass., Dec. 27, 1958; closed Shubert, Washington, D.C., Jan. 29, 1959); with George Justin and Harry Belafonte, presented, and designed settings for *Moonbirds* (Cort, N.Y.C., Oct. 9, 1959); and, in association with Seven Arts Associates Corp., produced, and designed settings and lighting for *Rhinoceros* (Longacre, Jan. 9, 1961).

He designed the settings, lights and costumes for the world premiere of Erwin Piscator's Neue Freie Volksbuehne production of *Der Stellvertreter (The Deputy)* (Theatre am Kurfuerstendamm, Berlin, Feb. 20, 1963). He was principal designer at Arena Stage, Washington, D.C. (1969–71), where he designed scenery for *You Can't Take It with You* (Dec. 4, 1969); *The Cherry Orchard* (Jan. 15, 1970); *The Chemmy Circle* (Mar. 4, 1970); *Dance of Death,* also lighting (Apr. 16, 1970); *No Place To Be Somebody,* also lighting (May 28, 1970); and *The Ruling Class* (American premiere, Jan. 15, 1971). In 1971, Mr. Kerz was production designer for the opening of Filene Center, Wolf Trap Farm Park, Vienna, Va.; he produced, with Allan Pepper and Stanley Snadowski, *Dance of Death* (Ritz Th., N.Y.C., Apr. 28, 1971); and he designed scenery for Center Stage, Baltimore, Md., productions of *The Seagull* (Oct. 31, 1971); *Andorra* (Feb. 6, 1972); and *Staircase,* also lighting and costumes (Mar. 12, 1972).

Films. Mr. Kerz was art director for *Guilty Bystander* (Film Classics, 1950); *Mr. Universe* (Eagle Lion, 1951); *This is Cinerama* (Cinerama, 1952); *Teresa* (MGM, 1951); *The Goddess* (Col., 1958); *Middle of the Night* (Col., 1959); production designer for *Odds Against Tomorrow* (UA, 1959); and designer of a documentary for NAJA, *Seeds of Discovery* (1966).

Television. He was staff designer for CBS (1949–54); designed sets for television films on New York Confidential (ABC, 1959); and was art director for the television film, *In What America?* for Esso World Theatre (1964).

Other Activities. He was assistant designer to architect Max Gerstl (Prague, Czech., 1934); designed government posters for the Central News Agency (Johannesburg, South Africa, 1938); taught and lectured at the Univ. of Witwatersrand (South Africa, 1938–39); conducted classes in stage design, costume design, lighting, and makeup at the Dramatic Workshop of the New Sch. for Social Research (N.Y.C., 1943–44); held private classes in designing for stage, films, and television (1962); and, as visiting professor at Montana State Univ., headed at the drama dept. of the Sch. of Fine Arts (Summer 1964), a seminar on "New Designs for Theatre," and lectured on "Recent Trends in Stage Designing." He taught a course, "Producing the Play, " at the New School, N.Y.C., in 1970, 1971, and 1972, and was visiting professor and lecturer at Illinois State Univ., Normal, Ill., in 1971.

Published Works. Mr. Kerz wrote "Scenery or Stage Setting?", NY *Times* (July 1954); "Brecht and Piscator," *Educational Theatre Journal* (Oct. 1968); and essays for *Theatre Arts* magazine.

Awards. He received the NY Music Critics Award for his direction of *Susannah* (1956); the Outer Circle Award for *Rhinoceros* (1961) as the most creative overall contribution to the Bway season; a partial grant from the US State Department's Cultural Exchange Program for travel through Poland, where he lectured at the Universities of Warsaw and Krakow and studied motion picture activities at the Film Acad. in Lodz (1963).

Recreation. Tennis, swimming, model building.

KESDEKIAN, MESROP. Director, producer, designer, teacher. b. Mar. 8, 1920, Philadelphia, Pa., to Avedis M. and Aznive (Tashjian) Kesdekian. Father, tailor. Educ. Harrington Grammar School; Shaw Jr. High, and West Philadelphia H.S.; grad. West Chester (Pa.) State Teachers Coll., B.S. 1948; Pennsylvania State Univ., M.A. 1950. Studied theatre with Miriam Phillips at Hedgerow Th. School. Served in US Air Corps (1942–45) as radio operator-mechanic; China-Burma-India campaigns (Air Medal with oak leaf cluster, CBI, 1945; Amer. Service Medal; Asiatic-Pacific Service Medal; Distinguished Flying Cross, CBI, 1945); highest rank, S/Sgt. Member of AEA; SSD&C. Address: 210 Riverside Dr., New York, NY 10025, tel. (212) UN 5-1090.

Pre-Theatre. Mr. Kesdekian taught in Philadelphia public schools (1948, 1949); was an acting instructor at Pennsylvania State Univ. (1949–53); the American Theatre Wing (1961–62); Hartford (Conn.) Univ. (1968); Univ. of South Florida, Tampa (1969, 1970–71, 1971–72); Lawrence Univ., Appleton, Wis. (1969–70, 1972–73); and Kalamazoo (Mich.) Coll. (1974).

Theatre. Mr. Kesdekian was designer at Mountain Playhouse, Jennerstown, Pa. (1949); costumer for *Othello* (Gate Th., Dublin, Ire., 1954); and, since 1952, has been producer-director at Green Hills Th., Reading, Pa., of such plays as *The Boy Friend, The Fantasticks, Pygmalion,* and *The Rose Tattoo.* He has also directed *Oasis in Manhattan* (Stage Society, Hollywood, Calif.); and was director of *Slaughter of the Innocents* and *The Earth a Trinket* (both Studio Th., Dublin, Ireland, 1954); *Blood Wedding* and *Saint Joan* (both University Players, Princeton, N.J., 1955). At Arena Stage, Washington, D.C., he directed the double bill *The Apollo of Bellac* and *The Browning Version* (Feb. 11, 1958) and designed *The Summer of the 17th Doll;* in N.Y.C., he designed an off-Bway production of *The Summer of the 17th Doll* (Players, Oct. 13, 1959) and directed Equity Library productions of *The Beautiful People* (Lenox Hill Playhouse, Dec. 11, 1959), *The Skin of Our Teeth* (Lenox Hill Playhouse, Oct. 11, 1960), and *Love's Old Sweet Song* (Master Institute, Oct. 21, 1961).

Me. Kesdekian directed the Theatre Guild American Repertory Co. production of *The Skin of Our Teeth* that toured Europe and Latin America under US State Dept. sponsorship (1960–61). At Bucks County Playhouse, New Hope, Pa., he directed *The Biggest Thief in Town* (1961), *Love Among the Platypi* (May 1962), *Time Out for Ginger* (1964), *Tom Jones,* and *Mary, Mary.* He also directed *The Caretaker* (Playhouse-in-the-Park, Cincinnati, Ohio, 1963); *The Hostage* (Center Stage, Baltimore, Md., Oct. 14, 1964); and *Thieves' Carnival* and the double-bill *The Typists* and *The Tiger* (all Pavilion Th., Pennsylvania State Univ., State College, Pa., 1964).

Awards. Mr. Kesdekian is a fellow of the International Institute of Arts and Letters (1960).

Recreation. Collecting sculpture and paintings.

KIDD, MICHAEL. Choreographer, director, dancer. b. Milton Greenwald, Aug. 12, 1919, New York City, to Abraham and Lillian Greenwald. Father, union official. Grad. New Utrecht H.S.,

Brooklyn, N.Y., 1936; attended City Coll. of New York, 1936–37 (Chem. engineering). Attended Sch. of American Ballet, N.Y.C., 1937–39; studied with Blanche Evan, Ludmilla Scholler, Muriel Stewart, and Anatole Vilzak. Married July 30, 1940, to Mary Heater, dancer; two daughters. Member of SSD&C; AGMA; SAG; SDG. Address: New City, NY.

Pre-Theatre. Copy boy for NY *Daily Mirror;* dance photographer.

Theatre. Mr. Kidd made his professional debut as understudy to Benjamin Zemach as the Adversary's Follower in *The Eternal Road* (Manhattan Opera House, N.Y.C., Jan. 7, 1937); appeared as a solo dancer in the Ballet Caravan's production of *Billy the Kid* (Chicago Opera House, world premiere Oct. 16, 1938).

He danced with Eugene Loring's Dance Players (Nov. 1941–Nov. 1942), in *Jinx* (Erie Th., Schenectady, N.Y., world premiere Apr. 9, 1942), *City Portrait, Harlequin for President,* and *The Man from Midian.*

From 1942–47, he was solo dancer with The Ballet Theatre, appearing in its productions of *Helen of Troy* and *Pillar of Fire* (Metropolitan Opera House, N.Y.C., world premiere Apr. 8, 1942), the title roles in *Petrouchka* and *Billy the Kid,* the Devil in *Three Virgins and a Devil;* and appeared in *Aurora's Wedding.*

He danced Another Reflection in *Dim Lustre* (Metropolitan Opera House, world premiere, Oct. 20, 1943); *Fancy Free* (Metropolitan Opera House, world premiere Apr. 18, 1944); and *Undertow* (Metropolitan Opera House, world premiere Apr. 10, 1945); danced in *Romeo and Juliet, Bluebeard, Tricorne, Giselle,* and *Coppelia.* He danced in *Interplay,* premiered in Billy Rose's *Concert Varieties* (Ziegfeld, June 1, 1945). He was scenarist and choreographer for *On Stage,* in which he also danced the role of Handyman (Boston Opera House, world premiere Oct. 4, 1945).

He choreographed and directed musical numbers for *Finian's Rainbow* (46 St. Th., N.Y.C., Jan. 10, 1947; Palace, London, Oct. 21, 1947); staged the dances and musical numbers for *Hold It!* (National, N.Y.C., May 5, 1948); choreographed *Love Life* (46 St. Th., Oct. 7, 1948); and *Arms and the Girl* (46 St. Th., Feb. 2, 1950); staged dances and musical numbers for *Guys and Dolls* (46 St. Th., N.Y.C., Nov. 24, 1950; Coliseum, London, May 28, 1953); and *Can-Can* (Shubert, N.Y.C., May 7, 1953).

With Norman Panama and Melvin Frank, he produced, directed, and choreographed *Li'l Abner* (St. James, Nov. 15, 1956); directed and choreographed *Destry Rides Again* (Imperial, Apr. 23, 1959); produced, with N. Richard Nash, and directed and choreographed *Wildcat* (Alvin, Dec. 16, 1960); was director and choreographer for *Subways Are for Sleeping* (St. James, Dec. 27, 1961); choreographed and staged the musical numbers of *Here's Love* (Shubert, Oct. 3, 1963); was associate director and choreographed *Wonderworld* (NY World's Fair, May 1964); co-produced, choreographed and directed *Ben Franklin in Paris* (Lunt-Fontanne, Oct. 27, 1964); staged the dances and musical numbers for *Skyscraper* (Lunt-Fontanne, Nov. 13, 1965); *Holly Golightly* (opened Forrest Th., Philadelphia, Oct. 10, 1966) which closed (Majestic, N.Y.C., Dec. 14, 1966) during previews under the title *Breakfast At Tiffany's;* and directed and choreographed *The Rothschilds* (Lunt-Fontanne, Oct. 19, 1970).

Films. Mr. Kidd choreographed *Where's Charley?* (WB, 1952); *The Band Wagon* (MGM, 1953); *Knock on Wood* (Par., 1954); *Seven Brides for Seven Brothers* (MGM, 1954); *Guys and Dolls* (MGM, 1955); danced in *It's Always Fair Weather* (MGM, 1955); directed *Merry Andrew* (MGM, 1958; *Star* (20th-Fox, 1969); and *Hello, Dolly* (20th-Fox, 1969).

Awards. Mr. Kidd received the Antoinette Perry (Tony) Awards for the choreography of *Finian's Rainbow* (1947); *Guys and Dolls* (1951); *Can-Can* (1954); *Li'l Abner* (1957); and *Destry Rides Again* (1959).

Recreation. Photography, operating a ski lodge, and house remodeling.

KILEY, RICHARD. Actor, singer. b. Richard Paul Kiley, Mar. 31, 1922, Chicago, Ill., to Leo J. and Leonore (McKenna) Kiley. Father, railroad statistician. Grad. Mt. Carmel H.S., Chicago, 1939; attended Loyola Univ., 1939–40. Married 1948 to Mary Bell Wood (marr. dis. 1967); two sons, four daughters; married 1968 to Patricia Ferrier. Served US Navy, 1943–46. Member of AEA; AFTRA; SAG; The Players. Address: (home) Warwick, NY 10990; (bus.) c/o Stephen Draper, 37 W. 57th St., New York, NY 10019, tel. (212) HA 1-5780.

Theatre. Mr. Kiley made his debut in stock at Michiana Shores, Mich. (Summer 1946); subsequently played in stock at the Pocono Playhouse (Mountainhome, Pa.), Norwich, Conn., and Princeton, N.J. (Summers, 1948, 1950); understudied and then succeeded Anthony Quinn as Stanley Kowalski in the national tour of *A Street Car Named Desire* (1948–50); and played Joe Rose in a pre-Bway tryout of *A Month of Sundays* (opened Shubert, Boston, Mass., Dec. 25, 1951; closed Forrest, Philadelphia, Pa., Jan. 26, 1952).

He made his N.Y.C. debut as Joey Percival in *Misalliance* (NY City Ctr., Feb. 18, 1953; moved to Ethel Barrymore Th., Mar. 6, 1953); subsequently played the Caliph in *Kismet* (Ziegfeld, Dec. 3, 1953); Ben Collinger in *Sing Me No Lullaby* (Phoenix, Oct. 14, 1954); Major Harry Cargill in *Time Limit!* (Booth, Jan. 24, 1956); James Tyrone in *A Moon for the Misbegotten* (Spoleto, Italy, June 1958); Tom Baxter in *Redhead* (46 St. Th., Feb. 5, 1959), in which he later toured (opened Shubert, Chicago, Mar. 23, 1960); Brig Anderson in *Advise and Consent* (Cort, Nov. 17, 1961); David Jordan in *No Strings* (54 St. Th., Mar. 15, 1962); Stan in *I Had a Ball* (Martin Beck Th., Dec. 15, 1964); Don Quixote and Cervantes in *Man of La Mancha* (ANTA Th., Nov. 22, 1965; Ahmanson Th., Los Angeles, Apr. 12, 1967; Piccadilly Th., London, June 10, 1969; and Vivian Beaumont Th., N.Y.C., June 22, 1972); Julius Caesar in *Her First Roman* (Lunt-Fontanne Th., Oct. 20, 1968); Enoch Soames and A. V. Laider in *The Incomparable Max* (Royale, Oct. 19, 1971); Robert in *Voices* (Ethel Barrymore Th., Apr. 3, 1972); and Miguel de Cervantes in *Cervantes* (on tour, Sept. 6, 1973–Dec. 11, 1973).

Films. Mr. Kiley has appeared in *The Mob* (Col., 1950); *The Sniper* (Col., 1951); *Eight Iron Men* (Col., 1952); *Pickup on South Street* (20th-Fox, 1954); *Phoenix City Story* (Allied, 1955); *Blackboard Jungle* (MGM, 1955); *Spanish Affair* (Par., 1958); *Pendulum* (Col., 1969); and *The Little Prince* (Par., 1974).

Television. Mr. Kiley has appeared on Playhouse 90 (CBS); US Steel Hour (ABC); Philco Television Playhouse (NBC); Studio One (CBS); Kraft Television Th. (NBC); *All the Way Home* (Hallmark Hall of Fame, NBC, 1971); *Murder Once Removed* (U); Mod Squad (ABC); Gunsmoke (CBS); Columbo (NBC); Cannon (CBS); *The 34th Star* (CBS); Night Gallery; and others.

Discography. Mr. Kiley has been on original cast recordings of *Man of La Mancha; No Strings; Redhead; Kismet;* and *I Had a Ball.* His other recordings include *Tall Tom Jefferson; Legend of the Twelve Moons* (Golden); *Greek Myths* (Spoken Arts); *The Happy Prince* (MGM); *Jungle Book* (MGM); and *Curtain Going Up* (MGM).

Awards. He received the *Theatre World* Award (1953) for his performance as Joey Percival in *Misalliance;* and for his performance as Tom Baxter in *Redhead,* he received the Antoinette Perry (Tony) Award (1960). He received the Tony, Drama League, and NY Critics Circle awards for his performance as Don Quixote in *Man of La Mancha* (1966).

Recreation. Carpentry, writing, jogging.

KILFOIL, THOMAS F. Curator-librarian. b. Thomas Kilfoil, Oct. 28, 1922, Hartford, Conn., to Thomas Clement and Anna (Doyle) Kilfoil. Father, printing executive. Grad. New Britain (Conn.) H.S., 1940; Holy Cross Coll., A.B. 1944; Columbia Univ., M.L.S. 1967. Served USN, 1942–46; rank, Lt. (j.g.). Member of Theatre Library Assn. Address: (home) 107 Buena Vista Rd., West Hartford, CT 06107, tel. (203) 521-9450; (bus.) West Hartford Public Library, 20 S. Main St., West Hartford, CT 06107, tel. (203) 236-4561.

Mr. Kilfoil was a teacher of play production at Fordham Univ. School of Education (1948); an instructor in English and speech at St. Peter's Coll., where he was also faculty adviser to the radio club (1955–60); librarian of Columbia Univ.'s collections of theatre and speech recordings (1960–68); acting curator of the Brander Matthews Dramatic Museum at Columbia Univ. (1963–68); assistant reference librarian (1968–69), head of circulation (1969–74), and head of reference (1974–to date) at the West Hartford (Conn.) Public Library.

KILIAN, VICTOR. Actor. b. Victor Arthur Kilian, March 6, 1891, Jersey City, N.J., to Henry and Josephine (Sauer) Kilian. Father, laundry owner. Attend. P.S. 8, Jersey City, N.J. Married Oct. 12, 1915, to Daisy Johnson (dec. Nov. 12, 1961); one son, Victor Kilian, Jr., television script writer. Member of AEA, (council, 1932–35; West Coast adv. bd., 1949–51); AFTRA; SAG.

Pre-Theatre. Longshoreman, brickmaker, ditchdigger.

Theatre. Mr. Kilian made his debut with a small repertory company in New England and Canada (1908); subsequently played in the touring company of *The Red Widow* (1912); made his Bway debut, succeeding (Jan. 12, 1925) Perry Ivins as Peter Cabot in *Desire Under the Elms* (Greenwich Village Th., Dec. 11, 1924; moved Earl Carroll Th., Jan. 12, 1925), and on tour for more than a year.

He appeared as Ben in *Beyond the Horizon* (Mansfield, N.Y.C., Nov. 30, 1926); Hasting in *Triple Crossed* (Morosco, May 5, 1927); Blake in *Nightstick* (Selwyn, Nov. 10, 1927); a Pirate in *The Black Crook* (Lyric, Hoboken, N.J., 1929); with the Bulgakov Associates, played Shamraev in *The Seagull* (Waldorf, N.Y.C., Apr. 9, 1929), and Bubnov in *At the Bottom* (Waldorf, Jan. 9, 1930); played Officer Hayes in *Hobo* (Morosco, Feb. 25, 1930); Second Questioner in *The One Man* (Oct. 21, 1930); a Songwriting Electrician in the pre-Bway tryout of *Once in a Lifetime* (1930); appeared as O'Keefe in *Cloudy with Showers* (Sept. 1, 1931); Klenitsch in *Collision* (Gaiety, Feb. 16, 1932); and succeeded Frank Craven as Detective Captain McKinley in *Riddle Me This* (John Golden Th., Feb. 25, 1932).

He made his London debut in *She Loves Me Not* (Adelphia, May 1, 1934); appeared as Otto Strumkopf in *Broomsticks, Amen!* (Little, N.Y.C., Feb. 1934); Hersch Kowritz in *The Bride of Torozko* (Henry Miller's Th., Sept. 13, 1934); Alcock in *Valley Forge* (Th. Guild, Dec. 10, 1934); Ben in *Solitaire* (Plymouth, Feb. 27, 1942); played Dr. Macquire and understudied Hugh Griffith as W. O. Gant, which he played for eight weeks, in *Look Homeward, Angel* (Ethel Barrymore Th., Mar. 28, 1957); portrayed Judge Corriglione in *The Gang's All Here* (Ambassador, Oct. 1, 1959); joined the cast of *All the Way Home* (Belasco, Nov. 30, 1960); played Abimelech in *Gideon* (Plymouth, Nov. 9, 1961), and succeeded Eric Berry as Shillem in the same play; and played Mr. Fineman in the pre-Bway tour of *What Makes Sammy Run?* (Philadelphia, Pa., 1964).

Films. Mr. Kilian appeared in *Ramona* (20th-Fox, 1936); *Seventh Heaven* (20th-Fox, 1937); *Only Angels Have Wings* (Col., 1939); *The Adventures of Huckleberry Finn* (MGM, 1939); *Dr. Cyclops* (Par., 1940); *Young Tom Edison* (MGM, 1940); *Reap the Wild Wind* (Par., 1942); *Johnny Come Lately* (UA, 1943); *Belle of the Yukon* (RKO, 1944); *Dangerous Passage* (Par., 1944); *Behind City Lights* (Rep., 1945); *Spellbound* (UA, 1945); *The Spanish Main* (RKO, 1945); *Smoky* (20th-Fox, 1946); *Gentleman's Agreement* (20th-Fox, 1947); *No Way Out* (20th-Fox, 1950); *The Flame and the Arrow* (WB, 1950); *Tall Target* (MGM, 1951); and *Unknown World* (Lippert, 1951).

KILTY, JEROME. Playwright, actor, director, producer. b. June 24, 1922, Pala Indian Reservation, Calif., to Harold and Irene (Zellinger) Kilty. Father, Indian agent. Grad. Lowell H.S., San Francisco, Calif., 1941; attended Guildhall Sch. of Drama, London, 1945–46; grad. Harvard Univ. B.A. 1949. Married to Cavada Humphrey, actress. Served WW II, USAAF, ETO; rank Capt.; received DFC, Air Medal with five clusters. Member of AEA; SWG; Society of Authors (Italy and France); AFTRA; Dramatists Guild; SSD&C; The Players; Signet Soc. (Harvard). Address: 7 W. 16th St., New York, NY 10011, tel. (212) AL 5-3822.

Theatre. Mr. Kilty was co-founder (1948) of the Brattle Th. (Cambridge, Mass.), where he served as director, producer, and actor (1948–52).

Since his N.Y.C. debut as Coupler in *The Relapse* (Morosco, Nov. 22, 1950), he has appeared as the King of France in *Love's Labour's Lost* (NY City Ctr., Feb. 4, 1953); Gunner in *Misalliance* (Ethel Barrymore Th., Mar. 6, 1963); Barrister in *A Pin to See the Peepshow* (Playhouse, Sept. 17, 1953); the Man in the Window in *Frogs of Spring* (Broadhurst, Oct. 20, 1953); and Rev. Spelvin in *Quadrille* (Coronet, Nov. 3, 1954).

From 1955–60, he was artistic director, director, and actor with the Group 20 Players (Wellesley, Mass.); with this company (NY City Ctr.), played Iago in *Othello* (Sept. 7, 1955); and Falstaff in *Henry IV, Part 1,* which he also directed (Sept. 21, 1955). He toured as Harry Kaye in *Will Success Spoil Rock Hunter?* (1955–56); appeared as Benedict in *Much Ado About Nothing* (Studebaker, Chicago, Ill., Jan. 20, 1957); and as the Actor in *The Guardsman,* which he also directed (Studebaker, Mar. 16, 1957).

He wrote *Dear Liar,* an adaptation for the stage, of the letters of Bernard Shaw and Mrs. Patrick Campbell; directed the N.Y.C. production of the latter, with Katherine Cornell and Briane Aherne (Billy Rose Th., Mar. 17, 1960), and the London production, in which he appeared with his wife, Cavada Humphrey (Criterion, June 14, 1960); with Elizabeth Bergner and O. E. Hasse, directed *Dear Liar* (Renaissance, Berlin, Germany, Oct. 1, 1960), and with Maria Casares and Pierre Brasseur (Athénée, Paris, Oct. 6, 1961).

He directed *Les Violons, Parfois* (Gymnase, Jan. 1962); appeared with his wife in *Dear Liar* (Th. Marquee, N.Y.C., Mar. 17, 1962); wrote *Ides of March,* which he directed (world premiere, Renaissance, Berlin, Germany, Nov. 10, 1962); directed *Dear Liar* (Quirino, Rome, Italy, Dec. 20, 1962); staged, with Elizabeth Bergner and O. E. Hasse, a German-language production of *Dear Liar* (Barbizon-Plaza, N.Y.C., May 3, 1963); staged an English-language production of his *Ides of March* (Haymarket, London, premiere, Aug. 8, 1963); toured South Africa as George in *Who's Afraid of Virginia Woolf?,* and repeated this role in matinee performances in London (Piccadilly, Feb. 6, 1964); and for the Boston (Mass.) Arts Festival, directed *St. Joan* (June 16, 1964), *Man and Superman* (June 23, 1964), and the *Ides of March* (American premiere, July 5, 1964).

Mr. Kilty directed the Italian productions of *O What a Lovely War* (Quirino, Rome, Italy, Dec. 20, 1964); wrote sketches for the revue *Nymphs and Satires* (Apollo, London, England, May 10, 1965); played the title role in *Dylan* (Goodman Memorial Th., Chicago, Ill., Feb. 18, 1966); appeared in the title role of *Falstaff* (American Shakespeare Festival, Stratford, Conn., June 18, 1966); played the Marquis de Sade in *Marat/Sade* (Goodman Memorial Th., Chicago, Ill., Oct. 21, 1966); and directed *Dear Liar* and *Man and Superman* (both American Conservatory Th., San Francisco, Calif., 1966).

He appeared in the title role of *Tartuffe* (Goodman Memorial Th., Chicago, Ill., Dec. 21, 1966); played Bernard Shaw in *Dear Liar,* which he again directed (American Conservatory Th., San Francisco, Nov. 3, 1967; Alley Th., Houston, Tex.); directed *Thieves' Carnival* (American Conservatory Th., San Francisco, Dec. 3, 1967); wrote and directed *Don't Shoot Mable, It's Your Husband* (world premiere, American Conservatory Th., Feb. 7, 1968); directed *Antigone* (American Shakespeare Festival, Stratford, Conn., June 18, 1967); and appeared as Sergeant Kite in *The Recruiting Officer* (Goodman Memorial Th., Chicago, Ill., 1968).

He wrote and directed *Long Live Life* (American Conservatory Th., 1968); directed a N.Y.C. production of *Don't Shoot Mable, It's Your Husband* (Bouwerie Lane Th., 1968); directed *Possibilities* (Players Th., N.Y.C., 1968); appeared as Sir Anthony Absolute in *The Rivals* (Yale Repertory Th., New Haven, Conn., Oct. 16, 1969); directed *Lascio Alle Miei Donne* (*I Leave to My Women*) (Morelli Stoppa Co., Milan, Italy, 1969); appeared as Robert Browning in *Dear Love* (Wellesley Coll., Mass., Nov. 7, 1969), which he also wrote, and made a national tour with the production (1970–71). He directed *Tartuffe* (Southwestern Theatre Festival, Normal, Okla., 1970); *A Midsummer Night's Dream* (Univ. of Texas, Austin, 1972); wrote *The Little Black Book* (adapted from Jean-Claude Carrière's *L'Aide Mémoire*) (Helen Hayes Th., N.Y.C., Apr. 25, 1972); directed *The Taming of the Shrew* (Kansas Shakespeare Festival, Lawrence, Kans., 1973); wrote *Look Away* (Playhouse Th., N.Y.C., Jan. 7, 1973); rewrote *Dear Love* for London (Comedy Th., May 15, 1973); and wrote *The Laffing Man* (1973).

Other Activities. In 1972, Mr. Kilty taught at the Univ. of Texas, Austin, and in 1974 he held the O'Conner Chair of Literature (Drama) at Colgate Univ.

Awards. For his play, *Dear Liar,* he received the Berlin (Germany) Festival Critics Award (1961), the Vienna (Austria) Critics Award (1962), the Baton du Brigadier (Paris, France, 1961–62), the Paume d'or (Bologna, Italy, 1962–63), and the Stanislavsky Cententerary Medal, (Moscow, USSR, Jan. 17, 1963).

His production of *Henry IV, Part 1* (NY City Ctr., Oct. 7, 1955) resulted in the Brattle Th. Co. being given the Stratford (Conn.) Shakespeare Award.

KIM, WILLA. Costume designer. b. Los Angeles, Calif. Studied at Chouinard Institute of Art. Married Raoul Pene du Bois, designer.

Theatre. Miss Kim designed the costumes for *Red Eye of Love* (Provincetown Playhouse, N.Y.C., June 12, 1961); *Fortuna* (Maidman, Jan. 3, 1962); the ballet, *Birds of Sorrow* (May 5, 1962); *The Saving Grace* (Writers' Stage Th., Apr. 19, 1963); the ballet *Gamelan* (premiere, Leningrad, USSR, Oct. 25, 1963; US premiere, Sept. 9, 1965); *Have I Got a Girl for You!* (Music Box, N.Y.C., Dec. 2, 1963); *Funnyhouse of a Negro* (East End Th., Jan. 14, 1964); *Dynamite Tonight* (York Playhouse, Mar. 15, 1964); the NY Shakespeare Festival's Mobile Th. production of *A Midsummer Nights's Dream* (June 29, 1964); *The Old Glory* (Amer. Place Th. at St. Clement's, Nov. 1, 1964); *Helen* (Bouwerie Lane Th., Dec. 10, 1964); a double-bill of plays by Arthur Kopit (Players Th., Mar. 15, 1965) that included *The Day the Whores Came Out To Play Tennis,* and *Sing to Me Through Open Windows; Game of Noah,* a ballet (The Netherlands, June 1, 1965); US premiere, Aug. 12, 1965); *The Stag King* (US premiere, Santa Fe, N.M., Opera Co., Aug. 6, 1965); *Malcolm* (Sam S. Shubert Th., N.Y.C., Jan. 11, 1966); *The Office* (Henry Miller's Th., closed in previews, Apr. 30, 1966); and, with Howard Bay, designed the costumes for the pre-Bway tryout of *Chu Chem* (Locust, Philadelphia, Nov. 15, 1966; closed there Nov. 19, 1966).

She was the costume designer for *Hail Scrawdyke!* (Booth, N.Y.C., Nov. 28, 1966); *Scuba Duba* (The New, Oct. 10, 1967); *The Ceremony of Innocence* (Amer. Place Th. at St. Clement's, Dec. 14, 1967); *Papp* (Amer. Place Th. at St. Clement's, May 5, 1969); *Promenade* (Promenade Th., June 4, 1969); *Operation Sidewinder* (Vivian Beaumont Th., Mar. 12, 1970); *Sunday Dinner* (Amer. Place Th. at St. Clement's, Oct. 16, 1970); *The Screens* (Chelsea Th. Ctr. of Brooklyn, Nov. 30, 1971); *Sleep* (American Place Th., Feb. 22, 1972); *Lysistrata* (Brooks Atkinson Th., N.Y.C., Nov. 13, 1972); *Jumpers* (Premiere, Kennedy Center, Washington, D.C., Feb 18, 1974; and Billy Rose Th., N.Y.C., Apr. 22, 1974); and *Goodtime Charley* (Palace, Mar. 3, 1975).

Miss Kim has also designed the costumes for the operas *The Magic Flute, Le Rossignol,* and *Help, Help, the Globolinks.* .

Television. For the Esso Repertory Theatre (NET), she designed the costumes for *St. Patrick's Day* (Nov. 24, 1964); *The Forced Marriage* (Jan. 8, 1965); and *The Beautiful People* (Jan. 28, 1965).

Awards. Miss Kim received the Off-Bway (Obie) Award (1964–65) for her contribution to *The Old Glory;* the Drama Desk Award (1969–70) for *Promenade* and *Operation Sidewinder;* and the Joseph Maharam Foundation Award (June 12, 1972), Drama Desk, and *Variety* NY Drama Critics Poll awards 1971–72) for *The Screens.*

KIMBROUGH, CLINTON. Actor. b. Feb. 14, 1936, Sandusky, Ohio, to Alfred Kent and Lucille Kimbrough. Father, businessman. Attended high schools throughout the US; studied acting at AADA, 1957; and with Lee Strasberg at The Actors Studio (N.Y.C. mbr., 1957–to date). Served US Army, 1954–56; Korea, eighteen months; rank, Cpl. Member of AEA; SAG; AFTRA.

Pre-Theatre. Summers: oil-field roughneck (N.D.); irrigation worker on cotton farm (Calif.).

Theatre. Mr. Kimbrough first performed as a professional in stock, playing the Waco Kid in *Saddle Tramps* (Cecil Woods Th., Fishkill, N.Y., Aug. 1957); subsequently appeared as George Gibbs in *Our Town* (Circle in the Square Th., N.Y.C., Mar. 23, 1959); Kilroy in *Camino Real* (St. Marks Playhouse, May 16, 1960); and as Dwight Taylor in the pre-Bway tryout of *Laurette* (opened Shubert, New Haven, Conn., Sept. 26, 1960; closed Forrest, Philadelphia, Pa., Oct. 1, 1960).

He made his Bway debut as Wain in *Look: We've Come Through!* (Hudson, Oct. 25, 1961); performed in *The Zoo Story* and *Time Remembered* (Peninsula Players, Fishcreek, Wis., Summer 1963); and with the Repertory Th. of Lincoln Ctr. (ANTA Washington Sq.) he appeared in *After the Fall* (Jan. 23, 1964); was Willard Prosper in *But for Whom Charlie* (Mar. 12, 1964); Pedro in *The Changeling* (Oct. 29, 1964); and Hoffman in *Incident at Vichy* (Dec. 3, 1964). He appeared with the Milwaukee (Wis.) Repertory Th. in *Saint Joan* (Oct. 28, 1965); *The Diary of a Scoundrel* (Nov. 18, 1965); *Mother Courage* (Jan. 13, 1966); and *Henry IV, Part 1* (Feb. 24, 1966); and was in *Marat/Sade* (Theatre Co. of Boston, Mass., Oct. 20, 1966); and *The Adventures of Jack and Max* (Actors Studio, Schoenberg Hall, Univ. of California, Los Angeles, 1967).

Films. Mr. Kimbrough appeared as Billy in *Hot Spell* (Par., 1958).

Television. He played Eugene in *Weston Strain* (Studio One, CBS, 1958); George Gibbs in *Our Town* (DuPont Show-of-the-Month, NBC, 1959); in *Last Dance* (GE Th., CBS, Nov. 1959); *Appointment at Eleven* (Alfred Hitchcock Presents, CBS, Dec. 1959); and in *A Special Summer* (US Steel Hour, CBS, Jan. 1960).

Recreation. Football, horses.

KING, EDITH. Actress. b. Edith N. Keck, White Haven, Pa., to John A. and Margaret Keck. Father, contractor. Attended East Orange (N.J.) H.S. Member of AEA (council, 1951–54); AFTRA; SAG. Address: 3140 Avenue A, Riviera Beach, FL 33404.

Theatre. Miss King first appeared on the stage as a Novice in *Marie-Odile* (Belasco, Washington, D.C., 1914); was understudy for *The Boomerang* (Belasco, N.Y.C., Aug. 10, 1915); played Lady Airdale in *The Great Pursuit* (Shubert, Mar. 22, 1916); Esther in *The Pipes of Pan* (Hudson, Nov. 6, 1917); and joined the company of *Blind Youth* (Republic, Dec. 3, 1917).

She appeared as Bobette in *Daddies* (Belasco, Sept. 5, 1918); Leila Archibald in *Bab* (Park, Oct. 18, 1920); Diane in *Thank You* (Longacre, Oct. 3, 1921); played in a season of stock (Lyric, Atlanta, Ga., 1924); portrayed June Lawler in *A Good Bad Woman* (Comedy, N.Y.C., Feb. 9, 1925); Belinda Perkins in *The Right to Love* (Wallack's, June 8, 1925); played in a season of stock with the Jessie

Bonstelle Co. (Detroit, Mich., 1926); appeared in stock (Portland, Me.; Columbus, Ohio; 1927–31); played Audrey in *White Flame*(Vanderbilt, N.Y.C., Nov. 4, 1929); Daisy Appleton in *Going Gay* (Morosco, Aug. 3, 1933); Leda in *Cross Ruff* (Masque, Feb. 19, 1935); on tour succeeded Helen Wesley in the roles of Curtis and the Widow and was understudy in *The Taming of the Shrew* (Guild, N.Y.C., Sept. 30, 1935).

Miss King played Amelia in *Halloween* (Vanderbilt, Feb. 20, 1936); succeeded (May 1936) Ethel Intropodi in the role of Julie Compton in *One Good Year*(Lyceum, Nov. 27, 1935); appeared in a season of stock at the St. Louis (Mo.) Municipal Opera (Summer, 1936); played Mrs. Thorne in *Frederika* (Imperial, N.Y.C., Feb. 4, 1937); with the Lunts, played Leda in *Amphitryon 38* (Shubert, Nov. 1, 1937), repeating the role in London (Lyric, May 17, 1938), Pauline in *The Seagull* (Shubert, N.Y.C., Mar. 28, 1938), and toured with them for two seasons, appearing in *Idiot's Delight*, as Pauline in *The Seagull*, and as The Widow in *Taming of the Shrew*, which played a one-week engagement in N.Y.C. (Alvin, Feb. 5, 1940). She played Margaret Eaves in *The Burning Deck* (Maxine Elliott's Th., Mar. 1, 1940); Mary Tibbs in *Popsy* (Playhouse, Feb. 10, 1941); Bertha Barnes in *Hope for a Harvest* (Guild, Nov. 26, 1941); the Godmother and Dr. Bodie in *A Kiss for Cinderella*(Music Box, Mar. 10, 1942); alternated with Margaret Webster as Bianca and Emilia in *Othello* (Shubert, Oct. 19, 1943), later (Mar. 1944) taking over the role of Emilia; played Madame Jourdain in *The Would-Be Gentleman* (Booth, Jan. 9, 1946); and succeeded Evelyn Varden as Lucy Allerton in *Dream Girl* (Coronet, Dec. 14, 1945).

She appeared as The Mother in *Eurydice* (Actor Th., Hollywood, 1946); in a production of *The Primrose Path*(Summer 1947); *The Glass Menagerie*(Summer 1947); repeated her role as The Mother in *Eurydice* (Coronet, Los Angeles, Oct. 1948); appeared in *Naughty Marietta* Los Angeles; San Francisco, 1948); played Mama in *The Guardsman* (Erlanger, Buffalo, N.Y., Jan. 1951); played the Mother in *Legend of Lovers*(Plymouth, N.Y.C., Dec. 26, 1951); Eugenie in *Ondine* (46 St. Th., Feb. 18, 1954); Mrs. Mackenzie in *Affair of Honor* (Ethel Barrymore Th., Apr. 6, 1956); Prudence in *First Night*(Sea Cliff, N.Y., Aug. 1956); Mrs. Ling in *Miss Isobel* (Royale, N.Y.C., Dec. 26, 1957); Charlotte Peloux in *Cheri*(Morosco, Oct. 12, 1959); Mrs. Sophie Bellop in *Saratoga* (Winter Garden, Dec. 7, 1959); Countess Emily O'Brien in *Wildcat* (Alvin, Dec. 16, 1960), repeating the role in a touring summer theatre production (1963); Madame Maille in *A Murderer Among Us* (Morosco, N.Y.C., Mar. 25, 1964); and appeared as The Mother in a tour of *Bachelor's Wife* (Summer 1964).

Films. Miss King has played in *Calcutta* (Par., 1947); *Blaze of Noon* (Par., 1947); *Belle Starr's Daughter*(20th-Fox, 1948); and *Gallant Blade* (Col., 1948).

Television. She has appeared in *Man and Superman*(Hallmark Hall of Fame, NBC, Nov. 25, 1956); in *Dodsworth* (Producer's Showcase, NBC, 1956); frequently on the Phil Silvers ("Sgt. Bilko") Show (CBS); as Maura in *The Guardsman* (Best of Broadway, CBS, Mar. 2, 1955); Mrs. Danvers in *Rebecca* (Robert Montgomery Presents, NBC); in *Who's Earnest*(Th. Guild, CBS); *Cyrano de Bergerac; The Easter Angel* (ABC, Apr. 10, 1966); and on Kraft Th. (NBC); Martin Kane (NBC); The Web (CBS); Studio One (CBS); Mama (CBS); Westinghouse Presents (CBS); Ellery Queen (NBC); and Doctors/Nurses (CBS).

KINGSLEY, SIDNEY.

Playwright, director, producer. b. Oct. 22, 1906, New York City. Grad. Townsend Harris Hall H.S., N.Y.C., 1924; Cornell Univ., B.A. 1928. Married July 1939 to Madge Evans, actress. Served US Army, 1939–43; rank Lt. Member of Dramatists Guild (former vice-pres., pres. emeritus); board of directors, Cafe La Mama. Address: (home) 79 Glengray Rd., Oakland, NJ 07436; (bus.) 108 Fifth Ave., New York, NY 10011.

Theatre. Mr. Kingsley first wrote *Men in White* (Broadhurst Th., N.Y.C., Sept. 26, 1933), which he directed in London (Lyric, June 28, 1934); directed his own play, *Dead End* (Belasco, N.Y.C., Oct. 28, 1935); produced and directed his plays *Ten Million Ghosts*(St. James, Oct. 23, 1936) and *The World We Make* (Guild, Nov. 20, 1939); wrote *The Patriots* (Natl., Jan. 29, 1943); and staged his own plays, *Detective Story*(Hudson, Mar. 23, 1949), *Darkness at Noon*(Alvin, Jan. 13, 1951), and *Lunatics and Lovers* (Broadhurst, Dec. 13, 1954); and, in association with Mr. Kirshner, produced and directed his own play, *Night Life* (Brooks Atkinson Th., Oct. 23, 1962).

Films. The following plays by Mr. Kingsley have been made into films: *Men in White*(MGM, 1934); *Dead End* (UA, 1937); and *Detective Story* (Par., 1951). In addition, he wrote the original story for *Homecoming* (MGM, 1946).

Awards. Mr. Kingsley received the Pulitzer Prize and the Theatre Club Award for his play, *Men in White*(1934); and the Theatre Club Award for *Dead End*(1936). For *The Patriots*(1943), he received the Drama Critics Circle Award, the Newspaper Guild Front Page Award and the Theatre Club Award. He received the Edgar Allen Poe Award for *Detective Story* (1949); and the NY Drama Critics Circle Award and Donaldson Award for *Darkness at Noon* (1951). He was awarded the Medal of Merit from the American Academy of Arts and Letters (1951); and a special citation from the Newspaper Guild.

KINOY, ERNEST.

Playwright.

Theatre. Mr. Kinoy wrote the book (based upon stories by James Mitchell) for *Bajour* (Shubert, N.Y.C., Nov. 23, 1964); and the book for *Golden Rainbow* (Shubert, Feb. 4, 1968).

Television. He wrote the pilot for a series, *Rx for the Defense* (ABC, 1973).

KIPNESS, JOSEPH.

Producer.

Theatre. Mr. Kipness produced, with Philip Waxman, *Star Spangled Family* (Biltmore, N.Y.C., Apr. 10, 1945); with Max Liebman, the pre-Bway tryout of *Shootin' Star* (opened Shubert, New Haven, Conn., Apr. 4, 1946; closed Shubert, Boston, Mass., Apr. 27, 1946); presented, with Monte Proser, *High Button Shoes* (Century, Oct. 9, 1947); produced, with John Pransky and Al Beckman, *That's the Ticket* (opened Shubert, Philadelphia, Pa., Sept. 24, 1948; closed there Oct. 2, 1948); presented, with Jack Hylton, *Women of Twilight*(Plymouth, N.Y.C., Mar. 3, 1952); Messrs. Shubert, by arrangement with Mr. Kipness and Jack Small, produced *Conscience* (Booth, May 15, 1952); Mr. Kipness and Alexander H. Cohen, in association with Morris K. Bauer, presented *Be Your Age* (48 St. Th., Jan. 14, 1953); Mr. Kipness presented, with David Merrick, the Jack Hylton production of *La plume de ma tante* (Royale, Nov. 11, 1958); and produced, with Richard W. Krakeur, in association with David Kaufman, *Have I Got a Girl for You!* (Music Box, Dec. 2, 1963).

Mr. Kipness produced the musical *I Had a Ball* (Martin Beck Th., N.Y.C., Dec. 15, 1964); with Arthur Lesser, produced *La Grosse Valise* (54 St. Th., Dec. 14, 1965); with Gerard Oestreicher and Harold Leventhal, produced *But, Seriously . .* . (Henry Miller's Th., Feb. 27, 1969); produced *Applause* (Palace, Mar. 30, 1970); *Father's Day* (John Golden Th., Mar. 16, 1971); *Inner City*(Ethel Barrymore Th., Dec. 19, 1971); *See Saw* (Uris, Mar. 18, 1973); and *No Hard Feelings*(Martin Beck Th., Apr. 8, 1973).

KIRBY, MICHAEL.

Educator, editor. Mr. Kirby is chairman (1971–to date) of the Graduate Drama Dept. of City College of New York; having previously served there as assistant professor in the Speech and Theatre Dept.

He is editor (1971–to date) and a frequent contributor to *The Drama Review*, published under the aegis of C.C.N.Y.

Published Works. Mr. Kirby is the author of *Happenings*, an illustrated anthology (Dutton, 1965).

KIRK, LISA.

Singer, actress. b. Elsie Marie Kirk, Feb. 25, 1926, Brownsville, Pa., to George and Elsie (Furlong) Kirk. Grad. Charleroi H.S., Roscoe, Pa., 1943. Married Apr. 17, 1949, to Robert Wells, lyricist, composer, writer. Address: c/o Heller Agency, 9220 Sunset Blvd., Los Angeles, CA 90069.

Theatre. Miss Kirk made her professional debut at the Pittsburgh (Pa.) Playhouse; in N.Y.C., subsequently appeared as a showgirl at the Folies Bergère and the Versailles night clubs; made her Bway debut as Vickie in *Good Night, Ladies* (Royale, Jan. 17, 1945); appeared in *Are You with It* (New Century, Nov. 10, 1945); and *Windy City* (Chicago, 1946); played Emily in *Allegro* (Majestic, N.Y.C., Oct. 10, 1947); Lois Lane in *Kiss Me, Kate* (New Century, Dec. 30, 1948); replaced Janis Paige (May 26, 1964) as Doris Walker in *Here's Love* (Sam S. Shubert Th., Oct. 3, 1963); appeared in *Riverwind*(Paramus, N.J., Playhouse, Summer 1966); and played Lottie Ames in *Mack and Mabel*(Majestic, N.Y.C., Oct. 6, 1974).

Television and Radio. At age fifteen, Miss Kirk had her own song show on KQV (Pittsburgh); and was frequently heard on WINS (N.Y.C.) in the late 1940s.

Her television appearances include The Ed Sullivan Show (CBS); The Dinah Shore Show (NBC); GE Th. (CBS); Studio One (CBS); *Tales from Shubert Alley;* A Salute to Cole Porter; A Tribute to Richard Rodgers; A Salute to Rodgers and Hammerstein; A Toast to Jerome Kern; Pontiac Star Parade; Batman; TV House (ABC); Front Row Center (CBS); Stagecoach West (ABC); and Bewitched (ABC).

Night Clubs. Miss Kirk made her night club debut at Le Ruban Bleu (N.Y.C., 1946). Subsequent appearances include The Maisonette of the St. Regis Hotel, and the Persian Room of the Waldorf-Astoria (N.Y.C.); Coconut Grove, and Ciro's (Hollywood); the Fairmont (San Francisco); the Caribe-Hilton (San Juan, Puerto Rico); the Shoreham (Washington, D.C.); the Palmer House (Chicago); the Americana (Miami Beach); the Shamrock (Houston); and the Monteleone (New Orleans).

Discography. Her recordings for RCA-Victor include "Lisa Kirk Sings Jimmy McHugh" (1951); and "Lisa Kirk at the Plaza" (1959).

KIRTLAND, LOUISE.

Actress. b. Louise Isabel Jelly, Aug. 4, 1910, Lynn, Mass., to Thomas Edgar and Hannah (Dukeson) Jelly. Attended Lynn (Mass.) English H.S. Married Dec. 13, 1951, to A. L. Alexander, radio and television producer. Member of AEA; AFTRA; SAG.

Theatre. Miss Kirtland made her stage debut as Miss Curtis in a school production of *The Charm School* (Lynn English H.S., Mass., 1924); and appeared in the John Marsh Stock Co. production of *The Golddiggers* (Lynn, Mass., 1926).

She made her N.Y.C. debut as Gladys Blake in *The Wicked Age*(Daly's Th., Nov. 4, 1927); followed by Peggy in *Night Hostess* (Martin Beck Th., Sept. 12, 1928); and succeeded (Feb. 1929) Marienne Francks as Tavie Ferguson in *That Ferguson Family* (Little, Dec. 22, 1928); played Dorothy Ruth in *Getting Even* (Biltmore, Aug. 19, 1929); Katie Zimmer in *Light Wines and Beer* (Waldorf, Nov. 10, 1930); Olly Frey in *A Church Mouse* (Playhouse, Oct. 12, 1931); Ethel in *Tell Her the Truth* (Cort, Oct. 28, 1932); Ninon Revelle in *Melody* (Casino, Feb. 14, 1933); Peggy Stetson in *Shady Lady* (Shubert, July 5, 1933); Lola Valette in *Her Man of Wax* (Shubert, Oct. 11, 1933); and played Jane McMurray in *The Only Girl* (44 St. Th., May 21, 1934).

She succeeded (June 1934) Olga Baclanova as Sonya Sonya in *Murder at the Vanities*(New Amsterdam Sept. 8, 1933); played Sister Pauline in *Few Are Chosen* (58 St. Th., Sept. 17, 1935); toured in *Pagan Lady* (1936); played Elaine Carley in *Love in My Fashion* (Ritz, N.Y.C., Dec. 3, 1937); toured in *My Maryland* (1938), "Payday Pauline" in *No! No! Nanette!* (1939), Grace Harrington in *Life of the Party* (1940), Beth in *Little Women* (1941); and in *Stage Door* (1943).

She appeared in the revues, *Along Fifth Avenue* (Broadhurst, N.Y.C., Jan. 13, 1949), and *Alive and Kicking* (Winter Garden, Jan. 17, 1950); succeeded (May 1952) Doris Patston as Andrée in *Gigi* (Fulton, Nov. 24, 1951); and toured as Lilly Sears in *Tea and Sympathy* (opened St. James, Asbury Park, N.J., Nov. 5, 1954).

She appeared as Mme. Dupont-Fredaine in *The Waltz of the Toreadors* (Coronet, N.Y.C., Jan. 17, 1957); succeeded (June 1957) Elisabeth Fraser as Alice Pepper in *The Tunnel of Love* (Royale, Feb. 13, 1957); played Birdie in *Winkelberg* (Renata, Jan. 14, 1958); Grace Davis in *Tovarich* (Bway Th., Mar. 18, 1963); Sister Berthe in *The Sound of Music* (State Fair Music Hall, Dallas, June 22, 1964); Aunt Polly in *Tom Sawyer* (Starlight Th., Kansas City, Mo., July 13, 1964); Grace Davis in *Tovarich* (tour, Summer 1964); Mrs. McGlone in *The Unsinkable Molly Brown* (Chastain Amphitheatre, Atlanta, Ga., July 12, 1965); Fanny Willoughby in *Quality Street* (summer stock tryout, Bucks County Playhouse, New Hope, Pa., Aug. 23, 1965); Sue in *Bells are Ringing* (Chastain Amphitheatre, Atlanta, Ga., July 26, 1966); Lily in *Take Me Along* (Paper Mill Playhouse, Millburn, N.J., Nov. 15, 1966); Mrs. Upson in *Mame* (national tour, 1967–68); directed *The Boy Friend* (Ivanhoe Th., Chicago, Ill., Apr. 26, 1968); and appeared as Maude in *Forty Carats* (tour, 1971).

Television. Miss Kirtland has appeared on the Kraft Television Th. (NBC); The Witness (NBC); Armstrong Circle Th. (CBS); The Aldrich Family (NBC); We the People (WOR Mutual); Mr. Peepers (NBC); I Spy (ABC); the Eddie Cantor (CBS), Bob Hope (NBC), Phil Silvers (CBS), and Milton Berle (NBC) shows; Play of the Week (WNTA); the Martha Raye Show (NBC); Your Show of Shows (NBC); and Car 54, Where Are You? (NBC).

KITT, EARTHA. Actress, singer, dancer. b. Eartha Mae Kitt, Jan. 26, 1930, North, S.C., to William and Mamie (Reily) Kitt. Father, farmer. Grad. New York Sch. of Performing Arts (studied drama with Mrs. Edith Banks), 1945. Married June 9, 1960, to William McDonald; one daughter. Member of AGVA; AEA; SAG.

Pre-Theatre. Seamstress.

Theatre. Miss Kitt made her Bway debut in the revue, *Blue Holiday* (Belasco, May 21, 1945); subsequently appeared in *Bal Nègre* (Belasco, Nov. 7, 1946) with which she toured Europe (1947); played Helen of Troy in Orson Welles' production of *Faust* (France, Germany, Belgium, 1951); appeared in *New Faces of 1952* (Royale, N.Y.C., May 16, 1952); as Teddy Hicks in *Mrs. Patterson* (Natl., Dec. 1, 1954); Mehitabel in *Shinbone Alley* (Bway Th., Apr. 13, 1957); and Jolly in *Jolly's Progress* (Longacre, Dec. 5, 1959).

Miss Kitt appeared in *Artists Against Apartheid* (Prince of Wales Th., London, Mar. 22, 1965); played Doris W. in the national touring production of *The Owl and the Pussycat* (opened Shubert Th., New Haven, Conn., Sept. 7, 1965; closed National Th., Washington, D.C., May 21, 1966); and played Miss Grace Daw in *High Bid* (Arnaud Th., Guildford, England, Oct. 1970; and Criterion, London, Dec. 1970).

Films. Miss Kitt made her debut in *New Faces* (20th-Fox, 1954); subsequently appeared in *St. Louis Blues* (Par., 1958); *The Mark of the Hawk* (U, 1958); played the title role in *Anna Lucasta* (UA, 1958); Betty Coleman in *Synanon* (Col., 1965); and was a Singer in *Onkel Tom's Huette (Uncle Tom's Cabin*, Nora, 1965).

Television. Miss Kitt has appeared on the Today Show (NBC, Apr. 28, 1953); All Star Review (NBC, Nov. 28, 1953); Colgate Comedy Hour (NBC, Jan. 3, 1954); Your Show of Shows (NBC, May 29, 1954); Jinx's Diary (NBC, Jan. 6, 1955); in the title role in *Salome* (Omnibus, CBS, Dec. 18, 1955); and as Oparre in *The Wingless Victory* (Play of the Week, WNTA, 1961).

In addition to *The Eartha Kitt Show* (Assoc. TV, London, 1965); and *Eartha Kitt in Australia* (Ind., 1966); she has made numerous appearances on such series as The Les Crane Show (ABC); The Rudy Vallee Show (CBS); The Regis Philbin Show (Ind.); Girl Talk (ABC); The Hy Gardner Show (Ind.); Burke's Law (ABC); Ben Casey (ABC); Memory Lane (Ind.); Juke Box Jury (BBC); The Merv Griffin Show (Ind.); I Spy (NBC); The Mike Douglas Show (Ind.); Hollywood Squares (NBC); Mission: Impossible (CBS); and Dial M For Music (CBS).

Night Clubs. Miss Kitt has appeared at the Karavansarey (Istanbul, Turk., 1951); the Latin Quarter (Boston, Mass., 1955); the Blue Angel, Village Vanguard, and La Vie en Rose (N.Y.C., 1954); Blinstrub's (Boston, 1956); the Latin Quarter and the Empire Room (N.Y.C., 1957); the Persian Room (N.Y.C. 1958–67); the Latin Quarter (Philadelphia, Pa., 1960); the Palmer House (Chicago, Ill., 1962–64); the Americana Hotel (San Juan, P.R., 1965); The Talk of the Town (London, 1965); The Cave (Vancouver, B.C., Canada, 1966); Crown Terrace Room of the Edgewater Inn (Seattle, Wash., 1966); and The Century Plaza (Los Angeles, 1966).

Published Works. Miss Kitt has written her autobiography, *Thursday's Child* (1956).

Discography. Miss Kitt has recorded the original cast album of *New Faces of 1952* (RCA Victor); and has made the solo albums, *Fabulous* (Kapp), *Bad, But Beautiful* (MGM), *That Bad Eartha* (RCA Victor), *Revisited* (Knapp), *Down to Eartha* (RCA Victor), *Eartha Kitt* (RCA Victor), *Somebody Stole the Wedding Bell* (RCA Victor), and *Thursday's Child* (RCA Victor).

Her single recordings include *Santa Baby, I Want to Be Evil, Monotonous* (her specialty from *New Faces of 1952)*, and *C'est Si Bon.*

Awards. For her performance in *Faust* (Paris, 1951), she received the Second Best Acting Award of France. She received the Golden Rose of Montreux for her performance in *Kaskade*, a spectacular on Swedish television (1962); and a NATAS (Emmy) Award nomination for her performance as Angel in *The Loser* (I Spy, NBC, Oct. 20, 1965).

Recreation. Golf, gardening, teaching dancing in spare time, bowling, sauna baths, swimming.

KLAVUN, WALTER. Actor, director. b. Waldemar Joseph Klavun, May 8, 1906, New York City, to Kurt and Johanne (Hoban) Klavun. Attended De La Salle Inst., N.Y.C., 1916–20; grad. St. Paul's Garden City, L.I., 1924; attended Yale Univ., 1925–26; grad. AADA, 1927; attended Neighborhood Playhouse Sch. of the Theatre, N.Y.C., 1947–48. Studied acting with Frances Robinson-Duff (1946–47); Psychodrama with Dr. J. L. Moreno (1957–63). Married July 9, 1931, to June Martel, actress (marr. dis. June 14, 1938); married June 25, 1938, to Elizabeth Beebe, sculptress (marr. dis. Nov. 9, 1954); one son, three daughters. Member of SAG; AFTRA; AEA; AGVA; The Players (bd. of dir., 1972). Address: (home) 32 Gramercy Park, New York, NY 10003; (bus.) c/o Actors' Equity Assn., 165 W. 46th St., New York, NY 10036.

Theatre. Mr. Klavun first appeared on the stage at age twelve, as Captain Miles Standish in *The First Thanksgiving*, staged in the family garage (Long Beach, L.I., N.Y., 1918).

Using the name of Bradley Cass, he made his Bway debut as Mr. Lincoln in *Say When* (Morosco, June 26, 1928); subsequently appeared in the revue, *Americana* (Mansfield, Oct. 30, 1928); as Prince Karl in *Old Heidelberg* (Rialto, Hoboken, N.J., Nov. 15, 1928); Capt. Chumley in *After Dark, of Neither Wife, Maid or Widow* (Rialto, Dec. 10, 1928); performed, with the Paris-American Repertory Co. (Comédie Caumartin, Paris, Fr.); appeared at the Cape Playhouse (Dennis, Mass., Aug. 25, 1930); in stock, with the Ivoryton (Conn.) Players (July–Aug. 1933); and played Oliver Allen in *No More Ladies* (Booth, N.Y.C., Jan. 23, 1934).

Using the name, Waldemar Klavun, he appeared as Otto in *A Journey By Night* (Shubert, Apr. 16, 1935); produced and directed at his own Theatre of II (Lincoln Th., New Haven, Conn., 1935); and directed for the Federal Th. (WPA) Project (New Haven and Bridgeport, Conn., Jan. 22, 1936–Feb. 10, 1937).

He took the name Walter Klavun, playing Nero in *Arms for Venus* (John Golden Th., N.Y.C., Mar. 10, 1937); and henceforth used this name in the theatre. He directed and played Dr. Hagget in an ELT production of *The Late Christopher Bean* (NY Public Libraries, 1941); replaced (1947) Cliff Dunstan as Mac, and (1948) Harry Bellaver as Chief Sitting Bull in *Annie Get Your Gun* (Imperial, May 16, 1946); appeared as Antonio in *Twelfth Night* (Empire, Oct. 3, 1949); Jim Lucas in *Dream Girl* (NY City Ctr., May 16, 1951); repeated his role as Jim Lucas in a touring production of *Dream Girl* (Summer 1952); as Buff Schneider in *The Grey-Eyed People* (Martin Beck Th., N.Y.C., Dec. 17, 1952); as Joe Ferguson in *The Male Animal* (Playhouse-in-the-Park, Philadelphia, Pa., June 29, 1953); as Jimmy Smith in *No! No! Nanette!* (St. Louis Municipal Th., Mo.); in an industrial touring production for Chevrolet (Oct.–Nov. 1955); as Theodore Swanson in *Morning's at Seven* (Cherry Lane Th., N.Y.C., June 22, 1955); as Ned Brinker in *Allegro* (St. Louis Municipal Th., Mo., Summer 1955); as Tristram Marden in *Dandy Dick* (Cherry Lane, N.Y.C., Jan. 10, 1956); and as a Frontiersman in *Show Boat* (Marine Th., Jones Beach, L.I., N.Y., Summer 1956).

Mr. Klavun played Claude Upson in *Auntie Mame* (Broadhurst, N.Y.C., Oct. 31, 1956); Morty Krebs in *Say, Darling* (ANTA, Apr. 3, 1958); Gen Horton in *A Desert Incident* (John Golden Th., Mar. 24, 1959); at the Ann Arbor (Mich.) Drama Festival (Summer 1961), Emory Wages in *The Bad Seed* (May 23), Arnold Nash in *Send Me No Flowers* (June 6), and Jim Dougherty in *The Pleasure of His Company* (June 12); repeated his role as Jim Dougherty in a touring company of *The Pleasure of His Company* (July–Aug. 1961); appeared in the national touring production of *A Thurber Carnival* (opened Center, Norfolk, Va., Sept. 22, 1961; closed Music Hall, Kansas City, Mo. Apr. 28, 1962); succeeded (Mar. 24, 1951) Paul Reed as Bratt in *How to Succeed in Business Without Really Trying* (46 St. Th., N.Y.C., Oct. 14, 1961); played H. L. Harrington in *What Makes Sammy Run?* (54 St. Th., Feb. 27, 1964); and was Ned in *Twigs* (Broadhurst, Nov. 14, 1971).

Films. Mr. Klavun has appeared in *The Mob* (Col., 1951); *It Should Happen to You* (Col., 1954); an industrial film for the Chrysler Corp. (1956); *The Boston Strangler* (20th-Fox, 1968); *Star!* (20th-Fox, 1968); and *Cops and Robbers* (EK Corp., 1972).

Television. Mr. Klavun has appeared on Kraft Television Theatre (NBC); Ellery Queen (1950); Star Time Theatre (1950); Colgate Comedy Hour (NBC, 1950); Martin Kane (CBS, 1951); The Aldrich Family (NBC, 1951); Man Against Crime (CBS, 1952); Secret Storm (CBS, 1954); *The Trap* (CBS, 1954); *Dream Girl* (NBC, 1955); Hallmark Hall of Fame (NBC, 1960); Armstrong Circle Theatre (NBC, 1960); Naked City (ABC, 1960); and CBS Workshop (1960); played Ed Mosler in *The Iceman Cometh* (WNTA, July 6, 1960); performed on The Defenders (CBS, 1962–63) and The Nurses (CBS, 1952–63); was Andrew Johnson in *The Impeachment of Andrew Johnson* (BBC; WNET, 1974); appeared in the Play of the Week *Enemy of the People;* and performed on As the World Turns (CBS, 1974) and A Life to Live (ABC, 1974).

Night Clubs. Mr. Klavun appeared as Mr. Knickerbocker (Old Knick, N.Y., 1948–49).

Recreation. The study of behavior, tennis, swimming, handicraft.

KLEIMAN, HARLAN PHILIP. Producer. b. Nov. 9, 1940, New York City, to Ira Arthur and Dorothy (Rosen) Kleiman. Father, retail merchant. Grad. Hunter Coll., B.A. 1962; Yale Univ., M.I.A. 1964. Married Sept. 30, 1968, to Sondra Lee, actress. Address: (home) 201 W. 77th St., New York, NY 10022, tel. (212) 724-5230; (bus.) 551 Fifth Ave., New York, NY 10017, tel. (212) 354-5720.

Theatre. Mr. Kleiman was producer for the Clinton (Conn.) Playhouse (1964); and co-founder (1965), and executive director (1965–67) of the Long Wharf Th. (New Haven, Conn.).

Off-Bway, he produced *Have I Got One For You* (Th. Four, Jan. 7, 1967); *Futz* (Th. de Lys, June 13, 1968); *Passing Through from Exotic Places* (Sheridan Square Playhouse, Dec. 7, 1969); and *The Ofay Watcher* (Stage 73, Sept. 15, 1969).

Other Activities. Mr. Kleiman served on the faculty, and was director of the theatre administration center at the NY Univ. Graduate Sch. of Arts (1968–70). He was director of the ANTA theatre management training program (1968–69); and executive producer of Teletronics International (1969–71). He is president (1971–to date) of Caravatt, Kleiman, Inc., a video-cassette and cable television company.

Published Works. "Video Communications: Less Is More and Usually Better" appeared in *Audio Visual Communication* (March 1974); and "Video Publishing: Communications Next Frontier" is included in *Cable Television and the University* (1974).

Awards. He was voted New Haven Man of the Year (1966); received the Margo Jones award for new plays presented at the Long Wharf Th. (New Haven, 1966); received the Village Voice Off-Bway (Obie) award for *Futz* (Th. de Lys, 1968); and the NY Film and Television Society award for best communication programs (1973).

KLEIN, ADELAIDE. Actress. b. July 4, 1904, New York City, to Morris and Sophie Klein. Father, cigar-maker, cigar salesman, real estate broker. Grad. Julia Richman H.S., N.Y.C.; attended Barnard Coll.; took night courses at Columbia Univ., New York Univ., Hunter Coll., and City Coll. of New York. Married to Louis S. Wattels, attorney (dec. 1943); married Apr. 1947 to Norman Annenberg, attorney. Member of AEA; SAG; AFTRA (founding mbr.); Actor's Fund; ANTA; Actors Studio. Address: 145 W. 55th St., New York, NY 10019, tel. (212) CO 5-6594.

Theatre. Miss Klein made her N.Y.C. debut as Lena Rose in *Brooklyn, U.S.A.* (Forrest Th., Dec. 21, 1941); subsequently appeared as Hester in *Uncle Harry* (Broadhurst, May 20, 1942); Fatima Birka in *Collector's Item* (Booth, Feb. 8, 1952); Sidma in *The Immoralist* (Royale, Feb. 8, 1954); Chana Bayle in *Once Upon a Tailor* (Cort, May 23, 1955); and Anna in the pre-Bway tryout of *One Foot in the Door* (opened Locust St. Th., Philadelphia, Pa., Nov. 6, 1957; closed Shubert, Boston, Mass., Nov. 23, 1957). She then toured with a USO company as Madame Arcati in *Blithe Spirit* (Italy, France, 1944–45); played Grace Poole in *Jane Eyre*, and was understudy to Blanche Yurka for the role of Mrs. Fairfax (Belasco, N.Y.C., May 1, 1958).

In stock, she played in *The Counting House* (Cecilwood Th., Fishkill, N.Y., 1960); appeared as the Palace Midwife in *The Secret Concubine* (Carnegie Hall Playhouse, N.Y.C., Mar. 21, 1960); toured as Ardeth Long in *There Must Be a Pony* (Summer 1962); and at the Woodstock (N.Y.) Playhouse, played Mrs. Baker in *Come Blow Your Horn*, Amalie Freud in *In a Far Country*, and the Fortune Teller in *The Skin of Our Teeth* (1963). She appeared as Mrs. Beckett-Jones, marathon fan, in *Marathon '33* (ANTA, N.Y.C., Dec. 22, 1963); in stock, appeared in *New Play* (Bucks County Playhouse, New Hope, Pa.); as Mrs. Coffman in *Come Back, Little Sheba;* Rosemary Disney in *Picnic;* and the Reporter's Wife in *The Front Page* (Playhouse in the Park, Philadelphia, Pa.); and she was in *Tartuffe* (Long Wharf Th., New Haven, Conn., Oct. 17, 1969).

Films. She played Mrs. Batory in *The Naked City* (U, 1948); the Candy Store Proprietor in *The Enforcer* (WB, 1951); Mrs. Hoffman in *C-Man* (Four Continents, 1949); the Italian Mother in *Splendor in the Grass* (WB, 1961); and the Senior Psychiatrist in *The Trouble-Maker* (1963).

Television and Radio. Miss Klein has acted on the major dramatic programs in radio and television.

Recreation. Sculpture, writing, reading, cooking, swimming.

KLOTZ, FLORENCE. Costume designer. b. to Philip and Hannah Klotz. Attended Parsons Sch. of Design. Member of United Scenic Artists. Address: 1050 Park Ave., New York, NY 10016, tel. (212) TR 6-4546.

Theatre. Miss Klotz designed the costumes for *A Call on Kuprin* (Broadhurst Th., May 25, 1961); *Take Her, She's Mine* (Biltmore, Dec. 21, 1961); *Never Too Late* (Playhouse, Nov. 27, 1962); *Nobody Loves an Albatross* (Lyceum, Dec. 19, 1963); *The Owl and the Pussycat* (ANTA Th., Nov. 19, 1964); *Mating Dance* (Eugene O'Neill Th., Nov. 3, 1965); *The Best Laid Plans* (Brooks Atkinson Th., Mar. 24, 1966); *It's A Bird. . . It's A Plane. . . It's Superman* (Alvin, Mar. 29, 1966); *Paris Is Out* (Brooks Atkinson Th., Jan. 19, 1970); *Follies* (Winter Garden, Apr. 4, 1971); *A Little Night Music* (Shubert, Feb. 25, 1973); and *Dreyfus in Rehearsal* (Ethel Barrymore Th., Oct. 17, 1974).

She has designed costumes for the ballets *Jazz Opus* and *Four Bagatelles;* and for the Jacobs Pillow dance group.

Films. She designed the costumes for *Something for Everyone* (National General, 1969).

Awards. For her costumes, Miss Klotz received the Drama Desk Award (1970–71), the Antoinette Perry (Tony) Award, and the Drama Critics Circle Award (1972) for *Follies;* and the Antoinette Perry (Tony) Award for *A Little Night Music* (1972–73).

KLUGMAN, JACK. Actor. Attended Carnegie Inst. of Technology; studied acting at Amer. Th. Wing, N.Y.C. Married 1946 to Brett Somers, actress (marr. dis.); one son, one daughter. Member of AEA; AFTRA; SAG.

Theatre. Mr. Klugman appeared in the ELT productions *Stevedore* (Feb. 18, 1949), *Saint Joan* (Nov. 5, 1949), and *Bury the Dead* (Jan. 21, 1950); and played Dowdy in the national tour of *Mister Roberts* (1950–51).

He made his Bway debut as Frank Bonaparte in *Golden Boy* (ANTA, Mar. 12, 1952); played the Sixth Citizen and the Second Volscian Servant in *Coriolanus* (Phoenix, Jan. 13, 1954); Carmen in *A Very Special Baby* (Playhouse, Nov. 14, 1956); Herbie in *Gypsy* (Broadway, May 21, 1959); succeeded (Apr. 1963) Anthony Quinn as Caesario Grimaldi in *Tchin-Tchin* (Plymouth, Oct. 25, 1962).

Mr. Klugman succeeded (Nov. 1, 1965) Walter Matthau in the role of Oscar Madison in *The Odd Couple* (Plymouth Th., N.Y.C., Mar. 10, 1965); played Horse Johnson in a staged reading of *The Sudden and Accidental Re-education of Horse Johnson* (Eugene O'Neill Memorial Th., Waterford, Conn., July 29, 1966); repeated the role of Oscar Madison in the London production of *The Odd Couple* (Queen's Th., London, Oct. 12, 1966); and repeated the title role in *The Sudden and Accidental Re-education of Horse Johnson* (Belasco, N.Y.C., Dec. 18, 1966).

Films. Mr. Klugman made his debut in *Time Table* (UA, 1956); subsequently appeared in *12 Angry Men* (UA, 1957); *Cry Terror* (MGM, 1958); *Hail, Mafia* (Fernand Rivers, 1965); *Good-bye, Columbus* (Par., 1969).

Television. He appeared in *Mrs. Gilling and the Skyscraper* (Alcoa Hour, NBC, June 9, 1957); wrote the television play, *The Big Break* (Kraft Television Th., NBC, July 17, 1957); appeared on Suspicion (NBC, Nov. 4, 1957); played in *The Dark Stairway* (NBC, Dec. 23, 1957); *Protegee* (Suspicion NBC, May 12, 1958); *The Man Who Asked for a Funeral* (Studio One, CBS, June 23, 1958); *The Time of Your Life* (Playhouse 90, CBS, Oct. 9, 1958); *Kiss Me, Kate* (Hallmark Hall of Fame, NBC, Nov. 20, 1958); *The Velvet Alley* (Playhouse 90, CBS, Jan. 23, 1959); *The Million Dollar Incident* (Jackie Gleason, CBS, Apr. 21, 1961); and *Look Up and Live* (CBS, July 28, 1963).

In addition to his series, The Odd Couple (ABC, 1970–75), Mr. Klugman has made numerous appearances on such programs as The Fugitive (ABC); Twilight Zone (CBS); Follow the Sun (Ind.); Great Adventure (CBS); The Untouchables (Ind.); The Johnny Carson Show (NBC); 90 Bristol Court (NBC); Bob Hope Presents (NBC); Kraft Suspense Th. (NBC); Ben Casey (ABC); Arrest and Trial (Ind.); The Defenders (CBS); Naked City (Ind.); Bob Hope Chrysler Theatre (NBC); Fame Is the Name of the Game (NBC); Alfred Hitchcock Presents (Ind.); Garrison's Gorillas (ABC); Name of the Game (NBC); Then Came Bronson (NBC); The Bold Ones (NBC); and Love, American Style (ABC).

Awards. Mr. Klugman received NATAS (Emmy) Awards for his performances in *Blacklist* (1964); and The Odd Couple (1971).

KNAUB, RICHARD K. Educator. b. Richard Keith Knaub, July 7, 1928, Springfield, Mo., to Norman K. and Bernice E. (Chesterson) Knaub. Father, teacher, insurance agent. Grad. Rensselaer (Ind.) H.S., 1946; Indiana Univ., A.B. 1950; Ph.D. 1962; State Univ. of Iowa, M.F.A. 1955. Married Dec. 20, 1953, to Joan Slaker, writer; one son, one daughter. Served US Army, 1950–52. Member of ATA (bd. of dir., 1972–73); Rocky Mountain Theatre Conference (pres., 1972–73); USITT. Address: (home) 4425 Osage Dr., Boulder, CO 80302, tel. (303) 494-8158; (bus.) Univ. of Colorado, University Theatre, Boulder, CO 80302, tel. (303) 492-7355.

In 1974, Mr. Knaub returned to the Univ. of Colorado as director of theatre, having spent 1973–74 as Fulbright Scholar to the Sherman Th., Univ. College, Cardiff, Wales, where he had been director and designer for Orbit Theatre. In Wales, he directed *How to Succeed in Business Without Really Trying*, and designed a production of *Cabaret*. From 1965 to 1973, Mr. Knaub was director of theatre and executive director, Colorado Shakespeare Festival, and from 1962 to 1965 was professor of speech and drama and technical director of the University Th., Univ. of Colorado, where he designed sets and lighting for dramatic and musical productions. Previously he was at Indiana Univ. (1957–62); and technical director at Allegheny Coll. (1955–57). At both schools he was designer and technical director for student productions, including *Of Thee I Sing, Abe Lincoln in Illinois, The Marriage of Figaro, Iolanthe, Dial "M" for Murder, Major Barbara*, and *The Crucible*. The first production for which he designed the sets and lighting was *Mrs. Mc Thing*, while he was a student at the State Univ. of Iowa.

Other Activities. Mr. Knaub is founder-producer of Colorado Caravan, a touring theatre group begun under Title III, ESEA.

Published Works. Mr. Knaub, with John Dolman, is author of *The Art of Play Production* (3rd ed., 1972), and he edited *On Shakespeare's Stage* (1967). He was editor (1967–72) of *Curtain Call*.

Awards. Mr. Knaub received the Gold Medal Award of the American Oil Company for theatre excellence in conjunction with the American College Theatre Festival.

Recreation. Golf.

KNICKERBOCKER, PAINE. Drama and film critic. b. William Paine Knickerbocker, Mar. 16, 1912, New York City, to Reginald Canning and Mary (Paine) Knickerbocker. Father, resident buyer. Grad. Scarsdale (N.Y.) H.S., 1929; Dartmouth Coll., A.B. 1933; Univ. of California at Berkeley, M.A. (English) 1939. Married June 12, 1940, to Nancy Burt; one son, one daughter. Served USNR, 1942–45; rank, Lt. Member of Amer. Newspaper Guild. Address: (home) 2600 Union St., San Francisco, CA 94123, tel. (415) FI 6-4364; (bus.) c/o San Francisco *Chronicle*, San Francisco, CA 94103, tel. (415) GA 1-1111.

Since 1955, Mr. Knickerbocker has been drama and film critic for the San Francisco *Chronicle*, which he joined in 1952.

He worked in advertising (1933–39); was assistant to the president of Mills Coll., Oakland, Calif. (1939–42); and wrote for the Oakland *Tribune* (1945–52).

Awards. Mr. Knickerbocker received the Film Critics Award from the Directors Guild of America (1963).

KNIGHT, SHIRLEY. Actress. b. July 5, 1936, Goessel, Kans. to Noel and Virginia (Webster) Knight. Father, oilman. Educ. Phillips Univ., Enid, Okla. Professional training with Lee Strasberg. Married Mar. 14, 1959, to Gene Persson, producer (marr. dis. 1969); two daughters; 1969 to John Hopkins, playwright. Member of SAG; AEA; AFTRA; Actors Studio. Address: (home) 1349 Marinette Rd., Pacific Palisades, CA 90272, tel. (213) 459-1454; (bus.) William Morris Agency, 151 El Camino, Beverly Hills, CA 90212, tel. (213) 274-7451.

Pre-Theatre. Assistant society editor, Wichita (Kans.) *Beacon* (1955–56); continuity, KAKE-TV, Wichita, 1956–57.

Theatre. Miss Knight first appeared on stage as Alison Porter in *Look Back in Anger* (Pasadena Playhouse, Pasadena, Calif., 1958); first appeared professionally off-Bway in N.Y.C. as Katherine in *Journey to the Day* (Th. de Lys, Nov. 11, 1963); and made her Bway debut as Irina in *The Three Sisters* (Morosco, June 22, 1964). She played Lula in *Dutchman* (Warner Playhouse, Los Angeles, Calif., Mar. 24, 1965); was in a program of two one-act plays billed as *Rooms*, playing Jenny in *Better Luck Next Time* and Helen in *A Walk in Dark Places* (Cherry Lane, N.Y.C., Jan. 27, 1966); played Constance in *We Have Always Lived in the Castle* (Ethel Barrymore Th., Oct. 19, 1966); Jean in *And People All Around* (Bristol Old Vic, Bristol, Eng., Oct. 31, 1967); Janet in *The Watering Place* (Music Box, N.Y.C., Mar. 12, 1969); Sara Melody in *A Touch of the Poet* (Gardner Arts Ctr., Univ. of Sussex, Brighton, Eng., 1970); made her London debut in *Antigone* (1971); and played the female lead in *Economic Necessity* (New Haymarket, Leicester, Eng., Oct. 1973).

Films. Miss Knight was in *Five Gates to Hell* (20th-Fox, 1959); *Ice Palace* (WB, 1960); *The Dark at the Top of the Stairs* (WB, 1960); *Sweet Bird of Youth* (MGM, 1962); *The Group* (UA, 1966); *Dutchman* (Continental, 1967); *Petulia* (WB, 1968); *The Rain People* (WB, 1968); and *Juggernaut* (UA, 1973).

Television. Miss Knight appeared on Buckskin; Staccato (both NBC); Hawaiian Eye (ABC, 1959); 77 Sunset Strip (ABC, 1960); *The Shape of the River* (Playhouse 90, CBS, May 2, 1960); Surfside 6 (ABC, 1960, 1961, 1962); Roaring 20's (ABC, 1961); Maverick (ABC, 1961); Cheyenne (ABC, 1961); Lawman (ABC, 1961); US Steel Hour (CBS, 1962, 1963); *The Broken Year* (Alcoa Premier, ABC, Apr. 4, 1963); *The Takers* (Dupont Show of the Month, NBC, Oct. 13, 1963); *Lost Yesterday* (The Virginian, NBC, July 1965); The Fugitive (ABC, 1965, 1966); *The Faceless Man* (Bob Hope Chrysler Th., NBC, May 4, 1966); *Shadow Over Elveron* (NBC, Mar. 5, 1968); *Walk Into the Dark* (BBC-2, England, Feb. 29, 1972); *Some Distant Shadow* (ITV, England, 1972); Alias Smith and Jones (ABC, 1972); *That Quiet Earth* (BBC, England, 1973); *The Country Girl* (Hallmark Hall of Fame, NBC, 1974); and *The Friendly Persuasion* (ABC, 1975).

Awards. Miss Knight was awarded the Volpi Cup at the 28th Venice Film Festival (1967) for her performance in *Dutchman*.

Recreation. Reading, playing piano, yoga.

KNILL, C. EDWIN. General manager.

Theatre. Mr. Knill was general manager of *The Day Before Spring* (National Th., N.Y.C., Nov. 22, 1945); subsequently was general manager of *Kiss Me, Kate* (New Century, Dec. 30, 1948); *Janus* (Plymouth, Nov. 24, 1955); *The Lovers* (Martin Beck Th., May 10, 1956); *The Square Root of Wonderful* (Natl., Oct. 30, 1957); The *Dark at the Top of the Stairs* (Music Box, Dec. 5, 1957); *J.B.* (ANTA, Dec. 11, 1958); and succeeded Herman Bernstein as general manager of *Masquerade* (John Golden Th., Mar. 16, 1959).

He was general manager of *The Tumbler* (Helen Hayes Th., Feb. 24, 1960); *Viva Madison Avenue!* (Longacre, Apr. 6, 1960); *Camelot* (Majestic, Dec. 3, 1960); *Look: We've Come Through!* (Hudson, Oct. 25, 1961); *Never Too Late* (Playhouse, Nov. 27, 1962; and national tour, 1964–65); *Barefoot in the Park* (Biltmore, Oct. 23, 1963; and national tours, 1964, 1965, 1966); the pre-Bway production of *Rich Little Rich Girl* (opened Walnut St. Th., Philadelphia, Oct. 26, 1964; closed there Nov. 7, 1964); *Zizi* (Broadway Th., N.Y.C., Nov. 21, 1964); *Mating Dance* (Eugene O'Neill Th., Nov. 3, 1965); *The Odd Couple* (Plymouth, Mar. 10, 1965; and three national tours, 1965–67); *The Star-Spangled Girl* (Plymouth, Dec. 21, 1966); *Love in E-Flat* (Brooks Atkinson Th., Feb. 13, 1967); *Dr. Cook's Garden* (Belasco, Sept. 25, 1967); *There's A Girl in My Soup* (Music Box, Oct. 18, 1967); *The Little Foxes* (Vivian Beaumont Th., Oct. 26, 1967); *The House of Flowers* (Th. de Lys, Jan. 28, 1968); *Weekend* (Broadhurst, Mar. 13, 1968); *Morningside Heights* (John Golden Th., Feb. 27, 1968); *The Last of the Red Hot Lovers* (Eugene O'Neill Th., Dec. 28, 1969; and national tour, 1970–71); *The Gingerbread Lady* (Plymouth, Dec. 13, 1970); *The Prisoner of Second Avenue* (Eugene O'Neill Th., Nov. 11, 1971; and national tours, 1972–74); and *Gigi* (Uris, Nov. 13, 1973).

KNOTT, FREDERICK. Playwright. b. to Cyril Wakefield and Margaret Caroline (Paull) Knott. Grad. Oundle Sch., England; Cambridge Univ., England, M.A. (honors). Married Nov. 10, 1953, to Ann Hillary, actress; one son. Served Royal Artillery, 1939–46; rank, Maj. Member of Dramatists Guild; WGA. Address: c/o Kay Brown, International Famous Agency, 1301 Ave. of the Americas, New York, NY 10019.

Theatre. Mr. Knott wrote *Dial 'M' for Murder* (Westminster Th., London, June 19, 1952; Plymouth, N.Y.C., Oct. 29, 1952); and subsequently wrote *Write Me a Murder* (Belasco, Oct. 26, 1961).

KNOX, ALEXANDER. Actor, writer. b. Jan. 16, 1907, Strathroy, Ontario, Canada, to William John and Jean (Crozier) Knox. Attended Univ. of Western Ontario, Canada. Married to Doris Nolan. Member of AEA; SAG; The Players.

Theatre. Mr. Knox played John Purdie in *Dear Brutus* (Peabody Playhouse, Boston, Mass., Feb. 12, 1929); subsequently made his London debut as Ferdinand Steinberg in *Smoky Cell* (Wyndham's, Dec. 16, 1930); played Dillon in *The Tiger* (Embassy, Sept. 1936); and Larry in *Anna Christie* (Westminster, Apr. 7, 1937).

With the Old Vic Co. (London), he appeared as Sir William Catesby in *Richard III* (Nov. 2, 1937); the Old Man and the Scotch Doctor in *Macbeth* (Nov. 26, 1937); Snout in *A Midsummer Night's Dream* (Dec. 27, 1937); Brabantio in *Othello* (Feb. 8, 1938); and Dr. McGlip in *The King of Nowhere* (Mar. 15, 1938). He played Robert Gillet in *Babes in the Wood* (Embassy, June 1938); the Judge in *Geneva* (Saville, Nov. 22, 1938); Jim Settle in *The Jealous God* (Lyric, Feb. 1939); and at the Malvern (England) Festival, he appeared in *Good King Charles's Golden Days*, and wrote and appeared in *Old Master* (Aug. 1939).

He played Friar Laurence in *Romeo and Juliet* (51 St. Th., N.Y.C., May 9, 1940); Dr. Paul Venner in *Jupiter Laughs* (Biltmore, Sept. 9, 1940); Jason Otis in *Jason* (Hudson, Jan. 21, 1942); Baron Tuzenbach in *The Three Sisters* (Ethel Barrymore Th., Dec. 21, 1942); and wrote *The Closing Door*, in which he played Vail Trahern (Empire, Dec. 1, 1949).

Mr. Knox played Gilbert Cotton in *Return to Tyassi* (Duke of York's, London, Nov. 29, 1950); Professor Thompson in *Cupid and Psyche* (King's, Edinburgh, Scotland, Mar. 1952); succeeded (Oct. 1952) Michael Redgrave as Frank Elgin in *Winter Journey* (St. James's, London, Apr. 3, 1952); played Cardinal Wolsey in *Henry VIII* (Old Vic, May 6, 1953); and John in *The Burnt Flower Bed* (Arts, Sept. 9, 1955; and Assembly Hall, Edinburgh, Scotland, Aug. 1968).

Films. Mr. Knox has appeared in *Four Feathers* (UA, 1939); *The Phantom Strikes* (Mono., 1939); *The Sea Wolf* (WB, 1941); *This Above All* (20th-Fox, 1942); *Commandos Strike at Dawn* (Col., 1942); *None Shall Escape* (Col., 1944); played the title role in *Wilson* (20th-Fox, 1944); appeared in *Over 21* (Col., 1945); *Sister Kenny* (RKO, 1946).

He appeared in, and collaborated on the screenplay of *Sign of the Ram* (Col., 1948); appeared in *The Judge Steps Out* (RKO, 1949); *Two of a Kind* (Col., 1951); *Man in the Saddle* (Col., 1951); *Saturday's Hero* (Col., 1951); *The Son of Dr. Jekyll* (Col., 1951); *I'd Climb the Highest Mountain* (20th-Fox, 1951); *Paula* (Col., 1952); *The Sleeping Tiger* (Astor, 1954); *Alias John Preston* (Assoc., 1955); *The Divided Heart* (Rep., 1955); *The Night My Number Came Up* (Continental, 1955); *Reach for the Sky* (Rank, 1957); *Chase a Crooked Shadow* (WB, 1958); *The Vikings* (UA, 1958); *The Two-Headed Spy* (Col., 1959); *The Wreck of the Mary Deare* (MGM, 1959); *Woman of Straw* (UA, 1964); *Crack in the World* (Par., 1965); *Mister Moses* (UA, 1965); *These Are the Damned* (Col., 1965); *Modesty Blaise* (20th-Fox, 1966); *The Psychopath* (Par., 1966); *Khartoum* (UA, 1966); *The 25th Hour* (MGM, 1967); and *Accident* (Ind., 1967).

Television. Mr. Knox's appearances include The Saint (NBC); The Vise (ABC); and The Hidden Truth (London). He wrote the script for *The Closing Door* (Play of the Week, NET).

Published Works. He is the author of *Bride of Quietness*; and *Totem Dream* (Viking, 1973); and has written detective novels.

KNUTSON, WAYNE S. Educator, director. b. Wayne Shafer Knutson, June 1, 1926, Roberts County, S.D., to Edward and Julia (Sanden) Knutson. Father, farmer. Grad. Sisseton (S.D.) H.S., 1944; Augustana Coll., B.A. 1950; State Univ. of South Dakota, M.A. 1951; Univ. of Denver, Ph.D. 1956. Married July 30, 1950, to Esther Marie Johnstad; two sons, one daughter. Served US Merchant Marines, 1944–46; rank, Cadet Midshipman; US Army, Korea, 1946–47. Member of AETA; AAUP; North Central Theatre Assn. (pres., 1959–60; advisory board, 1960–63); Natl. Collegiate Players. Address: (home) 1153 Valley View Dr., Vermillion, SD 57069, tel. (605) 624-3293; (bus.) State Univ. of South Dakota, Vermillion, SD 57069, tel. (605) 624-4411, ext. 256.

Mr. Knutson has taught at the Univ. of South Dakota since 1952; and is Dean of the Coll. of Fine Arts there.

Theatre. He joined (1951) the Black Hills Playhouse (Custer, S.D.) as assistant director and actor. During the Summers 1952–57, 1959–62, he was associate director and business manager of the Playhouse, and since 1961, has been a member of its board of directors.

KOBART, RUTH. Singer, actress. b. Ruth Maxine Kohn, Apr. 24, 1924, Des Moines, Iowa, to Morris L. and Sadie (Finkelstein) Kohn. Father, building contractor. Grad. Theodore Roosevelt H.S., Des Moines, 1942; American Conservatory of Music, Chicago, Ill., B. Mus. 1945; Hunter Coll., grad. study, 1959. Studied singing with Suzanne Sten, N.Y.C. Member of AEA; AGMA; AFTRA; SAG; Mu Phi Epsilon. Address: 2109 Broadway, New York, NY 10023, tel. (212) SU 7-3300.

Theatre. Miss Kobart first performed in a dance recital in Des Moines (Iowa) Community Center (1934); made her professional debut in N.Y.C. with the Lemonade Opera, as the Witch in *Hansel and Gretel* (Greenwich Mews Th., June 27, 1947); with the same company and at the same theatre, played the title role in *The Duenna* (June 1, 1948); Clarissa in *The Man in the Moon* (June 7, 1949); the Mother in *The Stranger* (Aug. 30, 1949); and Manuela in *Don Pedro* (June 1, 1953); with the Little Orchestra Society, at Hunter Coll. Aud., she appeared as the Old Lady in *Babar, the Elephant* (Dec. 28, 1953) and the Witch in *Hansel and Gretel* (Feb. 20, 1954).

Miss Kobart made her Bway debut in the chorus and understudied Helen Traubel as Fauna in *Pipe Dream*, playing the role about 20 times (Shubert, Nov. 30, 1955); toured with the NBC Opera Co. (Fall 1956, 1957); appeared with the Little Orchestra Society (N.Y.C.) as Hagga in *The Thirteen Clocks* (Mar. 8, 1958); with the NY City Opera Co., as Augusta Tabor in the N.Y.C. premiere of *The Ballad of Baby Doe* (NY City Ctr. Apr. 3, 1958), as Miss Todd in *The Old Maid and the Thief* (NY City Ctr., Apr. 30, 1958); and as Nettie in *Carousel*, Mrs. Ott in *Susannah*, and Agatha in *Maria Golovin* at the Brussels (Belgium World's Fair (Amer. Pavilion, Summer 1958).

With the NY City Ctr. Opera Co. at the NY City Ctr., Miss Kobart appeared in *Silent Woman* (Oct. 7, 1958) and *The Rape of Lucretia* (Oct. 23, 1958); played Agatha in the N.Y.C. premiere of *Maria Golovin* (Martin Beck Th., Nov. 5, 1958); Manuela in the Lemonade Opera Co.'s production of *Olè* (Greenwich Mews Th., Mar. 19, 1959); with the NY City Opera Co., at NY City Ctr., as Emma Jones in *Street Scene* (Apr. 2, 1959), Katisha in *The Mikado* (Sept. 29, 1959), and the Wife in *The Inspector General* (Oct. 19, 1959); toured with the NY City Opera Co. in the same roles (Spring 1960); with the Little Orchestra Society (N.Y.C.), appeared in *The Apothecary* (Oct. 5, 1960); and repeated her role as Katisha in *The Mikado* with the NY City Ctr. Opera (NY City Ctr., Jan. 17, 1961).

She played Miss Jones in *How To Succeed in Business without Really Trying* (46 St. Th., Oct. 14, 1961); Domina in *A Funny Thing Happened on the Way to the Forum* (Alvin, May 8, 1962); temporarily left this production to appear with the NY City Opera Co. at NY City Ctr. as Emma Jones in *Street Scene* (Apr. 26, 1963) and as Augusta Tabor in *The Ballad of Baby Doe* (Apr. 28, 1963).

She recreated her role as Domina in *A Funny Thing Happened on the Way to the Forum* (Riviera Hotel, Las Vegas, Nev., Sept. 15, 1964); sang Augusta Tabor in *The Ballad of Baby Doe* (NY City Ctr., Mar. 1965); played Caroline Willard, Madame de Villiers and Carrie Nation in *Mardi Gras* (Jones Beach Marine Th., L.I., N.Y., June 25, 1965); Aunt Eller in *Oklahoma!* (NY City Ctr., Dec. 15, 1965); and recorded the song used in *The Great Indoors* (Eugene O'Neill Th., Feb. 1, 1966).

In 1967, she joined ACT (the American Conservatory Th., Geary Th., San Francisco), playing Madame Pernelle in *Tartuffe* (Jan. 1967), Madame Pampinelli in *The Torchbearers* (Feb. 1967), Lady Hurf in *Thieves' Carnival* (Aug. 1968), Mommy in *The American Dream* (Dec. 1968); and for their N.Y.C. engagement at the ANTA Th., Olivia in *A Flea in Her Ear* (Oct. 3, 1969), and Anfisa in *The Three Sisters* (Oct. 9, 1969). She played Mistress Schermerhorn in *Knickerbocker Holiday* (Curran, San Francisco, May 11, 1971); and toured as Mrs. Margolin in *Forty Carats* (1970); the Maid in *Boeing, Boeing;* and Jeanette Fisher in *The Last of the Red Hot Lovers*. She acted again with ACT in their 1973–74 season in San Francisco.

Films. Miss Kobart played Miss Jones in *How To Succeed in Business without Really Trying* (UA, 1967), and a nun in *Petulia* (WB, 1968).

Television. Miss Kobart has appeared as Ciesca in *Gianni Schicchi* (1952), the Aunt in *The Marriage* (1953), the Gentlewoman in *Macbeth* (1953), Marcellina in *The Marriage of Figaro* (1954), and Agatha in *Maria Golovin* (1959), all for the NBC-TV Opera Company; she appeared as Vera Boronel in *The Consul* (Pay-TV, May 1960).

Awards. For her performance as Domina in *A Funny Thing Happened on the Way to the Forum*, Miss Kobart was nominated for the Antoinette Perry (Tony) Award (1963).

Recreation. Collecting contemporary art.

KOCH, FRED, JR. Educator, director. b. Frederick Henry Koch, Jr., Sept. 15, 1911, Grand Forks, N.D., to Frederick Henry and Jean (Hanigan) Koch. Father, educator and director of the Carolina Playmakers. Grad. Univ. of North Carolina, B.A. 1933, M.A. 1939. Married June 8, 1937, to Edna Bryant; three sons. Member of Amer. Assn. of Univ. Professors; NTC; Southeastern Th. Conf. (pres., 1956); AETA; Fla. Th. Conf. (founder, 1956); Phi Beta Kappa (pres., 1933). Address: (home) 7011 S.W. 83rd Place, Miami, FL 33143, tel. (315) 271-9433; (summer), Box 304, Burnsville, NC 28714; (bus.) Univ. of Miami, Coral Gables, FL 33146, tel. (315) 284-3354.

Since 1939, Mr. Koch has been professor of drama at the Univ. of Miami, where he teaches speech and drama. Previously he taught and directed at the Univ. of Virginia (Summers 1938–39). He was chairman of the Drama Dept. and director of theatres (The Box and The Ring) at the Univ. of Miami (1939–56).

He has directed more than fifty plays at the university and supervised the construction of the flexible-stage Ring Th. at the university (1951). He has also directed plays at the Parkway Playhouse (Burnsville, N.C., Summers 1951–to date).

KOHNER, SUSAN. Actress. b. Susanna Kohner, Los Angeles, Calif., to Paul and Lupita (Tovar) Kohner. Father, talent representative; mother, former actress. Grad. Westlake Sch. for Girls, Los Angeles, 1954; attended Univ. of California at Los Angeles, 1954–55; studied with Sanford Meisner, N.Y.C. Married Aug. 29, 1964, to John Weitz, designer. Relatives in theatre: two uncles, Walter Kohner, talent representative; Frederick Kohner, writer. Member of AEA; SAG; AFTRA.

Theatre. Miss Kohner made her stage debut as Mimi in an arena production of *The Girl on the Via Flaminia* (Circle Th., Hollywood, Calif., Oct. 1951); subsequently appeared as Rosa in *The Rose Tattoo* (Players Ring, Hollywood, Dec. 1954); Biagina in a pre-Bway tryout of *A Quiet Place* (opened Shubert, New Haven, Conn., Nov. 1955; closed Natl., Washington, D.C., 1955); Elma Duckworth in *Bus Stop* (La Jolla Playhouse, Calif., July 1956); Consuelo in *He Who Gets Slapped* (New England tour, Summer 1958); Fusima and the Maiden in a concert reading of *Back to Methuselah* (Fitz, Los Angeles, 1959); with the Theatre Group in summer repertory, played Inez in *Peribanez* and Annabella in *'Tis Pity She's a Whore* (Univ. of California at Los Angeles, 1963); Emily Whittaker in *Love Me Little* (Helen Hayes Th., N.Y.C., Apr. 15, 1958); Harriet Milbury in *Pullman Car Hiawatha* (Circle in the Square, Dec. 3, 1962); and the title role in *Saint Joan* at the International Drama Festival (Queen Elizabeth Th., Vancouver, Canada, 1963).

Films. Mis Kohner made her debut as Maria in *To Hell and Back* (UI, 1954); subsequently played in *The Last Wagon* (20th-Fox, 1956); *Trooper Hook* (UA, 1957); *Dino* (Allied, 1957); *Imitation of Life* (UI, 1959); *The Big Fisherman* (Buena Vista, 1959); *The Gene Krupa Story* (Col., 1959); *All the Fine Young Cannibals* (MGM, 1960); *By Love Possessed* (UA, 1961); and *Freud* (UI, 1962).

Television. Miss Kohner has appeared on Alcoa Hour (NBC), Matinee Th. (NBC), Schlitz Playhouse (CBS), Cavalcade Th., (ABC), Wagon Train (NBC), Climax! (CBS), Four Star Playhouse (CBS), Suspicion (NBC), Checkmate (NBC), Route 66 (CBS), Playhouse 90 (CBS), The Nurses (CBS), Hong Kong (ABC), Going My Way (ABC), Temple Houston (ABC) and The Dick Powell Th. (NBC).

Awards. Miss Kohner received an Academy (Oscar) Award nomination for her role as Sarah Jane in *Imitation of Life* (1960); *Film Daily* Filmdom's Famous Five Award (1957, 1959); the Exhibitors' Laurel Award (1959); two Hollywood Foreign Press Golden Globe Awards; International Star of Tomorrow (1959); and the Limelight Award for Best Supporting Actress (1960).

Recreation. Recording for the blind (N.Y.C.), modern jazz dance classes, tennis, swimming.

KOOK, EDWARD. Executive, designer of stage lighting equipment. b. Edward Frankel Kook, Mar. 5, 1903, New York City, to Philip and Leah (Frankel) Kook. Grad. H.S. of Commerce, N.Y.C., 1920; Pace Coll. of Accountancy, N.Y.C., 1926. Married Dec. 11, 1927, to Hilda H. Silverson; one daughter. Served WW II, US Army, O.S.S. Member of Illuminating Engineers Society (task comm., 1961–to date); AFTA; ANTA (vice-chairman, bd. of standards and planning, since 1957); IATSE; Phoenix Theatre (bd. of dir. 1957–63); Dept. of State Ad Hoc Drama Panel (comm., 1963–to date); The Lambs; International Institute of Th. Technology (pres., 1975).

Mr. Kook is vice-president and director of Progress Manufacturing Co., which purchased (1964) Century Lighting, Inc., founded (1929) by Mr. Kook, Saul Joseph, and Irving Levy, with offices in N.Y.C. and California, to provide lighting effects and lighting equipment for films and theatrical productions, and later television.

He is also founder and president of Portovox, a firm that makes permanent and portable wireless microphones and accompanying transmittal sound equipment.

With Joel W. Schenker, he produced *Love Me, Love My Children* (Mercer-O'Casey Th., N.Y.C., Nov. 3, 1971).

Other Activities. With his wife, he founded (1947) and is head of Arts of the Theatre Foundation, providing grants and fellowships for playwriting students and educational theatre projects. He has taught stage lighting at Columbia Univ. and Yale Drama School; and served on the board of directors of the Phoenix Th. (N.Y.C., 1957–63). Mr. Kook is a theatrical lighting consultant in partnership with Joe Mielziner.

Published Works. He wrote an article, "History of Stage Lighting," for *Encyclopedia Britannica;* an article, "The Idea of Living Light," for *The Best Plays of 1956–57;* and the book *Images in Light for the Living Theatre* (1963).

Awards. Mr. Kook received an Antoinette Perry (Tony) special citation award (1952) for "his contribution to and encouraging the development of stage lighting and electronics"; a Ford Foundation Grant (1961) for research in scenic projection through light; the Kelcey Allen Award (1962) for his contribution to the advancement of theatre lighting; and the USITT Founders Award (1974).

KOPIT, ARTHUR. Playwright. b. Arthur L. Kopit, May 10, 1937, New York City, to George and Maxine (Dubin) Kopit. Father, business executive. Grad. Lawrence (N.Y.) H.S., 1955; Harvard Univ., B.A. (Phi Beta Kappa, Shaw Travelling Fellowship) 1959. Married Mar. 24, 1968, to Leslie Ann Garis; one son. Member of WGA, East; Dramatists Guild; Actors Studio; Playwrights' Cooperative (founding mbr., 1973); ALA; Hasty Pudding; Signet Society; Harvard Club; Masons.

Theatre. Mr. Kopit wrote the following plays, which were first produced at Harvard Univ.; *The Questioning of Nick* (Oct. 1957); *Gemini* (Nov. 1957); and, with Wally Lawrence, *Don Juan in Texas*, which he also directed (Dec. 1957); subsequently wrote and directed the following plays, which were also initially presented at Harvard Univ.; *On the Runway of Life You Never Know What's Coming Off Next* (Apr. 1957), *Across the River and Into the Jungle* (Dec. 1958), and *Sing to Me Through Open Windows* (Apr. 1959).

He wrote *Oh Dad, Poor Dad, Mama's Hung You in the Closet and I'm Feelin' So Sad* which was presented at Harvard Univ. (Cambridge, Mass., Feb. 1960); in London (Lyric, Hammersmith, July 5, 1961); in N.Y.C. (Phoenix, Feb. 26, 1962; Morosco, Aug. 26, 1963); and in Paris, the production of which he also directed (Th. des Bouffes-Parisiens, Oct. 17, 1963).

Other works include *Asylum, or What the Gentlemen Are Up to, Not to Mention the Ladies* (closed in previews: Th. de Lys, N.Y.C., Mar. 1963); *As for the Ladies* (1964); *Chamber Music* (Society Hill Playhouse, Philadelphia, Pa., 1965); *The Day the Whores Came Out To Play Tennis* and *Sing to Me Through Open Windows* (Players Th., N.Y.C., Mar. 15, 1965); *Indians* (Aldwych, London, England, July 4, 1968; Amer. premiere: Arena Stage, Washington, D.C., May 6, 1969; Brooks Atkinson Th., N.Y.C., Oct. 13, 1969); *The Conquest of Everest* and *The Hero* (NY Th. Ensemble, May 18, 1973); and *The Questioning of Nick* (Manhattan Th. Club, Apr. 1974).

Television. Mr. Kopit directed and adapted for television his play *The Questioning of Nick* (WNHC, New Haven, Conn., June 1, 1959) and wrote for television *The Conquest of Everest* (NY Television Th., NET, Feb. 1966).

Published Works. He wrote *To Dwell in a Palace of Strangers*, the first act of which was published in the *Harvard Advocate* (May 1959).

Awards. He won (1956) the Leverett House Playwriting Contest; for *Oh Dad, Poor Dad, Mama's Hung*

You in the Closet and I'm Feelin' So Sad, he won the Adams House Playwriting Contest (1959), the Vernon Rice Award (1962), and the Outer Circle Award (1962). In 1969, he was awarded a Guggenheim Fellowship, and in 1971 he was elected to the American Acad. of Arts and Letters.

Recreation. Piano, photography.

KOPS, BERNARD. Playwright. b. Nov. 28, 1926, London, England, to Joel and Jenny (Zetter) Kops. Father, shoemaker. Attended elementary schools in London, 1933–39. Married Feb. 9, 1956, to Erica Gordon; one son, three daughters. Member of ALA; Dramatists Guild. Address: (home) 35 Canfield Gardens, London, N.W. 6, England; (bus.) c/o David Highams Assoc., 5/8 Lower John St., London, W.1, England tel. OL 437-7888.

Theatre. Mr. Kops wrote *The Hamlet of Stepney Green,* (Cricket Th., N.Y.C., Nov. 13, 1958), which had previously been produced in London (Lyric, Hammersmith, July 15, 1958).

He has also written *Goodbye World* (Guilford Th., Guilford Eng., Feb. 2, 1959); *Change for the Angel* (Arts Th., London, Mar. 1, 1960); *The Dream of Peter Mann,* for the Edinburgh (Scot.) Festival (Lyceum, Edinburgh, Sept. 5, 1960); for the Center 42 Arts Festival, *Enter Solly Gold* (Co-operative Hall, Wellingborough, Northamptonshire, Eng., Sept. 10, 1962, and Mermaid Th., London, 1969), and on tour.

The Hamlet of Stepney Green and *The Dream of Peter Mann* have also been presented in Athens, Milan, Barcelona, Buenos Aires, Budapest, Amsterdam, Goteborg, Dresden, Frankfurt, Munich, Toronto, and Sydney. *David, It Is Getting Dark* was presented in France by Le Comédie de l'Ouest (Rennes, 1970; Paris, 1972). Mr. Kops' other plays include *Stray Cats and Empty Bottles;* and the one-act plays *Home Sweet Honeycomb, The Lemmings,* and *The Boy Who Wouldn't Play Jesus.*

Television and Radio. Mr. Kops has also written *The Dark Ages,* commissioned by BBC-Radio; *I Want to Go Home* and *The Last Years of Brian Hooper,* commissioned by BBC-TV; and *Just One Kid,* a dramatized documentary commissioned by ATV (London).

Published Works. Mr. Kops wrote *The World Is a Wedding,* his autobiography (1963); and the novels, *Yes From No-Man's Land* (1965), *Awake for Mourning* (1958), *Motorbike* (1962), *The Dissent of Dominick Shapiro* (1967), *By the Waters of White Chapel* (1970), *The Passionate Past of Gloria Gaye* (1971), *Settle Down Simon Katz* (1973), and *Partners* (1975). His poetry includes *Poems and Songs* (1958), *An Anemone for Antigone* (1959), *Erica, I Want to Read You Something* (1967), and *For the Record* (1971).

Awards. He received an Arts Council of Great Britain Bursary (1958–59) as a promising new dramatist.

Recreation. Writing.

KORVIN, CHARLES. Actor, director. b. Geza Kaiser, Nov. 21, 1912, Pöstyen, Hungary, to Ede and Erna (Fischer) Kaiser. Father, restaurateur. Grad. Bulyovsky Real Sch., Budapest, 1929; Sorbonne, Paris, France, Belles Lettres 1935; attended école du Louvre, Paris, 1935–37. Emigrated to US, 1937; naturalized, 1957. Married May 17, 1957, to Anne Bogy; one son. Member of AEA; SAG; AFTRA.

Theatre. Mr. Korvin made his stage debut as Steven Gaye in *Accent on Youth* (Barter Th., Abingdon, Va., July 1940), followed by appearances there as Bluntschi in *Arms and the Man* (Summer 1941), and Appius Hadrian in *Family Portrait* (Summer 1942); played Jan in *Winter Soldiers* (12 St. Playhouse, N.Y.C., New Sch. for Social Research, Nov. 29, 1942); Niko in *Dark Eyes* (Belasco, Jan. 14, 1943); Turai in *The Play's the Thing* (Newport Casino, R.I., Summer 1950); Mario Volpe in the pre-Bway tryout of *Masquerade* (opened Court Square Th., Springfield, Mass., Apr. 9, 1953); William Herschel in *Miles of Heaven* (Deerlake Th., Deerlake, Pa., Summer 1953); Jean Gabriel in *Open House* (Alley Th., Houston, Tex., Summer 1954); the King in *The King and I* (Guber, Ford, and Gross Circuit, Summers 1955–56); Preston Mitchell in *For Love or Money* (Cherry County Playhouse, Saginaw, Mich., Summer 1956); Renato in *Time of the Cuckoo,* and Michael in *The Fourposter* (Festival, Saginaw, Mich., Summer 1957); the King in *The King and I* (Cheeseman Parr Th., Denver, Colo., July 1957); Barone Guido Belcredi in the pre-Bway tryout of *Enrico* (opened Erlanger, Philadelphia, Pa., Nov. 3, 1958; closed there Nov. 8, 1958); and repeated the role of the King in *The King and I* (St. Louis Municipal Opera, Mo., Summer 1963).

Films. During the Spanish Civil War, Mr. Korvin photographed and co-directed the documentary, *Heart of Spain* (UI, 1937); in 1941, he produced and directed the documentary *To Hear Your Banjo Play.* He made his screen debut in the title role of *Enter Arsène Lupin* (U, 1944); and has appeared in *This Love of Ours* (UI, 1945); *Temptation* (UI, 1946); *Berlin Express* (RKO, 1948); *The Killer That Stalked New York* (Col., 1950); *Lydia Bailey* (20th-Fox, 1952); *Tarzan's Savage Fury* (RKO, 1952); *Sangaree* (Par., 1953); *Thunderstorm* (AA, 1956); *Ship of Fools* (Col., 1965); and *The Man Who Has Power Over Women* (Avco-Embassy, 1970).

Television. Mr. Korvin has appeared on Studio One (CBS); Playhouse 90 (CBS); Dupont Show of the Month (CBS); Suspense (CBS); on the series Interpol Calling (ITC-Rank); US Steel Hour (CBS); Mr. Omm (NBC); Crime Hunt (Ind.); Memory Lane (Ind.); Zorro (Ind.); The Millionaire (Ind.); I Spy (NBC); and The F.B.I. (ABC).

Recreation. Skiing, tennis, sailing, swimming, mountain climbing, chess, cooking.

KOSARIN, OSCAR. Musical director, composer. b. Mar. 2, 1918, Munich, Germany, to Solomon and Rose (Rapaport) Kosarin. Parents, musicians. Grad. Stuyvesant H.S., N.Y.C., 1936; attended City Coll. of New York, 1936–37. Married Sept. 14, 1947, to Lyn Hopwood; one son. Member of AFM, Local 802.

Theatre. Mr. Kosarin was musical director for stock productions at the Lambertville (N.J.) Music Circus (Summers 1950–54); composed dance music for *A Tree Grows in Brooklyn* (Alvin, N.Y.C., Apr. 19, 1951), and *Pal Joey* (Broadhurst, Jan. 2, 1952). He succeeded (Mar. 5, 1953) Pembroke Davenport as musical director and wrote dance music for *Hazel Flagg* (Mark Hellinger Th., Feb. 11, 1953); and was musical supervisor for *Mr. Wonderful* (Bway Th., Mar. 22, 1956).

Mr. Kosarin was musical director in stock in Sacramento, Calif. (Summer 1957); succeeded (May 2, 1958) Jay Blackton as musical director for *Oh, Captain!* (Alvin, N.Y.C., Feb. 4, 1958); and was musical director for the Cape Cod (Mass.) Melody Tent (Summer 1958).

Mr. Kosarin succeeded (Nov. 4, 1963) Milton Rosenstock as musical director for *Oliver!* (Imperial, N.Y.C., Jan. 6, 1963); toured as musical director of *Do Re Mi, Carnival!* and *Stop the World—I Want to Get Off;* and conducted *To Broadway with Love* at the New York World's Fair (1964).

He was musical director for *Something More!* (Eugene O'Neill Th., N.Y.C., Nov. 10, 1964); assistant conductor for *Fade Out—Fade In* (re-opened Mark Hellinger Th., Feb. 15, 1965); *Sweet Charity* (Palace, Jan. 29, 1966), where he subsequently succeeded (July 1966) Fred Werner as conductor; and *Sherry* (Alvin, Mar. 28, 1967); musical director for *Arabian Nights* (Jones Beach Th., L.I., N.Y., July 2, 1967); musical director and vocal arranger for *The Happy Time* (Broadway Th., N.Y.C., Jan. 18, 1968); vocal and dance arranger and musical director for *Canterbury Tales* (Eugene O'Neill Th., Feb. 3, 1969); and *Park* (John Golden Th., Apr. 22, 1970); guest musical director with the Baltimore (Md.) Center Stage (1969–70 season); vocal arranger and musical director for *70, Girls, 70* (Broadhurst, N.Y.C., Apr. 15, 1971); and musical director for *The Sound of Music* (Jones Beach Th., L.I., N.Y., July 1, 1970; and July 8, 1971).

Other Activities. Mr. Kosarin was musical director for industrial shows sponsored by Cadillac, Plymouth, Lincoln-Mercury, Ford, and Comet.

KOZELKA, PAUL. Educator. b. Edwin Paul Kozelka, Sept. 11, 1909, Chicago, Ill., to Frank Joseph and Barbara (Cizek) Kozelka. Father, merchant. Grad. Harrison H.S., Chicago, Ill., 1927; Lawrence Coll. B.A. 1932; Northwestern Univ., M.A. 1937; Yale Univ., Ph.D. 1943. Served as assistant Field Dir., Amer. Red Cross, 1943–45. Married Sept. 4, 1943, to Faith Kuter; one son. Member of ATA (formerly AETA) (pres., 1961–65; 1st vice-pres. 1963–64; board member); ANTA (exec. comm., former board member); CTC (natl. dir., 1955–57); ASTR (secy. treas., 1956–61); Speech Assn. of the Eastern States (exec. council); Natl. Council of Teachers of English (comm. to revise "Guide to Play Selection"); Secondary Sch. Theatre Conf. (program chmn., annual meeting, 1955); Sigma Phi Epsilon. Address: (home) 100 La Salle St., New York, NY 10027; (bus.) Teachers College, Columbia Univ., New York, NY 10027, tel. (212) UN 5-6000.

Mr. Kozelka has been professor emeritus at Teachers College, Columbia Univ., since Sept. 1974. From 1957 until 1974, he was a professor of theatre there; previously he had been assistant professor (1947–50); and associate professor (1950–57). He has held academic positions at Rosary Coll. (dept. asst., 1937–40); and Allegheny Coll. (asst. prof., 1945–47).

In 1947, he established the Drama Workshop at Teachers Coll. (Columbia Univ.), where he designed the stage and auditorium, and he directed over 100 productions. He organized the work conference in Creative Drama, sponsored by the Speech Dept. of Teachers Coll. (Mar. 1957).

Mr. Kozelka was Theatre Specialist at the Arts Festival of West Virginia State Coll. (1962), and delivered lectures on the theatre at the American Embassy (London, Apr. 1961), Morgan State Coll. (Baltimore, Md., 1962), and the Language Arts Conference, St. Augustine Coll. (Raleigh, N.C., Mar. 1963).

Films. He edited a film strip for *Richard III* (Lopert, 1956).

Published Works. Mr. Kozelka is editor-in-chief of Theatre Student Series, of which twenty volumes are available; he wrote *Directing* (1968) for this series. Mr. Kozelka contributed the chapter on high-school drama to *History of Speech Education in America* (1954); edited *A Glossary to the Plays of Bernard Shaw* (1959); *Fifteen One-Act Plays* (1961); wrote articles on Jouvet, Max Reinhardt, and Rachel for the *Encyclopeadia Britannica;* and an article on Fanny Davenport for the *Directory of American Women.* He has contributed articles to *Players* Magazine, *Dramatics* Magazine, and *Audio-Visual Guide.*

Awards. Mr. Kozelka received the ATA Eaves Junior Award for 1961; was made a fellow of ATA in 1970; and received the Founders Award, Secondary School Theatre Conference in 1971.

Recreation. Attending theatre, collecting theatre memorabilia.

KRAFT, HY. Playwright. b. Hyman Solomon Kraft, April 30, 1899, New York City, to Abraham and Yetta Kraft. Father, tailor. Attended Townsend Harris H.S., N.Y.C. Married in 1938 to Reata; one daughter, Jill Kraft, actress. Member of Dramatists Guild. Address: 221 W. 82nd St., New York, NY 10024.

Pre-Theatre. Newspaper work; assistant to Sigmund Spaeth, musicologist.

Theatre. Mr. Kraft wrote *Ten Per Cent* (George M. Cohan Th., N.Y.C., Sept. 13, 1927); subsequently, with Thomas E. Jackson, produced *Gentlemen of the Press* (Henry Miller's Th., Aug. 27, 1928), and *Poppa* (Hudson, Dec. 24, 1928); wrote, with Peter Arno, the original story on which was based *The New Yorkers* (Bway Th., Dec. 8, 1930); wrote, with Messrs. Hellinger, Brown, and Henderson, *Hot-Cha* (Ziegfeld, Mar. 8, 1932); and Wrote, with Edward Chodorov, *Cue for Passion* (Royale, Dec. 19, 1940).

He wrote *Cafe Crown* (Cort. Jan. 23, 1942); and the book for *Top Banana* (Winter Garden, Nov. 1, 1951); with Eric Maschwitz, wrote *Summer Song* (Prince's Th., London, England, Feb. 16, 1956); and wrote the book for the musical version of his *Cafe Crown* (Martin Beck Th., Apr. 17, 1964).

Films. With Theodore Dreiser, he rewrote *An American Tragedy* (Par., 1932); with Billy Wilder, wrote the original story for *Champagne Waltz* (Par., 1933); wrote, with Oscar Hammerstein II, *Way of the River* (MGM, 1938); and wrote the original story and treatment of *Stormy Weather* (20th-Fox, 1942).

He wrote the screenplay for *Home Is the Hero* (Scoa 1961); with Theodore Dreiser wrote the original story (1933) for *Tobacco Story* (Garrick Films, 1964); and wrote screenplays for the Abbey Theatre presentations of *New Gossoon* and *Autumn Fire* (Emmett Dalton Productions).

Television and Radio. On radio, he was writer and originator, with Cy Howard, of Life with Luigi (CBS). For television, he has written scripts for Starlight Th. (CBS, 1951); Spectacular for Water Rats (BBC, 1956); *Robin Hood* (Granada, 1960); *Lancelot* (Granada, 1960); *Four Just Men* (Granada, 1960; and *Hercules* (Embassy TV).

Published Works. Mr. Kraft's published work includes *Skits and Sketches* (1938); *Six Anti-Nazi One-Act Plays* (1939); *Treasury Star Parade* (1942); *On My Way to the Theatre* (1971); and *Lyrics by Dorothy Field* (1974).

Awards. Mr. Kraft was cited by the US Treasury Dept. for services rendered (Treasury Star Parade, 1941–42).

KRAFT, JILL. Actress. b. Sept. 29, 1930, New York City. Father, Hy Kraft, playwright; mother, Reata Kraft, interior decorator. Grad. Beverly Hills (Calif.) H.S., 1948; attended Univ. of California at Los Angeles, 1948–49. Studied acting in N.Y.C., with Stella Adler, 1951; at the Curt Conway Workshop, 1954–55; Robert Lewis Workshop, 1959–60; and with Harold Clurman. Married Aug. 1950 to Louis Morheim, screen writer (marr. dis. 1952); married Dec. 1956 to Walter Marks, composer (marr. dis. May 1961). Member of AEA; SAG; AFTRA.

Theatre. Miss Kraft first appeared on stage as Emily in a high-school production of *Our Town* (1948); made her Bway debut in *Goodbye, My Fancy* (Fulton, Nov. 17, 1948); played Sylvia Craven in *The Philanderer* at the Westport (Conn.) Country Playhouse (July 1951); understudied Audrey Hepburn in the title role of *Gigi* (Fulton, Nov. 24, 1951); understudied the roles of Joan, Jeannie, and Ginger in *Time Out for Ginger* (Lyceum, Nov. 26, 1952); appeared as Cecily in a scene from *The Importance of Being Earnest* in an ANTA Album presentation (Empire, June 1953); and played Audrey in *Three Men on a Horse* in a tour of summer theatres (Summer 1953). She was understudy and played a Comedienne in *Cyrano de Bergerac* (NY City Ctr., Nov. 11, 1953); played Millie in *Picnic* and Jeannie in *Time Out for Ginger* (Playhouse-in-the-Park, Philadelphia, Pa., Summer 1955); and title role in *Sabrina Fair* (Grist Mill Playhouse, Andover, N.J., Summer 1955); Catherine in special afternoon performances (Winter 1956) of *A View from the Bridge* (Coronet, N.Y.C., Sept. 29, 1955); and subsequently repeated the role for the Group 20 Players (Wellesley, Mass., Summer 1956); played Myra in *Compulsion* (Bucks County Playhouse, New Hope, Pa., Summer 1958); succeeded Pat Stanley in the role of Lillian Bartley in *Blue Denim* (Playhouse, N.Y.C., Feb. 27, 1958); Miss Kraft understudied Joan Gray as Edmee in *Cheri* (Morosco, Oct. 12, 1959); at the Playhouse in the Park (Philadelphia, Pa.), played Sally Follet in *All the Way Home* (Summer 1961); Claire in *Here Today* in a tour of summer theatres (1962); and Debbie Hirsch in *Dear Me, the Sky Is Falling* (Music Box, N.Y.C., Mar. 2, 1963).

Films. Miss Kraft played the role of Carol in the film version of *Goodbye, My Fancy* (WB, 1951).

Television. She made her debut on the Gabby Hayes Show (NBC, 1951); and appeared on the Philco Playhouse (NBC, 1951); Starlight Th.; Man Behind the Badge; Big Story (NBC); *Millions of George* (Studio One, CBS); *Dashing White Sergeant* (Kraft Th., NBC); *Visit to a Small Planet* (Goodyear Playhouse, NBC); Colgate Comedy Hour (NBC); the Red Buttons Show (CBS); the Imogene Coca Show (NBC); Modern Romances (NBC); True Story (NBC); Edge of Night (CBS); As the World Turns (CBS); One Man's Family (NBC); and Valiant Lady (CBS).

Recreation. Interior decorating.

KRAMM, JOSEPH. Actor, director, playwright. b. Sept. 30, 1907, Philadelphia, Pa., to Samuel and Caecelia (Kramm) Kramm. Father, pharmacist. Grad. South Philadelphia (Pa.) H.S., 1924; Univ. of Pennsylvania, B.A. 1928. Married June 25, 1932, to Anna May Loevner, actress (marr. dis. 1938); married Oct. 11, 1940, to Isabel Bonner, actress (dec. July 1, 1955). Served US Army, 1943–45, ETO and PTO; rank, Sgt. t/4; five battle stars. Member of Dramatists Guild; SSD&C; AEA. Address: 169 Eighth Ave., New York, NY 10011.

Pre-Theatre. Journalist.

Theatre. Mr. Kramm first performed with the Mae Desmond Stock Co. in *Lilac Time* (Wm. Penn. Th., Philadelphia, Pa., Oct. 1928); was with Eva Le Gallienne's Civic Repertory Th. (N.Y.C., Oct. 1928 –June 1935); played Foresti in *L'Aiglon* (Broadhurst, Nov. 3, 1934), with the repertory company; a soldier in *Bury the Dead* (Ethel Barrymore Th., Apr. 18, 1936); Jake Psinski in the Federal Th. (WPA) Project production of *Processional* (Maxine Elliott's Th., Oct. 13, 1937); and made his London debut as Frank in *Golden Boy* (St. James's, Aug. 21, 1938).

He appeared as Dr. Stockmann in a tour of *An Enemy of the People* (Federal Th., US, 1939); Senator Talbot in *The Man Who Killed Lincoln* (Longacre, N.Y.C., Jan. 17, 1940); Linzman in *Liliom* (44 St. Th., Mar. 25, 1940); and Malachi in *Journey to Jerusalem* (Natl., Oct. 5, 1940).

He was director for the Sayville (N.Y.) Summer Th. (Summers 1946–47); directed *Hope Is the Thing with Feathers*, a one-act play in a triple bill, entitled *Six O'Clock Theatre* (Maxine Elliott's Th., N.Y.C., Apr. 11, 1948); and stock productions of *Twentieth Century* (Olney Th., Md., Summer 1948) and *Anna Christie* (Westport Country Playhouse, Conn., Summer 1948).

Mr. Kramm wrote *The Shrike* (Cort, N.Y.C., Jan. 15, 1952); dramatized *The Gypsies Wore High Hats* (Cape Playhouse, Dennis, Mass., Summer 1952); directed the national touring company of the play (opened Shubert, New Haven, Conn., Oct. 15, 1952; closed Erlanger, Chicago, Ill., Mar. 21, 1953), the London production (Prince's Th., Feb. 15, 1953), with Jose Ferrer, the N.Y.C. production (NY City Ctr., Nov. 25, 1953), and the West Coast production (Carthay Circle Th., Los Angeles, Calif., 1955).

He wrote *Build with One Hand* and directed it in association with Warren Enters (opened Shubert, New Haven, Conn., Nov. 7, 1956; closed Ford's Th., Baltimore, Md., Nov. 27, 1956); and wrote *Giants, Sons of Giants* (Alvin, N.Y.C., Jan. 6, 1962).

Awards. In 1952, Mr. Kramm received the Pulitzer Prize, the Donaldson Award, and the Front Page Award of the Newspaper Guild of Philadelphia, Pa., for his play *The Shrike.*

Recreation. Reading, swimming, walking, music.

KRASNA, NORMAN. Playwright, producer. b. Nov. 7, 1909, Corona, L.I., N.Y., to Benjamin and Beatrice (Mannison) Krasna. Attended New York Univ., 1927; Columbia Univ., 1928; St. John's Law Sch., 1929. Married Aug. 6, 1940, to Ruth Frazee, actress (marr. dis. Apr. 27, 1951); married Dec. 7, 1951, to Erle Galbraith Jolson, two daughters, one son. Served USAF, 1942–45; rank Maj. Member of Dramatists Guild; SWG. Address: Blonay, Switzerland.

Theatre. Mr. Krasna was assistant drama and film critic for the N.Y. *World* (1928); drama editor and critic for the N.Y. *Evening Graphic* (1929); and columnist for the trade periodical, *Exhibitors Herald-—World* (1930).

He wrote *Louder, Please* (Masque, N.Y.C., Nov. 12, 1931); *Small Miracle* (John Golden Th., Sept. 26, 1934); *The Man with Blonde Hair* (Belasco, Nov. 4, 1941); *Dear Ruth* (Henry Miller's Th., Dec. 13, 1944); and *John Loves Mary* (Booth, Feb. 4, 1947); collaborated with Groucho Marx on *Time for Elizabeth* (Fulton, Sept. 27, 1948); wrote *Kind Sir* (Alvin, Nov. 4, 1953); *Who Was That Lady I Saw You With?* (Martin Beck Th., Mar. 3, 1958); *Sunday in New York* (Cort, Nov. 29, 1961); *Watch the Birdie!* (Coconut Grove Playhouse, Miami, Fla., Summer 1954); *Love in E Flat* (Brooks Atkinson Th., N.Y.C., Feb. 13, 1967); *Blue Hour* (Comedy Th., Berlin, 1970); *Bunny* (Criterion Th., London, Dec. 18, 1972); and *We Interrupt This Program...* (Ambassador, N.Y.C., Apr. 1, 1975).

Films. Mr. Krasna adapted, with Alice Duer Miller, Faith Baldwin's story for the film, *Wife Versus Secretary* (MGM, 1939); wrote the story which Allen Rivlin and P. J. Wolfson adapted for *Meet the Baron* (MGM, 1932); wrote, with Jo Swerling, *Hollywood Speaks* (Col., 1932); wrote the screenplay, *That's My Boy* (Col., 1932), based on a novel by Francis Wallace; the screenplay for *Parole Girl* (Col., 1933), based on the story "Dance of the Millions"; author of story, screenplay, and dialogue for *So This Is Africa* (Col., 1933); author of the story and screenplay of *The Richest Girl in the World* (RKO, 1934); author with Don Hartman of the story for *Romance in Manhattan* (RKO, 1934).

He adapted his play *Small Miracle* into the film *Four Hours to Kill* (Par., 1935); collaborated with Vincent Lawrence and Herbert Fields on the screenplay for the film *Hands Across the Table* (Par., 1935); wrote the original screen story for *Fury* (MGM, 1936); collaborated with Groucho Marx on original screenplay for *The King and the Chorus Girl* (WB, 1937); wrote the story for *As Good as Married* (U, 1937); produced *The Big City* based on his story (MGM, 1937); produced *The First Hundred Years*, based on his story (MGM, 1938); produced *Three Loves Has Nancy* (MGM, 1938); wrote the story for *You and Me* (Par., 1938); the screenplay for *Bachelor Mother* (RKO, 1939); the screenplay for *It's a Date* (U, 1940); wrote, with Edward Buzzell, the screenplay for *Love, Honor and Oh, Baby!*, based on the play, *Oh, Promise Me* (U, 1940).

He wrote the original screenplay and story for *Mr. and Mrs. Smith* (RKO, 1941); for *The Devil and Miss Jones* (RKO, 1941), which he produced with Frank Ross; wrote *The Flame of New Orleans* (U, 1941); the screenplay, with Leo Townsend, for *It Started with Eve* (U, 1941); wrote and directed *Princess O'Rourke* (WB, 1943); supplied the story for *Bride by Mistake* (RKO, 1944), which was a remake of *The Richest Girl in the World*; and wrote the original screenplay of *Practically Yours* (Par., 1944). His play *Dear Ruth* was made into a film (Par., 1947); as was his play *John Loves Mary* (WB, 1949); and he wrote, produced, and directed *The Big Hangover* (MGM, 1950).

In 1950, he formed Wald-Krasna Productions, which distributed films through RKO, and produced *The Blue Veil* with Jerry Wald (RKO, 1950); *Behave Yourself* with Wald (RKO, 1951); and *Clash by Night* with Wald and Harriet Parsons (RKO, 1952). He sold his interest to Jerry Wald (May, 1952); later formed Monovale Productions (1956); wrote, produced and directed, *The Ambassador's Daughter* (UA, 1956); *Bachelor Mother* was remade as *Bundle of Joy* (RKO, 1956); wrote the screenplay for *Indiscreet* (WB, 1958), adapted from his play *Kind Sir*; collaborated on *White Christmas* (Par., 1954); wrote and produced *Who Was That Lady I Saw You With?*; wrote original screenplays for *Let's Make Love* (20th-Fox, 1961); *My Geisha* (Par., 1962); and for *Sunday in New York* (MGM, 1964), based on his play of the same name.

Awards. Mr. Krasna received the Academy (Oscar) Award (1943) for his original screenplay for *Princess O'Rourke*; and the Screen Writers Guild Laurel Award (1959) for his contribution to screen literature. He was nominated for Academy (Oscar) Awards for his writing of *The Richest Girl in the*

World (1935); *Fury* (1937); *The Devil and Miss Jones* (1942); and *Practically Yours* (1945).

KRAUS, TED M. Publisher, critic, editor, teacher. b. Theodore M. Kraus, Apr. 18, 1923, New York City, to Herman L. and Ruth J. (Weinberg) Kraus. Father, exporter. Grad. Lynbrook (N.Y.) H.S., 1940; Franklin and Marshall Coll., B.S. 1944; Columbia Univ., M.A. 1963. Member of the Drama Desk (secy., 1955–60; 1963–69); AETA; Amer. Community Theatre Assn. (bd. of dir., 1967–70). Address: 76 Fox Run, Poughkeepsie, NY 12603, tel. (914) 452-6184.

Mr. Kraus is the founder of the *Critical Digest*, a bi-weekly theatre newsletter service, for which he serves as publisher, editor, and official "Second Night Critic" (1950–to date). He is a former New York City contributing editor to *Players*, a bi-monthly publication of the National Thespian Assn. (1968–72).

He has lectured in English at Baruch Coll., CUNY (1963–69); the Fashion Institute of Technology (N.Y.C., 1966–67); and NY City Community Coll. (Brooklyn, N.Y., 1967–68); and in theatre arts at the Univ. of Maryland (Baltimore County, 1969–70). He has been an instructor in English and humanities at Dutchess Community Coll. (Poughkeepsie, N.Y., 1973–74); and at the Center for Continuing Education of State Univ. Coll. (New Paltz, N.Y., 1973–74), conducting seminars on current theatre and the theatre in London.

Other Activities. Mr. Kraus served as the senior faculty critic for summer sessions of the National Critics Institute (Waterford, Conn., 1968–70); presented a critique on the four-day educational meeting of the North West Theatre Conference (Univ. of Oregon at Eugene, 1970); and was a critique panelist for ASSITEJ, the Fourth International Children's and Youth Theatre Congress (Albany, N.Y., 1972).

Published Works. He is editor of *Theatre Trends* (1971), a workbook used in colleges in introductory theatre classes.

KRAWITZ, SEYMOUR. Press representative. b. Oct. 21, 1923, New York City, to Harry and Sarah (Epstein) Krawitz. Father, poultry dealer; mother, educator. Grad. Stuyvesant H.S., 1940; City Coll. of New York, B.S. (English) 1948; attended Columbia Univ., 1949–50; New York Univ., 1951–53. Married Mar. 23, 1958, to Patricia McLean, ballerina; one son. Relative in theatre: brother, Herman E. Krawitz, business manager, Metropolitan Opera Assn. Served US Army, ETO, PTO, 1943–46; rank, Sgt. Member of ATPAM. Address: (home) 230 W. 79th St., New York, NY 10024, tel. (212) TR 4-7813; (bus.) 850 Seventh Ave., New York, NY 10019, tel. (212) 247-1120.

Pre-Theatre. Truck driver, shoe salesman, copy boy, NY *Times*. .

Theatre. Mr. Krawitz sang in the chorus of a college production of *The Cradle Will Rock* (City Coll. of New York, Nov. 1940); was stage manager, press representative and co-producer of stock productions at the University Th. (Mashpee, Mass., Summers 1947–48); press representative for the Falmouth (Mass.) Playhouse (Summers 1949–50); the South Shore Music Circus (Cohasset, Mass., Summer 1951); and the Neptune (N.J.) Music Circus (Summer 1952).

In 1952, he joined the staff of Bill Doll, press representative, to do press work for the Bway productions of *New Faces of 1952;* in 1953, *Porgy and Bess, Room Service,* and summer stock productions of *A Night in Venice, The Strong Are Lonely,* and *Sherlock Holmes,* in 1954, for *The Starcross Story, The Immoralist, King of Hearts* and the six-month season at Bucks Co. Playhouse, New Hope, Pa. He then joined Richard Maney's staff, to work on *Dear Charles, The Reclining Figure, The Living Room,* and *Lunatics and Lovers;* rejoined Mr. Doll to work on *The Saint of Bleecker Street* and *Anastasia;* in 1955, on *Carmen Amaya and her Company, Deathwatch, Plain and Fancy, Macbeth,* and *Thesmophoriazusae;* in 1956, the pre-Bway tryout of *Strip for Action,* and the N.Y.C. productions of *Waiting for Godot, Wake Up Darling, New Faces of 1956,* and *The Threepenny Opera;* in 1957, the revival of *Waiting for Godot, The Potting Shed, A Moon for the Misbegotten,* and *Shoestring '57.*

In 1958, Mr. Krawitz was press representative for *The World of Suzie Wong,* and *La Plume de Ma Tante;* in 1959, *Gypsy,* and the pre-Bway tryout of *Juniper and the Pagans;* in 1960, the NY Shakespeare Festival production of *Henry V;* in 1961, *The Tiger Rag, Double Entry, Mary, Mary, A Far Country,* the NY Shakespeare Festival productions of *Much Ado About Nothing, A Midsummer Night's Dream,* and *Richard II,* and *Come Blow Your Horn.*

In 1962, he was press representative for *How To Succeed in Business without Really Trying,* and its subsequent tour (1963) the pre-Bway tryout of *The Umbrella,* Second City's *Seacoast of Bohemia* and *Alarums and Excursions, Little Me, The Pinter Plays, Half-past Wednesday,* the double bill, *A Portrait of the Artist as a Young Man* and *The Barroom Monks,* the NY Shakespeare Festival productions of *The Merchant of Venice, The Tempest,* and *King Lear;* in 1963, for *On an Open Roof,* Second City's *To the Water Tower, The Heroine, Mr. Simian, Nobody Loves an Albatross, The Riot Act,* and the NY Shakespeare Festival productions of *Antony and Cleopatra, As You Like It,* and *The Winter's Tale.* In 1964, he represented *Abraham Cochrane, Cafe Crown, Little Eyolf,* Second City's *The Third Ear,* the NY Shakespeare Festival's *Hamlet, Othello* and *Electra,* Second City's *A View from Under the Bridge,* and the Bway productions *Traveller Without Luggage, Absence of a Cello, The Sign in Sidney Brustein's Window, Bajour,* and *The Owl and the Pussycat,* and the NY Shakespeare Festival's touring productions of *The Puppet Theatre of Don Cristobal, The Shoemaker's Prodigious Wife,* and *A Midsummer Night's Dream.*

In 1965, Mr. Krawitz represented the Bway productions of *Peterpat,* and *And Things That Go Bump in the Night,* the pre-Bway tryout of *A Sign of Affection,* the tour of *From the Second City,* the NY Shakespeare Festival productions of *Love's Labour's Lost, Coriolanus, Troilus and Cressida, Henry V, The Taming of the Shrew,* and the off-Bway productions of *The New Cambridge Circus,* and *The Decline and Fall of the Entire World as Seen Through the Eyes of Cole Porter Revisited,* as well as the ANTA Matinee Series at the Th. de Lys; in 1966, he represented the Bway play *My Sweet Charlie,* the NY Shakespeare Festival's Spanish-language *Romeo and Juliet,* the off-Bway plays *Will Geer's Americana,* and *Command Performance,* and the ANTA Matinee Series; in 1967, the revival of *Marat/Sade, How To Be a Jewish Mother,* and the pre-Bway tryout of *The Hemingway Hero,* the ANTA Matinee Series, and was press representative in the US for the Montreal Expo '67 World Festival of Performing Arts.

In 1968, he represented *The Prime of Miss Jean Brodie;* in 1969, *A Teaspoon Every Four Hours,* NY City Ctr.'s *Fiesta in Madrid,* and the off-Bway plays *The Fourth Wall, Month of Sundays, Shoot Anything with Hair That Moves, Time for Bed— Take Me to Bed, Little Boxes,* and *The Moondreamers;* in 1970, *Sheep on the Runway,* NY City Ctr.'s *Rabelais,* and off-Bway, *Transfers, Lulu, The Rise and Fall of the City of Mahagonny,* and *The Effect of Gamma Rays on Man-in-the-Moon Marigolds;* in 1971, *Frank Merriwell, Soon,* and *Old Times,* and off-Bway, *One Flew Over the Cuckoo's Nest, And Who's Little Boy Are You?,* and *Leaves of Grass;* in 1972, *Lost in the Stars,* the off-Bway plays *God Says There Is No Peter Ott, Whitsuntide, A Quarter for the Ladies Room,* and *Blue Boys,* and the Queens (N.Y.) Playhouse productions of *Twelve Angry Men* and *Pygmalion.*

In 1973, Mr. Krawitz was press representative for *Finishing Touches, The Changing Room, Crown Matrimonial* and *A Moon for the Misbegotten,* as well as the off-Bway productions of *Oh Coward!, Crystal and Fox,* and *Spoon River Anthology;* in 1974, for *Henry Fonda as Clarence Darrow, James Whitmore in Will Rogers' USA, Cat on a Hot Tin Roof, Of Mice and Men,* and the URGENT Th. productions of *Entertaining Mr. Sloane* and *Break a Leg;* and in 1975, for *Don't Call Back* and *Rodgers and Hart*. .

Films. Mr. Krawitz was publicity manager for *Around the World in 80 Days* (UA, 1956); and press representative for *A Midsummer Night's Dream* and *Tomorrow Is My Turn* (Show corporation 1962).

Television. In 1952, Mr. Krawitz was a press representative for the Dumont Network, N.Y.C.

Recreation. Classical music, books, woodworking.

KRIMSKY, JOHN. Producer, advertising executive. b. July 7, 1906, New York City, to Dr. Joseph and Sophie Krimsky. Father, doctor. Grad. Erasmus Hall H.S., Brooklyn, N.Y.; attended Princeton Univ.; New York Univ.; Columbia Univ. Extension. Married Mar. 3, 1932, to Angela Atwell: two sons; one daughter, Angela Kathleen Krimsky, producer, director. Served OSS, Chief of the Entertainment Control Section, PWD-SHAEF, ETO, 1943–44. Member of League of NY Theatres; Washington Country Club, Conn; Lourel Bank Fishing Club. Address: Laurel River Rd., Roxbury, CT 06783.

Pre-Theatre. Banking for Lehman Bros. (1928–33).

Theatre. While still with Lehman Bros., Mr. Krimsky started the Play-of-the-Month Club (1927); produced, with Gifford Cochran, *The Threepenny Opera* (Empire, N.Y.C., US premiere Apr. 13, 1933); operated the American Music Hall, a cabaret-theatre on E. 55 St. 1936–40), where his productions included *Naughty Naught '00* (Jan. 23, 1937), *The Fireman's Flame* (Oct. 9, 1937), and *The Girl from Wyoming* (Oct. 29, 1938), all three written with his brother, Jerrold, under the pseudonym of John Van Antwerp.

He was director of entertainment of the NY World's Fair (1939–40); co-producer with Richard Charlton of *Cranks* (Bijou, N.Y.C., Nov. 26, 1956); took over the old El Morocco nightclub on E. 54th St. and remodeled it into the Strollers Theatre-Club, where he presented *Time Gentleman, Please!* (Nov. 1961), and with Peter Cook, produced the British revue, *The Establishment* (Jan. 19, 1963); and supervised the entertainment at the Seven-Up Pavilion at the NY World's Fair (1964).

Films. Mr. Krimsky presented the US premiere of the German film, *Maedchen in Uniform* (KAC, 1932); produced Eugene O'Neill's *The Emperor Jones* (UA, 1933); was a production executive for MGM studios (1943); and supervised the Shirley Temple and Will Rogers films for Fox Film Studios (1935–36).

Other Activities. Mr. Krimsky worked for the advertising agencies Buchanan and Co. (1940–49) and Donahue and Coe (1950–60). He is chairman of the Arts and Entertainment committee for Gov. Ella Grasso of Conn. (1975).

KROLL, LUCY. Literary and talent representative. b. Lucy Rosengardt, July 4, New York City, to Solomon and Esther Rosengardt. Father, dentist. Grad. P.S. 149, Brooklyn, N.Y.; Thomas Jefferson H.S., Brooklyn, N.Y.; Hunter Coll., B.A. 1933; Sch. for the Stage of Tamara Daykarhanova, two years, degree in acting, dance, theatre skills. Married Nov. 5, 1939, to Nathan Kroll, musician, film producer; one son. Member of TARA; Society of Authors' Representatives; Hunter Coll. Alumni Assn. Address: 390 West End Ave., New York, NY 10024, tel. (212) TR 7-0627.

Since 1945, Mrs. Kroll has been the sole owner of the Lucy Kroll Agency, which represents literary and theatrical talent, with offices in N.Y.C.

Before becoming an artists' representative, she was a member and co-producer of the American Actors Co. (1937–42); was engaged as a literary analyst for Warner Bros. studios (Hollywood, Calif., 1942–44); and taught drama and communications at Hunter Coll. (1944–45).

KRONE, GERALD. Producer, actor, director, lecturer. b. Gerald Sidney Krone, Feb. 25, 1933, Memphis, Tenn., to Irving and Eva (Sauer) Krone. Father, member of Florida State Hotel & Restaurant Commission; mother, attorney. Grad. Humes H.S., Memphis, Tenn., 1950 (Natl. Honor Society); Washington Univ., A.B. (honors) 1954;

attended Oxford Univ., Stratford, England, summer session, certificate 1954; Washington Univ., A.M. 1958. Served US Army Signal Corps, 1954–56; rank, S/3. Married April 1965 to Dorothy Olim (marr. dis. Feb. 1970). Member of League of Off-Bway Theatres & Producers (secy.-treas., Aug. 1963–April 1970); Assn. of Theatrical Producers and Managers; ATAS; Omicron Delta Kappa; Pi Epsilon Delta (pres.); Thyrsus (Washington Univ. drama organization, pres.). Address: (home) 160 West End Ave., New York, NY 10023; (bus.) 1540 Broadway, New York, NY 10036.

Theatre. Mr. Krone appeared in stock at the Avondale Playhouse (Laurel, Md., Summer 1952); was producer-director at the St. Louis (Mo.) Theatre-in-the-Round (June–Aug. 1957); and performed with the Dunes Summer Th. (Michiana, Ill., June 1958); and in *Blood Wedding* (Actors' Playhouse, N.Y.C., Mar. 3, 1958).

He produced and directed *No Trifling with Love* (St. Mark's Playhouse, Nov. 9, 1959); directed, and produced, with Dorothy Olim, *A Worm in Horseradish* (Maidman Th., Mar. 13, 1961); produced, with Miss Olim, *The Golden Apple* (York Playhouse, Feb. 12, 1962); presented, with Miss Olim and Irvin Dorfman, *The Lion in Love* (One Sheridan Sq., Apr. 25, 1963); and produced, with Miss Olim, *Pimpernel!* (Gramercy Arts, Jan. 6, 1964); and, with St. John Terrell, *I Must Be Talking to My Friends* (Orpheum Th., Nov. 16, 1967).

He was associate producer of St. John Terrell's Music Circus, Lambertville, N.J. (1963–68); founded, with Robert Hooks and Douglas Turner Ward, the Negro Ensemble Company (Apr. 1967), serving as its treasurer (1967–to date), administrative director (Apr. 1967–Sept. 1970), and consulting director (Oct. 1970–to date); and was executive administrator and producer of *The River Niger* (Brooks Atkinson Th., N.Y.C., Mar. 27, 1973).

Mr. Krone has been consultant to Loretto Hilton Th. (St. Louis, Mo.); Free Southern Th. (New Orleans, La.); and the Spring St. Players (N.Y.C.). He was manager of Morris Th. (Morristown, N.J.) and the Eleventh St. Th. (N.Y.C.), both in 1962–63. Among the thirty-two New York City productions that he has managed are: *Billy Liar* (Gate Th., Mar. 17, 1965); the double-bill *Happy Ending* and *Day of Absence* (St. Mark's Playhouse, Nov. 15, 1965); *America Hurrah* (Pocket Th., Nov. 6, 1966); *Viet Rock* (Martinique, Nov. 10, 1966); *MacBird!* (Village Gate, Feb. 22, 1967); *Fortune and Men's Eyes* (Actors Playhouse, Feb. 23, 1967); *Your Own Thing* (Orpheum, Jan. 13, 1968); *Tom Paine* (Stage 73, Mar. 25, 1968); the double-bill *Red Cross* and *Muzeeka* (Provincetown Playhouse, Apr. 28, 1968); *Collision Course* (Cafe au Go-Go, May 8, 1968); *Big Time Buck White* (Village South Th., Dec. 8, 1968); and *The Reckoning* (St. Mark's Playhouse, Sept. 4, 1969).

Films. Mr. Krone produced *The Inheritors* (Rome, Italy, 1972).

Television and Radio. Mr. Krone appeared on Radio Th. (WREC, Memphis, 1946). His first television appearance was on a panel show (WMC-TV, Memphis, 1950). He was executive producer of *Ceremonies in Dark Old Men* (ABC Theatre, ABC Network TV Special, 1974).

Other Activities. Mr. Krone was on the faculty of Washington Univ., St. Louis, Mo., from 1957 to 1959. From 1961 to 1969, he gave a series of lecture-discussions on "How To Produce Off-Bway," and from 1968 to 1970 he was president of Krone-Olim Advertising.

Awards. The Negro Ensemble Company received *Village Voice* Off-Bway (Obie) and Drama Desk-Vernon Rice awards in 1968; a Brandeis Univ. Creative Arts and Antoinette Perry (Tony) awards in 1969. *The River Niger* was awarded a Tony in 1974.

KRONENBERGER, LOUIS. Educator, writer, critic. b. Dec. 9, 1904, Cincinnati, Ohio, to Louis and Mabel (Newwitter) Kronenberger. Father, businessman. Grad. Hughes H.S., Cincinnati, Ohio, 1921; Univ. of Cincinnati, Litt. D. 1952. Married Jan. 29, 1940, to Emmy L. Plaut; one son, one daughter. Member of NY Drama Critics' Circle (vice-pres., 1942–44, 1949–61); Natl. Inst. of Arts and Letters (secy., 1953–56); Fellow of American Acad. of Arts and Sciences. Address: 1514 Beacon St., Brookline, MA 02146.

From 1953 to 1970, Mr. Kronenberger was professor of theatre arts, Brandeis Univ. (Waltham, Mass.)

He was drama critic for *Time Magazine* (1938–61), the newspaper *PM* (1940–48), and *Town and Country* Magazine (1948–49). He taught drama courses at Columbia Univ. (1950–51, 1959); City Coll. of New York (1953–54); Harvard Univ. (1959); Stanford Univ. (1963); and has lectured on drama at Oxford Univ. (1959) and at the Univ. of California at Berkeley (1968). He adapted Jean Anouilh's *Mademoiselle Colombe* (Longacre Th., N.Y.C., Jan. 6, 1954).

Pre-Theatre. Editor, Boni and Liveright, Inc.; Alfred A. Knopf, Inc.; *Fortune* Magazine.

Other Activities. Mr. Kronenberger served as Librarian of Brandeis Univ. (1963–67).

Published Works. Mr. Kronenberger wrote *Kings and Desperate Men* (1941); *The Thread of Laughter* (1952), a book on English stage comedy; *Company Manners* (1954); *The Republic of Letters* (1955); *Marlborough's Duchess* (1958); *A Month of Sundays* (1961); *The Cart and the Horse* (1964); *The Polished Surface* (1969); *No Whippings, No Gold Watches* (1970); *A Mania for Magnificence* (1972); *The Last Word* (1972); *The Extraordinary Mr. Wilkes* (1974); edited Burns Mantle's *Best Plays* series (1952–61); *Novelists on Novelists* (1960); general editor of the *Great Letters* series (1950) and of the *Masters of World Literature* series (first volumes, 1964); *Quality: Its Image in the Arts* (1969); *Atlantic Brief Lives: A Biographical Companion to the Arts* (1971); and has edited or written the introductions for the works of George Bernard Shaw, Oscar Wilde, William Congreve, Charles Greville, Alexander Pope, James Boswell, Samuel Johnson, Richard Sheridan, Ben Jonson, Oliver Goldsmith, Jane Austen, Henry Fielding, Ambrose Bierce, and others.

KRUPSKA, DANIA. Choreographer, director. b. Dania Krupska, Aug. 13, 1923, Fall River, Mass., to Bronislaw and Anna (Niementowska) Krupska. Attended Lankenau Sch. for Girls, Philadelphia, diploma (1929–30). In Philadelphia, studied at Ethel Phillips Dance Studio (1932–34), Mordkin Studio (1932–35); in N.Y.C., studied ballet at the Mordkin Studio (1936–39); Syvilla Fort (1954–64); and Aubrey Hitchens Studio (1948–64); acting and directing with Robert Lewis (1952–53); and dance with Egorova in Paris (1937). Married to Ted Thurston, actor. Member of AEA; AFTRA; SSD&C. Address: (home) 71 Toilsome Lane, East Hampton, NY 11937; (bus.) 564 W. 52nd St., New York, NY 10019.

Theatre. Miss Krupska began dancing in concerts at the age of six in Europe, using the name of Dania Darling. She continued her concerts every summer in Europe until the age of 13; on her return to the US, she joined the Catherine Littlefield Ballet (Philadelphia) for a European tour in 1937. Later she appeared with it at the Chicago Opera (season of 1938); became a member of the Balanchine's American Ballet Co. N.Y.C. in 1938, and performed on the Frank Fay Show and as soloist with the Radio City Music Hall Ballet. She succeeded Helen Craig in the part of Belinda in the national (touring) company of *Johnny Belinda* (1941); on Bway appeared in *Chauve Souris 1943* (Royale, Aug. 12, 1943); danced the role of Laurey in the dream sequence ballet in the national (touring) company of *Oklahoma!* (1943–45) and later on Bway (Sept. 1945–June 1946).

Miss Krupska was assistant to choreographer Agnes de Mille for *Allegro* (Majestic, Oct. 10, 1947); assisted Miss de Mille with her ballet, *Fall River Legend*, which was a part of the Ballet Th. repertoire (Metropolitan Opera House, premiere, Apr. 22, 1948), dancing the leading role (Metropolitan Opera House, Apr. 23, 1948); assisted Miss de Mille for *The Rape of Lucretia* (Ziegfeld, Dec. 29, 1948); and for *Gentlemen Prefer Blondes* (Ziegfeld, Dec. 8, 1949).

She choreographed *Seventeen* (Broadhurst, June 21, 1951); assisted Miss de Mille with the choreography for *Paint Your Wagon* (Shubert, Nov. 12, 1951); played Mimi and was assistant to choreographer Michael Kidd for *Can-Can* (Shubert, May 7, 1953); played Hattie Hopkins and was stand-by for Renee Jeanmaire as Lisette Gervais in *The Girl in Pink Tights* (Mark Hellinger Th., Mar. 5, 1954); performing in the role during the run.

Miss Krupska choreographed *Shoestring Revue* (President, Feb. 28, 1955); *The Most Happy Fella* (Imperial, May 3, 1956); and was choreographer for *Fanny, Annie Get Your Gun, Rose Marie, Guys and Dolls, Gentlemen Prefer Blondes, Oklahoma!, The King and I,* and *The Most Happy Fella* (State Fair, Dallas, Tex., Summers 1957–58). She choreographed the pre-Bway tryout of *The Carefree Heart* (opened Cass, Detroit, Mich., Sept. 30, 1957; closed Hanna, Cleveland, Ohio, Oct. 26, 1957; directed a revival of *The Most Happy Fella* (NY City Ctr., Feb. 10, 1959); *Oklahoma!* (Civic Light Opera, Philharmonic Aud., Los Angeles, Calif., June 1959); *The Gypsy Baron* (Metropolitan Opera House, N.Y.C., Nov. 25, 1959); a revival of *Oh, Kay!* (74 St. Th., Apr. 16, 1960); the ballet, *Pointes on Jazz*, for the American Ballet Th. (Bushnell Aud., Hartford, Conn., premiere, Jan. 16, 1961); *The Happiest Girl in the World* (Martin Beck Th., N.Y.C., Apr. 3, 1961); directed *Show Boat* (NY City Ctr., 1961); *Fiorello!* (NY City Ctr., June 13, 1962); choreographed *Apollo and Miss Agnes* (State Fair, Dallas, Tex., Aug. 5, 1963); *Rugantino* (Mark Hellinger Th., N.Y.C., Feb. 6, 1964); the premiere of *Her First Roman* (Lunt-Fontanne Th., N.Y.C., Oct. 20, 1968); choreographed *Zorba* (National Th., Reykjavik, Iceland, Jan. 1971); *Company* (Storan Th., Gothenberg, Sweden, Sept. 1971); directed and choreographed *The Fantasticks* (Scola Teater, Gothenberg, Sweden, Oct. 1971); *Oklahoma* (National Theatre, Reykjavik, Iceland, Jan. 1972); *Jacques Brel Is Alive and Well and Living in Paris* (North Shore Music Th., Beverly, Mass., July 1972); choreographed *No, No, Nannette* (Stads-Teater, Malmo, Sweden, Dec., 1972); choreographed and co-directed *Porgy and Bess* (Stads-Teater, Malmo, Sweden, Mar. 1973); directed and choreographed the American premiere of *Joseph and His Technicolor Dreamcoat* (Playhouse in the Park, Philadelphia, Pa., May 1974); *Kiss Me, Kate* and *Sugar* (North Shore Music Th., Beverly, Mass., July and August 1974); and choreographed *Becaud Tonight* (Studio Arena Th., Buffalo, N.Y., Dec. 3, 1974).

Television. Miss Krupska has choreographed for Buick Hour (NBC, 1953); Colgate Comedy Hour (NBC, 1954); *The Ballad of Tom Sawyer* (US Steel Hour, CBS, Nov. 21, 1956); *Burlesque* (Omnibus, ABC, 1957); *H.M.S. Pinafore* (Omnibus, NBC, 1959).

Recreation. "As Mrs. Ted Thurston, I enjoy raising my family and gardening at my home in East Hampton.".

KRUSCHEN, JACK. Actor. b. Mar. 20, 1922, Winnipeg, Canada, to Morris and Sophie Kruschen. Father, watchmaker. Grad. Hollywood (Calif.) H.S., 1938. Married Jan. 1947 to Marjorie Ullman, secy. (marr. dis. Dec. 1961); married Feb. 1963 to Violet R. Mooring (née Perruzzi). Served US Army, 1941–45; rank, T/Sgt. Member of AEA; SAG; AFTRA.

Theatre. Mr. Kruschen first appeared on the stage as Boris in a Hollywood H.S. production of *The Fortune Teller.*

He played Maurice Pulvermacher in the Bway production of *I Can Get It for You Wholesale* (Shubert, Mar. 22, 1962); was Dr. Dreyfuss in the English production of *Promises; Promises* (London, Oct. 2, 1969); and repeated the role in California (San Diego, May 11, 1970).

Films. He made his debut in *Red Hot and Blue* (Par., 1949); followed by *The Last Voyage* (MGM, 1960); *The Apartment* (UA, 1960); *Lover Come Back*

(UI, 1962); *McLintock* (UA, 1963); and *The Unsinkable Molly Brown* (MGM, 1964).

Television and Radio. He performed on the radio program, Christmas in Other Lands (CBS, 1938); during WW II was one of the founders of the Armed Forces Radio Service; operated a one-man carrier-wave station at the California Desert Training Center, and later was assigned to the Armed Forces Radio Service in the Pacific.

He performed on twenty shows for Lux Radio Th. (CBS, 1947–52); on both the radio and television versions of the Danny Thomas Show (CBS, 1947–58); and on Dragnet (NBC, 1950–57); during 1946–58, performed on such CBS radio shows as: Suspense, Sam Spade, Johnny Dollar, and as Detective Muggavan in Broadway Is My Beat. He has appeared on Bonanza (NBC) and I Spy (NBC).

He made his television debut with the Don Lee Experimental Station (W6 XAO, Los Angeles, 1939); and has appeared on The Rifleman (ABC); Wanted Dead or Alive (ABC); Our Miss Brooks (CBS); Colgate Comedy Hour (NBC); and played Tully in the Hong Kong series (ABC, 1960–61).

Awards. Mr. Kruschen was nominated for the Academy (Oscar) Award as best supporting actor for his performance in *The Apartment* (1961); and in the *Variety* Poll of London theatre critics (1969–70) he was named a best actor in a musical for his *Promises, Promises* performance.

L

LAHR, JOHN. Novelist, critic, dramaturg. b. July 12, 1941, Los Angeles, Calif., to Bert and Mildred (Schroeder) Lahr. Father, actor; mother, showgirl. Attended Yale Univ. and Worcester Coll., Oxford Univ. (England). Married Aug. 12, 1965, to Anthea Mander. Member of P.E.N. (bd. of dirs.); Choreo Concerts (bd. of dir.); Drama Critics Circle; Drama Desk; Theatre Development Fund; National Council of the Arts. Address: 418 E. 88th St., New York, NY 10028, tel. (212) 289-3533; 11A Chalcot Gardens, Englands Lane, London N.W. 3, England tel. 722-9485.

Theatre. Mr. Lahr was literary manager, Tyrone Guthrie Th. (1968) and literary manager, Repertory Th. of Lincoln Ctr. (1969–71).

Films. *Sticky My Fingers, Fleet My Feet* (Amer. Film Institute, 1970).

Television. Mr. Lahr has appeared on many talk shows.

Published Works. Mr. Lahr is the author of *Notes on a Cowardly Lion* (1969); *Up Against the Fourth Wall* (1970); *Astonish Me* (1973); and, with Jonathan Price, *Life-Show* (1973). He edited and wrote an introduction for *Showcase 1* (1969) and edited *A Casebook on Harold Pinter's 'The Homecoming'* (1971). He has also written criticism for *Arts Magazine, The Drama Review, Drama at Calgary, National Observer, Manhattan East, Evergreen Review,* the New York Times, New York Free Press, *The Times* (London), *The New Statesman, The Village Voice,* and *Vogue.* He was theatre editor of Grove Press (1969–71) and a contributing editor of *Evergreen Review* (1969–71).

Awards. He received the George Jean Nathan Award for Drama Criticism (1969).

Recreation. Fishing, squash, basketball.

LAMBERT, HUGH. Choreographer, dancer. Married Dec. 12, 1970, to Nancy Sinatra, singer; two daughters.

Theatre. Mr. Lambert appeared as a dancer in *Hazel Flagg* (Mark Hellinger Th., N.Y.C., Feb. 11, 1953); *Wonderful Town* (Winter Garden, Feb. 25, 1953); *Can-Can* (Shubert, May 7, 1953); *The Vamp* (Winter Garden, Nov. 10, 1955); and *Ziegfeld Follies* (Winter Garden, Mar. 1, 1957). He appeared as Beef Saunders in the industrial, Oldsmobile Announcement Show (1959); and was choreographer of *How To Succeed in Business without Really Trying* (46 St. Th., N.Y.C., Oct. 14, 1961).

Television. Mr. Lambert was choreographer on the Ed Sullivan Show (CBS), and directed the Frank Sinatra special *Ol' Blue Eyes Is Back* (Nov. 18, 1973).

LAMPELL, MILLARD. Playwright, author. b. Jan. 23, 1919, Paterson, N.J., to Charles and Bertha (Ungar) Lampell. Parents, milliners. Grad. Eastside H.S., Paterson, N.J., 1936; Univ. of West Virginia, B.S. 1940. Served USAAF, 1943–46; rank, Staff Sgt. Married Feb. 28, 1943, to Elizabeth Whipple (marr. dis.); one son, one daughter; married June 17, 1967, to Ramona Estep. Member of ALA; WGA; SWG; Dramatists Guild.

Pre-Theatre. Dye-worker, coal miner, folk singer with "The Almanacs" (1940–43).

Theatre. Mr. Lampell wrote *The Wall,* based on the novel by John Hersey (Billy Rose Th., N.Y.C., Oct. 11, 1960), which has been produced internationally. A revised version of the play was performed at the Arena Stage (Washington, D.C., Jan. 29, 1964). He wrote the book and lyrics (music by Earl Robinson) for *The Lonesome Train* (1943), which has been produced extensively (but never on Bway), including on a double bill with the premiere of Mr. Lampell's one-act play, *Hard Travelin'* (Arena Stage, Wash., D.C., May 27, 1965).

Films. Mr. Lampell wrote the screenplays for *Saturday's Hero* (Col., 1951); *Chance Meeting* (Par., 1960); *Escape From East Berlin* (MGM, 1962); a documentary, *The Inheritance* (Harold Mayer Prodns., 1964), as well as the lyrics for the film's theme song, "Pass It On"; *The Idol* (Embassy, 1966); *A Nice Girl Like Me* (Avco-Embassy, 1969); and for *Eagle in a Cage* (Natl. Gen., 1972), which he produced.

Television and Radio. *The Lonesome Train* was broadcast by CBS (1943), and Mr. Lampell wrote and directed a series of radio dramas for the USAAF (1945). He has written frequently for television including *Sometime Before Morning* (NBC, 1959); *No Hiding Place* (East Side / West Side, CBS); *The Street* (East Side / West Side, CBS, July 6, 1964); *Ballad of Isaac and Jacob* (Eternal Light, NBC, Dec. 13, 1964); *Eagle in a Cage* (Hallmark Hall of Fame, NBC, Oct. 20, 1965); *The Victims* (WNET, Apr. 3, 1967); *John Adams—Minister to England* (The Adams Chronicles, WNET, Feb. 10, 1976); and other programs.

Published Works. He is the author of *The Long Voyage Home,* a collection of his radio scripts (1946); *The Hero,* a novel (1949); *Journey to the Cape,* a book of poems (1959); and *A Public Nuisance in Two Acts,* a play (1966).

Awards. For his television writing, he has received the Peabody Award, for *Sometime Before Morning* (1959); the Sidney Hillman Award, for *No Hiding Place* (1964); and a NATAS (Emmy) Award, for *Eagle in a Cage* (1965–66).

LAMPERT, ZOHRA. Actress. b. May 13, 1937, New York City, to Morris and Rachil (Eriss) Lampert. Father, ironworker and architect. Grad. H.S. of Music and Art, N.Y.C.; Univ. of Chicago, Ill. Studied acting with Mira Rostova. Relative in theatre; uncle, Samuel Iris, actor. Member of AEA; AFTRA; AGVA; SAG. Address: c/o Harry Ufland, Creative Management Associates, 8899 Beverly Boulevard, Los Angeles, CA 90048, tel. (213) 278-8899.

Theatre. Miss Lampert (billed as Zohra Alton) succeeded Barbara Sohmers as Conchita in the pre-Bway tryout of *Dancing in the Chequered Shade* (opened McCarter Th., Princeton, N.J., Dec. 20, 1955; closed Wilbur, Boston, Mass., Dec. 31, 1955); appeared in a "side show" production of *Venice Preserv'd* (Phoenix, N.Y.C., 1955–56); played Mashenka in *Diary of a Scoundrel* (Phoenix, Nov. 4, 1956); and (billed as Zohra Lampert) succeeded Louise Latham in the role of Maid to Lady Britomart in *Major Barbara* (Martin Beck Th., Oct. 30, 1956), later following Sally Gracie in the role of Rummy Mitchens in the same production.

She played Adele in *Maybe Tuesday* (Playhouse, Jan. 29, 1958); was a member of the Playwright's Th. (Chicago, Ill.), which later became Second City; played Jennifer Lewison in *Look: We've Come Through!* (Hudson, N.Y.C., Oct. 25, 1961); Illyona in *First Love* (Morosco, Dec. 25, 1961); was a member of the Second City Company at Square East (July 1962–Jan. 1963); and played Kattrin in *Mother Courage and Her Children* (Martin Beck Th., Mar. 28, 1963).

With the Lincoln Center Repertory Company, she played Felice in *After the Fall* (ANTA Washington Sq. Th., Jan. 23, 1964) and Princess Kukachin in *Marco Millions* (ANTA Wash. Sq. Th., Feb. 20, 1964); she also played Rachel in *Nathan Weinstein, Mystic, Connecticut* (Brooks Atkinson Th., Feb. 25, 1966); Jane in *The Natural Look* (Longacre, Mar. 13, 1967); Brenda in *Lovers and Other Strangers* (Brooks Atkinson Th., Sept. 18, 1968); and Iris in revival (with music) of *The Sign in Sidney Brustein's Window* (Longacre, Jan. 26, 1972).

Films. Miss Lampert made her debut in *Pay or Die* (AA, 1960); followed by the role of Angelina in *Splendor in the Grass* (WB, 1961); appearances in *A Fine Madness* (WB, 1966) and *Bye Bye Braverman* (WB, 1968); and as Jessica in *Let's Scare Jessica to Death* (Par., 1971).

Television. She has appeared on Doctor Kildare (NBC); The Defenders (CBS); Sam Benedict (NBC); Alfred Hitchcock Presents (CBS); in Leonard Bernstein's *Carmen* (Omnibus, CBS); and in the series *The Reporter* (CBS). She played Jenny in *Better Luck Next Time* (London, Jan. 1964); appeared as Eve in a commercial for Cranapple (1969–73); the kidnap victim on The F.B.I. (ABC, 1970); Ellie in Where the Heart Is (CBS, 1970–71); in Love, American Style (ABC, 1972–73); as Hannah in *The Connection* (ABC Movie of the Week, 1972); as Janine on the Bob Newhart Show (CBS, 1973); and as Anne on The Girl with Something Extra (NBC, 1973–74).

Awards. She won the *Variety* NY Drama Critics Poll (1963) for her performance as Kattrin in *Mother Courage and Her Children;* was nominated for Antoinette Perry (Tony) awards for *Look: We've Come Through* and for *Mother Courage;* and received Andy awards for her Bankers Trust radio commercial (1969) and for her Enkasheer television commercial, "Girl in Lobby" (1970).

LANCHESTER, ELSA. Actress. b. Oct. 28, 1902, Lewisham, England, to James and Edith (Lanchester) Sullivan. Educated privately. Married 1918 to Charles Laughton (dec.). Member of AEA; SAG.

Theatre. Miss Lanchester founded the Children's Th. (Soho, London, 1918); founded the Cave of Harmony, where she presented *The Man with a Flower in his Mouth, The Queen, God Bless Her,* and *The King of the Jews.*

She made her professional debut as the Second Shop Girl in *Thirty Minutes in a Street* (Kingsway Th., Apr. 2, 1922); subsequently appeared as Larva in *The Insect Play* (Regent, May 5, 1923); Peggy in *The Way of the World* (Lyric, Hammersmith, Feb. 7, 1924); Sancho in *The Duenna* (Lyric, Hammersmith, Oct. 23, 1924); joined the cast as Sophie Binner in *Cobra* (Garrick, Aug. 18, 1925); performed in the revue *Riverside Nights* (Lyric, Hammersmith, Apr. 10, 1926); the Kid in *Cautious Campbell* ("Q," Nov. 15, 1926; received Royalty, July 26, 1927); Rosie Betts in *The Pool* (Everyman, Feb. 7, 1927); and Mimi Winstock in *Mr. Prohack* (Court, Nov. 16, 1927).

She was manager, with Harold Scott, of The Cave Harmony Cabaret (1927–1928); appeared as Anna in *The Outskirts* (Court, May, 1929); Mary Morgan in *Ten Nights in a Bar-Room* (Gate, Jan. 1, 1930); Cedric in *Little Lord Fauntleroy* (Gate, Jan. 7, 1931); and Winnie Marble in *Payment Deferred* (St. James's, May 4, 1931).

She made her N.Y.C. debut as Winnie Marble in *Payment Deferred* (Lyceum, Sept. 24, 1931); with the Old Vic-Sadler's Wells company (London), played Charlotta Ivanovna in *The Cherry Orchard*

(Oct. 9, 1933), the Singer in *Henry VIII* (Nov. 7, 1933), Juliet in *Measure for Measure* (Dec. 4, 1933), Ariel in *The Tempest* (Jan. 8, 1934), and Miss Prue in *Love for Love* (Mar. 6, 1934). She appeared in the title role in *Peter Pan* (Palladium, Dec. 26, 1936), and toured in the same role (1937). She played Emmy Baudine in *They Walk Alone* (John Golden Th., N.Y.C., Mar. 12, 1941); performed at the Turnabout Th. (Hollywood, Calif., 1942); and appeared in *Elsa Lanchester—Herself* (41 St. Th., N.Y.C., Feb. 2, 1961).

Films. Miss Lanchester made her debut in *Bluebottles* (1928); and has since appeared in *The Private Life of Henry VIII* (UA, 1933), *David Copperfield* (MGM, 1935), *Naughty Marietta* (MGM, 1935), *Bride of Frankenstein* (U, 1935), *The Ghost Goes West* (UA, 1936), *Rembrandt* (UA, 1936), *Ladies in Retirement* (Col., 1941), *Son of Fury* (20th-Fox, 1942), *Tales of Manhattan* (20th-Fox, 1942), *Lassie, Come Home* (MGM, 1943), *Passport to Destiny* (RKO, 1944), *Son of Lassie* (MGM, 1945), *The Spiral Staircase* (RKO, 1946), *The Razor's Edge* (20th-Fox, 1945), *The Bishop's Wife* (RKO, 1947), *Northwest Outpost* (Rep., 1947), *The Secret Garden* (MGM, 1949), *Come to the Stable* (20th-Fox, 1949), *The Inspector General* (WB, 1949), *Mystery Street* (MGM, 1950), *Frenchie* (U, 1950), *Petty Girl* (Col., 1950), *Buccaneer's Girl* (U, 1950); *Androcles and the Lion* (RKO, 1952), *Dreamboat* (20th-Fox, 1952), *Les Miserables* (20th-Fox, 1952), *The Girls of Pleasure Island* (Par., 1953), *Forever and a Day* (RKO, 1953), *Three Ring Circus* (Par., 1954), *Hell's Half Acre* (Rep., 1954), *The Glass Slipper* (MGM, 1955), *Witness for the Prosecution* (UA, 1957), and *Bell, Book and Candle* (Col., 1958), *Honeymoon Hotel* (MGM, 1964); *Mary Poppins* (BV, 1964); *Pajama Party* (AI, 1964); *That Darn Cat* (BV, 1965); *Easy Come, Easy Go* (Par., 1967); *Blackbeard's Ghost* (BV, 1968); *Rascal* (BV, 1969); *Me, Natalie* (Natl. Gen., 1969); *Willard* (Cinerama, 1971); *Arnold* (Cinerama, 1973); *Terror in the Wax Museum* (Cinerama, 1973); and *Murder By Death* (Col., 1976).

Television. Among Miss Lanchester's extensive appearances in television are Studio One (CBS, 1953); Ford Th. (NBC); Hallmark Hall of Fame (NBC); Lux Video Th. (NBC); Robert Montgomery Presents (NBC); GE Th. (CBS); Burke's Law (ABC); Alfred Hitchcock Th. (NBC); Ben Casey (ABC); The Man from U.N.C.L.E. (NBC); World of Disney (NBC); *In Name Only* (ABC); Night Gallery (NBC); Mannix (CBS); and It Takes a Thief (ABC); as well as the major talk shows.

Published Works. Miss Lanchester is the author of *Charles Laughton and I* (1938).

LANDIS, WILLIAM.

Producer, actor, director. b. William Lightner Landis, May 21, 1921, Minneapolis, Minn., to Willis E. and Ann E. Landis. Father, CPA. Grad. West H.S., Minneapolis, 1939; City Coll. of Los Angeles, A.A. 1947; Pacific Lutheran Coll., B.A. 1949; Univ. of Washington, M.A. 1950; attended New York Univ., 1961. Married July 16, 1955, to Elizabeth Engrav; two daughters, one son. Served USMC, 1940–43. Member of AEA. Address: (home) Main St., Sharon, CT 06069, tel. (203) 364-0271; (bus.) 132 E. 78th St., New York, NY 10021.

Pre-Theatre. Teacher.

Theatre. Mr. Landis made his debut as Bill Dowton in *The Drunkard* (Th. Mart, Los Angeles, Calif., 1944); subsequently appeared as Tallant in a stock production of *The Late Christopher Bean* (Cirque Playhouse, Seattle, Wash., May 1950); and played Montano and the Duke of Venice in *Othello* (Shakespearewrights, Oct. 1954).

Since 1955, Mr. Landis has been associated with the Downtown Th. (N.Y.C.), where he produced and played Morell in *Candida* (Feb. 16, 1955); produced *Man of Destiny* (Apr. 15, 1956); produced and directed *The Beaux' Stratagem* (July 12, 1957); produced and played Godfrey Kneller in *In Good King Charles' Golden Days* (Jan. 27, 1957); produced and played Bluntschli in *Arms and the Man* (Oct. 10, 1957); produced *The Boy Friend* (Feb. 15, 1958); produced, with Del Tenney, and played Leonard Charteris in *The Philanderer* (June 6, 1958); produced, with Del Tenney, and played Bohun in *You Never Can Tell* (July 2, 1958); produced and played Lickcheese in *Widowers' Houses* (Mar. 5, 1959); produced and played Aegisthus in *The Prodigal* (Feb. 11, 1960); played Manders in *Ghosts* (4th St. Th., N.Y.C., 1962); and appeared in *Rosmersholm* (4th St. Th., N.Y.C., 1962).

He has directed and acted in over twenty-five plays at the Sharon (Conn.) Playhouse (Summers 1968–74); and serves as the managing director of the Playhouse (1973–to date).

Awards. Mr. Landis received the Vernon Rice Award (1960) for his production of *The Prodigal*.

Recreation. Golf, tennis, swimming.

LANE, BURTON.

Composer. b. Burton Levy, Feb. 2, New York City, to Lazarus and Frances Levy. Father, builder in real estate. Attended H.S. of Commerce, N.Y.C. Studied at Dwight Sch. for Concentration, N.Y.C., six months; piano with Simon Bucharoff, N.Y.C., two years. Married June 28, 1935, to Marion Seaman (marr. dis. 1961); one daughter; married Mar. 5, 1961, to Lynn Daroff Kaye. Member of ASCAP (7th term pres., 1957–64; writers advisory comm.); AGAC (pres.); Dramatists Guild.

Theatre. Mr. Lane composed marches while in high school, and at age fifteen became a staff composer for a music publishing house.

He wrote the music for two songs in *Three's a Crowd* (Selwyn Th., Oct. 15, 1930); music for "Say the Word" which was included in the score of the revue, *The Third Little Show* (Music Box, June 1, 1931); music for the ninth edition of *Earl Carroll's Vanities* (Earl Carroll Th., Aug. 27, 1931); for two songs in *Singin' the Blues* (Liberty, Sept. 16, 1931); and music for "You're Not Pretty But You're Mine" in the revue *Americana* (Shubert, Oct. 5, 1932).

He composed the music for *Hold on to Your Hats* (Shubert, Sept. 11, 1940); lyrics, in collaboration with Al Dubin, and music for *Laffing Room Only* (Winter Garden, Dec. 23, 1944); and the music for *Finian's Rainbow* (46 St. Th., Jan. 10, 1947); and, with Alan Jay Lerner, *On a Clear Day You Can See Forever* (Mark Hellinger Th., Oct. 17, 1965).

Films. Mr. Lane began his career in motion pictures writing three songs for *Dancing Lady* (MGM, 1933), including "Everything I Have Is Yours"; and composed scores for *Babes on Broadway* (MGM, 1941), *Royal Wedding* (MGM, 1951), and *Give a Girl a Break* (MGM, 1953); and the film adaptation of *Finian's Rainbow* (WB-7 Arts, 1968).

Television. He composed the music for *Junior Miss* (1958); and has appeared as a guest on the Today Show (NBC); Merv Griffin Show (Ind.); and Lee Graham Show.

Awards. Mr. Lane was nominated for an Academy (Oscar) Award for the song "How About You" from the film *Babes on Broadway* (MGM, 1941).

He received the Essex Symphony Society Award for *Finian's Rainbow* (1947); and an Academy (Oscar) Award nomination for the song "Too Late Now" from the film, *Royal Wedding* (MGM, 1955).

Mr. Lane received a NARAS (Grammy) Award for his score, with Alan Jay Lerner, of *On a Clear Day You Can See Forever* (Best Score from an Original Cast Show Album, 1965); and was the recipient of the first ASCAP Sigmund Romberg Award (1966).

Recreation. Chess, golf.

LANG, PHILIP J.

Orchestrator, musician, composer, educator, writer. b. Philip Joseph Lang, Apr. 17, 1911, Bronx, N.Y., to Philip H. and Irene Veronica (Coleman) Lang. Father, salesman. Grad. Oceanside (N.Y.) H.S., 1929; Ithaca Coll., B.S. (orchestration and composition) 1933. Studied composition with Felix Deyo at Juilliard Sch. of Music, N.Y.C., 1934–35. Married Aug. 4, 1942, to Ruth E. Foote, teacher; two sons, one daughter. US Maritime Service, 1942–45; rank, Ensign. Member of ASCAP; AFM, Local 802; Amer. Bandmasters Assn.; Kappa Gamma Psi; Oracle. tel. (212) JU 6-0031; 231B Agawam Dr., Stratford, CT 06497, tel. (203) 378-3586.

Theatre. Mr. Lang was orchestrator for *Billion Dollar Baby* (Alvin, N.Y.C., Dec. 21, 1945); *Annie Get Your Gun* (Imperial, May 16, 1946); *High Button Shoes* (Century, Oct. 9, 1947); *Make A Wish* (Winter Garden, Apr. 18, 1951); *Two on the Aisle* (Mark Hellinger Th., July 19, 1951); *Three Wishes for Jamie* (Mark Hellinger Th., Mar. 12, 1952); *Can-Can* (Shubert, May 7, 1953); *Fanny* (Majestic, Nov. 4, 1954); *Plain and Fancy* (Mark Hellinger Th., Jan. 27, 1955); *My Fair Lady* (Mark Hellinger Th., Mar. 15, 1956); *Li'l Abner* (St. James, Nov. 15, 1956); *Redhead* (46 St. Th., Feb. 5, 1958); *Destry Rides Again* (Imperial, Apr. 23, 1959); and *Camelot* (Majestic, Dec. 3, 1960).

Also, *Carnival!* (Imperial, Apr. 13, 1961); *Kean* (Bway Th., Nov. 2, 1961); *Subways Are for Sleeping* (St. James, Dec. 27, 1961); *Hit the Deck* (Marine Th., Jones Beach, N.Y., Summer 1962); *Mr. President* (St. James, N.Y.C., Oct. 20, 1962); *Tovarich* (Bway Th., Mar. 18, 1963); *Around the World in Eighty Days* (Marine Th., Summers 1963–64); *Jennie* (Majestic, N.Y.C., Oct. 17, 1963); *Hello, Dolly!* (St. James, Jan. 16, 1964); and for the NY World's Fair, he orchestrated Spectacular (1964) and *To Broadway with Love* (Texas Pavilion, Apr. 22, 1964).

Mr. Lang did orchestrations for *Ben Franklin in Paris* (Lunt-Fontanne Th., N.Y.C., Oct. 27, 1964); *I Had a Ball* (Martin Beck Th., Dec. 15, 1964); *Pleasures and Palaces* (pre-Bway: Fisher Aud., Detroit, Mich., Mar. 11–Apr. 10, 1965); *The Roar of the Greasepaint—The Smell of the Crowd* (Sam S. Shubert Th., May 16, 1965); *Mardi Gras!* (Marine Th., Jones Beach, N.Y., June 26, 1965); *Hot September* (pre-Bway: Shubert Th., Boston, Mass., Sept. 14–Oct. 9, 1965); *Mame* (Winter Garden, N.Y.C., May 24, 1966); *I Do! I Do!* (47 St. Th., Dec. 5, 1966); *How Now, Dow Jones* (Lunt-Fontanne Th., Dec. 7, 1967); *George M!* (Palace, Apr. 10, 1968); *Maggie Flynn* (ANTA Th., Oct. 23, 1968); *Dear World* (Mark Hellinger Th., Feb. 6, 1969); *State Fair* (St. Louis, Mo., May 1969); *Rondelay* (Hudson West Th., N.Y.C., Nov. 5, 1969); *Applause* (Palace, Mar. 30, 1970); *Lovely Ladies, Kind Gentlemen* (Majestic, Dec. 28, 1970); *Ari* (Mark Hellinger Th., Jan. 15, 1971); *Sugar* (Majestic, Apr. 9, 1972); *Ambassador* (Lunt-Fontanne Th., Nov. 19, 1972); *Lorelei* (Palace, Jan. 27, 1973); *Cyrano* (Palace, May 13, 1973); *Mack & Mabel* (Majestic, Oct. 6, 1974); and *Good News* (St. James).

Films. Mr. Lang did the orchestrations for the motion pictures *The Night They Raided Minsky's* (UA, 1968) and *Hello, Dolly!* (20th-Fox, 1969).

Other Activities. He was associate professor of orchestration, Univ. of Michigan (Summers 1950–51); associate professor of orchestration, Univ. of Colorado (Summer 1953); and director of standard and educational music for E. H. Morris & Co. (1953–58).

Published Works. Mr. Lang wrote *Scoring for the Band*, a textbook on band arranging (1945) and has published over a hundred pieces for band, originals and arrangements.

Recreation. Photography, golf, boating, deep sea fishing.

LANGE, BARBARA PEARSON.

Educator. b. Barbara Wolfe Pearson, July 5, 1910, Swarthmore, Pa., to Paul Martin and Edna (Wolfe) Pearson. Father, educator; governor of Virgin Islands. Grad. Swarthmore (Pa.) H.S., 1927; Swarthmore (Pa.) Coll., 1927–29; Yale Univ. Sch. of Drama, 1929–31. Studied with George Pierce Baker and Alexander Dean at Yale Univ. Married June 1932 to Gordon Carlson Lange; one son, two daughters. Relatives in theatre: niece, Anne Pearson, actress; Leon Pearson, drama critic (dec.). Member of Kappa Alpha Theta. Address: (home) One Crum Ledge, Swarthmore, PA 19081, tel. (215) KI 3-3034; (bus.) Swarthmore Coll., Swarthmore, PA 19081, tel. (215) KI 3-0200.

Mrs. Lange is the associate dean of admissions at Swarthmore Coll. She was previously dean of women and director of dramatics. She supervised all dramatic activity and directed three student productions each year. Mrs. Lange has held academic positions at Scripps Coll., Claremont, Calif. (instructor of speech and acting, 1934–35) and at Stanford Univ. (speech therapist).

She has appeared in summer stock, with a Chautauqua (N.Y.) Th. Co. (Summers 1928–30); the Pasadena (Calif.) Playhouse (1934–35); and the 49'ers (Whitefield, N.H., Summer 1936). She appeared in *No More Frontier* (Provincetown Playhouse, N.Y.C., 1931).

Awards. She was given the Nason Award from Swarthmore Coll. for her contribution "beyond the scope of normal duties to the life of the college community" (1960).

LANGELLA, FRANK. Actor. b. Jan. 1, 1940, Bayonne, N.J., to Mr. and Mrs. Frank Langella. Father, business executive. Grad. Columbia H.S., Maplewood, N.J.; Syracuse Univ. Studied acting with Seymour Falk. Member of AEA; SAG; Berkshire Festival (bd. of dir.).

Theatre. Mr. Langella made his stage debut at age fifteen in a high school production of *The Goose Hangs High;* subsequently apprenticed at the Pocono Playhouse (Mountain Home, Pa.); at the Erie (Pa.) Playhouse (Fall 1960), played Heinzie in *Pajama Game,* Eugene Gant in *Look Homeward, Angel,* and appeared in *Macbeth;* was a member of the original Lincoln Center repertory training company (1963); made his off-Bway debut as Michel in *The Immoralist* (Bouwerie Lane Th., N.Y.C., Nov. 7, 1963); on a bill entitled *The Old Glory* (Amer. Place at St. Clement's, Nov. 1, 1964), that included *My Kinsman, Major Molineaux,* played the title role in *Benito Cereno;* the Young Man in *Good Day* (Cherry Lane Th., Oct. 18, 1965); Flaminco in *The White Devil* (Circle in the Square, Dec. 6, 1965); Jamie in *Long Day's Journey into Night* (Long Wharf Th., New Haven, Conn., May 6, 1966); at the Berkshire Th. Festival (Stockbridge, Mass., Summer 1966) appeared in *The Skin of Our Teeth* and *The Cretan Woman;* with the Repertory Co. of Lincoln Center, played Juan in *Yerma* (Vivian Beaumont Th., Dec. 8, 1966); appeared in the Center Th. Group's production of *The Devils* (Mark Taper Forum, Spring 1967); played the title role in *Dracula* (Berkshire Playhouse, Stockbridge, Mass., Aug. 8, 1967); played Achilles in *Iphigenia at Aulis* (Circle in the Square, N.Y.C., Nov. 21, 1967); and was a member of the company of the Cleveland (Ohio) Playhouse (1967–68 season); and the Long Island Festival Repertory (Mineola, N.Y., Apr. 30–June 23, 1968).

Returning to the Berkshire Festival (Stockbridge, Mass., Summer 1968), he played Will in *A Cry of Players;* repeating that role in the subsequent Repertory Co. of Lincoln Center production (Vivian Beaumont Th., N.Y.C., Nov. 14, 1968); made his directing debut with *John and Abigail* (Berkshire Th. Festival, Stockbridge, Mass., July 1, 1969); played the title role in *Cyrano de Bergerac* (Williamstown Th., Summer 1971); appeared with the Yale Repertory Th. (New Haven, Conn., 1971–72 season); with the Tyrone Guthrie Th. (Minneapolis, Minn.) played Oberon in *A Midsummer Night's Dream* (July 7, 1972) and Loveless in *The Relapse* (July 12, 1972); Hoss in *The Tooth of Crime* (McCarter Th., Princeton, N.J., Nov. 9, 1972); Petruchio in *The Taming of the Shrew* (Studio Arena, Buffalo, N.Y., Mar. 1, 1973); appeared in *The Seagull* (Williamstown (Mass.) Th., Summer 1974); in his Bway debut, played Leslie (a lizard) in *Seascape* (Shubert, N.Y.C., Jan. 26, 1975; and Los Angeles, Apr. 2, 1975); and appeared in *Ring Round the Moon* (Williamstown, Mass., July 3, 1975).

Films. Mr. Langella made his film debut as Bender in *The Twelve Chairs* (UMC, 1970); and played George Prager in *The Diary of a Mad Housewife* (U, 1970).

Television. His television appearances include *Good Day* (Experiment in Television, NBC); the title role in *The Mark of Zorro* (ABC, 1974); an episode on a series on Benjamin Franklin (CBS, 1974); and the televised version of the Williamstown (Mass.) Th. production of *The Sea Gull* (NET, 1975).

Awards. Mr. Langella received the Off-Bway (Obie) Award for *The Old Glory* (1964–65), *Good Day* (1965–66), and *The White Devil* (1965–66); the Drama Desk and Antoinette Perry (Tony) awards for his performance in *Seascape* (1974–75); and the National Society of Film Critics Award (1970) for *The Diary of a Mad Housewife.*.

LANGHAM, MICHAEL. Director, writer. b. Michael Seymour Langham, Aug. 22, 1919, Bridgwater, Somerset, England, to S. C. and Muriel (Andrews Speed) Langham. Father, gunny broker. Grad. Radley Coll., Abingdon, Eng., 1937; attended Univ. of London, 1937–39. Married July 8, 1948, to Helen Burns, actress; (marr. dis.) one son; married Nov. 25, 1972, to Elin Gorky. Served Gordon Highlanders, 1939–45 (France, 1939); P.O.W., 1939–45); rank, 2nd Lt. Member of SSD&C.

Theatre. Mr. Langham was at first director of the Midland Theatre Co., under the auspices of the Arts Council of Great Britain in Coventry. He first staged *Twelfth Night* (June 1946), and subsequently, *When We Were Married, Freda, Pygmalion, The Magistrate, Alice in Wonderland, Rope, Yes, Farewell, Tomorrow's Child, Anna Christie, It Depends What You Mean, Pink String and Sealing Wax, The Good Humored Ladies, Duet for Two Hands, The Petrified Forest, Othello, The Green Goddess, An Inspector Calls, The Doctor's Dilemma, While the Sun Shines,* and *French without Tears* (1946–48).

Later, he directed at the Birmingham Repertory Th., *Mourning Becomes Electra, A Modern Everyman, The Cassilis Engagement, Richard III, The Marvelous History of St. Bernard, The Diary of a Scoundrel, A Phoenix Too Frequent, The Glass Menagerie, The Importance of Being Earnest, Doctor's Delight,* and *Shadow and Substance* (Nov. 1948–Feb. 1950).

He directed, with Anthony Quale, *Julius Caesar* (Shakespeare Memorial Th., Stratford-upon-Avon, May 2, 1950); staged *Pygmalion* (Embassy, London, Jan. 23, 1951); *The Gay Invalid* (Garrick, Jan. 24, 1951); *Othello* (Old Vic, Oct. 31, 1951); *Richard Trois* (Belgium National Th., Brussels, Nov. 1951); and a Dutch production of *The Merry Wives of Windsor* (Haagsche Comedie Th. Hague, Netherlands, Jan. 1952).

Mr. Langham directed *The Other Heart* (Old Vic., London, Apr. 15, 1952); *The Noble Spaniard* (Guildford Rep. Th., May 1952); *The Beggar's Opera* (Tor and Torridge Festival, Barnstable, June 1953); became director of the Glasgow (Scotland) Citizens Th. (Sept. 1953–Apr. 1954), where he staged *The Thistle and the Rose, When We Were Married, The Diary of a Scoundrel, The Laird of Tarwattletie, Tapsalteerio, Witch Errant, The Road to the Isles, Right Royal, All in Good Faith,* and *Meeting by Night;* directed *The Beggar's Opera* (Sadlers Wells, London, Oct. 4, 1954); and *Witch Errant* ("Q" Th., Sept. 7, 1954).

He directed at the Crest Th. (Toronto, Canada), *The Diary of a Scoundrel* (Feb. 1955), *Meeting at Night* (Mar. 1955), and *When We Were Married* (Apr. 1955); directed *Julius Caesar* (June 1955) at the Stratford (Ontario) Shakespearean Festival, where he has been the artistic director (1955–to date); staged *Hamlet* (Memorial Th., Stratford-upon-Avon, England, Apr. 10, 1956); at the Stratford (Ontario) Shakespearean Festival, directed *Henry V* and *The Merry Wives of Windsor* (June 1956); directed *The Two Gentlemen of Verona* (Old Vic, London, Jan. 22, 1957); *Hamlet* (Stratford, Ontario, June 1957). *The Two Gentlemen of Verona* (Phoenix, N.Y.C., Mar. 18, 1958); *The Broken Jug* (Phoenix, Apr. 1, 1958); and at Stratford, Ontario, directed *Henry IV, Part I* (June 1958), and *Much Ado About Nothing* (June 1958).

Mr. Langham staged *The Merchant of Venice* (Memorial Th., Stratford-upon-Avon, Apr. 12, 1960); *Romeo and Juliet* (Stratford, Ontario, June 27, 1960); *A Midsummer Night's Dream* (Old Vic, London, Dec. 20, 1960); and *Much Ado About Nothing* (Royal Shakespeare Th., Stratford-upon-Avon, Apr. 1961); at Stratford, Ontario, staged *Coriolanus* (June, 1961) and *Love's Labour's Lost* (June 1961); and with actors from the Festival Co., directed *Two Programmes of Shakespearean Comedy,* which he adapted and which, sponsored by the Canadian government, toured universities in Canada (Feb. 1962–Mar. 1962); and at Stratford, Ontario, directed *The Taming of the Shrew* (June 1962), and his own adaptation of *Cyrano de Bergerac* (July 1962).

He staged *Andorra* (Biltmore, N.Y.C., Feb. 9, 1962); and at Stratford, Ontario, staged *Troilus and Cressida* (July 1963), *Cyrano de Bergerac* (June 1963), and *Timon of Athens* (July 1963); directed the Stratford Festival Co. in *Love's Labour's Lost* and *Timon of Athens* (Chichester Festival Th., England, Apr. 1964). He became artistic director (1964–67) of the Stratford Shakespearean Festival Foundation (Festival Th., Stratford, Ont., Canada), which presented *Richard II* (June 15, 1964); *Le Bourgeois Gentilhomme* (June 16, 1964); *King Lear,* which he directed (June 17, 1964); *The Yoeman of the Guard* (July 3, 1964); *Henry IV, Part 1* (June 14, 1965); *Falstaff (Henry IV, Part 2)* (June 15, 1965); *Julius Caesar* (June 16, 1965); *Mahagonny* (July 2, 1965); *The Marriage of Figaro* (July 6, 1965); *The Cherry Orchard* (July 26, 1965); *Henry V,* which he directed (July 6, 1966); *Henry VI* (June 7, 1966); *Twelfth Night* (June 8, 1966); *Don Giovanni* (July 8, 1966); *The Last of the Tsars,* which he directed (Avon, July 12, 1966); *The Dance of Death* (July 19, 1966); and *Rose La Tulipe* (Aug. 16, 1966).

He directed *Nicholas Romanov* (Theatre Centre, Winnipeg, Manitoba, Canada, Mar. 19, 1966); *The Prime of Miss Jean Brodie* (Helen Hayes Th., N.Y.C., Jan. 16, 1968); *A Play by Alexander Solzhenitsyn* (Tyrone Guthrie Th., Minneapolis, Minn., June 18, 1970); and became artistic director (1971–75) of The Tyrone Guthrie Th. (Minneapolis, Minn.), which presented *Cyrano de Bergerac, The Taming of the Shrew, Misalliance, A Touch of the Poet, The Diary of a Scoundrel,* and *Fables Here and Then* (1971–72); *A Midsummer Night's Dream, Of Mice and Men, The Relapse, An Italian Straw Hat, Oedipus the King* (world premiere of the Anthony Burgess translation and adaptation), and *A Christmas Carol* (1972–73); *Becket, Oedipus the King, The Government Inspector (The Inspector General), Juno and the Paycock, I, Said the Fly, Waiting for Godot,* and *The Merchant of Venice* (1973–74).

Television. Mr. Langham wrote the script and directed *The Affliction of Love* (Festival of the Arts, NBC, Apr. 1963); and, with Lorne Freed, co-directed Henry V (CTC, Toronto, 1967).

Other Activities. Under the sponsorship of the British Council, he toured Australia, lecturing on theatre (Sept. 1952–Feb. 1953); and was named editor of *Minnesota Drama Editions* (1972).

Awards. Mr. Langham received an honorary degree of D.Litt. from McMaster Univ. (1962) and, from The American Th. Assn., received the 1974 World Theatre Award.

Recreation. Cricket, walking, reading.

LANGHANS, EDWARD A. Director, designer, educator, theatre historian. b. Edward Allen Langhans, Mar. 11, 1923, Warren, Pa., to Allen M. and Frances (Allen) Langhans. Father, oil refiner. Grad. Warren H.S., 1940; Univ. of Rochester, A.B. 1948; M.A. 1949; Univ. of Hawaii, M.A. 1951; Yale Univ., Ph.D. 1955. Studied with Earle Ernst at the Univ. of Hawaii, 1949–51; Alois M. Nagler at Yale Univ., 1951–55. Married 1944 to Alice Jane Lougee (marr. dis. 1946); married 1950 to Joyce Gitelman (marr. dis. 1956). Served USAAC, ETO, 1942–45; awarded D.F.C., Distinguished Unit Citation, Air Medal with three clusters; served USAFR, 1947–63; rank, Maj. Member of ATA; Society for Theatre Research (US, exec. bd., 1957–60); Society for Theatre Research (England); Malone Society; Shakespeare Assn.; Honolulu Theatre for Youth (exec. bd., 1961–63). Address: (home) 1212 Punahou St. Apt. 3402, Honolulu, HI 96814; (bus.) c/o Univ. of Hawaii, Honolulu, HI 96822, tel. (808) 948-7677.

Theatre. Since 1957, Mr. Langhans has been professor of drama at the Univ. of Hawaii. Previously, he was director and designer of *The Country Wife* (Univ. of Hawaii Th., Apr. 1951); at the Woodbridge (Conn.) Players Th., directed *Two Blind Mice*

(Mar. 27, 1952); directed and designed *Angel Street* (Dec. 4, 1952); *Laura* (Indiana Summer Th., Pa., July 14, 1953); *The Madwoman of Chaillot* (Woodbridge Players Th., Mar. 26, 1954); and *Blithe Spirit* (Indiana Summer Th., Aug. 4, 1954).

At the Proscenium Th., London, England, he directed and designed *Come Back Little Sheba* (Mar. 8, 1955), *The Voice of the Turtle* (May 3, 1955), and *The Importance of Being Earnest* (June 6, 1955); at the Univ. of Texas Summer Th., Austin, directed and designed *The Alchemist* (July 15, 1956), and directed *Oedipus Rex* (June 12, 1957); at the Univ. of Hawaii Th., directed and designed *Antigone* (May 2, 1958), *The School for Wives* (Feb. 20, 1959), *Right You Are If You Think You Are* (July 27, 1960), *Oedipus Rex* (Sept. 27, 1960), and directed *The Rivals* (May 25, 1962), and *Tartuffe* (Sept. 25, 1962).

At the University of Hawaii, Mr. Langhans directed *The Man Who Came to Dinner* (Dec. 14, 1963); *The Way of the World* (Feb. 19, 1964); *Of Thee I Sing* (Oct. 28, 1964); *Volpone* (Feb. 17, 1965); *The Glass Menagerie* (June 25, 1965); *The Flies* (Jan. 7, 1966); *The School for Scandal* (May 13, 1966); *A Doctor in Spite of Himself* (July 8, 1966); *Lysistrata* (Oct. 14, 1966); *Look Back in Anger* (July 7, 1967); and *Play, Act Without Words I, All That Fall* (June 7, 1974).

At Tufts University, he directed *Antigone* (Apr. 19, 1968) and *The Miser* (July 17, 1968).

Published Works. He has prepared, with Philip H. Highfill and Kalman A. Burnim, *A Biographical Dictionary of Actors, Actresses, Musicians, Dancers, Managers, and Other Stage Personnel in London, 1660–1800* (1973); and has written "Notes on the Reconstruction of the Lincoln's Inn Field Theatre," *Theatre Notebook* (1956); "The Restoration Promptbook of Shirley's *The Sisters,*" *The Theatre Annual* (1956); "New Restoration Theatre Accounts," *Theatre Notebook* (1963); "Wren's Restoration Playhouse," *Theatre Notebook* (1964); "A Picture of the Salisbury Court Theatre," *Theatre Notebook* (1965); "The Dorset Garden Theatre in Pictures," *Theatre Survey* (1965); "Research Opportunities in Early Promptbooks," *Educational Theatre Journal* (1966); "Restoration Manuscript Notes in Seventeenth Century Plays," *Restoration and 18th Century Theatre Research* (1966); "Three Early Eighteenth Century Promptbooks," *Theatre Notebook* (1966); "Pictorial Material on the Bridges Street and Drury Lane Theatres," *Theatre Survey* (1966); "Restoration Theatre Scholarship 1960–66," *Restoration and 18th Century Theatre Research* (1967); "Three Early Eighteenth Century Manuscript Promptbooks," *Modern Philology* (1967); "The Vere Street and Lincoln's Inn Fields Theatres in Pictures," *Educational Theatre Journal* (1968); "New Early 18th Century Performances and Casts," *Theatre Notebook* (1972); "A Conjectural Reconstruction of the Dorset Garden Theatre," *Theatre Survey* (1972); "Players and Playhouses, 1695–1710 and Their Effect on English Comedy," *The Theatre Annual* (1973); and "New Restoration Manuscript Casts," *Theatre Notebook* (1973). He has published reviews and delivered several lectures before theatre groups.

Awards. Mr. Langhans received a Stirling Fellowship, Yale Univ. (1952–54), a Fulbright grant for research in theatre history in England (1954–55), National Endowment for the Humanities grants in 1968 and 1975; and Folger Shakespeare Library Fellowships in 1970, 1972, and 1973.

Recreation. Music.

LANGLEY, NOEL. Playwright, director, producer, author. Married Nov. 1937, to Naomi Mary Legate (marr. dis. 1954); three sons, two daughters; married Sept. 1959 to Pamela Margaret Deeming. Served Canadian Navy Voluntary Reserve. 1943–45, Special Services; rank, Lt. Member of WGA, East; Dramatists Guild. Address: c/o Writers Guild of America, East, 22 W. 48th St., New York, NY 10036.

Theatre. Mr. Langley wrote *Farm of Three Echoes* (Cort, N.Y.C., Nov. 28, 1939); *The Walrus and the Carpenter* (Cort, Nov. 8, 1941); with Robert Morley, *Edward, My Son* (Martin Beck Th., Sept. 30, 1948); and adapted *The Burning Bush* (Erwin Piscator Dramatic Workshop, 1950).

Films. Mr. Langley wrote screenplays for *Maytime* (MGM, 1937); *The Wizard of Oz* (MGM, 1939); *Florian* (MGM, 1940); *Unexpected Uncle* (RKO, 1941); *I Became a Criminal* (WB, 1948); *The Vicious Circle* (UA, 1948); *Edward, My Son* (MGM, 1949); *Trio* (Par., 1950); *Adam and Evelyn* (U, 1950); *Tom Brown's Schooldays* (UA, 1951); *A Christmas Carol* (UA, 1951); *Androcles and the Lion* (RKO, 1952); *The Prisoner of Zenda* (MGM, 1952); *Ivanhoe* (MGM, 1952); *The Pickwick Papers* (Mayer Kingsley, 1953), which he also produced and directed; *Knights of the Round Table* (MGM, 1953); *The Adventures of Sadie* (20th-Fox, 1955), which he also produced and directed; *Svengali* (MGM, 1955), which he also produced and directed; *The Vagabond King* (Par., 1956); *The Search for Bridey Murphy* (Par., 1956), which he also directed; and *Snow White and the Three Stooges* (20th-Fox, 1961).

Published Works. Mr. Langley wrote *Cage Me a Peacock* (1936) and *The Rift in the Lute* (1953).

Awards. With Robert Morley, Mr. Langley received the Donaldson Award for *Edward, My Son* (1949).

LANGNER, PHILIP. Producer. b. Aug. 24, 1926, New York City, to Lawrence and Armina (Marshall) Langner. Father, producer, lawyer; mother, producer. Grad. The Hotchkiss Sch., Lakeville, Conn., 1943; Yale Univ., B.S. 1948. Married Feb. 17, 1957, to Marilyn Clark, actress; two daughters. Served USN (two years). Member of League of NY Theatres, ATPAM; Amer. Shakespeare Festival Th. and Acad. (bd. of dir.). Address: (home) 135 Central Park West, New York, NY 10023; (bus.) 226 W. 47th St., New York, NY 10036, tel. (212) 265-6170.

Pre-Theatre. Foreign patent attorney.

Theatre. Since 1961, Mr. Langner has been co-director of the Theatre Guild, N.Y.C., which he joined as associate producer in 1956. He is owner of the Westport (Conn.) County Playhouse, and is director of The American Theatre Society, Inc.

He was managing director of the Westport Country Playhouse (Summers 1949–52; 1954–58); produced winter stock at the Bahama Playhouse (Nassau, B.W.I., 1951–52); and was managing director of the New Parsons Th. (Hartford, Conn., 1952–54).

Films. He was associate producer of *Judgment at Nuremburg* (UA, 1961); *A Child Is Waiting* (UA, 1963); produced *The Pawnbroker* (Landau, 1964); *Slaves* (Continental, 1969); and *Born to Win* (UA, 1971).

He is pres. of Theatre Guild Films, Inc., (NYC).

LANSBURY, ANGELA. Actress. b. Angela Brigid Lansbury, Oct. 16, 1925, London, England, to Edgar and Moyna (Macgill) Lansbury. Mother, actress. Attended S. Hampstead H.S. for Girls, London, 1934–39; Webber-Douglas Sch. of Dramatic Art, London, 1939–40; grad. Feagin Sch. of Drama, N.Y.C., 1942. Married Aug. 12, 1949, to Peter Pullen Shaw, film executive; one son, one daughter. Member of SAG; AEA; AFTRA.

Theatre. Miss Lansbury appeared in N.Y.C. as Marcelle in *Hotel Paradiso* (Henry Miller's Th., Apr. 11, 1957); Helen in *A Taste of Honey* (Lyceum, Oct. 4, 1960); as Cora Hoover Hooper in *Anyone Can Whistle* (Majestic, Mar. 26, 1964; played the title role in *Mame* (Winter Garden, May 24, 1966); Countess Aurelia in *Dear World* (Mark Hellinger Th., Feb. 6, 1969); and Mama Rose in the revival of *Gypsy* (London and Winter Garden, N.Y.C., Sept. 23, 1974).

Films. Miss Lansbury made her debut in *Gaslight* (MGM, 1944); subsequently appeared in *National Velvet* (MGM, 1944); *The Picture of Dorian Gray* (MGM, 1945); *The Hoodlum Saint* (MGM, 1946); *The Harvey Girls* (MGM, 1946); *Bel Ami* (UA, 1946); *Till the Clouds Roll By* (MGM, 1946); *If Winter Comes* (MGM, 1947); *State of the Union* (MGM, 1948); *The Three Musketeers* (MGM, 1948); *Samson and Delilah* (Par., 1949); *The Red Danube* (MGM, 1949); *Kind Lady* (MGM, 1951); *Mutiny* (UA, 1952); *Remains to Be Seen* (MGM, 1953); *A Lawless Street* (Col., 1955); *The Court Jester* (Par., 1956); *The Reluctant Debutante* (MGM, 1958); *The Long, Hot Summer* (20th-Fox, 1958); *The Dark at the Top of the Stairs* (WB, 1960); *A Breath of Scandal* (Par., 1960); *Blue Hawaii* (Par., 1961); *All Fall Down* (MGM, 1962); as Phyllis in *The Out of Towners* (WB, 1963); in *The Manchurian Candidate* (UA, 1963); *In the Cool of the Day* (MGM, 1963); *The World of Henry Orient* (UA, 1964); *Dear Heart* (WB, 1964); *The Greatest Story Ever Told* (UA, 1965); *The Amourous Adventures of Moll Flanders* (Par., 1965); *Harlow* (Par., 1965); *Mr. Buddwing* (MGM, 1966); *Something for Everyone* (Natl. Gen., 1970); and *Bedknobs and Broomsticks* (Buena Vista, 1971).

Television. Miss Lansbury has made numerous appearances on such series as The Danny Kaye Show (CBS); Alcoa Preview (ABC); The Man from U.N.C.L.E. (NBC); The Eleventh Hour (Ind.); The Trials of O'Brien (CBS); The Merv Griffin Show (Ind.); The Today Show (NBC); Suspense Th. (Ind.); The Perry Como Show (NBC); The Art of Film (NET); Robert Montgomery Presents (NBC); Video Th. (CBS); Ford Th. (NBC); Four Star Playhouse (CBS); GE Th. (CBS); Fireside Th. (NBC); and Climax (CBS).

Awards. Miss Lansbury was nominated for an Academy (Oscar) Award for performances in *Gaslight* (1944), *The Picture of Dorian Gray* (1945), and *The Manchurian Candidate* (1964). For the latter two films, she received Golden Globe awards from the Hollywood Press Assn.

She received the Antoinette Perry (Tony) Award for her performances in *Mame* (1966), *Dear World* (1969), and *Gypsy* (1974).

LANSBURY, EDGAR. Producer, scenic designer, art director. b. Edgar George McIlldowie Lansbury, Jan. 12, 1930, London, England, to Edgar Isaac and Moyna (Macgill) Lansbury. Father, Member of Parliament, Mayor of Poplar, lumber mill executive; mother, actress. Grad. Univ. H.S., West Los Angeles, Calif., 1947; attended Univ. of California at Los Angeles, 1947–50. Studied at Otis Art Inst., Los Angeles, 1947–50. Married Aug. 12, 1955, to Rose Anthony Kean; five sons; one daughter. Served US Army, Infantry, Korea, 1951–52; rank, Cpl. Relatives in theatre: brother, William Bruce Lansbury, playwright, television program executive; sister, Angela Shaw known as Angela Lansbury, actress; great uncle, Robert Mantell, actor. Member of United Scenic Artists, Society of Motion Picture Art Directors, League of NY Producers. Address: (home) 1220 Park Avenue, New York, NY 10029, tel. (212) TE 1-7928; (bus.) 1650 Broadway, New York, NY 10019, tel. (212) 765-5910.

Pre-Theatre. Sculptor.

Theatre. Mr. Lansbury started as an apprentice for summer productions at the Windham Playhouse (Salem, N.H., 1947), and later designed productions at this theatre (1953–54).

He designed the N.Y.C. productions of *The Wise Have Not Spoken* (Cherry Lane, Feb. 10, 1954), *A Sound of Hunting* (Cherry Lane, Spring 1954) and the ELT presentations of *The Master Builder* (Mar. 24, 1954), *Young Woodley* (Dec. 15, 1954), and *Misalliance* (Feb. 2, 1955).

He designed *Jackhammer,* for which he was an associate producer (Th. Marquee, Feb. 5, 1962); *Five Evenings* (Village South Th., May 9, 1963); produced and designed *The Subject Was Roses* (Royale, May 24, 1964); produced, with Stuart Duncan, *The Alchemist* (Gate, Sept. 9, 1964); produced, with Bruce Lansbury, *First One Asleep, Whistle* (Belasco Th., Feb. 26, 1966); produced *That Summer— That Fall* (Helen Hayes Th., Mar. 16, 1967); produced, with Stuart Duncan and Dina and Alexander E. Racolin, *Arms and the Man* (Sheridan Square Playhouse, June 22, 1967); produced, with Marc Merson, *Fragments* (Cherry Lane Th., Oct. 2, 1967); produced *The Only Game in Town* (Broadhurst, May 20, 1968); presented, with Harry Belafonte and Chic Schultz, *To Be Young, Gifted and Black* (Cherry Lane Th., Jan. 2, 1969); produced, with Marc Merson, *A Way of Life* (closed during previews; ANTA Th., Feb. 1, 1969); produced, with Joseph Beruh, *Promenade* (Promenade Th., June 4, 1969); produced, with Max J. Brown, Richard Lewine, and Ralph Nelson, *Look to the Lilies* (Lunt-Fontanne Th., Mar. 29, 1970); produced, with J. I. Rodale in association with Nan Pearlman, *The Engagement Baby* (Helen Hayes Th., May 21, 1970); produced, with Mark Wright and Joseph Beruh in association with Stuart Duncan and H. B. Lutz, a revival of *Waiting for Godot* (Sheridan Square Playhouse, Feb. 3, 1971); produced, with Jay H. Fuchs, Stuart Duncan, and Joseph Beruh, *Long Day's Journey Into Night* (Promenade Th., Apr. 21, 1971); produced, with Stuart Duncan and Joseph Beruh, *Godspell* (Cherry Lane Th., May 17, 1971), *Elizabeth I* (Lyceum, Apr. 5, 1972), and *Comedy* (pre-Bway tryout, Colonial Th., Boston, Mass., Nov. 6–18, 1972); produced *The Enclave* (world premiere, Washington Th. Club, Washington, D.C., Feb. 21, 1973); and produced a revival of *Gypsy* (Winter Garden, N.Y.C., Sept. 23, 1974).

Films. Mr. Lansbury was art director for *War Hunt* (UA, 1962) and produced on film *The Subject Was Roses* (MGM, 1969) and *Godspell* (Col., 1973).

Television. He was art director for ABC (1955); and for such CBS shows as The Red Skelton Show (1956–60), Playhouse 90 (1957, 1958), Climax! (1959), Studio One (1959), for Specials (1960–61), and The Defenders (1963).

He produced the pilot show, Star Witness (MGM, 1961); was executive art director for The Educational Broadcasting Co. (Channel 13, N.Y.C., 1961; and produced Coronet Blue (CBS, 1965).

Recreation. Skiing, painting, sailing, tennis, mountain climbing, and playing the violoncello.

LANSING, ROBERT. Actor. b. Robert Howell Brown, June 5, San Diego, Calif., to Robert G. Brown. Father, real estate broker. Attended Univ. H.S., West Los Angeles, Calif.; Beverly Hills (Calif.) H.S. Married June 6, 1956 to Emily McLaughlin, actress; one son. Member of AEA; AFTRA; SAG. Address: 13451 Erwin St., Van Nuys, CA.

Theatre. Mr. Lansing made his N.Y.C. debut succeeding (1951) Mark Roberts as Dunbar in *Stalag 17* (48 St. Th., May 18, 1948); subsequently toured in this role (opened Biltmore, Los Angeles, Calif., June 26, 1952; closed Natl., Washington, D.C., May 16, 1953); at the NY City Ctr., played a Cadet of Gascoyne in *Cyrano de Bergerac* (Nov. 11, 1953), the Marquis of Dorset in *Richard III* (Dec. 9, 1953), and Jack Chesney in *Charley's Aunt* (Dec. 22, 1953); played Herstal de la Crux in *The Lovers* (Martin Beck Th., May 10, 1956); Dr. Cukrowicz in *Suddenly, Last Summer,* which played on a double bill with *Something Unspoken,* under the title, *Garden District* (York, Jan. 7, 1958); Lloyd Hilton in *Cue for Passion* (Henry Miller's Th., Nov. 25, 1958); played in *All About Love* (Drury Lane, 1959); appeared as William A. Brown in *The Great God Brown* (Coronet, Oct. 6, 1959), Paul Carr in *Cut of the Axe* (Ambassador, Feb. 1, 1960); and in stock, played in *Under the Yum Yum Tree* (Playhouse-on-the-Mall, Paramus, N.J., Summer 1963).

He was Antony in *Antony and Cleopatra* (MacArthur Park, Los Angeles, Calif., Summer 1967); Daniel Brightower in *Brightower* (John Golden Th., N.Y.C., Jan. 28, 1970); Jeff Cooper in *Finishing Touches* (Plymouth, Feb. 8, 1973; Center Th. Group, Ahmanson Th., Los Angeles, Calif., Dec. 4, 1973); and the Captain in *The Father* (Roundabout Th., N.Y.C., Sept. 11, 1973).

Films. Mr. Lansing made his debut in *4-D Man* (U, 1959); subsequently appeared in *The Pusher* (UA, 1960); *A Gathering of Eagles* (U, 1963); *Under the Yum Yum Tree* (Col., 1963); and *The Grissom Gang* (Nat'l., Gen'l., 1971).

Television. Mr. Lansing appeared in *Shadow of Suspicion* (Kraft Th., NBC, Nov. 7, 1956); on the U.S. Steel Hour (CBS) in *The Square Egghead* (Mar. 11, 1959), *The Case of Julia Walton* (Sept. 9, 1959), *Big Doc's Girl* (Nov. 4, 1959), *The Great Gold Mountain* (June 29, 1960), *Wanted: Someone Innocent* (Oct. 17, 1962), and *Fair Young Ghost* (Jan. 23, 1963); played Detective Sgt. Steve Carella in the series 87th Precinct (NBC, 1961); and Gen. Frank Savage in 12 O'Clock High (ABC, 1964). Other programs on which he appeared include Sam Benedict (NBC, 1962, 1963); The Virginian (NBC, 1963, 1965, 1967); Wagon Train (ABC, 1964); Twilight Zone (CBS, 1964); The Man Who Never Was (ABC, 1966); Ironside (NBC, 1968); Name of the Game (NBC, 1969); Gunsmoke (CBS, 1969); Medical Center (CBS, 1969); Bonanza (NBC, 1970); Mannix (CBS, 1970, 1971); *Killer by Night* (ABC, 1972); and *The Astronaut* (ABC, 1972).

Recreation. Swimming, diving, painting.

LANTZ, ROBERT. Literary and talent representative, producer, playwright. b. July 20, 1914, Berlin, Germany, to Adolf and Ella Lantz. Father, screenwriter. Attended Goethe Schule, Berlin; Berlin Univ. Married Feb. 1950 to Sherlee Weingarten; one son. Member of Intl. P.E.N. (London). The Lantz Office, 114 E. 55th St., New York, NY 10022, tel. (212) 751-2107.

Mr. Lantz was head of the N.Y.C. office of Berg-Allenberg, artists reps. (1948–49); head of the stage and movie depts. of The Gale Agency, Inc. (N.Y.C., 1949–50); and since 1950 has had his own talent agency in N.Y.C., primarily representing literary artists.

Theatre. He produced *The Nervous Set* (Henry Miller's Th., N.Y.C., May 12, 1959); and *Kean* (Bway Th., Nov. 12, 1961).

He also wrote three plays which were produced in Vienna, Aust.: *L'Inconnue de la Seine, Das Geliebte Leben,* and *Voegelchen* (1933–35).

Films. He was story editor in London for 20th-Century Fox (1936–41); Columbia Pictures (1941–46); literary and talent representative in London for Universal Intl. Pictures (1946–47); and executive vice-pres. of Figaro, Inc. (N.Y.C., 1955–58).

Recreation. "Living.".

LARKIN, PETER. Designer of sets, costumes and lighting. b. Peter Sidney Larkin, Aug. 25, 1926, Boston, Mass., to Oliver W. and Ruth (McIntyre) Larkin. Father, educator, writer, designer. Grad. Deerfield (Mass.) Acad.; attended Yale Univ. Sch. of Drama, 1946–48. Studied with Oliver Larkin. Married Nov. 23, 1956, to Mary Ann Reeve. Served in USAAF. Member of United Scenic Artists, Local 829; The Players. Address: 66 Irving Place, New York, NY 10003, tel. (212) GR 3-2545.

Theatre. Mr. Larkin designed settings for *The Wild Duck* (NY City Ctr., Dec. 26, 1951); and *The First Lady* (NY City Ctr., May 28, 1952); designed the entire production of the ballet, *A Streetcar Named Desire* (Her Majesty's Th., Montreal, Can., Oct. 9, 1952); designed the setting and devised lighting for *Dial "M" for Murder* (Plymouth, N.Y.C., Oct. 29, 1952); and settings and lighting for *The Teahouse of the August Moon* (Martin Beck Th., Oct. 15, 1953).

He designed the settings for *Ondine* (46 St. Th., Feb. 18, 1954); *Peter Pan* (Winter Garden, Oct. 20, 1954); *Inherit the Wind* (Natl., Apr. 21, 1955); *No Time for Sergeants* (Alvin, Oct. 20, 1955); *Shangri-La* (Winter Garden, June 13, 1956); *New Faces of '56* (Ethel Barrymore Th., June 14, 1956); *Compulsion* (Ambassador, Oct. 24, 1957); *Miss Isobel* (Royale, Dec. 26, 1957); and settings and costumes for *Protective Custody* (Ambassador, Dec. 28, 1956).

He designed settings for *Good as Gold* (Belasco, Mar. 7, 1957); *Blue Denim* (Playhouse, Feb. 27, 1958); *Goldilocks* (Lunt-Fontanne, Oct. 11, 1958); *First Impressions* (Alvin, Mar. 19, 1959); *Greenwillow* (Alvin, Mar. 8, 1960); *Wildcat* (Alvin, Dec. 16, 1960); *Giants, Sons of Giants* (Alvin, Jan. 6, 1962); and *Marathon '33* (ANTA, Dec. 22, 1963); settings for the National Repertory Theatre's production *The Seagull* (Belasco, Apr. 5, 1964), and *The Crucible* (Belasco, Apr. 6, 1964); settings for the American Shakespeare Festival Theatre production of *Hamlet* (Stratford, Conn.); and the National Repertory Th. production of *She Stoops to Conquer* (Oct. 1964).

Mr. Larkin designed the sets for *The Porcelain Year* (opened Locust St. Th., Philadelphia, Oct. 11, 1965; closed Shubert Th., New Haven, Conn., Nov. 13, 1965); *The Great Indoors* (Eugene O'Neill Th., N.Y.C., Feb. 1, 1966); *Happily Never After* (Eugene O'Neill Th., Mar. 10, 1966); *Anna Christie* (Huntington Hartford Th., Los Angeles, May 2, 1966); *Hail Scrawdyke!* (Booth, N.Y.C., Nov. 28, 1966); *Scuba Duba* (New Th., Oct. 10, 1967); *Sheep on the Runway* (Helen Hayes Th., Jan. 31, 1970); *Les Blancs* (Longacre, Nov. 15, 1970); *Twigs* (Broadhurst, Nov. 14, 1971; and on national tour, 1972–73); *The Wise Child* (Helen Hayes Th., N.Y.C., Jan. 27, 1972); *Let Me Hear You Smile* (Biltmore, Jan. 16, 1973); *Turtlenecks* (opened Fisher Th., Detroit, Aug. 6, 1973; closed Forrest Th., Philadelphia, Sept. 22, 1973); and *Thieves* (Broadhurst, N.Y.C., Apr. 7, 1974).

Awards. Mr. Larkin received the Antoinette Perry (Tony) Award (1954) as outstanding designer, for his designs for *Teahouse of the August Moon* and *Ondine.* For his design for *Teahouse of the August Moon,* he received the Donaldson Award (1954). He received the Antoinette Perry (Tony) Award (1956) for his designs for *Inherit the Wind* and *No Time for Sergeants.*.

Recreation. Bugatti (automobile) Club.

LARSEN, WILLIAM. Actor. b. William Burton Larsen, Nov. 20, Lake Charles, La., to A. Marbry and Gertrude (Halpin) Jones. Father, contractor. Educ. Lamar H.S., Houston, Tex.; grad. Univ. of Texas, Austin, B.F.A. Served in Engineer Corps, US Army; staff sgt. Married to June Bennett. Member of AEA; AFTRA; SAG. Address: (home) 340 W. 87th St., New York, NY 10024, tel. (212) 787-7794; (bus.) c/o Jeff Hunter, 119 W. 57th St., New York, NY 10019, tel. (212) 757-4995.

Pre-Theatre. Service station attendant; drama teacher.

Theatre. Mr. Larsen made his stage debut as Sheridan Whiteside in *The Man Who Came to Dinner* (St. Denis Players, Natchitoches, La., Summer 1952). His first professional work was at the Alley Th., Houston, Tex., where he played Alan Seymour in *Picnic* (Oct. 19, 1954), the Nephew in *My 3 Angels* (Dec. 16, 1954), Frank Lubey in *All My Sons* (Dec. 25, 1954), George Tesman in *Hedda Gabler* (Feb. 25, 1956), and Endicott Sims in *Detective Story* (July 17, 1956). During the Summer 1957 he was at Antioch and Toledo, Ohio, where he appeared as Casca in *Julius Caesar,* as Peter Quince in *A Midsummer Night's Dream,* Antonio in *Twelfth Night,* and the Lord Chancellor in *Henry VIII.*

Mr. Larsen made his N.Y.C. debut off-Bway as Rev. Parris in *The Crucible* (Martinique, Mar. 11, 1958). This was followed by appearances as M. Henri in a revival of *Legend of Lovers* (41 St. Th., Oct. 27, 1959); the Boy's Father in *The Fantasticks* (Sullivan St. Playhouse, May 3, 1960); Max in *Anatol* (McCarter Th., Princeton, N.J., Sept. 1960); and, at the American Shakespeare Festival, Stratford, Conn., as Feste in *Twelfth Night* (Apr.–May 1961), the Laughing Lord in *As You Like It* (June 15, 1961), Mentieth in *Macbeth* (June 16, 1961), and Nestor in *Troilus and Cressida* (July 23, 1961). He appeared with the Association of Producing Artists (APA), Folksbiene Playhouse, N.Y.C., as Rowley in *The School for Scandal* (Mar. 17, 1962), Ilya Shamrayeff in *The Seagull* (Mar. 21, 1962), and the Sheriff in *The Tavern* (Apr. 4, 1962); was the Son in *The Exhaustion of Our Son's Love* (Festival of Two Worlds, Spoleto, Italy, July 1962); Casca in *Julius Caesar* (North Shore Music Th., Beverly Mass., May 1963); succeeded (Jan. 11, 1964) David Clarke as Henry Ford Crimp in *The Ballad of the Sad Cafe* (Martin Beck Th., N.Y.C., Oct. 30, 1963); played Chauvelin in *Pimpernel!* (Gramercy Arts Th., Jan. 6, 1964); and, again with APA (Phoenix Th.), played Willum in *The Tavern* (Mar. 5, 1964) and Bubnov in *The Lower Depths* (Mar. 30, 1964).

He appeared in a revival of *The Tragical Historie of Doctor Faustus* (Phoenix Th., Oct. 5, 1964); was Carshot in *Half a Sixpence* (Broadhurst, Apr. 25, 1965); played (July 1966) Florenz Ziegfeld in *Funny Girl* (Winter Garden, Mar. 26, 1964); Tiny Gilliatt-Brown in *Halfway Up the Tree* (Brooks Atkinson Th., Nov. 7, 1967); the Chairman of the Board in *Dear World* (Mark Hellinger Th., Feb. 6, 1969); and repeated his performance as the Boy's Father in *The Fantasticks* (Ford's Th., Washington, D.C., 1970).

He played Henry Baines in *Prettybelle* (pre-Bway: opened Shubert Th., Boston, Mass., Feb. 1, 1971; closed there Mar. 6, 1971); the Grand Master of Malta in *Caravaggio* (Playhouse in the Park, Cincinnati, Ohio, July 1, 1971); was standby for Max Showalter as Dr. Morris Ritz in *The Grass Harp* (Martin Beck Th., N.Y.C., Nov. 2, 1971); played Monsignor Polycarpe in *Murderous Angels* (Playhouse Th., Dec. 20, 1971); and at the American Shakespeare Festival, Stratford, Conn., Lepidus in *Julius Caesar*, Lepidus in *Antony and Cleopatra*, and Morrison in *Major Barbara* (all Summer 1972); and Barnardine in *Measure for Measure* (June 2, 1973); Siward in *Macbeth* (July 6, 1973) and Flavius and Lepidus in *Julius Caesar* (Aug. 1, 1973).

He repeated his performances as Siward in *Macbeth* and Barnardine in *Measure for Measure* (Eisenhower Th., Kennedy Ctr., Washington, D.C., Sept.–Oct. 1973); at the American Shakespeare Th., Stratford, Conn. (Summer 1974), was Lord Capulet in *Romeo and Juliet* and Dr. Baugh in *Cat on a Hot Tin Roof*, repeating the latter when the production moved to N.Y.C. (ANTA Th., Sept. 2, 1974), where he also substituted as Big Daddy on several occasions, and in Washington, D.C. (Opera House, Kennedy Ctr., Washington, D.C., Feb.–Mar. 1975). In 1975, Mr. Larsen appeared again at the American Shakespeare Th., Stratford, Conn., where he played Gloucester in *King Lear* (June 15), Dr. Gibbs in *Our Town* (June 16), and Antigonus in *The Winter's Tale* (July 30); and he appeared as Dr. Suit in *A Grave Undertaking* (McCarter Th., Princeton, N.J., Oct. 10, 1975).

Television. Mr. Larsen made his television debut on Armstrong Circle Th. (NBC) in 1958. He has also appeared on Kraft Th. (NBC); US Steel Hour (CBS) Alcoa Th. (NBC); The Defenders (CBS); Love of Life (CBS); Guiding Light (CBS); Directions (CBS); Lamp Unto My Feet (CBS); and repeated his performance as Bubnov in the televising of the APA production of *The Lower Depths* (NET).

Discography. Mr. Larsen is on the original cast recording of *The Fantasticks* (MGM, 1960).

Recreation. Reading.

LASTFOGEL, ABE. talent representative, executive. b. May 17, 1898, New York City. Married Apr. 6, 1927, to Frances Arms, actress. Member of USO (bd. of gov.); St. Jude Hospital (pres.); Natl. Jewish Welfare (bd. of dir.); Big Brothers of Greater Los Angeles (dir.); Amer. Th. Wing (honorary life mbr.); California Inst. of Tech. (assoc.). Pres. of USO camp shows during WW II.

In 1969, Mr. Lastfogel became board chairman of the William Morris Agency, Inc. He began his association with this agency in 1912 and became president in 1952.

Awards. He received the Medal of Freedom (1945); and a Presidential Certificate of Merit from President Harry S Truman (1946).

LATTIMORE, RICHMOND. Educator, translator, poet. b. Richmond Alexander Lattimore, May 6, 1906, Paotingfu, China, to David and Margaret (Barnes) Lattimore. Father, professor. Grad. Berkeley (Calif.) H.S., 1922; Dartmouth Coll., A.B. (Phi Beta Kappa) 1926; Oxford Univ. (England), A.B. (with honors) 1932; Univ. of Illinois, Ph.D. 1934; attended American Acad. (Rome, Italy), 1934–35. Married Aug. 31, 1935, to Alice Bockstahler; two sons. Served USN, 1943–46; rank, Lt. (jg). Member of American Philological Assn.; Archeological Inst. of America; American Philosophical Society; American Academy of Arts and Sciences; Merion Cricket Club. Address: (home) 149 Lowry's Lane, Rosemont, PA 19010; (bus.) c/o Bryn Mawr College, Bryn Mawr, PA 19010.

Mr. Lattimore was a professor of Greek at Bryn Mawr Coll. since 1948, where he had been a member of the faculty since 1935. He retired in 1971.

At the Univ. of Illinois, he was an assistant in Classics and English (1926–28) and in philosophy (1933–34); assistant professor at Wabash Coll. (1928–29); visiting lecturer at the Univ. of Chicago (1947) and Columbia Univ. (1948, 1950); Turnbull lecturer at Johns Hopkins Univ. (1956); Lord Northcliff lecturer at the Univ. of the Coll. of London (England, 1961); Fulbright Lecturer at Oxford University (England, 1963); visiting professor at Univ. of Toronto (Canada, 1966); and at UCLA (1974).

Published Works. Mr. Lattimore wrote *Themes in Greek and Latin Epitaphs* (1943); edited and translated *The Odes of Pindar* (1947), *The Iliad of Homer* (1951), *The Oresteia of Aeschylus* (1953); wrote *Greek Lyrics* (1955), *Poems* (1957), *The Poetry of Greek Tragedy* (1958); edited, with David Grene, *The Complete Greek Tragedies* (1959); translated *Hesiod* (1959), *The Revelation of John* (1962); wrote *Sestina for a Far-off Summer; Poems 1957–1962* (1962); translated *The Frogs of Aristophanes* (1962); translated *The Odyssey of Homer* (1967); Euripides', *Iphigeneia in Tauris* (1973); wrote *Poems from Three Decades* (1972); and contributed articles to scholarly journals, including *American Journal of Philology*, *Classical Philology*, *Classical Review*, and *The Phoenix*.

Awards. Mr. Lattimore received a Rockefeller Fellowship (1946); Fulbright Research Fellowship to Greece (1951–52); Award from the National Inst. of Arts and Letters (1954); honorary Litt.D. from Dartmouth Coll. (1958); Award from the American Council of Learned Societies (1959); and Fulbright Fellowship to Oxford (1963).

LAUGHLIN, SHARON. Actress. b. Sharon Joan Laughlin, Mar. 12, The Dalles, Ore., to Dale and Virginia (Morehouse) Laughlin. Educ. Wasco (Ore.) public schools; Marylhurst Coll., Univ. of Washington. Professional training with Niels Miller. Member of AEA; SAG. Address: c/o Stephen Draper Agency, 37 W. 57th St., New York, NY 10019, tel. (212) HA 1-5780.

Theatre. Miss Laughlin made her debut as the Pupil in *The Lesson* (Globe Studio, Jan. 1, 1962), and this was followed by her off-Bway debut as the Stenographer in *If Five Years Pass* (Stage 73, May 10, 1962). She subsequently appeared as Ophelia in *Hamlet* (Playhouse on the Mall, Paramus, N.J., Apr. 29, 1963); Jenny in *Jenny Kissed Me* (Bucks County Playhouse, New Hope, Pa., July 8, 1963); Emily in *Our Town* (Bucks County Playhouse, New Hope, Pa., Sept. 19, 1964); and, in her Bway debut, as Kathy in *One by One* (Belasco Th., N.Y.C., Dec. 1, 1964). She again played Ophelia (Pabst Th., Milwaukee, Wis., Mar. 30, 1965); appeared at the Playhouse in the Park, Cincinnati, Ohio, as Laura in *The Glass Menagerie* (June 27, 1965) and in *She Stoops to Conquer* (July 11, 1965) and at Center Stage, Baltimore, Md., played Cleopatra in *Caesar and Cleopatra* (Oct. 28, 1965); was in *Ardele* (Jan. 6, 1966); played the title role in *Miss Julie* (Feb. 6, 1966); the female lead in *Days Between* (Mar. 17, 1966); and Rosalind in *As You Like It* (May 26, 1966). At the NY Shakespeare Festival (Delacorte Th.), she was Lady Mortimer in *Henry IV, Part 1* (June 11, 1968) and Lady Northumberland in *Henry IV, Part 2* (June 18, 1968) and (Public Th.) Ramona in *Huui, Huui* (Nov. 16, 1968), Chris in *Mod Donna* (Apr. 24, 1970), and Natasha Fillipovna in *Subject to Fits* (Feb. 28, 1971).

She played the U.N. Attendant in *Murderous Angels* (Playhouse Th., Dec. 20, 1971); at the American Shakespeare Festival, Stratford, Conn., was Portia in *Julius Caesar* (June 22, 1972) and Charmian in *Antony and Cleopatra* (June 23, 1972); played Kate in *Old Times* (Goodman Memorial, Chicago, Ill., Oct. 8, 1972); toured in *Butley* (Sept. 10–Dec. 15, 1973); and played Elizabeth in *Four Friends* (Th. de Lys, N.Y.C., Feb. 17, 1975).

Films. Miss Laughlin played Nadine in *The Happy Hooker* (1974).

LAURENCE, PAULA. Actress, singer, writer, caricaturist. b. Jan. 25, Brooklyn, N.Y., to Benjamin and Lily (D' Alba) de Lugo. Father, broker. Attended Our Lady of Lourdes Sch. Married Feb. 22, 1953, to Charles Bowden, producer, director, lecturer. Member of AEA; AFTRA; SAG. Address: 263 West End Ave., New York, NY 10023, tel. (212) 873-8994.

Theatre. Miss Laurence made her stage debut as Agatha Entwhistle in a Federal Th. (WPA) Project production of *Horse Eats Hat* (Maxine Elliott's Th., N.Y.C., Sept. 22, 1936); subsequently for the Federal Th. Project, she played Helen of Troy in *Dr. Faustus* (Maxine Elliott's Th., Jan. 8, 1937), and appeared in the revue *Sing for your Supper* (Adelphi, Apr. 24, 1939).

She played Miss Preen in a stock production of *The Man Who Came to Dinner* (Maplewood, N.J., Aug. 1941); played Hilda in *Junior Miss* (Lyceum, N.Y.C., Nov. 18, 1941); Chiquita Hart in *Something for the Boys* (Alvin, Jan. 7, 1943); Molly Grant in *One Touch of Venus* (Imperial, Oct. 7, 1943); Miss Kiester and the Queen of Spain in *The Duchess Misbehaves* (Adelphi, Feb. 13, 1946); the Duenna in *Cyrano de Bergerac* (Alvin, Oct. 8, 1946); and toured as Olga in *Dark Eyes* (opened Yardley, Pa., July 14, 1947).

With the NY City Th. Co., at NY City Ctr., she played Lady Politic Would-be in *Volpone* (Jan. 8, 1948), Anna Smeyukin in *The Wedding* (Feb. 5, 1948), and the Female Beetle in *The Insect Comedy* (June 3, 1948); took over (July 1948) as Beatrice Lillie's standby in *Inside U.S.A.*, later substituting (Dec. 20, 1948) for Miss Lillie for two weeks (Century, Apr. 30, 1948); and in Chevy Chase, Ill., she played Mabel in *Three Men on A Horse* (July 11, 1949), Ethel Chichester in *Peg O' My Heart* (July 19, 1949), Frances Black in *Light Up the Sky* (July 26, 1949), Mavis Wilson in *Love from a Stranger* (Aug. 2, 1949), and Irene de Champigny in *The Man from Home* (Aug. 16, 1949).

She played Columbina in *The Liar* (Broadhurst, N.Y.C., May 18, 1950); Pauline in *No, No, Nanette!* (Lambertville Music Circus, N.J., Aug. 1950); Molly Burden in *A Season in the Sun* (Cort, N.Y.C., Sept. 28, 1950); toured as Morgan le Fay in *A Connecticut Yankee* (opened Somerset, Mass., June 1951); played Fernande Dupont in *Tovarich* (NY City Ctr., May 14, 1952); Signora Agazzi in *Right You Are If You Think You Are* (Westport Country Playhouse, Conn., Summer 1952); appeared in Baltimore, Md., as Miriam in *The Women* (Jan. 9, 1953), and Maria in *On Approval* (Jan. 27, 1953); and played Ingeborg Jensen in a summer tryout of *Second Fiddle* (Westport Country Playhouse, June 22, 1953; Cape Playhouse, Dennis, Mass., Aug. 4, 1953).

She repeated her role as the Duenna in *Cyrano de Bergerac* (NY City Ctr., Nov. 11, 1953); played Valeria in *Coriolanus* (Phoenix, Jan. 19, 1954); at the Westport Country Playhouse, appeared as Chevredent in *The Apollo of Bellac*, Hannah in *The Shewing Up of Blanco Posnet*, and the Baroness in *Candlelight* (Summer 1954). In Stamford, Conn., she appeared in scenes from *The Merchant of Venice* and *Henry V* (Aug. 29, 1954); played the Society Lady in *The Time of Your Life* (NY City Ctr., Jan. 19, 1955); toured as Madame Arcati in *Blithe Spirit* (opened Hinsdale, Ill., July 3, 1955); and as Countess Lina in *The Spa* (opened Camden, Me., July 30, 1956).

At the NY City Ctr., she played Public Opinion in *Orpheus in the Underworld* (Sept. 20, 1956); and Mrs. Coaxer in *The Beggar's Opera* (Mar. 13, 1957); then succeeded (June 24, 1957) Cynthia Latham as Madame Boniface in *Hotel Paradiso* (Henry Miller's Th., Apr. 11, 1957); played Sally Brass in a summer tryout of *Pound in Your Pocket* (John Drew Th., East Hampton, N.Y., Aug. 19, 1957); repeated her role as the Society Lady in *The Time of Your Life* at the Brussels (Belgium) World's Fair (Amer. Pavilion, Summer 1958); and as Sally Brass in *Pound in Your Pocket* (Palm Beach Playhouse, Fla., Mar. 9, 1959). She was standby for Bette Davis as Maxine Faulk in *The Night of the Iguana*, and played the role (Jan. 22–28, 1962) (Royale, N.Y.C., Dec. 28, 1961);

played Mae Peterson in *Bye Bye Birdie*(Lambertville Music Circus, Aug. 21, 1962); and succeeded (June 1, 1964) Jean Stapleton as Mrs. Strakosh in *Funny Girl*(Winter Garden, Mar. 26, 1964), played Mae Peterson in tour of *Bye Bye Birdie*, with Van Johnson (opened Shady Grove Music Fair, Gaithersberg, Md., July 27, 1965); appeared as Zinaida Savisha in *Ivanov*, with Sir John Gielgud and Vivien Leigh (opened Shubert Th., New Haven, Conn., Feb. 18, 1966; Shubert Th., N.Y.C., May 3, 1966); was standby for Geraldine Page, and played Miss Furnival (Nov. 1967) in *Black Comedy*(Ethel Barrymore Th., N.Y.C., Feb. 1967); played Varda Shimansky in *Seven Days of Morning* (Circle-in-the-Square, N.Y.C., Dec. 16, 1969); and appeared in *The Sea Gull*(Roundabout Th., N.Y.C., Jan. 23, 1974); and *Caesar and Cleopatra* (Sharon (Conn.) Playhouse, July 2, 1974).

Television. Miss Laurence has appeared in *The Cherry Orchard*(Play of the Week, NTA, 1959); *The Country Scandal*(Telemeter, 1960), and *Dark Shadows* (ABC). She has been associated with the Antoinette Perry (Tony) Award telecasts (1969–71).

Night Clubs. She has performed at Le Ruban Bleu, Brevoort Supper Club, Delmonico's, La Vie Parisienne, Le Directoire, and the Blue Angel (N.Y.C., 1939–49).

Other Activities. Miss Laurence's caricatures have been exhibited in the following N.Y.C. galleries: Assoc. Amer. Artists, NY City Ctr., United Nations; as well as the Univ. of Missouri, the Baltimore Museum of Fine Arts, the Westport (Conn.) Art Ctr., and the Natl. Gallery, Washington, D.C. They have been reproduced in *Vogue, Mademoiselle, Cue,* the NY *Herald Tribune*, and the Philadelphia (Pa.) *Evening Bulletin.* She has contributed articles and stories to *Playbill, Vogue, Harper's Bazaar,* Chicago (Ill.) *Daily News,* and *Mademoiselle.*

She has been a member of the auction committee for the Actors Fund of Amer. (1972–to date); and has served on the benefit committees for the New Dramatists Committee, and the Museum of the City of N.Y.

Published Works. She is the author of *Twenty-Five Years of "Tony" Awards* (1971), a kaleidoscopic view of concurrent world events.

Recreation. Cooking, reading. "Loathes sports—loves cats.".

LAURENTS, ARTHUR. Playwright, director, novelist. b. July 14, 1918, Brooklyn, N.Y., to Irving and Ada (Robbins) Laurents. Father, lawyer; mother, teacher. Grad. Cornell Univ., B.A. 1937. Served US Army, 1940–45; rank, Sgt. Member of Dramatists Guild (council); SWG; PEN; Motion Picture Academy of Arts and Sciences. Address: 9 St. Luke's Place, New York, NY 10014, tel. (212) CH 2-5465.

Pre-Theatre. Salesman, lumberjack.

Theatre. Mr. Laurents wrote *Home of the Brave* (Belasco Th., N.Y.C., Dec. 27, 1945); *Heartsong* (opened Shubert Th., New Haven, Conn., Feb. 27, 1947; closed Walnut St. Th., Philadelphia, Mar. 29, 1947); *The Bird Cage* (Coronet, Feb. 22, 1950); *The Time of the Cuckoo*(Empire, Oct. 15, 1952); *A Clearing in the Woods*(Belasco Th., Jan. 10, 1957); *Invitation to a March,* which he also directed (Music Box Th., Oct. 29, 1960); the book for *West Side Story* (Winter Garden, Sept. 26, 1957); *Gypsy*(Bway Th., May 21, 1959); directed *I Can Get It for You Wholesale* (Shubert Th., Mar. 22, 1962); and wrote the book for *Anyone Can Whistle,* which he also directed (Majestic, Apr. 4, 1964).

He wrote the books for the musicals, *Do I Hear a Waltz?*(46 St. Th., Mar. 15, 1965); and *Hallelujah, Baby!* (Martin Beck Th., Apr. 27, 1967). He wrote and directed *The Enclave*(Th. Four, Nov. 15, 1973); and directed *Gypsy*in England (Piccadilly Th., London, May 27, 1973), and for its N.A. tour (opened Royal Alexandra, Toronto, Canada, March 25, 1974; closed Winter Garden, N.Y.C., Sept. 23, 1974).

Films. Mr. Laurents wrote the screenplays for *Rope* (WB, 1948); *The Snake Pit*(20th-Fox, 1948); *Caught* (MGM, 1949); *Anastasia* (20th-Fox, 1956); *Anna Lucasta* (UA, 1958); *Bonjour Tristesse* (Col., 1958); and *The Way We Were* (Col., 1973).

Radio. He has written for the Screen Guild Th., Lux Radio Th., and for several series: Armed Forces Presents, Assignment: Home, and The Man Behind the Gun.

Published Works. Mr. Laurents wrote the novel *The Way We Were* (Harper & Row, 1972).

Awards. Mr. Laurents received the Sidney Howard Award and the American Academy of Arts and Letters Award for *Home of the Brave*(1945); and won the *Variety*NY Drama Critics Poll for the series Assignment: Home. He received the 1968 Antoinette Perry (Tony) Award for Best Musical for *Hallelujah, Baby!.*

Recreation. Skiing, water-skiing, bridge, tennis, and cooking.

LAVERY, EMMET. Writer. b. Emmet Godfrey Lavery, Nov. 8, 1902, Poughkeepsie, N.Y., to James A. and Katharine T. (Gilmartin) Lavery. Grad. Fordham Univ., LL.B. 1924. Admitted to N.Y. Bar (1925). Married Nov. 3, 1925, to Genevieve E. Drislane; one son, one daughter. Member of Natl. Catholic Th. Conference (co-founder, 1937); Hollywood Writers Mobilization (chairman, 1944–45); SWG (pres., 1945–47); MPAAS (vice-pres., 1946); ALA; Dramatists Guild; Society of Authors (Paris); Amer. Bar Assn.; The Players; Newman Club (Los Angeles); Board of Aldermen, Poughkeepsie, N.Y. (pres., 1929–33). Address: (home) 1075 Casiano Rd., Los Angeles, CA 90049; (bus.) Dramatists Guild, 234 W. 44th St., New York, NY 10036.

Theatre. Mr. Lavery wrote *The First Legion* (46 St. Th., Oct. 1, 1934); *Monsignor's Hour*(Josefstadt, Vienna, Austria, 1936); *The Magnificent Yankee* (Royale, N.Y.C., Jan. 22, 1946); *The Gentleman from Athens* (Mansfield, N.Y.C., Dec. 9, 1947); *Brother Petroc's Return* (State Th., Pforzheim, Germany, 1949), an adaptation from the novel by an anonymous English nun; collaborated with Ernst Krenek on the opera, *Tarquin* (Kammerspiele, Cologne Opera House, Germany, 1950); wrote *Fenelon* (State Th., Basel, Switzerland, 1956); *American Portrait* (Veterans Aud., San Francisco, Calif., June 9, 1959); *Hail to the Chief*(Pasadena Playhouse, Calif., 1958; State Th., Saarbrucken, Germany, 1959, under the title *The Indispensable Man*); *Dawn's Early Light* (Univ. of Oregon, 1959). He adapted *The Ladies of Soissons,* a novel by Sidney Cunliffe-Owen, (Pasadena Playhouse, Jan. 22, 1964). With the late Francis Poulenc, he is a co-licensor of the opera *Dialogues des Carmelites.*

Films. Mr. Lavery's screenplays include *Hitler's Children* (RKO, 1943); *Behind the Rising Sun* (RKO, 1943); *Guilty of Treason* (Eagle Lion, 1950); *The Magnificent Yankee* (MGM, 1950); *The First Legion* (UA, 1951); *The Bright Road* (MGM, 1953) from the story, *See How They Run* by Mary Elizabeth Vroman; *The Court Martial of Billy Mitchell,* in collaboration with Milton Sperling (WB, 1955); and *Williamsburg* (Par., 1957).

Television. Mr. Lavery wrote scripts for the television films *Continental Congress: 1976* (KNBC-TV, 1971) and *Prairie Lawyer* (NBC, 1974).

Other Activities. He has lectured on the drama at Fordham Univ. (1939), Smith College (1942), Univ. of Oregon (1959), and at Univ. of California (Los Angeles) in various years.

Published Works. His published plays include *Second Spring* (1938); *Kamiano,* in collaboration with Grace Murphy, published in the trilogy *Theatre for Tomorrow* (1940); *Brief Music* (1940); *Murder in a Nunnery,* from the novel by Eric Shepard (1944); *Song at the Scaffold,* from the novel by Gertrud von le Fort (1949).

Awards. Mr. Lavery received the Christopher Award (1953) for *Bright Road;* was nominated (1955) for an Academy (Oscar) Award for *The Court Martial of Billy Mitchell;* received the Dinneen Award (1957) of the National Catholic Theatre Conference; and received the American Bar Association's Gavel Award (1965) for the television production of *The Magnificent Yankee.* He was awarded an honorary L.H.D. degree from Mount St. Paul College in 1968.

LAVIN, LINDA. Actress. b. Oct. 15, 1939. Portland, Me., to David J. and Lucille (Potter) Lavin. Grad. Waynefleet Sch., Deering H.S., Portland, Me.; William and Mary Coll., B.A. 1959. Married Sept. 7, 1969, to Ron Leibman, actor. Member of AEA; SAG.

Theatre. While at William and Mary Coll. (Williamsburg, Va., 1955–59), Miss Lavin played Margot in *Dial "M" for Murder;* Rosalind in *As You Like It;* Juliet in *Romeo and Juliet;* and Dolly Levi in *The Matchmaker;* and, with the Restoration Players (Williamsburg, 1957–58), Miss Biddy in *Miss in Her Teens;* and Dorcas in *The Doctor in Spite of Himself.* As a resident principal actress at the Camden (N.J.) County Music Circus (Summer 1956) she appeared in *Plain and Fancy, South Pacific, Kismet, Annie Get Your Gun, Wish You Were Here, The Student Prince, Guys and Dolls,* and *The King and I;* subsequently appeared in the historical outdoor dramas, *The Common Glory* and *The Founders;* and, with the Charles Playhouse of Boston (at the Edgartown Summer Th., Cape Cod, Mass., Summer 1959) appeared as Cherie in *Bus Stop;* Rosa in *The Rose Tattoo;* Jean Tanner in *Separate Tables* Emma in *Summer of the Seventeenth Doll;* and Crazy Agnes in *The Drunkard.*

Miss Lavin made her off-Bway debut as Izzy in *Oh, Kay!* (E. 74 St. Th., N.Y.C., Apr. 16, 1960); appeared in *Gypsy* and *Flower Drum Song* (North Shore Music Th., Beverly, Mass., Summer 1961); made her Bway debut as Wilma in *A Family Affair* (Billy Rose Th., Jan. 27, 1962); subsequently replaced Rose Gregorio as Evelyn in *Kiss Momma* (Actors Playhouse, Oct. 1, 1964); appeared in the revues *Wet Paint* (Renata, Apr. 12, 1965), and *The Game Is Up* (Downstairs at the Upstairs, June 15, 1965); played Victoire in *Hotel Passionato* (E. 74 St. Th., Oct. 22, 1965); appeared in the revue *The Mad Show*(The New, Jan. 9, 1966); played Sydney in *It's a Bird . . It's a Plane . . It's Superman* (Alvin, Mar. 29, 1966); Daisy Gamble in a national touring company of *On a Clear Day You Can See Forever* (1966–67 season); Beth Nemerov in *Something Different* (Cort, N.Y.C., Nov. 28, 1967); was a member of the acting company of the Eugene O'Neill Playwrights' Unit (Waterford, Conn., Summer 1968); played Patsy Newquist in *Little Murders* (Circle in the Square, N.Y.C., Jan. 5, 1969); appeared in *Cop-Out* (Cort, Apr. 7, 1969); played Elaine Navazio in *The Last of the Red Hot Lovers* (Eugene O'Neill Th., Dec. 28, 1969); replaced Valerie Harper (Nov. 10, 1970) in *Story Theater* (Ambassador, Oct. 26, 1970); played Leah in *The Enemy Is Dead* (Bijou, Jan. 14, 1973); on a double-bill entitled *Love Two* (Billy Munk Th., May 23, 1974), played Sarah in *The Lover* and Sheila in *Score; and, for the NY Shakespeare Festival, played The Courtesan in The Comedy of Errors* (Delacorte, Summer 1975).

Films. Miss Lavin made her film debut in *The Story of a Patriot* (Par., 1956).

Television. While at William and Mary Coll., Miss Lavin played Rosalind in a televised production of *As You Like It* (WNOR, Norfolk, Va.). Subsequent appearances include *The Beggar's Opera* (NET); *Damn Yankees* (NBC); CBS Playhouse; The Nurses/The Doctors (CBS); Barney Miller (ABC); Rhoda (CBS); and three specials with Alan King.

Night Clubs. Miss Lavin has appeared at The Blue Angel (N.Y.C.).

Discography. She has recorded, as a single release, *The River Is Wide* (Cabot, 1968).

Awards. Miss Lavin was named *Theater World's* Most Promising Personality (1964–65) for her performance in *Wet Paint;* and was selected by *Best Plays* as best actress in a supporting role (1969–70) for *The Last of the Red Hot Lovers.* .

LAW, MOUZON. Educator, director, administrator. b. Walter Mouzon Law, Sept. 17, 1922, Texarkana, Ark., to Richard Green and Ettie M. (McWilliams) Law. Father, accountant. Grad. Texas H.S., Texarkana, 1939; Texarkana Junior Coll., A.A. 1941; Univ. of Texas, B.F.A. (with honors) 1948; Northwestern Univ., M.A. 1949; attended Columbia Univ., 1957–58; New York Univ., 1958–60. Member of AETA (exec. secy., treas., 1953–55; advisory council, 1953–58); Children's Th. Conference of AETA (bd. of gov., 1950–55; exec. secy., treas., 1953–55); TETA (secy., 1952–53); SWTC (program committee, 1956); ANTA (asst. exec. dir., 1957); NETC; NTC; the League of Professional Theatre Training Programs (vice-pres., 1971–to date); Alpha Epsilon Rho. Address: (home) 112 Pinckney St., Boston, MA 02114; (bus.) c/o Boston Univ. Theatre, 264 Huntington Ave., Boston, MA 02115, tel. (617) 353-3391.

Since 1974, Mr. Law has been the director of the School of Theatre Arts and professor of Theatre Arts at Boston Univ. From 1963 to 1973, he was chairman of the Division of Theatre Arts and professor of Theatre Arts at Boston Univ.

He was assistant professor of drama at the Univ. of Texas (1949–63); a guest professor at Birmingham Southern Coll. (1950); Tulane Univ. (1952); Sam Houston State Coll. (1955); Northwestern Univ. (1956); George Peabody Coll. (1957–59); Univ. of Illinois (1960); directed the children's theatre at the Sharon Creative Arts Foundation (1961); and was guest professor of drama at Syracuse Univ. (1962). He was the director of Boston University's Professional Playwrights Workshop at the Berkshire Music Center and the Berkshire Theatre Festival (1966–70).

Mr. Law, in association with Paul Libin, World Baker, and Franchot Productions, produced *The Crucible* (Martinique, N.Y.C., Mar. 11, 1958). He produced the Obie Award-winning play *Approaching Simone* (La Mama ETC, 1970).

He directed *Shall We Join the Ladies?* (Northwestern Univ., 1949); *Making the Bear* (Univ. of Texas, 1952); *Peter Pan* (Univ. of Texas); *No More Wars but the Moon* (Univ. of Texas, 1956); *The Innocents* (Univ. of Texas, 1957); *The Teahouse of the August Moon* (Univ. of Texas, 1959); *The Emperor's New Clothes* (Univ. of Texas, 1960); *The Land of the Dragon* (Univ. of Illinois, 1960; Sharon Playhouse, Conn., 1961); *Reynard the Fox* (Univ. of Texas, 1962); *Parade at the Devil's Bridge* (Syracuse Univ., 1962); and *The Thirteen Clocks* (Univ. of Texas, 1963).

Other Activities. He was managing editor of *Educational Theatre Journal* (1951–53); and consultant to NBC on educational television (1963).

Awards. Mr. Law was named an "Outstanding Educator of America" for 1972. He received a grant from the Whitney Foundation and the Sharon Creative Arts Foundation to institute and direct a program of drama for and with children at the Sharon (Conn.) Playhouse (1961). For special projects in connection with his professional theatre training program at Boston Univ., Mr. Law has received grants from the Rockefeller Foundation, the National Endowment for the Arts, the Shubert Foundation, and the League of Professional Theatre Training Programs.

LAWLER, RAY. Playwright, actor. b. 1921, Footscary, Australia. Married to Jacklyn Kelleher, actress; two sons, one daughter. Member of Dramatists League.

Pre-Theatre. Factory worker, messenger, ghost writer for Will Mahoney.

Theatre. Mr. Lawler was stage manager of the Variety Th., (Brisbane, Australia). At the National Th. (Melbourne, Australia), he directed and performed in their productions, wrote *Cradle of Thunder* (1949); and wrote children's shows (1950). Subsequently he wrote and played Barney Ibbot in *Summer of the Seventeenth Doll* which was presented in Australia under the auspices of the Elizabethan Th. Trust (Union Th., Melbourne Univ., 1956), in London (New Th., Apr. 30, 1957), and in N.Y.C. (Coronet Th., Jan. 22, 1958): Players Th., Oct. 13, 1959). He wrote *The Unshaven Cheek* (Lyceum, Edinburgh, Scotland, Aug. 19, 1963); and *The Piccadilly Bushman* (Palace Th., Watford, England, Sept. 28, 1965).

LAWRENCE, ELLIOT. Musical director, composer, orchestrator. b. Elliot Lawrence Broza, Feb. 14, 1925, Philadelphia, Pa., to Stan Lee and Esther (Malts) Broza. Father, band leader; mother, television/radio writer-producer. Grad. Berwyn (Pa.) H.S., 1941; Univ. of Pennsylvania, B.F.A. (cum laude) 1944. Studied piano with Erno Balogh, 1941–49; composition and music theory with Harl McDonald, 1942–44; Robert Elmore, 1942–44; conducting with Leon Barzin, 1943–45 (and was asst. cond. to him at the Natl. Orchestra Assn., N.Y.C.); Pierre Monteux, Hancock, Me., 1956–57. Married Jan. 3, 1954, to Amy Bunim; two sons, two daughters. Member of AFM, locals 802 and 77; ASCAP.

Theatre. Mr. Lawrence was musical director, vocal arranger, and contributed additional orchestrations to the Bway musicals, *Bye Bye Birdie* (Martin Beck Th., Apr. 14, 1960); *How To Succeed in Business without Really Trying* (48 St. Th., Oct. 14, 1961); *Here's Love* (Shubert, Oct. 3, 1963); *Golden Boy* (Majestic, Sept. 8, 1964); composed the title song for the pre-Bway tryout of *Everybody Out, the Castle is Sinking* (opened Colonial, Boston, Dec. 26, 1964; closed there Jan. 9, 1965); was musical director and vocal arranger for *Golden Rainbow* (Shubert, N.Y.C., Feb. 4, 1968); *Georgy* (Winter Garden, Feb. 26, 1970); wrote orchestrations for the pre-Bway tryout of *Prettybelle* (opened Shubert, Boston, Feb. 1, 1971; closed there Mar. 6, 1971); was musical director and vocal arranger for *Sugar* (Majestic, N.Y.C., Apr. 9, 1972); and provided orchestrations for *Music! Music!* (NY City Ctr., Apr. 11, 1974).

Films. He composed the scores for *The Violators* (U/RKO, 1957); a documentary for the French government, *You Are France to Me* (1963); and *Vertical and Horizontal*, which he also conducted.

Television and Radio. For radio, Mr. Lawrence was musical director for WCAU, Philadelphia, Pa. (1943–45); performed on his own radio show, Listen to Lawrence (CBS, 1944–45); was musical director and pianist on the Jack Sterling Show (WCBS, 1952–54); musical director and composer for the Philip Morris Playhouse (WCBS, WABC, 1953–55); musical director and arranger for the Jim Backus Show (WABC, 1955); On a Sunday Afternoon (WCBS, 1957); and Jazz Is My Beat (WCBS, 1959).

He was musical director and composer for the television version of the Philip Morris Playhouse (NBC, 1954); the Red Buttons Show (CBS, 1954–57); musical director and arranger for the Mel Torme-Teresa Brewer variety show, Summertime, U.S.A. (CBS, 1956); Wingo (NBC, 1957); the Ernie Kovacs Show (Dumont, 1957); musical director for a Victor Borge Special (NBC, 1957); musical director and arranger for the US Air Force variety show, Guide Right (Dumont, ABC, 1958–60); Laughline (ABC, NBC, 1958); the Ed Sullivan Moscow Special (CBS, 1959); and Autolite Specials (CBS, NBC, 1955–56). He was musical director for Calvalcade of Bands (NBC, 1952–53); the Robert Q. Lewis Show (CBS, 1953–54); and the Ed Sullivan Show (CBS, 1957–59). He composed the score for the documentary *City of Ships* (NBC, 1964), and for the cartoon series The Mighty Heroes (CBS).

Night Clubs. Mr. Lawrence, with his dance band, has performed at the Palladium (Hollywood, Calif., 1947); the Meadowbrook, N.J. (1947–50); Roosevelt Hotel (New Orleans, La., 1948–50); Statler Hotel (N.Y.C., 1948–50); Bop City (N.Y.C., 1949–50); the Blue Note (Chicago, Ill., 1950); and other locations.

Discography. Mr. Lawrence's recordings include *Moonlight on the Campus* (Decca, 1951); *Dream* (Fantasy, 1956); *Mulligan Arrangements* (1956); *Swinging at the Steel Pier* (1957); *Kahn and Mandel Arrangements* (1957); *Plays for Swinging Dancers* (1958); *Dream On, Dance On* (1958); and *Big Band Sound* (Fantasy, 1959).

Awards. He received the Thornton Oakley Award for creative achievement for his work, Suite for Animals (1944); and the Elliot Lawrence Dance Band was voted the favorite band of the nation's colleges in a *Billboard* poll (1948–49).

He was nominated for the Antoinette Perry (Tony) Award for his musical direction of *Bye Bye Birdie* (1960); and received the Antoinette Perry (Tony) Award for his musical direction of *How To Succeed in Business without Really Trying* (1961). He received a N.Y.C. chapter NATAS (Emmy) Award for his score for *City of Ships* (1964).

Recreation. Collecting primitive and Oriental art.

LAWRENCE, JEROME. Playwright, director, teacher. b. July 14, 1915, Cleveland, Ohio, to Samuel and Sarah (Rogen) Lawrence. Father, owner of printing co., baseball expert; mother, poet. Studied with Eugene C. Davis, Cleveland, 1930–33; grad. Glenville H.S., Cleveland, 1933; studied with Harlan Hatcher, Herman Miller, Robert Newdick, Ohio State Univ., B.A. (Phi Beta Kappa) 1937; graduate work Univ. of California at Los Angeles, 1939. Served in WW II as a consultant to the Secretary of War; rank, Staff Sgt.; Army correspondent, North Africa, Italy. Relatives in theatre: sister, Naomi Lawrence, actress; brother-in-law, David Robison, playwright. Member of Dramatists Guild (council mbr., 1969–74); Authors League (council mbr., 1972–to date); ASCAP; WGA, West (founding mbr., trustee); Amer. Guild of Authors & Composers; AMPAS; Amer. Playwrights Th. (co-fdr., trustee, pres., 1970–72); Radio Writers Guild of America (founding mbr., natl. pres., 1954–55); NATAS; ANTA (bd. of dir., 1964–67); natl. vice-pres., 1968–69); Eugene O'Neill Memorial Foundation (bd. of dir.); Bd. of Standards of the Living Th. (bd. of dir.); Natl. Rep. Th. (bd. of dir.); American Conservatory Th. (bd. of dir.); East-West Players (bd. of dir.); USDAN Center for the Creative and Performing Arts (bd. of dir.); Ohio State Univ. School of Journalism (adv. professional council); Ohio State Univ. Alumni Assn. (life mbr., bd. of dir.); Sigma Delta Chi; Zeta Beta Tau; The Players. Address: (home) 21056 Las Flores Mesa Dr., Malibu, CA 90265; (bus.) c/o Brandt & Brandt, 101 Park Ave., New York, NY 10017.

Pre-Theatre. Journalist, reporter, telegraph editor, of Ohio small town dailies, continuity editor-director. KMPC (Beverly Hills, 1938).

Theatre. Mr. Lawrence began his theatrical career as an actor in high school, college, and summer theatres, where he played such roles as Robert Mayo in *Beyond the Horizon*, Thomas Hayden in *Seven Keys to Baldpate*, Moser in *A Question of Honor*, Simon in *Hay Fever*, Runch in *Criminal Code*, Heine in *Laugh, God!* (written by Mr. Lawrence), a Striker in *Waiting for Lefty*, Robert Law in *Boy Meets Girl*, Leo Davis in *Room Service*, and Langlois in *Paths of Glory*. He also directed summer theatre productions of *Anything Goes*, *H. M. S. Pinafore*, *The Pirates of Penzance*, *Imaginary Invalid*, *Room Service*, *You Can't Take It with You*, *Androcles and the Lion*, *Green Pastures*, and *Boy Meets Girl*.

He wrote, in collaboration with Robert E. Lee, the book for *Look, Ma, I'm Dancin'!* (Adelphi Th., N.Y.C., Jan. 29, 1948); *Inherit the Wind* (National, Apr. 21, 1955), which has been translated into thirty languages; the book and lyrics, with James Hilton and Mr. Lee, for *Shangri-La* (Winter Garden, June 13, 1956), based on Mr. Hilton's novel *Lost Horizon;* with Mr. Lee, *Auntie Mame* (Broadhurst, Oct. 31, 1956); *The Gang's All Here* (Ambassador, Oct. 1, 1959); *Only in America* (Cort, Nov. 19, 1959); and *A Call on Kuprin* (Broadhurst, May 25, 1961). He wrote *Live Spelled Backwards* (Beverly Hills Playhouse, Beverly Hills, Calif., Jan. 14, 1966); and, with Mr. Lee, *Mame* (Winter Garden, N.Y.C., May 24, 1966), the first arena production of which he also directed (Sacramento Music Circus, Sacramento, Calif., Summer 1968); *Dear World* (Mark Hellinger Th., N.Y.C., Feb. 6, 1969); and *The Incomparable Max* (world premiere, Barter Th., Abingdon, Va., June 24, 1969, which he also directed; Royale, N.Y.C., Oct. 19, 1971). Mr. Lawrence and Mr. Lee's *The Night Thoreau Spent in Jail* has received more than 2,500 performances throughout the world since its premiere performance for American Playwrights Theatre as the Centennial Play, Ohio State Univ., Columbus, Ohio, Apr. 21, 1971; Mr.

Lawrence directed the Dublin (Scotland) Theatre Festival production (Mar. 1972). With Mr. Lee, Mr. Lawrence wrote *Jabberwock* for the official opening of the Thurber Th., Ohio State Univ., Columbus, Ohio, Nov. 18, 1972 (professional premiere directed by Mr. Lawrence, Dallas Th. Ctr., Dallas, Tex., Mar. 6, 1973).

Mr. Lawrence and Mr. Lee collaborated also on *Diamond Orchid* (Henry Miller's Th., N.Y.C., Feb. 10, 1965), which was revised and restaged as *Sparks Fly Upward* (McFarlin Aud., Southern Methodist Univ., Dallas, Tex., Dec. 3, 1967); and *The Laugh Maker* (Players Ring, Hollywood, Calif., Aug. 1952), rewritten and restaged as *Turn on the Night* (Playhouse-in-the-Park, Philadelphia, Pa., Aug. 1961), rewritten and restaged as *The Crocodile Smile* (premiere, directed by Mr. Lawrence, Stage Th., of N. Carolina, Flatrock, N.C., Aug. 1970).

Films. Screen adaptations were made of *Auntie Mame* (WB, 1958), *Inherit the Wind* (UA, 1960), and *Mame* (WB, 1974). Mr. Lawrence was also a scenario writer for Paramount (1941), for Samuel Goldwyn (1946), 20th Century-Fox (1965), and Hal Wallis Productions (1971–72).

Television and Radio. Mr. Lawrence was a senior staff writer for CBS (1939–41). He was one of the founders of Armed Forces Radio Service and a writer-director, with Robert E. Lee, of the official Army-Navy programs for D-Day, VE-Day, and VJ-Day, as well as Mail Call, Yarns for Yanks, Command Performance, Globe Theatre (including Know Your Enemy, Know Your Ally, and others), and many other programs. His other radio programs included the series Hollywood Showcase (CBS, 1940, 1941), They Live Forever (CBS, 1942), I Was There (CBS), and, with Mr. Lee, Columbia Workshop (CBS, 1941–42), The World We're Fighting For (1943), Request Performance (1945–46), Screen Guild Th. (1946), Favorite Story (CBS, 1946–49), Frank Sinatra Show (1947), The Railroad Hour (1948–54), Young Love (1949–50), Halls of Ivy (1950–51), and Hallmark Playhouse (1950–51). For television, Mr. Lawrence wrote, with Mr. Lee, *The Unexpected,* also called *Times Square Playhouse* (1951), *Song of Norway* (Railroad Hour, Feb. 1957), the pilot film *West Point* (1958), *Shangri-La* (Hallmark Hall of Fame, NBC, Oct. 24, 1960); *Inherit the Wind* (Hallmark Hall of Fame, NBC, Nov. 18, 1965); and *Lincoln the Unwilling Warrior* (Wolper Prod., 1974).

Other Activities. Mr. Lawrence has traveled to and studied theatre in almost a hundred countries. On his round-the-world trip in 1964, he initiated the cultural exchange tour of the Harold Clurman rehearsal panel of Eugene O'Neill's *Long Day's Journey into Night* for Japan. He has also lectured extensively in Thailand, Egypt, and Greece. He and Mr. Lee were guests of the Soviet Ministry of Culture as specialists in drama in the fall and winter of 1972.

Mr. Lawrence was a professor, Banff School of the Arts, Univ. of Alberta (1952–53); master playwright, NY Univ. (1966–68); visiting professor, Ohio State Univ. (1969); professor, Salzburg (Austria) Seminar in American Studies (1972); and visiting professor, Squaw Valley (Calif.) Community of Writers (1973). He has been guest lecturer at the Univ. of Southern California, The Univ. of California (Los Angeles), and Yale, Tufts, Villanova, California State, Boston, Ohio, and Kent State universities, the Eugene O'Neill Foundation, American Conservatory Theatre, Pasadena (Calif.) Playhouse, and Gorki Writers School, Leningrad, USSR. He was on the Drama Panel, US State Dept. Cultural Exchange Program (1963–71), a judge for the Hopwood Drama Award, Univ. of Michigan (1967); lecturer at the American College Theatre Festival (1970, 1971, 1974); keynote speaker at the American Univ. Playwrights Conference (1970); and judge for the Samuel Goldwyn Award, UCLA (1971). With Mr. Lee, he founded (1962) and is a judge for the Margo Jones Award.

Lawrence and Lee collections are at the Library and Museum of Performing Arts, Lincoln Center, N.Y.C., Ohio State, and Kent State universities.

Published Works. Mr. Lawrence is the author of *Oscar the Ostrich* (1940), *Off Mike* (1944), and *Actor: The Life and Times of Paul Muni* (1974). With Robert E. Lee, he wrote the one-act operas *Annie Laurie* (1954), *Roaring Camp* (1955), and *Familiar Stranger* (1956). He contributed to *The Spice of Variety* (1952), *The Language of Show Biz* (1973), and short stories and articles by him and Robert E. Lee have appeared in a variety of publications.

Discography. With Robert E. Lee, Mr. Lawrence dramatized and directed recordings of *Rip Van Winkle, The Cask of Amontillado,* and *A Tale of Two Cities* (all for Decca), and *One God* (Kapp).

Awards. Mr. Lawrence received the NY Press Award (1942); a special citation from the War Dept. (1945); City Coll. of NY Award (1948); Radio-TV Life Award (1948) and 1952); the Peabody Award (1949 and 1952); Radio-TV Mirror Award (1952 and 1953); *Variety* Showmanship Award (1954); five Antoinette Perry (Tony) Award nominations for *Inherit the Wind* (1955); the Donaldson Award (1955); the *Variety* NY Drama Critics Poll (1955); the Outer Circle Award (1955); the Ohioana Award (1955); Key to the City of Cleveland (1957); Playwrights of the Year, Baldwin-Wallace Coll. (1960); Ohio Press Club Award (1960); British Critics Award (1960); a citation from the Mayor of Philadelphia (1961); the Ben Franklin Award of the Poor Richard Club (1966); three Antoinette Perry (Tony) Award nominations for *Mame* (1966); the Moss Hart Memorial Award for Plays of the Free World (*Inherit the Wind*), 1967; the US State Dept. Medal (1969); the Ohio State Univ. Centennial Medal (1970); the Pegasus Award (1970); the Governor's Award, State of Ohio (1973); the Cleveland Playhouse Plaque as an "honorary member in perpetuity" (May 1973); a key to the city of Cleveland for the second time (1973); and honorary degrees of L.H.D. from Ohio State Univ. (1963), Litt.D. from Fairleigh Dickinson Univ. (1968), and D.F.A. from Villanova Univ. (1969).

Recreation. Photography, swimming, travel.

LAWRENCE, LAWRENCE SHUBERT JR.

Theatre executive. b. Feb. 18, 1916, Philadelphia, Pa., to Lawrence Shubert and Frances (Von Summerfield) Lawrence, Sr. Father, theatrical executive. Grad. Lawrenceville (N.J.) Sch., 1934; Univ. of Pennsylvania, B.A. 1938. Served USNR, 1944–46; rank, Lt. (jg). Relatives in theatre: great-uncles, Sam S. Shubert, Lee Shubert, and Jacob J. Shubert, founders of the Shubert theatrical chain; cousin, John Shubert, head of the Shubert theatrical chain. Member of Actors' Fund (trustee); ATS (Council of Living Theatre Play Selection Committee); ATPAM; Kappa Sigma; The Lambs. Address: Shubert Theatre Enterprises, 234 W. 44th St., New York, NY 10036, tel. (212) CI 6-9500.

Mr. Lawrence has been president and chief executive officer of the Shubert Theatre Enterprises. The company was founded by his great-uncles shortly after their arrival in N.Y.C. in 1900, and since that time has produced more than 500 plays. At one time the Shubert theatrical interests controlled as many as thirty-one theatres in New York, as well as sixty-three theatres in other American cities. They still control, in N.Y.C., the Ambassador, Ethel Barrymore Th., Belasco, Booth, Broadhurst, Bway Th., Cort, 54th St. Th., John Golden Th., Imperial, Longacre, Lyceum, Majestic, Music Box (fifty percent interest), Plymouth, Royale, Shubert, and the Winter Garden; in Philadelphia (Pa.), the Walnut St. Th. and the Forrest; in Chicago (Ill.), the Blackstone and the Shubert; in Boston (Mass.), the Shubert; in Cincinnati (Ohio), the Shubert and the Cox.

Mr. Shubert has also been responsible for the distribution of theatre tickets in Macy's stores at box office prices by Shubert theatres; the complete modernization of sixteen theatres in N.Y., and five theatres in other cities, and for the construction of a new theatre in Los Angeles.

Awards. Mr. Lawrence received the Bway Assn. Gold Medal for Greatest Achievement for the Advancement of Broadway, 1966, for his work in establishing post-graduate fellowships in playwriting in forty-nine colleges and universities.

LAWRENCE, STEVE.

Actor, singer. b. Sidney Liebowitz, July 8, 1935, Brooklyn, N.Y., to Emanuel and Anna (Gelb) Liebowitz. Grad. Thomas Jefferson H.S., Brooklyn. Married Dec. 29, 1957, to Eydie Gorme, singer; two sons, Member of AEA; AFTRA; AGVA; SAG; and the Friars (bd. of gov.).

Theatre. Mr. Lawrence toured stock theatres as Joey in *Pal Joey* (Summer 1962); appeared with his wife in a concert tour *An Evening with Steve Lawrence and Eydie Gorme* (Summer 1963); made his N.Y.C. debut as Sammy Glick in the musical, *What Makes Sammy Run?* (54 St. Th., Feb. 27, 1964); and was Larry Davis in *Golden Rainbow* (Sam S. Shubert Th., Feb. 4, 1968).

Television. Mr. Lawrence won first prize on Arthur Godfrey's Talent Scouts (CBS, 1950) and two years later began appearing on the Steve Allen Show (NBC). He was on the Tonight Show (NBC, 1953–58), on which, with Eydie Gorme, he substituted for Steve Allen for eight weeks (Summer 1958); co-hosted, also with Eydie Gorme, the Greater NY United Cerebral Palsy telethon (WOR-TV, 1960–69); was in *A Carol for Another Christmas* (ABC, Dec. 28, 1964); hosted his own show (CBS, 1965); was in *What It Was, Was Love* (Kraft Music Hall, NBC, Feb. 1969); and appeared on Medical Center (CBS, 1971); and Night Gallery (NBC, 1971).

Night Clubs. Mr. Lawrence has performed at the Copacabana (N.Y.C., 1957); and, with his wife, has appeared at many clubs, including the Coconut Grove (Los Angeles, Calif.), Diplomat Hotel, (Miami, Fla.), and the Copacabana (N.Y.C.).

Discography. Mr. Lawrence's recording of *Poinciana* (King Records, 1951) and his recordings of *Go Away Little Girl* and *Don't Be Afraid Little Darlin',* both of which sold over a million copies, were followed by *Everybody Knows* (Col.); *The Steve Lawrence Show* (Col.); and *What It Was, Was Love* (RCA). His other albums include *People Will Say We're in Love, About That Girl, Here's Steve Lawrence Sound, Portrait of My Love, Lawrence Goes Latin, The Very Best of Steve Lawrence, Come Waltz with Me, Winner, Swinging West, Academy Award Losers,* and *Everybody Knows.*

With Eydie Gorme, he has recorded *We Got Us Two on the Aisle, Golden Hits, Very Best, Cozy, To the Movies,* and *Steve and Eydie at the Movies* (Col.).

Awards. For his performance in *What Makes Sammy Run?,* Mr. Lawrence was named in the *Variety* NY Drama Critics Poll as best actor in a musical (1964).

LAWSON, JOHN HOWARD.

Playwright, author. b. Sept. 25, 1894, New York City, to Simeon Levy and Belle (Hart) Lawson. Father, journalist. Grad. Cutler Sch., N.Y.C., 1910; Williams Coll., A.B., 1914. Married Nov. 20, 1918, to Kathryn Drain (marr. dis. 1923); one son; married Aug. 5, 1925, to Susan Edmond; one son, one daughter. Served WW I, in Amer. Red Cross, with French and Italian Armies. Member of ALA (council mbr., c.1930–40); WGA, West; SWG (founding pres., 1933–34, exec. bd., c.1930–40).

Pre-Theatre. Cable editor, Reuter's Press Cables, N.Y.C., 1914–15.

Theatre. Mr. Lawson's first play to be produced was *Servant-Master-Lover* (Los Angeles, Calif., July 16, 1916); followed by *Standards,* which received a try-out production (Syracuse and Albany, N.Y., Nov. 23–30, 1916). He subsequently wrote *Roger Bloomer,* produced by Equity Players, Inc. (48 St. Th., N.Y.C., Mar. 1, 1923) and revived that season at the Greenwich Village Th.; for the Theatre Guild, wrote *Processional* (Garrick Th., Jan. 12, 1925); *Nirvana* (Greenwich Village, Mar. 3, 1926); for the New Playwright's Theatre, *Loud Speaker* (52 St. Th., Mar. 7, 1927), and *The International* (Cherry Lane, Jan. 12, 1928).

He wrote *Success Story* (Maxine Elliott's Th., Sept. 26, 1932), produced by the Group Theatre; *The Pure in Heart* (Longacre, Mar. 20, 1934); and *Gentlewoman* (Cort, Mar. 22, 1934); also produced by the Group Theatre; and *Marching Song* (Nora Bayes Th., Feb. 17, 1937) produced by the Theatre Union; *Processional* was revived by the Federal Th. (WPA) Project (Maxine Elliott's Th., Oct. 13, 1937).

Films. Mr. Lawson has written screen plays for *Dynamite* (MGM, 1930); *Blockade* (UA, 1938); *Algiers* (UA, 1938); *They Shall Have Music* (UA, 1939); *Four Sons* (20th-Fox, 1940); *Action in the North Atlantic* (WB, 1943); *Sahara* (Col., 1943); *Counterattack* (Col., 1945); and *Smash-Up, The Story of a Woman* (U, 1947).

Published Works. He has written *Theory and Technique of Playwriting* (1936); *Theory and Technique of Playwriting and Screenwriting* (1949); *The Hidden Heritage* (1950); *Film in the Battle of Ideas* (1953); and *Film: The Creative Process* (1964).

LAWSON, KATE. Scene designer, actress, costume designer, theatrical executive. b. Kathryn Drain, July 27, 1894, Spokane, Wash., to James Andrew and Ethel Mary (Marsland) Drain. Father, lawyer and banker. Grad. Western H.S., Washington, D.C., 1913; attended The Laurels, Canterbury, England, 1910–11; art schools in Paris, France, 1921–30. Married Nov. 20, 1918, to John Howard Lawson, playwright (marr. dis. 1924); one son, Alan Drain Lawson, sculptor and stage technician. Served WW I, Ambulance Americaine #1, Neuilly, France, 1917; WW II, Amer. Red Cross, India, 1943–45; Entertainment Production Unit, Special Services for 32 shows, staff director in Calcutta, 1945. Member of AEA (West Coast advisory board, 1956–to date); SAG; AFTRA; ANTA (natl. bd., 1958–to date; dir. of Region One, 1958–to date; secy., Greater Los Angeles chapter, 1960–61); AETA; United Scenic Artists, Local 892 (life member); Costume Designers Guild (secy., 1957–58); Radio and TV Women of Southern Calif.; CTC; Scene Designers Club, N.Y.C. (treas., 1935–36); TV Exploration Comm. (chairman, 1955–57); Pelican Production (exec. dir., 1947–48).

Theatre. Mrs. Lawson made her stage debut with an experimental group as a dancer in *Orpheus in Hades* (Grand Opera House, Paris, 1921). Her first assignment on Bway was with the Equity Players, Inc., as assistant stage manager and assistant to the designer for *Malvaloca* (48 St. Th., Oct. 2, 1922); subsequently was assistant to the designer for *Neighbors* (48 St. Th., Dec. 26, 1923); *The New Englander* (48 St. Th., Feb. 7, 1924); and *Macbeth* (48 St. Th., Mar. 15, 1924); designed costumes and scenery for *Old English* (Ritz, Dec. 23, 1924); was technical and art director for the Th. Guild (1925–31); appeared in some Th. Guild productions, including *The Chief Thing*, in which she played Ligia (Guild, Mar. 22, 1926); appeared in both editions of the *Garrick Gaieties* (Guild, June 4, 1930; Guild, Oct. 16, 1930), billed as Kate Drain Lawson, which she used thereafter in all her theatre work; was technical director for the London Th. Guild production of *Caprice* (St. James's Th., June 4, 1929); designed the costumes for a season of stock at the Berkshire Playhouse (Stockbridge, Mass.), for *Lute Song* and *Right You Are If You Think You Are* (Summer 1929); with Florine Stettheimer, designed the settings and costumes for *Four Saints in Three Acts* (44 St. Th., N.Y.C., Feb. 20, 1934); was costume designer and technical director for the Katharine Cornell touring productions of *Candida, The Barretts of Wimpole Street,* and *Romeo and Juliet* (1932–33), the latter of which was repeated in N.Y.C. (Martin Beck Th., Dec. 20, 1934).

Mrs. Lawson designed the setting for *A Slight Case of Murder* (48 St. Th., Sept. 11, 1935); headed the Bureau of Research and Publication and Chief Technical Officer for the Federal Th. (WPA) Project in N.Y.C. (1936); designed settings and costumes for *A Point of Honor* (Fulton, Feb. 11, 1937); was costume designer for the Suffern County (N.Y.) Playhouse (Summer 1937); designed the costumes for *Knights of Song* (51 St. Th., Nov. 17, 1938); settings and costumes for the West Coast productions of *Outward Bound, Broom for the Bride, Red Bumble Bee,* and *About Tomorrow* (Biltmore, Los Angeles, Calif., 1939–40); was costume designer for the Los Angeles Civic Light Opera Co. (Philharmonic Aud., 1939–42); designed the costumes for *Meet the People* (Assistant League Playhouse, Hollywood, Calif., Dec. 25, 1939); designed the costumes for the British War Relief production of *Tonight at 8:30* (El Capitan, Los Angeles, 1940); the costumes for the David Selznick summer theatre productions of *Lottie Dundass, Hello Out There, Anna Christie,* and *The Devil's Disciple* (Santa Barbara, Calif., Summer 1942); and was executive director of the Pelican Productions for John Housman at the Coronet Th., Los Angeles (1947–48).

Films. Mrs. Lawson appeared in *Ladies of the Big House* (Par., 1932); *Torchy Blaine* (WB, 1938); *Girls on Probation* (WB, 1938); *Remember the Night* (Par., 1940); *Phantom of the Opera* (U, 1943); *King of the Cowboys* (Rep., 1943); *They Raid by Night* (PRC, 1942); *Every Girl Should Be Married* (RKO, 1948); *Thelma Jordan* (Par., 1949); *The Bride of Vengeance* (Par., 1949); *M* (Col., 1951); and *How To Marry a Millionaire* (20th-Fox, 1953). She designed costumes for the Williamsburg, Va., documentary, *Story of a Patriot* (Par.).

Television. She organized the costume dept. for NBC, West Coast (1951); was costume designer for TV programs including *The Colgate Comedy Hour* (NBC, 1951–56), and Bob Hope's Shows (NBC, 1951).

Awards. Mrs. Lawson received the China, Burma, India campaign ribbon for service with the Amer. Red Cross in India (1943–46); the Merit Award from the Radio and TV Women of Southern Calif. (1958); the Dance Bus. Guild of Amer. Award (1961–62); and the Monte Meacham Award, Children's Th. Conf., AETA (1963).

LAYE, EVELYN. Actress. b. July 10, 1900, London, England, to Gilbert and Evelyn (Froud) Laye. Married to Sonnie Hale (marr. dis.); married to Frank Lawton. Member of AEA; SAG.

Theatre. Miss Laye made her debut as Nang-Ping in *Mr. Wu* (Th. Royal, Brighton, Aug. 1915); subsequently appeared in *Honi Soit* (East Ham Palace, Apr. 24, 1916); played Pyrrha in *Oh, Caesar!* (Lyceum, Edinburgh, Scotland, Dec. 1916); the title role in the pantomime, *Goody Two Shoes* (Th. Royal, Portsmouth, England, Dec. 25, 1917); took over for Moya Mannering as Leonie Bramble in *The Beauty Spot* (Gaiety, London, Feb. 14, 1918); also at the Gaiety Th., played Madeline Manners in *Going-Up* (May 22, 1918); Dollis Pym in *The Kiss Call* (Oct. 8, 1919); and Bessie Brent in *The Shop Girl* (Mar. 25, 1920).

She appeared in *The League of Notions* (New Oxford, Jan. 17, 1921); played Mollie Moffat in *Nightie Night* (Queen's, Mar. 1921); Mary Howells in *Mary* (Queen's, Apr. 27, 1921); appeared in *Fun of the Fayre* (London Pavilion, Oct. 17, 1921); played the Prologue and Helen in *Phi-Phi* (London Pavilion, Aug. 16, 1922); Sonia in *The Merry Widow* (Daly's, May 19, 1923); the title role in *Madame Pompadour* (Daly's, Dec. 20, 1923); Alice in *The Dollar Princess* (King's, Glasgow, Scotland, Dec. 1924; moved to Daly's, London, Feb. 4, 1925); the title role in *Cleopatra* (Daly's, June 2, 1925); Betty in *Betty in Mayfair* (Adelphi, Nov. 11, 1925); Molly Shine in *Merely Molly* (Adelphi, Sept. 1926); and succeeded (Mar. 1927) Winnie Melville as Princess Elaine in *Princess Charming* (Palace, Oct. 21, 1926).

She played Lili in *Lilac Time* (Daly's Dec. 23, 1927; Dec. 24, 1928); Marianne in *The New Moon* (Drury Lane, Apr. 4, 1929); made her N.Y.C. debut as the Marchioness of Shayne in *Bitter Sweet* (Ziegfeld, Nov. 5, 1929), and played this role in London (Lyceum, Apr. 13, 1931).

She toured in *Madame Pompadour* (July 1931); played the title role in *Helen!* (Adelphi, Jan. 30, 1932); Peggy in *Give Me a Ring* (London Hippodrome, June 22, 1933); appeared in *Bitter Sweet* (Shrine Aud., Los Angeles, Calif., Oct. 1935); and played Belinda Warren in *Sweet Aloes* (Booth, N.Y.C., Mar. 4, 1936).

She played Princess Anna in *Paganini* (Lyceum, London, May 1937); Natalie Rives in *Between the Devil* (Majestic, N.Y.C., Dec. 22, 1937); performed in English variety theatres (1938); and made her variety stage debut at the London Palladium (June 1938).

She appeared as Prince Florizel in the pantomime, *The Sleeping Beauty* (Theatre Royal, Birmingham, Dec. 1938); appeared in the revue *Lights Up* (Savoy, London, Feb. 9, 1940); played Violet Gray in *The Belle of New York* (Coliseum, Sept. 16, 1942); Marie Sauvinet in *Sunny River* (Piccadilly, Aug. 1943); the Prince in *Cinderella* (His Majesty's, Dec. 1943); Katherine in *Three Waltzes* (Prince's, Mar. 1, 1945), also touring in it; toured as Laura Kent in *Elusive Lady* (Apr.–July 1946); and Lady Teazle in *The School for Scandal* (1948).

She played Prince Charming in *Cinderella* (London Palladium, Dec. 1948); Marina Verani in *Two Dozen Red Roses* (Lyric, May 1949); toured as Stella in *September Tide* (Sept. 1950); played Joscelyn in *Queen of Hearts* (Wimbledon, Dec. 1950); toured Australia and New Zealand in *September Tide,* and *Bell, Book and Candle* (1951–52); appeared in *The Domino Revue* (Wimbledon, July 1953); played Mrs. Darling in Pat Hirkwood's *Peter Pan* (Scala, Dec. 23, 1953); Marcelle Thibault in *Wedding in Paris* (London Hippodrome, Apr. 3, 1954); Lady Marlowe in *Silver Wedding* (Cambridge, July 9, 1957); toured in the title role of *The Marquise* (Feb.–Sept. 1959); played Lady Fitzadam in *The Amorous Prawn* (Saville, Dec. 9, 1959); and toured in *Black Chiffon* (1963).

Miss Laye played Lady Catherine Champion-Cheney in *The Circle* (Savoy Th., London, June 14, 1965); Annie Besant in *Strike a Light!* (Alhambra, Glasgow, Apr. 1966; and Piccadilly Th., London, July 5, 1966); Lady Hadwell in *Charlie Girl* (Adelphi, London, Mar. 1969); Mrs. Fitzmaurice in *Phil the Fluter* (Palace Th., London, Nov. 1969); and appeared in *The Amorous Prawn* (tour of Great Britain, Sept. 1970); and *No Sex Please, We're British* (Strand Th., London, 1972–73).

Films. Miss Laye has appeared in *One Heavenly Night* (UA, 1930); *Evensong* (GB, 1934); and *Princess Charming* (GB, 1935).

Television. She has appeared in *Tony Draws a Horse* (ITV, London, July 25, 1958); and others.

LAYTON, JOE. Director, choreographer, dancer. b. Joseph Lichtman, May 3, 1931, New York City, to Irving and Sally (Fischer) Lichtman. Grad. H.S. of Music and Art, 1948; studied ballet and Spanish dance with Joseph Levinoff, 1943–48. Married Oct. 6, 1959, to Evelyn Russell, actress. Served US Army, Special Services, 1952–54; rank, Sgt. Member of SSD&C; AEA; AFTRA.

Theatre. Mr. Layton first performed in children's shows (Bklyn., 1937–41); subsequently made his N.Y.C. debut joining the cast (Dec. 1947) as a dancer in *Oklahoma!* (St. James Th., Mar. 31, 1943); toured in *High Button Shoes* (Sept.–Feb. 1949); in *Miss Liberty* (1950); joined the cast (1951) as a dancer in *Gentlemen Prefer Blondes* (Ziegfeld, Dec. 8, 1949); and danced in *Wonderful Town* (Winter Garden, Feb. 25, 1953).

While serving in the US Army, he directed and choreographed productions of *On the Town, Brigadoon, The Medium,* and *The Telephone,* and directed *The Moon is Blue.* He danced in and was choreographer for the Ballet Ho de George Reich (Paris and Cannes, France, 1954–55); choreographed stock productions (Camp Tamiment, Pa., Summer 1958); *On the Town* (Carnegie Hall Playhouse, N.Y.C., Jan. 16, 1959); *Once Upon a Mattress* (Phoenix, May 11, 1959); the Fashion Industrial Show for the Amer. Exhibition (Moscow, USSR, Aug. 1959).

He was choreographer for *The Sound of Music* (Lunt-Fontanne Th., N.Y.C., Nov. 16, 1959); *Greenwillow* (Alvin, Mar. 8, 1960); and the national tour of *Once Upon a Mattress* (opened Erlanger, Chicago, Ill., Sept. 1, 1960). He directed and choreographed *South Pacific* (Arena, Toronto, Canada, July

1960); and *Once Upon a Mattress* (Adelphi, London, Sept. 20, 1960).

Mr. Layton choreographed *Tenderloin* (46 St. Th., N.Y.C., Oct. 17, 1960); the national tour of *The Sound of Music* (opened Riviera, Detroit, Mich., Feb. 27, 1961), and also in London (Palace, Mar. 18, 1961); *Sail Away* (Broadhurst, N.Y.C., Oct. 3, 1961; Savoy, London, July 1962); directed and choreographed *No Strings* (54 St. Th., N.Y.C., Mar. 15, 1962); another tour of *The Sound of Music* (opened Community Th., Hershey, Pa., Sept. 17, 1962); and directed and choreographed *On the Town* (Prince of Wales's Th., London, May 1963).

He directed *The Girl Who Came to Supper* (Bway Th., N.Y.C., Dec. 8, 1963); revised and directed the historical pageant, *The Lost Colony* (Roanoke Island, N.C., June 25, 1964); directed and choreographed *South Pacific* (O'Keefe Ctr., Toronto, Canada, July 6, 1964); directed *Peterpat* (Longacre, N.Y.C., Jan. 6, 1965); directed and choreographed *Drat! The Cat!* (Martin Beck Th., Oct. 10, 1965); succeeded Morton da Costa and Ronald Field as director-choreographer of *Sherry!* (opened Colonial Th., Boston, Jan. 17, 1967; closed Feb. 5, 1967; and Alvin, N.Y.C., Mar. 28, 1967); staged *South Pacific* (NY State Th., June 12, 1967); was one of the directors for The National Theater of the Deaf (1967–69); directed and choreographed *George M!* (Palace, Apr. 10, 1967); *Dear World* (Mark Hellinger Th., Feb. 6, 1969); staged *Carol Channing and Her Ten Stout Hearted Men* (London, 1970); directed *Scarlet* (Tokyo, May 3, 1970; and Drury Lane Th., London, 1970); and *Two by Two* (Imperial, N.Y.C., Nov. 10, 1970); choreographed *Double Exposure* for the City Center Joffrey Ballet (NY State Th., Mar. 3, 1972); and *Grand Tour* for the Royal Ballet (London, 1972); choreographed the pre-Bway tryout of *Gone With the Wind* (opened Chandler Pavillion, Los Angeles, Aug. 28, 1973; closed Curran, San Francisco, Nov. 24, 1973); and staged the pre-Bway version of *Lorelei* (1973–74).

Films. Mr. Layton choreographed *Thoroughly Modern Millie* (U, 1967).

Television. He has danced in *Cinderella* (CBS, 1956); choreographed the Mary Martin Easter Show (NBC, Mar. 1959); *The Gershwin Years* (CBS, Dec. 1960); directed and choreographed *Once Upon a Mattress* (CBS, June 3, 1964); conceived, choreographed and staged *My Name Is Barbra* (CBS, 1965); *Color Me Barbra* (CBS, 1966); and *The Belle of 14th Street — Barbra Streisand* (CBS, 1967); produced *Jack Jones on the Move* (ABC, 1966); directed *On the Flip Side* (ABC, 1966); appeared in a special production of the Theater of the Deaf (NBC, 1967); directed *Androcles and the Lion* (1968); the Debbie Reynolds Special (1968); *Infancy* (1968); *The Littlest Angel* (1969); and the Raquel Welch Special (1974).

Night Clubs. Mr. Layton has performed as a dancer at the Latin Quarter (N.Y.C., 1950); and as a singer at One Fifth Avenue (N.Y.C., Mar. 1959).

Awards. He received the Antoinette Perry (Tony) Award for his choreography in *No Strings* (1961).

Recreation. Painting.

LEACH, WILFORD. Educator, director, playwright. b. Carson Wilford Leach, Aug. 26, 1929, Petersburgh, Va., to Carson Wilford and Louise (M.) Leach. Grad. Coll. of William & Mary, A.B. 1949; Univ. of Illinois, M.A. 1954, Ph.D. 1957. Served with US Army, 1952–54. Sarah Lawrence Coll., Bronxville, NY 10708, tel. (914) DE 7-0700.

Mr. Leach is a member of the theatre faculty at Sarah Lawrence Coll.

He wrote *In Three Zones*, the first play presented at the Forum Th., Lincoln Center, N.Y.C. (began previews Dec. 9, 1966; was withdrawn by the producers before the official opening); later produced at the Charles Playhouse, Boston (Oct. 1970).

Mr. Leach co-adapted and co-directed, with John Braswell (a fellow teacher at Sarah Lawrence Coll.), a double bill which evolved from their work at the coll., consisting of Yeats's *The Only Jealousy of Emer* and Stravinsky's *Renard* (La Mama ETC, N.Y.C., Feb. 1970; transferred to the Performing Garage, Mar. 19, 1970); became artistic director, with Mr. Braswell, of the 19-member La Mama ETC Th. Co. (1970–72); wrote the text of *Gertrude, or Would She Be Pleased To Receive It?* (La Mama ETC, Sept. 9, 1970), which he co-directed with Mr. Braswell; wrote the libretto and directed *Carmilla* (La Mama ETC, Nov. 25, 1970); directed a European tour of the La Mama ETC Th. Co., which performed the four above-mentioned plays (in Paris, Dubrovnik, Brussels, Berlin, Zurich, Cannes, Copenhagen; 1971); and presented a repertory season at La Mama ETC (Jan. 7, 1972–Mar. 19, 1972), consisting of *Gertrude, or Would She Be Pleased To Receive It?* with a new work which he wrote, *Demon* (Jan. 9, 1972), *Carmilla* (Jan. 16, 1972), and *The Only Jealousy of Emer* and *Renard* (Jan. 23, 1972), all five of which he co-directed with Mr. Braswell.

Discography. *Carmilla* was recorded (Vanguard, 1973).

Awards. He and Mr. Braswell received the *Village Voice* Off-Bway (Obie) Award for distinguished direction (of *The Only Jealousy of Emer*, 1972).

LEATHEM, BARCLAY. Educator, director. b. Barclay Spencer Leathem, Mar. 10, 1900, Philadelphia, Pa., to Thomas James and Mathilda (Schumacher) Leathem. Father, merchant. Grad. Northeast H.S., Philadelphia, 1917; Penn State Univ., A.B. 1922; Western Reserve Univ., LL.B. 1924; attended Max Reinhardt's Schauspiel und Regieseminar der Fachhochschule für Musik und darstellende Kunst, 1929–30. Married June 13, 1922, to Ruth Elton, artist; one daughter. Served SATC, 1918. Member of NTC (exec. secy., 1936–61); AETA (pres., 1937); City Club; Delta Upsilon; Hermit Club; Rowfant Club. Address: (home) 10217 Lake Shore Blvd., Cleveland, OH 44108, tel. (216) LI 1-3423; (bus.) Western Reserve University, Cleveland, OH 44106, tel. (216) CE 1-7700.

Mr. Leathem is now professor emeritus in the Dept. of Dramatic Arts at Western Reserve Univ., where he was previously instructor (1924–27), assistant professor (1928–31), associate professor (1931–42), and chairman (1942–72).

Awards. Mr. Leathem received a citation from the War Dept. for the establishment of the soldier shows program. From 1941 to 1945 he was civilian consultant to the Army and Navy Committee of Welfare and Recreation.

Recreation. Reading, bridge, cooking.

LEBOWSKY, STANLEY. Conductor, composer, arranger, pianist. b. Stanley Richard Lebowsky, Nov. 26, 1926, Minneapolis, Minn., to Morris and Katy (Sorkin) Lebowsky. Father, merchant. Grad. Los Angeles (Calif.) H.S., 1944; Univ. of Calif. at Los Angeles, B.A. 1949. Studied at MacPhail Coll. of Music, Minneapolis, 1939; piano with Mrs. R. Weber, Minneapolis, 1931–38; Mrs. A. Dillingham, Minneapolis, 1940–41; Ronald Buck, Los Angeles, 1942–44; voice with Seymour Osborne, N.Y.C., 1959; composition and harmony with Russ Carcia, Los Angeles, 1951–53; Asher Zlotnik, N.Y.C., 1958–59; conducting with Leon Barzan, N.Y.C., 1958. Married Mar. 8, 1959, to Barbara Warden, actress, dancer, choreographer; one daughter. Served US Army Medical Corps, Special Services, PTO, 1945–46; rank, T/5. Member of AGAC; Dramatists Guild; AFM, local 802 and 47; BMI; Phi Mu Epsilon.

Theatre. Mr. Lebowsky was musical director of *I Love Lydia* (Players' Ring Th., Los Angeles, Calif., Dec. 1950); subsequently was assistant musical director, and musical director of the touring company of *Guys and Dolls* (opened Curran, San Francisco, Calif., June 4, 1951; closed Detroit, Mich., May 1954); pianist and assistant musical director of *Jollyanna* (Philharmonic Aud., Los Angeles, Calif.; Curran, San Francisco, Calif., Summer 1952); *Carousel* (Philharmonic Aud., Los Angeles; Curran, San Francisco, Summer 1953); and musical director and pianist for *Look Ma, I'm Dancin'* (Players' Ring Th., Los Angeles, Winter 1952–53).

He composed the original music for the revue *Ring Around the Ring* (Players' Ring 1953); served as pianist for the pre-Bway tour of *Silk Stockings* (Nov. 1954–Mar. 1955); musical director for the touring production of *Can-Can;* for the tour of *The Boy Friend* (opened Shubert, New Haven, Conn., Nov. 28, 1955; closed Shubert, Philadelphia, Pa., Jan. 5, 1957); for the *1958 Ford Show* (West Coast tour, 1957); for *The Boy Friend* and *Best of New Faces* (Coconut Grove Playhouse, Miami, Fla., Spring 1957); *1959 Buick Show* (nation-wide tour, 1958); musical director and vocal arranger of *Whoop-Up* (Shubert, N.Y.C., Dec. 22, 1958); musical director of the *1960 Buick Show* (nation-wide tour, 1959); and served as musical director at the Carousel Th. (Framingham, Mass., Summer 1960), for such shows as *Kiss Me, Kate, Show Boat, Damn Yankees!, Annie Get Your Gun,* and *Kismet.*

Mr. Lebowsky was musical director and vocal arranger for *Irma La Douce* (Plymouth, Sept. 29, N.Y.C., 1960); *A Family Affair* (Billy Rose Th., Jan. 27, 1961); composer for the Colgate-Palmolive (industrial) Show (US tour, Dec. 1962); *Mile-A-Minute Malone* (Los Angeles, 1962–63); musical director and vocal arranger for *Tovarich* (Bway., N.Y.C., Mar. 18, 1963); and musical director and vocal arranger for *Wonder World* at the 1964 NY World's Fair.

He was musical director for *Half a Sixpence* (Broadhurst, N.Y.C., Apr. 25, 1965); musical director and vocal arranger for *Holly Golightly* (opened Forrest Th., Philadelphia, Oct. 10, 1966) which closed during previews under the title *Breakfast at Tiffany's* (Majestic, N.Y.C., closed Dec. 14, 1966); wrote the music for *Gantry* (George Abbott Th., Feb. 14, 1970); was vocal arranger and musical director for *Ari* (Mark Hellinger Th., Jan 15, 1971); and conductor for *Jesus Christ Superstar* (Mark Hellinger Th., Oct. 12, 1971); and *Pippin* (Imperial, Oct. 23, 1972).

Television. He has been a pianist on the Bob McGlaughlin Show (KLAC, Los Angeles, 1949); composed the music for *Let There Be Stars* (ABC, 1949); and was musical director for Best of New Faces (WNTA, 1961).

Night Clubs. He was musical director and pianist for Mary McCarty at the Mocambo, (Los Angeles, 1953); for Helen Traubel at the Mapes Hotel (Reno, Nev., 1954); and at the Copacabana (N.Y.C., 1955); and contributed to the music, lyrics, and sketches for *Pick a Number XV* (Plaza Nine, N.Y.C., Oct. 1965).

Other Activities. By request of President Lyndon B. Johnson, Mr. Lebowsky conducted excerpts from *Guys and Dolls* at the White House (Washington, D.C., Mar. 19, 1967).

Discography. More than 35 of Mr. Lebowsky's popular songs have been recorded between 1950 and 1953.

Awards. Mr. Lebowsky received the Blue Ribbon Citation from BMI for his composition, *The Wayward Wind* (1956); and was nominated for the Antoinette Perry (Tony) Award as musical director of *Irma La Douce* (1961).

Recreation. Swimming, antique collecting.

LECKY, ELEAZER. Educator. b. Dec. 28, 1903, Mars, Pa., to Bennett and Annie (Aronson) Lecky. Father, realtor. Grad. Schenley H.S., Pittsburgh, Pa., 1920; Univ. of Pittsburgh, A.B. 1923, LL.B. 1927; Harvard Univ. M.A. 1924; Cornell Univ. Ph.D. 1938. Married Oct. 24, 1930 to Margaret Thompson, teacher of bookbinding. Member of AAUP; MLA; Natl. Council of Teachers of English; Coll. English Assn.; Amer. Studies Assn.; Philological Assn. of the Pacific Coast. Address: 7029 Senalda Road, Los Angeles, CA 90068.

From 1938–70, Mr. Lecky was professor of English at the Univ. of Southern California, teaching courses in modern drama and dramatic theory. He is now emeritus professor of English (1970–to date). Previously, he was an instructor in English at the Univ. of Pittsburgh (1925–29) and at Columbia Univ. (1931–36).

Published Works. Mr. Lecky has contributed articles on the theatre to periodicals including the *Arizona Quarterly,* the *Tulane Drama Review, Modern Drama,* and *Teachers College Record.*

Awards. He received the Order of the Coif (1927).

Recreation. Book collecting.

LEDERER, FRANCIS. Actor, director. b. Frantisek Lederer, Nov. 6, 1906, Karlin, Prague, Czechoslovakia, to Joseph and Rose (Ornstein) Lederer. Father, leather merchant; mother, stationer. Attended the Gymnasium, Prague; Handelsacademie, Prague; grad. Academie Fuer Musik und Darstellende Kunst, Prague. Studied with Elia Kazan at Actors' Studio, 1951. Served WW I, Czechoslavakian artillery; rank, Cpl. Married to Ada Nejedly, opera singer (marr. dis.); married 1937 to Marguerita Bolando, known as Margo, actress, dancer (marr. dis. 1940); married July 10, 1941 to Marion Irvine. Member of AEA; SAG (bd. mbr. 1935–39; AFTRA; ANTA (former bd. mbr., dir. of Academy of Performing Arts, Los Angeles); Directors Guild of America; Motion Picture Relief Fund; San Fernando Coll. Arts Council.

Pre-Theatre. Apprentice and salesman; shop window decorator in Prague store.

Theatre. While attending the Academie in Prague, Mr. Lederer was an apprentice student at the New German Th., making his debut as a walk-on in *The Burning Heart*and appearing in many roles in classic and modern plays (1919–22). He joined a repertory company that toured Moravia and Silesia (1922); and subsequently was actor, stage manager, property man, and prompter with a touring company (Budapest, Hungary, 1922). From 1923–25, he played at the German theatres in Brno, Olmutz, and Marienbad in Czechoslovakia; using the name Franz Lederer, he played numerous roles (Breslau, Germany, 1925–27); and in Berlin, Germany, he made many appearances, including Romeo to Elizabeth Bergner's Juliet in the Max Reinhardt production of *Romeo and Juliet,* Prince Henry in *Henry IV, Part I,* and *Wonder Bar* (1928–30).

Mr. Lederer made his London debut as Fleuriot in *My Sister and I* (Streatham Hill, Feb. 9, 1931); subsequently played Andreas Steiner in *Autumn Crocus* (Lyric, Apr. 6, 1931); Mosca in *Volpone* (Garrick, Jan. 1932); and Victor Florescu in *The Cat and the Fiddle* (Palace, Mar. 4, 1932). He made his N.Y.C. debut repeating the role of Andreas Steiner in *Autumn Crocus* (Morosco, Nov. 19, 1932); and played the role again (El Capitan, Los Angeles, Calif., Jan. 1934; Curran, San Francisco, Calif., 1934); appeared as Joe Bonaparte in *Golden Boy* (Curran, Sept. 1937); played Chico in *Seventh Heaven* (Civic, Chicago, Ill., July 2, 1939); and succeeded (July 1939) Laurence Oliver in the role of Gaylord Esterbrook in *No Time for Comedy* (Ethel Barrymore Th., N.Y.C., Apr. 17, 1939).

He toured as Max Christman in *The Pursuit of Happiness* (1941); toured in *The Play's the Thing* (1942); and appeared at the Wilmington (Del.) Playhouse as General Bonaparte in *The Man of Destiny,* Kenneth Dovey in *The Old Lady Shows Her Medals,* and the Old Master in *Playgoers* (Nov. 1942); toured in *A Doll's House* (Oct. 1944); played Lafont in *Parisienne* (Fulton, N.Y.C., July 24, 1950); toured summer theatres in *The Silver Whistle* (1950); and played Captain Bluntschli in *Arms and the Man* (Arena Th., Edison Hotel, N.Y.C., Oct. 19, 1950). He appeared as Adrian Van Dyck in *Collector's Item* (Palace, Manchester, England, Apr. 1951); appeared in *Relative Values,* and *Nina* (Berlin, Germany); succeeded (Feb. 1955) Anton Walbrook in the role of Jacques Devallee in *Wedding in Paris* (Hippodrome, London, Apr. 3, 1954); toured as the Prince Regent in *The Sleeping Prince* (opened Huntington Hartford Th., Hollywood, Calif., Nov. 22, 1956); toured as Jacques Balard in *The Dazzling Hour* (1957); toured as Mr. Frank in *The Diary of Anne Frank* (1958); appeared as Paul Delville in *The Marriage-Go-Round,* and played in *The Pleasure of His Company, Three Curtains,* and *Watch on the Rhine.*

In 1973, Mr. Lederer founded The American National Academy of Performing Arts and in 1975 The American International Academy of Performing Arts, Washington, D.C., for promotion of his acting and coaching technique.

Films. Mr. Lederer appeared in *Refuge* (Ufa Studios, 1929); *Pandora's Box* (Moviegraphs, 1929); *Wonderful Lies of Nina Petrova* (UFA, 1930); *Man of Two Worlds* (RKO, 1934); *The Pursuit of Happiness* (Par., 1934); *Romance in Manhattan* (RKO, 1934); *The Gay Deception* (Col., 1935); *One Rainy Afternoon* (UA, 1936); *My American Wife* (Par., 1936); *It's All Yours* (Col., 1938); *Confessions of a Nazi Spy* (WB, 1939); *The Man I Married* (20th-Fox, 1940); *Voice of the Wind* (UA, 1944); *The Madonna's Secret* (Rep., 1946); *The Diary of a Chambermaid* (UA, 1946); *Million Dollar Weekend* Eagle-Lion, 1948); *Captain Carey, U.S.A.* (Par., 1950); *Stolen Identity* (Assoc. Independent Prod., 1953); *The Ambassador's Daughter* (UA, 1956); *Lisbon* (Rep., 1956); and *Maracaibo* (Par., 1958).

Television. Mr. Lederer was seen on *Turn the Key Deftly* (Breck Showcase, CBS, 1959).

Other Activities. Mr. Lederer is engaged in business and ranching. He is chairman of the advisory board of the Independent Bank of Canoga Park; a founding member of the Hollywood Museum; and has served on various committees to beautify Los Angeles and the surrounding area.

Awards. He is the recipient of many civic awards and is the Honorary Mayor of Canoga Park, Calif.

LEE, BRYARLY. Actress. b. Bryarly Elizabeth Lee, May 16, 1934, Westerly, R.I., to Howard M. and Winifred (Trask) Lee. Father, writer; mother, writer, public relations. Attended Thomas Sch., Rowayton, Conn.; grad. Fagin Sch. of Drama, N.Y.C., 1952. Studied acting with Peter Kass, N.Y.C., ten years; Actors' Studio (mbr. since 1957). Married June 1958 to Paul Clement Matthews, artist (marr. dis. 1963). Member of AEA; AFTRA.

Theatre. Miss Lee made her first stage appearance as Squeege in *The Goose That Laid the Golden Egg,* produced by herself in her backyard (1943).

As an apprentice in stock she was chosen to appear with Lillian Gish in *Miss Mabel* (July 1951); appeared with the Barter Th. (Abingdon, Va., June–Aug. 1952), and toured as Jessica in its production of *The Merchant of Venice* (Sept.–Dec. 1952); followed by a season with the Quarterdeck Th. (Atlantic City, N.J., Summer 1953). She played a Girl in the pre-Bway tryout of *Mardi Gras* (Jan. 1954); and subsequently toured in the title role of *Gigi* (1954). In stock, she appeared at the Windham (N.H.) Playhouse as Nellie in *Summer and Smoke* and Sherri in *Dead Pigeon* (Summer (1954); followed by a season as resident ingenue with the Robinhood Th. (Arden, Del., Summer 1955).

Miss Lee made her N.Y.C. debut as Martha in *Spring's Awakening* (Provincetown Playhouse, Oct. 9, 1955); followed by a season as resident ingenue at the Cincinnati (Ohio) Playhouse, appearing in *Blithe Spirit, Time of the Cuckoo, The Young and the Beautiful,* and *Anastasia* (Summer 1956). She played Nina in *The Seagull* (Fourth St. Th., N.Y.C., Oct. 22, 1956); Athena in the pre-Bway tryout of *Maiden Voyage* (opened McCarter Th., Princeton, N.J., Nov. 8, 1956; closed Locust St. Th., Philadelphia, Pa., Nov. 24, 1956); and Juliet in the NY Shakespeare Festival's *Romeo and Juliet* (Delacorte, June 1957). She was featured in a tryout production of *A Time To Be Rich* (John Drew Th., East Hampton, L.I., N.Y., Aug. 1957); and subsequently appeared in the ANTA Matinee Series productions as Rachel in *Christmas Oratorio,* and as the Young Mother in *Santa Claus* (Th. de Lys., N.Y.C., Dec. 1957).

She played Dilys in *A Power of Dreams* (Sullivan St. Playhouse, Feb. 1958); Ophelia in the ELT production of *Hamlet* (Lenox Hill Playhouse, 1960); Daisy in *The Summer of Daisy Miller* (Phoenix, May 27, 1963); followed by a tour as Viola in the NY Shakespeare Festival production of *Twelfth Night* (Oct.–Dec. 1963).

Miss Lee played Honey with both the evening and matinee companies in a touring production of *Who's Afraid of Virginia Woolf?* (opened Westport, Conn., Country Playhouse, Aug. 17, 1964), repeating the role in subsequent stock company tours (Summers 1965, 1966); played Jezebel in *The Recluse* on a double-bill with *So, Who's Afraid of Edward Albee?* (Village South, N.Y.C., June 1, 1964); Roxie in *The Silent Partner* (Actors Studio, May 11, 1972); Grandmother Kroner in *Siamese Connection* (Actors Studio, June 8, 1972); and Siamese Twin in *Soft Shoulders* (New Dramatists, Apr. 9, 1974).

Television. Miss Lee has performed in *Something Ventured* (Studio One Summer Th., CBS, 1956); appeared on the Goodyear Playhouse (NBC); Look Up and Live (CBS), 1957); played in scenes from *Romeo and Juliet* (Camera Three, CBS, 1957); Ismeme in *Antigone,* an educational televison film produced by ANTA (1958); Alison in *The Lady's Not for Burning* (Omnibus, NBC, 1958); appeared on From These Roots (CBS, 1958); and played Jezebel in *The Recluse,* one of three plays presented as *La Mama Playwrights* (NET Playhouse, 1967).

Recreation. Movie-going, kafee-klatching, learning to play the guitar, Robert Frost, and a small black scottie called Charlie.

LEE, EUGENE. Scenic and lighting designer. Married to Franne (Newman) Lee, costume designer.

Theatre. Mr. Lee designed the sets for *A Dream of Love* (Sept. 13, 1966), and costumes for *Beclch* (Dec. 20, 1966) for the Th. of the Living Arts (Philadelphia). For the Buffalo (N.Y.) Studio Arena, he designed the sets and lights for *The Threepenny Opera* (Sept. 28, 1967); *The Imaginary Invalid* (Nov. 2, 1967); *H.M.S. Pinafore* (Dec. 7, 1967); and *Enrico IV* (Jan. 11, 1967); and the lights for *A Delicate Balance* (Feb. 8, 1968). Subsequently, for the Trinity Square Repertory Co. (Providence, R.I.), he designed the sets for *The Threepenny Opera* (Oct. 5, 1967); *The Importance of Being Earnest* (Dec. 28, 1967); *Years of the Locust* (Feb. 8, 1968); *An Enemy of the People* (Mar. 21, 1968); *Phaedra* (Apr. 25, 1968); *Macbeth* (Jan. 2, 1969); *The Homecoming* (Feb. 13, 1969); *Billy Budd* (world premiere, Mar. 3, 1969); *Exiles* (Apr. 24, 1969); *The Old Glory* (Sept. 30, 1969); *House of Breathe, Black/White* (world premiere, Nov. 4, 1969); *Wilson in The Promise Land* (world premiere, Dec. 9, 1969; and Anta, N.Y.C., May 26, 1970); *The Skin of Our Teeth* (Jan. 20, 1970); and *Lovecraft's Follies* (world premiere, Mar. 10, 1970).

Mr. Lee designed the sets for *World War 2½* (Martinique, N.Y.C., Mar. 24, 1969); designed the production for *Slave Ship* (Brooklyn Acad. of Music, Nov. 18, 1969; and Th.-in-the-Church, Jan. 13, 1970); for the Th. of the Living Arts (Philadelphia), designed the sets for *The Recruiting Officer* (Oct. 31, 1969); *Harry Noon and Night* (Nov. 28, 1969); and *A Line of Least Existence* (Jan. 24, 1970). With Franne Newman, he co-designed *Alice in Wonderland* (The Extension, N.Y.C., Oct. 8, 1970); *Saved* (Brooklyn Acad. of Music, Oct. 28, 1970; and Cherry Lane Th., N.Y.C., Nov. 13, 1970); and *Mother Courage* (Arena Stage, Washington, D.C., Dec. 4, 1970).

For the Trinity Sq. Playhouse (Providence, R.I.), Mr. Lee designed the sets and lights for *You Can't Take It with You* (Oct. 14, 1970); and *The Good and Bad Times of Cady Francis McCullum and Friends* (world premiere, Feb. 17, 1971); sets for *Troilus and Cressida* (Nov. 1, 1971); sets for *Down By the River Where Water Lilies Are Disfigured Every Day* (world premiere, Dec. 20, 1971); and, for that company at the Rhode Island Sch. of Design Th., designed the sets for *Son of Man and The Family* (world premiere, Nov. 18, 1970); sets and lights for *The Taming of the Shrew* (Dec. 30, 1970); lights for *Love for Love* (Feb. 10, 1971); and sets and lights for *The Threepenny Opera* (Mar. 24, 1971).

With Franne Lee and Roger Morgan, he designed the production of *Dude* (Broadway Th., N.Y.C., Oct. 9, 1972); returned to the Trinity Sq. Playhouse (Providence, R.I.) where he designed the sets for *Old Times* (Sept. 24, 1972); *The Royal Hunt of the*

Sun (Jan. 10, 1973); and *Feasting with Panthers* (world premiere, Apr. 18, 1973); with Franne Lee, designed the Chelsea Th. Ctr. production of *Candide* (Brooklyn Acad. of Music, Dec. 11, 1973; Broadway Th., N.Y.C., Mar. 10, 1974); again with the Trinity Sq. Repertory Co., designed sets for *Brother To Dragons* (Oct. 24, 1973); *Ghost Dance* (world premiere, Nov. 1, 1973); scenery and environment for *Aimee* (world premiere, Dec. 6, 1973); and *A Man for All Seasons* (Feb. 21, 1974); sets for *Well Hung* (Amer. premiere, Oct. 31, 1974); and sets and lights for *Peer Gynt* (Jan. 7, 1975); *Tom Jones* (Mar. 4, 1975); and *Seven Keys to Baldpate* (Apr. 22, 1975).

In addition, he designed the sets for *Gabrielle* (Studio Arena, Washington, D.C., Dec. 9, 1974); and *The Skin of Our Teeth* (Kennedy Ctr., July 1975; Mark Hellinger, N.Y.C., Sept. 9, 1975).

Awards. With his wife, Franne Lee, he won the Drama Desk's "most promising scene designers" citation (1970–71) for *Alice in Wonderland*. For their designs for *Candide*, they received the Joseph Maharam Foundation, Antoinette Perry (Tony), and Drama Desk awards (1973–74).

LEE, FRANNE. Costume designer. b. Franne Newman. Married to Eugene Lee, set and lighting designer.

Theatre. Billed as Franne Newman, she designed the costumes for the Th. of the Living Arts (Philadelphia) productions of *Harry Noon and Night* (Nov. 28, 1969), and *A Line of Least Existence* (Jan. 24, 1970). With Eugene Lee, she co-designed *Alice in Wonderland* (The Extension, N.Y.C., Oct. 8, 1970); *Saved* (Cherry Lane Th., Nov. 13, 1970); and *Mother Courage* (Arena Stage, Washington, D.C., Dec. 4, 1970). Billed as Franne Lee, she designed the costumes for *The Good and Bad Times of Cady Francis McCullum and Friends* (world premiere, Trinity Square Th., Providence, R.I., Feb. 17, 1971); with Eugene Lee and Roger Morgan, co-designed *Dude* (Broadway Th., N.Y.C., Oct. 9, 1972); designed the costumes for *The Tooth of Crime* (Performing Garage, Mar. 7, 1973); with Eugene Lee, designed the Chelsea Th. Ctr. production of *Candide* (Brooklyn Acad. of Music, Dec. 11, 1973; moved to Broadway Th., Mar. 10, 1974); designed the costumes for *Love for Love* (Helen Hayes Th., Nov. 11, 1974); *Gabrielle* (world premiere, Studio Arena, Buffalo, N.Y.C., Dec. 9, 1974); and *The Skin of Our Teeth* (Kennedy Ctr., Washington, D.C., July 1975; and Mark Hellinger Th., N.Y.C., Sept. 9, 1975).

Awards. With Eugene Lee, she was co-winner of the Drama Desk Award (1970–71) for most promising new designer. For *Candide* (1973–74) she won *Best Play's* Citation and the Joseph Maharam Foundation, Antoinette Perry (Tony), and Drama Desk awards for costume design; and, with her husband, was co-winner of the Joseph Maharam, Antoinette Perry (Tony) and Drama Desk awards for set design.

LEE, JAMES. Playwright. b. James Henderson Lee III, Jan. 4, 1923, Detroit, Mich., to James Henderson, Jr., and Analdine (McCabe) Lee. Father, lawyer. Grad. Central H.S., Detroit, Mich., 1940; attended Colgate Univ., 1940–41; Harvard Coll., 1941–42; Univ. of Michigan, 1942–43. Married Sept. 13, 1957, to Neva Patterson, actress; one son, one daughter. Member WGA, East (council, 1959–63).

Theatre. Mr. Lee wrote *Career* (Seventh Ave. South Th., N.Y.C., Apr. 30, 1957).

Films. He wrote the screen adaptation of his play, *Career* (Par., 1959); the screenplay for *The Adventures of Huckleberry Finn* (MGM, 1960); and the screenplay for *Banning* (U, 1967).

Television. Mr. Lee wrote *Life of Samuel Johnson* (Omnibus, NBC, 1957); *Capital Punishment* (Omnibus, NBC, 1958); numerous plays for The Defenders series (CBS, 1961–65); *The Invincible Mr. Disraeli* (Hallmark Hall of Fame, NBC, 1963); *The Holy Terror* (Hallmark Hall of Fame, NBC, 1964); and an adaptation of *The Diary of Anne Frank* (England, 1967).

Awards. Mr. Lee won a Sylvania Award (1957), and a nomination for a NATAS (Emmy) Award (1957) for *Life of Samuel Johnson;* Mystery Writers Guild of America Award (1958) for *Capital Punishment;* and a NATAS (Emmy) nomination for *The Invincible Mr. Disraeli* (1963).

LEE, MICHELE. Actress, singer, dancer. b. Michele Lee Dusick, June 24, 1942, Los Angeles, Calif., to Jack and Sylvia Dusick. Father, make-up artist. Grad. Alexander Hamilton H.S., Los Angeles, Calif., 1960. Studied drama with Jeff Corey, Los Angeles; Frank Corsaro, N.Y.C.; voice with Paul Thompson, Los Angeles; Carmine Gagliardi, N.Y.C. Married Feb. 24, 1966, to James Farentino, actor; one son. Member of AEA; AFTRA; SAG; AGVA.

Theatre. Miss Lee made her first stage appearance in *Mike and Michele Variety Show* (Alexander Hamilton H.S., 1960); subsequently made her professional debut in *Vintage '60* (Ivar Th., Hollywood, Calif., Apr. 1960; Brooks Atkinson Th., N.Y.C., Sept. 12, 1960); subsequently appeared in *Parade Review* (Hollywood Circle, Calif., July 18, 1961); and appeared in the revue *Point of View* (Vine St. Th., Oct. 17, 1961). She succeeded Lois Leary as Rosemary in *How To Succeed in Business without Really Trying* (46 St. Th., N.Y.C., Oct. 14, 1961); played Miranda in *Bravo Giovanni* (Broadhurst, May 19, 1962); and Gittel Mosca in *Seesaw* (Uris, Mar. 18, 1973).

Films. Miss Lee repeated her role in *How To Succeed in Business without Really Trying* (UA, 1967); subsequently appeared in *The Love Bug* (BV, 1969), and *The Comic* (Col., 1969).

Television. Miss Lee has appeared on Dobie Gillis (CBS, 1961); Doctor Kildare (NBC); the Larry Findley Show (Los Angeles); the Jack Paar Show (NBC); American Musical Th. (CBS); Stump the Stars; the Today Show; the Jerry Lester Show (CBC); the Ed Sullivan Show (CBS); the Jerry Lewis Show; ABC Romp; Kraft Music Hall; *Roberta* (NBC); *Norman Rockwell's America* (NBC); the Glen Campbell Show; the Tom Jones Show; *USA* (PBS); *Of Thee I Sing;* and the Michele Lee Show (pilot, CBS, 1974).

Night Clubs. She has performed at Dino's (Hollywood, Calif., 1961); appeared in *Ben Blue's Revue* (Ben Blue's, Santa Monica, Calif., 1961); Harrah's Club (Lake Tahoe, Nev., 1961); The Persian Room (The Plaza, N.Y.C.); and The Miami Hilton Hotel.

Awards. Miss Lee is the recipient of *Screen World's* Most Promising Personality Award (1967); and, for her performance in *Seesaw*, the Outer Circle and Drama Desk awards (1972–73).

Recreation. Painting, sculpture, piano, writing, riding, swimming.

LEE, MING CHO. Scenic designer, lighting designer. b. Oct. 3, 1930, Shanghai, China, to Tsufa F. and Ing Tong (Yung) Lee. Father, insurance representative. Attended high schools in Shanghai and Hong Kong; grad. Occidental Coll. (Los Angeles) B.A. 1953; attended UCLA, 1953–54. Studied with Chinese water-colorist, Kuo-Nyen Chang, two years; apprentice and asst. designer to Jo Mielziner, five years. Married Mar. 21, 1958 to Elizabeth Rapport; three sons. Member of Th. Projects Comm. of the N.Y.C. Planning Commission; Amer. Th. Planning Bd.; Calif. Water Color Soc.; United Scenic Artists (Local 829, vice-pres., 1969–71). Address: 12 E. 87th St., New York, NY 10028, tel. (212) AT 9-0316.

Theatre. Mr. Lee's first scenic designs were for the production of *The Silver Whistle* (Occidental Coll., Los Angeles, Calif., Dec. 1951); his first professional designs were for *Guys and Dolls* (Grist Mill Playhouse, Andover, N.J., July 1955); subsequently was setting and lighting designer for *The Infernal Machine* (Phoenix, N.Y.C., Feb. 3, 1958); for the Metropolitan Opera Co., supervised the costumes for *Madame Butterfly* (Feb. 1958); designed the dance production of *Missa Brevis* (Juilliard Sch. of Music, Mar. 1958); designed setting and lighting for *The Crucible* (Martinique, Mar. 11, 1958); *Triad* (Th. Marquee, Nov. 1958); designed two short dances for the New London (Conn.) Dance Festival (Connecticut Coll., July 1959); and for the Metropolitan Opera Co., was assistant setting and lighting designer for *Il Trovatore* (Oct. 1959), and for *The Marriage of Figaro* (Nov. 1959).

For the Peabody Art Th. (Baltimore, Md.), he designed the sets and lighting for *The Turk in Italy* (Nov. 1959), *The Old Maid and the Thief* (Mar. 1960), *The Fall of the City* (Mar. 1960), and *La Bohème* (May 1960). For the Empire State Music Festival (N.Y., July 1960), he designed the setting and lighting for *Katya Kabanova*, and *Peter Ibbetson;* and for the Peabody Arts Th. designed *Amahl and the Night Visitors* (Feb. 1961), and three one-act operas by Offenbach (May 1961).

He was art director and designer in residence for the 1961 season of the San Francisco (Calif.) Opera Co.; designed the lighting for *Don Giovanni* (Peabody Arts Th., Baltimore, Md., Nov. 1961); the setting and lighting for *Tristan und Isolde* (Lyric Th., Baltimore, Md., Mar. 1962); for the Peabody Arts Th. (Baltimore, Md.), he designed the setting and lighting for *Werther* (Apr. 1962), *Hamlet* (Nov. 1962), and for a production of *Madame Butterfly*, which toured the Boston (Mass.) area schools (1962).

He designed the setting and lighting for *The Moon Besieged* (Lyceum, N.Y.C., Dec. 5, 1962); the sets for *Mother Courage* (Martin Beck Th., Mar. 28, 1963); sets and lighting for *Walk in Darkness* (Greenwich Mews Th., Oct. 28, 1963); sets and lighting for the pre-Bway tryout of *Conversations in the Dark* (opened Walnut St. Th., Philadelphia, Pa., Dec. 23, 1963; closed there Jan. 4, 1964).

He designed the scenery for *Slapstick Tragedy* (Longacre, N.Y.C., Feb. 22, 1966); *A Time for Singing* (Broadway Th., May 21, 1966); *Little Murders* (Broadhurst, Apr. 25, 1967); *Here's Where I Belong* (Billy Rose Th., Mar. 3, 1968); *King Lear* (Lincoln Center Rep. Co., Vivian Beaumont Th., Nov. 7, 1968); *Billy* (Billy Rose Th., Mar. 22, 1969); *La Strada* (Lunt-Fontanne, Dec. 14, 1969); *Gandhi* (Playhouse, Oct. 20, 1970); *Remote Asylum* (Ahmanson, Los Angeles, Dec. 1, 1970); the pre-Bway tryout of *Lolita* (opened Shubert, Philadelphia, Feb. 16, 1971; closed there Feb. 27, 1971; re-opened Shubert, Boston, Mar. 23, 1971; closed there Mar. 27, 1971); *Henry IV, Part I* (Mark Taper Forum, Los Angeles, 1972–73 season); and *All God's Chillun Got Wings* (Circle in the Square/Joseph E. Levine Th., Mar. 20, 1975).

Since 1962, Mr. Lee has designed prolifically for the NY Shakespeare Fest. at the Delacorte Th. in Central Park (N.Y.C.), including scenery and lighting for *The Merchant of Venice* (June 13, 1962); *The Tempest* (July 16, 1962); *King Lear* (Aug. 13, 1962); *Macbeth* (Heckscher Th., Nov. 15, 1962); *Antony and Cleopatra* (Delacorte, June 13, 1963); *As You Like It* (July 11, 1963); scenery for *The Winter's Tale* (Aug. 8, 1963); scenery and lighting for *Twelfth Night* (Heckscher Th., Sept. 1963); designed the Festival's Mobile Th. and, with Martin Aronstein, designed its control truck (1964); designed the scenery and lighting for *Hamlet* (Delacorte, June 16, 1964; Playhouse-in-the-Park, Philadelphia, Pa., July 13, 1964); scenery for *Othello* (Delacorte, July 14, 1964), subsequently moved to the Martinique Th., Oct. 12, 1964); scenery for *Electra* (Delacorte, Aug. 11, 1964); supervised design of scenery and costumes, and designed the lighting for the Mobile Th. tour of *The Puppet Theatre of Don Cristobal*, and *The Shoemaker's Prodigious Wife* (premiere Central Park Mall, Sept. 1, 1964); designed scenery and lighting for the Board of Education tour of *A Midsummer Night's Dream* (opened Heckscher, Oct. 5, 1964; closed Aviation Vocational H.S., Dec. 18, 1964).

Also, he designed the scenery for *Love's Labour's Lost* (Delacorte, June 9, 1965), *Coriolanus* (July 7, 1965), and *Troilus and Cressida* (Aug. 4, 1965); scenery for the Mobile Th. productions of *Henry V* (opened June 26, 1965; closed Aug. 22, 1965) and *The Taming of the Shrew* (opened June 27, 1965; closed Aug. 22, 1965); supervised design of the scenery and lighting for a Spanish language tour, by the Mobile Th., of *Romeo and Juliet* (opened Aug. 25, 1965); designed the scenery for *All's Well That Ends Well* (Delacorte, June 15, 1966); *Measure for*

Measure (July 12, 1966); *Richard III* (Aug. 9, 1966); *The Comedy of Errors* (June 7, 1967); *Titus Andronicus* (Aug. 2, 1967); *Henry IV, Part 1* (June 11, 1968); *Henry IV, Part 2* (June 18, 1968); *Romeo and Juliet* (Aug. 8, 1968); *Peer Gynt* (July 15, 1969); *Electra* (Mobile Th., Aug. 5, 1969); *Henry VI, Part 1* (Delacorte, June 23, 1970); *Henry VI, Part 2* (June 24, 1970); *Richard III* (June 25, 1970); *Sambo* (Mobile Th., July 14, 1970); *Timon of Athens* (Delacorte, June 30, 1971); *Two Gentlemen of Verona* (Delacorte, July 27, 1971; subsequently re-staged at the St. James, Dec. 1, 1971; and toured, opening at the O'Keefe, Toronto, Canada, Jan. 20, 1973); *Cymbeline* (Delacorte, Aug. 17, 1971); *Hamlet* (June 20, 1972); *Much Ado About Nothing* (Aug. 16, 1972; re-staged at the Winter Garden, Nov. 11, 1972); and re-designed *Two Gentlemen of Verona* for the Mobile Th. (July 31, 1973).

For the NY Shakespeare Festival's Public Th., Mr. Lee has designed *Hair* (Anspacher, Oct. 17, 1967); *Ergo* (Anspacher, Mar. 3, 1968); *Cities in Bezique* (Public, Jan. 4, 1969); *Invitation to a Beheading* (Public, Mar. 8, 1969); *Sambo* (Public, Dec. 21, 1969); *Jack MacGowran in the Works of Samuel Beckett* (Newman, Nov. 19, 1970); *Older People* (Anspacher, May 14, 1972); and *Wedding Band* (Newman, Oct. 26, 1972).

He was (1964–70) the principal designer for the Juilliard Opera Th. and Amer. Opera Ctr. of Juilliard Sch. of Music, designing *Katya Kabanova, Il Tabarro,* and *Gianni Schicchi* (1964); *Fidelio, The Magic Flute* (1965); *The Trial of Lucullus* (1966); *The Rape of Lucrezia* (1967); *The Barber of Seville,* and *L'Ormindo* (1968); and *The Rake's Progress* and *Il Giuramento* (1970).

For the Arena Stage (Washington, D.C.) he has designed sets for productions of *The Crucible* (Jan. 17, 1967); *The Tenth Man* (1967–68 season); *Room Service* (1967–68 season); *The Iceman Cometh* (Mar. 26, 1968); *The Night Thoreau Spent in Jail* (Oct. 23, 1970); and *Julius Caesar* (Feb. 21, 1975).

For the NY City Opera Co. at the NY State Th., he has designed sets for *Don Rodrigo* (Feb. 22, 1966); *Julius Caesar* (Sept. 27, 1966); *Le Coq d'Or* (1967); *Bomarzo* (1968); *Faust* (1968); *Roberto Devereux* (1970); *Tales of Hoffman; Idomeneo* (Mar. 17, 1975).

He has designed sets for *Madame Butterfly* (1965) and *The Marriage of Figaro* (1966), for the Metropolitan Opera National Co., and in 1974 designed *Boris Godunov* for the Metropolitan Opera at Lincoln Center; he has also designed sets for the Assoc. Opera Companies of America production of *Boris Godunov* (1967); sets for the world premiere of *Bomarzo* (Opera Society of Washington, D.C., Lisner Aud., May 19, 1967); *Julius Caesar* (1969) and *Lucia di Lammermoor* (1971) for the Staatsoper, Hamburg, Germany; and *Idomeneo* (Opera Society of Washington, D.C., Opera House, Kennedy Center, May 1974).

Mr. Lee has designed scenery for many ballets, notably for the Martha Graham Co. (*Three Short Dances,* 1959; *A Look at Lightning,* 1962; and *The Witch of Endor,* 1965); for the City Ctr. Joffrey Ballet (*Sea Shadow,* 1963; *Olympics,* world premiere Mar. 31, 1966, NY City Ctr.; *Night Wings,* 1966; *Elegy,* 1967; *Secret Places,* 1968; *Light Fantastic,* 1968; *Animus,* 1969; and *The Poppet,* 1969); for the Rebekah Harkness Ballet (*Ariadne,* 1965); for the Alvin Ailey Co. (*The Lady of the House of Sleep,* 1968); for the Natl. Ballet of Canada (*Whisper of Darkness,* 1974); and for the Royal Winnipeg Ballet (*Inquest of the Sun,* Jan. 1975).

Other Activities. Mr. Lee is on the faculty of the Yale Univ. School of Drama, and is the design advisor to the Yale Rep. Th. (1969 to date). He has also taught set design at the Washington Sq. Coll. of NYU.

For the NY Shakespeare Fest., he designed the Anspacher Th. and the Newman Th. (at the Public Th., 425 Lafayette St., N.Y.C.); designed the Garage Th., for the Harlem Sch. of the Arts; and was a consultant for the Performing Arts Ctr. of SUNY (Purchase, N.Y.), and the accoustical shell and proscenium arch of the Music Hall (Cincinnati, Ohio).

An exhibit of his work was shown at the Library and Museum for the Performing Arts (Lincoln Ctr., N.Y.C., Aug. 12, 1969), as well as in Los Angeles and other cities.

Awards. He received the Maharam Award (1965) for his designs for *Electra.*

Recreation. Painting.

LEE, ROBERT E. Playwright, director, producer, lecturer. b. Robert Edwin Lee, Oct. 15, 1918, Elyria, Ohio, to Claire Melvin and Elvira (Taft) Lee. Father, engineer; mother, teacher. Grad. Elyria (Ohio) H.S., 1935; attended Northwestern Univ., 1934; Ohio Wesleyan Univ., 1935–37; Drake Univ., 1943–44. Married Mar. 29, 1948, to Janet Waldo, actress; one son, one daughter. Appointed Expert Consultant to Secretary of War, 1942; served WW II, USAF, 1943–44; co-founder of Armed Forces Radio Service. Mr. Lee is a co-founder and trustee of Amer. Playwrights Th. (pres.) and Margo Jones Award, Inc. He is a member of Dramatists Guild; WGA West; AMPAS; NATAS; The Players; Theta Alpha Phi; Broadcasting and Film Commission, National Council of Churches (1962–to date); Alumni Assn., Ohio Wesleyan Univ. (pres., 1963–64). Address: (home) 15725 Royal Oak Rd., Encino, CA 91316; (bus.) MacGowan Hall, Univ. of California, Los Angeles, CA 90024, tel. (213) ST 4-6972.

Pre-Theatre. Mr. Lee was an executive with Young & Rubicam (1938–42) in N.Y.C. and Los Angeles.

Theatre. Mr. Lee wrote, with Jerome Lawrence, the book for *Look, Ma, I'm Dancin'* (Adelphi Th., Jan. 29, 1948), and the play *Inherit the Wind* (Natl., Apr. 21, 1955); wrote, with Mr. Lawrence and James Hilton, the book and lyrics for *Shangri-La* (Winter Garden, June 13, 1956); and, with Mr. Lawrence, *Auntie Mame* (Broadhurst, Oct. 31, 1956), *The Gang's All Here* (Ambassador, Oct. 1, 1959), *Only in America* (Cort, Nov. 19, 1959), *A Call on Kuprin* (Broadhurst, May 25, 1961); *Diamond Orchid* (Henry Miller's Th., Feb. 10, 1965), revised and restaged as *Sparks Fly Upward* (McFarlin Aud., Southern Methodist Univ., Dallas, Tex., Dec. 3, 1967); *Mame* (Winter Garden, N.Y.C., May 4, 1966); *Dear World* (Mark Hellinger Th., Feb. 6, 1969); *The Laugh Maker* (Players Ring, Hollywood, Cal., Aug. 1952), rewritten and restaged as *Turn on the Night* (Playhouse in the Park, Philadelphia, Aug. 1961), rewritten and restaged as *The Crocodile Smile* (State Th. of No. Carolina, Aug. 1970); *The Night Thoreau Spent In Jail* (premier perf. as Centennial Play, Ohio State Univ., Columbus, Ohio, Apr. 21, 1971; 150 productions through American Playwrights Th.; *The Incomparable Max* (Barter Th., State Th. of Virginia, Abingdon, June 24, 1969; Royale, N.Y.C., Oct. 19, 1971); *Jabberwock* (premier play in Thurber Th., Ohio State Univ., Columbus, Ohio, Nov. 18, 1972). By himself, Mr. Lee wrote *Ten Days That Shook The World* and directed its production in commemoration of the twenty-fifth anniversary of the Theatre Dept., Univ. of California at Los Angeles (MacGowan Hall, UCLA, May–June 1973).

Films. Mr. Lee was a director with the March of Time. Screen adaptations were made of *Auntie Mame* (WB, 1958), *Inherit the Wind* (UA, 1960), and *Mame* (WB, 1974).

Television and Radio. Mr. Lee wrote the radio series Empire Builders (1938), Flashbacks (1940–41), and Opened by Mistake (1940). He wrote also for such programs as Ceiling Unlimited (1942), Meet Corliss Archer (1942), Suspense (CBS, 1943), and The Saint (1945). He was a director of Screen Guild Theatre, The Aldrich Family, and the Jack Benny Show. He collaborated on many more radio and television programs with Jerome Lawrence, whose entry in this volume contains a detailed listing.

Other Activities. Mr. Lee was professor of playwriting, College of Theatre Arts of the Pasadena (Cal.) Playhouse (Feb.–June 1963) and lecturer in graduate playwriting, Univ. of California at Los Angeles (1966–74). He was keynote speaker at the 1972 national convention of ATA and has been guest lecturer at many colleges and universities throughout the world, including Univ. of Alberta (Banff School of Fine Arts); Gorky Institute (Moscow, USSR); East Washington State Coll.; Univ. of Washington; Brigham Young Univ.; Occidental Coll.; Univ. of Nevada; Redlands Univ.; Univ. of Colorado; Univ. of Southern Calif.; Oregon State Univ.; Univ. of Oklahoma; Univ. of Minnesota; Southern Methodist Univ.; Louisiana State Univ.; Ohio State Univ.; Ohio Wesleyan Univ.; Tufts Univ.; Villanova Univ.; Mercy College (Detroit); Chabot College (San Francisco); William Woods College (Fulton, Mo.); Nebraska Wesleyan Univ.; Mt. Berry College (Rome, Ga.); Heights College (Ottumwa, Ia.); Kent State Univ.; Utah State Univ.; Fisk Univ.; Union Theological Seminary; and others.

The Lawrence and Lee Collection of Theatre Manuscripts and Transcriptions is a gift to the NY Public Library at the Lincoln Center Library of the Performing Arts.

Published Works. He is the author of *Television: the Revolutionary Industry* (1944) and, with Mr. Lawrence, articles that have been published in various periodicals.

Discography. With Jerome Lawrence, Mr. Lee dramatized and directed recordings of *Rip Van Winkle, The Cask of Amontillado,* and *A Tale of Two Cities* (all for Decca), and *One God* (Kapp).

Awards. He has received the Peabody Award for a UN radio series (1948); with Mr. Lawrence, the Donaldson Award, Outer Circle Award, and *Variety* NY Drama Critics Poll for *Inherit the Wind* (1955); and Critics Award for Best Foreign Play for *Inherit the Wind* (London, 1960). He has received an honorary D.Litt. from Ohio Wesleyan Univ. (1962), and a M.A. in theatre from the Pasadena (Calif.) Playhouse Coll. of Theatre Arts (1963).

LEE, SONDRA. Actress, dancer. b. Sondra Lee Gash, Sept. 30, 1930, Newark, N.J., to David and Belle Gash. Father, manufacturer. Grad. South Side H.S., Newark. Studied dance at Tarossova Ballet, 1946; Metropolitan Opera House, N.Y.C.; with Eddie Caton, N.Y.C.; Nanette Charisse, N.Y.C. Married 1953, to Sidney Armus, actor (marr. dis. 1959). Married 1968 to Harlan P. Kleiman, producer-founder of Long Wharf Th. (New Haven, Conn.). Member of AEA; AFTRA; SAG; AGMA; AGVA.

Theatre. Miss Lee made her debut as a dancer at Times Hall, N.Y.C. (1947); subsequently danced and appeared as His Playmate in *High Button Shoes* (Century Th., Oct. 9, 1947); appeared in *Bloomer Girl* (St. Louis Municipal Opera, Mo., Summer, 1954); played Tiger Lily in Mary Martin's *Peter Pan* (Winter Garden, N.Y.C., Oct. 20, 1954); Louise in *Carousel* (Dallas, Summer Musicals, Tex., 1955); Gisella in the pre-Bway tryout of *Reuben Reuben* (opened Shubert, Boston, Mass., Oct. 10, 1955); appeared in *Ballet de Paris* (Th. de Paris, France, 1956–57); as Victoire in *Hotel Paradiso* (Henry Miller's Th., N.Y.C., Apr. 11, 1957); Ellen in *Winkleberg* (Renata, Jan. 14, 1958); and danced in *Ballet: U.S.A.* (Alvin Th., N.Y.C., Sept. 4, 1958).

At the Festival of the Two Worlds, she danced in Herbert Ross' Amer. Ballet Co. (Spoleto, Italy, 1958); appeared in *Album Leaves* (June 26, 1959); danced with John Butler's group in Europe (1959); appeared as the Serpent in *Adam and Eve Ballet* (Metropolitan Opera House, N.Y.C., Mar. 22, 1959); for three seasons played May Jones in *Street Scene* (NY City Center, Apr. 2, 1959); and played Cassandra in *The Trojan Women* (1963).

She played six roles in *Sunday in New York* (Cort, Nov. 29, 1961); and Minnie Fay in *Hello, Dolly!* (St. James, Jan. 16, 1964).

Since 1966, Miss Lee has taught acting at the Stella Adler Conservatory. She has also taught at New York Univ. and at the Metropolitan Opera Studio Co.

Films. Miss Lee played Sandra in *La Dolce Vita* (Astor, 1961).

Television. She has appeared in many major shows

for NET and is best known for her role as Tiger Lily in *Peter Pan* (NET).

Night Clubs. She performed at the Twin Tree Inn (Dallas, Tex., 1962).

Other Activities. Most recently, she has been a professional painter.

Awards. Miss Lee won the Dancers You Should Know Award (*Dance* Magazine).

LEE, WILL. Actor, director, drama teacher. b. Aug. 6, 1908, Brooklyn, N.Y., to George and Kate (Taisoff) Lee. Father, bookbinder. Grad. St. Clair McKelway J.H.S. P.S. 178, Brooklyn, N.Y., 1923; was a scholarship member of Group Theatre Studio, 1934, 1937, 1940; and member of the Group Th. acting company, 1938–41. Served US Army, Signal Corps, Special Services, 1942–45, PTO; rank T/5. Member of AEA; AFTRA; SAG. Address: 327 Central Park West, New York, NY 10025, tel. (212) UN 5-0108.

Pre-Theatre. Errand boy, shipping clerk, stock clerk, shoe salesman, men's furnishings, salesman, and assistant dental lab technician.

Theatre. Mr. Lee was a cofounder of the Workers Laboratory Th., which later became the Th. of Action, a Social Mobile Th. (1929–35), directing and acting in improvised skits and sketches, some of which he wrote.

He made his N.Y.C. debut as Beebie Menucci in *The Young Go First* (Park Th., May 28, 1935); followed by Nicolai Norton in *The Crime* (Civic Rep. Th., Mar. 1, 1936); for the Federal Th. (WPA) Project, appeared in *Triple A—Ploughed Under* (Biltmore, Mar. 14, 1936); as Harpagon in *The Miser* (Daly's, May 13, 1936); and in *Injunction Granted* (Biltmore, July 24, 1936).

Mr. Lee played a Photographer and Private Goldberger in the Group Th. production of *Johnny Johnson* (St. James, Nov. 19, 1936); succeeded (Mar. 8, 1937) Garson Kanin as Green in *Boy Meets Girl* (Cort, Dec. 11, 1935); in stock, played Mr. McBride in *Busman's Honeymoon* (Westport Th., Conn., July 1937), the same role at the Westchester Playhouse (Mt. Kisco, N.Y., July 1937); succeeded (Apr. 4, 1938) John Garfield as Siggie in *Golden Boy* (Belasco, N.Y.C., Nov. 4, 1937); appeared as Henry in *Plant in the Sun* (Nora Bayes Th., Apr. 24, 1938), presented on Sunday and matinee nights; as Siggie in *Golden Boy* (St. James's, London, June 21, 1938), and on tour in the US (1938–39); as Mendel in *Family Portrait* (Morosco, N.Y.C., Mar. 8, 1939); Willie in *The Time of Your Life* (Booth, Oct. 25, 1939); the Waiter in *Night Music* (Broadhurst, Feb. 22, 1940); Shorty Rocker in *Heavenly Express* (Natl., Apr. 18, 1940); and Shmelka in the pre-Bway tryout of *The White Haired Boy* (Plymouth, Boston, Oct. 28, 1940).

Mr. Lee helped found the Actor's Lab. Th. in Hollywood, Calif. (1941), appeared in some of its productions and was on the executive board (1941–49).

He appeared as Joe in *Lily of the Valley* (Windsor, N.Y.C., Jan. 26, 1942); Louis Liebens in *The Springs, My Lord, Are False* (Royale, May 19, 1942); in *The Lunch Hour Follies*, titled *Fun to Be Free*, performing in shipyards (American Th. Wing, June 22, 1942); with the Army, was a director of the GI Th. (Th. Royal, Brisbane, Australia, 1943–45); produced shows in Leyte and Manila, P.I.; directed the V-J Day Victory Program (Rizal Mem. Stadium, Manila, P.I., Sept. 5, 1945).

Mr. Lee rejoined the Actors' Lab Th., Hollywood, Calif., as actor and teacher, appearing as James Madison in *Declaration* (Feb. 1948); Willie, the Hackie, in *All You Need Is One Good Break* (July 1948); and Androcles in *Androcles and the Lion* (July 1948).

He directed *A Streetcar Named Desire* (Circle Th., Atlantic City, N.J., Aug. 13, 1951); appeared as Sam Tager in *The Shrike* (Cort, N.Y.C., Jan. 15, 1952); performed in four parts, a Teacher, the Malamed, Father Abraham and Uncle Maxel, in *The World of Sholem Aleichem* (Barbizon-Plaza Th., May 1, 1953); Mr. Carp in *Golden Boy* (Playhouse in the Park, Philadelphia, Pa., Aug. 2, 1954); and on tour as a Teacher, the Malamed, Father Abraham, and Uncle Maxel in *The World of Sholem Aleichem* (Parson Th., Hartford, Conn., Oct. 28, 1954; Mosque Th., Newark, N.J., Oct. 31, 1954; Walnut St. Th., Philadelphia, Pa., Nov. 1, 1954).

Mr. Lee played Eddie Brock in *Born Yesterday* (Playhouse in the Park, Philadelphia, Pa., July 4, 1955); Fez in the pre-Bway tryout of *Reuben Reuben* (opened Shubert, Boston, Mass., Oct. 10, 1955; closed there Oct. 22, 1955); appeared in a stock production of *The World of Sholem Aleichem* (Bucks County Playhouse, New Hope, Pa., June 25, 1956); as Peter Ilyitch Boroff in *Silk Stockings* (Colony Musical Tent, Latham, N.Y., July 1, 1958); Etienne in *Can-Can* (Colony Musical Tent, Aug. 5, 1958); Lou Kandall in *Wish You Were Here* (Pine Brook Show Tent, N.J., Aug. 20, 1959); understudied Jack Gilford as King Septimus in *Once Upon a Mattress* (Phoenix, May 11, 1959; moved Alvin, Nov. 25, 1959); succeeded (Aug. 4, 1959) Mr. Gilford in the role; appeared as Grobert in *Carnival!* (Imperial, Apr. 13, 1961); and the Man in a touring production of *The Millionairess* (opened Brown Th., Louisville, Ky., July 8, 1963).

Mr. Lee played summer stock in 1964, appearing as Doc in *West Side Story* (Westbury Music Fair, N.Y.; Camden County Music Fair, N.J.; Storrowtown Music Fair, Mass.; Painters Mill Music Fair; Valley Forge Music Fair, Pa.; Shady Grove Music Fair, N.J.); was Aufschnitt in *The Last Analysis* (Belasco Th., N.Y.C., Oct. 1, 1964); the Old Jew in *Incident at Vichy* (ANTA Washington Square Th., Dec. 3, 1964; Huntington Hartford Th., Hollywood, Cal., Oct. 25–Dec. 1965); the Foreman in *The Tenth Man* (Mineola Th., N.Y.; Playhouse on the Mall, N.J., Jan. 1966); repeated his role in *Incident at Vichy* (Playhouse in the Park, Philadelphia, Pa., June 13, 1966); was Estragon in *Waiting for Godot* and appeared in *The Merchant of Venice*, *Gabbo*, and *Tubal* (all Berkshire Th. Festival, Stockbridge, Mass., July–Aug. 1966); played Herman Teppis in *The Deer Park* (Th. de Lys, N.Y.C., Jan. 31, 1967); Jacob in *Awake and Sing* (Charles Playhouse, Boston, Mass., Nov. 2, 1967); appeared at the Eugene O'Neill Memorial Th., Waterford, Conn. (July–Aug. 1970); played Gregory Solomon in *The Price* (Long Wharf Th., New Haven, Conn., May 7, 1971); appeared as the Prompter in *A Swan Song* and the Greek Confectioner in *The Wedding* on the program *Troika: An Evening of Russian Comedy* (Long Wharf Th., New Haven, Conn., Mar. 17, 1972); was in the tryout of *The Opening* (Tappen Zee Playhouse, Nyack, N.Y., May 16, 1972); and played Kon in *Enemies* (Vivian Beaumont Th., N.Y.C., Nov. 9, 1972).

Films. Mr. Lee has appeared in *Whistling in the Dark* (MGM, 1941); *Ball of Fire* (RKO, 1941); *Her Honor* (MGM, 1941); *Temporary Bride* (U, 1941); *Babes on Broadway* (MGM, 1941); *Design for Scandal* (MGM, 1941); *Saboteur* (U, 1942); *Brute Force* (U, 1947); *A Song Is Born* (RKO, 1948); *They Live by Night* (RKO, 1948); *Casbah* (U, 1948); *Life of Reilly* (U, 1949); *M* (Col., 1951); *The Little Fugitive* (BST, 1953); and *An Affair of the Skin* (City Film, 1963).

Television. Mr. Lee was in the opera *From the House of the Dead* (PBS, 1969); created and played the character of Mr. Hooper on Sesame Street (PBS, 1969–to date); and played Kone in *Enemies* on the Theatre of America series (PBS, 1973).

Other Activities. Mr. Lee taught acting at the American Th. Wing (N.Y.C., 1950–59); the New School for Social Research (1961–to date); the Uta Hagen-Herbert Berghof (HB) Studio (1965–66); and at Boston Univ. (1967–68).

Awards. Mr. Lee received the Drama Desk-Vernon Rice Award for off-Bway achievement in 1967 for his performance in *The Deer Park*. .

Recreation. Swimming, tennis.

LEEDS, PHIL. Actor. Father, post office clerk. Grad. James Monroe H.S., Bronx, N.Y., attended City Coll. of New York. Married to Toby Brandt. Served US Army, Special Services, PTO, 1943–46; rank, Sgt. Member of AEA; AGVA; AFTR; SAG.

Pre-Theatre. Peanut vendor in Yankee Stadium and Polo Grounds.

Theatre. Mr. Leeds made his debut as a comedian in the revue, *Of V We Sing* (Concert Th., N.Y.C., Feb. 11, 1942); subsequently appeared as a comedian in the revue, *Let Freedom Sing* (Longacre, Oct. 5, 1942); and played comedy roles in summer stock productions at Camp Tamiment Th. (Pa. 1946).

He played Dr. Francel in *Make a Wish* (Winter Garden, N.Y.C., Apr. 18, 1951); appeared in *Curtain Going Up* (Forrest, Philadelphia, Pa., 1952); played Theophile and understudied Hans Conreid as Boris Adzinidzinadze in *Can-Can* (Shubert, N.Y.C., May 7, 1953); played Joe Scalan and the concertina-playing Gypsy in *The Matchmaker* (Royale, Dec. 5, 1955); the First Soldier in *Romanoff and Juliet* (Plymouth, Oct. 10, 1957); was standby for Bert Lahr and Shelley Berman in *The Girls Against the Boys* (Alvin, Nov. 2, 1959); played Uncle in *Christine* (46 St. Th., Apr. 28, 1960); and Simeon Moodis in *Smiling the Boy Fell Dead* (Cherry Lane, Apr. 19, 1961).

He played Sandor in *Bells Are Ringing* (State Fair Music Hall, Dallas, Tex., 1961); Peppy in *The Merry Widow* (South Shore Music Circus, Cohasset, Mass., 1961); appeared in *Song of Norway* (State Fair Music Hall, Dallas, 1961); played Oliver Badger in *The Banker's Daughter* (Jan Hus House, N.Y.C., Jan. 22, 1962); the Chinese Laundry Man and Hymie, the Waiter, in *Nowhere To Go But Up* (Winter Garden, Nov. 10, 1962); William Morris in *Sophie* (Winter Garden, Apr. 15, 1963); and Victor Talsey in *Nobody Loves an Albatross* (Lyceum, Dec. 19, 1963).

Mr. Leeds played Mr. Sawyer in the national tour of *Here's Love* (opened Philharmonic Aud., Los Angeles, Aug. 3, 1964; closed Curran, San Francisco, Dec. 19, 1964); Louis Lamont, Dominique You, and Louis the Guide in *Mardi Gras* (Jones Beach, N.Y. Marine Th., June 26, 1965); Benoit Penglet in *Hotel Passionato* (E. 74 St. Th., N.Y.C., Oct. 22, 1965); Ali Hakim in *Oklahoma!* (State Fair Music Hall, Dallas, July 11, 1966); Max Kane in *Dinner At Eight* (Alvin, N.Y.C., Sept. 27, 1966); and Lt. Miles Practice in *Little Murders* (Broadhurst, Apr. 25, 1967).

Films. He played Dr. Shand in *Rosemary's Baby* (Par., 1968); and Sam in *Don't Drink the Water* (Avco-Embassy, 1969).

Television and Radio. Mr. Leeds performed on radio as a guest comedian on the Jane Pickens Show (NBC, 1947).

On television, he appeared on Front Row Center (NBC, 1948); and as a guest comedian on the Milton Berle Show (NBC), the Jackie Gleason Show (CBS), the Jimmy Durante Show (NBC), Jack Paar (NBC), and Johnny Carson (NBC).

Other appearances include The Patty Duke Show (ABC); For the People (CBS); Car 54, Where Are You? (ABC); *Pins and Needles* (NET); This Proud Land (ABC); Trials of O'Brien (CBS); The Hero (NBC); The Dick Van Dyke Show (CBS); and The Monkees (NBC).

Night Clubs. He has appeared as a comedian at the Cafe Society (N.Y.C., 1942); Village Vanguard (N.Y.C., 1946); Blue Angel (N.Y.C., 1949–50); Club Charles (Baltimore, Md., 1949–50); hungry i (San Francisco, Calif., 1957); Mister Kelly's (San Francisco, Calif., 1957); and the Bon Soir (Chicago, Ill., 1957).

Recreation. Handball.

Le GALLIENNE, EVA. Actress, director, producer. b. Jan. 11, 1899, London, England, to Richard and Julie (Nörregaard) Le Gallienne. Father, writer; mother, journalist. Attended Coll. Sévigné, Paris, 1907–14; RADA, London, winter, 1914. Member of AEA; AFTRA; SAG; Dramatists Guild. Address: Hillside Road, Weston, CT 06880.

Theatre. Miss Le Gallienne made her debut in London as a Page in *Monna Vanna* (Queen's Th., July 21, 1914); subsequently played Elizabeth in *Laughter of Fools* (Prince of Wales's, May 29, 1915); and Victorine in *Peter Ibbetson* (His Majesty's, July 23, 1915).

She made her N.Y.C. debut as Rose in *Mrs. Boltay's Daughters* (Comedy, Oct. 23, 1915); followed by Jennie in *Bunny* (Hudson, Jan. 4, 1916); Mary Powers in *The Melody of Youth* (Fulton, Feb. 15, 1916); Patricia Molloy in *Mr. Lazarus* (Shubert, Sept. 5, 1916), in which she toured the West Coast (1917); and appeared in stock productions of *The Cinderella Man, Rio Grande,* and *Pierre of the Plains* (Alcazar, San Francisco, Calif., 1917).

Miss Le Gallienne played Dot Carrington in *Saturday to Monday* (Bijou, N.Y.C., Oct. 7, 1917); Ottiline Mallinson in *Lord and Lady Algy* (Broadhurst, Dec. 22, 1917); in Ethel Barrymore's company, the Duchess of Burchester in *The Off Chance* (Empire, Feb. 14, 1918) and Delia in *Belinda* (Empire, May 6, 1918); toured in *The Off Chance* (1918–19); appeared as Eithne in *Lusmore* (Henry Miller's Th., N.Y.C., Sept. 9, 1919); as the Parisienne in *Elsie Janis and Her Gang* (George M. Cohan Th., Dec. 1, 1919); and as Elsie Dover in *Not So Long Ago* (Booth, May 4, 1920), in which she toured (1920–21).

Miss Le Gallienne appeared as Julie in *Liliom* (Garrick, Apr. 20, 1921), in which she toured (1922–23); played Simonetta Vespucci in *Sandro Botticelli* (Provincetown Playhouse, Mar. 26, 1923); Julia in *The Rivals* (48 St. Th., May 7, 1923); Alexandra in *The Swan* (Cort, Oct. 23, 1923); Hannele in *The Assumption of Hannele* (Cort, Feb. 15, 1924); and Diane de Charence in *La Vierge Folle* (Gaiety, Mar. 21, 1924). *Hannele* and *La Vierge Folle* (in French) were given for special matinees during the run of *The Swan.* She played Alexandra in *The Swan* (Empire, Aug. 25, 1924) in which she toured (1924–25); played Marie in *The Call of Life* (Comedy, Oct. 1925); Hilda Wangel in her own production of *The Master Builder* (opened Maxine Elliott's Th., Nov. 10, 1925, for special matinees; moved to Princess Th., Dec. 21, 1925); and Ella Rentheim in her production of *John Gabriel Borkman* (Booth, Jan. 29, 1926), in which she toured (1926).

In 1926, Miss Le Gallienne founded the Civic Repertory Th., opening with *Saturday Night* (Oct. 25, 1926), which she directed and played Imperia; subsequently at the Civic Repertory Th., she directed and appeared as Hilda Wangel in *The Master Builder* (Nov. 1, 1926), Masha in *The Three Sisters* (Oct. 26, 1926), Ella Rentheim in *John Gabriel Borkman* (Nov. 9, 1926), Mirandolina in *The Mistress of the Inn* (Dec. 6, 1926), Viola in *Twelfth Night* (Dec. 20, 1926), Sister Joanna in *The Cradle Song* (Jan. 24, 1927), Aunt Isabel in *Inheritors* (Mar. 15, 1927), Jo in *The Good Hope* (OCt. 18, 1927), Sara Peri in *The First Stone* (Jan. 16, 1928), Princess Orloff in *Improvisations in June* (Mar. 5, 1928), the title role in *Hedda Gabler* (Mar. 26, 1928), Dorimène in *The Would-Be Gentleman* (Oct. 1, 1928), Marie Louise in *L'Invitation au voyage* (Oct. 4, 1928), and Varya in *The Cherry Orchard* (Oct. 15, 1928).

Also at the Civic Repertory Theatre, Miss Le Gallienne directed with J. Blake Scott and played the title role in *Peter Pan* (Nov. 26, 1928); directed a double bill, *The Lady from Alfaqueque* and *On the Hight Road* (Jan. 14, 1929) and *Katerina* (Feb. 25, 1929), directed and played Dona Laura in *A Sunny Morning* (Apr. 13, 1929), directed and played Masha in *The Seagull* (Sept. 16, 1929), directed *Mademoiselle Bourrat* (Oct. 7, 1929), played Anna Karenina in *The Living Corpse* (Dec. 6, 1929), directed another double bill and played Juanita in *The Women Have Their Way* and Lady Torminster in *The Open Door* (Jan. 27, 1930), directed and played Juliet in *Romeo and Juliet* (Apr. 21, 1930), directed *The Green Cockatoo* (Oct. 9, 1930), directed and appeared as Genevieve in *Siegfried* (Oct. 20, 1930), directed and played Elsa in *Alison's House* (Dec. 1, 1930), appeared as Marguerite in *Camille* (Jan. 26, 1931), directed and appeared as Julie in *Liliom* (Oct. 26, 1932), Cassandra Austen in *Dear Jane* (Nov. 14, 1932), and the White Chess Queen in *Alice in Wonderland* (Dec. 12, 1932), which she adapted with Florida Friebus.

Miss Le Gallienne toured with the Civic Repertory Th. in *Alice in Wonderland, A Doll's House, The Master Builder, Romeo and Juliet,* and *Hedda Gabler* (Fall 1933–Spring 1934).

She appeared as the Duke of Reichstadt in her production of *L'Aiglon* (Broadhurst, Nov. 3, 1934), which she also directed; revived her productions of *Hedda Gabler* (Broadhurst, Dec. 3, 1934) and *Cradle Song* (Broadhurst, Dec. 10, 1934); toured in repertory with the following plays in 1935, which opened at the Shubert Th. (N.Y.C.) on dates indicated, playing in repertory: *Rosmersholm* (Dec. 2); *Camille* (Dec. 4); the double bill, *The Women Have Their Way* and *A Sunny Morning* (Dec. 7).

She appeared as Angelica in *Love for Love* (Westport Country Playhouse, Conn., June 1936); Mathilda Wesendonck in *Prelude to Exile* (Guild, N.Y.C., Nov. 20, 1936); Mirandolina in *The Mistress of the Inn* (Westchester County Playhouse, Mt. Kisco, N.Y., June 1937); the title role in *Hamlet* (Cape Playhouse, Dennis, Mass., Aug. 1937); Marie Antoinette in *Madame Capet* (Cort, N.Y.C., Oct. 25, 1938); Juliet in the balcony scene in *Frank Fay's Music Hall* (44 St. Th., Mar. 1939); Amanda in *Private Lives* (Summer tour 1939); toured in *Hedda Gabler* and *The Master Builder* (1940–41).

She produced and directed *Ah, Wilderness!* (Guild, N.Y.C., Oct. 2, 1941); played Mrs. Malaprop (temporarily succeeding Mary Boland who was ill) in *The Rivals* (St. Louis, Mo., Dec. 1941) and directed the N.Y.C. production (Shubert, Jan. 14, 1942); played Lettie in *Uncle Harry* (Broadhurst, May 20, 1942); Lyubov Andreyevna in *The Cherry Orchard* (Natl., Jan. 25, 1944), which she also directed; and Therese Raquin in *Therese* (Biltmore, Oct. 9, 1945).

In 1946, with Cheryl Crawford and Margaret Webster, Miss Le Gallienne founded the American Repertory Th., and appeared at the International Th. as Queen Katherine in *Henry VIII* (Nov. 6, 1946), Comtesse de la Briere in *What Every Woman Knows* (Nov. 8, 1946), Ella Rentheim in *John Gabriel Borkman* (Nov. 12, 1946), and the White Queen in *Alice in Wonderland* (April 5, 1947).

Subsequently, she appeared as Mrs. Alving in *Ghosts* (Cort, N.Y.C., Feb. 24, 1948); Hedda Tesman in *Hedda Gabler* (Cort, Feb. 24, 1948); toured as Miss Moffat in *The Corn Is Green* (opened NY City Ctr., Jan. 11, 1950); played Signora Amaranta in *Fortunato* (Woodstock Playhouse, N.Y., July 1950); Lady Starcross in *The Starcross Story* (Royale, N.Y.C., Jan. 13, 1954); Marcia Elder in *The Southwest Corner* (Holiday, Feb. 3, 1955); presented a reading, *An Afternoon with Oscar Wilde* (Th. de Lys, Jan. 1957); and played Queen Elizabeth in *Mary Stuart* (Phoenix, Oct. 8, 1957), which later toured the US and Canada (1958–59); appeared as Lavinia Prendergast in a pre-Bway tryout of *Listen to the Mocking Bird* (opened Colonial, Boston, Mass., Dec. 27, 1958; closed Shubert, Washington, D.C., Jan. 29, 1959).

Miss Le Gallienne toured, with the National Repertory Th., playing Elizabeth, both in *Mary Stuart* (Acad. of Music, Northampton, Mass., Oct. 19, 1961) and in *Elizabeth, the Queen* (Acad. of Music, Oct. 20, 1961); toured in repertory as Madame Arkadina in *The Seagull* and Madame Desmortes in *Ring Round the Moon* (Oct. 1963–Apr. 30, 1964); appeared as Madame Arkadina in *The Seagull* (Belasco, N.Y.C., Apr. 5, 1964); directed *Liliom* and *Hedda Gabler* for the National Repertory Th. tour (1964–65); co-produced *The Bernard Shaw Story* (White Barn Th., Westport, Conn., 1965); toured with the National Repertory Th. as Aurelia in *The Madwoman of Chaillot* and Hecuba in *The Trojan Women* (1965–66); and co-produced *Come Slowly, Eden* and *Seven Ages of Bernard Shaw* (1966). For the Israeli Mime Theatre, she appeared in *The Effect of Gamma Rays on Man-in-the-Moon Marigolds*, for the APA Repertory Co. she played Queen Marguerite in *Exit the King* (Lyceum, Jan. 9, 1968) and translated and directed *The Cherry Orchard* (Lyceum, Mar. 19, 1968); and for the American Shakespeare Festival, Stratford, Conn., she played the Countess in *All's Well That Ends Well* (June 16, 1970).

Television. She has appeared in *Alice in Wonderland* (Hallmark Hall of Fame, NBC, Oct. 23, 1955); *The Corn Is Green* (Playhouse 90, CBS, Jan. 8, 1956); *The Bridge of San Luis Rey* (Dumont Show of the Month, CBS, Jan. 21, 1958); *Mary Stuart* (Kraft Television Playhouse, NBC, Mar. 1962); *Thérèse Raquin* (Playhouse 90); and *Memories of Duse* (Camera Three, 1972).

Other Activities. She gave a series of lectures on tour (1959); and taught acting at the White Barn Th. (Westport, Conn., Summers 1962–63 and Summers 1972–73).

Published Works. Miss Le Gallienne is the author of the autobiographies *At 33* (1934) and *With a Quiet Heart* (1953); a story for children, *Flossie and Bossie* (1949); an adaptation of *The Strong Are Lonely* (1953); translations of *Six Plays by Henrik Ibsen* (1957); translations of seven *Hans Christian Anderson Tales* (1959); translations of *The Wild Duck and Other Plays* (1961); Anderson's *The Nightingale* (1964); a study of Eleonora Duse, *The Mystic in the Theatre* (1966); and *Ibsen, The Lay Giant* (1971).

Discography. Miss Le Gallienne's recordings include *Romeo and Juliet* (Atlantic); *Hedda Gabler* (Th. Masterworks); *English and American Poetry* (Th. Masterworks); *An Evening with Will Shakespeare* (Th. Masterworks); *Les fleurs du mal,* in French (Caedmon); *Camille* (Caedmon); and *Hans Christian Anderson Tales* (Miller-Brody, 1973).

Awards. Miss Le Gallienne has received the Pictorial Review Prize (1926); Society of Arts and Sciences Gold Medal; The Town Hall Club Award (1934); American Academy of Arts and Letters Gold Medal for Good Speech; Norway's Cross of the Royal Order of St. Olav for work done in America for Ibsen (1961); the ANTA Award (1964); a special Antoinette Perry (Tony) Award (1964); and the Brandeis Univ. Award (1966). She was selected outstanding woman of the year (1947) by the Women's National Press Club of America and received a citation for distinguished work from the NY Drama League. She holds honorary degrees from Tufts Coll. (M.A. 1927), Smith Coll. (L.H.D. 1930), Russell Sage Coll. (D.Litt. 1930), Brown Univ. (D.Litt. 1933), Mt. Holyoke Coll. (D.Litt. 1937), Ohio Weslyan Univ. (L.H.D. 1953), Goucher Coll. (L.H.D. 1961), Univ. of N. Carolina (D.Litt. 1964), Bard College (D.H.L. 1965), and Fairfield Univ. (D.H.L. 1966).

Recreation. Gardening, carpentry, reading, weaving, horseback riding, calligraphy, fencing, languages (French, Danish, Russian, English).

LEIBERT, MICHAEL W. Director, actor, producer. b. Michael Williams Leibert, Apr. 24, 1940, San Francisco, Calif., to John Grant and Margaret Feiring (Atchley) Leibert. Father, contractor; mother, artist. Educ. Tamalpais H.S., Mill Valley, Cal.; Loomis Institute, Windsor, Conn.; Whitman Coll., Washington; Stanford Univ.; Univ. of California, Berkeley. Married 1966 to Alexa Peralta McGurrin (marr. dis. 1972); one son, one daughter. Member of AEA; California Theatre Council (pres., 1974–75); California Arts Commission (Theatre Panel mbr., 1974). Address: Berkeley Repertory Theatre, 2980 College Ave., Berkeley, CA 94705, tel. (415) 841-6108.

Mr. Leibert founded the Berkeley Repertory Theatre, Berkeley, Calif., in 1968 and has served as its producing director from that time to the present. His first appearance on any theatrical stage was in June 1946, when he played the Farmer's Son in *Distant Drums* (Ross Valley Players, Ross, Cal.). He made his first professional appearances with Hopkins Center Repertory, Hanover, N.H., in 1968, as Creon in *Antigone* (June), Orsino in *Twelfth Night,* and the Cook in *Mother Courage* (August). After that, working with the Berkeley Repertory Co., he played Pat in *The Hostage* (Oct. 1968); directed *The Importance of Being Earnest* (Dec. 14, 1968); produced Sophocles' *Electra* (Jan. 15, 1969); directed *The Time of Your Life* (Feb. 20, 1969); produced *Camino Real* (Apr. 5, 1969); directed *The Duchess of Malfi* (Sept. 20, 1969); produced *The Miser* (Nov. 15, 1969); directed *The Playboy of the Western World* (Jan. 10, 1970); produced *Hay Fever* (Mar. 1, 1970); and played Malvolio in *Twelfth Night* (May 10, 1970).

He directed *The Merry Wives of Windsor* (June 5, 1970); *The Plough and the Stars* (Sept. 20. 1970); played Creon in *Antigone* (Nov. 5, 1970); produced *The Wild Duck* (Jan. 10, 1971); directed *Idiot's Delight* (Feb. 26, 1971); *Angel Street* (Nov. 15, 1971); *Who's Happy Now?* (Feb. 10, 1972); and produced *Love's Labour's Lost* (Apr. 2, 1972). He also directed *Father's Day* (Sept. 20, 1972); *Loot* (Feb. 1, 1973); produced *Subject to Fits* (Mar. 15, 1973); played Trigorin in *The Seagull* (May 1, 1973); Joseph Surface in *The School for Scandal* (June 10, 1973); Hector in *Heartbreak House* (Oct. 10, 1973); Solness in *The Master Builder* (Nov. 15, 1973); directed *The Petrified Forest* (Jan. 15, 1974); played Claudius in *Hamlet* (University Th., Whitman Coll., Washington, Feb. 20, 1974); produced *Dracula—A Musical Nightmare* (Berkeley Rep. Th., Apr. 10, 1974); and directed *The Front Page* (June 7, 1974).

Awards. Mr. Leibert was awarded the Eisner Prize for outstanding creative achievement at the Univ. of California, Berkeley, in 1967.

LEIBMAN, RON. Actor. b. Oct. 11, 1937, New York City, to Murray and Grace (Marks) Leibman. Attended Columbia Grammar Sch. (N.Y.C.); Ohio Wesleyan Univ.; Amer. Academy of Dramatic Arts. Married Sept. 7, 1969, to Linda Lavin, actress. Member of Actors Studio; AEA; SAG.

Theatre. Mr. Leibman appeared with the Barnard Summer Th. (1959) playing Rodolfo in *A View from the Bridge,* and Kilroy in *Camino Real;* made his off-Bway debut as Orpheus in *Legend of Lovers* (41 St. Th., N.Y.C., Oct. 27, 1959); appeared in an Equity Library Th. production of *Dead End* (1960); succeeded George Furth (1962) in *The Premise* (Premise Th., opened Nov. 20, 1960); in his Bway debut, played Peter Nemo in *Dear Me, the Sky Is Falling* (Music Box, Mar. 2, 1963); subsequently played Rip Calabria in *Bicycle Ride to Nevada* (Cort, Sept. 24, 1963); and Capt. Salazer in *The Deputy* (Brooks Atkinson Th., Feb. 26, 1964). With the Theatre of the Living Arts (Philadelphia, Pa.), he appeared in *Galileo* (Jan. 6, 1965), played Alceste in *The Misanthrope* (Mar. 16, 1965), Clov in *Endgame* (Mar. 25, 1965), Mr. Puff in *The Critic,* appeared in *Uncle Vanya* (Nov. 16, 1965), and played Gordon Miller in *Room Service* (Nov. 1, 1966). He repeated his performance in *Room Service* (Mineola, N.Y., Playhouse, Summer 1967); played Teddy in *The Poker Session* (Martinique, N.Y.C., Sept. 19, 1967); appeared with the Yale Repertory Co. (1967–68 season), playing Sgt. Henderson in *We Bombed in New Haven,* Hermes in *Prometheus Bound,* Mosca in *Volpone,* and Solyony in *The Three Sisters.* He appeared in *Long Day's Journey into Night* (Springfield (Mass.) Th. Co., Apr. 4, 1968); was a member of the acting company of the Eugene O'Neill Playwright's Unit (Waterford, Conn., Summer 1968); repeated the role of Sgt. Henderson in *We Bombed in New Haven* (Ambassador, N.Y.C., Oct. 16, 1968); appeared in *Cop-Out* (Cort, Apr. 7, 1969); on a triple-bill (Village So. Th., Jan. 22, 1970), played Starr in the title play, *Transfers,* Bob in *The Rooming House,* and the title role in *Dr. Galley;* again played Gordon Miller in *Room Service* (Edison, May 12, 1970); on a double-bill entitled *Love Two* (Billy Munk Th., May 23, 1975), played Richard in *The Lover,* and Harry in *Score;* and appeared in *Rich and Famous* (Public/Newman, Feb. 19, 1976).

Films. He made his film debut as Sidney Hocheiser in *Where's Poppa?* (UA, 1970); played Murch in *The Hot Rock* (20th-Fox, 1972); Paul Lazzaro in *Slaughterhouse Five* (U, 1972); Greenberg in *The Super Cops* (UA, 1974); and Mike in *Your Three Minutes Are Up* (Cinerama, 1974).

Other Activities. While a member of the Yale Repertory Co. (1967–68), Mr. Leibman taught acting at Yale Drama School.

Awards. Mr. Leibman received the Drama Desk and Theatre World awards (1968–69) for his performance in *We Bombed in New Haven;* and the Off-Bway (Obie) and Drama Desk awards (1969–70) for *Transfers.*.

LEIGH, CAROLYN. Lyricist. b. Carolyn Rosenthal, N.Y.C., to Henry and Sylvia Rosenthal. Grad. Hunter College H.S.; attended Queens Coll. and New York Univ. Married 1959 to David Wynn Cunningham, Jr., attorney. Member of Dramatists Guild; ASCAP; NARAS (member of board).

Theatre. Miss Leigh was lyricist for *Peter Pan* (Winter Garden Th., N.Y.C., Oct. 20, 1954); *Ziegfeld Follies* (Winter Garden, Mar. 1, 1957); *Wildcat* (Alvin, Dec. 16, 1960); *Little Me* (Lunt-Fontanne, Nov. 17, 1962); and *How Now, Dow Jones* (Lunt-Fontanne Th., Dec. 7, 1967), for which she also conceived the idea.

Published Works. She wrote the songs "Young at Heart," "Witchcraft," "How Little We Know," "Firefly," "The Best Is Yet to Come," "It Amazes Me," and "Pass Me By" from the motion picture *Father Goose* (1964).

Awards. She was nominated for the NARAS Grammy and the Antoinette Perry (Tony) Award for her lyrics for *Little Me* (1963) and was nominated for a Tony as best lyricist (1967–68) for *How Now, Dow Jones.*

Recreation. Reading, photography.

LEIGH, MITCH. Composer, conductor, musician. b. Jan. 30, 1928, to David and Riva Michnick. Father, furrier. Grad. H.S. of Music and Art, N.Y.C.; Yale Univ., B.A. and M.A.; attended Yale School of Music (Paul Hindemith). Served US Army (1946–48). Married 1950 to Rene Goldman (marr. dis.), one son; married 1971 to Abby Kimmelman. Member of AFM; SAG; AFTRA; Dramatists Guild. Address: (home) 960 Ocean Ave., Seabright, NJ 07760, tel. (201) 747-0986; (bus.) c/o Music Makers, 3 E. 57th St., New York, NY 10022, tel. (212) CI 5-3737.

Mr. Leigh began his career as a jazz musician, usually playing bassoon. During the 1950's, he teamed with Art Harris for a daily radio show and a series of recordings. He is still active as a musician, playing with the Music Makers, and for commercials.

Theatre. He wrote the incidental music for *Too True To Be Good* (54 St. Th., N.Y.C., Mar. 1963); and *Never Live Over a Pretzel Factory* (Eugene O'Neill Th., N.Y.C., Feb. 1964); composed the music for *Man of La Mancha* (ANTA-Washington Square Th., N.Y.C., Nov. 22, 1965); and produced, and composed the music for *Cry for Us All* (Broadhurst, N.Y.C., April 8, 1970).

Other Activities. Mr. Leigh lectured at Yale Univ. in 1973.

Discography. Mr. Leigh, in conjunction with Art Harris, recorded *Jazz 1755, New Jazz in Hi-Fi, Jean Shepherd—Into the Unknown,* and *Modern Woodwind Expressions.* He subsequently recorded *Man of La Mancha, The Disadvantages of You,* and *Cry for Us All.*

Awards. For *Man of La Mancha,* Mr. Leigh received the Antoinette Perry (Tony) Award (1965–66); the Drama Critics Circle Award (1965–66); and the Variety Poll Award (1966). He received the Spanish Pavillion Award (1966) for his contribution to Spanish culture; the Yale Univ. School of Music Alumni Assn. Certificate of Merit (1967) in recognition of his distinguished service to the art and profession of music; and the Contemporary Classic award of the Songwriters Hall of Fame (1973) for "The Impossible Dream".

Recreation. Tennis, crossword puzzles.

LEIGH-HUNT, BARBARA. Actress. b. Dec. 14, 1935, Bath, England. Trained at Bristol (England) Old Vic Th. Sch.

Theatre. Miss Leigh-Hunt made her professional debut with the Old Vic company as a walk-on and understudy in a touring production of *A Midsummer Night's Dream;* appearing as Helena in that work in a later production (Old Vic, London, Dec. 20, 1960) also appearing as Bet Bouncer in *She Stoops to Conquer* (Nov. 8, 1960); in *Twelfth Night* (Apr. 18, 1961); and as Portia in *The Merchant of Venice* (May 30, 1961). As a member of the Bristol Old Vic Repertory Co. (Th. Royal), her roles included Beatrice in *Much Ado About Nothing* (1963); Rosemary in *A Severed Head* (May 7, 1963; and Criterion, London, June 27, 1963); Rosaline in *Love's Labour's Lost;* the title role in *Saint Joan* (1965); Lady Macbeth in *Macbeth;* Amanda in *Private Lives;* Ophelia in *Hamlet* (1967, and tour of North America), Isabella in *Measure for Measure;* The Woman in *Don Juan in Love;* and Anita Hill in *Mrs. Mouse, Are You Within?* (premiere Apr. 3, 1968). She played Madge Larrabee in *Sherlock Holmes* (Aldwych, London, Jan. 1974; and Broadhurst, N.Y.C., Nov. 12, 1974); and Lenin's Wife in *Travesties* (Aldwych, London, June 1974).

Films. Miss Leigh-Hunt has appeared in *Frenzy* (U, 1972); and, in England, *Henry VIII and His Six Wives;* and *A Bequest to the Nation.*.

Television. Her credits include the British productions of *The Search for the Nile; Macbeth; The Brontes;* and *Mrs. Mouse, Are You Within?.*

LeMASSENA, WILLIAM H. Actor. b. William Henry LeMassena, Jr., May 23, 1916, Glen Ridge, N.J., to William Henry and Margery (Lockwood) LeMassena. Father, broker. Grad. Glen Ridge (N.J.) H.S., 1934; New York Univ., B.F.A. 1939. Studied with William Hansen at the Amer. Th. Wing, 1948; Mira Rostova, 1949–51; Theodore Komisarjevsky, 1952. Served US Army, Anti-Aircraft Artillery, 1942–45; Armed Forces Radio Service, 1945–46; rank, T/Sgt. Member of AEA; AFTRA; SAG. Address: 132 W. 11th St., New York, NY 10011, tel. (212) OR 5-2566.

Theatre. Mr. LeMassena made his stage debut with the Washington Sq. Players of New York Univ. in *As You Like It* (New York Univ., 1935); subsequently appeared as the Priest in their production of *Twelfth Night* (New York Univ., 1935); made his Bway debut as a Pedant in *The Taming of the Shrew* (Alvin, Feb. 5, 1940); appeared as Frank Olmstead in *There Shall Be No Night* (Alvin, Apr. 29, 1940), in which he later toured; played in *Out of the Frying Pan* (Monomoy, Chatham, Mass., July, 1940); a Gold Shirt in *Mexican Mural* (Chanin, N.Y.C., 1941); and the Hermit in the pre-Bway tour of *The Pirate* (Sept. 1942).

He succeeded (Mar. 1946) Nelson Leigh as the Player King in *Hamlet* (Columbus Circle Th., N.Y.C., Dec. 13, 1945), and toured in the role; toured in the national company of *Call Me Mister* (1946–47); played a Guest in *The Wedding* (NY City Ctr., Feb. 5, 1948); appeared in the revue *Inside U.S.A.* (Century, Apr. 30, 1948); played William in *I Know My Love* on tour and in N.Y.C. (Shubert, Nov. 2, 1949); succeeded (Jan. 1950) Geoffrey Kerr as Frederic Chandler in *I Know My Love;* played a Radio Announcer, the District Attorney, and a Headwaiter in *Dream Girl* (NY City Ctr., May 9, 1951); Tom Hubbard in a stock production of *Kin Hubbard* (Westport County Playhouse, Conn., 1951); succeeded (Summer 1951) Irving Mitchell as Mr. Esmond, Sr., in *Gentlemen Prefer Blondes* (Ziegfeld, N.Y.C., Dec. 8, 1949); played M. Redon-La Mur in *Nina* (Royale, Dec. 5, 1951); Vaughan in the ELT production of *Fanny's First Play* (Lenox Hill Playhouse, Feb. 27, 1952); Pemberton Maxwell in *Call Me Madam* (State Fair Music Hall, Dallas, Tex., Summer 1952); toured as Roger Blakesley in *Point of No Return* (opened Ford's Th., Baltimore, Md., Nov. 24, 1954; closed Biltmore, Los Angeles, Calif., May 23, 1953); played a Lord and the Second Judge in *Ondine* (46 St. Th., N.Y.C., Feb. 18, 1954).

Mr. LeMassena toured as Mr. Jones in a stock production of *The Vegetable* (Aug. 1954); played Peterbono in *Thieves Carnival* (Cherry Lane, N.Y.C., Feb. 1, 1955); William Danbury in *Fallen Angels* (Playhouse, Jan. 17, 1956); Pawnee Bill in *Annie Get Your Gun* (NY City Ctr., Feb. 19, 1958); General St. Pé in *Ardele* (Cricket, Apr. 8, 1958); Howard Cavanaugh in *Redhead* (46 St. Th., Feb. 5, 1959), and on tour (opened Shubert, Chicago, Ill., Mar. 23, 1960); Bel-Kabbittu in *Susannah and the Elders* (Bway Chapel Th., N.Y.C., Oct. 18, 1959); a Nightclub Manager and Judge Callan in *The Conquering Hero* (ANTA, Jan. 16, 1961); Tullius in *Romulus* (Music Box Th., Jan. 10, 1962); and Hagedorn, Boris Pickwick, Emmett Stagg, Hennepin, and a Bailiff in *The Beauty Part* (Music Box Th., Dec. 26, 1962).

Mr. LeMassena assumed (1963) the role of Harry in *The Collection* (Cherry Lane Th., Nov. 26, 1972); was in *A Funny Thing Happened on the Way to the Forum* (Johannesburg, South Africa, 1964–65); played Sylvester in *The Coop* (Actors Playhouse, N.Y.C., Mar. 1, 1966); toured as Chitterlow in *Half a Sixpence* (1966–67); played Dr. Lloyd in a revival of *Life With Father* (NY City Ctr., Oct. 19, 1967); Mr. Lundi in a revival of *Brigadoon* (NY City Ctr., Dec. 13, 1967); Harrison Howell in *Kiss Me, Kate* (Mineola Playhouse, N.Y., Feb. 28, 1968; and tour to Toronto and Montreal); Francis Faucett in *Come Summer* (Lunt-Fontanne Th., N.Y.C., Mar. 18, 1969); and Prof. Perseus Smith in *Grin and Bare It* (Belasco Th., Mar. 16, 1970). At Meadow Brook Th., Rochester, Mich., he appeared in *Life with Father* (Dec. 3, 1970), *Tartuffe* (Feb. 4, 1971), and *A Thousand Clowns* (Apr. 29, 1971); he played Mr. Addams in *F. Jasmine Addams* (Circle in the Square, N.Y.C., Oct. 27, 1971); returned to Meadow Brook Th., where he was in *The Boy Friend* (Mar. 30, 1972), *The Front Page* (Oct. 12, 1972), *Right You Are If You Think You Are* (Feb. 1, 1973), the double bill *Bedtime Story* and *A Doctor in Spite of Himself* (Mar. 29, 1973), and played Heinrich Van Helsing in *Count Dracula* (Apr. 26, 1973). He understudied Eli Wallach as General St. Pé in *Waltz of the Toreadors* (Circle in the Square, N.Y.C., Sept. 13, 1973) and played Father Ambrose on tour with the same production (1974).

Films. He appeared as the Heavenly Friend in *Carousel* (20th-Fox, 1956); the Handwriting Witness in *The Wrong Man* (WB, 1957); and a Man in *The World of Henry Orient* (1964); and was in *Where's Poppa?* (UA, 1970).

Recreation. Motorcycling, traveling, photography.

LENARD, MARK. Actor. b. Oct. 15, 1927, Chicago, Ill. Grad. Univ. of Michigan, B.A.; attended Carnegie Inst. of Tech.; Biarritz (France) Amer. Univ., New Sch. for Social Research. Studied acting with Lee Strasberg, N.Y.C.; Uta Hagen, N.Y.C.; Mira Rostava. Married Ann, actress; one daughter. Served US Army. Member of AEA; AFTRA; SAG.

Theatre. Mr. Lenard made his professional debut as Digger in an ELT production of *The Hasty Heart;* subsequently played Richard in *Exiles* (Renata Th., N.Y.C., Mar. 12, 1957); appeared in an ELT presentation of *The Climate of Eden;* and was an understudy in *The Square Root of Wonderful* (National, Oct. 30, 1957).

He played George in an ELT production of *A Clearing in the Woods* (Sheridan Square Playhouse, Feb. 12, 1959); Conrad in *Much Ado About Nothing* (Lunt-Fontanne Th., Sept. 17, 1959); Platanov in *A Country Scandal* (Greenwich Mews, May 5, 1960); the Duke of Vienna in *Measure for Measure* (NY Shakespeare Festival, July 25, 1960); Loevborg in *Hedda Gabler* (Fourth St. Th., Nov. 9, 1960); Malchiel in *Gideon* (Plymouth, Nov. 9, 1961); General Pascal in the pre-Bway tryout of *We Take the Town* (opened Shubert, New Haven, Conn., Feb. 19, 1962; closed Shubert, Philadelphia, Pa., Mar. 17, 1962); Freud in the national tour of *A Far Country* (opened Playhouse, Wilmington, Del., Oct. 24, 1962; closed Hanna, Cleveland, Ohio, Jan. 12, 1963); Dr. Katz in *My Mother, My Father and Me* (Plymouth, Mar. 23, 1963); and was standby for Van Hefflin in the role of Sloane in *A Case of Libel* (Longacre, Oct. 10, 1963).

Mr. Lenard played Alfred Allmers in *Little Eyolf* (Actors Playhouse, N.Y.C., Mar. 16, 1964); Captain Delano in *Benito Cereno* (Th. de Lys, Jan. 14, 1965); the Rev. T. Lawrence Shannon in *The Night of the Iguana* (Purdue Univ. Th., West Lafayette, Ind., Dec. 3, 1965); appeared with the Center Theatre Group (Ahmanson, Los Angeles, 1966–67 season, 1967–68 season); the Actors Theatre of Louisville (Ky.) (1972–73 season); and appeared in Rosmersholm (McCarter Th., Princeton, N.J., Mar. 24, 1973).

Films. Mr. Lenard appeared in *The Greatest Story Ever Told* (UA, 1964); and *Hang 'Em High* (UA, 1968).

Television. Mr. Lenard has appeared on The Defenders (CBS); The Nurses (CBS); Directions '65 (ABC); Lamp Unto My Feet (CBS); Jericho (CBS); Star Trek (NBC); Iron Horse (ABC); Mission: Impossible (CBS), and *The Power and the Glory* (CBS).

LE NOIRE, ROSETTA. Actress, singer, dancer. b. Rosetta Olive Burton, Aug. 8, 1911, New York City, to Harold Charles and Marie (Jacques) Burton. Grad. Commerce H.S., N.Y.C., 1935; Betty Cashman Dramatic Sch., 1946; Amer. Theatre Wing, N.Y.C., 1950. Studied singing with Reginald Beane, Nat Jones, Kenneth Welch, Robert Gorman, 1947–to date; acting with Morris Carnovsky at ASFTA Dramatic Sch., 1955–58. Married Sept. 27, 1929, to William Le Noire (marr. dis. May 7, 1943); one son; married May 13, 1948, to Egbert F. Brown. Member of AEA; AFTRA; AGVA; SAG; Catholic Actors Guild of Amer.; Actors' Fund of Amer.; Catholic Actors St. Malachys Discussion Club; Negro Actors Guild of Amer.; NAACP; Club 12, (chairman of welfare comm.). . Address: 1037 E. 232nd St., Bronx, NY 10466, tel. (212) 881-4084.

Pre-Theatre. Bookkeeper, receptionist, hat designer, playground instructor, telephone operator.

Theatre. Miss Le Noire made her N.Y.C. debut as the First Witch in a Federal Th. (WPA) Project production of *Macbeth* (Lafayette Th., N.Y.C., Apr. 9, 1936), also touring in it; subsequently was a singer-dancer in the dance drama, *Bassa Moona* (Lafayette, Dec. 9, 1936); played the Crippled Girl in *Bluebird* (Lafayette, Feb. 1937); Pitti-Sing in *The Hot Mikado* (Broadhurst, Mar. 23, 1939; NY World's Fair, 1940), also touring in it (1941–42); and played Mrs. Sloan in *Head of the Family* (Westport Country Playhouse, Conn., Summer 1941).

She toured US Army bases as Emma in a USO production of *You Can't Take It with You* (1943); appeared as the Maid in a touring production of *Janie* (1943–44); appeared in *Decision* and *Three's A Family* (N.Y.C. Subway Circuit, June–July 1944); played Stella in *Anna Lucasta* (Mansfield, Aug. 30, 1944; Natl., Sept. 22, 1947); Annie in scenes from *The Easiest Way* in an ANTA Album production (Ziegfeld, N.Y.C., Mar. 6, 1949); played Hattie in *Kiss Me, Kate* (Dallas State Fair Music Hall, Tex., Summer 1950); Rose Bolton in *Four Twelves Are 48* 48 St. Th., N.Y.C., Jan. 17, 1951); appeared in a season of summer stock at the Corning (N.Y.) Glass Th., playing Queenie in *Show Boat,* Sherraloo in *Three's a Family,* appeared in *Here Today, Anything Goes, Happy Birthday,* and *A Streetcar Named Desire* (Summer 1951).

Miss Le Noire appeared in an ELT production of *O Distant Land* (at Lennox Hill Playhouse, N.Y.C., Mar. 26, 1952); at the Westport Country Playhouse, appeared in *Carmen Jones* (Summer 1952); played Vonie Oxendine in *Supper for the Dead* (Th. de Lys, N.Y.C., July 6, 1954); appeared in *The Feminine Touch* (Hilltop Parkway Th., Baltimore, Md., Jan. 16, 1955); played the 3rd Sharecropper ("Necessity" Girl) in *Finian's Rainbow* (NY City Ctr., May 18, 1955); Zanche in *The White Devil* (Phoenix, Mar. 17, 1955); Matumbi in *Mister Johnson* (Martin Beck Th., Mar. 29, 1956); Slave Girl in *Ceremonies of Innocence* (ANTA, June 1956); Christine in *Take a Giant Step* (Jan Hus, Sept. 25, 1956); the Mother in *Lost in the Stars* (NY City Ctr., Apr. 10, 1958); Clara in *Destry Rides Again* (Imperial, Apr. 23, 1959); the Grandmother in *The Bible Salesman* (Bway Congregational Church, Feb. 21, 1960); August in *La Belle Helene* (Westport Country Playhouse, Summer 1960); and Portia in *Fido* (Playhouse on the Mall, Paramus, N.J., Summer 1960).

In the double bill *Double Entry,* she repeated her role as the Grandmother in *The Bible Salesman,* and played Madame Scarlatina in *The Oldest Trick in the World* (Martinique, N.Y.C., Feb. 20, 1961); played Bloody Mary in *South Pacific* (NY City Ctr., Apr. 26, 1961); Clara in *Clandestine on the Morning Line* (Actors' Playhouse, Oct. 30, 1961); Mollie in *Sophie* (Winter Garden, Apr. 15, 1963); toured as Queenie in *Show Boat* and Bloody Mary in *South Pacific* (Summer 1963); played Essie Belle Johnson in *Tambourines to Glory* (Little, N.Y.C., Nov. 2, 1963); Petunia Jackson in *Cabin in the Sky* (Greenwich Mews, Jan. 21, 1964); Mother Henry in *Blues for Mr. Charlie* (ANTA, Apr. 23, 1964); Ma Maloney in *I Had a Ball* (Martin Beck Th., Dec. 15, 1964); Hattie Gaines in *The Great Indoors* (Eugene O'Neill Th., Feb. 1, 1966); repeated her role as Queenie in a revival of *Show Boat* (NY State Th., July 19, 1966); was Meg in *A Cry of Players* (Vivian Beaumont Th., Nov. 14, 1968); Grace Kumalo in a revival of *Lost in the Stars* (Imperial, Apr. 18, 1972); Mother Horn and Mom in *Lady Day* (Chelsea Th. Ctr. of Brooklyn, Brooklyn Acad. of Music, Oct. 17, 1972); a Woman in a revival of *A Streetcar Named Desire* (Vivian Beaumont Th., Apr. 26, 1973; St. James, Oct. 4, 1973); replaced (1974) Minnie Gentry as the Nurse in *The Sunshine Boys* (Broadhurst, Dec. 20, 1972) and toured in the same role (Summer 1974); and was Mady in *God's Favorite* (Eugene O'Neill Th., Dec. 11, 1974).

Miss Le Noire is the founder (1973) and artistic director of Amas Repertory Theatre, an interracial theatre group that conducts workshops for performers and playwrights and produces plays, preferably new ones.

Television and Radio. She performed on the radio programs, 21st Precinct (CBS), Counterspy (CBS), and David Harding (CBS).

On television, she has appeared on The Nurses (CBS), The Doctors and the Nurses, Love of Life (CBS), Armstrong Circle Th. (NBC), Lamp Unto My Feet (CBS), as Emma in Search for Tomorrow (CBS), Mrs. Noah in *The Green Pastures* (Hallmark Hall of Fame, NBC), Mrs. Evans in The Reporter (ABC), played in A World Apart (ABC, 1969), in The Guiding Light (CBS, 1971–72), in Another World (NBC, 1971–73), in Legacy of Blood (ABC-TV, 1973), and was Mrs. Gordon in Calucci's Department (CBS, 1973). She has also made television commercials for Comet Cleanser, Canada Dry, Puffs Tissue, Ohio Bell Telephone, Nationwide Insurance, Imperial Margarine, New York Telephone, Children's T.V. Th., and other organizations.

Discography. Miss Le Noire is on a recording of *A Streetcar Named Desire* and has recorded educational materials for Holt, Rinehart & Winston and Guidance Associates.

Awards. For her performance as Queenie in *Show Boat,* she received the Dallas, Tex., Blue Bonnet Musical Award (1963).

Recreation. Weaving, word games, participating in the Catholic Actors St. Malachys Discussion Club.

LENTHALL, FRANKLYN. Director, actor, producer, coach, theatre owner. b. Samuel Franklyn Leinthall, Jr., July 14, 1919, Nanticoke, Pa., to Samuel Franklyn and Lena (Fraunfelter) Lenthall. Father, electrician; mother, welfare worker. Grad. Laketon H.S., Harvey's Lake, Pa., 1937; Wyoming Seminary, 1938; attended Cornell Univ., 1942–44; grad. AADA, 1946. Studied for the theatre in N.Y.C. with Frances Robinson Duff, two years, Katherine Tyndal Dryer, one year, Fanny Bradshaw, one year, Dr. Stein, Hunter Coll., one year. Served US Army 1942–45; rank, Tech. Sgt. Member of AEA; SAG. Address: c/o Boothbay Playhouse, Boothbay, ME 04537, tel. (207) 473.

Theatre. Mr. Lenthall first performed in a Laketon H.S. production of *Betty, the Girl of My Heart* (1935); and made his professional debut as Vane in *Easy Virtue* (Harvey's Lake Th., Alderson, Pa., 1937).

He appeared in stock as Owen Turner in *Light Up the Sky* (Weston Playhouse, Weston, Vt., Summer 1950); as Dr. Paul Stronberg in *Flow to the Meadow* and Sheriff Weeks in *Sun-Up* (Gateway Summer Th., Gatlinburg, Tenn., 1951); produced and directed a bill of three one-acts, *Finders Keepers, The Happy Journey,* and *A Pair of Lunatics* (Pilgrim Th., N.Y.C., Dec. 1951); presented and staged *Personal Appearance* (Gray Gables Th., Kitchman, N.Y., 1953); founded and produced the Lenthall Players, an off-Bway group, whom he directed in such works as *Trespass, Daphne Laureola, The Mousetrap, The Holly and the Ivy, Castle in the Air, Down Came a*

Blackbird, Papa Is All, Don't Listen Ladies, High Ground, Black Chiffon, The Sign of Jonah, Hay Fever, Sun-Up, and *Monique* (St. Paul and St. Andrew Methodist Church, 1956–58).

In 1957, he bought the Boothbay (Me.) Playhouse, a summer theatre, where he produced and directed plays, including *The Reluctant Debutante, Gayden, Simon and Laura, High Ground, Don't Listen Ladies, Castle in Air, The Chalk Garden, Down Came a Blackbird,* and *The Tender Trap* (1957); *Holiday for Lovers, The Mousetrap, The Curious Savage, A Palm Tree in a Rose Garden, Book of the Month, Oliver, Oliver, Monique, Summer of the 17th Doll,* and *Fair and Warmer* (1958); *Up in Mable's Room, Dear Delinquent, Toward Zero, Wild Goose Chase, Home at Seven, The Tunnel of Love, Epitaph for George Dillon, The Iron Duchess, The Potting Shed,* and *Personal Appearance* (1959).

During the 1960 season he produced and directed at the same Boothbay (Me.) Playhouse, *Fashion, Third Best Sport, Murder Mistaken, Howie, The Warm Peninsula, Trespass, Plaintiff in a Pretty Hat, Charade,* and *George Washington Slept Here;* the 1961 season, *Sound of Murder, The Pleasure of His Company, Tony Draws a Horse, Five Finger Exercise, Trial and Error, Invitation to a March, A Touch of Fear,* and *Present Laughter;* during the 1962 season, *The Man in the Dog Suit, Write Me a Murder, Paddle Your Own Canoe, Critic's Choice, The Bald Soprano, The Lesson, Everybody Loves Opal, Sailor Beware, A Clean Kill,* and *Relative Values;* and during the 1963 season, *Come Blow Your Horn, Miranda, Kill Two Birds, The Grass is Greener, The Aspern Papers, Fool's Paradise, We Must Kill Toni, A Shot in the Dark,* and *The Torch Bearers.*

During the 1964 season, *Under the Yum-Yum Tree, The Big Killing, Fumed Oak, The Browning Version, A Thousand Clowns, Hedda Gabler, The Irregular Verb To Love, The Private Ear/The Public Eye, Oh Dad, Poor Dad, Hay Fever;* the 1965 season, *Mary Mary, The Whole Truth, The Holly and the Ivy, Beekman Place, The Physicists, Lunch Hour, Still Life, Never Too Late, The Poker Session, Nude with Violin;* during the 1966 season, *Brighten the Corner, Dangerous Corner, Ready When You Are, C. B., The Cocktail Party, Absence of a Cello, The Dance of Death, Boeing-Boeing, The Birthday Party, Fallen Angels;* during the 1967 season, *Barefoot in the Park, An Inspector Calls, On Approval, Daphne Laureola, The Odd Couple, A Delicate Balance, The Circle, A Walk on the Water, The Showoff;* during the 1968 season, Black Comedy, White Lies, The Promise, Skylark, Cue for Passion, The Seagull, Charlie, The Party, Enchanted Night, The Scandalous Affair of Mr. Kettle and Mrs. Moon, Variation on a Theme, and *Don't Listen Ladies.*

During the fall of 1968, Mr. Lenthall, as artistic director, Maine State Touring Theatre, toured 7,000 miles in Maine, producing *Hedda Gabler* and *Don't Listen Ladies.* Returning to Boothbay, he presented during the 1969 season *Blithe Spirit, The Night of the Iguana, The First Mrs. Fraser, The Prime of Miss Jean Brodie, Exit the King, Take My Wife, Hotel Universe, Suite in Three Keys, A Song at Twilight, Shadows of the Evening, Come into the Garden Maude;* during the 1970 season, *George Washington Slept Here, Another Language, The Innocents, The Complaisant Lover, The Adding Machine, Roar Like a Dove, The Constant Wife, Ethan Frome, Private Lives;* during the 1971 season, *Plaza Suite, Time and the Conways, The Letter, Yes, My Darling Daughter, All Over, The Late George Apley, The Chinese Prime Minister, The Vinegar Tree, The Skin of Our Teeth;* during the 1972 season, *The Royal Family, Come as You Are, The Heiress, How the Other Half Loves, Rules of the Game, The Effect of Gamma Rays on Man-in-the-Moon Marigolds, An Ideal Husband, The Return of Peggy Atherton, Design for Living;* during the 1973 season, *Norman, Is That You?, The Fatal Weakness, The Vortex, The School for Wives, The Philanthropist, The Three Sisters, The Play's the Thing, The Summer of the 17th Doll,* and *Present Laughter.* .

Films. Mr. Lenthall appeared in *Carnegie Hall* (UA, 1947); *Kiss of Death* (20th-Fox, 1947); *Portrait of Jenny* (Selznick, 1948); *The Marrying Kind* (Col., 1952); *The West Point Story* (WB, 1950); and *Naked City* (U, 1948).

Other Activities. Mr. Lenthall is curator of The Theatre Museum, Boothbay, America's only theatre museum. He is a director of the Maine State Ballet and was a member of the Governor's Commission on the Arts and Humanities, Maine (May 1967–May 1973). He is an instructor-director at AADA; an instructor at Katharine Long School, Metropolitan Opera House, N.Y.C.; and a member of the advisory board, Drama League of New York.

Recreation. Collecting theatre memorabilia, swimming, hiking, reading.

LENYA, LOTTE. Actress, singer. b. Karoline Blamauer, Oct. 18, 1900, Vienna, Austria, to Franz and Johanna (Teuschl) Blamauer. Father, coachman; mother, laundress. High School education. Studied ballet, drama, Zurich, Switzerland, 1914–20. Married February, 1926 to Kurt Weill, composer (dec. 1950); married 1951 to George Davis (dec. 1957) married Nov. 2, 1962, to Russell Detwiler (dec.). Member of AEA; SAG. Address: 116 S. Mountain Rd., New City, NY 10956.

Theatre. Miss Lenya first appeared in productions of Shakespeare (Berlin, Germany, 1920–33), during which time she also played in *Oedipus* (Stadttheater, Berlin, 1929); subsequently appeared in *Little Mahagonny* (Baden-Baden Festival, 1927); alternated in the roles of Jenny and Lucy in *The Threepenny Opera* (Theater-am-Schiffbauerdamm, Berlin, 1928); played in *Danton's Death* and *The Awakening of Spring* (Volksbuehne Th., Berlin, 1930); *Pioneer in Ingolstadt* (Theater-am-Schiffbauerdamm, 1930); *The Rise and Fall of the City of Mahagonny* (Theater-am-Kurfuerstendamm, Berlin, 1931); *Song of Hoboken* (Volksbuehne Th., 1932); and Anna I in *The Seven Deadly Sins* (Th. des Champs-Elysées, Paris, France, 1933).

She made her N.Y.C. debut as Miriam in *The Eternal Road* (Manhattan Opera House, Jan. 7, 1937); subsequently played Cissie in *Candle in the Wind* (Shubert, Oct. 22, 1941); Duchess in *The Firebrand of Florence* (Alvin, Mar. 22, 1945); Xantippe in *Barefoot in Athens* (Martin Beck Th., Oct. 31, 1951); Jenny in *The Threepenny Opera* (Th. de Lys, Mar. 10, 1954); Anna I in *The Seven Deadly Sins* (NY City Ctr., Dec. 5, 1958); appeared in *Brecht on Brecht* (Th. de Lys, Jan. 3, 1962; Royal Court, London, Sept. 1962); played the title role in *Mother Courage and Her Children* (Ruhr Festival, Recklinghausen, W. Germany, June 12, 1965); and Fraulein Schneider in *Cabaret* (Broadhurst, N.Y.C., Nov. 20, 1966).

Films. Miss Lenya appeared in *The Threepenny Opera* (Ufa, 1930); *The Roman Spring of Mrs. Stone* (WB, 1960); *From Russia with Love* (UA, 1964); and *The Appointment* (MGM, 1969).

Television. Miss Lenya appeared on the Personal Report series (Educ., 1964), *Brecht on Shakespeare* (Camera Three, CBS, 1964); Aaron Copland series (Educ., 1965); played the title role in *Mother Courage and Her Children* (2nd TV Network, Mainz, W. Germany, 1965); *Interregnum (Between the Wars)* (Educ., 1966); played the Gypsy in *Ten Blocks on the Camino Real* (NET Playhouse, 1966); appeared on the Today show (NBC, 1966); in *The World of Kurt Weill* (NET Playhouse, 1967); and narrated the George Grosz special (Creative Person series, Educ., 1967).

Other Activities. She has appeared in concerts at Town Hall (N.Y.C., 1951); Brandeis Univ. (Boston, 1953); Lewisohn Stadium (N.Y.C., 1958); Carnegie Hall (1959, 1960); and in Munich and Berlin, Germany (1960). She wrote the foreword for *The Threepenny Opera* (1964).

Discography. Miss Lenya's recordings include *Lotte Lenya Sings Kurt Weill* (1955); *The Seven Deadly Sins* (1956); *The Rise and Fall of the City of Mahagonny* (1956); *Johnny Johnson* (1956); *September Song* (1957); *The Threepenny Opera* (1958); *The Stories of Kafka* (1958); *Happy End* (1960); and *Brecht on Brecht* (1962).

Awards. She received an Academy (Oscar) Award nomination for her performance in *The Roman Spring of Mrs. Stone* (1961).

LEONE, LEONARD. Educator. b. Sept. 12, 1914, Highland Park, Mich., to Leonard and Mary (Catino) Leone. Grad. Berkley (Mich.) H.S., 1933; Wayne State Univ., B.A. 1936, M.A. 1937; attended Univ. of Florence, Italy, 1936; Univ. of Wisconsin, 1940. Married July 15, 1938, to Bertha A. Leone; one son, one daughter. Relative in theatre: cousin, Maria Leone, opera singer. Member of ATA (chairman, Overseas Touring Committee, 1963–64); ISTR; ASTR; ANTA; AAUP; NCP; Michigan Sch. Board Assn.; Mich. Cultural Commission (chmn.); USO (entertainment comm.); Amer. Coll. Th. Festival Central Committee (chmn., 1973–to date). Address: (home) 2111 Edgewood Blvd., Berkley, MI 48072, tel. (313) LI 2-4270; (bus.) c/o University Theatre, Wayne State University, Detroit, MI 48202, tel. (313) 577-2966.

Since 1946, Mr. Leone has been professor of speech and director of the University Th. at Wayne State Univ., Detroit, Mich., where he has been a faculty member since 1945. He has directed or produced more than 150 productions, including the world premiere of the Jan Meyerowitz opera, *Eastward in Eden* (Bonstelle Playhouse, Detroit, Mich., 1951).

He established and designed the Wayne University Circular Th. (1946); restored the Bonstelle Playhouse, Detroit, Mich., for the active use of Wayne State University Th.; and organized the Wayne State University Children's Th. and an Adult Touring Th. (1951).

He directed a tour of Wayne State Univ. students to India for the US State Dept. and ANTA (1958); under the joint sponsorship of the USO and AETA, toured Italy and Germany with the Wayne State Univ. production of *Where's Charley? (1962); and established (1964) the Hilberry Classic Th. at Wayne State Univ., with a resident graduate company of fellowship actors who appear in 140 repertory performances each season.*

Published Works. Mr. Leone has contributed articles to *Players* Magazine (1950) and *The Overlander* (1958), and was Michigan editor for *Players* Magazine.

He wrote "New Directions II: A State University Resident Theatre. An Outline for Exploration and Discussion," *Humanities and the Theatre;* and "New Direction in Educational Theatre," *Michigan Yearbook* (1963).

Awards. He was recipient of the Italian American Society Certificate of Esteem (1959); received from Wayne State Univ. the Distinguished Professor Award, and the Alumni Faculty Service Award (1964); ATA Fellow (1971); and Gold Medal Award by the Mich. Academy of Arts & Sciences (1972).

Recreation. Photography.

LEONTOVICH, EUGENIE. Actress, director, playwright, dramatic coach. b. Eugenie Konstantin Leontovich, Mar. 21, 1900, Moscow, Russia, to Konstantin and Ann (Joukovsky) Leontovich. Grad. Moscow Art Th. Married 1916 to Paul A. Sokoloff (marr. dis. 1922); married 1923 to Gregory Ratoff (marr. dis. 1946). Member of AEA; SAG; AFTRA. Address: (home) 660 El Medio, Pacific Palisades, CA 90272; (bus.) 45 W. 81st St., New York, NY 10024, tel. (212) 362-9200, ext. 609.

Theatre. Miss Leontovich made her N.Y.C. debut in *Revue Russe* (Booth Th., Oct. 5, 1922); subsequently toured for several seasons as Bella Bruna in *Blossom Time,* played Mrs. Pepys in *And So to Bed,* Sarah Bernhardt in *Fires of Spring,* and Maria in *Candle Light* (Chicago, 1929), repeating the latter role in N.Y.C. (Riviera, Mar. 1930); appeared as Grusinskaya in *Grand Hotel* (Natl., Nov. 13, 1930), also touring in it (1931–32); Lilly Garland in *Twentieth Century* (Broadhurst, Dec. 29, 1932); and Novia in *Bitter Oleander* (Lyceum, Feb. 11, 1935).

Miss Leontovich made her London debut as the Grand Duchess Tatiana in *Tovarich* (Lyric, Apr. 24, 1935); played Cleopatra in *Antony and Cleopatra*

(New, Oct. 1936); Tatiana in a touring production of *Tovarich* (US, 1937–38); Natasha in *Dark Eyes*, which she wrote with Elena Miramova (Belasco, N.Y.C., Jan. 14, 1943); played Mrs. Pepys in *And So to Bed* (Royal Alexandra Th., Toronto, Can., 1945); Nadya in *Obsession* (Plymouth, N.Y.C., Oct. 1, 1946); Gen. Tanya in *Caviar to the General*, which she wrote with George S. George (New Lindsey, London, Eng., Jan. 13, 1947); founded The Stage Th. in Los Angeles, Calif. (1948), where she acted in and directed productions (1948–52); and directed and played Mrs. Esther Jock in *The Web and the Rock* (Las Palmas, Calif., Oct. 1952).

She founded (1953) the Leontovich Workshop in Los Angeles, where she has directed and coached professional actors.

Miss Leontovich appeared as the Empress in *Anastasia* (Lyceum, N.Y.C., Dec. 29, 1954); also touring the US and Australia in it (1956); directed *A Month in the Country* (Studebaker, Chicago, Nov. 1956); and played the Queen in *The Cave Dwellers* (Bijou, N.Y.C., Oct. 19, 1957), and toured in it (1959–60). In 1963, she was artist-in-residence at the Sch. of Drama in Chicago where she conducted master classes for actors, directed their production of *The Three Sisters* (Nov. 1963), and played the title role in *Mother Courage* (May 9, 1964).

Miss Leontovich wrote, directed, and starred in *Anna K* (Actors Playhouse, N.Y.C., May 7, 1972); and directed *Media and Jason*, which she also adapted from the Robinson Jeffers version of *Media* by Euripides (Little Th., Oct. 1, 1974).

In 1973, she founded the Eugenie Leontovich Workshop for actors in N.Y.C.

Films. She has appeared in *Four Sons* (20th-Fox, 1940); and *Rains of Ranchipur* (20th-Fox, 1955).

Television. She has appeared on US Steel Hour (CBS), Naked City (ABC), Climax! (CBS), and Playhouse 90 (CBS).

Published Works. She translated and adapted *Cafe de Danse* from the French (1929); adapted *The Laughing Woman* (1934); and wrote *Anna K* (Samuel French, 1973).

LERMAN, OMAR K. Arts administrator/consultant. b. Omar Khayyam Lerman, Apr. 10, 1927, Pittsburgh, Pa., to Meyer Lewis and Fanny (Hoffman) Lerman. Father, men's clothing merchandising manager. Grad. Taylor Allerdice H.S., Pittsburgh, 1944; Pennsylvania State Coll., B.A. 1948; Graduate Sch., 1949. Married Nov. 4, 1955, to Martha Thomas Smallwood (marr. dis. 1967); one son. Served USN 1955–56, rank CMCBB 3/c. Member of Council of Resident Stock Theatres (pres., 1957–64); the Players; Fdtn. for American Dance (past pres.). Address: Box 51, Corning, NY 14830, tel. (607) 936-4634.

Theatre. Mr. Lerman made his debut in *George Washington Slept Here* (YM-YWHA Playhouse, Pittsburgh, Pa., 1940); subsequently was actor, business manager, and designer with the Town and Nine Players (Pennsylvania State Coll., University Pk., 1948); designer for the Pittsburgh (Pa.) Children's Th. (1949); technician for the Allenberry Playhouse (Boiling Springs, Pa., 1949) and its technical director (1950); property man, later producer with Dorothy Chernuck, at the Arena Th. (Rochester, N.Y., 1950–56); and producer, with Miss Chernuck, of 115 productions at the Corning (N.Y.) Summer Th. (1953–to date).

At the Phoenix Th., Mr. Lerman was assistant to the business manager (1957), associate managing director (1957–62), and director of its NY state tour of *The Matchmaker* (1962). Mr. Lerman is consultant to the NY State Council on the Arts (1962); associate producer of the sound and light production, *The American Bell* (Independence Hall, Philadelphia, Pa., 1962–63); associate producer of *The Firebugs* (Maidman Playhouse, N.Y.C., Feb. 11, 1963); administrator of the Professional Touring Performing Arts Program of the NY State Council on the Arts (1963–64); co-owner of the Pocket Th. (N.Y.C.); co-producer of national tours (1963) of *The Sound of Music* and *My Fair Lady;* managing director, A.C.T. (San Francisco, 1964); managing director, American Ballet Theatre (1966–67); and general manager of the City Center Joffrey Ballet (N.Y.C., 1968–72).

Other Activities. Mr. Lerman has served as consultant to the Associated Council on the Arts (1964–70); and the NY State Parks and Recreation Dept. (1973); and currently advises the Institute for Outdoor Drama, the National Endowment for the Arts, and State Univ. of NY For the NY State Council on the Arts, he has been assistant director and director of arts programs (1972–73); and research director of bicentennial programs (1974–to date). He is on the board of directors of the Paper Bag Players (1970–to date).

He has served as an independent consultant for arts organizations including Alvin Ailey, Alwin Nikolais, Murray Louis, and the Amer. Orchestra for Contemporary Music.

LERNER, ALAN JAY. Lyricist, producer, playwright. b. Aug. 31, 1918, New York City, to Joseph J. and Edith A. (Lloyd) Lerner. Father, founder of Lerner Stores. Grad. Choate Sch., Wallingford, Conn., 1936; Harvard Univ., B.S. 1940. Member of Dramatists Guild (pres., 1960–to date); ALA; Screen Writers Guild; ASCAP; The Lambs; The Players; Sands Point Golf Club. 10 E. 40th St., New York, NY 10022, tel. (212) 679-2211.

Theatre. Mr. Lerner was lyricist and author, with Arthur Pierson, of the revue, *What's Up?* (National, N.Y.C., Nov. 11, 1943); subsequently wrote the book and lyrics for *The Day Before Spring* (National, Nov. 22, 1945); *Brigadoon* (Ziegfeld, Mar. 13, 1947); *Paint Your Wagon* (Shubert, Nov. 12, 1951); *My Fair Lady* (Mark Hellinger Th., Mar. 15, 1956); *Camelot*, which he also produced, with Frederick Loewe and Moss Hart (Majestic, Dec. 1, 1960); *On a Clear Day You Can See Forever* with Burton Lane which he also co-produced (Mark Hellinger Th., Oct. 17, 1965); *Coco* (with André Previn (Mark Hellinger Th., Dec. 18, 1969); and *Gigi* with Frederick Loewe (Uris Th., Nov. 13, 1973).

Films. Mr. Lerner wrote the screenplay for *An American in Paris* (MGM, 1951); screenplay and lyrics for *Royal Wedding* (MGM, 1951); adapted *Brigadoon* (MGM, 1954); wrote the screenplay and lyrics for *Gigi* (MGM, 1958); and adapted *My Fair Lady* (WB, 1964); wrote the screenplay and lyrics for *Camelot* (WB, 1968); *Paint Your Wagon* which he also produced (Par., 1969); *On a Clear Day You Can See Forever* which he also co-produced (Par., 1970); and *The Little Prince* with Frederick Loewe (Par., 1974).

Awards. Mr. Lerner received the NY Drama Critics' Circle Award (1947) for *Brigadoon;* Academy (Oscar) Award (1951) for best original screenplay for *An American in Paris*, NY Drama Critics' Circle Award, Antoinette Perry (Tony) Award and the Donaldson Award for *My Fair Lady* (1956); and the Academy (Oscar) Award for best screen adaptation and best lyrics for *Gigi* (1958).

Recreation. Sailing, swimming, golf.

LERNER, ROBERT. Producer. b. Robert Warren Lerner, May 10, 1921, New York City, to Joseph J. and Edith (Lloyd) Lerner. Father, merchant. Attended Choate Sch., Conn., 1930–38; Grad. Hun Sch., N.J., 1939; Harvard Univ., A.B. 1942; Loyola Coll., LL.B. 1948. Married 1941 to Rosalind Gray (dec. 1942); married 1946 to Jan Clayton (marr. dis. 1960); one son, two daughters; married 1964 to Theresa Justman. Served WW II, US Army; rank, S/Sgt. Relative in theatre: brother, Alan Jay Lerner, author, lyricist. Address: (home) Sierra Ventana 650, Mexico 10 R.F., Mexico tel. 520-14-63; (bus.) Calle America 173, Mexico 21, D.F., Mexico tel. 549-31-00.

Pre-Theatre. Attorney.

Theatre. Mr. Lerner produces American plays in Spanish in Mexico City, Mexico; Buenos Aires, Argentina; and Rio de Janeiro and Sao Paolo, Brazil. He first produced *My Fair Lady* (Palacio de Bellas Artes, Mexico City, 1959); followed by *Sweet Bird of Youth, On Borrowed Time, Remains To Be Seen* (Sullivan Th., 1960); *Toys in the Attic* (Sullivan Th., 1961); and *Brigadoon* (Teatro del Bosque, 1961). He produced *My Fair Lady* (Teatro Nacional, Buenos Aires, 1961); *Marriage Go Round, Write Me a Murder* and *A Funny Thing Happened on the Way to the Forum* (Teatro de los Insurgentes, Mexico City, 1962). He produced the Portuguese language version of *My Fair Lady* (Teatro Carlos Gomes, Rio de Janeiro, 1962 and Teatro Paramount, Sao Paolo, 1962); *Mary, Mary* (Teatro de los Insurgentes, Mexico City, 1964); a Coco-Cola Industrial Show tour in Mexico (1964); *Wait Until Dark* (Teatro de los Insurgentes, Mexico City, 1966); *Forty Carats* (Teatro Manolo Fábregas, 1969); *Promises, Promises* (Teatro Manolo Fábregas, 1971); *No, No, Nanette* (Teatro Monolo Fábregas, 1972); *Kismet* (Teatro Manolo Fábregas, 1973); and *Mame* (Teatro de los Insurgentes, 1973–74).

Mr. Lerner is also a concert impresario. He presented Maurice Chevalier (Palacio de Bellas Artes, 1968); Nana Mouskouri (Palacio de Bellas Artes, 1971–72); Rudolf Nureyev (Palacio de Bellas Artes, 1972); Laurindo Almedia (Palacio de Bellas Artes, 1974); American Ballet Theatre (Palacio de Bellas Artes, 1974); and Dance Theatre of Harlem (Palacio de Bellas Artes, 1974).

LeROY, KEN. Actor, dancer. b. Kenneth Vladimir Klopfenstein, Aug. 17, 1927, Detroit, Mich., to Russell and LoLetta LeRoy. Father, pianist; mother, wardrobe mistress. Grad. Professional Children's Sch., N.Y.C., 1945. Studied at Neighborhood Playhouse Sch. of the Th., N.Y.C., 1950–52. Married Jan. 11, 1949, to Virginia Le Roy; two sons. Served WW II, US Army FETO. Relative in theatre: sister, Gloria LeRoy, singer, dancer. Member of SAG; AEA; AGVA; AFTRA.

Theatre. Mr. LeRoy made his N.Y.C. debut as a walk-on in *The American Way* (NY City Ctr., Jan. 12, 1939). Billed as Kenneth LeRoy, he played Hymie (as a Boy) in *Morning Star* (Longacre, Apr. 16, 1940); a Page in *Anne of England* (St. James, Oct. 7, 1941); was a dancer and understudied the role of Will Parker in *Oklahoma!* (St. James, Mar. 31, 1943); played Steve in *Land of Fame* (Belasco, Sept. 21, 1943); danced in the musical, *The Firebrand of Florence* (Alvin, Mar. 22, 1945); took over the role of the Bad Boy in the ballet in *Carousel* (Majestic, Apr. 19, 1945); alternated with Roland Guerard as a sword dancer, in *Brigadoon*, in which he understudied the role of Harry Beaton (Ziegfeld, Mar. 13, 1947); and danced in *Call Me Madam* (Oct. 12, 1950).

He joined the cast of *Pal Joey* (Broadhurst, Jan. 3, 1952); understudied and later took over Jimmy Mitchell's role as Pete Billings in *Paint Your Wagon* (Shubert, Nov. 12, 1951); danced in and understudied Frank Derbas as the Worker in *The Pajama Game* (St. James, May 13, 1954), later succeeding him (May 1954); took over for Eddie Philips as Sohovik in *Damn Yankees* (Adelphi, May 5, 1955); and danced in and played the First Henchman in the pre-Bway tryout of *The Amazing Adele* (opened Shubert, Philadelphia, Pa., Dec. 26, 1955; closed Shubert, Boston, Mass., Jan. 21, 1956).

Billed as Ken LeRoy, he played Bernardo in *West Side Story* (Winter Garden, Sept. 27, 1957; Her Majesty's Th., London, Dec. 12, 1958); Meyer Buskin in *I Can Get It for You Wholesale* (Shubert, N.Y.C., Mar. 22, 1962; and The Kralahome in *The King and I* (NY City Ctr., June 12, 1963).

Films. Mr. LeRoy appeared in *Back Door to Heaven* (Par., 1939); and *The Pajama Game* (WB, 1957).

Television. He has appeared on the Milton Berle Show (NBC), the Martha Raye Show (NBC, 1953); The Defenders (CBS, 1964); and The Nurses (CBS, 1964).

Night Clubs. He has appeared at La Martinique (N.Y.C., 1946).

LE ROY, WARNER. Producer, actor, director, writer. b. Warner Lewis Le Roy, Mar. 5, 1935, Los Angeles, Calif., to Merwyn and Doris (Warner) Le Roy. Father, motion picture producer-director. Grad. Chadwick H.S., 1952; Stanford Univ., B.A. 1956. Married June 25, 1970, to Kay O'Reilly. Member of AEA; SDG; SSD&C. Address: (home) 1 W. 72nd St., New York, NY 10023, tel. (212) SU 7-3551; (bus.) 320 E. 65th St., New York, NY 10021, tel. (212) 628-0100.

Theatre. Mr. Le Roy was stage manager and appeared as a Soldier in *Small War on Murray Hill* (Ethel Barrymore Th., N.Y.C., Jan. 3, 1957); produced, with John C. Wilson, the double bill, *Garden District,* which included *Something Unspoken* and *Suddenly Last Summer* (York Playhouse, Jan. 7, 1958); produced the San Francisco Actors Workshop production of *Waiting for Godot* (York Playhouse, Aug. 15, 1958), which subsequently played at the Brussels (Belgium) World's Fair (1958); produced, with Norman Twain, and directed *The Golden Six* (York Playhouse, N.Y.C., Oct. 25, 1958); produced, with Paul Libin, and was writer-director of *Between Two Thieves* (York Playhouse, Feb. 11, 1960); produced, with Paul Libin and Bunker Jenkins, and directed *Shadow of Heroes* (York Playhouse, Dec. 5, 1961); directed the pre-Bway tour of *Tchin-Tchin;* directed with Peter Glenville, and David Merrick, in association with Mr. Le Roy, produced the Bway production of *Tchin-Tchin* (Plymouth, Oct. 25, 1962).

Other Activities. Mr. Le Roy is the creator of and one-half owner of Maxwell's Plum Restaurant (N.Y.C.); part owner of Tavern-on-the-Green Restaurant; and is president of Great Adventure, an amusement complex (N.J.).

LESSAC, ARTHUR. Educator. b. Sept. 10, 1910, Haifa, Palestine. Grad. James Madison H.S., Brooklyn, N.Y., 1928; NY Univ., B.A. (speech educ.) 1953; M.A. (voice and speech and clinical science) 1956. Professional training at Music School Settlement House, N.Y.C., 1929–31; clinical certification in speech and voice, American Speech and Hearing Assn., 1958; Grotowski's body training, La Mama Th., N.Y.C.; Alexander technique and Tai Chi Chuan, N.Y.C.; workshop in international stage movement, San Francisco State Coll. Married to Bertha B. Lessac; one son, one daughter. Member of ATA; SAES; SCA; ASHA; SUNY Theatre Assn. Address: Dept. of Theatre, SUNY, Binghamton, NY 13901, tel. (607) 798-2567.

Since 1970, Mr. Lessac has been professor at the State Univ. of New York, Binghamton. He was previously in charge of voice and speech at the Jewish Theological Seminary of America (1951–70), and director of the Lessac Institute for Voice and Speech (1953–70), both in N.Y.C.

He was director of the Voice and Speech Workshop (N.Y.C., 1940); a member of the faculty of the Bard Coll. Summer Th. (Allendale, N.Y., 1941); director of the National Academy of Vocal Arts (N.Y.C., 1944–48); a voice and speech lecturer for ANTA (1951–52); and taught and directed the voice, speech, and singing program in the training program of the Repertory Th. of Lincoln Ctr. (May 1962–Jan. 1964). Among the many workshops, seminars, and demonstrations conducted by Mr. Lessac since 1964 are Lessac Training Institutes for teachers at SUNY, Binghamton, and Southern Methodist Univ., Dallas, Tex. (both 1970) and for teachers and performers at Trinity Univ., San Antonio, Tex. (1971) and SUNY, Binghamton (1972, 1973).

Mr. Lessac was in charge of voice, speech, dialogue, and ensemble coordination for *Pins and Needles* (Labor Stage, Nov. 27, 1937); *From Vienna* (Music Box, June 20, 1939); and *Reunion in New York* (Little, Feb. 21, 1940); director of the verse chorus in *Sing Out, Sweet Land* (Intl., Dec. 27, 1944); and produced, staged, and appeared in stock productions at Green Acres Playhouse (Lake Huntington, N.Y., Summers 1932–46).

Television and Radio. He was casting director for G&W Television Products (N.Y.C., 1945–47), and he was co-author, co-producer, and director of *Chizzlecrimp, In the Land of Anything* (WATV, 1951).

Published Works. Mr. Lessac wrote *The Use and Training of the Human Voice* (1960; 2d ed. 1967), and his articles have appeared in such periodicals as *Quarterly Journal of Speech, Players,* and the NY *Times Sunday drama section.*

Recreation. Tennis, handball, walking, squash, carpentry, clay-modeling.

LESTER, EDWIN. Producer, theatre executive. b. 1895, Providence, R.I. Attended Classical H.S., Providence, R.I. Married to Gertrude Duffy, singer. Served WW I US Army. Member of Dramatists Guild. Address: (home) 911 N. Rexford Dr., Beverly Hills, CA tel. BR 2-1936; (bus.) c/o Music Center, Los Angeles, CA.

Theatre. Mr. Lester was a child singer and actor in New England; went on to become a pianist and musical conductor; was general sales manager of the Platt Music Co. (Los Angeles, 1923–33); an artists' manager, specializing in singers (1933–35); and in 1935, organized the Los Angeles Light Opera Festival.

Mr. Lester founded the San Francisco Civic Light Opera Assn. (1937), and the Los Angeles Civic Light Opera Assn. (1938), and served as managing dir. of both, until his resignation late in 1975 (effective after the 1976 season).

Through the 1975 season, the Los Angeles Civic Light Opera Assn. had presented 159 musicals, 88 of them produced by Mr. Lester, inc. world premiers of *Song of Norway* (1944), *Gypsy Lady* (1946), *Magdelena* (1948), *Kismet* (1953), the Mary Martin production of *Peter Pan* (1954), *At the Grand* (1958), *Zenda* (1963), *Dumas and Son!* (1967), and *Gigi* (1973), which, with Saint-Subber, Mr. Lester also produced in N.Y.C. (Uris, Nov. 13, 1973).

Mr. Lester produced a tour of *Candide* (opened Curran, San Francisco, July 6, 1971; closed Kennedy Ctr., Washington, D.C., Nov. 13, 1971).

Night Clubs. He was producer and director of entertainment and conducted the orchestra at the Cafe Frontenac, Detroit, Mich.

Other Activities. Formerly sales manager of Platt Music Co. and branches in southern California.

Awards. Mr. Lester received a Los Angeles Drama Critics Circle Award (1974–75).

LETTON, FRANCIS. Teacher, actor, director, playwright. b. Francis Miot Letton, Dec. 8, 1912, Columbia, S.C., to James Best and Annie Randolph (Miot) Letton. Father, owner of livery stable. Grad. Columbia H.S., 1930; Univ. of South Carolina, B.A., 1935; AADA, diploma 1943. Studied with Charles Jehlinger, 1941–43; Edward Goodman, 1941–43; Uta Hagen, 1949–51. Married Oct. 30, 1937, to Jeannette Dowling, playwright, actress; one son, one daughter. Relative in theatre: Sara Letton, actress. Member of AEA; AFTRA; ALA; DGA. From 1960 until his retirement in 1975, Mr. Letton was associate director of AADA (Amer. Acad. of Dramatic Arts), where he had taught since 1953 and directed nearly 50 productions. He formerly taught theatre subjects and directed productions at the Th. Sch. (N.Y.C., 1947–48).

Theatre. Mr. Letton made his acting debut as Marchbanks in *Candida* (Town Th., Columbia, S.C., 1930); appeared in stock productions with the Guild Th. (Stamford, Conn., 1943–44); made his N.Y.C. debut as the Third Senator in a Guild production of *Othello* (NY City Ctr., May 22, 1945); played Charlie Harris in *Strange Fruit* (Royale, Nov. 29, 1945); a Meddler in *Cyrano de Bergerac* (Alvin, Oct. 8, 1946); and Luka and Yat in the double-bill, *The Bear* and *The Wedding* (NY City Ctr., Feb. 5, 1948).

Mr. Letton appeared in the revue *Come What May* (Weidman Studio, 1948); played The Father in *The Troublemakers* (President, 1954); directed *Hotel Universe* (Jan Hus, 1957); appeared in stock productions at the Putnam County Playhouse (Mahopac, N.Y., Summer 1959); with Jeannette Letton wrote *The Young Elizabeth* (Cambridge Th., London, England, Dec. 9, 1951; New Th., London, Apr. 2, 1952; and Bermuda in a special performance, which he directed, for Queen Elizabeth II (Bermudiana, Hamilton, Nov., 1954); directed, wrote, and appeared in plays for the Th. Wing Community Plays.

Television and Radio. Mr. Letton performed on radio for *The Big Show* (NBC); on television, Producer's Showcase (NBC) and Studio One (CBS); with Jeannette Letton, wrote *A Queen's Way* (NBC, 1955) and *Hold My Hand and Run* (NBC, 1956).

Published Works. He wrote, with his wife, the novel *The Young Elizabeth* (1953); and *The Robsart Affair* (1956).

Recreation. Gardening, painting, football.

LEVENE, SAM. Actor. b. Samuel Levine, Aug. 28, 1905, Russ. to Harry and Bethsheba (Weiner). Father, cantor. Grad. Stuyvesant H.S., N.Y.C. 1923. Studied acting at AADA, 1925; with Charles Jehlinger, 1925–27. Married 1953 to Constance Lena Hoffman; one son. Member of AEA; SAG; AFTRA. Address: Hotel St. Moritz, Central Park South, New York, NY 10019.

Pre-Theatre. Garment industry.

Theatre. Mr. Levene made his N.Y.C. debut as William Thompson in *Wall Street* (Hudson Th., Apr. 20, 1927); subsequently played a walk-on in *Jarnegan* (Longacre, Sept. 24, 1928); the Telephone Trouble Hunter in *Tin Pan Alley* (Biltmore, Nov. 1, 1928); the Gunman in *Solitaire* (Waldorf, Mar. 12, 1929); and joined (May 1929) the company of *Street Scene* (Playhouse, Jan. 10, 1929).

He appeared as Isadore Lipwitz in *Headquarters* (Forrest, Dec. 4, 1929); Rosso in *This Man's Town* (Ritz, Mar. 10, 1930); took over (Oct. 1930) the role of Kaplan in *The Up and Up* (Biltmore, Sept. 8, 1930); played Cooper in *Three Times the Hour* (Avon, Aug. 25, 1931); Schwartz in *Wonder Boy* (Alvin, Oct. 23, 1931); Max Kane in *Dinner at Eight* (Music Box, Oct. 22, 1932); Busch in *Yellow Jack* (Martin Beck Th., Mar. 6, 1934); and succeeded (May 1934) Leo Donnelly as Gabby Sloan in *The Milky Way* (Cort, May 8, 1934).

Mr. Levene played Milton in *Spring Song* (Morosco, Oct. 1, 1934); Patsy in *Three Men on a Horse* (Playhouse, Jan. 30, 1935); Gordon Miller in *Room Service* (Cort, May 19, 1937); Officer Finkelstein in *Margin for Error* (Plymouth, Nov. 3, 1939); directed *The Big Story* (opened Maplewood Th., N.J., Sept. 30, 1940); with Samuel Spewak, staged *Out West It's Different* (opened McCarter, Princeton, N.J., Dec. 7, 1940; closed there Dec. 1940); and, in Los Angeles (Calif.), appeared in a program of Grand Guignol plays (Belasco, June 1943).

He appeared as Pvt. Dino Collucci in *A Sound of Hunting* (Lyceum, N.Y.C., Nov. 20, 1945); Sidney Black in *Light Up the Sky* (Royale, Nov. 18, 1948), in which he subsequently toured the Subway Circuit (Flatbush Th., Brooklyn, N.Y., June 28, 1949; Windsor Th., Bronx, July 5, 1949); and Nathan Detroit in *Guys and Dolls* (46 St. Th., N.Y.C., Nov. 24, 1950). He made his London debut in the same role (Coliseum, May 28, 1953); followed by the role of Horace Vandergelder in *The Matchmaker* (Haymarket, Nov. 4, 1954).

He played Fred Stanley and was director of *The Hot Corner* (John Golden Th., N.Y.C., Jan. 25, 1956); and appeared as Louis Winkler in *Fair Game* (Longacre, Nov. 2, 1957). He played the Manufacturer in *Middle of the Night* in a summer stock tour (commenced July 1958); Sid Gray in *Make a Million* (Playhouse, N.Y.C., Oct. 23, 1958); Boss Mangan in *Heartbreak House* (Billy Rose Th., Oct. 18, 1959); Odilon in *The Good Soup* (Plymouth, Mar. 2, 1960); Dr. Aldo Meyer in *The Devil's Advocate* (Billy Rose Th., Mar. 9, 1961); Morris Seidman in *Seidman and Son* (Belasco, Oct. 15, 1962); and Hymie, the Busboy, in *Cafe Crown* (Martin Beck Th., Apr. 17, 1964).

He played Philip Bummidge in *The Last Analysis* (Belasco, N.Y.C., Oct. 1964); Felix Krebs in *Fidelio* (Playhouse on the Mall, Paramus, N.J., July 20, 1965; and John Drew Th., East Hampton, N.Y., Aug. 2, 1965); Nathan Detroit in *Guys and Dolls* (Paper Mill Playhouse, Millburn, N.J., Nov. 23, 1965); the title role in *Nathan Weinstein, Mystic, Connecticut* (Brooks Atkinson Th., N.Y.C., Feb. 25, 1966); succeeded (Aug. 22, 1966) Alan King in the role of Dr. Jack Kingsley in *The Impossible Years* (Playhouse, Oct. 13, 1965); played Jack Hollender in *Don't Drink the Water* (tour, 1968–69); Patsy in *Three Men on a Horse* (Lyceum, N.Y.C., Oct. 16, 1969); Daniel Brand in *Paris Is Out* (Brooks Atkinson Th., Jan. 19, 1970); Sidney Black in *Light Up the Sky* (tour, Summer 1970); Aaron in *A Dream Out of Time* (Promenade, N.Y.C., Nov. 9, 1970); Al Lewis in *The Sunshine Boys* (Broadhurst Th., Dec. 20, 1970; and on tour, 1973–74); and appeared in a revival of *The Royal Family* (tour, Winter 1975).

Films. Mr. Levene made his debut in *Three Men on a Horse* (1st Natl., 1936); and subsequently appeared in *After the Thin Man* (MGM, 1936); *Yellow Jack* (MGM, 1938); *The Shopworn Angel* (MGM, 1938); *The Mad Miss Manton* (RKO, 1938); *Golden Boy* (Col., 1938); *Married Bachelor* (MGM, 1941); *Shadow of the Thin Man* (MGM, 1941); *Grand Central Murder* (MGM, 1942); *Sunday Punch* (MGM, 1942); *The Big Street* (RKO, 1942); *Destination Unknown* (U, 1942); *I Dood It* (MGM, 1943); *Whistling in Brooklyn* (MGM, 1943); *Gung Ho!* (U, 1943); *Action in the North Atlantic* (WB, 1943); *The Purple Hearth* (20th-Fox, 1944); *The Killers* (U, 1946); *Boomerang* (20th-Fox, 1947); *Brute Force* (U, 1947); *The Babe Ruth Story* (AA, 1948); *Dial 1119* (MGM, 1950); *Three Sailors and a Girl* (WB, 1953); *The Opposite Sex* (MGM, 1956); *Sweet Smell of Success* (UA, 1957); *Designing Woman* (MGM, 1957); *Kathy O* (U, 1958); *Slaughter on Tenth Avenue* (U, 1957) and co-authored the screenplay for *Three Days of the Condor* (Par., 1975).

Television. Mr. Levene has appeared in *Fearful Decision* (US Steel Hour, ABC, June 25, 1954); played Ben Selig in *The Mother Bit* (Studio One, CBS, 1954); appeared in *Mrs. McThing* (Omnibus, NBC, Mar. 9, 1958); played Mendele in *The World of Sholom Aleichem* (Play of the Week, WNTA, Dec. 14, 1959); performed in *The Playwright and the Star* (Studio One, CBS, April 1957, 1958); and appeared on The Untouchables (ABC, 1960); Aquanauts (1960); The Mike Douglas Show (Ind., 1965–66); and Bob Hope Presents (NBC, 1966).

LEVIN, HERMAN. Producer. b. Dec. 1, 1907, Philadelphia, Pa., to Abraham and Jennie (Goldfin) Levin. Father, merchant. Attended Univ. of Pennsylvania, 1926; Univ. of Missouri, 1926; Dickinson Sch. of Law, 1926; grad. St. John's Univ. Law Sch., 1935. Married 1943, to Evelyne Kraft (marr. dis. 1948); one daughter; married Apr. 16, 1956, to Dawn McInerney. Member of League of NY Theatres (pres., 1955–57, 1962–63).

Pre-Theatre. Attorney.

Theatre. Mr. Levin represented Joseph Daltry, who produced a season of Gilbert and Sullivan operettas in repertory, including *The Gondoliers, The Mikado, The Pirates of Penzance,* and *Trial by Jury* (44 St. Th., N.Y.C., Sept. 30, 1940); produced with Melvyn Douglas, *Call Me Mister* (Natl., Apr. 18, 1946); with Oliver Smith, *No Exit* (Biltmore, Nov. 26, 1946); with Paul Faigay and Oliver Smith, the pre-Bway tryout of *Bonanza Bound!* (opened Shubert, Philadelphia, Pa., Dec. 26, 1947; closed there Jan. 3, 1948); produced *Richard III* (Booth, N.Y.C., Feb. 8, 1949); produced with Oliver Smith *Gentlemen Prefer Blondes* (Ziegfeld, Dec. 8, 1949), also its national tour (opened Palace, Chicago, Ill., Sept. 20, 1951); *Bless You All* (Mark Hellinger Th., N.Y.C., Dec. 14, 1950); produced *My Fair Lady* (Mark Hellinger Th., Mar. 15, 1956; Drury Lane, London, Apr. 30, 1958), and its national tour (opened Rochester Masonic Aud., N.Y., Mar. 18, 1957); *The Girl Who Came to Supper* (Bway Th., Dec. 8, 1963); *The Great White Hope* (Alvin, Oct. 3, 1968; and national tour, 1969–70); *Lovely Ladies, Kind Gentlemen* (Majestic, N.Y.C., Dec. 28, 1970); and *Tricks* (Alvin, Jan. 8, 1972).

LEVIN, IRA. Playwright, writer. b. Aug. 27, 1929, New York City, to Charles and Beatrice (Schlansky) Levin. Father, toy importer. Grad. Horace Mann Sch., N.Y.C., 1946; attended Drake Univ., 1946–48; graduated New York Univ., A.B. 1950. Married Aug. 20, 1960, to Gabrielle Aronsohn (marr. dis. 1968); three sons. Served US Army, 1953–55, wrote training films; rank, PFC. Member of Dramatists Guild; Authors Guild; and ASCAP. Address: c/o William Morris Agency (Howard Rosenstone), 1350 Avenue of the Americas, New York, NY 10019, tel. (212) 586-5100.

Theatre. Mr. Levin's first assignment was playwright-adapter of the Mac Hyman novel *No Time for Sergeants* (Alvin Th., N.Y.C., Oct. 20, 1955; Her Majesty's, London, Aug. 23, 1956).

His first original play produced was *Interlock* (ANTA, Feb. 6, 1958); followed by *Critic's Choice* (Ethel Barrymore Th., Dec. 14, 1960); *General Seeger* (Lyceum, Feb. 28, 1962); *Drat! The Cat!* (book and lyrics; music by Milton Schafer; Martin Beck Th., Oct. 10, 1965); *Dr. Cook's Garden* (Belasco Th., Sept. 25, 1967); and *Veronica's Room* (Music Box Th., Oct. 25, 1973).

Television. Mr. Levin's first play *The Old Woman,* was produced on the Clock series (NBC, 1950); subsequently wrote for the Clock and Lights Out series (NBC) and US Steel Hour (CBS); his adaptation of *No Time for Sergeants* was produced on the US Steel Hour (CBS) and led to his assignment by Maurice Evans and Emmett Rogers to write the stage adaptation.

Published Works. Mr. Levin wrote the novels *A Kiss Before Dying* (1953); *Rosemary's Baby* (1967); *This Perfect Day* (1970); and *The Stepford Wives* (1972); and several magazine short stories.

Awards. He received the Edgar Allan Poe Award for a first mystery from The Mystery Writers of Amer. for *A Kiss Before Dying* (1953).

LEVIN, MEYER. Playwright, author. b. Oct. 7, 1905, Chicago, Ill., to Joseph and Golda Levin. Father, tailor. Grad. Univ. of Chicago, Ph.B. 1924. Married 1934 to Mable Schamp, chemist (marr. dis. 1944); one son; married Mar. 25, 1948, to Tereska Szware, writer; two sons, one daughter. Member of Dramatists Guild; ALA; SWG.

Theatre. Mr. Levin adapted his novel, *Compulsion,* into the play of the same title (Ambassador Th., N.Y.C., Oct. 24, 1957).

He was creator and director of the Relic House Marionette Th. (Chicago, 1927–28); played Katz in *If I Were You* (Ambassador, N.Y.C., Sept. 23, 1931); was general understudy in *Counsellor-at-Law* (Plymouth, Sept. 12, 1932); director of the Marionette Th. at the New Sch. for Social Research (1933); and director of the Brookfield Players (Brookfield Center, Conn., June–July 1933).

Films. He was a contract writer for Columbia Pictures (1940); wrote, produced, and directed films for the Office of War Information (1942–44); wrote the story and screenplay for *My Father's House,* which he also co-produced with Herbert Kline (World View Films Levin, 1937); and wrote, produced, and directed the story-documentary film, *The Illegals* (MAB, 1948). His novel and play, *Compulsion,* was made into a film (20th-Fox, 1959).

Published Works. He wrote *Reporter* (1929); *Frankie and Johnny* (1930); *Yehuda* (1931); *The Golden Mountain* (1932); *The New Bridge* (1933); *The Old Bunch* (1936); *Citizens* (1940); *If I Forget Thee* (1947); *My Father's House* (1947); *In Search* (1950); *Compulsion* (1956); *The Good Old Days; Comedy of Manners* (1950); *Eva* (1959); *The Fanatic* (1964); *The Stronghold* (1965); *The Story of Israel for Young People* (1966); *Gore and Igor* (Simon and Schuster, N.Y.C., 1968); and *The Settlers* (1972).

Recreation. Household design, rough carpentry.

LEVINE, DAVID ELIOT. Executive. b. June 22, 1933, New York City, to Harry L. and Esther (Hartman) LeVine. Father, art director. Grad. Harvard Coll. A.B. 1955; Columbia Law Sch., LLB 1960. Married Sept. 16, 1956, to Stephanie D. Reichman (marr. dis.); married Mar. 1, 1974, to Barbara Ann Grande. Served USN, 1955–57; communications officer. Member of International Theatre Institute (bd. of dir., U.S. Ctr.); Harvard Club.

Mr. LeVine is executive director of the Dramatists Guild (1966–to date); previously having served there as administrative assistant (1959–62); and assistant executive director (1962–66).

Recreation. Swimming, antique map collecting.

LEVINE, JOSEPH I. Producer, attorney. b. Oct. 17, 1926, Brooklyn, N.Y., to Louis and Dorothy (Schiffman) Levine. Father, attorney, accountant. Grad. City Coll. of New York, B.B.A. 1951; New York Law Sch., L.L.B. 1954. Married Apr. 4, 1954, to Johnna Bernstein, attorney; two daughters. Served WW II, USAAF, rank, PFC. Address: (home) 498 West End Ave., New York, NY 10024, tel. (212) TR 4-5445; (bus.) 11 W. 42nd St., New York, NY 10036, tel. (212) 564-4330.

Pre-Theatre. Law and accounting.

Theatre. Mr. Levine was production associate of *Goldilocks,* produced by Producers' Theatre (Lunt-Fontanne Th., N.Y.C., Oct. 11, 1958); associate producer of *J. B.,* an Alfred de Liagre, Jr., production (ANTA, Dec. 11, 1958); associate to producer Alexander H. Cohen for *At the Drop of a Hat* (John Golden Th., Oct. 8, 1959); an associate to producers Lewis Allen and Ben Edwards for *Big Fish, Little Fish* (ANTA, Mar. 15, 1961); co-produced with wife, Johnna Levine, *Bob & Ray, The Two and Only* (John Golden Th., Sept. 24, 1970); and is owner-director of a theatrical investment syndicate.

LEVITT, SAUL. Playwright, writer. b. Mar. 3, 1913, Hartford, Conn., to Max and Leah (Migdal) Levitt. Father, hatmaker. Grad. Morris H.S., Bronx, N.Y., 1931; attended City Coll. of New York, 1931–33. Married Oct. 8, 1949, to Dena Glanz, film editor; one son. Served WW II USAAF, ETO; rank, Sgr. Member of WGA; Dramatists Guild. Address: 320 Riverside Dr., New York, NY 10025, tel. (212) MO 3-6495.

Theatre. Mr. Levitt wrote *The Andersonville Trial* (Henry Miller's Th., N.Y.C., Dec. 29, 1959); which also toured (opened Center, Norfolk, Va., Sept. 28, 1960; closed Community Ctr., Hershey, Pa., Apr. 15, 1961); was presented at various regional theatres including the Arena (Washington, D.C.), Atlanta Repertory (Ga.) and Dallas (Tex.); and also had productions in England, France, Germany, Scandinavia, Hungary, Holland, Finland and Poland.

He adapted for the stage Daniel Berrigan's *Trial of the Catonsville Nine* (Phoenix Th., Good Shepherd-Faith Ch., Feb. 7, 1971). It was presented at the Mark Taper Forum (San Francisco, Calif.) as well as abroad.

Films. He wrote the screenplay for *Last Frontier* (Col., 1955); the story and original screenplay for *The Major and the Private* (Chrislaw); and wrote, with Larry Marcus, *Covenant with Death* (WB, 1967).

Television. Mr. Levitt has written for Danger (CBS, 1952–53); You Are There (CBS, 1953–54); Wide Wide World (NBC, 1955); Climax (CBS, 1957); Westinghouse Th. (CBS, 1960); and Judd for the Defense (ABC).

He has written several specials for television including *Dispossessed* (CBS, 1960); *Seaway* (CBS, 1966); *Shepherd Murder Case* (U, 1973); and *The Andersonville Trial* (PBS, 1971).

Published Works. Mr. Levitt is the author of the novel *The Sun Is Silent* (1951). He was a correspondent for the US Army weekly newspaper, *Yank* (1944–45); and has contributed short stories and articles to *Harper's Atlantic Monthly, American Mercury, The Nation* and *Fortune.*

Awards. Mr. Levitt was the winner of an Emmy Award for the best dramatic presentation for *The Andersonville Trial* (1971).

Recreation. Fishing.

LEWINE, RICHARD. Composer, producer. b. July 28, 1910, New York City, to Irving and Jane (Weinberg) Lewine. Grad. Franklin Sch., N.Y.C., 1927; attended Columbia Univ., N.Y.C., 1927–30. Married Sept. 23, 1945, to Mary Haas (dec. 1968); one son, one daughter; married Nov. 27, 1970, to Elizabeth Rivers. Served US Army Signal Corps. (1942–46); rank, Capt. Member of Dramatists Guild (vice-pres; member council, 1950–to date); ASCAP. Address: 352 E. 69th St., New York, NY 10021.

Theatre. Mr. Lewine's first assignment was composing music for the revue *Fools Rush In* (Playhouse, N.Y.C., Dec. 25, 1934); subsequently composed one interpolated song for the *Gus Edwards Show Window* (Bway Th., Apr. 12, 1936); the full score of *Naughty Naught 'OO* (American Music Hall, Jan. 23, 1937); *The Fireman's Flame* (American Music Hall, Oct. 9, 1937); and *The Girl from Wyoming* (American Music Hall, Oct. 29, 1938); contributed additional music to *'Tis of Thee* (Maxine Elliott's Th., Oct. 26, 1940); composed the score for *Make Mine Manhattan* (Broadhurst, Jan. 15, 1948); *The Girls Against the Boys* (Alvin, Nov. 1, 1959); and was co-producer of *Look to the Lilies* (Mar. 29, 1970).

Films. Mr. Lewine was co-producer and composer of a short subject film, *The Days of Wilfred Owen* (1964), narrated by Richard Burton.

Television. Mr. Lewine produced the Noel Coward-Mary Martin Show (CBS-TV, Oct. 22, 1955); was network executive producer for the Ringling Brothers Circus (Sarasota, Fla., 1956; Madison Sq. Garden, N.Y.C., 1957); and for CBS-TV produced *Blithe Spirit* (1956), *This Happy Breed* (1956), *Cinderella* (1957), *Junior Miss* (1957), *Aladdin* (1957); and *My Name is Barbra* (1964). He produced for ABC the Hootenanny series (1963–64); *Rodgers and Hart Today* (1966); *On the Flip Side* (1966); and *Pinocchio* (1968).

He was director of special programs for CBS (1957–61), and executive producer for Crescendo (1957); the New York Philharmonic Young People's Concerts with Leonard Bernstein (1957–61), *Wonderful Town* (1958), *The Hasty Heart* (1958), Victor Borge Show (1958), *Hamlet* (1959), *Christmas at the Circus* (1959), and *The Fabulous Fifties* (1960).

Published Works. He is the author, with Alfred Simon, of *Encyclopedia of Theatre Music* (1962); and, again with Mr. Simon, *Songs of the American Theater* (1973).

Awards. Mr. Lewine won Spoleto and Edinburgh awards for *The Days of Wilfred Owen* (1964). In addition he won Emmy and Screen Producers Guild awards for best program of 1964–65 for *My Name is Barbra.*

LEWIS, ABBY. Actress. b. Camelia Albon Lewis, Jan. 14, 1910, Mesilla Park, N.M., to Hunter and Edith (Weymouth) Lewis. Father, missionary; mother, teacher, newspaper correspondent. Grad. Las Cruces (N.M.) Union H.S., 1928; Gunston Hall, Washington, D.C., 1930; New Mexico State Univ., B.A. 1932. Studied voice with Mary Bennett, N.Y.C., 1936–68, and Rolf Gerard, N.Y.C., 1962–to date; acting with Wendell Phillips, N.Y.C., 1943; Tamara Daykerhanova N.Y.C., 1944; Lee and Paula Strasberg, N.Y.C., 1954–69; at the Amer. Th. Wing, N.Y.C., 1957; at Lee Strasberg Th. Inst., N.Y.C., under John Strasberg, 1969–70; audition coaching for musicals with David Craig, N.Y.C., 1964, 1965; Dorothea Freitag, N.Y.C., 1970–to date. Married Apr. 22, 1951, to John D. Seymour, actor. Member of AEA; AFTRA; SAG (on council, 1961–64); Actors' Fund of Amer. (life member); Episcopal Actors Guild; Zeta Tau Alpha; New Mexico State Univ. Alumni Assn.; Rio Grande Historical Collections (bd. of dir., 1972–to date). Address: 25 Minetta Lane, New York, NY 10012, tel. (212) AL 4-0485, (212) SU 7-5400.

Pre-Theatre. Taught at Hillsboro (N.M.) H.S. (1932–33).

Theatre. Miss Lewis made her debut in the title role of *Saint Joan* (Little, Las Cruces, N.M., 1930–32).

In summer productions at Naples, Me., she played Marguise de St. Maur in *Caste,* Celia in *As You Like It,* Nanine in *Camille,* Mrs. Slade in *Ten Nights in a Bar Room,* Sarah Evans in *Footsteps,* and Ophelia in *Uncle Tom's Cabin* (1933).

She appeared as an understudy and walk-on in the pre-Bway tryout of *Ruy Blas* (opened Pittsfield, Mass., Oct. 1933; closed Ford's, Baltimore, Md., Oct. 1933); and for Walter Hampden's Repertory Co., toured the US and Canada as a walk-on in *Richelieu,* the Player Queen in *Hamlet,* and Fleance in *Macbeth* (Fall 1933–Spring 1934).

At the Playhouse (Martha's Vineyard, Mass.) she appeared as Jane Moonlight in *Mrs. Moonlight,* Aunt Min in *Her Master's Voice,* Ellen in *The Devil Passes,* and Martha Temple in *Dark Tower* (Summer 1934); and rejoined Walter Hampden's company, playing the Duchess of York in *Richard III,* in addition to her roles in *Richelieu, Hamlet,* and *Macbeth* (Fall 1934).

Billed as Albon Lewis, she made her N.Y.C. debut at the 44 St. Th., as the Player Queen in Walter Hampden's *Hamlet* (Dec. 25, 1934), and also at this theatre, appeared in Mr. Hampden's Repertory productions of *Macbeth, Richelieu,* and *Richard III* (Dec. 1934–Jan. 1935).

She was stage manager for production at Martha's Vineyard, where she also played Mrs. Quimby in *Seven Keys to Baldpate,* and May in *Post Road* (Summer 1935); played Mrs. Jones in *First Stones* (Lennox Hill Playhouse, N.Y.C., Dec. 1935); and appeared as a Comedienne, a Precieuse, and understudied Eliza Connolly as a Nun and Mabel Moore as the Duenna in *Cyrano de Bergerac* (New Amsterdam, Apr. 27, 1936).

At the Cragsmoor (N.Y.) Summer Th., she appeared in *Springtime for Henry, The Pursuit of Happiness, There's Always Juliet, Petticoat Fever, Smilin' Thru, Outward Bound, The Curtain Rises, Goodbye Again,* and *Three Cornered Moon* (1936).

As Abby Lewis, she understudied five roles in *You Can't Take It with You,* later appearing as Alice, Essie, and the Russian Duchess in this production (Booth, N.Y.C., Dec. 14, 1936); also played the Russian Duchess in a N.Y.C. subway circuit tour (Spring 1939); and at the Cragsmoor Summer Th., appeared in *The Women, Susan and God, Our Town, Boy Meets Girl, The Pursuit of Happiness, Three Men on a Horse, What a Life, Kiss the Boys Goodbye,* and *The Drunkard* (1939).

She played Kathy in *Gallivantin' Lady* (Beekman Tower, N.Y.C., Spring 1940); the Second Witch, and the Gentlewoman in Maurice Evans' *Macbeth* (National, Nov. 11, 1941), also touring military camps in this production (1942); and was understudy and production assistant for *The Willow and I* (48 St. Th., Dec. 10, 1942).

Miss Lewis understudied Kim Hunter as Ruby Hawes, Kim Stanley as Anna Reeves, and Nan McFarland as Mrs. Reeves in *The Chase* (Playhouse, Apr. 15, 1952); was standby for Ann Todd as Davina Mars and understudied Luella Gear as Audrey Pender and Ludmilla Toretzka as Mademoiselle in *Four Winds* (Cort, Sept. 25, 1957); played Martha Robinson and was standby for Peggy Conklin as Edith Simms in *Howie* (46 St. Th., Sept. 17, 1958); appeared as the Wife in *Proposals in Geneva* (Lambs Club, Feb. 1960); Sally in *Martin Matthews' Miracle* (Cosmopolitan Hotel, Denver, Colo., May 1961); Charlotte Shaw in *Fig Leaf in Her Bonnet* (Gramercy Arts, N.Y.C., June 14, 1961); was standby for Dorothy Stickney as Katie Delaney and Ruth Donnelly as Isabel Flynn in *The Riot Act* (Cort, Mar. 7, 1963); was Margaret in a revival of *Life With Father* (NY City Ctr., Oct. 19, 1967); and Mrs. McIllehenny, in *70, Girls, 70* (Broadhurst, Apr. 15, 1971).

Films. Miss Lewis has appeared in *The Queen Was in the Kitchen* (Dumont, 1945); *The Sleeping Beauty* and *The Three Wishes* (Haig Manoogian, 1947–48); *Journey to Reality, Geneva Convention, Charity* and *The Challenge* (US Army, Home Nursing Series, 1950–64); and appeared in 12 films for the Amer. Medical Assn. (1952–54).

She has also appeared in *Patterns* (UA, 1956); *Story of the America's Cup* (1958); *The Young Doctors* (UA, 1961); *Pleasure Island* (Vision Associates, 1962); *The Miracle Worker* (UA, 1962); *The Colonial Naturalist* (Williamsburg, Va., 1964); two Guideposts Films — *Love Story* (1967) and *Nets That Catch the Wind* (1968); *Brimstone, The Amish Horse* (1967); and in *It Can Happen to You* (National Rifle Assn., 1973).

Her voice was used in the sound track of the English dubbing for *Anna* (Italian Film Export, 1953); *Puccini* (Casolaro Films, 1958); *The Cranes Are Flying* (WB, 1959); and *Ballad of a Soldier* (Kingsley, 1960); and for "Sound and Light," Boscobel, Garrison, N.Y. (1964) and Independence Hall, Philadelphia, Pa. (1970).

Television and Radio. Since 1940, she has performed on the following radio programs: The Clock (ABC), Cavalcade of America (CBS), Young Widder Brown (NBC), Great Plays (NBC), Arthur Hopkins Presents (NBC), Big Town (CBS), Portia Faces Life (NBC), Famous Jury Trials (CBS), Suspense (CBS), Gangbusters (CBS), 21st Precinct (CBS), Road of Life (NBC), The Greatest Story Ever Told (NBC), Mr. Ace and Jane (CBS), School of the Air (CBS), Mystery Th. (CBS), Mr. Keen (CBS, NBC), Hearthstone of the Death Squad (CBS), David Harum (NBC), Our Gal Sunday (CBS), Helen Trent (CBS), Back Stage Wife (NBC), Just Plain Bill (NBC), Amanda of Honeymoon Hill (CBS), Valiant Lady (CBS), Front Page Farrell (NBC), Superman (WOR), Second Mrs. Burton (CBS), Nick Carter (WOR), Lorenzo Jones (NBC) and Mr. Chamelion (CBS), 21st Precinct (CBS), Hotel for Pets (NBC), and Theatre 5 (ABC).

For television, she played Helen Hayes in *An Impression of Helen Hayes* (NBC, 1940); was Mrs. Garrett in The Brighter Day (CBS, 1954); Miss Harley in Valiant Lady (CBS, 1955); Aunt Ella in Another World (NBC, 1965); Mary Jackson in As the World Turns (CBS, 1965–67); Dora in *Dr. Cook's Garden* (ABC Movie of the Week, 1970); and in *We, The Women* (American Parade, 1974). She has also appeared on The Doctors (NBC, 1963, 1966), Secret Storm (CBS, 1968, 1972), Love Is a Many Splendored Thing (CBS, 1969, 1971), and on the Ed Sullivan Show (CBS), Perry Como Show (NBC), The Defenders (CBS), US Steel Hour (CBS), Kraft Television Th. (NBC), I Remember Mama (CBS), True Story (NBC), Robert Montgomery Presents (NBC), Sgt. Bilko (CBS), the Jackie Gleason Show (CBS), and Brillo's Star Tonight (ABC).

Since 1953, Miss Lewis has also appeared in commercials.

Awards. Miss Lewis received the Distinguished Alumna Award (1964) of the New Mexico State Univ. Alumni Assn. She and her husband, John D. Seymour, were honored by the Lambs (July 10, 1973) for their devotion "to each other and to the theatre.".

Recreation. Swimming, theatre-going, creating and building with her husband such television game shows as "Whatsit" (for children) and "See the Sound.".

LEWIS, ALLAN. Educator, director, critic. b. Albert Ehrlich Lewis, June 30, 1908, New York City, to Barnett and Rebecca (Ehrlich) Lewis. Father, cigar maker. Grad. City Coll. of New York, A.B. 1927; attended New Sch. for Social Research, 1928–32; grad. Columbia Univ., A.M. 1929; attended Columbia Univ. and Univ. of Southern California, 1938–39; grad. Stanford Univ., Ph.D. 1943; Natl. Univ. of Mexico, D.Litt. 1954. Married June 15, 1934, to Matilda Ross (marr. dis. 1941); one daughter; married June 22, 1944, to Brooke Waring; one daughter. Served USAAF and Air Force Transport Command, CBI 1942–45; rank, 1st Lt. Member of AAUP; ATA; ANTA; New Dramatists Committee; Intl. Assoc. of Univ. Prof. of English; American Shakespeare Society. Address: (home) 4 Elwil Dr., Westport, CT 06880, tel. (203) 227-2462; (bus.) Shakespeare Institute, Univ. of Bridgeport, Bridgeport, CT 06602, tel. (203) 576-4214.

Since 1961 Mr. Lewis has been professor of Comparative Drama at the New Sch. for Social Research; and since 1965 Dir. of the Shakespeare Institute and Littlefield Professor of Shakespearean Studies at the Univ. of Bridgeport, Conn.

He was executive director of the New Dramatists Committee (1960–61); and since 1963, has been drama critic for the *New Haven Conn. Register.*

He taught English and drama in the N.Y.C. public schools (1927–36); was instructor of English at Compton Jr. Coll. (1937–38); at Stanford Univ. and Menlo Jr. Coll. (1940–42); and lectured on the history of drama at the Actors Laboratory Th. (Hollywood, Calif., 1946–47).

In 1948, he became chairman of the Drama Dept. at Bennington Coll.; in 1950, he became professor of Theatre History and director of the Univ. Th. and the Student Th. and at the Natl. Univ. of Mexico; in 1958, he joined the faculty at Briarcliff Coll. to teach English and Drama.

Dr. Lewis made his acting debut in Juvenile roles in stock productions of *Hay Fever, Cradle Snatchers,* and *Andorcles and the Lion* (Woodstock Th., N.Y., Summer 1929); subsequently appeared in Maya (Studio des Champs Elysées, Paris, Fr., 1932); in character roles in *Nathan the Wise, The Baker's Daughter, Home of the Brave,* and *Prometheus* (Actors Lab. Th., Hollywood, Calif., 1939–40; 1945–48); at the Players Th. and the Baker Workshop (Mexico City, 1950–58), he played Undershaft in *Major Barbara,* Captain Boyle in *Juno and the Paycock,* the title role in *Uncle Vanya,* the Narrator in *Six Characters in Search of an Author,* and Wang in *The Good Woman of Setzuan;* at the Baker Workshop (1955–57), he directed *A Sunny Morning, The Boor, The Toy Shop,* and *Major Barbara;* and at the University Th. (1956–58), directed *Bury the Dead, Volpone, Juno and the Paycock, Las Manos de Dios,* and others.

Films. He played the Sheriff in *Comanche* (UA, 1956); and appeared in *Sierra Baron* (20th-Fox, 1958). He also did voice dubbing, Spanish into English, and narrations for the Lerner Studios (Mexico City, 1955–57).

He has written eight film scripts, including *Canasta,* based on the short stories of B. Traven (Joe Kohn Prod., Mexico, 1957), and *The Tigress* (Mauricio de la Serna Prod., Mexico, 1958).

Television and Radio. In 1938–40, Mr. Lewis was program director for Keystone Broadcasting System (Chicago, Ill.). He was moderator of Under Discussion (Th. Today) (WNEW, N.Y.C., Sept. 1963); panelist on Books for our Time (WNDT, N.Y.C., Oct. 1963); wrote, directed, and narrated *The Green Room* (NBC, Aug. 1964), appeared on a special NBC Shakespeare program and panel discussion on the theatre (PBS, N.Y.C.); and has performed in commercials.

Published Works. Dr. Lewis wrote *El Teatro Moderno* (1955); *El Teatro* (1957); *The Contemporary Theatre* (1962); *The American Theatre To-day* (1965); and *Ionesco* (1973). He translated Raul F. Guerreco's *Five Mexican Painters* (1957).

His articles have appeared in *Contemporary Review, Texas Quarterly, The Nation, Cuadernos Americanos, Filosofia y Letras, College English, Educational Forum, Educational Theatre Journal, Contemporary Review, School and Society, Queen's Quarterly,* and *The Guardian.*

LEWIS, EMORY. Editor, writer, drama critic. b. Emory Charles Lewis, Mar. 15, 1919, Chincoteague Island, Va. to Nelson Emory and Elodie (Cherrix) Lewis. Father, oyster dealer. Grad. Chincoteague H.S., 1935; Coll. of Wm. and Mary, Va., B.A. 1939. Married 1940 to Edith Harris, writer (marr. dis. 1946); married June 1, 1957, to Lila Vigil, actress, photographer; one daughter. Served with US Army, 1944–45; awarded Bronze Star. Member of NY Drama Critics Circle; The Drama Desk (pres., 1960–62); Municipal Art Soc. (bd. of dir.). Address: 360 W. 22nd St., New York, NY 10011, tel. (212) AL 5-3715.

Mr. Lewis was an editor on *Newsweek* (1942–43); joined *Cue Magazine* as an editor (1946); and became its editor-in-chief and drama critic (1957–68). Since 1969, he has been the theater critic for *The Record,* a daily newspaper published in Hackensack, N.J.

Published Works. He has written *Cue's New York: A Leisurely Guide to Manhattan* (1963), *Stages: The fifty-year childhood of the American theatre* (1969), and articles in several publications.

Recreation. Exploring Manhattan, clamming, languages, bird-watching.

LEWIS, ROBERT. Director, actor, producer, writer, educator. b. Mar. 16, 1909, New York City, to Benjamin and Sadie (Boss) Lewis. Father, jeweler. Grad. Boys H.S., Brooklyn, N.Y.; attended City Coll. of New York; Juilliard Sch. of Music. Member of SSD&C. Address: (home) Cross River Rd., Katonah, NY 10536, tel. (212) CE 2-4009; (bus.) 25 Tudor City Pl., New York, NY 10017, tel. (212) TN 7-1682.

Theatre. Mr. Lewis made his first N.Y.C. appearance with the Civic Repertory Th. *The Would-Be Gentleman* (Sept. 21, 1929); subsequently for this company played a Redskin in *Peter Pan* (Nov. 2, 1929), a Waiter in *A Private Room in a Restaurant,* and a Doctor in *The Living Corpse* (Dec. 6, 1929), the Second Watchman, and Gregory, Servant to Capulet, in *Romeo and Juliet* (Apr. 21, 1930), and Capraro in *Gods of Lightning* (Provincetown Playhouse, Feb. 18, 1931); and Alf in *The House of Connelly* (Martin Beck Th., Sept. 28, 1931).

With the Group Th. Company, he appeared in *1931* (Mansfield, Dec. 10, 1931); as an Indian Slave in *Night Over Taos* (48 St. Th., Mar. 9, 1932); as Dr. Otis (Shorty) in *Men in White* (Broadhurst, Sept. 26, 1933); as Roxy Gottlieb in a Group Th. production of *Golden Boy* (Belasco, Nov. 4, 1937); and made his London debut in this role (St. James's, June 21, 1938).

He directed the national tour of *Golden Boy* (opened Chicago, Ill., 1938); *My Heart's in the Highlands* (Guild, N.Y.C., Apr. 13, 1939); *Heavenly Express* (Natl., Apr. 18, 1940); *Five Alarm Waltz* (Playhouse, Mar. 13, 1941); *Mexican Mural,* which he also produced (Chanin's Apr. 26, 1942); *Noah* (Actors Lab. Th., Los Angeles, Calif., 1945); *Land's End* (Playhouse, N.Y.C., Dec. 11, 1946); *Brigadoon* (Ziegfeld, Mar. 13, 1947); His Majesty's, London, Apr. 14, 1949); the opera *Regina* (46 St. Th., N.Y.C., Oct. 31, 1949; NY City Ctr., 1953); *The Happy Time* (Plymouth, Jan. 24, 1950), and its national tour (opened Cass, Detroit, Mich., Oct. 22, 1951; closed Blackstone, Chicago, Ill., Jan. 1, 1952).

Mr. Lewis directed *An Enemy of the People* (Broadhurst, N.Y.C., Dec. 28, 1950); *The Grass Harp* (Martin Beck Th., Mar. 27, 1952); *The Teahouse of the August Moon* (Martin Beck Th., Oct. 15, 1953); Her Majesty's, London, Apr. 22, 1954); *Witness for the Prosecution* (Henry Miller's Th., N.Y.C., Dec. 16, 1954); the pre-Bway tryout of *Reuben Reuben* (opened Shubert, Boston, Mass., Oct. 10, 1955; closed there Oct. 22, 1955); *Mister Johnson,* which he also produced with Cheryl Crawford, (Martin Beck Th., N.Y.C., Mar. 29, 1956); and the national tour of *The Teahouse of the August Moon* (opened Colonial, Boston, Apr. 2, 1956; closed National, Washington, D.C., July 7, 1956).

He directed *The Hidden River* (Playhouse, N.Y.C., Jan. 23, 1957); *Jamaica* (Imperial, Oct. 31, 1957); *A Handful of Fire* (Martin Beck Th., Oct. 1, 1958); *Candide* (Saville, London, Apr. 30, 1959); *Chéri,* which he produced with The Play Wrights' Co. (Morosco, N.Y.C., Oct. 12, 1959); the pre-Bway tryout of *Juniper and the Pagans* (opened Colonial, Boston, Dec. 10, 1959; closed Forrest, Philadelphia, Pa., Dec. 26, 1959); *Kwamina* (54 St. Th., N.Y.C., Oct. 23, 1961); *Foxy* (Ziegfeld, Feb. 16, 1964); and *Traveller without Luggage* (ANTA, Sept. 17, 1964); *On a Clear Day, You Can See Forever* (Mark Hellinger Th., Oct. 17, 1965); *Crimes and Crimes* (Yale Repertory Th., New Haven, Conn., Jan. 8, 1970); a double-bill of *The Lover* and *The Connection* (Center Stage, Baltimore, Md., Feb. 5, 1971); and *The Sea Gull* (Center Stage, Nov. 28, 1971).

Films. Mr. Lewis made his debut in *Tonight We Raid Calais* (20th-Fox, 1943); followed by *Dragon Seed* (MGM, 1944); *Son of Lassie* (MGM, 1945); *Ziegfeld Follies* (MGM, 1946); and *Monsieur Verdoux* (UA, 1947). He directed *The Tender Trap* (MGM, 1955); and *Anything Goes* (Par., 1956).

Television. He has appeared on *Excursion, 1953* (Ford Foundation, CBS, 1953); One Minute Please (1954); and the Jack Paar Show (NBC, 1961).

Other Activities. He was professor in the dept. of drama at Sarah Lawrence Coll. (Bronxville, N.Y., 1936–37); director of the Group Th. Studio (1938); professor in the Yale Univ. Sch. of Drama (1942, 1948); co-founder of the Actors Studio (1947); director of the Robert Lewis Th. Workshop (1952); director and teacher for the Lincoln Ctr. Repertory Co. Training Program (1962); and lectured at a theatre symposium, Univ. of Minnesota (1963).

Published Works. Mr. Lewis wrote *Method or Madness* (1958).

Awards. He received the NY Drama Critics' Circle Award for his direction of *The Teahouse of the August Moon* (1954).

LIBIN, PAUL. Producer, theatre operator. b. Dec. 12, 1930, Chicago, Ill., to Ely and Clara Libin. Father, manufacturer. Grad. Von Stuben H.S., Chicago, Ill., 1949; attended Univ. of Illinois, 1949–51; grad. Columbia Univ., B.F.A. 1955. Married Sept. 28, 1956, to Florence Rowe; one son, two daughters. Served US Army, 1953–55. Member of League of Off-Broadway Theatres and Producers (pres., 1959–74); Illinois Center Advisory Board (member-director, 1974). Address: Circle in the Square, 1633 Broadway, New York, NY 10019, tel. (212) 581-3270.

Theatre. Mr. Libin has operated the Martinique Th., N.Y.C., since 1958.

He presented, with Ward Baker, Mouzon Law and Franchot Productions, *The Crucible* (Martinique, Mar. 11, 1958); produced *Time of Vengeance* (York Playhouse, Dec. 10, 1959); produced, with Warner Le Roy, *Between Two Thieves* (York Playhouse, Feb. 11, 1960); with Warner Le Roy and Bunker Jenkins, *Shadow of Heroes* (York Playhouse, Dec. 5, 1961); with Claire Nichtern, *The Banker's Daughter* (Jan Hus House, Jan. 21, 1962); and with the Round Table Review, in association with Madeline Lee, a double-bill, consisting of *A Portrait of the Artist as a Young Man* and *The Barroom Monks* (Martinique, May 28, 1962). On Bway, he has produced *The Zulu and the Zayda, Morning, Noon, and Night, Hughie,* and *The Royal Hunt of the Sun.*

From 1963–to date, as managing director of Circle in the Square, he has produced, with Theodore Mann, such productions as *Six Characters in Search of an Author* (Circle in the Square, 1963); *Baal* (Martinique, 1965); and the following plays, all presented at Circle in the Square: *The White Devil* (1965), *Six from La Mama* (1966), *Eh?* (1966), *Little Murders* (1969), and *The White House Murder Case* (1969). At the Circle in the Square-Joseph E. Levine Th., he has presented, in association with Theodore Mann, *Mourning Becomes Electra* (1972); *Medea, Here Are Ladies, Uncle Vanya, Waltz of the Toreadors,* and *The Iceman Cometh* (all 1973); and *An American Millionaire, Scapino, The National Health,* and *Where's Charley?* (all 1974).

During his career, he has produced or managed over 125 Bway and off-Bway plays.

Other Activities. Mr. Libin has served as U.S. representative of the J. C. Williamson Theatres Limited (Australia) (1972–to date).

LIEBMAN, MAX. Producer, director, author. b. Aug. 5, 1902, to Harold and Sarah (Glazer) Liebman. Father, businessman. Attended Boys H.S., Brooklyn, N.Y. Married Aug. 17, 1935 to Sonia Veskova. Served USO. Member of ASCAP, Dramatists Guild, ALA. Address: (home) 27 E. 65th St., New York, NY 10021; (bus.) 130 W. 56th St., New York, NY 10019, tel. (212) PL 7-6533.

Pre-Theatre. Sketch writer, social director at summer camp.

Theatre. Mr. Liebman was first author, with Allen Boretz, of *Off to Buffalo* (Ethel Barrymore Th., N.Y.C., Feb. 21, 1939); subsequently contributed material to *Crazy with the Heat* (44th St. Th., Jan. 14, 1941); and *Let's Face It* (Imperial, Oct. 29, 1941); produced *Autumn Hill* (Booth, Apr. 13, 1942); was civilian director and sketch writer for USO camp shows (1943–44); and wrote, directed, and produced the tour of *Tars and Spars* for the US Coast Guard (1945).

With Joseph Kipness, he was producer of the pre-Bway tryout of *Shootin' Star* (opened Shubert, New Haven, Conn., Apr. 4, 1946; closed Shubert, Boston, Mass., Apr. 27, 1946); contributed material and directed sketches of *Make Mine Manhattan* (Broadhurst, N.Y.C., Jan. 15, 1948); contributed songs and material to *Along Fifth Avenue* (Broadhurst, Jan. 13, 1949); and *Tickets, Please* (Coronet, Apr. 27, 1950); and was producer, with Bernard Sahlins, Howard Alk, and Paul Sills, of *From the Second City* (Royale, Sept. 26, 1961).

Films. Mr. Liebman was writer and composer for *Up in Arms* (RKO, 1941), and *The Kid from Brooklyn* (RKO, 1946).

Television. He produced and directed Your Show of Shows (NBC, 1949–54); Bob Hope's television debut (Apr. 1950); and the Elgin-American's Thanksgiving Day Show (Nov. 1950); produced and directed various spectaculars (NBC, 1954–56), including *Ten from Your Show of Shows;* and special programs for the US Steel Hour (NBC, 1959–60).

Published Works. Mr. Liebman's articles on television have appeared in *Esquire, Hollywood Reporter, Variety,* and other publications.

Awards. For his production, Your Show of Shows, Mr. Liebman won the *Variety* showmanship citation (1950); the annual *Look* Magazine Awards (1951–52); the NATAS (Emmy) Award for the best variety show (1952); the Michaels Award of the Television Academy of Arts and Sciences for the year's best musical program (1952); an award from NBC for "bringing new talents and original methods to the field of television"; the *Motion Picture Daily* Award; and the Sylvania Award as the best TV producer. In 1953, he received the *Look* Magazine Award for "the individual who best organized and most creatively presented a TV series and who most effectively utilized the skills of actors and technicians in TV presentations.".

LIFF, SAMUEL. Talent representative, director, producer, stage manager. b. Apr. 14, 1919, Boston, Mass., to Morris and Rose (Rabinowitz) Liff. Father, restaurateur. Grad. Brookline (Mass.) H.S., 1937, Carnegie Inst. of Tech., B.F.A. 1941. Married May 15, 1947, to Arlene Friedrich, actress. Served with US Army, Signal Corps, 1941–46; rank, Capt. Member of AEA; IATSE, The Players.

Theatre. Mr. Liff was stage manager at the Playhouse (Nantucket, Mass., June 1940); subsequently stage manager at Bucks County Playhouse (New Hope, Pa., Summer 1941); at the Tamiment (Pa.) Playhouse (Summer 1946); of the national company of *Call Me Mister* (1946–47).

His first N.Y.C. assignment was assistant stage manager for *Strange Bedfellows* (Morosco Th., Jan 14, 1948); followed by *Along Fifth Avenue* (Broadhurst, Jan. 13, 1949); stage manager for Tamiment (Pa.) Playhouse (Summer 1949); *Gentlemen Prefer Blondes* (Ziegfeld, N.Y.C., Dec. 8, 1949); production stage manager for *Nina* (Royale, Dec. 5, 1951), and *Dear Barbarians* (Royale, Feb. 21, 1952); directed *Gentlemen Prefer Blondes* (tour, Jamaica and Brighton, L.I., 1952).

Mr. Liff was stage manager for *My Darlin' Aida* (Winter Garden, N.Y.C., Oct. 27, 1952); production stage manager of *Night in Venice* (Jones Beach Marine Th., N.Y., 1952), which he staged at the same theatre (1953).

He was production stage manager of *The Little Hut* (Coronet, N.Y.C., Oct. 7, 1953); *By the Beautiful Sea* (Majestic, Apr. 8, 1954); and *Lunatics and Lovers* (Broadhurst, Dec. 13, 1954), and director of the West Coast company (Carthay Circle Th., Los Angeles, Calif., Aug. 15, 1955); and was production stage manager of *The Matchmaker* (Royale, N.Y.C., Dec. 5, 1955).

He was production stage manager of *My Fair Lady* (Mark Hellinger Th., Mar. 15, 1956), and assisted Moss Hart as director of the national company (Masonic Aud., Rochester, N.Y., Mar. 18, 1957), was assistant director for the London production (Drury Lane, Apr. 30, 1958), directed the touring companies for Australia (Jan. 24, 1960), USSR (Apr. 4, 1961); a US touring company (Jan. 21, 1963), and the Tel Aviv production (Habimah Th., Israel, Feb. 1, 1964).

Mr. Liff was production stage manager of *Bravo Giovanni* (Broadhurst, N.Y.C., May 19, 1962); with Jerry Adler, produced *Moby Dick* (Ethel Barrymore Th., Nov. 28, 1962); was production stage manager of *The Lady of the Camellias* (Winter Garden, Mar. 20, 1963); *The Girl Who Came to Supper* (Bway Th., Dec. 8, 1963); and directed *My Fair Lady* (NY City Ctr., May 20, 1964).

On June 1, 1964, Mr. Liff became production supervisor and general casting director for producer David Merrick. He was production supervisor for *Oh, What a Lovely War* (Broadhurst Th., N.Y.C., Sept. 30, 1964); *A Severed Head* (Royale, Oct. 28, 1964); associate producer of *I Was Dancing* (Lyceum, Nov. 8, 1964); *The Roar of the Greasepaint—The Smell of the Crowd* (Sam S. Shubert Th., May 16, 1965); production supervisor for *Pickwick* (46 St. Th., Oct. 4, 1965); associate producer of *Inadmissible Evidence* (Belasco, Nov. 30, 1965); *Cactus Flower* (Royale, Dec. 8, 1965); production supervisor for *Marat/Sade* (Martin Beck Th., Dec. 27, 1965); *Philadelphia, Here I Come!* (Helen Hayes Th., Feb. 16, 1966); *The Loves of Cass McGuire* (Helen Hayes Th., Oct. 6, 1966); *Holly Golightly* (opened Forrest Th., Philadelphia, Oct. 10, 1966), which closed during previews under the title *Breakfast at Tiffany's* (Majestic, N.Y.C., closed Dec. 14, 1966); *We Have Always Lived in the Castle* (Ethel Barrymore Th., Oct. 19, 1966); *Don't Drink the Water* (Morosco, Nov. 17, 1966); *The Astrakhan Coat* (Helen Hayes Th., Jan. 12, 1967); *Cactus Flower* (national tour, opened Breakstone, Chicago, Oct. 7, 1967); *Rosencrantz and Guildenstern Are Dead* (Alvin, Oct. 16, 1967; and national tour, opened O'Keefe Ctr., Toronto, Jan. 6, 1969); *Hello Dolly!* (national tour, opened Indiana Univ. Aud., Bloomington, Ind., Nov. 14, 1967); *Mata Hari* (pre-Bway tryout, opened National, Washington, D.C., Nov. 18, 1967; closed there Dec. 9, 1967); *How Now, Dow Jones* (Lunt-Fontanne Th., N.Y.C., Dec. 7, 1967); *The Happy Time* (Broadway Th., Jan. 18, 1968); *The Seven Descents of Myrtle* (Ethel Barrymore Th., Mar. 27, 1968); *I Do! I Do!* (tour, opened Rochester, N.Y., Aud., Apr. 8, 1968); *Keep It in the Family* (Plymouth, N.Y.C., Sept. 27, 1968); *Rockefeller and the Red Indians* (Ethel Barrymore Th., Oct. 24, 1968); *Promises, Promises* (Sam S. Shubert Th., Dec, 1, 1968); *Forty Carats* (Morosco, Dec. 26, 1968; and national tour, opened Shubert, Cincinnati, Sept. 29, 1969); *Play It Again, Sam* (Broadhurst, N.Y.C., Feb. 12, 1969); national tour of *I Do! I Do!* (opened Playhouse, Wilmington, Del., Sept. 11, 1969; closed Santa Monica, Calif., Apr. 11, 1970); *A Patriot for Me* (Imperial, N.Y.C., Oct. 5, 1969); *The Penny Wars* (Royale, Oct. 15, 1969); *Private Lives* (Billy Rose Th., Dec. 4, 1969); and *Child's Play* (Royale, Feb. 17, 1970).

In addition, Mr. Liff directed a revival of *My Fair Lady* (NY City Ctr., June 13, 1969). On April 9, 1973, he was named head of the Theatre Department of the William Morris Agency.

He was production stage manager for industrials for the General Motors Motorama tour (1952); Buick (1959, 1960, 1961); Milliken (1959, 1960, 1961); Owens Corning (1960, 1961); and Nabisco (1960, 1961).

Television. Mr. Liff was unit manager for ABC (1948), and production manager of the Admiral Broadway Revue (NBC, 1948).

LILLIE, BEATRICE. Actress. b. Beatrice Gladys Lillie, May 29, 1903, Toronto, Canada, to John and Lucie (Shaw) Lillie. Father, schoolmaster. Studied with Harry Rich, 1906. Attended St. Agnes Coll., Belleville, Ont. 1913–14. Married Jan. 1920 to Sir Robert Peel (dec. 1934); one son (dec. 1942). During WW II, entertained (1939–45) Allied Armed Forces throughout Europe, Africa, and the Middle East; toured Great Britain in *Tonight at 8:30* (1940) and *Plays and Music* (Oct. 1940); toured Tokyo and Hong Kong entertaining Allied Forces in *An Evening with Beatrice Lillie* (Aug. 1954). Member of British AEA; AEA.

Theatre. Miss Lillie made her stage debut at the Chathaw Music Hall (1914); and in London appeared in *The Daring of Diane* (London Pavilion, Apr. 1914); joined (Oct. 1914) the revue *Not Likely* (Alhambra, May 4, 1914); appeared in *5064, Gerrard* (Alhambra, Mar. 19, 1915); and *Now's the Time!* (Alhambra, Oct. 13, 1915). She succeeded (Vaudeville, Mar. 1916) Mabel Russell in the revue *Samples* (Playhouse, Nov. 30, 1915); followed by *Some* (Vaudeville, June 29, 1916); *Cheep* (Vaudeville, Apr. 26, 1917); and *Tabs* (Vaudeville, May 15, 1918).

She played Jackie Sampson in *Oh! Joy* (Kingsway, Jan. 27, 1919); performed in the revue, *Bran-Pie* (Prince of Wales's, Aug. 28, 1919); played Geraldine Ainsworth in *Up In Mabel's Room* (Playhouse, Apr. 6, 1921); performed in the revues, *Now and Then* (Vaudeville, Oct. 1921), *Pot Luck* (Vaudeville, Dec. 24, 1921), *From A to Z* (Prince of Wales's, Sept. 1922), and *The Nine O'Clock Revue* (Little, Oct. 25, 1922).

Miss Lillie made her N.Y.C. debut in *Andre Charlot's Revue of 1924* (Times Square Th., Jan. 9, 1924); subsequently appeared (Mar. 1925) in *Charlot's Revue* (Prince of Wales's, London, Sept. 23, 1924); in *Charlot's Revue, 1926* (Selwyn, N.Y.C., Nov. 10, 1925); as Lily Valli in *Oh, Please* (Fulton, Dec. 17, 1926); and Tilly in *She's My Baby* (Globe, Jan. 3, 1928); sang at the London Palladium (1928); performed in *This Year of Grace* (Selwyn, N.Y.C., Nov. 7, 1928); and in a variety act (Palace, Feb 1930), which subsequently toured the US (Mar.–June 1930).

She played in *Charlot's Masquerade* (Cambridge, London, Sept. 1930); *The Third Little Show* (Music Box, N.Y.C., June 1, 1931); re-appeared in variety (Palace, Jan. 1932); portrayed the Nurse in *Too True To Be Good* (Guild, Apr. 4, 1932); appeared in *Walk a Little Faster* (St. James, Dec. 7, 1932); *Please!* (Savoy, London, Nov. 16, 1933); *At Home Abroad* (Winter Garden, N.Y.C., Sept. 19, 1935); at the London Palladium (Jan. 1935); in *The Show Is On* (Winter Garden, N.Y.C., Dec. 25, 1936); *Happy Returns* (Adelphi, London, May 1938); and *Set to Music* (Music Box, N.Y.C., Jan. 18, 1939).

She played in *All Clear* (Queen's, London, Dec. 20, 1939); *Tonight at 8:30* (Globe, July 1940); *Big Top* (His Majesty's, May 8, 1942); appeared as Frieda Appleby in an Oxford production of *Staff Dance* (New, Feb. 1944); performed in the revue, *Seven Lively Arts* (Ziegfeld, N.Y.C., Dec. 7, 1944); in *Better Late* (Garrick, London, Apr. 24, 1946); *Inside U.S.A.* (Century, N.Y.C., Apr. 30, 1948), and on the national tour (Ford's Th., Baltimore, Md., Apr. 4, 1949; Chicago, Ill., May 1949); and in England, performed before the Royal Family in charity performances (1951).

In the US, she toured summer theatres in *An Evening with Beatrice Lillie* (July 1952), subsequently appeared on Bway (Booth, Oct. 2, 1952), toured both the US and Canada (Sept. 1953–July 1954), opened in the English production in Liverpool (Court, Oct. 1954); followed by the London production (Globe, Nov. 24, 1954), toured the English provinces (Aug.–Sept. 1955); and returned to the US to perform in both Miami and Palm Beach (Fla.) in a revised edition of *An Evening with Beatrice Lillie* (Jan.–Feb. 1956). She toured the US in her one-woman stock production of *Beason's Fables* (June–Sept. 1956); appeared in *Ziegfeld Follies* (Winter Garden, N.Y.C., Mar. 1, 1957); succeeded (June 1958) Greer Garson in the title role in *Auntie Mame* (Broadhurst, Oct. 3, 1956), a role which she repeated in the London production (Adelphi, Sept. 10, 1958).

At the Edinburgh Festival, she appeared in *Late Evening with Beatrice Lillie* (Lyceum, Sept. 1960); performed in a benefit called *Lights On* (Carnegie Hall, N.Y.C., Dec. 1960); appeared in *An Evening of Highlights* (Tappan Zee Playhouse, Nyack, N.Y., June 25, 1963); and played Mme. Arcati in *High Spirits* (Alvin, N.Y.C., Apr. 8, 1964).

Films. Miss Lillie made her debut in *Exit Smiling* (MGM, 1926); followed by *Doctor Rhythm* (Par., 1938); *On Approval* (English Films, 1945); *Around the World in Eighty Days* (UA, 1956); and *Thoroughly Modern Millie* (U, 1967).

Television and Radio. She did a radio series for The Borden Milk Company (1935). She performed on radio and television both in the US and England (1946–47). In the US, she appeared on her own television series (Jan.–May 1951; Jan.–May, 1952); and from 1957–60 made many appearances, including the Bell Telephone Hour (NBC, 1959); Four for

Tonight (Pontiac Star Parade, Feb. 23, 1960); and Wagon Train (NBC, 1960). She appeared on the Dick Cavett Show (ABC, June 1969).

Night Clubs. She made her debut at Charlot's Rendezvous Club (1926); made frequent appearances in night clubs in London (1930–31), and at the Cafe de Paris, London, (Nov. 1933; May and Aug. 1934; 1938; June 1939; Nov.–Dec. 1950; June–July 1951).

Published Works. Miss Lillie wrote the autobiographical *Every Other Inch a Lady* (1972).

Awards. She received the Donaldson Award for her performance in *Seven Lively Arts* (1945); won the *Variety* NY Drama Critics Poll as best actress in a musical for *Seven Lively Arts* and *Inside U.S.A.* (1948); and received citations from the National Conference of Christians and Jews (1948) and the American Federation of Women's Philanthropies (1953); the Sarah Siddons Award (1953); and an Outer Circle Award (1964) "for consistently fine achievement in the Theatre." During WW II, she received the African Star for entertaining Allied troops.

Recreation. Walking, swimming, riding, shooting, electric canoeing, oil painting (signature, Beatrice van Gone).

LINDEN, HAL. Actor. b. Harold Lipshitz, Mar. 20, 1931, New York City, to Charles and Frances (Rosen) Lipshitz. Father, printer. Grad. H.S. of Music and Art, N.Y.C., 1948; attended Queen's Coll., 1948–50; grad. City Coll. of NY, B.B.A. 1952. Studied voice with Lou McCollogh, N.Y.C., 1953–56; acting at American Th. Wing, N.Y.C., 1954–55, and with Paul Mann, N.Y.C., 1956–60; voice with John Mace, N.Y.C., 1958–64; acting with Lloyd Richards, N.Y.C., 1962–63. Married Apr. 13, 1958, to Frances Martin, actress: two daughters. Served US Army, 1952–54; rank, Cpl. Member of AEA; AGVA; SAG; AFTRA; AFM, Local 802. Address: 470 West End Ave., New York, NY 10024, tel. (212) LY 5-1964.

Pre-Theatre. Musician.

Theatre. Mr. Linden made his debut in the chorus of a stock production of *Wonderful Town* (Cape Cod Melody Tent, Hyannis, Mass., July 1955); subsequently appeared in *Pleasure Dome* (closed during rehearsals); played Chuck in the pre-Bway tryout of *Strip for Action* (opened Shubert, New Haven, Conn., Mar. 17, 1956; closed Nixon, Pittsburgh, Pa., Apr. 14, 1956); appeared in stock (Oakdale Musical Th., Wallingford, Conn., Warwick Musical Th., R.I., 1957); was understudy to Sydney Chaplin as Jeff Moss in *Bells Are Ringing* (Shubert, Nov. 29, 1956), succeeded (July 1958) him, and toured in the role (opened Natl., Washington, D.C., Mar. 10, 1959; closed San Francisco, Calif., July 4, 1959).

Mr. Linden appeared in *Angel in the Pawnshop* (Playhouse-in-the-Park, Philadelphia, Pa., July 1960); appeared as Matt and understudied Keith Andes as Joe Dynamine in *Wildcat* (Alvin, Dec. 16, 1960); played Pinky Harris in *Wish You Were Here* (Cape Cod Melody Tent, Hyannis, Mass., July 1961); Jeff Moss in *Bells Are Ringing* (Univ. of Utah, Salt Lake City, Sept. 1961); and understudied Sydney Chaplin as Tom Bailey in *Subways Are for Sleeping* (St. James, N.Y.C., Dec. 27, 1961).

He played Billy Crocker in *Anything Goes* (Orpheum, May 15, 1962); Jess Moss in a tour of *Bells Are Ringing* (Summer 1962); appeared in industrial shows (Feb. 1963); played Sid Sorokin in *The Pajama Game* (Meadowbrook Dinner Th., N.J., July 1963); appeared in the American Motors industrial show (Aug. 1963); and *The Sign in Sidney Brustein's Window* (Longacre, N.Y.C., Oct. 16, 1964).

Mr. Linden was standby for Arthur Hill in the role of Bill Deems, and for Ronny Graham in the role of Monte Checkovitch, and played Dick in *Something More!* (Eugene O'Neill Th., N.Y.C., Nov. 10, 1964); he was standby for John Cullum in the role of Dr. Mark Bruckner and Clifford David in the role of Edward Moncrief in *On a Clear Day You Can See Forever* (Mark Hellinger Th., Oct. 17, 1965); played Waldo Walton in *Remains To Be Seen* (Royal Poinciana Playhouse, Palm Beach, Fla., Jan. 31, 1966; and Paper Mill Playhouse, Millburn N.J., Feb. 15, 1966); Antipholus of Syracuse in *The Boys from Syracuse* (Pocono Playhouse, Mountainhome, Pa., Aug. 1, 1966; and Paper Mill Playhouse, Millburn, N.J., July 11, 1966); took over the role of the Devil in *The Apple Tree* (Shubert, N.Y.C., Oct. 10, 1966); played No Face in *Illya, Darling* (Mark Hellinger Th., Apr. 11, 1967); Yissel Fishbein in *The Education of H*Y*M*A*N K*A*P*L*A*N* (Alvin, Apr. 4, 1968); Earnest in *The Love Match* (Ahmanson, Los Angeles, Nov. 1968); Charlie in *Three Men on a Horse* (Lyceum, N.Y.C., Oct. 16, 1969); and Mayer Rothschild in *The Rothschilds* (Lunt-Fontanne Th., Oct. 19, 1970).

Films. Mr. Linden played the Night Club Singer in *Bells Are Ringing* (MGM, 1959), and has appeared in industrial films.

Television. He appeared on the Jim Gibbons Show (WMAL, Washington, D.C., 1953); in the chorus of *The Ruggles of Red Gap* (NBC, 1956); in Car 54, Where Are You? (NBC, Jan. 1963); was the narrator for Saga of the Western World (ABC, 1963–64); and played the title role in his own series, Barney Miller (ABC).

Night Clubs. Mr. Linden appeared in Mimi Benzell's night club act (Hotel Seville, Miami, Fla., 1955; Hotel Savoy, London, England, 1956).

Awards. He received the Antoinette Perry (Tony) Award for best actor in a musical for his performance in The Rothschilds (1970).

Recreation. Bridge.

LINDEN, ROBERT. Production associate, stage manager. b. Robert Navra Jacobson, Mar. 23, 1912, Little Rock, Ark., to Charles and Dillie (Navra) Jacobson. Father, state senator, U.S. Commissioner, attorney. Grad. Little Rock H.S., 1928; attended John Murray Anderson-Robert Milton Sch. of the Th., N.Y.C., 1929. Served with USN, 1942–46; rank, CPO. Member of AEA. Address: (home) 400 E. 59th St., New York, NY 10022, tel. (212) 688-0361; (bus.) 445 Park Ave., New York, NY 10022, tel. (212) PL 5-8780.

Theatre. Since 1955, Mr. Linden has been production associate for Fryer & Carr, producers, in N.Y.C.

He made his debut as an actor in two seasons of stock (Somerville, Mass., 1928–29; 1929–30); subsequently played the Juvenile in *Subway Express* (Mason Th., Los Angeles, Calif., 1930); and appeared in stock (1931–39).

He was production manager with Sonja Henie's touring *Hollywood Ice Revue* (1938–41); and for Miss Henie's *It Happens on Ice* (Center, N.Y.C., Oct. 10, 1940; Apr. 4, 1941).

Mr. Linden was assistant stage manager for *Lady Windermere's Fan* (Cort, Oct. 14, 1946); stage manager for *Tonight at 8:30* (Natl., Feb. 20, 1948), a tour of *Happy Birthday* (opened Lobero, Santa Barbara, Calif., Nov. 1948); assistant stage manager for *The Wisteria Trees* (Martin Beck Th., NY.C., Mar. 29, 1950) and *Point of No Return* (Alvin, Dec. 13, 1951), and stage manager for its subsequent national tour (opened Ford's, Baltimore, Md., Nov. 24, 1952; closed Biltmore, Los Angeles, Calif., May 23, 1953); stage manager for *Kind Sir* (Alvin, Nov. 4, 1953), *Peter Pan* (Winter Garden, Oct. 20, 1954), *The Desk Set* (Broadhurst, Oct. 24, 1955), *Shangri-La* (Winter Garden, June 13, 1956) and *Auntie Mame* (Broadhurst, Oct. 31, 1956).

He was production manager for *Redhead* (46 St. Th., Feb. 5, 1959) and *There Was a Little Girl* (Cort, Feb. 29, 1960); production associate for *Finian's Rainbow* (46 St. Th., May 23, 1960), *Advise and Consent* (Cort, Nov. 17, 1960), *A Passage to India* (Ambassador, Jan. 31, 1962) and *Hot Spot* (Majestic, Apr. 19, 1963); assistant stage manager for *Double Dublin* (Little Theatre, Dec. 26, 1963); director for *An International Tribute Through the Arts* (Madison Square Garden, Jan. 27, 1964); and production associate for *Roar Like a Dove* (Booth, May 21, 1964); stage manager for *Cambridge Circus* (Plymouth Th., Oct. 6, 1964); production manager for *Sweet Charity* (Palace, Jan. 29, 1966 and Prince of Wales Th., London, Oct. 18, 1967), and *Sweet Potato* (Ethel Barrymore Th., N.Y.C., Sept. 19, 1968).

With the Center Theatre Group in Los Angeles (Calif.), Mr. Linden has been a production associate for *Design For Living* (Mar. 16, 1971), *A Funny Thing Happened On The Way to The Forum* (Oct. 12, 1971), *The Caine Mutiny Court Martial* (Nov. 30, 1971), *Richard II* (Mar. 7, 1972), *The Crucible* (Dec. 5, 1972), *A Streetcar Named Desire* (Mar. 20, 1973), *Cyrano de Bergerac* (Oct. 16, 1973), *St. Joan* (Jan. 19, 1974), and *The Time of the Cuckoo* (Apr. 2, 1974).

Films. Mr. Linden played the Juvenile in the film version of *Subway Express* (Col., 1931); danced and played in small roles in films (1931–38); and was assistant to the dance director at 20th-Century Fox for *Thin Ice* (1937); *You Can't Have Everything* (1937); *Happy Landing* (1938); *My Lucky Star* (1938); and *Second Fiddle* (1939).

Television. He was assistant to the director of *Peter Pan* (NBC, 1955).

LINDFORS, VIVECA. Actress. b. Elsa Viveca Torstensdotter Lindfors, Dec. 29, 1920, Upsala, Sweden, to Torsten and Karin (Dymling) Lindfors. Father, book publisher. Grad. Lyceum Sch. for Girls (with honors). Stockholm, 1940; appointed to Royal Dramatic Th. Sch., 1937–40. Married Jan. 1943 to Folke Rogard, lawyer (marr. dis. 1949); two daughters; married Sept. 1952 to Donald Siegel, director (marr. dis. Apr. 29, 1953); one son; married July 4, 1954, to George Tabori, novelist, playwright. Member of AEA; SAG; AFTRA; Actors Studio (1958–to date). Address: 172 E. 95th St., New York, NY 10028, tel. (212) 722-1458.

Pre-Theatre. Telephone operator.

Theatre. Miss Lindfors made her stage debut in Stockholm in a high school production of *Ann Sophie Hedvig* (1937); appeared at the Royal Dramatic Th. (Stockholm, 1940–46) in *French without Tears* (1940); the Bride in *Blood Wedding* (1943); and Olivia in *Twelfth Night* (1945).

She made her Bway debut as Inez Cabral in *I've Got Sixpence* (Ethel Barrymore Th., Dec. 2, 1952); toured in the Amer. Shakespeare Festival production of *An Evening with Will Shakespeare* (1952–53); in *Bell, Book and Candle* (Summer 1953); made her London debut as Sophia in *The White Countess* (Saville, Mar. 24, 1954); played Anna in *Anastasia* (Lyceum, N.Y.C., Dec. 29, 1954), and on tour (opened Ford's Th., Baltimore, Md., Sept. 26, 1955); Cordelia in *King Lear* (NY City Ctr., Jan. 12, 1956); and the title role in *Miss Julie*, presented on a double-bill with *The Stronger*, in which she played Missy (Phoenix, Feb. 21, 1956).

Miss Lindfors appeared as Anna in *The Rose Tattoo* (Fort Lee Playhouse, N.J., July 1958); Livia in *The Golden Six* (York Playhouse, N.Y.C., Oct. 25, 1958); Frieda in *I Rise in Flame, Cried the Phoenix* (Th. de Lys, Apr. 9, 1959), and Hebib, Sultana of Iluwayat, in *Brouhaha* (175 E. Bway Playhouse, Apr. 26, 1960).

She toured New England and South America as Catherine in *Suddenly, Last Summer*, Princess del Lago in *Sweet Bird of Youth*, Natalia in *I Am a Camera*, and the title role in *Miss Julie* (Summer 1961); appeared in *Brecht on Brecht* (Th. de Lys, N.Y.C., Jan. 3, 1962); toured as Elizabeth von Ritter in *A Far Country* (opened Playhouse, Wilmington, Del., Oct. 24, 1962; closed Hanna, Cleveland, Ohio, Jan. 12, 1963); played Vera Simpson in *Pal Joey* (NY City Ctr., May 29, 1963); and repeated her performance in *Brecht on Brecht* (Stockholm, Sweden, 1963).

In 1966 she founded the Berkshire Theatre Festival and the Berkshire Children's Theatre; formed and was artistic director of the Strolling Players, Inc. for college tours (1966–69); and was co-arranger, producer, actress for *I Am a Woman* (first presented Gotham Art Th., April, 1969, and again at Th. in Space Jan. 9, 1974). *I Am a Woman* also toured colleges and schools in the US and Sweden.

Films. Miss Lindfors has appeared in the Swedish motion pictures *The Crazy Family; If I Should Marry the Minister* (1941); *Appassionata* (1944); *Interlude* (1945); *Anna Lans*; and *The Saga of Singoalla* (1949).

She made her US film debut in *To the Victor*(WB, 1948); appeared in *Adventures of Don Juan* (WB, 1948); *Night Unto Night* (WB, 1949); *No Sad Songs for Me*(Col., 1950); *Dark City*(Par., 1950); *The Flying Missile*(Col., 1950); *Somewhere in the City; Journey into Light*(20th-Fox, 1951); *Four in a Jeep*(UA, 1951); *The Raiders* (U, 1952); *Moonfleet* (MGM, 1955); *Run for Cover*(Par., 1955); *I Accuse*(MGM, 1958); *Tempest*(Par., 1959); *The Riding Kid; King of Kings* (MGM, 1961); *Weddings and Babies* (1958); *No Exit*(ZEN, 1962); *Affair of the Skin;*and *The Way We Were* (Col., 1973).

Television. Miss Lindfors played Mata Hari on You Are There (CBS, May 1954); performed a scene from *Anastasia*(Toast of the Town, CBS, Jan. 25, 1955); appeared in *Kyrai Katina*(TV Playhouse, NBC, Feb. 12, 1956); *The Last Tycoon*(CBS, March 14, 1957); as Camilla in *The Bridge of San Luis Rey* (Dupont Show of the Month, CBS, Jan. 1958); in *Dangerous Interlude* (US Steel Hour, CBS, Jan. 1959); The Defenders (CBS); and The Nurses (CBS).

Awards. Miss Lindfors was cited by the Intl. Film Festival for her performance in *Four in a Jeep* (1951); received the Drama League Award for her performance as Anna in *Anastasia* (1955); and the Vasaordern from the King of Sweden.

LINN, BAMBI. Dancer, actress. b. Bambina Aennchen Linnemier, Apr. 26, 1926, Brooklyn, N.Y., to Henry William and Mary (Tweer) Linnemier. Father, accountant. Grad. Professional Children's Sch., N.Y.C., 1943. Studied with Mikhael Mordkin, N.Y.C., 1935; Helen Oakes, Brooklyn, 1932; dramatics with Violet Hill, Brooklyn, 1934; dance at Ballet Arts, N.Y.C., 1939; with Hanya Holm, N.Y.C., 1943; ballet with Helene Platava, N.Y.C., 1943; acting with Sanford Meisner at Neighborhood Playhouse Sch. of the Th., N.Y.C., 1943. Married Apr. 19, 1950, to Rod Alexander, dancer, choreographer (marr. dis. Oct. 1959); one daughter; married July 10, 1960, to Joseph De Jesus; two daughters, one son. Relative in theatre; brother, Ralph Linn, dancer, actor, stage manager. Member of AEA; SAG; AFTRA; AGVA. Address: 45 S. Compo Rd., Westport, CT 06880, tel. (203) CA7-0977.

Theatre. Miss Linn made her N.Y.C. debut as a dancer in the chorus of *Oklahoma!* (St. James Th., Mar. 31, 1943); subsequently played Alice in *Alice in Wonderland* (Intl., Apr. 5, 1947); the title role in *Sally* (Martin Beck Th., May 6, 1948); appeared in stock productions of *All the Way Home* (Clinton, N.J.; Ridgefield, Conn., Summer 1948); danced with the Ballet Th. (on tour, 1948; Metropolitan Opera House, N.Y.C., 1949); played Bonnie in *Great to Be Alive!* (Winter Garden, Mar. 23, 1950); Louise in *Carousel* (Majestic, Apr. 19, 1954); NY City Ctr., June 2, 1954 and Sept. 11, 1957); danced with the Dance Jubilee Co. (toured Eastern US, 1958–59), and with the American Ballet Co. (Spoleto, It., 1959); played Laurey in a stock production of *Oklahoma!* (Opera House, Dayton, Ohio, 1959); Essie Whimple in *Red Head* (Corning, Rochester, and Syracuse, N.Y., Summer 1960); and Blanche Bushkin in *I Can Get It for You Wholesale* (Shubert, N.Y.C., Mar. 22, 1962).

Films. Miss Linn appeared as Laurey in the ballet sequence of *Oklahoma!* (Magna, 1955); and was assistant choreographer for *Carousel* (20th-Fox, 1956), and *The Best Things in Life Are Free* (20th-Fox, 1956).

Television. She has appeared on the Kate Smith shows (NBC, 1948 and later); Your Show of Shows (NBC, 1952–54); the Max Liebman specials (NBC, 1955–57); Ding-Dong School (1956); Benny Goodman Special (1957); Arthur Murray's Dance Party (NBC, 1957–58); General Motor's 50th Anniversary Show (1958); The Verdict Is Yours (CBS, 1959); Peter Potter Show (1959); The Seven Lively Arts (1959); the Today Show (NBC, 1960); Andy Williams Special (1960); and several Ed Sullivan Shows (CBS).

Night Clubs. She has appeared at the Cocoanut Grove (Los Angeles, Calif., 1950); Park Plaza (St. Louis, Mo., 1950); Palmer House (Chicago, Ill., 1951, 1952, 1953); Caribe Hilton (San Juan, P.R., 1952); Persian Room (Plaza Hotel, N.Y.C., 1952–54); and in Las Vegas (Nev.), El Rancho Vegas (1954) and The Last Frontier (1956).

Other Activities. Miss Linn has taught ballet and modern ballet arts (Carnegie Hall, N.Y.C., 1960), and at the Weston (Conn.) Music School (1960–61); and at her own school, the Creative Arts Center (Westport, Conn.).

Awards. For her performance as Louise in *Carousel,* she received the Donaldson Award and the *Theatre World* Award (1945); The Award of Dance Educators of America (1956); and the Dance Award (1957) from NATAS.

Recreation. Living, jogging.

LINNEY, ROMULUS. Playwright, novelist. b. Philadelphia, Pa. Grad. Oberlin Coll., B.A. 1953; studied for the theatre at Yale Sch. of Drama, M.F.A. 1958. Married Margaret Andrews, actress; one daughter.

Pre-Theatre. Taught at Manhattan Sch. of Music.

Theatre. Mr. Linney wrote *The Sorrows of Frederick* (Mark Taper Forum, Los Angeles, June 23, 1967); *Democracy* and *Esther* (H B Studio, N.Y.C., 1969); *The Love Suicide at Schofield Barracks* (ANTA Th., Feb. 9, 1972); and *Holy Ghosts* (Cubiculo, Feb. 19, 1976).

Television. He wrote *The Thirty-fourth Star* (American Parade, CBS).

Published Works. Mr. Linney is the author of *Heathen Valley* (1962); and *Slowly By Thy Hand Unfurled* (1965).

LION, JOHN. Director. b. John Howard Lion, May 17, 1944, Baltimore, Md., to S. John, Jr., and Mary Francis (Aaron) Lion. Father, historical consultant; mother, stenographer. Grad. Baltimore City Coll. H.S., 1962; Univ. of Chicago, B.A. 1966; Univ. of Calif. at Berkeley, M.A. 1967. Studied in Chicago with Tyrone Guthrie, Morris Carnofsky, and Robert Bennidetti; studied in Berkeley with Jan Kott. Relative in theatre: Elmer Rice, playwright. Member of TCG (Experimental Th. Advisory Bd., 1971–74); University (of Chicago) Th. (pres., 1963–66). Address: (home) 1296 Union St., San Francisco, CA 94409; (bus.) 1615 Polk St., San Francisco, CA 94409, tel. (415) 441-8001.

Pre-Theatre. Mr. Lion worked with the cloud chamber group at Fermi Institute in Chicago, and at the Lawrence Radiation Laboratory in Berkeley; and wrote parapsychological biographies for *Who's Who in Chicago.* .

Theatre. Mr. Lion made his first stage appearance in the role of Tranio in *The Taming of the Shrew* (Court Th., Chicago, Sept. 1963); and subsequently played Gregory in *Romeo and Juliet* (Alumni Rep. Th., Berkeley, July 1967).

He is the founder and artistic director of The Magic Theatre, established in San Francisco in 1968. There, he directed *The Lesson* (Feb. 1968); *Jack*(Mar. 4, 1968); *Ubu Roi*(Mar. 6, 1968); *Victims of Duty* (Oct. 18, 1968); *Dutchman* (Jan. 31, 1969); *First Communion* (Mar. 29, 1969); *The Cherub* and *Meat Poem*(May 6, 1969); *The Pansy*(Aug. 8, 1969); *Botticelli*(Feb. 6, 1970); *The Shell, Snoutburbler, Apple Glove,* and *The Meatball* (May 5, 1970); wrote and directed *Sheriff Bill* (Aug. 3, 1970); directed *Beau, Stroganoff, Oppenheimer's Chair,* and *The Growl* (Feb. 22, 1971); *The Taming of the Shrew* (Aug. 1, 1971); *The Feather, The Pussy,* and *The Button* (Aug. 10, 1972); *Ball Game, Donald Duck, Intermission,* and *Fans*(Jan. 18, 1973); *Auto-Destruct*(Magic Th., Mar. 3, 1973, and NY Cultural Ctr., May 1973); *Spider Rabbit* and *The Beard* (Aug. 15, 1973); and *Gorf* (Jan. 16, 1974). For the Milwaukee Rep. Th., he directed *La Turista* (May 3, 1974).

Films. Mr. Lion was second unit director for *Space Is the Place* (1974).

Television and Radio. For television, he directed *Spider Rabbit* (PBS, 1969) and *The Feather* (PBS, 1972). His radio productions include *Snoutburbler* (KPFA, 1972) and *Peace Piece* (KPFA, 1974).

Published Works. Mr. Lion's article, "A Theatre of Iconography," was anthologized in *Breakout* (Swallow Press, Chicago, 1973).

Awards. Mr. Lion was elected to the Owl and Serpent Honor Society (Univ. of Chicago, 1966) for outstanding achievement in the arts; and, as artistic director of Magic Th., has been responsible for the disbursement of over $200,000 in awards from the National Endowment for the Arts, the Rockefeller Foundation, and OADE.

Recreation. Chess, music, travel.

LIPPMAN, MONROE. Educator, director. b. Dec. 10, 1905, Virginia, Minn., to Benjamin M. and Anne Juliet (Margulis) Lippman. Father, merchant. Grad. Lincoln H.S., Hibbing, Minn., 1922; Univ. of Michigan, A.B. 1926, M.A. 1929, Ph.D. 1937; attended Harvard Law Sch., 1926–27; State Univ. of Iowa, 1929. Married June 25, 1930, to Ruth Harriet Weeding. Relative in theatre: cousin, Leopold Jessner, director. Member of ATA (charter fellow and pres., 1950); ANTA (bd. of dir.); ASTR; NTC (bd. of trustees, 1953–55; 1964–66); SWTC (pres., 1954); TLA (bd. of dir., 1967–70); The Players Club; and the International Federation for Theatre Research. Address: (home) 1631 Ransom Rd., Riverside, CA 92506, tel. (714) 682-9707; (bus.) Dept. of Theatre, Univ. of Calif., Riverside, CA 92502, tel. (714) 787-3433.

Since 1973, Mr. Lippman has been a consultant for the theatre program of the Natl. Endowment for the Arts. He is professor Emeritus, Univ. of Calif. He was chairman, Dept. of Theatre, Univ. of Calif. (1970–73); chairman, Dept. of Drama, N.Y. Univ. (1967–70); served on the drama panel of the Cultural Exchange Program for the US State Dept. (1965–70); was head of the Dept. of Theatre and Speech at Tulane Univ. (1937–67); and was director of the college theatre at Southwest Texas State Coll. (San Marcos, Tex., 1929–35).

He served as the executive director of Le Petit Th. du Vieux Carré in New Orleans (1946–1953); has been guest director in summer sessions at Univ. of Texas, Univ. of Michigan, Univ. of Minnesota, and Mount Holyoke Coll. He has directed approximately 125 student and community theatre productions and has written articles on theatre for *Educational Theatre Journal, Tulane Drama Review, Theatre Survey, Theatre Arts, NY Times, Quarterly Journal of Speech* and *Southern Speech Journal.*

Awards. Mr. Lippman received a Guggenheim Fellowship (1956) and a Ford travel and study grant (1964).

Recreation. Spectator sports, poodles, jazz.

LIPPMANN, ZILLA. Theatre executive. b. Zilla Hymes, New York City, to M. L. and Nellie (Golden) Hymes. Father, realtor. Attended Ethical Culture Sch., N.Y.C., 1916–21; Vassar Coll., 1921–22; Cooper Union, 1922–25. Married Sept. 10, 1929, to Alfred Lippmann, advertising executive; one son, one daughter. Address: (home) 91 Central Park West, New York, NY 10023, tel. (212) EN 2-1415; (bus.) 246 W. 44th St., New York, NY 10036, tel. (212) BR 9-6994.

Since 1963, Mrs. Lippmann has been vice-president of the board of directors of the New Dramatists Committee and president of the John Golden Fund. She has been an associate of John Golden Associates (1955–to date).

Other Activities. Biochemist.

Recreation. Gardening, tennis, bird watching.

LIPSKY, DAVID. Press representative. b. David Isaac Lipsky, Mar. 23, 1907, New York City, to Louis and Charlotte Lipsky. Father, insurance executive; mother, interior decorator. Grad. Morris H.S., N.Y.C., 1925; attended Univ. of Pennsylvania, 1925–27; grad. Columbia Univ., B.A. 1929. Married Nov. 1941, to Ruth; one son, one daughter. Served US Army Corps of Engineers, ETO, 1943–45. Member of ATPAM. Address: (home) 251 W. 89th St., New York, NY 10024, tel. (212) TR 7-0458; (bus.) 1560 Broadway, New York, NY 10036, tel. (212) 575-1115.

Pre-Theatre. Columnist, syndicated in thirty suburban newspapers.

Theatre. Mr. Lipsky was press representative for *The Eternal Road* (1937); *The First Mrs. Fraser* (1947); *The Innocents* (1950); *Twentieth Century* (1950); *Stalag 17* (1951); *Cyrano de Bergerac* (1946); *The Girl on the Via Flaminia* (1954); *The Fragile Fox* (1954); *Seventh Heaven* (1955); *In Good King Charles' Golden Days* (1957); *Simply Heavenly* (1957); *Clerambard* (1957); *Make a Million* (1958); *An Enemy of the People* (1959); *Royal Gambit* (1959); *The Prodigal* (1960); *Come Share My House* (1960); *Greenwillow* (1960); *Machinal* (1960); *Greenwich Village U.S.A.* (1960); *Rape of the Belt* (1960); *The Mousetrap* (1960); *Donogoo* (1961); *The Tattooed Countess* (1961); *Let It Ride!* (1961); *All in Love* (1961); *Red Roses for Me* (1961); *New Faces of 1962* (1962); *A Chekov Sketchbook* (1962); *Rosmersholm* (1962); *King of the Whole Damn World!* (1962); *The Cherry Orchard* (1962); *The Living Room* (1962); *A Doll's House* (1963); *Too True To Be Good* (1963); *The Danny Kaye Show* (1963); *The Emperor* (1963); *A Month in the Country* (1963). Gilbert and Sullivan Repertory (1963); *Penny Change* (1963); *Walk in Darkness* (1963); *Habimah* (1963); *The Deputy* (1964); *Trumpets of the Lord* (1964); *Never Live Over a Pretzel Factory* (1964); *The Sunday Man* (1964); *Salad of the Mad Cafe* (1964); *A Dream of Swallows* (1964); *International Playgirls 1964* (1964); *One Is a Lonely Number* (1964); *The World of Kurt Weill* (1964); *Route 1* (1964); *The Cat and the Canary* (1964); *Pictures in the Hallway* (1965); *A View from the Bridge* (1964); the American Savoyards (1965); *Me and Thee* (1965); *The Pocket Watch* (1965); *The Porcelain Year* (1965); *Mame* (1965); *When We Dead Awaken* (1966); *Javelin* (1966); *Blizstein* (1966); *The Ox Cart* (1966); *Brother Jero* (1966); *Shoemaker's Holiday* (1967); Padraic Colum's *Carricknabauna* (1967); *A Warm Body* (1967); *Hello Dolly* (1967); *No Exit* (1967); *The Other Man* (1967); *Scarlet Lullaby* (1968); *Jericho-Jim Crow* (1968); the Puerto Rican Traveling Theatre (1968); *Before I Wake* (1968); *An Ordinary Man* (1968); *The Fig Leaves Are Falling* (1968); *Papers* (1968); *The Megillah* (1968); *The Village—A Party* (1969); Jimmy Roselli at the Palace (1969); *The Man with a Flower in His Mouth* (1969); *Three Men on a Horse* (1969); *The New Music Hall of Israel* (1969); *Love and Maple Syrup* (1969); *Mother Goose Go-Go* (1969); *Show Me Where the Good Times Are* (1969); *Contributions* (1969); *A Place for Polly* (1969); *A Slow Dance on the Killing Ground* (1970); *My House Is Your House* (1970); *Ari* (1970); *A Day in the Life of Just About Everyone* (1970); *Dance of Death* (1971); *Only Fools Are Sad* (1971); *Brothers* (1971); *Welcome to Andromeda* (1971); *The Soldier* (1973); *The Prisoner of Second Avenue* (B & T, 1973); and *The Sunshine Boys* (B & T, 1974–75).

He has handled publicity for the Circle in the Square Th.; The American Savoyards; a season of concerts and musicals produced by Michael Grace (Central Park, N.Y.C., 1957); benefit shows at Madison Square Garden, including *Night of Stars, Navy Relief Show, Fight for Freedom,* and *We Will Never Die;* Les Ballets de Paris; The Canadian Ballet; The Charles Weidman Dance Company; and The Ballet Society. Mr. Lipsky also handles personal publicity for performers.

Films. Mr. Lipsky was press representative for *Hill 24 Doesn't Answer* (CMP, 1955); Federico Fellini's *The White Sheik* (API, 1956); and *Tel Aviv Taxi* (GF, 1956). He has done promotional work for Universal, United Artists, 20th Century-Fox, Burstyn and Mayer, the Hollywood Victory Caravan, and the 55th St. Playhouse in N.Y.C.

Other Activities. Mr. Lipsky does publicity work for nontheatrical organizations, clubs, and businesses.

LITHGOW, ARTHUR W. Director, actor, administrator. b. Arthur Washington Lithgow, Jr., Sept. 9, 1915, Puerto Plata, Dominican Rep., to Arthur Washington and Ina Berenice (Robinson) Lithgow. Father, utilities executive; mother, nurse, rest home administrator. Grad. Melrose (Mass.) H.S., 1933; Antioch Coll., B.A. 1938; Cornell Univ., M.A. 1948. Married Jan. 13, 1939, to Sarah Jane Price; two sons, two daughters. Relative in theatre: son, John Lithgow, actor, director. Served US Army, 1946; rank, Pvt. Member of AEA. Address: (home) 54 Alexander St., Princeton, NJ tel. (201) WA 4-2275; (bus.) McCarter Th., Princeton Univ., Box 526, Princeton, NJ tel. (201) WA 1-8700.

Pre-Theatre. Publicity assistant, Toledo Museum of Art (1937–1938).

Theatre. From 1961–71, Mr. Lithgow was executive director of the McCarter Th. at Princeton Univ., where he directed and appeared in numerous productions.

He first performed as a Cherub in a Christmas pageant (Unitarian Church, Melrose, Mass., Dec. 1920); and appeared in student productions at Antioch Coll. (Yellow Springs, Ohio), including the title role in *The Drunkard* (July 1937).

He made his N.Y.C. debut as a Soldier in *Lorelei* (Longacre, Nov. 29, 1938). During July–Aug. 1951, he was associate producer of the Shaw Festival at the Rice Playhouse (Martha's Vineyard, Mass.), and appeared there as Alfred Doolittle in *Pygmalion,* the Elder Malone in *Man and Superman,* Colonel Popov in *Arms and the Man,* and Boss Mangan in *Heartbreak House.* He became executive director for the Antioch Coll. Shakespeare Festival (Yellow Springs, Ohio, Summer 1952), where he directed *King John* and appeared in it as Hugh de Burgh; played Henry Bolingbroke in *Richard II;* portrayed the title role in and directed *Henry IV, Part 1* and *Henry IV, Part 2;* played the Chorus in *Henry V;* directed *Henry VI; directed Richard III,* in which he played Tyrell; and appeared in the title role in *Henry VIII.* At Antioch Coll. as executive director each Summer until 1957, he continued to direct and act. In Summer 1956, the festival was sponsored by the college, in association with the Toledo (Ohio) Zoological Society, and the works were performed on the Antioch Coll. Festival (outdoor) stage and at the Toledo Zoological Garden Amphitheatre.

He played Claudius in *Macbeth* (Rooftop Th., N.Y.C., Oct. 7, 1955); directed *The Thesmophoriazusae* (Rooftop Th., Nov. 27, 1955); produced *Ah, Wilderness!, Pictures in the Hallway,* produced and directed *The Tempest* and *Charley's Aunt,* and appeared as Lawyer Hawkins in *The Devil's Disciple* (Toledo Zoo Indoor Th. Summer 1958). He was executive director of productions at the Stan Hywet Hall Outdoor Stage (Akron, Ohio, Summer 1958), where he presented *Richard II; Henry IV, Part 1; Henry IV, Part 2,* which he directed; and where he appeared as Essex in *Henry V.* He became executive director of productions at the Ohio Th., (Chuyahoga Falls, Ohio, Summer 1961), where he directed *The Taming of the Shrew,* directed and played Lennox in *Macbeth,* appeared as Antonio in *Twelfth Night,* and Peter Quince in *A Midsummer Night's Dream.* He was executive director for the Civic Aud. (Lakewood, Ohio, Summer 1962), where he directed *As You Like It, Othello,* and *Henry IV, Parts 1 and 2;* and where he was associate director of *Richard II,* in which he appeared as Salisbury and Gardener. He returned as executive director to the Civic Aud. (Summer 1963), where he directed *The Comedy of Errors, Romeo and Juliet,* and *Henry V* and appeared as Host of the Garter in *The Merry Wives of Windsor.*

At the Playhouse in the Park (Cincinnati), Mr. Lithgow was educational coordinator for *The Forced Marriage* and *The Doctor in Spite of Himself* (May 27, 1964), *Rhinoceros* (June 17, 1964), *A Moon for the Misbegotten* (July 8, 1964), *The Threepenny Opera* (July 29, 1964), and *The Fantasticks* (Aug. 19, 1964).

As executive director of the McCarter Th. (Princeton, N.J.), in association with the American Th. Co., he presented *Death of a Salesman* (Oct. 1, 1964); *The Great God Brown* (Oct. 9, 1964), which he also directed; *Three Men on a Horse* (Oct. 23, 1964); and *A Streetcar Named Desire* (Nov. 13, 1964). The McCarter Th. presented, with Mr. Lithgow as executive director, *The Rivals* (Feb. 20, 1965); *The School for Wives,* on a double-bill with *The Marriage Proposal,* which he directed (Feb. 27, 1965); *Macbeth* (Mar. 13, 1965), which he directed; *As You Desire Me* (Mar. 18, 1965); and *The Birds* (Apr. 3, 1965); subsequently presented *Mother Courage and Her Children* (Oct. 8, 1965), in which he played the Swedish Commander; and *Coriolanus* (Oct. 15, 1965), which he directed.

Mr. Lithgow was director of the Great Lakes Shakespeare Fest. which presented *The Taming of the Shrew* (June 30, 1964); *Hamlet* (July 7, 1964); *Much Ado About Nothing* (July 14, 1964); *Henri VI* (July 28, 1964); *Richard III* (Aug. 4, 1964); *Anthony and Cleopatra* (Aug. 18, 1964); *Macbeth* (June 25, 1965); *The Rivals* (June 29, 1965); *A Midsummer Night's Dream* (July 13, 1965); *The Marriage Proposal,* which he directed and in which he played Stepan Stepanovitch Tchubukov, on a double-bill with *The School for Wives* (July 27, 1965); *Henry VI* (Aug. 3, 1965), in which he played the Earl of Salisbury; and *Coriolanus* (Aug. 24, 1965).

Again, as executive director of the McCarter Th. (Princeton), he presented *Major Barbara* (Oct. 29, 1965); *An Enemy of the People* (Nov. 13, 1965), which he directed; *Lady Windemere's Fan* (Feb. 10, 1966); *A Midsummer Night's Dream* (Feb. 17, 1966), in which he played Quince; *Cox and Box,* on a double-bill with *Miss Julie* (Mar. 10, 1966), the former of which he directed; *Candida* (Mar. 18, 1966); *Arrah-Na-Pogue* (Apr. 1, 1966), which he directed; *Agamemnon* (Oct. 7, 1966); *A View from the Bridge* (Oct. 14, 1966); *Hamlet* (Oct. 21, 1966, and Feb. 26, 1967), which he directed; *Enrico IV,* which he directed (Nov. 3, 1967); *The Words upon the Window Pane,* which he directed, on a triple-bill with *It Should Happen to a Dog,* and *The Second Shepherd's Pageant* (Nov. 16, 1967); *The Merchant of Venice,* which he directed (Jan. 5, 1968); *The Tragical History of Doctor Faustus,* in which he appeared (Mar. 2, 1968); *The Birthday Party,* which he directed (Oct. 17, 1969); *Pygmalion,* in which he appeared (Oct. 24, 1969); *Troilus and Cressida,* which, with Tom Brennan, he co-directed (Mar. 28, 1970); *All My Sons,* which he directed (Oct. 16, 1970); *Macbeth,* in which he appeared (Jan. 31, 1971); and *Caesar at the Rubicon,* which he directed (Feb. 12, 1971).

Television. Mr. Lithgow appeared as Adam in *As You Like It* (KYW, Cleveland, Ohio, June 1963).

Recreation. Chess, reading, sketching, painting.

LITHGOW, JOHN. Actor, director. b. John Arthur Lithgow, Oct. 19, 1945, Rochester, N.Y., to Arthur and Sarah Lithgow. Father, producer; mother, teacher. Grad. Princeton (N.J.) H.S.; Harvard Coll.; London Acad. of Music and Dramatic Art. Married Sept. 10, 1966, to Jean Taynton; one son. Member of AEA; Phi Beta Kappa. Address: (home) 105 W. 73rd St., New York, NY 10023, tel. (212) 799-1604; (bus.) Brooks Atkinson Th., 256 W. 47th St., New York, NY 10036.

Pre-Theatre. Printmaker; founded Lithgow Graphics.

Theatre. Mr. Lithgow made his acting debut as Mustardseed in *A Midsummer Night's Dream* at the Antioch Shakespeare Festival (Ohio, 1953), and his Bway debut as Kendall in *The Changing Room* (Morosco, N.Y.C., 1973); he starred as Michael in *The Prodigal Daughter* (Kennedy Ctr., Washington, D.C., 1973); and appeared as James in *My Fat Friend* (Brooks Atkinson Th., N.Y.C., 1974). In stock and regional theatre, Mr. Lithgow appeared in fifteen Shakespearean roles at the Great Lakes Shakespeare Festival (Ohio, Summer 1963–64); as Bunthorne in *Patience,* Peachum in *Beggar's Opera,* Don Andres in *La Perichole,* and Lord Chancellor in *Iolanthe* (Highfield Th., Falmouth, Mass., Summer 1965); Henry Higgins in *Pygmalion,* Lennie in *Of Mice and Men,* and Achilles in *Troilus and Cressida* (McCarter Th., Princeton, N.J., 1969–70); Sir in *Roar of the Greasepaint,* Dr. Talacryn in *Hadrian VII,* and Capt. Vale in *The Magistrate* (Bucks County Playhouse, New Hope, Pa., Summer 1970); Kendall in *The Changing Room,* Kiper in *What Price Glory,* and Arthur in *Trelawny of the Wells* (Long Wharf Th., New Haven, Conn., Winter 1972). Mr. Lithgow has directed *As You Like It* (1968), *Much Ado About Nothing* (1969), and *The Way of the World* (1970) for the McCarter Th., Princeton, N.J.; *The Magistrate, Barefoot in the Park* (Bucks County Playhouse, New Hope, Pa., Summer 1970); *Abduction from the Seraglio* (Princeton, N.J., Opera Th., 1970); *Beaux' Stratagem* (Center Stage, Baltimore, Md., 1972); and the American premiere of *A Pagan Place* (Long Wharf Th., New Haven, Conn., 1973).

Films. Mr. Lithgow appeared in *Dealing* (WB, 1972).

Television. Mr. Lithgow co-starred as Paul Unger in *The Country Girl* (Hallmark Hall of Fame, NBC, Feb. 1974).

Radio. He wrote, produced, and acted in *Under the Gun*, his own radio show for WBAI-FM, N.Y.C. (1972–73).

Awards. Mr. Lithgow graduated magna cum laude from Harvard College in 1967. He was the recipient of a Fulbright Grant for study in London (1967–69) and received the Antoinette Perry (Tony) Award (1973) for best supporting actor in *The Changing Room*.

Recreation. Printmaking, sports, guitar, music.

LITTLE, CLEAVON. Actor. b. June 1, 1939, Chickasha, Okla., to Malachi and DeEtta Little. Father, gardener. Grad. San Diego (Calif.) State Coll., B.A., 1965; Amer. Academy of Dramatic Arts. Married Feb. 19, 1972, to Valerie Wiggins (marr. dis., 1974). Member of AEA; SAG.

Theatre. While attending college, Mr. Little appeared in *A Raisin in the Sun* (Globe, San Diego) and *The Skin of Our Teeth* (La Jolla, Calif., Playhouse). He made his NYC debut in a reading of *Americana* (Th. de Lys, Jan. 8, 1966), as part of the ANTA Matinee Series; subsequently appeared in the NY Shakespeare Festival Mobile Th. production of *Macbeth* (June 28, 1966); played Muslim Witch in *MacBird!* (Village Gate, Feb. 22, 1967); Foxtrot in *Scuba Duba* (New Th., Oct. 10, 1967); played the title role in *Hamlet* with the NY Shakespeare Festival Mobile Th., (Mar. 4, 1968); made his Bway debut as Lee Haines in *Jimmy Shine* (Brooks Atkinson Th., Dec. 5, 1968); played Paul Odum in *Someone's Comin' Hungry* (Pocket, Mar. 31, 1969); Rufus in *The Ofay Watcher*, (Stage 73, Sept. 15, 1969); the title role in *Purlie* (Bway Th., Mar. 15, 1970); Shogo in *Narrow Road to the Deep North* (Vivian Beaumont Th., Jan. 6, 1972); with the Negro Ensemble Co., replaced David Downing (Mar. 12, 1974) as Macdaddy in *The Great Macdaddy* (St. Mark's Playhouse, Feb. 12, 1974); played Corpie in *The Charlatan* (Mark Taper Forum, Los Angeles, Sept. 25, 1973); Lewis in *All Over Town* (Booth, N.Y.C., Dec. 29, 1974); and Willy Steppe in *The Poison Tree* (Ambassador, Jan. 8, 1976).

Films. He has appeared in *Three* (Impact Prods., 1967); *What's So Bad About Feeling Good?* (U, 1968); *John and Mary* (20th-Fox, 1969); *Cotton Comes to Harlem* (UA, 1970); *Vanishing Point* (20th-Fox, 1971); and *Blazing Saddles* (WB, 1974).

Television. He appeared on Felony Squad (ABC); All in the Family (CBS); and *The Homecoming* (CBS); and played Jerry Noland on Temperatures Rising (ABC).

Awards. Mr. Little won an ABC-TV sponsored scholarship to AADA (1965); received the Antoinette Perry (Tony) Award for Best Actor in a Musical (1970) for his performance in *Purlie* and was presented with the Key to the City of San Diego (June 22, 1973).

Recreation. Photography, reading.

LITTLE, GUY S., JR. Producer, director, manager. b. Feb. 13, 1935, Decatur, Ill., to Guy S. Little, Sr., and Inis (Mathew) Little. Father, farm manager; mother, teacher. Grad. Sullivan (Ill.) H.S., 1953; Univ. of Miami, B.A. 1956; attended Columbia Univ. 1957–58. Studied singing at Millikin Univ., 1950–53; acting at Amer. Th. Wing, 1956. Married June 9, 1954, to Jerili Romeo, actress, singer, director; one son, one daughter. Member of AEA; COST; CORST. Address: (home) Country Club Rd., Sullivan, IL 61951, tel. (217) 728-8522; (bus.) The Little Theatre on the Square, Sullivan, IL 61951, tel. (217) 728-7375.

Theatre. Since 1957, Mr. Little has been producer, director and manager of the Little Theatre (formerly, the Grand Theatre) in Sullivan, Ill. After purchasing the theatre in 1963, he renamed it The Little Theatre on the Square. There he has presented over 200 productions, from April to October each year, of recent Broadway releases—as well as popular revivals—featuring such stars as Ann Miller, Pat O'Brien, Eve Arden, Barbara Rush, Van Johnson, John Carradine, June Allyson, and many others.

Mr. Little made his professional debut at the Keene (N.H.) Summer Theatre, appearing as Ben Butler in *Lady in the Dark* (July 1951), and in *Die Fledermaus* and *Heaven Comes Wednesday* (Summer 1951); at the Gateway Playhouse (Somers Point, N.J.), played in *Brigadoon, Born Yesterday, Arsenic and Old Lace, Detective Story, Roberta, Carousel, The Desert Song, Annie Get Your Gun, The Merry Widow, Kiss Me, Kate, Song of Norway, Show Boat,* and *Gentlemen Prefer Blondes* (Summers 1952–53). At the Miami (Fla.) Opera Guild, he sang in the choruses of *Il Trovatore* and *Madame Butterfly* (1954), *Barber of Seville* and *Lucia di Lammermoor* (1955), and *Cosi Fan Tutti* (1956); and also appeared as Parpignol in *La Bohème* (Dade County Aud., Miami, Fla., Jan. 1956).

Recreation. Swimming, gardening.

LITTLE, STUART W. Writer, editor. b. Stuart West Little, Dec. 19, 1921, Hartford, Conn., to Mitchell Stuart and Elizabeth (Hapgood) Little. Father, manufacturer. Grad. Groton (Mass.) Sch., 1940; Yale Univ., B.A. 1946. Married Sept. 25, 1945, to Countess Anastazia Raben-Levetzan; one son, two daughters. Served WW II, USAAF, 1943–44; OSS, 1945; rank, Sgt. Member of The Drama Desk (vice-pres., 1960–62; pres., 1962–64); Century Club. Address: 165 E. 60th St., New York, NY 10022, tel. (212) TE 8-8458.

Mr. Little is the editor of The Authors Guild Bulletin; a director of the Theatre Development Fund; a member of the play selection committee of the Th. Guild-Amer. Th. Society; and a trustee of the Amer.-Scandinavian Foundation. From 1958–66, he was the theatre news reporter for the NY *Herald Tribune*. He joined the staff as a copy boy in 1946; served successively as NY correspondent, European edition; staff reporter; and until 1954, as assistant city editor.

Television. He wrote television news and documentaries, including Project 20 and Report from America (NBC, 1954–56).

Published Works. Mr. Little wrote the "Books in Communication" column for *Saturday Review* (1966–72). He is the author of *The Playmakers*, with Arthur Cantor (1970); *Off-Broadway: The Prophetic Theater* (1972); and *Enter Joseph Papp* (1974).

LIVINGSTON, JAY. Songwriter, composer. b. Jay Harold Livingston, Mar. 28, 1915, McDonald, Pa., to Maurice H. and Rose (Wachtel) Livingston. Father, merchant. Grad. McDonald (Pa.) H.S., 1933; Univ. of Pennsylvania, B.A. (Journalism) 1937. Studied piano and harmony with Harry Archer, Pittsburgh, Pa. Married Mar. 1947, to Lynne Gordon; one daughter. Served US Army, 1942–43, rank, Pvt. Member of NARAS (charter member; board of dir., two years); AMPAS (exec. comm., music branch, 1958–74); ASCAP; Composers and Lyricists Guild of Amer. (exec. bd.); Amer. Guild of Authors & Composers; Dramatists Guild; NARAS; Television Academy of Arts and Sciences. Address: 782 Tortuoso Way, Los Angeles, CA 90024.

Theatre. He made his N.Y.C. debut as rehearsal pianist and contributor of songs and material for Olsen & Johnson's *Hellzapoppin'* (46 St. Th., Sept. 22, 1938); and *Sons o' Fun* (Winter Garden, Dec. 1, 1941); followed by songs for *I Love Lydia* (Players Ring, Hollywood, Calif., 1952); wrote music and lyrics, with Ray Evans, for *Oh Captain!* (Alvin, N.Y.C., Feb. 4, 1958) and *Let It Ride!* (Eugene O'Neill Th., Oct. 12, 1961); and wrote the songs for *The Odyssey of Runyon Jones*, by Norman Corwin (Valley Music Th., Los Angeles, Dec. 16, 1972).

Films. Mr. Livingston wrote songs for *Swing Hostess* (PRC, 1944); *I Accuse My Parents* (PRC, 1944); *Why Girls Leave Home* (PRC, 1944); and *Crime, Inc.* (PRC, 1945); *Stork Club* (Par., 1945); *Kitty* (Par., 1945); *To Each His Own* (Par., 1946); *Monsieur Beaucaire* (Par., 1946); *Imperfect Lady* (Par., 1947); *My Favorite Brunette* (Par., 1947); *Golden Earrings* (Par., 1947); *Isn't It Romantic?* (Par., 1948); *The Paleface* (Par., 1948); *Streets of Laredo* (Par., 1949); *Sorrowful Jones* (Par., 1949); *Song of Surrender* (Par., 1949); *My Friend Irma* (Par., 1949); *The Great Lover* (Par., 1949); *Dear Wife* (Par., 1949); and *Samson and Delilah* (Par., 1949).

Also, *Copper Canyon* (Par., 1950); *Paid in Full* (Par., 1950); *Captain Carey, U.S.A.* (Par., 1950); *Fancy Pants* (Par., 1950); *My Friend Irma Goes West* (Par., 1950); *The Furies* (Par., 1950); *The Lemon Drop Kid* (Par., 1951); *The Mating Season* (Par., 1951); *The Cowboy and the Redhead* (Par., 1951); *Ace in the Hole* (Par., 1951); *Here Comes the Groom* (Par., 1951); *Aaron Slick from Pumpkin Crick* (Par., 1951); *A Place in the Sun* (Par., 1951); *Crosswinds* (Par., 1951); *When Worlds Collide* (Par., 1951); *My Favorite Spy* (Par., 1951); *Rhubarb* (Par., 1951); *That's My Boy* (Par., 1951); *Anything Can Happen* (Par., 1952); *Somebody Loves Me* (Par., 1952); *Son of Paleface* (Par., 1952); *The Great Houdini* (Par., 1952); *What Price Glory* (20th-Fox, 1952); *Thunder in the East* (Par., 1953); *Off Limits* (Par., 1953); *Sangaree* (Par., 1953); *Here Come the Girls* (Par., 1953); *The Stars Are Singing* (Par., 1953); *Three Ring Circus* (Par., 1954); *Red Garters* (Par., 1954); and *Casanova's Big Night* (Par., 1954).

Also, *Lucy Gallant* (Par., 1955); *Second Greatest Sex* (U, 1955); *The Scarlet Hour* (par., 1956); *The Man Who Knew Too Much* (Par., 1956); *Istanbul* (U, 1957); *Tammy and the Bachelor* (U, 1957); *The James Dean Story* (WB, 1957); *Raw Wind in Eden* (U, 1958); *The Big Beat* (U, 1958); *Saddle the Wind* (MGM, 1958); *This Happy Feeling* (U, 1958); *Another Time, Another Place* (Par., 1958); *Once Upon a Horse* (U, 1958); *Houseboat* (Par., 1958); *Vertigo* (Par., 1959); *Take a Giant Step* (UA, 1959); *A Private's Affair* (20th-Fox, 1959); *The Blue Angel* (20th-Fox, 1959); *All Hands on Deck* (20th-Fox, 1961); *Dear Heart* (WB, 1964); *Never Too Late* (WB, 1965); *The Third Day* (WB, 1965); *Harlow* (Par., 1965); *The Oscar* (Par., 1966); *This Property Is Condemned* (Par., 1966); *The Night of the Grizzly* (Par., 1966); *What Did You Do in the War, Daddy?* (Mirisch, 1966); *Wait Until Dark* (WB, 1967); *Love Is Forever* (Fedderson, 1974); and *The Tale of Two Mice* (Buena Vista).

Television. He wrote songs for *Satins and Spurs* (NBC, 1957); the theme music for Bonanza (NBC); Mister Ed (CBS); *The Good Guys* ( ); and *To Rome with Love* (CBS); and the score for *Odyssey in Progress* (Group W).

Night Clubs. Mr. Livingston wrote songs and special material for Betty Hutton's shows at the Palace Th. (N.Y.C.), and Desert Inn (Las Vegas, Nev., 1954); and special material for Mitzi Gaynor, Cyd Charisse, Tony Martin, Joel Grey, Polly Bergen and Sheila MacRae.

Awards. The songs, "Buttons and Bows," from the film, *The Paleface* (1948), "Mona Lisa" from *Captain Carey, U.S.A.* (1950), and "Whatever Will Be, Will Be" from *The Man Who Knew Too Much* (1956) received Academy (Oscar) awards; and the songs "Tammy," from *Tammy and the Bachelor* (1957), "Almost in Your Arms" from *Houseboat* (1958) and "Dear Heart" from the film of the same name (1964) received Academy (Oscar) Award nominations. In 1973, he was elected to the Songwriters Hall of Fame.

Recreation. Travel.

LIVINGSTON, ROBERT H. Director. b. Robert Henry Luria, Apr. 4, 1934, New York City, to Irving M. and Dorothy F. (Livingston) Luria. Father, lawyer. Attended P.S. 6 and Flushing H.S., N.Y.C.; grad. Carnegie Inst. of Tech., B.F.A. 1955. Married June 2, 1963, to Jeanne A. Epstein (marr. dis. 1974). Served US Army, Feb.–Aug. 1957. Member of SSDC (exec. bd. of dir., 1970–to date); AEA; DGA. Address: 16 E. 63rd St., New

York, NY 10021, tel. (212) 371-6250.

Theatre. Mr. Livingston began his professional career as stage manager for the Gateway Playhouse (Belport, N.Y., 1953); and made his Bway debut as assistant stage manager and understudy in *Time Limit* (Booth Th., N.Y.C., 1956). He subsequently stage managed the national tour of *Candide* (1958); and Bway and pre-Bway productions of *Kataki, The Little Glass Clock, Maybe Tuesday,* and *The Midnight Sons* (1955–59).

He directed a pre-Bway production of *The Interpreter* with Richard Kiley (Bucks County Playhouse, New Hope, Pa., 1961); and summer stock tours (1960–70) of *The Solid Gold Cadillac* and *A Girl Could Get Lucky,* with Imogene Coca; *The Miracle Worker; The Private Ear and The Public Eye,* with Dick Shawn; *Two for the Seesaw,* with Shelley Winters; *Anniversary Waltz,* with Lloyd Bridges; *Silk Stockings; Wedding Breakfast; Gentlemen Prefer Blondes;* and *The Matchmaker;* and *You Can't Take It with You,* with Imogene Coca (Loretto Hilton Rep. Th., St. Louis, Mo., 1969). He also directed the pre-Bway production of *The Selling of the President* (Feb. 1972); *The Fourposter,* with Imogene Coca (Texas Dinner Th., Apr. 1972); and a touring production of *The Effect of Gamma Rays on Man-in-the-Moon Marigolds* (Jan. 1973).

Off-Bway, Mr. Livingston directed *A Party for Divorce* and *Warm Play* (Provincetown Playhouse, Nov. 1965); and *How to Steal an Election* (Pocket Th., Sept. 1968). He subsequently wrote the book for, and directed, *The Me Nobody Knows,* first produced Off-Bway (Orpheum, May 18, 1970), and later moved to Bway (Helen Hayes Th., Dec. 1970); and directed later productions in Toronto (Crest Th., 1970), Chicago (Civic Th., 1971), and Baltimore (Center Stage, 1973). Other productions of the musical have been presented in London, Paris, and Munich (1970–73).

Television. Mr. Livingston was production assistant for *Captain Kangaroo* (CBS, 1959); production assistant, assistant director, and director on the CBS staff (1960–63), and has been a free-lance director for the major networks (1963–to date). He directed *It's a Nice Place to Visit* (NET, 1970), and segments of *Maude* and *All in the Family* (CBS, 1972).

Other Activities. Mr. Livingston is a cabinetmaker and makes personalized plastic items sold at leading N.Y.C. stores.

Discography. *The Me Nobody Knows* (Atlantic, 1970).

Awards. Mr. Livingston was awarded the 1970 Off-Bway (Obie) Award for best musical for *The Me Nobody Knows.* After its move to Bway, he was nominated for the 1970 Antoinette Perry (Tony) Awards in the best director of a musical, and best musical book categories.

Recreation. Photography, cabinetry, needlepoint.

LLOYD, JOHN ROBERT. Stage designer. b. Aug. 4, 1920, St. Louis, Mo. Grad. Roosevelt H.S., St. Louis, 1938; studied painting and drawing at Art Student's League, N.Y.C. 1939; Hadley Art Sch., St. Louis, 1940–1941; Washington Univ. 1941–1943; attended Univ. of Missouri, 1944–45. Married Dec. 24, 1943, to Karol Ann Fahnestock (marr. dis. 1946). Member of United Scenic Artists; AEA. Address: (home) Byram Lake Rd., Mt. Kisco, NY 10549, tel. (914) MK 6-4381; (bus.) 17 E. 45th St., New York, NY 10017, tel. (212) MO 1-2131.

Theatre. Mr. Lloyd first appeared on stage in the Italian production of *Ipaladini de Francia* (Song of Roland), in which he played the part of Christ (Brooklyn Acad., N.Y., June 1945), and on subsequent weekends at theatres in Italian-speaking communities in N.Y.C. He played small parts and was understudy to Ralph Clanton as the Genie in *Lute Song* where, as assistant to the designer, Robert Edmund Jones, he designed the masks and sculpture used in the production (Plymouth, Feb. 6, 1946); worked with Dr. Henry A. Murray of Harvard University's psychology dept. to design masks for Harvard's psycho-drama theatre (Mar.–June 1946); became (Summer 1946) resident designer at the Oqunquit (Me.) Playhouse, where he designed sets for *State of the Union, The Marquise, The Late Christopher Bean, Best Foot Forward, The Little Foyes, Caprice, The Happiest Years, The First Mrs. Frazer,* and *Joan of Lorraine;* and devised commedia sculpture for Lemuel Ayres, designer for *Cyrano de Bergerac* (Alvin, N.Y.C., Oct. 8, 1946), and for Jose Ferrer, who played the title role. Mr. Lloyd designed and executed Cyrano's special make up. He designed the Grecian sculptures for *Lysistrata* (Belasco, Oct. 17, 1946); and assisted Nat Karson, designer for *Ballet Ballads* (Maxine Elliott's Th., May 9, 1948).

He designed costumes, sets, and lighting for the opera *The Duenna* (Greenwich Mews Th., N.Y.C., May 1948); costumes for *Mrs. Gibbon's Boys* (Music Box, May 4, 1949); sets and costumes for *Touch and Go* (Broadhurst, N.Y.C., Oct. 13, 1949; Prince of Wales's, May 19, 1950); sets and lighting for *Stalag 17* (48 St. Th., May 8, 1951); costumes for the operas *I Pagliacci* and *Cavalleria Rusticana* (Metropolitan Opera House, Jan. 17, 1951); sets and lighting for *Bernardine* (Playhouse, Oct. 16, 1952); scenery and lighting at the Billy Rose Th. (Flushing Meadows) for the outdoor productions of *Hell-za-Splashin* (Summer 1953) and *Aqua Circus* (Summer 1954).

He designed the scenery and lighting for *Almost Crazy* (Longacre, N.Y.C., June 20, 1955); *Holiday for Lovers* (Longacre, Feb. 14, 1957); scenery for *Monique* (John Golden Th., Oct. 22, 1957); scenery and lighting for *Drink to Me Only,* which he produced in association with George Ross (54 St. Th., Oct. 8, 1958); scenery, costumes, and lighting for *The Man Who Never Died* (Jan Hus House, Nov. 21, 1958); and for *Dinny and the Witches* (Cherry Lane, Dec. 9, 1959), which he later directed (Univ. of Missouri, Dec. 12, 1961); designed scenery and lighting for *One Little Girl,* presented by Alfred Stern for the Camp Fire Girls (Manhattan Center Th., N.Y.C., Nov. 3, 1960); and settings and lighting for Stanley Holloway's one-man show, *Laughs and Other Events* (Ethel Barrymore Th., Oct. 10, 1960).

At the NY World's Fair (1964), he was lighting director for the Tower of Light, (Electric Power and Light Exhibit), and *All About Elsie* (Borden Exhibit); consulting art director for the re-design of the Hollywood Pavilion; and delivered a lecture series on theatre design at Pratt Institute (Brooklyn, N.Y., Dec. 1963–Feb. 1964).

Films. He was the N.Y. art director for *Reflections in a Golden Eye* (Par., 1967); art director for *The Night They Raided Minsky's* (UA, 1968); and production designer for *Midnight Cowboy* (UA, 1969); *John and Mary* (20th-Fox, 1969); *The Boys in the Band* (CBS, 1970); *The Owl and the Pussycat* (Col., 1970); *The Hot Rock* (20th-Fox, 1970); *They Might Be Giants* (U, 1971); *The Exorcist* (WB, 1973); and *Lovin' Molly* (Friedman-Lumet, 1974).

Television. Mr. Lloyd was staff designer at NBC (1950). He has been free-lance art director for live and film television productions, including the Aldrich Family (NBC, Oct. 1949–May 1953); Lux Video Th. (CBS, Oct. 1950–May 1951); Ford Festival (NBC, Apr. 1951–June 1952); Chrysler Medallion Th. (CBS, 1952); US Royal Showcase (NBC, Jan. 1952–June 1952); GE Th. (CBS, Feb. 1953–Sept. 1957); Campbell Sound Stage (NBC, June 1954–Sept. 1954); and Suspicion (NBC, Sept. 1957–Sept. 1959).

Mr. Lloyd was production designer for the film specials *The Trap of Solid Gold, Mark Twain Tonight!,* and *Dear Friends.*

Recreation. Swimming, pseudo-architecture, fiction writing.

LLOYD, NORMAN. Producer, actor, director. b. Nov. 8, 1914, Jersey City, N.J. Grad. Boys H.S., N.Y.C., 1930; attended New York Univ., 1930–32. Married June, 1936 to Peggy Craven; one son; one daughter, Josie Lloyd, actress. Member of AEA; SAG; SDG. Address: (home) 1813 Old Ranch Rd., Los Angeles, CA 90049; (bus.) c/o Hollywood Television Theatre, KCET, 4400 Sunset Dr., Los Angeles, CA 90027, tel. (213) 666-6500.

Theatre. Mr. Lloyd made his stage debut in N.Y.C. as a walk-on in *Liliom* (Civic Repertory Th., Oct. 26, 1932); subsequently played one of the Clubs (playing card) in *Alice in Wonderland* (Civic Repertory Th., Dec. 12, 1932); at the Apprentice Th. of the New Sch. for Social Research, played Fanères in *A Secret Life* (Dec. 1933), the title role in *Dr. Knock* (1934), and appeared in *Naked, Fear, The Armored Train* and *The Call of Life* (1934).

On Bway, he played Japhet in *Noah* (Longacre, Feb. 13, 1935); the title role in *Dr. Knock* and Kleist in *Gallery Gods* (Peabody Playhouse, Boston, Mass., 1935); appeared in three productions of the Living Newspaper Unit of the Federal Theatre, playing the Salesman and Judge Brandeis in *Triple-A Plowed Under* (Biltmore, N.Y.C., Mar. 14, 1936), the Clown in *Injunction Granted* (Biltmore, July 24, 1936) and the Consumer in *Power* (Ritz, Feb. 23, 1937); played stock at the Deertrees Th. (Harrison, Me., Summer 1937); appeared with Orson Welles's Mercury Theatre as Cinna the Poet in *Julius Caesar* (Mercury, N.Y.C., Nov. 11, 1937) and as Roger, commonly called Hodge, in *The Shoemaker's Holiday* (Mercury, N.Y.C., Jan. 1, 1938); played Johnny Appleseed in *Everywhere I Roam* (Natl., Dec. 29, 1938); Quack the Medicine Man in *Medicine Show* (New Yorker, Apr. 12, 1940); and one of the Four in *Liberty Jones* (Shubert, Feb. 5, 1941).

Also, Mr. Lloyd played Dawson the Reporter, in *Village Green* (Henry Miller's Th., Sept. 3, 1941); Sandy in *Ask My Friend Sandy* (Biltmore, Feb. 4, 1943); Mosca in *Volpone* (Las Palmas, Los Angeles, Calif., July, 1945); directed *The Road to Rome* (La Jolla Playhouse, Calif., 1948); played the Fool in *King Lear* (National, N.Y.C., Dec. 25, 1950); directed productions, including *The Cocktail Party* (La Jolla Playhouse, Calif., 1951–53); played the Devil in *Don Juan in Hell* (La Jolla Playhouse, Calif., 1953); played Mr. Dockwiler and directed, with Hume Cronyn, *Madam, Will You Walk* (Phoenix, N.Y.C., Dec. 1, 1953); directed *The Golden Apple* (Phoenix, Mar. 11, 1954; moved Alvin, Apr. 20, 1954); appeared as Lucio in *Measure for Measure* (ASFTA, Stratford, Conn., June 27, 1956); directed *The Taming of the Shrew* (ASFTA, Aug. 5, 1956); Lucio in *Measure for Measure* (Phoenix, N.Y.C., Jan. 22, 1957); directed *The Taming of the Shrew* (Phoenix, Feb. 20, 1957); and played Undershaft in *Major Barbara* (Mark Taper Forum, L.A., 1971).

Films. Mr. Lloyd made his film debut as Frye in *Saboteur* (UI, 1942); followed by the Nephew in *The Southerner* (UA, 1945); Archimbeau in *Walk in the Sun* (20th-Fox, 1945); appeared in *A Letter for Evie* (MGM, 1945); *Spellbound* (UA, 1945); played the Uncle in *The Green Years* (MGM, 1946); appeared in *Young Widow* (UA, 1946); *The Beginning or the End* (MGM, 1947); played Sturdevant in *No Minor Voices* (MGM, 1948); appeared in *Reign of Terror* (Eagle Lion, 1949); played Gordon in *Calamity Jane and Sam Bass* (UI, 1949); appeared in *Scene of the Crime* (MGM, 1949); *Buccaneer's Girl* (UI, 1950); played the Troubador in *Flame and the Arrow* (WB, 1950); appeared in *He Ran All the Way* (UI, 1951); *The Light Touch* (MGM, 1951); and played Bodalink in *Limelight* (UA, 1952).

Television. Mr. Lloyd made his first appearance in Streets of New York (NBC, 1939); subsequently directed *Mr. Lincoln* (Omnibus, NBC, 1952) and various productions for Revue (CBS, 1950–52); was associate producer (1957–61), producer (1962), and executive producer (1963–64) of Alfred Hitchcock Presents (CBS), directing and appearing in many of the segments; and directed *The Jail* (ABC, 1961), and *The Jar* (CBS, 1964).

For Universal, he produced and directed *The Smugglers* (1966), and *Companions in Nightmare* (1967); for 20th-Fox, produced and directed five episodes of *Journey to the Unknown* in London (1968); for Universal, produced the Anthony Franciosa segments of *The Name of the Game* (1969–70), and the Movie of the Week, *What's a Nice Girl Like You* (1971). For Hollywood Television Theatre (PBS), he appeared as Dickon in *Scarecrow* (1971); produced and directed *Awake and Sing* (1972), and Jean Renoir's *Carola* (1972); produced *Invitation to a March* (1972), *Another Part of the Forest* (1972), *Shadow of a Gunman* (1972), *Winesburg, Ohio* (1972), and *Steambath* (1973). In 1972, he became executive producer of HTT, serving in that capacity for the series "Conflicts," including *Double Solitaire; The Gondola*, in which he also appeared, *Me, The Man of Destiny*, and *Incident at Vichy*, and *The Carpenters* (1973), which he directed. He was executive producer of *The Sty of the Blind Pig* and *Nourish the Beast* (1974).

Recreation. Tennis.

LOCKE, SAM. Playwright. b. Samuel David Locke, Jan. 17, 1917, Peabody, Mass., to Maurice H. and Jenny (Djelysniak) Locke. Father, Hebrew teacher. Grad. James Madison H.S., Brooklyn, 1933; City Coll. of NY, B.S. 1937. Served USAAF, 1942–46; rank, PFC. Member of Dramatists Guild; SWG, West (TV branch). Address: 3043 Nichols Canyon Rd., Los Angeles, CA 90046, tel. (213) OL 6-6182.

Pre-Theatre. Newspaper reporter.

Theatre. Mr. Locke contributed material to the revue, *Sunday Night Varieties* (Club Mirador, N.Y.C., Apr. 9, 1939); wrote sketches for the revues, *Straw Hat Revue* (Ambassador Th., Sept. 29, 1939); *'Tis of Thee* (Maxine Elliott's Th., Oct. 10, 1940); *You Can't Sleep Here* (Barbizon-Plaza, Apr. 1941), *Of V We Sing* (Concert, Feb. 11, 1942); *Let Freedom Sing* (Longacre, Oct. 5, 1942); second edition of *Meet the People* (Los Angeles, Calif., 1943); and *Tidbits of 1946* (Plymouth, N.Y.C., July 8, 1946).

He wrote, with Paul Roberts, the play, *Woman with Red Hair* (Circle, Los Angeles, Calif., Feb. 1, 1955; as *La Donna dei Capelli Rossi* at Teatro dei Satiri, Rome, Italy, 1972); wrote, with John Latouche, the book for *The Vamp* (Winter Garden, N.Y.C., Nov. 10, 1955); and was author of *Fair Game* (Longacre, Nov. 2, 1957). He wrote, with Milton Sperling, the book of the musical *W. C.*, performed under auspices of Music Fair, Inc. in summer tent shows (1971).

Films. Mr. Locke wrote the commentary for the travelogue, *Deep-Sea Monsters* (1941), while in service, researched, wrote and assisted in the editing of training films, documentaries, and historical films; afterwards, was writer-advance man on a technical assistance film made for the E.C.A. (Marshall Plan, 1950); researched and wrote screen story for the Common Denominator series on forestry in Savannah, Ga., entitled *People of the Forest* (1951); was writer-liaison man to the State Dept. on the World Congress of Youth film at Cornell Univ. (1951); was writer-supervisor-advance man for a Congressional filmed tour of 63 countries (1951); wrote and directed in Africa, *Voice of the Drum* (1953); and wrote English commentary for and re-edited Austrian documentary entitled *Secret of Venus* (1955). Under the pseudonym of David Malcom, he wrote *Girls on the Beach* (Par., 1964); *Beach Ball* (Par., 1965); and *Wild, Wild Winter* (U, 1966).

Television and Radio. For radio, Mr. Locke wrote for First Nighters Playhouse, Grand Central Station, Inner Sanctum, Bulldog Drummond (1946–49); and for Travelin' Man (1946) and Gramps (NBC, 1947).

For television, he wrote and directed the comedy sketches for the revue Front Row Center (Dumont, 1949–50); comedy sketches for Garry Moore and Ed Wynn; scripts for The Web, Sure as Fats and the Westinghouse Summer Th. (CBS, 1951); wrote a serial, The Egg and I (CBS, 1952); the Red Buttons Show (CBS, 1952); *Bedroom A* (Schlitz Playhouse, CBS, 1952); *A Matter of Calculation* (Orient Express, CBS, 1953); collaborated on the Adventures of Colonel Flack (Dumont, 1953); wrote five segments of The Secret File series (1954); also *Men of the Clouds* (The Search, CBS, 1954); *Woman with Red Hair* (Alfred Hitchcock Presents, CBS, 1958); and segments for the series, Judge (1955), Charlie Farrell Racquet Club (1956), Bachelor Father (CBS, 1961), Peter Loves Mary (NBC, 1961), McKeever and the Colonel (1962), McHale's Navy (ABC, 1964), and the Donna Reed Show (ABC, 1964).

He wrote for the Chrysler Theatre Anthology; the Bill Dana Show (1963); *School for Bachelors* (Bob Hope Show, 1964); Gilligan's Island (Ind., 1966–67); Green Acres (1966); the Lucille Ball Show (1966); The Flying Nun (1969); The Ghost and Mrs. Muir (1969); *Shining Palace* (Bavarian Network, 1969); Julia (1970); Mayberry R.F.D. (CBS, 1970); The Brady Bunch (ABC, 1970–74); Love, American Style (ABC, 1971); All in the Family (CBS, 1972); *The Woman with Red Hair* (RAI-TV, Rome, Italy, 1972); and the Brian Keith Show (1973).

Published Works. Mr. Locke has contributed fiction and articles to *The Saturday Evening Post, True* and *Esquire*, and is the author of *Writing for Stage, Film & TV* (1955).

LOCKHART, JUNE. Actress. b. June Kathleen Lockhart, June 25, 1925, New York City, to Gene and Kathleen (Arthur) Lockhart, actors. Grad. Westlake School for Girls, Los Angeles, Calif., 1943. Married June 1951 to John S. Maloney, surgeon (marr. dis. Mar. 17, 1958); two daughters; Apr. 5, 1959, to John C. Lindsay, architect (marr. dis. Oct. 1970). Member of SAG; AEA; AFTRA; Academy of Television Arts and Sciences (secy., 1960). Address: c/o Milton H. Grossman Agency, 8730 Sunset Blvd., Los Angeles, CA 90069.

Theatre. Miss Lockhart made her stage debut as Mimsey in *Peter Ibbetson* (Metropolitan Opera House, N.Y.C., 1933); subsequently appeared as a dancer in *Die Meistersinger* (Metropolitan Opera House, 1934); and as Essie in a stock production of *The Devil's Disciple* (Lobero Th., Santa Barbara, Calif., Summer 1941).

She made her Bway debut as Janet Blake in *For Love or Money* (Henry Miller's Th., Nov. 4, 1947); played the title role in *Claudia* (Bucks County Playhouse, New Hope, Pa., Summer 1951); appeared in stock productions of *Sabrina Fair, Gramercy Ghost, Our Town, The Philadelphia Story* and *Claudia* (Empress Playhouse, St. Louis, Mo., 1953–55); and played Lucille Cotton in *The Grand Prize* (Plymouth, N.Y.C., Jan. 26, 1955).

Films. Miss Lockhart made her debut as Belinda in *A Christmas Carol* (MGM, 1938); subsequently played the Eldest Daughter in *All This and Heaven Too* (WB, 1940); Rosie in *Sergeant York* (WB, 1941); appeared in *Miss Annie Rooney* (1942); *Son of Lassie* (1945); *White Cliffs of Dover* (MGM, 1946); *Meet Me in St. Louis* (MGM, 1944); *Keep Your Powder Dry* (MGM, 1945); *The Yearling* (MGM, 1946); *It's a Joke, Son* (Eagle-Lion, 1947); *Bury Me Dead* (Eagle-Lion, 1947); *T-Men* (Eagle-Lion, 1947); and *Time Limit* (UA, 1957).

Television and Radio. She made her radio debut in *Cavalcade* (Lux Radio Th., CBS, 1938); subsequently appeared on the Charlie McCarthy Hour (CBS); Don Ameche Show (NBC, 1940–42); and Th. Guild of the Air (1951).

She made her television debut as Amy in *Little Women* (CBS, 1949); subsequently appeared in *One Sunday Afternoon* (CBS, 1951); on Robert Montgomery Presents (NBC, 1951–55); Schlitz Playhouse (NBC, 1951); Studio One (CBS, 1951–55); Th. Guild of the Air (CBS, 1952–57); Who Said That? (NBC, 1952–56); It's News to Me (NBC, 1952–56); Quick as a Flash (NBC, 1953); Playhouse 90 (CBS, 1956); Climax (CBS, 1956); Ford Th. (CBS, 1956); Peter Potter Platter Parade (NBC, 1956–60); Home Show (NBC, 1957); Tex and Jinx Show (NBC, 1957); as Ruth Martin in the Lassie series (CBS, 1958–64); on Zane Grey Th. (CBS, 1958); Cimarron City (ABC, 1958); Wagon Train (NBC, 1958–59); Rawhide (CBS, 1959); First Impression (NBC, 1963); You Don't Say (NBC, 1963); and Password (CBS, 1964).

Also on Perry Mason (CBS, 1964); Bewitched (ABC, 1964); Voyage to the Bottom of the Sea (ABC, 1964); The Man from U.N.C.L.E. (NBC, 1964); Branded (NBC, 1965); Alfred Hitchcock Th. (NBC, 1965); Mr. Novak (NBC, 1965); Lost in Space (CBS, 1965–66–67); Family Affair (CBS, 1968); Petticoat Junction (CBS, 1968, 1969); *But I Don't Want To Get Married* (ABC, 1970); Man and the City (ABC, 1971); and *I Never Said Goodbye* (ABC, Dec. 1973). She also served as hostess for telecasts of the Miss U.S.A. Beauty and Miss Universe pageants (both CBS, 1965–71).

Awards. For her performance as Janet Blake in *For Love or Money*, Miss Lockhart received an Antoinette Perry (Tony) Award, a *Theatre World* Award, an Associated Press Woman of the Year in Drama Award, and a Donaldson Award (1948). She was nominated for an NATAS (Emmy) Award for her role as Ruth Martin in the Lassie television series (1959).

Recreation. Swimming, traveling, cats, reading.

LODEN, BARBARA. Actress. b. Barbara Anne Loden, July 8, Marion, N.C., to George T., and Ruth (Sadur) Loden. Father, barber. Attended L. H. Edwards H.S., Ashville, N.C. Married to Elia Kazan, director; two sons. Member of AFTRA; SAG; AEA.

Theatre. Miss Loden made her Bway debut as Myra in *Compulsion* (Ambassador, Oct. 24, 1957); subsequently played Gaby in *Look After Lulu* (Henry Miller's Th., Mar. 3, 1959); and appeared with the Repertory Th. of Lincoln Ctr., as Maggie in *After the Fall* (ANTA, Washington Sq., Jan. 23, 1964).

Films. Miss Loden made her film debut as Betty Henderson in *Wild River* (20th-Fox, 1960); followed by Ginny Stamper in *Splendor in the Grass* (WB, 1961). She appeared in and directed *Wanda* (Bardene International, Mar. 1971).

Awards. Miss Loden received the Antoinette Perry (Tony) Award and the Outer Circle Award for her performance as Maggie in *After the Fall* (1964). She received the International Critics Prize for best film for *Wanda* at the Venice Film Festival (1970).

LOESSER, LYNN. Producer. b. Mary Alice Blankenbaker to Ralph Blankenbaker. Father, in advertising business. Married Oct. 19, 1936, to Frank Loesser, composer, lyricist, writer, producer, music publisher; one son, one daughter.

Theatre. With Kermit Bloomgarden, Miss Loesser produced the musical, *The Most Happy Fella*, for which her husband, Frank Loesser, wrote the words and music and adapted the book (Imperial Th., N.Y.C., May 3, 1956).

With Shamus Locke, she produced the pre-Bway tryout of *The Carefree Heart* (opened Cass, Detroit, Mich., Sept. 30, 1957; closed Hanna, Cleveland, Ohio, Oct. 26, 1957); with Robert Morley and Rubin Fox, *The Love Doctor* (Piccadilly, London, England, Oct. 12, 1959); in association with Sy Kasoff, the pre-Bway tryout of *High Fidelity* (opened Walnut, Philadelphia, Pa., Sept. 14, 1961; closed there Sept. 16, 1961); and *Chocolates* (Gramercy Arts Th., N.Y.C., Apr. 10, 1967).

LOGAN, JOSHUA. Director, producer, playwright. b. Joshua Lockwood Logan, Jr., Oct. 5, 1908, Texarkana, Tex., to Joshua Lockwood and Sue (Nabors) Logan. Grad. Culver (Ind.) Military Acad., 1927; attended Princeton Univ. Studied with Constantin Stanislavsky, Moscow, U.S.S.R., 1931. Married 1940 to Barbara O'Neill, actress (marr. dis. 1941); married 1945 to Nedda Harrigan, actress; one son, one daughter. Served WW II, USAAF; rank, Capt. Member of SDG; SSD&C; NY Athletic Club; The Players. c/o Fitelson and Mayers, 1212 Ave. of the Americas, New York, NY 10036, tel. (212) JU 6-4700.

Theatre. Mr. Logan was a founder of the University Players (Falmouth, Mass., Summer 1928), and directed and performed with the group at Falmouth (Summers 1928–32) and in Baltimore (Md., 1931–32; 1932–33). He also served as a member of the board of directors with Charles Leatherbee and Bretaigne Windust.

He made his N.Y.C. debut, playing Mart Strong in *Carry Nation* (Biltmore, Oct. 29, 1932); subsequently directed *Camille* (Colonial, Boston, Mass., 1933); *The Day I Forgot* (Globe Th., London, May

1933); produced, with J.H. Del Bondio, and directed *To See Ourselves* (Ethel Barrymore Th., N.Y.C., Apr. 30, 1935); directed *Hell Freezes Over* (Ritz, Dec. 28, 1935); appeared as Robert Humphreys in *A Room in Red and White*(46 St. Th., Jan. 18, 1936); directed *On Borrowed Time* (Longacre, Feb. 3, 1938), *I Married an Angel*(Shubert, May 11, 1938), *Knickerbocker Holiday*(Ethel Barrymore Th., Dec. 19, 1938), *Stars in Your Eyes*(Majestic, Feb. 9, 1939) and *Morning's at Seven* (Longacre, Nov. 30, 1939); directed the sketches for the revue, *Two for the Show*(Booth, Feb. 8, 1940); wrote, with Gladys Hurlbut, and directed *Higher and Higher* (Shubert, Apr. 4, 1940); directed *Charley's Aunt* (Cort, Oct. 17, 1940), *By Jupiter* (Shubert, June 3, 1942) and *This Is the Army* (Bway Th., July 4, 1942).

He staged *Annie Get Your Gun*(Imperial, May 16, 1946); *Happy Birthday* (Broadhurst, Oct. 3, 1946); produced, in association with Richard Rodgers and Oscar Hammerstein II, and directed *John Loves Mary* (Booth, Feb. 4, 1947); wrote with Thomas Heggan, and directed *Mister Roberts*(Alvin, Feb. 18, 1948); wrote with Mr. Hammerstein, produced with Richard Rodgers, Mr. Hammerstein, and Leland Hayward, and directed *South Pacific*(Majestic, Apr. 7, 1949).

Mr. Logan wrote, produced, with Leland Hayward, and directed *The Wisteria Trees*(Martin Beck Th., Mar. 29, 1950); wrote, with Harold Rome and Arthur Kober, produced with Leland Hayward, and directed *Wish You Were Here* (Imperial, June 25, 1952); produced, with the Theatre Guild, and directed *Picnic*(Music Box, Feb. 19, 1953); produced and directed *Kind Sir*(Alvin, Nov. 4, 1953); wrote, with S. N. Behrman, produced, with David Merrick, and directed *Fanny* (Majestic, Nov. 4, 1954); produced and directed *Middle of the Night*(ANTA, Feb. 8, 1956); directed *Blue Denim* (Playhouse, Feb. 27, 1958) and *The World of Suzie Wong* (Broadhurst, Oct. 14, 1958); produced, with David Merrick, *Epitaph for George Dillon* (John Golden Th., Nov. 4, 1958); directed *There Was a Little Girl* (Cort, Feb. 29, 1960), *All American* (Winter Garden, Mar. 19, 1962), *Mr. President*(St. James, Oct. 20, 1962); *Tiger Tiger Burning Bright* (Booth Th., Dec. 22, 1962); *Ready When You Are, C. B!* (Brooks Atkinson Th., Dec. 7, 1964); and *Look to the Lilies*(Lunt-Fontanne Th., March 29, 1970).

Films. Mr. Logan's first assignment was as dialogue director of *The Garden of Allah* (UA, 1936); subsequently, was dialogue director for *History Is Made at Night* (UA, 1937); co-director of *I Met My Love Again* (UA, 1938); director of *Picnic* (Col., 1955), *Bus Stop* (20th-Fox, 1956), *Sayonara* (WB, 1957), and *South Pacific* (Magna, 1958); producer and director of *Tall Story* (WB, 1960), *Fanny* (WB, 1961); producer, director and co-author of *Ensign Pulver*(WB, 1964); director of *Camelot* (WB, 1967), and *Paint Your Wagon* (Par., 1969).

Awards. Mr. Logan, Oscar Hammerstein II and Richard Rodgers received the Pulitzer Prize (1950) for their musical, *South Pacific.* He also received an honorary M.A. from Princeton Univ. (1953).

Recreation. Gardening, sculpting, travel.

LOGAN, NEDDA HARRIGAN.

Actress. b. c. 1900, Rumson, N.J., to Edward "Ned" and Anne Theresa (Braham) Harrigan. Father, comedian. Attended Natl. Park Seminary, Md. Married to Walter Connolly, actor (dec. 1940); one daughter; married 1945 to Joshua Logan, director, producer; one son, one daughter. Relative in theatre: brother, William Harrigan, actor. Member of AEA; SAG.

Theatre. Mrs. Logan appeared in *A Woman of No Importance*(Fulton, N.Y.C., Apr. 24, 1916); played the Sister in *The Children's Tragedy*(Greenwich Village Th., Oct. 10, 1921); Lisa Toselli in *Treat 'Em Rough* (Klaw, Oct. 4, 1926); Wells in *Dracula* (Fulton, Oct. 5, 1927); Janet Aiken in *Merry Andrew* (Henry Miller's Th., Jan. 21, 1929); Fifine in *Becky Sharp*(Knickerbocker, June 3, 1929); Estelle Fenley in *Monkey*(Mansfield, Feb. 11, 1932); Myra Crana in *Bidding High* (Nanderbilt, Sept. 28, 1932); succeeded (Jan. 1932); Jean Dixon as Frieda Chatfield in *Dangerous Corner*(Empire, Oct. 27, 1932); played Felicia Mitchell in *A Hat, a Coat and a Glove* (Selwyn, Jan. 31, 1934); and Natalia in *Field of Ermine* (Mansfield, Feb. 8, 1935).

She toured in *A Woman's a Fool-to Be Clever* (1938); and in stock, appeared in *Cardinal Richelieu* (Mohawk Drama Festival, Schenectady, N.Y., 1940).

Mrs. Logan played Donna Lucia D'Alvadorez in *Charley's Aunt* (Cort, N.Y.C., Oct. 17, 1940); and Edith Bolling Wilson in *In Time to Come*(Mansfield, Dec. 28, 1941).

Films. She has appeared in *I'll Fix It* (Col., 1934); *The Case of the Black Cat* (1st Natl., 1936); *Charlie Chan at the Opera* (Fox, 1936); *Fugitive in the Sky* (WB, 1937); *Thank You, Mr. Moto* (Fox, 1937); *A Trip to Paris*(Fox, 1938); *On Trial*(WB, 1939); *The Honeymoon's Over* (Fox, 1939); *The Castle on the Hudson* (WB, 1940); *Devil's Island* (WB, 1940), and others.

LOMBARDO, GUY.

Producer, bandleader. b. Gaetano Alberto Lombardo, June 19, 1902, London, Ont., Canada, to Gaetano and Lena (Palladino) Lombardo. Father, tailor. Grad. St. Peter's Sch., London, Ont., 1920. Dr. of Music, Univ. of Western Ontario, 1972. Married Sept. 11, 1926, to Lilliebell Glenn. Member of AFM; AGVA; AGMA; SAG; Amer. Power Boat Assn. (secy). Address: (home) 710 S. Grove St., Freeport, NY 11520; (bus.) 157 W. 57th St., New York, NY 10019, tel. (212) 581-4688.

Theatre. At the Marine Th., Jones Beach, L.I., N.Y., Mr. Lombardo produced *Arabian Nights*(June 25, 1954; June 26, 1955), *Show Boat* (1956, 1957), *Song of Norway*(1958), *Paradise Island*(1961, 1962), *Around the World in 80 Days* (1963), *Mardi Gras* (1965–66), *South Pacific* (1968–69), *The Sound of Music* (1970–71), *The King and I* (1972), *Carousel* (1973), and *Fiddler on the Roof* (1974).

He appeared with his orchestra at the Tipparilo Band Pavillion (NY World's Fair, May 30–Sept. 16, 1964).

Films. He played himself in *Many Happy Returns* (Par., 1934); and has appeared in *Stage Door Canteen* (UA, 1943); and *No Leave, No Love* (MGM, 1946).

Television and Radio. He made his debut with WTAM, Cleveland, Ohio (1938); performed on the Bob Burns Show (1930–35); the Lady Esther Show (1938–41); and Your Hit Parade (1941–45).

Mr. Lombardo played in the New Year from the Roosevelt Hotel (N.Y.C.) on CBS and NBC Radio (1930–54). In 1955 the show was moved from radio to television. From 1967 to the present, CBS has televised the show from the Waldorf Astoria.

Night Clubs. He has performed with his orchestra at the Clairmont Cafe (Cleveland, Ohio, 1924); Granada Cafe (Chicago, Ill., 1927); Roosevelt Hotel (N.Y.C., Winters 1929–61); Waldorf Astoria Hotel (N.Y.C., 1938–46); and the Coconut Grove in the Ambassador Hotel (Los Angeles, 1934–35; 1940).

Other Activities. Mr. Lombardo has been involved with speedboat racing. He broke all existing records, winning the Gold Cup at Detroit (1946); won the National Sweepstakes (1946; 1947; 1951); made new single engine record (119.7 mph) at Salton Sea, Calif. (May 1948); and was national champion in unlimited hydroplanes (1946–49). He retired from racing after winning a President's Cup in Washington, D.C. (1955).

Discography. Mr. Lombardo first recorded for Gennet Records (1924), followed by Columbia (1928–31), Brunswick (1932–34), Victor (1935–36), Decca (1937–56), and Capitol (1957–71).

LONEY, GLENN MEREDITH.

Drama critic, journalist, editor, educator. b. Dec. 24, 1928, Sacramento, Calif., to David Merton and Marion (Busher) Loney. Father, rancher; mother, teacher. Grad. Univ. of California at Berkeley, B.A. 1950; Univ. of Wisconsin at Madison, M.A. 1951; Stanford Univ., Ph.D. 1954. Served in US Army, 1953–55; infantry rifleman. Member of Drama Desk (recorder); Outer Critics Circle; ATA; CTC; USITT; ASTR; IFTR; AIDART (Advanced Institute for Development of American Repertory Theatre); TLA. Address: (home) 187 Hicks St., Brooklyn, NY 11201, tel. (212) UL 2-4826; (bus.) CUNY Graduate Center, Ph.D. in Theatre Program, Rm. 1229, 33 W. 42nd St., New York, NY 10036, tel. (212) 790-4464.

Mr. Loney became professor of theatre at Brooklyn College of the City Univ. of New York (CUNY) in 1961. Previously, he had taught at the Univ. of California (Berkeley), Stanford Univ., San Francisco State, Nevada Southern (Las Vegas), and the Univ. of Maryland Overseas (1956–59) and at Hofstra and Adelphi universities (1959–61).

He was performing arts correspondent for the *Christian Science Monitor*(1958–65), a staff member of *Theatre Arts* and a contributing editor (1961–63), drama critic for *Educational Theatre Journal* (1966–71), and off-Bway critic for the *New York Daily Column* (1968–70). In addition he has been a contributing editor to *Theatre Crafts, After Dark, Dance,* and *Theatre Today.*

Mr. Loney prepared the *Cue*-AIDART Interviews ("In the Words of. . .") with thirty-nine theatrical personalities, which appeared in *Cue* magazine (1969–71). He has published articles in a wide variety of periodicals, such as the New York *Times, Opera News, Musical America, Commonweal, Smithsonian, Scandinavian Review,* and *Theatre Design & Technology.* He edited *The House of Mirth* by Edith Wharton and Clyde Fitch and *The Authorized Peter Brook/Royal Shakespeare Production Book of 'A Midsummer Night's Dream'*(1974); edited and wrote an introduction to John Gassner's *Dramatic Soundings* (1968); wrote the chapter "The United States—American Theatre (1954–1967)" in George Freedley and John A. Reeve's *A History of the Theatre* (1968); contributed essays on operetta, musical comedy, Richard Wagner, Lorenzo Da Ponte, and Gilbert and Sullivan to *The Reader's Encyclopedia of World Drama* (1969); and prepared headnotes for three drama anthologies edited by Robert Corrigan: *Comedy* (1971); *Tragedy* (1971); and *The Forms of Drama* (1972). Mr. Loney also wrote *Briefing and Conference Techniques* (1959) and "Letters from a Soldier" (Adelphi Quarterly, Summer 1961).

Television and Radio. In 1970, Mr. Loney began contributing radio scripts on life in Germany to the "Germany Today" series. He wrote and was master of ceremonies for two Brooklyn College television series: *Exploring Your Museums* and *Meet the Professor.*.

Other Activities. Mr. Loney is acting archivist for AIDART and theatre editor for RILM International Music Bibliography project. He is a member of the steering committees for the Museum for the American Theatre Project and for the Preservation of Old Theatres Project.

Awards. Mr. Loney was made a fellow of the American-Scandinavian Foundation in 1962 for his study of the Swedish theatre. He received a CUNY grant for editing the plays of Edith Wharton (1967) and a *Cue* magazine grant for creation of an oral archive of contemporary performers (1969).

Recreation. Hiking, carpentry, photography, collecting theatre posters and programs.

LONG, AVON.

Actor, songwriter, singer, dancer. b. June 18, 1910, Baltimore, Md., to Charles and Bertha Long. Father, pianist; mother, seamstress. Grad. Douglass H.S., Baltimore, 1929. Studied at New England Conservatory, Boston, Mass., 1929; Allied Art Ctr., Boston, 1929; Sonya Koretna Sch. of Dance, Boston, 1929. Married Feb. 20, 1937, to Gretchen Cotton, secretary; three daughters. Entertained troops in USO tours during WW II. Member of AEA; AGMA; AGVA; SAG. Address: (home) 351 W. 114th St., New York, NY 10026, tel. (212) UN 6-2993; (bus.) c/o AEA, 165 W. 46th St., New York, NY 10036, tel. (212) PL 7-7660.

Theatre. Mr. Long toured in vaudeville with *Connie's Hot Chocolates* (Keith Circuit, 1934); appeared in *Gentlemen Unafraid*(St. Louis Opera House, Mo., 1938); played Sportin' Life in *Porgy and Bess* (Los Angeles Philharmonic Aud., 1938); Jackson in *Very*

Warm for May (Alvin Th., N.Y.C., Nov. 17, 1939); Orestes in *La Belle Helene* (Westport Country Playhouse, Conn., 1939); Sportin' Life in *Porgy and Bess* (Majestic Th., N.Y.C., Jan. 22, 1942); Windy in *Memphis Bound* (Bway Th., May 24, 1945); and the Fisherman in *Carib Song* (Adelphi, Sept. 27, 1945); Careless Love in *Beggar's Holiday* (Bway Th., Dec. 26, 1946); the First Man Angel in a revival of *The Green Pastures* (Broadway Th., Mar. 15, 1951); and Lt. Jim Crocker in *Shuffle Along* (Bway Th., May 8, 1952).

He was a featured artist with a symphony orchestra for a B'nai Brith scholarship benefit (Carnegie Hall, 1953); played Mr. D. in *Mrs. Patterson* (National Th., Dec. 1, 1954); played the Magician in *Ballad of Jazz Street* (Greenwich Mews, Nov. 11, 1959); William Piper in *Fly Blackbird* (Mayfair Th., Feb. 5, 1962); Mister Tambo in *Gentlemen, Be Seated* (NY City Ctr., Oct. 10, 1963); appeared in *Head of the Family* (Westport Country Playhouse, Conn.); and was the Narrator for *The Threepenny Opera* (Westport Country Playhouse, Nov. 19, 1963).

He toured the US as Sportin' Life in a revival of *Porgy and Bess* (1967); starred in the African tour of Mura Dehn's *Traditional Jazz Theatre;* appeared in stock presentations of *My Sister Eileen, Pajama Game, Kiss Me, Kate, Just Around the Corner, Bloomer Girl,* and *Carmen Jones;* and he has toured with his own concert groups, visiting college campuses and Canada, Alaska, and Trinidad. He joined (1972) the cast of *Ain't Supposed To Die a Natural Death* (Ethel Barrymore Th., N.Y.C., Oct. 20, 1971); was David in *Don't Play Us Cheap!* (Ethel Barrymore Th., May 16, 1972); played Jesus Fever in *Other Voices, Other Rooms* (world premiere, Studio Arena, Buffalo, N.Y., Oct. 4, 1973); and was in *The Jitney Vehicle* (Amas Rep. Th., Nov. 30, 1973).

Films. Mr. Long was in *Manhattan Merry-Go-Round* (Rep., 1937); *Centennial Summer* (20th-Fox, 1946); *Romance on the High Seas* (WB, 1948); *Finian's Rainbow* (1968); *Don't Play Us Cheap!* (Melvin Van Peebles, 1973); *The Sting* (Par., 1973); and *Harry and Tonto* (U, 1974).

Television. He appeared as a guest star on Garraway-At-Large (NBC, 1949, 1951); appeared on US Steel Hour (CBS, 1958); played Jim on The Big Story (CBS, 1959); and Caiu in *The Green Pastures* (Hallmark Hall of Fame, NBC, 1960). He has also been a guest on Black News; the Joe Franklin Show; the John Bartholomew Tucker Show; and Black Journal.

Night Clubs. He played Brown Boy in the *Cotton Club Revue* (Cotton Club, N.Y.C., 1931). He appeared with his concert trio, the Porgy and Bess Singers, at major clubs throughout the US and abroad during the 1960's.

Awards. He was selected by *Variety* as the Performer Most Likely to Succeed (1941); received a citation as the Best Broadway Male Actor of the Year for his performance as Sporting Life in *Porgy and Bess* (1942); and a certificate of merit from Henry Morgenthau for entertaining the armed forces (1942). He also received a citation from Emperor Haile Selassi of Ethiopia while on his African tour with Mura Dehn; was nominated (1973) for an Antoinette Perry (Tony) Award for best supporting actor in a musical for his role in *Don't Play Us Cheap!;* and won the *Focus* award for best performance of the year (1973) from the Studio Arena Th., Buffalo, N.Y.

Recreation. Roller-skating, making hooked rugs, crossword puzzles, oil painting, writing anecdotes and songs. Mr. Long is writing a musical about days of slavery.

LONG, SUMNER ARTHUR.

Playwright. b. Mar. 31, 1921, Boston, Mass., to Herman M. and Esther Long. Father, printer. Attended Roxbury Memorial H.S., Boston, Mass., 1935–37. Married July 23, 1956, to Beulah R. Grau, writer; one son, one daughter. Served USN, 1941–47, PTO; rank, AOM 1/C. Member of WGA, West; Dramatists Guild. Address: 1268 S. Camden Dr., Los Angeles, CA 90035.

Pre-Theatre. Television writer.

Theatre. Mr. Long is the author of *Never Too Late* (Playhouse Th., N.Y.C., Nov. 27, 1962; Prince of Wales's Th., London, Sept. 24, 1963); and *Angela* (Music Box Th., N.Y.C., Oct. 30, 1969).

Television. Mr. Long has written plays for Bigelow Th.; Ford Th. (CBS); Father Knows Best (CBS); Danny Thomas Show (CBS); Mickey Rooney Show; I Married Joan; Dobie Gillis; Lassie (CBS); Private Secretary; Life of Riley; the Dennis O'Keefe Show; the Donna Reed Show (ABC); and special material for Milton Berle.

Awards. He received the 38th Annual Gold Medal Award (1963) of the Theater Club, Inc., for *Never Too Late.*

Recreation. "Sports, hobbies and pastimes are incorporated in various methods of 'loafing.'".

LONGSTREET, STEPHEN.

Playwright, writer. b. Apr. 18, 1907, New York City, to Irwin and Sarah Longstreet. Grad. New Brunswick H.S., 1925; attended Rutgers Univ., 1926; Harvard Univ., 1927; grad. New York Sch. of Fine and Applied Art, M.A. 1929. Studied painting at Paris (Fr.), Rome (It.), London (Eng.), 1929–32. Married June 14, 1933, to Ethel Joan Godoff, television producer, educator, pianist; one son, one daughter. Created films for War Dept., WW II; awarded Citation of Meritorious Service. Member of Dramatists Guild; WGA; AFTRA; Screen Writers Film Society (bd. mbr., 1943–57); Los Angeles Art Assn. (trustee, 1952–64; pres. and historian, 1973–to date); Viewpoints Inst. (dir., 1964); Phi Sigma. Address: 1133 Miradero Rd., Beverly Hills, CA 90210.

Pre-Theatre. Painter, cartoonist, novelist, editor.

Theatre. Mr. Longstreet wrote *High Button Shoes* (Century, N.Y.C., Oct. 9, 1947); and *Gauguin* (Pasadena Playhouse, Calif., 1948).

Films. He wrote, in whole or in part, *The Gay Sisters* (WB, 1942); *The Imposter* (U, 1944); *Uncle Harry* (U, 1945); *The Jolson Story* (Col., 1946); *Duel in the Sun* (Selznick, 1946); *Stallion Road* (WB, 1947); *Silver River* (WB, 1948); *Stars and Stripes Forever* (20th-Fox, 1952); *The Greatest Show on Earth* (Par., 1952); *Houdini* (Par., 1953); *The Helen Morgan Story* (WB, 1957); *Untamed Youth* (WB, 1957); *Born Reckless* (WB, 1959); *Rider on a Dead Horse* (Allied, 1962); and *Man of Montmartre* (Allied, 1963).

Television and Radio. He has written radio shows for Rudy Vallee (1936); Deems Taylor (1936); John Barrymore (1937); Bob Hope (1936); and Ellery Queen (1939).

For television, he has written scripts for the Pulitzer Prize Th. (ABC); Big Town (CBS); Playhouse 90 (CBS); Readers' Digest Th.; Casey Jones, which he also created (1960); Agent of Scotland Yard (1959); The Sea (NBC), for which he also served as master of ceremonies (1960); and the award-winning *Young Man from Boston: "The John F. Kennedy Story"* (ABC, 1967).

Other Activities. He was film critic for the *Saturday Review of Literature* (1941); an editor on *Time* Magazine (1942); and literary critic for *Readers Syndicate* (1952–74).

He has been a lecturer at the Univ. of Southern California, the Univ. of California at Los Angeles, and Los Angeles City Coll. (1950–64). He has taught a course called "Advanced Writing" at Los Angeles City Coll. He has been a literary critic on the Los Angeles *Daily News.* He is at present a professor in the Dept. of Theatre Arts, Univ. of Southern California, teaching "The Disciplines of Writing.".

Published Works. He has written stories for such magazines as *Esquire, Liberty, Cosmopolitan,* and *Gourmet;* created cartoons for *Collier's, Saturday Evening Post, The New Yorker, College Humor, Life,* and *Judge.*

Under the pseudonym of Paul Haggard, he wrote Crime on the Cuff (1936); *Dead Is the Doornail* (1937); *Death Talks Shop* (1937); *Death Walks on Cat Feet* (1938); *Poison from a Wealthy Widow* (1938). As Stephen Longstreet, he wrote *Decade* (1940). As Thomas Burton, he wrote *And So Dedicated* (1940); *Bloodbird* (1941); *The Great Grab* (1941). As Stephen Longstreet, he wrote *The Golden Touch* (1941); *The Last Man Around the World* (1941); *The Gay Sisters* (1942); and *The Last Man Comes Home* (1942).

As David Ormsbee, he wrote *Sound of an American* (1942); *Chico Goes to the Wars* (1943). As Stephen Longstreet, he wrote *The Land I Live* (1943); *Nine Lives with Grandfather* (1944); *Free World Theatre; Nineteen New Radio Plays* (edited with A. Oboler, 1944); *Stallion Road* (1945); *The Sisters Liked Them Handsome* (dramatized as *High Button Shoes*) (1946); *Three Days* (1947); *The Crystal Girl* (1948); *The Pedlocks* (1951); *The Beach House* (1952); *A Hundred Years on Wheels* (1952); *The World Revisited* (1953); and *The Lion at Morning* (1954).

Mr. Longstreet wrote *Boy in the Model-T* (1956); *Promoters* (1957); *The Real Jazz, Old and New* (1958); *Crime* (1959); with his wife *Politicians* (1959); *Geisha* (1960); edited *Treasury of the World's Finest Prints* (1961); wrote *Flesh Peddlers* (1962); *Canvas Falcons* (1970); *War Cries on Horse Back* (1970); and *We All Went to Paris* (1972).

Awards. Mr. Longstreet received the *Billboard* Award (1948) for *High Button Shoes;* the *Photoplay* Gold Medal Gallup Poll Award (1948) for *The Jolson Story;* the California Golden Star (1949) for *Gauguin;* and was nominated for an Academy (Oscar) Award (1952) for *The Greatest Show on Earth.*

LOOS, ANITA.

Playwright, director. b. Apr. 26, 1893, Sisson, Calif., to Richard Beers and Minnie Ellen (Smith) Loos. Father producer. Attended high school, San Francisco, Calif. Married June 1915, to Frank Pallma, Jr. (marr. dis.); married to John Emerson, film director. Relative in theatre: niece, Mary Anita Loos, scenarist-novelist. Member of Dramatists Guild.

Theatre. Miss Loos made her first stage appearance in the title role of *Little Lord Fauntleroy;* subsequently appeared as Lady Barbara in *East Lynne,* played in *On the Yukon, The Prince Chap, The Jewess,* and performed as Mary Jane in *Mary Jane's Pa* (San Diego, Calif.).

She wrote the plays *The Whole Town's Talking* (Bijou, N.Y.C., Aug. 29, 1923); *The Fall of Eve* (Booth, Aug. 31, 1925); *Gentlemen Prefer Blondes* (Times Sq. Th., Sept. 28, 1926); wrote, and directed with John Emerson, *The Social Register* (Fulton, Nov. 9, 1931); *Happy Birthday* (Broadhurst, Oct. 31, 1946); wrote the book, with Joseph Fields, based on her collection of stories, for the musical version of *Gentlemen Prefer Blondes* (Ziegfeld, Dec. 8, 1949); adapted from the novel by Colette, the dramatization of *Gigi* (Fulton, Nov. 24, 1951); wrote the book for the pre-Bway tryout of *The Amazing Adele,* based on the French play by Pierre Barrillet and Jean-Pierre Gredy (opened Shubert, Philadelphia, Pa., Dec. 26, 1955; closed Shubert, Boston, Mass., Jan. 21, 1956); adapted from two novels by Colette, *Chéri* (Morosco, N.Y.C., Oct. 12, 1959); appeared with Carol Channing in *An Evening of Theatrical Reminiscences* (Gramercy Arts Th., May 1963); and

Gogo Loves You(Th. de Lys, Oct. 9, 1964); wrote *The King's Mare* (Garrick, London, July 6, 1966); and, with Joseph Fields, wrote *Lorilei, or Gentlemen Still Prefer Blondes* (Palace, N.Y.C., Jan. 27, 1974), a second musical adaptation based on her stories, *Gentlemen Prefer Blondes.*

Films. Beginning with the scenario and screenplay for *The New York Hat* (1906), Miss Loos wrote the screenplays for more than 400 short subjects, including *A Horse on Bill, Pa Says, The Hicksville Epicure, Highbrow Love, The Power of the Camera, The Suicide Pact, The Widow's Kids, A Fallen Hero, His Voodoo, The Lady in Black, The Wedding Gown, How the Day Was Saved, A Cure for Suffragettes, Bink's Vacation, False Colours, Billy's Revival, When the Road Parts, A Bunch of Flowers,* and *Gentleman Thief.* For Fine Arts-Triangle, she wrote the screenplays for *Little Liar*(1916), *His Picture in the Papers*(1916), *The Half Breed* (1916), *American Aristocracy* (1916), *The Social Secretary* (1916), and *The Americano* (1917). She wrote the screenplay for *In Again—Out Again* (Artcraft, 1917); *Reaching for the Moon* (Artcraft, 1917); *Wild and Wooly* (Artcraft, 1917); scenario and screenplay for *Goodbye Bill* (Par. 1918); *Come On In* (Par., 1918); screenplay for *Let's Get a Divorce*(Par., 1918); *Temperamental Wife,* which was based on the play, *Information Please,* which she wrote with John Emerson (1st Natl., 1919); wrote the screenplay for *Isle of Conquest* (Selznick, 1919); scenario for *Under the Top*(Artcraft, 1919); scenario and screenplay for *Oh, You Women!* (Par., 1919); *Getting Mary Married* (Select, 1919); *Virtuous Vamp* (1st Natl., 1919); screenplay for *The Branded Woman* (1st Natl., 1920).

Also wrote scenario and screenplay, with John Emerson, for *Perfect Woman* (1st Natl., 1920); *Dangerous Business* (1st Natl., 1920); screenplay, with John Emerson, for *In Search of a Sinner* (1st Natl., 1920); scenario and screenplay, with John Emerson, for *Woman's Place* (1st Natl., 1921); wrote scenario and screenplay for *Hold Your Man* (U, 1921); wrote screenplay for *Red Hot Romance* (1st Natl., 1921); wrote scenario and screenplay for *Polly of the Follies* (1st Natl., 1922); *Three Miles Out* (Assoc. Exhibitors, 1924); *Learning To Love* (1st Natl., 1925); *The Struggle* (UA, 1931); wrote screenplay for *Down to Earth* (20th-Fox, 1932); *Red Headed Woman* (MGM, 1932); *Blondie of the Follies* (MGM, 1932); *The Barbarian* (MGM, 1932); scenario for *Midnight Mary* (MGM, 1933); scenario and screenplay for *The Girl from Missouri*(MGM, 1934); screenplay for *Biography of a Bachelor Girl* (MGM, 1935); *Riffraff* (MGM, 1935); scenario and screenplay for *Mama Steps Out* (MGM, 1937); *Susan and God* (MGM, 1940); *They Met in Bombay* (MGM, 1941); and *I Married an Angel* (MGM, 1942).

Published Works. Miss Loos wrote the fictional works *Gentlemen Prefer Blondes* (1926), *But Gentlemen Marry Brunettes*(1928), *A Mouse Is Born*(1951), and *No Mother to Guide Her*(1962); with John Emerson, the nonfictional work, *Breaking Into the Movies;* her autobiography, *A Girl Like I* (1966); and *Kiss Hollywood Goodbye* (1974).

LOQUASTO, SANTO. Theatrical designer. b. Wilkes Barre, Pa. Grad. Kings College, Wilkes Barre; Yale Drama Sch.

Theatre. For the Hartford (Conn.) Stage Co., Mr. Loquasto designed the sets for *The Hostage* (Feb. 2, 1968); *The Rose Tattoo* (Nov. 22, 1968); *The Waltz Invention* (Jan. 3, 1969); *The Homecoming* (Feb. 14, 1969); sets and costumes for *A Delicate Balance* (Oct. 17, 1969); *The Farce of Scapin* (Nov. 28, 1969); sets for *A Day in the Death of Joe Egg* (Jan. 9, 1970); sets and costumes for *Misalliance* (Feb. 20, 1970); sets for *The Trial of A. Lincoln* (Apr. 3, 1970); sets and costumes for *Anything Goes* (May 15, 1970); *Rosencrantz and Guildenstern Are Dead* (Oct. 16, 1970); sets for *Ring Round the Moon* (Nov. 27, 1970); *A Gun Play* (Jan. 8, 1971); sets and costumes for *Long Day's Journey into Night* (Feb. 19, 1971). In addition, he designed the sets for *Tiny Alice* (Long Wharf Th., New Haven, Apr. 5, 1968); designed the sets for the Amer. premiere of *Narrow Road to the Deep North* (Charles Playhouse, Boston, Oct. 30, 1969); made his off-Bway debut as set designer for a double-bill which included *The Unseen Hand* and *Forensic and the Navigators* (Astor Place Th., N.Y.C., Apr. 1, 1970); designed costumes for *The Skin of Our Teeth* (Long Wharf Th., New Haven, Oct. 30, 1970); and, for the Yale Rep. Th. (New Haven) designed sets and costumes for *The Story Theatre: Gimpel the Fool, St. Julian the Hospitaler,* and *Olympian Games* (Oct. 8, 1970); sets for *The Revenger's Tragedy* (Nov. 19, 1970); and sets and costumes for the Amer. premiere of a double-bill including *The Little Mahagonny* and *The Seven Deadly Sins* (May 13, 1971; and Jan. 20, 1972).

For Arena Stage (Washington, D.C.), he designed the sets for *Wipe-out Games* (Apr. 9, 1971); *Pantagleize* (Oct. 22, 1971); *The House of Blue Leaves* (Jan. 7, 1972); and *Uptight* (Mar. 17, 1972). Beginning a long association with Joseph Papp, he designed the sets for *Sticks and Bones* (Public/Anspacher, N.Y.C., Nov. 7, 1971; moved to John Golden Th., Mar. 1, 1972); subsequently designed sets and costumes for *Henry V* (Hartford Stage Co., Nov. 26, 1971); sets for *That Championship Season* (Public/Newman, N.Y.C., May 2, 1972; moved to Booth, Sept. 14, 1974); *Old Times* (Mark Taper Forum, Los Angeles, May 25, 1972); *The Secret Affairs of Mildred Wild* (Ambassador, N.Y.C., Nov. 14, 1972); *Sunset* (Chelsea Th. Ctr., Dec. 5, 1972); *Siamese Connections* (Public/Annex, Jan. 9, 1973); *A Public Prosecutor Is Sick of It All* (Arena Stage, Washington, D.C., Jan. 31, 1973); *The Orphan* (Public/Anspacher, N.Y.C., Mar. 30, 1973); *As You Like It* (Delacorte, June 27, 1973); *King Lear* (Delacorte, July 31, 1973); *Boom Boom Room* (Vivian Beaumont Th., Nov. 8, 1973); *The Tempest* (Mitzi E. Newhouse Th., Feb. 10, 1974); *What the Wine-Sellers Buy* (Vivian Beaumont Th., Feb. 14, 1974); *The Dance of Death* (Vivian Beaumont Th., Apr. 4, 1974); sets and costumes for *Macbeth* (Mitzi E. Newhouse Th., closed during previews, Apr. 13, 1974); sets for *Pericles, Prince of Tyre* (Delacorte, June 20, 1974); *The Merry Wives of Windsor* (Delacorte, July 25, 1974); *King Richard III* (Mitzi E. Newhouse Th., Oct. 20, 1974); *Mert and Phil* (Vivian Beaumont Th., Oct. 30, 1974); *The Cherry Orchard* (Hartford Stage Co., Dec. 13, 1974); *A Midsummer Night's Dream* (Mitzi E. Newhouse Th., N.Y.C., Jan. 19, 1975); *A Doll's House* (Vivian Beaumont Th., Mar. 5, 1975); *The Comedy of Errors* (Delacorte, Summer 1975); *Kennedy's Children* (John Golden Th., Nov. 3, 1975); *Hamlet* (Vivian Beaumont Th., Dec. 17, 1975); *Murder Among Friends* (Biltmore, Dec. 28, 1975); and *Legend* (Ethel Barrymore Th., May 13, 1976).

Mr. Loquasto has also designed sets and costumes for the opera, *La Dafne* (Spoleto Fest. of Two Worlds, Italy, Summer 1973); and has designed for the San Diego Opera, the Opera Society of Washington, the San Francisco Spring Opera, and the Twyla Tharp Dance Foundation.

Awards. For *Sticks and Bones* and *That Championship Season,* Mr. Loquasto received the Drama Desk and the *Variety* Poll of N.Y. Drama Critics awards (1971–72).

LORD, BARBARA. Actress. b. Barbara Jeannette Gratz, Nov. 21, 1937, Chicago, Ill., to Charles T. and Manila (Scheski) Gratz. Father, hotel manager, Grad. Benedictine Acad., Paterson, N.J., 1955. Studied theatre at AADA, N.Y.C., 1955–57; acting with Morris Carnovsky and Fanny Bradshaw, 1956–57, and Sanford Meisner, N.Y.C., 1958–59. Married June 3, 1961, to John C. Warburton, M.D. Member of AEA; SAG; AFTRA. Address: (home) 330 Broadway, Paterson, NJ tel. 742-2809; (bus.) c/o Lester Lewis Agency, 15 E. 48th St., New York, NY 10016, tel. (212) PL 3-5082.

Theatre. Miss Lord made her stage debut as Jessica in *The Tender Trap* (Cherry County Playhouse, Traverse, Mich., Summer 1955); followed by her professional debut as Bianca in the American Shakespeare Festival production of *The Taming of the Shrew* (Stamford, Conn., Aug. 6, 1956); played in *The Reluctant Debutante* and *The Desperate Hours* (Westchester County Playhouse, N.Y.C., June–Aug. 1957) was understudy to Elizabeth Allen as Juliet in *Romanoff and Juliet* (Plymouth, N.Y.C., Oct. 10, 1957); appeared in stock production of 13 plays, including *Time Remembered* (Elitch Gardens, Denver, Colo., June–Aug. 1958); as Gina in *A Clearing in the Woods* (Sheridan Sq. Playhouse, N.Y.C., Feb. 12, 1959); and in stock productions of *The Chalk Garden, Love Me Little,* and *The Time of Your Life* (Elitch Gardens, Denver, Colo., June–Aug. 1959).

Miss Lord succeeded Diane Cilento as Ellie Dunn in *Heartbreak House* (Billy Rose Th., N.Y.C., Oct. 18, 1959); toured as Mary in *John Loves Mary* (Detroit, Mich.; Toronto, Canada; Warren, Ohio; Waltham, Mass.; July–Sept. 1960).

Films. She appeared in *The Bloody Brood* (Astor, 1962).

Television. Miss Lord made her debut in *The Night of April 14th* (Alcoa Presents, NBC, Mar. 1959); subsequently played Cecily Cardew in *the Importance of Being Earnest* (Ford Star Time, CBC, Canada, 1960); appeared in *Wingless Victory* (Play of the Week, WNTA, Apr. 1961); and in *The Long, Long Trail* (Gunsmoke, CBS, Sept. 1961).

Recreation. Skiing, skating, dancing, swimming, riding.

LOREN, BERNICE. Actress, director, writer, educator. b. Bernice Levine, Sept. 26, Montreal, Quebec, Canada, to Sam and Gertrude (Goldfine) Levine. Father, hat manufacturer. Educ. Guy Drummond School and Strathcona Acad., Montreal; McGill Univ., Montreal. Professional training at Dramatic Workshop of the New School, N.Y.C. (Erwin Piscator, Lee Strasberg, Reiken Ben-Ari, John Gassner); Margaret McCulloch (singing); Marian Rich (voice and speech); Katya Delakova, Nona Schurman, Valerie Bettis, William Burdick (dance); NY Univ. Radio-TV Workshop. Married 1951 to Duncan Tulk (marr. dis. 1952); married 1967 to Roland Frederick Bernhagen, director of expressions, scene and lighting designer, technical director. Member of AEA; IASTA. Address: 350 W. 55th St., New York, NY 10019, tel. (212) 586-8604.

Pre-Theatre. Miss Loren held various office and sales jobs, was a writer, researcher, and editor (assoc. ed., *Journal of Existential Psychiatry,* 1960).

Theatre. Miss Loren was co-director at the Drama Playhouse, Montreal, Quebec, Canada (Feb.–Mar. 1948), and she directed and appeared in summer stock at Center Stage, East Jordan, Mich. (Summers 1948, 1949). In 1950, she played Calpurnia in *Julius Caesar* (Everyman's Th., N.Y.C.), Mrs. McKee in *Johnny Belinda,* and Mrs. Brown in *Claudia* (both Centre Playhouse, Rockville Centre, N.Y.), and Peg in *The Way of the World* (Laughing Stock Co., N.Y.C.). She was in productions at the Palm Tree Playhouse, Sarasota, Fla. (Jan.–May 1952); directed Equity Library Theatre's *Hello Out There* (Lenox Hill Playhouse, Jan. 18, 1954); appeared in IASTA productions as Marthé in *Paris Impromptu* (1960), the Chorus of Women in Sophocles' *Electra* (Mar. 22, 1961), and the Chorus in *The Exception and the Rule* (May 18, 1961). For Stage 73, N.Y.C., she directed a professional workshop (1960–61), *The Enchanted Forest* (1962–63), and played Eurydice in *Antigone* (May 2, 1966).

Miss Loren is a director of Expressions, which, with Roland Bernhagen and Marilyn Lief Kramberg, she founded in 1972 as a nonprofit corporation and a center for the arts, including a theatre and a school for the theatre. For Expressions, Miss Loren directed and choreographed *Reverence,* aspects of guitar (June 16, 23, 1974) and directed *Aspects of Theatre* (June 25–27, 1974).

Television and Radio. Miss Loren appeared in *The Marble Faun* (Ford Th., CBS, 1950); as Hannee in *Domestic Happiness* (WATV, Newark, N.J. Nov. 1957). She has lectured on theatre over WNYC in N.Y.C.

Concerts. In 1958, Miss Loren appeared at the Carnegie Chapter Hall, N.Y.C., with the Spoken Music Ensemble in *Doctor Faustus Lights the Lights* (Jan. 18) and as a Voice in *Geographic Fugue for Four*

Voices (Mar. 9).

Other Activities. Miss Loren has taught acting, voice, and movement throughout her career as actress and director, at City College of New York; Center Stage in East Jordan, Mich.; the Palm Tree Playhouse, Sarasota, Fla.; and Drama Playhouse, Montreal; in community theatres; and as a private teacher. In 1969, she began teaching The Performing Art, acting, voice, and dance approached as a unit. She has also lectured on theatre at the NY Public Library.

Published Works. Miss Loren is author of *Effective Speaking* (1963).

Recreation. Music, art, reading, walking.

LORRING, JOAN. Actress. b. Dellie Madeline Ellis, Hong Kong, China, to Frederick and Ann (Bach) Ellis. Father, stockbroker. Attended Central British Sch., Hong Kong, 1938; Professional Sch., Hollywood, Calif., 1939; MGM Sch., Culver City, Calif; WB Sch., Burbank, Calif., 1946. Married Jan. 17, 1956, to Martin Sonenberg, M.D.; two daughters. Member of AEA; AFTRA; SAG. Address: c/o Jeff Hunter Agency, 119 W. 57th St., New York, NY 10019.

Theatre. Miss Lorring made her stage debut as a dancer and singer in benefit variety shows in Shanghai, China, and Hong Kong (1936–38); danced there with the Russian Ballet Co. (1936); made her debut on the American stage as Laura in *The Glass Menagerie* (Las Palmas Th., Hollywood, Calif., Spring 1945); and appeared in *A Free Hand* (Lake Whalom Playhouse, Fitchburg, Mass., Summer 1948).

Miss Lorring first appeared on Bway as Marie in *Come Back, Little Sheba* (Booth Th., Feb. 15, 1950); subsequently played Sophie in *Autumn Garden* (Coronet, Mar. 7, 1951); Sherry Parker in *Dead Pigeon* (Vanderbilt, Dec. 23, 1953); Ginna in *A Clearing in the Woods* (Belasco, Jan. 10, 1957); and Bessie in a revival of *Awake and Sing* (Bijou, May 27, 1970).

Films. Miss Lorring has appeared in *Song of Russia* (MGM, 1943); Bessie Watty in *The Corn Is Green* (WB, 1945); *The Verdict* (WB, 1946); *Three Strangers* (WB, 1946); *The Gangster* (AA, 1947); *The Lost Moment* (U, 1947); *Good Sam* (RKO, 1948); *The Other Love* (UA, 1947); and *Stranger On the Prowl* (UA, 1953).

Television and Radio. Miss Lorring's first radio engagement was in Dear John (NBC, 1941); followed by Lux Radio Th.; Suspense; Th. Guild on the Air; Ford Th.; and Cavalcade of America. In 1974, she played roles in CBS Radio Mystery Th., a revival of radio plays.

On television, she has appeared on Robert Montgomery Presents (NBC); Philco Television Playhouse (NBC); Motorola (ABC); Studio One (CBS); as Bessie Watty in *The Corn Is Green* (Hallmark Hall of Fame, NBC, 1957); and Alfred Hitchcock Presents (CBS).

Awards. Miss Lorring was nominated for an Academy (Oscar) Award for her performance as Bessie Watty in the film *The Corn Is Green* (1944); received the Donaldson Award for her performance as Marie in the play, *Come Back, Little Sheba* (1950); and for her portrayal of Bessie in the television production of *The Corn Is Green* (1957), she won the Sylvania Television Award.

Recreation. Cooking: American, French, Italian, Cantonese, Japanese, Near Eastern, East Indian, Russian, and Danish dishes, and baking various breads.

Miss Lorring is also a linguist who speaks Russian, French, Italian, some Danish, and studies Mandarin Chinese.

LORTEL, LUCILLE. Producer, former actress. b. Lucille Mayo, New York City, to Harry and Anna Mayo. Attended Adelphi Coll., 1920; AADA, 1920–21. Studied in Europe with Arnold Korf, actor; with Max Reinhardt in Berlin, Germany. Married Mar. 23, 1931, to Louis Schweitzer, chemical engineer (dec. Sept. 19, 1971). Member of ANTA (bd. of dir., Natl. & NY chapters); Natl. Repertory Th. (trustee, 1961–); IASTA (mbr., adv. comm., 1959–); New Dramatists Comm. (mbr., adv. council, 1955–); Office of Cultural Affairs for the City of NY (citizen's adv. council, 1963–); bd. of dir., Lincoln Center (Feb. 1971–to date); The Pickwick Club, London (hon. mbr.); The Ziegfeld Club; Woman Pays Club; Amer. Shakespeare Festival Th. & Acad. (co-founder, 1955). Address: "Fairweather", Cranbury Rd., Westport, CT 06880, tel. (203) CA 7-6816.

Theatre. MissLortel made her stage debut with a stock company (Albany, N.Y., 1924); toured as ingenue with the Merkle Harder Repertory Co. (1924); and played a season of stock (Lewiston, Me., Summer 1924).

She made her N.Y.C., debut in a minor role in *Two by Two* (Selwyn, Feb. 23, 1925); subsequently played a Handmaiden in the Th. Guild production of *Caesar and Cleopatra* (Guild, Apr. 13, 1925); and took over the role of Iras, for the last week of the run. She played Inez in a revival of *The Dove* (Empire, Aug. 24, 1925); Clara Rathbone in *One Man's Woman* (48 St. Th., May 25, 1926); succeeded (Feb. 1927) Dorothy Hall as Elsa in *The Virgin Man* (Princess, Jan. 18, 1927); succeeded Mary Duncan as Poppy during the national tour of *The Shanghai Gesture* (Kansas City, Mo., 1927).

In Nov. 1927, she played ingenue roles in stock productions (Paterson, N.J.). During 1928–29, she appeared in vaudeville as the Leading Lady in the playlet, *The Man Who Laughed Last* (Palace, N.Y.C.; Orpheum Circuit, US); subsequently, played the French Maid in *The Man Who Reclaimed His Head* (Broadhurst, N.Y.C., Sept. 8, 1932).

Miss Lortel is founder and artistic director of The White Barn Th. (Westport, Conn.), which, since 1947, has served as an experimental summer theatre for American and foreign plays and playwrights.

Miss Lortel is owner of the Th. de Lys (1955 to date), an off-Bway theatre (N.Y.C.). Its first production the *The Threepenny Opera* (Sept. 20, 1955), which was presented by Carmen Capalbo and Stanley Chase, in association with Miss Lortel, and ran for seven years, establishing long-run records for off-Bway. Subsequently, every production at the theatre has been presented "by arrangement with Lucille Lortel Productions, Inc."

At the Th. de Lys, Miss Lortel instituted (1956) a series of afternoon productions known as the Matinee Th. Series for the Greater NY Chapter of ANTA, serving as the series' artistic director. The series was discontinued in 1976.

Off-Bway, Miss Lortel produced, with Luther Green, *A Sleep of Prisoners* (St. James Church, Oct. 16, 1951); with Sanford Friedman and Henry Boettcher, *The River Line* (Carnegie Hall Playhouse, Jan. 2, 1957); with Paul Shyre and Howard Gottfried, *Cock-a-Doodle Dandy* (Carnegie Hall Playhouse, Nov. 12, 1958); with Circle in the Square, *The Balcony* (Circle in the Square, Mar. 3, 1960); produced alone, *Happy as Larry* (Martinique, Apr. 25, 1961); produced, with Arthur Cantor, *Put It in Writing* (Th. de Lys, May 12, 1963); with Sydney Bernstein, *The Blood Knot* (Cricket, Mar. 2, 1964); and in association with the American Place Th., revived the American Place Th. production of *The Old Glory: Benito Cereno* (Th. de Lys, Jan. 14, 1965).

On Bway, Miss Lortel produced, with Paul Shyre and Howard Gottfried, *I Knock at the Door* (Belasco, Sept. 29, 1957), which she subsequently presented for a limited run at the Th. de Lys (Nov. 24, 1964), followed by a limited run of *Pictures in the Hallway* (Th. de Lys, Dec. 16, 1964), both plays adapted by Paul Shyre from the works of Sean O'Casey.

Films. Miss Lortel made a series of shorts for Warner Bros. including her stage performance in *The Man Who Laughed Last* (WB, 1930).

Radio. She made her debut on Advice to the Lovelorn (WHN, N.Y.C., Mar. 8, 1935); and performed on Great Women of History (WHN).

Awards. Miss Lortel received a special citation from the *Village Voice* Off-Bway (Obie) awards "for fostering and furthering the spirit of theatrical experiment" (1958); the Greater NY Chapter of ANTA (1959) for "outstanding achievement as Artistic Director of the ANTA Matinee Series;" the Whistler Society Award (1960) for "outstanding merit in the field of theatre;" the Greater NY Chapter of ANTA Award (1961) for "unselfish devotion to the art of theatre," the National ANTA Award (1962) for "pioneering work fostering new playwrights, directors and actors," and the Margo Jones Award (1962) for "significant contribution to the dramatic art with hitherto unproduced plays."

Her productions, of *The Threepenny Opera* (1956) and *The Balcony* (1960), received the *Village Voice* Off-Bway (Obie) awards.

Recreation. Theatre.

LOTITO, LOUIS A. Theatre owner and manager. b. Louis Anthony Lotito, July 24, 1900, New York City, to Vincent and Rose Lotito. Father, tailor. Attended Stuyvesant H.S., N.Y.C., 1914–17. Married June 1, 1925, to Adeline Valerio; one son, one daughter. Member of League on NY Theatres (pres., 1958–61); ATPAM; NY Athletic Clubs; The Lambs; Grand St. Boys Club; Spring Lake (N.J.) Golf Club; Actors Fund of Amer. (treas.–pres.). Address: (home) 202 Tuttle Ave., Spring Lake, NJ 07762, tel. (201) GI 9-8668; (bus.) 1545 Broadway, New York, NY 10036, tel. (202) CI 6-2630.

Theatre. Mr. Lotito was the president of City Playhouse, Inc., the present owners of the Bway theatres, ANTA, 245 W. 52nd St.; Helen Hayes Th., 210 W. 46th St.; Martin Beck Th., 302 W. 45th St.; and Morosco, 217 W. 45th St., and the National Th., Washington, D.C. He is now retired.

Recreation. Golf.

LOUDON, DOROTHY. Actress. b. Sept. 17, 1933, Boston, Mass., to James E. Loudon, Jr., and Dorothy (Shaw) Loudon. Father, advertising manager. Relative in theatre: grandmother, Lola Albec (Loudon). Educ. Syracuse Univ.; Emerson Coll., Boston, Mass.; Alveini Acad. of Dramatic Arts, N.Y.C. Professional training at Alveini Acad. of Dramatic Arts; Sawyer Falk (Syracuse Univ.); Gertrude Binley Kay (Emerson). Married Dec. 18, 1971, to Norman Paris, musical arranger and conductor. Member of AEA; AGVA; SAG; AFTRA; Local 802, Musicians Union. Address: Lionel Larner Associates, 850 Seventh Ave., New York, NY 10019, tel. (212) 246-3105.

Theatre. Miss Loudon made her stage debut in vaudeville (Palace, N.Y.C., 1953) and first appeared in summer stock in a musical revue (Camp Tamiment, Pa., Summer 1959). She played Wilma Risque in *Nowhere to Go But Up* (Winter Garden, N.Y.C., Nov. 10, 1962); toured as Molly in *The Unsinkable Molly Brown* (Summer 1963); toured as Reno Sweeny in a revival of *Anything Goes* (Summer 1964); toured as Ellen Manville in the national company of *Luv* (Sept. 6, 1965–May 1966); starred in *Sweet Potato* (Ethel Barrymore Th., N.Y.C., Sept. 29, 1968); was Lillian Stone in *The Fig Leaves Are Falling* (Broadhurst, Jan. 2, 1969); Mabel in a revival of *Three Men on a Horse* (Lyceum, Oct. 16, 1969); toured as the female lead in *The Apple Tree* (Jan.–Feb. 1970); toured as the female lead in *You Know I Can't Hear You When the Water's Running* (Summer 1970); played Charlotte Haze in *Lolita, My Love* (pre-Bway, opened Shubert Th., Philadelphia, Pa., Feb. 15, 1971); closed Shubert Th., Boston, Mass., Mar. 27, 1971); toured as the female lead in *Plaza Suite* (Summer 1971); toured as Beatrice in *The Effect of Gamma Rays on Man-in-the-Moon Marigolds* (opened Detroit, Mich., Oct. 26, 1971; closed Mar. 1972) including engagement with American Conservatory Th., San Francisco, Calif.; and played Edith Potter in a revival of *The Women* (46 St. Th., N.Y.C., Apr. 25, 1973).

Television and Radio. Miss Loudon began performing on radio in 1952 (CBS) and was on the program The Big Time (1956). On television, she was a regular panelist on Laugh Line (NBC, 1959); appeared on the Dupont Show of the Month (NBC) in such programs as *Those Ragtime Years* (Nov. 1960), *Music of the Thirties* (Nov. 1961), and *Regards to George M. Cohan* (Mar. 1962); and was the female star on the Garry Moore Show (CBS) for two seasons (1962–64). In addition, from 1956 to 1972 she was a guest at various times on the Perry Como Show (NBC), the Dinah Shore Show (NBC), the Ed Sullivan Show (CBS), the Jonathan Winters Show (NBC), the Dean Martin Show (NBC), the Milton Berle Show (ABC), the Tonight Show (NBC), the Merv Griffin Show (CBS), and the Dick Cavett Show (ABC, 1969). Miss Loudon appeared on English television on the programs Granada at 9:00 and Sunday at the Palladium.

Night Clubs. Miss Loudon played several starring engagements at Le Ruban Bleu (1953–58) and the Blue Angel (1953–62), both in N.Y.C. She appeared at the Flamingo Hotel (1962) and the Sahara Hotel (1963), both in Las Vegas, Nev., and at Harrah's, Lake Tahoe, Nev. (1963); and has starred at Mr. Kelly's and the Palmer House, both in Chicago, and the Persian Room, Hotel Plaza, N.Y.C. (Spring 1964).

Discography. Miss Loudon recorded the album *Dorothy Loudon at the Blue Angel* (Decca, Fall 1960).

Awards. Miss Loudon was voted (1962) the "most promising newcomer to the television world" by the editors and publishers of *T.V. Mirror* and received two National Academy of Television Arts and Sciences (Emmy) awards nominations for her appearances on the Garry Moore Show. She received the *Theatre World* award as most promising musical star for her performance in *Nowhere to Go But Up;* for her performance in *The Fig Leaves Are Falling,* she won the Drama Desk Award and was nominated for an Antoinette Perry (Tony) Award as best musical actress; and she shared with the entire cast of *The Women* in the Outer Circle Critics Award for ensemble playing.

Recreation. Sewing, writing, collecting cranberry glass.

LOVE, BESSIE. Actress. b. Juanita Horton, Sept. 10, 1898 (?), Midland, Tex., to John Cross and Emma Jane (Savage) Horton. Father, chiropractor; mother, teacher. Attended public school, Los Angeles, Calif. Married Dec. 27, 1929, to William Ballinger Hawks (marr. dis. Dec. 1936); one daughter Patricia Hawks, actress. Served WW II with American Red Cross, England. Address: 42 Henderson Rd., London, S.W. 18, England.

Pre-Theatre. Miss Love began her career as a child, playing small parts and doing extra work in films.

Theatre. She first appeared on stage as Bonny in a West Coast tour of *Burlesque* (opened Geary, San Francisco, Mar. 5, 1928); subsequently toured cross-country as a variety performer, before making her N.Y.C., debut (Palace Th., 1931).

In 1935, she moved to England and later appeared in Grand Guignol productions as Julie in *Say It with Flowers* and as the Actress in *Zenobia* (Granville, Walham Green, Oct. 1945); succeeded (June 1945) Peggy Dear in the role of Miss Dell in *Love in Idleness* (Lyric, London, Dec. 20, 1944), and toured in the production, which was presented for the troops in France and Germany.

She appeared as Mrs. Hedges in *Born Yesterday* (Garrick, London, Jan. 23, 1947); Myrtle Keller in *The Male Animal* (Arts, May 18, 1949); the Laughing Woman in *Death of a Salesman* (Phoenix, July 28, 1949); Amanda Wingfield in *The Glass Menagerie* (Gaiety, Dublin, Ire., 1951); Lucy Barlow in *The Season's Greetings* ("Q," London, Sept. 29, 1953); Bessie Bockser in *The Wooden Dish* (Phoenix, July 27, 1954); Mrs. Prioleau in *South* (Arts, Mar. 30, 1955); Mrs. Kirke in *A Girl Called Jo* (Piccadilly, Dec. 15, 1955); and Mrs. Lilly Mortar in *The Children's Hour* (Arts, Sept. 19, 1956).

Miss Love played Babe in the premiere of her own play, *The Homecoming* (Perth Repertory Th., Scotland, Apr. 21, 1958); the Nurse in *Orpheus Descending* (Royal Court, London, May 14, 1959); Reba Spelding in *Visit to a Small Planet* (Westminster, Feb. 25, 1960); again played Mrs. Prioleau in *South* (Lyric, Hammersmith, Apr. 7, 1961); Mrs. Ella Spofford in *Gentlemen Prefer Blondes* (Princes, Aug. 20, 1962); Grace Kimbrough in *Never Too Late* (Prince of Wales, Sept. 24, 1963); "a worker" in *Saint Joan of the Stockyards* (Queen's, June 11, 1964); "the White Woman" in *In White America* (New Arts Th. Club, Nov. 16, 1964); Amanda in *The Glass Menagerie* (Palace, Watford, July 1966); Marguerite Oswald in *The Silence of Lee Harvey Oswald* (Hampstead Th. Club, London, Nov. 23, 1966); Aunt Nonnie in *Sweet Bird of Youth* (Palace, Watford, Nov. 1968); Mrs. Dekker in *West of Suez* (Royal Court, London, Aug. 17, 1971); and Aunt Pittypat in *Gone with the Wind* (Drury Lane, May 3, 1972).

Films. Miss Love appeared as a Swedish Servant Girl in *The Flying Torpedo* (Fine Arts-Triangle, 1916); subsequently appeared in *The Aryan* (Triangle, 1916); *Good Bad Man* (Fine Arts-Triangle, 1916); *Stranded* (Fine Arts-Triangle, 1916); *Reggie Mixes In* (Fine Arts-Triangle, 1916); *Hell to Pay in Austin* (Fine Arts-Triangle, 1916); *Intolerance* (Griffith, 1916); *A Sister of Six* (Fine Arts-Triangle, 1916); and *The Heiress at Coffee Dan's* (Fine Arts-Triangle, 1916).

She also played the title role in *Nina, the Flower Girl* (Fine Arts-Triangle, 1917); appeared in *Daughter of the Poor* (Fine Arts-Triangle, 1917); *Cheerful Givers* (Fine Arts-Triangle, 1917); *The Sawdust Ring* (Fine Arts-Triangle, 1917); *Little Reformer* (Triangle, 1917); *Persnickity Polly Ann* (Triangle, 1917); *The Great Adventure* (Pathé, 1918); *How Could You, Caroline?* (Pathé, 1918); *Little Sister to Everybody* (Pathé, 1918); *Dawn of Understanding* (Vitagraph, 1918); *Over the Garden Wall* (Vitagraph, 1919); *Enchanted Barn* (Vitagraph, 1919); *Wishing Ring Man* (Vitagraph, 1919); *Carolyn of the Corners* (Pathé, 1919); *Yankee Princess* (Vitagraph, 1919); *Little Boss* (Vitagraph, 1919); *Cupid Forecloses* (Vitagraph, 1919); and *Fighting Colleen* (Vitagraph, 1919).

Miss Love appeared in *Pegeen* (Vitagraph, 1920); *Bonnie May* (Federated, 1921); *The Midlander* (Federated, 1921); *Penny of Top Hill Trail* (Federated, 1921); *The Swamp* (FBO, 1921); *The Sea Lion* (1st Natl., 1922); *Forget Me Not* (Metro, 1922); *The Village Blacksmith* (20th-Fox, 1922); *Slave of Desire* (Goldwyn, 1923); *Human Wreckage* (FBO, 1923); *The Eternal Three* (Goldwyn, 1923); *Sundown* (1st Natl., 1924); *Tongues of Flames* (U, 1924); *The Woman on the Jury* (1st Natl., 1924); *Those Who Dance* (1st Natl., 1924); *The Lost World* (1st Natl., 1925); *The King on Main Street* (Par., 1925); *New Brooms* (Par., 1925); *Soul Fire* (1st Natl., 1925); *The Song and Dance Man* (Par., 1926); *Lovey Mary* (MGM, 1926); *Meet the Prince* (PDC, 1926); *Young April* (PDC, 1926); *Going Crooked* (20th-Fox, 1926); *The Rainmaker* (Par., 1927); *Rubber Tires* (PDC, 1927); *Dress Parade* (Pathé, 1927); *A Harp in Hock* (Pathé, 1927); *Matinee Idol,* (Col., 1928); *Sally of the Scandals* (FBO, 1928); *Anybody Here Seen Kelly?* (U, 1928); *The West Pointer* (MGM, 1928); and *The Idle Rich* (MGM, 1929).

In sound films, Miss Love appeared in the first of MGM's musicals, *Broadway Melody* (1929); followed by *Road Show* (MGM, 1929); *Hollywood Revue of 1929* (MGM); *The Girl in the Show* (MGM, 1930); *Chasing Rainbows* (MGM, 1930); *Good News* (MGM, 1930); *See America Thirst* (U, 1930); *They Learned About Women* (MGM, 1930); *The Swellhead* (Tiffany, 1930); and *Morals for Women* (Tiffany, 1931). Since moving to England, she has played Little Nell in *The Old Curiosity Shop* (Alliance, 1935); appeared in *Live Again* (Morgan, 1936); *Atlantic Ferry* (released in the US as *Sons of the Sea,* WB, 1941); *Take It Big* (Par., 1944); *Journey Together* (RKO, 1945); *No Highway in the Sky* (20th-Fox, 1951); *The Magic Box* (Rank, 1952); *The Barefoot Contessa* (UA, 1954); *Too Young To Love* (IFE, 1955); *Touch and Go* (re-released as *The Light Touch* (U, 1956); *The Story of Esther Costello* (Col., 1957); *Nowhere To Go* (MGM, 1959); *Next to No Time* (Show Corp., 1960); *The Greengage Summer* (released in US as *Loss of Innocence* (Col., 1961); *The Roman Spring of Mrs. Stone* (WB, 1962); *Children of the Damned* (MGM, 1964); *Promise Her Anything* (Par., 1966); *Hot Millions* (MGM, 1968); *The Battle Beneath the Earth* (MGM, 1968); *I'll Never Forget What's 'is Name* (U, 1968); *Isadora* (U, 1968; re-edited as *The Loves of Isadora,* U, 1969); *On Her Majesty's Secret Service* (UA, 1969); *Sunday, Bloody Sunday* (UA, 1971); and *Catlow* (MGM, 1971).

Television. Miss Love made her debut in 1946 and has since appeared in many British productions.

LOVE, PHYLLIS. Actress. b. Phyllis Ann Love, Dec. 21, 1925, Des Moines, Iowa, to Jack W. and Lois (Monroe) Love. Father, grocer. Grad. Roosevelt H.S., Des Moines, 1944; attended Lindenwood Coll., 1945; grad. Carnegie Tech., B.A. 1948; studied Actors Studio (1949–to date). Married Dec. 2, 1948, to James Vincent McGee, playwright, teacher. Member of AEA; AFTRA; SAG.

Pre-Theatre. Waitress.

Theatre. Miss Love made her stage debut playing the title role in *Claudia* (Kendall Little Th., Des Moines, 1942); made her N.Y.C. debut as a Neighbor Girl, and understudy to Julie Harris in the role of Frankie in *The Member of the Wedding* (Empire, Jan. 5, 1950); subsequently appeared as Nancy Stoddard in *The Country Girl* (Lyceum, Nov. 10, 1950); Rosa delle Rose in *The Rose Tattoo* (Martin Beck Th., Mar. 3, 1951); Lola McLaughlin in *Maggie Haggerty* (Brattle Th., Cambridge, Mass., 1952); Kate Pennypacker in *The Remarkable Mr. Pennypacker* (Coronet, Dec. 30, 1953); Elma Duckworth in *Bus Stop* (Music Box, Mar. 2, 1955); Eleanora in *Easter* (Fourth St. Th., Jan. 16, 1957); Sally Parsons in *The Egghead* (Ethel Barrymore Th., Oct. 9, 1957); Judy Cherry in *The Flowering Cherry* (Lyceum, Oct. 21, 1959); Waverly Greer in *A Distant Bell* (Eugene O'Neill Th., Jan. 13, 1960); and the Student in the Univ. of California at Los Angeles Th. Extension Group production of *The Lesson* (1960).

Films. Miss Love played Mattie Birdwell in *Friendly Persuasion* (Allied, 1956), and Mrs. Alexander in *The Young Doctors* (UA, 1961).

Television. She appeared on the Actors Studio television show (1949).

Awards. Miss Love received the Donaldson Award and the Clarence Derwent Award (1951) for her performance as Rosa delle Rose in *The Rose Tattoo.*

Recreation. Sailing, gardening.

LOW, CARL. Actor, director, designer. b. Carl A. Low, Oct. 30, 1916, Knoxville, Tenn., to Carl A. and Ruth (Miller) Low. Father, civil engineer. Attended Allegany H.S., Cumberland, Md., 1930–34. Married May 29, 1941, to Virginia Keffer; three daughters. Served WW II, US Army, ETO, Combat Engineers; rank, Staff Sgt. Member of AEA; SAG; AFTRA. Address: 237 N. Broadway, Nyack, NY 10960, tel. (914) EL 8-4489.

Theatre. Mr. Low made his debut as an Elf in a Christmas program at the Mt. Royal Sch. (Cumberland, Md., 1924); made his professional debut with the Paint Shop Players (Somerset, Pa.), as the Professor in *Blind Alley* (1938); subsequently played the Dutch Captain in *High Tor* (Mountain Playhouse, Jennerstown, Pa.); and was co-founder of the White Barn Th. (Irvin, Pa.), where he served as co-producer (1948–61).

He played the Moving Man in *Love Me Long* (48 St. Th., N.Y.C., Nov. 7, 1949); Charles Tutwell in *Touchstone* (Music Box, Feb. 3, 1953); Mr. Hobart in *King of Hearts* (Lyceum, Apr. 1, 1954); Drivinitz in *Anastasia* (Lyceum, Dec. 29, 1954); George in *A Very Special Baby* (Playhouse, Nov. 14, 1956); the Copy Chief in *Viva Madison Avenue!* (Longacre, Apr. 6, 1960); joined the company as a Delegate and a Reporter and understudied the role of Dr. Artinian in *The Best Man* (Morosco, Mar. 31, 1960), playing Dick Jensen in its tour (opened Hanna, Cleveland, Ohio, Sept. 18, 1961; closed Forrest, Philadelphia, Pa., Feb. 3, 1962); succeeded (Feb. 1963) George C. Scott as Ephraim Cabot in *Desire Under the Elms* (Circle in the Square, Jan. 8, 1963); and played Count Fontana in *The Deputy* (Brooks Atkinson Th., Feb. 26, 1964). He has acted in various experimental and showcase productions; and acted and directed dinner theatre productions in the Baltimore area.

Films. Mr. Low appeared in *Hud* (Par., 1963); and *America, America* (WB, 1963).

Television. He appears on *Search for Tomorrow* (CBS) as a regular performer (1965–to date).

Recreation. Golf, bridge.

LOWELL, ROBERT. Poet, playwright. b. Robert Traill Spence Lowell, Jr., March 1, 1917, Boston, Mass., to Robert Traill Spence and Charlotte (Winslow) Lowell. Grad. Harvard, Kenyon Coll., A.B. (summa cum laude), 1940. Married 1940 to Jean Stafford (marr. dis. 1948); married 1949 to Elizabeth Hardwick (marr. dis.), one daughter; married to Lady Caroline Blackwood; one son. Member of Amer. Academy of Arts and Letters.

Theatre. Mr. Lowell is the author of a trilogy of one-act plays, originally produced by the Amer. Place Th. (St. Clement's Church, N.Y.C.), with the overall title *The Old Glory,* which included *My Kinsman, Major Molineux* and *Benito Cereno* (Nov. 1, 1964), and *Endicott and the Red Cross* (Apr. 18, 1968). His adaptation of Aeschylus' *Prometheus Bound* was presented by the Yale Repertory Th. world premiere (New Haven, Conn., May 9, 1967); and Racine's *Phaedra,* as adapted by Mr. Lowell, was first produced by The Theatre of the Living Arts (Philadelphia, May 1967).

Television. Mr. Lowell read from his own poetry as part of a ninety-minute special program which included excerpts from The American Place Theatre's production of *The Old Glory,* and critical comment by Robert Brustein and Stanley Kunitz (NET, 1965).

Other Activities. Mr. Lowell worked for the publishing house, Sheed and Ward (N.Y.C., 1941–42), and served as a consultant in poetry to the Library of Congress (Washington, D.C., 1947–48). His teaching assignments include the Univ. of Iowa (1949–50; 1952–53); Salzburg Seminar in American Studies (1952); Boston Univ.; the New School for Social Research, Harvard Univ., and Yale Univ.

Published Works. Mr. Lowell's poetry includes *The Land of Unlikeness* (1944); *Lord Weary's Castle* (1946); *Poems 1938–1949* (1950); *The Mills of the Kavanaughs* (1951); *Life Studies* (1959); *Imitations* (1961); *For the Union Dead* (1964); *Selected Poems* (1967); *The Voyage and Other Versions of Poems by Baudelaire* (1968); *Notebook 1967–68* (1969); *For Lizzie and Harriet* (1973); *History* (1973); and *The Dolphin* (1973).

With Peter Taylor and Robert Penn Warren, he was editor of *Randall Jarrell 1914–1965* (1967).

Awards. Mr. Lowell has twice been the recipient of the Pulitzer Prize for Poetry (1946, 1974). In addition, he has received a National Institute of Arts and Letters grant (1947); a Guggenheim Fellowship (1947); The Harriet Monroe Poetry Award (1952); the Guinness Poetry Prize (1959); the National Book Award for Poetry (1960); the Harriet Monroe Memorial Prize (1961); the Levinson Prize (1963); the Ballinger Poetry Translation Award (1962); the Off-Bway (Obie) Award (1965) for *The Old Glory;* The Sarah Josepha Hale Award for Poetry (1966); and the Copernicus Award (1974).

LOWRY, W. MCNEIL. Foundation executive, journalist. b. Wilson McNeil Lowry, Feb. 17, 1913, Columbus, Kan., to Benedict Harrison and Helen Hannah (Graham) Lowry. Grad. Univ. of Illinois, A.B. (magna cum laude, Phi Beta Kappa) 1934. Ph.D. 1941, Litt.D. 1971. Married Aug. 31, 1936, to Elsa Alberta Koch; one son. Served USNR, 1943–46; rank, Lt. Member of Sigma Delta Chi; Century Club; Natl. Press Club (Washington, D.C.). Address: (home) 1161 York Ave., New York, NY 10021; (bus.) 320 E. 43rd St., New York, NY 10017.

Since June 1964, Mr. Lowry has been a vice-president of the Ford Foundation, with responsibility for the office of Policy and Planning, and the Humanities and the Arts program, which includes the Ford Foundation's activities in the professional theatre. Previously, he had been director of the Humanities and the Arts program (1957–June 1964) and director of Education (1953–57) for the Ford Foundation. Mr. Lowry has been an associate director of the International Press Inst. in Zurich, Switzerland (1952–53); chief of the Washington Bureau for the James M. Cox newspapers (1947–52); associate editor of the Dayton (Ohio) Daily News (1946); a writer for the Office of War Information (1942–43); and an instructor in the Dept. of English at the Univ. of Illinois (1936–42).

Awards. Mr. Lowry received an award from ANTA in 1961; and an Antoinette Perry (Tony) Special Citation Award "in behalf of the Ford Foundation for his and their distinguished support of the American theatre" (1963).

LUCAS, JONATHAN. Director, actor, producer, choreographer. b. Lucas Thomas Aco Giarraputo, Aug. 14, 1928, Sherman, Tex., to Luca and Florence (McCrady) Giarraputo. Father, importer. Attended Escoriala Prep. Sch., Salamanca, Spain; grad. Southern Methodist Univ., M.A. 1944; attended Amer. Ballet Sch., seven years; Amer. Th. Wing, two years. Served USN, 1942–45; rank, Lt.; received Purple Heart, Silver Star. Member of DGA; AEA; AFTRA; Delta Chi. Address: (home) 8690 Franklin Ave., Los Angeles, CA 90069, tel. (213) 654-8840; (bus.) C. G. Productions, 3630 Riverside Dr., Burbank, CA 91505, tel. (213) 849-2471.

Theatre. Mr. Lucas first appeared in the chorus of *A Lady Says Yes* (Broadhurst, Jan. 10, 1945), using his name of Lucas Aco; subsequently was a dancer in *Billion Dollar Baby* (Alvin Th., N.Y.C., Dec. 21, 1945); a Dancing Fella, an Assistant, and Jim in *Around the World* (Adelphi, May 31, 1946); and the First Geologist and understudy to David Wayne in the part of Og in *Finian's Rainbow* (46 St. Th., Jan. 19, 1947); subsequently using the name Jonathan Lucas, he appeared in *Small Wonder* (Coronet, Sept. 15, 1948); played Joe in *Me, the Sleeper* (Lenox Hill Playhouse, May 14, 1949); appeared in the revue *Touch and Go* (Broadhurst, Oct. 13, 1949; Prince of Wales Th., London, Eng., May 19, 1950).

He played Sam Jenkins in *Of Thee I Sing* (Ziegfeld, N.Y.C., May 5, 1952); and Paris in *The Golden Apple* (Phoenix, Mar. 11, 1954; moved to Alvin, Apr. 20, 1954); staged productions at the Sacramento (Calif.) Music Circus (Summer 1956); was choreographer for *First Impressions* (Alvin, N.Y.C., Mar. 19, 1959); choreographed and directed *Vintage '60* (Ivor Th., Los Angeles, Calif., 1960; Brooks Atkinson Th., N.Y.C., Sept. 12, 1960); succeeded James Mitchell (Oct. 5, 1962) as Marco the Magnificent in *Carnival!* (Imperial, Apr. 14, 1961), in which he later toured. He was choreographer for *The Beauty Part* (Music Box, Dec. 26, 1962); directed musical productions at Melodyland (Berkeley, Calif., Summer 1963); and was producer of the Hollywood Pavilion at the NY World's Fair (Apr.–Oct. 1964).

Films. Mr. Lucas choreographed the dances for the film *Happy Go Lovely* (RKO, 1951); *Two Little Bears* (20th-Fox); *Marriage on the Rocks* (WB); and *The Trouble with Girls* (MGM).

Television. He was choreographer for Celebrity Time (CBS, 1952); the Martha Raye Show (NBC, 1953); the Milton Berle Show (NBC, 1953); the Paul Winchell Show (NBC, 1954); the Imogene Coca Show (NBC, 1954); Melody Tour (ABC, 1954); director of the Royal Crown series (NBC, 1955); choreographer for the Jimmy Durante Show (NBC Special, 1956); the Ernie Kovacs Show (NBC, 1956); the Walter Winchell Show (NBC, 1956); the Eddie Fisher Show (NBC, 1957); director and choreographer for the *Esther Williams Aqua Spectacle* (NBC, 1957); choreographer for *Cinderella* (CBS, 1958); producer of *The Lively Ones* (NBC, 1963); directed *What's Up, America?* (NBC); *A Country Happening* (NBC); *Music Country, USA* (NBC, 1974); and *The Dean Martin Comedy Hour* (NBC, 1974).

Night Clubs. Mr. Lucas has appeared at Cafe de Paris (London), Palmer House (Chicago) and Mocambo (Los Angeles) in an act with Kay Thompson (1951). He was director of a show at The Upstairs at the Downstairs (N.Y.C., 1961); at 4 West (1963) and the *Society of Illustrators Show* (1963).

Awards. For his performance in *The Golden Apple,* Mr. Lucas received the Donaldson Award and the *Theatre World* Award (1954).

LUCE, CLAIRE. Actress. b. Syracuse, N.Y., to Frederick and Maud (Hinds) Luce. Studied dance at Denishawn Sch., N.Y.C.; with Michael Fokine and Florence Colebrook Powers. Married Clifford Warren Smith (dec.). Member of AEA; SAG; AFTRA. Address: 26 Gramercy Park South, New York, NY 10003, tel. (212) GR 5-6263.

Theatre. Miss Luce made her debut as a ballet dancer in Sol Hurok's Russian Opera Co. (1921). She appeared as a dancer in *Little Jessie James* (Longacre, N.Y.C., Aug. 15, 1923); played Clair in *Dear Sir* (Times Square Th., Sept. 23, 1924); danced in *The Music Box Revue* (Music Box, Dec. 1, 1924); replaced Mistinguett in *Casino de Paris* (Paris, Fr., June 1925), and appeared in *Ziegfeld Follies* (New Amsterdam, N.Y.C., Aug. 16, 1927).

She made her London debut as Bonny in *Burlesque* (Golder's Green, Nov. 26, 1928); played Nora Mason in the *Scarlet Pages* (Morosco, N.Y.C., Sept. 9, 1929); Judy Gelett in *Society Girl* (Booth, Dec. 30, 1931); Mimi in *Gay Divorce* (Ethel Barrymore Th., N.Y.C., Nov. 29, 1932; Palace, London, Nov. 2, 1933); Nina Popinot in *Vintage Wine* (Daly's, May 29, 1934); Maricousa in *Gay Deceivers* (Gaiety, May 23, 1935); appeared in *Follow the Sun* (Adelphi, Feb. 4, 1936); and *No Sleep for the Wicked* (Daly's, June 1937).

Miss Luce played Curley's wife in *Of Mice and Men* (Music Box, N.Y.C., Nov. 23, 1937; Gate, London, Apr. 12, 1939); and at the Open Air Th. (London), played Katherine in *The Taming of the Shrew* (Aug. 4, 1941), and Katherine in *Henry V* (Aug. 19, 1941).

During World War II, she toured with ENSA as Katherine in *The Taming of the Shrew,* Anna Christopherson in *Anna Christie,* Nora in *A Doll's House,* and Sadie Thompson in *Rain,* and with the USO, as Elvira in *Blithe Spirit.*

At the Shakespeare Memorial Th. (Stratford-upon-Avon), she played Viola in *Twelfth Night,* Beatrice in *Much Ado About Nothing,* Mistress Ford in *The Merry Wives of Windsor,* and Cleopatra in *Antony and Cleopatra* (Summer 1945).

She appeared as Mary Stuart in *Golden Eagle* (Whitehall, London, Jan. 29, 1946), and Becky in *Vanity Fair* ("Q," May 14, 1946).

Miss Luce played Tanis Talbot in *Portrait in Black* (Booth, N.Y.C., May 14, 1947); Rose Raymond in *With a Silk Thread* (Lyceum, Apr. 12, 1950); Effie in *The Devil Also Dreams* (Somerset Playhouse, Mass., July 1950); Katherine in *The Taming of the Shrew* (NY City Ctr., Apr. 25, 1951); Beatrice in *Much Ado About Nothing* (Music Box, May 1, 1952); and toured in a one-woman program, *Fashions in Love* (1956–59).

She appeared as Lucy Greer in *And So, Farewell* (Margo Jones Th., Dallas, Tex., Jan. 1958); appeared in a one-woman show *These Are My Loves* (Maidman Playhouse, N.Y.C., Apr. 18, 1960); Constance in *Feast of Panthers* (E. 74 St. Th., Mar. 20, 1961); toured universities in a one-woman show, *Woman* (1964 and subsequent years); played Flora Goforth in *The Milk Train Doesn't Stop Here Anymore* (1965; Barter Th., Abingdon, Va.; Studio, Miami, Fla.; both 1966); made several appearances in *The Time of the Cuckoo* (Ruth Foreman Playhouse, Miami, Fla., 1968); toured universities in *Tennessee Williams and Friends;* played the Tragic Queen in *The Cave Dwellers* (Highlands, N.C., Aug. 1970); and at the Globe Th., Odessa, Tex., appeared in *Dear Liar* (1972) and directed *Twelfth Night* (July 5, 1974).

Films. Miss Luce has appeared in *Up the River* (20th-Fox, 1930), and others.

Television. She has appeared in *The Queen Bee* (NBC); *Peer Gynt* (NBC); *Becky Sharpe* (Philco Television Playhouse, NBC); performed on Matinee Th. (NBC), and read Heinrich Heine poems (Camera Three, CBS, 1964).

Other Activities. Miss Luce's paintings have been exhibited in three one-woman shows at the Arthur Newton Gallery (N.Y.C., 1951, 1953,

1959). Her painting "Saint Joan" is the permanent collection of the Rochester (N.Y.) Museums, and her "Salome" in the Southampton (N.Y.) Museum.

She did the cover designs for her record albums, adapted the text of the *Colette's 'Music Hall Sidelights'* album, and the George Jean Nathan albums for Julie Haydon.

Miss Luce was a drama teacher on the NY Univ. faculty (1964–65).

Published Works. Miss Luce has published *Letters From Patrick* (1965).

Discography. She has recorded the folowing albums: *The Happy Prince, The Devoted Friend, Salome, Mary of Magdala, The Unfortunate Happy Lady, Flowers of Evil, Poems of Heinrich Heine, Lyrics and Sonnets of Lord Alfred Douglas, Colette's Music-Hall Sidelights'* (with Julie Haydon), *Gift from the Sea, Venus and Adonis, Woman* (two albums), *Cleopatra, a study in Moods, Jinny, a Portrait, In the Winter of Cities,* in which she set to music five of Tennessee Williams's poems, and *The Critical World of George Jean Nathan* (six albums).

LUCE, CLARE BOOTHE. Playwright. b. Ann Clare Boothe, Apr. 10, 1903, New York City, to William F. and Ann Clare (Snyder) Boothe. Father, violinist. Attended St. Mary's, Garden City, L.I., N.Y., 1915–17; grad. The Castle, Tarrytown, N.Y., 1919. Married Aug. 10, 1923, to George T. Brokaw (marr. dis. 1929, dec. May 28, 1935); one daughter (dec. Jan. 1944); married Nov. 23, 1935, to Henry R. Luce (dec., 1967), editor-in-chief of Time, Inc. Member of ANTA; Dramatists Guild; AMPAS; ALA; Acad. of Political Science; Museum of Modern Art (trustee); President's Advisory Committee on the Arts; International Rescue Committee (bd. of dir.); Amer. Institute for Foreign Trade; US Committee for Refugees (bd. of dir.); Amer. Friends of Captive Nations; Amer. Security Council (bd. of dir.); Amer. Society for Oceanography (advisory bd. member); Alfred E. Smith Memorial Foundation (trustee); Amer. Museum of Immigration (trustee); National Institute of Social Sciences (honorary life member); White House Preservation Committee; National Review Bd. East-West Center; Hawaii Foundation for Amer. Freedoms; Oceanic Foundation, Makapuu Oceanic Center (trustee); Former Members of Congress; Honolulu Acad. of Arts (trustee); Natl. Fed. of Press Women; International Platform Association; Society for Arts, Religion and Contemporary Culture (fellow); Bishop Trust Co. of Honolulu (dir.); Pan Amer. Medical Association (honorary member); The Library of Congress (honorary consultant in Amer. Letters); President's Foreign Intelligence Advisory Board; Commission on Critical Choices for Americans; National Committee on US-China Relations; US Strategic Institute (bd. of dir.); The Third Century Corporation (bd. of dir.); Accuracy in Media, Inc. (bd. of dir.); Encyclopedia Britannica (bd. of eds.); and US Capitol Historical Society (natl. adv. bd.). Address: 4559 Kahala Ave., Honolulu, HI 96816.

Pre-Theatre. Mrs. Luce was associate editor for *Vogue* (1930); associate editor (1931) and managing editor (1933) for *Vanity Fair* under the name Clare Boothe.

Theatre. Mrs. Luce wrote *Abide With Me* (Ritz Th., N.Y.C., Nov. 21, 1935); *The Women* (Ethel Barrymore Th., Dec. 16, 1936); *Kiss the Boys Good-Bye* (Henry Miller's Th., Sept. 28, 1938); *Margin for Error* (Plymouth, Nov. 3, 1939); *Child of the Morning,* which closed during a pre-Bway tryout (Shubert, Boston, Nov. 19, 1951) and had its first N.Y.C. staging at the Blackfriars Guild (Mar., 1958); and *Slam The Door Softly* (Mark Tapor Forum, Los Angeles, Calif., June 1971) which first appeared in *Life* magazine (Oct. 1970) under the title, "A Doll's House–1970.".

Films. Mrs. Luce wrote the scenario for *Come to the Stable* (20th-Fox, 1949).

Other Activities. Mrs. Luce was a war correspondent for *Life* (1940); correspondent for *Time, Life* and *Fortune* (1941–42); Congresswoman from Conn. (1943–47); and US Ambassador to Italy (1953–57).

Published Works. Mrs. Luce has written articles in *Sports Illustrated, Life, Jubilee,* a monthly column for *McCall's,* monthly conventions to Publishers Newspaper Syndicate monthly; the books *Stuffed Shirts* (1930); *Europe in the Spring* (1940); and edited *Saints for Now* (1952).

Awards. Mrs. Luce was nominated for an Academy (Oscar) Award (1949) for *Come to the Stable;* received the honorary degrees D.Litt. (1941) from Colby Coll.; LL.D. from Creighton Univ. (1948); LL.D. from Georgetown Univ. (1955); D.Litt. from Fordham Univ. (1957); LL.D. from Temple Univ. (1957); LL.D. from Mundelein Coll. (June 1964); and A.F.D. from St. John's Univ. (Jamaica, N.Y., June 1964).

She received the Dag Hammarskjold Medal for Diplomacy; the Laetare Medal (1947); Cardinal Newman Award (1951); the Poor Richard Club Gold Medal of Achievement (Philadelphia, Pa., Jan. 1955); George Washington Honor Medal Award, Freedoms Foundation (Valley Forge, Pa., 1956); was made a Dame of Magistral Grace of the Sovereign Military Order of Malta (Rome, It., Dec. 1956); Knight of the Grand Cross of the Order of Merit of the Italian Republic (Rome, Dec. 1956); Great Living Americans Award, US Chamber of Commerce, (Washington, D.C., Apr. 1957); Fourth Gimbel National Award (Philadelphia, Pa., Jan. 1957); Inst. of Social Sciences, Gold Medal Award (Dec. 1957); Cordell Hull Award (Dec. 1957); Distinguished Service Award, Natl. Society for Crippled Children and Adults (Nov. 1958); and the Annual Catholic Press Award (Feb. 1959); The Order of Lafayette's Freedom Award (1963); American Statesman Medal, from the Freedoms Foundation at Valley Forge (April 1972); Golden Plate Award, from American Academy of Achievement (July 1972); Fourth Estate Award, from the American Legion (Aug. 1973); and the Horatio Alger Award (May 1974).

Recreation. Skin diving, miscellaneous creative arts (painting, photography, mosaics, mobiles and collages).

LUDLAM, CHARLES. playwright, actor, director. Attended Hofstra Univ.

Theatre. Mr. Ludlam co-founded the Play-House of the Ridiculous (N.Y.C., 1966) for which he wrote *Conquest of the Universe* (1967). During this production Mr. Ludlam broke with the group and founded The Ridiculous Theatrical Company, rewriting *Conquest of the Universe* and retitling it *When Queens Collide* (Bouwerie Lane Th., Nov. 1967). He subsequently wrote, directed, and played Norma Desmond in *Big Hotel* (Gate Th., Nov. 24, 1967); directed and co-authored *Whores of Babylon* (Tambellini's Gate Th., Mar. 22, 1968); was co-author of *Turds in Hell* (Tambellini's Gate Th., Nov. 8, 1968); wrote, directed, and played The Fool in *The Grand Tarot* (Millenium Th., Oct. 13, 1969); wrote, directed, and played Baron Khanagar von Bluebeard in *Bluebeard* (La Mama ETC, Spring 1970; and CHristopher's End Th., 1970); directed and played The Fool in the revised version of *The Grand Tarot* (Gotham Art Th., Feb. 18, 1971); with his company, toured Europe (Fall 1971) with *Bluebeard, The Grand Tarot,* and *Eunuchs of the Forbidden City,* the last of which he wrote, directed, and appeared in (revived Th. for the New City, N.Y.C., Apr. 5, 1972). He wrote the book, directed, and played Paw Hatfield in the musical *Corn* (13th St. Th., Nov. 20, 1972); wrote the adaptation, directed, and played Marguerite Gautier in *Camille* (13th St. Th., May 2, 1973); wrote, directed and played Buck Armstrong in *Hot Ice* (Evergreen, Feb. 7, 1974); revived *Camille* (Evergreen, May 13, 1974); wrote, directed, and played Carleton Stone, Jr., in *Stage Blood* (Evergreen, Dec, 8, 1974); revived *Bluebeard* (Evergreen, Apr. 18, 1975); presented a Ludlam retrospective, *Tatu Tableax* (Evergreen, Nov. 2, 1975); and wrote and directed *Caprice* (Performing Garage, Feb. 1976).

Mr. Ludlam and The Ridiculous Theatrical Company were in residence at Connecticut Coll. (New London, Conn., Summer 1975), where he taught, and where the company performed.

Awards. Mr. Ludlam received a Guggenheim Fellowship (1971); and grants from the NY State Arts Council, and the National Endowment for the Arts (1972) for *Corn.*.

LUDLUM, ROBERT. Producer, actor, author. b. May 25, 1927, New York City, to George H. and Margaret (Wadsworth) Ludlum. Father, businessman. Grad. Rectory Sch., Pomfret, Conn., 1940; attended Kent (Conn.) Sch., 1940–41; grad. Cheshire (Conn.) Academy, 1945; Wesleyan Univ., B.A. 1951. Married 1951 to Mary Ryde, actress; two sons, one daughter. Served USMC, 1944–46. Member of AEA (Consultant to AEA, Committee to Extend the Professional Theatre, 1961–63); AFTRA; SAG; The Players; Alpha Delta Phi (vice-pres., Wesleyan chapter). Address: 125 Crescent Ave., Leonia, NJ 07605, tel. (201) 944-0752.

Theatre. He first played in a school production of *Outward Bound* (1941); later made his N.Y.C. debut when he succeeded (1943) Robert Willey in the role of Sterling Brown in *Junior Miss* (Lyceum, Nov. 18, 1941); and subsequently played Haskell Cummings in the national touring company (1943–44). He appeared in stock productions at the Canton (Conn.) Show Shop (Summer 1952); as a Soldier of the Spanish Army in *The Strong Are Lonely* (Broadhurst, Sept. 29, 1952); played in stock at the Ivoryton (Conn.) Playhouse (Summer 1953); appeared as the Third Messenger in *Richard III* (NY City Ctr., Dec. 9, 1953); Spartacus in *The Gladiator* (Amato, N.Y.C., 1954); performed in stock at the Cragsmoor (N.Y.) Playhouse (Summer 1954). He played a Policeman and later succeeded Ray Rizzo in the role of Cashel Byron in *The Admirable Bashville* (Cherry Lane, Feb. 20, 1956); and appeared in Saint Joan (Phoenix, Sept. 11, 1956), later succeeded Lee Richardson in the role of D'Estivet (when the production moved to Coronet, Dec. 24, 1956); and appeared in summer-theatre productions at the Olney (Md.) Theatre (Summer 1957).

In 1957, Mr. Ludlum became the producer of the North Jersey Playhouse in Fort Lee, N.J., which he operated until 1960, and in which he also appeared in productions. He was a founder of the Playhouse-on-the-Mall (Paramus, N.J., opened Sept. 1962), and was producer there until he resigned to write full time (June 1970).

Television. In the 1950's, Mr. Ludlum appeared on more than 200 television shows, including Treasury Men in Action (NBC); Studio One (CBS); Kraft Th. (NBC); Omnibus (CBS); Danger (CBS); Suspense (CBS); Robert Montgomery Presents (NBC); etc.

Published Works. Mr. Ludlum wrote the novels *The Scarlatti Inheritance* (1971); *The Osterman Weekend* (1972); *The Matlock Paper* (1973); *The Rhinemann Exchange* (1974); and *The Gemini Contenders* (1976).

Awards. He received the New England Professor of Drama Award (1951); an ANTA Grant (1959), an AEA Grant and a William C. Whitney Foundation Arts Grant (1960) for continuation of theatre activity; and an ANTA scroll of achievement (1960).

Recreation. Fishing, swimming, tennis, skiing.

LUKE, PETER. Playwright, director, television producer. b. Peter Ambrose Cyprion Luke, Aug. 12, 1919, St. Albans, Hertfordshire, England. Educated Eton Coll.; Byam Shaw Sch. of Art, London; Andre Lhote Workshop, Paris. Married, 1963, to June Tobin; three sons, four daughters. Served Royal Rifle Brigade, WW II, 1940–46; received the Military Cross. Member of Writers Guild of Great Britain. Address: c/o Harvey Unna, 14 Beaumont Mews, Marylebone High St., London W 1, England.

Pre-Theatre. Sub-editor of Reuters (1947); book critic, *Queens* Magazine; worked in the wine trade (1947–57).

Theatre. Mr. Luke is the author of *Hadrian VII* (Mermaid, London, Apr. 18, 1968; and Helen Hayes Th., N.Y.C., Jan. 8, 1969); and *Bloomsbury* (Phoenix, London, July 1974).

He made his theatrical directing debut with a production of *Hadrian VII* (Dublin, 1970).

Television. Mr. Luke served ABC-TV (London, 1958–63) in various capacities, including story editor (1958–60); and was drama producer for BBC-TV (1963–67). His plays for television include *Small Fish Are Sweet* (1959); *Pig's Ear with Flowers* (1960); *Roll On, Bloomin' Death* (1961); *A Man on Her Back* (written with William Sansom, 1966); *The Devil a Monk Wou'd Be* (1967); and the television films, *Anach Cuan; The Music of Sean O'Riada* (1967), and *Black Sound-Deep Song: The Andalusian Poetry of Federico Garcia Lorca* (1968), both of which he directed.

Mr. Luke also directed productions of *Fallen Angels* (1963); *Hamlet at Elsinore* (1963); *A Passage to India* (1966); and *Silent Song* (1967).

Published Works. He is the author of *Sisyphus and Reilly: An Autobiography* (1972); and has contributed articles and stories to *Envoy, The New Statesman (and Nation),* and *The Cornhill.*

Awards. Mr. Luke received the 1967 Italia Prize for Television Production for *Silent Song.*

LUMET, SIDNEY. Director. b. June 25, 1924, Philadelphia, Pa., to Baruch and Eugenia (Wermus) Lumet. Father, actor. Attended Professional Children's Sch., N.Y.C.; Columbia Univ. 1941–42. Married to Rita Gam, actress (marr. dis. July 14, 1955); married Aug. 27, 1956, to Gloria Vanderbilt, actress (marr. dis. Aug. 24, 1963); married Nov. 23, 1963, to Gail Jones. Served US Army, radar repairman, 1942–46; C.B.I., two years. Member of DGA, SSD&C, AMPAS, Acad. of TV Arts & Sciences. Address: (home) 68 Charles St., New York, NY 10014; (bus.) c/o Eli Landau, Time-Life Bldg., New York, NY 10036.

Theatre. Mr. Lumet made his stage debut as a child, with his father (Yiddish Th., N.Y.C., 1928).

He made his Bway debut as a Dead End Kid in *Dead End* (Belasco, Oct. 28, 1935); subsequently appeared as the Estranged One's Son in *The Eternal Road* (Manhattan Opera House, Jan. 7, 1937); Stanley in *Sunup to Sundown* (Hudson, Feb. 1, 1938); Mickey in *Schoolhouse on the Lot* (Ritz, Mar. 22, 1938); Johnny in *My Heart's in the Highlands* (Guild, Apr. 13, 1939); Leo in *Christmas Eve* (Henry Miller's Th., Dec. 27, 1939); Hymie Tashman in *Morning Star* (Longacre, Apr. 16, 1940); Joshua (Young Jesus) in *Journey to Jerusalem* (National, Oct. 5, 1940); was a replacement in *George Washington Slept Here* (Lyceum, Oct. 18, 1940); played Willie Berg in *Brooklyn, U.S.A.* (Forrest, Dec. 21, 1941); succeeded Marlon Brando as David in *A Flag Is Born* (Alvin, Sept. 5, 1946); and played Tonya in *Seeds in the Wind* (Empire, May 25, 1948).

Mr. Lumet's first assignment as director was the Phoenix production of *The Doctor's Dilemma* (Phoenix, Jan. 11, 1955); subsequently directed a stock production of *Picnic* (1955); *The Night of the Auk* (Playhouse, N.Y.C., Dec. 3, 1956); *Caligula* (54 St. Th., Feb. 16, 1960); and *Nowhere to Go But Up* (Winter Garden, Nov. 10, 1962).

Films. Mr. Lumet made his debut as a performer in *One Third of a Nation* (Par., 1939); as a director in *12 Angry Men* (UA, 1957); followed by *Stage Struck* (Buena Vista, 1958); *That Kind of Woman* (Par., 1959); *The Fugitive Kind* (UA, 1960); *A View from the Bridge* (Continental, 1962); *Long Day's Journey into Night* (Embassy, 1962); *Fail Safe* (Col., 1964); *The Pawnbroker* (AA, 1965); *Up from the Beach* (MGM, 1965); *The Hill* (MGM, 1965); *The Group* (UA, 1966); produced and directed *The Deadly Affair* (Col., 1967), *Bye Bye Braverman* (WB, 1968), and *The Seagull* (WB, 1968); directed *The Appointment* (MGM, 1970); *The Last of the Mobile Hot Shots* (WB, 1970); *The Anderson Tapes* (Col., 1971); *Childs Play* (Par., 1972); *The Offense* (UA, 1973); *Serpico* (Par., 1973); *Lovin' Molly* (Col., 1974); *Murder on the Orient Express* (Par., 1974); and *Dog Day Afternoon* (WB, 1975).

Television. Mr. Lumet first directed the Danger Series (CBS, 1951–53); subsequently directed more than 500 productions including *Mooney's Kid Don't Cry, The Last of My Gold Watches, This Property Is Condemned* (Kraft Television Th., Apr. 16, 1958); *The Hiding Place* (Playhouse 90, CBS, Mar. 18, 1960); *Sacco-Vanzetti Story* (NBC, June 3, 1960); *The Dybbuk* (Play of the Week, WNTA, Oct. 3, 1960); *John Brown's Raid* (NBC, Oct. 25, 1960); *The Iceman Cometh* (Play of the Week, WNTA, Nov. 14, 1960); *Rashomon* (Play of the Week, WNTA, Dec. 13, 1960); *Cry Vengeance* (NBC, Feb. 21, 1961); *The Dybbuk* (Play of the Week, WNTA, 1966); and the series, You Are There (CBS, 1952–53).

Awards. Mr. Lumet received the DGA and Academy (Oscar) Award nomination for *12 Angry Men* (1958); NATAS (Emmy) Award for *The Iceman Cometh* (1961); a NATAS (Emmy) nomination for *Sacco-Vanzetti Story* (1961) and a DGA Award for *Long Day's Journey into Night* (1963).

LUND, ART. Singer, actor. b. Arthur Earl Lund, Jr., Apr. 1, 1920, Salt Lake City, Utah, to Arthur Earl Lund, Sr., and Lillie Alma Lund. Father, realtor. Grad. South H.S., 1937; Westminster Jr. Coll., A.A. 1939; Eastern Kentucky State Coll., B.S. (mathematics, English) 1941; Naval Acad. Grad. Sch., M.S. (meteorology) 1944. Studied in Hollywood (Calif.) singing with Harriet Lee, acting with Florence Enright. Married July 26, 1940, to Kathleen Virginia (dec., Oct. 15, 1969); one son, one daughter. Served USN, 1942–46; rank, Lt. Member of AFTRA; AEA; SAG; AGVA. Address: (home) 10 Beechtree Lane, Bronxville, NY 10708, tel. (914) DE 7-2544; (bus.) c/o General Artists Corp., 640 Fifth Ave., New York, NY 10022, tel. (212) CI 7-7543.

Theatre. Mr. Lund made his first appearance in stock as Wreck in *Wonderful Town* (Lambertville Music Circus, N.J., Summer 1955); subsequently played the Zipper King in *Gentlemen Prefer Blondes* (Warwick Musical Th., R.I., Summer 1955); and Frank Butler in *Annie Get Your Gun* (Cape Cod Melody Tent, Hyannis, Mass., Summer 1955). He made his N.Y.C. debut as Joe in *The Most Happy Fella* (Imperial, May 3, 1956), and toured in this role (opened Riviera, Detroit, Mich., Dec. 23, 1957; closed Philharmonic Aud., Los Angeles, Calif., June 28, 1958). In stock, he played Billy Bigelow in *Carousel* (Starlight Th., Kansas City, Mo., July 1958); played Joe in *The Most Happy Fella* (Carter Barron Amphitheatre, Washington, D.C.; Starlight Th., Kansas City, Mo.; Carousel Th., Framingham, Mass., Summer 1958). He appeared as Lennie in the musical version of *Of Mice and Men* (Provincetown Playhouse, N.Y.C., Dec. 4, 1958); Joe in *The Most Happy Fella* (NY City Ctr., Feb. 10, 1959); in stock played Jeff in *Bells Are Ringing* (South Shore Music Circus, Cohasset, Mass.; Cape Cod Melody Tent, Hyannis, Mass., Summer 1959); and played Rue in *Summer of the Seventeenth Doll* (Bucks County Playhouse, New Hope, Pa., May 1959). He succeeded (Aug. 1959) Scott Brady as Kent in *Destry Rides Again* (Imperial, N.Y.C., Apr. 23, 1959); made his London debut as Joe in *The Most Happy Fella* (Coliseum, Apr. 21, 1960); played Sean Enright in *Donnybrook!* (46 St. Th., N.Y.C., May 18, 1961); and appeared in *Men Around the House* (Bucks County Playhouse, New Hope, Pa), Summer 1961).

Mr. Lund was standby for Robert Preston as Pancho Villa in the pre-Bway tryout of *We Take the Town* (opened Shubert, New Haven, Conn., Feb. 19, 1962; closed Shubert, Philadelphia, Pa., Mar. 17, 1962); played Ben Marino in *Fiorello!* (NY City Ctr., June 13, 1962); and, in stock, Frank Butler in *Annie Get Your Gun* (St. Louis Municipal Opera, Mo.; Meadowbrook Dinner Th., Cedar Grove, N.J.; Sombrero Th., Phoenix, Ariz., Summer 1962, Winter 1963). He played Frank Westphal in *Sophie* (Winter Garden, N.Y.C., Apr. 15, 1963); Wild Bill Hickok in *Calamity Jane* (State Fair Music Hall, Dallas, Tex., Summer 1963); and Johnny "Leadville" Brown in *The Unsinkable Molly Brown* (Starlight Th., Kansas City, Mo., July 1963; Civic Arena, Pittsburgh, Pa., Aug. 1963). He played David Jordan in *No Strings* (Her Majesty's, London, Dec. 30, 1963); Roy Bailey in *The Wayward Stork* (46 St. Th., N.Y.C., Jan. 19, 1966); Joe in *The Most Happy Fella* (NY City Ctr., May 11, 1966); and Doc Golightly in the pre-Bway tryout of *Breakfast at Tiffany's* (Forrest, Philadelphia, Oct. 15, 1966; closed during previews Majestic, N.Y.C., Dec. 14, 1966).

Films. He appeared in The Molly Maguires (Par., 1970).

Television. Mr. Lund has appeared on Texaco Star Th. (NBC); the Jackie Gleason Show (CBS); The Steve Allen Show (NBC); the Ernie Kovacs Show; the Ed Sullivan Show (CBS); the Jerry Lewis Show; the Dinah Shore Show (NBC); Wagon Train (NBC); Gunsmoke (CBS); and Wild Bill Hickok in *Calamity Jane.*

Night Clubs. Mr. Lund sang with the Benny Goodman Orchestra (1946).

Discography. Mr. Lund's recordings include the original cast albums of *The Most Happy Fella* (Col., 1963); and *Donnybrook!* (Kapp); as well as many singles including *Mam'selle; Peg o' My Heart; Sleepy Time Gal; Slowboat to China* and *Blue Skies,* all of which were gold record winners, selling over a million copies.

Awards. Mr. Lund was voted best male vocalist by the *Downbeat* Magazine Poll (1946; 1947); and best recording artist by *Billboard* Magazine (1947).

Recreation. Golf, tennis, swimming, all outdoor activities, cars.

LUNT, ALFRED. Actor, director. b. Aug. 19, 1892, Milwaukee, Wis., to Alfred and Harriet Washborn (Briggs) Lunt. Attended Carroll Coll., 1908. Married May 26, 1922, to Lynn Fontanne. Member of ANTA (drama adv. panel of Intl. Exchange Program, 1954); AEA; SAG; AFTRA; The Players. Address: Genesee Depot, WI 53127.

Theatre. Mr. Lunt made his stage debut as the Sheriff in a repertory production of *The Aviator* (Castle Sq. Th., Boston, Mass., Oct. 7, 1912); subsequently appeared with the company (1912–14) in such plays as *The Gingerbread Man* (Castle Sq. Th., 1913); toured with Margaret Anglin's Co. (1914–16), in *Medea, Green Stockings, Beverly's Balance, As You Like It,* and *Iphigenia in Tauris;* joined Lily Langtry in a touring vaudeville production of *Ashes* (1916); and again toured with Margaret Anglin's Co. (1916).

He made his N.Y.C. debut as Claude Estabrook in *Romance and Arabella* (Harris, Oct. 17, 1917); first appeared with Miss Fontanne in *A Young Man's Fancy* (Washington, D.C., June 16, 1919); played the title role in *Clarence* (Hudson, N.Y.C., Sept. 20, 1919); Ames in *The Intimate Strangers* (Henry Miller's Th., Nov. 7, 1921); the title role in *Banco* (Ritz, Sept. 20, 1922); Charles II in *Sweet Nell of Old Drury* (48 St. Th., May 18, 1923); David Peel in *Robert E. Lee* (Ritz, Nov. 20, 1923); and Mr. Prior in *Outward Bound* (Ritz, Jan. 7, 1924).

For the Theatre Guild, he played the Actor in *The Guardsman* (Garrick, Oct. 13, 1924); Capt. Bluntschli in *Arms and the Man* (Guild, Sept. 14, 1925); Juvan in *The Goat Song* (Guild, Jan. 25, 1926); Mr. Dermott in *At Mrs. Beam's* (Guild, Apr. 26, 1926); Maximilian in *Juarez and Maximilian* (Guild, Oct. 11, 1926); Babe Callahan in *Ned McCobb's Daughter* (John Golden Th., Nov. 29, 1926); Dmitri in *The Brothers Karamazov* (Guild, Jan. 3, 1927); Clark Story in *The Second Man* (Guild, Apr. 11, 1927); Louis Dubedat in *The Doctor's Dilemma* (Guild, Nov. 21, 1927); Marco Polo in *Marco Millions* (Guild, Jan. 9, 1928); Mosca in *Volpone* (Guild, Apr. 9, 1928); Counselor Albert von Eckhardt in *Caprice* (Guild, Dec. 31, 1928), which he repeated for his London debut (St. James's, June 4, 1929); Raphael Lord in *Meteor* (Guild, N.Y.C., Dec. 23, 1929); Earl of Essex in *Elizabeth the Queen* (Guild, Nov. 3, 1930); and Rudolf in *Reunion in Vienna* (Martin Beck Th., Nov. 16, 1931).

Mr. Lunt produced, with Miss Fontanne and Noel Coward, and played Otto in *Design for Living* (Ethel Barrymore Th., Jan 24, 1933); repeated his role and directed *Reunion in Vienna* (Lyric, London, Jan. 3, 1934); played Stefan in *Point Valaine* (Ethel Barrymore Th., N.Y.C., Jan. 16, 1935); Petruchio in *The Taming of the Shrew* (Guild, Sept. 30, 1935); Harry Van in *Idiot's Delight* (Shubert, Mar. 24, 1936); Jupiter in *Amphitryon 38* (Shubert, Nov. 1, 1937); Trigorin in *The Seagull* (Shubert, Mar. 28,

1938); repeated his role in *Amphitryon 38* (Lyric, London, May 17, 1938); toured the US in *Idiot's Delight, The Seagull,* and *Amphitryon 38* (1938–39); appeared as Petruchio in *The Taming of the Shrew* (Alvin, N.Y.C., Feb. 5, 1940); Dr. Kaarlo Valkonen in *There Shall Be No Night* (Alvin, Apr. 29, 1940); directed *Candle in the Wind* (Shubert, Oct. 22, 1941); and portrayed Serafin in *The Pirate* (Martin Beck Th., Nov. 25, 1942).

He played the retitled role of Karilo Vlachos (Dr. Kaarlo Valkonen) in *There Shall Be No Night* (Aldwych, London, Dec. 15, 1943); Sir John Fletcher in *Love in Idleness* (Lyric, Dec. 20, 1944), which he repeated in the N.Y.C. production, retitled *O Mistress Mine* (Empire, Jan. 23, 1946); Thomas Chanler in *I Know My Love* (Shubert, Nov. 2, 1949); directed and appeared in *Cosi Fan Tutte* (Metropolitan Opera House, Dec. 28, 1951); appeared as Axel Diensen in *Quadrille* (Phoenix, London, Sept. 12, 1952); directed *Ondine* (46 St. Th., N.Y.C., Feb. 18, 1954); repeated his role in *Quadrille,* which he also directed (Coronet, Nov. 3, 1954); played Rudi Sebastian in *The Great Sebastians* (ANTA, Jan. 4, 1956); toured England as Anton Schill in a tryout of *Time and Again* (opened at Theatre Royal, Brighton, Dec. 24, 1957) retitled *The Visit,* when presented in N.Y.C. (Lunt-Fontanne, May 5, 1958), and repeated this role on tour (1959–60), in the NY City Ctr. revival (Mar. 8, 1960), and in the London production (Royalty, June 23, 1960); directed *First Love* (Morosco, Dec. 25, 1961); and directed *La Traviata* (Sept. 24, 1966) for opening week of new Metropolitan Opera House, N.Y.C.

Films. Mr. Lunt appeared in *The Ragged Edge* (Goldwyn, 1923); *Backbone* (Goldwyn, 1923); *Second Youth* (MG, 1924); *Sally of the Sawdust* (1925); *The Man Who Found Himself* (1925); *Lovers in Quarantine* (1925); as the Actor in *The Guardsman* (MGM, 1931); and in *Stage Door Canteen* (UA, 1943).

Television. He played Rudi Sebastian in *The Great Sebastians* (Producers Showcase, NBC, Apr. 1, 1957); was the Narrator of *The Old Lady Shows Her Medals* (US Steel Hour, CBS, June 12, 1963) and of *Athens— Where the Theatre Began* (CBS, Sept. 11, 1963); was Mr. Justice Holmes in *The Magnificent Yankee* (Jan. 28, 1965; repeated Feb. 3, 1966); and appeared on the Dick Cavett Show with Fontanne and Noel Coward (ABC, Feb. 10, 1970; repeated June 1, 1970).

Awards. Mr. Lunt tied with Barry Fitzgerald in the *Variety* NY Drama Critics' Poll (1940) for his performance as Dr. Kaarlo Valkonen in *There Shall Be No Night.* He won the *Variety* NY Drama Critics' Poll (1943) for his performance as Serafin in *The Pirate,* and received Antoinette Perry (Tony) awards for his direction of *Ondine* (1954), and for his performance as Axel Diensen in *Quadrille* (1955). On Feb. 17, 1958, the Globe Th., N.Y.C. was renamed, in honor of Mr. Lunt and his wife, the Lunt-Fontanne Th. With his wife, Mr. Lunt received the Medal of Freedom in 1964, a special Antoinette Perry (Tony) Award (Apr. 19, 1970), the Brandeis Univ. Creative Arts Award (1972), the Actors' Fund Medal (1972), and the ANTA National Artist Award (1972).

He received honorary degrees from the Univ. of Wisconsin, Carroll Coll., Dartmouth Coll., New York Univ., Emerson Coll., Beloit Coll., and Yale Univ.

Recreation. Cooking, farming.

LUTZ, E. O. Certified public accountant, executive, educator. b. Edward Oscar Lutz, July 31, 1919, Brooklyn, N.Y., to A. George and Selma H. (Holtzmann) Lutz. Father, paper manufacturer. Grad. Bklyn. Technical H.S., 1936; attended New York Univ., 1936–38; grad. Columbia Coll., B.S. 1940; attended Golden Gate Law Sch., San Francisco, Calif., 1943–45; grad. Univ. of State of N.Y., C.P.A. 1947. Married Jan. 3, 1944, to Alice Lessem; two sons, one daughter. Served US Army, 1942–46; rank, 1st Lt. Member of Musical Theatres Assn. (exec. dir., 1956–70); NY Civil Liberties Union, Brooklyn Chapter (dir. and treas.); USITT (co-chairman, administration committee); American Th. Wing; G. B. Shaw Society (editorial board, Bulletin, 1950–59); Amer. Inst. of C.P.A.; Amer. Economic Assn.; Tax Inst., Inc.; NY Society of C.P.A.; Natl. Assn. of Accountants; NY Board of Trade; AAUP; Natl. Arbitration Panel; Amer. Arbitration Assn.; Variety Clubs of Amer. Address: (home) 2702 Ave. J, Brooklyn, NY 11210, tel. (212) CL 2-8985; (bus.) Economics Dept., Brooklyn College, Brooklyn, NY 11210, tel. (212) 780-5317.

Since 1948, Mr. Lutz has been professor of economics at Brooklyn Coll. He has also been a member of the American Th. Wing, N.Y.C. (1956–to date), and has taught a course in arts management at the New Sch. for Social Research and at the Inst. for Advanced Studies in the Th. Arts, N.Y.C. (1963–to date). He was founder and administrator of a theatre management course sponsored by MATA (1957–70); visiting professor of theatre management at Yale Drama Sch. (1970); and guest lecturer, PAMI (1971–72). He has served as an officer of the Professional Staff Congress (1972–to date); and was a member of the management negotiating team in collective bargaining for summer musical theatre contracts with AEA (1960–69). He is currently a consultant in financial and tax matters for various entertainment enterprises.

Published Works. He has written articles, including "Summer Theatre Accounting Procedures" (*N.Y. Certified Public Accountant,* Aug. 1950); "Limited Partnerships" (*Journal of Taxation,* May 1956); "Capital Formation of Speculative Enterprises" (*The Tax Magazine,* June 1956); "Tax Considerations for Promoters and Investors" (*Tax Ideas,* 1962); and has contributed articles to *Navarro Economica, Journal De La Comptabilita, Boekhoudkundig Nieuwsblad* and *Revista de Contabilidado e Comercio.* He is the author of *A Blueprint for Summer Theatre Management Quiz;* co-author of *Accountants Practice Management Handbook* (1961); and author of *Attorney's Guide to Practical Accounting* (1964). He co-authored, with William Herman, the chapter on theatre audits in *Encyclopedia of Auditing Techniques* (1966); was author of *Student's Manual* (2nd ed., 1967) for use in professional theatre management courses; was co-author of *Practical Accountants Handbook* (1970); and author of *Rights, Risks & Responsibilities* (1966).

Awards. He received an honorable mention from the Industrial Marketing Association for his article, "Summer Theatre Accounting Procedures" (1950).

LYNDE, PAUL. Actor, director, writer. b. Paul Edward Lynde, June 13, 1926, Mt. Vernon, Ohio, to Hoy C. and Sylvia (Bell) Lynde. Father, meat market proprietor. Grad. Mt. Vernon (Ohio) H.S., 1944; Northwestern Univ., B.S. 1948. Member of SAG; AFTRA; AEA; Phi Kappa Sigma; Deru Honorary Fraternity.

Theatre. Mr. Lynde made his debut at the Corning (N.Y.) Summer Th. (Summer 1951) as Pon in *Happy Birthday,* followed by Billy in *Anything Goes,* the District Attorney in *Dream Girl,* Steve in *Show Boat* and Steve in *A Streetcar Named Desire.*

He first appeared on Bway in the revue *New Faces of 1952* (Royale Th., May 16, 1952); subsequently wrote and directed sketches for *New Faces of '56* (Ethel Barrymore Th., June 14, 1956); in stock, repeated his performance in *New Faces of 1952* (Coconut Grove Playhouse, Miami, Fla., Apr. 1957); played Madame Lucy in *Irene* (St. Louis Municipal Opera, Mo., July 1957); Vivien Budd in *Panama Hattie* (Starlight Th., Kansas City, Mo., Aug. 1957); the General in *Visit to a Small Planet* (Bucks County Playhouse, New Hope, Pa., Summer 1958); the Electronics Expert in *Desk Set* (Bucks County Playhouse, Summer 1958); Paul Anderson in *Season in the Sun* (Bucks County Playhouse, Summer 1958); appeared in the revue *Dig We Must* (John Drew Th., East Hampton, L.I., N.Y., July 1959); as Maxwell Archer in *Once More, With Feeling* (Candlelight Cafe Playhouse, Washington, D.C., July 1959; Spa Summer Th., Saratoga Springs, N.Y., Sept. 1959); and as the General in *Visit to a Small Planet* (Coconut Grove Playhouse, Miami, Fla., Jan. 1959).

He played Harry Macafee in *Bye Bye Birdie* (Martin Beck Th., N.Y.C., Apr. 14, 1960); and wrote the sketches "The Reds Visit Mount Vernon" and with Tony Geiss "It Takes a Heap" for *New Faces of 1962* (Alvin, Feb. 1, 1962), which was repeated in *Wet Paint* (Renata Th., Apr. 12, 1965).

Films. Mr. Lynde made his debut in *New Faces* (20th-Fox, 1954); appeared in *Bye Bye Birdie* (Col., 1962); *Son of Flubber* (Buena Vista, 1962); *Under the Yum-Yum Tree* (Col., 1963); *For Those Who Think Young* (Par., 1963), *Send Me No Flowers* (U, 1964); *Beach Blanket Bingo* (Amer. Intl., 1965); *The Glass Bottom Boat* (MGM, 1966); and *How Sweet It Is* (Natl. Gen., 1968).

Television. Mr. Lynde appeared on the Ed Sullivan Show (CBS, 1952, 1960, 1961, 1962, 1963); Colgate Comedy Hour (NBC, 1954); the Martha Raye Show (NBC, 1954–55); the Red Buttons Show (NBC, 1954); Perry Como's Kraft Music Hall (NBC, 1959–60); and Andy Williams Show (NBC, 1963).

He was in *Henry Fonda and the Family* (CBS, June 23, 1964); on Celebrity Game (CBS, 1964–65); Steve Allen Show (Ind., 1964–65; CBS, 1967–68); Burke's Law, ABC, 1964, 1965); The Munsters (CBS, 1965); The Farmer's Daughter (ABC, 1965); Bewitched (ABC, 1965–67, 1970); Hollywood Palace (ABC, 1965–67); Gidget (ABC, 1966); the Mike Douglas Show (ABC, 1965–67); I Dream of Jeanie (NBC, 1966); Bob Hope Show (NBC, 1966); Hollywood Squares (NBC, 1966–68, 1971–76); Gypsy Rose Lee Show (ABC, 1966–68); Hey, Landlord! (NBC, 1967); Everybody's Talking (ABC, 1966–68); and the Patty Duke Show (Ind., 1967).

He appeared as a guest on The Flying Nun (ABC, 1969); was in *Gidget Grows Up* (ABC, 1969); *Gidget Gets Married* (ABC, 1972); and had his own program, the Paul Lynde Show (ABC, 1973). On The New Temperatures Rising (ABC, Sept.–Nov. 1973), he replaced James Whitmore as Dr. Campanelli (renamed Dr. Mercy), and he appeared again when the program was revived as Temperatures Rising (ABC, Summer 1974).

Night Clubs. Mr. Lynde won an amateur contest at Number One Fifth Avenue (N.Y.C., Nov. 1950) with his "African Hunter" sketch, and played in it there until early 1951. He appeared at Spivy's Roof (N.Y.C., Apr. 1951); in *What's New* (Statler Hotel chain, Nov. 1951); and in *Come As You Are* (Versailles, N.Y.C., Mar. 1955).

Recreation. Swimming, fishing.

LYNN, JEFFREY. Actor. b. Ragnar Godfrey Lind, Feb. 16, 1909, Auburn, Mass., to John A. and Hedvig (Edoff) Lind. Grad. South H.S., Worcester, Mass., 1926; Bates Coll., B.A. 1930. Studied drama in N.Y.C. with Theodora Irvine, 1934–35, Harold Clurman, 1956; in Hollywood (Calif.), with Frank Beckwith: voice with George Griffin, N.Y.C., 1957–58. Served 1942–46, US Army Signal Corps (photographic section); USAAF, combat and intelligence officer; rank, Capt.; awarded Air Medal, Bronze Star. Married Oct. 1946 to Robin Chandler Tippett (marr. dis. 1957); one son, one daughter; married Mar. 6, 1965, to Patricia Ciarlo, model and actress. Member of AEA; AFTRA; SAG; The Lambs. Address: Tarzana, CA 91356.

Pre-Theatre. Commercial representative for N.E. Telephone Co. (1930–32), high-school English teacher (1932–33).

Theatre. Mr. Lynn made his first professional appearance as David in a stock production of *The Silver Cord* (Barter Th., Abingdon, Va., July 1935); billed as Geoffry Lind, first appeared in N.Y.C. as a walk-on and assistant stage manager in *A Slight Case of Murder* (48 St. Th., Sept. 11, 1935); subsequently was a walk-on in *Stick-in-the-Mud* (48 St. Th., Nov. 26, 1935); was understudy and played walk-ons in a touring production of *Cyrano de Bergerac* (Feb.–June 1936); appeared in a stock production of *The Night of January 16th* (Bar Harbor, Me., July 1936); played in a touring production of *Lady Precious Stream* (Oct. 1936); and Harley Harrington in the national company of *Brother Rat* (Feb.–Dec.

1937).

Billed as Jeffrey Lynn, he played John in stock productions of *John Loves Mary* (Santa Fe Summer Th., N.M., July 1948; Chapel Playhouse, Guilford, Conn., Aug. 1948); C. K. Dexter-Haven in a summer-theatre touring production of *The Philadelphia Story* (June–Sept. 1949), and on a cross-country tour (Nov. 1949–Apr. 1950); repeated his role in *John Loves Mary* (Bahama Playhouse, Nassau, B.W.I., Feb. 1951); played Joe Adams in *The Long Days* (Empire, N.Y.C., Apr. 20, 1951); Dr. Robert Dorsey in *Lo and Behold!* (Booth, Dec. 12, 1951); appeared in *The Second Man* (Memphis Arena Th., Tenn., Mar. 1952); played David Naughton in *Claudia* (Bermudiana Th., Hamilton, Bermuda, May 1952), which he repeated in the US (Summer tour, 1952); and Peter Standish in *Berkeley Square* (Cape Playhouse, Dennis, Mass.; Triple Cities Playhouse, Binghamton, N.Y., July 1952).

He appeared in the title role in *Captain Carvallo* (Kennebunkport Playhouse, Me., July 1952); Lachlen in *The Hasty Heart* (Drury Lane Th., Chicago, Ill., Aug. 5, 1952); The Rev. Toop in *See How They Run* (Empress, St. Louis, Mo., Jan. 1953; Hollywood-by-the-Sea Playhouse, Hollywood, Fla., Feb. 1953); the title role in *Mister Roberts* (Summer tour, 1953); David Slater in *The Moon Is Blue* (York, Pa., Nov. 1953); repeated his role in *Mister Roberts* (Showcase Th., Evanston, Ill., Dec. 1953); Hilltop Th., Baltimore, Md., Jan. 1954); Sefton in *Stalag 17* (Fayetteville Playhouse, N.Y., July 5, 1954); Kenneth Bixby in *Goodbye Again* (Deer Lake Th., Pa., Aug. 1, 1954); repeated his role in *Mister Roberts* (Paper Mill Playhouse, Millburn, N.J., Oct. 1954); Linus in *Sabrina Fair* (Fred Miller Th., Milwaukee, Wis., Jan. 24, 1955); Lt. Maryk in *The Caine Mutiny Court-Martial* (Princess, Sydney, Australia, Mar. —Apr. 1955); Alan Coles in *Oh, Men! Oh, Women!* (Fred Miller Th., Milwaukee, Wis., June 1, 1955).

Mr. Lynn toured the eastern US as Lt. Greenwald in *The Caine Mutiny Court-Martial* (opened Pocono Playhouse, Mountainhome, Pa., July 1955; closed Playhouse-in-the-Park, Philadelphia, Pa., Sept. 1955); played the title role in *Mister Roberts* (Melody Circle, Allentown, Pa., June 11, 1956); appeared in *Champagne Complex* (Cincinnati Summer Playhouse, Ohio, June 25, 1956); played Constantine in *Call Me Madam* (Sacandaga Garden Th., N.Y., July 9, 1956); Richard in *The Seven Year Itch* (Legion Star Playhouse, Ephrata, Pa., July 23, 1956); Bud Walters in *Anniversary Waltz* (Capri Th., Atlantic Beach, N.Y., Aug. 5, 1956); repeated his role in *The Seven Year Itch* (Ivory Tower Playhouse, Spring Lake, N.J., Aug. 13, 1956); appeared as Alan Coles in *Oh, Men! Oh, Women!* (Myrtle Beach Playhouse, S.C., Aug. 20, 1956); as Bill Page in *The Voice of the Turtle* (Canal-Fulton Summer Th., Ohio, Sept. 10, 1956); as Grant in *State of the Union* (East Carolina Coll., Greenville, N.C., Oct. 29, 1956); Bud Walters in *Anniversary Waltz* (Blackstone Th., Chicago, Ill., Dec. 30, 1956); Alan Coles in *Oh, Men! Oh, Women!* (Royal Poinciana Playhouse, Palm Beach, Fla., Feb. 4, 1957); Bluntschli in *Arms and the Man* (Fred Miller Th., Milwaukee, Wis., Feb. 18, 1957), which he repeated with the Joe Jefferson Players (Mobile, Ala., May 29, 1957); Capt. Fisby in *The Teahouse of the August Moon* (Legion Star Playhouse, Ephrata, Pa., June 1957); Gil in *Janus* (Myrtle Beach Playhouse, S.C., July 16, 1957); Dan King in *Plain and Fancy* (Summer tour, Aug.–Sept. 1957); the title role in *Macbeth* (Bowling Green State Univ., Ohio, May 1958); Mr. Biddle in *The Happiest Millionaire* (Durham Star Playhouse, N.C., June 24, 1958); Mr. Malcolm and Major Pollock in *Separate Tables* (Long Beach Playhouse, N.Y., July 22, 1958); and Tony Wendice in *Dial 'M' for Murder* (Cape Playhouse, Dennis, Mass., Aug. 25, 1958).

He appeared as Jerry Ryan in a national tour of *Two for the seesaw* (opened Ford's Th., Baltimore, Md., Oct. 6, 1958; closed San Francisco, Calif., July 1959), and repeated the role at the end of the N.Y.C. production (Booth, Sept. 1959; closed Oct. 31, 1959); again repeated the role in summer theatres (June–Aug. 1960); played Jonathan Swift in *A Call on Kuprin* (Broadhurst, N.Y.C., May 25, 1961); Parker Ballantine in the national tour of *Critic's Choice* (opened Municipal Aud., Lafayette, La., Dec. 1, 1961; closed Paramount, Anderson, Ind., Mar. 28, 1962); repeated the role in stock (Summer 1962); played David in *Write Me a Murder* (Tappan Zee Playhouse, Nyack, N.Y., Aug. 20–25, 1962; Kennebunkport Playhouse, Me., Aug. 27–Sept. 1, 1962); Lakes Region Playhouse, Laconia, N.H., Sept. 3–8, 1962); and succeeded (Dec. 10, 1962) Lee Bowman as Dirk Winsten in a touring production of *Mary, Mary* (opened Central City Opera House, Colo., Aug. 6, 1962; closed Wheeling, W.Va., Dec. 1963).

Mr. Lynn played Henry Higgins in *My Fair Lady* (Charlotte Summer Th., N.C., Aug. 11, 1964); succeeded (Fisher Th., Detroit, Mich., May 24, 1965) Larry Parks as John Cleves in the natl. tour of *Any Wednesday*; played Jerry Ryan in *Two for the Seesaw* (Elitch Gardens Th., Denver, Colo., July 12, 1965); replaced temporarily (Aug. 2–Sept. 4, 1965) George Gaynes as John Cleves in the Bway Company of *Any Wednesday* (Music Box, Feb. 18, 1964); played Max Halliday in a tour of *Dial 'M' for Murder* (opened Municipal Th., Atlanta, Ga., Jan. 24, 1966; closed Paramus, N.J., Apr. 3, 1966); repeated the role of John Cleves in a stock tour of *Any Wednesday* (Summer 1966); and played Dr. J. Wayne Talbot in *Dinner at Eight* (Alvin, N.Y.C., Sept. 27, 1966).

Films. Billed as Jeffrey Lynn, he appeared in *Out Where the Stars Begin* (WB, 1938); *Cowboy from Brooklyn* (WB, 1938); *When Were You Born?* (WB, 1938); *Four Daughters* (WB, 1938); *Yes, My Darling Daughter* (WB, 1939); *Daughters Courageous* (WB, 1939); *Four Wives* (WB, 1939); *The Roaring Twenties* (WB, 1939); *Espionage Agent* (WB, 1939); *Money and the Woman* (WB, 1940); *The Fighting 69th* (WB, 1940); *It All Came True* (WB, 1940); *A Child Is Born* (WB, 1940); *My Love Come Back* (WB, 1940); *All This and Heaven Too* (WB, 1940); *Underground* (WB, 1941); *The Body Disappears* (WB, 1941); *Four Mothers* (WB, 1941); *Million Dollar Baby* (WB, 1941); *Law of the Tropics* (WB, 1941); *Flight from Destiny* (WB, 1941); *Whiplash* (WB, 1947); *Black Bart* (U, 1948); *Washington Girl* (U, 1948); *A Letter to Three Wives* (20th-Fox, 1948); *For the Love of Mary* (U, 1948); *Strange Bargain* (RKO, 1949); *Captain China* (Par., 1949); *Up Front* (U, 1951); *Home-Town Story* (MGM, 1951); *Lost Lagoon* (UA, 1958); *Butterfield 8* (MGM, 1960); and *Tony Rome* (20th-Fox, 1967).

Television. Mr. Lynn played in *Miracle in the Rain* (Studio One, CBS, May 1, 1950); on the Faye Emerson Show; in *The Silver Cord* (Pulitzer Prize Th., ABC, 1951); on Cameo Th. (NBC); the Fred Waring Show; the Ken Murray Show (CBS); US Steel Hour (CBS); Philco Television Playhouse (NBC); Lights Out (NBC); Lux Video Th. (CBS); Schlitz Playhouse of Stars (CBS); Robert Montgomery Presents (NBC); Tales of Tomorrow (ABC); Goodyear Playhouse (NBC); he was a regular on the summer series My Son Jeep (NBC, July–Aug., 1953); appeared on Kraft Television Th. (NBC); Frontiers of Faith (NBC); Danger (CBS); Modern Romances (NBC); The Verdict Is Yours (CBS); Philip Morris Playhouse (CBS); Suspense (CBS); Medallion Th. (CBS); Elgin Hour (ABC); True Story (NBC); in *The Spiral Staircase* (Th. 62, NBC, Oct. 4, 1961); *The Autumn Garden* (Showcase–Drama, Educ., May 22, 1966); was a regular on the daytime serial The Secret Storm (CBS, 1969); appeared on Ironside (NBC); The Bold Ones (NBC); and Matt Lincoln (ABC).

LYNN, MARA. Dancer, comedienne, actress, choreographer. b. Marilyn Mosier, July 17, 1929, Chicago, Ill., to Robert and Lauretta Mosier. Father, US foreign service officer; mother, educator. Grad. Muncie (Ind.) Central H.S., 1947; attended Brooklyn Coll., 1963. Studied dancing at Ballet Th., the Eugene Loring Sch., with Edward Caton, Mme. Nijinska, Henry Danton; acting with Charles Laughton and Arthur Kennedy; singing with Walter Greene. Married Oct. 1, 1950, to Harold Conrad; one son. Member of AEA; SAG; AFTRA; AGVA. Address: 205 W. 89th St., New York, NY 10024.

Theatre. Miss Lynn made her professional debut as the First Siren in the pre-Bway tour of *Bonanza Bound!* (opened Shubert Th., Philadelphia, Pa., Dec. 26, 1947; closed there Jan. 3, 1948); subsequently appeared in the revues *Inside U.S.A.* (Century, N.Y.C., Apr. 30, 1948), *Touch and Go* (Broadhurst, Oct. 13, 1949), and *Of All Things* (Los Angeles, Calif., 1950); performed in *I Love Lydia* (Players Ring, Hollywood, Calif., 1951); as Anna Christie in *New Girl in Town* (Sacandaga Summer Th., N.Y., 1959); Ninotchka in *Silk Stockings* (Pine Brook, N.J., 1959); the Yo-Yo Dance in the pre-Bway tryout of *The Amazing Adele* (opened Shubert, Philadelphia, Pa., Dec. 26, 1955; closed Shubert, Boston, Mass., Jan. 21, 1956); appeared in the touring company of the revue *What's the Rush?* (Playhouse-in-the-Park, Philadelphia, Pa.; Binghamton, N.Y.; Salt Creek Th., Hindsale, Ill.; Springfield, Ill., Summer 1956).

She understudied Gwen Verdon, played Katie and danced in *New Girl in Town* (46 St. Th., N.Y.C., May 14, 1957); at the Sacandaga (N.Y.) Summer Th., appeared as Mabel in *The Pajama Game, Maisie in The Boy Friend* Claudine in *Can-Can*, Jeannie in *Brigadoon*, and Helen in *Wonderful Town* (Summer 1957); played Gloria in *Body Beautiful* (Bway Th., N.Y.C., Jan. 23, 1958); appeared in stock as Dolly in *Rio Rita* (St. Louis Municipal Opera, Mo., 1958); toured as Lola in *Damn Yankees* (Camden County Fair, N.J.; Westbury Music Fair, L.I.; Valley Forge Music Fair, Devon, Pa., Summer 1959); played Essie Whimple in *Redhead* (Melody Fair, N. Tonawanda, N.Y., June 1960; Cleveland Tent, Ohio, Aug. 1960); Lola in *Damn Yankees* (Chicago Melody Fair, Ill., 1960); Gladys Bumps in *Pal Joey* (Starlight Th., Kansas City, Mo.; Niagara Melody Fair, July 1960); and Fay Fromkin in *Wish You Were Here*, and Lizette in *Naughty Marietta* (Melody Fair, N. Tonawanda, N.Y., July 1961).

Miss Lynn appeared in *This Was Burlesque* (Casino-East, N.Y.C., Mar. 6, 1962); as Claudine in *Can-Can* (NY City Ctr., May 16, 1962); toured in stock as Gladys Bumps in *Pal Joey* (Melody Fair, N. Tonawanda, N.Y.; Oakdale Musical Th., Wallingford, Conn.; Carousel Th., Framingham, Mass.; Warwick Musical Th., R.I., July 1962); played Gladys in *The Pajama Game* (Palace Th., San Francisco, Calif., 1962); understudied the roles of Melissa Peabody and Vera von Stovel in *Children from Their Games* (Morosco, N.Y.C., Apr. 11, 1963); and was Zenlia in *The Deer Park* (Th. de Lys, Feb. 1, 1967).

Miss Lynn has performed in industrial shows for Chevrolet, Ford, Edsel, Fruit of the Loom, and The Warners Fashion Show.

Films. Miss Lynn appeared in *Let's Make Love* (20th-Fox, 1960); *Last Train from Gun Hill* (Par., 1964); and *The Confession* (Wm. Marshall, Ltd.).

Television. Miss Lynn made her television debut on the Ed Sullivan Show (CBS, 1940); subsequently appeared on the Milton Berle Show (NBC, 1949); Dinah Shore Show (NBC, 1952); Jo Stafford Show (1952); Tony Martin Show (1952); Ritz Brothers (1952); Ben Blue (1952); Marx Brothers (1952); Colgate Comedy Hour (NBC, 1952–54); Red Skelton Show (CBS, 1953); *Svengali and the Blonde* (NBC, 1953); *Alice in Wonderland* (NBC, 1954); *The Taming of the Shrew* (NBC, 1954); Shower of Stars (CBS, 1954–55); Steve Allen Show (NBC, 1956); Car 54, Where Are You? (NBC, 1962); and Nuthouse (CBS, 1963).

Night Clubs. She has danced, with Nelson Barclift, at the Copacabana (N.Y.C.); Cocoanut Grove (Los Angeles, Calif.); Cal-Neva Lodge (Lake Tahoe, Calif.); performed in the Ray Bolger act (Sahara, Las Vegas, Nev.); Cesar Romero act (Top's, San Diego, Calif.); and her own act at the Chi-Chi (Palm Springs, Calif.); and appeared at the American Hotel (Miami Beach, Fla.); Arrowhead Springs Hotel (San Bernardino, Calif.); and the Dunes Hotel (Las Vegas, Nev.).

Recreation. Horseback riding, water skiing, canoeing, swimming, diving, sketching, poetry.

M

MABLEY, EDWARD. Playwright, educator. b. Mar. 7, 1906, Binghamton, N.Y., to Clarence W. and Mabelle C. (Howe) Mabley. Attended Wayne University, Detroit, Mich. Served US Army Signal Corps, 1941–43; rank, Sgt. Member of Dramatists Guild, ASCAP; DGA; WGA. c/o Brandt & Brandt, Dramatic Dept., 101 Park Ave., New York, NY 10017.

Theatre. Mr. Mabley's first Bway play was *Temper the Wind,* written with Leonard Mins (Playhouse, Dec. 27, 1946); subsequently he wrote *Glad Tidings* (Lyceum, Oct. 11, 1951), which had its premiere at the Somerset (Mass.) Playhouse (June 3, 1951); and *Red Sky at Morning,* with Joanna Roos (Olney Th., Md., 1953).

With Elie Siegmeister as composer, he wrote the book and lyrics for *The Mermaid in Lock No. 7,* first performed by the Amer. Wind Symphony (Pittsburgh, Pa., 1958); and *The Plough and the Stars,* a grand opera derived from Sean O'Casey's play (Louisiana State Univ., Baton Rouge, La., Mar. 16, 1969). With other composers he has also written *Bon Voyage,* a musical version of *Le Voyage de Monsieur Perrichon,* and many industrial shows and films, including *A Thousand Times Neigh* for the Ford Motor Co.'s ballet at the NY World's Fair (1940).

Television and Radio. Mr. Mabley has written more than seventy-five plays for radio and television, including the radio play *Created Equal* (CBS, Dec. 8, 1947) and the television play *Borderline of Fear,* written with Joanna Roos, for Danger (CBS-TV Nov. 21, 1950), which was beamed behind the Iron Curtain by the US State Dept. (RIAS, Berlin, c. 1951); adapted *The Silver Cord* (CBS 1949) and *Laburnum Grove* (CBS, 1949); the book for two original musicals, *The Box Supper* (CBS, 1950) and *Jasper* (NBC, 1950); and *The Woman at High Hollow* (NBC, 1958); with Ruth Friedlich, wrote The O'-Neills, a family situation comedy series (Dumont Network, 1949–50); directed radio and television at NBC and CBS.

Other Activities. Mr. Mabley was instructor of playwriting under John Gassner at the Dramatic Workshop of the New Sch. for Social Research (1946–49); and has taught playwriting at AADA and the New School for Social Research (1962–to date).

He was Mayor of the village of Pomona, N.Y., 1971–73.

Published Works. His published works include *Discrimination for Everybody!,* an adaptation for the stage of the radio play *Created Equal* (1948); *Glad Tidings* (1951); *Borderline of Fear,* which is included in *The Best Television Plays 1950–51* (1952), and in the anthology "Vanguard"; *Spring Journey* and *June Dawn,* written under the pseudonym John Ware; *The Motor Balloon "America"* (1969); and *Dramatic Construction,* a textbook of playwriting (1973).

Awards. He is the winner of two NTC fellowships in playwriting (1947–48).

MACDERMOT, GALT. Composer. b. Montreal, Canada, to Terrence and Elizabeth (Savage) MacDermot. Attended Capetown (South Africa) Univ. Married to Marlene Bruynzell; four children.

Pre-Theatre. Church organist, and dance orchestra musician.

Theatre. Mr. MacDermot wrote the music for *Hair* (Public Th., Oct. 17, 1967; moved to The Cheetah, Dec. 22, 1967; and Biltmore, Apr. 29, 1968). Again for the NY Shakespeare Festival, he wrote music for an adaptation of *Hamlet* (Public Th., N.Y.C., Dec. 26, 1967); music and lyrics for *Twelfth Night* (Delacorte, Aug. 12, 1969); the score for a musical adaptation of *Two Gentlemen of Verona* (Delacorte, July 22, 1971; and St. James Th., Dec. 1, 1971); incidental music for *The Tale of Cymbeline* (Delacorte, Aug. 12, 1971); and the music for the song "Baby, When I Find You" in *Sticks and Bones* (Public Th., Nov. 7, 1971; and John Golden Th., Mar. 1, 1972).

He composed the opera *Troilus and Cressida* (1969); wrote the music for *Isabel's a Jezebel* (Duchess, London, Dec. 15, 1970); subsequently composed the score for *Dude* (Broadway Th., N.Y.C., Oct. 9, 1972); *Via Galactica* (Uris, Nov. 28, 1972); contributed music to *The Maxi-Bar Tragedy* (London, 1972–73 season); wrote the book and music for *Aunt Harriet* (Th. for the New City, N.Y.C., Nov. 21, 1973); composed music for the ballet *La Novella-A Puerto Rican Soap Opera* (Clark Ctr. Th., Apr. 1973); wrote the music for *The Karl Marx Play* (Amer. Place Th., Apr. 2, 1973); wrote the score for *The Charlatan* (world premiere, Mark Taper Forum, Los Angeles, May 23, 1974); and contributed songs to *Straws in the Wind; A Theatrical Look Ahead* (Amer. Place Th., N.Y.C., Feb. 21, 1975).

Films. Mr. MacDermot wrote the background scores for *Cotton Comes to Harlem* (UA, 1970); *Fortune and Men's Eyes* (MGM, 1971); and *Rhinoceros* (Amer. Film Th., 1974).

Night Clubs. Mr. MacDermot appeared with his own group at The Village Gate (N.Y.C., Feb. 1974).

Other Activities. The world premiere of Mr. MacDermot's *Mass in F* was broadcast live from the Cathedral of St. John the Divine (N.Y.C., May 1971); the oratorio, *Take This Bread—A Mass in Our Time,* was performed at Madison Ave. Presbyterian Church (Feb. 26, 1975).

Discography. His recording credits include the original cast albums for *Hair* (RCA, 1968); and *Two Gentlemen of Verona* (ABC-Dunhill, 1971).

Awards. He won Grammy Awards for Best Jazz Composition of the Year (1961) for "African Waltz," and Best Score for an Original Cast Album (1968) for *Hair.*

He was named co-winner of the Vernon Rice and Drama Desk Awards (1967–68) for *Hair;* and received the Drama Desk and Critics' Circle Awards (1971–72) for *Two Gentlemen of Verona.*.

MacDOUGALL, ROGER. Playwright, director. b. Thomas Roger MacDougall, Aug. 2, 1910, Bearsden, Dunbartonshire, Scotland, to Thomas and Maggie (Doig) MacDougall. Parents, educators. Attended Bearsden Acad., 1913–26; grad. Glasgow Univ., B.L. 1929. Married Feb. 22, 1935, to Renée Jane Dalgleish Wallace Dunlop; one son, one daughter. Member of SWG, England (secy., 1940–50); League of Dramatists, England (exec. comm., council, 1950–60); Society of Authors, England; WGA; Dramatists Guild; Performing Rights Society.

Pre-Theatre. Musician, radio writer.

Theatre. Mr. MacDougall wrote *MacAdam & Eve* ("Q" Th., London, Feb. 7, 1950); *The Gentle Gunman* (Arts, Aug. 2, 1950); *To Dorothy, a Son* (Savoy, London, Nov. 23, 1950; John Golden Th., N.Y.C., Nov. 19, 1951); *Escapade* (St. James's, London, Jan. 20, 1953; 48 St. Th., N.Y.C., Nov. 18, 1953); *The Facts of Life* (Duke of York's, London, May 4, 1954); the pre-London tryout of *The Delegate* (opened Manchester Opera House, Summer 1955); and wrote with Ted Allen, *Double Image* (Savoy, London, Nov. 14, 1956); wrote with Stanley Mann, *Hide and Seek* (Ethel Barrymore Th., N.Y.C., Apr. 2, 1957); wrote *Tresor and Gog and Magog,* a translation of *Double Image* which ran 4 1/2 years in Paris; *Trouble with Father* (1964); and *Jack in the Box* (1971).

Films. Mr. MacDougall directed *Back to Normal* (Eng., 1947); *As Others See Us* (Eng., 1948); and *Designing Woman* (Eng., 1949).

He wrote the screenplays for *Midnight at Madam Tussaud's,* released in the US as *Midnight at the Wax Museum* (Par., 1936); *War on Wednesday* (Eng., 1938); *This Man Is News* (Par., 1938); *This Man in Paris* (Par., 1939); *Jimmy O'Dea* (Ealing); *Cheer Boys Cheer* (Ealing, 1939); *Spare a Copper* (Ealing, 1940); *The Bells Go Down* (Ealing, 1943); *The Man in the White Suit* (U, 1952); *The Gentle Gunman* (U, 1953); *Law and Disorder* (Court, 1958); *The Mouse That Roared* (Col., 1959); and *A Touch of Larceny* (Par., 1960).

Awards. Mr. MacDougall was nominated for an Academy (Oscar) Award for the screenplay of *The Man in the White Suit* (1952); and received a Bronze Plaque (Brussels Film Festival, 1949) for his direction of *As Others See Us.*

MacGRATH, LEUEEN. Actress, playwright. b. Leueen Emily MacGrath, July 3, 1914 (?), London, England, to Walter Michael Anthony and Jean (Martin) MacGrath. Father, mining engineer, recipient of D.S.O., M.C., Croix de Guerre. Attended Sacré Coeur, Lausanne, Switzerland; Farnborough Convent Coll., England; Les Tourelles, Brussels, Belgium; RADA, London, England. Served WW II, ENSA. Married to Christopher Burn (marr. dis.); married to Desmond Davis (marr. dis.); married May 1949 to George S. Kaufman (marr. dis. 1957); married Dec. 1961 to Dr. Stephen Goodyear. Member of AEA; British AEA; SAG.

Theatre. Miss MacGrath made her professional debut in London as Miss Cathcart in *Beggars in Hell* (Garrick Th., Apr. 17, 1933); subsequently played Benson in *The Night Club Queen* (Playhouse, Nov. 14, 1933); Hazel Graham in *The Laughing Woman* (New, Apr. 7, 1934); Helene Dupont in *Tovarich* (Lyric, Apr. 24, 1935); Jacqueline Vesey in *Love of Women* (Phoenix, June 2, 1935); Laura in *No Exit* (Embassy, Jan. 1936); Lydia Bennett in *Pride and Prejudice* (St. James's, Feb. 27, 1936); Lucretia Borgia in *Lucretia* (Arts, June 21, 1936); succeeded (Jan. 1937) Jessica Tandy as Jacqueline in *French without Tears* (Criterion, Nov. 6, 1936); and played Ellen Peter Burke in *The King's Breakfast* (Savoy, Dec. 12, 1937).

She appeared as Queenie in *Saloon Bar* (Wyndham's, Nov. 15, 1939); The Sphinx in *The Infernal Machine* (Arts, Sept. 5, 1940); Veronica Preston in *Deep Is the River* (Royal, Glasgow, Scot., Oct. 1941); Vicki in *Blossom Time* (Lyric, London, Mar. 17, 1942); Louise in *Salt of the Earth* (Vaudeville, July 9, 1942); and succeeded (Sept. 1942) Phylis Calvert as Patricia Graham in *Flare Path* (Apollo, Aug. 12, 1942).

She toured Europe and the Middle East for ENSA as Elvira in *Blithe Spirit* (1943–44); played the title role in *The Young Mrs. Barrington* (Winter Garden, London, Sept. 1945); played Leonora Yardly in *You Won't Need the Halo* (Arts, May 29, 1945); Gwennie in *Grim Fairy Tale* (Embassy, July 30, 1946); Maria Dean in *Bold Lover* ("Q," Oct. 1, 1946); Joan Chandler in *The Tightrope Walkers* ("Q," Mar. 4, 1947); and Eileen Perry in *Edward, My Son* (His Majesty's, May 30, 1947); repeated her role as Eileen Perry in her Bway debut in *Edward, My Son* (Martin Beck Th., Sept. 30, 1948).

She appeared as Isabel in *The Enchanted* (Lyceum, Jan. 18, 1950); collaborated with George S. Kaufman on *The Small Hours* (National, Feb. 15, 1951); played Sarat Carn in *The High Ground* (48 St. Th., Feb. 20, 1951); Amanda Phipps in *Fancy Meeting You Again* (Royale, Jan. 14, 1952), of which she was co-author with George S. Kaufman; and Donovan in *The Love of Four Colonels* (Shubert, Jan. 15, 1953); was librettist with George S. Kaufman and Abe Burrows, of *Silk Stockings* (Imperial, Feb. 24, 1955); appeared as Cassandra in *Tiger at the Gates* (Apollo, London, June 2, 1955; Plymouth, N.Y.C., Oct. 3, 1955); Sara Califer in *The Potting Shed* (Bijou, Jan. 29, 1957); Mrs. Shankland and Miss Railton-Bell in *Separate Tables* (Long Beach Playhouse, N.Y., July 22, 1958); Lucy in *Maidens and Mistresses at Home and at the Zoo* (Orpheum, Jan. 21, 1959); the Princess in *Lute Song* (NY City Ctr., Mar. 12, 1959); Louise Yeyder in a stock production of *Gilt and Gingerbread* (John Drew Th., East Hampton, L.I., N.Y., Aug. 24, 1959); repeated her role in *Maiden and Mistresses at Home and at the Zoo* (Festival of Two Worlds, Spoleto, Italy, Summer 1960); played Peonie Povis in *Farewell, Farewell Eugene* (Helen Hayes Th., N.Y.C., Sept. 27, 1960); Mrs. Alving in *Ghosts* (Fourth St. Th., Sept. 21, 1961); and Belke Worthmore in *The Love Nest* (Writers Stage Co., Jan. 25, 1963).

Miss MacGrath played Ruby in the premiere of *And Things That Go Bump in the Night* (Tyrone Guthrie Th., Minneapolis, Minn., Feb. 4, 1964); Luisa in a summer tryout of *So Much of Earth, So Much of*

Heaven (opened Westport, COnn., Country Playhouse, Aug. 30, 1965); The Lady in *On the Rocks* (Opera House, Manchester, England, Oct. 1969); and Lady Nelson in *A Bequest to the Nation* (Haymarket, London, Sept. 23, 1970).

Films. She made her debut in *Pygmalion* (MGM, 1938); subsequently appeared in *The Saint's Vacation* (RKO, 1941); *Edward, My Son* (MGM, 1949); and in *Three Cases of Murder* (Assoc., 1955).

Television. Miss MacGrath has appeared in *School for Scandal* (Th. Hour, CBS, Apr. 21, 1950); on Studio One (CBS); Robert Montgomery Presents (NBC); in *Angel Street* (Kraft Th., ABC, Mar. 25, 1954); on US Steel Hour (CBS); Pond's Th. (ABC); Alcoa Hour (NBC); Ellery Queen (NBC, 1959); as Cassandra in *Tiger at the Gates* (Play of the Week, WNTA, Feb. 8, 1960); and as Fanny Nightingale in *The Holy Terror* (Hallmark Hall of Fame, NBC, Apr. 7, 1965).

MACHIZ, HERBERT. Director, producer, acting teacher. b. Jan. 14, 1923, New York City, to Joseph and Eva (Myers) Machiz. Attended Washington and Lee Univ., 1948; New York Univ., 1949. Studied at the Amer. Th. Wing, N.Y.C., 1949. Served USAF, Special Services, 1943–46. Member of AEA; SSD&C. Address: 59 E. 73rd St., New York, NY 10021, tel. (212) RE 7-9838.

Theatre. Mr. Machiz directed shows while in the Special Services of the USAF (1943–46); after discharge, was managing dir. of the Riverside Th., Bridgton, Maine (Summer 1947); subsequently dir. an Equity Library Th. production of *Liliom* (Hamilton Grange Library, N.Y.C., May 17, 1952); directed a season of ten plays at the Surry (Me.) Playhouse (Summer 1952); dir., and designed scenery and lighting for a USAF production of *Down in the Valley* (Vienna, Austria, Summer 1952); dir. the opera, *The Tsar Has His Photograph Taken* (Provincetown Playhouse, N.Y.C., Fall 1952); and directed *The Glass Menagerie* for Equity Library Th. (Lenox Hill Playhouse, Nov. 19, 1952). He founded (N.Y.C., 1953) the Artists Theatre, and directed for it (1953–56): *The Love of Don Perlimplin and Belisa in the Garden; Try, Try; Auto da Fe; Red Riding Hood; Presenting Jane; The Death of Odysseus; Fire Exit; The Screen; The Heroes; The Bait; The Ladies Choice; Absalom;* and *The Ticklish Acrobat.*

He directed a stock production of *Cabin in the Sky* (Sea Cliff Summer Th., N.Y., 1953); a season of ten plays at the Lakeside Summer Th., Landing, N.J. (Summer 1954); *The Immortal Husband* (Th. de Lys, N.Y.C., Feb. 14, 1955); returned to direct another season of ten plays at the Lakeside Summer Th. (Summer 1955); directed a revival of *A Streetcar Named Desire,* starring Tallulah Bankhead (NY City Ctr., Feb. 15, 1956); *Eugenia* (Ambassador, Jan. 30, 1957); *Garden District* (York, Jan. 7, 1958); Arts, London, Sept. 16, 1958; and the US tour, opened Warren Th., Atlantic City, N.J., Mar. 11, 1959); directed, for the San Juan (Puerto Rico) Drama Fest. (1958–61), *Death of a Salesman, Gigi, The Man Who Came to Dinner, The Glass Menagerie, The Marriage-Go-Round,* and *Born Yesterday;* dir. *Street Scene* (NY City Ctr., Opera Co., Spring 1959); *The Pretender* (Cherry Lane, May 14, 1960); *Tambourines to Glory* (Westport Country Playhouse, Conn., Sept. 5, 1960); *Three Modern Japanese Plays* (Players Th., Feb. 3, 1961); and the world premiere of the opera, *The Harvest* (Chicago Lyric Opera, Nov. 25, 1961).

Mr. Machiz directed *The Automobile Graveyard* (41 St. Th., N.Y.C., Nov. 13, 1961); *A Pair of Paris* (Vandam, Apr. 24, 1962); the world premiere of *The Milk Train Doesn't Stop Here Anymore* (Fest. of Two Worlds, Spoleto, Italy, Summer 1962) and its Bway premiere (Morosco, N.Y.C., Jan. 16, 1963); *Just Wild About Harry* (Fest. of Two Worlds, Spoleto, Summer 1963); a stock tour of *the Wayward Stork* (Summer 1964); dir. and, with Leo B. Meyer as "Theatre: New York," prod. *The Wives* (Stage 73, N.Y.C., May 17, 1965); dir. *Elizabeth the Queen* (NY City Ctr., Nov. 3, 1966); withdrew during rehearsals, but remained billed as co-director (with the author, Ian Bernard) of *Chocolates* (Gramercy Arts, Apr. 10, 1967); dir. *In the bar of a Tokyo Hotel* (Eastside Playhouse, May 11, 1969); at Southampton (Long Island, N.Y.) Coll. dir. *Victor, or, The Children Take Over* (July 9, 1969), *Lady Laura Pritchett, American* (July 23, 1969), *The Waltz Invention* (Aug. 6, 1969); and *Gertrude Stein's First Reader* (Aug. 20, 1969), which he also conceived.

He produced and directed *In the Summerhouse* and *The Immortal Husband,* representing the US at the Dublin (Ireland) Intl. Th. Fest., Oct. 1969; re-staged his production of *Gertrude Stein's First Reader* (Astor Place Th., N.Y.C., Dec. 15, 1969); dir. *Madame de Sade* (ANTA Matinee Series, Th. de Lys, Oct. 30–31, 1972); *Henry's Daughter* (a one-Woman show performed and conceived by Cavada Humphrey, culled from the words of Queen Elizabeth I; premiere Manhattan Th. Club, Feb. 20, 1973; subsequently toured extensively by Miss Humphrey); and dir. *Scott and Zelda* (ANTA Matinee Series, Th. de Lys, Jan. 7–8, 1974).

Other Activities. He taught at the Amer. Th. Wing (1953–61).

Published Works. Mr. Machiz edited and wrote the introduction to *The Artists Theatre* (1960); and wrote the article, "The Challenge of a Poetic Theatre" (*Theatre Arts,* 1956).

Awards. He received a Fulbright Fellowship for theatre research in Paris (1948); and a Rockefeller Foundation Grant to direct *Three Modern Japanese Plays* in Brazil, and to lecture on American theatre, in South America (1962).

MACKAY, PATRICIA. Editor, journalist. b. Nov. 11, 1945, Niagara Falls, N.Y., to Thomas P. and Lois G. (Nicholson) MacKay. Father, airline pilot. Attended St. Nicholas Sch., Fleet, Hants, England; Smith Coll. Member of Drama Desk (publicity comm., 1974); U.S. Institute for Theatre Technology (bd. of dirs., 1972–74; vice-chairperson, N.Y. area, 1973–74); ATA.%

Ms. MacKay joined *Theatre Crafts* Magazine as an associate editor in 1970; became managing editor in 1973; and editor in 1974. While on the staff, she has written extensively on environmental theatre, street theatre, Shakespeare festivals in North America, children's theatre, and New York City's resident repertory companies, for special issues of the magazine. Her interviews, retrospectives and reports on regional repertory companies, university theatres, and professional designers appear regularly in the magazine.

Reprints of her articles have appeared in the *Group Four Programs:* Washington, D.C., and *Documents of American Theater History,* Vol. Two, by William C. Young (1973). Suite 815, 250 W. 57th St., New York, NY 10019, tel. (212) 582-4110.

Other Activities. Before joining *Theatre Crafts,* Ms. MacKay worked as an advertising copywriter with the Diners Club Creative Group; did publicity work for Marstellar, Inc., and freelanced in writing and editing.

Published Works. Articles by Ms. MacKay are included in *The Theatre Crafts Book of Costume,* edited by C. Ray Smith (1973); and *The Theatre Crafts Book of Makeup, Masks, and Wigs,* edited by C. Ray Smith (1974).

She is the co-author of *The Shakespeare Complex,* a guide to year-round repertory and summer festivals (1974).

MacKELLAR, HELEN. Actress. b. Feb. 13, 1891, Detroit, Mich., to Donald B. and Mary Ellen (Alexander) MacKellar. Attended Spokane (Wash.) H.S., Columbia Coll. of Expression, Chicago, Ill. Married George D. MacQuarrie. Member of AEA; SAG. Address: 11 E. 32nd St., New York, NY 10016, tel. (212) MU 4-1500.

Theatre. Miss MacKellar made her debut in a touring company of *Bought and Paid For* (1912); subsequently toured as Lily Wagner in *Today* (1913); appeared as Therese in *Woman on Her Own* (Hotel Plaza, N.Y.C., May 16, 1916); made her Bway debut as Georgianna Garrison in *Seven Chances* (George M. Cohan Th., Aug. 8, 1916); followed by Laura Bell in *Major Pendennis* (Criterion, Oct. 26, 1916); Tanya Huber in *A Tailor-Made Man* (Cohan and Harris Th., Aug. 27, 1917); Mrs. James Dawson in *The Unknown Purple* (Lyric, Sept. 14, 1918); Manette Fachard in *The Storm* (48 St., Oct. 2, 1919), and on tour.

Miss MacKellar took over the part of Ruth Atkins in *Beyond the Horizon* (Morosco, N.Y.C., Feb. 2, 1920); played Hester Bevins in *Back Pay* (Eltinge, Aug. 30, 1921); Virginia Blaine in a revival of *Bought and Paid For* (Playhouse, Dec. 7, 1921); Hester Dunnybrig in *The Shadow* (Klaw, Apr. 24, 1922); Diane Delatour in *The Masked Woman* (Eltinge, Dec. 22, 1922); Margaret "Maggie" Fortune in *The Desert Flower* (Longacre, Nov. 18, 1924); Eileen Donovan in *A Good Bad Woman* (Comedy, Feb. 9, 1925); Kate in *The Mud Turtle* (Bijou, Aug. 20, 1925); Eugenie Bellamy in *Open House* (Daly's, Dec. 14, 1925); Neena Dobson in *Romancin' Around* (Little, Oct. 3, 1927); and Inez Talbot in *Through The Night* (Masque, Aug. 18, 1930).

She succeeded (Oct. 1930) Ann Forrest as Frankie in *Frankie and Johnny* (Republic, Sept. 25, 1930); appeared as Greta in *Bloody Laughter* (49 St. Th., Dec. 4, 1931); Imilcea in *The Return of Hannibal* (Geary, San Francisco, Calif., Feb. 1937); succeeded Ruth McDevitt as Abby Brewster in *Arsenic and Old Lace* (Fulton, N.Y.C., Jan. 10, 1941); toured as Mame Phillips in *Ramshackle Inn* (1944–45); succeeded (July 1945) Phyllis Povah as Mrs. Edith Wilkins in *Dear Ruth* (Henry Miller's Th., N.Y.C., Dec. 13, 1944); and played Amanda Wingfield in a touring company of *The Glass Menagerie* (1946–47).

Films. Miss MacKellar has appeared in *A Man's Castle* (Col., 1933); *The Past of Mary Holmes* (RKO, 1933); *High School Girl* (BFP, 1935); *The Case of the Stuttering Bishop* (WB, 1937); *Crime School* (WB, 1938); and *Kansas City Cyclone* (Rep., 1941).

Television. Miss MacKellar has appeared on Dr. Christian (Hollywood) and The Show-Off (N.Y.C.).

MACKINTOSH, ROBERT. Costume designer. b. May 26, 1925. Attended Pratt Institute. Member of United Scenic Artists.

Theatre. Mr. Mackintosh designed the costumes for *Wish You Were Here* (Imperial, N.Y.C., June 25, 1952); *The Gambler* (Lyceum, Oct. 13, 1952); *At Home With Ethel Waters* (48 St. Th., Sept. 22, 1953); and *Anniversary Waltz* (Broadhurst, Apr. 7, 1954).

He was production supervisor of costumes for *The Boy Friend* (Royale, Sept. 30, 1954); designed the costumes worn by Hildegarde Neff and Gretchen Wyler in *Silk Stockings* (Imperial, Feb. 24, 1955); designed all the costumes for *Mr. Wonderful* (Broadway, Mar. 22, 1956); *Fair Game* (Longacre, Nov. 2, 1957); and *Interlock* (ANTA, Feb. 6, 1958); designed Celeste Holm's costumes for *Third Best Sport* (Ambassador, Dec. 30, 1958); and the costumes for *Masquerade* (John Golden Th., Mar. 1, 1959); executed Cecil Beaton's costume designs for *Saratoga* (Winter Garden, Dec. 7, 1959); and designed the costumes for *A Second String* (Eugene O'Neill Th., Apr. 13, 1960); *Hotel Passionato* (E. 74 St. Th., Oct. 22, 1965); *Mame* (Winter Garden, May 24, 1966); *Sherry!* (Alvin, Mar. 28, 1967); *How Now, Dow Jones* (Lunt-Fontanne Th., Dec. 7, 1967); *The Fig Leaves Are Falling* (Broadhurst, Jan. 2, 1969); *Butterflies Are Free* (Booth, Oct. 21, 1969); *The Enclave* (Th. Four, Nov. 15, 1973); Angela Lansbury's costumes for *Gypsy* (Winter Garden, June 23, 1974); and *Miss Moffatt* (pre-Bway tour, opened Shubert, Philadelphia, Oct. 7, 1974; closed there Oct. 18, 1974).

Since 1953, Mr. Mackintosh has designed the gowns for all of Lena Horne's theatre and nightclub appearances.

Television. He designed costumes for Holiday on Ice (1952–57); Tinsel Town; the Garry Moore Show (CBS, 1960–1964); and *Calamity Jane* (CBS, 1964); and executed Eugene Berman's designs for *Amahl and the Night Visitors* (NBC Opera).

Awards. For his costumes for *Mame,* Mr. Mackintosh won first place in the annual Variety New York Drama Critics Poll (Best Costumes, 1965–66).

MacLEISH, ARCHIBALD. Playwright, poet, writer. b. May 7, 1892, Glencoe, Ill., to Andrew and Martha (Hillard) MacLeish. Father, business executive. Grad. Hotchkiss Acad., Lakeville, Conn.; Yale Univ., B.A. (Phi Beta Kappa) 1915; Harvard Law Sch., LL.B. 1919. Married June 21, 1916, to Ada Hitchcock; four sons, one daughter. Served US Army, 1917–18; rank, Capt. (Decorated Comdr. Legion of Honor-France; Encomienda Order el Sol del Peru). Member of Amer. Acad. of Arts & Letters (pres. 1953–56); Century Club; Tavern Club; Somerset Club (Boston); Natl. Comm. for an Effective Congress; Commission on the Freedom of the Press. Address: Uphill Farm, Conway, MA 01341.

Pre-Theatre. Writer, educator, attorney.

Theatre. Mr. MacLeish wrote the libretto for the Federal Th. (WPA) Project production of the ballet, *Union Pacific* (St. James Th., Apr. 25, 1934); wrote *Panic* (Imperial, Mar. 14, 1935); *J.B.* (Yale School of Drama; Brussels World's Fair; ANTA Th., N.Y.C., Dec. 11, 1958; Phoenix, London, Mar. 23, 1961); *Scratch* (St. James, N.Y.C., May 6, 1971); and *The Great American Fourth of July Parade* (Carnegie Music Hall, Pittsburgh, Apr. 18, 1975).

He has also written a one-act play entitled *The States Talking* (1941); a one-act play, *The Admiral* (1944); a verse play, *Herakles* (1967); and *The Play of Herod* (1968).

Films. For a short film, *The Spanish Earth* (Contemporary Historians, Inc., 1937), narrated and mainly written by Ernest Hemingway, Mr. MacLeish contributed (with Lillian Hellman) additional material; he wrote and narrated the short film, *Grandma Moses* (Falcon Films, Inc., 1950); and wrote and partially narrated *The Eleanor Roosevelt Story* (dist. by Amer. Int., 1965).

Television and Radio. For radio, Mr. MacLeish wrote *The Fall of the City* (CBS, 1937); *Air Raid* (CBS, 1938); the American Story series (NBC, 1944), for which he also served as commentator; *The Son of Man* (CBS, 1947); and *The Trojan Horse* (BBC, London, 1952). For television, he wrote *The Secret of Freedom* (NBC, 1960) and *An Evening's Journey to Conway, Mass.* (WNET, Nov. 3, 1967). His radio script for *The Fall of the City* was presented on television (CBS, 1962). Mr. MacLeish appeared on the Today show (NBC, 1965).

Other Activities. Mr. MacLeish was a contributing editor to *Fortune* magazine and *The Nation;* poet in residence, Princeton Univ. (1936–37); Librarian of Congress (1939–44); dir. US Office of Facts and Figures (1941–42); asst. dir. Office of War Information (1942–43); Asst. Sec. of State (1944–45); Amer. del. to the Conf. of Allied Ministers of Education (London, 1944); Chmn., Amer. delegation, to the London Conf. to draw up the constitution for UNESCO (1945); Chmn., Amer. delegation, first Gen. Conf. of UNESCO (Paris, 1946); first Amer. mem. of Exec. Council, UNESCO (1946).

Mr. MacLeish was Rede lecturer at Cambridge Univ., England (1942); Boylston Prof. of Rhetoric and Oratory at Harvard Univ. (1949–62); and Simpson lecturer at Amherst Coll. (1963–67). In 1949, he became a trustee of Sarah Lawrence Coll.

Published Works. Mr. MacLeish is the author of *The Tower of Ivory* (1917); *The Happy Marriage* (1924); *The Pot of Earth* (1925); *Nobodaddy* (1925); *Streets in the Moon* (1925); *The Hamlet of A. MacLeish* (1928); *New Found Land* (1930); *Conquistador* (1932); *Frescoes for Mr. Rockefeller's City* (1933); *Poems* (1923–33); *Public Speech* (1936); *Land of the Free* (1938); *America Was Promises* (1939); *The Irresponsibles* (1940); *The American Cause* (1941); *A Time to Speak Out* (1941); *A Time to Act* (1942); *The Destroyers* (1942); *American Opinion and the War* (1942); *Actfive* (1948); *Poetry and Opinion* (1950); *Freedom is the Right to Choose* (1952); *Collected Poems, 1917–52* (1952); *This Music Crept by Me Upon the Waters* (1953); *Songs for Eve* (1954); *Poetry and Experience* (1960); *The Dialogues of Archibald MacLeish and Mark Van Doren* (Dutton, N.Y.C., 1964); *Herakles* (1967); *The Wild Old Wicked Man and Other Poems* (1968); *A Continuing Journey* (1968); *The Human Season: Selected Poems, 1926–72* and *The Great American Fourth of July Parade* (1975).

Awards. Mr. MacLeish received three Pulitzer prizes: for poetry, in 1932 *(Conquistador)* and 1953 *(Collected Poems, 1917–1952)*, and for drama, in 1959 *(J.B.)*. He received the Bollingen Prize in Poetry (1953) and the Nat. Book Award in poetry, both for *Collected Poems, 1917–52* (1953); the Boston Arts Festival Poetry Award (1956); the Antoinette Perry (Tony) Award, for *J.B.* (best play, 1959); and the Academy (Oscar) Award, for *The Eleanor Roosevelt Story* (best documentary, 1966). On Feb. 8, 1966, he was elected a Fellow of the Academy of American Poets. He has received honorary degrees from Tufts Coll. (M.A., 1932); Wesleyan Univ. (D. of Letters, 1938); Colby Coll. (1938); Yale (Litt. D., 1939); Dartmouth (L.H.D., 1940); Univ. of Pa. (1941); Johns Hopkins Univ. (LLD, 1941); Union Coll. (D.C.L., 1941); Williams Coll. (D.H.L., 1942); Univ. of Cal. (1943); Univ. of Ill. (1946); Queens Univ., Ontario, Canada (1948); Washington Univ. (1948); Rockford Coll. (1953); Univ. of Puerto Rico (1953); Columbia Univ. (1954); Harvard Univ. (1955); Carleton Coll. (1956); Univ. of Pittsburgh (1959); Amherst Coll. (1963); and Princeton Univ. (L.H.D., 1965).

MAC LIAMMÓIR, MICHEAL. Actor, director, playwright, costume designer, set designer. b. Oct. 25, 1899, Cork, Ireland, to Alfred Anthony and Mary (Lawler-Lee) Mac Liammóir. Educated at home and in the theatre; studied painting at Slade Sch., London, 1915–16. Relatives in theatre: nieces Sally Travers and Mary Rose McMaster, actresses. Member of Irish Equity; Gaelic League (Dublin and London); the Arts Club (Dublin). 4 Harcourt Terrace, Dublin 2, Ireland.

Theatre. Mr. Mac Liammóir's first appearance in the US, was at the Orson Welles's Woodstock (Ill.) Theatre Festival where he appeared in *Hamlet* (Summer 1934). His first N.Y.C. appearance was as Larry Doyle in the Dublin Gate Th. Co. production of *John Bull's Other Island* (Mansfield, Feb. 10, 1948); with this company, also played the Speaker in *The Old Lady Says "No!"*, for which he designed sets and costumes (Mansfield, Feb. 17, 1948); and Martin in his own play, *Where Stars Walk* (Mansfield, Feb. 24, 1948), all three of which he had played earlier in London (see below). He appeared as Don Pedro in John Gielgud's production of *Much Ado About Nothing* (Lunt-Fontanne, N.Y.C., Sept. 17, 1959); in his one-man show, *The Importance of Being Oscar,* which he adapted from Oscar Wilde's works (Lyceum, Mar. 14, 1961, and on tour); and in his second one-man show, *I Must Be Talking to My Friends* (Orpheum, N.Y.C., Nov. 16, 1967, and on tour).

Billed as Alfred Willmore, Mr. Mac Laimmóir made his first stage appearance as King Goldfish in *The Goldfish* (Little, London, Jan. 27, 1911); subsequently appeared as Macduff's Son in *Macbeth* (His Majesty's, Sept. 5, 1911); Michael Darling in *Peter Pan* (Duke of York's, Dec. 18, 1911); the title role in *Oliver Twist* (His Majesty's, June 11, 1912), John Darling in *Peter Pan* (Duke of York's, Dec. 18, 1912); Benjamin in *Joseph and His Brethren* (His Majesty's, Sept. 2, 1913); as John in *Peter Pan* (Duke of York's, Dec. 18, 1913); and Cornwallis in *Felix Gets a Month* (Haymarket, Feb. 1917). He returned to Dublin to paint and design for the Irish Th. and the Dublin Drama League (1918–21); and joined Anew McMaster's Co. (1927), where he played Shakespearean roles.

With Hilton Edwards, he opened the Galway Gaelic Th., in 1928 with his own play, *Diarmuid Agus Grainne.* Since then he has been director of it. That same year, again with Mr. Edwards, he founded the Dublin Gate Th., presenting *Peer Gynt* (Oct. 4, 1928) as the first production. Also in 1928, he became director of the government-sponsored Dublin Gaelic Th. Subsequently, he has directed and designed some 20 works at the Galway Gaelic Th., and has appeared in and designed approximately 300 works at the Dublin Gate Th. His roles at the latter include Romeo, Othello, Marc Antony, Faust, Peter in *Berkeley Square,* Liliom, Hsieh-Ping-Kuei in *Lady Precious Stream,* Raskolnikoff in *Crime and Punishment,* Francis in *The Marriage of St. Francis,* Oswald in *Ghosts,* and the title role in Pirandello's *Henry IV.*

With the Dublin Gate Th. Co., played the Speaker in *The Old Lady Says "No!"* and the title role in *Hamlet* (Westminster, June 1935); later played Lee in *Ill Met by Moonlight,* a play he wrote (Vaudeville, Feb. 5, 1947); Martin in his own comedy, *Where Stars Walk* (Embassy, Dec. 6, 1947); the Speaker in *The Old Lady Says "No!"* (Embassy, Dec. 9, 1947); and Larry Doyle in *John Bull's Other Island* (Embassy, Dec. 27, 1947).

Mr. Mac Liammóir played Mr. Wogan in his own comedy, *Home for Christmas* (Gate, Dublin, Dec. 1950); the title role in *Hamlet* (Kronberg Castle, Elsinore, Denmark, 1952); Brack in *Hedda Gabler* (Lyric, Hammersmith, London, Sept. 8, 1954); appeared in the revue, *Gateway to Gaiety* (Gaiety, Dublin, 1956), for which he designed the settings and costumes and also contributed material; played Don Cristovaw de Moura in *The Hidden King* at the Edinburgh (Scot.) Festival (Assembly Hall, Aug. 1957); Michael Marne in *The Key of the Door* (Lyric, Hammersmith, London, May 27, 1958); designed the setting and costumes for *The Heart's a Wonder* (Westminster, Sept. 18, 1958); appeared as Gypo Nolan in his own adaptation of *The Informer* from Liam O'Flaherty's novel (Olympia, Dublin, Nov. 1958), for which he also designed the settings; appeared in his one-man entertainment, *The Importance of Being Oscar* (Gaiety, Sept. 1960), which was presented in London (Apollo, Oct. 31, 1960; and again, at the Royal Court, Jan, 23, 1961), and in which he toured extensively, including the US (see above), Europe (inc. the Paris Fest., June 1961), South America (1961), South Africa (Apr.–July, 1962), etc., played Iago in *Othello* (Dublin Fest., Sept. 1962); again appeared in *The Importance of Being Oscar* (Aldwych, London, Apr. 23, 1963), followed by his new one-man show, *I Must Be Talking to My Friends* (Aldwych, May 2, 1963); designed and co-presented *The Last P.M.* (Dublin Fest., Sept. 1963); played Conrad Apfelbaum in *The Roses Are Real* (Dublin Fest., Oct. 1963; Vaudeville, London, Jan. 23, 1964); and toured Australia and New Zealand (Mar.–Aug. 1964) in *The Importance of Being Oscar.*

He co-presented, with Hilton Edwards, *Philadelphia, Here I Come!* (Dublin Fest., Sept. 28, 1964); again appeared in his two one-man shows (Queen's Th., London, Dec. 31, 1964), toured in *The Importance of Being Oscar* (Nov. 1965), and presented both shows in London again (Haymarket, Sept. 19, 1966); performed *I Must Be Talking to My Friends* in the US (see above); co-presented *Crystal and Fox* (Gaeity, Dublin, Nov. 1968); played Jonathan Swift in *Swift* (Dublin Fest., Oct. 1969) and translated *The Liar* from the Irish; designed *The Seagull* (Abbey, Dublin, Oct. 1970); appeared in and co-presented his new one-man show, *Talking About Yeats* (Arts, Cambridge, Sept. 1970; Duke of York's, London, Oct. 1971); and wrote *Prelude in Kazbek* (Gate, Dublin, Oct. 1973).

Films. Mr. Mac Liammóir played Iago in Orson Welles's production of *Othello* (UA, 1949); the "Irish Story Teller" in *30 is a Dangerous Age, Cynthia* (Col., 1968); and appeared in *What's the Matter With Helen?* (UA, 1971).

Television and Radio. He has written the television play, *The Liar,* and a musical, *The Speckledy Shawl.* In the US, he played the title role in *Othello* (NBC, 1947), and Potemkin in *Great Catherine* (NBC, 1947).

Published Works. Mr. Mac Liammóir has published in Gaelic, two short-stories, *Oicheanna Sidhe* and *La Agus Oiche;* an essay, *Ceo Meala La Seaca;* and a theatre diary, *Aisterorri Faoi dha,* published in an English translation by the author as *Each Actor on His Ass* (1962). Plays he has written in Gaelic include *Oiche Bhealtaine, Lulu,* and *Diarmuid Augus Grainne;* and in English *Diarmuid and Grainne,* translated by the author (1928); *The Ford of The Hurdles* (1929); *Dancing Shadow* (1941); *Portrait of Miriam* (1947); *The Mountains Look Different* (1948); *A Slipper for the Moon* (1952); *Saint Patrick* (1953); and *I*

Must Be Talking to My Friends (1963). He has written adaptations into English of *Jane Eyre, The Picture of Dorian Gray, A Tale of Two Cities,* and *Trilby.* His translations and adaptations into Gaelic include *Bean na Grnaige Duibbe* from Sacha Guitry's *Une villaine femme brune; Ag Iarraidh Mhna* from Chekov's *The Proposal; Ar Maidin go Moch* from Eugene O'Neill's *In the Morning* and *Gaisce Agus Gaiscioch* from Shaw's *Arms and the Man.* His translations into English include *Juliet in the Rain* from H. V. Lenormand's *Les Rates; An Apple a Day* from Jules Romain's *Dr. Knock,* and *Henry IV* from Pirandello's *Enrico IV.* Other published works in English include *All for Hecuba* (autobiography, 1946), *Put Money in Thy Purse* (1954), and a further autobiography, *An Oscar of No Importance* (Heinemann, London, 1968). He has published poetry in Gaelic, *Blath Agus Taibhse;* and has also written three ballets, *The Red Petticoat, The Enchanted Stream,* and *Full Moon for the Bride.*

Awards. Mr. Mac Liammóir received the Silver Award, Comhar Drama Tochta (1933); and the Gold Award, Comhar Drama Tochta (1934). He received the Douglas Hyde Prize (1952); the Medal of Kronberg for his performance as Hamlet at Elsinore (1952); the Lady Gregory Award from the Irish Academy of Letters (1960); and an honorary degree of LL.D. from Trinity Coll., Dublin (1962).

Recreation. Travel, "balletomania," languages.

MacMAHON, ALINE. Actress. b. May 3, 1899, McKeesport, Pa. Grad. Erasmus Hall H.S., N.Y.C. Attended Barnard Coll. Married Mar. 27, 1928, to Clarence S. Stein, architect-planner (dec. Feb. 7, 1975). Member of AEA; SAG; AFTRA. Address: 1 W. 64th St., New York, NY 10023, tel. (212) EN 2-8065.

Theatre. Miss MacMahon made her first professional appearance as Laura Huxtable in *The Madras House* (Oct. 29, 1921), at the Neighborhood Playhouse, N.Y.C., where she also played Matilda in *The Green Ring* (Apr. 4, 1922); made her Bway debut succeeding (June, 1922) Winifred Lenihan as Anne in *The Dover Road* (Bijou, Dec. 23, 1921); appeared as Miss Files in *The Exciters* (Times Square Th., Sept. 22, 1922); Molly Latimer in *Connie Goes Home* (49 St. Th., Sept. 6, 1923); Decima in *The Player Queen* (Oct. 16, 1923) at the Neighborhood Playhouse, where she also appeared as Babsy in *The Shewing-Up of Blanco Posnet* (Oct. 16, 1923), Mag Maggot in *This Fine-Pretty World* (Dec. 26, 1923), Riemke Van Eyden in *Time Is a Dream* (Apr. 22, 1924), and in *The Grand Street Follies* (May 20, 1924); performed in *Artists and Models* (Winter Garden, June 24, 1925); played Ruth Atkins in *Beyond the Horizon* (Mansfield, Nov. 30, 1926); Rosalie Kent in *Spread Eagle* (Martin Beck, Apr. 4, 1927); Hildegarde Maxon in *Her First Affair* (Nora Bayes Th., Aug. 22, 1927); and the Girl in the "Prolog" and Bella in *Maya* (Comedy, Feb. 21, 1928).

She played Tony Ambler in *Winter Bound* (Garrick, Nov. 12, 1929); May Daniels in a pre-Bway tryout of *Once in a Lifetime* (1930); repeated the latter role in Los Angeles (1930–31), and in a N.Y.C. revival (Plymouth, Aug. 3, 1931); appeared as Margaret Bryce in *If Love Were All* (Booth, N.Y.C., Nov. 13, 1931); in the title role of *Candida* (Berkshire Playhouse, Stockbridge, Mass., June, 1937); in *The Ghost of Yankee Doodle* (Lydia Mendelssohn Th., Ann Arbor, Mich., May 1938); and in *Away From It All* (Carmel, N.Y., June 1938); Mrs. Sullen in *The Beaux' Stratagem* (Dock St., Charleston, S.C., Mar. 24, 1939); Mary Fenet in *Kindred* (Maxine Elliott's Th., N.Y.C., Dec. 26, 1939); Betsy Graham in *Heavenly Express* (National, Apr. 18, 1940); Nell West in *The Eve of St. Mark* (Cort, Oct. 7, 1942); Queen Gertrude in *Hamlet* (Kronberg Castle, Elsinore, Denmark, June 17, 1949), in which she subsequently toured air bases in Germany; Countess Aurelia, the title role, in *The Madwoman of Chaillot* (Ivar Th., Los Angeles, Calif., Mar. 28, 1951); Mrs. Guzzard in *The Confidential Clerk* (Morosco, N.Y.C., Feb. 11, 1954); and Laura Anson in *A Day by the Sea* (ANTA, Sept. 26, 1955).

Miss MacMahon appeared in a staged reading of *Pictures in the Hallway* (Kaufmann Concert Hall, N.Y.C., May 1956) and in a reading of *I Knock at the Door* (Belasco, Sept. 29, 1957); played Mama Caparuta in the pre-Bway tryout of *The Poker Game* (opened Shubert, Washington, D.C., Jan. 16, 1959; closed Forrest, Philadelphia, Pa., Jan. 31, 1959); at the American Shakespeare Festival (Stratford, Conn.), played the Nurse in *Romeo and Juliet* (June 12, 1959) and the Countess of Rousillon in *All's Well That Ends Well* (July 29, 1959); played Aunt Hannah Lynch in *All the Way Home* (Belasco, N.Y.C., Nov. 30, 1960); and Countess Aurelia in *The Madwoman of Chaillot* (Arena Stage, Washington, D.C., Dec. 26, 1961).

She played Volumnis in *Coriolanus* (American Shakespeare Fest., Stratford, Conn., June 19, 1965); and for the Rep. Th. of Lincoln Center (Vivian Beaumont Th., N.Y.C.) played Tribulation Wholesome in *The Alchemist* (Oct. 13, 1966); Alegria in *Yerma* (Dec. 8, 1966); Mrs. Humphreys in *The East Wind* (Feb. 9, 1967); Mrs. Sarti in *Galileo* (Apr. 13, 1967); Mina in *Walking to Waldheim* (Forum, Nov. 10, 1967); Hecuba in *Tiger at the Gates* (Vivian Beaumont Th., Feb. 29, 1968); Mother Marguerite in *Cyrano de Bergerac* (Apr. 25, 1968); Mrs. Peeles in *The Inner Journey* (Forum, Mar. 20, 1969); Mrs. Casside in *Pictures in the Hallway* (Apr. 29, 1971); Hannah Kennedy in *Mary Stuart* (Vivian Beaumont Th., Nov. 1, 1971); Rebecca Nurse in *The Crucible* (Apr. 27, 1972); and Miss Trafalgar Gower in *Trelawny* (Oct. 15, 1975).

Beginning in 1950, she spent four seasons as "Artist in Residence" at Stanford Univ.; and in 1958, made a survey of theatre in open-air festivals, in France.

Films. Since her debut in *Five Star Final* (1st Natl., 1931), Miss MacMahon has appeared in *Heart of New York* (WB, 1932); *Week-End Marriage* (1st Natl., 1932); *The Mouthpiece* (WB, 1932); *Life Begins* (1st Natl., 1932); *Once In a Lifetime* (U, 1932); *One Way Passage* (WB, 1932); *Silver Dollar* (1st Natl., 1932); *The Life of Jimmy Dolan* (WB, 1933); *The Gold Diggers of 1933* (WB, 1933); *Heroes for Sale* (1st Natl., 1933); *The World Changes* (1st Natl., 1933); *Heat Lightning* (WB, 1934); *The Merry Frinks* (1st Natl., 1934); *Side Streets* (1st Natl., 1934); *Big Hearted Herbert* (WB, 1934); *Babbitt* (1st Natl., 1934); *While the Patient Slept* (1st Natl., 1935); *Mary Jane's Pa* (1st Natl., 1935); *I Live My Life* (MGM, 1935); *Ah, Wilderness!* (MGM, 1935); *Kind Lady* (MGM, 1935); *When You're in Love* (Col., 1937); *Back Door to Heaven* (Par., 1940); *Out of the Fog* (WB, 1941); *The Lady Is Willing* (Col., 1942); *Tish* (MGM, 1942); *Seeds of Freedom* (Artkino, 1943); *Dragon Seed* (MGM, 1944); *Stage Door Canteen* (UA, 1943); *Guest in the House* (UA, 1944); *The Mighty McGurk* (MGM, 1946); *Flame and the Arrow* (WB, 1950); *The Search* (MGM, 1948); *Roseanna McCoy* (Goldwyn, 1949); *The Eddie Cantor Story* (WB, 1953); *The Man from Laramie* (Col., 1955); *Cimarron* (MGM, 1960); *The Young Doctors* (UA, 1961); *Diamond Head* (Col., 1962); *The Lonely Stage* (UA, 1962); and *I Could Go On Singing* (UA, 1963).

Television. She has made numerous appearances, including the role of the Nurse in *Medea* (Play of the Week, WNDT, Oct. 12, 1959); in *Morning's at Seven* (Celanese Th. (ABC, 1952); Volumnia in *Coriolanus* (Esso Rep. Th., Ind., May 12, 1965); and on The Defenders (CBS); The Nurses (CBS); Pulitzer Prize Playhouse (ABC); Studio One (CBS); Frontiers of Faith (NBC); and as the Nurse in *Antigone* (NY Playhouse, WNET, Oct. 7, 1972).

MACY, GERTRUDE. General manager, producer. b. Gertrude Marguerite Macy, Oct. 8, 1904, Pasadena, Calif., to Lloyd R. and Mary Esther (Gill) Macy. Father, realtor. Grad. Private boarding sch., Piedmont, Calif., 1922; attended Bryn Mawr Coll., 1922–25. Member of ATPAM; AEA; Katherine Cornell Foundation (secy., 1934); Martha Graham Foundation (secy., 1943); ANTA (dir. of intl. cultural exchange service, 1960–63); Consultant on Cultural Affairs US State Dept. (1963); Cosmopolitan Club (N.Y.C.); B. de Rothschild Foundation for the Arts and Sciences (vice pres., 1951); Mayor Wagner's Citizens' Advisory Committee to the Office of Cultural Affairs; Natl. Committee for the Arts in America (founding member); NCAG. Address: Lawrence Lane, Palisades, NY 10964, tel. (914) EL 9-1579.

Pre-Theatre. Secretary to Katharine Cornell.

Theatre. Miss Macy began her career as assistant stage manager for *The Age of Innocence* (Empire, N.Y.C., Nov. 27, 1928); subsequently was understudy to Brenda Dahlen as Ella, the Maid, and assistant stage manager for *Dishonored Lady* (Empire, Feb. 4, 1930), and played Ella and was assistant stage manager for its tour (Oct. 1930–June 1931); was stage manager for *The Barretts of Wimpole Street* (Empire, Feb. 9, 1931) and company manager for its road tour; company manager and general manager for *Alien Corn* (Belasco, Feb. 20, 1933); general manager 1933–34) for a repertory tour of *The Barretts of Wimpole Street, Romeo and Juliet,* and *Candida.* At the Martin Beck Th., she served as general manager for *Romeo and Juliet* (Dec. 20, 1934); *The Barretts of Wimpole Street* (Feb. 25, 1935); *Flowers of the Forest* (Apr. 8, 1935); and *Saint Joan* (Mar. 9, 1936), and for its tour (opened Grand Opera House, Chicago, Ill., June 9, 1936; closed Curran, San Francisco, Calif., June 1936).

Miss Macy was general manager for *Wingless Victory* (Empire, N.Y.C., Dec. 23, 1936), *Candida* (Empire, Mar. 10, 1937) and the tour of *Herod and Marianne* (1938); co-produced, with Stanley Gilkey and Robert F. Cutler, *One for the Money* (Booth, N.Y.C., Feb. 4, 1939); was general manager for *No Time for Comedy* (Ethel Barrymore Th., Apr. 17, 1939), and its tour (Oct. 1939–June 1940); co-produced, with Stanley Gilkey, *Two for the Show* (Booth, N.Y.C., Feb. 8, 1940); was general manager for *The Doctor's Dilemma* (Shubert, Mar. 11, 1941); the tour of *Rose Burke* (opened Curran, San Francisco, Calif., Jan. 19, 1942; closed Erlanger, Buffalo, N.Y., Mar. 6, 1942); the revival of *Candida* (Shubert, N.Y.C., Apr. 27, 1942); *The Three Sisters* (Ethel Barrymore Th., Dec. 21, 1942); and *Lovers and Friends* (Plymouth, Nov. 29, 1943).

Miss Macy was general manager for the European tour of *The Barretts of Wimpole Street* (Italy, Holland, Belgium, 1944), its USO tour of military camps (July 1944), its Bway revival (Ethel Barrymore Th., Mar. 26, 1945), and subsequent tour (April–June 1945); produced the pre-Bway tryout of *Forever is Now* (opened Playhouse, Wilmington, Del., Sept. 7, 1945; closed Shubert, Philadelphia, Pa., Sept. 15, 1945); was general manager for *Antigone* (Cort, N.Y.C., Feb. 18, 1946); a revival of *Candida* (Cort, Apr. 3, 1946); and *Antony and Cleopatra* (Martin Beck Th., Nov. 26, 1947); produced *The Happiest Years* (Lyceum, Apr. 25, 1949); was general manager for *That Lady* (Martin Beck Th., Nov. 22, 1949); the tour of *Captain Carvallo* (Dec. 1950); and *The Constant Wife* (Natl., N.Y.C., Dec. 8, 1951), and its tour (opened Ford, Baltimore, Md., Oct. 13, 1952; closed Ann Arbor Festival, Mich., May 16, 1953).

She produced, in association with Walter Starcke, *I Am a Camera* (Empire, N.Y.C., Nov. 28, 1951), and its tour (opened Cass, Detroit, Mich., Sept. 1, 1952; closed Her Majesty's Th., Montreal, Can., May 2, 1953); was Katharine Cornell's personal manager for *The Prescott Proposals* (Broadhurst, N.Y.C., Dec. 16, 1953); general manager for *The Dark Is Light Enough* (ANTA, Feb. 23, 1955); *The Skin of Our Teeth* (Sarah Bernhardt Th., Paris, Fr., July 1955); the European tour of the All Star Group (Congressehalle, Berlin, Ger., Summer 1957); the Bway production of *The First Born* (Coronet, Mar. 30, 1958); and *Dear Liar* (Billy Rose Th., Mar. 17, 1960).

Other Activities. From 1941 to 1947, Miss Macy was executive producer of Martha Graham and her Dance Company. She is treasurer of *Plays for Living,* affiliated with the Family Service Assoc. of Amer.

Awards. Miss Macy received a citation from Douglas Dillon, Sr. for her volunteer services for the Navy League during WW II (1944); and a government civilian citation for services performed overseas during WW II (1945).

Recreation. Poodle dogs, traveling.

MADDEN, DONALD. Actor. b. Nov. 5, 1933, New York City, to Owen and Jane (Halloran) Madden. Grad. Coll. of the City of N.Y., 1955. Served US Army, 1955–57; rank, Cpl. Member of AEA; AFTRA; SAG.

Theatre. Mr. Madden made his professional debut at the University Playhouse (Mashpee, Mass., 1950); subsequently portrayed Edmund Kean in *Kean* (Brandeis Univ. Summer Th., US premiere 1955); toured with Linda Darnell, playing Al in a stock production of *Tea and Sympathy* (Summer 1956); appeared as Steve in *A Time To Be Rich* (John Drew Th., East Hampton, N.Y., Summer 1957); in *The Cantilevered Terrace* (White Barn Th., Westport, Conn., Aug. 31, 1957); understudied Kenneth Haigh as Jimmy Porter in *Look Back in Anger* (Lyceum, N.Y.C., Oct. 1, 1957), and made his Bway debut succeeding (June 30, 1958) Mr. Haigh in that role, subsequently playing it in the national tour; played Charles Bingley in *First Impressions* (Alvin, Mar. 19, 1959); and Marc Antony in *Julius Caesar* (NY Shakespeare Festival, Belvedere Lake Th., Aug. 3, 1959).

At the Phoenix Th., N.Y.C., he played Kinesias in *Lysistrata* (Nov. 24, 1959); appeared in *Picture in the Hallway* (Dec. 26, 1959); played Hotspur in *Henry IV, Part 1* (Mar. 1, 1960); Mr. Marlow in *She Stoops to Conquer* (Nov. 1, 1960); Lt. Langon in *The Plough and the Stars* (Dec. 6, 1960); and the title role in *Hamlet* (Mar. 16, 1961).

Mr. Madden appeared as Mark Hurlbird in *Step on a Crack* (Ethel Barrymore Th., Oct. 17, 1962); Lewis Elliot in *Time of Hope* (Playhouse-in-the-Park, Philadelphia, Pa., World premiere June 24, 1963); and Chris Flanders in the revised *The Milk Train Doesn't Stop Here Anymore* (Barter Th., Abingdon, Va., Sept. 16, 1963).

He played Jason Sample in *One by One* (Belasco, N.Y.C., Dec. 1, 1964); King Henry VIII in *A Man for All Seasons* (Coconut Grove Playhouse, Miami, Fla., Apr. 12, 1966); Elyot Chase in *Private Lives* (Studio Arena Th., Buffalo, N.Y., July 7, 1966); George Gregory in a pre-Bway tryout of a play by Pamela Herbert Chais, *Jack Be Nimble!* (Summer 1966); Frank in *White Lies* and Harold Gorringe in *Black Comedy* (Ethel Barrymore Th., N.Y.C., Feb. 12, 1967); King Ethelred in *The Ceremony of Innocence* (Amer. Place Th., Dec. 14, 1967); and the title role in *Richard II* (Amer. Place Th., Stratford, Conn., June 22, 1968).

He played Mark in *In the Bar of a Tokyo Hotel* (Eastside Playhouse, N.Y.C., May 11, 1969); Richard Ford in a stock tour of *Poor Richard* (August 1969); Richard, Duke of Gloucester (later King Richard III) in the NY Shakespeare Festival productions of *Henry VI, Part 2* (Delacorte, June 24, 1970) and *Richard III* (June 25, 1970); Torvald Helsner in *A Doll's House* (Jan. 13, 1971) and Eilert Lovborg in *Hedda Gabler* (Feb. 17, 1971), which played in repertory at the Playhouse Th., N.Y.C., and later toured; appeared in the premiere of Tennessee Williams' *Out Cry* (Ivanhoe, Chicago, July 8, 1971); in the title role of *The Resistible Rise of Arturo Ui* (Williamstown, Mass., Summer Th., July 18, 1972); as Deeley in *Old Times* (Goodman Th., Chicago, Oct. 8, 1972); and as Edmund in *King Lear* (May 17, 1975) and Leontes in *The Winter's Tale* (July 22, 1975), for the Amer. Shakespeare Th., Stratford, Conn.

Films. Mr. Madden made his debut as John Dickinson in *1776* (Col., 1972).

Television. Mr. Madden appeared on the daytime serials, As the World Turns and From These Roots (1957–59); in *The Old Lady Shows Her Medals* (US Steel Hour, NBC, June 12, 1963); in *Athens, Where the Theatre Began* (Roots of Freedom, CBS, Sept. 11, 1963); as Kilroy in *Camino Real* (Granada TV, London, Jan. 27, 1964); Victor in *Burning Bright* (Play of the Week, WNTA, Nov. 1959); on Dr. Kildare (NBC); Eleventh Hour (NBC); Espionage (Ind); Armstrong Circle Th. (NBC); and others.

Awards. He won a *Theatre World* Award (1960).

MAGARSHACK, DAVID. Writer, translator. b. Dec. 23, 1899, Riga, Latvia, to Benjamin and Charga Magarshack. Attended secondary school, Riga, 1911–18; grad. Univ. Coll., London (England) Univ., B.A. 1925. Married Apr. 16, 1926, to Elsie E.; two sons, two daughters. Address: 49 Willow Rd., Hampstead, London N.W. 3, England tel. OL-435-1046.

Published Works. Mr. Magarshack wrote *Stanislavsky, a Life* (1950), *Turgenev* (1954), *Gogol* (1957), *Chekhov, the Dramatist* (1960), *Dostoevsky* (1963), and *The Real Chekhov* (1972).

He has edited *The Storm and Other Russian Plays* (1960), and Stanislavski's *On the Art of the Stage* (1961), which he also translated.

Mr. Magarshack has also translated Dostoevsky's *The Brothers Karamazov, Crime and Punishment, The Idiot, The Devils and Occasional Writings* (1963); Chekhov's *The Seagull* (1947), *Uncle Vanya* (1960), *The Three Sisters* (1960), *The Cherry Orchard* (1960), *Selected Stories* (1964), and *Platonov* (unabridged, 1965); Turgenev's *Selected Tales* (1958), *Literary Reminiscences* (1958), and *The Torrents of Spring* (1959); Gogol's *Tales of Good and Evil* (1949), *The Government Inspector* (1960), *Dead Souls* (1961), and *Mirgorod* (1962); Tolstoy's *The Power of Darkness* (1960) and *Anna Karenina* (1961); Leskov's *The Amazon* and *The March Hare* (both 1949) and *Selected Tales* (1961); Goncharov's *Obiomov* (1954); and Ostrovsky's *Easy Money and Other Plays* (1944) and *The Storm* (1960).

MAGEE, PATRICK. Actor.

Theatre. In the U.S., Mr. Magee made his Bway debut as the Marquis de Sade in The Royal Shakespeare Co.'s production of *The Persecution and Assassination of Marat as Performed by the Inmates of the Asylum of Charenton under the Direction of the Marquis de Sade* (Martin Beck Th., N.Y.C., Dec. 27, 1965), a role he had originated in London (Aldwych, Aug. 1964); subsequently playing Frank Brady in *Keep It in the Family* (Plymouth, N.Y.C., Sept. 27, 1967); and Daniel Webster in *Scratch* (St. James Th., May 6, 1971).

He began his career in Ireland with Anew McMaster's company; in London, played Larry Slade in *The Iceman Cometh* (Arts, Jan. 1958; and Winter Garden, Mar. 1958); Max in *The Buskers* (Arts, Mar. 1959); Father Domineer in *Cock-a-Doodle Dandy* (Royal Court, Sept. 1959); Michael Carney in *A Whistle in the Dark* (Th. Royal, Stratford, England, Sept. 1961; and Apollo Th., London, Oct. 1961); and Hamm in *Endgame* (Paris, France, 1963).

With the Royal Shakespeare Co. (Aldwych, London), he played McCann in *The Birthday Party*, and Roche in *Afore Night Comes* (June, 1964); Hamm in *Endgame* (July 1964); de Sade in *Marat/Sade* (Aug. 1964); Matti in *Puntila* (July 1965); The Ghost in *Hamlet* (Stratford, Aug. 1965); and, again at the Aldwych, played de Sade in *Marat/Sade* (Nov. 1965); Wolfgang Schwitter in *The Meteor* (July 1966); Harry Leeds in *Staircase* (Dec. 1966); and Inspector Hawkins in *Dutch Uncle* (Mar. 1969).

Mr. Magee played Mark in *The Battle of Shrivings* (Lyric, London, Feb. 1970); and Cornelius Melody in *A Touch of the Poet* (Gardner Centre, Brighton, England, Feb. 1970).

Films. He has appeared in *Seance on a Wet Afternoon* (ARTIXO, 1964); *The Persecution and Assassination of Marat as Performed by the Inmates of the Asylum of Charenton under the Direction of the Marquis de Sade* (UA, 1967); *The Birthday Party* (Continental, 1968); *Hard Contract* (20th-Fox, 1969); and *Luther* (Amer. Film Th., 1974).

Television and Radio. In England, Mr. Magee has made frequent television appearances; and has read from the works of Samuel Beckett for radio.

Awards. Mr. Magee received an Antoinette Perry (Tony) Award for his performance in *Marat/Sade* (1965).

MAGUIRE, KATHLEEN. Actress. b. Kathleen Rita Maguire, Sept. 27, New York City, to Edward C. and Dorothea Maguire. Father, attorney. Grad. St. Lawrence Acad., N.Y.C.; attended Marymount Coll.; Neighborhood Playhouse Sch. of the Th. Studied acting with Sanford Meisner, Elia Kazan, Martin Ritt, Lee Strasberg, Actors' Studio. Married to Paul H. Krauss III; (marr. dis). Member of AEA; AFTRA; SAG.

Theatre. Miss Maguire appeared as Betty in the pre-Bway tryout of *Mary Had a Little* (opened Geary Th., San Francisco, Calif., July 15, 1946; closed Copley Th., Boston, Mass., Dec. 14, 1946). She made her N.Y.C. debut as Belle in *Sundown Beach* (Belasco, Sept. 7, 1948); subsequently appeared as Peggy Thomas in *The Greatest Man Alive!* (Ethel Barrymore Th., May 8, 1957); Ellen in *Miss Isobel* (Royale, Dec. 26, 1957); Leona Samish in *The Time of the Cuckoo* (Sheridan Square Playhouse, Oct. 27, 1958); Mabel Cantwell in *The Best Man* (Morosco, Mar. 31, 1960), and toured in the production (opened Hanna, Cleveland, Ohio, Sept. 18, 1961; closed Forrest Th., Philadelphia, Pa., Feb. 3, 1962); Connie in *The Sudden and Accidental Re-Education of Horse Johnson* (Belasco, N.Y.C., Dec. 18, 1968); and Bea Rockosy in *Ring Round the Bathtub* (Martin Beck Th., Apr. 29, 1972).

Miss Maguire also toured in summer theatre productions of *Harvey; Come Back, Little Sheba; Marcus in the High Grass; The Dragon Slayer;* and *The Desperate Hours.* At the Elitch Gardens (Denver, Colo.), she played in *The Chalk Garden, Anastasia, The Rainmaker, Love Me Little,* and *Nude with a Violin.*

Television. Miss Maguire appeared in *The Bachelor Party, The Catered Affair, Rabbit Trap,* and *Spring Reunion* (Philco Television Playhouse, NBC). She also performed on Studio One (CBS); Kraft Television Th. (NBC); The Defenders (CBS); The Nurses (CBS); Ben Casey (ABC); and East Side/West Side (CBS).

Awards. Miss Maguire received *The Village Voice* Off-Bway (Obie) Award (1958) for her performance as Leona Samish in *The Time of the Cuckoo.*

MAHARAM, JOSEPH. Executive. b. July 18, 1898, New York City, to Louis and Dora Maharam. Father, textile merchant. Attended Boys H.S., Brooklyn, N.Y.; grad. Erasmus Hall H.S., Bklyn., 1916; attended City Coll. of New York; Columbia Law Sch. Married 1949 to Roslyn Wendell (dec. 1956); one son, one daughter; married Feb. 1960 to Elsa Donath; one son, one daughter. Served Student Army Training Corps, 1918. Member of Amer. Theatre Wing; ANTA; Jewish Theatrical Guild; The Friars; The Lambs; Cinema Lodge of B'nai B'rith (trustee). Address: 45 Gefion Court, Lake Worth, Fl 33460; 176 E. 71st St., New York, NY 10021, tel. (212) UN 1-8589.

Mr. Maharam was president of the Maharam Fabric Corp. which designs, weaves and imports fabrics for theatrical and decorative purposes; supplies fabrics to theatres for drapes, stage curtains and wall coverings, and costume fabrics and accessories for theatre, ballet, opera, nightclub and television productions.

It has supplied fabrics to Bway theatres and for Bway productions since 1919, and has branches in Chicago, St. Louis, Los Angeles and San Francisco.

Mr. Maharam owned and operated the Cherry Lane Th. in N.Y.C. (1950–51).

Other Activities. Through his Joseph Maharam Foundation, Mr. Maharam contributes to various philanthropies and cultural projects, including annual awards for distinguished NY theatrical design, distributed by the American Theatre Wing, and national intercollegiate design awards for students, sponsored by Southern Illinois Univ.

Awards. Mr. Maharam has received plaques and citations for his philanthropic services from organizations including the United Jewish Appeal and the Federation of Jewish Philanthropies of New York.

Recreation. Sculpturing, painting, golf, theatre, traveling.

MAINBOCHER. Couturier, costume designer. b. Main Rousseau Bocher, Oct. 24, 1890, Chicago, Ill., to George R. and Luella (Main) Bocher. Grad. H.S., Chicago, 1903; Lewis Institute, 1907; attended Univ. of Chicago, 1911. Studied piano with Claire Osborn Reed at Columbia Sch. of Music, Chicago, 1907; design at Chicago Acad. of Fine Arts, 1908–09; Art Students League, N.Y.C., 1909–11; Koniglicae Kunstgwerbeschule, Munich, Germany, 1911–12; art with E.A. Taylor, Paris, France, 1913–14; piano with Frank La Forge, N.Y.C., 1914; voice with Henri Albers and Givlia Valda, N.Y.C., 1919. Served US Army, Intelligence Corps, 1918; rank, Sgt. Major.

Theatre. Mainbocher first designed for the theatre in France, where he created the costumes for acts one, three, and four of *La Fleur des Pois* (Th. de la Michodière, Paris, 1932). In N.Y.C., he designed costumes for Peggy Wood and Leonora Corbett in *Blithe Spirit* (Morosco, Nov. 4, 1941); Katharine Cornell and Doris Dudley in the pre-Bway tryout of *Rose Burke* (Curran, San Francisco, Calif., Jan. 19, 1942); Mary Martin in *One Touch of Venus* (Imperial, N.Y.C., Oct. 7, 1943); Ruth Chatterton in the pre-Bway tryout of *A Lady Comes Home* (Nixon, Pittsburgh, Pa., Dec. 15, 1943); Ruth Gordon in *Over Twenty-One* (Music Box, N.Y.C., Jan. 3, 1944); Betty Field in *Dream Girl* (Coronet, Dec. 14, 1945); Jean Arthur in the pre-Bway tryout of *Born Yesterday* (Shubert, New Haven, Conn., Dec. 20, 1945); Tallulah Bankhead in *Private Lives* (Plymouth, N.Y.C., Oct. 4, 1948); and Ethel Merman in *Call Me Madam* (Imperial, Oct. 12, 1950).

He designed costumes for *The Prescott Proposals* (Broadhurst, Dec. 16, 1950); *Point of No Return* (Alvin, Dec. 13, 1951); was costume consultant for *Wish You Were Here* (Imperial, June 25, 1952); designed costumes for Rosalind Russell in *Wonderful Town* (Winter Garden, Feb. 25, 1953); designed the costumes for *Kind Sir* (Alvin, Nov. 4, 1953); designed the costumes for Libby Holman in part one of *Blues, Ballads and Sin Songs* (Bijou, Oct. 4, 1954); Lynn Fontanne in *The Great Sebastians* (ANTA, Jan. 4, 1956); and Mary Martin in *The Sound of Music* (Lunt-Fontanne Th., Nov. 16, 1955); and the gowns for *Tiny Alice* (Billy Rose Th., Dec. 29, 1964).

Television. He appeared on television with Noel Coward in *Ninety Minutes Is a Long, Long Time* (1955); and designed Mary Martin's wardrobe for the television adaptation of *Born Yesterday* (NBC, 1956).

Other Activities. Mainbocher illustrated for *Harper's Bazaar* (Paris, 1922–23); was editor of *Vogue* (Paris, 1923–29); founded his own house of dress design in Paris (1930–39), and established (1940) Mainbocher, Inc., N.Y.C.

He designed the US Waves uniform (1942); Girl Scouts uniform (1946); American Red Cross uniform (1948); the nurse's uniform for Passavant Hospital, Chicago, Ill. (1949); and the US Marine Corps women's uniform (1951).

Recreation. Animals, theatre, music.

MAJOR, FRANK A. Business executive. b. Frank Adam Major, Apr. 1925, Oak Park, Ill., to Roscoe E. and Anna A. (Hunkeler) Major. Father, founder of Major Corp., Inc. Grad. Morgan Park Military Acad., Chicago, 1942; Univ. of Buffalo, B.S. 1949. Married Feb. 7, 1948, to Betty A. Westcott; three daughters. Served WW II, USAAF; rank, 2nd Lt. Member of Illuminating Engineering Society; Young Presidents Organization; Bd. of Trustees, Morningside Coll. (Sioux City, Iowa). Address: (home) 74 Balmoral, Northfield, IL 60093, tel. (302) HI 6-1948; (bus.) Major Corp., 4603 Fullerton Ave., Chicago, IL 60639, tel. (302) SP 2-7600.

Since 1956, Mr. Major has been president of Major Corp., with facilities in Chicago and Crystal Lake, Ill. The company manufactures stage lighting equipment and Alzak Aluminum Reflectors.

The Major Corp. owns the Lighting Equip. Co., Elk Grove, Ill., a manufacturer of architectural lighting.

Recreation. Golf, fishing, bridge.

MAKO. Actor, director, playwright. b. Makoto Iwamatsu, 1932, Kobe, Japan. Attended Los Angeles public schools; Pratt Inst., N.Y.C. Studied for the theatre at Pasadena (Calif.) Playhouse. Served U.S. Armed Forces. Married to Shizuko Hoshi, dancer, choreographer, dance teacher and actress; two daughters. Relative in theatre: sister, Momo Yashima, actress. Member of AEA; SAG; AFTRA.

Theatre. Mako is founder (1966) and artistic director of East West Players and Childrens' Workshop (Los Angeles), a company dedicated to the training and development of Oriental-American theatrical artists. With this group, Mako has directed, acted, and has written a play, *There's No Place Like a Tired Ghost.*

Elsewhere he played Taki in *A Banquet for the Moon* (Theatre Marquee, N.Y.C., Jan. 19, 1961); was guest artist with the Inner City Rep. Th. (Los Angeles, 1967–68 season); and made his Bway debut as The Reciter in *Pacific Overtures* (Winter Garden, N.Y.C., Jan. 11, 1976).

Films. His appearances include *Never So Few* (MGM, 1960); *The Ugly Dachsund* (BV, 1966); *The Sand Pebbles* (20th-Fox, 1966); *The Private Navy of Sgt. O'Farrell* (UA, 1968); *The Great Bank Robbery* (WB, 1969); *The Hawaiians* (UA, 1970); *Tora! Tora! Tora!* (20th-Fox, 1970); and *The Island at the Top of the World* (BV, 1975).

Television. Among his extensive appearances are Hawaiian Eye (ABC); The FBI (ABC); Ironside (NBC); Hawaii Five-O (CBS); Mannix (CBS); M*A*S*H (CBS); The Streets of San Francisco (ABC); and *Farewell to Manzanar* (NBC).

Awards. For his performance in *The Sand Pebbles* (1966), he received an Academy (Oscar) Award nomination for best supporting actor.

MALDEN, KARL. Actor, director. b. Mladew Sekulovich, Mar. 22, 1913, Chicago, Ill., to Peter and Minnie (Sebera) Sekulovich. Attended Emerson Sch., Gary, Ind. 1918–30; Art Inst., Chicago, 1933–36; Goodman Th. School, Chicago 1937–38. Married Dec. 18, 1938, to Mona Graham; two daughters—Mila, Carla. Served USAAF, 1943–45; rank, Cpl. Member of AEA; SAG (bd. mbr., 1963–66; dir., 1966–69); SDG; AFTRA. Address: 1845 Mandeville Canyon Rd., Los Angeles, CA 90049.

Theatre. Mr. Malden made his N.Y.C. debut as Barker in *Golden Boy* (Belasco Th., Nov. 4, 1937); subsequently appeared as Joe in *How To Get Tough About It* (Martin Beck Th., Feb. 8, 1938); Charlie Johnson in *Missouri Legend* (Empire, Sept. 19, 1938); Magruder in *The Gentle People* (Belasco, Jan. 5, 1939); Hunk in *Key Largo* (Ethel Barrymore Th., Nov. 27, 1939); Capt. George McNab in *Flight to the West* (Guild, Dec. 30, 1940); Ben in *Uncle Harry* (Broadhurst, May 20, 1942); Giltzparer in *Counterattack* (Windsor, Feb. 3, 1943); and Matthew Graves in *Sons and Soldiers* (Morosco, May 4, 1943).

While in the service, he appeared as Adams in the Air Force play, *Winged Victory* (44 St. Th., Nov. 20, 1943); later, played Andre Vauquin in *The Assassin* (National, Oct. 17, 1945); Stag in *Truckline Cafe* (Belasco, Feb. 27, 1946); George Deever in *All My Sons* (Coronet, Jan. 29, 1947); Mitch in *A Streetcar Named Desire* (Ethel Barrymore Th., Dec. 3, 1947); a Buttonmolder in *Peer Gynt* (ANTA, Jan. 28, 1951); Ephraim Cabot in *Desire Under the Elms* (ANTA, Jan. 16, 1952); Dan Hilliard in *The Desperate Hours* (Ethel Barrymore Th., Feb. 10, 1955); and Hank Parson in *The Egghead* (Ethel Barrymore Th., Oct. 9, 1957).

Films. Mr. Malden made his debut in *Boomerang* (20th-Fox, 1947); subsequently appeared in *The Kiss of Death* (20th-Fox, 1947); *Where the Sidewalk Ends* (20th-Fox, 1950); *The Gunfighter* (20th-Fox, 1950); *The Halls of Montezuma* (20th-Fox, 1950); *A Streetcar Named Desire* (WB, 1951); *Diplomatic Courier* (20th-Fox, 1952); *The Sellout* (MGM, 1952); *Operation Secret* (WB, 1952); *Ruby Gentry* (20th-Fox, 1952); *Take the High Ground* (MGM, 1953); *I Confess* (WB, 1953); *On the Waterfront* (Col., 1954); *Baby Doll* (WB, 1956); *Fear Strikes Out* (Par., 1957); *Bombers B-52* (WB, 1957); directed *Time Limit* (UA, 1957); appeared in *The Hanging Tree* (WB, 1959); *Parrish* (WB, 1960); *Pollyanna* (Buena Vista, 1960); *One-Eyed Jacks* (Par., 1961); *The Great Imposter* (U, 1961); *Birdman of Alcatraz* (UA, 1962); *All Fall Down* (MGM, 1962); *Gypsy* (WB, 1962); *How the West Was Won* (MGM, 1962); *Come Fly with Me* (MGM, 1963); *Dead Ringer* (WB, 1964); *Cheyenne Autumn* (WB, 1964); *The Cincinnati Kid* (MGM, 1965); *Nevada Smith* (Par., 1966); *Murderers' Row* (Col., 1965); *Hotel* (WB, 1967); *The Adventures of Bullwhip Griffin* (Buena Vista, 1967); *Billion Dollar Brain* (UA, 1967); *Hot Millions* (MGM, 1968); *Blue* (Par., 1968); *Patton* (20th-Fox, 1970); *The Cat O' Nine Tails* (Natl. Gen., 1971); and *Wild Rovers* (MGM, 1971).

Television. Mr. Malden starred as Lt. Mike Stone on the Streets of San Francisco series (ABC, 1972–to date).

Radio. He was a regular for one year on Our Gal Sunday.

Other Activities. Mr. Malden taught drama in a summer (1964) session at Emporia (Kansas) State College.

Awards. For his performance as Mitch in *A Streetcar Named Desire,* Mr. Malden received a NY Drama Critics' Circle Award (1948) and an Academy (Oscar) Award (1952) for his role in the screen version. He was nominated (1954) for an Academy (Oscar) Award for his performance in *On the Waterfront.*

MALINA, JUDITH. Actress, director, producer. b. June 4, 1926, Kiel, Germany, to Max and Rose (Zamora) Malina. Father, rabbi; mother, actress. Grad. Julia Richman H.S., N.Y.C., 1944; studied directing under Erwin Piscator at the Dramatic Workshop of the New Sch. for Social Research, 1945–47. Married Oct. 30, 1948, to Julian Beck, director, scenic designer, actor, producer; one son; one daughter. Member of AEA; SAG; AFTRA; NY Committee for General Strike for Peace; IWW. Address: c/o M. L. Beck, 800 West End Ave., New York, NY 10025.

Theatre. Miss Malina is co-director of the Living Theatre, which she founded in 1947 with her husband, Julian Beck; however, she did not begin production with this organization until 1951.

She made her acting debut as Cassandra in *Agamemnon* (President Th., N.Y.C., May 31, 1946); subsequently appeared as Maisie Madigan in *Juno and the Paycock* (Cherry Lane, June 23, 1947); Zenobia Frome in *Ethan Frome* (Cherry Lane, July 7, 1947); Mildred Luce in *The Dog Beneath the Skin* (Cherry Lane, July 21, 1947); and played Statira in *The Thirteenth God* (Cherry Lane, Mar. 20, 1951).

With Julian Beck, she presented a series of plays in the living room of their home, directing and playing in *Childish Jokes, He Who Says Yes and He Who Says No, Ladies' Voices* and *Dialogue of the Young Man and the Manikin* (Aug. 15, 1951).

With Mr. Beck, she presented the Living Theatre productions of *Doctor Faustus Lights the Lights* (Cherry Lane, Dec. 2, 1951), which she directed; *Beyond the Mountains* (Cherry Lane, Dec. 30, 1951), in which she played Phaedra, Iphigenia, and Berenike; *An Evening of Bohemian Theatre* (Cherry Lane, Mar. 2, 1952); a triple bill, which she also directed, including *Ladies' Voices,* in which she played Gertrude; *Desire;* and *Sweeney Agonistes;* directed *Faustina* (Cherry Lane, May 25, 1952); a double bill, *The Heroes and Ubu Roi* (Cherry Lane, Aug. 5, 1952); and a production of *R.U.R.* for the Dramatic Workshop (Capitol Th. Studio, Apr. 1953).

She produced, with her husband, at the Living Theatre Studio, 2641 Bway, *The Age of Anxiety* (Mar. 18, 1954), which she also directed and in which she was the Narrator; *The Spook Sonata* (June 3, 1954), which she directed; *Orpheus* (Sept. 30, 1954), which she directed and in which she played Death; *The Idiot King* (Dec. 2, 1954), in which she played the Nun; *Tonight We Improvise* (Feb. 17, 1955), in which she played Mommina; *Phaedra* (May 27, 1955), which she translated and in which she played the title role; and *The Young Disciple* (Oct. 12, 1955), in which she played the Old Crone;

and a double bill of operas, *Voices for a Mirror* and *The Curious Fern* (Master Inst. Th., June 5, 1957).

From 1959–63, Miss Malina produced with Mr. Beck, at the Living Theatre, *Many Loves* (Jan. 13, 1959), in which she played Alise, Seraphina, Breen, and Clara; *The Cave at Machpelah* (June 30, 1959), in which she played Sarah and Rebekah; *The Connection* (July 15, 1959), which she directed; *Tonight We Improvise* (Nov. 6, 1959), in which she played Mommina; *Madrigal of War* (Nov. 11, 1959); a triple bill, *All That Fall, Embers*, and *Act Without Words I & III* (Dec. 7, 1959); another triple bill, *Bertha, Theory of Comedy*, and *Love's Labour* (Dec. 28, 1959); *The Devil's Mother* (Feb. 1, 1960), which she directed; *Faust Foutu* (May 2, 1960); a double bill, *The Marrying Maiden*, which she directed, and *The Women of Trachis*, in which she played Daysair (June 22, 1960); a triple bill, *The Herne's Egg, Purgatory* and *A Full Moon in March* (Sept. 19, 1960); *The Election* (Nov. 4, 1960), in which she played a Stagehand; *In the Jungle of Cities* (Dec. 20, 1960), which she directed; *The Mountain Giants* (April 3, 1961), in which she played Countess Ilse; took over the role of Mary Garga in *In the Jungle of Cities* (April 15, 1961); *The Apple* (Dec. 7, 1961), which she directed; *Man Is Man* (Sept. 18, 1962), in which she played Leokadja Begbick; and *The Brig* (May 15, 1963), which she directed.

Miss Malina and Mr. Beck took the Living Theatre's productions of *The Connection, Many Loves*, and *In the Jungle of Cities* on tour in Italy, France, and Germany (June 1961); *The Connection, The Apple*, and *In the Jungle of Cities* on tour in France, Germany, Switzerland, the Netherlands, and Belgium (Apr.–May 1962). In 1964, they went with the Living Theatre to London, where they presented *The Brig* (Mermaid, Sept. 2–26), subsequently touring Europe (1964–68) and producing the following new works: *Mysteries and Smaller Pieces*, created collectively by the company under direction of Mr. Beck and Miss Malina (American Students and Artists Center, Paris, France, Oct. 26, 1964); *The Maids*, directed by Miss Malina with Mr. Beck playing Claire (Forum Th., Berlin, Feb. 26, 1965); *Frankenstein*, created collectively by the company under the direction of Miss Malina and Mr. Beck (Teatro La Perla, Venice, Italy, Sept. 26, 1965); Sophocles' *Antigone*, a translation by Miss Malina from the Bertolt Brecht version, with Miss Malina as Antigone and Mr. Beck as Creon (Stadttheater, Krefeld, Germany, Feb. 18, 1967); and *Paradise Now*, created collectively by the company under the direction of Mr. Beck and Miss Malina (Cloître des Carmes, Festival d'Avignon, France, July 20, 1968). The Becks then toured the US coast to coast with the Living Theatre productions *Mysteries, Antigone, Frankenstein*, and *Paradise Now* (tour opened Yale Univ. Th., New Haven, Conn., Sept. 16, 1968; closed Brooklyn Acad. of Music, N.Y.C., Mar. 28–29, 1969); followed by a return tour of Europe.

The Living Theatre changed its form in Jan. 1970 to concentrate on productions for street and non-theatre environments. Miss Malina and Mr. Beck went with the Living Theatre to Brazil (July 1970) and began production of the play cycle *The Legacy of Cain*, producing *Favela Project 1: Christmas Cake for the Hot Hole and the Cold Hole* (São Paulo, Dec. 1970); *Plaza Project 1: Rituals and Transformations* (Embu, Dec. 1970); *School Project 1: A Critical Examination of Six Dreams About Mother* (Saramenha, Brazil, May 1971). Further work on *The Legacy of Cain* cycle continued after the return of Miss Malina and Mr. Beck to the US (Sept. 1971) with production of *University Project 1: Seven Meditations on Political Sado-Masochism* (Chapel Hill, N.C., Apr. 1972) and *Strike Support Play 1: Strike Support Oratorium* (Brooklyn, N.Y., Mar. 1974).

Films. The Living Theatre production of *The Brig* was filmed onstage (1964). Miss Malina had roles in *Flaming Creatures* (1962); *Wheel of Ashes* (1967); and *Dog Day Afternoon* (1974); and appeared with the Living Theatre company in *Living and Glorious* (1965); *Amore, Amore* (1966); *Le Compromis* (1968); *Etre Libre* (1968); and *Paradise Now* (1969; 1970).

Published Works. Miss Malina has published *Conversations with Julian Beck and Judith Malina* (1969); *We, The Living*, with Julian Beck (1970); and *The Enormous Despair* (1972).

Awards. The Living Theatre received the Lola D'Annunzio Award for its contribution to the off-Bway theatre (1959); the Newspaper Guild of NY Page One Award (1960); *The Village Voice* Off-Bway (Obie) Award for *The Connection* (1960); the Brandeis Univ. Creative Arts Award Theatre Citation (1961); the Grand Prix de Théâtre des Nations, Paris, France (1961); the Médallion from the Paris Theatre Critics Circle (1961); the Prix de l'Université Paris (1961); the New England Th. Conference Award (1962); *The Village Voice* off-Bway (Obie) awards for direction and production of *The Brig* (1964); the Olympia Prize, Taormina, Italy, for *Antigone* (1967); and two Village Voice Off-Bway (Obie) awards in 1969 — for best new play, *Frankenstein*, and for acting in *Antigone*.

MALLORY, VICTORIA.

Actress, singer, dancer. b. Victoria Morales, Fort Lee, Va., to Marino and Ruby (Mallory) Morales. Father, trumpeter and bandmaster, US Army. Attended American Musical and Dramatic Acad., N.Y.C. Member of AEA.

Theatre. Miss Mallory has played Maria in *West Side Story* (NY State Th., N.Y.C., June 24, 1968); Lili in *Carnival!* (NY City Ctr., Dec. 12, 1968); Young Heidi in *Follies* (Winter Garden, Apr. 4, 1971); and Anne Egerman in *A Little Night Music* (Shubert, Feb. 25, 1973).

MALONE, DUDLEY FIELD.

Talent representative, producer. b. Dudley Field Malone, Jr., Jan. 1, 1931, New York City, to Dudley Field and Edna Louise (Johnson) Malone. Father, trial attorney. Tutored privately, London, England; Paris, France, 1946–50; studied French theatre and civilization, Sorbonne, Paris, 1950–52. Member of AEA, AFTRA, SAG. Address: (home) 419 E. 50th St., New York, NY 10022; (bus.) 343 E. 51st St., New York, NY 10022, tel. (212) 755-6110.

Mr. Malone is the head of his own agency, Dudley Field Malone, Inc. (1967–to date). Previously, he was a talent representative with Peter Witt Associates, and an associate to Peter Witt, president of that agency.

Theatre. Off-Bway, he produced *The Divorce of Judy and Jane* (Bijou, Apr. 26, 1972).

Television. Mr. Malone produced television commericals at Batten, Barton, Durstine and Osborne, Inc., N.Y.C. (1954–58).

Recreation. Swimming, water skiing.

MALTZ, ALBERT.

Playwright, novelist. b. Oct. 28, 1908, Brooklyn, N.Y., to Bernard and Lena (Sherry) Maltz. Father, builder. Grad. Erasmus H.S. Brooklyn, N.Y., 1926; Columbia Coll., A.B. (Phi Beta Kappa) 1930; attended Yale Univ. Sch. of Drama, 1930–32. Married Feb. 27, 1937, to Margaret Larkin, writer (marr. dis. Feb., 1964); one son, one daughter. Member of ALA (council, 1937–40). Address: c/o Roslyn Targ Literary Agency, 325 E. 57th St., New York, NY 10022, tel. (212) PL 3-9810.

Theatre. Mr. Maltz collaborated in the writing of *Merry-Go-Round* with George Sklar (Provincetown Playhouse, N.Y.C., Apr. 22, 1932); subsequently he and Mr. Sklar wrote *Peace on Earth*, the first production of the Th. Union, Inc., of which Mr. Maltz was a member of the executive board (Civic Rep. Th., Nov. 29, 1933); and *Black Pit*, also produced by the Theatre Union, Inc. (Civic Rep. Th., Mar. 20, 1935).

Films. Mr. Maltz, with W. R. Burnett, wrote the screenplay for *This Gun for Hire* (Par., 1942); wrote the commentary for the short film *Moscow Strikes Back* (Rep., 1942); with Delmer Daves, wrote *Destination Tokyo* (WB, 1943); *Pride of the Marines* (WB, 1945); collaborated with Ring Lardner, Jr., on *Cloak and Dagger* (WB, 1946); *The Naked City* (U, 1948); and *Two Mules for Sister Sara* (U, 1970); and under pseudonyms, wrote screenplays for other films.

Radio. Mr. Maltz wrote the radio script of *Red Head Baker* (CBS, 1937).

Published Works. He has written the one-act plays *Private Hicks* (1935), *Rehearsal* (1937), and *The Morrison Case* (1952); three volumes of short stories, *The Way Things Are* (1938), *Off-Broadway* (1960), and *Afternoon in the Jungle* (1971); the novels, *The Underground Stream* (1940), *The Cross and the Arrow* (1944), *The Journey of Simon McKeever* (1949), *A Long Day in a Short Life* (1956), and *A Tale of One January* (1964); and a book of essays, *The Citizen Writer* (1950).

Mr. Maltz has written articles and stories for magazines, including *The New Yorker, Harper's, New Masses, Southern Review*, and *Scholastic*. .

Awards. Mr. Maltz received the O. Henry Memorial Award for his short story, *The Happiest Man on Earth* (1938), and the Silver Medal from the Commonwealth Club for *The Journey of Simon McKeever* (1949).

Recreation. Swimming, walking, chess, study of American history.

MAMOULIAN, ROUBEN.

Director, producer, writer. b. Oct. 8, 1897, Tiflis (Georgia), Russia, to Zachary and Virginie (Kalantarian) Mamoulian. Father, banker; mother, actress, producer. Attended Lycée Montaigne, Paris, France; grad. Gymnasium, Tiflis (with Gold Medal); studied law at Univ. of Moscow, two years; studied theatre at Vakhtangov Studio of Moscow Art Th. Married Feb. 12, 1945, to Azadia Newman, painter. Member of DGA (founding member, board, 1936–39; 1944–46; 1952–53; board and 1st vice-pres., 1953–58); ALA. Address: 1112 Schuyler Rd., Beverly Hills, CA 90210.

Theatre. Mr. Mamoulian first worked as director of *The Beating on the Door* (St. James's Th., London, Eng., Nov. 6, 1922); subsequently at the Eastman Th. (Rochester, N.Y.), directed and produced a repertory of operas, operettas, and musical presentations, including *Rigoletto, Faust*, and *Carmen* (1923); *Boris Godounoff* (1924); and *Tannhauser, Pelleas and Melisande, Shanewis, The Merry Widow, The Count of Luxembourg, H.M.S. Pinafore, The Pirates of Penzance*, and *Sister Beatrice* (1925). For the Theatre Guild Sch., he directed stock productions of *Clarence, Enter Madame*, and *He Who Gets Slapped* (Scarborough, N.Y., 1926); and staged a matinee series of *Seven Keys to Baldpate* (Garrick, London, May 3, 1927).

He directed *Porgy* (Guild, N.Y.C., Oct. 10, 1927), which toured the US (1929–30) and was produced in London (His Majesty's, Apr. 10, 1929); *Marco Millions* (Guild, N.Y.C., Jan. 9, 1928); and *These Modern Women* (Eltinge, Feb 13, 1928); staged the pre-Bway tryouts of *Cafe Tomaza* (Cort, Jamaica, N.Y., Apr. 20, 1928) and *Women* (Adelphi, Philadelphia, Pa., Sept. 10, 1928); directed *Congai* (Sam H. Harris Th., N.Y.C., Nov. 27, 1928); *Wings Over Europe* (Martin Beck Th., Dec. 10, 1928); *The Game of Love and Death* (Guild, Nov. 25, 1929); and *R.U.R.* (Martin Beck Th., Feb. 17, 1930).

Mr. Mamoulian directed and adapted *A Month in the Country* (Guild, Mar. 17, 1930); directed the opera, *Die Glückliche Hand* (Metropolitan Opera House, N.Y.C., Apr. 22, 1930); *A Farewell to Arms* (Natl., Sept. 22, 1930); *Solid South* (Lyceum, Oct. 14, 1930); *Porgy and Bess* (Alvin, Oct. 10, 1935); which he directed and produced (Philharmonic Aud., Los Angeles and San Francisco, Calif., Spring 1938).

He directed *Oklahoma!* (St. James, N.Y.C., Mar. 31, 1943); directed and wrote, with Howard Dietz, the book for *Sadie Thompson* (Alvin, Nov. 16, 1944); directed *Carousel* (Majestic, Apr. 19, 1945); *St. Louis Woman* (Martin Beck Th., Mar. 30, 1946); *Oklahoma!* (Drury Lane, London, Apr. 30, 1947); *Leaf and Bough* (Cort, N.Y.C., Jan. 21, 1949); *Lost in the Stars* (Music Box, Oct. 30, 1949); *Arms and the Girl* (46 St. Th., Feb. 2, 1950); London production of *Carousel* (Drury Lane, June 7, 1950); staged *Oklahoma!* (Berlin Art Festival, Ger., Sept. 1951); directed and produced *Adolph's Zukor Golden Jubilee* (Palladium, Hollywood, Calif., May 1953); and directed *Carousel* (Civic Light Opera Co., Los Angeles and San Francisco, Calif., 1954) and *Oklahoma!*

(Paris, Fr.; Rome, Milan, Naples and Venice, It., May 1955). Mr. Mamoulian's *Shakespeare's Hamlet, A New Version* received its world premiere production in 1966 at Carrick Th., Lexington, Ky.

Films. Mr. Mamoulian directed *Applause* (Par., 1929); *City Streets* (Par., 1931); *Dr. Jekyll and Mr. Hyde* (Par., 1931); *Love Me Tonight* (Par., 1932); *Song of Songs* (Par., 1932); *Queen Christina* (MGM, 1933); *We Live Again* (UA, 1934); *Becky Sharp* (RKO, 1935); *The Gay Desperado* (U, 1936); *High, Wide and Handsome* (Par., 1937); *Golden Boy* (Col., 1938); *The Mark of Zorro* (20th-Fox, 1940); *Blood and Sand* (20th-Fox, 1941); *Rings on Her Fingers* (20th-Fox, 1942); *Summer Holiday* (MGM, 1948); *Silk Stockings* (MGM, 1957); and wrote, with Maxwell Anderson, *Never Steal Anything Small* (U, 1959).

Television and Radio. Mr. Mamoulian taped an interview for the Voice of America (1972) and has taped and filmed interviews for television at the Univ. of Utah, Salt Lake City, Utah (1972) and in London, England, for the BBC (1972).

Other Activities. Mr. Mamoulian served as vice-pres. of the jury, International Film Festival, Cannes, France (1963) and president of the international jury at the International Film Festival, San Sebastian, Spain (1973). In 1970, he conducted a seminar for US educators at the American Film Institute, Beverly Hills, Calif., and he participated in symposia at the Univ. of Southern California (1972) on "The Art of Survival" and at George Eastman House, Rochester, N.Y. (1973), on the "The Coming of Sound to the American Film, 1925–1940.".

Published Works. He wrote the book *Abigayil* (1964); contributed to *Scoundrels and Scalawags* (1968) and *Ararat* (1969); and wrote a foreword to the book *Chevalier* by Gene Ringgold and DeWitt Bodeen (1973).

Awards. At the Venice International Film festivals, Mr. Mamoulian received first prize (1931) for *Dr. Jekyll and Mr. Hyde* and a second award (1934) for *Queen Christina.* He received the diploma of cinema progress from the American Institute of Cinematography, Univ. of Southern California (1935); the NY Film Critics' Award (1936) for best direction of the year for *The Gay Desperado;* and he was made an honorary captain by the Mexico City chief of police (1936) and given the Golden Key to the City of San Francisco, Calif., by Mayor C. J. Rossi (1938). He received an award from the Venice International Film Festival (1941) for best color film for *Blood and Sand;* a citation for distinguished services rendered from the US Treasury Dept. (1943) for his radio broadcast opening the US War Savings Program; and honorary citizenship from the state of Oklahoma (1943) for the musical production *Oklahoma!* He received the Donaldson Award (1945) for best direction for *Carousel* (1945); an award from the Turin Technical Progress Festival (1955) for introducing color to the screen with *Becky Sharp;* and he was a guest of honor of the Italian government at the Venice International Film Festival (1955), where he received an honor citation, also for *Becky Sharp.* In 1955 also, he received the medal of the City of Paris and the plaque of the City of Versailles, France, for *Oklahoma!* He was guest of honor of the USSR at the 1961 International Film Festival in Moscow; in 1963 received a silver bowl from the Univ. of Southern California; and in 1966 a silver cup from the Univ. of Transylvania, Lexington, Ky. On the occasion of his 40th anniversary in films, the Gallery of Modern Art, N.Y.C., held a retrospective of all his films and awarded him a statuette (Oct. 10, 1967) and the City of New York gave him a citation for distinguished and exceptional services (1967). The National Film Theatre, London, England, screened a retrospective of his work in 1968 and a book of tribute was signed by 300 people. Retrospectives of Mr. Mamoulian's work were held in 1970 by the American Film Institute at the Center for Advanced Studies, Beverly Hills, Calif.; the National Gallery of Art, Washington, D.C.; the Metropolitan Museum of Art, N.Y.C.; and Sir George Williams Univ., Montreal, Canada. In 1971, he was guest of honor of the USSR at the International Film Festival, Moscow, and at the San Francisco (Calif.) International Film Festival, where there was a retrospective of his work, a polished agate tribute was presented to him by the Festival; and he received the Horace Walpole Gold Medal of the Count Dracula Society. Additional 1971 retrospectives of his work were screened at the Science Center, Toronto, Canada; the Museum of Science, Buffalo, N.Y.; the Univ. of California at Los Angeles; the Univ. of Southern Florida; and Yale Univ. In 1972, a retrospective of his musical films, *Musical Mamoulian,* was shown at the Academy of Motion Picture Arts and Sciences, Hollywood, Calif., and he was made an honorary member in the Alpha chapter from the Univ. of Southern California in Delta Kappa Alpha national honorary cinema fraternity. In 1973, the International Festival of Films, San Sebastian, Spain, and La Cinémathèque Française, Paris, France, each awarded him a silver plaque and held retrospectives of his work; there was a retrospective showing of his films at the Univ. of California at Los Angeles; and a special showing followed by a discussion of *Blood and Sand* (Filmex, Hollywood, May 23). In 1974, Mr. Mamoulian went to Australia as guest of honor at the Sidney and Melbourne International Film festivals, where there were retrospectives of his films and the Rouben Mamoulian Award for the best Australian short film was established in perpetuity.

Recreation. Horseback riding, tennis, gardening, chess, pressing flowers, stone collecting, writing poems, and other irrelevant distractions.

MANDEL, LORING. Playwright. b. May 5, 1928, Chicago, Ill., to Julius I. and Frieda (Okun) Mandel. Father, physician and surgeon. Grad. Senn H.S., Chicago, Ill., 1945; Univ. of Wisconsin, B.S. 1949. Married July 9, 1950, to Dorothy Bernstein; two sons. Served US Army, Korea, 1952–54. Member of Dramatists Guild; WGA; Natl. Collegiate Players. Huntington Arts Council (bd. of dir.).

Theatre. Mr. Mandel wrote *Advise and Consent* (Cort Th., N.Y.C., Nov. 17, 1960), based on the novel by Allen Drury, and which subsequently toured (opened Shubert, Cincinnati, Ohio, Oct. 2, 1961; closed American, St. Louis, Mo., May 5, 1962). His television play *Project Immortality* was presented as a stage play (world premiere, Arena Stage, Washington, D.C., Jan. 6, 1966).

Television. Mr. Mandel wrote *Shakedown Cruise* (Studio One, CBS, Nov. 7, 1955); *Fair Play* (Studio One, CBS, Dec. 26, 1955); *This Will Do Nicely* (Studio One, CBS, Apr. 2, 1956); *House of His Own* (NBC, June 14, 1956); with Mayo Simon, *Army Game* (Kaiser Hour, NBC, July 3, 1956); wrote *The Open Door* (Studio One, CBS, Oct. 15, 1956); *Rice Sprout Song* (Studio One, CBS, Apr. 15, 1957); *Blast in Centralia #5* (Seven Lively Arts, CBS, Jan. 26, 1958); *Hold for Release* (Armstrong Circle Th., CBS, June 11, 1958); *The Raider* (Playhouse 90, CBS, Feb. 19, 1959); *Project Immortality* (Playhouse 90, CBS, June 11, 1959); *Great Robbery I* (DuPont Show of the Month, NBC, May 27, 1962); *Great Robbery II* (Dupont Show of the Month, NBC, June 3, 1962); and *Ambassador at Large* (NBC, June 14, 1964).

He also wrote *Do Not Go Gentle into That Good Night* (CBS Playhouse, Oct. 17, 1967); *To Confuse the Angel* (Prudential's On Stage, NBC, Mar. 15, 1970); *Particular Men* (Playhouse New York, PBS, May 8, 1972); *The Whirlwind* (CBS, Dec. 12, 1974); *The Case Against Milligan* (American Parade, CBS, Jan. 22, 1975); *The Trial of Chaplain Jensen* (ABC, 1975); and *Crossing Fox River* (NBC, 1976).

Awards. Mr. Mandel received a Sylvania Award; was nominated for a NATAS (Emmy) Award for his *Project Immortality* (1959); and received an Emmy (1968) for outstanding achievement in dramatic writing for *Do Not Go Gentle into That Good Night.*

Recreation. Tennis, photography, carpentry.

MANKOWITZ, WOLF. Playwright, producer, author. b. Nov. 7, 1924, London, England, to Solomon and Rebecca Mankowitz. Father, retail tradesman. Grad. Downing Coll., Cambridge Univ., M.A., English tripos, 1946. Served during WW II as conscript coal miner and in British Army. Married Aug. 2, 1944, to Ann Margaret Seligmann; four sons. Address: Simmonscourt Castle, Donnybrook, Dublin, 4, Republic of Ireland.

Theatre. Mr. Mankowitz wrote the plays *The Bespoke Overcoat* (Arts, London, England, June 25, 1953; Embassy, Jan. 13, 1954) and *The Boychik* (Embassy, Jan. 13, 1954). In partnership with Oscar Lewenstein, he produced *The World of Sholem Aleichem* (Embassy, Jan. 11, 1955); *Moby Dick* (Duke of York's Th., Sept. 28, 1955); *The Threepenny Opera* (Royal Court, Feb. 9, 1956; Aldwych, Mar. 21, 1956); and he wrote *The Mighty Hunter* (New Lindsey, July 25, 1956). With Oscar Lewenstein, he produced *The Member of the Wedding* (Royal Court, Feb. 5, 1957); *Nekrassov* (Royal Court, Sept. 17, 1957); *The Public Prosecutor* (Arts, Oct. 15, 1957); *Expresso Bongo,* also written by Mr. Mankowitz and based on one of his own stories (Saville, Apr. 23, 1958); *The Party* (New, May 28, 1958); *The Hostage* (Royal, Stratford, Oct. 14, 1958; Wyndham's, London, June 11, 1959); *The Long and the Short and the Tall* (Royal Court, Jan. 7, 1959; New, Apr. 8, 1959); *A Taste of Honey* Th. Royal, Stratford, May 27, 1958 and Jan. 21, 1959; Wyndham's, London, Feb. 10, 1959); *Make Me an Offer,* with book by Mr. Mankowitz (Th. Royal, Stratford, Oct. 19, 1959; New, London, Dec. 16, 1959); *The Lily White Boys* (Royal Court, London, Jan. 27, 1960); *Rhinoceros* (Royal Court, Apr. 28, 1960; Strand, June 8, 1960); and *The Art of Living* (Criterion, Aug. 18, 1960).

Establishing his own production offices, Mr. Mankowitz presented *This Year, Next Year* (Vaudeville, Oct. 20, 1960); *The Lion in Love* (Royal Court, Dec. 29, 1960); and *Belle or the Ballad of Doctor Crippen,* which he wrote (Strand, May 4, 1961). He also wrote *Pickwick* (Saville, July 4, 1963; 46 St. Th., N.Y.C., Oct. 4, 1965); *Passion Flower Hotel* (Prince of Wales Th., London, Aug. 24, 1965); and produced, in association with Laurence Harvey, *Here Are Ladies* (Criterion, July 28, 1970; Estelle Newman Th., N.Y.C., Feb. 22, 1971). He wrote *The Notorious Cockney Highwayman* (Edinburgh, Scotland, Sept. 1972) and *Stand and Deliver* (Roundhouse, London, Eng., Oct. 24, 1972).

Films. Screenplays by Mr. Mankowitz are *The Bespoke Overcoat,* based on his play (Independent Film Distributors, 1955); *Make Me an Offer,* with W. P. Lipscomb (Dominant, 1956); *A Kid for Two Farthings,* based on his own novel (UA, 1956); and he was one of the writers for *Trapeze* (UA, 1956). His other film scripts include *Expresso Bongo* (Continental, 1960); *The Two Faces of Dr. Jekyll* (Col., 1960); *The Long and the Short and the Tall,* with Willis Hall (Cont., 1961); *The Millionairess,* with Riccardo Aragno (20th-Fox, 1961); *The Day the Earth Caught Fire,* with Val Guest (U, 1962); *The Waltz of the Toreadors* (Cont., 1962); *Where the Spies Are,* with Val Guest and James Leasor (MGM, 1965); *Casino Royale,* with John Law and Michael Sayers (Col., 1967); *The Twenty-Fifth Hour* (MGM, 1967); *The Assassination Bureau,* with Michael Relph (Par., 1969); *Bloomfield,* with Richard Harris (World Film Services-Limbridge, 1970), which, with John Heyman, he produced; *Black Beauty* (Par., 1971); *Treasure Island* Natl. Genl., 1972); *The Hebrew Lesson* (1972), which he also directed; *The Hireling* (Col., 1973); *Henry 8* (Levitt Pickman, 1973); and *The Hero* (Avco-Embassy, 1973), which, with John Heyman, he produced.

Television. Mr. Mankowitz's *Make Me an Offer* was televised as a play (Dec. 1952) and as a musical (BBC, 1966). *The Bespoke Overcoat* and *the Baby* were televised in 1954 and *The Girl* and *It Should Happen to a Dog* in 1955. Mr. Mankowitz wrote the series ABC of Show Business (BBC, Oct. 12, 1956); began conducting the weekly interview program Conflict on Jan. 3, 1958; wrote the series East End West End, based on his own stories (began Feb. 4, 1958), and the series The Killing Stones, based on his story *L.D.B.* (began Mar. 1958). He adapted *Wife of Thy Youth* for television as *The Model Marriage* (Armchair Th., ABC, June 1959) and wrote *A Cure for Tin Ear* (Love Story, ATV, Nov. 1965) and *The Battersea Miracle* (Armchair Th., ABC, 1966), both adapted from stories he had written.

Published Works. Fiction published by Mr. Mankowitz includes *Make Me an Offer* (1952); *A Kid for Two Farthings* (1953); *Laugh Till You Cry* (1955); *Majollika and Company* (1955); *My Old Man's a Dustman* (1956); *The Mendelman Fire and Other Stories* (1957); *Expresso Bongo* (1960); *Cockatrice* (1963); *The Biggest Pig in Barbados* (1965); *The Penguin Wolf Mankowitz* (1967); *The Samson Riddle* (1972); *The Blue Arabian Nights* (1972); and *The Ahakista Fables* (1972).

Among Mr. Mankowitz's other publications are *The Portland Vase and the Wedgwood Copies* (1952); *Wedgwood* (1953); *ABC Of Show Business* (1956); *A Concise Encyclopedia of English Pottery and Porcelain* (1957); and Twelve Poems (1971).

Awards. Mr. Mankowitz received the Society of Authors poetry award (1946). *The Bespoke Overcoat* won first prize as the best short story film at the Venice Film Festival, the diploma of merit at the Edinburgh Film Festival, the British Film Academy Award (all 1955), an Academy (Oscar) Award as the best two-reel short subject, the Film Council of America's Golden Reel Award, and the Jewish Audio-Visual Materials Award as the outstanding film of Jewish interest (all 1957). *Make Me an Offer* received the London *Evening Standard* drama award for best musical (1959); *The Day the Earth Caught Fire* received the British Film Academy Award as best British screenplay (1961); *The Hebrew Lesson* received the Critics' Prize (1972); and *The Hireling* received the Grand Prix at the Cannes Film Festival as best film (1973).

MANN, DANIEL. Director. b. Aug. 8, 1912, Brooklyn, N.Y., to Samuel and Helen Chugerman. Father, lawyer. Grad. Erasmus Hall H.S., Brooklyn, N.Y. Studied at Neighborhood Playhouse Sch. of Th., N.Y.C. Married 1948 to Kathleen Williams, actress; two sons, one daughter. Served US Army Infantry, 1942–46. Member of DGA; SDG. Address: 165 Mabery Rd., Santa Monica, CA 90402, tel. (213) GL 4-6825.

Pre-Theatre. Professional musician (clarinet); orchestra leader.

Theatre. Mr. Mann directed various productions in Canada (1939); appeared as a replacement in *Pins and Needles* (N.Y.C. and on tour, 1940); became a member of the production committee and a director at The Actors Lab (Los Angeles, 1940–42), and a director at Max Reinhardt's Workshop (Los Angeles, 1941–42), directed at the Los Palmas Th. (Hollywood, 1946–47); taught at the Amer. Th. Wing (N.Y.C., 1948–49); and directed several stock and off-Bway productions, including a summer tryout of *Come Back, Little Sheba* (Westport, Conn., Country Playhouse, Summer 1949), with which he made his Bway debut as a director (Booth Th., N.Y.C., Feb. 15, 1950).

He directed a revival of *A Streetcar Named Desire* (NY City Ctr., May 23, 1950); *The Rose Tattoo* (Martin Beck Th., Mar. 3, 1951), also its national tour (opened His Majesty's, Montreal, Can., Oct. 9, 1951; closed Curran, San Francisco, Apr. 5, 1952); *Paint Your Wagon* (Shubert, N.Y.C., Nov. 12, 1951), also its national tour (opened Hartman, Columbus, Ohio, Oct. 2, 1952; closed Blackstone, Chicago, Jan. 31, 1953); the pre-Bway tryout of *A Certain Joy* (opened Playhouse, Wilmington, Del., Feb. 12, 1953; closed Locust, Philadelphia, Feb. 21, 1953); *The Immoralist* (Royale, N.Y.C., Feb. 8, 1954); and *A Loss of Roses* (Eugene O'Neill Th., Nov. 28, 1959).

Films. Mr. Mann has directed *Come Back, Little Sheba* (Par., 1952); *About Mrs. Leslie* (Par., 1954); *The Rose Tattoo* (Par., 1955); *I'll Cry Tomorrow* (MGM, 1955); *The Teahouse of the August Moon* (MGM, 1956); *Hot Spell* (Par., 1959); *The Last Angry Man* (Col., 1959); *The Mountain Road* (Col., 1960); *Butterfield 8* (MGM, 1960); *Ada* (MGM, 1961); *Five Finger Exercise* (Col., 1962); *Who's Got the Action?* (Par., 1962); *Who's Been Sleeping in My Bed?* (Par., 1963); *Our Man Flint* (20th-Fox, 1966); *Judith* (Par., 1966); *For Love of Ivy* (Cinerama, 1968); *A Dream of Kings* (Natl. Gen., 1969); *Willard* (Cinerama, 1971); *The Revengers* (Natl. Gen., 1972); *Maurie* (Natl. Gen., 1973); *Interval* (Avco-Embassy, 1973); *Lost in the Stars* (Amer. Film Th., 1974); and *Journey into Fear* (Canadian; New World Prod., Ltd., 1975).

Awards. He received the Donaldson Award for his direction of *The Rose Tattoo* (1950); Academy (Oscar) Award nominations as Best Director for *Come Back, Little Sheba* (1952), *The Rose Tattoo* (1955), and *The Teahouse of the August Moon* (1956); and the *Look* Magazine Film Achievement Award (1955).

Recreation. Tennis, swimming.

MANN, DELBERT. Director, producer. b. Jan. 30, 1920, Lawrence, Kan., to Delbert and Ora (Patton) Mann. Father, professor of sociology; mother, teacher. Grad. Vanderbilt Univ., A.B. 1941; Yale Drama Sch. Married Jan. 13, 1942, to Ann Caroline Gillespie; one daughter, three sons. Served in WW II as B-24 pilot, in 8th Air Corps; and as Squadron Intelligence Officer. Member of Directors Guild of America (pres., 1967–71); Producers Guild of America; AEA. Address: Biography Productions Ltd., 303 N. LaPeer, Beverly Hills, CA 90211, tel. (213) 271-2356.

Pre-Theatre. Mr. Mann worked for General Shoe Corp. (Nashville, Tenn., 1941–42).

Theatre. After beginning his career as an actor (Nashville, Tenn., Community Playhouse, 1937) and stage manager (Wellesley Summer Th., 1947). Mr. Mann directed a touring production of *A Quiet Place* (1955) and made his Bway debut as director of *Speaking of Murder* (Royale, N.Y.C., 1956). He directed the opera, *Wuthering Heights* (NY City Ctr., 1959), and the play, *Zelda* (Ethel Barrymore Th., 1969).

Films. Mr. Mann directed *Marty* (Hecht-Lancaster and UA, 1954); *Bachelor Party* (Hecht-Lancaster and UA, 1956); *Desire Under the Elms* (Par., 1957); *Separate Tables* (Hecht-Lancaster and UA, 1958); *Middle of the Night* (Col., 1959); *The Dark at the Top of the Stairs* (WB, 1960); *The Outsider* (U, 1960); *Lover Come Back* (U, 1961); *That Touch of Mink* (U, 1961); *A Gathering of Eagles* (U, 1962); and *Dear Heart* (WB, 1963). He produced and directed *Quick Before It Melts* (MGM, 1964) and *Mr. Buddwing* (MGM, 1965); and directed *Kidnapped* (Omnibus Prod., 1971).

Television. Mr. Mann directed numerous productions for *Philco Playhouse* (NBC, 1947–55); he subsequently directed *Yellow Jack, Darkness at Noon, The Petrified Forest,* and *Our Town* (Producers Showcase, NBC, 1955); *Omnibus* (CBS and ABC, 1956–57); *The Day Lincoln Was Shot* (Ford Star Jubilee, CBS, 1956); *The Plot to Kill Stalin* and other productions (Playhouse 90, CBS, 1958–59); *Heidi* (Omnibus, NBC, 1967); *David Copperfield* (Omnibus, NBC, 1969); *Jane Eyre* (Omnibus, NBC, 1970); and *The Man Without a Country* (Rosemont Prod., ABC, 1972); and directed and produced *What Makes Sammy Run* (NBC, 1959) and *The First Woman President* (Wolper Prod., CBS, 1974).

Other Activities. Professorial Lecturer in Film Art, Claremont (Calif.) Men's College (1972–to date); member of the Board of Trustees at Vanderbilt Univ. (Nashville, Tenn., 1962–to date) and Coker Coll. (Hartsville, S.C., 1970–to date).

Awards. Mr. Mann was awarded an honorary L.L.B. from Northland College, Ashland, Wisc., in 1959; and received the Academy (Oscar) and Directors Guild awards (1955) for best director for the film *Marty.*.

MANN, EDWARD. Writer, director, producer. b. Edward Schulman, Oct. 7, 1924, to Samuel and Rachel Schulman. Father, businessman; mother, raconteur. Studied at NY Art Students League (painting and design); New Sch. for Social Research (directing and playwriting). Married to Marilyn Miller, pianist and composer (marr. dis., 1970); one son; one daughter. Relatives in theatre: grandfather, Nathan Schulman, producer and impressario, Yiddish Art Th. (1920's–30's); cousin Martha Scott, actress. Member of AGAC; WGAW. Address: 152 W. 58th St., New York, NY 10019, tel. (212) 582-7428.

Pre-Theatre. Mr. Mann was a professional artist and portrait painter while still in his teens. He then became the youngest syndicated cartoonist at that time, drawing *Dixie Dugan* (McNaught Syndicate); and *Blade Winter* (Publishers Syndicate).

Theatre. Mr. Mann first worked professionally as a designer and director at the Maverick Th. (Woodstock, N.Y., Summer 1946); subsequently played Tom in *The Glass Menagerie* (Woodstock, N.Y., Villetta Studio, and on tour, Summer 1947); and directed and designed Molière's *Le Mariage Farce* (Woodstock, N.Y., Playhouse, 1954). In association with Theodore Mann, Aileen Kramer, Jose Quintero, Emily Stevens, and Jason Wingreen, he founded (1949) and served as chairman of the board (1949–52) of the Circle in the Square Th. There, he appeared as Uncle Smelicue and was set designer and musical director for *Dark of the Moon* (Feb. 2, 1951); directed *Amata* (Mar. 16, 1951); and directed and wrote the theme music for *Bonds of Interest* (Nov. 30, 1951).

Films. He co-produced, wrote, and directed *Platero and I (1963),* a Spanish film based upon the Nobel Prize-winning book *Platero y Yo;* and *Hallucination Generation* (Amer. Intl., 1964); co-produced, wrote, directed, designed the costumes, and wrote the theme song, "There's a Certain Kind of Woman," for *Cauldron of Blood* (Cannon, 1966); wrote and directed *Hot Pants Holiday* (Avco-Embassy, 1968); and *Who Says I Can't Ride a Rainbow?* (Transvue, 1970); and was writer and production consultant for *The Killer Inside Me* (Col., 1974).

Television. In London, Mr. Mann directed J. P. McEvoy's *Little Rollo* (ITV, 1955).

Other Activities. Mr. Mann served as a volunteer with the Cartoonists Unit, entertaining the troops on USO tours.

Recreation. Cooking, music, drawing, languages, traveling, and real estate.

MANN, PAUL. Actor, director, acting teacher, educator. b. Yisrol Paul Mann Liebmann, Dec. 2, 1915, Toronto, Ontario, Canada, to Charles and Rose (Rachel Steinbok) Liebmann. Studied for the theatre at The Neighborhood Playhouse Studios, N.Y.C., 1932–34; The Group Theatre Studio, N.Y.C., 1937; The Michael Chekhov Studio, N.Y.C. Married Dec. 21, 1958, to Frances Rainer (marr. dis.), actress; married to Leonore Harris, speech coach and actress. Served WW II, OWI. Relative in theatre: brother, Larry Mann, actor. Member of AEA; SAG; AFTRA.

Theatre. Mr. Mann made his professional debut, billed as Yisrol Libman, in the roles of a Messenger and a Financier in a pre-Bway tryout of *Bring on the Girls* (closed National, Washington, D.C., Oct. 1934); made his first Bway appearance, billed as Paul Mann, in the role of the Second Man and, billed as Yisrol Libman, in the role of a Woodcutter in a Neighborhood Playhouse production of *Bitter Oleander* (Lyceum, Feb. 11, 1935); billed as Yisrol Libman, he appeared as a Member of the Delegation and one of the Chorus of the Unemployed in *Panic* (Imperial, Mar. 14, 1935); appeared with the Modern Dance Group and was one of the principals in the revue *Parade* (Guild, May 20, 1935); played the Guard in *The Green Bundle* and Bob Ingersoll in *The Crime,* a double-bill produced by the Theatre of Action (Civic Repertory Th., Mar. 1, 1936); Edstaston in a Federal Th. (WPA) Project production of *The Great Catherine* (Experimental Th., May 13, 1936); and danced the role of the Judge in the Charles Weidman production of *Candide* (Federal Dance Th., June 19, 1936).

Billed as Paul Mann, he played an Orderly and the German Priest in the Theatre Guild production of *Johnny Johnson* (44 St. Th., Nov. 19, 1936); toured as Killer Mears in *The Last Mile* (1936); appeared as George in a pre-Bway tryout of *The White-Haired Boy* (opened Plymouth, Boston,

Mass., Oct. 28, 1940; closed there Nov. 2, 1940); played Thomas Hickey in *Flight to the West* (Guild, N.Y.C., Dec. 30, 1940); appeared at the Studio Th. of the New Sch. for Social Research as Ottfried in *The Criminals*(Dec. 20, 1941) and as Prince Anatole Kuragin in *War and Peace* (May 21, 1942); with the Michael Chekhov Th. Co., played the Gangster in *Afton Water* (Elmhirst Th., Ridgefield, Conn., Aug. 15, 1942); appeared in a pre-Bway tryout of *Dancing in the Streets* (opened Shubert, Boston, Mar. 23, 1943; closed there Apr. 10, 1943); and succeeded (May 1947) Sanford Meisner in the role of Sergei Sinitsin in *The Whole World Over* (Biltmore, N.Y.C., Mar. 27, 1947). He was one of the founders of the New Stages Co., and played Father Firenzuola in *Lamp at Midnight* (New Stages Th., Dec. 21, 1947); appeared as a Murderer and Menteith in Michael Redgrave's production of *Macbeth* (National, Mar. 31, 1948); played the Doctor in *Bruno and Sidney* (New Stages Th., May 3, 1949); directed an ELT double-bill, *Plant in the Sun* and *Private Hicks* (Greenwich Mews Th., May 18, 1949); played Stefan Freund in *Flight into Egypt* (Music Box, Mar. 18, 1952); Japie Grobler in *Too Late the Phalarope* (Belasco, Oct. 11, 1956); and the Emperor Augustus in *The Golden Six* (York Playhouse, Oct. 25, 1958.

With the Repertory Th. of Lincoln Center at the ANTA-Washington Square Th., Mr. Mann played the Father in *After the Fall* (Jan. 23, 1964), Vermandero in *The Changeling* (Oct. 29, 1964) and Merchand in *Incident at Vichy* (Dec. 3, 1964); with that company at the Vivian Beaumont Th., played Collot d'Herbois in *Danton's Death* (Oct. 21, 1965); and The Fat Prince in *The Caucasian Chalk Circle* (Mar. 24, 1966); and appeared in *The Inspector General* (Arena Stage, Washington, D.C., Feb. 23, 1967). He was also director of the actors' training program for the Repertory Th. of Lincoln Center.

Films. Mr. Mann played the Father in *America America* (WB, 1963); and appeared in *Fiddler on the Roof* (UA, 1971).

Radio. He has been heard on many major dramatic radio programs, including The Philip Morris Playhouse (CBS, 1941–43); The Tallulah Bankhead series (CBS, 1942); and Columbia Presents Corwin (CBS, 1944).

Other Activities. Mr. Mann is professor of theatre in the Theatre Arts Dept., and artistic director of the Leonard Davis Center for the Performing Arts, City College of the City Univ. of N.Y. (1975–to date).

He has conducted classes for professional actors since 1949 and in 1953 founded the Paul Mann Actors Workshop, where he directed experimental productions using professional actors. He was founder and donor of scholarships in acting for Negro students, called the Ira Aldridge-Rose McClendon Memorial Scholarships, which were given through his school (1949–64); and was a delegate to the national convention of AFRA (Cleveland, Ohio, Aug. 25–27, 1944). In 1960 he was invited by the national centers of The International Theatre Institute (UNESCO) to lecture and study theatre techniques in Russia, Poland, and East and West Germany; in 1962 he was invited to Bulgaria, Yugoslavia, Romania, and Poland. He has lectured at Columbia Univ. Brander Matthews Dramatic Museum (1961); and has toured midwestern universities and colleges for ANTA. He has lectured and served as artistic consultant on the training of the actor at Stanford Univ., San Francisco Actors Workshop, and the Arena Stage in Washington, D.C.

Awards. In 1960, he was made an honorary member of the All-Russian Theatre Society (BTO); and an honorary member of the West German Genossenschaft Deutscher Bühnen Angehorigen and received its Silver Medallion (1960); received the Chekhov Medallion and the Sea Gull Medallion from the Moscow Art Theatre (1960); and the All-Russian Theatre Society's Stanislavsky Centennial Medallion (1962).

Recreation. Photography.

MANN, THEODORE. Producer, director. b. Theodore David Mann, May 13, 1924, Brooklyn, N.Y. to Martin M. and Qwen Goldman. Father, lawyer. Grad. Erasmus Hall H.S., Bklyn.; attended New York Univ.; grad Salinas Junior Coll. A.A.; Brooklyn Coll., LLB. Served USAF, 1943–45; rank, Sgt. Married Oct. 11, 1953, to Patricia Brooks, opera singer; two sons. Member of League of Off-Bway Theatres (bd. of dir.); League of NY Theatres.

Theatre. Mr. Mann produced *Alice in Wonderland* (Maverick Players, Woodstock, N.Y., Summer 1950).

Since 1950, he has been a producer at the Circle in the Square (N.Y.C.), where he has directed *Dark of the Moon* (Dec. 1950), *Amata* (1951), *The Enchanted* (June 1951), *Bonds of Interest* (1951), *Antigone* (1951), *The Cruelist Month* (July 1951), *Summer and Smoke* (Mar. 1952), *Burning Bright* (Sept. 1952), *Yerma* (1952), *Fortress of Glass* (1952), and *The Grass Harp* (Apr. 27, 1953).

He produced *Legend of Lovers* (Philadelphia, Pa., 1953); and at the Circle in the Square, produced *American Gothic* (Nov. 1953), *The Girl on the Via Flaminia* (Feb. 9, 1954; moved to 48 St. Th. Apr. 1, 1954), *The King and the Duke* (1955), and *La Ronde* (1955).

He was stage manager for *Once Upon a Tailor* (Cort, May 23, 1955); with Jose Quintero and Leigh Connell, produced *The Cradle Song* (Circle in the Square, Dec. 1, 1955); was associate producer of *The Innkeepers* (John Golden Th., Feb. 2, 1956); with Jose Quintero and Leigh Connell, produced *The Iceman Cometh* (Circle in the Square, May 8, 1956); *Long Day's Journey into Night* (Helen Hayes Th., Nov. 7, 1956); *Children of Darkness* (Circle in the Square, Feb. 28, 1958). Circle in the Square, and Banner Productions presented *The Quare Fellow* (Nov. 22, 1958); at the Circle in the Square, with Mr. Quintero and Mr. Connell, he presented *Our Town* (Mar. 23, 1959) and with Lucille Lortel, *The Balcony* (Mar. 3, 1956); he produced *Camino Real* (St. Mark's Playhouse, May 16, 1960); with Jose Quintero, produced *Under Milk Wood* (Circle in the Square, Mar. 29, 1961); and with George Kogel, produced *Smiling the Boy Fell Dead* (Cherry Lane, Apr. 19, 1961). He directed *The Fantasticks* (Bucks County Playhouse, New Hope, Pa., Summer 1961). With Mr. Quintero, produced *Plays for Bleecker Street*, three one-act works by Thornton Wilder; *Infancy*, *Childhood*, and *Someone from Assisi* (Circle in the Square, Jan. 11, 1962), and *Pullman Car Hiawatha* (1962); with the Th. of Michigan Co., he produced *General Seeger* (Lyceum, Feb. 28, 1962); and with Th. of Michigan and George C. Scott, produced *Great Day in the Morning* (Henry Miller's Th., Mar. 28, 1962). He directed *Period of Adjustment*, and *Gypsy* (Gateway Playhouse, Bellport, N.Y., Summer 1962), and *A Taste of Honey* Williamstown, Mass., 1962). With Mr. Quintero, he produced *Desire Under the Elms* (Circle in the Square, Jan. 8, 1963); and with Claude Geroux, *Six Characters in Search of an Author* (Martinique, Mar. 8, 1963). He directed *Pygmalion* (Casino-in-the-Park, Holyoke, Mass., Summer 1963); in association with Will B. Sandler, he produced *Trumpets of the Lord* (Astor Place Playhouse, N.Y.C., 1963); and produced *The Trojan Women* (Circle in the Square, Dec. 1963).

Mr. Mann, with Paul Libin, produced the NY Shakespeare Festival production of *Othello* (Martinique, N.Y.C., Oct. 12, 1964); with Joseph E. Levine, in association with Katzka-Berne Productions, produced *Hughie* (Royale, Dec. 22, 1964); and *And Things That Go Bump in the Night* (Royale, Apr. 26, 1965); with Paul Libin, presented *Bael* (Martinique, May 6, 1965); directed *Fidelio* (Playhouse-on-the-Mall, Paramus, N.J., July 20, 1965); with Howard J. Zuker in association with Frank Cassidy, presented the Theatre Co. of Boston production of *Live Like Pigs* (Actors' Playhouse, N.Y.C., June 7, 1965); co-produced *The Royal Hunt of the Sun* (ANTA, Oct. 26, 1965); with Dore Schary, produced *The Zulu and the Zayda* (Cort, Nov. 10, 1965); and produced *The White Devil* (Circle in the Square, Dec. 6, 1965). Joined by Paul Libin, managing director, Mr. Mann, as artistic director of Circle in the Square, presented *Six from La Mama* (Martinique, Apr. 11, and 12, 1966); *Eh?* (Circle in the Square, Oct. 16, 1966); *Drums in the Night* (Circle in the Square, May 17, 1967); *A Midsummer Night's Dream* (Th. de Lys, June 29, 1967); *Iphigenia in Aulis* (Circle in the Square, Nov. 21, 1967); produced and directed *A Moon for the Misbegotten* (Circle in the Square, June 12, 1968); *Morning, Noon and Night* (Henry Miller's Th., Nov. 28, 1968); and *Trumpets of the Lord* (Brooks Atkinson Th., Apr. 29, 1969).

At Circle in the Square, they produced *Little Murders* (Jan. 5, 1969); *Seven Days of Mourning* (Dec. 16, 1969); and *The White House Murder Case* (Feb. 18, 1970); subsequently produced *Chicago 70* (Martinique, May 25, 1970); and *Circle in the Square at Ford's Theatre* (Washington, D.C., Oct. 14, 1969 – Apr. 26, 1970), presenting *Ah, Wilderness!*, *Iphigenia in Aulis*, *Max Marath at the Turn of the Century*, and *The Fantasticks*; in association with John Berry, produced *Boesman and Lean* (Circle in the Square, June 22, 1970); produced *Circle in the Square at Ford's Theatre* (Washington, D.C., Sept. 15, 1970 – May 31, 1971), presenting *Will Rogers' USA*, *Arsenic and Old Lace*, *Festival at Ford's*, *John and Abigail*, *Max Marath at the Turn of the Century*, and *You're a Good Man, Charlie Brown*; and *The Last Analysis* (Circle in the Square, June 23, 1971), which Mr. Mann directed. He directed, and with G. Wood, wrote *F. Jasmine Adams* (Circle in the Square, Oct. 27, 1971), a musical adaptation of *The Member of the Wedding*.

At the new Joseph E. Levine Th., Circle in the Square (Paul Libin, managing director; Theodore Mann Artistic director) produced, and Mr. Mann directed, *Mourning Becomes Electra* (Nov. 15, 1972); subsequently produced *Medea* (Jan. 17, 1973); *Here Are Ladies*, an evening with Siobhan McKenna (Mar. 29, 1973); *Uncle Vanya* (June 4, 1973); *The Waltz of the Toreadors* (Sept. 13, 1973); and, directed by Mr. Mann, *The Iceman Cometh* (Dec. 13, 1973); and *An American Millionaire* (Apr. 20, 1974). The company presented the National Theatre of Great Britain's The Young Vic production of *Scapino* (May 19, 1974); produced a touring production of *The Waltz of the Toreadors* (opened Mechanic, Baltimore, Jan. 6, 1974; closed Huntington Hartford Th., Los Angeles, Apr. 21, 1974); at the Joseph E. Levine Th., presented The Long Wharf Th. production of *The National Health* (Oct. 10, 1974); produced *Where's Charley?*, directed by Mr. Mann (Dec. 20, 1974); produced *All God's Chillun Got Wings* (Mar. 20, 1975); *Death of a Salesman* (June 26, 1975); *Ah, Wilderness!* (Sept. 18, 1975); and *The Glass Menagerie* (Dec. 18, 1975), which Mr. Mann directed.

In addition, Mr. Mann has been a guest director with The Theater Co. of Boston (1967–68 season); and with The Dallas Theatre Center (1969–70 season).

Films. Mr. Mann, with Howard B. Kreitsek, produced *The Illustrated Man* (WB-7 Arts, 1969); and served as executive producer for *Buster and Billie* (Col., 1974).

Awards. The Circle in the Square received the Vernon Rice Award for its production of *The Iceman Cometh* (1956); and the theatre received the Page One Award (1961), and the *Village Voice* Off-Bway (Obie) Award for its production of *Six Characters in Search of an Author* (1962); and a congressional citation (1962).

Recreation. Tennis, basketball, baseball, script-reading.

MANNING, IRENE. Actress, singer, writer. b. Inez Harvuot, July 17, 1918, Cincinnati, Ohio, to Shirley Errett and Inez (Dunham) Harvuot. Father, real estate broker. Grad. Los Angeles (Calif.) H.S., 1935; Eastman Sch. of Music, B.A. 1939. Studied voice with Adelin Fermin and Emanuel Balaban, Rochester, N.Y., 1934–39; Yeatman Griffith, Los Angeles, 1940–41; Nina Davis Reynolds, London, Eng., 1948–51. Married May 29, 1940, to Het Manheim, television producer, writer (marr. dis. 1944); married Oct. 7, 1949, to Clinton Green (marr. dis. 1951); married Feb. 1, 1964, to

Maxwell W. Hunter, II, engineer. Relative in theatre: cousin, Clifford Harvuot, singer. Member of AEA; AFTRA; SAG; AGVA.

Theatre. Miss Manning made her debut as Margot in *The Desert Song* (Auditorium, Rochester, N.Y., Apr. 1939) and appeared in minor roles in summer productions at the St. Louis (Mo.) Municipal Opera (1939); billed as Hope Manning, she sang leading roles in *The Gypsy Baron, H.M.S. Pinafore, The Chocolate Soldier,* and *The Merry Widow* (Los Angeles Civic Light Opera Co., Summers 1939–41); and, as Irene Manning, toured England with her own four girl troupe for the USO (Nov. 1944–Feb. 1945).

She made her N.Y.C. debut as Katharine Townsend in *The Day Before Spring*(Natl., Nov. 22, 1945); for the Los Angeles Civic Light Opera Co., sang the title roles in *Rose Marie* 1946) and *Rosalinda* (May 1947); sang a leading role in *Ballaleika* (Pittsburgh Light Opera, Pa., June 1947); made her London debut as Jeanne in *The Dubarry* (Prince's, Oct. 8, 1947); toured English music halls in a variety act (Spring 1948); played Eleanor Barrett in *Serenade* (Empire, Edinburgh, Scotland, Aug. 1948); Mrs. Dunne in *Castle in the Air* (Adelphi, London, Dec. 7, 1949); toured the US as Mrs. Frayne in *The Second Man* (Mar.–Apr. 1952); played Vera Simpson in *Pal Joey* (Oakdale Music Th., Wallingford, Conn., July 1954; Circle Arts Th., San Diego, Calif., 1961); toured summer theatres in it (1962); toured summer musical tents as Anna in *The King and I* (1956); played this role at the Carousel Th. (Framingham, Mass., Sept. 8, 1958); toured summer theatres in *Holiday for Lovers* (May–Sept. 1958); appeared in it at the Palm Beach (Fla.) Music Th. (Jan.–Feb. 1959); played Ella, Countess Nattontorini, in *The Tattooed Countess*(Barbizon-Plaza Th., N.Y.C., Apr. 3, 1961), and Opal in *Everybody Loves Opal* (Saratoga Playhouse, Fla., Feb. 1962).

Films. Miss Manning made her debut as Fay Templeton in *Yankee Doodle Dandy* (WB, 1942); followed by the Warner Brothers films: *The Big Shot* (1942); *Spy Ship* (1942); *The Desert Song* (1943); *Shine on, Harvest Moon* (1944); *Make Your Own Bed* (1944); *The Doughgirls*(1944); and *Escape in the Desert*(1945); and appeared in *I Live in Grosvenor Square* (Rank, 1945).

Television and Radio. She performed on her own radio program in London. An American in England (BBC, 1951), and in the US, performed on a variety program (NBC, Aug. 1948), and in the series Mr. Broadway (1952).

On television, she played Mrs. Dodsworth in *Dodsworth* (CBS, 1963); and appeared in *The King and Mrs. Candle* (CBS, 1955).

Night Clubs. Miss Manning sang at the Casino Nacional (Havana, Cuba, 1940); Persian Room (Plaza Hotel, N.Y.C., 1941); and the Colony and Astor Clubs (London, July–Aug. 1953).

Other Activities. She wrote a newspaper column, "Girl About Town," for *Show Business*, London (1949–51); as an abstract expressionist painter, has exhibited her works in N.Y.C. and Washington, D.C. (1962–64).

MANNING, JACK. Actor, director, teacher. b. Jack Wilson Manning Marks, June 3, 1916, Cincinnati, Ohio, to J. L. and Irma (Davis) Marks. Grad. Hughes H.S., Cincinnati, 1934; Univ. of Cincinnati, B.A. 1938. Studied acting with Benno Schneider, N.Y.C., 1939; voice with Leola Lucey, 1944; acting with Robert Lewis, 1953, Harold Clurman, 1956; and speech with Marian Rich, 1955. Married Aug. 16, 1940, to Virginia Schuchardt; one daughter, Gale, television actress. Member of AEA; SAG; AFTRA; Omicron Delta Kappa; Sophos.

Theatre. Mr. Manning first appeared in stock with the New London (N.H.) Players, as George in *Our Town,* and Ed in *You Can't Take It with You* (June 1939). He first appeared in N.Y.C. as Albert Kunody in *Junior Miss* (Lyceum Th., Nov. 18, 1941); subsequently as Arthur Crochet in *The Great Big Doorstep* (Morosco, Nov. 26, 1942); Freddie Stowe in *Harriet*(Henry Miller's Th., Mar. 3, 1943); Roderigo in *Othello* (Shubert, Oct. 19, 1943); Choppy in *The Streets Are Guarded* (Henry Miller's Th., Nov. 20, 1944); Luther Cudworth in *The Mermaids Singing* (Empire, Nov. 28, 1945); Lee in *O'Daniel* (Princess, Feb. 23, 1947); Tweedle Dee and the Gryphon in the Amer. Repertory Th. production of *Alice in Wonderland* (International, Apr. 5, 1947); and Cockles in *Rip Van Winkle* (NY City Ctr., July 15, 1947).

He played Henry Straker in *Man and Superman* (Alvin, Oct. 8, 1947); Frank Gardner in *Mrs. Warren's Profession*(Bleecker St. Th., Oct. 3, 1950); Midshipman Gardner in *Billy Budd* (Biltmore, Feb. 10, 1951); Og (a Leprechaun) in a touring production of *Finian's Rainbow* (July–Aug. 1953). In Sept. 1954, he founded the Helen Hayes Equity Group in N.Y.C., later called the Helen Hayes Repertory Co., for which he directed plays including *Separate Tables, What Every Woman Knows, The Bear, As You Like It, Julius Caesar,* and *Write Me a Murder.* These were presented (1954–55) at colleges and universities, in the ANTA series (Th. de Lys, N.Y.C.), and at the John Drew Theatre (East Hampton, N.Y.).

In N.Y.C., he played Earl Lindquist in *The Tender Trap*(Longacre, Oct. 13, 1954); directed *Twelfth Night* (Brooklyn Acad. of Music, Oct. 10, 1955), *Macbeth* (Jan Hus House, Oct. 19, 1955), and *Othello* in which he also played Iago (Brooklyn Acad. of Music, Feb. 10, 1956). At the Ivy Tower Th. (Spring Lake, N.J.) he directed stock production of *Anyone for Love* (July 10, 1957), *The Reluctant Debutante* (July 17, 1957), and *Anastasia* (July 24, 1957). He played Pilot Roy Peters and was the standby for David Wayne in the role of Jack Jordan in *Say, Darling* (ANTA, N.Y.C. Apr. 3, 1958); directed a summer-theatre production of *Say, Darling* (Colonie Summer Th., Latham, N.Y., July 4, 1958); *Othello* (Washington Sq. Playhouse, N.Y.C. Nov. 15, 1960); and a production of *Lovers, Villains, and Fools*(Fulton Opera House, Lancaster, Pa., Apr. 12, 1964).

Mr. Manning played Mr. McIllhenny in *Do I Hear a Waltz?* (46 St. Th., N.Y.C., Mar. 18, 1965); directed the Helen Hayes Repertory Co. productions of *Lovers, Villains and Fools,* and *The Circle* (tour, Spring 1966); produced the first Bermuda Festival of the Arts (1967); and appeared in *The Little Foxes* (tour, 1967); and, with the Center Th. Group, *The Time of the Cuckoo* (Ahmanson Th., Los Angeles, 1973–74 season).

Films. Mr. Manning has appeared in *Walk East on Beacon* (Col., 1952); *The Owl and the Pussycat* (Col., 1970); *The Great Northfield Minnesota Raid* (U, 1972); *Melinda* (MGM, 1972); *The Thief Who Came to Dinner* (WB, 1973); and *Superdad* (BV, 1974).

Television and Radio. Since 1939, he has performed on radio programs including Mr. District Attorney, Theatre Guild on the Air, Cavalcade, Columbia Workshop, and World's Great Novels.

On television, he played the title role in *Hamlet* (Dumont, Jan. 5, 1953); Brutus in *Julius Caesar* (Dumont, Feb. 5, 1953); Sidney Carton in *A Tale of Two Cities*(Dumont, Feb. 19, 1953); Pip in *Great Expectations* (Dumont, Mar. 1, 1953). He directed Spotlight, a thirteen-week series of plays which included *Carmen in Harlem* and *Alice in Wonderland* (WOR-TV, 1954).

Other Activities. Since 1953, Mr. Manning has conducted acting classes at the Jack Manning Acting Laboratory and Theatre.

Awards. Mr. Manning received a *Variety* Award for his television show, Spotlight (1954).

Recreation. Swimming, collecting theatre books, gardening (Japanese gardens).

MANSFIELD, PORTIA. Educator. b. Nov. 17, 1887, Chicago, Ill., to Edward Ricker and Myra (Mansfield) Swett. Grad. Smith Coll. B.A. 1910; New York Univ., M.A. 1933; Ed. D. 1953. Member of Amer. Camping Assn. (pres., 1936); Western Assn. of Independent Camps. Address: (summer) Strawberry Park, Steamboat Springs, CO 80477; (winter), Box 4056, Carmel, CA 93921.

Since 1914, Miss Mansfield has been director, with Charlotte Perry, of the Perry-Mansfield Th. Sch. at Steamboat Springs, Colo., which operates during the Summer from June 28 to Aug. 19, and which, in 1964 became affiliated with Stephens Coll. At the school, she taught basic movement, ballet and modern. She first performed as a member of Pavley-Oukrainsky Ballet Co. (1914); later, in association with Charlotte Perry, organized the Perry-Mansfield Dancers and as director, conductor, and choreographer, toured with the dance companies in concert and on the Keith, Orpheum, and Pantages vaudeville circuits (1920–26).

She subsequently taught at Peabody Conservatory (Baltimore, Md.,) where she was director of dance.

After sixty years of co-directing and managing the school of theatre and dance, Miss Mansfield is now retired from active work in the theatre.

Films. She has made a series of color-sound films on the dance and horsemanship. In 1972 she commissioned the mountaineering film, *And the Ground Below,* shown in film festivals in Europe and Iran.

Other Activities. Miss Mansfield has been deeply interested in the outdoor life, and formed, in association with Charlotte Perry, the Perry-Mansfield Boys Camp, and School of Mountaineering, and the Perry-Mansfield School of Horsemanship.

Published Works. Miss Mansfield, in association with Louis Horst, has written six volumes of exercises in basic movement, *Dance and Rhythmic Body Mechanics* (1948–58).

Awards. She is rhe recipient of an award from Gov. John Love for leadership in the arts in Colorado (1971); and of the National Honor Award for leadership in camping (1974); and she has been honored by the Northern California section of ACA for pioneering in camping. She received the Golden Eagle award for her film on mountaineering, *And the Ground Below.*

Recreation. Travel, theatre, films, dance concerts.

MARASCO, ROBERT. Playwright. b. 1937, Bronx, N.Y. Grad. Fordham Univ.

Pre-Theatre. Copy-boy for the *New Yorker;* teacher.

Theatre. Mr. Marasco made his playwrighting debut with *Child's Play* (Royale, N.Y.C., Feb. 17, 1970).

Films. He has written the screenplays for *Child's Play* (Par., 1972); and *Burnt Offerings.*.

Published Works. Mr. Marasco is the author of the novel *Burnt Offerings* (1973).

Awards. The *Variety* Poll of NY Drama Critics named Mr. Marasco "most promising playwright" (1969–70) for *Child's Play.*.

MARCEAU, FELICIEN. Playwright, writer. b. Louis Albert Carette, Sept. 16, 1913, Cortenberg, Belgium, to Louis and Marie (Lefevre) Carette. Father, civil official. Attended Univ. of Louvain (Belgium) Sch. of Law, 1936. Married Dec. 30, 1953, to Bianca Licenziati. Member of Société Française des Auteurs; Dramatists Guild. Address: c/o Editions Gallimard, 5 Rue Sébastien-Bottin, Paris 7e, France.

Theatre. Mr.Marceau wrote the one-act play, *L'École des moroses* ("The School of Moroses") (Th. Hébertot, Paris, Fr., Oct. 10, 1952); subsequently wrote *Caterina*(Th. de l'Atelier, Oct. 20, 1954); *L'Oeuf*("The Egg") (Th. de l'Atelier, Dec. 18, 1956), which was translated by Robert Schlitt and presented (Cort, N.Y.C., Jan. 8, 1962); *La bonne soupe* ("The Good Soup") (Th. du Gymnase, Paris, Oct. 1, 1958), which was adapted and directed by Garson Kanin (Plymouth, N.Y.C., Mar. 2, 1960); *L'Étouffe-Chrétien* ("Nero") (Th. de la Renaissance, Paris, Oct. 31, 1960); *Les cailloux* ("The *Pebbles*") (Th. de L'Atelier, Jan. 27, 1962); *La preuve par quatre*("The Proof by Four") (Th. de la Michodière, Feb. 3, 1964); *Madame Princesse* (Th. du Gymnase, Sept. 3, 1965); *Un jour j'ai rencontré la vérité* ("One Day I Found the Truth") (Th. Comédie des Champs-Elysées, Jan. 21, 1967); *Le Babour* ("The Baby") (Th. de l'Atelier, Sept. 20, 1969); *L'Ouvre-boîte*("The Can Opener") (Th. de l'Oeuvre, Sept. 28, 1972); and *L'Homme en question* ("The Man in Question") (Th. de l'Atelier, Nov. 3, 1973).

Published Works. Mr. Marceau wrote the novelettes, *En de secretes noces* ("In Secret Nuptial") (1963); and *Les belles natures* ("The Good Kind") (1954); and the following novels: *Chasseneuil* ("By Invitation Only") (1948), translated by Arthur Rhodes; *Chair et cuir* ("The Flesh in the Mirror") (1951), translated by Margaret Crosland; *Capri petite ile* ("Capri, Little Island") (1951); *L'Homme du roi* ("The King's Man") (1952), translated by David Hughes and M. J. Mason; *Bergère légère* ("The China Shepherdess") (1953), translated by David Hughes and M. J. Mason; *Les élans du coeur* ("Heart Flights") (1955), translated by David Hughes and M. J. Mason; and *Creezy* ("Creezy ") (1969), translated by J. A. Underwood.

He has also written the essays, *Casanova ou l'anti-Don Juan* ("Casanova Against Don Juan") (1948); and *Balzac et son monde* ("Balzac and His World") (1955), translated by Derek Coltman; wrote, with Jean Giono and Georges Pillement, *Rome I Love* (1950); and wrote his memoirs, *Les années courtes* ("The Fleeting Years") (1968).

Awards. M. Marceau was awarded the 1969 Prix Goncourt for *Creezy.*.

MARCEAU, MARCEL. Mime. b. Mar. 22, 1923, Strasbourg, France, to Charles and Anne (Werzberg) Mangel. Attended Lycée de Strasbourg; Ecole d'arts Decoratifs. Studied with Charles Dullen and Etienne Decroux. Married to Huguette Malle, actress; two sons. Served WW II, French underground movement. Address: 14 rue Saussure, Paris 17, France.

Theatre. M. Marceau first appeared in Paris with the Renaud-Barrault Co. as Arlequin in *Baptiste* (Th. Maigny, 1946); and appeared in *Praxitele and the Golden Fish* (Sarah Bernhardt Th., 1946).

In 1947, he formed his own company, the Compagnie de Mime Marcel Marceau, and in his first program presented *Bip Goes to the Park* (Th. de Poche, 1947); later that year the company toured Switzerland, Holland, Belgium and Italy; in Paris, M. Marceau presented *Un jardin public* (1949); *Moriana et Galvin* (Th. de Poche, 1950); and *The Overcoat* and *Un Pierrot de Montmartre* (Studio des Champs Elysees, 1951).

M. Marceau played the Devil in his full-length mime, *L'Histoire du Soldat* (Stratford Festival, Avon, Ont., 1955); and made his N.Y.C. debut in *An Evening of Pantomime* (Phoenix, Sept. 20, 1955; moved to Ethel Barrymore Th., Oct. 4, 1955; revived, NY City Ctr., Feb. 1, 1956).

He presented *Mont du Piete,* and *14 Juillet* (Stratford, Summer 1956); an evening of varied mimes entitled *Marcel Marceau and His Partners* (NY City Ctr., Jan. 21, 1958); and performed in *Paris qui rit, Paris qui dort, Les matadors,* and *Le petit cirque* (Stratford, Conn., Summer 1958).

At the Cambridge (Mass.) Drama Festival, M. Marceau and his company presented his mimodrama *The Overcoat* (Aug. 30, 1960). He has returned frequently to the NY City Ctr. (1960; Jan. 1, 1963; Nov. 17, 1965; Apr. 7, 1970; Apr. 17, 1973); and has appeared at the McCarter Th. (Princeton, N.J., Dec. 26, 1962; Oct. 4, 1965).

In Paris, his company offered a program including *Don Juan,* and a "mime parade" (Th. Renaissance, Mar. 23, 1964). In London, appeared at the Adelphi (Aug. 10, 1964). In Los Angeles, at the Huntington Hartford Th. (Dec. 14, 1965). In recent years, he has performed in concert all over the world, with his company as well as solo.

Films. M. Marceau has appeared in film versions of his *Mic-Mac* (1950); *The Overcoat* (1951); *Pantomimes* (1954); and *Un jardin public* (1955). Also, in *Barbarella* (Par., 1968) and *Shanks* (Par., 1974).

Television. He has appeared on a Max Liebman spectacular (NBC, Dec. 4, 1955); the Ed Sullivan Show (CBS, 1956); the Red Skelton Show (CBS, Jan. 31, 1961; Feb. 2, 1965; Jan. 18, 1966); the Victor Borge Show (ABC, Feb. 26, 1963); and the Hollywood Palace Show (ABC, 1965; 1966).

Published Works. M. Marceau has written a book about his most famous mime character, entitled *The Story of Bip.*

Awards. M. Marceau received the Deburan Prize for *Mort avant L'Aube* (1948). In 1955, he received the NATAS ("Emmy") award for "Best Specialty Performer.".

Recreation. Drawing.

MARCHAND, NANCY. Actress. b. June 19, 1928, Buffalo, N.Y., to Raymond L. and Marjorie F. (Freeman) Marchand. Father, dentist; mother, pianist. Grad. Amherst H.S., Buffalo, 1945; Carnegie Inst. of Tech., B.F.A. 1949. Married July 7, 1951, to Paul Sparer; one son, two daughters. Member of AEA; AFTRA; SAG.

Theatre. Miss Marchand made her debut as the Reporter in *The Winslow Boy* (Falmouth Playhouse, Mass., Summer 1949); and her N.Y.C. debut as Hostess of the Tavern and Curtis in *The Taming of the Shrew* (NY City Ctr., Apr. 25, 1951). At the Brattle Th. (Cambridge, Mass.) she played The Princess in *Love's Labour's Lost;* Mrs. Dudgen in *The Devil's Disciple;* Tibueina in *The Critic;* the 1st witch in *Macbeth;* and Regan in *King Lear* (Summers 1950–52).

At the N.Y. City Center, she played the Princess of France in *Love's Labour's Lost* (Feb. 4, 1953) and Nerissa in *The Merchant of Venice* (Mar. 4, 1953); at the Antioch (Ohio) Shakespeare Festival, appeared as Kate in *The Taming of the Shrew;* the Nurse in *Romeo and Juliet;* and Amelia in *Othello* (Summer 1954). At the American Shakespeare Festival (Stratford, Conn.) played Paulina in *The Winter's Tale* (July 20, 1958); and Mistress Page in *The Merry Wives of Windsor* (July 8, 1959).

She appeared as Ursula in *Much Ado About Nothing* (Lunt-Fontanne, N.Y.C., Sept. 17, 1959); Irma in *The Balcony* (Circle-in-the-Square, Mar. 3, 1960); and with the association of Producing Artists (APA), at the Folksbiene Playhouse, N.Y.C., Lady Sneerwell in *The School for Scandal* (Mar. 17, 1962); and Irina Arkadina in *The Seagull* (Mar. 21, 1962); with the APA in Ann Arbor, Mich., she played Beatrice in *Much Ado About Nothing,* Amalia in *Right You Are,* and Vassilissa Karpovna in *The Lower Depths* (Winter 1963); and at the Phoenix Th., N.Y.C., Amalia in *Right You Are* (Mar. 4, 1964); the Woman in *The Tavern* (Mar. 5, 1964); and Vassilissa Karpovna in *The Lower Depths* (Mar. 30, 1964); also for the APA, she played Ann Whitefield in *Man and Superman* (Ann Arbor, Mich., Oct. 28, 1964; Phoenix, N.Y.C., Dec. 7, 1964).

Miss Marchand played The Old Lady in *Good Day* (Cherry Lane Th., N.Y.C., Oct. 18, 1965) presented on a double bill with *The Exhaustion of Our Son's Love;* Genevieve in *Three Bags Full* (Henry Miller's Th., Mar. 6, 1966; was one of the Women of Canterbury in *Murder in the Cathedral* (Amer. Shakespeare Fest. Th., Stratford, Conn., June 19, 1966); as a member of the Repertory Th. of Lincoln Center (Vivian Beaumont Th., N.Y.C.), played Dol Common in *The Alchemist* (Oct. 13, 1966), and Dolores in *Yerma* (Dec. 8, 1966); appeared in *The Sorrows of Frederick* (Mark Taper Forum, Los Angeles, June 1967); played Gertrude Forbes-Cooper in *After the Rain* (John Golden Th., N.Y.C., Oct. 9, 1967); The Duenna in Cyrano de Bergerac (Vivian Beaumont Th., Apr. 25, 1968), repeating that role with the Center Theatre Group (Mark Taper Forum, Los Angeles, 1968–69 season); Mrs. Latham in Forty Carats (Morosco, N.Y.C., Dec. 26, 1968); Ceil Adams in *And Miss Reardon Drinks a Little* (Morosco, Feb. 27, 1971); with the Repertory Theatre of Lincoln Center (Vivian Beaumont Th., N.Y.C.), played Queen Elizabeth in *Mary Stuart* (Nov. 1, 1971), Titania in *Enemies* (Nov. 4, 1972), and Bessie Burgess in *The Plough and the Stars* (Jan. 4, 1973); appeared in *Pal Joey* (Goodman Th. Ctr., Chicago, 1972–73 season); and was standby for Eileen Heckart as The Woman in *Veronica's Room* (Music Box, N.Y.C., Oct. 25, 1973).

Films. She has appeared in *Me, Natalie* (National General, 1969); *Tell Me That You Love Me, Junie Moon* (Par., 1970); and *The Hospital* (UA, 1971).

Television. Miss Marchand's appearances include The Defenders (CBS); Naked City (Ind.); The Southern Baptist Hour (NBC); Directions '66 (ABC); NYPD (ABC); Ana in *Don Juan in Hell* (Ind.); Vassilissa in *The Lower Depths* (NET); Elizabeth the Queen in *Dark Lady of the Sonnets* (NET); and Beacon Hill (CBS).

MARECHAL, JUDITH RUTHERFORD. Producer. b. Judith Rutherford, May 28, 1937, Worcester, Mass., to Richard James and Mildred Amanda (Horney) Rutherford. Father, pres. of Worcester Gas Co. Grad. Worcester (Mass) Classical H.S., 1955; Vassar Coll., B.A. 1959. Married Dec. 2, 1961, to Kelsey Marechal (marr. dis. Jan. 7, 1964). Member of League of Off-Bway Theatres and Producers (exec. comm., 1963–64).

Theatre. Mrs. Marechal first worked in the theatre as asst. to the casting director at the David Merrick office (Oct. 1959–Jan. 1960); subsequently was secretary to the producers, Theodore Mann and Jose Quintero, at the Circle in the Square Th. (Jan.–Oct. 1960).

She produced *Call Me By My Rightful Name* (One Sheridan Square Th., Jan. 31, 1961); produced with Ulu Grosbard, *The Days and Nights of Beebee Fenstermaker* (Sheridan Square Playhouse, Sept. 17, 1962); and presented *Cages* (York Playhouse, June 13, 1963). She produced *In White America* (Sheridan Square Playhouse, Oct. 31, 1963), co-produced it in London (New Arts Th., Nov. 16, 1964), and with Paul Libin presented a tour (opened Plainfield, N.J., Jan. 27, 1965; closed Mount Vernon, N.Y., May 15, 1965) and revival production of it in N.Y.C. (Players Th., May 18, 1965); she presented, with Josephine Forrestal and Seymour Litvinoff, *Leonard Bernstein's Theatre Songs* (Th. de Lys, June 28, 1965); presented, with Konrad Matthaei, in assn. with Jay Stanwyck, *An Evening's Frost* (Th. de Lys, Oct. 11, 1965); and presented, with Paul Libin and Jay Stanwyck, *Medea* (Martinique, Nov. 28, 1965).

Awards. She received the Margo Jones Award for her "encouragement of new playwrights" (1964).

MARGO. Actress, singer, dancer. b. Maria Margarita Guadalupe Bolado y Castilla, May 10, 1920, Mexico City, Mexico, to Emilio Bolado and Maria Castilla de Bolado. Studied dancing with Eduardo Cansino. Married Dec. 5, 1945, to Eddie Albert, actor; one son, one daughter. Served on bond tours and entertained troops in US, WW II. Relative in theatre: aunt, Carmen Castillo, singer. Member of AEA; SAG; AGVA.

Theatre. Margo made her stage debut at ten, singing and dancing at community affairs and at the Mexico Th., Los Angeles, Calif.

She made her N.Y.C. debut as Miriamne in *Winterset* (Martin Beck Th., Sept. 25, 1935); subsequently appeared as the Baroness in *Masque of Kings* (Shubert, Feb. 8, 1937); Virginia McKay in *The World We Make* (Guild, Nov. 20, 1939); and in dance concerts at the National Th. (Mexico City, Mexico, 1940).

She played Hessie McMorwa in *Tanyard Street* (Little Th., N.Y.C., Feb. 4, 1941); Tina in *A Bell for Adano* (Cort, Dec. 6, 1944); Bella Mannigham in *Angel Street* (Mexico City); and has appeared in summer stock as Lizzie McKaye in *The Respectful Prostitute* (1950), *Faust* and *Seventh Heaven.*.

Films. Margo made her debut at 15, as Carmen Brown in *Crime without Passion* (Par., 1934); subsequently appeared in *Rumba* (Par., 1935); *Robin Hood of El Dorado* (MGM, 1936); Miriamne in *Winterset* (RKO, 1936); *Lost Horizon* (Col., 1937); *Miracle of Main Street* (Col., 1940); *Behind the Rising Sun* (RKO, 1943); *Gangway for Tomorrow* (RKO, 1943); *The Leopard Man* (RKO, 1943); *Viva Zapata!* (20th-Fox, 1952); *I'll Cry Tomorrow* (MGM, 1955); *From Hell to Texas* (20th-Fox, 1958); and *Who's Got the Action?* (Par., 1963).

Television and Radio. On radio, Margo has performed on the *Camel Hour* (1942); and during Ww II was selected by the US government to make a series of goodwill shortwave broadcasts to South America. On television, she has appeared on the Ed Sullivan Show (CBS); the Steve Allen Show (NBC); Wagon Train (NBC); Westinghouse-Desilu Playhouse (CBS); Chevrolet Show (NBC); and Schlitz Playhouse (CBS).

Night Clubs. Before she was 15, Margo performed at the Cocoanut Grove (Los Angeles, Calif.); subsequently she appeared at the Waldorf-Astoria (N.Y.C.) and with Eddie Albert performed there again (1954); also at the Nautilus (Miami, Fla., 1954); The Last Frontier (Las Vegas, Nev., 1954); and Ciro's (Hollywood, Calif., 1954).

Awards. She received the Achievement Award for Voice, for her appearances on the Camel Hour (1942).

Recreation. Long walks along the ocean, reading, travel, playing musical instruments.

MARGOLIS, HENRY. Producer. b. Henry M. Margolis, Nov. 2, 1909, New York City, to Nathan and Dora (Boverman) Margolis. Grad. City Coll. of New York, B.S. 1929; New York Univ., J.D. 1932. Married Feb. 1, 1940, to Nexhmie Zaimi (marr. dis. 1950); one son; married May 21, 1956, to Irene Broza. Served with U.S.M.C., 1944–45. Member of League of NY Theatres. Address: (home) 785 Park Ave., New York, NY 10021, tel. (212) RE 4-5721; (bus.) 450 Park Ave., New York, NY 10022, tel. (212) PL 3-0636.

Pre-Theatre. Lawyer, industrialist.

Theatre. Mr. Margolis produced, with Martin Gabel, *Reclining Figure* (Lyceum Th., N.Y.C., Oct. 7, 1954); subsequently, with Mr. Gabel, he presented *Moby Dick* (Duke of York's, London, June 16, 1955); was one of the producers of *Tiger at the Gates* (Plymouth, N.Y.C., Oct. 3, 1955); *King Lear* (NY City Ctr., Jan. 12, 1956); with Mr. Gabel, produced *The Hidden River* (Playhouse, Jan. 23, 1957), and *Once More, With Feeling* (Natl., Oct. 21, 1958).

MARGULIES, DAVID. Actor, director, teacher. b. David Joseph Margulies, Feb. 19, 1937, New York City, to Harry D. and Runya Margulies. Father, lawyer. Educ. P.S. 173; J.H.S. 115; School of Performing Arts; De Witt Clinton H.S. (all N.Y.C.); grad. City Coll. of N.Y., B.A. 1958. Professional training at American Shakespeare Festival Acad. (Morris Carnovsky, Phoebe Brand); William Hickey. US Army, 1961–62. Married Mar. 17, 1969, to Carol Grant; one son. Member of AEA; SSD&C; AFTRA; Ensemble Studio Th., N.Y. (exec. bd., 1973–to date). Address: 320 W. 88th St., New York, NY 10024, tel. (212) 595-3491.

Theatre. Mr. Margulies made his theatrical debut as a young child, playing the fourth peddler in *Goldfarden's Dreams* (Shrub Oak Park Community Ctr., N.Y., 1941). He made his first professional appearance as a soldier in Cassio's Army in a NY Shakespeare Festival production of *Othello* (Playhouse in the Park, Philadelphia, Pa., June 1958; Belvedere Lake Th., N.Y.C., Aug. 6, 1958) and his off-Bway debut as Postumus in *The Golden Six* (York Th., Oct. 25, 1958). He was Grimaldi in *'Tis Pity She's a Whore* (Orpheum, Dec. 5, 1958); did walk-ons with the American Shakespeare Festival, Stratford, Conn., in *Romeo and Juliet, A Midsummer Night's Dream,* and *All's Well That Ends Well* (May 19–Sept. 13, 1959); and for American Shakespeare Festival's student season (Spring 1960) was assistant stage manager and the Gaoler, the Old Shepherd, the Mariner, and the Servant in *The Winter's Tale.* He played at Tenthouse Th., Highland Park, Ill., as Freddie in *The Disenchanted* (July 1960) and Orlov in *Who Was That Lady I Saw You With?* (Aug. 1960); and was Philostrate in American Shakespeare Festival's *A Midsummer Night's Dream* (Colonial Th., Boston, Mass., Sept. 1960).

Mr. Margulies was the stage manager and an understudy for *Under Milk Wood* (Circle in the Square, N.Y.C., Mar. 29, 1961); played David in *Six Characters in Search of an Author* (Martinique Th., Mar. 7, 1963); Benjamin in *Thistle in My Bed* (Gramercy Arts Th., Nov. 19, 1963); Sol Stern in *The Tender Trap* (Paper Mill Playhouse, Milburn, N.J.; Mineola, N.Y., Jan. 1964); and Clarin in *Life Is a Dream* (Astor Place Playhouse, N.Y.C., Mar. 17, 1964). He was the Girl's Father in a summer package of *The Fantasticks* (Westport Conn.; Coconut Grove, Fla.; Tappan Zee Playhouse, Nyack, N.Y.; and others, July–Aug. 1964); was the Pope and a Scholar in *The Tragical Historie of Dr. Faustus* (Phoenix Th., N.Y.C., Oct. 5, 1964); played the title role in an Equity Library Th. production of *Lorenzaccio* (Master Th., Mar. 12, 1965); and appeared with the American Conservatory Th., Pittsburgh (Pa.) Playhouse, as the Director in *Six Characters in Search of an Author* (July 28, 1965), Truffaldino in *The Servant of Two Masters* (Sept. 9, 1965), Apollo in *Apollo of Bellac* (Oct. 16, 1965), and Bernard in *Death of a Salesman.* He starred as Eisenring in *The Firebugs* (Studio Arena Th., Buffalo, N.Y., Jan. 6, 1966); was Elbow in *Measure for Measure* (NY Shakespeare Festival, Delacorte Th., N.Y.C., July 12, 1966); and was artistic director, Loft Th., N.Y.C. (Jan.–June 1967). At the Academy Playhouse, Wilmette, Ill., he was Cristoforu in *The Public Eye* (July 1967) and Berenger in *The Rhinoceros* (Aug. 1967). He played Davies in *The Caretaker* (Th. of the Living Arts, Philadelphia, Pa., Oct. 1967); directed *The Oresteia* (Company of the Southwark Th. School, Th. of the Living Arts, Mar. 1968); directed *Next* (Berkshire Th. Festival, Stockbridge, Mass., July 1968); was Arthur in *Tango* (Pocket Th., N.Y.C., Jan. 18, 1969); the Man in *The Man With the Flower in His Mouth* (Sheridan Sq. Playhouse, June 1969); and was Rev. Dupas (July 1969) in *Little Murders* (Circle in the Square, Jan. 5, 1969).

He appeared as Feivel Leishik in *Seven Days of Mourning* (Circle in the Square, Dec. 16, 1969); directed *The Christmas Dinner* (Berkshire Th. Festival, Stockbridge, Mass., July 1970); was Bertram, the Rat Catcher in *The Last Analysis* (Circle in the Square, N.Y.C., June 23, 1971); Dr. Rance in *What the Butler Saw* (Academy Playhouse, Lake Forest, Ill., Aug. 1971); Norman in *The Opening* (Tappan Zee Playhouse, Nyack, N.Y., May 1972); and directed *The Complete Works of Studs Edsel* (Folger Th. Group, Folger Mus., Washington, D.C., Dec. 12, 1972). He played Aaron Silver in *An Evening with the Poet-Senator* (Playhouse 2, N.Y.C., Mar. 21, 1973); played Hugo Kalmar in *The Iceman Cometh* (Circle in the Square, Dec. 13, 1973); directed the NY Shakespeare Festival's *The Merry Wives of Windsor* (Delacorte Th., July 30, 1974) and *Where Do We Go from Here?* (Newman, Public Th., Oct. 27, 1974); and played Harvey Appleman in *Kid Champion* (Anspacher, Public Th., Feb. 19, 1975).

Films. Mr. Margulies was the Acting Teacher in *Scarecrow in a Garden of Cucumbers* (1972).

Television. Mr. Margulies played David for a cable television version of *Six Characters in Search of an Author* (taped June 1964), and he was Pete in *A Mother for Janek* (PBS, 1965).

Night Clubs. Mr. Margulies was in the revue *The Second City* (Second City, Chicago, Ill., July 1962) and was a member of the company for *The Revue* (Moon, Easthampton, N.Y., July 1972).

Other Activities. Mr. Margulies taught acting at the Southwark Th. School, Th. of the Living Arts, Philadelphia, Pa. (1967–68); at the Circle in the Square Th. School, N.Y.C. (1969–72); and in the E.S.T. Artist-in-Residence Program, Johnson (Vt.) State Coll. (Summer 1973). He also gave private acting classes in N.Y.C. (1973) and was an artist in the schools under the Lincoln Ctr. Student Program (1969–75).

MARICLE, LEONA. Actress. b. Dec. 23, 1905, Wichita Falls, Tex. Grad. Texas State Coll. for Women, 1924; studied acting at AADA, N.Y.C., 1925. Married Aug. 13, 1928, to Louis Jean Heydt, actor. Member of AEA; SAG; AFTRA. Address: 234 E. 52nd St., New York, NY 10022, tel. (212) MU 8-4450.

Theatre. Miss Maricle made her N.Y.C. debut as Dagmar Lorne in *The Trial of Mary Dugan* (Natl. Th., Sept. 19, 1927); subsequently appeared as Gracie Turner in *First Mortgage* (Royale, Oct. 10, 1929); Vi Mudgeon in *Little Orchid Annie* (Eltinge, Apr. 21, 1930); Miss Leighton in *Once in a Lifetime* (Music Box, Sept. 24, 1930); succeeded (Apr. 1931) Veree Teasdale, as Jean in *The Greeks Had a Word for It* (Sam H. Harris Th., Sept. 25, 1930); played Lila Leroy-Gomez in *The Sex Fable* (Henry Miller's Th., Oct. 20, 1931); Marian Lane in *Bad Manners* (Playhouse, Jan. 30, 1933); Mari Fielding in *Under Glass* (Ambassador, Oct. 30, 1933); Daphne Martin in *The Dark Tower* (Morosco, Nov. 25, 1933); Margo Greshan in *First Episode* (Ritz, Sept. 17, 1934); Melisande Montgomery in *It's You I Want* (Cort, Feb. 5, 1935); and Audrey Quinn in *Slightly Married* (Cort, Oct. 25, 1943).

Miss Maricle toured as Ruth in *Blithe Spirit* (France; Italy, 1946); toured as Kay Thorndyke in *State of the Union* (1946–1947).

She played Margareta in *Harvest of Years* (Hudson, N.Y.C., Jan. 12, 1948); Pippa Shields in *The Small Hours* (National, Feb. 15, 1951); joined (1961) as Eulalie Shinn, the cast of *The Music Man* (Majestic, Dec. 19, 1957); played Grace Kimbrough in *Never Too Late* (Playhouse, Nov. 27, 1962); The Countess in *The Women* (Paper Mill Playhouse, Millburn, N.J., Mar. 22, 1966); Lilly in "The Coffee Lace," the first play of a double-bill entitled *Little Boxes* (New, N.Y.C., Dec. 3, 1969); and Mrs. Bramson in *Night Must Fall* (Actors Th. of Louisville, Ky., Nov. 11, 1971).

Films. Miss Maricle has appeared in *O'Shaughnessy's Boy* (MGM, 1935); *Theodora Goes Wild* (Col., 1936); *Women of Glamour* (Col., 1937); *Woman Chases Man* (UA, 1937); *Life Begins with Love* (Col., 1937); *Parole Racket* (Col., 1937); *Comet Over Broadway* (WB, 1938); *Lone Wolf in Paris* (Col., 1938); *Mad Miss Manton* (RKO, 1938); *Beauty for the Asking* (RKO, 1939); *Judge Hardy and Son* (MGM, 1939); *Curtain Call* (RKO, 1940); *Johnny Eager* (MGM, 1941); *This Thing Called Love* (Col., 1941); *Under Age* (Col., 1941); *The Hard Way* (WB, 1942); *Someone To Remember* (Rep., 1943); *My Pal, Wolf* (RKO, 1944); *Without Reservations* (RKO, 1946); *My Reputation* (WB, 1946); and *A Scandal in Paris,* also released as *Thieves' Holiday* (UA, 1946).

Television and Radio. On radio, Miss Maricle has performed on Lux Th. On television, she has appeared on Philco Television Playhouse (NBC); Studio One (CBS); Ellery Queen; Cameo Th. (NBC); Man Against Crime (CBS); and The Trials of O'Brien (CBS).

MARKEY, ENID. Actress. b. Enid Virginia Markey, Feb. 22, (1902?), Dillon, Colo., to John and Catherine Markey. Father, mining engineer. Attended St. Mary's Acad., Salt Lake City, Utah; Wolfe Hall, Denver, Colo. Studied at Egan Dramatic Sch., Los Angeles, Calif.; with Mary Agnes Doyle, Goodman Th., Chicago, Ill. Married Oct. 15, 1942, to George W. Cobb, Jr., exec., American Can Co. (dec. Mar. 13, 1948). Member of AEA; AFTRA; SAG. Address: 59 W. 44th St., New York, NY tel. (212) MU 7-4400.

Theatre. Miss Markey made her Bway debut as the Crybaby Bride in *Up in Mabel's* Room (Eltinge Th., Jan. 15, 1919), later playing the role for a year in Chicago (Cort, 1921); subsequently appeared as Ermintrude Marilley in *The Exciters* (Times Square Th., N.Y.C., Sept. 22, 1922); Mrs. Tuttle in *Barnum Was Right* (Frazee, Mar. 12, 1923); played a ten-month season of stock (Summerville Th., Mass., 1924); Josephine Dawson in *Bluffing Bluffers* (Ambassador, N.Y.C., Dec. 22, 1924); Amy Ralston in *Something To Brag About* (Booth, Aug. 13, 1925); Jane Potter in *Find Daddy* (Ritz, Mar. 8, 1926); Betty Hemmingworth in *The Blonde Sinner* (Cort, July 14, 1926); and in vaudeville, headlined as Bride in *Here Goes the Bride* (Palace, N.Y.C., 1927); with the Henry Duffy Players (Los Angeles, Calif.). She appeared in *Chickenfeed* and *The First Year;* appeared as Blanch Page in *Sisters of the Chorus* (Ritz, N.Y.C., Oct. 20, 1930); in the revue *After Such Pleasures* (Bijou, Feb. 7, 1934); in stock at Elitch Gardens (Denver, Colo., Summer 1934); succeeded (Feb. 1937) Ruth Hammond as Olga in *The Women* (Ethel Barrymore Th., N.Y.C., Dec. 26, 1936); played Amelia in *The Two Bouquets* (Windsor, May 31, 1938); Emily Terhune in *Run, Sheep, Run* (Windsor, Nov. 3, 1938); Myrtle Brown in *Morning's at Seven* (Longacre, Nov. 30, 1939); Della in *Beverly Hills* (Fulton, Nov. 7, 1940); Lilly Miller in a revival of *Ah, Wilderness!* (Guild, Oct. 2, 1941); Corinne Bassett in *Pie in the Sky* (Playhouse, Dec.

22, 1941); Estelle Benlow in *Mr. Sycamore* (ANTA, Nov. 13, 1942); Mrs. Brindle in *Sweet Charity* (Mansfield, Dec. 28, 1942); Mrs. Chubb in *Last Stop* (Ethel Barrymore Th., Sept. 5, 1944); Aunt Emily in *Snafu* (Hudson, Oct. 25, 1944); Tot in *Happy Birthday* (Broadhurst, Oct. 31, 1946); succeeded Doro Merande as Mrs. Hammer in *The Silver Whistle* (Biltmore, Nov. 24, 1948); played Daisy Sable in *Buy Me Blue Ribbons* (Empire, Oct. 17, 1951); and appeared in *Happy Birthday* (Calif., 1950).

She played Evva Lewis in *Mrs. McThing* (ANTA, N.Y.C., Feb. 10, 1952), and at the Central City (Colo.) Festival (Summer 1952); Vita Louise in a revival of *Harvey* (Biltmore, Los Angeles, Calif., 1954); the title role in *Mrs. Patterson* (Natl., N.Y.C., Dec. 1, 1954); Bea Cannon in *The Southwest Corner* (Holiday, Feb. 3, 1955); Gram in the pre-Bway tryout of *The Amazing Adele* (opened Shubert, Philadelphia, Dec. 26, 1955; closed Shubert, Boston, Jan. 21, 1956); Mrs. Tiffany in *Fashion* (Royal Playhouse, Jan. 20, 1959); Mrs. Archer-Loomis in *Only in America* (Cort, Nov. 19, 1959); Mrs. Candor in *The School for Scandal* (Mendelssohn Th., Ann Arbor, Mich., 1962); Emma Hale in *The Ballad of the Sad Cafe* (Martin Beck Th., N.Y.C., Oct. 30, 1963); Mrs. Bramson in *Night Must Fall* (Berkshire Playhouse, Stockbridge, Mass., Summer 1964); and Charlotte Cahill in *What Did We Do Wrong?* (Helen Hayes Th., N.Y.C., Oct. 22, 1967).

Films. Miss Markey first appeared in silent films, as William S. Hart's leading lady in *The Darkening Trail* (Inceville, 1915), *Between Men* (Inceville, 1915), *The Aztec God* (Inceville), and *The Fugitive* (Pat, 1916). She also appeared in *Jim Greinsbey's Boy* (Inceville, 1916); *Civilization* (Inceville, 1916); *War's Women* (Inceville); *Aloha Oea* (Inceville, 1916); starred in *Cheating the Public* (20th-Fox, 1918); *The Yankee Way* (20th-Fox, 1917); *Mother, I Need You* (Castleton-Shipman); appeared as Jane in the original *Tarzan of the Apes* with Elmo Lincoln (Intl., 1918); and as Jane in *Romance of Tarzan* (1st Natl., 1918).

She repeated her stage role in *Snafu* (Col., 1946), and appeared in *Naked City* (U, 1948).

Television and Radio. On radio, she has performed on Th. Guild of the Air; Grand Central Station; as Lillian Burke on the Women of Courage series (CBS, 1940–41), among others.

On television, she played Aunt Violet in the series Bringing Up Buddy (CBS, premiere Oct. 10, 1960); and has appeared on Armstrong Circle Th. (NBC); Philco Playhouse (NBC); Kraft Th. (NBC); Goodyear Playhouse (NBC); TV Hour (ABC); Alfred Hitchcock Presents (CBS); as Tot in *Happy Birthday* (Producers Showcase, NBC, June 25, 1956); on Suspense (NBC); True Story (NBC); *The Silver Whistle* (Playhouse 90, CBS, Dec. 24, 1959); on The Defenders (CBS); The Andy Griffith Show (CBS); in *The Wedding* (Esso Rep. Th., Inc., Apr. 21, 1965); on Ozzie and Harriet (ABC); Please Don't Eat the Daisies (NBC); Gomer Pyle, USMC (CBS); Omnibus (NBC); US Steel Hour (CBS); in *Mr. Sycamore* (Play of the Week, WNTA); and in *Morning's at Seven* (Play of the Week, WNTA).

Recreation. Concerts, theatre, opera, ballet, traveling.

MARKS, HERBERT E. Music publisher. b. Herbert Edward Marks, Apr. 21, 1902, New York City, to Edward B. and Miriam C. Marks. Father, music publisher, song writer. Grad. Dartmouth Coll., B.A. 1924. Married May 27, 1948, to Beatrice Landeck, writer; one son; one daughter. Served NY State Guard, 1918–19, 1941–45; rank, 1st Sgt. Relative in the theatre: cousin, Bosley Crowther, film critic. Member of Music Publishers Assn.; BMI. Address: (home) 33 W. 12th St., New York, NY 10011, tel. (212) WA 9-0079; 18 Stevens Lane, Westhampton Beach, NY 11978, tel. (516) 288-3978; (bus.) 1790 Broadway, New York, NY 10019, tel. (212) 247-7277.

Mr. Marks was president of the Edward B. Marks Music Corp. from 1945 to 1972. At present, he is the honorary chairman of the board.

Other Activities. He was reporter for *Variety* (1924–26).

MARLOR, CLARK S. Educator. b. Clark Strang Marlor, Nov. 18, 1922, Camden, N.J., to Alan Felten and Laura Mae (Strang) Marlor. Father, freight agent. Grad. Carnegie-Mellon Univ. (then Carnegie Institute of Technology), B.F.A. 1945; Univ. of Michigan, M.A. 1946; NY Univ., Ed. D. 1961. Member of ATA; SCA; Eastern States Communication Assn.; Salamagundi Club (honorary) (library comm. member); Long Island Historical Society (life member). Address: (home) 293 Sterling Place, Brooklyn, NY 11238; (bus.) Dept. of Speech Arts, Adelphi Univ., Garden City, NY 11530.

Mr. Marlor was appointed associate professor of speech and dramatic art, Adelphi Univ., Garden City, N.Y., in 1962. He had been instructor and technical director, Kalamazoo (Mich.) Coll. (1946–47); instructor and technical director, Miami Univ., Oxford, Ohio (1947–50); and tutor, City College of NY (1950–55). From 1956 to 1961, he was assistant professor of speech and dramatic art at Adelphi.

During his student years at Carnegie, Mr. Marlor played Homer in *Morning at Seven*, Benvolio in *Romeo and Juliet*, Mr. Twinkle in *Fashion*, Malvolio in *Twelfth Night*, and Nick in *Dear Octopus* (all 1943); Petulant in *The Way of the World*, Tsai-Yong in *Lute Song*, L'Abbe Bonnet in *Years of the Locust*, Parolles in *All's Well That Ends Well*, Anselme in *The Miser*, and Mr. Fair in *The Famous Mrs. Fair* (all 1944). At Kalamazoo, he was technical director of *Family Portrait* (1946) and *The Star Wagon* (1947), and he appeared as Beauvais in *Joan of Lorraine* (1947). At Miami Univ., he was technical director of *Scrap of Paper* and director of *The Father* (both 1947); technical director of *The Merchant of Venice* and *Fire Safe* and director of *Papa Is All* and *The Wandering Scholar* (all 1948); technical director of *Julius Caesar* and director of *Two Shepherds* (both 1949); and director of *I Like It Here* (1950). At Adelphi, he directed *Of Mice and Men* and *Summer and Smoke* (both 1957), *Imaginary Invalid* (1960), *Anne of a Thousand Days* (1962), *A Bachelor's Night* (1963), *The Gardener's Dog* (1965), *Goodbye, My Fancy* (1967), and *The Affected Young Ladies* (1973).

Published Works. Mr. Marlor is author of *A History of the Brooklyn Art Association*, which includes an index of the association's exhibitions (1970), and he wrote the article "John B. Whittaker: A Brooklyn Artist" (*Antiques*, Nov. 1971).

Awards. In conjunction with the publication of the book on the Brooklyn Arts Association, the Kennedy Galleries, N.Y.C., held a special exhibition.

Recreation. Reading, gardening, travel.

MARLOWE, HUGH. Actor. b. Hugh Herbert Hipple, Jan. 30, 1911, Philadelphia, Pa. Married 1941 to Edith Atwater, actress (marr. dis.); married 1946 to K. T. Stevens, actress. Member of AEA; SAG; AFTRA.

Theatre. Mr. Marlowe made his N.Y.C. debut as Donald Drake in *Arrest That Woman* (National Th., Sept. 18, 1936); followed by "Top" Rumson in *Kiss the Boys Good-bye* (Henry Miller's Th., Sept. 28, 1938); Jed Jones in *Young Couple Wanted* (Maxine Elliott's Th., Jan. 14, 1940); Wayne Kincaid in *The Land Is Bright* (Music Box, Oct. 28, 1941); and Charley Johnson in *Lady in the Dark* (Bway Th., Feb. 27, 1943).

He played Bill Page in *The Voice of the Turtle* (Chicago, 1944); Todd Frazier in *It Takes Two* (Biltmore, N.Y.C., Feb. 3, 1947); Mark McPherson in *Laura* (Cort, June 26, 1947); Stephen Cass in *Duet for Two Hands* (Booth, Oct. 7, 1947); Bud Walters in *Anniversary Waltz* (Alcazar, San Francisco, Calif., Apr. 6, 1956); Gil in *Janus* (Pasadena Playhouse, Calif., Nov. 14, 1957); appeared in *And Perhaps Happiness* (Central City Opera House, Colo., Aug. 3, 1958); and played Tucker Grogan in *Invitation to a March* (Moore, Seattle, Wash., 1961).

He was Parker Ballantine in *Critic's Choice* (Playhouse, Houghton Lake, Mich., July 21, 1964); Henry Higgins in *My Fair Lady* (Music Circus, Sacramento, Calif., Aug. 17, 1964; Music Circus, Fresno, Calif., Sept. 7, 1964); Shepherd Henderson in *Bell, Book and Candle* (Community Playhouse, Atlanta, Ga., Feb. 2, 1965); was in *The Rabbit Habit* (Denver Aud., Denver, Colo., Dec. 2, 1965); played David Shelby in *Good-By Ghost* (Royal Poinciana Playhouse, Palm Beach, Fla., Feb. 14, 1966); was in *Rain* (Renata Th., N.Y.C., May 1, 1966); played Charles Francis Eitel in *The Deer Park* (Th. de Lys, Jan. 31, 1967); was in *Postcards* (ANTA Matinee Th., Th. de Lys, Dec. 4, 1967); played Brigham Young in *Woman Is My Idea* (Belasco Th., Sept. 25, 1968); and Joe Keller in *All My Sons* (Roundabout Th., Sept. 27, 1974).

Films. Mr. Marlowe appeared in *Married Before Breakfast* (MGM, 1937); *Between Two Women* (MGM, 1937); *Marriage Is a Private Affair* (MGM, 1944); *Mrs. Parkington* (MGM, 1944); *Meet Me in St. Louis* (MGM, 1944); *Come to the Stable* (20th-Fox, 1949); *Twelve O'Clock High* (20th-Fox, 1947); *All About Eve* (20th-Fox, 1950); *Rawhide* (20th-Fox, 1951); *Mr. Belvedere Rings the Bell* (20th-Fox, 1951); and *The Day the Earth Stood Still* (20th-Fox, 1951).

Also, *Wait Til the Sun Shines, Nellie* (20th-Fox, 1952); *Bugles in the Afternoon* (WB, 1952); *Way of a Gaucho* (20th-Fox, 1952); *Monkey Business* (20th-Fox, 1952); *The Stand at Apache River* (U, 1953); *Casanova's Big Night* (Par., 1954); *Garden of Evil* (20th-Fox, 1954); *Illegal* (WB, 1955); *Earth Versus the Flying Saucers* (Col., 1956); *World without End* (AA, 1956); *The Black Whip* (20th-Fox, 1957); and *Elmer Gantry* (UA, 1960); *Castle of Evil* (World Entertainment, 1966); and *The Last Shot You Hear* (Lippert, 1969).

Television and Radio. Mr. Marlowe played the title role on the radio program Adventures of Ellery Queen (CBS, 1940), repeating his role on television. He made television appearances also on Alfred Hitchcock Presents (CBS, 1957); Arrest and Trial (ABC, 1964); The Virginian (NBC, 1964, 1966); Perry Mason (CBS, 1964, 1965, 1966); the Andy Griffith Show (CBS, 1965); Hazel (NBC, 1965); Alfred Hitchcock (Ind., 1966, 1967); Voyage (ABC); Dick Powell Th. (Ind., 1966); Rawhide (Ind., 1967); The Man from U.N.C.L.E. (NBC, 1968); Judd for the Defense (ABC, 1968); and Another World (NBC, 1970).

MARLOWE, JOAN. Publisher, writer. b. Jan. 7, 1920, Ithaca, N.Y., to Lionel E. and Mildred (Cole) Mintz. Father, editor of Ithaca *Journal News*. Grad. Ithaca (N.Y.) H.S., 1936; Stephens Jr. Coll., A.B. 1938; attended Cornell Univ., 1938–39. Married Jan. 24, 1941, to Ward Morehouse, author-critic (marr. dis. 1947); one son; married Sept. 13, 1952, to Roderic Warren Rahe, chemist; two sons. Member of The Drama Desk (treas., 1958–60); Outer Circle (recording secy., 1957–to date). Address: (home) 18 Tory Hole Rd., Darien, CT 06820, tel. (203) 655-9520; (bus.) Proscenium Publications, 4 Park Ave., Suite 21-D, New York, NY 10016, tel. (212) 532-2570.

Pre-Theatre. Editorial dept., *Newsweek*.

Theatre. Miss Marlowe has been editor and publisher, with Betty Blake, of *Theatre Information Bulletin* (est. 1944) a trade weekly announcing forthcoming New York productions, and of *New York Theatre Critics' Reviews* (1964–to date).

Miss Marlowe was a member of the editorial department at *Newsweek* magazine (1943); wrote *Broadway—Inside the Last Decade* (1954); and *The Keys to Broadway* (1951), both with Miss Blake.

Miss Marlowe appeared in the role of Jane Wilson in *Mr. and Mrs. North* (Belasco Th., N.Y.C., Jan. 12, 1941); and in stock (Miami Beach Playhouse, Fla., Winter 1939–40; Priscilla Beach, Plymouth, Mass., Summer 1939; Cape May Playhouse, N.J., Summer 1941); appeared in commercial films for Chesterfield cigarettes and Johns-Manville (1940–41).

Recreation. Tennis, cooking, boats.

MARRE, ALBERT. Director, producer. b. Sept. 20, 1925, New York City. Grad. Townsend Harris H.S., N.Y.C., 1939; Oberlin Coll., B.A. 1943; Harvard Univ., M.A., 1948. Married to Joan Diener, actress; one son, one daughter. Served USN 1943–46. Member of DGA; SSD&C. Address: 50 E. 64th St., New York, NY 10021.

Theatre. Mr. Marre was director of the Allied Repertory Th. (Berlin, Germany, 1946); and managing director of the Brattle Th. Co. (Cambridge, Mass.) where he produced 68 plays directing 45 of them (1948–52). He was director of *The Little Blue Light* (ANTA, Apr. 29, 1951); artistic director for the NY City Ctr. Drama Company (1952–53) for which he directed *Love's Labours Lost* (Feb. 4, 1953), and *Misalliance* (Feb. 18, 1953; moved to Ethel Barrymore Th., Mar. 6, 1953), and the touring production (1953–54); and directed *The Merchant of Venice* (Mar. 4, 1953). He directed *Kismet* (Ziegfeld, N.Y.C., Dec. 3, 1953), on tour (1955–57) and in London (Stoll, Apr. 20, 1955); Staged *Festival* (Longacre, N.Y.C., Jan. 18, 1955); *The Chalk Garden* (Ethel Barrymore Th., Oct. 26, 1955), and on tour (opened Lobero Th., Santa Barbara, Sept. 6, 1956; closed Feb. 16, 1957, McCarter Th., Princeton, N.J.); *Shangri-La* (Winter Garden, June 13, 1956); the opera *Die Fledermaus* (Los Angeles, Calif., Civic Light Opera Co., Summer 1956); *Saint Joan* (Phoenix, N.Y.C., Sept. 11, 1956); *Good as Gold* (Belasco, Mar. 7, 1957); *South Pacific* (Los Angeles Civic Light Opera Co., Los Angeles, San Francisco, Calif., Summer 1957); *Time Remembered* (Morosco, N.Y.C., Nov. 12, 1957); *At the Grand* (Los Angeles Light Civic Opera Co., Summer 1958); and *La Belle Helene* (Boston Arts Fest., Center Th., Summer 1960).

He produced *The Love Doctor* (Piccadilly, London, Oct. 12, 1959); directed *Rape of the Belt* (Martin Beck Th., N.Y.C., Nov. 5, 1960); *Milk and Honey* (Martin Beck Th., Oct. 10, 1961); *Too True to Be Good* (54 St. Th., Mar. 12, 1962); *Never Live Over a Pretzel Factory* (Eugene O'Neill Th., Mar. 28, 1964); and the Dublin (Ireland) Intl. Th. Festival's production of the revised version of *Laurette* (Olympia, Sept. 22, 1964).

Mr. Marre staged the book and musical numbers for his production of *Man of La Mancha* (Goodspeed Opera House, East Haddam, Conn., June 24, 1965; and ANTA-Washington Square, N.Y.C., Nov. 22, 1965); directed a revival of *The Great Waltz* (Music Center, Los Angeles, July 27, 1965); directed and staged the musical numbers for *Chu Chem* (opened Locust Th., Philadelphia, Nov. 15, 1966; closed there Nov. 19, 1966); was guest director with the Center Th. Group (Mark Taper Forum, Los Angeles, 1967–68 season); co-authored the book and staged the musical numbers for *Cry For Us All* (Broadhurst, N.Y.C., Apr. 8, 1970); directed *Knickerbocker Holiday* (tour, opened Curran, San Francisco, May 11, 1971); and the world premiere of *Halloween* (Bucks County Playhouse, New Hope, Pa., Summer 1972); and co-authored the book and directed *Home, Sweet Homer* (Palace Th., N.Y.C., Jan. 4, 1976).

Television. Mr. Marre directed *The Gambler, The Nun,* and *The Radio* (Buick-Hemingway series, ABC); *Androcles and the Lion* (Omnibus, ABC); and *Craig's Wife* (Best of Bway, ABC).

Awards. Mr. Marre received the Antoinette Perry (Tony) Award for his direction of *Man of La Mancha* (1966).

MARRONEY, PETER R. Educator, director. b. Peter Raulo Marroney, June 29, 1913, Pueblo, Colo., to Gerald and Constance (Guileramo) Marroney. Father, farmer. Grad. Central H.S. 1931; Univ. of Oklahoma, B.F.A. 1936; State Univ. of Iowa, M.A. 1939. Married Feb. 21, 1948, to Lenore Doster. Served USNR 1943–46; rank, Yeoman–3. Member of AETA; NTC; ANTA (reg. dir. 1956–59). Address: (home) 3823 Calle de Sota, Tucson, AZ 85721, tel. (602) EA 6-2065; (bus.) Dept. of Drama, Univ. of Arizona, Tucson, AZ 85721, tel. MA 4-8181.

He is also director of the Ariz. Corral (Community) Th., which he founded in 1950; he was education administrator of the Galler Th. Workshop (Los Angeles, 1946–47); and was on the technical staff of the Portland (Ore.) Civic Th. (1936–37).

Awards. Mr. Marroney was elected Tucson's Man-of-the-Year (1955).

Recreation. Gardening, woodworking, golf.

MARSHALL, ARMINA. Producer, actress, writer. b. Alfalfa County, Okla., to Chalmers and Elizabeth (Armina) Marshall. Grad. Anaheim (Calif.) H.S.; Univ. of California at Los Angeles. Studied theatre at AADA, N.Y.C. Married 1925 to Lawrence Langner, producer, playwright (dec. Dec. 26, 1962); one son, Philip, co-director of The Theatre Guild. Address: 227 w. 47th St., New York, NY 10036, tel. (212) 265-6170.

Theatre. Miss Marshall is co-director of the Theatre Guild (1955–to date); and a director and trustee (1951–to date) of The American Shakespeare Festival Th. and Academy (Stratford, Conn.), an organization founded by her husband, Lawrence Langner, in 1951.

She made her debut as an actress, appearing as a Nun in *The Tidings Brought to Mary* (Garrick Th., N.Y.C., Dec. 25, 1922); subsequently played Kari in *Peer Gynt* (Garrick, Feb. 5, 1923); a Maid in *The Race with the Shadow* (Garrick, Jan. 20, 1924); Mrs. Blazy in *Fata Morgana* (Garrick, Mar. 3, 1924); followed (Mar. 1925) Patricia Barclay as Old Maggie in *Processional* (Garrick, Jan. 25, 1925); appeared as Mary in *Ariadne* (Garrick, Feb. 23, 1925); Kati in *The Glass Slipper* (Guild, Oct. 19, 1925); Germine Bachelet in *Merchants of Glory* (Guild, Dec. 14, 1925); Signora Ponza in *Right You Are If You Think You Are* (Guild, Feb. 23, 1927); Anne in *Mr. Pim Passes By* (Garrick, Apr. 18, 1927); Emily Bender in *Man's Estate* (Biltmore, Apr. 1, 1929); May Williston in *Those We Love* (Golden, Feb. 19, 1930); Lona Hessel in *The Pillars of Society* (48 St. Th., Oct. 14, 1931); and Dorine in *The Bride the Sun Shines On* (Fulton, Dec. 26, 1931).

She wrote with Lawrence Langner, *The Pursuit of Happiness* (Avon, Oct. 9, 1933) and *On to Fortune* (Fulton, Feb. 4, 1935); subsequently appeared as Mrs. Gordon in *If This Be Treason* (Music Box, Sept. 23, 1935); and wrote, with Mr. Langner, *Suzanna and the Elders* (Morosco, Oct. 29, 1940).

During WW II, Miss Marshall was co-director of the Stage Door Canteen in Washington, D.C.; later was production supervisor of *Foolish Notion* (Martin Beck Th., N.Y.C., Mar. 13, 1945); and associate producer for *The Iceman Cometh* (Martin Beck Th., Oct. 9, 1946).

She is currently with Philip Langner, in association with the Theatre Guild, Miss Marshall produced *Absurd Person Singular* (Music Box, N.Y.C., Oct. 8, 1974); and *A Musical Jubilee* (St. James, Nov. 13, 1975).

Television and Radio. As co-director of the Theatre Guild, she headed its department of radio and TV and presented many dramatic broadcasts sponsored by US Steel (CBS).

MARSHALL, E. G. Actor. b. June 18, 1910, Owatonna, Minn., to Charles G. and Hazel Irene (Cobb) Marshall. Attended Carlton Coll., 1930; Univ. of Minnesota, 1932. Married Apr. 26, 1939, to Helen Wolf (marr. dis. 1953); two children.

Theatre. Mr. Marshall made his stage debut with the Oxford Players, a touring repertory company (1933); his Bway debut as Henry Onstott in the Federal Theatre (WPA) Project's production of *Prologue to Glory* (Ritz, Sept. 19, 1938), and on tour (Blackstone, Chicago, Ill., 1938; Walnut, Philadelphia, Pa., 1938); subsequently played Humphrey Crocker in *Jason* (Hudson, N.Y.C., Jan. 21, 1942); Mr. Fitzpatrick in *The Skin of Our Teeth* (Plymouth, Nov. 18, 1942); Brigadier in *Jacobowsky and the Colonel* (Martin Beck Th., Mar. 14, 1944); Dave in *Beggars Are Coming to Town* (Coronet, Oct. 27, 1945); Sims in *Woman Bites Dog* (Belasco, Apr. 17, 1946); Willie Oban in *The Iceman Cometh* (Martin Beck Th., Oct. 9, 1946); Finlay Decker in *The Survivors* (Playhouse, Jan. 19, 1948); Doc in *Hope Is the Thing with Feathers* (Maxine Elliot's Th., Apr. 11, 1948); and Emmet in a stock production of *The Silver Whistle* (Aug. 30, 1948).

Mr. Marshall played Ernest Bruni in *The Gambler* (Lyceum, N.Y.C., Oct. 13, 1952); Rev. John Hale in *The Crucible* (Martin Beck Th., Jan. 22, 1953), in which he subsequently succeeded (June 1953) Arthur Kennedy as John Proctor; played Brennan in *Red Roses for Me* (Booth, Dec. 28, 1955); Ferrante the King, in a special (Monday) performance of *Queen After Death* (Phoenix, Mar. 12, 1956); Vladimir in *Waiting for Godot* (John Golden Th., Apr. 19, 1956); Ephraim Cabot in *Desire Under the Elms* (Studebaker, Chicago, Ill., Nov., 1956); Walter Rafferty in *The Gang's All Here* (Ambassador, Oct. 1, 1959); Charles Bishop in the pre-Bway tryout of *This Winter's Hobby* (opened Shubert, New Haven, Conn., Mar. 23, 1966; closed Walnut St. Th., Philadelphia, Pa., Apr. 9, 1966); Felix Ungar in *The Odd Couple* (winter stock, 1966–67); Oscar Hubbard in *The Little Foxes* (Vivian Beaumont Th., N.Y.C., Oct. 26, 1967); and replaced (1968) George C. Scott in *Plaza Suite* (Plymouth, Feb. 14, 1968). He toured Scandinavia for the US State Dept. as Mr. Antrobus in *The Skin of Our Teeth* (1968); played the title roles in *The Imaginary Invalid* (Philadelphia Drama Guild, Nov. 1971); *Macbeth* (Virginia Museum Th., Richmond, Spring 1973); and *The Master Builder* (Long Wharf Th., New Haven, 1973), and appeared in *Nash at Nine* (Helen Hayes Th., N.Y.C., May 17, 1973).

Films. He has appeared in *The House on 92nd Street* (20th-Fox, 1945); *13 Rue Madeleine* (20th-Fox, 1946); *Call Northside 777* (20th-Fox, 1948); *The Caine Mutiny* (Col., 1954); *Pushover* (Col., 1954); *The Silver Chalice* (WB, 1954); *The Left Hand of God* (20th-Fox, 1955); *The Bamboo Prison* (Col., 1955); *The Mountain* (Par., 1956); *The Scarlet Hour* (Par., 1956); *The Bachelor Party* (UA, 1957); *Twelve Angry Men* (UA, 1957); *The Buccaneer* (Par., 1958); *The Journey* (MGM, 1959); *Compulsion* (20th-Fox, 1959); *Cash McCall* (WB, 1960); *Town without Pity* (UA, 1961); *The Chase* (Col., 1966); *The Bridge at Remagen* (UA, 1969); *Tora! Tora! Tora!* (20th-Fox, 1970); and *The Pursuit of Happiness* (Col., 1971).

Television and Radio. Mr. Marshall made his radio debut in 1932 in St. Paul, Minn., and Chicago, Ill.; and subsequently performed with the Th. Guild on the Air. He was host for the CBS Radio Mystery Th. (premiere, Jan. 6, 1974).

On television, he played Lawrence Preston on The Defenders series (CBS, premiere, Sept. 16, 1961 through Spring 1964), and was also a series regular on The Bold Ones (NBC, premiere, Sept. 15, 1969 through Spring 1973). By his own calculation, he has made more than 400 other television appearances since his debut in On Stage (NBC, 1947), including *The Little Foxes* (Hallmark Hall of Fame, NBC); *The Littlest Angel* (Hallmark, NBC); *The Cherry Orchard* (Play of the Week, WNTA); *The Master Builder* (Play of the Week, WNTA); *A Case of Libel* (ABC); *Look Homeward, Angel* (Playhouse 90, CBS); *The Plot to Kill Stalin* (Playhouse 90, CBS); and virtually every major series including Kraft Television Th. (NBC); Philco Playhouse (NBC); Studio One (CBS); Danger (CBS); The Web (CBS); Omnibus (CBS); You Are There (CBS); Pond's Theatre (ABC); The Brady Bunch (ABC); and Night Gallery (NBC).

Awards. For his performance as Lawrence Preston in The Defenders series, Mr. Marshall twice received the NATAS (Emmy) Award (1962, 1963).

Recreation. Writing, cycling.

MARSHALL, MORT. Actor. b. Mortimer Haig Lichtenstein, Aug. 17, 1918, New York City, to Perry M. and Louise M. (Cooke) Lichtenstein. Father, psychiatrist; mother, nurse. Grad. Rollins Coll., B.A. 1939; Yale Univ., M.F.A. 1942. Married June 11, 1950, to Anne S. Muir; two daughters. Served US Army, Special Services, Africa Middle East Theatre, 1942–46; rank, Capt. Member of AEA; SAG; AFTRA; The Players. Address: 363 E. 76th St., New York, NY 10021.

Theatre. Mr. Marshall first appeared in stock with

the Arena Players, playing in *Outward Bound, The Milky Way,* and *Petticoat Fever* (Franconia, N.H., June 1940). While in the US Army, he appeared in a revue, *Yalla Fever* (Ezbekiah Th., Cairo, Egypt, 1944).

He made his N.Y.C. debut as the Strange Man in *Crime and Punishment* (Natl., Dec. 22, 1947); subsequently appeared in the revue *Small Wonder* (Coronet, Sept. 15, 1948); played Robert Lemanteur in *Gentlemen Prefer Blondes* (Ziegfeld, Dec. 8, 1949); the Announcer and Chief Senate Clerk in *Of Thee I Sing* (Ziegfeld, May 5, 1952); Frobisher in *Men of Distinction* (48 St. Th., Apr. 30, 1953); appeared in the pre-Bway tryout of the revue *Ziegfeld Follies* (opened Shubert, Boston, Mass., Apr. 16, 1956; closed Shubert, Philadelphia, Pa., May 12, 1956); played Counsellor Nacella in *The Best House in Naples* (Lyceum, N.Y.C., Oct. 26, 1956); Pete in the pre-Bway tryout of *The Joker* (opened Shubert, New Haven, Conn., Mar. 6, 1957; closed Shubert, Washington, D.C., Mar. 30, 1957); Uncle Jocko and Mr. Goldstone in *Gypsy* (Bway Th., N.Y.C., May 21, 1959); succeeded (Dec. 18, 1959) Paul Ford as Mayor Shinn in *The Music Man* (Majestic, Dec. 19, 1957); played Fleisser and Coach Stockworth in *All American* (Winter Garden, Mar. 19, 1962); Bennie Buchsbaum in *Little Me* (Lunt-Fontanne Th., Nov. 17, 1962); succeeded (June 8, 1964) Frank McHugh as Senex in *A Funny Thing Happened on the Way to the Forum* (Alvin, May 8, 1962); played Al Sheen in *Minnie's Boys* (Imperial, 1971); and Senex in a revival of *A Funny Thing Happened on the Way to the Forum* (Lunt-Fontanne, 1972).

Films. Mr. Marshall was the emcee in *Go, Man, Go* (UA, 1954); and has appeared in *The Silver Chalice* (WB, 1954); *Target Earth* (Allied, 1955); *Pete Kelly's Blues* (WB, 1955); *Kiss Me Deadly* (UA, 1955); played the Australian Doctor in *Skullduggery* (U, 1968); Father Gregory in *Lovers and Other Strangers* (Cinerama, 1970); Heinei in *The Grissom Gang* (Natl. Gen., 1971); the Assistant Warden in *The Longest Yard* (Par., 1974); Hester Tate in *W. W. and the Dixie Dance Kings* (20th-Fox, 1974).

Television. Since 1947, he has appeared in over 250 major network TV productions, including the Ed Sullivan Show (CBS); the Dupont Show (NBC); Hallmark Hall of Fame (NBC); The Defenders (CBS); Studio One (CBS); Kraft Television Th. (NBC); Dragnet; Philco Television Playhouse (NBC); the Shari Lewis Show; and numerous spectaculars for CBS and NBC.

Recreation. Painting, writing, golf.

MARSHALL, SARAH. Actress. b. Sarah Lynn Marshall, May 25, 1933, London, England, to Herbert and Edna (Best) Marshall. Father, actor; mother, actress. Attended Westlake Sch., Hollywood, Calif., 1940–49. Studied acting with Constance Collier, 1948. Married June 13, 1952, to Mel Bourne (marr. dis. 1956); one son. Member of AEA; AFTRA; SAG.

Theatre. Miss Marshall made her N.Y.C. debut as a Monk in *The Browning Version* (Coronet Th., Oct. 12, 1949); subsequently played an Usher in *Dream Girl* (NY City Ctr., May 9, 1951); Anna in *Idiot's Delight* (NY City Ctr., May 23, 1951); a Maid in *Jane* (Coronet, Feb. 1, 1952); a Housemaid in *The Seagull* (Phoenix, May 11, 1954); Amy Spettigue in *Charley's Aunt* (NY City Ctr., Dec. 22, 1953); Bonnie Dee Ponder in *The Ponder Heart* (Music Box, Feb. 16, 1956); Ellen Spelding in *Visit to a Small Planet* (Booth, Feb. 7, 1957); Kay Fletcher in *The World of Suzie Wong* (Broadhurst, Oct. 14, 1958); Rusty Mayerling in *Goodbye, Charlie* (Lyceum, Dec. 16, 1959); and Connie Dayton in *Come Blow Your Horn* (Brooks Atkinson Th., Feb. 22, 1961); Karen Richards in *Applause* (London, England, Nov. 16, 1972); and appeared in *Children* (London season, 1973, 74).

Films. Miss Marshall has appeared in *The Long, Hot Summer* (20th-Fox, 1958); *Wild and Wonderful* (U, 1964); *A Rage To Live* (UA, 1965); *Lord Love a Duck* (UA, 1966); and *Embassy* (Hemdale, 1973).

Awards. Miss Marshall won the *Theatre World* Award and the *Variety* NY Drama Critics Poll for her performance as Bonnie Dee Ponder in *The Ponder Heart* (1956).

Recreation. Bridge.

MARSHALL, WILLIAM. Actor, director, singer. b. William Horace Marshall, Aug. 19, 1924, Gary, Ind., to Vereen and Thelma (Edwards) Marshall. Father, dentist. Grad. Roosevelt H.S., Gary, 1942. Studied at the Art Institute, Chicago, Ill., 1938–40, Art Students League, N.Y.C. 1944; American Th. Wing, N.Y.C., 1947; Actors Studio, N.Y.C., 1952–54; Neighborhood Playhouse, N.Y.C., 1958; Alliance Française, Paris, 1959–63. Served US Army, Infantry, 1943. Relative in theatre: cousin, Adelaide Marshall, night club performer. Member of AEA (recording secy., 1950–51); AGFA; AFTRA; SAG.

Pre-Theatre. Steel mill worker, stevedore, commercial artist.

Theatre. Mr. Marshall began as a singer in the chorus of *Carmen Jones* (Bway Th., N.Y.C., Dec. 2, 1944); subsequently understudied Ossie Davis in the title role in *Jeb* (Martin Beck Th., Feb. 21, 1946); toured in *Call Me Mister* (1948); played one of the Freed Men and understudied William Vesey as Joshua in *Our Lan'* (Royale, N.Y.C., Sept. 27, 1947); appeared in *Trial by Fire* (Blackfriars, 1947); played Sad-Act in *A Long Way from Home* (Maxine Elliott's Th., Feb. 8, 1948); Rolla Bennett in *Set My People Free* (Hudson, Nov. 3, 1948); Hlaben in *Lost in the Stars* (Music Box, Oct. 30, 1949); Cookson and understudied Boris Karloff as Captain Hook in *Peter Pan* (Imperial, Apr. 24, 1950); played the Lawd in *The Green Pastures* (Bway Th., Mar. 15, 1951); and Kelly in *Time To Go* (Yugoslavian Hall, 1952).

He appeared in the title role in *Othello*, which he also produced (Mother Zion Church and N.Y.C. schools, 1953); repeated the role at the Brattle Th. (Cambridge, Mass., 1955), at the NY City Ctr. (Sept. 7, 1955), and at the NY Shakespeare Festival (Belvedere Lake Th., Aug. 6, 1958).

He appeared in the title role in *Oedipus Rex* for the Chicago (Ill.) Playwrights Co. (1955); played Chief Uturo in *The Virtuous Island* (Carnegie Hall Playhouse, N.Y.C., Apr. 9, 1957); Henry Simpson in *Toys in the Attic* (Piccadilly, London, England, Nov. 10, 1960); the Bear Baiter in *When We Dead Awaken* (Gate Th., Dublin, Ireland, Feb. 1961); directed and appeared in *The Bear* and *The Marriage Proposal* at theatres on Air Force bases (France, 1961); directed *Long Voyage Home* (American Artists and Students Ctr., Paris, 1962); with the Dublin (Ireland) Th. Festival toured in the title role in *Othello* (Switzerland, Luxembourg, Belgium, and Holland, 1962–63); appeared as Saul in *Javelin* (Actors Playhouse, N.Y.C., Nov. 9, 1966); was Othello in *Catch My Soul* (Ahmanson Th., Los Angeles, Calif., Mar. 5, 1968); and the Captain in *Leviathan 99* (Samuel Goldwyn Studios, Nov. 24, 1972).

Films. Mr. Marshall made his debut as King Dick in *Lydia Bailey* (20th-Fox, 1952); subsequently appeared in *Demetrius and the Gladiators* (20th-Fox, 1954); *Something of Value* (MGM, 1957); *Sabu and the Magic Ring* (Allied, 1957); *Piedra de Toque* (Asturia Films, Madrid, Spain, 1953); *To Trap a Spy* (MGM, 1966); and *Blacula* (Amer. Intl., 1972).

Television and Radio. He played Yank in the radio play, *Bound East of Cardiff* (NBC, 1952); sang on the Lower Basin Street show (1952); was disc jockey for gospel and spiritual music (WLIB, N.Y., 1956); and played the title role in *The Emperor Jones* (BBC, London, 1959).

On television, he played the Battler in *The World of Nick Adams* (NBC, 1957); the Lawd in the London television presentation of *The Green Pastures* (BBC, London, 1958); Mr. Kano in the Danger Man series (MGM, London, 1959); and appeared in *The Big Pride* (BBC, 1961). He appeared on Alfred Hitchcock Presents (CBS); The Man from U.N.C.L.E. (NBC); Ben Casey (ABC); Secret Agent (CBS); was in *As Adam, Early in the Morning* (Repertoire Workshop, CBS, 1966); on Tarzan (NBC); and Daniel Boone (1967).

Night Clubs. He sang at the Moulin Rouge (Paris, 1962–63).

Recreation. Horseback riding, swimming, dancing, writing poetry.

MARTEL, FLORA. Theatre executive. b. Flora Ann Martel, Hartford, Conn., to Erennio and Madeline (Nettis) Martel. Attended Univ. of Connecticut; studied at New York Univ. and Columbia Univ.; studied drama at the Ann Randall School and Playhouse, Hartford. Member of ANTA; AEA; SAG.

From 1963 until 1969, Miss Martel was associate executive director of ANTA. She joined the organization in 1947, and was active in ANTA's Experimental Th. and Talent Workshop (1947–48).

She was a founder of the Mark Twain Masquers, a community theatre group in Hartford, Conn., and appeared with the company (1936); in stock, appeared at the Bolton (Conn.) Playhouse (Summers 1937–38); at the Canton (Conn.) Playhouse (Summer 1939–40); produced and appeared with the Little Th. (Hartford, Conn., 1939–40); appeared in *The Pursuit of Happiness* (N.Y.C. Subway Circuit, 1946); and was production manager for *The Little Foxes* (Unitarian Church, Brooklyn, N.Y., Dec. 1954, Jan. 1955).

MARTIN, CHRISTOPHER. Actor-manager, artistic director, producer. b. John Christopher Martin, Dec. 7, 1942, New York City, to Ian and Inge (Adams) Martin. Father, actor, writer, and director; mother, actress. Educ. Staples High School, Westport, Conn.; grad. NY Univ., B.S., M.A. Studied fencing with Christopher Tanner, mime with Richard Morse. Relatives in theatre: stepmother, Joen Arliss, actress; brother, Toby Martin, television producer; uncle, Claus Adam, cellist. Member Local #802, AFM; Off-Off Bway Alliance (pres., 1972–74). Address: (home) 564 Hudson St., New York, NY 10014, tel. (212) 691-4883; (bus.) CSC Repertory, 136 E. 13th St., New York, NY 10003, tel. (212) 477-5770.

Theatre. Mr. Martin made his stage debut as Kolenkhov in a high school production of *You Can't Take It with You* (Westport, Conn., 1960). In 1967, with Kathryn Wyman and Harris Laskawy, he founded the Classic Stage Company, later called CSC Repertory, and he has served since then as the group's artistic director. He made his professional acting debut as Thomas Mendip in a CSC production of *The Lady's Not for Burning* (Mar. 1967) and subsequently appeared in additional CSC productions: as Laertes and the Player King in *Hamlet* (Sept. 1967), as Jack Tanner and Don Juan in *Man and Superman* (Jan. 1968), as the Superintendent in *The Cavern*, which he also directed (Mar. 1968), and as Cleante in *Tartuffe*, which he directed (Apr. 1968). He was Astrov in *Uncle Vanya*, which he directed (Mar. 1969), directed *Poor Bitos* (Sept. 1969), *The Revenger's Tragedy*, also playing Vindice (Oct. 1969), *Moby Dick*, which he also adapted (Mar. 1970), *Hamlet* (Sept. 1970), designed *Twelfth Night* (Nov. 1970), directed *Rosencrantz and Guildenstern Are Dead* (Jan. 1971), *Pericles*, in which he also played Gower (May 1971), and *Marat/Sade* (Sept. 1971). He was fencing master for the ballet *Romeo and Juliet* (Pittsburgh, Pa., Ballet, Sept. 1971) and continued as artistic director for CSC, directing *Julius Caesar*, in which he played Mark Antony (Nov. 1971), and *Titus Andronicus* (Jan. 1972). He played the Mayor in *The Inspector General* (Apr. 1972), Max in *The Homecoming* (Sept. 1972), directed *The Tempest* (Oct. 1972), played the title role in *Macbeth* (Nov. 1972), directed *The Devils* (Jan. 1973), directed and choreographed *Rashomon*, in which he also played the Bandit (Apr. 1973), directed *Moby Dick*, in which he also played the Blacksmith, Boomer, and Peleg (Sept. 1973), played Alceste in *The Misanthrope* (Oct. 1973), designed *Miss Julie* (Nov. 1973), directed *The Revenger's Tragedy* (Jan. 1974), *Hedda Gabler*, in which he played Judge Brack (Mar. 1974), and *The Dwarfs* (Apr. 1974).

Television. Mr. Martin was producer of the program The Electric Village (WPIX, N.Y.C., Sept.–Nov. 1968).

Night Clubs. Mr. Martin appeared as singer and guitarist in the Metropole, N.Y.C., in 1962.

MARTIN, ELLIOT. Producer. b. Elliott Edwards Martin, Feb. 25, 1924, Denver, Colo., to Will H. and Elma A. (Harvey) Martin. Father, insurance broker. Grad. E. Denver (Colo.) H.S., 1942; attended Univ. of Denver, 1943–46. Married Oct. 7, 1949, to Marjorie E. Cuesta, singer; one son, one daughter. Member of AEA; The Players. Address: (home) Twin Gates, 94 Lyons Plain Rd., Weston, CT 06880; (bus.) 152 W. 58th St., New York, NY 10019.

Theatre. Mr. Martin first performed as an actor-singer in the London (Eng.) production of *Oklahoma!*, playing the role of Fred and understudying the role of Will Parker (Drury Lane, Apr. 30, 1947); subsequently toured as understudy for the role of Charlie in the national company of *Allegro* (opened Shubert, Philadelphia, Pa., Oct. 1948); appeared as a Prospector and a Neighbor in *Texas, Li'l Darlin'* (Mark Hellinger Th., N.Y.C., Nov. 25, 1949), for which he was also assistant stage manager. He became executive assistant of the Westport (Conn.) Country Playhouse (May 6, 1951) for the Summer season; manager of the Theatre Guild's Cherokee construction studio (Westport, Conn., Oct. 1951); manager-director of a season of stock productions at the Bahama Playhouse (Nassau, B.W.I., Jan. 1952); and was stage manager at the Westport (Conn.) Country Playhouse (June-Sept. 1952).

He was production stage manager of *At Home with Ethel Waters* (48 St. Th., N.Y.C., Sept. 22, 1953); *In the Summer House* (Playhouse, Dec. 29, 1953); *The Girl on the Via Flamina* (48 St. Th., Apr. 1, 1954); *Home is the Hero* (Booth, Sept. 22, 1954); *Portrait of a Lady* (ANTA, Dec. 21, 1954); *Phoenix '55* (Phoenix, Apr. 23, 1955); *The Heavenly Twins* (Booth, Nov. 4, 1955); *The Innkeepers* (John Golden Th., Feb. 2, 1956); and of *Little Glass Clock* (John Golden Th., Mar. 26, 1956).

He was managing director at the Famous Artists Country Playhouse (Fayetteville, N.Y., Summer 1956); production stage manager of *Long Day's Journey Into Night* (Helen Hayes Th., N.Y.C., Nov. 7, 1956); managed the Famous Artists Country Playhouse (Summers 1957, 1958); produced package touring productions of *Inherit the Wind* and *The Matchmaker* (Summer 1957); produced package productions of *Holiday for Lovers* and *The Remarkable Mr. Pennypacker* (Summer 1958); was production stage manager of *A Majority of One* (Shubert, N.Y.C., Feb. 16, 1959) and of *The Unsinkable Molly Brown* (Winter Garden, Nov. 3, 1960).

Mr. Martin produced, with Sonia Moore, *The Painted Days* (Th. Marquee, N.Y.C., Apr. 6, 1961); was an associate producer of *The Captains and the Kings* (Playhouse, Jan. 2, 1962); was production stage manager for *Great Day in the Morning* (Henry Miller's Th., Mar. 28, 1962); was an associate producer of *Seidman and Son* (Belasco, Oct. 15, 1962); produced, with Daniel Hollywood, *Never Too Late* (Playhouse, Nov. 27, 1962; Prince of Wales's Th., London, Sept. 24, 1963), and on tour (opened Central City, Colo., Aug. 3, 1963; closed Fisher, Detroit, Mich., March 21, 1964); with Philip Rose, *Nobody Loves an Albatross* (Lyceum, N.Y.C., Dec. 19, 1963); produced *Mating Dance* (Eugene O'Neill Th., Nov. 3, 1965); and, with Lester Osterman, produced Tyrone Guthrie's revival of *Dinner at Eight* (Alvin Th., Sept. 27, 1966). He was director (1966–71) of the Center Theatre Group, Music Center, Los Angeles, Calif., where he presented such attractions as Sir Laurence Olivier's National Theatre Company of Great Britain, the Royal Shakespeare Company, and sixteen of his own productions, including *Idiot's Delight, Captain Brassbound's Conversion,* and *Design for Living.* He also produced in N.Y.C. *More Stately Mansions* (Broadhurst, Oct. 31, 1967); *Abelard & Heloise* (Brooks Atkinson Th., Mar. 10, 1971); a revival of Pirandello's *Emperor Henry IV* (Ethel Barrymore Th., Mar. 28, 1973); with Lester Osterman, *A Moon for the Misbegotten* (Morosco, Dec. 1973); *When You Comin' Back, Red Ryder?* (Eastside Playhouse, Dec. 6, 1973); and a revival of *Of Mice and Men* (Brooks Atkinson Th., Dec. 18, 1974).

Television. Mr. Martin was the Coca Cola Man on the Freddy Robbins Show (WOR, Sept. 1952–Apr. 1953) and on the Eddie Fisher Show (NBC, Sept. 1953–Jan. 1954).

Other Activities. In June 1966, Mr. Martin was appointed executive manager of Jerome Robbins's American Musical Experimental Workshop, operating under a federal grant.

Awards. Mr. Martin shared with Lester Osterman in a special Antoinette Perry (Tony) Award for *A Moon for the Misbegotten,* named the outstanding production of the season. *When You Comin' Back, Red Ryder?* received a special Outer Circle Award for production.

Recreation. Golf, theatre.

MARTIN, ERNEST H. Producer, playwright. b. Ernest H. Markowitz, Aug. 28, 1919, Pittsburgh, Pa., to Samuel and Cecilia (Sklar) Markowitz. Grad. Univ. of California at Los Angeles, A.B. 1942. Married to Nancy Guild, actress; three daughters. Member of Dramatists Guild; League of N.Y. Theatres. Address: c/o Feuer and Martin Productions, Inc., 505 Park Ave., New York, NY 10022, tel. (212) PL 9-4004.

Theatre. With Cy Feuer, Mr. Martin has produced *Where's Charley?* (St. James Th., Oct. 11, 1948); *Guys and Dolls* (46 St. Th., Nov. 24, 1950); *Can-Can* (Shubert, May 7, 1953); *The Boy Friend* (Royale, Sept. 30, 1954); *Silk Stockings* (Imperial, Feb. 24, 1955); *Whoop-Up* for which they also wrote, with Dan Cushman, the libretto (Shubert, Dec. 22, 1958); *How to Succeed in Business Without Really Trying* (46 St. Th., Oct. 14, 1961); *Little Me* (Lunt-Fontanne, Nov. 17, 1962); and *The Goodbye People* (Ethel Barrymore Th., Dec. 3, 1968).

Messrs. Martin and Feuer are former owners of the Lunt-Fontanne Th. (N.Y.C., Aug. 1960–Apr. 1965).

Awards. *Guys and Dolls,* which he produced with Mr. Feuer, received the Antoinette Perry (Tony) Award and the NY Drama Critics Award (1951). Their production of *How to Succeed in Business Without Really Trying* received the Pulitzer Prize, the Antoinette Perry (Tony) Award and the NY Drama Critics Circle Award (1962).

MARTIN, HELEN. Actress. b. Helen Dorothy Martin, St. Louis, Mo., to William and Amanda Frankie (Fox) Martin. Father, minister. Grad. Pearl H.S., Nashville, Tenn.; attended Fisk Univ. and A&I State Coll. Member of AEA; SAG; AFTRA. Address: 50 Manhattan Ave., New York, NY 10025, tel. (212) UN 5-1278.

Theatre. Miss Martin made her stage debut with the Rose McClendon Players (N.Y.C., 1939); subsequently, as a charter member (1940) of the Amer. Negro Th., N.Y.C., appeared as Ruby Jackson in *Striver's Row;* in *Three's a Family;* and the variety show, *Hits, Bits and Skits.*

She made her Bway debut as Vera Thomas in *Native Son* (St. James, Mar. 24, 1941), and appeared in the role on tour and on the N.Y.C. Subway Circuit; played the Maid in *Three's a Family,* and Lissa, as a little girl, in *Mamba's Daughters* (N.Y.C. Subway Circuit, 1943); and appeared in *Chicken Every Sunday* (Blackstone, Chicago, Ill., 1944).

She played Honey Turner in *Deep Are the Roots* (Fulton, N.Y.C., Sept. 26, 1945; Wyndham's, London, July 8, 1947), and on tour (Scotland, North Wales); Della in *The Royal Family* and Paula in *The Petrified Forest* (Salt Creek Th., Hinsdale, Ill., July 1951); Poppy in *Take a Giant Step* (Lyceum, N.Y.C., Sept. 24, 1953); Rummy Mitchins in *Major Barbara* (Greenwich Mews, June 16, 1954); Rheba in a touring company of *You Can't Take It with You* (1954–55).

She appeared as Mrs. Tancred in *Juno and the Paycock* (Greenwich Mews, N.Y.C., Feb. 12, 1955); toured as Millie in *Anniversary Waltz* (opened Shubert, Cincinnati, Ohio, Sept. 26, 1955); played Jeniella in *King of Hearts* (Woodstock, N.Y., Summer 1956); Martha Lane in *A Land Beyond the River* (Greenwich Mews, N.Y.C., Mar. 28, 1957); Auntie Alice in a stock production of *Fever of Life* (Hyde Park, N.Y., and Westport Country Playhouse, Conn., Summer 1957); and Jessie in *The Ballad of Jazz Street* (Greenwich Mews, N.Y.C., Nov. 11, 1959).

Miss Martin played Maude Carter in *The Long Dream* (Ambassador, Feb. 17, 1960); Susie in *Period of Adjustment* (Helen Hayes TH., Nov. 10, 1960); Felicity Trollop Pardon in *The Blacks* (St. Marks Playhouse, May 4, 1961); Missy Judson in *Purlie Victorious* (Cort, Sept. 28, 1961); Essie in a stock production of *Critic's Choice* (Colonie Th., Latham, N.Y. and Playhouse-in-the-Park, Philadelphia, Pa., 1962); Hannah in *My Mother, My Father and Me* (Plymouth, Mar. 23, 1963); Adelaide Bobo in a tour of *The Blacks* (Chicago, Ill., Summer 1963), and succeeded (Oct. 1963); Vinnie Burrows as Bobo in the N.Y.C. production.

She played Ruby Grant in *One Is a Lonely Number* (Mermaid Th., N.Y.C., June 18, 1964); toured as Millie in *Happy Anniversary* (Summer 1964); was Maria Pleasant in *The Cat and the Canary* (Stage 73, N.Y.C., Jan. 4, 1965); Sister Douglas in *The Amen Corner* (Ethel Barrymore Th., Apr. 15, 1965; Lyceum, Edinburgh, Scot., Aug. 23, 1965; Saville, London, Eng., Oct. 12, 1965); toured as Rheba in *You Can't Take It with You* (Summer 1966); and was Ann Hall in the pre-Bway tryout of *What Do You Really Know About Your Husband?* (opened Shubert Th., New Haven, Conn., Mar. 9, 1967; closed there Mar. 11, 1967). She was understudy to Claudia McNeil as Sarah Goldfine in *Something Different* (Cort, N.Y.C., Nov. 28, 1967); again played Rheba in *You Can't Take It with You* (Arena Stage, Washington, D.C., Dec. 4, 1969); was Idella in *Purlie* (Broadway Th., N.Y.C., Mar. 15, 1970); Mrs. Johnson in *Raisin* (Arena Stage, Washington, D.C., May 23, 1973; 46 St. Th., N.Y.C., Oct. 18, 1973); and again played Idella in a revival of *Purlie* (Billy Rose Th., Dec. 27, 1972).

Films. Miss Martin appeared in *The Phoenix City Story* (Allied, 1955); *A Matter of Conviction* (1960); *Where's Poppa?* (UA, 1970); *Cotton Comes to Harlem* (UA, 1970); and *Death Wish* (Par., 1974). (1964).

Television and Radio. On radio, she played Honey Turner in *Deep are the Roots* (BBC, London, June 1947); subsequently was a disc jockey (WOV, US, Apr. 1953). On television, she appeared in *Green Pastures* (Hallmark Hall of Fame, NBC, 1959); *The Bitter Cup* (Frontiers of Faith, NBC, 1960); The Nurses (1964); and The Defenders (1964).

She was in the special *J.T.* (CBS Children's Hour, Dec. 13, 1969); the pilots *Wash and Dry* (WNYC, Ch. 31, 1974) and *Big Daddy* and has been on Maude (CBS) and Good Times (CBS).

Recreation. Attending the theatre, movies, reading.

MARTIN, HUGH. Composer, lyricist, accompanist.

Theatre. Mr. Martin made the musical arrangements for *Hooray for What?* (Winter Garden, N.Y.C., Dec. 1, 1937); was rehearsal pianist and appeared in the revue *One for the Money* (Booth, Feb. 4, 1939); and appeared in *Streets of Paris* (Broadhurst, June 19, 1939).

With Ralph Blane, he composed the music and lyrics for *Best Foot Forward* (Ethel Barrymore Th., Oct. 1, 1941), which was revived (Stage 73, Apr. 2, 1963); wrote the lyrics and music for *Look Ma, I'm Dancin'* (Adelphi, Jan. 29, 1948); *Make a Wish* (Winter Garden, Apr. 18, 1951); with Timothy Gray, wrote music and lyrics for *Love from Judy* (Saville, London, Sept. 26, 1952), which was presented in the US (Pittsburgh Playhouse, Pa.); and contributed lyrics to the revue, *Airs on a Shoestring* (Royal Court, London, Apr. 22, 1953).

He was accompanist for Eddie Fisher (Palladium, London, May 12, 1953) and for Judy Garland (Palace, N.Y.C.)

With Timothy Gray, Mr. Martin wrote music, lyrics, and book for *High Spirits* (Alvin, Apr. 7, 1964); music, lyrics, and sketches for *They Don't Make 'Em Like That Anymore* (Plaza 9 Music Hall,

June 8, (1972); with Buster Davis, vocal arrangements for *Lorelei* (Palace, Jan. 27, 1974); and, with Mr. Gray, was responsible for musical supervision and vocal arrangements for *Good News* (St. James, Dec. 23, 1974).

Films. Mr. Martin, with Ralph Blane, wrote the songs for *Meet Me in St. Louis* (MGM, 1944); made vocal arrangements for *The West Point Story* (WB, 1950); wrote songs for *Athena* (MGM, 1954); and music for the documentary film, *Grandma Moses.*

Television. Mr. Martin composed the music and lyrics for *Hans Brinker or The Silver Skates* (Hallmark Hall of Fame, NBC, Feb. 9, 1958).

MARTIN, LEILA. Actress, singer. b. Leila Markowitz, Aug. 22, 1936, New York City, to Seymour and Irma Markowitz. Studied acting with Lee Strasberg, N.Y.C., one year; Sanford Meisner, N.Y.C., two years. Married Dec. 24, 1955, to Leonard Green, manager, producer; one daughter, one son. Member of AEA; SAG; AFTRA.

Theatre. Miss Martin made her N.Y.C. debut as Gussie in *Wish You Were Here* (Imperial, June 25, 1952); subsequently played Sarah Brown in a revival of *Guys and Dolls* (NY City Ctr., Apr. 20, 1955); and appeared in the folk opera, *The Mermaid in Lock 7* with the American wind Symphony (Pittsburgh, Pa., July 1956).

She played Linda in *The Best House in Naples* (Lyceum, N.Y.C., Oct. 26, 1956); was standby for Sara Marshall as Ellen Spelding in *Visit to a Small Planet* (Booth, Feb. 7, 1957); toured in an industrial Coco Cola show (1959); was standby for Sandra Church as Louise in *Gypsy* (Bway Th., N.Y.C., May 21, 1959); played Maria in the national tour of *West Side Story* (opened Erlanger, Chicago, Ill., Oct. 8, 1959; closed Shubert, Boston, Mass., Apr. 23, 1960); Gwendolyn Fairfax in *Ernest in Love* (Gramercy Arts, N.Y.C., May 4, 1960); and appeared in stock as Magnolia in *Show Boat*, Polly in *The Boy Friend* and Teddy Stern in *Wish You Were Here* (Pinebrook Th., N.J., 1960).

Miss Martin played Rutka Mazur in *The Wall* (Billy Rose Th., N.Y.C., Oct. 11, 1960); was standby for Janice Rule as Diana and for Dran Seitz as Lysistrata in *The Happiest Girl in the World* (Martin Beck Th., Apr. 13, 1961); appeared as Dilla in *The Automobile Graveyard* (41 St. Th., Nov. 13, 1961); Maria in *West Side Story* (O'Keefe Center, Toronto, Can., 1962; Rainbow Stage, Winnipeg, Can., Aug. 1963); Dunreath Henry in *King of Hearts* (Playhouse-on-the-Mall, Paramus, N.J., Nov. 1963); and Lady Blakeney in *Pimpernel!* (Gramercy Arts, N.Y.C., Jan. 6, 1964).

She played Bellabruna in *Blossom Time* (Paper Mill Playhouse, Millburn, N.J., Oct. 18, 1966); was standby for Louise Lasser as Stella in *Henry, Sweet Henry* (Palace, Oct. 23, 1967); appeared as Gutele Rothschild in *The Rothschilds* (Lunt-Fontanne Th., Oct. 19, 1970); replaced (July 5, 1972) Kathleen Widdoes as Polly Peachum in *The Beggar's Opera* (Brooklyn Acad. of Music, Mar. 21, 1972; reopened McAlpin Roof Th., May 30, 1972); and was the Wife in *Philemon* (Portfolio Studio, Apr. 8, 1975).

Television. Miss Martin appeared in the serials, Golden WIndows (NBC, 1956); Modern Romances (CBS, 1957); the Max Liebman Spectaculars (NBC, 1957); True Story (CBS, 1957); Valiant Lady (CBS, 1957); the Patti Page Show (ABC, 1959); Naked City (ABC, 1963); The Doctors (NBC, 1963); and The Nurses (NBC, 1964–65).

MARTIN, MARY. Actress, singer. b. Mary Virginia Martin, Dec. 1, 1913. Weatherford, Tex., to Preston and Juanita (Presley) Martin. Father, judge. Attended Ward Belmont School for Girls, Nashville, Tenn. Married Nov. 3, 1930, to Benjamin J. Hagman (marr. dis. 1935); one son; married May 5, 1940, to Richard Halliday, producer (dec. Mar. 3, 1973); one daughter. Relative in theatre: son, Larry Hagman, actor. Member of AEA; SAG; AFTRA.

Pre-Theatre. Teacher of dance; night club singer.

Theatre. Miss Martin made her stage debut singing "When Apples Grow on the Lilac Trees" at age five at a firemen's ball in Weatherford, Tex.; made her Bway debut as Dolly Winslow in the musical, *Leave It to Me* (Imperial Th., Nov. 9, 1938); subsequently appeared in the pre-Bway tour of *Dancing in the Streets* (closed Shubert, Boston, Mass., Mar. 1943); played Venus in *One Touch of Venus* (Imperial, N.Y.C., Oct. 7, 1943), and on tour (1945); Tchao-Ou-Niang in *Lute Song* (Plymouth, N.Y.C., Feb. 6, 1946); made her London debut as Elena Salvador in *Pacific 1860* (Drury Lane, Dec. 19, 1946); and toured as Annie Oakley in *Annie Get Your Gun* (1947–48).

She appeared as Ensign Nellie Forbush in *South Pacific* (Majestic, N.Y.C., Apr. 7, 1949; Drury Lane, London, Nov. 1, 1951); appeared in her first nonsinging role as Jane Kimball in *Kind Sir* (Alvin, N.Y.C., Nov. 4, 1953); toured in the title role in *Peter Pan* (opened Curran, San Francisco, Calif., July 1954; Philharmonic Aud., Los Angeles, Calif., Aug. 1954; Winter Garden, N.Y.C., Oct. 20, 1954); played Sabina in *The Skin of Our Teeth* (Th. Sarah Bernhardt, Paris, June 1955) and on tour in the US (opened Natl., Washington, D.C., July 1955; closed Blackstone, Chicago, Ill., Aug. 1955) and in N.Y.C. (ANTA, Aug. 17, 1955); in revivals of *South Pacific* (June 1957) and *Annie Get Your Gun* (Curran Th., San Francisco, Calif., Aug. 1957); toured in a one-woman show, *Music with Mary Martin;* and played Maria Rainer in *The Sound of Music* (Lunt-Fontanne, N.Y.C., Nov. 16, 1959–Oct. 7, 1961).

She played the triple role of Our Melissa, Jennie Malone, and Shalamar in *Jennie* (Majestic, Oct. 17, 1963); toured the US and the world (Apr. 1965–Apr. 1966) as Dolly Gallagher Levi in the international touring company of *Hello, Dolly!*, including engagements in Okinawa, Korea, Japan (Sept. 1965), and South Vietnam (opened Bien Hoa, Oct. 10, 1965) before commencing the London, Eng., engagement (Th. Royal, Drury Lane, Dec. 2, 1965); and played Agnes in *I Do! I Do!* (46 St. Th., N.Y.C., Dec. 5, 1966), also touring in this part (Apr. 8, 1968–Apr. 1969).

Films. Miss Martin made her debut in *The Great Victor Herbert* (Par., 1939); subsequently appeared in *Rhythm on the River* (Par., 1940); *Love Thy Neighbor* (Par. 1940); *Kiss the Boys Goodbye* (Par., 1941); *New York Town* (Par., 1941); *Birth of the Blues* (Par., 1941); *Star Spangled Rhythm* (Par., 1942); *Happy Go Lucky* (Par., 1943); *True to Life* (Par., 1943); and *Night and Day* (WB, 1946).

Television and Radio. On radio, she appeared on Good News of 1938 (NBC, June 2–30, 1938); Rudy Vallee Show (Feb. 2, and 9, 1939); Good News of 1940 (NBC, March 7–Dec. 5, 1940); Jack Benny Show (CBS, Nov. 17, 1940); Kraft Music Hall (NBC, Jan. 1–Nov. 5, 1942); Tex and Jinx (July 2; Aug. 27, 1947); Bell Telephone Hour (NBC, May 16, 1949); Weekend (Oct. 4, 1953; Dec. 19, 1954; Mar. 27, 1955); Christmas Program (Dec. 4, 1955); Monitor (Paris Festival of Arts Interview, NBC, 1955); Biographies in Sound (Meet Mary Martin, Oct. 10, 1956); and Hungarian Relief Christmas Program (1956).

Miss Martin made her television debut on America Applauds (An Evening for Richard Rodgers, NBC, Mar. 4, 1951); subsequently, appeared on Ford 50th Anniversary (NBC-CBS, June 15, 1953); Rodgers and Hammerstein Cavalcade (NBC-CBS, Mar. 28, 1954); in *Peter Pan* (Producers Showcase, NBC, Mar. 7, 1955; Jan. 9, 1956; Dec. 8, 1960; Feb. 9, 1963); Ford Star Jubilee (CBS, Oct. 22, 1955); *The Skin of Our Teeth* (NBC, Sept. 11, 1955); *Born Yesterday* (Hallmark Hall of Fame, NBC, Oct. 28, 1956); *Together with Music* (NBC, 1959); *Annie Get Your Gun* (NBC, Nov. 27, 1957); *Magic with Mary Martin* (NBC, Mar. 29, 1959); and *Music with Mary Martin* (NBC, Mar. 29, 1959).

She also appeared in the title role in the *Peter Pan* special (NBC, 1960; repeated Jan. 21, 1966); was narrator of the *Hello, Dolly! 'Round the World* special (NBC, Feb. 7, 1966); was in the *Mary Martin at Eastertime* special (NBC, Apr. 3, 1966); and was co-host, with Robert Preston, of the 1967 Tony Award ceremonies (ABC, Mar. 26, 1967).

Published Works. Miss Martin wrote *Needlepoint* (1969).

Discography. Miss Martin has recorded for RCA Victor, Rodgers & Hammerstein's *Cinderella, Mary Martin Sings, Richard Rodgers Plays, Peter Pan; Jenny;* and *I Do! I Do!;* for Capitol, *Annie, Get Your Gun;* for Columbia, *The Bandwagon, Anything Goes, Babes in Arms, Girl Crazy, South Pacific,* and *The Sound of Music;* for Decca, *Ford 50th Anniversary Show, Lute Song,* and *On the Town;* for Disney, *Hi-Ho, Little Lame Lamb, The Sleeping Beauty* and *Mary Martin Sings a Musical Love Song;* and for Young People's Records, *Mary Martin sings for Children.*

Also, *Wait Till the Sun Shines, Nellie* (Brunswick); an album of lullabies; recordings with the late Eddie Duchin and his orchestra; "My Girl Back Home" and "Loneliness of Evening," dropped from the original *South Pacific; Get Out Those Old Records* and *You're Just in Love* (with son Larry Hagman); *My Heart Belongs to Daddy* and *Most Gentlemen Don't Like Love* (Brunswick).

Awards. Miss Martin won *Variety* NY Drama Critics Polls for her performances as Venus in *One Touch of Venus* (1944), Ensign Nellie Forbush in *South Pacific* (1949), Maria Rainer in *The Sound of Music* (1960); received Antoinette Perry (Tony) Awards for spreading theatre to the country while the originals are in New York as Annie Oakley in *Annie Get Your Gun* (1948), for her performance in the title role in *Peter Pan* (1955), and as Maria Rainer in *The Sound of Music* (1960); the NATAS (Emmy) Award for her television performance in the title role in *Peter Pan* (1955); and a Tony nomination (1967) for her performance in *I Do! I Do!*.

Recreation. Reading, painting, needlepoint.

MARTIN, NAN. Actress. b. Nan Clow Martin, Decatur, Ill., to Clarence and Frances (Clow) Martin. Father, musician; mother, musician. Grad. Santa Monica (Calif.) H.S.; attended Univ. of California at Los Angeles. Studied acting at Max Reinhardt Drama Sch.; Actors Studio. Married Mar. 17 to Robert Emmett Dolan, musician; one son. Member of AEA; SAG; AFTRA; Theatre Communications Group, Ford Foundation (advisory board); Drama Panel, US State Dept. (chairman). Address: Jay Wolf, c/o Frank Cooper Agency, 680 Fifth Ave., New York, NY 10018, tel. (212) PL 7-1100.

Theatre. Miss Martin made her Bway debut as Beatrice in *A Story for a Sunday Evening* (Playhouse, Nov. 17, 1950); subsequently played Marie-Louise Durham in *The Constant Wife* (Natl., Dec. 8, 1951); understudied the roles of Mrs. Anne Shankland in *Table by the Window* and Miss Railton-Bell in *Table Number 7* in the double-bill *Separate Tables* (Music Box, Oct. 25, 1956); performed in stock productions of *The Fourposter, Hatful of Rain,* and *Oh, Men! Oh, Women!* (Montreal, Canada, 1957); understudied Eva LeGallienne as Queen Elizabeth, and Irene Worth in the title role in *Mary Stuart* (Phoenix, N.Y.C., Oct. 8, 1957); understudied Eileen Herlie as Emilia Marty in *The Makropoulos Secret* (Phoenix, Dec. 3, 1957); played Carol Cutrere in *Orpheus Descending* (Coconut Grove Playhouse, Miami, Fla., March 1958); Mrs. Topaz in *The Saturday Night Kid* (Provincetown Playhouse, N.Y.C., May 15, 1958); and Blanche Du Bois in *A Streetcar Named Desire* (Hyde Park Playhouse, N.Y., Summer 1958).

She appeared as Sarah in *J. B.* (ANTA, N.Y.C., Dec. 11, 1958); Bertha Brett in *I Rise in Flame, Cried the Phoenix* as part of a double-bill with *Sweet Confession* (Th. de Lys, Apr. 14, 1959); Margaret in the Phoenix Th. production of *The Great God Brown* (Coronet, Oct. 6, 1959); the title role in *Lysistrata* (Phoenix, Nov. 24, 1959); Lady Percy in *Henry IV, Part 1* (Phoenix, Mar. 1, 1960); and Marguerite Gautier in the Circle in the Square production of *Camino Real* (St. Mark's Playhouse, May 16, 1960); and appeared in the Library of Congress, May 1960.

In stock, she appeared in *Memo for a Green Thumb* (Ogunquit Playhouse, Me.; Cape Playhouse, Dennis, Mass., Summer 1960); as Claire Zachanassian in *The Visit* (Williamstown Summer Th., Mass., August 1960); played Irene Wilson in *Under the Yum-Yum Tree* (Henry Miller's Th., N.Y.C., Nov.

16, 1960); Beatrice in the NY Shakespeare Festival production, *Much Ado About Nothing* (Wollman Memorial Skating Rink, N.Y.C., July 5, 1961); Helen Davis in the pre-Bway tryout of *A Short, Happy Life* (opened Moore Th., Seattle, Wash., Sept. 12, 1961; closed Huntington Hartford Th., Los Angeles, Calif., Oct. 21, 1961); in the title role in *Phaedra* (Natl. Arts Club, N.Y., 1962); as Elena in *Uncle Vanya* (Arena Stage, Washington, D.C., Mar. 1962); Portia in the NY Shakespeare Festival production of *The Merchant of Venice* (Delacorte Th., N.Y.C., June 13, 1962); and as Katherine in *The Taming of the Shrew* (Anderson Th., Mar. 6, 1963).

She played The Woman in *Hughie, And Others* (Duchess Th., London, England, June 18, 1963); Argia in *The Queen and the Rebels* (Alley Th., Dallas, Tex., Oct. 1963); Gertrude in *Hamlet* (Delacorte, N.Y.C., June 16, 1964); appeared in *Heart's Delight* (Westport Country Playhouse, Conn., Aug. 3, 1964); played Grace Easely in *The Slave* (St. Mark's Playhouse, Dec. 16, 1964); appeared in the pre-Bway tryout of *This Winter's Hobby* (opened Shubert, New Haven, Mar. 23, 1966; closed Philadelphia, Apr. 9, 1966); played Elizabeth in *Richard III* (Delacorte, N.Y.C., Aug. 9, 1966); and A Visitor in *Come Live with Me* (Billy Rose Th., Jan. 26, 1967); appeared in *The Marriage of Mr. Mississippi* (Washington, D.C., Th. Club, Feb. 16, 1967; and Ctr. Th. Group, Los Angeles, Aug. 25, 1967); replaced Constance Cummings as Gertrude in a touring production of *Hamlet* (July 9, 1969); and played Clytemnestra in *Agamemnon* (McCarter Th., Princeton, N.J., Oct. 26, 1972).

Films. Miss Martin appeared in the screen version of *Toys in the Attic* (UA, 1963).

Television. She has appeared in *People Kill People Sometimes* (Producers Showcase, NBC); *Heloise and Abelard* (Camera 3, CBS); *Richard II* (Camera 3, CBS); *Henry IV, Part 1* (Play of the Week, WNTA); *The Lonely Woman* (Purex Special); on The New Breed (ABC); Ben Casey (ABC); in *The Merchant of Venice* (CBS Special); on the US Steel Hour (CBS); Twilight Zone (CBS); The Untouchables (ABC); Eleventh Hour (NBC); The Defenders (CBS); The Fugitive (ABC); *Shakespeare's Women* (CBS); and in *Hamlet* (CBS Special).

MARTIN, VIRGINIA. Actress, singer. b. Chattanooga, Tenn. Attended Univ. of Chattanooga. Married to Joel O'Hayon, recording engineer. Member of AEA; AFTRA.

Theatre. Miss Martin made her N.Y.C. debut joining the cast of *South Pacific* (Majestic Th., Apr. 7, 1949); subsequently appeared in *The Pajama Game* (St. James, May 13, 1954); sang in the chorus and understudied Jane Kean as Wynne in *Ankles Aweigh* (Mark Hellinger Th., Apr. 18, 1955); appeared in the revue, *New Faces of 1956* (Ethel Barrymore Th., June 14, 1956); played Cheryl Merrill, and understudied Vivian Blaine as Irene Lovelle in *Say, Darling* (ANTA, Apr. 3, 1958); played Hedy in *How To Succeed in Business Without Really Trying* (46 St. Th., Oct. 14, 1961); Belle in *Little Me* (Lunt-Fontanne Th., Nov. 17, 1962; Blackstone Th., Chicago, Mar. 7, 1964); replaced (Feb. 8–27, 1965) Nancy Dussault as Emily Kirsten in *Bajour* (Shubert Th., Nov. 23, 1964); toured as Younger Belle and Baby in *Little Me* (Summer 1965); and appeared in *Buy Bonds, Buster!* (Th. de Lys, June 4, 1972).

Miss Martin has appeared in summer stock productions of *Best Foot Forward* and *Gentlemen Prefer Blondes* (Oakdale Musical Th., Wallingford, Conn.), *You Never Know* (Andover, Mass.), and *The Tender Trap* (Bucks County Playhouse, New Hope, Pa.).

Television. She has appeared on the Jack Paar Show (NBC) and The Gypsy Rose Lee Show; and was on Girl Talk (ABC, 1965–66); and Bewitched (ABC, Apr. 1966).

MARYAN, CHARLES. Director, producer, stage manager. b. Charles Peter Maryan, Dec. 30, 1934, Chicago, Ill., to Harry Oliver and Hazel (Sinaiko) Maryan. Father, doctor; mother, artist and teacher. Grad. Francis W. Parker Sch., Chicago; Dartmouth Coll., A.B. 1956. Studied at Goodman Th. (Chicago); Neighborhood Playhouse (with Sanford Meisner); and with Stella Adler. Married Feb. 1965, to Sarah Sanders (marr. dis. 1973). One daughter. Served US Army, 1957–59; Public Information Specialist, and editor of the command newspaper, *Along the Lines*. Member of AEA; SSDC. Address: (home) 777 West End Ave., New York, NY 10025, tel. (212) 886-8351; (bus.) tel. (212) LO 4-3250.

Theatre. Mr. Maryan took part in many school plays at Francis Parker Sch. in Chicago. He first worked professionally as a technician, and played small roles in *Sabrina Fair* (Shady Lane Playhouse, Marengo, Ill., 1955). He directed *The Emperor Jones* (The Blue Angel, Chicago, May 1959); was production stage manager for *The Days and Nights of Beebee Fenstermaker* (Sheridan Sq. Playhouse, N.Y.C., Sept. 17, 1962); The National Theatre of France (NY City Ctr., Feb. 1964); and *Absence of a Cello* (Ambassador, N.Y.C., Sept. 21, 1964); was production manager of *The Typist* and *The Tiger* (Globe Th., London, May 25, 1964); production stage manager for *Catch Me If You Can* (Morosco, N.Y.C., Mar. 9, 1965); and *A Hand Is on the Gate* (Longacre, N.Y.C., Sept. 21, 1966); directed *The Caretaker* (Th. of the Living Arts, Philadelphia, Pa., Nov. 1967); *Let Them Down Gently* (ANTA Matinee Series, Th. de Lys, N.Y.C., Jan. 8, 1968); *Mercy Street* (American Place Th., N.Y.C., Oct. 27, 1969); *A Day in the Death of Joe Egg* (Hartford Stage Co., Jan. 1970); directed a touring production of *Forty Carats*, (Oct. 1971); *The Blind Junkie* (street theatre production, N.Y.C., Aug. 1971); and *The Big Broadcast on East 53rd* (La Mama E.T.C., N.Y.C., June 2, 1974).

Television. He is associate producer of *Love of Life* (CBS, 1973–to date).

Awards. In 1972, Mr. Maryan received an award for Best Director for Summer Stock from the Council of Stock Theatres.

Recreation. Collecting art.

MARY ANGELITA, B.V.M, SISTER. Educator. b. Anne Merle Kramer, Aug. 30, 1912, Chicago, Ill., to John P. and Anne (Shannon) Kramer. Father, railroad employee. Grad. St. Mary's H.S., Chicago, Ill., 1929; Mundelein Coll., A.B. 1932; attended Loyola Univ., 1932–35; Clarke Coll., 1935–38; grad. Marquette Univ., M.A. 1949; attended St. Louis Univ., 1954; Northwestern univ., 1960; Univ. of Detroit, 1962; Univ. of Notre Dame, Summer 1964. Member of Natl. Catholic Theatre Conference (central regional chairman, 1951–53; vice-pres., 1953–55; pres., 1955–57; administrative vice-pres., 1957–65; chairman of natl. conventions, 1955, 1959, 1966); AETA (exec. committee, 1955–57; chairman audio-visual projects committee, 1961–64); North Central State Theatre Assn.; Natl. Thespian Soc.; Alpha Gamma Omega; Secondary Schools Th. Assn. (bd. of dirs.); SSTA (convention program chmn., 1974); Chimera Th. (founder and bd. of dirs.); Guthrie Th. (bd. of dirs.); Minneapolis Th. in the Round (bd. of dirs.). Address: (home) 40 N. Milton St., St. Paul, MN 55104, tel. (612) 225-8962; (bus.) 880 Portland Ave., St. Paul, MN 55104, tel. (612) 227-6000.

Since Sept. 1957, Sister Mary Angelita has taught drama and speech at Our Lady of Peace High School (St. Paul, Minn.)

Since 1964, she has led eight theatre tours to Europe. In November, 1973, she became theatre coordinator of the Minn. State Arts Council and the Audience Development director of the Children's Theatre Company (Minneapolis Soc. of Fine Arts; John C. Donahue Co.).

Before entering (Sept. 8, 1955) the religious order, the Sisters of Charity of the Blessed Virgin, she taught drama to private pupils (Chicago, Ill., 1930–35); directed for the Catholic Order of Foresters (Chicago, Ill. 1932–35); entertained clubs and groups; and had her own children's television program, and The Sunshine Hour (WGES, Chicago, Ill., 1929–32).

Awards. Sister Mary Angelita received the St. Genesius statuette from Mercy Coll. (1957); the National Catholic Theatre Conference Commander Award, Order of St. Genesius (1959), and was named to the National Catholic Theatre Conference Pilgrimage to Europe as a representative of Sisters who teach drama (1960).

MASON, MARSHA. Actress. b. Apr. 3, 1942, St. Louis, Mo., Father, James Mason, owner of printing company. Grad. Nerinx Hall (St. Louis); Webster Coll. Married 1964 to Gary Campbell, actor (marr. dis.); married Oct. 25, 1973, to Neil Simon, playwright.

Theatre. Miss Mason was the understudy for the role of Toni in *Cactus Flower* (Royale, N.Y.C., Dec. 8, 1965), and a replacement in the role of Botticelli's Springtime, subsequently playing the role of Toni in a national tour (1968); played Bobby in *The Deer Park* (Th. de Lys, N.Y.C., Feb. 1, 1967); played Joanna Dibble in *It's Called The Sugar Plum* on a double-bill with *The Indian Wants the Bronx* (Astor Place Th., Jan. 17, 1968); and Penelope Ryan in *Happy Birthday, Wanda June* (Th. de Lys, Oct. 7, 1970); and Edison, Dec. 22, 1970).

With the Eugene O'Neill Playwrights Conference (Waterford, Conn.), she played Masha in *Body and Soul* (July 16, 1971); Marion in *Respects* (July 22, 1971); Marjorie Bruce in *Bruce* (July 30, 1971); and Stat in *Ishtar* (Aug. 5, 1971). She appeared with the American Conservatory Th. (Geary Th., San Francisco) as Roxanne in *Cyrano de Bergerac* (Oct. 28, 1972); Jessica in *The Merchant of Venice* (Nov. 14, 1972); Nora in *A Doll's House* (Jan. 9, 1973); Alice in *You Can't Take It with You* (Jan. 30, 1973); and Abigail in *The Crucible* (Apr. 3, 1973); subsequently played various roles in *The Good Doctor* (Eugene O'Neill Th., N.Y.C., Nov. 27, 1973); and Lady Anne in *King Richard III* (Mitzi E. Newhouse Th., Oct. 20, 1974).

Films. She played Maggie Paul in *Cinderella Liberty* (20th-Fox, 1973); and Arlene in *Blume in Love* (WB, 1973).

Television. Miss Mason has appeared in a continuing role on Love of Life (CBS); on Dr. Kildare (NBC); and the ACT production of *Cyrano de Bergerac* (NET).

Awards. Miss Mason received the Golden Globe Award (1974) for her performance in *Cinderella Liberty.*.

MASON, MARSHALL W. Director, scenic and lighting designer, artistic director. b. Feb. 24, 1940, Amarillo, Tex., to Marvin M. and Lorine Chrisman (Hornsby) Mason. Father, cook; mother, realtor. Grad. Luling Elem. Sch.; Sam Houston Jr. H.S.; Amarillo (Tex.) H.S. (1957); Northwestern Univ., B.S. 1961. Studied with Lee Strasberg and Harold Clurman at the Actors Studio. Married Mar. 20, 1966, to Zita Litvinas (dec.). Member of SSDC. Address: (home) 165 Christopher St., New York, NY 10014; (bus.) 2307 Broadway, New York, NY 10024, tel. (212) 874-1080.

Theatre. While attending Northwestern Univ., Mr. Mason directed summer stock productions of *Mary Stuart, The Doctor's Dilemma,* and *Cyrano de Bergerac* (Eagles Mere, Pa., Playhouse, 1960–61). As his first professional production, he directed for Off-Off-Bway *The Rue Garden* (Caffe Cino, N.Y.C., July 1962), and subsequently directed productions of *The Clown, Romance D'Amour, The Haunted Host* (Caffe Cino, 1962–64); *Balm in Gilead, The Sand Castle, A Coffee Ground among Tea Leaves* (La Mama ETC, 1965–67); *One Room with Bath,* (13 St. Th., 1967); *Untitled Play* (Judson Poets' Th., 1968); and *Goodnight, I Love You* (Old Reliable Th., 1968). Off-Bway, he directed *Little Eyolf* (Actor's Playhouse, Mar. 16, 1964), *Arms and the Man* (East End Th., 1968), *Home Free* (Cherry Lane Th., Feb. 10, 1965), *Spring Play* (New Th., 1968), and *The Gingham Dog* (New Dramatists, 1968).

Mr. Mason is founder and artistic director of the Amer. Th. Project which produced *Home Free* and *The Madness of Lady Bright* for presentation abroad (Mercury Th., London, England; and Traverse Th., Edinburgh, Scotland, 1968); and of the Circle Th. Co. (1969–to date), where he directed *The Three Sisters* in simultaneous experimental and traditional productions (June 11, 12, 1970), *Sextet (Yes)* (Mar.

1971), *Elephant in the House* (Feb. 1972), *The Hot L Baltimore* (repeated at the Mark Taper Forum, Los Angeles, Calif., 1973), *Prodigal* (Dec. 1973), and *The Sea Horse* (Mar. 1974); and Tennessee Williams' *Battle of Angels* (Nov. 3, 1974). He produced *When You Comin Back, Red Ryder?* (Nov. 6, 1973). Mr. Mason also directed a production of *Come Back, Little Sheba*, starring Jan Sterling (Queens Playhouse, N.Y.C., Aug. 1974).

Awards. Mr. Mason received the Village Voice Off-Broadway (Obie) Award for Distinguished Direction 1972–73 for *The Hot L Baltimore*. .

Recreation. Mr. Mason enjoys rock music, opera, and films.

MASSEY, DANIEL. Actor. b. Daniel Raymond Massey, Oct. 10, 1933, London, England, to Raymond and Adrianne (Allen) Massey. Father, actor; mother, actress. Grad. Eton; Kings Coll., Cambridge. Married 1961 to Adrienne Corri (marr. dis. 1968). Relative in theatre: sister, Anna Massey, actress.

Theatre. Mr. Massey made his stage debut with the Cambridge Univ. Footlights Club in *Anything May* (June 1956); and his professional debut with the Worthing Repertory Co. playing Terry in *Peril at End House* (July 1956).

He made his first Bway appearance as Lt. Lord Frederick Beckenham in *Small War on Murray Hill* (Ethel Barrymore Th., Jan. 3, 1957); subsequently returned to England where he appeared with the Windsor Repertory Co.; made his London debut as Angier Duke in *The Happiest Millionaire* (Nov. 1957); was a leading player in the revue *Living for Pleasure* (July 1958); played Johnnie Jackson in *Dispersal* (Belgrade Th., Coventry, England, June 1959); Charlie in *Make Me an Offer* (Th. Royal, Stratford, Oct. 1959; and New Th., London, Dec. 1959); Charles Surface in *The School for Scandal* (Haymarket, Apr. 1962); and, at the Nottingham (England) Playhouse, played Athos in *The Three Musketeers* (Oct. 1962), and George Jacob Holyoake in *A Subject of Scandal and Concern* (Nov. 1962).

Mr. Massey appeared in the role of Georg Nowack in *She Loves Me* (Eugene O'Neill Th., N.Y.C., Mar. 1963); subsequently played Mark Antony in *Julius Caesar* (Royal Court, London, Apr. 1963); at the Yvonne Arnaud Th. (Guildford, England) played Beliaev in *A Month in the Country* (May 1965), and The Messenger in *Samson Agonistes* (June 1965); appeared in the role of Paul Bratter in *Barefoot in the Park* (Piccadilly, London, Nov. 1965); played Captain Absolute in *The Rivals* (Haymarket Th., Oct. 1966); John Worthing in *The Importance of Being Earnest* (Haymarket Th., Feb. 1968); and Howarth in *Spoiled* (Close Th. Club, Glasgow, Scotland); took over the role of Abelard in *Abelard and Heloise* (Wyndham's Th., Dec. 1970); and Gaston Lachailles in *Gigi* (Uris, N.Y.C., Nov. 13, 1973).

Films. Mr. Massey appeared in *Girls at Sea* (1957); played Graham in *The Entertainer* (Cont., 1960); and Noel Coward in *Star!* (20th-Fox, 1968).

Television. In the US, he has appeared as Saul Novick in *Shadow Game* (CBS Playhouse, 1969); and on the series Bonanza (NBC, 1971); and in the BBC productions of *Roads to Freedom* (NET), *The Golden Bowl* (NET), and *War and Peace* (NET). Other British appearances include *Venus Observed, On Approval*, and *Back to Beyond*.

MASSEY, RAYMOND. Actor, director, producer, writer. b. Raymond Hart Massey, Aug. 30, 1896, Toronto, Ontario, Canada, to Chester Daniel and Anna (Vincent) Massey. Father, manufacturer. Attended Appleby Sch., Ontario, Canada, 1910–14; Balliol Coll., Oxford England) Univ., 1919–21. Married 1921 to Margery Fremantle (marr. dis. 1929); one son; married Adrianne Allen, actress (marr. dis. 1939); one son, one daughter; married 1939 to Dorothy Ludington, lawyer. Relatives in theatre: son, Daniel Massey, actor; daughter, Anna Massey, actress. Served Canadian Field Artillery, 1915–19; CEF, 1916; instructor in gunnery with Princeton and Yale Univ. ROTC, 1917–18; in Siberia with C.F.A., 1918–19; rank, Capt. Served on staff of Adjutant-Genl. in Canadian Army, 1942–43; rank, Maj. Naturalized US citizen, 1944. Member of AFTRA; SAG; AEA (council, fifteen years; 1st vice-pres., five years); British Equity (original council member); Century Assn. (N.Y.C.); Garrick Club (London). Address: 913 N. Beverly Dr., Beverly Hills, CA.

Pre-Theatre. Sold agricultural machinery.

Theatre. Mr. Massey made his professional debut as Jack in *In the Zone* (Everyman Th., London, July, 1922); subsequently played James Bebb in *At Mrs. Beam's* (Royalty, Apr. 2, 1923); Smith in *The Rose and the Ring* (Wyndham's, Dec. 19, 1923), appeared with the Oxford Repertory Co., as Capt. Kerny in *Captain Brassbound's Conversion* (1923); played Stanley Pitt in *The Audacious Mr. Squire* (Criterion, London, Feb. 19, 1924); played Lt. Gaythorne in and directed *Tunnel Trench* (Prince's, Mar. 8, 1925); Jonty Drennan in *The Round Table* (Wyndham's, May 11, 1925); Capt. La Hire and Canon d'Estivet in *Saint Joan* (New, Mar. 26, 1924); and Capt. Rickman in *Prisoners of War* (Court, July 5, 1925).

With Allan Wade and George Carr, he was co-manager of the Everyman Th. (Jan. 1926), where he played Robert Mayo in, and directed *Beyond the Horizon* (Mar. 22, 1926); directed and played Rufe Pryor in *Hell-bent fer Heaven* (1926); appeared as Edmund Crowe in *The Rat Trap;* Mr. Man in *Br'er Rabbit;* and directed and played Tommy Luttrell in *The White Chateau* (Mar. 29, 1927).

Mr. Massey played Khan Aghaba in *The Transit of Venus* (Ambassadors', Apr. 26, 1927); directed and appeared as Rev. MacMillan in *An American Tragedy* (Apollo, June 26, 1927); appeared as Reuben Manassa in *The Golden Calf* (Globe, Sept. 14, 1927); directed *The Wolves* (New, Aug. 31, 1937); *The Crooked Billet* (Royalty, Oct. 13, 1928); *The Squall* (Nov. 15, 1927); played Austin Lowe in *The Second Man* (Playhouse, Jan. 24, 1928); Alistair Ballantyne in *Four People* (St. Martin's, May 10, 1928); directed and played Joe Cobb in *Spread Eagle* (New, June 27, 1928); Lewis Dodd in *The Constant Nymph* (Garrick, Sept. 27, 1928); directed *The Sacred Flame* (Playhouse, Feb. 8, 1929); *The Stag* (Globe, Apr. 2, 1929); appeared as Randolph Calthorpe in *The Black Ace* (Globe, May 9, 1929); directed *The Silver Tassie* (Apollo, Oct. 11, 1929); *Symphony in Two Flats* (New, Oct. 14, 1929); played Raymond Dabney in, and directed *The Man in Possession* (Ambassadors', Jan. 22, 1930); appeared in the title role in *Topaze* (New, Oct. 8, 1930); directed *Dishonored Lady* (Playhouse, May 8, 1930); *Lean Harvest* (St. Martin's, May 7, 1931); directed and played Randall in *Late Night Final* (Phoenix, June 25, 1931); and staged *Grand Hotel* (Adelphi, Sept. 3, 1931).

Mr. Massey made his N.Y.C. debut in the title role in *Hamlet* (Broadhurst, Nov. 5, 1931); played Smith in *Never Come Back* (Phoenix, London, Oct. 28, 1932); Dr. Maclean in *Doctor's Orders* (Globe, Jan. 31, 1933); Hugh Sebastian in *The Rats of Norway*, which he also directed (Playhouse, Apr. 6, 1933); Kurt von Hagen in *The Ace* (Lyric, Aug. 24, 1933); and Cleon in *Acropolis* (Lyric, Nov. 23, 1933).

He appeared as David Linden in *The Shining Hour* (Booth, N.Y.C., Feb. 13, 1934; St. James's, London, Sept. 4, 1934), directing the London production; staged *Ringmaster* (Shaftesbury, Mar. 11, 1935); *Worse Things Happen at Sea* (St. James's, Mar. 26, 1935); appeared in the title role in *Ethan Frome* National, N.Y.C., Jan. 21, 1936); directed *Heart's Content* (London, Dec. 23, 1936); *The Orchard Walls* (Feb. 3, 1937); and played Harry Van in *Idiot's Delight*, which he also directed (Apollo, Mar. 22, 1938).

Mr. Massey appeared as Abe Lincoln in *Abe Lincoln in Illinois* (Plymouth, N.Y.C., Oct. 15, 1938); Sir Colenso Ridgeon in *The Doctor's Dilemma* (Shubert, Mar. 11, 1941); James Mavor Morell in *Candida* (Shubert, Apr. 27, 1942); Rodney Boswell in *Lovers and Friends* (Plymouth, Nov. 29, 1943); toured the ETO as the Stage Manager in the USO production of *Our Town* (1945); played Prof. Henry Higgins in *Pygmalion* (Ethel Barrymore Th., N.Y.C., Dec. 26, 1945); Prof. Lemuel Stevenson in *How I Wonder* (Hudson, Sept. 30, 1947); appeared in and directed a stock production of *The Winslow Boy* (Summer 1949), staged *The Father*, in which he also played the Captain (Cort, N.Y.C., Nov. 16, 1949); and re-appeared in stock as the Stage Manager in *Our Town*.

Mr. Massey wrote *The Hanging Judge* (New, London, Sept. 23, 1952); appeared in a stage production *John Brown's Body*, on tour (1952–53), and in N.Y.C. (Century, Feb. 14, 1952); at the American Shakespeare Festival (Stratford, Conn., 1955), played Brutus in *Julius Caesar* (July 12) and Prospero in *The Tempest* (Aug. 1); played Abraham Lincoln in *The Rivalry* (Orpheum, Seattle, Wash., Sept. 1957), and on tour (1957); appeared as Mr. Zuss in *J. B.* (ANTA, N.Y.C., Dec. 11, 1958); and appeared as Tom Garrison in *I Never Sang for My Father* (London 1970).

Films. Since his debut in 1930, Mr. Massey has appeared in over seventy films, playing Sherlock Holmes in *The Speckled Band* (1st Division, 1931); appeared in *The Old Dark House* (U, 1932); as Chauvelin in *The Scarlet Pimpernel* (Korda, Eng., 1934); in *Things to Come* (UA, 1935); Philip II in *Fire Over England* (UA, 1937); Cardinal Richelieu in *Under the Red Robe* (20th-Fox, 1937); in *Dreaming Lips* (UA, 1937); Black Michael in *The Prizoner of Zenda* (UA, 1937); the Governor in *The Hurricane* (UA, 1937); Prince Ghul in *Drums* (UA, 1938); *Black Limelight* (Alliance, 1939); Abe Lincoln in *Abe Lincoln in Illinois* (RKO, 1940); John Brown in *Santa Fe Trail* (WB, 1940); in *Dangerously They Live* (WB, 1941); *The Invaders* (Col., 1942); *Desperate Journey* (WB, 1942); *Reap the Wild Wind* (Par., 1942); the Captain in *Action in the North Atlantic* (WB, 1943); Jonathan in *Arsenic and Old Lace* (WB, 1944); the District Attorney in *The Woman in the Window* (RKO, 1944); General Chennault in *God Is My Co-pilot* (WB, 1945); the General in *Hotel Berlin* (WB, 1945); in *Stairway to Heaven* (U, 1946); General Mannon in *Mourning Becomes Electra* (RKO, 1947); in *Possessed* (WB, 1947); *The Fountainhead* (WB, 1949); McCoy in *Roseanna McCoy* (RKO, 1949); in *Chain Lightning* (WB, 1950); *Barricade* (WB, 1950); *Dallas* (WB, 1950); *Sugarfoot* (WB, 1951); *Come Fill the Cup* (WB, 1951); as Nathan, the Prophet in *David and Bathsheba* (20th-Fox, 1951); in *Carson City* (WB, 1952); *The Desert Song* (WB, 1953); *Battle Cry* (WB, 1955); John Brown in *Seven Angry Men* (Allied, 1955); Junius Brutus Booth in *Prince of Players* (20th-Fox, 1955); Mr. Trask in *East of Eden* (WB, 1955); *Omar Khayyam* (Par., 1957); General Cummings in *The Naked and the Dead* (WB, 1958); the Abbot in *The Great Imposter* (U, 1960); in *The Fiercest Heart* (20th-Fox, 1961); and *The Queen's Guards* (Michael Powell, 1961).

Television. Mr. Massey made his debut as the Stage Manager in *Our Town* (1948), subsequently appeared as Dr. Gillespie in *Dr. Kildare* (NBC, 1961), and has been in countless television and radio productions. His play, *The Hanging Judge*, has been presented both on British and US television.

Awards. Mr. Massey has received the honorary degrees of D.Litt., Lafayette Univ. (1939); L.L.D., Queen's Univ., Kingston, Ont. (1949); D.Litt., Hobart Coll. (1953); D.F.A. from Northwestern Univ. (1959); L.H.D., Amer. International Coll. (1960); D.F.A., Ripon Coll. (1961); and D.H.L., College of Wooster (1966). He was awarded the Delia Austria Medal by the Drama League of New York for his performance as Abe Lincoln in *Abe Lincoln in Illinois* (1939).

Recreation. Golf, carpentry, reading.

MASSI, BERNICE. Actress. b. Bernice Dolores Massi, Aug. 23, Camden, N.J., to Vincent and Margaret (Scogna) Massi. Father, bartender. Attended Camden Catholic H.S. Married May 10, 1969, to Yuri Krasnapolsky, symphony conductor. Member of AEA; AFTRA; AGVA; SAG. Address: New York City, NY.

Theatre. Miss Massi made her first stage appearance as successor (Mar. 1952) to Joan Tangsrud in the role of Ensign Janet MacGregor in the national touring company of *South Pacific* (opened Shubert Th., Chicago, Ill., Nov. 14, 1950); subsequently joined (June 1953) *Wish You Were Here* (Imperial, N.Y.C., June 25, 1952) as understudy to Patricia Marand in the part of Teddy Stern; appeared in the chorus of *By the Beautiful Sea* (Majestic, Apr. 8, 1954); succeeded (Apr. 1955) Ruth Schueni as Gabrielle in *Can-Can* (Shubert, May 7, 1953); and sang in the chorus and was understudy to Patricia Hammerlee in the role of Elsie Chelsea in *The Vamp* (Winter Garden, Nov. 10, 1955). In stock, she played Lu Lu in *Hit the Deck* and Sara Brown in *Guys and Dolls* (Gateway Th., Somers Point, N.J., July–Aug. 1955); Teddy Stern in *Wish You Were Here* and appeared in *High Button Shoes* (Haddonfield Music Circus, N.J., Summer 1956).

In N.Y.C., she was understudy to Anne Bancroft as Gittel in *Two for the Seesaw* (Booth, Jan. 16, 1958); played Ethel in *Beg, Borrow or Steal* (Martin Beck Th., Feb. 10, 1960); with the Kenley Players (Columbus and Warren, Ohio, Aug. 1961), played Frenchy in *Destry Rides Again* and Gittel in *Two for the Seesaw;* appeared as Comfort O'Connell in *No Strings* (54 St. Th., N.Y.C., Mar. 15, 1962), Laurette Harrington in *What Makes Sammy Run?* (54 St. Th., Feb. 27, 1964); Nancy in *Oliver!* (Papermill Playhouse, Millburn, N.J., 1965); Crystal Allen in *The Women* (Papermill Playhouse, Millburn, N.J., 1966); Aldonza in *Man of La Mancha* (Martin Beck Th., N.Y.C., 1967–69); and appeared in *How The Other Half Loves* (Royale, N.Y.C., Mar. 29, 1971).

Television. Miss Massi has appeared singing with the Ray Charles Singers, and on the Perry Como Show (NBC, 1959–60). She has also appeared on *The Mike Douglas Show* (CBS); *The Tonight Show* (NBC); and *The Merv Griffin Show.*

Recreation. Piano, organ, swimming, reading, concerts, films, travel.

MASTEROFF, JOE. Playwright. b. Dec. 11, 1919, Philadelphia, Pa., to Louis P. and Rose Pogost Masteroff, Father, merchant. Grad. Overbrook H.S., Philadelphia, 1936; Temple Univ., B.S. 1940. Studied at Amer. Theatre Wing, 1949–51. Served USAAF, 1942–45; rank, Sgt. Member of Dramatists Guild, New Dramatists Committee (exec. comm., 1960–64). Address: 2 Horatio St., New York, NY 10014, tel. (212) 924-8165.

Theatre. Mr. Masteroff wrote *The Warm Peninsula* which toured nationally (opened Playhouse, Wilmington, Del., Oct. 29, 1958; closed Rochester Aud., N.Y., May 9, 1959), and opened on Bway (Helen Hayes Th., Oct. 20, 1959). He also wrote the book for the musical, *She Loves Me* (Eugene O'Neill Th., Apr. 23, 1963); for *Cabaret* (Broadhurst, Nov. 20, 1966); and adapted the book for *70, Girls, 70* (Broadhurst, Apr. 15, 1971).

Awards. *Cabaret* was named best musical (1966–67) by the NY Drama Critics Circle and by the Antoinette Perry (Tony) Award committee.

Recreation. Double-crostics.

MASTERSON, CARROLL. Producer. b. Isla Carroll Sterling, Apr. 8, 1913, Houston, Tex., to Frank Prior and Isla (Carroll) Sterling. Father, vice-pres., Humble Oil and Refining Co. Attended Holton Arms Sch., Washington, D.C., 1929–31. Married 1931, to Bert Farmer Winston (marr. dis. 1942); one son, one daughter; married 1943, to John A. Cowan (dec. 1949); married Jan. 17, 1951, to Harris Masterson. Member of Junior League, River Oaks Garden Club; Garden Club of Houston; Houston YWCA (vice-pres.); Alley Theatre Guild, Houston (vice-pres., pres., and founder); Mexico City Garden Club. Address: 1406 Kirby Dr., Houston, Tx 77019, tel. (713) JA 3-0524.

Theatre. Mrs. Masterson produced, together with her husband, Harris Masterson, and Charles R. Wood, *God and Kate Murphy* (54 St. Th., N.Y.C., Feb. 26, 1959); the Mastersons produced *The Villa of Madame Vidac* (Carnegie Hall Playhouse, Sept. 30, 1959); produced, with Eddie Bracken, *Beg, Borrow or Steal* (Martin Beck Th., Feb. 10, 1960); produced, with Leonard Sillman, *A Second String* (Eugene O'Neill Th., Apr. 13, 1960); produced the revue, *From A to Z* (Plymouth, Apr. 20, 1960); produced, with Stephen Mitchell, *Masterpiece* (Royalty, London, Jan. 26, 1961); produced the revue *New Faces of 1962* (Alvin, N.Y.C., Feb. 1, 1962); produced, with Norman Twain, *The Lady of the Camellias* (Winter Garden, Mar. 20, 1963); with Norman Twain, in association with ANTA, presented *Traveller Without Luggage* (ANTA, Sept. 17, 1964); with Norman Twain and Edward Padula, produced *Bajour* (Shubert Th., Nov. 23, 1964); and, with Norman Twain, presented *The Apparition Theatre of Prague* (Cort, Nov. 16, 1966).

In 1964, the Mastersons, with Norman Twain, took a long-term lease on the ANTA Th.

MASTERSON, HARRIS. Producer. b. July 9, 1914, Houston, Tex., to Neill Turner and Libbie (Johnston) Masterson. Father, rancher. Grad. New Mexico Military Inst., Roswell, N.M., 1931; Rice Univ., B.A. 1955. Married Jan. 17, 1951, to Carroll Sterling. Served WW II, US Army, 1941–45, ETO; rank, Capt.; attended Intelligence Sch., 1951–52. Member of Allegro Club; Ramada Club; Bolero Club; River Oaks Country Club; Texas Corinthian Yacht Club; 100 Clubs; Sons of the Republic of Texas; Chevaliers du Tastevin; Society of Americans of Royal Descent; SAR; Somerset Chapter of Magna Charta Barons; American Club, London; Mayfair Club (N.Y.C.); Houston Symphony (bd. of dir.); Houston Council for Retarded Children (pres., bd. of gov.); the Rienzi Foundation (pres.); Sons of the American Revolution; Colonial Order of the Crown; The Society of Descendents of Knights of the Most Noble Order of the Garter; Plantagenet Society; Kentucky Colonels (1958); Order of Washington; Houston Museum of Fine Arts (vice-pres.); Theatre-Under-the-Stars (vice-pres.); Houston Ballet Foundation (pres.); Riverside General Hospital (dir.); Miller Th. Advisory Council (pres.); Bayoo Bend Advisory Council (chmn.); Texas Fine Arts Society (dir.); Rice Univ. Arts Advisory Council; Houston Youth Symphony and Ballet (adv. bd.); and Houston Stock Show and Rodeo (dir.). Address: (home) 1406 Kirby Dr., Houston, TX 77002, tel. (713) JA 3-0524; (bus.) 1 W. 72nd St., New York, NY 10023, tel. (212) TR 3-5680.

Theatre. Mr. Masterson, together with his wife, Carroll Masterson and Charles R. Wood, produced *God and Kate Murphy* (54 St. Th., N.Y.C., Feb. 26, 1959); the Mastersons presented *The Villa of Madame Vidac* (Carnegie Hall Playhouse, Sept. 30, 1959); produced, with Eddie Bracken, *Beg, Borrow or Steal* (Martin Beck Th., Feb. 10, 1960); presented, with Leonard Sillman, *A Second String* (Eugene O'Neill Th., Apr. 13, 1960); produced the revue *From A to Z* (Plymouth, Apr. 20, 1960); produced with Stephen Mitchell, *Masterpiece* (Royalty, London, Jan. 26, 1961); presented the revue *New Faces of 1962* (Alvin, N.Y.C., Feb. 1, 1962); presented, with Norman Twain, *The Lady of the Camellias,* (Winter Garden, Mar. 20, 1963); with Norman Twain, in association with ANTA, presented *Traveller Without Luggage* (ANTA, Sept. 17, 1964).

In 1964, the Mastersons, with Norman Twain, took a long-term lease on the ANTA Th. and, with Mr. Twain, presented *Bajour* (Shubert, 1964); and *The Apparition Theatre of Prague* (Cort, 1966).

Other Activities. Mr. Masterson is an independent oil operator and rancher, as well as a director of the Bank of Texas, Assoc. Engineers, Diesel Corp., Winco, Travel Counselors of Houston, and Trade Company of America.

MATALON, VIVIAN. Director. b. Oct. 11, 1929, Manchester, England, to Moses and Rose (Tawil) Matalon. Educ. Munro Coll., Jamaica, Professional training, Neighborhood Playhouse, N.Y.C. (grad. 1950).

Theatre. Mr. Matalon began his theatrical career as an actor, appearing in summer stock at Lake George (N.Y.) Playhouse, Bucks County (New Hope, Pa.) Playhouse, and other theatres. In N.Y.C., he appeared off-Bway at Th. de Lys as a Man in *Maya* (June 9, 1953), Trip in *The School for Scandal* (June 23–28, 1953), and the Shampooer in *The Little Clay Cart* (June 30, 1953). In the mid-1950s, he went to London, England, where he played Signalman Urban in *The Caine Mutiny Court Martial* (Hippodrome, 1956); Apples in *A Hatful of Rain* (Princes, 1957); and Don Parritt in *The Iceman Cometh* (Arts, June 1958).

He began directing professionally with *The Admiration of Life* (Arts, Mar. 30, 1960) and later directed *Season of Goodwill* (Queen's, Sept. 16, 1964); *The Chinese Prime Minister* (Globe, May 20, 1965); *The Glass Menagerie* (Haymarket, Dec. 1, 1965); and *A Song at Twilight* (Queens's, Apr. 14, 1966), one of three plays by Noel Coward bearing the overall title of *Suite in Three Keys.* Mr. Matalon also directed productions of the other two plays: *Shadows of the Evening* and *Come into the Garden, Maud* (both Queen's, Apr. 25, 1966).

Other plays he directed include *After the Rain* (Hampstead Th. Club, Sept. 1, 1966); Duchess, Jan. 11, 1967; John Golden Th., N.Y.C., Oct. 9, 1967); *First Day of a New Season* (Th. Royal, Brighton, Eng., May 1967); *Two Cities* (Palace, London, Feb. 27, 1969); *Papp* (Hampstead Th. Club, Sept. 15, 1969); *Girlfriend* (Apollo, Feb. 17, 1970); *I Never Sang for My Father* (Duke of York's, May 27, 1970); *Noel Coward in Two Keys* (Ethel Barrymore Th., N.Y.C., Feb. 28, 1974), two of the plays that had been presented in London as *Suite in Three Keys;* and *P.S. Your Cat Is Dead* (John Golden Th., Apr. 7, 1975).

Television. In Sept. 1960, Mr. Matalon began directing television productions on the BBC, including *The Chopping Block, John Paddington, The Quails, A Case of Character, The Navigators,* and *Mr. Fowlds.* For commercial television in England, he was one of three directors (1961–63) of the hospital series Emergency in Ward 10.

MATHESON, MURRAY. Actor. b. Sidney Murray Matheson, July 1, 1912, Casterton, Victoria, Australia, to Kenneth Murray and Ethel Sunderland (Barrett) Matheson. Father, grazier. Attended Sandford (Victoria) State Sch., 1918–26. Served RAF, 1940–45; attached to British Embassy, Moscow, U.S.S.R., 1943–45. Member of AEA; AFTRA; SAG. Otter Lake, Parry Sound, Ontario, Canada tel. Fr 8-2243.

Theatre. Mr. Matheson first appeared on the stage as George in *Dangerous Corner* (Melbourne Little Th., Australia, July 4, 1933) and first appeared professionally in the chorus of *High Jinks,* followed by *Roberta* (His Majesty's Melbourne, 1934); played in a cross-country (Australia) ten-show tour of *Ten Minute Alibi, Tons of Money* and *While Parents Sleep;* and in *Billie* (Apollo, Melbourne, 1935).

In England, Mr. Matheson appeared with the Bournemouth Repertory Company (1936); subsequently played in a revue *And On We Go* (Savoy, London, March 3, 1937); Blenderband in *The Millionairess* (Th. Michel, Paris, France, May 14, 1937); appeared in *George and Margaret* (Charles, London, Aug. 14, 1937); toured as Charlie Parker in *Oscar Wilde* and Marchbanks in *Candida* (Berlin, Vienna, Brussels, Prague, Warsaw, Budapest, 1937–39); and played Eric in *The Human Element* (Th. de l'Oeuvre, Paris, May 14, 1939).

In London, he appeared in the musical revues *Band Wagon* (Palladium, Aug. 4, 1939), *Swinging the Gate* (Ambassadors', May 22, 1940), *Lights Up* (Savoy, Feb. 9, 1940); toured England in the revue *New Faces* (1940); appeared in the revue *Better Late* (Garrick, London, Apr. 24, 1946); toured Canada in the revue *There Goes Yesterday* (1948–50), which he wrote with John Pratt; toured in *The Drunkard;* and played a season at the Bahama Playhouse, Nassau.

Mr. Matheson made his Bway debut as Worthy in *The Relapse* (Morosco, Nov. 22, 1950); played Peter Henderson in *Escapade* (48 St. Th., Nov. 18, 1953); appeared in the pre-Bway tryout of *Down Came a Blackbird* (John Drew Th., East Hampton, L.I., N.Y., July 1955); played Felix Callender in *Third Person* (President, N.Y.C., Dec. 29, 1955); returned to the John Drew Th. to play in *Dead on Nine* (Aug. 13, 1956), *You Never Can Tell* (Aug. 20, 1956), and Simon in *Simon and Laura* (Aug. 12, 1957); toured in *The Cocktail Party;* toured in *Tonight at 8:30;* played Aegisthos in *Electra* and Arthur Gosport in *Harlequinade* (Rita Allen Th., N.Y.C.,

Feb. 13, 1959); Argan, the title role, in *The Imaginary Invalid* (Goodman Mem. Th., Chicago, May 3, 1959); and the Earl of Blandings in *Oh, Kay!* (E. 74 St. Th., N.Y.C., Apr. 16, 1960).

He played Sandor Turai in *The Play's the Thing* (Bucks County Playhouse, New Hope, Pa., May 2, 1964); Charles in *Blithe Spirit* (La Jolla Playhouse, Calif., Aug. 24, 1964); Denny in *Janus* (Paper Mill Playhouse, Millburn, N.J., Jan. 12, 1965); Dirk Winston in *Mary, Mary* (Bucks County Playhouse, May 17, 1965); Mr. Applegate in *Damn Yankees* (Melodyland, Berkeley, Calif., Aug. 3, 1965); appeared in *Yeats and Company: The Prose, Poetry and Plays of W. B. Yeats* (Th. Group, UCLA, Calif., Oct. 23, 1965); *Dial "M" For Murder,* as Captain Hook in *Peter Pan,* in *Heaven Can Wait,* and as "Sir" in *The Roar of the Greasepaint . .* (all in Calif.); as Von Mark in *The Student Prince* (Dorothy Chandler Pavilion, Los Angeles, July 26, 1966); Caesar in *Caesar and Cleopatra* (Goodman Th., Chicago, Jan. 12, 1968); in *Lock Up Your Daughters* (Pasadena Playhouse, Calif., 1968); as the butler, Tucker, in *The Ruling Class* (Goodman Th., Chicago, Mar. 7, 1972); and as Dr. Theodore Holley in the world premiere of the musical *The Charlatan* (Center Th. Group, Mark Taper Forum, Los Angeles, May 23, 1974).

Films. Mr. matheson made his debut in *Way to the Stars* (Rank, 1940); followed by *Journey Together* (Pinewood, 1945); *The Fool and the Princess* (Merton Park, 1946); *School for Secrets* (Two Cities, 1946); and in the US, *Hurricane Smith* (Par., 1952); *Plymouth Adventure* (MGM, 1952); *Botany Bay* (Par., 1953); *Flight to Tangier* (Par., 1953); *King of the Khyber Rifles* (20th-Fox, 1953); *Jamaica Run* (Par., 1953); *The Bamboo Prison* (Col., 1954); *Love Is a Many-Splendored Thing* (20th-Fox, 1955); *Wall of Noise* (WB, 1963); *Signpost to Murder* (MGM, 1965); *Assult on a Queen* (Par., 1966); *How To Succeed in Business without Really Trying* (UA, 1967); *In Enemy Country* (U, 1968); and *Star* (20th-Fox, 1968).

Television. Mr. Matheson has appeared as the Unidentified Guest in *The Cocktail Party* (CBC, Canada, 1949); on Adventures in Paradise (CBS, 1959); Alfred Hitchcock Presents (CBS); as Bunthorne in *Patience* (CBC, Canada, 1960); on Thriller (NBC); US Steel Hour (CBS); Alcoa Th. (NBC); King Magnus in *The Apple Cart* (CBC, Canada); The Fugitive (ABC); Suspense (NBC); Twilight Zone (CBS); Sam Benedict (NBC); Naked City (ABC); Route 66 (CBS); The Islanders (NBC); Laramie (CBS); Tall Man (NBC); in *Tiger at the Gates* (CBC, Canada); Studio One (CBS); Kraft Th. (NBC); Omnibus (NBC); The Man from U.N.C.L.E. (NBC); Get Smart (NBC); Perry Mason (CBS); 12 O'Clock High (ABC); The Defenders (CBS); Profiles in Courage (NBC); My Favorite Martian (CBS); One Step Beyond; The F.B.I. (ABC); Invaders (ABC); The Girl from U.N.C.L.E. (NBC); and other programs.

MATHEWS, CARMEN. Actress. b. Carmen Sylva Mathews, May 8, 1918, Philadelphia, Pa., to Albert Barns and Matilde (Keller) Mathews. Father, clothier. Grad. Bennett Jr. Coll., drama diploma, 1938; attended RADA, 1938–39. Member of AEA (council, 1953); AFTRA; SAG.

Theatre. Miss Mathews made her N.Y.C. debut as the Lady in Waiting in the Maurice Evans' production of *Hamlet* (St. James Th., Oct. 12, 1939), in which company she toured as Ophelia; and was the Queen in *Richard II* (1940). She appeared as Lady Madeleine in *The Seventh Trumpet* (Mansfield, N.Y.C., Nov. 21, 1941); Molly Morden in *The Moon is Down* (Martin Beck Th., Apr. 7, 1942); Mary Beech in *Harriet* (Henry Miller's Th., May 15, 1943); toured as Varya in *The Cherry Orchard* (1944); played Ida Stein in *The Assassin* (National, N.Y.C., Oct. 17, 1945); Mimi in *The Affairs of Anatol* (ELT, May 1946); Elsa Meredith in *Made in Heaven* (Henry Miller's Th., Oct. 24, 1946); Violet in *Man and Superman* (Alvin, Oct. 8, 1947); and Mrs. Sullen in a tour of *The Beaux' Stratagem* (Summer 1948).

Miss Mathews played Georgina in *The Ivy Green* (Lyceum, N.Y.C., Apr. 5, 1949); Miss Neville in *She Stoops to Conquer* (NY City Ctr., Dec. 28, 1949); Miss Ronberry in *The Corn Is Green* (NY City Ctr., Jan. 11, 1950); Theresa Tapper in *Courtin' Time* (National, June 3, 1951); Madame Ducotel in *My Three Angels* (Morosco, Mar. 11, 1953); sang the role of Contessa in *Candide* (Shubert, Boston, 1956); appeared as Mary Dean in *Holiday for Lovers* (Longacre, N.Y.C., Feb. 14, 1957); played the title role in *Candida* (Ann Arbor Drama Festival, Mich., May 1958); Eileen Stoddard in *The Man in the Dog Suit* (Coronet, N.Y.C., Oct. 30, 1958); Lady Utterword in *Heartbreak House* (Billy Rose Th., Oct. 18, 1959); Ceil in *Night Life* (Brooks Atkinson Th., Oct. 23, 1962); Maria in *Lorenzo* (Plymouth, Feb. 14, 1963); Louise in the pre-Bway tryout of *Zenda* (opened Curran, San Francisco, Calif., Aug. 5, 1963; closed Philharmonic Aud., Los Angeles, Calif., Nov. 1963); Mrs. Hutto in *The Yearling* (Alvin, N.Y.C., Dec. 10, 1965); Edna in *A Delicate Balance* (Martin Beck Th., Sept. 22, 1966); appeared in *My Mother, My Father, and Me* (Florida State Univ., Tallahassee, Feb. 1967); played Bathsheba in *I'm Solomon* (Mark Hellinger Th., N.Y.C., Apr. 23, 1968); Constance in *Dear World* (Mark Hellinger Th., Feb. 6, 1969); appeared in *All Over* (Washington, D.C. Th. Club, Nov. 3, 1971); played Mrs. Hanlon in *Ring 'Round the Bathtub* (Martin Beck Th., N.Y.C., Apr. 29, 1972); Gloriane in *Ambassador* (Lunt-Fontanne, Nov. 19, 1972); and appeared in *In Fashion* (Actors Th., St. Louis, Mo., Feb. 1973); and *Pygmalion* (Long Wharf Th., New Haven, Jan. 24, 1975).

Films. Miss Mathews has appeared in *A Rage To Live* (UA, 1965); *Rabbit, Run* (WB, 1970); and *Sounder* (20th-Fox, 1972).

Television. Among the programs on which Miss Mathews has appeared are Studio One (CBS); US Steel Hour (CBS); Hallmark Hall of Fame (NBC); Playhouse 90 (CBS); GE Th. (CBS); Twilight Zone (CBS); Ben Casey (ABC); The Fugitive (ABC); The F.B.I. (ABC); N.E.T. Playhouse (PBS); and Cannon (CBS).

Recreation. Farming.

MATHEWS, GEORGE. Actor. b. Oct. 10, 1911, New York City, to Joseph Patrick and Mary (O'Neill) Mathews. Attended schools in N.Y.C. Married to Guerita Donnelly (marr. dis.); married Sept. 6, 1951, to Mary Haynsworth, actress.

Theatre. Mr. Mathews made his professional debut as the Policeman in *The Thief of Mulberry Street* (Acad. of Music, Philadelphia, Pa., Nov. 1935). His first Bway appearance was as Dynamite Jim in *Processional* (Maxine Elliott's Th., Oct. 13, 1937); subsequently, played the First Marine in *Escape This Night* (44 St. Th., Apr. 22, 1938); and toured cross-country as Jack Armstrong in *Abe Lincoln in Illinois* (1939–40).

He played the Prizefighter in *Retreat to Pleasure* (Belasco, N.Y.C., Dec. 17, 1940); the Policeman in *Out of the Frying Pan* (Windsor, Feb. 11, 1941); the Safecracker in *The Night Before Christmas* (Morosco, Apr. 10, 1941); Sergeant Ruby in *The Eve of St. Mark* (Cort, Oct. 7, 1942); Memphis Jones in *The Streets Are Guarded* (Henry Miller's Th., Nov. 20, 1944); Gunner in *Kiss Them for Me* (Belasco, Mar. 20, 1945); Nick Palestro in *Beggars Are Coming to Town* (Coronet, Oct. 27, 1945); the First Guard in *Antigone* (Cort, Feb. 18, 1946); appeared in *Candida* (Cort, Apr. 3, 1946); played Tom Hutchinson in *Temper the Wind* (Playhouse, Dec. 27, 1946); Mitch in *A Streetcar Named Desire* (Ethel Barrymore Th., Dec. 3, 1947); Steve in *Hope Is the Thing with Feathers* (Playhouse, Apr. 11, 1948); Driscoll in *S.S. Glencairn* (NY City Ctr., May 20, 1948); and Emmett in *The Silver Whistle* (Biltmore, Nov. 24, 1948).

Mr. Mathews made his London debut as the Captain in *Mister Roberts* (Coliseum, July 19, 1950); subsequently played in *Twentieth Century* (ANTA, N.Y.C., Dec. 24, 1950); and, in stock, appeared as Hippolyte in *A Souvenir from Italy* (Olney Th., Md., July 1951); played Pausanias in *Barefoot in Athens* (Martin Beck Th., N.Y.C., Oct. 31, 1951); Cokey Mulqueen II in *One Eye Closed* (Bijou, Nov. 24, 1954); Robish in *The Desperate Hours* (Ethel Barrymore Th., Feb. 10, 1955); and Joe McDougall in *Holiday for Lovers* (Longacre, Feb. 14, 1957).

He appeared in the US Performing Arts Program production of *The Time of Your Life* (Brussels World's Fair, Belgium, Oct. 1958); played Adolphus Grigson in *The Shadow of a Gunman* (Bijou, N.Y.C., Nov. 20, 1958); and, in a program of one-act plays entitled *Triple Play,* appeared as Porter in *Portrait of a Madonna* and as a Policeman in *A Pound on Demand* (Playhouse, Apr. 15, 1959).

He played the Porter in *Macbeth* and Sir Toby Belch in *Twelfth Night* (Cambridge Drama Festival, Mass., July 1959); Frank Lilly in *Motel* (Wilbur, Boston, Mass., Jan. 1960); Fatso O'Rear in *Do Re Mi* (St. James, N.Y.C., Dec. 26, 1960); and appeared in the English-speaking premiere of *Joan of the Stockyards* (Dublin Festival, Ireland, Oct. 1961). Mr. Mathews followed (Nov. 26, 1963) Kenneth J. Warren as Hans in *Luther* (St. James, N.Y.C., Sept. 25, 1963); was one of the unnamed characters in *Catch Me If You Can* (Morosco, Mar. 9, 1965); played Cyfartha Lewis in *A Time for Singing* (Broadway Th., May 21, 1966); Walter Wishenant in *A Joyful Noise* (Mark Hellinger Th., Dec. 15, 1966); played Cap'n Dan in *The Great White Hope* (Arena Stage, Washington, D.C., Dec. 12, 1967); appeared at Barter Th. (Abingdon, Va.) in *A Gift for Cathy* (1968); and again played Cap'n Dan in *The Great White Hope* (Alvin Th., N.Y.C., Oct. 3, 1968).

Television. He has appeared on the CBS programs, The Defenders, Playhouse 90, Studio One, Suspense, and Glynis.

Recreation. Chess.

MATLAW, MYRON. Educator, theatre historian. b. May 21, 1924, Berlin, Germany. Grad. H.S. of Commerce, N.Y.C., 1941; Hofstra Coll., B.A. 1949; Univ. of Chicago, M.A. 1950, Ph.D. 1953. Married May 12, 1950, to Julia Moody; one son, one daughter. Served US Army, 1943–46; Officer, Military Intelligence. Member of ASTR; MLA. Address: (home) 43 W. 93rd St., New York, NY 10025, tel. (212) 663-6476; (bus.) c/o Dept. of English, Queens Coll. of CUNY, Flushing, NY 11351, tel. (212) 520-7331.

Dr. Matlaw has taught courses in drama and theatre history since 1953. He was a member of the faculty of the Univ. of Illinois (1953–55) and of Auburn Univ. (1955–56); and is Prof. of English at Queens Coll. and the Grad. Sch. of CUNY (1957–to date). He was visiting Prof. of English and Drama, Univ. of Hawaii (1967–68).

Published Works. Dr. Matlaw wrote, with James B. Stronks, *Pro and Con* (1960) and edited *Story and Critic* (1963) and *Nineteenth-Century American Drama* (1964); *Modern World Drama: An Encyclopedia* (1972).

He has contributed articles to *Modern Language Quarterly, Quarterly Journal of Speech, The Shavian, Modern Drama, Theatre Arts* Magazine, *Educational Theatre Journal, Theatre Annual, The Shaw Review, Symposium, The Regional,* and the *Encyclopedia Americana.* He has written book reviews for *Theatre Arts* Magazine and *Educational Theatre Journal* and other journals, magazines and newspapers; was a regular contributor to *Abstracts of English Studies* (1961–63), and was co-editor of *The Independent Shavian* (1962–67).

Awards. Dr. Matlaw received the American Council of Learned Societies Award for research on American vaudeville (1959).

MATTHAEI, KONRAD. Theatre executive, actor, producer. b. Detroit, Mich. Grad. Yale Univ., B.A.; Univ. of Michigan Grad. Sch. of Business Admin. Member of AEA; League of NY Th. Owners and Producers (bd. of dir.).

Pre-Theatre. Real estate salesman.

Theatre. Mr. Matthaei is president (May 1975–to date) of the American Shakespeare Th. (Stratford, Conn.), having previously served on that institution's board of trustees (1973–74; vice-pres., 1974–75). He is the owner of the Alvin Th. (N.Y.C.,

1967–to date), and a former co-owner of the Playhouse (N.Y.C., 1964–67).

Mr. Matthaei made his professional debut as Brick in *Cat on a Hot Tin Roof*(Groton, Conn., Summer Playhouse); debuted in N.Y.C. as a Servant in *She Stoops To Conquer* (Phoenix, Nov. 1, 1960); played David Scott in *Thirteen Daughters*(54 St. Th., Mar. 2, 1961); at Catholic Univ. (Washington, D.C.), appeared in *The Rivals, Hamlet,* and *Dr. Faustus;* played Zoilus in *The Thracian Horses* (Orpheum, N.Y.C., Sept. 27, 1961); appeared in the Equity Library Th. production of *Trelawney of the Wells* (Masters, Nov. 25, 1961); played the Grand Inquisitor in *Don Carlos* (Masque, Feb. 27, 1962); Jeraiah Jip in *A Man's a Man* (Masque, Sept. 19, 1962); was a replacement in *Riverwind*(Actors Playhouse, Dec. 13, 1962); appeared in *Luther* (St. James Th., Sept. 25, 1963); played the Stage Assistant in *The Milk Train Doesn't Stop Here Anymore* (Brooks Atkinson Th., Jan. 1, 1964); co-produced *An Evening's Frost*(Th. de Lys, Nov. 11, 1965); with David Black and Lorin E. Price, produced *George M!* (Palace, Apr. 10, 1968); replaced Lawrence Luckinbill (Jan. 25, 1969) in the role of Hank in *The Boys in the Band* (Th. Four, Apr. 15, 1968); again replaced Mr. Luckinbill (Mar. 10, 1969) in the national touring company of *The Boys in the Band;* played Otis in *A Place for Polly* (Ethel Barrymore Th., N.Y.C., Apr. 18, 1970); appeared in the NY Shakespeare Fest. production of *Trelawny of the Wells* (Public/Other, Nov. 11, 1970); appeared in the Center Th. Group production of *Othello* (Mark Taper Forum, Los Angeles, 1970–71 season); produced *Les Blancs* (Longacre, N.Y.C., Nov. 15, 1970); co-produced *The Love Suicide at Schofield Barracks* (ANTA Th., Feb. 9, 1972); on a double-bill, played Harris in *After Magritte,* and Simon in *The Real Inspector Hound* (Th. Four, Apr. 23, 1972); and, with Hale Matthews, presented the Goodman Th. Ctr. production of *The Freedom of the City* (Alvin, Feb. 17, 1974).

Films. He made his film debut in *Journey Out of Darkness* (Australia-American Pictures, 1967).

Television. He has appeared on the US Steel Hour; and Camera Three; and was a continuing character on The Secret Storm, As the World Turns, and Another World.

Other Activities. Mr. Matthaei is vice-president of Bayside Controls, Inc. (Queens, N.Y.); and was formerly associated with Amer. Metal Products Co. (Detroit, Mich.).

MATTHAU, WALTER. Actor. b. Walter Matthow, Oct. 1, 1920, New York City, to Melas and Rose (Berolsky) Matthow. Father, electrician. Grad. Seward Park H.S., N.Y.C., 1939. Studied with Erwin Piscator at the Dramatic Workshop of the New Sch. for Social Research, 1946–47. Married 1948 to Grace Geraldine Johnson (marr. dis. 1958); one son, one daughter. Married Aug. 21, 1959, to Carol Grace, actress; one son. Served USAAF, ETO, 1942–45; rank, Staff Sgt.; six battle stars. Member of AEA; SAG; AFTRA. Address: c/o William Morris Agency, 151 El Camino, Beverly Hills, CA 90212; c/o AEA, 226 W. 47th St., New York, NY 10036.

Pre-Theatre. File clerk, boxing instructor, basketball coach, radio operator.

Theatre. Mr. Matthau first appeared on stage at age four in a religious festival play presented at a N.Y.C. settlement house: made his professional debut as Sadovsky in the Dramatic Workshop of the New Sch. for Social Research production of *The Aristocrats* (President Th., 1946).

He made his first appearance on Bway as a Candle Bearer in *Anne of the Thousand Days* (Shubert, Dec. 8, 1948); played the Fourth Venetian Guard in *The Liar* (Broadhurst, May 18, 1950); was understudy to the role of Foreign Correspondent in *Season in the Sun* (Cort, Sept. 28, 1950); appeared as Sam Dundee in *Twilight Walk* (Fulton, Sept. 24, 1951); Sinclair Heybore in *Fancy Meeting You Again* (Royale, Jan. 14, 1952); George Lawrence in *One Bright Day* (Royale, Mar. 19, 1952); Charlie Hill in *In Any Language* (Cort, Oct. 7, 1952); John Hart in *The Gray-Eyed People* (Martin Beck Th., Dec. 17, 1952); and Andrew Lamb in the pre-Bway tryout of *A Certain Joy* (opened Playhouse, Wilmington, Del., Feb. 12, 1953; closed Locust, Philadelphia, Pa., Feb. 21, 1953).

Mr. Matthau played Paul Osgood in *The Ladies of the Corridor* (Longacre, N.Y.C., Oct. 21, 1953); Tony Lack in *The Burning Glass* (Longacre, Mar. 4, 1954); Yancy Loper in *The Wisteria Trees* (NY City Ctr., Feb. 2, 1955); Nathan Detroit in *Guys and Dolls* (NY City Ctr., Apr. 20, 1955); Michael Freeman in *Will Success Spoil Rock Hunter?* (Belasco, Oct. 13, 1955); Odysseus in the pre-Bway tryout of *Maiden Voyage* (opened Forrest, Philadelphia, Pa., Feb. 28, 1957; closed there Mar. 9, 1957); Maxwell Archer in *Once More with Feeling* (Natl., N.Y.C., Oct. 21, 1958); Potemkin in *Once There Was a Russian* (Music Box, Feb. 18, 1961); Benjamin Beaurevers in *A Shot in the Dark* (Booth, Oct. 18, 1961); Herman Halpern in *My Mother, My Father and Me* (Plymouth, Mar. 23, 1963); and Oscar Madison in *The Odd Couple* (Plymouth, Mar. 10, 1965).

Films. Mr. Matthau made his debut in *The Kentuckian* (UA, 1955); subsequently appeared in *The Indian Fighter* (UA, 1955); *Bigger Than Life* (20th-Fox, 1956); *A Face in the Crowd* (WB, 1957); *Slaughter on Tenth Avenue* (U, 1957); *Voice in the Mirror* (U, 1958); *Ride a Crooked Trail* (U, 1958); *King Creole* (Par., 1958); *Strangers When We Meet* (U, 1958); wrote and directed *Gangster Story* (Ind., 1959); played in *Island of Love* (WB, 1961); *Lonely Are the Brave* (U, 1962); *Who's Got the Action?* (Par., 1962); *Charade*(U, 1964); *Ensign Pulver*(WB, 1964); *Goodbye, Charlie* (20th-Fox, 1964); *Fail-Safe* (Col., 1964); *Mirage* (U, 1965); *Candy* (1965); *The Fortune Cookie* (UA, 1966); *A Guide for the Married Man* (20th-Fox, 1967); *The Odd Couple* (Par., 1968); *The Secret Life of an American Wife* (20th-Fox, 1968); *Hello, Dolly!* (20th-Fox, 1969); *Plaza Suite* (Par., 1969); *Kotch* (ABC Pictures, 1970); *New Leaf*(Par., 1971); *Cactus Flower* (Col., 1971); *Pete 'n Tillie* (U, 1972); *Charley Varrick* (U, 1972); *The Laughing Policeman* (20th-Fox, 1973); *The Taking of Pelham One Two Three* (UA, 1974); and *The Front Page* (U, 1974).

Awards. Mr. Matthau won the *Variety* NY Drama Critics' Poll for his performance as Maxwell Archer in *Once More, With Feeling* (1959); received the Antoinette Perry (Tony) Award for his performance as Benjamin Beaurevers in *A Shot in the Dark* (1961); the *Film Daily* Award for his role in *Lonely Are the Brave* (1962); the Antoinette Perry (Tony) Award for his performance in *The Odd Couple* (1965); an Academy (Oscar) Award for best supporting male actor for his performance in *The Fortune Cookie* (1966); was nominated for an Academy Award for his performance in *Kotch* (1970); and received British Academy awards for his performances in *Charley Varrick* and *Pete 'n Tillie* (1972).

MATTHEWS, INEZ. Singer, actress. b. Aug. 23, 1917, Ossining, N.Y., to Edward J. and Mary E. (Hamm) Matthews. Father, minister; mother, children's nurse. Grad. Ossining H.S., 1935. Studied voice with Mrs. Katherine Douglas until 1947; Robert Duke, 1947–50; Sara Lee, 1954; Mme. Paula Navikova, 1956; coached with Werner Singer, five years. Married Jan. 29, 1950, to Rev. Ulysses Jackson, Methodist minister; one daughter. Relative in theatre; brother, Edward Matthews (dec. Feb. 20, 1954), baritone, teacher of voice. Member of AEA (withdrawn); AGMA (withdrawn). Address: 25 Nassau Rd., Verona, NJ tel. (201) CE 9-4627.

Theatre. Miss Matthews made her Bway debut as the Maid to Isabella in *The Pirate* (Martin Beck Th., Nov. 25, 1942); was general understudy and later alternated in the title role in *Carmen Jones* (Bway Th., Dec. 2, 1943), in which she toured (US and Canada, Apr. 1944–Jan. 1946); appeared as Irina in *Lost in the Stars* (Music Box, N.Y.C., Oct. 30, 1949), in which she subsequently toured; played St. Theresa in *Four Saints in Three Acts* (Paris Art Festival, France, May–June 21, 1951); and repeated her role in *Four Saints in Three Acts* (Bway Th., N.Y.C., Apr. 16, 1952).

Films. Miss Matthews sang Serena for the sound track of *Porgy and Bess* (Col., 1959).

Radio. Miss Matthews made her debut as a singer in a chorus of twelve voices and a soloist for Leonard de Paur (Freedom's People, CBS, 1938–39); subsequently sang St. Settlement in a concert version of *Four Saints in Three Acts* (WEAF, May 1942); and was soloist with the Copenhagen Symphony (Denmark, 1954).

Concerts. She made her concert debut at Town Hall (N.Y.C., Nov. 1947); followed by concerts at Jordan Hall, Boston, Mass., and Kimball Hall, Chicago, Ill. (Nov. 1947). She toured Scandinavia twice, giving 15 concerts (1954) and 24 concerts (Feb. 1–Mar. 6, 1955); Alaska, giving 19 concerts (Sept. 1954); US and Canada with the De Paur Gala (1956–57; 1958–59); US (1960–61), including a performance of Verdi's *Requiem* (Southern Univ., Baton Rouge, La., 1961); and South America (Fall 1962).

Discography. She recorded *Four Saints in Three Acts* (1942); *Lost in the Stars* (1950); *Porgy and Bess* (1952, 1959); *Great New Voices of Today,* an album of spirituals (1954); *Die Schöne Müllerin* (1954); *Winterneise* (1954); and *Schwanengsang* (1954).

MATTHEWS, JESSIE. Actress, dancer. b. Mar. 11, 1907, London, England, to George E. and Jane (Townshend) Matthews. Father, fruiterer. Attended Pulteney Girls Sch., London. Married Henry Lytton, Jr. (marr. dis.); one daughter; married Sonny Hale (marr. dis.); married Brian Lewis (marr. dis.). Relative in theatre: nephew, Tony Hatch, musician. Member of AEA. Address: (home) 27 Penn Dr., Denham, Bucks, England tel. Denham 3012; (bus.) c/o Vincent Shaw, 23–24 Greek St., London, England tel. Gerrard 1135.

Theatre. Miss Matthews made her debut in *Bluebell in Fairyland* (Alhambra, London, Dec. 24, 1917); was the leading child dancer in *Dick Whittington* (Kennington Th., Dec. 27, 1920); appeared in *The Music Box Revue* (Palace, May 15, 1923); and in the chorus of *London Calling* (Duke of York's, Sept. 4, 1923).

She made her Bway debut as a member of the chorus and understudy to Gertrude Lawrence in *Andre Charlot's Revue of 1924* (Times Square Th., Jan. 9, 1924); which re-opened as *Andrew Charleton's Revue of 1924* (Selwyn, Apr. 21, 1924) and played Miss Lawrence's roles for several weeks (Toronto, Feb. 1925) during the subsequent tour; appeared in *The Charlot Show of 1926* (Prince of Wales's, Th., London, Oct. 5, 1926) and appeared in it on Bway when it was incorporated into *Earl Carroll's Vanities* (Earl Carroll Th., N.Y.C., Jan. 4, 1927), and on tour; for C. B. Cochran, appeared in *One Damn Thing After Another* (London Pavilion, May 19, 1927); played Melanie Page in *Jordan* (Strand Th., Jan. 22, 1928); appeared in the revues *This Year of Grace* (London Pavilion, Mar. 22, 1928); and *Wake up and Dream* (London Pavilion, Mar. 27, 1929; Selwyn, N.Y.C., Dec. 30, 1929); appeared in *Evergreen* (Adelphi, London, Dec. 3, 1930); played Paula Bond in *Hold My Hand* (Gaiety, Dec. 23, 1931); Sally in *Sally Who?* (Strand, May 30, 1933); toured as Sue Merrick and Gloria Grosvenor in *I Can Take It* (Jan. 1939); appeared in *Come Out to Play* (Wimbledon, Nov. 6, 1939; revised and re-opened, Phoenix, Mar. 19, 1940); played Jill Charters in the pre-Bway tryout of *The Lady Comes Across* (Shubert, New Haven, Dec. 1941; Philadelphia, Jan. 1941), but left before its Bway opening; played Sally in *Wild Rose* (Prince's, London, Aug. 6, 1942); appeared in *Maid to Measure* (King's, Hammersmith, Apr. 7, 1948); played Harriet Stirling in *Sweethearts and Wives* (Wyndham's, Feb. 22, 1949); Millie Crocker-Harris in *The Browning Version* and Edna Selby in *Harlequinade,* a double bill (Kings's, Hammersmith, May 1949); and joined (Aug. 1949) the *Sauce Tartare* Company (Cambridge, May 18, 1949).

She played Eliza Doolittle in *Pygmalion* (New, Hull, Apr. 1950; Aldershop, May 1950); toured as "Boss" Trent in *Castle in the Air* (Sept.–Dec., 1950);

played Madeleine in *Don't Listen, Ladies* ("Q," Apr. 1951); went to Australia and played Julia Lambert in *Larger Than Life* (Princess, Melbourne, June 1952) and Olivia Brown in *Love in Idleness* (Hippodrome, Preston, Dec. 1953); returned to England and directed *The Policeman and the Lady* (Royalty, Morecombe, Feb. 1955); played Amanda in *Private Lives* (Wimbledon, May 1955); and Denise Darvel in *Dear Charles* (Everyman Th., Cheltenham, Nov. 1955); returned to Australia and played Jessica in *Janus* (Th. Royal, Sydney, Dec. 1956); in England, played Gloria Faraday in *Nest of Robins* (Royal Court Th., Liverpool, July 1957); toured Austl. in several plays (Feb. 1958–60); toured Wales for the Arts Council as Louise Harrington in *Five Finger Exercise* (Oct.–Nov., 1960); played Fairy Snowflake in *Dick Whittington* (Bristol Old Vic Th., Dec. 1960); and played Nurse Wayland in *The Sacred Flame* (Royal, Northampton, Feb. 1961).

She toured as Alicia Storm in *Port in a Storm* (May–Aug., 1961); played Maggie Millward in *What a Racket!* (Pavilion, Torquay, June 1962); starred in two seasons of cabaret (Society, Mayfair, London, Apr. and Dec., 1964); appeared in *A Tribute to Jessie Matthews* (Huntington Hartford Museum, N.Y.C., Oct. 1965); played Violet Deakin in *A Share in the Sun* (Cambridge Th., London, Aug. 31, 1966); appeared in the revue, *Cockles and Champagne* (Th. Royal, Norwich, July 1969); played the Duchess of Monte Polo in *Puss in Boots* (Congress, Eastbourned, Dec. 1969); at the Palace Court (Bournemouth, June–Sept., 1970), played Judith Bliss in *Hay Fever* and Mrs. Bramson in *Night Must Fall;* played the title role in *The Killing of Sister George* (Welsh Th. Co., Casson, Cardiff, Wales, Jan. 1971); and "Mrs. Doasyouwouldbedoneby" in *The Water Babies* (Royalty, London, July 24, 1973).

Films. In England, Miss Matthews appeared in the silent film, *This England* (1923). She later appeared in *There Goes the Bride* (Gainsborough-Br. Lion, 1932); *Friday the Thirteenth* (Gainsborough, 1933); *The Good Companions* (Gaumont-Welsh-Pearson, 1933); *Waltzes From Vienna* (released in the US as *Strauss's Great Waltz;* Tom Arnold, 1934); and for Gaumont Studios appeared in *Evergreen* (1934), *First a Girl* (1935), *It's Love Again* (1936), *Head Over Heels* (1937), *Gangway* (1937); *Sailing Along* (1938), and *Climbing High* (1939); appeared in *Forever and a Day* (RKO, 1943); directed *Victory Wedding* (Gainsborough, 1944); and appeared in *Tom Thumb* (MGM, 1958).

Television and Radio. She played Mrs. Dale on the BBC radio serial The Dales (Mar. 1963 to Apr. 1969), and has made many other radio and television appearances.

Awards. Miss Matthews received the O.B.E. in 1970.

MATTOX, MATT. Dancer, actor, choreographer, singer, teacher. b. Harold Henry Mattox, Aug. 18, 1921, Tulsa, Okla., to Jack M. and Elsie M. (Wilbanks) Mattox. Father, luggage salesman; mother, saleslady. Attended San Bernardino (Calif.) H.S., 1934–36. Studied ballet with Ernest Belcher, Nico Charisso and Eugene Loring; tap dancing with Louis Da Pron, Evelyn Bruns and Teddy Kerr; modern jazz dancing with Jack Cole; voice with Keith Davis; and Drama with Wyn Handman. Served USAAF, 1942–44; rank, 2nd Lt. Member of SAG; SEG; AFTRA; AEA; SSD&C (exec. council, 1961).

Pre-Theatre. "Anything from box boy in a market to frying hamburgers in a White Castle.".

Theatre. Mr. Mattox (billed as Harold Mattox) first appeared with a dance group on a variety program at the Hippodrome Th. (Los Angeles, 1937).

He made his N.Y.C. debut (May 1946) as a dancer and member of the chorus in *Are You with It?* (Empire Th., Nov. 10, 1945); subsequently played Ted Woods in *Park Avenue* (Shubert, Nov. 4, 1946); and toured the US as a soloist in Edwin Lester's production of *Song of Norway* (July 1947); and appeared as Bailador (billed for the first time as Matt Mattox) in *Magdalena* (Ziegfeld, N.Y.C., Sept. 20, 1948).

In Australia, danced in touring productions of *Oklahoma!* (1949) and *Song of Norway* (1951), which he also choreographed; played Harry Beaton in the Los Angeles Civic Opera production of *Brigadoon* (Philharmonic Aud., 1952); danced the role of the Courier in *Carnival in Flanders* (New Century, N.Y.C., Sept. 8, 1953); played Charlie in *The Vamp* (Winter Garden, Nov. 10, 1955); danced in the pre-Bway tryout of *Ziegfeld Follies* (opened Shubert, Boston, Mass., Apr. 16, 1956; closed Shubert, Philadelphia, Pa., May 12, 1956); played Bill Calhoun in *Kiss Me, Kate* (South Shore Music Circus, Cohasset, Mass., Summer 1956); choreographed the ELT production of *Annie Get Your Gun* (Lenox Hill Playhouse, N.Y.C., Feb. 26, 1957); and played in stock at the Cape Cod Melody Tent (Hyannis, Mass., Summer 1957).

He choreographed and danced the role of Boris Reshevsky in *Say, Darling* (ANTA, N.Y.C., Apr. 3, 1958); choreographed the Metropolitan Opera Company production of *Aida* (Metropolitan Opera House, 1959); and danced in and choreographed the pre-Bway tour of *Pink Jungle* (opened Alcazar, San Francisco, Calif., Oct. 14, 1959; closed Shubert, Boston, Mass., Dec. 12, 1959).

Mr. Mattox played the Jester in *Once Upon a Mattress* (Phoenix, N.Y.C., May 11, 1959; moved Alvin, Nov. 25, 1959); produced and appeared in the *Matt Mattox Concert* (Kaufmann Aud., YMHA, 1960); choreographed the pre-Bway tryout of *A Short Happy Life* (opened Moore Th., Seattle, Wash., Sept. 12, 1961; closed Huntington Hartford Th., Los Angeles, Calif., Oct. 21, 1961); choreographed *Jennie* (Majestic, N.Y.C., Oct. 17, 1963); and did the musical staging of *What Makes Sammy Run?* (54 St. Th., Feb. 27, 1964).

Mr. Mattox choreographed and danced in *Dance Caravan '65,* a touring educational project of the Brooklyn Ballet Assn. of the Brooklyn Academy of Music (1965); was head of the Dance Department of The Neighborhood Playhouse Professional School (N.Y.C., Summer 1967); and choreographed and danced with the N.J. Ballet. Mr. Mattox lives and works in London (1970–to date) where he has founded "Jassart", a dance company which debuted at the Edinburgh Festival (1975).

Films. Mr. Mattox made his debut in the chorus of *Yolanda and the Thief* (MGM, 1945); followed by *Easy to Wed* (MGM, 1946); *'Til the Clouds Roll By* (MGM, 1946); *Good News* (MGM, 1947); *Something in the Wind* (U, 1947); *The Merry Widow* (MGM, 1952); *The I Don't Care Girl* (20th-Fox, 1953); *Gentlemen Prefer Blondes* (20th-Fox, 1953); *The Band Wagon* (MGM, 1953); played Caleb in *Seven Brides for Seven Brothers* (MGM, 1954); and appeared in *The Girl Rush* (Par., 1955).

Television. Mr. Mattox has been a dancer and choreographer for the Patti Page Show (ABC, 1958); Swinging into Spring with Benny Goodman (Texaco Special, NBC, 1959); The Good Years (DuPont Special NBC, 1962); *Golden Child* (Hallmark Hall of Fame, NBC, 1961); *Huck Finn* (US Steel Special, CBS); and the Bell Telephone Hour (CBS, 1963); *Arias and Arabesques* (CBS, 1963); played the Cat in *Pinocchio* (CBS); and Injun Joe in *Tom Sawyer* (US Steel Special, CBS); choreographed the Dinah Shore special (ABC, 1965); and various segments of the Bell Telephone Hour (NBC, 1964–66), on which he also appeared as a guest dancer (1964–65); and was a guest on the Mike Douglas Show (Ind., 1965–66).

Awards. He received the Dance Educators of America Award (1958) for his contribution to the dance.

Recreation. Golf, swimming, football, field and track, basketball and sketching.

MATTSON, ERIC. Producer, director. b. Rudolph Mattson, Jan. 8, 1908, Scranton, Pa., to Edward and Nellie (Johnson) Mattson. Father, policeman. Grad. Central H.S., Scranton, Pa., 1927; Muhlenberg Coll., A.B. 1935. Married May 12, 1930, to Margaret Mueller; one son, two daughters. Member of AEA; Phi Kappa Tau. Address: 35-15 75th St., Jackson Heights, NY 11372, tel. (212) IL8-9685..

Pre-Theatre. GMAC credit investigator.

Theatre. Mr. Mattson made his stage debut in N.Y.C. in the chorus of *Jumbo* (Hippodrome Th., Nov. 16, 1935); subsequently toured as soloist with Abe Lyman's orchestra (May 1936); appeared as soloist (Gay Nineties Club, N.Y.C., Oct. 1936); as tenor soloist (St. Louis Municipal Opera Co., Mo., June 1937); soloist (Los Angeles Civic Light Opera Co. Calif., May 1938); toured in operettas and musical comedies (San Francisco, Calif.; Dallas, Tex.; Detroit, Mich.; Memphis, Tenn.; Toledo, Ohio; St. Paul, Minn., 1938–41, 1943–44); and appeared as soloist for the Sigmund Romberg national concert tour (Sept. 1943).

He played Enoch Snow in *Carousel* (Majestic, N.Y.C., Apr. 12, 1945; national tour, May 1947; Drury Lane, London, June 7, 1950); and directed and appeared in production at the Theatre Under the Stars, Atlanta, Ga. (Summer 1953), where, beginning in 1954, he produced and directed musicals and operettas.

Radio. Mr. Mattson was soloist and an announcer for WOW, Omaha, Neb.

Recreation. Antiques, ornithology, numismatics, Civil War history.

MAUDE, MARGERY. Actress. b. Margery Kathleen Maude, Apr. 29, 1889, Wimbledon, England, to Cyril and Winifred (Emery) Maude. Father, actor, manager; mother, actress (known as Winifred Emery). Attended schools in London and Folkestone, England, and educated privately in Dresden, Germany, 1907. Studied at RADA, London, 1 1/2 terms. Married July 23, 1917, to Joseph W. Burde, investment counselor; one son, two daughters. Relative in theatre: cousin, John Emery, actor. Member of AEA; SAG; AFTRA; Episcopal Actors' Guild (bd. mbr.); English Speaking Union. Address: 10 E. 85th St., New York, NY 10028, tel. (212) BU 8-8970.

Theatre. Miss Maude first performed as a Lady-in-Waiting in *Rosencrantz and Guildenstern* (Lyceum, London, July 14, 1908); subsequently played Hesta in *The Toymaker of Nuremberg* (Playhouse, Mar. 15, 1910); Nerissa in *The Merchant of Venice* (Her Majesty's, 1910); Cynthia Dean in *D'Arcy of the Guards* (St. James's, Sept. 27, 1910); and the title role in *Little Cinderella* (Playhouse, Dec. 20, 1910).

She appeared as Titania in *A Midsummer Night's Dream* (His Majesty's, Apr. 17, 1911); Lucius in *Julius Caesar* (His Majesty's, May 22, 1911); Marjolaine Lachenais in *Pomander Walk* (Playhouse, June 29, 1919); Bunty in *Bunty Pulls the String* (Haymarket, July 18, 1911); Effie Pemberton in *The Blindness of Virtue* (Little, Jan. 29, 1912); appeared in *Love and What Then?* (Playhouse, May 22, 1912); played Mrs. Jesmond in *The Widow of Wasdale Head* (Duke of York's, Oct. 1912); Portia in *The Headmaster* (Playhouse, Jan. 22, 1913), and by Command of King George V, she appeared in this role in her father's company's production of this play (Balmoral Castle, Sept. 13, 1913).

She played Virginia Bullivant in *Grumpy* (Th. Royal, Glasgow, Scotland, Sept. 1913); accompanied her father on tour of Canada (Oct. 1913), appearing as Constance Jublyn in *Toodles,* Muriel Mannering in *The Second in Command,* and as Virginia in *Grumpy.*

She made her N.Y.C. debut as Muriel Mannering in a revival of *The Second in Command* (Wallack Th., Nov. 3, 1913); appeared in *Beauty and the Barge* (Wallack Th., Nov. 13, 1913); played Lady Windermere in *Lady Windermere's Fan* (Hudson, Mar. 30, 1914); Virginia Bullivant in *Grumpy* (New London, May 13, 1914); Gail in *Young Wisdom* (Playhouse, Sept. 1914); Minnie Templer in *A Message from Mars* (Apollo, Dec. 2, 1914); and Mary Sullivan in *A Quiet Rubber* (Drury Lane, Dec. 1914).

For the Actors Benevolent Fund, she played Maria in an all-star production of *The School for Scandal* (Covent Garden, Feb. 2, 1915); appeared as Phoebe Schmaltz in *Searchlight* (Savoy, Feb. 1915); Charlotte Watson in the Bway production of *Paganini* (Criterion, N.Y.C., Sept. 11, 1916), also touring in it; and toured as Lucy White in *Professor's Love Story.*

Miss Maude played Lydia Languish in the Bway production of *The Rivals* (Erlanger, Mar. 13, 1930); Janet Carnot in *The Great Adventure* (Mt. Kisco Playhouse, N.Y., June 1931); Juliet in *Romeo and Juliet* (Sept. 1933); and Mistress Page in *The Merry Wives of Windsor* (Sept. 1933).

She played Mrs. Sheeran in *The Old Foolishness* (Windsor, N.Y.C., Dec. 2, 1940); Mrs. Denvers in *Anne of England* (St. James, Oct. 7, 1941); Mrs. Barr in *Plan M* (Belasco, Feb. 20, 1942); Mrs. Shriver in *The Walking Gentlemen* (Belasco, May 7, 1942); Mrs. Latham in *The Two Mrs. Carrolls* (Booth, Aug. 3, 1943), also touring in it; and Polton in *O Mistress Mine* (Empire, Jan. 23, 1946).

She appeared in stock productions at the Westport (Conn.) Country Playhouse (1948) and Elitch Gardens (Denver, Colo., 1950); played the Mother Superior in *The High Ground* (48 St. Th., N.Y.C., Feb. 20, 1951); Belle Hardwick in *First Lady* (NY City Ctr., May 28, 1952); toured as Mrs. Cluver in *The Constant Wife* (opened Ford's, Baltimore, Md., Oct. 13, 1952); played Mrs. Hampden in *Escapade* (48 St. Th., Nov. 18, 1953); toured as Mrs. Higgins in *My Fair Lady* (opened Masonic Aud., Rochester, N.Y., Mar. 18, 1957), succeeding (Sept. 1962) Viola Roache in the role in N.Y.C. (Mark Hellinger Th., May 15, 1956), and appearing in it in two revivals (NY City Ctr., May 20, 1964; NY City Ctr., June 13, 1968). She also played Dona Elen Rivera in *Diamond Orchid* (Henry Miller's Th., Feb. 10, 1965).

Films. Miss Maude appeared in *You're Never Too Young* (Par., 1955) and *The Birds and the Bees* (Par., 1956).

Television and Radio. She has performed on radio programs with the Th. Guild on the Air; on the serial Our Girl Sunday, and others.

For television, she has appeared on Robert Montgomery Presents (NBC); Somerset Maugham Th. (ABC); Kraft Television Th. (NBC); and the Hallmark Hall of Fame (NBC); and The Defenders (CBS).

Recreation. Painting.

MAXTONE-GRAHAM, JOHN.

Production stage manager. b. John Kurtz Maxtone-Graham, Aug. 2, 1929, Orange, N.J., to Laurence Patrick and Ann (Taylor) Maxtone-Graham. Father, investment banker. Relatives in theatre: brother, Michael Maxtone-Graham, television director; cousin, Charles Smythe, composer, music director. Grad. Sedbergh (Yorkshire) Sch., Eng., 1946; Brown Univ., B.A. 1951. Served USMC, 1951–54; Korea, 1953; rank, Capt. Married June 4, 1955, to Katrina Kanzler, writer; one son, two daughters. Member of AEA; Dramatists Guild; ALA. Address: 126 E. 78th St., New York, NY 10021.

Theatre. Mr. Maxtone-Graham's first stage assignment was as assistant stage manager for the NY City Ctr. productions of *What Every Woman Knows* (Dec. 22, 1954) and *The Wisteria Trees* (Feb. 2, 1955). He was stage manager for *Gentlemen, The Queens!* (Ann Arbor Dramatic Festival, Univ. of Michigan, Lydia Mendelssohn Th., May 1955); and advance director for a touring production of *Champagne Complex* (Summer 1955).

At the NY City Ctr., he was stage manager for *King Lear* (Jan. 12, 1956) and *A Streetcar Named Desire* (Feb. 15, 1956); was production co-ordinator for the American Shakespeare Festival (Stratford, Conn., Mar. 1–June 1, 1956); at the NY City Ctr., was stage manager for *The Glass Menagerie* (Nov. 21, 1956); *Mister Roberts* (Dec. 5, 1956); *The Beggar's Opera* (Mar. 13, 1957); *Brigadoon* (Mar. 27, 1957); *The Merry Widow* (Apr. 10, 1957); and *South Pacific* (Apr. 24, 1957). He was production stage manager for *The Square Root of Wonderful* (Natl., Oct. 30, 1957); advance director for a summer theatre production of *Sabrina Fair* (Falmouth Playhouse, Mass.; Tappan Zee Playhouse, Nyack, N.Y., July 1958); was production stage manager (Morosco, Sept. 1, 1958) for *The Visit* (Lunt-Fontanne, N.Y.C., May 5, 1958); and for plays presented by Group 20 (Wellesley, Mass., June–Aug. 1959).

He was production stage manager for *Much Ado About Nothing* (Lunt-Fontanne, Sept. 17, 1959), replacing Keene Curtis for the final three weeks; for the pre-Bway tryout of *Motel* (opened Wilbur, Boston, Mass., Jan. 6, 1960; closed there Jan. 16, 1960); for *Duel of Angels* (Helen Hayes Th., N.Y.C., Apr. 19, 1960); *Big Fish, Little Fish* (ANTA, Mar. 15, 1961); *The Night of the Iguana* (Royale, Dec. 28, 1961); *The Ballad of the Sad Cafe* (Martin Beck Th., Oct. 30, 1963); for the Boston (Mass.) Arts Festival (Summer 1964); stage manager for a revival of *Brigadoon* (NY City Ctr., Dec. 23, 1964); production stage manager for *A Sign of Affection* (opened Shubert Th., New Haven, Conn., Mar. 10, 1965; closed Walnut St. Th., Philadelphia, Pa., Apr. 10, 1965); for a revival of *Kiss Me, Kate* (NY City Ctr., May 12, 1965); and for *The Right Honourable Gentleman* (Billy Rose Th., Oct. 19, 1965). He took over (Feb. 20, 1966) production stage manager's responsibilities for *Any Wednesday* (Music Box Th., Feb. 18, 1964) during the concluding months of that play's run at the George Abbott Th.

Films. In partnership (1966–69) with Lewis M. Allen in an independent film production company, Vineyard Films, Inc., Mr. Maxtone-Graham produced the documentary *The Queen.* .

Other Activities. Mr. Maxtone-Graham was associated as production manager with Jean Rosenthal's Th. Production Service, a firm that offers complete service and equipment for the theatre, and he designed and supervised mobile lighting systems for Chrysler Industrial Shows (1963 and 1964).

Published Works. Mr. Maxtone-Graham is author of a history of 20th-century Atlantic ocean liners, *The Only Way to Cross* (1972).

MAXWELL, ROBERTA.

Actress. b. Canada, to Mr. and Mrs. Richard Maxwell. Attended convent schools. Member of AEA; AFTRA.

Miss Maxwell's early experience includes work with the Stratford (Ontario, Canada) Festival, Manitoba Th. Centre, and provincial repertory companies in England. She made her US debut playing Ursula in *Two Gentlemen of Verona* with the Stratford (Ontario) Festival guesting at the Phoenix Th. (N.Y.C., Mar. 17, 1958); subsequently at Stratford, Ont., appeared in *Henry IV, Part 1, The Winter's Tale,* and played Ursula in *Much Ado About Nothing* (Summer 1958), played small parts in *As You Like It* (Summer 1959); Olivia in *Twelfth Night* (June 8, 1966), Marya in *The Government Inspector* (June 13, 1967), and Anne Page in *The Merry Wives of Windsor* (June 14, 1967); made her Bway debut playing a school girl and understudying Amy Taubin in *The Prime of Miss Jean Brodie* (Helen Hayes Th., N.Y.C., Jan. 16, 1968); with the American Shakespeare Fest. (Stratford, Conn.) played Hero in *Much Ado About Nothing* (June 18, 1969), Katharine in *Henry V* (June 19, 1969), and Natasha in *Three Sisters* (July 23, 1969); Betty Carney in *A Whistle in the Dark* (Mercury, N.Y.C., Oct. 8, 1969); repeated the role of Katharine in the American Shakespeare Festival production of *Henry V* (ANTA, Nov. 10, 1969); with the Minnesota Th. Co. in repertory at the Billy Rose Th., played in the Chorus of the trilogy, *The House of Atreus* (Dec. 17, 1969), and as Mrs. Dullfeet in *The Resistible Rise of Arturo Ui* (Dec. 22, 1969); appeard in *Antigone* (Charles Playhouse, Boston, Jan. 8, 1970); again with the ASF (Stratford, Conn.), played Helena in *All's Well that Ends Well* (June 16, 1970), and Desdemona in *Othello* (June 17, 1970; transferred to ANTA Th., N.Y.C., Sept. 14, 1970); Sorel Bliss in *Hay Fever* (Helen Hayes Th., N.Y.C., Nov. 9, 1970); Joanne in *Slag* (Public/Anspacher, Feb. 21, 1971); at the Guthrie Th. (Minneapolis) appeared in *Cyrano de Bergerac* (July 22, 1971, matinee), *The Taming of the Shrew* (July 22, 1971), and *Misalliance* (Sept. 24, 1971); played Lucienne in *There's One in Every Marriage* (Royale, N.Y.C., Jan. 3, 1972); Milliamont in *The Way of the World* (Long Wharf Th., New Haven, Feb. 18, 1972); at the Guthrie Th. (Minneapolis), played Titania and Hippolita in *A Midsummer Night's Dream* (July 7, 1972), Berenthia in *The Relapse* (July 12, 1972), and a Citizen of Thebes in *Oedipus* (Oct. 24, 1972); Nora Clitheroe in *The Plough and the Stars* (Vivian Beaumont Th., N.Y.C., Jan. 4, 1973); Jessica in *The Merchant of Venice* (Vivian Beaumont Th., Mar. 1, 1973); Julie in *Miss Julie* on a double-bill with *Dance of Death* (Long Wharf, New Haven, May 11, 1973); appeared in *The Marriage Brokers* (Stratford, Ontario, Canada, Festival, Aug. 3, 1973); played Clara in *The Widowing of Mrs. Holroyd* (Long Wharf, New Haven, Nov. 16, 1973); Nina in *The Seagull* (Long Wharf, Mar. 1, 1974); with the ASF (Stratford, Conn.) Maria in *Twelfth Night* (June 15, 1974), and Juliet in *Romeo and Juliet* (June 16, 1974); and Jill Mason in *Equus* (Plymouth, N.Y.C., Oct. 24, 1974).

Awards. Miss Maxwell is the recipient of the Tyrone Guthrie Award; the *Village Voice* Off-Bway (Obie) Award (1969–70) for *A Whistle in the Dark;* and the Drama Desk Award (1970–71) for *Slag.*

MAY, ELAINE.

Director, actress, playwright. b. Elaine Berlin, Apr. 21, 1932, Philadelphia, Pa., to Jack Berlin, Yiddish actor. Studied acting with Maria Ouspenskaya. Married 1949 to Marvin May (marr. dis.); one daughter, Jeannie Berlin, actress; married Apr. 1962 to Sheldon Harnick, lyricist (marr. dis. 1963); married 1963.

Theatre. Miss May was technical assistant for *Bruno and Sidney* (New Stages Th., N.Y.C., May 3, 1949). In Chicago, she performed with the Playwrights Th. Club (1953); then with the Compass Players (1954–57), an improvisational group that grew out of the Playwrights Th. Club; and, in cabaret, creating and performing sketches with Mike Nichols, who also had been a member of the Playwrights and Compass groups.

She made her Bway debut in the revue *An Evening with Mike Nichols and Elaine May* (John Golden Th., Oct. 8, 1960), in which she and Mr. Nichols performed their own material and created sketches *ad lib;* wrote *Not Enough Rope,* one of three one-act plays under the title of *3 by 3* (Maidman Playhouse, Mar. 1, 1962); wrote *A Matter of Position* (opened Walnut, Philadelphia, Sept. 29, 1962; closed there Oct. 13, 1962); wrote *Name of a Soup,* which was performed in a workshop production (H B Studio, N.Y.C., June 8, 1963); directed the revue *The Third Ear* (Premise Th., May 21, 1964); played Shirley in *The Office* (Henry Miller's Th., began previews Apr. 20, 1966; closed Apr. 30, 1966, before official opening); acted in a revised version of her play *A Matter of Position* (Berkshire Th., Stockbridge, Mass., June 1968); and wrote *Adaptation,* performed on a double-bill with Terrence McNally's *Next,* both of which she directed (Greenwich Mews Th., Feb. 10, 1969).

Miss May performed at the Inaugural Gala for President Lyndon B. Johnson (Natl. Guard Armory, Washington, D.C., Jan. 18, 1965).

Films. She played Ellen in *Luv* (Col., 1967); Angela in *Enter Laughing* (Col., 1967); wrote the screenplay, directed, and played Henrietta Lowell in *A New Leaf* (Par., 1971); is reputed to have written the screenplay (Esther Dale receiving the billing) for *Such Good Friends* (Par., 1971); and directed *The Heartbreak Kid* (20th-Fox, 1972).

Television. With Mike Nichols, Miss May made her debut on the Jack Paar Show (NBC, 1957), and in addition to playing subsequent engagements with Mr. Paar, the pair appeared on the Steve Allen Show (NBC, 1957); *Suburban Revue* (Omnibus, NBC, Jan. 15, 1958); *The Red Mill* (DuPont Show of the Month, CBS, Apr. 19, 1958); the Laugh Line series (NBC, Apr. 16–May 7, 1959); *The Fabulous Fifties* (CBS, Jan 31, 1960); the Perry Como Show (NBC); and the Dinah Shore Show (NBC).

In the early 1960s, the pair made weekly appearances on the NBC radio show, Monitor.

Night Clubs. Mike Nichols and Elaine May have performed at the Village Vanguard (N.Y.C., 1957); the Blue Angel (N.Y.C., 1957); Town Hall (N.Y.C., May 1, 1959); the Mocambo (Los Angeles, 1959); Mister Kelly's (Chicago); and Down in the Depths (Hotel Duane, N.Y.C.), among other night clubs.

Discography. Miss May and Mr. Nichols have recorded the comedy albums *Improvisations to Mu-*

sic, An Evening with Mike Nichols and Elaine May and *Mike Nichols and Elaine May Examine Doctors* (all Mercury Records).

Awards. For *Adaptation,* Miss May received (1969) a Drama Desk Award (as a promising playwright) and an Outer Circle Award (for direction and writing).

MAY, VAL. Director. b. Valentine May, July 1, 1927, Bath, Somerset, England, to Claude Jocelyn Delabere and Olive (Gilbert) May. Attended Cronleigh Sch.; Peterhouse Coll., Cambridge. Trained for the theatre at the Old Vic Th. Sch., London (1948–50). Married to Penelope Sutton.

Theatre. As director of productions, Mr. May made his professional debut at the Watergate Th. Club, London, directing *The Typewriter* (Nov. 1950); later directing *Medusa's Raft* (Jan. 1951); subsequently became assistant director (June 1951) of the Dundee (Scotland) Repertory Co.; associate director (Sept.–Dec. 1951) of the Salisbury (England) Arts Th.; and associate director (Sept. 1952–Apr. 1953), and director (Aug. 1953–July 1957) of the Ipswich (England) Repertory Th. He became director (Aug. 1957–Mar. 1961) of the Nottingham Playhouse, ending that affiliation with a production of *Celebration* (Mar. 1961; and Duchess Th., London, June 1961); became director (1961–75) of the Bristol Old Vic, where he directed productions of *War and Peace* (Feb. 1962; and Old Vic, London, June 1962); *Fiorello!* (Sept. 1962; and Piccadilly Th., London, Oct. 1962); *All Things Bright and Beautiful* (Oct. 1962; and Phoenix, London, Dec. 1962); *A Severed Head* (May 1963; and Criterion, London, July 1963; subsequently making his Bway debut when that production moved to Royale, N.Y.C., Oct. 28, 1964); *The Pavilion of Masks* (Oct. 1963; and The Little, London); *Love's Labour's Lost* (Apr. 1964; and Old Vic, London, Sept. 1964; and European tour); *Portrait of a Queen* (Feb. 1965; and Vaudeville, London, May 1965); *The Killing of Sister George* (Apr. 1965; moved to Duke of York's Th., London, June 1965; and Belasco, N.Y.C., Oct. 5, 1966); *She Stoops to Conquer* (at the Bath Festival, June 1965); *Cleo* (The Little, London, Nov. 1965); *Hamlet* (Oct. 1966; and NY City Ctr., Feb. 16, 1967); *Message from the Grassroots* (Bristol Old Vic, Apr. 1967); *The Pursuit of Love* (May 1967); *The Italian Girl* (Nov. 1967; and Wyndham's, London, Feb. 1968); *Mrs. Mouse, Are You Within?* (Apr. 1968; and Duke of York's Th., London, May 1968); *Brother and Sister* (May 1968); *Conduct Unbecoming* (Apr. 1969; and Ethel Barrymore Th., N.Y.C., Oct. 12, 1970); *It's a Two-Foot-Six-Inches Above-the-Ground World* (Nov. 1969; and Wyndham's, London, Jan. 1970); and *Poor Horace* (Feb. 1970; and Lyric, London, May 1970).

Elsewhere, he has directed *Richard II* (Old Vic, London, Nov. 1959); *Belle* (Strand Th., May 1961); *Sixty Thousand Nights* (Th. Royal, Bristol, May 1966), which he also devised; *Jarrocks* (New Th., London, Sept. 1966); *Portrait of a Queen* (Henry Miller's Th., N.Y.C., Feb. 28, 1968); and *They Don't Grow on Trees* (Prince of Wales Th., London, Nov. 1968).

Television. For the BBC, he directed *Last Day in Dreamland.*

Awards. Mr. May received the Cross of the British Empire, 1969.

MAYEHOFF, EDDIE. Actor, comedian. b. July 7, 1914 (?), Baltimore, Md., to M.N. and Maudie Mayehoff. Father, clothing manufacturer. Grad. Principia Jr. Coll. and Mil. Acad., St. Louis, Mo., 1928; grad. Yale Univ. Sch. of Music, 1932. Member of AEA; SAG; AFTRA.

Pre-Theatre. After graduating from Yale, Mr. Mayehoff organized his own orchestra, playing at various NY hotels (1933–39); subsequently became radio and night club performer.

Theatre. Mr. Mayehoff made his N.Y.C. debut in *Let Freedom Sing* (Longacre, Oct. 5, 1942); appeared in, and wrote material for, *Early to Bed* (Broadhurst, June 17, 1943); played Casanova in *Rhapsody* (Century, Nov. 22, 1944); appeared in *Billy Rose's Concert Varieties* (Ziegfeld, June 1, 1945); as Paul Anderson in *Season in the Sun* (Cort, Sept. 28, 1950); Gen. Tom Powers in *Visit to a Small Planet* (Booth, Feb. 7, 1957), playing the role again in a stock production (Fred Miller Th., Milwaukee, Wisc., Jan. 12, 1959); succeeded Tom Ewell in the revue *A Thurber Carnival* (ANTA, N.Y.C., Feb. 26, 1960); and played John T. Kodiak in *A Rainy Day in Newark* (Belasco, Oct. 22, 1963).

Films. Mr. Mayehoff first appeared in *That's My Boy* (Par., 1951); followed by *The Stooge* (Par., 1952); *Off Limits* (Par., 1953); *Artists and Models* (Par., 1955); *How To Murder Your Wife* (UA, 1965); and *Luv* (Col., 1967).

Television and Radio. Mr. Mayehoff appeared on the Norman Corwin radio show (1939); starred on and wrote the show, Broadway Document (1939); had his own shows—Words without Music, and Eddie Mayehoff On the Town (MBC, and Canadian Broadcasting System, 1940); and was quizmaster, for a while, of Beat the Band (NBC, 1944).

He starred on one of the earliest television comedy series, The Adventures of Fenimore J. Mayehoff (1946); for two seasons starred on That's My Boy (CBS, premiere Apr. 10, 1954); wrote, with David Swift, and appeared in *The Star Spangled Soldier* (Studio One, CBS, May 21, 1956); appeared in *Made in Heaven* (Playhouse 90, CBS, Dec. 6, 1956); and has appeared on the George Gobel Show (CBS); Bob Hope Presents (NBC); the Ed Sullivan Show (CBS); Kraft Television Th. (NBC); Lux Video Th.; Colgate Comedy Hour; and the Chrysler Shower of Stars.

Night Clubs. Mr. Mayehoff's many engagements include performances at the N.Y.C. clubs Le Ruban Bleu, Cafe Society, the Blue Angel, and Spivy's Roof.

MAYLEAS, RUTH. Theatre executive. b. Ruth Rothschild, Jan. 9, 1925, New York City, to Alfred and Anna Rothschild. Father, businessman, writer. Grad. Cornell Univ., A.B. 1946. Married May 4, 1952, to William Mayleas (marr. dis. 1964); one daughter. Member of ANTA; USITT.

Since 1966, Mrs. Mayleas has been affiliated with the National Endowment for the Arts From 1958 to 1966, she was director of the National Theatre Service Dept. of ANTA, and the editor of the ANTA *News Bulletin.* She has been assistant director of the International Theatre Institute, US Centre, and a member of the Advisory Council for Children's Theatre and of the board of directors of USITT.

Since 1958, she has also been the US correspondent for *World Premieres Mondiales,* published by the ITI in Paris.

Awards. She received a Ford Foundation Travel and Study Grant (1963); was selected as US delegate to the 10th International Theatre Inst. Congress (Warsaw, Poland, 1963) and received a 1973 National Theatre Conference Award.

MAYNARD, RUTH. Actress, music teacher. b. Ruth Maynard Coffin, May 29, 1913, Brookline, Mass., to William B. and Dorothy W. S. (Soule) Coffin. Father, architect. Grad. Beaver Country Day Sch., Chestnut Hill, Mass., 1931. Vassar Coll., A.B. 1935; attended Harvard Graduate Sch. of Education, 1936–38; Longy Sch. of Music, Cambridge, Mass., 1936–38; Harvard Univ. Summer Sch., 1937–39; studied for the theatre with Jeanne Tufts in Boston, Mass. (1946–48), Morris Carnovsky (1952–53), Herbert Berghof (1956–58), and Lee Grant (1958–62). Relative in theatre: sister, Barbara Coffin Morris, monologist. Member of AEA; SAG; AFTRA.

Pre-Theatre. Music teacher at the Beaver Country Day Sch., Chestnut Hill, Mass. (1938–50).

Theatre. Miss Maynard made her stage debut as Zenobia in an Actor's Th. production of *Ethan Frome* (Peabody Playhouse, Boston, Mass., Feb. 1947); subsequently appeared with the group as Maria in *Twelfth Night* (Peabody Playhouse, Jan. 1948), and in stock (Nantucket, Mass.); made her N.Y.C. debut in an ELT production of *You Can't Take it With You* (Lenox Hill Playhouse, 1951); appeared in ELT productions at the Lenox Hill Playhouse, of *Pygmalion* (1952), *Goat Song* (1954), and *The Heiress* (1955).

She made her Bway debut as a Lady of the Court in *The Lark* (Longacre Th., Nov. 17, 1955), in which she also understudied Rita Vale as Queen Yolande; appeared as the Countess in *The Smokeweaver's Daughter* (Fourth St. Th., Apr. 14, 1959); a Denizen of the Pink Jungle and understudy to Agnes Moorehead as the Shade of Eleanor West in the pre-Bway tryout of *The Pink Jungle* (opened Alcazar, San Francisco, Calif., Oct. 14, 1959; closed Shubert, Boston, Mass., Dec. 12, 1959).

Miss Maynard appeared as the Assistant to Dick Jensen, understudied Ruth McDevitt as Mrs. Gamadge in *The Best Man* (Morosco, N.Y.C., Mar. 31, 1960), and played the latter for 23 performances; succeeded (July 1961) Jean Stapleton as Mrs. Ochs in *Rhinoceros* (Longacre, Jan. 9, 1961); understudied Cathleen Nesbitt as Julia in *Romulus* (Music Box, Jan. 10, 1962); played Old Sally in *Oliver!* (Imperial, Jan. 6, 1963); and understudied Helena Carroll as Mrs. Sowerberry and succeeded (Dec. 1963) her, while still playing the part of Old Sally (1964). She toured as Old Sally and Mrs. Sowerberry in *Oliver!* (Summer 1966); played Frosine in *The Miser* (Front St. Th., Memphis, Tenn., Feb. 16, 1967); appeared in a production of *America Hurrah* (Long Wharf Th., New Haven, Conn., Jan. 10, 1969); was Julia Webber in the Washington (D.C.) Th. Club world premiere of *The Web and the Rock* (Feb. 24, 1971); and was in a Hartford (Conn.) Stage Co. production of *Arsenic and Old Lace* (Feb. 8, 1974).

Recreation. Swimming, sailing, playing piano, violin and viola.

MAYO, NICK. Producer, director. b. Nickoli Martoff, Oct. 31, 1922, Philadelphia, Pa., to Louis Martoff. Father, restaurateur. Grad. Los Angeles City Coll., B.A. (drama) 1941. First marriage dissolved; one daughter; married Oct. 5, 1952, to Janet Blair, actress, singer; one son, one daughter. Member of DGA; SSD&C. Address: (home) 2901 Antelo View Dr., Los Angeles, CA 90024, tel. GR 6-1265; (bus.) 20600 Ventura Blvd., Woodland Hills, CA 91364, tel. (213) ST 8-9104.

Theatre. Mr. Mayo took over as stage manager for *Catherine the Great* (Shubert Th., N.Y.C., Aug. 2, 1944); produced and directed summer productions (Brighton Beach, N.Y.; Montclair, N.J.), and directed two productions at Yale Univ. (1949).

He "acted in or stage managed thirteen consecutive Bway flops," before becoming production manager of the national tour of *South Pacific* (opened Shubert, Chicago, Ill., Nov. 14, 1950); was production manager for *A Girl Can Tell* (Royale, N.Y.C., Oct. 29, 1953); produced and directed *The Best House in Naples* (Lyceum, Oct. 26, 1956); and produced *A Shadow of My Enemy* (ANTA, Dec. 11, 1957); and co-produced a bus and truck tour of *Oklahoma!*

Mr. Mayo founded (with Randolph Hale and Art Linkletter), the Valley Music Th. (Woodland Hills, San Fernando Valley, Calif; opened June 1963).

Television and Radio. He was chief newscaster for radio station KIDO (Boise, Idaho, 1940–41); performed on radio in N.Y.C. (1941–45); and was producer-director of the television series The Witness (CBS).

Other Activities. He taught acting at the American Group Th. (N.Y.C., 1945).

Recreation. Tennis.

MAZZOLA, JOHN W. Executive, managing director, attorney. b. Jan. 20, 1928, Bayonne, N.J., to R. S. and Eleanor (Davis) Mazzola. Father, attorney. Grad. Admiral Farragut Acad., Pine Beach, N.J., 1945; Tufts Coll., B.A. 1949; Fordham Law Sch., LL.B. 1952. Married Mar. 7, 1959, to Sylvia Drulie, producer; two daughters. Served USNAF, 1945–46; US Army Counter Intelligence Corps, 1953–55. Member of Amer. Bar Assn.; Bar Assn. of the City of NY. Address: (home) 12 Beekman Place, New York, NY 10022; (bus.) c/o Lincoln Center for the Performing Arts, 1865

Broadway, New York, NY 10023, tel. (212) 765-5100.

Since 1970 Mr. Mazzola has been managing director for Lincoln Center for the Performing Arts, Inc.

Recreation. Cabinet making, gourmet cooking, sailing.

McBRYDE, DONALD M. b. May 27, 1937, Columbia, Miss. Grad. Mississippi Coll., B.A. 1958; Univ. of Mississippi, M.A. 1960; Univ. of Denver, Ph.D. (theatre) 1964. Served U.S. Army, 1959–60; Natl. Guard, 1960–65. Member of US Institute of Theatre Technology (bd. of dir., 1968–to date); Southeastern Th. Conf. (adv. council and chairman of th. arch. comm., 1964–to date); ATA. Address: Dept. of Speech, University of Mississippi, University, MS 38677.

Since 1960, Mr. McBryde has been a member of the faculty in the Dept. of Theatre at the Univ. of Mississippi, where he has held the positions of instructor (1960–62), asst. professor (1962–64), assoc. professor and chairman of the dept. (1964–68), and professor (1968–to date).

He has also acted as building consultant for the following projects in Mississippi: Wood Coll. auditorium (1964–65); Laurel Little Th. (1964–67); Cleveland Little Th. (1965–67); Natchez Little Th. (1967–73); and Lander Coll. auditorium (1967–73).

Published Works. He is the author of the article "Metal Theatre Building," (*Southern Theatre*, 1968).

McCALL, MONICA. Literary representative. b. Leicester, England, to John Henry and Gertrude (Sethsmith) McCall; immigrated to US, 1926; naturalized 1937. Married July 15, 1926, to Frank Howard Hodgkinson. Member of Society of Author's Representatives; Dramatists Play Service (bd. of dirs.). Address: (home) 230 E. 50th St., New York, NY 10022; (bus.) 1301 Sixth Ave., New York, NY 10019, tel. (212) 556-5740.

Miss McCall was the N.Y.C. representative, with Auriol Lee, for A. D. Peters of London (1928–29); joined Ann Watkins, Inc., N.Y.C. (1929); was head of the play and film dept. of Curtis Brown, Ltd., N.Y.C. (1936–39); opened her own firm, Monica McCall, N.Y.C. (1939–41); was associated with Myron Selznik, Inc., N.Y.C. (1941–45); and was president of Monica McCall, Inc., N.Y.C. (1946–68). In 1968, she sold the agency to Marvin Josephson Assoc., Inc. She is now affiliated with International Famous Agency, a division of Marvin Josephson Assoc., Inc.

Miss McCall is credited with originating the idea of linking sales and book-club selections to the asking price of motion picture rights, now known as escalator clauses. The first known instance of this practice was used with the novel *Escape* in 1939.

Recreation. Fishing, gardening, needlepoint.

McCALLY, DAVID. Director, actor, teacher. b. Charles David McCally, May 2, 1935, Fort Worth, Tex., to Travis William and Margaret Ann (Quattrochi) McCally. Father, typewriter service. Grad. Baylor Univ., B.A. 1957; M.A. 1963. He served in the US Navy Reserve. Married Sept. 2, 1954, to Regina Walker, actress; one son, one daughter. Member AEA; SAG; ATA; URTA. Address: (home) 2741 Cumberland, Odessa, TX tel. (915) 362-5251; (bus.) The Globe of the Great Southwest, 2308 Shakespeare Rd., Odessa, TX 79761, tel. (915) 332-4031.

Theatre. Mr. McCally began his theatrical career playing Col. William Barrett Travis in *The Drums of the Alamo* (Historical Th. of Texas, San Antonio, Tex., June–Aug. 1959, 1960). As a member of the resident company, Dallas (Tex.) Th. Center (Sept.–June, 1959–60; Sept.–June, 1960–61) and the National Repertory Company, N.Y.C. (Aug. 1961–Apr. 1962), he appeared in such plays as *Hamlet*, *Elizabeth the Queen*, and *Mary Stuart*. He presented ten plays during two seasons (Sept. 1963–June 1965) as producer-director of the Shakespeare Festival at the Trail of Six Flags Th., Victoria, Tex., including *A Midsummer Night's Dream* and *The Taming of the Shrew* (June–Aug. 1964). He appeared in *Tales of the South Pacific* and *The Music Man* (Casa Manana, Fort Worth, Tex., June–Aug. 1965) and was director-teacher and actor at the Ruth Taylor Th., Trinity Univ., San Antonio, Tex. (Sept.–Aug. 1965, 1966, 1966–67, 1967–68), where he directed *The Imaginary Invalid* (two productions), *The Boy Friend*, *Blood Wedding*, and acted in *The World of Carl Sandburg* and *A Different Drummer*.

In 1968, Mr. McCally became producer-director at the Globe of the Great Southwest, Odessa, Tex., site of the annual Odessa Shakespeare Festival. Plays he presented there include *Arms and the Man*, *Peter Pan*, *A Midsummer Night's Dream*, *The Taming of the Shrew*, *The World of Carl Sandburg*, *The Importance of Being Earnest*, *Pygmalion*, *Alice in Wonderland*, *Hamlet*, *As You Like It*, *Lady Precious Stream*, *A Thurber Carnival*, *God's Trombones*, *Julius Caesar*, *The Merchant of Venice*, *The Miser*, *Dracula*, *The Glass Menagerie*, *Dear Liar*, *The School for Wives*, *Romeo and Juliet*, *The Heiress*, *Macbeth*, *The Boy Friend*, *Antigone*, *Cyrano de Bergerac*, *The Tempest*, *The Comedy of Errors*, *Angel Street*, *Hay Fever*, *Oklahoma!*, *The Bald Soprano*, and *The Sandbox*. Mr. McCally directed and played Sergius in *Arms and the Man* (Mar. 1969), directed *The World of Carl Sandburg* (Oct.–Nov. 1969); directed and played Macduff in *Macbeth* (Sept.–Oct. 1970); directed and played Tom in *The Glass Menagerie* (Nov.–Dec. 1971); played the title role in *Cyrano de Bergerac* (June–Aug. 1972); and directed *Dear Liar* (Apr. 1972). In addition to these, Mr. McCally played the title role in *Hamlet* and directed *The World of Carl Sandburg* during a visit to the Lake District of England (July 5–Aug. 5, 1970).

Television. Mr. McCally first appeared on television as a Soldier in Rod Serling's *The Cause* (Matinee Th. Television, Jan. 1958); he played a medic on Combat (ABC, 1962); the Corporal in Gallant Men (1962); and the Cavalry Officer in The Tall Man (1962).

McCAMBRIDGE, MERCEDES. Actress. b. Charlotte Mercedes McCambridge, Mar. 17, 1918, Joliet, Ill., to John Patrick and Marie (Mahaffry) McCambridge. Grad. Mundelein Coll., A.B. (with honors) 1937. Married 1939 to William Fifield (marr. dis. 1946); one son; Feb. 19, 1950, to Fletcher Markle (marr. dis. 1962). Member of AEA; AFTRA; MPAS; Los Angeles Women's Bar Assn. (hon.); Phoenix (hon.). Address: c/o G.A.C., 640 Fifth Ave., New York, NY 10019.

Theatre. Miss McCambridge made her Bway debut as Mary Lorimer in *A Place of Our Own* (Royale Th., Apr. 2, 1945); subsequently appeared as Betty Lord in *Woman Bites Dog* (Belasco, Apr. 17, 1946); Mary in the pre-Bway tryout of *Twilight Bar* (opened Ford's, Baltimore, Md., Mar. 12, 1946; closed Walnut St. Th., Philadelphia, Pa., Mar. 23, 1946); Frances Morritt in *The Young and Fair* (Fulton, N.Y.C., Nov. 22, 1948); appeared in *Cages* (York, N.Y.C., June 13, 1963; Montreal, Canada, Sept. 30, 1963); at the Ann Arbor (Mich.) Drama Festival, she played Regina Giddens in *The Little Foxes* (Summer 1963); and replaced (Jan. 13, 1964) Uta Hagen as Martha in *Who's Afraid of Virginia Woolf* (Billy Rose Th., Oct. 13, 1962).

She replaced (July 7, 1963) Shelley Winters for six weeks in *Cages* (York, June 13, 1963); played Regina Giddens in *The Little Foxes* (Ann Arbor, Mich., Drama Festival, Summer 1963); replaced (Jan. 13, 1964) Uta Hagen as Martha in *Who's Afraid of Virginia Woolf?* (Billy Rose Th., Oct. 13, 1962); played Annie Sullivan in *The Miracle Worker* (Moorestown, N.J., Th., May 3, 1966); Nettie Cleary in *The Subject Was Roses* (Mineola Th., N.Y., July 11, 1966); Amanda in *The Glass Menagerie* (Mineola Th., Nov. 15, 1966); Lucy Lake in *The Love Suicide at Schofield Barracks* (ANTA Th., N.Y.C., Feb. 12, 1972); and the title role in *Medea* (Hartke Th., Catholic Univ., Washington, D.C., Jan. 5, 1973).

Films. Miss McCambridge made her debut in *All the King's Men* (Col., 1949); subsequently appeared in *The Scarf* (UA, 1951); *Lightning Strikes Twice* (WB, 1951); *Inside Straight* (MGM, 1951); *Johnny Guitar* (Rep., 1954); *Giant* (WB, 1956); *A Farewell to Arms* (20th-Fox, 1957); *Cimarron* (MGM, 1960); *Angel Baby* (Allied, 1961); *Run Home, Slow* (Joshua, 1964); and her voice was on the soundtrack of *The Exorcist* (WB, 1973) as the voice of Satan.

Television and Radio. Miss McCambridge has appeared on hundreds of radio programs including the Ford Th. and I Love a Mystery, for which she supplied all of the female voices. On daytime serials, she played the title role in Nora Drake and was Ruth in Big Sister (CBS, 1936). Since Jan. 1974, she has been in many CBS Radio Mystery Th. performances.

On television, she appeared on Tele-Theatre (NBC, 1950); Video Th. (CBS, 1950, 1952); Ford Th. (NBC, 1952); Studio One (CBS, 1953, 1956); Wire-Service (ABC, 1956); Loretta Young Show (NBC, 1956); Wagon Train (NBC, 1957); Jane Wyman Th. (NBC, 1958); Rawhide (CBS, 1959, 1960); Bonanza (NBC, 1962, 1970); Dr. Kildare (NBC, 1964); The Nurses (CBS, 1964); The Defenders (CBS, 1964); Lost in Space (CBS, 1966); Stage 67 (ABC, 1966); Bewitched (ABC, 1968); Medical Center (CBS, 1970); Name of the Game (NBC, 1971); Gunsmoke (CBS, 1971); *Killer by Night* (CBS, 1972); and *Two for the Money* (ABC, 1972).

Published Works. She is the author of an account of her world-wide tour with her son, *The Two of Us* (1960).

Awards. She received the Drama Award from Mundelein Coll. (1937); and for her performance as the Wife in *All the King's Men* (1949) she won the Academy (Oscar) Award, and the Associated Press Poll, the Look Award, Photoplay Award, and the Foreign Correspondents Award for best newcomer and best supporting actress. She has received a special citation from United Jewish Welfare, and two awards from the "City of Hope." In 1971, Mrs. Richard M. Nixon presented her with a certificate for her volunteer work for the National Council on Alcoholism, and she received the council's Gold Key Award (Kansas City, Mo., Apr. 12, 1972). She was nominated (1972) for an Antoinette Perry (Tony) Award as best supporting actress for her performance in *The Love Suicide at Schofield Barracks*..

McCARTHY, KEVIN. Actor. b. Feb. 15, Seattle, Wash., to Roy W. and Martha Therese (Preston) McCarthy. Attended Sch. of Foreign Service, Georgetown Univ., 1933–34; Univ. of Minn., 1936–38. Studied Actors Studio (charter mbr., 1947). Married Sept. 12, 1941, to Augusta Dabney, actress (marr. dis.); one son, two daughters. Served USAAF and USMP, 1942–45. Member of AEA; SAG; AFTRA.

Pre-Theatre. Newspaper circulation; news drama shows; newscasting.

Theatre. Mr. McCarthy first appeared on the stage as Sir Walter Blunt in *Henry IV, Part 1* at the Univ. of Minn. (1937); his first professional appearance was as Dan Crawford in *Brother Rat* (Warburton Sq. Playhouse, Yonkers, N.Y., 1938); made his Bway debut as Jasp and Phil in *Abe Lincoln in Illinois* (Plymouth, Oct. 15, 1938), which he subsequently played on tour; played Capt. Banning in *Flight to the West* (Guild, N.Y.C., Dec. 30, 1940); and appeared in *Mexican Mural* (Chanin Bldg. Penthouse Th., Apr. 1942).

While serving with the Air Force, he appeared as Ronny Meade in *Winged Victory* (44 St. Th., Nov. 20, 1943), and on tour (1944–45); played Maurice in *Truckline Cafe* (Belasco, N.Y.C., Feb. 27, 1946); Dunois in *Joan of Lorraine* (Alvin, Nov. 18, 1946); Morgan Decker in *The Survivors* (Playhouse, Jan. 19, 1948); Kurt Heger in *Bravo!* (Lyceum, Nov. 11, 1948); Biff in the London production of *Death of a Salesman* (Phoenix, July 28, 1949); Matt Burke in *Anna Christie* (NY City Ctr., Jan. 9, 1952); Berowne in *Love's Labour's Lost* (NY City Ctr., Feb. 4, 1953); succeeded (Mar. 1953) James Hanley as Freddie in *The Deep Blue Sea* (Morosco, Nov. 5, 1952), which he subsequently played on tour; played Boris Trigorin in *The Seagull* (Phoenix, N.Y.C., May 11, 1954); Ayamonn Breydon in *Red Roses for Me* (Booth, Dec.

28, 1955); Richard Morrow in *The Day the Money Stopped* (Belasco, Feb. 20, 1958); substituted one week (Mar. 1959) for Dana Andrews in the role of Jerry Ryan in *Two for the Seesaw* (Booth, Jan. 16, 1958); played Rupert Forster in *Marching Song* (Gate, Dec. 28, 1959); Jerry Ryan in *Two for the Seesaw* (Westport Country Playhouse, Conn.; Paper Mill Playhouse, Millburn, N.J.; Royal Poinciana Playhouse, Palm Beach, Fla., Summer 1960); Senator Van Ackerman in *Advise and Consent* (Cort, N.Y.C., Nov. 17, 1960); Capt. Dodd in *Something About a Soldier* (Ambassador, Jan. 4, 1962); made guest appearances during run of *Brecht on Brecht* (Th. de Lys, Jan. 3, 1962), also appeared in the Theatre Group (Univ. of California at Los Angeles) production (Oct. 22, 1963–Dec. 2, 1963); played Rev. Shannon in *Night of the Iguana* (Louisville, Ky., Feb. 1964); Vershinin in *The Three Sisters* (Morosco, N.Y.C., June 22, 1964); Jerry Ryan in *Two for the Seesaw* (tour, 1965–66); Homer in *A Warm Body* (Cort, N.Y.C., Apr. 15, 1967); Harold Ryan in *Happy Birthday, Wanda June* (opened Th. de Lys, Oct. 7, 1970; closed during the Equity strike and reopened at the Edison Th., Dec. 22, 1970); Dan in *The Children* (Public/Other, Nov. 28, 1972; Public/-Newman, Dec. 17, 1972); Gerte in *The Rapists* (New Dramatists, Mar. 12, 1974); and appeared in *Harry Outside* (Circle Repertory Th., May 11, 1975).

Films. Mr. McCarthy first appeared in *Death of a Salesman*, in which he played Biff (Col., 1951); followed by roles in *Drive a Crooked Road* (Col., 1954); *Gambler from Natchez* (20th-Fox, 1954); *Stranger on Horseback* (UA, 1955); *An Annapolis Story* (AA, 1955); *Invasion of the Body Snatchers* (AA, 1956); *Nightmare* (UA, 1956); *Forty Pounds of Trouble* (U, 1962); *Gathering of Eagles* (U, 1963); *The Prize* (MGM, 1963); *An Affair of the Skin* (City Films, 1963); *The Best Man* (WB, 1964); *Mirage* (U, 1965); *A Big Hand for the Little Lady* (WB, 1966); *Hotel* (WB, 1967); *The Hell with Heroes* (U, 1968); *If He Hollers, Let Him Go!* (Par., 1968); *Ace High* (Par., 1969); and *Kansas City Bomber* (MGM, 1972).

Television. Mr. McCarthy played Romeo in *Romeo and Juliet* (Cameo Th., NBC, Apr. 1949), and has subsequently appeared on such programs as Studio One (CBS); US Steel Hour (ABC); Goodyear Playhouse (NBC); *Antigone* (Omnibus, CBS); Climax (CBS); DuPont Th. (ABC); Kraft Television Th. (NBC); Twilight Zone (CBS); Ben Casey (ABC); Breaking Point (ABC); Dr. Kildare (NBC); Burke's Law (ABC); Alfred Hitchcock Th. (CBS); The Fugitive (ABC); The F.B.I. (ABC); The Man from U.N.C.L.E. (NBC); Judd for the Defense (ABC); Hawaii Five-O (CBS); The Name of the Game (NBC); Mission: Impossible (CBS); *A Great American Tragedy* (ABC); and *U.M.C.* (CBS).

Awards. Mr. McCarthy received a Village Voice Off-Bway (Obie) Award (1974–75) for his performance in *Harry Outside*.

McCARTHY, MARY.

Author, drama critic. b. Mary Therese McCarthy, June 21, 1912, Seattle, Wash., to Roy Winfield and Therese (Preston) McCarthy. Attended Forrest Ridge Convent, Seattle, Wash., 1918, 1923–24; grad. Annie Wright Seminary, Tacoma, Wash., 1929; Vassar Coll., B.A. 1933. Married June 21, 1933, to Harold Johnsrud, playwright, actor (marr. dis. 1936); married Feb. 15, 1938, to Edmund Wilson, critic (marr. dis. 1946); one son; married Dec. 18, 1946, to Bowden Broadwater (marr. dis. 1961); married Apr. 15, 1961, to James Raymond West. Relative in theatre: brother, Kevin McCarthy, actor. Member Natl. Institute of Arts and Letters. Address: c/o Castine, ME 04421.

Miss McCarthy was drama critic for *The Partisan Review* (1937–48).

She wrote the following works of dramatic criticism: *Sights and Spectacles* (1956) and *Mary McCarthy's Theatre Chronicles* (1963).

Other published works include: *The Company She Keeps* (1942); *The Oasis* (1949); *Cast a Cold Eye* (1950); *The Groves of Academe* (1952); *A Charmed Life* (1955); *Venice Observed* (1956); *Memories of a Catholic Girlhood* (1957); *The Stones of Florence* (1959); *On the Contrary* (1961); *The Group* (1963); *Vietnam* (1967); *Hanoi* (1968); *The Writing on the Wall* (1970); *Birds of America* (1971); *Medina* (1972); *The Mask of State* (1974); and *The Seventeenth Degree* (1974).

Awards. Miss McCarthy was awarded Guggenheim fellowships (1949–50 and 1959–60); a National Institute of Arts and Letters grant (1957); and the honorary degree of D. Litt. by Syracuse Univ. (1973) and Hull Univ. (England, 1974).

McCARTY, E. CLAYTON.

Educator, playwright. b. Edward Clayton McCarty, Jr., Aug. 14, 1901, Louisville, Ky., to Edward Clayton and Katherine Stella (Browning) McCarty. Father, research bio-chemist, educator. Grad. Intermountain Inst., Wieser, Idaho, 1920; attended Colorado State Coll. of A.&M.A., 1920–22; grad. Univ. of Colorado, A.B. 1924; attended Univ. of California at Berkeley, 1925–27; Univ. of Southern California, Summer 1927; Univ. of California at Los Angeles, Summer 1932; grad. Claremont Coll., M.A. 1938; attended Northwestern Univ., 1938–39; Stanford Univ., Summers 1940, 1942, 1945. Married Sept. 3, 1927, to Sara Sloane, writer; three daughters. Member of ALA; AETA. Address: Box 6058, Alpine, TX 79830.

From 1965–73, Mr. McCarty was asst. professor of Speech and chairman of the Department of Speech and Drama at Sul Ross State Coll. Previously, he was chairman of the Dept. of Speech and Drama at Trinity Univ. and director of Trinity Univ. Players (1944–62) and held academic positions at Reedley (Calif.) Joint Union H.S. (1927–29); Washington Junior H.S., Pasadena (1929–38); State Teachers' Coll. California, Pa., (1939–42); and New Mexico State Coll. of A.&M.A. (1942–44), at which he was director of the Coronado Th. In addition, he taught summer courses in playwriting and/or creative writing at Claremont Coll. Graduate Sch. (1936, 1937); Northwestern Univ. (1938); and was lecturer in radio writing at Stanford Univ.-NBC Radio Inst. (1945).

Mr. McCarty directed approximately three hundred student productions, of which about twenty were premieres. He also directed nearly two hundred short plays, most of which were originals by students; and produced approximately six hundred new plays by student playwrights. He retired from teaching in 1973.

Published Works. Mr. McCarty is the author of more than 50 short stories that have appeared in juvenile magazines (1930–38); two dozen plays, including *Three's a Crowd* (1936), *The Man on the Stairs* (1948), *Fog Island* (1949), *Not in a Thousand Years* (1950), *The Moon's Still Yellow* (1958), and *Behind This Mask* (1959); and two volumes of one-act plays, written in collaboration with his wife: *Star Bright and Other Plays* (1938), and *About Seventeen and Other Plays* (1941). He has contributed articles to *The Clearing House* (1936); *The Book of Knowledge* (1951 Annual); and *Dramatics* (1959).

Recreation. Music, growing roses.

McCORMACK, PATTY.

Actress. b. Patricia Ellen Russo, Aug. 21, 1945, New York City, to Frank and Elizabeth (McCormack) Russo. Father, fireman; mother, professional roller skater. Attended Wallard Mace Professional Children's Sch., N.Y.C.; New Utrecht H.S., Brooklyn. Studied speech with Eleanor Raab. Married to Bob Catania (restaurateur); one son, one daughter. Member of AEA; SAG; AFTRA.

Pre-Theatre. Child model.

Theatre. Miss McCormack played Cathy Roberts in *Touchstone* (Music Box, N.Y.C., Feb. 3, 1953); and Rhoda Penmark in *The Bad Seed* (46 St. Th., Dec. 8, 1954).

Films. Miss McCormack made her debut in *Two Gals and a Guy* (UA, 1951); subsequently appeared in *The Bad Seed* (WB, 1956); *Kathy-O* (U, 1958); *Jacktown; The Explosive Generation* (UA, 1961); *The Young Animals* (AI, 1968); *Maryjane* (AI, 1968); *The Mini-Skirt Mob* (AI, 1968); *Born Wild* (AI, 1968); and *The Young Runaways* (MGM, 1968).

Television and Radio. Miss McCormack was on the radio series, The Second Mrs. Burton.

Her television appearances include Mirror Th. (NBC, 1953); The Web (CBS); Armstrong Circle Th. (NBC); I Remember Mama (CBS); Climax (CBS); Playhouse 90 (CBS); Kraft Television Th. (NBC); Wagon Train (NBC); Peck's Bad Girl (CBS); US Steel Hour (CBS); Route 66 (CBS); Farmer's Daughter (ABC); Wild, Wild West (CBS); O'-Hara, US Treasury (CBS); and The Best of Everything (ABC).

McCOWEN, ALEC.

Actor. b. Alexander Duncan McCowen, May 26, 1925, Tunbridge Wells, Kent, England, to Duncan and Mary (Walkden) McCowen. Attended Skinner's Sch., Tunbridge Wells; Royal Academy of Dramatic Arts, London.

Theatre. Mr. McCowen made his acting debut as Micky in *Paddy, the Next Best Thing* (Repertory Th., Macclesfield, England, Aug. 1942); subsequently appeared in repertory (1943–45); toured India and Burma (1945) in *Love in a Mist;* returned to repertory (1946–49), playing one season at St. Johns, Newfoundland; made his London debut as Maxim in *Ivanov* (Arts, Apr. 20, 1950); played Georges Almaire in *The Mask and the Face* (Arts, Sept. 19, 1950); Kitts in *Preserving Mr. Panmure* (Arts, Nov. 15, 1950); appeared in *The Silver Box* (Lyric, Hammersmith, Jan. 1951); and Brian in *The Martin's Nest* (Westminister, Apr. 1951).

He made his American debut as The Messenger in *Antony and Cleopatra* (Ziegfeld, N.Y.C., Dec. 20, 1951); played Hugh Voysey in *The Voysey Inheritance* (Arts, London, May 6, 1952); The Announcer in *The Holy Terrors* (Arts, Nov. 20, 1952); Doventry in *Escapade* (St. James Th., Jan. 20, 1953); with The Repertory Players, played Larry Thompson in *Serious Charge* (Adelphi, Nov. 8, 1953), and Julian Heath in *Shadow of the Vine* (Wyndham's Feb. 14, 1954); subsequently played Henri de Toulouse-Lautrec in *Moulin Rouge* (The New, Bromley, June 1954); Barnaby Tucker in *The Matchmaker* (Haymarket, London, Nov. 4, 1954); Vicomte Octave de Clerambard in *The Count of Clerambarde* (Garrick, Sept. 6, 1955); Dr. Bird in *The Caine Mutiny Court Martial* (Hippodrome, June 13, 1956); Lancelot Berenson in *No Laughing Matter* (Arts, Jan. 24, 1957); and Michael Cloverton-Ferry in *The Elder Statesman* (Edinburgh Festival, Aug. 1958; and Cambridge Th., London, Sept. 25, 1958).

With the Old Vic Company (1959–60), he appeared as Mr. Brisk in *The Double Dealer;* Touchstone in *As You Like It;* Algernon Moncrieff in *The Importance of Being Earnest;* Ford in *The Merry Wives of Windsor;* The Dauphin in *Saint Joan;* and was a replacement in the title role in *Richard II;* subsequently (1960–61) played Mercutio in *Romeo and Juliet;* Oberon in *A Midsummer Night's Dream,* and Malvolio in *Twelfth Night.* Mr. McCowen appeared in the revue *Not To Worry* (Garrick, Feb. 22, 1962); played Sebastian in *Castle in Sweden* (Piccadilly Th., May 23, 1962); joined the Royal Shakespeare Company (Stratford-on-Avon), playing Antipholus of Syracuse in *The Comedy of Errors* (Sept. 11, 1962), and The Fool in *King Lear* (Nov. 6, 1962), appearing in both productions when they moved to London (Aldwych, Dec. 12, 1962). He appeared as Father Riccardo Fontana in *The Representative* (Stratford-on-Avon, Sept. 1963); repeated his performances in *The Comedy of Errors* (Aldwych, London, Dec. 11, 1963), and *King Lear* (Aldwych, Feb. 11, 1964), subsequently toured with both productions to the USSR, Europe, and the US (Feb.–June 1964), appearing at Lincoln Center (NY State Th., N.Y.C., May, 1964); played Ronald Gamble in *Thark* (Yvonne Arnaud Th., Guildford, England, July 1965; and Garrick, London, Aug. 3, 1965); The Author in *The Cavern* (Strand, Nov. 11, 1965); Arthur Henderson in *After the Rain* (Hampstead Th. Club, Sept. 1966; Duchess, London, Jan. 11, 1967; and Golden, N.Y.C., Oct. 9, 1967); Fr. William Rolfe in *Hadrian VII* (Birmingham Repertory, May 1967; Mermaid, London, Apr. 18, 1968; and Helen Hayes Th., N.Y.C., Jan. 8, 1969); appeared in the title role in *Hamlet* (Birmingham Repertory, Jan. 1970); played Philip in *The Philanthropist* (Royal Court,

London, Aug. 3, 1970; May Fair, Sept. 1970; and Ethel Barrymore Th., N.Y.C., Mar. 15, 1971); Martin Dysart in *Equus* (National Th. at The Old Vic, London, July 26, 1973); Professor Higgins in *Pygmalion* (Albery, May 16, 1974); and Alceste in *The Misanthrope* (Old Vic, London, Feb. 22, 1973; Kennedy Ctr., Washington, D.C., Feb. 11, 1975; and St. James Th., N.Y.C., Mar. 12, 1975).

Films. His film appearances include *The Cruel Sea* (UI, 1953); *A Night To Remember* (Rank, 1959); *The Loneliness of the Long Distance Runner* (Continental, 1963); *The Agony and the Ecstasy* (20th-Fox, 1965); and *Travels with My Aunt* (MGM, 1972).

Awards. For his performance in *Hadrian VII*, Mr. McCowen received the London *Evening Standard* Award for Best Actor (1968), the London Critics Award, the *Plays and Players* Award (1968); and was named best actor (1969) by the Drama League of N.Y. for the same role.

He received The Drama Desk Award (1970–71) for his performance in *The Philanthropist.*

Recreation. Writing and the piano.

McCREERY, BUD. Composer, lyricist, singer. b. Walker William McCreery, May 17, 1925, Benton, Ill., to Walker and Virginia (Murphy) McCreery. Father, insurance agent. Grad. Fairfax H.S., Los Angeles, Calif., 1941. In Los Angeles, studied theory and harmony with Gerald Dolin (1942–43), Dr. Julius Gold (1946–47); orchestration with Russell Garcia (1949–50). Served US Army, 1942–46, Infantry; special services; rank, T/Sgt. Member of AFM (Locals, 802, 47); SAG; AEA; ASCAP; ALA; Dramatists Guild; AGAC.

Pre-Theatre. Movie theatre usher.

Theatre. Mr. McCreery first composed for the music department of NBC-TV, Hollywood, Calif. His first score was for *Cage Me A Peacock* (Pelican Th., Los Angeles, Calif., April 23rd, 1942); for Bway, wrote "The Zither Song," sung in *An Evening with Beatrice Lillie* (Booth, Oct. 2, 1952); subsequently with Edw. C. (Bud) Redding, composed the score for *Stock in Trade* (Bermudiana Th., Hamilton, Bermuda, July 21, 1953); contributed sketches, songs and lyrics to *Shoestring Revue* (President, N.Y.C., Feb. 28, 1955); *The Littlest Revue* (Phoenix, May 24, 1956); *Shoestring '57* (Barbizon-Plaza, Nov. 14, 1956); *Put It in Writing* (Theatre de Lys, May 13, 1963); and composed music and lyrics for "Gold Medallion Home" and "Storybook Kitchen" (General Electric Exhibit, NY Worlds' Fair, 1954).

He wrote continuity and vocal material for *The Decline and Fall of the Entire World as Seen Through the Eyes of Cole Porter Revisited* (Square East, Mar. 30, 1965) and for the *New Cole Porter Revue* (Square East, Dec. 22, 1965).

Films. He was the voice of Ray McDonald singing the title song in *Til the Clouds Roll By* (MGM, 1946) and the voice of Marshall Thompson singing "Manhattan" in *Words and Music* (MGM, 1948). He appeared in *The West Point Story* (WB, 1950).

Night Clubs. Mr. McCreery has contributed material to the following cabaret revues: *Son of Four Below* (Downstairs Room, N.Y.C., Sept. 27, 1956); *Demi-Dozen* (Upstairs at the Downstairs, N.Y.C., Oct. 11, 1958); *Pieces of Eight* (Upstairs at the Downstairs, N.Y.C., Sept. 17, 1959); *Four Below Strikes Back* (Downstairs at the Upstairs, N.Y.C., Feb. 4, 1960); *Medium Rare* (Happy Medium, Chicago, Ill., June 29, 1960); *Put It In Writing* (Happy Medium, June 28, 1962); *A Dime a Dozen* (Plaza 9, Plaza Hotel, N.Y.C., Oct. 18, 1962; and *Baker's Dozen* (Plaza 9, Jan. 9, 1964).

Recreation. Tennis, swimming.

McDEVITT, RUTH. Actress. b. Ruth Thane Shoecraft, Sept. 13, 1895, Coldwater, Mich., to John B. and Elizabeth C. (Imber) Shoecraft. Father, security officer. Grad. Bowling Green (Ohio) H.S., 1912; attended Wooster Univ., 1912–13; Bowling Green Normal Coll., 1913–14. Studied at AADA, N.Y.C., 1916–17. Married Dec. 10, 1926, to Patrick John McDevitt, contractor (dec. 1936). Member of AEA (councillor, 1954–61); SAG; AFTRA; St. Petersburg (Fla.) Woman's Club (pres., 1933–34, life member).

Theatre. Miss McDevitt made her Bway debut as Ruth Thane McDevitt, playing Miss Muhlen in *Young Couple Wanted* (Maxine Elliott's Th., Jan. 24, 1940); subsequently, as Ruth McDevitt, appeared as a Female Boarder in *Goodbye in the Night* (Biltmore, Mar. 8, 1940); succeeded (1942) Josephine Hull as Abby Brewster in *Arsenic and Old Lace* (Fulton, Jan. 10, 1941); played Margaret MacGregor in *Meet a Body* (Forrest, Oct. 16, 1944); Sara in the pre-Bway tryout of *I'll Be Waiting* (opened Playhouse, Wilmington, Del., Mar. 29, 1945; closed Walnut St. Th., Philadelphia, Pa., Apr. 14, 1945); replaced (Summers 1945, 1946) Josephine Hull as Veta Louise Simmons in *Harvey* (48 St. Th., N.Y.C., Nov. 1, 1944); played Miss Brown in the pre-Bway tryout of *Darling, Darling, Darling* (opened McCarter, Princeton, N.J., Jan. 31, 1947; closed Wilbur, Boston, Mass., Feb. 8, 1947); Abby Brewster in a tour of *Arsenic and Old Lace* (Summer 1947); Mrs. Van Tassel in *Sleepy Hollow* (St. James, N.Y.C., June 3, 1948); Veta Louise Simmons in a tour of *Harvey* (Summer 1949); Mrs. Hanmer in a tour of *The Silver Whistle* (1950); and Helen Potts in *Picnic* (Music Box, N.Y.C., Feb. 19, 1953).

She succeeded (Music Box, Summer 1954) Josephine Hull as Mrs. Laura Partride in *The Solid Gold Cadillac* (Belasco, Nov. 5, 1953), also touring in the role (1955); played Madame Gloumova in *Diary of a Scoundrel* (Phoenix, N.Y.C., Nov. 5, 1956); Madame de Lere in *Clerambard* (Rooftop Th., Nov. 7, 1957); Mrs. Gamadge in *The Best Man* (Morosco, Mar. 31, 1960), also toured in it (opened Hanna, Cleveland, Ohio, Sept. 18, 1961; closed Forrest, Philadelphia, Pa., Feb. 3, 1962); and appeared as Gertrude in *Save Me a Place at Forest Lawn* (Pocket, N.Y.C., May 8, 1963).

Miss McDevitt played Emma Littlewood in *The Absence of a Cello* (Ambassador, N.Y.C., Sept. 21, 1964); and with the national tour (opened Clowes Hall, Indianapolis, Ind., Jan. 4, 1966; closed Huntington Hartford Th., Los Angeles, June 4, 1966); Mrs. Quigley in *The Man with a Perfect Wife* (Royal Poinciana Playhouse, Palm Beach, Fla., Mar. 22, 1965; and Coconut Grove Playhouse, Miami, Mar. 30, 1965); appeared in *Uncle Vanya* (Mark Taper Forum, Los Angeles, 1969–70); played Stella Livingston in *Light Up the Sky* (tour, opened Fisher Th., Detroit, Aug. 17, 1971; closed O'Keefe Center, Toronto, Canada, Dec. 11, 1971); and appeared in *Twenty-three Years Later* (Mark Taper Forum, Los Angeles, 1937–74).

Films. Miss McDevitt made her debut in *The Guy Who Came Back* (20th-Fox, 1951); subsequently appeared in *The Parent Trap* (Buena Vista, 1961); *Boys Night Out* (MGM, 1962); *Love Is a Ball* (UA, 1962); *The Birds* (U, 1962); *Dear Heart* (WB, 1964); *The Shakiest Gun in the West* (U, 1968); *Change of Habit* (U, 1969); *The Love God?* (U, 1969); *The War Between Men and Women* (Natl. Gen., 1972); *Homebodies* (Avco-Embassy, 1974); and *Mixed Company* (UA, 1974).

Television. She has appeared as Mom on the Mister Peeper series (NBC, 1953–54); on Route 66 (CBS, 1963); Dr. Kildare (NBC, 1963); The Nurses (CBS, 1953); played Mrs. Pfister in *The Cadaver* (Alfred Hitchcock Presents, CBS, 1964); and Miss Emmy in *The Gentleman Caller* (Alfred Hitchcock Presents, CBS, 1964); and performed on the Ed Sullivan Show (CBS).

Miss McDevitt played Grandma in Pistols 'n' Petticoats (CBS); and has appeared on The Doctors (NBC); Girl Talk (ABC); All in the Family (CBS); Room 222 (ABC); and The Night Stalker (ABC).

Recreation. People.

McDOWALL, RODDY. Actor. b. Roderick Andrew McDowall, Sept. 17, 1928, London, England, to Thomas Andrew and Winiefriede (Corcoran) McDowall. Grad. St. Joseph Coll., Beulah Hill, London, 1940; attended 20th-Century Fox Studio Sch., 1940–1947, grad. University H.S., Santa Monica, Calif., 1947. Studied acting with Edith Kingl, London, 1935–40; Mira Rostova, N.Y.C., 1952–57. Served in the Organized Reserve Corps, eight years. Member of AEA (council); SAG; AFTRA.

Theatre. Mr. McDowall made his stage debut touring in the title role in *Young Woodley* (Summer 1946); subsequently played Malcolm in Orson Welles' production of *Macbeth* (Salt Lake City Centennial, Utah, Summer 1947); Ninian in *The First Mrs. Fraser* (La Jolla Playhouse, Calif., 1948); and Lachie in *The Hasty Heart* (Lobero, Santa Barbara, Calif., 1948; Tucson, Ariz., 1949; Laguna Beach, Calif., 1950).

He appeared in *O Mistress Mine* (Laguna Beach, Calif., 1950; Sombrero Playhouse, Phoeniz, Ariz., 1951); as Richard in *The Youngest* (Cape Playhouse, Dennis, Mass., 1951; Playhouse-in-the-Park, Philadelphia, Pa., 1952; Pocono Playhouse, Mountainhome, Pa., 1952); and played Kialdo Walton in Remains to Be Seen (Alcazar, San Francisco, Calif., 1952).

He made his N.Y.C. debut as Bentley Summerhays in *Misalliance* (NY City Ctr., Feb. 18, 1953); appeared as Fancourt Baberly in *Charley's Aunt* (Playhouse-in-the-Park, Philadelphia, Pa., 1953); Dabney Featherstone in *Debut* (St. Louis Municipal Th., Mo., 1953); Daventry in *Escapade* (48 St. Th., N.Y.C., Nov. 18, 1953); in the revue, *Aboard the Band Wagon* (Bucks County Playhouse, New Hope, Pa., Summer 1954; Summer Playhouse, Andover, N.J., Summer 1954); and as Louis Dubedat in *The Doctor's Dilemma* (Phoenix, N.Y.C., Jan. 11, 1955).

He performed in two productions of the American Shakespeare Festival (Stratford, Conn.) as Octavius in *Julius Caesar* (July 12, 1955), and as Ariel in *The Tempest* (Aug. 1, 1955); played Ben Whitledge in *No Time for Sergeants* (Alvin, N.Y.C., Oct. 20, 1955); Yegor Gloumov in *Diary of a Scoundrel* (Phoenix, Nov. 5, 1956); Benjamin in *Good as Gold* (Belasco, Mar. 7, 1957); Artie Straus in *Compulsion* (Ambassador, Oct. 24, 1957); Pepe in *Handful of Fire* (Martin Beck Th., Oct. 1, 1958); Tarquin Medigales in *The Fighting Cock* (ANTA, Dec. 8, 1959); Marcel Blanchard in *Look After Lulu* (Henry Miller's Th., Mar. 3, 1959); the Boy-Next-Door in stock productions of *Meet Me in St. Louis* (Sacandaga, N.Y.; Toronto, Ontario, Canada); Mordred in *Camelot* (Majestic, N.Y.C., Dec. 3, 1960); Claud in *The Astrakhan Coat* (Helen Hayes Th., Jan. 12, 1967); and Babs Babberly in *Charley's Aunt* (PTP-Univ. of Michigan, Power Ctr. for the Performing Arts, Ann Arbor, Mich., May 14, 15, 16, 1976).

Films. Since his debut in *Scruffy* (Independent, 1937), Mr. McDowall has appeared in the following British films: *Murder in the Family* (Fox-Brit., 1937); *I See Ice* (Balcon, 1937); *John Halifax, Gentleman* (MGM-Brit., 1938); *Convict 99* (Gainsborough, 1938); *Hey! Hey! U.S.A.* (Gainsborough, 1938); *Sarah Siddons* (Butler, RKO, 1938); *The Outsider* (Butler, RKO, 1938); *Just William* (Assoc. Brit., 1938); *Poison Pen* (Assoc. Brit., 1938); *Dead Men's Shoes* (Assoc. Brit., 1938); *His Brother's Keeper* (Warner Brit., 1939); *Dirt* (Lever Bros., Balcon, 1939); *Saloon Bar* (Lever Bros., Balcon, 1939); *You Will Remember* (British Lion, 1940); and *This England* (Brit. Natl., 1940).

His American films include *Man Hunt* 20th-Fox, 1941); *How Green Was My Valley* (20th-Fox, 1941); *Confirm or Deny* (20th-Fox, 1941); *Son of Fury* (20th-Fox, 1941); *On the Sunny Side* (20th-Fox, 1941); *The Pied Piper* (20th-Fox, 1942); *My Friend Flicka* (20th-Fox, 1942); *Lassie Come Home* (MGM, 1942); *The White Cliffs of Dover* (MGM, 1943); *Keys of the Kingdom* (20th-Fox, 1944); *Thunderhead, Son of Flicka* (20th-Fox, 1944); *Molly and Me* (20th-Fox, 1944); *Holiday in Mexico* (MGM, 1945); *Macbeth* (Rep., 1947); *Rocky* (Mono., 1947); *Kidnapped* (Mono., 1948); *Tuna Clipper* (Mono., 1948); *Black Midnight* (Mono., 1950); *Killer Shark* (Mono., 1949); *Big Timber* (Mono., 1950); *The Steel Fist* (Mono., 1952); *The Subterraneans* (MGM, 1959); *Midnight Lace* (U, 1960); *The Longest Day* (20th-Fox, 1962); *Cleopatra* (20th-Fox, 1963); *The Greatest Story Ever Told* (UA, 1963); and *Shock Treatment* (20th-Fox, 1963).

He also appeared in *The Third Day* (WB, 1965); *The Loved One* (MGM, 1965); *That Darn Cat* (Buena Vista, 1965); *Lord Love a Duck* (UA, 1966); *Inside Daisy Clover* (WB, 1966); *The Defector* (Seven Arts, 1966); *The Cool Ones* (WB, 1967); *It* (WB-Seven Arts, 1967); *Five Card Stud* (Par., 1968); *Planet of the Apes* (20th-Fox, 1968); *Hello, Down There* (Par., 1969); *The Midas Run* (Cinerama, 1969); *Escape from the Planet of the Apes* (20th-Fox, 1971); *Conquest of the Planet of the Apes* (20th-Fox, 1972); *The Life and Times of Judge Roy Bean* (Natl. Gen., 1972); *The Poseidon Adventure* (20th-Fox, 1972); *Battle for the Planet of the Apes* (20th-Fox, 1973); *The Legend of Hell House* (20th-Fox, 1973); *Arnold* (Cinerama, 1973); and *Funny Lady* (Col., 1975).

Television. He has appeared in *Ah, Wilderness!* (1951) and *Buy Me Blue Ribbons* (Philco Television Playhouse, NBC, 1954); *Great Expectations* (Robert Montgomery Presents, NBC, 1954); *Philip Goes Forth* (Kraft Television Th., NBC, 1954); *The Silver Box* (Kraft Television Th., NBC, 1955); *The Good Fairy* (Maurice Evans Presents, 1956); *In the Days of Our Youth* (Goodyear Playhouse, NBC, 1956); *The Treasure Hunters* (Goodyear Playhouse, NBC, 1957); *Heart of Darkness* (Playhouse 90, CBS, 1958); *The Imposter* (1958); *Night of Betrayal* (US Steel Hour, CBS, 1959); *Too Bad About Sheila Troy* (Music Th., NBC, 1959); *Billy Budd* (Dupont, CBS, 1959); *The Tempest* (Hallmark Hall of Fame, NBC, 1960); *Not without Honor* (Our American Heritage, NBC, 1960); and the Art Carney Revue (1960).

He also appeared in *The Power and the Glory* (CBS, Oct. 1961); on Alfred Hitchcock Th. (CBS) in *The Gentleman Caller* (Apr. 1964) and *See the Monkey Dance* (Nov. 1964); on Bob Hope Chrysler Th. (NBC) in *Wake Up, Darling* (Feb. 1964), *Mr. Biddle's Crime* (Dec. 1964), and *The Fatal Mistake* (Nov. 1966); on Ben Casey (ABC, 1965); 12 O'Clock High (ABC, 1966); Batman (ABC, 1966); The Name of the Game (NBC, 1968, 1970); in *Saint Joan* (Hallmark Hall of Fame, NBC, Dec. 1967); on Felony Squad (ABC, 1968); It Takes a Thief (ABC, 1969); Medical Center (CBS, 1970); in *Terror in the Sky* (CBS, Sept. 1971); *No Taste of Evil* (ABC, Oct. 1971); on Ironside (NBC, 1971); in *What's a Nice Girl Like You?* (ABC, Dec. 1971); on Columbo (NBC, 1972); Delphi Bureau (ABC, 1972); Mission: Impossible (CBS, 1972); McCloud (NBC, 1972); Harry O (ABC, 1976); and Hollywood Squares (NBC, 1976).

Other Activities. He has been a professional photographer since 1955 and has had his photographs published in *Vogue, Paris Match, Life, Look, Ladies' Home Journal,* and *Harper's Bazaar;* he was an advisory editor for the last. *Double Exposure,* a book of his photographs, was published in 1966.

Discography. Mr. McDowall recorded, with Julie Harris, *Miracles: Poems Written by Children* (Caedmon, 1967).

Awards. Mr. McDowall has won *Box Office* Magazine awards and *Fame* Magazine awards during his childhood in films; the *Parents* Magazine Award (1942); the Antoinette (Tony) Award (1960) for his performance as Tarquin Mendigales in *The Fighting Cock;* and the NATAS (Emmy) Award (1960–61) for his performance in *Not without Honor.* .

Recreation. Riding, swimming.

McDOWELL, JOHN H. Educator. b. May 25, 1903, Tiffin, Ohio, to J. R. and Mary (Huber) McDowell. Father, merchant. Grad. Central H.S., Bowling Green, Ohio, 1921; Leland Powers Sch. of the Th., Boston, Mass., 1929; Boston Univ., B.S. 1929; Univ. of Wash., M.A. 1933; Yale Univ. (Univ. Scholar, 1935–37; Yale-Rockefeller Traveling Scholarship, Summer 1936) Ph.D. 1937. Married June 26, 1935, to Judith Walen; three daughters. Member of Section Internationale des Bibliothéques-Musées des Arts du Spectacle, 1960; Intl. Congress for Th. Research, 1948, ANTA; AETA (exec. comm., 1950–53; chmn., research comm., 1948–54; exhibits comm., 1960–64; th. collections comm., 1962–64; professional th. comm., 1951–52). Address: (home) 2006 Tewksbury Rd., Columbus, OH 43221, tel. 488-0889; (bus.) Dept. of Speech, Ohio State Univ., Columbus, OH 43210, tel. (614) CY 3-6241.

From 1945–54, Mr. McDowell was director of the Ohio State University Th.; director of the Stadium Theatre (1950–54); director of the Ohio State University Th. Collection and editor of the *OSU Theatre Collection Bulletin* (1950–to date); member of the Ohio State Univ. faculty (1945–to date); as assistant professor (1945–48); associate professor (1948–52); professor of speech (1952–73); and emeritus professor (1973–to date).

He was instructor at Leland Powers School (1929–30); instructor at Cornish Sch. of Th. (1930–34); assistant professor at Wellesley Coll. (1936); at Smith Coll. (1937–44); and at Manhattanville Coll. of the Sacred Heart (1944–45).

Awards. Mr. McDowell has received research grants from the Natl. Theatre Conference, Folger Shakespeare Library, and Ohio State Univ.; five Grants-in-Aid for the Ohio State Univ.; a grant from the Ohio State Univ. Development Fund; and a University grant to attend the Third Intl. Congress for Theatre Research (Paris, 1961).

McEWAN, GERALDINE. Actress. b. Geraldine McKeown, May 9, 1932, Old Windsor, Berkshire, England, to Donald and Norah (Burns) McKeown. Father, printer. Received General Cert. of Education, Windsor County (England) Girls' Sch., 1948. Married May 17, 1953, to Hugh Cruttwell, playwright, theatre director; one son, one daughter. Member of AEA. Address: 93 Abingdon Rd., London, W.8, England tel. 01-937-9726.

Theatre. Miss McEwan made her debut on Bway as Lady Teazle in *The School for Scandal* (Majestic Th., Jan. 24, 1963); subsequently appeared as Doreen and Belinda respectively, in the double-bill *The Private Ear* and *The Public Eye* (Morosco, Oct. 9, 1963), with which she toured the US.

She made her professional debut as an Attendant to Hippolyta in *A Midsummer Night's Dream,* with the Theatre Royal Repertory Co., Windsor, England; her first speaking role was with that company, as the Maid in *Life with Father* (Mar. 14, 1949); she subsequently played many roles with the company, inc. Catherine in *Little Lambs Eat Ivy* (June 1949), Catherine in *Northanger Abbey* (Oct. 1949), performing with them until Mar. 1951.

She made her London debut as Christina Deed in *Who Goes There!* (Vaudeville, Apr. 4, 1951); subsequently played Janet in *Sweet Madness* (Vaudeville, May 21, 1952); Janet Blake in *For Love or Money* ("Q," Sept. 30, 1952); Anne in *For Better, For Worse* (Comedy, Dec. 17, 1952); Julie Gillis in *The Tender Trap* (Saville, May 3, 1955); the title role in *Patience* (Royal, Brighton; Streatham Hill, July–Aug., 1955); and Francesca in *Summertime* (Apollo, Nov. 9, 1955); joined the Shakespeare Memorial Th. (Stratford-upon-Avon) to play the Princess of France in *Love's Labour's Lost* (July 3, 1956); played Frankie Adams in *The Member of the Wedding* (Royal Court, London, Feb. 5, 1957); succeeded (Dec. 1957), Joan Plowright as Jean Rice in *The Entertainer* (Palace, Sept. 10, 1957); returned to the Shakespeare Memorial Th. (Stratford-upon-Avon) to play Olivia in *Twelfth Night* (Apr. 22, 1958), repeating the role when the company toured USSR (Moscow, Leningrad, 1958); Marina in *Pericles* (Stratford-upon-Avon, July 8, 1958); and Hero in *Much Ado About Nothing* (Stratford-upon-Avon, Aug. 26, 1958); played Madame Renaud in *Change of Tune* (Strand, London, May 13, 1959); Olivia in the Shakespeare Memorial Th. production of *Twelfth Night* (Aldwych, Dec. 19, 1960); performed with the Royal Shakespeare Th. (the new name for the Shakespeare Memorial Th.) at Stratford-upon-Avon, as Beatrice in *Much Ado About Nothing* (Apr. 4, 1961); Ophelia in *Hamlet* (Apr. 11, 1961); and appeared in their production of *The Hollow Crown* (Aldwych, London, Mar. 19, 1961); played Jenny Action in *Everything in the Garden* (Duke of York's, May 16, 1962); in a revival of *The Hollow Crown* (Aldwych, 1962); Lady Teazle in *The School for Scandal* (Haymarket, Sept.–Oct. 1962), which she repeated on Bway (see above); and respectively Doreen and Belinda in the double-bill, *The Private Ear* and *the Public Eye* (Wimbledon, London, Sept. 1963), which she repeated on Bway (see above).

Miss McEwan returned to London to play Fay in *Loot* (Cambridge Arts, Feb. 1, 1965); became a member of the National Th. Co., playing The Lady in *Armstrong's Last Goodnight* (Chichester Fest., July 6, 1965); toured with the co. as Angelica in *Love for Love* (Moscow, Berlin, Sept. 1955); returned to London with the company, again playing The Lady in *Armstrong's Last Goodnight* (Old Vic, Oct. 12, 1965); and Angelica in *Love for Love* (Old Vic, Oct. 20, 1965; also, Aug. 9, 1966); Raymonde Chandebise in *A Flea in Her Ear* (Old Vic, Feb. 8, 1966; Queen's, Aug. 4, 1966); Alice in *The Dance of Death* (Old Vic, Feb. 21, 1967); toured Canada with the National Rep. Co. (inc. Expo 67), again playing the parts of Alice, Angelica and Raymonde (Oct.–Nov. 1967); returned to London with them, playing Queen Anne in Brecht's *Edward II* (Old Vic, Apr. 30, 1968); Victoria in *Home and Beauty* (Old Vic, Oct. 8, 1968); Ada in "Rites," one of four short plays by various women writers, in an evening entitled *An Evasion of Women* (Jeanetta Cochrane Th., National Th. Workshop season, Feb. 11, 1969); Millamant in *The Way of the World* (Old Vic, May 1, 1969); repeated the role of Ada in "Rites" on a double-bill with *Macrunes Guevara (as Realised by Edward Hotel)* (Old Vic, May 27, 1969); and played Vittoria Corombona in *The White Devil* (Old Vic, Nov. 13, 1969).

She played Alkmene in a revival of *Amphitryon 38* (1971); appeared in *Dear Love* (1972); played Zoe in *Not Drowning But Waving* (Greenwich Th., Sept. 20, 1973); Diana in *Chez Nous* (Globe, London, Feb. 6, 1974); and Susan in a revival of *The Little Hut* (1974).

Films. Miss McEwan appeared in *No Kidding* (Pinewood, 1960).

Television. She appeared in *George and Margaret* (ITV, London, 1956); *The Springtime of Others* (ITV, 1957); *The Witch* (ITV, 1958); *The Wind and the Rain* (ITV, 1959); *Tess* (ITV, 1960); *Man with a Conscience* (ITV, Dec. 1960); *Double Image* (Scottish TV, 1962); *Rhyme and Reason* (BBC, 1962); *The Tycoons* (BBC, 1962); *Separate Tables; Candida;* and other programs. In Canada, she appeared in *Roots* (CBC, May 1963).

In the US, she appeared as Jessie Benton Fremont in *The Thomas Hart Benton Story* (Profiles in Courage, NBC, Nov. 29, 1964).

McGAVIN, DARREN. Actor, director, producer. b. May 7, 1922, to Reed Delano and Grace (Bogart) McGavin. Gra. Galt (Calif.) Union H.S., 1940; attended Coll. of the Pacific, 1940–41. Studied acting at the Neighborhood Playhouse Sch. of the Theatre, N.Y.C., 1948; Actors' Studio (member 1950–to date). Married Mar. 20, 1944, to Melanie York, actress; (marr. dis.); one son, one daughter; married Dec. 31, 1968, to Kathie Browne, actress. Member of AEA; SAG; AFTRA; DGA; ANDA.

Theatre. Mr. McGavin first appeared on stage in a college production of *Lady Windermere's Fan* (1941); played the Judge Advocate, in *Liliom* (Actors Lab. Hollywood, Calif., 1945); played for six months in a USO tour of *The Late Christopher Bean* (1946); and produced and directed a stock season at the Spring Lake (N.J.) Community Th. (Summer 1947).

He made his N.Y.C. debut as a walkon in the Dublin Gate production of *The Old Lady Says No!* (Mansfield Th., Feb. 17, 1948); subsequently played Joe in *Cock-a-Doodle-Doo* (Lenox Hill Playhouse, Feb. 26, 1949); toured as Happy in the national co. of *Death of a Salesman* (Sept. 1949–June, 1951), later succeeding Cameron Mitchell in this role (Morosco, N.Y.C., Feb. 2, 1949); and played Heracles in *The Thracian Horses* (Brandeis Univ. 1951).

With David Heilweil and Robert N. Winter-Berger, he produced *Dark Legend* (President, Mar. 24, 1952); appeared as Alfred in *My 3 Angels* (Morosco, Mar. 11, 1953); Bill Starbuck in *The Rainmaker* (Cort, Oct. 28, 1954); the King in *The King and I* (St. Louis Municipal Opera, Mo., Summer 1955); Hal Carter in *Picnic* (Playhouse-in-the-Park, Philadelphia, Pa., Aug. 29, 1955); Matt Burke in a staged reading of *Anna Christie* (Phoenix, N.Y.C., Nov. 22, 1955); David McGregor in *The Innkeepers* (John Golden Th., Feb. 2, 1956); Chrysagon de la Crux in *The Lovers* (Martin Beck Th., May 10, 1956); Dick Pepper in *Tunnel of Love* (Royale, Feb. 13, 1957); and for the Theatre Guild directed a summer production of *With Respect for Joey.*

Mr. McGavin played the Wreck in *Wonderful Town* (US Pavilion, Brussels Worlds Fair, Belg., Summer 1958); 1st Lt. Stanley Poole in *Blood, Sweat and Stanley Poole* (Morosco, N.Y.C., Oct. 5, 1961); Prof. Harold Hill in *The Music Man* (Guber-Ford-Gross Circuit, Summer 1962); Joe Kelly in *The Happiest Man Alive,* which he also directed (Westport Country Playhouse, Conn., Summer 1962); and played the King in *The King and I* (NY State Th., July 6, 1964).

He played Murray Burns in a stock tour of *A Thousand Clowns* (Summer 1964), which he also directed; played Destry in *Destry Rides Again* (Meadowbrook Dinner Th., Cedar Grove, N.J., Sept. 17, 1964); Charlie Bickle in a pre-Bway tryout of *Here Lies Jeremy Troy* (Lakewood Th., Skowhegan, Me., Aug. 2, 1965); directed and appeared in the tryout of *Fairy Tale* (Royal Alexandra Th., Toronto, Ontario, Can., Jan. 25, 1966), written by his wife, Melanie York; played Larry Renault in an all-star revival of *Dinner at Eight* (Alvin, N.Y.C., Sept. 27, 1966); Harry Roat, Jr. in a winter stock tour of *Wait Until Dark* (Coconut Grove Playhouse, Miami, Fla., Feb. 28, 1967; Parker Playhouse, Fort Lauderdale, Fla., Mar. 20, 1967); and the title role in *Captain Brassbound's Conversion* (Ahmanson, Los Angeles, Fall 1968).

Films. Mr. McGavin made his screen debut in *A Song to Remember* (Col., 1945); subsequently appeared in *Kiss and Tell* (Col., 1945); *She Wouldn't Say Yes* (Col., 1945); *Counter-Attack* (Col., 1945); *Fear* (Monogram, 1946); *Queen for a Day* (UA, 1951): *Summertime* (UA, 1955); *The Court Martial of Billy Mitchell* (WB, 1955); *The Man with the Golden Arm* (UA, 1955); *Beau James* (Par., 1957); *The Delicate Delinquent* (Par., 1957); *The Case Against Brooklyn* (Col., 1958); *Bullet for a Bad Man* (U, 1964), *The Great Sioux Massacre* (Col., 1965); *Ride the High Wind* (Emerson, 1966); *Mission: Mars* (AA, 1968); *Mrs. Pollifax—Spy* (UA, 1971); through his production co., Taurean, prod. and dir. *Happy Mother's Day—Love, George* (Cinema 5, 1973); and appeared in *The Petty Story* (Rowland-Lasko, 1974).

Television. Mr. McGavin has starred in five television series: as Casey, Crime Photographer (CBS, premiere May 3, 1951); for two seasons, as Mike Hammer (first season, CBS: premiere Jan. 28, 1958; second season, in syndication); for two seasons as Grey Holden in Riverboat (NBC, premiere Sept. 13, 1959; overlapping his appearances as Mike Hammer); for a season as The Outsider (NBC, premiere Sept. 18, 1968); and for a season as The Night Stalker (ABC, premiere Sept. 1974, as Kolchak: The Night Stalker). He has appeared in numerous made-for-television movies, including the pilot for his series *The Night Stalker* (ABC, Jan. 11, 1972) and its sequel *The Night Strangler* (ABC, Jan. 16, 1973); the pilot films for two series, *Banyon* (NBC, Mar. 15, 1971) and *The Rookies* (ABC, Mar. 7, 1972); in *Sunset Boulevard* (Robert Montgomery Presents, NBC, Dec. 3, 1956); and on nearly a hundred other dramatic, comedy, and talk shows.

He directed the episodes entitled *Cousin Casey* and *Sally's Old Beau* (Buckskin, NBC, 1959); *Diamonds Ahead* (Riverboat, NBC, 1960); and *Queen of Spades* (Death Valley Days, 1960), etc.

McGAW, CHARLES. Educator, director. b. Charles James McGaw, Aug. 30, 1910, Grand Rapids, Mich., to Robert W. and Minnie (Clapp) McGaw. Father, salesman. Grad. Western Michigan H.S., Kalamazoo, 1925; Univ. of Michigan, B.A., M.A., Ph.D. 1928–40; studied at Amer. Th. Wing, 1948–49; studied with Valentine Windt, Lee Strasberg, Joseph Anthony, and Fanny Bradshaw. Served USN, 1943–46; rank, Lt. Member of ANTA; ATA (assoc. ed., *ETJ,* 1962–1966); SAA. Address: (home) 73 East Elm St., Chicago, IL 60611, tel. (312) 787-4059; (bus.) The Art Institute of Chicago, Monroe St. & Columbus Dr., Chicago, IL 60603, tel. (312) CE 6-7080.

In 1957, Mr. McGaw was appointed as head of education, senior director and professor of acting at the Goodman Memorial Th. and Sch. of Drama of The Art Inst. of Chicago (Ill.). Since 1966, he has been dean of the Goodman School of Drama.

He was assistant professor at Ithaca Coll. (N.Y., 1940–43); assistant professor at the Univ. of Michigan (Ann Arbor, Summer 1946); associate professor at Ohio State Univ. and administrative director of the Stadium Th. (Columbus, Ohio, 1946–56); visiting professor at the Sch. of Dramatic Arts, Columbia Univ. (N.Y.C., 1956–57); and lecturer in contemporary drama at the Univ. of Chicago (Ill., 1957–62).

Mr. McGaw was associate director of the Manhattan Th. Colony (Ogunquit, Me., Summer 1957); guest director at the San Diego (Calif.) Shakespeare Festival (Old Globe Th., Summer 1958); guest director at the Sch. of Theatre, Univ. of Bahia (Salvador, Brazil, Summers 1959, 1961); and visiting professor and production director at Northwestern Univ. (Evanston, Ill., Summers 1962, 1963).

He was visiting professor and director at Tulane Univ. (Spring semester 1965); the Univ. of Minnesota (Summer 1965); and the Univ. of Hawaii (Summer 1968); and was adjunct professor at the Univ. of Illinois at Chicago Circle (1974–to date).

Published Works. Mr. McGaw wrote *Acting Is Believing: A Basic Method for Beginners* (1955; rev. eds. 1966, 1975).

Recreation. Extensive travel in Europe, Asia, and South America.

McGINLEY, LAURENCE JOSEPH S.J. Priest, educator. b. Sept. 6, 1905, New York City, to James and Alice (McCabe) McGinley. Father, Commissioner of Accounts of the City of New York. Grad. Xavier H.S., N.Y.C., 1922; Woodstock Coll., B.A. 1928, M.A. 1935; Gregorian Univ., Rome, It., S.T.D. 1939. Address: (home) St. Peter Hall, 1641 Kennedy Blvd., Jersey City, NJ 07306; (bus.) tel. (201) 333-4400.

The Reverend McGinley serves on the board of directors of the Lincoln Ctr. for the Performing Arts. Since leaving his post at Fordham Univ., where he served as president (1949–63), Fr. McGinley has been assistant to the president of Saint Peter's Coll.

Awards. The Reverend McGinley has received the honorary degrees, LL.D. from Iona Coll.; Ph.D. from the Catholic Univ. of Santiago, Chile; L.H.D. from Manhattan Coll.; Litt. D. from St. Francis Coll.; D.Sc. from St. John's Univ.; D.C.L. from Pace Coll.; LL.D. from Manhattanville Coll.; L.H.D. from Clarkson College of Tech.; Litt. D. from Seton Hill Coll.; LL.D. from New York Univ.; L.H.D. from Saint Peter's Coll.; and LL.D. from Fordham Univ.

He received The American Irish Historical Society Gold Medal (1960); the Universal Brotherhood Award of the Jewish Theological Seminary of America (1960); US Army Outstanding Civilian Service Medal (1962); Civic Award in Education, the Bronx Board of Trade (1961); the Grand Gold Badge of Honor for Merits to the Republic of Austria (1963); and decorations from the governments of Peru, Brazil, Chile, and Italy.

Recreation. Golf, fishing.

McGINN, WALTER. Actor. b. Walter Vincent McGinn III, July 6, 1936, Providence, R.I., to Walter Vincent and Gertrude Elizabeth (Roe) McGinn. Father, real estate; mother, beautician. Educ. St. Raymond's Catholic Grammar School, Providence, R.I.; St. Raphael Academy High School, Pawtucket, R.I.; grad. School of Fine and Applied Arts, Boston (Mass.) Univ., B.A. 1959. Studied acting with Peter Kass and David Pressman, Theatre Dept., Boston Univ. Served in Finance Corps, US Army. Member of AEA; SAG; AFTRA. Address: 137 Riverside Drive, New York, NY 10024, tel. (212) 787-1031.

Theatre. Mr. McGinn's first stage appearance was at Boston Univ. Th.; he made his professional debut as Tom in *This Property Is Condemned* (Charles St. Playhouse, Boston, Mass., 1959); and, while serving in the Army, played the role of Moony in *Moony's Kid Don't Cry* (Frankfurt Playhouse, Frankfurt, Germany, 1961) and toured Germany with the play. In summer stock, he appeared in *Look Back in Anger* (Phoenicia Playhouse, N.Y., 1962) and in minor roles at the NY Shakespeare Festival in *Antony and Cleopatra, As You Like It,* and *The Winter's Tale* (all Summer 1963). He was Christy Mahon in *The Playboy of the Western World* (McCarter Th., Princeton, N.J., 1963); made his Bway debut replacing (Sept. 7, 1965) Martin Sheen as Timmy Cleary in *The Subject Was Roses* (Royale, May 25, 1964) and toured East Coast theatres with the production (Summer 1966). He toured as the Boy in *The Fantasticks* (1967); returned to N.Y.C. as Caleb Trask in *Here's Where I Belong* (Billy Rose Th., Mar. 3, 1968); played Jigger in *Carousel* (Dallas Music Fair, Dallas, Tex., and St. Louis Opera, Summer 1968); Tom Dart in *Spitting Image* (Th. de Lys, N.Y.C., Mar. 2, 1969); Bob in *Irma La Douce* (Dallas Music Fair, Summer 1969); toured as the Squire in *Canterbury Tales* (1970); replaced (Apr. 20, 1971) Jason Miller as Paryfon Rogozhin in *Subject to Fits* (Public Th., N.Y.C., Feb. 14, 1971); played Mickey in *The Basic Training of Pavlo Hummel* (Public Th., May 20, 1971); Mordred in *Camelot* (Dallas Music Fair, Summer 1971); Roscoe in *Manchineel* (The Cubiculo, Dec. 27, 1971); Tom Daley in *That Championship Season* (Public Th., May 2, 1972; Booth Th., Sept. 14, 1972); repeating this role in England (Garrick Th., London, 1974); and Willie Oban in *The Iceman Cometh* (Circle in the Square–Joseph E. Levine Th., N.Y.C., Dec. 13, 1973).

Films. Mr. McGinn's first film role was Jack Younger in *The Parallax View* (Par., 1974).

Television. Mr. McGinn made his television debut as a guest star in *Everybody Loved Him* (N.Y.P.D., ABC, 1967). He was in the series Another World (NBC, 1973); played Stephen Douglas in *Sandburg's Lincoln* (NBC, 1974); Martin Bronson in *The Best Judge Money Can Buy* (Kojak, CBS, 1974); and Eric Press in *Mortal Sin* (Harry O, ABC, 1974).

Awards. Mr. McGinn and the other members of the *That Championship Season* cast won NY Drama Desk awards for 1971–72 for outstanding performances; Mr. McGinn also received an Outer Circle Award and was a *Variety* poll winner for his work in the play.

Recreation. Magic.

McGOVERN, JOHN. Actor. Studied at AADA, N.Y.C. Member of AEA; AFTRA. Address: 160 West End Ave., New York, NY 10023, tel. (212) TR 3-3450.

Theatre. Mr. McGovern made his stage debut in *He Who Gets Slapped* (Neighborhood Playhouse, N.Y.C.); subsequently appeared in *Peer Gynt* (Garrick, Feb. 5, 1923); *The Devil's Disciple* (Garrick, Apr. 23, 1923); *Saint Joan* (Garrick, Dec. 28, 1923); played the Photographer in *The Glass Slipper* (Guild, Oct. 19, 1925); appeared in *Garrick Gaieties* (Garrick, May 10, 1926); and played Biondello in *The Taming of the Shrew* (Garrick, Oct. 25, 1927).

He played Professor Christian Gideon in *Double Dummy* (John Golden Th., Nov. 11, 1936); the Bartender in *Retreat to Pleasure* (Belasco, Dec. 17, 1940); Rieman in *Gabrielle* (Maxine Elliott's Th., Mar. 25, 1941); D'Arcy in *Uncle Harry* (Broadhurst, May 29, 1942); Pa Budd in *I'll Take the High Road* (Ritz, Nov. 9, 1943); Dr. Burian in *Thank You, Swoboda* (Mansfield, Mar. 1, 1944); Chet Blanchard in *Sophie* (Playhouse, Dec. 25, 1944); F. Neilson in *Kiss Them for Me* (Belasco, Mar. 20, 1945); Mr. Loomis in *January Thaw* (John Golden Th., Jan. 23, 1946); Dr. Jim Bayliss in *All My Sons* (Coronet, Jan. 29, 1947); Herbert Lee in *Tea and Sympathy* (Ethel Barrymore Th., Sept. 30, 1953); Judge Waite in *The Ponder Heart* (Music Box, Feb. 16, 1956); Dr. Hans Eberhart in *A Shadow of My Enemy* (ANTA, Dec. 11, 1957); Henry Gaxton in *The Man in the Dog Suit* (Coronet, Oct. 30, 1958); the Judge in *A Case of*

Libel on tour; and Dr. Lloyd in *Life with Father* on tour.

McGOWAN, JOHN (JACK). Playwright, actor, director. b. John McGowan, 1892, Muskegon, Mich., to George and Mary McGowan. Attended Muskegon High School, 1909. Member of AEA; Dramatists Guild. Address: Hotel Gramercy Park, Lexington and 21st St., New York, NY 10010, tel. (212) GR 5-4320.

Theatre. Mr. McGowan made his debut in vaudeville; subsequently appeared in *Midnight Revue* (Century Grove, Century Th., N.Y.C., May 4, 1918); *Take It from Me* (44 St. Th., Mar. 31, 1919); as Philip Scarsdale in *The Little Blue Devil* (Central, Nov. 3, 1919); Jack Keene in *Mary* (Knickerbocker, Oct. 18, 1920); Howard Rodney Smith in *The Rose of Stamboul* (Century, Mar. 7, 1922); in *George White's Scandals* (Globe, Aug. 28, 1922); as Bob Morgan in *The Rise of Rosie O'Reilly* (Liberty, Dec. 25, 1923); and succeeded (Sept. 1925) Roy Royston as Austin Bevans in *June Days* (Astor, Aug. 6, 1925).

He wrote, with Mann Page, *Mama Loves Papa* (Forrest, Feb. 22, 1926); with Lloyd Griscolm, *Tenth Avenue* (Eltinge, Aug. 15, 1927); wrote *Excess Baggage* (Ritz, Dec. 26, 1927), and played George McCarthy, replacing Harry Brown for one performance; with B. G. De Silva, wrote the book for *Hold Everything* (Broadhurst, Oct. 10, 1928); contributed sketches to *John Murray Anderson's Almanac* (Erlanger, Aug. 14, 1929); and wrote and directed *Big Shot* (Royale, Sept. 20, 1929).

With Paul Gerard Smith, Mr. McGowan wrote the book for *Heads Up* (Alvin, Nov. 11, 1929); with B. G. De Silva and Lew Brown, for *Flying High* (Apollo, Mar. 3, 1930); with Guy Bolton, *Girl Crazy* (Alvin, Oct. 14, 1930); billed as Jack McGowan, wrote *Singin' the Blues* (Liberty, Sept. 16, 1931); with Herbert Polesie, wrote *Heigh-Ho, Everybody* (Fulton, May 25, 1932); dialogue for *Earl Carroll Vanities* (Bway Th., Sept. 27, 1932); directed the book for *Pardon My English* (Majestic, Jan. 20, 1933); directed, and with Richard Jerome, wrote the sketches for *Strike Me Pink* (Majestic, Mar. 4, 1933); and wrote the book and co-produced with Ray Henderson, *Say When* (Imperial, Nov. 8, 1934).

Films. Mr. McGowan wrote screenplays for *Sitting Pretty* (Par., 1933); and *Little Nellie Kelly* (MGM, 1940).

McGRATH, PAUL. Actor. b. Paul Owen McGrath, April 11, 1904, Chicago, Ill., to Dennis Francis and Genevive (Sibley) McGrath. Father, realtor. Grad. Evander Childs H.S., N.Y.C., 1922; attended Carnegie Inst. of Tech. (theatre), 1922–24. Married Mar. 8, 1929, to Lulu Mae Hubbard, actress (marr. dis.); married June 27, 1968, to Anne Sargent, actress. Relatives in theatre: brother, Frank McGrath, playwright; brother, Byron McGrath, educator, former actor. Member of AEA (council); AFTRA; SAG; Delta Upsilon; The Players. Address: 77 Park Ave., New York, NY 10016, tel. (212) LE 2-5564.

Theatre. Mr. McGrath made his professional debut in the touring production of *The First Year* (Aug. 1924–Feb. 1925); subsequently appeared on Bway as Dr. Green in *In the Near Future* (Wallack's Th., Mar. 10, 1925); Larkin in *Made in America* (Cort, Oct. 14, 1925); Major Cromwell in *The Arabian* (Eltinge, Oct. 31, 1927); toured in Theatre Guild productions of *The Doctor's Dilemma, Ned McCobb's Daughter* and *John Ferguson* (1928); appeared in stock companies in Seattle, Wash.; San Francisco, Calif.; and Pittsburgh, Pa. (1929–31); played the Head Waiter in *The Good Fairy* (Henry Miller's Th., N.Y.C., Nov. 24, 1931); Spencer Grant in *Here Today* (Ethel Barrymore Th., Sept. 6, 1932); Franklyn Chase in *Pigeons and People* (Sam H. Harris Th., Jan. 16, 1933); Arthur Valois in *Three and One* (Longacre, Oct. 25, 1933); Douglas Allenby in *Lady Jane* (Plymouth, Sept. 10, 1934); and Dorlay in *Ode to Liberty* (Lyceum, Dec. 21, 1934).

He appeared as Mr. Dulcimer in a touring production of *The Green Bay Tree* (Nov. 1935); succeeded (Dec. 1935) Robert Shayne as Defense-Attorney Stevens in *The Night of January 16th* (Ambassador, N.Y.C., Sept. 16, 1935); played Cleonte Du Bois in a stock production of *The Would-Be Gentleman* (Westport Country Playhouse, Westport, Conn., Aug. 1936); John Clyde in *Seen But Not Heard* (Henry Miller's Th., N.Y.C., Sept. 17, 1936); and in stock productions of *The Inconstant Moon* and *As Husbands Go* (Newport, R.I., Aug. 1937).

Mr. McGrath played Barrie Trexel in *Susan and God* (Plymouth, N.Y.C., Oct. 7, 1937), and on tour (1938–39); Michael Carr in *Ring Two* (Henry Miller's Th., N.Y.C., Nov. 22, 1939); Kendall Nesbitt in *Lady in the Dark* (Alvin, Sept. 2, 1941); toured as Professor Michael Frame in *Tomorrow the World* (opened Selwyn Th., Chicago, Ill., 1943); played Jasper Doolittle in *In Bed We Cry* (Belasco, N.Y.C., Nov. 14, 1944); Ted Williamson in *Common Ground* (Fulton, Apr. 25, 1945); Brigadier General Clifton C. Garnett in *Command Decision* (Fulton, Oct. 1, 1947); Smiley Coy in *The Big Knife* (Natl., Feb. 24, 1949); Henry Mitchell in *Small Hours* (Natl., Feb. 15, 1951); Charles Warren in *Love and Let Love* (Plymouth, Oct. 19, 1951); Langdon Spaulding in *Touchstone* (Music Box, Feb. 3, 1953); and Mr. Benton in *A Girl Can Tell* (Royale, Oct. 29, 1953).

He first appeared on the London stage as Tom Chadwick in *Roar Like a Dove* (Phoenix, Sept. 26, 1957); in N.Y.C., played Charles Webster in *The Gang's All Here* (Ambassador, Oct. 1, 1959), in which he toured summer theatres (1960); Alex Wilkins in *Giants, Sons of Giants* (Alvin, N.Y.C., Jan. 6, 1962); George Quincy Fletcher in a stock production of *When the Beer Goes National* (Bucks County Playhouse, New Hope, Pa., Summer 1962); Jan Masaryk in *The Long Night* (Florida State Univ. Th., Feb. 1, 1963); Dr. Golka in *The Sound of Distant Thunder* (Playhouse-on-the-Mall, Paramus, N.J., Mar. 9, 1963); Victor in *Bicycle Ride to Nevada* (Cort, N.Y.C., Sept. 24, 1963); and succeeded (Mar. 2, 1964) Sidney Blackmer as Paul Cleary in *A Case of Libel* (Longacre, Oct. 10, 1963); and subsequent tour (Winter 1963, Spring 1964); appeared in *Don't Drink the Water* (Morosco, N.Y.C., Nov. 17, 1966); and in *Brightower* (John Golden Th., N.Y.C., Jan. 28, 1969).

Films. Mr. McGrath made his debut in *The Parole Fixer* (Par., 1940); followed by *This Thing Called Love* (Col., 1941); *No Time for Love* (Par., 1943); *A Face in the Crowd* (WB, 1957); *Advise and Consent* (Col., 1962); and *Pendulum* (Col., 1968).

Television and Radio. Mr. McGrath appeared on the radio program, *The Crime Doctor* (CBS, 1944–50); was host on *Inner Sanctum* (CBS, 1944–51); and played on the serial, *Big Sister* (CBS, 1944–54).

He made his television debut in *Susan and God* (NBC, 1938); followed by appearances on US Steel Hour (CBS, 1958); Hallmark Hall of Fame (NBC, 1959); Armstrong Circle Th. (CBS, 1959); Sunday Showcase (NBC, 1959); and Play of the Month (NBC, 1963).

He played the Chairman on *Witness* (CBS); and appeared in productions of the Philco Playhouse (NBC); and Studio One (CBS); and played leading roles on *Love of Life* (CBS); *The Guiding Light* (CBS); *Edge of Night* (CBS); *The Secret Storm* (CBS); and *Love Is a Many Splendored Thing* (CBS).

McGRAW, WILLIAM RALPH. Educator. b. Dec. 15, 1930, Martins Ferry, Ohio, to Ralph and Lois (Carmichael) McGraw. Father, salesman; mother, teacher. Grad. Senior H.S., Mansfield, Ohio, 1948; Coll. of Wooster, B.A. 1952; Ohio State Univ., M.A. 1953; Univ. of Minn., Ph.D. 1958. Married June 15, 1953, to Barbara Ward, teacher; five children. Relative in theatre: uncle, Dr. H. Keen Carmichael, theatre educator. Member of AETA (administrative vice-pres., 1963–65; vice-pres., programming, 1972; president, 1974–); SAA; NCP; Masonic Order. Address: 1469 Dogwood Avenue, Morgantown, WV 26505.

Since 1972, Mr. McGraw has been professor of drama and chairman of the division at West Virginia University. He was formerly at the Univ. of Minnesota (1955–58), the Univ. of Oregon (1958–61), the Univ. of Michigan (1961–66), and Ohio University (1966–72); and had directed numerous productions in university theatres.

Published Works. Mr. McGraw is the co-author of *Principles and Styles of Acting* (1970), and has written articles for *Educational Theatre Journal, Modern Drama, Dramatics* Magazine, *Studies in Scottish Literature,* and *Quarterly Journal of Speech.*

Awards. He received two commendations for his contributions to AETA.

Recreation. Tennis, travel.

McGUIRE, BIFF. Actor, playwright. b. William Joseph McGuire, Jr., Oct. 25, 1927, New Haven, Conn., to William Joseph Henry and Mildred Elizabeth (Dwyer) McGuire. Father, builder, rest home owner; mother, nurse. Grad. Hamden H.S., 1942; attended Univ. of Massachusetts, 1942; Shrivenham Univ., England, 1944; studied at Art Students' League, N.Y.C., 1948. Married Nov. 29, 1960, to Jeannie Carson, actress; one daughter. Served WW II, US Army, combat engineers, ETO; rank, Pfc. Member of AEA; SAG; AFTRA; SWG. Address: c/o Gloria Safier, 667 Madison Ave., New York, NY 10021, tel. (212) TE 8-4868.

Theatre. Mr. McGuire made his debut as Dudley in *The Time of Your Life* (Lyric, Hammersmith, London, Feb. 14, 1946); subsequently appeared in the revue *Make Mine Manhattan* (Broadhurst, N.Y.C., Jan. 15, 1948); played Bob McCaffrey in *South Pacific* (Majestic, Apr. 7, 1949); toured in *Miss Liberty* (May 1950); appeared in productions of *One Touch of Venus, Roberta,* and *Good News* (Summer 1952); succeeded (Mar. 17, 1953) Barry Nelson as Donald Gresham in *The Moon Is Blue* (Henry Miller's Th., Mar. 8, 1951), repeating the role in the London production (Duke of York's, July 7, 1953; and played Dudley in *The Time of Your Life* (NY City Ctr., Jan. 19, 1955).

He played Kenneth in *A Memory of Two Mondays,* which was part of the double-bill *A View from the Bridge* (Coronet, Sept. 29, 1955); Steve Boyle in *The Greatest Man Alive!* (Ethel Barrymore Th., May 8, 1957); Martin Donahue in *The Egghead* (Ethel Barrymore Th., Oct. 9, 1957); and Martin McKenrick in the pre-Bway tryout of *Listen to the Mockingbird* (opened Colonial, Boston, Mass., Dec. 27, 1958; closed Shubert, Washington, D.C., Jan. 29, 1959).

He played Daniel Halibut in *Bedtime Story* and Sammy in *A Pound on Demand,* a bill of one-act plays called *Triple Play* (Palm Beach, Fla., Mar. 1959), which he repeated on Bway, as well as playing the Elevator Boy in *Portrait of a Madona,* which was added to the bill of *Triple Play* (Playhouse, Apr. 15, 1959).

He played Craig Richards in *Happy Town* (54 St. Th., Oct. 7, 1959); Junior in *Beg, Borrow or Steal* (Martin Beck Th., Feb. 10, 1960); Woody Mahoney in a revival of *Finian's Rainbow* (NY City Ctr., Apr. 27, 1960); succeeded (July 1, 1963) Barry Nelson in *Mary, Mary* (Helen Hayes Th., Mar. 8, 1961); and played King Arthur in a national tour of *Camelot* (opened Shubert, New Haven, Conn., Oct. 3, 1963).

Mr. McGuire is the author of the play *Off Centre,* first produced at the Dell Th. (Toronto, Canada, Feb. 1963); appeared in *110 in the Shade* (national tour, 1965); played Julian in *Cactus Flower* (national tour, Sept. 20, 1968–Mar. 7, 1969); Tom in *The Time of Your Life* (Vivian Beaumont Th., N.Y.C., Nov. 6, 1969); Dr. Albert Rice in *Beggar on Horseback* (Vivian Beaumont Th., May 14, 1970); appeared in *A Man's a Man* (Guthrie Th., Minneapolis, Minn., Aug. 11, 1970, and Manitoba Th. Ctr., Winnipeg, Canada, Nov. 2, 1970); played Tom in *Father's Day* (John Golden Th., N.Y.C., Mar. 16, 1971); replaced Michael Kane (June 8, 1971) as Philip Berrigan in *The Trial of the Catonsville Nine* (Lyceum, June 2, 1971); appeared in *What the Butler Saw* (Manitoba Th. Ctr., Winnipeg, Canada, Oct. 25, 1971); played Morris Townsend in *Washington Square* (Washington Th. Club, Washington, D.C., Mar. 22, 1972); appeared in a bill of four one-act plays, *Present Tense,* including *Come Next Tuesday, Twas Brillig, So Please Be Kind,* and the title play (Sheridan Sq. Playhouse, N.Y.C., July 18, 1972); directed *A Thurber Carnival* (Manitoba Th. Ctr.,

Winnipeg, Canada, Nov. 27, 1972); appeared in *Promenade All!* (Seattle, Wash., Rep. Th., Mar. 6, 1973); replaced Philip Bosco as Mitch in *Streetcar Named Desire* (St. James Th., N.Y.C., Oct. 1973); and appeared in *That Championship Season* (Seattle, Wash., Rep. Th., Nov. 14, 1973); and in *Life with Father* (Seattle, Wash., Rep. Th., Dec. 11, 1973).

Films. His film appearances include *The Phoenix City Story* (AA, 1955); *Station Six-Sahara* (AA, 1964); *The Thomas Crown Affair* (UA, 1967); *The Heart Is a Lonely Hunter* (WB-7 Arts, 1967); *Serpico* (Par., 1973); and *Werewolf in Washington* (Diplomat, 1973).

Television. Mr. McGuire has appeared on Tele-Theatre (NBC, 1950); Studio One (CBS); Armstrong Circle Th. (NBC); Kraft Th. (ABC); Philco Playhouse (NBC); US Steel Hour (CBS); Alfred Hitchcock Presents (CBS); Goodyear Playhouse (NBC); Defenders (CBS); *The Typist* (BBC-TV); *Quillow and the Giant* (BBC-TV and NBC); wrote *On Top of the World* (BBC-TV); and appeared on Directions '66 (CBS); New York Television Th. (PBS); and NET Playhouse (PBS).

Recreation. Painting (two one-man shows).

McGUIRE, DOROTHY. Actress. b. Dorothy Hackett McGuire, June 14, 1918, Omaha, Nebr., to Thomas Johnson and Isabel (Flaherty) McGuire. Father, corporation lawyer. Attended Pine Manor Jr. Coll., 1935–37. Married July 18, 1943, to John Swope; one son, one daughter. Member of SAG; AEA; AFTRA.

Theatre. Miss McGuire first appeared in *A Kiss for Cinderella* (Little Th., Omaha, Nebr., 1930); made her N.Y.C. debut as understudy to Martha Scott as Emily in *Our Town* (Henry Miller's Th., Feb. 4, 1938), whom she succeeded (Sept. 1, 1938); toured as the eldest daughter in *My Dear Children* (Mar.–Aug., 1939); played Helena in *Swingin' the Dream* (Center, N.Y.C., Nov. 29, 1939); Ada in *Kind Lady* (Playhouse, Sept. 3, 1940); was general understudy for *The Time of Your Life* (Guild, Sept. 23, 1940); played the title role in *Claudia* (Booth, Feb. 12, 1941); toured in a USO production of *Dear Ruth* (1945); appeared as the Actress in *Legend of Lovers* (Plymouth, N.Y.C., Dec. 26, 1951); toured as Alma Winemiller in *Summer and Smoke* (opened La Jolla Playhouse, Calif., July 1950); and played Elizabeth Willard in *Winesburg, Ohio* (N.Y.C., Feb. 5, 1958).

Films. Miss McGuire made her debut in the title role in *Claudia* (20th-Fox, 1943); subsequently appeared in *A Tree Grows in Brooklyn* (20th-Fox, 1945); *The Enchanted Cottage* (RKO, 1945); *The Spiral Staircase* (RKO, 1946); *Claudia and David* (20th-Fox, 1946); *'Till the End of Time* (RKO, 1946); *Gentlemen's Agreement* (20th-Fox, 1947); *Callaway Went Thataway* (MGM, 1951); *I Want You* (RKO, 1951); *Make Haste to Live* (Rep., 1954); *Three Coins in the Fountain* (20th-Fox, 1954); *Trial* (MGM, 1955); *Friendly Persuasion* (Allied, 1956); *The Remarkable Mr. Pennypacker* (20th-Fox, 1959); *Old Yeller* (Buena Vista, 1957); *This Earth Is Mine* (U, 1959); *A Summer Place* (WB, 1959); *The Swiss Family Robinson* (Buena Vista, 1960); *The Dark at the Top of the Stairs* (WB, 1960); *Summer Magic* (Buena Vista, 1962); and played Mother Mary in *The Greatest Story Ever Told* (UA, 1965); and *Flight of the Doves* (Col., 1971); and supplied the Mother's voice in *Jonathan Livingston Seagull* (Par., 1973).

Television and Radio. She played the little sister, Sue, in the serial *Big Sister* (1937); and Ophelia in *Hamlet* (1951). Her television appearances include *Dark Victory* (Robert Montgomery Presents, NBC, 1951); US Steel Hour (ABC); Lux Video Th. (NBC); Climax (CBS); *Philadelphia Story* (Best of Broadway, CBS); *She Waits* (tele-film, CBS, 1972); and *Another Part of the Forest* (Hollywood Television Th., PBS, 1972).

Awards. She received a NY Drama Critics' Circle Award (1941) for her performance in *Claudia;* was named best actress by the National Board of Review (1955) for her performance in *Friendly Persuasion;* and she received the Academy (Oscar) nomination (1948) for her performance in *Gentlemen's Agreement.*

Recreation. Writing, swimming.

McHENRY, DON. Actor. b. Donald Evan McHenry, Feb. 25, 1908, Paterson, N.J., to Donald E. and Elizabeth E. McHenry. Father, engineer. Grad. Trenton (N.J.) Central H.S., 1924; Rutgers Coll. of Pharmacy, PH.G. 1926; Carleton Coll., B.A. 1929; N.Y. Sch. of Theatre, 1931. Served US Army, Medical Corps, N. Africa, Italy, 1942–45; rank, S/Sgt. Member of AEA; AFTRA; SAG. Address: 247 W. 10th St., New York, NY 10014, tel. (212) OR 5-7356, (212) PL 3-2310.

Pre-Theatre. Pharmacist.

Theatre. Mr. McHenry made his debut as a resident actor in summer productions at the Maverick Th. (Woodstock, N.Y., 1935–37), and appeared in productions at the Tamerack Th. (Lake Pleasant, N.Y., 1938); made his N.Y.C. debut as Murray Tserk in *Don't Throw Glass Houses* (Vanderbilt, Dec. 27, 1938); appeared in summer productions at the Woodstock (N.Y.) Playhouse (1939–42, 1947); and in repertory productions at the Brattleboro Th. (Brooklyn, N.Y., Winter 1939), and the Dayton (Ohio) Museum Th. (Winter 1940).

He toured as Ashley in *White Cargo* (opened Playhouse, Wilmington, Del., Dec. 31, 1941); appeared in productions at the John Drew Th. (East Hampton, N.Y.) and the Brattleboro (Vt.) Playhouse (Summer 1946); was assistant stage manager for *Temper the Wind* (Playhouse, N.Y.C., Dec. 27, 1946) and *Portrait in Black* (Booth, May 14, 1947); played the Tutor in *Medea* (Natl., Oct. 20, 1947); NY City Ctr., May 2, 1949; US State Dept. productions, Hebbel Th., Berlin, Ger., Sept. 1951; Sarah Bernhardt Th., Paris, Fr., June 14, 1956).

He appeared in productions at the Pocono Playhouse (Mountainhome, Pa.) and the Westchester Playhouse (Mt. Kisco, N.Y., Summer 1949); played the Porter in *The Tower Beyond Tragedy* (ANTA, N.Y.C., Nov. 26, 1950); for the Broadway Chapel Players, played the Fool in *The Hour Glass,* Tobit in *Tobias and the Angel,* the Captain in *Thunder Rock,* and appeared in *In April Once* (1951–53); played Capt. Fox Reddleman in *Venus Observed* (New Century, Feb. 13, 1952) and Herbert Reedbeck in this production at the Ann Arbor (Mich.) Drama Festival (Summer 1952); Ezekiel Cheever in *The Crucible* (Martin Beck Th., N.Y.C., Jan. 22, 1953); M. Brun in *Fanny* (Majestic, Nov. 4, 1954), also touring in it (opened Shubert, Boston, Mass., Dec. 25, 1957); was standby for George Relph as Billy Rice in *The Entertainer* (Royale, N.Y.C., Feb. 12, 1958); played Mayor Slade in *Destry Rides Again* (Imperial, Apr. 23, 1959); Mr. Perpetua in *The Cantilevered Terrace* (41 St. Th., Jan. 17, 1962); the Girl's Father in *The Fantasticks* (Goodspeed Opera House, East Haddam, Conn., Summer 1963); toured as Karl Miller in *Kind Sir* (opened Mineola Playhouse, N.Y., Dec. 26, 1963; closed Playhouse-on-the-Mall, Paramus, N.J., Apr. 19, 1964); made a guest appearance as Senator Canfield in *The Child Buyer* (Professional Th. Program, Univ. of Michigan, Feb. 1964); and played Harold Haskell in a tryout of *Watch the Birdie* (opened Coconut Grove Playhouse, Miami, July 14, 1964; closed Playhouse-on-the-Mall, Paramus, N.J., Aug. 16, 1964).

He was Ulysses in *Tiger at the Gates* (Th. of the Living Arts, Philadelphia, Pa., Feb. 9, 1965); played Lord Hastings in *Richard III,* the Doctor in *The Skin of Our Teeth,* and Monsewer in *The Hostage* (Pennsylvania State Univ. Festival of Professional Th., State College, Pa., July–Sept. 1965); Mr. Lundy in *Brigadoon* (Pabst Th., Milwaukee Wis., Dec. 16, 1965–Jan. 9, 1966); toured as Mr. Brownlow in *Oliver!* (opened Mineola Playhouse, N.Y., Mar. 16, 1966; closed North Tonawanda, N.Y., Sept. 4, 1966); played the Tutor in *Medea* (Houston, Tex., Music Th., Oct. 4, 1966); Lord Burleigh in *Elizabeth the Queen* (NY City Ctr., Nov. 3, 1966); toured as the Tragic Gentlemen in *Jacobowsky and the Colonel* (opened Mineola Playhouse, N.Y., June 20, 1967; closed Playhouse-on-the-Mall, Paramus, N.J., July 30, 1967); toured as Justice Worthy in *Lock Up Your Daughers* (opened Parker Playhouse, Fort Lauderdale, Fla., Feb. 12, 1968; closed Atlanta, Ga., Mar. 17, 1968); played Old John in *A Cry of Players* (Berkshire Th. Festival, Stockbridge, Mass., Summer 1968; in repertory, Vivian Beaumont Th., N.Y.C., 1968–69 season, with Attendant of Gloucester in *King Lear);* Gentleman and Brother Superior in *Hunger and Thirst* (Berkshire Th. Festival, Summer 1969); performed *A Passage to E. M. Forster,* readings from the novelist's works (Berkshire Th. Festival, Summer 1970); toured as Polonius in Dame Judith Anderson's *Hamlet* (opened Lobero Th., Santa Barbara, Calif., Sept. 24, 1970; closed American Th., St. Louis, Mo., Mar. 27, 1971); played Lord Bishop of Durham in *Vivat! Vivat Regina!* (Broadhurst, N.Y.C., Jan. 20, 1972); and Sen. Thaddeus Jones in *A Conflict of Interest* (U.R.G.E.N.T. Th., Oct. 3, 1973).

Television. Mr. McHenry made his debut on the Milton Berle Show (NBC, 1948); and has appeared in *Skylark* (CBS, 1950); *Abe Lincoln in Illinois* (Pulitzer Prize Th., ABC, 1950); *Berkeley Square* (CBS, 1950); *Macbeth* (Showtime U.S.A., CBS, 1950); on Schlitz Playhouse (CBS, 1950); the Colgate Comedy Hour (NBC, 1950); in *Return of Edward Barnard* (Somerset Maugham Th., ABC, 1952); and on Hallmark Hall of Fame (NBC, 1954).

Also, on Robert Montgomery Presents (NBC, 1954); US Steel Hour (ABC, 1954); Studio One (CBS, 1954); Excursion (CBS, 1954); in *Medea* (Play of the Week, WNTA, 1954); *Bernadette* (Desilu Playhouse, CBS, 1960); on The Secret Storm (CBS, 1960–63); Route 66 (CBS, 1963); The Nurses (CBS, 1964); The Defenders (CBS, 1964); The Edge of Night (CBS, 1966–69); in *The Crucible* (Xerox Playhouse, CBS, 1967); on Directions (ABC, 1967–70); in *Neither Are We Enemies* (Hallmark Hall of Fame, CBS, 1970); and on The Guiding Light (CBS, 1974).

McHUGH, FRANK. Actor. b. Francis Curry McHugh, May 23, 1898, Homestead, Pa., to Edward A. and Catherine (Curry) McHugh. Father, actor; mother, actress. Attended grade schools in various towns. Married July 22, 1933, to Dorothy Margaret Spencer; two sons, one daughter. Served USO tours, ETO, 1942–45. Relatives in theatre: brother, Edw. A., Jr., stage manager; brother, Matt, actor; brother, James (dec. 1928), actor; sister, Nora (dec. 1925), actress; sister Kathrun (dec. 1954), actress. Member of AEA; SAG; AFTRA; AGVA; The Players. Address: 8 White Birch Lane, Cos Cob, CT 06807.

Theatre. Mr. McHugh made his professional debut in stock at age 11 as Bobby in *For Her Children's Sake* (Opera House, Schuylerville, N.Y., Sept., 1909); subsequently appeared in a touring production of *Human Hearts* (1909); in stock repertory at the Gotham Th. (Bklyn., N.Y., 1909); in a touring company of *Rip Van Winkle* (1910); and in stock repertory with the Harry Davis Stock Co. (Duquesne Th., Pittsburgh, 1911). He toured in vaudeville (1911), and with the Virginia Duncan Stock Co. (1912); played with the Ralph W. Chambers (stock) Co. (Grand Opera House, Uniontown, Pa., 1911), and with the Virginia Duncan Stock Co. (Clarksburg, W.Va., 1913).

Mr. McHugh toured with Pollack's Juvenile Minstrels (1913); appeared in stock with the Marguerite Bryant Players (Orpheum, McKeesport, Pa., 1914); the Baker-Hill Stock Co. (Olympia Park, Versailles, Pa., 1914); the Altmeyer Stock Co. (Altmeyer Th., McKeesport, Pa., 1914); and the Frank Baker Stock Co. (Keagy Th., Greensburg, Pa., 1914).

He was actor and stage manager for the Marguerite Bryant Plays (Orpheum, McKeesport, Pa.; Duquesne, Pittsburgh, Pa.; Grand, Homestead, Pa.; Empire, East Liberty, Pittsburgh, Pa., 1915; and Orpheum, McKeesport, Pa., 1916); actor and stage manager with the Empire Stock Co. (Empire, East Liberty, Pittsburgh, Pa., 1916); appeared with the Academy Players (Academy of Music, Newport News, Va., 1916), and the Sherman Kelly Stock Co. on a Midwest tour (1916–17); toured in *The Marriage Question* (1918); *Unmarried Mother* (1918); *When Dreams Come True* (1918); appeared in vaudeville in a playlet, *Sweeties* (Orpheum Circuit, 1919);

appeared with the Shubert Theatre Stock Co. (Milwaukee, Wis., 1920); in vaudeville in the playlet, *The Man Hunt*(1920); and in productions of the Poli Stock Co. (Lyric, Bridgeport, Conn., 1921; Poli Th., Waterbury, Conn. 1922).

In 1923 Mr. McHugh appeared with the Carroll Stock Co. (Opera House, St. John, N.B., Can.); the Poli Players (Palace, Hartford, Conn.); the Century Players (Broad St. Th., Newark, N.J.); and the Princess Players (Princess Th., Des Moines, Iowa). In 1924, he appeared with the Poli Players (Palace, Hartford, Conn.), the Jefferson Th. Players (Birmingham, Ala.), toured in a musical, *Princess April;* and appeared with the Blaney Players (Yorkville Th., N.Y.C.).

Mr. McHugh understudied Ernest Truex as Johnnie Quinan in *The Fall Guy* (Eltinge Th., N.Y.C., Mar. 10, 1925), then succeeded (July 1925) Ralph Sipperly in the role of Dan Walsh; was understudy to James Gleason and Robert Armstrong as Hap and Chick, respectively, in *Is Zat So?* (Apollo, London, Feb. 1, 1926); and played Dan Walsh in *The Fall Guy* (Apollo, Sept. 20, 1926).

He played Scraggs in *Fog*(National, N.Y.C., Feb. 7, 1927); Curly Neff in *Tenth Avenue* (Eltinge, Aug. 15, 1927); Jimmy Dunn in *Excess Baggage* (Ritz, Dec. 26, 1927); appeared in the pre-Bway tryout of *Puffy*(1928); played Jimmy Dunn in a touring company of *Excess Baggage*(1928); Sgt. "Chink" Burt in *Conflict*(Fulton, N.Y.C., Mar. 6, 1929); appeared in *Show Girl* (Ziegfeld, July 2, 1929); and appeared in numerous stock productions, including *Ah, Wilderness!, Charley's Aunt, Harvey, Mister Roberts* and *Finian's Rainbow* (Summers 1929–52); and in USO tours (Europe, 1942–45).

Mr McHugh toured colleges in *The Best of Steinbeck* (1956); played in a stock production of *The Beast in Me*(Nash's Barn, Westport, Conn., Summer 1962); succeeded (Oct. 21, 1963); David Burns as Senex in *A Funny Thing Happened on the Way to the Forum* (Alvin, May 8, 1962); and played Finian McLonergan in a revival of *Finian's Rainbow* (NY City Ctr., Apr. 5, 1967).

Films. Mr. McHugh's film appearances include *M'lle Modiste* (1st Natl., 1926); a short, *If Men Played Cards as Women Do* (1928); *Top Speed* (1st Natl., 1930); *Toast of the Legion* (1930); *Flight Command*(1930); *Widow from Chicago*(1st Natl., 1930); *The Dawn Patrol*(1st Natl., 1930); *College Lovers*(1st Natl., 1930); *Little Caesar* (1st Natl., 1930); *Millie* (RKO, 1931); *Front Page*(UA, 1931); *Traveling Husbands*(RKO, 1931); *Corsair*(UA, 1931); *Men of the Sky*(1st Natl., 1931); *Going Wild*(WB, 1931); *Bright Lights*(1st Natl., 1931); *Bad Company*(Pathé, 1931); *Fires of Youth*(WB, 1931); *Up for Murder*(U, 1931); *Kiss Me Again* (1st Natl., 1931); *The Strange Love of Molly Louvain* (1st Natl., 1932); *Union Depot* (WB, 1932); *High Pressure* (WB, 1932); *The Crowd Roars* (WB, 1932); *Dark Horse* (1st Natl., 1932); *Life Begins*(1st Natl., 1932); *One Way Passage*(WB, 1932); *Blessed Event* (WB, 1932); *Wax Museum* (WB, 1933); *Grand Slam* (WB, 1933); *Parachute Jumper* (WB, 1933); *Elmer the Great*(1st Natl., 1933); *Lilly Turner* (1st Natl., 1933); *Footlight Parade* (WB, 1933); *Havana Widows*(1st Natl., 1933); *Convention City* (1st Natl., 1933); *Not Tonight, Josephine* (WB, 1933); *Son of a Sailor*(1st Natl., 1933); *House on 56th Street*(WB, 1933); *Private Jones*(U, 1933); *The Telegraph Trail* (WB, 1933); *Professional Sweetheart* (RKO, 1933); *The Mad Game* (20th-Fox, 1933); *Forty-second Street* (WB, 1933); *Tomorrow at Seven* (RKO, 1933); *Hold Me Tight* (20th-Fox, 1933); *Ex-Lady*(WB, 1933); *Grand Slam*(WB, 1933); *Let's Be Ritzy* (U, 1934); *Fashions of 1934* (1st Natl., 1934); *Heat Lightning*(WB, 1934); and *Smarty*(WB, 1934).

Also, *Merry Wives of Reno*(WB, 1934); *Return of the Terror* (1st Natl., 1934); *Here Comes the Navy* (WB, 1934); *Six Day Bike Rider* (1st Natl., 1934); *Happiness Ahead* (1st Natl., 1934); *Maybe It's Love* (1st Natl., 1935); *Devil Dogs of the Air*(WB, 1935); *A Midsummer Night's Dream*(WB, 1935); *Page Miss Glory*(WB, 1935); *The Irish in Us*(WB, 1935); *Stars Over Broadway*(WB, 1935); *Gold Diggers of 1935*(1st Natl., 1935); *Freshman Love* (WB, 1936); *Snowed Under*(1st Natl., 1936); *Bullets or Ballots*(1st Natl., 1936); *Stage Struck* (1st Natl., 1936); *Three Men on a Horse*(1st Natl., 1936); *Moonlight Murder*(MGM, 1936); *Marry the Girl* (WB, 1937); *Mr. Dodd Takes the Air*(WB, 1937); *Submarine D-1*(WB, 1937); *Ever Since Eve* (WB, 1937); *He Couldn't Say No* (WB, 1938); *Swing Your Lady* (WB, 1938); *Little Miss Thoroughbred* (WB, 1938); *Boy Meets Girl* (WB, 1938); *Valley of the Giants*(WB, 1938); *Four Daughters* (WB, 1938); *Wings of the Navy* (WB, 1939); *Dodge City*(WB, 1939); *Daughters Courageous*(WB, 1939); *Dust Be My Destiny*(WB, 1939); *The Roaring Twenties* (WB, 1939); *On Your Toes* (WB, 1939); *Four Wives*(WB, 1939); *Indianapolis Speedway*(WB, 1939); and *The Fighting Sixty-Ninth* (WB, 1940). Also, *Till We Meet Again* (WB, 1940); *Virginia City* (WB, 1940); *Love Me Again* (MGM, 1940); *City for Conquest* (WB, 1940); *Saturday's Children* (WB, 1940); *I Love You Again* (MGM, 1940); *Back Street* (U, 1941); *Four Mothers* (WB, 1941); *Manpower* (WB, 1941); *Her Cardboard Lover*(MGM, 1942); *All Through the Night*(WB, 1942); *Going My Way*(Par., 1944); *Marine Raiders* (RKO, 1944); *Bowery to Broadway*(U, 1944); *A Medal for Benny*(Par., 1945); *State Fair* (20th-Fox, 1945); *Third Avenue* (Par., 1945); *The Hoodlum Saint*(MGM, 1946); *Deadline for Murder* (20th-Fox, 1946); *Little Miss Big* (U, 1946); *The Runaround* (U, 1946); *Easy Come, Easy Go*(Par., 1947); *Carnegie Hall*(UA, 1947); *The Velvet Touch*(RKO, 1948); *Bitter Victory*(Wallis, 1948); *Mighty Joe Young* (RKO, 1949); *Miss Grant Takes Richmond* (Col., 1949); *Crackdown* (RKO, 1950); *The Tougher They Come* (Col., 1950); *Paid in Full* (Par., 1950); *The Pace That Thrills*(RKO, 1952); *My Son John* (Par., 1952); *A Lion Is in the Streets* (WB, 1953); *It Happens Every Thursday*(U, 1953); *There's No Business Like Show Business* (20th-Fox, 1954); *The Last Hurrah* (Col., 1958); *Say One for Me* (20th-Fox, 1959); *Career*(Par., 1959); *A Tiger Walks* (Buena Vista, 1964); and *Easy Come, Easy Go* (Par., 1967).

Television and Radio. On radio, Mr. McHugh performed in Finnegan (CBS, 1946–47), and Mr. Jolly's Home for Pets (1955).

On television, he has appeared in *The Orchard* (Dumont, 1954); *Center Stage* and *Heart of a Clown* (ABC, 1954); on Studio One (CBS, 1954); Elgin Th. (ABC, 1954); Justice (NBC, 1955); in *House of Hatred* (NBC, 1955); on Armstrong Circle Th. (NBC, 1955); Studio One (CBS, 1955, 1956, 1958); Alcoa Hour (NBC, 1956); Lamp Unto My Feet (CBS, 1956); US Steel Hour (CBS, 1957; 1959); Matinee Th. (NBC, 1957); Playhouse 90 (CBS, Apr. 18, 1957); Kraft Th. (NBC, 1957; 1958); and Ellery Queen (NBC, 1958).

He has also appeared on the Red Skelton Show (CBS, 1959); Buick Electra Playhouse (CBS, 1959); the Arthur Murray Show (NBC, 1960); in *Heaven Can Wait* (Dupont Show of the Month, CBS, 1960); on The Outlaws (NBC, 1961); Wagon Train (NBC, 1961); Theatre '62 (NBC, 1961); Route 66 (CBS, 1962); Dupont Show of the Week (NBC, 1962); Going My Way (ABC, 1962); The Nurses (CBS, 1962); Look Up And Live (CBS, 1963); played Willie on The Bing Crosby Show series (ABC, 1964–65); appeared on the Hollywood Palace show (ABC, 1964, 1965); F Troop (ABC, 1966); and others.

McILRATH, PATRICIA. Educator, director. b. Patricia Anne McIlrath, Jan. 25, 1917, Kansas City, Mo. to George David and Ethel (Howard) McIlrath. Father, lawyer. Grad. Pasco H.S., Kansas City, 1933; Grinnell Coll., B.A. 1937; Northwestern Univ., M.A. 1946; Stanford Univ.; Ph.D. 1951. Member of ATA (former mbr., adv. bd., CTC); SAA (mbr. of legislative assembly); Speech Assn. of Mo. (pres., 1958–59); ANTA; Mo. State Council on the Arts (adv. comm., 1964–74); Phi Kappa Phi; Chi Omega; Zeta Phi Eta; National Collegiate Players. Address: (home) 1300 E. 72nd St., Kansas City, MO 64108, tel. (816) JA 3-0875; (bus.) The University Playhouse, Univ. of Missouri, Kansas City, MO 64108, tel. (816) DE 3-7400.

Miss McIlrath is professor of theatre and director of the Univ. (of Missouri) Playhouse where she has directed both student and professional productions (1954–to date). In 1964, she founded a professional company, the Missouri Repertory Theatre, and, in 1968, added its touring wing, Missouri Vanguard Theatre.

She taught at the Univ. of Illinois (1946–54); and directed Sophocles' *Electra*(Rita Allen Th., N.Y.C., Feb. 13, 1959).

Other Activities. Miss McIlrath has been associate editor (theatre) for the *Quarterly Journal of Speech* (1963–1965).

Awards. She received the Award of Excellence from the American Theatre Assn. and American Air Lines in the 1972 regional American College Theatre Festival, and the Matrix award from Theta Sigma Phi, a professional sorority for women in communication.

Recreation. Theatre, traveling abroad, writing.

McKAY, SCOTT. Actor. b. Carl Chester Gose, May 28, 1915, Pleasantville, Iowa, to Chester Loring and Edith Edna (Shawver) Gose. Father, banker; mother, pianist. Grad. North Denver (Colo.) H.S., 1933; Univ. of Colorado, 1937. Married 1942 to Margaret Spickers, writer (marr. dis. 1953), two sons; married 1953 to Joan Morgan, actress (dec. 1963). Member of AEA (on council, 1950–55); AFTRA; SAG; Alpha Tau Omega.

Theatre. Mr. McKay made his professional debut in Federal Th. (WPA) Project productions of *Arms and the Man, See Naples and Die, Farmer Takes a Wife,* and *Fly Away Home*(Boston, Mass., 1937–38).

He appeared as a walk-on in *Good Hunting* (Hudson Th., N.Y.C., Nov. 11, 1938); *The American Way* (Center, Jan. 21, 1939); in stock, appeared in *The Three Sisters, Arms and the Man, Grass Is Always Greener,* and *Art and Mrs. Bottle* (Surrey, Me., Summer 1939); billed as Carl Gose, played Fedotik in *The Three Sisters* (Longacre, Oct. 13, 1939); toured as Sandy in *The Man Who Came to Dinner* (1940–41); and appeared in stock productions (Glen Rock, N.J., Summer 1941).

He played the Sophomore in *The Night Before Christmas* (Morosco, N.Y.C., Apr. 10, 1941); Hans in *Letters to Lucerne* (Cort, Dec. 23, 1941); Lt. Prackle in *The Moon Is Down* (Martin Beck Th., Apr. 7, 1942); Neil West in *Eve of St. Mark* (Cort, Oct. 7, 1942); Larry in *Dark Eyes* (Belasco, Jan. 14, 1943); and Lt. Don Mallory in *Pillar to Post* (Playhouse, Dec. 10, 1943).

Billed as Scott McKay, he played Eric in *Swan Song* (Booth, May 15, 1946); Oscar Hubbard in *Another Part of the Forest* (Fulton, Nov. 20, 1946); took over the role of Paul Verral in *Born Yesterday* (Lyceum, Feb. 4, 1946); played Leo Mack in *The Live Wire* (Playhouse, Aug. 17, 1950), also touring in it; Nicky Holroyd in *Bell, Book and Candle* (Ethel Barrymore Th., Nov. 14, 1950); George Flack in *Letter from Paris* (Aldwych, London, England, Oct. 10, 1952); and toured in *Josephine* (1953).

He played David in *Sabrina Fair* (National, N.Y.C., Nov. 11, 1953); succeeded (1954) John Forsythe as Capt. Fisby in *The Teahouse of the August Moon* (Martin Beck Th., Oct. 15, 1953); also touring in it (opened Hartman, Columbus, Ohio, Dec. 16, 1954); played Jeff Douglas in *Brigadoon* (NY City Ctr., Mar. 27, 1957); Voles in *Nature's Way* (Coronet, Oct. 16, 1957); played Mervyn in the pre-Bway tryout of *Odd Man In* (opened Playhouse, Wilmington, Del., Oct. 1, 1959; closed Memorial Aud., Burlington, Iowa, Mar. 5, 1960); succeeded (1962) Tom Poston as Bob McKellaway in *Mary, Mary* (Helen Hayes Th., N.Y.C., Mar. 8, 1961); played Ashley Robbins in *Once for the Asking* (Booth, Nov. 20, 1963), appeared in *Luv* (tour, 1966); replaced (Dec. 19, 1967) E. G. Marshall as Oscar Hubbard in *The Little Foxes* (Vivian Beaumont Th., N.Y.C., Oct. 26, 1967; and on tour); played Billy Boylan in *Forty Carats* (national tour, 1969–70); and Teddy in *A Breeze from the Gulf* (Eastside Playhouse, N.Y.C., Oct. 15, 1973).

Films. Mr. McKay has appeared in *30 Seconds Over Tokyo*(MGM, 1944); *Guest in the House*(UA, 1944);

Kiss and Tell (Col., 1945); and *Duel in the Sun* (SRO, 1946).

Recreation. Writing.

McKAYLE, DONALD. Choreographer, director, dancer, dance teacher. b. Donald Cohen McKayle, July 6, 1930, New York City, to Philip Augustus and Eva Wilhemina (Cohen) McKayle. Father, aviation mechanic. Grad. DeWitt Clinton H.S., N.Y., 1947; attended City Coll. of New York, 1947–49. Studied at the New Dance Group Studio, N.Y.C., 1947; Martha Graham Sch. of Contemporary Dance, N.Y.C., 1948; classical techniques with Nanette Charisse, N.Y.C., 1950; with Karel Shook, N.Y.C., 1955; ethnic forms with Pearl Primus, N.Y.C., 1947. Married Jan. 10, 1954, to Esta Beck, dancer (marr. dis.); two daughters; May 9, 1965, to Lea Vivante, flamenco dancer; one son. Member of AEA; AGMA; AFTRA; AGVA; SSD&C; Assn. of Amer. Dance Companies; Black Acad. of Arts and Letters (fellow). Address: (home) 3839 Davana Rd., Sherman Oaks, CA 91423; (bus.) William Morris Agency, 1350 Ave. of the Americas, New York, NY 10019, tel. (212) 586-5100; 151 El Camino, Beverly Hills, CA 90212, tel. (213) 274-7451.

Theatre. Mr. McKayle first performed as a dancer with the *New Dance Group Festival* (Mansfield, N.Y.C., Spring, 1948); subsequently was a dance soloist at the American Dance Festival (Palmer Aud., New London, Conn., 1948); with the Dudley-Maslow-Bales Dance Co. (1948–51); and was guest artist with the Jean Erdman Dance Co. (1948–53). In 1951, he founded the Donald McKayle Dance Co., directing its activities until 1970.

He danced in *Just a Little Simple,* for which he was also choreographer (Club Baron Th., N.Y.C., Fall 1950); danced with the N.Y.C. Dance Theatre (NY City Ctr., 1950); and in the revue *Bless You All* (Mark Hellinger Th., Dec. 14, 1950).

He choreographed *Games* (Hunter College Playhouse, May 25, 1951); *Her Name Was Harriet* (Hunter College Playhouse, Jan. 20, 1952); and *Saturday's Child* (Stage for Dancers, Brooklyn High School of Homemaking, Feb. 20, 1952); performed as a solo dancer in the opera, *The Dybbuk* (NY City Ctr., Spring 1952); was a guest artist with the Merce Cunningham Dance Co. (1952); danced at the B. de Rothschild Dance Festival (ANTA, Spring 1953); choreographed *Nocturne* (Jacob's Pillow Dance, Mass., Summer 1953), later performed in N.Y.C. with *Prelude to Action* and *The Street* (Brooklyn Acad. of Music, Feb. 17, 1954); danced in the full repertoire of the N.Y.C. Opera Co. (NY City Ctr., Spring 1954), and toured with the company (Spring 1954).

He was a soloist with the Anna Sokolow Dance Th. (1954–55); danced in *House of Flowers* (Alvin, Dec. 30, 1954); toured the Orient as a soloist with the Martha Graham Dance Co., under the auspices of the Intl. Exchange Program (Sankel Th., Tokyo, Japan, Nov. 1955–Mar. 1956); presented a revised version of *Her Name Was Harriet* (Hunter College Playhouse, N.Y.C., Nov. 24, 1956); was choreographer for *1-2-3 Follow Me* (The Merry-Go-Rounders, N.Y.C. 1957); *Out of the Chrysalis* (Juilliard Dance Th., N.Y.C., 1957); and danced in *Show Boat* (Marine Th., Jones Beach, L.I., N.Y., Summers 1957–58).

He was dance captain for *West Side Story* (Winter Garden, N.Y.C., Sept. 16, 1957); appeared as the Captain and was assistant choreographer for *Copper and Brass* (Martin Beck Th., Oct. 17, 1957); choreographed *Out of the Chrysalis* (Juilliard Dance Th. Group, Juilliard Concert Hall, Apr. 11, 1958); served as stage director for the national tour of *An Evening with Belafonte* (Pittsburgh, Pa., June 1958); associate choreographer for *Redhead* (46 St. Th., N.Y.C., Feb. 5, 1959); choreographed *Rainbow Round My Shoulder* (Kaufmann Auditorium, YM-YWHA, May 10, 1959); and was choreographer for *Semele* (Empire State Music Festival, Ellenville, N.Y., Summer 1959).

At the Festival of the Two Worlds (Spoleto, Italy, June–July 1960), Mr. McKayle directed *Album Leaves* and was choreographer for *New American Ballets,* including *Legendary Landscape;* was director and choreographer for the European tour of *Free and Easy* (1960); was choreographer, with Walter Nicks, for *Kicks and Co.* (McCormick Th., Chicago, Ill., 1961); danced in the Metropolitan Boston (Mass.) Fine Arts Festival (1961); was choreographer for the NY Shakespeare Festival's *The Tempest* (Delacorte Th., July 16, 1962); choreographed *District—Storyville* (Kaufmann Auditorium, Apr. 22, 1962); presented the US premiere of *Legendary Landscape* (Hunter College Playhouse, Nov. 10, 1962); was choreographer for the NY Shakespeare Festival's *Antony and Cleopatra* (Delacorte Th., June 13, 1963) and *As You Like It* (Delacorte Th., July 11, 1963); and choreographed *Blood of the Lamb* (July 27, 1963) and *Arena* (Aug. 3, 1963), both at Connecticut College, New London, Conn.

He was choreographer and danced in *August Fanfare* (Philharmonic Hall, Lincoln Ctr. for the Performing Arts, 1963); at the Rebecca Harkness Dance Festival (Delacorte Th., 1963); and at the Jacob's Pillow Dance Festival (Shawn Th., Lee, Mass., 1963); directed *Trumpets of the Lord* (Astor Place Playhouse, N.Y.C., Dec. 21, 1963); choreographed *Reflections in the Park* (Hunter College Assembly Hall, Mar. 6, 1964); at the invitation of the Batsheva Foundation choreographed *Daughters of the Garden* for the Batsheva Dance Co. (Israel, May 1964); was choreographer for *Golden Boy* (Majestic, N.Y.C., Sept. 25, 1964); and choreographed for American Dance Th. *Workout* (NY State Th., Nov. 18, 1964). He staged the US premiere of *Daughters of Eden* (new title of *Daughters of the Garden*) for his own company (Walt Whitman Auditorium, Brooklyn College, N.Y.C., Apr. 3, 1965); was choreographer for *A Time for Singing* (Broadway Th., May 21, 1966); and choreographed and directed *Black New World,* a production combining new material with the earlier *Rainbow Round My Shoulder, District —Storyville,* and *They Called Her Moses,* fomerly known as *Her Name Was Harriet* (Kaufmann Auditorium, YM-YWHA, N.Y.C., Feb. 8, 1967), which commenced a European tour at Wiesbaden, Germany, and visited the Holland, Edinburgh (Scotland), Zurich (Switzerland) June, Nervi (Italy), and Hamburg (Germany) festivals, and the Strand Th., London. He was choreographer for *The Four Musketeers* (Drury Lane, London, 1967); choreographed *Incantation* and *Wilderness* (both Brooklyn Acad. of Music, N.Y.C., Jan. 20, 1968); was choreographer for *I'm Solomon* (Mark Hellinger Th., N.Y.C., Apr. 23, 1968); staged *Nocturne* for Repertory Dance Th. (Salt Lake City, Utah, 1968); choreographed *Burst of Fists* (NY City Ctr., May 22, 1969); and in 1970 went to Los Angeles, Calif., where he was a co-founder of the Inner City Repertory Dance Co.

He staged *Games* for the Gloria Newman Dance Co. (Los Angeles, 1971) and *Rainbow Round My Shoulder* for the Alvin Ailey City Center Dance Th. (N.Y.C., 1972). Inner City Repertory Dance Co. made its N.Y.C. debut at the City Center American Dance Marathon (ANTA Th.) in 1972 and presented premieres of four new works by Mr. McKayle: *Sojourn* (Oct. 16), *Migrations* (Oct. 18), *Barrio* (Oct. 19), and *Songs of the Disinherited* (Oct. 19). Mr. McKayle was choreographer for *Mass* (Mark Taper Forum, Los Angeles, Jan. 4, 1973); staged *Daughters of Eden* for the Dance Theatre of Seattle, Wash. (1973); and was choreographer and director of *Raisin* (world premiere, Arena Stage, Washington, D.C., May 23, 1973; 46 St. Th., N.Y.C., Nov. 11, 1973).

Films. Mr. McKayle danced in *Edge of the City* (MGM, 1957); *Jazz on a Summer's Day* (1959); and in *On the Sound* (1960). He did choreography for *The Great White Hope* (20th-Fox, 1969); *Bedknobs and Broomsticks* (Disney Prod., 1970); and *Charlie and the Angel* (Disney Prod., 1972).

Television. He made his debut as a dance soloist on the Fred Waring Show (CBS, 1951, 1952); subsequently appeared as a dancer, singer, and choreographer in *Games* (Folio, CBC, Canada, 1957); choreographed and danced in *Rainbow Round My Shoulder* (Camera 3, CBS, 1959); *They Called Her Moses* (Camera 3, CBS, 1960); choreographer for *District—Storyville* (Quest, CBC, Can., 1962); choreographed and danced in *The Ghost of Mr. Kicks* (Repertory Workshop, CBS, 1963); choreographer for *Baseball Ballet* (Exploring, NBC, 1963); and choreographed and danced in *Amahl and the Night Visitors* (NBC Opera, 1963); choreographed *Fanfare* (CBS, 1965); *Jazz-Dance U.S.A.* (PBS, 1965); *The Strolling Twenties* (CBS, 1965); *Ten Blocks of the Camino Real* (PBS, 1966); and did choreography for segments of the Ed Sullivan Show (CBS, 1966, 1967). He also did choreography for *Black New World* (Sunday Showcase, WNDT, 1967); *The Bill Cosby Special* (NBC, 1967); *Soul* (NBC, 1968); *TCB* (NBC, 1968); *The Second Bill Cosby Special* (NBC, 1968); and *Sounds of Summer* (PBS, Aug. 10, 1969).

Mr. McKayle also choreographed and performed on a segment of Hollywood Palace (ABC, 1969); did choreography for the Leslie Uggams Show (CBS, 1969); *Dick Van Dyke and the Other Woman* (Dick Van Dyke Show, CBS, 1969); *And Beautiful* (Metro Media, 1969); the 43rd annual Oscar awards show (NBC, 1970); *Yesterday, Today and Tomorrow* (CBS, 1970); *The Super Comedy Bowl* (CBS, 1971); and *A Funny Thing Happened on the Way to a Special* (ABC, 1972). He did choreography for the annual Grammy awards ceremonies (ABC, 1973); The New Bill Cosby Show (CBS, 1972–73); staged *Angelitos Negros* for Black Omnibus (Metro Media, 1973); did choreography for *Free To Be You and Me* (ABC, 1974); and was director of Good Times (CBS, 1974).

Night Clubs. He was staging director for Rita Moreno's act at the El Rancho Vegas, (Las Vegas, Nev., 1957); Helen Gallagher's act at the Persian Room (Hotel Plaza, N.Y.C., 1958); and for the Belafonte Folk Choir at the Village Gate (N.Y.C., 1960).

Other Activities. Mr. McKayle is on the board of directors, National Center for Afro-American Artists, Roxbury, Mass., and New Dance Group, N.Y.C. He was a member of the board of directors of the Clark Ctr. for Performing Arts—YM-YWCA, N.Y.C.; the Modern Dance Foundation, Hackensack, N.J.; and the Dance Circle, Boston, Mass. He became a faculty member at the California Institute of the Arts, Valencia, Calif., in 1970, and he was formerly on the faculty of Bennington (Vt.) Coll. (1961–63); Bard Coll., Annandale-on-Hudson, N.Y. (1962–63); Sarah Lawrence Coll., Bronxville, N.Y. (1963, 1964); the Martha Graham School of Contemporary Dance, N.Y.C.; the new Dance Group Studio, Inc., N.Y.C.; American Dance Festival, Connecticut Coll., New London, Conn.; the Univ. of Oregon, Eugene, Ore.; Rubin Acad. of Music, Jerusalem, Israel (1970); Internationale Sommerakademie des Tanzes, Cologne, Germany (1970, 1971); Inner City Cultural Institute, Los Angeles, Calif. (1970–74); and Univ. of Washington, Seattle (1973).

In addition to his teaching activities, Mr. McKayle served in 1965 at the invitation of the government of Tunisia as an ex-officio advisor in the nation's cultural program. He also designs and executes fashions and costumes.

Published Works. Mr. McKayle wrote articles for *Modern Dance—Seven Points of View,* edited and compiled by Selma Jeanne Cohen (1965), and *The Dance Has Many Faces,* edited and compiled by Walter Sorrel (1966).

Discography. He was co-author, singer, and narrator for *Come and See the Peppermint Tree* (Washington, D.C., 1959); and sang in *Sometime, Anytime* (Washington, D.C., 1960).

Awards. Mr. McKayle received a scholarship to study dance at the New Dance Group Studio (1947); the Martha Graham Sch. of Contemporary Dance (1948); and was awarded the 12th Annual Capezio Dance Award (1963); the 4th Anniversary Award of the Waltann School of Creative Arts; he was nominated for Antoinette Perry (Tony) awards for his choreography for *Golden Boy* (1964) and for direction and choreography for *Raisin* (1974), which received a Tony as best musical of 1974. *Free To Be You and Me,* for which he did the choreography in 1974, received a NATAS (Emmy) Award as best children's special.

Recreation. Tropical fish, gourmet cooking.

MCKENNA, DAVID. Director, actor, public relations, stage manager. b. Nov. 5, 1949, Jersey City, N.J., to Joseph P. and Elizabeth (Nash) McKenna. Father, sales representative. Attended Bergen Catholic H.S.; studied at the Univ. of Texas with B. Iden Payne, Francis Hodge, and Webster Smalley, B.A. 1971; and at the Pacific Conservatory of Performing Arts with Alvina Krause and Gorden Peacock. Address: 616 Edel Ave., Maywood, NJ 07607, tel. (201) 843-5685.

Theatre. Mr. McKenna debuted as Wally in *The Impossible Years* with Don Porter (Playhouse-on-the-Mall, Paramus, N.J., July 1966) and served his apprenticeship from June 1966–May 1968 as actor, sound technician, assistant stage manager, and house manager at the same playhouse.

In Dec. 1970, he directed *Indian Wants the Bronx* (Student Rep. Co., Austin, Tex.); and the following year appeared as Jason in *Medea* (Zachary Scott Th., Austin, Tex., Feb. 1971); as McArdle in *Child's Play* (Trinity Sq. Rep. Co., Providence, R.I., Sept. 1971); directed *J. B.* (Cumberland Players, Austin, Tex., Apr. 1971); appeared as Dad and Bellboy in *Oh, Dad, Poor Dad...*; and served as assistant director for *Birthday Party*, assistant stage manager for *Mrs. Warren's Profession* (Loeb Drama Ctr., Harvard Univ., New Haven, Conn., July–Aug. 1971); and appeared in several roles in *Troilus and Cressida* (Trinity Sq. Rep. Co., Providence R.I., Nov. 1971). Later, he appeared as the Young Man in *Colette* and as Starbuck in *The Rainmaker* (Th. Three, Dallas, Tex., 1972). For the First Repertory Co. of San Antonio (Tex.) he appeared as Claudius in *Hamlet* (Sept. 1972), J. Carlyle Benson in *Boy Meets Girl* (Oct. 1972), John Cotton in *The Troublemaker* (premiere, Dec. 1973), the Chief of Police in *The Balcony* (Jan. 1973), and the Merchant in *Canterbury Tales* (Feb. 1973). For the same company he directed *Aesop's Fables* (tour, Nov. 1972) and *Desire Under the Elms* (Apr. 1973). Mr. McKenna also served as press agent for the company from July 1972–Apr. 1973 and again from Jan.–Mar. 1974.

He appeared as Master Page in *The Merry Wives of Windsor*, Lane in *The Importance of Being Earnest*, the Shriner in *Light Up the Sky* (Brown Brick Rep. Co., Rockford Coll., Ill., Summer 1973); directed *Dial "M" for Murder* and *Hogan's Goat* (First Rep. Co. of San Antonio (Tex.), Feb. and May 1974); and *Play It Again, Sam* (Plaza Dinner Th., San Antonio, Tex., Apr. 1974).

Published Works. Mr. McKenna was the film and theatre critic for the San Antonio *Gazette*.

Awards. Mr. McKenna graduated cum laude, B.A., Univ. of Texas, 1971.

Recreation. Reading, films, long-distance driving and running.

McKENNA, SIOBHAN. Actress. b. Siobhan Giollamhuire Nic Cionnaith, Belfast, Ireland, May 24, 1922, to Owen and Margaret (O'Reilly) McKenna. Father, professor of mathematical physics; mother, designer and buyer of millinery. Grad. Dominican Convent, Belfast, 1927; Dominican Convent, Galway, 1936; St. Louis Convent, Monaghan, 1939; National Univ., Galway, B.A. (scholarship, first honors) 1942; attended National Univ., Dublin, 1942–43. Married July 7, 1946, to Denis O'Dea, actor, one son. Member of Irish, British and U.S. AEA; AFTRA. Address: 23 Highfield Rd., Rathgar, Dublin, Ireland, 976837.

Theatre. Miss McKenna first appeared on stage as Charity in a school religious play (1930); from 1940–42, appeared with the Gaelic Repertory Theatre (An Taibhdhearc Th., Galway) in Gaelic-language productions, playing the title role in *Mary-Rose* (1940); Bessie Burgess in *The Plough and the Stars* (1940); Mrs. Grigson in *Shadow of a Gunman* (1940); the Wife in *Tons of Money* (1941); Miriamne in *Winterset* (1941); and Lady Macbeth in *Macbeth* (1941); and appearing in *The White Scourge* (1942); and as Bella in *Gaslight* (1942). She joined the Abbey Players (Abbey, Dublin) where she played Nicole in *Le Bourgeois Gentilhomme*; and appeared in *The End House*, *The Railway House*, *Marks and Mabel*, *The Countess Cathleen*, *The Far-off Hills*, and *Thy Dear Father* (1943–46).

Miss McKenna made her London debut as Nora Fintry in *The White Steed* (Embassy, Mar. 3, 1947); subsequently appeared as Helen Pettigrew in *Berkeley Square* ("Q" 1949); and Maura Joyce in *Fading Mansion* (Duchess, Aug. 31, 1949); played the title role in a Gaelic-language production of *Saint Joan* in Galway (An Taibhdhearc) and in Dublin (Gaiety); appeared as Regina in a London production of *Ghosts* (Embassy, June 12, 1951); at the Edinburgh (Scot.) Festival played Pegeen Mike in *The Playboy of the Western World* and appeared in *The White-Headed Boy*.

She played the title role of *Heloise* (Duke of York's Th., London, Nov. 14, 1951); Virgilia in *Coriolanus*, Celia in *As You Like It*, Lady MacDuff in *Macbeth*, and Virginia in *Volpone* at Stratford-upon-Avon (Royal Shakespeare Th., 1952); Avril in *Purple Dust* (Royal Glasgow, Scot., Apr. 1953); then later that year appeared at Dublin's Gaiety Th. as Beauty in *The Love of Four Colonels* and in the title role of *Anna Christie*; in 1954 she played *Saint Joan* (Gate, Dublin) and appeared at the Gaiety as Luka in *Arms and the Man* and Pegeen Mike in *The Playboy of the Western World*; then repeated the title role in *Saint Joan* (Arts, London, Sept. 20, 1954).

She made her American debut as Miss Madrigal in *The Chalk Garden* (Ethel Barrymore Th., N.Y.C., Oct. 26, 1955); appeared in the title role of *Saint Joan* (Sanders, Cambridge, Mass., Aug. 1956; Phoenix, N.Y.C., Sept. 11, 1956); as Viola in the Stratford (Ont.) Shakespeare Festival's production of *Twelfth Night* (June, 1957); played Margaret Hyland in *The Rope Dancers* (Cort, N.Y.C., Nov. 20, 1957); the title role in *Hamlet* (Th. de Lys. Jan. 28, 1959); repeated the role of Viola in *Twelfth Night* and played Lady Macbeth at the Cambridge (Mass.) Drama Festival (July, 1959) and appeared as Isobel in the pre-Bway tryout of *Motel* (opened Wilbur, Boston, Jan. 6, 1960; closed there Jan. 16, 1960); played Pegeen Mike in *The Playboy of the Western World* (Dublin Th. Festival, Sept. 1960; Piccadilly, London, Oct. 12, 1960); Anna in a London production of *To Play with a Tiger* (Comedy, 1962); at the Dublin Th. Festival, she played the title role of *Saint Joan of the Stockyards* (Gaiety, 1962); presented an evening of solo readings (Shelbourne Th., 1963); repeated her performance in *Saint Joan of the Stockyards* (Queen's, London, June 11, 1964); and the title role in the revised version of *Laurette* (Dublin International Theatre Festival, Olympia, Sept. 22, 1964). Subsequently she played Marie-Jeanne in *The Cavern* (Strand, London, Nov. 11, 1965); Juno in *Juno and the Paycock* (Gaiety, Dublin, Aug. 1, 1966); Cass in *The Loves of Cass McGuire* (Dublin Festival, Sept. 1967); Mme. Ranevsky in *The Cherry Orchard* (Dublin Festival, Oct. 1968); Pearl in *On a Foggy Day* (St. Martin's, London, July, 1969); Josie in *Best of Friends* (Strand, Feb. 19, 1970); and played in a revival of *The Chalk Garden* (Hub, Boston, May 2, 1971). She premiered her one-woman show, *Here Are Ladies*, at the Playhouse, Oxford, England, on Apr. 28, 1970, subsequently touring it extensively (Criterion, London, July 1970; N.Y. Shakespeare Fest. Newman Th., N.Y.C., Feb. 22, 1971; Circle-in-the-Square, Mar. 29, 1973; etc.). She directed *Playboy of the Western World* for the Long Wharf Th., New Haven, Conn. (Winter 1967–68).

Films. Since her screen debut as Kate in *Hungry Hill* (Rank, 1946), Miss McKenna has appeared as Emmy in *Daughter of Darkness* (Par., 1947); the Frenchwoman in *The Lost People* (Gainsborough, 1949); in *The Adventurers* (released in U.S. as *Fortune in Diamonds*, Rank, 1952); as the Virgin Mary in *The King of Kings* (MGM, 1961); Pegeen Mike in *The Playboy of the Western World* (Four Provinces, 1961); as Norah in *Of Human Bondage* (MGM, 1964); and as Anna in *Dr. Zhivago* (MGM, 1965).

Television. In the US, she played the Woman in *The Letter* (NBC, 1957); Sister Joanna in *The Cradle Song* (Hallmark Hall of Fame, NBC, 1957; re-staged 1960); Maggie in *What Every Woman Knows* (Dupont Show of the Month, CBS, 1959); in *The Winslow Boy* (Dupont Show of the Month, CBS, 1958); as Donna Ana in *Don Juan in Hell* (Play of the Week, WNTA, 1960); on the Hall of Kings special (ABC, 1967); on Girl Talk (ABC, 1965); *The Woman in White* (Great Mysteries, NBC, 1960); and *The Rope Dancers* (Play of the Week, WNTA, 1960).

Other Activities. Miss McKenna has translated into Gaelic, Shaw's *St. Joan*, Barrie's *Mary Rose*, and his *Peter Pan*. In Jan. 1975, she became the first woman nominated to Ireland's Council of State, a body advisory to the President.

Awards. She has received the London *Evening Standard* Award as Best Actress (1955) for her performance in *Saint Joan*, and was voted best international actress (Italy, 1961) for her performance as Pegeen Mike in *The Playboy of the Western World*. She was awarded an honorary degree of Doctor of Humane Letters from Wilson Coll., Chambersburg, Pa., and the Gold Medal of the Eire Society of Boston (1971).

Recreation. Reading, walking, talking, people and animals.

McKENZIE, JAMES B. Producer, manager. b. May 1, 1926, Appleton, Wis., to Basil F. and Helen McKenzie. Father, financier. Attended Campion Military Sch., Prairie du Chien, Wis., 1940–41; grad. St. Mary H.S., Menasha, Wis., 1944; attended Univ. of Wisconsin, 1944; grad. Univ. of Iowa, B.A. 1950; Columbia Univ., M.A. 1952. Married 1950, to Jeanne Bolan, actress; two sons, one daughter. Served USN, PTO, 1944–46; rank, RM 2/c. Member of League of NY Th. Owners and Producers; Independent Booking Org.; Council of Stock Theatres (pres., 1964–68); LORT (bd. of dirs.); Council of Resident Stock Theatres; TCG; ATPAM; AEA; IATSE (Local 479, Norwalk, Conn.; trustee, Local 16, San Francisco); NEA Th. Advisory Panel; Sigma Chi; Corinthians; Oceanic Society; National Oceanographic Inst. Address: (home) 44 Roseville Rd, Westport, CT 06880, tel. (203) 227-5138; (bus.) Producing Managers Co., 330 W. 45th St., New York, NY 10036, tel. (212) 581-2620.

Theatre. Mr. McKenzie began his professional career as an apprentice of Morton DaCosta (Port Players, Milwaukee, Wisc., 1942). For the Peninsula Players (Fish Creek, Wisc.), he subsequently served as carpenter, actor, stage manager, press agent, and director (1947–60); and producer (1961–to date). He has been producer of the Dobbs Ferry (N.Y.) Playhouse (1952–53); and the Lake George (N.Y.) Music Carnival (1954); and press agent for the U.S. Navy Band (1948); Shirt Sleeve Th. (Long Island, N.Y., 1950); Showcase Th. (Chicago, 1954); and the Fred Miller Th. (Milwaukee, Wisc., 1954–55). He worked as a stagehand at the Metropolitan Opera House (N.Y.C., 1956). He stage managed the MCA Industrial Theatre Dept. (1957–60); has been general manager (1959), co-producer (1960–63), and producer (1964–to date) of the Westport (Conn.) Country Playhouse; vice-president of the Lawrence-Henry Co. (1959); general manager of the Paper Mill Playhouse (Millburn, N.J., 1960–63); and of the Mineola (N.Y.) Playhouse (1962–63); secretary for TFK Plays, Inc. (1966–to date); general manager of Ballet Ballads (N.Y.C., 1961); producer for the Brown Th. (Louisville, Ky., 1963); general manager of the Little Theatre (N.Y.C., 1963); president of the Producing Managers Co. (1963–to date); co-producer of the Royal Poinciana Playhouse (Palm Beach, Fla., 1964–68); and the Bucks County Playhouse (New Hope, Pa., 1969–70); executive producer of the American Conservatory Theatre (San Francisco, 1969–to date; and, in N.Y.C., ANTA Th., 1969); co-producer of the Parker Playhouse (Ft. Lauderdale, Fla., 1972–to date); and producer of the first Greater Phoenix (Ariz.) Summer Festival (1973).

On Bway, he produced *The Girl in the Freudian Slip* (Booth, May 18, 1967); *And Miss Reardon Drinks a Little* (Morosco, Feb. 25, 1971); and *The Secret Affairs of Mildred Wild* (Ambassador, Nov. 14, 1972). He has produced or managed over one thousand plays in most states of the union during the past twenty-five years, including fifteen national tours of other Bway plays; and he has been general manager of numerous plays and musicals on Bway.

Television. Mr. McKenzie was a studio supervisor for over two hundred fifty network shows (NBC, 1950–52); and a teleprompter operator (CBS, 1956–57); and he has produced seven plays for NET since 1969, including the A.C.T. production of *Cyrano de Bergerac.*

Night Clubs. He was a trumpet player in mid-western territorial orchestras (1946–50); and was general manager of the Celebrity Room, Palm Beach (1964–68). He was permitee of the Westport, Conn. Players Tavern (1959–72); and has produced several legitimate comedies for Las Vegas clubs (1966–68).

Other Activities. Mr. McKenzie was a partner in the Merrill-McKenzie Advertising Agency (1946–50). He is treasurer of Port-O-Vox, Inc., a company dealing in theatrical sound systems; and co-owner of the Lake Cinema (Wis., 1967–to date), an independent art film house.

He was an active member of the Comm. to Advance Ethnic Minorities (1964–69); and is a panel member and lecturer on nonprofit regional theatre of today.

Recreation. Ocean yacht racing, billiards, poker, and motorcycle riding.

McLEOD, ARCHIBALD. Educator, director, producer. b. Nov. 5, 1906, Edinburgh, Scotland, to Thomas and Catherine S. (Wishart) McLeod. Father, marine engineer. Grad. Newark (N.J.) Prep. Sch., 1929; Oberlin Coll., B.A. 1933; State Univ. of Iowa, M.A. 1934; Cornell Univ., Ph.D. 1942. Married 1937, to Frances Gosney (marr. dis. 1943); married 1943, to Charlotte Samuels; one daughter. Member of ATA; NCP; Phi Kappa Phi; Ill. Speech Assn.; Theta Alpha Phi. Address: (home) 907 W. Schwartz, Carbondale, IL 62901, tel. (618) 457-7602; (bus.) Theatre Dept., Southern Illinois Univ., Carbondale, IL 62901, tel. (618) 543-5741.

Since 1947, Mr. McLeod has been professor and chairman of the Theatre Department, Southern Illinois Univ. He was instructor and technical director in the Speech Dept. of Kansas State Coll. (1934); associate professor and technical director at Texas State Coll. for Women (1935–39, 1941–43); assistant professor and technical director at Louisiana State Univ. (1943–47); founder (1955) and director (1955–56) of the Shepherd of the Hills Th., Branson, Mo.; and director-producer of the Kelso Hollow Th., New Salem Park, Springfield, Ill. (1957–58).

Awards. On a Fulbright Grant, Mr. McLeod was lecturer in dramatic art at Natya Sangh, Madras, India (1962–63).

Recreation. Photography, gardening.

McLERIE, ALLYN ANN. Actress, singer, dancer. b. Dec. 1, Grand'Mere, Quebec, Canada, to Allan Gordon and Vera (Stewart) McLerie. Father, aviator. Grad. Ft. Hamilton H.S., Brooklyn, N.Y., 1943. Studied at Lodge Professional Sch., N.Y.C., 1943–44; ballet with Nemchinova, 1941–45; Edward Caton, 1941–49; Agnes DeMille, 1942; Yudia-Nimura, 1941–45; Hanya Holm, 1946; Martha Graham, 1947; Sevilla Forte, 1963; acting with Tamara Daykarhanova, 1944; Lee Strasberg at Actors Studio, N.Y.C., 1952–60 (mbr., 1961–to date). Married Mar. 21, 1947, to Adolph Green, playwright, lyricist (marr. dis. May 1953); married Dec. 20, 1953, to George Gaynes, actor, singer; one son, one daughter. Member of AEA; AFTRA; SAG. Address: Los Angeles, CA.

Theatre. Miss McLerie first performed as a dancer in the ballet corps of the San Carlo Opera Repertoire Co. (Boston Opera House, Mass.; Center Th., N.Y.C., 1942); subsequently danced in the Bway production of *One Touch of Venus* (Imperial, Oct. 7, 1943); in the ensemble, and succeeded Sono Osato as Ivy in *On the Town* (Adelphi, Dec. 28, 1944); played Eustasia in the pre-Bway tryout of *Bonanza Bound!* (opened Shubert, Philadelphia, Pa., Dec. 26, 1947; closed there Jan. 3, 1948); Amy Spettigue in *Where's Charley?* (St. James, N.Y.C., Oct. 11, 1948; Bway Th., Jan. 29, 1951); Monique DuPont in *Miss Liberty* (Imperial, July 15, 1949); and toured Europe as a guest artist with the Ballet Th. (Aug.–Nov. 1950).

She appeared in a stock production of *You Never Can Tell* (La Jolla Playhouse, Calif., Summer 1952); *King of Hearts* (Fall River, Mass., July 1955); played Lady India in *Ring 'Round the Moon* (Hyde Park Playhouse, N.Y., July 1955); Corporal Jean Evans in *Time Limit!* (Booth, N.Y.C., Jan. 24, 1956); and at the Sacramento (Calif.) Music Circus (1957), appeared as Lola in *Damn Yankees,* Ninotchka in *Silk Stockings,* and Gladys in *The Pajama Game.*

She played Gwynn in *Bells Are Ringing* (Coliseum, London, Nov. 14, 1957); was standby for Gwen Verdon in *Redhead* (46 St. Th., N.Y.C., Feb. 5, 1959); appeared as Anita in *West Side Story* (Winter Garden, Apr. 20, 1960); Nellie Forbush in *South Pacific* (NY City Ctr., Apr. 26, 1961); Claudine in *Can-Can* (Garden Court Dinner Th., San Francisco, Calif., May 1962); and in various roles in the revue, *The Beast in Me* (Plymouth, N.Y.C., May 16, 1963).

Miss McLerie again played Anita in *West Side Story* (Melody Fair, Framingham, Mass.; Oakdale Musical Th., Wallingford, Conn.; Warwick Musical Th., R.I.; Melody Fair, N. Tonawanda, N.Y., Summer 1963); and toured, with her husband, as Eliza Doolittle in *My Fair Lady* (opened Westport Country Playhouse, Conn., June 12, 1964; closed John Drew Th., East Hampton, L.I., N.Y., Aug. 29, 1964).

She appeared as Ellie in *Show Boat* (State Th., N.Y.C., July 19, 1966); Tlimpattia in *Dynamite Tonight* (Martinique, Mar. 15, 1967); Elmire in *Tartuffe* (Inner City Rep. Co., Los Angeles, Calif., Sept. 16, 1967); Clytemnestra in *The Flies* (Inner City Rep. Co., 1967); as Irma in *Irma La Douce* and Anita in *West Side Story* (Sacramento Music Circus, Sacramento, Calif., 1967); as Lenore in *L.A. under Siege* (Mark Taper Forum, Los Angeles, Calif., Aug. 2, 1970); and as Alma Stone in *The Mind with the Dirty Man* (Mark Taper Forum, Mar. 15, 1973).

Films. She made her debut singing "Mountain Greenery" with Perry Como in *Words and Music* (MGM, 1948); subsequently appeared in *Where's Charley?* (ABPC, Elstree, 1951); *Calamity Jane* (WB, 1953); *Murder in the Rue Morgue* (WB, 1954); *Battle Cry* (WB, 1955); *The Reivers* (Nat'l Gen'l, 1969); *They Shoot Horses, Don't They?* (WB, 1969); *Monte Walsh* (1970); *Jeremiah Johnson* (WB, 1972); *The Cowboys* (WB, 1972); *The Magnificent Seven Ride* (U, 1972); *The Way We Were* (Col., 1973); *Cinderella Liberty* (20th-Fox, 1973); and *France—S.A.* (Albina Prod., Paris, France, 1973).

Television. Miss McLerie appeared in the television films *The Delphi Bureau* (ABC, Mar. 1972); *Shadow of a Gunman* (Hollywood Television Th., PBS, Dec. 1972); *A Tree Grows in Brooklyn* (NBC, 1974); and *Born Innocent* (NBC, 1974). She has made guest appearances on The Waltons (CBS); Cannon (CBS); The F.B.I. (ABC); Love Story (NBC); Ghost Story; Bonanza (NBC); My World and Welcome to It (NBC); Nichols; We'll Get By (ABC, 1975); Kodiak (ABC); and Young Dr. Kildare.

Night Clubs. She performed with John Butler at Ciro's (Hollywood, Calif., 1947); and at the Cotillion Room (N.Y.C., 1947).

Awards. Miss McLerie received the *Theatre World* Award (1948) for her performance as Amy Spettigue in *Where's Charley?.*

McLIAM, JOHN. Actor, director, playwright. b. John Joseph Williams, Jan. 24, 1920, Hayter, Alberta, Canada, to John Matthew and Johanna (Boland) Williams. Father, railroad foreman; mother, schoolteacher. Grad. St. Mary's H.S., Berkeley, Calif., 1935; St. Mary's Coll., 1939; attended Univ. of California at Berkeley, 1939–41; New Sch. for Social Research Dramatic Workshop, 1946–48; Amer. Th. Wing, 1948–50. Married Nov. 25, 1951, to Roberta Robinson, actress, teacher; one daughter. Served USN, PTO, 1942–46; rank Lt.; Bronze Star. Member of AEA; SAG; AFTRA; Dramatists Guild; Theatre West. Address: 5003 Alhama Dr., Woodland Hills, CA 91364.

Pre-Theatre. Reporter, advertising, teacher.

Theatre. Mr. McLiam made his stage debut as Shadow in *Winterset* (Arts Colony Th., San Francisco, Calif., June 1946); his professional debut in stock as Charlie in *Three Men on a Horse* (Pompton Lakes, N.J., June 1947); appeared as Grigson in *Shadow of a Gunman* (President, N.Y.C., Mar. 1947); the Farmer in *Desire Under the Elms* (ANTA, Jan. 16, 1952); toured as Brother Martin and Bertrand De Pouleny in *Saint Joan* (opened Natl., Washington, D.C., Sept. 20, 1954; closed Hartman, Columbus, Ohio, Nov. 6, 1954); succeeded Jack Bittner (1956) as Olpides in *Tiger at the Gates* (Plymouth, N.Y.C., Oct. 3, 1955), wrote *The Sin of Pat Muldoon* (Cort, Mar. 13, 1957); played Kelly, "Chips," in *One More River* (Ambassador, Mar. 18, 1960); performed in *The Cock May Crow,* which he also directed (Th. West, Apr. 1968); and in *Promises to Keep,* which he co-directed (Th. West, Feb. 1974).

Films. Mr. McLiam appeared as Harry in *My Fair Lady* (WB, 1964). He was in *In Cold Blood* (Col., 1967); *Cool Hand Luke* (WB, 1967); *The Reivers* (Natl. Gen., 1969); *Halls of Anger* (UA, 1970); *R.P.M.* (Col., 1970); *Monte Walsh* (National General, 1970); *riverrun* (Col., 1970); *Culpepper Cattle Company* (20th-Fox, 1972); *Showdown* (U, 1973); *The Iceman Cometh* (Amer. Film Th., 1973); and *The Dove* (EMI, 1974).

Awards. He received a drama fellowship to Stanford Univ. (1949).

Recreation. Camping, hiking.

McMARTIN, JOHN. Actor. b. Warsaw, Ind. Grad. Columbia Univ. Served US Army. Member of AEA; SAG.

Theatre. Mr. McMartin began performing at age fifteen as a straight man with a touring vaudeville company in Minnesota. He made his off-Bway debut as Cpl. "Billy" Jester in *Little Mary Sunshine* (Orpheum, N.Y.C., Nov. 18, 1959); appeared in summer stock in Bucks County, Pa., Newport, R.I., and Skowhegan, Me.; made his Bway debut as Forrest Noble in *The Conquering Hero* (ANTA, N.Y.C., Jan. 16, 1961); played Capt. Mal Malcolm in *Blood, Sweat and Stanley Poole* (Morosco, Oct. 5, 1961); Mr. Dupan in the pre-Bway tryout of *A Matter of Position* (closed Walnut St. Th., Philadelphia, Oct. 13, 1962); Edward L. Voorhees in *A Rainy Day in Newark* (Belasco, N.Y.C., Oct. 22, 1963); Mr. Billings in *Too Much Johnson* (Phoenix, Jan. 15, 1964); John Paul Jones in the pre-Bway tryout of *Pleasures and Palaces* (closed Fisher, Detroit, Apr. 10, 1965); Oscar in *Sweet Charity* (Palace, N.Y.C., Jan. 29, 1966); and Benjamin Stone in *Follies* (Winter Garden, Apr. 4, 1971); and appeared in *Forget-Me-Not-Lane* (Mark Taper Forum, Los Angeles, May 31, 1973).

With the New Phoenix Repertory Co., he has played Dion Anthony in *The Great God Brown* (Lyceum, N.Y.C., Dec. 10, 1972); Don Alonso in *Don Juan* (Lyceum, Dec. 11, 1972); Schill in *The Visit* (Ethel Barrymore Th., Nov. 25, 1973); Fedot in *Chemin de Fer* (Ethel Barrymore Th., Nov. 26, 1973); Foresight in *Love for Love* (Helen Hayes Th., Nov. 11, 1974); and Leone Gala in *The Rules of the Game* (Helen Hayes Th., Dec. 12, 1974).

Films. He made his film debut in *A Thousand Clowns* (UA, 1965).

Television. Mr. McMartin's appearances include Armstrong Circle Th. (NBC); DuPont Show of the Month (NBC); As the World Turns (CBS); *Ride with Terror* (NBC); The Nurses (CBS); Profiles in Courage (NBC); East Side/West Side (CBS); *The Lincoln Murder Case* (CBS); and Phyllis (CBS).

Awards. Mr. McMartin received *Theater World's* Most Promising Personality Award (1958–59); and received the Drama Desk Award (1972–73) for his performances in *The Great God Brown* and *Don Juan.*

McMULLAN, FRANK. Educator, writer, director. b. Frank Alonzo McMullan, Oct. 12, 1907, Jonesboro, Ga., to Wilson Henry and Birda Cornelia (Brown) McMullan. Father, farmer. Grad. Boy's H.S., Atlanta, Ga., 1925; Univ. of Georgia, B.A. 1928; Atlanta Law Sch., LL.B. 1930; Yale Univ. Sch. of Drama, M.F.A. 1934. Studied with George Pierce Baker; Alexander Dean; Allardyce Nicoll. Married Mar. 26, 1938, to Elizabeth Eckhard; two sons. Member of ATA Elizabethan Club (ret. July 1974); Chi Psi; and Fellow of Calhoun Coll., Yale Univ. Served US Army, Special Services, 1943–45; rank, Maj. Address: 12 Sunbrook Rd., Woodbridge, CT 06525, tel. (203) 387-7615.

Since 1934, Mr. McMullan has taught directing. He was co-director of the Stephens College Th. (1934–36); director of the Univ. of Vermont Sch. of Drama summer sessions (1937–40); acting chairman of the Drama Dept. (1941–43); acting chairman of the Drama Dept., Yale Univ. Sch. of Drama, head of the Directing Dept. (1939–65); and is presently associate professor emeritus of play production (Yale Univ. Sch. of Drama). Mr. McMullan has directed at the Yale Univ. Sch. of Drama; Wellesley (Mass.) Summer Th.; Southbury (Conn.) Playhouse; and Provincetown (Mass.) Playhouse; has been guest director at the Univ. of Arkansas; Ohio State Univ.; Univ. of Connecticut Summer Th.; Shakespeare Festival (Old Globe Th., San Diego, Calif.); Shakespeare Memorial Th. (Stratford-on-Avon, England); and the Champlain Shakespeare Festival (Burlington, Vt.); and has directed in Chile and Panama.

Films. He directed *Telephone Pioneers* for the Southern New England Telephone Co. (1950).

Television. Mr. McMullan's production of *The Merry Wives of Windsor* was televised for Omnibus (NBC, 1954). He appeared on his own weekly series in New Haven, Conn. (WNHC, 1956–57).

Other Activities. He was appointed head of the performing arts mission to the United Arab Republic (1962).

Published Works. Mr. McMullan has written articles for *Theatre Arts, Players Magazine,* and *Educational Theatre Journal;* and the books, *One World in Drama* (1950); *Play Interpretation and Direction* (1951), translated into Spanish (1959); *Producing Shakespeare* (1954); *Shakespeare: Of an Age and For All Time* (1954); *The Directorial Image* (1962); *The Director's Handbook* (1964); and *Directing Shakespeare in the Contemporary Theatre* (1974).

Awards. Mr. McMullan received a Fulbright Grant as guest director at the Teatro de Ensayo, Teatro Experimental (Santiago, Chile, 1958); the Chilean national award for directing (1958); and the Smith-Mundt grant to establish a theatre program at the Univ. of Panama (1959).

McNALLY, TERRENCE. Playwright. b. Nov. 3, 1939, St. Petersburg, Fla. Grad. Columbia Univ., B.A. 1960 (Phi Beta Kappa). Address: c/o William Morris Agency, 1350 Ave. of the Americas, New York, NY 10019.

Pre-Theatre. Tutor (1961–62).

Theatre. Mr. McNally adapted *The Lady of the Camellias* (Winter Garden, N.Y.C., Mar. 20, 1963), a play by Giles Cooper; subsequently wrote *And Things That Go Bump in the Night* (Royale, Apr. 26, 1965); *Tour,* presented on a bill entitled *Collision Course* (Cafe au Go-Go, May 8, 1968); *Sweet Eros* and *Witness* (Gramercy Arts Th., Nov. 21, 1968); *Noon,* on a bill entitled *Morning, Noon and Night* (Henry Miller's Th., Nov. 28, 1968); *Cuba Si!* (Th. de Lys, Dec. 9, 1968); *Next* on a double-bill with *Adaptation* by Elaine May, (Greenwich Mews Th., Feb 10, 1969); *Where Has Tommy Flowers Gone?* (world premiere, Yale Repertory Co., New Haven, Conn., Jan. 7, 1971; and Eastside Playhouse, N.Y.C., Oct. 7, 1971); *Whiskey* (Th. at St. Clements, Apr. 29, 1973); *Bad Habits* (Astor Place Th., Feb. 4, 1974; moved to Booth, May 5, 1974); and *The Tubs* (Yale Repertory Co., New Haven, Conn., Jan. 1974), which was revised and retitled *The Ritz* (Longacre, N.Y.C., Jan. 20, 1975).

In addition, Mr. McNally was a stage manager for the Actors Studio (1961).

Television. He is the author of *Botticelli* (1968); and *Last Gasps* (1969).

Published Works. Mr. McNally was a film critic for *The Seventh Art* (1963–65); and assistant editor of *Columbia College Today* (1965–66). His published, unproduced plays include *The Roller Coaster* (*Columbia Review,* 1960); *Apple Pie* (Dramatists Play Service, 1969), *Bringing It All Back Home,* included in *Three Plays: 1970* (Dramatists Play Service); and *Let It Bleed,* in *City Stops* (1972).

Awards. He has received the Stanley Award (1962) for *This Side of the Door* (unproduced); and two Guggenheim Fellowships (1966, 1969).

McNEIL, CLAUDIA. Actress. b. Aug. 13, 1917, Baltimore, Md., to Marvin and Annie Mae (Anderson) McNeil. Grad. Wadley H.S., N.Y.C. Studied acting with Maria Ouspenskaya; singing with Rhys Morgan. Member of AFTRA; AEA; SAG.

Pre-Theatre. Librarian.

Theatre. Miss McNeil made her first stage appearance at the Duxbury (Mass.) Playhouse, where she spent several seasons; followed by appearances at the Ann Arbor (Mich.) Drama Festival, and a South American tour as vocal soloist with the Katherine Dunham Dance Co.

She made her N.Y.C. debut as Mamie in *Simply Heavenly* (85 St. Playhouse, May 20, 1957); played Mary in *Winesburg, Ohio* (National, Feb. 5, 1958); Lena Younger in *A Raisin in the Sun* (Ethel Barrymore Th., Mar. 11, 1959), with which she toured (opened Wilbur, Boston, Mass., Sept. 12, 1960); Mama in *Tiger, Tiger Burning Bright* (Booth, N.Y.C., Dec. 22, 1962); Bernice in a touring production of *A Member of the Wedding* (1964); Sister Margaret in *The Amen Corner* for a US State Dept. tour (1965) which included Israel, Switzerland, Austria, France, Germany, Scotland, and England; played Sarah in *Something Different* (Cort, N.Y.C., Nov. 28, 1967); Ftatateeta in *Her First Roman* (Lunt-Fontanne Th., Oct. 20, 1968); Mrs. Deveraux in *The Wrong-Way Light Bulb* (John Golden Th., Mar. 4, 1969); as part of a triple-bill entitled *Contributions* (Tambellini's Gate, Mar. 9, 1970), played Martha in *Plantation,* and Mrs. Love in *Contributions;* and repeated her performance in *A Raisin in the Sun* (Hartford, Conn., Stage Co., Jan. 31, 1975).

Films. Miss McNeil made her screen debut in *The Last Angry Man* (Col., 1959); repeated the role of Lena Younger in the film version of *A Raisin in the Sun* (Col., 1961); and appeared in *There Was a Crooked Man* (WB, 1970); and *Black Girl* (Cinerama, 1972).

Television and Radio. Miss McNeil was program coordinator and entertainer for the Jamaican Broadcasting Co. (1951–52). Her television appearances include the role of Berenice Sadie Brown in *Member of the Wedding* (Dupont Show of the Month, NBC, 1958); *Express Stop from Lenox Avenue* (The Nurses, CBS, 1963); Look Up and Live (CBS, 1964); Profiles in Courage (NBC, 1965); *Do Not Go Gentle into that Good Night* (CBS, 1967); *Incident in San Francisco* (ABC, 1971); *To Be Young, Gifted and Black* (NET); Mod Squad (ABC, 1972); and *Moon of the Wolf* (1972).

Night Clubs. Miss McNeil made her supper club debut as The Black Cat (N.Y.C., 1933); and has performed at The Famous Door, The Onyx, and Greenwich Village Inn, all in N.Y.C.

Awards. Miss McNeil was nominated for the Antoinette Perry (Tony) Award for her performance as Mama in *Tiger, Tiger, Burning Bright* (1962); the NATAS (Emmy) Award for her performance in *Express Stop from Lenox Avenue* (The Nurses, CBS, 1963); and the London Critic's Poll award (1966) for her performance in *The Amen Corner..*

Recreation. Interior decorating, collecting milk glass, antiques, and rare books.

McNICHOL, EILEEN. Community theatre executive. b. Chicago, Ill., to Harry B. and Elizabeth (Brown) McNichol. Father, electrical engineer; mother, beautician, cosmetologist. Grad. Mt. St. Mary Acad. H.S.; Siena Heights Coll. Member of ANTA. Address: 612 N. Spring St., Elgin, IL 60120.

Miss McNichol was secretary-treasurer of the Illinois-Wisconsin Regional Conference of Community Theatres (1954–57), which later became the Illinois Community Theatre Association. She has been active in community theatre affairs since 1951, when she assisted in organizing the Elgin Community Theatre, subsequently becoming treasurer and head of the make-up department. In addition, she has performed in many of the group's productions including *Detective Story, The Philadelphia Story, The Robe, Suspect, The Curious Savage, The Girls in 509, Blithe Spirit, The Man Who Came to Dinner, Patterns, Rebecca, Arsenic and Old Lace, The Informer, Front Page,* and *The Effect of Gamma Rays on Man-in-the-Moon Marigolds.* She is also the director of the theatre's traveling company, supervises preparation of program books, and edits the organization's monthly newsletter, *Back Stage Call Board.*

In stock, she appeared with the Catholic Youth of Elgin Players in *Best Foot Forward, Hillbilly Courtship, Shadow and Substance, Drums of Death, Ramshackle Inn,* and directed *The Pirates of Penzance;* and, with the Boulder Hill Playhouse (Aurora, Ill.), appeared in *Ladies in Retirement, Anniversary Waltz, Inherit the Wind, Bell, Book and Candle, Papa Is All, O Mistress Mine, Sunrise at Campobello,* and *Pool's Paradise.* She is a board member of the Twilight Ridge Summer Stock Th. (Crystal Lake, Ill.), where she appeared in *The Torchbearers, Tally-Ho, Seven Nuns in Las Vegas* and *Breath of Spring.*

Recreation. Theatre.

McQUIGGAN, JACK. Producer, actor, director. b. John Alexander McQuiggan, Jan. 12, 1935, Detroit, Mich., to Paul F. and Elizabeth (Alexander) McQuiggan. Father, physician. Grad. Mercersburg (Pa.) Prep., 1952; Washington and Lee Univ., B.A. 1956. Attended Neighborhood Playhouse Sch. of the Th., 1957–59. Married to Mary Doyle, actress (marr. dis.); one daughter. Member of AEA; Phi Gamma Delta (pres., 1956); Omicron Delta Kappa.

Theatre. Mr. McQuiggan first appeared on a stage in a high-school production of *Christmas Eve Story* (Xenia, Ohio, Dec. 1948); made his professional debut as Robert Falconbridge in *King John* (Antioch Shakespeare Fest., Yellow Springs, Ohio, May 1952), followed by other appearances there (Summers 1953–55); and played in a drama school production of *The Italian Straw Hat* (Neighborhood Playhouse, N.Y.C., Apr. 6, 1958).

He was a founder (1960) and producer for the Association of Producing Artists (APA); appeared with the company in repertory productions of *The Seagull, Anatol* and *Man and Superman* (City Hall Th., Bermuda; McCarter Th., Princeton, N.J.; Bucks County Playhouse, New Hope, Pa. (Apr.–June 1960); was production stage manager for their productions of *A Midsummer Night's Dream, The Seagull, The Tavern, The School for Scandal,* and *Fashion* (Fred Miller Th., Milwaukee, Wis., 1961–62); and for the APA season at the Folksbiene Playhouse, N.Y.C., he was stage manager for *The School for Scandal* (Mar. 17, 1962), *The Seagull* (Mar. 21, 1962) and *The Tavern* (Apr. 4, 1962).

For the Fred Miller (resident) Th. (subsequently named the Milwaukee Rep. Th.), Milwaukee, Wis., Mr. McQuiggan was business manager (May 1962–May 1963); and genl. manager and producer (May 1963–May 1966), during which time the theatre presented *Charley's Aunt* (Apr. 1962); *Beyond the Horizon* (Oct. 24, 1962); *U.S.A.* (Nov. 14, 1962); *The Fantasticks* (Dec. 5, 1962); *Major Barbara* (Jan. 16, 1963); *As You Desire Me* (Feb. 6, 1963); *The Elder Statesman* (Feb. 27, 1963); *The Show-Off* (Mar. 20, 1963); *The Madwoman of Chaillot* (Nov. 20, 1963); *A Thurber Carnival* (Dec. 11, 1963); *The Comedy of Errors* (Dec. 26, 1963); *Tartuffe* (Jan. 8, 1964); *The Hostage* (Jan. 29, 1964); *Right You Are If You Think*

You Are (Feb. 19, 1964); *Long Day's Journey into Night* (Mar. 11, 1964); *The Fantasticks* (Apr. 1, 1964); *The Playboy of the Western World* (Oct. 28, 1964); *Oh, Dad, Poor Dad, Mama's s Hung You in the Closet and I'm Feelin' So Sad* (Nov. 18, 1964); *Once Upon a Mattress* (Dec. 9, 1964); *Uncle Vanya* (Jan. 6, 1965); *The Tempest* (Jan. 27, 1965); *Under Milk Wood* (Feb. 17, 1965); *Pantagleize* (Mar. 10, 1965); *Anatol* (Mar. 31, 1965); repeated with another cast, Apr. 14, 1966); *Saint Joan* (Oct. 28, 1965); *The Diary of a Scoundrel* (Nov. 18, 1965); *The Time of Your Life* (Dec. 9, 1965); *Mother Courage* (Jan. 13, 1966); *The Servant of Two Masters* (Feb. 3, 1966), which he adapted and directed; *Henry IV, Part 1* (Feb. 24, 1966); and *The Glass Menagerie* (Mar. 17, 1966), which he directed.

He became co-director, with Adrian Hall, of the Trinity Square Playhouse, Providence, R.I. (Summer 1966–resigned Jan. 21, 1967), during which time he organized Project Discovery, a professional theatre program for students and adults, sponsored by the state and local government of Providence, R.I.; and rejoined (Mar. 1967) APA as an assoc. director. He produced *Horseman, Pass By* (Fortune Th., N.Y.C., Jan. 15, 1969).

Television. Mr. McQuiggan's Milwaukee Rep. Th. production of *The Wedding* was televised (Esso Rep. Th., Educ., Apr. 21, 1965).

McWHINNIE, DONALD. Director. b. Oct. 16, 1920, Rotherham, Yorkshire, England, to Herbert and Margaret Elizabeth McWhinnie. Father, steel business executive. Grad. Rotherham Grammar Sch., 1938; Gonville and Caius Coll., Cambridge Univ., M.A. 1941. Served RAF, Intelligence, 1941–45, Entertainment and Welfare, 1945–46; rank, Flight Lt. Member of SSD&C; ACTT; Cambridge Univ. Amateur Drama Club (pres. 1940–41). Address: 16 Chepstow Place, London W.2, England tel. OL-229-2120.

Theatre. Mr. McWhinnie began his professional career as the director of the London production of *Krapp's Last Tape* (Royal Court Th., Oct. 28, 1958); subsequently, directed *The Caretaker* (Arts, Apr. 27, 1960); the Royal Shakespeare Co. production of the *Duchess of Malfi* (Aldwych, Dec. 15, 1960); *Three* (Arts, Jan. 18, 1961); and *The Tenth Man* (Comedy, April 1961). In N.Y.C., he again directed *The Caretaker* (Lyceum, Oct. 4, 1961), and also *A Passage to India* (Ambassador, Jan. 31, 1962).

He directed *Everything in the Garden* (Arts, London, Mar. 13, 1962); directed *Macbeth* (Royal Shakespeare Th., Stratford-on-Avon, Summer, 1962), *Rattle of a Simple Man* (Garrick, London, Sept. 1962), and *Doctors of Philosophy* (Arts, Oct. 1962). In N.Y.C. he again directed *Rattle of a Simple Man* (Booth, Apr. 17, 1963). He staged *The Doctor's Dilemma* (Haymarket Th., London, May 1963); *Alfie* (Mermaid, June 19, 1963); *Out of the Crocodile* (Phoenix, Oct. 29, 1963); *The Fourth of June* (St. Martin's, Jan. 30, 1964); *End Game* (Aldwych Th., July 1964); *All in Good Time* (Royale, N.Y.C., Feb. 18, 1965); *The Creeper* (St. Martin's, London, July 14, 1965); *The Cavern* (Strand, Nov. 11, 1965); *The Astrakhan Coat* (Helen Hayes Th., N.Y.C., Jan. 12, 1967); *Happy Family* (St. Martin's, London, Feb. 1967); *Hamlet* (Covent Garden Th., Apr. 18, 1969); *No Quarter* (Hampstead Th., June 9, 1969); *There'll Be Some Changes Made* (Fortune, Sept. 29, 1969); *The Applecart* (Mermaid, Mar. 5, 1970); and *Meeting at Night* (Duke of York's, Jan. 21, 1971).

Television and Radio. Mr. McWhinnie was a director for BBC Radio (London, 1947), and later was named script editor, and assistant head of the drama department (1952). He directed D. H. Lawrence's *Samson and Delilah* (BBC, 1960); also *Waiting for Godot*, and *Poor Bitos*.

He has directed numerous television productions, including Evelyn Waugh's trilogy, *Sword of Honour;* E. M. Forster's *Howard's End* and *Room with a View;* James Joyce's *The Dead* and *Stephen D; The Sinners; Country Matters;* and *Elizabeth R.*

Awards. Mr. McWhinnie for his direction of *The Caretaker*, won the *Variety* NY Drama Critics Poll (1962).

MEACHAM, ANNE. Actress. b. July 21, 1925, Chicago, Ill., to Florus David and Virginia (Foster) Meacham. Father, executive. Grad. New Trier H.S., Winnetka, Ill., 1942; attended Univ. of Rochester, 1942–44. Studied acting at Yale Univ. Sch. of Drama, 1944–45; and at Neighborhood Playhouse Sch. of the Theatre, 1945–47. Member of AEA; AFTRA; SAG.

Theatre. Miss Meacham first appeared on the stage as Grazia in a high school production of *Death Takes a Holiday* (1940). Her professional debut was as Mrs. Brown in *Claudia* (Bridgeton, Me., Summer 1946); subsequently toured as Penny in *The Fatal Weekness* (opened Buffalo, N.Y., Sept. 1947; closed Seattle, Wash., Jan. 1948). She joined the touring production of *The First Mrs. Fraser* as the second Mrs. Fraser (Philadelphia, Pa..; Washington, D.C.; Montclair, N.J.; Chicago, Ill.; and La Jolla Playhouse, Calif., 1948). She also appeared in stock at the Chevy Chase Th. (Wheeling, Ill., Summer 1949).

She made her N.Y.C. debut as Ensign Jane Hilton in *The Long Watch* (Lyceum, Mar. 20, 1952); subsequently played Marie in *Come Back, Little Sheba* (Ann Arbor Drama Festival, Mich., May 1952); Laura Bateman in the pre-Bway tryout of *Masquerade* (opened Court Square Th., Springfield, Mass., Apr. 9, 1953; closed Walnut St. Th., Philadelphia, Pa., Apr. 25, 1953); Violante in *Ondine* (46 St. Th., N.Y.C., Feb. 18, 1954); and Lorna Moon in *Golden Boy* (Arena Stage, Washington, D.C., Nov.–Dec. 1954).

Miss Meacham appeared as Aurora in *The Immortal Husband* (Th. de Lys, N.Y.C., Feb. 14, 1955); was the general understudy for *King Lear* (NY City Ctr., Jan. 12, 1956) and *A Streetcar Named Desire* (NY City Ctr., Feb. 15, 1956); understudied Gaby Rogers as Celia in *Mister Johnson* (Martin Beck Th., March 29, 1956); played Gertrude Wentworth in *Eugenia* (Ambassador, Jan. 30, 1957); Romaine in *Witness for the Prosecution* (Arena Stage, Washington, D.C., Apr.–May, 1957; toured Summer 1957); Catherine Holly in *Suddenly, Last Summer*, which was part of a double-bill entitled *Garden District* (York, N.Y.C., Jan. 7, 1958); Judith in *The Devil's Disciple* (Playhouse-in-the-Park, Philadelphia, Pa., Summer 1958); Lizzie Borden in *The Legend of Lizzie* (Adelphi, N.Y.C., Feb. 9, 1959); Elisa in *Moonbirds* (Cort, Oct. 9, 1959); Jere Halliday in *The Disenchanted* (Arena Stage, Washington, D.C., May 3, 1960); the title role in *Hedda Gabler* (4th St. Th., N.Y.C., Nov. 9, 1960); the title role in the ANTA Matinee series production of *The Lady Akane* (Th. de Lys, Nov. 15, 1960); Miss Adele Quested in *A Passage to India* (Ambassador, Jan. 31, 1962). With the APA, she played Dorcas Bellboys in *A Penny for a Song* (Bucks County Playhouse, New Hope, Pa., Aug. 6, 1962); Maria in *The School for Scandal* (Lydia Mendelssohn Th., Ann Arbor, Mich., Oct. 3, 1962); and The Woman in *The Tavern* (Lydia Mendelssohn Th., Oct. 17, 1962); The Unknown One in *As You Desire Me* (Fred Miller Th., Milwaukee, Wis., Jan. 1963); and Monica in *The Elder Statesman* (Fred Miller Th., Feb. 1963).

Miss Meacham joined the National Repertory Th. (Greensboro, N.C., Oct. 10, 1963), as Lady India in *Ring 'Round the Moon*, Nina in *The Seagull*, and Elizabeth Proctor in *The Crucible*. She repeated her roles in *The Seagull* and in *The Crucible* (Belasco, N.Y.C., Apr. 5–6, 1964). She appeared in a concert reading of *Pictures in the Hallway* (Greenwich Mews Th., Jan. 18, 1965); played Deianeira in *The Wives* (Stage 73, May 17, 1965); Emily Dickinson in *Come Slowly* (White Barn, Westport, Conn., July 1966); Penelope Gray in *Elizabeth the Queen* (NY City Ctr., N.Y.C., Nov. 3, 1966); Gertrude in *Rosencrantz and Guildenstern are Dead* (Alvin, Oct. 16, 1967); Countess Aurelia in *The Madwoman of Chaillot* (Playhouse-in-the-Park, Cincinnati; and tour, 1968); appeared in *Knights of the Round Table* and *Little Eyolf* (Artists Th., Southampton, England, 1968); played Madame Arcadina in *The Seagull* (Hartford, Conn., Stage Co., 1968–69); Miriam in *In the Bar of a Tokyo Hotel* (Eastside Playhouse, May 11, 1969); appeared in *Edith Stein* (world premiere, Arena Stage, Washington, D.C., Oct. 23, 1969); *Father's Day* (Arena Stage, May 5, 1971); and *The Importance of Being Earnest* (Goodman Th., Chicago, Dec. 20, 1971); and appeared in the name part in *The Latter Days of a Celebrated Soubrette (Central Arts Cabaret Th., N.Y.C., May 16, 1974), a new version of The Genadiges Fraulein.*

Films. Miss Meacham made her screen debut in *Lilith* (Col., 1964); and has subsequently appeared in *Dear Dead Delilah* (1971); and *Seizure* (Cinerama, 1974).

Television. She has appeared as Cathy in *Wuthering Heights* (Hollywood Screen Test); and has performed on The Brighter Day (CBS); *All the King's Men* (Kraft Television Th., NBC); *Face of a Hero* (Playhouse 90, CBS); The Defenders (CBS); The Virginians (NBC); The Nurses (CBS); and Dr. Kildare (NBC).

Awards. For her performance in *The Long Watch* (1952), Miss Meacham received the Clarence Derwent Award (1952); and for her performances in *Garden District* (1958) and Hedda Gabler (1961), she received two *Village Voice* off-Bway (Obie) awards.

Recreation. Music, horses, cats.

MEADE, JULIA. Actress. b. Dec. 17, 1928, Boston, Mass., to Adam and Caroline (Meade) Kunze. Father, businessman, mother, actress. Grad. Ridgewood, N.J., H.S. 1945; attended Yale Univ. Sch. of Drama, 1945–48. Married May 17, 1952, to Oliver Worsham Rudd, commercial artist; two daughters. Member of AEA; AFTRA; SAG.

Theatre. Miss Meade made her debut in the historical drama, *The Lost Colony* (Manteo, N.C., 1947); her Bway debut as Jessica Collins in *The Tender Trap* (Longacre Th., Oct. 12, 1954) subsequently, appeared as Gilian Holroyd in *Bell, Book and Candle* (Kennebunkport Playhouse, Me., 1956); Laura Reynolds in *Tea and Sympathy* (Newport Playhouse, R.I., Aug. 6, 1956); Dinah Lawrence in *Double in Hearts* (John Golden Th., N.Y.C., Oct. 16, 1956); Beauty in *The Love of Four Colonels* (Bucks County Playhouse, New Hope, Pa., July, 1957); Eleanor Winston in *Roman Candle* (Cort, N.Y.C., Feb. 3, 1960); Babe in *The Pajama Game* (Westbury Music Tent, L.I., N.Y., July 10, 1961); Ella Peterson in *Bells Are Ringing* (Cedar Grove, N.J., Nov. 1961); Dolly in *Once More, with Feeling* (Bucks County Playhouse, New Hope, Pa.; Ephrata Th., Pa., 1959); and appeared in *Send Me No Flowers* and *Pajama Game* (Sombrero Playhouse, Phoenix, Ariz., Mar. 13, 1962); succeeded (July 23, 1962) Barbara Bel Geddes as Mary in *Mary, Mary* (Helen Hayes Th., N.Y.C., Mar. 8, 1961); and succeeded (Aug. 13, 1962) Teresa Wright in this role on tour (opened Sacramento H.S. Aud., Calif., May 31, 1962), including an eleven-month engagement at the Blackstone Th., Chicago, Ill.

Miss Meade played Amalia Balash in *She Loves Me* (Charlotte (N.C.) Summer Th., July 21, 1964); Elizabeth in *Catch Me If You Can* (Playhouse in the Park, Philadelphia, Pa., Aug. 24, 1964); Doris Walker in *Here's Love!* (Little, Sullivan, Ill., July 6, 1965); Mary McKellaway in summer touring productions of *Mary, Mary* (North Shore Music Th., Beverly, Mass., Aug. 23, 1965; South Shore Music Circus, Cohasset, Mass., Aug. 30, 1965; and Cherry County, Mich., Playhouse, July 19, 1966); Suzy Hendrix in *Wait Until Dark* (Coconut Grove Playhouse, Miami, Fla., Feb. 27, 1967; Parker Playhouse, Ft. Lauderdale, Fla., Mar. 20, 1967); Mrs. Grant in *The Front Page* (Ethel Barrymore Th., N.Y.C., May 10, 1969); and appeared in a national tour of *Move Over, Mrs. Markham* (Sept. 18–Dec. 12, 1974).

Films. Miss Meade made her debut in *Pillow Talk* (U, 1959); subsequently, appeared in *Tammy Tell Me True* (UI, 1961); and *Zotz* (Col., 1962).

Television. Miss Meade has been a spokeswoman in television commercials (1952–to date); has appeared as an actress on Armstrong Circle Th. (CBS); The Christopher Program (Ind.); and Spotlight Playhouse (CBS); and has made guest appearances on Get the Message (ABC); and Girl Talk (ABC).

Awards. Miss Meade received the Sarah Siddons Award for her performance in the Chicago (Ill.) production of *Mary, Mary* (1963).

MEADOW, LYNNE. Artistic director, director. b. Carolyn Meadow, Nov. 12, 1946, New Haven, Conn., to Franklin and Virginia Meadow. Attended Bryn Mawr, B.A.; Yale Sch. of Drama.

Theatre. Miss Meadow is artistic director of the Manhattan Theatre Club, where she has produced seventy shows (1972–74). She directed *Jesus As Seen By His Friends* (Mar. 1973); *Shooting Gallery* (June 1973); and *The Wager* (Jan. 1974).

Recreation. Tennis, skiing.

MEDFORD, KAY. Actress. b. Kathleen Patricia Regan, Sept. 14, 1920, New York City, to James and Mary (Kelly) Regan. Father, laborer. Attended Morris H.S. Relatives in theatre: brother and sister-in-law, The Leonardos. Member of AEA; SAG; AFTRA. Address: 333 W. 56th St., New York, NY 10019, tel. (212) CI 7-6990.

Theatre. Miss Medford made her N.Y.C. debut as Madame Cherry in *Paint Your Wagon* (Shubert Th., Nov. 12, 1951); subsequently appeared in the revue, *John Murray Anderson's* Almanac (Imperial, Dec. 10, 1953); played Eadie in *Lullaby* (Lyceum, Feb. 3, 1954); Dr. Selda Barry in *Black Eyed Susan* (Playhouse, Dec. 23, 1954); appeared in the revue, *Almost Crazy* (Longacre, June 20, 1955); played Martha in *Wake Up, Darling* (Ethel Barrymore Th., May 2, 1956); and took over for Pat Marshall as Lil Campbell in *Mr. Wonderful* (Bway Th., Mar. 22, 1956).

She appeared as Sophie in *A Hole in the Head* (Plymouth, Feb. 28, 1957); Mrs. Mullin in *Carousel* (NY City Ctr., Sept. 11, 1957); Sylvi in *A Handful of Fire* (Martin Beck Th., Oct. 1, 1958); Mae Peterson in *Bye Bye Birdie* (Martin Beck Th., Apr. 14, 1960); Mary Buckley in *The Counting House* (Biltmore, Dec. 13, 1962); Oveta Turk in *The Tender Heel* (pre-Bway tryout, Curran, San Francisco, Sept. 30, 1963); Sylvia Barr in *The Heroine* (Lyceum, N.Y.C., Feb. 19, 1963); Melba Snyder in *Pal Joey* (NY City Ctr., May 29, 1963); Mrs. Brice in *Funny Girl* (Winter Garden, Mar. 26, 1964); Marion Hollander in *Don't Drink the Water* (Morosco, Nov. 17, 1966); and appeared in a summer stock production (1970) of *Light Up the Sky*.

Films. Miss Medford made her debut in *The War Against Mrs. Hadley* (MGM, 1942); followed by *Adventure* (MGM, 1945); *A Face in the Crowd* (WB, 1957); *Butterfield 8* (MGM, 1960); *The Rat Race* (Par., 1960); *Ensign Pulver* (WB, 1964); *A Fine Madness* (WB, 1966); *The Busy Body* (Par., 1967); *Funny Girl* (Col., 1968); *Angel in My Pocket* (U, 1969); and *Lola* (Amer. Inter., 1973).

Awards. Miss Medford received a *Theatre World* Award (1954); the *Variety* Poll Award (1963–64) for *Funny Girl;* and the Straw Hat Award for *Light Up the Sky* (1970–71).

MEDNICK, MURRAY. Playwright, director, poet, musician. b. Aug. 24, 1939, Brooklyn, N.Y., to Sol Joseph and Betty (Greenstein) Mednick. Father, movie projectionist. Educ. Fallsburgh (N.Y.) Central School; Brooklyn Coll., N.Y.C., 1957–60. Relative in theatre, sister, Blanche Mednick Olaik, playwright. Member of Dramatists Guild; NY Theatre Strategy (vice-pres., 1972–73; secy., 1973–74); Theatre Genesis (assoc. dir., 1971–to date). Address: c/o Theatre Genesis, St. Mark's Church, 2nd Ave. and 10th St., New York, NY 10003, tel. (202) OR 4-6377.

Theatre. Most of Mr. Mednick's work has been presented by Theatre Genesis at its theatre in St. Mark's Church, N.Y.C., beginning with *The Box* (Dec. 10, 1965), which was followed by *The Mark of Zorro* (June 17, 1966), *Guideline* (Nov. 18, 1966), *Sand* (Mar. 31, 1967), *The Hawk,* written with Tony Barsha (Oct. 13, 1967), *Willie the Germ* (May 10, 1968), and *The Hunter* (Oct. 11, 1968; Public Th., May 23, 1972). He wrote and directed *The Shadow Ripens* (Th. Five, San Diego, Calif., May 30, 1969); wrote *The Deer Kill* (Th. Genesis, N.Y.C., Apr. 30, 1970); *Cartoon* (Th. Genesis, Oct. 14, 1971); and wrote and directed *Are You Lookin'?* (Th. Genesis, Mar. 21, 1973).

Published Works. Mr. Mednick's poetry has been published in such periodicals as *The Evergreen Review, Trans-Atlantic Review,* and *Genre of Silence*.

Awards. Mr. Mednick received Rockefeller Foundation grants (1968, 1972); the Poetry Award of the National Council on the Arts (1968); the *Village Voice* off-Bway (Obie) for distinguished playwriting for *The Deer Kill* (1970); a Guggenheim Fellowship in playwriting (1973); and NY State Council on the Arts Public Service grant for playwriting (1973).

MEDOFF, MARK. Playwright, actor, teacher. b. Mark Howard Medoff, Mar. 18, 1940, Mt. Carmel, Ill., to Lawrence R. and Thelma (Butt) Medoff. Father, physician; mother, psychologist. Grad. Miami Beach (Fla.) H.S., 1958; Univ. of Miami, B.A. 1962; Stanford Univ., M.A. 1966. Married 1967 to Vicki Eisler (marr. dis.); married 1972 to Stephanie Zanotti; one daughter. Member of AEA; WGA. Address: (home) Las Cruces, NM 88001; (bus.) c/o Gilbert Parker, Curtis Brown, Ltd., 60 E. 56th St., New York, NY 10022, tel. (212) PL 5-4200.

Mr. Medoff has been associate professor of English, New Mexico State Univ., since 1966. He was previously supervisor of publications and assistant director of admissions, Capitol Radio Engineering Institute, Washington, D.C. (1962–64).

Theatre. Mr. Medoff's first produced play was *Doing a Good One for the Red Man* (New Playwrights Festival, Trinity Univ., San Antonio, Tex./Dallas Theatre Center, June 1969). Later works include *The Wager* (H B Playwrights Foundation, N.Y.C., Jan. 1973; Manhattan Th. Club, Mar. 1974; Eastside Playhouse, Oct. 21, 1974); *The Kramer* (American Conservatory Th., San Francisco, Calif., Mar. 1973; Mark Taper Forum, Los Angeles, Calif., Oct. 1973); and *When You Comin Back, Red Ryder?* (Circle Repertory Th. Co., N.Y.C., June and Nov. 1973; Eastside Playhouse, Dec. 1973). Mr. Medoff made his acting debut as Teddy in *When You Comin Back, Red Ryder?* (First Chicago Center, Ill., May 1974) and his N.Y.C. stage debut in the same role (Eastside Playhouse, July 1974).

Published Works. Among his published plays are *The Odyssey of Jeremy Jack* (1973); *Five Short Plays* (1974); and *When You Comin Back, Red Ryder?* (with *Home Movie,* a preface, 1975).

Awards. Mr. Medoff received a Guggenheim Fellowship in playwriting (1974); a *Village Voice* off-Bway (Obie) Award for distinguished playwriting (1974); the Outer Circle Critics Award for the best playwriting of the 1973–74 season; and the New Mexico State Univ. Westhofer Award for excellence in creativity (1974).

Recreation. Mr. Medoff lists his hobbies as needlepoint, guitar, and plants and says his recreation is "any sport in which there is a ball to be hit.".

MEEKER, RALPH. Actor. b. Ralph Rathgeber, Nov. 21, 1920, Minneapolis, Minn., to Ralph and Magnhild Senovia Haavig Meeker Rathgeber. Grad. Leelanau for Boys, Glen Arbor, Mich., 1938; attended Northwestern Univ., 1938–42. Studied with Alvina Krauss, 1941–42. Married July 20, 1964, to Salome Jens, actress (marr. dis. 1966). Served USN. Member of AEA; SAG; AFTRA; Rosicrucian Order A.M.O.R.C.

Pre-Theatre. Soda jerk.

Theatre. Mr. Meeker made his professional debut as the Bellboy in the national company of *The Doughgirls* (1943); and played Anthony Marston in a USO production of *Ten Little Indians* (Mediterranean area, 1944).

He was assistant stage manager, and later played Chuck in *Strange Fruit* (Royale Th., N.Y.C., Nov. 29, 1945); subsequently was assistant stage manager and understudy in *Cyrano de Bergerac* (Alvin, Oct. 8, 1946); played Mannion in *Mister Roberts* (Alvin, Feb. 18, 1947); Hal Carter in *Picnic* (Music Box, Feb. 19, 1953); Newton Reece in *Cloud 7* (John Golden Th., Feb. 14, 1958); and Sergeant Toat in *Something About a Soldier* (Ambassador, Jan. 4, 1962).

For the Lincoln Ctr. Repertory Th., he played Mickey in *After the Fall* (ANTA Washington Sq. Th., Jan. 4, 1964) and Charles Taney in *But for Whom Charlie* (ANTA Washington Sq. Th., Mar. 12, 1964); and he played Sam in *Mrs. Dally* (John Golden Th., Sept. 22, 1965) and replaced (July 6, 1971) Harold Gould as Artie Shaughnessy in *The House of Blue Leaves* (Truck and Warehouse Th., Feb. 10, 1971).

Films. He made his first appearance in *Teresa* (MGM, 1951); and was in *Four in a Jeep* (UA, 1951); *Shadow in the Sky* (MGM, 1951); *Somebody Loves Me* (Par., 1952); *The Naked Spur* (MGM, 1953); *Code Two* (MGM, 1953); *Big House U.S.A.* (UA, 1955); *Desert Sands* (UA, 1955); *Kiss Me Deadly* (UA, 1955); *A Woman's Devotion* (Rep., 1956); *Run of the Arrow* (U, 1957); *The Fuzzy Pink Nightgown* (U, 1957); *Paths of Glory* (UA, 1957); *Ada* (MGM, 1961); *Something Wild* (UA, 1961); *The Dirty Dozen* (MGM, 1967); *The St. Valentine's Day Massacre* (20th-Fox, 1967); *The Devil's Eight* (Amer. Internatl., 1969); *I Walk the Line* (Col., 1970); *The Anderson Tapes* (Col., 1972); and *The Happiness Cage* (Cinerama, 1972).

Television. He played Sergeant Dekker in *Not for Hire* (NBC, 1960); and other television programs on which he has appeared include the Loretta Young Show (NBC, 1964); Route 66 (CBS, 1964); The Doctors and the Nurses (CBS, 1964); Kraft Suspense Th., (NBC, 1964); Moment of Fear (NBC, 1965); The Long Hot Summer (ABC, 1966); FBI (ABC, 1966, 1967); Green Hornet (ABC, 1967); Custer (ABC, 1967); Tarzan (NBC, 1967); High Chaparral (ABC, 1967); Name of the Game (NBC, 1968); Ironside (NBC, 1968); Men from Shiloh (NBC, 1970); Police Surgeon (NBC, 1971); *Hard Traveling* (NET Playhouse, Feb. 4, 1971); *The Reluctant Heroes* (ABC, Nov. 23, 1971); *The Night Stalker* (ABC, Jan. 11, 1972); and The Rookies (ABC, 1975).

MEISER, EDITH. Actress, director, producer, playwright, writer. b. May 9, 1898. Grad. Liggett Sch., Detroit, Mich. Attended Kox Schule, Dresden, Germany, Ecole de la Cour de St. Pierre, Geneva, Switzerland; grad. Vassar Coll., 1921. Married 1927 to Tom McKnight, producer (marr. dis. 1943). Member of AEA; AFTRA; SAG; Cosmopolitan Club; Vassar Club. Address: 171 E. 62nd St., New York, NY 10021, tel. (212) 838-3297.

Theatre. Miss Meiser made her debut in productions with the Jessie Bonstelle Stock Co. in Detroit (June 1921) and in Providence, R.I. (1922–23); toured in *All Alone Susie* (1923); made her N.Y.C. debut as Matilda Mayhew in *The New Way* (Longacre, Dec. 4, 1923); subsequently played Katharine in *Fata Morgana* (Garrick, Mar. 3, 1924); Liesl in *The Guardsman* (Garrick, Oct. 13, 1924); appeared in the revue *Garrick Gaieties* (June 8, 1925); played the Lady with the Dog in *The Chief Thing* (Guild, Mar. 22, 1926); appeared in the second edition of *The Garrick Gaieties* (May 10, 1926); and played Dolores Barnes in *Peggy-Ann* (Vanderbilt, Dec. 27, 1926).

She appeared in vaudeville, singing songs from the *Garrick Gaieties*' revues (1927–28), including an appearance at the Palace, N.Y.C. (July 1927); played Martha Turner in *Airways, Inc.* (Grove St. Th., Feb. 20, 1929); appeared in the third edition of the *Garrick Gaieties* (Guild, June 4, 1930); played Glen Cornish in *Greater Love* (Liberty, Mar. 2, 1931); Miss Scoville in *He* (Guild, Sept. 21, 1931); and directed *Double Dummy* (Golden, Nov. 11, 1936); played Lydia Vaughn in *The Strangler Fig* (Lyceum, May 6, 1940), which she also adapted; Cornelia Abigail Pigeon in *Let's Face It* (Imperial, Oct. 29, 1941); Eadie Johnson in *Mexican Hayride* (Winter Garden, Jan. 28, 1944); Jane Daniels in *Round Trip* (Biltmore, May 29, 1945); Carrie in *The Rich Full Life* (Golden, Nov. 9, 1945); Senora Gonzales in the pre-Bway tryout of *Twilight Bar* (opened Ford's, Baltimore, Md., Mar. 12, 1946; closed Walnut, Philadelphia, Pa., Mar. 23, 1946); Melissa Morgan in the pre-Bway tryout of *The Magnificent Heel* (opened Erlanger, Buffalo, N.Y., Sept. 4, 1946; closed Natl., Washington, D.C., Sept. 14, 1946); Lydia in the pre-Bway tryout of *The Stars Weep* (opened Wilbur, Boston, Mass., Sept. 1, 1947; closed there Sept. 6, 1947); and Mrs. Clark in *I Gotta Get Out* (Cort, N.Y.C., Sept. 25, 1947).

She played Lesbia Grantham in *Getting Married* (ANTA, May 7, 1951), took over Luella Gear's role of Julia Ward McKinlock in *Sabrina Fair* (National, Nov. 11, 1953); appeared as Anita Harmon in *The Magic and the Loss* (Booth, Apr. 9, 1954); and as the Widow Yang in *The Carefree Tree* (Phoenix, Oct. 11, 1955); at the American Shakespeare Festival Th. and Academy (Stratford, Conn.), played Queen Elinor in *King John* (June 26, 1956) and Francisca in *Measure for Measure* (June 27, 1956).

Miss Meiser toured as Miss Addy in the national company of *Janus* (opened Rochester, N.Y., Aud., Sept. 27, 1956; closed Ford's, Baltimore, Md., Mar. 16, 1957); joined the company of *Happy Hunting* (Majestic, N.Y.C., Dec. 6, 1956); played Mrs. McGlove in *The Unsinkable Molly Brown* (Winter Garden, Nov. 3, 1960); returned to the American Shakespeare Festival, Stratford, Conn., as one of the Women of Canterbury in *Murder in the Cathedral* (June 19, 1966); and was in *Blithe Spirit* (Studio Arena, Buffalo, N.Y., Dec. 5, 1968).

she wrote *The Wooden O*, a play about the theatre which was presented at the 30th anniversary celebration of the Barter Theatre in Abingdon, Va., in 1962.

Films. She appeared in *Glamour Boy* (Par., 1941); *Go West, Young Lady* (Col., 1941); *Queen for a Day* (UA, 1951); *It Grows on Trees* (U, 1952); and *Middle of the Night* (Col., 1959).

Television and Radio. As a member of the production firm of McKnight and Jordan, Miss Meiser co-produced The Hall of Fame, Twenty Thousand Years in Sing-Sing, the Will Rogers Show, the Irving Berlin series, the D. W. Griffith series, the Blue Coal Mystery series and the Marx Brothers series. She wrote scripts for the Helen Hayes New Penny series, the Dr. Susan series, and the Sherlock Holmes series.

On television, she was Mrs. Miles in *The Club Bedroom* (NY Television Th., NET, Dec. 19, 1966).

Published Works. She wrote *Death Catches Up with Mr. Kluck*, which was made into a film, *Death on the Air* (Par., 1937); the novelette, *Log of a Lady on the Loose*, which was published in *Cosmopolitan* magazine, and the article, "Stranger in My Mirror," which was published in *Ladies' Home Journal*.

MEISNER, SANFORD. Teacher, actor, director. b. Aug. 31, 1905, Brooklyn, N.Y., to Herman and Bertha (Knoepfler) Meisner. Father, manufacturer. Grad. Erasmus Hall H.S., Brooklyn, N.Y.; Damrosch Inst. of Music (now Juilliard Sch. of Music), 1924; Th. Guild Sch. of Acting, 1926. Married 1940 to Peggy Meyer, actress (marr. dis. June 1947); married Dec. 17, 1947, to Betty Gooch (marr. dis. 1958). Member of AEA; SAG; AFTRA. Neighborhood Playhouse Sch.of the Theatre, 340 E. 54th St., New York, NY 10022, tel. (212) MU 8-3770.

Mr. Meisner joined the staff of the Neighborhood Playhouse Sch. of the Th. (N.Y.C.) in the fall of 1935, and became head of the school in 1936. He remained head until 1959, at which time he resigned to teach privately in Los Angeles, at the same time directing the new talent division of 20th Century-Fox (1959–61); headed the dept. of drama for the Amer. Musical Th. Acad. (N.Y.C., 1962–64); and returned to his former position as head of the Neighborhood Playhouse Sch. (1964–to date).

Theatre. Mr. Meisner made his stage debut as a Farmhand in *They Knew What They Wanted* (Garrick Th., N.Y.C., Nov. 24, 1924); appeared in the first *Garrick Gaieties* (Garrick, June 8, 1925); played Jeremy in his Th. Guild Sch. graduation class production of *Prunella* (Garrick, June 15, 1926); Blasio in *Juarez and Maximilian* (Guild, Oct. 11, 1926); Sid in *Four Walls* (John Golden Th., Sept. 19, 1927); appeared in *The Doctor's Dilemma* (Guild, Nov. 21, 1927); played a Papal Courier in *Marco Millions* (Guild, Jan. 9, 1928); and a Clerk of the Court in *Volpone* (Guild, Apr. 9, 1928).

He appeared in a revival of *Gods of the Lightning* (Provincetown Playhouse, Feb. 18, 1931). As an original member of the Group Th., he joined (Oct. 1931) the cast of their production of *The House of Connelly* (Martin Beck Th., Sept. 28, 1931); appeared in *1931* (Mansfield, Dec. 10, 1931); played Don Miguel in *Night Over Taos* (48 St. Th., Mar. 9, 1932); Henri in *American Dream* (Guild, Feb. 21, 1933); Dr. Wren and Mr. Smith in *Men in White* (Broadhurst, Sept. 26, 1933); Ortega and Guy Button, Jr., in *Gold Eagle Guy* (Morosco, Nov. 28, 1934); Sam Feinschreiber in *Awake and Sing!* (Belasco, Feb. 19, 1935); with the playwright, Clifford Odets, he directed *Waiting for Lefty* (Longacre, Mar. 26, 1935). On a double-bill, he repeated his role as Sam Feinschreiber in *Awake and Sing!*, and played the Second Henchman in *Waiting for Lefty* (Belasco, Sept. 9, 1935). He portrayed Julie in *Paradise Lost* (Longacre, Dec. 9, 1935); Wiggham in *The Case of Clyde Griffiths* (Ethel Barrymore Th., Mar. 13, 1936), an adaptation of the novel, *An American Tragedy;* played Captain Valentine in *Johnny Johnson* (44th St. Th., Nov. 19, 1936); succeeded (Jan. 17, 1938) Elia Kazan as Eddie Fuselli in *Golden Boy* (Belasco, Nov. 4, 1937); and played Gilbert Kromer in *All the Living* (Fulton, Mar. 24, 1938).

Mr. Meisner played Willie Wax in *Rocket to the Moon* (Belasco, Nov. 24, 1938); again played Sam Feinschreiber in *Awake and Sing!* (Windsor, Mar. 7, 1939); Gus-the-Hurrying-Salesman and Mr. Gilbert in *Night Music* (Broadhurst, Feb. 22, 1940); directed *The Criminals* (Erwin Piscator's New School Studio Th., Dec. 20, 1941); played Sam Simpkins in *They Should Have Stood in Bed* (Mansfield, Feb. 13, 1942); directed *The Playboy of Newark* (Provincetown Playhouse, Mar. 19, 1943); *I'll Take the High Road* (Ritz, Nov. 9, 1943); *Listen Professor!* (Forrest, Dec. 22, 1943); played Bichler in *Embezzled Heaven* (National, Oct. 31, 1944); Sergei Sinitsin in *The Whole World Over* (Biltmore, Mar. 27, 1947); Marmeladoff in *Crime and Punishment* (National, Dec. 22, 1947); Ferdy in *The Bird Cage* (Coronet, Feb. 22, 1950); directed a revival of *The Time of Your Life* (NY City Ctr., Jan. 19, 1955); and played Norbert Mandel in *The Cold Wind and the Warm* (Morosco, Dec. 8, 1958).

Films. Mr. Meisner played the Prosecuting Attorney in *The Story on Page One* (20th-Fox, 1959) and the Psychoanalyst in *Tender Is the Night* (20th-Fox, 1962).

MEISTER, BARBARA ANN. Singer, actress. b. Barbara Ann Meister, Nov. 12, Los Angeles, Calif., to Carl Eugene and Dorothy Cecelia Meister. Father, cameraman; mother, musician, teacher. Grad. Pueblo Catholic H.S., Colo.; Marycrest Coll., B.A. (Music education). Studied voice with Sister Sabina Mary, Iowa; with Leila Livian, Della Hayward, and Winifred Cecil, N.Y.C.; violin with William Heinigbaum, Davenport, Iowa; acting with Mary Tarcai, N.Y.C.; dance with Loya Leporska, N.Y.C. Married Dec. 1, 1960 to Theodore Ralph Morrill, singer, actor; one son. Member of AEA; AFTRA; AGMA; AFM, Local 802.

Theatre. Miss Meister made her N.Y.C. debut with the N.Y.C. Opera Co. (NY City Ctr.), as Micaela in *Carmen Burana* (Sept. 24, 1959), followed by Yum-Yum in *The Mikado* (Oct. 1, 1959), and Despina in *Cosi Fan Tutte* (Oct. 8, 1959); toured as Kathie in *The Student Prince* (July–Aug. 1960); with the N.Y.C. Opera Co., sang Yum-Yum in *The Mikado* (NY City Ctr., Jan. 17, 1961), and Casilda in *The Gondoliers* (NY City Ctr., Jan. 25, 1961); appeared as Despina in the Metropolitan Opera Studio Production of *Cosi Fan Tutte* (Spring 1961); was standby (Nov. 1961); sang Christmas songs on *The Sound of Music* (Lunt-Fontanne, Nov. 16, 1959), and succeeded (June 4, 1962) Florence Henderson in the role in the national touring company (opened Riviera, Detroit, Mich., Feb. 27, 1961).

Television. Miss Meister made her debut as a violinist with James Melton on the Ed Sullivan Show (CBS, 1958); subsequently sang on the Peter Lind Hayes Show (ABC, 1958); appeared as Yum-Yum in *The Mikado* (Bell Telephone Hour, NBC, Summer 1959); sang on The American Musical Th. (CBS, 1960); appeared as Maria in excerpts from *West Side Story* (Bell Telephone Hour, NBC, Mar. 1961); sang Christmas songs on *The Christmas Story* (NBC, 1962); and was guest singer on the Mike Douglas Show (ABC, Cleveland, Ohio, 1963).

Night Clubs. In 1957, Miss Meister appeared as violinist and singer with James Melton throughout the US, Canada, the Palladium (London, England), the Nacional (Havana, Cuba), and in concert at the Pueblo (Colo.) Civic Auditorium.

Recreation. Gourmet cooking, collecting antiques and Chinese art, flower arranging.

MEISTER, PHILIP. Director, producer. Married to Elaine Sulka, actress and theatre executive. Address: The Cubiculo, 414 W. 51st St., New York, NY 10019.

Pre-Theatre. In the early 1950s, he served an assistantship with Serge Kousevitsky of the Boston Symphony Orchestra.

Theatre. Mr. Meister made his theatrical debut in burlesque at the age of thirteen. He was resident director at the Lennox (Mass.) Playhouse, and the Newport (R.I.) Casino; and a directing fellow at the American Shakespeare Festival. At Circle in the Square (N.Y.C.), he replaced Michael Murray as the stage manager for *The Iceman Cometh* (opened May 8, 1956); and stage managed *Children of Darkness* (Feb. 28, 1958).

He directed, and with Lionel Kaplan, produced *The Breaking Wall* (St. Marks Playhouse, Jan. 25, 1960); directed *Hop, Signor!* (Cricket, May 7, 1962); and *Happy Ending* and *Day of Absence* (St. Marks Playhouse, Nov. 15, 1965).

In 1963, Mr. Meister and his wife, Elaine Sulka, began taking theatre readings to college campuses; subsequently forming the National Shakespeare Co. (1965–to date, Philip Meister, artistic director; Elaine Sulka, managing director), which performs full productions of Shakespeare and other classics (since 1967) for colleges, high schools and elementary schools. Productions Mr. Meister has directed include *Hamlet, King Lear*, and *Hedda Gabler*.

He is founder (1968) and artistic director of The Cubiculo (Elaine Sulka, managing director); and off-off Bway facility presenting plays, poetry, music and dance produced by various groups. There, Mr. Meister has directed *# * % ! & # ! Mother!* (1969–70 season); *Sundeck* (Dec. 3, 1970); *Motherlove* (Feb. 16, 1972); *Hedda Gabler* (Feb. 20, 1974); *Klytemnestra* (Apr. 18, 1974); *The Seagull* (Dec. 5, 1974); and *Blood Wedding* (Mar. 6, 1975).

MELFI, LEONARD. Playwright. b. Feb. 21, 1935, Binghamton, N.Y., to Leonard John and Louise Marie (Grennarelli) Melfi. Attended St. Bonaventure Univ., Olean, N.Y. Served U.S. Army, 1957–58. Member of Dramatists Guild; Author's League of Amer.; Eugene O'Neill Foundation; Actors Studio (Playwrights Unit). Address: (home) 320 E. 72nd St., New York, NY 10021; (bus.) c/o William Morris Agency, 1350 Ave. of the Americas, New York, NY 10019.

Pre-Theatre. Waiter, carpenter.

Theatre. Mr. Melfi's play *Night* is included in the triple-bill *Morning, Noon and Night* (Henry Miller's Th., N.Y.C., Nov. 28, 1968); and he contributed a sketch to *Oh! Calcutta!* (Eden, June 17, 1969).

Since 1965, Mr. Melfi's work has been produced by various workshop and experimental groups including La Mama ETC, Th. Club, Th. Genesis, Th. for the New City (Los Angeles), Actors Experimental Unit Th., N.Y. Th. Strategy, Drifting Traffic, Cafe au Go Go, and The Loft Workshop. His plays include *Lazy Baby Susan, Lunchtime, Birdbath, Ferryboat, Halloween, The Shirt, Times Square, Disfiguration, Pussies and Rookies, Stars and Stripes, The Breech Baby, Sunglasses, Up Tight All Right, Niagara Falls, Wet and Dry, To Be a Sweet Child, Alive, Stimulation, Jack and Jill, Horse Opera, The Jones Man, Cinque, Beautiful!, Having Fun in the Bathroom, The Raven*

Rock, Eddie and Susanna in Love, Ah! Wine!, and *Sweet Suite.* Many of the plays have been produced subsequently by experimental theatres throughout the US and abroad.

Mr. Melfi made his acting debut in the original production of *Sweet Suite* (Th. for the New City, Los Angeles, May 31, 1975).

Other Activities. He is one of the founders (1973) of NY Theatre Strategy, a group devoted to the futherance of new playwrights and new plays. Since 1967, he has conducted workshops and lectured on playwrighting.

Awards. He has been the recipient of the Eugene O'Neill Memorial Th. Foundation Award (1966); and two Rockefeller grants (1967, 1968).

MELNITZ, WILLIAM W. Educator, writer, director. b. Apr. 14, 1900, Cologne, Germany. Attended the Univ. of Berlin, Germany, 1923; Univ. of Cologne, Germany, 1920; grad. Univ. of California at Los Angeles, Ph.D. 1947. Address: (home) 10370 Rochester Ave., Los Angeles, CA 90024, tel. (213) CR 6-1338; (bus.) Univ. of California, Los Angeles, CA 90024, tel. (213) GR 8-9711.

From 1969 to 1973, when he retired as professor emeritus, Mr. Melnitz was professor of theatre and director of the Max Reinhardt Archive, State Univ. of NY at Binghamton. He had previously retired (July 1967) as dean, College of Fine Arts, Univ. of California at Los Angeles, and professor emeritus of theatre arts, having been associated with the Dept. of Theatre Arts at UCLA since 1947 and before that with the Dept. of Germanic Languages (1942–48). Mr. Melnitz was also professor of communications and director of performing arts, Annenberg School, Univ. of Pennsylvania (1967–68).

In Europe, he was director-producer at the Volkstheatre (Vienna, Austria, 1935–38), the Schauspielhaus (Bremen, Germany, 1930–35), and the Neues Th. (Frankfurt, Germany, 1925–30). He was also general manager and director of the Municipal Th. (St. Gall, Switzerland, 1938–39).

Following his retirement at Binghamton, Mr. Melnitz returned to UCLA, where he taught graduate courses and advanced seminars in modern European theatre, conducted the Max Reinhardt centennial celebrations, and staged Goethe's *Faust.* During the period 1947 to 1967 at UCLA, Mr. Melnitz directed *Don Carlos, The Theatre of George Bernard Shaw, Readings from Boccaccio, Teach Me How to Cry, The Grand Theatre of Oscar Wilde, Light of Love, The Winter's Tale,* and *The Deadly Game* (staged at Stanford Univ., Palo Alto, Calif.).

Published Works. He is the author of *Theatre Pictorial* (1955); *The Living Stage* (9th rev. ed., 1964); *Golden Ages of the Theatre* (1962); and he contributed the essay "The Theatre and Its Continuing Social Function" to *The Arts and Man,* a world view of the role and functions of the arts in society (UNESCO, 1969). In 1967, he became a contributor to the new Muret Sanders (English-German) dictionary and in 1968 an advisory to the *Encyclopedia Britannica.*

He has written numerous articles including "Studententheatre und Theaterstudenten in Amerika," written for a book sponsored by the Institut fur Theaterwissenschaft an der Universitat Köln Verbunden mit dem Theatermuseum; *War and Revolution on the Stages of the Weimar Republic* (UCLA, doctoral dissertation, 1947); and *Theatre Arts Publications in the United States, 1947–52* (AETA, Monograph 1, 1959).

Mr. Melnitz has contributed articles to the *Hollywood Quarterly, Western Speech, Educational Theatre Journal, The Modern Language Forum, Enciclopedia Dello Spettacolo, Italian Quarterly, Quarterly Journal of Speech,* and *Encyclopedia International.*

Awards. Mr. Melnitz received the Cross of Merit, First Class, from the German Federal Government (1959); and was invited by the German Government to tour German theatres (1960). In 1967, the Regents of the Univ. of California named the second unit of UCLA's theatre arts complex Melnitz Hall.

MENOTTI, GIAN-CARLO. Composer, director, librettist. b. July 7, 1911, Cadgliano, Italy, to Alfonso and Ines (Pellini) Menotti. Attended Milan Conservatory of Music, 1923–28. Studied composition with Rosario Scalero at the Curtis Inst. of Music, Philadelphia, Pa., 1928–33. Member of ASCAP.

Theatre. Mr. Menotti wrote the opera *Amelia Goes to the Ball,* his first work to be produced (Acad. of Music, Philadelphia, Pa., Apr. 1, 1937; Metropolitan Opera House, N.Y.C., Mar. 3, 1938). He also wrote *The Island God* (Metropolitan Opera House, Feb. 20, 1942); the score and scenario for the ballet *Sebastian* (world premiere, International, Oct. 30, 1944); the opera *The Medium* (premiere, Brander Matthews Th., Columbia Univ., May 8, 1946); later presented with *The Telephone* (Heckscher, Feb. 18, 1947; Ethel Barrymore Th., May 1, 1947); the score for Martha Graham's dance *Errand into the Maze* (Ziegfeld, Feb. 28, 1947); the operas *The Consul* (Shubert, Philadelphia, Pa., Feb. 22, 1950; Ethel Barrymore Th., N.Y.C., Mar. 15, 1950); *The Saint of Bleecker Street* (Bway Th., Dec. 27, 1954); and a madrigal opera, *The Unicorn, The Gorgon, and The Manticore* (Library of Congress, Washington, D.C., Oct. 21, 1956; NY City Ctr., Jan. 15, 1957).

He wrote the libretto for Samuel Barber's opera *Vanessa* (Metropolitan Opera House, Jan. 15, 1958); the opera *Maria Golovin* (American Pavilion, Brussels World's Fair, Belgium, Aug. 20, 1958; Martin Beck Th., N.Y.C., Nov. 5, 1958); the libretto for Barber's *A Hand of Bridge* (Festival of Two Worlds, Spoleto, Italy, June 17, 1959); and the operas *The Last Savage* (Opera-Comique, Paris, Oct. 22, 1963; Metropolitan Opera House, N.Y.C., Jan. 23, 1964); *Martin's Lie* (world premiere, Bristol (England) Cathedral, June 3, 1964); *Help, Help, the Globolinks* (American premiere, Santa Fe, N.Mex., Opera, Aug. 1969; and NY City Ctr., Dec. 22, 1969); *The Most Important Man* (NY State Th., N.Y.C., Mar. 12, 1971); *Tamu-Tamu* (world premiere, Studebaker Th., Chicago, Sept. 5, 1973); *The Hero* (Philadelphia Opera Co., June 1, 1976); and *The Egg* (Amer. premiere, Washington, D.C., Cathedral, June 17, 1976). Mr. Menotti has staged the premieres of many of his works, as well as directing his own and other operas in productions around the world. In addition, he wrote, directed and composed occasional music for his play *The Leper* (world premiere, Florida State Univ., Tallahassee, Apr. 20, 1970).

Mr. Menotti founded (1958) the Festival of Two Worlds (Spoleto, Italy) of which he is president (1968–to date), having served previously (1958–68) as general manager and artistic director.

Films. Mr. Menotti directed the film version of *The Medium* (Transfilm, 1951).

Television and Radio. His radio opera, *The Old Maid and the Thief,* was first broadcast by NBC (Apr. 22, 1939). He has written two operas for television, *Amahl and the Night Visitors* (NBC, Dec. 24, 1951), and *Labyrinth* (NBC, Mar. 3, 1963). Other televised works include *The Saint of Bleecker Street* (NBC, May 15, 1955); and *Martin's Lie* (CBS Opera, May 30, 1965).

Other Activities. Mr. Menotti taught composition at the Curtis Inst. of Music, Philadelphia, Pa. (1948–55).

He has composed such orchestral works as *Piano Concerto in F* (Boston Symphony Orchestra, Nov. 2, 1945); *Apocalypse* (Pittsburgh Symphony Orchestra, Oct. 19, 1951); *Violin Concerto in A Minor* (Philadelphia Orchestra, Dec. 5, 1952); *The Death of the Bishop of Brindisi* (Cincinnati Music Festival, May 18, 1963). His other works include *Poemetti,* piano pieces for children; *Trio for a House Warming Party,* for piano, cello, and flute; *The Hero,* a song for voice and piano (words by Robert Horan); *Ricercare and Toccata on a Theme from "The Old Maid and the Thief"* for piano; *Conti Bella Lontananza,* a seven-part song cycle; *Triple Concerto;* and his first symphony, *The Halcyon.*

Published Works. The following works have been published: *Poemetti* (1937); *Amelia Goes to the Ball* (1937); *The Old Maid and the Thief* (1941); *Sebastian Ballet Suite* (1947); *The Medium* (1947); *The Telephone* (1947); *Piano Concerto in F* (1948); *Amahl and the Night Visitors* (1952); *The Hero* (1952); *Ricercare and Toccata on a Theme from "The Old Maid and the Thief"* (1953); *Violin Concerto in A Minor* (1954); *The Saint of Bleecker Street* (1955); *Concerto for Violin and Orchestra* (1955); *The Unicorn, the Gorgon, and the Manticore* (1957); *Introductions and Good-Byes,* written with Lukas Foss (1961); and *The Last Savage.*

Discography. Recordings of works by Mr. Menotti include *Amahl and the Night Visitors, Amelia Goes to the Ball, The Consul, Maria Golovin, The Medium, The Saint of Bleecker Street, Sebastian Ballet Suite, The Telephone* and *The Unicorn, the Gorgon and the Manticore.*

Awards. Mr. Menotti received the Pulitzer Prize in music and the NY Music Critics Circle Award for The Consul (1950), and The Saint of Bleecker Street (1955); and the film version of *The Medium* was awarded a prize at the International Film Festival (Cannes, France).

He was the recipient (1945) of an honorary degree of B.M. from the Curtis Inst. of Music (Philadelphia); and was named honorary associate of the National Inst. of Arts and Letters (May 6, 1953), and a Member of the Academy of St. Cecilia of Rome (Mar. 1956).

MERANDE, DORO. Actress. Address: 115 E. 39th St., New York, NY 10016.

Theatre. Miss Merande made her Bway debut as Sophie Tuttle in *Loose Moments* (Vanderbilt, Feb. 4, 1935); subsequently played Sarah in *One Good Year* (Lyceum, Nov. 27, 1935); Mildred in *Fulton of Oak Falls* (Morosco, Feb. 10, 1937); Belle Smith in *Red Harvest* (Natl., Mar. 30, 1937); Bessie in *Angel Island* (Natl., Oct. 20, 1937); and Mrs. Soames in *Our Town* (Henry Miller's Th., Feb. 4, 1938).

She appeared as Leona Yearling in *Love's Old Sweet Song* (Plymouth, May 2, 1940); Miss White in *Beverly Hills* (Fulton, Nov. 7, 1940); Miss Hogben in *The More the Merrier* (Cort, Sept. 15, 1941); succeeded Paula Laurence as Hilda in *Junior Miss* (Lyceum, Nov. 18, 1941); played A Woman in *Hope for a Harvest* (Guild, Nov. 26, 1941); Adelaide in *Three's a Family* (Longacre, May 5, 1943); Myrtle McGuire in *The Naked Genius* (Plymouth, Oct. 21, 1943); repeated the role of Mrs. Soames in *Our Town* (NY City Ctr., Jan. 10, 1944); played Miss Porter in *Pick-up Girl* (48 St. Th., May 3, 1944); Mrs. Elfie Tunison in *Violet* (Belasco, Oct. 24, 1944); Mrs. Bassett in *Hope for the Best* (Fulton, Feb. 7, 1945), Stella Springer in *The Apple of His Eye* (Biltmore, Feb. 5, 1946); Mrs. Hanmer in *The Silver Whistle* (Biltmore, Nov. 24, 1948); Soda in *The Rat Race* (Ethel Barrymore Th., Dec. 22, 1949); Jane Dupre in *Four Twelves Are 48* (48 St. Th., Jan. 17, 1951); Minnetonka Smallflower in *Lo and Behold!* (Booth, Dec. 12, 1951); Lubinka in *Diary of a Scoundrel* (Phoenix, Nov. 5, 1956); Miss Kane in the pre-Bway tryout of *This Is Goggle* (opened McCarter, Princeton, N.J., Jan. 23, 1958; closed Shubert, Washington, D.C., Feb. 1, 1958); a revival of *Detective Story* (Philadelphia, 1969); a revival of *Our Town* (Huntington Hartford Th., Hollywood, 1970); a revival of *Front Page* (Ethel Barrymore Th., N.Y.C., May 10, 1969).

Films. Miss Merande played Mrs. Soames in the screen version of *Our Town* (UA, 1940); and appeared in *The Man with the Golden Arm* (UA, 1955); *The Seven Year Itch* (20th-Fox, 1955); *The Remarkable Mr. Pennypacker* (20th-Fox, 1959); *The Gazebo* (MGM, 1959); *The Cardinal* (Col., 1963); *Kiss Me Stupid* (Lopert, Dec., 1964); *The Russians Are Coming! The Russians Are Coming!* (U, May 1966); *Change of Habit* (U, Jan. 1970); *Making It* (20th-Fox, Jan. 25, 1971); and *Front Page* (U, 1974).

Television. Miss Merande's appearances include Sam Benedict (CBS, 1960); the Bringing Up Buddy series (CBS, 1961–63); and That Was the Week That Was (NBC, 1963–64).

MERCER, MARIAN. Actress, singer. b. Marian E. Mercer, Nov. 26, 1935, Akron, Ohio, to Samuel and Nelle Mercer. Grad. Garfield H.S., Akron, 1953; Univ. of Michigan, B. Mus., 1957. Studied voice with Frances Greer, N.Y.C. Married 1965 to Martin Cassidy, actor.

Theatre. Miss Mercer made her first appearance on a stage as Annie Oakley, in a Garfield H.S. production of *Annie Get Your Gun* (June 1953); and later appeared in *Gentlemen, the Queens* (Ann Arbor Dramatic Festival, Mich., May 1954). In stock she appeared in *The Happiest Millionaire, Holiday for Lovers,* and *A Hole in the Head* (Palmtree Playhouse, Sarasota, Fla., Oct. 1957–Apr. 1958); *The Ballad of Baby Doe, Showboat,* and *The Most Happy Fella* (Cleveland Musicarnival, Ohio, May–Sept. 1958); *The Waltz of the Toreadors* (Rickaway Th., Newark, N.J., Oct. 1958); *The Student Prince, Guys and Dolls,* and *The Pajama Game* (Palm Beach Musicarnival, Fla., Dec. 1958–May 1959); and toured summer theatres in *Bells Are Ringing* (Westport County Playhouse, Conn., Nyack, N.Y.; Philadelphia, Pa.; June–Aug. 1959).

She made her N.Y.C. debut as Marcelle in an ELT production of *Hotel Paradiso* (Lenox Hill Playhouse, Sept. 1959); appeared as a singer and understudied Elaine Swann as Maidy in *Greenwillow* (Alvin, Mar. 8, 1960); and appeared in summer stock productions of *The Tunnel of Love, Odd Man In,* and *Lady Be Good* (Totem Pole Playhouse, Fayetteville, Pa., June–Sept. 1960).

She joined (Sept. 1960) the cast of *Fiorello!* (Broadhurst, N.Y.C., Nov. 23, 1959); took over for Eileen Brennan as Mary in *Little Mary Sunshine* (Orpheum, Nov. 18, 1959); and appeared in *New Faces of '62* (Alvin, Feb. 1, 1962).

In stock, she played Mrs. Peterson in *Bye Bye Birdie* (Palm Beech Musicarnival, Fla., Mar. 1962); Mary in *Little Mary Sunshine* (Ann Arbor Dramatic Festival, Mich., June 1962); Tessie Tura in the Kenley Players production of *Gypsy* (Warren, Ohio, July–Aug. 1962); Mrs. Peterson in *Bye Bye Birdie* (Rochester, N.Y., Aug. 1962); Beatrice in *Much Ado About Nothing* (Shakespeare Summer Festival, Washington, D.C., June–Aug. 1963); and Mary in *Little Mary Sunshine* (Nutmeg Playhouse, Storrs, Conn., Aug. 1963).

She was in *Come to the Palace of Sin* (ANTA Matinee Th. Series, Th. de Lys, N.Y.C., Dec. 10, 1963); *. . .And in This Corner* (Downstairs at the Upstairs, Feb. 12, 1964); played Helena in *A Midsummer Night's Dream* and Beatrice in *Much Ado About Nothing* (Shakespeare Festival, Washington, D.C., Summer 1964); was in *The Game Is Up* (Upstairs at the Downstairs, N.Y.C., Sept. 29, 1964); played Marcelle Paillardin in *Hotel Passionato* (E. 74 St. Th., Oct. 22, 1965); and appeared at Loretto-Hilton Ctr. (St. Louis, Mo., 1966–67) in *Twelfth Night,* as Helena in *A Midsummer Night's Dream,* and in *Oh, What a Lovely War!* She was Olivia in *Your Own Thing* (Orpheum, N.Y.C., Jan. 13, 1968); Marge MacDougall in *Promises, Promises* (Sam S. Shubert Th., Dec. 1, 1968); Desdemona in *Othello* (Loretto-Hilton Ctr., St. Louis, Jan. 22, 1970); Polly in *A Place for Polly* (Ethel Barrymore Th., N.Y.C., Apr. 18, 1970); and Myra Arundel in a revival of *Hay Fever* (Helen Hayes Th., Nov. 9, 1970).

She appeared with the Trinity Square Rep. Co. (Providence, R.I.) as Katherina in *The Taming of the Shrew* (Dec. 30, 1970) and as The Woman and Dinah Darling in *The Good and Bad Times of Cady Francis McCullum and Friends* (Feb. 17, 1971); was in *And Miss Reardon Drinks a Little* (Seattle Rep. Th., Seattle, Wash., Jan. 10, 1972); appeared with the Center Th. Group (Los Angeles, Calif.) as Colomba in *Volpone* (Mark Taper Forum, Mar. 9, 1972) and as Colleen in *Tadpole* (New Th. for Now, Stage B, 20th Century-Fox, Sept. 18, 1973); was in a revival of *Three Men on a Horse* (Seattle Rep. Th., Dec. 19, 1973); played Lillian in *Travellers* (Playhouse in the Park, Cincinnati, Ohio, May 2, 1974); appeared in *Petrified Man* (Th. Vanguard, Los Angeles, Calif., Sept. 26, 1974); and in a revival of *The Waltz of the Toreadors* (Seattle Rep. Th., Jan. 8, 1975).

Films. Miss Mercer appeared in *John and Mary* (20th-Fox, 1969).

Television. Miss Mercer made her debut on the Dave Garroway Show (NBC, Apr. 1961); subsequently appeared on the Mike Wallace Show (Aug. 1961); and the Andy Williams Show (NBC, Sept. 1962; May 1963).

Night Clubs. She appeared in *Prickly Pair* at the Showplace (N.Y.C., July–Nov. 1961).

Awards. For her performance in *Promises, Promises,* Miss Mercer was a *Variety* NY Drama Critics Poll winner (1968–69) as best supporting actress and received an Antoinette Perry (Tony) Award as best supporting actress in a musical.

Recreation. Music, reading, antiques, art collecting.

MEREDITH, BURGESS. Actor, director, producer. b. Nov. 16, 1908, Cleveland, Ohio, to William George and Ida Beth (Burgess) Meredith. Father, physician. Attended Cathedral Choir Sch., N.Y.C., 1920–23; Hoosac Prep. Sch., Hoosac Falls, N.Y., 1923–25; Amherst Coll., 1926–28. Married 1923, to Mrs. Helen Berrien Derby (marr. dis. summer 1935; dec. Apr. 13, 1940); married Jan. 10, 1936, to Margaret Perry, actress (marr. dis. July 1938); married May 21, 1944, to Paulette Goddard, actress (marr. dis. 1950); married to Kaja Sundsten, ballet dancer; one son, one daughter. Served WW II, US Army, ETO. Member of AEA (vice-pres. and acting pres., 1938); Actors Studio West (exec. dir., 1972–to date); Merle Oberon Th., Los Angeles (artistic dir., 1972–to date); SAG; AFTRA. Address: Mt. Ivy, Rockland County, NY 10970; P.O. Box 757, Malibu, CA 90265.

Pre-Theatre. Businessman, seaman.

Theatre. Mr. Meredith began in the theatre as an apprentice in Eve Le Gallienne's Student Repertory Group at the Civic Repertory Th. (N.Y.C.), with whom he also made his professional debut as Peter in *Romeo and Juliet* (Apr. 21, 1930).

At the Westchester County Playhouse (Mt. Kisco, N.Y.), he played Saki in *Wedding Bells* (June 16, 1930), Marchbanks in *Candida* (June 23, 1930), and the Concierge in *The Guardsman* (July 1930); repeated his performance in *Candida* (Garrick, Philadelphia, July 15, 1930; Millbrook Th., N.Y., July 1930); at the Civic Repertory Th., N.Y.C., played Grain in *The Green Cockatoo* (Oct. 9, 1930), Kratz in *Siegfried* (Oct. 20, 1930), and a Dancing Dervish in *The Would-Be Gentleman* (Mar. 12, 1931); Wick Martin in *People on the Hill* (Princess, Sept. 25, 1931); a Peon in *Night Over Taos* (48 St. Th., Mar. 9, 1932); and at the Civic Repertory Th., played Young Hollunder in *Liliom* (Oct. 26, 1932), John Napoleon Darling in *Peter Pan* (Nov. 5, 1932), and the Duck, Tweedledee, and the Dormouse in *Alice in Wonderland* (Dec. 12, 1932).

Mr. Meredith appeared as Crooked Finger Jack in *The Threepenny Opera* (Empire, Apr. 13, 1933); Red Barry in *Little Ol' Boy* (Playhouse, Apr. 24, 1933); in stock, appeared in *I Am Laughing* (Red Bank, N.J., Summer 1933); played Lord Lebanon in *Criminal at Large* (Casino, Newport, R.I., July 7, 1933); appeared in *I Want Love* (John Drew Memorial Th., East Hampton, N.Y., Aug. 1933); and *Jack Be Nimble* (Westchester County Playhouse, Mt. Kisco, N.Y., Aug. 1933); played Buz Jones in *She Loves Me Not* (46 St. Th., Nov. 20, 1933); Jim Hipper in *Hipper's Holiday* (Maxine Elliott's Th., Oct. 18, 1934); Seaman Jones in *Battleship Gertie* (Lyceum, Jan. 18, 1935); Octavius Moulton in *The Barretts of Wimpole Street* (Martin Beck Th., Feb. 24, 1935); Leonard Dobie in *Flowers of the Forest* (Martin Beck Th., Apr. 8, 1935); at the North Shore Drama Festival, appeared in *Noah* (Central Sch. Th., Glencove, L.I., N.Y., June 31, 1935).

He played Mio in *Winterset* (Martin Beck Th., N.Y.C., Sept. 25, 1935); Van Van Dorn in *High Tor* (Martin Beck Th., Jan. 8, 1937); Stephen Minch in *The Star Wagon* (Empire, Sept. 29, 1937); Prince Hal and King Henry V in the pre-Bway tryout of Orson Welles' production of *The Five Kings* (opened Boston, Jan. 20, 1939; played Washington, D.C.; closed Philadelphia, Pa.); and the title role in a revival of *Liliom* (44 St. Th., N.Y.C., Mar. 25, 1940). While in the service, he was given permission to play Marchbanks in *Candida* (Shubert, Apr. 27, 1942), for a benefit of the Army and Navy Relief Fund. In London, he was the Speaker in *Lincoln Portrait* (Royal Albert Hall, July 1943); subsequently, appeared as Christopher Mahon in *The Playboy of the Western World* (Booth, N.Y.C., Oct. 26, 1946); and repeated the part of Mio in *Winterset* (Gaiety, Dublin, Ire., Aug. 1947).

He directed *Happy as Larry* and also played Larry (Coronet, N.Y.C., Jan. 6, 1950); toured as Elwood P. Dowd in *Harvey* (Summer 1950); directed *Season in the Sun* (Cort, N.Y.C., Sept. 28, 1950); directed the pre-Bway tryout of *Let Me Hear the Melody* (opened DuPont Playhouse, Wilmington, Del., Mar. 1951; closed Philadelphia, Pa., Apr. 1951); played Gandersheim in *The Little Blue Light* (ANTA Playhouse, Apr. 21, 1951); toured as Oliver Erwenter in *The Silver Whistle* (Summer 1951); directed *Lo and Behold!* (Booth, N.Y.C., Dec. 12, 1951); and succeeded (June 1952) Hume Cronyn as Michael in *The Fourposter* (Ethel Barrymore Th., Oct. 24, 1951).

Mr. Meredith staged *The Frogs of Spring* (Broadhurst, Oct. 20, 1953); played Pa Pennypacker in *The Remarkable Mr. Pennypacker* (Coronet, Dec. 30, 1953); directed *Macbeth* (Bermudiana Th., Hamilton, Bermuda, 1954); succeeded (1954) David Wayne as Sakini in *The Teahouse of the August Moon* (Martin Beck Th., N.Y.C., Oct. 15, 1953), and toured in the national company (opened Hartman, Columbus, Ohio, Dec. 16, 1954; closed Colonial, Boston, Mass., June 23, 1956); appeared in the title role in *Hamlet* (Baylor Univ. Th., Waco, Tex., May 5, 1956); played Adolphus Cusins in *Major Barbara* (Martin Beck Th., N.Y.C., Oct. 30, 1956); produced, with Courtney Burr, *Speaking of Murder* (Royale, Dec. 19, 1956); played Dr. Lao in *The Circus of Dr. Lao* (Edgewater Beach Playhouse, Chicago, Ill., July 1957); directed *Ulysses in Nighttown,* both in N.Y.C. (Rooftop Th., June 5, 1958) and in London (Arts, May 21, 1959).

He repeated Pa Pennypacker in *The Remarkable Mr. Pennypacker* (Edgewater Beach Playhouse, Chicago, June 1958); appeared in the title role in the pre-Bway tryout of *Enrico* (opened Erlanger, Philadelphia, Pa., Nov. 3, 1958; closed there Nov. 8, 1958); directed *God and Kate Murphy* (54 St. Th., N.Y.C., Feb. 26, 1959); played the Old Man in *The Death of Cuchulain* (Beekman Tower Hotel Th., Apr. 12, 1959); and performed in *The Vagabond King* (Dallas, Tex., June, 1959).

With the Actors Workshop (San Francisco, Calif.) he played Arnold St. Clair in *The Plaster Bambino* (Marines' Memorial Th., Sept. 22, 1959); subsequently adapted and directed *A Thurber Carnival* (ANTA, N.Y.C., Feb. 26, 1960); toured in *An Evening with Burgess Meredith* (1960–62, 1965); directed *Midgie Purvis* (Martin Beck Th., Feb. 1, 1961); *A Whiff of Melancholy* (Bucks Co. Playhouse, New Hope, Pa., Aug. 21, 1961); appeared as Mr. Kicks in the pre-Bway tryout of *Mr. Kicks & Co.* (opened Arte Crown Th., Chicago, Ill., Oct. 11, 1961; closed there Oct. 14, 1961); in the title role in Eugene O'Neill's *Hughie* (Bath, Eng., June 10, 1963); directed, in association with Harris Masterson, *Forest of the Night* for the Actors' Studio (N.Y.C., 1963); directed *Blues for Mr. Charlie* (ANTA, Apr. 23, 1964); played Daniel Considine in *I Was Dancing* (Lyceum, N.Y.C., Nov. 8, 1964); directed *Dutchman* and *The Toilet* (Warner Playhouse, Los Angeles, Calif., Mar. 24, 1965); *Of Love Remembered* (ANTA, Feb. 18, 1967); *The Latent Heterosexual* (Dallas Th. Ctr., Dallas, Tex., Mar. 20, 1968; Huntington Hartford Th., Los Angeles, Calif., 1968); and *Ulysses in Nighttown* (Winter Garden, N.Y.C., Mar. 10, 1974).

Films. Mr. Meredith made his debut as Mio in *Winterset* (RKO, 1936); subsequently appeared in *There Goes the Groom* (RKO, 1937); *Spring Madness* (MGM, 1938); *Idiot's Delight* (MGM, 1939); *Of Mice and Men* (UA, 1939); *Castle on the Hudson* (WB, 1940); *San Francisco Docks* (U, 1941); *Second Chorus* (Par., 1940); *The Forgotten Village* (Mayer-Burstin, 1941); *Street of Chance* (Par., 1942); produced and played in *Welcome to Britain* for O.W.I. (Dec. 1943); produced and appeared in *Salute to France* for the O.W.I. (Mar. 1944); wrote the screenplay, co-directed and played in *The Diary of a Chambermaid* (UA, 1946); played in *The Story of G.I. Joe* (UA, 1945); *The Magnificent Doll* (U, 1946); produced and appeared in *A Miracle Can Happen* (Par., 1947); directed and appeared in *The Man on the Eiffel Tower* (RKO, 1949); appeared in *The Gay Adventure* (Allied, 1953); played the title role in *Joe Butterfly* (U, 1957); narrated the documentaries *Universe* (Canadian government, 1961); and *The Gentle Doctor* (American Veterinary Assoc., 1962); played in *Advise and Consent* (Col., 1962); *The Cardinal* (Col., 1963); *Madame X* (U, 1966); *A Big Hand for the Little Lady* (WB, 1966); *The Torture Garden* (Col., 1966); *Batman* (20th-Fox, 1966); *Hurry Sundown* (Par., 1967); *Hard Contract* (20th-Fox, 1968); *There Was a Crooked Man* (WB, 1970); *Such Good Friends* (Par., 1971); and *Day of the Locust* (Par., 1975).

Television and Radio. Mr. Meredith first appeared on radio as Red Davis for the Beechnut Company (Oct. 1934); subsequently played *Hamlet* (WABC, July 13, 1937); appeared in his own one-act play, *Something About Love* (The Overcoat) (WABC, Apr. 20, 1939); in *Fall of the City* (CBS, Sept. 28, 1939); *Pursuit of Happiness* (CBS, Nov. 15, 1939); *Spirit of '41* and *Listen America!* (War Dept., 1941–42); Cavalcade of America (NBC, 1941); and Adventure (ABC, 1951).

His first assignment for television was as director for *The Christmas Tie* (Omnibus, CBS, Nov. 30, 1952); subsequently was host and producer of Junior Ford Omnibus (NBC, 1953); Excursion (CBS, 1953); Hand in Glove (NBC, Oct. 21, 1957); and he directed *Jet Propelled Couch* (Playhouse 90, CBS, 1958). He appeared on many television programs, including *The Human Comedy* (Dupont Show of the Month, CBS, 1959); Springtime Pause to Refresh (CBS, 1959); *Ah, Wilderness!* (Hallmark Hall of Fame, NBC, 1959); Twilight Zone (CBS, 1960, 1961, 1962, 1963); *Freedom Sings* (Bell Telephone Hour, NBC, Nov. 11, 1960); *Waiting for Godot* (Play of the Week, WNTA, 1961); and he narrated the American Medical Assoc. documentary *Dr. B.* (NBC, 1961).

Mr. Meredith also appeared on *Footnote to Fame* (Westinghouse Special, 1962); Naked City (ABC, 1962); Eleventh Hour (NBC, 1962); Sam Benedict (NBC, 1962); and Ben Casey (ABC, 1962). He played Vincent Marion in 77 Sunset Strip (ABC, Sept. 20, 1963); appeared on Breaking Point (ABC, 1963); Arrest and Trial (ABC, 1963); Burke's Law (ABC, 1963, 1964); Rawhide (CBS, 1963, 1964); Wagon Train (NBC, 1963); *The Square Peg* (Bob Hope Chrysler Th., NBC, Mar. 6, 1964); *John Peter Altgeld* (Profiles in Courage, NBC, Jan. 24, 1965); and narrated the documentaries *Story of Color, Copper, American Vision,* and the *UNICEF Christmas Show* (all CBS, 1965).

Other programs on which he appeared include Laredo (NBC, 1965); 12 O'Clock High (ABC, 1966); Ironside (NBC, 1966; 1972); The Invaders (ABC, 1967); and he narrated the documentaries *Down to the Sea in Ships* (Project 20, NBC, 1967) and *Twiggy* (ABC, 1967). He also appeared on Daniel Boone (NBC, 1969); narrated the documentary *Mirror of America* (Project 20, NBC, 1969); appeared on The Bold Ones (NBC, 1970); Name of the Game (NBC, 1970); Love, American Style (ABC, 1970); Night Gallery (NBC, 1970; 1972); Man from Shiloh (NBC, 1971); World of Disney (NBC, 1971); *The Man* (ABC, 1971); *Continental Congress of 1976* (NBC, 1971); *Lock, Stock and Barrel* (NBC, 1971); Man and the City (ABC, 1971); McCloud, (NBC, 1972); *Getting Away from It All* (Movie of the Week, ABC, Jan. 18, 1972); *Probe* (NBC, Feb. 21, 1972); Mannix (CBS, 1972); and *Why He Was Late to Work* (Of Men and Women, ABC, Dec. 17, 1972).

Mr. Meredith has also done a number of "voice-overs" for such companies as United Air Lines (1972–74), Stokeley Van Camp (1973–74), General Telephone & Electronics (1974), Ralston Purina (1974), and Papermate Pen (1974).

Concerts. Mr. Meredith appeared as host and narrator with the Honolulu Symphony Orchestra (1961) and directed the NY Symphony (Carnegie Hall, 1969).

Discography. Mr. Meredith narrated the albums *The Gold Rush* (Epic-Columbia 1961) and *The Ray Bradbury Stories* (Prestige, 1962); produced and directed the album *The Declaration of Independence* (1963); and narrated *The Wonderful O* (Colpix, 1965).

Awards. Mr. Meredith received an honorary M.A. from Amherst Coll. (Mar. 18, 1939) and was nominated for an Antoinette Perry (Tony) Award (1974) for his direction of *Ulysses in Nighttown.*

MERIVALE, JOHN. Actor. b. John Herman Merivale, Dec. 1, 1917, Toronto, Ontario, Canada, to Philip and Viva (Birkett) Merivale. Father, actor; mother, actress. Attended Rugby, Warwickshire, England, 1931–36; New Coll., Oxford Univ., 1936–37. Studied acting at Old Vic Sch., London, 1937–38. Married May 3, 1941, to Jan Sterling, actress (marr. dis. 1947). Served RCAF, 1942–46, Pilot; rank, Flying Officer. Member of AEA; SAG; AFTRA; The Players; Buck's Club (London); Middlesex County Cricket Club (London); The Lords Taverners (London). c/o Buck's Club, 18 Clifford St., London W.1, England; c/o The Players, 16 Gramercy Park, New York, NY 10003.

Theatre. Mr. Merivale made his debut as Lady Macbeth in a school production of *Macbeth* (Rugby Sch., 1935); subsequently toured Germany with the International Students Drama League, playing Richard in *Richard of Bordeaux* (1935); appeared as Sebastian in *Twelfth Night* (Oxford Univ. Drama Society); with the Old Vic Co., played Mentieth in *Macbeth* (New, Nov. 26, 1937) and the Herald in *Othello* (1937–38).

He appeared in four roles in *Money Talks* (Lyceum, 1938); as a walk-on in Shakespearean productions at the Open Air Th. (Regents Park, London, 1938); made his N.Y.C. debut as Robert in *Lorelei* (Longacre, Nov. 29, 1938); toured as Flossie Nightingale in *Bachelor Born* (1939); toured summer theatres as Raleigh in *Journey's End* (1939), also playing the role on Bway (Empire, Sept. 18, 1939); and played Tony Fox-Collier in *Spring Meeting* Locust Valley, N.Y., Summer 1939).

Mr. Merivale played Balthazar and understudied Laurence Olivier as Romeo in *Romeo and Juliet* (51 St. Th., N.Y.C., May 9, 1940); appeared in *Bird in the Hand* and *Fresh Fields* (Ridgefield, Conn., Summer 1940); was a walk-on and understudied Cecil Beaton as Cecil Graham in *Lady Windermere's Fan* (Cort, N.Y.C., Oct. 14, 1946); played Eric Birling in *An Inspector Calls* (Booth, Oct. 21, 1947), also toured in it (opened Baltimore, Md., Jan. 10, 1948); Aimwell in a stock tour of *The Beaux' Stratagem* (1948); and played Mark Smeaton in the N.Y.C. production of *Anne of the Thousand Days* (Shubert, N.Y.C., Dec. 8, 1948), and on tour (1949).

He played Ernest in *The Day After Tomorrow* (Booth, N.Y.C., Oct. 26, 1950); Cecil Sykes in *Getting Married* (ANTA, May 7, 1951); Edgar, the Marquis of Chanlock, in *Venus Observed* (Century, Feb. 13, 1952); Philip Welch in *The Deep Blue Sea* (1953); succeeded Paul Scofield as Paul Gardiner in *A Question of Fact* (Piccadilly, London, Dec. 10, 1953); played David Hoylake-Johnson in *The Reluctant Debutante* (Cambridge, England, May 24, 1955), and appeared in the role in N.Y.C. (Henry Miller's Th., Oct. 10, 1956).

He toured Great Britain as a Member of Parliament in *The Holiday* (1958); played Armand in *Duel of Angels* (Helen Hayes Th., N.Y.C., Apr. 19, 1960); and on tour (opened Huntington Hartford Th., Los Angeles, Calif., July 12, 1960; closed National, Washington, D.C., Oct. 15, 1960); with the Old Vic Co. on a world tour, played Sir Andrew Aguecheek in *Twelfth Night,* Armand Duval in *The Lady of the Camellias* and Armand in *Duel of Angels* (opened Australia, June 1961; closed Rio de Janerio, Brazil, May 1962); and succeeded Louis Demonds as Algernon Moncrieff in *The Importance of Being Earnest,* later taking over Michael Allison's role of John Worthing in this production (Madison Ave. Playhouse, N.Y.C., Feb. 25, 1963).

Films. Mr. Merivale made his debut as the Newsboy in *The Invisible Man* (U, 1933); followed by appearances in *If Winter Comes* (MGM, 1947); *The Battle of the River Plate* (Pinewood, 1955); *A Night to Remember* (Lopert, 1958); *Caltiki, the Immortal Monster* (Allied, 1960); *Circus of Horrors* (Amer. Intl., 1960); *The List of Adrian Messenger* (U, 1963); and *80,000 Suspects* (Par., 1963).

Television. He appeared in *Uncle Dynamite* (Philco Television Playhouse, NBC, 1950), and on other programs in the US and England.

Recreation. Golf, tennis, music.

MERKEL, UNA. Actress. b. Dec. 10, 1903, Covington, Ky., to Arno and Bessie (Phares) Merkel. Father, traveling salesman. Attended public school, Covington; Girls' Annex, Philadelphia, Pa., Studied dance at Alviene Dance Sch., N.Y.C. Married Jan. 1, 1932, to Ronald L. Burla, aviation designer (marr. dis. 1945). Member of AEA; SAG; AFTRA. Address: 1033 S. Curson Ave., Los Angeles, CA.

Theatre. Miss Merkel made her N.Y.C. debut playing a small role in *Two by Two* (Selwyn, Feb. 23, 1925); was an extra in *The Poor Nut* (Henry Miller's Th., Apr. 27, 1925); succeeded (May 1925) Rosemary Hilton as Lenore Hastings in *Pigs* (Little, Sept. 1, 1924); later taking over the role of Mildred Cushing for the national tour (commenced Sept. 1926). She succeeded (April 1927) Charlotte Denniston as Sarah Miller in *Two Girls Wanted* (Little, Sept. 9, 1926); played Anna Sterling in *The Gossipy Sex* (Mansfield, Apr. 19, 1927); Betty Lee Reynolds in *Coquette* (Maxine Elliott's Th., Nov. 8, 1927), and on tour (1928–29); and Marion Potter in *Salt Water* (John Golden Th., N.Y.C., Nov. 26, 1929).

In the early 1940's, Miss Merkel performed in stage shows, accompanying the showings of her films; succeeded (Little, N.Y.C., Apr. 1944) Ethel Owen as Irma Dalrymple in *Three's a Family* (Longacre, May 5, 1943); played Mrs. Winemiller in *Summer and Smoke* (La Jolla Playhouse, Calif., 1951); Aunt Jane Pennypacker in *The Remarkable Mr. Pennypacker* (Coronet, N.Y.C., Dec. 30, 1953); Edna Earle Ponder in *The Ponder Heart* (Music Box, Feb. 16, 1956); Faith Barrow in the pre-Bway tryout of *Listen to the Mocking-bird* (opened Colonial, Boston, Mass., Dec. 27, 1958; closed Shubert, Washington, D.C., Jan. 29, 1959); and Essie Miller in the musical, *Take Me Along* (Shubert, Oct. 22, 1959). She has also appeared in West Coast productions of *Cradle and All; Career* (La Jolla, Calif.); as Lola in *Come Back, Little Sheba* (La Jolla, Calif.; Phoenix, Ariz.); and in *My Sister Eileen* (Santa Fe, N.M.).

Films. Since her debut in *Abraham Lincoln* (UA, 1930), Miss Merkel has appeared in *Eyes of the World* (UA, 1930); *Command Performance* (Tiffany, 1931); *Daddy Long Legs* (20th-Fox, 1931); *The Bargain (You and I)* (1st Natl., 1931); *Don't Bet on Women* (20th-Fox, 1931); *The Maltese Falcon* (WB, 1931); *The Secret Witness* (Col., 1931); *Terror by Night* (Famous Attractions, 1931); *Private Lives* (MGM, 1931); *The Bat Whispers* (UA, 1931); *Six Cylinder Love* (20th-Fox, 1931); *Wicked* (20th-Fox, 1931); *The Impatient Maiden* (U, 1932); *Red-Headed Woman* (MGM, 1932); *She Wanted a Millionaire* (20th-Fox, 1932); *Man Wanted* (WB, 1932); *Huddle* (MGM, 1932); *They Call It Sin* (1st Natl., 1932); *The Silent Witness* (20th-Fox, 1932); *Midnight Mary* (MGM, 1933); *Beauty for Sale* (MGM, 1933); *Broadway to Hollywood* (MGM, 1933); *Clear All Wires* (MGM, 1933); *The Secret of Madame Blanche* (MGM, 1933); *Stage Mother* (MGM, 1933); *Reunion in Vienna* (MGM, 1933); *Bombshell* (MGM, 1933); *Day of Reckoning* (MGM, 1933); *Whistling in the Dark* (MGM, 1933); *Men Are Such Fools* (RKO, 1933); *42nd Street* (WB, 1933); *Clear All Wires* (MGM, 1933); *The Women in His Life* (MGM, 1933); *Her First Mate* (U, 1933); *Private Lives* (MGM, 1934); *Merry Widow* (MGM, 1934); *Cat's Paw* (20th-Fox, 1934); *Murder in the Private Car* (MGM, 1934); *This Side of Heaven* (MGM, 1934);

Have a Heart (MGM, 1934); *Paris Interlude* (MGM, 1934); *Bulldog Drummond Strikes Back* (UA, 1934); *Evelyn Prentice* (MGM, 1934); *Baby Face Harrington* (MGM, 1935); *Biography of a Bachelor Girl* (MGM, 1935); *The Night Is Young* (MGM, 1935); *Broadway Melody of 1936* (MGM, 1935); *It's in the Air* (MGM, 1935); *Murder in the Fleet* (MGM, 1935); *Riffraff* (MGM, 1935); *One New York Night* (MGM, 1935); *Speed* (MGM, 1936); *Born to Dance* (MGM, 1936); *He Went to College* (MGM, 1936); *The Good Old Soak* (MGM, 1937); *Don't Tell the Wife* (RKO, 1937); *True Confession* (Par., 1937); *Checkers* (20th-Fox, 1937); *Saratoga* (MGM, 1937); *Test Pilot* (MGM, 1938); *Destry Rides Again* (U, 1939); *On Borrowed Time* (MGM, 1939); *Some Like It Hot* (Par., 1939); *Four Girls in White* (MGM, 1939); *Saturday's Children* (WB, 1940); *The Bank Dick* (U, 1940); *Sandy Gets Her Man* (U, 1940); *Comin' Round the Mountain* (Par., 1940); *Double Date* (U, 1941); *Road to Zanzibar* (Par., 1941); *The Mad Doctor of Market Street* (U, 1942); *Twin Beds* (UA, 1942); *This Is the Army* (WB, 1943); *Sweethearts of the USA* (Monogram, 1944); a short, *To Heir Is Human* (1944); *It's a Joke, Son!* (Eagle Lion, 1947); *The Man from Texas* (Eagle Lion, 1948); *The Bride Goes Wild* (MGM, 1948); *Kill the Umpire* (Col., 1950); *Emergency Wedding* (Col., 1950); *My Blue Heaven* (20th-Fox, 1950); *Rich, Young and Pretty* (MGM, 1951); *Golden Girl* (20th-Fox, 1951); *A Millionaire for Christy* (20th-Fox, 1951); *With a Song in My Heart* (20th-Fox, 1952); *The Merry Widow* (MGM, 1952); *I Love Melvin* (MGM, 1953); *The Kentuckian* (UA, 1955); *The Kettles in the Ozarks* (U, 1956); *Bundle of Joy* (RKO, 1956); *The Girl Most Likely* (U, 1957); *The Fuzzy Pink Nightgown* (UA, 1957); *The Mating Game* (MGM, 1959); *Summer and Smoke* (Par. 1961); *The Parent Trap* (Buena Vista, 1961); *Summer Magic* (Buena Vista, 1963); *A Tiger Walks* (Buena Vista, 1964); and *Spinout* (MGM, 1966).

Television and Radio. Miss Merkel performed on the Texaco Star Th. radio series (CBS, 1938).

She has appeared on Studio One (CBS), Kraft Television Th. (NBC), Playhouse 90 (CBS), Climax! (CBS), played the Mother in *Aladdin* (CBS, Feb. 21, 1958); appeared on Destry (ABC); Burke's Law (ABC); the Cara Williams Show (CBS); The Real McCoys (CBS); I Spy (ABC); and others.

Awards. Miss Merkel received the Antoinette Perry (Tony) Award (1956) for her performance as Edna Earl Ponder in *The Ponder Heart;* and an Academy (Oscar) Award nomination for her performance as Mrs. Winemiller in *Summer and Smoke* (1961).

Recreation. Reading, walking, traveling.

MERLIN, JOANNA. Actress. b. Joann Ratner, July 15, 1931, Chicago, Ill., to Harry and Toni (Merlin) Ratner. Father, grocer. Attended Hyde Park H.S., Chicago, 1945; Univ. of Chicago Lab Sch. 1945–46; grad. Fairfax H.S., Los Angeles 1949; attended Univ. of California at Los Angeles, 1949–51; Amer. Shakespeare Festival Th., and Acad., N.Y.C., 1957–58. Studied in Los Angeles with Benjamin Zemach, 1947–50; and Michael Chekhov, 1950–1955; with Morris Carnovsky, 1 yr.; Uta Hagen, 1961; Fanny Bradshaw, 1957–58, and with Tamara Daykarhanova, 1962–to date. Married Dec. 17, 1950, to Martin Lubner, artist, teacher; (marr. dis. 1957); married Mar. 1, 1964, to David Dretzin, attorney. Member of AEA; AFTRA; SAG.

Pre-Theatre. Secretary.

Theatre. Miss Merlin first appeared on stage in a Chicago (Ill.) production of *Too Many Marys* (1942); and made her professional debut in Hollywood (Calif.) as Pilar in *Bullfight* (New Hampshire Playhouse, 1956).

In NYC, she played an Athenian Girl and was understudy for the role of Myrrhina in an ELT production of *Lysistrata* (Lenox Hill Playhouse, 1956); appeared as Gina in *The Pigeon* (Temple Th., 1957); and at the Amer. Shakespeare Festival (Stratford, Conn., 1958) in walk-on roles in *Hamlet,* (June 19) and *A Midsummer Night's Dream* (June 20); and played Emilia in *The Winter's Tale* (July 20).

At the Rockland County (N.Y.) Playhouse, she appeared as Isolde in *Tunnel of Love;* Mrs. Frank in *The Diary of Anne Frank;* Helena in *Look Back in Anger;* and Esther in *The Flowering Peach* (Summer 1959); played Barbara in *Major Barbara* (Murray Dodge Th., Princeton, N.J., July 1960); Catherine in *The Winslow Boy* (Tenthouse, Highland Park, Ill., Aug. 1960); Gina in *Right You Are,* with the APA (McCarter Th., Princeton, N.J., 1960); Rosetta in *No Trifling with Love* (St. Marks Playhouse, N.Y.C., Nov. 9, 1959); and Anita di Speranza in *The Breaking Wall* (St. Mark's Playhouse, Jan. 25, 1960).

She played Silia Gala in *The Rules of the Game* (Gramercy Arts, Dec. 19, 1960); made her Bway debut when she replaced (Feb. 1961) Dran Seitz as Gwendolyn in *Becket* (St. James, Oct. 5, 1960), on tour and continued in the part in the return engagement (Hudson, N.Y.C., May 8, 1961); succeeded (Sept. 1961) Salome Jens as Martha Freud in *A Far Country* (Music Box, Apr. 4, 1961), in which she later toured; appeared as Poppaea Sabina in *The Emperor* (Maidman, N.Y.C., Apr. 16, 1963); succeeded (July 1963) Maureen McNally as the Stepdaughter in *Six Characters in Search of an Author* (Martinique, May 7, 1963); played Dawnthea in *Thistle in My Bed* (Gramercy Arts, Nov. 19, 1963); Rachel Apt in *The Wall* (Arena Stage, Washington, D.C., Jan. 29, 1964); portrayed Tzeitl in *Fiddler on the Roof* (Imperial, N.Y.C., Sept. 22, 1964); Gertrude Glass in *The Bind, the Bear and the Actress* (Eugene O'Neill Memorial Th., Waterford, Conn., Aug. 6, 1966); Gloria in *Shelter* (John Golden Th., N.Y.C., Feb. 6, 1973); and was standby for Elizabeth Wilson as Sonya in *Uncle Vanya* (Circle in the Square, June 7, 1973).

Films. Miss Merlin played Jethro's Daughter in *The Ten Commandments* (Par., 1956); Myra in *The Key,* a documentary (Campus, 1957); Josie in *Weddings and Babies* (Morris Engel Assn., 1957); in *The Pusher* (UA, 1960); and in *Anatomy of a Disease,* a documentary (Vision Assn., 1962).

Television. She appeared in Great *Jewish Stories* (WOR, 1957); *The Oresteia* (Omnibus, NBC, 1960); *Seven Who Were Hanged* (CBS, 1960); as Delgado's Wife in *The Power and the Glory* (CBS, 1961); Gloria in *King Stainislaus and the Knights of the Round Table* (Naked City, ABC, 1962); Lucia Lopez in a pilot film for East Side/West Side (CBS, 1962); and as Mrs. Martinez in *The Bagman* (The Defenders, CBS, 1963).

Recreation. Folk guitar.

MERMAN, ETHEL. Singer, actress. b. Ethal Zimmerman, Jan. 16, 1909, Astoria, N.Y., to Edward and Agnes Zimmerman. Grad. William Cullen Bryant H.S., N.Y.C. Married Nov. 16, 1940, to William B. Smith (marr. dis. 1941); married 1941 to Robert D. Levitt (marr. dis. 1952; dec. 1958); one son, one daughter; married 1953 to Robert F. Six (marr. dis. 1960); married 1964 to Ernest Borgnine, actor (marr. dis. 1964). Member of AEA; SAG; AFTRA; AGVA.

Pre-Theatre. Stenographer.

Theatre. Miss Merman first performed in cabarets (1928); and appeared in vaudeville with Clayton, Jackson & Durante (Palace Th., N.Y.C., 1929).

She made her Bway debut as Kate Fothergill in *Girl Crazy* (Alvin, Oct. 14, 1930); appeared in the revue *George White's Scandals* (Apollo, Sept. 14, 1931); played Wanda Brill in *Take a Chance* (Apollo, Nov. 26, 1932); Reno Sweeney in *Anthing Goes* (Alvin, Nov. 21, 1934); "Nails" O'Reilly Duquesne in *Red, Hot and Blue!* (Alvin, Oct. 29, 1936) Jeannette Adair in *Stars in Your Eyes* (Majestic, Feb. 9, 1939); appeared in the title role in *DuBarry Was a Lady* (46 St. Th., Dec. 6, 1939); played Hattie Maloney in *Panama Hattie* (46 St. Th., Oct. 30, 1940); Blossom Hart in *Something for the Boys* (Alvin, Jan. 7, 1943); Annie Oakley in *Annie Get Your Gun* (Imperial, May 16, 1946); Mrs. Sally Adams in *Call Me Madam* (Imperial, Oct. 12, 1950); Liz Livingston in *Happy Hunting* (Majestic, Dec. 6, 1956); Rose in *Gypsy* (Bway Th., May 21, 1959), and also toured in it (opened Rochester, N.Y., Aud., Mar. 26, 1961; closed Amer., St. Louis, Dec. 9, 1961).

She again played Sally Adams in *Call Me Madam* (Valley Music Th., Los Angeles, Calif., July 1965); Annie Oakley in a slightly revised version of *Annie Get Your Gun* (State Th., N.Y.C., May 31–July 9, 1966), in which she toured before re-opening in N.Y.C. (Broadway Th., Sept. 21, 1966); again repeated her performance as Sally Adams in *Call Me Madam* (Coconut Grove Playhouse, Miami, Fla., 1968); replaced (Mar. 28, 1970); Phyllis Diller as Dolly Gallagher Levi in *Hello, Dolly!* (St. James Th., N.Y.C., Jan. 16, 1964); and appeared in concert (Palladium, London, England, Sept. 1974; Pavilion, Los Angeles, Calif., Nov. 1974).

Films. Miss Merman appeared in *The Big Broadcast* (Par., 1932); *We're Not Dressing* (Par., 1934); *Kid Millions* (UA, 1934); *The Big Broadcast of 1936* (Par. 1935); *Anything Goes* (Par., 1936); *Strike Me Pink* (UA, 1936); *Happy Landing* (20th-Fox, 1938); *Alexander's Ragtime Band* (20th-Fox, 1938); *Straight, Place and Show* (20th-Fox, 1938); *Stage Door Canteen* (UA, 1943); *Call Me Madam* (20th-Fox, 1953); *There's No Business Like Show Business* (20th-Fox, 1954); and *It's a Mad, Mad, Mad, Mad World* (WB, 1963).

Television and Radio. On radio, she appeared as a guest on The Big Show (NBC), and she had her own program, Rhythm at Eight (WABC, 1935).

She was on television in *Anything Goes* (Colgate Comedy Hour, NBC, Feb. 1954); *Panama Hattie* (Best of Broadway, CBS, Nov. 1954); the Ford 50th Anniversary Program (CBS, 1953); as a guest on the Judy Garland Show (CBS); on the pilot *Maggie Brown* (CBS, 1963); on The Lucy Show (NBC, 1964); Kraft Suspense Th., (NBC, 1965); *Annie Get Your Gun* (NBC, 1967); That Girl (ABC, 1967); Batman (ABC, 1967); Tarzan (ABC, 1967); That's Life (ABC, 1968); and she was on the special *Jack Lemmon in 'S Wonderful, 'S Marvelous, 'S Gershwin* (NBC, Jan. 1972).

Published Works. Miss Merman wrote her autobiography, *Who Could Ask for Anything More?* (1955).

Discography. In addition to appearing on original cast albums of stage shows, Miss Merman recorded *Merman Sings Merman* (London 1973).

Awards. Miss Merman received *Variety* NY Drama Critics awards for her performances in *Something for the Boys* (1943), *Annie Get Your Gun* (1946), and *Gypsy* (1959). She received a Donaldson Award (1947) for *Annie Get Your Gun;* an Antoinette Perry (Tony) Award (1951) for her performance in *Call Me Madam;* a Barter Theatre of Virginia Award (1957) for her performance in *Happy Hunting;* and a Drama Desk Award (1969–70) for her outstanding performance in *Hello, Dolly!* She received special homage at the 1972 Tony award ceremonies, at which she also sang; and she was guest of honor and sang at a benefit for Project HOPE, "A Salute to Ethel Merman" (Grand Ballroom, Plaza Hotel, N.Y.C., Nov. 25, 1975).

MERRILL, BOB. Composer, lyricist. b. May 17, 1920, Atlantic City, N.J. Father, candy mfg. Grad. Simon Gratz H.S., Philadelphia, Pa., 1938; attended Temple Univ., 1939. Served US Cavalry, 1941–43; rank, Sgt. Member of ASCAP; Dramatists Guild.

Theatre. Mr. Merrill first performed on the stage as a singer and mimic in night clubs and vaudeville (1935–41); subsequently wrote the lyrics and music for *New Girl in Town* (46 St. Th., N.Y.C., May 14, 1957); *Take Me Along* (Shubert, Oct. 22, 1959); *Carnival!* (Imperial, Apr. 13, 1961); wrote the lyrics for *Funny Girl* (Winter Garden, Feb. 27, 1964); the music and lyrics for *Holly Golightly* (opened Forrest Th., Philadelphia, Oct. 10, 1966), which closed during previews under the title *Breakfast at Tiffany's* (closed Majestic, N.Y.C., Dec. 14, 1966); and *Henry, Sweet Henry* (Palace, Oct. 23, 1967); the book and lyrics for the pre-Bway tour of *Prettybelle* (opened Shubert, Boston, Feb. 1, 1971; closed Mar. 6, 1971); and the lyrics for *Sugar* (Majestic, N.Y.C., Apr. 9, 1972).

Films. Mr. Merrill has served as dialogue director for 20 motion pictures; and has contributed lyrics and music for *The Wonderful World of the Brothers Grimm* (MGM, 1962); and lyrics for *Funny Girl* (MGM, 1962).

Television. Mr. Merrill supervised network writers (NBC, 1943–44); served as a director (CBS, 1950–51) and production consultant (Cunningham & Walsh Agency, 1949–56). He wrote the lyrics for *Mr. Magoo's Christmas Carol* (NBC, 1963); and the score for *The Dangerous Christmas of Red Riding Hood* (ABC).

Published Works. Mr. Merrill has written many popular songs, including "If I Knew You Were Coming, I'd Have Baked a Cake," "How Much Is That Doggie in the Window?," "My Truly, Truly Fair," "Mambo Italiano," "Honeycomb," "Sparrow in the Treetop," "Belle, Belle, My Liberty Belle," "Tina Marie," and "Make Yourself Comfortable.".

Awards. He received the NY Drama Critics Circle Award for his lyrics and music for *New Girl in Town* (1956–57) and *Carnival!* (1960–61); and the Anglo-American Award (1966) for his lyrics to Funny Girl.

MERRILL, GARY. Actor. b. Gary Franklin Merrill, Aug. 2, 1915, Hartford, Conn., to B. Gary and Hazel (Andrews) Merrill. Father, insurance business. Grad. Loomis Sch., Windsor, Conn., 1933; attended Bowdoin Coll., 1933–34; Trinity Coll., 1934–35; studied acting with Hilda Sprong, one year; with Benno Schneider, three years. Married Nov. 1941 to Barbara Leeds, actress (marr. dis. 1950); married July 1950 to Bette Davis, actress (marr. dis. 1960); one son, two daughters. Served USAAF, Special Services, 1941–45; rank, Sgt. Member of AEA; AFTRA; SAG; Portland Country Club; Portland Yacht Club.

Theatre. Mr. Merrill made his N.Y.C. debut as an extra in *External Road* (Manhattan Opera House, Jan. 7, 1937); succeeded (June 1937) Jose Ferrer as Don Crawford in *Brother Rat* (Biltmore Th., Dec. 16, 1936), left the cast (Sept. 1937); returned (Mar. 1938) toured in the same role (1938–39); played a season of stock (Pottsville, Pa., Summer 1939); appeared as Peter Russo in *See My Lawyer* (Biltmore, N.Y.C., Sept. 27, 1939); performed in *This Is the Army* (Bway Th., July 4, 1942); subsequently appeared as Capt. McIntyre in *Winged Victory* (44 St. Th., Nov. 20, 1943).

Mr. Merrill played Paul Verrall in *Born Yesterday* (Lyceum, Feb. 4, 1946); First Lt., Robert Johnson in *At War with the Army* (Booth, Mar. 8, 1949); toured in *The World of Carl Sandburg* (opened Bushnell Memorial Aud., Hartford, Conn., Oct. 16, 1959; closed Alcazar, San Francisco, Calif., Apr. 23, 1960); Dr. Bill Hurlbird in *Step on a Crack* (Ethel Barrymore Th., N.Y.C., Oct. 17, 1962); was Robert Jordan in *The Hemingway Hero* (pre-Bway: opened Shubert Th., New Haven, Conn., Feb. 21, 1967; closed Wilbur Th., Boston, Mass., Mar. 4, 1967); and appeared in USO shows in South Vietnam (Mar.–Aug. 1970).

Films. Mr. Merrill made his debut in *Slattery's Hurricane* (20th-Fox, 1949); subsequently appeared in *Twelve O'Clock High* (20th-Fox, 1949); *All About Eve* (20th-Fox, 1950); *Where the Sidewalk Ends* (20th-Fox, 1950); *The Frogman* (20th-Fox, 1951); *Another Man's Poison* (UA, 1951); *Night without Sleep* (20th-Fox, 1952); *Decision Before Dawn* (20th-Fox, 1952); *Witness to Murder* (UA, 1954); *The Human Jungle* (Allied, 1954); *The Black Dakotas* (Col., 1954); *Crash Landing* (Col., 1958); *The Pleasure of His Company* (Par., 1959); *Mysterious Island* (Col., 1961); *Farewell in Hong Kong* (Italian, 1961); and *A Girl Named Tamiko* (Par., 1962).

He was one of the narrators of *Strange Victory* (Thomas Brandon, 1964); was in *The Woman Who Wouldn't Die* (WB, 1965); *Cast a Giant Shadow* (UA, 1966); *Around the World Under the Sea* (MGM, 1966); *Ride Beyond Vengeance* (Col., 1966); *Destination Inner Space* (Magna, 1966); *Clambake* (UA, 1967); *The Incident* (20th-Fox, 1967); *The Last Challenge* (MGM, 1967); *The Power* (MGM, 1968); and *Huck Finn* (UA, 1974).

Television and Radio. He has performed on radio in Young Doctor Malone (CBS); Theatre Guild of the Air; Gangbusters (NBC); and Superman (WOR). On television, he has appeared on many programs, including Danger (CBS); The Mask (ABC); Justice (NBC); Ben Casey (NBC); Wagon Train (NBC); Sam Benedict (NBC); Laramie (ABC); Combat (ABC); Loretta Young Show (NBC); Outer Limits (ABC); Trailmaster (ABC); Twilight Zone (ABC); Rawhide (CBS); Alfred Hitchcock Presents; was in the documentary *A Splendid Misery* (CBS, Sept. 23, 1964); was John Marshall on Profiles in Courage (NBC, Apr. 18, 1965); was narrator on *In Search of Hart Crane* (U.S.A. — Poetry, NET, Sept. 22, 1966); and was on *The American Adventure* (CBS, Mar. 8, 1973).

MESERVE, WALTER JOSEPH JR. Educator, author. b. Mar. 10, 1923, Portland, Me., to Walter Joseph and Bessie Adelia (Bailey) Meserve. Father, electotyper. Grad. Deering H.S., Portland, 1941; Bates Coll., B.A. 1947; Boston Univ., M.A. 1948; Univ. of Washington, Ph.D. 1952. Married June 28, 1947, to Virginia L. Haynes; two sons, two daughers; married 1967 to Ruth I. Vikdal. Served Army Air Force, 1943–46. Member of ATA; ASTR; Assn. for Asian Studies; Asia Soc.; Authors' Guild. Address: (home) Box 63B, RR 1, Nashville, IN 47448, tel. (317) 988-7340; (bus.) Dept. of Theatre and Drama, Indiana Univ., Bloomington, IN 47401, tel. (812) 337-4080.

Mr. Meserve was engaged by Indiana Univ. as a visiting professor (1968), and subsequently joined the permanent faculty there as professor of dramatic literature (1969–to date), and director of the East Asian Studies Program (1971–72). He advanced from instructor to full professor in the Dept. of English of the Univ. of Kansas (1951–68); and was visiting professor at Manchester (England) Univ. (1959–60), and the Univ. of California at Santa Barbara (1967–68).

Published Works. Mr. Meserve is the author of *An Outline History of American Drama* (1965), and *Robert E. Sherwood, Reluctant Moralist* (1970). He edited *The Complete Plays of William Dean Howells* (1960), *Discussions of Modern American Drama* (1966), *American Satiric Comedies*, with William R. Reardon (1969), *Modern Drama From Communist China*, with Ruth I. Meserve (1970); and edited and introduced William Dean Howells' *The Rise of Silas Lapham* (1971), *Studies in Death of a Salesman* (1972), and *Modern Literature from China*, with Ruth I. Meserve (1974). He became associate editor of *Modern Drama*in 1960, his articles appearing in that periodical, as well as in *Comparative Drama, Players, American Quarterly*, and *Childrens Theatre Review;* and he has contributed essays on drama to the *American Literary Scholarship Annual* (1967–73).

Awards. Mr. Meserve was the recipient of an American Philosophical Society grant (1959–60) for his study, "Reception of American Drama in England". At the Univ. of Kansas, he was named "Hill Teacher" (1967) for excellence in teaching. From the National Endowment for the Humanities, he received a grant (1966–67) for his work on the Modern Language Assn. edition of Howells' *The Rise of Silas Lapham;* and an NEH senior fellowship (1974–75) for work on the first volume, *From the Beginnings to 1828*, of a proposed five-volume history entitled *The Drama of the American People.*

Recreation. Tennis, canoeing, travel.

MESHKE, GEORGE LEWIS. Educator, journalist, director. b. Oct. 7, 1930, Yakima, Wash., to George Joseph and Marye Elizabeth Meshke. Father, fruit rancher. Educ. Highland H.S., Cowiche, Wash.; Washington State Univ.; Univ. of the Americas; grad. Univ. of Washington, B.A., M.A., Ph.D. (drama). US Army, 1953–55; Adjutant General Corps, Salzburg, Austria. Member of ATA; Assn. of Higher Education; Arena; Washington Assn. of Theatre Artists (secy., two terms; bd. member, three terms); Washington State Speech Assn. (theatre coordinator, state council). Address: (home) 4010 West Chestnut, Yakima, WA 98902, tel. (509) GL 3-0356; (bus.) Yakima Valley College, 16th Nob Hill, Yakima, WA 98902, tel. (509) GL 3-0356.

Since 1970, Mr. Meshke has been professor of drama and speech at Yakima Valley (Wash.) Coll., where he now serves as chairman of the newly formed Dept. of Drama. He was theatre director (1956–70) at Federal Way (Wash.) H.S., where he presented forty-two full length shows, twelve touring productions of children's shows, and eight "evenings of one-acts."

He is the founder of the Yakima Valley Coll. Laboratory Th. (1974), an experimental theatre, which operates in conjunction with the traditional theatre.

Theatre. Mr. Meshke first appeared on stage as Warren Creamer in *The Late Christopher Bean*, and as Frank Lippencot in *My Sister Eileen* (Pacific Univ., Summer 1949). He played Sir Evelyn in *Anything Goes* (Old Brewery Th., Helena, Mont., Summer 1962); directed *Ah, Wilderness!, Auntie Mame, The King and I, Oliver!*, and *Peter Pan* (Old Brewery Th., Summers 1962–66); and produced and directed *The Prime of Miss Jean Brodie, A Streetcar Named Desire, The Imaginary Invalid, The Night Thoreau Spent in Jail, A Flea in Her Ear, America Hurrah, A Taste of Honey, The House of Blue Leaves, The Miser, Conduct Unbecoming, Look Homeward, Angel, Our Town*, and *Waiting for Godot* (Yakima Valley Coll., and on tour to high schools in the area).

Published Works. He is the author of *Guidelines for Teaching Drama in Secondary School* (1971); *The Rise of Neo-Expressionism in American Drama— The Post-Kennedy Years* (1972); and, for the Yakima (Wash.) *Herald Republic*, wrote "Insights" (1973–74), a weekly column of theatre criticism, and currently writes a bi-monthly news column on the arts.

Awards. Mr. Meshke was a Danforth finalist (1970) for drama research; and was awarded honorary citizenship by the city of Helena, Mont., for his contribution to the summer theatre and children's theatre of that area.

Recreation. Mountaineering, numismatics, books, and travel.

MESSEL, OLIVER. Designer, artist. b. Oliver Hilary Sambourne Messel, Jan. 13, 1904, London, England, to Leonard and Maud Frances (Sambourne) Messel. Studied at Slade Sch. of Art, London. Served with British Army, 1940–44; rank, Capt.

Theatre. Mr. Messel designed costumes and settings for *Cochran's Revue* (Pavilion, London, Apr. 29, 1926); *This Year of Grace* (Pavilion, Mar. 22, 1928); *Wake Up and Dream* (Pavilion, Mar. 27, 1929); *Cochran's 1930 Revue* (Pavilion, Mar. 27, 1930); *Cochran's 1931 Revue* (Pavilion, Mar. 19, 1931); *Helen!* (Adelphi, Jan. 30, 1932); *The Miracle* (Lyceum, Apr. 9, 1932); *Glamorous Night* (Drury Lane, May 2, 1935); *The Country Wife* (Old Vic, London, Oct. 6, 1936; Henry Miller's Th., N.Y.C., Dec. 1, 1936); the ballet *Francesca da Rimini* (world premiere, Royal Opera House, Covent Garden, London, July 15, 1937; American premiere, Metropolitan Opera House, N.Y.C., Oct. 24, 1937); *A Midsummer Night's Dream* (Old Vic, London, 1937); *The Tempest* (Old Vic, May 29, 1940); *The Infernal Machine* (Arts, Sept. 5, 1940); for the Sadler's Wells Co., the ballet *Comus* (New, 1941); *Big Top* (His Majesty's, May 8, 1942); *The Rivals* (Criterion, Sept. 25, 1945); the ballet *The Sleeping Beauty* (Royal Opera House, Covent Garden, 1946); and *The Magic Flute* (Royal Opera House, 1947).

He designed settings for *The Play's the Thing* (Booth, N.Y.C., Apr. 28, 1948); *The Lady's Not for Burning* (Globe, London, May 11, 1949); designed the production of *Tough at the Top* (Adelphi, July 15, 1949); *Ring 'Round the Moon* (Globe, Jan. 26, 1950); *Le bourgeois gentilhomme* (Glyndebourne Opera House, 1950); *Ariadne auf Naxos* (Glyndebourne, 1950); *The Little Hut* (Lyric, London, Aug. 23, 1950); and *The Queen of Spades* (Royal Opera House, 1950).

He designed settings and costumes for *Romeo and Juliet* (Broadhurst, N.Y.C., Mar. 10, 1951); *Under the Sycamore Tree* (Aldwych, London, Apr. 23, 1952); *La Cenerentola* (Glyndebourne Opera House, 1952); *Letter from Paris* (Aldwych, Oct. 10, 1952);

the ballet, *Homage to the Queen* (Royal Opera House, Convent Garden, London, 1953); *The Little Hut* (Coronet, N.Y.C., Oct. 7, 1953); and for the Glyndebourne Opera House, *The Barber of Seville* and *Le Comte d'Ory* (1954).

He designed *The Dark Is Light Enough* (Aldwych, London, Apr. 30, 1954; ANTA, N.Y.C., Feb. 23, 1955); *House of Flowers* (Alvin, Dec. 30, 1954); *The Marriage of Figaro* (Glyndebourne Opera House, England, Edinburgh Festival, Scotland, 1955); *Zemire et Azor* (Bath Festival, England, 1955); for the Glyndebourne Opera House, *Die Entführung aus dem Serail* and *The Magic Flute* (1956); *Breath of Spring* (Cambridge, London, Mar. 26, 1958); *The School for Scandal* (Det Ny Th., Copenhagen, Denmark, Sept. 19, 1958); and the opera *Samson* (Royal Opera House, London, Nov. 15, 1958).

He designed settings and costumes for *Rashomon* (Music Box, N.Y.C., Jan. 27, 1959); *Der Rosenkavalier* (Glyndebourne Opera House, 1959); the Metropolitan Opera production of *The Marriage of Figaro* (N.Y.C., Oct. 1959); created the interiors of the Billy Rose Th. (1959); designed the sets and costumes for *Traveller without Luggage* (ANTA, Sept. 17, 1964); and *Twang* (Shaftsbury, London, Dec. 20, 1965); and was scenic designer for *Gigi* (Uris, N.Y.C., Nov. 13, 1973).

Films. Mr. Messel designed for *The Private Life of Don Juan* (UA, 1934); *Romeo and Juliet* (MGM, 1936); *Caesar and Cleopatra* (UA, 1946); *The Queen of Spades* (Stratford, 1950); and *Suddenly, Last Summer* (Col., 1959).

Other Activities. Mr. Messel has had exhibitions of masks at the Claridge Galleries (1925); designs and maquettes at the Lefevre Gallery (1933) and the Leicester Galleries (1936); portrait paintings at the Leicester Galleries (1938), paintings at the Carol Carstairs Galleries (N.Y.C., 1938); designs for the film *Queen of Spades* at the Leicester Galleries (1949); paintings and designs at the Redfern Gallery (1951) and the Sagittarius Gallery (N.Y.C., 1959); and paintings at the O'Hana Gallery (1962).

Published Works. He is the author of *Stage Designs and Costumes* (1933); his designs appear in *Romeo and Juliet* (1936), in the Folio Society's *A Midsummer Night's Dream* (1957), and in *Delightful Food* by Adrienne Allen and Marjorie Salter (1958).

Awards. Mr. Messel received a decoration for Royal Command Performance for the President of France (Covent Garden, 1950); and for a Gala Performance for the King of Sweden (1954). He is a fellow of University Coll. (London, 1956) and an honorary associate of the Regional Coll. of Art (Manchester, England, 1960).

Recreation. Gardening.

METTEN, CHARLES. Educator, actor, director. b. Charles Leo Metten, Sept. 7, 1927, Fort Bragg, Calif., to Henry Leo and Leona (Bibert) Metten. Educ. Santa Rosa, Calif., public schools; Fordham Univ., 1948; grad. Univ. of Calif. (Los Angeles), B.A. (theatre arts) 1950; M.A. (theatre arts) 1951; State Univ. of Iowa, Ph.D. (theatre arts) 1960; studied summers with Arthur Hopkins, Lee Simonson, and Maria Manton. Professional training with Estelle Harmon and James Whitmore, Los Angeles; American Conservatory Th., San Francisco. Served US Army, 1945–48. Married 1949 to Patricia Horrigan; two sons, three daughters. Member of ATA; Rocky Mountain Th. Assn.; Western Speech Assn. Address: (home) 1111 East 820 North, Provo, UT 84601, tel. (801) 375-3372; (bus.) D581 HFAC, Brigham Young Univ., Provo, UT 84601, tel. (801) 374-1211, ext. 3406. as Constantine in *The Seagull*, and Orestes in *Daughters of Atreus*.

He directed, at Santa Barbara (Calif.) H.S. (1952–55), *The Late Christopher Bean, Carousel*, and *The Red Mill;* and, at Santa Barbara Repertory Th. (1955–57), *A Doll's House, The Time of Your Life, Of Mice and Men*, and *Saint Joan*. At the Univ. Th., Univ. of Iowa (1957–60), he was Vladimir in *Waiting for Godot*, Nat Miller in *Ah, Wilderness!*, and Orgon in *The Imaginary Invalid;* at the Univ. Th., Univ. of Nevada, Reno (1960–62), he directed *The Male Animal, Rashomon*, and *Our Town;* and for the Utah Shakespeare Festival, he directed *Julius Caesar* (1966). With the American Conservatory Th., San Francisco, Calif. (1969), he did walk-on parts in *Hamlet, Little Murders*, and *The Devil's Disciple* and was assistant stage manager for their productions of *The Three Sisters* and *The Architect and the Emperor of Assyria*.

At Brigham Young Univ. (1962–to date), Mr. Metten appeared in the title role of *King Lear*, as Shylock in *The Merchant of Venice*, and directed productions of *Macbeth, The Miser, The Skin of Our Teeth, Abe Lincoln in Illinois*, and *1776*. He also directed *Aida* (1968) for the university opera association.

Films. Mr. Metten worked (1960) in the Brigham Young Univ. motion picture studio on films for the Church of Jesus Christ of Latter-Day Saints.

Television. For KBYU-TV, Provo, Mr. Metten directed *In the Zone, Hello, Out There, The Happy Journey to Trenton and Camden, Riders to the Sea* (1970–73), and *An Enemy of the People* (1974).

Published Works. Mr. Metten's articles have appeared in *Western Speech Journal* (Spring 1962) and *Dramatics Magazine* (Feb. 1963).

Awards. At UCLA, Mr. Metten was named best supporting actor (1951) and at Brigham Young Univ., he received the Karl G. Maesar Creative Arts Award (1970) and was chosen as Honors Professor of the Year (1972).

Recreation. Gardening, reading, family.

MEYER, RICHARD D. Director, producer, educator. b. Richard DeWitt Meyer, Sept. 2, 1928, Springfield, Mo., to Eugene F. and Helen (O'-Doud) Meyer. Father, real estate salesman. Educ. Springfield (Mo.) H.S.; Univ. of Iowa (Summers, 1959, 1961); Columbia Univ. (Summers 1960, 1963); grad. Drury Coll., Springfield, Mo., B.A. 1950; Northwestern Univ., M.A. 1952. Married Sept. 19, 1952, to Nancy Hawkins; two sons, two daughters. Member of ATA; URTA (bd. member, 1973–to date); USITT. Address: (home) 3672 Frederick Drive, Ann Arbor, MI 48105, tel. (313) 769-6237; (bus.) Director of Theatre Programs, Mendelssohn Theatre, Univ. of Michigan, Ann Arbor, MI 48104, tel. (313) 764-0451.

Mr. Meyer was production assistant for *After the Fall* (premier: ANTA Washington Sq., N.Y.C., Jan. 23, 1964), and he directed *War Without End* (premier: Grinnell Th., Iowa, Feb. 1967) and *No Silver Saints* (Florida State Univ., Tallahassee, Fla., Feb. 1968). At the Asolo State Th., Tallahassee, Fla., he directed *Antigone* (June 1968), *Uncle Vanya* (July 1969), *The Price* (June 1970), and *The Subject Was Roses* (May 1971). He also directed *The Threepenny Opera* (Florida State Univ., Tallahassee, Fla., Apr. 1972); at Asolo State Th., *The Devil's Disciple* (June 1972) and *The Effects of Gamma Rays on Man-in-the-Moon Marigolds* (June 1973); and he produced *Up from Paradise* (Power Center for Performing Arts, Univ. of Michigan, Ann Arbor, Apr. 1974).

Published Works. Mr. Meyer wrote, with N. Meyer, the chapter "*After the Fall:* A View from the Director's Notebook" in *Theatre: Volume II* (1965), and his articles have appeared in *Educational Theatre Journal, Theatre Arts, Western Humanities Review, Players Magazine, A Hub Publication*, and *Theatre Design and Technology*.

MICHELL, KEITH. Actor. b. Keith Joseph Michell, Dec. 1, 1928, Adelaide, S. Austl., to Joseph and Alice Maud (Aslat) Michell. Father, furniture manufacturer. Grad. Port Pirie H.S., S. Austl., 1944; Port Adelaide Teachers Coll., S. Austl., 1948; S. Austl. Sch. of Arts and Crafts, Adelaide Univ., 1948; attended Old Vic Th. School, London, Eng., 1949–50. Married Oct. 18, 1957, to Jeannette Sterke; one son, one daughter. Member of British AEA. Address: c/o Chatto & Linnit Ltd., 113 Wardour St., London W. 1, England tel. 439-4371.

Pre-Theatre. Art teacher.

Theatre. Mr. Michell made his professional debut with the Young Vic Co., with whom he toured Eng. and Europe (1950–51) as Bassanio in *The Merchant of Venice*, as Duckworth in *Black Arrow*, and as Merrythought in *Knight of the Burning Pestle*. He made his London debut as Charles II in *And So to Bed* (New Th., Oct. 17, 1951).

With the Shakespeare Memorial Theatre Co., he toured Austl. (1952–53), appearing as Orlando in *As You Like It*, and as Hotspur in *Henry IV, Part 1;* in 1954, played with the same company at Stratford-upon-Avon (Eng.) as Petruchio in *The Taming of the Shrew;* as Theseus in *A Midsummer Night's Dream;* as Tybalt in *Romeo and Juliet;* and as Troilus in *Troilus and Cressida*. He then toured New Zealand with the New Zealand Players Co. as Thomas in *The Lady's Not for Burning*. During the 1955 season at Stratford-upon-Avon, he played Macduff in Laurence Olivier's *Macbeth;* Ford in *The Merry Wives of Windsor;* Orsino in *Twelfth Night;* and Parolles in *All's Well That Ends Well*. He appeared in the title role of *Don Juan* (Royal Court, London, May 15, 1956); subsequently joined the Old Vic Co. for two seasons in London, appearing as Benedick in *Much Ado About Nothing* (Oct. 23, 1956); as Proteus in *Two Gentlemen of Verona* (Jan. 22, 1957); Antony in *Antony and Cleopatra* (Mar. 5, 1957); and as Aaron in *Titus Andronicus* (Apr. 23, 1957).

Mr. Michell played Nestor-le-Fripe in *Irma La Douce* (Lyric, July 17, 1958), repeated this role for his U.S. debut (National Th., Washington, D.C., Sept. 1960) and his first appearance in N.Y.C. (Plymouth, Sept. 29, 1960); appeared as the Vicomte de Valmont in *The Art of Seduction* (Aldwych, London, Mar. 19, 1962); performed at the first Chichester (England) Festival as Don John in *The Chances* (July 3, 1962) and as Ithocles in *The Broken Heart* (July 9, 1962); played the Count in *The Rehearsal* (Royale, N.Y.C., Sept. 23, 1963); and toured Australia in *The First Four Hundred Years*, giving excerpts from Shakespeare (Mar.–Aug. 1964).

He played Robert Browning in *Robert and Elizabeth* (Lyric, London, Oct. 20, 1964); Kain Sutherland in *Kain*, which he co-presented (Yvonne Arnaud Th., Guildford, Jan. 1966); Henry the Eighth in *King's Mare* (Garrick Th., London, July 20, 1966); appeared in the anthology *The Fire of London* (Mermaid, Sept. 1966); played Don Quixote in *Man of La Mancha* (Piccadilly, Apr. 24, 1968) and assumed the same role in the N.Y.C. production (Dec. 22, 1970); played Peter Abelard in *Abelard and Heloise* (Wyndham's, London, May 19, 1970), which he repeated in the US (Ahmanson Th., Los Angeles, Calif., 1971; Brooks Atkinson Th., N.Y.C., Mar. 10, 1971); *Hamlet* (Bankside Globe, London, England, 1972); and appeared in *Dear Love* (Comedy, 1973).

Mr. Michell was appointed director of the Chichester Festival in 1973, replacing John Clements. During his first season (beginning May 1974), presentations included *Tonight We Improvise*, in which he appeared as the Director; *Oedipus Tyrannus*, in which he played Oedipus; *A Month in the Country;* and *The Confederacy*. .

Films. Mr. Michell appeared as Harry in *True as a Turtle* (Rank, 1956); played in *Dangerous Exile* (Rank, 1957); *The Gypsy and the Gentleman* (Rank, 1957); *Hellfire Club* (New World, 1959); as Cassius in *All Night Long* (Rank, 1961); as Malcolm in *Seven Seas to Calais* (MGM, 1961); in *Prudence and the Pill* (20th-Fox, 1968); *House of Cards* (U, 1969); *The Executioner* (Col., 1970); and *Moments* (1974).

Television. Mr. Michell played Prof. Higgins in *Pygmalion* (BBC, London, Nov. 1956); Rudolph in *Mayerling Affair* (BBC, Nov. 1956); Gaston in *Traveller Without Luggage* (ATV, 1959); Paul in *Guardian Angel* (ITV, Apr. 1960); Hector in *Tiger at the Gates* (ITV, July 1960); Heathcliff in *Wuthering Heights* (BBC, 1962); Clarry in *Shifting Heart* (ITV, 1962); Cordiner in *Bergonzi Hand* (BBC, 1963); and Antony in the Spread of the Eagle series' production of *Antony and Cleopatra* (BBC, 1963).

He also appeared in *Ring Round the Moon* (BBC, Aug. 4, 1964); *Loyalties;* repeated his stage role in *Kain;* and played Sir Robert Chiltern in *An Ideal Husband. The Six Wives of Henry VIII* (BBC), in which he played King Henry VIII, and *The Story of the Marlboroughs* (BBC), were both shown on American television. Additional television appearances include the *Keith Michell Special*, the *Keith Michell Christmas Show*, *Keith Michell at the Shows*, and *Keith Michell in Concert at Chichester*.

Other Activities. An art teacher and painter, Mr. Michell has had one-man shows in London (1961, 1962), held his first art exhibition in 1959 and has exhibited several times since in London at the John Whibley Gallery and in New York at the Wright Hepburn Webster Gallery. He has done silk screen and lithographic work as well as painting.

Discography. Mr. Michell recorded *Ancient and Modern*, *At the Shows*, and *Words Words Words*, all for Spark Records.

Recreation. Painting, photography, riding.

MIDDLETON, HERMAN D. Educator. b. Herman David Middleton, Mar. 24, 1925, Sanford, Fla., to Herman David and Ruby (Hart Davis) Middleton. Father, merchant; mother, motel operator. Grad. Seminole H.S., Sanford, 1942; attended Rollins Coll., 1942–43; grad. Columbia Univ., B.S. 1948, M.A. 1949; attended New York Univ., Summer, 1950; Northwestern Univ., Summer, 1951; Univ. of Florida, 1955–56; Summers, 1956, 1960, 1962; Ph.D. 1964. Married Dec. 12, 1945, to Amelia Eggart; one son, one daughter. Served USN, 1943–46; rank, Yeoman-2 c. Member of AAUP; ANTA (founder; bd. of dirs.; vice-pres., Piedmont chapter, 1957–60); ATA; SCA; SETC (vice-pres., 1961–62, 1964–65; chmn., coll.-univ. division, 1962–63; pres., 1965–66); Southern Speech Assn. (bd. of dir., 1957–59); Bway Theatre League of Greensboro (founder and bd. of dir. (1958–60); Greensboro Community Arts Council (bd. of dir., 1961–71); N.Y. Drama and Speech Assn. (pres., 1966–67); Guilford County, N.C., Bicentennial Celebration Commission (1969–70). University of North Carolina, Greensboro, NC 24712, tel. (919) BR 5-9371.

Mr. Middleton has been professor of drama and speech and head of the Dept. of Drama and Speech at the Univ. of North Carolina since 1956, and has been the director of the University Th. there. At his request, he was assigned to full-time teaching and research in 1974. Previously, he was a member of the faculty and technical director of the University Th. at the Univ. of Delaware (1951–55); and director of dramatics and speech at Maryville Coll. (1949–50).

He has participated in outdoor historical drama as the stage manager of *Unto These Hills* (Mountainside Th., Cherokee, N.C., Summers 1952–55); the set designer of *Chucky Jack* (Hunter Hills Th., Gatlingburg, Tenn., Summer, 1956); director-designer of another production of *Chucky Jack* (Summer 1957); and the technical director of *The Confederacy* (Virginia Beach, Va., Summer 1958).

At the Univ. of North Carolina at Greensboro, his productions have been selected by the Amer. Theatre Assn. for tours abroad under the sponsorship of the USO and the US Dept. of Defense. Productions selected were *The Women* (Far East, 1959); *The Pajama Game* (North Atlantic, 1962); and *Li'l Abner* (Europe, 1966). In a national competition sponsored by the Amer. Coll. Theatre Festival involving 350 college and university theatres, his production of the *Orestia* (which he edited and directed) was one of ten selected for presentation at the John F. Kennedy Center for the Performing Arts (Washington, D.C., 1974).

Other Activities. He was acting editor of the *Delaware Dramatic Center News* (1951–52); drama critic of the Wilmington (Del.) *Sunday Star;* and wrote a theatre column for the Greensboro (N.C.) *Daily News* (1959–61).

He has contributed articles to periodicals, including *Southern Theatre*, *Player's Magazine*, *North Carolina English Teacher*, and *Theatre Crafts*.

Mr. Middleton was appointed to the Commission of the North Carolina Arts Council by Gov. Terry Sanford (1964–66).

Recreation. Swimming, gardening.

MIDDLETON, RAY. Actor, singer. b. Raymond E. Middleton, Feb. 8, 1907, Chicago, Ill., to Almor C. and Lela (Owens) Middleton. Father, railroad executive. Grad. Calumet H.S., Chicago, Ill., 1925; Univ. of Illinois, B.Mus. 1930; attended Juilliard Sch. of Music, 1935. Served USAAF, 1942–45; rank, Sgt. Member of AEA; AFTRA; SAG; AGVA.

Theatre. Mr. Middleton made his debut as John Kent in *Roberta* (New Amsterdam, N.Y.C., Nov. 18, 1933); subsequently played Washington Irving in *Knickerbocker Holiday* (Ethel Barrymore Th., Oct. 19, 1938); appeared in *George White's Scandals* (Alvin, Aug. 28, 1939); *American Jubilee* (NY World's Fair, 1940); played Frank Butler in *Annie Get Your Gun* (Imperial, May 16, 1946); Sam Cooper in *Love Life* (46 St. Th., Oct. 7, 1948); succeeded (June 1, 1950), Ezio Pinza as Emile de Becque in *South Pacific* (Majestic, Apr. 7, 1949); toured the US as a lecturer in *America in Song and Story* (1957, 1963); and played Sergeant Fielding in *Too Good To Be True* (54 St. Th., Mar. 12, 1963); Emile de Becque in *South Pacific* (Coconut Grove Playhouse, Miami, Fla., May 4, 1965; NY City Ctr., June 2, 1965); The Governor and The Innkeeper in *Man of La Mancha* (Goodspeed Opera House, East Haddam, Conn., June 24, 1965; repeated Aug. 9, 1965; ANTA Washington Square, N.Y.C., Nov. 22, 1965; and Martin Beck Th., Mar. 19, 1968); and O'Dempsey in a musical version of *Purple Dust* (Goodspeed Opera House, East Haddam, Conn., July 22, 1965).

Films. Mr. Middleton has appeared in *Gangs of Chicago* (Rep., 1940); *I Dream of Jeanie* (Rep., 1952); and *Road to Denver* (Rep., 1955); and as Thomas McKean in *1776* (Col., 1972).

Television. Mr. Middleton appeared on a segment of *Children Talk To . . .* (NBC, 1965–66); and played Joe Boyd in the TV adaptation of *Damn Yankees* (NBC, Apr. 8, 1967).

MIELZINER, JO. Scene and lighting designer, designer, lecturer, theatre architecture consultant. b. Mar. 19, 1901, Paris, France, to Leo and Ella MacKenna (Friend) Mielziner. Father, portrait painter; mother, journalist. Attended Ethical Culture Sch., N.Y.C.; Pennsylvania Acad. of Fine Arts; NAD and Arts Students League, N.Y.C. Served USMC 1818–19; USAAF (OSS), 1943–45; rank Maj. Relative in theatre: brother, Kenneth MacKenna (dec. 1961), actor and director. Member of United Scenic Artists, Local 829; Amer. Th. Planning Bd. (chmn.); USITT (dir.); Society of British Th. Lighting Designers (hon. mbr.); Century Assn.; Living Th. (bd. of Standards and Planning; chmn.); Coffee House Club. Address: 1 W. 72nd St., New York, NY 10023, tel. (212) TR 4-4733.

Theatre. Mr. Mielziner first worked professionally as both actor and scene designer with the Jessie Bonstelle Stock Co. (Detroit, Mich., June 1921).

His first association on Bway was as actor and stage manager for the Th. Guild production of *The Failures* (Garrick Th., Nov. 19, 1923); the first Bway production for which he was scene designer was *The Guardsman* (Garrick, Oct. 13, 1924); subsequently he designed the sets and lighting for *Nerves* (Comedy, Sept. 1, 1924); *That Awful Mrs. Eaton* (Morosco, Sept. 29, 1924); *Mrs. Partridge Presents* (Belmont, Jan. 5, 1925); *First Flight* (Plymouth, Sept. 17, 1925); *Caught* (39 St. Th., Oct. 5, 1925); *The Call of Life* (Comedy, Oct. 9, 1925); *The Enemy* (Times Square Th., Oct. 20, 1925); *Lucky Sam McCarver* (Playhouse, Oct. 21, 1925); *Little Eyolf* (Guild, Feb. 2, 1926); *Masque of Venice* (Mansfield, March 2, 1926); the Actors Th. production of *The Wild Duck* (48 St. Th. Feb. 24, 1925); *Unseen* (1926); *Seed of the Brute* (Little, Nov. 1, 1926); *Pygmalion* (Guild, Nov. 15, 1926); *Saturday's Children* (Booth, Jan. 26, 1927); *Right You Are If You Think you Are* (Guild, Mar. 2, 1927); *Mariners* (Plymouth, Mar. 28, 1927); and *The Second Man* (Guild, Apr. 11, 1927).

He designed the sets and lighting for *Marquise* (Biltmore, Nov. 14, 1927); the Th. Guild production of *The Doctor's Dilemma* (Guild, Nov. 21, 1927); *Fallen Angels* (49 St. Th., Dec. 1, 1927); *Cock Robin* (48 St. Th., Jan. 12, 1928); *Strange Interlude* (John Golden Th., Jan. 30, 1928); *The Grey Fox* (Playhouse, Oct. 22, 1928); *The Jealous Moon* (Majestic, Nov. 20, 1928); *The Lady Lies* (Little, Nov. 26, 1928); *A Most Immoral Lady* (Cort, Nov. 26, 1928); *Street Scene* (Playhouse, Jan. 10, 1929); *The Sky Rocket* (Lyceum, Jan. 11, 1929); *Judas* (Longacre, Jan. 24, 1929); *Meet the Prince* (Lyceum, Feb. 25, 1929); *Young Alexander* (Biltmore, Mar. 12, 1929); *The First Little Show* (Music Box, Apr. 30, 1929); *Karl and Anna* (Guild, Oct. 7, 1929); *Jenny* (Booth, Oct. 8, 1929); *First Mortgage* (Broadhurst, Oct. 10, 1929); the pre-Bway tryout of *Dread* (opened Shubert-Belasco, Washington, D.C., Oct. 20, 1929; closed Majestic, Brooklyn, N.Y., Nov. 2, 1929); *The Amorous Antic* (Masque, N.Y.C., Dec. 2, 1929); *Mrs. Cook's Tour* (closed Chicago, Ill., 1929); *Uncle Vanya* (Cort, Apr. 15, 1930) the unproduced play, *The Red General; The Second Little Show* (Royale, N.Y.C. Sept. 2, 1930); *Mr. Gilhooley* (Broadhurst, Sept. 30, 1930); *Solid South* (Lyceum, Oct. 14, 1930); *Sweet and Low* (46 St. Th., Nov. 17, 1930).

He designed the sets and lighting for *Anatol* (Lyceum, Jan. 16, 1931); *The Barretts of Wimpole Street* (Empire, Feb. 9, 1931); *The House Beautiful* (Apollo, Mar. 12, 1931); *Billy Rose's Crazy Quilt* (44 St. Th., May 19, 1931); *The Third Little Show* (Music Box, June 1, 1931); *I Love an Actress* (Times Square Th., Sept. 17, 1931); *Brief Moment* (Belasco, Nov. 9, 1931); *Of Thee I Sing* (Music Box, Dec. 26, 1931); *Never No More* (Hudson, Jan. 7, 1932); *Distant Drums* (Belasco, Jan. 18, 1932); *Bloodstream* (Times Square Th., Mar. 30, 1932); *Bridal Wise* (Cort, May 30, 1932); *The Gay Divorce* (Ethel Barrymore Th., Nov. 29, 1932); *Biography* (Guild, Dec. 12, 1932); the opera, *The Emperor Jones* (Metropolitan Opera House, Jan. 8, 1933); *Champagne, Sec* (Morosco, Oct. 14, 1933); *Divine Drudge* (Royale, Oct. 26, 1933); *I Was Waiting for You* (Booth, Nov. 13, 1933); *The Dark Tower* (Morosco, Nov. 24, 1933); *The Lake* (Martin Beck Th., Dec. 26, 1933); *By Your Leave* (Morosco, Jan. 24, 1934); *Yellow Jack* (Martin Beck Th., Mar. 6, 1934); *The Pure in Heart* (Longacre, Mar. 20, 1934); the opera, *Merrymount* (Metropolitan Opera House, Feb. 10, 1934); *Dodsworth* (Shubert, Aug. 20, 1934); *Merrily We Roll Along* (Music Box, Sept. 29, 1934); *Spring Song* (Morosco, Oct. 1, 1934); the pre-Bway tryout of *Bird of Our Fathers* (opened Garrick, Philadelphia, Pa., Nov. 29, 1934; closed National, Washington, D.C., Dec. 8, 1934); Katharine Cornell's production of *Romeo and Juliet* (Martin Beck Th., N.Y.C., Dec. 20, 1934); *Accent on Youth* (Plymouth, Dec. 25, 1934); *De Luxe* (Booth, Mar. 5, 1935); *Panic* (Imperial, Mar. 14, 1935); *Flowers of the Forest* (Martin Beck Th., Apr. 8, 1935); *Kind Lady* (Longacre, Sept. 9, 1935); *Winterset* (Martin Beck Th., Sept. 25, 1935); *Jubilee* (Imperial, Oct. 12, 1935); *Pride and Prejudice* (Music Box, Nov. 5, 1935); *Hell Freezes Over* (Ritz, Dec. 28, 1935); *A Room in Red and White* 46 St. Th., Jan. 18, 1936); *Ethan Frome* (National, Jan. 21, 1936); *Co-Respondent Unknown* (Ritz, Feb. 11, 1936); and for *The Postman Always Rings Twice* (Lyceum, Feb. 25, 1936).

He designed the sets and lighting for Katharine Cornell's production of *Saint Joan* (Martin Beck Th., Mar. 9, 1936); *On Your Toes* (Imperial, Apr. 11, 1936); sets, lighting and costumes for *St. Helena* (Lyceum, Oct. 6, 1936); John Gielgud's production of *Hamlet* (Empire, Oct. 8, 1936); sets and lighting for *Daughters of Atreus* (44 St. Th., Oct. 14, 1936); *The Wingless Victory* (Empire, Dec. 23, 1936); *The Women* (Ethel Barrymore Th., Dec. 26, 1936); *High Tor* (Martin Beck Th., Jan. 9, 1937); *The Star-Wagon* (Empire, Sept. 29, 1937); *Susan and God* (Plymouth, Oct. 7, 1937); sets, lighting and costumes for *Antony and Cleopatra* (Mansfield, Nov. 10, 1937); sets and lighting for *Too Many Heroes* (Hudson, Nov. 15, 1937); *Father Malachy's Miracle* (St. James, Nov. 17, 1937); *Barchester Towers* (Martin Beck Th., Nov. 30, 1937); *Yr. Obedient Husband* (Broadhurst, Jan. 10, 1938); *On Borrowed Time* (Longacre, Feb. 3, 1938); *Save Me the Waltz* (Martin Beck Th., Feb. 28, 1938); *I Married an Angel* (Shubert, May 11, 1938); *Sing Out the News* (Music Box, Sept. 24, 1938); *Abe Lincoln in Illinois* (Plymouth, Oct. 15, 1938); *Knickerbocker Holiday* (Ethel Barrymore Th., Oct. 19,

1938); *The Boys from Syracuse* (Alvin, Nov. 23, 1938); sets, lighting, and costumes for *Mrs. O'Brien Entertains* (Lyceum, Feb. 8, 1939); sets and lighting for *Stars in Your Eyes* (Majestic, Feb. 9, 1939); and for *No Time for Comedy* (Ethel Barrymore Th., Apr. 17, 1939).

Mr. Mielziner designed the sets and lighting for *Too Many Girls* (Imperial, Oct. 18, 1939); *Key Largo* (Ethel Barrymore Th., Nov. 27, 1939); *Mornings at Seven* (Longacre, Nov. 30, 1939); *Christmas Eve* (Henry Miller's Th., Dec. 29, 1939); *Two on an Island* (Broadhurst, Jan. 22, 1940); *Higher and Higher* (Shubert, Apr. 4, 1940); the pre-Bway tryout of *Little Dog Laughed*, which closed out of town (Aug. 20, 1940); *Journey to Jerusalem* (Natl., N.Y.C., Oct. 5, 1940); *Pal Joey* (Ethel Barrymore Th., Dec. 25, 1940); *Flight to the West* (Guild, Dec. 30, 1940); *Mr. and Mrs. North* (Belasco, Jan. 12, 1941); *The Cream in the Well* (Booth, Jan. 20, 1941); *The Talley Method* (Henry Miller's Th., Feb. 24, 1941); *Watch on the Rhine* (Martin Beck Th., Apr. 1, 1941); *The Wookey* (Plymouth, Sept. 10, 1941); *Best Foot Forward* (Ethel Barrymore Th., Oct. 1, 1941); *Candle in the Wind* (Shubert, Oct. 22, 1941); *The Land Is Bright* (Music Box, Oct. 28, 1941); *The Seventh Trumpet* (Mansfield, Nov. 21, 1941); *Solitaire* (Plymouth, Feb. 27, 1942); the ballet, *Pillar of Fire* (Metropolitan Opera House, Apr. 8, 1942); and for *By Jupiter* (Shubert, June 3, 1942).

He designed the sets and lighting for *Foolish Notion* (Martin Beck Th., Mar. 18, 1945); *The Firebrand of Florence* (Alvin, Mar. 22, 1945); *The Glass Menagerie* (Plymouth, Mar. 31, 1945); *Carousel* (Majestic, Apr. 19, 1945); *Hollywood Pinafore* (Alvin, May 31, 1945); *Carib Song* (Adelphi, Sept. 27, 1945); *Beggars Are Coming to Town* (Coronet, Oct. 27, 1945); and *The Rugged Path* (Plymouth, Nov. 10, 1945).

After designing the settings and lighting for the pre-Bway production of *St. Lazare's Pharmacy* (closed Chicago, Ill., Dec. 1945); Mr. Mielziner designed *Dream Girl* (Coronet, N.Y.C., Dec. 14, 1945); followed by the settings and lighting for *Jeb* (Martin Beck Th., Feb. 21, 1946); the pre-Bway tryout of *Windy City* (opened Shubert, New Haven, Conn., Apr. 18, 1946; closed Great Northern, Chicago, Ill., June 6, 1946); *Annie Get Your Gun* (Imperial, N.Y.C., May 16, 1946); *Happy Birthday* (Broadhurst, Oct. 31, 1946); *Another Part of the Forest* (Fulton, Nov. 20, 1946); *The Big Two* (Booth, Jan. 8, 1947); the musical version of *Street Scene* (Adelphi, Jan. 9, 1947); *Finian's Rainbow* (46 St. Th., Jan. 10, 1947); the unproduced revue *The Fourth Little Show* (1947); *The Chocolate Soldier* (Century, Mar. 12, 1947); sets and lighting for *Barefoot Boy with Cheek* (Martin Beck Th., Apr. 3, 1947); *Command Decision* (Fulton, Oct. 1, 1947); *Allegro* (Majestic, Oct. 10, 1947); *A Streetcar Named Desire* (Ethel Barrymore Th., N.Y.C., Dec. 3, 1947; Aldwych, London, Oct. 11, 1948); *Mister Roberts* (Alvin, N.Y.C., Feb. 18, 1948); the ballet, *Shadow of the Wind* (Metropolitan Opera House, Apr. 14, 1948); *Legend of Sleepy Hollow* (St. James, June 3, 1948); *Summer and Smoke* (Music Box, Oct. 6, 1948); *Anne of the Thousand Days* (Shubert, Dec. 8, 1948); *Death of a Salesman* (Morosco, Feb. 10, 1949); *South Pacific* (Majestic, Apr. 7, 1949); *The Man* (Fulton, Jan. 19, 1950); *Dance Me a Song* (Royale, Jan. 20, 1950); *The Real McCoy* (Catholic Univ., Washington, D.C., Dec. 2, 1950); *The Innocents* (Playhouse, N.Y.C., Feb. 1, 1950); *The Wisteria Trees* (Martin Beck Th., Mar. 29, 1950); *Burning Bright* (Broadhurst, Oct. 18, 1950); *Guys and Dolls* (46 St. Th., Nov. 24, 1950); *The King and I* (St. James, Mar. 29, 1951); *A Tree Grows in Brooklyn* (Alvin, Apr. 19, 1951); *Top Banana* (Winter Garden, Nov. 1, 1951); *Point of No Return* (Alvin, Dec. 13, 1951); and for the pre-Bway tryout of *A Month of Sundays* (closed Forrest Th., Philadelphia, Pa., Jan. 26, 1952).

He designed the sets and lighting for *Flight into Egypt* (Music Box, N.Y.C., Mar. 18, 1952); *Wish You Were Here* (Imperial, June 25, 1952); *The Gambler* (Lyceum, Oct. 13, 1952); *Picnic* (Music Box, Feb. 19, 1953); *Can-Can* (Shubert, N.Y.C., May 7, 1953; Coliseum, London, Oct. 14, 1954); *Me and Juliet* (Majestic, N.Y.C., May 28, 1953); *Tea and Sympathy* (Ethel Barrymore Th., Sept. 30, 1953); *Kind Sir* (Alvin, Nov. 4, 1953); *By the Beautiful Sea* (Majestic, April 8, 1954); *All Summer Long* (Coronet, Sept. 23, 1954); *Fanny* (Majestic, Nov. 4, 1954); *Silk Stockings* (Imperial, Feb. 24, 1955); *Cat on a Hot Tin Roof* (Morosco, Mar. 24, 1955); *Island of Goats* (Fulton, Oct. 4, 1955); *The Lark* (Longacre, Nov. 17, 1955); *Pipe Dream* (Shubert, Nov. 30, 1955); *Middle of the Night*, assisted by John Harvey (ANTA, Feb. 8, 1956); *The Most Happy Fella* (Imperial, May 3, 1956); *Happy Hunting* (Majestic, Dec. 6, 1956); the pre-Bway tryout of *Maiden Voyage* (opened Forrest, Philadelphia, Pa., Feb. 28, 1957; closed there Mar. 9, 1957).

Mr. Mielziner designed the sets and lighting for *Miss Lonelyhearts* (Music Box, N.Y.C., Oct. 3, 1957); *Square Root of Wonderful* (National, Oct. 30, 1957); *Look Homeward, Angel* (Ethel Barrymore Th., Nov. 28, 1957); *Oh, Captain!* (Alvin, Feb. 4, 1958); *The Day the Money Stopped* (Belasco, Feb. 20, 1958); *Handful of Fire* (Martin Beck Th., Oct. 1, 1958); *The World of Suzie Wong* (Broadhurst, Oct. 15, 1958); *The Gazebo* (Lyceum, Dec. 12, 1958); *Whoop-up!* (Shubert, Dec. 22, 1958); the lighting for *Rashomon* (Music Box, Jan. 27, 1959); the sets and lighting for *Sweet Bird of Youth* (Martin Beck Th., Mar. 10, 1959); *Gypsy* (Bway Th., May 21, 1959); *The Gang's All Here* (Ambassador, Oct. 1, 1959); *Silent Night, Lonely Night* (Morosco, Dec. 3, 1959); *There Was a Little Girl* (Cort, Feb. 29, 1960); *The Best Man* (Morosco, Mar. 31, 1960); *Christine* (46 St. Th., Apr. 28, 1960); *Period of Adjustment* (Helen Hayes Th., Nov. 10, 1960); *Little Moon of Alban* (Longacre, Dec. 1, 1960); the pre-Bway tryout of *White Alice*, which closed out of town (Dec. 26, 1960); *The Devil's Advocate* (Billy Rose Th., N.Y.C., Mar. 9, 1961); *Everybody Loves Opal* (Longacre, Oct. 11, 1961); *A Short Happy Life* (opened Moore, Seattle, Wash., Sept. 12, 1961; closed Huntington Hartford, Los Angeles, Calif., Oct. 1961); *All American* (Winter Garden, N.Y.C., Mar. 19, 1962); *Mr. President* (St. James, Oct. 20, 1962); *The Milk Train Doesn't Stop Here Anymore* (Morosco, Jan. 16, 1963); and the Lincoln Ctr., Repertory's *After the Fall* (ANTA-Washington Square Th., N.Y.C. Jan. 23, 1964) and *But for Whom Charlie* (ANTA-Washington Square Th., Mar. 12, 1964); the national tour of *After the Fall* (opened Playhouse, Wilmington, Del., Oct. 19, 1964); and for *The Owl and the Pussycat* (ANTA Th., N.Y.C., Nov. 18, 1964).

Mr. Mielziner designed scenery and lighting for *Danton's Death* (Vivian Beaumont Th., Oct. 21, 1965); *The Playroom* (Brooks Atkinson Th., Dec. 5, 1965); *Venus Is* (preview, Billy Rose Th., Apr. 9, 1966); *Don't Drink the Water* (Morosco, Nov. 17, 1966); *My Sweet Charlie* (Longacre, Dec. 6, 1966); *The Paisley Convertible* (Henry Miller's Th., Feb. 11, 1967); *That Summer—That Fall* (Helen Hayes Th., Mar. 16, 1967); and the setting for *The Unemployed Saint* (Royal Poinciana Playhouse, Palm Beach, Fla., Mar. 20–25, 1967). He did scenery and lighting for *Daphne in Cottage D* (Longacre, N.Y.C., Oct. 15, 1967); *Mata Hari* (pre-Bway, National Th., Washington, D.C. Nov. 18–Dec. 9, 1967); *The Prime of Miss Jean Brodie* (Henry Miller's Th., N.Y.C., Jan. 11, 1968); *I Never Sang for My Father* (Longacre, Jan. 25, 1968); *The Seven Descents of Myrtle* (Ethel Barrymore Th., Mar. 27, 1968); and scenery for the NY City Ballet version of the ballet *Slaughter on Tenth Avenue* (NY State Th., May 2, 1968).

He also designed scenery and lighting for *Possibilities* (Players Th., Dec. 4, 1968); *1776* (46 St. Th., Mar. 16, 1969); *The Conjuror* (Univ. of Michigan Professional Th. Program, Ann Arbor, Mich., Nov. 5, 1969); *Galileo* (Univ. of Illinois, Urbana, Ill., 1969); the NY City Ballet's *Who Cares?* (NY State Th., N.Y.C., Feb. 7, 1970); *Child's Play* (Royale, Feb. 17, 1970); *Georgy* (Winter Garden, Feb. 26, 1970); *Look to the Lilies* (Lunt-Fontanne Th., Mar. 29, 1970); *1776* (New, London, England, June 16, 1970); *Father's Day* (John Golden Th., N.Y.C., Mar. 16, 1971); and the ballet *PAMTGG* for NY City Ballet (NY State Th., June 17, 1971). He did scenery and lighting for *Caravaggio* (Playhouse in the Park, Cincinnati, Ohio, July 1, 1971); scenery for *Love Me, Love My Children* (Mercer-O'Casey Th., N.Y.C., Nov. 3, 1971); sets and lighting for *Children! Children!* (Ritz Th., Mar. 7, 1972); *Voices* (Ethel Barrymore Th., Apr. 3, 1972); *Sugar* (Majestic, Apr. 9, 1972); a revival of *The Crucible* (Vivian Beaumont Th., Apr. 27, 1972); and *Out Cry* (Lyceum, Mar. 1, 1973).

Films. He executed the color art direction for *Picnic* (Col., 1955).

Other Activities. In May 1945, Mr. Mielziner was commissioned by the US State Dept. to design the setting and lighting for the first meeting of the United Nations at San Francisco, Calif. In the early days of television, he was a consultant on lighting to CBS. At the NY World's Fair (1964), he produced and designed the AT&T show and designed the setting and lighting for Michelangelo's "Piéta" at the Vatican Pavilion. In 1965, he designed a special portable stage for use in the East Room of the White House, Washington, D.C.

Mr. Mielziner designed, with Edward Barnes, "A Lyric Theatre for Intimate Musical Drama" under a Ford Foundation Ideal Theatres grant in 1960. He designed the interior of the ANTA-Washington Square Th., N.Y.C. (opened Jan. 23, 1964); with the late Eero Saarinen, the Vivian Beaumont and Forum theatres, Lincoln Center, N.Y.C.; and, with Kevin Roche, John Dinkeloo and Associates, the theatre at the Univ. of Michigan, Ann Arbor. He was consultant on the Loretto-Hilton Th., Webster Groves, Mo. (opened 1965); special consultant to Welton Becket on construction of the Mark Taper Forum Th. (opened 1967) of the Los Angeles (Calif.) Music Center; consultant to Hellmuth, Obata & Kassabaum on Communications Bldg. Th., Southern Illinois Univ., Edwardsville, Ill.; consultant to Harrison and Abramowitz on the Krannert Center for the Performing Arts, Univ. of Illinois; and special theatre consultant and co-designer, with Edward F. Kook, of two theatres for Wake Forest Univ., Winston-Salem, N.C.

Mr. Mielziner's stage designs have been exhibited at the Research Library and Museum of the Performing Arts, Lincoln Ctr., N.Y.C.; Brandeis Univ., Waltham, Mass.; and the Coffee House Club, N.Y.C. (all in 1966); at the Virginia Museum of Fine Arts, Richmond, Va. (1967); on the International Exhibitions Foundation tour (1968, 1969); at the Toneelmuseum, Amsterdam, Netherlands (1972); and at Amherst (Mass.) Coll. (1973).

Published Works. Mr. Mielziner is author of *Designing for the Theatre* (1965) and *The Shapes of Our Theatre* (1970).

Awards. Mr. Mielziner received Donaldson awards for his scene designs for *Dream Girl* (1946), *A Streetcar Named Desire* (1948), *Death of a Salesman* (1949), *The Innocents* (1950), *The King and I* (1951), and a special award for distinguished contribution to the theatre (1952). He won the *Variety* NY Drama Critics Poll as best scenic designer for *Dream Girl* (1946), *Another Part of the Forest* (1947), *A Streetcar Named Desire* (1948), *Death of a Salesman* (1949), *The Innocents* (1950), *The King and I* (1951), *Flight into Egypt* (1952), *Can-Can* (1953), and *The Most Happy Fella* (1956).

He received five Antoinette Perry (Tony) awards: for his work of the season 1948–49, for *The Innocents*, for *The King and I*, and two for *Child's Play*—for scene design and for lighting design; he received Tony nominations for scene design for *1776* and *Father's Day*. Mr. Mielziner's other awards include an Academy (Oscar) Award in 1955 for color art direction of *Picnic*, the Drama Desk Award for outstanding scene design for *Child's Play*, and Joseph Maharam Foundation awards for scene design for a musical (1969) for *1776* and for straight play design (1970) for *Child's Play*. He received the New England Theatre Conference's first award (1957) for creative achievement in the American theatre; the Charlotte Cushman Award (1958); the Lotus Club Award of Merit (1961); the Brandeis Univ. Award (1963) for creative achievement in the theatre; and he was made a Benjamin Franklin Fellow of the Royal Society of Arts in 1969. He received honorary degrees of D.F.A. from Fordham Univ. (1947) and the Univ. of Michigan (1971) and of L.H.D. from Otterbein Coll. and the Univ. of Utah (1972).

MILES, JULIA. Producer, actress. b. Julia Hinson, Pelham, Ga., to John and Saro (Jones) Hinson. Father, farmer. Attended Pelham (Ga.) Grade Sch.; Brenan Acad.; Northwestern Univ. (1948–52). Studied with Lee Strasberg (acting). Married 1950 to William Miles (marr. dis.); one son, one daughter; married 1962 to Samuel C. Cohn; one daughter. Member of AEA; ATPAM. Address: (home) 25 Central Park W., New York, NY 10023, tel. (212) JU 2-6794; (bus.) 111 W. 46th St., New York, NY 10036, tel. (212) CI 6-3730.

Theatre. Miss Miles is associate producer of The American Place Th. (N.Y.C., 1964–to date), where she has worked on thirty-eight full productions and over one hundred workshop presentations of works-in-progress.

Previously, with Theatre Current (St. Ann's Church, Brooklyn, N.Y., 1957–60), she acted and produced under the name Julia Miles Cohn. She was co-producer of *The Red Eye of Love* (Living Th., N.Y.C., June 12, 1961); *Fortuna* (Maidman Playhouse, N.Y.C., Jan. 3, 1962); and *Not Enough Rope* and *George Washington Crossing the Delaware* (Maidman Playhouse, N.Y.C., Jan. 3, 1962).

Recreation. Theatre, movies, reading, tennis.

MILES, SYLVIA. Actress, comedienne. b. Sept. 9, 1932, New York City. Grad. Washington Irving H.S., N.Y.C., 1946. Studied art and stage design at Pratt Inst., N.Y.C., 1946–47, attended Dramatic Workshop, New Sch. for Social Research, N.Y.C.; studied acting with Harold Clurman; N. Richard Nash; Lee Strasberg; Joe Anthony; Frank Corsaro; and with Erwin Piscator, Stella Adler, and Ben Ari, Dramatic Workshop of the New Sch., N.Y.C. Married 1952 to Gerald Price, actor (marr. dis. 1958); married 1963 to Ted Brown, radio and television performer. Member of AEA; AFTRA; SAG; Manhattan Chess Club.

Theatre. Miss Miles made her debut as Lampito in the Dramatic Workshop production of *Lysistrata* (President, N.Y.C.); played a season as comedienne at Tamiment (Pa.) Playhouse (Summer 1949); played June in a summer touring production of *Made in Heaven* (1949); and was understudy for the role of Ellie in a national touring company of *Show Boat* (1950).

She played Arlene in *A Stone for Danny Fisher* (Downtown Natl., N.Y.C., Oct. 21, 1954). In stock, she played Ruthie in *Wedding Breakfast* (Capri Th., L.I., N.Y., Summer 1955); the Shoplifter in *Detective Story* (Great Neck Summer Th., N.Y., Summer 1955); succeeded Gloria Scott Backé as Margie in *The Iceman Cometh* (Circle in the Sq., May 8, 1956); played Lizzie Curry in *The Rainmaker* (Drury Lane, Chicago, Ill., June 1959); Ninotchka in *Silk Stockings* (Casa Mañana, Ft. Worth, Tex., Summer 1959); Rita Marlowe in *Will Success Spoil Rock Hunter?* (Candlelight, Washington, D.C., Summer 1959); the Thief in *The Balcony* (Circle in the Sq., N.Y.C., Mar. 3, 1960); Bessie in *Man Around the House* (Bucks County Playhouse, New Hope, Pa., Summer 1961); and Katrin in *The Marriage-Go-Round* (British Colonial Th., Nassau, Bahamas; Coconut Grove Playhouse, Miami, Fla.). She played Raisa in *The Witch*, a part of *A Chekhov Sketchbook*, which included *The Vagrant* and *The Music Shop* (Gramercy Arts, N.Y.C., Feb. 15, 1962).

Miss Miles made her Bway debut as Rosie in *The Riot Act* (Cort, Mar. 7, 1963); in stock, played Mrs. Boker in *Infancy* and The Nurse in *Pullman Car Hiawatha*, in the double bill called *Plays for Bleecker Street* (Olney Playhouse, Md., Summer 1963); Mildred Turner in *Oh, Men! Oh, Women!* (No. Shore Playhouse, Beverly, Mass., Summer 1963); and Windy Hill in a summer tour of *The Glass Rooster* (1964).

She played Stella Rizzo in *Matty and the Moron and Madonna* (Orpheum, N.Y.C., Mar. 29, 1965); appeared in *Play That on Your Old Piano* (Renata Th., Oct. 14, 1965); played Monique in *The Kitchen* (81 St. Th., June 13, 1966); appeared in *Luv* and *The Owl and the Pussycat* (Hampton, N.Y., Playhouse, Summer 1967); played the title role in *The Killing of Sister George* (Santa Fe, New Mex., Th., Summer 1969); Sylvie in *Rosebloom* (Eastside Playhouse, N.Y.C., Jan. 5, 1972); Martha in *Who's Afraid of Virginia Woolf?* (Pittsburgh Playhouse, Nov. 16, 1972); Nellie in *Nellie Toole and Co.* (Th. Four, N.Y.C., Sept. 24, 1973); and appeared in *American Night Cry* (Actors Studio, Mar. 7, 1974).

Films. Miss Miles made her screen debut as The Girl in the Phone Booth in *Murder, Inc.* (20th-Fox, 1960); and has subsequently appeared in *Parrish* (WB, 1961); *Violent Monday* (Del Tenney Assoc., 1961); *The Truant* (Barbro Prod., 1962); *Pie in the Sky* (Baron, 1964; AA, 1965); *Psychomania* (Emerson, 1964); *Midnight Cowboy* (UA, 1969); *Who Killed Mary What's 'Ername?* (Cannon, 1971); *Heat* (Warhol, 1972); and *Farewell, My Lovely* (Avco Embassy, 1975).

Television. Her debut was in a comedy sketch on the Bob Hope Show (NBC, 1950), followed by three more appearances on the same show. She has since appeared on The Mask (ABC); the Steve Allen Show (NBC); US Steel Hour (CBS); Edge of Night (NBC); Love of Life (CBS); Search for Tomorrow (CBS); Sgt. Bilko (CBS); CBS Workshop (CBS); *Uncle Harry* (Play of the Week, WNTA); The Defenders (CBS); Route 66 (CBS); Naked City (ABC); and Car 54, Where Are You? (NBC). In addition, she has made guest appearances on the major talk shows.

Recreation. Chess (US Female Championship Contender), antiquing and finishing furniture, carpentry, and construction of apartments.

MILLER, ARTHUR. Playwright, novelist. b. Oct. 17, 1915, New York City, to Isadore and Augusta (Barnett) Miller. Grad. Univ. of Michigan, A.B. 1938. Married Aug. 5, 1940, to Mary Grace Slattery (marr. dis.); one son, one daughter; married June 1956, to Marilyn Monroe (marr. dis.; dec. Aug. 1962); married Feb. 1962, to Ingeborg Morath; one daughter. Member of Dramatists Guild; Natl. Inst. of Arts and Letters. Address: Roxbury, CT 06783.

Theatre. Mr. Miller wrote *They Too Arise* (not yet produced in N.Y.C.); *The Man Who Had All the Luck* (Forrest Th., N.Y.C., Nov. 23, 1944); *All My Sons* (Coronet, Jan. 29, 1947); *Death of a Salesman* (Morosco, Feb. 10, 1949); an adaptation of Henrik Ibsen's *An Enemy of the People* (Broadhurst, Dec. 28, 1950); *The Crucible* (Martin Beck Th., Jan. 22, 1953; and Martinique, Mar. 11, 1958); *A View from the Bridge* and *A Memory of Two Mondays* (Coronet, Sept. 29, 1955); *After the Fall* (ANTA-Washington Square Th., Jan. 23, 1964); *Incident at Vichy* (ANTA-Washington Square Th., Dec. 3, 1964; Phoenix, London, Jan. 26, 1966); revised and expanded his one-act *A View from the Bridge* into a full-length play (Sheridan Sq. Playhouse, N.Y.C., Jan. 28, 1965); wrote *The Price* (Morosco, Feb. 7, 1968), which he subsequently directed for London (Duke of York's Th., Mar. 4, 1969) and for a US national tour (opened Shubert, New Haven, Sept. 24, 1969; closed Studebaker, Chicago, Apr. 25, 1970); and wrote *The Creation of the World and Other Business* (Shubert, N.Y.C., Nov. 30, 1972).

For the academic year 1973–74, he was an assoc. prof. of drama at the Univ. of Mich., during which time he worked on a play entitled *An American Clock* (not yet produced in N.Y.C.), and revised *The Creation of the World and Other Business*, presented as *Up from Paradise* (Power Center, Ann Arbor, Mich., April 1974).

Films. The following of Mr. Miller's plays have been adapted to the screen: *All My Sons* (U, 1948); *Death of a Salesman* (Col, 1951); *The Crucible* (French; released as *The Witches of Salem*, Kingsley-Int., 1958); and *A View from the Bridge* (Cont., 1962). He wrote the story and screenplay for *The Misfits* (UA, 1961).

Television and Radio. Mr. Miller has appeared on the Lincoln Center Day special (CBS-TV, Sept. 20, 1964); the Eugene O'Neill documentary, *The Face of Genius* (WBZ-TV, Boston, 1966); and on the New Comment radio show (Third Network, London, 1966). His work has often been broadcast in excerpt, and the list of his plays televised in entirety includes *A View from the Bridge* (ITV, London, Apr. 4, 1966); *Death of a Salesman* (CBS, N.Y.C, May 8, 1966); *An Enemy of the People* (NET Playhouse, WNET, Dec. 2, 1966); *The Crucible* (CBS, May 4, 1967); *A Memory of Two Mondays* (NET Playhouse, WNET, Jan. 28, 1971); *The Price* (Hallmark Hall of Fame, NBC, Feb. 3, 1971); *Incident at Vichy* (produced for Hollywood Television Th., KCET, Los Angeles; shown by PBS stations; on WNET, N.Y.C., Dec. 8, 1973); and *After the Fall* (NBC, Feb. 10, 1974).

Other Activities. Mr. Miller was president of P.E.N. (an association of poets, essayists, and novelists) from 1965 until he resigned, Sept. 15, 1969. He read at the *Poets for Peace* rally (Town Hall, N.Y.C., Nov. 12, 1967).

Published Works. Mr. Miller's published work includes *Situation Normal* (1944); a novel, *Focus* (1945); a children's book, *Jane's Blanket;* a collection of short stories, *I Don't Need You Any More* (1967); and a volume of photographs and comment, in collaboration with Inge Morath, entitled *In Russia* (1969).

Discography. Mr. Miller reads from and speaks about *The Crucible* and *Death of a Salesman* on an album (Spoken Arts 704) recorded in 1956.

Awards. He received the Hopwood Award for Playwrighting from the Univ. of Michigan (1936); the Th. Guild Natl. Award (1938); NY Drama Critics' Circle awards for *All My Sons* (1947) and *Death of a Salesman* (1949); the Pulitzer Prize for *Death of a Salesman* (1949); the Antoinette Perry (Tony) Award for *The Crucible* (1953); the Gold Medal for Drama from the Natl. Institute of Arts and Letters (1959); one of the first annual Anglo-American Awards "for outstanding contributions to the British Theatre" (London, June 3, 1966); and the Brandeis Univ. Creative Arts Award (1970). He received an honorary D.H.L. from the Univ. of Mich. (1956).

MILLER, BUZZ. Dancer, actor, choreographer. b. Vernal Philip Miller, 1928, Snowflake, Ariz., to Allen K. and Philena (Hunt) Miller. Father, rancher. Grad. Arizona State Coll., B.A. Served US Army, Infantry; awarded Bronze Star, Purple Heart. Member of AEA; AFTRA; AGMA. Address: 8 W. 9th St., New York, NY 10011, tel. (212) GR 7-6491.

Theatre. Mr. Miller first appeared on stage in the third grade as a singer in a musical version of *A Christmas Carol.*

He made his professional debut as dancer in *Magdalena* (Philharmonic Hall, Los Angeles, Calif., July 1948) and on Bway (Ziegfeld, Sept. 20, 1948); and appeared with the Jack Cole Dancers (Acad. of Music, Philadelphia, Pa., Dec. 1948). He performed as singer-dancer in *Pal Joey* (Broadhurst, Jan. 3, 1952); and as a dancer in *Two's Company* (Alvin, Dec. 15, 1952), *Me and Juliet* (Majestic, May 28, 1953), and *the Pajama Game* (St. James, Mar. 13, 1954). In Aug. 1954, he toured as a singer-dancer with an Oldsmobile industrial show; danced in *Arabian Nights* (Marine Th., Jones Beach, N.Y., June 1955); and toured with a Buick industrial show (Aug. 1955). He appeared in *La Chambre* with the Ballets de Paris (London, Paris, Vienna, Munich, Berlin, 1956); was an assistant choreographer for an Oldsmobile industrial show (US, Aug. 1956); performed as the Count in *The Unicorn, the Gorgon and the Manticore* (George Washington Univ., Washington, D.C., and Massachusetts Inst. of Tech., Cambridge, Mass., Apr. 1957); in *Seven Faces of Love* (Phoenix, N.Y.C., May 1957); and succeeded (June 17, 1957) Peter Gennaro in the role of Carl in *Bells Are Ringing* (Shubert, Nov. 29, 1956).

Mr. Miller appeared at the Festival of Two Worlds in four chamber ballets, played T. Stedman Harder in José Quintero's production of *A Moon for the Misbegotten* (Spoleto, Italy, June 1958); and the Jailer in *Redhead* (46 St. Th., N.Y.C., Feb. 5, 1959); danced the role of Reverend Davidson in Roland Petit's ballet *Rain* performed in *An Evening with Zizi Jeanmaire* (Royalty, London, Nov. 2, 1960); was assistant choreographer for an Oldsmobile industrial show (US, July 1961); was assistant choreographer and played Dino, the Night Club Manager, and the Head Chef in *Bravo Giovanni* (Broadhurst, N.Y.C., May 19, 1962). He appeared as Rami and Pulski in *Hot Spot* (Majestic, Apr. 19, 1963); danced in *A Portrait of Billie* (Delacorte, Sept. 1963); played Snub Taylor and Ben in *Funny Girl* (Winter Garden, Mar. 26, 1964); and was dance soloist in a Bartok concerto at the Caramoor Music Festival (Katonah, N.Y., June 26–27, 1964); and at the inauguration of President Lyndon B. Johnson (1965); principal dancer and understudy to Jack Cole in *Chu Chem* (pre-Bway tryout, opened Locust St. Th., Philadelphia, Nov. 15, 1966, closed Nov. 20, 1966); was soloist in *Catulli Carmini* (Coromoor Festival, 1967); principal dancer and choreographer for *Bomarzo* (Washington, D.C., Opera Society, 1967; and NY City Ballet, NY State Th., Lincoln Ctr., Mar. 14, 1968); choreographer and assistant director for *Moondreamer* (La Mama Experimental Th., N.Y.C., 1968); as special guest with the Carmen De Lavallade company, performed in *Villon, Portrait of Billie* and the premiere of Bertram Ross' *Ballet* (March 8–9, 1968); at the Israel Festival (1968), was soloist with the American Th. of Dance in *Banda*, and *Portrait of Billie;* performed *Bomarzo* (Los Angeles, and Lincoln Ctr., N.Y.C., 1968); danced the title role in *Dracula* (Judson Church, N.Y.C., Nov. 16, 1969); danced *Bomarzo* (Lincoln Ctr., N.Y.C., 1969); was soloist in *Songs of Catullus* (Lincoln Ctr., N.Y.C., 1969); principal dancer and assistant choreographer for Menotti's *The Unicorn, The Gorgon* and *the Manticore* at the Spoleto (Italy) Festival of Two Worlds (1970); associate director, with Julie Bovasso, of her play *Monday on the Way to the Mercury Island* (La Mama Experimental Th., N.Y.C., 1971); taught at George Balanchine's Sch. of Amer. Ballet (1970); with Gemze Delappe, choreographed *Patterns* for the Zina Bethune company (Nov. 1970); choreographed a new production of *Aida* (Berlin (Germany) State Opera, Jan. 26, 1972); and performed in *Shuberts Serenade* (Apr. 2, 1974). In addition, Mr. Miller teaches at an actors-dancers workshop with Julie Bovasso.

Films. He made his screen debut as a member of a dance team in *On the Riviera* (20th-Fox, 1951); subsequently appeared in *No Business Like Show Business* (20th-Fox, 1954); *Anything Goes* (Par., 1956); and *The Pajama Game* (WB, 1957).

Television. Mr. Miller first appeared on a closed circuit program for members of Parliament (BBC, London, 1950). Subsequently, he performed on *The Big Record* (US, CBS, 1958); the Arthur Godfrey Show (CBS, 1959); and Ed Sullivan Show (CBS, 1961). He choreographed *Postures* (CBS, 1961) and was assistant choreographer and dancer in *Home for the Holidays* (ABC, 1961); assistant choreographer of *The Broadway of Lerner and Loewe* (NBC, 1962); danced on *Music for the Young* (ABC, 1962); and in two half-hour ballets, *Arias and Arabesques* and *Brief Dynasty* (CBS, 1962).

He performed on a television special with Mary Hinkson and Matt Maddox (1963); was a soloist in *Psalms* (1963); soloist in *Ants-USA* (1965); assistant choreographer of The Bell Television Hour (ABC, 1965); soloist in *Jeptha's Daughter,* and *The Captive Lark* (1966); solo dancer and choreographer for Lincoln Center-Stage 5 (1967); soloist in the Gunter Schuker special (1968), and on Camera Three (CBS, 1968).

Night Clubs. He performed with the Jack Cole Dancers (Copa City, Miami, Fla., Jan. 1949); with Kay Thompson and Co. (Beverly Country Club, New Orleans, La., Dec. 1949); and in an act called "Carol Haney with Buzz Miller and Joe Milan" (Fontainebleau, Miami, Fla.; Flamingo, Las Vegas, Nov., Oct. 1956).

Recreation. Painting, photography, tennis.

MILLER, JAMES HULL. Theatre design consultant, scenic designer. b. June 21, 1916, Sewickley, Pa., to James Roberts and Texas (Niswanger) Miller. Father, lawyer; mother, librarian. Grad. Princeton Univ., B.A. 1938. Married July 10, 1942, to Dorothy Davies, director; one son, two daughters. Served US Army, 1941–45; rank, Sgt. Member of USITT (bd. of dir., 1963–to date); AETA (former chmn., Theatre Architecture, Technical Developments Projects; member, Advisory Council, 1955–58). Address: 3415 Reily Lane, Shreveport, LA 71105, tel. (318) 865-1521.

Theatre. Mr. Miller was technical designer in stock for the East Hampton (L.I., N.Y.), Locust Valley (N.Y.), and Stockbridge (Mass.) theatres; in charge of lighting for the Graff Ballet national tour (1940–41); assistant business manager for the Goodman Th. (Chicago, Ill., 1945–46); taught at the Univ. of New Mexico (Albuquerque, 1946–1955); and Centenary Coll. of Louisiana (Shreveport, La., 1955–58).

He founded the Arts Lab in Shreveport, La., an institute for the research and development and stagecraft for open stage theatres (1958) and where he conducts intensive training courses in self-supporting scenery. He has been consulting designer for theatres particularly small community, high school and community college theatres of which he has made a specialty. He has been guest professor for courses in this area in colleges and universities. In the fall of 1972 he gave forty workshops for the County Education Authorities in Great Britain.

Published Works. Mr. Miller is the author of *Self-Supporting Scenery for Children's Theatre—and Grown-ups', Too* (1973), and has contributed articles on theatre design to *AIA Journal, American School and University, Theatre Arts, Progressive Architecture, Tulane Drama* Review, *RIBA Journal, Recreation, Hub Electric Company Bulletins,* and *Tabs.*

MILLER, JASON. Playwright, actor. b. Apr. 22, 1939, Scranton, Pa., to John and Mary Miller. Father, electrician; mother, teacher. Grad. St. Patrick's H.S. (Scranton); Scranton Univ., 1961; Catholic Univ. (Washington, D.C.). Married 1963 to Linda Gleason (marr. dis.); three children.

Theatre. A bill of three short plays by Mr. Miller, *Lou Gehrig Did Not Die of Cancer, Perfect Son,* and *The Circus Lady,* was produced off-off Bway (Triangle, N.Y.C., Feb. 23, 1967); followed by *Nobody Hears a Broken Drum* (Fortune, Mar. 19, 1970); and *That Championship Season* (Estelle Newman Th., May 2, 1972; and Booth, Sept. 14, 1972).

As an actor, he played Pip in *Pequod* (Mercury, N.Y.C., June 29, 1969); the Assistant in *The Happiness Cage* (Estelle Newman Th., Oct. 4, 1970); Paryfon Rogozhin in *Subject to Fits* (Public Th., Feb. 14, 1971); and, at Catholic Univ. (Hartke Th., Washington, D.C., 1971), played Edmund Tyrone in *Long Day's Journey into Night,* and appeared in *Juno and the Paycock.*

He has also performed with the Champlain Shakespeare Festival (Burlington, Vt.); the Cincinnati (Ohio) Shakespeare Festival; and Baltimore Center Stage. He wrote the first draft of *That Championship Season* while appearing at the Windmill Dinner Th. (Ft. Worth, Texas, 1970).

Films. Mr. Miller played Father Karvas in *The Exorcist* (WB, 1973); and Cooper in *The Nickel Ride* (20th-Fox, 1975).

Awards. Mr. Miller received the high school playwriting award for his first effort, *The Winner.* For *That Championship Season,* he won the NY Drama Critics' Circle Award (1971–72); the Antoinette Perry (Tony) Award (1972–73); and the Pulitzer Prize (1973). In 1974, he was nominated for the Academy (Oscar) Award for Best Supporting Actor for his performance in *The Exorcist.*.

MILLER, JONATHAN. Director, actor, writer, journalist, doctor. b. Jonathan Wolfe Miller, July 21, 1934, to Emanuel and Betty (Spiro) Miller. Father, doctor; mother, writer. Attended St. Paul's Sch., London, Eng., 1948–53; grad. St. John's Coll., Cambridge, Eng., M.B., B. Chir. 1959. Married July 27, 1956, to Helen Rachel Collet, doctor of medicine; two sons, one daughter. Member of British AEA; British Medical Assn. Address: 63 Gloucester Crescent, London, N.W.1, England tel. 01-485-6973.

Pre-Theatre. Doctor.

Theatre. Dr. Miller made his first stage appearance in the Cambridge Footlights Club revue, *Out of the Blue* (Phoenix, London, July 6, 1954); subsequently appeared in the London production of *Between the Lines* (Scala, July 1955); the revue, *Beyond the Fringe,* of which he was also co-author (Edinburgh Festival, Lyceum Th., Aug. 1960; Arts Th., Cambridge, Apr. 24, 1961; Fortune Th., London, May 10, 1961; John Golden Th., N.Y.C., Oct. 27, 1962); directed *Under Plain Cover* (Royal Court, London, July 19, 1962); *The Old Glory* (American Place Th., N.Y.C., Nov. 1, 1964); *Come Live with Me* (Billy Rose Th., Jan. 26, 1967; withdrew as director during New Haven tryout, but remained billed as "production associate"); directed *Benito Cereno* (Part I of *The Old Glory*) in London (Mermaid, Mar. 8, 1967); and directed William Alfred's *Prometheus Bound* (Yale Repertory Th., New Haven, May 9, 1967).

For the Nottingham Playhouse (Nottingham, England) he directed *The School for Scandal* (1968); *The Seagull* (Nov. 27, 1968); and *King Lear* (1969; Old Vic Th., Feb. 10, 1970). For the second annual US tour of the Oxford and Cambridge Shakespeare Co., he directed *Twelfth Night* (toured US six weeks, inc. Hunter Coll. Playhouse, N.Y.C., Dec. 29, 1969). He directed the National Th. production of *The Merchant of Venice* (Old Vic, London, Apr. 28, 1970); directed *The Tempest* (Mermaid, June 15, 1970); the Oxford and Cambridge Shakespeare Co. production of *Hamlet* (Arts Th., Cambridge, Oct. 1970; subsequent US tour inc. Columbia Univ. Playhouse, N.Y.C., Dec. 4–5, 1970, and Hunter Coll. Playhouse, Dec. 26, 1970 to Jan. 3, 1971). He again directed William Alfred's *Prometheus Bound* (Mermaid, London, June 24, 1971).

In the US, he directed *Richard II* (Ahmanson Th., Los Angeles, Feb. 1972); for the Oxford and Cambridge Shakespeare Co., *Julius Caesar* (US tour inc. Loeb Th., Cambridge, Mass., Jan. 1972; returned to England and played at the New Th., London, Mar. 1972); and for the Nottingham Playhouse Co., *The Malcontent* (Nottingham, England, Apr. 1973).

Dr. Miller was appointed an assoc. dir. of the National Th. in England, in 1973, for whom he directed *Measure for Measure.* He resigned in Mar. 1975. He is currently (1975) an associate director of the Greenwich Th., England, for whom he has directed *Ghosts* (1974), *The Seagull* (1974), *Hamlet* (1974), *The Importance of Being Earnest* (Mar. 20, 1975), *All's Well That Ends Well* (July 1975), and *Measure for Measure* (July 1975).

He has also directed the operas, *Arden Must Die* (Sadler's Wells Th., London, 1974); *Cosi fan Tutte* (Kent Opera, Congress Th., Eastbourne, England, Oct. 23, 1974); and *The Cunning Little Vixen* (Glyndebourne, Sussex, England, May 1975).

Films. Mr. Miller played Kirby Groomkirby in *One Way Pendulum* (Par., 1965). He directed *Take a Girl Like You* (Col., 1970).

Television. In the US, Dr. Miller appeared in a comedy sketch on the Jack Paar Show (NBC, Dec. 1962); directed *What's Going on Here?* (WNEW, Apr. 1963); appeared in *A Trip to the Moon* (CBS, Feb. 12, 1964); was a guest on the Johnny Carson Show (NBC, 1964–65) and the Books for Our Times series (Educ., 1964); wrote *The Anne Hutchinson Story* (Profiles in Courage, NBC, Jan. 10, 1965); and was a guest on the David Susskind Show (Ind., 1966–67). His *Plato's Dialogues* (see below) was shown on NET (1971).

In England, Dr. Miller has appeared in comedy sketches on the Tonight Show (BBC, Apr. 1958) and on the Tempo show (A.T.V., Oct. 1961). He was seen in the telecast of *Beyond the Fringe* (BBC-2, Dec. 19, 1964); was editor of the Monitor series (BBC-1, 1964–65); and appeared on the Intimations series (BBC-2, 1965–66) and the Sunday Night series (BBC-1, Feb. 6, 1966). He produced and directed films of *Plato's Dialogues* (BBC-1, July 3, 1966); wrote and directed a version of *Alice in Wonderland* (BBC-1, Dec. 28, 1966); and directed *From Chekhov with Love; Whistle and I'll Come to You;* and *King Lear* (BBC).

Other Activities. Dr. Miller was the film and

television critic for *The New Yorker* (1963).

Published Works. Dr. Miller is the author of *Maculuhan* (1970). He has contributed articles to *The New Yorker,* the New York *Herald Tribune, The Partisan Review, Commentary,* the London *Observer, Spectator, The New Statesman,* and other periodicals.

Awards. *Beyond the Fringe* received the Evening Standard Award for Best Revue or Musical (1961), the Antoinette Perry (Tony) Award Special Category (1963), and the NY Drama Critics' Circle Award (Special Citation, 1963).

Recreation. Sleeping.

MILLER, WYNNE. Actress, singer. b. Velna Lou Miller, Sept. 29, 1935, Greeley, Colo., to E. Deane and Velna L. Miller. Father, dentist; mother, organist. Grad. Greeley (Colo.) H.S., 1953; attended Colo. State Coll., 1953–54. Relative in theatre: uncle, Glenn Miller, band leader. Member of AEA; AFTRA; AFM, Local 802.

Theatre. Miss Miller was the first female to perform at The Lambs, N.Y.C., appearing in Eddie Dowling's *Mr. Dooley* (1956).

She played Nancy in *By Hex* (Tempo Playhouse, N.Y.C., June 18, 1956); subsequently succeeded (1958) Edie Adams as Daisy Mae in *Li'l Abner* (St. James, Nov. 15, 1956), in which she toured (opened Riviera Hotel Las Vegas, Nev., Sept. 1, 1958; closed Royal Alexandra, Toronto, Canada, Jan. 3, 1959); appeared in *A Thurber Carnival* (ANTA, N.Y.C., Feb. 26, 1960); and played Laura in *Tenderloin* (46 St. Th., Oct. 17, 1960).

Television. Miss Miller appeared as Mary Weldon on *Our Five Daughters* (NBC, 1962), and was a guest singer on the Perry Como Show (NBC, 1963).

Awards. She received the *Theatre World* Award (1958) for her performance as Daisy Mae in *Li'l Abner.*

Recreation. Golf, interior decorating, cooking.

MILLINGTON, RODNEY. Publisher, actor. b. London, England, Aug. 15, 1905, to Walter S. and Adelaide (Hall) Millington. Father, owner of paper manufacturing company. Grad. Malvern Coll., 1924; Lincoln Coll., Oxford, 1926. Member of British AEA, Actors' Charitable Trust (member, exec. comm., edu. and welfare sub-committees); The Royal General Theatrical Fund Assn. (vice-pres.). Address: c/o The Spotlight, Ancaster House, 43, Cranbourn St., London, W.C.Z.H 7AP, England tel. 01 437 7631.

Since 1935, Mr. Millington has been managing director, owner, and publisher of *The Spotlight Casting Directory* (London). His association with The Spotlight, Ltd. began as director in July 1931.

Mr. Millington made his acting debut as Morris in *Magic* at the Cambridge (Eng.) Th. Festival (Sept. 1926), followed by appearances there as Mr. Zero in *The Adding Machine* and Tattle in *Love for Love* (1927). He made his London debut succeeding Milton Rosmer as Bernard Ravenscroft in *The World's End* (Everyman Th., May 9, 1928); subsequently played Cotton in *Holding Out the Apple* (Globe, June 1928); spent a season with the Hull Repertory Co. (1928); and a season with the Northampton Repertory Co. (1929). He played Willie Ward in *The Misdoings of Charley Peace* (Ambassadors', London, Sept. 12, 1929); the Young Soldier in *Suspense* (Duke of York's, Apr. 8, 1930); a Journalist in *Mr. Eno, His Birth, Death and Life* (Arts, Oct. 22, 1930); Warwick Entwhistle in *The Rising Generation* (Embassy, Jan. 12, 1931); the Mechanic in *Sea Fever* (New, June 30, 1931); Sulieman Ali in *Port Said* (Wyndham's, Nov. 1, 1931); Sulieman Ali in a revival of *Port Said,* retitled *Vessel's Departing* (Embassy, July 3, 1933); Dr. Chrisp in *Men in White* (Lyric, June 28, 1934); Lob in *Dear Brutus* and Tom Pryor in *Outward Bound* (Aberdeen Repertory Co., Scot., 1939).

Films. Mr. Millington has appeared in *Channel Crossing* (Gaumont-British, 1934) and *Bella Donna* (Olympic, 1935).

Recreation. Travel, driving.

MINER, JAN. Actress. b. Janice Miner, Oct. 15, 1919, Boston, Mass., to Walter Curtis and Ethel Lindsey (Chase) Miner. Father, dentist; mother, painter. Attended Beaver Country Day School, Chestnut, Mass.; Vesper George School of the Arts, Boston. Studied acting with Lee Strasberg, David Craig, Ira Cirker, Don Richardson. Married May 5, 1963, to Richard Merrell, writer. Member of AEA; AFTRA; SAG (bd. mbr.); Variety Arts. Address: (home) Bethel, CT 06801, tel. (203) 748-2519; (bus.) c/o Lester Lewis Associates, 156 E. 52nd St., New York, NY 10022, tel. (212) PL 3-5082.

Theatre. Miss Miner made her debut as Frances Black in *Light Up the Sky* (Playhouse, Cincinnati, Ohio; Webster Playhouse, Mass., Summer 1958) and first appeared in N.Y.C. as Maria Louvin in *Obbligato* (Th. Marquee, Feb. 18, 1958). She was Peggy in *Viva Madison Avenue* (Longacre, Apr. 6, 1960); Pampina in *The Decameron* (E. 74th St. Th., Apr. 12, 1961); Alice Lampkin in *Dumbell People in a Barbell World* (Cricket, Feb. 14, 1962); Yvonne in *Intimate Relations* (Mermaid, Nov. 1, 1962); Prudence in *The Lady of the Camellias* (Winter Garden, Mar. 20, 1963); the Third Woman in *The Wives* (Stage 73, May 17, 1965; and she appeared at the American Shakespeare Festival, Stratford, Conn., as Mistress Quickly in *Falstaff* (June 18, 1966) and a woman of Canterbury in *Murder in the Cathedral* (June 19, 1966).

She was Nancy Reed in *The Freaking Out of Stephanie Blake* (previews: Eugene O'Neill Th., N.Y.C., Oct. 30–Nov. 1, 1967); appeared at the American Shakespeare Festival as Megaera in *Androcles and the Lion* (June 25, 1968); was in *The Autograph Hound* (Jan Hus Playhouse, N.Y.C., Dec. 13, 1968); understudied Eileen Heckart as Mrs. Baker in *Butterflies Are Free* (Booth Th., Oct. 21, 1969); returned to the American Shakespeare Festival, where she was the Widow of Florence in *All's Well That Ends Well* (June 16, 1970) and Emilia in *Othello* (June 17, 1970), which transferred to Bway (ANTA Th., Sept. 14, 1970); played the Countess de Lage in a revival of *The Women* (46 St. Th., Apr. 25, 1973); appeared at the American Shakespeare Festival as Mistress Quickly in *The Merry Wives of Windsor* (June 12, 1971) and as Lady Britomart Undershaft in *Major Barbara* (June 27, 1973); and played Aunt Meme in *Saturday Sunday Monday* (Martin Beck Th., Nov. 21, 1974).

In addition to *Light Up the Sky,* Miss Miner has appeared in other summer packages and tours; she was Lottie Lacey in *The Dark at the Top of the Stairs* (Cape Playhouse, Dennis, Mass., July 1960) and a Reporter in *There Must Be a Pony* (Mineola Playhouse, N.Y., Aug. 1962).

Films. Miss Miner appeared in *Ten Girls Ago* (filmed 1962; unreleased); *The Swimmer* (Col., 1968); and *Lenny* (Par., 1975).

Television and Radio. Miss Miner played Della Street on Perry Mason, Julie on Hilltop House, and starred in many other evening and daytime radio shows, including Boston Blackie, Casey, Crime Photographer, and Dimension X.

She has also played leading roles on many television shows, including Robert Montgomery Presents (NBC, 1954); the Jackie Gleason Show (CBS); N.Y.P.D. (WPIX-Ind.); The Defenders (CBS); The Nurses (CBS); Naked City (ABC); Alcoa Playhouse (NBC); Lux Video Theatre (CBS); Schlitz Playhouse of Stars; and Friends and Lovers (CBS, 1974).

She has appeared as Madge the Manicurist for Colgate-Palmolive Liquid since 1965, doing the commercials in French, German, and Italian, as well as English. She has also done "voice-overs" for numerous national brand products.

Awards. Miss Miner won the "Best Dramatic Actress Award" (radio) for nine consecutive years.

MINER, WORTHINGTON. Director, producer, writer. b. Worthington Cogswell Miner, Nov. 13, 1900, Buffalo, N.Y., to Worthington Cogswell and Margaret Willard (Cammann) Miner. Father, lawyer. Grad. Kent Sch., Kent, Conn., 1917; Yale Univ., B.A. 1922; attended Magdalene Coll., Cambridge Univ., England, 1922–24. Married Mar. 30, 1929, to Frances Fuller, actress; one son, two daughters. Served US Army, 1917–19. Member of DGA; AFTRA (ret.); AEA (ret); Century Assn.; AADA (vice-pres). Address: (home) 1 W. 72nd St., New York, NY 10023, tel. (212) TR 7-2388; (bus.) Worthington Miner Prod., 1 W. 72nd St., New York, NY 10023, tel. (212) SU 7-4195; c/o Landau Company, Time & Life Building, New York, NY 10020, tel. (212) LT 1-8990.

Theatre. Mr. Miner first appeared on the stage in a school production of *Man without a Country* (1910); made his Bway debut, temporarily replacing (Nov. 1925) Gordon Ash as Hilary Townsend in *The Green Hat* (Broadhurst, N.Y.C., Sept. 15, 1925); subsequently directed a touring company of *Front Page* (Chicago, Ill.; Los Angeles, Calif., 1928); *Weekend* (John Golden Th., N.Y.C., Oct. 22, 1929); *Uncle Vanya* (Cort, Apr. 15, 1930); *Up Pops the Devil* (Masque, Sept. 1, 1930); *Five Star Final* (Cort, Dec. 30, 1930); *The House Beautiful* (Selwyn, Mar. 12, 1931); *Reunion in Vienna* (Martin Beck Th., Nov. 16, 1931); *Wild Waves* (Times Square Th., Feb. 19, 1932); *I Loved You Wednesday* (Sam Harris Th., Oct. 11, 1932); *Both Your Houses* (Royale, Mar. 6, 1933); *Her Master's Voice* (Plymouth, Oct. 23, 1933); *Revenge with Music* (New Amsterdam, Nov. 28, 1934); *Let Freedom Ring* (Broadhurst, Nov. 6, 1936); *One Act Play Cycle* (Th. Union, 1936); *On Your Toes* (Imperial, Apr. 11, 1936); *Bury the Dead* (Ethel Barrymore Th., Apr. 18, 1936); *Blind Alley* (Windsor, Oct. 15, 1936); *Two Hundred Were Chosen* (48 St. Th., Nov. 20, 1936); *Excursion* (Vanderbilt, Apr. 9, 1937); *Father Malachy's Miracle* (St. James, Nov. 17, 1937); *Dame Nature* (Booth, Sept. 26, 1938); and *Suzanna and the Elders* (Morosco, Oct. 29, 1940).

Films. He directed *Let's Try Again* (RKO, 1934); *Hat, Coat and Glove* (RKO, 1934); and *The Pawnbroker* (Landau, 1964).

Television. Mr. Miner was director of program development for CBS (1939). He produced *Toast of the Town,* 1948); was producer-playwright for Studio One (CBS, 1948); produced and directed The Goldbergs (CBS, 1949); and produced *Mr. I. Magination* (CBS, 1949). He made his initial television appearance in the Studio One production of *Away from It All* (CBS, 1951). He was executive producer of Medic (NBC, 1953); Frontier (NBC, 1954); and Play of the Week (NTA, 1959).

Awards. Mr. Miner's series, Studio One, received two NATAS (Emmy) Awards (1950, 1951). He received the NATAS (Emmy) Award for Best Producer (1950).

Recreation. Tennis, architecture, painting, carpentry.

MINNELLI, LIZA. Actress, singer, dancer. b. Liza May Minnelli, Mar. 12, 1946, Los Angeles, Calif., to Vincente and Frances (Gumm) Minnelli. Father, film director; mother, known as Judy Garland, actress, singer, dancer. Grad. Scarsdale (N.Y.) H.S., 1962; attended Univ. of Paris (de la Sorbonne), 1962–63. Studied acting at HB Studio, N.Y.C. Married 1967 to Peter Allen, singer, song-writer (marr. dis. 1974); married Sept. 15, 1974, to Jack Haley, Jr., movie producer. Member of AEA; AFTRA; SAG.

Theatre. Miss Minnelli made her debut at the Cape Cod Melody Top, Hyannis, Mass. in *Take Me Along* and *The Flower Drum Song* (July 1962).

She made her N.Y.C. debut as Ethel Hofflinger in *Best Foot Forward* (Stage 73, Apr. 2, 1963); toured as Lili in *Carnival!* (Mineola Playhouse, N.Y., Jan. 28, 1964); played the title role in *Flora, the Red Menace* (Alvin, N.Y.C., May 11, 1965); appeared in her one-woman show *Liza* (Winter Garden, Jan. 6, 1974); and substituted for Gwenn Verdon in *Chicago* (46 St. Th., Aug. 8, 1975–Sept. 15, 1975).

Films. Miss Minnelli has appeared in leading roles in *Charles Bubbles* (Regional, 1968); *The Sterile Cuckoo* (Par., 1969); *Tell Me That You Love Me, Junie Moon* (Par., 1970); *played Sally Bowles in Cabaret* (AA, 1972); and appeared in *Lucky Lady* (20th-Fox, 1975). She appeared in *That's Entertainment* (UA, 1974); and *Journey Back to Oz* (Filmation, 1974).

Television. She has appeared on Mr. Broadway

(NBC); *The Dangerous Christmas of Red Riding Hood* (ABC); That's Life (ABC); the Keefe Brasselle Show (NBC); with her mother on The Judy Garland Show (CBS); *Liza* (NBC); and *Liza, with a "Z"* (CBS); as well as the major variety and talk shows.

Night Clubs. She has appeared at the Shoreham Hotel (Washington, D.C.); Olympia Th. (Paris); Talk of the Town (London); Chequers Club (Sydney, Australia); Empire Room, Waldorf-Astoria (N.Y.C.); Eden Roc (Miami); and Coconut Grove (Los Angeles); as well as several appearances in Las Vegas and Monte Carlo.

Discography. Among her recordings are *Liza Minnelli* (A&M Records); *Come Saturday Morning* (A&M); *It Amazes Me* (Capitol); and *There Is a Time* (Capitol).

Awards. For her performance in *Best Foot Forward*, she received the *Theatre World* Award (1963); and subsequently received *Best Plays'* citation as best new performer in a musical for her performance in *Flora, the Red Menace* (1964–65); the Di Donatello Award for Best Foreign Actress of the Year (1970) for her performance in *The Sterile Cuckoo;* an Academy (Oscar) Award for her performance in *Cabaret* (1972); and the Las Vegas Entertainer of the Year Award (1972).

MINNELLI, VINCENTE. Director, designer. b. Feb. 28, Chicago, Ill. Attended St. Mary's H.S. and Willis H.S., Delaware, Ohio; studied painting at Chicago Art Inst. Relatives in theatre: father, tent show impressario, musician, conductor; mother, actress, singer, dancer; daughter Liza, actress, singer, dancer. Married June 15, 1945, to Judy Garland, actress (marr. dis. 1951), one daughter; married Feb. 1954 to Georgette Magnani (marr. dis. 1958), two daughters; married Dec. 31, 1960, to Denise Gigante (marr. dis. Aug. 1971). Member of Society of Painters and Paper Hangers (1931–to date); DGA.

Pre-Theatre. Window dresser; photograher.

Theatre. At age three, Mr. Minnelli made his theatrical debut as Little Willie in the Minnelli Bros. Dramatic and Tent Show production of *East Lynn*, playing opposite his mother, Mina Gennell. He toured throughout Ohio with this company, co-owned by his father and uncle, until, as a teenager, he was employed as a set and costume designer for the weekly stage shows which accompanied motion picture bookings in the Chicago-based Baleban and Katz theatre circuit. When the firm relocated in NYC, Mr. Minnelli moved with them, designing the stage shows at the Paramount movie theatre (1930–31). He subsequently designed special settings for the *Earl Carrol Vanities* (Earl Carrol Th., Sept. 7, 1931); sets and costumes for *The Du Barry* (George M. Cohan Th., Nov. 22, 1932); staged tableaux for Paramount movie th. stage shows (1933); became art director at Radio City Music Hall (1933–35), directing certain of, and designing costumes, sets and lights for all weekly stage shows; directed and designed sets, lights and costumes for *At Home Abroad* (Winter Garden, Sept. 19, 1935); designed sets and costumes for *The Ziegfeld Follies* (Winter Garden, Jan. 30, 1936); conceived, staged and designed *The Show Is On* (Winter Garden, Dec. 25, 1936); directed and designed sets, costumes and lights for *Hooray for What!* (Winter Garden, Dec. 1, 1937); and staged and designed sets, costumes and lights for *Very Warm for May* (Alvin, Nov. 17, 1939). After an absence of twenty-eight years, Mr. Minnelli returned to the theatre to direct *Mata Hari* (closed prior to Bway opening, National Th., Washington, D.C., Nov. 18, 1967).

Films. In 1937, Mr. Minnelli, under contract to Paramount Pictures, went to Hollywood as associate producer of musicals. Given no projects, he returned to New York. Again in Hollywood (1940), he began his long association with Metro-Goldwyn-Mayer as a production assistant, staging, without screen credit, musical numbers for Lena Horne, Judy Garland and Mickey Rooney in various films. He made his motion picture directorial debut with *Cabin in the Sky* (1943); subsequently directed *I Dood It* (1943); *Meet Me in St. Louis* (1944); *The Clock* (1945); *Yolanda and the Thief* (1945); the Judy Garland segments of *Til the Clouds Roll By* (no screen credit, 1945); *Undercurrent* (1946); The Pirate (1948); *Madame Bovary* (1949); *Father of the Bride* (1950); *An American in Paris* (1951); *Father's Little Dividend* (1951); the fashion show sequences of *Lovely to Look At* (no screen credit, 1952); *The Bad and the Beautiful* (1952); the "Mademoiselle" sequence in *Story of Three Loves* (1952); *The Band Wagon* (1953); *The Long, Long Trailer* (1954); *Brigadoon* (1954); *The Cobweb* (1955); *Kismet* (1955); *Lust for Life* (1956); *Tea and Sympathy* (1956); *Designing Woman* (1957); *Gigi* (1958); *The Reluctant Debutante* (1958); *Some Came Running* (1958); *Home from the Hill* (1960); *Bells Are Ringing* (1960); *Four Horsemen of the Apocolypse* (1962); *Two Weeks in Another Town* (1962); *The Courtship of Eddie's Father* (1963); and *The Sandpiper* (1965). For other studios, he also directed *Goodbye, Charlie* (20th-Fox, 1964); and *On a Clear Day You Can See Forever* (Par., 1970).

Published Works. Mr. Minnelli illustrated *Casanova's Memoirs* (1931); and, with Hector Arce, wrote his autobiography, *I Remember It Well* (Doubleday, 1974).

Awards. He received the Academy (Oscar) Award (1958) for his direction of *Gigi*.

MINSKOFF, JEROME. Theatre owner, producer, realtor. 1350 Ave. of the Americas, New York, NY 10019, tel. (212) 765-9700.

Theatre. Mr. Minskoff, with Albert Selden, co-produced the pre-Bway tryout of *Halloween* (Bucks County Playhouse, New Hope, Pa., Sept. 20, 1972; closed there Oct. 1, 1972); and *The Lincoln Mask* (Plymouth, N.Y.C., Oct. 30, 1972).

With his brothers, Henry and Myron, he is director of Sam Minskoff & Sons, the builders and owners of the Minskoff Th. (opened Mar. 13, 1973).

Films. He is a co-founder (1969) of Phillip Waxman-Jerome Minskoff Productions, Inc. Releases include *Tell Them Willie Boy Is Here* (U, 1970); and *The Old Man's Place* (Cinerama).

MINTZ, ELI. Actor. b. Edward Satz, Mar. 1, 1904, Lemberg, Austria, to Mende and Feige (Freuntlich) Satz. Father, tailor. Relative in theatre: brother, Ludwig Satz. Educ. in public elementary schools in Europe and by American private tutors; had private dancing and singing lessons. Married Sept. 25, 1943, to Hasha Saks, pianist and teacher: two daughters. Member of AEA; AFTRA; SAG; AGVA. Address: 86-11 Kingston Pl., Jamaica, NY 11432, tel. (212) OL 8-7159.

Theatre. Mr. Mintz made his theatrical debut on the Yiddish stage at Gimpel's Th., Lemberg, Austria, as the Groom in *Moses' Torah* (Sept. 1916), following this with the Groom in *The Dybbuk* (1917–18). From 1918 to 1924, he appeared in twenty-five different plays in repertory (Bochenska Th., Lemberg) and from 1924 to 1927, he was a member of the Yiddish Peretz Rep. Group (Danzig Free State Th.).

Following his emigration to the US in 1927, Mr. Mintz appeared in seven productions with the Maurice Schwartz Art Th., N.Y.C. (1928–29); in sixty-two productions in a thirty-two-weeks season at the Franklin Park Th., Dorchester, Mass. (1929–30); played the Thief in *God's Thieves* and Rep in *Electric Chair* (both Bronx Art Th., N.Y.C., 1930–31); Surogalsky in *Between Two Fires* (Littman's People's Th., Detroit, Mich., 1932); and was a featured character actor in classical repertory, Maurice Schwartz Art Th., N.Y.C. (1933–34) and in ten productions with the Beaux Arts Th., Los Angeles, Calif. (1935–37).

He toured extensively in Yiddish repertory (1935–48) and made his debut on the English-speaking stage as Esdras in *Winterset* (Writer's Club Th., Hollywood, Calif., 1937); was again a featured character actor in Yiddish theatre in twenty productions at Douglas Park Th., Chicago, Ill. (1937–38); and in fifty productions in N.Y.C., Los Angeles, San Francisco, and other cities (1939–48). He made his Bway debut as Uncle David in *Me and Molly* (Belasco Th., Feb. 26, 1948); subsequently played Max Pincus in *The Fifth Season* (Hyde Park Playhouse, N.Y., 1956–57); Simon Lowe in *The 49th Cousin* (Ambassador Th., N.Y.C., Oct. 27, 1960); Yonkel Feinberg in *A Worm in Horse Radish* (Maidman Playhouse, 1961); Al Gottlieb in *I Was Dancing* (Lyceum, Nov. 8, 1964); Mr. Foreman in *Enter Laughing* (Playhouse in the Park, Philadelphia, Pa., 1964); Sidney in *Catch Me If You Can* (Morosco, N.Y.C., Mar. 9, 1965); Gittleman in *Enemies* and the Tutor in *Friends* (Theater East, Sept. 19, 1965); was in *The World of Sholem Aleichem* (Roosevelt Playhouse, Miami Beach, Fla., 1966); played Mr. Lepke in *Jimmy Shine* (Brooks Atkinson Th., Dec. 5, 1968); Mr. Blum in *Midnight Ride of Alvin Blum* (Gateway Playhouse, L.I., 1968); and Uncle David in *Molly* (Alvin, N.Y.C., Nov. 1, 1973).

Films. Mr. Mintz made his motion picture debut in *She* (Par., 1935) and appeared also in *Molly* (Par., 1951); *Proud Rebel* (Buena Vista, 1958); and *Murder, Inc.* (20th-Fox, 1960).

Television and Radio. On radio and television, Mr. Mintz played Uncle David in The Goldbergs (NBC, 1950–51). Since 1950, he has been on many television shows, including Kraft Th. (NBC); Play of the Week; Steve Allen Show (NBC); Johnny Carson Show (NBC); Ford Startime (NBC); Ben Casey (ABC); Jack Paar Show (NBC); Merv Griffin; US Steel Hour (CBS); I Spy (NBC); Naked City (ABC); Hallmark Hall of Fame (NBC); Dr. Kildare (NBC); Studio One (CBS); and he has made various commercials.

Night Clubs. In the 1930s, Mr Mintz was a singing waiter and standup comic at Catskill Mts. (N.Y.) resorts.

Concerts. Mr. Mintz has visited colleges and cultural centers from coast to coast, presenting monologues in Yiddish and English based on the writings of such famous Yiddish authors as Sholem Aleichem and I. L. Peretz.

Awards. Mr. Mintz was nominated in the *Variety* NY drama critics poll for giving the best Performance by an actor in a supporting role for his depiction of Al Gottlieb in *I Was Dancing* (1964).

Recreation. Mr. Mintz has special interest in wardrobe and makeup. He is an avid reader, collects books, became interested in music because of his wife's work as pianist and teacher, and paints portraits with greasepaints.

MITCHELL, JAMES. Actor, dancer. b. James H. Mitchell, Feb. 29, 1920, Sacramento, Calif., to John and Edith (Burne) Mitchell. Grad. Turlock (Calif.) Union H.S., 1937; Los Angeles City Coll., A.A.; Empire State Coll., B.A. 1974. Member of AEA; SAG; AFTRA; AGMA. Address: 6 W. 77th St., New York, NY 10024, tel. (212) 787-4247.

Theatre. Mr. Mitchell made his N.Y.C. debut as a dancer in *Bloomer Girl* (Shubert Th., Oct. 5, 1944); subsequently appeared as Rocky in *Billion Dollar Baby* (Alvin, Dec. 21, 1945); and Harry Beaton in *Brigadoon* (Ziegfeld, Mar. 13, 1947).

He was guest soloist during the Ballet Theatre's European tour (1950) appearing in *Pillar of Fire, Fall River Legend, Rodeo* and *Facsmilie;* played Pete Billings in *Paint Your Wagon* (Shubert, N.Y.C., Nov. 12, 1951); appeared as guest soloist in the ballet *Rib of Eve* (Metropolitan Opera House, 1951); played Harry Beaton in *Brigadoon* (St. Louis Municipal Opera, Mo., Summer 1952); and toured with the Agnes de Mille Dance Th. (1953–54). At the Kennebunkport (Me.) Playhouse, he played File in *The Rainmaker*, Sakini in *The Teahouse of the August Moon* (Summer 1955); and Jeff in *Bells Are Ringing* (Summer 1956). He took over (Fall 1956) the role of Mack the Knife in *The Three-penny Opera* (Th. de Lys, N.Y.C., Sept. 20, 1955); played the Soldier in *L'Histoire du Soldat* (NY City Ctr., Oct. 16, 1956); Injun Joe in *Livin' the Life* (Phoenix, Apr. 27, 1957); Jigger Craven in *Carousel* (NY City Ctr., Sept. 11, 1957); the Enemy in *Winkelberg* (Renata, Jan. 14, 1958); and Capt. Wickham in *First Impressions* (Alvin, Mar. 19, 1959).

Mr. Mitchell appeared in a stock production of *Tonight at 8:30* (Coconut Grove Playhouse, Miami, Fla., Summer 1959); Marco the Magnificent in *Car-*

nival! (Imperial, N.Y.C., Apr. 13, 1961), a role he played with the Civic Light Opera Assn. (Los Angeles, San Francisco, Calif., Summer 1962), and repeated in London (Lyric, Feb. 8, 1963). He appeared as Dominic in the Santa Fe (N. Mex.) Opera Co. production of *Jeanne d'Arc au Bucher* (July 1963); played the Doctor in *The Deputy* (Brooks Atkinson Th., N.Y.C., Feb. 26, 1964); and Dr. Ostermork in *The Father* (Roundabout Th., N.Y.C., 1973).

Films. Mr. Mitchell made his debut in *Colorado Territory* (WB, 1949); subsequently appeared in *Border Incident* (MGM, 1949); *Stars in My Crown* (MGM, 1950); *The Band Wagon* (MGM, 1953); *Deep in My Heart* (MGM, 1954); *The Prodigal* (MGM, 1955); *Oklahoma!* (Magna, 1955); and *The Peacemaker* (UA, 1956).

Television. He has played in *Rashomon* and *The Enchanted* (Play of the Week, WNTA); appeared on Omnibus (NBC); the series Edge of Night (CBS); Armstrong Circle Th. (CBS); Camera Three (CBS); Twilight Zone (CBS); Stakeout; Andy Williams Show; Seven Lively Arts; performed on *An Evening with Cyd Charisse;* and appeared in the series Where the Heart Is (CBS, 1968–1973).

MITCHELL, JOHN D. Theatre executive, director. b. John Dietrich Mitchell, Nov. 3, 1917, Rockford, Ill., to John Dennis R. and Dora (Schroeder) Mitchell. Grad. Rockford H.S., 1935; attended Univ. of Illinois, 1935–37; grad. Northwestern Univ., B.S. 1939, M.A. 1940; Columbia Univ., Ed. D. 1956. Studied with Alfred Dixon, N.Y.C., 1943. Married Aug. 25, 1956, to Miriam Picairn, actress, co-founder and vice-pres. of IASTA; two sons, one daughter. Member of AAUP; AEA; ATA; IASTA (pres.); Beneficia Foundation (bd. mbr.); Council of Performing Arts, Univ. of Pa. (trustee); Comm. for Fine Arts, Fairleigh Dickinson Univ.; RTDG; Nippon Club; The Players. Address: (home) Creek Rd., Bryn Athyn, PA 19009, tel. (215) WI 7-0924; (bus.) IASTA, 310 W. 56th St., New York, NY 10023, tel. (212) 581-3133.

Mr. Mitchell and his wife founded the Institute for Advanced Studies in Theatre Arts (IASTA) in 1958, of which Mr. Mitchell is president and a member of the board of trustees. IASTA, a non-profit educational institution chartered by the Board of Regents of the Univ. of the State of New York, is a center providing advanced training for people in professional and educational theatre through workshop productions of theatre classics, directed by leading foreign directors in English-language versions.

He was producer-director of IASTA's international theatre festivals, given at the Wharf Th. (Nantucket, Mass., 1961) and the Univ. of Denver (Colo., 1963). In Nantucket, Mr. Mitchell directed *The Heiress* and *Antigone*, and in Denver, *The False Confessions, Knight from Olmedo*, and the world premiere of Richard Wilbur's translation of *Tartuffe*. Mr. Mitchell produced IASTA's *Phèdre* (Greenwich Mews Th., N.Y.C., Feb. 10, 1966), also at the Festival of American Arts and Humanities (American Embassy Th., London, England, June 1966) and *The Butterfly Dream* (Greenwich Mews Th., N.Y.C., May 1966); produced *House of Fools*, of which he was also co-translator (Greenwich Mews Th., Apr. 1972); the Peking Opera *White Snake*, which he also directed (Asia House, N.Y.C., Jan. 1972); and he was artistic director and executive producer of *Your Own Thing* (Fourth International Festival of Arts, Monte Carlo, Monaco, Aug. 1973).

He made his stage debut playing Eddie in *Spring Again* (Henry Miller's Th., N.Y.C., Nov. 10, 1941; moved to Playhouse, Jan. 12, 1942).

He was associate professor of dramatic arts at Manhattan Coll. and director of the Manhattan (N.Y.C.) Players Th. (1948–58), and was guest director at the Wharf Th. (Nantucket, Mass., Aug. 1959).

He was the US delegate to the Fifth Congress of the International Theatre Institute at The Hague (Neth., 1953); delegate and president of the committee on theatre and youth at the World Conference on Theatre (Bombay, India, 1956); and U.S. delegate to the Second Congress of the International Amateur Theatre Association (The Hague, Neth., 1953).

Radio. Mr. Mitchell was co-producer and director of the Metropolitan Opera Broadcasts and the Boston Symphony broadcasts (ABC, 1943–48).

Other Activities. Mr. Mitchell was a delegate to the Conference on Soviet-US Cultural Exchange (Institute of International Education, N.Y.C.); a delegate to the US-Japan Cultural Exchange Conference (Washington, D.C., 1964); chairman of the Fulbright Theatre Committee (1961); and a delegate to the conferences on exchange in performing arts with the People's Republic of China, National Committee on US-China Relations (Asia House, N.Y.C., Nov. 1973–Jan. 1974).

Published Works. He is the author of *Andre Gide: Rebel and Conformist* (1958); editor and a translator of *Red Pear Garden* (1974); co-editor of *Wild Boar Forest* (1974); and co-translator of *Verlaine's Unpublished Erotic Poems*.

Awards. He received the Medal for Research in Russian Theatre from the Moscow Art Theatre (1963).

Recreation. Swimming, languages, archaeology.

MITCHELL, LEE. Educator, writer. b. Oct. 24, 1906, Washington, D.C., to Joseph Donald and Irene (Helbling) Mitchell. Grad. Carnegie Inst. of Tech., B.A. 1929; Northwestern Univ., M.A., Ph.D. 1941. Married June 8, 1940, to Maurine Morgan. Served Army, US Corps of Engineers, 1942–46; rank, Capt. Member of AETA (pres., 1951; chmn., bd. of research 1954–55); ANTA (bd. of dir. 1956–58; treas., Chicago chapter 1959); MLA; SAA; AAUP. Address: Dept. of Speech and Theatre, Western Kentucky University, Bowling Green, KY 42101.

Since 1971, Mr. Mitchell has been distinguished professor of the theatre at Western Kentucky Univ. From 1929–71, he had been a member of the faculty at Northwestern Univ. (instructor, 1929–38; asst. professor, 1938–47; assoc. professor, 1947–52; professor, 1952–71, and chairman of the Dept. of Theatre and director of University Th., 1951–71).

Published Works. With William P. Halstead and H. Darkes Albright, he wrote *Principles of Theatre Art* (1955).

He has been associate editor of *Educational Theatre Journal* since 1960; and has contributed articles to the *Educational Theatre Journal, Theatre Arts, Quarterly Journal of Speech* and *Speech Monographs*.

Awards. He received the Otto H. Kahn Prize for dramatic production at the Carnegie Inst. of Tech. (1929).

Recreation. Military miniatures.

MITCHELL, LOFTEN. Playwright. b. Apr. 15, 1919, Columbus, N.C., to Ulysses Sanford and Willia (Spaulding) Mitchell. Father, laborer. Grad. DeWitt Clinton H.S., Bronx, N.Y., 1937; attended City Coll. of New York, 1937–38; grad. Talladega Coll., A.B. 1943. Studied playwriting with John Gassner, Columbia Univ., 1947–51; studied with John Bunn of the Salem Community Dramatizers, N.Y.C., 1936–37, and Dick Campbell of the Rose McClendon Players, N.Y.C., 1937–39. Married Sept. 30, 1948, to Helen Marsh; two sons. Relative in theatre: brother, Louis D. Mitchell, composer. Served USNR, since 1945; rank, Seaman 2/c. He teaches at the State University of New York at Binghamton and is a member of Dramatists Guild (New Dramatists Comm.); Amer. Society of African Culture; NAACP; St. Marks-in-the-Bouwerie Episcopal Church; Harlem Cultural Committee (vice-chairman, literary division). Address: c/o Ann Elmo, 52 Vanderbilt Ave., New York, NY 10017.

Pre-Theatre. Social work, writing.

Theatre. Mr. Mitchell made his stage debut as Victor in the Pioneer Drama Group production, *Cocktails* (Elks Th., N.Y.C., Jan. 16, 1938); subsequently played Aaron in *Having a Wonderful Time* (Rose McClendon Players Workshop Th., Nov. 1938); an Angel in the cooperative players production of *The Black Messiah* (Nora Bayes Th., June 1939).

Mr. Mitchell's first play to be produced was *Blood in the Night* (115 St. Library, N.Y.C., Mar. 1946); followed by *The Bancroft Dynasty* (Harlem Showcase, Mar.–June 1948), which was revived (1949, 1950); and *The Cellar* (Harlem Showcase, Nov.–Apr. 1953).

His play *A Land Beyond the River* was produced at the Greenwich Mews Th. (Mar. 28, 1957), and on tour (1958–59); he wrote, with Irving Burgie, *Ballad for Bimshire* (Mayfair, Oct. 15, 1963); and, with John Oliver Killens, *Ballad for the Winter Soldiers*, a dramatic documentary, presented as a benefit show for the Congress on Racial Equality (Philharmonic Hall, Lincoln Ctr., Sept. 28, 1964). *Ballad for Bimshire* was rewritten and produced (Karamu Th., Cleveland, Ohio, Sept. 29, 1964); and he wrote the book for *Bubbling Brown Sugar*, a musical (Philadelphia, Pa., 1975).

Films. Mr. Mitchell wrote *Young Man of Williamsburg* (YM-YWHA, Williamsburg, Va., 1955); *Integration Report One* (Andover Productions, 1959); and *I'm Sorry* (1965).

Television and Radio. For radio, he wrote *Tribute to C.C. Spaulding*, a special program for WLIB (N.Y.C., 1952); a daily program, Friendly Advisor (WWRL, N.Y.C., 1955); and a weekly program, The Later Years (WNYC, 1959–62).

For television, he wrote *Tell Pharoah*, a documentary commissioned by the American Negro Emancipation Centennial Authority (Cleveland, Ohio, 1963).

Other Activities. He served as editor for the *NAACP Freedom Journal*, which was published in May 1964.

Published Works. Mr. Mitchell's play *Star of the Morning: Scenes in the Life of Bert Williams* was published in *Black Drama Anthology* (1971). Other works include *Black Drama: The Story of the American Negro in the Theatre* (1967); a novel, *The Stubborn Old Lady* (1972); and *Voices of The Black Theatre* (1975). Mr. Mitchell has also contributed articles to *The Negro in the Theatre; Theatre Arts* (1953); has written "Negro Spettacolo" for *Encyclopedia Della Spettacolo* (Rome, It., 1961), "An Anglican from Harlem" for the *Episcopalian* Magazine (1962); "The Negro in the Theatre Since 1948" for the *Oxford Companion* (1962); "The History of the Negro Theatre" for *Freedomways* Magazine (1963); "Report from Riot-Torn Harlem" for the Salvation Army *War Cry* (1964); "What's It Really Like?," "The Need for a Harlem Theatre," "Crash Corner," and "Elston Howard Night" for *The Amsterdam News* (Summer 1964); and "Harlem Reconsidered; Memories of My Native Land" for *Freedomways* Magazine (Nov. 1964).

He collaborated, with Langston Hughes, William Branch, and others, on *The American Negro Writer and His Roots* (May 1959).

Awards. He received a Guggenheim Award for "creative writing in the drama" (1958–59), a Rockefeller Grant through the New Dramatists Committee (1961); and a Harlem Cultural Committee Award (1969).

MITCHELL, RUTH. Production stage manager, director. b. Ruth Kornfeld, Sept. 24, 1919, Newark, N.J., to Arthur and Miriam (Mitchell) Kornfeld. Father, salesman. Relative in theatre: Lewis Mitchell, director, stage manager, playwright. Grad. West Side H.S., Newark, N.J., 1937. Member of AEA.

Theatre. Miss Mitchell made her stage debut as a dancer and an actress (Mohawk Drama Festival, Schenectady, N.Y., 1936); subsequently appeared in the touring production of *Pinocchio* (Clare Tree Major's children's theatre, 1937); and in a touring production of *Rio Rita* (1938); and was assistant stage manager of stock productions of *The Second Mrs. Tanqueray* and *Her Cardboard Lover* (Summers 1942–43).

She was assistant to the director of *Annie Get Your Gun* (Imperial Th., N.Y.C., May 16, 1946); stage manager for *Memphis Bound* (Bway, May 24, 1945); *Happy Birthday* (Broadhurst, Oct. 31, 1946); *Mister*

Roberts (Alvin, Feb. 18, 1948); and *The King and I* (St. James Th., Mar. 29, 1951), with which she toured as production stage manager (1954). She was stage manager of *Pipe Dream* (Shubert, N.Y.C., Nov. 30, 1955); *Bells Are Ringing* (Shubert, Nov. 29, 1956); production stage manager of *West Side Story* (Winter Garden, Sept. 26, 1957; Her Majesty's Th., London, England, Dec. 12, 1958); *Gypsy* (Bway, N.Y.C., May 21, 1959); *Fiorello!* (Broadhurst, Nov. 23, 1959); *Tenderloin* (46 St. Th., Oct. 17, 1960); and *A Call on Kuprin* (Broadhurst, May 25, 1961). She directed a production of *West Side Story* (O'-Keefe Center, Toronto, Canada, July 10, 1961).

Miss Mitchell was production stage manager of *Take Her, She's Mine* (Biltmore, N.Y.C., Dec. 31, 1961); *A Funny Thing Happened on the Way to the Forum* (Alvin, May 8, 1962; Strand, London, Oct. 3, 1963); assistant director of the national touring company of *Fiorello!* (opened State Fair Music Hall, Dallas, Tex., Aug. 8, 1960; closed Erlanger, Philadelphia, Pa., Mar. 31, 1962); production stage manager of *She Loves Me* (Eugene O'Neill Th., N.Y.C., Apr. 23, 1963; Lyric, London, Apr. 29, 1964); *Fiddler on the Roof* (Imperial, N.Y.C., Sept. 22, 1964; and national tour, 1966); *Poor Bitos* (Cort, N.Y.C., Nov. 14, 1964); and *Baker Street* (Broadway Th., Feb. 16, 1965); and production supervisor for *Flora, the Red Menace* (Alvin, May 11, 1965).

Harold Prince, in association with Miss Mitchell, presented *It's a Bird, It's a Plane, It's Superman* (Alvin, Mar. 29, 1966), and *Cabaret* (Broadhurst, Nov. 20, 1966), for which productions she also served as production stage manager. She and Mr. Prince subsequently presented *Zorba* (Imperial, Nov. 11, 1968); *Company* (Alvin, Apr. 26, 1970; and national tour, 1971–72); and *Follies* (Winter Garden, Apr. 4, 1971), for which Miss Mitchell was production supervisor. She was assistant director for *The Great God Brown* (Lyceum, Dec. 10, 1972); production supervisor for *A Little Night Music* (Shubert, Feb. 25, 1973); assistant director for *The Visit* (Ethel Barrymore Th., Nov. 25, 1973); and *Candide* (Chelsea Th. Ctr., Brooklyn Acad. of Music, Dec. 11, 1973); was production supervisor, and with Harold Prince, co-produced the national tour of *A Little Night Music* (1974); and was production supervisor for *Candide* when it moved to Bway (Broadway Th., Mar. 5, 1974).

Recreation. Photography, water skiing, ice skating.

MOE, CHRISTIAN H. Playwright, educator. b. Christian Hollis Moe, July 6, 1929, New York City, to Henry Allen and Edith (Monroe) Moe. Father, foundation executive. Attended Putney Sch. 1944–45; grad. Blair Acad., Blairstown, N.J., 1947; Coll. of William and Mary, A.B. 1951; studied at Columbia Univ., Summer 1951; grad. Univ. of North Carolina, M.A. 1955; Cornell Univ., Ph.D. 1958; post-doctoral study, London, and research, Oxford, 1968. Married May 7, 1952, to Carolyn Forman; two sons. Served USN 1950–55. Member of ATA (chmn., pres. comm. on touring exhibits, 1960–61; chairman, art museums and theatres project, 1962–64; chairman, publications committee, 1966–71; assn. bibliographer, 1972–to date); New Playwriting Awards Chairman, Midwest Region, American College Theatre Festival (1973–to date); The Institute of Outdoor Drama, Chapel Hill, N.C. (mbr., adv. bd., 1965–to date); Illinois Arts Council (th. adv. comm., 1967–68; SCA: Illinois Speech Assn.; Southeastern Theatre Conference; Illinois State Historical Society; Phi Beta Kappa; Omicron Delta Kappa; Theta Alpha Phi; National Collegiate Players. Address: (home) 1203 South Cherry St., Carbondale, IL 62901, tel. (618) 457-5130; (bus.) Theatre Dept. Southern Illinois University, Carbondale, IL tel. (618) 453-5741.

Mr. Moe is professor and associate director of theatre at Southern Illinois University, where he also directs student productions.

He wrote *Gomennasai* (Univ. of North Carolina, Chapel Hill, Jan. 12–13, 1955; Cornell Univ., Ithaca, N.Y., May 26, 1957); *The Finer Performance* (Univ. of North Carolina, Chapel Hill, May 18–19, 1955); *Stranger in the Land* (Univ. of North Carolina, Chapel Hill, Mar. 27–31, 1957; St. Felix St. Playhouse, N.Y.C., Nov. 15–16, 1957); *Hark Upon the Gale* (350th Anniversary of Jamestown, Va., at Coll. of William and Mary, Williamsburg, Va., Oct. 23–25, 1957); *The Strolling Players*, written with Darwin Reid Payne (Southern Illinois Univ., Carbondale, Nov. 1962); *Make Her Wilderness Like Eden* (Illinois State Sesquicentennial Drama, Museum of Science and Industry, Chicago, Dec. 26–29, 1967); *Between the Tower and the Town* (Mississippi River Tricentennial Celebration, Grand Tower, Ill., July 6–8, 1973); *How Santa Claus Came to Simpson's Crossing*, adapted with Cameron Garbutt (Southern Illinois Univ., Dec. 5–8, 1973). His publications also include the books *Creating Historical Drama*, written with George McCalmon, Southern Illinois University Press, 1965; *Six New Plays for Children*, edited and written with Darwin Reid Payne, Southern Illinois University Press, 1971; and contributions to *The William and Mary Theatre: A Chronicle, 1926–56*, Althea Hunt, ed., The Dietz Press, 1968; *Bibliographic Annual of Speech Communication*, 1973; *Contemporary Dramatists*, James Vinson, ed., St. James Press, 1974; and various newspapers, speech and theatre journals.

He appeared in two outdoor symphonic dramas, *The Common Glory* (Matoaka Lake Th., Williamsburg, Va., Summers 1949–50, 1957), and *Unto These Hills* (Mountainside Th., Cherokee, N.C., Summers 1954–55).

Awards. Mr. Moe received the Frederick H. Koch Memorial Scholarship for Playwriting, Univ. of North Carolina, 1955; won awards in the Samuel French Collegiate Playwriting Contest, 1956, 1957; won the Encore Players' National Playwriting Contest, 1957; received The Joseph D. Feldman Award in Playwriting, 1957; won the Humboldt National Children's Play Contest, 1966; and received a special citation presented by the Governor of Illinois, 1968.

Recreation. Tennis.

MOFFAT, DONALD. Actor, director. b. Dec. 26, 1930, Plymouth, England, to Walter George and Kathleen Mary (Smith) Moffat. Father, insurance agent. Grad. King Edward VI Sch., Totnes, England, 1949; attended Dartington Hall, Devon, 1951–52. Studied at RADA, London, 1952–54. Married May 22, 1954, to Anne Murray, actress; (marr. dis. 1968) one son, one daughter. Married May 1969, Gwen Arner, actress. Served British Army, Royal Artillery, 1949–51; rank; Bombardier. Member of AEA; AFTRA; SAG; SSDC. Address: 223 33rd St., Hermosa Beach, CA 90254, tel. (213) 376-3875.

Theatre. Mr. Moffat made his first stage appearance as the Earl of Loam in a King Edward VI Sch. production of *The Admirable Crichton* (1947); subsequently appeared as the First Murderer in *Macbeth* (Edinburgh Festival, Scotland, Aug. 23, 1954; Old Vic Th., London, Sept. 9, 1954). In stock, he played Albini in *Adelaise* (Ashburton, Devon, 1954); and served as stage manager for the London production of *Salad Days* (Vaudeville, Aug. 8, 1954). At the Old Vic Th. in London, he portrayed Sir Stephen Scroop in *Richard II* (Jan. 18, 1955), the Earl of Douglas in *Henry IV, Part 1* (April 27, 1955), and the Earl of Warwick in *Henry IV, Part 2* (Apr. 28, 1955). He was stage manager for *Romanoff and Juliet* (Piccadilly, May 17, 1956), and *The Skin of Our Teeth* (University Players, Princeton, N.J., 1957).

He made his N.Y.C. debut as Mr. Ogmore and Nogood Boyo in *Under Milk Wood* (Henry Miller's Th., Oct. 15, 1957); subsequently appeared as Mr. Martin in *The Bald Soprano* and Grandfather Jack in *Jack* (Sullivan St. Playhouse, 1958); Detective-Inspector Bruton in the pre-Bway tryout of *Listen to the Mocking Bird* (opened Colonial, Boston, Mass., Dec. 27, 1958; closed Shubert, Washington, D.C., Jan. 29, 1959); and succeeded (Feb. 1959) Roberts Blossom as Shabyelsky in *Ivanov* (Renata, N.Y.C., Oct. 7, 1958).

He played Verges in *Much Ado About Nothing* (Lunt-Fontanne, Sept. 17, 1959); George in *The Tumbler* (Helen Hayes Th., Feb. 24, 1960); the Clerk of Court in *Duel of Angels* (Helen Hayes Th., Apr. 19, 1960); and at the Akron (Ohio) Shakespeare Festival (1960), he played the title role in *Richard II*, the Earl of Worcester in *Henry IV, Part I*, Justice Shallow in *Henry IV, Part 2* and Chorus in *Henry V*; played Pat in the national tour of *The Hostage* (opened O'Keefe Center, Toronto, Canada, Jan. 30, 1961); at the McCarter Th. for APA (Princeton, N.J. 1961), he played Laudisi in *Right You Are*, Geronte in *Scapin* and the Rev. Canon Chasuble in *The Importance of Being Earnest*.

At the Akron (Ohio) Shakespeare Festival (1961), he played the title role in *Macbeth*, Malvolio in *Twelfth Night*, Gremio in *The Taming of the Shrew* and directed *A Midsummer Night's Dream*; played Mr. Tarlton in *Misalliance* (Sheridan Sq. Playhouse, N.Y.C., Sept. 25, 1961); Sam McBryde in *A Passage to India* (Ambassador, Jan. 31, 1962); at the Great Lakes Shakespeare Festival, Cleveland, Ohio (1962), appeared in the title role of *Richard II* and played Touchstone in *As You Like It*; portrayed Julian Sheffington in *The Affair* (Henry Miller's Th., N.Y.C., Sept. 20, 1962); and at the Playhouse-in-the-Park (Cincinnati, Ohio, 1963), played Dick Dudgeon in *The Devil's Disciple*, A and B in *Act Without Words* and Henry IV in *The Emperor*.

Mr. Moffat repeated his role of Gremio in *The Taming of the Shrew* (Phoenix, N.Y.C., Mar. 6, 1963); and at the Great Lakes Shakespeare Festival (1963), served as artistic associate and director of *Julius Caesar* and *The Merry Wives of Windsor*, and played the title role in *Henry V* and Duke Vincentio in *Measure for Measure*.

He played Aston in *The Caretaker* (Jan. 1964); rejoined APA repertory to play alternately Octavius Robinson and Jack Tanner in *Man and Superman* (Univ. of Mich. and Phoenix 74th St., N.Y.C., 1964); Andrei in *War and Peace* (1965); Martin Vanderhoff in *You Can't Take It with You* (Lyceum, 1965). Subsequently he directed *Miss Julie* (McCarter Th., Princeton, N.J., 1966), and played in repertory at Royal Alexandra, Toronto, Canada; Huntington Hartford, Los Angeles, Calif.; Univ. of Mich., Ann Arbor; and Montreal, Canada, in the roles of Lamberto Laudisi in *Right You Are* (Nov. 1966); Hjalmar Ekdal in *The Wild Duck* (Feb. 1967); Granpa Vanderhoff in *You Can't Take It with You* (Mar. 1967); and Andrei in *War and Peace*. He played Joseph Surface in *School for Scandal* (Lyceum, N.Y.C., June 1967); Lopahin in *Cherry Orchard* (Lyceum, Jan. 1969); co-directed and played Sailor Mahan in *Cock-a-Doodle-Dandy* (Lyceum, Mar. 1969); played Horatio in *Hamlet* (June 1969) and Chanal in *Chemin de Fer* (June 1970) at the Mark Taper Forum, Los Angeles; played in *Hadrian VII* and the title role in *The Magistrate* (Bucks County Playhouse, Pa., 1970); Richard in *Father's Day* (Mark Taper Forum, Oct. 1970); directed and repeated the role of Richard in *Father's Day* (Golden Th., N.Y.C., Mar. 1971); played Thomas Melville in *Trial of Catonsville Nine* (Mark Taper Forum, May 1971); Boniface in *Hotel Paradiso* (Dec. 1971), and Vagabond in *The Tavern* (Feb. 1973) at the Seattle Rep. Th.; Joseph Malley in *Child's Play* (Studio Arena Th., Buffalo, N.Y., Apr. 1973); Charles in *Forget-Me-Not-Lane* (Mark Taper Forum, May 1973); and Harpagon in *The Miser* (Studio Arena Th., Mar. 1974).

Films. Mr. Moffat played Swanston in *Pursuit of the Graf Spee* (Rank, 1957); Rachel's Father in *Rachel, Rachel* (WB, 1968); Manning in *Great Northfield, Minnesota, Raid* (U, 1970): played in *R.P.M.* (Col., 1970); Thomas Melville in *Trial of Catonsville Nine* (1971); Art in *Showdown* (U, 1972); and McPherson in *Terminal Man* (WB, 1973).

Television. He appeared in *Ad Astra* (Camera 3, CBS, 1958), and played Jimmy in *You Can't Have Everything* (US Steel Hour, CBS, 1961).

He has made various guest appearances in *Hawaii Five-O*, Bonanza, High Chapparal, Ironside, Mission: Impossible, Mannix, and Gunsmoke. He appeared as the Reverend Lundstrom in *The New Land* (ABC, 1974).

MOFFATT, JOHN. Actor. b. Albert John Moffatt, Sept. 24, 1922, Badby, Daventry, England, to Ernest George and Letitia (Hickman) Moffatt. Father and mother, servants to the royal family. Educated in England. Member of AEA. Address: 59 Warrington Crescent, London W.9, England tel. CUN 1091.

Pre-Theatre. Bank clerk.

Theatre. Mr. Moffatt made his debut touring as Karl in a Children's Theatre production of *The Snow Queen* (Oct. 1944).

During 1945–49, he appeared in 200 repertory productions in Perth and Oxford; at the Perth (Scot.) Repertory Th., he played Sebastian in *Twelfth Night* (1945), Richard Dudgeon in *The Devil's Disciple,* Louis Dubedat in *The Doctor's Dilemma,* Laertes in *Hamlet,* Frank Gibbon in *The Happy Breed,* Bassanio in *The Merchant of Venice* and Alfred Doolittle in *Pygmalion* (1946–47); for the Oxford (Eng.) Repertory Co., he played the Stage Manager in *Our Town,* Mr. Puff in *The Critic,* Konstantin Treplev in *The Seagull,* Waldo Lydecker in *Laura,* Otto in *Design for Living,* Gribaud in *The Duke in Darkness,* the title role in *Mother Goose,* Gerald Popkiss in *Rookery Nook,* Tesman in *Hedda Gabler,* Marchbanks in *Candida,* and the Angel in *Tobias and the Angel* (1947–49).

He appeared in six productions for the Bristol (Eng.) Old Vic Co. (Jan.–June 1950); made his London debut as Loyale in *Tartuffe* (Lyric, Hammersmith, June 27, 1950); followed by the Hotel Waiter in *Point of Departure* (Lyric, Hammersmith, Nov. 1, 1950); Verges in *Much Ado About Nothing* (Phoenix, Jan. 11, 1952); Paulina's Steward in *The Winter's Tale* (Phoenix, June 27, 1952); Frank Ford in *The Square Ring* (Lyric, Hammersmith, Oct. 21, 1952); and Nicobar in *The Apple Cart* (Haymarket, May 7, 1953).

Mr. Moffat played Ambrose Applejohn in *Ambrose Applejohn's Adventure* (Oxford Playhouse, Dec. 1953); toured as Jakob in *The Light Is Dark Enough* (Jan. 1954), also played this role in London (Aldwych, Apr. 30, 1954); and for the Marlowe Th. Repertory Co., appeared as the Ugly Sister in a pantomine production of *Cinderella* (Canterbury, Dec. 1954).

For the Hornchurch Repertory Co. (Queen's Th.), he played Richard Greatham in *Hay Fever,* the Wicked Fairy in *The Love of Four Colonels,* Ben in *The Little Foxes,* and Claude in *The Confidential Clerk* (1955).

He played Dr. Grenock in the London production of *Mr. Kettle and Mrs. Moon* (Duchess, Sept. 1, 1955), also toured England in it; at the Royal Court Th., played Dr. Bitterling in *Cards of Identity* (June 26, 1956), the Second God in *The Good Woman of Setzuan* (Oct. 31, 1956), Mr. Sparkish in *The Country Wife* (Dec. 12, 1956), the Secretary in *Apollo of Bellac* (May 14, 1957), Mr. Fairbrother in *The Making of Moo* (June 25, 1957), and Edwin Goosebell in *How Can We Save Father?* (Aug. 5, 1957).

He made his N.Y.C. debut as Mr. Sparkish in *The Country Wife* (Adelphia, Nov. 27, 1957); for the Richmond (Eng.) Th. Co., played Otto Frank in *The Diary of Anne Frank* (Feb. 1958), Sebastian in *Nude with Violin* (Apr. 1958), toured England as Saxman in *The Holiday* (Sept. 1958), and played Widow Twankey in the Guildford Repertory Th. pantomine production of *Aladdin,* which he wrote (Dec. 1958).

For the Old Vic Co., he played Le Beau in *As You Like It* (Sept. 3, 1959), the Bishop of Carlisle in *Richard III* (Nov. 17, 1959), Dr. Caius in *The Merry Wives of Windsor* (Dec. 22, 1959), Chaplain de Stogumber in *Saint Joan* (Feb. 9, 1960), Mr. Venables in *What Every Woman Knows* (Apr. 12, 1960), and the Dauphin and Burgundy in *Henry V* (May 31, 1960). He also toured Great Britain with the Old Vic Co., playing Chaplain de Stogumber in *Saint Joan,* Algernon Moncrieff in *The Importance of Being Earnest,* and a Witch in *Macbeth* (Sept. 1960), and appeared in these productions in Russia and Poland (Jan. 1961).

He played Jacques' Father in *Jacques* (Royal Court, London, Mar. 1961); Cardinal Cajetan in *Luther* (Royal Court, London, July 1961; St. James, N.Y.C., Sept. 25, 1963); the Queen in the Leatherhead Repertory pantomine, *Puss in Boots* (Dec. 1962); Lord Foppingham in *Virtue in Danger* (Mermaid, Apr. 10, 1963); at the Oxford Playhouse, appeared as Kuligin in *The Three Sisters* and Orestes in *The Twelfth Hour* (May 1964). He played Dame Trot in the pantomime *Jack and the Beanstalk,* which he also wrote (Marlowe Th., Canterbury, 1964); Ilya Kotchkaryov in *The Marriage Brokers* (Mermaid Th., London, 1965); appeared in *Victorian Music Hall,* which he also devised and directed (Canterbury; Hampstead Th. Club; Ipswich); played Nurse Tickle in *The Babes in the Wood,* which he also wrote (Canterbury, 1965); Chief Inspector Warren in *The Beaver Coat* (Mermaid Th., London, 1966); toured England in *Victorian Music Hall* (1966); repeated his performance as Widow Twankey in the pantomime *Aladdin* (Canterbury, 1966); played Lord Fancourt-Babberley in *Charley's Aunt* (Bury Saint Edmunds, 1967); Henry in *The Fantasticks* (East Grinstead, 1967); repeated his performance as Dame Trot in *Jack and the Beanstalk* (Guildford, 1967); and played Jan Letzeresco in *Dear Charles* (Duchess Th., London, 1967).

As a member of the National Theatre, London (Feb. 1968–Jan. 1971), Mr. Moffatt played Fainall in *The Way of the World,* De Histingua in *A Flea in Her Ear,* Monticelso in *The White Devil,* Judge Brack in *Hedda Gabler,* Geronte in *Scapino* (Young Vic Th.), Von Schlettow, Krakauer, and the Chief of Police in *The Captain of Kopernick,* Menenius in *Coriolanus,* and Sir Joshua in *Tyger.* After leaving the National Th., Mr. Moffatt played Bishop de Sylva in *The Beheading* (Apollo Th., London, Feb. 1971); was in *Cowardy Custard* (Arts Th., Cambridge, June 1972); and again appeared as Dame Trot in *Jack and the Beanstalk* (Christmas 1973).

Films. Mr. Moffatt played a Barman in *Loser Take All* (1957), and appeared in *Tom Jones* (Lopert, 1963), *Julius Caesar* (1971), and *Lady Caroline Lamb* (1972).

Television. He made his debut as Zhukov in *Curtain Down* (BBC, 1953); followed by Grebeauval in *The Public Prosecutor* (BBC, 1953); Eddie Fuselli in *Golden Boy* (BBC, 1953); Diaghilev in *The Man Who Made People* (BBC, 1956); Malvolio in *Twelfth Night* (BBC, Apr. 1957); Brush in *The Clandestine Marriage* (BBC, 1958); and the title role in the series Ben Gunn (BBC, 1958).

Also, the Police Inspector in *The Fourth Wall* (BBC, 1958); the Stranger in *Picnic at Sakkara* (BBC, 1959); Casca in *Julius Caesar* (BBC, 1959); Joseph Surface in *The School for Scandal* (BBC, 1959); Boyd in *The Long Memory* (BBC, 1962); Cyril in *Call Oxbridge 2000* (ATV, 1962); and Fred Johnson in *The Seventh Wave* (ATV, 1963).

Mr. Moffatt has also appeared on television as Sir William Pitt in *The Rules That Jack Made,* Professor Grainger in *Sullavan Brothers,* Mr. Lone in *Kipling,* and Aubrey Drummond in *Sergeant Cork* (all 1964); Mr. Stotman in *Alice,* Gray in *The Body Snatchers,* Marquis d'Harmonville in *The Flying Dragon,* and Edward Cosgrove in *Dismissal Leading to Lustfulness* (all 1965); the Investigator in *The Single Passion* and Joseph Sedley in *Vanity Fair* (both 1966); Andrew Aguecheek in *Twelfth Night* and Don Diego in *Man in Room 17* (both 1967); Teng Kan in *Judge Dee* (1968); Aragon in *The Merchant of Venice* (1971); Captain Brazen in *The Recruiting Officer* and Bobby Southcott in *England, Their England* (both 1973); and Jackie Jackson in *The Deep Blue Sea* and Count von Aerenthal in *Fall of Eagles* (both 1974).

Awards. Mr. Moffatt received the Clarence Derwent Award (1962) as best supporting actor for his performance as Cardinal Cajetan in *Luther.*

Recreation. Collecting old and rare phonograph recordings of theatre personalities.

MOISEIWITSCH, TANYA. Scenic designer. b. Dec. 3, 1914, London, England, to Benno and Daisy (Kennedy) Moiseiwitsch. Father, pianist. Attended schools in England. Studied for the theatre at Central Sch. of Arts and Crafts, London. Married Felix Krish (dec.).

Theatre. Miss Moiseiwitsch designed at first, *The Faithful* (Westminster Th., London, 1934); subsequently went to the Abbey Theatre (Dublin, Ireland) to design *Deuce o' Jacks* (Sept. 1935), and then designed more than 50 productions for the Abbey Players (1935–39).

She designed the settings for *The Golden Cuckoo* (Duchess, London, Jan. 2, 1940); she was resident designer at the Oxford Playhouse (1941–44). She became designer for the Old Vic Co. (1944), for such productions as *The School for Scandal, Dr. Faustus,* and *John Gabriel Borkmann* (Playhouse, Liverpool, 1944–45); *Twelfth Night* and *Beaux' Stratagem* (Th. Royal, Bristol, 1945–46); and at the New Th. (London) for *Uncle Vanya* (Jan. 16, 1945), *The Critic* (Oct. 18, 1945), and *Cyrano de Bergerac* (Oct. 24, 1946).

Miss Moiseiwitsch designed *The Time of Your Life* (Lyric, Hammersmith, London, Feb. 14, 1946); *Bless the Bride* (Adelphi, Apr. 26, 1947); *The Beggar's Opera* (Sadler's Wells, Sept. 6, 1948); the Old Vic production of *The Cherry Orchard* (New, Nov. 25, 1948); *Henry VIII* (Shakespeare Memorial Th., Stratford-upon-Avon, Summer 1949); *Treasure Hunt* (Apollo, London, Sept. 14, 1949); the Old Vic production of *A Month in the Country* (New, Nov. 30, 1949); *Home at Seven* (Wyndham's, Mar. 7, 1950); *The Holly and the Ivy* (Lyric, Hammersmith, Mar. 28, 1950); and *Captain Carvallo* (St. James's, Aug. 9, 1950.

With Alix Stone, she designed at the Shakespeare Memorial Th. (Stratford-upon-Avon), *Henry IV, Part 1* (Apr. 3, 1951), *Henry IV, Part 2* (May 8, 1951), and *Henry V* (July 31, 1951); designed *The Passing Day* (Lyric, Hammersmith, London, Mar. 20, 1951); *Figure of Fun* (Aldwych, Oct. 16, 1951); *A Midsummer Night's Dream* (Old Vic, Dec. 26, 1951); *The Deep Blue Sea* (Duchess, Mar. 5, 1952); designed the Shakespeare Memorial Th. touring production of *Othello* (Australia and New Zealand, 1952); for the Old Vic (London), designed *Julius Caesar* (Feb. 24, 1952), and sets and costumes for *Henry VIII* (May 6, 1953); for the inaugural season of the Stratford Shakespearean Festival (Ontario, Can.), designed, with Tyrone Guthrie, the theatre tent and the productions of *Richard III* and *All's Well That Ends Well* (Summer, 1953); and designed *Measure for Measure, The Taming of the Shrew,* and *King Oedipus* (June 20, Aug. 21, 1954).

She designed settings and costumes for *The Matchmaker* (Edinburgh Festival, Scotland, Aug. 1954; Haymarket, London, Nov. 4, 1954); Royale, N.Y.C., Dec. 5, 1955); at the Stratford Shakespearean Festival, designed *Julius Caesar* and *The Merchant of Venice* (June 27–Aug. 27, 1955); designed *A Life in the Sun* (Edinburgh Festival, Aug. 1955); *The Cherry Orchard* (Piccolo Teatro, Milan, Italy, 1955); at the Stratford Shakespearean Festival, designed *The Merry Wives of Windsor* and *Henry V* (June 18–Aug. 18, 1956); at Shakespeare Memorial Th. (Stratford-upon-Avon), designed *Measure for Measure* (Aug. 14, 1956); and designed *The Two Gentlemen of Verona* (Old Vic, London, Jan. 22, 1957). Miss Moiseiwitsch designed, with Tyrone Guthrie, the new theatre for the Stratford (Ontario, Canada) Shakespearean Festival, which was erected in 1957, and designed *Twelfth Night* (July 1–Sept. 7, 1957); for the company's tour and N.Y.C. appearance, designed *The Two Gentlemen of Verona* (Phoenix, Mar. 18, 1958) and *The Broken Jug* (Phoenix, Apr. 1, 1958); and at Stratford, Canada, designed *The Winter's Tale* and, with Marie Day, *Henry IV, Part 1* (June 23–Sept. 13, 1958).

At the Shakespeare Memorial Th. (Stratford-upon-Avon), she designed *Much Ado About Nothing* (Aug. 26, 1958); designed *The Bright One* (Winter Garden, London, Dec. 10, 1958); *The Merchant of Venice* (Habimah Th., Tel-Aviv, Israel, 1958–59); *All's Well That Ends Well* (Shakespeare Memorial Th., Stratford-upon-Avon, Apr. 21, 1959); the opera *Don Giovanni* (Covent Garden, London, (Oct., 1959); *The Wrong Side of the Park* (Cambridge, Feb. 3, 1960); at the Stratford (Canada) Shakespearean Festival designed *Romeo and Juliet* and *King John* (June 27–Sept. 17, 1960); *Coriolanus* and *Love's Labour's Lost* (June 19–Sept. 23, 1961); designed *Ondine* (Aldwych, London, 1961); and at Stratford,

Canada, redesigned the festival stage with Brian Jackson and designed, with Desmond Hegley, *Cyrano de Bergerac* (June 18–Sept. 29, 1962).

Miss Moiseiwitch has been a principal designer with the Minnesota Theatre Co. (Tyrone Guthrie Th., Minneapolis, 1963–to date) where her work has included designs for *Hamlet, The Miser,* and *The Three Sisters* (May 7–Sept. 22, 1963); *Volpone* and *Saint Joan* (May 11–Oct. 10, 1964); *The Way of the World, The Cherry Orchard* and *The Miser* (May 11–Sept. 7, 1965); *The Skin of Our Teeth,* and *As You Like It* (May 31–Sept. 10, 1966); and *the House of Atreus* (Summer 1968), which was subsequently presented on Bway (Billy Rose Th., N.Y.C., Dec. 17, 1968).

In addition, she designed the sets for the American Shakespeare Festival production of *Antony and Cleopatra* (Stratford, Conn., July 31, 1967); was a guest designer with the Center Th. Group (Mark Taper Forum, Los Angeles, 1967–69 season); and designed the settings for *Volpone* (National Th. at the Old Vic, London, 1968).

Films. Miss Moiseiwitsch designed the film version of the Stratford (Canada) Shakespearean Festival production of *Oedipus Rex* (MPD, 1957).

Recreation. The piano.

MONKS, JOHN JR. Playwright. b. Brooklyn, N.Y., 1910, to John and Emily Frances Monks. Father, actor, insurance executive. Grad. Virginia Military Inst., A.B. 1932 (commissioned 2nd Lt. US Army Cavalry Reserve). Married to Margaret Josephine; one daughter. Served WW II, USMC; rank, Maj. Member of Dramatists Guild; SWG; WGA; The Players. Address: 1058 Napoli Dr., Pacific Palisades, CA 90272.

Theatre. Mr. Monks wrote, with Fred Finklehoff, *Brother Rat* (Biltmore Th., N.Y.C., Dec. 16, 1936).

Films. Mr. Monks and Mr. Finklehoff, wrote *Brother Rat* (WB, 1938); *Brother Rat and Baby* (WB, 1940); *Strike Up the Band* (MGM, 1940); *About Face* (MGM, 1940); and *Babes on Broadway* (MGM, 1941). While in the service, Mr. Monks wrote, directed, and appeared in the documentary film, *We Are the Marines* (20th-Fox, 1942.) He also wrote *The House on 92nd Street* (20th-Fox, 1945); *13 Rue Madeleine* (20th-Fox, 1946); *Wild Harvest* (Par., 1947); *Knock On Any Door* (Col., 1949); *The West Point Story* (WB, 1950); *The People Against O'Hara* (MGM, 1951); *Where's Charley* (WB, 1952); and *So This Is Love* (WB, 1953). With Richard Goldstone, he formed Gold Coast Productions, Inc., and wrote, produced, and directed with Mr. Goldstone, *No Man Is An Island* (U, 1962).

Television. For Climax! (CBS), Mr. Monks wrote *The Gioconda Smile* and *A Box of Chocolates.* He also wrote *Miracle on 34th Street* (20th-Fox Hour), and *High Tor.*

Published Works. He wrote a book on jungle warfare, *A Ribbon and a Star* (1945).

MONTEL, MICHAEL. Director. b. Michael Joseph Montel, Jan. 26, 1939, New York, N.Y., to Joseph Irwin and Gertrude (Michael) Montel. Father, chemical engineer; mother, interior decorator. Educ. Public School 131, N.Y.C.; High School of Performing Arts, N.Y.C.; Jamaica (L.I.) High School; Syracuse Univ., B.S.; graduate study at Hunter Coll., N.Y.C. Professional training with Sawyor Falk, Charles Elson. Member of SSD&C; past member of SAG; AEA. Address: New Phoenix Repertory Co., Lyceum Theatre, 149 W. 45th St., New York, NY 10036, tel. (212) 765-1620.

Theatre. Mr. Montel directed *Oedipus and Jocasta* (Hunter College Playhouse, N.Y.C., Nov. 1963); at the 1965 National Shakespeare Festival, Old Globe Th., San Diego, Calif., was assistant director of *The Merry Wives of Windsor* (June 15), played Capucius in *King Henry VIII* (June 23), and played the Senator in *Coriolanus* (July 13), of which he was also assistant director. He was assistant director of *The Rose Tattoo* (Studio Arena Th., Buffalo, N.Y., Nov. 18, 1965); *After the Fall* (Coconut Grove, Miami, Fla., Jan. 1966; Bucks County Playhouse, New Hope, Pa., June 1966); another production of *The Rose Tattoo* (NY City Ctr., Oct. 20, 1966; moved to Billy Rose Th., Nov. 9, 1966); *Funny Girl* and *On a Clear Day* (both Coconut Grove, Miami, Fla., and Parker Playhouse, Fort Lauderdale, Fla., Jan.–Mar. 1967); *The Glass Managerie* (Mineola, N.Y., Spring 1967); *Incident at Vichy,* in which he also played the Detective (Playhouse in the Park, Philadelphia, Pa., June 1967); *Lion in Winter,* for which he was also advance director (both Coconut Grove, Miami, Fla., and Bucks County Playhouse, New Hope, Pa., July–Aug. 1967); and he was assistant director for the overland tour of *Lion in Winter* (Jan. 17–May 5, 1968).

He was casting director for the Center Theatre Group, Los Angeles, Calif., from May 1968 to March 1972; casting director for the tour of *A Day in the Death of Joe Egg* (Sept. 1968); assistant director for *Beatrice and Benedict* (Dorothy Chandler Pavilion, Los Angeles, May 1970); director of *Father's Day* (New Theatre for Now Workshop, Mark Taper Forum, Los Angeles, Calif., Oct. 1970); *Jeanne d'Arc au bûcher* (Dorothy Chandler Pavilion, Apr. 1971); *Aubrey Beardsley, The Neophyte* (New Theatre for Now, Mark Taper Forum, July 1971).

Mr. Montel has been artistic director, New Phoenix Repertory Co., N.Y.C. since Apr. 1972 and managing director since Sept. 1973. During that period, the company presented *The Great God Brown* (Lyceum, Dec. 10, 1972) and *Don Juan* (Lyceum, Dec. 11, 1972); *The Visit* (Ethel Barrymore Th., Nov. 25, 1973); *Chemin de Fer* (Ethel Barrymore Th., Nov. 26, 1973); and *Holiday,* which Mr. Montel also directed (Ethel Barrymore Th., Dec. 26, 1973). Mr. Montel was also producer (Dec. 1972–May 1974) of the New Phoenix Repertory Sideshows: *A Meeting by the River,* which he also directed (Edison Th., Dec. 12, 1972); *Strike Heaven on the Face* (Bijou, Jan. 15, 1973); *Games* and *After Liverpool* (Bijou, Jan. 22, 1973); *The Government Inspector* (Bijou, Jan. 28, 1973); *Miracle Play* (Playhouse II, Dec. 30, 1973); *The Removalists,* which he also directed (Playhouse II, Jan. 20, 1974); *In the Voodoo Parlor of Marie Leveau,* a program of one-act plays, of which Mr. Montel directed *Gris-Gris* (Playhouse II, Apr. 19, 1974); *Energy Crisis;* and *Pretzels* (Playhouse II, May 17, 1974).

Mr. Montel also directed a production of the opera *Barber of Seville* (Corpus Christi, Tex., Feb. 1973) and the plays *The Second Man* and *A Trip to Niagara* (both Williamstown, Mass., Th., July 1973).

MONTGOMERY, EARL. Actor. b. Aug. 17, 1921, Memphis, Tenn., to Earl and Augusta (McColour) Montgomery. Father, salesman. Grad. South Kent (Conn.) Sch., 1939; Harvard Coll., B.A. 1943. Member of AEA; AFTRA; SAG.

Theatre. Mr. Montgomery first appeared on stage at the age of eight, playing Prince Charming in an elementary-school production of *The Sleeping Beauty* (Memphis, 1929). He made his professional debut as Simon Jenkins in a stock production of *Room Service* (Gretna Playhouse, Mount Gretna, Pa., Summer 1947); and his first Bway appearance as the Mathematician in *Galileo* (Maxine Elliott's Th., Dec. 7, 1947).

He played Roger Doremus in *Summer and Smoke* (Music Box, Oct. 16, 1948); Dr. Bull in *The Relapse* (Morosco, Nov. 22, 1950); Tupman in *Mr. Pickwick* (Plymouth, Sept. 17, 1952); Boyet in *Love's Labour's Lost* (NY City Ctr., Feb. 4, 1953); Salario in *The Merchant of Venice* (NY City Ctr., Mar. 4, 1953); Liebermann in *The Strong Are Lonely* (Broadhurst, Sept. 29, 1953); the Inspector in *Heavenly Twins* (Booth, Nov. 4, 1955); the Abbot in *The Lovers* (Martin Beck Th., May 10, 1956); de Stogumber in *Saint Joan* (Phoenix, Sept. 11, 1956; moved to Coronet, Dec. 25, 1956); the Camerman in *Visit to a Small Planet* (Booth, Feb. 7, 1957), also, succeeded (July 1957) Philip Coolidge as Roger Spelding in the same play a role which he repeated in the national touring production (opened Playhouse, Wilmington, Del., Feb. 5, 1958; closed Geary, San Francisco, Calif., June 28, 1958); and succeeded (June 1959) Henderson Forsythe as Peter Stockman in *An Enemy of the People* (Actors Playhouse, N.Y.C., Feb. 4, 1959).

Mr. Montgomery appeared as Oudatte in *Look After Lulu* (Henry Miller's Th., Mar. 3, 1959); Ramsden in the APA production of *Man and Superman* (Hamilton Th., Bermuda, May 1960); the Bishop of London in *Becket* (St. James, N.Y.C., Oct. 5, 1960); understudied Stubby Kaye in the role of Solomon in *Everybody Loves Opal* (Longacre, Oct. 11, 1961); played Zeno in *Romulus* (Music Box, Jan. 10, 1962); performed in *Atti Unici* (Festival of the Two Worlds, Spoleto, It., 1962); portrayed Ribaud in *The Lady of the Camellias* (Winter Garden, N.Y.C., Mar. 20, 1963); succeeded C.K. Alexander (Apr. 1, 1963) as M. Chauffourier Dubieff in *Tovarich* (Bway Th., Mar. 18, 1963); and played Demiens in *The Rehearsal* (Royale, Sept. 23, 1963).

At the Charles Playhouse (Boston, Mass.), Mr. Montgomery played Sir Anthony Absolute in *The Rivals* (Nov. 11, 1964), Ladislav Sipos in *She Loves Me* (Dec. 23, 1964), and The President in *The Madwoman of Chaillot* (Feb. 3, 1965); Victor in *Gigi* (Summer tour, 1965); with the Repertory Theatre of Lincoln Center (Vivian Beaumont Th., N.Y.C.), he played various roles in *The Caucasian Chalk Circle* (Mar. 24, 1966), Ananias in *The Alchemist* (Oct. 13, 1966), Mr. Crockett in *The East Wind* (Feb. 9, 1967), The Mathematician and Informer in *Galileo* (Apr. 13, 1967); Pothinus in *Her First Roman* (Lunt-Fontanne Th., Oct. 20, 1968); was a member of Studio Arena Th. Repertory Co. (Buffalo, N.Y., 1967–69); and played Father Ambrose in *The Waltz of the Toreadors* (Circle in the Square, N.Y.C., Sept. 13, 1973).

Films. He appeared as Alexander Woollcott in *Act One* (WB, 1963).

Television. Mr. Montgomery made his debut in Love of Life (CBS, 1952); subsequently, appeared on Kraft Television Theatre (NBC); Omnibus (CBS); Robert Montgomery Presents (NBC); and the Jackie Gleason Show (CBS).

Recreation. Handicrafts, antique refinishing.

MONTGOMERY, ELIZABETH. Designer. b. Feb. 15, 1904, Oxfordshire, England to William and Marta (Corbett) Montgomery. Father, educator. Attended Westminster Sch. of Art, London, England. Married 1945 to Pat Wilmot, writer; one son. Member of United Scenic Artists. Address: 27 Grumann Hill Rd., Wilton, CT 06897, tel. (203) PO 2-3874.

Pre-Theatre. Illustrator.

Theatre. Elizabeth Montgomery, known together with Audrey Sophia Harris (dec.) Mar. 1966) and Margaret F. Harris as Motley, designed costumes for *Romeo and Juliet* (Oxford Univ. Dramatic Society, England, 1932); *Men About the House* (Globe, London, 1932); *Strange Orchestra* (St. Martin's, Sept. 27, 1932); *The Merchant of Venice* (Old Vic, Dec. 12, 1932); *Richard of Bordeaux* (New, Feb. 2, 1933); *A Midsummer Night's Dream* (Open Air, July 5, 1933); *Ball at the Savoy* (Sept. 8, 1933); *Spring 1600* (Shaftsbury, Jan. 31, 1934); a tour of *Jack and Jill* (1934); John Gielgud's *Hamlet* (New, London, Nov. 14, 1934) the ballet, *The Haunted Ballroom* (Sadler's Wells, 1934); *The Old Ladies* (New, Apr. 3, 1935); *Noah* (1935); *Dusty Ermine* (Comedy, Mar. 6, 1936); *Aucassin and Nicolette* (Duke of York's, 1936); *Richard II* (Oxford Univ. Dramatic Society, 1936); *Happy Hypocrite* (His Majesty's, London, Apr. 8, 1936); *Farewell Performance* (1936); *Charles the King* (Lyric, Oct. 9, 1936); *The Witch of Edmonton* (Old Vic, Dec. 8, 1936); *Henry V* (Old Vic, Apr. 6, 1937); *He Was Born Gay* (Queen's, 1937); *Great Romance* (New, 1937); *Richard II* (Old Vic, Sept. 6, 1937; *The School for Scandal* (Queen's, Nov. 25, 1937); *Macbeth* (Old Vic, Nov. 26, 1937); *The Three Sisters* (Queen's, Jan. 28, 1938); *The Merchant of Venice* (Queen's, Apr. 21, 1938); *Dear Octopus* (Queen's, Sept. 14, 1938); *The Importance of Being Earnest* (Globe, 1939); *Rhonda Roundabout* (Globe, May 31, 1939); a tour of *Weep for Spring* (1939); *Great Expectations* (Rudolf Steiner Hall, Dec. 7, 1939); and *The Beggar's Opera* (Haymarket, London, Mar. 5, 1940).

Motley designed costumes for *The Doctor's Dilemma* (Shubert, N.Y.C., Mar. 11, 1941); also for its London production (Haymarket, Mar. 4, 1942); *The Cherry Orchard* (New, London, Aug. 28, 1941); *Watch on the Rhine* (Aldwych, Apr. 22, 1942); *The Three Sisters* (Ethel Barrymore Th., N.Y.C., Dec. 21, 1942); *Richard III* (Forrest, Mar. 24, 1943); *Lovers and Friends* (Plymouth, Nov. 29, 1943); *The Cherry Orchard* (Natl., Jan. 25, 1944); *A Highland Fling* (Plymouth, Apr. 28, 1944); *A Bell for Adano* (Cort, Dec. 6, 1944); *The Tempest* (Alvin, Jan. 25, 1945); *Hope for the Best* (Fulton, Feb. 7, 1945); *The Wind of Heaven* (St. James's, London, Apr. 12, 1945); *You Touched Me!* (Booth, N.Y.C., Sept. 25, 1945); *Carib Song* (Adelphi, Sept. 27, 1945); *Skydrift* (Belasco, Nov. 13, 1945); *Pygmalion* (Ethel Barrymore Th., Dec. 26, 1945); *Antony and Cleopatra* (Piccadilly, London, Dec. 20, 1946); *The Importance of Being Earnest* (Royale, N.Y.C., Mar. 3, 1947); *Anne of the Thousand Days* (Shubert, Dec. 8, 1948); *The Heiress* (Haymarket, London, Feb. 1, 1949); *Antigone* (New, Feb. 10, 1949); *South Pacific* (Majestic, N.Y.C., Apr. 7, 1949); *Miss Liberty* (Imperial, July 15, 1949); *Happy as a Lark* (Coronet, Jan. 6, 1950); *The Innocents* (Playhouse, Feb. 1, 1950); Jean Arthur's *Peter Pan* (Imperial, Apr. 24, 1950); *The Liar* (Broadhurst, May 18, 1950); *Bartholomew Fair* (Old Vic, London, Dec. 18, 1950); *Hassan* (Cambridge, May 9, 1951); Orson Welles' *Othello* (St. James's, June 18, 1951); *Paint Your Wagon* (Shubert, N.Y.C., Nov. 12, 1951); *The Grand Tour* (Martin Beck Th., Dec. 10, 1951); and *The Happy Time* (St. James's, London, Jan. 30, 1952).

Also, *Candida* (National, N.Y.C., Apr. 22, 1952); *To Be Continued* (Booth, Apr. 23, 1952); *The Innocents* (Her Majesty's, London, July 3, 1952); *The River Line* (Strand, Oct. 28, 1952); *Midsummer* (Vanderbilt, N.Y.C., Jan. 21, 1953); *Paint Your Wagon* (Her Majesty's, London, Feb. 11, 1953); *Can-Can* (Shubert, N.Y.C., May 7, 1953); *King John* (Old Vic, London, Oct. 27, 1953); *Antony and Cleopatra* (Princes', Nov. 4, 1953); *Mademoiselle Colombe* (Longacre, N.Y.C., Jan. 6, 1954); and *The Immoralist* (Royale, Feb. 8, 1954).

Also, *Charley's Aunt* (New, London, Feb. 10, 1954); *I Capture the Castle* (Aldwych, Mar. 4, 1954); *Wedding in Paris* (London, Hippodrome, Apr. 3, 1954); *Can-Can* (Coliseum, Oct. 14, 1954); *Peter Pan* (Winter Garden, N.Y.C., Oct. 20, 1954); *The Honeys* (Longacre, Apr. 28, 1955); *The Merry Wives of Windsor* (Old Vic, London, Sept. 27, 1955); *The Young and the Beautiful* (Longacre, N.Y.C., Oct. 1, 1955); *Island of Goats* (Fulton, Oct. 4, 1955); *Middle of the Night* (ANTA, Feb. 8, 1956); *A Likely Tale* (Globe, London, Mar. 22, 1956); *The Mulberry Bush* (Royal Court, Apr. 2, 1956); *The Crucible* (Royal Court, Apr. 9, 1956); and *The Most Happy Fella* (Imperial, N.Y.C., May 3, 1956).

Motley designed the costumes for a Shakespeare Memorial Th. production of *Othello* (Stratford-upon-Avon, Eng., May 29, 1956); *Cards of Identity* (Royal Court, London, June 26, 1956); *The Seagull* (Savoy, Aug. 2, 1956); *Long Day's Journey into Night* (Helen Hayes Th., N.Y.C., Nov. 7, 1956); *The Magic Flute* and *Eugene Onegin* (Sadler's Wells Ballet, London, 1957); *As You Like It* (Shakespeare Memorial Th., Apr. 2, 1957); *Shinbone Alley* (Bway Th., N.Y.C., Apr. 13, 1957); *South Pacific* (NY City Ctr., Apr. 24, 1957); *The First Gentleman* (Belasco, Apr. 25, 1957); *Julius Caesar* (Shakespeare Memorial Th., Stratford-upon-Avon, England, May 28, 1957); *The Merchant of Venice* (Amer. Shakespeare Festival, Stratford, Conn., July 10, 1957); *Look Back in Anger* (Lyceum, London, Oct. 1, 1957); *Requiem for a Nun* (Royal Court, Nov. 26, 1957; John Golden Th., N.Y.C., Jan. 30, 1959).

Also, *The Country Wife* (Adelphi, Nov. 27, 1957); *Look Homeward, Angel* (Ethel Barrymore Th., Nov. 28, 1957); *A Majority of One* (Shubert, Feb. 16, 1958); *Love Me Little* (Helen Hayes Th., Mar. 15, 1958); *Romeo and Juliet* (Shakespeare Memorial Th., Stratford-upon-Avon, Apr. 8, 1958); *Jane Eyre* (Belasco, N.Y.C., May 1, 1958); *Hamlet* (Shakespeare Memorial Th., Stratford-upon-Avon, June 3, 1958); *Much Ado About Nothing* (Shakespeare Memorial Th., Stratford-upon-Avon, Aug. 26, 1958); *The Cold Wind and the Warm* (Morosco, N.Y.C., Dec. 8, 1958); *Eugene Onegin* (Sadler's Wells, London, Jan. 1959); *The Rivalry* (Bijou, N.Y.C.; Feb. 7, 1959); *The Magistrate* (Old Vic, London, Mar. 18, 1959); *The Merry Wives of Windsor* (Amer. Shakespare Festival, Stratford, Conn., July 8, 1959); *The Aspern Papers* (Queen's, London, Aug. 12, 1959); *King Lear* (Shakespeare Memorial Th., Stratford-upon-Avon, Aug. 18, 1959); *Rosmersholm* (Royal Court, London, Nov. 18, 1959); *Il Trovatore* (Metropolitan Opera House, N.Y.C., 1959); *Ross* (Haymarket, London, May 2, 1960); *A Man for All Seasons* (Globe, July 1, 1960); *Waiting in the Wings* (Duke of York's, Sept. 7, 1960); *Becket* (St. James, N.Y.C., Oct. 5, 1960); *Simon Boccanegra* (Metropolitan Opera House, 1960); and the Russian tour of *Caprice* (1960).

For the American Shakespeare Festival, Motley designed the costumes for *As You Like It* (June 15, 1961); *Macbeth* (June 16, 1961); and *Troilus and Cressida* (July 23, 1961); for *Ross* (Eugene O'Neill Th., N.Y.C., Dec. 26, 1961); for the pre-Bway tryout of *We take the Town* (opened Shubert, New Haven, Conn., Feb. 19, 1962); *Richard II* (Amer. Shakespeare Festival, Stratford, Conn., June 16, 1962); *Henry IV, Part 1,* (Amer. Shakespeare Festival, June 17, 1962); the opera *Idomeneo* (Sadler's Wells, London, England, Oct. 1962); *Lorenzo* (Plymouth, N.Y.C., Feb 14, 1963); *Tovarich* (Bway, Th., Mar. 18, 1963); the opera *Cosi Fan Tutte* (Sadler's Wells, London, Eng., Mar. 22, 1963); *Mother Courage and Her Children* (Martin Beck Th., N.Y.C., Mar. 28, 1963); *110 in the Shade* (Broadhurst, Oct. 24, 1963); the opera *Faust* (Sadler's Wells, London, England, Sept. 16, 1964); *Ben Franklin in Paris* (Lunt-Fontanne Th., N.Y.C., Oct. 27, 1964); *Baker Street* (Bway Th., Feb. 16, 1965); and *The Devils* (Bway Th., Nov. 16, 1965).

Recreation. Small boat sailing.

MOODY, RICHARD. Educator, writer, theatre historian. b. Richard Anselm Moody, Sept. 30, 1911, Des Moines, Iowa, to Carl Eric and Josephine (Peterson) Moody. Grad. Drake Univ., B.A. 1932, M.A. 1934; attended Yale Univ., 1932–33, 1934–35; Cornell Univ., Ph.D. 1942. Married Feb. 26, 1937, to Carol Martin; one son, one daughter. Served USNR, 1943–46; rank, Lt. Member of AETA; NTC; SAA; American Soc. for Theatre Research; British Soc. for Theatre Research; Theatre Communications Group; Speech Assn. Amer.; Phi Beta Kappa. Address: Red Ridge, RR 1, Bloomington, IN 47401.

Since 1942, Mr. Moody has been associated with Indiana Univ., as assistant professor of speech and theatre (1942–43); associate professor (1946–55); and professor (1955–to date). He was director of the Ind. Univ. Th. (1958–70).

Published Works. Mr. Moody wrote *America Takes the Stage* (1955); *The Astor Place Riot* (1958); *Edwin Forrest, First Star of the American Stage* (1960); *Dramas From the American Theatre, 1762–1909* (1966); and *Lillian Hellman, Playwright* (1972). He has contributed articles to *Quarterly Journal of Speech, American Heritage* Magazine, *Educational Theatre Journal, Compton's Encyclopedia, World Book Encyclopedia,* and *Enciclopedia Della Spettacolo.* .

Awards. Mr. Moody was a National Th. Conference Fellow (1940–42); a Guggenheim Fellow (1959–60); received the Distinguished Alumni Award from Drake Univ. (May 1961); and two of his books, *Edwin Forrest* and *America Takes the Stage* were chosen for the White House Library (Aug. 1963).

MOORE, CARROLL. Playwright. b. Carroll Byron Moore, Jr., May 4, 1913, Somerville, Mass., to Carroll Byron and Helen (Totten) Moore. Grad. Medfield (Mass.) H.S., 1930); Dean Acad., Franklin, Mass., 1931. Married Nov. 29, 1936, to Catherine George; one daughter. Served USN, 1942–45. Member of Dramatists Guild; WGA, West. Address: 32-17 165th St., Flushing, NY 11358.

Theatre. Mr. Moore wrote, with Norman Barasch, *Make a Million* (Playhouse, N.Y.C., Oct. 23, 1958) and *Send Me No Flowers* (Brooks Atkinson Th., Dec. 5, 1960).

Films. *Send Me No Flowers* was made into a Universal film, starring Doris Day and Rock Hudson.

Television and Radio. Since 1946, he has written scripts for the Henry Morgan Show; the Herb Shriner Show; the Fred Allen Show; the Steve Allen Show; and the Garry Moore Show. Later television credits include The Danny Kaye Show, Kraft Music Hall, specials starring Alan King, and Lotsa Luck, (producer), all in collaboration with Norman Barasch. Mr. Moore and Mr. Barasch were script consultants for the series Rhoda (1974–75 season).

Published Works. *Beginner's Luck* and *Daddy, Dear Daddy,* written by Mr. Moore and Norman Barasch, have been published by Samuel French.

MOORE, CHARLES WERNER. actor, director, Educator, 22. b. Sept. 9, 1920, Stafford Springs, Conn., to Charles H. and Harriet (Werner) Moore. Father, retail lumberman. Grad. Westminster Sch., Simsbury, Conn., 1939; Williams Coll., B.A. 1943; Yale Univ., M.F.A. 1950. Married 1945 to Fay Mowery (marr. dis. 1956); married 1962 to Marjorie Anne Battles, actress. Served US Army, 1943–46; rank, 1st Lt. Member of AETA; Alpha Delta Phi.

Mr. Moore was asst. director at the Univ. of Kansas City Playhouse (1950–52); prof. of drama, and director of student productions, at Carnegie-Mellon Inst. of Tech. (Pittsburgh, Pa., 1952–63); and is currently prof. of th. arts at Brandeis Univ. (Waltham, Mass.).

He played Capt. Stanhope in a Westminster (Conn.) school production of *Journey's End* (Jan., 1939); was actor, director, and production stage manager at the Provincetown (Mass.) Playhouse (1947–50), where he played the Sheriff in *Desire Under the Elms,* the Gentleman Caller in *The Glass Menagerie,* Gradeau in *No Exit,* which he also directed, Benedick in *Much Ado About Nothing,* and the Captain in *Gold.* He also directed premiere productions of Conrad Aiken's *Mr. Arcularis* and Dennis Johnston's *Me Golden Cuckoo.* In summer stock, he acted and directed at the Sharon (Conn.) Playhouse (Summers 1958, 1959); was resident director at the Berkshire Playhouse (Stockbridge, Mass., 1959); directed productions at the Theatre-by-the-Sea (Matunuck, R.I., 1960); played Macduff in *Macbeth* (Pittsburgh Playhouse, Pa., 1962); and Rossi in *Time of the Cuckoo,* and Mr. Gibbs in *Our Town* (Sharon Playhouse, Conn., 1963).

Mr. Moore directed the premiere of *Fire!* (Brandeis Univ., Spingold Th., Waltham, Mass., May 1, 1968), and made his Bway debut directing the same play (Longacre, N.Y.C., Jan. 28, 1969); subsequently directed, for the Rep. Th. of the Loretto-Hilton Center, St. Louis, Mo., *The Devils* (Jan. 8, 1971), and *The Rivals* (Mar. 15, 1972); and wrote the book for, with Priscilla B. Dewery, and directed, *Two If By Sea* (Circle in the Square, N.Y.C., Feb. 6, 1972).

Among other productions he has directed at the Spingold Th., Brandeis Univ., are the premiere of *Does a Tiger Wear a Necktie? The Importance of Being Earnest* (Feb. 7, 1968), *The Duchess of Malfi* (Oct. 30, 1968), *Home Monster* (Apr. 30, 1969), *All the King's Men* (Oct. 17, 1973), *Oedipus the King* (Apr. 23, 1974), and the premiere of a musical based on Percy MacKaye's play, *The Scarecrow,* entitled *Lord Scarecrow* (Apr. 22, 1975).

Mr. Moore has written many plays, articles, reviews and television scripts.

Recreation. Trout fishing, carpentry.

MOORE, DENNIE. Actress. b. Florence Moore, Dec. 31, 1907, New York City to Philip and Mary Moore. Father, night watchman. Attended Sacred Heart H.S., N.Y.C.; Paulist Fathers H.S., N.Y.C. Studied acting at AADA, Sargent Dramatic Sch. Married Apr. 30, 1943, to S. Simm (marr. dis. 1960). Member of AEA; SAG.

Pre-Theatre. Child model.

Theatre. Miss Moore made her stage debut in the *Ziegfeld Follies* (New Amsterdam Th., N.Y.C., June

24, 1924); succeeded Justine Johnstone as Kathleen Forrest in *Hush Money* (49 St. Th., Mar. 15, 1926); appeared as Moll in *A Lady in Love* (Lyceum, Feb. 21, 1927); Mary Harris in *The Trial of Mary Dugan* (Natl., Sept. 19, 1927); Sally in *Jarnegan* (Longacre, Sept. 24, 1928), succeeded (Nov. 1928) Beatrice Kay as Velma in the same production; played Mary Bishop in *Conflict* (Fulton, Mar. 6, 1929); a Girl in *Cross Roads* (Morosco, Nov. 11, 1929); Edna Kinsey in *Torch Song* (Plymouth, Aug. 27, 1930); Lorraine Fortier in *East Wind* (Manhattan, Oct. 27, 1931); Chonchon in *The Man Who Reclaimed His Head* (Broadhurst, Sept. 8, 1932); Jackie in *The Great Magoo* (Selwyn, Dec. 2, 1932); Anita Highland in *Twentieth Century* (Broadhurst, Dec. 29, 1932); and Renee Brennan in *Man Bites Dog* (Lyceum, Apr. 25, 1933).

She made her London debut as Meg in *The Pursuit of Happiness* (Avon Th., Oct. 9, 1933); appeared as Aimee Bates in the musical, *Say When* (Imperial, N.Y.C., Nov. 8, 1934); toured as Mabel in a production of *Three Men on a Horse* (1935–36); played Cookie McGinn in *Swing Your Lady* (Booth, N.Y.C., Oct. 18, 1936); Miss Schwartz in *Hitch Your Wagon* (48 St. Th., Apr. 8, 1937); Polly La Varre Brewer in *In Clover* (Vanderbilt, Oct. 13, 1937); Belle in *Ah, Wilderness!* (Guild, Oct. 2, 1941); Mrs. Foley in *Over 21* (Music Box, Jan. 3, 1944); appeared in the revue, *The Seven Lively Arts* (Ziegfeld, Dec. 7, 1944); played Gwen Purchase in *Star Spangled Family* (Biltmore, Apr. 10, 1945); Edie Kerry in *The Rat Race* (Ethel Barrymore Th., Dec. 22, 1949); and Mrs. Van Daan in *The Diary of Anne Frank* (Cort, Oct. 5, 1955).

Films. Miss Moore made her film debut as Maudie Tilt in *Sylvia Scarlett* (RKO, 1935); subsequently performed in *The Perfect Specimen* (1st Natl., 1937); *Boy Meets Girl* (WB, 1938); *The Women* (MGM, 1939); *Saturday's Children* (WB, 1940); *Dive Bomber* (WB, 1941); *Anna Lucasta* (Col., 1949); and *The Model and the Marriage Broker* (20th-Fox, 1951).

Recreation. Dancing, roller skating.

MOORE, DICK. Actor, director, writer, editor. b. John Richard Moore, Jr., Sept. 12, 1925, Los Angeles, Calif., to John R. and Nora Eileen (Orr) Moore. Father, banker. Attended Los Angeles State Coll., 1946–47. Studied at Actors' Lab., Los Angeles, one year; with Florence Enright, Los Angeles, one year; with Uta Hagen, N.Y.C., two years; voice with Marian Rich, N.Y.C., two years. Married Dec. 14, 1949, to Patricia Dempsey (marr. dis. 1954); one son; married Nov. 8, 1959, to Eleanor Donhowe Fitzpatrick; one son. Served US Army, Correspondent for *Stars and Stripes*, PTO, 1944–46; rank, Sgt. Member of AEA; SAG; AFTRA; Amer. Newspaper Guild; Natl. Council on the Arts and Govt. (1957–to date); State Dept. Professional Th. (advisory panel for Intl. Culture Exchange Program, 1962–to date). Address: (home) 865 West End Ave., New York, NY 10025, tel. UN 6-3005; (bus.) Dick Moore and Associates, Inc., 850 Seventh Ave., New York, NY 10019.

Theatre. Billed as Dickie Moore, Mr. Moore made his debut as Jigger in *The Stone Jungle* (Coronet Th., Los Angeles, Calif., Aug. 1948); subsequently toured as Marco Polo in a children's theatre production of *The Adventures of Marco Polo* (opened Chicago, Ill., 1949); appeared in *Hay Fever* (Tenthouse Th., Chicago, Summer 1951); played Frederick Ellis in the national company of *The Autumn Garden* (opened Playhouse, Wilmington, Del., Oct. 26, 1951); Danny in *Night Must Fall* (Birmingham, Ala., Summer 1953); Michael in a tour of *The Fourposter* (Jan.–Apr. 1954); and Lachie in *The Hasty Heart* (Myrtle Beach, S.C., Summer 1954). At Glens Falls, N.Y., he directed *Bell, Book and Candle*, and *The Fourposter* (Summer 1955); at the Cincinnati (Ohio) Summer Th., directed *The Rainmaker* (Summer 1955), *Dial 'M' for Murder*, *On Borrowed Time*, and *Goodbye, My Fancy* (Summer 1956); and at Glens Falls, N.Y., directed *Dial 'M' for Murder*, and *The Hasty Heart* (Summer 1956).

Billed as Dick Moore, he made his N.Y.C. debut as Brother Martin Ladvenu in Siobhan McKenna's *Saint Joan* (Phoenix, Sept. 11, 1956); for the Peggy Wood Reading Group, he directed *The Hasty Heart* (Philadelphia, Pa., 1957), and *No Exit* (Brooklyn Acad. of Music, N.Y., 1958); and for the Equity and USO sponsored overseas tour, he directed *Angel Street* and *The Fourposter*.

Films. He made his debut at the age of 11 months in *Beloved Rogue* (UA, 1927); subsequently appeared in the *Our Gang* series (Hal Roach, 1930–32); *From Rags to Riches; Slice of Life; Obey the Law* (Col., 1927); *Timothy's Quest* (Gotham, 1929); *Lawful Larceny* (RKO, 1930); *Aloha* (Tiffany, 1933); *The Passion Flower* (MGM, 1930); *Son of the Gods* (1st Natl., 1930); *The Squaw Man* (MGM, 1931); *Seed* (U, 1931); *And God Smiles; Manhattan Parade* (WB, 1932); *Union Depot* (1st Natl., 1932); *Fireman, Save My Child* (1st Natl., 1932); *Disorderly Conduct* (20th-Fox, 1932); *No Greater Love* (Col., 1932); *Blond Venus* (Par., 1932); *So Big* (WB, 1932); *The Expert* (WB, 1932); *Gabriel Over the White House* (MGM, 1933); *A Man's Castle* (Col., 1933); *Gallant Lady* (UA, 1933); *Swell Head* (Col., 1933); *Oliver Twist* (Mono., 1933); *Human Side* (U, 1934); *Little Men* (Mascot, 1934); *In Love with Life* (Chesterfield, 1934); *The Story of Louis Pasteur* (WB, 1935); *Peter Ibbetson* (Par., 1935); *The Life of Emile Zola* (WB, 1937); *The Arkansas Traveler* (Par., 1938); *My Bill* (WB, 1938); *A Dispatch from Reuters* (WB, 1940); *Sergeant York* (WB, 1941); *Miss Annie Rooney* (UA, 1942); *The Song of Bernadette* (20th-Fox, 1943); *Are These Our Children?* (RKO, 1942); *Together Again* (Col., 1944); *Sweet and Lowdown* (20th-Fox, 1944); *The Eve of St. Mark* (20th-Fox, 1944); *Out of the Past* (RKO, 1947); *16 Fathoms Deep* (Mono., 1948); *Tuna Clipper* (Mono., 1949); *The Boy and the Eagle*, which he produced (RKO, 1949); *Cody of the Pony Express* (Col., 1951); *Eight Iron Men* (Col., 1952); *The Member of the Wedding* (Col., 1952); and others.

Television and Radio. Mr. Moore directed the series Time and the Play (KMPC, Los Angeles, Calif., 1942). For television, he wrote *The Jewel Box* (Matinee Th., NBC, Sept. 1958).

Other Activities. During Apr. 1957–May 1964, he was editor of *Equity* Magazine, published by Actors' Equity Assn., and public relations director and legislative liaison for AEA. He taught acting and lectured on the theatre at the Amer. Acad. of Dramatic Art, N.Y.C. (1957).

From 1964 to 1966, he was Director of Meetings and Shows Dept. of S.C.I. division of Communications Affiliates, Inc. (interpublic group of companies). From 1966 to 1967, he was senior associate at Hal Leyshon Associates, a public relations firm, and from 1967 to present, he has been president of Dick Moore and Associates, Inc., a public relations firm active in entertainment and the arts.

Published Works. Mr. Moore wrote *Opportunities in Acting* (1962); and *The Relationship of Amateur to Professional in the American Theatre*, commissioned by the Rockefeller Foundation (1963).

MOORE, DUDLEY. Pianist, performer, composer. b. Apr. 19, 1935, Dagenham, Essex, England, to John and Ada Francis Moore. Attended Guildhall Sch. of Music, 1947–53; grad. Magdalen Coll., Oxford Univ., B.A. 1957; B. Mus. 1958. Member of British AEA; AEA; SAG; Equity; Writers' Guild; PRS.

Theatre. Mr. Moore made his first stage appearance with the Oxford Univ. Drama Society (1955), and in 1959, appeared in the US as pianist with Vic Lewis' Jazz Band throughout the country. After this he played in the John Dankworth Band for a year.

He made his London debut in *Beyond the Fringe* (Edinburgh Festival, Scot., premiere, Aug. 1960; Fortune, London, May 10, 1961; John Golden Th., N.Y.C., Oct. 27, 1962).

He performed in a one-man concert (Royal Festival Hall, London, Dec. 1960); for the Royal Shakespeare Th., composed incidental music for *Caucasian Chalk Circle* (Aldwych, London, Mar. 29, 1962); for the ballet, *The Owl and the Pussycat* (Western Th. Ballet Co., London, premiere, July 1962); also composed incidental music for several productions of the English Stage Co. (Royal Court, London), among which were *Serjeant Musgrave's Dance* (Oct. 22, 1959), *One-Way Pendulum* (Dec. 22, 1959), and *Platonov* (Oct. 13, 1960); and for the Gillian Lynne Dance Co. (Saville, 1963).

Mr. Moore adapted Woody Allen's screenplay *Play It Again, Sam* and played the title role (Globe Th., London, 1970); wrote and performed with Peter Cook in *Behind the Fridge* touring Australia and New Zealand (late 1971 to April 1972; Cambridge Th., London, 1972–73). The production was then redesigned, partly rewritten, retitled *Good Evening* and opened (Plymouth Th., N.Y.C., Nov. 14, 1973) for a year's limited run prior to a tour of the rest of the U.S.

Television. Mr. Moore appeared in *A Trip to the Moon* (CBS, Feb. 12, 1964); the Jack Paar Show (NBC); the Johnny Carson's Tonight Show (NBC); and, in England, had his own jazz series program, called Strictly for the Birds.

He appeared with Peter Cook in three series of seven programs, each entitled *Not Only . . But Also* (BBC, 1964, 66, 70); one series of three programs, each entitled *Goodbye Again* (ITV, 1968); and various appearances as a guest on the shows of Cilla Black, Bruce Forsyth, Val Doonican, Harry Secombe, Sacha Distel, Dusty Springfield; appeared in the Royal Variety Performance (BBC, 1965); and a series *Here's Lulu . . Not to Mention Dudley Moore* (BBC, 1972).

Night Clubs. He appeared at the Establishment Club (London, 1961); as pianist for two weeks at The Blue Angel (N.Y.C., July 22, 1963); at the Village Vanguard (Mar. 24–Apr. 5, 1964) at the Rainbow Grill (May–June, 1964); at Small's (London, 1973); and at Michael's Pub (N.Y.C., 1974).

MOORE, EDWARD JAMES. Actor, director, playwright. b. Robert James Moore, June 2, 1935, Chicago, Ill., to Irwin J. and Mary Elizabeth (Kase) Moore. Father, truck driver. Educ. Nobel Grammar School, Chicago; Washburne Trade School, Chicago. Professional training at Goodman Memorial Th. and School of Drama, Chicago; HB Studios (Uta Hagen), N.Y.C. Served in US Navy, 1954–58; machinist's mate, 3rd class. Member of AEA; SAG; AFTRA; Dramatists Guild, Inc. Address: 11 Carmine St., New York, NY 10014, tel. (212) 989-6438 or (212) LO 4-3250.

Theatre. Mr. Moore first performed at the Goodman Memorial Th., Chicago, beginning in 1960, as Robert Moore and later as Edward Moore. He played a Palace Guard in *Hippolytus* (Jan. 3, 1960), the Gendarme in *The Inspector* (May 8, 1960), the Drum Major in *Woyzeck* (Feb. 12, 1961), Mayor Berger in *Hannele* (Mar. 1, 1961), and Orsino in *Twelfth Night* (May 15, 1961). At the Red Barn Th., Saugatuck, Mich. (Summer 1961), Mr. Moore played Mr. Akins in *Send Me No Flowers* (June 26), Roger Henderson in *The Pleasure of His Company* (July 10), was in *Sunrise at Campobello* (July 17), played Lt. Rooney in *Arsenic and Old Lace* (July 24), and Sandy Dean in *Brigadoon* (July 31). Returning to the Goodman Th. in Chicago, he played Centuri in *Right You Are* (Jan. 30, 1962), Hal Carter in *Picnic* (Feb. 18, 1962), Tom in *Dinny and the Witches* (Mar. 14, 1962), Cornelius Hackl in *The Matchmaker* (Apr. 14, 1962), and Bo Decker in *Bus Stop* (May 31, 1962).

Mr. Moore made his professional debut, in stock with the Peninsula Players, Fish Creek, Wis. (Summer 1962), first playing Dion Kapakos in *Critic's Choice*, following with performances as Mr. Tibbit in *Write Me a Murder* (July 10), Freddie Vanderstuyt in *Romanoff and Juliet* (July 17), Foley Thorndike in *Armored Dove* (July 24), Anagnos in *The Miracle Worker* (July 31), Anniello in *Hotel Paradiso* (Aug. 7), and Ready-Money Matt in *The Threepenny Opera* (Aug. 21). Returning again to the Goodman Th. in Chicago, Mr. Moore played the Duke of Arundel in *Becket* (Oct. 28, 1962), Ronny Heaslop in *A Passage to India* (Jan. 13, 1963), Sergis Saranoff in *Arms and the Man* (Mar. 25, 1963), and Captain Absolute in *The Rivals* (May 12, 1963). He toured as Edward

West in *Good Housekeeping* (Aug. 4, 1963); appeared at the Cleveland (Ohio) Playhouse as the Policeman in *The Madwoman of Chaillot* (Sept. 23, 1964), Matti in *Galileo* (Oct. 21, 1964), Number 12 in *Twelve Angry Men* (Jan. 27, 1965), Roger in *Enter Laughing* (Feb. 10, 1965), and Murillo in *The Physicists* (Apr. 21, 1965); and at the Candlelight Playhouse, Summit, Ill., as Phil Matthews in *Nobody Loves an Albatross* (May 16, 1965) and Irvin Blanchard in *No Time for Sergeants* (June 1965).

He was Tom Stark in *All the King's Men* (Cleveland Playhouse, Nov. 18, 1965); the Executioner in *The Balcony* (Hartford Stage Co., Hartford, Conn., Mar. 11, 1966); the Young Man in *The American Dream* (Playhouse in the Park, Cincinnati, Ohio, Apr. 28, 1966); again played Roger in *The Pleasure of His Company* (Coconut Grove Playhouse, Miami Beach, Fla., Aug. 2, 1966); was understudy for the role of Tony Batch in *After the Rain* (John Golden Th., N.Y.C., Oct. 9, 1967); appeared again at the Candlelight Playhouse, Summit, Ill., as John Ken O'Dunc in *MacBird!* (Mar. 1968), Captain Fisby in *The Teahouse of the August Moon* (June 1968), and Arthur Brooks in *The Tenth Man* (Aug. 1968). He played Lt. Cutler in *The White House Murder Case* (Circle in the Square, N.Y.C., Feb. 18, 1970); Andrew Mayo in *Beyond the Horizon* (McCarter Th., Princeton, N.J., Sept. 10, 1974); and he was Harry Bales in *The Sea Horse*, which he also wrote (Circle Rep. Th. Co., Mar. 3, 1974; Westside Th., Apr. 15, 1974).

Films. Mr. Moore played the Scout Master in *Lady in a Cage* (Par., 1964).

Television. Mr. Moore made his television debut as Dr. Hale in *Love Is a Many Splendored Thing* (CBS, 1967); was Mr. Broadway in *Smelling Like a Rose;* was in *Smile;* played Dr. Kelly in All My Children (ABC, 1970); was the Courtier in *Soldier in Love* (Hallmark Hall of Fame, NBC); Rick Latimer in Love of Life (CBS, 1971–72); and Sam English in The Edge of Night (CBS, 1973–74).

Other Activities. In 1973, Mr. Moore founded the Greenwich Village Playwrights' Workshop.

Published Works. Mr. Moore's play, *The Sea Horse*, was published in 1975.

Awards. Mr. Moore received a Vernon Rice Drama Desk Award as an outstanding new playwright (1974) for *The Sea Horse.*

Recreation. Boxing, weightlifting, hiking, theatre, opera, motor cycle racing.

MOORE, LAURENS. Actor, educator. b. Laurens Potter Moore, Dec. 2, 1919, Gaffney, S.C., to Henry Carlton and Eloise (Potter) Moore. Educ. Gaffney public schools; Wofford Coll., Spartanburg, S.C. Married May 25, 1937, to Mary Haynes Fultz; one son, one daughter. Served in USNR, 1943–46. Member of AFTRA (editorial bd., 1960–62); SAG; AEA; ANTA; NATAS; South Carolina Th. Assn. (bd. of dir., 1972–75); South Carolina Arts Comn. (advisory bd., 1972–73). Address: 500 S. Petty St., Gaffney, SC 29340, tel. (803) 489-6216.

Pre-Theatre. Mr. Moore was chief accountant for an automobile financing company (1937–40) and executive vice-pres. of Palmetto Broadcasters (1948–55).

Theatre. Mr. Moore was professor of theatre arts, Limestone Coll., Gaffney, S.C., from 1967 to 1974, resigning in order to continue professional acting full-time. His first appearance on stage was as a nine-year-old, when he played the Schoolboy in a production of *Quality Street* (Limestone Coll., Nov. 1929). His first professional experience was with the Dock St. Th., Charleston, S.C., where he made his debut as the Stage Manager in *Our Town* (Mar. 1950), following with appearances as Elwood Dowd in *Harvey* (Oct. 15, 1950), Descius Heiss in *The Shop at Sly Corner* (Jan. 3, 1951), Beacham in The Chiltern Hundreds (Nov. 10, 1951), a repeat of his role as the Stage Manager in *Our Town* (Mar. 1952), Brig. Gen. Dennis in *Command Decision* (Oct. 1953), and Michael in *The Fourposter* (Feb. 1954).

He appeared in summer stock as Richard Sherman in *The Seven Year Itch* (Grossinger's, N.Y., 1957); made his first N.Y.C. appearance as the Psychiatrist in an off-Bway production of *Nightmare* (Davenport Th., Oct. 1957); toured (Mar.–June 1958) as Evans-Rogers in *No Time for Sergeants;* first performed on the Bway stage as the Legislator in *Only in America* (Cort, Nov. 19, 1959); was Jim Trawley in *Ding Dong Bell* (pre-Bway, Aug. 19, 1961); Willy Loman in *Death of a Salesman* (Mint Museum Drama Guild, Charlotte, N.C., Apr. 1966); played the title role in *Jonah!* (Stage 73, N.Y.C., Sept. 21, 1967); John Middleton in *The Constant Wife* (Centenary Th., Hackettstown, N.J., Nov. 1967); Burns in *Don't Drink the Water* (Charlotte Summer Th., July 1968); again played the Stage Manager in *Our Town* (Centenary Th., Hackettstown, N.J., Nov. 1968); was Augie Poole in *Tunnel of Love* (Centenary Th., May 1969); and began touring (Oct. 1970) in a one-man show, *Washington Irving, Man of Legends.*

Films. Mr. Moore was Emory Slade in *North by Northwest* (MGM, 1959); played Wendell Terman in *The Last American Hero* (20th-Fox, 1972); and Barton C. Taylor in *Challenge* and *The Big Brass Ring* (both Cinemation, 1974).

Television. Mr. Moore first appeared on television as the body servant to Pontius Pilate in *The Trial of Pontius Pilate* (Robert Montgomery Presents, NBC, Mar. 1957). He has also been on Camera Three (CBS, Apr. 1957); Studio One (CBS, July 1957); Kitty Foyle (CBS, Feb. 1958); The Naked City (CBS, Oct. 1958); *The Moon and Sixpence* (NBC, Dec. 1958); the US Steel Hour (CBS, Apr. 1959); For the People (CBS, Jan. 1965); and *The Impeachment of Andrew Johnson* (BBC, PBS, CBC, June 1974).

Recreation. Reading, deep-sea fishing.

MOORE, ROBERT. Director, actor. b. Aug. 7, 1929, Washington, D.C. Grad. Roosevelt H.S., Washington, D.C.; attended Catholic Univ., Washington, D.C. Served US Navy.

Theatre. Billed as Brennan Moore, he appeared in the pre-Bway tryout of *Magnolia Alley* (Mansfield Th., N.Y.C., Apr. 18, 1949); and made his Bway debut as Owen Parkside in *Jenny Kissed Me* (Hudson, Dec. 23, 1949); played Ron Bronson in *Alley of the Sunset* (Jan Hus Th., Dec. 30, 1959); and Lewis Codman in *The Tiger Rag* (Cherry Lane Th., Feb. 16, 1961).

During the 1950's, billed as Robert Moore, he acted with a touring repertory group, playing Edmund in *King Lear*, Christie in *The Playboy of the Western World*, Orsino in *Twelfth Night*, Cleante in *The Miser*, Horace in *The School for Wives*, Dick Dudgeon in *The Devil's Disciple*, Almoviva in *The Barber of Seville*, Lodovico in *Othello*, and Mosca in *Volpone*. He was resident director for two seasons with the Royal Poinciana Playhouse (Palm Beach, Fla.), where he presented *Janus*, *The Rainmaker*, *Write Me a Murder*, *Under the Yum-Yum Tree*, and *Light Up the Sky*, and played the Deafmute in *The Madwoman of Chaillot.* At Playhouse on the Mall (Paramus, N.J.), he directed productions of *Compulsion*, *Tunnel of Love*, *Born Yesterday*, *Critic's Choice*, *The Anniversary Waltz*, *Stalag Seventeen*, *Good-bye, My Fancy*, and *Write Me a Murder;* and played Jimmy Porter in *Look Back in Anger*, Hogan in *Under the Yum-Yum Tree*, Nevil in *Towards Zero*. He was resident director for eight seasons with the Olney (Md.) Th., presenting *The Fantasticks*, *Roshomon*, *Leave It to Jane*, *Plays for Bleecker Street*, *The Cave Dwellers*, *A Phoenix Too Frequent*, *Time Remembered*, *Thieve's Carnival*, *Royal Gambit*, *Caesar and Cleopatra*, *The Shadow of A Gunman*, *Holiday for Lovers*, *Say, Darling*, *Sabrina Fair*, *The Hidden River*, *King of Hearts*, *Bespoke Overcoat* and *Cecile*, and *Teahouse of the August Moon;* and appeared as Freddy in *Pygmalion*, Philip in *You Never Can Tell*, Patrice in *Ring Around the Moon*, Tullius in *Romulus*, Cousin in *The Power and the Glory*, and the Ghost in *The Enchanted.*

At the Playhouse (Winnooski Park, Vt.), he played Leo in *The Little Foxes*, Randall in *Heartbreak House*, Charley in *Charley's Aunt*, and Hadrian in *You Touched Me;* directed *You Never Know* at the Ogunquit (Me.) Playhouse; *Little Mary Sunshine* (tour, Paper Mill Playhouse, Millburn, N.J.; and Mineola (N.Y.) Playhouse); and *Critics' Choice* and *Sunday in New York* (Bucks County Playhouse, New Hope, Pa., Summer 1964).

Returning to Bway, he understudied Alan Alda as F. Sherman in *The Owl and the Pussycat* (ANTA, N.Y.C., Nov. 18, 1964); played Harvey in *Cactus Flower* (Royale, Dec 8, 1965); and Jack in *Everything in the Garden* (Playhouse, Nov. 29, 1967).

Mr. Moore made his off-Bway directing debut with *The Ticket-of-Leave Man* (Midway, N.Y.C., Dec. 22, 1961); subsequently directed *The Boys in the Band* (Th. Four, Apr. 14, 1968); *Promises, Promises* (Shubert, Dec. 1, 1968); *The Last of the Red Hot Lovers* (Eugene O'Neill Th., Dec. 28, 1969); *The Gingerbread Lady* (Plymouth, Dec. 13, 1970); *Lorelei* (Palace, Jan. 27, 1974); and *My Fat Friend* (Brooks Atkinson Th., Mar. 31, 1974).

Films. Mr. Moore played Warren in *Tell Me That You Love Me, Junie Moon* (Par., 1970).

Awards. Mr. Moore received The Drama Desk-Vernon Rice Award (1967–68) for his direction of *The Boys in the Band.*

MOORE, SONIA. Author, director, producer, coach. b. Sophie Sonia Shatzov, Dec. 4, Gomel, Russia, to Evser and Sophie (Pasherstnik) Shatzov. Attended Univ. of Kiev, Univ. of Moscow; Drama Studio of the Kiev Solovtzov Th.; Studio of the Moscow Art Th. (Vakhtangov Th.); grad. Alliance Francaise, Paris, diploma 1927; Instituto Interuniversitario Italiano, Rome, diploma, 1938; Royal Conservatory of Music, Sta. Cecilia, Rome, diploma 1939; Royal Philharmonic Acad. of Rome, diploma 1939. Married May 2, 1926, to Leon Moore, diplomat, businessman; one daughter, Irene Moore, Actress. Member of SSD&C; Authors League; ATA; Internatl. Federation for Th. Rsch.; TLA; International Biographical Assn. Address: (home) 485 Park Ave., New York, NY 10022, tel. (212) PL 5-5120; (bus.) Sonia Moore Studio of the Theatre, 139 W. 13th St., New York, NY 10011, tel. (212) PL 5-5120.

Theatre. Mrs. Moore was an actress in the Russian Th. (Berlin, Ger., 1923–1926); and taught drama and coached at her Dramatic Workshop (Rome, It., 1935–1940). With Elliot Martin, she produced *The Painted Days*, which she also directed (Th. Marquee, N.Y.C., Apr. 6, 1961); and directed *Sharon's Grave*, produced by the Irish Players (Maidman Playhouse, Nov. 8, 1961).

Mrs. Moore founded the American Center for Stanislavski Theatre Art, Inc., in 1964. She has been president since that time and has been artistic director of the Center's repertory company, ACSTA 1 since 1971, when she directed its productions of *The Cherry Orchard*, *Desire Under the Elms*, and *Birdbath* and supervised ACSTA 1's tour of underprivileged areas of N.Y.C. under sponsorship of the Mayor's Office of Neighborhood Government. In 1972, the company continued to present *The Cherry Orchard* and *Desire Under the Elms*, and Mrs. Moore directed new productions of *The Slave*, *The Stronger*, and *The Man with the Flower in His Mouth;* all 1972 productions continued in 1973, and Mrs. Moore directed *The Anniversary*, *The Boor*, and *The Marriage Proposal;* and in 1974, the company continued with all 1973 productions, and Mrs. Moore directed *A Deed from the King of Spain* and *The Crucible.* .

Television and Radio. Mrs. Moore has appeared on interviews about Stanislavsky. She gave a series of lecture-demonstrations on the Stanislavski system on WNYC-FM (1968–69; 1973) and directed ACSTA 1 productions for WNYC Radio (1971, 1972, 1973).

Other Activities. Mrs. Moore is director of the Sonia Moore Studio of the Th., where she has taught since 1961. In 1967–68, she gave a series of lecture-demonstrations at the Library and Museum of the Performing Arts, Lincoln Ctr., N.Y.C., and supervised a Stanislavski system workshop under the auspices of the Recreation and Cultural Affairs Administrator, City of New York. In 1969 and again in

1973 she gave a seminar under the sponsorship of the Cultural Development Branch, Dept. of the Provincial Secretary, Alberta, Can.; she lectured at the ATA convention, Washington, D.C., in 1970 and has lectured at NY Univ., Pace Univ., Swarthmore Coll., and other institutions.

Published Works. Mrs. Moore wrote *The Stanislavski Method* (1960); *The Stanislavski System* (1965; rev. ed. 1974); *Training an Actor* (1968); and *Stanislavski Today* (1973); an article on the Stanislavski centennial that appeared in London's *Stage* (Jan. 17, 1963); and has contributed articles to *Tulane Drama Review* and *The Drama Review, The Secondary School Theatre, Players Magazine,* and the *Encyclopedia Britannica.*

Awards. Mrs. Moore received the John F. Kennedy Library American Heritage Award in 1974.

MORAN, JIM. Publicist, performer, author, photographer, musician. b. James Sterling Moran, Nov. 24, 1909, Woodstock, Va., to James Sterling Moran. Father, attorney for U.S. Dept. of Agriculture. Grad. Western H.S., Washington, D.C., 1926; attended Geo. Washington Univ.; studied classical guitar with Sophocles Papas. Member of AFTRA; SAG; AFM, Local 802. Address: 300 West End Ave., New York, NY 10023, tel. (212) 787-4964.

Mr. Moran is presently president of Jim Moran Associates, publicity and public relations counsellors. He was publicity counsellor to David Merrick (1954–66), involved in special publicity for all his productions during this period; and was press agent for Fred Waring's Orchestra (1938–40).

Pre-Theatre. Lecturer on sightseeing busses (Washington, D.C.); salesman of humidifying radiator covers for the home; guitar teacher; pilot for Luddington Airlines (1930–32); state airport engineer for Virginia (1933).

Films. He appeared in *The Body Snatchers* (RKO, 1945); *The Spectre of the Rose* (Rep., 1946); *Youngblood Hawke* (WB, 1964); and *Is There Sex After Death?* (Univ. Marion Corp., 1972).

He was press representative for *The Egg and I* (U, 1947); *The Third Man* (SRO, 1950); *Rhubarb* (Par., 1951); *The Mouse That Roared* (Col., 1959); *The Mask,* in which he also appeared (WB, 1961); *The Mouse On the Moon* (UA, 1963); *John Goldfarb, Please Come Home* (20th-Fox, 1965); *Blindfold* (U, 1966); *Casino Royale* (Col., 1967); *Myra Breckenridge* (20th-Fox, 1970); and *That's Entertainment!* (UA, 1974).

Television and Radio. In radio, he wrote, directed and starred in the Professor Rhinelander Briggs Show, and the Whak's Museum (WJSV, Washington, D.C., 1940–42); the Professor Rhinelander Briggs Show (KECA, Hollywood, 1943–44); and the Ivan Black Talk Show (WVNJ, N.Y.C., 1950–51).

On television, Mr. Moran made over one hundred appearances on *The Tonight Show* (NBC) while Steve Allen and Jack Paar were hosts. He made twenty-six weekly appearances on *The Home Show* (NBC, 1954) as a pet and wild animal expert; has appeared approximately seventy-five times on the *Today* show (NBC); made twelve regular appearances on the David Frost Show (Syndicated); and has made numerous appearances on the Mike Douglas Show (CBS).

David Wolper produced the documentary film *The Story of a Press Agent,* based on Mr. Moran's life (NBC, 1962); Victor Borge and Jeff Selden produced the film documentary, *The Way-Out World of Jim Moran* (Syndicated, 1963); and Pan-American Airways produced a documentary for Japanese television, *The Magnificent American,* in which Mr. Moran starred with Kannetaka.

Other Activities. He is an officer of U.S. Pet Registration, Inc., and, as a professional photographer, has sold twelve photos to *Popular Photography* magazine.

Published Works. He wrote *Sophocles the Hyena* (1954), which was set to music by Tom Scott and performed by the NY Philharmonic Orchestra (Carnegie Hall, N.Y.C., 1957) and by the Vienna (Austria) State Orchestra.

He wrote *Miserable* (1957); and *Miff the Mole* (1960).

He wrote *Why Men Shouldn't Marry* (1969); *Houleton on Vaimoton* (1971); *The Classic Woman,* a collection of his photography of women (1971); and *How I Became an Authority on Sex* (1973).

Discography. Mr. Moran wrote and narrated *Don't Make Waves* (London Records, 1967); and composed *George Washington Bridge* (copyright 1950).

Recreation. Gourmet cooking; party giving; collecting, among other things, beautiful girls; playing the guitar; world traveling; photography; and kite flying.

MORDECAI, BENJAMIN. Producer, director, teacher. b. Dec. 10, 1944, New York City, to Allen Lewis and Florence Mordecai. Father, realtor. Educ. P.S. 135 and Friends Seminary, N.Y.C.; Morristown (N.J.) Preparatory. Grad. Buena Vista Coll., B.A.; Eastern Michigan Univ., M.A.; additional graduate study at Indiana Univ. Studied mime with Franz Reynders. Married July 20, 1974, to Sherry Lynn Morley, costumer. Member of ATA; League of Resident Theatres (chmn., Children's Th. Comm.). Address: (home) 425 E. Walnut, Indianapolis, IN 46204, tel. (317) 635-1831; (bus.) 411 E. Michigan, Indianapolis, IN 46204, tel. (317) 635-5277.

Theatre. Mr. Mordecai is producing director and a co-founder of the Indiana Repertory Theatre, Indianapolis, which opened Oct. 18, 1972, with a production of *Charley's Aunt.* Other presentations of the 1972–73 season were *Fables Here and There* (Nov. 23–Dec. 17, 1972), also directed by Mr. Mordecai; *The Scamp* (Dec. 21, 1972–Jan. 7, 1973); *The House of Blue Leaves* (Jan. 11–28, 1973), directed by Mr. Mordecai; *The Glass Menagerie* (Feb. 1–18, 1973); and *Count Dracula* (Feb. 22–Mar. 11, 1973), directed by Mr. Mordecai.

The 1973–74 season included *Our Town* (Nov. 1–24, 1973), directed by Mr. Mordecai; *What the Butler Saw* (Nov. 29–Dec. 22, 1973); *Of Mice and Men* (Dec. 27, 1973–Jan. 19, 1974); *Jacques Brel . . .* (Jan. 24–Feb. 16, 1974), directed by Mr. Mordecai; *The Servant of Two Masters* (Feb. 28–Mar. 23, 1974); and *Sherlock Holmes* (Mar. 28–Apr. 20, 1974).

The 1974–75 season included *Harvey* (Oct. 24–Nov. 16, 1974); *The Little Foxes* (Nov. 21–Dec. 13, 1974); *One Flew Over the Cuckoo's Nest* (Dec. 19, 1974–Jan. 11, 1975); *The Taming of the Shrew* (Jan 23–Feb. 15, 1975); *The Rainmaker* (Feb. 20–Mar. 15, 1975); and *A Bird in the Hand* (Mar. 20–Apr. 12, 1975), directed by Mr. Mordecai.

Television. Mr. Mordecai directed and narrated *The Story of Mime* (Spring 1968).

Other Activities. Mr. Mordecai is on the board of directors of Hospital Audience, Inc., Indianapolis, and is a consultant for the Foundation for the Extension and Development of the American Professional Theatre.

MORENO, RITA. Actress. Address: 2211 Broadway, New York, NY 10024, tel. (212) PL 9-6300.

Theatre. Miss Moreno made her debut under the stage name Rosita Cosio in the role of Angelina in *Skydrift* (Belasco Th., Nov. 13, 1945). She later played Sally Bowles in *I Am a Camera* (Edgewater Th., Chicago, Ill., 1960; Ilona Ritter in *She Loves Me* (Lyric, London, England, Apr. 29, 1964); played Doris in *The Owl and the Pussycat* (Coconut Grove Playhouse, Miami, Fla., 1965); Lola in *Damn Yankees* (Houston, Tex., 1967); Serafina in *The Rose Tattoo* (Ivanhoe Th., Chicago, Ill., 1968); Charlotte in *The Magistrate* (Williamstown Playhouse, Williamstown, Mass., 1969); Annie Sullivan in *The Miracle Worker* (Ivanhoe Th., Chiago, Ill., 1970); replaced (July 27, 1970) Linda Lavin as Elaine Navazio in *Last of the Red Hot Lovers* (Eugene O'Neill Th., N.Y.C., Dec. 28, 1969); was in *Have You Ever Been Blue?* (Berkshire Th., Stockbridge, Mass., 1971); played the Shoplifter in a revival of *Detective Story* (pre-Bway: opened Paramus Playhouse, N.J., Feb. 18, 1973; closed Shubert Th., Philadelphia, Pa., Mar. 24, 1973); Adelaide in *Guys and Dolls* (Melody Th., Milwaukee, Wis., 1974); Edna Edison in *The Prisoner of Second Avenue* (North Shore Music Th., Beverly, Mass., 1974); Staff Nurse Norton in *The National Health* (Long Wharf Th., New Haven, Conn., Apr. 5, 1974; Circle in the Square/Joseph E. Levine Th., N.Y.C., Oct. 10, 1974); and Googie Gomez in *The Ritz* (Longacre, Jan. 20, 1975).

Films. Miss Moreno made her motion-picture debut in *So Young, So Bad* (UA, 1950). Her other films include *The Toast of New Orleans* (MGM, 1950); *Pagan Love Song* (MGM, 1950); *Singin' in the Rain* (MGM, 1952); *Cattle Town* (WB, 1952); *Latin Lovers* (MGM, 1953); *Yellow Tomahawk* (UA, 1954); *Jivaro* (Par., 1954); *Garden of Evil* (20th-Fox, 1954); *Untamed* (20th-Fox, 1955); *Seven Cities of Gold* (20th-Fox, 1955); *The Lieutenant Wore Skirts* (20th-Fox, 1956); *The King and I* (20th-Fox, 1956); *This Rebel Breed* (WB, 1960); *West Side Story* (UA, 1961); *Summer and Smoke* (Par., 1962); *Cry of Battle* (Allied Artists, 1963); *Marlowe* (MGM, 1967); *The Night of the Following Day* (U, 1969); *Popi* (UA, 1969); and *Carnal Knowledge* (Avco-Embassy, 1971).

Television. Miss Moreno is regularly featured on the educational series The Electric Company (PBS, Oct. 1971–to date).

Night Clubs. Miss Moreno performed in a night-club act in Las Vegas, Nev., in 1963.

Awards. Miss Moreno received an Academy of Motion Picture Arts and Sciences (Oscar) Award for best supporting actress in 1961 for her performance as Anita in *West Side Story,* and she received the Joseph Jefferson Award in 1969 as best actress for her performance as Serafina in *The Rose Tattoo.*

Recreation. Sewing, needlework, cooking.

MORGAN, AGNES. Director. b. 1901, LeRoy, N.Y., to Frank H. and Sarah L. (Cutler) Morgan. Father, editor; mother, teacher. Grad. Radcliffe Coll., A.B. 1901; A.M. 1903; attended George Baker's 47 Workshop, Harvard Univ., 1904. Member of AEA. Address: (home) 51 Short Hills Circle, Millburn, NJ 07041, tel. (201) DR 9-3369; (bus.) Paper Mill Playhouse, Millburn, NJ 07041, tel. (201) DR 9-3636.

Theatre. Miss Morgan wrote and staged *When We Two Write History* for George Arliss (Chicago, Ill., May 9, 1910); translated, and with Paul M. Potter, wrote the book for *The Man with Three Wives* (Weber & Fields Th., N.Y.C., Jan. 23, 1913); and with H. Harry Benrimo, adapted *Taking Chances* (39 St. Th., Mar. 17, 1915).

Miss Morgan was an executive staff member of the Neighborhood Playhouse, a producing theatre group, and a director of its productions (Neighborhood Playhouse, N.Y.C., 1915–27), directing the double bill of *Tethered Sheep* and, with Alice Lewisohn, *The Maker of Dreams* (Mar. 3, 1915); *The Glittering Gate* (1915); with Alice Lewisohn, *The Waldies* (1915); staged *Captain Brassbound's Conversion* (1915); *The Subjection of Kezia* (1916); the Gertrude Kingston Co. productions of *The Inca of Jerusalem, Great Catherine,* and, with Alice Lewisohn, *The Queen's Enemies* (Nov. 14, 1916; moved Maxine Elliott's Th., Dec. 18, 1916); and directed *A Night at an Inn* (1916).

At the Neighborhood Playhouse, with Alice Lewisohn, directed *Black 'Ell* (1917); staged *A Sunny Morning* (1917), *The People* (1917); with Alice Lewisohn, *Pippa Passes* (1917), *Tamara* (1918), and *Fortunato* (1918), adapted and, with Alice Lewisohn, directed *Guibour* (1918); staged *Free* (1918), *The Eternal Megalosaurus* (1918), *The Noose* (1918); with Alice Lewisohn, directed *Everybody's Husband* (1919); staged *The Mob* (1920); adapted and directed *The Beautiful Sabine Women* (Feb. 14, 1920); directed *Innocent and Annabel* (1920); with Alice Lewisohn, directed *The Madras House,* in which she played Minnie Huxtable (Oct. 29, 1921); and wrote *The Suicides in the Rue Sombre* (1921).

With Alice Lewisohn, Miss Morgan directed parts I and II of *Back to Methuselah* for the Th. Guild (Garrick, Feb. 27, 1922); at the Neighborhood Playhouse, her play *The Little Legend of the Dance* was produced (1923); also, at the Neighborhood Playhouse, with Alice Lewisohn, she directed *This Fine-Pretty World* (Dec. 26, 1923); wrote the book, contributed lyrics and directed the first edition of *The Grand Street Follies* (June 16, 1922); wrote the book and lyrics and appeared in *The Grand Street Follies* (May 20, 1924); with Irene Lewisohn, directed *The Little Clay Cart* (Dec. 5, 1924); directed *Exiles* (Feb. 19, 1925); wrote and directed *The Legend of the Dance* (Mar. 31, 1925); with Ian Maclaren, directed *The Critic* (May 8, 1925); wrote sketches and lyrics, directed, and performed in the third edition of *The Grand Street Follies* (June 18, 1925); directed *The Romantic Young Lady* (May 4, 1926); wrote sketches and lyrics and directed and appeared in the fourth edition of *The Grand Street Follies* (June 15, 1926); directed *The Lion Tamer* (Oct. 7, 1926); wrote sketches, lyrics, directed, and appeared in the fifth edition of *The Grand Street Follies* (May 19, 1927; moved to Little, May 31, 1927); and directed *Lovers and Enemies* (special matinees, Little, Sept. 20, 1927).

Miss Morgan was president and a director of the Actor-Managers, Inc. (1927–39), for which she staged *If* (Little, Oct. 25, 1927), *The Love Nest* (Comedy, Dec. 22, 1927), and *Maya* (Comedy, Feb. 21, 1928).

She wrote the book, contributed lyrics, and staged the sixth edition of *The Grand Street Follies* (Booth, May 28, 1928); *The Grand Street Follies of 1929* (Booth, May 1, 1929); wrote *If Love Were All*, under the pseudonym of Cutler Hatch, and directed it (Booth, Nov. 13, 1931); directed productions at the Westchester County Playhouse (Mt. Kisco, N.Y., Summers 1930–33). She directed (Summers 1935–39) works at the Casino Th. (Newport, R.I.), including *The Critic* (1936), *Inconstant Moon* (Aug. 17, 1937) and her own plays, *Grandpa* (Aug. 13, 1938); and *Behind the Verdict*; for the Popular Price Th., Federal Theatre (WPA) Project (N.Y.C.) was director for *American Holiday* (Manhattan Th., Feb. 21, 1936) and *Class of '29* (Manhattan Th., May 15, 1936).

Miss Morgan has been a co-producer and a director at the Paper Mill Playhouse (Millburn, N.J., 1940–to date), a year-round stock theatre, where she was co-director of *Jeannie* (Nov. 12, 1940); with Frank Carrington, directed *Papa Is All* (Guild, N.Y.C., Jan. 6, 1942) and *I Killed the Count*, which she produced with Mr. Carrington and the Shuberts (Cort, Sept. 4, 1942).

MORGAN, AL. Playwright, writer, television producer. b. Albert Edward Morgan, Jan. 16, 1920, New York City, to Albert Edward and Julia (Britt) Morgan. Father, businessman. Grad. Bryant H.S., N.Y.C., 1937; attended New York Univ., 1937–40. Married Dec. 19, 1945, to Martha Jones, actress, known as Martha Falconer; one son, two daughters. Served US Army, 1943–45, ETO; rank, Sgt.; awarded Silver Star, Croix de Guerre, Purple Heart, Presidential Citation. Member of Dramatists Guild; AFTRA; ALA. Address: (home) 53 Wilgarth Rd., Bronxville, NY 10708, tel. (914) DE 7-3388; (bus.) Children's Television Workshop, One Lincoln Plaza, New York, NY 10023, tel. (212) 595-3456.

Theatre. Mr. Morgan wrote, with Jose Ferrer, the book for *Oh, Captain!* (Alvin, N.Y.C., Feb. 4, 1958); and *Minor Miracle* which he adapted from his novel of the same name (Henry Miller's Th., Oct. 7, 1965).

Films. He wrote the screenplay for *The Great Man* (U, 1956), in which he also appeared.

Television and Radio. Mr. Morgan is presently senior producer of the Health Series (PBS) Children's Television Workshop. He was dramatic director for the Armed Forces Network (Paris, 1945); he wrote and produced the radio documentary on race relations, *The High Mountain* (CBS, 1953).

He made his first television appearance as an interviewer for Night Beat (Dumont, 1956); subsequently appeared as interviewer for Entertainment Press Conference (Dumont, 1957); and was the producer of the Today Show (NBC, 1962–68).

Published Works. Mr. Morgan has written *The Great Man* (1955), *Cast of Characters* (1956), *One Star General* (1957), *A Small Success* (1958), *A Minor Miracle* (1960), *The Six-Eleven* (1963), *To Sit on a Horse* (1964), *The Whole World Is Watching* (1973), and *Anchor-Woman* (1974). He has written book reviews for the NY *Herald Tribune* and the *Saturday Review* and is a regular contributor to major magazines.

Awards. He received the Ohio State Award for Journalism for the CBS radio documentary, *The High Mountain*, and an Emmy Award for excellence in programming (1967–68).

MORIARTY, MICHAEL. Actor. b. Apr. 5, 1942, Detroit, Mich. Graduated Dartmouth Coll.; attended London Academy of Music and Dramatic Arts. Married to Françoise Martinet; one son.

Theatre. Mr. Moriarty made his professional debut with the NY Shakespeare Festival (Delacorte, N.Y.C.) playing Octavius Caesar in *Antony and Cleopatra* (June 13, 1963) and Florizel in *The Winter's Tale* (Aug. 8, 1963); subsequently appearing there as Longaville in *Love's Labour's Lost* (June 9, 1965), and Helenus in *Troilus and Cressida* (Aug. 4, 1965).

He appeared in *Major Barbara* (Charles Playhouse, Boston, Jan. 19, 1966); joined the resident company at the Minneapolis Theatre Co. (Tyrone Guthrie Th., 1966–70), where he appeared in various productions including *Enrico IV* (Crawford Livingston Th., St. Paul, Minn., Feb. 16, 1968); *The House of Atreus* (Tyrone Guthrie Th., June–Dec. 1968; and Billy Rose Th., N.Y.C., Dec. 17, 1968), in which he was a member of the chorus and an understudy; *The Resistible Rise of Arturo Ui* (Tyrone Guthrie Th., Minneapolis, June–Dec. 1968; and Billy Rose Th., N.Y.C., Dec. 22, 1968), in which he played Rag, Fish, and Dullfeet; *Mourning Becomes Electra* (Tyrone Guthrie Th., Minneapolis, Aug. 19, 1969); and *The Alchemist* (Crawford Livingston Th., St. Paul, Apr. 11, 1970).

Mr. Moriarty appeared in *In the Jungle of Cities* (Charles St. Th., Boston, Feb. 12, 1970); played Man in *Peanut Butter and Jelly* (Univ. of the Streets Th., N.Y.C., May 9, 1970); and appeared in *The Night Thoreau Spent in Jail* (Alley Th., Houston, Jan. 14, 1971).

He replaced (Apr. 20, 1971) Richard Jordan in the role of George Mische in *The Trial of the Catonsville Nine* (Good Shepherd Church, N.Y.C., opened Feb. 7, 1971; moved to Lyceum, June 2, 1971); played Julian Weston in *Find Your Way Home* (Brooks Atkinson Th., Jan. 2, 1974); played the title role in the NY Shakespeare Festival at Lincoln Center production of *King Richard III* (Mitzi E. Newhouse Th., Oct. 20, 1974); and James Tyrone, Jr., in *Long Day's Journey Into Night* (Brooklyn Acad. of Music, Jan. 27, 1976).

Films. Mr. Moriarty made his film debut in the role of Henry Wiggen in *Bang the Drum Slowly* (Par., 1973); and appeared in *The Last Detail* (Col., 1974); and *Report to the Commissioner* (UA, 1975).

Television. He played The Gentleman Caller in *The Glass Menagerie* (ABC, 1973).

Other Activities. A self-taught jazz pianist, Mr. Moriarty has appeared at Michael's Pub (N.Y.C., Apr. 1975).

Awards. He was the recipient of a Fulbright Scholarship to The London Academy of Music and Dramatic Arts; and for his performance in *Find Your Way Home*, received the Antoinette Perry (Tony) Award for Best Actor (1974).

MORISON, PATRICIA. Actress, singer. b. Mar. 19, 1915, New York City, to William and Selena (Carson) Morison. Father, playwright, actor. Grad. Washington Irving H.S., N.Y.C. Studied acting at Neighborhood Playhouse Sch. of the Th., N.Y.C.; design at Ecole des Beaux Arts, Paris, Fr. Member of AEA; SAG; AGMA; AFTRA.

Pre-Theatre. Dress designer.

Theatre. Miss Morison made her N.Y.C. debut as Helen in *Growing Pains* (Ambassador Th., Nov. 23, 1933); subsequently was an understudy in *Victoria Regina* (Broadhurst, Dec. 26, 1935); played Laura Rivers in *The Two Bouquets* (Windsor, May 31, 1938); and Marcia Mason Moore in *Allah Be Praised* (Adelphi, Apr. 20, 1944).

She appeared as Lilli Vanessi (Kate) in *Kiss Me, Kate* (New Century, Dec. 30, 1948; Coliseum, London, Eng., Mar. 8, 1951), and also played this role in summer stock (St. Louis Municipal Opera Company, Mo.). She succeeded (Feb. 22, 1954) Constance Carpenter as Anna in *The King and I* (St. James, N.Y.C., Mar. 29, 1951), and also toured in it (opened Community Th., Hershey, Pa., Mar. 22, 1954). She appeared as the Baroness in *The Sound of Music* (L.A. Civic Light Opera, 1972); starred in *Pal Joey* (San Diego, 1973); and *Oh, Coward* (Columbia Concerts Tour, 1974).

Films. Miss Morison made her debut in *Persons in Hiding* (Par., 1939); and has since appeared in *I'm from Missouri* (Par., 1939); *The Magnificent Fraud* (Par., 1939); *Romance of the Rio Grande* (20th-Fox, 1941); *One Night in Lisbon* (Par., 1941); *Night in New Orleans* (Par., 1942); *Beyond the Blue Horizon* (Par., 1942); *Are Husbands Necessary?* (Par., 1942); *Hitler's Madman* (MGM, 1943); *The Song of Bernadette* (20th-Fox, 1943); *The Fallen Sparrow* (RKO, 1943); *Dressed to Kill* (U, 1946); *Queen of the Amazons* (SCG, 1947); *Song of the Thin Man* (MGM, 1947); *Return of Wildfire* (SCG, 1948); *Sofia* (FCL, 1948); and *Song Without End* (Col., 1960).

Television. She has appeared in excerpts from *The King and I* (Mar. 28, 1954); repeated her role in *Kiss Me, Kate* (Hallmark Hall of Fame, NBC, Nov. 20, 1958); appeared on the Voice of Firestone (CBS, Mar. 1959); and *Ben Franklin in Paris* (CBS, 1974).

Recreation. Painting.

MORLEY, ROBERT. Actor, director, playwright. b. Robert Adolph Wilton Morley, May 26, 1908, Semley, Wiltshire, England, to Robert Wilton and Gertrude Emily (Fass) Morley. Father, army officer. Attended Wellington Coll.; additional schooling in France, Germany, and Italy; RADA. Married Joan Buckmaster; two sons, one daughter. Relatives in the theatre: mother-in-law, Gladys Cooper, actress, (dec.); brother-in-law, John Buckmaster, actor. Member of British AEA; Garrick Club; Buck's. Address: (home) Fairmans, Wargrave, Berkshire, England; (bus.) 235 Regent St., London, W.1, England.

Theatre. Mr. Morley made his N.Y.C. debut in the title role of *Oscar Wilde* (Fulton, Oct. 10, 1938). His play, *Short Story*, was produced at the Heckscher Th. (N.Y.C., Mar. 13, 1940); with Noel Langley, he wrote *Edward, My Son*, in which he appeared as Arnold Holt (Martin Beck Th., Sept. 30, 1948). He appeared in a one-man show, *An Evening with Robert Morley*, at the 92 St. YM-YWHA (N.Y.C., Mar. 8, 1964).

He made his professional debut in *Dr. Syn* (Hippodrome, Margate, England, May 28, 1928); and his first appearance in London as a Pirate in *Treasure Island* (Strand, Dec. 26, 1929). He was assistant stage manager in the touring company of *And So to Bed* (1930); played in repertory (Oxford Playhouse, 1931); and at the Cambridge Arts Festival (1933); he appeared as Oakes in *Up in the Air* (Royalty, London, Nov. 1933); toured in H. V. Nielson's Shakespearean Co. (1934); played the Rev. Vernon Isopod in a touring production (1934) of *Late Night Final* (entitled in the US, *Five Star Final);* and Gloucester in *Richard of Bordeaux* (1935); with Peter Bull, organized and played in a repertory company (Perranporth, Cornwall, 1935). His play, *Short Story* was produced in London (Queen's, Nov. 2, 1935); later he appeared in the title role in *Oscar Wilde* (Gate Th., Sept. 1936), and in N.Y.C. (see above); as Alexandre Dumas in *The Great Romancer* (Strand, London, May 1937); and Henry Higgins in *Pygmalion* (Old Vic, Sept. 21, 1937). His play, *Goodness, How Sad!* was staged in London (Vaudeville, Oct. 18, 1938); he played Henry Dewlip in *Springtime for Henry* (Perranporth, Cornwall, July 1939); Decius Hess in *Play with Fire* (Royal, Brighton, Feb. 1941); and Sheridan Whiteside in *The Man Who*

Came to Dinner (Savoy, London, Dec. 4, 1941).

He toured England, playing Charles, in his play, *Staff Dance* (Feb.–Apr. 1944); portrayed the Prince Regent of England in *The First Gentleman* (Savoy, London, July 18, 1945); Arnold Holt in *Edward, My Son* (His Majesty's Th., 1947), and in N.Y.C. (see above), also on tour in Australia and New Zealand (1949–1950). He appeared as Philip in *The Little Hut* (Lyric, London, Aug. 23, 1950); Hippo in *Hippo Dancing*, which he adapted from André Roussin's *Les oeufs de l'autruche* (Lyric, Apr. 7, 1954); produced, with H. M. Tennent, *A Likely Tale*, in which he appeared as Oswald Petersham (Globe, Mar. 22, 1956); played Panisse in *Fanny* (Drury Lane, Nov. 15, 1956); directed and co-authored (with Ronald Gow) *The Full Treatment* ("Q", Feb. 3, 1957); wrote, with Dundas Hamilton, *Six Months' Grace* (Phoenix, June 11, 1957); directed *The Tunnel of Love* (Her Majesty's, Dec. 3, 1957); appeared as Sebastian Le Boeuf in *Hook, Line and Sinker* (Piccadilly, Nov. 19, 1958), which he adapted from a play by André Roussin; directed *Once More, With Feeling* (New July, 9, 1959); played Mr. Asano in *A Majority of One* (Phoenix, Mar. 9, 1960); and the Bishop in *A Time to Laugh* (Piccadilly, Apr. 24, 1962).

He played the Prince Regent in a *son et lumiere* pageant (Royal Pavilion grounds, Brighton, June 26, 1965); toured Australia in his one-man show, *The Sound of Morley* (Phillip Th., Sydney, Feb. 4, 1967; Princess, Melbourne, Mar. 7, 1967); played Sir Mallalieu Fitzbuttress in *Halfway Up the Tree* (Queen's Th., London, Nov. 8, 1967); Frank Foster in *How the Other Half Loves* (Lyric, Aug. 5, 1970); and appeared in his own play (written with Rosemary Ann Sisson), *A Ghost on Tiptoe* (Savoy, Apr. 25, 1974).

Films. Mr. Morley made his debut as Louis XVI in *Marie Antoinette* (MGM, 1938); subsequently appeared in *You Will Remember* (British Lion, 1940); *The Big Blockade* (Ealing, 1940); played Undershaft in *Major Barbara* (UA, 1941); appeared in *This Was Paris* (WB, 1942); *The Foreman Went to France* (WB, 1942); *The Young Mr. Pitt* (20th-Fox, 1942); *I Live in Grosvenor Square* (1945); *The Ghosts of Berkeley Square* (British Natl., 1947); *Edward, My Son* (MGM, 1949); *Curtain Up* (Rank, 1950); *African Queen* (UA, 1951); *The Small Black Room* (Snader, 1952); *Outcast of the Islands* (UA, 1952); *Gilbert and Sullivan* (UA, 1953); *Melba* (UA, 1953); *The Final Test* (Rank, 1954); *Beat the Devil* (UA, 1954); *The Rainbow Jacket* (Rank, 1954); as Prince Regent in *Beau Brummel* (MGM, 1954); in *The Good Die Young* (UA, 1955); *Quentin Durward* (MGM, 1955); *Around the World in 80 Days* (UA, 1956); *Loser Takes All* (DCA, 1957); *Sheriff of Fractured Jaw* (20th-Fox, 1958); *The Doctor's Dilemma* (MGM, 1958); *Law and Disorder* (Continental, 1958); *The Journey* (MGM, 1959); *Libel* (MGM, 1959); *The Battle of the Sexes* (Continental, 1960); Oscar Wilde in *Oscar Wilde* (FAW, 1960); *Go to Blazes* (Elstree, 1961); *The Young Ones* (Elstree, 1961); *Nine Hours to Rama* (20th-Fox, 1961); *The Story of Joseph and His Brethren* (Italian, 1960; Colorama, USA, 1962); *The Road to Hong Kong* (UA, 1962); *Old Dark House* (Hammer, 1962); *Murder at the Gallop* (MGM, 1963); *Ladies Who Do* (Continental, 1963); *Take Her, She's Mine* (20th-Fox, 1963); *Hot Enough for June* (Cont., 1964); Dr. Jacobs in *Of Human Bondage* (MGM, 1964); Cedric Page in *Topkapi* (UA, 1964); Emperor of China in *Genghis Khan* (Col., 1965); Lord Rawnsley in *Those Magnificent Men in Their Flying Machines* (20th-Fox, 1965); Sir Ambrose Abercrombie in *The Loved One* (MGM, 1965); Tiffield in *Life at the Top* (Col., 1965); in *Agent 8 3/4* (Cont., 1965); Mycroft Holmes in *A Study in Terror* (Col., 1966); Hastings in *The Alphabet Murders* (MGM, 1966); Henri Cot in *Hotel Paradiso* (MGM, 1966); Edward in *Tendre Voyou* (Prodis, 1966) released in US as *Tender Scoundrel* (Embassy, 1967); Harold Quonset in *Way, Way Out!* (20th-Fox, 1966); Dr. Xavier in *Woman Times Seven* (Embassy, 1967); Colonel Roberts in *Finders Keepers* (UA, 1968); in *Hot Millions* (MGM, 1968); as the Duke of Argyll in *Sinful Davey* (UA, 1969); in *Twinky* (Rank, 1969); as Hubert in *The Trygon Factor* (WB, 1969); Berg in *Song of Norway* (Cinerama, 1970); the Earl of Manchester in *Cromwell* (Col., 1970); Miss Mary in *Some Girls Do* (UA, 1971); Sir Arthur in *When Eight Bells Toll* (Cinerama, 1971); Judge Roxburgh in *Lola* (Amer. Int., 1973); and in *Theatre of Blood* (UA, 1973).

Television. Mr. Morley has appeared on British television in the Charge series, and on the Bringing Up Parents series (BBC, 1952). He was host for the Golden Drama special (ATV, 1965) and appeared in *An Evening with Robert Morley* (The Creative Urge, BBC-2, 1965). In the US, he has appeared in *Edward, My Son* (US Steel Hour, CBS, 1955); *Misalliance* (Playhouse 90, CBS, 1959); *Oliver Twist* (Du-Pont Show of the Month, CBS, 1959); on Alfred Hitchcock Presents (CBS); in *Heaven Can Wait* (Du-Pont Show of the Month, CBS, 1960); on the Dick Powell Th. (NBC); Espionage (NBC); the Jo Stafford special (Ind.); the Jack Paar Show (NBC); the Danny Kaye Show (CBS); the Today Show (NBC); the Mike Douglas Show (Ind.); the David Susskind Show (Ind.); Book Beat (Educ.); the Festival of Performing Arts (WNEW); and *The Bluffers* (NBC, May 28, 1971).

Night Clubs. He has performed at the Cafe de Paris (London, 1957).

Published Works. Mr. Morley wrote (with Sewell Stokes) his autobiography, published in England as *A Responsible Gentleman* (1966), and in the US as *Robert Morley, A Reluctant Autobiography* (1967). He has been a frequent contributor to *Punch* and other magazines.

Awards. The Order of Commander of the British Empire (C.B.E.) was conferred upon him in 1957.

Recreation. Discussion, horse racing.

MORLEY, RUTH. Costume designer.

Theatre. Miss Morley was costume designer for *Mrs. Warren's Profession* (Bleecker St. Playhouse, N.Y.C., Oct. 25, 1950); *The Cellar and the Well* (ANTA, Dec. 10, 1950); *Billy Budd* (Biltmore, Feb. 10, 1951); costume supervisor for *The Scarecrow* (Th. de Lys, June 16, 1953); with Dale Clement, costume designer for *The Little Clay Cart* (Th. de Lys, June 30, 1953); designed the costumes for *A Pin To See the Peepshow* (Playhouse, Sept. 17, 1953); *Take a Giant Step* (Lyceum, Sept. 24, 1953); *The Night of the Burning Pestle* (Th. de Lys, Oct. 23, 1953); selected the costumes for *The Troublemakers* (President, Dec. 20, 1954); and was assistant to Ben Edwards, costume designer for *Anastasia* (Lyceum, Dec. 29, 1954).

Miss Morley designed the costumes for *The Merchant of Venice* (Club Th., Jan. 7, 1955); *The Miser* (Downtown Natl., Mar. 24, 1955); *Inherit the Wind* (Natl., Apr. 21, 1955); the pre-Bway tryout of *Dancing in the Chequered Shade* (opened McCarter, Princeton, N.J., Dec. 20, 1955; closed Wilbur, Boston, Mass., Dec. 31, 1955); *A Moon for the Misbegotten* (Bijou, May 2, 1957); was costume supervisor for a revival of *Pajama Game* (NY City Ctr., May 15, 1957); designed the costumes for *The Cave Dwellers* (Bijou, Oct. 19, 1957); *Clerambard* (Rooftop, Nov. 7, 1957); *Who Was That Lady I Saw You With?* (Martin Beck Th., Mar. 3, 1958); was costume supervisor for *Wonderful Town* (NY City Ctr., Mar. 5, 1958; Brussel's World's Fair, July 1958); *The Most Happy Fella* (NY City Ctr., Feb. 10, 1959) and *Lute Song* (NY City Ctr., Mar. 12, 1959).

She was costume designer for *The Miracle Worker* (Playhouse, Oct. 19, 1959); *Only in America* (Cort, Nov. 19, 1959); *Roman Candle* (Cort, Feb. 3, 1960); *Toys in the Attic* (Hudson, Feb. 25, 1960); *Brouhaha* (115 E. Bway Playhouse, Apr. 26, 1960); for the operas *The Crucible* (NY City Ctr., Oct. 24, 1961); *Lucia de Lammermoor* (Metropolitan Opera House, Nov. 26, 1961), and *The Golem* (NY City Ctr., Mar. 22, 1962); and the play *A Thousand Clowns* (Eugene O'Neill Th., Apr. 5, 1962); the pre-Bway tryout of *A Matter of Position* (opened Walnut St. Th., Philadelphia, Pa., Sept. 29, 1962; closed there, Oct. 17, 1962); the opera *The Passion of Jonathan Wade* (NY City Ctr., Oct. 11, 1962); the play *In the Counting House* (Biltmore, Dec. 13, 1962); was costume supervisor for another revival of *Wonderful Town* (NY City Ctr., Feb. 13, 1963); designed the costumes for *Dylan* (Plymouth, Jan. 18, 1964); for the NY City Opera Co. (NY City Ctr.), designed productions of *Carmina Burana, St. Joan at the Stake*, and *The Good Soldier Schweik*.

Miss Morley designed the costumes for *Die Dreigroschenoper* (NY City Ctr., N.Y.C., Mar. 11, 1965); *Square in the Eye* (Th. de Lys, May 19, 1965); *Xmas in Las Vegas* (Ethel Barrymore Th., Nov. 4, 1965); *Wait Until Dark* (Ethel Barrymore Th., Feb. 2, 1966; and national tour, 1967); and *Dialogues of the Carmelites* (NY State Th., Mar. 1966); was costume supervisor for the Bavarian State Th., Munich, productions of *Wozzeck* (NY City Ctr., Apr. 5, 1966) and *Die Ratten* (NY City Ctr., Apr. 12, 1966); designed the costumes for *Here's Where I Belong* (Billy Rose Th., Mar. 3, 1968); *The Cannibals* American Place Th., Oct. 17, 1968); *The Rise and Fall of the City of Mahagonny* (Anderson Th., Apr. 28, 1970); and *Pinkville* (American Place Th., Mar. 17, 1971); was costume consultant for *The Silent Partner* (Actors Studio, May 11, 1972); and designed costumes for *Twelve Angry Men* (Queens Playhouse, Dec. 3, 1972); and *Bread* (American Place Th., Jan. 28, 1974).

Films. Miss Morley designed costumes for *The Young Doctors* (UA, 1961); *The Hustler* (20th-Fox, 1961); *The Connection* (FAW, 1962); *The Miracle Worker* (UA, 1962); *Lilith* (Col., 1964); *A Thousand Clowns* (UA, 1965); *The Brotherhood* (Par., 1967); *The Hot Rock* (20th-Fox, 1972); and *To Find a Man* (Col., 1972).

Television. Miss Morley designed for the NBC-TV Opera; the Paul Winchell Variety Show (CBS); and Cosmopolitan Theatre (ABC).

Awards. Miss Morley was nominated for an Academy (Oscar) Award for her costumes for *The Miracle Worker* (1963).

MOROSS, JEROME. Composer. b. Aug. 1, 1913, Brooklyn, N.Y., to Samuel and Mollie (Greenberg) Moross. Father, realtor. Grad. DeWitt Clinton H.S., Bronx, N.Y., 1928; New York Univ., B.S. 1932; Juilliard Grad. Sch., N.Y.C., 1932. Married 1939 to Hazel Aframs; one daughter. Member of AFM, Locals 802, 47; ASCAP; Dramatists Guild.

Theatre. Mr. Moross, at first, composed music for *Parade* (Guild Th., N.Y.C., 1935); subsequently composed the ballet *Frankie and Johnny*, sponsored by the Chicago (Ill.) Federal Th. (WPA) Project (1938); *Ballet Ballads* (Maxine Elliott's Th., N.Y.C., May 9, 1948; revived East 74 St. Th., Jan. 3, 1961); music for *The Golden Apple* (Phoenix Th., Mar. 11, 1954; moved Alvin, Apr. 20, 1954; revived York Playhouse, Feb. 12, 1962); and the opera *Gentlemen Be Seated* (NY City Ctr., Oct. 10, 1963).

Films. Mr. Moross wrote the music for *The Cardinal* (Col., 1963); *The War Lord* (U, 1965); *Rachel, Rachel* (WB-Seven Arts, 1968); *Hail, Hero!* (Natl. Gen., 1969); and *The Valley of Gwangi* (WB-Seven Arts, 1969).

MORRILL, PRISCILLA. Actress. b. Priscilla Alden Morrill, June 4, 1927, Medford, Mass., to Joseph Henry and Reina H. (Messer) Morrill. Father, advertising dept. of Boston *Herald*. Grad. Winchester H.S., Mass., 1945; Carnegie Inst. of Technology, B.F.A. 1949. Studied acting with Norma Woodward, Somerville, Mass., five years; Marjorie Oxnard, Somerville, Mass., five years. Married March 7, 1954, to Paul Hendley Bryson. Relative in theatre: cousin, Walter Prichard Eaton (dec. 1957), writer; drama critic for the N.Y. *Sun*; professor of playwriting at Yale Univ., and Univ. of North Carolina. Member of AEA; AFTRA; SAG.

Theatre. Miss Morrill first appeared as the Housekeeper in a stock production of *Angel Street* (New London Playhouse, N.H., Summer 1946); and made subsequent appearances there (Summers 1947, 1948); played Portia in *Julius Caesar* (Brattle Th., Cambridge, Mass., July 5, 1950); made her Bway debut as Abigail and understudied Madge Elliott as Berintha in *The Relapse or Virtue in Danger* (Morosco Th., Nov. 22, 1950); subsequently was understudy to Audrey Christie as Liz Kendall in *Buy Me Blue Ribbons* (Empire, Oct. 17, 1951); appeared in stock at the White Barn Th. (Irwin, Pa., Summer 1952); played Jacquenetta in *Love's Labour's Lost* (NY City Ctr., Feb. 4, 1953); succeeded (Dec. 1953) Jan Farrand as Hypatia Tarleton in the tour of *Misalliance* (opened Selwyn, Chicago, Ill., Dec. 22, 1953; closed Erlanger, Buffalo, N.Y., Feb. 1954); played Julie in a stock production of *New Moon* (Dallas State Fair, Musicals, Tex., July 1953); Mrs. Fainall in *The Way of the World* (Cherry Lane, N.Y.C., Oct. 2, 1954); appeared in a season of stock (Corning Summer Th., N.Y., Summer 1954); played Donna Anna in *Don Juan in Hell* (Rochester Arena, N.Y., Winter 1955); appeared at the Totem Pole Playhouse (Fayetteville, Pa., Summers 1955–57; 1959); and at the Playhouse on the Green (Columbus, Ohio, Summer 1955).

Miss Morrill was general understudy for *Diary of a Scoundrel* (Phoenix, N.Y.C., Nov. 5, 1956), succeeding Josephine Brown as a Gypsy Fortune Teller during the run; played Cariola in *The Duchess of Malfi* (Phoenix, Mar. 19, 1937); Vera Charles in a summer tour of *Auntie Mame* (1958) and at the Coconut Grove Playhouse (Miami, Fla., Nov. 1958); understudied Barbara Baxley as Cora Flood and Audrey Christie as Lottie Lacy in the national tour of *The Dark at the Top of the Stairs* (opened Playhouse, Wilmington, Del., Jan. 21, 1959; closed Pabst, Milwaukee, Wis., May 16, 1959); appeared in a summer tryout of *Babylon by Candlelight* (Cincinnati Summer Playhouse, Ohio, Aug. 31, 1959); played Ann Taft in *Alley of the Sunset* (Jan Hus, N.Y.C., Dec. 30, 1960); Anne Cinquefoil in *The Sudden End of Ann Cinquefoil* (East End, Jan. 10, 1961); Lavinia in *The Cocktail Party*, and Inez in *No Exit* (Charles Th., Boston, Mass., Mar. 28, 1961); and Penelope Grey in *Elizabeth the Queen* (Boston Arts Fest., Aug. 23, 1961); and succeeded Jane Hoffman as Mommy (Nov. 1961) in *The American Dream* (Cherry Lane, N.Y.C., Sept. 17, 1961).

Miss Morrill succeeded Shelly Winters as Maxine Faulk (Sept. 1962) in *The Night of the Iguana* (Royale, Dec. 28, 1961); then played Deedee Grogan in *Invitation to a March* (Playhouse-on-the-Mall, Paramus, N.J., Dec. 4, 1962); and Babette Biederman in *The Firebugs* (Maidman, N.Y.C., Feb. 11, 1963). For the National Shakespeare Festival, San Diego, Calif., she played Lady Macbeth in *Macbeth*, Mistress Overdone in *Measure for Measure*, Margaret in *Much Ado About Nothing*, in repertory (Old Globe, June 9–Sept. 13, 1964); the Nurse in *Romeo and Juliet* (June 14, 1966); Iris in *The Tempest* (June 22, 1966); Lucetta in *Two Gentlemen of Verona* (July 14, 1966); and Calpurnia in *Julius Caesar* (Summer 1969).

She played Nora Melody in *A Touch of the Poet* (ANTA Th., N.Y.C., May 2, 1969); appeared as a guest artist with the Meadow Brook Theater (Rochester, Mich., 1970–71), and the Seattle (Wash.) Repertory Theatre (1971–72); and appeared with the Center Theatre Group in *Richard II* (Ahmanson Th., Los Angeles, 1971–72).

Television. Miss Morrill made her debut as an extra in *Hamlet* (Hallmark Hall of Fame, NBC, 1953); and has appeared on The Seeking Heart (CBS, 1954); played Claire in *Dream Girl* (Hallmark Hall of Fame, NBC, 1955); Evelyn in an episode of The Defenders (CBS, 1963); Vera in an episode of Outer Limits (ABC, 1963); and Phyllis in an episode of The Nurses (CBS, 1964).

Recreation. Travel, tennis, reading.

MORRIS, JOHN. Composer, conductor, arranger, orchestrator. b. John Leonard Morris, Oct. 18, 1926, Elizabeth, N.J., to Thomas Arthur and Helen (Sherratt) Morris. Father, architect-engineer. Grad. Bosse H.S., Evansville, Ind., 1944; attended Jordan Conservatory, Indianapolis, 1944–45; Juilliard Sch. of Music, N.Y.C. (scholarship), 1945–47; Univ. of Washington, Summer 1946; New Sch. for Social Research, 1947. Studied piano (scholarship) with Alfred Mirovitch, 1943–48; conducting and composing with Victor Kolar, 1944–45. Married 1949 to Francesca Bosetti; one son, one daughter. Member of AFM; ASCAP; Dramatists Guild. Address: 317 Millwood Rd., Chappaqua, NY 10514.

Theatre. Mr. Morris made his debut as a concert pianist in recitals in the Midwest and with the Evansville (Ind.) Philharmonic and the Indianapolis (Ind.) Symphony Orchestra (1945); had his first assignment in N.Y.C. as arranger for the dance music of *Carnival in Flanders* (Century, Sept. 8, 1953); arranged the dance music and was assistant conductor for *Peter Pan* (Winter Garden, Oct. 20, 1954); composed ballet music for *Phoenix '55* (Phoenix, Apr. 23, 1955); conducted and arranged dance music for the summer-theatre productions at the Valley Forge Music Fair (Devon, Pa., Summer 1956); composed additional dance arrangements for *Shangri-La* (Winter Garden, N.Y.C., June 13, 1956); composed incidental scoring and arranged dance music for *Bells Are Ringing* (Shubert, Nov. 29, 1956); composed additional musical routines for *Shinbone Alley* (Bway Th., Apr. 13, 1957); conducted at the Cape Cod Melody Tent (Hyannis, Mass., Summers 1957–58); arranged dance music for *Copper and Brass* (Martin Beck Th., N.Y.C., Oct. 17, 1957); *First Impressions* (Alvin, Mar. 19, 1959); conducted and arranged for *Dig We Must* (John Drew Th., East Hampton, L.I., N.Y., Summer 1959); arranged dance music for *The Girls Against the Boys* (Alvin, N.Y.C., Nov. 2, 1959); arranged dance music and was associate conductor for *Bye-Bye Birdie* (Martin Beck Th., Apr. 14, 1960); conducted and arranged the songs and dance music of *Wildcat* (Alvin, Dec. 16, 1960); composed the ballet music in *Kwamina* (54 St. Th., Oct. 23, 1961); conducted and arranged dance music for *All American* (Winter Garden, Mar. 19, 1962); composed incidental music for *My Mother, My Father and Me* (Plymouth, Mar. 23, 1963); arranged dance music for *The Boys from Syracuse* Th. Four, Apr. 15, 1963); and with Trude Rittman, arranged dance and vocal music for *Hot Spot* (Majestic, Apr. 19, 1963).

He composed incidental music for NY Shakespeare Festival productions (both Delacorte Th.) of *As You Like It* (July 11, 1963) and *Electra* (Aug. 11, 1964); dance music for *Baker Street* (Bway Th., Feb. 16, 1965); music for *The Day the Whores Came Out To Play Tennis* and *Sing To Me Through Open Windows* (Players Th., Mar. 15, 1965); and he wrote songs and music for the NY Shakespeare Festival's *Love's Labour's Lost* (Delacorte Th., June 9, 1965). he was co-author, with Gerald Freedman, of the book and lyrics for and composed music for *A Time for Singing* (Bway Th., May 21, 1966); composed music for *Sherry!* (Alvin Th., Mar. 27, 1967); and for NY Shakespeare Festival productions (both Delacorte Th.) of *The Comedy of Errors* (June 7, 1967) and *Titus Andronicus* (Aug. 2, 1967).

At the NY Shakespeare Festival's Public Th., he was musical director for *Hair* (Oct. 29, 1967), for *Hamlet* (Dec. 26, 1967), composed music and a sound score for *Ergo* (Mar. 3, 1968), and composed music for *The Memorandum* (May 5, 1968); for NY Shakespeare Festival productions at the Delacorte Th., he wrote songs and music for *Henry IV, Part 1* (June 11, 1968), *Henry IV, Part 2* (June 18, 1968), and composed music for *Romeo and Juliet* (Aug. 7, 1968); and, again with Gerald Freedman, he wrote the NY Shakespeare Festival's Mobile Th. children's show *Take One Step* (June 25, 1968). Also for the NY Shakespeare Festival, Mr. Morris wrote music and supervised the sound score for *Cities in Bezique* (Public, Jan. 4, 1969); composed music for *Invitation to a Beheading* (Public, Mar. 8, 1969); wrote songs and music for *Peer Gynt* (Delacorte Th., July 8, 1969); and was musical supervisor for *Sambo* (Public, Dec. 12, 1969).

Mr. Morris also composed dance music for *Dear World* (Mark Hellinger Th., Feb. 6, 1969); *Look to the Lilies* (Lunt-Fontanne Th., Mar. 29, 1970); did dance arrangements for *Lolita, My Love* (opened Shubert Th., Philadelphia, Pa., Feb. 15, 1971; closed Shubert Th., Boston, Mass., Mar. 18, 1971); was musical supervisor for *Blood* (Public Th., N.Y.C., Mar. 7, 1971); composed music for the NY Shakespeare Festival's *Hamlet* (Delacorte Th., June 20, 1972); for American Shakespeare Festival (Stratford, Conn.) productions of *Julius Caesar* (June 22, 1972) and *Antony and Cleopatra* (June 23, 1972); was musical supervisor for *Much Ado About Nothing* (Winter Garden, N.Y.C., Nov. 11, 1972); composed music for the NY Shakespeare Festival's *The Cherry Orchard* (Public, Dec. 7, 1972); made orchestral arrangements and was musical supervisor for *Nash at Nine* (Helen Hayes Th., May 17, 1973); composed music for the American Shakespeare Festival's *Measure for Measure* (Stratford, Conn., June 2, 1973); and composed dance and incidental music for *Mack and Mabel* (Majestic, N.Y.C., Oct. 6, 1974).

Films. Mr. Morris composed the score for the documentary film, *With Wings of Eagles* (New Dimensions, 1963); composed and conducted music for *The Producers* (Embassy, 1968); *The Twelve Chairs* (UMC, 1970); *The Gamblers* (U-M, 1970); *Blazing Saddles* (WB, 1974); *The Bank Shot* (UA, 1974); and *Young Frankenstein* (20th-Fox, 1974).

Television. He arranged dance music for *Ruggles of Red Gap* (NBC, 1957); *Mr. Broadway* (NBC, 1957); *Hans Brinker* (NBC, 1958); the Garry Moore Show (CBS, 1958); *Peter Pan.* for which he was also assistant conductor (NBC, 1958); composed ballet music for the Steve Allen Show (NBC, 1958); arranged dance music for *Meet Me in St. Louis* (CBS, 1959); Hallmark Christmas Festival (NBC, 1959); Bell Telephone Hour (ABC, 1960); *Four for Tonight* (NBC, 1960); and Hallmark Christmas Tree (NBC, 1960).

Other television shows on which Mr. Morris worked include *The Littlest Angel; Cole Porter in Paris; the Desperate Hours* (ABC, Dec. 13, 1967); *Annie, The Women in the Life of a Man* (CBS, Feb. 18, 1970); and *'S Wonderful, 'S Marvelous, 'S Gershwin* (NBC, Jan. 17, 1972). He was musical supervisor for the televising of the NY Shakespeare Festival *Much Ado About Nothing* (CBS, Feb. 2, 1973); and arranged music for *Annie and the Hoods* (ABC, Nov. 1974) and *The Canterville Ghost.* Mr. Morris also wrote theme music for Thalassa Cruso's Making Things Grow program; the Julia Child "French Chef" theme; and the ABC "After School Special" theme.

Awards. Mr. Morris received a NATAS (Emmy) Award for music for *Annie, The Women in the Life of a Man* and the ASIFA East Award for his "After School Special" theme.

Recreation. Serious cooking, home on Pemaquid Point, Me.

MORRIS, WILLIAM, JR. Theatrical enterprises. b. Oct. 22, 1899, New York City, to William and Emma (Berlinghoff) Morris. Father, talent agency representative. Grad. N.Y.C. public schools. Married Dec. 28, 1949, to Ruth Bachman. Address: (home) Solstice, 26044 Pacific Coast Highway, Malibu, CA 90265, tel. (213) 456-2493; (bus.) William Morris Agency, Inc., 1350 Ave. of the Americas, New York, NY 10019, tel. (212) JU 6-5100.

Since 1952, Mr. Morris has been a director of the William Morris Agency, Inc.; was president of William Morris Agency, Inc. (1932–52); and a partner in the organization (1915–32).

Recreation. Innovations in theatre presentation, and electronic laser music.

MORRISON, HOBE. Drama editor, critic. b. Mar. 24, 1904, Philadelphia, Pa., to J. I. and Agnes (Millar) Morrison. Father, railroad executive. Grad. Cheltenham H.S., Elkins Pk., Pa., 1924. Married Mar. 15, 1946, to Elizabeth Augun; (marr. dis. 1962); three sons; married Nov. 20, 1964, to Toni Darnay, actress. Address: (home) 7 W. 16th St., New York, NY 10011; (bus.) c/o Variety, 154 W. 46th St., New York, NY 10036, tel. (212) JU 2-2700.

Since 1948, Mr. Morrison has been drama editor of *Variety.*

He joined the Philadelphia *Record* (1930) as staff reporter; became drama editor (1934); and served as second-string drama critic, film, dance and music critic, and night club columnist (1934–1937).

He became Philadelphia correspondent for *Variety* (1935); joined the staff in New York City, covering theatre and radio (1937); was a member of the radio department at Young & Rubicam advertising agency (1944–47); and returned to *Variety* (1947).

He is also the N.Y.C. drama critic for the *Herald-News,* Passaic, N.J., and writes a daily entertainment column for the *Herald-News* and the *Westchester Rockland Newspapers,* White Plains, N.Y., a unit of the Gannett Newspapers.

MORRISON, JACK. Educator, foundation executive. b. Jack Sherman Morrison, Dec. 17, 1912, Santa Barbara, Calif., to Charles Pacific and Anna Marie (Sandberg) Morrison. Father, motion picture producer. Grad. Hollywood H.S., 1930; Univ. of Calif. at Los Angeles (Calif.) B.A. 1934, M.A. 1951; attended Univ. of Vienna, 1935; grad. Univ. of Southern Calif., Ed.D. 1962. Married August 1938 to Martha Louise Godfrey, teacher (marr. dis. 1949); one daughter, one son; married June 6, 1953, to Jeanne Carolyn Cagney, actress (marr. dis. 1973); two daughters. Served with Amer. Natl. Red Cross as program director and entertainment liaison officer for No. Africa, WW II. Member of AETA (admin. vice-pres., 1951–56; pres. 1957); American Playwrights Th. (member, bd. of gov., 1966–72); Amer. Ed. Research Assn.; Amer. Natl. Th. and Academy (bd. mbr., 1968–to date); SAG; Phi Kappa Psi; Players Club (N.Y.C.). Address: (home) 61 W. 90th St., New York, NY 10024; (bus.) JDR 3rd Fund, 50 Rockefeller Plaza, New York, NY 10020.

Presently, Mr. Morrison is associate director of the Arts in Education Program, JDR 3rd Fund, New York. He was Dean, College of Fine Arts, Ohio Univ. (Athens, 1966–70); was a member of the faculty at the Univ. of California at Los Angeles (from 1947) where he had been director of theatre activities (1938–47); member of board of directors, UCLA Theatre Group (1958–62); head of theatre division (1959–61); vice-chairman of theatre department (1960–61); and is associate professor of Theatre Arts. He has directed many student productions, including the American premiere of Albert Camus' *The Just* (Theatre 170, 1960).

Mr. Morrison made his acting debut as the Sick Child in the film, *Damaged Goods* (Amer. Film Co., 1913), and has appeared as Thomas in the *Pilgrimage Play* Pilgrimage Play Th., Hollywood, Calif., Summer 1947).

He serves as consultant for theatre and fine arts at Univ. of Maryland, Univ. of Hawaii, Hofsta Univ., Syracuse Univ., Purdue Univ., York Univ. (Toronto and Ontario, Canada), and for the states of New Jersey and South Carolina.

Published Works. Mr. Morrison has written a book, *The Rise of the Arts on the American Campus* (1973), a report for the Carnegie Commission on higher education. He has contributed articles to the *Educational Theatre Journal; Quarterly Journal of Speech; Journal of Motion Picture and TV Engineers; Arts in Society,* and others.

Awards. Mr. Morrison has received an AETA citation for his leadership in the arts, and a Ford Foundation Fellowship, through the New Dramatists Committee, as director-observer on the George Abbott production, *Take Her, She's Mine.*

He received the Amer. Th. Assoc. Award of Merit (1966) and was made a Fellow (1968); was made a Founding Fellow of the American Council for the Arts in Education (1972).

Recreation. Skiing, photography.

MORRISON, PAUL. Scenic, lighting, costume designer, executive. b. Paul Patrick Morrison, July 9, 1906, Altoona, Pa., to Patrick L. and Catherine (Murphy) Morrison. Father, hotel owner and manager. Grad. Altoona H.S., 1923; Lafayette Coll., B.A. 1927. During WW II, designed and supervised USO overseas productions. Member of AEA; United Scenic Artists, Local 829.

Pre-Theatre. Designer of advertising layout, newspaper reporter.

Theatre. Mr. Morrison performed with the Theatre Guild (1929–30); and was an actor and stage manager with the Group Theatre (1931–34). The settings for the Group Theatre productions of *Till the Day I Die* and *Waiting for Lefty* (Longacre Th., N.Y.C., Mar. 26, 1935) were designed from his suggestions. During 1935–36, he was technical director and design supervisor of the Chicago (Ill.) Division of the Federal Theatre (WPA) Project.

He designed the costumes for *Thunder Rock* (Mansfield, N.Y.C., Nov. 14, 1939); scenery, lighting, and costumes for *Walk into My Parlor* (Forrest, Nov. 19, 1941); scenery and lighting for *Hedda Gabler* (Longacre, Jan. 29, 1942); costumes for *Apology* (Mansfield, Mar. 22, 1943); scenery, lighting, and costumes for *I'll Take the High Road* (Ritz, Nov. 9, 1943); scenery and lighting for *Mrs. January and Mr. X* (Belasco, Mar. 31, 1944), *That Old Devil* (Playhouse, June 5, 1944), *Love on Leave* (Hudson, June 20, 1944), and *What Every Woman Knows* (Repertory Th., Nov. 8, 1946).

He created the scenery, lighting, and costumes for *John Gabriel Borkman* (Repertory Th., Nov. 12, 1946); costumes for *All My Sons* (Coronet, Jan. 29, 1947); scenery and lighting for *The Young and Fair* (Fulton, Nov. 22, 1948), *The Closing Door* (Empire, Dec. 1, 1949), and *Affairs of State* (Royale, Sept. 25, 1950); scenery, lighting, and costumes for *Arms and the Man* (Arena, Oct. 19, 1950); scenery and lighting for *The Cellar and the Well* (ANTA, Dec. 10, 1950), and *Billy Budd* (Biltmore, Feb. 10, 1951); scenery, lighting, and costumes for *Getting Married* (ANTA, May 7, 1951); and scenery and lighting for *Twilight Walk* (Fulton, Sept. 24, 1951).

He designed the scenery and lighting for *Faithfully Yours* (Coronet, Oct. 18, 1951); scenery, lighting, and costumes for *Golden Boy* (ANTA, Mar. 12, 1952), *Four Saints in Three Acts* (Bway Th., April 16, 1952), and *On Borrowed Time* (48 St. Th., Feb. 10, 1953); was technical scenic director for *Cyrano de Bergerac* (NY City Ctr., Nov. 11, 1953); designed the scenery, lighting, and costumes for *The Confidential Clerk* (Morosco, Feb. 11, 1954); scenery and lighting for *The Tender Trap* (Longacre, Oct. 13, 1954); scenery, lighting, and costumes for *Abie's Irish Rose* (Holiday, Nov. 18, 1954); lighting and costumes for *Bus Stop* (Music Box, Mar. 2, 1955); and lighting and costumes for *Once Upon a Tailor* (Cort, May 23, 1955).

He was lighting and supervising designer for the NY production of *Tiger at the Gates* (Plymouth, Oct. 3, 1955); scenic supervisor and lighting designer for both *Joyce Grenfell Requests the Pleasure*. . . (Bijou, Oct. 10, 1955), and *Tamburlaine* (Winter Garden, Jan. 19, 1956); designed scenery, lighting, and costumes for *The Loud Red Patrick* (Ambassador, Oct. 3, 1956); scenery and lighting for *Sixth Finger on a Five Finger Glove* (Longacre, Oct. 8, 1956); was scenic supervisor and lighting designer for *Separate Tables* (Music Box, Oct. 25, 1956), and *Cranks* (Bijou, Nov. 26, 1956); and created lighting for *Candide* (Martin Beck Th., Dec. 1, 1956), *Ziegfeld Follies* (Winter Garden, Mar. 1, 1957), and *The Sin of Pat Muldoon* (Cort, Mar. 13, 1957).

He designed the scenery and lighting for *Maybe Tuesday* (The Playhouse, Jan. 29, 1958); was scenic supervisor and lighting designer for *The Visit* (Lunt-Fontanne, May 5, 1958); designed the scenery and lighting for *Make a Million* (The Playhouse, Oct. 23, 1958), *Masquerade* (John Golden Th., Mar. 16, 1959), and *Jeanette* (Maidman, Mar. 24, 1959); lighting for *Kataki* (Ambassador, Apr. 9, 1959); and scenery and lighting for *The Nervous Set* (Henry Miller's Th., May 12, 1959).

He was lighting and supervising designer for *Much Ado About Nothing* (Lunt-Fontanne, Sept. 17, 1959); designed lighting for *Happy Town* (54 St. Th., Oct. 7, 1959), *The Flowering Cherry* (Lyceum, Oct. 21, 1959), *Lysistrata* (Phoenix, Nov. 24, 1959), *A Thurber Carnival* (ANTA, Feb. 26, 1960), *Duel of Angels* (Biltmore, Apr. 19, 1960), and *Invitation to a March* (Music Box, Oct. 29, 1960); designed *The Mousetrap* (Maidman, Nov. 5, 1960); scenery and lighting for *Rape of the Belt* (Martin Beck Th., Nov. 5, 1960); lighting for *South Pacific* (NY City Ctr., Apr. 26, 1961), and *Porgy and Bess* (NY City Ctr., May 17, 1961); was scenic supervisor and lighting designer for *The Caretaker* (Lyceum, Oct. 4, 1961); and created lighting for *The Complaisant Lover* (Ethel Barrymore Th., Nov. 1, 1961), and *A Man for All Seasons* (ANTA, Nov. 22, 1961).

He was tehnical director and lighting designer for the Theatre Guild American Repertory Theatre tour of Europe (1961), during which he designed the scenery, lighting and costumes for *The Skin of Our Teeth* (1961). He designed the scenery, lighting, and costumes for *The Cantilevered Terrace* (41 St. Th., N.Y.C., Jan. 17, 1962); scenery, lighting, and costumes for the pre-Bway tryout of *Banderol* (opened Forrest, Philadelphia, Pa., Sept. 17, 1962; closed there Sept. 22, 1962); lighting for *Parnassus '63* (ANTA, N.Y.C., Dec. 16, 1962); scenery and lighting for the Bway production of *Too True to Be Good* (54 St. Th., Mar. 12, 1963); lighting for *The Student Gypsy* (54 St. Th., Sept. 30, 1963); and directed and designed the National Performing Art tour of *A Man for All Seasons* (opened Rochester Aud., N.Y., Oct. 5, 1963).

Mr. Morrison designed the sets and lighting for *Babes in the Wood* (Orpheum Th., N.Y.C., Dec. 28, 1964); and the sets for *The Cat and the Canary* (Stage 73, Jan. 4, 1965). Under the U.S. Department of State's cultural presentation program, Mr. Morrison was one of a coaching team which worked with the members of the Kumo Gekidan (Tokyo, Japan) to present *Long Day's Journey into Night* (Sept.–Oct. 1965); subsequently executed the sets for *After the Rain* (John Golden Th., N.Y.C., Oct. 9, 1967); lighting for *The Price* (Morosco, Feb. 7, 1968); was production supervisor for *Conduct Unbecoming* (Ethel Barrymore Th., Oct. 12, 1970); and designed the sets and lighting for *The Jockey Club Stakes* (Cort, Jan. 24, 1973).

Other Activities. Since May 5, 1963, Mr. Morrison has been executive director of the Neighborhood Playhouse School of the Theatre. From 1936–41, he was head of the Theatre Dept., Bard Coll., Annandale-on-Hudson, N.Y.

Recreation. Theatre, traveling.

MORSE, BARRY. Actor, director. b. Barry Herbert Morse, June 10, 1919, London, England, to Charles Hayward and Mary Florence (Hollis) Morse. Father, tobaccanist. Attended Royal Academy of Dramatic Arts, London, 1935–36. Married 1939 to Sydney Sturgess; son, Hayward Morse, actor; daughter, Melanie Morse, actress.

Theatre. From 1937–41, Mr. Morse toured the provinces of England with fourteen various repertory companies, playing more than two hundred roles. He made his professional debut playing the French Herald in *If I Were King* (Peoples' Palace, East London); and his West End debut in *School for Slavery* (Westminster Th., 1941); subsequently appeared in *Escort* (Lyric, 1942); *War and Peace* (Phoenix, 1943); *Crisis in Heaven* (1944); *The Assassin* (Savoy Th., 1945); and *Written for a Lady* (Garrick, 1948); and produced, directed and played the lead in *The Voice of the Turtle* (tour, England, 1948).

Mr. Morse and his family moved to Canada in 1951, where he produced and directed the North American premiere of *Salad Days,* which was later presented in NYC (Barbizon-Plaza, Nov. 10, 1958). He made his Bway debut in the role of Tom Richards in *Hide and Seek* (Ethel Barrymore Th., Apr. 2, 1957); played Davies in a touring production of *The Caretaker* (opened Sombrero Playhouse, Phoenix, Ariz., Oct. 16, 1962); directed *Staircase* (Biltmore, N.Y.C., Jan. 10, 1968); and replaced Alec McCowen (Sept. 1, 1969) as Fr. William Rolfe in *Hadrian VII* (Helen Hayes Th., Jan. 8, 1969).

Mr. Morse has appeared in various Canadian and American repertory companies in productions such as *Cyrano de Bergerac, Man and Superman, Much Ado About Nothing,* and *Oedipus Rex.* .

Television. In addition to his frequent appearances on major Canadian (1951–to date) and American (1958–to date) networks, he has played Dr. Austin Sloper in *The Heiress* (CBS, 1961); Lt. Philip Gerard on The Fugitive (ABC, 1963–67); and Prof. Victor Bergman in Space: 1999 (Ind., 1975).

Awards. Mr. Morse played the title role in *Henry V* in a command performance (1936) before King George VI and Queen Elizabeth of England. He was named best actor in Canadian television (1954,

1956, 1961, 1962); and received the Gold Award (1955) of the Canadian Council of Authors and Artists for "consistently high artistic achievement.".

MORSE, ROBERT. Actor. b. Robert Alan Morse, May 18, 1931, Newton, Mass., to Charles and May (Silver) Morse. Father, assistant manager of record store. Grad. Newton (Mass.) H.S., 1952. Married Apr. 8, 1961, to Carole Ann D'Andrea; three daughters. Served USN, 1951; rank, Sonarman-2. Relative in theatre: brother, Richard Morse, actor, teacher. Member of AEA; SAG; AFTRA.

Theatre. Mr. Morse directed and appeared in a high school production of *Sing Out, Sweet Land* (1951); made his professional debut in *Our Town* (Peterborough Players, Peterborough, N.H., Summer 1949); his Bway debut as Barnaby Tucker in *The Matchmaker* (Royale Th., Dec. 5, 1955), and repeated the role in the national touring company (opened Shubert, Detroit, Mich., Feb. 4, 1957); played the part of Ted Snow in *Say, Darling*(ANTA, N.Y.C., Apr. 3, 1958); Richard Miller in *Take Me Along*(Shubert, Oct. 22, 1959); J. Pierpont Finch in *How To Succeed in Business without Really Trying*(46 St. Th., Oct. 14, 1961); and Jerry in *Sugar*(Majestic, Apr. 9, 1972).

Films. He appeared in *The Proud and the Profane* (Par., 1956); played Barnaby Tucker in *The Matchmaker* (Par., 1958); appeared in *Honeymoon Hotel* (1964); *Quick Before it Melts*(1964); played Dennis Barlow in *The Loved One*(MGM, 1965); J. Pierpont Finch in *How To Succeed in Business without Really Trying*(UA, 1967); Jonathan in *Oh Dad, Poor Dad, Mamma's Hung You in the Closet and I'm Feeling So Sad*(Par., 1967); Ed Stander in *Guide for the Married Man* (20th-Fox, 1967); Waldo Zane in *Where Were You When the Lights Went Out?*(MGM, 1968); and Ensign Garland in *The Boatniks* (Buena Vista, 1970).

Television. Mr. Morse appeared on Naked City (ABC); the Shirley Temple Show; the Perry Como Show (NBC); the Jack Paar Show (NBC); *People and Other Animals* (Ind.); To Tell the Truth (CBS); the Mike Douglas (Ind.), Red Skelton (CBS), and Clay Cole (Ind.) shows; I've Got a Secret (CBS); Hollywood Squares (NBC); The Today Show (NBC); the Smothers Brothers Comedy Hour (CBS); and Alias Smith and Jones (ABC).

Recreation. All sports, cooking, amateur photography.

MOSEL, TAD. Playwright. b. George Ault Mosel, Jr., May 1, 1922, Steubenville, Ohio, to George A. and Margaret (Norman) Mosel. Father, advertising executive. Attended Mt. Hermon Sch. for Boys, Northfield, Mass., 1937–38; New Rochelle (N.Y.) H.S., 1938–40; Amherst Coll., B.A. 1947; Yale Univ. Sch. of Drama, 1947–49; Columbia Univ. M.A. 1953. Served USAAF, 1943–46, Weather Service; and edited Weather Squadron newspaper (Manila, Philippines); rank, Sgt. Member of WGA (council member, 1963–65); The Players; Theta Delta Chi.

Theatre. Mr. Mosel wrote *The Happiest Years*, his first play, which he also directed (Kirby Th., Amherst Coll., Mass., Aug. 1942). His play, *All the Way Home*(Belasco, Nov. 30, 1960), was based on James Agee's novel, *A Death in the Family*. He also wrote the book for the musical, *Madame Aphrodite* (Orpheum, Dec. 29, 1961).

Films. Mr. Mosel wrote the screenplays for *The Out-of-Towners*(WB, 1964); *Dear Heart*(WB, 1964); and *Up the Down Staircase* (WB, 1967).

Television. Mr. Mosel wrote *Jinxed* (Chevrolet Th., NBC, Jan., 1949); adapted James Thurber's stories: *The Figgerin' of Aunt Wilma, This Little Kitty Stayed Cool* and *The Remarkable Case of Mr. Bruhl* (Omnibus, CBS, Spring, 1953); wrote *Ernie Barger Is Fifty* and *Other People's Houses* (Philco-Goodyear Playhouse, NBC, Aug. 1953); *The Haven* (Philco-Goodyear Playhouse, NBC, Oct. 1953); *Madame Aphrodite* (Philco-Goodyear Playhouse, NBC, Dec. 1953); *The Lawn Party, Star in the Summer Night* and *Guilty Is the Stranger* (Philco-Goodyear Playhouse, NBC, 1954); *My Lost Saints*(Philco-Goodyear Playhouse, NBC, 1955); *The Waiting Place* (Playwrights '56, NBC, 1955); *The Five Dollar Bill* and *The Morning Face*(Studio One, CBS, 1957); *The Presence of the Enemy*(Studio One, CBS, 1958); *The Innocent Sleep* (Playhouse 90, CBS, 1958); *A Corner of the Garden* (Playhouse 90, CBS, 1959); *Sarah's Laughter* (GE Theatre, CBS, 1959); *The Invincible Teddy* (American Heritage, NBC, 1960); *That's Where the Town's Going* (Westinghouse Presents, CBS, 1962); wrote the original story for *Who Has Seen the Wind*(ABC, 1965); and wrote *Secrets* (CBS Playhouse, 1968).

Awards. Mr. Mosel received the Pulitzer Prize in Drama and the NY Drama Critics Circle Award for his play *All the Way Home*(1961); and an honorary degree (Litt.D.) from the Coll. of Wooster (1963).

Recreation. Collecting clocks and rare books.

MOSER, MARGOT. Actress, singer. b. Margot Ann Moser, Aug. 15, 1930, Reading, Pa., to Alvin Clair and Marion (Edwards) Moser. Father, director of Pennsylvania State Educ. Assn.; mother, teacher. Grad. Lower Paxton Township H.S., Harrisburg, 1945; attended Juilliard Sch. of Music, 1945–47. Studied singing with William Herman, N.Y.C., two years; Susan Migliaccio, N.Y.C., 1957; acting with David Le Grant, 1958. Married June 25, 1949, to Raymond E. Jacobson, electronics company executive (marr. dis. Aug. 1955); married Dec. 11, 1955, to Michael Kuttner, second violinist, Hungarian String Quartet (marr. dis. Nov. 1960). Member of AEA; AFTRA; SAG; AGMA; AGVA.

Pre-Theatre. Secretary, piano teacher.

Theatre. Miss Moser began as a member of the chorus of the London production of *Oklahoma!* (Drury Lane, Apr. 30, 1947); subsequently made her N.Y.C. debut (Nov. 1947) as Giggling Gertie Cummings in *Oklahoma!*, in which she also understudied Mary Hatcher as Laurey and Shelley Winters as Ado Annie Carnes (St. James, March 31, 1943); appeared as Carrie in *Carousel*(NY City Ctr., Jan. 25, 1949), repeated the role in the London production (Drury Lane, June 7, 1950), and in stock (Paper Mill Playhouse, Millburn, N.J., Summer 1951).

From 1951 to 1959, Miss Moser appeared with many stock companies in such roles as Sarah Brown in *Guys and Dolls*; and Marsinah in *Kismet*; understudied Barbara Cook as Cunegonde in *Candide* (Martin Beck Th., N.Y.C., Dec. 1, 1956); followed by her appearance as Sweet Betsy in *Sweet Betsy from Pike*, one of three one-act operas, entitled *Triad* (Th. Marquee, Nov. 1958). With the NY City Opera Co., she sang Alexandra in *Regina* (NY City Ctr., Apr. 19, 1959); subsequently played Sarah Brown in *Guys and Dolls* (Th. in the Park, July 21, 1959); appeared as soloist in *A Gilbert and Sullivan Evening* (Lewisohn Stadium, July 23, 1960); succeeded (Jan. 1961) Pamela Charles, as Eliza Doolittle in *My Fair Lady*(Mark Hellinger Th., March 15, 1956); and produced and appeared in a benefit for the Summerhill Sch. (Alvin, N.Y.C., May 13, 1962).

She appeared as Julie, her first non-singing role, in *Write Me a Murder* (Playhouse-on-the-Mall, Paramus, N.J., Nov. 1962); played Marian in *The Music Man* (Garden Court Dinner Th., Palace Hotel, San Francisco, Calif., Dec. 1962); and played Laurey in *Oklahoma!* (Gladiators Music Arena, Totowa, N.J., Aug. 1963).

Miss Moser played Eliza Doolittle in *My Fair Lady* (tour, Summer 1964); Queen Guenevere in *Camelot* (Paper Mill Playhouse, Millburn, N.J., Nov. 3, 1964; Mineola Playhouse, L.I., N.Y., Mar. 4, 1965); Rosabella in *The Most Happy Fella* (Paper Mill Playhouse, Millburn, N.J., Apr. 20, 1965); repeated the role of Guenevere in *Camelot* (Starlight Th., Kansas City, Mo., June 21, 1965; Municipal Th., St. Louis, Mo., Aug. 16, 1965); played Marion Paroo in *The Music Man* (Municipal Th., St. Louis, Mo., June 6, 1966); Julie Jordan in *Carousel* (Music Circus, Sacramento, Calif., Aug. 8, 1966; Music Circus, Fresno, Calif., Aug. 15, 1966); subsequently made US State Department tour of Mexico and South America in that role (Fall 1966); and, at NY City Center, appeared as Fiona in *Brigadoon* (Dec. 13, 1967), Mabel in *The Pirates of Penzance*(Apr. 25, 1968), and Elsie Maynard in *The Yoeman of the Guard* (May 8, 1968).

Television. Miss Moser made regular appearances on Easy Does It (NBC, 1949); and has been a guest on the Kate Smith Show (NBC, 1950–51); appeared as one of the five sisters in *Bloomer Girl* (NBC, 1956); *Cinderella*(CBS, 1958); the title role in *Sweet Betsy from Pike* (Music for a Spring Night, ABC, 1960); was guest panelist on To Tell the Truth (CBS, 1961); appeared on The Doctors (NBC, 1963); the Tonight Show (NBC, 1953); and the Bell Telephone Hour (NBC, 1963).

Awards. For her performance as Eliza Doolittle in *My Fair Lady*, Miss Moser won the Outer Circle Award (1962).

Recreation. Swimming, skiing, ice skating, reading.

MOSES, GILBERT. Director, actor, playwright, editor. b. 1943, Cleveland, Ohio. Attended Oberlin Coll.; the Sorbonne, Paris. Married 1963 to Denise Nocholos, actress (marr. dis. 1966); married 1968 to Wilma Butler (marr. dis.).

Pre-Theatre. Guitarist with The Street Choir; guitarist with Chaka (Columbia Records).

Theatre. Mr. Moses gained his earliest theatrical experience as a child with the Karamu Th., an integrated settlement house theatre in Cleveland, Ohio; subsequently appeared in *The Good Soldier Schweik* (Gate Th., N.Y.C., Apr. 8, 1963); wrote *Roots* (Afro-American Studio, 1969–70 season); for the Chelsea Th. Ctr., directed *Slave Ship* Brooklyn Acad. of Music, Third Stage, Nov. 18, 1969; Theatre-in-the-Church, Jan. 13, 1970); directed *In New England Winter* (Th. Co. of Boston, 1969–70 season); *The Blood Knot*(Amer. Conservatory Th., San Francisco, Apr. 14, 1970); at Arena Stage (Washington, D.C.), *No Place To Be Somebody* (May 28, 1970); and *Mother Courage* (Dec. 4, 1970); with Jerry Adler, co-directed *Charlie Was Here and Now He's Gone* (Eastside Playhouse, N.Y.C., June 6, 1971); directed *Ain't Supposed To Die a Natural Death*(Ethel Barrymore Th., Oct. 20, 1971; Ambassador, Nov. 17, 1971); *Don't Let It Go to Your Head* (Henry Street Th., Jan. 17, 1972); *The Taking of Miss Janie*(Mitzi E. Newhouse Th., May 4, 1975); *Every Night When the Sun Goes Down*(American Place Th., Feb. 15, 1976); and, with George Faison, co-directed and choreographed *Sixteen Hundred Pennsylvania Avenue* (Mark Hellinger Th., May 4, 1976).

With John O'Neal, he co-founded (1963) and was artistic director (1963–68) of the Free Southern Th., a professional repertory company started in Jackson, Miss., and relocated in New Orleans, La.

Films. Mr. Moses wrote the music and lyrics, and directed *Willie Dynamite* (U, 1974).

Published Works. He is co-author of *The Free Southern Theatre* (Bobbs-Merrill); and editor of *The Mississippi Free Press* and *The Fort Green Drum* (Brooklyn).

Awards. Mr. Moses received the Off Bway (Obie) Award for Distinguished Direction (1969–70); the Drama Desk "Most Promising Director" Award (1971–72) for *Ain't Supposed to Die a Natural Death*; and the Off-Bway (Obie) Award (1974–75) for *The Taking of Miss Janie*.

MOSS, ARNOLD. Actor, director, producer, writer, educator. b. Jan. 28, 1910, Brooklyn, N.Y., to Jack and Essie (Joseph) Moss. Father, pianist. Grad. Boys' H.S., Brooklyn, 1924; Coll. of the City of New York, B.A. cum laude (Phi Beta Kappa) 1928; Columbia Univ., M.A., 1934; New York Univ., Ph.D., 1973. Married 1933 to Stella Reynolds, writer; one son, one daughter. Member of AEA (on council); AFTRA (local natl. board); SAG; The Players. Address: 30 Beekman Place, New York, NY 10022, tel. (212) PL 5-2683.

Theatre. Mr. Moss first performed as an Indian in *Peter Pan* (Eva Le Gallienne's Civic Repertory Th., N.Y.C., 1929) and appeared in productions with this group (1929–31).

He made his Broadway debut as the Page Boy in *Wonder Boy*(Alvin, Oct. 23, 1931); followed by Antonio in *The Fifth Column* (Alvin, Mar. 6, 1940); Fernando in *Hold On to Your Hats* (Shubert, Sept. 11, 1940); Ishmael in *Journey to Jerusalem* (Natl., Oct. 5, 1940); Howard Ingram in *Flight to the West* (Guild, Dec. 30, 1940); Count Czarniko in *The Land Is Bright* (Music Box, Oct. 25, 1941); Prospero in *The Tempest*(Alvin, Jan. 25, 1945); Walter Burns in *The Front Page*(Royale, Sept. 4, 1946); Malvolio in *Twelfth Night*(Empire, Oct. 3, 1949); Gloucester in Louis Calhern's *King Lear* (Natl., Dec. 25, 1950); Col. Janek in *The Dark Is Light Enough* (ANTA, Feb. 23, 1955); George Bernard Shaw in *Back to Methusaleh*, which Mr. Moss adapted and, with the Th. Guild, produced (Ambassador, Mar. 26, 1958); and Dimitri Weissmann in *Follies* (Winter Garden, Apr. 4, 1971).

He played Creon in the Salute to France production of *Medea* with Judith Anderson (Th. Sarah Bernhardt, Paris, June 1955) and the Society Man in *Time Of Your Life* at the American Pavillion of the Brussels World's Fair (Oct. 1958).

For the American Shakespeare Festival (Stratford, Conn.), he played the King of France in *King John*, and the Duke of Vienna in *Measure for Measure* (June 1956), and repeated the latter role (Phoenix, N.Y.C., Jan. 22, 1957). He was also director of the Professional Acad. Workshop.

For the Whitall Poetry and Literature Series, he produced, directed, and appeared in Walt Whitman's *Leaves of Grass* (Library of Congress, Washington, D.C., 1956); produced, directed, and played Prospero in *The Tempest*(1957); the Duke of Vienna in *Measure for Measure* (1958); Armado in *Love's Labour's Lost* (1959), was the Narrator and played Mark in E. A. Robinson's *Tristram*(1960), appeared in the title role in *King Lear* (1960), Malvolio in *Twelfth Night* (1961), in the title role in *Macbeth* (1962), and in several roles in *Come, Woo Me!* (1963).

These were followed by an annual succession of twenty different programs devised and directed by Mr. Moss through 1973. He appeared in all of them.

At various times he has toured the country in a succession of one-man shows including *Seven Ages of Man, A Goodly Heritage, Windows on America*, and *The Trembling Years*. He headed the Shakespeare Festival Players in a national tour sponsored by Sol Hurok (1959).

He represented the State Dept. as an American specialist in theatre on a five-month tour of seven Latin American nations (1961), and in French-speaking Africa (1964).

Mr. Moss appeared on the concert stage with the Boston Symphony orchestra as Frère Dominique in Honegger's *Jeanne D'Arc au Bûcher*(Boston, Mass.); served as narrator and director for Stravinsky's *L'Histoire du Soldat* (Boston); narrator for Honegger's *La Danse des Morts* (Boston; Berkshire Music Festival, Tanglewood, Mass.; Carnegie Hall, N.Y.C.); Debussy's *Le Martyre de St. Sébastien* (Boston); and for the Detroit (Mich.) Symphony Children's Concert series, narrated Johnson's *Chuggy and the Blue Caboose*. He has also been seen with the Milwaukee Symphony Orchestra in a program based on music inspired by the work of William Shakespeare.

Films. He made his debut as Lt. Achmed in *Temptation* (U, 1946); subsequently appeared in *The Loves of Carmen* (Col., 1948); *Reign of Terror*(Eagle-Lion, 1949); *Border Incident* (MGM, 1949); *Kim* (MGM, 1949); *Mask of the Avenger*(Col., 1951); *My Favorite Spy* (Par., 1951); *Quebec* (Par., 1951); *Viva Zapata!* (20th-Fox, 1952); *Salome* (Col., 1950); *Casanova's Big Night* (Par., 1954); *Bengal Brigade* (U, 1954); *Jump Into Hell* (WB, 1955); *Hell's Island* (Par., 1955); *The 27th Day* (Col., 1957); *The Fool Killer* (Landau Prods., 1965); and *Caper of the Golden Bulls* (Par., 1967).

Television and Radio. On radio, he served as a staff announcer for CBS (1931); and performed on such programs as N.Y. Philharmonic Symphony, Columbia Workshop, Great Novels, Spoon River Anthology, Archibald MacLeish Program, Thomas Jefferson Series; was heard in roles in the Great Plays Series, and also performed in daytime radio serials.

He performed on the first color television dramatic shows for NBC and CBS, and has appeared as guest star on over one hundred shows including Studio One (CBS), Suspense (CBS), Th. Guild on the Air (CBS), G.E. Th. (CBS), You Are There (CBS), Alfred Hitchcock Presents (CBS), The Rifleman (ABC), Going My Way (ABC), Star Trek, Bonanza (NBC), and Hallmark Hall of Fame (NBC).

Other Activities. In 1973–74, Mr. Moss was distinguished visiting professor, Dept. of Dramatic Arts, Univ. of Connecticut. He was a staff member, Speech and Theatre Department, Brooklyn (N.Y.) College (1933–40), where he taught courses in speech, acting, directing, and, on the graduate level, phonetics and comparative linguistics. He also supervised the building of the college's first theatre and first radio studio. At other universities, he has from time to time conducted brief seminars in various aspects of theatre, and he was one of the two directors at the American Shakespeare Th. and Acad., Stratford, Conn., who helped train thirty professional actors to form the nucleus of the professional company.

Published Works. Mr. Moss is the author of *The Professional Actor as Performing Guest Artist in American Colleges and Universities* and articles that have been published in the NY *Times*, the *Educational Theatre Journal, Equity News*, and other periodicals.

Discography. Mr. Moss acted the role of Jason in *Medea* and adapted Stravinsky's *L'Histoire du Soldat* (1961). In the album, *Come, Woo Me!*, he narrated, directed, and played in a series of courtship scenes from the works of William Shakespeare (1964).

He recorded for the educational series *Many Voices*, as well as in the Parnassus Series *A Treasury of The Spoken Word*. Since 1962, he has recorded more than seventy-five books for the *Talking Book* series of the American Foundation for the Blind.

Awards. The College of the City of New York awarded Mr. Moss its James K. Hackett Medal in 1968 for "distinguished achievement in dramatic arts," and NY University awarded him its Founders' Day Certificate for achieving "the highest bracket of scholastic preferment" in the field of theatre study.

Recreation. Walking, clamming, cooking, carpentry, cabinetmaking, and the construction of crossword puzzles, twelve of which have appeared in the NY *Times* Sunday Magazine or in Simon and Schusters *Crossword Puzzle Book*.

MOSTEL, ZERO. Actor. b. Samuel Joel Mostel, Feb. 28, 1915, Brooklyn, N.Y., to Israel and Celia (Druchs) Mostel. Father, rabbi, vintner of sacramental wines. Grad. Seward Park H.S., N.Y.C., 1931; City Coll. of New York, B.A. (Art) 1935; attended New York Univ., graduate art study, 1936. Married July 2, 1944, to Kathryn Harkin, dancer; two sons. Served WW II, US Army Infantry, 1943; rank, Pvt. Member of AEA; AFTRA; SAG; Actors Studio (1950–to date). Address: c/o Sidney E. Cohn, 10 E. 56th St., New York, NY 10022, tel. (212) PL 3-4200.

Pre-Theatre. Factory and dock worker; art teacher and lecturer; painter.

Theatre. Mr. Mostel first appeared on stage in satirical sketches in Greenwich Village night clubs and made his Bway debut in a vaudeville production, *Keep 'Em Laughing* (44 St. Th., Apr. 24, 1942); subsequently appeared in *Concert Varieties*(Ziegfeld, June 1, 1945); as Hamilton Peachum in *Beggar's Holiday* (Bway Th., Dec. 26, 1946); Glubb in *Flight into Egypt* (Music Box, Mar. 18, 1952); played in his own adaptation of *The Imaginary Invalid* (Brattle Th., Cambridge, Mass., July 1952); Maxie Fields in *A Stone for Danny Fisher* (Downtown Natl. Th., N.Y.C., Oct. 21, 1954); Dan Cupid in a touring production of *Lunatics and Lovers*(Calif., 1955); Shu Fu in *The Good Woman of Setzuan* (Phoenix, N.Y.C., Dec. 18, 1956); Doc Penny in *Good as Gold* (Belasco, Mar. 7, 1957); Leopold Bloom in *Ulysses in Nighttown* (Rooftop, June 5, 1958, and US tour); John in *Rhinoceros*(Longacre, N.Y.C., Jan. 9, 1961); Prologus in *A Funny Thing Happened on the Way to the Forum* (Alvin, May 8, 1962); Tevye in *Fiddler on the Roof* (Imperial, Sept. 22, 1964); the title role in *The Latent Heterosexual* (Kalita Humphreys Th., Dallas, March 1968); and Leopold Bloom in *Ulysses in Nighttown* (Winter Garden, Mar. 10, 1974).

Films. Mr. Mostel made his debut as Paliostro and Rami in *Du Barry Was a Lady*(MGM, 1943); subsequently appeared in *Panic in the Street* (20th-Fox, 1950); *The Enforcer*(WB, 1951); *The Guy Who Came Back*(20th-Fox, 1951); *Sirocco*(Col., 1951); *Mr. Belvedere Rings the Bell* (20th-Fox, 1951); *The Model and the Marriage Broker*(20th-Fox, 1951); and *Zero* (England, 1959); *A Funny Thing Happened on the Way to the Forum* (UA, 1966); *The Producers* (Embassy, 1967); *Great Catherine* (WB-Seven Arts, 1968); *The Great Bank Robbery* (WB-Seven Arts, 1969); *The Angel Levine* (UA, 1970); and *The Hot Rock* (20th-Fox, 1972).

Television. Mr. Mostel has appeared in "A Tale of Chelm" on *The World of Sholom Aleichem* (Play of the Week, WNTA, 1960); *Waiting for Godot*(Play of the Week, WNTA, 1961); and in a one-man show on Festival of the Performing Arts (WNTA, Apr. 1963).

Night Clubs. Mr. Mostel has appeared in N.Y.C. at the Cafe Society Downtown (Feb. 16, 1942); and at La Martinique (1942).

Awards. He received *The Village Voice* Off-Bway (Obie) Award for his performance as Leopold Bloom in *Ulysses in Nighttown* (1959); was named best actor at the International Th. Festival in Paris (1959); received Antoinette Perry (Tony) awards for his performance as John in *Rhinoceros* (1961), and as Prologus in *A Funny Thing Happened on the Way to the Forum* (1963); and the NY Drama Critics Award, 1964–65, for his performance in *Fiddler on the Roof*. .

Recreation. Collecting pre-Colombian, Peruvian and Coptic art; modern art.

MOTTER, CHARLOTTE KAY. Educator, director. b. Oct. 21, 1922, Henry, Ill., to Charles Harold and Opal (Euard) Motter. Grad. Ponce de Leon H.S., Coral Gables, Fla., 1940; Univ. of Miami, A.B. 1944; Univ. of Southern California, teaching certificate 1947; Univ. of Michigan, M.A. 1956. Member of AETA (natl. exec. committee, board of dir., 1961–63; Southern Calif. District, secondary sch. vice-pres., 1957; adv. council, 1957–61; So. Calif. Dist., pres., 1966); ANTA (Los Angeles, Calif., chapter, board of dir. 1960–62); Secondary Sch. Th. Conference (natl. exec. dir., 1961–63); Drama Teachers Assn. of Southern Calif. (pres., 1955–56); Amer. Federation of Teachers; Sigma Kappa; Panhellenic; Theta Alpha Phi; and Calif. Educational Th. Assoc. (founding pres., 1967–70). Address: (home) 12938 Greenleaf St., N. Hollywood, CA 91604, tel. (213) ST 9-7078; (bus.) c/o Canoga Park High Sch., 6850 Topanga, Canoga Park, CA 91303, tel. (213) DI 0-3221.

Since 1950, Miss Motter has taught dramatics at Canoga Park High Sch., where she has directed approximately 50 plays including *Medea, Hamlet, The Skin of Our Teeth*, and *The Miser* which won So. Calif. High School Th. Festival Award (1972).

She has lectured on high-school drama at the Univ. of Calif. at Los Angeles, Dept. of Th. Arts (1952–63); directed teacher training workshops in theatre (Summer 1960–62); was guest lecturer at San Fernando Valley State Coll. (Spring, Summer 1957), where she directed *Alice in Wonderland* (July 1957) and *Lady Precious Stream* (Aug. 1957); and lectured at Los Angeles City Coll. (Fall 1959).

She was director of a summer workshop in directing high school theatre (1966) at Southern Methodist Univ.; directing teacher at Furman Univ. under the EPDA (Education Professions Development Act) for high school drama teachers (1968); assoc. director (EPDA) for high school drama teachers at Western Wash. State Coll. (1969); guest professor of theatre arts at Long Beach State Univ. (Summer 1972); and guest director (directing *Born Yesterday*) at Foothill Coll., Los Altos, Calif. (Summer 1973).

She has been guest lecturer for Illinois State Univ., Univ. of Iowa, Univ. of Oregon, the Texas Th. Assoc., New Mexico Th. Guild and the National Assoc. of Secondary Sch. Administrators. She has been the director for Educational Th. Laboratory and Inner City Repertory Co., Los Angeles, Calif. (1968–69). She was a judge of the Amer. Coll. Th. Festival of the Pacific South Region (1972–73; 1973–74).

Miss Motter toured army camps in Southern Florida as Edith Potter in a USO production of *The Women* (Mar. 1943); billed as Charlotte Kay, with the Horshoe Th. (N. Hollywood, Calif.), she was business manager (1947), played Mame in *Moondown* (Apr. 1948), Lucille Cooke in *Ex Marks the King* (June 1948), directed *Outward Bound* (Jan. 1948), and *Aunt Margaret* (July 1948).

She was publicity director and business manager at the Encore Playhouse (Downey, Calif., Summer 1952).

Published Works. Miss Motter has written articles on drama for *The Secondary School Theatre Conference Newsletter, Educational Theatre Journal, Education Theatre News* and was secondary school editor for the *Educational Theatre Journal* (1959–61). She has written a college textbook entitled *Theatre in High School: Planning, Teaching, Directing* (1970).

Awards. She won the Valley Forge Classroom Teachers Medal for the presentation to the students of Canoga Park H.S. of a series of plays under the theme, "We hold these truths," including *An Enemy of the People, The Devil's Disciple, Harriet,* and *The Male Animal* (May 1962). She was elected to the Coll. of Fellows, American Th. Assoc. (1969); and received the Amer. Coll. Th. Festival Award of Excellence, Gold Medallion (1972) presented by American Oil Co. for outstanding contributions to educational theatre.

Recreation. Travel, reading.

MOULTON, ROBERT. Educator, director, choreographer, dancer. b. Robert Darrell Moulton, July 20, 1922, Dodge Center, Minn., to Edwin and Ethel Jane (Pendergast) Moulton. Father, butcher; mother, educator. Grad. Central H.S., Duluth, Minn., 1940; Univ. of Minnesota, B.S. 1947, M.A. 1949, Ph.D. 1957. Studied at Connecticut Coll. of Dance, 1951; choreography with Louis Horst, N.Y.C., 1951–53; at Martha Graham Sch. of Dance, N.Y.C., 1952–53; choreography with Audrey de Vos, London, Eng., 1962. Married June 19, 1948, to Marion Skowland; one son, one daughter. Served US Army Cavalry, 1943–46; rank, Pfc. Member of SSD&C; AETA; AAUPHER, C.O.R.D., Phi Epsilon Delta (pres., 1947). Address: (home) 48 Melbourne Ave., S.E., Minneapolis, MN 55414, tel. (612) 333-6772; (bus.) Dept. of Theatre Arts, 249 Middlebrook, Univ. of Minnesota, Minneapolis, MN 55414, tel. (612) 373-4841.

Since 1961, Mr. Moulton has been associate professor of speech and theatre arts at the Univ. of Minnesota; and since 1962, he has been artistic director at the Stagecoach Th. (Shakopee, Minn. 1961–1971). For the Royal Winnipeg Ballet Company, Winnipeg, Can., he choreographed the ballets, *Grassland* (Oct. 1958); *Brave Song* (Dec. 1959); and *Beggars' Ballet* (Dec. 1963). For the Canadian Contemporary Dancers, he choreographed *Rondo ad Absurdum* (1967); *True Believer* (1968); *Bach Is Beautiful* (1970); and *7 Rituals* (1972). For the Calgary Dance Theatre, he choreographed *Nickel Dances* (1971) and *Bachanelle* (1972); and for the Duluth Civic Ballet, *Turned on Bach* (1973). He directed and choreographed productions at the Rainbow Stage (Winnipeg, Can., Summers 1959–62).

Awards. He received the Charles Nichols Service Award (1943) from the Univ. of Minnesota Th.; the Univ. of Minnesota Gopher Award (1950); a fellowship from the School of American Dance at Connecticut Coll. (1951); was chosen one of the ten outstanding young men in American Educational Theatre by AETA (1957); and received a Univ. of Minnesota fellowship (1961–62) to study dance in Sweden and England. In 1972, he was named master teacher by the National Endowment of the Arts, and in 1973 he received the first Dance Fellowship awarded by Minnesota State Arts Council.

MUIR, KENNETH. Educator. b. Kenneth Arthur Muir, May 5, 1907, London, England, to Robert D. and Edith (Barnes) Muir. Father, physician. Grad. Epsom Coll., 1926; Oxford Univ., A.B. 1930. Married 1936, to Mary Ewen, teacher; one son, one daughter. Relatives in theatre: brother, Douglas Muir, actor; sister-in-law, Miriam Muir, actress; niece, Gillian Muir, actress. Served Officer in Charge, War Room, N.E. Regional Control 1939–40. Member of Assn. of Univ. Teachers (chmn., Liverpool Branch, 1953–54). Address: (home) 6 Chetwynd Rd., Oxton, Birkenhead, England tel. CLA 3301; (bus.) c/o Univ. of Liverpool, Liverpool, England tel. ROY 6022.

From 1951–74, Mr. Muir was professor of English literature at the Univ. of Liverpool; he was formerly visiting professor at Wayne Univ., Detroit, Mich. (1959); visiting fellow at the Folger Shakespeare Library, Washington, D.C. (1957); and Andrew Mellon Professor at the Univ. of Pittsburgh (1962–63).

In 1928, he appeared in amateur productions as Antipholus of Syracuse in *The Comedy of Errors,* Cusins in *Major Barbara,* Vershinin in *The Three Sisters,* Orcino in *Twelfth Night,* Gloucester in *King Lear,* the Stranger in *After the Fire; Prospero in The Tempest,* the King in *Cymbeline,* was director (1933–37) for the York Settlement Community Players of *Rosmersholm, Twelfth Night, Troilus and Cressida, Hamlet, King Lear, Shadow of Evil* and *The Misanthrope;* translating the latter two; directed the Leeds (England) Univ. Th. Group's productions of *All for Love, Heartbreak House, The Trojan Women, Coriolanus* (1932–43); and directed *Measure for Measure.* (Liverpool Univ., 1954).

Published Works. Mr. Muir has edited Shakespeare's plays, including *Macbeth* (1951), *King Lear* (1952), *Richard II* (1963); and *Othello* (1968); has written several works on Shakespeare, including: *Shakespeare's Sources* (1957), *Shakespeare as Collaborator* (1960); and *Shakespeare: Hamlet* (1963); has contributed articles on Marlowe, Congreve, Shaw, Lenormand and other dramatists to *Stratford-on-Avon Studies* and other periodicals; and has translated *Five Plays of Jean Racine* (1960), Calderon's *A House with Two Doors* (1963); and Corneille's *Le Cid* (1967).

MULHARE, EDWARD. Actor. b. 1923.

Theatre. Mr. Mulhare made his debut at the Opera House (Cork, Ireland) in *The First Mrs. Fraser* and as Cassio in *Othello* (1942).

With the Dublin Th. Guild, he played Bill Walker in *Major Barbara,* Horace Giddens in *The Little Foxes,* and La Hire in appeared St. Joan.

During 1950, he appeared with the Liverpool (Eng.) Repertory Co. as Max de Winter in *Rebecca;* played Lodovico in *Othello* (St. James's, London, Oct. 18, 1951); and Sidney Willis, M.P., in *The Night of the Ball.*

Mr. Mulhare made his N.Y.C. debut succeeding (Feb. 4, 1957) Rex Harrison as Henry Higgins in *My Fair Lady* (Mark Hellinger Th., Mar. 15, 1956), also playing this role in USSR (Apr.–June 1960); appeared as Paul Delville in *The Marriage-Go-Round* (Bucks County Playhouse, New Hope, Pa., Sept. 12, 1960); Giacomo Nerone in *The Devil's Advocate* (Billy Rose Th., N.Y.C., Mar. 9, 1961); and replaced (Dec. 1961) Michael Wilding as Dirk Winsten in *Mary, Mary* (Helen Hayes Th., Mar. 8, 1961). He was in *A Man for All Seasons* (Mummers Th., Oklahoma City, Okla., Dec. 4, 1970); and was the Devil in a revival of *Don Juan in Hell* (Palace, N.Y.C., Jan. 15, 1973), then touring with the production (Sept. 1974–Feb. 1975).

Films. Mr. Mulhare has appeared in *Hill 24 Doesn't Answer* (MP, 1955).

Television. He appeared in the British series, Robin Hood and in the US played Larry Darant in *The First and the Last* (Kraft Television Th., NBC, July 10, 1957); and Earnest in *Who's Earnest? (CBS, Oct. 9, 1957). He appeared in episodes of The Ghost and Mrs. Muir (NBC, 1968, 1969) and Streets of San Francisco (ABC, 1972) and in the television movie Gidget Grows Up* (ABC, 1969).

MUNDY, MEG. Actress. b. London, England, to John and Clytie (Hine) Mundy. Father, cellist; mother, singing teacher. Grad. Wadleigh H.S., N.Y.C.; Inst. of Musical Art, N.Y.C. Studied at Amer. Th. Wing, N.Y.C. Married 1952 to Dino Yannopoulos (marr. dis. 1962); one son. Member of AEA; SAG; AFTRA. Address: Bridgewater, CT 06752.

Theatre. Miss Mundy made her debut as a concert singer, appearing as soloist with the NY Philharmonic Orchestra.

She played the Secretary in *Ten Million Ghosts* (St. James Th., N.Y.C., Oct. 23, 1936); appeared in the chorus of *Hooray for What!* (Winter Garden, Dec. 1, 1937); *The Fabulous Invalid* (Broadhurst, Oct. 8, 1938); and *Three to Make Ready* (Adelphi, Mar. 7, 1946). She played Lisa in *How I Wonder* (Hudson, Sept. 30, 1947); Lizzie McKaye in *The Respectful Prostitute* (Cort, Mar. 16, 1948); appeared in *The Time of Your Life* (Westport Country Playhouse, Conn., 1948); and played Mary McLeod in *Detective Story* (Hudson, N.Y.C., Mar. 23, 1949).

She played Rosalind in *Love's Labour's Lost* (NY City Ctr., Feb. 4, 1953); Laurie Trumbull in *Love Me Little* (Helen Hayes Th., Mar. 15, 1958); and the title role in *Lysistrata* (E. 74 St. Th., May 19, 1959).

She appeared as Basil Rathbone's leading lady in summer tours of *The Winslow Boy* (1960) and *The Gioconda Smile* (1961); and opposite Ben Gazzara in a summer tour of *Epitaph for George Dillon* (1962). Other stock and regional engagements include leads in *Bell, Book and Candle, The Rainmaker, The Respectful Prostitute, Misalliance* and *Summer and Smoke.*

Television. Miss Mundy has appeared on Suspense (CBS), Studio One (CBS), Naked City (ABC), The Defenders (CBS), Playhouse 90 (CBS), US Steel Hour (NBC), Ford Th. (CBS), Alfred Hitchcock Presents (CBS), and a running part on the daytime drama The Doctors (NBC, 1972–74).

Other Activities. Miss Mundy was the associate beauty editor of *Vogue* magazine (1961–64); beauty editor for *Mademoiselle* magazine (1964–66); fashion director for Klopman Mills-Burlington Industries (1966–70); and market editor for *House and Garden* magazine (1970–72).

Recreation. Cooking, music.

MUNSELL, WARREN P. Theatre executive, actor, director, general manager. b. Warren Perry Munsell, June 16, 1889, Jefferson, Iowa, to Chester Elmer and Agnes Belle (Forbes) Munsell. Married Jan. 7, 1913, to Jeanette Noot, known as Jean Newton, actress; one son. Served US Army WW I, ETO, 1917–19; rank, Maj.; WW II, ETO, 1942–46; rank, Col. Organized London Stage Door Canteen and Paris Stage Door Canteen for Amer. Th. Wing, WW II. Member of Actors' Fund of Amer. ATPAM, The Lambs, The Players. Address: (home) 1 Fifth Ave., New York, NY 10003; (bus.) 1501 Broadway, New York, NY 10036, tel. (212) 221-7300.

Since 1954, Mr. Munsell has been executive secretary and general manager of the Actors' Fund of Amer., for which he was trustee, 1937–54. Since 1959, he has been director of The Percy Williams Home.

Theatre. He made his acting debut in stock productions in Brainard, Minn. (1908); appeared in productions with the Lyric Th. Stock Co. (Minneapolis, Minn., 1909); and also during 1909, appeared in productions at the Opera House (Findlay, Ohio), and at the Amer. Th. (Toledo, Ohio).

He made his N.Y.C. debut as John in *The Talker* (Sam H. Harris Th., Jan. 8, 1912), also touring in it; took over John Cromwell's role as Joe in *Sinners* (Playhouse, Jan. 7, 1915), and directed and appeared in touring productions of this play.

He appeared in *Any House* (Cort, Feb. 14, 1916); and in productions at Keith's Th., Portland, Me. (1916–17); managed the Alhambra and Hamilton

Theatres (N.Y.) for the Keith-Albee vaudeville circuit (1919–21); and was business manager for the Th. Guild (N.Y.C. 1921–42).

He directed a stock production of *By Any Other Name* (McCarter, Princeton, N.J., July 29, 1940); produced, with Herman Bernstein, *Love Goes to Press* (Biltmore, N.Y.C., Jan. 1, 1947); and was general manager for the following productions: *Leaf and Bough* (Cort, Jan. 21, 1949), *Darkness at Noon* (Alvin, Jan. 13, 1951), *A Date with April* (Royale, Apr. 15, 1953), and *The Righteous Are Bold* (Holiday, Dec. 22, 1955).

Recreation. Gardening, bridge.

MURPHY, DONN B. Educator, director. b. 1931, San Antonio, Tex., to Arthur M. and Clare F. Murphy. Father, college president; mother, writer. Grad. Benedictine Coll., Atchison, Kans., B.A.; Catholic Univ., M.F.A.; Univ. of Wisconsin, Ph.D. Professional training, Moreno Institute for Psychodrama; US Army Entertainment Program. Served US Army, 1950–54; military police in Japan. Relative in theatre, nephew, David Murphy, actor. Member of ATA (pres., Mid-Atlantic chap., 1972); Natl. Catholic Th. Conference (vice-pres., 1971); USITT; International Institute for Theatre Technology. Address: (home) 2323 North Utah St., Arlington, VA 22207, tel. (703) 524-1616; (bus.) 3630 P St., N.W., Washington, DC 20007, tel. (202) 625-4960.

At Georgetown Univ. (Washington, D.C.), where he has directed over fifty productions, Dr. Murphy has served as instructor of English (1954); director of theatre (1955–to date); and professor of Fine Arts (1960–to date). He is also director of theatre at Chestnut Lodge Psychiatric Hospital (Rockville, Md.).

Theatre. Dr. Murphy appeared in summer stock in 1954; was lighting director for twenty musicals at Starlight Th. (Kansas City, 1955, 1956); directed six musicals for the Amer. Light Opera Co. (Washington, D.C.); and was theatrical consultant to Mrs. John F. Kennedy, and Mrs. Lyndon B. Johnson for opera, theatre, and ballet performances in the White House. He is the author of the environmental theatre piece, *Creation of the World.*

Published Works. He wrote *A Director's Guide to Good Theatre* (1968).

Awards. Dr. Murphy was named best director (1960, 1961) by the Washington, D.C. Theatre Alliance; received Ford Foundation Fellowships in international theatre (1963, 1964); and was included in the 1965 edition of *Outstanding Young Men in America.* In 1968 and 1970, he received US Army Theatre Project awards.

Recreation. Motorcycling, photography, travel.

MURPHY, ROSEMARY. Actress. b. Jan. 13, Munich, Germany, to Robert D. and Mildred (Taylor) Murphy. Father, diplomat. Attended Convent of the Sacred Heart, N.Y.C.,: Notre Dame de Sion, Kansas City, Mo. Studied at the Neighborhood Playhouse Sch. of the Th., N.Y.C.; Actors Studio, N.Y.C. (mbr. since 1954). Member of AEA; SAG; AFTRA. Address: 220 E. 73rd St., New York, NY 10021, tel. (212) RH 4-3712.

Theatre. Miss Murphy made her debut as The Woman in Green in *Peer Gynt* (Schlosspark Th., Berlin, Germany, 1949). She made her first US appearance as Mary Boleyn in a NY Subway Circuit production of *Anne of the Thousand Days* (opened Flatbush Th., Brooklyn, N.Y., June 1950); followed by one of the Townspeople in *The Tower Beyond Tragedy* (ANTA, Nov. 26, 1950); Jane Pugh in *Clutterbuck,* and Liserle in *Candle-Light* (Memphis Arena Th., Tenn., Summer 1952); appeared in *Red Sky at Morning* (Olney Th., Md., Aug. 1953); and *The Women* (Norwich Playhouse, Conn., July 1954).

At the Myrtle Beach (S.C.) Playhouse, she played Lizzie Curry in *The Rainmaker* (July 5, 1955), and Rosemary Sydney in *Picnic* (Aug. 2, 1955); appeared as Lady Isabel Welwyn in *The Ascent of F6* (Davenport, N.Y.C., Feb. 23, 1955); Lady Macduff in *Macbeth* (Rooftop, Oct. 7, 1955); toured as Olivia in *The Chalk Garden* (opened Lobero Th., Santa Barbara, Calif., Feb. 16, 1957); and played Helen Gant Barton in *Look Homeward, Angel* (Ethel Barrymore Th., N.Y.C., Nov. 28, 1957).

Also, Hannah Jelkes in the world premiere of *The Night of the Iguana* (Festival of Two Worlds, Spoleto, Italy, July 1959); Dorothea Bates in *Period of Adjustment* (Helen Hayes Th., N.Y.C., Nov. 10, 1960); took over (June 1962) for Viveca Lindfors in *Brecht on Brecht* (Th. de Lys, Jan. 3, 1962); with the Amer. Shakespeare Festival (Stratford, Conn.), played Goneril in *King Lear* (June 9, 1963), and a Courtesan in *Comedy of Errors* (June 11, 1963); and appeared as Dorothy Cleves in *Any Wednesday* (Music Box, N.Y.C., Feb. 18, 1964); Claire in *A Delicate Balance* (Martin Beck Th., Sept. 11, 1966); appeared in *Week-End* (Broadhurst Th., Mar. 13, 1968); and played Mrs. Baker in *Butterflies Are Free* (Booth Th., Oct. 21, 1969).

Films. Miss Murphy has appeared in *Berlin Express* (RKO, 1948); *Der Ruf* (The Call) (Germany, 1949); *The Night* (Lopert, 1962); *To Kill a Mockingbird* (U, 1962); *Any Wednesday* (WB, 1966); *Ace Eli and Rodger of the Skies* (20th-Fox, 1972); *A Fan's Notes* (20th-Fox, 1972); *You'll Like My Mother* (U, 1973); and *Walking Tall* (Bing Crosby Prod., 1973).

Television. She has appeared in *The Long Way Home* (Robert Montgomery Presents, NBC, 1956); in *Way Out* (Studio One, CBS, 1962); The Secret Storm (CBS, 1969); Cannon (CBS, 1972); Banyon (CBS, 1973); Medical Center (CBS, 1973); Streets of San Francisco (ABC, 1973); Colombo (NBC, 1974); Lucas Tanner (NBC, 1974); Movie of the Week, "A Case of Rape" (NBC, 1974); *The Lady's Not for Burning* (PBS, 1974); and on Thriller, Wide Country and The Virginian (NBC).

Awards. Miss Murphy received the Clarence Derwent Award, the Outer Circle Award, and won the *Variety* NY Drama Critics Poll for her performance as Dorothea Bates in *Period of Adjustment* (1961).

She has received Antoinette Perry (Tony) nominations for *Period of Adjustment* (1962); *Any Wednesday* (1964); and *A Delicate Balance* (1967).

Recreation. Skiing, sailing.

MURRAY, BRIAN. Actor, director. b. Brian Bell, Oct. 10, 1937, Johannesburg, South Africa, to Alfred and Mary Dickson (Murray) Bell. Father, professional golfer. Grad. King Edward VII Sch., Johannesburg.

Pre-Theatre. Radio announcer, editor.

Theatre. At age twelve, he made his acting debut playing Taplow in *The Browning Version* (Hofmeyer Th., Capetown, South Africa, July 1950); subsequently appeared in various children's roles (Johannesburg, 1950–54); and, prior to his immigration to England (1957), played Bo in *Bus Stop,* Bruno in *Dear Charles,* Peter in *The Diary of Anne Frank,* and Father Oros in *The Strong Are Lonely.*

Mr. Murray made his London debut as Harry Lomax in *Last Day in Dreamland* (Lyric, Hammersmith, Nov. 1959); played Conrad Mayberry in *Visit to a Small Planet* (Westminster, Feb. 1960); Wade in *Roger the Sixth* (Westminster, May 1960); at the Royal Shakespeare Th. (Stratford-upon-Avon), appeared as Richmond in *Richard III* (1961), Romeo in *Romeo and Juliet* (1961), Horatio in *Hamlet* (1961), Cassio in *Othello* (1961), Malcolm in *Macbeth* (1962), Edgar in *King Lear* (1962), Guiderius in *Cymbeline* (1962), and Lysander in *A Midsummer Night's Dream* (May 14, 1963); with the Royal Shakespeare Co., made his US debut (NY State Th., N.Y.C.) playing Edgar in *King Lear* (May 18, 1964), and appearing in *The Comedy of Errors* (May 20, 1964); in his Bway debut, succeeded (June 9, 1964) George Segal as Tolen in *The Knack* (Royale, May 27, 1964); played Arthur Felton in *All in Good Time* (Royale, Feb. 18, 1965); with the Bristol (England) Old Vic, played Philip in *The Spiral Bird* (Sept. 1965), Bassanio in *The Merchant of Venice* (Oct. 1965), and Claudio in *Measure for Measure* (Mar. 1966); made his directorial debut with *Beauty and the Beast* (Civic Th., Torquay, Dec. 1965); played Mike in *Wait Until Dark* (Strand, London, July, 1966); Rosencrantz in *Rosencrantz and Guildenstern Are Dead* (Alvin, N.Y.C., Oct. 16, 1967; moved to Eugene O'Neill Th., Jan. 8, 1968); repeated that role in Canada (O'Keefe Th., Toronto, Jan. 6, 1969); and directed *A Scent of Flowers* (Martinique, N.Y.C., Oct. 30, 1969).

He played Donny in a touring production of *A Present from Harry* (England, Apr. 1970); subsequently directed a double-bill of *A Slight Ache* and *Oldenburg* (Playhouse in the Park, Cincinnati, Ohio, 1970–71 season); repeated that double-bill at Long Wharf Th. (New Haven, Conn., Nov. 20, 1970); directed *A Place Without Doors* (Stairway Th., N.Y.C., Dec. 22, 1970); again staged that production (Goodman Th., Chicago, Sept. 21, 1971); replaced Donal Donnelly (Mar. 27, 1972) as Milo Tindle in *Sleuth* (Music Box, N.Y.C., Nov. 12, 1970); played the BBC Voice in *The Real Inspector Hound* (Th. Four, Apr. 23, 1972); directed *The Waltz of the Toreadors* for the Philadelphia Drama Guild (1972–73 season), a production repeated at Kennedy Ctr. (Washington, D.C., June 19, 1973), the Circle in the Square/Joseph E. Levine Th. (N.Y.C., Sept. 13, 1973), and on tour (opened Mechanic, Baltimore, Jan. 6, 1974; closed Hartford Th., Los Angeles, Apr. 21, 1974); subsequently directed *The Cherry Orchard* (Goodman Th. Ctr., Chicago, Oct. 4, 1974); and *Enter a Free Man* (Th. at St. Clement's, N.Y.C., Dec. 14, 1974); appeared in *The Philanthropist* (Goodman Th. Ctr., Chicago, Feb. 14, 1975); wrote *On the Inside, On the Outside* (staged reading, Long Wharf, New Haven, May 19, 1975); and directed a revival of *Endicott and the Red Cross,* and *My Kinsman, Major Mollineux* on the bill entitled *The Old Glory* (Amer. Place Th., N.Y.C., Apr. 18, 1976).

MURRAY, JOHN. Playwright, composer, lyricist. b. Oct. 12, 1906, New York City, to Morris and Kate Pfeferstein. Father, grocer. Grad. De Witt Clinton H.S., N.Y.C., 1924; attended City Coll. of New York, and Columbia Univ., 1925–28. Served WW II, Signal Corps; rank, Capt. Married Oct. 20, 1941, to Joan Loewi; one son. Member of ASCAP; Dramatists Guild; Amer. Guild of Authors and Composers.

Theatre. Mr. Murray contributed songs and sketches to the revues *Ziegfeld Follies, American,* and *Earl Carroll Vanities.*

He wrote, with Allen Boretz, *Room Service* (Cort Th., N.Y.C., May 19, 1937); wrote sketches for the revue *Sing for Your Supper* (Adelphi, Apr. 24, 1939); songs and sketches for *Straw Hat Revue* (Ambassador, Sept. 29, 1939); and *Alive and Kicking* (Winter Garden, Jan. 17, 1950). He produced and wrote the West Coast revue *Sticks and Stones;* produced, in association with Bernard Hart and Don Hershey, *Room Service* (Playhouse, N.Y.C., Apr. 6, 1953); and co-produced *Room Service* (Edison Th., May 12, 1970); and *Charley's Aunt* (Brooks Atkinson Th., July 4, 1970).

Television and Radio. Mr. Murray was head writer for radio shows of Eddie Cantor and Phil Baker. For television he has written scripts for Hallmark Hall of Fame (NBC), Schlitz Playhouse (CBS), and Ford Th. (CBS).

Other Activities. Mr. Murray has written popular songs, including "If I Love Again," "Have a Little Dream on Me," "It Can't Happen Here," "Oh, What a Thrill to Hear It from You," and "If I Were You.".

Published Works. Mr. Murray wrote *Mystery Plays for Teen-Agers* (1956); *Comedies and Farces for Teen-Agers* (1959); *One Act Plays for Young Actors* (1959); and *Modern Monologues for Young People* (1961).

Recreation. Swimming, bicycling, reading, "especially history and current events.".

MURRAY, MICHAEL. Producer, director. b. Michael William Murray, Mar. 31 1932, Washington, D.C., to William M. and Sally (Stock) Murray. Father, president of paper products company. Grad. Priory Sch., Washington, D.C., 1950; attended Univ. of Notre Dame, 1950–51; grad. Catholic Univ. of America, B.A. 1954; Boston

Univ., M.F.A. 1955. Married Oct. 15, 1962, to Jane Campbell, actress; one daughter, one son. Member of AEA. Cincinnati Playhouse in the Park, Cincinnati, OH 45202; 704 West End Ave., New York, NY 10025.

Theatre. In 1975, Mr. Murray was appointed producer of the Cincinnati (Ohio) Playhouse in the Park. He had been a co-founder (1957) and artistic director (until 1968) of the Charles Playhouse, Boston, Mass., where he directed over forty productions; had been a guest director at the Hartford (Conn.) Stage Co.; Center Stage, Baltimore, Md.; and Playhouse in the Park; and artistic director, American Heritage Festival, Lancaster, Pa., in 1974.

Mr. Murray made his first stage appearance as the First Citizen in a high school production of *Julius Caesar* (Nov. 1946). His first professional assignment was as stage manager for *The Iceman Cometh* (Circle in the Square Th., N.Y.C., May 8, 1956); subsequently directed *House of Breath* (Circle in the Square, May 1957).

Other Activities. Mr. Murray was visiting professor of drama in the humanities at Massachusetts Institute of Technology (1968–70) and also taught (1972–74) at Hunter Coll. and the New School for Social Research, both in N.Y.C.

Published Works. Mr. Murray is author of *The Videotape Book* (1975) and is a columnist for *Commonweal* magazine.

MUSSER, THARON. Lighting designer. b. Tharon Myrene Musser, Jan. 8, 1925, Roanoke, Va., to George C. and Hazel (Riddle) Musser. Father, clergyman. Grad. Marion (Va.) H.S., 1942; Berea Coll., B.A. 1946; Yale Univ. Sch. of Drama, M.F.A. 1950. Member of United Scenic Artists, Local 829; AGMA; USA Lighting Comm. to organize Lighting Associates (chmn., 1962–63). Address: 21 Cornelia St., New York, NY 10014, tel. (212) CH 3-9076.

Theatre. While at Berea Coll., Miss Musser was designer for its production of *Ghosts* (1943); and was assistant to the manager at the Wellesley (Mass.) Summer Th. (Wellesley Coll., 1947).

At the Provincetown Playhouse (N.Y.C.), she was on the production staff of *The Father* (Summer 1949), and *Naked* (Sept. 6, 1950), and served as lighting designer and stage manager for dance concerts at the 92 St. YMHA (N.Y.C., 1950–51).

She toured as lighting designer and stage manager for the José Limon Dance Co. (Jordan Hall, Boston, Mass., 1953; Municipal Th., Buenos Aires, Argentina, Nov. 1954); and was stage manager for the Amer. Dance Festival (ANTA, N.Y.C., May 3, 1955).

She was lighting designer for *Long Day's Journey into Night* (Helen Hayes Th., Nov. 7, 1956); *Shinbone Alley* (Bway Th., Apr. 13, 1957); *Much Ado About Nothing* (Amer. Shakespeare Festival and Acad., Stratford, Conn., Aug. 3, 1957); *Monique* (John Golden Th., N.Y.C., Oct. 22, 1957); and at the Phoenix Th. for *The Makropoulos Secret* (Dec. 3, 1957), *The Chairs* and *The Lesson* (Jan. 9, 1958); and *The Infernal Machine* (Feb. 3, 1958).

She was lighting designer for *The Entertainer* (Royale, Feb. 12, 1958); *The Firstborn* (Coronet, Apr. 30, 1958), *A Midsummer Night's Dream* (ASFTA, Stratford, Conn., June 20, 1958); and for the Israeli production of *The Firstborn* (Habimah, Tel Aviv, July 1958).

Also, for *Murder in the Cathedral* (Carnegie Hall, N.Y.C., Sept. 1958), *Shadow of a Gunman* (Bijou, Nov. 20, 1958), *J. B.* (ANTA, Dec. 11, 1958), *The Beaux' Strategem* (Phoenix, Feb. 24, 1959), *Once Upon a Mattress* (Phoenix, May 11, 1959); and at the ASFTA for *Romeo and Juliet* (June 12, 1959), *A Midsummer Night's Dream* (June 20, 1959), and *The Merry Wives of Windsor* (July 8, 1959).

Also, for *The Great God Brown* (Coronet, N.Y.C., Oct. 6, 1959); *Only in America* (Cort, Nov. 19, 1959); *Five Finger Exercise* (Music Box, Dec. 2, 1959); *Peer Gynt* (Phoenix, Jan. 12, 1960); *The Long Dream* (Ambassador, Feb. 17, 1960); *The Tumbler* (Helen Hayes Th., Feb. 24, 1960); and at the ASFTA for *Twelfth Night* (June 8, 1960), *The Tempest* (June 19, 1960), and *Antony and Cleopatra* (July 31, 1960).

She was lighting designer for the Amer. Repertory Company's State Dept. sponsored tours of *The Glass Menagerie, The Skin of Our Teeth*, and *The Miracle Worker* (Europe, South America, 1961); at the ASFTA for *As You Like It* (June 27, 1961), and *Macbeth* (June 28, 1961); and at the Amer. Festival (Boston, Mass.), for *The Turn of the Screw* (July 5, 1961), *Anatol* (Aug. 1, 1961), and *Elizabeth the Queen* (Aug. 22, 1961).

Also, for the tour of *Advise and Consent* (opened Shubert, Cincinnati, Ohio, Oct. 2, 1961; closed Amer. Th., St. Louis, Mo., May 5, 1962), the Natl. Repertory Th. tours of *Mary Stuart* and *Elizabeth the Queen* (opened Acad. of Music, Northampton, Mass., Oct. 1961); *Garden of Sweets* (ANTA, N.Y.C., Oct. 31, 1961), *Giants, Sons of Giants* (Alvin, Jan. 6, 1962), and at the Boston (Mass.) Arts Festival for *H.M.S. Pinafore*, and *Androcles and the Lion* (June 1962).

Also, for *Calculated Risk* (Ambassador, N.Y.C., Oct. 31, 1962); *Nowhere To Go But Up* (Winter Garden, Nov. 10, 1962); *Andorra* (Biltmore, Feb. 9, 1963); *Mother Courage and Her Children* (Martin Beck Th., Mar. 28, 1963); at the ASFTA for *King Lear* (June 9, 1963), *The Comedy of Errors* (June 11, 1963), and *Henry V* (June 12, 1963); *Here's Love* (Shubert, N.Y.C., Oct. 3, 1963); for the Natl. Repertory Th. tours of *Ring 'Round the Moon, The Seagull*, and *The Crucible* (1963–64); *The Seagull* (Belasco, N.Y.C., Apr. 5, 1964); *The Crucible* (Belasco, Apr. 6, 1964).

Also, for *Marathon '33* (ANTA, Dec. 22, 1963); *Any Wednesday* (Music Box, Feb. 18, 1964); at the ASFTA for *Much Ado About Nothing* (June 9, 1964), *Richard III* (June 10, 1964), and *Hamlet* (July 2, 1964); and for the Natl. Repertory Th. tour of *Hedda Gabler, Liliom*, and *She Stoops To Conquer* (Greensboro, N.C., Oct. 9, 1964).

Also, for *Golden Boy* (Majestic Th., N.Y.C., Oct. 20, 1964); *Alfie* (Morosco, Dec. 17, 1964); *Kelly* (Broadhurst, Feb. 6, 1965); *All in Good Time* (Royale, Feb. 18, 1965); *Flora, the Red Menace* (Alvin Th., May 11, 1965); at the ASFTA for *Romeo and Juliet* (June 19, 1965), *Coriolanus* (June 20, 1965), *The Taming of the Shrew* (June 23, 1965), and *King Lear* (June 24, 1965).

Also, for *Mais Oui* (Casino du Leban, Beirut, Lebanon, July 1965); *Minor Miracle* (Henry Miller's Th., N.Y.C., Oct. 7, 1965); for the Natl. Repertory Th. tour of *The Rivals* and *The Madwoman of Chaillot* (Greensboro, N.C., Oct. 8, 1965) and *The Trojan Women* (Columbus, Ohio, Nov. 5, 1965); for *Malcolm* (Shubert Th., N.Y.C., Jan. 11, 1966); *Great Indoors* Eugene O'Neill Th., Feb. 1, 1966); *The Lion in Winter* (Ambassador, Mar. 3, 1966); *Mame* (Winter Garden, May 24, 1966); at the ASFTA for *Falstaff* (June 18, 1966), *Murder in the Cathedral* (June 19, 1966), *Twelfth Night* (June 21, 1966), and *Julius Caesar* (June 22, 1966); for *A Delicate Balance* (Martin Beck Th., N.Y.C., Sept. 22, 1966); and for the Natl. Repertory Th. tour of *Tonight at 8:30* and *A Touch of the Poet* (Greensboro, N.C., Oct. 14, 1966) and *The Imaginary Invalid* (Columbus, Ohio, Nov. 8, 1966).

Also, for *Hallelujah, Baby* (Martin Beck Th., N.Y.C., Apr. 26, 1967); *The Imaginary Invalid* (ANTA, May 1, 1967); *A Touch of the Poet* (ANTA, May 2, 1967); *Tonight at 8:30* (ANTA, May 3, 1967); at the ASFTA for *Midsummer Night's Dream* (June 17, 1967), *Antigone* (June 18, 1967), and *The Merchant of Venice* (June 20, 1967); for *The Birthday Party* (Booth Th., N.Y.C., Oct. 3, 1967); *After the Rain* (Golden Th., Oct. 9, 1967); and for the Natl. Repertory Th. tour of *John Brown's Body* and *A Comedy of Errors* (Greensboro, N.C., Oct. 16, 1967).

Also, for *The Promise* (Henry Miller's Th., N.Y.C., Nov. 14, 1967); *Everything in the Garden* (Plymouth Th., Nov. 29, 1967); *House of Flowers* (Th. de Lys, Jan. 28, 1968); for the CBS special on the re-opening of Ford's Th., Washington, D.C. (Jan. 30, 1968); for *Catch My Soul* (Ahmanson Th., Los Angeles, Calif., Mar. 5, 1968); *Man and the Universe* (HemisFair Exhibit, San Antonio, Tex., Apr. 1968); *Golden Boy* (Palladium, London, England, June 5, 1968); at the ASFTA for *As You Like It* (June 23, 1968); and *Androcles and the Lion* (June 25, 1968); for *Lovers* (Vivian Beaumont Th., Lincoln Ctr., N.Y.C., July 25, 1968); *Maggie Flynn* (ANTA, Oct. 23, 1968); *Fig Leaves Are Falling* (Broadhurst, Jan. 2, 1969); *Mame* (Drury Lane Th., London, England, Feb. 20, 1969); *The Gingham Dog* (Golden Th., Apr. 23, 1969); *Spofford* (tour, Fisher Th., Detroit, Mich., Sept. 8, 1969); *Fedora* (Dallas Civic Opera, Dallas, Tex., Nov. 24, 1969); *Blood Red Roses* (Golden Th., N.Y.C., Mar. 22, 1970); *Applause* (Palace, Mar. 30, 1970); *The Boy Friend* (Ambassador, Apr. 14, 1970); and for the Center Th. Group, Mark Taper Forum, Los Angeles, Calif., *Dream On Monkey Mountain* (Aug. 27, 1970) and *Rosebloom* (Nov. 5, 1970).

Also, for the Dallas Civic Opera, Dallas, Tex., *The Merry Widow* (Nov. 6, 1970), *Madame Butterfly* (Nov. 13, 1970), *Il Tabarro* and *Carmina Burana* (both Nov. 21, 1970); for *Follies* (Winter Garden, N.Y.C., Apr. 4, 1971); *Trial of the Catonsville Nine* (Lyceum, June 2, 1971); for the Center Th. Group, Mark Taper Forum, Los Angeles, Calif., *Trial of the Catonsville Nine* (June 17, 1971) and *Major Barbara* (Aug. 26, 1971); for *On the Town* (Imperial, N.Y.C., Oct. 31, 1971); *Prisoner of Second Avenue* (Eugene O'Neill Th., Nov. 11, 1971); for the Dallas Civic Opera, Dallas, Tex., *Fidelio* (Nov. 18, 1971); for *Night Watch* (Morosco, N.Y.C., Feb. 28, 1972); and for the Center Th. Group, Mark Taper Forum, Los Angeles, Calif., *Old Times* (May 25, 1972).

Also, for *Dream on Monkey Mountain* (Kammerspiele Th., Munich, Germany, July 31, 1972); *Applause* (Her Majesty's Th., London, England, Nov. 1972); *The Creation of the World and Other Matters* (Shubert Th., N.Y.C., Nov. 30, 1972); for the Dallas Civic Opera, Dallas, Tex., *Lucia di Lammermoor* (Dec. 1, 1972); for *The Great God Brown* (Lyceum, N.Y.C., Dec. 10, 1972); *Don Juan* (Lyceum, Dec. 11, 1972); *The Sunshine Boys* (Broadhurst, Dec. 20, 1972); *A Little Night Music* (Shubert Th., Feb. 25, 1973); *The Orphan* (Public Th., Anspacher Th., Apr. 17, 1973); for the Center Th. Group, Mark Taper Forum, Los Angeles, Calif., *Forget-Me-Not Lane* (May 31, 1973); for *The Good Doctor* (Eugene O'Neill Th., N.Y.C., Nov. 27, 1973); for the Dallas Civic Opera, Dallas, Tex., *Andre Chenier* (Nov. 30, 1973); for the Center Th. Group, Ahmanson Theatre, Los Angeles, Calif., *Saint Joan* (Jan. 29, 1974); for *Candide* (Broadway Th., N.Y.C., Mar. 10, 1974); for the Miami (Fla.) Opera Guild, *The Pearl Fishers* (Apr. 1, 1974); and for the Center Th. Group, Mark Taper Forum, Los Angeles, Calif. *The Charlatan* (May 23, 1974).

Other Activities. Miss Musser has lectured on the theatre at the NY Teachers' Assn. (1957–58); ANTA Natl. Convention (1958); Vassar Coll. (1961); Yale Univ. Drama Dept. (1962); the Polakov Studio of Design (1962–64); Bridgeport (Conn.) Univ. Student Center (Aug. 10, 1967); Yale Drama School (Apr. 28, 1969); State Univ. of NY at Purchase, N.Y. (Dec. 1, 1969); Bucknell Univ., Lewisburg, Pa. (Apr. 5, 1973); and Rhode Island Coll., Providence, R.I. (Apr. 26, 1974); and she was on the visiting committee, Loeb Drama Center, Harvard Univ. (1974–76).

She has also served as theatrical consultant for Webb & Knapp, Radcliffe Coll., Amer. Acad. of Dramatic Arts, and the NY Council on the Arts.

Awards. Miss Musser received the Antoinette Perry (Tony) Award for best lighting design for 1971–72 for *Follies* and was nominated for Tony's for best lighting design for *Applause* (1969–70), *A Little Night Music* (1972–73), and *The Good Doctor* (1973–74). On July 21, 1973, Berea (Ky.) College gave her its Distinguished Alumna Award.

Recreation. Traveling.

MYERS, PAUL. Theatre librarian. b. Paul H. Myers, Mar. 5, 1917, New York City, to J. Franklin and Miriam (Heimerdinger) Myers. Grad. Trinity Sch., 1934; New York Univ., B.F.A. 1938; Pratt Inst. Sch. of Library Service, M.L.S. 1960. Married Aug. 14, 1948, to Elizabeth Burke; one daughter. Member of Th. Library Assn.; Drama Desk; the National Theatre Conference; and the American Society for Theatre Research. Address: (home) 13 W. 13th St., New York, NY 10011, tel. (212) 242-2874; (bus.) Theatre Collection, N.Y. Public Library, 111 Amsterdam Ave., New York, NY 10023, tel. (212) 799-2200, ext. 204.

Since 1945, Mr. Myers has been librarian for the Theatre Collection of the N.Y. Public Library and became curator in 1967.

During 1936–38, he appeared in and was stage manager for productions of the Washington Square Players at New York Univ. He made his N.Y.C. debut in minor roles in *First American Dictator* (Nora Bayes Th., Mar. 14, 1939); and toured as actor and stage manager with the James Hendrickson-Claire Bruce Shakespearean Repertory Co. (Dec. 1940 –Mar. 1941).

He was associated with *Stage* magazine (1941); and was docent at the Cooper Union Museum of the Arts of Decoration (N.Y.C., 1941–42).

Published Works. Mr. Myers wrote, with Roy Stallings, *A Guide to Theatre Reading* (1949), and collaborated on *Performing Arts Collections, An International Handbook* (Paris, Editions du Centre National de la Recherche Scientifique, 1960).

MYERS, RICHARD. Producer, composer. b. Richardson Myers, Mar. 25, 1901, Philadelphia, Pa., to Milton and Alice (Foster) Myers. Father, executive. Attended William Penn Charter Sch., Philadelphia, 1910–17. Married May 25, 1929, to Carolin Smith (dec. 1948); married June 25, 1949, to Suzanne Royer (dec. 1963); married July 5, 1966, to Henriette Georgette Bisserier, author. Member of ASCAP; Dramatists Guild; The Travellers (Paris); Piping Rock Club (Locust Valley, N.Y.).

Theatre. Mr. Myer's first assignment was composing the music for a song, "Whistle Away Your Blues" in *Greenwich Village Follies* (46 St. Th., N.Y.C., Dec. 24, 1925); subsequently composed the music for "The Life of the Party" in *Greenwich Village Follies* (Shubert, Mar. 15, 1926); with Phillip Charig, wrote the music for *Allez-Oop* (Earl Carroll Th., Aug. 2, 1927); contributed music to *Night Hostess* (Martin Beck Th., Sept. 12, 1928); composed the music for *Hello Yourself* (Casino, Oct. 30, 1928) which included the song, "Jericho"; with Nicholas Kemper and Sam Timberg wrote the music for *The Street Singer* (Shubert, Sept. 17, 1929); contributed music to *Ruth Selwyn's 9:15 Revue* (George M. Cohan Th., Feb. 11, 1930); *Garrick Gaieties* (Guild, June 4, 1930); composed, with Johnny Green, the score for *Here Goes the Bride* (46 St. Th., Nov. 3, 1931); *Earl Carroll Vanities* (Bway, Sept. 27, 1932); composed music for *Americana* (Shubert, Oct. 5, 1932); with Edward Heyman, wrote music and lyrics for *Murder at the Vanities* (New Amsterdam, Sept. 12, 1933); wrote additional lyrics and music for *Ziegfeld Follies* (Winter Garden, Jan. 4, 1934); and composed the music for *The Pure in Heart* (Longacre, Mar. 20, 1934).

Mr. Myers was one of the producers of *Lorelei* (Longacre, Nov. 29, 1938); produced, with Richard Aldrich, *The Importance of Being Earnest* (Vanderbilt, Jan. 12, 1939); *Margin for Error* (Plymouth, Nov. 3, 1939); *My Dear Children* (Belasco, Jan. 31, 1940); *Cue for Passion* (Royale, Dec. 19, 1940); *Plan M* (Belasco, Feb. 20, 1942); with Max Reinhardt and Norman Bel Geddes, *Sons and Soldiers* (Morosco, May 4, 1943); and presented *Mrs. January and Mr. X* (Belasco, Mar. 31, 1944).

Mr. Myers produced, with Lester Meyer, *Calico Wedding* (Natl., Mar. 7, 1945); with Richard Aldrich in association with Julius Fleischmann, *Caesar and Cleopatra* (Natl., Dec. 21, 1949); *The Moon Is Blue* (Henry Miller's Th., Mar. 8, 1951); with Richard Aldrich and the Theatre Guild, *The Love of Four Colonels* (Shubert, Jan. 15, 1953); and with Richard Aldrich in association with Julius Fleischmann, *A Girl Can Tell* (Royale, Oct. 29, 1953); *Dear Charles* (Morosco, Sept. 15, 1954); and *Little Glass Clock* (John Golden Th., Mar. 26, 1956).

He contributed music to *Ziegfeld Follies* (Winter Garden, Mar. 1, 1957); was one of the producers of *Hotel Paradiso* (Henry Miller's Th., Apr. 11, 1957); *Interlock* (ANTA, Feb. 6, 1958); and produced, with the Theatre Guild and Julius Fleischmann, *Requiem for a Nun* (John Golden Th., Jan. 30, 1959).

Films. The film *Susan Slept Here* (RKO, 1954) contained Mr. Myers' song "Hold My Hand.".

Published Works. Mr. Myer's first published song was the title song from the David Belasco play *Lulu Belle* (Belasco, Feb. 9, 1926).

Awards. Mr. Myers received an Academy (Oscar) Award nomination for the song, "Hold My Hand," from *Susan Slept Here* (1954).

Recreation. Tennis, bridge.

MYRTIL, ODETTE. Actress. b. Odette Quignard, June 28, 1898, Paris, France, to Charles and Marguerite Quingnard. Attended school in France. Married June 1916 to Bob Adams (marr. dis.); one son, Roger Adams, composer, pianist; married 1926 to Stanley Logan. Member of SAG; AEA. Address: Chez Odette, New Hope, PA tel. 862-2432.

Theatre. Miss Myrtil made her debut as a violinist (Olympia, Paris, France, 1911) and subsequently toured Europe, made her Bway debut in *Ziegfeld Midnight Frolics* (Sept. 1914); and appeared in the *Ziegfeld Follies of 1915* (New Amsterdam, June 21, 1915); made her London debut as a vocalist and violin virtuoso (Alhambra, Feb. 28, 1916); performed in *The Bing Boys Are Here* (Alhambra, Feb. 28, 1916); toured Eng. in *Ciro's Frolics* (1917); played in *Bubly* (Comedy, London, May 5, 1917); *Tabs* (Vaudeville, May 15, 1918); *Tails Up* (Comedy, June 1, 1918); Cora Merville in *The Officers' Mess* (St. Martin's, Nov. 1918); and in *Bran Pie* (Prince of Wales's, Aug. 28, 1919), with which she toured in 1921.

She played Venus in *La ceinture de Venus* (Apollo, Paris, Dec. 1920); appeared in *Dover Street to Dixie* (London Pavilion, May 31, 1923); performed in the Bway production of *Vogues of 1924* (Shubert, Mar. 27, 1924); played Hortense in *The Love Song* (Century, Jan. 13, 1925); succeeded (Mar. 1926) Yvonne George in the revue, *A Night in Paris* (Casino de Paris, Jan. 5, 1926); appeared as Manja in *Countess Maritza* (Shubert, Sept. 18, 1926; revived Century, Apr. 9, 1928); Mme. George Sand in *White Lilacs* (Shubert, Sept. 10, 1928); Marian Lavarre in *Broadway Nights* (44 St. Th., July 15, 1929); and Odette in *The Cat and the Fiddle* (Globe, Oct. 15, 1931).

She succeeded (July 1934) Lyda Roberti in the role of Clementina Scharwenka in *Roberta* (New Amsterdam, Nov. 18, 1933); appeared as Mme. La Fleur in *The Red Mill* (Ziegfeld, Oct. 16, 1945); the Countess in a stock production of *Miss Liberty* (Green Th., Los Angeles, Calif., Summer 1950); succeeded (Jan. 1952) Diosa Costello as Bloody Mary in *South Pacific* (Majestic, N.Y.C., Apr. 7, 1949); portrayed Mme. Marstonne in *Maggie* (Natl., Feb. 18, 1953); and Belle Piquery in *Saratoga* (Winter Garden, Dec. 7, 1959).

Films. Miss Myrtil has appeared in about 50 films, among which are: *Dodsworth* (UA, 1936); *Kitty Foyle* (RKO, 1940); *Out of the Fog* (WB, 1941); *I Married an Angel* (MGM, 1942); *Dark Waters* (UA, 1944); *Rhapsody in Blue* (WB, 1945); *The Fighting Kentuckian* (Rep., 1949); and *Here Comes the Groom* (Par., 1951).

Night Clubs. She has appeared at The Blue Angel (N.Y.C.) and at the Statler hotels.

Other Activities. She was a dress designer in Beverly Hills, Calif. (1930–36), and owns a restaurant called Chez Odette in New Hope, Pa.

Recreation. Walking, reading.

N

NADEL, NORMAN. Critic, editor, writer, lecturer. b. Norman Sanford Nadel, June 19, 1915, Newark, N.J., to Louis D. and Sara (Fiverson) Nadel. Father, engineer. Grad. John Marshall H.S., Rochester, N.Y., 1933; Denison Univ., A.B. (psychology) 1938; Univ. of Chicago, graduate study (psychology) 1943. Married Feb. 8, 1941, to Martha Smith, children's librarian; two sons, one daughter. Served with US Army, 1942–45. Member of NY Drama Critics Circle; Dutch Treat Club (N.Y.C.); Phi Mu Alpha Sinfonia; N.Y.C. Cultural Council; ACTA (bd. of gov.); Foundation for the Community of Artists (bd. of dir.); Theatre Guild-American Theatre Soc. (play selection comm.); Richmond County (N.Y.) and White's Point Yacht clubs. Address: (home) 234 College Ave., Staten Island, NY 10314, tel. (212) SA 7-3693; (bus.) Scripps-Howard Newspapers, 200 Park Ave., New York, NY 10017, tel. (212) 867-5000.

Since Nov. 1967, Mr. Nadel has been critic, cultural affairs editor, and writer for the Scripps-Howard newspapers, covering all performing and visual arts. He was drama critic, NY *World Telegram & Sun* (1961–66) and in 1966 was named drama critic of the *World Journal Tribune.* Mr. Nadel has served also as arbiter of disputes between Actors' Equity and the League of NY Theatres and Producers over employment of foreign actors.

Previously, he was founder; member, board of directors; and trombonist of the Columbus (Ohio) Philharmonic Orchestra (1940); and taught journalism at Ohio State Univ. He joined the staff of the Columbus (Ohio) *Citizen* as make-up editor (1939), and later served as radio columnist (1940), music critic (1942), drama, music and movie critic, and theatre editor (1947–61).

Mr. Nadel originated newspaper-sponsored (Columbus *Citizen*) long-distance theatre-plane and theatre-train tours (1952), and headed twenty-four New York and several European trips in 1970. Since 1947, he has lectured on the theatre throughout the US.

Published Works. Mr. Nadel is author of *A Pictorial History of the Theatre Guild* (1970). From 1967 to 1970, he was a consultant to the Theatre Guild and editor of the Guild magazine, *Critic's Choice.* He has contributed articles to the *Saturday Review,* the NY *Times, Together, Ohio Boating, Lakeland Yachting, Bravo, Minutes, Theatre Arts, Yachting, Boating, Rudder, American-Scandinavian Review,* Los Angeles *Times,* and other periodicals.

Awards. Mr. Nadel won the rebel-class national championship in sailing (1951); received the Variety Spotlight Award for service to the American theatre in originating theatre-trains (1956); a Natl. Federation of Music Clubs Citation for music criticism (1957); won four times, the Scripps-Howard Story-of-the-Month Prize; and received from Denison Univ. its Alumni Citation (1963) and the honorary degree of D.H.L. (1967).

Recreation. Sailing, canoeing, photography, camping, music.

NAGLER, A. M. Educator, drama critic, theatrical historian. b. Alois M. Nagler, Sept. 14, 1907, Graz, Austria, to Alois and Auguste (Schupp) Nagler. Grad. Univ. of Graz; Univ. of Vienna, Ph.D. 1930. Married Aug. 19, 1933, to Erna Scheinberger. Member of Intl. Federation for Theatrical Research (pres., 1959–63); Austrian Acad. of Arts and Sciences (mbr.); ASTR (past chairman). Address: (home) 174 Linden St., New Haven, CT 06511; (bus.) c/o School of Drama, Yale Univ., New Haven, CT 06520.

Mr. Nagler is a professor of dramatic history and criticism at Yale Univ., where he has been a member of the faculty since 1946. Before coming to the US, Mr. Nagler was a drama critic in Berlin, Germany (1930–32) and in Vienna, Austria (1932–38).

Published Works. He has written *Frederick Hebbel and Music* (1928); *Ferdinand von Saar as a Short*

Story Writer (1930); edited *Sources of Theatrical History* (1952); wrote *Shakespeare's Stage* (1958); and *Theatre Festivals of the Medici* (1964).

Awards. Mr. Nagler received a Rockefeller Research Fellowship (1940); and a Rockefeller Foundation Grant (1949). In 1967, he was awarded the Austrian Cross of Honor for Sciences and Art.

NAISMITH, LAURENCE. Actor. b. Laurence Bernard Johnson, Dec. 14, 1908, Thames-Ditton, England, to Bernard and Beatrice Johnson. Attended All Saints Choir Sch., London. Married Oct. 30, 1939, to Vera Christine Bocca, actress; one son. Served Royal Army, 1939–45, gunner to battery commander. Member of British AEA; AEA; Garrick Club (London); NY Century Assn.; Lotus Club (N.Y.).

Pre-Theatre. Merchant seaman.

Theatre. Mr. Naismith first appeared on stage in a school production of *The Taming of the Shrew* (Old Memorial Th., Stratford-upon-Avon, 1922); and made his professional debut in the chorus of *Oh, Kay!* (His Majesty's Th., London, Sept. 21, 1927). After appearing in England in various repertory companies as well as managing his own company, he played the Salesman in *Rocket to the Moon* (St. Martin's, London, Mar. 20, 1948); followed by Wilson in *Larger Than Life* (Duke of York's, Feb. 7, 1950); Lagarde in *Colombe* (New, Dec. 13, 1951); Proteus in *The Apple Cart* (Haymarket, May 7, 1953); Montagu Winthrop in *The Burning Glass* (Apollo, Feb. 18, 1954); Cauchon in *The Lark* (Lyric, Hammersmith, May 11, 1955); Dvorak in *Summer Song* (Princes's, Feb. 16, 1956); Dr. Pangloss and Martin in *Candide* (Saville, Apr. 30, 1959); Sir Oliver Surface in *The School for Scandal* (Haymarket), the role in which he made his Bway debut (Majestic, Jan. 24, 1963); Kris Kringle in *Here's Love* (Shubert, Oct. 3, 1963); Gwillym Morgan (Dada) in *A Time for Singing* (Broadway Th., May 21, 1966); and Capt. Edward Vere in *Billy* (Billy Rose Th., Mar. 22, 1969).

Films. Since his debut in *High Treason* (1947), Mr. Naismith has appeared in *Richard III* (Lopert, 1956); *The Man Who Never Was* (20th-Fox, 1956); *A Night To Remember* (Lopert, 1958); *The Angry Silence* (Valient, 1960); *Sink the Bismarck!* (20th-Fox, 1960); *Greyfriar's Bobby* (Buena Vista, 1961); *The Three Lives of Tomasina* (Buena Vista, 1963); *Gypsy Girl* (Cont.-Rank, 1966); *Deadlier Than the Male* (U, 1967); *The Long Duel* (Rank, 1967); and *Camelot* (WB, 1967).

Television. Mr. Naismith appeared on Danger Man (Ind., 1964); Twelve O'Clock High (ABC, 1965); played John Adams on Profiles in Courage (NBC, Apr. 11, 1965); was on The Fugitive (ABC, 1965, 1966, 1967); played George Mason on another segment of Profiles in Courage (NBC, May 2, 1965); was Gordon Knight in *The Fatal Mistake* (Bob Hope Presents, NBC, Nov. 30, 1966); and Lord Hertford in *The Prince and the Pauper* (Walt Disney's World, NBC, Apr. 1967).

Recreation. Swimming, water skiing, bridge, casinos.

NASH, N. RICHARD. Playwright, producer. b. Nathaniel Richard Nusbaum, June 7, 1913, Philadelphia, Pa., to S. L. and Jennie (Singer) Nusbaum. Father, bookbinder. Grad. S. Philadelphia H.S., 1930; Univ. of Pennsylvania, B.S. 1934. Married Mar. 1935 to Helena Taylor (marr. dis. 1954); one son; married Mar. 1956 to Janice Rule, actress (marr. dis. 1956); married Nov. 1956 to Katherine Copeland; two daughters. Member of Dramatists Guild; WGA, West; ALA; AMPAS.

Theatre. Mr. Nash wrote *Second Best Bed* (Ethel Barrymore Th., N.Y.C., June 3, 1946); *The Young and Fair* (Fulton, Nov. 22, 1948); *See the Jaguar* (Cort, Dec. 3, 1952); *The Rainmaker* (Cort, Oct. 28, 1954); *Girls of Summer* (Longacre, Nov. 19, 1956); *Handful of Fire* (Martin Beck Th., Oct. 1, 1958); the book for the musical, *Wildcat*, which he also produced, with Michael Kidd (Alvin, Dec. 16, 1960); adapted his play, *the Rainmaker*, for the musical stage as *110 in the Shade* (Broadhurst, Oct. 24, 1963; Palace Th., London, Feb. 8, 1967); wrote the book for *The Happy Time* (Bway Th., N.Y.C., Jan. 18, 1968); and wrote *Echoes* (Bijou, Feb. 26, 1973).

Films. He wrote with Arthur Sheekman, *Welcome Stranger* (Par., 1947); wrote *Nora Prentiss* (WB, 1947); and the screenplay for *Porgy and Bess* (Col., 1959).

Television. He wrote the scripts for *House in Athens* (Philco Playhouse, NBC); adapted *The Rainmaker* (Philco Playhouse, NBC); *The Brownstone* (Philco Playhouse, NBC); *The Happy Rest* (Philco Playhouse, NBC); adapted *The Young and Fair* (Philco Playhouse, NBC); wrote *The Arena* (Philco Playhouse, NBC); *Welcome Home* (Theatre Guild of the Air, ABC); and *The Joker* (Philco Playhouse, ABC).

Awards. Mr. Nash received the Maxwell Anderson Verse Drama Award (1940); for *Parting at Imsdorf;* the International Drama Award (Cannes, France) and Prague (Czechoslovakia) Award (1954) for *See the Jaguar;* the Karl Gosse Award (Germany) for *The Rainmaker* (1957); and the Archer Award (Canada) for *Handful of Fire* (1960).

Recreation. Furniture making.

NASSAU, PAUL. Composer, Lyricist. b. Jan. 30, 1930, Brooklyn, N.Y., to Harry and Lillian (Brinberg) Nassau. Father, salesman; mother, antique dealer. Attended James Madison H.S., Bklyn., N.Y., 1944–45; grad. Cherry Lawn Sch., Darien, Conn., 1947; attended Western Reserve Univ., 1947–49; grad. Oberlin Coll., B.A. 1953. Married Dec. 23, 1953, to Chloe Anderson; one son, one daughter. Address: 201 W. 86th St., New York, NY 10024, tel. (212) TR 4-7268.

Theatre. Mr. Nassau was a composer-lyricist of material presented in the revue, *New Faces of '56* (Ethel Barrymore Th., N.Y.C., June 14, 1956); subsequently was composer-lyricist for original summer-stock productions at Tamiment, Pa. (July–Sept. 1957). With Martin Charnin and Robert Kessler, he wrote the music and lyrics for *Fallout* (Renata, N.Y.C., May 20, 1959); wrote additional music and lyrics for *Happy Town* (54 St. Th., Oct. 7, 1959); with Oscar Brand, wrote music and lyrics for *A Joyful Noise* (Mark Hellinger Th., N.Y.C., Dec. 14, 1966), and *The Education of Hyman Kaplan* (Alvin, N.Y.C., Apr. 4, 1968); and contributed material to *New Faces of 1968* (Booth, N.Y.C., May 2, 1968).

Television. He composed the theme music for *Exploring* (NBC, Oct. 1962).

NASSIF, S. JOSEPH. Producer, actor, director, educator. b. Shakeeb Joseph Nassif, Aug. 30, 1938, Cedar Rapids, Iowa, to Samuel Joseph and Mary (Slaman) Nassif. Father, real estate. Grad. Grinnell (Iowa) College, B.A.; School of Drama, Yale Univ., M.F.A.; Univ. of Denver, Ph.D. 1973. Professional training with John Gassner, Alois Nagler, Martin Feinstein, F. Curtis Canfield, Tyrone Guthrie, Maria Ley Piscator, Columbia Studios Workshop, Westinghouse Broadcasting Company. Married Aug. 29, 1964, to Michelle Marie McKenna; one son, one daughter. Relative in theatre: cousin, Fred Nassif. Member of AEA; ATA; SAA; National Broadcasters Assn.; Piscator Foundation (trustee). Address: (home) 5122 Pembroke Place, Pittsburgh, PA 15232, tel. (412) 681-0115; (bus.) Pittsburgh Playhouse, 222 Craft Ave., Pittsburgh, PA 15213, tel. (412) 621-6695; (412) 621-4445.

Dr. Nassif has been guest professor of English and Drama at St. Bonaventure Univ. (1963–64); visiting professor of Drama at the Univ. of Montana (1965–66); associate professor of English and Drama at the Univ. of Southern California (1967); and professor and chairman of the Dept. of Theatre Art, Point Park Coll. (1969–to date). He is general manager of the Pittsburgh (Pa.) Ballet Theatre.

Theatre. Off-Bway, he appeared in the Chorus of *John Brown's Body* (Cherry Lane Th., N.Y.C., July 1959); subsequently directed and played Don Juan in a college tour of *Don Juan in Hell* (1959–60); at the Yale School of Drama, appeared as Scandal in *Love for Love* (Nov. 1960); Count Jolimaitre in *Fashion* (Jan. 1961); and the Burgermaster in *The Visit* (Mar. 1963). At the Williamstown (Mass.) Th. he appeared as Glogauer in *Once in a Lifetime,* Lodovico in *Othello,* the Comforter in *J. B.,* and the Pope of Rome in *Becket* (Summer 1961). He was producer-director of the Montowese Summer Th. (Branford, Conn.), presenting *The Country Girl* and *Don Juan in Hell* (June–Aug. 1962); and of the Yale Summer Th. (New Haven, Conn., June–Aug. 1963, 1964) where his productions included *Under the Gaslight, Bus Stop, The Barber of Seville, Pygmalion, The Fantasticks, The American Dream* and *Zoo Story, Dial 'M' for Murder, A View from the Bridge, The Threepenny Opera, The Bald Soprano* and *The Lesson, Two for the Seesaw, Babes in Arms, Night Must Fall,* and *Period of Adjustment.*

With the Univ. of Denver (Colo.) Repertory Co., he appeared as Jean in *Rhinoceros* (Sept. 1964); Jourdain in *The Bourgeois Gentleman* (Nov. 1964); and Tyrone in *Long Day's Journey into Night* (Mar. 1965). He played Duncan in *Macbeth* (Intl. Alliance of Theatrical Stage Employees, Denver, Colo., June 1965), directed *Who's Afraid of Virginia Woolf?* (Nov. 1965), and *Hay Fever* (June 1966) for the Montana Repertory Co. (Missoula, Mont.); directed *The Bartered Bride* (Sch. of Music, Univ. of Montana, July 1966); and was director-producer of *The Streets of New York* (Hollywood Th., Los Angeles, Jan. 1967). He was executive producer, Pittsburgh Playhouse (May 1969–June 1973), where plays presented included *Gypsy, The Owl and the Pussycat, The Hostage, A Day in the Death of Joe Egg, The Streets of New York,* in which he also played Badger, *Irma La Douce, Man of La Mancha, The Boys in the Band, Your Own Thing, Everything in the Garden, The Lion in Winter, The Serpent, Tom Paine, Carousel, Who's Afraid of Virginia Woolf?, Salvation, Forty Carats, Cactus Flower, Guys and Dolls, Room Service, Plaza Suite, You Can't Take It with You, Alfred the Great,* and *A Streetcar Named Desire.* For the American Academy in Paris (France), he directed *Tartuffe* (1971).

Films. Dr. Nassif directed workshop films at Columbia Studios, Hollywood, (Sept. 1966).

Television. He was producer-director of the Marie Torre Show (KDKA-TV, Pittsburgh, Pa., Sept. 1967–69); *The Business of Culture* (Westinghouse Broadcasting Co., 1968); and *Public Enemy #1* (Westinghouse Broadcasting Co.).

Night Clubs. He produced and directed musical revues at Iron Springs Chateau, (Colorado Springs, Colo., Summer 1965).

Published Works. He is author of *Antonin Artaud: The Man and His Work* (1963); *Beaumarchais: French Middle Class Comedy* (1963); and *A History of the Pittsburgh Playhouse* (1973).

Awards. He received the Outstanding Educator in America Award (1974) for his contribution to theatre education.

Recreation. Tennis, real estate.

NATHAN, VIVIAN. Actress. b. Vivia Firko, Oct. 26, 1921, New York City, to Hipolit and Anna (Marczak) Firko. Grad. St. Nicholas Seminary, N.Y. Studied dance with Anna Sokolow; voice with Frances Robinson-Duff; Actors Studio (member 1948–to date). Married to Nathan Schwalb. Member of AEA; AFTRA; SAG. Address: 95 Christopher St., New York, NY 10014, tel. (212) CH 2-8323.

Theatre. Miss Nathan made her Bway debut as Helen in *Sundown Beach* (Belasco, Th., Sept. 7, 1948); subsequently played Mathilde in *Montserrat* (Fulton, Oct. 29, 1949); Pepina in *The Rose Tattoo* (Martin Beck Th., Feb. 3, 1951); and La Madrecita do los Perdidos in *Camino Real* (National, Mar. 19, 1953).

She played Josefina in *Bullfight* (Th. de Lys, Jan. 12, 1954); the Charwoman in *Anastasia* (Lyceum, Dec. 29, 1954); Clothide in *The Lovers* (Martin Beck Th., May 10, 1956); Maxine in *The Night of the Iguana* and Mrs. Crosby in *Tiny Closet* (Festival of Two Worlds, Spoleto, Italy, Summer, 1959); Marie Duschene in *Semi-Detached* (Martin Beck Th., N.Y.C., Mar. 10, 1960); a Witness for the Prosecution in *The Investigation* (Ambassador, Oct. 4, 1966);

Margaret Young, the Mother, in *The Watering Place* (Music Box, Mar. 12, 1969); and Mary Tyrone in *Long Day's Journey into Night* (Center Stage, Baltimore, Md., 1969–70 season; and again, at the Actors Studio, N.Y.C., Dec. 10, 1973).

Films. Miss Nathan appeared in *Teacher's Pet* (Par., 1958); *The Young Savages* (UA, 1961); *The Outsider* (U, 1961); and *Klute* (WB, 1971).

Television. She has appeared on Playhouse 90 (CBS); Studio One (CBS); The Nurses (CBS); Breaking Point (ABC); Arrest and Trial (ABC); Pursuit (CBS); Tyranny (ABC); Alfred Hitchcock Presents (CBS); and re-created her Bway role in a television adaptation of *The Investigation* (NBC, Apr. 14, 1967).

Awards. Miss Nathan received the Clarence Derwent Award, for best performance in a non-featured role, for *Anastasia* (1955).

NATWICK, MILDRED. Actress. b. June 19, 1908, Baltimore, Md., to Joseph and Mildred Marion (Dawes) Natwick. Attended Bryn Mawr Sch., Baltimore; Bennett Sch., Millbrook (N.Y.). Address: 1001 Park Ave., New York, NY 10028, tel. (212) TR 9-6416.

Theatre. Miss Natwick made her stage debut as Widow Quin in *The Playboy of the Western World* (Vagabond Th., Baltimore, Md., 1929); followed by appearances with the Natl. Junior Theatre Co., Washington, D.C.

She made her N.Y.C. debut as Mrs. Noble in *Carry Nation* (Biltmore, Oct. 29, 1932), and her London debut as Aunt Mabel in *The Day I Forgot* (Globe, May 12, 1933).

She played Drusilla Thorpe in *Amourette* (Henry Miller's Th., N.Y.C., Sept. 27, 1933); Pura in *Spring in Autumn* (Henry Miller's Th., Oct. 24, 1933); Mrs. McFie in *The Wind and the Rain* (Ritz, Feb. 1, 1934); Mrs. Venables in *The Distaff Side* (Booth, Sept. 25, 1934); May Beringer in *Night in the House* (Booth, Nov. 7, 1935); Mrs. Wyler in *End of Summer* (Guild, Feb. 17, 1936); Ethel in *Love from a Stranger* (Fulton, Sept. 29, 1936); Miss Proserpine Garnett in *Candida* (Empire, Mar. 10, 1937); the Widow Weeks in *Missouri Legend* (Empire, Sept. 19, 1938); Bess in *Stars in Your Eyes* (Majestic, Feb. 9, 1939); Mother McGlory in *Christmas Eve* (Henry Miller's Th., Dec. 27, 1939); Milly in *The Lady Who Came to Stay* (Maxine Elliott's Th., Jan. 2, 1941); and Madame Arcati in *Blithe Spirit* (Morosco, Nov. 5, 1941).

Miss Natwick repeated her role as Miss Proserpine Garnett in *Candida* (Shubert, Apr. 27, 1942; Cort, Apr. 3, 1946); Widow Quin in *The Playboy of the Western World* (Booth, Oct. 26, 1946); and Dolly Talbo in *The Grass Harp* (Martin Beck Th., Mar. 27, 1952).

She appeared as Volumnia in *Coriolanus* (Phoenix, Jan. 19, 1954); Madame St. Pe in *The Waltz of the Toreadors* (Coronet, Jan. 17, 1957); Kathie Morrow in *The Day the Money Stopped* (Belasco, Feb. 2, 1958); Miriam in *The Firstborn* (Coronet, Apr. 30, 1958); the Mother of Marie-Paule, Angele, and Armand's Mother in *The Good Soup* (Plymouth, Mar. 2, 1960); Charlotte Orr in *Critic's Choice* (Ethel Barrymore Th., Dec. 14, 1960); Mrs. Banks in *Barefoot in the Park* (Biltmore Th., Oct. 23, 1963); appeared in *Our Town* (ANTA, N.Y.C., Nov. 27, 1969); and *Landscape* (Forum, Lincoln Ctr., N.Y.C., Apr. 2, 1970); and played Ida in *70 Girls 70* (Broadhurst, N.Y.C., Apr. 15, 1971).

Films. Miss Natwick has appeared in *The Long Voyage Home* (UA, 1940); *The Enchanted Cottage,* (RKO, 1945); *Yolanda and the Thief* (MGM, 1945); *The Late George Apley* (20th-Fox, 1947); *A Woman's Vengeance* (U, 1947); *Three Godfathers* (MGM, 1948); *The Kissing Bandit* (MGM, 1948); *She Wore a Yellow Ribbon* (RKO, 1949); *Cheaper by the Dozen* (20th-Fox, 1950); *The Quiet Man* (Rep., 1952); *Against All Flags* (U, 1952); *The Trouble with Harry* (Par., 1955); *The Court Jester* (Par., 1956); *Teenage Rebel* (20th-Fox, 1956); *Tammy and the Bachelor* (U, 1957); *Barefoot in the Park* (Par., 1966); *If It's Tuesday, This Must Be Belgium* (UA, 1969); *Trilogy* (AI, 1969); *The Maltese Bippy* (MGM, 1969); and *Daisy Miller* (Par., 1974).

Television and Radio. On radio, she played in *Diary of a Saboteur* (Cavalcade of America, NBC, Mar. 1, 1943). On television, she appeared as Martha Brewster in *Arsenic and Old Lace* (Hallmark Hall of Fame, NBC, Feb. 5, 1962); appeared as Madame Arcati in *Blithe Spirit;* played in *Eloise; The House without a Christmas Tree* (CBS); *Thanksgiving Treasure* (CBS); *Money to Burn* (CBS); and *Do Not Fold, Spindle, or Mutilate* (NBC); and, with Helen Hayes, co-starred in her own series, The Snoop Sisters (NBC).

Recreation. Swimming, tennis, reading, theatre-going.

NEAGLE, ANNA. Actress, producer, singer. b. Marjorie Robertson, Oct. 20, 1904, London, England, to Herbert William and Florence (Neagle) Robertson. Father, Capt., British Maritime Service. Attended St. Alban's H.S., Herts, England; Wordsworth's Physical Training Coll. Studied dancing with Mme. Espinosa dnd Gwladys Dillon. Married Aug. 9, 1943, to Herbert Wilcox, C.B.E., film producer, director. Relative in theatre: brother, Stuart Robertson, songwriter, singer. Member of AEA; SAG; F.A.N.Y. Regimental Club; King George V Memorial Foundation (mbr. of exec. council, 1953); Edith Cavell Homes of Rest for Nurses (mbr. of council).

Pre-Theatre. Dance instructor, gym instructor.

Theatre. Miss Neagle made her debut as a dancer in *The Wonder Tales* (Ambassadors', London, Dec. 22, 1917); appeared in the chorus of *Charlot's Revue* (Prince of Wales's, Sept. 23, 1924); in *Rose Marie* (Drury Lane, Mar. 20, 1925); a revival of *Bubbly* (Duke of York's, June 29, 1925); *The Charlot Show of 1926* (Prince of Wales's, Oct. 5, 1926); *The Desert Song* (Drury Lane, Apr. 7, 1927); *This Year of Grace* (London Pavilion, Mar. 22, 1928); danced in *Wake Up and Dream* (London Pavilion, Mar. 27, 1929), and made her N.Y.C. debut in this production (Selwyn, Dec. 30, 1929).

Miss Neagle played Mary Clyde-Burkin in *Stand Up and Sing* (London Hippodrome, Mar. 5, 1931); Olivia in *Twelfth Night* (Open Air, May 28, 1934); Rosalind in *As You Like It* (Open Air); and the title role in *Peter Pan* (London Palladium, Dec. 24, 1937); during WW II, toured England and the Continent for ENSA, appearing in such productions as *Victoria Regina* and *French Without Tears;* toured as Emma Woodhouse in *Emma* (1944), also playing this role in London (St. James's, Feb. 7, 1945); toured as Carol Beaumont, Nell Gwyn, Victoria and Lillian Grey in *The Glorious Days* (1952), and also played these roles in London (Palace, Feb. 28, 1953); appeared as Stella Felby in *The More the Merrier* (Strand, Feb. 2, 1960); Ruth Peterson in a tryout of *Nothing Is for Free* (Royal, Brighton, May 29, 1961); and Jane Canning in a six month, pre-West End tour of *Person Unknown* (1963).

Miss Neagle played Lady Hadwell in *Charley Girl* (Adelphi, London, Dec. 15, 1965) for 2047 of the production's 2,202 performances (over five years), then played the show in Australia (Her Majesty's, Melbourne, Sept. 25, 1971); played Sue Smith in *No, No, Nanette* (Drury Lane, London, May 15, 1973); and succeeded (Duke of York's, Feb. 1975) Celia Johnson as Dame Sybil Hathaway in *The Dame of Sark* (Wyndham's, Oct. 17, 1974), also playing this role on a British and Canadian tour (including O'Keefe Ctr., Toronto, Canada, Oct. 13–25, 1975).

Films. Miss Neagle appeared in thirty-six films, all but four of which (note *) were produced and directed by Herbert Wilcox, her husband. She made her debut in *Should a Doctor Tell** (British Lion, 1930), followed by *The Chinese Bungalow** (Neo-Art, 1930); *Good Night Vienna* (British and Dominion Film Corp., 1932; titled *Magic Night,* in the US); *Flag Lieutenant* (Brit. & Dom., 1932); *The Little Damozel* (Brit. & Dom., 1933); *Bitter Sweet* (Brit. & Dom., 1933); *The Queen's Affair* (Brit. & Dom., 1934; US, *Runaway Queen*); *Nell Gwyn* (Brit. & Dom., 1935); *Limelight* (Wilcox, 1935; US, *Backstage*); *Peg of Old Drury* (Brit. & Dom., 1935); *The Three Maxims* (Cie Pathe), 1935; US, *The Show Goes On*); *Victoria the Great* (Imperator, 1937); *London Melody* (Wilcox, 1937; US, *Girls in the Street*); *Sixty Glorious Years* (Imperator, 1938; US, *Queen of Destiny*); *Nurse Edith Cavell* (RKO, 1939); *No, No, Nanette* (RKO, 1940); *Irene* (RKO, 1940); *Sunny* (RKO, 1941); *They Flew Alone* (Imperator, 1942; US, *Wings and the Woman*); *Forever and a Day** (RKO, 1943); *The Yellow Canary* (Imperator, 1943); *I Lived in Grosvenor Square* (Assoc. Brit., 1945; US, *A Yank in London*); *Piccadilly Incident* (Assoc. Brit., 1946); *The Courtneys of Curzon Street* (Imperadio, 1947; US, *The Courtney Affair*); *Spring in Park Lane* (Imperadio, 1948); *Elizabeth of Ladymead* (Imperadio, 1949); *Maytime in Mayfair* (Imperadio, 1949); *Odette* (Imperadio, 1950); *The Lady with the Lamp* (Imperadio, 1951); *Derby Day* (Imperadio, 1952; US, *Four Against Fate*); *Lilacs in the Spring* (Everest, 1954; US, *Let's Make Up*); *The King's Rhapsody* (Everest, 1955); *My Teenage Daughter* (Everest, 1956; US, *Teenage Bad Girl*); *No Time for Tears** (Assoc. Brit., 1957); produced with her husband, who also directed, *These Dangerous Years* (Everest, 1957; US, *Dangerous Youth*) and *Wonderful Things!* (Everest, 1958); appeared in *The Man Who Wouldn't Talk* (Everest, 1958); produced with her husband, who also directed, *The Heart of a Man* (Everest, 1959); and appeared in, as well as co-produced with her husband, who directed, *The Lady Is a Square* (Everest, 1959).

Night Clubs. Miss Neagle danced at the Trocadero (London, 1928–29).

Published Works. She wrote her autobiography, *There's Always Tomorrow* (W. H. Allen, London, 1974).

Awards. She received the Cup of Nations Award (Vienna, Austria) for her performance in *Victoria the Great* (1937); the National Film Awards for her performances in *Spring in Park Lane* (1949) and *Odette* (1951).

The Order of Commander of the British Empire (C.B.E.) was conferred upon her in the New Year's Honours (1952), and she was created a Dame of the British Empire in the Birthday Honours (1970).

NEAL, PATRICIA. Actress. b. Patsy Louise Neal, Jan. 20, 1926, Packard, Ky., to William B. and Eura (Petrey) Neal. Father, transportation manager. Grad. Knoxville (Tenn.) H.S., 1943; attended Northwestern Univ., 1943–45. Studied acting with George Shdanoff, Calif., 1948–52; Actors Studio, N.Y.C. (member, 1947–to date). Married July 2, 1953, to Roald Dahl, writer; one son, three daughters. Member of AEA; AFTRA; SAG; Pi Beta Phi.

Pre-Theatre. Doctor's assistant, employee in hotels and restaurants.

Theatre. Miss Neal first performed at the Barter Th. (Abindon, Va., 1942); subsequently appeared at the Eaglesmere (Pa.) Playhouse (Summer 1945). Her first Bway assignment (Oct. 1945) was as understudy to Martha Scott as Sally, and to Vicki Cummings as Olive in *The Voice of the Turtle* (Morosco, Dec. 5, 1943); was understudy for K. T. Stevens as Sally in the Chicago (Ill.) Co., of the same play, replacing (Dec. 31, 1945) Vivian Vance in the role of Olive for three weeks. She appeared as Claire Walker in the pre-Bway tryout of *Bigger Than Barnum* (opened Wilbur, Boston, Mass., Apr. 22, 1946; closed there Apr. 27, 1946); and as "Wildcat" in the summer stock tryout of *Devil Take a Whittler* (Westport Country Playhouse, Conn., Summer 1946).

Miss Neal made her Bway debut as Regina Giddens in *Another Part of the Forest* (Fulton, Nov. 20, 1946); spent a season at Elitch Gardens (Denver, Colo., Summer 1947). She played Martha Dobie in *The Children's Hour* (Coronet, N.Y.C., Dec. 18, 1952); Lady Teazle in *The School for Scandal* (Th. de Lys, June 1953); and the Blacksmith in *The Scarecrow* (Th. de Lys, June 16, 1953).

She appeared as Nancy Fallon in *Roomful of Roses* (Playhouse, N.Y.C., Oct. 17, 1955); Catherine Holly in *Suddenly, Last Summer* (Arts, London, Sept. 16, 1958); and Mrs. Keller in *The Miracle Worker* (Playhouse, N.Y.C., Oct. 19, 1959).

Films. Miss Neal made her debut in *John Loves*

Mary(WB, 1949); and appeared in *The Fountainhead* (WB, 1949); *The Hasty Heart* (WB, 1949); *Three Secrets* (WB, 1950); *Bright Leaf* (WB, 1950); *The Breaking Point*(WB, 1950); *Weekend with Father*(U, 1951); *The Day the Earth Stood Still* (20th-Fox, 1951); *Diplomatic Courier* (20th-Fox, 1952); *Something for the Birds* (20th-Fox, 1952); *The Washington Story* (MGM, 1952); *La Tua Donna* (1955); *A Face in the Crowd* (WB, 1957); *Breakfast at Tiffany's*(Par., 1961); *Hud* (Par., 1963); *Psyche 59* (Col., 1964); *In Harm's Way* (Par., 1965); *The Subject Was Roses* (MGM, 1968); *The Roadbuilder* (1970); *The Night Digger* (MGM, 1971); and *Baxter!* (Natl. Gen., 1973).

Television. She appeared in *The Stronger* (Play of the Week, WNTA, 1960); *The Magic and the Loss* (Play of the Week, WNTA, 1961); The Untouchables (Ind., 1964); Espionage (Ind., 1965); Ben Casey (ABC, 1966); Checkmate (Ind., 1967); *The Homecoming* (CBS, 1971); *Life, Death and the American Woman* (ABC, 1972); *Things in Their Season* (GE Th., CBS, Nov. 27, 1974); and as the Mother in *Eric* (NBC, Nov. 1975). She has also appeared on Playhouse 90 (CBS).

On English television, she played roles in *Clash by Night; The Country Girl; The Royal Family; Biography;* and *The Days and Nights of Bee-Bee Fenstermaker.*

Awards. For her performance as Regina Giddens in *Another Part of the Forest,* Miss Neal received the Antoinette Perry (Tony) Award, the *Look* Magazine Award, the *Theatre World* Award, the Donaldson Award for debut performance, and won the *Variety* NY Drama Critics Poll (1947). In 1962, she was voted the most outstanding woman under forty from Tennessee. For her performance in *Hud* (1963), she received the NY Film Critics Award, the Academy (Oscar) Award, and was voted best foreign actress by the British Academy. She was again voted best foreign actress by the British Academy for her performance in *In Harm's Way* (1965).

NEAL, WALTER. Stage manager, actor, account executive. b. Walter Lee Neal, Mar. 22, 1920, Frostburg, Md., to James E. and Mary (Cook) Neal. Father, contractor, bricklayer; mother, seamstress, amateur actress. Grad. Univ. of Md., College Park, B.A. (Charles B. Hale award) 1942; attended Catholic Univ. of America, Summer 1941. Studied at Amer. Th. Wing, N.Y.C., 1946–47. Served USN, 1942–46; rank, Lt. (d) USNR Ret. Member of AEA; SAG; AFTRA; The Lambs (1950–63); Omicron Delta Kappa; Alpha Psi Omega. Address: (home) 61 W. 9th St., New York, NY 10011, tel. (212) GR 3-7396; (bus.) Marketing Concepts, Inc., 598 Madison Ave., New York, NY 10022, tel. (212) PL 1-4060.

Pre-Theatre. Journeyman meat-cutter.

Theatre. Mr. Neal made his debut as a child in *Uncle Tom's Cabin* (Lyric Th., Frostburg, Md., 1926); his Bway debut as a walk-on in the American Repertory Co. productions of *Henry VIII* (International, Nov. 6, 1946); *Yellow Jack* (International, Feb. 27, 1947); and *Alice in Wonderland* (International, Apr. 5, 1947), in which he was understudy for both ends of the White Knight's horse; Tweedledum and the Frog Footman (Boston Opera House, Mass., 1947); toured as stage manager for the Amer. Wing Hospital Tour series (1946–47); in stock, appeared and was stage manager at the Chapel Playhouse, Great Neck, L.I., N.Y. (Summer 1947); Berwyn Playhouse, Pa., (Winter 1947–48); performed and was manager and producer at the Sail Loft Th., Germantown, N.Y. (Summer 1948); performed and was lighting designer and stage manager at the Grist Mill Playhouse, Andover, N.J. (Summers 1950–54); Empress Playhouse, St. Louis, Mo., (Winter 1951–52); and Savoy Th., Asbury Park, N.J. (1953).

He was stage manager for the national tour of *My Three Angels* (opened Playhouse, Wilmington, Del., 1953; closed Harris, Chicago, Ill., 1954); and the western tour of the Ford Tractor (industrial) Show (1950); assistant stage manager for *Peter Pan* (Winter Garden, N.Y.C., Oct. 20, 1954); production manager for *The Diary of Anne Frank* (Cort, Oct. 5, 1955), and the national tour (opened Huntington Hartford, Hollywood, Calif., July 29, 1957; closed Owens Aud., Charlotte, N.C., Dec. 20, 1958); *Small War on Murray Hill* (Ethel Barrymore Th., N.Y.C., Jan. 3, 1957); and assistant stage manager for *A Hole in the Head* (Plymouth, Feb. 28, 1957). He was stage manager, lighting designer and appeared at the John Drew Th. (Easthampton, L.I., N.Y., Summer 1958); stage manager for *The Nervous Set* (Henry Miller's Th., N.Y.C., May 12, 1959); assistant stage manager for *The Cold Wind and the Warm* (Morosco, Dec. 8, 1959); stage manager for *The Fighting Cock* (ANTA, Dec. 8, 1959); *A Thurber Carnival* (ANTA, Feb. 26, 1960); *Once There Was a Russian* (Music Box, Feb. 18, 1961); and *Kean* (Bway Th., Nov. 2, 1961).

Films. He appeared as the Husband in a March of Time film, *Wanted: More Homes* (1946); and as the Service Manager in a General Motors training film (1960).

Television. He made his debut on the Fred Waring Show (NBC, 1949); was stage manager of *Peter Pan* (NBC, 1956); appeared on the Hallmark Hall of Fame production of *The Joke and the Valley* (NBC, 1962); *Cyrano de Bergerac* (NBC, 1963); and in commercials (1962–63).

Other Activities. Mr. Neal has been stage manager, operations director, and now senior vice-president of Marketing Concepts, Inc. (1962–to date). He is also vice-president of Visamation, Inc., and a director of Associated Marketing Concepts Limited of London, England.

Recreation. Cooking.

NEDERLANDER, JAMES. Theatre owner. b. James Morton Nederlander, Mar. 31, 1922, Detroit, Mich., to David and Shara Nederlander. Father, theatre owner. Grad. Pontiac H.S., Mich.; attended Detroit (Mich.) Inst. of Tech.; University of North Dakota. Married Fed. 12, 1968, to Charlene Saunders; one son. Served WW II, USAAF. Member of ATPAM; IATSE; Actors' Fund (life mbr.); The Lambs; Variety Club of Detroit; Franklin Hills Country Club; Standard City Club; League of New York Theatres (former mbr. of bd. of gov.). Address: (home) 5233 E. Arroyo Rd., Scottsdale, AZ 85253; (bus.) 1564 Broadway, New York, NY 10036, tel. (212) 765-3906.

Theatre. Mr. Nederlander has been the owner of the Fisher Th. (Detroit, Mich.); Shubert Th. (Detroit, Mich.); Lyceum Th. (Minneapolis, Minn.); Erlanger Th. (Chicago, Ill.); the McVickers Th. (Chicago, Ill.); and The Palace, Brooks Atkinson and Uris Ths. (N.Y.C.). He has also been a director of the Independent Booking Office, and was treasurer (1963).

Mr. Nederlander was on the managerial staff of the USAAF's production, *Winged Victory* (44 St. Th., N.Y.C., Nov. 20, 1943).

Other Activities. Mr. Nederlander is a member of the board of America Ship Building (Cleveland) and is a partner in the New York Yankees.

Recreation. Golf and tennis.

NELSON, BARRY. Actor. b. Robert Nielson, Oakland, Calif., to Trygve and Betsy (Christophsen) Nielson. Grad. Univ. of California, at Berkeley, B.A. Married to Teresa Celli. Served USAAF; rank, Staff Sgt. Member of AEA; AFTRA; SAG; AGVA. Address: William Morris Agency Inc., 1350 Ave. of the Americas, New York, NY 10019, tel. (212) 586-5100.

Theatre. Mr. Nelson made his N.Y.C. debut as Bobby Grills in *Winged Victory* (44 St. Th., Nov. 20, 1943); succeeded Lloyd Bridges as Joe Bannion in the pre-Bway tryout of *Heartsong* (opened Shubert, New Haven, Conn., Feb. 27, 1947; closed Walnut St. Th., Philadelphia, Pa., Mar. 29, 1947); subsequently played Peter Sloan in *Light Up the Sky* (Royale, N.Y.C., Nov. 18, 1948); Gus Hammer in *The Rat Race* (Ethel Barrymore Th., Dec. 22, 1949); Donald Gresham in *The Moon Is Blue* (Henry Miller's Th., Mar. 8, 1951); and Don Emerson in *Wake Up, Darling* (Ethel Barrymore Th., May 2, 1956). He played Will Stockdale in *No Time for Sergeants* (Her Majesty's, London, Aug. 23, 1956); Bob McKellaway in *Mary, Mary* (Helen Hayes Th., N.Y.C., Mar. 8, 1961); and appeared in *Cactus Flower* (Royale, N.Y.C., Dec. 8, 1965); *The Only Game in Town* (Broadhurst, N.Y.C., May 20, 1968); and *Seascape* (Shubert, N.Y.C., Jan. 26, 1975).

Films. Mr. Nelson has appeared in *A Guy Named Joe* (MGM, 1943); *Winged Victory* (20th-Fox, 1944); *The Man with My Face* (UA, 1951); *The First Traveling Lady* (RKO, 1956); *Mary, Mary* (WB, 1963); *Airport* (U, 1970); and *Pete 'n' Tillie* (U, 1973).

Television. Mr. Nelson starred in the series The Hunter; and My Favorite Husband (CBS).

Recreation. Traveling, reading, the arts.

NELSON, KENNETH. Actor. b. Kenneth Barro Nelson, Mar. 24, 1930, Rocky Mount, N.C., to Frederick and Rachel (Barro) Nelson. Father, civil court judge. Grad. Brackenridge H.S., San Antonio, Tex., (with honors) 1950. Studied acting with Paul Baker at Baylor Univ., 1950–51; Uta Hagen, N.Y.C., 1953–58; singing with Keith Davis, N.Y.C. (1958–to date). Member of AEA; SAG; AFTRA; AGVA.

Theatre. Mr. Nelson made his Bway debut as Willie Baxter in *Seventeen* (Broadhurst Th., June 21, 1951); played the title role in the pre-Bway tour of *Solomon Grundy* (opened Rochester, N.Y., Aud., Aug. 1953), which closed out of town; appeared in the dual role of Twins in Jean Cocteau's *The Typewriter* (Tempo, N.Y.C., Sept. 1955); the revue *Kaleidoscope* (Provincetown Playhouse, Mass., Jan. 13, 1957); played the Boy in *The Fantasticks* (Sullivan St. Playhouse, N.Y.C., May 3, 1960); was standby for Anthony Newley as Littlechap in *Stop the World—I Want To Get Off* (Shubert, Oct. 3, 1962), for whom he substituted (Feb. 22, 1963, matinee), and on four other occasions, and in which role he succeeded (Playhouse, Wilmington, Del., Sept. 30, 1963) Joel Gray in the national touring company (opened Pabst, Milwaukee, Wis., Mar. 25, 1963; closed, Forrest, Philadelphia, Pa., Apr. 18, 1964).

Mr. Nelson co-directed and played Littlechap in *Stop the World—I Want To Get Off* (Music Circus, Sacramento, Calif., Aug. 3, 1964); played Bob in *Royal Flush* (pre-Bway tour, Dec. 31, 1964–Jan. 23, 1965); Arthur in *Camelot* (Music Circus, Sacramento, Calif., June 17, 1965); directed and played Littlechap in *Stop the World, I Want To Get Off* (Coconut Grove Playhouse, Miami, Fla., July 3, 1965; Paper Mill Playhouse, Millburn, N.J., Nov. 9, 1965); played Cocky in *The Roar of the Greasepaint—The Smell of the Crowd* (Coconut Grove Playhouse, Miami, Fla., June 28, 1966; Paper Mill Playhouse, Millburn, N.J., Aug. 1, 1966); Arthur Kips in *Half-a-Sixpence* (tour, Summer 1966); repeated his performance in *Half-a-Sixpence* (Coconut Grove Playhouse, Miami, Fla., Summer 1967); played Michael in *The Boys in the Band* (Theatre Four, N.Y.C., Apr. 14, 1968); and Sakini in *Lovely Ladies, Kind Gentlemen* (Majestic, Dec. 28, 1970).

Films. He made his debut playing Michael in *The Boys in the Band* (Natl. Gen., 1970).

Television. He made his debut as Henry Aldrich in The Aldrich Family (NBC, Jan. 1952–Nov. 1952); has appeared on Studio One (CBS, 1954, 1955, 1956, 1957) and Kraft Th. (NBC, 1955, 1956, 1957); in *New York Scrapbook* (Play of the Week, WNTA, 1961); and on an Art Carney Special, *All About Love* (CBS, Sept. 1960).

Night Clubs. He performed in the revue *Night-Cap* (The Showplace, N.Y., Apr.–Dec. 1958); and at the Hotel Carillon (Miami Beach, Fla., June 1959–Jan. 1960).

Recreation. Swimming, horseback riding, painting, reading.

NELSON, NOVELLA. Actress, director, producer, singer. b. Novella Christine Nelson, Dec. 17, 1939, Brooklyn, N.Y., to James A. and Evelyn Elizabeth (Hines) Nelson. Educ. Brooklyn public schools; Brooklyn Coll. Professional training at American Academy of Dramatic Arts; the American Mime Th. under the direction of Paul Curtis; Richard Altman. Relatives in theatre: cousins,

Hines & Hines & Dad, nightclub and vaudeville act. Member of AEA; AFTRA; SAG; SSD&C. Address: (home) 160 W. 95th St., New York, NY 10025, tel. (212) 850-5445; (bus.) NY Shakespeare Festival, 425 Lafayette St., New York, NY 10003, tel. (212) 677-1750.

Pre-Theatre. Miss Nelson was executive secretary and then administrator, Oak Hill Industries.

Theatre. Miss Nelson first appeared on stage at Brooklyn Coll. (1958–59). She made her professional debut touring as Flossie in *To Follow the Phoenix* (Dec. 1961–Apr. 1962); went on tour (Jan. 28, 1964) as the Woman in *In White America;* repeated the role in the play's return engagement off-Bway (Players Th., N.Y.C., May 18, 1965) and with the American Conservatory Th., Pittsburgh, Pa. (June 1965). She appeared with the American Conservatory Th. as Doriana in *Tartuffe* (Seattle, Wash., Nov. 1965); was Madame Tango in a revival of *House of Flowers* (Th. de Lys, N.Y.C., Jan. 28, 1968); first appeared on Bway (St. James, July 1968) as standby for Pearl Bailey as Dolly in *Hello, Dolly!;* was Vanity in *Horseman, Pass By* (Fortune Th., Jan. 15, 1969); and appeared with the Theatre Company of Boston in a program of Ed Bullins's plays, creating the role of Stella in *The Corner* (May 22, 1969). She also played Lucy Brown in *The Threepenny Opera* (Atlanta Repertory, Atlanta, Ga., Sept. 1969); Missy in *Purlie* (Broadway Th., Mar. 15, 1970); and directed *Nigger Nightmare* (Public Th., Nov. 1970).

Miss Nelson has been a consultant to the producer, Public Th. (Sept. 21, 1971–to date); was executive producer of the Sunday afternoon theatre series at Public Th. (1971–72); directed *Sister Son/ji* on the program Black Visions (Public Th., Apr. 4, 1972); again played Stella in *The Corner* (Public Th., Apr. 1973); and directed *Les Femmes Noires* (Public Th., Feb. 21, 1974).

Television. Miss Nelson appeared in *Harriet Tubman* (CBS, 1965).

Night Clubs. Miss Nelson appeared at the hungry i (San Francisco, Calif., 1966); Hilly's (N.Y.C., 1968); Village Vanguard (N.Y.C., Nov. 1969); and Reno Sweeney (N.Y.C., Apr., Aug., Nov.–Dec. 1973; Mar. 4–15, 1975).

Concerts. In 1968, Miss Nelson made her concert debut at Philharmonic Hall (later Avery Fisher Hall), N.Y.C.; sang on a national college tour (1973–74); appeared with Freddie Hubbard as special guest (Avery Fisher Hall, Apr. 20, 1975).

Published Works. Among her published works are the poems "Deep" and "I" (both 1974) and the songs "Silences," "Dear, Gee, See!," and "Words, Ooh" (all 1974).

Discography. Miss Nelson recorded the album *Novella Nelson* (Arcana, 1970).

NELSON, RAYMOND. House manager, treasurer. b. Raymond Jacob Nelson, Nov. 16, 1898, Chicago, Ill., to Henry Peter and Margaret Nelson. Father, sea captain. Grad. Berendo H.S., Los Angeles, Calif., 1916; Isaac Woodbury Bus. Coll., Los Angeles, Calif., 1918. Married Dec. 28, 1925, to Florence Nelson; one son. Served USN, 1923; rank, Seaman. Member of Treasurers Union, ATPAM. Address: (home) 4373 Irvine Ave., Studio City, CA tel. (213) 762-4381; (bus.) 427 W. 5th St., Los Angeles, CA 90052, tel. (213) MA 5-2581.

Pre-Theatre. Railroad work, engineering.

Theatre. From 1954–68 Mr. Nelson was house manager for the Los Angeles Civic Light Opera Association. Since his retirement in 1968, he has been associated with Opera in English, sponsored by the Los Angeles Bd. of Education, which plays to about 60,000 school children each Spring.

His first work in the theatre was as assistant treasurer of the Figueroa Playhouse (Los Angeles, Calif.), becoming treasurer in 1926. He was treasurer at the Vine St. Theatre in Hollywood (1928); at the El Capitan Theatre (1929–42); for the Hollywood Playhouse (1942–50), becoming manager as well as treasurer in 1949. Mr. Nelson was also manager and treasurer for a production of *Life with Father* (Hollywood Music Box Th., 1942).

NEMIROFF, ROBERT. Playwright, producer. b. New York City. Grad. New York Univ., M.A. Married 1953 to Lorraine Hansberry (dec.). Member of Artists Civil Rights Assistance Fund (bd. of dir.).

Pre-Theatre. Publishing, songwriting.

Theatre. Mr. Nemeroff was co-producer, with Burton C. D'Lughoff, of *Kicks and Company* (Arie Crown Th., Chicago, Oct. 11, 1961) which he wrote with Oscar Brown, Jr. With Mr. D'Lughoff and J. I. Jahre, he subsequently presented *The Sign in Sidney Brustein's Window* (Longacre, N.Y.C., Oct. 15, 1964); wrote and, with Mr. D'Lughoff, produced *Postmark Zero* (Brooks Atkinson Th., Nov. 1, 1965); adapted, and, with Mr. D'Lughoff and others, produced *To Be Young, Gifted and Black* (Cherry Lane Th., Jan. 2, 1969); adapted the final text of Lorraine Hansberry's *Les Blancs* (Longacre, Nov. 15, 1970); and, with Charlotte Zaltzberg, wrote the book for the musical comedy *Raisin* (world premiere, Arena Stage, Washington, D.C., May 23, 1973), which he subsequently produced in its move to Bway (46 St. Th., N.Y.C., Oct. 18, 1973; moved to Lunt-Fontanne, Jan. 14, 1975).

Discography. Mr. Nemiroff wrote "Cindy, Oh Cindy.".

Awards. Mr. Nemiroff received the Antoinette Perry (Tony) Award (1973–74) for *Raisin*.

NESBITT, CATHLEEN. Actress. b. Cathleen Mary Nesbitt, Nov. 24, 1888, Liskeard, Eng., to Capt. Thomas and Cathrine (Parry) Nesbitt. Father, Naval Officer. Attended Victoria Sch., Belfast, Ire., 1900–04; Ecole Secondaire, Lisieux, Fr., 1905–06; Univ. of Paris, 1906–07; Univ. of London, 1908–09. Studied for stage with Rosina Filippi (1910–11). Married Nov. 30, 1922, to Cecil B. Ramage; one son, one daughter. Relatives in theatre; brother, Tom Nesbitt, (dec. 1926), actor; niece, Prudence Nesbitt, television producer. Member of AEA; AFTRA; SAG.

Theatre. Miss Nesbitt made her stage debut as Angela in *The Cabinet Minister* (Court Th., London, Oct. 21, 1910); played Mrs. Wilton in *John Gabriel Borkman* (Court, Jan. 26, 1911); and Mrs. Borlasse in *The Master of Mrs. Chilvers* (Royalty, Apr. 1911).

With the Irish Players (1911–12), she toured the US as Molly Byrne in *The Well of the Saints,* Honor Brady in *The Playboy of the Western World,* and Nora Burke in *The Shadow of the Glen;* and appeared with the company in Dublin, as Mrs. Carrigher in *The Family Failing* (Abbey, Mar. 1912).

She performed in *The Workhouse Ward* (Prince of Wales's, London, 1912); played Marcelle de Rochefort in *The Escape* and Vivien in *The Temptation of Sir Galahad* (Court, June 25, 1912); Perdita in *The Winter's Tale* (Savoy, Sept. 21, 1912); Freda in Galsworthy's *The Eldest Son* (Kingsway, Nov. 25, 1912); Euphemia in *The Waldies* (Haymarket, Dec. 8, 1912); Mary Ellen in *General John Regan* (Apollo, Jan. 9, 1913); and Madge Cray in *The Perfect Cure* (Apollo, June 17, 1913); Viola in *Twelfth Night* (Th. des Deux Masques, Paris, June 1913); the title role in *Deirdre of the Sorrows* (Little, London, 1913); Alice Whistler in *The Harlequinade* (St. James's, Sept. 1, 1913); Phoebe in *Quality Street* (Duke of York's, Nov. 25, 1913); Mrs. Denbigh in *Daughters of Ishmael* (King's Hall, Covent Garden, Mar. 1, 1914); and Peggy in a touring production of *A Butterfly on the Wheel* (commencing Aug. 1914).

Miss Nesbitt appeared as Martha in *Exchange* (Little, London, May 2, 1915); Mary Dean in *Mater* (Playhouse, June 4, 1915); Mabel Dredge in a stock production of *Quinneys* (Court, Liverpool, Sept. 1915); repeated the role (Maxine Elliott's Th., N.Y.C., Oct. 18, 1915); played Ruth Honeywill in *Justice* (Candler, Apr. 3, 1916); Julie Laxton in *Hush!* (Little, Oct. 3, 1916); and Leslie Crankshaw in *Such Is Life* (Princess, Nov. 25, 1916); with the Gertrude Kingston Repertory Co., appeared in two of five plays as the Queen in *The Queen's Enemies,* and as Varinka in *Great Catherine* (Maxine Elliott's Th., Dec. 18, 1916–Jan. 1917); Patricia Carleon in *Magic,* one of a double bill (Maxine Elliott's Th., Feb. 12, 1917); Kathleen in *The Very Minute* (Belasco, Apr. 9, 1917); in Chicago, appeared as Nan Carey and Ruth Brokton in *Cheating Cheaters* (1917–18); and played the Mermaid in *The Garden of Paradise* (Playhouse, N.Y.C., July, 1918); toured as Betty in *General Post* (1918); and appeared as Susan Blaine in *The Saving Grace* (Empire, N.Y.C., Sept. 30, 1918).

She played Jessica in *The Merchant of Venice* (Court, London, Oct. 9, 1919); the title role in *The Duchess of Malfi* (Lyric, Hammersmith, Nov. 23, 1919); Doralice in *Marriage à la Mode* (Lyric, Hammersmith, Feb. 8, 1920); Pamela in *Grierson's Way* (Ambassadors', Mar. 10, 1920); Marjorie Corbett in *The Grain of Mustard Seed* (Ambassadors', Apr. 20, 1920); Melisande in *The Romantic Age* (Comedy, Oct. 18, 1920); Belvidera in *Venice Preserved* (Lyric, Hammersmith, Nov. 28, 1920); appeared in Oxford as Cleopatra in *Antony and Cleopatra* Audrey in *Sweet William* (Shaftesbury, London, May 4, 1921); Ginevra in *The Love Thief* (Comedy, Sept. 6, 1921); Myrtle Carey in *The Rattlesnake* (Shaftesbury, Jan. 1922); Margaret Orme in *Loyalties* (St. Martin's, Mar. 8, 1922); Mrs. Dubedat in *The Doctor's Dilemma* (Everyman, Apr. 2, 1923); Amarillis in *The Faithful Shepherdess* (Shaftesbury, June 24, 1923); Hilda Norbury in *The Eye of Siva* (New, Aug. 8, 1923); Yasmin in *Hassan* (His Majesty's, Sept. 20, 1923); and Vera Farington in *This Marriage* (Comedy, May 7, 1924).

She played Emma Hunter in *The Blue Peter* (Prince's, Oct. 11, 1924); Mona in *Spring Cleaning* (St. Martin's, Jan. 29, 1925); Jessica Madras in *The Madras House* (Ambassadors', Nov. 30, 1925); Julia Dwyer in *Confessions* (Court, July 18, 1926); Malia in *Down Hill* (Prince's, July 26, 1926); and Florence Churchill in *The Constant Nymph* (New, Sept. 14, 1926).

Miss Nesbitt appeared as Rayetta Muir in *Diversion* (49 St. Th., N.Y.C., Jan. 11, 1928; Arts Th. Club, London, Sept. 26, 1928; Lily Shane in *The House of Women* ("Q", Sept. 3, 1928); Lady Myrtle in *Fame* (St. James's, Feb. 20, 1929); Mother Goddam in *The Shanghai Gesture* (Scala, May 12, 1929); Margaret Fairfield in *A Bill of Divorcement* (St. Martin's, July 9, 1929); Lady Panniford in *The Calendar* (Wyndham's, Sept. 18, 1929); Greta in *After All* (Arts, March 30, 1930); Stella de Gex in *His Excellency the Governor* (Kingsway, Apr. 28, 1930); Lady Porter in *The Way to Treat a Woman* (Duke of York's, June 11, 1930); Cora Drew in *Good Losers* (Whitehall, Feb. 16, 1931); and Lady Lebanon in *The Case of the Frightened Lady* (Wyndham's, Aug. 18, 1931).

She played Lady Paulina in *Sentenced* (Comedy, Feb. 15, 1932); Eloise Fontaine in *Marriage by Purchase* (Garrick, Mar. 24, 1932); Eunice Malvinetti in *Somebody Knows* (St. Martin's, May 12, 1932); Margaret Orme in *Loyalties* (Garrick, Aug. 22, 1932); appeared as Fraülein Von Nordeck in *Children in Uniform* (Duchess, Oct. 7, 1932); Lucia Brignac in *Maternité* (Daly's, Oct. 19, 1933); Enid Deckle in *The World of Light* (Playhouse, Dec. 4, 1933); Manuella in *Secret Orchard* (Arts, Apr. 29, 1934); Elizabeth in *King Richard III* (Open Air Th., June 26, 1934); Katherine in the Old Vic production of *The Taming of the Shrew* (Sadler's Wells, Jan. 1, 1935); Mrs. Hardcastle in *Love on the Dole* (Garrick, Jan. 30, 1935); Hilda Lester in *Ringmaster* (Shaftesbury, Mar. 11, 1935); succeeded (Mar. 1936) Louise Hampton as Harriet in *The Two Mrs. Carrolls* (Garrick, Feb. 24, 1936); played Mrs. Morant in *London After Dark* (Apollo, Apr. 7, 1937); Judith in *Land's End* (Westminster, Feb. 23, 1938); Madame Gautier in *Money Talks* (Lyceum, May 4, 1938); Countess Isabel in *Trumpeter, Play!* (Garrick, June 13, 1938); and Therese Raquin in *Thou Shalt Not . .* (Playhouse, Aug. 24, 1938).

She toured as Miss Rimmer in *The King of Nowhere* (opened Oct. 1938); toured Europe and Egypt with the Old Vic Co. (Jan.–Apr. 1939), as the Queen in *Hamlet,* the Queen of France in *Henry V,* and Lady Loddon in *Libel;* played Beatrice in *Much Ado About Nothing* (Open Air Th., London, June 3, 1939); Dionyza in *Pericles, Prince of Tyre* (Open Air Th., June 20, 1939); Alinda Howard in *Under One Roof* (Richmond, Mar. 11, 1940); Goneril in *King*

Lear (Old Vic, Apr. 15, 1940); Mrs. Cliveden-Banks in *Outward Bound* (New, Aug. 30, 1940); Mrs. Wislack in *On Approval* (Aldwych, Feb. 10, 1942), in which she had previously toured for 14 months; Mrs. Gordon in *We Are the People* ("Q", Aug. 25, 1942); and Delia Channing of *A Murder for Valentine* (Lyric, Mar. 22, 1944).

In 1944–45, she toured as Lady Lebanon in *The Case of the Frightened Lady* and as Lady Panniford in *The Calendar;* appeared as Mathilde Heiss in *The Shop at Sly Corner* (St. Martin's, London, Apr. 11, 1945); Principessa della Cercola in *Our Betters* (Playhouse, Oct. 3, 1946); Discretion in *The Pilgrim's Progress* (Covent Garden, July 19, 1948); the Nurse in *Medea* (Edinburgh Festival, Scot.; Globe, London, Sept. 29, 1948); and as Mrs. Mannering in *Breach of Marriage* (Duke of York's, Jan. 25, 1949).

Miss Nesbitt played Julia in *The Cocktail Party* (Henry Miller's Th., N.Y.C., Jan. 21, 1950); Alicia de St. Ephlam in *Gigi* (Fulton, Nov. 24, 1951); Margaret Dowager Duchess of Burgundy, in *The Player King* (Royal Court, Liverpool, Eng., Aug. 1952), which was also presented at the Edinburgh Festival; Lady Lannion in *The Uninvited Guest* (St. James's, London, May 27, 1953); and Maude Larrabee in *Sabrina Fair* (Natl., N.Y.C., Nov. 11, 1953; Palace, London, Aug. 4, 1954).

She appeared as Countess Gemini in *Portrait of a Lady* (ANTA, N.Y.C., Dec. 21, 1954); succeeded (Aug. 1955) Eugenie Leontovitch as the Dowager Empress in *Anastasia* (Lyceum, Dec. 29, 1954); played Mrs. Higgins in *My Fair Lady* (Mark Hellinger Th., Mar. 15, 1956); the Grand Duchess in *The Sleeping Prince* (Coronet, Nov. 1, 1956); succeeded Ruth Chatterton in the role of Mrs. St. Maugham in the national touring production of *The Chalk Garden* (opened Lobero, Santa Barbara, Calif., Sept. 6, 1956; closed McCarter, Princeton, N.J., Feb. 16, 1957); toured as Mrs. Venable in *Suddenly, Last Summer* (opened Warren, Atlantic City, N.J., Mar. 11, 1959; closed Civic, Chicago, Ill., May 30, 1959); in stock, played the Duchess in *Time Remembered,* Amanda in *The Glass Menagerie,* and Queen Sophie in *Royal Enclosure;* appeared as Clara in *A Second String* (Eugene O'Neill Th., N.Y.C., Apr. 13, 1960); and as Julia in *Romulus* (Music Box, Jan. 10, 1962).

She was Juliana Bordereau in *A Garden in the Sea* (Playhouse in the Park, Philadelphia, Pa., June 1962); the Dowager Lady Headleigh in *The Claimant* (Comedy Th., London, England, Apr. 30, 1964); the Mother in *Amazing Grace* (Mendelssohn Th., Ann Arbor, Mich., Dec. 1967); Amy in *The Family Reunion* (Yvonne Arnaud Th., Guildford, England, Mar. 1968); repeated her performance as Mrs. Higgins in *My Fair Lady* (Los Angeles Civic Light Opera, Music Ctr., Los Angeles, Calif., May–June 1969); played Fanny Cavendish in *The Royal Family* (Goodman Memorial Th., Chicago, Ill., Jan. 25, 1972); repeated her performance as Maude Larrabee in *Sabrina Fair* (Playhouse in the Park, Philadelphia, Pa., July 1972); and was Mrs. Voinitsky in *Uncle Vanya* (Circle in the Sqaure—Joseph E. Levine Th., N.Y.C., June 4, 1973).

Films. Since her debut as Lady Lebanon in *The Case of the Frightened Lady* (Eng., 1932), she has performed in *A Day at the Fair; Three Coins in the Fountain* (20th-Fox, 1954); *Desiree* (20th-Fox, 1954); *An Affair to Remember* (20th-Fox, 1957); *Separate Tables* (UA, 1959); *The Trygon Factor* (WB, 1969); and *Family Plot* (U, 1976).

Television. She has appeared on British television as Mrs. Alving in *Ghosts* (BBC, 1946); Mrs. Borkman in *John Gabriel Borkman* (BBC); in *The Style of the Countess* (Granada, Aug. 1970); and she was interviewed on Rupert Brooke (BBC, Jan. 1972).

In the US, she appeared on Studio One (CBS) in *You're Only Young Twice, Strange Companion, Split Level* (all 1955), *The Playwright and the Star* and *Bend in the Road* (both 1957); in *Reunion in Vienna* (Producers Showcase, NBC, 1955); on the Alcoa Hour (NBC) in *Undertow* (1955), *Sister* (1956), and *No License to Kill* (1957); on the US Steel Hour (CBS) in The Reward (1958), *A Time to Decide* (1960), and *Fair Young Ghost, The Old Lady Shows Her Medals,* and *The Many Ways of Heaven* (all 1963); on Play of the Week (NET) in *Thieves' Carnival* (1959), *The House of Bernardo Alba* (1960), and *The Wingless Victor* (1961); and in such specials as *Mrs. Miniver* (CBS, 1960) and *The Crucible* (CBS, May 4, 1967).

She also appeared in episodes of such series as Bronco (ABC, 1960); Adventures in Paradise (NBC, 1961); Naked City (ABC, 1961); Dr. Kildare (NBC, 1961); and regularly on The Farmer's Daughter (ABC, 1963–65).

NETTLETON, LOIS. Actress. b. Lois June Nettleton, Oak Park, Ill., to Edward L. and Virginia (Schaffer) Nettleton. Father, stationary engineer. Grad. Senn H.S., Chicago; studied at Goodman Memorial Th. Sch.; and Actors Studio (mbr., 1951–to date). Married Dec. 3, 1960, to Jean Shepherd, actor, humorist, writer (marr. dis.). Relative in theatre: cousin, John Nettleton, actor. Member of AEA; SAG; AFTRA.

Theatre. Miss Nettleton made her stage debut at eleven as the Father in the operetta *Hansel and Gretel* (Greenbriar Community Ctr., Chicago, Ill.); her Bway debut as Laurie Hutchins in *The Biggest Thief in Town* (Mansfield Th., N.Y.C., Mar. 30, 1949); succeeded (1951) Kim Hunter as Luba in *Darkness at Noon* (Alvin, Jan. 13, 1951), in which she toured (opened McCarter, Princeton, N.J., Sept. 28, 1951); understudied Barbara Bel Geddes as Maggie in *Cat on a Hot Tin Roof* (Morosco, N.Y.C., Mar. 24, 1955), which she played several times; played Shelagh O'Connor in *God and Kate Murphy* (54 St. Th., Feb. 26, 1959); and Janet in *Silent Night, Lonely Night* (Morosco, Dec. 3, 1959).

At the American Shakespeare Festival, Miss Nettleton appeared as Nerissa in *The Merchant of Venice* and Hero in *Much Ado About Nothing* (Stratford, Conn., Summer 1957); and in stock, played Elektra in Giraudoux' *Elektra* (Olney Playhouse, Md., Summer 1960). She was Mrs. Julia Stevens in *The Wayward Stork* (46 St. Th., Jan. 19, 1966); played the roles of Catherine, Diane, Dorothy, and Maria in the pre-Bway tryout of *The Hemingway Hero* (opened Shubert Th., New Haven, Conn., Feb. 21, 1967; closed Wilbur, Boston, Mass., Mar. 4, 1967); replaced (June 19, 1973) Rosemary Harris as Blanche Du Bois in a revival of *A Streetcar Named Desire* (St. James Th., N.Y.C., Oct. 4, 1973); and was Amy in a Phoenix Th. revival of *They Knew What They Wanted* (Playhouse, Jan. 27, 1976).

Films. Miss Nettleton made her film debut in *Period of Adjustment* (MGM, 1962); subsequently, appeared in *Come Fly with Me* (MGM, 1963); *Mail Order Bride* (MGM, 1964); *Valley of Mystery* (U, 1967); *Bamboo Saucer* (World Entertainment, 1968); *The Good Guys and the Bad Guys* (WB, 1969); *Dirty Dingus Magee* (MGM, 1970); *Pigeons* (MGM, 1970); and *The Honkers* (UA, 1972).

Television and Radio. Miss Nettleton played Patsy in the radio-television simulcast of *The Brighter Day* (CBS 1954–56); and on television appeared in *Portrait of Emily Dickinson* and *Rendezvous* (both Camera Three, CBS, 1956); *Incident of Love* (Studio One, CBS, 1956); *The Complex Mummy* and *Accused of Murder* (both Armstrong Circle Th., CBS, 1958); the special *Meet Me in St. Louis* (CBS, 1959); *Duet for Two Hands* and *Emmanuel* (both Play of the Week, WNTA, 1960); *The Mind's Eye* (CBS TV Workshop, 1960); *The Woman in White* (Great Mysteries, NBC, 1960); *The Light That Failed* (Family Classics, CBS, 1961); and other television dramas.

She also performed on such series as Naked City (ABC, 1960, 1961); Twilight Zone (CBS, 1961); Route 66 (CBS, 1961, 1963); Gunsmoke (CBS, 1961, 1967, 1971); The Nurses (CBS, 1963); East Side/West Side (CBS, 1963); Dr. Kildare (NBC, 1964); Fugitive (ABC, 1964, 1966); The Doctors and the Nurses (CBS, 1964); Mr. Novak (NBC, 1965); Bonanza (NBC, 1966); The FBI (ABC, 1966, 1970); The Virginian (NBC, 1965, 1968); Then Came Bronson (NBC, 1969); Medical Center (CBS, 1970, 1972); and Name of the Game (NBC, 1970).

Awards. Miss Nettleton is the recipient of the Clarence Derwent Award for her performance as Shelagh O'Connor in *God and Kate Murphy* (1959) and the Laurel Award as one of the "top ten new female movie personalities" (1963).

NEVILLE, JOHN. Actor, director, theatre administrator. b. May 2, 1925, Willesden, London, England, to Reginald Daniel and Mabel Lillian (Fry) Neville. Father, truck driver. Attended Willesden Country Sch.; Chiswick Country Sch.; Royal Acad. of Dramatic Arts, 1947. Married Dec. 9, 1949, to Caroline Hooper, actress; three sons, three daughters. Served WW II, Royal Navy, two years. Member of British AEA. Address: Totteridge, Hertfordshire, England; 92 Hadley Road, New Barnet, Hertfordshire, England.

Pre-Theatre. Retail clerk.

Theatre. Mr. Neville made his N.Y.C. debut with the Old Vic Co. (Winter Garden Th.), portraying the title role in *Richard II* (Oct. 23, 1956); Romeo in *Romeo and Juliet* (Oct. 24, 1956); Macduff in *Macbeth* (Oct. 29, 1956); and Thersites in *Troilus and Cressida* (Dec. 26, 1956); and subsequently toured the US. He again toured the US with the Old Vic Co. (Sept. 1958–Feb. 1959), playing Sir Andrew Aguecheek in *Twelfth Night* (Broadway Th., N.Y.C., Dec. 9, 1958), the title role in *Hamlet* (Bway, Dec. 16, 1958), and Angelo in *Measure for Measure;* played Humbert Humbert in the pre-Bway tryout of the musical *Lolita* (opened Shubert, Philadelphia, Feb. 16, 1971; closed there for revision Feb. 27, 1971; re-opened Shubert, Boston, Mar. 23, 1971; closed there Mar. 27, 1971); and succeeded (May 13, 1975) Patrick Horgan, who succeeded John Wood, in the title role of *Sherlock Holmes* (Broadhurst, N.Y.C., Nov. 12, 1974).

He made his stage debut as a walk-on in an Old Vic production of *Richard II* (New, London, Apr. 23, 1947); at the Open Air Th., London, appeared as Chatillon in *King John* (July 6, 1947) and Lysander in *A Midsummer Night's Dream* (July 27, 1947); toured in *Justice* (Bergen and Oslo, Norway, 1948); played in repertory performances at Lowestoft (Mar. 1948–Dec. 1948); and with the Birmingham Repertory Th. (Jan. 1949–Mar. 1950). He appeared with the Bristol Old Vic Co. (Th. Royal, Bristol, Sept. 1950–June 1953), playing Gregers Werle in *The Wild Duck,* both Hugo and Frederic in *Ring Round the Moon,* Marlow in *She Stoops to Conquer,* Richard in *The Lady's Not for Burning,* (Dunois in *Saint Joan,* Edgar in *Venus Observed,* Valentine in *Two Gentlemen of Verona,* the Duke in *Measure for Measure* and the title role in *Henry V,* which subsequently played at the Old Vic, London (June 20, 1953). He became a member of the Old Vic Co. (Old Vic Th., London), portrayed Fortinbras in *Hamlet* (Sept. 14, 1953), Bertram in *All's Well That Ends Well* (Sept. 15, 1953), Lewis, the Dauphin in *King John* (Oct. 27, 1953), Orsino in *Twelfth Night* (Jan. 6, 1954), Cominius in *Coriolanus* (Feb. 23, 1954), Ferdinand in *The Tempest* (Apr. 13, 1954), Macduff in *Macbeth* (Sept. 9, 1954), Berowne in *Love's Labour's Lost* (Oct. 19, 1954), the title role in *Richard II* (Jan. 18, 1955), Orlando in *As You Like It* (Mar. 1, 1955), Henry Percy in *Henry IV, Part I* (Apr. 27, 1955), Pistol in *Henry IV, Part II* (Apr. 28, 1955), Marc Antony in *Julius Caesar* (Sept. 7, 1955), Autolycus in *The Winter's Tale* (Nov. 1, 1955), Chorus in *Henry V* (Dec. 13, 1955), alternated, with Richard Burton, as Iago (Feb. 21, 1956) and Othello (Feb. 22, 1956) in *Othello,* played Troilus in *Troilus and Cressida* (Apr. 3, 1956), Romeo in *Romeo and Juliet* (June 12, 1956), and the title role in *Richard II* (July 3, 1956).

After he made his Bway debut with the Old Vic Co. and toured the US (1956–57, see above), he played Angelo in *Measure for Measure* (Old Vic, Nov. 19, 1957); the title role in *Hamlet* (Old Vic, Dec. 18, 1957; and at the Brussels, Belgium, World Fair, July 1958); Sir Andrew Aquecheek in *Twelfth Night* (Old Vic, Apr. 1, 1958); directed *The Summer of the Seventeenth Doll* (Th. Royal, Bristol, 1958). He again toured the US (see above), and then appeared as Victor Fabian in *Once More, with Feeling* (New London, July 9, 1959); succeeded (Oct. 1959) Keith Michell as Nestor in *Irma La Douce* (Lyric, July 17, 1958); directed *Henry V* (Old Vic, May 31, 1960); played Jacko in *Naked Island* (Arts Th., Sept. 29,

1960); the Stranger in *The Lady from the Sea* (Queen's, Mar. 15, 1961); and the Evangelist in *The Substitute* (Palace, Watford, May 1961).

He joined (Sept. 1961) the Nottingham Playhouse Co., playing the title role in *Macbeth* and Sir Thomas More in *A Man for All Seasons;* toured Malta in both plays (Oct. 1961); was named assoc. dir. of the company (Dec. 1961), and played Petruchio in *The Taming of the Shrew* (early 1962); played Joseph Surface in *A School for Scandal* (Haymarket, London, Apr. 5, 1962); left the cast to open the Chichester Festival as Don Frederick in *The Chances* (July 3, 1962), followed by Orgilus in *The Broken Heart* (July 9, 1962); returned to the Nottingham Playhouse, where he directed *Twelfth Night* (Oct. 1962); co-adapted and played D'Artagnan in a musical of *The Three Musketeers* (Oct. 1962); directed *A Subject of Scandal and Concern* (Nov. 13, 1962); toured West Africa with the company, for the British Council, playing Ross in *Macbeth* (Feb. 1963); played the title role in *Alfie* (Mermaid, London, June 19, 1963); was named joint theatre director of the Nottingham Playhouse Co., and left the *Alfie* cast to appear in the opening production at the new Nottingham playhouse as *Coriolanus* (Dec. 11, 1963); subsequently performed in repertory with the company as John Worthing in *The Importance of Being Earnest* (Dec. 18, 1963), which he co-directed; as Bernard Shaw in *The Bashful Genius* (Feb. 12, 1964); directed *The Mayor of Calamea* (Mar. 11, 1964); directed *Memento Mori* (May 13, 1964); directed *Listen to the Knocking Bird* (Sept. 30, 1964); played Moricet in *The Bird Watcher* (Nov. 9, 1964); the title role in *Oedipus the King* (Nov. 25, 1964); and the title role in *Richard II* (Jan. 27, 1965; repeated Oct. 8, 1965), which he also directed.

At Nottingham, he directed, with Ronald Magill, *The Collapse of Stout Party* (Feb. 10, 1965); played Mosca in *Volpone* (Apr. 7, 1965); directed the revue *Changing Gear* (June 23, 1965); *Measure for Measure* (Sept. 22, 1965); directed with Michael Rudman, *Schweyk in the Second World War* (Nov. 3, 1965); directed *Saint Joan* (Mar. 2, 1966); played Barry Field in *The Spies Are Singing* (Apr. 27, 1966); played the title role in *Doctor Faustus* (May 25, 1966); directed, with Ronald Magill, *Moll Flanders* (June 22, 1966); with Michael Rudman, *Julius Caesar* (Sept. 21, 1966), and *Antony and Cleopatra* (Oct. 12, 1966), in both of which he played Mark Antony; directed *Jack and the Beanstalk* (Dec. 21, 1966); played He, Kolpakov, Fiance, Maxime, and Pavlovitch in *Beware of the Dog* (Feb. 15, 1967; St. Martin's, London, June 7, 1967); Willy Loman in *Death of a Salesman* (Sept. 1967); Iago in *Othello* (Oct. 1967); G. B. Shaw in *Boots with Strawberry Jam* (Feb. 28, 1968); Charles Dyer in *Staircase* (Spring 1968); and directed *All's Well That Ends Well* (Spring 1968). He resigned from the playhouse, July 31, 1968.

Mr. Neville played Henry Gow in *Mr.* and Alec Harvey in *Mrs.* in the double-bill, *Mr. and Mrs.* (Palace, London, Dec. 11, 1968); directed *Honour and Offer* (Park Th. Co., Fortune Th., May 12, 1969); played King Magnus in *The Apple Cart* (Mermaid, Mar. 5, 1970); Garrick in *Boswell's Life of Johnson* and Benedick in *Much Ado About Nothing* (Edinburgh Fest., Aug. 1970); came to the US to appear in *Lolita* (Spring 1971, see above); at the Natl. Arts Centre, Ottawa, Canada, directed *The Rivals* (Nov. 28, 1972), and several other plays; appeared in *Hedda Gabler* (Manitoba Th. Ctr., Winnipeg, Can., Jan. 8, 1973); and became artistic director of the Citadel Th., Edmonton, Alberta, Can. (June 1, 1973 to date).

Films. Mr. Neville has appeared in *Oscar Wilde* (FAW, 1960); *Billy Budd* (Allied, 1962), *I Like Money* (20th-Fox, 1962); *The Unearthly Stranger* (Amer. Intl., 1964); and as Sherlock Holmes in *A Study in Terror* (Col., 1966).

Television. He has appeared frequently on British television, including in the title role of *Henry V* (BBC, Jan. 1958); in *Poor Bitos* (BBC-2, Feb. 7, 1965); in *The Order* (BBC-1, Jan. 18, 1967).

In the US, he first appeared as Romeo in the Old Vic production of *Romeo and Juliet* (NBC, Mar. 4, 1957); next, in the title role of the Old Vic *Hamlet* (Dupont Show of the Month, CBS, Feb. 24, 1959); and as the Duke of Marlborough in *The First Churchills* (Masterpiece Th., WNET; first shown in England).

Awards. Mr. Neville received the O.B.E. in the Queen's Birthday Honours List (June 12, 1965).

NEWAY, PATRICIA. Singer, actress. b. Brooklyn, N.Y., 1919. Grad. Notre Dame Coll. for Women, S.I., N.Y. 1942. Married Morris Gesell.

Pre-Theatre. Piano student, choral singer.

Theatre. Miss Neway made her N.Y.C. debut, alternating with Brenda Lewis as the Female Chorus in *The Rape of Lucretia* (Ziegfeld Th., Dec. 29, 1948); subsequently played Magda Sorel in *The Consul* (Ethel Barrymore Th., Mar. 15, 1950), a role which she has repeated more than 500 times; appeared at the NY City Ctr., with the N.Y.C. Opera Co. as Leah in *The Dybbuk* (Oct. 4, 1951), Santuzza in *Cavalleria Rusticana* (Oct. 14, 1951), and Marie in *Wozzeck* (Apr. 3, 1952).

She appeared in Paris in the title role in *Tosca* (Th. Natl. de l'Opéra-Comique, 1953), and in *The Resurrection* (1954); played the Old Woman in *Lord Byron's Love Letter* (New Orleans, La., Jan. 1955); Magda Sorel in *The Consul* (Sadler's Wells, London, Oct. 1957); Laura Gates in *Tale for a Deaf Ear* (NY City Ctr., Apr. 6, 1958); directed her opera workshop production of *Chanticleer* (Apr. 21, 1958); played Madame Flora in *The Medium* (NY City Ctr., May 1, 1958); and the Mother in *Maria Golovin* (Martin Beck Th., Nov. 5, 1958) which she repeated at the NY City Ctr. (Mar. 30, 1959).

At NY City Ctr., she appeared as Miriam in *The Scarf* (Apr. 5, 1959), and Nelly in *Wuthering Heights* (Apr. 9, 1959); played the Mother Abbess in her first musical comedy, *The Sound of Music* (Lunt-Fontanne, Nov. 16, 1959); directed three productions of her opera workshop (Kaufmann Aud.) *The Mother, Goodbye to the Clown,* and *A Hand of Bridge* (May 22, 1960); appeared as the Governess in *Turn of the Screw* (NY City Ctr., Mar. 25, 1962); the Mother in *Morning Sun* (Phoenix, Oct. 6, 1963); Lady Thiang in *The King and I* (NY State Th., July 6, 1964); Nettie Fowler in *Carousel* (NY City Ctr., Dec. 15, 1966); and the Queen in *The Leper* (Florida State Univ., April 1970).

Television. Miss Neway first appeared as Madame de Croissy in the NBC-TV Opera Th. production of *Dialogues of the Carmelites* (Dec. 8, 1957); subsequently played Martha in *Golden Child* (Hallmark Hall of Fame, NBC, Dec. 16, 1960). In addition to her performance in *The Consul* (CBS, 1961), she has appeared in *Maria Golovin, Wozzeck,* and *Macbeth;* and on the Ed Sullivan Show (CBS) and Jack Paar's Tonight Show (NBC).

Awards. She received the Donaldson Award and won the Variety NY Drama Critics Poll for her performance as Magda Sorel in *The Consul* (1950); and received the Antoinette Perry (Tony) Award for her performance as the Mother Abbess in *The Sound of Music* (1959).

NEWHALL, PATRICIA. Actress, director, producer. b. Detroit, Mich. Grad. Kingswood H.S., Bloomfield Hills, Mich.; attended Univ. of California at Los Angeles; Univ. of Michigan; Neighborhood Playhouse Sch. of the Th., 1951–52. Studied painting and sculpture at Cranbrook Art Acad.; dance with Martha Graham. Member of AEA; SAG; AFTRA.

Theatre. Miss Newhall played Erna in a USO tour of *Letters to Lucerne* (1945); subsequently appeared as Katherine in the pre-Bway tryout of *The Wise Have Not Spoken* (1953); Mrs. Gogan in *The Plough and the Stars* (Cherry Lane Th., N.Y.C., 1953); Julie in *Liliom* (Bklyn. Acad. of Music, 1954); toured as Maggie in *Cat on a Hot Tin Roof;* produced, with Hans Weigert, and directed *No Exit* (Th. East, N.Y.C., Aug. 14, 1956); directed *Three Plays by John Millington Synge,* a triple bill including *In the Shadow of the Glen, The Tinker's Wedding,* and *Riders to the Sea* (Th. East, Mar. 6, 1957); *Does Poppy Live Here?* (Actors Playhouse, Dec. 18, 1957); and directed and produced *Blood Wedding* (Actors Playhouse, Mar. 3, 1958).

With Krishna Shah, in association with Carol Davies, she produced *Shakuntala* (St. Mark's Playhouse, Sept. 9, 1959); produced, with Hans Weigert in association with Frank Rohrbach, directed, and succeeded (June 14, 1960) Mindy Carson as the Wife in *La Ronde,* which she had also translated with Hans Weigert (Th. Marquee, May 9, 1960); in association with Van Joyce and Harold Leventhal, produced *The King of the Dark Chamber* (Jan Hus House, Feb. 9, 1961); directed the New Repertory Co. production of *Don Carlos* (Masque, Feb. 27, 1962); and directed *Goa* (Martinique, Feb. 22, 1967).

Films. She played the Sister in *Metamorphosis;* and appeared in *Prince of Foxes* (20th-Fox, 1949).

Awards. Miss Newhall received the Vernon Rice Award (1958) as the most promising young producer-director for *Blood Wedding.* .

Recreation. Riding, sculpting, designing jewelry, writing, languages, travel.

NEWLEY, ANTHONY. Actor, director, playwright, composer, lyricist, singer. b. Anthony George Newley, Sept. 24, 1931, Hackney, London, England, to George Anthony and Frances Grace Newley. Studied with Dewsbury (England) Repertory Co. Married 1956 to Anne E. Lynn, actress (marr. dis. 1963); married May 27, 1963, to Joan Collins, actress (marr. dis. Aug. 13, 1971); one daughter, one son. Member of AEA; AFTRA; British AEA.

Theatre. Mr. Newley made his professional debut as Gwynn in *Winds of Heaven* (Colchester Repertory Th., England, Apr. 1946); subsequently appeared in a season of plays (Empire Th., Dewsbury, Mar. 1950); as Peter Howard in a touring production of *Lady of the House* (Her Majesty's Th., Brighton, Mar. 1953); made his London debut in *Cranks* (Watergate, Dec. 19, 1955); his N.Y.C. debut in the same production (Bijou, Nov. 26, 1956); produced, directed, wrote, with Leslie Bricusse, and appeared as Littlechap in *Stop the World—I Want To Get Off* (Queens, London, July 20, 1961; Shubert, N.Y.C., Oct. 3, 1962); wrote, with Leslie Bricusse, the book, music, and lyrics for *The Roar of the Greasepaint—The Smell of the Crowd,* which he also directed and in which he played Cocky (Sam S. Shubert Th., May 16, 1965); wrote, with Leslie Bricusse, book, music, and lyrics for *The Good Old Bad Old Days,* in which he also played Bubba (Prince of Wales Th., London, England, Dec. 20, 1972); and wrote the book and, with John Taylor, the music for *Royalty Folies* (Royalty Th., London, Mar. 1974).

Films. Mr. Newley made his debut as Dusty Bates in *The Adventures of Dusty Bates,* (Elstree, 1946); subsequently appeared as Johnnie in *Little Ballerina* (Nettleford, 1947), Dick Bultitude in *Vice Versa* (Denham, 1948); the Artful Dodger in *Oliver Twist* (MGM, 1948); Miles Minor in *The Guinea Pig* (1948); Dudley in *Vote for Huggett* (Islington, 1949); Jimmy Knowles in *Don't Ever Leave Me* (Shepherds Bush, 1949); Charlie Ritchie in *A Boy, a Girl and a Bike* (Shepherds Bush, 1949); Arab Street Urchin in *Golden Salamander* (Pinewood, 1950); Dispensary Assistant in *Madeleine* (Pinewood, 1950); Wireless Operator in *Highly Dangerous* (Ealing, 1950); Bob Twigg in *Those People Next Door* (The Film Studios, 1952); Percy in *Top of the Form* (Pinewood, 1953); Bob in *Weak and the Wicked* (Elstree, 1954); Tommy in *Up to His Neck* (Pinewood, 1954); X2 Engineer in *Above Us the Waves* (Pinewood, 1955); Marine Clerk in *Cockleshell Heroes* (Shepperton, 1955); Sparrow in *Blue Peter* (Beaconsfield, 1955); Pedro in *Port Afrique* (Boreham Wood with MGM, 1956); Gaskin in *Last Man To Hang* (Nettleford, 1956); Pte. Spider Web in *X, the Unknown* (Bray, 1956); Wireless Operator in *Battle of the River Plate* (Pinewood, 1956); Milbrau in *The Good Companions* (Elstree, 1957); Miguel in *Fire Down Below* (Elstree with MGM, 1957); Edward in *How To Murder a Rich Uncle* (Shepperton, 1957); Roger Endicott in *High Flight* (Elstree, 1957); Noakes in *No Time To Die* (Elstree, 1958); Ernest in *The Man Inside* (Elstree, 1958); Stokes in *The Bandit of Zhobe* (Twickenham, 1959); Freddy in *The Lady Is a Square* (Elstree, 1959); Jeep Jackson in *Idle on Parade* (Shepperton, 1959); Johnnie in *Heart of a Man* (Pinewood, 1959); Hooky in *Killers of Kilimanjaro* (Shepperton, 1959); Bert in *Jazz Boat* (Boreham Wood, 1959); Dr. Newcombe in *In the Nick* (Boreham Wood, 1960); Dicky in *Let's Get Married* (Elstree, 1960); Sammy in *The Small World of Sammy Lee* (Shepperton, 1963); and, with Leslie Bricusse, wrote lyrics for the title song for *Goldfinger* (UA, 1964). He played Matthew Mugg in *Doctor Doolittle* (20th-Fox, 1967); Heironymus Merkin in *Can Heironymus Merkin Ever Forget Mercy Humppe and Find True Happiness?*, which he also produced and directed (Regional, 1969); Charlie Blake in *Sweet November* (WB, 1968); directed *Summertree* (Col., 1971); and, with Leslie Bricusse, wrote music and lyrics for *Willy Wonka and the Chocolate Factory* (Par., 1971).

Television. On British television, Mr. Newley played the title role in *Sammy* (BBC, Mar. 1958); had his own series, The Strange World of Gurney Glade (1960–61); appeared on Sunday Night Palladium; Saturday Spectaculars; The Johnny Darling Show (1962); and Lucky in London (1966); and in the US appeared on *The Anthony Newley Show* (ABC, Feb. 1972) and on the special *Burt Bacharach!* (ABC, Nov. 1972).

Night Clubs. Mr. Newley appeared at Caesar's Palace, Las Vegas, Nev. (1969); the Empire Room, Waldorf-Astoria, N.Y.C. (1969); Harrah's, Lake Tahoe, Calif. (1970); and other clubs.

Concerts. Mr. Newley appeared with Buddy Hackett (Fisher Th., Detroit, Mich., Apr.–May 1971); with Henry Mancini (Uris Th., N.Y.C., Oct. 31, 1974); with Burt Bacharach (Westbury Music Fair, N.Y., June 21–27, 1976); and has made other concert appearances.

Discography. Mr. Newley's recordings include the album *In My Solitude* (RCA, 1964); songs from *The Roar of the Greasepaint* (RCA, 1965); songs from *Doctor Doolittle* (RCA, 1967); and *Ain't It Funny* (GM-Verve, 1973).

Awards. With Leslie Bricusse, he won the Ivor Novello and BMI awards for the song "What Kind of Fool Am I?" (1962) from *Stop the World—I Want To Get Off.*

Recreation. Photography.

NEWMAN, HOWARD. Publicist, writer. b. Dec. 22, 1911, New York City, to Samuel and Gussie (Farber) Newman. Father, academic executive. Educ. Columbia Univ.; City Coll. of NY. Professional training with George Pierce Baker (playwriting); Jose Quintero (directing). Member of ATPAM; Screen Publicists Guild; AMPAS. Address: (home) 205 W. 57th St., New York, NY 10019, tel. (212) 245-6866; (bus.) 250 W. 57th St., New York, NY 10019, tel. (212) 765-2566.

Theatre. Mr. Newman's association with the theatre began on Oct. 1, 1929, when he went to work as a receptionist in the office of Dwight Deere Wiman. The following year he directed and performed in *Get a Doctor* (Cherry Lane Th., N.Y.C., 1930). He adapted *Squaring the Circle* (Lyceum, Oct. 3, 1935) and wrote *Man with the Pink Slip* (Wheeling, W. Va., Little Th., 1950). With *Claudia* (N.Y.C., 1941), Mr. Newman first worked as a theatrical publicist. He was press representative in 1944 for the Th. Guild *Othello* (tour); in 1945–46 for *O Mistress Mine* (N.Y.C.) and for *The Tempest* (Chicago); in 1946 for *Pygmalion* (tour); in 1947–48 for *The Heiress* (tour); in 1948–49 for *State of the Union* (tour); in 1949 for *That Lady* (N.Y.C.); and in 1950 for *The Madwoman of Chaillot* (N.Y.C. and tour). In 1950–51, he was press representative for *Kiss Me Kate* (national tour); in 1952 for *The Devil's Disciple* (Calif.) and for Jose Greco (first national tour); in 1953 for *Paint Your Wagon* (tour) and the first N.Y.C. season of the Phoenix Th.; in 1954 for *My 3 Angels* (tour); in 1954–55 for *Wonderful Town* (tour); in 1955–56 for *the Pajama Game* and *Damn Yankees* (both N.Y.C.). He was associate publicist in 1956 for *The Teahouse of the August Moon* (tour) and *Candide* (N.Y.C.); in 1957 for *The Girl of the Golden West* (N.Y.C.); in 1958 for *Auntie Mame, Two for the Seesaw,* and *The Music Man* (all in N.Y.C.); and in 1960 for *The Poker Game* (Philadelphia).

As a member of the Gifford-Wallace Agency, N.Y.C., Mr. Newman was publicist in 1971 for *The James Joyce Memorial Liquid Theatre, Lenny,* and *Hair* (all N.Y.C.) and *Godspell* (N.Y.C. and Boston); and in 1973 he was publicist for *Nellie Toole & Co.* and, with Jeffrey Richards, for *Don Juan in Hell* (both N.Y.C.).

Films. Mr. Newman was publicist for *Spellbound* (UA, 1945); field publicist for Michael Todd's *Around the World in 80 Days* (1956); unit press representative for *Happy Anniversary* (UA, 1959); publicist for Wolf Mankowitz for *Expresso Bongo* (Cont., 1960); N.Y.C. publicity manager for *Porgy and Bess* (Col., 1960); national director of field activities for *Spartacus* (U, 1960); and national publicity manager for *El Cid* (Allied Artists, 1961). From 1962 to 1964, Mr. Newman was studio publicity head for Samuel Bronston in Madrid, Spain, during the filming of *The Fall of the Roman Empire, Circus World,* and *55 Days at Peking,* and in 1964 he was publicity director for Eli Landau's *The Pawnbroker* and *Umbrellas of Cherbourg.* In 1966–67, as publicity director for Twentieth Century-Fox, he covered thirty to forty films including international publicity for the company's *Star!* (1967). From 1968 to 1970, he was publicity director, Paramount Pictures, also covering between thirty and forty films. Mr. Newman later did publicity for *A Separate Peace* (Par., 1971); *The Godfather* (Par., 1971); *Shamus* (Col., 1972); *Tomorrow* (Filmgroup, 1972); *Amazing Grace* (UA, 1973); *The Gambler* (Par., 1973); *Cops and Robbers* (UA, 1973); *The Exorcist* (WB, 1973); and *The Savage Is Loose* (Campbell Devon Prod., 1974).

Television. Mr. Newman's first work in television was as publicist for Mr. Wizard (NBC, 1958). He was also publicist for Armstrong Circle Theatre (CBS, 1958), the NBC special *Hansel and Gretel* (1958), and for the Kate Smith Show (CBS, 1960).

Published Works. Mr. Newman is author of *The Exorcist: The Strange Story Behind the Film* (1974).

Recreation. Travel.

NEWMAN, PHYLLIS. Actress. b. Mar. 19, 1935, Jersey City, N.J., to Arthur and Rachael Newman. Father, music teacher. Grad. Lincoln H.S., Jersey City; attended Western Reserve Univ.; Columbia Univ. Studied acting with Wynn Handman. Married Jan. 31, 1960, to Adolph Green; one son, one daughter. Member of AEA; AFTRA; SAG.

Theatre. Since her debut as Sarah in *Wish You Were Here* (Imperial Th., June 25, 1953), Miss Newman has appeared as a principal in the revue *I Feel Wonderful* (Th. de Lys, Oct. 18, 1954); was a standby for Judy Holliday in *Bells Are Ringing* (Shubert, Nov. 29, 1956); played Jane Bennett in *First Impressions* (Alvin, Mar. 19, 1959); Martha Vail in *Subways Are for Sleeping* (St. James, Dec. 27, 1961); Sura in *Pleasures and Palaces* (pre-Bway tour, March–Apr. 1965); played the matinee performances (commencing Nov. 23, 1966), and substituted (July 10–29, 1967) for Barbara Harris in *The Apple Tree* (Shubert Th., N.Y.C., Oct. 18, 1966); played Claire in *On the Town* (Imperial, Oct. 31, 1971); replaced Barbara Barrie in the role of Edna in *The Prisoner of Second Avenue* (Eugene O'Neill Th., Nov. 11, 1971); and directed *Straws in the Wind: A Theatrical Look* (American Place Th., Feb. 21, 1975).

Films. She appeared as Juanita in *Picnic* (Col., 1955); Lulu in *Vagabond King* (Par., 1956); and Chris in *Let's Rock* (Col., 1958).

Television. Miss Newman was a panelist on To Tell the Truth (CBS, 1964–66); appeared on That Was the Week That Was (NBC, 1964–65); Decoy (CBS, 1964); and Mr. Broadway (CBS, 1964); was a guest on Password (CBS, 1965–66, 1967–68); Match Game (NBC, 1965–68); appeared on The Man from U.N.C.L.E. (NBC, 1965); Amos Burke (ABC, 1965); Gypsy (Ind., 1965–66); was a guest panelist on What's My Line? (CBS, 1966–68); The Face Is Familiar (CBS, 1966–67); appeared on Stage 67 (ABC, 1966); Wild, Wild West (CBS, 1966); Snap Judgement (NBC, 1966–68); and Personality (NBC, 1967–68); and has been a frequent guest on The Johnny Carson Show (NBC, 1965–to date), and The Mike Douglas Show (CBS).

Awards. Miss Newman received an Antoinette Perry (Tony) Award for her performance as Martha Vail in *Subways Are for Sleeping* (1962).

NEWMAR, JULIE. Actress, singer, dancer. b. Julia Charlene Newmeyer, Aug. 16, 1935, Los Angeles, Calif., to Don and Helene (Jesmer) Newmeyer. Father, engineer, football coach; mother, Ziegfeld Girl (1920). Grad. John Marshall H.S., Los Angeles, Calif.; attended Univ. of California at Los Angeles. Studied acting with Lee Strasberg, N.Y.C.; dance with Bronislava Nijinska; Carmelita Maracci, Ruth St. Denis; voice with Augusta Weiss, Sue Seton. Member of AEA; SAG; AFTRA. Address: (home) 12 Beekman Place, New York, NY 10022, tel. (212) 688-3965; (bus.) c/o Jeff Hunter, 119 W. 57th St., New York, NY 10019, tel. (212) 757-4995.

Theatre. Miss Newmar made her debut as a dancer in concerts and operas (Los Angeles Philharmonic and Los Angeles Opera Company): her Bway debut as Vera in *Silk Stockings* (Imperial, Feb. 24, 1955); followed by Stupefyin' Jones in *Li'l Abner* (St. James, Nov. 15, 1956); Katrin Sveg in *The Marriage-Go-Round* (Plymouth, Oct. 29, 1958); Sura in *There Once Was a Russian* (Music Box, Feb. 18, 1961); toured in *Stop the World—I Want to Get Off* (opened Pabst, Milwaukee, Wis., Mar. 25, 1963; closed Rochester, N.Y., Oct. 1963); and has appeared in touring productions of *Dames at Sea,* and *Irma La Douce.*.

Films. She was dance director at Universal Studios; appeared in *Seven Brides for Seven Brothers* (MGM, 1954); *Li'l Abner* (Par., 1959); *Marriage-Go-Round* (20th-Fox, 1960); *For Love or Money* (UI, 1963); and *Mackenna's Gold* (Col., 1969).

Television. Miss Newmar has appeared on Columbo (NBC); Love, American Style (ABC); The Jonathan Winters Show (CBS); The Danny Kaye Show (CBS); Route 66 (CBS); My Living Doll (ABC); Wide World of Sports (ABC); and Batman (ABC).

Awards. Miss Newmar received the Antoinette Perry (Tony) Award for her performance as Katrin Sveg in *The Marriage-Go-Round* (1959).

Recreation. Painting, designing, piano, skiing, tennis, horseback riding.

NICHOLS, MIKE. Director, comedian, actor, writer. b. Michael Igor Peschkowsky, Nov. 6, 1931, Berlin, Germany, to Paul and Brigitte (Landauer) Peschkowsky. Father, physician. Attended Univ. of Chicago, 1950–53. Studied with Lee Strasberg. Married 1957 to Patricia Scot (marr. dis. 1960); married 1963 to Margot Callas (marr. dis. 1974); one daughter. Member of AEA; AFTRA; SSD&C; AGVA; SAG; WGA.

Theatre. Mr. Nichols made his stage debut in *An Evening with Mike Nichols and Elaine May* (John Golden Th., Oct. 8, 1960); subsequently appeared as Howard Miller in *A Matter of Position* (opened Walnut St. Th., Philadelphia, Sept. 29, 1962; closed there Oct. 13, 1962); directed *Barefoot in the Park* (Biltmore, N.Y.C., Oct. 23, 1963; and national tour, opened Central City (Colo.) Opera House, July 28, 1964); *The Knack* (New Th., N.Y.C., May 28, 1964); and *The Odd Couple* (Plymouth, Mar. 10, 1965); contributed special material for *The Carol Burnett Show* (Greek Th., Los Angeles, Aug. 8, 1966); directed *The Apple Tree* (Shubert, N.Y.C., Oct. 18, 1966); *The Little Foxes* (Vivian Beaumont, Oct. 26, 1967); *Plaza Suite* (Plymouth, Feb. 14, 1968); *The Prisoner of Second Avenue* (Eugene O'Neill Th., Nov. 11, 1971); and *Uncle Vanya* (Circle in the Square/Joseph E. Levine Th., June 4, 1973).

Films. Mr. Nichols has directed *Who's Afraid of Virginia Woolf?* (WB, 1966); *The Graduate* (Embassy, 1967); *Catch-22* (Par., 1970; *Carnal Knowledge* (Avco-Embassy, 1971); *The Day of the Dolphin* (Avco-Embassy, 1973); and *The Fortune* (Col.,

1975).

Television. He has appeared on the Jack Paar Show (NBC, 1957); The Fabulous Fifties (CBS, Jan. 31, 1960); the Perry Como Show (NBC); the Dinah Shore Show (NBC); and The Today Show (NBC).

Night Clubs. He has appeared at the Blue Angel (N.Y.C., 1957).

Other Activities. By presidential request, Mr. Nichols performed at the Inaugural Gala for Pres. Lyndon B. Johnson (National Guard Armory, Washington, D.C., Jan. 18, 1965).

Awards. For *The Odd Couple* and *Luv*, Mr. Nichols won first place in the Annual *Variety* New York Drama Critics Poll (Best Direction, 1964–65) and an Antoinette Perry (Tony) Award. He received an Outer Circle Award "for directing four current hits" (1965); the Sam S. Shubert Foundation Award "for his outstanding individual contribution to the New York legitimate theater for the 1964–65 season" (1965); and was voted the fifth winner in the annual "Entertainer of the Year" Awards chosen by the editors of *Cue* magazine "in recognition of his directorial achievements" (Dec. 29, 1965). In the Filmdom's Famous Fives poll he was voted the year's Outstanding Director for *Who's Afraid of Virginia Woolf?* (Feb. 1967) which received the British Film Academy Award as the Best Film From Any Source (1966); and he received The Academy Award and the New York Film Critics Award for *The Graduate* (1967).

Recreation. Raising Arabian horses.

NICHOLSON, ANNE P. General manager, playwright, writer. b. Anne Preston Nicholson, Chicago, Ill., to Frank G. and Annie (Jackson) Nicholson. Father, railroad exec. Grad. Faulkner H.S., Chicago, 1938; Pine Manor Jr. Coll., certificate 1940; studied radio and television, Northwestern Univ.; playwrighting with Charlotte Chorpenning at Goodman Th., Chicago, 1943–45. Member of AETA; ANTA; Arts Club of Chicago; Women's Athletic Club; Flossmoor Country Club; Chicago Drama League (vice-pres., 1957–61; board); Illinois Arts Council (vice-chmn., 1965–71); Sarah Siddons Society (gov.). Address: 100 E. Bellevue Pl., Chicago, IL 60611.

Miss Nicholson was promotion manager (1959–66), and general manager (1962–66) of the Goodman Th. In 1966, under a Title III grant, she managed a statewide tour of the National Th. of the Deaf. She served as chairman of the audience development program for the initial Chicago appearance of the Stratford (Ontario) Shakespeare Festival (1969); and was manager of the Ravinia (Ill.) Festival (Summer 1970), which included the first US appearance of the Birmingham (England) Repertory Co.

She is the subject of regularly scheduled author interviews at the Pump Room in Chicago.

She wrote the play, *Exclusive Story* (Univ. of Seattle Th., 1955).

Radio. She has written scripts for *Books Bring Adventure* (1950); and *Scoop Ryan . . . Cub Reporter!* (CBS, Detroit, Mich., 1951–58).

Published Works. She has written the following children's plays: *The Magic Horn, Captain Kidd's Treasure, The Snow Maiden, Joan of Arc,* and *Scoop Ryan . . . Cub Reporter!* and has adapted Esther Forbes' novel, *Johnny Tremain.*

She writes a monthly column for *Chicagoland* magazine, in addition to other free-lance writing.

Awards. Miss Nicholson received the Billboard Award (1953) for writing the radio series, Scoop Ryan . . . Cub Reporter!.

Recreation. Golf, cooking, traveling.

NICHTERN, CLAIRE. Producer, director. b. Claire Joseph, May 10, 1920, New York City, to Fred and Rebecca (Brumer) Joseph. Father, jewelry designer. Grad. Union (N.J.) H.S., 1936; attended N.Y. University, 1951–53. Married June 4, 1944, to Sol Nichtern, physician, (marr. dis. 1968); one son, one daughter. Member of League of Off-Bway Theatres and Producers; ANTA. Address: 61 W. 9th St., New York, NY 10011, tel. (212) 254-3536.

Pre-Theatre. Housewife.

Theatre. Mrs. Nichtern's first professional assignment was as production assistant for *Saint Joan* (Phoenix Th., Sept. 11, 1956); subsequently was production assistant for the Phoenix Th. productions of *Diary of a Scoundrel* (Nov. 5, 1956), *Good Woman of Setzuan* (Dec. 18, 1956), *Measure for Measure* (Jan. 22, 1957), *The Taming of the Shrew* (Feb. 20, 1957), *The Duchess of Malfi* (Mar. 19, 1957) and *Livin' the Life* (Apr. 27, 1957). She was casting director for the Phoenix Theatre (1957–58), including productions of *Mary Stuart* (Oct. 8, 1957), *The Makropoulos Secret* (Dec. 3, 1957), *The Chairs* and *The Lesson* (Jan. 9, 1958) and *The Infernal Machine* (Feb. 3, 1958).

She was assistant to the general manager of *The Pleasure of His Company* (Longacre, Oct. 22, 1958); *Edwin Booth* (46 St. Th., Nov. 24, 1958); *Cue for Passion* (Henry Miller's Th., Nov. 25, 1958); *The Gazebo* (Lyceum, Dec. 12, 1958); *Look after Lulu* (Henry Miller's Th., Mar. 3, 1959); and *Juno* (Winter Garden, Mar. 9, 1959). From 1959–61, she was executive assistant to the producer for eleven productions of the Phoenix Theatre.

Mrs. Nichtern presented, with Paul Libin, *The Banker's Daughter* (Jan Hus House, Jan. 22, 1962); produced *The Typists* and *The Tiger* (Orpheum, Feb. 4, 1963; also, with H. M. Tennent, Ltd., Globe, London, May 25, 1964); *Luv* (Booth Th., N.Y.C., Nov. 19, 1963); in association with Zev Bufman, *Jimmy Shine* (Brooks Atkinson Th., Dec. 5, 1968) and *The Trial of A. Lincoln* (Huntington Hartford Th., Los Angeles, Cal., Apr. 7, 1971); was producing consultant, Nantucket (Mass.) Stage Co. (Summer 1973); associate director for the revival of *The Waltz of the Toreadors* (Circle in the Square-Joseph E. Levine Th., N.Y.C., Sept. 13, 1973); and producing consultant, E.T.C. Theatre Co. productions of *Waiting for Lefty* (NY Newspaper Guild, Mar. 14, 1964) and *Break a Leg* (U.R.G.E.N.T. Th., May 13, 1974).

Other Activities. In 1965, Mrs. Nichtern served on a special jury for the National Endowment for the Arts Playwrights Experimental Theatre Program and was a judge for the Annual National Collegiate Playwriting Contest. She was director of admissions and producer-in-residence, American Academy of Dramatic Art (Sept. 1970–Apr. 1973) and in Feb. 1974 became assistant professor, Richmond College, C.U.N.Y., teaching craft of the theatre and directing *Feiffer's People.*

Awards. Mrs. Nichtern won the Antoinette Perry (Tony) Award for best producer of a straight play in 1965 for *Luv*..

NICKOLE, LEONIDAS. Educator. b. Leonidas Anesty Nickole, Feb. 13, 1929, Saugus, Mass., to Anesty and Olga Nickole. Grad. Saugus (Mass.) H.S., 1945; Emerson Coll., A.B. 1950; Columbia Univ. (scholarship), M.A. 1950; attended Lehigh Univ., 1950–51; Harvard Univ., 1953–54; Indiana Univ. (doctoral program in theatre history), 1963–65. Served US Army, 1951–53; rank, Top Sgt.; awarded three Bronze Service Stars, UN Service Medal. Member of ANTA; ATA; NETC (pres., 1970–71); SCA; AAUP; National Society of Arts and Letters; Eastern Communication Assn.; William Sutton Lodge, Phi Tau Alpha; Alpha Pi Theta; Towncriers Community Th. (pres., 1974, Saugus, Mass.). Address: (home) 123 Forest St., Saugus, MA 01906, tel. (617) CE 3-0894; (bus.) Emerson College, 130 Beacon St., Boston, MA 02116, tel. (617) 262-2010.

Prof. Nickole organized, and is chairman (1966–to date) of the Theatre Education Dept. at Emerson Coll., where he has served as instructor (1953–57); assistant professor (1957–61); professor (1961–to date); and chairman of the Dept. of Theatre Arts (1961–66).

Since 1954, in addition to directing plays at Emerson Coll., Mr. Nickole has directed Emerson's annual spring musicals, including *Lady in the Dark; Finian's Rainbow; Wonderful Town; Guys and Dolls; The Pajama Game; Bloomer Girl; Brigadoon; Bells Are Ringing; Wildcat; South Pacific; Carnival!; Anything Goes; Fiorello; West Side Story; Cabaret; Fiddler on the Roof; Applause!;* and *No, No, Nanette.*

He directed for the Civic Little Th., Allentown, Pa., *Light Up The Sky* and *Ten Little Indians* (1950), and *Two Blind Mice* and *Rebecca* (1951); for Martha's Vineyard Summer Th., Mass., he directed *Laura, Time Out for Ginger,* and *See How They Run* (1955); *The Rainmaker, The Tender Trap, The Seven Year Itch* and *Road Show* (1956); in Boston, Mass., directed *The Devil's Discourse* (Image Th., 1961) and *Liberty Under Law* for the Amer. Bar Assn. (1953); directed *You Can't Take It with You,* and *Guys and Dolls* for the Deertrees Th. (Harrison, Me., 1964); and directed *How To Succeed in Business without Really Trying* (1967), *Never Too Late* (1969), and *Oklahoma* (1973) in community theatre in the Greater Boston Area.

Awards. Mr. Nickole received the President's Scholar scholarship to Columbia Univ. (1949), an Honorary Master's Degree from Emerson Coll. (1963), the Musical Theatre Society Citation for distinguished service to musical theatre (1970), the St. George's Award for distinguished service to the community (1972), and the Emerson Coll. President's Award for distinguished service to the college and community (1973).

NICOL, ALEX. Actor, director. b. Alexander Livingston Nicol, Jr., Jan. 20, 1919, Ossining, N.Y., to Alexander L. Nicol, Sr. Father, prison guard. Attended Ossining H.S.; Faegin Sch. of Dramatic Arts, N.Y.C. Studied drama with Al Sax, N.Y.C., 1946–47; Elia Kazan, 1948; Lee Strasberg, 1949–50. Married Sept. 17, 1948, to Jean Fleming, actress; two sons, one daughter. Served WW II, US Army, Cavalry and Intelligence; rank, Tech. Sgt. Relative in theatre: aunt, Florence Nicol, actress. Member of AEA; SAG; SDG; AFTRA; Actors Studio. Address: 10601 Ohio Ave., Los Angeles, CA 90024.

Pre-Theatre. Newspaper sports editor.

Theatre. Mr. Nicol first appeared on stage in a high school production of *For the Love of Mike* (1937); made his professional debut in *Rope's End* (Summer 1938); and his first Bway appearance as a walk-on in Maurice Evans' *Henry IV, Part 1* (St. James Th., Jan. 30, 1939); subsequently was a walk-on in Evans' *Hamlet* (44 St. Th., Dec. 4, 1939), and *King Richard II* (St. James, Apr. 1, 1940).

He played Gene Morton in the pre-Bway tryout of *You Twinkle Only Once* (Shubert, New Haven, Conn., Jan. 3, 1946; closed Wilbur, Boston, Mass., Jan. 19, 1946); the Young Chemist in a N.Y.C. revival of *Waiting for Lefty* (1946); the 1st Air Force Pilot in *Sundown Beach* (Belasco, Sept. 7, 1948); and was understudy to William Prince as David Gibbs in *Forward the Heart* (48 St. Th., Jan. 28, 1949).

Mr. Nicol appeared in *South Pacific* (Majestic, Apr. 7, 1949); succeeded Jack Lord as Mannion in *Mr. Roberts* (Alvin, Feb. 18, 1948); followed Ben Gazzara in the role of Brick in *Cat on a Hot Tin Roof* (Morosco, Mar. 24, 1955), and toured in the role (opened National, Washington, D.C., Nov. 26, 1956); played the Young Man in the pre-Bway tryout of *The Saturday Night Kid* (opened Westport Country Playhouse, Conn., Sept. 9, 1958; closed Locust St. Th., Philadelphia, Pa., Sept. 28, 1958); and directed *The Best Man* (Los Angeles); and *La Ronde* (Los Angeles).

Films. Mr. Nicol made his debut in *Sleeping City* (U, 1950); subsequently appeared in *Tomahawk* (U, 1951); *Target Unknown* (U, 1951); *Air Cadet* (U, 1951); *The Raging Tide* (U, 1951); *Meet Danny Wilson* (U, 1952); *Red Ball Express* (U, 1952); *The Redhead from Wyoming* (U, 1952); *Because of You* (U, 1952); *Law and Order* (U, 1953); *Lone Hand* (U, 1953); *Champ for a Day* (Rep., 1953); *Dawn at Socorro* (U, 1954); *About Mrs. Leslie* (Par., 1954); *Black Glove* (Lippert, 1954); *Heat Wave* (Lippert, 1954); *Strategic Air Command* (Par., 1955); *Sincerely Yours* (WB, 1955); *The Man from Laramie* (Col., 1955); and *Great Day in the Morning* (RKO, 1956).

He appeared in *The Gilded Cage; Five Branded Women* (Par., 1960); *Under Ten Flags* (Par., 1960); *Gunfighters of Casa Grande* (MGM, 1965); *The Bru-*

tal Hand (MGM); *Hell Black Night; Tutti a Casa; Brandy; The Aging Gunfighter; Via Margutta;* and *Homer* (National General, 1970).

Mr. Nicol directed *The Screaming Skull* (AI, 1958); produced and directed *Then There Were Three* (Ind., 1961); and directed *Point of Terror,* and various Air Force training films.

Television. He made his debut on the Lux Video Th. (ABC, 1948); subsequently appeared on Studio One (CBS); Kraft Television Th. (NBC); Climax! (CBS); and Matinee Th. (NBC); Schlitz Playhouse (CBS); and Alfred Hitchcock Presents (CBS).

Mr. Nicol has directed numerous segments of such series as Tarzan (NBC); Wild, Wild West (CBS); The Wackiest Ship in the Army; Jesse James; Daniel Boone; and the pilot film for *Survival.*

Awards. In Spain, he received the award for best foreign actor (1964) for his performance in *Brandy.*

Recreation. Golf, swimming, camping, traveling, photography.

NICOLL, ALLARDYCE. Theatre historian. b. Allardyce John Nicoll, June 28, 1894, Glasgow, Scotland, to David Binny and Elsie (Allardyce) Nicoll. Grad. Stirling H.S., Glasgow; Glasgow Univ., Scotland, M.A. Married to Josephine Calina (dec. Nov. 1962); Married Dec. 1963 to Maria Dubno. Member of the Society for Th. Research (hon. pres.); Shakespeare Birthplace Trustees (life trustee); Modern Language Assoc. of Amer. (hon. mbr.); Accademia Ligure di Scienza e Lettore (hon. mbr.). Address: Wind's Acre, Colwall, Malvern, Worcester, England tel. Colwall 310.

Mr. Nicoll is a historian of the theatre and of drama. He was a professor of English language and literature at the Univ. of London, Eng. (1926–33); was professor of the history of drama, and chairman of the department of drama (Yale Univ., 1933–45); was professor of English and director of the Shakespeare Inst., Univ. of Birmingham (England, 1945–61); Mallon Visiting Professor in English (Univ. of Pittsburgh, Pa., 1963–64, 1965, 1967 and 1968).

Published Works. Mr. Nicoll is the author of numerous books, most of which are concerned with theatrical or dramatic themes. Among these are: *British Drama* (1925; 1962); *The Development of the Theatre* (1927; 1966); *Studies in Shakespeare* (1927); *The English Stage* (1928); *The Theory of Drama* (1931); *Masks, Mimes and Miracles* (1931); *Film and Theatre* (1936); *Stuart Masques and the Renaissance Stage* (1937); *The English Theatre* (1936); *World Drama: From Aeschylus to Anouilh* (1949; 1974); *Shakespeare* (1952); *The Elizabethans* (1957); *The Theatre and Dramatic Theory* (1962); *The World of Harlequin* (1963); a six-volume series, *A History of English Drama, 1660–1900* (1952–1959), with later editions of most volumes); *English Drama, 1900–1930: The Beginnings of the Modern Period* (1973).

He was editor of *Shakespeare Survey* from the first volume in 1948 to the eighteenth volume in 1965, and he has also edited several other volumes, notably *The Works of Cyril Tourneur* (1930) and *Chapman's Homer* (1957).

Awards. Mr. Nicoll has received honorary doctorates from the Univ. of Toulouse (France, 1950), the Univ. of Montpellier (France, 1953), the Univ. of Glasgow (Scotland, 1964); the Univ. of Durham (Eng., 1964); and Brandeis Univ. (1965).

NIMS, LETHA. Executive. b. Letha Ione Parrott, Sept. 10, 1917, Lemmon, S.D., to Ralph Leon and Ethel (Lowe) Parrott. Father, wool grower. Grad. Santa Barbara (Calif.) H.S., 1934; Northwestern Univ., B.A. (speech) 1938. Studied acting with E. Clayton McCarty, Pasadena, Calif., 1929–32; Alvina Krause, 1936–38. Married Dec. 17, 1938, to William H. Nims; one son, one daughter. Member of Zeta Phi Eta. Address: (home) 21 Claremont Ave., New York, NY 10027, tel. (212) MO 2-1306; (bus.) c/o The New Dramatists, Inc., 424 W. 44th St., New York, NY 10036.

Mrs. Nims retired as executive director of New Dramatists, Inc., in 1972. She is now a member of its board of directors.

NIZER, LOUIS. Lawyer, writer. b. Feb. 6, 1902, London, England, to Joseph and Bella Nizer. Grad. Boys H.S., Brooklyn, N.Y., 1919; Columbia Coll., B.A. 1922; Columbia Law Sch., LL.B. 1924. Married July 31, 1939, to Mildred Mantel. Member of Association of the Bar of the City of N.Y.; NY State and American Bar Associations; Independent Order of Odd Fellows; ASCAP; Lotos Club. Address: (home) 180 W. 58th St., New York, NY 10019; (bus.) 40 W. 57th St., New York, NY 10019, tel. (212) 977-9700.

Mr. Nizer is senior partner in the law firm of Phillips, Nizer, Benjamin, Krim & Ballon.

Published Works. Louis Nizer is the author of *The Implosion Conspiracy, The Jury Returns, My Life in Court, Commentary and Analysis of Official Warren Commission Report, What To Do with Germany, Thinking on Your Feet, Between You and Me,* and *New Courts of Industry.* The chapter "Reputation" from *My Life in Court* was dramatized in the play *A Case of Libel* (Longacre, N.Y.C., Oct. 10, 1963).

Awards. Mr. Nizer received the Golden Plate Award of the Academy of Achievement (1962) and was Literary Father of the Year (1962). His paintings have won awards at the annual New York City Bar Association Art Exhibitions.

Recreation. Golf, painting, writing.

NOBLE, WILLIAM. Playwright, teacher, screenwriter. b. Aug. 30, 1921, Spokane, Wash., to Ronald and May (Hart) Noble. Attended Univ. of Washington, 1940. Served US Army, 1944–47; rank, Staff Sgt.

Pre-Theatre. Teacher.

Theatre. Mr. Noble wrote, with James Leo Herlihy, *Blue Denim* (Playhouse Th., N.Y.C., Feb. 27, 1958); and was author of the play *Snapfinger Creek.*

Mr. Noble has directed and taught playwriting at the Tryout Th. (Seattle, Wash.), of which he was also a founder, and at the Pasadena Playhouse.

Films. He was screenwriter for his play *Faculty Row,* which was released as *Young Ideas* (MGM, 1943); and he was a contract writer for MGM for five years.

Television. He has written numerous scripts for major networks.

Awards. Mr. Noble received a Kraft Television Playwriting Award for an adaptation of his play *Snapfinger Creek* (1956).

NOEL, CRAIG R. Producer, director. b. Rupert Craig Noel, Aug. 25, 1915, Demmino, N.M., to Luther and Catherine Noel. Father, railroad inspector. Attended San Diego (Calif.) H.S., 1933–35; San Diego State Coll., 1936–37. Served US Army, 1944–45; rank, T/Sgt.; 1st director, Ernie Pyle Th., Tokyo. Member of AEA; ANTA; ATA (member, community theatre board, 1959); California Theatre Council (co-chmn., 1974). Address: (home) 3688 Jackdaw, San Diego, CA 92103, tel. (714) 298-4723; (bus.) c/o Old Globe Theatre, El Prado, Balboa Park, P.O. Box 2171, San Diego, CA 92112, tel. (714) 234-3601.

Theatre. Mr. Noel directed (1939–41) at the San Diego Community Th., *Of Mice and Men, Yes, My Darling Daughter, The Firebrand, Here Today, Hay Fever, Margin for Error, A World Elsewhere, Mad Hopes.*

Mr. Noel was producing director, Old Globe Theatre, San Diego, Calif. (1947–74) and has been producing director, San Diego National Shakespeare Festival (1949–to date), staging three hundred plays at the theatre, including seventy for the Festival and personally directing 161, including The *Time of Your Life, Kiss and Tell, Ladies in Retirement, Loser Take All, Another Part of the Forest, State of the Union, Petrified Forest, Dream Girl, Laura, The Little Foxes, Junior Miss, The Corn is Green, Chicken Every Sunday, John Loves Mary, Rain, Caught in the Act I, The Beautiful People, A Christmas Carol, Our Hearts Were Young and Gay, One Is a Crowd, Montserrat, Strange Bedfellows, Belvedere, Caught in the Act II, At War With the Army, Harvey, The Son, Lady in the Dark, The Bat, The Madwoman of Chaillot, The Constant Wife, The Cricket on the Hearth, Twentieth Century, The Curious Savage, Goodbye My Fancy, Caught in the Act III, Angel in the Pawnshop, Ladies of the Jury, Death of a Salesman, Light Up the Sky, Born Yesterday, Bell, Book and Candle, Mr. Roberts, Caught in the Act IV, The Silver Whistle, Gigi, Cheaper by the Dozen, Lo and Behold, The Great Catherine, A Phoenix Too Frequent, Stalag 17, The Play's the Thing, Ten Little Indians, Affairs of State, Dear Ruth, My Three Angels, Caught in the Act V, Taming of the Shrew, The Caine Mutiny Court Martial, Sabrina Fair, Time Out for Ginger, The Moon Is Blue, The Remarkable Mr. Pennypacker, Caught in the Act VI, Volpone, The Solid Gold Cadillac, Tea and Sympathy, The Lady's Not for Burning, Janus, Witness for the Prosecution, Teahouse of the August Moon, The Seven Year Itch, On the Town, Anniversary Waltz, Time of Your Life, Knight of the Burning Pestle, Macbeth, The Boy Friend, The Happiest Millionaire, The Importance of Being Earnest, The Waltz of the Toreadors, A Streetcar Named Desire, The Man Who Came to Dinner, A Visit to a Small Planet, Live It Up, The Reluctant Debutante, The Matchmaker, A View from the Bridge, The Girls in 509, Golden Fleecing, Picnic, Children of Darkness, The Mousetrap, Holiday for Lovers, Under the Yum-Yum Tree, The Gazebo, The Pleasure of His Company, A Raisin in the Sun, Thieves' Carnival, The American Dream, The Zoo Story, The Fantasticks, Take a Giant Step, Man in the Dog Suit, Becket, Six Characters in Search of an Author, Sunday in New York, The Night of the Iguana, A Far Country, The Crucible, A Sleep of Prisoners, A Thousand Clowns, A Man for All Seasons, Galileo, The Hostage, Oh Dad, Poor Dad, Mama's Hung You in the Closet and I'm Feelin' So Sad, Inherit the Wind, The Rose Tattoo, Dark of the Moon, The Caretaker, A Case of Libel, Any Wednesday, You Can't Take It With You, Catch Me If You Can, The Birthday Party, Philadelphia Here I Come, Barefoot in the Park, Long Days' Journey into Night, Under Milk Wood, King John, The Innocents, Blithe Spirit, The Unknown Soldier and His Wife, The Balcony, Slightly Higher on the West Coast, The Star Spangled Girl, The Skin of Our Teeth, Don't Drink the Water, Slow Dance on the Killing Ground, Charley's Aunt, The Night Thoreau Spent in Jail, Harvey, The Face of Violence, Play It Again, Sam, The House of Blue Leaves, The Trial of the Catonsville Nine, Beyond the Fringe, Child's Play, What the Butler Saw, One Flew Over the Cuckoo's Nest, Getting Married, Private Lives, I Do! I Do!, Summer and Smoke, The Threepenny Opera, And Miss Reardon Drinks a Little.*

Films. He served as dialogue director for *Guadalcanal Diary* (20th-Fox, 1943) and was the test director and dialogue director for *The Lodger* (20th-Fox, 1944).

Awards. Mr. Noel received an honorary M.A. degree from the Pasadena (Cal.) Playhouse in 1968.

Recreation. Swimming.

NOLAN, LLOYD. Actor. b. Aug. 11, San Francisco, Calif., to James and Margaret (Shea) Nolan. Father, shoe manufacturer. Grad. Santa Clara (Calif.) Prep Sch.; attended Stanford Univ. Studied at the Pasadena Playhouse (1927). Married May 23, 1933, to Mell Efird, actress; one son (dec.); one daughter. Member of SAG; AEA; AFTRA. Address: 239 N. Bristol Ave., Los Angeles, CA 90049, tel. (213) CR 4-7633.

Theatre. Mr. Nolan made his debut in a vaudeville sketch *The Radio Robot* (Keith-Albee circuit, Worcester, Mass., 1925); subsequently worked at the Cape Playhouse, Dennis, Mass., as a stagehand and appeared in *The Lower Road, Romeo and Juliet, You Never Can Tell,* and as a Pirate in the chorus of *Cape Cod Follies* (Summer 1928); he made his Bway debut in *Cape Cod Follies* (Bijou, Sept. 18, 1929); appeared in a revival of *The Blue and the Gray* or *War Is Hell* (Old Rialto, Hoboken, N.J., Dec. 23, 1929); played Holloway in *Sweet Stranger* (Cort, N.Y.C., Oct. 21, 1930); Emil in *Reunion in Vienna* (Martin Beck Th., Nov. 16, 1931); appeared in the revue *Americana* (Shubert, Oct. 5, 1932); played Biff

Grimes in *One Sunday Afternoon* (Little, Feb. 15, 1933); Geoffrey Carver in *Ragged Army* (Selwyn, Feb. 26, 1934); and Rudy Flannigan in *Gentlewoman* (Cort, Mar. 22, 1934).

Mr. Nolan played Oliver Erwenter in the national company of *Silver Whistle* (1950); Samuel Rilling in the pre-Bway tour of *Courtin' Time* (opened Shubert, Boston, Mass., Apr. 9, 1951; closed Forrest, Philadelphia, Pa., Apr. 20, 1951); Lt. Commander Philip Francis Queeg in *The Caine Mutiny Court-Martial* (Plymouth, Jan. 20, 1954), in which he toured the US (opened Blackstone, Chicago, Ill., Jan. 31, 1955; closed Huntington Hartford Th., Los Angeles, Calif., Apr. 30, 1955), and played the role in the London production which he directed (Hippodrome, June 13, 1956); and appeared as Johnny Condell in *One More River* (Ambassador, N.Y.C., Mar. 18, 1960).

Films. Mr. Nolan made his film debut in *Stolen Harmony* (Par., 1935); subsequently appeared in *Bataan* (MGM, 1943); *Guadalcanal Diary* (20th-Fox, 1943); *Captain Eddie* (20th-Fox, 1945); *The House on 92nd Street* (20th-Fox, 1945); *Circumstantial Evidence* (20th-Fox, 1945); *A Tree Grows in Brooklyn* (20th-Fox, 1945); *Somewhere in the Night* (20th-Fox, 1946); *Two Smart People* (MGM, 1946); *Lady in the Lake* (MGM, 1946); *Wild Harvest* (Par., 1947); and *Green Grass of Wyoming* (20th-Fox, 1948).

Also, *Street With No Name* (20th-Fox, 1948); *Bad Boy* (AA, 1949); *Easy Living* (RKO, 1949); *The Sun Comes Up* (MGM, 1949); *The Lemon Drop Kid* (Par., 1951); *We Joined the Navy* (Dial, 1962); *Island in the Sky* (WB, 1953); *Crazy Legs* (Rep., 1953); *Last Hunt* (MGM, 1956); *Santiago* (WB, 1956); *Peyton Place* (20th-Fox, 1956); *Abandon Ship!* (Col., 1957); *A Hatful of Rain* (20th-Fox, 1957); *Portrait in Black* (U, 1960); *Susan Slade* (WB, 1961); *Circus World* (Par., 1964); *Never Too Late* (WB, 1965); *The Double Man* (WB, 1968); *Sergeant Ryker* (U, 1968); *Ice Station Zebra* (MGM, 1969); *Airport* (U, 1970); and *Earthquake* (U, 1974).

Television. Mr. Nolan appeared as Capt. Queeg in *The Caine Mutiny Court-Martial* (CBS, Nov. 19, 1955); performed in *Ah, Wilderness!;* on Martin Kane, Private Eye (NBC, 1952–53); was a regular on the series Julia (NBC); and made many appearances as a guest star in TV series.

Awards. Mr. Nolan received the Donaldson Award, and won the Variety N.Y. Drama Critics poll for his performance as Capt. Queeg in *The Caine Mutiny Court-Martial* (1954); and the NATAS (Emmy) Award for his performance in the same role in television version (1956).

Recreation. Golf, archaeology.

NOLTE, CHARLES. Actor, director, playwright. b. Charles Miller Nolte, Nov. 3, 1926, Duluth, Minn., to Julius and Mildred (Miller) Nolte. Father, dean of Univ. of Minnesota. Grad. Wayzata (Minn.) H.S., 1941; Yale Univ., B.A. 1946; Univ. of Minnesota, M.A., 1963. Served USN, 1942–45. Address: Box 71, Wayzata, MN 55391, tel. (612) GR 3-7738.

Theatre. He made his acting debut at age ten as Tranio in *The Taming of the Shrew* (Old Log, Minn., 1936). His first professional appearance was as Greg Talbot in the American Negro Th. production of *Tin Top Valley* (ANT Playhouse, Harlem, N.Y., Feb. 27, 1947).

He made his Bway debut as Silius in Katharine Cornell's *Antony and Cleopatra* (Martin Beck Th., Nov. 26, 1947); played Billy Budd in the ANTA production of *Uniform of Flesh* (Lenox Hill Playhouse, Jan. 29, 1949); a soldier in *Caesar and Cleopatra* (National, Dec. 20, 1949); William Clitherow in *Design for a Stained Glass Window* (Mansfield, Jan. 23, 1950); was a replacement (1950) in the role of Payne in *Mister Roberts* (Alvin, Feb. 18, 1948); played the title role in *Billy Budd* (Biltmore, Feb. 10, 1951), which was a re-written version of *Uniform of Flesh;* and played Willy Keith in *Caine Mutiny Court Martial* (Plymouth, Jan. 20, 1954).

He played Slave in *Medea* (Th. Sarah Bernhardt, Paris, 1955); made his London debut as Charlie in one of his own plays, *The Summer People* (Golder's Green Th., 1962); the latter play was also presented at the Pembroke Th. (London, 1962), and at the Univ. of Minnesota (1963).

He wrote and directed *Alexander's Death* (produced by Univ. of Minnesota (1963); wrote and played Crawford in *Do Not Pass Go* (Cherry Lane Th., N.Y.C., Apr. 19, 1965), which was subsequently produced in London (Hampstead Th. Club, June 6, 1966); adapted and directed *The Bacchae '65* (Univ. of Minn., Scott Hall Aud., Minneapolis, July 7, 1965); and at the Meadow Brook Th., Rochester, Mich., has directed and appeared in *The Andersonville Trial* (Nov. 11, 1971); directed *The Front Page* (Oct. 12, 1972); *Inherit the Wind* (Nov. 9, 1972); *A Streetcar Named Desire* (Nov. 8, 1973); directed the world premiere of his own adaptation of *Oedipus Rex* (Jan. 3, 1974); and directed *Death of a Salesman* (Jan. 2, 1975).

Mr. Nolte became an instructor at the Univ. of Minnesota, Minneapolis, in 1963.

Films. He made his debut in *Warpaint* (UA, 1953); subsequently appeared in *Steel Cage* (UA, 1954); *Ten Seconds to Hell* (UA, 1959); *Under Ten Flags* (Par., 1960); and *Armored Command* (AA, 1961).

Television. Mr. Nolte has appeared on Kraft Th. (NCB, 1950); in the title role of *Billy BUdd* (Schlitz Playhouse of Stars, CBS, Jan. 11, 1952); and on summer Studio One (CBS). His play, *Do Not Pass Go* was adapted for presentation on *The Unpleasant Play (USA—Satire,* Educ., May 5, 1966).

Awards. He received a *Th. World* Promising Personality Award for his performance in *Design for a Stained Glass Window* (1950); a McNight Foundation Humanities Award, for his play, *The Summer People* (Univ. of Minnesota, Minneapolis, 1962); and won the Charles H. Sergel Drama Contest, for his play *Do Not Pass Go* (Univ. of Chicago, 1965).

NOONAN, JOHN FORD. Playwright. b. Oct. 7, 1943, New York City. Father, physician. Grad. Fairfield Preparatory Sch., Greenwich, Conn., 1959; Brown Univ., A.B. 1964; Carnegie Institute of Technology, M.F.A. 1966. Married 1962 to Marcia Lunt (marr. dis., 1965); three children. Member of Ensemble Studio Th. (exec. comm.). Address: c/o Joan Scott, Inc., 162 W. 56th St., New York, NY 10019.

Pre-Theatre. Construction worker, go-go dancer, basketball coach, accountant, housepainter, dockhand, truck loader, stockbroker.

Theatre. Mr. Noonan is the author of *The Year Boston Won the Pennant* (Forum, N.Y.C., May 22, 1969); *Lazarus Was a Lady* (1970); *Rainbows for Sale* (1971); *Concerning the Effects of Trimethyl Chloride* (Old Reliable, Mar. 29, 1971); *Older People* (Public/Anspacher, May 14, 1972); *Good-Bye and Keep Cold* (1973); *A Sneaky Bit to Raise the Blind,* and *Pick, Pack, Pock, Puck,* presented as a double bill entitled *Two More from Jimmy Ray's* (Cubiculo, May 9, 1974); *Where Do We Go from Here?,* produced in workshop form (Public/Martinson Hall, Apr. 28, 1974), and subsequently given full production (Public/Newman, Oct. 24, 1974); and *Getting Through the Night* (Ensemble Studio Th., Feb. 12, 1976).

In addition, he was a stagehand at the Fillmore East Rock Th. (1969–71).

Films. He has written the screenplays for *Septuagenarian Substitute Ball* (1970); and *The Summer the Snows Came* (1972).

Other Activities. Mr. Noonan taught English, Latin and history at Buckley Country Day Sch. (North Hills, N.Y., 1966–69); was professor of drama at Villanova Univ. (1972–73); and has taught playwriting at the Circle in the Square Th. Sch.

Awards. He was the recipient of a basketball scholarship to Brown Univ.; and a Rockefeller Grant (1973).

NORTH, ALEX. Composer. b. Dec. 4, 1910, Chester, Pa., to Jesse and Bela (Soifer) North. Father, blacksmith. Grad. Chester (Pa.) H.S., 1927; attended Juilliard Sch. of Music (scholarship), N.Y.C., 1929–32; Moscow (USSR) Conservatory (scholarship), 1933–35. Studied composition with Aaron Copland, N.Y.C., 1936–38; and Ernst Toch, N.Y.C., 1938–40. Married Dec. 19, 1941, to Sherle Hartt (marr. dis.); one son, one daughter; married Mar. 25, 1972, to Annemarie Hoellger; one son. Served US Army, War Dept., Special Services, 1942–46; rank, Capt. Member of Screen Composers Assn.; Composers and Lyricists Guild; AFM; Dramatists Guild; ASCAP. Address: 911 Gateway West, Los Angeles, CA 90067.

Pre-Theatre. Teacher of music for the dance at Finch Coll., Briarcliff Coll., Sarah Lawrence Coll., and Bennington Coll. (1935–38).

Theatre. Mr. North composed, at first, music for ballets; *Ballad in a Popular Style* (1933), *Case History* (1933), *Into the Streets* (1934), *Song of Affirmation* (1934), *Facade* (1935), and *War Is Beautiful* (1936); wrote music for the play, *Dog Beneath the Skin* (1936); wrote music for the ballets *Slaughter of the Innocents* (premiere, Guild Th., N.Y.C., Nov. 14, 1937); Martha Graham's *American Lyric* (premiere, Guild, Dec. 26, 1937; moved Jan. 2, 1938); *The Last Waltz* (1937); *Exile* (premiere, Mansfield, Mar. 3, 1941); *Golden Fleece* (premiere, Mansfield, Mar. 17, 1941); and *Inquisition* (1938).

He contributed music to *The Life and Death of an American* (Maxine Elliott's Th., May 19, 1939); and, as musical director, accompanied the ballet troupe of Anna Sokolow to Mexico, where he also conducted concerts at the Palace of Fine Arts (Mexico City). He wrote music for the revue, *'Tis of Thee* (Maxine Elliott's Th., N.Y.C., Oct. 26, 1940); for the ballets, *Lupe* (1940), and *Design for Five* (1941); for the children's musical, *Danny Dither* (1941); two revues, *You Can't Sleep Here* (Barbizon-Plaza, Apr. 26 and 27; May 10, 11–17, 1941), and *Of V We Sing* (American Youth Th., Oct. 25, 1941); the ballet *Clay Ritual* (Avery Museum, Hartford, Conn., May 20, 1942); the pageant *Song of Our City* (1946); composed incidental music for *O'Daniel* (Princess, Feb. 23, 1947); and *The Great Campaign* (Princess, Mar. 30, 1947); the ballet *Intersection* (1947); the plays, *Death of a Salesman* (Morosco, Feb. 10, 1949); and *The Innocents* (Playhouse, Feb. 1, 1950); and the musical *Queen of Sheba* (1950). He wrote the music for the ballet, *A Streetcar Named Desire* (Her Majesty's Th., Montreal, Quebec, Canada, Oct. 9, 1952; Century, N.Y.C., Dec. 8, 1952); incidental music for *Richard III* (NY City Ctr., Dec. 9, 1953); and *Coriolanus* (Phoenix, Jan. 19, 1954); and two ballets, *Daddy Long Legs Dream Ballet* (1955), and *Mal de Siècle* (Brussels World's Fair, Belgium, July 3, 1958).

Films. Mr. North composed background music for *The Thirteenth Letter* (20th-Fox, 1951); *A Streetcar Named Desire* (WB, 1951); *Death of a Salesman* (Col., 1951); *Viva Zapata!* (20th-Fox, 1952); *Member of the Wedding* (Col., 1952); *Les Miserables* (20th-Fox, 1952); *Pony Soldier* (20th-Fox, 1952); *Desirée* (20th-Fox, 1954); *Go Man Go* (UA, 1954); *The Racers* (20th-Fox, 1955); *I'll Cry Tomorrow* (MGM, 1955); *The Rose Tattoo* (Par., 1955); *Unchained* (UA, 1955); *Man with the Gun* (UA, 1955); *The Rainmaker* (Par., 1956); *The Bad Seed* (WB, 1956); *Four Girls in Town* (U, 1956); *A King and Four Queens* (UA, 1957); *Bachelor Party* (UA, 1957); *Stagestruck* (Buena Vista, 1958); *Hot Spell* (Par., 1958); *South Seas Adventure* (Stanley Warner Cinema Corp., 1958); *The Long, Hot Summer* (20th-Fox, 1958); *The Sound and the Fury* (20th-Fox, 1959); *The Wonderful Country* (UA, 1959); *Spartacus* (U, 1960); *The Misfits* (UA, 1961); *Sanctuary* (20th-Fox, 1961); *All Fall Down* (MGM, 1962); *The Children's Hour* (UA, 1962); *Cleopatra* (20th-Fox, 1963); *Cheyenne Autumn* (WB, 1964); *The Outrage* (MGM, 1964); *The Agony and the Ecstasy* (20th-Fox, 1965); *Who's Afraid of Virginia Woolf?* (WB, 1966); *The Shoes of the Fisherman* (MGM, 1968); *The Devil's Brigade* (UA, 1968); *Hard Contract* (20th-Fox, 1969); *A Dream of Kings* (Natl. Gen., 1969); *Willard* (Cinerama, 1971); *Pocket Money* (UA, 1972); *Once Upon a Scoundrel* (Carlyle Prod., 1972); *Rebel Jesus* (Amer. Intl., 1972); and *Shanks* (Par., 1974). Mr. North was musical director for *Lost in the Stars* (Amer. Film Th., 1973).

His scores for documentary films include *China Strikes Back* (1936); *Heart of Spain* (1937); *People of Cumberland* (1938); *Venezuela: (a) Election, (b)*

Sports, (c) Recreation (1939); *Recreation* (Dept. of Agriculture, 1939); *Mount Vernon* (1940); *Rural Nurse* (1940); *City Pastorale* (1942); *Decision for Chemistry* (1953); and *The American Road* (1953).

Television. Mr. North wrote music for the ballet, *Wall Street* (Show of Shows, NBC, premiere 1953). He has composed music for the Billy Rose Show (1950); the theme music for Playhouse 90 (CBS, 1960); music for the F.D.R. series (ABC, 1961); for the special *Africa* (ABC, 1969); the Christmas special *Silent Night* (ABC, 1970); and the series The Man and the City (Univ., 1972).

Published Works. He wrote the music for such songs as "To My Son" (1936), "Valley Forge" (1938), "Down in the Clover" (1941); "Elegy" (1946), "There's a Nation" (1942), "I Belong to You " (1953), with Hal David, "Vino Vino" (1955); with Paul Francis Webster, "Handful of Dreams" (1958); with Sam Cahn, "Hey Eula" (1959) and "The One Love" (1960); with Johnny Mercer, "Out of Time, Out of Space" (1960); with Harold Adamson, "Restless Love" (1961); "World of Love" (1963); and with Johnny Mercer, "The Nile" (1963).

Nr. North's other published compositions include *Revue* for clarinet and orchestra, written for Benny Goodman; *Pastime Suite,* for clarinet and piano; *Twelve Dance Preludes,* for solo piano; the children's musical *The Hither and Thither of Danny Dither;* and, for narrator and orchestra, *Little Indian Drum* and *The Waltzing Elephant.*

Awards. Mr. North received a Guggenheim Fellowship in Composition (1947); and was nominated for Academy (Oscar) awards for musical scoring of *A Streetcar Named Desire* (1951); *Death of a Salesman* (1951); *Viva Zapata!* (1952); *The Rose Tattoo* (1955); for the theme song for *Unchained Melody* (1956); *The Rainmaker* (1958); *Spartacus* (1960); *Cleopatra* (1963); *The Agony and the Ecstasy* (1965); *Who's Afraid of Virginia Woolf?* (1966); and *The Shoes of the Fisherman* (1968). He received the *Downbeat* magazine Award for his ballet, *Daddy Longlegs Dream Ballet* (1955); "Unchained Melody" was selected as best song by the Band Stand Revue (1956); received Exhibitor Laurel awards for top film composer (1957, 1966, 1967, and 1971); and the first annual award (1964) from the Composers and Lyricists Guild of America for the best film score for *Cleopatra.* Mr. North also received the Golden Globe Award for *The Shoes of the Fisherman,* and his score for *Who's Afraid of Virginia Woolf?* received National Academy of Recording Arts and Sciences (NARAS) award nominations for best original score and best instrumental theme.

Recreation. Sporting events, electronic music, zoological research, skin diving, American jazz and folk music, antiques.

NORTON, ELLIOT. Drama critic, lecturer. b. William Elliot Norton, May 17, 1903, Boston, Mass., to William Laurence and Mary E. Norton. Grad. Boston (Mass.) Latin school, 1922; Harvard Univ., B.A. 1926; Emerson Coll., M.A. 1955. Married Sept. 9, 1934, to Florence E. Stelmach; one son, two daughters. Member of ANTA (dir., 1957, Drama Advisory Panel to US State Dept., 1959–63); ATA; New England Th. Conference (pres., 1951–53; dir., 1953–72); Boston Press Club (pres., 1951–53); National Th. Conference (honorary member); Amer. Academy of Arts and Sciences (fellow); Mass. Council on the Arts and Humanities (vice-chmn., 1966–72). Address: (home) 126 Church St., Watertown, MA 02172, tel. (617) 924-7731; (bus.) Boston *Herald American* , Boston, MA 02106.

Mr. Norton is the drama critic (1972–to date) of the Boston *Herald American,* and the Boston *Sunday Herald Advertiser.* Formerly, he was drama critic for the Boston *Record American* and the Boston *Sunday Advertiser* (1956–72); and the Boston *Post* (1934–56). He wrote a column for *Boston* Magazine, contributed the Boston chapter to the annual *Best Plays* series; and has contributed articles to *Theatre Arts* Magazine, *Shakespeare Quarterly,* and various anthologies, including *A College in a Yard* (1957), and *The Passionate Playgoer* (1958). Since 1958, he has conducted a weekly television program, *Elliot Norton Reviews* (Boston).

Mr. Norton has also taught theatre courses at Emerson Coll. (1943–63); Boston Coll. (1943–63); Harvard Univ. (Summer 1962); and Boston Univ. (1947–74), where he was adjunct professor of dramatic literature.

Awards. Mr. Norton has received the Boston Coll. Citation of Merit (1947) "for distinguished criticism in the field of journalism"; the Connor Memorial Award, Emerson Coll. (1956) "for creative criticism of the drama"; the Rodgers and Hammerstein Coll. Pres. Award (1962) "for the person who has done most for theatre in Boston"; the George Foster Peabody Award (1963) for his television show, Elliot Norton Reviews; the George Jean Nathan Award (1963–64) "for best dramatic criticism written during the year"; the Antoinette Perry (Tony) Award (1971) "for his services to the American theatre"; the Humanities Award of the National Council of Teachers of English (1971); and the Gold Medal Award of Excellence of the American College Theater Festival (1973).

He has received the honorary degrees of L.H.D. from Fairfield Univ. (1964), and Boston Coll. (1970); D.Litt. from Northeastern Univ. (1966); D.J. and D.Litt. from St. Francis Coll. (1970).

NOTO, LORE. Producer, actor. b. Lorenzo Noto, June 9, 1923, New York City, to Antonino and Maria Antoinette (Savona) Noto. Father, laborer; billiard academy proprietor. Grad. N.Y. Sch. of Industrial Art, N.Y.C., 1940. Attended AADA, and David Ross' Th. Workshop (N.Y.C.). Married Sept. 14, 1947, to Mary Luzzi; three sons, one daughter. Served US Merchant Marines, 1943–45; rank, Able-bodied Seaman (Purple Heart, 1944); US Maritime Service, 1945–46; rank, Chief Petty Officer. Member of AEA; League of Off-Bway Theatres and Producers; Dramatists Guild. Address: 24 Ascan Ave., Forest Hills, Queens, NY 11375, tel. (212) 544-9796.

Pre-Theatre. Representative for commercial artists.

Theatre. During the 1940's, Mr. Noto acted in more than 100 Off-Bway amateur and professional productions, beginning with an appearance as an old man in a production of *The Master Builder* (Public Library, N.Y.C., 1940), and including performances in *Chee Chee;* as a Temple Guard and Carpus in *The Time Predicted* (Madison Ave. Presbyterian Church); Wilbur Albright in *Bomb Shelter* (Little Th., June 10, 1941); for the Blackfriars Guild, in *Armor of Light; Truce of the Bear;* and as the Second Captor and the Examining Officer in *Shake Hands with the Devil* (Oct. 20, 1949); etc. He played Servant and Corporal in the David Ross production of *The Italian Straw Hat* (4th St. Th., Sept. 30, 1958); Mr. Van Daan in *The Diary of Anne Frank* (Cecilwood Summer Th., Fishkill, N.Y., July 7, 1959); and was associated with David Ross in the production of, and played the Police Commissioner in, *The Failures* (Fourth St. Th., N.Y.C., Jan. 5, 1959).

Mr. Noto produced *The Fantasticks* (Sullivan St. Playhouse, May 3, 1960), which is still running and has become the longest running play in the history of Amer. Th.; and produced and, with Herbert Martin, wrote the book for *The Yearling* (Alvin, Dec. 10, 1965). He assumed the role of "The Boy's Father" in *The Fantasticks* for a single performance in 1960, occasionally thereafter (including July 20, 1966–Aug. 1, 1966), and has been playing that role continuously since Jan. 1972.

Awards. He won the AADA Award of Achievement (Oct. 6, 1966).

NOVA, LOU. Actor, comedian. b. Jay Louis Nova, Mar. 16, 1920 (?), Los Angeles, Calif., to Jay Louis and Wanda Belle (Parker) Nova. Father, concert pianist; mother, nurse. Grad. Alameda (Calif.) H.S., 1936; attended Sacramento Jr. Coll.; Univ. of California. Studied at Ben Bard's Dramatic Sch., Hollywood, Calif. Married Hertha Marie Robbins (marr. dis. 1951); three sons, one daughter. Served Calif. Natl. Guard, 1941–42; rank, 1st Lt. Relative in theatre: cousin, Joe Parker, director. Member of SAG; AEA; AGVA; AFTRA; The Lambs. Address: c/o The Lambs, 130 W. 44th St., New York, NY 10036.

Pre-Theatre. Prizefighter; US and world amateur heavyweight champion (1935); challenger for professional heavyweight championship of the world (1941).

Theatre. Mr. Nova made his acting debut in the role of a boxer in a production of *Is Zat So?* (Th. of the 15, Coral Gables, Fla., Feb. 1942); played many stock roles in succeeding years; and made his N.Y.C. debut as Big Jule in a revival of *Guys and Dolls* (NY City Ctr., Apr. 20, 1955). He played "the Wreck" in a stock tour of *My Sister Eileen* (Summer 1955); O'Malley in *The Happiest Millionaire* (Lyceum, N.Y.C., Nov. 20, 1956); and appeared in *Rosalie* (Central Park, N.Y.C., 1957).

Films. Through 1969, Mr. Nova had made, by his own count, twenty-eight pictures, including *Swing Fever* (MGM, 1943); *The Prizefighter and the Cowboy; Joe Palooka, Champ* (Monogram, 1946); *Somewhere in the Night* (20th-Fox, 1946); *The Red Badge of Courage* (MGM, 1951); *Salome* (Col., 1953); *Prince Valiant* (20th-Fox, 1954); *World for Ransom* (AA, 1954); *The Leather Saint* (Par., 1956); *What a Way to Go* (20th-Fox, 1964); *Thoroughly Modern Millie* (U, 1967); and *Blackbeard's Ghost* (Buena Vista, 1968).

Television and Radio. Mr. Nova had his own radio sports program; and has made appearances on many television shows, including US Steel Hour (CBS); Dupont Show of the Month (NBC); Kraft Television Th. (NBC); The Ed Sullivan Show (CBS); the Red Skelton Show (CBS); and Get Smart (NBC).

Night Clubs. He has performed at Cafe Society (N.Y.C.) and the Chez Paree (Chicago), among others.

Other Activities. Mr. Nova gave frequent poetry recitals in the 1950's, including two performances at Carnegie Recital Hall (N.Y.C., May 8, 1956; May 14, 1957); toured for the USO, in *The Lou Nova Show* (including a Korean and Pacific hospital tour, Summer 1969); invented the Yogi Nova, a health aid; has been an after-dinner speaker; and has written magazine and newspaper articles.

Awards. Mr. Nova received the C. B. deMille Award as America's most versatile entertainer (1959).

NOYES, THOMAS. actor, Producer, 7. b. Thomas Ewing Noyes, Oct. 24, 1922, Washington, D.C., to Newbold and Alexandra Ewing Noyes. Father, journalist. Grad. St. Paul's Sch., Concord, N.H., 1941; Yale Univ., B.A. 1947. Married Dec. 19, 1944, to Ann Lilienthal (marr. dis. 1951); married Feb. 22, 1952, to Elizabeth Ross, actress; two sons, one daughter. Served USNAC, 1942–43; rank, Ensign. Member of AEA; Newspaper Guild; The Players; Yale Club; Coffee House Club. Address: 2811 Chesterfield Pl., N.W., Washington, DC 20008, tel. (202) 362-0668.

Theatre. Mr. Noyes made his stage debut as Mr. Bonaparte in a Yale Univ. Dramatic Association production of *Golden Boy* (1946); subsequently produced, with the Yale Players, a season of plays (Siasconset, Mass., Summer 1946); produced, with his wife, Ann Noyes, the pre-Bway tryout of *The Innocents* (Pocono Playhouse, Mountainhome, Pa., Sept. 1949); appeared as the Second Gendarme and the Second Seaman in *Now I Lay Me Down to Sleep* (Broadhurst Th., N.Y.C., Mar. 2, 1950); Carter Reynolds in *The Small Hours* (Natl., Feb. 15, 1951); and succeeded (May 1951) Robert McQueeney as Duncan in *Billy Budd* (Biltmore, Feb. 10, 1951).

Mr. Noyes produced, with Lyn Austin, *Take a Giant Step* (Lyceum, Sept. 24, 1953); produced, with Lyn Austin and in association with Robert Radnitz and Robert Sagalyn, *The Frogs of Spring* (Broadhurst, Oct. 20, 1953); produced, with Lyn Austin and The Producers Theatre, *Portrait of a Lady* (ANTA, Dec. 2, 1954); produced, with Lyn Austin and Roger Stevens, the pre-Bway tryout of *Blue Denim* (Westport Country Playhouse, Conn., July

18, 1955); and produced, with Lyn Austin and The Producers Theatre, *Joyce Grenfell Requests the Pleasure . .* (Bijou, Oct. 10, 1955); presented, with Lyn Austin and Roger Stevens, *The Crystal Heart* (Saville Th., London, Feb. 19, 1957); and produced with Lyn Austin and in association with Anderson Lawler, *Copper and Brass* (Martin Beck Th., N.Y.C., Oct. 17, 1957).

Television. Mr. Noyes appeared on Lux Video Th. (NBC, Fall 1951); was associated with Arthur Penn and Fred Coe in the preparation (Winter 1958–Spring 1959) of a projected dramatic series, entitled *Biography*, for CBS, which was never produced.

Other Activities. Mr. Noyes is also a freelance writer and was a newspaper reporter with the *Long Island Press* (Jamaica, N.Y.) from 1959 to 1964, when he joined the staff of *The Evening Star* (Washington, D.C.).

Recreation. Photography, flying, sailing.

NUGENT, ELLIOTT. Actor, director, producer, playwright. b. Elliott John Nugent, Sept. 20, 1899, Dover, Ohio, to John Charles and Grace Mary (Fertig) Nugent. Father, actor, playwright known as J. C. Nugent; mother, actress. Grad. Dover H.S., Ohio, 1915; Ohio State Univ., B.A. 1919. Studied acting with father, and Madame Alberti, one year. Married Oct. 15, 1921, to Norma Lee Nugent, actress; three daughters. Relatives in theatre: sister, Ruth Nugent, actress; daughter, Nancy Nugent, actress-producer; brother-in-law, Alan Bunce, actor; son-in-law, John Gerstad, actor, director. Served USNR, 1918–19, Great Lakes Naval Tng. Sta. Member of AEA (council member, 1941–43); AFTRA; DGA; Phi Kappa Psi; The Lambs; The Players. Address: 333 E. 57th St., New York, NY 10022.

Pre-Theatre. Journalist.

Theatre. Mr. Nugent made his stage debut at four, when he joined his parents in their vaudeville act (Orpheum, Los Angeles, Calif., 1904); his Bway debut as Tom Sterrett in *Dulcy* (Frazee Th., Aug. 13, 1921); wrote *Kempy*, with his father, and appeared in the title role (Belmont, May 15, 1922); followed by *A Clean Town*, written with his father (1922); played Jim Dolf in *The Breaks* (Klaw, Apr. 16, 1923); appeared in *The Dumb-Bell* (Belmont, Nov. 26, 1923); played Eddie Hudson in *The Wild Westcotts* (Frazee, Dec. 24, 1923); with his father, wrote *The Rising Sun*, in which he played Ted Alamayne (Klaw, Oct. 27, 1924); appeared as John Miller in *The Poor Nut* (Henry Miller's Th., Apr. 27, 1925); in *Human Nature* (Liberty, Sept. 24, 1925); and *The Trouper* (52 St. Th., Mar. 8, 1926).

Mr. Nugent played Kempy James in a revival of *Kempy* (Hudson, May 11, 1927); toured in *Hoosiers Abroad* (1927); with his father, Elaine S. Carrington, and John Wray, wrote *Nightstick* (Selwyn, N.Y.C., Nov. 10, 1927); with his father, wrote *By Request* and played William Abbott (Hudson, Sept. 27, 1928); succeeded (Nov. 1928) Eddie Buzzell as Walter Meakin in *Good Boy* (Hammerstein's, Sept. 5, 1928); played Bing Allen in *Fast Service*, which he wrote with his father (Selwyn, Nov. 17, 1931); and *The World's My Onion*, which he wrote with his father (Pasadena Community Th., Calif., 1934–35).

Mr. Nugent played Tommy Turner in *The Male Animal*, which he wrote with James Thurber (Cort, N.Y.C., Jan. 9, 1940); directed and produced, with Robert Montgomery and Jesse Duncan, *All in Favor* (Henry Miller's Th., Jan. 20, 1942); played Patrick Jamieson in *Without Love* (St. James, Nov. 10, 1942); directed *Tomorrow the World* (Ethel Barrymore Th., Apr. 14, 1943); played Bill Page in *The Voice of the Turtle* (Morosco, Dec. 8, 1943); wrote and directed *A Place of Our Own*, produced by John Golden, in association with Mr. Nugent and Robert Montgomery (Royale, Apr. 2, 1945).

Mr. Nugent and Mr. Montgomery, by arrangement with David Bramson, produced *The Big Two* (Booth, Jan. 8, 1947); directed, with George Schaefer, the pre-Bway tryout of *Darling, Darling, Darling*, originally titled *The First Hundred Years*, (opened McCarter Th., Princeton, N.J., Jan. 31, 1947; closed Wilbur Th., Boston, Mass., Feb. 8, 1947); directed *Message for Margaret* (Plymouth, N.Y.C., Apr. 16, 1947); toured in *The Fundamental George* (Summers 1947–49); played Ambrose Atwater in *Not for Children* (Coronet, N.Y.C., Feb. 13, 1951); and appeared in *The Male Animal* (NY City Ctr., Apr. 30, 1952).

He produced *The Seven Year Itch* with Courtney Burr and succeeded (1954) Tom Ewell as Richard Sherman (Fulton, Nov. 20, 1952); supervised the national tour of *The Seven Year Itch* (opened Cass Th., Detroit, Mich., Sept. 7, 1953); with Courtney Burr and John Byram, produced *The Wayward Saint* (Cort, N.Y.C., Feb. 17, 1955); played Dr. Brothers in the pre-Bway tour of *Build with One Hand* (opened Shubert, New Haven, Conn., Nov. 7, 1956; closed Ford Th., Baltimore, Md., Nov. 27, 1956); and directed *The Greatest Man Alive!* which he produced with Frederic Fox and John Gerstad (Ethel Barrymore Th., N.Y.C., May 8, 1957).

Films. Mr. Nugent began acting, writing, and directing for films (1929); directed *Three Cornered Moon* (Par., 1933); *She Loves Me Not* (Par., 1934); *The Cat and the Canary* (Par., 1939); *The Male Animal* (WB, 1942); *Up in Arms* (RKO, 1944); *Welcome Stranger* (Par., 1947); *My Favorite Brunette* (Par., 1947); *The Great Gatsby* (Par., 1949); and *Just for You* (Par., 1952).

Published Works. Mr. Nugent is the author of *Of Cheat and Charmer* (1962) and *Events Leading Up to the Comedy* (1965).

Awards. He won the *Variety* NY Drama Critics Poll for his portrayal of Bill Page in *The Voice of the Turtle* (1944).

Recreation. Swimming, photography, golf.

NUGENT, NANCY. Actress, producer, coach. b. Nancy Elliott Nugent, Feb. 10, 1938, Los Angeles, Calif., to Elliott and Norma (Lee) Nugent. Father, actor, director, playwright; mother, actress. Studied at Art Students League, N.Y.C., 1956–57; voice with Kathryn Meisle (1962), Oly Olsen, Royal Hinman, Donald Haywood, Phyllis Grandy, Joe Bousard; jazz dance with Dave Harris, Ron Forella, Luigi, Frank Wagner, Betsy Haug, Timmy Everett, Charles Kelley; Hindu dance with Beatrice Krafft; ballet with Don Farnworth, Armgard von Bardeleben, Job Sanders; musical comedy with David Craig. Married May 29, 1958, to Douglas S. Crawford (marr. dis., March 28, 1961); one son, one daughter. Relative in theatre: brother-in-law, John Gerstad, director, producer, actor, writer. Member of AEA; AFTRA; SAG. Address: 890 West End Ave., New York, NY 10025.

Theatre. Miss Nugent made her Bway debut at age 10 as Pat Frame in *Tomorrow the World* (Ethel Barrymore Th., Apr. 14, 1943); subsequently was stage manager for *The Devil in Boston* (Circle, Hollywood, Calif., Dec. 1951); played Patricia Stanley in *The Male Animal* (NY City Ctr., Apr. 30, 1952); and Nurse Evans in a summer theatre tryout of *The Automobile Man* (Bucks County Playhouse, New Hope, Pa., July 1954).

She succeeded (Sept. 1954) Paulette Girard in the role of Marie-What-Ever-Her-Name-Was in *The Seven Year Itch* (Fulton, N.Y.C., Nov. 20, 1952); and appeared in repertory production (American Th., Rome, Italy, Spring 1955); and at the Helen Hayes Workshop (N.Y.C.), played Viola in *Twelfth Night*, Lady Anne in *Richard III*, Katherine in *The Taming of the Shrew*, and appeared in staged readings of *Lovers, Villains and Fools* (1957).

She played Secretary and The Other Woman in a touring production of *Witness for the Prosecution* (Summer 1957); in association with her husband, Douglas Crawford, produced a revival of *On the Town* (Carnegie Hall Playhouse, Jan. 15, 1959); was casting director and production assistant at the Dayton (Ohio) Memorial Th., where she also appeared in Summer productions (1959); played Mrs. Cargill in *Time Limit!* (Th. East, Bromley, England, Oct. 1960); succeeded (Jan. 1961) Carrie Nye as Regina Engstrand in *Ghosts* (Fourth St. Th., N.Y.C., Sept. 21, 1961); played Agatha Higginson in *Billygoat Eddie* (Writers Stage Th., Apr. 20, 1964); was featured in *A Thurber Carnival* (Bucks County Playhouse, New Hope, Pa., 1965); and toured as Sarah in *Company* (Summer 1972).

Films. She appeared in *Vistavision Goes to Spain* (Par., 1955).

Television. Miss Nugent has done "voice-overs" for Sony Industrial Film Strips and a commerical for Bayer aspirin.

Other Activities. Miss Nugent taught improvisation and dance at the Central YMCA, Bronx, N.Y., in 1965. She was an assistant to Lester Lewis, talent representative in 1970; in 1973–74, she assisted the director of the Puerto Rican Theatre, Henry Street Playhouse, N.Y.C., and conducted classes in "presence" for the International Model's Union, Local #1, and for Columbia Attractions, Inc. During the same period, she was guest lecturer on theatre at the State Univ. of New York (New Paltz), Henry St. Playhouse, Adelphi College, Brooklyn (N.Y.) Community College, and was an adjunct lecturer teaching speech at John Jay College, N.Y.C.

Recreation. Tennis, swimming, yoga, ballet and modern dance, painting, people-watching, child-appreciation, laughing, meditation, teaching yoga.

NYE, CARRIE. Actress. Attended Stephens Coll., Columbia, Mo.; Yale Drama Sch. Married to Dick Cavett, television entertainer. Member of AEA; SAG.

Theatre. Miss Nye has been a professional actress since age 14, making her N.Y.C. debut as Inez in *A Second String* (Eugene O'Neill Th., Apr. 13, 1960). The following season she appeared in the title role in the ELT production of *Ondine* (Lenox Hill Playhouse, Apr. 25, 1961); and replaced (Feb. 1962) Betsy Von Furstenberg as Tiffany Richards in *Mary, Mary* (Helen Hayes Th., Mar. 8, 1961). At the American Shakespeare Festival (Stratford, Conn.), she played Celia in *As You Like It* (June 27, 1961), Lady Macduff in *Macbeth* (June 28, 1961), and Cressida in *Troilus and Cressida* (July 23, 1961). She played Regina Engstrand in *Ghosts* (Fourth St. Th., N.Y.C., Sept. 21, 1961); Cecily Cardew in *The Importance of Being Earnest* (Madison Ave. Playhouse, Feb. 25, 1963); returned to the American Shakespeare Festival (Stratford, Conn.), where she played Regan in *King Lear* (June 9, 1963), Adriana in *The Comedy of Errors* (June 11, 1963), and Cleopatra in *Caesar and Cleopatra* (July 30, 1963); was in *A Plumb Line* (Village South Th., N.Y.C., Nov. 24, 1963); and played Cassandra in *The Trojan Women* (Circle in the Square, Dec. 23, 1963).

She was Helen Walsingham in *Half a Sixpence* (Broadhurst, Apr. 25, 1965); Ursula Bailey in *A Very Rich Woman* (Belasco Th., Sept. 30, 1965); Vittoria Corombona in *The White Devil* (Circle in the Square, Dec. 6, 1965); Beatrice in *Much Ado About Nothing* (Goodman Memorial Th., Chicago, Ill., Feb. 17, 1967); Lady Macbeth in *Macbeth* (American Shakespeare Festival, Stratford, Conn., July 30, 1967); Eleanor of Aquitaine in *The Lion in Winter* (Studio Arena, Buffalo, N.Y., Oct. 31, 1968); Margaret Ross-Hughes in *Home Fires* on the bill *Cop-Out* (Cort, Apr. 7, 1969); Thelma in *After Magritte* and Cynthia in *The Real Inspector Hound* (Th. Four, Apr. 23, 1972); and Blanche in *A Streetcar Named Desire* (Playhouse in the Park, Cincinnati, Ohio, Mar. 29, 1973).

NYPE, RUSSELL. Actor, singer. b. Russell Harold Nype, Apr. 26, 1924, Zion, Ill., to William and Elizabeth (Huisinga) Nype. Grad. Lake Forest Coll., B.A. 1943. Married Mar. 9, 1953, to Diantha Lawrence; one son. Served WW II, USAAF, 1943–46; rank, Sgt. Member of AEA; AFTRA; SAG; AGVA. Address: 1290 Madison Ave., New York, NY 10028, tel. (212) TE 1-5708.

Theatre. Mr. Nype made his N.Y.C. debut as Leo Hubbard in *Regina* (46 St. Th., Oct. 31, 1949); subsequently appeared as Freddie in *Great To Be Alive!* (Winter Garden, Mar. 23, 1950); Kenneth Gibson in *Call Me Madam* (Imperial, Oct. 12, 1950); and Bud Walters in the West Coast company of *Anniversary Waltz* (Alcazar, San Francisco, Calif.; Ritz, Los Angeles, Calif., 1954).

He has also played Charlie Reader in the national touring company of *The Tender Trap* (opened McCarter Th., Princeton, N.J., Jan. 21, 1955); Deerfield Prescott in *Wake Up, Darling* (Ethel Barrymore Th., N.Y.C., May 2, 1956); Enoch Snow in *Carousel* (NY City Ctr., Sept. 11, 1957); George Randolph Brown in *Goldilocks* (Lunt-Fontanne, Oct. 11, 1958); Stitch Allenstock in *Brouhaha* (175 E. Bway Playhouse, Apr. 26, 1960); Albert Peterson in *Bye Bye Birdie* (Coconut Grove Playhouse, Miami, Fla.); Hogan in the touring production of *Under the Yum-Yum Tree* (June–Oct. 1962), Jeff Douglas in *Brigadoon* (NY City Ctr., Jan. 30, 1963); Freddy Eynsford-Hill in *My Fair Lady* (NY City Ctr., May 20, 1964); Felix Sherman in *Owl and the Pussycat* (national tour, 1965–66); Alec Rice in *Girl in the Freudian Slip* (Booth Th., May 18, 1967); Elyot Chase in *Private Lives* (Th. de Lys, May 19, 1968); Cornelius Hackl in *Hello, Dolly!* (St. James Th., 1970); Tyler Rayburn in *Light Up the Sky* (Los Angeles, 1971); Jack Worthing in *The Importance of Being Earnest* (Goodman Th., Chicago, 1972) Capt. Robert Audley in *Lady Audley's Secret* (Eastside Playhouse, N.Y.C., 1972); Reginald Bridgenorth in Shaw's *Getting Married* (Hartford Stage Co., Hartford, Conn., 1973); Mr. Pincus in *The Front Page* (Los Angeles, 1974); and Jimmy Smith in *No, No, Nanette* (Parker Playhouse, Ft. Lauderdale, Fla., and Coconut Grove Playhouse, Miami, Fla., 1974).

Films. He appeared as the Assistant Dean of Harvard in *Love Story* (Par., 1970).

Television and Radio. On radio, he performed on the Big Show (NBC, 1951); MGM Th. of the Air (ABC, 1951); and Bandstand (NBC, 1954). On television, he has performed on the Ed Sullivan Show (CBS, 1950–58); Milton Berle Show (NBC, 1951); the role of Rodney in *One Touch of Venus* (NBC, 1957); appeared on Bell Telephone Hour (NBC, 1958); Ford Startime (CBS, 1959); *Omnibus* (NBC, 1960); and the June Allyson Show (CBS, 1961).

Night Clubs. Mr. Nype's first professional engagement as a singer was in the club, Number One Fifth Avenue (N.Y.C.); subsequently has performed at the Plaza Hotel (N.Y.C.); the Radisson Hotel (Minneapolis, Minn.); the El Rancho Hotel (Las Vegas, Nev.); and the Edgewater Beach Hotel (Chicago, Ill.).

Awards. For his performance as Kenneth Gibson in *Call Me Madam,* he received the Antoinette Perry (Tony) Award, the Donaldson Award, and the *Theatre World* Award (1951); and for his role as George Randolph Brown in *Goldilocks,* received an Antoinette Perry (Tony) Award (1959).

Recreation. Tennis, piano, horseback riding.

O

OBER, PHILIP. Actor. b. Philip Nott Ober, Mar. 23, 1902, Fort Payne, Ala., to Frank Willis and Emily (Nott) Ober. Father, International Committee, YMCA. Grad. Roger Ascham H.S., Hartsdale, N.Y., 1917; The Peddie Sch., 1919; attended Princeton Univ., 1919–21. Married June 14, 1923, to Phyllis Roper (marr. dis. 1941); one daughter; married Aug. 22, 1941, to Vivian Vance, actress (marr. dis. 1958); married Dec. 30, 1961, to Jane Westover, writer. During WW I, served with Red Cross, 1918; during WW II, USO. Member of AEA)council, 1947–52); SAG (bd. of gov., 1955–57); AFTRA; AMPAS; NATAS; McCarter Th. at Princeton Univ. (Professional Advisory Council); Veterans of the 7th Regiment Engineer Corps.

Pre-Theatre. Assistant advertising manager, Brooklyn Edison Co.

Theatre. Mr. Ober spent five seasons with The Beechwood Players (Scarborough-on-Hudson, N.Y.); made his Bway debut as Joe Fiske in *The Animal Kingdom* (Empire Th., Jan. 12, 1932); subsequently appeared as Henry Broughton in *She Loves Me Not* (46 St. Th., Nov. 20, 1933); Bud in *Personal Appearance* (Henry Miller's Th., Oct. 17, 1934); Walter Beckett in *Spring Dance* (Empire, Aug. 25, 1936); Mr. Jevries in *Without Warning* (Natl., May 1, 1937); appeared at Elitch Gardens (Denver, Colo., Summer 1937); played Brent in *The Hill Between* (Little, N.Y.C., Mar. 11, 1938); Ted Strong in *Eye on the Sparrow* (Vanderbilt, May 3, 1938); Horace Rand in *Kiss the Boys Goodbye* (Henry Miller's Th., Sept. 28, 1938); Humphrey Williams in *Out from Under* (Biltmore, May 4, 1940); Lt. Weigand in *Mr. and Mrs. North* (Belasco, Jan. 12, 1941); Harry Graves in *Junior Miss* (Lyceum, Nov. 18, 1941); Michael Fox in *Another Love Story* (Fulton, Oct. 12, 1943); and Dr. William Lathrop in *Doctor's Disagree* (Bijou, Dec. 28, 1943).

Mr. Ober appeared as Max Wharton in the USO production of *Over 21* (North Africa, Italy, 7 mos., 1944); toured as Judge Wilkins in *Dear Ruth* (Biltmore Th., Los Angeles, Calif.; Geary, San Francisco, Calif. Sept. 1944–Mar. 1945); appeared as Walter Craig in *Craig's Wife* (Playhouse, N.Y.C., Feb. 12, 1947); and Owen Turner in *Light Up the Sky* (Royale, Nov. 18, 1948).

Films. Mr. Ober made his debut as Jim Strong in *Chloe, Love Is Calling* (Pinnacle, 1934); subsequently appeared in *The Secret Fury* (RKO, 1950); *Never A Dull Moment* (RKO, 1950); *The Magnificent Yankee* (MGM, 1950); *The Washington Story* (MGM, 1952); *Come Back Little Sheba* (Par., 1952); *From Here to Eternity* (Col., 1953); *About Mrs. Leslie* (Par. 1954); *Broken Lance* (20th-Fox, 1954); *Tammy and the Bachelor* (U, 1957); *Escapade in Japan* (U, 1957); *The High Cost of Loving* (MGM, 1958); *Ten North Frederick* (20th-Fox, 1958); *Torpedo Run* (MGM, 1958); *North by Northwest* (MGM, 1959); *The Mating Game* (MGM, 1959); *Beloved Infidel* (20th-Fox, 1959); *Let No Man Write My Epitaph* (Col., 1960); *Elmer Gantry* (UA, 1960); *The Facts of Life* (UA, 1960); *Go Naked in the World* (MGM, 1960); *The Ugly American* (U, 1963); *The Brass Bottle* (U, 1964); *The Ghost and Mr. Chicken* (U, 1966); and *Assignment to Kill* (WB-7 Arts, 1969).

Television. Mr. Ober has appeared on Alfred Hitchcock Presents (CBS); Climax! (CBS); Lux Video Th. (NBC); I Love Lucy (CBS); Thriller; Ripcord; Sugarfoot; Whirleybirds; Desilu Playhouse (CBS); Mr. Lucky; Perry Mason; Death Valley Days; Outlaws (NBC); Loretta Young Show; The Real McCoys (NBC); Hercule Poiret; Danny Thomas Show (ABC); Sam Benedict (NBC); Cain's Hundred; Hazel (NBC); Empire (NBC); Bonanza (NBC); Twilight Zone (CBS); Temple Houston; the Investigators; Grindl (NBC); Moment of Fear (NBC); 90 Bristol Court (NBC); The Farmer's Daughter (ABC); Trails West (Ind.); Walt Disney's World (NBC); Profiles in Courage (NBC); The Munsters (CBS); No Time for Sergeants (ABC); I Dream of Jeannie (NBC); Tammy (ABC); Honey West (ABC); Hazel (CBS); I Spy (NBC); The Dick Van Dyke Show (CBS); The Tammy Grimes Show (ABC); Family Affair (CBS); Iron Horse (ABC); McHale's Navy (Ind.); Perry Mason (Ind.); and The Monkees (NBC).

Recreation. Tennis, bridge, cooking.

OBERLIN, RICHARD. Theatre administrator, actor, director, producer. b. Richard Paul Oberlin, Aug. 16, 1928, Dayton, Ohio, to Robert Charles and Lois Ruth (Young) Oberlin. Grad. Coll. of Wooster (Ohio), B.A. (honors in drama) 1952; postgraduate study at Indiana Univ., 1952–53. Served USNR, 1946–48. Married May 28, 1966, to Shirley Joan Cousins. Member of Theatre Panel, Ohio Arts Council (1970–to date); NTC; League of Resident Theatres. Address: (home) 13401 Lake Shore Blvd., Bratenahl, OH 44110; (bus.) Cleveland Play House, 2040 E. 86th St., Cleveland, OH 44106.

Theatre. Mr. Oberlin has been associated with the Cleveland Play House throughout his theatrical career, starting there in 1955 as an actor, a capacity in which he continued, concurrent with other responsibilities, until 1973. He became coordinating director in Sept. 1967, production director in Sept. 1968, managing director in Jan. 1971, and was named director in 1972.

At the Play House, Mr. Oberlin played Oliver in *As You Like It* (1956–57); Fra Timotheo in *The Love Apple* (Jan. 22, 1958); Hugh Barton in *Look Homeward, Angel* (Jan. 17, 1961); the First Scholar in *Dr. Faustus* (1960–61), in which he also toured (1961); Rev. Morell in *Candida* (1960–61); Mr. Martin in *The Bald Soprano* and Daddy in *The American Dream* (Dec. 12, 1962); Leo Herman in *A Thousand Clowns,* which he also stage managed (Dec. 16, 1964); Mr. Webb in *Our Town* (Apr. 13, 1966); and Mr. Antrobus in *The Skin of Our Teeth* (Nov. 2, 1966). He directed *The Hostage* (Feb. 8, 1967); *Barefoot in the Park,* in which he also played Victor Velasco (Mar. 29, 1967); *The Inspector General* (Sept. 29, 1967); performed in *Luv* (Oct. 13, 1967); in *Morning's at Seven* (Nov. 17, 1967); directed *Generation* (Jan. 19, 1968); *Dear Liar* (Mar. 15, 1968); *The Merry Wives of Windsor* (Mar. 27, 1968); was in *Waiting for Godot* (Apr. 19, 1968); directed *The Birthday Party* (Nov. 22, 1968); was in *Thieves' Carnival* (Jan. 17, 1969); directed *Money* (Mar. 2, 1969); appeared in *The Male Animal* (Apr. 11, 1969); directed *Bea, Frank, Richie and Joan* and *Black Comedy* (Dec. 19, 1969); *Fallen Angels* (Oct. 23, 1970); played the Warden in *Gallows Humor* (Oct. 30, 1970); directed *The White House Murder Case* (Jan. 29, 1971); and was in *Johnny No-Trump* (Nov. 24, 1972).

Mr. Oberlin was also resident director and producer at Chautauqua (N.Y.) Repertory Th. (Summers 1968, 1969).

Other Activities. Mr. Oberlin has taught in the theatre department, Cleveland State Univ. (1970–to date) and at Case Western Reserve Univ. (1970–to date).

Awards. Mr. Oberlin was a guest of the West German government in 1973 for a work-study tour of German theatres.

OBOLER, ARCH. Playwright, director, producer. b. Dec. 7, 1909, Chicago, Ill., to Leo and Clara Oboler. Father, engineer. Attended Hyde Park H.S., Chicago; Univ. of Chicago. Married Eleanor Helfand; four sons. Member of ALA; Dramatists Guild; WGA; Radio Writers Guild (past pres.). Address: Rt. 4, Malibu, CA 90265.

Theatre. Mr. Oboler wrote *The Night of the Auk* (Playhouse, N.Y.C., Dec. 3 1956).

Films. Mr. Oboler's first film assignment was as writer and director of *Strange Holiday* (Ind., 1939); subsequently wrote the script for *Escape* (MGM, 1940); wrote and directed *Bewitched* (MGM, 1945); and *The Arnelo Affair* (MGM, 1946); produced, wrote, and directed *Five* (Col., 1950); *Bwana Devil,* the first 3-D feature (UA, 1952); *1+1* (Selected Pictures, 1961); produced, directed and wrote *The Bubble* (Arch Oboler, 1966); and *Arigato* (Sharpix, 1972).

Television. Mr. Oboler wrote and directed *African Adventure.* .

Radio. He was, at first, a writer and director of the radio program, *Lights Out* (NBC, 1938–39); then, writer-director for *Arch Oboler's Plays* (NBC, 1940–45). He is the author of *Night, The Old Boy,* and *Johnny Got His Gun,* to be performed on tape for 190 college stations (NER, Educ., recorded at San Diego State Coll., Apr. 1965).

Published Works. Mr. Oboler's plays for radio have been published under the following titles: *Ivory Tower* (1940), *This Freedom* (1941); *Plays for Americans* (1942); *Free World Theatre* (1944); *Oboler Omnibus* (1945); and *House on Fire* (1969).

Awards. He received the Ohio Univ. Award, 1941; the thirteenth Institute for Education by Radio Award, 1942; the Peabody Award, 1945; first annual A.S.F. Radio Award, 1945; and the first award of the Acad. of Stereoscopic Arts and Sciences, 1952.

O'BRIEN, LIAM. Playwright, producer. b. Liam Francis Xavier O'Brien, Mar. 7, 1913, New York City, to James Alfred and Bridget Agnes (Baldwin) O'Brien. Father, butcher. Grad. Regis H.S., N.Y.C., 1930; attended Fordham Univ., 1931–33; grad. Manhattan Coll., B.A. 1935. Married Jan. 18, 1958, to Claudette Thornton, actress, dancer; two sons. Relatives in theatre: brother, Edmond O'Brien, actor; nephew, Edward Waters, TV and screen writer. Served US Army, 1943–45; rank, 1st Lt. Member of WGA, West; Dramatists Guild; AMPAS (nominating committee, 1961–62); Beverly Hills Tennis Club (bd. of dir., 1961–63).

Pre-Theatre. Union organizer, cartoonist.

Theatre. Mr. O'Brien wrote *The Remarkable Mr. Pennypacker* (Coronet Th., N.Y.C., Dec. 3, 1953), which was produced in London (New, May 18, 1955) and in Vienna, Paris, and Rotterdam (1958–60). He also wrote *The Masculine Principle.*.

Films. His first screenplay was *Chain Lightning* (WB, 1950). He wrote the story, and with Robert Riskin and Myles Connelly, the screenplay for *Here Comes the Groom* (Par., 1951); the story, and with Casey Robinson, the screenplay for *Diplomatic Courier* (20th-Fox, 1952); the story and screenplay for *The Stars Are Singing* (Par., 1953); the story and, with Jonathan Latimer, the screenplay for *Gentleman and Redhead* (Par., 1952); the story, and with Julius Epstein, the screenplay for *Young at Heart* (WB, 1954); the story for *Trapeze* (UA, 1956); the screenplays for *The Great Imposter* (U, 1960), and *Devil at 4 O'Clock* (Col., 1961); and adapted for the screen his play, *The Masculine Principle* (MGM).

Television. Mr. O'Brien has written *The Town That Slept with Lights On* (NBC, 1961) and *The Agitator* (Insight, CBS, 1962).

Awards. He was nominated for an Academy (Oscar) Award for best original motion picture story for *Here Comes the Groom* (1951).

Recreation. Tennis, baseball.

O'BRIEN, PAT. Actor. b. William Joseph Patrick O'Brien, Nov. 11, 1899, Milwaukee, Wis. Grad. Milwaukee (Wis.) H.S.; Marquette Univ.; studied for the theatre at Sargeant Sch. of Drama, N.Y.C. Married Jan. 21, 1931, to Eloise Taylor, actress; two sons, two daughters. Served USN, 1918. Member of AEA; SAG; AFTRA; AGVA; Harlequin of the Masquers; The Players; Knights of Columbus; The Lambs.

Theatre. Mr. O'Brien made his professional debut on tour in *Way Down East* (Summer c. 1920); made his Bway debut (billed as Fred O'Brien) as a gentleman of the ensemble in the musical, *Adrienne* (George M. Cohan Th., May 28, 1923); succeeded Robert Gleckler as Charlie Groff in *A Man's Man* (52 St. Th., Oct. 13, 1925), in which he subsequently toured; appeared (billed as W.J.P. O'Brien) as Hewitt Lysacht in *You Can't Win* (Klaw, N.Y.C., Feb. 26, 1926); as Pat O'Brien, played Anthony Alexander in *Henry—Behave* (Nora Bayes Th., Aug. 23, 1926); Steve in *Gertie* (Nora Bayes Th., Nov. 15, 1926); and succeeded Robert Gleckler as Steven Crandall in *Broadway* (Broadhurst, Sept. 16, 1926).

He played Hennessy in *Danger* (Bronx Opera House, N.Y., Oct. 15, 1928); succeeded to the role of Walter Burns in *The Front Page* (Times Sq. Th., N.Y.C., Aug. 14, 1926); Bill Post in *This Man's Town* (Ritz, N.Y.C., Mar. 10, 1930); Curly in *The Up and Up* (Biltmore, Sept. 8, 1930); Mazim in *Overture* (Longacre, Dec. 5, 1930); Ernie in the pre-Bway tryout of *Strike a Match* (opened Alcazar, San Francisco, Calif., Dec. 9, 1952); William Spain in *Miss Lonely Hearts* (Music Box, N.Y.C., Oct. 3, 1957); Mr. Banks in a stock production of *Father of the Bride* (Drury Lane, Chicago, Ill., Summer 1960; Swan, Milwaukee, Wis., Summer 1961); the Captain in *Mister Roberts*)New Braunfeld, Tex., July 24, 1963); and was in *Skip and Go Naked* (Drury Lane, Chicago, July 1975).

Films. Mr. O'Brien made his debut in a short subject (Vitaphone); subsequently appeared in *Fury of the Wild* (RKO, 1929); *The Freckled Rascal* (RKO, 1929); *The Front Page* (UA, 1931); *Consolation Marriage* (RKO, 1931); *Honor Among Lovers* (Par., 1931); *Flying High* (MGM); *The Strange Case of Clara Deane* (Par., 1932); *American Madness* (Col., 1932); *Hollywood Speaks* (Col., 1932); *Air Mail* (U, 1932); *Virtue* (Col., 1932); *Laughter in Hell* (U, 1932); *The Final Edition* (Col., 1932); *Hell's House* (Capitol, 1932); and *Scandal for Sale* (U, 1932).

He also appeared in *Destination Unknown* (U, 1933); *Bombshell* (MGM, 1933); *The World Gone Mad* (Majestic, 1933); *College Coach* (WB, 1933); *Bureau of Missing Persons* (1st Natl., 1933); *Gambling Lady* (WB, 1934); *20 Million Sweethearts* (1st Natl., 1934); *Flirtation Walk* (1st Natl., 1934); *Here Comes the Navy* (WB, 1934); *Flaming Gold* (RKO, 1934); *I've Got Your Number* (WB, 1934); *Personality Kid* (WB, 1934); *I Sell Anything* (1st Natl., 1934); *Oil for the Lamps of China* (WB, 1935); *Devil Dogs of the Air* (WB, 1935); *The Irish in Us* (WB, 1935); *Page Miss Glory* (WB, 1935); *Ceiling Zero* (WB, 1935); *In Caliente* (1st Natl., 1935); *Stars Over Broadway* (WB, 1935); *I Married a Doctor* (1st Natl., 1936); and *Back in Circulation* (WB, 1937).

Also, *Women Are Like That* (WB, 1938); *Garden of the Moon* (WB, 1938); *Angels with Dirty Faces* (WB, 1938); *Flowing Gold* (WB, 1940); *Knute Rockne—All American* (WB, 1940); *The Iron Major* (RKO, 1943); *Bombardier* (RKO, 1943); *His Butler's Sister* (U, 1943); *Secret Command* (Col., 1944); *Marine Raiders* (RKO, 1944); *Having Wonderful Crime* (RKO, 1945); *Man Alive* (RKO, 1945); *Perilous Holiday* (Col., 1946); *Crack-Up* (RKO, 1946); *Riffraff* (RKO, 1947); *The Boy with Green Hair* (RKO, 1948); *Fighting Father Dunne* (RKO, 1948); *Off the Record* (WB, 1949); *A Dangerous Profession* (RKO, 1949); *The Fireball* (20th-Fox, 1950); *Johnny One-Eye* (UA, 1950); *Criminal Lawyer* (Col., 1951); *The People Against O'Hara* (MGM, 1951); *Okinawa* (Col., 1952); *Ring of Fear* (WB, 1954); *Jubilee Trail* (Rep., 1954); *Inside Detroit* (Col., 1955); *The Last Hurrah* (Col., 1958); and *Some Like It Hot* (UA, 1959).

Television and Radio. On radio, Mr. O'Brien performed in *Alias Jimmy Valentine* (Lux, CBS, Nov. 9, 1936); on the series The Sea Has a Story (CBS, 1945); and in *The Barker* (Th. Guild, CBS, Mar. 10, 1946).

On television, he appeared on Video Th. (CBS) in *The Irish Drifter* (Feb. 1951), *Tin Badge* (Dec. 1951), *The Fires of Autumn* (Nov. 1952), and *One for the Road* (Mar. 1953); in *Tomorrow's Men* (Ford Th., NBC, Oct. 1953); on Climax (CBS, 1955, 1956); in *Newspaper Man* (Rheingold Th., NBC, Apr. 1955); *Dinner at Eight* (Front Row Center, CBS, June 1955); on Studio 57 in *Who's Calling?* (Feb. 1956), *Exit Laughing* (Apr. 1956), and *Strange Query* (Feb. 1957); Crossroads (ABC) in *Strange Bequest* (Feb. 1956), *Holiday for Father Jim* (June 1956), *Riot* (Apr. 1957), and *Circus Priest* (July 1957); in *The Brotherhood of the Bell* (Studio One, CBS, Jan. 1958); *Eddie* (Kraft Television Th., NBC, Jan. 1958); and on Harrigan and Son (ABC, 1960).

Also on The Virginian (NBC, 1964, 1967); on Kraft Suspense Th. (NBC) in *Threatening Eye* (Mar. 1964) and *The Jack Is High* (Nov. 1964); Bob Chrysler Th. (NBC, 1964, 1965); on Hazel (CBS, 1966); in *The Over-the-Hill Gang* (ABC, 1969); *The Adventures of Nick Carter* (ABC, 1972); and on Banyon (NBC, 1972).

Night Clubs. Mr. O'Brien appeared in Las Vegas, Nev. (1951) and at the Statler-Hilton (Dallas, Tex., Feb. 13, 1964).

Published Works. Mr. O'Brien wrote his autobiography, *The Wind at My Back* (1964).

Awards. Mr. O'Brien was made a Knight of Malta in 1974. He is an honorary member of B'nai B'rith; received the Decency in Entertainment Award, Notre Dame Univ. (1966); the Catholic Youth Organization Award; Knights of Columbus Achievement Award; the Amer. Acad. of Dramatic Arts Alumni Achievement Award (1972); and the honorary degrees of Litt. D. from Marquette Univ. and LL. D. from Loretto Coll.

Recreation. Spectator sports, collecting Irish literature and music.

O'CONNELL, ARTHUR. Actor. b. Arthur Joseph O'Connell, Mar. 29, 1908, New York City, to Michael and Julia (Byrne) O'Connell. Father, headwaiter. Grad. St. John's H.S., Brooklyn, N.Y., 1926; attended St. John's Coll., Brooklyn, N.Y., 1926–28. Married June 23, 1962, to Anne Hall Dunlop; one stepson; two stepdaughters. Served US Army, Signal Corps Training Films (1941–45); rank, Sgt. Member of AEA; AFTRA; SAG; The Players; The Navy League; Columbia Country Club (Washington, D.C.).

Theatre. Mr. O'Connell made his debut in *The Patsy* (Franklin Park Th., Dorchester, Mass., Dec. 1929); subsequently appeared in vaudeville in Harry Delf's act *Any Family* and as a stooge for Bert Walton, Roy Sedley, and Bert Lahr (1931–34); played Pepper White in *Golden Boy* (St. James's, London, Sept. 7, 1938); made his N.Y.C. debut as an Orderly in the US Army production of *The Army Play by Play,* which he directed (46 St. Th., June 14, 1943); performed for the Army Emergency Relief, which gave a performance for President Franklin D. Roosevelt and Queen Wilhelmina (Hyde Park, N.Y., June 19, 1943); directed *Brighten the Corner* (Lyceum, N.Y.C., Dec. 12, 1945); toured with the Margaret Webster Shakespeare Co. as Polonius in *Hamlet,* and Banquo and Siward in *Macbeth* (opened Buffalo, N.Y., Sept. 28, 1948; closed Philadelphia, Pa., Apr. 26, 1949).

He appeared as the Postman in *Anna Christie* (NY City Ctr., Jan. 9, 1952); Pepper White in *Golden Boy* (ANTA, Mar. 12, 1952); Howard Bevins in *Picnic* (Music Box, Feb. 19, 1953); Will Harrison in *Lunatics and Lovers* (Broadhurst, Dec. 13, 1954); Charlie Lawton in *Come a Day* (Ambassador, Nov. 6, 1958); and Cornelius V. Stolts in the pre-Bway tryout of *The Umbrella* (opened Locust St. Th., Philadelphia, Pa., Jan. 20, 1962; closed there, Jan. 29, 1962). In Feb.-Mar. 1968, he toured Vietnam and Thailand for the USO.

Films. Mr. O'Connell made his debut in *Murder in Soho* (Assn. British Pictures, 1938); subsequently appeared in short comedy subjects (RKO, 1938); in *Citizen Kane* (RKO, 1941); *Law of the Jungle* (Mono., 1942); *Man from Headquarters* (Mono., 1942); *Picnic* (Col., 1955); *The Solid Gold Cadillac* (Col., 1956); *The Man in the Grey Flannel Suit* (20th-Fox, 1956); *The Monte Carlo Story* (UA, 1957); *The Proud Ones* (20th-Fox, 1956); *Bus Stop* (20th-Fox, 1956); *The Violators* (U, 1957); *April Love* (20th-Fox, 1957); *Voice in the Mirror* (U, 1958); *Man of the West* (UA, 1958); *Gidget* (Col., 1959); the *Hound Dog Man* (20th-Fox, 1959); *Anatomy of a Murder* (Col., 1959); *Operation Petticoat* (U, 1959); *Cimarron* (MGM, 1960); *A Thunder of Drums* (MGM, 1961); *The Great Imposter* (U, 1960); *Follow that Dream* (UA, 1962); *Misty* (20th-Fox, 1961); *Pocketful of Miracles* (UA, 1961); *Kissin' Cousins* (MGM, 1963); *The Seven Faces of Dr. Lao* (MGM, 1964); *Nightmare* (U, 1964); *Your Cheating Heart* (MGM, 1964); and *Fantastic Voyage* (20th-Fox, 1966).

Television. Mr. O'Connell has appeared on television in many plays and in episodes of series, including *Summer Had Better Be Good* (Comedy Th., ABC, July 1950); Kraft Th. (ABC, 1954); Lamp Unto My Feet (CBS, 1955); Omnibus (ABC, 1956); The New Breed (ABC, 1962); Breaking Point (ABC, 1963); The Greatest Show on Earth (ABC, 1964); Fugitive (ABC, 1964, 1965); Wagon Train (ABC, 1965); Shenandoah (ABC, 1966); Gunsmoke (CBS, 1967); My Three Sons (CBS, 1968); Ironside (NBC, 1969); Name of the Game (NBC, 1969); Men from Shiloh (NBC, 1971); Cannon (CBS, 1971); Night Gallery (NBC, 1971); McCloud (NBC, 1971); and Alias Smith and Jones (ABC, 1972).

Other Activities. Mr. O'Connell shows and races horses.

Awards. Mr. O'Connell was nominated for the Academy (Oscar) Award for his performances as Howard Bevins in *Picnic* (1955) and as Parnell McCarthy in *Anatomy of a Murder* (1959); was voted one of Filmdom's Famous Fives for *April Love* (1957); was made an Honorary Kentucky Colonel (1957); and received the Citizens Award from the NY Democratic Party (1961).

Recreation. Horses, gardening, cooking.

O'CONNOR, KEVIN. Actor, director. b. May 7, 1938, Honolulu, Hawaii. Attended Hawaii Univ.; Univ. of Calif. Studied acting at the Neighborhood Playhouse, and with Uta Hagen and Lee Strasberg. Member of AEA; SAG; AFTRA.

Theatre. Mr. O'Connor worked extensively with LaMama ETC, and Theatre Genesis before playing Harry in *Up to Thursday* on a triple-bill with *Balls* and *Home Free* (Cherry Lane, N.Y.C., Feb. 10, 1965); Subsequently played several roles in *Six from La Mama* (Martinique, Apr. 11, 1966); Bill Maitland in *Inadmissible Evidence* (Woodstock, NY, Th., Summer 1966); Walter in *The Rimers of Eldritch* (Cherry Lane Th., N.Y.C., Feb. 20, 1967); Sir Andrew Aguecheek in *Twelfth Night* (Baltimore Ctr. Stage, 1968); the title role in *Tom Paine* (Stage 73, N.Y.C., Mar. 25, 1968); Dionysus in *The Bacchae* (Charles Playhouse, Boston, Fall 1968); Toby in *Boy on the Straight-Back Chair* (Amer. Place Th., Feb. 14, 1969); made his Bway debut as Julius Esperanza in *Gloria and Esperanza* (ANTA, Feb. 4, 1970); on a double-bill played Alex Koonig in *Dear Janet Rosenberg, Dear Mr. Koonig* and Jake in *Jakey Fat Boy* (Gramercy Arts Th., Apr. 5, 1970); appeared in *As You Like It* (Milwaukee Repertory Th. Co., Dec. 18, 1970); and played Glendenning in *The Contractor* (Chelsea Th. of Manhattan, Oct. 17, 1973); and James in *The Morning After Optimism* (Manhattan Th. Club, 1974–75 season).

For the Eugene O'Neill Memorial Th. Playwright's Unit (Waterford, Conn.) he has played Man 3 in *American Triptych* (July 14, 1971); Sir Owen Hopton in *Campion* (July 20, 1971); B in *African Star* (July 23, 1971); William Wallace in *Bruce* (July 30, 1971); Cop in *Lonnie, James, Bernhardt and Zoowolski* (Aug. 6, 1971; Antrocius in *The General Brutus* (July 12, 1972); # 3 in *The Executioners* (July 19, 1972); Street Vendor in *Artists for the Revolution* (July 22, 1972; the title role in *Warren Harding* (July 29, 1972); Will in *Alfred the Great* (Aug. 4, 1972); Mr. Ryan in *A Grave Undertaking* (July 24, 1974); Marc in *She's Bad Today* (Aug. 7, 1974); and Aaron Burr in *Founding Father* (Aug. 1, 1974).

Mr. O'Connor was artistic director (1972–74) of the off-off-Bway Th. at St. Clements where he played Abe in *Eyes of Chalk* (June 7, 1972); appeared in *The Funny Men Are in Trouble* on a bill entitled *Two By Paul Austin* (Nov. 20, 1972); directed *Whiskey* (Apr. 29, 1973), and *Winging It!* (May 29, 1973); directed and played the Kid in *Alive and Well in Argentina* (Mar. 4, 1974); and played the Man in *Duet* and *Trio* (Mar. 28, 1974) which was retitled *Figures in the Sand*, and reopened (Oct. 9, 1975).

Television. His appearances include *Apple Pie* (NET); Hidden Faces; and The Doctors.

Awards. Mr. O'Connor received the Drama Desk Vernon Rice Awards, and the *Village Voice* Off-Bway (Obie) Award (1965–66) for his performance in *Six from La Mama;* and the Drama Desk Award (1973–74) for *The Contractor.*

OESTREICHER, GERARD. Producer. b. July 29, 1916, New York City, to Carl and Lucile (Peiser) Oestreicher. Grad. Columbia Univ., B.A. 1937. Married 1938 to Toby Ruby (marr. dis. 1957); one son, two daughters; married Apr. 11, 1958, to Irma Kaplan. Served US Army, 1944–46; rank, 1st Lt. Member of City Athletic Club; Harmonie Club; Sunningdale Country Club; Cavendish Club; League of NY Theatres; Zeta Beta Tau. Address: (home) 680 Madison Ave., New York, NY 10021, tel. (212) 838-3000; (bus.) 444 Madison Ave., New York, NY 10017, tel. (212) 688-1050.

Mr. Oestreicher owns and manages real estate.

Theatre. Mr. Oestreicher produced *Milk and Honey* (Martin Beck Th., N.Y.C., Oct. 10, 1961), and its national tour (opened Shubert, Philadelphia, Jan. 28, 1963); closed Biltmore, Los Angeles, Sept. 7, 1963); the pre-Bway tryout of *La Belle* (based on Offenbach's *La Belle Helene;* opened Shubert, Philadelphia, Aug. 13, 1962; closed there, Aug. 25, 1962); produced, with Laurence Feldman, in assoc. with Idar Productions, *A Girl Could Get Lucky* (Cort, N.Y.C., Sept. 20, 1964); produced, with the Th. Guild, the summer tryout of *So Much of Earth, So Much of Heaven* (Westport, Conn., Country Playhouse, Aug. 30, 1965; Bucks County Playhouse, New Hope, Pa., Sept. 6, 1965); produced, with the Th. Guild and Theodore Mann, in assoc. with Hope Abelson, *The Royal Hunt of the Sun* (ANTA, Oct. 26, 1965), and its national tour (opened Rajah Th., Reading, Pa., Oct. 11, 1966; closed McVickers, Chicago, Jan. 21, 1967); and produced, with Joseph Kipness and Harold Leventhal, and was production supervisor for, *But Seriously. . .* (Henry Miller's Th., N.Y.C., Feb. 27, 1969).

Mr. Oestreicher is a silent partner in the Nederlander Th. and Producing Operation, which owns the Uris, Palace, Brooks Atkinson, and Alvin Th. (N.Y.C.); Fisher, Pine Knob, and Vest Pocket Th. (Detroit); McVickers and Studebaker Th. (Chicago); Mechanic Th. (Baltimore); Palace West Th. (Phoenix, Ariz.); National Th. (Washington, D.C.); and Meriwether Post Pavilion (Maryland), among others. For the Nederlanders, Mr. Oestreicher has managed the Uris Th., since its opening (Nov. 1972).

O'HEARN, ROBERT. Designer. b. July 19, 1921, Elkhart, Ind., to Robert O'Hearn, Sr., and Ella May (Stoldt) O'Hearn. Father, advertising executive. Grad. Central H.S., South Bend, Ind., 1939; Indiana Univ., B.A. 1943; attended Art Students League, N.Y.C., 1945–46. Member of United Scenic Artists. Address: 59 Fifth Ave., New York, NY 10003, tel. (212) AL 5-8570.

Theatre. Mr. O'Hearn designed 60 productions for the Brattle Th. (Cambridge, Mass., 1948–52). His first Bway assignment was as designer for sets and costumes for *The Relapse* (Morosco Th., Nov. 22, 1950); subsequently designed scenery for *Love's Labour's Lost* (NY City Ctr., Feb. 4, 1953) and *A Date with April* (Royale, Apr. 15, 1953); sets and lighting for *Festival* (Longacre, Jan. 18, 1955); sets for *Othello* (NY City Ctr., Sept. 7, 1955) and *Henry IV, Part 1* (Sept. 21, 1955); scenery and lighting for *Child of Fortune* (Royale, Nov. 13, 1956) and *The Apple Cart* (Plymouth, Oct. 18, 1956).

From 1959–63, he designed nine operatic productions for the Central City (Colo.) Opera House; and in Nov. 1960, designed scenery and costumes for *L'Elisir d'Amore* for the (N.Y.) Metropolitan Opera Association.

For the American Shakespeare Festival Theatre and Academy (Stratford, Conn.), Mr. O'Hearn created scenery for *As You Like It* (June 27, 1961), *Macbeth* (June 28, 1961) and *Troilus and Cressida* (July 23, 1961). He designed sets and costumes for the Metropolitan Opera Association's new production of *Die Meistersinger* (Oct. 1962), for their new production of *Aida*, (Oct. 1963); designed scenery and lighting for *Abraham Cochrane* (Belasco, Feb. 5, 1964); sets and costumes for the Metropolitan Opera Association production of *Samson and Delilah* (Oct. 1964); and sets and costumes for the Ballet Th. production of *La Sylphide* (San Antonio, Tex., Nov. 1964).

For the Metropolitan Opera, he designed the sets for *Pique Dame* (1965); *La Ventana* (1966); *Die Frau Ohne Schatten* (1966); *Hansel and Gretel* (1967); *Der Rosenkavalier* (1969); *Parsifal* (1970); and *Marriage of Figaro* (1975). He designed the scenery for *Porgy and Bess* (Vienna Volksoper, 1965); *Othello* (Boston Opera, also Hamburg State Opera, 1967); *The Nutcracker Suite* ballet (San Francisco Ballet, 1967); *La Traviata* (Santa Fe Opera, 1968); *Rosalinda* (Los Angeles Civic Light Opera, 1968); *Tallis Fantasia* (N.Y.C. Ballet, 1969); *Porgy and Bess* (Bregenz Festspiel, Austria, 1971); *Falstaff*, and *The Marriage of Figaro* (Central City, Colo., Opera, 1972); *The Mind with the Dirty Man* (Mark Taper Forum, Los Angeles, Calif., 1973); *The Enchanted* (Kennedy Center, Washington, D.C., 1973); *The Barber of Seville*, and *Gianni Schicci* (Central City, Colo., Opera, 1973); *The Pearl Fishers* (Miami, Fla., Opera, 1974); *Carmen* (Strasbourg, France, Opera, 1974); *A Midsummer Night's Dream* (Central City, Colo., Opera, 1974); and *Copelia* (Ballet West, 1974).

Films. He designed the scenery for *A Clerical Error* (Paris Cinema, 1955).

Recreation. Music.

O'HORGAN, TOM. Director, composer, singer, musician. b. May 3, 1926, Chicago, Ill. Father, newspaper owner. Grad. DePaul Univ., Chicago, B.A., M.A. (music major). Address: c/o Mike Rosenfeld, William Morris Agency, 151 El Camino Dr., Beverly Hills, CA 90212.

Pre-Theatre. Mr. O'Horgan sang in churches and played the harp in symphony orchestras before going into the theatre.

Theatre. Mr. O'Horgan made his theatrical debut in the off-Bway revue *Fallout* (Renata Th., N.Y.C., May 31, 1959); composed music for a production of *The Tempest* (E. 74 St. Th., Dec. 27, 1959); composed and played music for the Second City revue *To the Water Tower* (Square East, Apr. 4, 1963); wrote and directed *Love and Vexations* (Caffe Cino, Aug. 29, 1963); and composed and played music for three more Second City revues (all at Square East): *When the Owl Screams* (Sept. 12, 1963), *Open Season at the Second City* (Jan. 22, 1964), and *The Wrecking Ball* (Apr. 15, 1964).

Mr. O'Horgan began directing with a production of *The Maids* (Cafe La Mama, Oct. 21, 1964). He directed and composed music for a group of plays billed as *Six from La Mama*, in which members of the La Mama company toured Europe (Fall 1965–Spring 1966), followed by N.Y.C. presentation (Martinique, Apr. 11, 12, 1966); was director for a second European tour by the company (Fall 1966); directed *The Hessian Corporal* (Cafe La Mama, Dec. 21, 1966); directed and wrote music for *Futz!* (Cafe La Mama, Mar. 1, 1967); for *Tom Paine* (Cafe La Mama, Apr. 27, 1967); and directed a third La Mama European tour (Summer 1967), during which the company developed Mr. O'Horgan's stagings of *Futz!* and *Tom Paine.*

He directed another N.Y.C. production of *Tom Paine* (Stage 73, Mar. 25, 1968); directed *Hair* (Biltmore, Apr. 29, 1968; also US national companies and European productions); another production of *Futz!* (Th. de Lys, June 13, 1968); and at Waltham, Mass., he directed, designed and wrote music for *Massachusetts Trust* (Interact, Spingold Th., Brandeis Univ., Aug. 21, 1968).

In March 1969, Mr. O'Horgan was named artistic director of La Mama, which became La Mama Experimental Theatre Club (La Mama ETC) the following month. Other productions directed by Mr. O'Horgan include *Lenny* (Brooks Atkinson Th., May 26, 1971), for which he also composed music; *Jesus Christ Superstar*, which he conceived (Mark Hellinger Th., Oct. 12, 1971); *Inner City*, which he also conceived and co-produced (Ethel Barrymore Th., Dec. 19, 1971); *Dude* (Broadway Th., Oct. 9, 1972); and *The Leaf People* (Booth Th., Oct. 20, 1975).

Films. Mr. O'Horgan performed in *All Men Are Apes* (Adelphia, 1965); directed and composed music for the motion picture *Futz!* (Commonwealth United, 1969); composed music for *Alex in Wonderland* (MGM, 1970); and composed music for *Rhinoceros* (AM Film Th., 1974).

Television. Mr. O'Horgan played the percussion accompaniment for and directed *!Heimskringla! or the Stoned Angels* (NET, 1969).

Night Clubs. Mr. O'Horgan first appeared as a night club entertainer at the hungry i, San Francisco, Calif. (Jan. 1958). He later repeated this performance in N.Y.C., at the Village Gate (Sept. 1959) and Bon Soir (Mar. and June 1972).

Awards. Mr. O'Horgan received a *Village Voice* off-Bway (Obie) Award (1967) for his direction of *Futz!;* an Antoinette Perry (Tony) nomination (1968) for his direction of *Hair;* the Brandeis Univ. Creative Arts Award (1968) for his work as a director; and Drama Desk awards for directing *Tom Paine* (1968) and *Lenny* (1971).

Recreation. Collecting and playing antique and modern musical instruments.

OLAF, PIERRE. Actor. b. Pierre-Olaf Trivier, July 14, 1928. Cauderan (Gironde), France, to Pierre and Anne Marie (Lenglet) Trivier. Father, insurance agent. Attended Lycée J. Decour, Paris, France, 1943–46. Member of AEA; AFTRA; SAG.

Theatre. Mr. Olaf made his debut in the dual roles of the Spanish Soldier and the Innkeeper in *Les Espagnols au Danemark* (Th. de Poche, Paris, June 1947); subsequently, appeared as the Bell Boy in *The Skipper Next to God* (Th. des Arts, 1948), which he repeated in Brussels, Belgium (Th. de Parc, Feb. 1949), and Geneva, Switzerland (Mar. 1949); played Evariste in *La tour Eiffel qui tue* (Vieux-Colombier, Paris, 1949); Damis in *Tartuffe* (Th. Athenée, 1949); appeared in eight roles in the revue *Dugudu* (La Bruyere, 1951); Jonathas in *Folies Douces* (Quartier Latin, 1953); repeated Evariste in *La tour Eiffel qui tue* (Quartier Latin, 1954); played six roles in the revue, *Jupon vole* (Th. des Variétés, 1954); and Philippe in *Orvet* (Th. de la Renaissance, 1955).

He played eight roles in the revue *La plume de ma tante* (Garrick, London, Nov. 3, 1955); nine roles in *Pommes à l'Anglaise* (Th. de Paris, Paris, 1957); repeated his roles in *La plume de ma tante* (Royale, N.Y.C., Nov. 11, 1958); played Jacquot in *Carnival!* (Imperial, Apr. 13, 1961); in stock he appeared as Passepartout in *Around the World in 80 Days* (Municipal Opera, St. Louis, Mo.; Starlight Th., Kansas City, Kans., Summer 1963); the Golux in *The 13 Clocks* (Barter, Abingdon, Va., Summer 1963); Ferdinand Goddard in *That Hat!* (Theatre Four, N.Y.C., Sept. 23, 1964); and Raphael Bonnardon in a pre-Bway tryout of *Madame Mousse* (Westport, Conn., Country Playhouse, Aug. 16, 1965); substituted (July 5–17, 1966) for Irving Jacobson in the role of Sancho Panza in *Man of La Mancha* (ANTA Washington Square, N.Y.C.); and played Jacquot in *Carnival* (NY City Ctr., Dec. 12, 1968); and Quillery in *Idiot's Delight* (Ahmanson Th., Los Angeles, Mar. 17, 1970).

Films. Mr. Olaf has appeared in *Miquette et sa mere* (Discina, 1951); *Three Women* (Times, 1952); *Virgile* (1952); *French Can-Can* (UMP, 1956); *Monsieur Cognac* (U, 1964); *Allez France* (Prodis, 1964); *The Art of Love* (U, 1965); *The Counterfeit Constable* (Seven Arts, 1966); *Camelot* (WB-Seven Arts, 1967); *Don't Drink the Water* (Avco-Embassy, 1969); and *The Gamblers* (UM, 1970).

Television. Mr. Olaf has appeared in *He Who Gets Slapped* (Play of the Week, WNTA, 1961); played Dr. Gombault in *The Enchanted Nutcracker* (ABC, 1961); and appeared on the Jack Paar Show (NBC, 1962); Perry Como Show (NBC, 1963); and Shari Lewis Show (NBC, 1963); and *The Trials of O'Brien* (CBS, 1966).

Recreation. Painting, writing.

O'LEARY, JOHN. Actor. b. May 5, 1926, Mass., to Dr. Joseph J. and Marion (Fitzgerald) O'Leary. Father, physician. Grad. Northwestern Univ., B.S. 1951. Address: New York City, NY tel. (212) 799-4261.

Theatre. On Bway, Mr. O'Leary has appeared in *General Seeger* (Lyceum, Feb. 28, 1962); *More Stately Mansions* (Broadhurst, Oct. 31, 1967); *Georgy* (Winter Garden, Feb. 26, 1970); and *Moon for the Misbegotten* (Morosco, Dec. 29, 1973).

OLESEN, OSCAR. General manager, company manager. b. Oscar Ernest Olesen, Sept. 28, 1916, England, to Ernest and Ann Olesen. Grad. Duke Univ., A.B. 1938. Married Oct. 5, 1951, to Terry Fay, casting director; one son, two daughters. Served RCAF; Amer. Field Service. Member of ATPAM. Address: (home) Trinity Pass, Pound Ridge, NY 10576, tel. (914) PO 4-4231; (bus.) Whitehead-Stevens Productions, Inc., 1564 Broadway, New York, NY 10036, tel. (212) 757-5100.

Theatre. Mr. Olesen was general manager for *The Emperor's Clothes* (Ethel Barrymore Th., Feb. 9, 1953); *The Remarkable Mr. Pennypacker* (Coronet, Dec. 30, 1953); *The Confidential Clerk* (Morosco, Feb. 11, 1954); *Portrait of a Lady* (ANTA, Dec. 21, 1954); *The Flowering Peach* (Belasco Th., Dec. 28, 1954); *Bus Stop* (Music Box Th., Mar. 2, 1955); the US State Dept. production of *The Skin of Our Teeth* (Sarah Bernhardt Th., Paris, Fr., June 1955); *Joyce Grenfell Requests the Pleasure* (Bijou, N.Y.C., Oct. 10, 1955); *Tamburlaine the Great* (Winter Garden, Jan. 19, 1956); *Separate Tables* (Music Box Th., Oct. 25, 1956); *Major Barbara* (Martin Beck Th., Oct. 30, 1956); *The Waltz of the Toreadors* (Coronet, Jan. 17, 1957); *Orpheus Descending* (Martin Beck Th., Mar. 21, 1957); *The Day the Money Stopped* (Belasco Th., Feb. 20, 1958); *The Visit* (Lunt-Fontanne Th., May 5, 1958); *A Touch of the Poet* (Helen Hayes Th., Oct. 2, 1958); *Goldilocks* (Lunt-Fontanne Th., Oct. 11, 1958); *The Cold Wind and the Warm* (Morosco, Dec. 8, 1958); *Much Ado About Nothing* (Lunt-Fontanne Th., Sept. 17, 1959); company manager for *Duel of Angels* (Helen Hayes Th., Apr. 19, 1960); general manager for *The Conquering Hero* (ANTA Th., Jan. 16, 1961); *Midgie Purvis* (Martin Beck Th., Feb. 2, 1961); *Big Fish, Little Fish* (ANTA Th., Mar. 15, 1961); *A Man for All Seasons* (ANTA Th., Nov. 22, 1961); *The Ballad of the Sad Cafe* (Martin Beck Th., Oct. 30, 1963).

He was also general manager of the Repertory Th. of Lincoln Ctr. (1963–64); and for the first American tour of the Royal Shakespeare Co. and its productions of *King Lear* and *Comedy of Errors* (1964); and general manager for *The Prime of Miss Jean Brodie* (Helen Hayes Th., Jan. 16, 1968); *The Price* (Morosco, Feb. 7, 1968); *Indians* (Brooks Atkinson Th., Oct. 13, 1969); *Sheep on the Runway* (Helen Hayes Th., Jan. 31, 1970); *Candide* (Kennedy Center, Washington, D.C., Oct. 26, 1971); *Old Times* (Billy Rose Th., N.Y.C., Nov. 20, 1971); *The Creation of the World and Other Business* (Sam S. Shubert Th., Nov. 30, 1972); *Finishing Touches* (Plymouth, Feb. 8, 1973); *The Prodigal Daughter* (Kennedy Center, Washington, D.C., Nov. 16, 1973); and *Freedom of the City* (Alvin Th., N.Y.C., Feb. 17, 1974).

OLIM, DOROTHY. Producer, general manager, advertising executive. b. Oct. 14, 1934, New York City, to Sol and Esther (Kessel) Olim. Father, merchant Attended Juilliard Sch. of Music, N.Y.C., 1949–50; grad. Battin H.S., Elizabeth, N.J., 1951; attended St. John's Coll., Annapolis, Md., 1951–53; Neighborhood Playhouse Sch. of the Th., N.Y.C., Summer 1953. Grad. Columbia Univ., Sch. of Dramatic Arts, B.F.A. 1955. M.F.A. 1956. Member of Association of Theatrical Press Agents and Managers; League of Off-Bway Th. Owners and Producers (secy.-treas.). Address: 1540 Broadway, New York, NY 10036, tel. (212) 869-8282.

Miss Olim is president of Krone-Olim Advertising, Inc., a theatrical advertising agency.

Theatre. Miss Olim made her stage debut as the Sorceress in *The Boys from Syracuse* (Lambertville Music Circus, N.J., Summer 1953), serving also as the company's assistant treasurer; and appeared as the Signora in *Tonight We Improvise* (Living Th., N.Y.C., Feb. 1954).

Subsequently she produced *The One-Eyed Man is King* (Th. East, N.Y.C., May 1956). She produced forty-five plays at the Saranac Lake (N.Y.) Summer Th. (1956–60); was general manager at St. John Terrell's Music Circus (Sterling Forest Gardens, Tuxedo, N.Y., Summer 1960); and directed *The Glass Menagerie* (Flagcourt Playhouse, N.Y., 1960).

Miss Olim served as associate producer, with Lore Noto and Sheldon Baron, of *The Fantasticks* (Sullivan St. Playhouse, N.Y.C., May 3, 1960); and produced, with Gerald Krone, *A Worm in Horseradish* (Maidman Playhouse, Mar. 13, 1961). She was general manager (1961–62) at the E. 11 St. Th.; produced with Gerald Krone, *The Golden Apple* (York Playhouse, Feb. 12, 1962); *The Lion in Love* (One Sheridan Sq. Th., Apr. 25, 1963); and *Pimpernel!* (Gramercy Th., Jan. 6, 1964); and produced, with St. John Terrell and Gerald Krone, *I Must Be Talking to My Friends* (Orpheum, Nov. 16, 1967).

Miss Olim was a member of the board of directors of the Negro Ensemble Company, N.Y.C. (1967–71). She has been general manager of over fifty Broadway and off-Broadway productions, among them *The River Niger, Bob & Ray, The Two and Only, Your Own Thing, America Hurrah, MacBird!, Fortune and Men's Eyes, Viet Rock, Collision Course, Red Cross and Muzeeka, Tom Paine, Happy Ending and Day of Absence, We Bombed in New Haven, You Never Know, Rosebloom, Big Time Buck White, El Hajj Malik, Sensations, Gandhi, The Reckoning, Lime Green Khaki Blue, The Firebugs, The Poker Session, Billy Liar,* and others.

Other Activities. Miss Olim has lectured around the country on the subject of "How To Produce Off-Broadway." She is a member of the board of governors of the League of Advertising Agencies, of which her agency, Krone-Olim Advertising, Inc., is a member. She is also president and founder of Dorothy Olim Travel Associates (1971–74).

Recreation. Sailing, reading science fiction, cooking, travel.

OLIVER, EDITH. Drama critic, writer. b. Aug. 11, 1913, New York City, to Samuel and Maude (Biow) Goldsmith. Grad. Horace Mann H.S., N.Y.C., 1931; attended Smith Coll., 1931–33; studied acting with Mrs. Patrick Campbell, Laura Elliott, and Frances Robinson Duff. Address: c/o The New Yorker Magazine, 25 W. 43rd St., New York, NY 10036, tel. (212) OX 5-1414.

Miss Oliver was, at first, an actress-apprentice at The Berkshire Playhouse, Stockbridge, Mass., and later became assistant to the director (1932–33). She was casting director for the Biow Agency (1944–66). In 1947, she joined the editorial staff of *The New Yorker* magazine where she is the reviewer of off-Bway plays (1961–to date).

Radio. From 1937–41, she performed on radio in such programs as Gangbusters; True Detective (WNEW); Crime Doctor (CBS); Philip Morris Playhouse (CBS) and others. In 1938, she wrote the questions and answers for a quiz show called True or False (WOR), at the J. Walter Thompson Agency. She also wrote and, for a while, produced Take It or Leave It and the $64 Question (CBS, NBC; 1940–52).

OLIVER, ROCHELLE. Actress. b. Rochelle Olshever, Apr. 15, 1937, New York City, to Sol and Bess (Goldsmith) Olshever. Grad. Steward Park H.S., N.Y.C., 1954; attended Brooklyn Coll., 1954–1956. Studied acting and dance at the Henry St. Playhouse; acting with Uta Hagen, 1954–57. Member of AEA; AFTRA; SAG.

Theatre. Miss Oliver appeared as Fenya and understudy to Eileen Ryan in the role of Grushenka in *The Brothers Karamazov* (Gate Th., N.Y.C., Dec. 6, 1957); followed by the role of the Girl in a stock production of *The Cave Dwellers* (Olney Playhouse, Md., Summer 1958); Lolly Hester in *Jackknife* (Royal Playhouse, N.Y.C., Sept. 22, 1958); Anne in *The Diary of Anne Frank* (Playhouse on the Green, Columbus, Ohio, 1959); and Marie in *Vincent* (Cricket, N.Y.C., Sept. 30, 1959).

She played Lily Berniers in *Toys in the Attic* (Hudson, Feb. 25, 1960); at the John Drew Th. (East Hampton, L.I., N.Y., Summer, 1961), appeared as Nellie in *Summer and Smoke,* Allison in *The Lady's Not for Burning,* and the Maid in *The Bald Soprano;* played Claire in *The Maids* (Playwright's Th. at Second City, Chicago, Ill., Nov.–Jan. 1961); Iris in *Harold* (Cort, N.Y.C., Nov. 29, 1962); and succeeded (Mar. 27, 1963) Avra Petrides at matinees and (Apr. 1, 1963) Melinda Dillon at evening performances as Honey in *Who's Afraid of Virginia Woolf?* (Billy Rose Th., Oct. 13, 1962). She was Mary Kingsley in *Happily Never After* (Eugene O'Neill Th., Mar. 10, 1966); Lonesome Sally in *Terrible Jim Fitch,* one of three one-act plays on the program *Stop, You're Killing Me* (Stage 73, Mar. 19, 1969); Eleanor in *The Enclave* (Washington Th. Club, Washington, D.C., Feb. 21, 1973; Th. Four, N.Y.C., Nov. 15, 1973); and was standby for Ellen Burstyn as Doris in *Same Time, Next Year* (Brooks Atkinson Th., Mar. 13, 1975).

OLIVIER, LAURENCE (CR. BARON 1970; KT. 1957). Actor, director, producer. b. Laurence Kerr Olivier, May 22, 1907, Dorking, England, to Gerard Kerr and Agnes Louise (Crookenden) Olivier. Father, clergyman. Attended All Saint's Sch., London; St. Edward's Sch., Oxford. Studied acting with Elsie Fogerty. Married 1930, to Jill Esmond, actress (marr. dis. 1940), one son; married Aug. 30, 1940, to Vivien

Leigh, actress (marr. dis. 1960); married Mar. 17, 1961, to Joan Plowright, actress; one son, two daughters. Served WW II, with Fleet Air Arm, rank, Lt. Member of British AEA; The Garrick Club; The Green Room. Address: (home) 4 Royal Crescent, Brighton, England; (bus.) 33/34 Chancery Lane, London W.C.2, England tel. 836-7932.

Theatre. Laurence Olivier first appeared on stage while at Oxford as Brutus in *Julius Caesar* (c.1918); played Katherine in a school production of *The Taming of the Shrew* (Shakespeare Festival Th., Stratford-upon-Avon, Apr. 1922); made his professional debut as the Suliot Officer in *Byron* (Century, London, Nov. 1924); played Thomas of Clarence and Snare in *Henry IV, Part 2* (Regent, Feb. 8, 1925); appeared in both *Henry VIII* and *The Cenci* (Empire, Dec. 23, 1925); and with the Birmingham Repertory Co. (1926–28); played the Minstrel in *The Marvellous History of Saint Bernard* (Kingsway, Apr. 7, 1926); toured as Richard Coaker in *The Farmer's Wife* (July, 1926); appeared in repertory productions as the Young Man in *The Adding Machine*, Malcolm in *Macbeth* (modern dress), Martellus in *Back to Methuselah*, the title role in *Harold*, and the Lord in *The Taming of the Shrew* (modern dress), (Court, Jan.–Apr., 1928); played Gerald Arnwood in *Bird in Hand* (Royalty, June 1928); Captain Stanhope in *Journey's End* (Apollo, Dec. 9, 1928); the title role in *Beau Geste* (His Majesty's, Jan. 30, 1929); Prince Po in *The Circle of Chalk* (New, Mar. 14, 1929); Richard Parish in *Paris Bound* (Lyric, Apr. 30, 1929); and John Hardy in *The Stranger Within* (Garrick, June 20, 1929).

He made his N.Y.C. debut as Hugh Bromilow in *Murder on the Second Floor* (Eltinge, Sept. 11, 1929); subsequently appeared, as Jerry Warrender in *The Last Enemy* (Fortune, London, Dec. 19, 1929); Ralph in *After All* (Arts, Mar. 30, 1930); Victor Prynne in *Private Lives* (Phoenix, London, Sept. 24, 1930; Times Square Th., N.Y.C., Jan. 27, 1931).

Steven Beringer in *The Rats of Norway* (Playhouse, Hollywood, Calif., Apr. 6, 1933); Julian Dulcimer in *The Green Bay Tree* (Cort, N.Y.C., Oct. 20, 1933); Richard Kurt in *Biography* (Globe, London, Apr. 25, 1934); Bothwell in *Queen of Scots* (New, June 8, 1934); Anthony Cavendish in *Theatre Royal* (Lyric, Oct. 23, 1934); Peter Hammond in *Ringmaster* (Shaftesbury, Mar. 11, 1935); produced, and played Richard Harben in *Golden Arrow* (Whitehall, May 30, 1935); appeared as Romeo in *Romeo and Juliet* (New, Oct. 17, 1935) and Mercutio the following month in the same production. He was producer, with Ralph Richardson, of *Bees on the Boatdeck* (Lyric, May 5, 1936), in which he played Robert Patch.

With the Old Vic Co. (1937) he played the title role in *Hamlet* (Jan. 5), Sir Toby Belch in *Twelfth Night* (Feb. 23), King Henry in *Henry V* (Apr. 6), repeated Hamlet with the company at Kronborg Castle, Elsinore, Denmark (June 1937), and played the title role in *Macbeth* (Nov. 26), later repeated at the New Th. (Dec. 24); in 1938, appeared as Iago in *Othello* (Feb. 8); Vivaldi in *The King of Nowhere* (Mar. 15); and Caius Marcius in *Coriolanus* (Apr. 19). In N.Y.C., played Gaylord Easterbrook in *No Time for Comedy* (Ethel Barrymore Th., Apr. 17, 1939); produced, and played Romeo, in *Romeo and Juliet* which he directed with Robert Ross (51 St. Th., May 9, 1940).

He was named co-director of the Old Vic Co., with whom he appeared at the New Th. as the Button Moulder in *Peer Gynt* (Aug. 31, 1944), Sergius Saranoff in *Arms and the Man* (Sept. 5, 1944), the Duke of Gloucester in *Richard III* (Sept. 13, 1944), and Astrov in *Uncle Vanya* (Jan. 16, 1945). He produced *The Skin of Our Teeth* (Phoenix, London, May 16, 1945); and appeared with the Old Vic Co. in Paris (Comédie-Française, July 1945) in *Peer Gynt*, *Arms and the Man*, and *Richard III;* played Hotspur in *Henry IV, Part 1* (London, Sept. 26, 1945); Justice Shallow in *Henry IV, Part 2* (Oct. 3, 1945), and the title role in *Oedipus* (Oct. 18, 1945), presented on a double-bill with *The Critic*, in which he played Puff.

In May, 1946, he appeared with the Old Vic Co. at the Century Th., N.Y.C. repeating his roles in repertory productions of *Henry IV, Part 1* (May 6), *Henry IV, Part 2* (May 7), *Uncle Vanya* (May 13), and *Oedipus* and *The Critic* (May 20); then played the title role and directed their production of *King Lear* (New, London, Sept. 24, 1946); and presented *Born Yesterday* (Garrick, London Jan. 23, 1947); with the Old Vic Co. toured Australia and New Zealand in *The School for Scandal, Richard III*, and *The Skin of Our Teeth* in which he played Mr. Antrobus; appeared at the New Th., London, with the company, as Sir Peter Teazle in *The School for Scandal* (Jan. 20, 1949) which he also directed; played the title role in *Richard III* (Jan. 26, 1949); directed and played the Chorus in *Antigone*, presented on a double-bill with *The Proposal*, which he also staged (Feb. 10, 1949).

He produced *A Streetcar Named Desire* (Aldwych, London, Oct. 12, 1949); played the Duke of Altair in *Venus Observed* (St. James's, Jan. 18, 1950) which he also produced; presented *Captain Carvallo* (St. James's, Aug. 9, 1950); at St. James's Th. produced and played Caesar in *Caesar and Cleopatra* (May 10, 1951), and Antony in *Antony and Cleopatra* (May 11, 1951); produced *Othello* (St. James's, Oct. 18, 1951); repeated his roles in *Caesar and Cleopatra* and *Antony and Cleopatra* (Ziegfeld, N.Y.C., Dec. 19, 20, 1951); with Gilbert Miller, co-produced *The Happy Time* (St. James's London, Jan. 30, 1952); staged *Venus Observed* (New Century, N.Y.C., Feb. 13, 1952); produced *Anastasia* (St. James's, London, Aug. 5, 1953); played the Grand Duke in *The Sleeping Prince* (Phoenix, Nov. 5, 1953); produced *Waiting for Gillian* (St. James's, London, Apr. 21, 1954); and *Meet a Body* (Duke of York's Th., July 21, 1954); at the Royal Shakespeare Th., Stratford-upon-Avon (1955) played Malvolio in *Twelfth Night* (Apr. 12); and the title role in *Macbeth* (June 7); and *Titus Andronicus* (Aug. 16). He produced *Double Image* (Savoy, London, Nov. 14, 1956); played Archie Rice in *The Entertainer* (Royal Court, London, Apr. 10, 1957); produced *The Summer of the Seventeenth Doll* (New, Apr. 30, 1957); toured Eastern Europe in the title role of *Titus Andronicus* (June, 1957); repeated the role (Stoll, London, July 1, 1957); again played Archie Rice in *The Entertainer* (Palace, London, Sept. 10, 1957; Royale, N.Y.C., Feb. 12, 1958); and at Stratford-upon-Avon played the title role in *Coriolanus* (July 7, 1959).

He produced *The Shifting Heart* (Duke of York's Th., London, Sept. 14, 1959); was co-producer of *The Tumbler* (Helen Hayes Th., N.Y.C. Feb. 24, 1960); and *A Lodging for a Bride* (Westminster, London, Apr. 18, 1960); played Berenger in *Rhinoceros* (Royal Court, Apr. 28, 1960); was co-producer of *Over the Bridge* (Prince's, May 4, 1960); and appeared in the title role of *Becket* (St. James, N.Y.C., Oct. 5, 1960); toured as Henry II in *Becket* (opened Colonial, Boston, Mass., March 29, 1961; closed Shubert, Philadelphia, Pa., May 6, 1961), and returned to N.Y.C. in the same role (Hudson, May 8, 1961) for a three-week limited engagement.

He was appointed director of the Chichester Festival Th., Sussex, England, in 1961; where he staged *The Chances* (July 3, 1962); directed and played Bassanes in *The Broken Heart* (July 9, 1962), and directed and played Astrov in *Uncle Vanya* (July 16, 1962). In London, he played Frank Midway in *Semi-Detached* (Saville, Dec. 5, 1962); at the Chichester Festival Th., directed, and played Astrov in *Uncle Vanya*.

He was director, National Theatre of Great Britain (1963–73) and associate director (1973–to date); directed the National's opening production, *Hamlet* (National, Oct. 22, 1963); staged and played Astrov in *Uncle Vanya* (National, 19, 1963); played Captain Brazen in *The Recruiting Officer* (National, Dec. 10, 1963); played the title role in *Othello* (National, Apr. 21, 1964), which was repeated during the 1964 season at the Chichester Festival Th.; replaced (Nov. 17, 1964) Michael Redgrave as Halvard Solness in *The Master Builder* (National, June 9, 1964); directed *The Crucible* (National, Jan. 19, 1965); toured (Sept. 1965) with the National Th. company in *Othello* and *Love for Love* (Kremlevsky Th., Moscow, USSR; Freie Volksbuhne, West Berlin, Germany); played Tattle in *Love for Love* (National, Oct. 20, 1965); directed *Juno and the Paycock* (Alexandra Th., Birmingham, England, Apr. 4, 1966; National, London, Apr. 26, 1966); played Edgar in *Dance of Death* (National, Feb. 21, 1967); directed *The Three Sisters* (National, July 4, 1967); took over the role of Etienne in *A Flea in Her Ear* (National, July 18, 1967). He toured Canada with the National, Th. company in *Love for Love, A Flea in Her Ear*, and *Dance of Death* (Oct.–Nov. 1967); co-directed *The Advertisement* (Royal, Brighton, England, Sept. 17, 1968; National, London, Sept. 24, 1968); directed *Love's Labour's Lost* (National, Dec. 19, 1968); replaced Arthur Lowe as A. B. Raham in a revival of *Home and Beauty* (National, Jan. 30, 1969); played Chebutikin in *The Three Sisters* (National, Apr. 10 and 18, 1969; Royal, Brighton, Sept. 29–Oct. 1, 1969); played Shylock in *The Merchant of Venice* (National, Apr. 28, 1970); directed *Amphitryon 38* (New, Oxford, June 15, 1971; National, London, June 23, 1971); played James Tyrone in *Long Day's Journey into Night* (National, Dec. 14, 1971); Antonio in *Saturday Sunday Monday* (National, Oct. 23, 1973); John Tagg in *The Party* (National, Dec. 18, 1973); and directed *Eden End* (Richmond, Mar. 25, 1974; National, London, Apr. 2, 1974).

Films. Since his film debut in *Too Many Crooks* (Par., 1927), he has appeared in *Friends and Lovers* (RKO, 1931); *The Yellow Ticket* (20th-Fox, 1931); *Perfect Understanding* (UA, 1933); *No Funny Business* (Principal, 1934); *Fire over England* (UA, 1937); *Moscow Nights* (Lenauer, 1938); *The Divorce of Lady X* (UA, 1938); *Wuthering Heights* (UA, 1939); *Rebecca* (UA, 1940); *Pride and Prejudice* (MGM, 1940); *The 49th Parallel; That Hamilton Woman* (UA, 1941); *Henry V* (UA, 1946), which he directed; *Hamlet* (U, 1948), which he directed and produced; *Carrie* (Par., 1952); *The Demi-Paradise; The Magic Box* (Rank, 1952); *The Beggar's Opera* (WB, 1953); *Richard III* (Lopert, 1956); *The Prince and the Showgirl* (WB, 1957), which he directed; *The Devil's Disciple* (UA, 1959); *Spartacus* (U, 1960); *The Entertainer* (Continental Distributing, 1960); *Term of Trial* (WB, 1963); *Bunny Lake Is Missing* (Col., 1965); *Othello* (WB, 1966); *Khartoum* (UA, 1966); *Dance of Death* (1968); *Shoes of the Fisherman* (MGM, 1968); *Oh! What a Lovely War* (Par., 1969); *Battle of Britain* (UA, 1969); *The Three Sisters* (1969), which he also directed; narrated *Tree of Life* (1971); and appeared in *Nicholas and Alexandra* (Col., 1971); *Sleuth* (20th-Fox, 1973); and *Lady Caroline Lamb* (UA, 1974).

Television. Mr. Olivier appeared in the title role of *John Gabriel Borkman* (BBC, Nov. 1958); played Strickland in *The Moon and Sixpence* (NBC, Oct. 30, 1959); the Priest in *The Power and the Glory* (CBS, Oct. 1961); Astrov in *Uncle Vanya* (BBC, 1963); was in *David Copperfield* (NBC, Mar. 15, 1970); played James Tyrone in *Long Day's Journey into Night* (1972); Shylock in *The Merchant of Venice* (1973); narrated *World at War* (1973); and played Sir Arthur Granville-Jones in *Love Among the Ruins* (ABC, Mar. 6, 1975).

Awards. He received the Academy (Oscar) Award for his performance in the title role of *Hamlet*, and the film *Hamlet*, which he produced-directed, received the Academy (Oscar) Award for the Best Production of the Year (1948). He also received NATAS (Emmy) awards for his performances as Strickland in *The Moon and Sixpence* (1960), James Tyrone in *Long Day's Journey into Night* (1973), and Sir Arthur Granville-Jones in *Love Among the Ruins* (1975). He was awarded the Sonning Prize (Denmark, 1966) and the gold medallion of the Swedish Academy of Literature (1968).

He was knighted in birthday honours (England, 1947) and created baron (1970); was made a commander of the Order of Dannebrog (Denmark, 1949); an Officer of the Légion d'Honneur (France, 1953); a Grand Officer of the Ordine al Merito della Republica (Italy, 1954); was awarded honorary degrees of D.Litt. by Oxford Univ. (1957), Edinburgh Univ. (1964), and the Univ. of London (1968) and LL.D. by the Univ. of Manchester (1968). He received the Selznick Golden Laurel Trophy "for contributions to international goodwill" (1956); and was made president of the Actors' Orphanage (1956).

Recreation. Tennis, swimming, gardening.

O'LOUGHLIN, GERALD. Actor. b. Gerald Stuart O'Loughlin, Dec. 23, 1921, New York City, to Gerald S. and Laura (Ward) O'Loughlin, Sr. Grad. Blair Acad., Blairstown, N.J., 1941; attended Univ. of Rochester 1943–44; Lafayette Coll., B.S. (Mech. England) 1948. Studied at Neighborhood Playhouse Sch. of the Th., 1948–50, with Sanford Meisner, David Pressman, Martha Graham; at Actors Studio, with Lee Strasberg and Alice Hermes, 1951–to date; with Albert Malver, voice coach, N.Y.C.; David Craig, singing, N.Y.C.; Nick Colasanto, acting, N.Y.C. Married 1967 to Meryl Abeles, television casting director; one son, one daughter. Relatives in theatre: cousin, Judy Robinson, actress; cousin, Charles Robinson, actor. Served USMC, 1942–46; rank, 1st Lt. Member of AEA; SAG; AFTRA; Theta Delta Chi. Address: c/o William Morris Agency, 151 El Camino Dr., Beverly Hills, CA 90212.

Pre-Theatre. Cabinet-maker, mechanical engineer, photographer, auto mechanic.

Theatre. Mr. O'Loughlin made his stage debut in stock as Harry Brock in *Born Yesterday* and as Joe Keller in *All My Sons* (Crystal Lake Lodge, N.Y., June 1949); first appeared in N.Y.C. as the Bucket Boy in the ANTA production of *Golden Boy*(ANTA Th., Mar. 12, 1952); subsequently appeared as Stanley Kowalski in *A Streetcar Named Desire* (NY City Ctr., Feb. 15, 1956); temporarily replaced (Aug. 11–Sept. 1, 1958) Frank Overton as Morris Lacey in *The Dark at the Top of the Stairs* (Music Box, Dec. 5, 1957), and played Rubin Flood in a stock production (Playhouse-in-the-Park, Philadelphia, Pa., Aug. 1960); succeeded (Erlanger, Chicago, Ill., July 1957) John Anderson as Gooper in a national tour of *Cat on a Hot Tin Roof*(opened National, Washington, D.C., Nov. 26, 1956).

Mr. O'Loughlin played Seamus Shields in *Shadow of a Gunman* (Bijou, N.Y.C., Nov. 20, 1958); succeeded (Jan. 1959) Tom Clancy as Mickey Maloy in *A Touch of the Poet*(Helen Hayes Th., Oct. 2, 1958); appeared as Richard Roe in *Machinal* (Gate, Apr. 7, 1960); Goober in *A Cook for Mister General* (Playhouse, Oct. 19, 1961); William Medlow in *Calculated Risk* (Ambassador, Oct. 31, 1962); Albert Cobb in *Who'll Save the Plowboy?* (Phoenix, Jan. 9, 1962); Charles Cheswick in *One Flew Over the Cuckoo's Nest* (Cort, Nov. 13, 1963) in *Harry, Noon and Night* (Pocket Th., May 5, 1965); and as Johnny in *Lovers and Other Strangers* (Brooks Atkinson Th., Sept. 18, 1968).

Films. Following his debut in *Lovers and Lollipops* (Trans-Lux, 1956) Mr. O'Loughlin appeared in *A Hatful of Rain* (A.F., 1957); *Cop Hater* (UA, 1958); *Mister Pulver and the Captain* (WB, 1963); *A Fine Madness* (WB, 1966); *In Cold Blood* (Col., 1967); *Ice Station Zebra* (MGM, 1967); *The Riot* (Par., 1968); *Desperate Characters* (Par., 1970); *The Organization* (UA, 1971); and *The Valachi Papers* (Col., 1972).

Television. He made his debut on Cameo Th. (NBC, June 1950); subsequently appeared in *A Piece of Blue Sky* (Play of the Week, WNTA, Apr. 1960) and *A Clearing In The Woods* (Play of the Week, WNTA, Jan. 1961); on Ben Casey (ABC, May 1962); The Defenders (CBS, Jan. 19, 1963); Naked City (ABC, Mar. 1963); Alcoa Premiere (ABC, Apr. 1963); Guiding Light (CBS, Jan. 1963); The Doctors (NBC, 1963); Dr. Kildare (NBC, May 1964); Run for Your Life (1966); The F.B.I. (ABC, 1966, 1969, 1971); Green Hornet (1966); Felony Squad (1967); Cimarron Strip (1967); Mission: Impossible (CBS, 1968, 1971); Mannix (CBS, 1968); Judd for the Defense (1968); Hawaii Five-O (CBS, 1968, 1970); Ironside (NCB, 1969, 1970); Medical Center (CBS, 1969); The Virginians (1969); Storefront Lawyers (also called Men at Law (1969)); Bronson (1969); The Senator (1970); Young Lawyers (1970); Dan August (1970); Owen Marshal (1971); Sarge (1971); Nichols (1971); Cade's County (1971); Room 222 (NBC, 1972–73–74); Cannon (CBS, 1972–73–74); and The Rookies (ABC, 1972–73–74).

Other Activities. Mr. O'Loughlin is a faculty member at the Lee Strasberg Theatre Institute, Hollywood, Calif.

Awards. Mr. O'Loughlin received *The Village Voice* Off-Bway (Obie) Award for his performance as Albert Cobb in *Who'll Save the Plowboy?.*

OLSON, NANCY. Actress. b. Nancy Ann Olson, July 14, 1928, Milwaukee, Wis., to Henry J. and Evelyn B. (Bergstrom) Olson. Father, physician. Grad. Wauwatosa H.S., Milwaukee, Wis., 1946; attended Univ. of Wisconsin, 1946–47; Univ. of California at Los Angeles, 1947–49. Married Mar. 19, 1950, to Alan Jay Lerner, playwright, lyricist (marr. dis. 1957); two daughters; married Sept. 1, 1962, to Alan W. Livingston, pres., Capitol Records; one son. Member of AEA; SAG; AFTRA. Address: 945 North Alpine Dr., Beverly Hills, CA 90210, tel. (213) CR 3-2690.

Theatre. Miss Olson made her first N.Y.C. appearance as Isolde Poole in *The Tunnel of Love* (Royale Th., Feb. 13, 1957); subsequently played Judy Kimball in *Send Me No Flowers* (Brooks Atkinson Th., Dec. 5, 1960); and temporarily replaced Barbara Bel Geddes for a month (Feb. 1962) as Mary McKellaway in *Mary, Mary*(Helen Hayes Th., Mar. 8, 1962).

Films. Miss Olson made her debut in *Canadian Pacific* (20th-Fox, 1949); subsequently appeared in *Sunset Boulevard* (Par., 1950); *Mr. Music* (Par., 1950); *Union Station* (Par., 1950); *Submarine Command* (Par., 1951); *Force of Arms* (WB, 1951); *Big Jim McLain* (WB, 1952); *So Big* (WB, 1953); *Boy from Oklahoma* (WB, 1954); *Battle Cry* (WB, 1955); *Pollyanna* (Buena Vista, 1960); *The Absent-Minded Professor* (Buena Vista, 1961); *Son of Flubber* (Buena Vista, 1962); *Snowball Express* (Buena Vista, 1972); and *Airport 1975* (U, 1974).

Awards. For her performance in *Sunset Boulevard,* Miss Olson received an Academy (Oscar) Award nomination (1950).

Recreation. Music, playing piano.

O'MALLEY, J. PAT. Actor. b. James Patrick O'Malley, Mar. 15, 1904, Burnley, England, to Francis and Frances Elizabeth (Lea) O'Malley. Attended Christ's Coll., England, 1917–21. Married Jan. 13, 1936, to Margeret Mullen; one son, one daughter. Member of AEA; SAG; AFTRA; The Lambs; Del Mar Beach Club (Santa Monica, Calif.).

Theatre. Mr. O'Malley appeared on Bway as Ben Griggs in *But Not Goodbye* (48 St. Th., Apr. 11, 1944); Blore in *Ten Little Indians* (Broadhurst, June 27, 1944); played Cob O'Brien in the pre-Bway tryout of *Portrait in Black* (opened Shubert, New Haven, Conn., Dec. 27, 1945; closed Nixon, Pittsburgh, Pa., Jan. 12, 1946); Francis X. Gilhooley in a revival of *Of Thee I Sing* (Ziegfeld, N.Y.C., May 5, 1952); Able Seaman Badger in *Seagulls Over Sorrento* (John Golden Th., Sept. 11, 1952); succeeded John Williams (July 1953) as Inspector Hubbard in *Dial M for Murder* (Plymouth, Oct. 12, 1952); and played Dovetail in *Home Is the Hero* (Booth, Sept. 22, 1954).

Films. Mr. O'Malley made his debut in *Paris Calling* (U, 1941); and has since appeared in *Over My Dead Body* (20th-Fox, 1942); *Thumbs Up* (Rep., 1943); *Lassie, Come Home* (MGM, 1943); *The Long Hot Summer* (20th-Fox, 1957); *Blueprint for Robbery* (Par., 1960); and *A House Is Not a Home* (Par., 1964).

Television. Mr. O'Malley has appeared on Philco Television Playhouse (NBC); Kraft Television Th. (NBC); Suspense (CBS); Studio One (CBS); Playhouse 90 (CBS); Bonanza (NBC); Ben Casey (ABC); Dr. Kildare (NBC); Wagon Train (NBC); Have Gun Will Travel (CBS); The Danny Thomas Show (ABC); The Dick Van Dyke Show (CBS); My Favorite Martian (CBS); and Wendy and Me (ABC).

O'MORRISON, KEVIN. Playwright, actor, stage manager. b. St. Louis, Mo., to S. E. and Dori (Adams) O'Morrison. Father, farmer. Educ. Illinois Military School (later Roosevelt Military Acad.). Professional training with Robert Lewis; Harold Clurman's playwrights' seminars. Married to Janet Lord (marr. dis.); married Apr. 30, 1966, to Linda Soma. Member of Dramatists Guild; Authors League of America; WGA, East; AEA; SAG; AFTRA; The Players. Address: 239 E. 18th St., New York, NY 10003; The Players, 16 Gramercy Park, New York, NY 10003, tel. (212) GR 5-6116.

Theatre. Mr. O'Morrison made his theatrical debut as Firk in a production of *The Shoemakers' Holiday* (Little Th., St. Louis, Mo., Sept. 1936) and his professional debut as a walk-on and understudy in the Mercury Th. production of *Julius Caesar* (Jan. 1938). He first appeared in summer stock at Stony Creek, Conn., where he played juvenile leads for ten weeks (beginning June 1938); played a Senator and was an understudy in the Mercury Th. production of *Danton's Death* (Nov. 2, 1938); played six parts in *Railroads on Parade* (Railroad Pavilion, NY World's Fair, May 1939; May 1940); toured as the juvenile lead in *Second Helping* (Shubert Th., New Haven, Conn., Sept. 1940); played in ten weeks of stock at Mt. Tom, Holyoke, Mass. (beginning June 1941) and at Syracuse (N.Y.) Summer Th. (beginning June 1942); was a Soldier and general understudy in *The Eve of St. Mark* (Cort, N.Y.C., Oct. 7, 1942); Ed and general understudy in *Winged Victory* (44 St. Th., Nov. 1943) and toured with it (War Memorial, San Francisco, Calif., Oct. 1944).

He played the Prosecutor in *The Caine Mutiny Court Martial* (Mt. Kisco Th., Mt. Kisco, N.Y., June 1954); played leads in stock for ten weeks, Clinton (Conn.) Th. (beginning June 1955), including Ed McKeever in *The Solid Gold Cadillac;* was standby for Denis O'Dea in *The Righteous Are Bold* (Forum, N.Y.C., Dec. 22, 1955); was stage manager for eight weeks of *Sing, Man, Sing,* starring Harry Belafonte (opened: Hanna Th., Cleveland, Ohio, Mar. 1956); was Fergus in *Deirdre of the Sorrows* (Gate Th., N.Y.C., Oct. 14, 1959); and played the Doctor in a revival of *The Rose Tattoo* (NY City Ctr., Oct. 20–30, 1966; Billy Rose Th., Nov. 9, 1966).

Mr. O'Morrison wrote *Three Days Before Yesterday* (Chelsea Th. Ctr., N.Y.C., Sept. 1965), presented later as *The Long War* (Triangle Th., Trinity Church, N.Y.C., Mar. 1969); *The Morgan Yard* (O'-Neill Ctr., Waterford, Conn., Aug. 3, 1971; Mercury Th., Colchester, England, Mar. 5, 1974; Olympia, Dublin, Eire, Sept. 30, 1974); and *The Realist* (Attic Th., Trinity Univ., San Antonio, Tex., Oct. 16, 1974).

Films. Mr. O'Morrison's first film was *Dear Ruth* (Par., 1947); followed by *The Set-Up* (RKO, 1949); *The Young Lovers* (Eagle-Lion, 1950); and *The Golden Gloves Story* (Eagle-Lion, 1950).

Television. Mr. O'Morrison made his television debut in the title role of *Charlie Wild* (CBS, Jan. 1951). He wrote *The House of Paper* (NBC, Feb. 15, 1959); *And Not a Word More* (CBS, July 3, 1960); and *A Sign for Autumn* (NBC, Mar. 11, 1962).

Awards. Mr. O'Morrison has received a CAPS Fellowship Award (1974–75).

Recreation. Sailing, traveling, walking.

O'NEAL, FREDERICK. Actor, director, lecturer. b. Frederick Douglas O'Neal, Aug. 27, 1905, Brooksville, Miss., to Ransome James and Ninnie Bell (Thompson) O'Neal. Father, merchant, teacher; mother, teacher. Attended Waring School, St. Louis, Mo., 1922; New Theatre Sch., N.Y.C. 1936–40; Amer. Theatre Wing. Studied with Komisarjevsky. Married Apr. 18, 1942, to Charlotte Talbot Hainey, administrative assistant. Served US Army (AGO) 1942–43; rank, Pvt. Member of AEA (1st and 3rd vice-pres., councillor, pres., 1964; pres. emeritus, 1964–73); SAG; AFTRA; Negro Actors' Guild (pres., 1961–64); Catholic Actors' Guild (vice-pres.); NATAS; ANTA; Actors Fund; Associated Actors and Artists of America (intl. pres., 1970–to date); AFL-CIO (vice-pres., 1969); AFL-CIO Civil Rights Committee (chmn., 1970);

Harlem Cultural Council Advisory Board (chmn.); A. Philip Randolph Institute (vice-pres.); Schomburg Collection of Black History, Literature & Art, Inc. (pres., chmn. of the bd.); NYC Central Labor Council (coordinator, Job Placement Program; vice-pres., Black Trade Unionists Leadership Comm.); Ira Aldridge Soc. (bd. member); Amer. Veterans Comm.; NAACP; Catholic Interracial Council (vice-pres.); Knights of St. Peter Claver; The Players; The Lambs. Address: 165 W. 46th St., New York, NY 10036.

Theatre. Mr. O'Neal made his first stage appearance in a recitation at the Brooksville (Miss.) School (Apr. 1, 1913); in 1927, founded the Aldridge Players, and made his professional debut as Charles and Sylvius in *As You Like It* (Odeon Th., St. Louis, Mo., Oct. 1927); was a cofounder of the American Negro Th. (1940) where he appeared as the Father in *Strivers Row*, Preacher in *Natural Man*, the Father in *Three's A Family*, and the title role in *Henri Christophe* (1940–45).

He made his Bway debut as Frank in *Anna Lucasta* (Mansfield, Aug. 20, 1944), repeated the role in Chicago (Civic, 1945–46), in London (His Majesty's, Oct. 29, 1947), in Scotland (1948), and staged the revival that played in London (Prince of Wale's, Aug. 24, 1953), and toured England and Ireland (1953); and helped organize the British Negro Th. (1948). Mr. O'Neal appeared as Paul Freeman in the pre-Bway tryout of *A Lady Passing Fair* (opened Lyric Th., Bridgeport, Conn., Jan. 3, 1947; closed Newark Opera House, N.J., Jan. 11, 1947); played Father in *Head of the Family* (Westport Country Playhouse, Conn., Sept. 1950); Lem in *Take a Giant Step* (Lyceum, N.Y.C., Sept. 24, 1954); Judge Samuel Addison in *The Winner* (Playhouse, Feb. 17, 1954); the Hougan in *House of Flowers* (Alvin, Dec. 30, 1954); Bednar in *The Man with the Golden Arm* (Cherry Lane, May 21, 1956); John Kumalo in the NY City Opera Co. production of *Lost in the Stars* (NY City Ctr., Apr. 10, 1958); at the Cambridge Arts Festival, played Antonio in *Twelfth Night* (July 1959); and in N.Y.C., the Minister in *Shakespeare in Harlem* (41 St. Th., Feb. 9, 1960). He taught as visiting professor and played Ceasar in the Southern Illinois Univ. production of *Marseilles* (Oct. 1962); also taught and played Willie in the Clark Coll. production of *Death of a Salesman*, (Atlanta, Ga., Apr. 1963); played Captain Neddie Boyce in the first production of the New Group, *Ballad for Bimshire* (Mayfair, Oct. 15, 1963); was in *The Iceman Cometh* (Arena Stage, Washington, D.C., Mar. 26, 1968); and played in a revival of *The Madwoman of Chaillot* (Sokol Th., N.Y.C., Mar. 22, 1970).

Films. Mr. O'Neal made his film debut as Jake in *Pinky* (20th-Fox, 1949); subsequently appeared as the Doctor in *No Way Out* (20th-Fox, 1950); Bulam in *Tarzan's Peril* (RKO, 1951); Adam in *Something of Value* (MGM, 1957); Frank in *Anna Lucasta* (UA, 1958); Lem in *Take a Giant Step* (UA, 1959); Chief Bnderga in *The Sins of Rachel Cade* (WB, 1961); and as Ernie Jones in *Free, White, and 21* (Falcon-Intl. 1962).

Television. Mr. O'Neal appeared as the Preacher in *God's Trombones* (Fred Waring Show, CBS); and Moses in *Green Pastures* (Hall of Fame, NBC, Oct. 1959); narrated *New York Illustrated* (NBC, Dec. 1962); and played Patrolman Wallace in Car 54, Where Are You? (NBC, 1961–62) and the Motor Pool Sargeant in the Sgt. Bilko series.

Awards. For his performance as Frank in *Anna Lucasta* he received the Clarence Derwent Award (1944–45), won the Variety NY Drama Critics Poll for best supporting actor (1944–45); a nomination for the Donaldson Award, Dutch Treat Disc; and tied as Best Actor in Chicago for the Critics' Award (1945–46 season). He received an award for courage and leadership toward integration in the performing arts (1954); the Motion Picture Critics Award for his performance in the film *Anna Lucasta* (1959); and an Ira Aldridge Citation for leadership toward integration in performing arts (Feb. 1963). He also received the Hoey Award of the Catholic Interracial Council (1964); the David W. Petegorsky Award for civic achievement of the American Jewish Congress (1964); the National Urban League E.O.D. Award (1965); the Distinguished Service Award of the NYC Central Labor Council (1967); the George W. Norris Civil Rights Award of the American Veterans Committee (1970); the Frederick Douglass Award of the NY Urban League (1971); the Canada Lee Foundation Award; an honorary D.F.A. degree from Columbia College, Chicago (1966); a citation from Loeb Student Center, NY Univ. (1967); and honorary membership in Kappa Delta Pi.

Recreation. Outdoor sports, photography, cooking.

O'NEAL, JOHN. Playwright, actor, director, producer, teacher. b. John Milton O'Neal, Jr., Sept. 24, 1940, Mound City, Ill., to John Milton, Sr., and Rosetta (Crenshaw) O'Neal. Educ. Lovejoy Senior H.S., Mound City; grad. Southern Illinois Univ., 1962. Alternative to military service performed as conscientious objector to the draft. Married Feb. 10, 1965, to Mary Felice Lovelace (marr. dis. Aug. 15, 1968); June 10, 1972, to Marilyn Norton; one daughter. Relative in theatre: first cousin, Ron O'Neal, actor. Address: (home) 1014 St. Claude Ave., New Orleans, LA 70116, tel. (504) 523-3117; (bus.) 1328 Dryades St., New Orleans, LA 70113, tel. (504) 581-5091.

Mr. O'Neal was field secretary, Student Non-Violent Coordinating Committee (SNCC) (1960–65), and field secretary, Committee for Racial Justice, United Church of Christ (1966–68).

Theatre. Mr. O'Neal is producing director, Free Southern Theater, Inc. (FST), founded by him and Gilbert Moses in 1963 as the Tougaloo Drama Workshop at Tougaloo College, near Jackson, Miss., to encourage development of theatrical expression among Southern blacks. In Sept. 1964, FST moved to New Orleans, La., and began building a repertory company to visit black communities in Southern states.

In White America toured Miss. (July–Aug. 1964); a double bill of *Purlie Victorious* and *Waiting for Godot* toured Miss., Tenn., Ga., and La., (Nov. 1964–Feb. 1965); *The Rifles of Senora Carrar* toured La. and Miss. (Aug. 1965); *Roots, I Speak of Africa*, and *Does Man Help Man?* toured La., Miss., Ala., and Ga. (July–Sept. 1966); *Happy Ending, Uncle Tom's Second Line Funeral*, and *The Lesson* toured in New Orleans, in Ga., and visited college campuses (Apr.–Aug. 1967). A new professional company was brought from N.Y.C. in 1969. Among the new presentations were *Slave Ship, The Black Liberation Army, Proper and Fine*, and *Fanny Lou Hammer's Entourage* (Jan.–Oct. 1969); *East of Jordan*, which opened in New Orleans and toured Tex., Miss., La., Ala., Ga., and Tenn. (1969); *Snapshot, Feathers and Stuff, Ritual Murder, The Pill, Mama, The Picket*, and *To Kill or Die* (Nov. 1969–June 1970); *The Warning—A Theme for Linda* (New Orleans, Oct. 1971) and tour in La. and Miss.; *The Picket, To Kill a Devil*, and *Minstrel Quintet* (New Orleans, Jan. 1972); *Rosalee Pritchett, Edifying Further Elaborations on the Mentality of a Chore* toured La. and Ga. (Apr.–May 1972); *Black Love Song* and *Daddy Gander Raps* (New Orleans, May 1972); *A Raisin in the Sun* (July–Sept. 1972); *We Are the Suns* (Oct. 1972–Apr. 1973); *Terraced Apartment* and *One Last Look* (Dec. 1972); and *The Hurricane Season*, also written by Mr. O'Neal (Feb.–Mar. 1973).

Television and Radio. FST began producing Nation-Time, a biweekly magazine-type television show in 1972 over WYES-TV and in 1973 started Plain Talk, a weekly radio show, over WNNR.

Other Activities. In May 1971, FST started the Black Theater Workshop to train individuals interested in working in the black theatre, and the Coffee House was inaugurated in Feb. 1972 as a center where speakers on black issues could be heard and black talent could have an audience.

O'NEAL, PATRICK. Actor. b. Patrick Wisdom O'Neal, Sept. 26, 1927, Ocala, Fla., to Coke Wisdom and Martha O'Neal. Father, citrus grower. Grad. Riverside Military Academy, Gainesville, Ga., Univ. of Fla. Studied acting at the Neighborhood Playhouse, N.Y.C. Married to Cynthia Baxter; two sons. Served U.S. Air Force (1952–53). Member of AEA; SAG; AFTRA; Actors Studio.

Theatre. Mr. O'Neal made his acting debut in *The Glass Menagerie*; and debuted professionally in the juvenile lead in a try-out production of *The Violin Messiah* (Chevy Chase Summer Th., Chicago, 1951). Off-Bway, he played Walter Schwarz in *Lulu* (Fourth St. Th., N.Y.C., Sept. 29, 1958); toured in *Oh, Men! Oh, Women!*; played John Gilbert in the pre-Bway tryout of *Laurette* (opened Shubert, New Haven, Sept. 26, 1960; closed there, Oct. 1, 1960); made his Bway debut as Frederick Wohlmuth in *A Far Country* (Music Box, N.Y.C., Apr. 4, 1961); played Rev. T. Lawrence Shannon in *The Night of the Iguana* (Royale, Dec. 28, 1961), a role in which he had appeared previously at the Festival of Two Worlds (Spoleto, Italy), and the Actors Studio; and Sebastian Belfe Dangerfield in *The Ginger Man* (Orpheum, N.Y.C., Nov. 21, 1963).

Films. His appearances include *The Mad Magician* (Col., 1954); *The Black Shield of Falworth* (U, 1954); *From the Terrace* (20th-Fox, 1960); *A Matter of Morals* (1961); *The Cardinal* (Col., 1963); *In Harm's Way* (Par., 1965); *King Rat* (Col., 1965); *A Fine Madness* (WB, 1966); *Alvarez Kelly* (Col., 1966); *Where Were You When the Lights Went Out?* (UA, 1966); *Chamber of Horrors* (WB-Seven Arts, 1967); *A Big Hand for the Little Lady* (WB-Seven Arts, 1967); *Matchless* (UA, 1967); *Assignment To Kill* (WB, 1969); *The Secret Life of an American Wife* (20th-Fox, 1969); *Castle Keep* (Col., 1969); *Stiletto* (Avco, 1969); *The Kremlin Letter* (20th-Fox, 1969); *Joe* (Cannon, 1970); *El Condor* (Natl. Gen., 1970); *The Sporting Club* (Abco, 1971); *Corky* (MGM, 1972); *The Way We Were* (Col., 1973); *Silent Night, Bloody Night* (Cannon, 1974); and *The Stepford Wives* (Col., 1975).

Television. Mr. O'Neal's extensive television appearances include Hallmark Hall of Fame (NBC); Philco Playhouse (NBC); Studio One (CBS); ABC Playhouse (ABC); Alcoa Hour (NBC); The Millionaire (CBS); The Ann Sothern Show (CBS); Play of the Week (Synd.); Naked City (ABC); The Defenders (CBS); Dr. Kildare (NBC); Route 66 (CBS); Twilight Zone (CBS); The F.B.I. (ABC); *Companions in Nightmare* (NBC, film); McCloud (NBC); Columbo (NBC); Marcus Welby, M.D. (ABC); Cannon (CBS); and *Cool Million* (NBC, film).

Other Activities. Mr. O'Neal, in partnership with members of his family, owns several restaurants in N.Y.C., including The Ginger Man, O'Neal's Balloon, O'Neal Bros., The Liberty Ice Cream Concern, and Aunt Fish.

OPATOSHU, DAVID. Actor, author, radio announcer. b. David Opatovsky Opatoshu, Jan. 30, 1918, New York City, to Joseph (Opatovsky) and Adele Opatoshu. Father, novelist; mother, teacher. Grad. Morris H.S., Bronx, N.Y., 1935. Studied acting at the Benno Schneider Studio, N.Y.C. Served USAAF, 1942–45, PTO; rank, Sgt. Married June 10, 1941, to Lillian Weinberg, psychiatric social worker (marr. dis.); one son. Married May 25, 1970, to Peggy O'Shea, author. Member of AEA; AFTRA; SAG. Address: 190 Riverside Dr., New York, NY 10024, tel. (212) TR 7-0065.

Pre-Theatre. Silk-screen printer.

Theatre. Mr. Opatoshu made his first appearance as Mr. Carp in a stock production of *Golden Boy* (Shubert, Newark, N.J., Sept. 19, 1938). He made his Bway debut as the Sleeping Man and the Blind Man in *Night Music* (Broadhurst Th., Feb. 22, 1940); subsequently, appeared as Dan in *Clinton Street* (Mercury, 1940); Ralph in *Man of Tomorrow* (Natl., 1941); Mr. Mendel in *Me and Molly* (Belasco, Feb. 26, 1948); Tewfik Bey in *Flight into Egypt* (Music Box, Mar. 18, 1952); Denesco in *Reclining Figure* (Lyceum, Oct. 7, 1954); Bibinski in *Silk Stockings* (Imperial, Feb. 24, 1955); and in the national tour (opened Curran, San Francisco, Calif., Apr. 23, 1956); Luca in the pre-Bway tryout of *At the Grand* (opened Philharmonic Aud., Los Angeles, Calif., July 7, 1958; closed Curran, San Francisco, Calif.,

Sept. 13, 1958); and succeeded (Mar. 15, 1959) Joseph Buloff as Maxwell Archer in *Once More, With Feeling* (National, Oct. 21, 1958); played Pan Apt in *The Wall* (Billy Rose Th., Oct. 11, 1960); Amedeo in *Bravo Giovanni* (Broadhurst, May 19, 1962); Filippo in *Lorenzo* (Plymouth, Feb. 16, 1963); appeared in *Does a Tiger Wear a Necktie* (Belasco, Feb. 25, 1969); and *Yoshe Kalb* (Eden, Oct. 22, 1972); and wrote the book, directed, and played Shimele Soroker in the musical *The Big Winner* (Eden, 1974).

Films. Mr. Opatoshu made his film debut as Fishke in *The Light Ahead* (Ultra, 1939); subsequently appeared as Detective Ben in *Naked City* (UI, 1948); Frenchy in *Thieves' Highway* (20th-Fox, 1949); the Accountant in *The Goldbergs* (Par., 1950); Slim in *Public Enemy No. 1* (Jacques Barr Prod., France, 1953); Capt. Snegyarov in *The Brothers Karamazov* (MGM, 1958); Sol Levy in *Cimarron* (MGM, 1960); Akiva in *Exodus* (UA, 1960); the Chief of Police in *King of Naples* (Dino de Laurentiis Prod., Italy, 1961); Capt. Bernasconi in *The Best of Enemies* (Col., 1962); President Riverra in *Guns of Darkness* (WB, 1962); appeared in *The Fixer* (MGM, 1968); and wrote the screenplay for *Romance of a Horse Thief* (Allied Artists, 1971).

Television and Radio. On radio, Mr. Opatoshu was a newscaster for WEVD, N.Y.C. (1941, 1946–55).

He made his television debut as Mr. Dutton on The Goldbergs (CBS, 1949); subsequently appeared in *Rivierra* (Studio One, CBS, 1949); the Father in *The Big Deal* (Goodyear Playhouse, NBC, 1953); the Friend in *Six O'Clock Call* (ABC, 1954); Finkle in *Finkle's Comet* (Alcoa Hour, NBC, 1956); the Brother-in-law in *The Mother* (Philco Television Playhouse, NBC, 1956); the Father in *Bricoe: Mayor Dublin* (Playhouse 90, CBS, 1957); the Bookie in *On the Nose* (Alfred Hitchcock Presents, CBS, 1958); appeared on Ellery Queen (NBC, 1958); played the Mayor in *Hidden Valley* (Alfred Hitchcock Presents, CBS, 1962); the Diplomat in *The Traitor* (Alcoa Premiere, ABC, 1962); Dulong in *The Magic Show* (Alfred Hitchcock Presents, CBS, 1963).

Published Works. Mr. Opatoshu is the author of *Mid Sea and Sand* (1947).

Awards. For his performance as Akiva in *Exodus* he won the Limelight Award for best supporting actor (1961). He has also received the Distinguished Artist Award (State of Israel Bonds, Los Angeles, Calif., 1961).

OPP, PAUL F. Educator. b. Paul Franklin Opp, Oct. 2, 1894, Forest, Ohio, to Joseph and Whilhelmina (Heuberger) Opp. Father, farmer. Grad. Forest H.S., 1914; Mt. Union Coll., B.A. 1918; Columbia Univ., M.A. 1923; Univ. of Toronto, Ph.D. 1933. Studied ballet and theatre with Madame Bosse-Lassare (Toronto, 1929–30). Married Oct. 30, 1935, to Helen C. Crawford; three sons. Served USN, 1918–21; rank, Ensign. Member of National Thespian Society (exec. secy., 1929–31); AETA (advisory council, 1957–63); Phi Kappa Tau; Alpha Psi Omega (natl. exec. secy., 1929–1964); Delta Psi Omega; Kappa Sigma Kappa (grand pres., 1955). Address: (home) 1317 Peacock Lane, Fairmont, WV 26554, tel. (304) 363-3368; (bus.) Fairmont State College, Fairmont, WV 26554.

Mr. Opp founded the National Thespian Society (1929) and *Dramatics* magazine (1930). He edited *The Playbill,* a college theatre publication (1925–64).

Since 1923, Mr. Opp has been associate professor of Speech and English at Fairmont State Coll. He directed the Fairmont State College Theatre from 1923–29.

Published Works. He is the author of the booklet, *Value-Showing First-Round Bidding in Contract Bridge* (1963). Since retirement (1965), Dr. Opp has contributed articles on stage speech and theatre personalities of the past to *Dramatics* magazine.

Recreation. Contract Bridge.

OPPENHEIMER, GEORGE. Drama critic, playwright. b. George Seligman Oppenheimer, Feb. 7, 1900, New York City, to Julius and Ida (Adler) Oppenheimer. Father, jeweler. Attended Franklin Sch., N.Y.C., 1915; Tome Sch., Port Deposit, Md., 1916; Williams Coll., B.A. 1920; and attended Harvard Univ., 1921. Served WW I, Field Artillery, OTC; WW II, was member of First Motion picture Unit SEAC staff (India); wrote, produced, and directed training films and documentaries: rank, Capt. Member of Dramatists Guild; Drama Desk, N.Y. Critics' Circle, Players Club Coffee House, Savile Club (London). Address: 15 E. 64th St., New York, NY 10021, tel. (212) TR 9-7337.

Pre-Theatre. Publishing.

Theatre. Mr. Oppenheimer wrote *Here Today* (Ethel Barrymore Th., N.Y.C., Sept. 6, 1932); wrote, with Arthur Kober, *A Mighty Man Is He* (Cort, Jan. 6, 1960); and Sunday drama critic of *Newsday* (1955–to date).

Films. Mr. Oppenheimer is the author or co-author of 30 screenplays, including *Roman Scandals* (UA, 1933); *Libeled Lady* (MGM, 1936); *Day at the Races* (MGM, 1938); *A Yank at Oxford* (MGM, 1938); *Broadway Melody of 1940* (MGM, 1940); *Two-Faced Woman* (MGM, 1941); *The War Against Mrs. Hadley* (MGM, 1942); and *A Yank at Eton* (MGM, 1942).

Television. He wrote the pilot of the Topper series for UA and 29 segments (CBS, later syndicated, 1953).

Published Works. Mr. Oppenheimer is editor-author of *The Passionate Playgoer,* a collection of theatre articles (1958; paperback edition, 1962); and has written a book of reminiscences, *A View from the Sixties* (1965). He also edited *Well, There's No Harm in Laughing,* selected letters and pieces by Frank Sullivan; and co-edited *The Best in The World,* a selection of material from the NY *World.*

Awards. He received an Academy (Oscar) Award nomination for the screenplay of *The War Against Mrs. Hadley* (1942).

ORBACH, JERRY. Actor, singer. b. Jerome Orbach, Oct. 20, 1935, Bronx, N.Y., to Leon and Emily Orbach. Father, restaurant manager; mother, greeting card manufacturer. Grad. Waukegan Township H.S., Ill., 1952; attended Univ. of Illinois, 1952–53; Northwestern Univ., 1953–55. Studied acting in N.Y.C. with Herbert Berghof, Mira Rostova, Lee Strasberg; singing with Hazel Schweppe. Married June 21, 1958 to Marta Curro, actress, writer; two sons. Member of AEA; SAG; AFTRA. Address: 232 W. 23rd St., New York, NY 10011, tel. (212) PL 9-8180.

Theatre. Mr. Orbach made his professional debut as the Typewriter Man in *Room Service* (Chevy Chase Tent, Wheeling, Ill., June 1952); appeared in more than 40 productions as resident actor at the Show Case Th. (Evanston, Ill., Summers 1953–54); followed by *Picnic,* and *The Caine Mutiny Court Martial* (Gristmill Playhouse, Andover, N.J., 1955).

He made his N.Y.C. debut as the Streetsinger and Mack the Knife in *Threepenny Opera* (Th. de Lys, Sept. 20, 1955); in resident stock, played Mannion in *Mr. Roberts,* Kralohome in *The King and I,* Dr. Sanderson in *Harvey,* Benny in *Guys and Dolls,* appeared in *The Student Prince* (Dayton Municipal Aud., Ohio; Shubert, Cincinnati, Ohio, 1959); appeared as El Gallo, the Narrator, in *The Fantasticks* (Sullivan St. Playhouse, May 3, 1960); Paul, the Puppeteer, in *Carnival!* (Imperial, Apr. 13, 1961), repeating the role in the Chicago, Ill., company (Shubert, Nov. 1963); played Charlie Davenport in *Annie Get Your Gun* NY State Th., May 31, 1966); Sky Masterson in *Guys and Dolls* (NY City Ctr., June 8, 1966); Harold Wonder in *Scuba Duba* (The New Th., N.Y.C., Oct. 10, 1967); Chuck Baxter in *Promises, Promises* (Shubert Th., Dec. 1, 1968); and Paul Friedman in *6 Rms Riv Vu* (Helen Hayes Th., Oct. 17, 1972).

Films. He appeared in *Please Come Home* (20th-Fox, 1964); *The Gang That Couldn't Shoot Straight* (MGM, 1971); and *A Fan's Notes* (WB, 1974).

Television. Mr. Orbach has appeared on the Shari Lewis Show (NBC), the Jack Paar Show (NBC), The Nurses (CBS, 1963), and Bob Hope Presents (NBC, 1964); Love American Style (ABC); *Diana* (NBC) and the Mitzi Gaynor special, *Mitzi . . A Tribute to the American Housewife* (CBS).

Awards. Mr. Orbach received the New March of Dimes Horizon Award (1961); the Actors' Fund Award of Merit (1961); and the 1968 Antoinette Perry (Tony) Award for Best Actor in a Musical (Promises Promises).

Recreation. Pocket billiards, fishing, poker, tennis.

ORLOB, HAROLD. Composer, producer, playwright, lyricist, scenarist. b. Harold Fred Orlob, June 3, 1885, Logan, Utah, to Christian A. F. and Metha Jorgine (Jensen) Orlob. Father, merchant. Grad. Univ. of Utah, 1903; Michigan Conservatory of Music, 1905. Member of ASCAP (charter, 1914); AGAC (charter); AFM, Local 104 (hon.). Address: 636 W. 174th St., New York, NY 10033, tel. (212) WA 7-1469.

Theatre. Mr. Orlob composed his first operetta at the age of 16, which was entitled *The Prince and the Peasant* (Salt Lake Th., Utah, May 1901; Grand Opera House, Salt Lake City, Utah, June 1901); followed by the music for the operetta, *The Merry Grafters* (Whitney Opera House, Detroit, Mich., May 1904; Salt Lake Th., Utah, June 1907).

His first N.Y.C. job was as rehearsal pianist for the Shuberts at $20 per week. He was assistant musical director for De Wolfe Hopper's *Happyland* (Lyric, Oct. 2, 1905); wrote the interpolated songs for the English extravaganza, *Babes in the Woods,* retitled *The Babes and the Baron* (Lyric, Dec. 25, 1905); composed the score for *Seminary Girl* which toured (1906); composed the theme song for the play, *The Boys of Company "B"* (Lyceum, N.Y.C., Apr. 8, 1907); wrote the interpolated songs for *The Maid and the Millionaire* (Madison Square Garden Roof, June 22, 1907); composed the score for *Look Who's Here* which toured (1907); composed the music for *Anita the Singing Girl* which toured (1908); composed, with Joe Howard, the music for *Miss Nobody from Starland* (Princess, Chicago, Ill., 1910); composed with Mr. Howard, the music for *The Flirting Princess* (La Salle, Chicago, Ill., 1911); and wrote the complete score for *The Heart Breakers* (Princess, Chicago, Ill., 1912).

Mr. Orlob composed the music for *A La Broadway,* which was presented with *Hello, Paris* (Folies Bergère, N.Y.C., Sept. 22, 1911); contributed songs to the revue, *The Passing Show of 1912* (Winter Garden, June 22, 1912); composed the score for *The Red Canary* (Lyric, Apr. 13, 1914); *Ned Wayburn's Town Topics* (Century, Sept. 23, 1915); wrote the theme song for *Johnny Get Your Gun* (Criterion, Feb. 12, 1917); composed the music for John Cort's touring production of *The Masked Model* (1917); with Ned Wayburn, wrote songs for the revue, *Hitchy Koo of 1918* (Globe, N.Y.C., June 6, 1918); composed the score for *Listen, Lester* (Knickerbocker, Dec. 23, 1918); collaborated with Sigmund Romberg on the music for the touring production of *The Melting of Molly* (1918); composed the score for *Nothing But Love* (Lyric, N.Y.C., Oct. 14, 1919); *Just a Minute* (Cort, Oct. 27, 1919); composed music for the touring production of *Ned Wayburn's Town Gossip* (1921); contributed material to the touring production of *Take a Chance* (opened Boston, Mass., Sept. 4, 1923); produced his own musical, *Ginger* (Daly's, N.Y.C., Oct. 16, 1923); composed music for *Suzanne* (1926); wrote interpolated songs for the tour of *Yes, Yes, Yvette* (1926); with Stephen Jones, wrote the score for *Talk About Girls* (Waldorf, N.Y.C., June 14, 1927); wrote book, music, and lyrics for *Making Mary* (1931); and wrote book, music, and lyrics for *Hairpin Harmony* (Natl., Oct. 1, 1943).

Mr. Orlob's symphonic suite, *Recreation,* was premiered in N.Y.C. (Carnegie Hall, May 28, 1949); and an all-Orlob concert was presented by the Salt Lake Symphony Orchestra and Choir (Salt Lake City, Utah, 1961).

Films. Mr. Orlob produced and wrote the theme song, "That's How Dreams Should End" for *One Third of a Nation* (Par., 1939); wrote the screenplay and theme song, "Saint Frances Cabrini," for *Citizen Saint* (Par., 1948); and distributed the Paramount film, *Back Door to Heaven* (1940).

Other Activities. Mr. Orlob was president of AAA Productions (1938); and president of Adams Records (1950–55).

Published Works. Mr. Orlob collaborated on the song "I Wonder Who's Kissing Her Now" (1909); wrote the music for "Take It from Me" (1915), "Johnny Get Your Gun" (1916), "Waiting" (1918), "When the Shadows Fall" (1918), "I Was a Very Good Baby in the Daytime" (1918), "Little by Little" (1919), and "Maybe I Will Let You Baby Me" (1927); wrote the lyrics for "Gypsy of Love" (1933) and "Lehua" (1933); wrote the words and music for "Children's Day" (1933), "That's How Dreams Should End" (1938); "God Is My All" (1944), "If You Should Stop Caring" (1949), and "I Always Knock on Wrong Doors" (1950); wrote the music for "I Saw You Smile" (1950) and "Glorious New York Town" (1953); wrote music and lyrics for "No More Talk But Much More Love" (1953), "When Love is Young" (1955), "University of Utah" (class song) (1957), "When Mother Sang Her Lullaby" (1958), and "Polka Man" (1958); wrote the lyrics for "Why Did You Tell Those Lies" (1959), "I Would, Would You" (1959), and "Carolina" (1959); composed the music for "Bring Back the Old Hurdy Gurdy" (1959); collaborated on the Ted Mack Amateur Hour Theme Song entitled "Stand By" (1960); wrote music and lyrics for "I'm Going Single" (1960) and "Never Mind" (1960); and wrote the lyrics for "Part-time Romance" (1963). He also composed "This Is Utah" (1964), the official song of "The Pioneers of 47"; "Mister Million" (1964), the official song celebrating Utah's attaining a population of one million; and "Symphonic Suite" for full orchestra, vocal soloists, and choir (1950).

Awards. The mayor of Salt Lake City, Utah, declared Sept. 26 and 27, 1961, Harold Orlob Days. In 1972, Mr. Orlob received the Music Publishers' "Hall of Fame" Award for writing "I Wonder Who's Kissing Her Now." On Feb. 27, 1974, the occasion of ASCAP's sixtieth anniversary, he was celebrated as a charter member.

ORR, MARY. Actress, playwright, novelist. b. Mary Caswell Orr, Dec. 21, Brooklyn, N.Y., to Chester Andrew and Jessica (Caswell) Orr. Father, pres., Union Metal Mfg. Co.; mother, educator. Attended Mrs. Dow's Sch., Briarcliff Manor, N.Y.; grad. Ward Belmont H.S., Nashville, Tenn.; attended Syracuse Univ.; AADA. Married March 26, 1947, to Reginald Denham, director, playwright. Member of AEA; SAG; AFTRA; Dramatists Guild; ALA; Gamma Phi Beta. Address: 100 W. 57th St., New York, NY 10019, tel. (212) CI 7-1094.

Theatre. Miss Orr first appeared on stage in the Syracuse Univ. production of *New Toys* (1934). She made her professional debut as Mary Norton in *Seven Keys to Baldpate* (Ivoryton Playhouse, Conn., Summer 1935); and subsequently, in a pre-Bway tryout, played Mary Lou Gregg in *Julie the Great* (opened National, Washington, D.C., Jan. 14, 1936; closed there Jan. 18, 1936).

She returned to the Ivoryton (Conn.) Playhouse (Summer 1936) to appear as Olly Frey in *A Church Mouse,* Nancy Lee Faulkner in *The Night of January 16th,* Stonewall Jackson in *Sailor, Beware!* Audrey in *Three Men on a Horse,* and Claire in *Co-Respondent Unknown.*

Miss Orr understudied Claire Luce as Curley's Wife in *Of Mice and Men* (Music Box Th., N.Y.C., Nov. 23, 1937); made her Bway debut succeeding (Lyceum, June 1, 1938) Helen Trenholme as Rosemary in *Bachelor Born* (Morosco, Jan. 25, 1938); and toured as Curley's Wife in *Of Mice and Men* (opened Brighton Beach Th., N.Y., June 1, 1939; closed Steel Pier, Atlantic City, N.J., Sept. 30, 1939).

She played Jennie in *Jupiter Laughs* (Biltmore, N.Y.C., Sept. 9, 1940); Blanche in a stock production of *Jeannie* (Paper Mill Playhouse, Millburn, N.J., Summer 1941); Corinne Mahon in *Malice Domestic* (Stony Creek, Conn., Summer 1942); Alda in *Death Takes a Holiday* (Milford Summer Th., Conn., Summer 1942); and Alma Kent in *Evening Rise* (Woodstock Playhouse, N.Y., Summer 1942); toured as Margaret in *Play With Fire* (opened Hartford Aud., Conn., Oct. 1942; closed Cox Playhouse, Cincinnati, Ohio, Dec. 1942); appeared as Hazel in a pre-Bway tour of *The Wife Takes a Child* (Wilbur, Boston, Mass., Dec. 25, 1942); in the summer of 1943, played Ada in *The Late Christopher Bean* (Erlanger, Buffalo, N.Y.), and Martha Ladd in *Without Love* (Adams, Newark, N.J.).

She appeared as Ruth Hennicut in *Wallflower* (Cort, N.Y.C., Jan. 26, 1944); and Coral Platt in *Dark Hammock* (Forrest, Dec. 11, 1944). During the summer of 1948, in stock, she played Ann Marvin in *This Thing Called Love* (Ivoryton Playhouse, Conn.); Emily Blackman in *Chicken Every Sunday* (Olney Th., Md.); and Liz Imbrie in *The Philadelphia Story,* and Anne Rogers in *Goodbye Again* (Chapel Playhouse, Guilford, Conn.). During the summer of 1952, she appeared at Elitsche Gardens Th. (Denver, Colo.) as Shirley in *Love and Let Love,* Alicia Christie in *Black Chiffon,* Maud Abbott in *Glad Tidings,* Alice in *The Number,* and Liz Kendall in *Buy Me Blue Ribbons.*

She played Miss Alice Dunbar in *Sherlock Holmes* (New Century, N.Y.C., Oct. 30, 1953); Miss Swift in *The Desperate Hours* (Ethel Barrymore Th., Feb. 10, 1955); Mrs. Lincoln in *Abraham Lincoln* and Lucienne Ravinel in *Monique* (John Drew Th., East Hampton, L.I., N.Y., Summer 1958); toured as Edith Lambert in *Never Too Late* (opened Comedy Th., Melbourne, Australia, Apr. 27, 1964; closed Christ Church, N.Z., Sept. 19, 1964); and played Mrs. Bradman in Noel Harrison's tour of *Blithe Spirit* (opened Elitsche Gardens Th., Denver, Colo., June 1970; closed Westport, Conn., Aug. 1970).

With her husband, Reginald Denham, she has written *Wallflower* (Cort, N.Y.C., Jan. 26, 1944); *Dark Hammock* (Forrest, Dec. 11, 1944); *Round Trip* (Biltmore, May 29, 1945); and *Be Your Age* (48 St. Th., Jan. 14, 1953). In London, three of their plays were produced: *The Platinum Set* (Saville, Mar. 30, 1950); *Sweet Peril* (St. James's, Dec. 3, 1952); and *Minor Murder* (Savoy, London, July 26, 1967).

Miss Orr's short story, *The Wisdom of Eve,* combined with the film *All About Eve,* formed the basis for the Antoinette Perry (Tony) Award winning musical, *Applause* (Palace, N.Y.C., March 30, 1970).

Films. The film *All About Eve* (20th-Fox, 1950) was based on Miss Orr's short story, *The Wisdom of Eve,* published in *Cosmopolitan* magazine.

Television. With her husband, Miss Orr has written approximately 40 television scripts. Many of her short stories have been adapted for television presentation. On television, she has appeared in Suspect (NBC, 1942), the first full-length play presented on television; subsequently performed on Studio One (CBS); Philco Television Playhouse (NBC); Colgate Th. (NBC); and others.

Published Works. In addition to her short stories published in *Cosmopolitan, Ladies Home Journal, Woman's Day,* and *Friday's Woman,* Miss Orr is the author of the novels *Diamond in the Sky* (1956), *A Place to Meet* (1961), and *The Tejera Secrets* (1974).

Awards. She received the Screen Writer's Guild Award (1950) for the original story, *The Wisdom of Eve,* the basis for the film *All About Eve,* which won the Academy (Oscar) Award (1950).

ORZELLO, HARRY. Producer, actor. b. Oct. 23, 1940, Hughestown, Pa., to Harry and Grace (Hoban) Orzello. Father, owner of small construction firm. Educ. Hughestown H.S.; Univ. of Maryland (overseas). Studied at Gene Frankel Workshop; American Mime (Paul Curtis); Circle in the Square (Gladys Vaughn); Twickenham (England) Repertory. Served in US Air Force. Member of AEA; AFTRA. Address: 120 Thompson St., New York, NY 10012, tel. (212) 966-7105.

Theatre. Mr. Orzello, with Virginia Aquino and Daniel P. Dietrich, founded the Workshop of the Players Art (WPA) Theatre in 1968, and since that time, as a co-producer with the organization, has produced over a hundred plays. He has also directed a number of WPA productions.

Mr. Orzello has also been active as a performer, making his stage debut in a small role at the Old Reliable Tavern Th., N.Y.C. (Oct. 1967). He made a dinner theatre tour in the southern US in *My Three Angels* and *Joseph* (1967); appeared in several roles in summer stock as a resident character actor with the Plymouth (Mass.) Playhouse; and played Gen. O'Grady in *The Triumph of Robert Emmett* (Frances Adler Th., May 7, 1969).

Films. Mr. Orzello appeared in *Week-End with Strangers* (Ind.).

Television. In 1973, Mr. Orzello played Father O'Keene in The Secret Storm (CBS).

OSATO, SONO. Dancer, actress. b. Aug. 29, 1919, Omaha, Nebr., to Shoji and Frances (Fitzpatrick) Osato. Father, photographer. Studied ballet with Adolph Bolm and Bernice Holmes in Chicago, Ill. Member of AGMA; AEA.

Theatre. Miss Osato was a member of the corps de ballet and soloist with the original Ballet Russe de Monte Carlo (1934–40), dancing in *Scheherezade, Symphonie Fantastique, Le Pressage, Choreartium, Jeux d'enfants, The Three-Cornered Hat, Aurora's Wedding, The Firebird, Petroushka, Prince Igor, Le coq d'or,* and *The Prodigal Son.*

For the Ballet Theatre (N.Y.C., 1941–43), she danced in *Romeo and Juliet, Les Sylphides, Swan Lake, The Lilac Garden,* and *Pillar of Fire.*

She made her Bway debut as premiere danseuse in *One Touch of Venus* (Imperial, Oct. 7, 1943); subsequently played Ivy in *On the Town* (Adelphi, Dec. 28, 1944); Cocaine Lil in *Willie the Weeper,* part of *Ballet Ballads* (Maxine Elliott's Th., May 9, 1948); Anitra in *Peer Gynt* (ANTA, Jan. 28, 1951); Vasantasana in *The Little Clay Cart* (Th. de Lys, June 1953); and appeared in the revue, *Once Over Lightly* (Barbizon-Plaza, 1955).

OSBORN, PAUL. Playwright. b. Sept. 4, 1901, Evansville, Ind., to Edwin Faxon and Bertha (Judson) Osborn. Father, minister. Grad. Univ. of Michigan, B.A. 1923; M.A. 1924; attended Yale Univ., George P. Baker's 47 Dramatic Workshop, 1927. Married May 10, 1939, to Millicent Green; one daughter. Member of ALA; WGA; Dramatists Guild (council). Address: 1165 Park Ave., New York, NY 10028.

Pre-Theatre. English teacher (Univ. of Michigan, 1925–27; Yale Univ., 1928).

Theatre. Mr. Osborn wrote *Hotbed* (Klaw Th., N.Y.C., Nov. 8, 1928); *A Ledge* (Assembly, Nov. 18, 1929); *The Vinegar Tree* (Playhouse, Nov. 19, 1930); *Oliver, Oliver* (Playhouse, Jan. 5, 1934); *On Borrowed Time* (Longacre, Feb. 3, 1938); *Morning's at Seven* (Longacre, Nov. 30, 1939); *The Innocent Voyage* (Belasco, Nov. 15, 1943); *A Bell for Adano* (Cort, Dec. 6, 1944); *Point of No Return* (Alvin, Dec. 13, 1951); and *The World of Suzie Wong* (Broadhurst, Oct. 14, 1958).

He is also the author of *Maiden Voyage,* which closed during its pre-Bway tryout (Philadelphia, Pa., 1957); and *Film of Memory,* with Vivien Leigh (London, 1965).

Films. Mr. Osborn has written the screenplays for the following films: *Young in Heart* (UA, 1938); *Madame Curie* (MGM, 1943); *Cry Havoc* (MGM, 1943); *The Yearling* (MGM, 1946); *Homecoming* (MGM, 1947); *Forever* (MGM, 1948); *Portrait of Jennie* (SRO, 1948); *East of Eden* (WB, 1955); *Sayonara* (WB, 1957); *South Pacific* (MTC, 1958); *Wild River* (20th-Fox, 1960), and *John Brown's Body* (20th-Fox, 1967).

OSBORNE, JOHN. Playwright, actor, producer. b. John James Osborne, Dec. 12, 1929, London, England, to Thomas Godfrey and Nellie Beatrice (Grove) Osborne. Father, commercial artist; mother, barmaid. Married 1951 to Pamela Elizabeth Lane, actress (marr. dis. 1957); 1957 to Mary Ure, actress (marr. dis. 1962; dec.); one son; 1963 to Penelope Gilliatt, drama and film critic (marr. dis. 1967); one daughter; Apr. 19, 1968, to Jill Bennett, actress.

Pre-Theatre. Journalist.

Theatre. Mr. Osborne first performed as Mr. Burrells in *No Room at the Inn* (Empire, Sheffield, Eng., Mar., 1948); made his London debut as Antonio in *Don Juan* and as Lionel in *The Death of Satan* with the English Stage Co. (Royal Court, May 15, 1956); subsequently appeared with the English Stage Co. as Dr. Scavenger, the Custodian, and an Aunt in *Cards of Identity* (Royal Court, June 26, 1956); Lin To in *The Good Woman of Setzuan* (Royal Court, Oct. 31, 1956); the Commissionaire in *The Apollo de Bellac* (Royal Court, May 14, 1957); and Donald Blake in *The Making of Moo* (Royal Court, June 25, 1957).

He wrote *Look Back in Anger* (Royal Court, London, May 8, 1956; Lyceum, N.Y.C., Oct. 1, 1957; World Youth Festival, Moscow, USSR, July 1957); *The Entertainer* (Royal Court, London, Apr. 10, 1957; Royale, N.Y.C., Feb. 12, 1958); *Epitaph for George Dillon,* with Anthony Creighton (Oxford Experimental Th. Club, Oxford, England, Feb. 26, 1957; Royal Court, London, Feb. 11, 1958; Golden Th., N.Y.C., Nov. 4, 1958); *The World of Paul Slickey,* which he also directed (Pavilion, Bournemouth, England, Apr. 14, 1959; Palace, London, May 5, 1959); *Luther* (Th. Royal, Nottingham, June 26, 1961; Royal Court, London, July 27, 1961; St. James, N.Y.C., Sept. 25, 1963); *The Blood of the Bambergs* and *Under Plain Cover* (both Royal Court, London, England, July 19, 1962).

Mr. Osborne also wrote *Inadmissible Evidence* (Royal Court, Sept. 9, 1964; revived Wyndham's, Mar. 17, 1965; Belasco Th., N.Y.C., Nov. 30, 1965); played Claude Hickett in *A Cuckoo in the Nest* (Royal Court, Oct. 22, 1964); directed *Meals-on-Wheels* (Royal Court, May 19, 1965); wrote *A Patriot for Me* (Royal Court, June 30, 1965; Imperial, N.Y.C., Oct. 5, 1967); *A Bond Honoured* (Old Vic, London, June 6, 1966); *Time Present* (Royal Court, May 23, 1968); *The Hotel in Amsterdam* (Royal Court, July 3, 1968); *West of Suez* (Royal Court, Aug. 17, 1971); *A Sense of Detachment* (Royal Court, Dec. 4, 1972); adapted *Hedda Gabler* (1972); wrote *The End of Me Old Cigar* (Greenwich Th., Jan. 16, 1975); and adapted *The Picture of Dorian Gray* (Greenwich Th., Feb. 13, 1975).

Films. Mr. Osborne wrote the screenplays for *Look Back in Anger* (WB, 1959); *The Entertainer* (Cont., 1960); *Tom Jones* (Woodfall, 1963); *The Charge of the Light Brigade* (UA, 1968); and scripts for *Living in Sin* (Woodfall) and *Moll Flanders.* Mr. Osborne appeared in *First Love* (UMC, 1970) and *Carter* (UMC, 1971).

Television. Mr. Osborne's plays for television include *A Subject of Scandal and Concern* (BBC, 1960); *The Right Prospectus* (Assoc. TV, 1968); *Very Like a Whale* (Assoc. TV, 1968); *The Gift of Friendship* (ITV, 1974); and *Jill and Jack* (1974). Mr. Osborne appeared on television in *The Parachute* (BBC, 1967), *First Night of Pygmalion* (1969), and *Brainscrew.* .

Awards. *Look Back in Anger* won the NY Drama Critics Circle Award (1958) as best foreign play, and *Luther* won as best play in 1964; Mr. Osborne received an Antoinette Perry (Tony) Award (1964) for writing *Luther,* and that play was awarded a Tony as best play. *Inadmissible Evidence* won first place in the annual London Critics' Poll as best new British play (1964–65), and it received a Tony as best play (1966). Mr. Osborne received an AMPAS (Oscar) Award (1964) for *Tom Jones,* chosen as best movie script.

O'SHAUGHNESSY, JOHN. Director, actor. b. John Ambrose Patrick O'Shaughnessy, Sept. 20, 1907, Spokane, Wash., to Malachy and Maud (Calvey) O'Shaughnessy. Father, construction foreman; mother, seamstress. Grad. Gonzaga H.S., Spokane, 1926; attended Univ. of Washington, 1928–29; grad. Cornish Sch., Seattle, Wash., 1932. Served US Army, 1942–46; rank, M/Sgt. Member of AEA; SSD&C.

Pre-Theatre. Newspaper reporter for the Spokane *Press* (1926–28).

Theatre. Mr. O'Shaughnessy made his first stage appearance singing and dancing in a St. Patrick's Day show at his church in Spokane (Mar. 17, 1922); played T-Bone in the Will Maylon Stock Co.'s production of *The Barker* (Hippodrome, Spokane, Feb. 1928); made his N.Y.C. debut as a dancer in *Six Miracle Plays* (Guild, Dec. 16, 1933); was understudy and appeared in minor roles in the revue, *Parade* (Guild, May 20, 1935); played Tom Stevens in *Let Freedom Ring* (Broadhurst, Nov. 6, 1935); the First Soldier in *Bury the Dead* (Ethel Barrymore Th., Apr. 18, 1936); and Michael in a summer production of *Lover's Meeting* (Straight Wharf Th., Nantucket, Mass., 1936).

He appeared as Shaw in *200 Were Chosen* (48 St. Th., N.Y.C., Nov. 20, 1936); a Passenger in *Excursion* (Vanderbilt, Apr. 9, 1937); the Clerk and Senator Ransom in *Washington Jitters* (Guild, May 2, 1938); Aegeon in *The Boys from Syracuse* (Alvin, Nov. 23, 1938); and was a narrator for the N.Y. World's Fair pageant, *Railroads on Parade* (1940); directed the United Nations War Relief Benefit (Convention Hall, Philadelphia, Pa., Apr. 1941; Madison Square Garden, N.Y.C., Nov. 1942), and the United Nations Flag Day Benefit (Boston Garden, Mass., June 1941); was a member of the resident company at the Monomy Th. (Chatham, Cape Cod, Mass., Summers 1941–42); directed an ELT production of *One-Man Show* (Hudson St. Branch, NY Public Library, N.Y.C., May 1946); directed summer productions at Yardley, Pa. (1946); and the American premiere of *The Black Eye* (Mt. Kisco, N.Y., Aug. 28, 1946); and the ELT production of *Paths of Glory* (145 St. Branch, N.Y. Public Library, Feb. 1947).

Mr. O'Shaughnessy directed *Command Decision* (Fulton, Oct. 1, 1947); *The Last Dance* (Belasco, Jan. 27, 1948); *Church Street,* which was part of a double-bill entitled *An Evening of Two Plays* (New Stages, Feb. 9, 1948); *Afternoon Storm,* which was part of a triple bill entitled *Six O'Clock Theatre* (Maxine Elliott's Th., Apr. 11, 1948); *Sleepy Hollow* (St. James, June 3, 1948); *A Phoenix too Frequent* and *Freight,* a double bill (Fulton, Apr. 26, 1950); as resident director of the Pocono Playhouse (Mountainhome, Pa.), he staged *Vicious Circle* (Aug. 22, 1950), *Debut* (July 28, 1953), *The Sin of Pat Muldoon* (Aug. 17, 1953), *The Other Devil* (Aug. 25, 1954), and *A House in the Country* (Aug. 22, 1956); directed the American premiere of *Red Roses for Me* (Playhouse, Houston, Tex., Apr. 26, 1951), also in N.Y. (Booth, Dec. 28, 1955); the premiere of *The Open Door* (Sombrero Playhouse, Phoenix, Ariz., Mar. 11, 1954); and at the Arena Stage (Washington, D.C.), directed *The Three Sisters* (1956), *The Doctor's Dilemma* (1956), *The Plough and the Stars* (1958), and *The Hostage* (1963); directed *Asmodee* (Th. 74, N.Y.C., Mar. 25, 1958); Charlton Heston's *Macbeth* (Ann Arbor Drama Festival, Mich., May 11, 1958); *Cut of the Axe* (Ambassador, N.Y.C., Feb. 1, 1960); and *Kinderspiel,* under the auspices of the Ford Foundation Program for Playwrights (Boston Univ., 1960).

He succeeded (Aug. 1962) Alan Nunn as Pat in *The Hostage* (One Sheridan Sq., N.Y.C., Dec. 12, 1961); directed *Figure in the Night* and *The Moon Shines on Kylenamoe,* a double bill (Th. de Lys, Oct. 30, 1962); and *The Chinese Wall* at the Pennsylvania State Univ. where he was visiting director for Theatre Arts (Apr.–June 1963).

At the Theatre of the Living Arts (Philadelphia, Pa.), Mr. O'Shaughnessy played several roles in *Galileo* (Jan. 6, 1965) and directed *Tiger at the Gates* (Feb. 10, 1965). He subsequently played Phil Hogan in *A Moon for the Misbegotten* (Studio Arena Th., Buffalo, N.Y., Oct. 7, 1965); and, at the Pennsylvania State Univ. Summer Festival of Professional Theatre (State College, Pa.), directed *The Tragedy of Richard III* (Playhouse, July 6, 1965), *The Skin of Our Teeth* (Pavilion, Aug. 5, 1965), *The Hostage* (Pavilion, Aug. 26, 1965), *The Physicists* (Pavilion, July 12, 1966), *Blood Wedding* (Playhouse, Aug. 2, 1966), and *Oh, What a Lovely War!* (Playhouse, Aug. 23, 1966). He replaced David Hooks in the role of Creon in *Medea* (Martinique Th., N.Y.C., Nov. 28, 1965).

Films. Mr. O'Shaughnessy directed *The Sound of Laughter* (Union Films, 1963).

Television. He appeared as Cassius in *Julius Caesar* (CBS, 1948).

Recreation. Gardening.

O'SHEA, MILO. Actor, director. b. June 2, 1926, Dublin, Ireland. Father, vocalist; mother, harpist, ballet teacher. Married 1974 to Kitty Sullivan.

Theatre. Mr. O'Shea began his career with the D'Alton Company in Ireland (1943); subsequently joined the Langford Company (Gate Th., Dublin, 1944); played William Burke in *Treasure Hunt* (Apollo, London, Sept. 14, 1949); and toured the US with the Dublin Players (1951–52).

At the White Barn Th. (Westport, Conn., Summer 1952), he appeared in *Londonderry Air, The Tempest, The Skin of Our Teeth, The Lottery,* and *Brewsie and Willie.* In N.Y.C., he appeared off-Bway as Rory in *Out West, 1940,* the Bartender in *Paris, 1945,* and the Second Hood in *The City Zoo* on a triple-bill entitled *Which Way Is Home?* (Th. de Lys, Apr. 5, 1953).

In Dublin, Mr. O'Shea was director of the Globe Th. Co.; subsequently acted and sang in the revue *Dublin Pike Follies* (Lyric, Hammersmith, London, Nov. 25, 1957); played Shawn Keogh in *The Heart's a Wonder* (Westminster, London, Sept. 18, 1958); the King in *Once Upon a Mattress* (Adelphi, London, Sept. 20, 1960); Piper Best in *Glory Be* (Th. Royal, Stratford, England, Apr. 3, 1961); directed *Janus* (Elbana, Dublin, July 1, 1963); played Danny Nolan in *Carrie* (Olympia, Dublin, Sept. 30, 1963); in N.Y.C., made his Bway debut playing Harry Leeds in *Staircase* (Biltmore, Jan. 10, 1968); and played the Sewerman in *Dear World* (Mark Hellinger Th., Feb. 6, 1969).

Films. He has appeared in *Never Put It in Writing* (Seven Arts, 1965); *Carry On, Cabbie* (Warner-Pathé, 1967); *Ulysses* (Continental, 1968); *Barbarella* (Par., 1969); *Romeo and Juliet* (Par., 1969); *Sacco and Vanzetti* (UMC, 1972); *Loot* (Cinevision, 1973); *Theatre of Blood* (UA, 1974); and *Digby, the Biggest Dog in the World* (Cinerama, 1975).

Television. Mr. O'Shea's television appearances include *Do You Know the Milky Way?* (NET, 1967); Journey to the Unknown (ABC); *Silent Song* (NET); and The Protectors (CBS).

OSTERMAN, LESTER. Producer, theatre owner. b. Lester Osterman, Jr., Dec. 31, 1914, New York City, to Lester Osterman, Sr., and Adrienne (Pinover) Osterman. Father, merchandising executive; mother, actress. Grad. Columbia Grammar H.S., N.Y.C., 1931; attended Univ. of Virginia, 1931–33. Married June 3, 1937, to Marjorie Korn, author; one son, one daughter. Member of League of NY Theatres (bd. of gov.); CLT.

Mr. Osterman is president of the Coronet Theatre Corp. which owns and operates the 46 St. Th., the Eugene O'Neill Th. (sold, Dec. 1964) and the Alvin Th., all in N.Y.C. He is president and treasurer of Lester Osterman Productions, Inc.; and chairman of the board of On Stage Productions, Inc., a company he formed with Jule Styne.

Pre-Theatre. Stock market.

Theatre. Mr. Osterman produced, in association with Jule Styne and George Gilbert, *Mr. Wonderful* (Bway Th., N.Y.C., Mar. 22, 1956); presented, in association with Ethel Linder Reiner, *Candide* (Martin Beck Th., Dec. 1, 1956); produced, with Alfred R. Glancy, Jr., in association with Diana Green, *Lonelyhearts* (Music Box, Oct. 3, 1957); presented, with Jule Styne, *Say, Darling* (ANTA, Apr. 3, 1958); and produced *Brouhaha* (Aldwych, London, Aug. 27, 1958).

Mr. Osterman produced *A Loss of Roses* Eugene O'Neill Th., N.Y.C., Nov. 28, 1959); *The Cool World* (Eugene O'Neill Th., Feb. 22, 1960); *Face of a Hero* (Eugene O'Neill Th., Oct. 20, 1960); presented, in association with Shirley Bernstein, *Isle of Children* (Cort, Mar. 16, 1962); produced, with Robert Fletcher and Richard Horner, *High Spirits* (Alvin, Apr. 7, 1964); and presented *Fade Out—Fade In* (Mark Hellinger Th., May 25, 1964); produced *Something More!* (Eugene O'Neill Th., Nov. 10, 1964); in association with Lawrence Kasha, produced *The Coffee Lover* (pre-Bway tour, Summer 1966); co-produced *Dinner at Eight* (Alvin, N.Y.C., Sept. 27, 1966); with Saint-Suber, co-produced *Weekend* (Broadhurst, Mar. 13, 1968); co-produced *A Mother's Kisses* (pre-Bway tour, opened Shubert, New Haven, Conn., Sept. 23, 1968; closed Mechanic, Baltimore, Md., Oct. 19, 1968); *Hadrian VII* (Helen Hayes Th., N.Y.C., Jan. 8, 1969); *The Rothschilds* (Lunt-Fontanne Th., Oct. 19, 1970; national tour, 1972); *Butley* (Morosco, Oct. 31, 1972); by arrangement with his company, Lester Osterman Productions, *The Women* was presented (46 St. Th., Apr. 25, 1973); co-produced *Crown Matrimonial* (Helen Hayes Th., Oct. 2, 1973); *A Moon for the Misbegotten* (Morosco, Dec. 29, 1973); and *James Whitmore in Will Rogers' U.S.A.* (Helen Hayes Th., May 6, 1974).

Other Activities. He was owner of the Bristol Owls a minor league baseball club (1946–49).

Recreation. Football, baseball, tennis, gardening.

OSTERTAG, BARNA.

Artists' representative, actor. b. Bernard Ostertag, June 6, 1902, Piqua, Ohio, to Louis and Rose (Steinhart) Ostertag. Father, clothier. Grad. Piqua H.S., 1920; Western Reserve Univ., A.B., B.S. 1924. Studied at Goodman Memorial Th., Chicago, Ill., 1925–30. Member of TARA (exec. bd., 1963); AFTRA; SAG; life member of AEA; Actors Fund of America. Address: (home) 250 W. 22nd St., New York, NY 10011, tel. (212) WA 9-7475; (bus.) 501 Fifth Ave., New York, NY 10017, tel. (212) OX 7-6339.

Since 1950, Miss Ostertag has been an artists' representative with offices in N.Y.C.

Theatre. Miss Ostertag helped found the Goodman Memorial Th. (1925), and as a member of the company (1925–30), appeared in 50 productions, including *The Critic, She Stoops to Conquer, The Rivals, Romeo and Juliet, The Dybbuk,* and *Escape.* She toured in *Broken Dishes* (1930–31–34); appeared in stock productions at the Provincetown (Mass.) Playhouse, Mass.; Cape Playhouse, Dennis, Mass., Cohasset Th., Mass.; and Ogunquit Playhouse, Me.

Miss Ostertag made her N.Y.C. debut as Janet in *The Anatomist* (Bijou, Oct. 24, 1932); played Annie in *Nine Pine Street* (Longacre, Apr. 27, 1933); the Fifth Woman of Canterbury in *Murder in the Cathedral* (Manhattan, Mar. 20, 1936); succeeded Janet Fox as Bernice Niemeyer in *Stage Door* (Music Box, Oct. 22, 1936), and toured in the role (1937–38); and played Margaret, Carleton's Secretary, in *The Fabulous Invalid* (Broadhurst, Oct. 8, 1938).

Other Activities. She was founder and team captain of the Stage Door Canteen; a member of the Overseas American Red Cross Mobile Unit, S.W. Pacific Area (1943–46); and assistant to Oscar Serlin (1946–49).

OSTERWALD, BIBI.

Actress. b. Margaret Virginia Osterwald, Feb. 3, New Brunswick, N.J., to Rudolf and Dagmar (Kvastad) Osterwald. Father, hotel owner. Grad. Central H.S., Washington, D.C., 1937; Washington Sch. for Secretaries, 1940; attended Catholic Univ., 1941–44. Studied voice with Keith Davis, N.Y.C., six years; acting with David Pressman, N.Y.C. Married Jan. 14, 1951, to Edward J. Arndt, bassist; one son. Member of AEA (council, 1956); AFTRA; AGVA; SAG; Natl. Honor Society. Address: 853 7th Ave., New York, NY 10019, tel. (212) CO 5-5856.

Pre-Theatre. Secretary for US Govt.; telephone operator.

Theatre. Miss Osterwald made her N.Y.C. debut as Texas Guinan in *Sing Out Sweet Land* (Intl., Dec. 27, 1944); subsequently appeared in the revue, *Three to Make Ready* (Adelphi, Mar. 7, 1946), and also on tour; Lily Bedlington in *Sally* (Martin Beck Th., May 6, 1948); and Maybelle in *Magnolia Alley* (Mansfield, Apr. 18, 1949).

Miss Osterwald, as standby for Carol Channing, played Lorelei Lee (1950–51) in *Gentlemen Prefer Blondes* (Ziegfeld, Dec. 8, 1949); appeared as Lovey Mars in *The Golden Apple* (Phoenix, Mar. 4, 1954; Alvin, Apr. 20, 1954); Bessie Bisco in *The Vamp* (Winter Garden, Nov. 10, 1955); succeeded (Winter Garden, 1956) Elaine Stritch as Grace in *Bus Stop* (Music Box, Mar. 2, 1955); played Madame Elizabeth in *Look Homeward, Angel* (Ethel Barrymore Th., Nov. 28, 1957); Miss Lumpe in *Family Affair* (Billy Rose Th., Jan. 27, 1962); was standby for Carol Channing in *Hello, Dolly!* (St. James, Jan. 16, 1964) and starred in *Gallows Humor* (Academy Playhouse, Highland Park, Ill., Summer 1973).

Films. Miss Osterwald appeared as Rosie in *Parrish* (WB, 1961); Boothy in *The World of Henry Orient* (Meyerberg, 1964); appeared in *A Fine Madness* (1967); *Tiger Makes Out* (1968); and as Mums in *Bank Shot* (1973).

Television. Since 1948, Miss Osterwald has performed on Kraft Playhouse (NBC), Studio One (CBS), Philco Television Playhouse (NBC), Route 66 (CBS), Naked City (ABC), The Nurses (CBS), American Musical Th. (CBS), Martin Kane, Private Eye (CBS), the Milton Berle Show (NBC), Jackie Gleason Show (CBS), Red Buttons Show (CBS, NBC), Front Row Center (Dumont, 1949–50), the Imogene Coca Show (NBC, 1955); and played Sophie Steinberg in the series Bridget Loves Bernie (ABC, 1972–73).

Night Clubs. Miss Osterwald appeared at the Village Vanguard (N.Y.C., 1946); and Julius Monk's Revue (Le Ruban Bleu, 1951–53).

Awards. She received The Outer Circle Award for her performance as Lovey Mars in *The Golden Apple* (1954).

Recreation. Swimming, cooking, dance class, symphonic music, church work.

OSTROW, STUART.

Producer. b. Feb. 8, 1932, New York City, to Abe and Anna Ostrow. Educ. P.S. 80, N.Y.C.; High School of Music and Art, N.Y.C.; YMHA School of Music, N.Y.C.; and NY Univ. (music educ.). Served in US Air Force, 1952–55. Married May 1957 to Ann Elizabeth Gilbert; two daughters, one son. Member of League of NY Theatres (bd. of gov., 1968–74). Address: Box 188, Pound Ridge, NY 10576, tel. (914) 764-4412.

Pre-Theatre. Mr. Ostrow was vice-president and general manager of Frank Music Corp.

Theatre. Mr. Ostrow produced *We Take the Town* (pre-Bway: opened Shubert Th., New Haven, Conn., Feb. 19, 1962; closed Shubert Th., Philadelphia, Mar. 17, 1962); *Here's Love,* which he also directed (Sam S. Shubert Th., N.Y.C., Oct. 3, 1963); *The Apple Tree* (Sam S. Shubert Th., Oct. 18, 1966); *1776* (46 St. Th., Mar. 16, 1969; New, London, England, June 16, 1971); *Scratch* (St. James Th., N.Y.C., May 6, 1971); and *Pippin* (Imperial, Oct. 23, 1972; Her Majesty's, London, Oct. 30, 1973).

Other Activities. Mr. Ostrow is president of the Stuart Ostrow Foundation for the furtherance of musical theatre. From 1968 to 1974, he was on the Play Selection Committee, Theatre Guild.

Awards. *1776* received an Antoinette Perry (Tony) Award as best musical and was chosen as best musical by the NY Drama Critics.

OSWALD, GENEVIEVE.

Librarian. b. Genevieve Mary Oswald, Aug. 24, 1923, Buffalo, N.Y., to Charles T. and Jeannette (Glenn) Oswald. Father, traffic consultant. Grad. Buffalo Acad. of the Sacred Heart, 1941; Univ. of North Carolina, B.S. (music) 1945. Studied singing at Juilliard Sch. of Music, 1945–46; musicology at New York Univ., 1947–48. Married 1949 to Dean L. Johnson, musician, teacher; one son, one daughter. Member of the Amer. Library Assn. Address: (home) 45 Overton Rd., Scarsdale, NY 10583, tel. (914) 723-0741; (bus.) c/o NY Public Library, Fifth Ave. and 42nd St., New York, NY 10018, tel. (212) OX 5-4200.

Since 1947, Miss Oswald has been Curator of the Dance Collection of the NY Public Library, New York City, which she organized. She has sung professionally and written music.

She has taught the American Dance Heritage course at New York University School of Graduate Studies. She is editor of *Dance Bibliographies* and Bicentennial Publications Arts in America from Colonial to Modern Times and co-editor of a bibliography of projected theses and project titles for dance. She completed a ten-volume computer-produced dance book catalog published in 1975.

Awards. Miss Oswald received the Capezio Award (1956); the American Dance Guild Award (1970) and the Dance Masters of America, New York Chapter Award (1972).

Recreation. Dance, interior decorating, singing, 19th-century literature, art.

OSWALD, VIRGINIA.

Singer, actress. b. Brooklyn, N.Y. Attended Bishop McDonnell H.S., Brooklyn; grad. Bay Ridge H.S., Brooklyn. Studied at Neighborhood Playhouse Sch. of the Th., two years. Member of AGVA; AEA; AFTRA.

Pre-Theatre. Factory worker.

Theatre. Miss Oswald's first assignment on Bway was as understudy for the role of Laurie in *Oklahoma!* (St. James, Mar. 31, 1943), later succeeding to the role, and played the part on tour; was understudy to Marion Bell as Fiona MacLaren in *Brigadoon* (Ziegfeld, N.Y.C., Mar. 13, 1947); and appeared in the revue, *Small Wonder* (Coronet, Sept. 15, 1948).

In stock, she performed in *The Merry Widow;* as Nina in *Song of Norway* (Paper Mill Playhouse, Millburn, N.J., Apr. 18, 1949). Subsequently she played Fiona MacLaren in *Brigadoon* (NY City Ctr., May 2, 1950), and in stock (Municipal Open Air Th., St. Louis, Mo., June 8, 1950); appeared as Nadino Popoff in *The Chocolate Soldier* (Paper Mill Playhouse, Millburn, N.J., 1952, 1956); in *Desert Song;* played Sarah Millick, the Marchioness of Shayne, in *Bittersweet* (Melody Tent, Hyannis, Mass., July 1954); Fiona MacLaren in *Brigadoon* (NY City Ctr., Mar. 27, 1957); and was a singer in the chorus of *Greenwillow* (Alvin, Mar. 8, 1960); *Wildcat* (Alvin, Dec. 16, 1960); and *Hot Spot* Majestic, Apr. 19, 1963).

Radio. Miss Oswald was a singer at age 12 on Milton Cross' Children's Hour, remaining on the show for five years (NBC).

Night Clubs. She was a singer at Spivy's Roof (N.Y.C., 1948).

Recreation. Reading.

OWENS, ROCHELLE.

Playwright, poet. b. Rochelle Bass, Apr. 2, 1936, Brooklyn, N.Y., to Max and Molly (Adler) Bass. Father, postal clerk. Educ. N.Y.C. public schools. Married 1962 to George D. Economou, poet, educator. Relative in theatre: cousin, Morris Engel, film-maker. Member of Dramatists Guild; AEA; New Dramatists Comm.; American Soc. of Composers, Authors and Publishers; Authors Guild. Address: 606 W. 116th St., New York, NY 10027, tel. (212) UN 4-4374.

Theatre. The Judson Poets' Th., N.Y.C., produced Miss Owens's *The String Game* (Feb. 12, 1965) and *Istanboul* (Sept. 12, 1965), both at Judson Memorial Church. Other plays include *Futz* (Tyrone Guthrie Workshop, Minneapolis, Minn., Oct. 10, 1965; La Mama Th., N.Y.C., Mar. 1, 1967); *Beclch* (Th. of the Living Arts, Philadelphia, Pa., Dec. 20, 1966; Gate Th., N.Y.C., Dec. 16, 1968); *Homo* (Cafe La Mama E.T.C., Apr. 11, 1969); and *The Karl Marx Play* (American Place Th., Apr. 2, 1973; also at the Berlin Festival, 1973).

Films. Miss Owens's *Futz* was made into a motion picture (Commonwealth United, 1970).

Television. Portions of *The String Game* have been on television (CBS, 1968), and *Beclch* was televised on WNET (PBS).

Other Activities. Miss Owens has lectured and given poetry readings at Princeton, Columbia, and NY universities and in many other places throughout the US.

Published Works. Miss Owens has published *I Am the Babe of Joseph Stalin's Daughter* (1971), *The Joe 82 Creation Poems* (1974), and articles in such publications as *The Partisan Review* and *The Village Voice.*

Discography. Miss Owens has made recordings of early and archaic poetries of the world, including Mesopotamian and various Eskimo and African languages (Folkways), and the songs and lyrics from *The Karl Marx Play* have been recorded.

Awards. The premiere workshop production of *Futz* (1965) was done under an OADR grant, and *Beclch* was produced (1967) with a Ford Foundation grant to the theatre. Miss Owens received a *Village Voice* off-Bway (Obie) Award for distinguished playwriting (1966–67) and an Obie nomination in 1973 for best play; an ABC-Yale Sch. of Drama Award for film (1969); a Guggenheim Fellowship (1971); a Creative Artists Public Service Grant (1973); the ASCAP award for lyrics; a National Endowment for the Arts grant in 1974; and she was honored by the NY Drama Critics Circle for *The Karl Marx Play* in 1973.

Recreation. Film, collage-making, painting, collecting art and first editions, music, walking, swimming.

P

PADULA, EDWARD. Producer, director, writer. b. Edward Victor Padula, Jan. 24, 1916, Newark, N.J., to James V. and Catherine Padula. Father, banker, realtor. Grad. Columbia H.S., Maplewood, N.J.; attended Univ. of Pennsylvania, Yale Univ. Sch. of Drama. Married 1942 to Thelma A. Prescott, screenwriter, producer, director. Member of AEA; League of NY Theatres; NY Athletic Club; Delta Kappa Epsilon.

Theatre. Mr. Padula was stage manager for the Westport (Conn.) Country Playhouse; stage manager and Lawrence Langner's assistant for productions of the Th. Guild; and assisted John C. Wilson in his productions. He directed the book for the musical, *The Day Before Spring* (National, Nov. 22, 1945); was production stage manager for *No Time for Sergeants* (Alvin, Oct. 20, 1955); *Rumple* (Alvin, Nov. 6, 1957); and *God and Kate Murphy* (54 St. Th., Feb. 26, 1959). He produced with L. Slade Brown, *Bye Bye Birdie* (Martin Beck Th., Apr. 14, 1960); and *All American* (Winter Garden, Mar. 19, 1962); co-produced *Bajour* (Shubert, Nov. 23, 1964); produced and wrote the book for *A Joyful Noise* (Musicarnival, Cleveland, Ohio, June 20, 1966), which he subsequently directed (Mark Hellinger Th., N.Y.C., Dec. 15, 1966); presented *Red, White and Maddox* (Cort, Jan. 26, 1969); *Park* (John Golden Th., Apr. 22, 1970); and co-presented, with Arch Lustberg, Vinnette Carroll's Urban Arts Corps production of *Don't Bother Me, I Can't Cope* (Playhouse Th., Apr. 19, 1972; moved to Edison, June 13, 1972).

Films. Mr. Padula was dialogue director for Paramount Pictures, and 20th Century-Fox.

Television. He has written, directed, and produced for NBC; and has been a guest on the major talk shows.

PAGE, GERALDINE. Actress. b. Geraldine Sue Page, Nov. 22, 1924(?), Kirksville, Mo., to Leon Elwin and Edna Pearl (Maize) Page. Father, osteopathic physician and surgeon. Grad. Englewood H.S., Chicago, Ill., 1942; grad. Goodman Th. Sch., Chicago, 1945. Studied with Sophia Swanstrom Young, Chicago (1940); Uta Hagen, N.Y.C. (1949–56); Mira Rostova, N.Y.C. (1950). Married briefly while living in Chicago (marr. dis.); married to Alexander Schneider, violinist (marr. dis.); married to Rip Torn, actor, director; one daughter, twin sons. Member of AEA; SAG; AFTRA; Actors Studio. c/o Stephen Draper Agency, 37 W. 57th St., New York, NY 10019, tel. (212) HA 1-5780.

Theatre. Miss Page first appeared on stage at age seventeen in a church production of *Excuse My Dust* (Englewood Methodist Ch., Chicago, Ill., May 1940); subsequently appeared in summer stock productions at the Lake Zurich (Ill.) Playhouse (Summers, 1945–48); made her N.Y.C. debut as The Sophomore in *Seven Mirrors* (Blackfriars Guild, Oct. 25, 1945); played in winter stock productions (Woodstock Opera House, Ill., 1946–48); and in summer stock (Shady Lane Playhouse, Marengo, Ill., 1949, 1950).

She played The Pagan Crone in the Loft Players production of *Yerma* (Circle in the Square, N.Y.C., Feb. 7, 1952); Alma Winemiller in *Summer and Smoke* (Circle in the Square, Apr. 24, 1952); Lily in *Midsummer* (Vanderbilt, Jan. 21, 1953); Marcelline in *The Immoralist* (Royale, Feb. 8, 1954); Lizzy Curry in *The Rainmaker* (Cort, Oct. 28, 1954), with which she later toured (1955), and in which she made her London debut (St. Martin's Th., May 31, 1956); appeared as Amy McGregor in *The Innkeeper* (John Golden Th., N.Y.C., Feb. 2, 1956); at the Studebaker Th., Chicago, played in repertory, Abbie Putnam in *Desire Under the Elms*, Natalia Islaev in *A Month in the Country*, and Marcelline in *The Immoralist* (Oct.–Dec., 1956); and succeeded (July 1, 1957) Margaret Leighton as Sybil and Anne in *Separate Tables* (Music Box, Oct. 25, 1956), with which she later toured (opened Locust St. Th., Philadelphia, Sept. 30, 1957; closed Blackstone, Chicago, Feb. 1, 1958).

Miss Page played Alexandra del Lago, the Princess Kosmonopolis, in *Sweet Bird of Youth* (Martin Beck Th., N.Y.C., Mar. 10, 1959), with which she also toured; Sister Bonaventure in the pre-Bway tryout of *The Umbrella* (opened New Locust, Philadelphia, Jan. 18, 1962; closed there Jan. 27, 1962); Nina Leeds in the Actors Studio production of *Strange Interlude* (Hudson, N.Y.C., Mar. 11, 1963); Olga in the Actors Studio production of *The Three Sisters* (Morosco, June 22, 1964), succeeding (Sept. 4, 1964) Kim Stanley as Masha in that production; played Julie Cunningham in *P.S. I Love You* (Henry Miller's Th., Nov. 19, 1964); and Oriane Brice in *The Great Indoors* (Eugene O'Neill Th., Feb. 1, 1966).

She played Sophie, Baroness Lemberg, in *White Lies*, and Clea in *Black Comedy* (Ethel Barrymore Th., Feb. 12, 1967); succeeded Anne Bancroft as Regina Giddens in a tour of *The Little Foxes* (opened Fisher, Detroit, Mar. 11, 1968); played Angela Palmer in *Angela* (Music Box, N.Y.C., Oct. 30, 1969); appeared in a summer tour of *Marriage and Money*, three one-act plays (Chekhov's *The Proposal* and *The Bear*, and Alfred Sutro's *A Marriage Has Been Arranged)*, with, and directed by, her husband, Rip Torn (Summer 1971); played Mary Todd Lincoln in *Look Away* (Playhouse, N.Y.C., Jan. 7, 1973); Regina Giddens in *The Little Foxes* (Walnut St. Th., Philadelphia; Chicago, Summer 1974); and Marion in *Absurd Person Singular* (Music Box, N.Y.C., Oct. 8, 1974).

Films. Miss Page has appeared in *Out of the Night* (Moody Bible Inst., Chicago, 1947); *Taxi* (20th-Fox, 1953); *Hondo* (WB 1953); *Summer and Smoke* (Par., 1961); *Sweet Bird of Youth* (MGM, 1962); *Toys in the Attic* (UA, 1963); *Dear Heart* (WB, 1964); the Actors Studio production of *The Three Sisters* (Ely Landau, 1965); *You're a Big Boy Now* (Seven Arts, 1966); *The Happiest Millionaire* (Buena Vista, 1967); *Whatever Happened to Aunt Alice?* (Cinerama, 1969); *Trilogy* (three short works written by Truman Capote and first shown on television, including *A Christmas Memory*, cf. below; AA, 1969); *The Beguiled* (U, 1971); *J. W. Coop* (Col., 1972); *Pete 'N' Tillie* (U, 1972); and *The Day of the Locust* (Par., 1975).

Television. Since her debut as the Virgin Mary in *Easter Story* (WBBM-TV, Chicago, 1946), Miss Page has appeared in *The Turn of the Screw* (Omnibus, CBS, Feb. 13, 1955); as Xantippe, Socrates' wife, in *Barefoot in Athens* (Hallmark Hall of Fame, NBC, Nov. 11, 1966); Miss Sook ("Sookie") in Truman Capote's *A Christmas Memory* (Stage 67, ABC, Dec. 21, 1966); again as Miss Sook in Mr. Capote's *The Thanksgiving Visitor* (ABC, Nov. 28, 1968); in *Montserrat* (Hollywood Television Th., KCET, PBS, Mar. 21, 1971); in *Look Homeward, Angel* (CBS Playhouse, Feb. 25, 1972); and on Playhouse 90 (CBS); Goodyear Playhouse (NBC); Omnibus (CBS); Studio One (CBS); Kraft Television Th. (NBC); US Steel Hour (CBS); Robert Montgomery Presents (NBC); Philco Playhouse (NBC); Windows (CBS); Sunday Showcase (NBC); The Long Hot Summer (ABC); The Name of the Game (NBC); Night Gallery (NBC); Medical Center (CBS); and Ghost Story (NBC).

Awards. For her performance in *Mid-Summer*, Miss Page received the Donaldson Award, the *Theatre World* Award, and tied with Shirley Booth in the *Variety* NY Drama Critics Poll (1953). For her performance in *Sweet Bird of Youth* she won the *Variety* poll again (1959), and the Sarah Siddons Award in Chicago (1960). She received the Who's Who of American Women Award as the outstanding woman of the year in the theatre (1960); and the *Cue* Magazine Award as best actress of 1961. For her performance in the film *Summer and Smoke*, she received the Cinema Nuova Gold Plaque (Venice, 1961), the Natl. Board of Review of Motion Pictures Award (1961), and the Golden Globe of the Hollywood Foreign Press Assn. Award (1962); for her performance in *Sweet Bird of Youth*, she again won the Golden Globe Award, and the Donatello Award (1963); and for her performance in *Dear Heart*, the Golden Globe Award (1964).

Miss Page has been nominated three times for the Academy (Oscar) Award; best supporting actress (*Hondo*, 1953); best actress (*Summer and Smoke*, 1961); and best actress (*Sweet Bird of Youth*, 1962).

She has twice won the NATAS (Emmy) Award as Best Actress: for *A Christmas Memory* (1967), and for *The Thanksgiving Visitor* (1969).

PAIGE, JANIS. Actress. b. Donna Mae Jaden, Sept. 16, 1923, Tacoma, Wash. Grad. Stadium H.S., Tacoma. Married Frank Martinelli, restaurateur (marr. dis. 1951); Jan. 18, 1956, to Arthur Stander, television producer and writer (marr. dis. June 1957); Aug. 30, 1962, to Ray Gilbert, composer (dec. Mar. 3, 1976). Member of AEA; AFTRA; SAG; AGVA. Address: c/o International Famous Agency, 9255 Sunset Blvd., Los Angeles, CA 90069.

Theatre. Miss Paige made her N.Y.C. debut as Jody Revere in *Remains to Be Seen* (Morosco Th., Oct. 3, 1951); subsequently played Babe Williams in *The Pajama Game* (St. James, May 13, 1954); Doris Walker in *Here's Love* (Shubert Th., Oct. 3, 1963); played Charity in *Sweet Charity* (Packard Aud., Cleveland, Ohio, July 1967); replaced (Apr. 1, 1968) Angela Lansbury in the title role of *Mame* (Winter Garden, N.Y.C., May 24, 1966); and was Ann Stanley in *Forty Carats* (Playhouse on the Mall, Paramus, N.J., Feb. 8, 1972).

In summer stock, she appeared as Miss Adelaide in *Guys and Dolls* (Dallas Summer Musicals, Tex.; Philharmonic Aud., Los Angeles, Calif.), appeared in *High Button Shoes* (Dallas Summer Musicals, Tex.); and as Annie Oakley in *Annie Get Your Gun* (Starlight Th., Kansas City, Mo.).

Films. She appeared in *Hollywood Canteen* (WB, 1944); *Of Human Bondage* (WB, 1946); *The Time, the Place and the Girl* (WB, 1946); *Two Guys from Milwaukee* (WB, 1946); *Her Kind of Man* (WB, 1946); *Cheyenne* (WB, 1947); *Love and Learn* (WB, 1947); *Winter Meeting* (WB, 1948); *One Sunday Afternoon* (WB, 1948); *Romance on the High Seas* (WB, 1948); *House Across the Street* (WB, 1949); *The Younger Brothers* (WB, 1949); *Mr. Universe* (EL, 1951); *Two Gals and a Guy* (UA, 1951); *Fugitive Lady* (Rep., 1951); *Silk Stockings* (MGM, 1957); *Please Don't Eat the Daisies* (MGM, 1960); *Bachelor in Paradise* (MGM, 1961); *Follow the Boys* (MGM, 1963); *The Caretakers* (UA, 1963); and *Welcome to Hard Times* (MGM, 1967).

Television. Miss Paige has appeared on Bob Hope Specials and Christmas Shows (NBC), the Jack Benny Program (CBS), the Garry Moore Show (CBS), the Perry Como Show (NBC), the Red Skelton Show (CBS), Desilu Playhouse (CBS), Wagon Train (NBC), Dinah Shore Show (NBC), the George Gobel Show (NBC).

She appeared on her own series, It's Always Jan (CBS, 1955–56); was on Lux Video Th. (NBC, 1957); in *The Happiest Day* (Chevy Show, NBC,

Apr. 1961); on Dick Powell Th. (NBC, 1963); Fugitive (ABC, 1964); in *Roberta* (NBC, 1969); on Columbo (NBC, 1972); and Banacek (NBC, 1972).

Night Clubs. She has performed at the Copacabana (N.Y.C.), New Frontier (Las Vegas, Nev.), Ambassador Hotel (Los Angeles, Calif.), Raddison Room (Minneapolis, Minn.), Statler Hotel (Dallas, Tex., and the Nautilus (Miami Beach, Fla.).

Recreation. Languages, knitting, tennis.

PALERMO, ALEX. Director, actor, choreographer. b. Alfonse Lawrence Palermo, Oct. 25, 1929, Brooklyn, N.Y., to Alfonso L. and Angela Jean (Gerone) Palermo. Father, building contractor. Grad. Midwood H.S., Brooklyn, N.Y., 1948. Studied dancing at Dance Circle, N.Y.C., with Sonia Dobrovynskya, three years; and Nanette Charisse, five years. Member of AEA; AFTRA.

Pre-Theatre. Window display designer.

Theatre. Mr. Palermo made his professional debut as a dancer in *Kiss Me, Kate* (St. John Terrell Music Circus, Miami, Fla., Jan. 1953); subsequently appeared as Uncle Willie in *High Button Shoes* (Carter-Barron Amphitheatre, Washington, D.C., June 1953). He first appeared in N.Y.C. as the Sleepy Man in an ELT production of *The Doughgirls* (Lenox-Hill Playhouse, Nov. 17, 1954); and was a supernumerary at the Metropolitan Opera Co. (1953–54).

He toured as the Tailor in a stock production of *The Boys from Syracuse* (June 1954); was assistant choreographer, dancer, and singer at the Flint (Mich.) Musical Tent (June 1955); performed and was a choreographer at the British Colonial Playhouse (Nassau, B.W.I., Jan. 1956); and appeared at the Flint (Mich.) Musical Tent (June 1956) as Bill Calhoun in *Kiss Me, Kate,* Frank in *Show Boat,* and Speedy in *Wonderful Town.*

He directed and choreographed two productions of the Junior League's *Follies* (Kankakee, Ill., Sept. 1956; Greensboro, N.C., 1957) and at the Flint (Mich.) Musical Tent, choreographed six productions (June 1957).

Mr. Palermo was assistant choreographer and dancer at the Malmo (Sweden) Stadsteater for *Silk Stockings, La Bohème,* and *Don Juan* (Aug. 1957); choreographer at the Flint (Mich.) Musical Tent and at the Detroit (Mich.) Music Th. (June 1958); danced in the ELT production of *On the Town* (Lenox Hill Playhouse, N.Y.C., Jan. 1959); and in stock was advance director for *Say, Darling* (Corning, N.Y.; Cleveland, Ohio; Binghamton, N.Y.; Pocono Playhouse, Mountainhome, Pa., June 1959).

He played four roles in, and was choreographer for, *Miss Emily Adam* (Th. Marquee, N.Y.C., Mar. 29, 1960); was ensemble director at the Starlight Th. (Kansas City, Mo., June 1960); staged and choreographed the ELT production of *The Golden Apple* (Lenox Hill Playhouse, N.Y.C., Feb. 5, 1961); the musical number in *The Tattooed Countess* (Barbizon-Plaza, Apr. 3, 1961); directed and choreographed ten productions at the Town and Country Musicals (East Rochester, N.Y., June 1961); and for ELT, directed *Paint Your Wagon* (Masters Inst., N.Y.C., Feb. 24, 1961).

He was director and choreographer for *Guys and Dolls* and *Damn Yankees* (Spa Summer Th., Saratoga Springs, N.Y., June 1962), and of the Ford Tractor Show (Detroit, Mich., Aug. 1962); for ELT, directed and choreographed *Out of This World* (Masters Inst., N.Y.C., Nov. 30, 1962); directed and staged the nightclub revue *4 Faces East* (The Roundtable, N.Y.C., Nov. 1962).

Mr. Palermo staged and choreographed *Kismet* (Westchester Dinner Th., N.Y.); directed *The Most Happy Fella* (Meadowbrook Dinner Th., Cedar Grove, N.J., Jan. 1963); *Oh, Captain!* (Meadowbrook Dinner Th., Feb. 1963); *Brigadoon* (Westchester Dinner Th., N.Y., Mar. 1963); *Do Re Mi* (Westchester Dinner Th., April 1963; Meadowbrook Dinner Th., N.J., May 1963); and *The Pajama Game* (Meadowbrook Dinner Th., June 1963).

He directed and choreographed a Chrysler industrial show (Ford Aud., Detroit, Mich., July 1963; Oakland, Calif., Aug. 1963); staged and choreographed *Li'l Abner* (Meadowbrook Dinner Th., N.J., Nov. 1963); directed and choreographed *The Athenian Touch* (Jan Hus House, N.Y.C., Jan. 14, 1964); directed *Gypsy* (Meadowbrook Dinner Th., N.J., Feb. 1964), and *Wish You Were Here* (Meadowbrook Dinner Th., May 1964); directed *No Strings* (Lambertville Music Circus, N.J., June 1964); *My Fair Lady* (Meadowbrook Dinner Th., N.J., July 1964); and a Dodge-Chrysler industrial show (Aug. 1964).

At the Meadowbrook Dinner Th. (Cedar Grove, N.J.), Mr. Palermo directed *Fanny* (Apr. 2, 1964), *Wish You Were Here* (May 27, 1964); directed and choreographed *My Fair Lady* (July 8, 1965; Oct. 8, 1964); and directed *Gypsy* (Dec. 2, 1964). He directed *Fade Out—Fade In* (Tivoli, Sydney, Australia, Feb. 1965); and, at the North Shore Music Theatre (Beverly, Mass.), directed and staged *A Funny Thing Happened on the Way to the Forum* (July 5 and Aug. 2, 1965), and *The Music Man* (July 19, 1965), productions which were repeated at the South Shore Music Circus (Cohasset, Mass., July 12, and July 26, 1965).

Television. Mr. Palermo appeared as an actor and dancer in *Cinderella* (Studio 72, CBS, 1957) and on the Arthur Murray Dance Party (NBC, 1959).

Recreation. Tennis, history, auctions, music.

PALMER, BETSY. Actress. b. Patricia Betsy Hrunek, Nov. 1, 1929, East Chicago, Ind., to Vincent R. and Marie (Love) Hrunek. Father, chemist; mother, business college owner and teacher. Grad. Roosevelt H.S., 1944; attended East Chicago Business Coll., 1944; Indiana Univ. 1946; grad. De Paul Univ., B.D.A. 1949. Studied at Actor's Studio (mbr., 1964–to date). Married May 8, 1954, to Vincent J. Merendino, physician (marr. dis. 1975); one daughter. Member of AFTRA; AEA; SAG; Pi Gamma Mu.

Pre-Theatre. Secretary.

Theatre. Miss Palmer was resident ingenue in stock at Lake Geneva, Wis. (Summer 1950); and spent six months in stock at Woodstock, Ill. (Winter 1950–51).

She made her N.Y.C. debut as Kate Wilson in *The Grand Prize* (Plymouth, Jan. 26, 1955); subsequently played Sally MacKenzie in *Affair of Honor* (Ethel Barrymore Th., Apr. 6, 1956); Lorelei Lee in *Gentlemen Prefer Blondes* (Kenley Players, Warren and Columbus, Ohio, Summer 1962); the title role in *Maggie* (Paper Mill Playhouse, Millburn, N.J.; Mineola Playhouse, L.I., N.Y.; Ogunquit Playhouse, Me., Summer 1963); Nellie Forbush in a tour of *South Pacific* (opened Phoenix Star Musical Th., Ariz., Summer 1963); Anna in *The King and I* (Paper Mill Playhouse, Mineola Playhouse, Summer 1963); Lady Dungavel in *Roar Like a Dove* (Booth, N.Y.C., May 21, 1964); again played Nellie Forbush in *South Pacific* (NY City Ctr., June 2, 1965); replaced (Oct. 17–Oct. 24, 1966) Lauren Bacall as Stephanie in *Cactus Flower* (Royale, Dec. 8, 1965), later playing the role for a year (Nov. 20, 1967–Oct. 1968); appeared often at the Paper Mill Playhouse, where her parts included the title role in *The Prime of Miss Jean Brodie* (Sept. 1969), Mary in *Mary, Mary* (Feb. 21, 1973), and Nellie Forbush (Spring 1974). In addition, Miss Palmer has toured extensively in those and other productions, including *Gentlemen Prefer Blondes, The King and I, Peter Pan, Hello, Dolly!,* and *The Innocents.*.

Films. Miss Palmer has appeared in *The Long Gray Line* (Col., 1955); *Mr. Roberts* (WB, 1955); *Queen Bee* (Col., 1955); *The Tin Star* (Par., 1957); *The Other Life of Lynn Stewart* (Col.); and *The Last Angry Man* (Col., 1959).

Television. She made her television debut on the Miss Susan Show (WPTZ-TV, Philadelphia, Pa., 1951); and has appeared on Studio One (CBS), Philco Television Playhouse (NBC), US Steel Hour (CBS), Playhouse 90 (CBS), and Climax! (CBS). She has been a regular panelist on I've Got a Secret (CBS, 1955–66); succeeded (1967) Virginia Graham as hostess on Girl Talk (ABC); appeared in *A Punt, a Pass, and a Prayer* (Hallmark Hall of Fame, NBC, Nov. 1968); and on Love, American Style (ABC, 1972).

Awards. For her performance in *The Prime of Miss Jean Brodie,* Miss Palmer was awarded the Council of Stock Theaters' Straw Hat Award (1969–70) for best starring performance by an actress.

PALMER, PETER. Actor, singer. b. Peter Webster Palmer, Sept. 20, 1931, Milwaukee, Wis., to Allen Drury and Marian (Kastern) Palmer. Father, sales engineer. Grad. Clayton (Mo.) H.S., 1950; Univ. of Illinois, B.Mus. 1954. Studied singing with Carlo Menotti, 1956–60; Richard Cammalucci, 1960–to date; Joe Baque, 1956–to date; acting with Nick Colasanto, 1958–to date. Married Dec. 15, 1954, to Jaca Lee Gleason; three sons, two daughters. Served US Army 1955–57; rank, PFC. Member of AEA; AFTRA; SAG; Kappa Sigma.

Theatre. Mr. Palmer made his Bway debut in the title role in *Li'l Abner* (St. James Th., Nov. 15, 1956), and on tour (opened Riviera, Las Vegas, Nev., Sept. 1, 1958; closed Royal Alexandra, Toronto, Canada, Jan. 3, 1959); subsequently appeared as Robert in *The New Moon* (Circle Arts, San Diego, Calif., June 15, 1960); and Tom Baxter in *Redhead* (St. Louis Municipal Th., Mo., Aug. 15, 1960).

At NY City Ctr., he played Tommy Albright in *Brigadoon* (May 30, 1961); in stock, Prince Karl Franz in *The Student Prince* (Circle Arts, San Diego, Calif., June 15, 1962); Curly in *Oklahoma!* (Little Th., Sullivan, Ill., July 15, 1962; St. Louis Municipal Th., Mo., Aug. 3, 1962); Tommy Albright in *Brigadoon* (NY City Ctr., Jan. 30, 1963); Prince Karl Franz in *The Student Prince* (Garden Court Dinner Th., San Francisco, Calif., Feb. 5, 1963); Curly in *Oklahoma!* (NY City Ctr., Feb. 27, 1963; return engagement May 15, 1963); and appeared as Billy Bigelow in *Carousel* (Circle Arts, San Diego, Calif., June 14, 1963); Johnny "Leadville" Brown in *The Unsinkable Molly Brown* (Packard Music Hall, Warren, Ohio; Veterans Memorial Aud., Columbus, Ohio, June 1963); Sky Masterson in *Guys and Dolls* (County Fairs, Ohio, Mich., Ind., Ill., Wis., July 1963); and Joe McCall in *The Tender Trap* (Little Th., Sullivan, Ill., Sept. 1963).

He played the title role in *Li'l Abner* (Westchester Th., N.Y., Dec. 10, 1963), and in stock (San Diego, Calif., Summer 1964); and in stock, appeared as Sid in *The Pajama Game* (Little Th., Sullivan, Ill., Summer 1964); and as Will Stockdale in *No Time for Sergeants* (Charlotte, N.C., Summer 1964).

He repeated the title role in *Li'l Abner* (New Circle Arts Th., San Diego, Calif., June 30, 1964); at Presidential request, played Curly in a 35-minute digest of *Oklahoma!* (The White House, Washington, D.C., July 27, 1964); played Sid Sorokin in *The Pajama Game* (Little Th., Sullivan, Ill., July 28, 1964); Will Stockdale in *No Time for Sergeants* (Charlotte, N.C., Summer Th., Aug. 18, 1964); Tommy Albright in *Brigadoon* (NY City Ctr., N.Y.C., Dec. 23, 1964); Bill Starbuck in *110 in the Shade* (Little Th., Aug. 3, 1965); Tom Marlowe in *Good News* (Municipal, St. Louis, Mo., June 20, 1966); and Billy Bigelow in *Carousel* (Little Th., N.Y.C., July 19, 1966). At the Music Circus (Fresno, Calif.), he alternated in the roles of Billy Bigelow in *Carousel* (Aug. 15, 1966) and Gaylord Ravenal in *Show Boat* (Aug. 22, 1966), subsequently made a US State Department tour of Mexico and South America with the productions (opened Mexico City, Sept. 27, 1966; closed Bogota, Colombia, Dec. 4, 1966); and played Gus Edmond in *Lorelei* (national pre-Bway tour opened Civic Ctr., Music Hall, Oklahoma City, Feb. 26, 1973; opened at the Palace Th., N.Y.C., Jan. 27, 1974).

Films. Mr. Palmer made his debut in the title role in *Li'l Abner* (Par., 1959).

Television. He has appeared on the Perry Como Show (NBC); the Ed Sullivan Show (CBS); the Ford Show (NBC); the Red Skelton Show (CBS); US Steel Hour (CBS); the Bell Telephone Hour (NBC); the Today Show (NBC); the Tonight Show (NBC); the Bill Dana Show (NBC); *American Landscape* (Kraft Special, NBC); Ford Fair Time (CBS); the opera *Trouble in Tahiti* (CBC); and The John Forsythe Show (NBC).

Night Clubs. He has performed at the Drake Hotel (Chicago, Ill.); Raddison Room (Minneapolis, Minn.); Lotus Club (Washington, D.C.); Shamrock Hilton Hotel (Houston, Tex.); Adolphus Hotel (Dallas, Tex.); La Fiesta Night Club (Juarez, Mex.); Holiday House (Pittsburgh, Pa.); and the Chevron Hilton (Sydney, Australia).

Awards. He won first place in the singing competition of the All Army Entertainment Contest (1956); and received the *Theatre World* Award (1957) for his performance in the title role in *Li'l Abner*.

Recreation. Football, golf, carpentry, painting.

PANAMA, NORMAN. Playwright, director, producer. b. Apr. 21, 1914, Chicago, Ill., to Herman and Tessie (Nevins) Panama. Father, merchant. Grad. Univ. of Chicago, Ph. B., 1936. Married 1940 to Marcia Engel; one son, one daughter. Member of Dramatists Guild; SWG; SDG. Address: (home) 80 Eaton Place, London S.W.1, England tel. Belgravia 5643; (bus.) 8 Grosvenor St., London W.1, England tel. Grosvenor 1427.

Theatre. Mr. Panama collaborated on the sketches for the revue *Keep off the Grass* (Broadhurst Th., N.Y.C., May 23, 1940); wrote with Melvin Frank, the book, and produced, with Mr. Frank and Michael Kidd, *Li'l Abner* (St. James, November 15, 1956).

Films. Mr. Panama wrote, with Melvin Frank, the screenplay for *My Favorite Blonde* (Par., 1942); *Happy Go Lucky* (Par., 1943); *Star-Spangled Rhythm* (Par., 1942); *Thank Your Lucky Stars* (WB, 1943); *And the Angels Sing* (Par., 1944); *The Road to Utopia* (Par., 1945); *Duffy's Tavern* (Par., 1945); *Our Hearts Were Growing Up* (Par., 1946); *Monsieur Beaucaire* (Par., 1946); *It Had To Be You* (Col., 1947); and *The Return of October* (Col., 1948).

With Mr. Frank, he collaborated on the screenplay and produced *Mr. Blandings Builds His Dream House* (RKO, 1948); collaborated on story, produced and directed *The Reformer and the Redhead* (MGM, 1950), *Strictly Dishonorable* (MGM, 1951), *Callaway Went Thataway* (MGM, 1951), *Above and Beyond* (MGM, 1952), and *Knock on Wood* (Par., 1954).

With Mr. Frank, he collaborated on the story and screenplay of *White Christmas* (Par., 1954); collaborated on the story and screenplay, and produced *The Court Jester* (Par., 1956); collaborated, produced, and directed *That Certain Feeling* (Par., 1956); and *The Trap* (Par., 1959); co-produced *The Jayhawkers* (Par., 1959); co-produced and collaborated on the screenplay of *Li'l Abner* (Par., 1959) and *Facts of Life* (UA, 1960); was co-author, director and co-producer of *The Road to Hong Kong* (UA, 1962); and was co-author and co-producer of *Strange Bedfellows* (U, 1965).

He produced and directed (and with Mr. Frank, wrote the story and screenplay for) *Not with My Wife, You Don't* (WB, 1966); directed *The Maltese Bippy* (MGM, 1969); and directed *How To Commit Marriage* (Cinerama, 1969).

Radio. Mr. Panama was writer for the Bob Hope Show (NBC, Hollywood, 1938); and Phil Baker Show (CBS, N.Y.C., 1939); and Rudy Vallee Show (NBC, Hollywood, 1940); and consultant for Armed Forces Radio Command Performance.

Awards. He was nominated for Academy (Oscar) Awards for *The Road to Utopia* (original screenplay, 1946); *Knock on Wood* (story and screenplay, 1954); and *The Facts of Life* (original screenplay, 1960).

PAPP, JOSEPH. Producer, director. b. Joseph Papirofsky, June 22, 1921, Brooklyn, N.Y., to Shmuel and Yetta (Morris) Papirofsky. Father, trunk maker; mother, seamstress. Grad. Eastern District H.S., Brooklyn, 1938; Actors Laboratory, Hollywood, Calif., 1948. First marriage (at age 18) dissolved; one daughter; second marriage (to Sylvia –) dis.; one son; married Nov. 27, 1951, to Peggy Marie Bennion (marr. dis.); one son, one daughter; married Jan. 18, 1976, to Gail Merrifield. Served USN, 1942–46; rank, C.P.O. Member of AEA; DGA; Intl. Th. Inst.; Adv. Comm. to NY State Educ. Dept. of Eng. Lang. Arts; Harlem Cultural Comm. (dir.); ANTA (pres., 1969; prof. panel of Bd. of Dirs.); Natl. Screening Comm., Fulbright-Hays Awards (1962–67); adv. comm. NY Educ. Task Force on Perf. Arts Ctrs. (1962–to date); Th. Adv. Panel Natl. Endowment for the Arts (1971–72); playwrights nominating comm., Rockefeller Found. (1971–to date); Sch. of Th. Arts, Brandeis Univ. (overseer). Public Theater, 425 Lafayette St., New York, NY 10003, tel. (212) 677-6350.

Theatre. Mr. Papp was managing director of the Actors Laboratory Th. (Hollywood, 1948–50); joined (Aug. 1950) the national tour of *Death of a Salesman* as understudy for the roles of Happy and Biff, and also was assistant stage manager. He was director-producer of the One-Act Play Company (Lake Arrowhead, N.Y., 1951); directed the ELT production of *Deep Are the Roots* (Lenox Hill Playhouse, 1952); directed and produced *Bedtime Story* and *Hall of Healing*, and produced *Time To Go*, three one-act plays by Sean O'Casey (Yugoslav Hall, N.Y.C., Spring 1952); and was production stage manager for *Comes A Day* (Ambassador, Nov. 6, 1958). At the Peabody Institute, Baltimore, Md., he directed an operatic version of *Hamlet* (Nov. 9, 1962); and Mozart's opera, *Idomeneo*, for which he also adapted the libretto (Nov. 22, 1963); directed *Stock Up on Pepper Cause Turkey's Going to War* (La Mamma ETC, N.Y.C., Feb. 1, 1967); and adapted the libretto for David Amram's opera, *Twelfth Night* (Lake George Opera Fest., Glens Falls, N.Y., Aug. 1968).

Mr. Papp is the producer and founder of the NY Shakespeare Festival (see article on same), which had its origins in the Shakespearean Th. Workshop, founded in 1954 by Mr. Papp at Emmanuel Presbyterian Church (729 E. 6th St., N.Y.C.). There he produced *As You Like It, Much Ado About Nothing, Cymbeline* (which he also directed, July 1955), *Titus Andronicus, An Evening with Shakespeare and Marlowe, Shakespeare's Women* (Jan. 1955), *Romeo and Juliet* (Dec. 15, 1955), and *The Changeling* (which he directed, Apr. 1956). Mr. Papp's Shakespearean Th. Workshop first presented free outdoor productions at the East River Park Amphitheater (E. River Drive and Grand St., N.Y.C.), beginning with *Julius Caesar* (June 29, 1956), followed by *The Taming of the Shrew* (July 27, 1956). He produced a second outdoor season (Belvedere Lake, Central Park, N.Y.C.) consisting of *Romeo and Juliet* (June 27, 1957), *Two Gentlemen of Verona* (July 22, 1957), and *Macbeth* (Aug. 15, 1957). The *Macbeth* was transferred indoors in the fall (Heckscher Th., 1230 Fifth Ave., N.Y.C., Sept. 18, 1957), followed by *Richard III* (Nov. 25, 1957) and *As You Like It* (Jan. 20, 1958). He has continued to produce for the NY Shakespeare Fest., at the Belvedere Lake Th. (Summers 1958–60), at the Wollman Memorial Skating Rink (Summer 1961), and finally at the Delacorte Th. (Central Park, N.Y.C., Summer 1962–to date).

In 1967, Mr. Papp established the NY Shakespeare Festival Public Th., at the former Astor Place Library (425 Lafayette St., N.Y.C.). The building contains six theatres, workshop spaces, the Festival's main offices, as well as a th. across the street (the Annex).

In 1973, Mr. Papp took over the management of the Vivian Beaumont Th. and the Forum Th. (renamed the Mitzi E. Newhouse Th., dedicated Dec. 2, 1973) at Lincoln Ctr., on behalf of the NY Shakespeare Fest., where he has continued to produce (to date).

In 1975, Mr. Papp rented the Booth Th. (N.Y.C.) for the NY Shakespeare Fest., but cancelled a scheduled season of five plays after the first production, *The Leaf People* (Booth, Oct. 20, 1975).

In addition to being producer for all of the NY Shakespeare Fest. productions (see Theatre Group Biographies for complete list), Mr. Papp has directed the Festival's productions of *Twelfth Night* (Belvedere Lake Th., Aug. 6, 1958); a reading of *Antony and Cleopatra* (Heckscher Th., Jan. 13, 1959); *Henry V* (Belvedere Lake, June 29, 1960); *Much Ado About Nothing* (Wollman Mem. Skating Rink, July 5, 1961); *Julius Caesar* (Heckscher, Feb. 19, 1962); *The Merchant of Venice* (Delacorte Th., June 19, 1962); *King Lear* (Delacorte, Aug. 13, 1962); *Antony and Cleopatra* (Delacorte, June 13, 1963); *Twelfth Night* (Heckscher, Oct. 8, 1963); *Hamlet* (Delacorte, June 16, 1964); *Henry V* (Mobile Th. tour, June 26, 1965); *The Taming of the Shrew* (Mobile Th. tour, June 28, 1965); *Troilus and Cressida* (Delacorte, Aug. 4, 1965); *All's Well That Ends Well* (Delacorte, June 15, 1966); *King John* (Delacorte, July 5, 1967); *Hamlet* (Anspacher Th., Dec. 26, 1967); *The Memorandum* (Anspacher, Apr. 23, 1968); *Hamlet* (Mobile Th. tour, June 25, 1968); *Romeo and Juliet* (Delacorte, Aug. 8, 1968); *Huui, Huui* (Anspacher, Nov. 24, 1968); *Twelfth Night* (Delacorte, Aug. 12, 1969); *Mod Donna* (Anspacher, Apr. 24, 1970); *As You Like It* (Delacorte, June 27, 1973); *Boom Boom Room* (Vivian Beaumont Th., Nov. 8, 1973); and *Mert and Phil* (Vivian Beaumont, Oct. 30, 1974).

Television. Mr. Papp was stage manager for CBS-TV (1952–60). Three of the plays he directed for the NY Shakespeare Festival were televised by CBS: *The Merchant of Venice* (June 21, 1962); *Antony and Cleopatra* (June 20, 1963); and *Hamlet* (June 16, 1964). Also televised were the NY Shakespeare Fest. productions of *Much Ado About Nothing* (CBS, Feb. 2, 1973); *Sticks and Bones* (CBS, Aug. 17, 1973); and *Wedding Band* (ABC, Apr. 25, 1974). Mr. Papp has appeared frequently on various discussion shows and documentaries including Eye on New York and Camera Three both CBS.

Other Activities. Mr. Papp has been Visiting Fellow in Humanities (Colo. Univ., Feb. 1965); gave a Distinguished Lecture series (Long Island Univ., 1965–66); was Adjunct Prof. of Play Production (Yale Univ. Sch. of Drama, 1966–67); Adjunct Prof. of Play Directing (Columbia Univ., 1967–69); and visiting critic in directing (Yale Univ. School of Drama, 1974–75). He has contributed articles to various magazines.

Published Works. Stuart Little wrote a book about Mr. Papp, entitled *Enter Joseph Papp* (1974).

Awards. Mr. Papp received *The Village Voice* off-Bway (Obie) Award (1955–56); American Shakespeare Festival Th. and Acad. Award (1957); Amer. Theatre Wing (Tony) Award for Distinguished Service to Theatre (1957–58); Shakespeare Club of N.Y.C. Award for Unusual Service in Bringing Shakespeare to the People (1958); Teachers Union Annual Award for Distinguished Service in the Cause of Education. Cultural Freedom and the Arts (1962); Brandeis Univ. Creative Arts Award (1963); NETC Award for Outstanding Creative Achievement in the American Theatre (1963); American Jewish Congress (Queen's Women's Division) Distinguished Citizen Award (1964); the NY State Natl. Poetry Day Award (1964); Long Island Univ. Award for Outstanding Contribution to the th. (1964); CCNY Alumni Assn. Finley Award (1964); Fedn. Jewish Philanthropies citation (1965); ANTA Award (1965); Lotus Club Award of Merit (1968); was named Man of the Year by the Natl. Th. Conf. (1969); received the N.Y.C. Handel Medallion (1971); the Margo Jones Award for encouragement of new playwrights (1971); and on behalf of the NY Shakespeare Fest., received a special 20 year *Village Voice* "Obie" Award (1975).

PARELLA, ANTHONY. Producer, director. b. Anthony John Panzarella, May 3, 1915, New York City, to Elia and Raffaela (Romano) Panzarella. Father, clothing contractor. Attended Westwood (N.J.) H.S., 1930–32; grad. Richmond Hill (N.Y.) H.S., 1933. Studied speech with Eileen Stantial, N.Y.C., three years; acting with Joseph Gallino, N.Y.C., four years. Married June 28, 1934, to Beatrice Biazzo; three sons, one daughter. Served as a civilian with US Army, Engineers Corps, North Atlantic, 1941–44. Relative in theatre: Armando Romano, Italian playwright. Member of the League of NY Theatres. Address: 1545 Broadway, New York, NY 10036, tel. (212) CI 6-8538.

Pre-Theatre. Speech teacher, realtor.

Theatre. Mr. Parella first produced and directed at

the Deer Lake (Pa.) Th. (1941), such stock productions as *The Male Animal* (June 23), *Out of the Frying Pan* (June 30), *Love Rides the Rail* (July 14), *Smilin' Through* (July 21), *Dracula* (July 28), *Burlesque* (Aug. 4), and *White Cargo* (Aug. 18); subsequently produced at the Brighton Th. (Brooklyn, N.Y., 1945), the *Jazz Singer* (June 28), *All for All* (July 3), *Burlesque* (July 10), and *My Dear Children* (July 17); at the Sea Cliff (N.Y.) Th. (1947), he produced and staged *Personal Appearance* (June 24), *Portrait of Irish* (July 5), *Dear Ruth* (July 12), *Angel Street* (July 19), *The Second Man* (Aug. 2), *Yes, My Darling Daughter* (Aug. 16); and produced at the Lazzara Playhouse (Paterson, N.J., 1949), *The Show Off* (Sept. 23), and *John Loves Mary* (Oct. 1), directed *Home of the Brave* (Oct. 8), and *Dangerous Corner* (Oct. 15).

He produced *The Sacred Flame* (President, N.Y.C., Oct. 7, 1952); *Whistler's Grandmother* (President, Dec. 11, 1952); the pre-Bway tryout of *Mardi Gras* (opened Locust Th., Philadelphia, Pa., Jan. 13, 1953); and *Harbor Lights* (Playhouse, N.Y.C., Oct. 4, 1956). He was the co-producer of a summer tour of *The Indoor Sport* (Mineola Playhouse, L.I., N.Y., June 24, 1963; Paper Mill Playhouse, Millburn, N.J., July 9; Bergen Mall Playhouse, Paramus, N.Y., July 22; Brown Th., Louisville, Ky., July 29; Arts Playhouse, Fayetteville, N.Y., Aug. 5; Falmouth Playhouse, Mass., Aug. 12; Westport Country Playhouse, Conn., Aug. 19; and Coconut Grove Playhouse, Miami, Fla., Aug. 26).

Films. Since 1957, he has been the American representative for Vanguard Film (Rome, Italy) and Euro-International (Rome, Italy).

Radio. Mr. Parella was the producer-director of Stardust Variety Show (WILB, N.Y.C., Sept. 1947–51).

Other Activities. From 1947 to 1951, Mr. Parella was on the staff of the speech and drama departments of the Scotti Studios (NYC).

Recreation. Baseball, golf, bowling, photography.

PARKER, GILBERT. Talent representative. b. Gilbert Parker Albrecht, Jr., Feb. 4, 1927, Philadelphia, Pa., to Gilbert Parker and Clara (Rumpp) Albrecht. Father, manufacturers' representative. Grad. Germantown Friends Sch., Philadelphia, Pa., 1944; Wesleyan Univ., B.A. (cum laude) 1948; Fordham Univ., M.F.A. (cum laude) 1952. Served USNR, 1944–45. Member of Soc. of Authors Reps.; Dramatists Play Service (bd. of dir.). Address: (home) 360 E. 55th St., New York, NY 10022; (bus.) Curtis-Brown, Ltd., 60 E. 56th St., New York, NY 10022, tel. (212) PL 5-4200.

Since 1969, Mr. Parker has been vice-president of Curtis-Brown, Ltd., and Collins-Knowlton-Wing, Inc., in charge of the theatre, motion picture, and television department of those related agencies, where he represents authors, playwrights, composers, and directors. He has served as personal assistant to Audrey Wood, play agent, at Liebling-Wood Agency, N.Y.C. (1951–52); head of the subsidiary rights department of the Play Dept. (1954–57); play agent at MCA Artists, Ltd., N.Y.C. (1957–62); a partner in the theatrical agency Savan-Levinson-Parker, Inc. (1962–65); a vice-president of the Agency for the Performing Arts, Inc. (1965–67); and head of the Play Dept. at General Artists Corporation (1967–68).

Mr. Parker was a member of the resident acting company at the Cleveland (Ohio) Playhouse (1949–50).

PARKER, JOHN WILLIAM. Educator. b. Oct. 16, 1909, Murfreesboro, N.C., to John Reuben and Brownie Gertrude Parker. Father, merchant. Grad. Murfreesboro (N.C.) H.S., 1926; attended Wake Forest Coll., 1926–27; grad. Univ. of North Carolina, B.A. (education) 1930. M.A. (dramatic art) 1937. Married June 14, 1936, to Darice Lee Jackson; one son. Served USAAF, 1942–46, rank, Capt. Member of AETA; Southeastern Th. Conf. (exec. secy. and treas.); Historic Murfreesboro (bd. mbr.); Inst. of Outdoor Drama (bd. mbr.); Carolina Dramatic Assn. (exec. secy., 1936–69). Address: (home) 1 Brierbridge Lane, Chapel Hill, NC 27514, tel. (919) 942-3578; (bus.) Univ. of North Carolina, 212 Graham Memorial, Chapel Hill, NC 27514, tel. (919) 933-1133.

Mr. Parker has been professor of dramatic art at the Univ. of North Carolina since 1934; associate director and business manager of the Carolina Playmakers (1936–69); director of the Junior Carolina Playmakers since 1938; and director of the Bureau of Community Drama at the Univ. of North Carolina, since 1946.

He was director of the Acorn Players (Four Oaks, N.C., 1930–31); director of the Green Mask, a theatre group (High Point, N.C., 1931–34) and director of the Little Th. (Danville, Va., 1932–34); and subsequently served as director and manager of Pageantry for the North Carolina Educational Centennial (1936–37).

Mr. Parker directed and was manager of the outdoor drama, *The Highland Call* (Fayetteville, N.C., 1939–41); and general manager of the outdoor drama, *The Lost Colony* (Manteo, N.C., 1948–51). He has also directed more than 30 productions in educational theatre.

Published Works. Mr. Parker was assistant editor and business manager of *The Carolina Playbook* (1934–42); and editor of the *Carolina Stage* (1936–40), *Adventures in Playmaking* (U.N.C. Press, 1968), and *The Carolina Playbook* (commemorative issue, 1973). He is the author of the following plays: *Itching Heel* (1937); *Pine Song* (1930); and *Sleep On, Lemuel* (1932).

PARKER, W. OREN. Educator, designer. b. Wilford Oren Parker, Dec. 1, 1911, Lansing, Mich., to Wilford E. and Alice (Oren) Parker. Father, supt. of schools; mother, teacher. Grad. Rochester (Mich.) H.S., 1929; Univ. of Michigan Sch. of Architecture, B.S. of D. 1934; Yale Univ., M.F.A. 1940. Married April 10, 1937, to Thelma F. Teschendorf; one son, one daughter. Member of United Scenic Artists; AETA; Connecticut Acad. of Arts and Sciences; Silvermine Guild of Artists; Michigan M. Club; Michigan Union; Trigon; Yale Univ. Alumni Assn.; Yale Dramatic Assn.; Yale Drama Alumni Assn. Address: (home) 1732 Wightman St., Pittsburgh, PA 15219, tel. 421-2419; (bus.) Dept. of Drama, Carnegie-Mellon Univ., Pittsburgh, PA 15213.

Since 1963, Mr. Parker has been a professor of drama at Carnegie-Mellon Univ. From 1946–63, he was a member of the faculty at Yale Univ. School of Drama.

He has designed for CBS-TV (1951); for the Westport, Conn., Country Playhouse (Summer 1952); for the Pittsburgh Civic Light Opera (1963 and 1972); and for Coca-Cola, American Motors, and General Motors industrial shows. He has been architectural consultant on theatres for Mount Lebanon H.S.; McKeesport Little Th.; Chatham Coll.; and Sweckley Academy.

Published Works. He is the author of *Scenic Graphic Techniques* (1958) and co-author of *Scene Design and Stage Lighting* (1963), and of the revised and third edition of *Scene Design and Stage Lighting* (1974).

Awards. He received a Rockefellow Fellowship (1938–39).

PARKS, HILDY. Actress, Producer. b. Hildy de Forrest Parks, Mar. 12, Washington, D.C., to Steve McNeill and Cleo (Scanland) Parks. Father, H.S. principal; mother, concert singer. Grad. Thomas Jefferson H.S., Richmond, Va., 1942; Univ. of Virginia, B.A. 1945; attended Danbury State Teachers Coll., 1963–64. Married Mar. 1946 to Sidney Morse, talent representative (marr. dis. 1949); married Mar. 1950 to Jackie Cooper, actor (marr. dis. 1951); married Feb. 24, 1956, to Alexander H. Cohen, producer; two sons. Member of AEA; AFTRA; SAG; Dramatists Guild.

Theatre. Miss Parks made her stage debut as Curley's Wife in *Of Mice and Men* (Dramatic Workshop, New Sch. for Social Research, N.Y.C., 1945); made her Bway debut as Shari in *Bathsheba* (Ethel Barrymore Th., Mar. 26, 1947); subsequently appeared as a Girl in *Summer and Smoke* (Music Box, Oct. 6, 1948); Joadie in *Magnolia Alley* (Mansfield, Apr. 18, 1949); Lt. Ann Girard in *Mister Roberts* (Coliseum Th., London, July 19, 1950); Alice in *To Dorothy, a Son* (John Golden Th., N.Y.C., Nov. 19, 1951); Gwendolyn Holly in *Be Your Age* (48 St. Th., Jan. 14, 1953); succeeded Elizabeth Fraser (Oct. 1957) in the role of Alice Pepper in *The Tunnel of Love* (Royale, Feb. 13, 1957); and played in *The Time of Your Life* (Brussels World's Fair, 1958).

She was production associate for *Baker Street* (Bway Th., N.Y.C., Feb. 16, 1965); *The Devils* (Broadway Th., Nov. 16, 1965); *Ivanov* (Sam S. Shubert Th., May 3, 1966); *A Time for Singing* (Bway Th., May 21, 1966); *Black Comedy* and *White Lies* (Ethel Barrymore Th., Feb. 12, 1967); and *Little Murders* (Broadhurst, Apr. 25, 1967); associate producer of *The Unknown Soldier and His Wife* (Vivian Beaumont Th., July 6, 1967); *Halfway Up the Tree* (Brooks Atkinson Th., Nov. 7, 1967); and *Dear World* (Mark Hellinger Th., Feb. 6, 1969); production associate for *Home* (Morosco, Nov. 17, 1970); associate producer of the pre-Bway tryout of *Prettybelle* (Shubert, Boston, Feb. 1, 1971; closed there Mar. 6, 1971); production associate for *Fun City* (Morosco, N.Y.C., Jan. 2, 1972); and *6 Rms Riv Vu* (Helen Hayes Th., Oct. 17, 1972); producer of *The Unknown Soldier and His Wife* (London, England, Jan. 11, 1973); and production associate for *Ulysses in Nighttown* (Winter Garden, N.Y.C., Mar. 10, 1974); *Who's Who in Hell* (Lunt-Fontanne, Dec. 9, 1974); and *We Interrupt This Program* (Ambassador, Apr. 1, 1975).

Films. Miss Parks appeared in *The Night Holds Terror* (Col., 1955); and *Seven Days in May; Fail Safe* (Col., 1964); and *The Group* (UA, 1966).

Television. Miss Parks performed from 1946–47 on Studio One (CBS); Armstrong Circle Th. (NBC); Philco Television Playhouse (NBC); Kraft Televison Th. (NBC, 18 shows); Danger (CBS); The Defenders (CBS); Suspense (CBS); The Web (CBS); appeared as a panelist on To Tell the Truth (CBS) and Down You Go; and for five years, played in the serial Love of Life (CBS).

Recreation. Running a farm, raising poodles.

PARSONS, ESTELLE. Actress. b. Nov. 20, 1927, Lynn, Mass., to Eben and Elinor (Mattson) Parsons. Father, attorney. Grad. Oak Grove Sch. for Girls, Vassalboro, Me., 1945; Conn. Coll. for Women, B.A. 1949; attended Boston Univ. Law Sch., 1949–50. She has been a member of the Actors Studio since 1963. Married Dec. 19, 1953, to Richard Gehman, writer (marr. dis. 1958); two daughters. Served WW II, Women's Land Army, London, England. Member of AEA; SAG; AFTRA; AGVA. Address: 505 West End Ave., New York, NY 10024, tel. (212) 362-1289.

Pre-Theatre. Politics.

Theatre. Miss Parsons made her N.Y.C. debut as the Girl Reporter in *Happy Hunting* (Majestic Th., Dec. 6, 1956); subsequently appeared in stock as Cleo in *The Most Happy Fella* (North Shore Th., Beverly, Mass., 1958); was an understudy in *Whoop-Up* (Shubert, N.Y.C., Dec. 22, 1958); appeared in the revues, *Demi-Dozen* and *Pieces of Eight* (Upstairs at the Downstairs, 1959); as Ollie in *Beg, Borrow or Steal* (Martin Beck Th., Feb. 10, 1960); Coaxer in *The Threepenny Opera* (Th. de Lys, 1960) and Mrs. Peachum in the same play (Los Angeles, and San Francisco, Calif., 1960). In stock, she appeared as Nellie Forbush in *South Pacific* (Chautauqua Opera Assn., N.Y., Summer 1961); played Lasca in *The Automobile Graveyard* (41 St. Th., N.Y.C., Nov. 13, 1961); performed in the revue *Put It in Writing* (Royal Poinciana Playhouse, Palm Beach, Fla., Summer 1962); and in *Hey You, Light Man!* (Theatre-by-the-Sea, Matunuck, R.I., Summer 1962).

Miss Parsons played Mrs. Dally in *Mrs. Dally Has a Lover* (Cherry Lane, N.Y.C., Oct. 1, 1962); was understudy for the roles Mother Courage and Yvette in *Mother Courage and Her Children* (Martin Beck Th., Mar. 28, 1963); played Polly Seedystockings in *The Millionairess* (Theatre Guild tour, Summer 1963); Lizzie in *Next Time I'll Sing to You* (Phoenix, N.Y.C., Nov. 27, 1963); was in *Come to the Palace of Sin* (ANTA Matinee Th. Series, Th. de Lys, Dec. 10, 1963); was Gertrude Eastman-Cuevas in *In the Summer House* (Little Fox, Mar. 25, 1964); Felicia in *Ready When You Are, C. B.!* (Brooks Atkinson Th., Dec. 7, 1964); appeared at the Playhouse in the Park, Cincinnati, Ohio, in *Major Barbara* (May 19, 1965), *Summer of the Seventeenth Doll* (June 9, 1965), and *She Stoops To Conquer* (June 30, 1965); played Laureen in *Malcolm* (Sam S. Shubert Th., N.Y.C., Jan. 11, 1966); was on the program *Monopoly* as Shirley in *Princess Rebecca Birnbaum* (Stage 73, Mar. 5, 1966); and performed at the Stockbridge (Mass.) Drama Festival in *The Skin of Our Teeth* (Summer 1966).

She was Doris in *The East Wind* (Vivian Beaumont Th., N.Y.C., Feb. 9, 1967); Virginia in *Galileo* (Vivian Beaumont Th., Apr. 13, 1967); Ruth in *We Bombed in New Haven* (Yale School of Drama Rep., New Haven, Conn., Dec. 1967); Myrtle in *The Seven Descents of Myrtle* (Ethel Barrymore Th., N.Y.C., Mar. 27, 1968); and was Helen in *A Taste of Honey* (Playhouse in the Park, Philadelphia, Pa., July 8, 1968) and summer theatre tour.

She appeared in *Honor and Offer* (Playhouse in the Park, Cincinnati, Ohio, Nov. 21, 1968); played Janice Krieger in *A Way of Life* (previews: ANTA Th., N.Y.C., Jan. 18–Feb. 1, 1969); Aase in *Peer Gynt* (Delacorte Th., July 8, 1969); Leocadia Begbick in *Mahagonny* (Anderson Th., Apr. 28, 1970); Catherine Reardon in *And Miss Reardon Drinks a Little* Morosco, Feb. 25, 1971); Milly in *People Are Living There* (Forum, Nov. 18, 1971); Guinevere in *Barbary Shore* (Public, Dec. 18, 1973); was in *Oh Glorious Tintinnabulation* (Actors Studio, May 23, 1974); and played Mert in *Mert and Phil* (Vivian Beaumont Th., Oct. 30, 1974).

Films. Miss Parsons made her film debut in *Ladybug, Ladybug* (UA, 1963); and was in *Bonnie and Clyde* (WB, 1967); *Rachel, Rachel* (WB, 1968); *Don't Drink the Water* (Avco Embassy, 1969); *I Never Sang for My Father* (Col., 1970); *Watermelon Man* (Col., 1970); *I Walk the Line* (Col., 1970); *Two People* (U, 1973); and *For Pete's Sake* (Col., 1974).

Television. Miss Parsons was the "girl Friday" (1953–55) on Dave Garroway's Today Show (NBC) and also appeared on The Verdict Is Yours (CBS, 1957); Faith for Today (1958); The Nurses (CBS, 1962–63); The Defenders (CBS); *The Gambling Heart* (Dupont Show, Feb. 23, 1964); Patty Duke Show (ABC, Feb. 26, 1964); *The Front Page* (Ind., Jan. 31, 1970); *Memory of Two Mondays* (NET Playhouse, Jan. 28, 1971); Medical Center (CBS, 1972); June Moon (1973); and *Terror on the Beach* (ABC, 1974).

Awards. Miss Parsons received the *Theatre World* Award (1963) for her performance in *Mrs. Dally Has a Lover;* a *Village Voice* off-Bway (Obie) citation (1964) for her outstanding performance in *Next Time I'll Sing to You;* an AMPAS (Oscar) Award for best supporting actress (1967) for her performance in *Bonnie and Clyde;* and Antoinette Perry (Tony) nominations for best actress for her performances in *The Seven Descents of Myrtle* and *And Miss Reardon Drinks a Little.*

Recreation. Swimming, skiing, "getting out into the wilderness by canoe or on foot.".

PARTINGTON, REX. Theatre administrator, actor, producer, stage manager. b. Newark, N.J. Educ. Syracuse Univ. Served World War II as parachute infantryman in Europe. Member of NTC. Address: Barter Th., Abingdon, VA 24210, tel. (703) 628-2281.

Theatre. Mr. Partington began his theatrical career as a performer, and he appeared at the Barter Th., Abingdon, Va., as Max Lawrence in *The Vinegar Tree* (June 1950); Dr. Haggett in *The Late Christopher Bean* (July 1950); Dan McCorn in *Broadway* (Aug. 1951); and Rufe Cagle in *Sun-Up,* in which he toured (1951). In 1952–53, he was a member of the acting company, Memphis (Tenn.) Arena Th., where he played Mingo in *Home of the Brave* (Dec. 23, 1952) and Michael Gosselyn in *Theatre* (Feb. 17, 1953). He toured (1953) as Sandor Turani in *The Play's the Thing* and appeared in N.Y.C. as the Groom in *Lunatics and Lovers* (Broadhurst, Dec. 13, 1954).

He was stage manager for *The Matchmaker* (Royale Th., Dec. 5, 1955); *Child of Fortune* (Royale, Nov. 13, 1956); *The First Gentleman,* in which he also played a Footman (Belasco Th., Apr. 25, 1957); became (Nov. 1958) stage manager for *My Fair Lady* (Mark Hellinger Th., Mar. 15, 1956); and was stage manager for *Moby Dick* (Ethel Barrymore Th., Nov. 28, 1962). Mr. Partington was stage manager for the first production of the Minnesota Th. Co., a modern-dress *Hamlet* (Tyrone Guthrie Th., May 7, 1963), and he remained with that organization as stage manager through the season of 1966–67. He became producer for Heartland Productions, Marshall, Minn. (Oct. 4, 1968) and from 1969 to 1971 was associated with the Cleveland (Ohio) Play House, as associate director (Dec. 1969), managing director (May 1970), and consultant (Jan. 1971). Since 1971, he has been with the Barter Th., Abingdon, Va., as stage manager (Apr. 1971), producing director (Oct. 28, 1971), artistic director and manager (Apr. 1973), and producing director (Apr. 1974).

PATRICK, JOHN. Playwright. b. May 17, 1907, Louisville, Ky. Attended St. Edward's Sch., Austin, Texas, and southern boarding schools; Holy Cross Coll.; Columbia Univ.; Harvard Univ. Served WW II, Amer. Field Service, British Army; rank, Capt. Member of SWG; Dramatists Guild (on council); Intl. Inst. of Arts and Letters. Address: Fortune Mill Estate, P.O. Box 3537, St. Thomas, U.S. Virgin Islands 00801.

Theatre. Mr. Patrick wrote *Hell Freezes Over* (Ritz Th., N.Y.C., Dec. 28, 1935); *The Willow and I* (Windsor, Dec. 10, 1942); *The Hasty Heart* (Hudson, Jan. 3, 1945); *The Story of Mary Surratt* (Henry Miller's Th., Feb. 8, 1947); *The Curious Savage* (Martin Beck Th., Oct. 24, 1950); *Lo and Behold!* (Booth, Dec. 12, 1951); *The Teahouse of the August Moon* (Martin Beck Th., Oct. 15, 1953); *Good as Gold* (Belasco, Mar. 7, 1957); *Juniper and the Pagans* (opened Coloniel, Boston, Mass., Dec. 10, 1959; closed, Forrest, Philadelphia, Pa., Dec. 26, 1959); *Everybody Loves Opal* (Longacre, N.Y.C., Oct. 11, 1961); *Love Is a Time of Day* (Music Box, N.Y.C., Dec. 22, 1969); and *Lovely Ladies, Kind Gentlemen* (Majestic, N.Y.C., Dec. 28, 1970).

Scandal Point (1969), and *A Barrel Full of Pennies* (May 12, 1970) were staged at the Paramus (N.J.) Playhouse; *The Dancing Mice* (1972), *The Enigma* (June 12, 1972) and *Roman Conquest* (July 25, 1973) at the Baldwin-Wallace Summer Th. (Berea, Ohio); *The Savage Dilemma* at the Community Th. (Long Beach, Calif., May 19, 1972); and *Opal Is a Diamond* (July 27, 1971), *MacBeth Did It* (July 1972), and *Opal's Baby* (June 26, 1973) at the State Th. of N.C. (Flatrock, N.C.).

Films. For Twentieth Century-Fox, he wrote the screenplays for *Educating Father, High Tension, Thirty-Six Hours to Kill,* and *15 Maiden Lane* (1936); *One Mile from Heaven, Midnight Taxi, Sing and Be Happy, Born Reckless, Big Town Girl,* and *The Holy Terror* (1937); and *Look Out, Mr. Moto,* and *International Settlement* (1938). He also wrote *Enchantment* (RKO, 1948); *The President's Lady* (20th-Fox, 1953); *Three Coins in the Fountain* (20th-Fox, 1954); *Love Is a Many Splendored Thing* (20th-Fox, 1955); *The Teahouse of the August Moon* (MGM, 1956); *High Society* (MGM, 1956); *Les Girls* (MGM, 1957); *Some Came Running* (MGM, 1958); *The World of Suzie Wong* (Par., 1960); *Gigot* (20th-Fox, 1962); *Main Attraction* (7 Arts, 1963), and *The Shoes of the Fisherman* (MGM, 1968).

Radio. Mr. Patrick wrote scripts for Helen Hayes' programs and several hundred radio plays, in which he acted and directed. For Hallmark Hall of Fame, he wrote *The Small Miracle* (NBC, 1973).

Other Activities. He is a breeder of Aberdeen-Angus cattle, Saanen goats, and Suffolk sheep.

Awards. Mr. Patrick received the Pulitzer Prize, the NY Drama Critics Circle Award, the Antoinette Perry (Tony) Award, the Aegis Club Award, and the Donaldson Award for his adaptation of *The Teahouse of the August Moon* (1954); and the Screenwriters Guild Award, and the Foreign Correspondents Award for *Les Girls* (1957). *Les Girls* was presented as a Command Performance for Queen Elizabeth of England. He is the recipient of an honorary Ph.D. in Fine Arts from Baldwin Wallace Coll., Berea, Ohio.

PATRICK, LEE. Actress. b. Lee Salome Patrick, Nov. 22, New York City, to Warren and Marie S. (Conrad) Patrick. Father, journalist. Attended Hyde Park H.S., Chicago, Ill. Married Apr. 1, 1937, to Thomas Wood, writer. Member of AEA; AFTRA; SAG. Address: (home) 1619 Comstock Ave., Los Angeles, CA 90024, tel. (213) CR 1-1691; (bus.) Kumin-Olenick Agency, 400 S. Beverly Dr., Beverly Hills, CA 94712.

Theatre. Miss Patrick made her stage debut with the Henry Duffy stock company (Washington, D.C., 1923); her Bway debut as Elsie Chandos in *The Green Beetle* (Klaw, Sept. 2, 1924); appeared as Helen Mills in *The Undercurrent* (Cort, Feb. 3, 1925); Mrs. Kennedy in *The Backslapper* (Hudson, Apr. 11, 1925); Mary Bowing in *Bachelor's Brides* (Cort, May 28, 1925); Maida Spencer in *It All Depends* (Vanderbilt, Aug. 10, 1925); Angele in *The Kiss in a Taxi* (Ritz, Aug. 25, 1925); Caroline Wendham in *The Shelf* (Morosco, Sept. 27, 1926); Zoie in *Baby Mine* (Chanin's 46 St. Th., June 9, 1927); Juliette Corton in *The Matrimonial Bed* (Ambassador, Oct. 12, 1927); Joan Manning in *Nightstick* (Selwyn, Nov. 10, 1927); "Bobo" Astor in *The Common Sin* (Forrest, Oct. 15, 1928); Eileen in *June Moon* (Broadhurst, Oct. 9, 1929); Jacqueline Emontin in *Room of Dreams* (Empire, Nov. 3, 1930); Mayme Taylor in *Privilege Car* (48 St. Th., Mar. 3, 1931); Louise Dale in *Friendship* (Fulton, Aug. 31, 1931); Meg in *Little Women* (Playhouse, Dec. 7, 1931); Gladys Price in *Blessed Event* (Longacre, Feb. 12, 1932); the Girl in *The Girl Outside* (Little, Oct. 24, 1932); and Meg in a special matinee performance of *Little Women* (Playhouse, Dec. 23, 1932).

She played Eileen in *June Moon* (Ambassador, May 15, 1933); Flo Curtis in *Shooting Star* (Selwyn, June 12, 1933); Millicent Hargraves in *Slightly Delirious* (Little, Dec. 31, 1934); Pat Moran in *Knock on Wood* (Cort, May 28, 1935); Julia Field in *Abide with Me* (Ritz, Nov. 21, 1935); Judith Canfield in *Stage Door* (Music Box, Oct. 22, 1936); Nan McNeil in *Michael Drops In* (John Golden Th., Dec. 27, 1938); toured (pre-Bway) as Myrtle Valentine in *The Skylark* (Boston, Toronto, Baltimore, Washington, D.C., and Selwyn Th., Chicago, all in 1939); and toured as Peg Costello in *The Desk Set* (opened Carthay Circle Th., Los Angeles, Calif., July 16, 1956).

Films. Miss Patrick made her film debut in *Strange Cargo* (Pathé, 1929); subsequently appeared in *Border Cafe* (RKO, 1937); *Crashing Hollywood* (RKO, 1937); *Music for Madame* (RKO, 1937); *Night Spot* (RKO, 1937); *Law of the Underworld* (RKO, 1938); *Condemned Women* (RKO, 1938); *The Sisters* (WB, 1938); *Saturday's Children* (WB, 1939); *Fisherman's Wharf* (RKO, 1939); *Invisible Stripes* (WB, 1940); *Money and the Woman* (WB, 1940); *Father Is a Prince* (WB, 1940); *South of Suez* (WB, 1940); *The Maltese Falcon* (WB, 1941); *Footsteps in the Dark* (WB, 1941); *Honeymoon for Three* (WB, 1941); *Million Dollar Baby* (WB, 1941); *The Nurse's Secret* (WB, 1941); *The Smiling Ghost* (WB, 1941); *Dangerously They Live* (WB, 1941); *Somewhere I'll Find You* (MGM, 1942); *Now, Voyager* (WB, 1942); *In This Our Life* (WB, 1942); *George Washington Slept Here* (WB, 1942); *A Night to Remember* (Col., 1943); *Jitterbugs* (20th-Fox, 1943); *Nobody's Darling* (Rep., 1943); *Larceny with Music* (U, *Moon Over Las Vegas* (U, 1944); *Gambler's Choice* (Par., Faces in the Fog (Rep., 1944); *Mrs. Parkington* (MGM, 1944); *Over 21* (Col., 1945); *Keep Your Powder Dry* (MGM, 1945); *Mildred Pierce* (WB, 1945); *See My Lawyer* (U, 1945); *The Walls Came Tumbling Down* (Col., 1946); *Wake Up and Dream* (20th-Fox, 1946); *Mother Wore Tights* (20th-Fox, 1947); *Strange Journey* (20th-Fox, 1947); *Inner Sanctum* (Film Classics, 1948); *The Snake Pit* (20th-Fox, 1948); *The Doolins of Oklahoma* (Col., 1949); *The Lawless* (Par., 1950); *Caged* (WB, 1950); *The Fuller Brush Girl* (Col.,

1950); *Tomorrow Is Another Day* (WB, 1951); *Take Me to Town* (U, 1953); *There's No Business Like Show Business* (20th-Fox, 1954); *Vertigo* (Par., 1958); *Auntie Mame* (WB, 1958); *Pillow Talk* (U, 1959); *Visit to a Small Planet* (Par., 1960); *Summer and Smoke* (Par., 1961); *Goodbye Again* (UA, 1961); *A Girl Named Tamiko* (Par., 1962); *Wives and Lovers* (Par., 1963); *The New Interns* (Col., 1963); and *The Seven Faces of Dr. Lao* (MGM, 1964).

Television. Miss Patrick played Mrs. Topper on the Topper series (CBS, 1953–55); appeared in The Backbone of America (NBC, 1953); Mr. Adams and Eve series (CBS, 1956–57); and the Boss Lady series (CBS, 1952). She appeared as a guest on many shows, including Hazel, The Farmer's Daughter, The Real McCoys, Studio One, Wagon Train (NBC), The Mail Order Bride, the Joan Davis Show, The Wally Cox Show, Adventure in Paradise, The Thin Man, The Pat O'Brien Show, and The Rifleman.

PATRICK, ROBERT. Playwright, actor, director, composer, poet. b. Robert Patrick O'Connor, Sept. 27, 1937, Kilgore, Tex., to Robert Henderson and Beulah Adele Jo (Goodson O'Connor Durkee Hawkins Bobo Henson) O'Connor. Educ. Webb School for Boys; Eastern New Mexico Univ. Professional training with Joe Cino, Charles Stanley, Maggie Dominic, Neil Flanagan. Served in USAF. Member of NY Theatre Strategy; Playwrights Cooperative; Actors' Studio West; National Playwrights Co. Address: c/o La Mama ETC, 74 E. 4th St., New York, NY 10003.

Pre-Theatre. Autopsy typist, miniature golf-course manager; dishwasher; accounts correspondent.

Theatre. Mr. Patrick's theatrical career in N.Y.C. began at the off-off-Bway Caffe Cino, which he helped manage and where he was a waiter, actor, and director. At Cafe Cino he developed and staged "comic book" story-plays and had his first play produced, *Haunted Host* (Dec. 6, 1964). It was followed by *Mirage* (La Mama ETC, July 8, 1965); at Caffe Cino in 1966, *Lights Camera Action* (June 6), *Indecent Exposure* (Sept. 29), and *Hallowe'en Hermit; Sleeping Bag* (Playwrights Workshop, 1966); and, at Caffe Cino in 1967, *Warhol Machine* (Sept. 21) and *Cornered.* Productions at the Old Reliable in 1968 included *Un Bel Di* and *Help, I Am* (both Mar. 11), *See Other Side* (Apr. 1), *Absolute Power Over Movie Stars* (May 13), *Preggin and Liss* (June 17), *The Overseers* and *Angels in Agony* (both July 1); at the Playbox Studio, *Still-Love* (July 18); and, at the Old Reliable, *Salvation Army* (Sept. 23) and *Dynel* (Dec. 16). Mr. Patrick's *Camera Obscura,* originally part of *Lights Camera Action,* was also produced in 1968, as one of the eleven one-act plays by different playwrights on the program *Collision Course* (Cafe au Go-Go, May 8).

Productions at the Old Reliable in 1969 included *Fog* (Jan. 20), *I Came to New York to Write* (Mar. 24), *Joyce Dynel* (Apr. 7), *The Young of Aquarius* (Apr. 28), *Ooooooops!* (May 12), *Lily of the Valley of the Dolls* (June 30), *One Person* (Aug. 25); at other theatres were *Robert Patrick's Cheap Theatricks* (Playbox Studio) and *The Arnold Bliss Show* (Village Vanguard and NY Th. Ensemble). In 1970 the Old Reliable presented *The Golden Animal* and *Angel, Honey, Baby, Darling, Dear* (July 20); the Dove Co. presented *A Bad Place To Get Your Head, Bead Tangle,* and *Picture Wire;* La Mama ETC *The Richest Girl in the World Finds Happiness* (Dec. 24); and The Open Space *I Am Trying To Tell You Something.*

Later plays include *A Christmas Carol* (La Mama ETC, Dec. 22, 1971); *Shelter* (Playbox, 1971); *Valentine Rainbow* (Caffe Cino, Jan. 25, 1972); *Play-by-Play* (La Mama ETC, Dec. 28, 1972); and *The Golden Circle* (Spring St. Co., 1972). Also, in 1973, *Mercy Drop* (Feb. 24), *Happy as a Lark,* and *Cleaning House* (all Workshop of the Players Art); *Something Else* (NY Th. Ensemble, Jan. 19); *Simultaneous Transmissions* (Seventy-Four Below, Trinity Church); *Kennedy's Children* (Clark Ctr., May 30); and, in 1974 at La Mama, Hollywood-Los Angeles, Calif., *How I Came To Be Here Tonite* and *Orpheus & Amerika.*

Mr. Patrick directed most of the preceding as well as numerous additional productions of his plays by other off-off-Bway groups, was also a frequent performer in a number of them, and wrote songs for them. He also directed *BbAaNnGg!* (Nov. 3, 1965), a program of twenty-five three-minute sketches, each by a different playwright, presented to raise funds for La Mama ETC.

Television. Works by Mr. Patrick seen on television include *Camera Obscura* (PBS) and *Simultaneous Transmission* (cable TV).

Published Works. Mr. Patrick's articles have appeared in *Saturday Review, Cineaste, Sybil Leek's Astrology Journal, Astrology Today,* and *Off-Off.* He is a columnist for *Proscenium* magazine, and his poetry has been published in *Calliope, Things,* and *M.E.A.L.*

Awards. Mr. Patrick received the *Show Business* award as best playwright of the 1968–69 season for *Fog, Salvation Army,* and *Joyce Dynel;* was nominated (1973) for a special *Village Voice* Off-Bway (Obie) award for *The Golden Circle, Mercy Drop, Play-by-Play, Something Else,* and *Simultaneous Transmission;* and in 1974 received a Rockefeller grant for distinguished achievement in playwriting and won first prize of the Citizen's Th., Glasgow, Scotland, worldwide new play contest for *Kennedy's Children.*

PATTERSON, NEVA. Actress. b. Neva Louise Patterson, Feb. 10, Nevada, Iowa, to George Louis and Marjorie Zoa (Byers) Patterson. Father, farmer. Grad. Nevada H.S.; attended American Institute of Business (Des Moines, Iowa), 3 mons. Studied acting with Isabel Merson, N.Y.C., 1944–49. Married Mar. 1953, to Michael Ellis, producer (marr. dis.); married Sept. 13, 1957, to James Lee, playwright; one son, one daughter. Member of AEA (council, 1957–59); AFTRA; SAG; AGVA. Address: 12 Blind Brook Rd., Westport, CT 06880, tel. (203) 227-4609.

Pre-Theatre. Singer with dance bands; model.

Theatre. Miss Patterson made her professional debut in a small role in Jose Ferrer's *Cyrano de Bergerac,* but the role was eliminated during the pre-Bway tryout (opened Shubert, New Haven, Conn., May 17, 1946); she subsequently appeared as the Player Queen in Maurice Evans' cross-country tour of *Hamlet* (Aug. 1946–May 1947).

She made her N.Y.C. debut as Brenda Maddox in *The Druid Circle* (Morosco, Oct. 23, 1947); at the NY City Ctr., appeared as a walk-on in *Volpone* (Jan. 8, 1948), was understudy to Uta Hagen as Mrs. Menningham in *Angel Street* (Jan. 22, 1948), and played a small role in *The Wedding* (Feb. 5, 1948).

She succeeded Joan Tetzel as Clarissa Blynn Cromwell in *Strange Bedfellows* (Morosco, Jan. 14, 1948); played Baroness Angela Burdette-Coutts in *The Ivy Green* (Lyceum, Apr. 5, 1949); replaced (Mar. 1950, for four weeks) Ann Sargent as Eleanor Peabody in *I Know My Love* (Shubert, Nov. 2, 1949); played Diana Messerschman in *Ring 'Round the Moon* (Martin Beck Th., Nov. 23, 1950); Ann Adams in *The Long Days* (Empire, Apr. 20, 1951); Faith McNairn in *Lace on Her Petticoat* (Booth, Sept. 4, 1951); toured with Estelle Winwood and Dennis King in *The Cocktail Party* (1952); played Helen Sherman in *The Seven Year Itch* (Fulton, N.Y.C., Nov. 20, 1952); Nan Waterhouse in *Double in Hearts* (John Golden Th., Oct. 16, 1956); Connie Ashton in *Speaking of Murder* (Royale, Dec. 19, 1956); and Claire Manning in *Make a Million* (Playhouse, Oct. 23, 1958).

Films. Miss Patterson made her motion picture debut in *Taxi* (20th-Fox, 1953); appeared in *The Solid Gold Cadillac* (Col., 1956); *The Desk Set* (20th-Fox, 1957); *An Affair to Remember* (20th-Fox, 1957); *Too Much, Too Soon* (WB, 1958); *The Spiral Road* (U, 1962); *David and Lisa* (Cont., 1962); *Dear Heart* (WB, 1964); and *Counterpoint* (U, 1968).

Television. Miss Patterson was a regular performer for two seasons (as secretary to "the Governor," played by Dan Dailey) on The Governor and J. J. (CBS, premiere Sept. 23, 1969); and was a regular on the James Garner series, Nichols (NBC, premiere Sept. 16, 1971). She has appeared in *Satins and Spurs* (NBC Spectacular, Sept. 12, 1954); *The Philadelphia Story* (Best of Broadway, CBS, Dec. 8, 1954); *Dear Brutus* (Omnibus, CBS, Aug. 1956); *The Man in the Dog Suit* (NBC, Jan. 8, 1960); and on various other shows, including Kraft Television Th. (NBC, 1948–1955); Rocky King (Dumont, 1950); Elgin Hour (ABC); Philco Television Playhouse (NBC); Goodyear Playhouse (NBC); Studio One (CBS); Playhouse 90 (CBS); The Defenders (CBS); Ben Casey (ABC); US Steel Hour (CBS); The Nurses (CBS); Man Against Crime (CBS); Suspense (CBS); Danger (CBS); The Web (CBS); the Patty Duke Show (ABC); Naked City (ABC); The Lieutenant (NBC); Felony Squad (ABC); Owen Marshall (ABC); Cannon (CBS); and Moment of Fear (NBC).

PAULSON, ARVID. Actor, author, translator. b. Arvid Paulsson, Feb. 14, 1888, Helsingborg, Sweden, to Hans and Anna Christina (Müller) Paulsson. Father, real estate and insurance broker. Attended Ebba Lundberg Private School, Helsingborg, Sweden, 1894–98; State Preparatory School, Helsingborg, 1898–1903; tutored privately, 1903–04. Relative in theatre: cousin, Inga-Bodil Vetterlund (Fru Taro Gadelius), Swedish stage and film actress. Served US Army, WW I; rank, Sgt. Member of AEA; AFTRA; Dramatists Guild; ANTA; Sidney Rankin Drew Post, Amer. Legion (1920–until its dissolution); Green Room Club (1925–28); Ibsen Memorial Comm. (chmn. 1928–31); Circus Saints and Sinners Clubs of Amer. (co-founder, resigned); City Club (1934–45); Comm. of Hosts, Stage Door Canteen and Merchant Marine Canteen (1940–44); Steinberg Soc., Stockholm (life); V.F.W. (former J. Commander, Floyd Gibbons Post); Amer. Museum of Natural History (assoc.); Amer. Swedish Historical Foundation and Museum, Philadelphia (life); American Scandinavian Foundation (NY chapter, 1912–70); First Editions Club; Swedish Colonial Society (life); P.E.N. American Center; Museum of Modern Art; NY Univ. Faculty Club; American Translators Assn.; A.A.R.P. Address: 5606 Ninth Ave., Brooklyn, NY 11220.

Pre-Theatre. Associate editor, *SVEA,* Swedish weekly, Worcester, Mass. (1906–08).

Theatre. Mr. Paulson made his first appearance on the stage as Placide in a private charity benefit performance of *Les Deux Sourds* (Villa Gunnebo, Helsingborg, Sweden, 1901). His debut in America was as Philip in a Swedish-language production of *Laughter and Tears* (Worcester, Mass., Th., 1907); followed by appearances in *I Marry—Never;* and as Erik in *Värmlänningarne* (Männerchor Hall, N.Y.C., 1908); subsequently appeared in professional Swedish-language productions, as the Page Boy in *The Servant in the House* and Charley in *Charley's Aunt* (Carnegie Lyceum, N.Y.C., 1909); was stage manager and played Sune in *The Wedding at Ulfsa* (Carnegie Lyceum, N.Y.C.; Jordan Hall, Boston; 1909); and the Old Custodian in *A Night Off* (Carnegie Lyceum, 1910).

Mr. Paulson thereafter played in English, as the Second Soldier in *Salomé* (Miner Th., N.Y.C., 1910); Nikolas Kromeski in a touring company of *The Beauty Spot* (1910–11); in summer stock, played Freddie Tatton in *The Liars* (Worcester, Mass., 1911); was Dr. Hartmann in a tour of *The Three Twins* (1911–12); was assistant stage manager and played the Attendant and Consul Sharpless in *Madame Butterfly* (Orpheum circuit, Summer 1912); played Sydney in *The Elopement* (Little Th., Washington, D.C.; Young's Pier, Atlantic City, N.J., 1912); Oku in *Bought and Paid For* (Princess Th., Chicago, Ill., 1913); the Innkeeper in *His Majesty the Fool* (Little Th., Philadelphia, Pa., 1914); Walter Wallace and Louis in *The Young Idea* (tryout tour, Atlantic City, N.J.; Wilmington, Del.; Star Th., Buffalo, N.Y.; Hollis St. Th., Boston, Mass., 1914); and Benjamin in *Easter,* and Cléante in *The Miser* (Professional Women's League Th., N.Y.C., 1914–15).

He appeared with the Washington Square Players in their first season, as the Wazir in *The Shepherd in the Distance* (Bandbox, N.Y.C., Mar. 25, 1915); and, later the same season, played the English Lord in

Andreyev's *Love of One's Neighbor* (American premiere); directed Strindberg's *The Stronger* and *Simoon*, in the latter of which he also played Lt. Guimard (Professional Women's League Th., Apr., 1915); played Dmitri in The Modern Stage's production of Hauptmann's *Elga* (American premiere, Garrick Th., Feb. 23, 1915). His translation of Bjornson's *When the Young Vine Blooms* was performed in New York (American premiere, Madison Square Garden Th., Nov. 16, 1915); he played the Traveling Salesman in *The Weavers* (American premiere, Madison Square Garden Th., Dec. 14, 1915); translated *Poor Little Girl* (American premiere, Brooklyn, N.Y., Repertory Th., 1916); played Stan in *The Peasant's Revolt* (American premiere, People's Th., N.Y.C., 1916); the Shrieve in *Brand* (Brinckerhoff Th., Columbia Univ., N.Y.C., 1916); directed Swedish-language productions of Strindberg's *In the Face of Death* and Ibsen's *An Enemy of the People*, in which he played Dr. Stockmann (Brevoort Hall, N.Y.C., 1916); was co-director and played Count von Asterberg in *Old Heidelberg* (Lyceum Th., New London, Conn., 1916); played Cyril Lord in a pre-Bway tryout of *Mother Carey's Chickens* (Poughkeepsie, N.Y.; Springfield, Mass.; Manchester, N.H., 1917); Nogo in *The Willow Tree* (Cohan and Harris Th., N.Y.C., Mar. 6, 1917).

After his return from war service in France and with the Army of Occupation in Germany, he was seen as Li Sing in a pre-Bway tryout of *Mommer* (1919); Ching Wong in *Curiosity* (Greenwich Village Th., Dec. 18, 1919); with the Stuart Walker company, he played Baptiste in *The Wolf*, and the General in *Civilian Clothes* (Murat Th., Indianapolis, Ind., 1921); played Peter Mortensgaard in *Rosmersholm* (Little Lenox Th., N.Y.C., 1923); appeared as Ching Wong in a pre-Bway tryout of *Tiger Lily* (1923); in N.Y.C., he appeared as Clisby in *Madame Melissa* (Mimer's Little Th., 1927); directed *Five Ghosts* (John Wanamaker Aud., 1928); appeared as Serjent Durant (in French) in *Goin' Home* (Hudson Th. and Masque Th., Aug. 23, 1928); as Swede in *This Man's Town* (Ritz, Mar. 10, 1930); Saki in a pre-Bway tryout of *A Well-Known Woman* (Providence, R.I.; Broad St. Th., Philadelphia, Pa., 1931); appeared in *Tiger Hour* (Harmon, N.Y., 1931); on Bway, he played Tokem in *Pigeons and People* (Sam H. Harris Th., Jan. 16, 1933); and appeared in *Yoshe Kalb* (National, Dec. 28, 1933).

He appeared in repertory as Oswald in *Ghosts*, Ulfheim in *When We Dead Awaken*, and the Sea Captain in *Love and Friendship* (Master Th., N.Y.C., 1934) then on tour of Midwest colleges and universities, 1934; as the Japanese Ambassador in *Madame President* (Jackson Heights, N.Y., 1936); Jungquist in *The Night of January 16* (Jamaica, N.Y., 1936); Billy in *The Bat* (Majestic, N.Y.C., May 31, 1937); Blanqui in a pre-Bway tryout of *Flight to the West* (McCarter Th., Princeton, N.J.; National Th., Wash., D.C., Fall 1940); the Swedish Sea Captain (in Swedish) in *The Innocent Voyage* (Belasco Th., N.Y.C., Nov. 15, 1943); and Anderson in a tryout of *Kicked Upstairs* (Boston, 1945).

Mr. Paulson's translation of Strindberg's *The Great Highway* had its American premiere at the Pasadena Playhouse (Pasadena, Calif., Mar. 25, 1952); other Strindberg translations of his that have been performed include *Crimes and Crimes* (Times Th. Lab., McBurney Th., N.Y.C., Nov. 16, 1956) and *Miss Julie* (McCarter Th., Princeton, N.J.; Theatre of the Living Arts, Philadelphia, Pa., Spring 1966).

His translations of plays by Ibsen, Strindberg, and other Scandinavian playwrights have been performed in university, college, and community theatres in America and abroad.

Television and Radio. For radio, Mr. Paulson adapted, produced, directed, and played the title role in the world radio premiere of Ibsen's *Peer Gynt* (WGBS, May 1925; repeated on the Eveready Hour, WEAF, 1925; WOR, 1932). He produced, directed, and acted in *Eyes That Cannot See* (WGBS, 1925; WEAF, 1926); gave poetry readings on radio and television at the Radio World's Fair (Madison Square Garden, N.Y.C., 1926); appeared in Oscar Wilde's *The Happy Prince* (WABC, 1927); enacted the title role in *Paul Bunyan and His Big Axe* (WCBS); gave poetry reading from the Stockholm radio station in Swedish, English, and French (1933). He produced, directed, and acted in scenes and excerpts from the following Strindberg plays: *Lucky Per's Journey* (WHN, 1938); *The Great Highway* (WNYC, 1949, 1960, 1962, 1966); *The Father, The Stronger*, and *Miss Julie*, and read from *Letters of Strindberg to Harriet Bosse* (WNYC, 1962). His translations of *Miss Julie* and *The Stronger* were presented on Play of the Week (WNTA, 1960–70).

Other Activities. During National Poetry Week, he delivered readings from English, French, and Swedish literature in the original languages (Town Hall, N.Y.C., May 25, 1932). Mr. Paulson was invited by the Library of Congress to give readings from his Strindberg translations (1962); presented his collection of Strindberg first editions to NY Univ. (1971); and has lectured on and given readings from Strindberg and Ibsen at colleges and universities.

Published Works. He is the author of *The Story of Don Quixote;* with Clayton Edwards (1922); and a contributor to *Luck* by Lothrop Stoddard (1929). He translated and edited *Letters of Strindberg to Harriet Bosse* (1959, 1961); translated Strindberg's *Easter, The Father, Miss Julie, The Stronger, The Bond, Comrades, Crimes and Crimes* (1960); *A Dream Play* (1960, 1965, 1972); *To Damascus*, Part I (1960); Ibsen's *Hedda Gabler, The Master Builder, Rosmersholm, John Gabriel Borkman*, and *When We Dead Awaken* (1962, 1973); Strindberg's *To Damascus*, Parts I to III, *Lucky Per's Journey, The Keys of Heaven, A Dream Play, The Great Highway* and *The Ghost Sonata* (1965, 1972); Strindberg's one-act prose plays: *The Outlaw, Creditors, Pariah, Simoon, Debit and Credit, The First Warning, The Pelican, The Bond, Miss Julie, The Stronger, Motherlove, In the Face of Death, Playing with Fire* (1969); *The Dance of Death*, parts I and II (1971); *The Strindberg Reader* (1968); Strindberg's world-historical plays (1971): *The Nightingale of Wittenberg (Luther), Through Deserts to Ancestral Lands (Moses), Hellas (Socrates), The Lamb and the Beast (Christ);* and the Strindberg novels: *The Natives of Hemsë* (1965, 1967, 1973), *The Scapegoat* (1967), *Days of Loneliness* (1971), and *The Dance of Death*, parts I and II (1974). He has contributed articles on the theatre to newspapers, periodicals, and books in Sweden and America.

Awards. He was awarded knighthood, first class, Order of Vasa, by the King of Sweden (1962); received the Gold Medal of the Royal Swedish Academy of Letters (1964); the V.F.W. merit award (1964); was awarded honorary membership in Gillet Gamla Helsingborg; received a citation from the Governor of Scania (1969); received the Merit Award of the Performing Arts Review (1971); and received the honorary degree of Doctor of Literature from Upsala Coll. (East Orange, N.J., 1973).

Recreation. Fencing, horseback riding, tennis; bookbinding, book collection.

PAVETTI, SALLY THOMAS. Curator. b. Aug. 15, 1936, New York, N.Y., to John B. and Godiva A. Thomas. Father, school superintendent. Grad. Riverhead (N.Y.) H.S.; Wellesley Coll., B.A.; Yale Univ., M.A. (Ford Foundation Fellow). Professional training in theatre librarianship under George Freedley, Columbia Univ. (scholarship, 1966). Married 1958 to Francis J. Pavetti, attorney; one daughter. Member TLA (bd. mbr., 1973–77); Connecticut Comn. on the Arts, 1969–77 (exec. comm.; policy rev. comm.; bicentennial comm.). Address: (home) Strand Rd., Goshen Pt., Waterford, CT 06385, tel. (203) 443-3564; (bus.) 305 Great Neck Rd., Waterford, CT 06385, tel. (203) 443-5378.

Mrs. Pavetti is curator, Eugene O'Neill Th. Ctr., Waterford, Conn. In 1967, she organized a major O'Neill exhibition at the Lyman Allyn Museum, New London, for the international meeting of ITI.

PAXTON, GLENN. Composer. b. Glenn Gilbert Paxton, Jr., Dec. 7, 1931, Chicago, Ill., to Glenn G. and Florence (Nosek) Paxton. Father, lawyer. Grad. New Trier H.S., Winnetka, Ill., 1949; Princeton Univ., B.A. 1953. Studied piano with Mr. and Mrs. Hans Hess, Chicago, 1941–49; and composition with Max Wald at the Chicago Musical Coll., 1945–47. Married Dec. 8, 1962, to Leslie H. Davis, actress; one daughter. Served with USCG, 1953–56; rank, Lt. (jg). Member of ASCAP; Dramatists Guild; AFM, Local 802.

Pre-Theatre. Advertising.

Theatre. Mr. Paxton composed the score for the Princeton Univ. Triangle Club's *Ham 'n Legs* (McCarter Th., Princeton, N.J., Dec. 1952); and for *First Impressions* (Alvin, N.Y.C., Mar. 19, 1959).

Television. Mr. Paxton was composer of *Ballet for a Sunday Morning* (CBS, May 8, 1961); composed ballet music for the television film *Look Up and Live* (1963); the score for the documentary *The Art of Collecting* (NBC, Jan. 1964); for *A Bird's Eye View of America* (One of a Kind, CBS, Jan. 1964); and for *The Stately Ghosts of England* (NBC, Jan. 1965).

Published Works. He is the composer of *Four Character Pieces* for piano (1963).

PEDI, TOM. Actor. b. Thomas Pedi, Sept. 14, 1913, New York City, to Angelo and Carmela Pedi. Father, finisher. Grad. New Utrecht H.S., Brooklyn, N.Y., 1931. Served WW II, US Army, ETO, and N. Africa; 1st under-secy. to director of labor, Port of Safi, French Morocco. Member of AEA; SAG; AFTRA.

Theatre. Mr. Pedi made his N.Y.C. debut playing Mussolini in the revue *Pins and Needles* (Labor Stage Th., Nov. 27, 1937); subsequently appeared in *Brooklyn, U.S.A.* (Forrest, Dec. 21, 1941); *Beggars Are Coming to Town* (Coronet, Oct. 27, 1945); played Joe in the pre-Bway tryout of *You Only Twinkle Once* (opened Shubert, New Haven, Conn., Jan. 3, 1946; closed Wilbur, Boston, Mass., Jan. 19, 1946); and Stony in the pre-Bway tryout of *Windy City* (opened Shubert, New Haven, Apr. 18, 1946; closed Great Northern, Chicago, Ill., June 6, 1946).

He played Rocky Pioggi in *The Iceman Cometh* (Martin Beck Th., N.Y.C., Oct. 9, 1946), and toured in it; played Stanley in *Death of a Salesman* (Morosco, N.Y.C., Feb. 10, 1949); Harry the Horse in *Guys and Dolls* (46 St. Th., Nov. 24, 1950), repeated the role in London (Coliseum, May 28, 1953), and in stock (Valley Forge Music Fair, Pa., June 25, 1955).

Mr. Pedi played the 2nd Gangster in *Kiss Me, Kate* (NY City Ctr., May 9, 1956); Mike in *Pal Joey* (Valley Forge Music Fair, Pa., June 1956); Lenny in *A Hole in the Head* (Plymouth, N.Y.C., Feb. 28, 1957); Wolfie in *Simon and Laura* (John Drew Th., East Hampton, N.Y., Aug. 12, 1957); and Hippo in *Comic Strip* (Barbizon-Plaza Th., N.Y.C., May 14, 1958).

He played Frank in the pre-Bway tryout of *Poker Game* (opened Shubert, Washington, D.C., Jan. 16, 1959; closed Forrest, Philadelphia, Pa., Jan. 31, 1959); Rosey in the pre-Bway tryout of *One for the Dame* (opened Ford's, Baltimore, Md., Mar. 24, 1960; closed Colonial Boston, Mass., Apr. 2, 1960); in stock, played Harry the Horse in *Guys and Dolls* (Carousel, Framingham, Mass., June 1960; Oakdale Music Tent, Conn., June 1960; Camden Music Fair, N.J., Aug. 1960; Westbury Music Fair, N.Y., Aug. 1960; Painters Mill Music Fair, Md., Sept. 1960); the 2nd Gangster in *Kiss Me, Kate* (Carousel, Framingham, Mass., Sept. 1960); and Hippo in *Comic Strip* (Academy Playhouse, Palm Beach, Fla., Dec. 1960).

He played the Stage Manager in *A Stage Affair* (Cherry Lane, N.Y.C., Jan. 17, 1962); Hippo in *King of the Whole Damn World!*, the musical version of *Comic Strip* (Jan Hus House, Apr. 12, 1962); Tonio Crazzo in *My Mother, My Father and Me* (Plymouth, Mar. 23, 1963); the First Bodyguard in *Arturo-Ui* (Lunt-Fontanne Th., Nov. 11, 1963); Frank in *Kiss Mama* (Actors Playhouse, Oct. 1, 1964); Harry the Horse in *Guys and Dolls* (NY City Ctr., Apr. 28, 1965); Stewpot in *South Pacific* (NY City Ctr., June

2, 1965); repeated his role in *Guys and Dolls* (NY City Ctr., June 8, 1966); appeared in *The Investigation* (Ambassador, Oct. 4, 1966); played Paul in *Mike Downstairs* (Hudson, Apr. 18, 1968); and appeared in *The Sunshine Boys* (Manitoba Th. Ctr., Winnipeg, Canada, Oct. 18, 1974).

Films. Mr. Pedi first appeared as Perelli in *The Naked City* (U, 1948); subsequently appeared in *State of the Union* (MGM, 1948); *Criss-Cross* (U, 1949); *Sorrowful Jones* (Par., 1949); *Death Trap* (1949); *The Iceman Cometh* (Amer. Film Th., 1973); and *The Taking of Pelham One, Two, Three* (UA, 1974).

Television. He has appeared on the Eddie Cantor Show (NBC); Bob Hope Show (NBC); Philco Television Playhouse (NBC); The Big Story (NBC); Mr. Peepers (NBC); as Mr. Ferris in *Stanley* (Pall Mall, NBC, 1956); a Policeman in *Merry Christmas, Mr. Baxter* (NBC, 1956); and Maxie in *Odds Against the Jockey* (Decoy, 1957).

He also appeared as Charlie in the Dash Soap commercial (1958–63).

Awards. Mr. Pedi received the Screen Album Oscar Award for his performance as Once-Over Sam in *Sorrowful Jones* (1949).

Recreation. Baseball, swimming, reading.

PEDICORD, HARRY WILLIAM. Educator, clergyman. b. Mar. 23, 1912, Benwood, W.Va., to Harry Lewis and Aletha (Bell) Pedicord. Father and mother, educators. Grad. Washington and Jefferson Coll., B.A. 1933, M.A. 1934; Princeton Theological Seminary, Th. B. 1937; Univ. of Pennsylvania, Ph.D. 1949. Married Aug. 23, 1938, to Adah Alison; one daughter. Member of ASTR (chairman, 1960–1970); BSTR; MLA; The English Inst.; AAUP; SAA; Delta Tau Delta; The Pittsburgh Cleric: Col. Henry Bouquet Lodge, F. & A.M. 787 (past-master); Valley of Pittsburgh, A.A.S.R.; Syria Temple, A.A.O.N.M.S.; Tancred Commandery #48, Knights Templar; Grand Lodge of Pa. (Grand Chaplain).%

Since 1963, Mr. Pedicord has been professor of English and chairman of the English Dept. at Thiel Coll. Address: (home) R.D. #3, Greenville, PA tel. (412) 588-8305; (bus.) Dept. of English, Thiel Coll., Greenville, PA 16125, tel. (412) 588-7700 ext. 255.

Theatre. He wrote a comedy, *Jack and Jill* (Kilbuck Th., Pittsburgh, Pa., Jan. 9–July 20, 1937).

He was founder and director of The Covenant Players (Erie, Pa., 1938–42); and The Hiland Players (Pittsburgh, Pa., 1947–63).

Other Activities. He has been Assistant Pastor, First Presbyterian Church (Bridgeport, Conn., 1937–38), Pastor (1942–47); Executive Minister, The Church of the Covenant (Erie, Pa., 1938–42); and Pastor, Hiland Presbyterian Church (Ross Township, Pa., 1947–63).

Mr. Pedicord is a US voting delegate to the Plenary Comm. of the International Federation of Societies for Theatre Research (IFTR) (1970–to date); a member of the Comm. for the Venice Institute for Theatre Research, Casa Goldoni (1970–to date); and chairman of the editorial board of *Theatre Survey*, an ASTR periodical.

Published Works. He wrote *The Theatrical Public in the Time of David Garrick* (1954); and *The Course of Plays 1940-42* (1958); and edited *The Tragedy of Jane Shore* by Nicholas Rowe (Regents Restoration Drama Series, Univ. of Nebraska Press, 1974). He has also published articles in such periodicals as: *Church Management, Modern Language Association*, the *Bulletin of the John Rylands Library, Theatre Survey, Philological Quarterly, Theatre Research* (IFTR), and *Kleine Schriften der Gesellschaft fü r Theatergeschichte*.

Awards. Mr. Pedicord received an honorary D.D. from Waynesberg Coll. (1949); a Litt.D. from Washington and Jefferson Coll. (1961); and a citation for theatrical works by the Comm. on the Law of the Theatre, Federal Bar Assn. of N.Y., N.J., and Conn. (1969). He is an honorary fellow of the Consular Law Society (1969); and a fellow of the Folger Shakespeare Library (1973).

Recreation. Golf; water color painting; collecting theatre memorabilia, rare books, and prints; amateur stage direction.

PENE du BOIS, RAOUL. Costume and scenic designer. b. Raoul-Henri Charles Pene du Bois, Nov. 29, 1914, New York City, to Raoul-Georges-Gontran and Bessie (Hetherington) Pene du Bois. Father, banker. Privately educated. Member of United Scenic Artists. Address: 9 W. 75th St., New York, NY 10023, tel. (212) SC 4-4387.

Theatre. Mr. Pene du Bois designed the costumes for *Life Begins at 8:40* (Winter Garden Th., N.Y.C., Aug. 27, 1934); *Jumbo* (Hippodrome, Nov. 16, 1935); *The Two Bouquets* (Windsor, May 31, 1938); *Leave It to Me* (Imperial, Nov. 9, 1938); sets and costumes for *One for the Money* (Booth, Feb. 4, 1939); costumes for *Too Many Girls* (Imperial, Oct. 18, 1939), and *Aquacade* (NY World's Fair, 1939).

He designed the sets and costumes for *Du Barry Was a Lady* (46 St. Th., Dec. 6, 1939); *Two for the Show* (Booth, Feb. 8, 1940); *Panama Hattie* (46 St. Th., Oct. 30, 1940); costumes for *Carmen Jones* (Bway Th., Dec. 2, 1943); *The Firebrand of Florence* (Alvin, Mar. 22, 1945); and *Are You with It?* (Century, Nov. 10, 1945).

Also, sets and costumes for *Lend an Ear* (National, Dec. 16, 1948); *Alive and Kicking* (Winter Garden, Jan. 17, 1950); *Call Me Madam* (Imperial, Oct. 12, 1950); *Make a Wish* (Winter Garden, Apr. 18, 1951); sets for *New Faces of 1952* (Royale, May 16, 1952); sets and costumes for *In Any Language* (Cort, Oct. 7, 1952); *Wonderful Town* (Winter Garden, Feb. 25, 1953); and sets for *John Murray Anderson's Almanac* (Imperial, Dec. 10, 1953).

Mr. Pene du Bois was production designer for *Charley's Aunt* (NY City Ctr., Dec. 22, 1953); designed sets and costumes for *Mrs. Patterson* (National, Dec. 1, 1954); *Plain and Fancy* (Mark Hellinger Th., Jan. 27, 1955); *The Vamp* (Winter Garden, Nov. 10, 1955); *Bells Are Ringing* (Shubert, Nov. 29, 1956); *Ziegfeld Follies* (Winter Garden, Mar. 1, 1957); costumes for *The Music Man* (Majestic, Dec. 19, 1957); *Gypsy* (Bway Th., May 21, 1959); decor and lighting for *Maurice Chevalier* (Ziegfeld, Jan. 28, 1963); sets and costumes for *The Student Gypsy or The Prince of Liederkrantz* (54 St. Th., Sept. 30, 1963); sets for *Wonderful Town* (NY City Ctr., May 17, 1967); costumes for *Darling of the Day* (George Abbott Th., Jan. 27, 1968); sets for *Rondelay* (Hudson West, Nov. 5, 1969); sets and costumes for *No, No, Nanette* (46 St. Th., Jan. 19, 1971); costumes for *Rain* (Astor Place Th., Mar. 23, 1972); and sets and costumes for *Irene* (Minskoff, Mar. 13, 1973).

Films. Mr. Pene du Bois designed for *Louisiana Purchase* (Par., 1941); *Dixie* (Par., 1943); *Frenchman's Creek* (Par., 1944); *Lady in the Dark* (Par., 1944); and *Kitty* (Par., 1945).

Awards. He received the Donaldson and the Antoinette Perry (Tony) award for his sets and costumes in *Wonderful Town* (1952); and the 1970–71 Drama Desk, Antoinette Perry (Tony), and Joseph Maharam awards for his costumes for *No, No, Nanette.*.

PENN, ARTHUR. Director. b. Sept. 27, 1922, Philadelphia, Pa. Attended Black Mountain Coll., 1946; Univ. of Florence (Italy), 1951; Univ. of Perugia (Italy), 1951. Studied at Actors' Studio, N.Y.C.; with Michael Chekhov, Los Angeles, Calif. Married 1956 to Peggy Maurer, actress; one son, one daughter. Served WW II, US Army Infantry, ETO. Member of AEA; SSD&C. Address: 1860 Broadway, New York, NY 10023.

Theatre. Mr. Penn directed *Two for the Seesaw* (Booth, N.Y.C., Jan. 16, 1958); *The Miracle Worker* (Playhouse, Oct. 19, 1959); *Toys in the Attic* (Hudson, Feb. 25, 1960); *An Evening with Nichols and May* (Belasco, Nov. 30, 1960); *In the Counting House* (Biltmore, Dec. 13, 1962); *Lorenzo* (Plymouth, Feb. 14, 1963); and *Golden Boy* (Majestic, Oct. 21, 1964).

Films. He directed *The Left-Handed Gun* (WB, 1958); *The Miracle Worker* (UA, 1962); *Mickey One* (Col., 1964); *The Chase* (Col., 1965); *Bonnie and Clyde* (WB, 1967); *Alice's Restaurant* (WB, 1968); and *Little Big Man* (Cinema Ctr. Films, 1970).

Television. Since 1951, Mr. Penn has directed about 200 productions, including *The Miracle Worker* (Playhouse 90, CBS, 1957).

Awards. He received the Sylvania Award for his television direction of *Man on a Mountaintop* and *The Miracle Worker* (1959); the Antoinette Perry (Tony) Award (1959) for his direction of the latter on Bway.

PERELMAN, S. J. Playwright, author. b. Sidney Joseph Perelman, Feb. 11, 1904, Brooklyn, N.Y., to Joseph and Sophia (Charren) Perelman. Grad. Brown Univ., B.A., 1925. Married July 4, 1929, to Laura West, writer (dec. Apr. 10, 1970); one son, one daughter. Member of Dramatists Guild; SWG; Natl. Inst. of Arts and Letters.

Theatre. Mr. Perelman contributed sketches to *The Third Little Show* (Music Box Th., N.Y.C., June 1, 1931); subsequently collaborated with Robert MacGunigle on the sketches for *Walk a Little Faster* (St. James, Dec. 7, 1932); with his wife, Laura Perelman, wrote *All Good Americans* (Henry Miller's Th., Dec. 5, 1933); and wrote the sketches for *Two Weeks with Pay*, which toured summer theatres (1940).

With his wife, he wrote *The Night Before Christmas* (Morosco, Apr. 10, 1941); with Ogden Nash, the book for *One Touch of Venus* (Imperial, Oct. 7, 1943); with Al Hirschfeld, the book for *Sweet Bye and Bye* (opened Shubert, New Haven, Conn., Oct. 10, 1946; closed, Erlanger, Philadelphia, Pa., Nov. 5, 1946); and wrote *The Beauty Part* (Music Box, Dec. 26, 1962), which was revived by The American Place Th. (Oct. 23, 1974).

Films. Since 1930, Mr. Perelman has written sketches and screenplays for motion pictures, including: *Paris Interlude* (MGM, 1963); *Ambush* (Par., 1939); *The Golden Fleecing* (MGM, 1940); *Larceny, Inc.* (WB, 1942); *One Touch of Venus* (U, 1948); and, with John Farrow and James Poe, the screenplay for *Around the World in 80 Days* (UA, 1956).

Television. He was a staff writer for Omnibus (NBC, 1957–58) and has written *Aladdin* (CBS); contributed material to the Seven Lively Arts (CBS); and wrote *The Changing Ways of Love* (CBS); and *Elizabeth Taylor's London* (CBS).

Published Works. He wrote for *Judge* (1925–29); *College Humor* (1929–30); and since 1934, has contributed humorous material to *The New Yorker* and *Holiday*. He wrote *Dawn Ginsbergh's Revenge* (1929); *Parlor Bedlam and Bath* (1930); *Strictly from Hunger* (1937); *Look Who's Talking* (1940); *The Dream Department* (1943); *Crazy Like a Fox* (1944); *Keep It Crisp* (1946); *Acres and Pains* (1947); *The Best of S. J. Perelman* (1947); *Westward Ha! or, Around the World in Eighty Clichés* (1948); *Listen to the Mocking Bird* (1949); *The Swiss Family Perelman* (1950); *The Ill-Tempered Clavichord* (1953); *Perelman's Home Companion* (1955); *The Road to Miltown* (1957); *The Rising Gorge* (1961); *Chicken Inspector No. 23* (1966); and *Vinegar Puss* (1975).

Awards. With John Farrow and James Poe, Mr. Perelman received the NY Film Critics Award, and the Academy (Oscar) Award for their adaptation of *Around the World in 80 Days* (1956).

PERKINS, ANTHONY. Actor, director. b. Apr. 4, 1932, New York City, to Osgood and Janet Esselton (Rane) Perkins. Father, actor. Grad. Browne and Nichols Sch., Cambridge, Mass., 1950; attended Rollins Coll., 1951–52; Columbia Univ., 1952–53. Married Aug. 1973 to Berinthia Berenson, photographer; two sons. Relative in theatre: sister-in-law, Marisa Berenson, actress. Member of AEA; AFTRA; SAG; Kappa Alpha.

Theatre. Mr. Perkins was an apprentice at the Brattleboro (Vt.) Summer Th. (1947). At the Robin Hood Th. (Arden, Del.), he appeared as Awyas Beudish in *Sarah Simple*, in *George and Margaret*, *My Sister Eileen*, and as Fred Whitmarsh in *Years Ago* (1948–50); and toured in a production of *Theatre* (Saratoga Springs, N.Y., Summer 1951).

Mr. Perkins made his N.Y.C. debut succeeding (May 31, 1954) John Kerr as Tom Lee in *Tea and Sympathy* (Ethel Barrymore Th., Sept. 30, 1953); subsequently played Eugene Gant in *Look Homeward, Angel* (Ethel Barrymore Th., Nov. 28, 1957); Gideon Briggs in *Greenwillow* (Alvin, Mar. 8, 1960); the title role in *Harold* (Cort, Nov. 29, 1962); and Andy Hobart in *The Star-Spangled Girl* (Plymouth, Dec. 21, 1966).

He directed, at the Milwaukee (Wis.) Repertory Th., *The Imaginary Invalid* (Dec. 20, 1968) and *The Burgomaster* (Nov. 7, 1969); played Tandy in *Steambath*, which he also directed (Truck and Warehouse Th., N.Y.C., June 30, 1970); directed *Angel Street* (Playhouse in the Park, Cincinnati, Ohio, May 1, 1971); directed *The Wager* (Eastside Playhouse, Oct. 21, 1974); and succeeded (July 1975–Feb. 16, 1976) Anthony Hopkins as Martin Dysart in *Equus* (Plymouth, Oct. 24, 1974) and, in the same role, replaced (May 11, 1976) Richard Burton.

Films. Mr. Perkins made his debut as Fred Whitmarsh in *The Actress* (MGM, 1953); subsequently appeared in *Friendly Persuasion* (Allied, 1956); *The Lonely Man* (Par., 1957); *Fear Strikes Out* (Par., 1957); *The Tin Star* (Par., 1957); *This Angry Age* (Col., 1958); *Desire Under the Elms* (Par., 1958); *The Matchmaker* (Par., 1958); *Green Mansions* (MGM, 1958); *On the Beach* (UA, 1959); *Tall Story* (WB, 1960); *Psycho* (Par., 1960); *Goodbye Again* (UA, 1961); *Phaedra* (Lopert, 1962); *Five Miles to Midnight* (UA, 1962); *The Trial* (Gibraltar, 1963); *Two Are Guilty* (MGM, 1963); *The Fool Killer* (Ely Landau, 1964); and *The Adorable Fool* (Belle-Rives, 1964).

His other films include *A Ravishing Idiot* (French, 1965); *Is Paris Burning?* (Par., 1966); *The Champagne Murders* (U, 1968); *Pretty Poison* (20th-Fox, 1968); *WUSA* (Par., 1970); *Catch-22* (Par., 1970); *Ten Days Wonder* (Levitt-Pichman, 1972); *The Life and Times of Judge Roy Bean* (Natl. Gen., 1972); and *Play It As It Lays* (U, 1972). He wrote, with Stephen Sondheim, and directed *The Last of Sheila* (WB, 1973); and appeared in *Murder on the Orient Express* (Par., 1974); *Lovin' Molly* (Col., 1974); and *Mahogany* (Motown, 1975).

Television. Mr. Perkins first appeared on television in *Joey* (Alcoa-Goodyear, NBC, 1953); subsequently in *The Missing Year* (Kraft Th., NBC, 1954); *The Fugitive* (Armstrong Circle Th., NBC, 1954); *Mr. Blue Ocean* (GE Th., CBS, 1955); *Home Is the Hero* (Kraft Th., NBC, 1956); *The Silent Gun* (Studio One, CBS, 1956); and *How Awful About Allan* (ABC, 1970).

Awards. He received the *Theatre World* Award for his performance as Tom Lee in *Tea and Sympathy* (1954–55); the Cannes Film Festival Award for his performance in *Goobye Again* (1961–62); and has twice received the French "Victoire du Cinema" (1961, 1962).

Recreation. Piano, tennis, murder mysteries, puzzles.

PERLMAN, PHYLLIS. Press representative. b. Jan. 8, New York City, to Abraham and Flora (Baker) Perlman. Father, realtor. Grad. Wadleigh H.S., N.Y.C.; attended Barnard Coll.; grad. Columbia Univ., B.Litt. 1917. Married Nov. 26, 1930, to Theron Bamberger, producer (dec. 1953). Member of ATPAM. Address: 240 Central Park South, New York, NY 10019, tel. (212) CI 6-7913.

Pre-Theatre. Magazine editor and publicist.

Theatre. Miss Perlman was first a press representative with the Shubert Press Dept. (1930); subsequently has been press representative for *Fifty Million Frenchmen* (1930); *Counsellor-at-Law* and *The Left Bank* (1931); *Fly Away Home* (1935); *Yes, My Darling Daughter* (1937); *Too Many Girls* (1939); *Kiss and Tell* (1943); *Snafu* (1944); *Mr. Cooper's Left Hand* (1945); *St. Louis Woman, The Haven,* and *A Family Affair* (1946); *Under the Counter* and *An Inspector Calls* (1947); *The Hallams* and *Minnie and Mr. Williams* (1948); *Leaf and Bough* (1949); *Out West of Eighth* (1951); *Gertie, Curtain Going Up,* and *The Seven Year Itch* (1952); *Wonderful Town* (1953); *The Desperate Hours* and *The Wayward Saint* (1955); *Little Glass Clock, The Happiest Millionaire, Speaking of Murder,* and *No Exit* (1956); *Three Plays by John Millington Synge,* and *Hotel Paradiso* (1957); and the West Coast productions of *Nude with Violin* and *Present Laughter,* which starred Noel Coward (1959).

Miss Perlman is now retired.

Other Activities. Miss Perlman assisted her husband, Theron Bamberger, in the operation of the Bucks County Playhouse (New Hope, Pa., 1940–53) and the John B. Kelly Playhouse-in-the-Park (Philadelphia, Pa., 1951–53). Miss Perlman's recollections were used in *The Difference Began at the Footlights,* Gilda Morigis' book about the Bucks County Playhouse.

Recreation. Travel, foreign languages.

PERRIE, ERNESTINE. Director. b. Ernestine Minciotti, July 3, 1912, San Francisco, Calif., to Silvio and Esther (Cunico) Minciotti. Father, actor; mother, actress. Grad. Bay Ridge H.S., Brooklyn, N.Y., 1930–33; attended Hunter Coll., 1962–63. Married Dec. 31, 1939, to David Perrie, musician; (dec. 1968); one daughter. Member of AEA. Address: 25 W. 54th St., New York, NY 10019, tel. (212) 247-6654.

Theatre. Mrs. Perrie made her stage debut as an infant in an Italian repertory company (La Moderna Co., Washington Square, San Francisco, Calif., 1913) with which she later played children's parts; subsequently appeared as an Italian Child in *They Knew What They Wanted* (Curran Th., San Francisco, 1923).

In N.Y.C., she was assistant stage manager for *Craig's Wife* (Playhouse, Feb. 12, 1947); and *Strange Bedfellows* (Morosco, Jan. 14, 1948); stage manager for *The Shop at Sly Corner* (Booth, Jan. 18, 1949); *Gayden* (Plymouth, May 10, 1949); and the pre-Bway tryout of *House on the Cliff* (opened Shubert, New Haven, Conn., Apr. 13, 1950; closed Locust St. Th., Philadelphia, Pa., Apr. 27, 1950); directed a stock production of *Goodbye, My Fancy* (Sea Cliff Th., N.Y., Summer 1951); an ELT production of *The Enchanted* (Lenox Hill Playhouse, N.Y.C., 1950–51); was assistant to the director of *Dear Barbarians* (Royale, Feb. 21, 1952); in stock, directed *The Lady's Not for Burning* and *Years Ago* (Hillsdale Th., Chicago, Summer 1953); *Mister Roberts, A Streetcar Named Desire, Camino Real, The Long Street, On Cobweb Twine,* and *Chintz and Chippendale* (Sea Cliff Th., N.Y., Summers 1953–54).

She played Maria, was stage manager, and was Italian coach for the cast, in the pre-Bway tryout of *A Quiet Place* (opened Shubert, New Haven, Conn., Nov. 23, 1955; closed National, Washington, D.C., Dec. 21, 1955); directed *The Enchanted* (Renata, N.Y.C., Apr. 22, 1958); directed a six-month season at the Hedgerow Th. (Moylan, Pa., 1958); staged *Beautiful Dreamer* (Madison Ave. Playhouse, N.Y.C., Dec. 27, 1961), and *The Worlds of Shakespeare,* which she arranged with Marchette Chute, (Carnegie Hall, Dec. 4, 1963).

Other Activities. Since 1955, Mrs. Perrie has directed the annual productions of Theatre in Education, a touring group which performs in schools. She is currently engaged by the Smithsonian Institution as a consultant on Italian cultural affairs for the bicentennial.

Published Works. With Marchette Chute, she co-authored *Worlds of Shakespeare.*

PERRY, ELAINE. Actress, director, producer. b. Elaine Storrs Frueauff, Mar. 12, 1921, New York City, to Frank W. and Antoinette (Perry) Frueauff. Father, investment banker; mother, director. Grad. Miss Hewitt's Sch., N.Y.C., 1938. Member of AEA; League of NY Theatres; Amer. Theatre Wing; Council of Resident Stock Theatres; NY Junior League; Colorado Cattlemen's Assn.; Amer. Quarter Horse Assn.

Theatre. Miss Perry's first professional appearance onstage was at the Braddock Heights (Md.) Th. (1939); subsequently she was understudy to Ingrid Bergman in the role of Julie in *Liliom* (44 St. Th., N.Y.C., Mar. 25, 1940); played a Strange Girl in *Glamour Preferred* (Booth, Nov. 15, 1940); sang in the chorus of *No for an Answer* (Mecca Temple, 1941); appeared in *The Trojan Women* (Cort, 1941); played in stock at the Lakewood Th. (Skowhegan, Me., Summer 1941); appeared with the American Theatre Wing audience-participation shows in hospitals in N.Y.C., New England and Ohio (1942–44); and as Frances Bass in *Pillar to Post* (Playhouse, N.Y.C., Dec. 10, 1943).

She was stage manager of the USO touring production of *The Barretts of Wimpole Street* (ETO), Aug. 1944–Mar. 1945); *The Barretts of Wimpole Street* (Ethel Barrymore Th., N.Y.C., Mar. 26, 1945); and the pre-Bway tryout of *The Magnificent Heel* (Philadelphia, Pa.; Buffalo, N.Y., 1946); appeared in summer-stock productions at the Lakewood Th., (Skowhegan, Me., 1947); produced *Touchstone* (Music Box, N.Y.C., Feb. 3, 1953); produced *The Paradise Question* (Lakewood Th., Skowhegan Me., Summer 1953), and its pre-Bway tryout (closed Walnut St. Th., Philadelphia, Fall 1953).

Miss Perry produced *King of Hearts* (Lyceum, N.Y.C., Apr. 1, 1954); *Anastasia* (Lyceum, Dec. 29, 1954); produced and directed stock productions at the Cragsmoor (N.Y.) Th. (Summers 1955–57); directed several plays at the White Barn Th. (Irwin, Pa., Summer 1958); *The Girls in 509* (Poinciana Playhouse, Palm Beach, Fla., 1960); and *The Late Christopher Bean* (1960); produced and directed the pre-Bway tryout of *Catstick* (opened Shubert, New Haven, Conn., Jan. 4, 1961; closed Wilbur, Boston, Mass., Jan. 14, 1961); and directed a Theatre International production of *Never Too Late* (Johannesburg Civic Th., South Africa, May 29, 1964); directed *A Race of Hairy Men!* (Henry Miller's Th., Apr. 29, 1965); and with Charles Hollereth, Jr., produced *How's the World Treating You?* (Music Box, Oct. 24, 1966).

Films. Miss Perry, with Sidney Buchman, wrote the screenplay for *The Deadly Trap* (Natl. Gen., 1972).

Television. She performed in *Charlotte Corday* (NBC, 1940).

Recreation. Riding, deep-sea fishing, bridge, music, languages, writing, reading.

PERRY, MARGARET. Actress, director, playwright. b. Margaret Hall Frueauff, Feb. 23, 1913, Denver, Colo., to Frank W. and Antoinette (Perry) Frueauff. Father, financier; mother, Antoinette Perry, actress, director. Grad. Miss Hewitt's Classes, N.Y.C., 1929. Married 1933 to Winsor B. French II, newspaper columnist (marr. dis. 1934); married 1935 to Burgess Meredith, actor, director (marr. dis. 1937); married 1943 to Paul P. Fanning, scenic artist (marr. dis. 1950); two sons, two daughters. Relative in theatre: sister, Elaine Perry, producer. Member of AEA; ALA; Denver Country Club, Colo.

Theatre. Miss Perry made her N.Y.C. debut succeeding (Dec. 18, 1929) Muriel Kirkland for several performances as Isabelle in *Strictly Dishonorable* (Avon, Sept. 18, 1929), later succeeded (July 1930) Mary Cullinan in the part and repeated it on tour (1930); subsequently played Phyl in *After All* (Booth, Dec. 3, 1931); Tommy Thomas in *Ceiling Zero* (Music Box Th., Apr. 10, 1935); Grace Dosher in *Now You've Done It* (Henry Miller's Th., Mar. 5, 1937); and Kitty in *The Greatest Show on Earth* (Playhouse, Jan. 5, 1938).

She was production assistant for *Craig's Wife* (Playhouse, Feb. 12, 1947); assistant to the producer in *The First Mrs. Fraser* (Shubert, Nov. 5, 1947); and production assistant in a touring production of *On Approval* (opened Shubert, New Haven, Conn., May 13, 1948; closed Selwyn, Chicago, Ill., June 5, 1948); staged *The Passing of the Third Floor Back* (Henry St. Settlement, N.Y.C., 1948); adapted and directed a touring production of *The Virginian* (1949); directed *The Shop at Sly Corner* (Booth, N.Y.C., Jan. 18, 1949); and with Brock Pemberton, directed *Love Me Long* (48 St. Th., Jan. 31, 1950).

Films. Miss Perry played in *New Morals for Old* (MGM, 1932) and *Go West, Young Man* (Par., 1936).

Radio. She played Ophelia in *Hamlet* (Los Angeles, 1936).

Recreation. Knitting, gardening, reading.

PERRY, MARTHA. Theatre administrator. b. Martha Falknor, Seattle, Wash. Grad. Univ. of Washington, B.A. (drama, cum laude) 1946. Attended Pasadena Playhouse, Calif. Married July 13, 1946, to James C. Perry; one son, one daughter. Member of CTC. Address: 433 86th St. N.E., Bellevue, WA 98004.

Mrs. Perry was regional chairman, for Wash. and Ore. of the Children's Theatre Conference (CTC, 1961–63); and has been a board member (1957–to date) and program chairman (1961–to date) of the Seattle Junior Programs. She is editor of the CTC newsletter for Region Three.

PERSOFF, NEHEMIAH. Actor. b. Aug. 14, 1920, Jerusalem, Israel, to Samuel and Puah (Holman) Persoff. Father, jeweler. Grad. Hebrew Technical Inst., N.Y.C., 1937. Studied at Actors' Studio (member since 1948); with Stella Adler; Brett Warren; John O'Shaunessy; Peter Frye; Peggy Wood; Elia Kazan; Lee Strasberg. Married Aug. 22, 1951, to Thia Persov; three sons, one daughter. Served Coast Artillery, Airborne Inf., 1942–45. Member of SAG; AEA; AFTRA.

Pre-Theatre. Electric motor repairman, signal department of N.Y.C. subway system.

Theatre. Mr. Persoff first appeared in summer theatre productions at the Haverhill (Mass.) Bayhouse, as Candy in *Of Mice and Men,* Dean Frederick Damon in *The Male Animal,* Dick Dudgeon in *The Devil's Disciple,* and in *Hay Fever* (Summer 1947); he played Andrea in *Galileo* (Maxine Elliott's Th., N.Y.C., Dec. 7, 1947); Cecil in *Sundown Beach* (Belasco, Sept. 7, 1948); Tyrell in *Richard III* (Booth, Feb. 8, 1949); Antonanzas in *Montserrat* (Fulton, Oct. 29, 1949); Cecco in *Peter Pan* (Imperial, Apr. 24, 1950); the Duke of Cornwall in *King Lear* (Natl., Dec. 25, 1950); the Troll King in *Peer Gynt* (ANTA, Jan. 28, 1951); and the Younger Arab in *Flahooley* (Broadhurst, May 14, 1951).

In Tel-Aviv, Israel, he appeared at the Chamber Th. as Tom in *The Glass Menagerie* and as Mosca in *Volpone* (1952); played the First Street Cleaner in *Camino Real* (Natl. N.Y.C., Mar. 19, 1953); appeared in summer theatre productions at the Playhouse-in-the-Park (Philadelphia, Pa.), as Charlie in *Detective Story* and in *The Road to Rome* (Summer 1953); subsequently played the Hair Dresser in *Mademoiselle Colombe* (Longacre, N.Y.C., Jan. 6, 1954); returned to the Playhouse-in-the-Park to appear as Eddie Fuseli in *Golden Boy* (Summer 1954); played Dr. Hickey in *Reclining Figure* (Lyceum, N.Y.C., Oct. 7, 1954); Topman in *Tiger at the Gates* (Plymouth, Oct. 3, 1955); Harry Golden in *Only in America;* (Cort, Nov. 19, 1959); the title role in *Rosebloom* (Mark Taper Forum, Los Angeles, Calif., Nov. 5, 1970); and appeared in a one-man show, *Aleichem Sholem - Sholem Aleichem* (Oxford Th., Los Angeles, Calif., Aug. 11, 1971).

Films. Mr. Persoff has appeared in *Naked City* (U, 1948); *A Double Life* (U, 1948); as the Taxi Driver in *On the Waterfront* (Col., 1954); the Bookkeeper in *The Harder They Fall* (Col., 1956); Kicks in *The Wild Party* (UA, 1956); Sgt. Lewis in *Men in War* (UA, 1957); the Bar Owner in *Street of Sinners* (UA, 1957); the Brother in *The Wrong Man* (WB, 1957); the Mexican Miner in *Badlanders* (MGM, 1958); Albert in *This Angry Age* (Col., 1957); Pinneli in *Never Steal Anything Small* (U, 1958); the Storekeeper in *Green Mansions* (MGM, 1959); Johnny Torio in *Al Capone* (Allied, 1959); Little Bonaparte in *Some Like It Hot* (UA, 1959); a Cowhand in *Day of the Outlaw* (UA, 1959); the Comanchero Chief in *The Comancheros* (20th-Fox, 1961); the Circus Owner in *The Big Show* (20th-Fox, 1961); the Captain in *The Hook* (MGM, 1962); Segura in *A Global Affair* (MGM, 1963); Sawyer in *Fate Is the Hunter* (20th-Fox, 1964); and the Chief Rabbi in *The Greatest Story Ever Told* (UA, 1964). Other of his films are *Dangerous Days of Kiowa Jones* (MGM, 1966); *The Money Jungle* (Commonwealth United, 1968); *Panic in the City* (Commonwealth United, 1968); *The Power* (MGM, 1968); *The Girl Who Knew Too Much* (Commonwealth United, 1969); *The People Next Door* (Avco Embassy, 1970); *Mrs. Pollifax Spy* (WB, 1970); *Red Sky at Morning* (U, 1970); and *Kirlian Effect* (Mars, 1974).

Television. Mr. Persoff has appeared on many television shows, including Captain Video (Dumont); Shirley Temple Storybook (NBC); Producer's Showcase (NBC); Playwrights '56 (NBC); Clash by Night (BBC, 1958); as Pablo in *For Whom the Bell Tolls* (Playhouse 90, CBS, 1958); *Tiger at the Gates* (CBC, 1958); Dracula (CBC); Philco-Goodyear Playhouse (NBC); Kraft Television Th. (NBC); Thriller; Wagon Train (NBC); Bus Stop (ABC); Twilight Zone (CBS); Dick Powell Th. (NBC); You Are There (CBS); Danger (CBS); I Spy (NBC); Appointment with Adventure (CBS); Mr. Lucky; Five Fingers (NBC); Red Buttons Show; Naked City (ABC, 1961–63); The Untouchables (ABC, 1961–63); Route 66 (CBS, 1961); *The Last Days of Benito Mussolini* (Playhouse 90, CBS); Rawhide (CBS, 1963–64); Bob Hope Presents (NBC, 1964).

Also Marcus Welby (ABC); Hawaii Five-0 (CBS); Gunsmoke (CBS); Gilligan's Island (CBS); Search; McMillan and Wife; Bill Cosby Show; The New Breed (ABC); Burke's Law (ABC); Police Surgeon (ABC); Manley and the Mob (pilot); Cutter's Trail (pilot); pilot for the Barbara Eden Show; Mr. Novak (NBC); Big Valley (ABC); Chicago Teddy Bears; Convoy; Disney's Wonderful World of Color; Ben Casey (ABC); Police Story (NBC); Wild, Wild West (CBS); Mission: Impossible (CBS); Love American Style (ABC); Adam-12 (NBC); Mannix (CBS); The Streets of San Francisco (ABC); Tarzan; Cool Millions; McCloud (NBC); the Danny Thomas Show (CBS); It Takes a Thief (ABC); Name of the Game (NBC); Honey West; Dan August (ABC); Trials of O'Brien (CBS); Mod Squad (ABC); The Man from U.N.C.L.E. (NBC); The Flying Nun (ABC); Alfred Hitchcock Presents (NBC). He has also appeared on the Joey Bishop, Merv Griffin, and Virginia Graham talk shows, and he was in the television films *Destination Mindanao* (Universal) and *Sex Symbol* (Screen Gems, 1973).

Awards. Mr. Persoff received the Sylvania Award (1958) for his performance as Pablo in the television production of *For Whom the Bell Tolls* and a special award from Los Angeles drama critics (1971) for his one-man show, *Aleichem Sholem - Sholem Aleichem.*

Recreation. Tennis, swimming, chess, vegetable gardening.

PETERS, BERNADETTE. Actress, singer, dancer. b. Bernadette Lazzara, Feb. 28, 1948, Ozone Park, Queens, N.Y., to Peter and Marguerite (Maltese) Lazzara. Father, bakery salesman. Grad. P.S. 58 (Queens); Quintano Sch. for Young Professionals; trained with David LeGrant Sch. (acting); James Gregory (musical comedy). Member of AFTRA; SAG; AEA. Address: (home) c/o Thomas Hammond, 8651 Pinetree Pl., Los Angeles, CA 90069, tel. (213) 657-2958; (bus.) International Famous Agency, 9255 Sunset Blvd., Los Angeles, CA 90069, tel. (213) CR 3-8811.

Theatre. Ms. Peters first appeared on the stage professionally as Tessie in *The Most Happy Fella* (NY City Ctr., Feb. 1959); and subsequently toured in the roles of Dainty June and Agnes in *Gypsy* (national company, 1961); Alice Burton in *This Is Google,* a pre-Bway production (1962); Jenny in *Riverwind* (Summer 1966); and Carolotta Monti in *W. C.* (Summer 1971).

Off-Bway, she played Cinderella in *The Penny Friend* (Stage 73, Dec. 1966); Alice in *Curley McDimple* (Bert Wheeler Th., Nov. 1967); and Ruby in *Dames at Sea* (Bouwerie Lane Th., Dec. 1968).

On Bway, she served as understudy in *The Girl in the Freudian Slip* (Booth Th., May 1967); played Bettina in *Johnny No-Trump* (Cort Th., Oct. 1967); Josie Cohan in *George M* (Palace, Apr. 1968); Gelsomina in *La Strada* (Lunt-Fontanne Th., Dec. 1969); Hildy in a revival of *On the Town* (Lunt-Fontanne Th., Oct. 1971); and Mabel in *Mack and Mabel* (Majestic, Oct. 1974). Outside of N.Y.C., she has appeared as Dorine in *Tartuffe* (Walnut St. Th., Philadelphia, Pa., Dec. 1972).

Films. She played Allison in *Ace Eli & Rodger of the Skies* (20th-Fox, 1971); and Hildagarde in *The Longest Yard* (Par., 1973).

Television. She has performed on *Horn & Hardhardt's Children's Hour* (CBS, 1953–54); the *Carol Burnett Show* (CBS, 1969 and 1974); and *The Bing Crosby Special* (CBS, 1970). She played Josie Cohan in *George M!* (NBC, 1970); Lady Larkin in *Once Upon a Mattress* (CBS, 1972); and Doris in the made-for-television movie, *The Owl and the Pussycat* (Screen Gems, 1974).

Recreation. Tennis, painting, yoga.

PETERS, BROCK. Actor, singer. b. July 2, 1927, New York City, to Sonnie and Alma A. (Norford) Fisher. Father, sailor. Grad. Music and Art H.S., N.Y.C., 1941; attended Univ. of Chicago, 1944–1945; City Coll. of New York, 1945–1947. Studied acting with Betty Cashman, N.Y.C., one year; Michael Howard, N.Y.C., one year; Robert Lewis, N.Y.C., two years; Harry Wagstaff Gribble, Chicago, Ill., two years. Married July 29, 1961, to Dolores Daniels, television producer and public relations consultant; one daughter. Member of AEA; SAG; AFTRA; AGVA.

Pre-Theatre. YMCA instructor, N.Y.C. Parks Dept. instructor, hospital orderly, shipping clerk.

Theatre. Mr. Peters made his N.Y.C. debut, succeeding William C. Smith as Jim in *Porgy and Bess* (44 St. Th., Sept. 13, 1943), and on tour (1943–44); subsequently appeared in *South Pacific* (Cort, N.Y.C., Dec. 29, 1943); and played Lester and Rudolph in *Anna Lucasta* (Mansfield, Aug. 30, 1944; Civic, Chicago, Ill., Sept. 1944–June 1945).

During 1947–50, he was bass soloist with the De-Paur Infantry Chorus, which toured the US and Canada; played Wheat in *My Darlin' Aida* (Winter Garden, N.Y.C., Oct. 27, 1952); "Rhythm" Nelson in a Summer tryout of *Head of a Family* (Westport Country Playhouse, Conn., Sept. 1950); Autumn in *The Year Round* (N.Y.C.); Ajali in *Mister Johnson* (Martin Beck Th., Mar. 29, 1956); the King in *King of the Dark Chamber* (Jan Hus House, Feb. 1961); and Obitsebi in *Kwamina* (54 St. Th., Oct. 23, 1961).

In addition to numerous stock engagements, he played the title role in *Othello* (Arena Stage, Washington, D.C., Apr. 10, 1963); The Storyteller in *The Caucasian Chalk Circle* (Vivian Beaumont Th., N.Y.C., Mar. 24, 1966); Jack Jefferson in *The Great White Hope* (national tour, opened Sept. 15, 1969); and Stephen Kumalo in *Lost in the Stars* (Imperial, N.Y.C., Apr. 18, 1972).

Films. Mr. Peters made his debut as Sergeant Brown in *Carmen Jones* (20th-Fox, 1954); subsequently appeared as Crown in *Porgy and Bess* (Col., 1959); Tom Robinson in *To Kill a Mockingbird* (U, 1962); in *Heavens Above* (Brit. Lion, 1962); *The L-Shaped Room* (Col., 1963); *The Pawnbroker* (Landau, 1965); *Major Dundee* (Col., 1965); *The Incident* (20th-Fox, 1968); *P. J.* (U, 1968); *Daring Game* (Par., 1969); *Ace High* (Par., 1969); *The McMasters* (Chevron, 1970); narrated *Jack Johnson* (Big Fights, Inc., 1971); appeared in *Black Girl* (Cinerama, 1972); *Soylent Green* (MGM, 1973); *Five on the Black Hand Side* (UA, 1973); *Slaughter's Big Ripoff* (Amer. Intl., 1973); and *Lost in the Stars* (Amer. Film Th., 1974).

Television. He made his debut as a singer on Arthur Godfrey's Talent Scouts (CBS, 1953); has appeared as guest singer on such shows as The Hit Parade (NBC), the Garry Moore Morning Show (CBS), Music for a Summer Night (NBC), Music for a Spring Night (ABC), the Garry Moore Show (CBS), the Tonight Show (NBC), and Hootenanny (ABC).

He appeared on Adventures in Paradise (ABC); played in *Bloomer Girl* (NBC Special); *The Snows of Kilimanjaro* (Buick Playhouse, CBS); appeared on Sam Benedict (NBC); Great Adventure (CBS); and Eleventh Hour Series (NBC); Doctors/Nurses (CBS); Rawhide (CBS); Loner (CBS); Trials of O'-Brien (CBS); Run for Your Life (NBC); The Girl from U.N.C.L.E. (NBC); Mission: Impossible

(CBS); Tarzan (NBC); Judd for the Defense (ABC); It Takes a Thief (ABC); Felony Squad (ABC); Outcasts (ABC); Gunsmoke (CBS); Mannix (CBS); Longstreet (ABC); Mod Squad (ABC); and *Welcome Home, Johnny Bristol* (tele-film, CBS).

He appeared as a guest singer on Show Time (BBC, London, 1961), and on two one-man shows (BBC, 1961).

Night Clubs. He has performed at various times at the Village Gate (N.Y.C.); The Gate of Horn (Chicago, Ill.); The Purple Onion (Toronto, Ontario, Canada); The Copa (Pittsburgh, Pa.); The Troubadour (Los Angeles, Calif.); and others throughout the US and Canada.

Awards. Mr. Peters received the All American Press Assn. Award for best supporting actor; the Box Office Blue Ribbon Award; the Allen AME Award; and the American Society of African Culture Emancipation Award for his performance as Tom Robinson in *To Kill a Mockingbird* (1962); and the Drama Desk Award (1971–72) for his performance in *Lost in the Stars.*

He also received the Douglas Jr. H.S. (Higher Horizon School of N.Y.) man of the year award (1964).

Recreation. Basketball, track, swimming, table tennis, hiking, reading.

PETERSON, LENKA. Actress. b. Betty Ann Isacson, Oct. 16, 1925, Omaha, Nebr., to Sven Edward and Lenke (Leinweber) Isacson. Father, physician; mother, secretary, therapist. Grad. Central H.S., Omaha, 1942; attended State Univ. of Iowa, 1942–45; Northwestern Univ., H.S. Speech Inst., 1944. Studied acting at Actors' studio, N.Y.C. (member, 1947–to date); singing with Henry Jacobi, N.Y.C., 1956–to date; mime with Etienne de Croux, N.Y.C., 1958–59; musical comedy technique with David Craig, 1962–63; dance with Mimi and Patricia Kellerman, 1962–63. Married May 8, 1948, to Daniel P. O'Connor, television producer; four sons, one daughter. Member of AEA; AFTRA; SAG; C.O.R.E.; P.T.A.; Iona Prep. Sch. Mother's Club. Address: 82 Elk Ave., New Rochelle, NY tel. (914) NE 6-1820.

Pre-Theatre. NBC guidette, Summer 1945.

Theatre. Miss Peterson first appeared on stage with the Omaha Community Playhouse; and first appeared professionally as Corliss Archer in a USO production of *Kiss and Tell* (PTO, 1945–46); subsequently played at the Berkshire Playhouse (Stockbridge, Mass., Summer 1946).

She was understudy to Patricia Kirkland as Ruth and assistant stage manager in *Years Ago* (Mansfield, N.Y.C., Dec. 3, 1946); played Orphie in *Bathsheba* (Ethel Barrymore Th., Mar. 26, 1947); played at the Berkshire Playhouse (Stockbridge, Mass., Summer 1947); appeared as Jenny Nelson in *Harvest of Years* (Hudson, N.Y.C., Jan. 12, 1948); Ella in *Sundown Beach* (Belasco, Sept. 7, 1948); Selma Keeney in *The Young and Fair* (Fulton, Nov. 22, 1948); Maude Riordan in *The Grass Harp* (Martin Beck Th., Mar. 27, 1952); Kitty Duval in *The Time of Your Life* (NY City Ctr., Jan. 19, 1955); Binnie Brookman in *Girls of Summer* (Longacre, Nov. 19, 1956); and succeeded (Apr. 1958) Frances Hyland as Laura James in *Look Homeward, Angel* (Ethel Barrymore Th., Nov. 28, 1957).

She played Sally Follett in *All the Way Home* (Belasco, Nov. 30, 1960) and succeeded (Apr. 1961) Colleen Dewhurst as Mary Follett; succeeded (Aug. 1962) Barbara Baxley in *Brecht on Brecht* (Th. de Lys, Jan. 3, 1962); played Edna in *The Rapists* (Washington, D.C., Th. Club, Washington, D.C., Nov. 8, 1972); was in *Detective Story* (Loretto-Hilton Rep. Ctr., St. Louis, Mo., Oct. 19, 1973); in *Thunder in the Index* on the program *American Night Cry* (Actors Studio, N.Y.C., Mar. 7, 1974); in *Mrs. Minter* on the program *People of the Shadows* (Actors Studio, Apr. 18, 1974); and played Mary Mercer in *Leaving Home* (Th. of the Riverside Church, Nov. 1974).

Films. Miss Peterson appeared in *Answer for Ann* (Caravel, 1948); *Panic in the Streets* (20th-Fox, 1950); *Take Care of My Little Girl* (20th-Fox, 1951); *The Phoenix City Story* (Allied, 1955); and *Black, Like Me* (Hilltop, 1964).

Television and Radio. Miss Peterson first performed on radio on WOW (Omaha, Neb. 1941); subsequently on Road of Life (CBS); My True Story (ABC); Grand Central Station (CBS); the Romance of Helen Trent (CBS); Henry Aldrich (NBC).

On television, she appeared on *I, Bonino* (NBC, 1953); Love of Life (CBS, 1954); Young Dr. Malone (NBC, 1959–61); Search for Tomorrow (CBS, 1962–to date); Philco Television Playhouse (NBC); Actors Studio Playhouse (ABC); Westinghouse Th. (CBS); Kraft Television Th. (NBC); CBS Workshop; US Steel Hour (CBS); Armstrong Circle Th. (CBS); Pulitzer Prize Playhouse (ABC); Studio One (CBS); the Ed Sullivan Show (CBS); The Defenders (CBS); The Nurses (CBS); Route 66 (CBS); Robert Montgomery Presents (NBC); Suspense (CBS); Look Up and Live (CBS); Lamp Unto My Feet (CBS); Danger (CBS); The Web (CBS); Inner Sanctum (CBS); and My True Story (NBC).

Awards. Miss Peterson received the Dorothy Maguire Award (1942) for best actress of the year from the Omaha (Neb.) Community Playhouse.

Recreation. Reading, playing the piano, swimming, driving.

PETERSON, LOUIS. Playwright, actor. b. Louis Stamford Peterson, Jr., June 17, 1922, to Louis Stamford Sr., and Ruth (Conover) Peterson. Father, banker. Grad. Bulkeley H.S., Hartford, Conn., 1940; Morehouse Coll., B.A. 1944; attended Yale Univ. Sch. of Drama, 1944–45; New York Univ., M.A. 1947; studied with Sanford Meisner at the Neighborhood Playhouse Sch. of the Th., N.Y.C., 1948–49; Clifford Odets, 1950–51, and Lee Strasberg, 1950–52, Actors' Studio. Married July 21, 1952, to Margaret Mary Feury (marr. dis. 1961). Member of Omega Psi Phi (pres., 1943–44); Dramatists Guild; WGA, East; AEA. Address: (home) 138 Standish St., Hartford, CT 06114, tel. (203) 246-2100; (bus.) 194 Third Ave., New York, NY 10003, tel. (212) OR 7-3321.

Theatre. Mr. Peterson made his first stage appearance in N.Y.C., playing Emanuel Price in *Our Lan'* (Royale Th., Sept. 27, 1947); played Honey Camden Brown in the national tour of *Member of the Wedding* (opened Cass, Detroit, Mich., Sept. 3, 1951; closed Shubert, New Haven, Conn., May 3, 1952).

He wrote *Take a Giant Step* (Lyceum, N.Y.C., Sept. 24, 1953; revived Jan Hus House, Sept. 25, 1956); *Entertain a Ghost* (Actors' Playhouse, Apr. 9, 1962).

Films. Mr. Peterson wrote the screenplays for *The Tempest* (Cinecitta, 1957); and *Take a Giant Step* (UA, 1959).

Television. Mr. Peterson has written *Padlocks* (Danger, CBS, Nov. 1954); *Class of '58* (Goodyear, NBC, Dec. 1954); *Joey* (Goodyear, NBC, Mar. 1956); the *Emily Rossiter Story* (Wagon Train, NBC, Sept. 1957); and *Hit and Run* (Dr. Kildare, NBC, Dec. 1961).

Awards. Mr. Peterson received the Benjamin Brawley Award for Excellence in English (1944). He was nominated for a NATAS (Emmy) Award (1956) for his play *Joey.*.

PETINA, IRRA. Singer, actress. b. Irra Stephany Petina, Apr. 18, 1914, Petrograd, Russia, to Stephan I. and Alexandra A. Petina. Grad. Oksakovsky Sch., Harbin, China (Gold Medal) 1930; Curtis Inst. of Music, Philadelphia, Pa., B.Mus. 1935. Studied singing with Harriet van Emden, Philadelphia, five years; and with Elena Gerhard, London; coached in N.Y.C. with Laslo Halasz, Silven Levin, Eliza Fiedler, Edwin MacArthur, Boris Goldowsky, Erich Leinsdorf, and Wilfred Pelletier. Married Sept. 3, 1944, to Frank R. Bussey, physician; one son. Member of AGMA; AFTRA; AEA; Friends of New York Philharmonic; Woman's Auxiliary, Suffolk County Medical Society; Friends of City Center; Amer. Theatre Wing; Metropolitan Opera Guild; Music Lover's Club of Long Island; Sigma Alpha Iota (hon. mbr.). Address: 130 Wagstaff Lane, West Islip, NY 11795, tel. (516) JU 7-8505.

Theatre. Miss Petina made her debut with the Metropolitan Opera Co. as Schweitleite in *Die Walküre* (Dec. 29, 1933), where she remained until 1944, appearing in the title roles in *Carmen* (1943) and *Mignon* (Mar. 31, 1944); also appeared with the Teatro Colon (Buenos Aires, Argentina) as Octavian in *Der Rosenkavalier,* Nicklausse in *The Tales of Hoffman,* Suzuki in *Madame Butterfly* and Maddelena in *Rigoletta* (1936).

She made her debut with the New York City Opera Co. in the title role of *Carmen* (NY City Ctr., Apr. 10, 1947); subsequently appeared with the Metropolitan Opera as Marfa in *Khovantchina,* Octavian in *Der Rosenkavalier,* Berta in *The Barber of Seville,* and Feodor and Marina in *Boris Goudounov* (1947–50); and with the San Francisco (Calif.) Opera, Cincinnati (Ohio) Opera, Philadelphia (Pa.) La Scala Opera, and Teatro alla Scala, Milan, Italy; made concert tours in the US and Europe; and played Masha in *The Chocolate Soldier* (1941), Frieda in *Music in the Air* (1942), and Czipra in *The Gypsy Baron* (1943), with the Los Angeles Civic Light Opera (Philharmonic Hall, Los Angeles; Curran Th., San Francisco; Music Circus, Sacramento, Calif.).

She made her Bway debut as the Countess Louisa Giovanni in *Song of Norway* (Imperial, Aug. 21, 1944), and played it on tour (1946–47); subsequently played Teresa in *Magdalena* (Ziegfeld, N.Y.C., Sept. 20, 1948); in stock, Sonia in *The Merry Widow* (Melody Fair, Danbury, Conn., Summer 1951); the Countess in *Song of Norway* (Music Fair, Toronto, Canada, 1951); Rosalinda in a summer-theatre tour of *Die Fledermaus* (Summer 1951); and appeared as soloist in the *Night in Vienna* concert (Lewisohn Stadium, N.Y.C., 1951); Sonia in *The Merry Widow* (Tulsa Opera House, Okla., 1951); the title role in a concert version of *Carmen* (Minneapolis Symphony Orchestra, Minn., 1952); Sonia in *The Merry Widow* and the Countess Olga Baranskaja in *The Great Waltz* (Music Fair, Toronto, Summer 1952); appeared as a soloist in a Cole Porter concert (Hollywood Bowl, Calif., 1952); Sonia in *The Merry Widow* (Washington Light Opera, D.C., 1953); Bellabruna in *Blossom Time* (St. Louis Municipal Opera, Mo., Summer 1953); the Countess in *Song of Norway* and Frieda in *Music in the Air* (Music Fair, Toronto, Summer 1953); the Countess in *Song of Norway* (St. Louis Municipal Opera, Mo., Summer 1954); and the Countess in *The Great Waltz* (Arena Garden, Toronto, Summer 1954).

She was soloist in a concert tour of *The Immortal Music of Romberg* (1954); played Lucy Vernay in *Hit the Trail* (Mark Hellinger Th., N.Y.C., Dec. 2, 1954); the Countess in *The Great Waltz* and Katisha in *The Mikado* (Music Circus, Sacramento, Calif., Summer 1955); the Countess in *Song of Norway* (Civic Light Opera, Pittsburgh, Pa., Summer 1955); Frieda in *Music in the Air* and Sonia in *The Merry Widow* (Music Circus, Sacramento, Calif., Summer 1956); Madame de la Fleur in *The Red Mill* (Greek Th., Hollywood, Calif., Summer 1956); the Old Lady and Mme. Sofronia in *Candide* (Martin Beck Th., N.Y.C., Dec. 1, 1956); the Countess in *Song of Norway* (Univ. of Utah, Salt Lake City, Utah; Musicarnival, Cleveland, Ohio; Musicarnival, Palm Beach, Fla.; 1957) the Countess in *The Great Waltz* (Musicarnival, Cleveland, Summer 1959); and the Countess in *Song of Norway* (Cape Cod Melody Top, Hyannis, Mass., Summer 1959; Marine Th., Jones Beach, N.Y., Summer 1959; North Shore Music Th., Beverly, Mass., Summer 1960; Charlotte Music Th., N.C., Summer 1961; Musicarnival, W. Palm Beach, Fla., 1964); Katerina in *Anya* (Ziegfield Th., 1965); the Grand Duchess in *The Student Prince* (Civic Light Opera, Los Angeles and San Francisco, Summer 1966); the Old Lady in *Candide* in concert form (Grand Park Symphony, Chicago, Summers 1967; 1968; New York Philharmonic, 1968); Orlovsky in *Die Fledermaus* (Seattle Opera, Wash., Summer 1969); and Miss Todd in Menotti's opera *The Old Maid and the Thief* with the Boris Goldovsky Opera Theater (Staten Island and West Point, N.Y., 1974).

Other Activities. Miss Petina enjoys teaching young people with vocal and dramatic potential.

Awards. Miss Petina was nominated for the Antoinette Perry (Tony) Award for her performances as the Countess in *Song of Norway* (1945), and as Mme. Sofronia in *Candide* (1957).

Recreation. Painting, boating, horseback riding, tennis.

PETRIE, DANIEL M. Director, actor. b. Glace Bay, Nova Scotia, Canada, to William M. and Mary Ann (Campbell) Petrie. Father, soft drink manufacturer. Grad. St. Francis Xavier Univ., Antigonish, Nova Scotia, B.A. 1942; Columbia Univ., M.A. 1945; attended Northwestern Univ., 1947–48. Married Oct. 27, 1946, to Dorothea Grundy; two sons, two daughters. Served Royal Canadian Army, Artillery, 1942–43; rank, Lt. Member of DGA, SSD&C, NATAS. Address: (home) 13201 Haney Place, Los Angeles, CA 90049, tel. (213) 451-9157; (bus.) Jack Gilardi, International Creative Management, 9255 Sunset Blvd., Los Angeles, CA 90069, tel. (213) 273-8811.

Pre-Theatre. Actor, university professor.

Theatre. Mr. Petrie made his Bway debut as Charlie in *Kiss Them For Me* (Belasco Mar. 20, 1945); subsequently was stage manager for an ELT production of *The Affairs of Anatol* (1945); understudied the part of Nels and later played it in a national touring production of *I Remember Mama* (1946–47).

He directed *The Cherry Orchard* (Sombrero Playhouse, Phoenix, Ariz., Jan. 25, 1959; Royal Poinciana Playhouse, Palm Beach, Fla., Feb. 9, 1959); *A Shadow of My Enemy* (ANTA, N.Y.C., Dec. 11, 1957); *Who'll Save the Plowboy* (Phoenix, Jan. 9, 1962); *Morning Sun* (Phoenix, Oct. 6, 1963); the pre-Bway tryout of *Conversations in the Dark* (opened Walnut St. Th., Philadelphia, Pa., Dec. 30, 1963; closed there Jan. 11, 1964); and (Walnut St. Th., Philadelphia, 1972).

Films. Mr. Petrie directed *The Bramble Bush* (WB, 1960); *A Raisin in the Sun* (Col., 1961); *The Main Attraction* (MGM, 1962); *Stolen Hours* (UA, 1962); *The Idol* (Par., 1965); *The Spy With a Cold Nose* (Par., 1966); *The Neptune Factor* (20th-Fox, 1972); *Buster and Billie* (Col., 1973); and *Lifeguard* (Par., 1974).

Television. Mr. Petrie has directed *Studs Place* and *Hawkins Falls* (NBC, Chicago, Jan. 1950); the Billy Rose Show (ABC, Oct. 1950–May 1951); Somerset Maugham Th. (ABC, 1951); Treasury Men in Action (NBC, 1952); Excursion (CBS, 1953); Omnibus (CBS, 1953); Revlon Mirror Th. (CBS, 1953), Justice (NBC, 1954); Armstrong Circle Th. (NBC, 1954); Elgin Th. Hour (ABC, 1955); Alcoa Goodyear Th. (NBC, 1956); US Steel Hour (ABC, CBS, 1955–58); Dupont Show of the Month (CBS, 1958–61); East Side/West Side (CBS, 1963); *One Day in the Life of Ivan Denisovich* (Bob Hope Chrysler Show, NBC, 1963); *The Benefactor* (The Defenders, CBS, 1962); and the following television movies: *Silent Night, Lonely Night* (Univ. World Premiere, 1969); *Big Fish, Little Fish* (Hollywood TV Th., PBS, 1970); *The City,* a pilot (ABC, 1971); *A Howling in the Woods* (Univ. World Premiere, 1971); *A Stranger in Town* (ABC Movie of the Week, 1972); *Moon of the Wolf* (ABC Movie of the Week, 1972); *Hec Ramsey,* a pilot (Univ. World Premiere, 1973); *Mousey* (ABC Movie of the Week); *The Gun and the Pulpit* (ABC Movie of the Week, 1974); and *Returning Home* (ABC Movie of the Week, Apr. 29, 1975).

Awards. Mr. Petrie received the Directors Guild of America Award for his direction of the film, *A Raisin in the Sun* (1961); the Christopher Award for his direction of *The Prince and the Pauper* (Dupont Show of the Month, CBS); TV Directors Guild of America awards in 1963 for *The Benefactor,* in 1969 for *Silent Night, Lonely Night,* and in 1970 for *Hands of Love;* and the Western Heritage Award in 1972 for outstanding Western fiction television for *Hec Ramsey.* In 1973, Mr. Petrie was awarded the honorary degree of L.H.D. by St. Francis Xavier Univ., Antigonish, Nova Scotia.

PHELPS, LYON. Playwright, poet. b. Chengtu, Szechwan Province, China, to Dryden Linsley and Margaret (Hallenbeck) Phelps. Father, Ch'an (Zen) poet, scholar, religious teacher; mother, musician. Attended Canadian School, Chengtu; Phillips Acad., Andover, Mass.; Swarthmore Coll. (peace program training), 1944; grad. Harvard Coll. (Phi Beta Kappa, 1950), A.B. 1951. Professional training as apprentice, Cleveland (Ohio) Playhouse, 1944; acting with Montgomery Clift, N.Y.C. (1944–46); dance and choreography with Sylvia Dick Karas, Nora Shattuck (1954); James Waring (1968); Merce Cunningham. Member of AEA (1962); New Dramatists, N.Y.C.; American Acad. in Rome; Signet Soc., Harvard (secy., 1951); Harvard Club (Monterey, Calif.). Address: Big Sur P.O., CA 93920.

Theatre. Mr. Phelps is a founder of the Poets' Th. (Cambridge, Mass., 1950), where he served as playwright, director, and actor (1950–56), vice-president (1952), president (1953), manager in residence (1954), and a member of the board of directors (1960–62). He was on the playwriting faculty of the Herbert Berghof Studio, N.Y.C. (1961, 1962).

Winter, from his play cycle *A House in a Grain of Sand,* was presented as a dance ode by the Boston Conservatory of Music and the Jan Veen Dance Studio (May 16, 1950); his *Three Words in No Time* was acted by the Brattle Th. on the opening bill of the Poets' Th. (Christ Church, Cambridge, Mass., Feb. 26, 1951). Subsequent Poets' Th. productions of Mr. Phelps's work were *Autumn,* also from the play cycle (Apr. 23, 1951); *A Bottle of Wine* (Feb. 20, 1952); and *Speak If You Can* (May 14, 1952); the text of the last was withdrawn. The Fellowship Players, San Francisco, Cal., first performed *The Gospel Witch* (July 7, 1954), and the Poets' Th. presented it in the East (Cambridge, Mass., Feb. 14, 1955; outdoor version, Boston Arts Festival, June 9, 1955). Mr. Phelps was assistant to the producer of *Too Late the Phalarope* (Belasco Th., N.Y.C., Oct. 11, 1956); the Arts Council, Natl. Council of Churches, commissioned him to write *Midnight Jury* (Kiel Aud., St. Louis, Mo., Dec. 9, 1959); he directed a Poets' Th. revival of *Three Words in No Time,* presented in repertory with *Christopher C.,* his adaptation of Michel de Ghelderode's *Cristophe Columb* (Provincetown Playhouse on the Wharf, Provincetown, Mass., July 29, 1961); he wrote lyrics for *Do You Know the Milky Way?* (Internatl. Festival, Vancouver, B.C., Can. Aug. 15, 1961; Billy Rose Th., N.Y.C., Oct. 16, 1961); *Christopher C.* was presented in Chicago (Goodman Memorial Th., Feb. 10, 1963). Other productions and readings of Mr. Phelps's plays included *The Jungle's Edge* (text withdrawn) and *The Takeoff* by the Poets' Th. (Agassiz Th., Cambridge, Mass., Mar. 30, 1964) and *Game* (reading by Actors' Workshop, San Francisco, Cal., July 26, 1964; and, as *Crosslots,* Th. for the New City, N.Y.C., Feb. 1972). Mr. Phelps staged a reading of Sophocles' *The Eumenides* (John Steinbeck Th., Monterey, Cal., 1965); wrote *Vanozza* (reading by The Old Reliable, N.Y.C.; Judson Poets' Th., Nov. 11, 1970; Feb. 18, 1971); and coordinated and staged women's rights plays (Jane St. Th., N.Y.C., Apr. 8, 1971).

Other Activities. Mr. Phelps was one of the organizers of the Verse-Music Quartet, which gave peace readings in California (1963–65); he gave poetry readings for peace in Europe with various musicians (1964–68); was active in the Th. for the New City peace program at the Westbeth Community, N.Y.C. (1971, 1972); and participated in the peace vigils (1963, 1964, 1965, 1973).

Published Works. Mr. Phelps's poetry has been published in such periodicals as *Atlantic, The Dodo, Epocha, The Friends Journal, The New Yorker, Poetry,* and *The Phoenix.*

Awards. Mr. Phelps held the poet-resident scholarship at the Centre Culturel de France, Royauemont, Chantilly, France (1948); was class poet at Harvard (1951); and Phi Beta Kappa poet, Alpha Chapter (1961). *The Gospel Witch* was named by the NY *Times* as one of the "hundred best books of 1955"; Mr. Phelps received a grant for the managership of the Poets' Th. (1954); he was dramatist-in-residence, American Academy in Rome (1965) and poet-in-residence, Westbeth Artists' Community, N.Y.C. (1970, 1971) under a NY State Council of the Arts grant.

Recreation. Classical archaeology; music.

PHILBRICK, NORMAN. Educator. b. Norman Douglas Philbrick, Apr. 30, 1913, Fort Wayne, Ind., to George Andrew and Stella (Mossman) Philbrick. Grad. Pomona Coll., B.A. 1935; attended Yale Univ., 1935–36; Pasadena Community Playhouse, 1936–37; grad. Stanford Univ., M.A. 1942; Cornell Univ., Ph.D. 1949. Married Sept. 10, 1941, to Geraldine Womack, teacher; one son, three daughters. Member of NTC; ASTR; BSTR; IFTR; Intl. Inst. of Arts and Letters; AETA (exec. secy., treas., 1949–52; 2nd vice-pres., 1959; 1st vice-pres., 1960; pres., 1961); Bohemian Club; Menlo Country Club; Univ. Club of Palo Alto; Palo Alto Club; The Players; Grolier Club; Roxburghe Club; Book Club of Calif. Address: 25855 Westwind Way, Los Altos Hills, CA 94022, tel. (415) 948-8241.

From 1943 to 1968, Mr. Philbrick was a member of the faculty of Stanford Univ. From 1954–1962, he was head of the Dept. of Speech and Drama. Previously, he held academic positions at Pasadena Community Playhouse (1937–38), Scripps Coll. (1937–39), and Pomona Coll. (1937–41).

In 1962, he directed and taught at the Univ. of New South Wales. He directed a professional Australian company in *Saint Joan* for the second Adelaide Festival of Arts in South Australia (Mar. 1962), which later toured Australia; he directed *The Skin of Our Teeth* for the Univ. of New South Wales (May 1962).

He is founder and director of the Philbrick Library, specializing in books and memorabilia of the eighteenth century English and American theatre.

Published Works. Mr. Philbrick wrote "Act and Scene Division in the First Edition of Shakespeare" in *Theatre Annual* (Th. Library Assn, N.Y.C., 1944); the introduction to *History of the American Theatre* by George O. Seilhamer (Benjamin Blom, Inc., N.Y.C., 1968); "Of Books and the Theatre," in *Garrick's London* (Stanford Univ. Libraries, Stanford, Calif., Oct. 1969); "The Theatrical Scholar," in *Ifan Kyrle Fletcher, A Memorial Tribute* (The Society for Theatre Research, London, Eng., 1970); "The Spy as Hero: An Examination of *Andre* by William Dunlap," in *Studies in Theatre and Drama; Essays in Honor of Hubert C. Heffner* (Mouton, 1972); and "Blanche Bates," in *Dictionary of American Biography* (Charles Scribner's Sons, N.Y.C., 1973). He was an editor and annotator for *Trumpets Sounding: Propaganda Plays of the American Revolution* (Benjamin Blom, Inc., N.Y.C., 1972).

Awards. Mr. Philbrick received a Fulbright Scholarship (1962).

PHILIPS, MARIE L. Community and professional theatre actress, director, producer, educational theatre teacher and director, administrator, adjudicator, publicist. b. Marie Lucia Philips, Aug. 12, 1925, Waltham, Mass., to Thomas and Adeline Philips. Father, retired lumber company dispatcher. Grad. St. Mary's H.S., Waltham, Mass., 1942; attended Boston Univ. Sch. of Public Relations & Communication (1957–58). Studied art at Notre Dame Convent, Waltham (1938–1941) and at Harvard Univ. (1942–1943); voice with Clara Shear, Boston (1958–59); courses on publicity & promotion at Univ. of Wisconsin, Madison, and Publicity Club of Boston; and on supervisory management at Northeastern Univ., Boston. Member of ATA (chairman of Region 1, 1963–73 and chairman of New England Region for American College Theatre Festival of ATA (1968–73)); New England Theatre Conference (exec. secy., 1957–58; exec. secy.-treas., 1958–to date; editor of NETC *News,* 1972–to date); USITT (secy.-treas. of New England section, 1969–to date); NCTC; Arlington (Mass.) Friends of the Drama (1958–to date); Massachusetts Inst. of Tech. Community Players (1958–to date); Hovey Players (1946–58); Tufts Community Players (1953–65); Industrial Photographers of New England; Little Theatre League of Mass. (advisory board, program chairman, *Bulletin* editor, public relations chairman, 1951–59); Waltham (Mass.) Summer Theatre (advisory board, 1971); Weston (Mass.) Drama Workshop Summer Theatre (bd. of dir., 1970–73); Theatre Ensemble of Boston (1967–69); Metropolitan Cultural Alliance of Boston; Eugene O'Neill Memorial Foundation, Waterford, Conn.; Waltham Choral Group (1953); Waltham Musical Club (1955–57); St. Mary's Dramatic Club (1942–47). Address: (home) 50 Exchange St., Waltham, MA 02154, tel. (617) 893-3120; (bus.) M.I.T. Lincoln Laboratory, 244 Wood St., Lexington, MA 02173, tel. (617) 862-5500.

Theatre. Miss Philips has been active in community, professional, and educational theatre.

She acted and directed for the Hovey Players (Waltham, Mass.), was corresponding secretary (1948–50), publicity chairman (1950–56), recording secretary (1955–56), and president and business manager (1956–58); and she wrote and directed *Gay Nineties Revue*, performed before civic and church groups to raise funds for an annual drama scholarship presented by the Hovey Players (1951).

She acted for the St. Kevin Players (Dorchester, Mass.) in an annual Passion Play (1958–59) and was publicity and promotion director (1958–63); acted and directed for the M.I.T. Community Players (Cambridge, Mass.) and was program chairman (1958–59), 1960–61, and 1970–71), president (1961–63 and 1964–65), publicity director (1962–63 and 1966–67), and corres. secy. (1967–68); acted and directed for the Arlington (Mass.) Friends of the Drama and was program director (1960–61); acted and directed for the Tufts Community Players (Medford, Mass., 1958–65).

She acted and sang in minstrel shows and musicals produced by St. Mary's Dramatic Club (Waltham, Mass.) (1942–47), the Waltham Choral Group (1953), and the Waltham Musical Club (1955–57). She played in stock productions at the Boothbay (Me.) Playhouse (Summer 1953); was resident manager at the Deertrees Th. (Harrison, Me., Summer 1954), and appeared in its productions (Summers 1954, 1956, 1959).

She formed a theatre group, the Make-Believers (1958–to date), which tours the Boston area under her direction, and appeared in its productions of *How He Lied to Her Husband, The Menu, Box and Cox, A Marriage Proposal, No Exit, The Lesson, A Slight Ache*, and *Gallows Humor.*

She was a founding member of The Theatre Ensemble (Boston), a coffee house and touring company, and was actress, producer, and publicity chairman (1967–69). She directed for the Weston (Mass.) Drama Workshop Summer Theatre (1970), and was publicity and promotion director for the Waltham (Mass.) Summer Theatre (1972–73).

Miss Philips has been an adjudicator for drama festivals in New England. She has also judged play scripts for the Unitarian-Universalist Assn. Chancel Drama Competition and NETC's John Gassner Memorial Playwriting Award.

She has been a panelist or speaker on various subjects for New England theatre groups and conferences, and she has conducted acting workshops for drama groups.

Television. Miss Philips appeared on WGBH-TV (Cambridge, Mass.), in the *Inevitable Monday* segment of *Epitaph for Jim Crow* (1962); on *The Precinct* segment of the series, *Practical Politics;* and on *What's Happening, Mr. Silver,* (1968). She produced, wrote, and acted in TV pilot films in partnership with TD Associates, Harrison, Me. (1954–55), shown over WGAN-TV (Portland, Me.).

Awards. Miss Philips received a Special Award from the New England Th. Conference for her services to NETC (1962); Amoco Oil Company gold medal Award of Excellence for 5-year service as New England chairman of American College Theatre Festival (1974).

Recreation. Bowling, knitting, choral singing, reading, writing, skiing, collecting antiques, sight-seeing, and travel.

PHILLIPS, MARGARET. Actress. b. July 6, 1923, Cwmgwrach, South Wales. Studied acting with Cecil Clovelly. Emigrated to US, 1939. Member of AEA; AFTRA; SAG.

Theatre. Miss Phillips first performed at the Woodstock (N.Y.) Summer Th. (1941, 1942); and appeared in productions at the Barter Th. (Abingdon, Va., 1942).

She made her N.Y.C. debut as Sue in *Proof Through the Night* (Morosco, Dec. 25, 1942), in which she subsequently toured (when the play was entitled *Cry Havoc*); followed by Agnes Willing in *The Late George Apley* (Lyceum, Nov. 23, 1944); Birdie Bagtry in *Another Part of the Forest* (Fulton, Nov. 20, 1946); Alma Winemiller in *Summer and Smoke* (Music Box, Oct. 6, 1948); the title role (Catherine Sloper) in *The Heiress* (NY City Ctr., Feb. 8, 1950); and succeeded (June 1950) Irene Worth as Celia Coplestone in *The Cocktail Party* (Henry Miller's Th., Jan. 1, 1950). She played Miranda Bolton in *Second Threshold* (Morosco, Jan. 2, 1951); in stock, Jeannie in *A Case of Scotch* (Bahama Playhouse, Nassau, B.W.I., Feb. 18, 1952); appeared in *Venus Observed* (Ann Arbor, Mich., June 9, 1952); played Portia in *The Merchant of Venice* (NY City Ctr., Mar. 4, 1953); succeeded (Dec. 7, 1953) Gusti Huber as Margot Wendice in *Dial "M" for Murder* (Plymouth, Oct. 29, 1952), with which she toured (opened Walnut St. Th., Philadelphia, Mar. 1, 1954; closed Biltmore, Los Angeles, May 29, 1954); played Jane Danbury in *Fallen Angels* (Playhouse, Jan. 17, 1956); Jennet Jourdemayne in *The Lady's Not for Burning* (Carnegie Hall Playhouse, Feb. 21, 1957); and the Queen in *Under the Sycamore Tree* (Cricket Th., Mar. 7, 1960).

With the Amer. Shakespeare Festival (Stratford, Conn.), she played Olivia in *Twelfth Night* (June 1960), toured as Titania in *A Midsummer Night's Dream* (opened Colonial, Boston, Sept. 26, 1960; closed National, Washington, D.C., Feb. 25, 1961); and succeeded (Aug. 1961) Jessica Tandy as Lady Macbeth in *Macbeth;* appeared as Marion Dangerfield in *The Ginger Man* (Orpheum, N.Y.C., Nov. 21, 1963); at the Amer. Shakespeare Fest., played Gertrude in *Hamlet* (June 16, 1964) and Margaret in *Richard III* (June 17, 1964); and played Judith Bliss in *Hay Fever* (Bucks County Playhouse, New Hope, Pa., June 14, 1965).

She played Jane Danbury in a stock production of *Fallen Angels* (Paper Mill Playhouse, Millburn, N.J., Aug. 15, 1966); was standby for Geraldine Page as Sophie, in *White Lies* (Ethel Barrymore Th., N.Y.C., Feb. 12, 1967), presented on a double-bill with *Black Comedy;* toured as Queen Eleanor in *The Lion in Winter* (opened Cochran Aud., Johnstown, Pa., Jan. 17, 1968; closed May 5, 1968); played Elvira in *Blithe Spirit* (Studio Arena Th., Buffalo, N.Y., Dec. 5, 1968); with the Minnesota Th. Co., played Calpurnia in *Julius Caesar* (Tyrone Guthrie Th., Minneapolis, June 26, 1969), Christine Mannon in *Mourning Becomes Electra* (Tyrone Guthrie Th., Aug. 19, 1969), and appeared in *Ardele* (Crawford Livingston Th., St. Paul, Apr. 12, 1970); on a double bill, played Stella in *The Collection* and Sarah in *The Lover* (Center Stage, Baltimore, Md., Feb. 5, 1971); and appeared in *Getting Married* (Seattle Repertory Th., Wash., Dec. 29, 1971).

Miss Phillips played Gladys Wagner in the pre-Bway tryout of *Keep Off the Grass* (opened Maurice Mechanic Th., Baltimore, Md., Apr. 3, 1972; closed Hanna Th., Cleveland, Ohio, Apr. 22, 1972); Mrs. Manningham in *Angel Street* (Arlington Park, Ill., Th., 1972); and Birdie Bagtry in *The Little Foxes* (Indiana Rep. Th., Indianapolis, Nov. 21, 1974; Syracuse Stage, Syracuse, N.Y., Mar. 14, 1975).

Films. Miss Phillips made her debut in *A Life of Her Own* (MGM, 1950) and appeared in *The Nun's Story* (WB, 1959).

Television. She has appeared on Philco Playhouse (NBC, Jan. 22, 1950); Starlight Th. (CBS); Studio One (CBS); Masterpiece Th. (NBC) in *Hedda Gabler* (July 23, 1950) and *The Importance of Being Earnest* (Aug. 20, 1950); as Juliet in scenes from *Romeo and Juliet* (Kate Smith Hour, NBC, Nov. 6, 1950); on Kraft Th. (NBC); Goodyear Playhouse (NBC); Robert Montgomery Presents (NBC); Tales of Tomorrow (ABC); as Regan in *King Lear* (Omnibus, CBS, Oct. 18, 1953); Danger (CBS); US Steel Hour (ABC); Appointment with Adventure (CBS); Climax (CBS); Five Fingers (NBC); Alcoa Premiere (ABC); Rawhide (CBS); in *The Picture of Dorian Gray* (CBS, Dec. 6, 1961); on One Step Beyond (ABC); The Third Man; Checkmate (CBS); The Investigators (NBC); Lamp Unto My Feet (CBS); Armstrong Circle Th. (CBS); and Route 66 (CBS).

Awards. Miss Phillips won a *Theatre World* Award (1945) for *The Late George Apley,* and a Clarence Derwent Award (1946) for *Another Part of the Forest.*

PHILLIPS, WENDELL K. Actor, director, playwright, designer. b. Wendell Keith Phillips, Nov. 27, 1907, Blandinsville, Ill., to Donald A. and Ethel Grace Phillips. Father, realtor. Attended Senn H.S., Chicago, Ill., 1923–24; Elgin Acad., Ill., 1924–28; Goodman Sch. of Th., Chicago, 1930–32. Studied acting with Lee Strasberg, N.Y.C., 1937–41; Michael Chekov, N.Y.C., 1941. Married 1933 to Odielein Pearce (marr. dis. 1949; dec. 1961); two sons; married 1950 to Jean Shelton; two sons; one daughter. Relative in theatre: son, Wendell K. Phillips, Jr., actor. Member of AEA; SAG; AFTRA; AGVA.

Pre-Theatre. Carpenter, plumber, mason, plasterer, electrician, blacksmith, sheet metal worker.

Theatre. Mr. Phillips first performed as Joe Hennig in a school production of *The Fool* (Elgin Acad., Dec. 1926); made his professional debut as a walk-on in *Incubator* (Boulevard Jackson Heights, N.Y., 1932); and appeared in the N.Y.C. production (Avon, Nov. 1, 1932). He played Jim, the Fifth Passerby, and the Fourth Producer in *Fantasia* (Provincetown Playhouse, Jan. 3, 1933); designed sets and lighting for three one-act plays and *Black Diamond* (Provincetown Playhouse, Feb. 24, 1933); and was set designer for three one-act plays, and wrote *Illusion* (Playmiller's Th., Mar. 1933), where he appeared as one of the Lung Twins in *The Chalk Circle* (Aug. 22, 1933).

He played a Sailor in *Sailors of Catarro* (Civic Rep. Th., Dec. 10, 1934); the Boy in *Till the Day I Die* and a Cab Driver in *Waiting for Lefty,* a double bill (Longacre, Mar. 26, 1935); Ben Schermer in *Mother Sings* (58 St. Th., Nov. 12, 1935); a Party Guest in *The Case of Clyde Griffiths* (Ethel Barrymore Th., Mar. 13, 1936); Doremus Jessup in a Federal Th. (WPA) Project's production of *It Can't Happen Here* (Majestic, Brooklyn, Oct. 17, 1936); Adolph in *Till the Day I Die* and Phillips, the Actor, in *Waiting for Lefty* (N.Y.C. Subway Circuit, Dec. 1, 1936); Sam Feinschrieber in *Awake and Sing* (Subway Circuit, Feb. 1937); and Morgan Grange in *Many Mansions* (Biltmore, Oct. 27, 1937). He directed a Current Th. production of *Fingers* (Artef, Mar. 1938); played Herndon in *Abe Lincoln in Illinois* (Plymouth, Oct. 15, 1938); and a Soldier from New York in *The Fifth Column* (Alvin, Mar. 6, 1940).

At the Hilltop Playhouse, Baltimore, Md., Mr. Phillips directed nine plays (June 1941) and played Richard Kurt in *Biography* (July 14, 1941). He appeared as Grandpa Crane in *Comes the Revelation* (Al Jolson's Th., N.Y.C., May 26, 1942) and the Crook in *Yours, A. Lincoln* (Shubert, July 9, 1942); in stock, repeated his role as William Herndon in *Abe Lincoln in Illinois* (Providence, R.I., July 1942); played the Texan in *Stage Door* at the same th. (Aug. 1942); Primus in *R.U.R.* (Ethel Barrymore Th., N.Y.C., Dec. 3, 1942); directed a touring production of *It's Only the Beginning* (June 1943); appeared as Alan Squire in *The Petrified Forest* (New Amsterdam Roof, N.Y.C., Nov. 1, 1943); Captain Dunlap in the drama *South Pacific* (Cort, Dec. 29, 1943); directed *War President* (Shubert, Apr. 24, 1944); staged seven plays for the Hunterdon Hills Playhouse (June 1945); directed ELT productions of *Those Endearing Young Charms* (Lenox Hill Playhouse, N.Y.C., Dec. 1945) and *Rosmersholm* (Lenox Hill Playhouse, Mar. 1946); played Frank in the pre-Bway tour of *Brigadoon* (1946); and directed a summer theatre production of *Doctors Are People* (Falmouth, Mass., July 1946).

He played Thomas Cromwell in *Anne of the Thousand Days* (Shubert, N.Y.C., Dec. 8, 1948), in which he later toured; Jeeter Lester in *Tobacco Road* (Smithtown, N.Y., July 1949); directed (June 1950) at Norwich, Conn.; directed *Detective Story* (Montreal, Canada, Aug. 1950); played the Doctor in *The Small Hours* (National, N.Y.C., Feb. 15, 1951); repeated his role in *Tobacco Road* (Keene, N.H., June 1951); at Putnam Co. (N.Y.) Playhouse, directed *Too Much Amphitryon* (July 1951), and played Doc in *Come Back, Little Sheba* (Aug. 1951); appeared in London, Ontario, Canada, as Jeeter Lester in *Tobacco Road* (Grande, Aug. 1951); directed the ELT production of *Hotel Universe* (Lenox Hill Playhouse, N.Y.C., Sept. 1951) and played Spence Douthit in an October production of *Tragic Ground* (Memphis, Tenn., 1952). He appeared as Alfred Metcalfe in *The Solid Gold Cadillac* (Belasco, N.Y.C., Nov. 5, 1953); Edward Worthmore in *The Love Nest* (Writers' Stage Th., Jan. 25, 1963); one of the Accused in *The Investigation* (Ambassador, Oct. 4, 1966); Francis Nurse in a revival of *The Crucible* (Vivian Beaumont Th., Apr. 27, 1972); and directed *L'Été* (Cherry Lane Th., Apr. 9, 1973).

Films. Mr. Phillips appeared as Johnny Scalza in *The Glass Case* (Par., 1939); directed and wrote USN training films (1943); appeared in *The Burglar* (Eagle-Lion, 1946); *Kiss of Death* (20th-Fox, 1947); *Close-Up* (Eagle-Lion, 1948); and *The Fool Killer* (Landau, 1964).

Television. Since his debut on *The Copperhead* (NBC, Oct. 1941), he has appeared on The Secret Storm (CBS, 1957–58); and during 1961–63), on Naked City (ABC), Westinghouse Th. of the Air (CBS), The Defenders (CBS), and East Side/West Side (CBS).

Other Activities. He was founder, with Lazlo Bird, and directed the Actors Repertory Th. Workshop (N.Y.C., 1955–61).

Recreation. Tennis, swimming, poetry, carpentry, clay modeling.

PIACENTINI, VINCENT. Theatre consultant, stage director, set and lighting designer. b. June 1, 1922, St. Louis, Mo., to Vincent and Josephine (Davis) Piacentini. Father, architect. Grad. Washington Univ., St. Louis, B.F.A. (design), 1945. Member of USITT (bd. of dir., 1969–71); SSD&C; United Scenic Artists; Illuminating Engineering Soc. Address: Bolt, Beranek and Newman, Inc., 235 Wyman St., Waltham, MA 02154, tel. (617) 890-8440.

Mr. Piacentini became supervisory consultant with Bolt, Beranek and Newman, Inc., in 1967. He is in addition principal consultant and partner, Piacentini/Auerbach Associates, N.Y.C. and San Francisco, and The Production Group, N.Y.C. He has been consultant for many projects throughout the US and abroad, including comprehensive theatre planning and equipment consultation, orchestra shell design, audiovisual facilities planning, and special lighting projects. He was a theatre consultant and designer, Morris Th., Morristown, N.J. (1964); Theatre Atlanta (Ga.) (1965–66); and theatre consultant, Cultural Center of the Philippines, Manila (1967–69); Norfolk (Va.) Convention and Cultural Center (1967–70); Sacramento (Calif.) Civic Ctr. (during the design phase, 1968–69); Hamilton Place, Hamilton, Ontario, Canada (1968–73); and Fair Park Music Hall renovation, Dallas, Tex. (1969–72). He has also been special theatre consultant, Teatro National de Santo Domingo (1970–to date); designer and theatre consultant, Corfu (Greece) Festival of the Arts (1972–73); theatre consultant for Centro de Bellas Artes Puerto Rico (1970–to date); special theatre consultant, Victorian Arts Centre, Melbourne, Australia (1974–to date); and designer of orchestra shells for Saskatoon Centennial Auditorium, Canada (1968–to date); Saskatchewan Centennial Auditorium (1969–70); Le Grand Theatre de Quebec, Canada (1969–70); Fair Park Music Hall, Dallas, Tex. (1971); Onondaga County (NY) Civic Ctr. (1972–73); Northwestern Univ. Concert Hall (1973–74); and Tulsa (Okla.) Performing Arts Ctr. (1973–to date).

Films. Mr. Piacentini was art director and assistant film director of *Diamonds for Dixie* (Pathe, 1960).

Other Activities. Mr. Piacentini was visiting designer and lecturer, Maryville Coll., St. Louis, Mo. (1949–50) and Penn. State Univ. (1966–67). He has lectured extensively throughout his career at professional conventions and symposia.

Published Works. Mr. Piacentini was associate editor, *Players' Magazine* (1950–52) and community theatre editor (1952–55, 1958–61). Among papers he has published are *Ft. Wayne Civic Theatre, Spaces and Facilities* (1965); with T. DeGaetani, *Space and Facilities Study, Hamilton—Auditorium and Convention Trade Center* (1969); with T. DeGaetani, *Nashville and the Arts* (1969); and *Sites and Feasibility, A Festival of the Arts on Corfu* (1970).

PIAZZA, BEN. Actor, writer. b. Benito Daniel Piazza, July 30, 1934, Little Rock, Ark., to Charles D. and Elfreida Piazza. Father, shoemaker. Grad. Central H.S., Little Rock, 1951; Princeton Univ., B.A. 1955. Studied at Actors' Studio, N.Y.C. (member since 1958). Member of AEA; AFTRA; SAG.

Theatre. Mr. Piazza made his N.Y.C. debut as George Willard in *Winesburg, Ohio* (Natl. Th., Feb. 5, 1958); subsequently played Alvin in *Kataki* (Ambassador, Apr. 9, 1959); Paul in *A Second String* (Eugene O'Neill Th., Apr. 13, 1960); and the Young Man in *The American Dream* (York, Jan. 24, 1961).

He toured South America with the American Repertory Co., playing Isherwood in *I Am a Camera*, Jerry in *The Zoo Story*, and Chance Wayne in *Sweet Bird of Youth* (June–Aug. 1961); in Barr and Wilder's Theatre of the Absurd, he played the Young Man in *The American Dream*, Green Eyes in *Death Watch*, Clov in *Endgame*, and Jerry in *The Zoo Story* (Cherry Lane, N.Y.C., Feb. 11, 1962).

He appeared as Leopold in *The Fun Couple* (Lyceum, Nov. 26, 1962); succeeded (Feb. 4, 1963) George Grizzard as Nick in *Who's Afraid of Virginia Woolf?* (Billy Rose Th., Oct. 13, 1962); played Jerry in *The Zoo Story* (Cherry Lane Th., June 8, 1965); Tom in *The Glass Menagerie* (Huntington Hartford Th., Los Angeles, 1966/67); Aristobulo in *Song of the Grasshopper* (ANTA Th., N.Y.C., Sept. 28, 1967); the Intern in *The Death of Bessie Smith* (Studio Arena, Buffalo, and Billy Rose Th., N.Y.C., Oct. 2, 1968); Jerry in *The Zoo Story* (Studio Arena, Sept. 17, 1968 and Billy Rose Th., Oct. 9, 1968); wrote *Lime Green Khaki Blur* (two one-act plays) (Provincetown Playhouse, N.Y.C., Mar. 26, 1969); directed *Long Day's Journey into Night* (Center Stage, Baltimore, Dec. 17, 1969); and played Mark Crawford in *Savages* (Amer. premiere, Mark Taper Forum, Los Angeles, Aug. 15, 1974).

Films. Mr. Piazza made his debut in *Dangerous Age* (Ajay, 1959); appeared in *The Hanging Tree* (WB, 1959); and *No Exit* (Zenith, 1962); *Tell Me that You Love Me, Junie Moon* (Par., 1970); and *The Candy Snatchers* (GFC, 1973).

Television. He has appeared on The Defenders (CBS); Stoney Burke (ABC); Kraft Television Th. (NBC); Naked City (ABC); Dick Powell Th. (NBC); and Ben Casey (ABC).

Published Works. He is the author of the novel *The Exact and Very Strange Truth* (1964).

Awards. He won the *Theatre World* Award (1959) for his performance as Alvin in *Kataki*.

PICON, MOLLY. Actress. b. Feb. 28, 1898, New York City, to Louis and Clara (Ostrow) Picon. Father, shirtmaker; mother, wardrobe mistress. Attended William Penn H.S., Philadelphia, Pa., 1911–14. Married June 29, 1919, to Jacob Kalich, producer, author. Member of AEA; Hebrew Actors Union; AGVA; AFTRA; ASCAP; SAG; Yiddish Theatrical Alliance; Jewish Theatrical Guild; Guild for The Blind; Amer. Red Cross. Address: P.O. Box 199, Mahopac, NY 10541, tel. (914) MA 8-2114.

Theatre. Miss Picon made her debut as Baby Margaret in a vaudeville act which played nickelodeon theatres (Philadelphia, Pa., Summer 1904); subsequently in Yiddish repertory, appeared in *Gabriel, The Silver King, Uncle Tom's Cabin, Sappho,* and *Shulamith* (Columbia Th., Philadelphia, 1904–07); *Girl of the West, God of Revenge, Medea, King Lear,* and *The Kreutzer Sonata* (Arch St. Th., Philadelphia, 1908–12); performed a song and dance act in nickelodeon theatres (Philadelphia, Pa.; Camden and Red Bank, N.J.; 1912–15); in stock, appeared in *Broadway Jones* and *Bunty Pulls the Strings* (Chestnut St. Th., Philadelphia, Summer 1915); and toured cross-country in the vaudeville act, *Four Seasons* (Gus Sun Time, Ackerman Harris Time, 1918–19).

She appeared in Yiddish repertory with her husband's company at the Boston (Mass.) Grand Opera House (1919–20); also touring Europe with this company (1920–22).

At the 2nd Ave. Th. in N.Y.C., she appeared in *Yankee* (Dec. 1923), *Tzipke* (Sept.–Dec. 1924), *Schmendrile* (Dec. 1924–Apr. 1925), *Gypsy Girl* (Sept. 1925–Apr. 1926), *Rabbi's Melody* (Nov. 1926), *Little Devil* (Dec. 1926–May 1927), *Little Czar* (Sept.–Dec. 1927), *Raizele* (Dec. 1927–May 1928), *Mazel Brocke* (Sept.–Dec. 1928), and *Hello Molly* (Dec. 1928–Apr. 1929).

She appeared in *Girl of Yesterday* (Molly Picon Th., Sept. 1931); in vaudeville at the Palace Th. (N.Y.C.), and throughout the US; appeared in *Love Thief* (Molly Picon Th., N.Y.C., Dec. 1931); in *Yankele,* and *Mamale* (Buenos Aires, Arg., 1932); appeared in vaudeville in Paris, France, and Johannesburg, South Africa (1932); a concert tour of Israel, Poland, and Russia (1933); and appeared in *Here Runs the Bride* (2nd Ave. Th., N.Y.C., Sept. 19, 1934). She performed in vaudeville (London Palladium, May 1937), and on tour in England; and toured America, Canada, and Israel in concert (1939).

Miss Picon made her Bway debut as Becky Felderman in *Morning Star* (Longacre, Apr. 16, 1940); followed by a world concert tour (1941); appeared in *Oy Is Das a Leben* (Molly Picon Th., N.Y.C., Oct. 12, 1942); toured the US and Canada in vaudeville (1943); performed at US Military Camps and D.P. Camps in Europe (1944–45); and in vaudeville and concerts in the US and Africa (1946–47). She played Mrs. Rubin in *For Heaven's Sake, Mother!* (Belasco, N.Y.C., Nov. 16, 1948); at the 2nd Ave. Th., appeared in *Sadie Was a Lady* (Jan. 27, 1949), *Abi Gezunt* (Oct. 3, 1949), *Mazel Tov Molly* (Sept. 30, 1950), and *Take It Easy* (Dec. 1950); toured Korea and Japan for the USO (1951); made an Israel Bond tour (US; Canada; 1952); and appeared in vaudeville (Alhambra, Paris, Fr., March 24, 1953).

She appeared in *Make Momma Happy* (Walnut St. Th., Philadelphia, Pa., Summer 1953); toured in Yiddish plays (London, Eng.; Israel; Catskills, N.Y.; Bronx, N.Y.; 1955); appeared in *Farblonjet Honeymoon* (Palace, Brooklyn, N.Y., Sept. 26, 1956); appeared with her husband, Jacob Kalich, in *The World of Sholem Aleichem* (Capri Th., Atlantic Beach, N.J., July 9, 1957); played Peppy in *The Kosher Widow* (Anderson Th., N.Y.C., Oct. 31, 1959); Mrs. Jacobi in *A Majority of One* (Phoenix, London, Mar. 9, 1960); in the US, repeated the role in stock (Paper Mill Playhouse, Millburn, N.J.; Westport Country Playhouse, Conn.; Coconut Grove Playhouse, Miami, Fla., Summer 1961); played Clara Weiss in *Milk and Honey* (Martin Beck Th., N.Y.C., Oct. 10, 1961); also touring in it (opened Shubert, Philadelphia, Pa., Jan. 29, 1963; closed Biltmore, Los Angeles, Calif., Sept. 7, 1963) and repeated the role in stock (Starlight Th., Kansas City, Mo., June 1964; Municipal Opera, St. Louis, Mo., July 1964; Music Fair, Valley Forge, Pa., Aug. 1964; Guber-Lee-Ford summer circuit; Coconut Grove Playhouse, Miami, Fla.; Melody Land, Hollywood, Calif., all Summer 1964); repeated her performance in *A Majority of One* (Royal Poinciana Playhouse, Palm Beach, Fla.; Sombrero Th., Phoenix, Ariz., Mar. 1965); appeared in *Madame Mousse* (Westport Country Playhouse, Conn., Aug. 16, 1965; Paramus, N.J., Aug. 24, 1965; Mineola Playhouse, L.I., N.Y., Sept. 14, 1965); again played her role in *A Majority of One* (Mill Run, Niles, Ill., Oct. 4, 1965; Roosevelt, Miami, Fla., Feb. 15, 1966); appeared in *Dear Me, the Sky Is Falling* (Pheasant Run, Chicago, Ill., 1966; Playhouse-in-the-Park,

Philadelphia, June 20, 1966; Paramus, N.J., July 5, 1966); again appeared in *Milk and Honey* (Melody Tent, Milwaukee, Wis., Aug. 2, 1966); appeared in *The Rubiyat of Sophie Klein* (Westbury Music Fair, N.Y., May 2, 1967); *Funny Girl* (John Kenley Circuit, Ohio, June 12–18, 1967); repeated her performance in *The Rubiyat of Sophie Klein* (Playhouse-in-the-Park, Philadelphia, Sept. 2, 1967); appeared in *How to Be a Jewish Mother* (pre-Bway: Oct.–Dec. 1967; Hudson Th., N.Y.C., Dec. 28, 1967); appeared in the Milliken Show (Waldorf-Astoria, N.Y.C., May 27, 1968); repeated her performance in *Milk and Honey* (Summer 1968); appeared in *The Solid Gold Cadillac* (Pheasant Run, Ill., Apr. 1969; Candlelight, Windsor, Conn., June 1969); repeated her performance in *Milk and Honey* (Summer 1969); replaced (Dec. 1, 1969) Helen Hayes as Jenny in *The Front Page* (Ethel Barrymore Th., N.Y.C., Dec. 1, 1969); played Hortense Brand in *Paris Is Out!* (Brooks Atkinson Th., Jan. 19, 1970); appeared in the Milliken Show (Waldorf-Astoria, June 1, 1971); *Hello, Dolly!* (North Shore Music, Beverly, Mass., July 2, 1971); repeated her performance in *Paris Is Out!* (Playhouse-in-the-Park, Philadelphia, Aug. 16, 1971); appeared in concert for the International Ladies' Garment Workers Union (Carnegie Hall, N.Y.C., Nov. 3 and 16, 1970); repeated her performance in *Hello, Dolly!* (Tappan Zee Playhouse, Nyack, N.Y., Apr. 28, 1972; Playhouse-in-the-Park, Philadelphia, Pa.) May 22, 1972; Hyde Park, N.Y., June 12, 1972; Warren, Dayton, Columbus, Ohio, Aug. 1–14, 1972); played in *Come Blow Your Horn* (Carillon Dinner Th., Miami Beach, Fla., Jan. 1973); and repeated her performance in *A Majority of One* (Carillon Dinner Th., Feb. 1974).

Films. Miss Picon appeared in two Yiddish films produced in Warsaw, Pol.; *Yiddle and His Fiddle* (1936), and *Mamale* (1938); and in *Come Blow Your Horn* (Par., 1963); *Fiddler on the Roof* (UA, 1970); and *For Pete's Sake* (Col., 1973).

Television and Radio. She performed on radio in Maxwell House Coffee Time (WMCA-WEVD, N.Y.C., 1951); for television, she has appeared on Car 54, Where Are You? (NBC, 1961); the Ed Sullivan Show (CBS, 1961); the Jack Paar Show (NBC, 1961); the Mike Wallace Show; Dr. Kildare (NBC, 1961); and the Johnny Carson Show (NBC, 1961); the Merv Griffin Show (June 1, 1965; Jan. 20, 1966; July 25, 1966); was co-host on the Mike Douglas Show (CBS, Feb. 13–17, 1967); appeared on the Gomer Pyle Show (CBS, Sept. 9, 1968); My Friend Tony (Sept. 20, 1968); the Jack O'Brien Show (Dec. 3, 1968); the David Frost Show (Dec. 2, 1969); the Merv Griffin Show (Dec. 9, 1969); and the Mike Douglas Show (CBS, Apr. 1971).

Published Works. Miss Picon wrote *So Laugh a Little* (1963).

Recreation. Walking, gardening.

PINE, RALPH. Publisher. b. Ralph Jonathan Pine, Apr. 30, 1939, Paterson, N.J., to Maurice M. and Molly Pine. Father, dentist. Educ. Fair Lawn (N.J.) public schools; Rutgers Univ.; Emerson Coll., Boston, Mass.; Boston Univ.; grad. Univ. of California (Los Angeles), M.A. Member of The Players; USITT; ATA; Assn. of American Publishers; Institute for Acting Rsch. (bd. of dir.). Address: (home) 151 E. 80th St., New York, NY 10021, tel. (212) 249-9368; (bus.) 150 W. 52nd St., New York, NY 10019, tel. (212) JU 2-1475.

Mr. Pine is president and editor in chief of Drama Book Specialists/Publishers, N.Y.C. He was previously a theatrical and literary agent in N.Y.C.; has written plays that were produced (non-AEA) in Los Angeles and Boston; has also written for radio and television; and his poetry has been published in several periodicals.

Recreation. Playing oboe, flute, and recorder; cooking; cats; fish; backgammon.

PINTER, HAROLD. Playwright, actor, director. b. Oct. 10, 1930, Hackney, East London, England, to Hyman Jack and Frances (Mann) Pinter. Father, tailor. Educ. Hackney Downs Grammar School. Studied at RADA (1948); Central School of Speech and Drama (1951). Married 1956 to Vivien Merchant, actress; one son. Member of AEA.

Theatre. Mr. Pinter began his career as an actor; he toured Ireland with the Anew McMaster repertory co. (Sept. 1951–Fall 1952); appeared with the Donald Wolfit Co. (King's Th., Hammersmith, London, England) as Jaques in *As You Like It* (Feb. 16, 1954), an Officer in *Twelfth Night* (Feb. 25, 1953), Solanio in *The Merchant of Venice* (Mar. 9, 1953), the Second Murderer in *Macbeth* (Mar. 19, 1953), and in other roles; and, using the name David Baron, toured provincial repertory theatres in England (1954–57). The first production of a play that he had written was *The Room* in 1957 (see below).

The first of Mr. Pinter's plays to be seen in the US was *The Birthday Party* (Encore Th., San Francisco, Calif., July 15, 1960); followed by *The Caretaker* (Lyceum, N.Y.C., Oct. 4, 1961); and *The Dumb Waiter* (Univ. of Wisconsin Summer Arts Festival, Madison, Wis., July 10, 1962). In N.Y.C. double-bills were presented of *The Collection* and *The Dumb Waiter* (Cherry Lane, Nov. 26, 1962); *The Lover* and Samuel Beckett's *Play* (Cherry Lane, Jan. 4, 1964). *The Room* was produced in Canada (Le Hibou, Ottawa, Aug. 1964) and *A Slight Ache* in Boston, Mass. (Th. Co. of Boston, Oct. 15, 1964), and both plays, billed as *The New Pinter Plays*, were produced in N.Y.C. (Writers Stage Th., Dec. 9, 1964).

Later N.Y.C. productions of Mr. Pinter's plays include *The Homecoming* (Music Box, Jan. 5, 1967); *The Birthday Party* (Booth Th., Oct. 3, 1967); the double-bill *Tea Party* and *The Basement*, both originally television plays (Eastside Playhouse, Oct. 15, 1968); the double bill *Landscape* and *Silence* (Forum, Apr. 2, 1970); and *Old Times* (Billy Rose Th., Nov. 16, 1971). Mr. Pinter also directed the N.Y.C. production of *The Man in the Glass Booth* (Royale, Sept. 26, 1968).

The Room, the first play by Mr. Pinter that was produced (Drama Dept., Bristol Univ., Bristol, England, 1957; Bristol Old Vic., Dec. 30, 1957), was followed by *The Birthday Party* (Arts, Cambridge, Apr. 28, 1958; Lyric, Hammersmith, London, May 19, 1958); and *The Dumb Waiter* (world premiere, in German, at Frankfurt-am-Main, Germany, Feb. 28, 1959). Mr. Pinter contributed sketches and lyrics to the revues *One to Another* (Lyric, Hammersmith, London, July 15, 1959) and *Pieces of Eight* (Apollo, Sept. 23, 1959); directed a production of *The Room*, which was on a double-bill with *The Dumb Waiter* (Hampstead Th., Club, Jan. 21, 1960; transferred to Royal Court, Mar. 8, 1960); and wrote *The Caretaker* (Arts, Apr. 27, 1960; moved to Duchess Th., May 30, 1960), in which Mr. Pinter replaced (Feb. 21–Mar. 19, 1961) Alan Bates as Mick.

Mr. Pinter also wrote (originally for radio) *A Slight Ache*, produced on the triple bill *Three* (Arts Th. Club, Jan. 18, 1961), and *A Night Out* (Gate Th., Dublin, Ireland, Sept. 17, 1961), which was presented in London on the triple bill *Counterpoint* (Comedy Th., Oct. 2, 1961). He wrote (originally for television) and, with Peter Hall, directed *The Collection* (Aldwych, June 18, 1962); wrote (originally for television) and directed *The Lover* and wrote (originally for radio) and, with Guy Vaesen, directed *The Dwarfs*; *The Lover* and *The Dwarfs* were presented on a double-bill (Arts Th. Club, Sept. 18, 1963). He also directed a revival of *The Birthday Party* (Aldwych, June 18, 1964); wrote *The Homecoming* (Aldwych, June 3, 1965); directed *The Man in the Glass Booth* (St. Martin's, July 27, 1967); wrote *Night*, presented on the program *Mixed Doubles* (Comedy Th., Apr. 9, 1969); *Landscape* and *Silence* (Aldwych, July 2, 1969); directed *Exiles* (Mermaid, Nov. 12, 1970; transferred to Aldwych); wrote *Old Times* (Aldwych, June 1, 1971); directed *Butley* (Criterion, July 15, 1971); wrote *No Man's Land* (Old Vic, Apr. 23, 1975); and directed *Otherwise Engaged* (Queen's Th., July 1975).

In 1973, Mr. Pinter became an associate director of the National Theatre.

Films. Motion pictures of Mr. Pinter's plays include *The Caretaker*, retitled *The Guest* (Janus, 1963) and adapted by Mr. Pinter; *The Birthday Party* (Continental, 1968), also adapted by Mr. Pinter; and *The Homecoming* (Amer. Film Th., 1973). He wrote scripts for *The Servant* (Landau, 1964); *The Pumpkin Eater* (Royal Intl., 1964); *The Quiller Memorandum* (20th-Fox, 1967); *Accident* (Cinema V, 1967); and *The Go-Between* (Col., 1971); and he directed the film *Butley* (Amer. Film Th., 1974).

Television and Radio. In addition to occasional television appearances in his own plays (see below), Mr. Pinter performed on radio on the BBC Home Service (Sept., Oct. 1950) and the BBC Third Programme, for which he played Abergavenny in *Henry VIII* (Feb. 9, 1951). For the Third Programme also, he read his story "The Examination" (Sept. 7, 1962); nine of his sketches were produced (Feb. 1964); and he read his story "Tea Party" (June 2, 1964).

Plays written by Mr. Pinter for radio include *A Slight Ache* (BBC, July 29, 1959); *A Night Out* (BBC, Mar. 1, 1960), in which he played Seeley; and *The Dwarfs* (BBC, Dec. 2, 1960). He rewrote for radio (1966) his television play *Night School* (see below). The first performance of his play *Landscape* was on radio (BBC, Apr. 25, 1968).

On television, he played Garcin in *In Camera* (BBC, Nov. 15, 1964); and he was on American television on the series The Art of Film (NET, 1966–67) and interviewed on The Scene (Ind., 1966–67). Plays by Mr. Pinter or excerpts from them seen on American television include scenes from *The Room* and *A Slight Ache* (Camera Three, CBS, Jan. 31, 1965); *The Dumb Waiter* (Repertory Th., Ind., Mar. 10, 1965).

Mr. Pinter adapted for television his play *A Night Out* (ABC-TV, Apr. 24, 1960) and wrote for television *Night School* (Associated Rediffusion, July 21, 1960); *The Collection* (Associated Rediffusion, May 11, 1961); *The Lover* (Associated Rediffusion, Mar. 28, 1963); *Tea Party* (BBC, Mar. 25, 1965); *The Basement* (BBC, Feb. 28, 1967), in which he played Stott; and *Monologue* (1972). Other works of Mr. Pinter's seen on British television include *The Birthday Party* (Associated Rediffusion, Mar. 22, 1960) and *A Slight Ache* (BBC, Feb. 1967).

Awards. Mr. Pinter was named C.B.E. in Birthday Honours (June 1966); received a Whitbread Anglo-American Theater Award (1967) for British contributions to the Bway stage; the Shakespeare Prize in Hamburg, Germany (1970); and the Austrian State Prize for European literature (1973).

For *The Caretaker*, he received the London Drama Critics Award for the best play of the season and *The Evening Standard* Award for the best new play (both 1960); for the screenplay of *The Servant*, he received the British Screenwriters' Guild Award (1962) and the NY Film Critics Award (1964); for the script of *The Lover* (1963), he received the Guild of British Television Producers and Directors Award for the best original television play of the year; for his adaptation of *The Pumpkin Eater*, he received the British Film Academy Award for best screenplay (1964); for *The Homecoming*, he received a NY Drama Critics' Circle Award (best play, 1966–67) and an Antoinette Perry (Tony) Award (play, author, and producer, 1967); he received a Tony nomination for his direction of *The Man in the Glass Booth* (1969); and *Old Times* received a Tony nomination as best play (1972).

PIPPIN, DON. Musical director, conductor, composer, pianist, vocal arranger, orchestrator. b. Donald W. Pippin, Nov. 25, Macon, Ga., to Earl C. and Irene Louise (Ligon) Pippin. Father, businessman. Attended Baylor School for Boys (Chattanooga, Tenn.); Univ. of Alabama; Univ. of Chattanooga; Julliard School of Music; studied piano with James Friskin (Julliard); composition with Tibor Serly; and conducting with Victor Bay and George Schick. Married Jan. 27, 1974, to Marie Santell, actress-singer. Member of AF of M, Locals 802 and 47; BMI. Relative in theatre: cousin, Bill Pippin, with The Nashville Brass. Served U.S. Army, 181st Infantry Div. Address: (home) 350 W. 57th St., New York, NY 10019, tel. (212) 581-1436; (bus.) c/o Samuel Liff, William Morris Agency,

1350 Ave. of the Americas, New York, NY 10019, tel. (212) JU 6-5100.

Pre-Theatre. Mr. Pippin was a staff pianist for ABC Television and Radio (1949–53) and a free-lance musician for NBC and CBS.

Theatre. He made his debut as assistant conductor at the Lambertville (N.J.) Music Circus. On Bway, he was musical director of *Irma La Douce* (Plymouth, 1960); *Oliver* (Imperial, 1963); *110 in the Shade* (Broadhurst Th., 1963); *Foxy* (Ziegfeld Th., 1964); and vocal arranger and musical director for *Ben Franklin in Paris* (Lunt-Fontanne Th., 1965); *Mame* (Wintergarden, 1966); *Dear World* (Mark Hellinger Th., 1968); *Applause* (Palace, 1970); *Seesaw* (Uris Th., 1973); and *Mack and Mabel* (Majestic, 1974).

Off-Bway, he composed the scores for *Contrast* (East Side Playhouse, 1973); and *Fashion* (McAlpin Th., 1974). He also composed *Dr. Fidibus* which was performed in Bonn, Germany (1972).

Films. He wrote the song, "Hold Me in Your Arms" for the film, *Young at Heart* (WB, 1952).

Published Works. The score of *Contrast* (E. H. Morris, 1973).

Discography. "Hold Me in Your Arms" (Columbia, 1953).

Awards. Mr. Pippin received the Antoinette Perry (Tony) Award for best musical director, 1963, for *Oliver*. .

Recreation. Electronics, pets, "do-it-yourselfing" at his country home.

PISCATOR, MARIA LEY. Teacher, director. b. Maria Czada, Aug. 1, Vienna, Austria, to Edmund V. and Friedericke Brunswick (de Corrompa) Czada. Father, architect. Educated in private schools in Vienna. Studied dance with Cerri, Mme. Alevandr, and Mme. Egrova, Paris; grad. Handel's Acad., Vienna; Univ. of Paris, M.A. 1933, D.Litt., 1935; attended graduate school at Columbia Univ., 1950–51. Married Apr. 10, 1928, to Frank Gerhardt Deutsch (dec. Sept. 1934); married Apr. 17, 1937, to Erwin Piscator, director, Intendant of the Freie Volksbuehner, Berlin (dec. Mar. 30, 1966). Member of Pen Club, Vienna; AEA. Address: 17 E. 76th St., New York, NY 10021, tel. (212) RE 7-4202..

Theatre. Maria Ley Piscator, with her husband, Erwin Piscator, founded the Dramatic Workshop of the New Sch. for Social Research in 1938 and since that time has been a member of the faculty of the New Sch.; has been director of Evening Sessions of the Dramatic Workshop; chairman of the Acting Dept.; chairman of Evening Productions; co-chairman, with John Gassner, of New Plays in Work; associate director of Sayville (L.I., N.Y.) Playhouse, and Great Neck (L.I.) Chapel Th. (summer sessions, 1944–46); and Adirondacks Drama Festivals (Lake Placid, N.Y., 1949–50), during which time, in addition to staging plays, presented pianist Jose Iturbi in outdoor concerts.

Mme. Piscator was founder-director of the Junior Dramatic Workshop, first at the New Sch., at Master Inst. and Walt Whitman Sch. (1942–49); American Th. for Young Folks (1944); Poets Th., Inc. (1947); Maria Piscator Inst. (1954–60); and is presently director of Actors Workshop at the New Sch.

She staged *The Imaginary Invalid* (President, N.Y.C., 1942), *Romeo and Juliet* (Rooftop, 1943, 1948), *Bobino* (Adelphi, 1944), *Petrified Forest* (Sayville Summer Th., L.I., N.Y., 1945; Adirondacks Drama Festival, Lake Placid, N.Y.); *Pinocchio* (Rooftop, N.Y.C., 1945); *Blithe Spirit* (Great Neck Chapel Th., L.I., N.Y., 1946; Adirondacks Drama Festival, 1951); *Emile and the Detectives*, which was her own translation of *Nights of Wrath* (President, N.Y.C., 1947); *Tom Sawyer* (Museum of Natural History, 1947); *Alice in Wonderland* (President, 1948); *Ballad of the Mississippi* (Engineers Inst., 1948); *Hope of the World* (Metropolitan Opera House, 1948); *Two Noh Plays* by Paul Goodman (YMHA Th., 1949); *A Midsummer Night's Dream* (Th. Workshop, 1947–48); *Twilight Crane* (Studio Th. and Finch Coll. Th., 1959–60); *Call of the City* and *Objective Case* by Lewis John Carlino (New Sch., 1963–64); and Duerrenmatt's *Night Talk with a Contemptible Visitor* and *The Great Man* and Ring Lardner's *Letters from Chi. to N.Y.* (New Sch., 1964).

The Poet Th., Inc., presented a subscription series of experimental plays and films, notably *Twilight Crane* (see above), wherein live actors were integrated for the first time with painting on film, through the cooperation of Andre Girard's Theatre of Light and the mime Etienne Decroux.

Under the name of Maria Ley, she made her stage debut in Vienna (1920); subsequently performed for ten years with her own company in leading concert halls and theatres of all European capitals as well as in South America; choreographed Max Reinhardt's productions of *A Midsummer Night's Dream*, *The Imaginary Invalid*, *A Servant of Two Masters*, and other plays (Vienna and Salzburg Festivals, Austria, 1924–29); appeared under aegis of Otto Kahn as guest star in New York (1928); was supervisor of dance movement for the Group Th. (N.Y.C., 1939); was chairman of the March of Dance Series (New Sch. and Rooftop Th., 1940–49); and was chairman of the Dance Dept. of the Dramatic Workshop (New Sch., 1939–52).

Published Works. Mme. Piscator's published works include a volume of poetry entitled *Das Tanzende Ich (The Dance Within Me)* (German, 1925; English, 1930); the essays, *Theatre au dixhuitième siècle* (French, 1934): *Les queux chez Victor Hugo*, her doctoral thesis (French, 1934); *Le role d'intelligence dans le théâtre moderne* (French, 1934); and a translation from the German of Hugo von Hoffmanstthal's *Essai sur Victor Hugo* (French, 1937). She is the author of the novels *Grace Bennett* (1932) and *Lot's Wife* (1954); the one-act play *Lendemain* (1933) which was produced in Paris (Champs-Elysées Th., 1933); the three-act play *Le chien dangereux* (1934) which was also presented in Paris (Th. de la Madeleine, 1934); a translation of Armand Salacrou's *L'Inconnu d'Arras* in German (1934); and a translation of Salacrou's *Nuits de colère* into English, *Nights of Wrath* (1937). She has also written an adaptation of Kleist's novel *Michael Kohlhaas;* Kafka's story *Metamorphosis;* and *Total Theatre*, the story of the Dramatic Workshop of the New Sch., 1939–42.

Awards. She received the Odéon prize for her one-act play *Lendemain* (Paris, 1933).

PITKIN, WILLIAM. Scenic designer. b. July 15, 1925, Omaha, Neb., to Loren H. and Letha M. (Risk-Wimmer-Jarrell) Pitkin. Father, independent oil producer; mother, rancher. Attended Thomas Jefferson H.S., San Antonio, Tex., 1938–40; grad. M.B. Lamar H.S., Houston, Tex., 1941; attended Universidad Nacional de Mexico, 1941; Southwestern Univ., 1941–42; Univ. of Texas, 1942–43; Univ. of New Mexico, 1943; Bard Coll., B.A., 1949. Served USAAF, 1943–46. Member of United Scenic Artists, Local 829. Address: 799 Lexington Ave., New York, NY 10021, tel. (212) PL 8-2545.

Theatre. Mr. Pitkin was the designer for ten productions at the Woodstock (N.Y.) Playhouse (Summer 1947); went to Italy to design the productions of *Born Yesterday* and *Napoleone, Unico* for the Rome Th. Guild (1950); and designed 10 productions for the Paul Bunyan Drama Festival (Brainerd, Minn., 1951). He designed the settings and supervised the costumes for *The Threepenny Opera* (Th. de Lys, Sept. 20, 1955); designed the costumes for *Child of Fortune* (Royale, Nov. 13, 1956); the settings for *The Potting Shed* (Bijou, Jan. 29, 1957); *A Moon for the Misbegotten* (Bijou, May 2, 1957); *The Cave Dwellers* (Bijou, Oct. 19, 1957); *Marriage of Figaro* for the Washington Opera Society (Lisner Aud., Nov. 1958); supervised designs for *The Good Soup* (Plymouth, N.Y.C., Mar. 2, 1960); designed the setting for *Invitation to a March* (Music Box, Oct. 29, 1960); and designed the settings, with Jean Rosenthal, for *The Conquering Hero* (ANTA, Jan. 15, 1961).

Mr. Pitkin designed the Theatre Guild production of *The Glass Menagerie* for its State Department tour of Europe and South America (1961); designed the settings and costumes for *Something About a Soldier* (Ambassador, N.Y.C., Jan. 4, 1962); designed *Seidman and Son* (Belasco, Oct. 15, 1962); designed the settings and lighting for *The Beauty Part* (Music Box, Dec. 26, 1962); and was production designer for *La Fille Mal Gardée* presented by the Robert Joffrey Th. Ballet on its tour of Asia and the US (Winter 1962). For the American Shakespeare Festival (Stratford, Conn.), he designed the settings and costumes for *Henry V* (June 12, 1963); and, for the NY City Ctr. Opera, designed the settings for *Gentlemen, Be Seated* (NY City Ctr., world premiere Oct. 10, 1963).

He designed the sets for *Die Fledermaus* (NY City Opera, 1964); *Madama Butterfly* (Washington, D.C., Opera Society, 1964); *The Taming of the Shrew* (Amer. Shakespeare Festival, Stratford, Conn., 1965); and *The Impossible Years* (Playhouse, N.Y.C., Oct. 13, 1965). For the Joffrey Ballet (1966), he designed *Cake Walk*, *These Three*, and *Donizetti Variations;* and *Scotch Symphony* (1967). For the National Repertory Theatre's inaugural season at the reconstructed Ford's Th. (Washington, D.C., 1967–68), he designed *John Brown's Body*, *A Comedy of Errors* and *She Stoops To Conquer;* designed the sets for *The Guide* (Hudson, N.Y.C., Mar. 6, 1968); for the Berkshire Th. Festival (Stockbridge, Mass., Summer, 1968), he designed *A Matter of Position* and *Adaptation* and *Next* (again at the Greenwich Mews Th., N.Y.C., Feb. 10, 1969); and *Hunger and Thirst* and *Encounters* (Summer 1969).

With Bernard Daydee, he co-designed The Joffrey Ballet's *The Lesson* (NY City Ctr., 1969); did the sets for *The Chinese and Dr. Fish* (Ethel Barrymore Th., Mar. 10, 1970); designed *Schubertiade* for the San Francisco Ballet (1970); did the sets for *Buy Bonds, Buster* (Th. de Lys, N.Y.C., June 4, 1972); designed the sets and costumes for *Comedy* (Colonial Th., Boston, Oct. 1972); the sets for *Dear Oscar* (Playhouse, N.Y.C., Nov. 16, 1972); *Forty-two Seconds from Broadway* (Playhouse, N.Y.C., Mar. 11, 1973); and, in association with IASTA, *Your Own Thing* at the August Festival of the Arts (Casino Th., Monte Carlo, 1973) at the invitation of the Royal Family of Monaco.

For the opening season (1974) of the Syracuse (N.Y.) Stage Co., he designed productions of *Waiting for Lefty*, *Of Mice and Men*, and *Noon*. .

Recreation. Swimming, kite-flying and building, photography, archaeology, and Egyptology.

PITOT, GENEVIEVE. Arranger, composer. b. Genevieve Marie Pitot, May 20, New Orleans, La., to Henri Clement and Helena Marie (Chalaron) Pitot. Studied with Alfred Cortot, Paris, France. Married Dec. 22, 1941, to Joseph Patrick Sullivan, Hi-Fi technician (dec. May 7, 1961). Member of AFM, Local 802.

Theatre. Miss Pitot was a concert pianist and composer for Helen Tamiris with the Federal Th. (WPA) Project (1937–39). She also arranged the dance music for *Inside U.S.A.* (Century Th., N.Y.C., Apr. 30, 1948); *Kiss Me, Kate* (Century, Dec. 30, 1948); *Miss Liberty* (Imperial, July 15, 1949); *Touch and Go* (Broadhurst, Oct. 13, 1949); *Great to Be Alive* (Winter Garden, Mar. 23, 1950); *Call Me Madam* (Imperial, Oct. 12, 1950); *Out of This World* (Century, Dec. 21, 1950); *Two on the Aisle* (Mark Hellinger Th., July 9, 1951); *Two's Company* (Alvin, Dec. 15, 1952); *Can-Can* (Shubert, May 7, 1953); *By the Beautiful Sea* (Majestic, Apr. 8, 1954); *Silk Stockings* (Imperial, Feb. 24, 1955); *Shangri-La* (Winter Garden, June 13, 1956); and *Li'l Abner* (St. James, Nov. 15, 1956).

She arranged the dance music for *Livin' the Life* (Phoenix, Apr. 27, 1957); for the Ballet Workshop, composed music for *This Property Is Condemned* (Phoenix, May 13 1957) and *Winesburg* (Jacobs's Pillow, Lee, Mass., Summer 1958); arranged the dance music for *The Body Beautiful* (Bway Th., N.Y.C., Jan. 23, 1958); *Destry Rides Again* (Imperial, Apr. 23, 1959); *Saratoga* (Winter Garden, Dec. 7, 1959); *Milk and Honey* (Martin Beck Th., Oct. 10, 1961); the pre-Bway tryout of *La Belle* (opened Shubert, Philadelphia, Pa., Aug. 13, 1962); *Sophie* (Winter Garden, N.Y.C., Apr. 15, 1963); *The Girl Who Came to Supper* (Bway Th., Dec. 8, 1963); composed dance music for *Cool Off!* (pre-Bway, opened Forrest Th., Philadelphia, Pa., Mar. 31, 1964; closed there, Apr. 4, 1964); arranged dance music for the NY City Ctr. Light Opera Co. revival of *Kiss Me, Kate* (NY City Ctr., May 12, 1965); and composed dance music for *Drat! The Cat!* (Martin Beck Th., Oct. 10, 1965).

PLEASENCE, DONALD. Actor, director, producer, playwright. b. Oct. 5, 1919, Worksop, Nottinghamshire, Eng., to Thomas Stanley and Alice (Armitage) Pleasence. Father, railway station master. Attended The Grammar School, Eccleseld, Yorkshire, England, 1931–37. Married Aug. 8, 1941, to Miriam Raymond, actress (marr. dis. 1957); two daughters; married May 15, 1958, to Josephine Crombie; two daughters (marr. dis. 1971); married 1971 to Meira Shore; one daughter. Served in RAF, 1942–46; P.O.W. 1944–46. Member of British and American AEA; SAG; the Arts Club (London); Royal Automobile Club (London). Address: (home) Strand on the Green, London, W.4, England; (bus.) Regina House, 124 Finchley Rd., London N.W. 3, England.

Pre-Theatre. Railway clerk.

Theatre. Mr. Pleasence made his N.Y.C. debut as the Major-Domo in *Caesar and Cleopatra* (Ziegfeld, Dec. 19, 1951); played Lemprius Euphronius, a Soothsayer, in *Antony and Cleopatra* (Ziegfeld, Dec. 20, 1951); and Davies in *The Caretaker* (Lyceum, Oct. 4, 1961).

Mr. Pleasence made his stage debut as Hareton in *Wuthering Heights* (Playhouse Th., Jersey, Channel Islands, Eng., May 1939); his London debut as Curio in *Twelfth Night* (Arts Th. Club, June 10, 1942); played Mavriky in *The Brothers Karamazov* (Lyric, Hammersmith, June 4, 1946); the Bellboy in *Vicious Circle* (titled in the US as *No Exit*) (Arts Th. Club, July 17, 1946), Steen in *Tangent* (Mercury, Sept. 1946); Starkey in *Peter Pan* (Scala, Dec. 20, 1946); appeared with the Birmingham Repertory Th. (1948–50); the Bristol Old Vic Co. (Royal Th., 1950–51); played Sherman in *Right Side Up* (Arts Th. Club, London, Aug. 16, 1951); the Rev. Giles Aldus in *Saint's Day* (Arts Th. Club, Sept. 5, 1951); and William Mossop in *Hobson's Choice* (Arts Th. Club, June 4, 1952).

Mr. Pleasence played Huish in his own dramatization of a short story by Robert L. Stevenson, *Ebb Tide* (Edinburgh Festival, Scot., 1952; Royal Court, London, Sept. 16, 1952); Horst Bratsch in *High Balcony* (Embassy, Nov. 19, 1952); appeared for a season at the Shakespeare Memorial Th. (Stratford-upon-Avon, 1953); with the company, played Diomedes and Lepidus in *Antony and Cleopatra* (Prince's London, Nov. 4, 1953); appeared as Maccario in *The Impressario from Smyrna* (Arts Th. Club, May 26, 1954); Leone Gola in *The Rules of the Game* (Arts Th. Club, Jan. 13, 1955); the Dauphin in *The Lark* (Lyric, Hammersmith, May 11, 1955); the Man in *Misalliance* (Lyric, Hammersmith, Feb. 8, 1956); M. Tarde in *Restless Heart* (St. James's, May 8, 1957); Davies in *The Caretaker* (Arts Th. Club, Apr. 27, 1960); (Duchess Th., June 1960; and Lyceum Th., N.Y.C., Oct. 4, 1961); and the title role in *Poor Bitos* (Arts Th. Club, Nov. 13, 1963; Duke of York's Th., Jan. 7, 1964, and the Cort Th., N.Y.C., Nov. 16, 1964); starred in *The Man in the Glass Booth* (St. Martin's Th., London, 1967, and Royale, N.Y.C., Sept. 26, 1968); appeared in *Tea Party* and *The Basement* (Eastside Playhouse, N.Y.C., Oct. 15, 1968, and Duchess Th., London, 1970); and *Wise Child* (Helen Hayes Th., Dec. 1967).

Films. Mr. Pleasence has appeared in *The Big Day* (Mayer-Kingsley, 1952); *The Beachcomber* (UA, 1955); *The Man in the Sky* (1956); *The Black Tents* (Rank, 1957); *Manuela* (Ind., 1957); *A Tale of Two Cities* (Rank, 1958); *The Man Inside* (Col., 1958); *Heart of a Child* (Rank, 1958); *Look Back in Anger* (WB, 1959); *The Shakedown* (U, 1960); *Wind of Change* (Ind., 1960); *The Horsemasters* (Disney, 1960); *No Love for Johnny* (Emb., 1961); *Lisa* (20th-Fox, 1962); *The Great Escape* (UA, 1962); *Doctor Crippen* (ABC, 1962); *The Caretaker* (Caretaker Films Ltd., 1962) which he co-produced; *The Greatest Story Ever Told* (UA, 1965); *Halleluja Trail* (UA, 1965); *Fantastic Voyage* (20th-Fox, 1966); *Cul-de-Sac* (Sigma III, 1966); *Will Penny* (Par., 1968); *Soldier Blue* (Avco-Embassy, 1970); *Wedding in White* (Avco-Embassy, 1973); *Mutations* (Col., 1974); and *The Black Windmill* (U, 1974). He has completed three as yet unreleased films: *The Rainbow Boys, Death Line* and *Hearts of the West.*

Television. Mr. Pleasence made his debut in London in *I Want To Be a Doctor* (1946); subsequently appeared in *Misalliance; One; Man in a Moon; No Flags for Geebang; A House of His Own; The Millionairess; The Silk Purse; The Scarf;* a serial, Fate and Mr. Browne; *Small Fish Are Sweet; Double Indemnity; The Cupboard; Machinal;* and produced his own Sunday night drama series, Armchair Mystery Th. (Summer 1960). He has appeared in *Occupations; The Cafeteria; The Joke; Skin Deep; The Fox Trot;* and *Captain Rogers.* In the US, he has appeared in the musical *Jekyll and Hyde* and *Columbo* (NBC).

Awards. Mr. Pleasence was voted Actor of the Year (1958) by the London Guild of Film and Television Producers and Directors; received the London Critics Award for Best Stage Performance (1960–61) for *The Caretaker;* and the Variety Award for Best Stage Actor (1967); and was a nominee for the Antoinette Perry (Tony) Award for Best Actor for his performances in *The Caretaker, Poor Bitos, The Man in the Glass Booth,* and *Wise Child.*

Recreation. "Having dinner with good friends and talking too much.".

PLOWRIGHT, JOAN. Actress. b. Joan Anne Plowright, Oct. 28, 1929, Scunthorpe, Brigg, Lincolnshire, England, to William Ernest and Daisy Margaret (Burton) Plowright. Attended Scunthorpe Grammar Sch., 1943–48. Studied at the Laban Art of Movement Studio, Manchester, 1949–50; Old Vic Theatre Sch., 1950–52. Married Sept. 1954 to Roger Gage, actor (marr. dis. 1960); married Mar. 17, 1961, to Baron (then Sir Laurence) Olivier, actor, director; one son, two daughters. Member of AEA; SAG. Address: 33/34 Chancery Lane, London, W.C. 2, England.

Theatre. Miss Plowright toured South Africa in productions for the Old Vic Co. (1952); played Hope in the Croydon Repertory Co. production of *If Four Walls Told* (Sept. 1952); and Alison in the Bristol Old Vic production of *The Merry Gentlemen* (1954).

She made her London debut as Donna Clara in *The Duenna* (Westminster, July 28, 1954); played Pip in the Orson Welles' production of *Moby Dick* (Duke of York's, June 16, 1955); appeared in repertory productions at the Playhouse (Nottingham, 1955–56); and at the Royal Court Th., played the following roles for the English Stage Co.; Mary Warren in *The Crucible* (Apr. 9, 1956), Baptista in *Don Juan* and the Receptionist in *The Death of Satan* (May 15, 1956), Miss Tray in *Cards of Identity* (June 26, 1956), Mrs. Shin in *The Good Woman of Setzuan* (Oct. 31, 1956), Mrs. Margery Pinchwife in *The Country Wife* (Dec. 12, 1956; moved Adelphi, Feb. 4, 1957), the Old Woman in *The Chairs* (May 14, 1957), and Elizabeth Compton in *The Making of Moo* (June 25, 1957).

Miss Plowright appeared as Jean Rice in *The Entertainer* (Palace, Sept. 10, 1957); after which she made her N.Y.C. debut as the Old Woman in *The Chairs* and the Pupil in *The Lesson* (Phoenix, Jan. 9, 1958); and her Bway debut as Jean Rice in *The Entertainer* (Royale, Feb. 12, 1958). In London again, she repeated her roles in *The Chairs* and *The Lesson* (Royal Court, June 18, 1958); played the title role in *Major Barbara* (Royal Court, Aug. 28, 1958); Arlette in *Hook, Line and Sinker* (Piccadilly, Nov. 19, 1958); Beatie Bryant in *Roots* (Belgrade, Coventry, May 25, 1959; Royal Court, June 30, 1959); and Daisy in the Orson Welles' production of *Rhinoceros* (Royal Court, Apr. 28, 1960).

Miss Plowright played Josephine in *A Taste of Honey* (Lyceum, N.Y.C., Oct. 4, 1960), and at the Chichester (England) Festival Th., played Constantia in *The Chances* (July 2, 1962); Sonya in *Uncle Vanya* (July 16, 1962); and the title role in *Saint Joan* (June 24, 1963).

For the National Theatre she repeated her roles as Sonya in *Uncle Vanya* (Old Vic, Oct. 30, 1963) and the title role in *Saint Joan* (Old Vic, Nov. 19, 1963); she played Maggie in *Hobson's Choice* (National, Jan. 8, 1964); Hilda Wangel in *The Master Builder* (National, Nov. 17, 1964); took over the role of Beatrice in *Much Ado About Nothing* (National, Mar. 21, 1967); played Masha in *Three Sisters* (National, July 4, 1967); Dorine in *Tartuffe* (National, Nov. 21, 1967); Teresa in *The Advertisement* (Royal, Brighton, Sept. 17, 1968; and National, Sept. 24, 1968); Rosaline in *Love's Labour's Lost* (National, Dec. 19, 1968); directed *Rites* (Jeannetta Cochrane Th., Feb. 11, and National, May 27, 1969); she was the Voice of Lilith in *Back to Methuselah* (National, July 29, 1969); co-directed *The Travails of Sancho Panza* (New Th., Dec. 18, 1969); played Portia in *The Merchant of Venice* (New Th., Apr. 28, 1970); Anne in *A Woman Killed with Kindness* (New Th., Apr. 6, 1971); Silia in *Rules of the Game* (New Th., June 15, 1971); Jennifer Dubedat in *The Doctor's Dilemma* (Chichester Festival, May 17, 1972); Katherina in *The Taming of the Shrew* (Chichester Festival, July 5, 1972); Rebecca West in *Rosmersholm* (Greenwich Th., May 17, 1973); Rosa in *Saturday, Sunday, Monday* (Richmond Th., Oct. 23, 1973); and Stella Kirby in *Eden End* (Richmond Th., Mar. 25, and National, Apr. 2, 1974).

Films. Miss Plowright has appeared in *Moby Dick* (WB, 1956); *Time without Pity* (Astor, 1957); *The Entertainer* (Continental, 1960); and *Three Sisters* (British Lion, 1969).

Television. In London she has appeared in *Odd Man Out* (BBC, 1958); *The School for Scandal* (BBC, 1959), repeated in the US (June 3, 1964); and *The Secret Agent* (BBC, 1959); *Twelfth Night* (BBC, 1967); *The Plastic People* (BBC, 1969); and *The Merchant of Venice* (BBC, 1973).

Recreation. The children, reading, music, entertaining.

PLUGGE, MARY LOU. Educator. b. Mary Lou Kromer, May 16, 1906, Youngwood, Pa., to Jacob and Mary Louise (Hitchman) Kromer. Father, businessman. Grad. Hurst H.S., Mt. Pleasant Township, Pa., 1925; Curry Sch. of Expression, Boston, Mass., 1925–27; AADA, 1927–28; Columbia Univ., B.S. 1932, M.A. 1935; attended New York Univ., Summer 1947. Married June 14, 1928, to Domis Edward Plugge, educator, actor, known as Daniel Poole. Member of ASAA; Speech Assn. of the Eastern States; Ny State Assn. (secy.-treas.); Long Island Speech Assn. (vice-pres.); Long Island Arts Ctr. (drama comm.); AEA; Columbia Th. Assn. (exec. comm. 1936–60).

From 1954 until her retirement in 1968, Mrs. Plugge was chairman of the department of speech and dramatic arts at Adelphi Univ., where she has been teaching since 1940. She also served as chairman of the arts division, 1945–50. Her previous academic positions include assistant in theatre to Milton Smith at Columbia Univ. (Summers 1931–36); instructor of oral interpretation of literature at Columbia Univ. Teachers Coll. (Summers 1936–40); teacher and director of speech and dramatics at Miss Beard's Sch. (Orange, N.J., 1936–40).

Mrs. Plugge made her professional debut as Dorothy in *The American Tragedy* (2nd Ave. Th., N.Y.C., May 1928); subsequently appeared in a minor role in *Crime* (2nd Ave. Th., May 1928); as the Ingenue in a stock production of *The Night Hawk* (Union City, N.J., May 1928); played the remainder of the 1928 season and the entire 1929 season at the Canton (Ohio) Opera House. She played Mary Adams in Elmer Rice's *Left Bank* (Little, N.Y.C., Oct. 5, 1931).

At Miss Beard's Sch. (1936–40), Mrs. Plugge directed *Pride and Prejudice,* and *A Kiss for Cinderella;* while a student at Columbia Univ., was a member of the Morningside Players, and played numerous roles in original plays written in Hatcher Hughes' playwriting classes, directed by Milton Smith (1931–36).

For the Adelphi Univ. Little Th., she directed *Children in Uniform* (May 1941); an original adaptation of *Alice in Wonderland and Through the Looking Glass* (May 1942); *Twelfth Night* (May 1944); *Iphigenia in Tauris* (May 1945); played Mrs. Phelps in *The Silver Cord* (Oct. 1947); directed *Winterset* (Nov. 1948); played Miss Moffat in *The Corn Is Green* (Summer 1949); with Victor Jacoby, directed *A Midsummer Night's Dream* (Dec. 1952); and with Richard Clemo, directed *Hamlet* (May 1956).

Recreation. Gardening, traveling, collecting early American speech books.

PLUMMER, CHRISTOPHER. Actor. b. Arthur Christopher Orme Plummer, Dec. 13, 1929, Toronto, Ontario, Canada, to John and Isabella Mary (Abbott) Plummer. Father, secy. to Dean of Science, McGill Univ. Attended Montreal H.S; Jennings Private Sch., Montreal; studied speech with Iris Warren, London; voice with C. Herbertcaesari, London, 1964. Married 1956 to Tammy Lee Grimes, actress, singer (marr. dis.); one daughter; married, May 4, 1962, to Patricia Audrey Lewis, journalist, writer (marr. dis.). Relatives in theatre: cousin, Guy Du Maurier author and playwright; cousin, Nigel Bruce, actor. Member of AEA; AFTRA; SAG; The Players; The Garrick Club (London).

Theatre. Mr. Plummer's first assignment was as lighting designer for a high school production of *A Midsummer Night's Dream.* His stage debut was as Lt. Victor O'Leary in *John Loves Mary* with the Canadian Repertory Theatre (Ottawa, Canada, 1950); subsequently appeared with the company in about 100 roles. He played with the Bermuda Repertory Theatre (Winter 1952), as Old Mahon in *The Playboy of the Western World;* Gerard in *Nina;* Anthony Cavendish in *The Royal Family;* Ben in *The Little Foxes;* Duke Manti in *The Petrified Forest;* the Father in *George and Margaret;* Hector Benbow in *Thark;* and Bernard Kersal in *The Constant Wife;* understudied John Emery in the role of Bernard Kersal with the natl. touring company of *The Constant Wife* (opened Ford's Th., Baltimore, Md., Oct. 13, 1952).

He made his N.Y.C. debut as George Phillips in *The Starcross Story* (Royale, Jan. 13, 1954); appeared as Manchester Monaghan in *Home Is the Hero* (Booth, Sept. 22, 1954); Count Peter Zichy in *The Dark Is Light Enough* (ANTA, Feb. 23, 1955); at the International Festival, played Jason in *Medea* (Th. Sarah Bernhardt, Paris, France, June 1955); played with the American Shakespeare Festival (Stratford, Conn.), as Mark Antony in *Julius Caesar* (July 12, 1955), and as Ferdinand in *The Tempest* (Aug. 1, 1955).

He appeared as the Earl of Warwick in *The Lark* (Longacre, N.Y.C., Nov. 17, 1955); at the Stratford (Ontario, Canada) Shakespearean Festival in the title role in *Henry V* (Summer 1956), repeating the role at the Edinburgh (Scotland) Festival (Assembly Hall, Aug. 1956); played the Narrator in *L'Histoire du soldat* (NY City Ctr., Oct. 16, 1956); and Lewis Rohnen in *Night of the Auk* (Playhouse, Dec. 3, 1956); with the Stratford (Ontario, Canada) Shakespearean Festival, performed in the title role in *Hamlet;* as Sir Andrew Aguecheek in *Twelfth Night* (Summer 1957); and as Bardolph in *Henry IV, Part I;* as Leontes in *The Winter's Tale;* and as Benedick in *Much Ado About Nothing* (Summer 1958).

He played Nickles in *J. B.* (ANTA, N.Y.C., Dec. 11, 1958); with the Stratford (Ontario, Canada) Shakespearean Festival, appeared as Philip the Bastard in *King John,* and Mercutio in *Romeo and Juliet* (Summer 1960); and appeared at the Royal Shakespeare Th. (Stratford-upon-Avon, Summer 1961), as Benedick in *Much Ado About Nothing,* and in the title role in *Richard III,* and played Henry II in *Becket* (Aldwych, London, 1961). He appeared with the Stratford (Ontario, Canada) Shakespearean Festival in the title roles in *Macbeth* and *Cyrano de Bergerac* (Summer 1962); played the title role in *Arturo Ui* (Lunt-Fontanne, N.Y.C., Nov. 11, 1963); played Francisco Pizarro in *The Royal Hunt of the Sun* (ANTA Th., Oct. 26, 1965); Anthony in *Anthony and Cleopatra* (Festival Th., Stratford, Ontario, Canada, July 31, 1967); Danton in *Danton's Death* (New Th., London, 1971–72); the title role in *Cyrano* (world premiere, Guthrie Th., Minneapolis, Jan. 23, 1973; and Palace, N.Y.C., May 13, 1973); appeared in *Love and Master Will* (Opera House, John F. Kennedy Center, Washington, D.C., Sept. 11, 1973); and in *The Good Doctor* (Eugene O'Neill Th., N.Y.C., Nov. 27, 1973).

Films. Mr. Plummer made his debut in the role of the Playwright in *Stage Struck* (Buena Vista, 1958); appeared in *Wind Across the Everglades* (WB, 1958); as Commodus in *Fall of the Roman Empire* (Par., 1964); and as Captain Von Trapp in *The Sound of Music* (20th-Fox, 1965); appeared in *Inside Daisy Clover* (WB, 1965); *The Night of the Generals* (Col., 1967); *Oedipus the King* (Regional, 1968); *The High Commissioner* (Cinerama, 1968); *Lock Up Your Daughters* (Col., 1969); *The Battle of Britain* (UA, 1969); *The Royal Hunt of the Sun* (Natl. Gen., 1969); *Waterloo* (Par., 1971); *The Pyx* (Cinerama, 1973); and *The Man Who Would Be King* (AA, 1975).

Television and Radio. Mr. Plummer has performed in many roles on radio in Canada (CBS, 1951–62). His first television appearance was as Montano in *Othello* (CBC, 1951); followed by many performances in the US, including the title role in *Oedipus Rex* (Omnibus, CBS, 1956); the Soldier in *Little Moon of Alban* (Hallmark Hall of Fame, NBC, 1958); Helmer in *A Doll's House* (Hallmark Hall of Fame, NBC, 1959); the title role in *Captain Brassbound's Conversion* (Hallmark Hall of Fame, NBC, 1960); the Doctor in *Johnny Belinda* (Hallmark Hall of Fame, NBC, 1958); the title role in *Cyrano de Bergerac* (Hallmark Hall of Fame, NBC, 1962); Agamemnon and Orestes in *Oreseia* (Omnibus, CBS, 1959); Thomas Mendip in *The Lady's Not for Burning* (Omnibus, CBS, 1958); Mike in *The Philadelphia Story* (DuPont Show of the Month, NBC, 1959); Rassendyl in *The Prisoner of Zenda* (DuPont Show of the Month, NBC, 1961); Miles Hendon in *The Prince and the Pauper* (DuPont Show of the Month, NBC, 1957); and Prince in *Time Remembered* (Hallmark Hall of Fame, NBC, 1961).

His performance as the title role in *Macbeth* at the Stratford (Ontario, Can.) Shakespearean Festival was transmitted by Telestar (1962); and he appeared as Hamlet in *Hamlet at Elsinore* (Kronborg Castle, Elsinore, Denmark, BBC and Danish World Television Distribution, 1964).

Awards. Mr. Plummer received a *Theatre World* Award (1955) for his performance as Count Peter Zichy in *The Dark Is Light Enough; The Evening Standard* Award (London, 1961) for his performance as Henry II in *Becket;* the *Best Plays* citation (1963–64) for his performance in *Arturo Ui;* the Outer Circle and Drama Desk awards, and *Best Plays* citation (1972–73); and the Antoinette Perry (Tony) Award (1973–74) for his performance in *Cyrano.* Mr. Plummer was named Companion of the Order of Canada (Oct. 28, 1969).

Recreation. Tennis, skiing, music (piano).

POCKRISS, LEE. Composer. b. Lee Julian Pockriss, Jan. 20, 1927, New York City, to Joseph and Ethel (Price) Pockriss. Father, businessman. Grad. Erasmus Hall H.S., Brooklyn, 1942; Brooklyn Coll., B.A. 1948; attended New York Univ., 1949–51; studied composition with Aaron Copeland, Tanglewood Music Festival, 1948–49; with Stefan Wolpe, four years; with Tibor Serly, two years; with Max Persin, one year. Relative in theatre: cousin, Sam Pokrass, composer. Member of AFM; Dramatist Guild; ASCAP. Address: 160 W. 73rd St., New York, NY 10023, tel. (212) TR 7-6700.

Pre-Theatre. Pianist, arranger, orchestrator.

Theatre. Mr. Pockriss' first professional work involved composing special musical material for the Latin Quarter night club (N.Y.C., 1949); subsequently wrote revues at Camp Tamiment (Pa., Summers 1951–52).

He composed the ballet music for *Top Banana* (Winter Garden, N.Y.C., Nov. 1, 1951), and for *Three Wishes for Jamie* (Mark Hellinger Th., Mar. 21, 1952); wrote the complete score for *Ernest in Love* (Cherry Lane, May 4, 1960), which was produced in Brussels, Belgium, under the title, *Ernest En Constant* (Th. de Quatsous, May 1963); and the score for *Tovarich* (Bway Th., N.Y.C., Mar. 18, 1963). He wrote the music for *Split Lip* by John Cromwell, produced and directed by Gene Frankel (Th. in Space, N.Y.C., Mar. 1974).

Films. He wrote the songs for *The Phantom Tollbooth* (MGM); and the background score for *The Subject Was Roses* (MGM, 1968).

Television. Mr. Pockriss composed the music, ballets, and songs for the Milton Berle Show (NBC, 1953–56) and for the Martha Raye Show (NBC, 1953–57).

Awards. In 1950, he won first prize in the National Contest for Young American Composers, sponsored by the American Federation of Music Clubs, for his work, "Little Suite for Oboe and Strings." In 1958, he received an award from the National Association of Recording Arts and Sciences for his song, "Catch a Falling Star," and subsequently wrote and produced "Playground in My Mind," for which he received a Gold Record in 1973.

Recreation. Horseback riding, French, travel.

POITIER, SIDNEY. Actor, director, producer. b. Feb. 20, 1924, Miami, Fla., to Reginald and Evelyn (Outten) Poitier. Attended Governor's H.S., Nassau, British West Indies. Studied acting with Paul Mann and Lloyd Richards, N.Y.C. Married 1951, to Juanita Hardy, dancer (marr. dis. 1965); four daughters; married Feb. 4, 1976, to Joanna Shimkus, actress; two children. Served US Army, 1943–44. Member of AEA; SAG; AFTRA.

Pre-Theatre. Dishwasher, longshoreman, construction worker.

Theatre. Mr. Poitier made his debut with the Amer. Negro Th. Harlem, N.Y.C., (1945), appearing in *Days of Our Youth, On Strivers Row, You Can't Take It with Your, Rain, Freight, The Fisherman, Hidden Horizon, Riders to the Sea,* and in *Sepia Cinderella.*

He played Polydorus in the all-Negro production of *Lysistrata* (Belasco, N.Y.C., Oct. 17, 1946); Lester in *Anna Lucasta,* in which he was also a general understudy (National, Sept. 22, 1947), and touring in it (Civic Th., Chicago, Ill.); and played Walter Lee Younger in *A Raisin in the Sun* (Ethel Barrymore Th., N.Y.C., Mar. 11, 1959).

Films. He made his debut in a US Army documentary, *From Whom Cometh Help* (1949); subsequently appeared in *No Way out* (20th-Fox, 1950); *Cry, the Beloved Country* (UA, 1952); *Red Ball Express* (U, 1952); *Go, Man, Go* (UA, 1954); *The Blackboard Jungle* (MGM, 1955); *Good-Bye My Lady* (WB, 1956); *Something of Value* (MGM, 1957); *Edge of the City* (MGM, 1957); *Band of Angels* (WB, 1957); *The Defiant Ones* (UA, 1958); *The Mark of the Hawk* (U, 1958); *Porgy and Bess* (Col., 1959); *All the Young Men* (Col., 1960); *A Raisin in the Sun* (Col., 1961); *Paris Blues* (UA, 1961); *Pressure Point* (UA, 1962); *Lilies of the Field* (UA, 1963); *The Long Ships* (Col., 1964); *The Greatest Story Ever Told* (UA, 1965); *The Bedford Incident* (Col., 1965); *A Patch of Blue* (MGM, 1965); *The Slender Thread* (Par., 1965); *Duel at Diablo* (UA, 1966); *The Heat of the Night* (UA, 1967); *Guess Who's Coming to Dinner* (Col., 1967); *To Sir, With Love* (Col., 1967); *For Love of Ivy,* which he also produced (Cinerama, 1968); *The Lost Man* (U, 1969); *They Call Me Mr. Tibbs* (UA, 1970); *Brother John* (Col., 1971); *The Organization* (UA, 1971); *Buck and the Preacher,* which he also directed (Col., 1972); *A Warm December* (Natl. Gen., 1973); and *Uptown Saturday Night* which he also produced and directed (WB, 1974).

Television. He has appeared on Pond's Th., (ABC, 1955); Philco Playhouse (NBC); and the major talk shows.

Awards. He received the Venice Film Festival Georgio Cini Award (1958) for his performance in the film, *Something of Value;* the Berlin Film Festival Award (1959) for *The Defiant Ones;* and the Academy (Oscar) Award (1964) for his performance in *Lilies of the Field.*

POLAN, LOU. Actor. b. Louis Polan, June 15, 1904, Ukraine, Russia, to Joseph and Faga Polan. Grad. P.S. 109, Brooklyn, N.Y., 1916; attended Manual Training H.S., Brooklyn, 1917; New Lots Evening H.S., 1917–19; studied at the Neighborhood Playhouse Sch. of the Th., 1919–21; grad. NY Sch. of Theatre, 1922. Member of AEA; SAG; AFTRA. Address: 45 W. 69th St., New York, NY 10023, tel. (212) EN 2-5834.

Theatre. Mr. Polan first appeared in N.Y.C. as the Shopkeeper in *La Boutique Fantasque* and as a member of the mob in *The Mob* (Neighborhood Playhouse, 1920); made his Bway debut as a walk-on in *R.U.R.* (Garrick, Oct. 9, 1922); played Lubetsky in *The Bootleggers* (39 St. Th., Nov. 27, 1922); toured the Keith vaudeville circuit as the Clown in a sketch "Heart of a Clown" (1923); subsequently appeared as a Pirate in *The Jolly Roger* (Natl., N.Y.C., Nov. 1, 1923); D'Artagnan in *Cyrano de Bergerac* (Natl., Nov. 1, 1923), with which he toured (1923–24); played a Gentleman of Cyprus in *Othello* (Shubert, N.Y.C., Jan. 10, 1925); several small roles in *Hamlet* (Hampden, Oct. 10, 1925); one of the Indians in *The Fountain* (Greenwich Village Th., Dec. 10, 1925); a Charcoal Burner in *Goat Song* (Guild, Jan. 25, 1926); a Sailor Spy in *The Immortal Thief* (Hampden, Oct. 2, 1926); Montini in *Caponsacchi* (Hampden, Oct. 26, 1926); Pylades in Margaret Anglin's *Electra* (Metropolitan Opera House, May 3, 1927); Charles, wrestler to Frederick, in *As You Like It* (N.Y.C. high schools, 1927); Montjoy in *Henry V* (Hampden, Mar. 15, 1928); Devadatta, Prince of Koli in *The Light of Asia* (Hampden, Oct. 9, 1928); Mr. Vik in *An Enemy of the People* (Hampden, Nov. 5, 1928); the Comte de Guiche in *Cyrano de Bergerac* (Hampden, Dec. 25, 1928); the Captain in *The Bonds of Interest* (Hampden, Oct. 14, 1929); Gaston, Duke of Orleans in *Richelieu* (Hampden, Dec. 26, 1929); the Prince of Morocco in *The Merchant of Venice* (Times Sq. Th., Dec. 2, 1930), with which he toured (1931); and as Pfeiffer in *The Firebird* (Empire, N.Y.C., Nov. 21, 1932).

Mr. Polan toured as Antonio in *Twelfth Night* (1933); played the Rabbi of Lizhan in *Yoshe Kalb* (Natl., N.Y.C., Dec. 28, 1933); a Top Sergeant in *The Young Go First* (Park, May 28, 1935); Loretti in *Sweet Mystery of Life* (Shubert, Oct. 11, 1935); toured as a Producer in *The Great Julie* (1936); appeared as the Chain Gang Captain in *Hymn to the Rising Sun* (Ritz, N.Y.C., May 6, 1937); Colonel Roche in *Haiti* (Lafayette, Mar. 2, 1938); Victor Piazzi in *All the Living* (Fulton, Mar. 24, 1938); Roxy Gottleib in *Golden Boy* (St. James's, London, June 21, 1938), and toured the US in it (1938–40); played Teddy in *Night Music* (Broadhurst, N.Y.C., Feb. 22, 1940); one of the Dictators in *Liberty Jones* (Shubert, Feb. 5, 1941); Nich in *Walk into My Parlor* (Forrest, Nov. 19, 1941); Looie in *Cafe Crown* (Cort, Jan. 23, 1942); toured as Sergeant Ruby in *The Eve of St. Mark* (1943), and as the Laundry Man in *The White-Haired Boy* (1943); played Jud in a national touring company of *Oklahoma!* (1943–44), and in a USO production in the Pacific (1945).

He appeared as Delcorte in the pre-Bway tryout of *You Twinkle Only Once* (opened Shubert, New Haven, Conn., Jan. 3, 1946; closed Wilbur, Boston, Mass., Jan. 19, 1946); Colonel Ivanov in *The Whole World Over* (Biltmore, N.Y.C., Mar. 27, 1947); Mike Rykowski in *The Gentleman from Athens* (Mansfield, Dec. 9, 1947); Bob Kressner in *The Golden State* (Fulton, Nov. 25, 1950); Simeon Cabot in *Desire Under the Elms* (ANTA, Jan. 16, 1952); Titus Lartius and the First Lord in *Coriolanus* (Phoenix, Jan. 19, 1954); the Cook and was understudy to George Voskovec as Dr. Dorn in *The Seagull* (Phoenix, May 11, 1954); Captain La Hire in a pre-Bway tryout of *Saint Joan* (opened Natl., Washington, D.C., Sept. 20, 1954; closed Hartman, Columbus, Ohio, Nov. 6, 1954); Will Masters in *Bus Stop* (Music Box, N.Y.C., Mar. 2, 1955); Ilya Afanasyevitch Shamraev in *The Seagull* (4th St. Th., Oct. 22, 1956); Harvey L. Gruber in *Drink to Me Only* (54 St. Th., Oct. 18, 1958); Marshall Haynes in *The Legend of Lizzie* (54 St. Th., Feb. 9, 1959); the First Moving Man in the pre-Bway tryout of *One for the Dame* (opened Ford's Th., Baltimore, Md., Mar. 24, 1960; closed Colonial, Boston, Mass., Apr. 2, 1960); Mr. Magnuson in the national touring company of *Seidman and Son* (opened Locust St. Th., Philadelphia, Pa., Oct. 7, 1963; closed Geary, San Francisco, Feb. 22, 1964); with the NY Shakespeare Festival, played the Ghost of Hamlet's father in *Hamlet* (Delacorte, June 10, 1964); Schlissel in *The Tenth Man* by Paddy Chayefsky (NY City Ctr., 1967); the Father in *After the Fall* (Philadelphia Playhouse and Bucks County, Pa., Playhouse, 1970); and Azrael (the Angel of Death) in *The Creation of the World and Other Business* (Shubert Th., N.Y.C., 1972).

Films. Mr. Polan has appeared as the Taxi Driver in *Fourteen Hours* (20th-Fox, 1951); a Detective in *You Never Can Tell* (U, 1951); Louis Capone in *Murder, Incorporated* (20th-Fox, 1960); a Mafia Don in *Brotherhood* (Par., 1967); Dr. Einhorn in *The Hospital* (Sinica, 1971); and Carmine Coltello in *The Seven Ups* (Di Antonio–20th-Fox, 1973).

Television. He has performed on The Untouchables (ABC); Car 54, Where Are You? (NBC); Big Story (NBC); Big Town (CBS); Danger (CBS); Casey-Crime Photographer (CBS); Philco Television Playhouse (NBC); Studio One (CBS); Somerset Maugham Th. (ABC); The Web (CBS); Arnie (NBC); and Store Front Lawyers (CBS).

POLLOCK, NANCY R. Actress. b. Nancy Reiben Feb. 10, 1907, Brooklyn, N.Y., to Philip and Rachel (Gelbrass) Reiben. Studied drama at Columbia Univ., New York Univ.; speech at Brooklyn Coll. Married Feb. 10, 1925, to Herbert H. Pollock; two daughters. Member of AEA; AFTRA; SAG. Address: 98 Riverside Dr., New York, NY 10024, tel. (212) TR 4-4592.

Theatre. Mrs. Pollock first appeared on stage in a school production of *Little Bo Peep* (Dec., 1912); made her professional debut in Spanish-language repertory, as Stella Tabera in *Star of Seville*, and Sister Theresa in *The Cradle Song* (El Teatro Nacional, Havana, Cuba, 1925–27); appeared in English-language repertory, as Ilona in *The Play's the Thing*, Roxane in *Cyrano de Bergerac*, and Melisande in *The Romantic Age* (Teatro de Chapultepec, Chapultepec Hts., Mex., 1927–29); in Spanish-language repertory, played many roles, including Acacia in *The Passion Flower* (Teatro Grande, Barcelona, Sp., 1930–35).

She first appeared in N.Y.C. as Bessie Berger in *Awake and Sing* (Hudson Park Library, Mar. 1947); subsequently played a season of stock with the Hampton Players, appearing as the Princess of San Luca in *Death Takes a Holiday*, Essie Stuyvesant in *The Walrus and the Carpenter*, Madame Daruschka in *Claudia*, and Abby Brewster in *Arsenic and Old Lace* (Bridgehampton, L.I., Summer 1946); played Mrs. Bodine in *A World Elsewhere* (Master Inst., N.Y.C., 1947); Lucy Allerton in *Dream Girl*, appeared in *Made in Heaven*, and played Mrs. Chisholm in *The Petrified Forest* (Casino Th., Newport, R.I., Summer 1947); appeared as Mrs. Lucy de Lacy in *Church Street* (New Stages, N.Y.C., Feb. 9, 1948); Amanda Wingfield in *The Glass Menagerie*, Mrs. Wilkins in *Dear Ruth*, and Alice Forster in *Senor Bananas* (Rockaway Park Th., L.I., N.Y., Summer 1948); played the Neighbor Woman in *Blood Wedding* (New Stages, N.Y.C., Feb. 6, 1949); Vashnee in *The Sun and I* (New Stages, Mar. 20, 1949); and appeared in stock as Mrs. Barnes in *The Winslow Boy* (North Shore Players, Marblehead, Mass., Summer 1949).

In stock at the Southbury (Conn.) Playhouse, she appeared as Mrs. Bramson in *Night Must Fall* and Lucy Allerton in *Hay Fever* (Summer 1950); later succeeded Miriam Goldina in the role of Rita in *Diamond Lil* (Coronet, Feb. 5, 1949), in which she toured (1951); understudied the role of Sheila; Prescott in *One Bright Day* (Royale, N.Y.C., Mar. 19, 1952); played Circe in *The Heroes* and the Mother in *Red Riding Hood* (Comedy Club, May 18, 1952); in stock at the Lakeside Summer Th., appeared as Emilie Docoutel in *My 3 Angels*, Aunt Alicia in *Gigi*, played in *A Summer's Day*, and portrayed Leona Samish in *The Time of the Cuckoo* (1952); played Mrs. Stanley in a summer theatre production of *The Man Who Came to Dinner* (Astor, Syracuse, N.Y., 1953); was an understudy for *In the Summer House* (Playhouse, N.Y.C., Dec. 29, 1953); appeared as Violet in *The Family Reunion* (YMHA, 1954); Sarah Shapiro in *The Grass Is Always Greener* (Downtown Natl. Th., Feb. 15, 1955); Lucille Dudley in *This Here Emerson* (New Dramatists Workshop, May 5, 6, 1955); and Mrs. Muriven in *The River Line* (White Barn Th., Westport, Conn., July 24, 1955).

Mrs. Pollock played the Sister in *Middle of the Night* (ANTA, N.Y.C., Feb. 8, 1956), in which she toured (opened Shubert, New Haven, Conn. Oct. 9, 1957); Matroyna in *Power of Darkness* (York, N.Y.C., Sept. 29, 1959); with Peggy Wood's concert reading group; appeared in a concert of poetry-readings, *Equity Stars Present* (1959); played the Mother roles in *Too Close for Comfort* and *The Gay Apprentice* (ANTA Matinee Series, Th. de Lys, Feb. 2, 1960); Mrs. McGillicuddy in *Period of Adjustment* (Helen Hayes Th., Nov. 10, 1960); toured summer theatres as Charlotte Orr in *Critic's Choice* (1961); appeared as Vera Stern in *In the Counting House* (Biltmore, N.Y.C., Dec. 13, 1962); Mrs. Baker in *Come Blow Your Horn* (Playhouse-on-the-Mall, Paramus, N.J., Summer 1963); played Rose Garfield in *Have I Got a Girl for You!* (Music Box, N.Y.C., Dec. 2, 1963); portrayed Olla Robinson in *A Dream of Swallows* (Jan Hus House, Apr. 14, 1964); was in a revival of *Pictures in the Hallway* (Th. de Lys, Dec. 15, 1964); was Alfreda in *The Ceremony of Innocence* (American Place Th., Jan. 1, 1968); replaced (1968) Joan Hickson as Grace in *A Day in the Life of Joe Egg* (Brooks Atkinson Th., Feb. 1, 1968); and was Mrs. Rosen in *The Wrong Way Light Bulb* (John Golden Th., Mar. 4, 1969).

Films. She appeared in *The Last Angry Man* (Col., 1959); *Go Naked in the World* (MGM, 1961); *The Pawnbroker* (Landau, 1964); and *Such Good Friends* (Par., 1971).

Television and Radio. Mrs. Pollock performed on radio for ten years; and has appeared on television on such programs as the Ford Show (CBS); the Nash and Colgate shows (NBC); Robert Montgomery Presents (NBC); The Goldbergs; Kraft Television Th. (NBC); The World of Mr. Sweeney (NBC); Armstrong Circle Th. (NBC); Man Against Crime (CBS); Claudia; Ethel and Albert (ABC); Treasury Men in Action (NBC); Love of Life (CBS); the Ed Sullivan Show (CBS); As the World Turns (CBS); Lamp Unto My Feet (CBS); The Nurses (CBS); Brenner (NBC); and The Doctors (NBC).

Recreation. Music, art, literature, cooking.

PONS, HELENE. Costume designer. b. Weinncheff, in Tiflis, Russia. Married to George Pons (dec. 1959). Member of United Scenic Artists. Address: 165 W. 66th St., New York, NY 10021, tel. (212) 362-4767.

Theatre. She designed and executed the costumes for *The Ivory Door* (Charles Hopkins Th., N.Y.C., Oct. 18, 1927); *Berkeley Square* (Lyceum, Nov. 4, 1929); with Raymond Sovey, designed the costumes for *The Second Little Show* (Royale, Sept. 2, 1930); designed the costumes for *Marseilles* (Henry Miller's Th., Nov. 17, 1930); *Tonight or Never* (Belasco, Nov. 18, 1930); *The Wives of Henry VIII* (Avon, Nov. 11, 1931); *Hey! Nonny Nonny* (Shubert, June 6, 1932); *Empress Eugenie* (Lyceum, Nov. 22, 1932); *Gay Divorce* (Ethel Barrymore Th., Nov. 29, 1932); *The Mad Hopes* (Broadhurst, Dec. 1, 1932); *Alien Corn* (Belasco, Feb. 2, 1933); *Run Little Children* (Lyric, Mar. 1, 1933); *The Loves of Charles II* (48 St. Th., Dec. 27, 1933); *Moorborn* (Playhouse, Apr. 3, 1934); *The Golden Journey* (Booth, Sept. 15, 1936); *Towarich* (Plymouth, Oct. 15, 1936); *Babes in Arms* (Shubert, Apr. 14, 1937); *Edna His Wife* (Little, Dec. 7, 1937); *Our Town* (Henry Miller's Th., Feb. 4, 1938); *Two on an Island* (Broadhurst, Jan. 22, 1940); *Flight to the West* (Guild, Dec. 30, 1940); *The Talley Method* (Henry Miller's Th., Feb. 24, 1941); *Five Alarm Waltz* (Playhouse, Mar. 13, 1941); *Watch on the Rhine* (Martin Beck Th., Apr. 1, 1941); *Distant City* (Longacre, Sept. 22, 1941); *The Man with the Blonde Hair* (Belasco, Nov. 4, 1941); *Theatre* (Hudson,

Nov. 12, 1941); and *Violet* (Belasco, Oct. 24, 1944); *La Tosca* (Center, May 6, 1946).

She designed and executed costumes for *The Skin of Our Teeth* (ANTA, Aug. 17, 1955); *The Diary of Anne Frank* (Cort, Oct. 5, 1955); *The Heavenly Twins* (Booth, Nov. 4, 1955); *Holiday for Lovers* (Longacre, Feb. 14, 1957); *Romanoff and Juliet* (Plymouth, Oct. 10, 1957); *Monique* (John Golden Th., Oct. 22, 1957); *A Lovely Light* (Hudson, Feb. 8, 1961); *Sail Away* (Broadhurst, Oct. 3, 1961); *Daughters of Silence* (Music Box, Nov. 30, 1961); and *Love and Kisses* (Music Box, Dec. 18, 1963).

Films. She designed costumes for the *Richest Man in the World,* originally titled *Father's Day* (MGM, 1930); *The Smiling Lieutenant* (Par., 1931); and *White Christmas* (Par., 1954).

Other Activities. Mrs. Pons's paintings were exhibited at the Panoras Gallery, N.Y.C. (Sept. 1966) and The Wright-Hepburn-Webster Gallery, N.Y.C. (Oct. 1970).

Recreation. Painting.

POOLE, ROY. Actor. b. Roy Neil Poole, Mar. 31, 1924, San Bernardino, Calif., to Roy Warren and Isabel (Trudgen) Poole. Father, grain merchant. Educ. Univ. of Redlands; Stanford Univ. Served in US Army in World War II. Married Sept. 6, 1946, to Marie Blanche Côté. Member of AEA; SAG; AFTRA; The Lambs. Address: c/o Jeff Hunter, 119 W. 57th St., New York, NY 10019, tel. (212) 757-4995.

Theatre. Mr. Poole made his stage debut as Prof. Scallop in *The Dark House* (San Bernardino High School, 1939); trouped in *Volpone* and *Hay Fever* through the European theatre of operations as a member of US Army Special Services (1946); appeared at the National Theatre Conference as David in *Still Life* and Jaques in *As You Like It* (YMHA, N.Y.C., 1948); was Faulkland in the Equity Library Theatre (ELT) production of *The Rivals* (1949); first appeared on the professional stage as Jean in *Now I Lay Me Down to Sleep* (Broadhurst, N.Y.C., Mar. 2, 1950); and played Devery in *Born Yesterday* (Charleston, W.Va., Summer 1950).

He played Shadow in ELT's *Winterset* (Lenox Hill Playhouse, Dec. 17, 1952); Lucifer in ELT's *Dr. Faustus* (Lenox Hill Playhouse, Apr. 1953); was a member of the original cast of *Under Milk Wood* (YMHA Poetry Center, 1953); was the Messenger in *Cretan Woman* (Provincetown Playhouse, July 7, 1954); Mr. Steele in *Clandestine Marriage* (Provincetown Playhouse, Oct. 2, 1954); Leroy in *The Bad Seed* (46 St. Th., Dec. 8, 1954); La Trémouille in *St. Joan* (Phoenix, Sept. 11, 1956); played the title role in *Macbeth* (Shakespeare in the Park, Summer 1957); played various roles in *I Knock at the Door* (Belasco Th., Sept. 29, 1957); was the Second Workman in *Purple Dust* (Cherry Lane Th., Dec. 27, 1957); the Hard Case in *The Quare Fellow* (Circle in the Square, Oct. 20, 1958); David Bowman in *Flowering Cherry* (Lyceum, Oct. 21, 1959); the Chief of Police in *The Balcony* (Circle in the Square, Mar. 3, 1960); Att'y.-Gen'l. Knox in *Face of a Hero* (Eugene O'Neill Th., Oct. 20, 1960); Dobelle in *Moon in the Yellow River* (East End, Feb. 6, 1961); the Baron in *Witches' Sabbath* (Madison Ave. Playhouse, Apr. 19, 1962); Starbuck in *Moby Dick* (Ethel Barrymore Th., Nov. 28, 1962); Danton in *Poor Bitos* (Cort, Nov. 14, 1964); Stephen Hopkins in *1776* (46 St. Th., Mar. 16, 1969); and Seth Petersen in *Scratch* (St. James Th., May 6, 1971).

Films. Mr. Poole made his motion picture debut as Owen Bradley in *Experiment in Terror* (Col., 1962). He appeared also as McHabe in *Up the Down Staircase* (WB, 1967); was the Editor in *Gaily, Gaily* (UA, 1969); the Union President in *Sometimes a Great Notion* (Univ., 1972); and Stephen Hopkins in *1776* (Col., 1972).

Television. Mr. Poole's first television appearance was on Kay Kyser's Kollege of Musical Knowledge (NBC, 1948). He has been a guest star on Banacek; Toma; The F.B.I. (ABC); Saree; The Invaders; The Defenders (CBS); Naked City (ABC); Armstrong Circle Theatre (NBC); Kraft Mystery Th. (NBC); Omnibus (CBS); Philco Playhouse (NBC); Dundee and the Culhane; Hallmark Hall of Fame (NBC); and other programs. He has also been on such daytime serials as Search for Tomorrow (CBS); As the World Turns (CBS); A Time for Us; Secret Storm; Edge of Night (CBS); Love Is a Many Splendored Thing (CBS); and Where the Heart Is. He was the District Attorney in *The Whole World Is Watching* (NBC, Mar. 11, 1969); Mister Robert in *The Autobiography of Miss Jane Pittman* (CBS, Jan. 31, 1974); and co-starred in *A Cry from the Wilderness* (1974).

POPE, CURTIS L. Educator. b. Curtis Lamar Pope, Jan. 19, 1919, Alba, Tex., to William Floyd and Roda Lillian (Dollar) Pope. Father, cattleman. Grad. Alba H.S.; East Texas State Univ., B.S. 1941; State Univ. of Iowa, M.A. 1949, Ph.D. 1957; attended Univ. of Texas, 1953; Univ. of Missouri, 1955. Married 1951 to Mary Mildred Lowrey, pianist, teacher. Served WW II, US Army, PTO; rank, Capt. Member of ATA; Texas Educational Th. Assn.; Texas Speech Assn. (exec. comm.); Alpha Psi Omega. Address: (home) 1505 Bois d'Arc, Commerce, TX 75428, tel. (214) 886-3382; (bus.) c/o East Texas State Univ., Commerce, TX 75428, tel. (214) 468-2202.

Dr. Pope has been professor and head of the Dept. of Speech and Drama, East Texas State Univ., and director of the Univ. Playhouse, E.T.S.U. He has directed and designed student productions and has been consultant in theatre design and technical facilities. He has also been director-manager of the Jefferson (Tex.) Playhouse.

He wrote the book and lyrics for three original musicals: *Gold and Blue* (1953); *Ye Gods* (1954); and *Thumbs Up* (1960).

Other Activities. Dr. Pope has conducted historical research into operations of Opera Houses in nineteenth-century Texas and the Southwest.

Awards. He received the Purple Mask Award for excellence in theatre at the Univ. of Iowa (1957). His productions for the Amer. Coll. Th. Festival were selected to represent Texas at the Region V ACTF (1971–73), and on two occasions were nominated to advance to the national finals. His production of *The Time of Your Life* (Ford Th., Washington, D.C., 1971) was named one of the ten best college theatre productions in America.

POPE, KARL THEODORE. Setting and lighting designer. b. May 7, 1937, Vernal, Utah, to Lloyd Theodore and Oris (Powell) Pope. Father, welder. Grad. Brigham Young Univ., Provo, Utah; Wayne State Univ. Married Jan. 11, 1960, to Connie (Lundell) Pope; three daughters, three sons. Member of ATA; SAA. Address: (home) 476 East 2950 North, Provo, UT 84601, tel. (801) 374-8083; (bus.) Dept. of Speech and Dramatic Arts, Brigham Young Univ., Provo, UT 84601, tel. (801) 374-1211, Ext. 2284.

Mr. Pope is graduate coordinator and designer, Dept. of Drama, Brigham Young Univ. He started work as a setting and lighting designer for a production at the university of *Carousel* (1962). Subsequently, he was setting and lighting designer for productions at Kearney (Neb.) State Coll. of *The Time of Your Life* and *Harvey* (Dec. 8–11, 1965), *Medea* (Mar. 9–12, 1966), and *Inherit the Wind* (May 11–14, 1966). He was setting designer at Brigham Young for *Dear Me, the Sky Is Falling* (Oct. 12–29, 1966), *Abe Lincoln: New Salem Days* (Nov. 14, 1966), *Lute Song* (Jan. 4–16, 1967), *The Dragon* (May 1–18, 1967), and *La Bohème* (May 1–6, 1967). He was setting and lighting designer for *Barefoot in the Park* (Sept. 20–29, 1967), *The Barretts of Wimpole Street* (Oct. 13–28, 1967), *Macbeth* (Dec. 8–20, 1967), *The Little Foxes* (Jan. 4–16, 1968), *A Majority of One* (Mar. 1–16, 1968), *La Perichole* and *Harry's Boat* (May 8–11, 1968), *Arsenic and Old Lace* (July 10–13, Sept. 20–28, 1968), *Richard III* (Oct. 18–Nov. 2, 1968), *The Comedy of Errors* (Jan. 13–18, 1969), *Walking Happy* (Feb. 12–15, 1969), *Pilgrim's Progress* (Apr. 28–May 3, 1969), *The Taming of the Shrew* (June 25–28, 1969), *Joan of Lorraine* (1969), *Korihor* (1969), *Stolen Sword* (1969), *The Imaginary Invalid* (Feb. 27–Mar. 14, 1970), *Treasure Island* (1970), *Pilgrim's Progress* (Apr. 22–25, 1970), *Once Upon a Mattress* (Apr. 17–May 2, 1970), *Night Must Fall* (Sept. 24–Oct. 3, 1970), *Mary, Mary* (Oct. 15–31, 1970), and *The Wizard and the Wand* (1970).

He also designed *The Birds* (Jan. 7–19, 1971), *Abe Lincoln in Illinois* (Feb. 25–Mar. 13, 1971), *Aladdin* (1971), *The Late Christopher Bean* (Aug. 11–14, 1971), *Hello, Dolly!* (1971), *The Taming of the Shrew* (1971), *Beauty and the Beast* (1971), *Move On!* (1971), *Star Spangled Girl* (Oct. 21–Nov. 6, 1971), *Dance on a Country Grave* (Dec. 2–17, 1971), *Play the Drums Again* (Mar. 16–31, 1972), *You're a Good Man, Charlie Brown* (Apr. 27–May 13, 1972), the operas *Pagliacci* (Apr. 19–22, 1972) and *Gianni Schicchi* (Apr. 19–22, 1972), *Twelfth Night* (1972), *Move On!* (1972), *Good Night, Good Knight* (1972), *Julius Caesar* (Oct. 13–28, 1972), *Madama Butterfly* (Nov. 1–4, 1972), *Stone Tables* (Mar. 16–31, 1973), *Cinderella* (1973), *Lucy the Forsaken* (1973), *Hello, Dolly!* (Jan. 18–26, 1973), *The Departure* (1973), *Dido and Aeneas* (1973), *Noye's Fludde* (1973), *Fiddler on the Roof* (1973), *A Midsummer Night's Dream* (June 6–15, 1974), *Family Portrait* (Oct. 10–25, 1974); and *A Man for All Seasons* (Dec. 4–14, 1974).

Television. In 1968, Mr. Pope did the designs for three one-act plays on television and since that time he has worked on numerous other television shows.

Published Works. Mr. Pope prepared a syllabus for students of voice, diction, and interpretation.

Recreation. Antique automobiles, art.

PORTER, DON. Actor. b. Sept. 24, 1912, Miami, Okla., to Jesse Bradley and Hazel Margaret (Wills) Porter. Father, banker. Grad. Oregon Inst. of Technology. Studied acting with Bess Whitcomb and the Portland (Ore.) Civic Th. Sch. Married to Peggy Converse; one son; one daughter, Melissa Murphy, actress. Served U.S. Army Signal Corps, WW II. Member of AEA; SAG; DGA.

Pre-Theatre. Bank teller, office manager, salesman, reporter.

Theatre. Mr. Porter made his acting debut playing a messenger in *Elizabeth the Queen* (Civic Th., Portland, Oregon, 1936); appeared in numerous West Coast productions including *Another Part of the Forest, The Philadelphia Story, Dream Girl, Who Was that Lady I Saw You With, Black Chiffon, Two Blind Mice, And So to Bed, Blithe Spirit, O Mistress Mine, The First Mrs. Fraser,* and *This Happy Breed;* toured with Dame Judith Anderson in companies of *Family Portrait,* and *Tower Beyond Tragedy;* played Aubrey Piper in *The Show-Off* (Eighteen Actors Co., Los Angeles, 1954); J. Malcolm and Major Pollack in *Separate Tables* (West Coast tour, 1958); William Russell in *The Best Man* (tour, opened Festival Th., Stratford, Conn., Jan. 7, 1962; closed Hartman, Columbus, Apr. 28, 1962); replaced Roland Winters (Nov. 19, 1962) as Malcolm Turnbull in *Calculated Risk* (Ambassador, N.Y.C., Oct. 31, 1962); played John Cleves in *Any Wednesday* (Music Box, Feb. 18, 1964); succeeded Barnard Hughes as Jim Bolton in *Generation* (tour, opened Fisher, Detroit, Aug. 8, 1966); closed Hanna, Cleveland, Mar. 8, 1967); replaced Dan Dailey (May 24, 1969) as Sam Nash in *Plaza Suite* (Plymouth, N.Y.C., Feb. 14, 1968); and played McCue, City Press, in a revival of *The Front Page* (Ethel Barrymore Th., May 10, 1969).

Films. He made his screen debut in *Eagle Squadron* (U, 1942); subsequently appearing in *Madame Spy* (1942); *Top Sergeant* (UI, 1942); *Night Monster* (UI, 1942); *Keep 'Em Slugging* (UI, 1943); *Eyes of the Underworld* (UI, 1943); *Danger Woman* (UI, 1946); *She-Wolf of London* (UI, 1946); *Cuban Pete* (UI, 1946); *Wild Beauty* (UI, 1946); *Buck Privates Come Home* (UI, 1947); *711 Ocean Drive* (Col., 1950); *The Racket* (RKO, 1951); *The Savage* (Par., 1952); *Because You're Mine* (MGM, 1952); *The Turning Point* (Par., 1952); *Cripple Creek* (Col., 1952); *Our Miss Brooks* (WB, 1956); *Who Done It?* (UA, 1956); *Bachelor in Paradise* (MGM, 1961); *Gidget Goes to Rome* (CPT, 1963); *Youngblood Hawke* (WB, 1964); *Live a Little, Love a Little* (MGM, 1969); *The Candidate* (WB, 1972); *Forty Carats* (Col., 1973); *Mame* (WB, 1974); and *White Line Fever* (Col., 75).

Television. Mr. Porter's appearances include Private Secretary (CBS); The Ann Sothern Show

(CBS); Gidget (ABC); I Love My Doctor (CBS); Judd for the Defense (ABC); Love, American Style (ABC); Mod Squad (ABC); Green Acres (CBS); Banacek (NBC); The Rookies (ABC); and Cade's County (CBS).

PORTER, STEPHEN. Director, actor, producer, designer, teacher, translator. b. Stephen Winthrop Porter, Ogdensburg, N.Y., July 24, 1925, to Charles Talbot and Anna Martin (Newton) Porter. Father, engineer; mother, teacher. Grad. Yale Coll.; Yale Drama School. Member of AEA; SSD&C; DGA.

Theatre. Mr. Porter began his work as a theatrical director and designer at McGill Univ., Montreal, Quebec, Canada, where he directed and designed productions of *Hippolytus* (Mar. 1952), *Measure for Measure* (Mar. 1953), *The Caprice of Marianne* (Oct. 1953), *The Cenci* (Mar. 1954), *The Seagull* (Oct. 1954), and *Much Ado About Nothing* (Mar. 1955).

His first professional work was his own production of *The Misanthrope*, which he also directed (Th. East, N.Y.C., Nov. 12, 1956). He directed and designed a production of *The Country Wife* (Renata Th., June 26, 1957); directed summer stock productions of *Mr. Roberts, Cat on a Hot Tin Roof, The Matchmaker, Inherit the Wind, Auntie Mame, Room at the Top*, and other plays (Red Barn Th., Northport, N.Y., 1958, 1959); *Dark of the Moon* and *Our Town* (Fred Miller Th., Milwaukee, Wis., Nov.–Dec. 1959); and, at the McCarter Th., Princeton, N.J., Association of Producing Artists (APA) repertory productions of *Right You Are* (Oct. 13, 1960), *Scapin* (Nov. 3, 1960), *King Lear* (Feb. 3, 1961), and *Twelfth Night* (Feb. 23, 1961); *The Alchemist* (Apr. 6, 1962) and *Antigone* (1962); *Caligula, Galileo*, and *Julius Caesar* (1963). At the Playhouse in the Park, Cincinnati, Ohio (1962–65), he directed *The Lady's Not for Burning, The Hostage, The Devil's Disciple, The Burnt Flower Bed* (May 13, 1964), *The Doctor in Spite of Himself, Major Barbara* (May 19, 1965), and *Sodom and Gomorrah* (May 25, 1966).

He directed *Tartuffe* (Fred Miller Th., Milwaukee, Wis., Jan. 8, 1964); *The Alchemist* (Gate Th., N.Y.C., Sept. 14, 1964); *The Tempest* (Fred Miller Th., Milwaukee, Wis., Jan. 27, 1965); *The School for Wives* (McCarter Th., Princeton, N.J., Feb. 27, 1965); *The Birds* (McCarter Th., Princeton, N.J., Apr. 3, 1965); *The Diary of a Scoundrel* (Fred Miller Th., Milwaukee, Wis., Nov. 18, 1965); *Twelfth Night* (Trinity Square Rep. Co., Providence, R.I., Jan. 6, 1966); *Henry IV, Part 1* (Fred Miller Th., Milwaukee, Wis., Feb. 24, 1966); *Phaedra* (Th. of the Living Arts, Philadelphia, Pa., May 16, 1967); *Thieves' Carnival* (Tyrone Guthrie Th., Minneapolis, Minn., June 2, 1967); *Enrico IV* (Studio Arena, Buffalo, N.Y., Jan. 11, 1968); *The Master Builder* (Tyrone Guthrie Th., Minneapolis, Minn., June 20, 1968); *As You Like It* (American Shakespeare Festival, Stratford, Conn., June 23, 1968); *The Wrong Way Light Bulb* (John Golden Th., N.Y.C., Mar. 4, 1969); *Chemin de Fer* (Mark Taper Forum, Los Angeles, Calif., June 5, 1969); and *The Guardsman* (Shaw Festival, Niagara on the Lake, Ontario, Can., Aug. 1969).

In addition to the preceding, Mr. Porter toured continuously from 1960 to 1969 with APA Rep. (Toronto, Ontario, Canada; N.Y.C.; Ann Arbor, Mich.; Los Angeles), whose presentations included productions directed by Mr. Porter of *Scapin*, which he also translated (Trueblood Th., Ann Arbor, Oct. 17, 1963; Phoenix, N.Y.C., Mar. 9, 1964); *A Phoenix Too Frequent* (Trueblood Th., Oct. 17, 1963); *Right You Are* (Trueblood Th., Nov. 17, 1963; Phoenix, N.Y.C., Mar. 4, 1964; Lyceum, Nov. 22, 1966); *Impromptu at Versailles* (Phoenix, Mar. 9, 1964); *Man and Superman* (Ann Arbor, Sept. 30, 1964; Phoenix, Dec. 6, 1964); *The Hostage* (Ann Arbor, Oct. 14, 1964); *The Wild Duck* (Ann Arbor, Oct. 6, 1965; Lyceum, N.Y.C., Jan. 11, 1967); *The Show-Off* (Ann Arbor, Oct. 17, 1967; Lyceum, Dec. 5, 1967); *The Misanthrope* (Ann Arbor, Sept. 17, 1968; Lyceum, Oct. 9, 1968); *King Lear; Twelfth Night;* and *Private Lives* (Ann Arbor, Oct. 14, 1969; Billy Rose Th., N.Y.C., Dec. 4, 1969).

He also directed a revival of *Harvey* (ANTA, N.Y.C., Feb. 24, 1970); *Richard II* (Old Globe Th., San Diego, Calif., June 12, 1970); *The School for Wives* (Phoenix Th. Co., Ann Arbor, Mich., Jan. 26, 1971; Lyceum, N.Y.C., Feb. 16, 1971); *An Italian Straw Hat* (Avon Th., Stratford Festival, Ontario, Can., July 2, 1971); and *Captain Brassbound's Conversion* (Kennedy Ctr., Washington, D.C., Mar. 13, 1972; Ethel Barrymore Th., N.Y.C., Apr. 17, 1972). For the New Phoenix Rep. Co., he directed *Don Juan*, which he also adapted (Lyceum, Dec. 11, 1972); *Chemin de Fer* (Ethel Barrymore Th., Nov. 26, 1973); and *The Rules of the Game* (Helen Hayes Th., Dec. 12, 1974).

Other productions directed by Mr. Porter include *The Enchanted* (Mar. 2, 1973) and *The Prodigal Daughter* (Nov. 1, 1973), both at the Kennedy Ctr., Washington, D.C.; *The School for Wives* and *Born Yesterday* (both Royal Poinciana Playhouse, Palm Beach, Fla., 1973); *The Lady's Not for Burning* (Goodman Th., Chicago, Ill., Apr. 1, 1973); and *You Never Can Tell* (McCarter Th., Princeton, N.J., Mar. 28, 1974).

Television. He directed, with Kirk Browning, *A Touch of the Poet* (PBS, Apr. 24, 1974).

Awards. Mr. Porter was nominated for an Antoinette Perry (Tony) Award (1971) for his direction of *The School for Wives*.

POSTON, TOM. Actor. b. Oct. 17, 1927, Columbus, Ohio, to George and Margaret Poston. Father, dairy chemist, liquor salesman. Attended Bethany Coll., 1938–40. Studied for the theatre at AADA, N.Y.C., 1945–47. Married 1955 to Jean Sullivan; one daughter; married June 8, 1968, to Kay Hudson; one daughter, one son. Served USAAF WW II, pilot. Member of AEA; AFTRA; SAG.

Theatre. Mr. Poston first performed as a tumbler with "The Flying Zebley" (c. 1930); succeeded (1947) to a role in *Cyrano de Bergerac* (Alvin, N.Y.C., Oct. 8, 1946); and played Otakar and Quartermaster in *The Insect Comedy* (NY City Ctr., June 3, 1948).

He produced a season of stock (Rehoboth Beach, Del., Summer 1948), appearing in several productions; played the Herald in Louis Calhern's *King Lear* (Natl., N.Y.C., Dec. 25, 1950); Pvt. Turnipseed in *Stockade* (President, Feb. 4, 1954); Edward Martin in *The Grand Prize* (Plymouth, Jan. 26, 1955); succeeded (1955) Orson Bean in the role of George MacCauley in *Will Success Spoil Rock Hunter?* (Belasco, Oct. 13, 1955); appeared as Arthur Westlake in *Goodbye Again* (Helen Hayes Th., Apr. 24, 1956); and in *Best of Burlesque* (Carnegie Hall Playhouse, Sept. 29, 1957).

He succeeded (June 30, 1958) Peter Ustinov as the General in *Romanoff and Juliet* (Plymouth, Oct. 10, 1957); played Miles Pringle in *Drink to Me Only* (54 St. Th., Oct. 8, 1958); Lt. Ferguson Howard in *Golden Fleecing* (Henry Miller's Th., Oct. 15, 1959); Cornelius in *Come Play with Me* (York Playhouse, Apr. 30, 1959); Woodrow Truesmith in *The Conquering Hero* (ANTA, Jan. 16, 1961); in stock, the title role in *Destry Rides Again* (Dallas, Tex.; St. Louis, Mo.; Summer 1961); succeeded (July 1962) Hal March in the role of Alan Baker in *Come Blow Your Horn* (Brooks Atkinson Th., N.Y.C., Feb. 22, 1961); and succeeded (Nov. 1962) Barry Nelson in the role of Bob McKellaway in *Mary, Mary* (Helen Hayes Th., Mar. 8, 1961); appeared in *The Butter and Egg Man* (Ivanhoe Th., Chicago, Sept. 26, 1967); replaced Murray Hamilton (Dec. 22, 1969) as Billy Boylan in *Forty Carats* (Morosco, N.Y.C., Dec. 26, 1968); played Walter London in *But, Seriously. . .* (Henry Miller's Th., Feb. 27, 1969); replaced Phil Silvers (Aug. 9, 1972) as Pdseudolus in *A Funny Thing Happened on the Way to the Forum* (Lunt-Fontanne, Mar. 30, 1972); appeared in *Lovers and Other Strangers* (Playhouse in the Park, Philadelphia, Summer 1973); played Lenny in *Of Mice and Men* (Bucks County Playhouse, New Hope, Pa., Oct. 1973); and, at the McCarter Th. (Princeton, N.J.) appeared in *Mother Courage and Her Children* (Feb. 13, 1975); and *Romeo and Juliet* (Mar. 27, 1975).

His appearances in summer stock and touring productions include *The Odd Couple; Easy Does It; Any Wednesday; Bye, Bye, Birdie; The Fantasticks;* and *Catch Me If You Can*.

Films. Mr. Poston has appeared in *The City That Never Sleeps* (Rep., 1953); *Zotz!* (Col., 1962); *The Old Dark House* (Col., 1963); and *Cold Turkey* (UA, 1971).

Television. He was the emcee for the series, Entertainment (ABC, premiere Feb. 26, 1955); appeared in *You Sometimes Get Rich* (Playwrights '56, NBC); performed regularly on the Steve Allen Show (NBC, 1956–58); played the title role in *The Change in Chester* (US Steel Hour, CBS); became a regular panelist on To Tell the Truth (CBS); appeared in *Merman on Broadway* (NBC); *The Enchanted* (Play of the Week, PBS); *The Tempest* (Hallmark Hall of Fame, NBC); and The Bob Newhart Show (CBS).

Awards. Mr. Poston received a NATAS (Emmy) Award in connection with his appearances on the Steve Allen Show (1959).

POTTER, H. C. Director, producer. b. Henry C. Potter, New York City, Nov. 13, 1904, to Alonzo and Elzie (Nicholas) Potter. Father, investment banker. Grad. St. Mark's Sch., Southborough, Mass., 1922; Yale Univ., B.A. 1926; studied with George Pierce Baker, 47 workshop; Yale Sch. of Drama, 1926–28. Married Sept. 25, 1926, to Lucilla Wylie; three sons. Served US Army Air Transport Command, 1943–44. Member of DGA (bd. mbr., 1953–to date; natl. secy.; 1956–58); SSD&C; Century Assn.; Racquet and Tennis Club; Labrador Retriever Club (bd. of dir.). Address: 166 E. 63rd St., New York, NY 10021, tel. (212) TE 8-3564.

Theatre. Mr. Potter made his stage debut in the Yale Dramatic Assn. production of *Out of Luck* (Shubert, New Haven, Conn., 1925), with which he toured; with George Haight, Mr. Potter founded the Hampton Players (Southampton, L.I., N.Y., 1927) and co-produced and directed *Dover Road* and four plays each successive summer (1927–33).

He was assistant stage manager for *Marco Millions* (Guild, N.Y.C., Jan. 9, 1928); assistant stage manager for the tour of *Marco Millions* and *Volpone* (opened Nixon, Pittsburgh, Pa., Sept. 3, 1928); directed *Overture* (Longacre, N.Y.C., Dec. 5, 1930); produced, with George Haight, and directed *Double Door* (Ritz, Sept. 21, 1933); *Wednesday's Child* (Longacre, Jan. 16, 1934); *Post Road* (Masque, Dec. 4, 1934); and *Kind Lady* (Booth, Apr. 23, 1935).

Mr. Potter directed *A Bell for Adano* (Cort, Dec. 6, 1944; Phoenix, London, Sept. 19, 1945); *Anne of the Thousand Days* (Shubert, N.Y.C., Dec. 8, 1948); *Point of No Return* (Alvin, Dec. 13, 1952); and *Sabrina Fair* (National, Nov. 11, 1953).

Films. Mr. Potter began as a film director with *Beloved Enemy* (UA, 1936); followed by *Wings over Honolulu* (UA, 1937); *Romance in the Dark* (Par., 1938); *The Cowboy and the Lady* (UA, 1938); *Shopworn Angel* (MGM, 1938); *The Story of Vernon and Irene Castle* (RKO, 1939); *Blackmail* (MGM, 1939); *Congo Maisie* (MGM, 1940); *Second Chorus* (Par., 1940); *Hellzapoppin'* (U, 1941); *Victory Through Air Power* (UA, 1943); *Mr. Lucky* (RKO, 1943); *The Farmer's Daughter* (RKO, 1947); *A Likely Story* (RKO, 1947); *The Time of Your Life* (UA, 1948); *You Gotta Stay Happy* (U, 1948); *Mr. Blandings Builds His Dream House* (RKO, 1948); *The Miniver Story* (MGM, 1950); *Three for the Show* (Col., 1955); and *Top Secret Affair* (WB, 1957).

Other Activities. Mr. Potter was a civilian airline captain and civilian RAF flight instructor (1941–43).

POTTS, NANCY. Costume designer. Attended Washington Univ., St. Louis, Mo. Member of United Scenic Artists (1963–to date).

Pre-Theatre. Fashion designer.

Theatre. For the Association of Producing Artists (APA) at the Phoenix Th., N.Y.C., Miss Potts designed the costumes for *Right You Are If You Think You Are* (Mar. 4, 1964), *The Tavern* (Mar. 5, 1964), a double-bill of *Scapin* and *Impromptu at Versailles*

(Mar. 9, 1964), and *The Lower Depths* (Mar. 30, 1964). For the next several years, APA spent part of each year in residence at the Univ. of Michigan, Ann Arbor, where productions were prepared and performed prior to opening in N.Y.C. Miss Potts designed *War and Peace* (Ann Arbor, Sept. 23, 1964; Phoenix Th., N.Y.C., Jan. 11, 1965); *Man and Superman* (Sept. 30–Dec. 6, 1964); *Judith* (Oct. 28, 1964–Mar. 24, 1965); *You Can't Take It with You* (Sept. 29–Nov. 23, 1965); *The Wild Duck* (Oct 6, 1965–Jan. 11, 1967); *Herekles* (Ann Arbor only, Oct. 27, 1965); *The School for Scandal* (Sept. 20–Nov. 2, 1966); *We Comrades Three* (Oct. 18 –Dec. 20, 1966); *Pantagleize* (Sept. 19–Nov. 30, 1967); *Exit the King* (Oct. 10, 1967–Jan. 9, 1968); *The Show-Off* (Oct. 17–Dec. 5, 1967); *The Cherry Orchard* (Lyceum, N.Y.C., only, Mar. 19, 1968); *The Misanthrope* (Sept. 17–Oct. 9, 1968); *Hamlet* (Oct. 1, 1968–Mar. 3, 1969); *The Cocktail Party* (Lyceum only, Oct. 7, 1968); *Cock-a-Doodle Dandy* (Oct. 15, 1968–Jan. 20, 1969); *Macbeth* (Ann Arbor only, Sept. 16, 1969); *The Chronicles of Hell* (Ann Arbor only, Sept. 1969); *Private Lives* (Ann Arbor only, Oct. 14, 1969); *The Criminals* (Ann Arbor only, Jan. 26, 1970); *Harvey* (Ann Arbor only, Feb. 2, 1970); and *The School for Wives* (Jan. 26–Feb. 16, 1971).

For other companies, Miss Potts has designed costumes for *Sgt. Musgrave's Dance* (Arena Stage, Washington, D.C., Mar 17, 1966); *The Magistrate* (Arena Stage, Dec. 6, 1966); *The Crucible* (Arena Stage, Jan. 17, 1967); *Hair* (Biltmore, N.Y.C., Apr. 29, 1968); *Horseman, Pass By* (Fortune, Jan. 15, 1969); *La Strada* (Lunt-Fontanne, Dec. 14, 1969); *Harvey* (ANTA Th., Feb. 24, 1970); *The Criminals* (Sheridan Sq. Playhouse, Feb. 25, 1970); *The Persians* (St. George's Church, Apr. 15, 1970); *The Grass Harp* (Martin Beck Th., Nov. 2, 1971); *The Selling of the President* (Shubert, Mar. 22, 1972); *Don Juan* (Lyceum, Dec. 11, 1972); *Rainbow* (Orpheum, Dec. 18, 1972); *Medea* (Circle in the Square/Joseph E. Levine Th., Jan. 17, 1973); *Detective Story* (pre-Bway tour, opened Paramus, N.J., Playhouse, Feb. 18, 1973; closed Shubert, Philadelphia, Mar. 24, 1973); *A Streetcar Named Desire* (Vivian Beaumont Th., N.Y.C., Apr. 26, 1973; reopened St. James Th., Oct. 4, 1973); *Veronica's Room* (Music Box, Oct. 25, 1973); *Chemin de Fer* (Ethel Barrymore Th., Nov. 26, 1973); *Total Eclipse* (Chelsea Th. Ctr. at Brooklyn Acad. of Music, Feb. 23, 1974); *Guys and Dolls* (Goodman Memorial Th., Chicago, May 10, 1974); *Who's Who in Hell* (Lunt-Fontanne, N.Y.C., Dec. 9, 1974); *The Rules of the Game* (Helen Hayes Th., Dec. 12, 1974); *Present Laughter* (Eisenhower Th., John F. Kennedy Ctr., Washington, D.C., Apr. 29, 1975); *Edward II* (Harkness Th., N.Y.C., Oct. 21, 1974); and *The Time of Your Life* (Harkness Th., Oct. 27, 1975).

Awards. Miss Potts received the *Best Plays* Award as best costumer of a Bway musical (1967–68) for *Hair;* the Joseph Maharam Foundation Award (1967–68) for her designs for APA; and the *Saturday Review of Literature* Award for her designs for *Pantagleize*.

POVAH, PHYLLIS. Actress. b. Phyllis Seely Povah, Detroit, Mich., to Edwin H. and Anne Roberta (Godard) Povah. Attended Central H.S., Detroit, Mich.; Bishop Bethune Sch., Oshawa, Ontario, Canada; grad. Univ. of Michigan, B.A. Married Mar. 14, 1921, to James E. Shields (marr. dis.); one daughter; married Aug. 2, 1930, to Henry E. Drayton; one son. Member of AEA; SAG; ANTA.

Pre-Theatre. Advertising.

Theatre. Miss Povah made her Bway debut as Margot Haser in *The Light of the World* (Lyric Th., Jan. 6, 1920); subsequently appeared as Dinah in *Mr. Pim Passes By* (Garrick, Feb. 28, 1921); Muriel in *Hospitality* (48 St. Th., Nov. 13, 1922); Jane Crosby in *Icebound* (Sam H. Harris Th., Feb. 10, 1923); Faith Bly in *Windows* (Garrick, Oct. 8, 1923); Nettie Minick in *Minick* (Booth, Sept. 24, 1924); Vilma in *A Tale of the Wolf* (Empire, Oct. 7, 1925); and Ruth in *The Virgin* (Maxine Elliott's Th., Feb. 22, 1926).

She made her London debut in the role of Grace Livingstone in *The First Year* (Apollo, Nov. 1926); returned to Bway as Julia Jones in *Blood Money* (Hudson, Aug. 22, 1927); and appeared as Marie Tobin in *Marriage on Approval* (Wallack's, Mar. 1, 1928); Ann Carter in *Vermont* (Erlanger, Jan. 7, 1929); Hope Ames in *Hotel Universe* (Martin Beck Th., Apr. 14, 1930); Grace Manning in *Re-Echo* (Forrest, Jan. 10, 1934); Claire Hammond in *Co-Respondent Unknown* (Ritz, Feb. 11, 1936); Edith Potter in *The Women* (Ethel Barrymore Th., Dec. 26, 1936); and Margery Harvey in *Dear Octopus* (Broadhurst, Jan. 11, 1939).

She appeared as Ellen Kincaid in *The Land Is Bright* (Music Box, Oct. 28, 1941); Belle Newell in *Broken Journey* (Henry Miller's Th., June 23, 1942); Pancy in *Naked Genius* (Plymouth, Oct. 21, 1943); Edith Wilkins in *Dear Ruth* (Henry Miller's Th., Dec. 13, 1944); Stella Livingston in *Light Up the Sky* (Royale, Nov. 18, 1948); Monica Bare in *Gently Does It* (Playhouse, Oct. 28, 1953); and Mrs. Gans in *Anniversary Waltz* (Broadhurst, Apr. 7, 1954).

Films. Miss Povah made her debut as Edith Potter in *The Women* (MGM, 1939); subsequently, she appeared in *Let's Face It* (Par., 1943); *The Marrying Kind* (Col., 1952); *Pat and Mike* (MGM, 1952); and as Mrs. Gans in *Happy Anniversary* (UA, 1959).

POWYS, STEPHEN. Playwright. b. Virginia de Lanty, 1907, Los Angeles, Calif., to John Mark and Mary Virginia (Durnall) de Lanty. Attended Ward Seminary, Nashville, Tenn., 1922–24. Married to Guy Reginald Bolton, playwright. Address: Shore Rd., Remsenburg, L.I., NY 11960, tel. (516) 325-0206.

Theatre. Miss Powys wrote *Wise To-Morrow* (Biltmore Th., N.Y.C., Oct. 15, 1937; Lyric, London, England Feb. 17, 1937); and *Three Blind Mice* (Duke of York's, Apr. 26, 1938), which was adapted into a musical by Guy Bolton, Parke Levy, and Alan Lipscott, entitled *Walk with Music* (Ethel Barrymore Th., N.Y.C., June 4, 1940); and, with Mr. Bolton, adapted from a play by Sacha Guitry, *Don't Listen, Ladies!* (St. James's, London, Sept. 2, 1948; Booth, N.Y.C., Dec. 28, 1948). She also wrote *There's Always To-Morrow* (1940) and *The Girl in the Swing* (1965).

PREMICE, JOSEPHINE. Actress, singer, dancer. b. July 21, 1926, Brooklyn, N.Y. Grad. Columbia Univ.; attended Cornell Univ. Married Nov. 14, 1958, to Timothy Fales; one son; one daughter. Member of AEA; AGMA; AGVA.

Theatre. Miss Premice made her N.Y.C. debut in the revue, *Blue Holiday* (Belasco, May 21, 1945); appeared in *Caribbean Carnival* (International, Dec. 5, 1947); played Tulip in the pre-Bway tryout of *House of Flowers* (opened Erlanger, Philadelphia, Nov. 25, 1954), but withdrew before the N.Y.C. opening (Alvin, Dec. 30, 1954); played Bamm in *Mister Johnson* (Martin Beck Th., Mar. 29, 1956); and Ginger in *Jamaica* (Imperial, Oct. 31, 1957).

Miss Premice resided in Italy from 1960 to 1966; returned to the US, and performed her one-woman show, *Here's Josephine Premice* (E. 74 St. Th., N.Y.C., Apr. 25, 1966); appeared in *An Evening of Negro Poetry and Folk Music* (Delacorte Th., Central Park, Aug. 15, 1966), which was subsequently presented as *A Hand is On the Gate* (Longacre, Sept. 21, 1966); played Madame Fleur in the revival of *House of Flowers* (Th. de Lys, Jan. 28, 1968); Madame Xenia, the fortune teller, in a summer stock production of *The Killing of Sister George;* Clytemnestra in *Electra* (NY Shakespeare Fest. Mobile Th., N.Y.C., Aug. 5, 1969); Charlotta in *The Cherry Orchard* (Public/Anspacher Th., Jan. 11, 1973); in a workshop production of Phillip Hayes Dean's one-act play, *This Bird Dawning All Night Long* (Actors Studio, Mar. 7, 1974); and in the revue, *Bubbling Brown Sugar* (ANTA, Mar. 2, 1976).

Television. Miss Premice has appeared in *Pins and Needles* (Educ., Mar. 21, 1966); frequently on the Merv Griffin Show (Ind., 1966–67); on Girl Talk (ABC); and in *A Nice Place to Visit* (Showcase-Music, Educ., May 14, 1967).

Night Clubs. She has performed extensively all over the world, inc. N.Y.C. (Village Vanguard, 1947; Blue Angel); Los Angeles (Mocambo, Interlude); Las Vegas (Frontier); Chicago (Mr. Kelly's, 1958); Montreal (Samovar; Ritz Carlton, 1964); London; Paris (Chez Florence); Madrid; and Rio de Janiero.

Awards. She was nominated for an Antoinette Perry (Tony) Award for her performance in *A Hand is On the Gate* (best actress in a featured or supporting role, musical, 1967).

PREMINGER, OTTO. Producer, director. b. Otto Ludwig Preminger, Dec. 5, 1906, Vienna, Austria, to Marc and Josefa Preminger. Father, lawyer. Grad. Univ. of Vienna, LL.D. 1928. Married Aug. 3, 1932, to Marion Mill (marr. dis. Aug. 19, 1949); married Dec. 4, 1951, to Mary Gardner (marr. dis. Mar. 4, 1959); married 1960 to Hope Bryce; one son, one daughter. Relatives in theatre; brother, Ingo Preminger, literary agent. Member of AMPAS; League of NY Theatres; SDG; AFTRA. Address: (home) 129 E. 64th St., New York, NY 10021, tel. (212) PL 5-8700; (bus.) 711 Fifth Ave., New York, NY 10022, tel. (212) PL 5-8700.

Theatre. Mr. Preminger made his professional debut in Vienna in Max Reinhardt's production of *A Midsummer Night's Dream* (Th. in der Josefstadt, 1922). He first directed *Libel* (Henry Miller's Th., N.Y.C., Dec. 20, 1935); subsequently, *Outward Bound* (Playhouse, Dec. 22, 1938); directed, and played Karl Baumer in *Margin for Error* (Plymouth, Nov. 3, 1939); directed *My Dear Children* (Belasco, Jan. 31, 1940); directed, and produced with Laurence Schwab, *Beverly Hills* (Fulton, Nov. 7, 1940); directed *Cue for Passion* (Royale, Dec. 19, 1940); directed, and produced with Norman Pincus, *The More the Merrier* (Cort, Sept. 15, 1941); and produced and directed *In Time to Come* (Mansfield, Dec. 28, 1941).

He directed *The Moon Is Blue* (Henry Miller's Th., N.Y.C., Mar. 8, 1951); and produced and directed *Critic's Choice* (Ethel Barrymore Th., Dec. 14, 1960); and *Full Circle* (ANTA, Nov. 7, 1973).

Films. Mr. Preminger appeared in *Pied Piper* (20th-Fox, 1942); *They Got Me Covered* (RKO, 1943); and *Margin For Error,* which he also directed (20th-Fox, 1943). He produced and directed *Laura* (20th-Fox, 1944); *In The Meantime, Darling* (20th-Fox, 1944); *Fallen Angel* (20th-Fox, 1945); directed *A Royal Scandal* (20th-Fox, 1945); produced and directed *Centennial Summer* (20th-Fox, 1946); *Daisy Kenyon* (20th-Fox, 1947); and directed *Forever Amber* (20th-Fox, 1947).

He produced and directed *Whirlpool* (20th-Fox, 1949); *Where the Sidewalk Ends* (20th-Fox, 1950); *The Thirteenth Letter* (20th-Fox, 1951); *Angel Face* (RKO, 1952); *The Moon Is Blue* (UA, 1953); and appeared in *Stalag 17* (Par., 1953). He directed *River of No Return* (20th-Fox, 1954); produced and directed *Carmen Jones* (UA, 1954); *The Man with the Golden Arm* (UA, 1955); directed *The Court Martial of Billy Mitchell* (WB, 1955); produced and directed *Saint Joan* (UA, 1957); *Bonjour Tristesse* (Col., 1958); *Anatomy of a Murder* (Col., 1959); directed *Porgy and Bess* (Col., 1959); produced and directed *Exodus* (UA, 1960); *Advise and Consent* (Col., 1962); *The Cardinal* (Col., 1963); *In Harm's Way* (Par., 1964); *Bunny Lake Is Missing* (Col., 1965); *Hurry Sundown* (Par., 1967); *Skidoo* (Par., 1968); *Tell Me That You Love Me, Junie Moon* (Par., 1970); *Such Good Friends* (Par., 1971); and *Rosebud* (UA, 1975).

Television. He has made guest appearances on Suspense (CBS); and Batman (ABC).

Other Activities. Mr. Preminger was associate professor at Yale Univ., 1938–41.

Awards. He received the Grand Cross of the Republic of Austria for contribution to the arts and culture (1961); and the Grand Cross of Merit, Knights of the Holy Sepulchre (1963).

Recreation. Collecting art.

PRENSKY, LESTER H. Attorney, former union executive. b. New York City to Joseph M. and Regina (Rosenberg) Prensky. Father, lawyer. Grad. Univ. of Penn., B.A. 1937; Harvard Law Sch., L.L.B. 1946. Relative in theatre: cousin, Bertram Ross, dancer. Served USAAF, 1941–45; rank, Warrant Officer. Address: (home) 35 E. 84th St., New York, NY 10028; (bus.) 40 W. 57th St., New York, NY 10019, tel. (212) 586-2000.

Since 1969, Mr. Prensky has been a lawyer for Broadcast Music, Inc. (BMI).

Other Activities. From 1955 to 1965, he was associated with the late New York attorney, Erwin Feldman. The firm's practice was principally in the labor and theatrical fields, and among its clients were United Scenic Artists (Local 829), the Screen Directors International Guild, and the Society of Stage Directors and Choreographers. From 1962 to 1965, he was the executive secretary of the Society of Stage Directors and Choreographers. From 1965 to 1969, he was associated with the New York law firm of Cramer & Hoffinger. The firm specialized in copyright law in the entertainment field, among other things.

PRESSMAN, DAVID. Director, actor, educator. b. Oct. 10, 1913, Tiflis (Caucasus) Russia, to Solomon and Natalie (Shenker) Pressman. Father, musician; mother, actress, singer. Grad. George Washington H.S., N.Y.C., 1931; attended Seth Low Jr. Coll. of Columbia Univ., 1931–34. Studied at Neighborhood Playhouse Sch. of the Theatre, N.Y.C., 1934–36; Actors Studio, N.Y.C., (member since 1947). Married May 22, 1941, to Sasha Katz; three sons. Served US Army, WW II; awarded two Purple Hearts; rank, S/Sgt. Relatives in theatre; Jacques Press, composer; son, Michael Pressman, director and writer; son, Eugene Pressman, actor. Member of AEA; DGA; SSD&C; VFW. Address: 333 Central Park West, New York, NY 10025, tel. (212) RI 9-7512.

During 1958–64, Mr. Pressman was head of the acting dept. at the Neighborhood Playhouse Sch. of the Theatre, where he was assistant instructor (1938–43). In 1954, he was on the staff of the theatre arts dept. of Boston Univ. as teacher and director. He also teaches acting at the Actors Studio.

Theatre. Mr. Pressman made his debut as a child actor in the Russian Grand Opera Company's tour of *The Snow Maiden* (1922); made his N.Y. debut, taking over Ian MacLaren's role of Snout in the Shakespeare Repertory Company's production of *A Midsummer Night's Dream* (Al Jolson's Th., Nov. 17, 1932); also appearing at this theatre as Malcolm in *Macbeth* (Jan. 5, 1933); Gregory in *Romeo and Juliet* (Feb. 1, 1933); Rugby in *The Merry Wives of Windsor* (Feb. 17, 1933); and the Second Gentleman in *Othello* (Mar. 31, 1933).

With the Toronto (Can.) Theatre of Action, he appeared in and directed *Bury the Dead* (Hart House Th., Oct. 1936); *Roar China* (Hart House Th., Jan. 1937); *Steel* (T. Eaton Th., Oct. 1937); and *Class '29* (T. Eaton Th., Jan. 1938); directed and appeared in stock productions of *Boy Meets Girl* and *Of Thee I Sing* (Camp Unity, Wingdale, N.Y., Summer 1940); directed the revue, *You Can't Sleep Here* (Barbizon-Plaza, N.Y.C., Mar. 1941); was assistant director and actor in productions at the Suffern (N.Y.) Summer Playhouse (Summer 1941); played Tony Mazzini in *Brooklyn, U.S.A.* (Forrest, N.Y.C., Dec. 21, 1941); Pvt. Shevlin in *The Eve of St. Mark* (Cort, Oct. 7, 1942); and Luigi in *Dream Girl* (Coronet, Dec. 14, 1945).

He directed and appeared in productions at Camp Unity (Summer 1947); directed the pre-Bway tryout of *Josephine* (opened Playhouse, Wilmington, Del., Jan. 8, 1953; closed Selwyn, Chicago, Ill., Feb. 7, 1953); a revival of *The Emperor's Clothes* (Greenwich Mews, N.Y.C., Nov. 14, 1953); *The Pony Cart* (Theatre de Lys, Sept. 14, 1954); and for the Boston (Mass.) Arts Festival at the Boston Common, directed *The Skin of Our Teeth* (June 15, 1956), and *The Devil's Disciple* (June 22, 1957).

For the NY City Opera Co. at NY City Ctr., he directed *La Bohème*, *La Traviata* and *Die Fledermaus* (1956–57); directed Chicago productions of *The Immoralist* (Dec. 26, 1956); and *The Flowering Peach* (Apr. 24, 1957); *The Disenchanted* (Coronet, N.Y.C., Dec. 3, 1958); the national tour of *Look Homeward, Angel* (opened Playhouse, Wilmington, Del., Oct. 21, 1959); *Roman Candle* (Cort, N.Y.C., Feb. 3, 1960); *A Cook for Mr. General* (Playhouse, Oct. 19, 1961); the pre-Bway tryout of *A Gift Horse* (opened Mineola Playhouse, N.Y., Feb. 1963; closed Paper Mill Playhouse, Millburn, N.J.); and *Summertree* (Forum Th. at Lincoln Ctr., Mar. 3, 1968).

Television. Mr. Pressman has directed the Actors Studio Television Program (ABC, 1948); T-Men in Action (ABC, 1950); Nash Airflyte Theatre (CBS, 1951); Cosmopolitan Theatre of the Air (Dumont, 1951); and Comedy Theatre (CBS, 1951). In Boston he directed *The Scarecrow* (WGBH); and for the Festival of Performing Arts (WNDT, 1962–63). He directed *This Town Will Never Be the Same* (NBC); and *Neither Are We Enemies* (NBC); and the daytime serials, *The Nurses* (ABC); *Another World* (NBC); and *One Life to Live* (ABC); and has directed segments for *The Defenders* (CBS); *The Nurses* (ABC); *Coronet Blue* (CBS); and *NYPD* (CBS).

Awards. As director of Theatre of Action in Toronto, Mr. Pressman received First Prize in the Canadian Drama Festival (1936). He won the Peabody Award for his direction of the Actors Studio Television Program (1949).

Recreation. Photography, sailing, music, art, travel.

PRESTON, ROBERT. Actor. b. Robert Preston Meservey, June 8, 1918, Newton Highlands, Mass., to Frank W. Meservey, Sr., and Ruth (Rea) Meservey. Father, in garment business. Grad. Lincoln H.S., Los Angeles, Calif., 1935; attended Pasadena Playhouse Coll. of Theatre Arts, 1936–38. Married Nov. 8, 1940, to Catherine (Feltus) Craig, actress. Served USAAF, 1942–45; rank, Capt. Member of SAG; AFTRA; AEA (council member). Address: Greenwich, CT 06830.

Theatre. Mr. Preston first performed in *Kearney from Killarney* (Los Angeles, Calif., 1932); subsequently played with the Patia Power Co. in *Julius Caesar* (Los Angeles, 1936); at the Pasadena Playhouse (Calif.) appeared in Shakespeare Festival plays, and in *Montezuma, Murder in the Cathedral, Night Over Taos, Ethan Frome, Knights of Song, Idiot's Delight, Star of Navarre,* and *The Girl of the Golden West* (1937–38); and with the 18 Actors Co., appeared in *The Play's the Thing* (1949).

He made his Bway debut succeeding (June 1951) Jose Ferrer as Oscar Jaffe in *Twentieth Century* (ANTA, Dec. 24, 1950); subsequently played Joe Ferguson in *The Male Animal* (NY City Ctr., May 11, 1952); Peter Hogarth in *Men of Distinction* (48 St. Th., Apr. 30, 1953); Clem Scott in *His and Hers* (48 St. Th., Jan. 7, 1954); George Wilson in *The Magic and the Loss* (Booth, Apr. 9, 1954); Joe McCall in *The Tender Trap* (Longacre, Oct. 12, 1954); Gil in *Janus* (Plymouth, Nov. 24, 1955); Jean Monnerie in *The Hidden River* (Playhouse, Jan. 23, 1957); Harold Hill in *The Music Man* (Majestic, Dec. 19, 1957); Pancho Villa in the pre-Bway tryout of *We Take the Town* (opened Shubert, New Haven, Conn., Feb. 19, 1962; closed Shubert, Philadelphia, Pa., Mar. 17, 1962); the Burglar (Aubrey) in *Too True to be Good* (54 St. Th., Mar. 12, 1963); Nat Bentley in *Nobody Loves an Albatross* (Lyceum, Dec. 19, 1963); the title role in *Ben Franklin in Paris* (Lunt-Fontanne Th., Oct. 13, 1964); Henry II in *The Lion in Winter* (Ambassador Th., Mar. 3, 1966); Michael in *I Do! I Do!* (46 St. Th., Dec. 5, 1966; national tour 1968–69); and Mack in *Mack and Mabel* (Majestic, Oct. 6, 1974).

Films. Mr. Preston made his debut in *King of Alcatraz* (Par., 1938); subsequently appeared in *Illegal Traffic* (Par., 1938); *Disbarred* (Par., 1939); *Union Pacific* (Par., 1939); *Beau Geste* (Par., 1939); *Moon Over Burma* (Par., 1940); *Typhoon* (Par., 1940); *Northwest Mounted Police* (Par., 1940); *New York Town* (Par., 1941); *The Lady from Cheyenne* (U. 1941); *The Night of January 16th* (Par., 1941); *Parachute Battalion* (RKO, 1941); *Midnight Angel* (Par., 1941); *Reap the Wild Wind* (Par., 1942); *Pacific Blackout* (Par., 1942); *This Gun for Hire* (Par., 1942); *Wake Island* (Par., 1942); *Night Plane from Chunking* (Par., 1943); *Wild Harvest* (Par., 1947); *The Macomber Affair* (UA, 1947); *Variety Girl* (Par., 1947); *Whispering Smith* (Par., 1948); *Blood on the Moon* (RKO, 1948); *The Big City* (MGM, 1948); *The Lady Gambles* (U, 1949); *Tulsa* (Eagle Lion, 1949); *The Sundowners* (Eagle Lion, 1949); *My Outlaw Brother* (Eagle Lion, 1951); *When I Grow Up* (Eagle Lion, 1951); *The Best of the Bad Men* (RKO, 1951); *Face to Face* (RKO, 1952); *Cloudburst* (UA, 1952); *The Last Frontier* (Col., 1955); *The Dark at the Top of the Stairs* (WB, 1960); *The Music Man* (WB, 1962); *How the West Was Won* (MGM, 1962); *Island of Love* (WB, 1963); *All the Way Home* (Par., 1963); *Junior Bonner* (ABC-Cinerama, 1972); *Child's Play* (Par., 1972) and *Mame* (WB, 1974).

Television. Mr. Preston made his debut in 1951 on the series, Blockade. He has since appeared on numerous dramatic programs, including Robert Montgomery Presents (NBC); Lux Video Th. (CBS); US Steel Hour (CBS); and Omnibus (NBC). He played opposite Carol Burnett on Carol and Company (CBS, Feb. 23, 1963); and subsequently appeared in the series *This Proud Land* (ABC, 1965); and in *My Father's House*, a made-for-television movie (ABC, 1974).

Awards. Mr. Preston received the Antoinette Perry (Tony) Award and won the *Variety* NY Drama Critics Poll for his performances as Harold Hill in *The Music Man* (1958); and as Michael in *I Do! I Do!* (1967).

PRICE, JOHN L. JR. Producer, actor, director. b. John Lemar Price, Jr., May 29, 1920, Cleveland, Ohio, to John Lemar and Emma (Moskopp) Price. Father, broker; mother, lecturer. Grad. Cleveland Heights H.S., 1938; Western Reserve Univ., B.A. 1942. Studied for the stage at Cain Park Th., Cleveland Heights, 1937–42. Married Sept. 6, 1947, to Constance Mather, set designer, actress; two sons, two daughters. Served USN, ETO, 1942–46; rank, Lt. Relatives in theatre: cousin, Agnes Moorehead, actress; son, John L. Price, III, radio newscaster; daughter, Diana Price, theatre business manager. Member of AEA; AFTRA (Cleveland board, 1951–52); SAG; AGVA; MATA; Delta Upsilon. Address: (home) 13301 Lake Shore Blvd., Cleveland, OH 44108, tel. (216) GL 7-7754; Bahia Lodge, Box 537, Tavernier, FL 33070, tel. (305) 852-2361; (bus.) Musicarnival, P.O. Box 22102, Cleveland, OH 44122, tel. (216) 663-8400.

Theatre. Since 1954, Mr. Price has been producer of the Musicarnival, a summer musical-arena theatre in Cleveland. Previously he played at the Cain Park Th. in *The Importance of Being Earnest* (1939), *The American Way* (1940), *Fashion, Julius Caesar, Mary of Scotland,* and *The Petrified Forest* (1942); wrote and directed *Army Red!* which was produced by the Office of Civil Defense (Sept. 1942); and appeared in *Hawk Island* (Weymouth, Eng., Apr. 1945).

He appeared at the Cain Park Th. as Harry Binton in *Room Service* (July 1946); played Gene Tuttle in *Personal Appearance* (Ring Th., Allerton Hotel, Cleveland, Summer 1950); Noah in *Anna Lucasta* (Bolton Square Th., Cleveland, 1950); Patrick Buckingham in *Libel* (Cleveland Playhouse, 1951); and Banjo in *The Man Who Came to Dinner* (Hanna Th., Cleveland, 1951).

Since 1954, Mr. Price has appeared in productions at the Musicarnivals in Cleveland and Palm Beach. Annually, he does a one-man reading of Dickens' *Christmas Carol* (1938–to date).

Films. He wrote the screenplay for the American Cancer Society documentary film, *New Voices* (1950).

Television and Radio. Mr. Price wrote, produced, directed and performed on the Cain Park Theatre of the Air radio programs (WHK and WGAR, Cleveland, 1940–42); wrote and directed Men of the Navy (WBST, South Bend, Ind., 1940–42); performed on Duffy's Tavern (NBC, 1948); and the Gene Autry Show (CBS, 1948–50).

He had three weekly television shows in Cleveland: The Troubador, Rowena, the Minstrel Girl and Golden Wedding, which he wrote, produced, and directed (WNBK, NBC, 1948–49); directed *Hansel and Gretel* (WNBK, NBC-TV, 1949); wrote, produced and appeared on Mr. Weather-Eye (WEWS, Cleveland, 1951–55); and appeared on the Bob Hope Show (NBC, 1954).

Night Clubs. During 1947–49, he adapted, produced, directed and appeared in musicals at the Alpine Village Nightclub, Cleveland, where he also wrote and produced *Baseball Review* (1947); *Football Review* (1948); and adapted *A Christmas Carol*, in which he appeared as Scrooge (1948).

Awards. Mr. Price received a citation from the Office of Civil Defense for his play, *Army Red!* (1942); a citation from Cuyahoga County (Ohio) Council of Mayors for outstanding service to the Northeast Ohio area by Musicarnival (1954–63); and was cited by MATA for outstanding quality productions (1963).

Recreation. Fishing, Shakespeare, Elizabethan life and times, nature photography and theatrical photography.

PRICE, LORIN ELLINGTON. Theatrical producer. b. Apr. 1, 1921, New York City, to Victor and Hattie Price. Father, business executive. Grad. Cheshire (Conn.) Academy (1939); Yale Univ., B.A. 1944; attended Yale Graduate Sch. (Govt. and International Relations) 1946. Married July 4, 1948 to Alice L. Holm (marr. dis. 1956), one son, one daughter; married Nov. 26, 1968 to Barbara Lee Horn, three step-sons, one step-daughter. Served US Marine Corps Reserve (1942–43); US Army Air Force (1944–46). Member of the Yale Club; past member of Cheshire Academy Alumni Assn. (pres. and bd. mbr.); Bayport Lions Club (treas.); Washington Sq. Village Tenants Assn. (pres.); Greenwich Village Lions Club. Address: (home) 345 E. 52nd St., New York, NY 10022; (bus.) Paramount Th. Bldg., 1501 Broadway, Rm. 2009, New York, NY 10036, tel. (212) 765-0665.

Pre-Theatre. Mr. Price was associated with the N.Y. Merchandise Co., Inc. (1946–59), an import-export firm handling annual volume in excess of thirty million dollars. He started as a salesman and later became export manager and director. He traveled extensively throughout the Caribbean, and Central and South America in connection with his work.

Theatre. Off-Bway, he produced *Alley of the Sunset* (Jan Hus Th., Jan. 1960); *The Mime and Me* (Gramercy Arts, Apr. 1960); *The Tiger Rag* (Cherry Lane Th., Jan. 1961); *To Clothe the Naked* (Sheridan Sq. Playhouse, June 1967); and *Show Me Where the Good Times Are* (Edison Th., Mar. 1970). His Bway productions include *The Moon Besieged* (Lyceum Th., Dec. 1962); *The Natural Look* (Longacre Th., Mar. 1967); *George M* (Palace, Apr. 1968); *Seesaw* (Uris Th., Mar. 1973); and *No Hard Feelings* (Martin Beck Th., Apr. 1973).

Films. He produced *Free* (formerly entitled *Power of the People*) (P.O.P. Films Ltd., Sept. 1972).

Awards. He was presented the Key to the City of New York by Mayor John V. Lindsay in appreciation of his production of *Seesaw* (April 24, 1973).

PRICE, VINCENT. Actor. b. May 27, 1911, St. Louis, Mo., to Vincent Leonard and Margaret Cobb (Willcox) Price. Father, president of National Canday Co. Attended Community Sch., St. Louis, Mo.; Grad. student, 1933; London (England) Univ. (fine arts) Louis Country Day Sch.; Yale Univ., B.A. 1935. Married to Edith Barrett (marr. dis., 1948); one son; married Aug. 25, 1949, to Mary Grant, designer (marr. dis.); one daughter; married to Coral Browne, actress. Member of AEA; SAG.

Theatre. Mr. Price made his London debut as a Policeman in *Chicago* (Gate Th., Mar. 13, 1935); subsequently played Prince Albert in *Victoria Regina* (Gate, May 1, 1935); and Max in *Anatol* (Gate, Oct. 9, 1935).

He made his N.Y.C. debut as Prince Albert in *Victoria Regina* (Broadhurst, Dec. 26, 1935); appeared as Jean in *The Lady Has a Heart* (Longacre, Sept. 25, 1937); Master Hammon in *The Shoemaker's Holiday* (Mercury, Jan. 1, 1938); Hector Hushabye in *Heartbreak House* (Mercury, Apr. 29, 1938); and Rev. William Duke in *Outward Bound* (Playhouse, Dec. 22, 1938).

He appeared in stock (Summer 1939), in *What Every Woman Knows*, *Elizabeth the Queen*, *The Wild Duck*, *The Passing of the Third Floor Back*, and *Parnell*. He played Saint in *Mamba's Daughters* (Biltmore, Los Angeles, Calif., Sept. 10, 1941); Mr. Manningham in *Angel Street* (John Golden Th., N.Y.C., Dec. 5, 1941); Arthur Winslow in *The Winslow Boy* (Las Palmas Playhouse, Calif., Nov. 1950); toured as An Unidentified Guest in *The Cocktail Party* (opened Curran, San Francisco, Calif., Oct. 15, 1951); and succeeded Charles Laughton as the Devil in *Don Juan in Hell* on tour (opened Curran, San Francisco, Calif., Sept. 22, 1952; closed Civic Opera House, Chicago, Ill., Dec. 15, 1952); and appeared as the Duke of Buckingham in *Richard III* (NY City Ctr., Dec. 9, 1953); and as Dr. Nicholas Marsh in *Black-Eyed Susan* (Playhouse, Dec. 23, 1954), and Priam Farll in *Darling of the Day* (George Abbott Th., Jan. 27, 1968).

Films. He has appeared in *Service de Luxe* (U, 1938); *The Private Lives of Elizabeth and Essex* (WB, 1939); *Tower of London* (U, 1939); *Green Hell* (U, 1940); *The House of the Seven Gables* (U, 1940); *The Invisible Man Returns* (U, 1940); Hudson's Bay (20th-Fox, 1940); *The Song of Bernadette* (20th-Fox, 1943); *The Eve of St. Mark* (20th-Fox, 1944); *Wilson* (20th-Fox, 1944); *The Keys of the Kingdom* (20th-Fox, 1944); A Royal Scandal (20th-Fox, 1945); *Dragonwyck* (20th-Fox, 1946); *The Long Night* (RKO, 1947); *The Web* (U, 1947); *Up in Central Park* (U, 1948); *The Three Musketeers* (MGM, 1948); *Curtain Call at Cactus Creek* (U, 1950); *Champagne for Caesar* (U, 1950); *His Kind of Woman* (RKO, 1951); *Adventures of Captain Fabian* (Rep., 1951); *The Las Vegas Story* (RKO, 1952); *The Naked Terror* (Brenner, 1951); *House of Wax* (WB, 1953); *Casanova's Big Night* (Par., 1954); *Dangerous Mission* (RKO, 1954); *The Mad Magician* (Col., 1954); *Son of Sinbad* (RKO, 1955); *Serenade* (WB, 1956); *While the City Sleeps* (RKO, 1956); *The Ten Commandments* (Par., 1956); *The Story of Mankind* (WB, 1957); *The Fly* (20th-Fox, 1958); *House on Haunted Hill* (Allied, 1958); *The Return of the Fly* (20th-Fox, 1959); *The Bat* (Allied, 1959); *The Big Circus* (Allied, 1959); *House of Usher* (Amer. Intl., 1960); *The Tingler* (Col., 1959); *The Master of the World* (Amer. Intl., 1961); *The Pit and the Pendulum* (Amer. Intl., 1961); *Poe's Tales of Terror* (Amer. Intl., 1962); *Convicts 4* (Allied, 1962); *Confessions of an Opium Eater* (Allied, 1962); *Tower of London* (UA, 1962); *The Comedy of Terrors* (Amer. Intl., 1963); *The Last Man on Earth* (Amer. Intl., 1964); *Masque of the Red Death* (Amer. Intl., 1964); *The Tomb of Ligeia* (Amer. Intl., 1965); narrated *Taboos of the World* (Amer. Intl., 1965); appeared in *Dr. Goldfoot and the Bikini Machine* (Amer. Int., 1965); *Dr. Goldfoot and the Girl Bombs* (Amer. Int., 1966); *House of 1,000 Dolls* (Amer. Intl., 1967); *The Conqueror Worm* (Amer. Intl., 1967); *The Oblong Box* (Amer. Intl., 1969); *The Trouble with Girls* (MGM, 1969); *More Dead than Alive* (UA, 1969); *Cry of the Banshee* (Amer. Intl., 1970); *Scream and Scream Again* (Amer. Intl., 1970); *The Abominable Dr. Phibes* (Amer. Intl., 1971); *Dr. Phibes Rises Again* (Amer. Intl., 1972); *Theatre of Blood* (UA, 1973); and *Madhouse* (Amer. Intl., 1974); and narrated *The Devil's Triangle* (Maron, 1974).

Television and Radio. Mr. Price played Torvald in a radio presentation of *A Doll's House* (Great Plays, WJZ, Feb. 1939); on television he has appeared on Lux Video Th. (CBS, 1951); subsequently appearing on such programs as Lights Out (NBC); Playhouse 90 (CBS); Climax (CBS); GE Th. (CBS); Alcoa Hour (NBC); Alfred Hitchcock Presents (CBS); *Angel Street* (Matinee Th., NBC); *The Three Musketeers* (Family Classics, CBS); The Man from U.N.C.L.E. (NBC); Batman (ABC); Love, American Style (ABC); Mod Squad (ABC); Night Gallery (NBC); *What's a Nice Girl Like You . . ?* (tele-film, ABC, 1971); and the Jimmy Stewart Show (NBC).

Other Activities. Mr. Price is an art and food critic and has authored books and articles on both subjects.

Recreation. Art collecting (paintings).

PRICKETT, OLIVER B. Theatre manager, actor, producer. b. Oliver Bettle Prickett, Apr. 4, 1905, Centralia, Ill., to Charles Fillmore and Ruth (Bettle) Prickett. Father, pharmacist. Grad. Pasadena (Calif.) H.S., 1923; attended Univ. of California at Berkeley, 1923–26. Married Sept. 14, 1930, to Margaret (Gaynor) Prickett (dec. 1969); one daughter; married 1970 to Katharine Frost. Relatives in theatre: brother, Charles Prickett, theatre mgr. (dec. 1954); sister-in-law, Maudie Prickett, actress. Member of AEA; SAG; AFTRA; Kappa Alpha; Salvation Army (advisory council, 1960–to date); Players Club of Santa Barbara; California Alumni Association; Overland Club of Pasadena; Rotary Club; Huntington Memorial Clinic Auxiliary. Address: 1180 Banyan St., Pasadena, CA 91103, tel. (213) SY 2-1605.

From 1967–70, Mr. Prickett served as trustee of the IATSE Health, Welfare & Pension fund, Local 33.

Theatre. Since 1964, Mr. Prickett has been general manager of the Pasadena (Calif.) Playhouse. He was production manager of the Biltmore and Greek Theatres, Los Angeles (1959–64); production coordinator of the Pasadena Playhouse (1951–58); publicity director, Pasadena Playhouse (1937–50); manager of the Padua Hills Theatre (Claremont, Calif., 1935–36); publicity director of the Lobero Theatre (Santa Barbara, Calif., 1934); and owner-operator of two California film theatres; the Alcazar in Carpenteria, and the Ojai in the town of that name.

He made his debut in 1917 at the Pasadena Playhouse as Billy Wiggs in *Mrs. Wiggs of the Cabbage Patch*, and during 1917–58, has appeared there in over 100 productions.

He made his first New York appearance as Tom McDow in *All the Comforts of Home* (Longacre, May 25, 1942); appeared as Obadiah Latch in *Mr. Adam* (Royale, May 25, 1949); and played Billy Jackrabbit in a touring company of *The Girl of the Golden West* (Playhouse, Pasadena; Lobero, Santa Barbara; Curran, San Francisco; July–Nov. 1947).

From 1966–69, he served on the managerial staff of the Los Angeles Music Center Operation Company.

Mr. Prickett retired from active theatre work in 1970.

Films. Mr. Prickett first appeared in *New York Town* (Par., 1940); and subsequently performed in *Shadow of the Thin Man* (MGM, 1941); *H. M. Pulham, Esq.* (MGM, 1941); *Design for Scandal* (MGM, 1941); *I Married an Angel* (MGM, 1942); *Saboteur* (U, 1942); *The Postman Didn't Ring* (20th-Fox, 1942) *Casablanca* (WB, 1942); *Mark Twain* (WB, 1942); *Reunion in France* (MGM, 1942); *Get Hep to Love* (U, 1942); *Mission to Moscow* (WB, 1943); *Sweet Rosie O'Grady* (20th-Fox, 1943); *Greenwich Village* (20th-Fox, 1943); *Up in Arms* (Goldwyn, 1943); *National Barn Dance* (Par., 1943); *Gypsy Wildcat* (U, 1943); *Corvette* (U, 1943); *Horn Blows at Midnight* (WB, 1944); *Mask of Dimitrious* (WB, 1944); *Doughgirls* (WB, 1944); *Stranger in the Midst* (WB, 1944); *The Thin Man* (MGM, 1944); *Col. Effingham's Raid* (20th-Fox, 1944); *Jungle Queen* (U, 1944); *Enchanted Voyage* (20th-Fox, 1945); *Murder Mansion* (U, 1945); *Rhapsody in Blue* (WB, 1945); *Conflict* (WB, 1945); *A Medal for Benny* (Par., 1945); *My Reputation* (WB, 1946); *Inside Job* (U, 1946); *Blonde Alibi* (U, 1946); *Ginger* (Mono., 1946); *Live and Learn* (WB, 1946); *The Mighty McGurk* (MGM, 1946); *The Guilty* (Mono., 1947); *Out of the Past* (RKO, 1947); *Merton of the Movies* (MGM, 1947); *The Senator Was Indiscreet* (U, 1947); *Nightmare Alley* (20th-Fox, 1947); *Road to Rome* (20th-Fox, 1947); *Miracle of the Bells* (RKO, 1947); *Arch of Triumph* (UA, 1948); *The Pirate* (MGM, 1948); *Good Sam* (RKO, 1948); *Walls of Jericho* (20th-Fox,

1948); *Summer Holiday* (MGM, 1948); *The Challenge* (20th-Fox, 1948); *Moonrise* (Rep., 1948); *Livewire* (Eagle-Lion, 1948); *Shed No Tears* (Equity, 1948); *Long Denial* (RKO, 1948); *The Girl from Jones Beach* (WB, 1949); *Colorado Territory* (WB, 1949); *Pa & Ma Kettle* (U, 1949); *Ma and Pa Kettle Go to Town* (U, 1950); *Father of the Bride* (MGM, 1950).

Also, *Let's Dance* (Par., 1950); *Ma & Pa Kettle Back on the Farm* (U, 1951); *The Lemon Drop Kid* (Par., 1951); *Rhubarb* (Par., 1951); *Come Fill the Cup* (WB, 1951); *Chain of Circumstances* (Col., 1951); *Ma & Pa Kettle at the Fair* (U, 1952); *The Stooge* (Par., 1952); *The Greatest Show on Earth* (Par., 1952); *Room for One More* (WB, 1952); *The Belle of New York* (MGM, 1952); *Son of Paleface* (Par., 1952); *The Iron Mistress* (WB, 1952); *Back to Broadway* (WB, 1952); *Grace Moore Story* (WB, 1952); *Bowery Boys* (Mono., 1952); *Ma & Pa Kettle on Vacation* (U, 1953); *Caesar* (MGM, 1953); *Houdini* (Par., 1953); *Man of Wax* (WB, 1953); *So Big* (WB, 1953); *Casanova* (WB, 1953); *Ma & Pa Kettle at Home* (U, 1954); *The Long Long Trailer* (MGM, 1954); *Susan Slept Here* (RKO, 1954); *Brigadoon* (MGM, 1954); *Drum Beat* (WB, 1954); *Ma & Pa Kettle at Waikiki* (U, 1955); *Moonfleet* (MGM, 1955) *Cobweb* (MGM, 1955); *The Seven Little Foys* (Par., 1955); *Bar Sinister* (MGM, 1955); *Lust for Life* (MGM, 1955); *Raintree County* (MGM, 1957); *The Beast* (Screen, 1957); *Onionhead* (WB, 1958); *The Fear Makers* (UA, 1958); *Jesse James-Hope* (Par., 1958); *Bells Are Ringing* (MGM, 1960).

Television and Radio. Mr. Prickett's television credits include appearances on the Hal Roach Series (1950); Stu Erwin Show (1951); Space Patrol (1952); Irene Dunne Show (1952); Gangbusters (1952); Racket Squad (ABC, 1952); I Love Lucy (CBS, 1953); Schlitz Playhouse (CBS, 1954); Father Knows Best (CBS, 1954); Lassie (CBS, 1955); Producers Showcase (NBC, 1956); Desilu (CBS); The Brothers (CBS, 1956–57); December Bride (CBS, 1956); Maverick (ABC, 1957); The Pied Piper (NBC, 1957); Rin Tin Tin (CBS, 1958); Mark of Zorro (ABC, 1958); and Alcoa Hour (NBC, 1958).

Other Activities. In 1962 and 1964, he was director of the Tournament of Roses (Pasadena, Calif.).

Awards. Mr. Prickett received an honorary degree of Master of Theatre Arts from the Pasadena Playhouse Coll. of Theatre Arts (1955), and the 1974 "Man of the Year" Community Service Award from the Salvation Army.

Recreation. Baseball, tennis.

PRIDEAUX, TOM. Drama editor, writer. b. May 9, 1908, Hillsdale, Mich., to William and Rolla (Robards) Prideaux. Grad. Yale Univ., Ph.B. 1930. Served USAAF, WW II, rank, Capt.; Legion of Merit. Member of Skull and Bones; Delta Kappa Epsilon; Coffee House (N.Y.C.); Elizabethan Club (Yale).

Mr. Prideaux was theatre and amusements editor of *Life* Magazine for some year's before that publication's demise in 1972. He is the author of *Another Man's Poison* (tryout, Tamiment, Pa., Summer 1934); *Gallivanting Lady* (tryout, Farragut Playhouse, Rye Beach, N.H., July 26, 1938); and the teleplay *The Milwaukee Rocket*.

Published Works. Mr. Prideaux is the author of *World Theatre in Pictures* (1954). Other works include *Never to Die, The Egyptians in Their Own Words* (1938), written with Josephine Mayor; and *The World of Eugene Delacroix* (1968).

PRIESTLEY, J. B. Playwright, novelist. b. John Boynton Priestley, Sept. 13, 1894, Bradford, England, to Jonathan Priestley. Attended Bradford Sch.; Trinity Hall, Cambridge Univ., M.A. Married to Patricia Tempest (dec. 1925); married to Mary Wyndham Lewis (marr. dis.); married to Jacquetta Hawkes. Served WW I, Duke of Wellington's and Devon regiments, 1914–19. Member of International Theatre Inst. (pres.); British Theatre Conference (chmn., 1948); International Theatre Conference (chmn., Paris, 1947; Prague, 1948). Address: Kissing Tree House, Alveston, Stratford-upon-Avon, Warwickshire, England.

Theatre. Mr. Priestley wrote, with Edward Knoblock, *The Good Companions* (His Majesty's Th., London, May 14, 1931; 44 St. Th., N.Y.C., Oct. 1, 1931); wrote *Dangerous Corner* (Lyric, London, May 17, 1932; Empire, N.Y.C., Oct. 27, 1932); *Laburnum Grove* (Duchess, London, Nov. 28, 1933; Booth, N.Y.C., Jan. 14, 1935); *Eden End* (Duchess, London, Sept. 13, 1934; Masque, N.Y.C., Oct. 21, 1935; revived Duchess, London, Aug. 26, 1948); *Cornelius* (Duchess, Mar. 20, 1935); *Duet in Floodlight*, which he directed, with Cedric Hardwicke (Apollo, June 4, 1935); *Bees on the Boatdeck* (Lyric, May 5, 1936); *Springtide*, under the pen name, Peter Goldsmith (Duchess, July 15, 1936).

He also wrote *Time and the Conways* (Duchess, London, Aug. 26, 1937; Ritz, N.Y.C., Jan. 3, 1938); *I Have Been Here Before* (Royalty, London, Sept. 22, 1937; Guild, N.Y.C., Oct. 13, 1938); *People at Sea* (Apollo, London, Nov. 24, 1937); *When We Are Married* (St. Martin's, London, Oct. 11, 1938; Lyceum, N.Y.C., Dec. 25, 1939); *Johnson Over Jordan* (New, London, Feb. 22, 1939); *Music at Night* (Westminster, Oct. 10, 1939); *Goodnight Children* (New, Feb. 5, 1942); *They Came to a City* (Globe, Apr. 21, 1943); *Desert Highway* (Playhouse, Feb. 10, 1944); *How Are They at Home?* (Apollo, May 4, 1944); *The Long Mirror* (Gateway, Nov. 6, 1945); *An Inspector Calls* (New, London, Oct. 1, 1946; Booth, N.Y.C., Oct. 21, 1947); *Ever Since Paradise* (Winter Garden, London, June 4, 1947); *The Linden Tree* (Duchess, London, Aug. 15, 1947; Music Box, N.Y.C., Mar. 2, 1948); *Home Is To-Morrow* (Cambridge, London, Nov. 4, 1948); and *Summer Day's Dream* (St. Martin's, Sept. 8, 1949).

Mr. Priestley wrote the libretto for the opera, *the Olympians* (Covent Garden, Sept. 29, 1949); wrote *Bright Shadow* (Intimate, Palmer's Green, Apr. 10, 1950); *Treasure on Pelican* (Golder's Green Hippodrome, Feb. 25, 1952); wrote, with Jacquetta Hawkes, *Dragon's Mouth* (Winter Garden, London, May 13, 1952; Cherry Lane, N.Y.C., Nov. 16, 1955); and *The White Countess* (Saville, London, Mar. 24, 1954); wrote *Mr. Kettle and Mrs. Moon* (Duchess, Sept. 1, 1955); and for the Crest Th. (Toronto, Ontario, Canada, 1957), wrote *The Thirty-First of June* and *The Glass Cage*, the latter of which was also produced in London by the Crest Th. (Piccadilly, Apr. 26, 1957). With Iris Murdoch, he wrote *A Severed Head*, produced first in London (1964) and then in N.Y.C. (Royale Th., Oct. 28, 1964).

Mr. Priestley was co-manager of the Duchess Th. (1934–35, 1937), when *Eden End, Cornelius*, and *Time and the Conways* were presented; also the Royalty (1937), during *I Have Been Here Before;* St. Martin's (1938), during *When We Are Married;* Prince's (1939); and Saville (1939), during *Johnson Over Jordan*. He was also a director of the Mask Th., which played at the Westminster (1938–39), and he was appointed a member of the board of directors of the National Theatre, London (Nov. 1965).

His plays have been translated into several languages and have been produced throughout the world.

Films. Mr. Priestley wrote the screenplays for *The Foreman Went to France;* and *The Last Holiday* (Stratford, 1950).

Television and Radio. During World War II, Mr. Priestley had his own radio program, Postscripts. On television, he wrote and was narrator of *1940* (BBC, London, Sept. 19, 1965); was host of the series The English Novel (Associated TV, London, 1965–66; and appeared on An Evening With. .(BBC, Sept. 21, 1973).

Published Works. In addition to his plays, Mr. Priestley wrote many magazine articles and works of fiction and nonfiction, including *The Good Companions* (1929); *Angel Pavement* (1930); *English Journey* (1934); *Midnight on the Desert* (1937); *Blackout in Gretley* (1942); *Bright Day* (1946); *Festival* (1951); *Last Holiday* (1952); *Journey Down a Rainbow*, with Jacquetta Hawkes (1955); *The Art of the Dramatist* (1957); *Literature and Western Man* (1960); *Saturn Over the Water* (1961); *The Thirty-First of June* (1961); *The Shapes of Sleep* (1962); *Margin Released* (1963); *Man and Time* (1964); *Lost Empires* (1965); *Salt Is Leaving* (1966); *It's an Old Country* (1967); *The Image Men*, 2 vols. (1968); *Essays of Five Decades* (1969); and *The Prince of Pleasure* (1969).

PRINCE, HAROLD. Producer, director. b. Harold Smith Prince, Jan. 30, 1928, New York City, to Milton and Blanche (Stern) Prince. Father, stock broker. Grad. Franklin H.S., N.Y.C., 1944; Univ. of Pennsylvania, B.A. 1948. Married Oct. 26, 1962, to Judy Chaplin; one son, one daughter. Served US Army 1950–52. Member of League of NY Theatres (pres., 1963–June 15, 1965); SSD&C; Coffee House Club. Address: (home) 45 E. 66th St., New York, NY 10021, tel. (212) TR 9-7996; (bus.) 1 Rockefeller Plaza, New York, NY 10020, tel. (212) 582-0600.

Theatre. Mr. Prince was assistant stage manager for *Tickets, Please* (Coronet Th., N.Y.C., Apr. 27, 1950); and subsequently for *Wonderful Town* (Winter Garden, Feb. 25, 1953). He was producer, in partnership with F. Brisson and R. E. Griffith, for *The Pajama Game* (St. James, May 13, 1954); *Damn Yankees* (46 St. Th., May 5, 1955); and *New Girl in Town* (46 St. Th., May 14, 1957). With Mr. Griffith, he produced *West Side Story* (Winter Garden, Sept. 26, 1957); the pre-Bway tryout of *A Swim in the Sea* (opened Walnut Th., Philadelphia, Sept. 15, 1958; closed there Sept. 27, 1958); the London production of *West Side Story* (Her Majesty's, Dec. 12, 1958); the London production of *Two for the Seesaw* (Haymarket, Dec. 17, 1958; presented by H. M. Tennent Ltd., and Mr. Prince and Mr. Griffith, in association with Fred Coe); *Fiorello!* (Broadhurst, N.Y.C., Nov. 23, 1959); *Tenderloin* (46 St. Th., Oct. 17, 1960); and *A Call on Kuprin* (Broadhurst, May 25, 1961).

Mr. Prince produced *Take Her, She's Mine* (Biltmore, Dec. 21, 1961); directed *A Family Affair* (Billy Rose Th., Jan. 27, 1962); produced *A Funny Thing Happened on the Way to the Forum* (Alvin, May 8, 1962; Strand, London, Oct. 3, 1963); directed a statewide tour, for the Phoenix Th., of *The Matchmaker* (Spring 1963), sponsored by the NY State Council on the Arts; and directed and produced, with Lawrence N. Kasha and Phillip C. McKenna, *She Loves Me* (Eugene O'Neill Th., Apr. 23, 1963). He directed a tryout of Lonnie Coleman's *She Didn't Say Yes* (Falmouth Th., Coonamessett, Mass., July 23, 1963; produced by Sidney Gordon, in association with Mr. Prince and Howard Erskine); directed the London production of *She Loves Me* (Lyric, Apr. 29, 1964); and produced *Fiddler on the Roof* (Imperial, N.Y.C., Sept. 22, 1964; first national company opened San Diego Civic Th., Calif., Apr. 11, 1966; second national company opened State Fair Music Hall, Dallas, Texas, Aug. 27, 1968; third national company opened Dade County Aud., Miami, Fla., Dec. 27, 1969; London company, produced with Richard Pilbrow, opened Her Majesty's, Feb. 16, 1967). The original N.Y.C. production of *Fiddler on the Roof* closed on July 2, 1972 after 3242 performances, the longest run by any play in Bway history.

Mr. Prince produced, in association with Michael Codron and Pledon Ltd., *Poor Bitos* (Cort, N.Y.C., Nov. 14, 1964); he directed *Baker Street* (Broadway Th., Feb. 16, 1965); produced *Flora, the Red Menace* (Alvin, May 11, 1965); and directed and produced *It's a Bird . . It's a Plane . . It's Superman!* (Alvin, Mar. 29, 1966).

Mr. Prince produced (in association with Ruth Mitchell) and directed *Cabaret* (Broadhurst, Nov. 20, 1966; first national company opened Shubert, New Haven, Dec. 23, 1967; second national company opened State Fair Music Hall, Dallas, Texas, Aug. 19, 1969; London company, produced with Richard Pilbrow, opened Palace, Feb. 28, 1968); he produced, with Richard Pilbrow, *The Beggar's Opera* (Apollo, London, Sept. 12, 1968); produced (in association with Ruth Mitchell) and directed *Zorba* (Imperial, N.Y.C., Nov. 17, 1968; first national company opened Forrest, Philadelphia, Dec. 26, 1969; second national company opened Bushnell Aud., Hartford, Conn., Sept. 11, 1970); *Company* (Alvin, N.Y.C., Apr. 26, 1970; national company opened Ahmanson, Los Angeles, May 20, 1971;

London company, produced with Richard Pilbrow, opened Her Majesty's, Jan. 18, 1972); *Follies*, co-directed with Michael Bennett (Winter Garden, N.Y.C., Apr. 4, 1971; national company opened Shubert, Century City, Calif., July 22, 1972); *A Little Night Music* (Shubert, N.Y.C., Feb. 25, 1973; national company opened Forrest, Philadelphia, Feb. 26, 1974; London co., produced with Richard Pilbrow, opened Adelphi, Apr. 15, 1975); he directed *Candide*, produced by and at the Chelsea Th. (Brooklyn Academy of Music, N.Y., Dec. 11, 1973; re-mounted at Broadway Th., N.Y.C., Mar. 5, 1974, produced by the Chelsea Th. Ctr., in conjunction with Mr. Prince and Ruth Mitchell); and he produced (in association with Miss Mitchell) and directed *Pacific Overtures* (Winter Garden, Jan. 11, 1976).

Mr. Prince is an artistic director of the New Phoenix Rep. Co., for which he has directed *The Great God Brown* (Lyceum, N.Y.C., Dec. 10, 1972); *The Visit* (Ethel Barrymore Th., Nov. 25, 1973); and *Love for Love* (Helen Hayes Th., Nov. 11, 1974).

Films. Mr. Prince directed *Something for Everyone* (Natl. Gen., 1970).

Published Works. He has written a memoir entitled *Contradictions: Notes on Twenty-Six Years in the Theatre* (1974).

Awards. Mr. Prince received Antoinette Perry (Tony) Awards (as producer of the best musical) for *The Pajama Game* (1955), *Damn Yankees* (1956), *Fiorello!* (tied with *The Sound of Music*, 1960), *A Funny Thing Happened on the Way to the Forum* (1963), *Fiddler on the Roof* (1965), *Cabaret* (1967), *Company* (1971), and *A Little Night Music* (1973). *Candide*, ineligible for the best musical award, received a special Tony (1974).

He received the NY Drama Critics Circle Award (as producer of the best musical) for *Fiorello!* (1960), *Fiddler on the Roof* (1965), *Cabaret* (1967), *Company* (1970), *Follies* (1971), *A Little Night Music* (1973), and *Candide* (1974).

Mr. Prince received Antoinette Perry (Tony) awards as best director of a musical for *Cabaret* (1967), *Company* (1971), *Follies* (1972), and *Candide* (1974).

Fiorello! received the Pulitzer Prize (1959).

PRINCE, WILLIAM. Actor. b. William LeRoy Prince, Jan. 26, 1913, Nichols, N.Y., to Gorman and Myrtle (Osborne) Prince. Father, salesman; mother, office nurse. Grad. Binghamton (N.Y.) Central H.S., 1930; attended Cornell Univ., 1930–34; studied acting with Tamara Daykarhanova, 1936–37. Married Oct. 27, 1934, to Dorothy Huass (marr. dis. 1964); two sons, two daughters. Member of AEA (council, 1949–52); SAG; AFTRA (mbr. of bd., 1954–56).

Theatre. Mr. Prince made his N.Y.C. debut as a walk-on in *The Eternal Road* (Manhattan Opera House, Jan. 7, 1937); subsequently appeared in stock (Barter Th., Abingdon, Va., Summer 1937); in the Maurice Evans production of *Richard II* (tour 1937–38); in the Maurice Evans productions of *Hamlet* (St. James, N.Y.C., Oct. 12, 1938) and *Henry IV, Part 1* (St. James, Jan. 30, 1939); and appeared in stock (Playhouse, Eagles Mere, Pa., Summer 1940).

He played Richard in *Ah, Wilderness!* (Guild, N.Y.C., Oct. 2, 1941); Dan Proctor in *Guest in the House* (Plymouth, Feb. 24, 1942); Callaghan Mallory in *Across the Board on Tomorrow Morning* (Belasco, Aug. 17, 1942); Private Quizz West in *The Eve of St. Mark* (Cort, Oct. 7, 1942); David Rice in the pre-Bway tryout of *Judy O'Connor* (opened Shubert, New Haven, Conn., Mar. 21, 1946; closed Copely, Boston, Mass., Mar. 30, 1946); and David Gibbs in *Forward the Heart* (48 St. Th., Jan. 28, 1949). Mr. Prince appeared as Orlando in *As You Like It* (Cort, Jan. 26, 1950); Chris Isherwood in *I Am a Camera* (Empire, Nov. 28, 1951); Captain Tom Cochran in *Affair of Honor* (Ethel Barrymore Th., Apr. 6, 1956); Dr. Jonas Lockwood in *Third Best Sport* (Ambassador, Dec. 30, 1958); Dr. Robert Leigh in *The Highest Tree* (Longacre, Nov. 4, 1959); Alec Grimes in *Venus at Large* (Morosco, Apr. 12, 1962); Charles Marsden in *Strange Interlude* (Hudson, Mar. 11, 1963); and Henry Macy in *The Ballad of the Sad Cafe* (Martin Beck Th., Oct. 30, 1963).

He replaced (June 22, 1964) Wayne Carson as Bob McKellaway in *Mary, Mary* (Helen Hayes Th., Mar. 8, 1961); was William Marshall in a revival of *The Little Foxes* (Vivian Beaumont Th., Oct. 26, 1967); Arthur in *Mercy Street* (American Place Th., St. Clements Church, Oct. 11, 1969); appeared in *Long Day's Journey into Night* (Center Stage, Baltimore, Md., Dec. 17, 1969); *The Silent Partner* (Actors Studio, N.Y.C., May 11, 1972); *In the Matter of J. Robert Oppenheimer* (Goodman Memorial Th., Chicago, Ill., Jan. 7, 1973); was Davies in *The Caretaker* (Roundabout Th. Co., N.Y.C., June 23, 1973); and replaced (Apr. 7, 1975) Barry Nelson as Charlie in *Seascape* (Ahmanson Th., Los Angeles, Calif., Apr. 2, 1975).

Films. Mr. Prince appeared in *Destination Tokyo* (WB, 1943); *Hollywood Canteen* (WB, 1944); *Objective Burma!* (WB, 1945); *Pillow to Post* (UA, 1945); *Cinderella Jones* (WB, 1946); *Carnegie Hall* (UA, 1947); *Lust for Gold* (Col., 1949); *Cyrano de Bergerac* (UA, 1950); and *Macabre* (Allied, 1958).

Television. Plays and series in which Mr. Prince has appeared include Philco Playhouse (NBC) productions of *The Second Oldest Profession* (Mar. 1950), *Pretend I Am a Stranger* (July 1951, and *Night of the Vulcan* (Aug. 1951); Armstrong Circle Th. (NBC) productions of *A Man and His Conscience* (Aug. 1952), *A Volcano Is Dancing Here* (Nov. 1952), *Two Prisoners* (Sept. 1953), *John Doe 154* (Nov. 1957), and *The Meanest Crime in the World* (Mar. 1958); in *Babylon Revisited* (Th. for You, Oct. 1953); on episodes of The Mask (ABC, 1954); in *The Man Who Came to Dinner* (Best of Broadway, CBS, Oct. 1954); Justice (NBC, 1955); Modern Romances (NBC, 1956, 1957, 1958); and True Story (NBC, 1957).

He was in *All the King's Men* (Kraft Television Th., NBC, 1958); appeared on Young Dr. Malone (NBC, 1960); The Nurses (CBS, 1964); in *An Enemy of the People* (NET Playhouse, Dec. 1966); and *Father Uxbridge Wants to Marry* (NY Television Th., PBS, Feb. 1970).

Recreation. Sailing, skiing, tennis.

PRINE, ANDREW. Actor. b. Andrew Louis Prine, Feb. 14, 1936, Jennings, Fla., to Randy and Florence (Riviere) Prine. Father, Pullman conductor; mother, teacher. Grad. Jackson H.S., Miami, Fla., 1954; attended Miami Univ., 1954–56. Studied acting at Welch Workshop, N.Y.C. Member of AEA; SAG; AFTRA.

Pre-Theatre. Newsboy, farm worker.

Theatre. Mr. Prine made his debut in stock as Jimmy in *The Rainmaker* (Roosevelt Th., Miami Beach, Fla., Sept. 1956); and appeared in *Mrs. Patterson* (Davenport, N.Y.C., 1956).

He succeeded (1958) Anthony Perkins as Eugene Gant in *Look Homeword, Angel* (Ethel Barrymore Th., Nov. 28, 1957); played Lt. John Borak in *Borak* (Martinique, Dec. 13, 1960); John Creighton in *Distant Bell* (Eugene O'Neill Th., Jan. 13, 1960); and appeared in *The Caine Mutiny Court-Martial* (Center Th. Group, Ahmonson, Los Angeles, Nov. 30, 1971).

Films. Mr. Prine has appeared in *The Miracle Worker* (UA, 1962); *Advance to the Rear* (MGM, 1964); *Texas Across the River* (U, 1966); *Bandolero!* (20th-Fox, 1968); *The Devil's Brigade* (UA, 1968); *This Savage Land* (U, 1969); *Generation* (Avco Embassy, 1969); *Chisum* (WB, 1970); *Simon, King of the Witches* (Fanfare, 1971); *Squares* (Plateau Intl., 1972); *Crypt of the Living Dead* (Atlas, 1973); *One Little Indian* (BV, 1973); *The Centerfold Girls* (Gen. Film, 1974); and *Terror Circus* (CNC, 1974).

Television. Mr. Prine's extensive work in this medium includes appearances on US Steel Hour (CBS, 1957); Playhouse 90 (CBS); Overland Mail (NBC); *Roughing It* (NBC special); Peter Gunn (NBC); Wide Country (series regular, NBC); Alfred Hitchcock Th. (NBC); The Defenders (CBS); Ben Casey (ABC); Gunsmoke (CBS); Wagon Train (ABC); Dr. Kildare (NBC); Bonanza (NBC); Road West (series regular, NBC); Tarzan (NBC); Invaders (ABC); Ironside (ABC); The F.B.I. (ABC); The Name of the Game (NBC); *Along Came a Spider* (tele-film, ABC); *Night Slaves* (tele-film, ABC); Dan August (ABC); *Another Part of the Forest* (Hollywood Television Th., PBS); and The World of Disney (NBC).

Awards. He received the Century Th. Award for his performance as Eugene Gant in *Look Homeward, Angel* (1958) and the Outstanding Citizen Award of Miami (1959).

Recreation. Swimming, painting, reading.

PRITNER, CALVIN LEE. Educator. b. Aug. 23, 1935, Kansas City, Kans., to Ward E. and Losson M. Pritner. Educ. Washington H.S., Bethel, Kans.; grad. Kansas State Teachers Coll., B.S., 1957; Univ. of Illinois, M.A. 1961; Ph.D. 1964. Served in US Navy, 1958–60; journalist 3rd class. Married 1954 to Jacquelyn Elaine Adair; one son, one daughter. Member of ASTR; AAUP; ATA (bd. of dir. and exec. comm., 1971–74); UCTA (pres., 1973–74). Address: (home) 103 Lawrence, Normal, IL 61761, tel. (309) 452-4384; (bus.) Dept. of Theatre, Illinois State Univ., Normal, IL 61761, tel. (309) 436-6683.

Mr. Pritner has been professor and chairman, Dept. of Theatre, at Illinois State Univ., Normal, Ill., since 1971. Previously, he was a graduate assistant at the university (1960–64); assistant professor, Southern Illinois Univ. (1964–66); and associate professor of speech, Illinois State (1966–71). He taught high school in Missouri in 1957 and in Kansas in 1957–58.

He directed Univ. Th. productions of *The Playboy of the Western World, The Waltz of the Toreadors, A Tale of Chelm, The Devil's Disciple, Windows, The Subject Was Roses, Juno and the Paycock, The Glass Menagerie,* and *A Real Fast Caterpillar* and Chamber Th. productions of *Why I Live at the P.O.* and *The Strength of God,* and he played the role of George in *Who's Afraid of Virginia Woolf?* (Illinois State Univ., Aug. 1970) and was Sam Nash and Jesse Kiplinger in *Plaza Suite* (Illinois State Univ., Summer 1973).

Other Activities. Mr. Pritner was a drama consultant, Illinois Mid-State Educational Center (1967–70), was project director of a survey of the status of theatre in US high schools under a US Office of Education grant to ATA (1969–71), and has conducted workshops for elementary teachers in the uses of creative drama in the classroom.

Published Works. Mr. Pritner was chairman of a committee that edited *A Selected and Annotated Bibliography for the Secondary School Theatre Teacher and Student* (ATA, 1970). His articles on aspects of the theatre and reviews of plays and books about theatre have appeared in such publications as *Central States Speech Journal, Theatre Survey, Pennsylvania Magazine of History and Biography, Secondary School Theatre,* and *Dramatics.*.

Awards. Mr. Pritner received the Amoco award of merit (1974) for his contributions to the American College Theatre Festival.

Recreation. Tennis, reading.

PROCTOR, JAMES D. Press representative. b. James Durant Proctor, July 8, 1907, New York City, to Thomas D. and Rachel Proctor. Grad. Cornell Univ., A.B. 1929. Served WW II, US Merchant Marine. Member of ATPAM. Address: 123 E. 37th St., New York, NY 10016, tel. (212) MU 9-5973.

Pre-Theatre. N.Y.C. correspondent for Boston *Evening Transcript*, magazine editor.

Theatre. Mr. Proctor has been press representative for such productions as *Americana* (1932), *Hold Your Horses* (1933), *Double Door* (1933), *Wednesday's Child* (1934), *Life Begins at 8:40* (1934), *Kind Lady* (1935), *At Home Abroad* (1935), *Something Gay* (1935), *Ten Million Ghosts* (1936), *Reflected Glory* (1936), *Co-Respondent Unknown* (1936), *Journeyman* (1938), *I Married an Angel* (1938), *On Borrowed Time* (1938), *Stars in Your Eyes* (1939), *Thunder Rock* (1939), *Night Music* (1940), *Retreat to Pleasure* (1940), *Heavenly Express* (1940), *Brooklyn U.S.A*

(1941), and *Five Alarm Waltz* (1941), *Lower North* (1944), *The Man Who Had All the Luck* (1944), *Kiss Them for Me* (1945), *Marinka* (1945), *Mr. Strauss Goes to Boston* (1945), *Deep Are the Roots* (1945), *Truckline Cafe* (1946), *Woman Bites Dog* (1946), *You Twinkle Only Once* (1946), and *Shootin' Star* (1946).

He produced, with Barney Josephson, the pre-Bway tryout of *Barnaby and Mr. O'Malley* (opened Playhouse, Wilmington, Del., Sept. 6, 1946; closed Ford's Th., Baltimore, Md., Sept. 14, 1946).

Mr. Proctor was press representative for *All My Sons* (1947), *Bathsheba* (1947), *Tenting Tonight* (1947), *Carrot and Club* (1947), *Topaze* (1947), *Death of a Salesman* (1949), *The Man* (1950), *The Gioconda Smile* (1950), *Legend of Sarah* (1950), *An Enemy of the People* (1950), *The Shrike* (1952), *The Brass Ring* (1952), *The Chase* (1952), *The Crucible* (1953), *A Certain Joy* (1953), *Lullaby* (1954), *Wedding Breakfast* (1954), *A View from the Bridge*, and *A Memory of Two Mondays* (1955), *The Diary of Anne Frank* (1955), *Johnny Johnson* (1956), *Maiden Voyage* (1957), *Look Homeward, Angel* (1957), *Cloud 7* (1958), and *A Raisin in the Sun* (1959), *Semi-Detached* (1960), *One for the Dame* (1960), *The Good Soup* (1960), *Becket* (1960), *Borak* (1960), *Purlie Victorious* (1961), *General Seeger* (1962), *Great Day in the Morning* (1962), *Bravo Giovanni* (1962), *Nowhere To Go But Up* (1962), *Pullman Car Hiawatha* (1962), *Under Milk Wood* (1962), *Come On Strong* (1962), *A Gift of Time* (1962), *Desire Under the Elms* (1963), *The Rehearsal* (1963), *Anyone Can Whistle* (1964), Richard Burton's *Hamlet* (1964), *Comedy in Music* (1964), *Baker Street* (1965), *The Devils* (1965), *The Playroom* (1965), *Ivanov* (1966), *A Time for Singing* (1966), *The Homecoming* (1967), *Black Comedy* (1967), *Illya, Darling* (1967), *Little Murders* (1967), *The Deer Park* (1967), *Halfway Up the Tree* (1967), *The Unknown Soldier and His Wife* (1967), *The Price* (1968), *Dear World* (1969), *Home* (1970), *Prettybelle* (1971), *Fun City* (1972), *6 Rms Riv Vu* (1972), and *The Creation of the World and Other Business* (1972). He served as public relations consultant to the Antoinette Perry (Tony) Awards (1968–1972).

Other Activities. Mr. Proctor has also been a film publicist and an industrial public relations writer.

Published Works. He wrote the novel, *The Man on the Couch* (1951).

Awards. He received the *Theatre World* Award (1953).

PRYCE-JONES, ALAN. Critic, dramatist, editor. b. Alan Payan Pryce-Jones, Nov. 18, 1908, London, England, to Col. Henry and Marion Vere (Dawnay) Pryce-Jones. Father, army officer. Attended Eton, 1926; Magdalen Coll., Oxford Univ., 1927–28. Married Dec. 24, 1934, to Thérèse Carmen May Fould-Springer (dec. 1953); one son. Relatives in theatre: brother, Adrian Pryce-Jones, director of London theatrical agency; son, David Pryce-Jones, London theatre critic. Served British Army, 1939–45; rank, Lt. Col. Member of the Newspaper Guild; Century Association, N.Y.C.; Spouting Rock Club, Newport, R.I.; The Travellers; Garrick; Beefsteak; Arts Theatre; Pratts; the Marylebone Cricket Club, London.

Pre-Theatre. Editor of the London *Times* Literary Supplement (1948–59).

Theatre. Mr. Pryce-Jones wrote the libretto for the opera *Nelson* (Sadler's Wells, London, Sept. 15, 1954); and was co-author of the book and lyrics for the musical *Vanity Fair*, adapted from Thackeray's novel (Queen's Th., London, Nov. 22, 1962).

He has been drama critic for the London *Observer;* drama critic for *Theatre Arts* magazine 1960–61; 1962–64); was program associate of the Arts and Humanities Division of the Ford Foundation (1961–63); and a member of the board of the Theatre Development Fund (1967–68).

Other Activities. He has been a book reviewer on the staff of the NY *Herald Tribune* (1963–66); *World Journal Tribune* (1966–to date); and has written articles for the London *Times*, the NY *Times*, the *New Statesman* and *Nation*, the *Spectator, Harper's Bazaar, Harper's, Mademoiselle, Vogue*, and the *Saturday Review.*

Published Works. He is the author of *The Spring Journey* (1931); *Hot Places* (1932); *Beethoven* (1933), a biography; *27 Poems* (1935); *Private Opinion* (1936); and *Pink Danube* (1939).

Awards. He received the *Prix Denyse Clairouin* in the field of the arts (Paris, Fr., 1955); and the *Prix Plaisir de France* for Anglo-French cooperation (Paris, 1956).

PRYOR, NICHOLAS. Actor. b. Nicholas David Probst, Jan. 28, 1935, Baltimore, Md., to J. Stanley and Dorothy (Driskill) Probst. Father, pharmaceutical manufacturer. Grad. Gilman Sch., Baltimore, 1952; Yale Univ., B.A. 1956. Married Dec. 21, 1958, to Joan Epstein, actress (marr. dis. 1968); married Feb. 27, 1968, to Melinda Plank, dancer-actress. Member of AEA; AFTRA; SAG; WGA, East. c/o Ronald Muchnick and Yvette Schumer, Suite 1102, 1697 Broadway, New York, NY 10019.

Theatre. Mr. Pryor first performed as Peter in *Light Up the Sky;* Trock in *Winterset;* Haimon in *Antigone;* John in *John Loves Mary;* Loevborg in *Hedda Gabler;* in *The Father;* and *Peg O' My Heart* (Drummond Players, Baltimore, Md., Summer 1951); appeared as the Lord Chancellor in *Iolanthe;* Arthur Kindred in *Detective Story;* Randy Curtis in *Lady in the Dark;* the Singer in *My Heart's in the Highlands;* Cromwell in *Henry VIII;* Gremio in *The Taming of the Shrew;* and Owen in *Jenny Kissed Me* (Camden Hills Th., Me., Summer 1952).

In the Summer of 1953 he performed at the Ashland (Ore.) Shakespeare Festival as Launcelot Gobbo in *The Merchant of Venice;* Hortensio in *The Taming of the Shrew;* and Suffolk in *Henry IV, Part I;* and in *Coriolanus.* He played Paul Verrall in *Born Yesterday*, Ernest in *The Importance of Being Earnest*, Turk in *Come Back, Little Sheba*, Arthur in *Detective Story*, Don in *The Moon Is Blue*, and Simon in *Hay Fever* (Star Th., Minneapolis, Minn., Summer 1954).

Mr. Pryor first appeared on Bway (billed as Nicholas Probst) as Captain Dupont in *Small War on Murray Hill* (Ethel Barrymore Th., Jan. 3, 1957); subsequently played John in *The Old Maid* (John Drew Th., East Hampton, L.I., N.Y., July 1957); Roger Parson in *The Egghead* (Ethel Barrymore Th., N.Y.C., Oct. 9, 1957); Bill in *Love Me Little* (Helen Hayes Th., Apr. 15, 1958); Bezano in *He Who Gets Slapped* (Falmouth Playhouse, Mass., July 1958); appeared as Jimmie Keefe in *Howie* (46 St. Th., N.Y.C., Sept. 17, 1958); was understudy to Robert Redford and subsequently succeeded him (Oct. 13, 1959) in the role of Buzz in *The Highest Tree* (Longacre, Oct. 4, 1959); played Fredericks in *Craig's Wife* (Tappan Zee Playhouse, Nyack, N.Y., July 1960); Schuyler Grogan in *Invitation to a March* (Ogunquit Playhouse, Me., July 1961); at the Bucks County Playhouse (New Hope, Pa.), he played Ed Hughes in *The Advocate* (July 1962), and Jimmy Keller in *The Miracle Worker* (Aug. 1962); Romeo in *Romeo and Juliet* (Casino Park Playhouse, Holyoke, Mass., Aug. 1963); and the Young Man in *Moments of Love* (Westport Country Playhouse, Conn., Sept. 1963).

He was understudy to Ben Piazza in *Who's Afraid of Virginia Woolf?* (Billy Rose Th., N.Y.C., Jan.–Apr. 1964); played Barney in *A Party for Divorce* (Provincetown Playhouse, N.Y.C., Oct. 1966); Tiger in *The Rehearsal* (Th. of Living Arts, Philadelphia, Pa., Jan.–Apr. 1968); Alan in *The Boys in the Band* (Wilbur Th., Boston, May 1970; National Th., Washington, July 1970; Caesars Palace, Las Vegas, Sept. 1970; Th. Four, N.Y.C., Oct. 1970); played Tom Daley (Sept. 1973) and James Daley (Oct. 1973–Apr. 1974) in *That Championship Season* (Booth Th., N.Y.C.); and Gordon in *Thieves* (Broadhurst Th., Sept. 11, 1974).

Television. He made his debut as Tom in *Star for Tonight* (NBC, Sept. 1955); subsequently appeared on *Kraft Television Th.* (NBC, Dec. 1955); *US Steel Hour* (CBS, 1958); *Omnibus* (ABC, 1958); *The Dupont Show of the Month* (NBC, 1960); *Hallmark Hall of Fame* (NBC, 1959); *Ford Startime* (NBC, 1960); *Alfred Hitchcock Presents* (NBC, 1961); as Ernie in Young Dr. Malone (NBC, March–August 1959); as Rex Stern in The Brighter Day (CBS, Sept. 1960–April 1961); as Johnny Ellis in The Secret Storm (CBS, Mar.–Nov. 1963); as Tom Baxter in Another World (NBC, May 1964); as Ken Cora in The Nurses (ABC, Sept. 1965–Apr. 1967); as Paul Bradley in Love Is a Many Splendored Thing (CBS, Sept.–Dec. 1968); as Lincoln Tyler III in All My Children (ABC, Nov. 1971–May 1972); and as Joel Gantry in The Edge of Night (CBS, Apr.–Dec. 1973).

Awards. Mr. Pryor was National Scholarship holder, Oregon Shakespeare Festival (1953); and was the first recipient of the RCA-NBC Drama Scholarship, Yale Univ. (1955–56).

PSACHAROPOULOS, NIKOS. Director, educator, theatre administrator. b. Jan. 18, 1928, Athens, Greece, to Konstantin and Helen Psacharopoulos. Emigrated to US in 1947. Grad. Oberlin Coll., B.A. 1951; Yale Univ., M.F.A. 1954. Member of directors' unit of the Actors Studio (1960–to date). Address: 4 Gramercy Park West, New York, NY 10010, tel. (212) GR 5-2398.

Mr. Psacharopoulos taught at Amherst (Mass.) Coll. (1954); was director of the Rangeley Lakes, Me., Summer Th. (1954); visiting lecturer at Williams (Mass.) Coll. (1955); taught at Columbia Univ. (1961); and since 1956, has taught directing at the Graduate Sch. of Drama at Yale Univ. Among the productions he has directed there are *Legend of Lovers* (Nov. 5, 1958) *Agamemnon* (Jan. 21, 1959); *He Who Must Die* (Mar 16, 1960); *The Flowering Peach* (Nov. 2, 1960); *Man Better Man* (Jan 24, 1963); *The Visit* (Mar. 13, 1963); *Arms and the Man* (Mar. 17, 1965); and *Peer Gynt* (Jan. 19, 1966).

He directed the NY Pro Musica production of *The Play of Daniel* (Cloisters, N.Y.C., Jan. 2, 1958), and a subsequent European tour (Festival of Two Worlds, Spoleto, Italy, June 16, 1960; Maggio Musicale, Florence, Italy, June 26, 1960; Royaumont, France, July 9, 1960; and Th. des nations, Paris, France, July 12, 1960); directed *Tambourines to Glory* (Little Th., N.Y.C., Nov. 2, 1963); *The Play of Herod*, for the NY Pro Musica (Cloisters, Dec. 9, 1963); for the NY City Opera, directed *Lizzie Borden* (NY City Ctr., world premiere Mar. 25, 1965), *Cavalleria Rusticana* (NY State Th., premiere Oct. 1965), *Miss Julie* (NY State Th., premiere Nov. 1965), and *Dialogues of the Carmelites* (NY State Th., Mar. 3, 1966); dir. *Androcles and the Lion* (Amer. Shakespeare Fest., Stratford, Conn., June 25, 1968); and *The Lion in Winter* (Studio Arena Th., Buffalo, N.Y., Oct. 31, 1968).

He helped found the Williamstown (Mass.) Theatre Foundation (1955), became its executive dir. (1956), and since then has directed more than sixty productions for its annual summer seasons (at the 479-seat Adams Mem. Th., Williams Coll.), including *The Seagull, Rhinoceros, Once Upon a Mattress, The Visit, Time Remembered, Our Town, The Skin of Our Teeth, Toys in the Attic, The Madwoman of Chaillot, A Streetcar Named Desire, Othello, Becket, Man and Superman, The Cherry Orchard, Pal Joey, A View from the Bridge, A Man for All Seasons, Ondine, Cyrano de Bergerac, Once in a Lifetime, Mary Stuart, Saint Joan, Caesar and Cleopatra, Two for the Seesaw*, and *The Flowering Peach.*.

Television. Mr. Psacharopoulos directed *Night of the Auk* (Play of the Week, WNTA, 1960); *Agamemnon* (Hartford, Conn., 1960); and *The Play of Daniel* (WNET, Jan. 1966).

Awards. He received a Ford Foundation grant to teach at Amherst Coll. (1954).

PUGLIESE, RUDOLPH E. Educator. b. Rudolph Edward Pugliese, June 14, 1918, Cleveland, Ohio, to Joseph and Felicia (Peluso) Pugliese. Father, machinist. Grad. West Technical H.S., Cleveland, 1937; Miami Univ., B.A. 1947; Catholic Univ. of America, M.F.A. 1949; Ohio State Univ., Ph.D. 1961. Married Jan. 1942 to Betty Haberer; one son. Served USAF, 1941–45; rank, Capt. Member of AETA; Speech Assn. of Eastern States; NCP (advisor); Omicron Delta Kappa, National Men's Collegiate Honorary. Address: (home) 7806 Adelphi Ct., Adelphi, MD tel. (301) 422-3227; (bus.) Dept. of Speech and Dramatic Arts, Univ. of Maryland, College Park, MD tel. (301) 454-2541.

Since 1967, Dr. Pugliese has been a professor of drama in the Dept. of Speech and Dramatic Arts at the Univ. of Maryland, where previously he has been instructor (1948–57); and assistant professor (1957–62).

He was associate director of the University Th. (1961–69); and is currently director of the Th. Division (1969–to date); established the Children's Th. at the Univ.; established the student experimental theatre (1954); founded and directed the Summer Th. on the campus (1955); and is co-founder of the Maryland Drama Assn.

Dr. Pugliese acted at the Barter Th. (Abingdon, Va., 1949); was stage manager for *Faith of Our Fathers* (National Capital Sesquicentennial, 1950–51); director of public relations at the Olney (Md.) Th. (1956–57); and has published articles and reviews in journals and bulletins related to his field.

Films. He appeared in *Within Man's Power* (1954) and *Die Universitaet Von Maryland* (1956).

Radio. Dr. Pugliese was an announcer and producer for WMOH Radio (Hamilton, Ohio) and WJEL Radio (Springfield, Ohio, 1947).

PYLE, RUSSELL. Set and lighting designer, theatre manager. b. George Russell Pyle, Oct. 29, 1941, El Centro, Calif., to George Wilton and Mary Emma (Van Duzer) Pyle. Father, dairyman. Attended California State Univ., Los Angeles. Studied acting and directing with Jim Kirkwood. Married June 21, 1969, to Roxan Mary Pyle. Address: (home) 674 The Village, Redondo Beach, CA 90277, tel. (213) 376-1356; (bus.) El Camino College, via Torrance, CA 90506, tel. (213) 532-3670, ext. 347 or; Company Theatre, 1024 South Robertson Boulevard, Los Angeles, CA 90035, tel. (213) 652-3499.

Mr. Pyle is a founding member (1972); chairman of the board (1972–to date); and principal designer and technical director of the Company Theatre of the Company Theatre Foundation; and manager of the theatre at El Camino Coll. (Torrance, Calif., 1968–to date).

Theatre. For the Company Th., Mr. Pyle did the sets and lighting for *Johnny Johnson* (Dec. 1967); and lighting for *Antigone* (Feb. 1968), *Keep Tightly Closed in Cool Dry Place* (Mar. 1968), and *Comings and Goings* (Mar. 1968). *Sport of My Mad Mother* (Jan. 1969), lighting for *The James Joyce Memorial Liquid Theatre* (Apr. 1969), sets and lighting for *Red Cross* and *Voyages* (both May 1969), *The Emergence* (Sept. 1969), and *Such as We Are for as Long as It Lasts* (Oct. 1969).

He did the sets and lighting for *The Roar of the Grease Paint, the Smell of the Crowd* (P.V. Playhouse, Feb. 1970); *Man of La Mancha* (El Camino Coll., May 1970); directed *Amahl and the Night Visitors* (El Camino Coll., Dec. 1970); and, for Company Th., did sets and lighting for *The Plague* (Mar. 1971), sets for *Caliban* (Nov. 26, 1971), lighting for *Chamber Music* and *The Gloaming, Oh My Darling* (Jan. 13, 1972), and sets and lighting for *Mother of Pearl* (June 1972). In addition, he did the sets for *Revolution* (Mark Taper Forum, Los Angeles, Calif., Oct. 4, 1972); and *A Booth Called War* (Mark Taper Forum, Oct. 7, 1972); sets and lighting for *Endgame* (Company Th., Nov. 24, 1972); *Grabbing of the Fairy Button* (Company Th., Nov. 1972); *Soon* (Pilgrimage Th., Mark Taper Laboratory, Los Angeles, Fall 1972); *Mary Stuart* (Company Th., Feb. 1973); and *The Hashish Club* (Company Th., Apr. 28, 1973; and Bijou, N.Y.C., Jan. 4, 1975); lighting for *As You Like It* (Pilgrimage Th., Los Angeles, Sept. 3, 1973); sets for *The Tooth of Crime* (Mark Taper Forum, Sept. 19, 1973) and *The Kramer* (Stage B, Mark Taper Laboratory, Oct. 9, 1973); sets and lighting for *The Beast and the Rose* (Company Th., Dec. 1973); sets for *The Nutcracker* (El Camino Coll., Dec. 1973); lighting for the 1973 tour of Gene Marinaccio's American Concert Ballet productions of *Into the Night We Shall Return*, and *Cantique de la Vie;* for the Company Th., did sets and lighting for *The Derby* (Zephyre Th., July 1974); and lighting for *The Basic Training of Pavlo Hummel* (Los Angeles Inner City Cultural Ctr., Aug. 1974).

Night Clubs. Mr. Pyle did the sets and lighting for the rock group Fanny (Troubadour, Los Angeles, Calif., Oct. 1974).

Awards. Mr. Pyle received the Los Angeles Drama Critics Circle Award for sets and lighting (1969), for outstanding contribution to Los Angeles theatre (1972), and for lighting (1973); and received the Margaret Harford Award (1972) for outstanding contribution to the Los Angeles theatre.

Recreation. Building a 48-foot sailing ketch, backpacking, water skiing, weightlifting.

Q

QUAYLE, ANNA. Actress. b. Anna Veronica Quayle, Oct. 6, 1936, Birmingham, England, to Douglas and Katy (Parke) Quayle. Father, actor, producer. Attended Convent of Jesus and Mary, London, 1948–54. Studied acting at RADA (Gilbert Prize for Comedy) 1954–56; and with father. Relative in theatre: brother, John Quayle, actor. Member of AEA; AGVA; AFTRA. Address: c/o Elspeth Cochrane, 1, The Pavement, Clapham Common, London, W4, England.

Theatre. Miss Quayle made her debut in England at age five in *Quality Street* (Th. Royal, Lincoln, 1941); subsequently appeared as a Child in a touring production of *Lisbon Story* (1946); with the Th. Royal (Lincoln, 1951) played the Second Witch in *Macbeth*, the title role in *Johnny Belinda*, Emily Brontë in *Wild December*, and Meg in *Little Women;* appeared in *Better Late* (Oxford Th. Group, Edinburgh, Scotland, 1956); and as the Duchess of Barleycorn in the pantomime *Mother Goose* (Arts, Cambridge, England, Dec. 1956).

Miss Quayle's first London assignment was as stage manager and general understudy in *Malatesta* (Lyric, Hammersmith, Mar., 1957); subsequently she played a season of stock (Pavilion, Isle of Wight, England, 1957); Miss Lush in *Listen to the Wind* (Arts, Cambridge, Dec. 1957); Lucie in a pre-London tour of *A Fig for Glory* (opened Nottingham, Sept. 1958; closed Golder's Green, Oct. 1958); performed in *Ridgeway's Late Joys* (Players, London, May 1959); *Do You Mind?* (Palladium, Edinburgh, Scotland, Aug. 1959); *Look Who's Here* (Fortune, London, Jan. 21, 1960); *And Another Thing* (Fortune, Oct. 6, 1960); as Evie in *Stop the World—I Want to Get Off* (Queen's, London, July 20, 1961; Shubert, N.Y.C., Oct. 3, 1962); appeared in *Homage to T. S. Eliot* (Globe, London, June 13, 1965); in *Full Circle*, which she also wrote (Apollo Th., Dec. 1970); in *Bristow* (I.C.A., London, 1971); and in *Out of Bounds* (Bristol Old Vic, Dec. 1973).

Films. Miss Quayle made her debut in *A Hard Day's Night* (UA, 1964) and appeared also in *Sandwich Man; Drop Dead Darling* (Par., 1966); *Casino Royale* (Col., 1967); *Smashing Time* (Par., 1967); *Chitty Chitty Bang Bang* (UA, 1968); *Up the Chastity Belt* (1971); and *Mistress Pamela* (1972).

Television. She has appeared on Laughline (BBC, London, July 1960); *Flying High* (ITV, May 1961); the Sammy Davis, Jr., Show (ITV, Oct. 1961); Jack Paar Show (NBC, US, 1962); Merv Griffin Show (NBC, Feb. 1963); Juke Box Jury (BBC, London, 1963); Not Only But Also (BBC-1, June 1965); *Knock on Any Door* and *Guests of Honour* (ATV, Oct. 1965); *Tempo International* (BBC, Oct. 1965); The Avengers (Rediffusion, Mar. 1967); Spate of Speight (ITV, May 1969); Join Jim Dale (ATV, July 1969); Girls About Town (Thames, Oct. 1969); The Beauty Operators (Thames, Nov. 1969); Late Night Lineup (BBC, Feb. 1971); A Degree of Frost (BBC, Feb. 1973); What's My Line? (BBC, Aug. 1973); and Grub Street (BBC, June–July, 1973).

Night Clubs. Miss Quayle has entertained at the Sandown Theatre Club (Isle of Wight, Dec. 1958); at The Lost World Ball (Royal Festival Hall, London, May 1960); and the RADA Theatre Ball (Savoy Hotel, Jan. 1962). She was selected as solo artiste to entertain at the Midnight Cabaret for the Theatrical Ball (Lyceum, London, Mar. 31, 1974).

Awards. Miss Quayle received the British Drama Critics Award (1962) and the Antoinette Perry (Tony) Award (1963) for her performance as Evie in *Stop the World—I Want to Get Off.* .

Recreation. Reading, collecting records, writing verse, Siamese cats, Pekinese dogs.

QUAYLE, ANTHONY. Actor, director. b. John Anthony Quayle, Sept. 7, 1913, Ainsdale, Lancashire, England, to Arthur and Esther (Overton) Quayle. Attended Rugby Sch. (1927–30); Royal Academy of Dramatic Art (1930–31). Married to Hermione Hannen (marr. dis.); married June 3, 1947, to Dorothy Hyson, actress; one son, two daughters. Served Royal Artillery, 1939–45; rank, Maj. Member of British AEA; BSAG; Garrick Club.

Theatre. Mr. Quayle made his N.Y.C. debut as Mr. Harcourt in *The Country Wife* (Henry Miller's Th., Dec. 1936); subsequently played the title role in *Tamburlaine the Great* (Winter Garden, Jan. 19, 1956); directed *The Firstborn*, in which he portrayed Moses (Coronet, Apr. 29, 1958); played the title role in *Galileo* (Vivian Beaumont Th., Apr. 13, 1967); was General Fitzbuttress in *Halfway Up the Tree* (Brooks Atkinson Th., Nov. 7, 1967); directed *Tiger at the Gates* (Vivian Beaumont Th., Feb. 29, 1968); repeated his London performance (see below) as Andrew Wyke in *Sleuth* Music Box, Nov. 12, 1970; Ahmanson Th., Los Angeles, Calif., Jan. 11, 1972); and directed and played Pavel Andrejev in *The Headhunters* (Clarence Brown Th., Knoxville, Tenn., April 1974; Eisenhower Th., Kennedy Ctr., Washington, D.C., May 1, 1974).

Mr. Quayle became a visiting professor at the Univ. of Tennessee, Knoxville, in 1974 and a director and actor in the university's Clarence Brown Co., appearing with it in the title roles of *Everyman* (Oct. 17, 1974); *Macbeth* (1975); and *Rip Van Winkle* (Jan. 2, 1976).

He made his professional debut in vaudeville (London, 1931); followed by the roles of both Richard Coeur de Lion and Will Scarlett in *Robin Hood* ("Q," London, Dec. 28, 1931); Hector in *Troilus and Cressida* (Festival Th., Cambridge, 1932); Aumerle in *Richard of Bordeaux* (New, London, June 26, 1932); Ferdinand in *Love's Labour's Lost* (Westminster, July 6, 1932); as a member of the Old Vic Co. (Sept. 1932), he played various minor roles; appeared in Shakespearean roles (Chiswick Empire, 1933); portrayed Bennie Edelman in *Magnolia Street* (Adelphi, London, Mar. 8, 1934); Mat Burke in *Anna Christie* (Imperial Inst., July 3, 1934); Guildenstern in *Hamlet* (New, Nov. 14, 1934); Captain Courtine in *The Soldier's Fortune* (Ambassadors', Oct. 1, 1935); St. Denis in *St. Helena* (Old Vic, Feb. 4, 1936); and Mr. Wickham in *Pride and Prejudice* (St. James's, Feb. 27, 1936).

After making his Bway debut in *The Country Wife* (see above), he played Laertes in *Hamlet* (Kronberg Castle, Elsinore, Denmark, June 1937); Horatio in *Hamlet* (Westminster, London, July 9, 1937); Duke of Surrey in *Richard II* (Queen's, Sept. 6, 1937); Beppo in *The Silent Knight* (St. James's, Nov. 16, 1937); Demetrius in *A Midsummer Night's Dream* (Old Vic, Dec. 27, 1937); Cassio in *Othello* (Old Vic, Feb. 8, 1938); Robert Devereux, Earl of Essex in *Elizabeth, la femme sans homme* (Gate, Mar. 11, 1938); Ferdinand Godd in *Trelawny of the Wells* (Old Vic, Sept. 20, 1938); Laertes in *Hamlet* (Old Vic, Oct. 11, 1938); John Tanner in *Man and Superman* (Old Vic, Nov. 21, 1938); Capt. Jack Absolute in *The Rivals* (Old Vic, Dec. 6, 1938); and during an Old Vic tour of Europe and Egypt, appeared in the title role in *Henry V* (Jan.–Apr. 1939).

Mr. Quayle played Capt. Jack Absolute in *The Rivals* (Criterion, London, Sept. 25, 1945); directed *Crime and Punishment* (Wimbledon, June 18, 1946); portrayed Enobarbus in *Antony and Cleopatra* (Piccadilly, Dec. 20, 1946); Iago in *Othello* (Piccadilly, Mar. 26, 1947); and directed *The Relapse* (Lyric,

Hammersmith, Dec. 17, 1947).

He became a member of the Shakespeare Memorial Theatre Co. (Stratford-upon-Avon), in 1948 and in October was named director. At the Shakespeare Memorial Th., he played Philip Falconbridge in *King John* (1948); Iago in *Othello* (1948); Claudius in *Hamlet* (1948); Petruchio in *The Taming of the Shrew* (1948); directed and played Hector in *Troilus and Cressida* (1948); and directed *The Winter's Tale* (1948). He directed *Harvey* (Prince of Wales's, London, Jan. 5, 1949); at the Shakespeare Memorial Th., played the title role in *Henry VIII* (1949); and directed *Macbeth* (1949).

He headed the company's tour of Australia and New Zealand (Oct. 1949–Feb. 1950), playing the title roles in *Macbeth* and *Henry VIII*, and Benedick in *Much Ado About Nothing*. At Stratford-upon-Avon, directed, with Michael Langham, and played Antony in *Julius Caesar* (May 2, 1950); and directed, with John Gielgud, *King Lear* (July 18, 1950); and staged *Who Is Sylvia?* (Criterion, London, Oct. 24, 1950). He had overall charge of a Cycle of the Histories (Shakespeare Memorial Th.), in which he directed *Richard II* (Mar. 24, 1951); staged, with John Kidd, and played Falstaff in *Henry IV, Part 1* (Apr. 3, 1951); appeared as Falstaff in *Henry IV, Part 2* (May 8, 1951); and directed *Henry V* (July 31, 1951). Also at the Shakespeare Memorial Th., he played the title role in *Coriolanus* (Mar. 13, 1952); Mosca in *Volpone* (1952); and Jaques in *As You Like It* (Dec. 2, 1952).

Mr. Quayle again toured Australia and New Zealand with the Shakespeare Memorial Th. Co. (Jan.–Oct. 1953) in productions of *As You Like It*, *Henry IV, Part 1*, and *Othello*; and at Stratford-upon-Avon, directed and appeared in the title role in *Othello* (Mar. 16, 1954); portrayed Bottom in *A Midsummer Night's Dream* (Mar. 23, 1954); Pandarus in *Troilus and Cressida* (July 13, 1954); Falstaff in *The Merry Wives of Windsor* (July 12, 1955); and Aaron in *Titus Andronicus* (Aug. 16, 1955).

After he appeared in *Tamburlaine the Great* in N.Y.C. (see above), he directed a Shakespeare Memorial Th. Co. (Stratford-upon-Avon) production of *Measure for Measure* (Aug. 14, 1956); appeared as Eddie in the London production of *A View from the Bridge* (Comedy, Oct. 11, 1956); left the directorship of the Shakespeare Memorial Th. in Nov. 1956; toured as Aaron in *Titus Andronicus* (Paris Festival, May 1957; Venice, Belgrad, Zagreb, Vienna, and Warsaw), and repeated the role in London (Stoll, July 1, 1957).

After directing and appearing in the Bway production of *The Firstborn* (see above), he repeated his performance in Israel (Habimah Th., Tel-Aviv, July 1958); appeared as James Tyron in an Edinburgh (Scotland) Festival production of *Long Day's Journey into Night* (Sept. 1958), and in London (Globe, Sept. 24, 1958); played Marcel Blanchard in *Look After Lulu* (Royal Court, July 29, 1959); Cesareo Grimaldi in *Chin-Chin* (Wyndham's, Nov. 3, 1960); appeared as Nachtigall in *The Power of Persuasion* (Garrick, Sept. 19, 1963); played Sir Charles Dilke in *The Right Honourable Gentleman* (Her Majesty's Th., May 28, 1964); Leduc in *Incident at Vichy* (Phoenix, Jan. 26, 1966); directed *Lady Windermere's Fan* (Phoenix, Oct. 13, 1966); played Andrew Wyke in *Sleuth* (St. Martin's, Feb. 12, 1970); and directed the National Th. production of *The Idiot* (Old Vic, July 15, 1970).

Films. Mr. Quayle appeared in *Saraband for Dead Lovers; Hamlet* (U, 1948); *Oh, Rosalinda!* (Powell and Pressburger, 1955); *No Time for Tears* (ABPC, 1956); *Pursuit of the Graf Spee* (Rank, 1957); *The Wrong Man* (WB, 1957); *Woman in a Dressing Gown* (WB, 1957); *Ice Cold in Alex* (ABPC, 1957); *Serious Charge* (Alva Films, 1958); *Tarzan's Greatest Adventure* (Par., 1959); *The Challenge* (Alexandra, 1959); *The Man Who Wouldn't Talk* (Showcorporation, 1960); *The Guns of Navarone* (Col., 1961); *H.M.S. Defiant* (GW Films, 1961); *Lawrence of Arabia* (Col., 1962); *The Fall of the Roman Empire* (Par., 1964); *East of Sudan* (Col., 1964); *Operation Crossbow* (MGM, 1965); *Fog* (Col., 1965); *A Study in Terror* (Col., 1966); *Mackenna's Gold* (Col., 1969); *Before Winter Comes* (Col., 1969); *Anne of the Thousand Days* (U, 1970); *Everything You Always Wanted to Know About Sex* (UA, 1972); *The Tamarind Seed* (Avco-Embassy, 1974); and *Moses* (Avco-Embassy, 1976).

Television. He appeared in *The Man with the Gun* (Suspicion, NBC, US, June 1958); *The Barretts of Wimpole Street* (Producers Showcase, Apr. 2, 1956); directed *Caesar and Cleopatra* (Producers Showcase, Mar. 3, 1956); was in *The Rose Affair* (Armchair Th., ABC, 1961); *Any Other Business* (ATV, England, 1961); *Miss Hanago* (ATV, 1964); *The Rules of the Game* (ITV, 1965); *A Fearful Thing* (ATV, 1965); *The Poppy Is Also a Flower* (UN Drama, ABC, N.Y.C., 1966); *Barefoot in Athens* (Hallmark Hall of Fame, NBC, 1966); and Strange Report (NBC, 1971).

Published Works. He is the author of *Eight Hours from England* (1945) and *On Such a Night* (1947).

Discography. Mr. Quayle has recorded readings from classical literature for Caedmon.

Awards. The order of Commander of the British Empire (C.B.E.) was conferred upon him in 1952, and he received Outer Circle and Drama Desk awards (1971) for his performance in *Sleuth*.

Recreation. Sailing.

QUAYLE, CALVIN. Educator, director, scenic designer. b. Calvin King Quayle, July 22, 1927, Logan, Utah, to Joseph L. and Mabel (Hillman) Quayle. Father, farmer, salesman. Grad. Logan Sr. H.S., 1945; Utah State Univ., B.S. 1950, M.S. 1954; attended Univ. of Wisconsin, 1950; grad. Univ. of Minnesota, Ph.D. 1958. Married Aug. 4, 1949, to Virginia Winget; one son, two daughters. Served US Army, 6th Constabulary Squadron, 1945–47; rank, Staff Sgt.; ROTC Quartermaster Corps, 1950; rank, 2nd Lt. Member of AETA (vice-chmn. Musical Th. Proj., 1962–63). Address: Dept. of Speech, University of Wisconsin, Eau Claire, WI 54701.

Since 1965, Mr. Quayle has been professor of speech and chairman of the dept. at the Univ. of Wisconsin-Eau Claire. Previously, he had been assistant professor of speech at the Univ. of Michigan and designer at the university theatre (1963–65). He taught speech and English at Preston (Idaho) H.S. and directed and designed six productions (1951–53); and was instructor, assistant professor, and associate professor of speech at Chico (Calif.) State Coll. (1956–63), where he designed forty productions and directed seven.

Radio. He was a radio announcer at KVNU (Logan, Utah, 1948–49).

Recreation. Spectator sports, woodworking, reading.

QUINBY, GEORGE H. Educator, director. b. George Hunnewell Quinby, Mar. 26, 1901, Newton, Mass., to John Murray and Mary (Thayer) Quinby. Father, interior decorator. Grad. Wellesley (Mass.) H.S., 1919; Bowdoin Coll., A.B. 1923; Yale Univ. Sch. of Drama, M.F.A. 1946. Married June 28, 1939, to Clarice (Guthrie) Quinby. Member of ANTA; AETA (co-chairman, Architectural Project, 1948); AAUP; USITT; Psi Upsilon (faculty adviser, clerk of house assn.). Address: (home) 26 McKeen St., Brunswick, ME 04011, tel. (207) 725-2565; (bus.) Bowdoin College, Brunswick, ME 04011, tel. (207) 725-8731.

Since 1934, Mr. Quinby has been director of dramatics at Bowdoin Coll. (instructor, 1934–36; assistant professor, 1936–46; associate professor, 1946–49; professor, 1949; and professor emeritus, 1969–to date). He taught courses in playwriting; has directed 80 plays in the Memorial Hall Th. and 18 plays in the Pickard Th.; has held academic positions at Lafayette Coll. (instructor, 1923–25); Queens Univ. in Canada (visiting professor, 1956); Univ. of Teheran (Smith Mundt Grant as lecturer on American theatre, 1956–57; Fulbright Grant as lecturer on American theatre, 1962–63); in Teheran, directed plays in English and in Farsi, including *Long Day's Journey into Night* (1962); and at Maine Maritime Academy (1971–72).

Mr. Quinby was University Theatre consultant for three theatres and seven play groups at the University of Michigan (June 1930); under a Rockefeller Grant, he included 40 theatres in 30 different institutions as part of a study on college and university theatres built from 1930 to 1943 (1944). On sabbatic leave from Bowdoin Coll., he studied 20 ancient theatres in France, Italy, Sicily, and Greece (1955); as U.S. State Dept. specialist to report on Afghan theatre, he studied three theatre groups in Kabul, Afghanistan (1958); and is on theatre consultant lists for ANTA, AETA, and USITT.

Mr. Quinby performed at the Portland (Me.) Th. of Art (Summer 1922); acted and stage-managed plays for the University Players (Southampton, L.I., N.Y., 1927) and the Hampton Players (Southampton, L.I., Summer 1928–30); and directed 14 plays for the Savannah (Ga.) Town Theatre (1928–30).

Mr. Quinby was stage manager and played several small roles in *Grand Hotel* (Natl., N.Y.C., Nov. 13, 1930) and on tour; was stage manager and played William in *Double Door* (Ritz, Sept. 21, 1933) and on tour; was production manager (Summer 1933) and actor and stage manager (Summer 1934) for the Barnstormers (Tamworth, N.H.); and performed for the Arena Players (Franconia, N.H., Summer 1941).

In 1973, he became founder and first president of the Theatre Association of Maine and joined the advisory council for Pinetree Players of Brunswick, Me.; in 1974, he joined the advisory council of the New England Theatre Conference; and was a guest-delegate to the 8th annual Iranian Festival of Arts at Shiraz and Persepolis (Aug. 15–23, 1974).

Published Works. Mr. Quinby has written articles on Iranian and Afghan theatres for *Educational Theatre Journal*, on fifty years of Shakespeare at Bowdoin for the *Shakespeare Quarterly*, and on orientation of ancient Greek theatres to sun and prevailing wind for *Theatre Design and Technology*.

QUINTERO, JOSE. Director, producer, author. b. Jose Benjamin Quintero, Oct. 15, 1924, Panama City, Panama, to Carlos Rivira and Consuelo (Palmorala) Quintero. Father, cattleman, politician. Grad. LaSalle H.S., Panama; attended Los Angeles (Calif.) City Coll.; grad. Univ. of Southern California, Los Angeles, B.A. 1948. Studied at Goodman Th. Sch., Chicago, Ill., 1948–49.

Theatre. Mr. Quintero first directed *The Glass Menagerie* and *Riders to the Sea* (Woodstock Summer Th., N.Y., 1949); subsequently at the Circle in the Square, directed *Dark of the Moon* (Dec. 1950); *The Bonds of Interest; The Enchanted* (June 1951); *Yerma; Burning Bright* (Nov. 1951); *Summer and Smoke* (Apr. 24, 1952); *The Grass Harp* (Apr. 27, 1953); and *The Girl on the Via Flaminia* (Feb. 1954).

He directed *In the Summer House* (Playhouse, N.Y.C., Dec. 29, 1953); *Portrait of a Lady* (ANTA, Dec. 21, 1954); and, at the Circle in the Square, he directed *La Ronde* (June 27, 1955), and *Cradle Song* (Dec. 1, 1955).

He directed *The Innkeepers* (John Golden Th., Feb. 2, 1956); directed and produced, with Leigh Connell and Theodore Mann, *The Iceman Cometh* (Circle in the Square, May 8, 1956); with Messrs. Connell and Mann *Long Day's Journey Into Night* (Helen Hayes Th., Nov. 7, 1956), and its tour (opened Hanna, Cleveland, Ohio, Dec. 13, 1957; closed Biltmore, Los Angeles, Calif., May 17, 1958); he directed a production of *The Iceman Cometh* (Amsterdam, Holl., 1957); *Children of Darkness* (Circle in the Square, N.Y.C., Feb. 28, 1958); *A Moon for the Misbegotten* (Festival of the Two Worlds, Spoleto, Italy, Summer 1958); an operatic production of *Lost in the Stars* and *The Triumph of St. Joan* (NY City Ctr., Apr. 10, 1958); and staged a double bill of *Cavalleria Rusticana* and *I Pagliacci* (Metropolitan Opera House, Nov. 7, 1958).

At the Circle in the Square, he directed *The Quare Fellow* (Nov. 28, 1958); *Our Town* (Mar. 23, 1959); *The Balcony* (Mar. 3, 1960); staged *Camino Real* (St. Marks Playhouse, May 16, 1960); the pre-Bway tryout of *Laurette* (opened Shubert, New Haven, Conn., Sept. 26, 1960; closed there Oct. 1, 1960).

Mr. Quintero produced, with Theodore Mann, *Under Milk Wood* (Circle in the Square, N.Y.C., Mar. 29, 1961); directed *Look, We've Come Through* (Hudson, Oct. 25, 1961); three one-act plays presented as *Plays for Bleecker Street* (Circle in the Square, Jan. 11, 1962); *Great Day in the Morning* (Henry Miller's Th., Mar. 28, 1962); at Circle in the Square, produced, with Theodore Mann, a double bill, *Under Milk Wood* and *Pullman Car Hiawatha* (Dec. 23, 1962); and *Desire Under the Elms* (Jan. 8, 1963); for the Actors Studio Co., he directed *Strange Interlude* (Hudson, Mar. 11, 1963); and for the Repertory Co. of Lincoln Ctr., he directed *Marco Millions* (ANTA Washington Sq. Th., Feb. 20, 1964).

He also directed *Hughie* (Royale, Dec. 22, 1964); *Diamond Orchid* (Henry Miller's Th., Feb. 10, 1965); *Matty and the Moron and Madonna* (Orpheum, Mar. 29, 1965); *A Moon for the Misbegotten* (Studio Arena, Buffalo, N.Y., Oct. 7, 1965); *Pousse-Cafe* (46 St. Th., N.Y.C., Mar. 20, 1966); *More Stately Mansions* (Ahmanson Th., Los Angeles, Calif., Sept. 12, 1967; Broadhurst, N.Y.C., Oct. 31, 1967); *The Seven Descents of Myrtle* (Ethel Barrymore Th., Mar. 27, 1968); *Episode in the Life of an Author* and *The Orchestra* (Studio Arena, Buffalo, N.Y., Sept. 16, 1969); *Gandhi* (Playhouse, N.Y.C., Oct. 20, 1970); a revival of *Johny Johnson* (Edison Th., Apr. 11, 1971); *A Moon for the Misbegotten* (Morosco, Dec. 29, 1973); *Gabrielle*, which he also wrote (Studio Arena, Buffalo, N.Y., Dec. 9, 1974); and *The Skin of Our Teeth* (Eisenhower Th., John F. Kennedy Ctr., Washington, D.C., July 9, 1975; Mark Hellinger Th., Sept. 9, 1975).

Films. He directed *The Roman Spring of Mrs. Stone* (WB, 1961).

Television. He directed *Medea* (Play of the Week, WNTA, 1959); *Our Town* (NBC, 1959); *The Thunder of Ernie Bass* (The Nurses, CBS, 1962); *A Strange and Distant Place* (The Nurses, CBS, 1962); and *A Moon for the Misbegotten* (ABC, May 1975).

Published Works. Mr. Quintero wrote *If You Don't Dance They Beat You* (1974).

Awards. Mr. Quintero received the Vernon Rice Award (1956) for *The Iceman Cometh;* the *Variety* and Antoinette Perry (Tony) awards for *Long Day's Journey into Night* (1956); the NY Newspaper Guild (Page One) Award as the outstanding theatre personality (1957); the Grand Prix du Television (1959) at the Monte Carlo Festival for *Medea;* the Lola d'Annunzio Award (1960); and for *A Moon for the Misbegotten,* he received Antoinette Perry (Tony) and Drama Desk awards (1973–74).

Recreation. Reading.

R

RABE, DAVID. Playwright. b. Mar. 10, 1940, Dubuque, Iowa, to William and Ruth (McCormick) Rabe. Father, H.S. teacher. Grad. Loras Coll., Dubuque, B.A. 1962; Villanova Univ., M.A. (Drama and film) 1968. Married 1969 to Elizabeth Pan; one son. Served US Army, 1965–67. Address: c/o Th., Dept., Villanova Univ., Villanova, PA 19085.

Pre-Theatre. Journalist (New Haven, Conn., *Register,* 1969–70).

Theatre. Mr. Rabe wrote *The Basic Training of Pavlo Hummel* (NY Shakespeare Fest., Newman Th., May 20, 1971); *Sticks and Bones* (NY Shakespeare Fest., Anspacher Th., Nov. 7, 1971; moved to John Golden Th., Mar. 1, 1972); *The Orphan* (NY Shakespeare Fest., Anspacher Th., Mar. 30, 1973); *Boom Boom Room* (NY Shakespeare Fest., Vivian Beaumont Th., Nov. 8, 1973; revised and presented as *In the Boom Boom Room,* Anspacher Th., Nov. 20, 1974); *Burning* (performed in a workshop production, NY Shakespeare Fest., Martinson Hall, Apr. 13, 1974); and *Streamers* (Long Wharf Th., New Haven, Conn., Jan. 30, 1976; NY Shakespeare Fest., Newhouse Th., Apr. 6, 1976).

Television. *Sticks and Bones* was televised (CBS, Aug. 17, 1973).

Other Activities. Mr. Rabe was an asst. prof. at Villanova Univ. (1970–72), and since 1972 has taught playwriting there.

Awards. For *The Basic Training of Pavlo Hummel,* Mr. Rabe received (1971) a *Village Voice* Off-Bway (Obie) Award, a Drama Desk Most Promising Playwright Award, a *Variety* Poll of NY Drama Critics Most Promising Playwright Award, and a Dramatists Guild Elizabeth Hull-Kate Warriner Award. For *Sticks and Bones,* he received (1972) the Antoinette Perry (Tony) Award for best Amer. play, a NY Drama Critics Circle citation, the Outer Circle Award, and a second *Variety* Poll of NY Drama Critics Most Promising Playwright Award. *Boom Boom Room* was nominated (1974) for an Antoinette Perry (Tony) Award as best play.

Mr. Rabe received a Rockefeller Grant (1967), and won (1970) an Associated Press Award for his New Haven *Register* articles on the Daytop drug rehabilitation program.

RACHOW, LOUIS A. Performing arts librarian. b. Louis August Rachow, Jan. 21, 1927, Shickley, Nebr., to John Louis and Mable Louise (Dondlinger) Rachow. Father, farmer. Educ. Strang (Nebr.) H.S.; grad. York (Nebr.) Coll., B.S. 1948; School of Library Service, Columbia Univ., M.L.S. 1959. Served in US Army, 1954–56; adjutant general librarian (specialist 3d class), V Corps Hq., Frankfurt, Germany, 1955–56. Member of ALA; SLA (secy.-treas., Museum Group, N.Y.C. chap., 1964–66); TLA (recording secy., 1966–67; pres., 1967–72); ANTA; ASTR; ATA; Archons of Colophon; Council of Natl. Library Assns. (secy.-treas., 1970–71; bd. of dir., 1974–to date); NYLA; NY Library Club (council, 1973–77); NY Technical Services Librarians; Eugene O'Neill Memorial Theater Center (library advisory bd., 1966–to date). Address: (home) 528 W. 114th St., New York, NY 10025, tel. (212) MO 2-4150; (bus.) The Walter Hampden Memorial Library, 16 Gramercy Park, New York, NY 10003, tel. (212) 228-7610.

Mr. Rachow became librarian of The Walter Hampden Memorial Library at The Players, N.Y.C., in 1962. Previously, he had been librarian, York (Neb.) College (1949–54); instructional library assistant, Queens College, N.Y. (1946–57); serials acquisition assistant, Columbia Univ. Law Library (1957–58); and assistant librarian, University Club, N.Y.C. (1958–62). In addition to those posts, he served as a consultant to the Theatre Section, Univ. of California Libraries (San Diego) New Campuses Program (1964); the Theatre Division, Toronto (Ontario) Public Library System, Ash Survey of Book Resources (1965); and the Theatre Section, Queens Borough (N.Y.C.) Public Library System, N.Y., Ash Survey of Book Resources (1969).

Published Works. Mr. Rachow has contributed numerous articles and reviews to professional library and performing arts publications.

Awards. Mr. Rachow received the NY Library Club Scholarship Award in 1957.

RADO, JAMES. Actor, producer, playwright, composer, lyricist. b. James Radomski, 1932, Los Angeles, Calif., to Dr. and Mrs. Alexander Radomski. Father, professor and sociologist. Studied acting with Lee Strasberg, N.Y.C.

Theatre. Mr. Rado made his New York acting debut appearing in *Marathon '33* (ANTA, N.Y.C., Dec. 22, 1963); subsequently played the Ringmaster in the revue *Hang Down Your Head and Die* (Mayfair, Oct. 18, 1964); Georg Novak in *She Loves Me* (Charles Playhouse, Boston, Dec. 23, 1964); appeared in the pre-Bway musical *Quality Street* (Bucks County Playhouse, New Hope, Pa., Aug. 23, 1965); replaced George Segal (June 13, 1965) as Tolan in *The Knack* (The New, N.Y.C., May 27, 1964); played Richard in *The Lion in Winter* (Ambassador, Mar. 3, 1966); Wiley in *The Infantry* (81 St. Th., Nov. 14, 1966); with Jerome Ragni, co-authored the book and lyrics for *Hair* (Public/Anspacher, Oct. 17, 1967; Cheetah, Dec. 22, 1967), and played Claude when the production was moved to Bway (Biltmore, Apr. 22, 1968), and in the Los Angeles company (Nov. 22, 1968); wrote the music and lyrics, and, with his brother, Ted Rado, co-authored the book and produced *Rainbow* (Orpheum, N.Y.C., Dec. 18, 1972); and appeared in a revised and retitled version called *The Rainbow, Rainbeam, Radio, Roadshow* (American Th., Washington, D.C., Jan. 22, 1974).

Awards. With Jerome Ragni, he won (1967–68) the *Variety* NY Drama Critics Poll as best lyricist for *Hair.*

RAE, CHARLOTTE. Actress, comedienne, singer. b. Charlotte Rae Lubotsky, Apr. 22, Milwaukee, Wis., to Meyer and Esther (Offenstein) Lubotsky. Grad. Shorewood (Wis.) H.S.; Northwestern Univ., B.S. Studied acting with Mary Tarcai. Married Nov. 4, 1951, to John Strauss, composer, arranger, pianist, conductor; two sons. Member of AEA; AFTRA; SAG; AGVA.

Theatre. Miss Rae made her Bway debut as Tirsa Shanahan in *Three Wishes for Jamie* (Mark Hellinger Th., March 21, 1952); subsequently played Mrs. Peachum in *The Threepenny Opera* (Th. de Lys, Mar. 10, 1954); Mrs. Juniper in the Phoenix Th. production of *The Golden Apple* (Alvin, Apr. 20, 1954); appeared in *The Littlest Revue* (Phoenix, May 22, 1956); as Mammy Yokum in *Li'l Abner* (St. James, Nov. 15, 1956); Molly Brazen in *The Beggars Opera* (NY City Ctr., Mar. 13, 1957); Gloria Krumgold, Mrs. Younghusband, Rowena Inchcape and Mrs. Lafcadio Mifflin in *The Beauty Part* (Music Box, Dec. 26, 1962); the Caretaker in *The New Tenant* and Madeleine in *Victims of Duty,* a double-bill (Writers Stage, May 24, 1964).

She played Mrs. Bardell in *Pickwick Papers* (46 St. Th., Oct. 4, 1965); appeared at the 1968 NY Shakespeare Festival (Delacorte Th.) as Hostess Quickly in *Henry IV, Part 1* (June 11) and *Henry IV, Part 2* (June 18) and as the Nurse in *Romeo and Juliet* (Aug. 7); was Gertrude in *Morning,* Beryl in *Noon,* and Filigree Bones in *Night,* a program of three one-act plays (Henry Miller's Th., Nov. 28, 1968); Charlotte Mendelsohn in *Dr. Fish* on the program *The Chinese and Dr. Fish* (Ethel Barrymore Th., Mar. 10, 1970); Lola in *Come Back, Little Sheba* (Playhouse in the Park, Cincinnati, Ohio, July 16, 1970); Mother Sweet in the pre-Bway tryout of *Prettybelle* (opened Shubert Th., Boston, Mass., Feb. 1, 1971; closed there Mar. 6, 1971); Tia Maria in *Whiskey* (St. Clement's Ch., N.Y.C., Apr. 29, 1973); Helen in *Boom Boom Room* (Vivian Beaumont Th., Nov. 8, 1973); and was in the Center Th. Group production of *The Time of the Cuckoo* (Ahmanson Th., Los Angeles, Calif., Apr. 2, 1974).

Television. Miss Rae appeared on the Colgate Comedy Hour (NBC, 1954); the Garry Moore Show (CBS, 1954); the Martha Raye Show (NBC, 1954); the US Steel Hour (ABC, 1954); Kraft Television Playhouse (NBC, 1955); Philco Television Playhouse (NBC, 1955); Appointment with Adventure (CBS, 1955); the Ed Sullivan Show (CBS, 1956); played Myrtle Mae in *Harvey* (Dupont Show of the Month, NBC, 1957); appeared on Camera Three (CBS, 1957); *The World of Sholom Aleichem* (Play-of-the-Week, WNTA, 1958); Look Up and Live (CBS, 1963); Girl Talk (ABC, 1963); played Sylvia Schnauser in Car 54, Where Are You? (NBC, 1962–63); appeared on NY Television Th. (NET) in *The Immovable Gordons* (Nov. 1966) and *Apple Pie* (Mar. 1968); was in *Pinocchio* (Hallmark Hall of Fame (NBC, Dec. 1968); *Foul* (NET Playhouse, PBS, Nov. 1970); in episodes of Sesame Street (PBS, 1971–72); Love, American Style (ABC, 1972); and Hot l Baltimore (ABC, 1975).

Night Clubs. As a singing comedienne, Miss Rae appeared in N.Y.C. at the Sawdust Trial (1949); Old Knick Music Hall (1949); the Village Vanguard (1950); Cafe Society (1950); Blue Angel (1951, 1952); Village Vanguard (1952); Carnival Room (Sherry-Netherland Hotel, 1954); Bon Soir (1954); and, in Chicago, at the Empire Room (Palmer House, Chicago, Ill., 1957).

Awards. Miss Rae received Antoinette Perry (Tony) Award nominations, as best supporting actress in a musical (1965–66) for her role in *Pickwick Papers* and as best dramatic actress (1968–69) for her performance in *Morning, Noon and Night.*

Recreation. Housewife, mother, attempting to further state, city, and foundation subsidy for mentally ill children's schools.

RAEDLER, DOROTHY. Director, producer, manager. b. Dorothy Florence Raedler, Feb. 24, New York City, to Charles C. and Florence Elizabeth (Radley) Raedler. Father, civil service inspector. Grad. Bryant H.S., N.Y.C., 1934; Hunter Coll., B.A. 1942. Member of AEA; AGMA; NY Gilbert & Sullivan Society (hon. mbr.).

Pre-Theatre. Market researcher, insurance claims adjuster.

Theatre. Miss Raedler made her debut as producer, director, stage manager, and conductor for the Masque and Lyre Light Opera Co. productions of *The Mikado, H.M.S. Pinafore, The Pirates of Penzance, Iolanthe,* and *The Gondoliers* (Jan Hus House, N.Y.C., Aug. 1949); subsequently toured Eastern states as producer-director of the American Savoyards Co. productions of *The Mikado* and *Patience* (Oct. 1952), and presented the program at the Carter Barron Amphitheatre (Washington, D.C., June 1953).

She presented eight operettas at the Gilbert and Sullivan Festival Th. (Monmouth, Me., June 1953); she toured the mid-west with her company (Sept. 1953); presented the company in repertory (President, N.Y.C., Sept. 1953); in an appearance at the Carter Barron Amphitheatre (Washington, D.C., June 1954); Gilbert and Sullivan Festival Th. (Monmouth, Me., June 28, 1954); a tour of Eastern and Southern states (Oct. 1954); the Toledo (Ohio) Univ. Th. (Nov. 21, 1954); the Las Palmas Th. (Hollywood, Calif., Feb. 8, 1955); a Canadian-US tour (Oct. 1955); the Phillipe Park Amphitheatre (Safety Harbor, Fla., Mar. 12, 1956); the Gilbert and Sullivan Festival (Monmouth, Me., June 25, 1956); the Univ. of Wisconsin Th. (Madison, Oct. 12, 1956); and the Coconut Grove Playhouse (Miami, Fla., Nov. 1956).

With Donald Goldman, she was producer of a repertory engagement of Gilbert and Sullivan operettas in N.Y.C. (Shakespearewrights, Feb. 26, 1957); presented her company in 12 operettas (Monmouth, Me., July 1957); with Virginia Card, produced a series of six contemporary one-act operas, entitled *From Here to There,* which she also directed (Sullivan St. Playhouse, N.Y.C., Apr. 23, 1958); presented a program of Gilbert and Sullivan operettas to which were added *Firefly* and *Musical Threesome,* which was a group of three one-act operas (Monmouth, Me., June 1958); at Monmouth, produced and staged engagements of works by Gilbert and Sullivan, and such other operettas as *Sweethearts, The Grand Duke, The Vagabond King, Bittersweet,* and *Naughty Marietta* (Summer 1959).

She directed *The Mikado* (NY City Ctr., Oct. 3, 1959); was producer, with Michael E. Vogel, of a Gilbert and Sullivan repertory series (Jan Hus House, Jan. 28, 1960); and produced and staged an English-language adaptation of *La Traviata* (Jan Hus House, July 10, 1960); toured the Eastern states and Canada as producer-director of Gilbert & Sullivan works; staged *The Mikado* and *The Pirates of Penzance* (NY City Ctr., Sept. 30, 1960); and directed *The Gondoliers* (NY City Ctr., Jan. 17, 1961).

With Stella Holt and David Lipsky, she was producer of a repertory program of Gilbert and Sullivan operettas (Greenwich Mews Th., Apr. 26, 1961); toured Canada and the US as producer-director of *The Student Prince* (July 25, 1961); directed *The Mikado* (NY City Ctr., Oct. 1961); was producer, with David Lipsky, of a program of musical repertory, which she also directed (Jan Hus House, Oct. 26, 1961); staged three Gilbert and Sullivan operettas (NY City Ctr., Apr. 10, 1962); was producer, with Jeff Britton, of other engagements of this program (Actors Playhouse, N.Y.C., Aug. 7, 1962; Lyric, Baltimore, Md., Feb. 23, 1963); and directed *Cavalleria Rusticana* and *I Pagliacci* (Lyric, Baltimore, Md., Mar. 8, 1963).

She produced, with Mr. Britton, a Gilbert and Sullivan engagement, which she staged (Jan Hus House, N.Y.C., May 28, 1963); directed *Madame Butterfly* and *The Mikado* (NY City Ctr., Oct. 6, 1963); a Gilbert and Sullivan season of *The Mikado, Iolanthe, The Gondoliers, The Pirates of Penzance,* and a new production of *Patience* (NY City Ctr., Mar. 1964); and directed *Carmen* (Baltimore Civic Opera Co., Md., Apr. 1964).

She directed an American Savoyards series of Gilbert and Sullivan operettas (Jan Hus House): *Iolanthe* (May 18, 1965), *H.M.S. Pinafore* (May 20, 1965), *THe Mikado* (May 22, 1965), *The Gondoliers* (May 23, 1965), *The Yeomen of the Guard* (July 7, 1965), and *Ruddigore* (Aug. 26, 1965). As artistic director of American Savoyards, she directed (Jan Hus House) *The Pirates of Penzance* (May 23, 1966), *Princess Ida* (May 26, 1966), *The Mikado* (June 1, 1966), *Trial by Jury* and *H.M.S. Pinafore* (June 7, 1966); and, as executive director, American Savoyards, directed (Jan Hus House) *Patience* (Oct. 12, 1967), *H.M.S. Pinafore* (Oct. 17, 1967), *The Gondoliers* (Oct. 18, 1967), *The Mikado* (Oct. 24, 1967), and *Iolanthe* (Oct. 31, 1967).

Awards. Miss Raedler received the Show Business Awards as a director (1951) and as a musical director (1954).

RAGNI, GEROME. Playwright, actor, lyricist. b. Canada to Mr. and Mrs. Lawrence Ragni. Attended Georgetown Univ. and Catholic Univ., Washington, D.C. Studied acting with Philip Burton. Married May 18, 1963, to Stephanie; one son.

Theatre. Mr. Ragni made his theatrical debut as Father Corr in *Shadow and Substance* (Washington, D.C., 1954); subsequently appeared in *War* (Village South Th., N.Y.C., Dec. 2, 1963); *Hamlet* (Lunt-Fontanne, Apr. 9, 1964); the revue, *Hang Down Your Head and Die* (Mayfair Th., Oct. 19, 1964); replaced Brian Bedford (July 26, 1965) as Tom in *The Knack* (New Th., opened Apr. 27, 1964); and appeared in *Viet Rock* (Martinique, Nov. 10, 1966).

Mr. Ragni played the part of Berger, and, with James Rado, wrote the book and lyrics for *Hair* (Public Th., N.Y.C., Oct. 29, 1967; Biltmore, Apr. 29, 1968); subsequently wrote the book and lyrics for *Dude, The Highway Life* (Broadway Th. Oct. 9, 1972).

Films. Mr. Ragni has appeared in *Hamlet* (WB, Electronovision, 1964); and *Lions in Love* (Raab, 1969).

Night Clubs. He appeared at the Village Gate (N.Y.C., Feb. 4, 1974).

Awards. Mr. Ragni is the recipient of the Barter Th. (Abbingdon, Va.) Award for Outstanding Actor (1963); and, with Mr. Rado, the *Variety* Poll of NY Drama Critics Award for best lyricist (1967–68) for *Hair.*

RAGOTZY, JACK. Director, actor, producer. b. Jack Peyton Ragotzy, Dec. 16, 1921, Kalamazoo, Mich., to Floyd R. and Mary Louise (Gordon) Ragotzy. Father, printer; mother, seamstress. Grad. Central H.S., Kalamazoo, 1939; Kalamazoo Coll., B.A. 1948; Univ. of California at Los Angeles, M.A. 1949; grad. studies at New York Univ., 1949–51. Married Feb. 5, 1946, to Betty Ebert, actress; one son. Served USAAF, radar bombardier, 1942–46; rank, 1st Lt. Member of AEA; Directors Guild; SSD&C; SAG; AFTRA; CORST (bd., 1955–to date).

Pre-Theatre. Truck driver, retail clothing salesman, store manager, magazine salesman.

Theatre. Mr. Ragotzy made his debut as the Old Man in an elementary school production of *Where There Is Love There Is God* (Kalamazoo, Mich., Dec. 1931); subsequently, while stationed with the USAAF in Texas, directed the Midland (Tex.) Civic Players (1943–44); worked with a Special Service unit, writing, producing and directing soldier shows (Tinian Is., Jap., 1945).

He founded, with his wife, the Barn Th., Augusta, Mich., where he has been actor, producer and director (June–Sept. 1946–to date); produced *Country Mile,* which he had written for his M.A. at UCLA (Barn Th. Augusta, Mich., Summer 1949); was assistant stage manager for and the Military Policeman in the final national touring company of *Mister Roberts* (opened Washington, D.C.; closed Philadelphia, Pa., 1954).

Mr. Ragotzy directed the ELT productions of *Mamba's Daughters* (Lenox Hill Playhouse, N.Y.C., Mar. 1953), *Point of No Return* (Lenox Hill Playhouse, Apr. 3, 1957) and *The Time of the Cuckoo* (Lenox Hill Playhouse, Mar. 26, 1958).

He was assistant director of *Portofino* (Adelphi, Feb. 21, 1958); director at Sheridan Square Playhouse of *The Time of the Cuckoo* (Oct. 27, 1958) and *A Clearing in the Woods* (Feb. 12, 1959); *A Piece of Blue Sky* (North Jersey Playhouse, Fort Lee, N.J., Summer 1959); *Come Share My House* (Actors Playhouse, N.Y.C., Feb. 18, 1960); *Happy Ending* (Bucks County Playhouse, New Hope, Pa., July 1960); *King of the Whole Damn World* (Jan Hus House, N.Y.C., Apr. 12, 1962); *High Fidelity* (Walnut St. Th., Philadelphia, Pa., Sept. 14, 1962); and *Angela* (Music Box, N.Y.C., Oct. 30, 1969).

Television. Mr. Ragotzy wrote the adaptation of his play *Country Mile,* entitled *The Lovelorn Hiker* (CBC, Canada, 1955); directed on Play of the Week (WNTA), *Mornings at Seven* (Apr. 1960), *The Rope Dancers* (May 1960), *The Wooden Dish* (Mar. 1961) and *Close Quarters* (May 1961); and was also script editor for Play of the Week (1961). He has appeared in episodes of such programs as The Nurses (CBS); The Defenders (CBS); I Spy (NBC); and Dragnet (NBC).

Awards. Mr. Ragotzy received the *Village Voice* Off-Bway (Obie) Award for his direction of *The Time of the Cuckoo* and *A Clearing in the Woods* (1959).

Recreation. Baseball, as player and spectator.

RAIDY, WILLIAM ANTHONY. Drama critic, writer. b. Feb. 24, 1923, New York City, to William A. and Frances (O'Reilly) Raidy. Father, business executive. Attended Georgetown Univ.; Long Island Univ.; NY Univ. Graduate Sch.; NY Univ. Institute of Fine Arts; Univ. of Paris (Sorbonne). Member of NY Drama Critics Circle; Second Act Club; NY Newspaper Guild. Address: 25 Central Park West, New York, NY 10023, tel. (212) 247-5873.

During 1943–45, he served with the Office of War Information (OWI), and during 1945–46 with the Dept. of International Culture, US Dept. of State.

He has contributed to the *Paris Herald-Tribune,* the *Chicago Daily News,* the *Los Angeles times,* the *Washington Post,* and the *St. Louis Globe-Democrat,* and during 1966–70 he was a syndicated columnist for the *Los Angeles Times.*

He is also the author of magazine articles, television scripts and documentary films.

Recreation. Travel, collecting art.

RAINE, JACK. Actor. b. Thomas Foster Raine, May 18, 1897, London, England, to Thomas and Jenny Raine. Father, merchant. Attended Cranleigh Sch., Surrey, England, 1909–12. Married 1924 to Binnie Hale, actress (marr. dis. 1933); one daughter, Patricia Hale, actress; married 1935 to Sonia Somers, actress (marr. dis. 1942); married 1943 to Theodora Wilson. Served Royal Army, 1916–19; rank, 1st Lt.; RAF, 1940–44; rank, Wing Commander. Member of AEA; SAG; AFTRA.

Pre-Theatre. Banking.

Theatre. Mr. Raine made his London debut in *U.S.* (Ambassadors', Nov. 28, 1918); subsequently appeared in *Bird of Paradise* (Lyric, Sept. 11, 1919); *Paddy the Next Best Thing* (Savoy, Apr. 5, 1920); toured in *Eliza Comes to Stay* (1921); and he played Hank P. Dipper in *The Dippers* (Criterion, Aug. 22, 1922).

He played Sir Harry Fenton in *Mr. Garrick* (Court, Sept. 1922); Rev. Lewis Abbot in *Jack Straw* (Criterion, Apr. 18, 1923); Charles Bonipard in *Enter Kiki!* (Playhouse, Aug. 2, 1923); Mr. Darling in *Peter Pan* (Adelphi, Dec. 20, 1923); appeared in *The Odd Spot* (Vaudeville, July 30, 1924); played Van Herbert and Joe in *DeLuxe Anni* (Duke of York's, Sept. 3, 1925); Captain Harry Wythes in *Sweet Pepper* (Everyman, Dec. 1, 1925); Reginald Ridgley in *Aloma* (Adelphi, May 21, 1926); Hon. Harold Green in *The Blue Train* (Prince of Wales's, May 10, 1927); Harry Shaftesbury in *The Big Drum* ("Q," Oct. 17, 1927); Henry Reade in *Lady Mary* (Daly's, Feb. 23, 1928); and Gilbert Rand in *Little Accident* (Apollo, Apr. 3, 1929).

He made his N.Y.C. debut as Gordon McIlvaine in *Fast Service* (Selwyn, Nov. 17, 1931); subsequently appeared as Saunderson in *Chase the Ace* (Westminster, London, Mar. 1935); James Jago in *Anthony and Anna* (Whitehall, Nov. 8, 1935); Commander Musbury in *The Dog Watches* (King's, Hammersmith, Nov. 14, 1944); Jack Kurton in *The Third Visitor* ("Q," June 12, 1945); Inspector Pembury in *Dear Murderer* (Aldwych, July 31, 1946); and Captain Ponsford-Beckett in a revival of *Sweethearts and Wives* ("Q," Sept. 28, 1948); repeated his role as Inspector Pembury in *Dear Murderer* (Beverly Th., Los Angeles, Calif., 1953); and played Dr. Watson in *Sherlock Holmes* (New Century, N.Y.C., Oct. 30, 1953).

In stock, he played Champion Cheny in *The Circle* (Pasadena Playhouse, Calif., July 1956); the Lover and Manager in *An Evening with Noel Coward* (Sombrero Playhouse, Phoenix, Ariz., Oct. 1957); the Actor's Agent in *Epitaph for George Dillon* (1959); Dr. Bruce in the national tour of *Hilary* (opened Playhouse, Wilmington, Del., Oct. 14, 1959; closed Geary, San Francisco, Calif., Dec. 19, 1959); Defense Counsel in *The Deadly Game* (Pasadena Playhouse, Calif., Feb. 1961); the Father in *Five Finger Exercise* (Pasadena Playhouse, Aug. 1962); McPherson, the Scottish Engineer in *Time for Elizabeth* (Sombrero Playhouse, Phoenix, Ariz., May 1963); and he played Father Bonaventura in *'Tis Pity She's a Whore* and the Constable in *Peribanez* (UCLA Th. Group, July 1963).

Films. Mr. Raine made his debut as a Ship's Captain in *Les Miserables* (20th-Fox, 1952); subsequently appeared in *Saddles to Gobi* (20th-Fox, 1952); *Rogue's March* (MGM, 1952); *The Happy Time* (Col., 1952); *Holiday for Sinners* (MGM, 1952); *Above and Beyond* (MGM, 1952); *The Desert Rats* (20th-Fox, 1963); *Botany Bay* (Par., 1953); *Bengal Rifles* (U, 1953); *Dangerous When Wet* (MGM, 1953); *Young Bess* (MGM, 1953); *Julius Caesar* (MGM, 1953); *Elephant Walk* (Par., 1954); *The Silver Chalice* (WB, 1954); *Three Loves* (MGM, 1954); *Rhapsody* (MGM, 1954); *Moonfleet* (MGM, 1955); *Interrupted Melody* (MGM, 1955); *Not as a Stranger* (UA, 1955); *Soldier of Fortune* (20th-Fox, 1955); *The Girl in the Red Velvet Swing* (20th-Fox, 1955); *The Power and the Prize* (MGM, 1956); *An Affair to Remember* (20th-Fox, 1957); *Woman Obsessed* (20th-Fox, 1959); *My Fair Lady* (WB, 1964); *Strange Bedfellows* (U, 1964); and in *The Americanization of Emily* (MGM, 1964).

Television and Radio. During 1949–51, Mr. Raine was an actor and staff announcer for the Australian Broadcasting Corp.

On television, he appeared as Charles in *Man in Possession* (US Steel Hour, CBS, Dec. 1955); appeared in *A Christmas Carol* (Kraft Television Th., NBC, Dec. 1955); on the Perry Mason Show (CBS, Dec. 1957); played Omar Khayyam in *Arabian Nights* (Chevrolet Spectacular, Mar. 1958); Lord Dundreary in *The Day Lincoln Was Shot* (NBC, Dec. 1958); appeared on Death Valley Days (NBC, 1959); One Step Beyond (June, 1960); Sunset Strip (ABC, June 1960; Feb. 1963); played the title role in *The Meanest Professor* (Father Knows Best, CBS, Aug. 1960); appeared on the Burns and Allen Show (CBS, Nov. 1960); Hong Kong (ABC, Apr. 1961); Mr. Ed (CBS, Jan. 1962); Fair Exchange (CBS, Feb.–Mar.–Apr. 1963); the Dobie Gillis Show (1963); and Outer Limits (ABC, 1963); played the Butler in the series The Rogues (NBC, premiere Sept. 1964); appeared on Burke's Law (ABC, June 1964); 12 O'Clock High (ABC, 1964); and in a three-part story on Day in Court (ABC, Sept. 1964).

RAINEY, FORD. Actor. b. Aug. 8, 1908, Mountain Home, Idaho, to Archie Coleman and Vyrna (Kinkade) Rainey. Father, ship-fitter, woodsman, farmer, "jack of all trades"; mother, teacher, secretary. Grad. Centralia (Wash.) H.S., 1927; Centralia Jr. Coll., 1930; Cornish Drama Sch., Seattle, Wash., 1932. Studied with Alexandre Koiransky, Seattle, Wash., two years; Michael Chekhov, Ridgefield, Conn., two years; in Hollywood, Calif., one year. Married 1942 to Mary Lou Taylor (marr. dis. 1950); married Mar. 4, 1954, to Sheila Hayden, actress; two sons, one daughter. Served US Coast Guard, 1942–45; rank, Boatswain's Mate 2/c. Member of AEA; SAG; AFTRA. Address: 16751 Livorno Dr., Pacific Palisades, CA tel. (213) GL 4-7340.

Pre-Theatre. Logger, fisherman, construction worker, carpenter.

Theatre. Mr. Rainey first performed in the title role in *Copperhead* (Centralia H.S., Washington, 1927); and made his professional debut as Orgon in the Cornish Drama Sch. Repertory's tour of *Love and Chance* (1932).

He first appeared on Bway as a member of Verkhovenski's Organization in *The Possessed* (Lyceum Th., Oct. 24, 1939); subsequently played Sir Toby Belch in *Twelfth Night* (Little, Dec. 2, 1941); the title role in a touring production of *King Lear* (1941); 1st Customer and John B. Sherman in *The Wanhope Building* (Princess, N.Y.C., Feb. 9, 1947); in summer stock productions at Saratoga Spa (Saratoga, N.Y., June 1947); and in the title role in *Macbeth* (Las Palmas Th., Hollywood, Calif., Mar. 1948).

Mr. Rainey understudied Fredric March in *Long Day's Journey into Night* (Helen Hayes Th., N.Y.C., Nov. 7, 1956); appeared as Deputy Governor Danforth in *The Crucible* (Martinique, Mar. 11, 1958); played the prompter, understudied the title role and Mr. Zuss, and later succeeded Pat Hingle in the title role in *J. B.* (ANTA, Dec. 11, 1958); played Pilate in *Between Two Thieves* (York Playhouse, Feb. 11, 1960); James Tyrone in *Long Day's Journey into Night* (Fred Miller Th., Milwaukee, Wis., Mar. 1964); and appeared in *The Crucible* (Ahmanson, Los Angeles, Dec. 5, 1972).

Films. Mr. Rainey made his debut in *White Heat* (WB, 1949); subsequently appeared in *3:10 to Yuma* (Col., 1957); *Badlanders* (MGM, 1958); *John Paul Jones* (Col., 1958); *Parrish* (WB, 1961); *Claudelle Inglish* (WB, 1961); *Ada* (MGM, 1961); *Two Rode Together* (Col., 1961); *40 Pounds of Trouble* (U, 1962); *Kings of the Sun* (UA, 1963); *The Sand Pebbles* (20th-Fox, 1966); *The Gypsy Moths* (MGM, 1969); *The Traveling Executioner* (MGM, 1970); *My Sweet Charlie* (U, 1970); *My Old Man's Place* (Cinerama, 1971); and *Like a Crow on a Junebug* (Futurama, 1974).

Television. Mr. Rainey played Abraham Lincoln in *Miss Curtis Goes to Washington* (Hallmark Hall of Fame, NBC, 1953); from 1955–60 appeared on US Steel Hour (CBS), Philco Television Playhouse (NBC), Kraft Television Th. (NBC), Goodyear Playhouse (NBC), Camera Three (CBS), The Catholic Hour (NBC), Robert Montgomery Presents (NBC), Hallmark Hall of Fame (NBC), and Studio One (CBS); played the Editor on the series Window on Main Street (CBS, 1961). Between 1960–63, he performed on Route 66 (CBS), Bonanza (NBC), Rawhide (CBS), The Detectives (NBC), Empire (NBC), Gunsmoke (CBS), Perry Mason (CBS), Have Gun, Will Travel (CBS), The Untouchables (ABC), Mr. Novak (NBC), The Virginian (NBC), and The Nurses (CBS); and appeared on Perry Mason (CBS, Apr.–June 1964). He was also a member of the Richard Boone Repertory Co. (NBC, 1963–64).

Recreation. Tennis, chess.

RAISON, CHARLES W. Educator. b. Charles William Raison, May 1, 1936, Detroit, Mich., to Oscar Everett and Lillian (Walker) Raison. Grad. Michigan State Univ., BA, 1959; Tulane Univ., MFA, 1961. Married July 12, 1958, to Diane Millicent Deuvall; three children. Member of Commonwealth Playhouse Foundation (bd. of dir.); ASA; ATA; NCPA; Theta Alpha Pi. Address: (home) 1234 Stony Brook Lane, Mountainside, NJ 07092; (bus.) American Academy of Dramatic Arts, 120 Madison Ave., New York, NY 10016.

Pre-Theatre. Communications consultant.

Theatre. Mr. Raison joined the faculty of Lycoming Coll. (Williamsport, Pa.), serving as instructor and head of the Theatre Department (1961–63); assistant professor (1963–68); and associate professor (1968–69). There, he was the founder (1961) and producer-director of the Arena Theatre of Williamsport.

On June 15, 1969, Mr. Raison became executive director of the American Academy of Dramatic Arts (N.Y.C.); and was subsequently appointed director (1974–to date) of that institution.

RAITT, JOHN. Actor, singer. b. John Emmet Raitt, Jan. 29, 1917, Santa Ana, Calif., to Archie John and Stella (Walton) Raitt. Father, YMCA secretary. Grad. Fullerton (Calif.) H.S., 1935; attended Univ. of Southern California, 1935–36; grad. Univ. of Redlands, A.B. 1939; studied voice with Richard Cummings, twenty years. Married Dec. 28, 1942, to Marjorie Haydock (marr. dis. 1971); two sons, one daughter; married June 25, 1972, to Kathleen Smith Landry. Member of AEA; SAG; AFTRA; AGVA; Kappa Sigma Sigma; Society of Friends. Address: (home) 10787 Wilshire Boulevard #1102, Los Angeles, CA 90024; (bus.) John Raitt Productions, Inc., Box 1187, Carlsbad, CA 92008, tel. (714) 438-1807.

Pre-Theatre. YMCA secretary.

Theatre. Mr. Raitt made his debut as Dr. Falke in *Die Fledermaus* (Greek Th., Univ. of Redlands, June 1936); subsequently appeared in the chorus of *H.M.S. Pinafore* (Curran, San Francisco, Calif., May 1940; and sang Figaro in *The Barber of Seville* (Civic Aud., Pasadena, Calif., Sept. 2, 1941), where he also sang Count Almavida in *The Marriage of Figaro* (1942), and Escamillo in *Carmen* (1943).

He played Curly in the national tour of *Oklahoma!* (opened Erlanger, Chicago, Ill., Mar. 10, 1944); Billy Bigelow in *Carousel* (Majestic, N.Y.C., Apr. 19, 1945); Pedro in *Magdalena* (Ziegfeld, Sept. 20, 1948); Jim in *Rose Marie* (Civic Aud., State Fair Grounds, June 1949); Robert in *The New Moon* (Greek Th., Los Angeles, Calif., July 1949); Jamie in *Three Wishes for Jamie* (Curran, San Francisco, Philharmonic Aud., Los Angeles, May 1951; Mark Hellinger Th., N.Y.C., Mar. 21, 1952); the Duke in *Carnival in Flanders* (New Century, Sept. 8, 1953); Sid Sorokin in *The Pajama Game* (St. James, May 13, 1954); and Frank Butler in *Annie Get Your Gun* (Curran, San Francisco; Civic Aud., Los Angeles, 1957).

During the summer of 1960, he played Billy Bigelow in *Carousel* (Oakdale Musical Th., Wallingford, Conn.; Carousel Th., Framingham, Mass.; Warwick Musical Th., R.I.); Curly in *Oklahoma!* (Melody Fair, Chicago, Ill.; Kenley Players, Warren, Ohio); and Tom Destry in *Destry Rides Again* (Philharmonic Aud., Los Angeles; Curran, San Francisco); played Sid Sorokin in *The Pajama Game* (Old Globe, San Diego, Calif., 1961; Oakdale Musical Th., 1962; Warwick Musical Th., 1962; Carousel Th., Framingham, Mass., 1962); Curly in *Oklahoma!* and Billy in *Carousel* (St. Paul Aud., Minn., 1962); Sid in *The Pajama Game* (Sheraton Palace, San Francisco, 1962); toured as Billy in *Carousel* (Curran Th., San Francisco, Apr. 22, 1963) and played the role in a N.Y.C. revival (NY State Th., Aug. 10, 1965); was Shade Motley in *A Joyful Noise* (Mark Hellinger Th., Dec. 15, 1966); Dr. Mark Brucker in the bus-and-truck national tour of *On a Clear Day* (Dec. 31, 1967–May 26, 1968); and played the title role on the road in *Zorba* (opened Philadelphia, Pa., Dec. 26, 1969). His own company, John Raitt Productions, Inc., produced *Carousel*, which he directed and in which he toured as Billy (Jan. 27, 1972–May 27, 1972); *Camelot* (Feb. 1–Apr. 9, 1974); *Kiss Me, Kate* (1973); and *Seesaw* (1974–75), in which he also starred.

Films. Mr. Raitt has appeared in *Flight Command* (MGM, 1940); *Billy the Kid* (MGM, 1941); *Ziegfeld Girl* (MGM, 1941); *Minstrel Man* (PRC, 1944); and *The Pajama Game* (WB, 1957).

Television. He made his television debut as John Ringling North on the Buick Circus Hour (NBC, 1951–52); has appeared on the Ed Sullivan Show (CBS); and This Is Show Business (1951–52); played Frank Butler in *Annie Get Your Gun* (NBC, Nov. 27, 1957); was host and performed on the Summer Chevy Show (NBC, 1958, 1959); has made several guest appearances on the Bell Telephone Hour (NBC, 1960–63) and on such variety and talk shows as Merv Griffin, Mike Douglas, David Frost, and the Dinah Shore Show (1973–74).

Night Clubs. He has performed at the Riverside Hotel (Reno, Nev.); Fairmount Hotel (San Francisco); the Chi Chi (Palm Springs, Calif.); the Nugget (Reno, 1963); and the Desert Inn Hotel (Las Vegas, Nev., 1969), where he starred in the musical *Many Happy Returns*. .

Discography. Mr. Raitt has recorded for Decca, Capitol, and other companies. *John Raitt/Today* is a recent album.

Awards. Mr. Raitt received an honorary D.Mus. from the Univ. of Redlands; the Donaldson Award (1945) for his performance as Billy in *Carousel;* the San Francisco Drama Critics Award (1957); and the National Collegiate Athletic Award (1965).

Recreation. Water skiing, golf, camping, landscaping, construction on home.

RALL, TOMMY. Dancer, actor, choreographer, singer. b. Thomas Edward Rall, Dec. 27, 1929, Kansas City, Mo., to Edward M. and Margaret (Patterson) Rall. Father, magician, businessman; mother, teacher. Grad. Hollywood (Calif.) Professional H.S., 1944; attended Chouinard Art Inst., 1957–58. Studied dancing with Carmelita Maracci and David Lichine (Los Angeles, Calif.), and Oboukhoff (Sch. of American Ballet, N.Y.C.); acting at HB (Herbert Berghof) Studios (N.Y.C.), with Jack Kosslyn (Los Angeles); singing with Robert Weede and Sylvan Robert. Married Oct. 13, 1959, to Monte Amundsen, singer, actress. Member of AEA; AGMA; SAG; AFTRA. Address: (home) 917 5th St., Santa Monica, CA 90403, tel. (213) EX 5-8927; (bus.) c/o Ray C. Smith Assoc., 1869 Broadway, New York, NY 10023, tel. (212) JU 2-1412.

Theatre. Mr. Rall first appeared in a tap and tumbling act (Palomar Th., Seattle, Wash., 1938); performed throughout the Northwest at theatres, night clubs and convention halls (1938–40); and toured as a member of the corps de ballet with the Ballet Th. (1944).

He made his N.Y.C. debut as the Tyrolean Boy in *Graduation Ball* (Metropolitan Opera House, 1944); appeared in a specialty dance act in the *Ken Murray Blackouts* (El Capitan, Hollywood, Calif., Summer 1944); rejoined the Ballet Th. as a soloist (1945–47); sang in *Louisiana Purchase* (Los Angeles Philharmonic Aud., Calif., 1947); played Tommy in *Look Ma, I'm Dancin'* (Adelphi, N.Y.C., Jan. 29, 1948); appeared in the revue *Small Wonder* (Coronet, Sept. 15, 1948); played the Boy in *Miss Liberty* (Imperial, July 15, 1949); and danced in *Call Me Madam* (Imperial, Oct. 12, 1950).

He appeared as Johnny Boyle in *Juno* (Winter Garden, Mar. 9, 1959); appeared as a soloist with the Ballet Th. for the duration of the 1959 season at the Metropolitan Opera House; sang at the Berkshire Music Festival (Tanglewood, Mass., Summer 1960); made his operatic debut as Jean in *The Juggler of Notre Dame* (Wilbur, Boston, Mass., Feb. 1961); subsequently appeared as the Prince in *Cinderella* (Cleveland, Ohio, 1961); and David in *Milk and Honey* (Martin Beck Th., N.Y.C., Oct. 10, 1961), and also toured in it (opened Shubert, Philadelphia, Pa., Jan. 29, 1963); toured as Mario in the Boris Goldovsky Grand Opera Company's production of *Tosca* (Oct. 1963); played David Cole in *Cafe Crown* (Martin Beck Th., N.Y.C., Apr. 17, 1964); and Petey Boyle in *Cry for Us All* (Broadhurst, Apr. 8, 1970).

Films. Mr. Rall made his film debut in *Give Out, Sisters* (U, 1942); subsequently appeared in *Mr. Big* (U, 1943); *Kiss Me, Kate* (MGM, 1953); *Seven Brides for Seven Brothers* (MGM, 1954); *My Sister Eileen* (Col., 1955); *The Second Greatest Sex* (U, 1955); *World in My Corner* (U, 1956); *Walk the Proud Land* (U, 1956); *Invitation to the Dance* (MGM, 1956); *Merry Andrew* (MGM, 1958); and *Funny Girl* (Col., 1968).

Television. Mr. Rall was choreographer for the Faye Emerson Show (NBC, 1951–52); danced on the Ford Special (CBS, 1959), and appeared as a guest star on the Bell Telephone Hour (NBC, 1961, 1962).

Awards. He received the Outer Circle Critics Award for his performance as Johnny Boyle in *Juno* (1959).

Recreation. Painting, drawing.

RAMIN, SID. Composer, conductor, arranger. b. Sidney Norton Ramin, Jan. 22, 1924, Boston, Mass., to Ezra and Beatrice (Salamoff) Ramin. Father, in advertising. Grad. Memorial H.S., Boston; attended New England Conservatory of Music; Boston Univ.; Columbia Univ. Studied theory with Leonard Bernstein, Boston, Mass., 1933–42. Married to Gloria Bright, singer, model; one son. Served US Army, 1941–46; rank, Sgt. Member of ASCAP; AMPAS; AFM; Composers and Lyricists Guild of America. Address: 140 W. 57th St., New York, NY 10019, tel. (212) JU 2-5885.

Theatre. Mr. Ramin orchestrated, with Leonard Bernstein and Irwin Kostal, *West Side Story* (Winter Garden, N.Y.C., Sept. 26, 1957); with Robert Ginzler, *Gypsy* (Bway Th., May 21, 1959); orchestrated *The Girls Against the Boys* (Alvin, Nov. 2, 1959); arranged and orchestrated, with Robert Ginzler, *Wildcat* (Alvin, Dec. 16, 1960); arranged and orchestrated *The Conquering Hero* (ANTA, Jan. 16, 1961); orchestrated, with Irwin Kostal, for *Kwamina* (54 St. Th., Oct. 23, 1961); orchestrated the entire score of *I Can Get It for You Wholesale* (Shubert, Mar. 22, 1962); with Irwin Kostal, for *A Funny Thing Happened on the Way to the Forum* (Alvin, May 8, 1962); and orchestrated the chamber-orchestra version of Leonard Bernstein's *Mass* (Mark Taper Forum, Los Angeles, Calif., January, 1973).

Films. He orchestrated, with Saul Chaplin, Johnny Breen, and Irwin Kostal, the score of *West Side Story* (UA, 1961); and composed the score for *Too Many Thieves* (UA, 1967).

Television. He was musical arranger for the Milton Berle Show (NBC, 1949–56); musical director for Candid Camera (CBS, 1963–66); and composer for the Patty Duke Show (CBS, 1964–66); Trials of O'Brien (CBS, 1966); Miracle on 34th Street (CBS, Dec., 1973); and was composer/arranger/conductor for many radio and television commercials.

Awards. He received the Academy (Oscar) Award for his participation in the best scoring of a musical, and the "Grammy" Award for best soundtrack album, for *West Side Story* (1961); received a "Clio" for best musical scoring of the Johnson and Johnson Band-Aid commercial (1964), of the Diet Pepsi ad (1965–69), and of the Ford Pinto ad (1972) from Amer. Television Commercial Festival.

RAMSEY, LOGAN. Actor, director. b. Logan Carlisle Ramsey, Jr., Mar. 21, 1921, Long Beach, Calif., to Logan C. and Harriet Lillian (Kilmartin) Ramsey. Father, Rear Adm., USN (ret'd.). Grad. Friends' Central, Philadelphia, 1940; 1940); St. Joseph's Coll., B.S. 1943. Studied with Jasper Deeter, Hedgerow Theatre Repertory Company, Moylan, Rose Valley, Pa., 1940–44; Actors Studio (mbr., 1951–to date). Married June 26, 1954, to Anne Mobley, actress. Served USN, ETO, PTO, 1942; rank, Lt. (jg). Member of AEA; AFTRA; SAG.

Pre-Theatre. Advertising copywriter.

Theatre. During 1940–43, Mr. Ramsey appeared with the Hedgerow Theatre Repertory Co., Moylan, Pa. His debut was as Bardolph in *Henry IV, Part I*, followed by Christy in *The Devil's Disciple*, Valere in *The Physician in Spite of Himself*, Eben in *Family Portrait*, the Witch Doctor in *The Emperor Jones*, Malcolm in *Macbeth*, and appeared in *Arms and the Man;* at the American National Theatre Conference, he appeared as Wolf in *Liliom*, the Tycoon in *Midnite at Eight*, and the Egyptian in *Daughters of Atreus* (Hunter Coll., N.Y.C., 1947).

Mr. Ramsey made his Bway debut as Christy in *The Devil's Disciple* (NY City Ctr., Feb. 5, 1950; moved to Royale, Feb. 21, 1950); subsequently played Willy Pentridge in *The High Ground* (48 St. Th., Feb. 20, 1951); Lionel in *In the Summer House* (Playhouse, Dec. 29, 1953); the Second God in *The Good Woman of Setzuan* (Phoenix, Dec. 18, 1956); George Scudder in *Sweet Bird of Youth* (Martin Beck Th., Mar. 10, 1959); Shnozz in the Actors Studio production of *Marathon 33* (ANTA, Dec. 22, 1963); the Tavern Keeper in *My Kinsman, Major Molineux* on the program *The Old Glory* (Amer. Place Th., Nov. 1, 1964); was in *The Last Days of Lincoln* (ANTA Matinee Th. Series, Th. de Lys, Apr. 20, 1965); played Willy Kane in *The Great Indoors* (Eugene O'Neill Th., Feb. 1, 1966); and directed *The Seagulls of 1933* (Sherman Oaks Playhouse, Los Angeles, Calif., Feb. 15, 1975).

Films. Mr. Ramsey played a television director in *A Face in the Crowd* (WB, 1957); and George McHale in *The Hoodlum Priest* (UA, 1961).

Television. He has appeared on three hundred shows, including Hallmark Hall of Fame (NBC); Omnibus (CBS); Pulitzer Prize Playhouse (ABC); Ford Th. (CBS); Kraft Television Th. (NBC); Edge of Night (CBS); Ben Casey (ABC); The Defenders (CBS); Naked City (ABC); and Route 66 (CBS).

Awards. Mr. Ramsey received the Clarence Derwent Award for his performance as Willy Pentridge in *The High Ground* (1951).

Recreation. Painting.

RANDALL, BOB. Playwright, dramatist. b. Stanley B. Goldstein, Aug. 20, 1937, New York City, to Jerome and Bessie (Chiz) Goldstein. Father, salesman. Attended P.S. 104; Jr. H.S. 82; Music and Art H.S.; New York Univ. Married Mar. 11, 1962, to Ruth Gordon; one daughter, one son. Member of Dramatists Guild; Writers Guild. Address: 50 E. 78th St., New York, NY 10021, tel. (212) 249-7478.

Pre-Theatre. Television commercial writer.

Theatre. Mr. Randall is the author of *6 Rms Riv Vu* (Helen Hayes Th., N.Y.C., Oct. 17, 1972); and *The Magic Show* (Cort, N.Y.C., May 28, 1974).

Television. He wrote the script for the pilot *Mo and Joe* (CBS, 1974); and adapted *6 Rms Riv Vu* for television (CBS, 1974).

Awards. Mr. Randall received the Drama Desk Most Promising Playwright Award (1972–73) for *6 Rms Riv Vu* and the NATAS (Emmy) and Amer. Academy of Humor nominations for best special for his television adaptation of that play.

RANDALL, TONY. Actor. b. Anthony L. Randall, Feb. 26, 1920, Tulsa, Okla., to Philip and Julia (Finston) Randall. Grad. Tulsa H.S.; attended Northwestern Univ., Columbia Univ., Neighborhood Playhouse Sch. of the Th., 1938–40. Married (1939) to Florence Gibbs. Served US Army, Signal Corps, 1942–46; rank, 1st Lt. Member of AEA; AFTRA; SAG.

Theatre. Mr. Randall first performed in productions at the Upper Ferndale (N.Y.) Country Club (Summer 1939); and subsequently directed and played in productions at the Sussex County Playhouse (Culvers Lake, N.J.).

He made his N.Y.C. debut as the Brother in *The Circle of Chalk* (New Sch. for Social Research, Mar. 1941); followed by Marchbanks in a summer-theatre production of *Candida* (North Shore Players, Marblehead, Mass., Aug. 1941); and as a Miner in a N.Y.C. Subway Circuit production of *The Corn Is Green* (Bklyn., Bronx, Passaic, Scarsdale, July

1942); at the Olney (Md.) Th., directed and played in various productions (Summer 1946); and toured as Octavius Moulton-Barrett in *The Barretts of Wimpole Street* (Detroit, Mich.; Salt Lake City, Utah; Omaha, Nebr.; Los Angeles, Calif., May 1947).

Mr. Randall made his Bway debut as Scarus in *Antony and Cleopatra* (Martin Beck Th., N.Y.C., Nov. 26, 1947); played Adam in *To Tell You the Truth* (New Stages, Apr. 18, 1948); the Major Domo in *Caesar and Cleopatra* (Natl., Dec. 21, 1949); succeeded (July 1954) Gig Young as Arthur Turner in *Oh, Men! Oh, Women!* (Henry Miller's Th., Dec. 17, 1953); appeared as E. K. Hornbeck in *Inherit the Wind* (Natl., Apr. 21, 1955); Capt. Henry St. James in *Oh, Captain!* (Alvin, Feb. 4, 1958); and in summer stock productions of *Arms and the Man* (Westport Country Playhouse, Conn., 1960), and *Goodbye Again* (Detroit, Mich.; Chicago, Ill., 1961). He played J. Francis Amber in *UTBU* (Helen Hayes Th., N.Y.C., Jan. 4, 1966); and appeared as Felix Unger in various productions of *The Odd Couple* (Las Vegas, Nev., 1970?; Drury Lane Th., Chicago, 1970?; Summer tour, 1974; California tour, Summer 1975).

Films. Mr. Randall made his debut as Grant Cobbler in *Oh, Men! Oh, Women!* (20th-Fox, 1957); followed by *Will Success Spoil Rock Hunter?* (20th-Fox, 1957); *No Down Payment* (20th-Fox, 1957); *The Mating Game* (MGM, 1959); *Pillow Talk* (U, 1959); *Adventures of Huckleberry Finn* (MGM, 1960); *Let's Make Love* (20th-Fox, 1960); *Lover Come Back* (U, 1961); *Boys' Night Out* (MGM, 1962); *Island of Love* (WB, 1963); *The Brass Bottle* (U, 1963); *The Seven Faces of Dr. Lao* (MGM, 1964); *Send Me No Flowers* (U, 1964); *Fluffy* (U, 1965); *The Alphabet Murders* (MGM, 1966); *Bang, Bang, You're Dead* (Amer. Intl., 1967); *Hello Down There* (Par., 1969); and *Everything You've Always Wanted to Know About Sex* But Were Afraid to Ask* (UA, 1972).

Television and Radio. He was a radio announcer for WTAG (Worcester, Mass., June 1941–June 1942), and performed on various dramatic radio shows (1946–55), including continuing roles as Reggie on I Love a Mystery; on Portia Faces Life; When a Girl Marries; and Life's True Story.

Mr. Randall made his first television appearance as Mac, the Sailor, on One Man's Family (NBC, 1949); he played the continuing role of Harvey Weskit on the Mr. Peepers series (NBC, premiere Sept. 3, 1952; through Summer 1955); and Felix Unger on The Odd Couple Series (ABC, premiere Sept. 24, 1970; through Spring 1975). His many other appearances include performances on The Max Liebman Spectaculars (NBC); as Jonathan Brewster in *Arsenic and Old Lace* (Hallmark Hall of Fame, NBC, Feb. 5, 1962); in *The Littlest Angel* (Hallmark Hall of Fame, NBC, Dec. 12, 1971); and on Here's Lucy (CBS); Love, American Style (ABC); Checkmate (CBS); GE Th. (CBS); Sunday Showcase (NBC); Philco Playhouse (NBC); The Web (CBS); Kraft Th. (NBC); Goodyear Playhouse (NBC); Motorola TV Hour (ABC); Armstrong Circle Th. (NBC); Appointment with Adventure (CBS); Alcoa Hour (NBC); Studio One (CBS); Playhouse 90 (CBS); and many other panel, talk and game shows.

Discography. He has recorded two albums of "nostalgia" songs (one entitled *Vo, Vo, De, Oh, Do;* 1967); and with Jack Klugman, an album entitled *The Odd Couple Sings* (London, 1973).

Awards. Mr. Randall received the NATAS (Emmy) Award as Best Actor in a Comedy Series for his work on The Odd Couple (1975).

RANDELL, RON. Actor. b. Ronald Egan Randell, Oct. 8, 1923, Sydney, Australia, to Ernest Barrie and Louisa Maria (Egan) Randall. Father, importer. Grad. Clunes H.S., Victoria, Australia, 1928; attended St. Mary's Coll., North Sydney, New South Wales, 1933–40. Married July 27, 1957, to Laya Raki, actress. Served Australian Military Forces, 1941–42; rank, Lance Corporal. Member of AEA; SAG; AFTRA.

Theatre. Mr. Randell first appeared on stage, as Lt. Raleigh in *Journey's End* (Conservatorium of Music, Sydney, Australia, 1938); subsequently at the Minerva Th., Sidney appeared in *Quiet Wedding* (1938), played George in *Of Mice and Men* (1939), and Robert in *Dangerous Corner* (1940); appeared as Mr. North in *Mr. and Mrs. North* (Trivoli, San Francisco, Calif., Oct. 1942); and at the Minerva Th., Sidney, Australia, played Mahoney in *While the Sun Shines* (1943), and Bill Page in *The Voice of the Turtle* (1944).

He made his N.Y.C. debut as Frank Hunter in *The Browning Version* (Coronet, N.Y.C., Oct. 12, 1949); subsequently played the Rev. James Morell in *Candida* (National, Apr. 22, 1952); Chester Ames in *Sweet Peril* (St. James's, London, England, Dec. 3, 1952); Linus Larrabee, Jr., in *Sabrina Fair* (Palace, Aug. 4, 1954); Ben Jeffcoat in *The World of Susie Wong* (Broadhurst, N.Y.C., Oct. 14, 1958); Dirk in *Mary, Mary* (Queen's, London, Feb. 27, 1963); was standby for Alan Bates in the title role of *Butley* (Morosco, N.Y.C., Oct. 31, 1972) and played the part at matinees; and replaced (Feb. 4, 1975) Nicholas Selby as James Larrabee in *Sherlock Holmes* (Broadhurst, Nov. 12, 1974).

Films. Mr. Randell first appeared as Smitty in *Pacific Adventure* (Col., 1947); subsequently appeared in *A Son Is Born* (Porter Studios, Australia, 1947); *Bulldog Drummond at Bay* (Col., 1947); *It Had to Be You* (Col., 1947); *Sign of the Ram* (Col., 1948); *The Loves of Carmen* (Col., 1948); *The Mating of Millie* (Col., 1948); *Lorna Doone* (Col., 1951); *Mississippi Gambler* (U, 1953); *Kiss Me, Kate* (MGM, 1953); *I Am a Camera* (DCA, 1955); *The Story of Esther Costello* (Col., 1957); *The Girl in Black Stockings* (UA, 1957); *Beyond Mombasa* (Col., 1957); *King of Kings* (MGM, 1961); *Follow the Boys* (MGM, 1962); and *Gold for the Caesars* (MGM, 1962).

Television and Radio. He performed in *Lives of the Bengal Lancers* (Lux Radio Th., Station 2 U.W., Sydney, Australia, 1938); and played the Doctor in *Dad and Dave* (Station 2 U.W., Sydney, 1938).

Television programs on which Mr. Randell appeared include *Ever Since the Day* (Ford Th., NBC, Dec. 1953); *The Lovely Place* (Rheingold Th., NBC, Dec. 1954); *Man of the Law* (20th-Fox Hour, CBS, Feb. 1957); *Contact* (Alcoa Premiere, ABC, May 1960); and *Thou Still Unravished Bride* (Alfred Hitchcock Th., NBC, Mar. 1965). He also appeared regularly on the series O.S.S. (ABC) and in episodes of other series, such as The Millionaire (CBS); Gunsmoke (CBS); Tales of Wells Fargo (NBC); Espionage (NBC); Perry Mason (CBS); Outer Limits (ABC); Bonanza (NBC); Wild, Wild West (CBS); Mission: Impossible (CBS); and Mannix (CBS).

RANDOLPH, JOHN. Actor, producer, playwright. b. Emanuel Hirsch Cohen (changed at age 12 by stepfather, Joseph Lippman, to Mortimer Lippman), June 1, 1915, Bronx, N.Y., to Louis and Dorothy (Schorr) Cohen. Father, milliner. Grad. DeWitt Clinton H.S., N.Y.C., 1932; attended City Coll. of New York, 1932–34. Studied acting with Stella Adler at the Dramatic Workshop of the New Sch. for Social Research, 1940–42; and with William Hansen at the Amer. Th. Wing, 1947; Actors Studio, 1948–54. Married Jan. 3, 1942, to Sarah E. Cunningham, actress; one son, one daughter. Served USAAF, 1942–46; rank, Cpl. Relatives in theatre: nephew, Peter Lippman; cousin, Robert Hilliard, actor, educator, writer. Member of AEA (council member, 1968–72); AFTRA; SAG; Philadelphia Drama Guild (artistic consultant, 1971–74). Address: (home) 561 W. 163rd St., New York, NY 10032, tel. (212) SW 5-9610; 1811 N. Whitley Ave., Hollywood, CA 90028, tel. (213) 465-7657, 464-5191; (bus.) tel. (212) SU 7-5400.

Pre-Theatre. Soda-jerk, paint salesman.

Theatre. Mr. Randolph made his stage debut with the Ibsenians as Engstrand in *Ghosts* (E. Houston St. Th., N.Y.C., Mar. 7, 1935). He joined the Theatre Collective in N.Y.C. and appeared as a Private in *Private Hicks* and as the Old Man in *You Can't Change Human Nature* (both Provincetown Playhouse, Mar. 21–29, 1936). He appeared with the Federal Th. (WPA) Project as Tuff in *Revolt of the Beavers* (Adelphi, May 20, 1937) and the Weaver in *The Emperor's New Clothes* (June 1937); in repertory productions, played the *Times* Reporter in *Captain Jinks of the Horse Marines*, Jacob in *No More Peace*, and the Roman Herald in *Coriolanus* (Maxine Elliott's Th., Jan.-Feb., 1938); with the Federal Th. (WPA) Project (Salem, Mass.), he played St. Bernard H. Blackwood in *The Great Barrington* (Empire, N.Y.C., Apr. 1938) and the Second Beau in *Created Equal* (Empire, May 1938). He directed *Plant in the Sun* (Brattle Th., Cambridge, Mass., May 26, 1938); founded (1938), with Frank Silvera, the Transit Th. of Boston, for whom he directed *Transit* and another production of *Plant in the Sun* (Peabody Playhouse, Boston, Mass., Sept. 26, 1938).

He appeared as Mac in *Medicine Show* (New Yorker, Apr. 12, 1940); the Radio Announcer in *Hold on to Your Hats* (Shubert, Sept. 11, 1940); for the Erwin Piscator Dramatic Workshop at the New Sch. for Social Research (N.Y.C.), played the title role in *Wozzeck* (May 1941) and Rudolf Dvoracek in *Any Day Now* (June 1941); followed by a national tour as Jan Erlone in *Native Son* (1941–42).

Mr. Randolph appeared at the Sayville (N.Y.) Playhouse in *My Sister Eileen* and *The Bishop Misbehaves* (June-Sept. 1946); as Endicott in *Front Page* (Civic, Chicago, Ill., Feb. 14, 1947); Lt. Jake Goldberg in *Command Decision* (Fulton, N.Y.C., Oct. 1, 1947); Dan in *The Sun and I* (New Stages, Mar. 20, 1949); Fred in *The Respectful Prostitute* (Harris, Chicago, Ill., May 1949; East Hartford (Conn., Oct. 1949); at the Westport (Conn.) Country Playhouse, played Longshoreman McCarthy in *The Time of Your Life* (June 1949) and the Milkman in a summer tryout of *Come Back, Little Sheba* (Aug. 18, 1949).

He played Joe Williamson in *The Golden State* (Fulton, N.Y.C., Nov. 25, 1950); Aslak, a Voice, and Herr Trompetstaale in *Peer Gynt* (ANTA, Jan. 28, 1951); Mike Mooney in *Paint Your Wagon* (Shubert, Nov. 12, 1951); the Milkman in *Come Back, Little Sheba* (Booth, Feb. 15, 1952); Lofty in *Seagulls Over Sorrento* (John Golden Th., Sept. 11, 1952); the Delivery Man in *The Grey-Eyed People* (Martin Beck Th., Dec. 17, 1952); Gordon Miller in *Room Service* (Playhouse, Apr. 6, 1953); and a Sailor in *Maya* (Th. de Lys, June 9, 1953).

In stock, Mr. Randolph played Sir Lawrence Wargrave in *Ten Little Indians* (Cecilwood Th., Fishkill, N.Y., July 1953); Mike Mooney in *Paint Your Wagon* (State Fair Music Hall, Dallas, Tex., Aug. 1953); Officer Mallon in *Madam, Will You Walk?* (Phoenix, N.Y.C., Dec. 1, 1953); Junius Brutus in *Coriolanus* (Phoenix, Jan. 19, 1954); Sgt. Fielding in *Too True To Be Good* (Playhouse-in-the-Park, Philadelphia, Pa., July 5, 1954); and at the Cecilwood Th. (Fishkill, N.Y.), played Joe Rugg in *The Farmer's Hotel* (July 1954) and Rev. Davidson in *Rain* (Aug. 1954).

He played Harry in *All Summer Long* (Coronet, N.Y.C., Sept. 23, 1954); subsequently Gus Kennedy in *Glad Tidings* (Shubert, Washington, D.C., 1954); McCarthy in *The Time of Your Life* (NY City Ctr., Jan. 19, 1955); succeeded (Feb. 1955) Ray Walston as Capt. Jonas in *House of Flowers* (Alvin, Dec. 30, 1954); and played Nathan Detroit in *Guys and Dolls* (NY City Ctr., May 31, 1955); played Ed Devery in *Born Yesterday* (Playhouse-in-the-Park, Philadelphia, Pa., July 1955); at the Brattle Shakespeare Festival, Don Pedro in *Much Ado About Nothing* (Cambridge, Mass., Aug. 1955); Ed Mason in *The Wooden Dish* (Booth, N.Y.C., Oct. 6, 1955); toured as Rev. Jeremiah Brown in the national company of *Inherit the Wind* (opened Blackstone, Chicago, Ill., Feb. 8, 1956; closed Ford's Th., Baltimore, Md., Jan. 19, 1957); toured high schools in the title role of the Connecticut Th. in Education's production of *Macbeth* (Mar. 1957) and played Doc Earl in *Fever for Life* (Hyde Park Playhouse, N.Y., Aug. 1957).

Mr. Randolph appeared as Howard in *Miss Isobel* (Royale, N.Y.C., Dec. 26, 1957); Chief of Police Shultz in *The Visit* (Lunt-Fontanne, May 5, 1958); Mr. Abrams in *Portrait of a Madonna*, one of three one-act plays presented under the title *Triple Play* (Playhouse, Apr. 15, 1959); Franz in *The Sound of Music* (Lunt-Fontanne, Nov. 16, 1959); was producer and adaptor, with Phoebe Brand and Frederic Ewen, of *A Portrait of the Artist as a Young Man*

(Martinique, May 28, 1962); played the Recruiting Officer in *Mother Courage and Her Children* (Martin Beck Th., Mar. 28, 1963); Dennis Corcoran in *A Case of Libel* (Longacre, Oct. 10, 1963); and joined (June 17, 1964) the NY Shakespeare Festival as the First Gravedigger in *Hamlet* (Delacorte, June 10, 1964).

He was the Narrator for *An Evening's Frost* (Th. de Lys, Oct. 11, 1965); played Mickey in *After the Fall* (Playhouse-in-the-Park, Philadelphia, Pa., Aug. 15, 1966); Treadwell in *My Sweet Charlie* (Longacre, N.Y.C., Dec. 6, 1966); Hofrat Behrens in *The Magic Mountain,* which he adapted with Frederick Ewen and Phoebe Brand (Brandeis Univ., Waltham, Mass., Feb. 9, 1967); Judge Jerome Stern in *Little Murders* (Wilbur Th., Boston, Mass., Mar. 25, 1967); Art Steinmiller in *The Peddler* and Russ Nowack in *The Dodo Bird* (Martinique, N.Y.C., Dec. 8, 1967); repeated in London, England, his role in *The Magic Mountain* (Camden Group Th., Mar. 25, 1968); played at the Mark Taper Forum, Los Angeles, Calif., as John Landsdale in *In the Matter of J. Robert Oppenheimer* (May 24, 1968), Louis in *Dance Next Door* (July 29, 1969), The President of the United States in *God Bless* (Oct. 12, 1969), and Fleming in *Line* (Oct. 13, 1969); was Editor Webb in *Our Town* (ANTA Th., N.Y.C., Nov. 27, 1969; Huntington Hartford Th., Los Angeles, Calif., Mar. 1970); repeated his role as Fleming in *Line* (Th. de Lys, N.Y.C., Feb. 15, 1971); played Andrew Creed in *Motive* (Playhouse-in-the-Park, Philadelphia, Pa., Aug. 9; Corning, N.Y., Aug. 17; Kennebunkport, Me., Aug. 30, all 1971); Harry Brock in *Born Yesterday* (Walnut St. Th., Philadelphia, Pa., Jan. 18, 1972); Charley in *Death of a Salesman* (Arlington Heights Th., Ill., May 18, 1972); Dr. Bonfant in *The Waltz of the Toreadors* (Walnut St. Th., Philadelphia, Pa., Jan. 9, 1973; Royal Poinciana, Palm Beach, Fla., Jan. 30, 1973); Mario in *Baba Goya* (American Place Th., N.Y.C., May 21, 1973); Mario in *Nourish the Beast* (Cherry Lane Th., Oct. 3, 1973); and again played Charley in *Death of a Salesman* (Walnut St. Th., Philadelphia, Apr. 28, 1974).

Films. Mr. Randolph appeared as a Radio Operator in *Naked City* (U, 1948); the Fire Chief in *Fourteen Hours* (20th-Fox, 1951); the role of V.P. in Charge of Labor in *Partners in Production* (20th Century Fund, 1952); the Disk Jockey in *Night Song* (Ind., 1965); Arthur Hamilton in *Seconds* (Par., 1965); narrated *Like a Beautiful Child* (Local 1199, 1967); was Azenauer in *Pretty Poison* (20th-Fox, 1967); Father Harvey in *Gaily, Gaily* (Mirisch, 1968); the Prosecutor in *Smith* (Walt Disney, 1968); Coach Jim Southern in *Number One* (UA, 1969), Cyrus McNutt in *There Was a Crooked Man* (WB, 1970); the Chairman of the Presidential Inquiry Commission in *Escape from the Planet of the Apes* (20th-Fox, 1970); Mr. Chamberlain in *Little Murders* (20th-Fox, 1971); Mr. Victor in *The Victors* (NY Univ., 1971); the Chairman in *Conquest of the Planet of the Apes* (20th-Fox, 1972); Inspector Sid Green in *Serpico* (Par., 1973); the Mayor of Los Angeles in *Earthquake* (U, 1974); and he was in the documentary *The Rehearsal* (Jules Dassin, 1974).

Television and Radio. He performed on radio in such roles as Hitler and Joshua on Five Star Final (WMCA, July 1934); was announcer for WORL and WHDH (Boston, Mass., 1938) and WHN (N.Y.C., 1939) and appeared on Americans at Work (CBS, Oct. 1939).

He has appeared on television on Captain Video (Dumont, 1947); Treasury Men in Action (NBC, 1947–49); The Web (CBS, 1947–49); the Actors Studio production of *My Three Brothers* (World Video, Nov. 1945); Hands of Murder (WARB, Dec. 1949); *Bulletin 120,* and the *Floyd Collins Story* (Philco Television Playhouse, NBC, 1950); Kraft Television Th. (NBC, 1950); in *Mrs. McThing* (Omnibus, CBS, 1958); on East Side/West Side (CBS, 1963); The Defenders (CBS, 1964); Ed Sullivan Show (CBS, 1964); Reporter (1964); Another World (NBC, 1964–66); For the People (1965); *Yiddish Stories of Two Worlds,* which he also adapted with Frederic Ewen and Phoebe Brand (Camera Three, CBS, 1965); the Patty Duke Show (CBS, 1965); Slattery's People (1965); *Inherit the Wind* (Hallmark Hall of Fame, NBC, 1965); Mr. O'Brien (1965); As the World Turns (CBS, 1965–66); N.Y.P.D. (Ind., 1965–67); *Unknown Chekhov,* which he also adapted with Frederic Ewen and Phoebe Brand (Camera Three, CBS, 1967); The Invaders (1967); Mission Impossible (CBS, 1967); Mannix (CBS, 1967–69–73); Judd for the Defense (1968); Bonanza (NBC, 1968–70–72); Hawaii Five-O (CBS, 1969); *Trail of Tears (PBS, 1969); Lawyers* (Bold Ones, NBC, 1969–72); *The Senator* (Bold Ones, NBC, 1970–71); Step Out of Line (CBS, 1970); Night Gallery (1970); Bracken's World (1970); The Name of the Game (1970); The Interns (1970); *The Cable Car Murder* (CBS, 1971); *The Death of Innocence* (CBS, 1971); O'Hara, Treasury Agent (1971); Topper Returns (NBC, 1972); Judge and Jake Wyler (1972); Family Rico (CBS, 1972); Rookies (ABC, 1972); All in the Family (CBS, 1973); Young Dr. Kildare (ABC, 1973); Partners in Crime (1973); *The Pueblo Incident* (ABC, 1973); Secret Storm (1973); Bob Newhart Show (CBS, 1973); Police Story (NBC, 1974); Wide World of Entertainment (ABC, 1974); Columbo (CBS, 1974); *Tell Me Where It Hurts* (GE Th., CBS, 1974); *Anne in Blue* (ABC, 1974); and *Nourish the Beast* (PBS, 1974).

Awards. Mr. Randolph received the Richard Watts (NY *Post*) Stardust Citation (1951) for his performance as the Milkman in *Come Back, Little Sheba.*

Recreation. Collecting stamps.

RANDOLPH, ROBERT.

Designer. b. Robert Stephen Randolph, Mar. 9, 1926, Centerville, Iowa, to Charles W. and Saide M. (Walker) Randolph. Grad. Centerville H.S., 1944; State Univ. of Iowa, B.F.A. 1950, M.F.A. 1953. Served with USAAF, 1944–46. Member of United Scenic Artists, Local 829.

Pre-Theatre. Architectural and industrial designer; instructor, State Univ. of Iowa.

Theatre. Mr. Randolph designed the scenery and costumes for *The Saint of Bleecker Street* (Bway Th., N.Y.C., Dec. 27, 1954); costumes for *The Desperate Hours* (Ethel Barrymore Th., Feb. 10, 1955); scenery for *Bye Bye Birdie* (Martin Beck Th., Apr. 14, 1960); scenery and lighting for *How To Succeed in Business Without Really Trying* (46 St. Th., Oct. 15, 1961); and setting and lighting for *Bravo Giovanni* (Broadhurst, May 19, 1962).

Mr. Randolph also designed the scenery for *Calculated Risk* (Ambassador, Oct. 12, 1962); scenery and lighting for *Little Me* (Lunt-Fontanne, Nov. 17, 1962); *Sophie* (Winter Garden, Apr. 15, 1963); *Foxy* (Ziegfeld, Feb. 16, 1964); scenery for *Any Wednesday* (Booth, Feb. 18, 1964); scenery and lighting for *Funny Girl* (Winter Garden, Mar. 26, 1964); *Something More!* (Eugene O'Neill Th., Nov. 10, 1964); a revival of *The Saint of Bleecker Street* (NY City Ctr., Sept. 29, 1965); scenery for *Minor Miracle* (Henry Miller's Th., Oct. 7, 1965); scenery and lighting for *Xmas in Las Vegas* (Ethel Barrymore Th., Nov. 4, 1965); *Skyscraper* (Lunt-Fontanne Th., Nov. 13, 1965); scenery for *Anya* (Ziegfeld Th., Nov. 29, 1965); scenery and lighting for *Sweet Charity* (Palace, Jan. 29, 1966); *It's a Bird It's a Plane It's SUPERMAN* (Alvin Th., Mar. 29, 1966); a revival of *How To Succeed in Business Without Really Trying* (NY City Ctr., Apr. 20, 1966); *Walking Happy* (Lunt-Fontanne Th., Nov. 26, 1966); *Sherry* (Alvin, Mar. 27, 1967); *Henry, Sweet Henry* (Palace, Oct. 23, 1967); scenery for *How To Be a Jewish Mother* (Hudson Th., Dec. 28, 1967); scenery and lighting for *Golden Rainbow* (Sam S. Shubert Th., Feb. 4, 1968); scenery for *Teaspoon Every Four Hours* (ANTA, June 14, 1969); scenery and lighting for *Angela* (Music Box, Oct. 30, 1969); scenery for *Applause* (Palace, Mar. 30, 1970); *Ari* (Mark Hellinger Th., Jan. 15, 1971); scenery and lighting for *70, Girls, 70* (Broadhurst, Apr. 15, 1971); *No Hard Feelings* (Martin Beck Th., Apr. 8, 1973); *Good Evening* (Plymouth, Nov. 14, 1973); *The Enclave* (Th. Four, Nov. 15, 1973); scenery for *Words and Music* (John Golden Th., Apr. 16, 1974); and scenery and lighting for a revival of *Gypsy* (Winter Garden, Sept. 23, 1974).

For the Los Angeles Civic Light Opera, Mr. Randolph did scenery and lighting for productions of *The Sound of Music, The King and I, Porgy and Bess* and lighting for productions of *Fiddler on the Roof, Sugar,* and *Camelot.*

Television. Mr. Randolph did scenery and lighting for *Liza With a "Z"* (NBC, Oct. 10, 1972); for the musical series That's Life (ABC); and designed the settings of the annual Antoinette Perry (Tony) awards ceremonies (1968–to date).

Awards. Mr. Randolph received Antoinette Perry (Tony) Award nominations for scene design for *Golden Rainbow* (1968) and *Applause* (1970).

RAPHAELSON, SAMSON.

Playwright, director, writer. b. Mar. 30, 1899, New York City, to Ralph and Anna (Marks) Raphaelson. Father, cap manufacturer. Grad. Univ. of Ill., B.A. 1917. Married Dec. 24, 1927, to Dorothy Wegman; one son, one daughter. Member of Dramatists Guild. Address: c/o Samuel French, 25 W. 45 St., New York, NY 10036.

Pre-Theatre. Advertising, journalism, teaching, photography.

Theatre. Mr. Raphaelson wrote *The Jazz Singer* (Fulton Th., N.Y.C., Sept. 14, 1925); *Young Love* (Masque, Oct. 30, 1928); *The Wooden Slipper* (Ritz, Jan. 23, 1934); *Accent on Youth* (Plymouth, Dec. 25, 1934); *White Man* (National, Oct. 17, 1936); *Skylark,* which he also directed (Morosco, Oct. 11, 1939); *Jason,* which he also directed (Hudson, Jan. 21, 1942); *The Perfect Marriage,* which he also directed (Ethel Barrymore Th., Oct. 26, 1944); and *Hilda Crane* (Coronet, Nov. 1, 1950).

Films. Mr. Raphaelson wrote the screenplays for *That Lady in Ermine;* (20th-Fox, 1947); *The Smiling Lieutenant* (Par., 1931); *The Magnificent Lie* (Par., 1931); *One Hour With You* (Par., 1932); *Broken Lullabye* (Par., 1932); *Trouble in Paradise* (Par., 1932); *Caravan* (20th-Fox, 1934); *Servant's Entrance* (20th-Fox, 1934); *Accent on Youth* (Par., 1935); with Robert Ellis and Helen Logan, *Ladies Love Danger* (20th-Fox, 1935); wrote *Angel* (Par., 1937); with Leon Gordon and Monckton Hoffe, *The Last of Mrs. Cheyney* (MGM, 1937); wrote *The Shop Around the Corner* (MGM, 1940); *Suspicion* (RKO, 1941); *Heaven Can Wait* (20th-Fox, 1943); with Edmund Beloin, Nathaniel Curtis, Harry Crane, and James O'Hanlon, *The Harvey Girls* (MGM, 1946); wrote *Green Dolphin Street* (MGM, 1947); *In the Good Old Summertime* (MGM, 1949); *Mr. Music* (Par., 1950); *The Merry Widow* (MGM, 1952); *The Jazz Singer* (WB, 1952); *Main Street to Broadway* (MGM, 1953); and *But Not For Me* (Par., 1959).

Other Activities. Mr. Raphaelson was visiting professor at the Univ. of Illinois (1948). He studied and practised photography as a professional, writing for *Modern Photography* and *Popular Photography;* his photographs appeared in various annuals and prize-winning publications.

Published Works. He is the author of more than 50 short stories, some of which were included in Martha Foley's *Best American Short Stories,* Herbert Mayes' *Editor's Choice,* and other collections. He also wrote *The Human Nature of Playwriting* (1949), and a novel, *Skylark* (1939). His plays have all been published: *The Jazz Singer* and *Young Love* by Brentano's; the rest by Random House. Burns Mantle's annual *10 Best Plays* include: *Accent on Youth* (1934–35), *Skylark* (1939–40), and *Jason* (1941–42).

RATTIGAN, TERENCE.

Playwright. b. Terence Mervyn Rattigan, June 10, 1911, London, England, to William Frank Arthur and Vera (Houston) Rattigan. Father, diplomatic service. Grad. Harrow, 1930; Trinity Coll., Oxford Univ., 1933. Served WW II, RAF, gunnery. Member of Royal and Ancient, London; M.C.C,; St. James's.

Theatre. While a student at Oxford, Mr. Rattigan appeared in the Dramatic Society production of *Romeo and Juliet.*

He first wrote, with Philip Heimann, *First Episode* ("Q" Th., London, Sept. 11, 1933; revived Comedy, Jan. 26, 1934; revived Garrick, Dec. 7, 1934), subsequently produced in N.Y.C. (Ritz, Sept. 17, 1934); wrote *French Without Tears* (Criterion, London, Nov. 6, 1936; Henry Miller's Th., N.Y.C., Sept. 28, 1937); *After the Dance* (St. James's, London, June 21, 1939); wrote with Anthony Maurice, *Follow My Leader* (Apollo, Jan. 16, 1940); wrote, with Hector Bolitho, *Grey Farm* (Hudson, N.Y.C., May 3, 1940); wrote *Flare Path* (Apollo, London, Aug. 13, 1942; Henry Miller's Th., N.Y.C., Dec. 23, 1942); *While the Sun Shines* (Globe, London, Dec. 24, 1943; Lyceum, N.Y.C., Sept. 19, 1944); *Love in Idleness* (Lyric, London, Dec. 20, 1944), presented in N.Y.C. under the title, *O Mistress Mine* (Empire, Jan. 23, 1946); and *The Winslow Boy* (Lyric, London, May 23, 1946; Empire, N.Y.C., Oct. 29, 1947).

Mr. Rattigan also wrote *The Browning Version* and *Harlequinade* (Phoenix, London, Sept. 8, 1948; Coronet, N.Y.C., Oct. 12, 1949); *Adventure Story* (St. James's, London, Mar. 17, 1949); *Who Is Sylvia?* (Criterion, London, Oct. 24, 1950); *The Deep Blue Sea* (Duchess, London, Mar. 6, 1952; Morosco, N.Y.C., Nov. 5, 1952); *The Sleeping Prince* (Phoenix, London, Nov. 5, 1953; Coronet, N.Y.C., Nov. 1, 1956); the double bill, *Table By the Window* and *Table Number Seven*, produced under the title *Separate Tables* (St. James's, London, Sept. 22, 1954; Music Box, N.Y.C., Oct. 25, 1956); *Variations on a Theme* (Globe, London, May 8, 1958); *Ross* (Haymarket, London, May 12, 1960; Eugene O'Neill Th., N.Y.C., Dec. 26, 1961); *Joie de Vivre*, a musical based on *French Without Tears* (Queen's, London, July 14, 1960); and *Man and Boy* (Queen's, London, Sept. 4, 1963; Brooks Atkinson Th., N.Y.C., Nov. 12, 1963); *A Bequest to the Nation* (Haymarket, London, Sept. 23, 1970); and *In Praise of Love* (Duchess, Sept. 1973; Morosco, N.Y.C., Dec. 10, 1974). The musical, *The Girl Who Came to Supper* (Bway Th., N.Y.C., Dec. 8, 1963), with book by Harry Kurnitz, was based on Mr. Rattigan's play, *The Sleeping Prince.*

Films. Mr. Rattigan wrote the screenplays for *Quiet Wedding* (U, 1942); *The Day Will Dawn* (Kirsos, 1942), issued in the US as *The Avengers* (Par., 1942); *Uncensored* (Gainesboro, 1942); *The Way to the Stars* (Two Cities, 1945); issued in the US as *Johnny in the Clouds* (UA, 1945); *Breaking the Sound Barrier* (UA, 1952); *The Final Test* (ATC, 1953; and Rank, 1954); *The Man Who Loved Redheads* (UA, 1955); *The Deep Blue Sea* (London Films, 1955; and 20th-Fox, 1955); *The VIP's* (MGM, 1963); *The Yellow Rolls-Royce* (MGM, 1965); and the musical *Goodbye, Mr. Chips* (MGM, 1969). Filmed versions of his plays include *French without Tears* (Par., 1940); *The Winslow Boy* (Eagle Lion, 1950); *The Browning Version* (U, 1951); *The Prince and the Showgirl* (WB, 1957); based upon *The Sleeping Prince; Separate Tables* (UA, 1958); and *The Nelson Affair* (U, 1973), based upon *A Bequest to the Nation.* .

Television and Radio. His first radio play was *Cause Célèbre* (BBC, 1975). In England, his television productions include *The Final Test* (BBC, 1962); *Heart to Heart* (BBC, 1962); *Nelson* (ATV, 1966); *Variations on a Theme* (ITV, 1966); *The Browning Version* (ITV, 1966); *Harlequinade* (BBC, 1973); and *In Praise of Love* (1976).

In the US, his produced works include *Ninety Years On* (WOR-TV, 1964).

Awards. Mr. Rattigan received the Ellen Terry Award, London, for *The Winslow Boy* (1946) and for *The Browning Version* (1948); and a NY Drama Critics Circle Special Citation for *The Winslow Boy* (1948). A Commander of the British Empire (C.B.E.) was conferred upon him in the Queen's Birthday Honours (1958); and he was Knighted in the Queen's Birthday Honours (1971).

Recreation. Watching cricket, golf.

RAWLINS, LESTER. Actor. b. Sept. 24, 1924, Sharon, Pa. Grad. Miami (Fla.) H.S., 1942; Carnegie Inst. of Tech., B.F.A. (Drama, Summa Cum Laude) 1950. Studied at American Shakespeare Festival and Acad. Sch., Stratford, Conn., 1963. Served USAAF, 1943–46; rank, 1st Sgt. Member of AEA; AFTRA; SAG; Phi Kappa Phi. Address: 33-B, One Sherman Square, New York, NY 10023, tel. JU 6-6300; c/o Smith-Stevens Representatives, Ltd., 1650 Broadway, New York, NY 10019, tel. (212) JU 2-8040.

Pre-Theatre. Hash slinger, stock clerk, waiter, gas company, dispatcher.

Theatre. Mr. Rawlins made his first stage appearance at age six as the Dwarf in *The Birthday of the Infanta* (Farrell, Pa., 1930) where he also played Scrooge in *A Christmas Carol* (1935); appeared as Maxie in *June Moon* (Chapel Playhouse, Guilford, Conn., 1948); served as stage manager and appeared in productions at this theatre (Summer 1949); appeared in 30 productions at the Arena Stage (Washington, D.C., Aug. 1950–Jan. 1952; Jan. 1954–June 1955); played the Nephew in *The Golden State* (Pasadena Playhouse, Calif., 1953); and at the Brattle Th. (Cambridge, Mass.), appeared as Lodovico in *Othello*, Conrade in *Much Ado About Nothing* and Worcester in *Henry IV, Part 1* (June-Sept. 1955).

Mr. Rawlins made his N.Y.C. debut as Lodovico in *Othello* (NY City Ctr., Sept. 18, 1955); played Worcester in *Henry IV, Part 1* (NY City Ctr., Sept. 21, 1955); Lenox in *Macbeth* (Jan Hus House, Dec. 19, 1955); Gloucester in Orson Welles' *King Lear* (NY City Ctr., Jan. 12, 1956); Friar Lawrence in *Romeo and Juliet* (Jan Hus House, Feb. 23, 1956); and Escavalon in *The Lovers* (Martin Beck Th., May 10, 1956).

At the Antioch (Ohio) Shakespeare Festival, he played Dogberry in *Much Ado About Nothing*, Angelo in *Measure for Measure*, and Gloucester in *King Lear* (Sept. 1956); played Polonius in Philip Lawrence's *Hamlet* (Shakespearewrights Th., N.Y.C., Oct. 27, 1956); understudied James Daly as Tom Wingfield and Lonny Chapman as the Gentleman Caller in *The Glass Menagerie* (NY City Ctr., Nov. 21, 1956); played the Cardinal in the American premiere of *The Prisoner* (Arena Stage, Washington, D.C., Jan. 1957); Pop in *The Pajama Game*, the Artist in *Can-Can*, Mr. Moon in *Anthing Goes*, Jeff in *Brigadoon*, the Devil in *Damn Yankees*, and Luther Billis in *South Pacific* (Flint Musical Tent, Mich.; Detroit Musical Tent, Mich., June-Sept. 1957); David Slater in *The Moon Is Blue* (North Jersey Playhouse, Fort Lee, N.J., Oct. 1957); Clarence in the NY Shakespeare Festival production of *Richard III* (Heckscher, N.Y.C., Nov. 25, 1957); Hamm in *Endgame* (Cherry Lane, Jan. 28, 1958); Shunderson in *Dr. Praetorius* (North Jersey Playhouse, Apr. 1958); toured as the Devil in *Damn Yankees* (June-Sept. 1958); played Ensign Pulver in *Mister Roberts* (Flint Musical Tent, Sept. 1958); Regan in *The Quare Fellow* (Circle in the Square, N.Y.C., Nov. 22, 1958); Sir Nathaniel in *Love's Labour's Lost* (Library of Congress, Washington, D.C., Apr. 1959); toured summer theatres as Jack Jordan in *Say, Darling* (June-July 1959), and as Papa in *The Happy Time* (July-Aug., 1959), also playing this role at the Coconut Grove Playhouse (Miami, Fla., Feb. 1960); appeared as Lord Byron in *Camino Real* (St. Marks Playhouse, N.Y.C., May 16, 1960); Poppet in *Redhead* and Bennie in *The Desert Song* (Rochester and Syracuse Musical Theatres, N.Y., June-July 1960); and Fender in *The Bespoke Overcoat*, Grigson in *Shadow of a Gunman*, and Beggar in *Elektra* (Olney Th., Md., July-Aug. 1960).

Mr. Rawlins played Tesman in *Hedda Gabler* (Fourth St. Th., N.Y.C., Nov. 9, 1960); Cranmer, and understudied Paul Scofield as Thomas More, in *A Man for All Seasons* (ANTA, Nov. 21, 1961); played Don Felipe in the pre-Bway tryout of *We Take the Town* (opened Shubert, New Haven, Conn., Feb. 19, 1962; closed Shubert, Philadelphia, Pa., Mar. 17, 1962); at the American Shakespeare Festival, Stratford, Conn., played the Fool in *King Lear* (June 9, 1963); Angelo in *Comedy of Errors* (June 11, 1963); and Fluellen in *Henry V* (June 12, 1963). He appeared at the Festival of the Two Worlds (Spoleto, It., June 19, 1964–July 20, 1964).

Most recently, he has appeared on- and off-Bway in *The Lovers, Winterset, Nightride, The Reckoning, Richard III*, and *He Who Gets Slapped.*

Films. Mr. Rawlins has appeared as a Reporter in *Mr. Congressman* (MGM, 1951); the Editor in *Within Man's Power* (Natl. Tuberculosis Assn., 1954); and in *They Might Be Giants* (1971); and *Diary of a Mad Housewife* (1972).

Television. He made his debut as a dancer on the Dinah Shore Show (CBS, 1953); and has appeared on Studio One (CBS, 1956); Look Up and Live (CBS, 1961); played Rysdale on Secret Storm (CBS, June 1962–Jan. 1963); appeared in *The Life of Samuel Johnson* (Omnibus, NBC); *Salome* (Omnibus, CBS); on The Defenders (CBS); The Nurses (CBS); Camera Three (CBS); in *Eye on New York* (CBS); *Portraits in Verse* (CBS); *John Brown's Body* (CBS); and *Russian Special* (CBS). He has also appeared on Banacek, Apple's Way, The Snoop Sisters, Police Woman, and played Orin Hellyer in the series The Edge of Night (CBS).

Awards. Mr. Rawlins received the Norman Apell Award and the Goldbloom Memorial Award for "development and contribution" at Carnegie Inst. of Tech. (1950), and Village Voice off-Bway (Obie) awards for his performances as Regan in *The Quare Fellow* (1958), Tesman in *Hedda Gabler* (1960), and Captain Delano in *Benito Cereno* (1965). He also received the Drama Desk Award for *Nightride* (1972).

Recreation. Reading, driving, swimming, cooking, and raising six foster children and four cats (Abyssinian, Hunalayan, and Burmese).

RAWLS, EUGENIA. Actress. b. Mary Eugenia Rawls, Sept. 11, 1916, Macon, Ga., to Hubert Fields and Louise (Roberts) Rawls. Father, lawyer. Studied acting with Anne Chenauet Wallace, Macon, Ga.; and Dr. Edna West, Dublin, Ga.; attended Univ. of North Carolina, 1932–33. Married Apr. 5, 1941, to Donald Seawell, lawyer, producer; one son, Brockman Seawell, actor; one daughter, Brook Seawell, actress. Member of AEA; AFTRA; SAG. Address: 510 E. 84th St., New York, NY 10028, tel. (212) RH 4-7553.

Theatre. Miss Rawls acted with the Clare Tree Major's Children's Th. (N.Y.C., 1933–34); subsequently played Peggy in *The Children's Hour* (Maxine Elliott's Th., Nov. 20, 1934); Jane Bennett in a national tour of *Pride and Prejudice;* Tomasa in *To Quito and Back* (Guild, N.Y.C., Oct. 6, 1937); Dene Horey in *Journeyman* (Fulton, Jan. 29, 1938); appeared in *Susannah and the Elders* and *The Inner Light* (Westport Country Playhouse, Conn., Summer 1938); with Margaret Webster's Shakespearean Co., played Celia in *As You Like It*, Titania in *A Midsummer Night's Dream*, and Bianca in *The Taming of the Shrew* (NY World's Fair, Apr.–July 1939).

She succeeded (Oct. 1939) Florence Williams as Alexandra in *The Little Foxes* (National, N.Y.C., Feb. 15, 1939); subsequently played the role on tour (Feb. 5, 1940–Apr. 5, 1941); appeared as Ellean in a stock production of *The Second Mrs. Tanqueray* (June 1940); Alexandra in *The Little Foxes* (Newport Playhouse, R.I., July 1941); the ingenue in *Curtain Going Up* (Westport Country Playhouse, Conn.); the title role in *Harriet* (Univ. of Syracuse, N.Y., Nov. 1942); and succeeded (Spring 1942) Mary Anderson as Evelyn Heath in *Guest in the House* (Plymouth, N.Y.C., Mar. 24, 1942), with which she also toured (through June 1942).

Miss Rawls appeared as Connie in *Cry Havoc* (Studebaker Th., Chicago, Ill., Feb. 1943), with which she toured (through May 1943); toured as Mrs. de Winter in *Rebecca* (1944; Summer 1945), and in stock (Ogunquit Playhouse, Me., Summer 1944); played Hester Falk in Arthur Miller's first play, *The Man Who Had All the Luck* (Forrest, N.Y.C., Nov. 23, 1944); Harriet Harris in *Strange Fruit* (Royale, Nov. 29, 1945); succeeded (May 1952) Judith Evelyn as Ann Downs in *The Shrike* (Cort, Jan. 15, 1952); played Mrs. Czerney in *The Great Sebastians* (ANTA, Jan. 4, 1956); Catherine in *All the Way Home* (Playhouse-in-the-Park, Philadelphia, Pa., July 1961); was standby for the role of Nina Kecew in *First Love* (Morosco, N.Y.C., Dec. 25, 1961); played Emily Bindix in *A Case of Libel* (Longacre, Oct. 10, 1963); Amanda in *The Glass*

Menagerie (Playhouse in the Park, Cincinnati, Ohio, Aug. 11, 1965); appeared in *Our Town* (Repertory Th., New Orleans, La., Feb. 23, 1967); was Mrs. Beavis in *The Poker Session* (Martinique, N.Y.C., Sept. 19, 1967); and was Amande Mangebois in *The Enchanted* (Kennedy Ctr., Washington, D.C., Mar. 2, 1973).

She appeared in her one-woman show, *Affectionately Yours, Fanny Kemble*, in England (Arts, London, Oct. 5, 1969) and Ireland (Abbey Th., Dublin, Feb. 1972); presented another one-woman show, *Tallulah, A Memory*, in Ireland (American Embassy, Dublin, May 1972); appeared again in *Affectionately Yours, Fanny Kemble* in England (Bath Festival, May 27, 1972; Soc. for Th. Research, London, Mar. 19, 1974) and in *Tallulah, A Memory* (American Embassy, London, Mar. 21, 1974); and toured the US in both one-woman shows (Town Hall, N.Y.C., Feb. 12, 1974; Washington Club, Washington, D.C., Apr. 4, 1974; Playmakers Th., Chapel Hill, N.C., Apr. 6, 1974).

As artist-in-residence, Univ. of Northern Colorado, Greeley, Colo. (Summers 1971–73), Miss Rawls appeared in *Mother Courage, The Show-Off, Family Portrait, The Glass Menagerie, Butterflies Are Free*, and *The Lion in Winter*.

Films. She has appeared in documentary films.

Television and Radio. She played Mrs. Elvsted in *Hedda Gabler* (US Steel Hour, CBS, 1954); and has appeared on Armstrong Circle Th. (CBS); Dupont Show of the Month (CBS); in *The Great Sebastians* (NBC, 1957); played Margaret on Road to Reality (ABC, 1960–61); has performed on The Doctors (NBC, 1963); The Nurses (CBS, 1963); was in *The Magnificent Yankee* (Hallmark Hall of Fame, NBC, 1965); played Elaine Harris in Love of Life (CBS, 1966, 1967); was in *A Punt, a Pass, and a Prayer* (Hallmark Hall of Fame, NBC, 1968); and played Grace Burton on As the World Turns (CBS, 1972-73). She has made transcription recordings of *Arrowsmith* and *Look Homeward, Angel* for radio broadcast on Voice of America.

Other Activities. Miss Rawls has contributed to two cookbooks, and she cooperated with Brendan Gill in preparing the book *Tallulah* (1973). She has recorded 96 talking books for the blind.

Recreation. "Farm on Maryland's Eastern Shore;" and travel "especially to London and the Hebrides." She enjoys writing poetry.

RAY, ANDREW. Actor. b. Andrew Alden Ray, May 31, 1939, Southgate, London, England, to Ted and Sybil (Stevens) Ray. Father, comedian; mother, show girl. Grad. Highgate (England) Sch., 1955; Christ's Coll., Oxford Univ., 1959. Married Aug. 25, 1959, to Susan Burnet, actress; one daughter. Relative in theatre: brother, Robin Ray, television producer. Member of AEA; British AEA; SWG.

Pre-Theatre. Photographer.

Theatre. Mr. Ray made his London debut as Bibi in *The Happy Time* (St. James's , Jan. 30, 1952); subsequently appeared as Thomas Mortmain in *I Capture the Castle* (Aldwych, Mar. 4, 1954); Chris Walker in *Ring for Catty* (Lyric, Feb. 14, 1956); Gio in *Less Than Kind* (Arts, June 27, 1957); and Tom Cherry in *The Flowering Cherry* (Haymarket, Nov. 21, 1957), which he repeated for his Bway debut (Lyceum, Sept. 21, 1959).

He played Norman in *A Chance in Life* at the Cheltham (England) Festival (May 1960); Geoffrey in *A Taste of Honey* (Lyceum, N.Y.C., Oct. 4, 1960); Jonathan in *Oh Dad, Poor Dad, Mama's Hung You in the Closet and I'm Feelin' So Sad* (Lyric, Hammersmith, London, July 5, 1961); the Waiter in *Incident at Vichy* (Phoenix Th., London, Jan. 26, 1966); Leonard in *Howard's End* (Cambridge Arts, July 20, 1966; New, Feb. 28, 1967); Dave in *Staring at the Sun* (Vaudeville Th., Mar. 13, 1968); and was in *The Feydeau Farce Festival of 1909* (Greenwich Th., Feb. 14, 1972).

Films. Mr. Ray appeared as Wheeler in *The Mudlark* (20th-Fox, 1950); Joey in *Yellow Balloon* (Allied, 1953); Nicky in *Escape by Night* (Tempean, 1953); in *A Prize of Gold* (Col., 1955); *Escapade* (D. Angel, 1955); Alan in *The Woman in a Dressing Gown* (WB, 1957); Bill in *The Young and the Guilty* (A.B.P.L., 1957); P. C. Witty in *Gideon of Scotland Yard* (Col., 1959); Ricky in *Serious Charge* (Anglo, 1959); Ginger in *Private Pooley* (D.E.F.A., Berlin, 1961); Chris in *Twice Around the Daffodils* (1961); and Willie in *The System* (Bryanston, 1963).

Television. Mr. Ray played Mark in *Inquest on a Hero* (BBC, London); Finch in *Whiteoak Chronicles* (BBC, 1955); Jonathan in *The Son and I* (BBC, 1955); Taplow in *The Browning Version* (BBC, 1955); performed on Discan of Back Green (BBC, 1956); Escapade (BBC, 1959); appeared as Pie Face in *Fly Away Peter* (ITA, 1959); Henry in *The Girl in the Road* (ABC, US); Chips Kirby in *The Sentimental Agent* (ITA, London, 1963); was on Maupassant Th. (Granada, 1963); was on Suspense (BBC, 1963); and Good Night, Mrs. Dill (ATV, 1967).

Awards. He received the *Empire News* Award (1959) for best supporting actor and the *Daily Citizen* Award (1958) for the best performance by a teenager in films.

Recreation. Photography, football, boxing.

RAY, JAMES. Actor. b. Jan. 1, 1932, Calgra, Okla., to Sherman Gentry and Ora Catherine (Mitchell) Ray. Father, rancher. Attended Oklahoma A & M; studied acting with Uta Hagen, 1957–60; Fanny Bradshaw, 1958–61. Member of AEA; AFTRA; SAG. Address: c/o International Famous Agency, 1301 Avenue of the Americas, New York, NY 10019, tel. (212) MU 8-8330.

Theatre. Mr. Ray made his stage debut as Friar John in *Romeo and Juliet* (Margo Jones Th., Dallas, Tex., 1949); and appeared at Circle in the Square, N.Y.C., as the Witch Boy in the Loft Player's premiere production *Dark of the Moon* (Dec. 1950) and Vernon in *Summer and Smoke* (Apr. 24, 1952); followed by a season of stock (Straight Wharf Th., Nantucket, Mass., Summer 1952).

He made his Bway debut in *Compulsion* (Ambassador, Oct. 24, 1957); toured as the First Roustabout in *J. B.* (opened Shubert, New Haven, Conn., Oct. 28, 1959; closed Locust, Philadelphia, Pa., Mar. 26, 1960); played in the NY Shakespeare Festival production of *Henry V* (Belvedere Lake Th., N.Y.C., June 29, 1960); and appeared in *Macbeth* (Cambridge Drama Festival, Mass., Summer 1959).

He played Katz in *The Wall* (Billy Rose Th., N.Y.C., Oct. 11, 1960); and at the American Shakespeare Festival Th. and Academy, Stratford, Conn., appeared as Malcolm in *Macbeth*, Diomedes in *Troilus and Cressida*, and Oliver in *As You Like It* (1961).

He played Adolf in *The Creditors* (Mermaid, N.Y.C., Jan. 25, 1962); at the ASFTA, appeared as Prince Hal in *Henry IV, Part 1* and Mowbray in *Richard II* (Stratford, Conn., 1962); and played James in *The Collection*, which, with *The Dumbwaiter*, was presented as *The Pinter Plays* (Cherry Lane, N.Y.C., Nov. 26, 1962).

At the American Shakespeare Festival (Stratford, Conn.), he played Edgar in *King Lear* (June 9, 1963), the title role in *Henry V* (June 12, 1963), and Apollodorus in *Caesar and Cleopatra* (July 30, 1963); and Brinnin in *Dylan* (Plymouth, N.Y.C., Jan. 18, 1964).

He played Dr. Faustus in *Mefistofiles* (Phoenix, N.Y.C., Oct. 6, 1964); Navarre in *Love's Labours Lost* (Delacorte, N.Y.C., Summer 1965); and, for the Goodman Th. (Chicago, Ill.), played Marat in *The Persecution and Assassination of Marat as Performed by the Inmates of the Asylum at Charenton under the Direction of the Marquis de Sade* (1966); and Benedick in *Much Ado About Nothing* (1967); Henry IV in *Henry IV*, Parts I and II (Delacorte, N.Y.C., Summer 1968); Stott in *The Basement* (Eastside Playhouse, N.Y.C., Oct. 15, 1968); Macheath in *Three Penny Opera* (Alliance, Atlanta, Ga., Summer 1969); appeared in various new plays at the O'Neill Playwrights Conference (Waterford, Conn., Summers 1969, 1971, 1973); starred in *This Way to the Rose Garden* (Alliance, Atlanta, Ga., Summer 1970); appeared in *Sensations* (Th. Four, N.Y.C., Oct. 25, 1970); played the Son in *All Over* (Martin Beck Th., N.Y.C., Mar. 27, 1971); appeared in *Jacques Brel Is Alive and Well and Living in Paris* (Alliance, Atlanta, Ga., Summer 1971); played Dr. Rank opposite Claire Bloom in *A Doll's House* (North Amer. tour beginning Sept. 13, 1971); played Brutus in *Julius Caesar* and Snobby Price in *Major Barbara* (Amer. Shakespeare Festival, Stratford, Conn., Summer 1972); Cleante in *Tartuffe* (Walnut, Philadelphia, Winter 1972); Prospero in *The Tempest*, Deeley in *Old Times*, von Berg in *Incident at Vichy* and Mitch in *A Streetcar Named Desire* (Playhouse-in-the-Park, Cincinnati, Ohio, 1973).

REA, OLIVER. Producer, theatre executive. b. Oct. 20, 1923, New York City, to Henry Oliver and Margaret (Moorhead) Rea. Father, realtor. Grad. Culver (Ind.) Military Acad., 1942; Dartmouth Coll., 1946. Married May 6, 1948, to Elizabeth Wilson (marr. dis.); one son, two daughters. Served US Army, American Field Service, 1943–44; rank, 2d Lt.

Theatre. Mr. Rea was a co-founder (1962), president, and managing director of the Minnesota Theatre Company Foundation at the Tyrone Guthrie Theatre in Minneapolis (1962–66), and he has been president of the Theatre Communications Group (TCG).

Mr. Rea was associated with Paul Killiam, producer, in the presentation of *Naughty Naught '00* (Old Knickerbocker Music Hall, N.Y.C., Oct. 19, 1946); subsequently produced, with Robert Whitehead, *Medea* (Natl., Oct. 20, 1947), which was revived by Guthrie McClintic, by arrangement with Messrs. Whitehead and Rea (NY City Ctr., May 2, 1949); presented, with Mr. Whitehead, *Crime and Punishment* (Natl., Dec. 22, 1947); produced, with Mr. Whitehead and Stanley Martineau, *Member of the Wedding* (Empire, Jan. 5, 1950) and the national tour (opened Cass, Detroit, Mich., Sept. 3, 1951; closed Shubert, New Haven, Conn., May 3, 1952); with the Playwrights' Co. and Oliver Smith, *Juno* (Winter Garden, N.Y.C., Mar. 9, 1959); and, with the Chelsea Theater Ctr., *Slave Ship* (Theater-in-the-Church, Jan. 13, 1970).

Awards. Mr. Rea received the American Shakespeare Festival Award (1963).

Recreation. Travel, reading.

READER, RALPH. Actor, director, producer, choreographer, composer, lyricist, librettist, writer. b. William Henry Ralph Reader, May 25, 1903, Somerset, England, to William Henry and Emma (Frost) Reader. Father, store owner. Attended Boarding Sch., Somerset, Eng., 1910–18; St. John's, Cardiff, Wales. Served RAF, Squadron Leader. Member of British AEA; Performing Rights Society; Song Writers Guild; Grand Order of the Water Rats. Address: "Round Corners", 2 Sherrock Gardens, London, N.W.4, England tel. Sunnyhill 1517.

Theatre. Mr.Reader first performed as a chorus boy in the Bway musical, *Sharlee* (Daly's Th., Nov. 22, 1923); subsequently appeared in *The Passing Show of 1924* (Winter Garden, Sept. 3, 1924); *Big Boy* (Winter Garden, Jan. 7, 1925), and played Butler in *June Days* (Astor, Aug. 6, 1925).

He performed in vaudeville shows in the Keith Circuit and at the Palace Th. (N.Y.C., 1924–26); served as choreographer for *Artists and Models* (Winter Garden, June 24, 1925); appeared in *Bad Habits of 1926* (Greenwich Village Th., Apr. 30, 1926); choreographed *Gay Paree* (Winter Garden, Nov. 9, 1926); *Yours Truly* (Shubert, Jan. 25, 1927); *Night in Spain* (44 St. Th., May 3, 1927); *Take the Air* (Waldorf, Nov. 22, 1927); and *The Greenwich Village Follies* (Winter Garden, Apr. 9, 1928).

He played Tom Marlowe in *Good News* (Carlton, London, Aug. 15, 1928); produced *Virginia* (Palace, Oct. 24, 1928); was choreographer for *Merry Merry* (Carlton, Feb. 28, 1929); *Hold Everything* (Palace, June 12, 1929); *Dear Love* (Palace, Nov. 14, 1929); *Silver Wings* (Dominion, Feb. 14, 1930); and *The Cochran Revue of 1930* (Pavilion, Mar. 27, 1930); and produced *Artists and Models* (Majestic, N.Y.C., June 10, 1930).

He was choreographer for *Sons O' Guns* (Hippodrome, June 26, 1930); *Song of the Drum* (Drury Lane, Jan. 1931); *Tommy Tucker* (Daly's Th., Mar. 17, 1931); *The Hour Glass* (Victoria Palace, May 7, 1931); and produced *Viktoria and Her Hussar* (Palace, Sept. 17, 1931).

Since 1932, Mr. Reader has been associated with the annual London revue, *The Gang Show*, serving at various times as author, producer, and songwriter. During 1932–38, he wrote and produced each edition.

He produced *Yes, Madam?* (Hippodrome, Sept. 27, 1934); produced, with Jack Waller, *Please, Teacher!* (Hippodrome, Oct. 2, 1935); produced *Rise and Shine* (Drury Lane, Apr. 3, 1936); *Certainly, Sir!* (Hippodrome, Sept. 17, 1936); and *Big Business* (Hippodrome, Feb. 18, 1937).

He served as choreographer for *Crest of the Wave* (Drury Lane, Sept. 1, 1937); appeared as Lt. Jack Prentiss in *The Fleet's Lit Up* (Hippodrome, Aug. 17, 1938); and was choreographer for the pantomime *Babes in the Wood* (Drury Lane, Christmas 1938).

He has produced 145 shows at the Royal Albert Hall (London), writing the musical score for many of these presentations, including *Voyage of the Venturer* (1957); *Boy Scout* (1943); and *Battle for Freedom* (1941). For the Admiralty, he produced *Heart of Oak* (1942); for the Air Ministry, *Per Adua Ad Astra* (1944); and at the Royal Albert Hall, directed *Remembrance Festival* (1944–74); *The Proudest Badge* (1950); and *Ranger Pageant* (1951).

He produced and appeared in another production of *The Gang Show* (Stoll, May 10, 1946; King's Th., Hammersmith, Dec. 2, 1950), and in a special performance of the same revue for the Queen of England (1954).

He played Buttons in *Cinderella* (Hippodrome, Lewisham, Dec. 20, 1947); produced *The Pilgrim's Progress* (Covent Garden Opera House, July 12, 1948); played Wishee-Washee in *Aladdin* (Grenada, Tooting, Dec. 20, 1948); Simple Simon in *Babes in the Wood* (Empire, Croydon, Dec. 17, 1949); and in 1950, formed the National Light Opera Co., producing new versions of the musicals *Chu Chin Chow* (Apr. 7, 1953); *Merrie England* (Mar. 2, 1953); and *The Lilac Domino* (May 20, 1953).

He directed and wrote the lyrics for *Wild Grows the Heather* (Hippodrome, London, May 3, 1956); and produced his own musical, *Summer Holiday* (Open Air Th., Scarborough, York, Summer 1960).

He has appeared in three Royal Command Performances at the London Palladium.

Films. Mr. Reader has appeared in *The Red Robe* (Par., 1924); and for Herbert Wilcox Productions, *The Gang Show* (1937); *Derby Day; Lilacs in the Spring;* and *Splinters in the Air.* He also appeared in *Limelight* (UA, 1952).

Television and Radio. He performed on British radio in Services Calling (BBC, 1939–45); Housewives Choice (BBC, 1948–50); Pick of the Week (BBC, 1950–60); Town Tonight (BBC, 1959–64); Startime (1971); Desert Island Discs (1971); and Meet My Guests (1974). On television, he appeared on Chance of a Lifetime (Assoc. Rediffusion, 1951); Wonderful Life (BBC, June–Dec. 1959); Flying High (ATV, May, 1960); Tune In (Granada, June 1961); Meet the Gang (ATV, Oct. 1962); and It's All Yours (ATV, July 1963). He has also appeared on The Gang Show; Scenes Familiar; Beat the Clock; and This Is Your Life (1967–1974).

Other Activities. Chief Scouts Commissioner.

Published Works. Mr. Reader wrote *It's Been Terrific* (1958); *Oh Scouting Is a Boy* (1960); *This is the Gang Show* (1961); *Ralph Reader, My Life— "And It's All Been Worth It"* (1974).

Awards. He received an M.B.E. from King George VI (1941); and a Commander of the British Empire (C.B.E.) from Queen Elizabeth II (1957).

Recreation. Football, reading, motoring, dancing, writing.

REDGRAVE, LYNN. Actress. b. Lynn Rachel Redgrave, Mar. 8, 1943, London, England, to Sir Michael and Rachel (Kempson) Redgrave. Father, actor; mother, actress. Educ. Queensgate School, London. Professional training at Central School of Speech and Drama, London. Married Apr. 2, 1967, to John Clark; one son, one daughter. Relatives in theatre: sister, Vanessa Redgrave, actress; brother, Corin Redgrave, actor. Address: 205 W. 57th St., New York, NY 10019, tel. (212) 489-0597.

Theatre. Miss Redgrave made her theatrical debut as a Shepherd in a performance of the *Nativity Play* at Queensgate School, London (1951). She first appeared professionally as Helena in *A Midsummer Night's Dream* (Royal Court Th., London, Jan. 1962); played Portia in *The Merchant of Venice* (Dundee Repertory, Scotland, Feb. 1962); toured in England as Barbara in *Billy Liar* (Apr. 1962); and was Sarah in *The Tulip Tree* (Haymarket Th., London, Sept. 1962). For the National Th. of Great Britain (Sept. 1963–July 1966) she played Rose in *The Recruiting Officer*, Barblin in *Andorra*, Jackie in *Hay Fever*, Margaret in *Much Ado About Nothing*, Kattrin in *Mother Courage*, and Miss Prue in *Love for Love*. She appeared in the last in Berlin, Germany, and Moscow, USSR (Sept. 1965). She made her Bway debut as Carol Melkett in *Black Comedy* (Ethel Barrymore Th., Feb. 12, 1967); played Maeve in *Zoo Zoo Widdershins Zoo* (Lyceum Th., Edinburgh, Scotland, Sept. 1969); the female lead in *The Two of Us* (Garrick Th., London, June 1970); Joanne in *Slag* (Royal Court Th., Apr. 1971); Stella in *A Better Place* (Gate Th., Dublin, Ireland, 1972); Billie Dawn in *Born Yesterday* (Greenwich Th., London, 1973); and Vicky in *My Fat Friend* (Brooks Atkinson Th., N.Y.C., Mar. 31, 1974).

Films. Miss Redgrave made her motion picture debut as Susan in *Tom Jones* (UA, 1963), followed by appearances as Baba in *Girl with Green Eyes* (UA, 1963); Georgy in *Georgy Girl* (Col., 1966); Yvonne in *Smashing Time* (Par., 1967); the Virgin in *A Deadly Affair* (Col., 1967); Philippa in *The Virgin Soldiers* (Col., 1969); Myrtle in *The Last of the Mobile Hot-Shots* (WB, 1970); Nanny in *Every Little Crook and Nanny* (MGM, 1972); the Queen in *Everything You Wanted to Know About Sex* (UA, 1972); Nurse Sweet and Nurse Martin in *The National Health* (Col., 1973); and Mary in *Don't Turn the Other Cheek* (Internatl. Amusement Corp., 1974).

Television. Miss Redgrave first appeared on television in London in *The Power and the Glory* (ABC, Mar. 1963). She played Queen Victoria as a young woman in *Hall of Kings* (ABC, Feb. 14, 1967); Eliza in Pygmalion (Play-of-the-Month, BBC, Dec. 1973); Berta in *Vienna 1900* (BBC 2, Jan. 1974); and Miss Cubberly in *The Turn of the Screw* (Wide World of Mystery, ABC, Apr. 1974).

Awards. For her performance in the film *Georgy Girl*, Miss Redgrave received the NY Film Critics Award, the Golden Globe Award of the Hollywood Foreign Press Association, the Independent Film Importers and Distributors of America Award, and was nominated for Academy (Oscar) Award as best actress in 1967.

Recreation. Horseback riding, cooking, child-rearing.

REDGRAVE, SIR MICHAEL. Actor, director, writer. b. Michael Scudamore Redgrave, Mar. 20, 1908, Bristol, England, to George Ellsworthy (Roy) and Margaret (Scudamore) Redgrave. Father, actor; mother, actress. Grad. Clifton Coll., Bristol, England, 1926; Magdalene Coll., Cambridge, England, M.A. 1931. Married July 18, 1935, to Rachel Kempson, actress; one son, Corin, actor; two daughters, Vanessa, actress; Lynn, actress. Served WW II with the Royal Navy, 1941–42; rank, Seaman. Member of British AEA (councillor, 1943–44); English Speaking Board (pres., 1953–to date): British Film Inst. (governor, 1954–57); Michael Redgrave Productions Ltd. (founded Oct. 1957; director); F.E.S. (Fred E. Sadoff) Plays Ltd. (founded Feb. 1959; director). Address: 35 Lower Belgrave St., London, S.W.1, England tel. Kensington 9572; Wilks Water, Odiham, Hampshire, England.

Pre-Theatre. Schoolmaster, Cranleigh Sch., 1931–34.

Theatre. Michael Redgrave made his Bway debut in the title role in *Macbeth* (National Th., Mar. 31, 1948); followed by Hector in *Tiger at the Gates* (Plymouth, Oct. 3, 1955); Shylock in the Tubal scene in *The Merchant of Venice* (Helen Hayes midnight matinee, Waldorf-Astoria, Dec. 1955); directed *A Month in the Country* (Phoenix, April 3, 1956); directed and played the Regent in *The Sleeping Prince* (Coronet, Nov. 1, 1956); appeared as Victor Rhodes in *The Complaisant Lover* (Ethel Barrymore Th., Nov. 1, 1961); and appeared with the Royal Shakespeare Co. in *The Hollow Crown* (Central City, Col., Sept. 1973), then touring the US in it and appearing at the Brooklyn Acad. of Music, N.Y.C. (Apr. 18, 1974) in it and in *Pleasure and Repentance* (Apr. 21, 1974).

As a member of English amateur productions, he directed and played Ralph Rackstraw in *H.M.S. Pinafore* (Cranleigh Sch., Nov. 1932); directed and appeared in the title role in *Samson Agonistes* (Cranleigh Sch., Mar. 6, 1933); directed and portrayed the title role in *Hamlet* (Cranleigh Sch., June 29, 1933); directed and played John Worthing in *The Importance of Being Earnest* (Guildford Repertory Co., Oct. 6, 1933); Menelaus in *The Trojan Women* (Guildford Repertory Co., Nov. 17, 1933); directed and portrayed Prospero in *The Tempest* (Cranleigh Sch., Nov. 30, 1933); Clive Champion-Cheney in *The Circle* (Guildford Repertory Co., Feb. 9, 1934); Young Marlow in *She Stoops to Conquer* (Guildford Repertory Co. Mar. 9, 1934); directed and played the title role in *King Lear* (Cranleigh Sch., June 28, 1934); and Mr. Browning in *The Barretts of Wimpole Street* (Guildford Repertory Co., July 6, 1934).

He made his professional debut with the Liverpool Repertory Th., as Roy Darwin in *Counsellor-at-Law* (Liverpool Playhouse, Aug. 30, 1934); Dr. Purley in *A Sleeping Clergyman* (Liverpool Playhouse, Oct. 10, 1934); Charles Hubbard in *The Distaff Side* (Liverpool Playhouse, Sept. 19, 1934); the Man in *The Perfect Plot* (Liverpool Playhouse, Oct. 31, 1934); Mr. Bolton in *Sheppey* (Liverpool Playhouse, Nov. 21, 1934); Ernest Hubbard in *Heaven on Earth* (Liverpool Playhouse, Dec. 12, 1934); Melchior Feydak in *Biography* (Liverpool Playhouse, Jan 23, 1935); Gaston in *Villa for Sale* (Liverpool Playhouse, Feb. 13, 1935); Sir Mark Loddon in *Libel* (Liverpool Playhouse, Mar. 6, 1935); Richard Newton-Clare in *Flowers of the Forest* (Liverpool Playhouse, Mar. 27 1935); Horatio in *Hamlet* (Liverpool Playhouse, Apr. 17, 1935); Bill Clarke in *Too Young to Marry* (Liverpool Playhouse, May 8, 1935); wrote the *Seventh Man* (Liverpool Playhouse, May 8, 1935); and played Oliver Maitland in *The Matriarch* (Liverpool Playhouse, May 29, 1935).

He portrayed Sir Mark Loddon in *Libel* (Winter Gardens, New Brighton, June 17, 1935); Charles McFadden in *Counsellor-at-Law* (Winter Gardens, New Brighton, June 24, 1935); Bill Clarke in *Too Young to Marry* (Winter Gardens, New Brighton, July 1, 1935); Randolph Warrender in *Youth at the Helm* (Liverpool Playhouse, Aug. 29, 1935); Richard Barnet in *Barnet's Folly* (Liverpool Playhouse, Sept. 18, 1935); Robert Murrison in *Cornelius* (Liverpool Playhouse, Oct. 9, 1935); Richard Brinsley Sheridan in *Miss Linley of Bath* (Liverpool Playhouse, Oct. 30, 1935); Max in *The Copy* (Liverpool Playhouse, Nov. 20, 1935); Trino in *A Hundred Years Old* (Liverpool Playhouse, Nov. 20, 1935); Gilbert Raymond in *The Wind and the Rain* (Liverpool Playhouse, Dec. 11, 1935); wrote and appeared as the BBC Official in *Circus Boy* (Liverpool Playhouse, Dec. 24, 1935); played Rev. Ernest Dunwoody in *Boyd's Shop* (Liverpool Playhouse, Feb. 19, 1936); a Radio Announcer in *And So to War* (Liverpool Playhouse, Mar. 11, 1936); Richard II in *Richard of Bordeaux* (Liverpool Playhouse, Apr. 1, 1936); Richard Burdon in *Storm in a Teacup* (Liverpool Playhouse, Apr. 29, 1936); Tom Lambert in *Painted Sparrows* (Liverpool Playhouse, May 20, 1936); and Malvolio in *Twelfth Night* (Liverpool Playhouse, June 5, 1936).

He made his London debut with the Old Vic Company as Ferdinand, King of Navarre, in *Love's Labour's Lost* (Old Vic, Sept. 14, 1936); and subsequently appeared as Mr. Horner in *The Country Wife* (Old Vic, Oct. 6, 1936); Orlando in *As You Like It* (Old Vic, Nov. 10, 1936); Warbeck in *The Witch of Edmonton* (Old Vic, Dec. 8, 1936); and Laertes in *Hamlet* (Old Vic, Jan. 5, 1937). He played Orlando in *As You Like It* (New, Feb. 11, 1937); Anderson in *The Bat* (Embassy, Mar. 29, 1937); Iachimo in a Shakespeare Birthday Festival performance of a scene from *Cymbeline* (Old Vic, Apr. 23, 1937); succeeded (Apr. 26, 1937) Marius Goring as Chorus in *Henry V* (Old Vic, Apr. 6, 1937); portrayed Christopher Drew in *A Ship Comes Home* (St. Martin's, May 15, 1937); Larry Starr in *Three Set Out* (Embassy, June 22, 1937); Bolingbroke in *Richard II* (Queen's, Sept. 6, 1937); Charles Surface in *The School for Scandal* (Queen's, Nov. 25, 1937); Baron Tusenbach in *The Three Sisters* (Queen's, Jan. 28, 1938); Chorus in *Henry V* in a Shakespeare Birthday performance (Old Vic, Apr. 25, 1938); and Orlando in the 10th Ellen Terry Anniversary Performance of scenes from *As You Like It* (The Barn Th., Smallhythe, Eng., July 24, 1938).

He played Alexei Turbin in *The White Guard* (Phoenix, London, Oct. 6, 1938); Sir Andrew Aguecheek in *Twelfth Night* (Phoenix, Dec. 1, 1938); Harry Monchensey in *The Family Reunion* (Mar. 21, 1939); Henry Dewlip in a touring production of *Springtime for Henry* (Oct. 1939); Macheath in *The Beggar's Opera* (Haymarket, London, Mar. 5, 1940); Romeo in a scene from *Romeo and Juliet* (Palace, charity matinee, Mar. 12, 1940); and Charleston in *Thunder Rock* (Neighborhood, June 18, 1940).

He directed *Lifeline* (Duchess, July 2, 1942); directed and played Gribaud in *The Duke in Darkness* (St. James's, Oct. 8, 1942); Rakitin in *A Month in the Country* (St. James's, Feb. 11, 1943); directed and portrayed Lafont in *Parisienne* (St. James's, June 7, 1943); directed *Blow Your Own Trumpet* (Playhouse, Aug. 11, 1943); and *The Wingless Victory* (Phoenix, Sept. 8, 1943); directed, with William Armstrong, and played Harry Quincey in *Uncle Harry* (Garrick, Mar. 29, 1940); directed and portrayed Colonel Tadeusz Bolesley Stjerbinsky in *Jacobowsky and the Colonel* (Wimbledon, May 21, 1945); and appeared in the title role in *Macbeth* (Aldwych, Dec. 18, 1947).

After he made his Bway debut in *Macbeth* (see above), he appeared as the Captain in *The Father* (Embassy, London, Nov. 30, 1948); adapted, with Diana Gould, directed, and played Etienne in *A Woman in Love*, originally entitled *Amoureuse* (Embassy, Apr. 26, 1949); with the Old Vic Company appeared as Berowne in *Love's Labour's Lost* (New, Oct. 11, 1949); Young Marlow in *She Stoops to Conquer* (New, Oct. 8, 1949); Rakitin in *A Month in the Country* (New, Nov. 30, 1949); and the title role in *Hamlet* (New, Feb. 2, 1950; Kronberg Castle, Elsinore, Denmark, June 7, 1950); subsequently played Filmer Jesson in a scene from *His House in Order* (Drury Lane, London, charity matinee, Nov. 6, 1950); toured Holland in solo performances of Shakespeare (Dec. 1950); joined the Shakespeare Memorial Th. Co. (Stratford-upon-Avon) and played the title role in *Richard II* (Mar. 24, 1951); Hotspur in *Henry V, Part I* (Apr. 3, 1951); directed *Henry IV, Part 2* (May 8, 1951); and played Prospero in *The Tempest* (June 26, 1951); and again appeared in solo performances of Shakespeare at the Holland Festival (July 14, 1951); and with the Shakespeare Memorial Th., played Chorus in *Henry V* (Stratford-upon-Avon, July 31, 1951). He appeared as Frank Elgin in *Winter Journey* (St. James's, London, Apr. 3, 1952); with the Shakespeare Memorial Th. (Stratford-upon-Avon), Shylock in *The Merchant of Venice* (Mar. 17, 1953), Antony in *Antony and Cleopatra* (Apr. 28, 1953), and the title role in *King Lear* (July 16, 1953); Antony in *Antony and Cleopatra* (Prince's, London, Nov. 4, 1953), which he repeated when the Shakespeare Memorial Th. Co. toured Holland, Belgium, and Paris (Jan. 1954); and portrayed Hector in *Tiger at the Gates* (Apollo, London, June 2, 1955).

After he appeared on Bway in *Tiger at the Gates* and the scene from *The Merchant of Venice*, directed *A Month in the Country*, and directed and played in *The Sleeping Prince*, he portrayed Philip Lester in *A Touch of the Sun* (Saville, London, Jan. 31, 1958); at the Shakespeare Memorial Th. (Stratford-upon-Avon) played the title role in *Hamlet* June 3, 1958), and Benedick in *Much Ado About Nothing* (Aug. 28, 1958), both of which he repeated in Moscow and Leningrad, USSR; adapted from the novel by Henry James, and played "H.J." in *The Aspern Papers* (Queen's, London, Aug. 12, 1959); and played Jack Dean in *The Tiger and the Horse* (Queen's, Aug. 24, 1960). In N.Y.C., David Black by arrangement with Peter Daubeny, Michael Redgrave Productions, and F.E.S. Plays Ltd. presented *The Aspern Papers* (Playhouse, N.Y.C., Feb. 7, 1962). After he played in the Bway production of *The Complaisant Lover*, he appeared at the 1st Chichester (England) Festival in the title role in *Uncle Vanya* (July 16, 1962); as Lancelot Dodd in *Out of Bounds* (Wyndham's, London, Nov. 8, 1962); at the 2nd Chichester (England) Festival, in the title role in *Uncle Vanya* (July 1, 1963); and for the first National Th. season, played Claudius in *Hamlet* (Oct. 22, 1963), the title role in *Uncle Vanya* (Nov. 19, 1963), Henry Hobson in *Hobson's Choice* (Jan. 7, 1964), and Halvard Solness in *The Master Builder* (June 9, 1964).

Mr. Redford directed the opening of the festival at the Yvonne Arnaud Th., Guildford, England, in 1965 and played Rakitin in *A Month in the Country* (June 2, 1965) and the title role in *Samson Agonistes* (June 16, 1965), then appearing as Rakitin in London (Cambridge Th., Sept. 23, 1965). He directed for the Glyndebourne (Sussex) Opera Co. *Werther* (May 31, 1966) and *La Bohème* (May 21, 1967); was Mr. Jaraby in *The Old Boys* (Mermaid, London, July 29, 1971); succeeded Alec Guiness as the Father in *A Voyage Round My Father* (Haymarket, Apr. 11, 1972); played that role in Canada (Royal Alexandra Th., Toronto, Oct. 30, 1972) and in Australia (Melbourne, Mar. 1973; Adelaide, Apr. 1973; Sydney, May 1973); and appeared in the US in *The Hollow Crown* and *Pleasure and Repentance* (see above).

Films. Michael Redgrave made his film debut as Gilbert in *The Lady Vanishes* (Gaumont-British, 1938); subsequently appeared as Alan Mackenzie in *Stolen Life* (Par., 1939); Nicholas Brooke in *Climbing High* (20th-Fox, 1939); Peter in *A Window in London* (1940); David Fenwick in *The Stars Look Down* (MGM, 1941); the title role in *Kipps*, released in the US as *Remarkable Mr. Kipps* (20th-Fox, 1942); Charles MacIver in *Atlantic Ferry*, released in the US as *Sons of the Sea* (WB, 1941); Stanley Smith in *Jeannie;* the Russian in *The Big Blockade* (1942); Charleston in *Thunder Rock* (English Films, 1943); Flight-Lt. Archdale in *The Way to the Stars* (1945); Maxwell Frere in *Dead of Night* (U, 1946); Michael Wentworth in *The Years Between* (U, 1947); Karel Hasek in *The Captive Heart* (U, 1947); Carlyon in *The Man Within*, released in the US as *The Smugglers* (Eagle Lion, 1948); Orin Mannon in *Mourning Becomes Electra* (RKO, 1948); Mark Lamphere in *Secret Beyond the Door* (U, 1948); Hamer Radshaw in *Fame Is the Spur* (Oxford, 1949).

Also, Andrew Crocker-Harris in *The Browning Version* (U, 1951); John Worthing in *The Importance of Being Earnest* (U, 1952); Maître Déliot in *The Green Scarf* (Assoc., 1955); Air Commodore Waltby in *The Sea Shall Not Have Them* (UA, 1955); Colonel Eisenstein in *Oh, Rosalinda! !* (Assoc. Brit. Pathé, 1955); the Air Marshall in *The Night My Number Came Up* (Continental, 1955); Barnes Wallis in *The Dam Busters* (WB, 1955); Trebitsch in *Confidential Report* (WB, 1955); O'Connor in *1984* (Col., 1956); David Graham in *Time Without Pity* (Astor, 1957); General Medworth in *The Happy Road* (MGM, 1957); Fowler in *The Quiet American* (UA, 1958); Percy Brand in *Law and Disorder* (Continental, 1958); the General in *Shake Hands with the Devil* (UA, 1959); Defence Counsel in *The Wreck of the Mary Deare* (MGM, 1959); Sir Arthur Benson Gray in *Behind the Mask* (Showcorporation, 1960); Sir Matthew Carr in *No, My Darling Daughter* (Rank, 1961); the Uncle in *The Innocents* (20th-Fox, 1961); and the Prison Governor in *The Loneliness of the Long Distance Runner* (Continental, 1962).

Later films in which he appeared include *The Hill* (MGM, 1965); *The Heroes of Telemark* (Col., 1966); *Assignment K* (Col., 1968); *Goodbye, Mr. Chips* (MGM, 1969); *Oh! What a Lovely War* (Par., 1969); *Battle of Britain* (UA, 1969); *Connecting Rooms* (1970); *Goodbye, Gemini* (Cinerama Inter., 1970); *The Go-Between* (MGM-EMI, 1971); and *Nicholas and Alexandra* (Col., 1971).

Television and Radio. He made his debut in 1937, when he appeared as Romeo in an abbreviated version of *Romeo and Juliet* (BBC, London). He appeared as Philip Lester in *A Touch of the Sun* (Tennent, May 1959); followed by Tesman in *Hedda Gabler* (BBC, London; CBS, US, 1962); and General Cavendish in *Return to the Regiment* (Tennent, 1963). He was the Caterpillar in *Alice in Wonderland* (BBC-1, 1966); the Ghost in *The Canterville Ghost* (ABC, 1966); Charles Dickens in *Mr. Dickens of London* (ABC, 1967); M. Barnett in *Monsieur Barnett* (BBC-1, 1968); Prospero in *The Tempest* (BBC-1, 1968); Mr. Peggotty in *David Copperfield* (NBC, Mar. 15 1970); Polonius in *Hamlet* (Hallmark Hall of Fame, NBC, Nov. 17, 1970); the Commander in *Don Juan in Hell* (BBC-1, 1971); and starred on BBC radio in *The Pump* (1972).

Other Activities. He was Rockefeller Foundation Lecturer at Brisol Univ. (1952–53), and the Theodore Spencer Memorial lecturer at Harvard Univ. (1956).

Published Works. He has written *The Actor's Ways and Means* (1953), *Mask or Face* (1958), *The Mountebank's Tale* (1959).

Awards. In 1947, he received the Natl. Board of Film Review Award and was nominated for an Academy (Oscar) Award for his role of Orin Mannon in *Mourning Becomes Electra*. In 1951, he won the Cannes Film Festival Award and the Finnish Film Journalists Assn. Award for his performance as Andrew Crocker-Harris in *The Browning Version;* received the Film Club of Buenos Aires Award (1953) for the same film.

He received the *Evening Standard* Drama Award and the Variety Club of Great Britain Award for both *A Touch of the Sun* (1958) and *Uncle Vanya* (1963) and was awarded the Prix Femina Belge du Cinema for his performance in *Connecting Rooms* (1971).

The order of Commander of the British Empire (C.B.E.) was conferred upon him in 1952. He was made Commander of the Order of Dannebrog (Denmark) on (Mar. 25, 1955) for services to Danish art and literature; and was knighted in the Queen's Birthday Honours (Eng., July 7, 1959); and was awarded the honorary degree of Litt. D. by the Univ. of Bristol (1966).

Recreation. Music, singing.

REDMAN, JOYCE. Actress. b. 1918, County Mayo, Ireland. Studied at RADA, London. Married 1949 (?) to Charles Wynne Roberts.

Theatre. Miss Redman made her London debut as the First Tiger Lily in *Alice Through the Looking Glass* (Playhouse, Dec. 23, 1935), subsequently appeared as Mrs. Cricket in *The Insect Play* (Little, June 23, 1936); the title role in *Lady Precious Stream* (Little, Nov. 24, 1936); Katherine Carew in *The King's Pirate* (St. Martin's, June 10, 1937); repeated the role of Cricket in *The Insect Play* (Playhouse, Apr. 27, 1938); followed by the role of Suzanne in *Thou Shalt Not— (Therese Requin)* (Playhouse, Aug. 24, 1938).

She played Hsiang Fei in *The Fragrant Concubine* (Little, Oct. 2, 1938); Hung Niang in *The Western Chamber* (Torch, Dec. 7, 1938); Alice in *Alice in Wonderland and Through the Looking Glass* (Playhouse, Dec. 21, 1938); Emanuelle in *Asmodee* (Gate, Feb. 23, 1939); Laura in *Drawing Room* (Streatham Hill, May 29, 1939); repeated the title role in *Lady Precious Stream* (Kingsway, Dec. 7, 1939); appeared as Essie in *The Devil's Disciple* (Piccadilly, July 24, 1940); Maria in *Twelfth Night* (Arts, June 10, 1942); Roberta in *The House of Jeffreys* (Orpheum, Golder's Green, Oct. 12, 1942); Wendy Darling in *Peter Pan* (Winter Garden, Dec. 24, 1942); Brigid in *Shadow and Substance* (Duke of York's, May 25, 1943); and succeeded Pamela Brown in the title role in *Claudia* (St. Martin's, Sept. 17, 1943), and on tour (1944).

Miss Redman played, with the Old Vic Co., as Solveig in *Peer Gynt* (New, Aug. 31, 1944); Louka in *Arms and the Man* (New, Sept. 5, 1944); Lady Anne in *Richard III* (New, Sept. 13, 1944); and Sonya in *Uncle Vanya* (New, Jan. 16, 1945); and appeared with the company at the Comédie Française in Paris (July 1945). She played Doll Tearsheet in *Henry IV, Part 2* (New, London, Oct. 3, 1945); and in a double-bill, an Attendant to Jocasta in *Oedipus Rex*, and the Confidante in *The Critic*, (New, Oct. 18, 1945).

She made her Bway debut with the Old Vic, repeating her roles in *Henry IV, Part 2*, (Century, May 7, 1946), *Uncle Vanya* (May 13, 1946); *Oedipus Rex*, and *The Critic* (May 20, 1946). With the Old Vic, she played Cordelia in *King Lear* (New London, Sept. 24, 1946), and Dol Common in *The Alchemist* (New, Jan. 14, 1947); appeared as Valentine North in *Angel* (Strand, June 6, 1947); Abigail Sarclet, in *Duet for Two Hands* (Booth, N.Y.C., Oct. 7, 1947); as Jessica in *Crime Passionnel* (Lyric, Hammersmith, London, June 14, 1948); and Anne Boleyn in *Anne of the Thousand Days* (Shubert, N.Y.C., Dec. 8, 1948).

Miss Redman played Gay Butterworth in *Count Your Blessings* (Wyndham's, London, Mar. 7, 1951); the title role in *Colombe* (New, Dec. 13, 1951); and Irene Elliott in *Affairs of State* (Cambridge, Aug. 21, 1952). With the Shakespeare Memorial Th. (Stratford-upon-Avon), she appeared as Helena in *All's Well That Ends Well* (Apr. 26, 1955) and Mistress Ford in *The Merry Wives of Windsor* (July 12, 1955); played Fay Edwards in *The Long Echo* (St. James's, London, Aug. 1, 1956); Titania in the Old Vic production of *A Midsummer Night's Dream* (New, Dec. 23, 1957); Frances Brough in *The Party* (New, May 28, 1958); Hippolyte in *The Rape of the Belt* (Martin Beck Th., N.Y.C., Nov. 5, 1960); succeeded (Oct. 1961) Joan Greenwood as Hedda Rankin in *The Irregular Verb to Love* (Criterion, London, Apr. 11, 1961); played Therese in *Power of Persuasion* (Garrick, Sept. 19, 1963); and Laura in *The Father* (Piccadilly, Jan. 14, 1964).

With the National Th., she played Emilia in *Othello* (Old Vic, Apr. 23, 1964; Chichester Fest., July 21, 1964); Crispinella in *The Dutch Courtesan* (Chichester Fest., July 14, 1964; Old Vic, Oct. 14, 1964); Elizabeth Proctor in *The Crucible* (Old Vic, Jan. 19, 1965); toured as Emilia in *Othello*, Mrs. Frail in *Love for Love*, and in *Hobson's Choice* (Moscow and Berlin, Sept. 1965); recreated the role of Mrs. Frail in *Love for Love* (Old Vic, Oct. 20, 1965; revived Aug. 9, 1966); and played Juno Boyle in *Juno and the Paycock* (Old Vic, Apr. 26, 1966).

She replaced (June 1969) Rosemary Harris in her three roles in *Plaza Suite* (Lyric, Feb. 18, 1969); and played Vivian Fairleigh in *The Lionel Touch* (Lyric, Nov. 5, 1969).

Films. Miss Redman appeared in *One of Our Aircraft Is Missing* (Brit. Natl., 1942); *Tom Jones* (UA, 1963); as Emilia to Sir Laurence Olivier's *Othello* (WB, 1965); and in *Prudence and the Pill* (20th-Fox, 1968).

REEVE, ALEX. Educator, director. b. Alexander Reeve, May 16, 1900, London, England, to Albert Alexander and Louisa Jane (Newsam) Reeve. Father, architect. Attended English Schools, 1906–16. Married Oct. 18, 1924, to Constance A. Robertson; one daughter. Served British Army, WW I; rank, Pvt.; Civil Defense Sector Warden, WW II. Relatives in theatre; aunt, Dame Madge Kendall, actress; uncle, T. W. Robertson, playwright. Member of Texas Educational Theatre Assn. (exec. sec., 1960–63); Interscholastic League (judge); British Guild of Drama Adjudicators (1943–60); Theta Alpha Phi (past Historian, National Council). Address: 1201 Cottage St., Brownwood, TX 76801, tel. (915) 646-3032.

Before his retirement in 1971, Mr. Reeve was professor of speech and English (1951–71); chairman of the Dept. of Speech and Drama (1966–71); and director of theatre at Howard Payne Coll., Brownwood, Tex. His productions have included the "Texas-style" *A Midsummer Night's Dream*, which toured Britain, and was part of the International Festival of Univ. Drama, Bristol, 1959. Since 1920, he has been engaged in theatre as an actor and director.

During 1943–56, he was director of productions at the Royal Th. and Opera House, Northampton, Eng., where he directed approximately 300 productions, including thirty world premieres. In 1952, he represented the Council of Repertory Theatres at the International Theatre Institute World Congress, The Hague, The Netherlands; and in 1953–54, was guest professor of drama at Vanderbilt Univ., Nashville, Tenn.

Since retiring, he has been active as a guest lecturer, director, and artist in residence at various colleges, including Georgia Southern Coll., where he taught and directed a six-week workshop (Summer 1974).

Other Activities. In his capacity as Historian, Mr. Reeve wrote a brief account of the first fifty years of Theta Alpha Phi for the anniversary edition of that honor society's journal.

Awards. In 1935, Mr. Reeve directed the winning play, *Not this Man*, by Sydney Box, in the National Festival of British Drama at Old Vic, London; and in 1951, directed one of the Arts Council of Great Britain Festival of Britain award winning plays *Mansfield Park*, by Constance Cox. He is the recipient of the Distinguished Faculty Member Award (1970) from Howard Payne Coll.; and of the Texas Educational Th. Assn. Citation Award (1972) for distinguished services to the association and theatre in Texas.

Recreation. Theatre and allied arts.

REGAN, SYLVIA. Playwright, actress. b. Sylvia Hoffenberg, Apr. 15, 1908, New York City, to Louis and Esther (Hoffenberg) Hoffenberg. Father, in shoe business. Grad. Hillhouse H.S., New Haven, Conn., 1925. Married Feb. 11, 1931, to James J. Regan (marr. dis. 1936); married Nov. 7, 1940, to Abraham Ellstein, composer (dec. 1963). Relative in theatre: brother, Arthur Hoffe, film and TV producer. Member of ALA, Dramatists Guild. Address: 70 E. 10th St., New York, NY 10003, tel. (212) 473-0125.

Theatre. Miss Regan made her Bway debut, under the name Sylvia Hoffman, as Anna in *We Americans* (Sam H. Harris Th., Oct. 12, 1926); subsequently played Elizabeth in *The Waltz of the Dogs* (Cherry Lane, April 25, 1928; moved to 48 St. Th., May 7, 1928); and Marjorie in *Poppa* (Biltmore, Dec. 24, 1928).

She was promotion and public relations manager, under the name Sylvia Regan, for the Theatre Union at the Civic Repertory Th. (1932–36) and the Mercury Th. Co. (1936–38).

Miss Regan wrote the play *Morning Star* (Longacre, April 16, 1940); the book, with Walter Bullock, for the musical *Great To Be Alive!* (Winter Garden, Mar. 23, 1950); the play *The Fifth Season* (Cort, Jan. 23, 1953); the libretto for the opera *The Golem* by her husband, Abraham Ellstein (NY City Ctr., Mar. 22, 1962); and the play *Zelda* (Ethel Barrymore Th., Mar. 5, 1969).

Recreation. Painter.

REICH, JOHN. Director, producer, educator, adaptor. b. Johannes Theodor Reich, Sept. 30, 1906, Vienna, Austria, to Leopold and Martha (Baxter) Reich. Father, industrialist. Grad. Realgymnasium I, Vienna, Austria, B.A. 1928; Graduate Sch. of Business, Univ. of Vienna, 1929; The Max Reinhardt Seminary of the Univ. of Vienna, directing diploma 1931; Cornell Univ., Ph.D. 1944. Married Oct. 23, 1932, to Karoline Friederike von Kurzweil (dec. Feb. 2, 1945); married July 8, 1957, to Karen Ruth Lasker-Lester. Member of ATA; NTC; The Cliff Dwellers Club (Chicago, Ill.). Address: 724 Bohemia Parkway, Sayville, NY 11782, tel. (516) 589-5997.

Theatre. Mr. Reich was producer, director, and head of the Goodman Memorial Th. and Sch. of Drama (1957–1972). During 1957–58 and 1958–59, he produced six plays each season, using local professionals. Since 1959, the theatre has employed equity performers and Bway stars. He produced there *The Merchant of Venice, The Cave Dwellers, Hippolytus*, produced and directed Pirandello's *Henry IV*, produced *The Good Woman of Setzuan*, and *The Inspector General* (1959–60); produced *The Taming of the Shrew*, produced and directed *Venus Observed*, produced *Royal Gambit, Under Milk Wood, Uncle Vanya* and *On Borrowed Time* (1960–61); produced and directed *Faust*, produced *The Lark, My Heart's in the Highlands, Hedda Gabler, The American Dream*, and produced and directed *The Caucasian Chalk Circle* (1961–62).

There he produced and directed *Becket*, produced *A Passage to India*, produced and directed *Christopher C.*, produced *The Lesson* and *The Rivals* (1962–63); produced and directed *The Millionairess*, produced *The Three Sisters, The Glass Menagerie, King Lear, Mother Courage*, and produced and directed *A Far Country* (1963–64); produced and directed *The Madwoman of Chaillot;* produced *Macbeth, The Ballad of the Sad Cafe, Rashomon, The Barrets of Wimpole Street, Anna Karenina* (1964–65); produced and directed *The Cocktail Party*, produced *The Winter's Tale, The Pedestrian in the Air, Dylan, The Skin of Our Teeth, Galileo* (1965–1966); produced and directed *Tartuffe* and *A Dream Play*, produced *Marat-Sade, The Eccentricities of a Nightingale, Much Ado About Nothing; Oh, What a Lovely War!* (1967–67); produced and directed *The Miser*, produced *The Balcony, Caesar and Cleopatra, Othello, A Man's a Man, A Flea in Her Ear* (1967–68); directed and produced *The Salzburg Great Theatre of the World, The Death and Life of Sneaky Fitch*, produced *Red Roses for Me, Measure for Measure, Tom Paine, The Recruiting Officer* (1968–69); produced *Soldiers, You Can't Take It with You, The Tempest, The Basement* and *Tea Party, The Man in the Glass Booth, Heartbreak House* (1969–70); *The Three Penny Opera, Twelfth Night, The Night Thoreau Spent in Jail, Marching Song, Poor Bitos, Lady Audley's Secret* (1970–71); *A Place Without Doors, Assassination, 1865, The Importance of Being Earnest, The Royal Family, The Ruling Class, The Boys from Syracuse* (1971–72). He also produced and directed an all-star production of *The Misanthrope* at the Univ. of Chicago Law auditorium (1966), and at the Ravinia Festival (1968).

Mr. Reich first directed *Swanwhite* (Th. in Schoenbrunn Castle, Vienna, Austria, Mar. 1930); subsequently was assistant director of *The Robbers* (Burgtheatre, Vienna, Sept. 1931); also at the Burgtheatre, was assistant director of *The Tempest* (Jan. 1932); directed *As Husbands Go* (Mar. 1932); and *Measure for Measure* (May 1932). He directed *The Passion Play* (Circus Renz, Apr. 1933); and at the Salzburg (Austria) Festival, was assistant director (1934) and director (1935–37) of *Faust I;* at the Theatre in der Josefstadt (Vienna), directed *Tiger at the Gates* (1936); *The First Legion* (1937); *Black Limelight* (1937); and *Espionage* (1938).

He directed twenty productions in US universities and summer festivals (1938–45); directed *The Imaginary Invalid* (Brander Matthews Th., N.Y.C., Dec. 5, 1945); *The Dream* (Berkshire Festival, Mass., Aug. 1946); *Faust I* (Equity Library Th., N.Y.C., Oct. 1946); *Henry IV* (Greenwich Mews, May 12, 1947); and *Hippolytus* (Lenox Hill Playhouse, Nov. 21, 1948); directed Pirandello's *Henry IV* (Sea Cliff Summer Th., N.Y., Summer 1950); *Mrs. Warren's Profession* (Bleecker St. Playhouse, N.Y.C., Oct. 25, 1950); at the Plymouth Opera Festival (Plymouth Rock Center, Mass.), directed *Trial by Jury* (July 26, 1951); *Down in the Valley* (July 26, 1951); *The Marriage of Figaro* (Aug. 8, 1951); *The Magic Flute* (Aug. 14, 1952); directed *The Sacred Flame* (President, N.Y.C., Oct. 6, 1952); and, at the Caramoor Festival (Katonah, N.Y.), *The Abduction from the Seraglio* (Aug. 30, 1953). At the Plymouth Opera Festival (Plymouth Rock Center, Mass.), he directed *Don Giovanni* (Aug. 1954); and *The Dream* (Brander Matthews Th., N.Y.C., Mar. 1957).

Television. Mr. Reich produced and directed a dramatic documentary series, The Doctor Looks

(CBS, 1945); directed *The Imaginary Invalid* (CBS, 1946); *Untitled* (CBS, 1946); *The Shelleys* (CBS, 1951); and *The Missus Goes Shopping* (CBS, 1945).

Awards. He received the Ford Foundation Award (1959) for producing directors; ANTA, Chicago Theatre Man-of-the-Year (1960); and the award from the Governor of Illinois for outstanding contribution by a foreign-born American citizen (1961); received the order, Chevalier des Arts et Lettres (1964); and the Grand Badge of Honor from Austria (1968).

Recreation. Mountain climbing, hiking, piano.

REID, ELLIOTT. Actor. b. Edgeworth Blair Reid, Jan. 16, 1920, New York City, to Blair L. and Christine (Challenger) Reid. Father, Foreign Dept., Chemical Bank and Trust; mother, fashion artist. Grad. Professional Children's H.S., 1938. Studied acting with Robert Lewis (1947–48), Daniel Mann (1950–51). Served USN, 1943–46; rank, Spec.(x)3/C. Member of AEA; AFTRA; SAG; AGVA; Actors' Studio (1947–to date). Address: 40 W. 53rd St., New York, NY 10019.

Theatre. Mr. Reid made his N.Y.C. debut with Orson Welles' Mercury Th., as Cinna in *Julius Caesar* (Nov. 11, 1937) and Ralph in *Shoemaker's Holiday* (Jan. 1, 1938); succeeded (June 1942) Henry Jones as Frank Lippincott in *My Sister Eileen* (Biltmore Th., Dec. 26, 1940); played Malcolm in *Macbeth* (National, Mar. 31, 1948); Ensign Jamison in *Two Blind Mice* (Cort, Mar. 2, 1949); Granny Schenk in *The Live Wire* (Playhouse, Aug. 17, 1950); and appeared in the revue, *Two on the Aisle*, in which he played in a satirical sketch about the Kefauver Crime Committee hearings (Mark Hellinger Th., July 19, 1951); performed at the Roxy Th. (N.Y.C., Summer 1952); and performed his own comedy material at Radio City Music Hall (Summer 1956).

Mr. Elliott appeared in the pre-Bway tryout of *Ziegfeld Follies* (opened Shubert, Boston, Mass., Apr. 16, 1956; closed Shubert Philadelphia, Pa., May 12, 1956); in the revue *From A to Z* (Plymouth, N.Y.C., Apr. 20, 1960); was Felix Unger in the national company of *The Odd Couple* (Blackstone Th., Chicago, 1967–68); made a national tour in *There's a Girl in My Soup* (1969); and was Uncle Jimmy in the national company of *No, No, Nanette* (Chicago, 1973). He has also made dinner theatre and summer stock appearances.

Films. Mr. Reid made his debut in *The Story of Dr. Wassell* (Par., 1944); subsequently appeared in *Gentlemen Prefer Blondes* (20th-Fox, 1952); *Vicki* (20th-Fox, 1953); *A Woman's World* (20th-Fox, 1954); *Inherit the Wind* (UA, 1960); *The Absent Minded Professor* (Buena Vista, 1961); *Son of Flubber* (Buena Vista, 1961); *The Thrill of It All* (U, 1963); *Who's Been Sleeping in My Bed?* (Par., 1964); *The Wheeler Dealers* (MGM, 1964); *Move Over, Darling* (20th-Fox, 1964); *Follow Me, Boys!* (Disney, 1966); *Blackbeard's Ghost* (Disney, 1968); and *Some Kind of a Nut* (UA, 1969).

Television and Radio. Mr. Reid performed on the radio programs, The March of Time (NBC), Theatre Guild on the Air (NBC) and others.

On television, he has appeared on The Defenders (CBS); Alfred Hitchcock Presents (CBS); I Love Lucy (CBS); the Loretta Young Show (NBC); Kraft Television Th. (NBC); Alcoa Goodyear (NBC); US Steel Hour (CBS); Surfside Six (ABC); The Roaring 20's (ABC); Danny Thomas Show (CBS); To Tell the Truth (CBS); The Odd Couple (ABC); Lotsa Luck!; Afternoon Playbreak (ABC); Love American Style (ABC); and many others. In 1972, he wrote a script for The Odd Couple. Performing his own comedy material, he has appeared on the Ed Sullivan Show (CBS); Jackie Gleason Show (NBC); Jack Paar Show (NBC); Dinah Shore Show (NBC); and That Was the Week That Was (NBC).

Night Clubs. In 1962, Mr. Reid appeared at the Cocoanut Grove (Los Angeles, Calif.).

REID, FRANCES. Actress. b. Dec. 9, Wichita Falls, Tex., to Charles William and Anna May (Priest) Reid. Father, banker. Grad. Anna Head Sch., Berkeley, Calif., 1932; Pasadena Playhouse Sch. of the Theatre, Calif., 1936. Married June 27, 1940, to Philip Bourneuf. Member of AEA (AEA rep. to TVA, the organization which preceded AFTRA); SAG; AFTRA. Address: 129 S. Bowling Green Way, Los Angeles, CA 90049, tel. (213) GR 2-3875.

Theatre. Miss Reid made her professional debut as Helene Dupont in the West Coast touring production of *Tovarich* (Lobero Playhouse, Santa Barbara, Calif.; Curran Th., San Francisco, Calif.; Biltmore Th., Los Angeles, Calif., 1937); subsequently played ten wks. of stock at the Rise Playhouse (Martha's Vineyard, Mass., 1938); and appeared in *Dracula* (Brooklyn, N.Y., 1938).

She made her Bway debut as Juliette Lecourtois in *Where There's a Will* (John Golden, Th., Jan. 17, 1939); followed by appearances in stock productions at Maplewood, N.J. (Feb.–Mar. 1939), and Ridgefield, Conn. (July–Sept. 1939); was understudy to Arlene Francis and Helen Shields in the roles of Catherine Daly and Cora Bedell, respectively, in *Young Couple Wanted* (Maxine Elliott's Th., N.Y.C., Jan. 24, 1940); appeared in stock at Ridgefield, Conn. (Summer 1940); played in the pre-Bway tryout of *The White-Haired Boy* (opened Plymouth, Boston, Mass., Oct. 28, 1940; closed there Nov. 2, 1940); in stock, appeared in *Western Union Please* (Paper Mill Playhouse, Millburn, N.J., and Studebaker Th., Chicago, Ill., 1941).

In N.Y.C., Miss Reid played Julia in the Theatre Guild production of *The Rivals* (Shubert Th., Jan. 14, 1942); Martha in *The Patriots* (Natl., Jan. 29, 1943); Nina Alexandrovna in *Listen, Professor!* (Forrest, Dec. 22, 1943); the Angel, Jeannie Mackenzie, in *A Highland Fling* (Plymouth, Apr. 28, 1944); and Beth in *Little Women* (NY City Ctr., Dec. 12, 1944); in the pre-Bway tryout of *Clover Ring* (opened Plymouth, Boston, Mass., Feb. 5, 1945; closed there Feb. 10, 1945); as Sally Jones in *Star Spangled Family* (Biltmore, N.Y.C., Apr. 10, 1945); Jean in *The Wind Is 90* (Booth, June 21, 1945); Ophelia in Maurice Evans' GI *Hamlet* (Columbus Circle Th., Dec. 13, 1945), and on tour; Roxanne in the Jose Ferrer revival of *Cyrano de Bergerac* (Alvin, Oct. 8, 1946); Minnie in *Rip Van Winkle* (NY City Ctr., July 15, 1947); and Elena Popova in *The Bear* (NY City Ctr., Feb. 5, 1948).

For the Utah Drama Festival, she appeared as Raina in *Arms and the Man* (Univ. of Utah, 1948); in stock, as Gwendolyn in *The Importance of Being Earnest* (Olney Th., Md., 1948); as Ann in Richard Whorf's production of *Richard III* (Booth, N.Y.C., Feb. 8, 1949); Viola in *Twelfth Night* (Empire, Oct. 3, 1949), in which she had previously played at the Ann Arbor (Mich.) Drama Festival (Lydia Mendelssohn Th., 1949); toured as Judith in Maurice Evans' production of *The Devil's Disciple* (Central City, Colo., 1950); Lady Utterwood in *Heartbreak House* (opened Brattle Th., Cambridge, Mass., 1953); appeared at the Boston Arts Festival as Mrs. Antrobus in *The Skin of Our Teeth* (Public Gardens, Boston, Mass., Summer 1955); toured for the Chicago Society as Lavinia in *Androcles and the Lion* (Studebaker Th., Chicago, Ill., 1956); and for Columbia Univ. as Renata in *Last Five Minutes* (1957); in stock, played Ranata in *Lease on Love* (Bucks County Playhouse, New Hope, Pa., 1957).

Miss Reid succeeded Edith Atwater (1957), as Comtesse Louise de Clerambard in *Clerambard* (Rooftop Th., N.Y.C., Nov. 7, 1957); subsequently toured as Mlle. de St. Euverte in *The Waltz of the Toreadors* (Summer 1958); performed in repertory as Nora in *A Touch of the Poet*, Solange in *The Maids, and Lina in Misalliance* (Marine's Memorial Th., San Francisco, Calif., 1960–61); appeared in *When the Bear Goes National* (Bucks County Playhouse, New Hope, Pa., 1962); as Mrs. Russell in *The Best Man* (Kelley Memorial Th., Fairmont Park, Philadelphia, Pa., 1962); and as Miss Swanson in *Lord Pengo, which toured summer theatres (1963).*

Films. Miss Reid appeared in *Seconds* (Par., 1966).

Television and Radio. She made her radio debut in *Charlotte Corday* (NBC, 1939); subsequently appeared on *Prologue to Glory* and *Little Women* (NBC, 1939–40). On television, she has been seen as Roxanne in *Cyrano de Bergerac* (NBC, 1948); as Olivia in *Twelfth Night* (NBC, 1949); played Portia for the series Portia Faces Life (CBS, 1954); Grace Baker in the series As the World Turns (CBS, 1959–60); appeared on Suspense, Danger, You Are There (CBS, 1951–52); Cameo Th., Philco Television Playhouse, Hallmark Hall of Fame (NBC, 1951–52); Matinee Th. (NBC, 1955–56); Telephone Time (NBC, 1956); Alfred Hitchcock Presents (CBS, 1961); Dear Rose Pollack in the series Edge of Night (CBS, 1964); Wagon Train (NBC); Ben Casey (ABC); Eleventh Hour (NBC); The Defenders (CBS); Perry Mason (CBS); Armstrong Circle Th. (CBS); and as the continuing character Mrs. Thomas Horton on *The Days of Our Lives serial (NBC, 1965–to date).*

Awards. Miss Reid received the Fanny Morrison Award from the Pasadena (Calif.) Playhouse.

REID, KATE. Actress. b. Daphne Kate Reid, Nov. 4, 1930, London, England, to Walter Clarke and Helen Isabelle (Moore) Reid. Father, soldier. Attended Havergal Coll.; Toronto (Ont., Can.) Conservatory of Music; Univ. of Toronto. Studied acting at the Herbert Berghof (HB) Studio, N.Y.C., with Uta Hagen and Herbert Berghof. Married July 13, 1953, to Austin Willis, actor (marr. dis. 1962); one son, one daughter. Member of ACTRA; AFTRA; AEA. Address: 14 Binscarth Rd., Toronto, Ontario, Canada tel. (416) WA 5-5015.

Theatre. Miss Reid made her stage debut as Ruth in *Years Ago* (Straw Hat Players, Gravenhurst, Ontario, Canada, Summer 1948); subsequently played numerous roles in stock and on tour in Canada (appearing frequently at the Crest Th., Toronto) and in Bermuda; toured England as Lizzie in *The Rainmaker;* and made her West End debut as Catherine Ashland in *The Stepmother* (St. Martin's Th., London, Nov. 11, 1958). She returned to Canada to join the Stratford (Ontario) Shakespearean Festival, for which she played Celia in *As You Like It*, and Emilia in *Othello* (June 29–Sept. 19, 1959); the Nurse in *Romeo and Juliet*, and Helena in *A Midsummer Night's Dream* (June 27–Sept. 17, 1960); Queen Katherine in *Henry VIII*, Jacquenetta in *Love's Labour's Lost*, and Elly Cassady in *The Canvas Barricade* (June 19–Sept. 23, 1961); and Katharina in *The Taming of the Shrew*, and Lady Macbeth in *Macbeth* (June 18–Sept. 29, 1962). She made a Canadian university tour (Feb. 1962), appearing in *Two Programs of Shakespearean Comedy.*

Miss Reid made her N.Y.C. debut as Martha in the matinee company of *Who's Afraid of Virginia Woolf?* (Billy Rose Th., Oct. 13, 1962); at the Stratford (Ontario) Shakespeare Festival, played Adriana in *The Comedy of Errors*, Cassandra in *Troilus and Cressida*, and both Lisa and Sister Marthe in *Cyrano de Bergerac* (June 17–Sept. 28, 1963). Subsequently, she appeared in the role of Caitlin Thomas in *Dylan* (Plymouth, N.Y.C., Jan. 18, 1964).

She played Martha in *Who's Afraid of Virginia Woolf?* (Manitoba Th. Ctr., Winnipeg, Canada, Apr. 7, 1965); at the Stratford (Ontario) Shakespearean Fest., played Portia in *Julius Caesar* (June 16, 1965) and Mme. Ranevskaya in *The Cherry Orchard* (July 26, 1965); played Celeste in "The Mutilated" and Molly in "The Gnadiges Fraulein" in *Slapstick Tragedy* (Longacre, N.Y.C., Feb. 22, 1966); the Medical Officer in *The Adventures of Private Turvey* and the Mayor's Wife in *The Ottawa Man* (Confederation Memorial Ctr., Charlottetown, Prince Edward Island, Canada, July 1966); the Writer's Wife in the pre-Bway tryout of *What Do You Really Know About Your Husband?* (opened Shubert, New Haven, Mar. 9, 1967; closed there Mar. 11, 1967); Lady Kitty in *The Circle* (Shaw Fest., Court House Th., Niagara-on-the-Lake, Ontario, July 19, 1967); and Esther Franz in *The Price* (Morosco, N.Y.C., Feb. 7, 1968; Duke of York's Th., London, Mar. 4, 1969).

For the American Shakespeare Fest. (Stratford, Conn., US), Miss Reid played Gertrude in *Hamlet* and Masha in *The Three Sisters* (Summer 1969). She returned to Toronto to play Esther in Arnold Wesker's *The Friends* (Stratford, Ontario, Shakespearean Fest., Summer 1970); and later appeared as Juno in *Juno and the Paycock* (Philadelphia Drama

Guild, 1973–74 season); Lily in *Freedom of the City* (Eisenhower Th., Kennedy Ctr., Washington, D.C., Jan. 25, 1974; Alvin, N.Y.C., Feb. 17, 1974); and for the American Shakespeare Fest. (Stratford, Conn.), she played the Nurse in *Romeo and Juliet* and Big Mama in *Cat on a Hot Tin Roof* (Summer 1974), repeating the latter role in the same production when it transferred to N.Y.C. (ANTA Th., Sept. 24, 1974).

Films. Miss Reid has appeared in *One Plus One* (Selected, 1961); *This Property Is Condemned* (Par., 1966); *Pigeons* (MGM, 1970); *The Andromeda Strain* (U, 1971); as Claire, the Sister, in *A Delicate Balance* (Amer. Film Th., 1973); and in *The Rainbow Boys* (Mutual, Canada, 1973).

Television. Miss Reid's more than 200 television appearances in Canada include roles in *Candida*, *Little Women*, *A Month in the Country*, *Queen After Death*, *Unburied Dead*, and *Hamlet*. In the US, she has appeared as Queen Victoria in *The Invincible Mr. Disraeli* (Hallmark Hall of Fame, NBC, 1963); Mary Todd Lincoln in *Abe Lincoln in Illinois* (Hallmark Hall of Fame, NBC, Feb. 5, 1964); in *The Holy Terror* (Hallmark Hall of Fame, NBC, Apr. 7, 1965); *An Enemy of the People* (NET Playhouse, WNET, Dec. 2, 1966); *Neither Are We Enemies* (Hallmark Hall of Fame, NBC, Mar. 13, 1970); and *Enemies* (NET Playhouse, WNET, 1974).

Awards. She was twice nominated for the Antoinette Perry (Tony) Award as best actress (for *Dylan*, 1964, and *Slapstick Tragedy*, 1966); and was twice nominated for the NATAS (Emmy) Award as best actress for her television roles in *The Invincible Mr. Disraeli* (1963) and *Abe Lincoln in Illinois* (1964).

REIFSNEIDER, ROBERT. Educator. b. Robert Daniel Reifsneider, May 20, 1912, Pottstown, Pa., to Daniel E. and Alice G. (Erb) Reifsneider. Father, purchasing agent. Grad. Plainfield H.S., N.J., 1928; Emerson Coll., B.A. 1938; Univ. of Mich., M.A. 1943; attended Amer. Th. Wing, N.Y.C., 1950; Jacob's Pillow, 1955; Paul Curtis' American Mime Th., 1952; Lilias Courtney Sch. of Ballet, Louisville, Ky., 1943–45; studied with Eduard DeBuron, Boston, Mass., 1938; Betty Jane Dittmar, Pa. State Coll., 1954–to date. Served US Army, Armored Forces S–2; Fort Knox, Ky., 1942–46; rank, T/4. Member of AETA; ANTA; AAUP. Address: 243 Ridge Ave., State College, PA 16801, tel. (814) 238-6926.

Mr. Reifsneider retired as full professor in 1972. He was guest professor at Florida Atlantic Univ. during the 1973–74 winter term.

From 1946–72, Mr. Reifsneider was a member of the faculty at Pennsylvania State Univ. and was associate professor of theatre arts.

In stock, he appeared at Plymouth Th., Westford, Mass. (1936); Orangeburg Playhouse, Orangeburg, N.Y. (1950); Globe Playhouse, San Diego, Calif. (1951); Green Hills Th., Reading, Pa. (1953); Mateer Playhouse, Standing Stone, Pa. (1961); directed at Plainfield Th. Guild, Plainfield, N.J. (1934–36); Bradford Junior Coll., Haverhill, Mass. (1940–42); and Pennsylvania State Univ. (1946–to date).

Mr. Reifsneider made a survey of the teaching of theatre subjects in professional and educational institutions in England, Scotland, and the US (1960–61).

REILLY, CHARLES NELSON. Actor, singer, teacher of acting. b. Jan. 13, 1931, New York City, to Charles Joseph and Signe Elvira (Nelson) Reilly. Father, commercial artist. Grad. Weaver H.S., Hartford, Conn., 1948; attended Univ. of Connecticut, 1948–49. Studied acting with Herbert Berghof and Uta Hagen, HB Studio, N.Y.C.; singing with Keith Davis, five years. Member of AEA; AFTRA; AGVA; SAG.

Pre-Theatre. Mail clerk, usher, stock boy, hospital aide.

Theatre. Mr. Reilly appeared in school plays while attending P.S. 163, Bronx, N.Y. He made his professional debut with the Metropolitan Players as the Detective in *Broken Dishes* (Tiverton, R.I., 1950); performed in stock at the Newport (R.I.) Casino Th. (Summers 1950–51); at the Starlight Th. (Kansas City, Mo., 1954–60); at the Playhouse on the Mall (Paramus, N.J.); the Woodstock (N.Y.) Playhouse; and the Matunuck (R.I.) Th.

He has appeared in the ELT production of *Best Foot Forward* (Lenox Hill Playhouse, N.Y.C., Feb. 22, 1956); *Saintliness of Marjory Kempe* (York Playhouse, Feb. 2, 1959); *Fallout* (Renata, May 20, 1959); *Lend an Ear* (Renata, Sept. 24, 1959); *The Billy Barnes Revue* (Carnegie Hall Playhouse, Oct. 20, 1959); *Parade* (Players, Jan. 20, 1960); in the ELT production of *The Inspector General* (Chanin Aud.); in the three one-act plays, *Three Times Three*, *The Apollo of Bellac*, and *Nightcar* (H B Studio, Apr. 10, 1956).

Mr Reilly made his Bway debut as Mr. Henkel in *Bye Bye Birdie* (Martin Beck Th., Apr. 14, 1960), and was understudy to Dick Van Dyke as Albert Peterson and to Paul Lynde as Mr. MacAfee, playing their roles 35 times. He appeared as Bud Frump in *How to Succeed in Business Without Really Trying* (46 St. Th., Oct. 14, 1961); and subsequently appeared as Cornelius Hakle in *Hello, Dolly!* (St. James, Jan. 16, 1964); Roger Summerhill in *Skyscraper* (Lunt-Fontanne Th., N.Y.C., Nov. 13, 1965); and the Messenger in *God's Favorite* (Eugene O'Neill Th., N.Y.C., Dec. 11, 1974).

Mr. Reilly taught a course in acting for musical comedy and opera at the HB (Herbert Berghof) Studio (N.Y.C.); and, on the West Coast, founded a drama school called The Faculty (Los Angeles, 1971).

Films. Mr. Reilly has appeared in *A Face in the Crowd* (WB, 1957); *Two Tickets to Paris* (Col., 1962); and *The Tiger Makes Out* (Col., 1967).

Television. He has appeared on the Ed Sullivan Show (CBS); Jack Paar Show (NBC); Tonight (NBC); Sid Caesar Show (CBS); Steve Allen Show (NBC); *The Broadway of Lerner and Loewe* (CBS); Car 54, Where Are You? (NBC); the Patty Duke Show (ABC); Farmer's Daughter (ABC); What's My Line? (CBS); the Les Crane Show (ABC); the Dean Martin Show (NBC); The Gold Diggers (NBC); played Claymore Gregg in The Ghost and Mrs. Muir (ABC); Hoo Doo in Lidsville (NBC); appeared in *First Miseries* (CBS); and is a regular on Match Game 1975 (CBS).

Night Clubs. He has performed in *Nightcap* (Showplace, N.Y.C., 1958); an act with Eileen Brennan, *Brennan and Reilly;* and wrote the night club act, *A Party with Andy Thomas* (Bon Soir, N.Y.C., Feb. 25, 1964).

Awards. Mr. Reilly has received the Antoinette Perry (Tony) Award (1962) for his performance as Bud Frump in *How to Succeed in Business Without Really Trying;* won the *Variety* NY Drama Critics Poll; Wheel Award (Carriage Club Award); and was nominated for an Antoinette Perry (Tony) Award (1964) for his performance as Cornelius Hakle in *Hello, Dolly!*.

REMICK, LEE. Actress. b. Lee Ann Remick, Dec. 14, 1935, Boston, Mass., to Frank E. and Margaret Patricia (Waldo) Remick. Father, retail store business; mother, actress. Grad. Hewitt Sch., N.Y.C., 1953; attended Barnard Coll., 1953. Married Aug. 3, 1957, to William A. Colleran (marr. dis. Nov. 23, 1969); one son, one daughter; Dec. 18, 1970, to William Rory Gowans, director. Member of AEA; SAG; AFTRA. Address: c/o Ashley-Famous Agency, 1301 Avenue of the Americas, New York, NY 10019.

Theatre. Miss Remick made her professional debut in stock, dancing in musicals (Cape Cod Melody Tent, Hyannis, Mass., Summer 1952); subsequently made her N.Y.C. debut as Lois Holly in *Be Your Age* (48 St. Th., Jan. 14, 1953).

She appeared in *Brigadoon* (Cape Cod Melody Tent; South Shore Music Circus, Cohasset, Mass., July 1953); danced in *Paint Your Wagon* (State Fair Music Hall, Dallas, Tex., Aug. 1953); appeared in *Show Boat*, *Annie Get Your Gun* and played Ado Annie in *Oklahoma!* (Fox River Valley Th., St. Charles, Ill., Aug. 1954); played the title role in a New England tour of *Jennie Kissed Me* (1955); the Girl in a New England tour of *The Seven Year Itch* (1956); Fay Apple in *Anyone Can Whistle* (Majestic, N.Y.C., Apr. 4, 1964); Susy Hendrix in *Wait Until Dark* (Ethel Barrymore Th., Feb. 2, 1966); and Grace in *Bus Stop* (Phoenix, London, Eng., May 12, 1976).

Films. Miss Remick made her film debut as Betty Lou in *A Face in the Crowd* (WB, 1957); subsequently appeared in *The Long Hot Summer* (20th-Fox, 1958); *These Thousand Hills* (20th-Fox, 1959); *Anatomy of a Murder* (Col., 1959); *Wild River* (20th-Fox, 1960); *Sanctuary* (20th-Fox, 1961); *Experiment in Terror* (Col., 1962); *Days of Wine and Roses* (WB, 1962); *The Running Man* (Col., 1963); *The Wheeler Dealers* (MGM, 1964); *Baby, the Rain Must Fall* (Col., 1965); *The Hallelujah Trail* (UA, 1965); *No Way to Treat a Lady* (Par., 1968); *The Detective* (20th-Fox, 1968); *Hard Contract* (20th-Fox, 1969); *A Severed Head* (Col., 1971); *Sometimes a Great Notion* (U, 1971); *Loot* (Cinevision, 1972); *A Delicate Balance* (Amer. Film Th., 1973); and *Hennessy* (Amer. Internatl., 1975).

Television. Among the many television productions in which Miss Remick appeared are *The Tempest* (Hallmark Hall of Fame (NBC, 1960); *Damn Yankees* (NBC, 1967); *The Man Who Came to Dinner* (Hallmark Hall of Fame, NBC, 1972); *Of Men and Women* (ABC, 1972); *And No One Could Save Her* (ABC, Feb. 1973); *The Blue Knight* (NBC, Nov. 1973); *QB VII* (ABC, Apr. 1974); *A Girl Named Sooner* (NBC, 1975); *Hustling* (ABC, Feb. 1975); and *Jennie: Lady Randolph Churchill* (Thames Television, England, 1975; PBS, Oct. 1975).

Awards. Miss Remick was nominated for an Academy (Oscar) Award for her performance in *Days of Wine and Roses* (1962); nominated for an Antoinette Perry (Tony) Award (1966) for her performance in *Wait Until Dark;* and in 1975 was named best actress by the British Society of Film and Television Arts.

RENAUD, MADELEINE. Actress. b. Feb. 21, 1900, Paris, France, to Louis and Pauline (Derignon) Renaud. Father, professor. Grad. Paris Conservatoire, 1923. Married to Charles Granval (marr. dis.); married Sept. 5, 1940, to Jean-Louis Barrault, director, actor. Address: 18 Avenue de President-Wilson, Paris 16e, France.

Theatre. In the US, with the Renaud-Barrault Co., Miss Renaud has appeared in three tours. For their first engagement (1952), at the Ziegfeld Th. (N.Y.C.), she appeared as Araminte in *Les fausses confidences* (Nov. 12); La Statue in *Baptiste* (Nov. 12–15; Dec. 8–13); Leni in *Le procès* (Nov. 17–19); Alcmène in *Amphitryon* which was presented on the same bill with *Les fourberies de Scapin* (Scapin's Pranks) (Nov. 20–22; Dec. 15–20); Amélie in *Occoupe-toi d'Amélie* (Nov. 24–26); and La Comtesse in *La répétition, ou l'amour puni* (Nov. 27–29). Their second engagement in the US was at the Winter Garden Th. (N.Y.C., 1957), where they presented *Christophe Colomb*, in which she played Isabelle, the Catholic (Jan. 30–Feb. 2); appeared as Celimène in *Le Misanthrope* (Feb. 7–9); Pierrette Bazire in *Les nuits de la colère (Nights of Fury)*, and Yvonne in *Feu la mère de madame (Dear Departed Mother-in-law)*, presented on the same bill (Feb. 11–13); Comtesse Diane de Belflor in *Le chien du jardinier* (Feb. 18). The third engagement was at NY City Ctr. (1964), where she played the Countess in *Le mariage de Figaro* (The Marriage of Figaro (Feb. 25); and a Narrator, Celimène, and Madeleine Bejart in *Salut à Molière*, which was presented on the same bill as *Le piéton de l'air* (The Pedestrian of the Air), in which she played Mme. Berenger (Mar. 3).

Mlle. Renaud has since appeared in the US as Winnie in *Oh! Les beaux jours* (Happy Days) for a two-week engagement (Cherry Lane Th. N.Y.C., Sept. 14, 1965); again in that role at the Barbizon-Plaza (Apr. 24, 1970); and as Claire Lannes in *L'Amante Anglaise* (Barbizon-Plaza, Apr. 14, 1971), which was later presented as *A Place without Doors*, with Mildred Dunnock.

Miss Renaud made her debut as Agnès in the Comédie Française production of *L'Ecole des femmes* (Paris, 1923); subsequently appeared with the same company in works by Molière, Marivaux, and Musset both in Paris and on tour. She played Ophelia in *Hamlet* (Paris, 1932); appeared in *Le chandelier; Les fausses confidences;* returned to the Comédie Française (1940) and appeared in their productions of *Les mal aimés, Le soulier de satin, La reine morte, Feu la mère de madame,* and *Les fiancés du Havre.*

In 1946, she and her husband, Jean-Louis Barrault, established their own company, Theatre de France. At the Th. de Marigny (Paris), they presented such plays as *Les fausses confidences,* in which she played Araminte; *Bacchus; Le procès* (The Trial), in which she played Leni; *Amphitryon,* in which she played Alcmène; *Occupe-toi d'Amélie* (Keep Your Eye on Amelie), in which she played Amélie; *La répétition, ou l'amour puni* (The Rehearsal or Love Punished), in which she played La Comtesse; *La Cerisaie* (The Cherry Orchard); *Le chien du jardinier* (The Gardner's Dog), in which she played Comtesse Diane de Belflor; *La vie parisienne; Le Misanthrope,* in which she played Celimène; *Christophe Colomb,* in which she played Isabelle, the Catholic; and *Judith.*

With the Th. de France, Mlle. Renaud has also played Mme. Beranger in *Le piéton de l'air (The Pedestrian of the Air;* Mar. 3, 1964); Winnie in *Oh! Les beaux jours (Happy Days),* including a single performance at the World's Fair (Brussels, Belgium, July 1964); Claire in *Il faut aller par les nuages (One Must Pass by the Clouds;* Th. de l'Odéon, Paris, Oct. 22, 1964); the Countess in *Le Mariage de Figaro* (Feb. 25, 1964); at the World Th. Season (Aldwych, London), played Mme. Berenger in *Le piéton de l'air* and Clarisse Ventroux in *Ne te promène donc pas toute nue (Don't Walk in the Nude);* on a double-bill together (Mar. 25, 1965), the Moon in *Le soulier de satin* (Apr. 1, 1965) and Winnie in *Oh! Les beaux jours* (Apr. 3, 1965); and in Paris, played the Mother in *Des journées entières dans les arbres (Whole Days in the Trees;* Dec. 22, 1965); Warda in *Les paravents (The Screens;* Apr. 18, 1966); Agnes in *A Delicate Balance;* in *Le Silence* and *Le Mensonge* (1966); and *Le tentation de S. Antoine* (1967).

In 1968, Mlle. Renaud and M. Barrault formed a new co., whose first production was M. Barrault's adaptation of *Rabelais* (Salle Firmin Gémier, Th. Natl. Populaire), followed by *L'Amante Anglaise,* in which Mlle. Renaud played Claire. Since then, Mlle. Renaud has played the title role in *La Mère* (Th. Récamier, 1970–71 season); appeared in *Where the Cows Drink* (Th. Récamier, 1972–73 season); in *Sous le vent des Baléares (Beneath the Balearic Wind;* performed in a tent beside the Gare d'Orsay, 1972–73 season); and as Maude in *Harold and Maude,* translated by Jean-Claude Carrière from the English play of Colin Higgins (1973–74 season).

Films. Mlle. Renaud has appeared in *Jean de la lune* (1932); *La belle marinière* (1932); *La Couturière de Luneville* (1932); *Mistigri* (1933); *La Maternelle* (1933); *Maria Chapdelaine* (1934); *Le ciel est à vous; Hélène* (1936); *L'Étrange M. Victor* (1938); *Remarques* (1940); *Lumière d'été* (1942); *Le plaisir (The House of Madame Tellier;* 1954); *Dialogues des Carmelites; The Longest Day* (20-Fox, 1962); and *The Devil by the Tail* (Lopert, 1969).

Awards. Mlle. Renaud received the rosette of the Chevalier de la Légion d'Honneur (France, 1965). For her role in the film, *Maria Chapdelaine,* she received Le Grand Prix du Cine (France, 1934); and in the US, she received a Drama Desk Award for her performance in the play *L'Amante Anglaise* (1971).

RENSHAW, EDYTH. Educator, director. b. Edyth May Renshaw, Nov. 10, 1901, Hennessey, Okla., to Charles T. and Julia Anne (Merris) Renshaw. Father, contractor, builder. Grad. Hennessey (Okla.) H.S., 1919; Southern Methodist Univ., A.B. (Phi Beta Kappa) 1923, M.A. 1924; Columbia Univ., Ph.D. 1950; attended New York Univ., 1927; State Univ. of Iowa, 1935. Member of SAA (admin. council, 1954–57, chairman of the committee on History of Speech Education 1954–57, chairman of Interest Group in History of Speech Education 1957–59, member of the Legislative Assembly, 1962–65); AETA; Southern Speech Assoc. (editor, book review section, *Southern Speech Journal,* 1952–54); Southwest Th. Conf.; Pi Lambda Theta; Kappa Delta Pi; AAUW; Zeta Phi Eta (3rd natl. vice-pres., 1930–34); Mortar Board; McCord Museum of the Th. of Dallas, Tex. (bd. of dir., 1932; chmn. of bd., 1950; curator, 1960–to date). Address: 3317 Rankin St., Dallas, TX 75205, tel. (214) 363-1005.

Miss Renshaw was director of theatre at Southern Methodist University from 1926, where she directed more than ninety-five student productions. She retired as professor emeritus in 1967, and was visiting professor at the Univ. of Washington (1967–68) and at South Dakota State Coll. (1971–72).

For the Alfresco Players (Dallas, Tex.), she was director, designer, and producer of *The Fan* (1933); director and producer of *The Would-Be Gentleman, Pygmalion and Galatea,* and *Mary Tudor* (1934). For the Civic Playhouse (Dallas, Tex.), she was director of *The Mad Woman of Chaillot* (1950), *Sailor Beware* (1951), and *Second Threshold* (1951).

For Zeta Phi Eta Dallas' Readers Theatre, Miss Renshaw has arranged and directed programs of light verse including Benét's *Western Star* and Kipling's *Just So Stories* (1953–71). For South Dakota State College Children's Theatre, Miss Renshaw directed her dramatization of *Wind in the Willows* (1971).

Published Works. Miss Renshaw published some poems in *The Prairie Pegasus* (1924), and wrote the section on "Five Private Schools of Speech" in *History of Speech Education in America* (1954).

Awards. She received a Carnegie Research Grant in 1950.

Recreation. Collecting theatre memorabilia, traveling.

RESNIK, MURIEL. Playwright. Married 1962 to Wallace Litwin, photographer (sep. 1969). Member of ALA; Authors Guild; PEN; Dramatists Guild; WGA, West.

Pre-Theatre. Novelist.

Theatre. Miss Resnik wrote *Any Wednesday* (Music Box Th., N.Y.C., Feb. 18, 1964).

Published Works. She wrote the novels *Life without Father, House Happy,* and *The Girl in the Turquoise Bikini.*

She has also had published *Any Wednesday* and *Son of Any Wednesday;* and her articles have appeared in *Vogue, Harper's Magazine, New York, Saturday Review* and *Town and Country.*

REVERE, ANNE. Actress. b. June 25, 1903, New York City, to Clinton Tristram and Harriette (Winn) Revere. Father, stock broker and writer. Grad. Westfield (N.J.) H.S., 1922; Wellesley Coll., B.A. 1926. Studied at the American Laboratory Th., 1926–28. Married April 11, 1935, to Samuel Rosen, director. Member of AFTRA; AEA; SAG (bd. mem., 1943–50; treas., 1945–46). Address: 9 Fox Lane, Locust Valley, NY 11560, tel. (516) 671-3718.

Theatre. Miss Revere made her stage debut as Lee Sin in *The Yellow Jacket* (Wellesley Coll. Th., Mass., Dec. 9, 1924); subsequently appeared as a walk-on in *The Bridal Veil* (American Laboratory Th., N.Y.C., Jan. 26, 1928); appeared in stock productions as Marcella in *Some Baby* (Montclair Th., N.J., Dec. 3, 1928); and Stella in *Mary's Other Husband* (Thornton, Riverpoint, R.I., Dec. 25, 1928).

With the Stuart Walker Stock Co., she appeared at the Taft Auditorium (Cincinnati, Ohio) as Francesca in *Enchanted April* (Apr. 1, 1929); Sylvia Marco in *Burlesque* (May 6, 1929); the Maid in *The Silver Cord* (June 3, 1929); Manuella in *The Squall* (June 10, 1929); Madame Pasquier in *Peter Ibbetson* (Oct. 21, 1929); Janet Ingleby in *Adriadne* (Dec. 17, 1929); Julia Murdoch in *The Goose Hangs High* (Dec. 23, 1929); Julia Seton in *Holiday* (Dec. 30, 1929); Mrs. Preston in *Enter Madame* (Jan. 27, 1930); Jane West in *The Perfect Alibi* (Mar. 8, 1930); Mrs. Farraday in *The Wisdom Tooth* (Mar. 17, 1930); Meg in *Little Women* (Mar. 24, 1930); Martha Winslow in *The Youngest* (Apr. 14, 1930); Miss Kittridge in *Secret Service* (Apr. 21, 1930); and in *Let Us Be Gay* (Apr. 29, 1930).

Miss Revere made her Bway debut as Katie in *The Great Barrington* (Avon, Feb. 19, 1931); at the Millbrook Th., N.Y., played Julia Seton in *Holiday* (June 22, 1931), Alice Peabody in *Its a Wise Child* (June 29, 1931), Lucille in *June Moon* (July 6, 1931), and June West in *Perfect Alibi* (July 13, 1931). She played Miss Pelt and a Nurse in *The Lady with a Lamp* (Maxine Elliott's Th., N.Y.C., Nov. 19, 1931); Miss Lehman in *Wild Waves* (Times Square Th., Feb. 19, 1932); appeared in stock as Lucille in *June Moon* (Westchester Playhouse, N.Y., June 13, 1932); Mammy Pleasant in *The Cat and the Canary* (Hampton Players, Southampton, L.I., N.Y., Aug. 1, 1932); and Freda in *Dangerous Corner* (Greenwich Th., Conn., July 31, 1933).

She appeared as Caroline Van Bret in *Double Door* (Ritz, N.Y.C., Sept. 21, 1933); and in stock at the County Th., Suffern, N.Y. (June 19, 1934), where she also played Cora Beale in *Round Trip* (July 3, 1934); Caroline Van Bret in *Double Door* (Cape Playhouse, Dennis, Mass., July 17, 1934; Nantucket Th., Mass., July 24, 1934); and Freda Chatfield in *Dangerous Corner* (County Th., Suffern, N.Y., Aug. 7, 1934).

She played Martha Dobie in *The Children's Hour* (Maxine Elliott's Th., N.Y.C., Nov. 20, 1934), and on tour (Sept. 1936–Jan. 1937); with her husband, organized the Surry Players (1937), appearing with them (Surry Th., Me., Summers 1937–39) as Candida in *Candida;* Celia in *As You Like It,* a role which she played on Bway (Ritz, Oct. 30, 1937); Mrs. Muskat in *Liliom;* the title role in *Hedda Gabler;* Kniertje in *The Good Hope;* Celia in *Art and Mrs. Bottle;* Mama Petkoff in *Arms and the Man;* and Masha in *The Three Sisters,* which she played on Bway (Longacre, Oct. 14, 1939). With her husband, she organized the Phoenix-Westwood Th. (Los Angeles, Calif., Sept., 1945), where she produced four plays, opening with *Candida,* in which she played the title role.

Miss Revere played Nellie Bawke in *Four Twelves Are 48* (48 St. Th., N.Y.C., Jan. 17, 1951); appeared in stock as Lady Cicely in *Captain Brassbound's Conversion* and Anita Alvero in *The Idea* (Brattle, Cambridge, Mass., Jan.–Feb. 1952); the Mother in *The World of Sholom Aleichem* (11 St. Th., Chicago, Ill., Feb. 25, 1954); the Mother in *The Illustrious Uncle* (Circle Th., Hollywood, Calif., Feb. 27, 1955); Mrs. Casside in *I Knock at the Door* (White Barn, Westport, Conn., Aug. 18, 1956); and Amanda in *The Glass Menagerie* (Durham Playhouse, N.C., June 30, 1958).

She appeared as Mattie Haines in *Cue for Passion* (Henry Miller's Th., N.Y.C., Nov. 25, 1958); Emma Ford in *Jolly's Progress* (Longacre, Dec. 5, 1959); Anna Bernier in *Toys in the Attic* (Hudson, Feb. 25, 1960), and on national tour (opened Playhouse, Wilmington, Del., Sept. 27, 1961; closed Biltmore, Los Angeles, Calif., Feb. 10, 1962); played Albertine Prine in *Toys in the Attic* (Williamstown Coll., Williamstown, Mass., Aug. 15, 1961); Aunt Hannah in *All the Way Home* (Playhouse-in-the-Park, Philadelphia, Pa., July 10, 1961); and at the Arena Stage (Washington, D.C.), Amanda in *The Glass Menagerie;* Aunt Rachel in a solo performance of a short story by Mark Twain, "A True Story"; the Mother in *The High School;* and Aunt Hannah in *All the Way Home* (1962–63).

She conducted a seminar on acting at Vassar Coll. (1962); appeared in *Mother Courage* (Purdue Univ., 1963); played the Nurse in *Romeo and Juliet* at Purdue Univ. and appeared again in *Mother Courage* in Olney, Md., (1964); played the Nurse in *Romeo and Juliet* and Mrs. Loman in *Death of a Salesman* (Atlanta, Ga., 1965); made a tour of O'Casey readings, *Night of the Dunce,* (Cherry Lane Th., N.Y.C., 1966); and appeared in *Long Day's Journey Into Night* (Purdue Univ., 1967).

Films. She made her film debut as Caroline Van Bret in *Double Door* (Par., 1934); subsequently appeared in *One Crowded Night* (RKO, 1940); *The Howards of Virginia* (Col., 1940); *Men of Boys Town* (MGM, 1941); *The Devil Commands* (Col., 1941); as Nadine Price in *Remember the Day* (20th-Fox,

1941); in *Flame of New Orleans* (U, 1941); *The Gay Sisters* (WB, 1942); *Are Husbands Necessary?* (Par., 1942); *Star Spangled Rhythm* (Par., 1942); *The Falcon Takes Over* (RKO, 1942); *Meet the Stewarts* (Col., 1942); *Old Acquaintance* (WB, 1942); Mother Soubirous in *The Song of Bernadette* (20th-Fox, 1943); *The Meanest Man in the World* (20th-Fox, 1943); *Standing Room Only* (Par., 1944); *Sunday Dinner for a Soldier* (20th-Fox, 1944); as the Queen in *Rainbow Island* (Par., 1944); Mrs. Brown in *National Velvet* (MGM, 1944); Crazy Mary in *The Thin Man Goes Home* (MGM, 1944); in *Keys of the Kingdom* (20th-Fox, 1944); *Fallen Angel* (20th-Fox, 1945); *Dragonwyck* (20th-Fox, 1946); as Mrs. Greene in *Gentleman's Agreement* (20th-Fox, 1947); in *The Shocking Miss Pilgrim* (20th-Fox, 1947); *Carnival in Costa Rica* (20th-Fox, 1947); as Madame Redcap in *Forever Amber* (20th-Fox, 1947); Mother in *Body and Soul* (UA, 1947); in *Scudda Hoo! Scudda Hay!* (20th-Fox, 1948); *The Secret Beyond the Door* (U, 1948); *Deep Waters* (20th-Fox, 1948); as Aunt Jane in *You're My Everything* (20th-Fox, 1949); Ma James in *The Great Missouri Raid* (Par., 1950); Mother in *A Place in the Sun* (Par., 1951); *Tell Me That You Love Me, Junie Moon* (Preminger Prod., 1969); and *Birch Interval* (Radnitz Mattel, 1974).

Television. Miss Revere made her television debut as Celia Bottle in *Art and Mrs. Bottle* in an experimental project (1939); subsequently played Bernarda Alba in *The House of Bernarda Alba* (WNTA, 1960); and the Mother in *The Purification* in *Four by Tennessee* (Play of the Week, WNTA, 1961). She also appeared in the TV serials A Time for Us (ABC, 1965–66); Edge of Night (CBS, 1969–70); Search for Tomorrow (CBS, 1970–71); and Guiding Light (1972); and in Two for the Money (ABC, 1971) and Six Million Dollar Man (U, 1974).

Awards. She received Academy (Oscar) Award nominations for her performance as Mother Soubirous in *The Song of Bernadette* (1943); as Mrs. Greene in *Gentleman's Agreement* (1947); an Academy (Oscar) Award for her performance as Mrs. Brown in *National Velvet* (1945); and won an Antoinette Perry (Tony) Award for her role as Anna Bernier in *Toys in the Attic* (1960).

Recreation. Swimming, walking, knitting.

RHODES, ERIK. Actor, director, singer. b. Ernest Rhoades Sharpe, Feb. 10, 1906, El Reno, Okla., to Ernest A. and Virginia (Rhoades) Sharpe. Father, insurance business, farm broker. Grad. Central H.S., Okla. City; Univ. of Oklahoma, A.B. (modern languages, music). Studied singing with William Schmidt, Univ. of Oklahoma; Sarah Robinson-Duff, N.Y.C.; Edouard Lippe, N.Y.C., two years; Harold Hurlbut, Hollywood, Calif., three years; piano with Josef Noll, Univ. of Oklahoma; dramatics with Frances Robinson-Duff, N.Y.C., three years. Served USAAF, PTO; rank, Capt. Member of AEA; SAG; AGVA; Phi Beta Kappa, Phi Delta Theta (pres. of chapter).

Theatre. Mr. Rhodes made his N.Y.C. debut, billed as Ernest Sharpe, in the role of Pedro in *A Most Immoral Lady* (Cort Th., Nov. 26, 1928); subsequently appeared in the revue *The Little Show* (Music Box, Apr. 30, 1929); and *Hey, Nonny, Nonny!* (Shubert, June 6, 1932).

As Erik Rhodes, he played Tonetti in *Gay Divorce* (Ethel Barrymore Th., N.Y.C., Nov. 29, 1932; Palace, London, Nov. 2, 1933); succeeded Gene Sheldon as Solomon Bundy during the pre-Bway tryout of *Sweet Bye and Bye* (opened Shubert, New Haven, Conn., Oct. 10, 1946; closed Erlanger, Philadelphia, Pa., Nov. 5, 1946); played Sidney Gat in *The Great Campaign* (Princess, N.Y.C., Mar. 30, 1947); appeared in the revue *Dance Me a Song* (Royale, Jan. 20, 1950); played Sir Cecil Pond in *Collector's Item* (Booth, Feb. 8, 1952); Hilaire Jussac in *Can-Can* (Shubert, May 7, 1953), and on a tour of summer theatres; Tyrone T. Tattersal in *Shinbone Alley* (Bway Th., N.Y.C., Apr. 13, 1957); the Governor in *Jamaica* (Imperial, Oct. 31, 1957); appeared in *Song of Norway* (Marine Th., Jones Beach, L.I., N.Y., 1958); repeated his role as Hilaire Jussac in *Can-Can* (Theatre-in-the-Park, N.Y.C., July 25, 1959), and on a tour of summer theatres (1959); appeared in *The King and I* (Beverly, Mass., Summer 1960); *Knights of Song* (St. Louis Opera, Mo.); *Can-Can* (Warren, Ohio); and played Anson Lee in *How To Make a Man* (Brooks Atkinson Th., N.Y.C., Feb. 2, 1961).

He played in *The King and I* (Lambertville Music Circus, N.J., 1961); toured in *Gentlemen Prefer Blondes* (1961); repeated his role as Hilaire Jussac in *Can-Can* (Meadowbrook Dinner Th., N.J.); appeared in *Around the World in Eighty Days* (St. Louis Municipal Opera, Mo., world premiere 1962); and in *Can-Can* (Pittsburgh Civic Light Opera, Pa.).

He appeared in *Witness for the Prosecution* (Canal Fulton, Ohio); repeated his role in *Can-Can* (Totowa, N.J.); appeared in *Call Me Madam* (Atlanta, Ga.); and again appeared in *Can-Can* (Framingham, Mass.; Wallingford, Conn.; Warwick, R.I.); and succeeded (Sept. 9, 1963) John Carradine as Lycus in *A Funny Thing Happened on the Way to the Forum* (Alvin, N.Y.C., May 8, 1962) and on tour. He was Benjamin Goodman in *Remains To Be Seen* (Royal Poinciana Playhouse, Palm Beach, Fla., Jan. 31, 1966; Paper Mill Playhouse, Millburn, N.J., Feb. 15, 1966); was Florenz Ziegfeld, Jr. in *Funny Girl* (Coconut Grove Playhouse, Miami, Fla., Mar. 14, 1967; Parker Playhouse, Fort Lauderdale, Fla., Apr. 3, 1967); Dr. Conrad Fuller in *On a Clear Day You Can See Forever* (Parker, Apr. 10, 1967; Coconut Grove, Apr. 18, 1967); played Zoltan Karpathy in a revival of *My Fair Lady* (NY City Ctr., June 13, 1968); the Captain, Max, George Wague, and the Reporter in *Colette* (Ellen Stewart Th., Oct. 14, 1970); and Pyotr Sorin in *The Seagull* (Roundabout Th., Dec. 18, 1973).

Films. Mr. Rhodes appeared in *The Gay Divorcee* (RKO, 1934); *A Night at the Ritz* (WB, 1935); *Top Hat* (RKO, 1935); *Woman Chases Man* (UA, 1937); *One Rainy Afternoon* (UA, 1937); *Fight for Your Lady* (RKO, 1937); and *On Your Toes* (WB, 1939).

Television. He first appeared in *Great Catherine;* appeared on his own shows, Wonder Boy and Second Cup of Coffee; and on the series, The Secret Storm (CBS, 1962–63).

Night Clubs. He appeared in N.Y.C. at One Fifth Ave., The Living Room (1959), and the Waldorf-Astoria (1962); and in St. Louis (Mo.), at the Chase-Park Plaza Hotel (1962).

Other Activities. He was guest reader at the Walt Whitman Centennial (Camden, N.J., 1955).

Recreation. Swimming, horseback riding, music.

RHYNSBURGER, H. DONOVAN. Educator. b. Henry Donovan Rhynsburger, Apr. 15, 1903, Pella, Iowa, to H. S. and Grace Edith (Wolf) Rhynsburger. Father, poultry processor. Grad. Oskaloosa (Iowa) H.S., 1921; Univ. of Iowa, B.S. (commerce) 1925; attended Chicago Arts Sch., 1927; grad. Yale Univ. Sch. of Drama, M.F.A. 1938. Married Aug. 12, 1931, to Gertrude Eleanor Minton; one daughter. Member of ANTA; AETA; AAUP; Rotary Club (pres., 1951); Omicron Delta Kappa. Address: 1018 Westwinds Court, Columbia, MO 65201, tel. (314) 449-5748.

Mr. Rhynsburger was chairman of the department of speech and dramatic art at the Univ. of Missouri (1957–61), where he has been instructor (1925–28); assistant professor (1928–40); associate professor (1940–45); and professor of speech and dramatic art (1945–to date).

From 1941–73, Mr. Rhynsburger was director of dramatics at the Univ. of Missouri and directed productions including *Wind in the Stars*, by Mary Paxton Keeley (1932), *Bachelor Beware*, by Anne Ferring Weatherly (1940). He retired in May 1973 as professor emeritus.

Recreation. Gardening, refinishing old furniture.

RIBMAN, RONALD. Playwright. b. May 28, 1932, New York City, to Samuel and Rosa (Lerner) Ribman. Father, attorney. Educ. Brooklyn Coll., 1950–51. Grad. Univ. of Pittsburgh, B.B.A. 1954; M. Litt. 1958; Ph.D. 1962. US Army, 1954–56. Married 1967 to Alice Rosen; one son, one daughter. Member of P.E.N.; WGA; Dramatists Guild. Address: (home) 50 W. 96th St., New York, NY 10025, tel. (212) 865-9814; (bus.) Flora Roberts Agency, 116 E. 59th St., New York, NY 10022, tel. (212) EL 5-4165.

Pre-Theatre. Mr. Ribman was assistant professor of English at Otterbein Coll.

Theatre. Mr. Ribman's produced plays include *Harry, Noon and Night* (St. Clements Ch., N.Y.C., Mar. 17, 1965; Pocket Th., May 5, 1965); *The Journey of the Fifth Horse* (St. Clements Ch., Apr. 21, 1966); *The Ceremony of Innocence* (St. Clements Ch., Jan. 1, 1968); *Passing Through from Exotic Places* (Sheridan Square Playhouse, Dec. 7, 1969); *Fingernails Blue as Flowers* (American Place Th., Dec. 6, 1971); *A Break in the Skin* (World premiere, Yale Rep. Th., New Haven, Conn., Oct. 13, 1972); and *The Poison Tree* (Theater in the Park, Philadelphia, Pa., 1973).

Films. Mr. Ribman wrote the script for *The Angel Levine* (UA, 1970).

Television. Plays by Mr. Ribman that have been seen on television include *The Journey of the Fifth Horse* (PBS, 1966); *The Final War of Olly Winter* (CBS Playhouse, 1967); *The Most Beautiful Fish* (PBS, 1969); and *The Ceremony of Innocence* (PBS, 1970; Granada TV, England, 1974).

Awards. Mr. Ribman received Rockefeller (1966, 1968), Guggenheim (1970), C.A.P.S. (1972), and National Foundation for the Arts (1973) grants in playwriting and a Rockefeller Foundation Award (1975) for "sustained contribution to the American theatre." *The Journey of the Fifth Horse* received a *Village Voice* Off-Bway (Obie) Award as the best off-Bway play of 1965–66; *The Final War of Olly Winter* received an Antoinette Perry (Tony) Award nomination (1969); and *The Poison Tree* won the Strawhat Award (1973) as best play of the summer stock season.

RICHARDS, BEAH. Actress. b. Vicksburg, Miss. Attended Dillard Univ. Studied at San Diego (Calif.) Community Th. Member of AEA; SAG.

Theatre. Miss Richards appeared as the Grandmother in *Take a Giant Step* (Jan Hus House, N.Y.C., Sept. 25, 1956); subsequently understudied Claudia McNeil as Lena Younger in *A Raisin in the Sun* (Ethel Barrymore Th., Mar. 11, 1959); played Viney in *The Miracle Worker* (Playhouse, Oct. 19, 1959); and Idella Landy in *Purlie Victorious* (Cort, Sept. 28, 1961); appeared as Sister Margaret in the world premiere of *The Amen Corner* (Robertson Playhouse, Los Angeles, 1963–64 season); played The Woman in *Arturo Ui* (Lunt-Fontanne, N.Y.C., Nov. 11, 1963); repeated her performance in *The Amen Corner* (Ethel Barrymore Th., Apr. 15, 1965); played Addie in *The Little Foxes* (Vivian Beaumont Th., Oct. 26, 1967); again played Sister Margaret in *The Amen Corner* (Th. of Being, Los Angeles, 1966–67 season); Lena Younger in *A Raisin in the Sun* (Inner City Rep. Co., Oct. 1968); and appeared in *The Crucible* (Ahmanson, Dec. 5, 1972).

Films. She has appeared in *The Miracle Worker* (UA, 1962); *Gone Are the Days* (Hammer, 1964); *Guess Who's Coming to Dinner* (Col., 1967); *In the Heat of the Night* (UA, 1967); *Hurry Sundown* (Par., 1967); *The Great White Hope* (20th-Fox, 1970); and *The Biscuit Eater* (BV, 1972).

Television. Miss Richards' appearances include Dr. Kildare (NBC); The Big Valley (ABC); I Spy (NBC); Hawaii Five-O (CBS); Ironside (ABC); Room 222 (ABC); It Takes a Thief (ABC); On Stage (ABC); Sanford and Son (NBC); *Footsteps* (CBS); and *The Autobiography of Miss Jane Pittman*. .

Other Activities. In her one-woman show, *An Evening with Beah Richards*, she includes poetry from her collection entitled *A Black Woman Speaks*. .

Awards. She received *Best Plays' citation for her performance in The Amen Corner.* .

RICHARDS, DAVID BRYANT. Drama critic. b. Oct. 1, 1942, Concord, Mass., to Gordon Draper and Elizabeth Wilson (Crabb) Richards. Father, building contractor. Attended Occidental College, B.A.; Middlebury College, M.A.;

Catholic Univ., M.A. Member of AFTRA; Newspaper Guild. Address: (home) 1734 P St., N.W., Apt. 26, Washington, DC 20036, tel. (202) 667-8709; (bus.) Washington *Star-News, Washington, DC 20003, tel. (202) 484-4320.*

Mr. Richards is drama critic for the Washington (D.C.) *Star-News* (1972–to date). He was formerly articles editor (1971–72) for that newspaper's Sunday supplement, *Washington.* Prior to his positions with the newspaper, he was a radio announcer for The Voice of America; critic-at-large for WGMS radio, Washington, D.C.; college professor at Howard Univ.; and a Peace Corps volunteer to the Ivory Coast.

Awards. Mr. Richards is a member of Phi Beta Kappa.

Recreation. Swimming.

RICHARDS, LLOYD. Director, actor, educator. b. Lloyd George Richards, Toronto, Ontario, Can., to Albert George and Rose (Coote) Richards. Father, carpenter. Grad. Northwestern H.S., Detroit, Mich.; Wayne State Univ., B.A. (theatre arts) 1944. Studied acting at Paul Mann Actors Workshop, N.Y.C. (1949–52); assistant dir. (1952–60). Married Oct. 11, 1957, to Barbara Davenport; two sons. Served with USAAF, 1944–45; rank, Cadet Pilot. Member of AEA; SAG; SSD&C (pres., 1970–to date). Address: (home) 18 W. 95th St., New York, NY 10025; (bus.) National Playwrights Conference, O'Neill Center, 1860 Broadway, New York, NY 10023, tel. (212) 246-1485.

Mr. Richards is artistic director of the O'Neill Center National Playwrights Conference (1969–to date); professor in the Department of Theatre and Cinema at Hunter Coll. (N.Y.C., 1972–to date); and teacher at the National Theatre Institute (1970–to date). Previously, he taught at his own studio (1962–72); was head of actor training at NY Univ. School of the Arts (1966–72); taught for the Conn. Commission on the Arts training program (1970); The Negro Ensemble Co. (1967–68); Rhode Island Univ. (1967); Boston Univ. (1967); and was assistant director and teacher with Paul Mann's Actor's Workshop (N.Y.C., 1952–62).

Pre-Theatre. Social work.

Theatre. Mr. Richards made his N.Y.C. debut as Pee Wee in an ELT production of *Plant in the Sun* (Wideman Studios, 1948); subsequently appeared as Oz in *Freight* (Fulton, Apr. 26, 1950); as Iago in William Marshall's *Othello,* a stage reading (played churches in greater N.Y.C.); and as Carr in *Winterset* (ELT).

As resident director of the Great Lakes Drama Festival (1954), he staged nine productions. From 1955–57, he was resident director at the Northland Playhouse (Detroit, Mich.); played Perry Hall in *The Egghead* (Ethel Barrymore Th., N.Y.C., Oct. 9, 1957); directed *A Raisin in the Sun* (Ethel Barrymore Th., Mar. 11, 1959; Adelphi, London, Eng., Aug. 4, 1959); *The Long Dream* (Ambassador, N.Y.C., Feb. 17, 1960); *The Moon Besieged* (Lyceum, N.Y.C., Dec. 5, 1962); and in stock, directed *Desperate Hours* (Mineola Playhouse, L.I., N.Y.; Westport Country Playhouse, Conn.).

Mr. Richards directed *I Had a Ball* (Martin Beck Th., N.Y.C., Dec. 15, 1964); *Lower Than the Angels* (American Place Th., Jan. 30, 1965); *Ghosts* (Playhouse in the Park, Cincinnati, Apr. 7, 1965); *The Amen Corner,* which came under the aegis of the US Department of State's cultural presentation program, its tour including Israel (Habimah Hall, Tel Aviv, Aug. 8, 1965), Switzerland, Austria (Vienna Festival), France (Théâtre des Nations, Paris), Germany, Scotland, (Edinburgh Festival, Lyceum Th., Aug. 23, 1965), and England (Saville, London, Oct. 12, 1965); *The Yearling* (Alvin, N.Y.C., Dec. 10, 1965); *Bedford Forest* (Eugene O'Neill Memorial Th., Waterford, Conn., Aug. 5, 1966); *Who's Got His Own* (American Place Th., N.Y.C., Sept. 30, 1966); *The Ox Cart* (Greenwich Mews, Dec. 19, 1966; and the Puerto Rican Traveling Th., (opened Aug. 2, 1967; closed Aug. 26, 1967, N.Y.C.); *Freeman* (American Place Th., Feb. 5, 1973); "The Past Is the Past" and "Going Through Changes," billed as *Two Plays by Richard Wesley* (Billie Holliday Th., N.Y.C., Dec. 29, 1973).

For the O'Neill Memorial Theatre Center (Waterford, Conn.), he directed (1966–68) *Don't End My Song Before I Sing; Redemption Center; Summertree; Just Before Morning; A Man Around the House;* and *Bedford Forrest;* and, for the Tanglewood (Mass.) Writer's Conference (1967), directed *That's the Game, Jack.*

Mr. Richards directed *The Hide and Seek Odyssey of Madeline Gimple* for the Conn. School System's Project Create (1969); and created and directed The Amer. Shakespeare Festival's theatre demonstration programs (1971–74).

He has been guest director at the NADSA Conf. (Tuskegee, Ala., 1961); Boston (Mass.) Univ. (1962); St. Mary's Coll. (Notre Dame, Ind., 1963–64); and Univ. of No. Carolina (1973).

Mr. Richards directed the NAACP tribute to Duke Ellington, *Sold on Soul* (1970); and The Miss Black America Pageant (Madison Sq. Garden, N.Y.C., 1969–70).

He was a founding member of two theatres: "These 20 People," which became The Actors Co., a repertory theatre (Detroit, Mich.) and the Greenwich Mews Th. (N.Y.C.).

Television and Radio. Mr. Richards began his radio career with the Wayne Univ. Radio Guild (Detroit, Mich.); was narrator for the Little Church on the Air (WWJ, Detroit); and a disc jockey (WJLB, Detroit). In N.Y.C., he performed on Helen Trent; The Greatest Story Ever Told; Theatre Guild of the Air; Up for Parole; Jungle Jim; My True Story; Inheritance; Murder by Experts; Mysterious Traveller; Front Page Drama; and Mr. Joll's Hotel for Pets.

On television, he has appeared on Studio One (CBS); The Guiding Light (CBS); Silver Th. (NBC); Philco Television Playhouse (NBC); We the People; Lux Video Th. (CBS); Famous Jury Trials; The Web (CBS); Hallmark Hall of Fame (NBC); Pulitzer Television Playhouse; and the Somerset Maugham Playhouse (ABC).

He has directed Wide World of Entertainment (ABC); GE Theatre; You Are There (CBS); and Visions (KCET).

Other Activities. Mr. Richard is a charter fellow of the Black Academy of Arts and Letters; has served on the theatre panel of the National Endowment of the Arts (co-chmn.); and the NY State Council on the Arts; as secretary of board of directors of the Theatre Development Fund; as a member of the Rockefeller Foundation Playwrights Selection Committee; is on the advisory councils for the Theatre Hall of Fame, the Bicentennial at Kennedy Center, The National Council on Theatre and the Humanities, The Street Theatre, Inc., and Double Image Theatre; and on the board of the US Bicentennial World Theatre Festival.

He has lectured extensively to academic and theatre groups, and, as an American theatre specialist for the cultural presentations division of the US Dept. of State, conducted a fact-finding theatre survey of, and lectured in, Uganda, Zambia, Kenya, and Ghana.

Awards. Mr. Richards received the Wayne Univ. Alumni Award (1962) for theatre achievement.

RICHARDSON, HOWARD. Playwright, actor, director, producer, educator. b. Howard Dixon Richardson, Dec. 2, 1917, Spartanburg, S.C., to Frank Howard and Clara (Dixon) Richardson. Father, physician. Grad. Asheville Farm Sch., Swananoah, N.C., 1934; attended Mars Hill Coll., 1934–36; grad. Univ. of North Carolina, A.B. 1938; attended Alliance Française, Paris, Fr., diplomé degré avancé, 1939; Univ. of North Carolina, M.A. 1940; State Univ. of Iowa, playwriting fellowship, 1940–42; Univ. of Paris (de la Sorbonne), 1949–50; State Univ. of Iowa, Ph.D. 1960. Studied playwriting with Frederick H. Koch and Paul Green, Univ. of North Carolina. Relatives in theatre: great-uncle, Thomas Dixon, Jr., playwright. Served USAAF, 1941–42; Field Rep., OWI, 1942–45. Member of Dramatists Guild; AEA; New Dramatists Committee; ANTA; ELT; Intl. Brotherhood of Magicians. Address: 207 Colombus Ave., New York, NY 10023, tel. (212) TR 4-2616.

Theatre. While a student at Mars Hill (N.C.) Coll., Mr. Richardson made his acting debut as Tesman in *Hedda Gabler* (Sept. 1935), and wrote his first play, *Top Hats and Tenements* (Apr. 1936). He played Jelliwell in a stock production of *Springtime for Henry* (Town Players, North Leeds, Me., July 1940). He wrote *Barbara Allen* (Univ. Th., Iowa City, Iowa, 1942); and with William Berney, rewrote and retitled it *Dark of the Moon* (Brattle Hall, Cambridge, Mass., July 1944; 46 St. Th., N.Y.C., Mar. 14, 1945; Lyric, Hammersmith, London, Mar. 9, 1949), which was revived as the first production of the Loft Players, later known as Circle in the Square (Circle in the Square Th., Dec. 1950); and again by Temple Productions (Carnegie Hall Playhouse, Feb. 26, 1958; and the Mercer Shaw Arena Th., April 3, 1970).

Mr. Richardson wrote, with Frances Goforth, *Catch on the Wing* (Playhouse, New Milford, Conn., July 1948); wrote with Mr. Berney, *Sodom, Tennessee* (Hayloft, Allentown, Pa., July 1949), and *Design for a Stained Glass Window* (Mansfield, N.Y.C., Jan. 23, 1950); with Mr. Goforth, wrote *Le chat dans le cage* (Th. Noctambule, Paris, Feb. 12, 1951), produced in the U.S. as *The Cat in the Cage* (Hayloft, Allentown, Pa., July 1953); and *Widow's Walk* (Barter Th., Abingdon, Va., July 1952); wrote with Mr. Berney, *Mountain Fire* (Royal Court, Liverpool, May 1954; Haymarket, London, Feb. 3, 1955); *Protective Custody* (Ambassador, N.Y.C., Dec. 28, 1956); *Giselle* (Mountainview, London, July 9, 1957); and *Birds of Prey* (Guthsville Th., Pa., Aug. 1962). His play, *The Laundry,* was adapted from David Guerdon's *La Buanderie* (Gate, N.Y.C., Feb. 13, 1963). He has also written *Brink of Brimstone* (Clemson Univ., S.C., Nov. 1973).

Television. He adapted his play, *Dark of the Moon* (NBC, 1946); wrote and adapted scripts for the Circle Th. (NBC, 1946–47); wrote, with William Berney, *My Friends the Birds* (Heinz Playhouse, ABC, 1954); was author and, with Robert Wild, associate producer of the American Inventory series (NBC, Jan.–Dec. 1956); wrote, with Frances Goforth, *Ark of Safety* (Goodyear Playhouse, NBC, Apr. 1958); and wrote with Ella Gerber, *Aftermath of a Conviction* (True Story, NBC, Mar. 1960).

Other Activities. Mr. Richardson has been an associate professor in the department of drama at San Fernando Valley State Coll. (1964–65); and in the department of speech at the Univ. of Oregon (1963–64). Previously, he was an instructor in playwriting at the Abbe Drama Sch., (N.Y.C., 1946–48); a visiting lecturer for ANTA at colleges, theatre clubs, etc. (1952–to date); and a lecturer at Queens Coll. (1961–62).

For the Upward Bound Program, he served as head of the Speech Dept. at the Coll. of the Virgin Islands (St. Thomas, Summer 1966); and was artist in residence at the State Univ. of No. Dakota (1972). He has led conducted tours through Europe and the Orient for various commercial agencies, and for the US State Dept. (1966–to date).

Awards. Mr. Richardson received the Carolina Playmaker Mask for playwriting (Univ. of North Carolina, 1938); the Purple Mask for playwriting (State Univ. of Iowa, 1941); the Maxwell Anderson Award for best poetic drama of 1942 for his play, *Barbara Allen,* later revised with W. Berney, as *Dark of the Moon; Dark of the Moon* received several off-Bway awards (1951).

Recreation. Magic, experimental hypnotism in speech therapy and instructing in yoga.

RICHARDSON, JACK. Playwright, novelist. b. Jack Carter Richardson, Feb. 18, 1935, New York City, to Arthur and Marjorie Richardson. Grad. Collegiate Sch., N.Y.C., 1951; Columbia Univ., B.A. 1957; Univ. of Munich, Ger., 1958. Married Aug. 24, 1957, to Anne Gail Roth; one daughter. Served with US Army. Member of Dramatists Guild, WGA. Address: 32 W. 69th St., New York, NY 10023, tel. (212) SU 7-1360.

Theatre. Mr. Richardson wrote *The Prodigal* (Downtown Th., N.Y.C., Feb. 11, 1960); *Gallows Humor* (Gramercy Arts, Apr. 11, 1961; Cherry Lane, Feb. 18, 1962); *Lorenzo* (Plymouth, Feb. 14, 1963); and *Xmas in Las Vegas*(Ethel Barrymore Th., Nov. 4, 1965).

Television. Mr. Richardson's *Gallows Humor* was produced for New York Television Theater (NET, 1965).

Published Works. *The Prison Life of Harris Filmore* (NY Graphic Soc., 1969).

Awards. For *The Prodigal*, Mr. Richardson won the Vernon Rice Award and *The Village Voice* off-Bway (Obie) Award (1960).

RICHARDSON, LEE. Actor. b. Lee David Richard, Sept. 11, 1926, Chicago, Ill., to Jacob and Mamie (Golden) Richard. Father, artist, musician. Grad. Sullivan H.S., Chicago, Ill., 1944; attended Loyola Univ., 1944; Univ. of Illinois, 1946–47; grad. Goodman Memorial Th. Sch. of Drama, B.F.A. 1951. Studied acting with Uta Hagen (four years). Married Feb. 12, 1961, to Elane Rower, actress. Served USAAF, 1944–46. Relative in theatre; aunt, Helen Golden, opera singer. Member of AEA (council mbr., 1963–68); AFTRA; SAG.

Theatre. Mr. Richardson first appeared at the Goodman Memorial Th. Sch. of Drama, in *Hamlet, Oedipus Rex, Arms of the Man, All My Sons, Joan of Lorraine, Jason, This Happy Breed*, and *The Linden Tree* (1948–51). During this period he appeared in stock productions at the Lake Zurich (Ill.) Th. (Summer 1948); the Pinetop Th. (Elkhart Lake, Wis., Summer 1949); and Luzerne Th. (Lake Geneva, Wis., Summer 1950); and performed at the Chevy Chase Th. (Chicago, Ill., Summer 1951) in *There's Always Juliet; Come Back, Little Sheba; Skylark;* and *John Loves Mary.*

His first N.Y.C. appearance was as John Buchanan, Jr., in *Summer and Smoke* (Circle in the Square, Apr. 24, 1952); subsequently played Joey Percival in the national tour of *Misalliance* (Oct. 1953–Feb. 1954); performed in stock in *The Cocktail Party* (Barter Th., Abingdon, Va., June 1954); and *Quiet Wedding*(John Drew Th., East Hampton, L.I., N.Y., July 1954); appeared as Bertrand De Poulengey and succeeded Earl Hyman as Dunois in *Saint Joan* (Phoenix, N.Y.C., Sept. 11, 1956); played Leone in *Volpone* (Rooftop, Jan. 7, 1957); Reverend Phipps in *The Legend of Lizzie* (54 St. Th., Feb. 9, 1959), Ross in *Macbeth*(Cambridge Drama Festival, Mass., Aug. 1959); Ben Gant in the national tour of *Look Homeward, Angel* (opened Playhouse, Wilmington, Del., Oct. 21, 1959); was standby for Anthony Quinn as Henry II in *Becket* (St. James, N.Y.C., Oct. 5, 1960); played the Intern in *The Death of Bessie Smith*, as part of the bill with *The American Dream* and *Bartleby*(York Playhouse, Jan. 24, 1961); and Father Francis in *Someone from Assisi*, as part of the bill, entitled *Plays for Bleecker Street* (Circle in the Square, Jan. 11, 1962).

With the NY Shakespeare Festival Co., he played Bassanio in *The Merchant of Venice*(Delacorte, June 13, 1962) and Edgar in *King Lear*(Delacorte, Aug. 9, 1962). He appeared as Wilfred Oliver in *Lord Pengo* (Royale, Nov. 19, 1962); joined the Minnesota Th. Co. (Tyrone Guthrie Th., Minneapolis, Minn.), where he played Claudius in *Hamlet* (May 7, 1963); Roday in *The Three Sisters*(June 18, 1963); Biff in *Death of a Salesman* (July 16, 1963); the Bishop of Beauvais in *Saint Joan* (May 12, 1964); Tom in *The Glass Menagerie* (June 1, 1964); Henry Tudor in *Richard III* (May 10, 1965); Lopahin in *The Cherry Orchard* (June 15, 1965); Valere in *The Miser* (Sept. 7, 1965); Mr. Antrobus in *The Skin of Our Teeth* (May 31, 1966); and was in *The Doctor's Dilemma* (Sept. 6, 1966).

He was in *The Eccentricities of a Nightingale* (Goodman Memorial Th., Chicago, Ill., Feb. 5, 1967); appeared with the Minnesota Th. Co. (Tyrone Guthrie Th.) in *The Shoemaker's Holiday* (June 1, 1967); *THieves' Carnival* (June 2, 1967); and *The House of Atreus* (June 21, 1967), in which he played the Watchman in *Agamemnon* and Apollo in *The Furies*, roles he repeated during the N.Y.C. engagement of the company (Billy Rose Th., Dec. 17, 1968). Mr. Richardson also appeared with the Minnesota Th. Co. (Crawford Livingston Th., St. Paul, Minn.) in *Tango*(Dec. 29, 1967) and *Enrico IV*(Feb. 16, 1968); and (Tyrone Guthrie Th., Minneapolis) played Max in *The Homecoming* (July 8, 1969); Mannon in *Mourning Becomes Electra* (Aug. 19, 1969); and Astrov in *Uncle Vanya* (Oct. 7, 1969). He was at the American Shakespeare Festival, Stratford, Conn., as Iago in *Othello*(June 17, 1970; transferred to ANTA Th., N.Y.C., Sept. 14, 1970) and Anderson in *The Devil's Disciple* (June 19, 1970); appeared with Yale Repertory Th., New Haven, Conn., in *The Revenger's Tragedy* (Nov. 19, 1970) and *Macbeth* (Feb. 18, 1971); and at Stratford, Conn., was Ford in *The Merry Wives of Windsor* (June 12, 1971) and Mannon in *Mourning Become Electra*(June 16, 1971). He played Lord Bothwell in *Vivat! Vivat Regina!* (Broadhurst, N.Y.C., Jan. 20, 1972); returned to the American Shakespeare Theatre (formerly Festival), Stratford, Conn., to play Undershaft in *Major Barbara* (June 27, 1972) and Enobarbus in *Antony and Cleopatra* (June 23, 1972); and appeared as Lord Green in *The Jockey Club Stakes* (Cort, Jan. 24, 1973). Again at Stratford, Conn., he was in *Measure for Measure*(June 2, 1973); *Macbeth* (July 6, 1973); and *Julius Caesar* (Aug. 1, 1973); he played Alan Harrison in *Find Your Way Home*(Brooks Atkinson Th., N.Y.C., Jan. 2, 1974); was in *Mother Courage and Her Children* (McCarter Th., Princeton, N.J., Feb. 13, 1975); and at the American Shakespeare Th., Stratford, Conn., played Kent in *King Lear* (June 14, 1975) and Mr. Webb in *Our Town* (June 16, 1975).

Films. Mr. Richardson appeared in *Middle of the Night* (Col., 1959).

Television. He made his debut as a member of the Omnibus repertory company (CBS 1954) appearing in *The Man Who Married a Dumb Wife, Contrasts, The Diamond*, and *The John Adams Story;* subsequently performed in *Almanac of Liberty* (Studio One, CBS, 1954); *Contrasts* (Omnibus, CBS, 1954); and in *The Silent Women* (Studio One, CBS, 1955); and has appeared on the series, The Brighter Day (CBS, 1958); and played Dr. Walton on the series, Search for Tomorrow (CBS, 1960–61).

Awards. Mr. Richardson was nominated for an Antoinette Perry (Tony) Award as best supporting actor (1972) for his performance in *Vivat! Vivat Regina!*

Recreation. Music, photography, art.

RICHARDSON, SIR RALPH. Actor. b. Ralph David Richardson, Dec. 19, 1902, Cheltenham, Gloucestershire, England, to Arthur and Lydia (Russell) Richardson. Father, artist. Attended Xaverion Coll., Brighton, England. Married 1922, to Muriel Hewitt (dec. 1942); married 1944, to Meriel Forbes, one son. Served British Fleet Arm, 1939–44; rank, Lt. Comdr. Member of AEA; SAG; Arts Council of Great Britain (1951–to date). Address: (home) 1 Chester Terrace, London N.W.1, England; (bus.) International Famous Agency, New York City and London.

Theatre. Sir Ralph Richardson made his first appearance in the US playing Mercutio and the Chorus in *Romeo and Juliet* (Martin Beck Th., Dec. 23, 1935), also touring in it; with the Old Vic Co., at the Century Th., he played Sir John Falstaff in *Henry IV, Part 1* (May 6, 1946), and *Henry IV, Part 2*(May 7, 1946), Voynitsky in *Uncle Vanya*(May 13, 1946), Tiresias in *Oedipus*, and Lord Burleigh in *The Critic* (May 20, 1946); General St. Pé in *The Waltz of the Toreadors* (Coronet, Jan. 17, 1957); and Sir Peter Teazle in *The School for Scandal* (Majestic, Jan. 24, 1963).

He made his debut with F. R. Growcott's St. Nicholas Players (St. Nicholas Hall, Brighton, England, playing a Gendarme in *Jean Valjean* (Jan. 10, 1921); Cuthbert in *The Farmer's Romance* (Jan. 18, 1921); Banquo and Macduff in *Macbeth* (Mar. 29, 1921); the Father in *The Moon-Children*, and Tranio in *The Taming of the Shrew* (May 25, 1921); appeared in these roles with Growcott's Repertory Co. (Shakespearean Playhouse, Brighton); also playing Malvolio in *Twelfth Night* (June 24, 1921), Mr. Bumble and Bill Sikes in *Oliver Twist*(July 18, 1921), and Defarge Stryver, and the Marquis in *A Tale of Two Cities* (Aug. 1, 1921).

With the Charles Doran Shakespeare Co., he toured England and Ireland, as Lorenzo in *The Merchant of Venice*(opened Marina Th., Lowestoff, Aug. 29, 1921), Guilderstern and Bernardo in *Hamlet*, a Pedant in *The Taming of the Shrew*, a Soothsayer and Strato in *Julius Caesar*, Oliver in *As You Like It*, Scroop and Gower in *Henry V*, Angus and Macduff in *Macbeth*, Francisco and Antonio in *The Tempest*, Lysander in *A Midsummer Night's Dream*, and Curio and Valentine in *Twelfth Night;* made a second tour with Charles Doran Shakespeare Co. (Jan.–June 1922), during which he played Vincentio in *The Taming of the Shrew* (Borough Th., Stratford, Feb. 13, 1922); made a third tour with Charles Doran Shakespeare Co. (Sept.–Dec. 1922), playing Lucentio in *The Taming of the Shrew* and Sebastian in *Twelfth Night;* and during the fourth tour, added the roles of Cassio in *Othello*, Antonio and Gratiano in *The Merchant of Venice*, and Marcus Antonius in *Julius Caesar.*

He joined the Earle Grey Co. (Abbey Th., Dublin), playing Sir Lucius O'Trigger in *The Rivals*, and Bobby in *The Romantic Age* (July–Aug. 1923); toured with Charles Doran Shakespeare Co. (Sept.–Nov. 1923); played Henry in *Outward Bound* (Winter Garden, New Brighton, Jan. 7, 1924), also touring in it (to June 1924); played Fainall in *The Way of the World* (Prince's, Manchester, Aug. 4, 1924); Richard Cooker in *The Farmer's Wife* (New, Cambridge, Feb. 16, 1925); joined the Birmingham Repertory Th., playing Dick Whittington in *The Christmas Party*(Dec. 26, 1925), Geoffrey Cassilis in *The Cassilis Engagement* (Jan. 1926), Christopher Pegrum in *The Round Table* (Feb. 1926), a Gentleman in *He Who Gets Slapped* (Feb. 1926), Lane in *The Importance of Being Earnest*(Mar. 1926), Robert Blanchard in *Devonshire Cream* (Mar. 1926), Albert Prosser in *Hobson's Choice* (Apr. 1926), Mr. Dearth in *Dear Brutus* (Apr. 1926), Frank Taylor in *The Land of Promise* (May 1926), and Dr. Tudor Bevan in *The Barber and the Cow* (June 1926).

He played the Stranger in a Greek Play Society production of *Oedipus at Colonus* (Scala, London, July 10, 1926); rejoined the Birmingham Repertory Co., playing Robert Blanchard in *Devonshire Cream* (Prince's, Manchester, Aug. 23, 1926), also touring in it; played Arthur Varwell in *Yellow Sands* (Haymarket, London, Nov. 3, 1926), and during this run, performed on Sundays with various groups, as Harold Devril in *Sunday Island* (Apr. 24, 1927), John Bold in *The Warden* (June 12, 1927), Sphus Meyer in *Samson and Delilah* (July 17, 1927), Frank Kiddell in *Chance Acquaintance*(Sept. 11, 1927), and Albert Titler in *At Number Fifteen* (Oct. 16, 1927).

He played Zozim in Part IV and Pygmalion in Part V of *Back to Methuselah* (Royal Court, Mar. 5, 1928); Gurth in *Harold*(Royal Court, Apr. 2, 1928); Tranio in a modern dress production of *The Taming of the Shrew*(Royal Court, Apr. 30, 1928); Hezekiah Brent in *Prejudice* (Arts, June 17, 1928); Ben Hawley in *Aren't Women Wonderful?* (Royal Court, Aug. 14, 1928); Alexander Magnus in *The First Performance* (Strand, Sept. 23, 1928); David Giles in *Arms and the Maid or Rustic Ribaldry* (Queen's Oct. 7, 1928); James Jago in *The Runaways* (Garrick, Nov. 14, 1928); and David Llewellyn Davids in *The New Sin* (Epsom Little Th., Jan. 1929).

He toured South Africa with Gerald Lawrence's Co. (Apr.–Aug. 1929), appearing as the Duke of Winterset in *Monsieur Beaucaire*, Joseph Surface in *The School for Scandal*, and Squire Chivy in *David Garrick;* played Gilbert Nash in *Silver Wings* (Dominion, London, Feb. 14, 1930); followed by Edward in *Cat and Mouse*(Queen's, Feb. 23, 1930); and Roderigo in *Othello* (Savoy, May 19, 1930); joined the Old Vic Co., playing Henry, Prince of Wales, in *Henry IV, Part 1* (Old Vic, Sept. 13, 1930), Caliban in *The Tempest* (Old Vic, Oct. 6, 1930), Sir Harry Beagle in *The Jealous Wife* (Old Vic, Oct. 27, 1930), Bolingbroke in *Richard II* (Old Vic, Oct. 6, 1930), Tom Holt in *Under the Table*(Strand, Dec. 7, 1930),

Sir Toby Belch in *Twelfth Night*(Sadler's Wells, Jan. 6, 1931), Bluntschli in *Arms and the Man* (Old Vic, Feb. 16, 1931), Don Pedro in *Much Ado About Nothing* (Old Vic, Mar. 16, 1931), Earl of Kent in *King Lear*(Old Vic, Apr. 13, 1931), and Sir Toby Belch and Don Pedro in scenes from Shakespeare (Old Vic, Apr. 23, 1931); appeared as John Morrison in *Revenge*(Strand, May 3, 1931); and David Regan in *The Mantle* (Arts, May 13, 1931).

At the Malvern (England) Festival, he played Matthew Merrygreek in *Ralph Roister Doister*(Aug. 3, 1931), Mr. Courtall in *She Would If She Could* (Aug. 5, 1931), and Viscount Pascal in *The Switchback* (Aug. 8, 1931); rejoined the Old Vic Co., as Philip the Bastard in *King John*(Sadler's Wells, Sept. 15, 1931); John Morrison in *Revenge*(Arts, Sept. 20, 1931); Petruchio in *The Taming of the Shrew* (Sadler's Wells, Oct. 13, 1931); Bottom in *A Midsummer Night's Dream* (Old Vic, Nov. 2, 1931); the title role in *Henry V*(Old Vic, Nov. 30, 1931); Ralph in *The Knight of the Burning Pestel*(Old Vic, Jan. 4, 1932); Brutus in *Julius Caesar* (Old Vic, Jan. 25, 1932); General Grant in *Abraham Lincoln* (Old Vic, Feb. 15, 1932); Iago in *Othello* (Old Vic, Mar. 7, 1932); Sir Toby Belch in *Twelfth Night* (Old Vic, Mar. 29, 1932); appeared in special performances of the revue, *Willy's Choice or An Author in Search of Some Characters* (Old Vic, Apr. 23, 1932); and the Ghost and First Gravedigger in *Hamlet*(Old Vic, Apr. 25, 1932).

Again at the Malvern Festival, he played Matthew Merrygreek in *Ralph Roister Doister,* and Face in *The Alchemist* (Aug. 2, 1932), the title role of *Oroonoko* (Aug. 3, 1932), and Sergeant Fielding in *Too True to Be Good* (Aug. 6, 1932), repeating the latter role in London (New, Sept. 13, 1932); played Collie Stratton in *For Services Rendered* (Globe, Nov. 1, 1932); Dirk Barclay in *Head-on-Crash* (Queen's, Feb. 1, 1933); Shylock in scenes from *The Merchant of Venice*(Old Vic, Apr. 23, 1933); Arthur Bell in *Wild December*(Apollo, May 26, 1933); and the title role in *Sheppey* (Wyndham's, Sept. 14, 1933).

He produced *Beau Nash* (Th. Royal, Bath, Nov. 1933); played Captain Hook and Mr. Darling in *Peter Pan* (Palladium, London, Dec. 23, 1933); John MacGregor in *Marriage Is No Joke* (Globe, Feb. 6, 1934); Charles Appleby in *Eden End* (Duchess, Sept. 13, 1934); the title role in *Cornelius*(Duchess, Mar. 20, 1935); Emile Delbar in *Promise* (Shaftesbury, Feb. 26, 1936); Sam Gridley in *Bees on the Boat,* which he directed with Laurence Olivier (Lyric, May 5, 1936); Dr. Clitterhouse in *The Amazing Dr. Clitterhouse* (Haymarket, Aug. 6, 1936); Peter Agardi in *The Silent Knight*(St. James's, Nov. 16, 1937); Bottom in *A Midsummer Night's Dream* (Old Vic, Dec. 27, 1937); the title role in *Othello*(Old Vic, Feb. 8, 1939); Johnson in *Johnson Over Jordan*(New, Feb. 22, 1939); Henry in scenes from *Henry V*for a Red Cross matinee (Palace, Mar. 12, 1940); appeared in scenes from Shakespeare on the *Theme of Time* (Old Vic, Apr. 23, 1940); narrated "Salute to the Red Army" (Royal Albert Hall, Feb. 24, 1943); *Ship-Shape Show*(H. M. Troopship, May 1943); and read "The Little Ships" from *Seascape,* by J. B. Priestley, for ENSA (Royal Albert Hall, Sept. 12, 1943).

In Aug. 1944, he became joint director of the Old Vic Co., with Laurence Olivier, a position he held until May 1947; with the Old Vic Co., he played the title role in *Peer Gynt* (New, Aug. 31, 1944), Bluntschli in *Arms and the Man* (New, Sept. 13, 1944), Earl of Richmond in *Richard II* (New, Sept. 13, 1944), and Voynitsky in *Uncle Vanya*(New, Jan. 16, 1945); toured for ENSA with the Old Vic Co., appearing in Antwerp and Ghent, Belgium; Hamburg, Germany; and Paris, France (May–July 1945); also with the Old Vic Co., played Sir John Falstaff in *Henry IV, Part 1* (New, London, Sept. 26, 1945), Falstaff in *Henry IV, Part 2* (New, Oct. 3, 1945), Tiresias in *Oedipus,* and Lord Burleigh in *The Critic* (New, Oct. 18, 1945), Inspector Goole in *An Inspector Calls* (New, Oct. 1, 1946); and the title role in *Cyrano de Bergerac* (New, Oct. 24, 1946); for the Brighton Philharmonic Society, he was Narrator for *Interlude and Serenade for Voice and Orchestra* (The Dome, Brighton, Dec. 14, 1946); with the Old Vic, played Face in *The Alchemist* (New, London, Jan. 14, 1947), and John of Gaunt in *Richard II* (New, Apr. 23, 1947); was the Narrator in a Remembrance Day Concert (Royal Albert Hall, Nov. 6, 1947); appeared as Marcus Ivanirex in *Royal Circle,* which he also directed (Wyndham's, Apr. 27, 1948); Dr. Sloper in *The Heiress* (Haymarket, Feb. 1, 1949); appeared in a special performance of excerpts from Shakespeare, "Three Thoughts on Time" and ". . . Merely Players" (London Coliseum, Nov. 20, 1949); played David Preston in *Home at Seven* (Wyndham's, Mar. 7, 1950); the Orator in a Halle Orchestra concert (King's Hall, Belle Vue, Manchester, Apr. 16, 1950); Vershinin in *The Three Sisters*(Aldwych, London, May 3, 1951); and Narrator in *Salute to Ivor Novello* (London Coliseum, Oct. 7, 1951).

At the Shakespeare Memorial Th. (Stratford-upon-Avon), he played Prospero in *The Tempest* (Mar. 25, 1952) and the title roles in *Macbeth* (June 10, 1952), and *Volpone* (Oct. 1952); presided at the opening of the Kenya National Th. (Kenya, Nairobi, Africa, Nov. 1952); appeared as John Greenwood in *The White Carnation* (Globe, London, Mar. 20, 1953); Dr. Farley in *A Day by the Sea* (Haymarket, Nov. 26, 1953); toured Australia and New Zealand as the Grand Duke in *The Sleeping Prince,* and Mr. Martin in *Table by the Window*and Major Pollock in *Table Number Seven,* a double bill entitled *Separate Tables*(Spring–Fall 1955); played the title role in an Old Vic Co. production of *Timon of Athens*(Old Vic, London, Sept. 5, 1956); Cherry in *Flowering Cherry* on tour (Oct. 1956) and in London (Haymarket, Nov. 21, 1957); Victor Rhodes in *The Complaisant Lover*(Globe, June 18, 1959); Edward Portal in *The Last Joke*(Phoenix, Sept. 28, 1960); Sir Peter Teazle in *School for Scandal* (Haymarket, 1962); appeared in *Six Characters in Search of an Author* (Mayfair, June 1963); on a South American tour (March–May 1964), played Shylock in *The Merchant of Venice,* and Bottom in *A Midsummer Night's Dream;* and played the Father in *Carving a Statue* (Haymarket, London, Sept. 17, 1964).

He played the Waiter in *You Never Can Tell*(Haymarket Th., London, Jan. 1966); Sir Anthony Absolute in *The Rivals* (Haymarket Th., Mar., 1967); Shylock in *The Merchant of Venice* (Haymarket Th., Sept. 1967); The Professor in *What the Butler Saw* (Queen's Th., Mar. 1969); Jack in *Home* (Royal Court, London, June 1970; and Morosco, N.Y.C., Nov. 1970); the Author in *Best of Luck* (London, 1971); and the General in *Lloyd George Knew My Father* (Savoy, London, 1972; and on tour).

Films. Sir Ralph made his debut as Nigel Hartley in *The Ghoul* (Gaumont-British, 1933); followed by roles in *Friday the 13th* (Gaumont-British, 1934); *The Return of Bulldog Drummond* (1934); *Java Head* (First Division, 1935); *King of Paris* (1935); *Bulldog Jack* (1935); *Things to Come* (UA, 1936); *The Man Who Worked Miracles* (1937); *Thunder in the City* (Col., 1937); *South Riding* (UA, 1938); *Divorce of a Lady* (UA, 1938); *The Citadel* (MGM, 1938); *Q-Planes* (1939); *Four Feathers*(UA, 1939); *The Lion Has Wings* (UA, 1940); *On the Night of the Fire* (U, 1940); *The Day Will Dawn* (1942); *The Silver Fleet* (PRC Pictures, 1945); *The Fallen Idol* (20th-Fox, 1945); *School of Secrets* (1946); *Anna Karenina* (20th-Fox, 1948); *The Heiress* (Par., 1949); *Outcast of the Islands* (UA, 1952); *Home at Seven,* which he also directed (1952); *Breaking the Sound Barrier* (UA, 1952); *The Holly and the Ivy* (Pacemaker, 1953); *Richard III*(Lopert, 1956); *Smiley*(20th-Fox, 1957); *Passionate Stranger*(Rank, 1956); *Our Man in Havana* (Col., 1960); *Lion of Sparta* (1960); *Long Day's Journey into Night* (Emb., 1962); *Woman of Straw* (Rank, 1963); *Doctor Zhivago* (MGM, 1966); *Khartoum* (WB, 1966); *The Wrong Box* (Col., 1966); and *A Doll's House* (Par., 1973).

Television. His appearances include roles in *Hedda Gabler* (CBS, 1963); *David Copperfield* (NBC, 1970); and *Home* (NET, 1971).

Awards. Sir Ralph received an honorary D.Litt. from Oxford Univ. (1969).

RICHARDSON, TONY. Director. b. Cecil Antonio Richardson, June 5, 1928, Shipley, England, to Clarence Albert and Elsie (Campion) Richardson. Father, chemist. Attended Ashville Coll., Harrogate, England, 1939–46; grad. Wadham Coll., Oxford Univ., B.A., 1951. Married April 28, 1962, to Vanessa Redgrave, actress; one daughter (marr. dis. 1967). Member of SDG; ACTT; SSD&C. Address: (home) 30 St. Peter's Sq., London W.6, England; (bus.) 11a Curzon St., London W.1, England tel. HYD 2361.

Theatre. Mr. Richardson first directed productions of the Oxford Univ. Dramatic Soc., of which he was pres. (1949–51), including *The Duchess of Malfi* (1949); *Peer Gynt* (1950); *Romeo and Juliet* (1951); and *King John* (1951).

As associate artistic director of The English Stage Company (1955–to date), he directed, at the Royal Court Th., (London), *Look Back in Anger* (May 8, 1956; Mar. 11, 1957); *Cards of Identity* (June 26, 1956); *Member of the Wedding* (Feb. 2, 1957); *The Entertainer* (Apr. 10, 1957); *The Apollo of Bellac,* presented on a double bill with *The Chairs* (May 14, 1957); and *The Making of Moo* (June 25, 1957).

His first N.Y.C. directing assignment was *Look Back in Anger* (Lyceum, Oct. 1, 1957); subsequently directed *Requiem for a Nun* (Royal Court, London, Nov. 26, 1957); the double-bill *The Lesson* and *The Chairs* (Phoenix, N.Y.C., Jan. 9, 1958); and *The Entertainer*(Royale, Feb. 12, 1958); at the Royal Court Th. (London), *Flesh to a Tiger* (May 21, 1958), *The Lesson,* and *The Chairs* (June 18, 1958); and at the Shakespeare Memorial Th. (Stratford-upon-Avon), *Pericles* (July 8, 1958).

He directed *Requiem for a Nun* (Golden, N.Y.C., Jan. 30, 1959); *Othello* (Shakespeare Memorial Th., Stratford-upon-Avon, Apr. 7, 1959); at the Royal Court Th. (London) *Orpheus Descending* (May 14, 1959), and *Look After Lulu* (July 29, 1959); with George Devine, directed *A Taste of Honey* (Lyceum, N.Y.C., Oct. 4, 1960); at the Royal Court Th. (London) directed *The Changeling* (Feb. 21, 1961), *Luther* (July 27, 1961), and *A Midsummer Night's Dream* (Jan. 24, 1962); and *Semi-Detached* (Saville, Dec. 5, 1962).

Mr. Richardson directed *Natural Affection* (Booth, N.Y.C., Jan. 31, 1963); *Luther* (St. James, Sept. 25, 1963); *Arturo Ui*(Lunt-Fontanne, Nov. 11, 1963); *The Milk Train Doesn't Stop Here Anymore* (Brooks Atkinson Th., Jan. 1, 1964); *The Seagull* (Queen's, London, Mar. 12, 1964); *St. Joan of the Stockyards* (Queen's, June 11, 1964); and *Hamlet* (Lunt-Fontanne, N.Y.C., May 1, 1969).

Films. He directed *Momma Don't Care* (1953); directed and produced, with John Osborne, *Look Back in Anger* (WB, 1959) and *The Entertainer* (Continental Distributing, 1960); and produced *Saturday Night and Sunday Morning* (Continental Distributing, 1961).

He directed and produced, with Mr. Osborne, *A Taste of Honey* (Continental Distributing, 1962), *The Loneliness of the Long Distance Runner* (Continental Distributing, 1963), and *Tom Jones* (UA, 1963); and was executive producer of *Girl with the Green Eyes.*

Mr. Richardson directed *The Loved One* (MGM, 1965); *Mademoiselle* (Lopert-Woodfall, 1966); collaborated on the screenplay and directed *The Sailor from Gibraltar* (Lopert, 1967); directed *The Charge of the Light Brigade* (UA, 1968); *Laughter in the Dark* (Lopert, 1969); *Ned Kelly* (UA, 1970); *A Delicate Balance* (Amer. Film Th., 1973); and co-authored the screenplay for *Dead Cert* (1974).

Awards. Mr. Richardson received the Academy (Oscar) Award and the NY Film Critics' Award (1963) for his direction of *Tom Jones;* and, for his direction of *The Loneliness of the Long Distance Runner,* he received a Porretta Terme Festival of Free Cinema Award, 1963.

RICHMAN, MARK. Actor. b. Marvin Jack Richman, Apr. 16, 1927, Philadelphia, Pa., to Benjamin and Yetta Dora (Peck) Richman. Grad. South Philadelphia H.S., 1945; Philadelphia Coll. of Pharmacy and Science, B.S. 1951. Studied acting with Lee Strasberg 1952–54; at Actors Studio (mbr.,

1954–to date; mbr., Directors' group, 1960–to date). Married May 10, 1953, to Theodora Landress, actress, known, as Teddi Landress; two sons, one daughter. Served USN, 1944–46; rank, Seaman 2/c. Member of AEA; AFTRA; SAG; Alpha Zeta Omega.

Pre-Theatre. Pharmacist and professional football player in the Eastern Conference.

Theatre. Mr. Richman acted in amateur productions in Philadelphia, beginning with the role of Santa Claus in a grammar school play, *Christmas Cantata* (1934); later played Billy in *This Happy Breed* (1947), and the title role in *Liliom* (Philadelphia Neighborhood Players, 1949); played a season of stock at Grove Theatre (Nuangola, Pa., 1952), appearing in *Lo and Behold*, as Jarvis Addams in *The Member of the Wedding*. Alvaro Mangiacavallo in *The Rose Tattoo*, Ben Goodman in *Remains To Be Seen*, Horace William Dodd in *Season in the Sun;* Owen O'Malley in *20th Century*, Clark Wilson in *Twilight Walk*, Matt Burke in *Anna Christie*, Eliot in *Private Lives*, in *Apron Strings*, as Charles Steward in *Gramercy Ghost*, Sinclair Heybore in *Fancy Meeting You Again*, and Steve in *Pretty Lady*.

He played Stefanowski in *Mister Roberts* and Joe Feinson in *Detective Story* (Westchester Playhouse, Mt. Kisco, N.Y., 1953); followed by a summer tour as Mannion in *Mister Roberts* (Fayetteville Playhouse, N.Y., and Syracuse Playhouse, N.Y.).

Mr. Richman made his New York debut as Larrence Corger in *End as a Man* (opened Theatre de Lys, Sept. 15, 1953; moved to Vanderbilt, Oct. 14, 1953); subsequently played a season of stock at the Guthsville Playhouse (Pa., 1954), directing and appearing as the Gentleman Caller in *The Glass Menagerie;* playing Mr. Manningham in *Angel Street*, Harry Binion in *Room Service*, and Charles Grant in *The Family Upstairs;* and directing *Apple of His Eye*.

He played File, the Sheriff, in *The Rainmaker* which toured summer theatres in New England (Summer 1955); succeeded Robert Dowdell as Channon in *The Dybbuk* (Fourth St. Th., N.Y.C., Oct. 26, 1954); succeeded Steve McQueen (Aug. 1956) as Johnny Pope in *A Hatful of Rain* (Lyceum, Nov. 9, 1955), and played this role on tour (opened Selwyn, Chicago, Ill., Oct. 15, 1956; closed Plymouth, Boston, Mass., May 4, 1957); appeared as Sergius in a summer stock production of *Arms and the Man* (Drury Lane, Chicago, Ill., June–July 1957); played Jimmy Porter in *Look Back in Anger* (Atlantic Beach Playhouse, N.J., 1959); Ralph Glenville in *Masquerade* (John Golden Th., Mar. 16, 1959); Jerry in *The Zoo Story* (Provincetown Playhouse, Mass., Jan. 14, 1960). During the summer of 1962, he played David in *Write Me a Murder* (Ogunquit Playhouse, Me.; Cape Playhouse, Dennis, Mass.); Glen Griffin in *Desperate Hours* (Deertrees Th., Harrison, Me.) and Senator Joe Cantwell in *The Best Man* (Playhouse-in-Park, Philadelphia, Pa.). He played Joe Garfield in the pre-Bway tryout of *Have I Got a Girl for You!* (opened Biltmore, Los Angeles, Calif., Jan. 24, 1963; closed there Feb. 16, 1963); Shannon in *The Night of the Iguana* (Playhouse-in-the-Park, Philadelphia, Pa., Summer 1963); and was in *The Deputy* (Theater Group-Univ. of California, Los Angeles, Aug. 13, 1965).

Films. Mr. Richman played Gard Jordan in *Friendly Persuasion* (AA, 1956); Laurence Corger in the film version of *End As a Man*, called *The Strange One* (Col., 1957); and Noble in *the Black Orchid* (Par., 1959).

Television. Mr. Richman made his debut in the series, Papa Pietro's Place (WPTZ-TV, Philadelphia, Pa., 1950). He has since appeared on many programs, including Philco Playhouse (NBC) presentations of *Middle of the Night* (Sept. 19, 1954) and *The Bold and the Brave* (Sept. 17, 1955); Goodyear Playhouse presentations (NBC) of *Star in the Night* (July 22, 1954), *Backfire* (Feb. 27, 1955), and *The House* (Sept. 8, 1967); and Kraft Theatre (NBC) presentations of *Sheriff's Man* (Mar. 27, 1957) and *Death Wears Many Faces* (July 30, 1958). He was in *The Last Man* (Playhouse 90, CBS, Jan. 9, 1958); on Alfred Hitchcock Presents (CBS) in *Man with a Problem* (Nov. 16, 1958) and *The Cure* (Jan. 24, 1960); on the US Steel Hour (CBS) in *The Hours Before Dawn* (Sept. 23, 1959), *Act of Terror* (Dec. 30, 1959), *Shame of Paula Marsten* (Apr. 19, 1961), and *You Can't Escape* (June 13, 1962). He appeared in *Ruth and Naomi* (June Allyson Show (CBS, Sept. 21, 1959); *A Question of Chairs* (CBS, Jan. 15, 1961); *Therese Raquin* (Play of the Week, NET, Mar. 13, 1961); and played in episodes of many series, such as Stoney Burke (ABC, 1963); Ben Casey (ABC, 1963); Outer Limits (ABC, 1963); The Virginian (NBC, 1963, 1964); Combat (ABC, 1964), 1966); Fugitive (ABC, 1964, 1966); The F.B.I. (ABC, 1965, 1968, 1970); Daniel Boone (NBC, 1967); The Man from U.N.C.L.E. (NBC, 1968); Bonanza (NBC, 1968); Gunsmoke (CBS, 1968); Name of the Game (NBC, 1968, 1969); It Takes a Thief (ABC, 1968, 1969); Hawaii Five-O (CBS, 1969); Mannix (CBS, 1970); Mission: Impossible (CBS, 1970); and Longstreet (ABC, 1971).

Recreation. Photography, movie direction and photography, oil painting, gardening.

RIGBY, HARRY. Producer, adaptor. b. Feb. 21, 1925, Pittsburgh, Pa., to Howard and Anne (Halpen) Rigby. Father, publicist. Attended Haverford Sch.; Univ. of North Carolina. Member of Dramatists Guild; League of NY Theatres. Address: (home) 420 W. 24th St., New York, NY 10011, tel. (212) 675-9039; (bus.) 1650 Broadway, Rm. 312, New York, NY 10019, tel. (212) 757-3903.

Theatre. Mr. Rigby was co-producer of *Make a Wish* (Winter Garden, N.Y.C., Apr. 18, 1951); *John Murray Anderson's Almanac* (Imperial, N.Y.C., Dec. 10, 1953); *Half-a-Sixpence* (Broadhurst, N.Y.C., Apr. 25, 1965); *Hallelujah, Baby* (Martin Beck Th., Apr. 26, 1967); *Riot* (Bway United Church, N.Y.C., Dec. 19, 1968); subsequently conceived the revival of *No, No, Nanette* (46 St. Th., N.Y.C., Jan. 19, 1971); adapted and co-produced *Irene* (Minskoff, N.Y.C., Mar. 13, 1973); and produced the revival of *Good News* (St. James, N.Y.C., Dec. 23, 1974).

Films. Mr. Rigby produced *Pound* (UA, 1970).

Awards. Mr. Rigby received the Antoinette Perry (Tony) Award for Best Musical (1967) for his production of *Hallelujah, Baby*.

RILEY, LAWRENCE. Playwright. b. 1897, Bradford, Pa., to James and Best Riley. Married 1941 to Virginia Sweeney. Member of Dramatists Guild; WGA. Address: Riverside, CT 06878.

Pre-Theatre. Newspaper work.

Theatre. Mr. Riley wrote *Personal Appearance* (Henry Miller's Th., N.Y.C., Oct. 17, 1934); *Return Engagement* (John Golden Th., Nov. 1, 1940); and *Kin Hubbard* (Westport, N.Y., 1951).

Films. His screenplays include *Stolen Harmony* (Par., 1935); *Go West, Young Man* (Par., 1936), and adaptation of his play, *Personal Appearance; Ever Since Eve* (WB, 1937); *The Perfect Specimen* (1st Natl., 1937); and *On Your Toes* (WB, 1939).

Television. Mr. Riley has written several plays for this medium.

Published Works. Mr. Riley has written stories published in *Saturday Evening Post* and other magazines.

RILL, ELI. Actor, director, playwright, teacher. b. Elias Maxwell Schectman, May 26, 1926, New York City, to Benjamin and Edith (Rill) Schectman. Father, butcher. Grad. Townsend Harris H.S., N.Y.C., 1942. Studied with Lee Strasberg at Actors' Studio, N.Y.C. (member 1953–to date). Married June 30, 1953, to Janine Manatis, writer; one son. Served USMC, FETO, 1943–46; rank, PFC. Member of AEA; AFTRA; SAG.

Theatre. Mr. Rill made his first stage appearance at age six as "October" in *The Months* (P.S. 162, N.Y.C., 1932); and subsequently made his professional debut as Nathaniel Francis in *Nat Turner* (Eldridge Th., Dec. 1950).

He directed and played Stanley in *Monday's Heroes* (Greenwich Mews, 1952); played the First Orderly in *End As a Man* (Th. de Lys, Sept. 15, 1953; moved Lyceum, Oct. 14, 1953); directed *Village Wooing* (Greenwich Mews, Aug. 11, 1955); and understudied and played Japie Grobler in *Too Late the Phalarope* (Belasco, Oct. 11, 1956).

Mr. Rill adapted and directed *Conversation at Midnight* (Actors' Studio, June 6, 1957); directed *Franklyn Barnabas* for the Shaw Society of America (Grolier Club, Mar. 24, 1959); at the Festival of the Two Worlds (Spoleto, Italy, Summer 1960), directed *Lady of Larkspur Lotion, I Rise in Flame Cried the Phoenix* and *Maidens and Mistresses at Home in the Zoo;* wrote and directed *The Closet* (Drama Workshop, Toronto, Canada, Jan. 4, 1961); directed *Village Wooing* (Poor Alex Th., Toronto, July 9, 1964).

Films. Mr. Rill was assistant director for *The Harder They Fall* (Col., 1956).

Other Activities. He was instructor at Actors' Studio (1957–60) and in 1957 began conducting a workshop for actors, writers, and directors in Toronto, Ontario, Canada, where he settled in 1964.

Awards. Mr. Rill received a Ford Foundation Grant to observe theatre in Europe (1960).

Recreation. Violin.

RINDLER, MILTON. Theatrical accountant, treasurer for theatrical funds and foundations. b. July 4, 1898, New York City, to Julius and Jennie (Goldsmith) Rindler. Father, newspaper circulation manager. Grad. H.S. of Commerce, N.Y.C., 1915; attended City Coll. of New York, 1915–16; Columbia Univ., 1916–17; New Sch. for Social Research, 1925–28. Married Oct. 30, 1921, to Sonia Levitt; two daughters. Served US Army, 1917–19; rank, Pvt. Member of John Golden Fund (director); New Dramatists, Inc. (director). Address: (home) 4805 Gulf of Mexico Drive, Sarasota, FL 33577, tel. (813) 383-3133; (bus.) 274 Madison Ave., New York, NY 10016, tel. (212) MU 5-1194.

Mr. Rindler became a theatrical accountant in 1923, and currently operates his own firm, Milton Rindler and Company, N.Y.C. He was an original member and has been director-treasurer of the John Golden Fund, Inc. (1946–to date), and director-treasurer of the New Dramatists, Inc. (1960–69); director (1960–to date).

Other Activities. Mr. Rindler has written articles on taxation for magazines and the NY *Times*.

He became vice-president of the Ringling Art Museum Council, Sarasota, Fla. (vice-pres. and dir., 1969–to date); and was elected a director of the Asolo Th. Festival Co. operating the Asolo Th., a repertory theatre in Sarasota, Fla. (1969–to date).

Recreation. Growing dahlias, golf, swimming, playing the piano, reading play scripts for John Golden Fund Playwright's Committee.

RIPLEY, PATRICIA. Actress. b. Mary Patricia Ripley, Aug. 15, 1926, Evanston, Ill., to C. T. and Mabel (Thomson) Ripley. Father, mechanical engineer; mother, nurse. Grad. Bennington Coll., B.A. 1948; studied acting with Theodore Komisarjevski, two years; Francis Ferguson, three years. Member of AEA; AFTRA; SAG. Address: (home) 115 W. 86th St., New York, NY 10024, tel. (212) EN 2-1853; (bus.) c/o Actors' Equity Assn., 165 W. 46th St., New York, NY 10036.

Theatre. Miss Ripley made her N.Y.C. debut as Jocasta in *The Infernal Machine* (Provincetown Playhouse, June 17, 1948); subsequently appeared as Maolia in *The Seagull* and Oliva in *Twelfth Night* (Brattle Th., Cambridge, Mass.); Catherine Sloper in *The Heiress* and Gwendolyn in *The Importance of Being Earnest* (Holiday Stage, Tustin, Calif., July 18, 1949); and as Miss Preen in the Max Gordon touring production of *The Man Who Came to Dinner* (1950–51).

She played Abigail in *Be Your Age* (48 St. Th., N.Y.C., Jan. 14, 1953); played Ellie in *The Ticklish Acrobat* (Amato Opera Th., Mar. 8, 1954); Col. Baines in *Major Barbara* (Martin Beck Th., Oct. 30, 1956); appeared at the Cambridge (Mass.) Drama Festival, as Queen Isabel in *Henry V* and Betty in *The Beggar's Opera* (1957); succeeded (1957) Barbara Sohmers in the role of Betty in *The Threepenny Opera* (Th. de Lys, N.Y.C., Sept. 20, 1955); succeeded (June 1958) Sylvia Stone in the role of Cornelia Scott in *Garden District* (York Playhouse,

Jan. 7, 1958); played Beulah Binnings in *Orpheus Descending*(Coconut Grove Playhouse, Miami, Fla., Mar. 1958); and Agnes in *A Memory of Two Mondays* and Luisa in *The Purification* (Arena Stage, Washington, D.C., Nov. 19, 1958).

Miss Ripley played Mrs. Anthony in *The Great God Brown* (Coronet, N.Y.C., Oct. 6, 1959); the Maid in *Sweet Bird of Youth* (Martin Beck Th., March 10, 1959); the Leader of the Chorus in *Lysistrata* (Phoenix, Nov. 24, 1959); Kari in *Peer Gynt* (Phoenix, Jan. 12, 1960); joined the Assn. of Producing Artists (APA), playing Violet in *The Tavern* and Signora Cini in *Right You Are If You Think You Are*(McCarter Th., Princeton, N.J., Oct. 1960); appeared as the Step-daughter in *Six Characters in Search of an Author*(Arena Stage, Washington, D.C., 1961); Miss Gilchrist in *The Hostage*(One Sheridan Square, N.Y.C., Dec. 12, 1961); Miss Skilton in a stock production of *See How They Run* (Bucks County Playhouse, New Hope, Pa., Summer 1961); and as Mrs. Shedar in *Hey You, Light Man* (Th. by the Sea, Matunuck, R.I., Summer 1962).

She played the Photographer in *The Beauty Part* (Music Box, N.Y.C., Dec. 26, 1962), in which she also understudied Alice Ghostley and Charlotte Rae; toured as Marfa in *Romanoff and Juliet*(opened Playhouse-in-the-Park, Philadelphia, Pa., and played seven other theatres, Summer 1963), played Mrs. Botting in *Half-a-Sixpence* (Broadhurst Th., Apr. 25, 1965); was standby for Colleen Dewhurst in *Ballad of the Sad Cafe*(Martin Beck Th., Oct. 30, 1963); played Duchess in *Love Match* (pre-Bway tour, 1968); she appeared in *Success in America*, a National Humanities tour (1973); and played Pauline in a tour of *The Prisoner of Second Avenue* (1973–74).

Films. Miss Ripley made her screen debut in *Splendor in the Grass* (WB, 1961); and played the President's wife in *Hail* (Cine-Globe, 1974).

Television. She has appeared on The Defenders (CBS); The Jackie Gleason Show (CBS); Car 54, Where Are You? (NBC); Mister Peepers (NBC); and The Goldbergs.

Other Activities. From 1960–63, Miss Ripley was playreader for Brandt and Brandt, and since 1963, has served in that capacity for the William Morris Agency, Flora Roberts Agency, International Famous Agency, The Mark Taper Forum, and independent producers.

RITCHARD, CYRIL. Actor, director. b. Cyril Trimnell-Ritchard, Dec. 1, 1897, Sydney, Austrl., to Herbert and Margaret (Collins) Trimnell-Ritchard. Attended St. Aloysius Coll., Sydney; Sydney Univ. Married Sept. 16, 1935, to Madge Elliott (dec. Aug. 8, 1955); one son. Member of AEA; AFTRA; AGMA; SAG; SDG; N.Y. Athletic Club; Coffee House Club; Knickerbocker Club. Address: (home) "Lone Rock", Danbury Rd., Ridgefield, CT 06877, tel. (212) ID 8-8108; (bus.) 135 Central Park West, New York, NY 10023, tel. (212) EN 2-1208.

Theatre. Mr.Ritchard made his stage debut in Sydney, Australia, in productions for J. C. Williamson, Ltd. (1917–24).

He made his N.Y.C. debut in the revue, *Puzzles of 1925* (Fulton, Feb. 2, 1925); subsequently made his London debut in the revue, *The Charlot Show of 1926*(Prince of Wales's, Oct. 5, 1926); performed in *Lady Luck*(Carlton, Apr. 27, 1927); *Love Lies*(Gaiety, Mar. 20, 1929); *The Love Race*(Gaiety, June 25, 1930); and played the Hon. Aubrey Forsyth in *Millionaire Kid*(Gaiety, May 20, 1931). From 1932–35, Mr. Ritchard appeared in the following Australian productions, *Blue Roses, Roberta, Gay Divorce, Blue Mountain Melody, Our Miss Gibbs, The Quaker Girl,* and *High Jinks.*

He performed in *Nine Sharp*(Little, London, Jan. 26, 1938); *The Little Revue*(Little, Apr. 21, 1939); *Big Top* (His Majesty's, May 8, 1942); *The Importance of Being Earnest*(Phoenix, Oct. 14, 1942); appeared as Prince Danilo, and directed *The Merry Widow*(His Majesty's, Mar. 4, 1943), and toured in it (Egypt, Italy, Feb.–June 1944); returned to London (Coliseum, Sept. 19, 1944), and toured again (France, Belgium, Holland, Dec. 1944).

He Played Gabriel von Eisenstein in *Gay Rosalinda* (Palace, London, Eng., Mar. 8, 1945); performed in *Sigh No More*(Piccadilly, Aug. 22, 1945); played Tattle in *Love for Love*(Royale, N.Y.C., May 26, 1947); Sir Novelty Fashion in *The Relapse* (Phoenix, London, Jan. 28, 1948); and Georgie Pillson in *Make Way for Lucia* (Cort, N.Y.C., Dec. 22, 1948).

He played Hubert Manning in *Ann Veronica*(Piccadilly, London, May 20, 1949); the Hon. Vere Queckett in *The School Mistress* (Saville, Feb. 1, 1950); directed and played Lord Foppington in *The Relapse*(Morosco, N.Y.C., Nov. 22, 1950); directed *Jane* (Morosco, Feb. 1, 1952); and played Adrian Blunderbland in *The Millionairess* (New, London, June 27, 1952).

Mr. Ritchard directed *Misalliance*(NY City Ctr., Feb. 18, 1953); appeared in the revue, *High Spirits* (London Hippodrome, May 13, 1953); directed the sketches for the revue, *John Murray Anderson's Almanac* (Imperial, N.Y.C., Dec. 10, 1953); played Captain Hook in *Peter Pan*(Winter Garden, Oct. 20, 1954); directed *The Heavenly Twins*(Booth, Nov. 4, 1955); *The Reluctant Debutante*(Henry Miller's Th., Oct. 10, 1956); directed and played Kreton in *Visit to a Small Planet*(Booth, Feb. 7, 1957), and toured in it (opened Playhouse, Wilmington, Del., Feb. 5, 1958; closed Geary, San Francisco, Calif., June 28, 1958); directed and played Biddeford Poole in *The Pleasure of His Company*(Longacre, N.Y.C., Oct. 22, 1958), with which he later toured (opened Forrest, Philadelphia, Pa., Nov. 23, 1959; closed Erlanger, Chicago, Ill., May 28, 1960), and subsequently toured Australia in it (June–Dec. 1960).

He directed *Look After Lulu*(Henry Miller's Th., N.Y.C., Mar. 3, 1959); directed and played the Chief of State, Pluto, a Heckler, a Gay Blade, a Wine Smuggler, the Pied Piper of Hamelin, a Playwright, and an Ambassador in *The Happiest Girl in the World*(Martin Beck Th., Apr. 3, 1961); directed *Everybody Loves Opal*(Longacre, Oct. 11, 1961); appeared in the title role in *Romulus*(Music Box, Jan. 1, 1962); Colonel Tallboys in *Too True to Be Good* (54 St. Th., Mar. 12, 1963); and played Felix Rankin and directed *The Irregular Verb to Love*(Ethel Barrymore Th., Sept. 18, 1963).

He appeared in *The Country Wife* (Cambridge, Mass.); and directed a summer stock tour of *The Mackerel Plaza.* At the Metropolitan Opera House (N.Y.C.), he directed new versions of *La Perichole, The Gypsy Baron* (1960–61), *The Barber of Seville* (1961–62), *The Marriage of Figaro* (1961–62), and *The Tales of Hoffman* (1962–63).

Mr. Ritchard directed and played Felix Rankin in a tour of *The Irregular Verb to Love*(Summer 1964); played Sir in *The Roar of the Greasepaint, The Smell of the Crowd* (Shubert, N.Y.C., May 16, 1965); directed the US tour of *Where's Charley?* (1966); for the American Shakespeare Festival (Stratford, Conn.), directed and played Bottom, Oberon, and Pyramus in *A Midsummer Night's Dream* (Summer 1967); appeared in *Lock Up Your Daughters*(Parker Playhouse, Ft. Lauderdale, Fla., Feb. 12, 1968); was the Narrator for *Peter and the Wolf*(NY City Ctr., Mar. 1969); directed and played Don Andres in *La Perichole*(Metropolitan Opera House, N.Y.C., Dec. 1970–Jan. 1971); and directed *The Jockey Club Stakes*(Cort, N.Y.C., Jan. 24, 1973).

Films. Mr. Ritchard did the voice of the Sandman in *The Daydreamer*(Embassy, 1966).

Television. Mr. Ritchard played Captain Hook in *Peter Pan*(NBC); played the title role in *Mr. Scrooge* (CBC, 1964); directed *The Anne Hutchinson Story*for Profiles in Courage (NBC, 1965); played Valentine Silepzki in *The Man Who Bought Paradise* (CBS, 1965); played Felix Rankin in *The Irregular Verb to Love*(NET, 1965); Lone T. Wolf in *The Dangerous Christmas of Red Riding Hood*(ABC, 1965); and has made various appearances on Dr. Kildare (NBC, 1964); the Alcoa Preview series (ABC, 1965); The Mike Douglas Show (1965); The Merv Griffin Show (1965–66); The Today Show (1965–66); The Danny Kaye Show (CBS, 1965–66); The Bell Telephone Hour (NBC, 1966); and Talent Scouts (CBS, 1966).

Awards. He received an Antoinette Perry (Tony) Award and two Donaldson Awards (1955) for his performance as Captain Hook in *Peter Pan* (NBC).

Recreation. Swimming, tennis, horseback riding.

RITMAN, WILLIAM. Set, lighting, and costume designer. Grad. Goodman Th. Sch., Chicago.

Theatre. Mr. Ritman designed the sets and lights for *Zoo Story* and *Krapp's Last Tape*(Provincetown Playhouse, N.Y.C., Jan. 14, 1960); sets and costumes for *Russell Patterson's Sketch Book*(Maidman Playhouse, Feb. 6, 1960); scenery and lights for *The Killer*(Seven Arts Th., Mar. 22, 1960); decor for *Kukla, Burr and Ollie* (Kuklapolitan Room, Astor Hotel, Oct. 31, 1960); sets and lights for *The Sudden End of Anne Cinquefoil* (East End Th., Jan. 10, 1961); sets, lights, and costumes for *The American Dream* (York Playhouse, Jan. 24, 1961); designed *Gallows Humor*(Gramercy Arts Th., Apr. 18, 1961); sets, lights, and costumes for *The Death of Bessie Smith* (Cherry Lane Th., May 23, 1961); designed *Happy Day* (Cherry Lane Th., Sept. 17, 1961); sets and lights for *Fortuna*(Maidman Playhouse, Jan. 3, 1962); for the Theatre 1962 production of a bill of plays under the collective title *Theatre of the Absurd,* designed sets, lights, and costumes (Cherry Lane Th., Feb. 11, 1962); designed the lights for *King of the Whole Damned World* (Jan Hus Th., Apr. 12, 1962); sets, lights, and costumes for the double-bill *Whisper in My Good Ear* and *Mrs. Daley Has a Lover* (Cherry Lane Th., Oct. 1, 1962); *Who's Afraid of Virginia Woolf?* Billy Rose Th., Oct. 13, 1962; and national tour); and a double-bill entitled *The Pinter Plays,* which included *The Dumbwaiter* and *The Collection* (Cherry Lane Th., Nov. 26, 1962).

He designed the sets for *The Riot Act* (Cort, N.Y.C., Mar. 7, 1963); sets, lights, and costumes for *Corruption in the Palace of Justice*(Cherry Lane Th., Oct. 8, 1963; and Village South Th., Dec. 22, 1963); sets for a double-bill of *Play* and *The Lover*(Cherry Lane Th., Jan. 4, 1964); sets and lights for *Funnyhouse of a Negro*(East End Th., Jan. 14, 1964); sets, lights, and costumes for *Three at the Cherry Lane* (Cherry Lane Th., Mar. 24, 1964); sets and lights for *The Place for Chance*(Stage 73, May 14, 1964); sets for *A Midsummer Night's Dream*(Delacorte, June 26, 1964); sets and lights for *Absence of a Cello*(Ambassador, Sept. 21, 1964; and national tour); sets, lights, and costumes for *The Giants' Dance* (Cherry Lane Th., Nov. 16, 1964); a double-bill of *Zoo Story* and *Dutchman* (Cherry Lane Th., Nov. 24, 1964); *Tiny Alice*(Billy Rose Th., Dec. 29, 1964); *Do Not Pass Go* (Cherry Lane Th., Apr. 19, 1965); a double-bill of *Zoo Story* and *Krapp's Last Tape* (Cherry Lane Th., June 8, 1965); *Entertaining Mr. Sloane* (Lyceum, Oct. 12, 1965); *Play That on Your Old Piano*(Renata, Oct. 14, 1965); and *Malcolm* (Sam S. Shubert Th., Jan. 11, 1966); sets for *A Delicate Balance* (Martin Beck Th., Sept. 22, 1966; and national tour). He was production supervisor for Catherine Browne's sets for *The Killing of Sister George* (Belasco, Oct. 5, 1966); designed the sets, lights, and costumes for *Night of the Dunce*(Cherry Lane Th., Dec. 28, 1966); sets and lights for *Come Live with Me*(Billy Rose Th., Jan. 26, 1967); and sets, lights, and costumes for *The Rimers of Eldritch*(Cherry Lane Th., Feb. 20, 1967).

For the Pittsburgh Playhouse, he designed the sets for *The Tavern* (Sept. 30, 1967); *After the Fall* (Oct. 14, 1967); *Henry IV, Part 1* (Nov. 18, 1967); *Arms and the Man* (Dec. 16, 1967); *Rashomon* (Jan. 20, 1968); *Three Men on a Horse*(Feb. 17, 1968); and *Galileo* (Apr. 17, 1968). He designed the sets and costumes for *The Birthday Party* (Booth, N.Y.C., Oct. 3, 1967); sets, lights, and costumes for *Johnny No-Trump*(Cort, Oct. 8, 1967); sets for *The Promise* (Henry Miller's Th., Nov. 14, 1967); sets and costumes for *Everything in the Garden*(Plymouth, Nov. 29, 1967); sets, lights, and costumes for *A Delicate Balance*(Studio Arena, Buffalo, N.Y., Feb. 8, 1968); sets for *Box Mao Box*(Studio Arena, Mar. 6, 1968; and Spoleto, Italy, Festival of Two Worlds, Summer 1968); sets and lights for *Loot* (Biltmore, N.Y.C., Mar. 18, 1968); sets for *Lovers* (Vivian Beaumont Th., July 25, 1968; and Music Box, Sept. 17, 1968); sets and lights for *Theatre 1969 Playwrights' Repertory*

(Studio Arena, Buffalo, Sept. 15, 1968; and Billy Rose Th., N.Y.C., Sept. 30, 1968); sets for *We Bombed in New Haven* (Ambassador, Oct. 16, 1968); *Play It Again, Sam* (Broadhurst, Feb. 12, 1969; and national tour); *The Gingham Dog* (John Golden Th., Apr. 23, 1969); and *The Three Sisters* (American Shakespeare Fest., Stratford, Conn., July 23, 1969); sets, lights, and costumes for *Hello and Goodbye* (Sheridan Square Playhouse, N.Y.C., Sept. 18, 1969); sets for *The Penny Wars* (Royale, Oct. 15, 1969); and *Crimes of Passion* (Astor Place Th., Oct. 26, 1969); sets and lights for *The Mundy Scheme* (Royale, Dec. 11, 1969); sets for *Nature of the Crime* (Bouwerie Lane Th., Mar. 23, 1970); sets and lights for *How Much, How Much?* (Provincetown Playhouse, Apr. 20, 1970); sets, lights, and costumes for *What the Butler Saw* (McAlpin Rooftop Th., May 4, 1970); sets for *The Devil's Disciple* (American Shakespeare Fest., Stratford, Conn., June 19, 1970); and *Bob and Ray— The Two and Only* (John Golden Th., N.Y.C., Sept. 24, 1970); lights for *Sleuth* (Music Box, Nov. 12, 1970; and national tour); sets for *Long Day's Journey into Night* (Manitoba Th. Ctr., Winnipeg, Nov. 30, 1970); sets, lights, and costumes for *Waiting for Godot* (Sheridan Sq. Playhouse, N.Y.C., Feb. 3, 1971); sets for *Little Murders* (Manitoba Th. Ctr., Apr. 5, 1971); sets for *Mourning Becomes Electra* (American Shakespeare Fest., Stratford, Conn., June 16, 1971); sets and lights for *What the Butler Saw* (Manitoba Th. Ctr., Oct. 25, 1971); sets for *Moon Children* (Arena Stage, Washington, D.C., Oct. 29, 1971); lights for *Sleuth* (Ahmanson Th., Los Angeles, Calif., Jan. 11, 1972); sets for *The Sign in Sidney Brustein's Window* (Longacre, N.Y.C., Jan. 26, 1972); sets for *Moon Children* (Royale, Feb. 21, 1972); a double-bill of *The Real Inspector Hound* and *After Magritte* (Th. Four, Apr. 23, 1972); *An Evening with Richard Nixon and . .* (Sam S. Shubert Th., Apr. 30, 1972); *Major Barbara* (American Shakespeare Fest., Stratford, Conn., June 27, 1972); and *6 Rms Riv Vu* Helen Hayes Th., N.Y.C., Oct. 17, 1972; Lunt-Fontanne, Jan. 30, 1973); sets and lights for *Sleuth* (Manitoba Th. Ctr., Winnipeg, Oct. 30, 1972); *The Last of Mrs. Lincoln* (ANTA, N.Y.C., Dec. 12, 1972); *Detective Story* (pre-Bway tryout, opened Shubert, Philadelphia, Mar. 10, 1973; closed there Mar. 24, 1973); sets for *Measure for Measure* (American Shakespeare Fest., Stratford, Conn., June 2, 1973); and *Find Your Way Home* (Brooks Atkinson Th., N.Y.C., Jan. 2, 1974); sets and lights for *Noel Coward in Two Keys* (Ethel Barrymore Th., Feb. 28, 1974; and national tour); sets for *My Fat Friend* (Brooks Atkinson Th., Mar. 31, 1974; and national tour); *Zalman, or The Madness of God* (Arena Th., Washington, D.C., May 3, 1974; Lyceum, N.Y.C., Mar. 17, 1976); and *God's Favorite* (Eugene O'Neill Th., Dec. 11, 1974); for *P.S., Your Cat Is Dead* deisgned the sets (world premiere Studio Arena, Buffalo, Mar. 6, 1975) and sets and lights (John Golden Th., N.Y.C., Apr. 7, 1975); designed the sets for *Same Time, Next Year* (Brooks Atkinson Th., Mar. 13, 1975; and national tours); and sets and lights for the revival of *Who's Afraid of Virginia Woolf?* (Music Box, Apr. 1, 1976).

Mr. Ritman has served as staff designer for the Westport (Conn.) Country Playhouse, and the John Drew Th. (Easthampton, N.Y.); and was executive producer for the Rebeccah Harkness Dance Festival (Central Park, N.Y.C., Summers 1962–67).

Television. Before beginning his career in the theatre, Mr. Ritman was a designer for numerous productions, including the Steve Allen Show, Matinee Th., and Kukla, Fran and Ollie.

Awards. He received the *Best Plays* Award (1972–73) for his sets for *The Last of Mrs. Lincoln.*

RITT, MARTIN. Director, actor. b. Mar. 2, 1920, New York City, to Morris and Rose Ritt. Attended Elon Coll. Studied with Group Theatre, N.Y.C. Served WW II, USAAF, Special Services; rank, Pfc. Member of AEA; SAG; AFTRA; SDG.

Theatre. Mr. Ritt first performed as Sam and served as assistant stage manager for *Golden Boy* (Belasco, N.Y.C., Nov. 4, 1937); subsequently appeared as Tony in *Plant of the Sun* (Mercury, Mar. 6, 1938); the Polack and the Clerk in *The Gentle People* (Belasco, Jan. 5, 1939); Samuel Brodsky in *Two on an Island* (Broadhurst, Jan. 22, 1939); the Second Man in *They Should Have Stood in Bed* (Mansfield, Feb. 13, 1942); and Private Glinka in *The Eve of St. Mark* (Cort, Oct. 7, 1942).

As a member of the US Armed Forces, he played Gleason in the Air Force production of *Winged Victory* (44 St. Th., N.Y.C., Nov. 20, 1943), and on tour; directed *Mr. Peebles and Mr. Hooker* (Music Box, Oct. 10, 1946); *Yellow Jack* (International, Feb. 27, 1947); *The Big People* (Lyric, Bridgeport, Conn., Sept. 20, 1947, Falmouth Playhouse, Coonamessett, Mass., 1947); *Set My People Free* (Hudson, N.Y.C., Nov. 3, 1948); *The Man* (Fulton, Jan. 19, 1950); *Cry of the Peacock* (Mansfield, Apr. 11, 1950); played August Volpone in *Men of Distinction* (48 St. Th., Apr. 30, 1953); Ernest in *Maya* (Th. de Lys, June 9, 1953); and directed *Golden Boy, Boy Meets Girl* and *The Front Page* (Playhouse-in-the-Park, Philadelphia, Pa., 1954).

He played Shem in *The Flowering Peach* (Belasco, N.Y.C., Dec. 28, 1954); Harry Brock in *Born Yesterday* (Playhouse-in-the-Park, Philadelphia, Pa., July 1955); and directed *A View from the Bridge* and *A Memory of Two Mondays* (Coronet, N.Y.C., Sept. 25, 1955).

Films. Mr. Ritt has appeared in *Winged Victory* (20th-Fox, 1944); directed *Edge of the City* (MGM, 1957); *No Down Payment* (20th-Fox, 1957); *The Long Hot Summer* (20th-Fox, 1958); *The Sound and the Fury* (20th-Fox, 1959); *The Black Orchid* (Par., 1959); *Five Branded Women* (Par., 1960); *Paris Blues* (UA, 1961); *Hemingway's Adventures of a Young Man* (20th-Fox, 1962); directed and produced, with Paul Newman, *Hud* (Par., 1963); and directed *The Outrage* (MGM, 1964).

He also directed *The Spy Who Came In From the Cold,* which he also produced (Par., 1966); *Hombre,* which, with Irving Ravetch, he also produced (20th-Fox, 1967); *The Brotherhood* (Par., 1968); *The Molly Maguires* (Par., 1970); *The Great White Hope* (20th-Fox, 1970); *Sounder* (20th-Fox, 1972); *Pete 'n' Tillie* (U, 1972); and *Conrack* (20th-Fox, 1974).

Television. Mr. Ritt directed the series Danger (CBS); has directed for the US Steel Hour (CBS), Playwrights Th., Actors Studio Th.; and has appeared on Danger (CBS) and Starlight Th. (CBS).

Awards. He received a Peabody Award; also an Academy (Oscar) Award nomination for *Hud* (1964); and *The Spy Who Came In From the Cold* received the British Film Academy Award as best British film (1966).

Recreation. Tennis, horse-racing.

RITTMAN, TRUDE. Composer, arranger. b. Gertrud Rittman, Mannheim, Germany, to Adolf and Rosa (Bacharach) Rittman. Father, businessman. Grad. Hochschule fur Musik, Cologne, Ger. Studied composition with Ernst Toch and Philip Tarnach, piano with Hans Bruch and Eduard Erdmann. Member of AFM, Local 802. Address: (home) 2160 Center Ave., Fort Lee, NJ 07024, tel. (201) 461-5614; (bus.) c/o Deborah Coleman Agency, 667 Madison Ave., New York, NY 10019, tel. (212) TE 8-0734.

Pre-Theatre. Concert pianist, composer.

Theatre. During 1937–41, Miss Rittmann served as musical director of the touring Ballet Caravan. She directed the chorus of the NY City Ctr. production of *No for an Answer* (Jan. 5, 1941); was rehearsal pianist for *One Touch of Venus* (Imperial, Oct. 7, 1943); arranged the dance music for *Bloomer Girl* (Shubert, Oct. 5, 1944); played for the rehearsals of *The Tempest* (Alvin, Jan. 25, 1945); arranged dance music for *Carousel* (Majestic, Apr. 19, 1945); was rehearsal pianist for *Billion Dollar Baby* (Alvin, Dec. 21, 1945); arranged the dance music for *Finian's Rainbow* (46 St. Th., Jan. 10, 1947); was rehearsal pianist for *Brigadoon* (Ziegfeld, Mar. 13, 1947); arranged the ballet music for *Allegro* (Majestic, Oct. 10, 1947); wrote the original ballet "Mademoiselle Marie" and the ballet arrangements for *Look Ma, I'm Dancing* (Adelphi, Jan. 29, 1948).

Miss Rittman arranged the musical continuity for *South Pacific* (Majestic, Apr. 7, 1949); wrote additional ballet music for *Miss Liberty* (Imperial, July 15, 1949); arranged the dance music for *Gentlemen Prefer Blondes* (Ziegfeld, Dec. 8, 1949); arranged incidental and dance music for Jean Arthur's *Peter Pan* (Imperial, Apr. 24, 1950); and wrote the incidental music for *Out of this world* (Century, Dec. 21, 1950). She arranged the ballet sequences for *The King and I* (St. James, Mar. 29, 1951); the dance music for *Paint Your Wagon* (Shubert, Nov. 12, 1951); and musical continuity for *Wish You Were Here* (Imperial, June 25, 1952); composed incidental music for *The Climate of Eden* (Martin Beck Th., Nov. 6, 1952); arranged the music for the transcontinental tour of Agnes De Mille's Dance Theatre (1953); composed the ballet music for *The Girl in Pink Tights* (Mark Hellinger Th., N.Y.C., Mar. 5, 1954); composed incidental music, with Elmer Bernstein, for Mary Martin's *Peter Pan* (Winter Garden, Oct. 20, 1954); arranged dance and incidental music for *Fanny* (Majestic, Nov. 4, 1954); dance music for *My Fair Lady* (Mark Hellinger Th., Mar. 15, 1956); dance and incidental music for the pre-Bway tryout of *At the Grand* (opened Philharmonic Aud., Los Angeles, Calif., July 7, 1958; closed Curran, San Francisco, Calif., Sept. 13, 1958).

She wrote additional ballet music for *Juno* (Winter Garden, N.Y.C., Mar. 9, 1959); choral arrangements for *The Sound of Music* (Lunt-Fontanne, Nov. 16, 1959); arranged the dance and vocal music for *Christine* (46 St. Th., Apr. 28, 1960) and *Camelot* (Majestic, Dec. 3, 1960); arranged background music and continuity for *All American* (Winter Garden, Mar. 19, 1963); dance music and vocal arrangements for *Hot Spot* (Majestic, Apr. 19, 1963) and *Jennie* (Majestic, Oct. 17, 1963); arranged vocal and background music for *On a Clear Day You Can See Forever* (Mark Hellinger Th., Oct. 17, 1965); wrote dance arrangements for *Darling of the Day* George Abbott Th., Jan. 27, 1968) and *Maggie Flynn* (ANTA, Oct. 23, 1968); arranged vocal and music continuity for *Come Summer* (Lunt-Fontanne Th., Mar. 18, 1969); wrote dance, vocal, and music continuity arrangements for *Scarlett* (Rome, Italy; Tokyo, Japan; 1970) and for *Gone with the Wind* (London, 1972; Dorothy Chandler Pavilion, Los Angeles, Calif., Aug. 28, 1973); arranged dance and vocal music for *Two by Two* (Imperial, Nov. 10, 1970); and wrote dance arrangements for *Ambassador* (Lunt-Fontanne Th., Nov. 19, 1972) and *Gigi* (Uris Th., Nov. 13, 1973). Miss Rittman's ballet composition, *The Four Marys,* was premiered by American Ballet Theater (State Th., N.Y.C., Mar. 1965) and was included with her compositions *Goldrush, The Cherry Tree Legend,* and *Hell on Wheels* in the repertory of the Agnes de Mille American Heritage Dance Theatre on US tour (1973–74).

Films. Miss Rittman arranged the ballet music for *The King and I* (20th-Fox, 1956) and the dance music for *Camelot* (WB, 1967).

RIVERA, CHITA. Actress, singer, dancer. b. Dolores Conchita Figueroa del Rivero, Jan. 23, 1933, Washington, D.C., to Julio and Katherine del Rivero. Grad. Taft H.S., Bronx, N.Y., 1951; attended Amer. Sch. of Ballet, N.Y.C., 1950–51. Married Dec. 1, to Anthony Mordente, actor; one daughter. Member of AFTRA; AEA; SAG. Address: (home) 15 W. 75th St., New York, NY 10023; (bus.) c/o Hasseltine, Bookman and Seff, Ltd., 200 W. 57th St., New York, NY 10019, tel. (212) LT 1-8850.

Theatre. Miss Rivera made her N.Y.C. debut as a dancer in *Guys and Dolls* (46 St. Th., Nov. 24, 1950); subsequently billed as Conchita Del Rivero, danced in the national touring company of *Call Me Madam* (opened Natl., Washington, D.C., May 5, 1952); appeared as a dancer in *Can-Can* (Shubert, N.Y.C., May 7, 1953); billed as Chita Rivera, performed in *Shoestring Review* (President, Feb. 28, 1955); played the singing and dancing role of Fifi in *Seventh Heaven* (ANTA, May 26, 1955); appeared as Rita Romano in *Mr. Wonderful* (Bway Th., Mar. 22, 1956); and Anita in *West Side Story* (Winter Garden,

N.Y.C., Sept. 26, 1957; Her Majesty's, London, England, Dec. 12, 1958).

She played Rosie in *Bye Bye Birdie* (Martin Beck Th., N.Y.C., Apr. 14, 1960), and repeated the role in London (Her Majesty's), and in summer theatre productions (Paper Mill Playhouse, Millburn, N.J.; Mineola Playhouse, L.I., N.Y., Starlight Th., Kansas City, Mo.); and appeared as Athena Constantine in the pre-Bway tryout of *Zenda* (opened Curran, San Francisco, Calif., Aug. 5, 1963; closed Pasadena Civic Aud., Calif., Nov. 16, 1963); appeared in the title role in a national touring production of *Sweet Charity* (Fall 1967); played The Leader in the national tour of *Zorba* (opened Philadelphia, Dec. 26, 1969); and Velma in *Chicago* (46 St. Th., N.Y.C., June 3, 1975).

Films. Miss Rivera appeared in *Sweet Charity* (U, 1969).

Television. Miss Rivera has appeared on the Garry Moore Show (CBS); the Ed Sullivan Show (CBS); the Arthur Godfrey Show (CBS); the Sid Caesar Show (NBC); the Dinah Shore Show (NBC); General Motors' 50th Anniversary Show; the Imogene Coca Show (NBC, 1954); Max Liebman (NBC); and, in London, on the Palladium Show.

Night Clubs. Her appearances include the Grand Finale (N.Y.C., 1975), and Studio One (Los Angeles, 1975).

Other Activities. She has made two tours for the Oldsmobile Industrial Show.

Awards. Miss Rivera is the recipient of the English Theatre Award and received *Best Plays'* Citation for her performance in *Bajour.*

ROBARDS, JASON. Actor. b. July 26, 1922, Chicago, Ill., to Jason and Hope Maxine (Glanville) Robards. Father, actor. Grad. Hollywood (Calif.) H.S., 1940; attended AADA, 1946; studied acting with Uta Hagen. Married May 7, 1948, to Eleanor Pitman (marr. dis. 1958); two sons, one daughter; married to Rachel Taylor (marr. dis.); married July 4, 1961, to Lauren Bacall (marr. dis. 1969); one son; married 1970 to Lois O'Connor; one daughter, one son. Served USN, 1940–46, PTO. Member of AFTRA; AEA; SAG; The Players; AADA (bd. mbr.).

Theatre. Mr. Robards made his debut as Nick in an AADA production of *Holiday* (1946); subsequently appeared in stock with Del-York Players (Rehoboth, Del., Summer 1947); with the Children's World Theatre (Barbizon-Plaza, N.Y.C., Winter 1947); and as Buoyant in *Buoyant Billions* (23rd St. YMCA, 1947).

He made his Bway debut as a walk-on with the D'Oyly Carte Opera Co. (Century Th.) in *The Mikado* (Dec. 29, 1947), *Iolanthe* (Jan. 12, 1948) and *The Yeomen of the Guard* (Feb. 2, 1948); was assistant stage manager and understudy for *Stalag 17* (48 St. Th., May 8, 1951); asst. stage manager for *The Chase* (Playhouse, Apr. 15, 1952); and was stage manager and played Witherspoon in the national touring company of *Stalag 17* (opened Biltmore, Los Angeles, Calif., June 26, 1952; closed Natl., Washington, D.C., May 16, 1953).

Mr. Robards played Ed Moody in *American Gothic* (Circle in the Square, N.Y.C., Nov. 10, 1953); and appeared in stock productions of *Stalag 17, The Philadelphia Story* and *Oh, Men! Oh, Woman!* (Playhouse-in-the-Park, Philadelphia, Pa.; Grist Mill Playhouse, Andover, N.J.; Stamford, Conn., Summer 1955).

He played Theodore Hickman (Hickey) in *The Iceman Cometh* (Circle in the Square, N.Y.C., May 8, 1956); James Tyrone, Jr., in *Long Day's Journey into Night* (Helen Hayes Th., Nov. 7, 1956); Hotspur in *Henry IV, Part 1* and Polixenes in *The Winter's Tale* (Stratford Shakespearean Festival, Can., Summer 1958); Manley Halliday in *The Disenchanted* (Coronet, N.Y.C., Dec. 3, 1958); and the title role in *Macbeth* (Cambridge, Mass., Drama Fest., Metropolitan Boston Arts Ctr., July 30–Aug. 16, 1959).

He portrayed Julian Berniers in *Toys in the Attic* (Hudson, N.Y.C., Feb. 25, 1960); William Baker in *Big Fish, Little Fish* (ANTA, Mar. 15, 1961); Murray Burns in *A Thousand Clowns* (Eugene O'Neill Th., Apr. 5, 1962); and, with the Repertory Th. of Lincoln Ctr., played Quentin in *After the Fall* (ANTA Washington Square, Jan. 23, 1964) and Seymour in *But for Whom Charlie* (ANTA Washington Square, Mar. 12, 1964).

He played "Erie" Smith in *Hughie* (Royale, Dec. 22, 1964; Huntington Hartford Th., Los Angeles, Feb. 22, 1965; and on tour); Father Urbain Grandier in *The Devils* (Broadway Th., N.Y.C., Nov. 16, 1965); Capt. Starkey in *We Bombed in New Haven* (Ambassador, Oct. 16, 1968); Frank Elgin in *The Country Girl* (Eisenhower Th., Washington, D.C., Nov. 1971; Billy Rose Th., N.Y.C., Mar. 15, 1972; Huntington Hartford Th., Los Angeles, May 15, 1972); James Tyrone, Jr., in *A Moon for the Misbegotten* (Academy Th., Lake Forest, Ill., June 1973; Eisenhower Th., Washington, D.C., Dec. 5, 1973; Morosco, N.Y.C., Dec. 29, 1973; Ahmanson, Los Angeles, Fall 1974); and directed and played James Tyrone, Sr., in *Long Day's Journey into Night* (Mendelssohn Th., Ann Arbor, Mich., Dec. 9, 1975; Eisenhower Th., Washington, D.C., Dec. 16, 1975; Opera House, Brooklyn Acad. of Music, Jan. 27, 1975).

Films. Mr. Robards appeared in *The Journey* (MGM, 1959); *By Love Possessed* (UA, 1961); *Tender Is the Night* (20th-Fox, 1962); as James Tyrone, Jr., in *Long Day's Journey into Night* (EMB, 1962); George S. Kaufman in *Act One* (WB, 1963); Murray Burns in *A Thousand Clowns* (UA, 1965); in *A Big Hand for the Little Lady* (WB, 1966); John Cleves in *Any Wednesday* (WB, 1966); in *Divorce, American Style* (Col., 1967); Al Capone in *The St. Valentine's Day Massacre* (20th-Fox, 1967); in *The Night They Raided Minsky's* (UA, 1968); *The Hour of the Gun* (UA, 1967); as Paris Singer in *Isadora;* re-cut and released as *The Loves of Isadora,* 1969); in *Once Upon a Time in the West* (Par., 1969); *The Ballad of Cable Hogue* (WB, 1970); *Tora! Tora! Tora!* (20th-Fox, 1970); *Fools* (Cinerama, 1970); *Johnny Got His Gun* (Cinemation, 1971); *Jud* (Maron, 1971); Brutus in *Julius Caesar* (Amer. Intl., 1971); in *Murders in the Rue Morgue* (Amer. Intl., 1971); *The War Between Men and Women* (Natl. Gen., 1972); and in *Pat Garrett and Billy the Kid* (MGM, 1973).

Television and Radio. On radio, he performed on Pepper Young's Family, Perry Mason, and Rosemary (CBS and NBC, 1948–50).

Mr. Robards has appeared on television as Roberto in *For Whom the Bell Tolls* (Playhouse 90, CBS, Mar. 12 and 19, 1959); in *Billy Budd* (Dupont Show of the Month, CBS, May 25, 1959); Dr. Rank in *The Doll's House* (Hallmark Hall of Fame, NBC, Nov. 15, 1959); in *The Bat* (Great Mysteries, NBC, Mar. 31, 1960); as Hickey in *The Iceman Cometh* (Play of the Week, WNTA, Nov. 14 and 21, 1960); the title role in *One Day in the Life of Ivan Denisovich* (Bob Hope Chrysler Th., NBC, Nov. 8, 1963); the title role in *Abe Lincoln in Illinois* (Hallmark Hall of Fame, NBC, Feb. 5, 1964); as the Father in the three specials, *The House without a Christmas Tree* (CBS, Dec. 3, 1972), *A Thanksgiving Visitor* (CBS, Nov. 1973), and *The Easter Promise* (CBS, Mar. 26, 1975); as Frank Elgin in *The Country Girl* (Hallmark Hall of Fame, NBC, Feb. 5, 1974); and as James Tyrone, Jr., in *A Moon for the Misbegotten* (ABC, May 27, 1975).

He has also appeared on The Alcoa Hour (NBC); Studio One (CBS); The Web (CBS); Suspense (CBS); Philco Television Playhouse (NBC); Ford Th. (CBS); Big Story (NBC); Treasury Men in Action (NBC); Armstrong Circle Th. (NBC); Justice (NBC); Appointment with Adventure (CBS); Goodyear Playhouse (NBC); Omnibus (NBC); ABC Stage 67; Ghost Story (NBC); Westinghouse Presents (CBS); and The Deputy (ABC), among others.

Awards. Mr. Robards received *The Village Voice* Off-Bway (Obie) Award for his performance as Hickey in *The Iceman Cometh* (1956); the 1956–57 NY Drama Critics Award as the Most Promising Actor (for *Long Day's Journey into Night*); the *Variety* NY Drama Critics Poll and the Antoinette Perry (Tony) Award for his performance as Manley Halliday in *The Disenchanted* (1959); won the *Variety* NY Drama Critics Poll for his performance as Julian Berniers in *Toys in the Attic* (1960), and again for his performance as Frank Elgin in *The Country Girl* (1972); received the US Film Exhibitors Award (1963), and the Achievement Award from the AADA (1963).

ROBBINS, CARRIE F. Costume designer. b. Carrie Mae Fishbein, Feb. 7, 1943, Baltimore, Md., to Sidney W. and Bettye A. (Berman) Fishbein. Father, high school history teacher. Educ. Forest Park H.S., Baltimore, Md. Grad. (Phi Beta Kappa) Pennsylvania State Univ., State College, Pa., with degree in art education and theatre arts; Drama School, Yale Univ., M.F.A. Professional training at Baltimore art schools from age three through high school; also, after Yale, Parsons, Traphagen, School of Visual Arts, and National Acad., all in N.Y.C. Married Feb. 15, 1969, to Richard D. Robbins, M.D. Member of United Scenic Artists; Natl. Soc. of Interior Designers; Amer. Inst. of Interior Designers. Address: 22 E. 36th St., Apt. 5A, New York, NY 10016, tel. (212) 532-5291.

Pre-Theatre. During her years in school, Miss Robbins designed book jackets, program covers, record album jackets, and posters. She also did drafting at George Izenour's theatre lab and sang and performed in reviews, particularly at the Hofbrau House, New Haven, Conn.

Theatre. Miss Robbins began her theatre work as an undergraduate, designing scenery and playing leads in Penn State Thespians' productions of *Bells Are Ringing* (Feb. 1962) and *Bye Bye Birdie* (Mar. 1963). At the Playhouse and Pavilion theatres, State College, Pa., she was resident set designer for *A Midsummer Night's Dream* (Mar. 3, 1964), *Come Back, Little Sheba* (Oct. 20, 1964), *The Hostage* and *The Merry Widow* (both Summer 1965). At the Yale Drama School she was assistant to Michael Annals on costumes for *Prometheus Bound* (1965) and did costumes for *Tartuffe* (Oct. 4, 1966) and *Pantagleize* (Mar. 1967). She started working in the professional theatre at the Studio Arena, Buffalo, N.Y., where she designed costumes for *The Mikado* (Dec. 18, 1966), *The Lesson* and Anouilh's *Antigone* (both Apr. 2, 1967), a production with the Buffalo Philharmonic of *The Barber of Seville* (Feb. 25, 1968), and *The Lion in Winter* (Oct. 31, 1968). At the Inner City Cultural Center, Los Angeles, Calif., she was resident costume designer (June–Dec. 1968), doing costumes for *Tartuffe, The Flies, The Glass Menagerie,* and *The Seagull.*

Her first work for the Bway stage was costumes for Leda Had a Little Swan (previews: Cort, Mar. 29–Apr. 10, 1968) and off-Bway for *Trainer, Dean, Liepolt and Company* (St. Clement's Ch., Dec. 12, 1968). Subsequent work included costumes for *The Millionairess* (Sheridan Square Playhouse, Mar. 2, 1969); *Inner Journey* Forum, Mar. 20, 1969); *The Year Boston Won the Pennant* (Forum, May 22, 1969); *Julius Caesar* (Tyrone Guthrie Th., Minneapolis, Minn., June 26, 1969); *The Time of Your Life* (Vivian Beaumont Th., N.Y.C., Nov. 6, 1969); *Look to the Lilies* (Lunt-Fontanne Th., Mar. 29, 1970); *The Good Woman of Setzuan* (Vivian Beaumont Th., Nov. 5, 1970); *An Enemy of the People* (Vivian Beaumont Th., Mar. 11, 1971); *Narrow Road to the Deep North* (Vivian Beaumont Th., Jan. 6, 1972); *Grease* (Eden, Feb. 14, 1972; Broadhurst, June 7, 1972); *The Beggar's Opera* (Brooklyn Acad. of Music, Mar. 21, 1972); *The Crucible* (Vivian Beaumont Th., Apr. 27, 1972); and *The Hostage* (Good Shepherd-Faith Church, Oct. 9, 1972).

Also, *The Secret Affairs of Mildred Wild* (Ambassador, Nov. 14, 1972); *Sunset* (Brooklyn Acad. of Music, Dec. 5, 1972); the bus and truck tour of the national company of *Grease* (Jan. 3, 1973); *The Plough and the Stars* (Vivian Beaumont Th., Jan. 4, 1973); *Let Me Hear You Smile* (Biltmore, Jan. 16, 1973); the Washington Opera Co.'s *The Rake's Progress* (Opera House, Kennedy Ctr., Washington, D.C., Feb. 5, 1973); the London production of *Grease* (New, London, June 1973); *Sisters of Mercy* (Shaw Festival, Canada, June 1973; Th. de Lys, N.Y.C., Sept. 25, 1973); *The Beggar's Opera* (Performing Arts Ctr., Saratoga, N.Y., July 1973; Billy

Rose Th., N.Y.C., Dec. 22, 1973); *Molly* (Alvin Th., Nov. 1, 1973); a revival of *The Iceman Cometh* (Circle in the Square/Joseph E. Levine Th., Dec. 13, 1973); *Over Here!* (Sam S. Shubert Th., Mar. 6, 1974); *The Merry Wives of Windsor* (Delacorte Th., July 28, 1974); *The Taming of the Shrew* (Good Shepherd-Faith Church, Sept. 1974); *Yentl—The Yeshiva Boy* (Brooklyn Acad. of Music, Dec. 20, 1974); and *Polly* (Brooklyn Acad. of Music, May 8, 1975).

Films. Miss Robbins designed costumes for Bell Telephone's *Flight of Fantasy* (June 1970).

Television. Miss Robbins designed costumes for two productions of WNET's Theatre in America series: *In Fashion* (PBS, Feb. 1974) and *The Seagull* (PBS, Jan. 1975).

Other Activities. Miss Robbins's work has been exhibited at the Wright-Hepburn Gallery, N.Y.C., and was included in the ITI touring exhibit, *Contemporary Stage Design—U.S.A.* In addition to her theatre work, Miss Robbins teaches costume design and history as a member of the faculty, Design Dept., NY Univ.

Awards. Miss Robbins was nominated for Antoinette Perry (Tony) awards as best costume designer for *Grease* (1971–72) and *Over Here!* (1973–74). She received the Drama Desk Award as most promising costume designer for *Grease* and *The Beggar's Opera* (1971–72) and the Drama Desk Award for her costumes for *Over Here!* and *The Iceman Cometh* (1973–74).

Recreation. Miss Robbins gives her hobbies as: "looking—at magazines; stores of any kind, anywhere; museums; buses; fabrics; tap dancing (alone in well-tiled bathrooms) in class when time permits; looking after my husband, dog, two cats, and plants.".

ROBBINS, EDWARD E. Artists' representative. b. Jan. 20, 1930, Brooklyn, N.Y., to Morris and Sophie (Brinen) Robbins. Grad. Metropolitan Vocational H.S., N.Y.C., 1948. Served US Army, Special Services, 1953–55; rank, PFC. Member of TARA; Jewish Theatrical Guild; B'nai B'rith. Address: (home) 25 Central Park West, New York, NY 10023; (bus.) 1350 Avenue of the Americas, New York, NY 10019, tel. (212) JU 6-5100.

Recreation. Theatre, art, music, and travel.

ROBBINS, JEROME. Director, producer, choreographer, dancer. b. Jerome Rabinowitz, Oct. 11, 1918, New York City, to Harry and Lena (Rips) Rabinowitz. Father, corset manufacturer. Grad. Woodrow Wilson H.S., Weehawken, N.J., 1935; attended New York Univ., 1935–36. Studied ballet with Ella Daganova, H. Platova, Eugene Loring, Anthony Tudor; modern dance with the New Dance League, N.Y.C.; Spanish dance with Helene Veola. Member of AEA; AGMA; DGA. 117 E. 81st St., New York, NY 10028.

Theatre. Mr. Robbins made his debut as a dancer, with the Sandor-Sorel Dance Ctr. (1937); subsequently danced in *Great Lady* (Majestic Th., N.Y.C., Feb. 9, 1939); *The Straw Hat Revue* (Ambassador, Sept. 29, 1939); *Keep Off the Grass* (Broadhurst, May 23, 1940); and danced and choreographed at Camp Tamiment, Pa. (1938–41).

He joined the corps de ballet of Ballet Th. (1940), appearing as Hermes in *Helen of Troy* (Detroit, Mich., world premiere Nov. 29, 1942); the Moor in *Petrouchka;* the Youth in *Three Virgins and a Devil;* and Benvolio in *Romeo and Juliet* (Metropolitan Opera House, world premiere N.Y.C., Apr. 6, 1943). Mr. Robbins choreographed *Fancy Free,* for the Ballet Th., in which he danced the role of one of the Sailors (world premiere, Metropolitan Opera House, Apr. 18, 1944); choreographed *On the Town,* which was based on *Fancy Free* (Adelphi, Dec. 28, 1944); created and danced in the ballet, *Interplay,* in *Concert Varieties* (world premiere, Ziegfeld, June 1, 1945); and appeared in Ballet Th. repertoire (Metropolitan Opera House, Oct. 17, 1945).

Mr. Robbins choreographed and staged the musical numbers for *Billion Dollar Baby* (Alvin, Dec. 21, 1945); created and danced in *Facsimile* for Ballet Th. (world premiere, Bway Th., Oct. 24, 1946), choreographed *Pas de Trois* for the Original Ballet Russe (world premiere, Metropolitan Opera House, Mar. 26, 1947); created the dances and staged the musical numbers in *High Button Shoes* (Century, Oct. 9, 1947); and for the Ballet Th., choreographed and danced in *Summer Day* (world premiere, NY City Ctr., Dec. 2, 1947).

He wrote the book, directed with George Abbott, and created the choreography for *Look, Ma, I'm Dancin'* (Adelphi, Jan. 29, 1948); directed the pre-Bway tryout of *That's the Ticket* (opened Shubert, Philadelphia, Pa., Sept. 24, 1948; closed there, Oct. 2, 1948); joined the NY City Ballet Co. (1949), became associate artistic director (1950), for which he choreographed *The Guests* (world premiere, NY City Ctr., Jan. 20, 1949); created the choreography and directed the musical numbers for *Miss Liberty* (Imperial, July 15, 1949); danced in Balanchine's *Bourrée Fantasque* (world premiere, NY City Ctr., Dec. 1, 1949); danced the title role in Balanchine's *The Prodigal Son* (NY City Ctr., Feb. 23, 1950); choreographed and danced in *The Age of Anxiety* (world premiere, NY City Ctr., Feb. 26, 1950); and, with Mr. Balanchine, choreographed *Jones Beach* (world premiere, NY City Ctr., Mar. 9, 1950).

He directed and choreographed *Call Me Madam* (Imperial, Oct. 12, 1950); choreographed *The King and I,* for which he created the ballet, *The Small House of Uncle Thomas* (St. James, Mar. 29, 1951); for the NY City Ballet Co., choreographed *The Cage* (world premiere, NY City Ctr., June 10, 1951); in Israel, was associated with the Yemenite company, Inbal (Summers 1951, 1952, 1953); choreographed and danced in *The Pied Piper* (NY City Ctr., Dec. 4, 1951); choreographed and staged the musical numbers for *Two's Company* (Alvin, Dec. 4, 1951); and for the NY City Ballet Co., choreographed *Wonderful Town* (Winter Garden, Feb. 25, 1953); *Afternoon of a Faun* (NY City Ctr., May 14, 1953); *Fanfare* (world premiere, NY City Ctr., June 2, 1953), which he restaged for the Royal Danish Ballet (1956); and *Quartet* (world premiere, NY City Ctr., Feb. 18, 1954).

Mr. Robbins choreographed the opera, *The Tender Land,* for the NY City Opera Co. (world premiere, NY City Ctr., Apr. 1, 1954); directed with George Abbott, *Pajama Game* (St. James, May 13, 1954); adapted, directed, and choreographed Mary Martin's *Peter Pan* (Winter Garden, Oct. 20, 1954); choreographed and directed *The Bells Are Ringing,* staging the dances and musical numbers with Bob Fosse (Shubert, Nov. 29, 1956); and conceived, directed, and choreographed *West Side Story* (Winter Garden, Sept. 26, 1957; Her Majesty's, London, Dec. 12, 1958).

Mr. Robbins formed his own company, *Ballets: U.S.A.* which performed at the Spoleto (Italy) Festival of Two Worlds, the Brussels (Belgium) World's Fair, toured the US (1958), and performed in N.Y.C. (Alvin, Sept. 4, 1958).

He choreographed and directed *Gypsy* (Bway Th., May 21, 1959); toured Europe for the State Dept. with *Ballets: U.S.A.* (1959, 1961), and played in N.Y.C. (ANTA, Oct. 8, 1961); directed *Oh Dad, Poor Dad, Mama's Hung You in the Closet and I'm Feelin' So Sad* (Phoenix, Feb. 26, 1962); *Mother Courage and Her Children* (Martin Beck Th., Mar. 28, 1963); and directed and choreographed *Fiddler on the Roof* (Imperial, Sept. 22, 1964).

He choreographed *Les Noces* (Amer. Ballet Th., 1965 and Royal Swedish Ballet, 1969); *Moves* (Joffrey Ballet, 1967; Batsheva Dance Co., 1969; and Nederlands Dans Th. (premiered at Venice Festival), 1973); *N. Y. Export: Opus Jazz* (Harkness Ballet, 1969; and Joffrey Ballet, 1974); *Dances at a Gathering* (NY City Ballet, 1969; and Royal Ballet, 1970); *In the Night* (NY City Ballet, 1970; and Royal Ballet, 1973); choreographed one section of George Balanchine's new version of *Firebird* (NY City Ballet, 1970); *The Goldberg Variations* (NY City Ballet, 1971); revived *The Concert* (NY City Ballet, 1971); choreographed *Afternoon of a Faun* (Royal Ballet, 1971); *Watermill* (NY City Ballet, 1972); *Scherzo Fantastique* and *Circus Polka* (NY City Ballet, 1972; and Paris Opera, 1974); *Dunbarton Oaks* (NY City Ballet, 1972); with George Balanchine, choreographed a new version of *Pulcinella* (NY City Ballet, 1972); choreographed *Requiem Canticles* (NY City Ballet, 1972; and Bayerischen Staadsper, Munich, Germany, 1974); *Interplay* (Joffrey Ballet, 1972); *An Evening's Waltzes* (NY City Ballet, 1973); and *Celebration: The Art of the Pas de Deux* (Spoleto, Italy, 1973).

Under a US government grant, Mr. Robbins formed the American Theatre Laboratory, Inc. (1966–68), to explore theatre forms involving dance, song, and speech.

Films. Mr. Robbins choreographed the film version of *The King and I* (20th-Fox, 1956); and choreographed and co-directed *West Side Story* (UA, 1961).

Television. He directed and choreographed the Ford 50th Anniversary Show with Mary Martin and Ethel Merman (1953); and directed and choreographed the three telecasts of Mary Martin's *Peter Pan* (NBC, 1955, 1956, 1960).

Awards. Mr. Robbins received the Donaldson awards for *Billion Dollar Baby* (1945), *High Button Shoes* (1947), *The King and I* (1951); *Two's Company* (1952); and *The Pajama Game* (1954); and the Antoinette Perry (Tony) awards for *High Button Shoes* (1947) and *West Side Story* (1957). He received the *Look* Magazine Award for *Peter Pan* (1956); and the *Dance* Magazine award for Outstanding Achievement (1950, 1957). He received the Sylvania Award for the Ford 50th Anniversary Show (1953); the NATAS (Emmy) Award for *Peter Pan* (1955); a Box Office Blue Ribbon Award for *The King and I* (1956); the London *Evening Standard* Drama Award for *West Side Story* (1958); a City of New York Citation by Mayor Wagner for *Ballets: U.S.A.* (1959); Thâåtre des Nations Award for best choreography (1959); SBI Gold Owl for *West Side Story* (1961); Screen Directors Guild Award for *West Side Story* (1961); and Academy (Oscar) awards for choreography and direction of *West Side Story* (1961). He was named Chevalier of the Order of Arts and Sciences (France, 1964); received the Drama Critics Circle Award for best musical for *Fiddler on the Roof* (1965); and, at the International Dance Festival (Paris, France), received the City of Paris Award for *Les Noces* (1971).

Recreation. Photography.

ROBERTS, BEVERLY. Actress, director, executive. b. Beverly Louise Roberts, May 19, 1914, Brooklyn, N.Y., to Arthur K. and Mary Louise (Genner) Roberts. Father, sales manager. Grad. Girls H.S., Bklyn., 1930. Studied art at Pratt Inst., 1928–29; apprenticed at Civic Rep. Th., N.Y.C., 1931–32; singing with Al Segal, Hollywood, Calif., 1939–40; Marguerite Haymes, N.Y.C., 1943–45; dancing with Mme. Chamie of the Diaghilev Ballet, N.Y.C., 1944–45; fencing with Miltiades, N.Y.C., 1944–45. Member of AEA (on council, 1951–54); AFRA; AFTRA (bd. mbr., 1949–53); Television Authority (1952); SAG. 485 Fifth Ave., New York, NY 10017, tel. (212) MU 2-4215.

Theatre. Miss Roberts directed three Eugene O'Neill one-act plays (Madison Square Boys Club, N.Y.C., 1931); played Lady Bridget Manners in *The Passionate Pilgrim* (48 St. Th., N.Y.C., Oct. 19, 1932); understudied Florence Williams as Manuela in *Girls in Uniform* (Booth, Dec. 30, 1932); appeared in *Paris* (Newport Casino, R.I., Summer 1941); played Rosalind in *Heart of a City* (Henry Miller's Th., N.Y.C., Feb. 12, 1942); and Lucy in *Uncle Harry* (Broadhurst, May 20, 1942). At the Newport Casino, she played Lydia in *Skylark* (Summer 1942); succeeded Claudia Morgan as Vera Claythorne in *Ten Little Indians* (Broadhurst, N.Y.C., June 27, 1944), which she later directed in various summer stock theatres (1945); and directed and appeared in a stock tour of *Blithe Spirit* (Atlantic City, N.J.; Fairhaven, Mass.; Summer 1946).

Films. Miss Roberts has appeared in *China Clipper* (1st Natl., 1936); *The Singing Kid* (1st Natl., 1936);

Two Against the World (1st Natl., 1936); *God's Country and the Woman* (WB, 1936); *The Perfect Specimen* (1st Natl., 1937); and more than 18 films for Columbia, Universal, and Republic (1938–40).

Television and Radio. Miss Roberts has performed on more than 60 radio programs, among them: Woodbury Playhouse (1936–37); Hollywood Hotel (1936–37); Lux Radio Th. (1937–38); Screen Guild of the Air (1937–38); John Barrymore's *Hamlet* (1938); *Icebound* (1938); *Animal Kingdom* (1938); Kate Smith Hour (1940); Society Girl (1941–42); Silver Th. (1942); Romance (1947); Light of the World (1947–48); Portia Faces Life (1948); and Our Gal Sunday (1949).

She has appeared on the following television programs: Celanese Th. (ABC); Studio One (CBS, 1949–52); Westinghouse Th. (CBS, 1949–52); NBC Playhouse; Martin Kane (CBS, 1949–50); Kraft Television Th. (NBC, 1950–51); Americana (NBC); Think Fast (1950–51); Great Day; Once Upon a Tune (1951); Ethel and Albert (ABC, 1952–53); and Schlitz Playhouse (CBS).

Night Clubs. Miss Roberts has performed at the Cafe aux Noctambules (Paris, 1932); in N.Y.C., at the House of Lords (1934), Town Casino (1935), and Versailles (1941–42); and the Chez Paree (Chicago, 1941).

Other Activities. Since 1954, Miss Roberts has been executive secretary of the US Theatre Authority, an amalgam of the theatrical performers' unions including AEA, AFTRA, AGMA, AGVA and SAG, which regulates the appearances of performers at fund-raising events such as benefit dinners and telethons throughout the US.

Recreation. Painting, sculpture, archaeology, astronomy, mountaineering, undersea exploration. Polynesian and Peruvian peoples (ancient and modern), Biblical history and civilizations.

ROBERTS, DORIS. Actress. b. Nov. 4, 1930, St. Louis, Mo. Mother, Ann Roberts, theatrical stenographer. Educ. P.S. 19; Washington Irving H.S.; New York Univ.; all in N.Y.C. Professional training with Sanford Meisner at Neighborhood Playhouse and Lee Strasberg at Actors' Studio. Married Nov. 10, 1963, to William Goyen, author; one son by previous marriage. Member of AEA; SAG; AFTRA. Address: 277 West End Ave., New York, NY 10023, tel. (212) 877-9397.

Theatre. Miss Roberts first appeared on stage as an undergraduate at New York Univ. She made her professional debut in 1953 at Ann Arbor, Mich., and appeared in summer stock at Chatham, Mass., in 1955. Her first N.Y.C. performance was as the Prostitute in a revival of *The Time of Your Life* (NY City Ctr., Jan. 19, 1955), followed by appearances as Miss Rumple in *The Desk Set* (Broadhurst, Oct. 24, 1955); the Nurse in *The Death of Bessie Smith* (York, Feb. 28, 1961); the Other Woman in *Natural Affection* (Phoenix, Ariz., 1962); and Minnalou in American Place Theatre's *Christy* (1962). She was in the production *Color of Darkness* as Mrs. Klein in *Don't Call Me By My Right Name* and Jennie in *You Reach for Your Hat* (Writers' Stage, Sept. 30, 1963); was Rae Wilson in *Marathon '33* (ANTA, Dec. 22, 1963); standby for Ruth White as Madame Girard in *Malcolm* (Sam S. Shubert Th., Jan. 11, 1966); Miss Punk in *The Office* (previews: Henry Miller's Th., Apr. 20, 1966); standby for Shelley Winters in *Under the Weather* (Cort, Oct. 27, 1966); Edna in *The Natural Look* (Longacre, Mar. 11, 1967); the Mother in *A Matter of Position* (Stockbridge, Mass., Summer 1968); Jeanette Fisher in *Last of the Red Hot Lovers* (Eugene O'Neill Th., Dec. 28, 1969); Miss Manley in *The Secret Affairs of Mildred Wild* (Ambassador, Nov. 14, 1972); and was Dolly Scupp in *Ravenswood* and Nurse Hedges in *Dunelawn*, both plays on the program *Bad Habits* (Astor Place Th., Feb. 4, 1974); Booth Th., May 5, 1974).

Films. Miss Roberts made her motion picture debut in *Something Wild* (UA, 1961), following with performances in *Barefoot in the Park* (Par., 1967); *No Way to Treat a Lady* (Par., 1968); *A Lovely Way to Die* (U, 1968); *Honeymoon Killers* (Cinerama, 1970); *A New Leaf* (Par., 1971); *Such Good Friends* (Par., 1971); *Little Murders* (20th-Fox, 1971); *Heartbreak Kid* (Par., 1972); *Hestor Street* (1974); and *The Taking of Pelham, One, Two, Three* (UA, 1974).

Television. Miss Roberts made her television debut on Studio One (CBS, 1950). She appeared in *The Mad Dog* (The Defenders, CBS, 1959); *The Lady of Larkspur Lotion* (Play of the Week, WNTA, Feb. 6, 1961); *Shadow-Game* (CBS Playhouse, 1968); *Look Homeward, Angel* (CBS Playhouse 90, Feb. 25, 1972); the Neil Simon Comedy Hour (NBC, 1973); and the Lily Tomlin Comedy Hour (ABC, 1974).

Awards. Miss Roberts received the Outer Critics Circle Award in 1974 for her performance in *Bad Habits*.

Recreation. Painting, needlepoint.

ROBERTS, JOAN. Actress, Singer. b. Josephine Seagrist, July 15, 1922, New York City, to Julius and Mary Seagrist. Grad. Cathedral H.S., N.Y.C., 1939; attended Fordham Sch. of Adult Education, 1943–45. Studied voice with Raphael del la Marca, N.Y.C., two years; Estelle Liebling, N.Y.C., seven years; drama with Claudia Franck, N.Y.C., three years; Ballet Art School, N.Y.C., two years; Rockville Dance Academy, Rockville Ctr., N.Y., two years. Married May 5, 1946, to John Donlon, physician (dec.); married to Alexander Peter, dentist; one son. Served WW II, USO. Member of ASA; SAG; AGVA. Address: 141 Hempstead Ave., Rockville Ctr., NY 11570, tel. (516) RO 6-4473.

Theatre. Miss Roberts made her professional debut as Kathy in *The Student Prince* (Dallas Under the Stars, Tex., June 1, 1940); subsequently appeared (Dallas, Tex.) in the title role in *Irene*, as Marsha in *The Chocolate Soldier* and in *Too Many Girls* (June–July 1940); played Nanette in *No! No! Nanette!* (St. Louis Municipal Opera, Mo., Oct. 11, 1940); Loo Loo in *Hit the Deck* (Philharmonic Aud., Los Angeles, Calif., Oct. 1941); and made her N.Y.C. debut as Madeleine Caresse in *Sunny River* (St James, Dec. 4, 1941).

She played Madeleine in *New Orleans* (St. Louis Municipal Opera, Mo., June 4, 1942); the title role in *Naughty Marietta* (Louisville Light Opera Co., Ky., July 1942); appeared as Laurey in *Oklahoma!* (St. James, N.Y.C., Mar. 31, 1943); in the title role in *Marinka* (Winter Garden, July 18, 1945); as Vivian Reilly in *Are You With It?* (Century, Nov. 10, 1945); succeeded Nanette Fabray as Sara Longstreet in *High Button Shoes* (Century, Oct. 9, 1947); repeated the role of Sara Longstreet in *High Button Shoes* and also appeared in *Show Boat* (Pittsburgh Opera Co., Pa., July 1952); played the title role in *No! No! Nanette!* Evalina in *Bloomer Girl*, and appeared in *Show Boat* (Miami Tent Th., Fla., 1954); played in *Lady in the Dark* (Long Beach Th., N.Y., 1955); as Evalina in *Bloomer Girl* (Louisville Light Opera Co., Ky., 1955; Guthsville Playhouse, Allentown, Pa., 1956); as a singer with the Pittsburgh (Pa.) Symphony Orchestra (Sept. 1959); in *Dinner for Three* (Houston Th. in the Round, Tex., 1960); and in a tent-theatre touring production of *Take Me Along* (1962).

Television. Miss Roberts appeared on the Texaco Star Th. (NBC, 1947); Fireside Playhouse (1948); on her own show, Joan Roberts Sings (WOR, 1951); on the Steve Allen Show (NBC, 1952); and with the Prince Street Players in *Jack and the Beanstalk* (CBS, 1966).

Night Clubs. She appeared at the Persian Room (Plaza Hotel, N.Y.C., 1950); and toured the US and Canada in an act which included James Eiler and Bill Nuss (1959–60).

Discography. Miss Roberts has recorded albums for Columbia in 1965 and 1967).

Awards. Miss Roberts received an Oklahoma State Citation from Governor Kerr (1944); Mayor LaGuardia Citation for her work in charitable causes (1945); Red Cross Citation (1946); Armed Forces Citation for her work with the USO (1946).

Recreation. Sewing, painting, cooking, horseback riding, ice-skating.

ROBERTS, LOUISE. Theatre executive, producer. b. Naomi Louise Roberts, May 18, 1911, Boston, Mass., to Maurice and Clara (Levine) Roberts. Father, dentist and manufacturer. Attended Boston and New York public schools; grad. Hunter Coll., B.A. (political sci.) 1931; attended Columbia Univ., N.Y.U. Th. Program. Married 1942 to Paul Ziporkis (dec.); one daughter, Karen De Francis, stage manager and lighting designer. Relative in theatre: cousin, Samuel Golding, playwright (dec.). Address: (home) 71 Lexington Ave., New York, NY 10010, tel. (212) MU 6-4637; (bus.) Clark Center for the Performing Arts, 939 Eighth Ave., New York, NY 10019, tel. (212) 246-4818.

Pre-Theatre. Guidance councellor at Rikers Island Prison; Peace Corps consultant.

Theatre. As director (Mar. 1970–to date) of the Clark Center for the Performing Arts, Miss Roberts founded (1971) Playwrights Horizons, where, until 1974, some one hundred and twenty new plays were presented. She has subsequently produced *Clark Center Dance Festival—The Mall* (June 1975 and July–Aug. 1976) at City Univ.

Other Activities. At the invitation of the Tunisian government, she and Donald McKayle toured that country and co-authored (1964–65) a report on its indigenous dance.

Awards. For Clark Center, she has been the recipient of grants from The National Endowment for the Arts; The NY State Council on the Arts; The Chase Manhattan Bank; and The Shubert, Clark, and Mobil foundations.

Recreation. College.

ROBERTS, MEADE. Playwright. b. Stanley Robert Mednick, June 13, 1930, New York City, to Jacob D. and Lillian (Patterson) Mednick. Father, architectural engineer. Relatives in theatre: cousin, Peter Daniels, composer-pianist; cousin, Anita Yager, actress. Grad. Erasmus Hall H.S., Brooklyn, 1947; New York Univ., B.A. 1950. Member of WGA, Dramatists Guild. Address: (home) 215 E. 68th St., New York, NY 10021, tel. (212) BU 8-3530; (bus.) c/o Frank Cooper Associates, 680 Fifth Ave., New York, NY 10021.

Theatre. Mr. Roberts wrote *A Palm Tree in a Rose Garden* (Pocono Playhouse; Bucks County Playhouse; Falmouth Playhouse, July 1955; Cricket Th., N.Y.C., Nov. 26, 1957), which toured Germany and Austria (Jan. 1959); subsequently wrote *Maidens and Mistresses at Home at the Zoo* (Orpheum, N.Y.C., Jan. 21, 1959; Festival of Two Worlds, Teatro Caio Melisso, Spoleto, Italy, June 1960); and *Icarus at Noon.*.

Films. Mr. Roberts, with Tennessee Williams, wrote the screenplays for *The Fugitive Kind* (UA, 1960) and *Summer and Smoke* (Par., 1961); wrote the screenplays for *In the Cool of the Day* (MGM, 1963) *The Stripper* (20th-Fox, 1963); *Blue* (Par., 1968); and *Danger Route* (UA, 1968).

Television and Radio. Mr. Roberts wrote for the Radio City Playhouse (NBC Radio, Sept. 1948). For television, he wrote *A Lovely Night for a Birthday* (NBC, Sept. 1951); *Sound of Waves Breaking* (Lux Video Th., CBS, Jan. 1952); *Rainy Day in Paradise Junction* (Columbia TV Workshop, CBS, Apr. 1952); *Circus Story* (Suspense, CBS, Sept. 1953); *The Rose Garden* (Kraft Television Th., NBC, Dec. 1953); *All Our Yesterdays* (Kraft Television Th., NBC, Apr. 1954); *Hickory Limb* (Ponds Th., ABC, Jan. 1955); *A Domestic Dilemma* (Windows, CBS, July 1955); *The Wings of the Dove* (Playhouse 90, CBS, Jan. 1959); *The Impossible Dream* (Alfred Hitchcock Presents, CBS, 1959); and *Misalliance* (Playhouse 90, CBS, Oct. 1959).

Recreation. Traveling, walking, music, frequenting coffeehouses the world over.

ROBERTS, TONY. Actor. b. David Anthony Roberts, Oct. 22, 1939, New York City, to Kenneth and Norma Roberts. Father, announcer; mother, cartoon animator. Educ. P.S. 6 and High School of Music and Art, both in N.Y.C. Grad. Northwestern Univ., B.S.S. 1961. Studied acting with Alvina Krause and also during two seasons of amateur stock repertory at Eaglesmere Playhouse, Pa. Relative in theatre: cousin, Everett Sloane. Married Dec. 14, 1969 (marr. dis. 1975); one daughter. Served in US Army, 1962. Member of AEA (governing council, 1968–74).

Theatre. Mr. Roberts made his stage debut as a child in 1950, when he appeared as Calpurnia in *Julius Caesar* at a summer camp in New Hampshire. He made his Bway debut as the Air Cadet in *Something About a Soldier* (Ambassador, Jan. 4, 1962); replaced (1962) Walter Moulder as Richard Gluck in *Take Her, She's Mine* (Biltmore, Dec. 21, 1961); toured as Buddy in the national company of *Come Blow Your Horn* (Philadelphia, Detroit, Washington, D.C., 1962); replaced (1963) Orson Bean as Charlie in *Never Too Late* (Playhouse, Nov. 27, 1962); appeared off-Bway in a revival of *The Cradle Will Rock* (1963); was Paul Braher in *Barefoot in the Park* (Biltmore, Oct. 23, 1963); Max Bummidge in *The Last Analysis* (Belasco Th., Oct. 1, 1964); Axel Magee in *Don't Drink the Water* (Morosco, Nov. 17, 1966); Charlie Matson in *How Now, Dow Jones* (Lunt-Fontanne Th., Dec. 7, 1967); and Dick Christie in *Play It Again, Sam* (Broadhurst, Feb. 12, 1969). He made his London, England, debut as Chuck Baxter in *Promises, Promises* (Prince of Wales Th., Oct. 2, 1969); toured the US in the same role in the national company of *Promises, Promises* (opened San Diego, Calif., May 11, 1970); replaced (Oct. 26, 1970–Apr. 11, 1971) Jerry Orbach as Chuck Baxter in the N.Y.C. production (Sam S. Shubert Th., Dec. 1, 1968); was Joe and Josephine in *Sugar* (Majestic, Apr. 9, 1972); appeared in 1973 with the Yale Repertory Th., New Haven, Conn., as Antonio in *The Tempest* (Oct. 5) and Richard in *Darkroom* (Oct. 19); and was Geoffrey in *Absurd Person Singular* (Kennedy Ctr., Washington, D.C., Sept. 1974; Music Box, N.Y.C., Oct. 8, 1974).

Films. Mr. Roberts first appeared in films in *The Million Dollar Duck* (Buena Vista, 1971), following with performances in *Star Spangled Girl* (Par., 1971); *Play It Again, Sam* (Par., 1971); *Serpico* (Par., 1973); and *The Taking of Pelham, One, Two, Three* (UA, 1974).

Television. Mr. Roberts made his television debut as Lee Pollock on The Edge of Night (CBS, 1963–65) and was the Doctor in *The Messiah on Mott Street* (Night Gallery, NBC, 1967). His other television appearances include Love American Style (ABC); Let's Celebrate (ABC); The Defenders (CBS); and The Trials of O'Brien (CBS).

Awards. Mr. Roberts received Antoinette Perry (Tony) Award nominations for *Play It Again, Sam* and for *How Now, Dow Jones*, and he won the London Critics Poll Award for *Promises, Promises*.

Recreation. Chess, sailing, photography.

ROBERTS, VERA MOWRY. Educator, director. b. Vera Lilian Mowry, Oct. 21, 1918, Pittsburgh, Pa., to Joseph E. and Emma (Steinmann) Mowry. Father, painting contractor. Grad. Univ. of Pittsburgh, B.S. 1936; M.A. 1940; Ph.D. 1950. Also trained as teacher, secretary, and in public relations. Married Jan. 4, 1951, to Pernell Roberts, actor (marr. dis. 1959); one son. Served USN (WAVES); 1943–46; rank, Lt. Member of ATA (chmn., International Liaison; pres., N.Y. dist., 1960–61; national pres., 1973; fellow, 1972–to date); ANTA; Speech Assn. of Amer.; AEA; Phi Delta Gamma (natl. ed., Phi Delta Gamma Jour., 1947–49; natl. pres., 1950–52). Address: (home) 303 W. 66th St., New York, NY 10023; (bus.) c/o Hunter College, 695 Park Ave., New York, NY 10021, tel. (212) 360-2704.

Pre-Theatre. Secretary.

Theatre. Dr. Roberts made her debut as Titania in a high school production of *A Midsummer Night's Dream* (Oct. 1930); her professional debut in Pittsburgh (Pa.) was as a speaking extra in Ethel Barrymore's *The Kingdom of God* (Nixon Th., Dec. 1932).

She was director and stage manager for the Mount Vernon Players (Washington, D.C., 1945–48); assistant director for *Alice in Wonderland* and *Peter Pan* (Children's Th., Washington, D.C., 1947–48), where she directed *The Merry Devil of Edmonton* for the Southeast Dramatics Assn. (May, 1948); staged *Port Tobacco Flames* for the State of Maryland Pageant (1949); *The Jealous Wife* (Little Th., Alexandria, Va., Apr. 1950); and directed her first stock production, Hoyt's *A Texas Steer* (Cross Roads Th., Alexandria, Va., July 1950).

Dr. Roberts was a co-founder of the Arena Stage (Washington, D.C.) and was active in thirty six productions as designer, director, costume designer, or publicity director (Aug. 1950–June 1954); and was stage manager for ten plays produced by the Port Players (Oconomowoc, Wis., Summer 1954).

Dr. Roberts has been associated with Hunter Coll. where she is presently professor and chairman of the Dept. of Theatre and Cinema, and a member of the Doctoral Faculty of the City Univ. of N.Y. (1955–to date), and has staged *The Grass Harp* (Nov. 1955); *Dear Brutus* (Mar. 1956); *Maedchen in Uniform* (Nov. 1956); Giraudoux's *Electra* (Apr. 1957); *The Cradle Song* (Nov. 1957); *In the Summer House* (Apr. 1958); *Down in the Valley* (May 1958); *Tiger at the Gates* (Nov. 1958); *The Lowland Sea* (Dec. 1958); *Yerma* (Apr. 1959); *The Cave Dwellers* (Oct. 1959); *The Skin of Our Teeth* (Apr. 1960); *Arms and the Man* (Nov. 1960); *The Children's Hour* (Apr. 1961); *The Prodigal* (Oct. 1962); *You Can't Take It with You* (Oct. 1963); Sophocles' *Antigone* (Apr. 1963); *Sing Out Sweet Land* (Nov. 1963); *Othello* (Apr. 1964); *The Cave Dwellers* (Apr. 1965); *The Lady's Not for Burning* (Apr. 1966); *The Madwoman of Chaillot* (May 1967); and *The Italian Straw Hat* (May 1968); directed three plays for the Magic Circle Children's Th. (Medford, Mass., Summer 1960); and directed *Father Oxbridge Wants to Marry* (Act IV Experimental Th., Provincetown, Mass., July 1968).

Published Works. Dr. Roberts is the author of *On Stage: A History of Theatre* (1962; 2nd ed., 1974); *The Nature of Theatre* (1972); and has contributed various articles to periodicals and encyclopedias.

Recreation. Collecting rare books, hiking, handicrafts.

ROBIN, LEO. Lyricist. b. Apr. 6, 1899, Pittsburgh, Pa. Attended Univ. of Pittsburgh c. 1920; Carnegie Inst. of Technology. Married to Estelle Clarke, actress. Member of ASCAP; Song Writers Protective Assn.; AMPAS; Dramatists Guild.

Theatre. Mr. Robin wrote the lyrics, with Clifford Grey, for *Hit the Deck* (Belasco, N.Y.C., Apr. 25, 1927); wrote the lyrics for *Gentlemen Prefer Blondes* (Ziegfeld, Dec. 8, 1949); *The Girl in Pink Tights* (Mark Hellinger Th., Mar. 5, 1954). His lyrics were included in *The Harold Arlen Songbook* (Stage 73, Feb. 28, 1967); and he wrote lyrics for *Lorelei* (National Th., Washington, D.C., May 15, 1973; Palace, N.Y.C., Jan. 27, 1974).

Films. He wrote lyrics for *Innocents of Paris* (Par., 1929); *Monte Carlo* (Par., 1930); *One Hour with You* (Par., 1932); *Blonde Venus* (Par., 1932); *All of Me* (Par., 1934); *Kiss and Make Up* (Par., 1934); *She Loves Me Not* (Par., 1934); *Little Miss Marker* (Par., 1934); *The Big Broadcast of 1935* (Par., 1935); *The Big Broadcast of 1937* (Par., 1936); *The Devil Is a Woman* (Par., 1937); *Waikiki Wedding* (Par., 1937); *Angel* (Par., 1937); *The Big Broadcast of 1938* (Par., 1938); *Tropical Holiday* (Par., 1938); *St. Louis Blues* (Par., 1939); *Paris Honeymoon* (Par., 1939); *Gulliver's Travels* (Par., 1939); *Tall, Dark and Handsome* (20th-Fox, 1941); *My Sister Eileen* (Col., 1942); *My Gal Sal* (20th-Fox, 1942); *Coney Island* (20th-Fox, 1943); *The Gang's All Here* (20th-Fox, 1943); *The Time, the Place and the Girl* (WB, 1946); *The Way of Love* (Burstyn, 1951); *Meet Me After the Show* (20th-Fox, 1951); *Just for You* (Par., 1952); *Small Town Girl* (MGM, 1953); *Latin Lovers* (MGM, 1953); and *Hit the Deck* (MGM, 1955).

Published Works. Mr. Robin often collaborated with the composer Ralph Rainger. Among songs for which Mr. Robin wrote lyrics are "Hallelujah" (1927); "Louise" (1929); "My Ideal" (1930); "Beyond the Blue Horizon" (1930); "Prisoner of Love" (1931); "One Hour with You" (1932); "Love in Bloom" (1934); "Love Is Just Around the Corner" (1934); "June in January" (1934); "Moonlight and Shadows" (1936); "Blue Hawaii" (1937); "A Gal in Calico" (1946); "This Is the Moment" (1948); and "Diamonds Are a Girl's Best Friend" (1949).

Awards. Mr. Robin received an Academy (Oscar) Award (1938) for his lyrics to "Thanks for the Memory" from *The Big Broadcast of 1938*.

ROBINSON, CHARLES. Playwright. b. Charles Knox Robinson, Jr., Apr. 28, 1909, New York City, to Charles Knox and Elizabeth Alberta (Lyons) Robinson. Attended Lawrenceville Sch., N.J.; Peddie Sch., Hightstown, N.J.; Staunton Mil. Acad., Va.; Columbia Univ. Sch. of Journalism. Married to Geraldine Constance O'Loughlin; one son, Charles Robinson, Jr., actor; two daughters. Member of Dramatists Guild; WGA, East; The Players.

Pre-Theatre. Wrote for NY *Herald Tribune* (1930).

Theatre. Mr. Robinson wrote, with Kenyon Nicholson, *Sailor, Beware!* (Lyceum, N.Y.C., Sept. 18, 1933); *Swing Your Lady* (Booth, Oct. 18, 1936); *The Flying Gerardos* (Playhouse, Dec. 29, 1940); *Apple of His Eye* (Biltmore, Feb. 5, 1946); *Heart's Delight;* and *Pigeon on the Boardwalk*.

Films. Mr. Robinson was a screenwriter in Hollywood, Calif. (1931).

Television. During the early 1950s, he wrote and produced more than 140 television shows.

ROBINSON, HORACE. Educator, director, theatre architecture consultant. b. Horace William Robinson, Oct. 26, 1909, Apache, Okla., to William Wesley and Ora (Moran) Robinson. Father, office manager. Grad. Classen (Okla.) H.S., 1927; Oklahoma City Univ., A.B. 1931; State Univ. of Iowa, M.A. 1932; attended Stanford Univ. (on Field-Hotling Scholarship), 1947 and 1952. Married Dec. 29, 1932, to Gwendolyn West; two sons, one daughter. Member of AETA (pres., 1954); ANTA (bd. of dir., 1963–66); SCA; Western Speech Assn.; NTC; NWDC (exec. sec.); NAST (pres., 1973–to date); NCP. Address: (home) 1671 Sylvan St., Eugene, OR 97403, tel. (503) 345-2529; (bus.) c/o University Theatre, Univ. of Oregon, Eugene, OR 97403, tel. (503) 686-4197.

Since 1933, Mr. Robinson has been a member of the faculty at the Univ. of Oregon, and is presently professor of speech and a director in the University Theatre. He has taught at Oklahoma City Univ. (1932–33); Montana State Univ., and at the Univ. of California at Los Angeles (1955–56).

He has directed more than 70 student productions, as well as eight professional pageants: Oregon Trail Pageant (Eugene, Ore., 1937, 1940, 1947, 1950); Oregon Statehood Pageant (Salem, Ore., c. 1941); Klamath Falls Centennial (Klamath Falls, Ore.); Umpqua Cavalcade (Roseburg, Ore., 1952); and Plywood Age (Portland, Ore., c. 1953). Many of his unpublished plays were produced in educational theatre.

He made three trips to the Orient, one trip to Europe, and one trip to Greenland and Iceland for USO-AETA-Defense Dept. program presenting plays in Japan, Korea, Okinawa, the Philippine Islands, Guam, and Hawaii.

Mr. Robinson was theatre architecture consultant for the theatres at the Univ. of Oregon; Modesto (Calif.) Coll.; Stockton (Calif.) Coll.; Univ. of New Hampshire; Catawba Coll.; Coll. of the Desert, Palm Desert, Calif.; Civic Auditorium, Redding, California; and the Univ. of Sydney in Australia. He has been architectural advisor to the Los Angeles City Schools.

Published Works. Mr. Robinson has contributed articles to *Theatre Arts* Magazine, *Educational Theatre Journal, Bulletin of Secondary School Superintendents, Players Magazine,* and *Dramatics Magazine.* His short play, *The Promised Land,* was included in *Amateur Acting and Play Production.*

Mr. Robinson also wrote the book *Architecture for the Educational Theatre* (1969).

Awards. Mr. Robinson received a Fulbright Lecture Grant to Australia (1957) a Fulbright Research Grant to Finland (1963); and the American College

Theatre Award of Excellence (1973).

Recreation. Building.

ROBINSON, JAY. Actor. b. April 14, 1930, New York City, to Stanley and Barbara (Breslaw) Robinson. Father, board of directors of Van Heusen Shirts; mother, dancer known as Bobbie Breslaw. Grad. Miami Beach (Fla.) H.S., 1945; attended Professional Children's Sch., N.Y.C., 1945. Married Feb. 8, 1960, to Pauline Flowers; one son. Member of AEA; SAG. Address: 199 E. 7th St., New York, NY 10003, tel. OR 4-9189.

Theatre. Mr. Robinson made his stage debut at the Hawthorne Inn Playhouse, E. Gloucester, Mass., as Henry Aldrich in *What a Life*, (July 8, 1946), also played Dexter Franklin in *Kiss and Tell* (July 22, 1946), and in the title role of *Young Woodley* (July 29, 1946). He repeated his role of Henry Aldrich in *What a Life* (Mt. Gretna Playhouse, Pa., July 2, 1947); at Lake Summit Playhouse (Tuxedo, N.C.), played Henry Aldrich in *What a Life* (July 22, 1947), and the Young Editor in *Parlor Story* (July 22, 1947).

For the Broadway Players (Daytona Beach, Fla.), he appeared as Henry Aldrich in *What a Life* (Jan. 15, 1948), the Young Baron in *A Churchmouse* (Jan. 22, 1948), and Danny in *Night Must Fall* (Jan. 29, 1948); and at Williamsport (Pa.) Playhouse, played Marchbanks in *Candida* (July 3, 1948), and the Boy in *Fata Morgana* (July 17, 1948).

Mr. Robinson made his N.Y.C. debut as Archie in *The Shop at Sly Corner* (Booth, Jan. 18, 1949); subsequently played the title role in *Gayden* (Plymouth, May 10, 1949); Le Beau in *As You Like It* (Cort, Jan. 26, 1950); and Jordan Sable in *Buy Me Blue Ribbons*, which he also produced (Empire, Oct. 17, 1951); and Borachio in *Much Ado About Nothing* (Music Box, May 1, 1952).

At the Biltmore Playhouse (Miami, Fla.), he played Danny in *Night Must Fall* (Sept. 24, 1954) and Jordan Sable in *Buy Me Blue Ribbons* (Nov. 15, 1954); repeated the role of Jordan Sable in *Buy Me Blue Ribbons* (Player's Ring, Hollywood, Calif., Mar. 25, 1957; Encore Th., San Francisco, Calif., June 1, 1958); and Danny in *Night Must Fall* (Hollywood Ctr. Th., Calif., Dec. 28, 1959).

At Actors Studio (Miami, Fla.), he appeared in the title role in *Caligula* Jan. 15, 1962), Merton in *Merton of the Movies* (Mar. 28, 1962), and as Howard in *The Man* (May 6, 1962); in his own reminiscences, *Echoes and Encores* (Coconut Grove Playhouse, Miami, Fla., Aug. 17, 1962); in the title role in *Hamlet* (Southern Shakespeare Festival, Univ. of Miami, Fla., July 4, 1962); and Lord Henry in *The Picture of Dorian Grey* (Showboat, N.Y.C., Aug. 28, 1963). He appeared in *Shakespeare Scene by Scene*, which toured high schools in North Carolina and Connecticut.

Films. Mr. Robinson has appeared in *The Robe* (20th-Fox, 1953); *Demetrius and the Gladiators* (20th-Fox, 1954); *The Virgin Queen* (20th-Fox, 1955); *The Wild Party* (UA, 1956); *The Tower* (UA, 1957); Vincent in *My Man Godfrey* (U, 1957); the Barber in *Tell Me in the Sunlight* (Movie-Rama, 1967); and Norman in *Shampoo* (Col., 1975).

Television. Mr. Robinson appeared on The Men from Shiloh (NBC, Sept. 26, 1970); Bewitched (ABC); Judd for the Defense (ABC); Mannix (CBS); Wild, Wild West (CBS); and Doc (CBS, Oct. 4, 1975).

Night Clubs. Mr. Robinson has starred in a one-man show, *An Evening with Jay Robinson* at the Fontainbleau Hotel (Miami, Fla., Sept. 15, 1962). Eden Roc Hotel (Miami, Oct. 1, 1962), Hotel Seville (Miami, Oct. 15, 1962), Hotel British Colonial (Nassau, Bahamas, March 3, 1963), and Hotel Essex House (Newark, N.J., June 24, 1963).

Recreation. Raising and breeding monkeys and apes.

ROBINSON, WAYNE. Television editor, writer. b. Sept. 19, 1916, Syracuse, N.Y. Served WW II, US Army, overseas. Address: The Philadelphia *Bulletin*, Philadelphia, PA 19104.

Mr. Robinson joined the news staff of The Philadelphia *Bulletin* in 1936; became theatrical editor of the newspaper in 1954; and was appointed television editor in 1972.

Published Works. He has written the novel, *Barbara* (1962), and several articles for *Theatre Arts* magazine.

ROBSON, DAME FLORA. Actress. b. Mar. 28, 1902, South Shields, Durham, England, to David Mather and Eliza (McKenzie) Robson. Grad. Palmer's Green H.S.; attended RADA.

Theatre. Flora Robson made her first appearance on the N.Y.C. stage as Ellen Creed in *Ladies in Retirement* (Henry Miller's Th., Mar. 26, 1940); subsequently appeared as Sarah, Duchess of Marlborough (Mrs. Freeman), in *Anne of England* (St. James, Oct. 7, 1941); toured summer theatres, playing the title role in *Elizabeth the Queen* (1942); played Rhoda Meldrum in *The Damask Cheek* (Playhouse, N.Y.C., Oct. 22, 1942); in a series of Grand Guignol one-act plays entitled *Horror Tonight* (Belasco, Los Angeles, Calif., June 1943); Lady Macbeth in *Macbeth* (Natl., N.Y.C., Mar. 31, 1948); and Alicia Christie in *Black Chiffon* (48 St. Th., Sept. 27, 1950), in which she had appeared previously in London (see below).

She made her London debut as Queen Elizabeth in *Will Shakespeare* (Shaftesbury, Nov. 17, 1921); subsequently joined the Ben Greet Players and appeared in Shakespearean repertory (1922); performed in repertory under the direction of J. B. Fagan (Oxford Playhouse, 1923); played Annie in *Fata Morgana* (Ambassadors', Sept. 15, 1924); joined the Anmer Hall's Co. (Festival Th., Cambridge, Oct. 1929) and, with the company, played in repertory.

She appeared as Tatiana in *Betrayal* (Little, London, Jan. 7, 1931); Abbie in *Desire Under the Elms* (Gate, Feb. 24, 1931); Herodias in *Salomé* (Gate, May 27, 1931); Mary Paterson in *The Anatomist* (Westminster, Oct. 24, 1931); the Stepdaughter in *Six Characters in Search of an Author* (Westminster, Feb. 18, 1932); Bianca in *Othello* (St. James, Apr. 4, 1932); Olwen Peel in *Dangerous Corner* (Lyric, May 17, 1932); Mercia in *The Storm Fighter* (St. Martin's, June 12, 1932); Eva Ardsley in *For Services Rendered* (Globe, Nov. 1, 1932); Lady Audley in *Lady Audley's Secret* (Arts, Jan. 22, 1933); Ella Downey in *All God's Chillun Got Wings* (Embassy, Mar. 13, 1933); and Narouli Karth in *Vessels Departing* (Embassy, July 3, 1933).

She joined (Oct. 1933) the Old Vic-Sadler's Wells Co. and appeared as Varya in *The Cherry Orchard* (Oct. 9, 1933), Queen Katharine in *Henry VIII* (Nov. 7, 1933), Isabella in *Measure for Measure* (Dec. 4, 1933), Gwendolen Fairfax in *The Importance of Being Earnest* (Feb. 5, 1934), Mrs. Foresight in *Love for Love* (Mar. 6, 1934), Lady Macbeth in *Macbeth* (Apr. 2, 1934), and Ceres in *The Tempest* (Jan. 8, 1934).

She appeared as Elizabeth Enticknap in *Touch Wood* (Haymarket, May 16, 1934); in the title role in *Mary Read* (His Majesty's, Nov. 21, 1934); Liesa Bergmann in *Close Quarters* (Embassy, June 25, 1935); the title role in *Mary Tudor* (Streatham Hill, Nov. 18, 1935); Anna in *Anna Christie* (Westminster, Apr. 7, 1937); Mrs. Ellen de Meyer in *Satyr* (Shaftesbury, June 16, 1937); Lady Catherine Brooke in *Autumn* (St. Martin's, Oct. 15, 1937); and Anya in *Last Train South* (St. Martin's, Aug. 11, 1938). After appearing in the US (see above), she returned to London as Thérèse Raquin in *Guilty* (Lyric, Hammersmith, Apr. 18, 1944); toured England in the title role in *Ethel Fry* (Feb. 1945); appeared as Agnes Isit in *A Man About the House* (Piccadilly, London, Feb. 27, 1946); Margaret Hayden in *Message for Margaret* (Westminster, Aug. 28, 1946); Lady Cicely Waynflete in *Captain Brassbound's Conversion* (Lyric, Hammersmith, Oct. 13, 1948); Alicia Christie in *Black Chiffon* (Westminster, May 3, 1949), which she repeated on Bway (see above); Lady Brooke in *Autumn* ("Q" Th., London, Apr. 24, 1951); Paulina in *The Winter's Tale* (Phoenix, June 27, 1951); Miss Giddens in *The Innocents* (Her Majesty's, July 3, 1952); Sister Agatha in *The Return* (Duchess, Nov. 7, 1953); on tour, appeared as Rachel Lloyd in *No Escape* (1954); Sarah Ashby in *A Kind of Folly* (Duchess, London, Feb. 15, 1955); Janet in *The House by the Lake* (Duke of York's, May 9, 1956), and toured Australia in this part (1957).

She played Mrs. Alving in *Ghosts* (Old Vic, London, Nov. 12, 1958); appeared as Miss Tina in *The Aspern Papers* (Queen's, Aug. 12, 1959); toured South Africa with the Cockpit Players, appearing as Miss Tina in *The Aspern Papers* (Sept.–Dec. 1960), and as Miss Moffat in *The Corn Is Green* (1961–62); toured England as Liesa Bergmann in *Close Quarters* (1963); appeared as Gunhild Borkman in *John Gabriel Borkman* (Duchess Th., London, Dec. 4, 1963); Lady Bracknell in *The Importance of Being Earnest* (Flora Robson Playhouse, Newcastle-on-Tyne, 1964); Hecuba in *The Trojan Women* (Assembly Hall, Edinburgh, Scotland, Aug. 29, 1966); toured as Winifred Brazier in *Brother and Sister* (Apr. 1967); played Miss Prism in *The Importance of Being Earnest* (Haymarket, London, England, Feb. 8, 1968); the Mother in *Ring 'Round the Moon* (Haymarket, Oct. 30, 1968); Agatha Payne in *The Old Ladies* (Westminster, Nov. 4, 1969); and appeared at the Edinburgh (Scotland) Festival in the title role of *Elizabeth Tudor, Queen of England* (Aug. 1970).

Films. Miss Robson appeared in *Dance Pretty Lady* (Wardour, 1932); *One Precious Year* (Par., 1933); *Catherine the Great* (UA, 1934); *Fire Over England* (UA, 1937); *Farewell Again* (UA, 1937); *Wuthering Heights* (UA, 1939); *We Are Not Alone* (WB, 1939); *The Lion Has Wings* (UA, 1940); *Invisible Stripes* (WB, 1940); *The Sea Hawk* (WB, 1940); *Poison Pen* (Reformation, 1941); *Bahama Passage* (Par., 1941); *Saratoga Trunk* (WB, 1945); *Caesar and Cleopatra* (UA, 1946); *Great Day* (RKO, 1946); *The Years Between* (U, 1947); *Frieda* (U, 1947); *Black Narcissus* (U, 1947); *Holiday Camp* (U, 1948); *Saraband* (Eagle Lion, 1949); *Good Time Girl* (Film Classics, 1950); *Malta Story* (UA, 1954); *Romeo and Juliet* (UA, 1954); *High Tide at Noon* (Rank, 1957); *No Time for Tears* (Assoc. Brit. Picture Corp., 1957); *The Gypsy and the Gentleman* (Rank, 1958); *55 Days at Peking* (Allied, 1963); *Murder at the Gallop* (MGM, 1963); *Guns at Batasi* (20th-Fox, 1964); and *Young Cassidy* (MGM, 1965).

She appeared in *Those Magnificent Men in Their Flying Machines* (20th-Fox, 1965); *Seven Women* (MGM, 1965); was the voice of Queen Mary in *A King's Story* (Cont., 1967); was in *The Eye of the Devil* (MGM, 1967); *The Shuttered Room* (WB-7 Arts, 1968); *Cry in the Wind* (Cont., 1958); *Fragment of Fear* (Col., 1971); and *The Beloved* (Curtwel, 1971).

Television. She appeared in *The Cherry Tree* (BBC, Feb. 1959); *Close Quarters* (Nov. 1959); *Nurse Cavell; Romeo and Juliet; The Corn Is Green; Message for Margaret.*

Awards. She was created Commander of the British Empire (C.B.E.) in 1952 and Dame of the British Empire (D.B.E.) in the Queen's Birthday Honours (1960). She also received the London *Evening Standard* Award for her performance as Miss Tina in *The Aspern Papers* (1960).

Recreation. Swimming, gardening.

ROCKEFELLER, KAY. Producer, actress, director. b. Katherine Terry Rivett, May 14, 1918, Omaha, Neb., to Harry Logan and Julia (Bednar) Rivett. Father, lumberman; mother, teacher. Attended Omaha Central H.S.; Northwestern Univ.; Univ. of Chicago; Carnegie Institute of Technology. Studied modern dance with Martha Graham; choreography with Louis Horst. Married 1941, to Kenneth Rockefeller; two daughters. Relatives in theatre: husband, Kenneth Rockefeller, television and theatre producer, director, actor; daughter, Terry Rockefeller, television producer. Member of AEA; Producers Assn. of Children's Theatre; ATA. Address: 104 Northampton Dr., White Plains, NY 10603, tel. (914) 946-5289.

Theatre. Mrs. Rockefeller made her acting debut as Celia in *As You Like It* (Omaha, Neb., Community Playhouse, 1935); appeared with several USO tours during WW II, including a European tour of

The Patsy (1945–46); and was a member of the company for the Duxbury (Mass.) Playhouse (Summers 1946–48); and The Artillery Lane Playhouse (St. Augustine, Fla., Winters 1947–48). On Bway, she was associate producer of *Wallflower* (Cort, Jan. 26, 1944).

Since 1948, she has been director at the YMHA's Kaufmann Aud. (N.Y.C.). Mrs. Rockefeller, with her husband, is producer and director of The Traveling Playhouse (1949–to date), a children's theatre company which tours annually, and which has presented thousands of performances before millions of children. Their productions include *Pinocchio; The Wizard of Oz; Cinderella; The Prince and the Pauper; Tom Sawyer; The Secret Treasure Room; Aladdin and His Magic Lamp; Snow White and the Seven Dwarfs; Rip Van Winkle; The Golden Goose; The Magic Fiddle; Rumpelstiltskin; The Emperor's New Clothes; Robin Hood; Greensleeves; Marco Polo; Jack and the Beanstalk;* and *Mr. Popper's Penguins.*

Television. Mrs. Rockefeller produced *The Wizard of Oz* (NBC, 1965); and co-authored *Robin Hood* (NBC, 1966).

Discography. She has produced the original cast recordings of the Traveling Playhouse productions of *The Wizard of Oz, Snow White and the Seven Dwarfs,* and *Pinocchio.*

Awards. Mrs. Rockefeller received a Rockefeller Foundation grant-in-aid to direct theatre productions at the Baltimore (Md.) Museum of Art (1940–42).

Recreation. Travel.

RODD, MARCIA. Actress, singer. b. July 8, Lyons, Kansas. Grad. Northwestern Univ., BA, 1963. Married 1963 to Dale Hagen. Member of AEA; AFTRA; SAG.

Theatre. Miss Rodd made her off-Bway debut as a chorus singer in *Oh, Say Can You See* (Provincetown Playhouse, N.Y.C., Oct. 8, 1962); sang and acted in the Bway Show League revue, *Talent '64* (Booth, Apr. 6, 1964); was a replacement singer in the revue, *Cambridge Circus* (Square East, Feb. 1965); replaced (Jan. 18, 1966) Linda Lavin in *The Mad Show* (The New Th., Jan. 9, 1966).

She played Lottie in the pre-Bway tryout of *Chu Chem* (opened New Locust, Philadelphia, Nov. 15, 1966; closed there Nov. 19, 1966); Bea in *Love in E-Flat* (Brooks Atkinson Th., N.Y.C., Feb. 13, 1967); was a replacement in the role of Viola in *Love and Let Love* (Sheridan Sq. Playhouse, Jan. 3, 1967); replaced (shortly after opening) Marian Mercer in the role of Olivia in *Your Own Thing* (Orpheum, Jan. 13, 1967; and Huntington Hartford Th., Los Angeles, Aug. 2, 1968); played Bobby Michele in *The Last of the Red Hot Lovers* (Eugene O'Neill Th., Dec. 28, 1969); Maud in *Shelter* (John Golden Th., Feb. 6, 1973); the voice of Mrs. Blustone in a puppet theatre production of *Pinocchio* (Bil Baird Th., Dec. 15, 1974); and Mistress Page in the NY Shakespeare Festival's production of *The Merry Wives of Windsor* (Delacorte, July 25, 1974).

Miss Rodd directed an off-off Bway production of *After We Eat the Apple* (Cubiculo, N.Y.C., Aug. 10, 1972).

Films. She played Patsy Newquist in *Little Murders* (20th-Fox, 1972); and Dayle in *T. R. Baskin* (Par., 1972).

Television. Miss Rodd's appearances include All in the Family (CBS); Johnny Carson (NBC); Ed Sullivan (CBS); Wednesday Revue (NET); CBS Repertory Theatre (CBS); and The Dumplings (CBS).

RODGERS, EILEEN. Actress, singer. b. Eileen Mary Rodgers, July 10, 1933, Pittsburgh, Pa., to Emil and Mary (Anderson) Rodgers. Father, restaurateur. Attended St. Paul's Cathedral H.S. for Girls, Pittsburgh, Pa. Married Aug. 18, 1958, to William J. Thompson, Jr., sales executive. Member of AEA; SAG; AFTRA; AGVA; Cresthaven Yacht Club (Whitestone, L.I., N.Y.).

Theatre. Miss Rodgers made her N.Y.C. debut in the revue *Chic* (Orpheum Th., May 19, 1959); subsequently played Mitzi in *Fiorello!* (Broadhurst, Nov. 23, 1959); Nita in *Tenderloin* (46 St. Th., Oct. 17, 1960); Georgia Motley in a stock production of *Billion Dollar Baby* (State Fair Music Hall, Dallas, Tex., Aug. 7, 1961); Reno Sweeney in *Anything Goes* (Orpheum, N.Y.C., May 15, 1962) and repeated the role (Thunderbird Hotel, Las Vegas, Nev., Dec. 4, 1963); played Mama in *High Button Shoes* (Thunderbird Hotel, May 8, 1964); was Fay Cherry in *Kelly* (Broadhurst, N.Y.C., Feb. 6, 1965); standby for Ethel Merman as Annie Oakley in the Music Th. of Lincoln Ctr. revival of *Annie Get Your Gun* (State Th., May 31, 1966; transferred to Broadway Th., Sept. 21, 1966); and appeared in the concert *George Gershwin's Theatre* (Philharmonic Hall, Lincoln Ctr., Jan. 23, 1966; repeated Mar. 27, 1966).

Television. She has appeared on the Ed Sullivan Show (CBS); the Tonight Show (NBC); the Jack Paar Show (NBC); Bell Telephone Hour (NBC); Dupont Show of the Month (NBC); Chevrolet 50th Anniversary Show (NBC).

Night Clubs. Miss Rodgers has performed at the Eden Roc and Fontainebleau hotels (Miami Beach, Fla.); the Hilton (Dallas, Texas); The Blinstrubs (Boston, Mass.); The Town Casino (Buffalo, N.Y.); and the Holiday House (Pittsburgh, Pa.).

Discography. Miss Rodgers has made numerous recordings for Columbia.

Awards. She received the Blue Bonnet Award (Dallas, 1962) for her performance as Georgia Motley in *Billion Dollar Baby.*

Recreation. Collecting clown paintings, boating.

RODGERS, MARY. Composer. b. Jan. 11, 1931, N.Y.C., to Richard and Dorothy (Feiner) Rodgers. Father, composer; mother, author, inventor. Grad. the Brearley School, N.Y.C., 1948; attended Wellesley Coll. 1948–51; Mannes Coll. of Music, N.Y.C., 1943–48. Married Dec. 7, 1951, to Julian B. Beaty, Jr., attorney (marr. dis. Feb. 1958); one son, two daughters; married Oct. 14, 1961, to Henry A. Guettel, producer; two sons. Member of ASCAP; Dramatists Guild. Address: 115 Central Park West, New York, NY 10023, tel. (212) TR 7-3997.

Theatre. Miss Rodgers was composer of the score for Bil Baird's marionette show *Davy Jones's Locker* (Morosco, Mar. 28, 1959); and wrote scores for *Once Upon a Mattress* (Phoenix, N.Y.C., May 11, 1959; Alvin, Nov. 25, 1959); *Hot Spot* (Majestic, Apr. 19, 1963); *The Mad Show* (New, Jan. 10, 1966); and for Bil Baird's Marionette show *Pinocchio* (Dec. 15, 1973).

Television. Miss Rodgers was script editor and assistant to the producer of the NY Philharmonic Young People's Concerts (CBS, 1957–63). She has also worked as composer, script writer and lyricist for the Mary Martin Spectaculars (NBC, Mar. 1959), and composed for *Feathertop* (ABC, Sept. 1961).

Other Activities. She was script writer for six concerts of the Little Orchestra Society at Hunter Coll. (1958–59).

Published Works. She is the author of *The Rotten Book* (1969); *Freaky Friday* (1972); *A Word to the Wives,* with Dorothy Rodgers (1970); and wrote a monthly column, *Of Two Minds,* for *McCall's* magazine (1972).

Recreation. Croquet, reading, movies, theatre, games.

RODGERS, RICHARD. Composer, producer, lyricist. b. Richard Charles Rodgers, June 28, 1902, New York City, to William and Mamie (Levy) Rodgers. Father, physician. Attended Columbia Univ., 1919–21,, Inst. of Musical Art Juilliard Sch. of Music), N.Y.C., 1921–23. Married Mar. 5, 1930, to Dorothy Feiner; two daughters. Relative in the theatre, daughter, Mary Rodgers, composer. Partner, Rodgers and Hammerstein Productions; partner, Williamson Music, Inc. Member of Actors Fund of Amer. (bd. of trustees, since 1949); ASCAP (bd. mbr., 1929–30; 1941–47; 1960–74); Authors League of Amer.; Dramatists Guild (pres., 1943–47); Philharmonic Symphony Soc. of NY (1954–to date); Bd. of Dirs., Juilliard Sch. of Music (1959–to date); Natl. Council on the Arts (1964–to date); trustee, John F. Kennedy Center for Performing Arts (1964–to date); Natl. Assn. for American Composers and Conductors; Amer. Theatre Wing (mbr., bd. of dir., 1941–to date); Dutch Treat Club; The Players; Century Assn. Address: 598 Madison Ave., New York, NY 10022, tel. (212) 486-7373.

Theatre. Mr. Rodgers began his career as composer for *One Minute Please,* an amateur musical presented by a New York Boys' Club (Plaza Hotel, Dec 29, 1917); and commenced his collaboration with lyricist Lorenz Hart as composer of the song "Any Old Place with You," introduced on Aug. 26, 1919, into *A Lonely Romeo* (Shubert, June 10, 1919).

They wrote the score for the Columbia Univ. Varsity Show, *Fly with Me* (Astor Hotel, Mar. 24, 1920), which Mr. Rodgers conducted; seven of their songs were sung in *Poor Little Ritz Girl* (Central, July 28, 1920); wrote the score for Columbia Univ. Varsity Show, *You'll Never Know* (Astor Hotel, Apr. 20, 1921); with Herbert Fields and Mr. Hart, he wrote *The Melody Man* (Ritz, May 13, 1924) under the collective name Herbert Richard Lorenz.

Collaborating with Mr. Hart, he composed the music for *The Garrick Gaieties* (Garrick, May 17, 1925; regular run, June 8, 1925); *Dearest Enemy* (Knickerbocker, Sept. 18, 1925); the night club revue, *The Fifth Avenue Follies* (Fifth Ave. Club, Jan. 1926); *The Girl Friend* (Vanderbilt, Mar. 17, 1926); *The Garrick Gaieties* (Garrick, May 10, 1926); *Lido Lady* (Gaiety, London, Dec. 1, 1926); *Peggy-Ann* (Vanderbilt, N.Y.C., Dec. 27, 1926; Daly's, London, July 29, 1927); *Betsy* (New Amsterdam, Dec. 28, 1926); the London revue *One Dam Thing After Another* (London Pavilion May 20, 1927).

Mr. Rodgers wrote the music for *A Connecticut Yankee* (Vanderbilt, Nov. 3, 1927; produced in London under the title *A Yankee in the Court of King Arthur,* (Daly's, Oct. 10, 1929), which Mr. Rodgers later revived (Martin Beck Th., Nov. 17, 1943); *She's My Baby* (Globe, Jan. 3, 1928); *Present Arms* (Mansfield, Apr. 26, 1928); *Chee-Chee* (Mansfield, Sept. 25, 1928); *Spring Is Here* (Alvin, Mar. 11, 1929); *Heads Up!* (Alvin, Mar. 11, 1929); Palace, London, May 1, 1930); *Simple Simon* (Ziegfeld, Feb. 18, 1930); *Ever Green* (Adelphi, London, Dec 3, 1930); *America's Sweetheart* (Broadhurst, Feb. 10, 1931); *Jumbo* (Hippodrome, Nov. 16, 1935); *On Your Toes* (Imperial, Apr. 11, 1936; Palace, London, Feb. 5, 1937; revived 46th St. Th., Oct. 11, 1954), for which he was also librettist with George Abbott and Mr. Hart; composed the music for *Babes in Arms* (Shubert, Apr. 14, 1937), for which he was librettist with Mr. Hart; wrote the music for *I'd Rather Be Right* (Alvin, Nov. 2, 1937); *I Married an Angel* (Shubert, May 11, 1938), for which he was librettist with Mr. Hart; *The Boys from Syracuse* (Alvin, Nov. 23, 1938; revived Th. Four, Apr. 15, 1963; Th. Royal, Drury Lane, London, Nov. 12, 1939); *Too Many Girls* (Imperial, N.Y.C., Oct. 18, 1939); composed the music for *Higher and Higher* (Shubert, Apr. 4, 1940); *Pal Joey* (Ethel Barrymore Th., N.Y.C., Dec. 25, 1940; revived Broadhurst, Jan. 3, 1952; Prince's, London, Mar. 31, 1954; NY City Ctr., May 31, 1961; NY City Ctr., May 29, 1963); and *By Jupiter* (Shubert, June 2, 1942; revived Th. Four, Jan. 19, 1967; Palace, Manchester, Eng., July 31, 1944), for which he wrote the book with Mr. Hart), and which he produced with Dwight Deere Wiman in association with Richard Kollmar.

Mr. Rodgers began a professional association with Oscar Hammerstein II as his lyricist with *Oklahoma!* (St. James, N.Y.C., Mar. 31, 1943; Drury Lane, London, Apr. 30, 1947; revived NY City Ctr., Aug. 31, 1953; Mar. 19, 1958; Feb. 27, 1963, reopened May 15, 1963; Dec. 15, 1965; NY State Th., June 23, 1969).

Mr. Hammerstein wrote the lyrics and Mr. Rodgers composed the music for *Carousel* (Majestic, N.Y.C., Apr. 19, 1945; Drury Lane, London, June 7, 1950; revived NY City Ctr., Jan. 25, 1949; June 2, 1954; Sept. 11, 1957; NY State Th., Aug. 10, 1965; NY City Ctr., Dec. 15, 1966; Jones Beach Th., June 22, 1973); *Allegro* (Majestic, Oct. 10,

1947); *South Pacific* (Majestic, N.Y.C., Apr. 7, 1949; Drury Lane, London, Nov. 1, 1951; revived NY City Ctr., May 4, 1955; Apr. 24, 1957; Apr. 26, 1961; June 2, 1965; NY State Th., June 12, 1967; Jones Beach Th., June 27, 1968; July 3, 1969), producing the original NY production with Messrs. Hammerstein, Logan, and Leland Hayward.

Mr. Rodgers wrote the music for, and produced the original Bway production, with Mr. Hammerstein, of *The King and I* (St. James, N.Y.C., Mar. 29, 1951; Drury Lane, London, Oct. 8, 1953; revived NY City Ctr., Apr. 18, 1956; May 11, 1960; June 10, 1963; NY State Th., July 6, 1964; NY City Ctr., May 20, 1968; Jones Beach Th., June 28, 1972); *Me and Juliet* (Majestic, N.Y.C., May 28, 1953); *Pipe Dream* (Shubert, Nov. 30, 1955); composed the music and produced, with Mr. Hammerstein, in association with Joseph Fields, *Flower Drum Song* (St. James, N.Y.C., Dec. 1, 1958; Palace, London, Mar. 24, 1960); wrote the music and produced, with Mr. Hammerstein, Leland Hayward, and Richard Halliday, *The Sound of Music* (Lunt-Fontanne, N.Y.C., Nov. 16, 1959; Palace, London, Mar. 18, 1961; revived NY City Ctr., Apr. 26, 1967; Jones Beach Th., July 1, 1970; July 8, 1971).

A pantomime version of their television musical, *Cinderella*, was produced in London (Coliseum, Dec. 18, 1958).

Mr. Rodgers and Mr. Hammerstein produced *I Remember Mama* (Music Box, Oct. 19, 1944); *Annie Get Your Gun* (Imperial, May 16, 1946); *Happy Birthday* (Broadhurst, Oct. 31, 1946); in association with Joshua Logan, *John Loves Mary* (Booth, Feb. 4, 1947); *The Happy Time* (Plymouth, N.Y.C., Jan. 24, 1950); *The Heart of the Matter* (Wilbur, Boston, Feb. 20, 1950); and *Burning Bright* (Broadhurst, N.Y.C., Oct. 18, 1950).

Mr. Rodgers composed the music and wrote the lyrics for *No Strings* (54 St. Th., N.Y.C., Mar. 15, 1962; Her Majesty's, London, Dec. 30, 1963), which he produced in association with librettist Samuel Taylor; produced and composed the music (with lyrics by Stephen Sondheim) for *Do I Hear a Waltz?* (46 St. Th., N.Y.C., Mar. 18, 1965); produced and composed the music (with lyrics by Martin Charnin) for *Two by Two* (Imperial, Nov. 10, 1970); and produced and composed the music (with lyrics by Sheldon Harnick) for *Rex* (1976).

Mr. Rodgers was pres. and producing dir. of the Music Th. of Lincoln Center for the Performing Arts (1964–69), for which he presented, at the NY State Th., *The King and I* (July 6, 1964), *The Merry Widow* (Aug. 17, 1964), *Kismet* (June 22, 1965), *Carousel* (Aug. 10, 1965), *Annie Get Your Gun* (May 31, 1966), *Showboat* (July 19, 1966), *South Pacific* (June 12, 1967), *West Side Story* (June 24, 1968), and *Oklahoma!* (June 23, 1969).

He produced, in association with Morris Jacobs and Jerome Whyte, *Avanti* (Booth, Jan. 31, 1968).

Touring companies of Rodgers and Hart musicals include *The Garrick Gaieties* (opened Weiting, Syracuse, Nov. 1, 1926; closed Garrick, Detroit, Nov. 20, 1926); *The Girl Friend* (opened Shubert, Brooklyn, Dec. 27, 1926; closed Adelphi, Philadelphia, Feb. 26, 1927); *Peggy-Ann* (opened Majestic, Bklyn., Oct. 31, 1927; closed Detroit Th., Detroit, Mar. 3, 1928); *She's My Baby* (opened Ohio Th., Cleveland, Mar. 5, 1928; closed Illinois Th., Chicago, May 5, 1928); *Present Arms* (opened Wood's, Chicago, Sept. 2, 1928; closed Erlanger, Philadelphia, Oct. 6, 1928); *A Connecticut Yankee* (opened Majestic, Boston, Oct. 29, 1928; closed Boulevard, Jackson Hts., Apr. 5, 1930), revival (opened Erlanger, Buffalo, Mar. 13, 1944; closed Colonial, Boston, Apr. 22, 1944); *Simple Simon* (opened Shubert, Newark, Oct. 13, 1930; closed Shubert, Boston, Apr. 18, 1931); *On Your Toes* (opened Nixon, Pittsburgh, Jan. 25, 1937; closed Natl., Washington, Mar. 13, 1937); *Babes In Arms* (opened Forrest, Philadelphia, Dec. 24, 1937; closed Shubert, Newark, Mar. 12, 1938); *I'd Rather Be Right* (opened Forrest, Philadelphia, Oct. 3, 1938; closed Playhouse, Wilmington, Feb. 25, 1939) *I Married an Angel* (opened Nixon, Pittsburgh, Feb. 28, 1939; closed Curran, San Francisco, Jan. 28, 1940); *Too Many Girls* (opened Opera House, Chicago, Aug. 31, 1939; closed Sept. 21, 1939); *Pal Joey* (opened Shubert, Boston, Dec. 1, 1941; closed Cass, Detroit, Feb. 28, 1942; revived Shubert, Washington, Apr. 20, 1953; closed Nixon, Pittsburgh, Nov. 28, 1953). Touring companies of Rodgers and Hammerstein musicals include *Oklahoma!*, the national company (opened Shubert, New Haven, Oct. 5, 1943; closed Shubert, Philadelphia, May 1, 1954), N.Y.C. touring company (opened Opera House, Boston, May 31, 1948; closed Auditorium, Barre, N.H., May 21, 1949); *Carousel* (opened Shubert, Chicago, May 29, 1947; closed Majestic, N.Y., Mar. 5, 1949); *Allegro* (opened Shubert, Philadelphia, Nov. 5, 1948; closed Great Northern, Chicago, June 11, 1949); *South Pacific* (opened Hanna, Cleveland, Apr. 24 1950; closed Opera House, Chicago, Mar. 26, 1955); *The King and I* (opened Community Th., Hershey, Pa., March 22, 1954; closed Shubert, Philadelphia, Dec 17, 1955); *Me and Juliet* (opened Shubert, Chicago, Apr. 7, 1954; closed May 29, 1954); *The Sound of Music* (opened Riviera, Detroit, Feb. 27, 1961; closed O'-Keefe Centre, Toronto, Ontario, Canada, 23, 1963); the touring company of Mr. Rodgers' musical *No Strings* (opened Shubert, Boston, Aug. 5, 1963; closed Curran, San Francisco, Jan. 4, 1964); and of *Two by Two* (opened Dupont Th., Wilmington, Del., Sept. 11, 1972; closed Memorial Hall, Dayton, Ohio, Mar. 11, 1973). Touring companies of Rodgers and Hammerstein productions include *I Remember Mama* (opened Erlanger, Buffalo, Sept. 26, 1946; closed Studebaker, Chicago, Dec. 7, 1946); *Annie Get Your Gun* (opened Fair Park Aud., Dallas, Oct. 3, 1947; closed Cass, Detroit, May 28, 1949); *John Loves Mary* (opened Harris, Chicago, Feb. 9, 1948; closed Nixon, Pittsburgh, Oct. 16, 1948); and *Happy Time* (opened Nixon, Pittsburgh, Sept. 24, 1951; closed Blackstone, Chicago, Jan. 12, 1952).

A review, *Rodgers & Hart* (Helen Hayes Th., N.Y.C., May 13, 1975), presented excerpts from nearly one hundred of the composers' songs.

Films. In collaboration with Mr. Hart, Mr. Rodgers composed the scores for *The Hot Heiress* (1st Natl., 1931); *Love Me Tonight* (Par., 1932); *The Phantom President* (Par., 1932); *Hallelujah! I'm a Bum!* (UA, 1933); *Dancing Lady* (MGM, 1933); *Manhattan Melodrama* (MGM, 1934); *Hollywood Party* (MGM, 1934); *Mississippi* (Par., 1935); *Dancing Pirate* (RKO, 1936); *Fools for Scandal* (WB, 1938), *They Met in Argentina* (RKO, 1941); in collaboration with Mr. Hammerstein, *State Fair* (20th-Fox, 1945, remade, 1962), *Word and Music* (MGM, 1948) was a biographical film dealing with Messrs. Rodgers and Hart.

Rodgers-Hart stage musicals which were adapted for the Screen include *The Melody Man* (Col., 1930); *Leathernecking (Present Arms)* (Radio, 1930); *Spring Is Here* (1st Natl., 1930); *Heads Up!* (Par., 1930); *Evergreen* (Gaumont-British, 1934); *On Your Toes* (WB, 1939); *Babes in Arms* (MGM, 1939); *The Boys from Syracuse* (U, 1940); *Too Many Girls* (RKO, 1940); *I Married an Angel* (MGM, 1942); *Higher and Higher* (RKO, 1944); *Pal Joey* (Col., 1957); and *Jumbo* (MGM, 1962).

Rodgers-Hammerstein stage musicals which were adapted for the screen include *Oklahoma!* (Magna, 1955), which they also produced; *Carousel* (20th-Fox, 1956); *The King and I* (20th-Fox, 1956); *South Pacific* (Magna-Fox, 1958), which they also produced); *Flower Drum Song* (U, 1961); and *The Sound of Music* (20th-Fox, 1965), for which Mr. Rodgers wrote additional lyrics.

Television. Mr. Rodgers composed the background score for *Victory at Sea* (NBC, 1952–53). The Television versions of Rodgers and Hart musicals were *A Connecticut Yankee* (NBC, Mar. 12, 1955) and *Dearest Enemy* (NBC, Nov. 26, 1955). With Mr. Hammerstein, he wrote the score for *Cinderella* (CBS, Mar. 31, 1957; re-produced, CBS, Feb. 26, 1966); wrote the background score for *Winston Churchill—The Valiant Years* (ABC, Nov. 17, 1960); and the music and lyrics for *Androcles and the Lion* (NBC, Nov. 15, 1967).

Carousel was adapted as a special (ABC, May 7, 1967).

Published Works. Mr. Rodgers wrote an autobiography, *Musical Stages* (Random House, 1975).

Awards. Mr. Rodgers received a special Pulitzer Prize for *Oklahoma!* in 1944, and the Pulitzer Prize for drama for *South Pacific* in 1950; Donaldson awards for best score for *Carousel* (1945), *Allegro* (1948), *South Pacific* (1949), and *Pal Joey* (1952); Antoinette Perry (Tony) Awards for *South Pacific* (1950), *The King and I* (best score, 1952), and *No Strings* (1962); NY Drama Critics' awards for *Carousel* (1946), *South Pacific* (1949), and *Pal Joey* (1952); a Motion Picture Academy (Oscar) Award for the song "It Might as Well Be Spring" from the film *State Fair* 1945); and for *The Sound of Music*, which won the Academy (Oscar) Award as Best Picture of the Year (1965); a NATAS (Emmy) Award and US Navy Distinguished Service Award for *Victory at Sea* (1953); Christopher Award for *The King and I* (1956); a NATAS (Emmy) Award for *Winston Churchill—The Valiant Years* (1962); and the NARAS (Grammy) Award for *No Strings*. The 1963 revival of *The Boys from Syracuse* received the Vernon Rice Award and the *Village Voice* Off-Bway (Obie) Award for best musical presented off-Broadway.

He was elected a member of the Natl. Institute of Arts & Letters (1955); received the Columbia Medal of Excellence (1949); 100 Year Association Gold Medal (1950); Columbia College Award (1952); Alexander Hamilton Medal, Columbia (1956); Dutch Treat Club distinguished Achievement Award (1957); Natl. Conference of Christians and Jews Human Relations Award (1959); Advertising Federation of America Award (1960); Poor Richard Gold Medal (1960); Broadway Association Award (1961); Antoinette Perry (Tony) Special Award (1962); Mary MacArthur Memorial Fund Award (1963); Holland Society Award (1964); City of Boston Medal for Distinguished Achievement (1964); Sam S. Shubert Foundation Award, in recognition of this contribution to the Amer. Th. (1966); and the Brandeis Univ. Creative Arts Award (1968).

Mr. Rodgers has received the following honorary degrees: Drury Coll., LL.D. 1949; Columbia Univ., Mus.D. 1954; Univ. of Mass., D.H.L. 1954; Univ. of Bridgeport, Mus.D. 1962; Univ. of Maryland, Mus.D. 1962; Hamilton Coll., 1965; and Brandeis Univ., 1965. He is a trustee of Barnard Coll., Juilliard Sch. of Music, and N.Y. Philharmonic. The following special scholarships were conferred on Mr. Rodgers: Permanent Scholarship, Juilliard (inaugurated 1953); Max Dreyfus Annual Scholarship, Juilliard (given with Hammerstein) inaugurated 1954); two scholarships, American Theatre Wing (Rodgers and Hammerstein Foundation, inaugurated 1955); Rodgers and Hammerstein Annual Award to individual who has done most for the theatre in Boston area (inaugurated 1959); Rodgers and Hammerstein Annual Award to individual who has done most for theatre in Southwest (inaugurated 1960).

ROE, PATRICIA. Actress. b. Sept. 18, 1932, New York City, to Raymond and Christina Roe. Father, civil engineer. Grad. Mark-Ken H.S., Los Angeles, Calif., Univ. of Southern California; Columbia Univ. Studied acting in N.Y.C. at Amer. Th. Wing, Actors' Studio, with Robert Lewis, Lee Strasberg and Paul Mann. Member of AEA; SAG: AFTRA; Natl. Honor Society; Zeta Psi Eta (hon.).

Theatre. Miss Roe made her N.Y.C. debut as a citizen of Verona and understudied Olivia de Havilland as Juliet in *Romeo and Juliet* (Broadhurst Th., Apr. 10, 1951); subsequently appeared in the chorus of *By the Beautiful Sea* (Majestic, Apr. 8, 1954); joined (June 1956) the cast of *Cat on a Hot Tin Roof* as understudy to Barbara Bel Geddes as Maggie, and Madeleine Sherwood as Sister Woman, playing the latter role for three weeks (Morosco, Mar. 25, 1955). She played the Girl on the Telephone and the Second Girl in *Compulsion* (Ambassador, Oct. 24, 1957); a Lady of the Evening in *Night Circus* (John Golden Th., Dec. 2, 1958); and was general understudy in *Look After Lulu* (Henry Miller's Th., Mar. 3, 1959).

She played Barrett Greer in *A Distant Bell* (Eugene O'Neill Th., Jan. 13, 1960); Miss Judith Fellowes in *The Night of the Iguana* later taking over Margaret Leighton's role as Hanna Jelkes (Royale, Dec. 28, 1961); Stella in *The Collection*, which appeared on a double-bill with *The Dumb Waiter* (Cherry Lane, Nov. 26, 1962).

For the Repertory Th. of Lincoln Ctr. (ANTA Washington Square Th.) she was Elsie in *After the Fall* (Jan. 23, 1964), Naomi Saunders in *But For Whom Charlie* (Mar. 12, 1964), and Mme. Pernelle in *Tartuffe* (Jan. 14, 1965). She played Flo Owens in the pre-Bway tryout of *Hot September* (opened Shubert Th., Boston, Mass., Sept. 14, 1965; closed there Oct. 9, 1965); replaced (June 26, 1967) Lynn Farleigh as Ruth in *The Homecoming* (Music Box, N.Y.C., Jan. 5, 1967); was the Talking Woman in *Bananas* (Forum Th., Lincoln Ctr., Dec. 5, 1968); and Elie in *The Rooming House* on the program *Transfers* (Village South Th., Jan. 22, 1970).

Films. She appeared in *A Face in the Crowd* (WB, 1957).

Television. Miss Roe has appeared on Robert Montgomery Presents (NBC), Philco Playhouse (CBS), and Studio One (CBS).

Recreation. Horseback riding, swimming, sculpting, painting.

ROEBLING, PAUL. Actor. b. Mar. 19, Philadelphia, Pa., to Siegfried and Mary (Gindhart) Roebling. Mother, banker. Attended Episcopal Acad., Philadelphia, Pa., 1948–50; grad. Valley Forge (Pa.) Military Acad., 1952; attended Columbia Univ., 1952. Studied acting at HB (Herbert Berghof) Studio, N.Y.C., 1952–62; speech with Beatrice Desfosses, N.Y.C. Married Aug. 24, 1961, to Olga Bellin, actress. Member of AEA; AFTRA.

Theatre. Mr. Roebling made his debut as a Newsboy in *The Vegetable* at the Princeton (N.J.) Univ. Intime Th. (July 1949), where he spent two seasons in stock (1949–50); subsequently appeared at the Ivy Tower Playhouse (1951–53); the Royal Poinciana Playhouse (Palm Beach, Fla., Jan. 1953); was understudy for *A Girl Can Tell* (Royale, N.Y.C., Oct. 29, 1953); and appeared in *The Homeward Look* (Th. de Lys, June 1954).

Mr. Roebling appeared as Stefan in *The Dark Is Light Enough* (ANTA, Feb. 23, 1955); the Dauphin in *The Lark* (Longacre, Nov. 17, 1955); Sir Mark Grahame in *A Desert Incident* (John Golden Th., Mar. 24, 1959); Romeo in *Romeo and Juliet* (Heckscher Th., Dec. 1960), which toured the N.Y.C. public schools; at the Vancouver (Canada) Intl. Festival, he played the Angel in *Men, Women and Angels* (Queen Elizabeth Th., Aug. 1961); played Amory in *This Side of Paradise* (Sheridan Sq. Playhouse, N.Y.C., Feb. 21, 1962); at the Festival of the Two Worlds (Spoleto, Italy), played Christopher Flanders in the original version of Tennessee Williams' *The Milk Train Doesn't Stop Here Any Mcre* (Teatro Nuovo, June 1962), which he repeated in N.Y.C. (Morosco, Jan. 16, 1963) was Adam in *The Four Seasons* (Th. Four, Mar. 14, 1968); and appeared (1973–74) as a guest artist with the Seattle (Wash.) Repertory Th.

Television. Mr. Roebling appeared in *Mrs. Miniver*; on Playwright at Work (CBS, 1962); and in *Romeo and Juliet* (WNEW, Apr. 1964).

Awards. Mr. Roebling received the *Theatre World* Award (1959) for his performance as Sir Mark Grahame in *The Desert Incident* and *The Village Voice* Off-Bway (Obie) Award (1962) for his performance as Amory in *This Side of Paradise*.

ROERICK, WILLIAM. Actor, director, playwright. b. William G. Roehrich, Dec. 17, 1912, Hoboken, N.J., to William George and Josephine (Clark) Roehrich. Father, publisher. Educ. N.Y.C. public schools; grad. Hamilton Coll., B.S. 1934. Professional training at Berkshire Drama School, Stockbridge, Mass. (1935). Served US Army (1942–45). Member of AEA (council mbr., 1962–to date); SAG; AFTRA; Dramatists Guild; Emerson Literary Soc. (Clinton, N.Y.). Address: "Lost Farm", Tyringham, MA 01264, tel. (413) 243-2579.

Theatre. Mr.Roerick made his debut on the stage as Count Paulo del Magiore with Ethel Barrymore in *Déclassée* (Berkshire Playhouse, Stockbridge, Mass., Aug. 1935), and he first appeared on the Bway stage as Balthasar in the Katherine Cornell-Maurice Evans *Romeo and Juliet* (Martin Beck Th., Dec. 23, 1935). He followed this with performances as Gilles de Rais in Katherine Cornell's *Saint Joan* (Martin Beck Th., Mar. 9, 1936), in which he also toured; Guildenstern in John Gielgud's *Hamlet* (Empire, N.Y.C., Oct. 8, 1936), a production in which he replaced (Jan. 1937) John Emery as Laertes, then touring in the latter role; and the Baseball Player in *Our Town* (Henry Miller's Th., Feb. 4, 1938), in which he later toured as George.

Mr. Roerick also played Algernon Moncrieff in *The Importance of Being Earnest* (Vanderbilt Th., N.Y.C., Jan. 12, 1939); toured in *Easy Virtue* (1939); was Theodore Kincaid in *The Land Is Bright* (Music Box, Oct. 28, 1941); and Bob Ferguson in *Autumn Hill* (Booth Th., Apr. 13, 1942). While serving in the US Army, he appeared in the Irving Berlin revue *This Is the Army* (Broadway Th., July 4, 1942), then touring throughout the world with the production until 1945, during which time he made his London debut (Palladium, 1943).

He was Mr. Palmer in *The Magnificent Yankee* (Royale, N.Y.C., Jan. 22, 1946); John in *The Great Campaign* (Princess, Mar. 30, 1947); appeared with Gertrude Lawrence in *Tonight at 8:30* (National, Feb. 20, 1948) and on tour; replaced (June 1948) Peter Cookson as Morris Townsend in *The Heiress* (Biltmore, N.Y.C., Sept. 29, 1947), later touring as Arthur Townsend in the same play. Mr. Roerick wrote, with Thomas Coley, *The Happiest Years* (Lyceum, N.Y.C., Apr. 25, 1949); appeared as Father Christy in *Madam Will You Walk* (Phoenix, Dec. 1, 1953); Gerry Hardlip in *The Burning Glass* (Longacre, Mar. 4, 1954); and replaced (1955) Hugh Reilly as Jeffrey in *Dear Charles* (Morosco, Sept 15, 1954), then going on tour with the play.

He toured with Judith Anderson as Jason in *Medea* and in the title role of *Macbeth* (1962–63); played Roebuck Ramsden in *Man and Superman* (Charles Playhouse, Boston, Mass., Feb. 5, 1964); played Joseph Chamberlain in *The Right Honourable Gentleman* (Billy Rose Th., N.Y.C., Oct. 19, 1965); was Sir Walter Raleigh in a revival of *Elizabeth the Queen* (NY City Ctr., Nov. 3, 1966); and Father in *Come Slowly, Eden* (ANTA Matinee Series, Th. de Lys, Dec. 5–6, 1966).

He played the Marquis de Sade in a revival of *Marat/Sade* (Majestic, Jan. 3, 1967), in which he went on tour (Feb. 20, 1967); replaced (Oct. 16, 1967) Paul Rogers as Max in *The Homecoming* (Music Box, N.Y.C., Jan. 5, 1967), then touring in that part (1967–68); was The Major in *We Bombed in New Haven* (Ambassador, N.Y.C., Oct. 16, 1968); played Max in another production of *The Homecoming* (Studio Arena, Buffalo, N.Y., Feb. 6, 1969); appeared in *A Passage to E. M. Forster*, which, with Thomas Coley, he also compiled and which he directed (Th. de Lys, Oct. 26 & 27, 1970), later appearing in the production at the Berkshire Th. Festival, Stockbridge, Mass., and the McCarter Th., Princeton, N.J., both in 1971. He played Dr. Bonfant in *The Waltz of the Toreadors* (Circle in the Square-Joseph E. Levine Th., Sept. 13, 1973), later making a national tour with the production (1974); and was Gaev in *The Cherry Orchard* and directed *The Importance of Being Earnest* (both Goodman Th., Chicago, Ill., 1974).

Films. Mr. Roerick made his motion picture debut in *This Is the Army* (WB, 1943). Other films in which he appeared include *The Harder They Fall* (Col., 1956); *Flight to Hong Kong* (UA, 1956); *Not of This Earth* (Allied Artists, 1957); *The Sporting Club* (Avco-Embassy, 1971); *The Love Machine* (Col., 1971); *A Separate Peace* (Par., 1972); and *92 in the Shade* (MGM, 1975).

Television. Programs on which Mr. Roerick has appeared include Climax (CBS); Playhouse 90 (CBS); Dr. Kildare (NBC); Perry Mason (CBS); We the People; and Clear Horizon. With Thomas Coley, he has written scripts for episodes of I Remember Mama; Claudia; Ben Casey (ABC); and Climax.

Published Works. Mr. Roerick wrote the essay "Forster in America" in *Aspects of E. M. Forster* (1969).

Awards. Mr. Roerick was awarded an honorary D.F.A. by Hamilton Coll. (1971).

Recreation. Gardening, carpentry, books, pictures, and music.

ROGERS, ANNE. Actress. b. Agnes Anne Rogers, July 29, 1933, Liverpool, England. Attended St. John's C. of E., Cheshire, Eng.; studied at the Sch. of Dance, Hanley, England. Married Mar. 24, 1956, to Mike Hall, actor; two sons. Member of British AEA; The Players (London). Address: (home) 5 Middle Field St., St. John's Wood Park, London N.W. 8, England; (bus.) c/o Henry Hall, Steinway Hall, 1-2 St. George St., London W.1, England tel. Mayfair 1892.

Theatre. Miss Rogers made her debut as Snow White in *Snow White and the Seven Dwarfs* (Theatre Royal-Burnley, Lancashire, Eng., 1950; toured, 1950–53); subsequently appeared as Polly Browne in *The Boy Friend* (Players' Th., London, Apr. 14, 1953).

In the US, she played Eliza Doolittle in the natl. tour of *My Fair Lady* (opened Rochester Aud., N.Y., Mar. 18, 1957); left the cast in Chicago to succeed (Aug. 1959) Julie Andrews (Drury Lane Th., London, Apr. 6, 1962); appeared as Queen Flavia in *Zenda* (opened Curran Th., San Francisco, Calif., Aug. 5, 1963; closed Civic Aud., Pasadena, Calif., Nov. 16, 1963); played Amalia Balash in *She Loves Me* (Lyric, London, April 29, 1964); played Anne in *Half-a-Sixpense* (N.Y.C., San Francisco, and Los Angeles, 1966); Maggie in *Walking Happy* (N.Y.C., San Francisco, and Los Angeles, 1967); Agnes in *I Do, I Do* (Lyric, London, 1968); Josefa Lantenay in *A Shot in the Dark* (Ivanhoe Th., Chicago, 1970); and Lucille in *No, No, Nanette* (Th. Royale and Drury Lane, London, 1973).

Television. Miss Rogers made her debut in *Anne Rogers Sings* (BBC, London, 1955). Her American debut was in *Elizabeth the Queen* (Hallmark Hall of Fame, NBC). She appeared in *Hogan's Heroes* (CBS); played Elizabeth in *Birds on the Wing* (BBC, 1971); and appeared in *Song of Songs* (BBC, 1972).

Awards. Miss Rogers received the Sarah Siddons Award (1958) for her performance as Eliza Doolittle in *My Fair Lady*. She was nominated for the Sarah Siddons and Jeff Awards for her performance as Josefa Lantenay in *A Shot in the Dark* (1970).

ROGERS, PAUL. Actor. b. Mar. 22, 1917, Plympton, Devon, England, to Edwin and Dulcie Myrtle (Collier) Rogers. Father, headmaster; mother, teacher. Attended Plympton Grammar Sch., 1928; Newton Abbot Grammar Sch., Newton Abbot, 1936; studied at Nichael Checkhov Th. Studio, Dartington Hall, 1936–38. Married 1939, to Jocelyn Wynne (marr. dis., June 1955); two sons; married July 7, 1955, to Rosalind Boxall, actress; two daughters. Served WW II, Royal Navy, 1940–46; rank, Lt. Member of British AEA. Address: 9 Hillside Gardens, London N.6, England tel. May 8721.

Theatre. Mr. Rogers made his first appearance on Bway with the Old Vic Co., appearing as John of Gaunt in *Richard II* (Winter Garden, Oct. 23, 1956); subsequently, at the same theatre, performed with the company as Mercutio in *Romeo and Juliet* (Oct. 24, 1956); the title role in *Macbeth* (Oct. 29, 1956); and Pandarus in *Troilus and Cressida* (Dec. 26, 1956); and appeared as Reginald Kinsale, Esq., in *Photo Finish* (Brooks Atkinson Th., Feb. 12, 1956).

He made his London debut as Charles Dickens in *The Bird's-Eye View of Valour* (Scala, Dec. 1938); subsequently appeared with the Shakespeare Memorial Th. (Stratford-upon-Avon) in minor roles and as understudy in *Othello*, *The Taming of the Shrew*, *Richard III*, *As You Like It*, and *Twelfth Night* and was also assistant stage manager (Apr.–Sept. 1939); was a member of the repertory company in Colchester (Albert Hall, Oct. 1939–Oct. 1940), where he later appeared in roles that included Montague in *Romeo and Juliet*, Boanerges in *The Apple Cart*, and General Andrei Cherevenki in *House of Regrets* (Aug. 1946–Jan. 1947).

He appeared as Jonathan Kail and the Shepherd in *Tess of the D'Urbervilles* (Piccadilly, London, May 20, 1947); joined (Sept. 1947–July 1949) the Bristol Old Vic Co. (Th. Royal), where he appeared as the Earl of Gaversham in *An Ideal Husband*, Alfred Lockhart in *The Linden Tree*, Roderigo in *Othello*, Troke in *Rein on the Just*, Joe Gargery in *Great Expectations*, Widow Twankey in the Pantomine, *Aladdin*, and Polonius and the Priest in *Hamlet*, which was also presented in London (St. James's, July 13, 1948).

Also at the Bristol Old Vic Co., he played Sir George Orreyed, Bart., in *The Second Mrs. Tanqueray*, Tobias in *Tobias and the Angel*, Judge Brack in *Hedda Gabler;* the Writer in *You Never Can Tell*, Sir Anthony Absolute in *The Rivals*, Bottom in *A Midsummer Night's Dream*, Esdras in *Winterset*, Lord Porteous in *The Circle*, Tybalt in *Romeo and Juliet*, Denys Reynolds in *Wilderness of Monkeys*, also presented (Embassy, London, July 12, 1949), Sir Harry Beagle in *The Jealous Wife* and Captain Bluntschli in *Arms and the Man*.

Mr. Rogers joined the Old Vic Co. (New Th., London), where he played Dull in *Love's Labour's Lost* (Oct. 11, 1949), and later Don Armado in the same play; Stingo in *She Stoops To Conquer* (Oct. 18, 1949); Schaaf in *A Month in the Country* (Nov. 30, 1949); La Fleche in *The Miser* (Jan. 17, 1950); and Osric, Lucianus and the First Player in *Hamlet* (Feb. 2, 1950); the Stage-keeper and Trouble-all in *Bartholomew Fair* (Edinburgh Festival, Scotland, Aug. 1950; Old Vic, London, Dec. 18, 1950); Malvolio in *Twelfth Night* (Old Vic, Nov. 14, 1950); Lew and the Duke of Burgundy in *Henry V* (Jan. 30, 1951); Aegisthus in *Electra* and Fyodor Yakovlevitch Revunov-Karaulov in *The Wedding* a double-bill (Mar. 13, 1951); Dr. Caius in *The Merry Wives of Windsor* (May 31, 1951); Iago in *Othello* (Oct. 31, 1951); Bottom in *A Midsummer Night's Dream* (Dec. 26, 1951); and William Villon in *The Other Heart* (Apr. 15, 1952). In the latter play he repeated his role on a South African tour with the Old Vic Co., where he also appeared as Iago, Bottom, and the Third Witch in *Macbeth* (May–Oct. 2, 1952).

With the Old Vic Co., London, he appeared as Tardiveau in *An Italian Straw Hat* (Nov. 18, 1952); Shylock in *The Merchant of Venice* (Jan. 8, 1953); Cassius in *Julius Caesar* (Feb. 24, 1953); The First Knight in *Murder in the Cathedral* (Mar. 31, 1953); and in the title role in *Henry VIII* (May 6, 1953). He toured England (June–Aug. 1953); appeared as Sir Claude Mulhammer in *The Confidential Clerk* (Edinburgh Festival, Lyceum Th., Aug. 1953; Lyric, London, Sept. 16, 1953); with the Old Vic, London, played in the title role in *Macbeth* (Sept. 9, 1954); Don Armado in *Love's Labour's Lost* (Oct. 19, 1954); Petruchio in *The Taming of the Shrew* (Nov. 30, 1954); Touchstone in *As You Like It* (Mar. 1, 1955); Falstaff in *Henry IV, Part 1* (Apr. 27, 1955) and in *Henry IV, Part 2* (Apr. 28, 1955); Brutus in *Julius Caesar* (Sept. 7, 1955); Falstaff in *The Merry Wives of Windsor* (Sept. 27, 1955); Leontes in *The Winter's Tale* (Nov. 1, 1955); Pandarus in *Troilus and Cressida* (Apr. 3, 1956); the title role in *Macbeth* (May 22, 1956); Mercutio in *Romeo and Juliet* (June 12, 1956); and John of Gaunt in *Richard II* (July 3, 1956).

Mr. Rogers appeared in N.Y.C. with the Old Vic Co. (see above) and toured the US and Canada (Oct. 1956–Feb. 1957); toured Australia with the New Elizabethan Th. Co., appearing in the title role in *Hamlet* and as Lord Foppington in *The Relapse* (Mar.–Dec. 1957). He appeared with the Old Vic Co. London, in the title role in *King Lear* (Feb. 19, 1958); as Lord Claverton in *The Elder Statesman* (Edinburgh Festival, Aug. 1958; Cambridge, London, Sept. 25, 1958); played Cecil Fox in *Mr. Fox of Venice* (Piccadilly London, Apr. 15, 1959); Johnny Condell in *One More River* (Duke of York's Oct. 6, 1959); and Richard Medway in *A Shred of Evidence* (Duchess, Apr. 27, 1960). On tour with the Old Vic Co., he appeared in Moscow and Leningrad (USSR) and Warsaw (Poland), playing the title role in *Macbeth* and the Bishop of Beauvais in *Saint Joan* (Fall 1960). He appeared as Nickles in *J. B.* (Phoenix, London, Jan. 1961); Sam Old in *Photo Finish* (Saville, Apr. 1962), also appearing in the play in N.Y.C. (see above); and played Zorin in *The Seagull* (Queen's, London, Mar. 12, 1964).

Mr. Rogers played Oscar Portman in *Season of Goodwill* (Queen's Th., London, Sept. 16, 1964); Max in *The Homecoming* (Aldwych, London, June 3, 1965; and Music Box, N.Y.C., Jan. 5, 1967); for the Royal Shakespeare Co. (Stratford-on-Avon) played Apermantus in *Timon of Athens* (July, 1965), and Falstaff in *Henry IV, Parts 1 and 2* (Apr. 6, 1966); appeared as the Mayor in *The Inspector General* (Aldwych, London, Jan. 19, 1966); Sam Nash, Jesse Kiplinger, and Roy Hubley in *Plaza Suite* (Billy Rose Th., N.Y.C., Jan. 1968); Charles Murray in *The Happy Apple* (Apollo, London, Mar. 1970); and took over the role of Andrew Wyke in *Sleuth* (St. Martin's Th., London, Sept. 1970).

Films. Mr. Rogers appeared as the Fourth Knight in *Murder in the Cathedral* (Hoellening, 1950); the Prince in *A Prince for Cynthia* (Munnel Box, 1953); William Pitt in *Beau Brummell* (MGM, 1954); Taffy in *Svengali* (MGM, 1955); the Reverend Owen Jones in *The Beachcomber* (UA, 1955); *Our Man in Havana* (Col., 1960); *Trials of Oscar Wilde* (WAK, 1960); *Destruction Test* (20th-Fox); *No Love for Johnnie* (Embassy, 1961); *The Mark* (Continental, 1961); Henry VIII in *The Prince and the Pauper* (Buena Vista, 1961); Lieut. Seymour in *Billy Budd* (Allied, 1962); the Prison Governor in *The Pot Camera* (Assoc. Brit.); *Life for Ruth* (Saracen); *The Third Secret* (Hubris); played Superintendent Taylor in *He Who Rides a Tiger* (Lion, 1966); Hart Jacobs in *Walk in the Shadow* (Walter Reade, 1966); and appeared in *The Reckoning* (Col., 1969); and *The Looking Glass War* (Col., 1970).

Television. Mr. Rogers played Cardinal York in *Count Albany* (BBC, 1954); Vershinin in *The Three Sisters* (BBC, 1954); Iago in *Othello* (BBC, 1956); appeared in *The Cherry Orchard* (BBC, Jan. 1958); *Three Winters* (BBC, 1958); *For Services Rendered* (ABC, Apr. 26, 1958); *Statue of David* (BBC, 1958); played Bottom in *A Midsummer Night's Dream* (BBC, Nov. 1958); appeared in *The Deaf Heart* (ABC, Dec. 1958); played King Charles I in *The Killing of the King* (ABC, Dec. 1958); appeared in *The Model Husband* (ABC, May 1959); *Justice* (BBC, Jan. 1960); *The Temble Choice* (Assoc. Rediffusion, Jan. 1960); *The Conquering Hero* (BBC, Feb. 1960); played Pastor Manders in *Ghosts* (BBC, Feb. 1961); appeared in *Nora* (Assoc. Rediffusion, 1961); *The Candidate* (BBC, 1962); *The Duel* (BBC, 1963); *The Rose Garden* (Tennent, 1963); played Henry VIII in *The White Falcon* (BBC); Pastor Manders in *Ghosts* (BBC); and Sam in *Photo Finish* (BBC); appeared in *The Living Room* (BBC); and played Henry VIII in *The Prince and the Pauper* (NBC).

Awards. He received the Clarence Derwent Award (1952) for his performance as William Villove in *The Other Heart;* the best actor award (1954) from the Guild of Television Producers and Directors for his performance as Cardinal York in *Count Albany*, and Vershinin in *The Three Sisters;* a Whitbread Anglo-American Theatre Award (1967) for British contributions to the Bway stage; and the Antoinette Perry (Tony) Award for best actor (1967) for his performance in *The Homecoming*. .

Recreation. Music, gardens, making things.

ROGOFF, GORDON. Drama critic, producer, educator. b. Gordon Myles Rogoff, May 17, 1931, New York City, to Bernard M. and Hazel (Hirsch) Rogoff. Father, teacher, retired; mother, office manager, bookkeeper. Grad. H.S. of Music & Art, N.Y.C., 1948; Yale Univ., B.A. 1952; attended Central Sch. of Speech & Drama, London, 1952–53; Shakespeare Inst., Univ. of Birmingham, Stratford-upon-Avon, Summer 1952.%

Mr. Rogoff is chairman, Dept. of Theatre, School of Performing Arts, Brooklyn Coll., CUNY. Previously, he was a faculty member at the New School for Social Research, N.Y.C. (1963–64); head of the directing department, Yale School of Drama (1966–69); and teacher, director, and administrator at SUNY (Buffalo, N.Y.), where he established the Ctr. for Theatre Research as an independent branch of the Department of Theatre. Address: 27 W. 96th St., New York, NY 10025, tel. (212) 866-0732.

Theatre. Mr. Rogoff made his acting debut in summer stock (Milford, Pa., July–Aug. 1954), as Ensign Pulver in *Mister Roberts*, followed by the Doctor in *A Streetcar Named Desire*, Sen. Norval Hedges in *Born Yesterday*, Judge Omar Gaffney in *Harvey*, and Ed Anderson in *Come Back, Little Sheba;* subsequently succeeded Dutton Van Alstyne (June 10, 1958) as the Bride's Father in *Jack* and followed Donald Moffat (July 1958) as Mr. Martin in *The Bald Soprano* (Sullivan St. Playhouse, N.Y.C., June 3, 1958).

He was administrative director of Actors' Studio (May 1959–Jan. 1961); a partner in Writers' Stage Co., Ltd., N.Y.C., he co-produced at the Writers' Stage, *P.S. 193* (Oct. 30, 1962), *Three by Me* (Nov. 19, 1962), and *The Love Nest* (Jan. 25, 1963); and he produced, with Shirley Broughton, *Cliche, U.S.A.* (Theatre for Ideas, May 1964).

Television. Mr. Rogoff was assistant story editor for GE Th. (CBS) and Campbell's Star Stage with M.C.A. (May 1955–56).

Other Activities. Mr. Rogoff was co-founder and editor of *Encore* magazine, London, England (1956–57); drama critic and contributing editor for the *Tulane Drama Review* (later *The Drama Review)*, 1963–68; New York correspondent for *Plays and Players* magazine, London; and managing editor of *Theatre Arts Magazine* (Nov. 1961–Aug. 1962). He has contributed articles to *The New Leader, The Village Voice, The Nation*, and *The Commonweal*.

Awards. He received a Ford Fellowship for further study in the creative arts and for a study of the Actors' Studio (1961), and he has been awarded Rockefeller and Guggenheim grants.

Recreation. Music: piano and clarinet.

ROKER, ROXIE. Actress. b. Miami, Fla., to Albert and Bessie Roker. Father, laborer. Grad. Howard Univ., MA. Married to Sy Kravitz, television network assignment editor; one son.

Pre-Theatre. Office clerk, secretary, television production assistant.

Theatre. Miss Roker made her stage debut in the chorus of *Faith of Our Fathers* (Rock Creek Amphitheatre, Washington, D.C.); appeared off-off Bway as Irene in *The Dreamy Kid* on a bill entitled *Three by O'Neill* (West End Collegiate Chapel, N.Y.C., Sept. 19, 1957); replaced Maya Angelou as Queen in The Negro Ensemble Co. production of *The Blacks* (St. Marks Playhouse, May 4, 1961), a role she played for almost two years; again with NEC (St. Marks Playhouse), played Dorothea Ellen (Dorry) Sanders in *Rosalee Pritchett* (Jan. 21, 1970), and was a member of the company of *Ododo* (Nov. 17, 1970).

She played Desiree Vanderkellan in *Behold! Cometh the Vanderkellans* (Th. de Lys, N.Y.C., Mar. 31, 1971); Viola Caine Robinson in *Jamimma* (New Federal Th., Mar. 16, 1972); and, with NEC, Mattie Williams in *The River Niger* (St. Mark's Playhouse, Dec. 5, 1972; and Brooks Atkinson Th., Mar. 27, 1973).

Television. Miss Roker appears as Helen Willis on The Jeffersons series (CBS, 1975–76); and played Mama in *Change at 125th Street* (CBS).

Previously, she was associate producer for Family Living (NBC, 1962–69); and co-hostess for Inside Bedford Stuyvesant (WNEW, 1968).

Night Clubs. She was a featured singer in *Caribbean Fantasy* at El Morocco (Montreal).

Awards. Miss Roker was nominated for The Antoinette Perry (Tony) Award, and received The Off-Bway (Obie) Award (1973–74) for her performance in *The River Niger*. .

ROLF, FREDERICK. Actor, director. b. Aug. 14, 1926, Berlin, Ger., to Theodor and Ilse (Kadisch) Friedrichs. Father, physician. Attended City of Bath England) Boys' Sch. 1939–41. Member of AEA; AFTRA; SAG.

Theatre. Mr. Rolf made his first stage appearance as Captain Frederick de Foenix in *Trelawny of the Wells* (Grand Th., Halifax, England, June 1946); and subsequently played with repertory theatres in England (1946–48).

In the US, he appeared with the Margaret Webster touring company as Rosencrantz in *Hamlet* and Seyton in *Macbeth* (1948–49), and as Caesar in *Julius Caesar*, and Gremio in *The Taming of the Shrew* (1949–50); played the Man from Bellac in a stock production of *The Apollo of Bellac* (Woodstock Playhouse, N.Y., Summer 1950); and toured with Eva Le Gallienne in *Scenes from Great Plays* (1950).

He made his Bway debut as the Inquisitor in *Saint Joan* (Cort, Oct. 4, 1951); First Citizen in *Coriolanus* (Phoenix, Jan. followed by Arago in *The Strong Are Lonely* (Broadhurst, Sept. 29, 1953); the 19, 1954); Laomedon and Memnon in *The Immortal Husband* (Th. de Lys, Feb. 14, 1955); Will Shakespeare in *The Dark Lady of the Sonnets* (Cherry Lane, Feb. 20, 1956); at the Amer. Shakespeare Festival (Stratford, Conn.), played the Pedant in *The Taming of the Shrew* (Aug. 5, 1956); and directed *Titus Andronicus* for Joseph Papp's Shakespeare Workshop (Emmanuel Presbyterian Church, N.Y.C., 1956).

He played Theophilus in *Time Remembered* (Morosco, Nov. 12, 1957); the Count in *The Smokeweaver's Daughter* (Fourth St. Th., Apr. 14, 1959); Judas in *Between Two Thieves* (York, Feb. 11, 1960); Gaev in *The Cherry Orchard* (IASTA, June 1960); Nicola in *The Burnt Flower Bed* (Westport Country Playhouse, Conn., Summer 1960); Judge Brack in *Hedda Gabler* (Fourth St. Th., Nov. 9, 1960); directed an ELT production of *The Corn Is Green* (Masters Inst., Sept. 30, 1961); played The Doctor, Raffard, and Dugommier in *The Egg* (Cort, Jan. 8, 1962); the title role in *Uncle Vanya* (Charles Playhouse, Boston, Mass., Mar.–Apr. 1962); directed the ELT production of *The Vegetable* (Masters Inst., Oct. 26, 1963); in stock, directed *The Deadly Game* (Playhouse-on-the-Mall, Paramus, N.J., Jan. 21, 1964); and, in N.Y.C., played Duncan in *The Day the Whores Came Out to Play Tennis* (Actors' Studio, Mar. 16, 1964); Harry Payne in *Play with a Tiger* (Renata Th., Dec. 30, 1964); and directed *Hogan's Goat* (American Place Th., Nov. 11, 1965); and *The Winner* (U.R.G.E.N.T., Dec. 12, 1973).

Television. Mr. Rolf has appeared as King Priam in *The Iliad* (Omnibus, CBS, 1955); Richard in *Darkness at Noon* (Producers' Showcase, NBC, 1955); Senator James Mason in *The Constitution* (Omnibus, CBS, 1956); Iago in *A Double Life* (Alcoa Hour, NBC, 1957); Frederick the Great in *The Craft of Kings* (Camera Three, CBS, 1957); Dr. Joseph Breuer in *The Wound Within* (U.S. Steel Hour, CBS, 1958); Adolf Eichmann in *The Adolf Eichmann Story* (Armstrong Circle Th., CBS, 1960); and Judas in *The Death of Judas* (Directions '62, ABC, 1962).

Published Works. He has published an English adaptation of Schiller's drama, *Love and Intrigue* (1962).

ROLLE, ESTHER. Actress. b. Nov. 8, Pompano Beach, Fla., attended Spellman Coll. (Atlanta, Ga.); Hunter Coll. (N.Y.C.); New Sch. for Social Research (N.Y.C.). Married 1968 to Oscar Robinson (marr. dis.).

Theatre. For ten years, Miss Rolle was a dancer with Asada Dafora's Shogola Obola Dance Co. (1950's); a singer-dancer with the *African Holiday* troupe; toured Scandinavia with a production of *The Skin of Our Teeth;* and sang and danced in a touring production of *Calypso* (1954) and in *Carousel* (Open Door Th., N.Y.C., May 10, 1954).

She made her off-Bway debut with The Negro Ensemble Co. (St. Mark's Playhouse, N.Y.C.), replacing Brunetta Barnett as Felicity Trollop Pardon in production of *The Blacks* (opened May 4, 1961), playing that role for two years; subsequently toured Australia and New Zealand (Fall-Winter 1964) as the Narrator in *Black Nativity;* again at St. Marks Playhouse (N.Y.C.), played Ellie in *Happy Ending*, and the Clubwoman in *Day of Absence* on a double-bill (Nov. 15, 1965); played Pearl Cunningham in *The Summer of the Seventeenth Doll* (Feb. 20, 1968); Cannibal in *God Is a (Guess What?)* (Dec. 17, 1968), Mrs. Beverly in *String* and Katy Jones in *Contribution* on a double-bill entitled *An Evening of One-Acts* (Apr. 1, 1969); Alice Sugar in *Man Better Man* (July 2, 1969); Maybelle (Belle) Johnson in *Rosalee Pritchett* (Jan. 12, 1971); Faye in *Ride a Black Horse* (May 25, 1971); and Shouter Woman in *a Ballet Behind the Bridge* (Mar. 15, 1972).

In addition, she appeared in *The Crucible* (Arena Stage, Washington, D.C., Jan. 17, 1966); repeated her performance as Felicity Trollop Pardon in *The Blacks* (Th. Co. of Boston, 1969-70 season); played Aide and Market Wife in *The Dream on Monkey Mountain* on a double-bill with *Brotherhood* (Center Th. Group, Ahmanson, Los Angeles, Aug. 27, 1970; reopened Mar. 9, 1971); replaced Mimmie Gentry (Oct. 5, 1971) as Mu'Dear in *Black Girl* (Th. de Lys, N.Y.C., June 16, 1971); and played Miss Maybell in *Don't Play Us Cheap!* (Ethel Barrymore Th., May 16, 1972).

Films. Miss Rolle has appeared in *To Kill a Mocking Bird* (UI, 1963); *Nothing But a Man* (Cinema V, 1964); and *The Learning Tree* (WB-Seven Arts, 1969).

Television. Her television credits include East Side, West Side (CBS); The Guiding Light (CBS); One Life to Live (ABC); Dinah's Place (NBC); Maud (CBS); and her own series, Good Times (CBS).

ROMAN, LAWRENCE. Playwright. b. May 30, 1921, Jersey City, N.J., to Isadore Irving and Bessie Dora (Roud) Roman. Father, grocer. Grad. Washington H.S., Los Angeles, Calif., 1935; Univ. of California at Los Angeles, B.A. 1943. Married Apr. 29, 1946, to Evelyn Mildred Zirkin; one son, one daughter. Member of Dramatists Guild; WGA, West. 9157 Sunset Blvd., Los Angeles, CA 90069, tel. (213) CR 5-3747.

Theatre. Mr. Roman wrote *Under the Yum-Yum Tree* (Henry Miller's Th., N.Y.C., Nov. 16, 1960); *P.S. I Love You* (Henry Miller's Th., Nov. 19, 1964); *Buying Out* (Studio Arena Th., Buffalo, N.Y., Nov. 4, 1971); and *Crystal, Crystal Chandelier* (Berkshire Th., Stockbridge, Mass., July 31, 1973).

Films. Mr. Roman wrote, with David Swift, the screenplay for *Under the Yum-Yum Tree* (Col., 1963). He also wrote the screenplay for *Paper Lion* (UA, 1969); and the original screenplays for *A Warm December* (1st Artists, 1973) and *Mc Q* (WB, 1974).

ROME, HAROLD. Composer, lyricist. b. May 27, 1908, Hartford, Conn., to Louis and Ida (Aaronson) Rome. Attended Trinity Coll., 1924–26; grad. Yale Univ. B.A. 1929; attended Yale Univ. Sch. of Law, 1929–30; Grad. Yale Univ. Sch. of Architecture, B.F.A., 1934. Studied piano with Arthur Lloyd and Loma Roberts; composition with Joseph Schillinger, Lehman Engel and Meyer Kupferman. Married 1939, to Florence Miles; one son, one daughter. Served WW II, US Army 1943–45, rank, Cpl. Member of ASCAP, Player's Club (member, bd. of dir.), Dramatists Guild, AFTRA, AGAC. Address: (home) 1035 Fifth Ave., New York, NY 10028; (bus.) c/o Chappel & Co., 609 Fifth Ave., New York, NY 10017.

Pre-Theatre. Architect.

Theatre. Mr. Rome wrote the words and music for the revue, *Pins and Needles* Labor Stage Th., N.Y.C., Nov. 27, 1937; Apr. 20, 1939); *Sing Out the News* (Music Box, Sept. 24, 1938); contributed lyrics to the revue, *Streets of Paris* (Broadhurst, June 19, 1939); was composer of *The Little Dog Laughed* (opened Garden Pier, Atlantic City, N.J., July 1940; closed Shubert, Boston, Mass., Aug. 24, 1940); contributed songs to *Star and Garter* (Music Box, N.Y.C., June 24, 1942); *Let Freedom Sing* (Longacre, Oct. 5, 1942); and a sketch to the *Ziegfeld Follies* (Winter Garden, Apr. 1, 1943).

He wrote material for a series of touring Army shows in the US and the PTO (1943–44); wrote the lyrics and music for *Call Me Mister* (Natl., N.Y.C., Apr. 18, 1946); music for the pre-Bway tryout of *That's the Ticket* (opened Shubert, Philadelphia, Pa., Sept. 24, 1948; closed there Oct. 2, 1948); contributed lyrics and music to *Alive and Kicking* (Winter Garden, N.Y.C., Jan. 17, 1950); *Michael Todd's Peep Show* (Winter Garden, June 28, 1950); wrote words and music for *Bless You All* (Mark Hellinger Th., Dec. 14, 1950); *Wish You Were Here* (Imperial, June 25, 1952); and *Fanny* (Majestic, Nov. 4, 1954).

He wrote incidental music for *Romanoff and Juliet* (Plymouth, Oct. 10, 1957); words and music for *Destry Rides Again* (Imperial, Apr. 23, 1959); and *I Can Get It for You Wholesale* (Shubert, Mar. 22, 1962); wrote music and lyrics for *The Zulu and the Zayda* (Cort Th., N.Y.C., Nov. 10, 1965); wrote English lyrics for *La Grosse Valise* (N.Y.C., Nov. 25, 1965); wrote music and lyrics for *Scarlett* (Imperial Th., Tokyo, Japan, Jan. 3, 1970); and *Gone with the Wind* (Drury Lane Th., London, Eng., May 3, 1972; and Dorothy Chandler Pavilion, Los Angeles, Calif., Aug. 28, 1973).

Films. Mr. Rome's score for *Fanny* was used as background music for the screen version (WB, 1961).

Other Activities. He wrote material for a series of revues entitled *Lunchtime Follies*, presented in defense plants during WW II. There was a one-man show of his paintings at the Marble Arch Gallery (Nov. 1964). His second one-man show of paintings appeared at the Bodley Gallery, N.Y.C., (Mar. 1970).

Awards. Mr. Rome received the ASCAP awards for his songs "Sunday in the Park" in *Pins and Needles* (1937), and "Franklin D. Roosevelt Jones" in *Sing Out the News* (1940); and the Music Critics' Award for his recordings, *Harold Rome Sings Fanny* 1955.

Recreation. Collecting African sculpture. He has world's outstanding collection of African heddle-pullies; and one of the largest collections of African Tribal Sculpture in US. He also collects books on African Sculptures.

ROMOFF, WOODY. Actor. b. Woodrow Wilson Romoff, Oct. 16, 1918, New York City, to Joseph and Rose (Freed) Romoff. Father, monotype machinist. Attended De Witt Clinton H.S., Bronx, N.Y., 1936; Neighborhood Playhouse Sch. of the Th., 1944–46. Served US Army, 1941–45; rank, 1st Lt. Relatives in theatre: brother, Colin Romoff, coach, musical director; brother, Dick Romoff, musician. Member of AEA; AFTRA; SAG. Address: 372 Central Park West, New York, NY 10025, tel. (212) 864-7531; tel. (212) PL 3-2310.

Theatre. During 1946–52, Mr. Romoff appeared at the Barter Th. (Abingdon, Va.), in approximately 75 summer stock productions, including such roles as Shylock in *The Merchant of Venice;* the title role in the world premiere of *Mr. Thing* (which was produced in N.Y.C. as *Mrs. McThing*), and directed and performed in *Trial by Jury, H.M.S. Pinafore, The Mikado, Iolanthe,* and *The Gondoliers.*

He made his N.Y.C. debut as Gadshill in *Henry IV, Part 1* (NY City Ctr., Sept. 21, 1955); subsequently understudied Henry Lascoe as Vadim Romanoff in *Romanoff and Juliet* (Plymouth, Oct. 10, 1957), in which he toured as the Second Soldier (opened Royal Alexandra, Toronto, Canada, Sept. 15, 1958; closed Blackstone, Chicago, Ill., Jan. 3, 1959); and also toured in it as Vadim Romanoff (opened H.S. Aud., Topeka, Kans., Jan. 17, 1959; closed Rochester, N..Y., Aud., Mar. 14, 1959).

He understudied Henry Lascoe as Mr. Schlegel in *Carnival!* (Imperial, N.Y.C., Apr. 13, 1961); was stage manager for the national tour of *Irma La Douce* (opened Colonial, Boston, Mass., Jan. 4, 1962); played the Headwaiter in *She Loves Me* (Eugene O'Neill Th., N.Y.C., Apr. 23, 1963); Mr. Schlegel in a touring production of *Carnival!* (Mineola Playhouse, N.Y.; Paper Mill Playhouse, Millburn, N.J.; Westchester Dinner Th., Yonkers, N.Y., Jan. 19–Feb. 8, 1964); Mendel Polan in *Cafe Crown* (Martin Beck Th., N.Y.C., Mar. 20, 1964); in stock, Rough in *Angel Street* (Westchester County Playhouse, Dobbs Ferry, N.Y., June 23–July 5, 1964); and Counselor Khadja in *The Merry Widow* (NY

State Th., N.Y.C., Aug. 17, 1964).

Mr. Romoff played Victor Velasco in *Barefoot in the Park* (national company, 1966; and Biltmore, N.Y.C., 1967); and subsequently played Victor Velasco and directed fifteen productions (1967–74) of *Barefoot in the Park* with Sylvia Sidney, Vivian Vance, Vivian Blaine, Thelma Ritter, Tab Hunter, Ann Sothern, and Joan Bennett. He appeared in a touring production of *The Student Prince* (Summer 1966); played Herr Schultz in the national company of *Cabaret* (1969), and on two tours with Joel Grey (1970–71); toured with the national company of *Cactus Flower* (1970); played Inspector Levine in *Catch Me If You Can* (Meadowbrook Dinner Th., Cedar Grove, N.J., 1971); played the Doctor in *Promises, Promises* (Meadowbrook Dinner Th., Cedar Grove, N.J., 1972; and Melody Top Music Th., Milwaukee, Wis., 1973); played the title role in *Dracula* (Barter Th., Abingdon, Va., May 1972; and Windmill Dinner Ths., Ft. Worth and Dallas, Tex., Sept. 1972); appeared in *Wonderful Town* (Melody Top Music Th., Milwaukee, Wis.); appeared in *A Funny Thing Happened on the Way to the Forum, Bells Are Ringing,* and *Sugar* (Casa Mañana, Ft. Worth, Tex.); played Lou in the national company of *Twigs* (1974); and directed and played Victor Velasco in *Barefoot in the Park* (Granny Dinner Th., Dallas, Tex., Oct.–Dec. 1974).

Television. Mr. Romoff has appeared on Omnibus (NBC), Studio One (CBS), and Kraft Television Th. (NBC).

Recreation. Playing cello and flute.

RONELL, ANN. Composer, lyricist, librettist. Grad. Radcliffe Coll., B.A. Studied with Edward Ballantine; Archibald Davison; Walter Piston; George Gershwin; Richard Lert. Member of Dramatists Guild; AGAC; ASCAP; SWG; Natl. Music Camp Arts Acad. (dir. of natl. adv. bd., 1963); Natl. Council of Women of the U.S., Inc.; Radcliffe Club of N.Y. Address: 630 Fifth Ave., New York, NY 10020, tel. (212) CI 6-3040.

Theatre. Miss Ronell composed the score for *Trojan Women* (Wheaton Coll., Norton, Mass., 1927); and wrote the lyrics for *College Is the Place for Me* (Choral Group Show, Paramount, N.Y.C.).

She wrote the music and lyrics for *Down by the River* (Radio City Music Hall, N.Y.C., 1929); *Love and I* (Ziegfeld Roof Show, 1929); wrote the song "Let's Go Out in the Open Air" for the revue *Shoot the Works* (George M. Cohan Th., July 21, 1931); and wrote the music and lyrics for *Ile de France Revue* (Th. Champs-Elysées, Paris, 1932).

She performed her songs at the Paramount Th. (Los Angeles, Calif., 1935) and the Paramount Th. (Omaha, Nebr., 1935); was composer-lyricist for the opera *The Magic Spring* (Paramount Th., Los Angeles, 1935); was co-lyricist of the English versions of *The Magic Flute,* and *La Serva Padrona* (Los Angeles Jr. Coll., 1937), *The Merry Wives of Windsor,* and *The Barber of Seville* (Los Angeles Jr. Coll., 1938), and *Tales of Hoffman* (Los Angeles City Coll., 1938); co-writer of the song "Who's Afraid of the Big Bad Wolf," sung in the *New Ziegfeld Follies* (Winter Garden, N.Y.C., 1937); lyricist for *King With the Umbrella* (Boston, Mass., 1937); and was librettist, with Vicki Baum, for the opera *Martha* (Hollywood Bowl, Calif., 1939; Chicago Opera Assn., Ill., 1940).

She wrote the lyrics for new songs added to *The Chocolate Soldier* (Los Angeles Civic Light Opera Assn., Calif., 1941); contributed music and lyrics to *Count Me In* (Ethel Barrymore Th., N.Y.C., Oct. 8, 1942); wrote music and lyrics and was adaptor for a revised version of *The Gypsy Baron* (Los Angeles Civic Light Opera Assn., Calif., 1943); and for *The Open Road* (St. Louis Park Th., Mo., 1944); wrote the lyrics for a folk opera *Oh, Susanna!* (Pasadena Playhouse, Calif., 1947; Cleveland Play House, Ohio, 1949); wrote the song "The Lullaby," for *The Crucible* (Martin Beck Th., N.Y.C., Jan. 22, 1953); and was librettist and adaptor of an English version of the opera *Martha* (Metropolitan Opera House, N.Y.C., 1961).

Films. Miss Ronell wrote songs for *The Last Yacht* (RKO, 1935); *The Big Broadcast* (Par., 1936); and *Champagne Waltz* (Par., 1937); was lyricist for *The River Is So Blue* (UA); *Blockade* (UA, 1938); and *Algiers* (UA, 1938); and wrote songs for *You Can't Cheat an Honest Man* (U, 1939).

She wrote songs and adapted musical classics for *Magic in Music* (Par., 1940); served as musical production assistant for *Ladies in Retirement* (Col., 1941); *Commandos Strike at Dawn* (Col., 1942); music director for *Tomorrow the World* (UA, 1944); wrote lyrics and was co-composer of the music for *The Story of G.I. Joe* (UA, 1945); composed the music, wrote the lyrics, and was music director for *One Touch of Venus* (U, 1948); *Love Happy* (UA, 1949); and *Main Street to Broadway* (MGM, 1953).

Television and Radio. Miss Ronell has written program songs for the radio and television appearances of Helen Jepson, John Raitt, Nadine Connor, Grace Moore, Frank Sinatra, Steve Lawrence, Andy Williams, Louis Armstrong, Ella Fitzgerald, June Christy, Vivian Della Chiesa, Mary Martin, and Gladys Swarthout.

Published Works. Her published songs include "The Candy Parade," "Baby's Birthday Party," "Rain on the Roof," "Beach Boy," "On the Merry-Go-Round," "Andy Panda," "Mickey Mouse," "Minnie's in Town," "Fireflies on Parade," "Who's Afraid of the Big Bad Wolf," "Love Happy," "The Great Adventure," "Linda," "The Woman Behind the Gun," "Just a Girl," "Don't Look Now, But My Heart Is Showing," "The Commandos March," "Buy a Buddy Poppy," "At the ANTA Ball," "Some Folks Say," words and music for "Willow Weep for Me," "C'est la vie," "Beloved," "You're Lovely," "The Infantry March," "The River," "Too Big a Price," "Ticketyboo," "Dark Moon," and "Hondo."

Her published works include "Open Road, Open Sky," "Love Can Be Dreamed," "Your Eyes Shine in My Own," "Sleepy-Bye," "The Girls of Cadiz," "April of Nostalgia," "When Lovers Meet," "Flirtation Intermezzo," "The Deanna Durbin Favorite Arias Songbook," "One Lonely Night," "The Judy Garland Songbook," and choral arrangements from *Gypsy Baron, Magic of Spring, Martha,* and *Oh, Susanna!.*

Awards. Miss Ronell received an Academy (Oscar) Award nomination for the best musical score for *The Story of G.I. Joe* (1945); and for the best song "Linda," (1945); her muscial band number, "The Infantry March," was adopted by the US Army Ground Forces (1945); and she received the best film score prize by *Film Music* Magazine for "Love Happy," (1949).

Recreation. Hockey, basketball, ballet, piano playing.

ROOS, JOANNA. Actress, playwright. b. Brooklyn, N.Y., to John A. and Mary Elizabeth (Graham) Roos. Married to Edmond W. Rickett, composer, musical director, (dec. Mar. 14, 1957); one son, Peter John Rickett, musical director. Member of AEA; SAG; AFTRA; Dramatists Guild. Address: 340 E. 50th St., New York, NY 10022, tel. (212) EL 5-2179.

Theatre. Miss Roos made her debut at the Neighborhood Playhouse of the Th., N.Y.C., appearing in *Alice in Wonderland, The Harlequinade,* and as Sonia in *The Green Ring* (1921).

She played Esther in *The Idle Inn* (Plymouth, Dec. 20, 1921); and at the Neighborhood Playhouse of the Th., appeared as the Wife of the 3rd Countryman, and a Page in *The Player Queen,* and Jessie in *The Shewing-Up of Blanco Posnet,* a double-bill (Oct. 16, 1923), Goldie Shoop in *This Fine-Pretty World* (Dec. 26, 1923), and appeared in the revue, *Grand Street Follies* (May 20, 1924, June 18, 1925).

She played Kristina in *The Makropoulous Secret* (Charles Hopkins Th., Jan. 21, 1926); Norah Halpin in *Loggerheads* (Cherry Lane, Feb. 9, 1926); Aglaia Epanchin in matinee performances of *The Strange Prince* (Booth, Dec. 7, 1926); Elaine Carleton in *Stigma* (Cherry Lane, Feb. 10, 1927); appeared in the revue *Grand Street Follies* (Little, May 31, 1927); and in matinee performances of *Lovers and Enemies* (Little, Sept. 20, 1927).

She joined the cast during the run of *Grand Street Follies* (Booth, May 28, 1928); took over for Beatrice Ames as Delia during the run of *Holiday* (Plymouth, Nov. 26, 1928); played Allie Smith in *Veneer* (Sam H. Harris Th., Nov. 12, 1929); joined the cast during the run of *Rebound* (Plymouth, Feb. 3, 1930); played Sonia in *Uncle Vanya* (Cort, Apr. 15, 1930); Naomi Bradshaw in *Schoolgirl* (Ritz, Nov. 20, 1930); succeeded (Dec. 1930) Anita Kerry as Penelope Gray in *Elizabeth the Queen* (Guild, Nov. 31, 1930); played Mary Grove in *Washington Heights* (Maxine Elliott's Th., Sept. 29, 1931); Beth in *Little Women* (Playhouse, Dec. 7, 1931); and Grace Sutton in *Life Begins* (Selwyn, Mar. 28, 1932).

Also, Emmeline in *Uncle Tom's Cabin* (Alvin, May 29, 1933); a Girl in *Panic* (Imperial, Mar. 14, 1934); Vera in *Picnic* (Natl., May 2, 1934); Sallie Tabor in *Tight Britches* (Avon, Sept. 11, 1934); Katherine in *Black Widow* (Mansfield, Feb. 12, 1936); Elektra in *Daughters of Atreus* (44 St. Th., Oct. 14, 1936); Lettie in the pre-Bway tryout of *Uncle Harry* (Cohasset, Mass., July 1938); succeeded (Nov. 1939) Muriel Kirkland as Mary Todd in *Abe Lincoln in Illinois* (Plymouth, N.Y.C., Oct. 15, 1938); was in the tryout of *Lottie Dandass* (Lobero Th., Santa Barbara, Calif., 1941); played the 1st Mrs. Carroll in the pre-Bway tryout of *The Two Mrs. Carrolls* (Philadelphia, Pa., 1942); Bessie in the pre-Bway tryout of *The Willow and I* (Philadelphia, Pa., and Boston, Mass., Nov. 1942); and played Mrs. Lincoln in matinee performances of *War President* (Shubert Th., N.Y.C., Apr. 1944); St. Margaret in *Joan of Lorraine* (Alvin Th., Nov. 18, 1946); and Elizabeth Barrett in *The Barretts of Wimpole Street* (Bridgehampton Th., Bridgehampton, N.Y., 1947).

With Alexander King and Lehman Engle, she wrote the musical, *Mooncalf* (Karamu Th., Cleveland, Ohio, May 1953); at the Th. de Lys, she played Mama in *Maya* (June 9, 1953), and Mrs. Candour in *The School for Scandal* (June 16, 1953); with Edward Mabley, adapted *Comes the Comrade* (Olney Th., Md., Aug. 1953); played Vee Talbot in *Orpheus Descending* (Martin Beck Th., N.Y.C., Mar. 21, 1957); and Isabella Wilson in *Maidens and Mistresses at Home at the Zoo* (Orpheum, Jan. 21, 1959).

At the San Diego (Calif.) Shakespeare Festival, Miss Roos appeared at the Old Globe in 1959 as Mistress Quickly in *Henry IV, Part 1* (July 7) and as the Nurse in *Romeo and Juliet* (July 17); and she played Aase in *Peer Gynt* (Phoenix, N.Y.C., Jan. 12, 1960).

In 1960, Miss Roos was a founding member of the Association of Producing Artists (APA) and appeared with the company that year at the McCarter Th., Princeton, N.J., as Signora Frola in *Right You Are* (Oct. 13) and Miss Prism in *The Importance of Being Earnest* (Nov. 10). At the San Diego Shakespeare Festival, she played Maria in *Twelfth Night* (June 27, 1961) and Queen Margaret in *Richard III* (July 26, 1961).

In 1962, she appeared with APA at the Folksbiene Playhouse, N.Y.C., as Mrs. Candour in *The School for Scandal* (Mar. 17), Paulina Shamrayeff in *The Seagull* (Mar. 21), and Mrs. Lamson in *The Tavern* (Apr. 4) and then toured summer theatres as Charlie in *Critic's Choice* (1962).

At the Fred Miller Th., Milwaukee, Wis., she played Lady Britomart Undershaft in *Major Barbara* (Feb. 1963), and Mrs. Carghill in the tryout of *The Elder Statesman* (Mar. 1963); she was Lady Bracknell in *The Importance of Being Earnest* (Robin Hood Th., Philadelphia, Pa., July 15, 1963); appeared with APA at Trueblood Th., Ann Arbor, Mich., as Doto in *A Phoenix Too Frequent* (Oct. 17, 1963), Signora Frola in *Right You Are* (Nov. 7, 1963), and Anna in *The Lower Depths* (Nov. 21, 1963); with APA at Phoenix Th., N.Y.C., as Signora Frola (Mar. 4, 1964), Mrs. Lamson in The Tavern (Mar. 5, 1964), Mlle. Du Parc in *Impromptu at Versailles* (Mar. 9, 1964); with APA at Ann Arbor as Countess Rostova in *War and Peace* (Sept. 23, 1964), Mrs. Whitefield in *Man and Superman* (Sept. 30, 1964), and Miss Gilchrist in *The Hostage* (Oct. 14, 1964); then repeating at the Phoenix in N.Y.C. her performances as Mrs. Whitefield (Dec. 6, 1964) and Countess Rostova (Jan. 11, 1965).

She played at the NY Shakespeare Festival, Delacorte Th., as Countess Rossillion in *All's Well That Ends Well* (June 15, 1966); was Essie in *Ah, Wilderness!* (Trinity Square Repertory Co., Providence, R.I., Jan. 17, 1967); appeared at the Univ. of Missouri Festival (Summer 1967) as Dr. Van Zahnd in *The Physicists* and Miss Prism in *The Importance of Being Earnest;* was Juno Burke in *The Heir Apparent* (New Dramatists, N.Y.C., Nov. 19, 1967); and Grace Sky in *Buying Out* (Studio Arena, Buffalo, N.Y., Nov. 4, 1971).

Films. Miss Roos has appeared in *Patterns* UA, 1956); *Splendor in the Grass* (WB, 1961); and *Two Weeks in Another Town* (MGM, 1962).

Television. With Edward A. Mabley, she wrote *Borderline of Fear* (Danger, CBS); played Meg in *Little Women* (NBC, 1941); in Oct. 1967 began playing Sarah Caldwell in Love of Life (CBS); and was Mary in *The Rimers of Eldritch* (PBS, Nov. 4, 1972).

Published Works. Miss Roos wrote "So You Want To Go on the Stage" (1934), which won a Reader's Digest Prize; "Among Ourselves" (1944), which won the Olga Shapiro Prize; and "The Stepmother" (1950), which won Stanford University's Thomas Wood Stevens Award.

ROOT, LYNN. Playwright, actor, writer. b. Apr. 11, 1905, Morgan, Minn., to Charles B. and Edith (Butterfield) Root. Attended Univ. of Minnesota, 1924 (Business Administration). Married 1934 to Helen Walter. Member of Dramatists Guild. Address: 470 So. Camden Dr., Beverly Hills, CA 90212.

Pre-Theatre. Advertising.

Theatre. Mr. Root first performed in a touring production of *Strictly Dishonorable;* made his Bway debut as Brady in *City Haul* (Hudson, Dec. 30, 1929); played Herbert Flint in *Blessed Event* (Feb. 12, 1932).

He wrote, with Harry Clork, *The Milky Way* (Cort Th., May 8, 1934); with Frank Fenton, wrote *Stork Mad,* in which he also played Harry Dever (Ambassador, Sept. 30, 1936); and wrote the book for *Cabin in the Sky* (Martin Beck Th., Oct. 25, 1940; revived Greenwich Mews, Jan. 21, 1964).

Films. With Frank Fenton, Mr. Root wrote the scenarios for *Woman Chases Man* (UA, 1937); *The Saint Takes Over* (RKO, 1940); *Millionaires in Prison* (RKO, 1940); *The Golden Fleecing* (MGM, 1940); *The Gay Falcon* (RKO, 1941); *Highways by Night* (RKO, 1942); *The Sky's the Limit* (RKO, 1943); *Lady Luck* (RKO, 1946); and *The Kid From Brooklyn* (RKO, 1946).

Recreation. Music, gardening.

ROSE, GEORGE. Actor. b. George Walter Rose, Feb. 19, 1920, Bicester, England, to Walter John Arthur and Eva Sarah (Rolfe) Rose. Father, butcher. Grad. City of Oxford H.S. for Boys, 1936; Central Sch. of Speech and Drama, London, 1944–45. Studied with Gwynneth Thurburn, Audrey Bullard, London. Member of AEA; British AEA; AFTRA.

Pre-Theatre. Secretary to the bursar, Wadham Coll., Oxford, England (1937–40).

Theatre. Mr. Rose made his first appearance in N.Y.C. as Peto in the Old Vic Company production of *Henry IV, Part 1* (Century, May 6, 1946); subsequently appeared as Dogberry in John Gielgud's production of *Much Ado About Nothing* (Lunt-Fontanne, Sept. 17, 1959), which previously had played at the Cambridge (Mass.) Arts Festival (Aug. 1959); The Common Man in *A Man for All Seasons* (ANTA, N.Y.C., Oct. 22, 1961), in which he also toured cross-country (1963–64); and as the First Grave Digger in Richard Burton's *Hamlet* (Lunt-Fontanne, Apr. 9, 1964).

He was Glas in *Slow Dance on the Killing Ground* (Plymouth, Nov. 30, 1964); Martin Ruiz in *The Royal Hunt of the Sun* (ANTA Th., Oct. 26, 1965); Henry Horatio Hobson in *Walking Happy* (Lunt-Fontanne Th., Nov. 26, 1966); Alfred P. Doolittle in a revival of *My Fair Lady* (NY City Ctr., June 13, 1968); Drinkwater in *Captain Brassbound's Conversion* (Center Th. Group, Mark Taper Forum, Los Angeles, Calif., Summer 1968); the Steward, the Carpenter, and January in *Canterbury Tales* (Eugene O'Neill Th., N.Y.C., Feb. 3, 1969); Louis Greff in *Coco* (Mark Hellinger Th., Dec. 18, 1969), in which he later toured; and Mr. Booker in *Wise Child* (Helen Hayes Th., N.Y.C., Jan. 27, 1972).

He toured (Sept. 1972–Mar. 1973) as Andrew Wyke in *Sleuth* and replaced (Apr. 9, 1973) Patrick Macnee in the part in the N.Y.C. production (Music Box, Nov. 12, 1970); played Lutz in the pre-Bway tryout of a revival of *The Student Prince* (opened Academy of Music, Philadelphia, Pa., June 5, 1973); closed State Fair, Dallas, Tex., Oct. 21, 1973); was Henry in *My Fat Friend* (Brooks Atkinson Th., Mar. 31, 1974), in which he later toured (1974–75); and repeated his performance as Alfred Doolittle in another revival of *My Fair Lady* (St. James, N.Y.C., Mar. 25, 1976).

He made his first professional appearance with the Old Vic Co. as a walk-on in *Peer Gynt* (New, London, Aug. 31, 1944); appeared with the Old Vic as Peto in *Henry IV, Part 1* (New, Sept. 26, 1945); Thomas, Duke of Clarence, Lord Bardolph, and Mouldy in *Henry IV, Part 2* (New, Oct. 3, 1945); as Sir Christopher Hatton in *The Critic* and appeared in the Chorus of *Oedipus Rex* (New, Oct. 18, 1945); The Duke of Burgundy and a Captain in *King Lear* (New, Sept. 24, 1946); Montfleury in *Cyrano de Bergerac* (New, Oct. 24, 1946); Kastril in *The Alchemist* (New, Jan. 14, 1947); the Duke of Surrey and Keeper in *Richard II* (New, Apr. 23, 1947); Lucentio in *The Taming of the Shrew* (New, Nov. 4, 1947); the English Soldier in *Saint Joan* (New, Dec. 3, 1947); Zemlyanika in *The Government Inspector* (New, Feb. 3, 1948); and a Roman Herald in *Coriolanus* (New, Mar. 31, 1948).

He then played Dickie Miles in *People Like Us* (Wyndham's, July 6, 1948), and appeared with The High Wycombe Repertory Co. as Tiresias in *Oedipus Rex* and George in *Peace Comes to Peckham* (High Wycombe Rep. Th., Oct.–Nov. 1948), and in the revue, *1066 and All that* for the Royal Artillery Rep. Co. (Royal Artillery Th., Woolwich, Dec. 17, 1948).

Mr. Rose performed with the Royal Shakespeare Co. (Memorial Th., Stratford-upon-Avon), as Lennox in *Macbeth,* Dogberry in Gielgud's production of *Much Ado About Nothing* (in which he subsequently appeared on Bway, see above), Snug in *A Midsummer Night's Dream,* Belarius in *Cymbeline,* Brabantio in *Othello,* the First Gentleman in *Henry VIII,* Pompey in *Measure for Measure,* Casca in *Julius Caesar,* and as Oswald in *King Lear,* (1949–50).

He played Harry in *Nothing Up My Sleeve* (Watergate, London, Dec. 5, 1950); William Humpage in *A Penny for a Song* (Haymarket, Mar. 3, 1951); Autolycus in *The Winter's Tale* (Phoenix, June 27, 1951); Dogberry in *Much Ado About Nothing* (Phoenix, Jan. 11, 1952); Sailor in *The Square Ring* (Lyric, Hammersmith, Oct. 21, 1952); Boanerges in *The Apple Cart* (Haymarket, May 7, 1953); Krogstad in *A Doll's House* (Lyric, Hammersmith, Sept. 8, 1953); Jules in *My 3 Angels* (Lyric, May 12, 1955); Maitland in *The Chalk Garden* (Haymarket, Apr. 12, 1956); appeared in a revue *Living for Pleasure* (Garrick, July 10, 1958); played the Burgomaster in *The Visit* (Royalty, June 23, 1960); appeared in a bill of two one-act plays, *Trials by Logue,* in which he appeared as Creon in *Antigone* and the Magistrate in *The Trial of Cobb & Leach* (Royal Court, Nov. 23, 1960); The Common Man in *A Man for All Seasons* (Globe, Jan. 1, 1960), which he also played in the US (see above); and appeared in a revue *On the Avenue* (Globe, June 17, 1961).

Films. Mr. Rose made his debut as the Coachman in *The Pickwick Papers* (Kingsley, 1953); and subsequently appeared in *The Square Ring* (Rank, 1953); *Wicked Wife* (Allied, 1955); *The Sea Shall Not Have Them* (UA, 1955); *The Shiralee* (Rank, 1955); *Barnacle Bill* (MGM, 1956); *Panic in the Parlor* (DCA, 1956); *The Third Key* (Rank, 1957); *A Tale of Two Cities* (Rank, 1958); *The Good Companions* (Stratford, 1958); *A Night to Remember* (Lopert, 1958); *The Devil's Disciple* (UA, 1959); *The Heart of a Man* (Rank, 1959); *Jack the Ripper* (Par., 1960); *No Love for Johnnie* (Embassy, 1961); and *Hawaii* (UA, 1966).

Television. His credits include Noah in *Before the Flood* (BBC, 1951); two programs of short stories (BBC, 1954); the Sergeant in *The Face of Love* (ATV, 1954); the Tax Inspector in *Both Ends Meet* (ATV, 1955); Trock in *Winterset* (ATV, 1957); Fred in *The Pier* (ITV, Manchester, 1957); Ericson in *The Family First* (ATV, 1960); and Salinas in *Top Secret* (ARTV, 1961).

In the US he appeared as the Prisoner in *The Dock Brief* and the Husband in *What Shall We Tell Caroline?* (Play of the Week, WNTA, 1959); the Magistrate in *Oliver Twist* (Dupont Show of the Month, NBC, 1959); George in *The Fifth Column* (Buick Electra Playhouse, CBS, 1960); Owen in *The Citadel* (Dupont Show of the Month, NBC, 1960); Ben Gunn in *Treasure Island* (Dupont Show of the Month, NBC, 1960); Drinkwater in *Captain Brassbound's Conversion* (Hallmark Hall of Fame, NBC, 1960); the Porter in *Macbeth* (Hallmark Hall of Fame, NBC, 1960); Raguneau in *Cyrano de Bergerac* (Hallmark Hall of Fame, NBC, 1962); Doolittle in *Pygmalion* (Hallmark Hall of Fame, NBC, 1963); on Stage 2 (CBS, Nov. 1964); in *Eagle in a Cage* (Hallmark Hall of Fame, Oct. 1965); and as Lassiter in Beacon Hill (CBS, 1975).

Awards. Mr. Rose received an Antoinette Perry (Tony) Award (1975–76) as best actor in a musical for his performance as Doolittle in the revival of *My Fair Lady.* He was nominated for a Tony award (1969–70) for best supporting actor in a musical for his performance in *Coco.* He received a Drama Desk Award (1973–74) for his outstanding performance in *My Fat Friend* and was nominated for a Tony (1974–75) for the same performance in the best supporting actor category, a nomination which he asked to have withdrawn.

Recreation. Records, photography.

ROSE, PHILIP. Producer, director, playwright. b. Philip Rosenberg, July 4, 1921, New York City, to Max and Esther Rosenberg. Father, businessman. Attended Seward Park H.S., N.Y.C., 1937. Married 1946 to Doris Belack, actress. Member of AEA; AGVA; AFTRA. Address: (home) 50 Central Park West, New York, NY 10023, tel. (212) TR 7-5593; (bus.) 157 W. 57th St., New York, NY 10019, tel. (212) CI 5-2255.

Theatre. Mr. Rose produced, with David J. Cogan, *A Raisin in the Sun* (Ethel Barrymore Th., N.Y.C., Mar. 11, 1959); produced *Semi-Detached* (Martin Beck Th., May 10, 1960); *Purlie Victorious* (Cort, Sept. 28, 1961); *Bravo Giovanni* (Broadhurst, May 19, 1962); produced, with Elliot Martin, *Nobody Loves an Albatross* (Lyceum, Dec. 19, 1963); and produced *Cafe Crown* (Martin Beck Th., Apr. 20, 1964).

Also *The Owl and the Pussycat* (ANTA Th., Nov. 18, 1964); with Herschel Bernardi and Jeanne Otto, *Nathan Weinstein, Mystic, Connecticut* (Brooks Atkinson Th., Feb. 25, 1966); produced and directed *The Ninety-Day Mistress* (Biltmore, Nov. 6, 1967); produced, with Huntington Hartford in association with Jay Weston, *Does a Tiger Wear a Necktie?* (Belasco Th., Feb. 25, 1969); produced and directed *Purlie,* for which, with Ossie Davis and Peter Udell, he also wrote the book (Broadway Th., Mar. 15, 1970; revival, Billy Rose Th., Dec. 27, 1971); and produced, with Gloria and Louis K. Sher, and directed *Shenandoah,* for which, with James Lee Barrett and Peter Udell, he also wrote the book (Alvin, Jan. 7, 1975).

Mr. Rose began as a singer, and sang with the St. Louis (Mo.) Municipal Opera (Summer 1945).

Awards. *A Raisin in the Sun,* which Mr. Rose co-produced, received the NY Drama Critics' Circle Award (1959). *Purlie,* which he produced and directed and for which he collaborated on the book, was nominated for an Antoinette Perry (Tony) Award as best musical (1969–70), and Mr. Rose received a Tony nomination as best director for the same production. *Shenandoah,* of which he was co-producer and co-author and which he directed, received a Tony for best book of a musical (1974–75) and was nominated for a Tony as best musical.

ROSE, REGINALD. Playwright. b. Dec. 10, 1920, New York City, to William and Alice (Obendorfer) Rose. Father, lawyer. Grad. Townsend Harris H.S., N.Y.C., 1937; attended City Coll. of New York, 1937–38. Married Sept. 5, 1943, to Barbara Langbart (marr. dis. May 20, 1963); four sons; married July 6, 1963, to Ellen McLaughlin; two sons. Served US Army, Quartermaster Corps, 1942–46; rank, 1st Lt. Member of Dramatists Guild; WGA, East. Address: (home) 30 Kingston House North, Prince's Gate, London, S.W.7, England; (bus.) Defender Productions c/o David W. Katz & Co., 10 E. 40th St., New York, NY 10016, tel. (212) 685-4700.

He is the president of Defender Productions, Inc.

Pre-Theatre. Advertising copywriter.

Theatre. Mr. Rose adapted three of his television plays for the theatre: *Black Monday* (Vandam Th., N.Y.C., Mar. 6, 1962), *Twelve Angry Men* (Queen's, London, Eng., July 9, 1964; and *Dear Friends* (Edinburgh Festival, 1968).

Films. He was adaptor and co-producer of his *Twelve Angry Men* (UA, 1957); wrote *Crime in the Streets* (AA, 1956); *Dino* (AA, 1957); *Man of the West* (UA, 1958); *The Man in the Net* (UA, 1959); and *Baxter* (EMI, 1973).

Television. He wrote *The Bus to Nowhere* (Out There, CBS, 1951); *Twelve Angry Men* (Studio One, CBS, 1954); *Thunder on Sycamore Street* (Studio One, CBS, 1954); *The Incredible World of Horace Ford* (Studio One, CBS, 1955); *Crime in the Streets* (Elgin Hour, ABC, 1955); *Tragedy in a Temporary Town* (Alcoa Hour, NBC, 1956); *A Quiet Game of Cards* (Playhouse 90, CBS, 1959); *The Sacco-Vanzetti Story* (Sunday Showcase, NBC, 1960); *The Cruel Day* (Playhouse 90, CBS, 1959); and *Dear Friends* (CBS Playhouse, 1968). He created the series The Defenders (CBS).

Awards. He received three NATAS (Emmy) Awards for his television play, *Twelve Angry Men* (1958); for his film of the same play, The Writers Guild of Amer. Award (1958); the Mystery Writers of Amer. Edgar Allan Poe Award (1958); a citation at the Berlin Film Festival (1958); and NATAS (Emmy) Awards for The Defenders (1961 and 1962).

ROSENBERG, MARVIN. Educator, writer. b. Nov. 6, 1912, Fresno, Calif., to Leon and Anna (Davidson) Rosenberg. Father, businessman. Grad. Sacramento (Calif.) H.S., 1929; Univ. of California, Berkeley, A.B. 1933; M.A. 1936; Ph.D. 1951. Member of Amer. Society for Th. Research; AETA; Shakespeare Assn.; MLA; Amer. Society for Aesthetics. Address: (home) 945 King Dr., El Cerrito, CA 94530; (bus.) Univ. of California at Berkeley, Berkeley, CA 94720, tel. (415) 642-1677.

Since 1948, Mr. Rosenberg has been a member of the faculty of the Univ. of California at Berkeley, where he has been professor of dramatic arts (1960–to date). Previously, he was chief of the Siam Section of the State Department's Intl. Broadcasting Division. During WW II, he had been an editor for the Office of War Information.

Published Works. He has written *The Masks of Othello* and *The Masks of King Lear;* and essays in such scholarly and critical journals as *PMLA, Theatre Notebook, Theatre Arts, Shakespeare Quarterly, Studies in Philology, Modern Drama, Educational Theatre Journal, Philological Quarterly,* and *Journal of English and German Philology.* .

Awards. Mr. Rosenberg received the Dramatists Alliance Etherege Award (1958) for comedy; and the Catawba Coll. Production Award (1961).

The Masks of King Lear was selected for inclusion in the Modern Language Association's Scholar's Library.

Recreation. Tennis, golf, squash, touch football.

ROSENBLUM, M. EDGAR. Producer, manager. b. Morton Edgar Rosenblum, Jan. 8, 1932, Brooklyn, N.Y., to Jacob and Pauline (Feldman) Rosenblum. Father, physician; mother, nurse, social worker. Grad. Midwood H.S., Brooklyn, 1949; attended Bard Coll., 1952–56. Married May 1, 1960, to Cornelia Hartmann, painter. Served US Army, 1953; rank, Pvt. Member of AGMA; CORST; League of Resident Theatres. Address: c/o Long Wharf Theatre, 222 Sargent Dr., New Haven, CT 06511.

Pre-Theatre. Copywriter, music manager for National Music League; director of Polari Art Gallery (N.Y.C.; Woodstock, N.Y.).

Theatre. Mr. Rosenblum was, at first, secretary to designer, Norman Bel Geddes (1956); subsequently, at the American Scandinavian Foundation, produced *Let Man Live* (1958); produced, with Arnold Tager, and was company manager for a tour of *When I Was a Child* and its N.Y.C. production (41 St. Th., Dec. 8, 1960).

For fourteen years, Mr. Rosenblum was producer and manager of the Woodstock (N.Y.) Playhouse, which he bought in 1960. Among his numerous presentations there were the American premieres of Michel de Ghelderode's *Barabbas* (Aug. 1, 1961) and *Schweik in the Second World War* and various folk concerts, recitals, and childrens shows. He was stage manager for tours of the Robert Joffrey Ballet (1961), and the Benjamin Britten opera, *The Turn of the Screw* (Winter 1963). Mr. Rosenblum has also been producer of the Hyde Park (N.Y.) Playhouse and executive director of the Hudson Valley Repertory Th.

Since 1970, when he became executive director of the Long Wharf Th., New Haven, Conn., the theatre has staged American premieres of *Country People* (Jan. 9, 1970); *A Place without Doors* (Nov. 20, 1970); *Yegor Bulichov* (Dec. 18, 1970); *The Contractor* (Nov. 17, 1971); *The Country Woman* (Mar. 17, 1972); *The Changing Room* (Nov. 17, 1972); *Forget-Me-Not Lane* (Apr. 6, 1973); and the double-bill *Sizwe Banzi Is Dead* and *The Island* (Oct. 11, 1974); plus world premieres of *Solitaire/Double Solitaire* (Feb. 12, 1971) and *Patrick's Day* (May 12, 1972).

ROSENSTOCK, MILTON. Musical director. b. Milton Max Rosenstock, June 9, 1917, New Haven, Conn., to Osios and Sophie Rosenstock. Father, building contractor. Grad. Stuyvesant H.S., N.Y.C. (NY Philharonic scholarship student), 1935; attended Inst. of Musical Art (scholarship), 1935–38; Juilliard Sch. of Music (conducting fellowship), 1938–41; composition fellowship, 1945–46. Married 1941 to Lillian Libove; one son, two daughters. Served in US Army, 1941–45; rank, Master Sgt. Member of AFM, Local 802. Address: 780 Riverside Dr., New York, NY 10032, tel. (212) AU 1-5442.

Pre-Theatre. Symphonic conductor.

Theatre. Mr. Rosenstock's first assignment in the theatre was as conductor of *This Is the Army* (Bway Th., N.Y.C., July 4, 1942); subsequently succeeded Max Goberman as conductor of the touring company of *On the Town;* and succeeded (June 1946) Mr. Goberman as conductor of *Billion Dollar Baby* (Alvin, N.Y.C., Dec. 21, 1945).

Mr. Rosenstock was musical director of *Finian's Rainbow* (46 St. Th., Jan. 10, 1947); *Barefoot Boy with Cheek* (Martin Beck Th., Apr. 3, 1947); *High Button Shoes* (Century, Oct. 9, 1947); *Gentlemen Prefer Blondes* (Ziegfeld, Dec. 8, 1949); *Make a Wish* (Winter Garden, Apr. 18, 1951); the pre-Bway tour of *Curtain Going Up* (opened Forrest, Philadelphia, Pa., Feb. 15, 1952; closed there Apr. 1, 1952); *Two's Company* (Alvin, N.Y.C., Dec. 15, 1952); *Can-Can* (Shubert, May 7, 1953); *The Vamp* (Winter Garden, Nov. 10, 1955); *Bells Are Ringing* (Shubert, Nov. 29, 1956); *Gypsy* (Bway Th., May 21, 1959); *Subways Are for Sleeping* (St. James, Dec. 27, 1961); *Stop the World–I Want to Get Off* (Shubert, Oct. 3, 1962); *Hot Spot* (Majestic, Apr. 19, 1963); *Oliver!* (Imperial, Jan. 6, 1963); and *Funny Girl* (Winter Garden, Mar. 26, 1964).

He wrote the vocal arrangements and was musical director for the pre-Bway tryout of *Hot September* (opened Shubert, Boston, Sept. 14, 1965; closed there Oct. 9, 1965); musical director for *Come Summer* (Lunt-Fontanne, N.Y.C., Mar. 18, 1969); *Jimmy* (Winter Garden, Oct. 23, 1968), for which he also supplied vocal arrangements; and *Look to the Lilies* (Lunt-Fontanne, Mar. 29, 1970); musical supervisor for *Echoes of the Left Bank* (Ford's, Washington, D.C., Jan. 4, 1972); musical director for a revival of *On the Town* (Imperial, N.Y.C., Oct. 31, 1971); musical and vocal director for a revival of *A Funny Thing Happened on the Way to the Forum* (Lunt-Fontanne, Mar. 30, 1972); musical director for *Lorelei* (Palace, Jan. 27, 1974); wrote the music for *Nash at Nine* (Helen Hayes Th., May 17, 1973); and was musical director for a revival of *Gypsy* (Winter Garden, Sept. 23, 1974).

Television. Mr. Rosenstock was musical director of Gene Kelly's program, *Dancing Is a Man's Game* (CBS, 1962); directed and conducted Kurt Weill's *Huckleberry Finn* and Gershwin's *Girl Crazy* for German television (1964).

Other Activities. He was conductor of the Brooklyn Symphony Orchestra (1938–40); directed four concerts of the Gotham Small Orchestra (Town Hall, 1952–54, 1957); and has been musical director of the Lyric Chamber Th. and the Shirt-sleeve Opera Co. (1960–64).

Awards. He received the Alice Ditson Award in conducting (1945).

ROSENTHAL, ANDREW. Playwright, composer, novelist. b. July 11, 1917, Columbus, Ohio, to Monroe and Celia (Kahn) Rosenthal. Father, wool merchant. Attended Ecole Pascal, Paris; grad. Hun Sch., Princeton, N.J.; Exeter Academy; attended Univ. of Pennsylvania, two years. Member of Dramatists Guild; Screenwriters Guild. Address: 9 E. 62nd St., New York, NY 10022.

Pre-Theatre. Newspaper copy boy and cub reporter (1935–36).

Theatre. With Ethel Frank, Mr. Rosenthal wrote *Dear Family* (Stony Creek Th., Conn., July 11, 1938); his first play to be produced on Bway was *The Burning Deck* (Maxine Elliott's Th., Mar. 1, 1940); followed by *Broken Journey* (Henry Miller's Th., June 23, 1942). He wrote the book, lyrics, and music for *The Best of Friends* (Boston Summer Music Hall, Mass., Aug. 5, 1946; Cambridge Summer Th., Mass., Aug. 12, 1946).

Mr. Rosenthal wrote *Third Person* (Criterion, London, Jan. 3, 1952; and President, N.Y.C., Dec. 29, 1955); *Red Letter Day* (Garrick, Feb. 21, 1952); *Horses in Midstream* (Royale, N.Y.C., Apr. 2, 1953; Vaudeville, London, Sept. 22, 1960); and *Sense of Guilt* (Kings Th., Glasgow, Scotland, Nov. 12, 1953), which toured the major cities of Great Britain for ten weeks. He is the author of *Red Letter Day* (tour, Summer 1959); *Happenstance* (Tappan Zee Playhouse, Nyack, N.Y., Aug. 23, 1960); *Horses in Midstream* (Vaudeville, London, Sept. 23, 1960); the musical, *Innocent as Hell,* for which he wrote the book, lyrics and music (Lyric, Hammersmith, England, June 29, 1960); *The Strangers* (Westport (Conn.) Country Playhouse, Nov. 5, 1963); and *Gathering of the Clan* (Cheltenham, England, Repertory Th., Sept. 1973).

Published Works. Under the pseudonym Andrew Warren, Mr. Rosenthal and Warren Tate wrote the novel *This Time Next October* (London, 1971).

Recreation. Painting, tennis, racing cars.

ROSENTHAL, LAURENCE. Composer. b. Nov. 4, 1926, Detroit, Mich., to Albert and Hannah (Lazarow) Rosenthal. Father, tire distributor. Grad. Central H.S., Detroit, Mich., 1944; Eastman Sch. of Music, Univ. of Rochester, B. Mus. 1948, M. Mus. 1951; Mozarteum, Salzburg, Austria, 1949; Conservatoire, Nationale, Paris, France, 1950. Studied composition with Nadia Boulanger, Paris and Fontainebleau, France, 1948–50. Married Jan. 20, 1952, to Barbara Stander, musician; two daughters. Served USAF, Documentary Film

Squadron, 1951–55; rank, Staff Sgt. Member of ASCAP; AFM, Local 802; Screen Composers Assn.; Composers and Lyricists Guild of America.

Theatre. For Bway productions, Mr. Rosenthal composed the incidental music for *A Clearing in the Woods* (Belasco Th., Jan. 10, 1957); the dance music arrangements for *The Music Man* (Majestic, Dec. 19, 1957), and for *Goldilocks* (Lunt-Fontanne, Oct. 11, 1958); the incidental music for *Rashomon* (Music Box, Jan. 27, 1959); the ballet and incidental music for *Take Me Along* (Shubert, Oct. 22, 1959); the incidental music for *Becket* (St. James Th., Oct. 5, 1960); the ballet music arrangements and orchestrations for *Donnybrook!* (46 St. Th., May 18, 1961); music for *Dylan* (Plymouth, Jan. 18, 1964); *Sherry!* (Alvin Th., Mar. 27, 1967); was musical supervisor for *George M!* (Palace, Apr. 10, 1968); and composed music for *Indians* (Brooks Atkinson Th., Oct. 13, 1969).

Films. Mr. Rosenthal composed the scores for *A Raisin in the Sun* (Col., 1961); *The Miracle Worker* (UA, 1962); *Requiem for a Heavyweight* (Col., 1962); *Becket* (Par., 1964); and *The Return of a Man Called Horse* (UA, 1976).

Television. Mr. Rosenthal composed the score for *The Power and the Glory* (Hallmark Hall of Fame, NBC, 1961).

Awards. Mr. Rosenthal is the recipient of the ASCAP-John Philip Sousa Award (1954) for his US Air Force Parade March, *The Thunderjet.*

ROSQUI, TOM. Actor. b. Thomas Francis Rosqui, June 12, 1928, Oakland, Calif., to Thomas Anthony and Sally (Jardin) Rosqui. Father, traffic manager; mother, saleswoman. Attended Walla Walla (Wash.) H.S., 1942–44; grad. Alameda (Calif.) H.S., 1946; Sacramento City Coll., A.A. 1948; Univ. of the Pacific, B.A. 1951. Studied with Lloyd Sisler, Alameda H.S. (1945–46); and De Marcus Brown, Univ. of the Pacific (1950–51). Married Aug. 18, 1963, to Erica Fishman, actress; one stepson, one stepdaughter. Relatives in theatre: mother-in-law, Sonia Bierman, actress; father-in-law, Jacob Fishman, actor, director. Served USN, 1952–54. Member of AEA; SAG; Delta Psi Omega; Omega Phi Alpha.

Theatre. Mr. Rosqui first appeared on the stage as Dick in *Janie* (Alameda H.S., Calif., Nov. 1945). He made his professional debut as the Caterer's Man in the national touring company of *The Cocktail Party* (opened Curran, San Francisco, Calif., Oct. 15, 1951), later playing the role of Peter Quilpe (Biltmore, Los Angeles, Calif., Dec. 10, 1951).

He appeared as Salarino in *The Merchant of Venice* (Club Th., N.Y.C., Jan. 7, 1955); and performed at the Red Barn Th. (Westboro, Mass., 1955) as Michael in *The Fourposter* (May), Elgin in *The Country Girl* (May), Uncle in *The Golddiggers* (June), Witch Boy in *The Dark of the Moon* (July), Steve Stackhouse in *Separate Rooms* (July), Slater in *The Moon Is Blue* (Aug.), the Husband in *Meet the Wife* (Aug.), Freddy in *Getting Gertie's Garter* (Sept.), Chesney in *Charlie's Aunt* (Sept.), the Husband in *Apron Strings* (Sept.), the Psychiatrist in *Champagne Complex* (Sept.), Jose in *Cradle Snatchers* (Oct.), Levison in *East Lynne* (Oct.), Billings in *The Happiest Day of Your Life* (Oct.), and Jake in *Sailor Beware* (Oct.).

He played Johnny in a stock production of *Lullaby* (Studio Th., Washington, D.C. Jan. 1956); appeared at the White Barn Th. (Irwin, Pa., Summer 1956) as Prescott in *Wake Up, Darling,* Serensky in *Anastasia,* Ferelli in *The Fifth Season,* Bo Decker in *Bus Stop,* Heathcliffe in *Wuthering Heights,* Lefty McShane in *The Hot Corner,* Glenn Griffin in *The Desperate Hours,* Harris in *Tea and Sympathy,* Jay in *A Roomful of Roses,* and also appeared in *The Solid Gold Cadillac* and *The Seven Year Itch.*

At the Fred Miller Th. (Milwaukee, Wis., 1956–57), he played Callahan in *Detective Story,* Michael in *Jenny Kissed Me,* Tom in *The Glass Menagerie,* Sanders in *Harvey,* Pugh in *Clutterbuck,* Sergius in *Arms and the Man,* Jay in *A Roomful of Roses,* Jarvis in *The Member of the Wedding,* and Nicky in *Bell, Book and Candle* (1956–57). At the Red Barn Th. (Saugatuck, Mich., Summer 1957), he appeared as Michael in *The Fourposter,* Bud in *Anniversary Waltz,* Uncle Ben in *The Little Foxes,* the Count in *Candlelight,* Gil in *Janus,* Carl in *Bus Stop,* Stanley Kowalski in *A Streetcar Named Desire,* Don Juan in *Don Juan in Hell,* Johnny in *Roberta,* and appeared in *Peg o' My Heart* and *Write Me a Murder.* He toured (Pa., Me., N.Y., Sept.–Oct. 1957), in a production of scenes from Irish plays, playing Christy in *The Playboy of the Western World* and Canon in *Shadow and Substance.*

In 1958, Mr. Rosqui joined the Actor's Workshop, San Francisco, Calif., and he appeared there the same year as Paul in *A Gift of Fury,* Hicky in *The Iceman Cometh,* Biff in *Death of a Salesman,* Cleante in *The Miser,* Harry in *Prometheus Found,* Dr. Bonfant in *The Waltz of the Toreadors,* Oedipus in *The Infernal Machine,* Dr. Sugar in *Suddenly, Last Summer,* The Messenger in *Cock-a-Doodle Dandy,* Clov in *Endgame,* Judge Hathorne in *The Crucible,* Muscari in *The Busy Martyr;* in 1959, as George Dillon in *Epitaph for George Dillon;* in 1960, as Dick Dudgeon in *The Devil's Disciple,* Christian Melrose in *Saints' Day,* Eugene d'Ettouville in *The Rocks Cried Out;* and in 1961, as Jerry in *The Zoo Story,* Edgar in *King Lear,* John Tarleton in *Misalliance,* Edmund in *King Lear,* Serjeant Musgrave in *Serjeant Musgrave's Dance,* the title role in *Becket,* and Douglas in *Henry IV, Part 1.*

He appeared as Jerry in a summer theatre production of *Two for the Seesaw* (Tunn Th., Redwood City, Calif., July 1962). He returned to the Actor's Workshop (1962) to play Malvolio in *Twelfth Night* and Tom in *The Glass Menagerie;* in 1963, Jack in *Telegraph Hill,* the Inquisitor in *Galileo,* Theobald in *The Underpants,* Sir Politick in *Volpone,* the Lord of the Inn in *The Taming of the Shrew,* Aston in *The Caretaker,* Ashuwa in *The Caucasian Chalk Circle,* Dangerfield in *The Ginger Man,* Shannon in *Night of the Iguana,* and Prometheus in *The Birds;* in 1964, he repeated his performances in *The Ginger Man, Night of the Iguana,* and *The Birds;* and in 1965, he appeared in *Uncle Vanya.*

He left San Francisco in 1965 to become a member of the Repertory Th. of Lincoln Ctr. Company (Vivian Beaumont Th., N.Y.C.), where he played Citizen Barère and was understudy to Alan Bergmann as George Danton in *Danton's Death* (Oct. 21, 1965), was in *The Country Wife* (Dec. 9, 1965); played Frantz in *The Condemned of Altona* (Feb. 3, 1966); and was the Limping Man and understudy to John Devlin as Shalva Tzereteli and to Ronald Weyand as Shauwa in *The Caucasian Chalk Circle* (Mar. 24, 1966).

He toured as Jean-Paul Marat in *Marat/Sade* (Summer 1966); and, at the Vivian Beaumont Th., was a Neighbor and understudy to Robert Symonds as Jeremy Butler in *The Alchemist* (Oct. 13, 1966), Victor in *Yerma* (Dec. 8, 1966), and Vitek and one of the people of London in *The East Wind* (Feb. 9, 1967). Mr. Rosqui appeared in six of the eleven plays on the program *Collision Course* (Cafe au Go-Go, May 8, 1968): as He in *Wandering,* Henry James in *Stars and Stripes,* the Man in *Skywriting,* Mr. Wilson in *Tour,* He in *Camera Obscura,* and Jebbie in *Rats.* He was Tom Jason in *Brotherhood* (St. Marks Playhouse, Mar. 10, 1970); Sergeant Match in *What the Butler Saw* (McAlpin Rooftop Th., May 4, 1970); Saul in *L.A. Under Siege* (Studio Arena, Buffalo, N.Y., Dec. 29, 1970); and Capt. Paul Barrett in *Defender of the Faith* and Harry in *Eli, the Fanatic* on the program *Unlikely Heroes: 3 Philip Roth Stories* (Plymouth, N.Y.C., Oct. 26, 1971).

He was standby for Tom Aldredge as Ozzie and for Charles Siebert as the Priest in *Sticks and Bones* (John Golden Th., Mar. 1, 1972); replaced Anthony Holland as Lucky in *Waiting for Godot* (Sheridan Square Playhouse, Feb. 3, 1971); played William Herndon in *The Lincoln Mask* (Plymouth, Oct. 30, 1972); replaced (June 1, 1973) Robert Symonds as Steve Hubbel in *A Streetcar Named Desire* (Vivian Beaumont Th., Apr. 26, 1973; and was in *Whiskey* (St. Clement's Ch., Apr. 29, 1973).

Films. Mr. Rosqui appeared in *Crazy Quilt* (Continental, 1966).

Television. Mr. Rosqui played roles in *The Office Party* (Kraft Television Th., NBC, Oct. 1954); *The Counsel* (Kraft Television Th., Nov. 1955); *No Room at the Inn* (Nov. 1957); and *Lineup* (CBS, Jan. and Mar. 1960). He was the voice of Edward Weston in *How Young I Was* and *The Strongest Way of Seeing* (U.S.A.—Photography, NET, Apr. 1966) and played Phil in *A Party for Divorce* (NT Television Th., NET, 1967).

ROSS, DOROTHY. Press representative. b. Dorothy Applebaum, July 21, 1912, New York City, to Jacob and Mamie (Zieph) Applebaum. Father, jeweler. Grad. George Washington H.S., N.Y.C., 1929; attended Hunter Coll., 1929–31. Married May 24, 1932, to George Ross, journalist, press agent (marr. dis. 1952); one son, one daughter; married Nov. 1, 1952, to Harlan Jackson, artist (marr. dis. 1962). Founding member of ATPAM. Address: (home) El Alhambra, Bloque 3 Apt. 6D, Los Boliches, Spain tel. 952-46 32 27; (bus.) c/o Gardner, 108 Wyckoff St., Brooklyn, NY 11201, tel. (212) 858-3319.

Theatre. Miss Ross began her theatrical career at the age of six, touring the eastern circuit as Little Uncle Sammy in David Belasco's *Daddies.* At Hunter Coll., she was active in the theatrical group, the Make-Up Box. Her first work as a press representative was as assistant to Bernard Simon for the N.Y.C. productions of *Another Language, Carry Nation* and *Goodbye Again* (1932). She was press representative for *Hilda Cassidy* (1933); *Take a Bow* and *Sophie* (1944); *Are You with It?* (1945); *Call Me Mister* and *If the Shoe Fits* (1946); the double-bill *The Telephone* and *The Medium* (1947); *Kiss Me, Kate* (1948); *The Consul* and *Out of This World* (1950); *Borscht Capades* and *Saint Joan* (1951); *Venus Observed, The Grass Harp,* and *Four Saints in Three Acts* (1952); *House of Flowers* (1954); *Third Person* (1955); *The Square Root of Wonderful* and *The Girl of the Golden West* (1957); *The Nervous Set* (1959); *Viva Madison Avenue!* (1960); the pre-Bway tryout, *Kicks and Co.* (1960); on Bway, *Sail Away* (1961); *The Affairs* (1962); *Enter Laughing* and *The Beast in Me* (1963); *Chips with Everything* (1963); and *The White House* (1964).

Also for *P.S. I Love You* (1964); *The Killing of Sister George* (1966); *The Promise* and *Come Live with Me* (1967); *Lovers* and *We Bombed in New Haven* (1968); *The Mundy Scheme* (1969); and *Sleuth* (1970). Miss Ross was also press representative for the Circle Repertory Co., N.Y.C. (1970–72); has been personal press representative to Lena Horne, Hildegarde, Morton Downey, Eddy Duchin, Vaughan Monroe, Frankie Laine, Woody Allen, Joan Rivers, and Bill Cosby; and, 1965, a stringer for *Variety,* first at East Hampton, N.Y., and currently Costa del Sol, Spain.

Recreation. Raising Scottish terriers, collecting paintings, flora and fauna, writing, sunbathing, and photography.

ROSS, ELIZABETH. Actress. b. Aug. 28, 1928, Morristown, N.J., to Eugene Phillips Ransom and Louise (Brooks) Ross. Father, personnel director; mother, teacher. Grad. Woodrow Wilson H.S., Washington, D.C., 1944; attended Catholic Univ. of Amer., 1944–45. Married July 1, 1946, to Robert E. Vetault (marr. dis. 1950); married Feb. 2, 1952, to Thomas E. Noyes, journalist, former theatrical producer; two sons, one daughter. Member of AEA; AFTRA; SAG. Address: 2811 Chesterfield Pl., N.W., Washington, DC 20008.

Theatre. Miss Ross made her stage debut as Bernadette in *The Song of Bernadette* (Catholic Univ. Th., Aug. 1944); repeated the role in her first Bway appearance (Belasco, Mar. 26, 1946); played Anna Surratt in *The Story of Mary Surratt* (Henry Miller's Th., Feb. 8, 1947); was standby for Patricia Kirkland (May 1947) as Ruth Gordon Jones in *Years Ago* (Mansfield, Dec. 3, 1946); played Eva Strachan in *Pink String and Sealing Wax* (John Drew Th., East Hampton, N.Y., Aug. 1947); Gladys in *Minnie and Mr. Williams* (Morosco, Oct. 27, 1948); toured as Alexandra in *The Little Foxes* (Summer 1948), and as Laura in *The Glass Menagerie* (Summer 1949); appeared as Darinka in *The Burning Bush* (Rooftop

Th., N.Y.C., Dec. 16, 1949); Ginger in the pre-Bway tryout of *Season With Ginger* (Ogunquit Playhouse, Me., June 1952); toured as Audrey Trowbridge in *Three Men on a Horse* (Summer 1953); and played Molly in *In the Summer House* (Playhouse, N.Y.C., Dec. 29, 1953).

Television. Miss Ross has appeared on more than 50 network dramas, including a repeat of her role as Anna Surratt in *The Story of Mary Surratt* (Philco Television Playhouse, NBC, 1948); Naked City (ABC); Kraft Television Th. (NBC); Armstrong Circle Th. (CBS); Lux Playhouse (ABC); Big Story (ABC); Danger (NBC); and a TV special, Atomic Attack (ABC).

Awards. Miss Ross won a Kraft TV Award (1955).

Recreation. Writing, entertaining at home.

ROSS, GEORGE. Producer, playwright, press representative. b. Aug. 4, 1911, New York City, to Solomon and Pauline Ross. Attended N.Y.C. schools. Married Dec. 21, 1958, to Madi Blitzstein, press representative. Served WW II, civilian director, USO Camp Shows. Member of ATPAM; Dramatists Guild; Newspaper Guild; League of NY Theatres.

Theatre. Mr. Ross' first assignment was as assistant to Daniel H. Frohman, founder and president of the Actors' Fund of Amer., and he was assistant to Lee Shubert, producer and theatre owner.

With Rose C. Feld, he wrote *Sophie*, which he produced with Meyer Davis (Playhouse, N.Y.C., Dec. 25, 1944); was press representative for the N.Y.C. productions of *Hilarities* and *Kiss Me, Kate* (1948); *How Long Till Summer?* (1949); *Alive and Kicking, The Consul, Jane Eyre* (1950); the pre-Bway tryout of *The House on the Cliff*, the N.Y.C. production of *Pride's Crossing*, and *Out of This World* (1950); *The Green Bay Tree, Ti-Coq*, and *Billy Budd* (1951); for Uta Hagen's *Saint Joan* (1951); *Venus Observed, Time Out for Ginger*, and *See the Jaguar* (1952); and *My Three Angels* (1953).

He produced with Edward Choate, by arrangement with Wauna Paul, *Gently Does It* (Playhouse, Oct. 28, 1953); was press representative for the pre-Bway tryouts of *The Suspects, Josephine*, and *Masquerade* (1953); the N.Y.C. productions of *The Girl in Pink Tights* (1954), *The Grand Prize*, and *Ankles Aweigh* (1955); the national tour of *Anastasia* (1955–56); *The Hot Corner* and *Goodbye Again* (1956); *Exiles, Holiday for Lovers, Shinbone Alley, The Greatest Man Alive, Monique*, and *Conversation Piece* (1957).

With John Robert Lloyd, Mr. Ross produced *Drink to Me Only* (54 St. Th., Oct. 8, 1958); was press representative for *The Big Knife* (1959); company manager for *Kataki* (Ambassador, Apr. 9, 1959) and press representative for its off-Bway production (1959); press representative for *A Thurber Carnival* and Marcel Marceau (NY City Ctr., 1960); *How to Make a Man, Beautiful Dreamer*, and *Two by Saroyan* (1961); and for *The Amorous Flea* (1964).

Other Activities. He was columnist and drama editor for the NY *World Telegram* (1933–34); and syndicated columnist for the Scripps-Howard Newspaper Enterprise Assn.

ROSS, HERBERT. Choreographer, director, dancer. b. Herbert David Ross, May 13, 1927, Brooklyn, N.Y., to Louis Chester and Martha (Grundfast) Ross. Attended Miami Beach (Fla.) H.S. Studied dance in N.Y.C. with Doris Humphrey, Helene Platova and Laird Leslie; acting with Herbert Berghof (1943–50). Married, Aug. 21, 1959, to Nora Kave, ballerina. Member of SSD&C; AGMA; SAG; AEA. Address: Sneden's Landing, Palisades, NY 10964, tel. (914) EL 9-5460.

Theatre. Mr. Ross made his debut performing in a touring Shakespearean Repertory company, as the Third Witch in *Macbeth;* Laertes in *Hamlet*, and the Duke of Venice in *Othello* (1942–43).

He played the Bartender in *Across the Board on Tomorrow Morning* (N.Y.C., Sept. 1943); danced in *Follow the Girls* (Century, Apr. 8, 1944); joined the cast during the run of *Bloomer Girl* (Shubert, Oct. 5, 1944); danced in *Laffing Room Only* (Winter Garden, Dec. 23, 1944); *Beggar's Holiday* (Bway Th., Dec. 26, 1946); *Look, Ma, I'm Dancing* (Adelphi, Jan. 29, 1948); *Inside U.S.A.* (Century, Apr. 30, 1948).

He choreographed and danced in a Ballet Theatre production of *Caprichos* (Hunter College, Playhouse, Jan. 29, 1950); choreographed and danced in *Ballet's d'Action* (Jacob's Pillow, Lee, Mass., 1951); choreographed a Ballet Th. production of *The Thief Who Loved a Ghost* (Metropolitan Opera House, Apr. 11, 1951); choreographed *A Tree Grows in Brooklyn* (Alvin, Apr. 19, 1951); choreographed and directed the musical numbers in *House of Flowers* (Alvin, Dec. 30, 1954); for the Ballet Th., choreographed *Paean, The Maids, Tristan, Concerto* and *Ovid Metamorphoses* (1958); for the Metropolitan Opera Ballet Co., choreographed *The Exchange* (1959); and supervised the production of *Wonderful Town* (NY City Ctr., 1959; Brussel's World's Fair, Belgian production, 1958).

At the Festival of the Two Worlds (Spoleto, It.), he choreographed the ballets, *Serenade for Seven Dancers, Angel Head, Rashomon*, and *Dark Song* (1959); choreographed the musicals *Rinaldo in Campo, Rascel in Aria*, and *Delia Scala* (Teatro Sistina, Rome, 1960); directed and choreographed *Finian's Rainbow* (NY City Ctr., Apr. 27, 1960); danced with his own company (Berlin Festival, Sept. 1960); choreographed directed the musical numbers in *The Gay Life* (Shubert, N.Y.C., Nov. 18, 1961); *I Can Get It for You Wholesale* (Shubert, Mar. 22, 1962); *Tovarich* (Bway Th., Mar. 18, 1963); directed the dances and musical numbers in *Anyone Can Whistle* (Majestic, Mar. 4, 1964); and choreographed *Do I Hear a Waltz?* (46 St. Th., Mar. 18, 1965); and *On A Clear Day You Can See Forever* (Mark Hellinger Th., Oct. 17, 1965).

Films. Mr. Ross choreographed and directed the musical numbers for *Carmen Jones* (20th-Fox, 1954); *The Young One* (Vitalite, 1961); and was a director for the English film, *Summer Holiday* (1962).

He provided choreography for *Inside Daisy Clover* (WB, 1966); *Who's Afraid of Virginia Woolf?* (WB, 1966); and *Funny Girl* (Col., 1968); and directed *Dr. Dolittle* (20th-Fox, 1967); *Good-bye, Mr. Chips* (MGM, 1969); *The Owl and the Pussycat* (Col., 1970); *T.R. Baskin* (Par., 1971); *Play It Again, Sam* (Par., 1972); produced and directed *The Last of Sheila* (WB, 1973); and directed *Funny Lady* (Col., 1975).

Television. He was choreographer and producer for the Martha Raye Show, and the Milton Berle Show (NBC, 1952–57); choreographed *Meet Me in St. Louis* (NBC, 1959); directed and choreographed *Wonderful Town* (NBC, 1959); choreographed and staged the musical numbers for Hallmark Hall of Fame's Christmas Special (NBC, 1959); and the Jerome Kern Special (NBC, 1960); directed and choreographed the Bea Lillie and Cyril Ritchard Show (NBC, 1960); choreographed and staged the musical numbers for Bell Telephone Hour (NBC, 1963); produced the Robert Goulet Special (Bell Telephone Hour, NBC, July 1964); and directed *The Fantasticks* (Hallmark Hall of Fame, NBC).

Night Clubs. Mr. Ross was writer-director of night club acts for Eddie Albert and Margo (1955); Marguerite Piazza (1956); Patrice Munsel (1956); Constance Bennett (1957); Imogene Coca (1957); Genevieve (1962); and Leslie Uggams (1964).

ROSSET, BARNEY. Editor. b. Barnet Lee Rosset, Jr., May 28, 1922, Chicago, Ill., to Barnet Lee and Mary (Tansey) Rosset. Father, banker. Grad. Univ. of Chicago, Ph.B., 1947; New Sch. for Social Research, New York City, B.A. 1952. Married Aug. 1953 to Hannelore Eckert (marr. dis. 1957); one son; married Mar. 11, 1965, to Cristina Agnini; two sons. Served WW II, US Army, Signal Corps, 1942–46; rank, 1st Lt. Member of P.E.N. Club; Overseas Press Club. Address: (home) 203 W. Houston St., New York, NY 10014; (bus.) Grove Press, 64 University Pl., New York, NY 10003, tel. (212) OR 4-7200.

Mr. Rosset founded The Grove Press, publishers of plays and other theatrical works, in 1951, and since that year has served as its publisher and editor. Since 1957, he has been the editor of *The Evergreen Review;* and since 1963, has been pres. of Evergreen Theatre, Inc.

ROSTEN, NORMAN. Playwright, poet. b. Jan. 1, 1914, New York City. Grad. Brooklyn Coll., B.A. 1935; New York Univ., M.A. 1936; attended Univ. of Michigan 1937–38. Member of Dramatists Guild; WGA. Address: 84 Remsen St., Brooklyn, NY 11201.

Theatre. Mr. Rosten wrote *This Proud Pilgrimage* (Heckscher Th., N.Y.C., June 8, 1940); *First Stop to Heaven* (Windsor, Jan. 5, 1941); *Mardi Gras* (Walnut St. Th., Philadelphia, Pa., Jan. 11, 1954), which closed during its pre-Bway tryout; *Mister Johnson* (Martin Beck Th., N.Y.C., Mar. 29, 1956), which was later presented in London (Lyric, Hammersmith, Sept. 29, 1960), and revived by ELT (Masters Institute, N.Y.C., Oct. 5, 1963); *The Golden Door* (H B Playwrights Foundation, N.Y.C. Apr. 21, 1966); *Come Slowly, Eden* (Th. de Lys, N.Y.C. Dec. 5, 1966; earlier at Nassau Community College, May 3, 1966, and Library of Congress, Nov. 28, 1966).

Films. Mr. Rosten wrote the screenplay for *A View from the Bridge* (Continental, 1962).

Published Works. Mr. Rosten is the author of several volumes of poetry; *Return Again, Traveler* (1940); *Return Again, Traveler* (1941); *The Fourth Decade* (1943); *The Big Road* (1946); *Songs for Patricia* (1951); *The Plane and the Shadow* (1953); and *Thrive Upon the Rock* (1965). His play, *Mister Johnson*, was included in the anthology edited by John Chapman entitled *Theatre '56* (1956). His play *Come Slowly, Eden* was published in 1967.

He is the author of two novels: *Under the Boardwalk* (1968) and *Over and Out* (1972), and a non-fiction work, *Marilyn: An Untold Story* (1973).

Awards. Mr. Rosten received the Avery Hopwood (Poetry and Drama) Award, Univ. of Mich. (1938); the Yale Series of Younger Poets Award (1940); a Guggenheim Fellowship (1941); the American Academy of Arts and Letters Award (1945); and a Ford Foundation Grant (1965).

ROTH, LILLIAN. Actress. b. Dec. 13, 1910, Boston, Mass., to Arthur and Kate Roth. Father, salesman. Grad. Professional Childrens Sch., N.Y.C., 1923; attended Clark Sch. of Concentration, 1924. Married William Scott (marr. dis. 1930); married Jan. 29, 1933, to Ben Shalleck, jurist (marr. dis.); married 1940 to Mark Harris (marr. dis. 1940); married 1941 to Edward Leeds (marr. dis.); married 1947 to Burt McGuire (marr. dis. 1963). Member of AEA; AGVA; AFTRA; SAG.

Theatre. Miss Roth made her debut in vaudeville at age eight, with her sister Ann, in an act "Lillian Roth and Co.," which later became "The Roth Kids" (B. F. Keith Circuit). She appeared in a solo act at the Palace Th. (N.Y.C.), and on cross-country vaudeville tours.

Miss Roth joined the cast during the run of *The Inner Man* (Lyric, Aug. 13, 1917); appeared in *Penrod* (Globe, Sept. 2, 1918); as Tyltyl's Grandchild in *The Betrothal* (Shubert, Nov. 18, 1918); Barbara Armstrong in *Shavings* (Knickerbocker, Feb. 16, 1920); performed in *Artists and Models* (Shubert, Chicago, Ill., 1925); *Padlocks of 1927* (Shubert, N.Y.C., July 5, 1927); *Vanities* (Earl Carroll Th., Aug. 6, 1928); and *Midnight Frolics* (New Amsterdam Roof, 1928).

In stock, Miss Roth played Lottie Gibson in *By the Beautiful Sea* (Starlight Th., Kansas City, Mo., Summer 1957); Emma Wallace in *The Primrose Path* (Spa Summer Th., Saratoga Springs, N.Y., Aug. 5, 1957); and Ruth in *Wonderful Town* (Westbury Music Fair, N.Y., Aug. 19, 1958). She played Mrs. Bogen in *I Can Get It for You Wholesale* (Shubert, N.Y.C., Mar. 22, 1962); toured as Mrs. Brice in *Funny Girl* (opened State Fair Music Hall, Dallas, Tex., Oct. 8, 1965); appeared in *70, Girls, 70* (Broadhurst, N.Y.C., Apr. 15, 1971); and toured as Catherine Reardon in *And Miss Reardon Drinks a Little* (opened Powers Aud., Youngstown, Ohio, Jan. 25, 1973; closed Masonic Aud., Scranton, Pa., Apr. 8, 1973).

Films. Miss Roth has appeared in *The Love Parade* (Par., 1929); *The Vagabond King* (Par., 1930); *Honey* (Par., 1930); *Paramount on Parade* (Par., 1930); *Animal Crackers* (Par., 1930); *Sea Legs* (Par., 1930); *Madam Satan* (MGM, 1930); *Take a Chance* (Par., 1933); *Ladies They Talk About* (WB, 1933); and a documentary, *The Sound of Laughter* (1964). The film, *I'll Cry Tomorrow* was based on Miss Roth's autobiographical book of the same title (MGM, 1955).

Television. She played Elaine Hollander in *Outcast* (US Steel Hour, CBS, Nov. 9, 1955); and has appeared on Playhouse 90 (CBS); Matinee Th. (NBC); the Ed Sullivan Show (CBS); and Witness.

Night Clubs. Miss Roth appeared at the Grand Finale (N.Y.C., 1974).

Published Works. Miss Roth wrote *I'll Cry Tomorrow* (1953); and *Beyond My Worth* (1958).

ROTHMAN, LAWRENCE. Theatre manager, producer, press agent. b. Aug. 29, 1934, New York City, to Benjamin and Helen (Waga) Rothman. Father, theatrical press representative, producer; mother, seam-stress. Grad. Seward Park H.S., N.Y.C., 1951; attended New York Univ., 1951–52; Coll. of the City of N.Y., 1955–60. Member of ATPAM (bd. of govs., 1962–72). Address: (home) 311 W. 24th St., New York, NY 10011, tel. (212) WA 9-3634; (bus.) Trans-Lux Corp., 625 Madison Ave., New York, NY 10022, tel. (212) PL 1-3110.

Theatre. From 1953–57, Mr. Rothman owned and operated the President Theatre (N.Y.C.). With his father, he presented *Sands of the Negev* (President Th., Oct. 19, 1954). He was drama critic on the Anglo-Jewish weekly publication, *American-Examiner* (N.Y.C., 1955–56). He produced, with his father, a touring production of *The World of Sholom Aleichem* (Royal Alexandra Th., Toronto, Canada; Her Majesty's Th., Montreal, Canada, Mar. 1959). Mr. Rothman owned and operated the Carnegie Hall Playhouse (N.Y.C., 1959–60); was company manager for *Top Secret* (Barbizon-Plaza, N.Y.C., Sept. 1, 1960); treasurer for the Clairidge Cinerama Th. (Montclair, N.J., 1960–63); house manager (Little Th., N.Y.C.) for *Tambourines to Glory* (Nov. 2, 1963), *Double Dublin* (Dec. 26, 1963), and *Baby Want a Kiss* (Apr. 19, 1964); general manager for Habimah, The National Theatre of Israel (Little Th., N.Y.C.) which presented *The Dybbuk* (Feb. 3, 1964), *Children of the Shadows* (Feb. 26, 1964), and *Each Had Six Wings* (Mar. 11, 1964); house manager for *The Subject Was Roses* (Winthrop Ames Th. formerly Little Th., Sept. 7, 1964); general manager and company manager for *Let's Sing Yiddish* (Brooks Atkinson Th., N.Y.C., Nov. 9, 1966); company manager for the Jewish State Theatre of Poland (Billy Rose Th., N.Y.C., Oct. 19, 1967), which presented *Mirele Efros*, and *Mother Courage* in repertory; general manager and company manager for *The Megilla of Itzik Manger* (Golden, N.Y.C., Oct. 9, 1968; on tour, Jan., 1969; and Longacre, N.Y.C., Apr. 19, 1969); general manager for *The End of All Things Natural* (Village South Th., N.Y.C., Sept. 11, 1969); general manager and company manager for *The Trees Die Standing* (Roosevelt Th., N.Y.C., Oct. 12, 1969), *Mirele Efros* (Roosevelt Th., N.Y.C., Dec. 25, 1969), and *Light, Lively and Yiddish* (Belasco, N.Y.C., Oct. 27, 1970); company manager for *Dance of Death* (Ritz Th., N.Y.C., Apr. 28, 1971); general manager and company manager for a touring production of *The Grand Music Hall of Israel* (Jan.–June 1973; and company manager for *Israel Folk Festival '74* (Felt Forum, Madison Sq. Garden, N.Y.C., and on tour, Sept.–Dec. 1974).

He was press assistant to Reuben Rabinovitch for *Only in America* (Cort, N.Y.C., Nov. 19, 1959), *Out of the Axe* (Ambassador, N.Y.C., 1960), and *Bye Bye Birdie* (Martin Beck Th., N.Y.C., Apr. 14, 1960); press representative for *Judy Garland at Carnegie Hall* (Carnegie Hall, N.Y.C., Apr. 23, 1961); and for the Roundabout Repertory Theatre Co.'s productions of *Pins and Needles* and *The Father* (Roundabout, N.Y.C., May 19, 1967), *Waiting for Lefty* and *The Bond* (Masque, N.Y.C., Dec. 13, 1967), *The Importance of Being Earnest* (Roundabout, N.Y.C., June 1, 1968), *Journey's End* (Roundabout, N.Y.C., Dec. 4, 1968), *King Lear* (Roundabout, N.Y.C., Nov. 29, 1968), and *Candida* (Roundabout, N.Y.C., Feb. 2, 1969).

Mr. Rothman served as consultant to *Jazz on Broadway* (Little Th., N.Y.C., Apr. 1964), the Chuck Berry Concert (Village Th., N.Y.C., Nov. 23, 1965); and the National Israeli Chassidic Song Festival (on tour, Oct. 1973). He is group sales director for *The New York Experience* (Trans-Lux Experience Th., N.Y.C., June 1974–to date).

Films. Mr. Rothman produced the full-length documentary film, *The Last Chapter* (Ben-Lar, 1966).

ROUNDS, DAVID. Actor. b. Oct. 9, 1930, Bronxville, N.Y., to Harry MacDonald and Beatrice (Beveridge) Rounds. Father, insurance broker. Grad. Bronxville (N.Y.) public schools; Denison Univ., B.A. 1952. Studied acting with Joseph Hardy. Served U.S.N.R., Lt. (j.g.). Member of AEA; AFTRA; SAG.

Theatre. Mr. Rounds made his stage debut at the age of twelve, singing in a variety show at Sebasie Estates, a resort in Maine, where his mother was social director. He made his professional debut as Tom Lee in *Tea and Sympathy* (North Jersey Playhouse, June 1957); subsequently played Harry in *The Time of Your Life* (Sharon, Conn.) Playhouse, July 1957); and designed the sets and played Philip in *You Never Can Tell* (Downtown Th., N.Y.C., June 16, 1958); and Inspector Sterling in *Foxy*, starring Bert Lahr (Ziegfeld, N.Y.C., Feb. 16, 1964). He appeared in various roles in repertory with Center Stage (Baltimore, Md., 1966–67), and with Theatre-of-the-Living-Arts (Philadelphia, Pa., 1968); played Ernst Ludwig in *Cabaret* (national company tour, 1969); Father George Penny in *Child's Play* (Royale, N.Y.C., Feb. 17, 1970); Nathan in *The Rothschilds* (Lunt-Fontanne, N.Y.C., Oct. 19, 1970); Robert Lincoln in *The Last of Mrs. Lincoln* (ANTA, N.Y.C., Dec. 12, 1972); and Moon in *The Real Inspector Hound* (Th. Four, N.Y.C., Apr. 23, 1972).

With the Amer. Shakespeare Th. (Stratford, Conn., 1973–74), he appeared as Sparkish in *The Country Wife;* Lucio in *Measure for Measure;* Sir Andrew Aguecheek in *Twelfth Night;* and Mercutio in *Romeo and Juliet.* He subsequently played George Reilly in *Enter a Free Man* (St. Clement's Church, N.Y.C., Dec. 17, 1974); and Harry Glassman in *Chicago* (46 St. Th., N.Y.C., May 12, 1975).

Films. Mr. Rounds recreated the role of Father George Penney in *Child's Play* (Par., 1972).

Television. He appeared as Philip Holden in Love of Life (CBS, 1963–66), and played Terrance O'Hara in Beacon Hill (CBS, 1975).

Night Clubs. He played Harry in the revue, *Money* (Upstairs at the Downstairs, 1963).

Published Works. With Madeleine Edmondson, Mr. Rounds wrote *The Soaps: Daytime Serials of Radio and TV* (1973).

Awards. He received the Theatre World Award (1970) for his performance in *Child's Play.*

ROUSSIN, ANDRÉ. Playwright. b. André Jean Paul Marie Roussin, Jan. 22, 1911, Marseilles, France, to Honore and Suzanne (Gardair) Roussin. Father, insurance agent. Grad. Institution Melizan M.A. (philosophy) 1928. Member of the Société des Gens des Lettres; Société des Auteurs et Compositeurs Dramatiques.

Theatre. M. Roussin's works for the stage include *Am-Stram-Gram* (Athénée, 1943); *Une grande fille toute simple* (Ambassadeurs, 1944); *Jean-Baptiste le mal-aimé* (Vieux-Colombier, 1945); *La sainte famille* (Th. Saint-Georges, 1946); *La petite hutte* (Th. des Nouveautés, 1947) which was produced as *The Little Hut* (Lyric, London, Aug. 23, 1950; Coronet, N.Y.C., Oct. 7, 1953); *Les oeufs de l'autruche* (Th. de la Michodière, 1948); *L'Ecole des dupes* (Th. de la Michodière, 1948); *Nina* (Buffes Parisiens, 1949; Royale, N.Y.C., Dec. 5, 1951); *Bobosse* (Th. de la Michodière, 1950); *Lorsque l'enfant paraît* (Th. des Nouveautés, 1951); *La main de César* (Th. de Paris, 1951); collaborated with Madeleine Gray on *Hélène ou la joie de vivre* (Th. de la Madeleine, 1952); *Le marié, la femme et la mort* (Ambassadeurs, 1954); *L'Amour fou ou la première surprise* (Th. de la Madeleine, 1955); *La mamma* (Th. de la Madeleine, 1960); *Une femme qui dit la vérité* (Th. de la Madeleine, 1960); *L'Ecole des autres* (Th. de l'Oeuvre, 1962); *Un amour qui ne finit pas* (Th. de la Madeleine, 1963); *La voyante* (Th. de la Madeleine, 1963); *La locomotive*, which he also directed (Th. Marigny, Dec. 18, 1966); *On ne sait jamais* (1969); *Le tombeau d'Achille* (1970); and *La claque* (1972).

Awards. M. Roussin was elected to the Académie Française, Apr. 11, 1973.

ROWLANDS, GENA. Actress. b. Gena Catherine Rowlands, June 19, Cambria, Wis., to Edwin Merwin and Mary Allen (Neal) Rowlands. Father, banker; mother, painter. Attended Washington and Lee H.S., Arlington, Va.; Univ. of Wisc. (1952–53); AADA (N.Y.C., 1953). Married Mar. 19, 1954, to John Cassavetes, actor and director; one son, two daughters. Member of AEA; AFTRA; SAG; AGVA. Address: 7917 Woodrow Wilson Dr., Hollywood, CA 90046.

Theatre. Miss Rowlands was Mistress of Ceremonies for the musical *All About Love* (Versailles Night Club, N.Y.C., Oct. 17, 1951); acted at the Provincetown Playhouse (N.Y.C.), other Off-Bway theatres, and in stock (1951–53); played Elaine, one of the Dream Girls, in the natl. company of *The Seven Year Itch* (opened Cass Th., Detroit, Mich., Sept. 7, 1953), making her Bway debut (Apr. 1954) in that role, with the N.Y.C. company; she played the Girl in *Middle of the Night* (ANTA, Feb. 8, 1956).

Films. Miss Rowlands has appeared in *The High Cost of Loving* (MGM, 1958); *Lonely Are the Brave* (U, 1962); *A Child Is Waiting* (UA, 1962); *Spiral Road* (U, 1962); *Tony Rome* (20th-Fox, 1967); *Faces* (Cont., 1968); *Machine Gun McCain* (Col., 1970); as Minnie in *Minnie and Moskowitz* (U, 1971); and as Mabel Longhetti in *A Woman Under the Influence* (Faces Int., 1974).

Television. Miss Rowlands has appeared on many television shows, including Philco Playhouse (NBC); Armstrong Circle Th. (NBC); Studio One (CBS); Goodyear Playhouse (NBC); Robert Montgomery Presents (NBC); Appointment with Adventure (CBS); GE Th. (CBS); Staccato (NBC); Danger (CBS); Suspense (CBS); Martin Kane (NBC); US Steel Hour (CBS); Riverboat (NBC); Adventures in Paradise (ABC); Markham (CBS); The Tab Hunter Show (NBC); The Islanders (ABC); as Teddy Carella, the deaf-mute, in the 87th Precinct series (NBC, premiere Sept. 25, 1961); on Target: Corrupters (ABC); Dick Powell Th. (NBC); 77 Sunset Strip (ABC); The Lloyd Bridges Show (NBC); Alfred Hitchcock Presents (CBS); Bob Hope Chrysler Show (NBC); Dr. Kildare (NBC); Bonanza (NBC); The Virginian (NBC); Kraft Mystery Th. (NBC); Run for Your Life (NBC); The Long Hot Summer (ABC); Road West (NBC); The Girl from U.N.C.L.E. (NBC); as Adrienne Van Leyden (Aug. 1967–68) on the Peyton Place series (ABC); on Breaking Point (ABC); Burke's Law (ABC); Medical Center (CBS); Garrison's Gorillas (ABC); and Ghost Story (NBC).

Awards. For her role in *A Woman Under the Influence*, Miss Rowlands received nominations for the NY Film Critics Award and the Academy (Oscar) Award (1975).

ROWLES, POLLY. Actress. b. Jan. 10, Mary Elizabeth Rowles, Philadelphia, Pa., to Ralph and Mary (Dick) Rowles. Father, steel executive. Grad. Carnegie Inst. of Technology, B.A. 1936. Studied acting with B. Iden Payne, four years; E. Hickman, four years; Elizabeth Kimberly, Chester Wallace, four years. Married Dec. 8, 1938, to Franklin Snyder, television executive (marr. dis. 1944); one daughter. Member of AEA (council member, 1953–58); AFTRA; SAG. Address: Actors Equity Association, 165 W. 46th St., New York, NY 10036.

Theatre. Miss Rowles made her Bway debut succeeding (Apr. 1938) Evelyn Allen as Calpurnia in *Julius Caesar* (Mercury Th., Nov. 11, 1937); and her London debut as Natasha Rapakovich in *Dark Eyes* (Strand Th., Mar. 24, 1948).

With the Copley Square Th. Repertory Co. (Boston, Mass.) she appeared as Lavinia in *The Road to Rome*, Lady Eutterword in *Heartbreak House*, and Sabrina in *The Skin of Our Teeth* (1949); played Elizabeth in *Richard III* (Booth, N.Y.C., Feb. 8, 1949); Lucy McLean in *The Small Hours* (National, Feb. 15, 1951); in *Time Out for Ginger* (Lyceum, Nov. 26, 1952); and Calpurnia in *Julius Caesar* (American Shakespeare Festival, Stratford, Conn., July 12, 1955).

She played Clara Dennison in *The Wooden Dish* (Booth, N.Y.C., Oct. 6, 1955); Anne Rodgers in *Goodbye Again* (Helen Hayes Th., Apr. 24, 1956); Vera Charles in *Auntie Mame* (Broadhurst, Oct. 31, 1956); Claire in *Look After Lulu* (Henry Miller's Th., Mar. 3, 1959); Phyllis in *A Mighty Man Is He* (Cort, Jan. 6, 1960); and Mollie Plummer in *No Strings* (44 St. Th., Mar. 15, 1962). Subsequently, she played Mme. Xenia in *The Killing of Sister George* (Belasco, Oct. 5, 1966) and toured in it with the national company for five months; played Mrs. Margolis in *Forty Carats* (Morosco, Dec. 24, 1968); appeared in *Older People* (Public Th., May 14, 1972); played Lucy in a revival of *The Women* (46 St. Th., Apr. 25, 1973); and toured as Pauline in *No, No, Nanette* (Fall, 1973).

Films. She appeared in *The Group* (1964).

Television. Miss Rowles has appeared on Playhouse 90 (CBS); Alcoa Premiere (ABC); Philco Playhouse (NBC); Kraft Television Th. (NBC); Alfred Hitchcock Presents (CBS); US Steel Hour (CBS); Jamie (ABC, 1954–56); The Defenders (CBS, 1961); The Nurses (CBS, 1964); played Helen Hunt on Love of Life (1970–72); and Freida Lang on Somerset (1973–to date). She has also appeared in numerous television commercials.

ROYAL, TED. Orchestrator, arranger, composer. b. Ted Royal Dewar, Sept. 6, 1904, Skedee, Okla., to Clyde and Maude (Boylan) Dewar. Grad. Arkansas City (Kan.) H.S., 1921; attended Univ. of Kansas, 1922–23. Studied theory and counterpoint with Aldrich Kidd, Houston, Tex., 1927–28; clarinet with Dr. Cloud, Houston, Tex., 1929–30; composition with Joseph Schillinger, N.Y.C., 1939–42. Member of AFM, Local 802; ASCAP; AGAC; The Lambs; Masons. Address: 210 Turn of River Rd., Stamford, CT 06905, tel. (203) DA 2-1560.

Theatre. Mr. Royal was orchestrator for *Too Many Girls* (Imperial, N.Y.C., Oct. 18, 1939); subsequently orchestrated *Du Barry Was a Lady* (46 St. Th., Dec. 6, 1939); *Higher and Higher* (Shubert, Apr. 4, 1940); *Panama Hattie* (46 St. Th., Oct. 30, 1940); *Pal Joey* (Ethel Barrymore Th., Dec. 25, 1940); *Something for the Boys* (Alvin, Jan. 7, 1943); *Mexican Hayride* (Winter Garden, Jan. 28, 1944); *Bloomer Girl* (Shubert, Oct. 5, 1944); *St. Louis Woman* (Martin Beck Th., Mar. 30, 1946); *Annie Get Your Gun* (Imperial, May 16, 1946); *Around the World in 80 Days* (Adelphi, May 31, 1946); *Brigadoon* (Ziegfeld, Mar. 13, 1947); *Make Mine Manhattan* (Broadhurst, Jan. 15, 1948); *Where's Charley?* (St. James, Oct. 11, 1948); *As the Girls Go* (Winter Garden, Nov. 13, 1948); *Guys and Dolls* (46 St. Th., Nov. 24, 1950); *Paint Your Wagon* (Shubert, Nov. 12, 1951); *John Murray Anderson's Almanac* (Imperial, Dec. 10, 1953); *The Boy Friend* (Royale, Sept. 30, 1954); *House of Flowers* (Alvin, Dec. 30, 1954); and *Mr. Wonderful* (Bway Th., Mar. 22, 1956).

He has arranged music for the bands of Wayne King (1934–40), Ted Weems (1935–39), Abe Lyman (1937), Jimmy Dorsey (1937), Paul Whiteman (1938), Ben Bernie (1938), Emil Coleman (1939–40), Harry James (1940), and Ruby Newman (1941). He has also arranged, orchestrated, and conducted the music for the Westinghouse national industrial shows (1952, 1957). Mr. Royal retired from active theatre work in 1962.

Films. Mr. Royal orchestrated the Mary Martin-Richard Rodgers-Oscar Hammerstein sequence in *Main Street to Broadway* (MGM, 1953); composed, arranged, and orchestrated the music for *When Comedy Was King* (20th-Fox, 1960); and orchestrated the motion picture score of *Days of Thrills and Laughter* (20th-Fox, 1961).

Television and Radio. He arranged music for the radio shows of Paul Whiteman (1939), Gustave Haenschen (1940–41), Victor Arden (1940–42), and Lyn Murray (1941–42); and has orchestrated for television, including Your Show of Shows (NBC, 1950–55).

Other Activities. Mr. Royal taught arranging and orchestration at the Juilliard School of Music, N.Y.C. (Summers 1945–47).

RULE, JANICE. Actress, dancer. b. Mary Janice Rule, Aug. 15, 1931, Norwood, Ohio, to John Christopher and Kathleen Frances (Forbes) Rule. Father, dealer in industrial diamonds. Attended Glenbard H.S., Glen Ellyn, Ill. Studied acting at the Chicago (Ill.) Professional Sch. Married to Ben Gazzara, actor; two daughters. Relative in theatre: brother, Charles Rule, actor, singer, dancer. Member of AEA; SAG; AGVA; AFTRA (NY board, 1955). Address: (home) 67 Riverside Dr., New York, NY 10024; (bus.) c/o J. Julien, 9 E. 41st St., New York, NY 10017.

Theatre. Miss Rule first appeared in N.Y.C. as a dancer in *Miss Liberty* (Imperial Th., July 15, 1949); subsequently was a dancer and understudied Bambi Lynn as Bonnie in *Great to Be Alive!* (Winter Garden, Mar. 23, 1950); played Madge Owens in *Picnic* (Music Box, Feb. 19, 1953); played Rachel in *The Flowering Peach* (Belasco, Dec. 28, 1954); in stock, appeared in *Ondine* (Olney Th., Md., Summer 1955); *Bus Stop* (Cherry Grove Th., Summer 1955); and *The Minotaur* (Westport Country Playhouse, Conn., Summer 1955); played the Princess in *The Carefree Tree* (Phoenix, N.Y.C., Oct. 11, 1955); Daphne Bau in *Night Circus* (John Golden Th., Dec. 2, 1958); Diana in *The Happiest Girl in the World* (Martin Beck Th., Apr. 3, 1961); and Ruth in Pinter's *The Homecoming* (Bijou, Apr. 18, 1971).

Films. Miss Rule made her debut in *Goodbye, My Fancy* (WB, 1951); subsequently appeared in *Holiday for Sinners* (MGM, 1952); *Rogue's March* (MGM, 1952); *A Woman's Devotion* (Rep., 1956); *Gun for a Coward* (U, 1957); *Invitation to a Gunfighter* (Stanley Kramer, 1963) *The Chase* (Col., 1966); *Ambushers* (Col., 1967); *Doctors' Wives* (20th-Fox, 1968); *Gumshoe* (Col., 1970); and *Kid Blue* (20th-Fox, 1973).

Television. Since 1951, Miss Rule has appeared on Philco Television Playhouse (NBC); Goodyear Playhouse (NBC); G.E. Th. (CBS, 1956); Playhouse 90 (CBS); The Defenders (CBS); Dr. Kildare (NBC); Jimmy Durante Special; Bob Hope Th. (NBC); *Ben Casey* (ABC); *The Fugitive* (ABC); *Run for Your Life* (NBC); *Orsen Wells Mystery Th.* (syndicated); *Profiles in Courage* (NBC); *The Name of the Game* (NBC); and many made-for-television movies.

Night Clubs. Miss Rule first appeared as a solo dancer at the Chez Paree (Chicago, Ill., 1946); later was a dancer in the chorus at the Copacabana (N.Y.C., 1947), and at the Riviera (N.Y.C., 1947).

RUMLEY, JERRY. Educator, director, choreographer. b. Jerry Bruce Rumley, Nov. 3, 1930, Denver, Colo., to Melville Franklin and Mae Veronica (Cousins) Rumley. Father, safety supervisor; mother, millinery designer. Grad. Holy Family H.S., 1949; attended Regis Coll., 1949–52; grad. Univ. of Denver, B.A. 1955; Univ. of Minnesota, M.A. 1958, Ph.D. 1969. Studied dance in Denver with Lillian Covillo, 1952–55; Friede Ann Parker, 1952–55; Lillian Cushing, 1946–52; and Martha Wilcox, 1952–55. Married Dec. 27, 1955, to Elva Mae Rumley; three sons, two daughters. Relative in theatre: Cyrus Rumley, rider and marksman, Buffalo Bill Wild West Show. Member of AGVA; ATA; Natl. Collegiate Players (pres., Minn. chapter, 1956). Address: (home) 2490 S. Milwaukee St., Denver, CO 80210, tel. (303) 756-0536; (bus.) Theatre Dept., Univ. of Denver, Denver, CO 80210, tel. (303) 753-2510.

Since 1962, Mr. Rumley has been associate professor, associate director of dance, and director of undergraduate studies in theatre in the theatre department of the Univ. of Denver. He also teaches jazz at the Lillian Cushing Sch., Denver. Previously, he was an instructor (1959–62) and costumer (1961–62) at the Univ. of Minnesota.

He has danced in, directed, and choreographed student and professional productions; appeared with the ballet company of the Central City Opera, Denver, Colo. (1946); performed in summer stock (Elitch's Gardens, Denver, Colo., 1951); performed as dance soloist with the Denver Symphony (Red Rocks Amphitheatre, July 1953); appeared with Maurice Evans's national company of *The Devil's Disciple;* and was in the Minnesota Centennial Showboat productions (1959–60).

Awards. Mr. Rumley won the 1,000-hour Service Award, USO (1945); Wyndat Theatre Award for Most Outstanding Theatre Graduate, Univ. of Denver (1955); and the Ski-U-Mah (Service Award) from the Univ. of Minnesota for directing the *All Univ. Show* (1958–59).

Recreation. Sculpture, decorative furniture construction, wildlife conservation, cooking.

RUSSELL, ANNA. Actress, composer, lyricist, singer. b. Anna Claudia Russell-Brown, Dec. 27, 1911, London, England, to Col. Claude and Beatrice (Tandy) Russell-Brown. Father, British army officer. Grad. St. Felix Sch., Southwold, England, 1929; Royal Coll. of Music, London, A.R.C.M. 1935. Married Sept. 7, 1934 to John L. Denison, theatre executive (marr. dis. 1946); married May 17, 1948, to Charles Goldhammer, educator (marr. dis. 1954). Member of Musicians Union Local 149; AEA; British AEA; AGMA; ASCAP; Toronto (Ontario, Canada) Zonta Club (intl. mbr.).

Theatre. Miss Russell made her N.Y.C. debut in a one-woman show (Town Hall, 1948), with which she has toured the US, England, Australia, New Zealand, So. Africa, the Orient and Canada.

She wrote the lyrics and music for *Anna Russell's Little Show* (Vanderbilt, N.Y.C., Sept. 7, 1953); played the Witch in the opera, *Hansel and Gretel* (NY City Ctr., Oct. 14, 1953), and also with the San Francisco (Calif.) Opera Co. (1957–58).

In stock, she appeared in *Traveller's Joy* (Berkshire Playhouse, Stockbridge, Mass., Summer 1954); performed at the Johannesburg (Africa) Music Festival (1956); and at the Edinburgh (Scotland) Festival (1957, 1959). She played Lady Bracknell in *Half in Earnest* (Bucks County Playhouse, New Hope, Pa., Summer 1957); Aunt Lily in *The Children's Hour* (Bucks County Playhouse, New Hope, Pa., Summer 1958); Myra Gantry in *One Way Pendulum* (E. 74 St. Th., N.Y.C., Sept. 18, 1961); and composed the music, wrote the lyrics, and played Lady Audley in *Lady Audley's Secret or Who Pushed George?* (Berkshire Playhouse, Stockbridge, Mass., Summer 1963).

Miss Russell appeared in her one-woman show, *All by Myself* (41 St. Th., N.Y.C., June 17, 1964); played Lady Audley and was co-producer of *Lady Audley's Secret* (Beechnut Th., NY World's Fair, Summer 1964); played Alicia de St. Ephlom in a touring production of *Gigi* (Summer 1965); and Mary Welloughby in the world premiere of *Quality Street* (Bucks County Playhouse, New Hope, Pa., Aug. 23, 1965); and wrote an adaptation of *The Ladies Game* (Town Hall, N.Y.C., Oct. 31, 1966). In Australia, she played Madame Armfeldt in *A Little Night Music* (Her Majesty's Th., Sydney, 1973).

Since 1943, Miss Russell has appeared as a soloist on the concert stage in Can. with the Toronto (Ontario) Symphony Orchestra and in the US, with the Cincinnati (Ohio) Symphony, the New York Philharmonic, the Little Orchestra Society, the Dallas (Tex.) Symphony, the Indianapolis (Ind.) Symphony and the San Francisco (California) Symphony. She has also sung in England with the London Symphony Orchestra, the London Philharmonic; in Australia with the Melbourne Symphony, and the Sydney Symphony. She appeared in concert on a sixteen-month tour sponsored by the Australian Arts Council (early 1970s); and in the US, was seen in concert at Avery Fisher Hall (N.Y.C., Mar. 10, 1974) and Carnegie Hall (Mar. 28, 1976).

Films. She was the voice of the Witch in the puppet version of *Hansel and Gretel* (RKO, 1954).

Television and Radio. She was a folk singer on radio (BBC, London, 1931); in Can. a singer on Round the Marble Arch (CFRB, Toronto, 1940); and Jolly Millertime (CBC, 1946); and conducted an interview program, Sid and Anna (Dominion Network, 1946). In London, she appeared on the world premiere of Musical Send-Ups Home Network, Jan. 31, 1966).

On US television, she played Lady Bracknell in *The Importance of Being Earnest* (Kraft Television Th., NBC, 1947); and appeared on the Mike Douglas Show (Ind., 1965–66); and the Today Show (NBC, 1966–67).

Other Activities. She is president of the B & R Music Publishing Co.

Published Works. Miss Russell is the author of *The Power of Being a Positive Stinker* (1955); and the *Anna Russell Songbook.* (1958); and wrote her versions of plot synopses for the program notes of the Australian Opera Co.'s productions at the new opera house in Sydney.

Discography. She has composed, written, and performed her own material on the Columbia recordings *Anna Russell Sings?; Anna Russell Sings? Again! Guide to Concert Audiences; Square Talk on Popular Singing; Anna Russell in Darkest Africa;* and *A Practical Banana Promotion.*

Awards. She received the Canadian Women's Press Club Award (1956) as best Canadian comedy writer of the year.

RUSSELL, ROSALIND.

Actress. b. June 4, 1912, Waterbury, Conn., to James and Clara (McKnight) Russell. Father, trial lawyer; mother, fashion editor, *Vogue* magazine. Attended Notre Dame Acad., Waterbury, Conn.; Marymount Coll., Tarrytown, N.Y., 1926–28; grad. AADA, N.Y.C., 1929. Married Oct. 25, 1941, to Frederick Brisson, producer; one son. Served WW II, USO, Hollywood Canteen. Member of AEA; SAG; AFTRA; AMPAS; ALA, West; Natl. Cultural Center (Chairman, Southern Calif.); CTG (dir.); Nat. Council of the Arts; Sister Elizabeth Kenny Inst. and Foundation (founder, bd. of dir.); Arthritis and Rheumatism Foundation (natl. campaign chmn.).

Theatre. Miss Russell made her debut with E. E. Clive's British Co. (Copley Th., Boston, Mass.); subsequently appeared in a stock production of *Goodbye Again* (Lake Placid, N.Y.); made her Bway debut in *The Garrick Gaieties* (Guild Th., Oct. 16, 1930), in which she toured; toured in *Roar China;* played Miss Mallory in *Company's Coming* (Lyceum, N.Y.C., Apr. 20, 1931); followed by the pre-Bway tryout of *Talent,* which closed during previews (N.Y.C., Dec. 1933); and Monica Grey in *The Second Man* (Boulevard Jackson Heights, Apr. 9, 1934).

She toured as Gillian in *Bell, Book and Candle* (Playhouse, Wilmington, Del., Dec. 21, 1951); played Ruth in *Wonderful Town* (Winter Garden, N.Y.C., Feb. 25, 1953); the title role in *Auntie Mame* (Broadhurst, Oct. 31, 1956); and she appeared in a one-woman show, *A Tribute to Rosalind Russell* (Town Hall, Sept. 22, 1974; Ford's Th., Washington, D.C., Dec. 3–8, 1974).

Films. Miss Russell made her debut in *Evelyn Prentice* (MGM, 1934); followed by *The President Vanishes* (Par., 1934); *Forsaking All Others* (MGM, 1934); *West Point of the Air* (MGM, 1935); *Reckless* (MGM, 1935); *Casino Murder Case* (MGM, 1935); *China Seas* (MGM, 1935); *Rendezvous* (MGM, 1935); *It Had To Happen* (20th-Fox, 1936); *Under Two Flags* (20th-Fox, 1936); *Trouble for Two* (MGM, 1936); *Craig's Wife* (Col., 1936); *Night Must Fall* (MGM, 1937); *Live, Love and Learn* (MGM, 1937); *Manproof* (MGM, 1938); *Four's a Crowd* (WB, 1938); *The Citadel* (MGM, 1938); *Fast and Loose* (MGM, 1939); and *The Women* (MGM, 1939).

Also *His Girl Friday* (Col., 1940); *Hired Wife* (U, 1940); *No Time for Comedy* (WB, 1940); *This Thing Called Love* (Col., 1941); *They Met in Bombay* (MGM, 1941); *The Feminine Touch* (MGM, 1941); *Design for Scandal* (MGM, 1941); *Take a Letter, Darling* (Par., 1942); *My Sister Eileen* (Col., 1942); *Flight for Freedom* (RKO, 1943); *What a Woman* (Col., 1943); *Roughly Speaking* (WB, 1945); *She Wouldn't Say Yes* (Col., 1945); *Sister Kenny* (RKO, 1946); *The Guilt of Janet Ames* (Col., 1947); *Mourning Becomes Electra* (RKO, 1947); *The Velvet Touch* (RKO, 1948); and *Tell It to the Judge* (Col., 1949).

Also *Woman of Distinction* (Col., 1950); *Never Wave at a WAC* (RKO, 1952); *The Girl Rush* (Par., 1955); *Picnic* (Col., 1955); *Auntie Mame* (WB, 1958); *A Majority of One* (WB, 1961); *Five Finger Exercise* (Col., 1962); *Gypsy* (WB, 1962); *The Trouble with Angels* (Col., 1966); *Rosie* (U, 1967); *Oh Dad, Poor Dad, Mama's Hung You in the Closet and I'm Feeling So Sad* (Par., 1967); *Where Angels Go, Trouble Follows* (Col., 1968); and *Mrs. Pollifax—Spy* (UA, 1971).

Television and Radio. Miss Russell played Beatrice in *Much Ado About Nothing* (CBS Radio Shakespeare Series); and performed on Silver Th. (CBS, Oct. 3, 1937). She made her television debut in *Never Wave at a WAC* (Schlitz Playhouse, CBS); subsequently appeared in *Wonderful Town* (1958); a Ford Spectacular; NBC Music Spectacular (NBC); GE Th. (CBS); What's My Line (CBS); the Ed Sullivan Show (CBS); *Wonderful Town* (CBS, Nov. 1958); *The Crooked Hearts* (ABC, Nov. 1972); and she was hostess on the special *Women of the Year, 1973* (CBS).

Published Works. Miss Russell wrote the original story for the film *The Unguarded Moment* (U, 1956); and contributed articles to *Readers' Digest* (1957), and the *Saturday Evening Post* (1962).

Awards. For her performance as Ruth in *Wonderful Town* (1953), Miss Russell won an Antoinette Perry (Tony) Award, the NY Drama Critics Circle Award, the Outer Circle Critics Award, the *Variety* NY Drama Critics Poll, the Donaldson Award, the Knickerbocker Award, and the Barter Theatre Award. She received The Lambs' certificate (1957); AADA's annual achievement awards (1962, 1974); the National Artist Award of ANTA (1974); and the Council of Stock Theaters Straw Hat Achievement Award (1975). Miss Russell is a four-time Academy (Oscar) Award nominee, for her performances as Ruth in *My Sister Eileen* (1942), the title role of *Sister Kenny* (1946), Lavinia in *Mourning Becomes Electra* (1947), and the title role in *Auntie Mame* (1959), received the Golden Globe Award of Merit from the Hollywood Foreign Press Assn., for her performances in *Sister Kenny* (1946), *Mourning Becomes Electra* (1947), *Auntie Mame* (1951); *Gypsy* (1963); won the Laurel Award for *Mourning Becomes Electra* (1948), *Picnic* (1956), *Auntie Mame* (1959); the Blue Ribbon Award from the *Box Office Magazine* for *The Citadel* (1938), *Sister Kenny* (1946) and *A Majority of One* (1962); the *Parents* Magazine Medal for *Sister Kenny* (1946); *Look* Magazine's Gold Plaque (1947) and the Film Critics Circle Award, given by the NY Foreign Language Press for *Sister Kenny* (1946) and *Mourning Becomes Electra* (1947); and the SAG annual award in 1974.

Miss Russell has frequently been elected to the Ten Best Dressed Women lists of both the NY Dress Inst. and the NY Fashion Acad. She has also received a citation from the Sister Kenny Foundation (1945); the Citation for Distinguished Service by the Community Chest of America (1947); and the Certificate of Service Award by the Hollywood Guild for work in social service and recreation for veterans of WW II; the Medallion of the Woman's Division of the Conference of Christians and Jews for work in brotherhood and human relations (1962); and the certificate of honor of the American Red Cross for her work in the 1962 fund campaign; the Floyd B. Odlum Award of the Arthritis Foundation (1971); and the Jean Hersholt Humanitarian Award (1973).

Recreation. Riding, swimming, tennis, golf, designing clothes.

RYDER, ALFRED.

Actor, director. b. Alfred Jacob Corn, Jan. 5, 1919, New York City, to Max and Zelda (Baruchin) Corn. Father, dentist. Grad. Professional Children's Sch., N.Y.C., 1933. Studied with Benno Schneider, Robert Lewis, and Lee Strasberg, N.Y.C. Married Aug. 1, 1958, to Kim Stanley, actress; one daughter. Relative in theatre: sister, Olive Deering, actress. Served WW II, USAAF. Member of Actor's Studio, both actors and directors units; AEA; AFTRA; SAG.

Theatre. Mr. Ryder first appeared on stage in a recitation of *Hiawatha* (P.S. 70, N.Y.C.). Billed as Alfred Corn, he made his professional debut as Curly in *Peter Pan* (Civic Repertory Th., Nov. 26, 1928), and on tour; subsequently played Benny Solomon in *East of Broadway* (Belmont, N.Y.C., Jan. 26, 1932); Etienne du Bois in *Another Love* (Vanderbilt, Mar. 19, 1934); Billy Harrison (as a Young Man) in *Come What May* (Plymouth, May 15, 1934); billed as Alfred Ryder, played a Baseball Player in *Our Town* (Henry Miller's Th., Feb. 4, 1938); Alec Jenkins in *All the Living* (Fulton, Mar. 24, 1938); and Baruch in *Jeremiah* (Guild, Feb. 3, 1939); and appeared in stock at the Westport (Conn.) Country Playhouse (Summer 1938).

He played Ralphie in *Awake and Sing* (48 St. Th., N.Y.C., Mar. 7, 1939); performed in two Sunday preview productions of *Quiet City* (Belasco, Apr. 16 & 23, 1939); played Dr. Young in *Medicine Show* (New Yorker, Apr. 12, 1940); the Knight Templar in *Nathan the Wise* (Belasco, Apr. 3, 1942); Milhauser in the USAAF production of *Winged Victory* (44 St. Th., Nov. 20, 1943); and Sgt. Robert A. Kane in *Sky Drift* (Belasco, Nov. 13, 1945). During 1946–47, he taught at the Actor's Lab. (Las Palmas Th., Hollywood, Calif.), where he also directed *The Long Goodbye* and *Mooney's Kid Don't Cry,* played Ralphie in *Awake and Sing,* and Mosca in *Volpone.* He appeared as Lazear in *Yellow Jack* (International, N.Y.C., Feb. 27, 1947); Oswald in *Ghosts* (Cort, Feb. 24, 1948); the title role in *Hamlet* for Margaret Webster's Shakespeare Co. (cross-country tour, 1949–50); Mark Antony in *Julius Caesar* (Arena Th., Edison Hotel, N.Y.C., June 20, 1950); and Orestes in *The Tower Beyond Tragedy* (ANTA, Nov. 26, 1950).

Mr. Ryder succeeded (June 11, 1956) Franchot Tone as Astroff in *Uncle Vanya* (Fourth St. Th., Jan. 31, 1956); appeared as Mosca in *Volpone* (Rooftop, Jan. 7, 1957); was standby for Sir Laurence Olivier as Archie Rice in *The Entertainer* (Royale, Feb. 12, 1958); for the ANTA Matinee Series, portrayed D. H. Lawrence in *I Rise in Flame, Cried the Phoenix* and directed the curtain raiser *Sweet Confession* (Th. de Lys, Apr. 4, 1959); repeated his role in *I Rise in Flame, Cried the Phoenix,* and played both Laurence and the Writer in *The Lady of Larkspur Lotion* (Fest. of Two Worlds, Spoleto, Italy, 1960); and played Sewell, the First Mate, in *One More River* (Ambassador, N.Y.C., Mar. 18, 1960), which he directed for the national tour.

He directed *A Far Country* (Music Box, N.Y.C., Apr. 4, 1961), and also the national tour (opened Playhouse, Wilmington, Del., Oct. 24, 1962; closed Hanna, Cleveland, Ohio, Jan. 12, 1963); played Berenger in the touring company of *Rhinoceros* (opened Alcazar, San Francisco, Calif., Oct. 3, 1961; closed Huntington Hartford Th., Los Angeles, Calif., Nov. 11, 1962); directed and played Ashley Knight in *Hey You, Light-Man!* (Mayfair, N.Y.C., Mar. 1, 1963); appeared in the title role in the NY Shakespeare Fest. production of *Hamlet* (Delacorte, June 10, 1964); directed *An Evening of Williams, Pinter and Schisgal* (Schoenberg Hall Aud., U.C.L.A., Los Angeles, Calif., June 4, 1965), in which he appeared as D. H. Lawrence in *I Rise in Flame, Cried the Phoenix;* directed *The Exercise* (John Golden Th., N.Y.C., Apr. 24, 1968); directed at the Arena Stage (Washington, D.C., 1968–70), where productions included *Dance of Death,* which subsequently moved to Bway (Ritz, N.Y.C., Apr. 28, 1971); and, at Center Stage (Baltimore, Md., Oct. 1971–Apr. 1972), where he also appeared in *Staircase.* .

Films. Mr. Ryder appeared in *Winged Victory* (20th-Fox, 1944); played Tony in *T-Men* (Eagle-Lion, 1947); the Husband in *Story on Page One* (20th-Fox, 1959); Doc Barker in *Invitation to a Gunfighter* (UA, 1964); and Capt. Yolles in *Hotel* (WB, 1967).

Television and Radio. On radio, he played Sammy in The Rise of the Goldbergs (NBC, 1930–33); and during a ten-year period, appeared on dramatic shows, specials, and soap operas.

He has appeared on television since 1950, in such roles as John Wilkes Booth, Hamlet, Iago, Tiberius, and Mark Antony; and in plays by such authors as Fitzgerald, Dostoevsky, James, and Schnitzler. He also played Claggart in *Billy Budd* (Dupont Playhouse, CBS, 1959); and repeated his original roles in *I Rise in Flame, Cried the Phoenix* and *The Lady of Larkspur Lotion* (Play of the Week, WNTA, 1960).

In addition, Mr. Ryder has appeared in episodes of various series, including Greatest Show (ABC); The Rogues (NBC); Decoy (CBS); One Step Beyond (Ind.); The Defenders (CBS); Ben Casey (ABC); Profiles in Courage (NBC); Bob Hope Presents (NBC); The Man from U.N.C.L.E. (NBC); Slattery's People (CBS); Alfred Hitchcock Presents (NBC); Route 66 (Ind.); The Long, Hot Summer (ABC); Wild, Wild West (CBS); Gunsmoke (CBS); Voyage (ABC); Star Trek (NBC); Dr. Kildare (Ind.); The Virginian (NBC); The F.B.I. (ABC); Laredo (NBC); and The Invaders (ABC).

Other Activities. He also taught acting at the Dramatic Workshop (N.Y.C., 1958–60).

Awards. Mr. Ryder received *The Village Voice* Off-Bway (Obie) Award (1960) for his performance as D. H. Lawrence in *I Rise in Flame, Cried the Phoenix.* .

Recreation. Drawing, reading, sunbathing.

RYSKIND, MORRIE. Playwright, columnist. b. Oct. 20, 1895, New York City, to Abraham and Ida (Etelson) Ryskind. Father, storekeeper. Grad. Townsend Harris H.S., N.Y.C., 1912; Columbia Univ., B.Litt. 1917. Married Dec. 1929 to Mary House; one son, one daughter. Relative in theatre: niece, Linda Ashkin, writer, composer. Member of Dramatists Guild (formerly on bd. of dir.). Address: 605 N. Hillcrest Rd., Beverly Hills, CA 94705.

Pre-Theatre. Reporter, press agent.

Theatre. Mr. Ryskind wrote sketches and lyrics for *The '49'ers* (Punch and Judy Th., N.Y.C., Nov. 7, 1922); and for the first *Garrick Gaieties* (Garrick Th., June 8, 1925).

He assisted George S. Kaufman in the preparation of the script for *The Cocoanuts* (Lyric, Dec. 8, 1925); wrote, with Mr. Kaufman, *Animal Crackers* (44 St. Th., Oct. 23, 1928); and wrote lyrics for the songs in *Americana* (Belmont, July 26, 1926); wrote, with Howard Dietz, sketches and lyrics for *Merry-Go-Round* (Klaw Th., May 31, 1927); adapted Mr. Kaufman's libretto for *Strike Up the Band* (Times Sq., Jan. 14, 1930); collaborated with Mr. Kaufman on the librettos of the George and Ira Gershwin musicals, *Of Thee I Sing* (Music Box Th., Dec. 26, 1931; return engagement Imperial, May 15, 1933; revived Ziegfeld, May 5, 1952), and *Let 'Em Eat Cake* (Imperial, Oct. 21, 1933); and adapted the libretto for the Irving Berlin musical, *Louisiana Purchase* (Imperial, May 28, 1940).

Films. Mr. Ryskind wrote the screenplays for *The Cocoanuts* (Par., 1929); *Animal Crackers* (Par., 1933); *A Night at the Opera* (MGM, 1935); *My Man Godfrey* (U, 1936); *Stage Door* (RKO, 1937); *Penny Serenade* (Col., 1941); *Claudia* (20th-Fox, 1943); and *Where Do We Go from Here?* (20th-Fox, 1945).

Other Activities. Since 1960, he has written a syndicated column for the Los Angeles *Times* entitled "The Morrie Ryskind Column." Since 1966, the column has been syndicated by the Washington (D.C.) *Star.*

Published Works. Mr. Ryskind wrote *Unaccustomed As I Am* (1920), a collection of light verse; and *The Diary of an Ex-President* (1932).

Awards. He received the Pulitzer Prize for his collaboration on the libretto of the musical *Of Thee I Sing* (1933).

S

SAARI, CHARLES. Actor. b. Charles Lee Saari, June 23, 1944, New York City, to Carl and Lenore (Brady) Saari. Father, dancer; mother, dancer. Grad. Professional Children's Sch., N.Y.C., 1962; New York Univ., B.S. 1966; Ohio State Coll. of Law, J.D. 1971. Studied acting with Helen Bonstelle, N.Y.C., 1956–63; singing with Bill Russell, N.Y.C., 1957–62; Shakespearean acting with Fanny Bradshaw, N.Y.C., 1960–63; speech with Alice Hermes, N.Y.C., 1961; singing with Jack Prenner, N.Y.C., 1962–63; voice and speech with Henry Jacobi, N.Y.C., 1963–64. Member of AEA; AFTRA; SAG. Address: 360 W. 55th St., New York, NY 10019, tel. (212) JU 2-5098.

Theatre. Mr. Saari made his N.Y.C. debut as one of the children in *Music in the Air* (Ziegfeld, Oct. 8, 1951); subsequently appeared in stock as Sergei in *Love in Upper Sandusky* (Lake Whalom, Mass., June 29, 1953); Little Jake in *Annie Get Your Gun* (Lake Whalom, Mass., July 6, 1953); was an understudy in *King of Hearts* (Lyceum, N.Y.C., Mar. 11, 1954); appeared in *Angel on the Loose* (Norwich Playhouse, Conn., July 11, 1955); as Norman in *King of Hearts* (Paper Mill Playhouse, Millburn, N.J., Aug. 2, 1955); Billy in the Amer. Th. Wing production of *Point of Beginning* (Greater N.Y.C. area, 1955–57); and Larry Fallon in *Room Full of Roses* (Playhouse-in-the-Park, Philadelphia, Pa., June 25, 1956; Northland Playhouse, Detroit, Mich., July 1956; Ivy Tower Playhouse, Spring Lake, N.J., July 1956).

He played Sonny Flood in *The Dark at the Top of the Stairs* (Music Box, N.Y.C., Dec. 5, 1957), and on tour (opened Playhouse, Wilmington, Del., Jan. 21, 1959; closed Pabst, Milwaukee, Wis., May 16, 1959); appeared as Bernie in *Behind the Wall* (Jan Hus House, N.Y.C., Oct. 31, 1960); and Billy in the pre-Bway tryout of *Journey to the Day* (opened Westport Country Playhouse, Conn., Aug. 28, 1961).

Television and Radio. Mr. Saari performed on radio on Five Star Matinee (NBC, 1954); The Guiding Light (CBS, 1954); Whispering Streets (ABC, 1955); Papa Married a Mormon (NBC, 1955); and Aunt Jennie (CBS, 1955).

On television, he appeared on Ranger Ranch Round-Up (ABC, 1950); Texaco Star Th. (NBC, 1950); I Remember Mama (CBS, 1950); Cameo Th. (NBC, 1951); Armstrong Circle Th. (NBC, 1951); Cosmopolitan Th. (ABC, 1951); the Steve Allen Show (CBS, ABC, 1951); Studio One (CBS, 1952); Ken Murray Show (CBS, 1952); US Royal Showcase (NBC, 1952); Hallmark Hall of Fame (NBC, 1952); Kate Smith (NBC, 1952); Curtain Call (NBC, 1952); Schlitz Playhouse (CBS, 1952); Omnibus (CBS, 1952); Jackie Gleason Show (CBS, 1952); George Jessel Show (ABC, 1953); Danger (CBS, 1953); Red Skelton Show (CBS, 1953); Ed Sullivan Show (CBS, 1953); Robert Montgomery Presents (NBC, 1954); US Steel Hour (ABC, 1954); Caesar's Hour (NBC, 1954); Garry Moore Show (NBC, 1954); Kraft Television Th. (NBC, 1954); The World of Mr. Sweeney (NBC, 1954); Your Show of Shows (NBC, 1955); Ethel and Albert Show (NBC, 1955); Big Story (Dumont, 1957); played Ferike in *The Emperor's Clothes* (Play of the Week, WNTA, 1960); appeared on the Phil Silvers Special, *Summer in N.Y.* (CBS, 1960); Tab Hunter Show (NBC, 1960); 25 Years of Life (NBC, 1961); and The Defenders (CBS, 1962).

Night Clubs. During his pre-school days, Mr. Saari performed in hotels with the dance act of his parents, "Lenore and Charles.".

Recreation. Figure skating, swimming, collecting books and records.

SABINSON, HARVEY B. Writer, teacher, press representative, theatre consultant. b. Oct. 24, 1924, New York City, to Samuel and Sarah (Slutzker) Sabinson. Father, dental mechanic, salesman. Grad. Townsend Harris H.S., N.Y.C., 1940; attended Ohio State Univ., 1943; Amer. Th. Wing, 1946; grad. Queens Coll., B.S. 1947. Married Aug. 15, 1944, to Sarah S. Shaub, teacher; two sons. Served US Army, ETO, 1943–46; rank, 1st Lt. Relative in theatre: brother, Lee Sabinson, producer. Member of ATPAM (bd. of gov., 1959–60; 1962–74). Address: 67-82 Selfridge St., Forest Hills, NY 11375, tel. (212) LI 4-6378.

Theatre. Mr. Sabinson was a partner in the publicity firm of Solters and Roskin, Inc. He has been press representative for over two hundred Bway, off-Bway, and regional theatre productions.

In 1949, he served as associate press representative for *The Biggest Thief in Town;* in 1950, *Guys and Dolls;* in 1951, for *Twilight Walk, Faithfully Yours,* and *Don Juan in Hell;* in 1952, *Three Wishes for Jamie, Shuffle Along,* and *My Darlin' Aida;* in 1953, *On Borrowed Time, Comedy in Music* (Victor Borge), *John Brown's Body, Can-Can,* and *Jamaica;* in 1955, *Silk Stockings, Three for Tonight, Tiger at the Gates,* and *A Hatful of Rain;* in 1956, *Catch a Star;* subsequently, in 1956 was press representative for *The Best House in Naples,* and *Li'l Abner;* in 1957, *The First Gentleman, Look Back in Anger, The Egghead, Romanoff and Juliet, The Dark at the Top of the Stairs,* and *A Shadow of My Enemy;* in 1958, *Oh Captain!, Interlock, Lulu, The Entertainer, The Man in the Dog Suit, Epitaph for George Dillon, Maria Golovin,* and *Ages of Man;* in 1959, *Triple Play, Destry Rides Again, The Failures, Our Town, And the Wind Blows,* the tour of *The Dark at the Top of the Stairs, Heartbreak House, Take Me Along, The Tenth Man, A Loss of Roses,* and *Mark Twain Tonight.*

In 1960, Mr. Sabinson represented *Parade, The Balcony, An Evening with Mike Nichols and Elaine May, The Fantasticks, 41 in a Sack, Camino Real, A Mighty Man Is He, The Deadly Game, The Cool World, Face of a Hero, Period of Adjustment, Little Moon of Alban,* and *Wildcat;* in 1961, *Rhinoceros, Once There Was a Russian, Big Fish, Little Fish, The Caretaker, Carnival!, Do You Know the Milky Way?, Look: We've Come Through!, The Garden of Sweets, Kean, Sunday in New York, Ross,* and *Subways Are for Sleeping,* and the American Shakespeare Festival productions of *Troilus and Cressida, As You Like It,* and *Macbeth;* in 1962, *A Family Affair, Isle of Children, The Perfect Setup, Calculated Risk, Harold, The Days and Nights of Beebee Fenstermaker,* the pre-Bway tryout of *We Take the Town,* the American Shakespeare Festival production of *Shakespeare Revisited,* the tour of *The Caretaker,* and with Lee Solters, *I Can Get It for You Wholesale, Venus at Large, Stop the World—I Want To Get Off,* and *In the Counting House;* in 1963, *The Rehearsal, Luther, Here's Love, Barefoot in the Park, 110 in the Shade, Mother Courage and Her Children, Cages,* and with Lee Solters, *Rattle of a Simple Man, Oliver!,* and *The Milk Train Doesn't Stop Here Anymore;* and in 1964, *Hello Dolly!, Dylan, Any Wednesday, High Spirits,* and *Fade Out—Fade In.* In 1964, he was general press representative for *The Physicists, Ben Franklin in Paris, Golden Boy, A Severed Head, I Was Dancing,* the pre-Bway tryout of *Rich Little Rich Girl,* and *Slow Dance on the Killing Ground.*

In 1965, *Alfie, The Odd Couple, The Roar of the Greasepaint—The Smell of the Crowd, Mrs. Dally Has a Lover, Minor Miracle, Pickwick, Cactus Flower, The Yearling, Marat/Sade.* In 1966, *Philadelphia, Here I Come, Hostile Witness, Happily Never After, Mark Twain Tonight* (ret.), *The Loves of Cass McGuire, We Have Always Lived in the Castle, The Apple Tree, Don't Drink the Water, I Do! I Do!, The Star-Spangled Girl.* In 1967, *The Astrakhan Coat, You Know I Can't Hear You When the Water's Running, Dr. Cook's Garden, Keep It in the Family, Daphne in Cottage D, Rosencrantz and Guildenstern Are Dead, There's a Girl in My Soup, Henry, Sweet Henry, The Little Foxes, How Now, Dow Jones.* In 1968, *The Happy Time, I Never Sang for My Father, Plaza Suite, Carry Me Back to Morningside Heights, The Guide, Weekend, The Seven Descents of Myrtle, The Education of Hyman Kaplan, The Flip Side, Maggie Flynn, Rockefeller and the Red Indians, Up Eden, The Sudden Education of Horse Johnson, Promises, Promises, Forty Carats.* In 1969, *Hadrian VII, Celebration, Canterbury Tales, Play It Again Sam, The Watering Place, 1776, Billy, A Patriot for Me, Indians, The Penny Wars, Private Lives, Coco, Last of the Red Hot Lovers.* In 1970, *Child's Play, Norman, Is*

That You?, The Chinese and Dr. Fish, Borstal Boy, Cry for Us All, Bob and Ray, the Two and Only, Opium, Conduct Unbecoming, Saved, Orlando Furioso, The Gingerbread Lady. In, 1971, *A Midsummer Night's Dream, And Miss Reardon Drinks a Little, Four on a Garden, The Philanthropist, How the Other Half Loves, Scratch, The Proposition, Solitaire/Double Solitaire.* In 1972, *There's One in Every Marriage, Twigs, Moonchildren, Night Watch, The Prisoner of Second Avenue.* In 1972, *Sugar, Hurry, Harry, Pippin, The Secret Affairs of Mildred Wild, Via Galactica, The Sunshine Boys.* In 1973, *Shelter, Status Quo Vadis, Rainbow, Out Cry, An Evening with the Poet Senator, Echoes.*

Other Activities. Mr. Sabinson was visiting professor of theatre administration, Yale University School of Drama (1966–70), and he has been adjunct associate professor of speech and drama, Queensborough Community College, City Univ. of NY (1973–to date).

Recreation. Tennis, baseball, reading.

SABINSON, LEE. Producer, company manager. b. Lee S. Sabinson, Nov. 11, 1911, Bronx, N.Y., to Samuel Sabinson. Father, actor, salesman. Attended Coll. of the City of New York. Married to "Bily" Lindenauer; two daughters. Relative in theatre: brother, Harvey Sabinson, press representative. Member of League of NY.

Theatre. Mr. Sabinson produced *Counterattack* (Windsor Th., N.Y.C., Feb. 3, 1943); *Trio* (Belasco, Dec. 29, 1944); with William R. Katzell, produced *Home of the Brave* (Belasco, Dec. 27, 1945) and *Finian's Rainbow* (46 St. Th., Jan. 10, 1947); produced *The Biggest Thief in Town* (Mansfield, Mar. 30, 1949); and was company manager for *Lace on Her Petticoat* (Booth, Sept. 4, 1951).

SACHAROW, LAWRENCE. Director, educator. b. Oct. 10, 1937, New York City, to Samuel and Belle Sacharow. Father, taxi driver; mother, insurance clerk. Educ. Tilden H.S., N.Y.C.; Brooklyn Coll., B.A.; Mexico City Coll. Professional training at Circle in the Square Theatre School (Alan Schneider); Actors' Studio Directors Unit (Lee Strasberg); observer, Brecht Berliner Ensemble Theatre, East Berlin. Served in US Army, 1956–58. Married Dec. 25, 1967, to Rochelle Perelson; one daughter. Member of SSD&C; AAUP. Address: (home) 463 West St., New York, NY 10014, tel. (212) 989-7063; (bus.) c/o Bard College, Annandale-on-Hudson, NY 12504, tel. (914) 758-4194.

Theatre. Mr. Sacharow's first work in the theatre was done off-Bway at Cafe Cino, where he arranged and directed *38 Haikus* (June 1964) and directed *The Vaseline Photographer* (Sept. 1964) and *The Run to the Sea* (Dec. 1964). He directed *Center for Death* (Spencer Church, N.Y.C., Apr. 1965); was assistant director, NY Shakespeare Festival (Summer 1965); at Judson Poets' Theatre directed *After Closing* (Oct. 1965) and *Three Thousand Red Ants* (Jan. 1966); and at Cafe La Mama directed *The Cantilever Rainbow* (Mar. 1966) and *The Madonna in the Orchard* (May 1966). He directed a street theatre production of *The Exception and the Rule*, which played in Harlem (NYC) parks and churches and a children's theatre production of *Open House for Butterflies*, which also played in Harlem parks (both Summer 1966); directed *God Bless Us, Everyone* (Cafe La Mama, Feb. 1967); *Images* (Th. East, June 1967); *Endgame* (Daytop Village, Staten Island, N.Y.C., Dec. 1967); and conceived and directed *The Concept* (Sheridan Square Playhouse, May 1968) and *CONCEPT II*, which toured universities (Mar. 1969).

Mr. Sacharow also conceived and directed *Primitives* (Cafe La Mama, Sept. 1969); directed *Denouement* (Hunter Playhouse, Feb. 1970); conceived and directed *Where Is Everyone?* (Museum of the City of NY, Apr. 1970); *The Journey* (Th. for the New City, Nov. 1971); *Tabula-Rasa* (Brooklyn Acad. of Music, Mar. 1972); directed *The Tempest* (WPA Th., May 1972); *The Tooth of Crime* (Bard Coll., Annandale-on-Hudson, N.Y., May 1973); conceived and directed *L.A. W.O.M.A.N.* (Mark Taper Forum, Los Angeles, Calif., Sept. 20, 1973); and directed *The Three Sisters* (Bard Coll., Mar. 1974).

Television. Mr. Sacharow was subject-consultant for *L.A. W.O.M.A.N.*, a documentary on group process (KCET-TV, Los Angeles, Calif., June 1974).

Other Activities. Mr. Sacharow is an assistant professor of drama, Bard Coll., Annandale-on-Hudson, N.Y.; an instructor in theatre directing, New School for Social Research, N.Y.C.; and director of The Theatre Company. He is a trainer in group dynamic skills; a sensitivity group leader; consultant to drug prevention and rehabilitation programs; and a body awareness workshop leader in growth centers. He has been a workshop consultant at the National Training Workshop, Germany (environmentalist); at Naval Drug Training Workshops (group leader) in San Diego, Calif., and Jacksonville, Fla.; at Addiction Services Agency, Phoenix Institute (training consultant); at Bucks County (Pa.) Seminar House, Grow Institute, SPARK program (theatre games workshop); and he was associate professor, Adelphi Univ. (National Drug Institute) and director of education and culture, Daytop Village, Staten Island, N.Y.

Published Works. Mr. Sacharow's article "Theatre as Therapy" appeared in *British International Theatre Quarterly* (Oct.–Dec. 1972).

Awards. Mr. Sacharow received grants from the National Endowment on the Arts and the NY State Arts Council (1971, 1972) to produce new theatre works using the collective group process approach with a company; *The Journey, Tabula-Rasa*, and *The Tempest* were produced.

Recreation. Anthropology, religion.

SACKLER, HOWARD. Playwright, screenwriter, director, poet. b. Dec. 19, 1929, Bronx, N.Y., to Martin and Evelyn (Rapaport) Sackler. Father, real estate agent. Grad. Brooklyn Coll.; BA, 1950. Married 1963 to Greta Lynn Lungren, two children. Address: London, England; Ibiza, Spain.

Theatre. Mr. Sackler's plays include *Mr. Welk and Jersey Jim* (Actors Studio, N.Y.C., 1960; and Arena Stage, Washington, D.C., Apr. 21, 1966), one segment of a four-part work entitled *A Few Enquiries*, which also includes *The Nine O'Clock Mail* (Charles Playhouse, Boston; and Direct Th., N.Y.C., Sept. 1974) and *Sara*, and *Skippy; The Yellow Loves* (Pacts Th., Cambridge, Mass., Feb. 1, 1962); *The Great White Hope* (Arena Stage, Washington, D.C., Dec. 7, 1967; and Alvin, N.Y.C., Oct. 3, 1968); *The Pastime of Monsieur Robert* (Hempstead Th. Club, London, Feb. 17, 1968; and ACT, Los Angeles, June 4, 1968); and *Uriel Acosta* and *The Man Who Stammered* (unproduced to date).

At the New Sch. for Social Research (N.Y.C.), Mr. Sackler directed dramatic readings of *King John* (Mar. 1953), *Women of Trachis* (Feb. 1954), and *Family Reunion* (Nov. 1954). In England he has directed *Chin-Chin* (Wyndham's Th., London, Nov. 3, 1960); and *Suzanna Adler* (Yvonne Arnaud Th., Guilford, Oct. 1971; and Aldwych, London, Mar. 1972).

Films. He wrote the screenplay for *Fear and Desire* (Stanley Kubrick Prods., 1953); adapted and directed *A Midsummer Night's Dream* (Showcorp, 1962); and, based on his play, wrote the screenplay for *The Great White Hope* (20th-Fox, 1971).

Television. Mr. Sackler directed *Soul of An Age* (NBC).

Other Activities. Mr. Sackler is the founder and production director (1953–to date) of Caedmon Records (London), a firm specializing in readings of plays and poetry.

Published Works. His poetry has appeared in *Poetry* Magazine, *Commentary, The Hudson Review*, and *New Directions Annual*, and a volume entitled *Want My Shepherd: Poems.*.

Awards. He has received a Rockefeller Foundation grant (1953); a Littnaur grant (1954); the Maxwell Anderson Award (1954) for *Uriel Acosta;* the Sergei Award (1959) for *The Yellow Loves;* and the Pulitzer Prize, the NY Drama Critics Circle Award, and the Antoinette Perry (Tony) Award for *The Great White Hope* (1969).

SADDLER, DONALD. Choreographer, director, dancer. b. Donald Edward Saddler, Jan. 24, 1920, Van Nuys, Calif., to Elmer Edward and Mary Elizabeth (Roberts) Saddler. Father, farmer. Grad. David Starr Jordan H.S., Los Angeles, 1937; attended Los Angeles City Coll., 1939. Served US Army, 1943–45; rank, Sgt. Member of AEA; SSD&C.

Theatre. Mr. Saddler made his debut as a dancer in *Grand Canyon Suite* (Hollywood Bowl, Calif., 1937); subsequently appeared with the Ballet Th. (N.Y.C., 1940–43; 1946–47); performed with the Ballet Theatre the title role in *Bluebeard*, Alias in *Billy the Kid*, Benno in *Swan Lake*, the Rose Cavalier in *Aurora's Wedding*, the White Cavalier in *Les patineurs*, the Hussar in *Lilac Garden*, Partner to Italian Ballerina in *Gala Performance*, Paris in *Romeo and Juliet*, and the Head Hunter in *Peter and the Wolf.*

He made his N.Y.C. debut succeeding Paul Godkin (Nov. 1, 1947) as Uncle Willie in *High Button Shoes* (Century, Oct. 9, 1947); then appeared as a principal dancer in *Dance Me a Song* (Royale, Jan. 20, 1950); *Bless You All* (Mark Hellinger Th., Dec. 14, 1950); and, in stock, appeared in *The Song of Norway* (Dallas, Tex., Aug. 1951).

His first assignment as a choreographer was for the Markova-Dolin Co. production of *Blue Mountain Ballads* (1948); subsequently choreographed *Wonderful Town* (Winter Garden, N.Y.C., Feb. 25, 1953); *John Murray Anderson's Almanac* (Imperial, Dec. 10, 1953); *Tobia la Candida Spia* (Teatro Sistina, Rome, Italy, Dec. 30, 1954); and *La Patrona di Raggio di Luna* (Teatro Sistina, Rome, Dec. 10, 1955); *Wonderful Town* (Prince's, London, Feb. 24, 1955), and also for the Greek Th. production, which he also directed (Los Angeles, Calif., July 1955).

Mr. Saddler made a guest appearance in the Fifteenth Anniversary Programme of Ballet Th. (1955); choreographed *Shangri-La* (Winter Garden, N.Y.C., June 13, 1956); and the dances for *Buona Notte Bettina* (Teatro Lirico, Milan, Italy, Nov. 14, 1956); and *L'Adorabile Giulio* (Teatro Sistina, Rome, Italy, 1957). Mr. Saddler directed the State Fair musicals (State Fair Music Hall, Dallas, Tex., 1957, 1959); and a season at Carousel Th. (Framingham, Mass., Summer 1958); choreographed *Un Trapezio per Lisistrata* (Teatro Sistina, Rome, Dec. 18, 1958); headed his own company at Jacob's Pillow (Lee, Mass., 1958), providing choreography for, and appearing as Rev. Curtis Brown in *Winesburg, Ohio*, and choreography for *This Property Is Condemned* (July 1958).

He choreographed *When in Rome* (Adelphi, London, Dec. 26, 1959); with the Valerie Bettis Co., he appeared as Macbeth in *The Golden Round* and in *Early Voyagers*, based on Truman Capote's *Other Voices, Other Rooms* (Jacob's Pillow, Lee, Mass., Aug. 2–6, 1960); danced at the Boston (Mass.) Arts Festival in *The Castle Period* (June 12–17, 1961); and for the Robert Joffrey Ballet Co., choreographed *Dreams of Glory* (1961).

He choreographed *Milk and Honey* (Martin Beck Th., N.Y.C., Oct. 10, 1961); *Sophie* (Winter Garden, Apr. 15, 1963); *Morning Sun* (Phoenix, Oct. 7, 1963); and *To Broadway with Love* (Texas Pavilion, NY World's Fair, Apr. 22, 1964).

From 1964 to 1970, Mr. Saddler was associated with the Harkness Ballet, first as assistant director and later as artistic director.

On Bway, he staged dances and musical numbers for the revival of *No, No, Nanette* (46 St. Th., Jan. 19, 1971); staged dances for the NY Shakespeare Festival's *Much Ado About Nothing* (Delacorte Th., Aug. 10, 1972); Winter Garden, Nov. 11, 1972); staged the off-Bway production *Berlin to Broadway with Kurt Weill* (Th. de Lys, Oct. 1, 1972); and created choreography for *Tricks* (Alvin, Jan. 8, 1973). Mr. Saddler choreographed *Fanfare Gala* (NY City Ctr., Oct. 1973), celebrating the 30th anniversary of the City Ctr.; he created choreography for the NY Shakespeare Festival production of *The Merry Wives of Windsor* (Delacorte Th., July 26, 1974); supervised musical staging for the pre-Bway tryout of *Miss Moffat* (opened Shubert Th., Philadelphia, Pa., Oct. 7, 1974; closed there, Oct. 18, 1974); staged musical numbers in a revival of *Good News* (St. James Th., N.Y.C., Dec. 23, 1974); for the NY Shakespeare Festival production of *A Midsummer Night's Dream* (Mitzi E. Newhouse Th., Jan. 19, 1975); choreographed the tarantella in *A Doll's House* (Vivian Beaumont Th., Mar. 5, 1975); did choreography for *Rodgers & Hart* (Helen Hayes Th., May 13, 1975); and for *The Robber Bridegroom* (Harkness Th., Oct. 7, 1975).

Films. Mr. Saddler choreographed *April in Paris* (WB, 1952); *By the Light of the Silvery Moon* (WB, 1953); *Young at Heart* (WB, 1954); and *The Main Attraction* (7 Arts, 1963).

Television. He has choreographed for the Bell Telephone Hour (NBC, 1961–64); Holiday Hotel (ABC, 1950); and in Italy, for Canozionissima (Rome, Dec. 1959, Jan.–Feb. 1960). He restaged *Much Ado About Nothing* for television (CBS, Feb. 2, 1973).

Night Clubs. Mr. Saddler appeared at the International Casino (N.Y.C., May 1939).

Awards. He received the Antoinette Perry (Tony) Award for his choreography for *Wonderful Town* (1953) and the Maschera d'Argento for *Tobia la Candida Spia* (1954). For his choreography for *No, No, Nanette*, he received Drama Desk and Antoinette Perry (Tony) awards (both 1971), and he was nominated for a Tony for his choreography for *Much Ado About Nothing* (1973).

SADOFF, FRED E. Actor, director, producer. b. Fred Edward Sadoff, Oct. 21, 1926, Bklyn., N.Y., to Henry and Bertha (Leib) Sadoff. Father, motion picture operator. Grad. Lafayette H.S., Bklyn., 1942; attended Brooklyn Coll., 1942–44. Studied acting at HB (Herbert Berghof) Studio, N.Y.C., 1944; with Sanford Meisner at Neighborhood Playhouse Sch. of the Th., N.Y.C., 1945–47; with Lee Strasberg, N.Y.C., 1947–49; Actors' Studio (member 1949–to date). Served USN, 1944–45; rank, Yeoman 3/C. Member of AEA; British AEA; AFTRA; SAG; Society of West End Theatre Managers (London, England).

Theatre. Mr. Sadoff first performed as an actor in stock at the Tappan Zee Playhouse (Nyack, N.Y., Summer 1945); subsequently appeared at the Bennington (N.Y.) Drama Festival (1946); and at the Maverick Th. (Woodstock, N.Y., 1947).

He made his Bway debut as the Professor in *South Pacific* (Majestic, Apr. 7, 1949); appeared in stock in *The School for Scandal* (Westport Country Playhouse, Conn.; Playhouse-in-the-Park, Philadelphia, Pa. 1952); and played Marvin in *Wish You Were Here* (Imperial, N.Y.C., June 25, 1952).

At the Actors' Studio during 1953, he adapted, directed, and performed in *The Catcher in the Rye* and *The Thirteen Clocks;* directed and appeared in a tour of the latter production (Summer 1954). He played the Second Street Cleaner in *Camino Real* (Natl., N.Y.C., Mar. 19, 1953); directed at the Hyde Park (N.Y.) Playhouse (Summer 1955); directed *The Terrible Swift Sword* (Phoenix, N.Y.C., Nov. 15, 1955); and served as assistant director of *A Month in the Country* (Phoenix, Apr. 3, 1956).

Mr. Sadoff directed *The Young and the Beautiful* (Arts, London, Oct. 15, 1956); directed and produced *The Sound of Murder* (Aldwych, Aug. 5, 1959); co-produced *The Aspern Papers* (Queen's, Aug. 12, 1959); directed *My Friend Judas* (Arts, Oct. 21, 1959); produced *The Importance of Being Oscar* (Apollo, Oct. 3, 1960); and with Michael Redgrave, in association with Sol Hurok and Roger L. Stevens, presented the latter production (Lyceum, N.Y.C., Mar. 14, 1961).

He produced *Waiting in the Wings* (Duke of York's, London, Sept. 7, 1960); Irene Mayer Selznick in association with H. M. Tennent Ltd., Donald Albery, and F.E.S. (Fred E. Sadoff) Plays, Ltd., presented *The Complaisant Lover* (Ethel Barrymore Th., N.Y.C., Nov. 1, 1961); directed and produced *The Jackhammer* (Theatre Marquee, Feb. 5, 1962); David Black by arrangement with Peter Daubeny, Michael Redgrave Productions and F.E.S. (Fred E. Sadoff) Plays, Ltd., presented *The Aspern Papers* (Playhouse, Feb. 7, 1962); directed and produced the English-speaking world premier of Eugene O'Neill's *Hughie* (Duchess, London, June 1963); toured South Africa for four weeks as Nick in *Who's Afraid of Virginia Woolf?* (Durban, Sept. 10, 1963); and appeared as Jamie and Daniel Wallace in and directed his own two one-act plays, *Games* (Arts, London, Sept. 29, 1964).

Films. He performed in *Viva Zapata!* (20th-Fox, 1952); and in *The Quiet American* (UA, 1958).

Television. Mr. Sadoff has appeared on such shows as Omnibus (CBS, 1952); Philco Television Playhouse (NBC, 1952); Robert Montgomery Presents (NBC, 1952); and on The Big Story (NBC, 1952).

In London, he adapted *The Thirteen Clocks* (Motorola TV, 1954); and appeared on the series Suspense (BBC, 1963).

Night Clubs. He performed at the Village Vanguard (N.Y.C., 1950).

Recreation. Swimming, reading, music.

SAIDY, FRED. Playwright, director, lyricist, writer. b. Fareed Milhem Saidy, Feb. 11, 1907, Los Angeles, Calif., to Milhem A. and Nejiba (Ablan) Saidy. Father, importer; mother, business woman. Grad. Manual Training H.S., Brooklyn, N.Y., 1924; New York Univ., B.C.S. (Journalism) 1927. Married Nov. 25, 1935, to Marie Mallouk; two sons, one daughter. Member of Dramatists Guild; ALA.

Pre-Theatre. Journalism, import business.

Theatre. Mr. Saidy contributed, with Paul Francis Webster, Arthur Ross, and others, sketches to the revue, *Rally Round the Girls* (Assistance League Playhouse, Hollywood, Calif., Feb. 5, 1942); with Sig Herzig, wrote the book for *Bloomer Girl* (Shubert Th., N.Y.C., Oct. 5, 1944); and, with E. Y. Harburg, wrote the book for *Finian's Rainbow* (46th St. Th., Jan. 10, 1947); with Mr. Harburg, wrote and directed *Flahooley*, which they also produced, in association with Cheryl Crawford (Broadhurst, May 14, 1951); with Mr. Harburg, wrote *Jollyanna* (Philharmonic Aud., Los Angeles, Calif.; Curran, San Francisco, Calif., Summer 1952) and *Jamaica* (Imperial, N.Y.C., Oct. 31, 1957); with Henry Myers, collaborated on the book for *The Happiest Girl in the World* (Martin Beck Th., Apr. 3, 1961); and with Mr. Harburg, wrote the book for *I Got a Song* (pre-Bway: opened Studio Arena, Buffalo, N.Y., Sept. 26, 1974; closed there Oct. 20, 1974).

Films. Mr. Saidy contributed material to *Star Spangled Rhythm* (Par., 1942); collaborated on the screenplays for *I Dood It* (MGM, 1943) and *Meet the People* (MGM, 1944); and wrote Ed Wynn's narration for *The Sound of Laughter* (1963).

Television and Radio. He has been a guest panelist on both radio and television shows (NBC, CBS, 1946–to date). He was staff writer for NBC-TV musical spectaculars (1954–55), and appeared on Championship Bridge (ABC, 1961) as guest expert.

Published Works. Mr. Saidy has contributed articles and verse to *Stage, Saturday Review*, NY *World*, NY *Herald Tribune*, NY *Times*, and has been columnist on *Broadway* magazine.

Awards. For *Finian's Rainbow*, Mr. Saidy and Mr. Harburg won the Donaldson (1946–47) and the George Jean Nathan (1946–47) awards. He also received the Essex (N.J.) County Symphony Society Achievement Award (1948).

Recreation. Contract bridge, light verse writing.

SAINT-SUBBER, ARNOLD. Producer. b. Feb. 18, 1918, Washington, D.C., to Saul and Rose Subber. Father and mother, ticket brokers. Member of League of NY Theatres.

Theatre. Mr. Saint-Subber was assistant stage manager for *Hellzapoppin* (46 St. Th., N.Y.C., Sept. 22, 1938); was assistant to John Murray Anderson for Billy Rose's Aquacade (NY World's Fair, 1939), and the Ringling Brothers Circus (1942); assistant to producer Otto Preminger for *Woodrow Wilson;* and *The More the Merrier* (Cort, Sept. 15, 1941); assistant to Mr. Anderson for *Ziegfeld Follies* (Winter Garden, Apr. 1, 1943), and *The Firebrand of Florence* (Alvin, Mar. 22, 1945); and production supervisor for *Hollywood Pinafore* (Alvin, May 31, 1945), and *Park Avenue* (Shubert, Nov. 4, 1946). With Lemuel Ayers, he produced *Kiss Me, Kate* (New Century, Dec. 30, 1948), and *Out of This World* (New Century, Dec. 21, 1950).

Mr. Saint-Subber produced, in association with Rita Allen, *The Grass Harp* (Martin Beck Th., Mar. 27, 1952); with Rita Allen and Archie Thomson, *My Three Angels* (Morosco, Mar. 11, 1953); produced *House of Flowers* (Alvin, Dec. 30, 1954); produced with Figaro, Inc., *The Square Root of Wonderful* (National, Oct. 30, 1957); produced with Elia Kazan, *The Dark at the Top of the Stairs* (Music Box, Dec. 5, 1957); and with Arthur Cantor, *The Tenth Man* (Booth, Nov. 5, 1959).

He produced, with Lester Osterman, *A Loss of Roses* (Eugene O'Neill Th., Nov. 28, 1959); with Frank Prince in association with David Black, *Look: We've Come Through* (Hudson, Oct. 25, 1961); in association with Ben Edwards and Wigwam Productions, *Harold* (Cort, Nov. 29, 1962); and produced *Barefoot in the Park* (Biltmore, Oct. 23, 1963).

He also produced *The Star-Spangled Girl* (Plymouth, Dec. 21, 1966); *Dr. Cook's Garden* (Belasco Th., Sept. 25, 1967); supervised the Repertory Th. of Lincoln Ctr. revival of *The Little Foxes* (Vivian Beaumont Th., Oct. 26, 1967); produced a revival of *House of Flowers* (Th. de Lys, Jan. 28, 1968); produced *Plaza Suite* (Plymouth, Feb. 14, 1968); *Carry Me Back to Morningside Heights* (John Golden Th., Feb. 27, 1968); with Lester Osterman, *Weekend* (Broadhurst, Mar. 13, 1968); produced *Last of the Red Hot Lovers* (Eugene O'Neill Th., Dec. 28, 1969); *The Gingerbread Lady* (Plymouth, Dec. 13, 1970); *The Prisoner of Second Avenue* (Eugene O'Neill Th., Nov. 11, 1971); and *Gigi* (Uris Th., Nov. 13, 1973).

Awards. *Last of the Red Hot Lovers* and *The Prisoner of Second Avenue* received Antoinette Perry (Tony) Award nominations as best plays of their respective seasons.

SAKS, GENE. Actor, director. b. Jean Michael Saks, Nov. 8, 1921, New York City, to Morris J. and Beatrix (Lewkowitz) Saks. Father, shoe wholesaler. Grad. Hackensack (N.J.) H.S., 1939; Cornell Univ., A.B. 1943. Studied theatre at Dramatic Workshop, N.Y.C., 1946–48; with Lee Strasberg, Sanford Meisner and David Pressman at Actors Studio (member 1948–to date). Married May 28, 1950, to Beatrice Arthur, actress, singer; two sons. Served US Navy, 1943–46, ETO, FETO; rank, Lt. (jg). Member of AEA; AFTRA; SAG; SSD&C.

Theatre. Mr. Saks made his first stage appearance as Lord Fancourt Babberley in a high school production of *Charley's Aunt* (1939); he formed, with Kim Stanley and Michael Gazzo, a co-op company which rented the Cherry Lane Th. (N.Y.C.), and made his professional debut as Joxer Daly in that company's production of *Juno and the Paycock* (June, 1947); appearing in their subsequent productions as the Vicar, the Poet, and in other roles in *The Dog Beneath the Skin* (July 21, 1947), the Engineer in *Gas* (Aug. 1947), the title role in Pirandello's *Henry IV* (Sept. 1947), and Rene St. Gall in *The Watched Pot* (Oct. 28, 1947).

He played the Butler in *Topaze* (Morosco, Dec. 27, 1947); and with the afore-mentioned co-op company, played at the Provincetown Playhouse in repertory, as the Old Shepherd in *The Infernal Machine*, the Park Attendant in *Within the Gates*, and the Doctor in *him* (from June, 1948); and played a third season (at the Cherry Lane Th.) as the German in *Yes is for a Very Young Man* (June, 1949), the Professor of Religion in *Too Many Thumbs* (Aug. 1949), and Monsieur Jordan in *The Bourgeois Gentleman* (Sept. 1949). He played Sam, the Second Discusser and Marty's double in *All You Need Is One Good Break* (Mansfield, Feb. 9, 1950); toured as Stefanowski in *Mister Roberts* (May 30, 1950–May 30, 1951); and played a season of stock at the Circle Th. (Chelsea Hotel, Atlantic City, N.J., June–July 1951) as the Baron in *Candlelight*, the Chauffeur in *Personal Appearance*, Bill Page in *The Voice of the Turtle*, Wilbur in *For Love or Money*, and appeared in *Missouri Legend*.

He succeeded (Fall 1951) Sidney Armus as the Professor during the run of *South Pacific* (Majestic, Apr. 7, 1949); played the Servant in *Coriolanus* (Phoenix, Jan. 19, 1954); appeared as a comedian in a revue at the Camp Tamiment (Pa.) Th. (July 1954); played the Wicked Duke in *The Thirteen Clocks* (Westport Country Playhouse, Conn.; Mt. Kisco, N.Y.; Somerset, Mass., Summer 1954); Billy Gordon in *Late Love* (Westchester Playhouse, N.Y., Aug. 1954); Ragnar Brovik in *The Master Builder* (Phoenix, Mar. 1, 1955); the Professor in *South Pacific* (NY City Ctr., May 4, 1955); Charlie Reader in *The Tender Trap* (Westchester Playhouse, Aug. 1955); Richard Sherman in *The Seven Year Itch* (Westchester Playhouse, June 1956); Del Rio in *The Gimmick* (Westport Country Playhouse, July 1956); Dr. Mohodan, Pvt. Jessel and other roles in *Johnny Johnson* (Carnegie Hall Playhouse, Oct. 21, 1956); the First God in *The Good Woman of Setzuan* (Phoenix, Dec. 18, 1956); succeeded (Feb. 1957) Martin Balsam as the Son-in-Law in *Middle of the Night* (ANTA, Feb. 8, 1956); played the Marquis of Forlipopli in *The Mistress of the Inn* (Bucks County Playhouse, New Hope, Pa., July 1957); Charlie Reader in *The Tender Trap* (Cape Playhouse, Dennis, Mass., July 1957); the Officer in *The Infernal Machine* (Phoenix, Feb. 3, 1958); the Professor in *Howie* (46 St. Th., Sept. 17, 1958); appeared in *A Circle of Wheels* (Lester Horton Dance Th., Mar. 1959); and appeared in various roles in *Album Leaves* at the Festival of Two Worlds, (Ciai Melisso Th., Spoleto, Italy, June 1959).

Mr. Saks played the Rabbi in *The Tenth Man* (Booth, N.Y.C., Nov. 5, 1959); Norman Yarrow in *Love and Libel* (Martin Beck Th., Dec. 7, 1960); Morestan in *A Shot in the Dark* (Booth, Oct. 18, 1961); and Leo Herman (Chuckles) in *A Thousand Clowns* (Eugene O'Neill Th., Apr. 5, 1962). He directed *Enter Laughing* (Henry Miller's Th., Mar. 13, 1963); a summer tour of *The Millionairess* (1963); *Nobody Loves an Albatross* (Lyceum, N.Y.C., Dec. 19, 1963); *Half a Sixpence* (Broadhurst, Apr. 25, 1965; national company opened Curran, San Francisco, July 26, 1966); *Generation* (Morosco, Oct. 6, 1965); *Mame* (Winter Garden, May 24, 1966; first national company opened Mechanic, Baltimore, Md., Aug. 29, 1967; second national company opened Curran, San Francisco, Apr. 30, 1968); the pre-Bway tryout of *A Mother's Kisses* (opened Shubert, New Haven, Sept. 23, 1968; closed Mechanic, Baltimore, Oct. 19, 1968); *Sheep on the Runway* (Helen Hayes Th., N.Y.C., Jan. 31, 1970); *How the Other Half Loves* (Royale, Mar. 29, 1971); and *Same Time, Next Year* (Brooks Atkinson Th., Mar. 13, 1975).

Films. Mr. Saks appeared as Leo ("Chuckles") in *A Thousand Clowns* (UA, 1965). The first film he directed was *Barefoot in the Park* (Par., 1967); followed by *The Odd Couple* (Par., 1968); *Cactus Flower* (Col., 1969); *Last of the Red Hot Lovers* (Par., 1972); and *Mame* (WB, 1974). He appeared as the Brother in *The Prisoner of Second Avenue* (WB, 1975).

Television. Mr. Saks has appeared on the Actors Studio Series (1949); US Steel Hour (CBS); Armstrong Circle Th. (CBS); Camera Three (CBS); You Are There (CBS); Brenner; Bachelor Father (NBC); Philco Television Playhouse (NBC); Goodyear Playhouse (NBC); Kaiser Aluminum Hour (NBC); Producers Showcase (NBC); Playwrights '55; Playwrights '56; and Studio One (CBS).

SALMI, ALBERT. Actor. b. 1928. Grad. Haaren H.S., N.Y.C. Studied acting at Dramatic Workshop, N.Y.C.; Amer. Th. Wing, N.Y.C.; Actors Studio, N.Y.C. Married May 10, 1956, to Peggy Ann Garner, actress; one daughter. Member of AEA; SAG; AFTRA.

Pre-Theatre. Pinkerton detective.

Theatre. Mr. Salmi made his stage debut in *The Scarecrow* (Th. de Lys, N.Y.C., June 16, 1953); subsequently played Roger Gatt in *End as a Man* (Th. de Lys, Sept. 15, 1953; moved Vanderbilt, Oct. 14, 1953); Jim Curry in *The Rainmaker* (Cort, Oct. 28, 1954); Bo Decker in *Bus Stop* (Music Box, Mar. 2, 1955), also touring in it (opened Aud., Central City, Colo., Aug. 15, 1955); Yank Sun in *The Good Woman of Setzuan* (Phoenix, N.Y.C., Dec. 18, 1956); the title role in *Howie* (46 St. Th., Sept. 17, 1958); He in *The Failures* (Fourth St. Th., Jan. 5, 1959); John Paul Jones in *Once There Was a Russian* (Music Box, Feb. 18, 1961); Matt Burke in *Anna Christie* (Huntington Hartford Th., Hollywood, Calif., May 2, 1966); succeeded (Oct. 14, 1968) Pat Hingle as Victor Franz in *The Price* (Morosco, N.Y.C., Feb. 7, 1968); and repeated that role in London (Duke of York's Th., Mar. 4, 1969).

Films. Mr. Salmi appeared in *The Brothers Karamazov* (MGM, 1958); *The Unforgiven* (UA, 1960); *The Bravados* (20th-Fox, 1958); *Wild River* (20th-Fox, 1960); *The Outrage* (MGM, 1964); and *The Flim-Flam Man* (20th-Fox, 1967).

Television. He appeared as Holmes in *Survival* (US Steel Hour, CBS, Nov. 7, 1956); Putnam Cox in *Most Blessed Woman* (Kraft Television Th., NBC, Jan. 23, 1957); in *Man Under Glass* (CBS, July 15, 1958); as Peter Sheeran in *The Old Foolishness* (Play of the Week, WNTA, Mar. 6, 1961); in *Noon on Doomsday* (Th. Guild, CBS); and in *The Mary S. McDowell Story* (Profiles in Courage, NBC, Nov. 15, 1964).

He has also appeared on such series as Destry (ABC); The Defenders (CBS); The Fugitive (ABC); Rawhide (CBS); Daniel Boone (NBC); Eleventh Hour (Ind.); Trailmaster (ABC); Stoney Burke (Ind.); Twilight Zone (CBS); Naked City (Ind.); The Virginian (NBC); I Spy (NBC); Laredo (NBC); Untouchables (ABC); Shenandoah (ABC); Gunsmoke (CBS); The Big Valley (ABC); Voyage (ABC); Jesse James (ABC); Route 66 (Ind.); The FBI (ABC); 12 O'Clock High (ABC); Petrocelli (NBC); and Kung Fu (ABC).

Awards. For his performance in *The Price*, Mr. Salmi tied with Harold Gary for best male supporting performance in a play in the 1968–69 *Variety* poll of London critics.

Recreation. Painting.

SAMROCK, VICTOR. Theatre manager, producer. b. Gabriel Victor Samrock, Sept. 5, 1907, New York City, to Samuel and Yetta (Sole) Samrock. Grad. Boys H.S., Brooklyn, N.Y., City Coll. of New York, B.S. 1932. Married Sept. 7, 1937, to Hyla Roberts; one son, one daughter. Member of ATPAM (bd., 1946–49); League of NY Theatres (bd. of gov.); Actors' Fund of America. Address: (home) 16 W. 77th St., New York, NY 10024; (bus.) 745 Fifth Ave., New York, NY 10022, tel. (212) PL 1-1290.

Theatre. Mr. Samrock was general manager of *Double Door* (Ritz, Sept. 21, 1933); *Wednesday's Child* (Longacre, Jan. 16, 1934); and *Kind Lady* (Booth, Apr. 23, 1935). He was company manager at the Cape Playhouse (Dennis, Mass., 1936); and general manager for *Yes, My Darling Daughter* (Playhouse, N.Y.C., Feb. 9, 1937). During 1937–55, he was general manager and vice-president of the Playwrights Company.

Mr. Samrock was also general manager and associate producer for Roger L. Stevens, presenting such productions as *The Best Man* (Morosco, N.Y.C., Mar. 31, 1960); *Mary, Mary* (Helen Hayes Th., Mar. 8, 1961); *A Far Country* (Music Box, Apr. 4, 1961); *The Caretaker* (Lyceum, Oct. 4, 1961); *The Private Ear and the Public Eye* (Morosco, Oct. 9, 1963); and *A Case of Libel* (Longacre, Oct. 10, 1963). Since 1963, Mr. Samrock has acted as manager and associate for such producers as Joel Schenker, Mary Frank; for Richard Gregson for *Cyrano* (Palace, N.Y.C., May 13, 1973); Harold Fielding for *Gone with the Wind* (Dorothy Chandler Pavilion, Los Angeles, Calif., Aug. 28, 1973); and the Theatre Guild for *Absurd Person Singular* (Music Box, N.Y.C., Oct. 8, 1974).

SAND, PAUL. Actor. b. Pablo Sanchez, Mar. 5, 1935, Santa Monica, Calif. Studied acting with Viola Spolins, Los Angeles; mime with Marcel Marceau, France and Switzerland.

Theatre. Mr. Sand began his career as a dancer with Judy Garland in her touring show (c. 1958). With the improvisational Second City troupe (Chicago, Ill.), he appeared in *Too Many Hats* (Feb. 15, 1960); *The Third Programme* (July 1960); *The Seacoast of Bohemia* (1960); *From the Second City* (Royale, N.Y.C., Sept. 26, 1961); and *The Water Tower* (Second City at Square East, Apr. 3, 1963).

He played Arthur in *Journey to the Day* (Th. de Lys, N.Y.C., Nov. 11, 1963); appeared in the musical revue *Wet Paint* (Renata, Apr. 12, 1965); played Max in *Hotel Passionato* (East 74 St. Th., Oct. 22, 1965); appeared in *The Mad Show* (New, Jan. 9, 1966); replaced Richard Benjamin (July 1, 1967) in the role of Norman Conell in *The Star Spangled Girl* (Plymouth, Dec. 21, 1966); and appeared with Paul Sills' *Story Theatre* (Ambassador, Oct. 26, 1970).

Mr. Sand wrote and performed in a one-act play entitled *Luis from Work* at the Festival of Two Worlds (Spoleto, Italy, Summer 1963).

Films. Mr. Sand played Morrie in *A Great Big Thing* (Aarofilm, 1968); Moreno in *Viva Max!* (Commonwealth United, 1970); Greenberg in *Hot Rock* (20th-Fox, 1973); and Benny Napkins in *Every Little Crook and Nanny* (MGM, 1972).

Television. He appeared with Sid Caesar on *As Caesar Sees It* (ABC); with *The Story Theatre* (ABC); was a guest on The Carol Burnett Show (CBS); appeared on The Mary Tyler Moore Show (CBS); and played Robert Dreyfus in the series Paul Sand in Friends and Lovers (CBS).

Awards. Mr. Sand received the Antoinette Perry (Tony) Award for Best Supporting Actor (1970–71) for his performance in *Story Theatre*..

SANDLE, FLOYD. Educator. b. Floyd Leslie Sandle, July 4, 1913, Magnolia, Miss., to Leslie and Essie (Hampton) Sandle. Grad. Dillard Univ. B.A. 1937; Univ. of Chicago, M.A. 1947; attended New York Univ., 1951–52; Louisiana State Univ., Ph.D. 1959. Married June 17, 1941, to Marie Johnson; two sons, three daughters. Served USN, 1943–45, PTO; rank, Boatswain's Mate 2/C. Member of AETA; SAA; SSA; NADSA (pres., 1955–57; publicity dir., 1959–63); Omega Psi Phi; Kappa Delta Pi. Address: (home) 102 Richmond Dr., Grambling, LA 71245, tel. (318) CH 7-3787; (bus.) Grambling College, Box 43, Grambling, LA 71245, tel. (318) CH 7-3761.

Since 1963, Mr. Sandle has served as Dean of the Division of General Studies at Grambling Coll., where he has been a member of the faculty since 1938 (instructor, 1937–38; asst. professor of social sciences and English, 1945–47; head of the dept. of speech and drama, 1947–49, 1950–68; acting dean of the college, (1949–50). During 1972–73, he was visiting professor of speech at Louisiana State Univ., Baton Rouge.

Published Works. He has contributed articles to *Speech Teacher* and *Developments in Speech*.

SANDOR, ALFRED. Actor. b. Alfred Heymann Sandwina, Nov. 5, 1918, Budapest, Hungary, to Maximillian Heymann and Katerina (Brummbach) Sandwina. Father, circus acrobat and equestrian; mother, billed as world's strongest woman with Barnum and Bailey Circus. Attended public school in Berlin, Germany, 1924–29; London, England, 1929–30; grad. P.S. 69, Queens, N.Y., 1934; attended Newtown H.S., Queens, 1934–35; Univ. of Pennsylvania, 1941–42. Studied for the theatre with Max Reinhardt, Salzburg Festspielhaus, 1926; MacGowan Acad. and Wolter Acad., N.Y.C., 1937–40. Married Apr. 7, 1956, to Tanagra Markham, writer; one son. Served US Army Air Corps, 1941–43, aviation cadet; Counter Intelligence Corps, special agent Seventh Army, 1943–45; rank, Sgt. Member of AEA; AFTRA; SAG.

Theatre. Mr. Sandor's first appearance on a stage was as Theseus, Duke of Athens, in a grade-school production of *A Midsummer Night's Dream* (June 1934). Billed as Al Sandwina, he made his professional debut in N.Y.C. as Patsy in *Three Men on a Horse* (Cherry Lane, Aug. 1939), which he followed by portraying Donald Meadows in *The Bishop Misbehaves* (65 St. Th., Jan. 1940). He played Mannion and Dowdy in a national touring company of *Mister Roberts* (opened Klein Aud., Bridgeport, Conn., Sept. 13, 1951; closed Ford's, Baltimore, Md., May 24, 1952); produced, directed, and played Matthew in *Murder Without Crime* (Central Plaza, N.Y.C., Oct. 1952); changed his name to Alfred Sandor and played a season of stock in roles that included Mr. Cherry in *The Silver Whistle*, Preacher Haggler in *Dark of the Moon*, and Shepherd Henderson in *Bell, Book and Candle* (Totem Pole Playhouse, Caledonia State Park, Fayetteville, Pa., Summer 1953); played Giacoppetti in *Detective Story* (Hilltop Th., York, Pa., Oct. 26, 1963); replaced one of the Waiters (Nov. 23, 1953) in *Wish You Were Here* (Imperial, N.Y.C., June 25, 1952), and played the same role and understudied the part of Pinky Harris in the Chicago company (Shubert, Dec. 8, 1953).

He appeared as Colonel Izquierdo in an ELT production of *Montserrat* (Lenox Hill Playhouse, Apr. 7, 1954; moved Barbizon-Plaza, May 25, 1954); played a season of stock in roles that included Geoffrey in *The Two Mrs. Carrolls*, Renato Di Rossi in *The Time of the Cuckoo*, and Detective McLeod in *Detective Story* (Lakeside Summer Th., Lake Hopatcong, N.J., Summer 1954); appeared as John Brown in *In Splendid Error* (Greenwich Mews, N.Y.C., Oct. 26, 1954); played a season of winter stock in roles that included John Buchanan, Jr., in *Summer and Smoke*, Joseph in *My Three Angels*, and Renato Di Rossi in *The Time of the Cuckoo* (Palm Tree Playhouse, Sarasota, Fla., Jan.–Apr. 1955); appeared as Lt. Stephan Maryk in a summer touring production of *The Caine Mutiny Court Martial* (1955); Capt. Gus Jablonski and was understudy to Arthur Kennedy in the role of Lt. Col. William F. Edwards in *Time Limit!* (Booth, N.Y.C., Jan. 24, 1956); played a season of winter stock in roles that included Joe McCall in *The Tender Trap*, Lt. Stephan Maryk in *The Caine Mutiny Court-Martial*, Max Pincus in *The Fifth Season*, Edward L. McKeever in *The Solid Gold Cadillac*, Prince Bounine in *Anastasia*, and Will in *Bus Stop* (Palm Tree Playhouse, Sarasota, Fla., Feb.–Apr. 1956).

Mr. Sandor played Pinky Harris in *Wish You Were Here* (Cape Cod Melody Tent, Hyannis, Mass., June 1956); succeeded (July 1956) Ed Peck in the role of the Captain and was understudy to Royal Beal as General Pollard in *No Time for Sergeants* (Alvin, N.Y.C., Oct. 20, 1955); succeeded (Dec. 1957) Sydney Walker in the title role in the Shakespearewrights' production of *Julius Caesar* (Shakespearewrights' Th., Oct. 23, 1957); played General Pollard and the Captain in a summer touring production of *No Time for Sergeants* (1958); was general understudy in *Third Best Sport* (Ambassador, N.Y.C., Dec. 30, 1958); played Jefferson Davis in *The Confederates* (Th. Marquee, Sept. 28, 1959); Oliver in an ANTA matinee series production of *This Music Crept By Me Upon the Waters* (Th. de Lys, Nov. 24, 1959); directed *Duet for Two Hands* (Th. Cyclorama, St. John's in the Village, Apr. 22, 1960); played Agamemnon in *The Prodigal* (Boston Arts Festival, June 3, 1960); the Judge in *Han's Crime* and Toyama in *The Damask Drum*, two of *Three Modern Japanese Plays* (Players Th., N.Y.C., Feb. 3, 1961); and directed Chekhov's *The Boor* on a program entitled *Cuttings in Style* (E. 74 St. Th., Feb. 13, 1961).

He succeeded (Mar. 20, 1961) Richard Porter in the role of Pastey in *Gypsy* (Bway Th., May 21, 1959); played Herbie in the Bway national touring company of *Gypsy* (opened Rochester, N.Y., Aud., Mar. 29, 1961; closed American, St. Louis, Mo., Dec. 9, 1961); repeated the role of Herbie in a Guber, Ford, and Gross touring production of *Gypsy* (Aug.–Oct. 1962); again played Herbie in *Gypsy* (Paper Mill Playhouse, Millburn, N.J., Oct. 29, 1962); played Otto Vidor in *On an Open Roof* (Booth, N.Y.C., Jan. 28, 1963); was understudy for Walter Matthau in the role of Herman Halpern in *My Mother, My Father and Me* (Plymouth, Mar. 23, 1963); became standby (Apr. 22, 1963) for Jack Klugman in the role of Caesario Grimaldi in *Tchin-Tchin* (Ethel Barrymore Th., Oct. 25, 1962); played Herbie in *Gypsy* (St. Louis Municipal Opera, Mo., Aug. 5, 1963); played the Reader and understudied Peter Bull in the role of Tetzel in *Luther* (St. James, N.Y.C., Sept. 25, 1963), and played the Prior and Eck in the touring company (opened Natl., Washington, D.C., Mar. 30, 1964; closed Blackstone, Chicago, Ill., June 13, 1964). He played the Duke of Norfolk in *A Man for All Seasons* (Playhouse-in-the-Park, Philadelphia, Pa., July 27, 1964); Paul Cantrell in *No Sometime Thing* (Adelphi Coll. Summer Th., Garden City, L.I., N.Y., Aug. 13, 1964); and Cajetan and the Prior in the national touring company of *Luther* (opened Center Th., Norfolk, Va., Oct. 2, 1964).

He succeeded Paul Dooley as Speed in *The Odd Couple* (Plymouth, N.Y.C., Mar. 10, 1965), was standby for Walter Matthau as Oscar in the same production, and succeeded (Nov. 1965) Mr. Matthau; was standby for George C. Scott in *Plaza Suite* (Plymouth, Feb. 14, 1968) and played the triple role (May 13–22, 1968) during Mr. Scott's illness; and played Elliott Hartman in *Zelda* (Ethel Barrymore Th., Mar. 5, 1969).

Television and Radio. Mr. Sandor was radio program director at Shaw Field (Sumter, S.C., 1943). He made his TV debut as a Policeman on Danger (CBS, 1951), which was followed by appearances on such programs as The Web (CBS, 1951); Suspense (CBS, 1951); Casey Crime Photographer (CBS, 1952); the Phil Silvers Show (CBS, 1958); The Verdict Is Yours (CBS, 1959–60); played the Insurance Lawyer on Our Five Daughters (CBS, June–July, 1959); appeared on *Shadow of a Soldier* (American Heritage, NBC, Feb. 1960); *Honeyman* (American Heritage, NBC, Jan. 1961); and *To Spend, to Give, to Want* (The Nurses, CBS, June 1964).

Recreation. Softball, antique collecting.

SANDS, DOROTHY. Actress, director, teacher. b. Cambridge, Mass., Mar. 5, 1893, to Frank Edgar and Lydia Reynolds (Phipps) Sands. Father, flour merchant. Grad. Cambridge Latin Sch., 1911; Radcliffe Coll., B.A. 1915. Studied at Curry Sch. of Expression, Boston, Mass., 1918; Central Sch. of Speech and Drama, London, 1920; studied drama with George Pierce Baker, Harvard 47 Workshop, 1913–15, 1919–23; phonetics with Dr. William Tilly, 1915–16; speaking voice with Prof. Irvah Winter, 1914–15, Richard Wood Cone, 1915, and Laura Elliot, 1924–28; acting with Maria Ouspenskaya, 1927; singing with Esther Mathieu, 1938–40, H. Wellington Smith, 1952–55 and Keith Davis, 1963. Member of AEA (council, 1956–71; pres. of ELT bd. of dir., 1964–67 and bd. mbr., 1964–to date); AFTRA; ANTA; IASTA (mbr., adv. bd.); SAG; Cosmopolitan Club; Radcliffe Club of N.Y.C.

Theatre. Miss Sands made her debut as Pansy Purple in a Cambridge Latin Sch. production of *Miss Buzby's Boarders* (1910); subsequently wrote and directed a historical pageant, *The Spirit of Niagara* (Niagara Falls, N.Y., July 4, 1919); made her professional debut as Jane in the national touring production of *Children of the Moon* (Studebaker, Chicago, Ill., Dec. 12, 1923); and her Bway debut as Nautcha Tenneych in *Catskill Dutch* (Belmont, May 6, 1924).

She joined the Neighborhood Playhouse Repertory company and appeared with it at the Neighborhood Playhouse as Radanika and Vasantasena's Mother in *The Little Clay Cart* (Dec. 5, 1924); Beatrice Justice in *Exiles* (Feb. 19, 1925); a dancer in *The Legend of the Dance* (Mar. 31, 1925); Mrs. Dangle and the Confidant in *The Critic* (May 8, 1925); an impersonator in *The Grand Street Follies* (June 18, 1925), an annual satirical revue; Frade in *The Dybbuk* (Dec. 15, 1925); Grilletta in an adaptation of Haydn's opera *The Apothecary* one of a triple-bill (Mar. 16, 1926); Dona Barbarita in *The Romantic Young Lady* (May 4, 1926); in another edition of *The Grand Street Follies* (June 15, 1926); Arabella in *The Lion Tamer* (Oct. 7, 1926); The Jane in *Pinwheel* (Feb. 3, 1927); Isabella in *Commedia dell'Arte*, part of a triple-bill titled *Lyric Drama* (Apr. 5, 1927); and in another edition of *The Grand Street Follies* (May 19, 1927).

She appeared on Bway as Clotilde in *The Stairs* (Bijou, Nov. 7, 1927); in another edition of *The Grand Street Follies* (Booth, May 28, 1928); and as the Nightclub Hostess in the musical, *Well, Well, Well*, titled *Pleasure Bound*, on its pre-Bway tryout (Philadelphia, Pa., Feb. 1929).

Miss Sands appeared as Irina Arkadin in *The Seagull* (Comedy, N.Y.C., Apr. 9, 1929); in the final edition of *The Grand Street Follies* (Booth, May 1, 1929); as Helena Grey in *Half Gods* (Plymouth, Dec. 21, 1929); Emily Coster in *Many-a-Slip* (Little, Feb. 3, 1930), and on tour; Dona Barbarita in a stock production of *The Romantic Young Lady* (Westchester County Playhouse, Mt. Kisco, N.Y., July 1930); Winifred Satterlee Dexter in *Rock Me, Julie* (Royale, N.Y.C., Feb. 3, 1931); Julie Cavendish in *The Royal Family* (Shubert-Riviera, Apr. 1931); in stock, at the Mt. Vernon (N.Y.) Playhouse, played Alda in *Death Takes a Holiday*, Alice Peabody in *It's a Wise Child*, and Miss Krail in *Philip Goes Forth* (May–June 1931); Prossy in *Candida* (Red Barn Th., Locust Valley, N.Y., July 1931); and Mrs. Dangle and the Confidant in *The Critic* (Westchester County Playhouse, Mt. Kisco, N.Y., July 1931).

She presented her one-woman show, *Styles in Action* (Booth, N.Y.C., Sunday evenings, Apr. 3 and 10, 1932), and on tour; appeared in another one-woman presentation, *Our Stage and Stars* (Little, Nov. 11, 1933), and on tour (US, Canada, 1933–36).

Miss Sands appeared as Lady Teazle in *The School for Scandal* (Millbrook Summer Th., N.Y., July 1934); the title role in *Candida* (Barnstormers Th., Tamworth, N.H., July 1937); *The Inconstant Moon* (Newport Casino Th., R.I., Aug. 1937); Phoebe Eldredge in *Rain From Heaven* at the Ann Arbor (Univ. of Michigan) Dramatic Festival (Lydia Mendelssohn Th., June 1938); Gertrude in *Fashion* (Newport Casino Th., R.I., July 1938); Prossy in a touring production of *Candida* (1939–40); in stock, Miss Shoe in *At Mrs. Beam's*, Lady Grace Pierson in *Not in Our Stars*, and Rose in *Madame X* (Newport Casino Th., R.I., July–Aug. 1940); Mrs. Whitelaw and Mrs. Murdoch in *Jeannie* (Paper Mill Playhouse, Millburn, N.J., Nov. 1940); Emily in *Ladies in Retirement* (Bucks County Playhouse, New Hope, Pa., June 1941); Ellen Smith in *By Your Leave* (Ogunquit Playhouse, Me., July 1941); Barbara Fawcett in *The Constant Wife* (Marblehead Playhouse, Mass., July 1941); and Laura Merrick in *The Vinegar Tree* (Larchmont Th., Toledo, Ohio, Aug. 1941).

She appeared as Mrs. Yoder in *Papa Is All* (Guild, N.Y.C., Jan. 6, 1942); Josephine Bender in *All the Comforts of Home* (Longacre, May 25, 1942); in the title role in *The Duenna* (Cape Playhouse, Dennis, Mass.; McCarter Th., Princeton, N.J., July 1942); as Cornelia Van Gorder in *The Bat* (Cape Playhouse, Dennis, Mass., Aug. 1942); Jessie Frame in *Tomorrow the World* (Ethel Barrymore Th., N.Y.C., Apr. 14, 1943); in stock, Mrs. Mopply in *Too True To Be Good* (Lakewood Playhouse, Barnesville, Pa.; Playhouse-in-the-Park, Philadelphia, Pa., July 1945); Tina in *A Joy Forever* (Biltmore, N.Y.C., Jan. 7, 1946); in stock, Mrs. Apley in *The Late George Apley* (Cape Playhouse, Dennis, Mass.; Bucks County Playhouse, New Hope, Pa., July 1946); Martha Brewster in *Arsenic and Old Lace* (Bucks County Playhouse, July 1947); Abby in *The Late Christopher Bean* and Annie Jones in *Years Ago* (Clinton Summer Th., N.J., Aug. 1947); and Lady Catherine Champion-Cheney in *The Circle* (Brattle Th., Cambridge, Mass., July 1948).

She appeared in her one-woman presentation of *American Theatre Highlights* (Little, N.Y.C., May 10, 1949; Mercury, London, June 12, 1949), and in Germany, under the auspices of the State Dept., as part of the reorientation program (Heidelberg, Berlin, Comburg, Frankfurt, Munich, July 2–13, 1949); played Princess Beatrice in a stock production of *The Swan*, and Grace Winslow in *The Winslow Boy* (Bucks County Playhouse, New Hope, Pa., Aug. 1949); Mother Hildebrand in *The Velvet Glove* (Bucks County Playhouse, July 1950); Countess Lister in *Yes, M'Lord* (South Shore Music Circus, Cohasset, Mass.; Brattle Th., Cambridge, Mass.,

July 1950); and Mrs. Tarleton in *Misalliance* (Brattle Th., Cambridge, Mass., Aug. 1950).

Miss Sands appeared as Maud Mayo in *The Cellar and the Well* (ANTA, N.Y.C., Dec. 10, 1950); Aunt Queenie in a touring production of *Bell, Book and Candle* (1952–53); Mrs. Tarleton in *Misalliance* (NY City Ctr., Feb. 18, 1953); Octavia, Countess of Bonnington, in *Quadrille* (Coronet, Nov. 3, 1954); Aaronetta Gibbs in *Morning's at Seven* (Bucks County Playhouse, New Hope, Pa., July 1955); Cornelia Knight in *The First Gentleman* (Belasco, N.Y.C., Apr. 25, 1957); Lavinia Penniman in *The Heiress* (Paper Mill Playhouse, Millburn, N.J., Sept. 1957); Hannah Kennedy in *Mary Stuart* (Phoenix, N.Y.C., Oct. 8, 1957); and succeeded (Jan. 1958) Helen Hayes as the Duchess in *Time Remembered* (Morosco, Nov. 12, 1957). On a Rockefeller Foundation grant, she directed *Ah, Wilderness!* in Turkey (Turkish Natl. Th., Ankara, Mar.–Apr. 1958); played Mrs. Olcott in *Boston Love Story* (Bucks County Playhouse, New Hope, Pa., Aug. 1958); Ivy in *The Family Reunion* (Phoenix, N.Y.C., Oct. 20, 1958); in stock, Mrs. Elliot in *Epitaph for George Dillon* (Capri Th., Atlantic Beach, N.J., July 1959); Madame Bobignot in *Moonbirds* (Cort, N.Y.C., Oct. 8, 1959); as Tot in *Happy Birthday* (Lydia Mendelssohn Th., Univ. of Michigan, Ann Arbor, May 1960); Miss Austin in a touring production of *Craig's Wife* (June–Aug. 1960); Mary Herries in *Kind Lady* (Cape Playhouse, Dennis, Mass., Aug. 1960); and Little Pigeon in *Whisper to Me* (Players Th., N.Y.C., Nov. 21, 1960).

Miss Sands appeared in the Theatre Guild-ANTA touring productions under the auspices of the State Dept., as a Convener, a standby for Helen Hayes as Mrs. Antrobus, and for Helen Menken as the Fortune Teller in *The Skin of Our Teeth*, in which she later appeared as the Fortune Teller; was a standby for Miss Hayes as Amanda in *The Glass Menagerie;* and played Aunt Ev in *The Miracle Worker* (Palm Beach, Fla.; Washington, D.C.; Europe and Latin America; Jan.–June, Aug.–Nov. 1961).

She appeared as Queen Tartaglioni in *The Green Bird* (IASTA Th., N.Y.C., Feb. 18–25, 1962); Mrs. Mary Ellis in *The Autumn Garden* (Charles Playhouse, Boston, Mass., Apr. 1962); in stock at the Robin Hood Th., (Ardentown, Del.), played Mrs. Levi in *The Matchmaker* (June 1962) and Mrs. Tarleton in *Misalliance* (July 1962); Mrs. Visserthooft in *The Moments of Love* (Westport Country Playhouse, Conn., Oct. 29, 1963); Mrs. Goolsby in *Once for the Asking* (Booth, N.Y.C., Nov. 19, 1963); and Mrs. Pearce in *My Fair Lady* (NY City Ctr., May 19, 1964); replaced (Feb. 28, 1966) Mildred Dunnock as Oenone in *Phèdre* (Greenwich Mews Th., Feb. 10, 1966), which she repeated in Denver and Aspen, Colo. (Aug. 1966); was Martha Brewster in *Arsenic and Old Lace* (Bonfils Th., Denver, Colo., July 1967); Mrs. Miles in *The Club Bedroom* (ANTA Matinee Th. Series, Th. de Lys, N.Y.C., Dec. 11, 1967); and, while actress in residence at the Univ. of Denver (Colo.), she appeared as Mrs. Hardcastle in *She Stoops to Conquer* (Apr. 1968). She was also Mrs. Meserve in *Come Summer* (Lunt-Fontanne Th., N.Y.C., Mar. 18, 1969); Hattie Fields in *Paris Is Out!* (Brooks Atkinson Th., Jan. 19, 1970); and Signora Frola in *Right You Are* (Roundabout Th., Sept. 12, 1972).

Television. Miss Sands has appeared as Aaronetta Gibbs in *Morning's at Seven* (NBC, 1948); Mrs. Pearce in *Pygmalion* (Hallmark Hall of Fame, NBC, Feb. 6, 1963); and in the title role in *Colette* (Camera 3, CBS, Feb. 16, 1964).

Other Activities. Miss Sands taught classic acting at the American Th. Wing, professional training program (1945–1960); and has been a member of the advisory board of drama at Union Theological Seminary, N.Y.C. (1960–to date).

Awards. Miss Sands received an honorary A.A. degree from the Curry School of Expression, (Boston, Mass., 1949); an honorary membership in Phi Beta Kappa from Radcliffe Coll. (June 18, 1940); a Rockefeller grant (1958); and an Antoinette Perry (Tony) Award for her teaching at the American Theatre Wing (1959). In 1972, AEA awarded Miss Sands a certificate for her years of service to the association and in commemoration of her 50th anniversary in the professional theatre.

Recreation. Gardening, travel.

SANG, LEONARD B. Public relations, theatre manager. b. Dec. 23, 1900, Buffalo, N.Y., to Paul and Helene (Goldstein) Sang. Father, sales manager. Attended Masten Park H.S., 1914–17. Married Oct. 21, 1937, to Lillian Passman. Member of ATPAM; Jewish Theatrical Guild (exec. secy., 1957–63); The Lambs. Address: (home) 235 West End Ave., New York, NY 10023, tel. (212) TR 3-6171; (bus.) 236 W. 44th St., New York, NY 10036, tel. (212) CI 6-9500.

Pre-Theatre. Sales promotion.

Theatre. Mr. Sang first worked as a theatre manager in Buffalo (N.Y., 1927).

From 1938–41, he managed various N.Y.C. theatres for the Shubert management; subsequently managed the Independent Shubert Th. (New Haven, Conn., 1941–46); the Belasco (N.Y.C., 1947); and the Lyceum (N.Y.C., 1950); which were operated independently; and various N.Y.C. theatres, also for the Shubert management.

From 1953, Mr. Sang was associated with the Shubert office in the press and public relations department. He is now retained on a consultant basis.

Recreation. Sports, travel for pleasure, manuscript reading.

SARNOFF, DOROTHY. Singer, actress. b. May 25, 1919, New York City, to Dr. Jacob and Belle (Roosin) Sarnoff. Father, surgeon. Grad. Berkeley Inst., Bklyn.; Cornell Univ. Married March 15, 1957, to Milton Harold Raymond. Address: 40 W. 59th St., New York, NY 10019, tel. (212) PL 9-3996.

Miss Sarnoff is the president of Speech Dynamics, Inc., N.Y.C., where she directs courses in effective verbal communication. She has also served as a consultant to many major corporations and has lectured at numerous conferences, universities, and conventions.

Theatre. Miss Sarnoff made her N.Y.C. debut in the title role in *Rosalinda* (44 St. Th., Oct. 28, 1942); subsequently appeared as Maria in *Magdalena* (Ziegfeld, Sept. 20, 1948); Lady Thiang in *The King and I* (St. James, Mar. 29, 1951); and Jessica Farrow in *My Darlin' Aida* (Winter Garden, Oct. 27, 1952). In stock, she has played in *Maytime* and *Gypsy* (St. Louis Municipal Opera, Mo.); and *Desert Song, The Vagabond King, Magdalena,* and *The Great Waltz* (Los Angeles Civic Opera, Calif., San Francisco Light Opera, Calif.).

Miss Sarnoff has sung the operatic roles Marguerite in *Faust* (Philadelphia Opera Co., Pa.); Nedda in *Pagliacci* (Philadelphia Opera Co.); Rosalinda in *Die Fledermaus* (New Orleans Opera Co., La.); Mimi in *La Bohème,* and the title roles in *Aida* and *Tosca* (NY City Opera Co.). She has appeared as soloist with the San Francisco Symphony, The National Symphony, the New York Philharmonic Symphony, the Baltimore Symphony, the Toronto Symphony, and the Philadelphia Orchestra.

Television. She has appeared on the Ed Sullivan Show (CBS); the Tonight Show (NBC); the Jack Paar Show (NBC); the Today Show (NBC, 1963, 1970); Girl Talk (ABC, 1963); the Kup Show (1970–71); the Mike Douglas Show (1972); AM New York with John Bartholomew Tucker (ABC, 1971–72); and the CBS Morning Show (1973).

Night Clubs. Miss Sarnoff has appeared at the Waldorf-Astoria, Plaza (Persian Room), and Pierre Hotels (N.Y.C.); the Fontainebleau, Carillon, Americana, and Eden Roc hotels (Miami, Fla.); and the Drake hotel (Chicago, Ill.).

Published Works. Miss Sarnoff wrote *Speech Can Change Your Life* (1970; 1972).

Awards. Miss Sarnoff received The Spirit of Achievement Award of the Albert Einstein Coll. of Medicine (Apr. 13, 1964).

Recreation. Golf, oriental antiques, cooking, sewing.

SAROYAN, WILLIAM. Playwright, author. b. Aug. 31, 1908, Fresno, Calif., to Armenak and Takoohi Saroyan. Attended Emerson Public School, Fresno. Married Feb. 20, 1943, to Carol Marcus (marr. dis. Nov. 16, 1949); one son, one daughter. Served US Army. Address: 2729 W. Griffith Way, Fresno, CA 93705.

Theatre. The first of Mr. Saroyan's plays to be produced on Bway was *My Heart's in the Highlands* (Guild Th., Apr. 13, 1939). He subsequently wrote *The Time of Your Life,* which he directed with Eddie Dowling (Booth, Oct. 25, 1939); the book for the ballet *The Great American Goof* (Center Th., Jan. 11, 1940); wrote and, with Eddie Dowling, directed *Love's Old Sweet Song* (Plymouth, May 2, 1940); and wrote *Sweeney in the Trees, The Hero of the World,* and *Something About a Soldier,* all of which were produced in stock (1940).

He wrote, produced, and directed *The Beautiful People* (Lyceum, Apr. 21, 1941); and also the double-bill *Across the Board on Tomorrow Morning* and *Talking to You* (presented by the Saroyan Th. at Belasco Th., Aug. 17, 1942); wrote *Hello, Out There* (Belasco, Sept. 29, 1942); *Get Away Old Man* (Cort, Nov. 24, 1943); *The Hungerers* and *The Ping Pong Players,* which were presented on a triple-bill with *Hello, Out There* (Provincetown Playhouse, Aug. 23, 1945); *Don't Go Away Mad* (Master Inst. Th., May 9, 1949); *The Son* (Circle Th., Los Angeles, Calif., 1950); and *Opera, Opera,* presented with *The Hungerers* on a double-bill, *Floydada to Matador* (Amato Th., N.Y.C., Dec. 21, 1955).

Mr. Saroyan also wrote *The Cave Dwellers* (Bijou, Oct. 19, 1957); *Ever Been in Love with a Midget?* (Congress Hall, Berlin, Ger., Sept. 20, 1957); *Sam, the Highest Jumper of Them All,* which he also directed (Th. Royal, Stratford, England, Apr. 6, 1960); *High Time Along the Wabash,* which he also produced and directed while spending six weeks at Purdue Univ. (Lafayette, Ind., Dec. 1, 1961); and *The Rebirth Celebration of the Human Race at Artie Zabala's Off-Broadway Theatre* (Shirtsleeve Th., N.Y.C., July 10, 1975).

Films. Mr. Saroyan wrote and directed *The Good Job* (1943) and co-adapted for motion pictures his novel *The Human Comedy* (MGM, 1943). The film *The Time of Your Life* (UA, 1948) was based on Mr. Saroyan's play of the same title.

Television. Many plays by Mr. Saroyan have been presented on television, including *My Heart's in the Highlands* (Playhouse 90, CBS; Omnibus, NBC, Oct. 28, 1956) *Ah Sweet Mystery of Mrs. Murphy* (Omnibus, NBC, Mar. 1, 1959); and *The Unstoppable Grey Fox* (GE Th., CBS).

Other Activities. In collaboration with his cousin, Ross Bagdsarian, he wrote both the music and the lyrics for the song, "Come-on-a-My-House" (1951). He wrote the text for the cantata (music by Peter Racine Fricker), *Ah Man* (BBC Concert, Aldeburgh Festival, England, June 21, 1962).

Published Works. Mr. Saroyan wrote *The Man with the Heart in the Highlands, Jim Dandy, The Violin Messiah, A Decent Birth; A Happy Funeral, The Slaughter of the Innocents, Once Around the Block, Sam Ego's House, Razzle Dazzle* and other plays. His other works include *The Daring Young Man on the Flying Trapeze* (1934); *My Name Is Aram* (1939); *Dear Baby* (1944); *The Adventures of Wesley Jackson* (1946); *The Twin Adventures* (1950) *The Assyrian and Other Stories* (1950); *Tracy's Tiger* (1951); *Rock Wagram* (1951); *The Bicycle Rider in Beverly Hills* (1952); *The Laughing Matter* (1953); *Little Children* (1953); *Mama I Love You* (1956); *The Whole Voyald* (1956); *Papa You're Crazy* (1957); *Here Comes, There Goes, You Know Who* (1961); *Boys and Girls Together* (1963); *Not Dying* (1963); and many other books.

Awards. Mr. Saroyan received the NY Drama Critics' Circle Award and the Pulitzer Prize (which he rejected) for his play *The Time of Your Life* (1940); and an Academy (Oscar) Award for *The Human Comedy* (1943).

SARTRE, JEAN-PAUL. Playwright, philosopher. b. Jean-Paul Charles Aymard Sartre, June 21, 1905, Paris, France, to Jean-Baptiste and Anne-Marie (Schweitzer) Sartre. Grad. Lycée Henri IV, Paris, baccalaureat; Ecole Normale Supérieure, Agrégé de Philosophie, 1929. Served WW II, French Army; rank, Pvt. Member of Amer. Acad. of Arts and Sciences. Address: 42 rue Bonaparte, Paris 6, France.

Pre-Theatre. M. Sartre was a teacher of philosophy in French secondary schools. At the start of WW II, he enlisted in the French army (Sept. 1939) and served for nine months before being taken prisoner by the Germans (1940–41). He escaped nine months later, and worked as a journalist with the resistance movement for the duration of the war (1941–44).

Theatre. His first dramatic work was *Les Mouches,* which was presented in Paris during the German occupation (Th. Sarah Bernhardt, 1942); and first produced in N.Y.C. by the Dramatic Workshop of the New Sch. for Social Research, translated by Stuart Gilbert as *The Flies* (President Th., Apr. 17, 1947). He then wrote *Huis-Clos.* (Th. du Vieux-Colombier, Paris, May 1944), first performed in English, translated by Marjorie Gabain and Joan Swinstead, as *The Vicious Circle* (Arts Th. Club, London, July 17, 1946), and adapted by Paul Bowles as *No Exit* (Biltmore, N.Y.C., Nov. 26, 1946).

M. Sartre wrote *La putain respectueuse* (Th. Antoine, Nov. 8, 1946), which was adapted from the French by Eva Wolas and produced in N.Y.C. by New Stages, Inc., as *The Respectful Prostitute;* originally paired with *Church Street,* it was later presented with *The Happy Journey to Trenton and Camden* as *An Evening of Two Plays* (New Stages Th., Feb. 9, 1948; moved Cort, Mar. 16, 1948). His *La putain respectueuse* was translated and adapted by Kitty Black as *The Respectful Prostitute* (Lyric, Hammersmith, London, July 17, 1947), and presented on a double bill with *Men without Shadows,* translated and adapted by Miss Black from his *Mort sans sepulture* (Th. Antoine, 1947). *Mort sans sepulture* had its first New York production as *The Victors,* adapted by Thornton Wilder (New Stages Th., Dec. 26, 1948).

He wrote *Les mains sales* (Th. Antoine, Paris, Apr. 2, 1948), translated by Miss Black as *Crime Passionnel* (Lyric, Hammersmith, London, June 17, 1948), and adapted by Daniel Taradash as *The Red Gloves* (Mansfield, N.Y.C., Dec. 4, 1948); *Le diable et le bon Dieu* (Th. Antoine, Paris, June 7, 1951); *Kean,* based on a play by Alexandre Dumas (Th. Sarah Bernhardt, Paris, Nov. 17, 1953), which subsequently served as the basis for the N.Y.C. musical of the same name (Bway Th., Nov. 2, 1961); *Nekrassov* (Th. Antoine, Paris, June 8, 1955), and translated by Sylvia and George Leeson (Royal Court, London, Sept. 17, 1957); *Les sequestres d'Altona* (Th. de la Renaissance, Paris, Sept. 24, 1959), translated by Justin O'Brien as *The Condemned of Altona,* and first presented in the US by the Lincoln Center Rep. Co. (Vivian Beaumont Th., N.Y.C., Feb. 3, 1966); and adapted Euripides' *The Trojan Women* (Théâtre National Populaire, Paris, Mar. 17, 1965).

Films. Sartre wrote the scenarios for *Les jeux sont faits* (France, 1944), released in the US as *The Chips Are Down* (Lopert, 1949); *L'Engrenage* (France, 1948); *Les mains sales* (France, 1951), released in the US under the same title (McDonald, 1954); *La putain respectueuse* (France, 1952), in the US, *The Respectful Prostitute* (T.F.C., 1957); *Les faux nez* (France, 1952); the story, on which the screenplay was based, for *Les orgueilleux* (France, 1953), released in the US as *The Proud and the Beautiful* (Kingsley, 1956); *Huis Clos* (France, 1955); wrote the screenplay for a film version of Arthur Miller's *The Crucible,* entitled *Les sorcières de Salem* (France, 1958), released in the US as *The Witches of Salem* (Kingsley-Intl., 1958); and *Les sequestres d'Altona* (France), shown in the US as *The Condemned of Altona* (20th-Fox, 1963). His *Huis Clos* was filmed a second time, adapted into English by George Tabori, as *No Exit* (Zenith Intl., 1962).

Television and Radio. Three of his novels (*The Age of Reason, The Reprieve,* and *Troubled Sleep*) were adapted into a thirteen-week serial entitled *The Roads to Freedom* (premiêred in England on BBC-2, Oct. 4, 1970; premiered US, WNET, Nov. 13, 1972). His play *No Exit* was seen on the Play of the Week series (WNET, Feb. 28, 1961).

Other Activities. He has contributed articles and essays to such publications as *Les lettres françaises, La nouvelle revue française,* and *Combat.* In 1946, he founded the revue *Les temps modernes,* and has since served as its editor.

Published Works. M. Sartre's works published in English include *Being and Nothingness* (1947); *The Reprieve* (1947); *Existentialism* (1947); *The Age of Reason* (1947); *Anti-Semite and Jew* (1948); *The Wall,* a collection of short stories (1948); *Emotions, Outline of a Theory* (1948); *The Psychology of Imagination* (1948); *What Is Literature?* (1949); the novels *Nausea* (1949); *Intimacy* (1950); *Baudelaire* (1950); *Troubled Sleep* (1950); the introduction for Genet's *Our Lady of the Flowers* (1951); *Existential Psychoanalysis* (1953); *Saint Genet: Actor and Martyr* (1963); *Essays in Aesthetics* (1963); an autobiography, *The Words* (1964); the forward for Genet's *The Thief's Journal* (1964); a collection of essays, *Situations: The Artist and His Conscience* (1965); *The Philosophy of Existentialism* (1965); *Of Human Freedom* (1966); *On Genocide* (1969); *Between Existentialism and Marxism* (trans. by John Mathews, 1974); *Art and Faith,* correspondence with Jacques Maritain; and *Death in the Soul.* He completed and had published three volumes of a study of Flaubert, under the general title of *L'Idiot de la Famille* (*The Idiot of the Family*), but announced in 1975 that he had to abandon work on the fourth and final volume, due to worsening blindness.

Awards. The N.Y.C. production (*No Exit*) of his play *Huis Clos,* received a Donaldson Award (1947). He also was awarded, but refused, the Nobel Prize for Literature (1964).

SAVAGE, GEORGE. Educator, playwright. b. George Milton Savage, Jr., Apr. 25, 1904, Tacoma, Wash., to George Milton and Annie Simmons (Sibley) Savage. Father, contractor. Grad. Philip Exeter Acad., 1923; Univ. of Washington, A.B. 1927, M.A. 1927. Ph.D. (English) 1935. Married Sept. 8, 1929, to Gladys C. Ferrier, college counselor; two sons. Member of NTC; Dramatists Guild; AETA; TLA; Sigma Delta Chi; Hammer and Coffin; Society for Theatre Research (England); Intl. Theatre Research; AAUP; Chi Psi (pres.); Military Order of the Loyal Legion Faculty Center Evergreen Stage Company; LOLAT; Emeriti. Address: (home) 1818 Overland Ave., Los Angeles, CA 90025, tel. (213) 474-9689; (bus.) Dept. of Theatre Arts, Macgowan Hall, University of Calif., Los Angeles, CA 90024, tel. (213) 478-9711.

From 1951–71, Mr. Savage was a professor in the Dept. of Theatre Arts at the Univ. of California at Los Angeles, where he taught courses in playwriting and was responsible for the production of 280 original plays (30 three-act, 250 one-act). He retired as professor emeritus in July 1971.

From 1930–51, he was a member of the faculty at the Univ. of Washington (associate, 1930–35; instructor, 1935–39; assistant professor, 1939–45; associate professor, 1945–51).

He was visiting professor at the State Univ. of Iowa (Summer, 1955); conducted the Playwright's Workshop at the Idyllwild Arts Foundation (Idyllwild, Calif., Summers 1953–62); was Fulbright Senior Lecturer and visiting professor at the Univ. of Bristol (England, 1958–59); Dramatische Werkstaat, Salzburg (Austria, Summer 1959); was appointed to the Inst. for Creative Arts, Univ. of California (1963–64).

From 1943–51, he worked with new playwrights at the Tryout Th. (Seattle, Wash.), an experimental community theatre, where more than 50 new full-length plays were performed. He also served on the board of trustees of the Inner City Cultural Center (1966–to date) and the advisory board of the Los Angeles Junior Programs and the California Junior Programs (1953–to date).

Mr. Savage is the author of *See How They Run,* which was produced by the Federal Th. (WPA) Project (Alcazar Th., San Francisco, Calif., Sept. 5, 1938; 12 St. Th., Oakland, Calif., Sept. 19, 1938; Metropolitan, Seattle, Wash., Sept. 19, 1938); *American Family Robinson,* also produced by the Federal Th. (Federal Th., San Diego, Calif., 1938).

He wrote, with George Taylor, *Phoenix and the Dwarfs* (Th. of All Nations, Hunter Playhouse, N.Y.C., 1945); wrote, with Zoe Schiller, *The Expensive Wench,* produced by the Red Barn Th. (Summer 1945); with William Noble, wrote *Fire Shall Forgive* (Theatre-in-the-Dale, New Milford, Conn., 1946); with Gladys Charles, wrote *Verily I Do* (River Oaks Th., Houston, Tex., Nov. 30, 1949); wrote, with George Savage, Jr., *Western Trilogy* (Sheridan Sq. Playhouse, N.Y.C., 1962; Theatre Shack, Arlington, N.J., May 20, 1964); collaborated with George Savage, Jr., and Olympic productions on *Editorial Conference* (Beverly Hills, Calif., Aug. 3, 1962); wrote, with George Savage, Jr., *The Young Scooter* (Norfolk Little Th., Va., June 13, 1964); wrote *The Garbage Hustler* (Las Palmas, Dec. 1964–65; and Th. L'Homme Dieux, 1966); *Days of Wakefield's Bar* (Cellar Th., Apr.–July 1973); and *The Legend of Bodie Rose* (Nevada City Th., Aug.–Sept. 1973).

Awards. Mr. Savage received the Arthur A. Denny Fellowship (1933); Dramatists Guild-Federal Theatre Award (first place, 1938); with Barrett Clark, Dramatists Guild-Federal Theatre Fellowship (1938); Dramatists Alliance Award (1942); Theatre of all Nations Award (1945); Paul Bunyan Award (1957); Natl. Theatre Conference Fellowship (1944, 1951); the Third Annual Margo Jones Award in the University Theatre Division (1964) for his work with new plays and playwrights. He and his son, George Savage, Jr., won first prize in the experimental theatre playwriting contest of the Norfolk (Va.) Little Th. (1964) for their play, *The Young Scooter.*

Recreation. Seeing plays.

SAVAN, BRUCE. Talent Representative. b. Bruce Sheldon Savan, July 11, 1927, Portland, Ore., to Joseph and Florence (Anthone) Savan. Father, jeweler. Grad. Lincoln H.S., Portland, Ore., 1944; Univ. of Southern California, B. Mus. (cum laude) 1950. Studied music with Carl Ebert, Frank Baxter, William DeMille, Benjamin Britten, Ernst Toch, Alice Ehlers, Univ. of Southern California; conducting with Jacques Gershkowitz; piano with Jesse Lewis, Portland, Ore., Ignatz Hilsberg, Emanuel Bay, Tarnowski, Los Angeles, Calif. Served US Army, 1945–47; rank, Sgt. Member of TARA; AEA; AFM, local 802; Zeta Beta Tau; Phi Mu Alpha Simphonia. Address: (home) 151 E. 37th St., New York, NY 10016, tel. (212) MU 5-1722; (bus.) c/o A.P.A., 120 W. 57th St., New York, NY 10019, tel. (212) LT 1-8860.

Mr. Savan has been a talent representative with the William Morris Agency, Inc. (1954–57), and Lenny-Debin, Inc. (1957–59), and has been president of Savan-Levinson-Parker, Inc., a theatrical agency in N.Y.C. (1959–64, and vice-president of the Agency for the Performing Arts in N.Y.C. (1964–to date).

Theatre. He first performed on stage as Tiny Tim in *A Christmas Carol* (Civic, Portland, Ore., Dec. 1932); subsequently appeared with the Portland Junior Symphony Orchestra as pianist, timpanist, and conductor (Civic, Portland, Ore., 1940, 1944).

He was co-producer of *Ballet Ballads* (Century Th., Los Angeles, Calif., Oct. 14, 1950); stage manager for the Players Ring Th. (Hollywood, Calif., 1950); choral director and stage manager at the Sacramento (Calif.) Music Circus (Summer 1951); stage manager for the national tour of *The Cocktail Party* (opened Curran, San Francisco, Calif., Oct. 15, 1951; closed, Royal Alexandre, Toronto, Can., May 22, 1952); for the Cape Cod Melody Tent (Hyannis, Mass., Summer 1952); for *Time Out for Ginger* (Lyceum, N.Y.C., Nov. 26, 1952); and for *The Girl in Pink Tights* (Mark Hellinger Th., Mar. 5, 1954).

Films. Mr. Savan was musical director for Republic Studios (1949–50).

Published Works. He wrote *Your Career in the Theatre* (1961).

SAWYER, CARL. Producer, manager. b. Carl Schreuer, May 2, 1921, Chicago, Ill., to Carl and Katherine (Arlen) Schreuer. Father, engineer. Grad. Columbia Univ., B.S. 1942. Married Jan. 24, 1944, to Barbara Bel Geddes, actress (marr. dis. Apr. 1951); one daughter; married Sept. 1, 1951, to Helen Rhinelander, writer. Member of AEA; ATPAM; The Lambs.

Pre-Theatre. Electrical engineer for marine architects.

Theatre. Since 1959, Mr. Sawyer, with Gray McHugh, has owned and operated the Meadowbrook (N.J.) Dinner Th., and since 1962, the Westchester (N.Y.) Dinner Th. They also owned and operated the Bradford Dinner Th., Boston, Mass. (1961–62).

Mr. Sawyer was on the production staff for *Song of Norway* (Booth, N.Y.C., Apr. 15, 1948); was general manager of the Sacramento (Calif.) Music Circus (1953–55) and the Camden County (N.J.) Circus, a summer theatre which he also built; general manager for the productions of Anna Deere Wiman at the Shakespeare Th., Liverpool, England (1958); production supervisor for *13 Daughters* (54 St. Th., N.Y.C., Mar. 2, 1961); and business manager for *Love and Kisses* (Music Box, Dec. 18, 1963).

Recreation. Theatre, food.

SCHAEFER, GEORGE. Director, producer. b. George Louis Schaefer, Dec. 16, 1920, Wallingford, Conn., to Louis and Elsie (Otterbein) Schaefer. Father, salesman. Grad. Oak Park (Ill.) H.S., 1937; Lafayette Coll., B.A. (magna cum laude) 1941; attended Yale Univ. Sch. of Drama, 1942. Married Feb. 5, 1954, to Mildred Trares, actress. Served with US Army, Special Services, PTO, 1942–45; rank, Sgt. Member of DGA (natl. bd. of dir., 1960–75; vice-pres., 1961–74); AMPAS; ATAS; ANTA, West (bd. of dir.); and Variety Clubs International. Address: (home) 1040 Woodland Dr., Beverly Hills, CA 90210, tel. (213) 274-6017; (bus.) c/o Compass Productions, Inc., 1801 Ave. of Stars, Los Angeles, CA 90067, tel. (213) 553-6205.

Theatre. Mr. Schaefer began as a director with the Pastime Players (Oak Park, Ill., 1947–51) for the US Army Special Services, directed more than 50 musicals, plays, and vaudeville productions (Honolulu, 1942–45).

His first assignment as director was for Maurice Evans' GI version of *Hamlet* (Columbus Circle Th., Dec. 13, 1945), which also toured cross-country (1946–47), and played at NY City Ctr. (June 4, 1946). He was director of the pre-Bway tour of *Darling, Darling, Darling* (opened McCarter Th., Princeton, N.J., Jan. 31, 1947; closed Wilbur, Boston, Mass., Feb. 8, 1947); with Maurice Evans, he was associate director of *Man and Superman* (Alvin, N.Y.C., Oct. 8, 1947), toured cross-country (1948–49), and played at NY City Ctr. (May 16, 1949); and director of *The Linden Tree* (Music Box, Mar. 2, 1948).

He was executive producer (1949–51) and artistic director (1950–52) of the NY City Ctr. Co., for whom he staged *The Heiress* (Feb. 8, 1950), and *Idiot's Delight* (May 23, 1951). With Maurice Evans, he produced *The Teahouse of the August Moon* (Martin Beck Th., Oct. 15, 1953), two national tours (opened Hartman, Columbus, Ohio, Dec. 16, 1954; and opened Colonial, Boston, Mass., Apr. 2, 1956; closed National, Washington, D.C., July 7, 1956), and the London production (Her Majesty's, Apr. 22, 1954).

Mr. Schaefer has also directed 28 musical productions at the State Fair Music Hall (Dallas, Tex., 1952–56; 1958); and *Kiss Me, Kate* for the Los Angeles Civic Light Opera Co. (Los Angeles Philharmonic, Calif., May 2, 1955).

He staged *The Southwest Corner* (Holiday, N.Y.C., Feb. 3, 1955); *The Apple Cart* (Plymouth, Oct. 18, 1956), and on tour (opened National, Washington, D.C., Mar. 4, 1957; closed Huntington Hartford, Hollywood, Calif., June 29, 1957); and *The Body Beautiful* (Bway Th., Jan. 23, 1958). He produced and directed *Write Me a Murder* (Belasco, N.Y.C., Oct. 26, 1961; Lyric, London, Mar. 28, 1962); produced, with Edwin Lester, and directed the pre-Bway tour of *Zenda (opened Curran, San Francisco, Calif., Aug. 5, 1963; closed Civic Aud., Pasadena, Calif., Nov. 16, 1963); and produced To Broadway with Love* (Texas Pavilion, NY World's Fair, Apr. 22, 1964).

In addition, he directed *The Great Indoors* (O'Neill Memorial Th. Ctr., Feb. 1, 1966); *The Last of Mrs. Lincoln* (opened Kennedy Ctr. Opera House, Nov. 13, 1972; opened ANTA Th., N.Y.C., Dec. 12, 1972); and the revival *The Student Prince* (opened Academy of Music, Philadelphia, Pa., June 4, 1973; tour closed Dallas, Tex., Oct. 21, 1973).

Films. Mr. Schaefer produced and directed a technicolor motion picture of *Macbeth* (1960), which was shown twice on the Hallmark Hall of Fame. He also directed *Pendulum* (Col., 1969); *Generation* (Avco-Embassy, 1970); *Doctors' Wives* (Col., 1971); and *Once Upon a Scoundrel* (1972).

Television. Among the productions which Mr. Schaefer has directed for the Hallmark Hall of Fame (NBC) are: *Hamlet* (1953); *Richard II* and *Macbeth* (1954); and *Alice in Wonderland, The Devil's Disciple, Dream Girl, The Corn Is Green, The Good Fairy, The Taming of the Shrew,* and *The Cradle Song* (1955–56). He directed and produced *Man and Superman, The Little Foxes, The Lark, There Shall Be No Night,* and *The Yeomen of the Guard,* and produced *Born Yesterday* (1956–57); directed and produced *Green Pastures, On Borrowed Time, Little Moon of Alban,* and *Dial 'M' for Murder* (1957–58); directed and produced *Johnny Belinda, Kiss Me, Kate,* and *Berkeley Square* (1958–59); directed and produced *Winterset, A Doll's House, The Borrowed Christmas* (Christmas Festival), *The Tempest, The Cradle Song,* and *Captain Brassbound's Conversion* (1959–60); directed and produced *Shangri-La, Macbeth, Time Remembered, Give Us Barabbas,* and *The Joke and the Valley,* and produced *Golden Child* (1960–61).

He directed and produced *Victoria Regina* and *Arsenic and Old Lace* (1961–62); directed and produced *The Teahouse of the August Moon, Cyrano de Bergerac, Pygmalion* and *The Invincible Mr. Disraeli* (1962–63); directed and produced *The Patriots, A Cry of Angels,* and *Abe Lincoln in Illinois* (1963–64).

Mr. Schaefer has also directed *One Touch of Venus* (NBC, 1955); *Harvey* (CBS, 1958); *Gift of the Magi* (CBS, 1958); and *Meet Me in St. Louis* (CBS, 1959); *Turn the Key Deftly* (Breck Showcase, NBC, 1960); *Hour of the Bath* (Alcoa, ABC, 1962), and *The Hands of Donofrio* (Fred Astaire Premiere, ABC, 1962).

He directed and produced *The Fantasticks, The Magnificent Yankee,* and *The Holy Terror* (1964–65); *Eagle in a Cage, Inherit the Wind,* and *Lamp at Midnight* (1965–66); *Barefoot in Athens, Blithe Spirit, Anastasia,* and *Soldier in Love* (1966–67); and *Do Not Go Gentle into That Good Night, Saint Joan, Elizabeth the Queen, The Admirable Crichton,* and *My Father and My Mother* (1967–68). He directed *The File on Devlin* (1970), *U.S.A.* (1971), *A War of Children* (1972), *F. Scott Fitzgerald and the Last of the Belles* (1973); was executive producer of Love Story series and directed two episodes (1973–74); and directed and produced *Carl Sandburg's Lincoln* (1974–75).

Awards. *The Teahouse of the August Moon* won the NY Drama Critics' Circle Award, Pulitzer Prize, and Antoinette Perry (Tony) Award (1954). The Hallmark Hall of Fame received the Sylvania Award as the outstanding dramatic series and the George Foster Peabody Award for outstanding television entertainment (1958); Mr. Schaefer received the Sylvania Award for his contribution as producer-director of the Hallmark show; *Green Pastures* received the *Look* Magazine Award (1957) and the *Radio-Television Daily* Award; and Mr. Schaefer received the *Radio-Television Daily* Award as director of the year. In 1959, *Johnny Belinda* received the *Radio-Television Daily* Award, and *Little Moon of Alban* received the Sylvania Award, the Peabody Award, the Christopher Award, and four NATAS (Emmy) awards, including one to Mr. Schaefer for best direction of a single dramatic program. In 1961, Mr. Schaefer received the Directors Guild of America Award and the *Radio-Television Daily* Award as director of the year; and *Macbeth* received the *TV Guide* Award for the best single dramatic program on television, the *Radio Television Daily* Award for the dramatic show of the year and five NATAS (Emmy) awards, including one to Mr. Schaefer for outstanding directorial achievement in drama; *Victoria Regina* received the *Saturday Review's* Special Commendation for Notable Production (1961) and three NATAS (Emmy) awards, including one as program of the year. In 1963 Mr. Schaefer received the *Radio-Television Daily* All-American Award as director of the year and producer of the year; *The Invincible Mr. Disraeli* received two NATAS (Emmy) awards; the Directors Guild Award for best TV director (1964, 1968, 1969); the Radio-TV Daily Award for best director (1964, 1965); and NATAS (Emmy) awards were won by *The Magnificent Yankee* (five Emmys, 1965), *Elizabeth the Queen* (four Emmys, 1968), and *A War of Children* (1972). He received an honorary D.Litt. degree (1963) from Lafayette Coll.; the Dineen Award (1964) from the National Catholic Th. Conference and an honorary L.H.D. degree from Coker Coll. (1973).

Recreation. Contract bridge, travel, theatre-going.

SCHAFER, NATALIE. Actress. b. Nov. 5, 1912, Red Bank, N.J., to Charles and Jane (Tim) Schafer. Father, stock broker. Attended Oaksmere Sch., Mamaroneck, N.Y. Married Apr. 20, 1934, to Louis Calhern, actor (marr. dis. 1942; dec. May 12, 1956). Member of AEA; SAG; AFTRA.

Theatre. Miss Schafer played Eleanor Stafford in *Trigger* (Little, N.Y.C., Dec. 6, 1927); Ethel in *March Hares* (Little, Apr. 2, 1928); Edith Major in *These Few Ashes* (Booth, Oct. 30, 1928); Helen Bent in *The Nut Farm* (Biltmore, Oct. 14, 1929); Marjorie Kellam in *The Rhapsody* (Cort, Sept. 15, 1930); Annabelle Barrington in *The Great Barrington* (Avon, Feb. 19, 1931); Viva North in *Perfectly Scandalous* (Hudson, May 13, 1931); Constance Carroll in *New York to Cherbourg* (Forrest, Feb. 19, 1932); Margaret Kenny Brown in *So Many Paths* (Ritz, Dec. 6, 1934); The Princess of the Western Regions in *Lady Precious Stream* (Booth, Jan. 27, 1936); succeeded Vera Allen as Irene Burroughs in *Susan and God* (Plymouth, Oct. 7, 1937).

She appeared as Alison Du Bois in *Lady in the Dark* (Alvin, Jan. 23, 1941); Sylvia in *The Doughgirls* (Lyceum, Dec. 30, 1942); Allora Eames in *A Joy Forever* (Biltmore, Jan. 7, 1946); Mrs. Marion Gibbs in *Forward the Heart* (48 St. Th., Jan. 28, 1949); the Leading Lady in *Six Characters in Search of an Author* (Phoenix, Dec. 11, 1955); Beulah Moulsworth in *Romanoff and Juliet* (Plymouth, Oct. 10, 1957); Susan Ashe in *The Highest Tree* (Longacre, Nov. 4, 1959); Mrs. Mercy Croft in *The Killing of Sister George* (national tour, 1967–68); appeared in *The Front Page* (Huntington Hartford Th., Hollywood, Calif., Jan. 1974); and played Lady Kitty in *The Circle* (Roundabout, N.Y.C., Apr. 17, 1974).

Films. Miss Schafer made her debut in *Marriage Is a Private Affair* (MGM, 1944); subsequently appeared in *Keep Your Powder Dry* (MGM, 1945); *Wonder Man* (RKO, 1945); *Molly and Me* (20th-Fox, 1945); *Repeat Performance* (Eagle-Lion, 1947); *Dishonored Lady* (UA, 1947); *Secret Beyond the Door* (U, 1948); *The Time of Your Life* (UA, 1948); *The Snake Pit* (20th-Fox, 1948); *Caught* (MGM, 1949); *Callaway Went Thataway* (MGM, 1951); *Take Care of My Little Girl* (20th-Fox, 1951); *The Law and the Lady* (MGM, 1951); *Payment on Demand* (RKO, 1951); *Anastasia* (20th-Fox, 1956); *Oh, Men! Oh, Women!* (20th-Fox, 1957); *Susan Slade* (WB, 1961); played Mrs. Adams in *Forty Carats* (Col., 1973); and Mrs. Jennings in *The Day of the Locust* (Par., 1975).

Television. She has appeared on Kraft Television Th. (NBC); Philco Television Playhouse (NBC); Lux Video Playhouse (CBS); Schlitz Playhouse of Stars (CBS); Mr. and Mrs. North (CBS); Robert Montgomery Presents (NBC); I Love Lucy (CBS); Armstrong Circle Th. (CBS); Ann Sothern Show (CBS); Topper (NBC); and Studio One (CBS). She has performed in the series Gilligan's Island (CBS, premiere Sept. 24, 1964); The Survivors (ABC); Mannix (CBS); Gomer Pyle (CBS); The Brady Bunch (ABC); Search for Tomorrow (CBS); and Diana (NBC); and did the voice of Lovely for the cartoon series Adventures of Gilligan.

Recreation. Traveling, decorating.

SCHARY, DORE. Playwright, director, producer, business executive. b. Aug. 31, 1905, Newark, N.J., to Herman Hugo and Belle (Drachler) Schary. Grad. Newark Central H.S. Married Mar. 5, 1932, to Miriam Svet; one son, Jeb Schary, stage manager; two daughters. Member of League of NY Theatres; Dramatists Guild (pres. of fund, 1962–63); ALA; Amer. Th. Wing (bd. of dir.); SDG; SPG; SSD&C; SWG; AMPAS; Hollywood Museum Assn. (fdr.); Anti-Defamation League of B'nai B'rith (natl. chmn., 1963–69); Brandeis Univ. (bd. of trustees); Eleanor Roosevelt Memorial Foundation (bd. of trustees); Natl. Committee for a Sane Nuclear Policy (sponsor); US Committee for United Nations (advisory council); Americans for Democratic Action (natl. bd.); United World Federalists (honorary vice-pres.). Address: 50 Sutton Place S., New York, NY 10022, tel. (212) 838-6540.

Pre-Theatre. Camp counsellor; newspaperman; publicity man.

Theatre. Mr. Schary wrote *Sunrise at Campobello*, which he produced with the Th. Guild (Cort, Jan. 30, 1958); *A Majority of One*, which he directed (Shubert, Feb. 16, 1959); produced a program of three short plays and a monologue entitled *Triple Play* (Playhouse, Apr. 15, 1959); wrote *The Highest Tree*, which he also produced and directed (Longacre, Nov. 4, 1959); and produced *The Unsinkable Molly Brown*, which he also directed (Winter Garden, Nov. 3, 1960).

In association with Walter Reilly, Mr. Schary produced *The Devil's Advocate*, which he also adapted and directed (Billy Rose Th., Mar. 9, 1961); in association with the Th. Guild by arrangement with Herbert Brodkin, produced *Something About a Soldier*, which he also directed (Ambassador, Jan. 4, 1962); produced and directed *Love and Kisses* (Music Box, Dec. 18, 1963); wrote, produced and directed *One by One* (Belasco Th., Dec. 1, 1964); produced, with Theodore Mann, and directed *The Zulu and the Zayda* (Cort, Nov. 10, 1965); wrote *Brightower* (John Golden Th., Jan. 28, 1970); and wrote special material for *Antiques* (Mercer-O'Casey Th., June 19, 1973).

Films. Mr. Schary has written 40 screenplays since 1932, including *Boys Town* (MGM, 1938); *Young Tom Edison* (MGM, 1940); and *Edison the Man* (MGM, 1940).

He was executive producer for 350 films, including *Joe Smith, American* (MGM, 1942); *Journey for Margaret* (MGM, 1942); *The War Against Mrs. Hadley* (MGM, 1942); *Lassie Come Home* (MGM, 1943); *Bataan* (MGM, 1943); *The Spiral Staircase* (RKO, 1946); *Till the End of Time* (RKO, 1946); *The Farmer's Daughter* (RKO, 1947); and *The Bachelor and the Bobby-Soxer* (RKO, 1947).

As vice-president in charge of production at RKO Pictures, he produced *Crossfire* (1947); *Mr. Blandings Builds His Dream House* (1948); *The Window* (1949); and *The Set-Up* (1949).

He became executive producer (1948), vice-president in charge of production (1951) at MGM, where his films included *Battleground* (1949); *The Next Voice You Hear* (1950); *Go for Broke* (1951); *Bad Day at Black Rock* (1954); *The Last Hunt* (1956); *The Swan* (1956); and *Designing Woman* (1957); adapted, produced and directed *Sunrise at Campobello* (WB, 1960); and *Act One* (WB, 1964).

Television. Mr. Schary has been president of Schary Productions, Inc. (1959–to date); Theatre Vision, Inc. (1972–to date); and was president of Schary Television Productions, Inc. He produced *Blueprint for Biography* (1959), *Where Were You?* (NBC, 1960), and *Sound of the Sixties* (NBC, 1961).

Other Activities. Mr. Schary served during the Mayor John V. Lindsay administration as commissioner, N.Y.C. Parks, Recreational, and Cultural Affairs Administration. He has lectured at universities on theatre, films, and television.

Published Works. He wrote *Case History of a Movie* (1950); *For Special Occasions* (1962); with Sinclair Lewis, *Storm in the West* (1963); and contributed articles and stories to the NY *Times*, NY *Herald-Tribune*, *This Week*, *Commonweal*, *Atlantic Monthly*, and *The Reporter*.

Awards. Mr. Schary received the Academy (Oscar) Award for *Boys Town* (1938); two Antoinette Perry (Tony) Awards as playwright and co-producer of *Sunrise at Campobello* (1958); the Barney Balaban Human Relations Award of the Motion Picture Division of B'nai B'rith Anti-Defamation League (1971); an honorary D.H.L. from the College of the Pacific (1951); Wilberforce University (1951); and an honorary D.F.A. from Lincoln College (1960).

SCHATTNER, MEYER. Publisher. b. Martine Schattner, June 15, 1911, New York City, to Abraham L. and Hannah (Fixler) Schattner. Father, businessman. Grad. Bushwick H.S., Brooklyn, N.Y., 1928; attended Univ. of Georgia, 1928–29; Columbia Univ., night school 1930–31; New York Univ., night school 1931–35; Univ. of Florida, 1936. Married Oct. 31, 1952, to Lenore Tobin, theatre party agent. Member of Phoenix Theatre, Inc.; City Ctr. for Music and Drama. Address: (home) RFD #2, Pound Ridge, NY 10576, tel. (914) SO 3-3094; (bus.) 246 W. 44th St., New York, NY 10036, tel. (212) 564-5180.

Since 1960, Mr. Schattner has been the publisher of *Stubs*, the seating plan guide. He was previously distributor-sales manager of the publication (1949–60).

Recreation. Gardening, travel, opera, ballet, concerts.

SCHEAR, ROBERT. Producer, casting director, artists representative, stage manager. b. Robert L. Schear, Mar. 26, 1936, Brooklyn, N.Y., to Emanuel and Sylvia Schear. Father, stock broker. Grad. Thomas Jefferson H.S., Brooklyn, 1954; attended Drake Business Sch., N.Y.C., one year. Member of AEA. Address: 405 E. 54th St., New York, NY 10022, tel. (212) PL 1-5331.

Theatre. As an artists' representative, Mr. Schear was assistant agent and served as head of the off-Bway dept. at the William Morris Agency, Inc., N.Y.C. (1954–57); as casting director for Yvette Schumer Productions, N.Y.C. (1957); and for the Lenny-Debin Agency, N.Y.C., cast winter and summer productions at the Bucks County Playhouse, New Hope, Pa.; Coconut Grove Playhouse, Miami, Fla.; and the Cleveland (Ohio) Musicarnival (1957–58).

He was staff associate for *The World of Susie Wong* (Broadhurst, N.Y.C., Oct. 14, 1958); *La Plume de Ma Tante* (Royale, Nov. 11, 1958); assistant to the producer for *The Ages of Man* (46 St. Th., Dec. 28, 1958); staff associate for *Destry Rides Again* (Imperial, Apr. 23, 1959); personal assistant to John Gielgud for *Much Ado About Nothing* (Lunt-Fontanne, Sept. 17, 1959); staff associate for *Take Me Along* (Shubert, Oct. 22, 1959); the pre-Bway tryout of *Juniper and the Pagans* (opened Colonial, Boston, Mass., Dec. 10, 1959; closed Forrest, Philadelphia, Pa., Dec. 26, 1959); assistant casting director for *The Good Soup* (Plymouth, N.Y.C., Mar. 2, 1960); staff associate for *Vintage '60* (Brooks Atkinson Th., Sept. 12, 1960); assistant casting director for *Irma La Douce* (Plymouth, Sept. 29, 1960); *A Taste of Honey* (Lyceum, Oct. 4, 1960); *Becket* (St. James, Oct. 5, 1960); and assistant production supervisor for *Do Re Mi* (St. James, Dec. 26, 1960).

He was production associate for *Carnival!* (Imperial, Apr. 13, 1961); assistant casting director for the touring company of *Gypsy* (opened Shubert, Detroit, Mich., Sept. 14, 1961; closed Hanna, Cleveland, Ohio, Jan. 20, 1962); production associate for *Subways Are for Sleeping* (St. James, Dec. 27, 1961); stage manager for *I Can Get It for You Wholesale* (Shubert, Mar. 22, 1962); casting director for its tour (opened Aud., Rochester, N.Y., Nov. 13, 1962); assistant casting director for *Oliver!* (Imperial, Jan. 6, 1963); assistant to Norman Jewison for *Here's Love* (Shubert, Oct. 3, 1963); assistant casting director for *110 in the Shade* (Broadhurst, Oct. 24, 1963); and stage manager for the NY World's Fair presentation of *Wonderworld* (Amphitheatre, Apr. 22, 1964).

He was also stage manager of the N.Y. World's Fair Dupont Show, *The Wonderful World of Chemistry* (1964–65); general manager of the American Place Th., N.Y.C. (1965); agent for the legitimate theatre and concert department at the Agency of the Performing Arts, N.Y.C. (1966); stage manager of *The Impossible Years* (Playhouse Th., N.Y., 1967); production manager of two all-star musical productions of Variety Clubs International: *Salute to Prince Phillip* (Americana Hotel, N.Y.C., Mar. 19, 1966) and *The Cancer Fund Memorial Tribute to Judy Holliday* (Americana Hotel, N.Y.C., May 15, 1966); stage manager of Dallas Summer Th. musicals, *South Pacific*, *Sweet Charity*, *Camelot*, and *Brigadoon;* stage manager of *Celebration* (Ambassador Th., N.Y.C., Jan. 22, 1969); *The Boys in the Band* (Th. Four, opened Apr. 14, 1968) and for its national tour (opened Studebaker Th., Chicago, Ill., Jan. 18, 1970); *No, No, Nanette* (46 St. Th., Jan. 19, 1971); producer of *Mourning in a Funny Hat* (ten-week summer tour opened Gilford Playhouse, Gilford, N.H., July 3, 1972); stage manager of *Irene* (Minskoff Th., Mar. 13, 1973); coordinator of The Actors Fund of America: *Special Benefit Performance of Bette Midler* (Palace Th., Dec. 23, 1973); stage manager of *A Gala Tribute to Richard Rodgers* (Imperial Th., Mar. 26, 1972); and *A Gala Tribute to Joshua Logan* (Imperial Th., Mar. 9, 1975).

Recreation. Collecting musical comedy and opera records, ticket stubs, theatre programs, and theatrical and historical autographs and pictures; opera; classical music; swimming, travel to far-away places.

SCHECHNER, RICHARD. Editor, educator, writer, director, producer, playwright. b. Aug. 23, 1934, Newark, N.J., to Sheridan and Selma (Schwarz) Schechner. Father, banker. Grad. Columbia H.S., Maplewood, N.J., 1952; Cornell Univ., B.A. 1956; attended Johns Hopkins Univ., 1956–57; grad. State Univ. of Iowa, M.A. 1958; Tulane Univ., Ph.D. 1962. Served US Army, 1958–60.

Mr. Schnechner is professor of drama at NY Univ. School of the Arts (1966–to date); and the founder (1968), producer and director of the Performance Group, an off-off-Bway experimental repertory theatre, which grew out of his work at NY Univ. The group's productions include *Dionysus in '69* (1968); *Macbeth* (1969); *Government Anarchy* (1970); *Commune* (1970); *Don Juan* (1971); *The Beard* (1972); and *The Tooth of Crime* (1972).

Previously, he directed and produced *Miss Julie*, *The Lesson*, *Woman of Paris*, *Philoctetes*, *Riders to the Sea*, *Purgatory*, and *When We Dead Awaken* (East End Players, Provincetown, Mass., Summers 1958–61); wrote *Blessing of the Fleet* (East End Players, Provincetown, Mass., Aug. 1958; Playwrights Showcase, New Orleans, May 1961); *Briseis and the Sergeant* (Tulane Univ. Th., May 1962); and directed *The Maids* (Tulane Univ. Th., Apr. 1963).

Mr. Schechner was one of three producing directors of the Free Southern Th., an integrated professional company with headquarters in New Orleans and touring facilities in Mississippi, Tennessee, Louisiana, and Alabama. He directed the FST's production of *Purlie Victorius* (Nov. 1964).

Published Works. Mr. Schechner has been editor of both the *Tulane Drama Review* (1962–67), and the re-located and renamed *Drama Review* (NY Univ., N.Y.C., 1967) from which he resigned in 1969. He contributed regularly to both publications, including such articles as "The Inner and the Outer Reality" and "Who's Afraid of Edward Albee?" (Spring 1963), "Intentions, Problems and Proposals" (Summer 1963), and "Stanislavski at School" (Winter 1964); and to the *Educational Theatre Journal*, *Yale French Studies*, the NY *Times*, the *Village Voice*, and *Theatre Quarterly*. He is the author of *Tonesco and Comic Theory* (1965); *Public Domain* (1969); *The Free Southern Theatre* (1969); *Environmental Theatre* (1973); and a monograph "Aspects of Training at the Performance Group", which is included in the Institute for Research in Acting publication, *Actor Training I.*

Awards. Mr. Schechner received a Guggenheim Fellowship Grant (Spring 1975) for the study of traditional performance in Asian theatre and experimental forms in American theatre.

SCHECHTMAN, SAUL. Musical director, composer, vocal arranger. b. Sept. 4, 1924, Winchester, Conn., to Isidore and Clara (Goodman) Schechtman. Father, businessman. Grad. Boys H.S., Brooklyn, NY, 1940; Brooklyn Coll., B.A. 1947; post-grad. diploma, Juilliard Sch. of Music, 1949. Studied piano with Celia Saloman, 1942; and Jerome Rappaport 1941; conducting with Edgar Schenkman, 1947; Dean Dixon, 1948; Jean Morel, 1949–51. Married July 31, 1952, to Carolyn Raney, voice teacher and musicologist; two daughters. Served USAAF and 16th Inf. Reg. ETO, 1943–46. Member of AFM, local 802; The Bohemians. Address: 4702 Underwood, Baltimore, MD 21212.

Theatre. Mr. Schechtman was a founder of the Co-Opera Inc. summer theatre (Green Mansions, Warrensburg, N.Y.) and its musical director for two seasons (1949–50). He was associate musical director (Juilliard Opera Th., N.Y.C.) of *The Magic Flute* (Nov. 1949), *Gianni Schicchi* (Feb. 1950), *Rigoletto* (Apr. 1950), *Le Pauvre Matelot* (Nov. 1950), *The Marriage of Figaro* (Feb. 1951), and musical director for *The Enchanted Pear Tree* (Apr. 1951), and a program of modern dance (May 1951).

He was assistant conductor for the pre-Bway tryout of *A Month of Sundays* (opened Shubert, Boston, Mass., Dec. 25, 1951; closed Forrest, Philadelphia, Pa., Jan. 26, 1952); and for *Wish You Were Here* (Imperial, N.Y.C., Apr. 1952); choral director for a repertory engagement of Gilbert and Sullivan operettas (Mark Hellinger Th., Oct. 20, 1952); musical director at the Miami (Fla.) Music Circus (Jan. 1953); for summer stock productions at the Fox Valley Playhouse (St. Charles, Ill., June 1954; June 1955); of the pre-Bway tryout of *The Amazing Adele* (opened Shubert, Philadelphia, Dec. 26, 1955; closed Shubert, Boston, Jan. 21, 1956); composed incidental music for *Auntie Mame* (Broadhurst, Oct. 31, 1956); was assistant conductor for rehearsals and the pre-Bway tour of *Li'l Abner* (St. James, Nov. 15, 1956); musical director for the Soviet Union tour of *My Fair Lady* (Spring 1960); joined (Apr. 4, 1960) the Bway production as musical director of *My Fair Lady* (Mark Hellinger Th., Mar. 15, 1956); was musical director at the Cass Th. (Detroit, Mich., Sept.–Oct. 1959); for the Kenley Players (Warren, Ohio, June–July 1960); standby conductor for rehearsals and the pre-Bway tour of *Camelot* (Majestic, Dec. 3, 1960); musical director and vocal arranger for *Carnival!* (Imperial, Apr. 13, 1961); musical director for *Kiss Me, Kate* (Iceland Natl. Th., Reykjavik, May 1958); musical director of the summer tour of *Music Fair* (May, 1963); for *How to Succeed in Business Without Really Trying* (Paris, France, Jan.–Feb. 1964); *Ice-Travaganza* (NY World's Fair, Apr. 1964); the national company of *Hello Dolly!* (Nov. 1966–Aug. 1967); and for the Bway company (St. James Th., N.Y.C., Aug. 1967–Dec. 1970).

Films. He composed a portion of the score for *Auntie Mame* (WB, 1958).

Television. He was associate conductor for six presentations on Omnibus, (CBS, Dec. 1953–Nov. 1957).

Other Activities. Mr. Schechtman was an arranger and member of the Air Force Band and made his concert debut as conductor and musical director at an orchestral concert (Carnegie Recital Hall, Feb. 1949); was assistant conductor of the Juilliard Orchestra (N.Y.C., 1949–1951); at Columbia Univ., conducted a concert of modern American music (June 1950); a piano recital of his works was given at Town Hall, N.Y.C. (Feb. 1951); he conducted an orchestral concert at Columbia Univ. (May 1951); and was musical director for the Bronx (N.Y.) Symphony Orchestra (Sept. 1953–56).

He was musical dir. for the Teaneck (N.J.) Symphony Orchestra (Dec. 1957–60); his vocal compositions were presented in a recital at the Carnegie Recital Hall (Apr. 1961); his organ works at the Union Theological Seminary (N.Y.C., June 1963). He was choral director for the *Chrysler Press Show* (Detroit, Mich., Sept. 1955); and musical director for the *Milliken Fashion Show* (Statler Hotel, N.Y.C., May 1956–July 1956, and May 1957–July 1957); *Chrysler Press Show* (Detroit, Mich., Sept. 1956); and *The March of Dimes* (Waldorf-Astoria, N.Y.C., Jan. 1959).

He was guest conductor, Danish Radio Symphony Orchestra (1964), Norwegian Radio Orchestra (1965), Baltimore Symphony Orchestra (1968), and the Netherlands Radio Chamber Orchestra (1973).

Published Works. A number of Mr. Schechtman's compositions have been published by MCA, Galaxy, and Boston Music Co.

Discography. Mr. Schechtman was musical director for the original cast album of *Carnival!;* for the Paris company's recording of *How To Succeed in Business without Really Trying;* and for the Pearl Bailey company recording of *Hello, Dolly!.*

Awards. He received a Greenwich House Music Sch. piano scholarship (1941–43); and a Juilliard Fellowship in orchestral conducting (1949–51).

Recreation. Travel.

SCHEEDER, LOUIS W. Director, producer. b. Dec. 26, 1946, New York City, to Louis W. and Julia (Callery) Scheeder. Father, insurance agent; mother, rental agent. Grad. Immaculate Conception Grammar Sch. (N.Y.C.); Regis H.S. (N.Y.C.); Georgetown Univ. (Washington, D.C.), B.A. 1968. Studied with Joseph Papp (directing), Jenny Egan (acting), and Albert Bermel (theatre history and criticism) at Columbia Univ. Sch. of the Arts (1968–69). Married June 14, 1969, to Donna Wills. Member of AEA; SSD&C. Address: (home) 12 Third St., S.E., Washington, DC 20003, tel. (202) 544-1344; (bus.) Folger Theatre Group, 201 E. Capitol St., S.E., Washington, DC 20003, tel. (202) 547-3230.

Pre-Theatre. Ice cream salesman, messenger, garment district runner, sanitationman, etc.

Theatre. Mr. Scheeder made his theatre debut playing Green in a high-school production of *Richard II;* and subsequently appeared as The Boy in *The Rapists* (Gate, N.Y.C., June 28, 1966). He served as a journeyman stage manager with the Arena Stage (Washington, D.C., 1969–70); was resident director for the Theatre Lobby (Washington, D.C.), where he was responsible for productions of *We Bombed in New Haven, The Rimers of Eldritch,* and *America Hurrah* (Summer 1969), the original productions of *If I Had a Yardstick, Harry, Noon and Night,* and *The White House Murder Case* (Summer 1970); and directed weekly staged readings of new plays (Washington Th. Club, Apr.–Nov. 1970).

For the Folger Theatre Group (Washington, D.C.), where he has served as associate artistic director (Apr. 1971–Feb. 1973), associate producer (Feb.–Aug. 1973), and producer (Aug. 1973–to date), he directed *Happy Days* (Jan. 1971); *Twelfth Night* (Apr. 1971); *The Promise* (May 1971); *Landscape* and *Silence* (Oct. 1972); the American premiere of *Total Eclipse* (Oct. 1972); *The Revenger's Tragedy* (Dec. 1972); *The Winter's Tale* (Feb. 1973); and the American premiere of *Creeps* (Oct. 1973), which he subsequently directed off-Bway (Playhouse II, N.Y.C., Dec. 4, 1973). At The Little Theatre on the Square (Sullivan, Ill.), he directed *1776* (June 1972) and *Applause* (July 1973).

Other Activities. Mr. Scheeder has served on the faculty of the Fine Arts Dept. of Georgetown Univ. (Jan.–May 1974).

Awards. He was awarded the Georgetown Univ. Dixon Medal (1968) for his outstanding contribution to dramatic arts.

Recreation. Music, basketball.

SCHENKER, JOEL. Producer, educator, business executive. b. Joel W. Schenker, Nov. 24, 1903, New York City, to Barnet L. and Bertha (Deutsch) Schenker. Father, restaurateur. Attended Sch. of Law, Univ. of St. Lawrence. Married June 17, 1931, to Janet Blau; four daughters. Served WW II, ETO, PTO, 1943–45. Member of ASFTA (dir., vice-pres.); League of NY Theatres (bd. of gov.); AADA (trustee); Amer. Theatre Wing (Trustee); The Lambs; Woodmere (N.Y.) Country Club; Jewish Theological Seminary of America (dir.). Address: (home) 211 Central Park West, New York, NY 10024, tel. (212) SC 4-0287; (bus.) 165 W. 46th St., Rm. 805, New York, NY 10036, tel. (212) JU 2-4031.

Theatre. Mr. Schenker was a founder of the Lenox Hill Players in 1929, and appeared there in *Androcles and the Lion, Foundations, The Power of Darkness,* and *The Cenci.* He wrote with Allan Fleming, *This Is Our House* (58 St. Th., N.Y.C., Dec. 10, 1935); and produced, with Cheryl Crawford, by arrangement with the Actors' Studio, *Shadow of a Gunman* (Bijou, Nov. 20, 1958); produced, with Miss Crawford, *The Rivalry* (Bijou, Feb. 7, 1959); produced, with Miss Crawford, in association with October Productions, Inc., *The Long Dream* (Ambassador, Feb. 17, 1960); presented with Roger L. Stevens, *A Far Country* (Music Box, Apr. 4, 1961); produced, with Theatre Guild Productions, Inc., *The Captains and the Kings* (Playhouse, Jan. 2, 1962); produced *Venus at Large* (Morosco, Apr. 12, 1962); *If Five Years Pass* (Stage 73, May 10, 1962); produced, with Alan Pakula and Eleanor Brissinger, the tryout of *There Must Be a Pony* (opened Ogunquit Playhouse, Me., July 16, 1962); presented, with Theatre Guild Productions, Inc., in association with Michael Kanin and Elliot Martin, *Seidman and Son* (Belasco, N.Y.C., Oct. 15, 1962); and produced *A Case of Libel* (Longacre, Oct. 10, 1963).

From 1964 until his resignation in 1968, Mr. Schenker was a managing director, with Armina Marshall and Philip Langner, of the Theatre Guild, as well as one of the major stockholders in the producing firm. He produced, with the Theatre Guild, *Darling of the Day* (George Abbott Th., Jan. 27, 1968); with Lyn Austin, Oliver Smith, and Roger L. Stevens, *Indians* (Brooks Atkinson Th., Oct. 13, 1969); and the Guthrie Th. Co. (Minneapolis, Minn.) produced, by arrangement with Mr. Schenker and George W. George, *A Play by Aleksandr Solzhenitsyn* (Guthrie Th., Oct. 13, 1970). Mr. Schenker also produced a revival of *The Homecoming* (Cherry Lane Th., N.Y.C., May 17, 1971); with Edward F. Kook, *Love Me, Love My Children* (Mercer-O'Casey Th., Nov. 3, 1971); produced *An Evening with the Poet-Senator* (Playhouse 2, Mar. 21, 1973); and, with Claire Nichtern, *I Got a Song* (pre-Bway: opened Studio Arena, Buffalo, N.Y., Sept. 26, 1974; closed there, Oct. 20, 1974).

In 1976, Mr. Schenker was appointed adjunct professor of modern theatre at Windham Coll. (Putney, Vt.).

Radio. In 1966, Mr. Schenker conducted a program on theatre on WNCN-FM (N.Y.C.).

Other Activities. Mr. Schenker has been a real estate developer and builder. He was director of Foreign Shelter for the Public Housing Authority (1944–45); was president, Roth-Schenker Corp., builders and developers; and in 1967 was appointed president, Starrett Bros. and Eken Development Corp. (N.Y.C.), builders and construction engineers.

Awards. He received a World Brotherhood Award (1953) and other communal, Jewish, and hospital organization awards. *Indians* was nominated for an Antoinette Perry (Tony) Award as best play of the season 1969–70. In 1975, Mr. Schenker was awarded an honorary D.F.A. degree by California Western Univ., Santa Ana, Calif.

SCHIRMER, GUS JR. Director, talent representative, packager. b. Gustave Schirmer, Jr., Oct. 18, 1918, New York City, to Gustave Schirmer, Sr., and Florence (Powers) Schirmer. Father, music publisher; mother, businesswoman. Attended

Browning Sch. for Boys, N.Y.C., 1926–32; Lawrenceville Academy, 1932–34; Pasadena Playhouse, 1935–38. Member of AEA; SSD&C. Address: 1403 N. Orange Grove Ave., Los Angeles, CA 90046, tel. (213) 876-5044.

Theatre. Mr. Schirmer established the Musical Comedy Dept. at MCA Artists Ltd. (1945) and served as agent until 1946; talent agent since 1948; opened his own talent agency in New York City, representing clients in all entertainment media (1951–to date).

He made his Bway debut in the revue *New Faces of 1934* (Fulton, Mar. 15, 1934); subsequently appeared in *You Never Know* (Winter Garden, Sept. 21, 1938); was casting assistant for *Madame Capet* (Cort, Oct. 25, 1938), *Here Come the Clowns* (Booth, Dec. 7, 1938), and *The White Steed* (Cort, Jan. 10, 1939); produced and directed the USO all-girl voluntary revue *Look Boys-Girls* (1942–45); and at the Strand Th., Stamford, Conn., presented stock productions of *Private Lives* (Summer 1944) and *Candida* (Summer 1945).

He was producer for the Greenwich (Conn.) Playhouse (Summer 1946); stage manager for *Burlesque* (Belasco, N.Y.C., Dec. 25, 1946); packaged summer touring productions of *The Philadelphia Story* (1948); *Harvey* (1949); *Second Man* (1949); packaged and directed *Pal Joey* (1951); directed the national touring company of *A Tree Grows in Brooklyn* (opened Klein Aud., Bridgeport, Conn., Oct. 10, 1952; closed Shubert, Chicago, Ill., Nov. 29, 1952); directed summer touring productions of *One Touch of Venus* (1952), *Three to One* (1952), *Gentlemen Prefer Blondes* (1953); packaged and directed *The Boys from Syracuse* (1954); packaged *Dear Charles* (1954); packaged and directed *Wonderful Town* (1955); packaged *The Rainmaker* (1955); *Sabrina Fair* (1955); packaged and directed *Plain and Fancy* (1956); directed *The Boy Friend* (John Drew Th., East Hampton, L.I., 1957; Downtown Th. N.Y.C., Jan. 25, 1958); supervised the revue *Diversions* Downtown Th., Nov. 7, 1958); directed *Monday Nights at Nine,* a program presented on Monday nights at the Cherry Lane Th., consisting of *The Art of Mabel Mercer* (Oct. 1958) and *A Party with Betty Comden and Adolph Green* (Nov. 1958); directed *Gay Divorce* (Cherry Lane, Apr. 3, 1960); for Dallas (Tex.) summer musicals, directed *West Side Story* (1960), *Redhead* (1960), and the 1961–62 summer seasons, including *Gypsy, South Pacific, Carousel, The Merry Widow, Take Me Along, Destry,* and *Brigadoon.*

Mr. Schirmer directed *Pal Joey* (NY City Ctr., May 31, 1961); *Can-Can* (NY City Ctr., May 16, 1962); *Wonderful Town* (NY City Ctr., Feb. 13, 1963); for the Guber, Ford and Gross Music Fairs, staged *The King and I* and *Pal Joey* (Summer 1963); directed a summer touring production of *Kind Sir* (1963); directed *Double Dublin* (Little Th., N.Y.C., Dec. 26, 1963); staged the opera *The Mother of Us All* for the American Opera Soc. (Carnegie Hall, Mar. 31, 1964); and directed the Kenley Players (Summer 1964).

For the NY City Ctr. Light Opera Co., he directed (all at NY City Ctr.) *Guys and Dolls* (Apr. 28, 1965), *The Music Man* (June 16, 1965), *How To Succeed in Business without Really Trying* (Apr. 20, 1966), *Guys and Dolls* (June 8, 1966), *Carousel* (Dec. 15, 1966), *Finian's Rainbow* (Apr. 5, 1967), *Wonderful Town* (May 17, 1967), *Brigadoon* (Dec. 13, 1967), and *Carnival!* (Dec. 12, 1968). He also directed a revival of *Life with Father* (NY City Ctr., Oct. 19, 1967); a summer touring production of *Desk Set* (Summer 1968); *The Boy Friend* (Ambassador, N.Y.C., Apr. 14, 1970); *Guys and Dolls* (Denver, Colo., 1971); and *Pal Joey* (German Th., Chicago, Ill., 1972).

Television. Mr. Schirmer was executive producer of the *Sandy Duncan Special* (CBS, 1974).

Night Clubs. Mr. Schirmer was producer-director for Tallulah Bankhead (Sands Hotel, Las Vegas, Nev., 1952).

Recreation. Cooking.

SCHISGAL, MURRAY.

Playwright. b. Nov. 25, 1926, Brooklyn, N.Y. Educ. Brooklyn Conservatory of Music; Long Island Univ.; grad. Brooklyn Law School, LL.B. 1953; New School for Social Research, B.A. 1959. Served in US Navy, 1944–46. Married 1958 to Reene Schapiro; one daughter, one son. Address: 275 Central Park West, New York, NY 10024.

Pre-Theatre. Mr. Schisgal worked as a musician (1947–50); practised law (1953–55); taught in private and public schools (1955–59); and has concentrated on writing since 1960.

Theatre. Mr. Schisgal's *The Typists, The Postman,* and *A Simple Kind of Love Story* were produced in London, England (British Drama League, Dec. 1960), as was his *Ducks and Lovers* (Arts, Oct. 19, 1961). *The Typists* was presented off-Bway in N.Y.C. on a double bill with *The Tiger* (Orpheum, Feb. 4, 1963), and *Knit One, Purl Two* in Boston, Mass., by the Boston Poets Th. (Hotel Bostonian, Mar. 27, 1963). *Luv* (New Arts, London, Eng., Apr. 24, 1963; Booth Th., N.Y.C., Nov. 11, 1964) was followed by the double-bill *Fragments* and *The Basement* (Cherry Lane Th., N.Y.C., Oct. 2, 1967); *Jimmy Shine* (Brooks Atkinson Th., Dec. 5, 1968); another double-bill. *The Chinese and Dr. Fish* (Ethel Barrymore Th., Mar. 10, 1970); *An American Millionaire* (Circle in the Square/Joseph E. Levine Th., Apr. 20, 1974); and *All Over Town* (Booth Th., Dec. 29, 1974).

Films. Mr. Schisgal wrote the screenplay for *The Tiger Makes Out* (Col., 1967).

Television. Mr. Schisgal wrote *The Love Song of Barney Kempinski* (ABC Special, 1966).

Other Activities. In addition to his writing, Mr. Schisgal has lectured and taught playwriting at universities since 1960.

Awards. For *The Typists* and *The Tiger,* Mr. Schisgal received the Vernon Rice and Outer Circle awards (1963).

SCHMIDT, CHARLES A.

Educator. b. Charles Albert Schmidt, Jr., Feb. 17, 1923, Ben Hur, Tex., to Charles Albert and Jewell (Herod) Schmidt. Father and mother, teachers. Grad. Thornton (Tex.) H.S., 1939; Univ. of Texas, B.F.A. 1943, M.F.A. 1949; attended Univ. of Wisconsin, Summer, 1950; Univ. of Houston, Summer 1951; Louisiana State Univ., Summer 1955; grad. Univ. of Denver, Ph.D. 1963. Served US Army, 1943–46. Member of ATA; Texas Educational Theatre Assn. (secy., 1958–60; pres., 1968–70). Address: (home) Sunset Lake, Huntsville, TX 77340, tel. (713) 295-7687; (bus.) Dept. of Speech & Drama, Sam Houston State Coll., Huntsville, TX 77340, tel. (713) 295-6211, ext. 2877.

Mr. Schmidt is chairman of the Dept. of Speech and Drama at Sam Houston State Coll., where he has been a member of the faculty (1949–to date). He supervises and writes screenplays for the motion picture production program, and directs eight or nine stage productions annually, presented either on the college's proscenium or modified thrust stage. Mr. Schmidt also directs some of the college's television productions, transmitted in color from the local CATV studio (Ch. 7). In addition, the Dept. of Speech and Drama has participated since 1972 in a summer session program at the Point Th., Ingram, Tex., offering college credit in cooperation with the Hill County Arts Foundation.

SCHMIDT, DOUGLAS W.

Scenic designer, costume designer. b. Douglas Wocher Schmidt, Oct. 4, 1942, Cincinnati, Ohio, to Robert Wocher and Jean (Murdoch) Schmidt. Father, president of surgical supply company. Educ. High Mowing School, Wilton, N.H.; Boston (Mass.) Univ. Studied with Horace Armistead, Raymond Sovey, Dept. of Th. Arts, Boston Univ.; Lester Polakov at the Studio and Forum of Stage Design, N.Y.C. Member of USA, Local 829; American Soc. of Interior Designers (professional affiliate member). Address: 5 W. 86th St., New York, NY 10024, tel. (212) TR 3-5565.

Theatre. Mr. Schmidt directed and designed a production of *The Thirteen Clocks* (Feb. 1960) while a student at High Mowing School. His first professional work was as stage manager and designer for a summer stock production of *The Importance of Being Earnest* (Monmouth Repertory Th., Monmouth, Me., July 1961), and he subsequently designed sets for Monmouth productions of *The Devil's Disciple* (July 17, 1961), *Othello* (July 24, 1961), and *Androcles and the Lion* (Aug. 7, 1961); for Boston Univ. Th. he designed the set for *Blood Wedding* (Apr. 3, 1963).

In 1965, Mr. Schmidt designed sets for Playhouse in the Park, Cincinnati, Ohio, productions of *Ghosts* (Apr. 7), *The Collection* and *The Lover* (Apr. 28), *Major Barbara* (May 19), *The Summer of the Seventeenth Doll* (June 9), *She Stoops To Conquer* (June 30), and *The Glass Menagerie* (Aug. 11). He designed the Festival Stage for Baltimore (Md.) Center Stage and the set for Center Stage's production of *Caesar and Cleopatra* (Oct. 28, 1965); for *La Bohème* (Juilliard Opera Th., N.Y.C., Mar. 3, 1966); and again for a series of Cincinnati's Playhouse in the Park productions (all 1966); *Man and Superman* (Apr. 6), *Benito Cereno* and *The American Dream* (Apr. 28), *Charley's Aunt* (June 16), *Eh?* (July 13), and *The Skin of Our Teeth* (Aug. 4).

He was set designer for the off-Bway production *The Ox Cart* (Greenwich Mews Th., N.Y.C., Dec. 19, 1966); for two more Juilliard Opera Th. productions in N.Y.C.: *The Marriage of Figaro* (Jan. 17, 1967) and *The Mines of Sulphur* (Mar. 16, 1967); for *A Clearing in the Woods* (Riverside Ch., Mar. 1, 1967); *The Importance of Being Earnest* (Playhouse in the Park, Cincinnati, Apr. 13, 1967); *To Bury a Cousin* (Bouwerie Lane, N.Y.C., May 16, 1967); *The Cavern* (Playhouse in the Park, Cincinnati, June 8, 1967); *King John* (Delacorte Th., N.Y.C., July 5, 1967); *Anatol* (Playhouse in the Park, Cincinnati, Aug. 31, 1967); *Father Uxbridge Wants to Marry* (American Place Th., N.Y.C., Oct. 12, 1967); *The Entertainer* (Th. of the Living Arts, Philadelphia, Pa., Nov. 1, 1967); and *The Great White Hope* (Arena Stage, Washington, D.C., Dec. 7, 1967).

Mr. Schmidt was also set designer for *Silent Night, Lonely Night* (Riverside Ch., N.Y.C., Mar. 12, 1968); for the Jose Limón ballet *Tonantzintla* (Juilliard Th., Mar. 28, 1968); *Misalliance* (Playhouse in the Park, Cincinnati, Apr. 4, 1968); *The Memorandum* (Public Th., Apr. 23, 1968); for *Camino Real* (Playhouse in the Park, Cincinnati, July 18, 1968); *The Madwoman of Chaillot* (Playhouse in the Park, Aug. 29, 1968); for *Huui, Huui* (Public Th., Nov. 24, 1968); for *Trainer, Dean, Liepolt & Co.* (American Place Th., Dec. 12, 1968); *Geese* and *Parents and Children* (Players Th., Jan. 12, 1969); and the Jose Limón company ballet *La Piñata* (Juilliard Th., Mar. 20, 1969).

He designed scenery for *The Inner Journey* (Forum Th., Mar. 20, 1969); *Julius Caesar* (Tyrone Guthrie Th., Minneapolis, Minn., June 26, 1969); *The Homecoming* (Tyrone Guthrie Th., July 8, 1969); *Twelfth Night* (Delacorte Th., N.Y.C., Aug. 12, 1969); *The Time of Your Life* (Vivian Beaumont Th., Nov. 6, 1969); and for *Paris Is Out!* (Brooks Atkinson Th., Jan. 19, 1970). Also for *The Disintegration of James Cherry* (Forum, Jan. 29, 1970); *Operation Sidewinder* (Vivian Beaumont Th., Mar. 12, 1970); *Mod Donna* (Public Th., May 3, 1970); for *The Good Woman of Setzuan* (Vivian Beaumont Th., Nov. 5, 1970); and sets and costumes for *The Playboy of the Western World* (Vivian Beaumont Th., Jan. 7, 1971). He was set designer for *An Enemy of the People* (Vivian Beaumont Th., Mar. 11, 1971); for the opera *The Losers* (Juilliard Th., Mar. 26, 1971); set and costume designer for *Pictures in the Hallway* (Forum, Apr. 29, 1971); set designer for *Antigone* (Vivian Beaumont Th., May 13, 1971); *Huckleberry Finn* (Juilliard Th., May 20, 1971); *Play Strindberg* (Forum, June 3, 1971); and for the American Shakespeare Festival *The Merry Wives of Windsor* (Stratford, Conn., June 12, 1971).

He was set designer for operas given at Tanglewood, Lenox, Mass., in 1971: *Croquefer* and *Mahagonny* (July 21) and *Down by the Greenwood Side* and *Socrate* and *Aventures et Nouvelles Aventures* (all Aug. 8); designed sets for *Mary Stuart* (Vivian Beaumont

Th., N.Y.C., Nov. 12, 1971); for *The Country Girl* (Eisenhower Th., Washington, D.C., Nov. 16, 1971); *People Are Living There* (Forum, N.Y.C., Nov. 18, 1971); and for the NY Shakespeare Festival *Iphigenia* (Public Th., Dec. 16, 1971). Also for *Narrow Road to the Deep North* (Vivian Beaumont Th., Jan. 6, 1972); *The Love Suicide at Schofield Barracks* (ANTA Th., Feb. 9, 1972); *Grease* (Eden, Feb. 14, 1972) and for Australian, British, and two American touring companies; *Twelfth Night* (Vivian Beaumont Th., Mar. 2, 1972); *The Country Girl* (Billy Rose Th., Mar. 15, 1972); *Suggs* (Forum, May 4, 1972); and the Berkshire Festival *And Miss Reardon Drinks a Little* (Stockbridge, Mass., June 30, 1972).

He again designed sets for operas given at Tanglewood, Lenox, Mass.: *Der Jasager* and *Chocorua* (both Aug. 2, 1972) and *L'Incoronazione di Poppaea* (Aug. 13, 1972); designed sets for the City Center Acting Co's tours of *The School for Scandal* (Sept. 18, 1972), *The Hostage* (Oct. 1, 1972), *Women Beware Women* (Oct. 17, 1972), and *The Lower Depths* (Oct. 24, 1972); for *Enemies* (Vivian Beaumont Th., Nov. 9, 1972); *Happy Days* and *Act without Words I* (Forum, Nov. 20, 1972); *Krapp's Last Tape* and *Not I* (Forum, Nov. 22, 1972); and for the opera *Mahagonny* (Opera House, Kennedy Ctr., Washington, D.C., Dec. 15, 1972). He also designed sets for *The Plough and the Stars* (Vivian Beaumont Th., Jan. 4, 1973); for the operas *Aventures et Nouvelles Aventures* and *Satyricon* (Circustheatre, Scheveningen, Netherlands, Mar. 16, 1973); for *A Streetcar Named Desire* (Vivian Beaumont Th., Apr. 26, 1973; and for the American Shakespeare Festival *Macbeth* (Stratford, Conn., June 28, 1973).

He designed sets for City Ctr. Acting Co's *Measure for Measure* (Saratoga Spa Th., Saratoga, N.Y., July 9, 1973; Billy Rose Th., N.Y.C., Dec. 26, 1973) and *The Three Sisters* (Saratoga Spa Th., Saratoga, N.Y., July 16, 1973; Billy Rose Th., N.Y.C., Dec. 19, 1973); for *A Breeze from the Gulf* (Eastside Playhouse, N.Y.C., Oct. 15, 1973); *Veronica's Room* (Music Box, Oct. 25, 1973); and for the opera *Il Ritorno d'Ulisse in Patria* (Opera House, Kennedy Ctr., Washington, D.C., Jan. 18, 1974). Also for *An American Millionaire* (Circle in the Square, Mar. 1, 1974); *Over Here!* (Shubert Th., Mar. 6, 1974); and for City Ctr. Acting Co's (all at Saratoga Spa Th., Saratoga, N.Y.) *Love's Labour's Lost* (July 8, 1974), *Play* and *Orchestra* (both July 22, 1974), and *Edward II* (July 29, 1974).

Mr. Schmidt was also set designer for City Ctr. Acting Co's *The Taming of the Shrew* (Art Park, Buffalo, N.Y., Sept. 7, 1974) and *The Time of Your Life* (Mendelssohn Th., Ann Arbor, Mich., Nov. 7, 1974); for *Fame* (Golden Th., Nov. 18, 1974); *Who's Who in Hell* (Lunt-Fontanne Th., Dec. 9, 1974); *Our Late Night* (Public Th., Jan. 9, 1975); the NY City Opera's *Salome* (State Th., Mar. 2, 1975); and *Kid Champion* (Public Th., Mar. 19, 1975).

Television. Mr. Schmidt was set designer for *Antigone* (Playhouse New York, PBS, Oct. 7, 1972) and *Enemies* (Th. in America, PBS, Jan. 23, 1974).

Published Works. Mr. Schmidt's designs appear in *Stage Design Since 1960* (1972) and in ITI's *Contemporary Stage Design USA* (1974).

Awards. Mr. Schmidt received a Maharam Foundation Award (1972–73) for best scenic design for *Enemies* and a Drama Desk Award for his set designs for *Veronica's Room* and *Over Here!.*

SCHMIDT, HARVEY. Composer. b. Harvey Lester Schmidt, Sept. 12, 1929, Dallas, Tex., to the Rev. E. C. and Edna (Wieting) Schmidt. Father, Methodist minister. Grad. Univ. of Texas, B.F.A. 1952. Served US Army, 1953–55. Member ASCAP.

Pre-Theatre. Painter.

Theatre. With his collaborator (dating from college days), playwright and lyricist Tom Jones, Mr. Schmidt composed music for *Shoestring '57* (Barbizon-Plaza Hotel, N.Y.C., Nov. 5, 1956); *Kaleidoscope* (Provincetown Playhouse, N.Y.C., June 13, 1957); and *The Fantasticks*, first presented as a one-act musical (Barnard Summer Th., N.Y.C., 1959) and later expanded to full length (Sullivan St. Playhouse, May 3, 1960). In June 1976, *The Fantasticks*, already the long-run record holder for the American theatre, began its seventeenth off-Bway season; in addition there have been productions in every state, as well as in over fifty foreign countries.

Mr. Schmidt also wrote the music for *110 in the Shade* (Broadhurst, N.Y.C., Oct. 24, 1963); and *I Do! I Do!* (46 St. Th., Dec. 5, 1966); *Celebration* (Ambassador Th., Jan. 22, 1969); and *Colette* (Ellen Stewart Th., May 6, 1970).

Mr. Schmidt and Tom Jones established The Portfolio Studio in N.Y.C. as an experimental theatre workshop and are its artistic directors. Works by them presented at Portfolio include *Portfolio Revue* (Dec. 6, 1974); two original musicals: *Philemon* (Jan. 3, 1975; reopened Apr. 8, 1975) and *The Bone Room* (Feb. 28, 1975); and a revival of *Celebration* (Jan. 31, 1975).

Films. With Tom Jones, Mr. Schmidt wrote the film short *A Texas Romance—1909* (1964).

Television. Mr. Schmidt wrote the music for *New York Scrapbook* (Play of the Week, WNTA, 1961).

Night Clubs. Mr. Schmidt collaborated with Tom Jones in creating material for Julius Monk's revues in the late 1950's.

Other Activities. Mr. Schmidt's paintings and drawings have appeared in several periodicals, including *Life*, *Esquire*, *Fortune*, *Harper's Bazaar*, and *Sports Illustrated*.

Published Works. Mr. Schmidt collaborated with Robert Benton on the *In and Out Book* (1958) and *The Worry Book* (1962), and he illustrated *The Mighty Ones* (1959).

Awards. He received, with Tom Jones, the Vernon Rice Award (1961) for *The Fantasticks*, and they were nominated for an Antoinette Perry (Tony) Award (1967) as best composer and lyricist for *I Do! I Do!.* The Portfolio Studio received the Outer Critics' Circle Award (1975) for outstanding contributions to the musical theatre. Their film short, *A Texas Romance—1909* won first prize at the San Francisco Film Festival. Mr. Schmidt received the gold medal of the NY Soc. of Illustrators in 1959, 1960, and 1963.

SCHNABEL, STEFAN. Actor, singer. b. Feb. 2, 1912, Berlin, Germany, to Artur and Therese Schnabel. Father, pianist; mother, musician. Attended Univ. of Bonn (Germany); Gruening Sch. of Acting. Married 1947 to Marion Kohler, actress; one son, one daughter. During Ww II, served two years with the OSS in the underground in England, Germany, France, and Holland, for which he received a Certificate of Merit. Member of AEA; AFTRA; SAG; AGMA.

Theatre. Mr. Schnabel made his professional debut as an offstage wind noise in *The Tempest* (Old Vic, London, 1933); subsequently, at the Old Vic, played the Third Murderer in *Macbeth* (Apr. 2. 1934); the Soothsayer in *Anthony and Cleopatra* (Sept. 17, 1934); and Lord Willoughby in *King Richard II* (Oct. 15, 1934); the Second Player in *The Taming of the Shrew* (Old Vic at Sadler's Wells, Jan. 1, 1935); Morrison in *Major Barbara* (Old Vic, London, Mar. 4, 1935); the Porter in *Henry IV* (Old Vic, Mar. 25, 1935); Krumpaker in *Sweeney Agonestes* (Westminster Th., London, Oct. 1, 1935); the Messenger, Sheriff, and Murderer in *King Richard III* (Old Vic, Jan. 14, 1936); Grabatern in *The Dog Beneath the Skin* (Westminster Th., Jan. 30, 1936); the Doctor in *King Lear* (Old Vic, Apr. 7, 1936); Bergriffenfeldt in *Peer Gynt* (Sadler's Wells, May 5, 1936); Charles in *As You Like It* (Old Vic, Nov. 10, 1936); and Hamluc in *The Witch of Edmonton* (Old Vic, Dec. 8, 1936).

In New York, he appeared as Metellus Cimber in *Julius Caesar* (Mercury, Nov. 11, 1937); A Dutch Skipper in *Shoemaker's Holiday* (Mercury, Jan. 1, 1938); Nicholas Jarga in *Glamour Preferred* (Booth, Nov. 5, 1940); Lieutenant Werner in *Land of Fame* (Belasco, Sept. 21, 1943); Lopakin in *The Cherry Orchard* (National, Jan. 25, 1944); Avery Jevitt, an Arab Spy, the Clown, and the Medicine Man in *Around the World in 80 Days* (Adelphi, May 31, 1946); M. Hufnagel and Don Modesto in *Now I Lay Me Down to Sleep* (Broadhurst, Mar. 2, 1950); Dr. Waldersee in *Idiot's Delight* (NY City Ctr., May 23, 1951); Col. Alexander Ikonenko in *The Love of Four Colonels* (Shubert, Jan. 15, 1953; and national tour, opened Community Th., Hershey, Pa., Oct. 2, 1953); Papa Yoder in *Plain and Fancy* (Mark Hellinger Th., N.Y.C., Jan. 27, 1955; and national tour, opened Forrest, Philadelphia, Mar. 6, 1956); Gen. Graf Van Donop in *Small War on Murray Hill* (Ethel Barrymore Th., N.Y.C., Jan. 3, 1957); and Baron Gray in *The Grand Duchess of Gerolstein* (Town Hall, Jan. 21, 1958).

Mr. Schnabel played Stomil in the off-Bway production of *Tango* (Pocket, N.Y.C., Jan. 18, 1969); subsequently appeared as Hans Bethe in *In the Matter of J. Robert Oppenheimer* (Vivian Beaumont Th., Mar. 6, 1969); Gen. Conrad von Hotzendorf in *A Patriot for Me* (Imperial, Oct. 5, 1969); Dubufay, Dunbar, Bubber, Sidney, Bob, and Howardina's Brother in *Older People* (Public Th., May 14, 1972); Gen. Pechenegov in *Enemies* (Vivian Beaumont Th., Nov. 9, 1972); off-off-Bway, played Vlrik Brendel in *Rosmersholm* (Roundabout, Dec. 3, 1974); and, with the NY Shakespeare Festival, Willie Schmidt in *Little Black Sheep* (Vivian Beaumont Th., May 7, 1975).

Films. Mr. Schnabel made his film debut in *Journey into Fear* (RKO, 1942); subsequently appeared in *The Iron Curtain* (20th-Fox, 1948); *The Barbary Pirate* (Col., 1949); *Diplomatic Courier* (20th-Fox, 1953); *Houdini* (Par., 1953); *Crowded Paradise* (Tudor, 1955); *The 27th Day* (Col., 1957); *The Mugger* (UA, 1959); *The Secret Ways* (U, 1962); *Counterfeit Traitor* (Par., 1962); *Two Weeks in Another Town* (MGM, 1963); *The Ugly American* (U, 1964); *Rampage* (WB, 1964); and *A Very Rich Woman* (Supervision, 1965).

Television and Radio. Mr. Schnabel performed on over three thousand network radio broadcasts, including The Mercury Th. presentation of *The War of the Worlds* (CBS). Subsequent appearances include Big Sister (CBS); Columbia Workshop (CBS); Gang Busters (CBS); The Story of Mary Marlin (CBS); Against the Storm (NBC); Portia Faces Life (NBC); Revlon Th. (NBC); and Th. Guild (ABC).

His television appearances number over one hundred, including Kraft Th. (NBC); Ford Th. (CBS); Studio One (CBS); Lux Video Th. (CBS); You Are There (CBS); and Suspense (CBS).

SCHNEIDEMAN, ROBERT IVAN. Educator, director. b. June 23, 1926, Bay City, Mich., to Louis and Frances Schneideman. Father, merchant. Grad. Central H.S., Bay City, 1944; Northwestern Univ., B.S. (speech and theatre) 1948, M.A. (speech and oral interpretation) 1949, and Ph.D. (theatre) 1956. Studied dance with Hanya Holm; directing with Lee Strasberg and Lee Mitchell; acting with Alvina Krause; and lighting with Theodore Fuchs. Member of AETA (exec. secy.-treas., 1962–64); AAUP; James Joyce Society. Address: (home) 1500 Oak Ave., Apt. 2F, Evanston, IL 60201, tel. (312) DA 8-8555; (bus.) Northwestern Univ., Sch. of Speech, Evanston, IL 60201, tel. (312) 492-7281.

Mr. Schneideman began as an instructor in dramatic production at Northwestern Univ. (1953), and became professor of dramatic production (1968). While at Northwestern, he has directed plays for the university theatre that include *The Imaginary Invalid*, *Fashion*, *The Birds*, *Oedipus Rex*, *The Caucasian Chalk Circle*, *Galileo*, *Mother Courage*, *Waiting for Godot*, *Endgame*, *The Time of your Life*, *Awake and Sing*, *The Beggar's Opera*, *The Servant of Two Masters*, *Lute Song*, *Noah*, *The Quare Fellow*, *The White Devil*, *The Tempest*, *Danton's Death*, and *Hotel Paradiso*. He also chaired the Theatre Dept. (1968–71), and served on the advisory board of the Hull House Assn., theatre division. Since 1961, he has been director of an advanced stage directors' course in Ontario (Canada), sponsored annually by the Canadian Dept. of Education.

With the Natl. Youth Th., Mr. Schneideman has toured cross-country in the title role in *Merlin, the Magician* (1949–50). He directed *Stewed Prunes* (Gate of Horn, Chicago, Ill., Oct. 1961); and for the Playwrights, *Krapp's Last Tape* (Second City, May

1962). Since 1949, he has presented a solo concert version of Mann's *Mario and the Magician* (Midwest and Can.).

Television. He has appeared on network and local dramatic programs, including *Vistas* (CBS, 1962), and panel shows (WTTW, 1955–to date).

Recreation. Antique collecting, magic, tropical fish breeding, painting miniatures, and hand crafts.

SCHNEIDER, ALAN. Director. b. Abram Leopoldovich Schneider, Dec. 12, 1917, Kharkov, Russia, to Leo V. and Rebecca L. (Malkin) Schneider. Father and mother, physicians. Grad. Forest Park H.S., Baltimore, Md., 1935; studied at the Maryland Inst. of Art, Baltimore, 1932–33; attended Johns Hopkins Univ., 1935–36; Univ. of Maryland, Summer 1936; grad. Univ. of Wisconsin, B.A. (magna cum laude, elected to Phi Beta Kappa, 1939); Cornell Univ., M.A., 1941. Studied with Lee Strasberg at the American Th. Wing, 1948. Married Mar. 23, 1953, to Eugenie Muckle; one son, one daughter. Served WW II, OWI (domestic branch). Member of AEA; SSD&C (exec. bd.); DGA; Drama Panel, Office of Cultural Presentations, Bureau of Educational and Cultural Affairs, US Dept. of State; Fulbright Exchange Program (theatre selection bd.); ITI (US delegate to international conferences: Warsaw, Tel-Aviv, New York City, Budapest, Moscow); NY State Language Arts Advisory Comm.; Mayor's Comm. (N.Y.C.) for the 25th anniversary of the UN; Mayor's Comm. (N.Y.C.) for New Theatre Planning; N.Y.C. Committee for Westbeth (housing for artists); Westchester (N.Y.) Council on the Arts; consultant, Rockefeller Foundation; consultant, Div. of Humanities and Arts, The Ford Foundation; Arts Society (adv. bd.); IASTA (adv. council); Creative Arts Council, Hastings-on-Hudson, N.Y.; Actors Studio and Actors Studio Th. (mbr., prod. bd.); Theatre Communications Group (mbr., exec. bd.); Provost Committee for Establishment of Fine Arts Center at Long Island Univ.'s Zeckendorf Campus (mbr., exec. bd.); New Dramatists Committee (mbr., adv. bd.); *Tulane Drama Review* (mbr., adv. bd.); Board of Standards and Planning for the Living Th. (ANTA). Address: 30 Scenic Dr., Hastings-on-Hudson, NY 10706.

Pre-Theatre. Reporter (1936–39); radio announcer (1939); in public relations (1940).

Theatre. Mr. Schneider has been associate director (1971–to date), Arena Stage, Washington, D.C., where he was previously artistic director (1952–53), associate director (1961–63), and acting producer (1973–74). He was also associate director, Minnesota Theatre Co. (1964). Mr. Schneider first appeared as an actor, playing Magee in a Forest Park H.S. production of *Seven Keys to Baldpate* (June 1935). His first professional assignment as a director was *Jim Dandy* (The Catholic Univ. of America, Washington, D.C., Oct. 29, 1941); subsequently, for The Catholic Univ. of America he directed *Athaliah* (Mar. 17, 1942); *Jim Dandy* (July 15, 1942); *Child's Play* (world premiere, Aug. 20, 1942); *The Romancers* (Aug. 4, 1943); *The Doctor in Spite of Himself* (Aug. 9, 1944); *Lute Song* (Nov. 19, 1944); *The Tidings Brought to Mary* (Feb. 18, 1945); *The Importance of Being Earnest* (Aug. 5, 1945); *Electra* (Nov. 30, 1945); *That's Where the Money Goes* (world premiere, May 10, 1946) and *State Occasion* (world premiere, Nov. 29, 1946). He made his first professional acting appearance as Winkle in the Playwrights Co. production of *Storm Operation* (Belasco Th., Jan. 11, 1944). At the Cain Park Th. (Cleveland Heights, Ohio), he directed *You Can't Take It with You* (July 1, 1947) and *Sing Out, Sweet Land* (Aug. 5, 1947).

His first directorial assignment on Bway was *A Long Way from Home* (Maxine Elliott's Th., Feb. 8, 1948); subsequently directed *The Long Goodbye* (Studio 63 of Theatre Inc., Apr. 8, 1948); again at the Cain Park Th. (Cleveland Heights, Ohio), directed *Lute Song* (July 6, 1948), *Reluctant Lady* (world premiere, July 27, 1948), and *The Taming of the Shrew* (Aug. 17, 1948); directed *My Heart's in the Highlands* (Barn Th., Dartington Hall, England, July 1, 1949); and *Oedipus the King* (Mar. 17, 1950); in stock, *Born Yesterday* (Cape Playhouse, Dennis, Mass., July 3, 1950); at the Falmouth Playhouse (Coonamassett, Mass.), *Over 21* (July 31, 1950), *Harvey* (Aug. 7, 1950), and *Post Road* (Aug. 14, 1950).

For Players, Inc., Mr. Schneider directed *Macbeth* (Washington, D.C., Sept. 30, 1950); for The Catholic Univ. of America, *The Madwoman of Chaillot* (Oct. 27, 1950) and *Othello* (Mar. 2, 1951); directed *The Glass Menagerie* (Apr. 10, 1951; May 22, 1951, Arena Stage, Washington, D.C.); *Primrose Path* (Playhouse Th., Houston, Tex., Aug. 8, 1951); *The Cherry Orchard* (The Catholic Univ. of America, Nov. 30, 1951); *Pullman Car Hiawatha* (The Neighborhood Playhouse, N.Y.C., Jan. 30, 1952); *Macbeth* (The Catholic Univ. of America, Washington, D.C., Mar. 21, 1952); at the Arena Stage (Washington, D.C.), *The Hasty Heart* (June 17, 1952) and *Desire Under the Elms* (Oct. 7, 1952); *The Skin of Our Teeth* (The Catholic Univ. of America, Washington, D.C., Dec. 5, 1952); at the Arena Stage, he directed *Lady Precious Stream* (Dec. 9, 1952), *All Summer Long* (world premiere, Jan. 13, 1953), *Our Town* (Mar. 16, 1953), *The Country Girl* (May 18, 1953), *My Heart's in the Highlands* (Aug. 11, 1953), *The Happy Journey* (Sept. 1, 1953), and *The Bad Angel* (world premiere, Oct. 20, 1953).

He directed *Hide and Seek* (world premiere, Neighborhood Playhouse, N.Y.C., Apr. 21, 1953); *The Remarkable Mr. Pennypacker* (Coronet, Dec. 30, 1953); and *Summer and Smoke* (Arena Stage, Washington, D.C., Feb. 9, 1954); *All Summer Long* (Coronet, N.Y.C., Sept. 23, 1954); *Anastasia* (Lyceum, Dec. 29, 1954); *Tonight in Samarkand* (Morosco, Feb. 16, 1955); the Salute to France production of *The Skin of Our Teeth* (Th. Sarah Bernhardt, Paris, France, June 28, 1955), on tour (Chicago, Ill.; Washington, D.C.) and in New York (ANTA, Aug. 17, 1955); *Waiting for Godot* (American premiere, Coconut Grove Playhouse, Miami, Fla., Jan. 3, 1956); *The Little Glass Clock* (John Golden Th., N.Y.C., Mar. 26, 1956); *The Trip to Bountiful* (Arts Th. Club, London, England, July 4, 1956); a revised version of *A View from the Bridge* (American premiere, Arena Stage, Washington, D.C., Nov. 7, 1956); *The Glass Menagerie* (NY City Ctr., Nov. 21, 1956); *The Enchanted* (Boston Univ., Mass., May 3, 1957); *The Circus of Dr. Lao* (world premiere, Edgewater Beach Playhouse, Chicago, Ill., July 9, 1957); *Miss Lonelyhearts* (Music Box, N.Y.C., Oct. 3, 1957); *Endgame* (American premiere, Cherry Lane Th., Jan. 28, 1958); *Summer of the 17th Doll* (Arena Stage, Washington, D.C., Apr. 29, 1958); *Wilder and Wilder*, a double bill consisting of *Pullman Car Hiawatha* and *The Happy Journey* (Brooklyn Coll., N.Y., 1958); directed the world premiere of *The Deserters*, which toured England (1958); *Kataki* (Ambassador, N.Y.C., Apr. 9, 1959).

Mr. Schneider staged *Epitaph for George Dillon* (Arena Stage, Washington, D.C., May 5, 1959); *Waiting for Godot* (Alley Th., Houston, Tex., Sept. 9, 1959); *Summer of the 17th Doll* (Players Th., N.Y.C., Oct. 13, 1959); *Clandestine on the Morning Line* (world premiere, Arena Stage, Nov. 24, 1959); *The Cherry Orchard* (Arena Stage, Jan. 12, 1960); *Krapp's Last Tape* (Provincetown Playhouse, N.Y.C., Jan. 14, 1960); *Detective Story* (Boston Univ., Mass., Feb. 24, 1960); *Two for the Seesaw* (Royal Poinciana Playhouse, West Palm Beach, Fla., Mar. 28, 1960); the American stage premiere of *Twelve Angry Men* (Bucks County Playhouse, New Hope, Pa., May 23, 1960); for the NY Shakespeare Festival, *Measure for Measure* (Belvedere Lake Th., N.Y.C., July 25, 1960); directed the pre-Bway tryout of *Rape of the Belt* (Wilbur Th., Boston, Mass., Oct. 20, 1960); *Twinkling of an Eye* (world premiere, Actors Workshop, San Francisco, Calif., Jan. 11, 1961); *The American Dream* (world premiere, York, N.Y.C., Jan. 24, 1961); *Krapp's Last Tape* (Arena Stage, Washington, D.C., Apr. 4, 1961); *Uncle Vanya* (Goodman Memorial Th., Chicago, Ill., Apr. 9, 1961); *The Bald Soprano* and *Pullman Car Hiawatha* (Hofstra Coll., L.I., N.Y., May 12, 1961); *The Chairs, The Lottery*, and *The Dock Brief* (Univ. of Wisconsin-Milwaukee, Milwaukee, Wis., July 25, 1961); *Happy Days* (world premiere, Cherry Lane, N.Y.C., Sept. 17, 1961); the American professional premiere of *The Caucasian Chalk Circle* (Arena Stage, Washington, D.C., Oct. 30, 1961); *The American Dream* and *What Shall We Tell Caroline?* (Arena Stage, Nov. 28, 1961); *Endgame* (Cherry Lane, N.Y.C., Feb. 11, 1962); *The American Dream* (Cherry Lane, Mar. 1, 1962); and at the Arena Stage, directed *The Burning of the Lepers* (world premiere, Mar. 20, 1962), *Uncle Vanya* (Apr. 17, 1962), and *The Time of Your Life* (May 15, 1962).

Mr. Schneider directed the triple-bill *The Dumbwaiter, Act without Words II* (American premieres), and *Pullman Car Hiawatha* (Univ. of Wisconsin-Milwaukee, Fred Miller Th., Milwaukee, Wis., July 10, 1962); he directed *Man Is Man* (Stanford Univ., Palo Alto, Calif., Aug. 9, 1962); *Who's Afraid of Virginia Woolf?* (Billy Rose Th., N.Y.C., Oct. 13, 1962) and the matinee company (Billy Rose Th., Oct. 31, 1962); *The Pinter Plays*, consisting of *The Dumbwaiter* and *The Collection* (American premiere, Cherry Lane, Nov. 26, 1962); at the Arena Stage, *All the Way Home* (Mar. 12, 1963), *Othello* (Apr. 10, 1963) and *The Threepenny Opera* (May 14, 1963); directed the national touring company of *Who's Afraid of Virginia Woolf?* (opened Colonial Th., Boston, Mass., Sept. 12, 1963); *The Ballad of the Sad Cafe* (Martin Beck Th., N.Y.C., Oct. 30, 1963); the double-bill *Play* and *The Lover* (American premiere, Cherry Lane, Jan. 4, 1964); *Who's Afraid of Virginia Woolf?* (Piccadilly, London, Feb. 6, 1964); *The American Dream* (Cherry Lane, N.Y.C., Apr. 21, 1964); *The Glass Menagerie* (Tyrone Guthrie Th., Minneapolis, Minn., June 1, 1964); bus and truck touring company of *Who's Afraid of Virginia Woolf?* (opened Westport Country Playhouse, Westport, Conn., Aug. 17, 1964); and *Tiny Alice* (Billy Rose Th., N.Y.C., Dec. 29, 1964).

He also directed *Do Not Pass Go* (Cherry Lane, Apr. 19, 1965); the double bill *Krapp's Last Tape* and *The Zoo Story* (Cherry Lane, June 8, 1965); *Happy Days* (Cherry Lane, Sept. 28, 1965); *Entertaining Mr. Sloane* (Lyceum, Oct. 12, 1965); *Herakles* (APA-Phoenix, Professional Th. Program, Univ. of Michigan, Ann Arbor, Mich., Oct. 27, 1965); *Malcolm* (Sam S. Shubert Th., N.Y.C., Jan. 15, 1966); *Slapstick Tragedy* (Longacre, Feb. 22, 1966); *You Know I Can't Hear You When the Water's Running* (Ambassador, Mar. 13, 1967); *A Delicate Balance* (Martin Beck Th., Sept. 22, 1967); *The Birthday Party* (Booth Th., Oct. 3, 1967); and *I Never Sang for My Father* (Longacre, Jan. 25, 1968). At the Studio Arena Th., Buffalo, N.Y., he directed *Box-Mao-Box* (world premiere, Mar. 6, 1968; Sept. 15, 1968), the double-bill *Krapp's Last Tape* and *The Zoo Story* (Sept. 17, 1968), and *Happy Days* (Sept. 20, 1968); and at the Billy Rose Th., N.Y.C., *Box-Mao-Box* (Sept. 30, 1968), *Krapp's Last Tape* (Oct. 9, 1968), and *Happy Days* (Oct. 12, 1968). He also directed *The Watering Place* (Music Box, N.Y.C., Mar. 12, 1969); *The Gingham Dog* (John Golden Th., Apr. 23, 1969); *La Strada* (Lunt-Fontanne Th., Dec. 14, 1969); *Blood Red Roses* (John Golden Th., Mar. 22, 1970); *Inquest* (Music Box, Apr. 23, 1970); *Saved* (American premiere, Chelsea Th. Ctr., Brooklyn Academy of Music, N.Y.C., Oct. 28, 1970); and a revival of *Waiting for Godot* (Sheridan Square Playhouse, Feb. 3, 1971).

He directed *Moonchildren* (American premiere, Arena Stage, Washington, D.C., Nov. 13, 1971); a revival of *The Sign in Sidney Brustein's Window* (Longacre, N.Y.C., Jan. 26, 1972); *Moonchildren* (Royale, Feb. 21, 1972); *Uptight* (American premiere, Arena Stage, Washington, D.C., Mar. 22, 1972); *The Foursome* (American premiere, Arena Stage, Nov. 8, 1972); at the Forum Th., N.Y.C., two double-bills: *Happy Days* and *Act without Words I* (Nov. 20, 1972) and *Krapp's Last Tape* and the world premiere of *Not I* (Nov. 22, 1972); and at Arena Stage *Our Town* (Dec. 20, 1972) and *Enemies* (Mar. 21, 1973). He also directed *Jabberwock* (Missouri Repertory Th., Kansas City, Mo., Aug. 9, 1973); and, at Arena Stage, Washington, D.C., *Krapp's Last Tape* and *Not I* (Sept. 18, 1973), *Our Town* (Oct. 24, 1973), *Tom* (American premiere, Dec. 14, 1973), and *Zalmen, or the Madness of God* (world premiere, May 8, 1974). In 1973, Arena Stage's cultural exchange tour of the USSR included Mr. Schneider's staging of *Our Town* (Moscow, Oct. 3; Leningrad, Oct. 10).

Films. In 1964, Mr. Schneider directed Samuel Beckett's *Film* (Evergreen Th., Inc.), which was first shown Sept. 14, 1965, at the NY Film Festival.

Television and Radio. On radio, Mr. Schneider directed *Mister Roberts* (Voice of America, 1961). For television, he directed *Pullman Car Hiawatha* (CBS, Washington, D.C., Feb. 1951); *Oedipus the King* (Omnibus, NBC, Dec. 1956); *The Life of Samuel Johnson* (CBS, Dec. 1957); *The Years Between* (CBS, Feb. 1958); *The Secret of Freedom* (NBC Documentary Film, May 1959); and Samuel Beckett's *Waiting for Godot* (Play of the Week, WNTA, Sept. 1960); *Eh Joe* (PBS, Apr. 18, 1966); *Act without Words II* (1965); and *Krapp's Last Tape* (1971).

Other Activities. Mr. Schneider is University Professor and professor of theatre arts, Boston Univ. (1972–to date). He was an instructor (1941–47) and assistant professor (1949–52) of speech and drama, The Catholic Univ. of America, and he has lectured at numerous universities, including Cornell, Wisconsin, Texas, Boston, Minnesota, Yale, Harvard, California, Oregon, North Carolina, Johns Hopkins, and Smith and Hunter colleges.

Published Works. Mr. Schneider wrote "A Tale of Two Cities" in *Ten Talents in the American Theatre* (1957) and also contributed to *Futures in The American Theatre* and *The Arts and the Public.* He is the author of "On Directing *Film,* " in the published edition of Samuel Beckett's *Film* (1969); was drama critic for the *New Leader* (1962–63); and his articles have appeared in the NY *Times, Theatre Arts, Village Voice, Saturday Review,* and its successor *Saturday Review/World.* .

Awards. Mr. Schneider received a Rockefeller Foundation Grant through the National Theatre Conference for the Study of European theatre (1949); a Guggenheim Grant for the study of the open stage (1956); a Ford Foundation Director's Grant for work in regional theatre (1958); and the Washington Board of Trade Award "for outstanding contribution to professional community theatre in the nation's capital as production director of Arena Stage, Inc." In 1963, for his direction of *Who's Afraid of Virginia Woolf?,* Mr. Schneider received the Antoinette Perry (Tony) and Outer Circle awards and won the *Variety* NY Drama Critics Poll as best director, and for his direction of *The Pinter Plays,* he won the *Village Voice* Off-Bway (Obie) Award. He received Tony nominations for his direction of *Tiny Alice* (1965), *A Delicate Balance* (1967), and *You Know I Can't Hear You When the Water's Running* (1968). *Film* won the diploma of merit at the Venice Biennale in 1965, was named an outstanding film the same year at the London and NY film festivals, and won prizes in 1966 at the Tours (France), Oberhausen (Germany), Krakow (Poland) and Sidney (Australia) film festivals.

Recreation. The family, reading, music, walking.

SCHNITZER, ROBERT C. Theatre administrator, actor, producer, educator, general manager. b. Sept. 8, 1906, New York City, to Louis and Clara (di Billiani) Schnitzer. Father, managing editor, *The New Yorker Staats Zeitung.* Grad. Horace Mann Sch. for Boys, N.Y.C., 1923; Columbia Univ., A.B. 1927. Married June 7, 1953, to Marcella Abels Cisney, director, producer. Member of ATA (fellow, 1974); URTA (fdr., exec. dir., 1969–73); AEA; ANTA; ATPAM; National Council on Arts and Government; Fulbright Selection Comm. on Theatre Arts (1955–59); Michigan State Council for the Arts (1966–72); NTC; ITI; USITT; The Players. Address: 6 Woods End Lane, Westport, CT 06880; Loggerhead Cay, Sanibel Island, FL 33957.

From 1961 to 1973, when he retired, Mr. Schnitzer was professor of speech and director of the Univ. of Michigan's Professional Theatre Program, which he established. He was appointed to emeritus status in 1974. Mr. Schnitzer was responsible for engaging the APA to perform as resident acting company at the university, a continuing association for two to three months a year. He also instituted the University's Great Star Series, Distinguished Lecture Series, and a playwright-in-residence program to produce new scripts.

Theatre. Mr. Schnitzer made his Bway debut in *The Brothers Karamazov* (Guild Th., Jan. 3, 1927), then joining Walter Hampden's repertory seasons at the Hampden Th., N.Y.C., and on national tours. He appeared in and stage managed *Hamlet, An Enemy of the People, Richelieu, Henry V, Richard III, Caponsacchi, Macbeth,* and *Cyrano de Bergerac.* During this time, he also owned, operated, and directed productions at Robin Hood Summer Th. (Arden, Del., Summers 1931–40).

From 1936 to 1939, he was Delaware state director and deputy national director of the Federal Th. (WPA) Project. In 1939, he administered the theatre program at the San Francisco (Calif.) World's Fair, and was executive director of the Civic Th. (Kalamazoo, Mich., 1939–40).

Mr. Schnitzer taught drama courses at Vassar Coll. (1941–42), and at Smith Coll. (1942–43). From 1945 to 1949, he served as consultant to the Martha Graham Sch. of Dance, the Rollins Sch. Th., Randall Sch. Th., the Dramatic Workshop of the New Sch. for Social Research, Denver Red Rocks Th., the Utah Centennial and the NTC program for veterans.

In 1946, Mr. Schnitzer helped establish the ANTA Experimental Th., and served as general manager (1946–47). From 1948 to 1954 he was an instructor at Columbia Univ. Sch. of Dramatic Arts. In Europe, he was general manager for the US company that presented *Hamlet* (Elsinore, Den., 1949); and for the Ballet Th.'s first European tour (1950); returned to the US as general manager for the 1951 ANTA Album; arranged the US performances of the Greek Natl. Th.; and was general manager for the US participation in the Berlin (Ger.) Festivals (1951–53); and for the US production of *Four Saints in Three Acts* (Congress of Cultural Freedom Festival, Paris, Fr., 1952). He was general manager for Cheryl Crawford's productions (1952–53); Gilbert Miller's productions (1953–54) and for ANTA's Salute to France production of *The Skin of Our Teeth* (Th. Sarah Bernhardt, Paris, June 28, 1955).

From 1954 to 1960, Mr. Schnitzer was general manager of the US State Dept.-ANTA Intl. Exchange Program. Under his administration, the President's Special Intl. Program for Cultural Presentations sent 150 attractions, ranging from drama to jazz bands to 102 foreign countries. In 1960–61, he was general manager of the Th. Guild-American Repertory Co., which was sponsored by the State Dept. and presented productions of *The Skin of Our Teeth, The Glass Menagerie,* and *The Miracle Worker,* in Europe and Latin America.

Other Activities. Mr. Schnitzer was a delegate to the US Natl. Conference for UNESCO (1953, 1955, 1957); and to the first Inter-American Conference on Exchange of Persons, 1958); and he was guest theatre expert for the German government in 1965 under the German Foreign Office cultural exchange program.

Awards. For his work in establishing the ANTA Experimental Th., Mr. Schnitzer received the Sydney Howard Award of the Playwrights' Co. in 1947, and he held a Rockefeller Foundation Fellowship in 1948. In 1971, the National Business Committee on the Arts gave him its Career Service Award for Arts Management, and he received the Univ. of Michigan's President's Citation. In 1974, he was made a fellow of ATA in recognition of his services to the national theatre, and the Univ. of Michigan established a special fellowship in theatre administration and named it for him.

SCHOENBAUM, DONALD. Managing director, actor, director, producer. b. Donald H. Schoenbaum, Jan. 3, 1926, Yonkers, N.Y., to Irving and Beatrice Schoenbaum. Father, stockbroker. Educ. Yonkers Central H.S.; NY Univ.; Univ. of Southern California. Served in US Army Air Corps, 1944–46. Married 1947 to Geraldine Cain, costume designer, landscape architect; three sons. Member of AEA; OADR (exec. comm., 1966–to date); League of Resident Theatres (exec. comm., secy., 1971–to date); Theatre Communications Group, (resident theatre panel member, 1974–to date). Address: (home) 705 Kenwood Parkway, Minneapolis, MN 55403, tel. (612) 374-5078; (bus.) Tyrone Guthrie Theatre, 725 Vineland Place, Minneapolis, MN 55403, tel. (612) 377-2824.

Theatre. Mr. Schoenbaum is executive vice-president and managing director, Guthrie Theatre Foundation, Minneapolis, Minn. He became managing director of the Tyrone Guthrie Th. in 1965. Previously, he was producer-director, The Repertory Players, Omaha, Neb. (1960–64) and managing director, Trinity Square Repertory Th., Providence, R.I. (1964–65).

He made his theatrical debut as Petruchio in *The Taming of the Shrew* (Univ. of Southern Calif., 1946), and he played Eben in *Desire Under the Elms* (Laguna Playhouse, Laguna, Calif., 1947). From 1948 to 1960, he appeared in various theatres, where he played over fifty roles, including Stanley in *A Streetcar Named Desire,* the title role in *Mr. Roberts,* Sakini in *The Teahouse of the August Moon,* Haemon in Sophocles' *Antigone,* Archy in *Archy and Mehitabel,* and Jack Jordan in *Say, Darling.* .

Awards. Mr. Schoenbaum received Ford Foundation grants to study the feasibility of establishing a repertory theatre in Honolulu, Hawaii (1963), and to study theatre administration (1965).

SCHULBERG, BUDD. Playwright, producer, writer, educator, editor. b. Budd Wilson Schulberg, Mar. 27, 1914, New York City, to Benjamin and Adeline (Jaffe) Schulberg. Father, chief of productions, Paramount Studios; mother, artists and literary representative. Grad. Dartmouth Coll., B.A. (cum laude) 1936. Married 1936 to Virginia Ray (marr. dis. 1942); one daughter; married 1943 to Victoria Anderson, actress (marr. dis. 1964); two sons; married June 1964 to Geraldine Brooks, actress. Served USN, O.S.S., ETO; awarded Army and Navy Commendation Ribbons; rank, Lt. (j.g.). Relative in theatre: brother, Stuart Schulberg, playwright, producer. Member of Dramatists Guild, WGA, ALA (member of council of the Authors' Guild, 1958–60), ASCAP, American Civil Liberties Union. Address: c/o Ad Schulberg, 300 E. 57th St., New York, NY 10022, tel. (212) PL 9-1341.

Theatre. Mr. Schulberg was author, with Harvey Breit, of *The Disenchanted* (Coronet Th., N.Y.C., Dec. 3, 1958); and, with Stuart Schulberg, of the book for the musical *What Makes Sammy Run?* (54 St. Th., Feb. 27, 1964).

Films. Mr. Schulberg wrote some of the dialogue for the first filming of *A Star Is Born* (UA, 1937). He wrote original stories and collaborated on screenplays for *Winter Carnival* (UA, 1939) and *City Without Men* (Col., 1943); wrote *On the Waterfront* (Col., 1954); and *A Face in the Crowd* (WB, 1957); with Stuart Schulberg, he wrote and produced *Wind Across the Everglades* (WB, 1958). A motion picture was made of his novel *The Harder They Fall* (Col., 1956).

Television. He was author, with Stuart Schulberg, of the television adaptation of *What Makes Sammy Run?* (NBC, Sunday Showcase, 1959; repeated 1960).

Other Activities. Mr. Schulberg was first boxing editor of *Sports Illustrated.* With Stuart Schulberg, Mr. Schulberg, started Douglass House Writers' Workshop in the Watts area of Los Angeles, Calif., in 1965. He has also lectured on writing at Frederic Douglass Creative Arts Ctr., Harlem, N.Y.C., and he has served on the boards of directors of Westminster Neighborhood Association, Watts, and the Inner City Cultural Ctr., Los Angeles.

Published Works. Mr. Schulberg wrote: *What Makes Sammy Run?* (1941); *The Harder They Fall* (1947); *The Disenchanted* (1950); *Some Faces in the Crowd,* which consisted of a novelette, *Your Arkansas Traveler,* and short stories (1953); *On the Waterfront* (1955); *Sanctuary V* (1969); and *Loser and Still Champion: Muhammad Ali* (1972). He edited and wrote an introduction for *From the Ashes: Voices of Watts* (1967).

He has also written short stories and articles for *The Saturday Evening Post, The New Yorker, The New Republic, Times Book Review, Sports Illustrated, Esquire, Playboy,* and *Holiday.*

Awards. Mr. Schulberg received the Christopher Award (1954) for his novel, *On the Waterfront;* an Academy (Oscar) Award (1955) for best story and screenplay, *On the Waterfront;* and the German Film Critics Award (1957) for *A Face in the Crowd.* He also received an honorary LL.D. degree from Dartmouth Coll. (1960).

Recreation. Deep-sea fishing, archeology, pigeon racing, farming (pig raising), boxing, traveling, bird watching.

SCHULMAN, ARNOLD. Playwright. b. Aug. 11, 1925, Philadelphia, Pa., to H. and Eva (Blank) Schulman. Father, innkeeper. Attended Univ. of North Carolina, 1942–43, 1945–46. Married June 27, 1954, to Jean Alexander, one daughter. Served WW II, USN, as aerial photographer; rank Pho. M1/c. Member of Dramatists Guild; WGA, West.

Theatre. Mr. Schulman wrote the play, *A Hole in the Head* (Plymouth, N.Y.C., Feb. 28, 1957); and the book for the musical *Jennie* (Majestic, Oct. 17, 1963).

He previously appeared as the Messenger Boy in *Come Back Little Sheba* (Booth, N.Y.C., Feb. 15, 1950) and as the Village Idiot in Arthur Miller's adaptation of *An Enemy of the People* (Broadhurst, Dec. 28, 1950).

Films. Mr. Schulman wrote the screen versions of *Wild Is the Wind* (Par., 1957); *A Hole in the Head* (UA, 1959); and *Love with the Proper Stranger* (Par., 1963).

Television. From 1950–56, Mr. Schulman wrote sixty seven teleplays for major live dramatic programs, including *Lost* and *The Heart's a Forgotten Hotel* (Playwrights '56, NBC); *Lady on the Rock* (Danger, CBS); Philco Playhouse (NBC); Studio One (CBS); Omnibus (NBC); and Kraft Television Th. (NBC); and was associate producer for the GE Theatre series (CBS, 1954–55).

SCHUMER, YVETTE. producer, Manager, 24. b. Yvette Gold, Sept. 10, 1921, New York City, to Morton B. and Marth Gold. Father, broker. Grad. Linden Hall Sch., Lititz, Pa., 1937; attended Cornell Univ., 1937–38; grad. New York Univ., B.S. (Education, Drama, Journalism) 1940. Married Jan. 27, 1946, to Henry Schumer, theatrical-warehouser and hauler, producer, investor (div. 1967). During WW II, served on the Entertainment Committee, Halloran Hospital. Relative in theatre: niece, Sandra Hochman, actress. Address: 155 W. 68th St., New York, NY 10023.

Pre-Theatre. Advertising, promotion.

Theatre. Miss Schumer produced with her husband, Henry Schumer, a season of stock at the Stratford Summer Playhouse (Middletown, N.Y., Summer 1946); produced, with Richard Kollmar and James W. Gardiner, *Plain and Fancy* (Mark Hellinger Th., N.Y.C., Jan. 27, 1955), and its tour (opened Forrest, Philadelphia, Pa., Mar. 6, 1956; closed Nixon, Pittsburgh, Pa., May 5, 1956); with Leonard Sillman and John Roberts, produced *New Faces of '56* (Ethel Barrymore Th., N.Y.C., June 14, 1956); with the Saba Co., produced *Winesburg, Ohio* (Natl., Feb. 5, 1958); produced *Dancing Heiress* (Lyric, Hammersmith, London, Mar. 15, 1960); a season of stock at the Off Beach Th. (Westhampton, L.I., N.Y., Summer 1961); and *New York Coloring Book* (Cafe Society, N.Y.C., Apr. 9, 1962).

Since 1963, she has been active in the development and management of new talent for Bway and television.

Recreation. Golf, writing, cooking.

SCHWARTZ, ARTHUR. Composer, producer. b. Nov. 25, 1900, Brooklyn, N.Y., to Solomon S. and Dora (Grossman) Schwartz. Father, lawyer. Grad. New York Univ., B.A. (Phi Beta Kappa) 1920; Columbia Univ., M.A. 1921; J.D. 1924. Married July 7, 1934, to Katherine Carrington, actress (dec. 1953); one son; married 1954 to Mary O'Hagan Scott, actress (professional name, Mary Grey); one son. Served WW I, USN. Member of ASCAP; Natl. Assn. of American Composers and Conductors; ALA; League of NY Theatres (pres., 1951–54); Pi Lambda Phi.

Pre-Theatre. Lawyer, taught high school English.

Theatre. Mr. Schwartz composed the music for *Grand Street Follies* (Neighborhood Playhouse, June 15, 1926); *The New Yorker* (Edyth Totten Th., Mar. 10, 1927); and with lyricist Howard Dietz, composed the music for *The Little Show* (Music Box, Apr. 30, 1929).

Forming a partnership with Mr. Dietz, he composed the music for *Here Comes the Bride* (Piccadilly, London, England, Feb. 20, 1930); music for *Second Little Show* (Royale, N.Y.C., Sept. 2, 1930); *Princess Charming* (Imperial, Oct. 13, 1930); *Three's a Crowd* (Selwyn, Oct. 15, 1930); *The Band Wagon* (New Amsterdam, June 3, 1931); *Flying Colors* (Imperial, Sept. 15, 1932); and *Nice Goings On* (Strand, London, Sept. 13, 1933).

Mr. Schwartz was the composer of *Revenge with Music* (New Amsterdam, N.Y.C., Nov. 28, 1934); *At Home Abroad* (Winter Garden, Sept. 19, 1935); *Follow the Sun* (Adelphi, London, Feb. 4, 1936); composed the music and was author, with Howard Dietz, of the book for *Between the Devil* (Imperial, N.Y.C., Dec. 22, 1937); composer of *Stars in Your Eyes* (Majestic, Feb. 9, 1939); *American Jubilee* (NY World's Fair, 1940); *Park Avenue* (Shubert, Nov. 4, 1946); produced and composed the music for *Inside U.S.A.* (Century, Apr. 30, 1948); produced *Hilda Crane* (Coronet, Nov. 1, 1950); composed the music for *A Tree Grows in Brooklyn* (Alvin, Apr. 19, 1951); *By the Beautiful Sea* (Majestic, Apr. 8, 1954); *The Gay Life* (Shubert, Nov. 18, 1961); *Jennie* (Majestic, Oct. 17, 1963); *Many Happy Returns: A Re-View of Revues* (Playhouse in the Park, Cincinnati, Ohio, June 18, 1970); and for *That's Entertainment* (Edison Th., N.Y.C., Apr. 14, 1972).

Films. Mr. Schwartz composed the music for *Under Your Spell* (20th-Fox, 1936); *That Girl from Paris* (RKO, 1936); *Navy Blues* (WB, 1941); *Thank Your Lucky Stars* (WB, 1943); produced *Cover Girl* (Col., 1944); *Night and Day* (WB, 1946); composed the music for *The Time, the Place and the Girl* (WB, 1946); *Excuse My Dust* (MGM, 1951); *Dangerous When Wet* (MGM, 1953); *The Band Wagon* (MGM, 1953); and *You're Never Too Young* (Par., 1955).

Television and Radio. He composed the music for the radio series, The Gibson Family (1934).

For television, he produced and composed the music for the first 90-minute special, *Suprise for Santa* (CBS, 1948); produced and composed the music for *High Tor* (CBS, 1956); and composed the score for *A Bell for Adano* (CBS, 1956).

SCHWARTZ, STEPHEN. Composer, lyricist. b. 1950, Long Island, N.Y. Attended Mineola (N.Y.) H.S.; Juilliard (studied music, composition, piano); Carnegie Tech., BFA, 1968.

Pre-Theatre. "Artist and repertoire" man for RCA records.

Theatre. Mr. Schwartz wrote revue material for the Washington (D.C.) Th. Club (1969–70 season); composed the title song for *Butterflies Are Free* (Booth, N.Y.C., Oct. 21, 1969); was musical supervisor for *The Survival of St. Joan* (Anderson, Feb. 28, 1971); composer and lyricist for *Godspell* (Cherry Lane Th., May 17, 1971; moved to Promenade, Aug. 10, 1971); lyricist for Leonard Bernstein's *Mass* (Kennedy Ctr., Washington, D.C., Sept. 8, 1970); and composer and lyricist for *Pippin* (Imperial, N.Y.C., Oct. 23, 1972); and *The Magic Show* (Cort, May 23, 1974).

He spent three summers as director, choreographer, and musical director for the New London (N.H.) Playhouse.

Films. Mr. Schwartz wrote additional musical material for the filming of *Godspell* (Col., 1973), which was the opening presentation of the Cannes (France) Film Festival (May 1973).

Television. Mr. Schwartz participated in the presentation of the documentaries *The Gospel of Godspell* (ABC, 1970); and *According to Godspell* (HSV-7, Melbourne, Australia, 1972).

Discography. Mr. Schwartz' recording credits include the cast albums of *Godspell* (Columbia, 1971); *Pippin* (Motown, 1973); and *The Magic Show* (Bell, 1974). In addition, he was the producer of the cast albums of *The Last Sweet Days of Isaac* and *The Survival of St. Joan.*.

Awards. For *Godspell,* he received the *Variety* Critics' Poll Award for best composer (1970–71); The Drama Desk Award for most promising composer (1970–71); the Grammy Award for best score from an original cast album; and, for the film version, the Grand Prix of the International Catholic Film Office, and the National Theatre Arts Conference Dineen Award.

SCOFIELD, PAUL. Actor. b. David Paul Scofield, Jan. 21, 1922, King's Norton, England, to Edward H. and Mary (Wild) Scofield. Attended Varndean Sch. for Boys, Brighton, Eng., 1933–39. Studied for theatre at London Mask Th. Sch., Westminster Th., England. Married May 15, 1943, to Joy Parker, actress; one son, one daughter. Member of AEA; AEA (Brit.); AEA (Canada). Address: The Gables, Balcombe, Sussex, England tel. 378.

Theatre. Mr. Scofield made his Bway debut as Sir Thomas More in *A Man for All Seasons* (ANTA Th., Nov. 22, 1961); followed by the title role in the Royal Shakespeare Th. Co.'s production of *King Lear* at Lincoln Ctr. (NY State Th., May 18, 1964), which he also played in Washington, D.C.; Boston, Mass.; and Philadelphia, Pa.

He made his stage debut at age 14 in a touring production of *The Only Way* passing through Brighton (Th. Royal, 1936); as a student at the London Mask Th. Sch. Westminster Th., London), he appeared in *Desire Under the Elms* (Jan. 24, 1940) and played the Third Clerk and First Soldier in *Abraham Lincoln* (Apr. 16, 1940); joined the Birmingham Rep. Th. (1942); played Alex Morden in *The Moon is Down* (Whitehall, London, June 8, 1943); again appeared with the Birmingham Rep. Th. (1944–46); played Reginald in *Getting Married* (1944), the Prince in *The Circle of Chalk* (1944), the Clown in *The Winter's Tale* (1944), William D' Albini in *The Empress Maud* (1944), Valentine in *Doctor's Delight* (1945), Konstantin in *The Seagull* (1945), John Tanner in *Man and Superman* (1945), and Philip, the Bastard in *King John* (1945).

At the Shakespeare Memorial Th. (Stratford-upon-Avon, 1946) he played the title role in *Henry V,* Don Armando in *Love's Labour's Lost,* Malcolm in *Macbeth,* Lucio in *Measure for Measure,* and Cloten in *Cymbeline;* and appeared as Tegeus-Chromis in *A Phoenix Too Frequent* (Arts, London, Nov. 20, 1946).

At Stratford (1947), he played the title role in *Pericles,* Bassanio in *The Merchant of Venice,* and Mephistopheles in *Dr. Faustus,* Sir Andrew Aguecheek in *Twelfth Night,* and Mercutio in *Romeo and Juliet;* repeated the latter two roles in London (His Majesty's Oct. 1947); played Young Fasion in *The Relapse* (Lyric, Hammersmith, Dec. 17, 1947); At Stratford (1948), played King Philip of France in *King John,* Roderigo in *Othello,* the Clown in *The Winter's Tale,* Troilus in *Troilus and Cressida,* and the title role in *Hamlet.*

Mr. Scofield appeared as Alexander in *Adventure Story* (St. James's, London, Mar. 17, 1949); Treplef in *The Seagull* (Lyric, Hammersmith, Oct. 4, 1949); and Hugo and Frederic in *Ring Round the Moon* (Globe, Jan. 26, 1950); subsequently produced, and played the title role in *Pericles* (Rudolph Steiner Hall, July 2, 1950); played Don Pedro in *Much Ado About Nothing* (Phoenix, Jan. 11, 1952); Philip Strugess in *The River Line* (Edinburgh Festival, Scotland, 1952; Lyric, Hammersmith, London, Sept. 2, 1952); appeared in London with Sir John Gielgud's repertory company at the Lyric, Hammersmith, in the title role of *Richard II* (Sept. 24, 1952), as Witwood in *The Way of the World* (Feb. 19, 1953), and Pierre in *Venice Preserved* (May 15, 1953); played Paul Gardiner in *A Question of Fact* (Piccadilly, Dec. 10, 1953); Prince Albert Troubiscol in *Time Remem-*

bered (Lyric, Hammersmith, Dec. 2, 1954); the title role in *Hamlet* (Moscow, Nov. 1955; and in repertory, Phoenix Th. London, Dec. 8, 1955), where he also appeared as the Priest in *The Power and the Glory* (Apr. 5, 1956), and Lord Monchensey in *The Family Reunion* June 7, 1956). He played Fred Dyson in Rodney Ackland's *A Dead Secret* (Piccadilly, May 30, 1957); Johnnie in *Expresso Bongo* (Saville, Apr. 23, 1957); Clive Root in *The Complaisant Lover* (Globe, June 18, 1959); and Sir Thomas More in *A Man for All Seasons* (Globe, July 1, 1960).

At the Stratford (Ontario) Shakespeare Festival (1961) he played the title role of *Coriolanus* (June 1961), and Don Armado in *Love's Labour's Lost* (June 1961)).

With the Royal Shakespeare Th. Co. he played the title role in *King Lear* (Nov. 6, 1962), later performing the role in London (Aldwych, Dec. 12, 1962), in the US and in West Berlin, Prague, Belgrade, Budapest, Warsaw, Bucharest, Helsinki, Leningrad, and Moscow; appeared in *Timon of Athens* (Stratford upon Avon, 1965); *The Government Inspector* (Aldwych Th., 1966); *Staircase* (Aldwych, 1966–67); *Macbeth* (Stratford upon Avon and Aldwych Th. (1967–68); *Hotel in Amsterdam* (Court Th. and New Th., 1968); and *Uncle Vanya* (Royal Court Th., 1970). With the National Theatre Company (1971–72), he appeared in *The Captain of Kopenick* and Pirandello's *Rules of the Game;* and in *Savages* (Royal Court Th., and Comedy Th., 1973).

Films. Mr. Scofield has appeared in *Carve Her Name with Pride* (1954); played Philip II in *That Lady* (20th-Fox, 1955); appeared in *The Train; A Man for All Seasons* (1966); *King Lear* (1969); *Bartleby* (1970); *Scorpio* (1972); and *A Delicate Balance* (1973).

Awards. He was made a Commander of the Order of the British Empire (C.B.E.) in 1955; received the London *Evening Standard* Drama Award for his performances in *The Power and the Glory* (1956); the Antoinette Perry (Tony) Award for his performance as Sir Thomas More in *A Man for All Seasons* (1962); and the London *Evening Standard* Drama Award for his performances in the title role in *King Lear* (1962). He received the Academy (Oscar) Award (1967) for his role as Sir Thomas More in *A Man For All Seasons;* the Danish Film Award for *King Lear* (1968); and the Shakespeare Prize (Hamburg, Germany, 1972). He also received an honorary L.L.D. degree from Glasgow Univ. (1968) and an honorary D.Litt. degree from the Univ. of Kent, England (1973).

SCOTT, A. C. Writer, educator. b. Dec. 3, 1909, Leeds, Yorkshire, England, to A. L. and Evelyn (Roe) Scott. Grad. Leeds (Eng.) Modern H. S., 1928; Leeds Coll. of Art; Royal Coll. of Art, A.R.-C.A. 1934. Married Sept. 1936 to Dorothea Hayward, librarian, lecturer; one son. Served RAF, 1941–46; S.E.A.C., 1942–46; rank F/Lt. Member of Society of Authors (London); ATA; Assn. for Asian Studies; English Speaking Union. Address: Dept. of Theatre and Drama Vilas Hall, Univ. of Wisconsin, Madison, WI 53706, tel. (608) 262-2329.

Mr. Scott was on the staff of the British Council for Cultural Relations as assistant representative (Nanking, China, 1946–49; Hong Kong, 1950–52). With the permission of the Shochiku Company, he did theatre research at the Kabukiza (Tokyo, Japan, 1952–54); and in 1956, he surveyed theatre developments in Communist China. As a member of a government-invited group connected with Hong Kong Univ., he surveyed the theatre in Taiwan, Formosa (1957); and the following year, received a Rockefeller Travel Grant to research the puppet theatre in Japan (1958). He was a staff member of the Modern China Research Project, Columbia University (1960–62); and in New York directed a Chinese Th. Workshop at IASTA, assisted by two Chinese actors (Autumn 1961). In 1963, he inaugurated a new program of Asian Theatre at the Univ. of Wisconsin. In 1964, he surveyed theatre/dance training schools in India, Thailand, and Hong Kong. Since 1965, he has directed an annual production for students of the university's actor training program including *Twilight Crane, Butterfly Dream, Love of Tojuro, The Father Returns,* and *Encounter.*.

Published Works. Mr. Scott's publications include *The Kabuki Theatre of Japan* (1955), *The Classical Theatre of China* (1956), *Traditional Chinese Plays,* translated and annotated (vol. 1, 1967; vol. 2, 1969; vol. 3, 1974), and *The Theatre in Asia* (1972). Mr. Scott has also contributed articles to a number of journals.

Awards. Mr. Scott received a Rockefeller travel grant to Japan for research on puppet theatre (1958) and a Guggenheim Fellowship for research in Indonesia (1970). He is an honorary member of Phi Beta Kappa.

SCOTT, ALLAN. Playwright, producer. b. Laurence Allan Scott, Jr., May 23, 1909, to Laurence Allan Scott, Sr., and Mary Cecelia Scott. Grad. Mercersburg Acad., Pa., 1925; Amherst Coll., B.A. 1929; Jesus Coll., Oxford Univ., B.A. and M.A. 1932. Married 1934 to Laura Straub, actress; one son, David Scott, scientist, writer, producer; one daughter, Pippa Scott, actress. Served WW II, OWI; produced propaganda films. Member of WGA, West; AMPAS.

Theatre. Mr. Scott wrote, with George Haight, *Goodbye Again* (Masque Th., Dec. 28, 1932; revived New Amsterdam Roof, Nov. 9, 1943; revived Helen Hayes Th., Apr. 24, 1956); and wrote *In Clover* (Vanderbilt, Oct. 13, 1937); *Joy to the World* (Plymouth, Mar. 18, 1948); *Doubloon, The Piper's Son, Third Side of the Coin,* and *Memo* (opened Shubert, New Haven, Conn., Feb. 27, 1963; closed Wilbur, Boston, Mass., Mar. 9, 1963); and, with Alice and Bob Banner, wrote the book for *Apollo and Miss Agnes* (State Fair Music Hall, Dallas, Tex., Aug. 5, 1963), for which he also wrote lyrics.

Films. Mr. Scott wrote the screenplays for *Top Hat* (RKO, 1935); *Roberta* (RKO, 1935); *Village Tale* (RKO, 1935); *Follow the Fleet* (RKO, 1936); *Quality Street* (RKO, 1937); *Joy of Living* (RKO, 1938); *Carefree* (RKO, 1938); *Fifth Avenue Girl* (RKO, 1939); *Man about Town* (Par., 1939); *Lucky Partners* (RKO, 1940); *Skylark* (Par., 1941); *Remember the Day* (20th-Fox, 1941); *So Proudly We Hail* (Par., 1943); *I Love a Soldier* (Par., 1944); *Here Come the Waves* (Par., 1944); *Notorious* (RKO, 1946); *Blue Skies* (Par., 1946); *By Your Leave* (Par., 1946); *Let's Dance* (Par., 1950); *The Fourposter* (Col., 1952); *The 5000 Fingers of Dr. T.* (Col., 1953); *Top Secret Affair* (WB, 1957); and *Imitation of Life* (U, 1959).

Awards. Mr. Scott received an Academy (Oscar) Award nomination for *So Proudly We Hail* (1943).

SCOTT, GEORGE C. Actor, director. b. George Campbell Scott, Oct. 18, 1927, Wise, Virginia. Father, executive. Grad. Redford H.S., Detroit, 1944. Attended Univ. of Missouri, 1950. Married to Carolyn Hughes (marr. dis.); one daughter; married to Patricia Reed, actress (marr. dis.); one daughter, one son; married 1960 to Colleen Dewhurst, actress (marr. dis. July 1965; re-married July 4, 1967; marr. dis. Feb. 2, 1972); two sons; married Sept. 14, 1972, to Trish Van Devere, actress. Served USMC, 1944–48. Member of AEA; SAG; AFTRA.

Pre-Theatre. Truck driver, bricklayer.

Theatre. While a student at the Univ. of Missouri, Mr. Scott played the Barrister in *The Winslow Boy* (1950); subsequently appeared as Chester Norton in *Personal Appearance* (Stephens Playhouse, Columbia, Mo.); after playing more than 150 roles in stock, made his N.Y.C. debut in the title role in *Richard III* for the NY Shakespeare Festival (Heckscher Th., Nov. 25, 1957); followed by the role of Jacques in *As You Like It* (Heckscher, Jan. 20, 1958).

He appeared as Lord Wainright in *Children of Darkness* (Circle in the Sq., Feb. 28, 1958); Tydings Glenn in *Comes a Day* (Ambassador, Nov. 6, 1958); Antony in the NY Shakespeare Festival concert version of *Antony and Cleopatra* (Heckscher, Jan. 13, 1959); and Lt. Col. Chipman in *The Andersonville Trial* (Henry Miller's Th., Dec. 29, 1959).

He played Shylock in *The Merchant of Venice* (Salt Lake City, Utah, 1960); Dolek Berson in *The Wall* (Billy Rose Th., N.Y.C., Oct. 11, 1960); founded (1961), with Theodore Mann, Theatre of Michigan Co., Inc., which co-produced (with Mr. Mann) *General Seeger* (Lyceum, Feb. 28, 1962), which Mr. Scott directed and in which he played the title role; and which also produced *Great Day in the Morning* (Henry Miller's Th., N.Y.C., Mar. 28, 1962); appeared with the NY Shakespeare Festival as Shylock in *The Merchant of Venice* (Delacorte, June 13, 1962). He played Ephraim Cabot in *Desire Under the Elms* (Circle in the Sq., Jan. 8, 1963).

Mr. Scott played Vershinin in the Actors Studio production of *The Three Sisters* (for the World Th. Season, Aldwych Th., London, May 12, 1965); Henry II, King of England, in a stock tour of *The Lion in Winter* (Summer 1966); directed, but withdrew during rehearsals, *Dr. Cook's Garden* (Belasco, N.Y.C., Sept. 25, 1967); played Benjamin Hubbard in *The Little Foxes* (Vivian Beaumont Th., Oct. 26, 1967); Sam Nash, Jessie Kiplinger, and Roy Hubley in *Plaza Suite* (Plymouth, Feb. 14, 1968); Dr. Michael Astrov in *Uncle Vanya* (Circle in the Sq., Joseph E. Levine Th., June 4, 1973); dir., but withdrew during rehearsals, *Death of a Salesman* (Philadelphia Drama Guild, Walnut St. Th., Feb. 28, 1974); dir. *All God's Chillun Got Wings* (Circle in the Sq., Joseph E. Levine Th., N.Y.C., Mar. 20, 1975); and dir. and played Willy Loman in *Death of a Salesman* (Circle in the Sq., Joseph E. Levine Th., June 26, 1975).

Films. Mr. Scott made his debut as Grubb in *The Hanging Tree* (WB, 1959); subsequently appeared in *Anatomy of a Murder* (Col., 1959); *The Hustler* (20th-Fox, 1961); *The List of Adrian Messenger* (U, 1963); *Dr. Strangelove* (Col., 1964); *The Yellow Rolls-Royce* (MGM, 1965); *Not With My Wife, You Don't* (WB, 1966); as Abraham in *The Bible* (20th-Fox, 1966); in *The Flim-Flam Man* (20th-Fox, 1967); *Petulia* (WB, 1968); as Gen. George S. Patton, Jr. in *Patton* (20th-Fox, 1970); in *They Might Be Giants* (U, 1971); *The Last Run* (MGM, 1971); *The Hospital* (U, 1971); *The New Centurions* (Col., 1972); *Rage* (WB, 1972), which he also directed; *Oklahoma Crude* (Col., 1973); *The Day of the Dolphin* (Avco-Embassy, 1973); *The Bank Shot* (UA, 1974); *The Savage is Loose* (1974), which he also directed, and produced (through his own prod. co., Campbell Devon); and *The Hindenburg* (U, 1975).

Television. He played in *A Tale of Two Cities* (Dupont Show of the Month, CBS, Mar. 27, 1958); the Gardener in *I Haven't Seen Her Lately* (Kraft Mystery Th., NBC, Aug. 20, 1958); appeared in *The Empty Chair* (Omnibus, NBC, Dec. 7, 1958); played Juan in *Target for Three* (Playhouse 90, CBS, Oct. 1, 1959); the Devil in *Don Juan in Hell* (Play of the Week, WNTA, Feb. 15, 1960); Trock in *Winterset* (Hallmark Hall of Fame, NBC, Oct. 26, 1959); Karl Anderson in *I Remember a Lemon Tree* (Ben Casey, ABC, Oct. 23, 1961); in *The Power and the Glory* (CBS, Oct. 29, 1961); Lord Henry in *The Picture of Dorian Gray* (CBS, Dec. 6, 1961); played the continuing role of Brock in the East Side/West Side series (CBS, premiere Sept. 23, 1963) with ran for two seasons; played in *A Time for Killing* (Bob Hope Th., NBC, Apr. 30, 1965); John Proctor in *The Crucible* (CBS, May 4, 1967); in *Mirror, Mirror on the Wall* (On Stage, NBC, Nov. 21, 1969); directed *The Andersonville Trial* (made by KCET, Los Angeles, for PBS, shown on WNET, May 17, 1970); played Walter Franz in *The Price* (Hallmark Hall of Fame, NBC, Feb. 3, 1971); Rochester in *Jane Eyre* (NBC, Mar. 24, 1971); narr. *From Yellowstone to Tomorrow* (NBC, Apr. 1972); appeared in a sketch, "The Man Who Got a Ticket," on a comedy special written by Neil Simon, *The Trouble with People* (NBC, Nov. 12, 1972); and played Louis Nizer in *Fear on Trial* (CBS, Oct. 2, 1975).

He has also appeared on US Steel Hour (NBC); Great Mysteries (NBC); Naked City (ABC); The Virginian (NBC); Eleventh Hour (NBC); Road West (NBC); Open End (Ind.); the Red Skelton Show (CBS); Hollywood Squares (NBC); etc.

Other Activities. By presidential request, Mr. Scott appeared with Colleen Dewhurst in a program entitled *The Voices of Ireland* (East Room, White House, Washington, D.C., 1964).

Awards. For his performance as Lord Wainright in

Children of Darkness, he received the Clarence Derwent Award (1958) for most promising young actor, and the Vernon Rice Award (1958) for outstanding contribution to off-Bway theatre. He received the *Theatre World* Award (1958) for his performance in the title role in *Richard III*; *The Village Voice* Off-Bway (Obie) Award for best actor, for his performance in the title role in *Richard III*, Jacques in *As You Like It*, and Lord Wainright in *Children of Darkness* (1958); and again (1963) for his performance as Ephraim Cabot in *Desire Under the Elms*.

He was nominated twice for the Academy (Oscar) Award as best supporting actor (for *Anatomy of a Murder*, nom. 1960; and *The Hustler*, nom. 1962). He won, but refused to accept, the Academy Award in 1971 as Best Actor (for his role in *Patton*).

He was nominated for a NATAS (Emmy) Award (1962) for his performance as Karl Anderson in *I Remember a Lemon Tree;* and won two Emmy Awards for the 1970–1971 season: one for directing (*The Andersonville Trial*) and the other for acting (in *The Price*).

SCOTT, HELENA. Actress, singer. b. Helen Schurgot, Philadelphia, Pa., to Emil and Helena Schurgot. Attended Juilliard Sch. of Music. One daughter. Member of AEA; AFTRA.

Theatre. Miss Scott made her N.Y.C. debut, billed as Helena Schurgot, as an Usherette and a Reporter in *Hold It* (National Th., May 5, 1948); subsequently sang in the chorus of *All for Love* (Mark Hellinger Th., Jan. 22, 1949); appeared as Ensign Bessie Noonan in *South Pacific* (Majestic, Apr. 7, 1949); and played one of the King's Wives and was understudy to Stephanie Augustine in the role of Tuptim (1952) in *The King and I* (St. James, Mar. 29, 1951); billed as Helena Scott, appeared as Lily in *Me and Juliet* (Majestic, May 28, 1953); Scheherazade, and the Chinese Princess in *Arabian Nights* (Marine Th., Jones Beach, L.I., N.Y., June 24, 1955); and Natalie in *The Merry Widow* (NY City Ctr., Apr. 10, 1957); in stock, she played the title role in *Fanny* (Guber, Ford and Gross Circuit, Summer 1957); Nina Hagerup in *Song of Norway* (Marine Th., Jones Beach, L.I., N.Y., Summers 1958–59).

She made her operatic debut as Musetta in *La Bohème* (NY City Ctr., Nov. 2, 1958); appeared in *Street Scene* (NY City Ctr., Apr. 2, 1959); played Rosabella in *The Most Happy Fella* (Coliseum, London, Apr. 21, 1960); served as standby and vacation replacement (1962) for Julie Andrews as Guenevere in *Camelot* (Majestic, N.Y.C., Dec. 3, 1960); and appeared as Alida Bloodgood, in *The Banker's Daughter* (Jan Hus House, Jan. 22, 1962).

Television. Miss Scott has made appearances on the Ernie Kovacs Show; the Kate Smith Show (NBC); and appeared in the opera *War and Peace* (NBC Opera, Jan. 13, 1957).

SCOTT, MARTHA. Actress. b. Martha Ellen Scott, Sept. 22, Jamesport, Mo., to Walter and Letha (McKinley) Scott. Father, farmer and maintenance engineer. Grad. Westport H.S., Kansas City, Mo.; Univ. of Michigan, B.A. 1934. Married Sept. 16, 1940, to Carleton W. Alsop, radio-film producer (marr. dis. July 23, 1946); one son; married 1946 to Mel Powell, composer, pianist, educator; two daughters. Member of AEA; AFTRA; SAG; Delta Gamma Sorority, Zeta Phi Eta.

Theatre. Miss Scott joined the Globe Th. at the World's Fair (Chicago, Ill., 1934), which presented condensations of Shakespearean plays, and played Cordelia in *King Lear;* Bianca in *The Taming of the Shrew;* Hermia in *A Midsummer Night's Dream;* Celia in *As You Like It;* a Witch in *Macbeth;* and Hero in *Much Ado About Nothing;* appeared in stock in Detroit, Lansing, and Kalamazoo, Mich.; in *Please Do Not Disturb* (Locust Valley Playhouse, N.Y.); and in stock (Cape Playhouse, Dennis, Mass., 1937).

She made her Bway debut as Emily Webb in *Our Town* (Henry Miller's Th., Feb. 4, 1938); repeated that role and appeared in *Seventh Heaven* (Bucks County Playhouse, New Hope, Pa., Aug. 1939); played The Girl in *Foreigners* (Belasco, N.Y.C., Dec. 5, 1939); Mara in *The Willow and I* (Windsor, Dec. 10, 1942); Kate in *Soldier's Wife* (John Golden Th., Oct 4, 1944); succeeded (Sept. 1945) Margaret Sullavan as Sally in *The Voice of the Turtle* (Morosco, Dec. 8, 1943); played Connie Frazier in *It Takes Two* (Biltmore, Feb. 3, 1947); Margaret in *Design for a Stained Glass Window* (Mansfield, Jan. 23, 1950); succeeded (July 1951) Sarah Churchill as Nancy Willard in *Gramercy Ghost* (Morosco, Apr. 26, 1951); played Sylvia in *The Number* (Biltmore, Oct. 30, 1951); Ellen Turner in the revival of *The Male Animal* (NY City Ctr., Apr. 30, 1952; Music Box, May 15, 1952) and on tour (opened Nixon, Pittsburgh, Pa., Mar. 9, 1953; closed Blackstone, Chicago, Ill., May 2, 1953).

She played Mrs. Pennypacker in *The Remarkable Mr. Pennypacker* (Coronet, N.Y.C. Dec. 30, 1953); Mary Reese in *Cloud 7* (John Golden Th., Feb. 14, 1958); Lucy Greer in *A Distant Bell* (Eugene O'Neill Th., Jan. 13, 1960); Nina in *The Tumbler* (Helen Hayes Th., Feb. 24, 1960); Fanny Lowe in *The 49th Cousin* (Ambassador, Oct. 27, 1960); Lillian Hudson in *Future Perfect* (Cape Playhouse, Dennis, Mass., July 1961); toured in stock as Mary in *The Complaisant Lover* (Summer 1962); played Mattie Martin in *Open Book* (Pasadena, Calif., Playhouse, Apr. 1963); toured as Pamela Pew-Pickett in *Tchin-Tchin* (Summer 1963); succeeded (Apr. 27, 1964) Maureen O'-Sullivan as Edith in *Never Too Late* (Playhouse, Nov. 27, 1962); replaced (July 5, 1965) Irene Dailey as Nettie Cleary in *The Subject Was Roses* (Royale, May 25, 1964); and toured in the play; and was Mrs. Antrobus in a revival of *The Skin of Our Teeth* (Eisenhower Th., John F. Kennedy Ctr., Washington, D.C., July 9, 1975; Mark Hellinger Th., N.Y.C., Sept. 9, 1975).

In Aug. 1969, Miss Scott was one of a group of thirty individuals who organized the Plumstead Playhouse for the purpose of presenting classics of the American theatre; she was also a director of the group. The inaugural production was a revival of *Our Town* (ANTA Th., Nov. 27, 1969).

Films. Miss Scott made her film debut in *Our Town* (UA, 1940); subsequently appeared in *The Howards of Virginia* (Col., 1940); *Cheers for Miss Bishop* (UA, 1941); *One Foot in Heaven* (WB, 1941); *War of the Wildcats* (Rep., 1943); *Hi Diddle Diddle* (UA, 1943); *So Well Remembered* (RKO, 1947); *Strange Bargain* (RKO, 1949); *The Desperate Hours* (Par., 1955); *The Ten Commandments* (Par., 1956); *Sayonara* (WB, 1957); *Ben Hur* (MGM, 1959); and *Airport 1975* (U, 1974).

Television and Radio. Miss Scott made her radio debut as a "ten buck scream" on a ghost story with Orson Welles (CBS); subsequently appeared on such radio serials as The Career of Alice Blair (Mutual, 1937–38); John's Other Wife (NBC, 1937–38); and Pepper Young's Family (NBC, 1937).

On television, she appeared as narrator and hostess on the daytime series Modern Romances (NBC, 1954–57); on Omnibus (CBS, 1955); in *Give and Take* (Robert Montgomery Presents, NBC, Jan. 1957); *A Trip to Paradise* (Playhouse 90, CBS, Mar. 1959); *The Wooden Dish* (Play of the Week, WNTA, Mar. 1961); on Route 66 (CBS, 1962); The Nurses (CBS, 1963); Greatest Show on Earth (ABC, 1963); in *Two Faces of Treason* (Dupont Show of the Month, NBC, 1963); Cimarron Strip (CBS, 1967); The F.B.I. (ABC, 1967); Ironside (NBC, 1969); Paris 7000 (ABC, 1970); Longstreet (ABC, 1971); in *Lemonade* (Hollywood Television Th., PBS, Oct. 1971); on Delphi Bureau (ABC, 1972); in *Murder in the First Person Singular* (ABC, June 1974); and on various occasions on the Bob Newhart Show (CBS), as Mr. Newhart's mother.

Awards. Miss Scott was nominated for an Academy (Oscar) Award for her performance as Emily Webb in *Our Town* (1940).

SCOURBY, ALEXANDER. Actor. b. Nov. 13, 1913, Brooklyn, N.Y., to Constantine and Bessie Scourby. Attended Univ. of W. Virginia, 1931–32. Married May 12, 1943, to Lori March, actress; one daughter. Member of AEA; AFTRA; SAG; AGMA.

Theatre. Mr. Scourby was an apprentice with the Civic Repertory Th. (1932); made his N.Y.C. debut as the Player King in Leslie Howard's *Hamlet* (Imperial, Nov. 10, 1936); played the same role in Eva Le Gallienne's *Hamlet* (Cape Playhouse, Dennis, Mass., Aug. 1937); Rosencrantz in Maurice Evans' *Hamlet* (St. James, N.Y.C., Oct. 12, 1938); the Earl of Westmoreland in *Henry IV, Part 1* (St. James, Jan. 30, 1939); in stock, he played Sandor Turai in *The Play's the Thing*, and Henry Abbott in *Kind Lady* (Masonic Temple, Long Beach, L.I., N.Y., 1939); appeared as Green in *Richard II* (St. James, Apr. 1, 1940); succeeded (Music Box, 1946) Ruth Chatterton as the Speaker in *A Flag Is Born* (Alvin, Sept. 5, 1946); played Jacques Dubois in *The Deputy of Paris* (Henry St. Playhouse, Mar. 21, 1947); Dmitri Prokovitch Razoumikhin in *Crime and Punishment* (National, Dec. 22, 1947); Tami Giacoppetti in *Detective Story* (Hudson, Mar. 23, 1949); Ivanoff in *Darkness at Noon* (Alvin, Jan. 13, 1951); Peter Cauchon in Uta Hagen's *Saint Joan* (Cort, Oct. 4, 1951); and Paul Tabourier in *Tonight in Samarkand* (Morosco, Feb. 16, 1955).

Mr. Scourby played Ratikin in *A Month in the Country* (Phoenix Th., Apr. 3, 1956); succeeded Ian Keith as Peter Cauchon in Siobhan McKenna's *Saint Joan* (Phoenix, Sept. 11, 1956); played Claudius in *Hamlet* (Phoenix, Mar. 16, 1961); Gorothchenko in *Tovarich* (Broadway, Mar. 9, 1963); Senator Orton in *Sparks Fly Upward* (McFarlin Auditorium, SMU, Dallas, Dec. 3, 1965); Walt Whitman in *A Whitman Portrait* (Gramercy Arts Th., N.Y.C., Oct. 11, 1966); and in *Walt Whitman's America* (Feb. 12, 1968); the Narrator in *L'Histoire du Soldat* (Caramoor, N.Y., Festival, July 5, 1968); and John Knox in *Vivat! Vivat Regina!* (Broadhurst, N.Y.C., Jan. 20, 1972).

Films. Mr. Scourby made his screen debut in *Affair in Trinidad* (Col., 1952); appeared in *The Glory Brigade* (20th-Fox, 1953); and was the narrator for *Victory at Sea* (UA, 1954).

Television. Mr. Scourby has appeared on Playhouse 90 (CBS); Armstrong Circle Th. (NBC); US Steel Hour (CBS); the Defenders (CBS); and Naked City (ABC); was narrator of *The Innocent Years* (NBC, Nov. 21, 1957); *The Coming of Christ* (NBC, Dec. 21, 1960); *World of Bob Hope* (NBC, Oct. 29, 1961); *World of Sophia Loren* (NBC); played in *The Man Who Refused To Die* (CBS, Mar. 14, 1962); *Death of the Hired Man* (Americans: A Portrait in Verses, CBS, Aug. 1962); narrated *The World of Jacqueline Kennedy* (NBC, Nov. 30, 1962); *The World of Benny Goodman* (NBC, Jan. 24, 1963); *The World of Maurice Chevalier* (NBC, Feb. 22, 1963); and Project 20 (NBC, 1953–60).

His other television appearances include Mr. Novak (NBC); The Christopher Program (Ind.); The Man from U.N.C.L.E. (NBC); The Rogues (NBC); Daniel Boone (NBC); Herald of Truth (ABC); Zane Grey (Ind.); and The Defenders (Ind.). He has served as narrator for The Southern Baptist Hour (NBC); *Jonathan and the Movies* (NBC); *The Winging World of Jonathan Winters* (NBC); *The Inheritance* (NBC); *The World of James Bond* (NBC); *Ready on Arrival* (CBS); *The Investigation* (NBC); *The Law and the Prophets* (NBC); *Child of Darkness, Child of Light* (CBS); *Childhood: The Enchanted Years* (NBC); and various National Geographic specials (CBS).

Discography. Mr. Scourby has recorded approximately 250 books for the blind (1937–to date), including the *Bible*, *War and Peace*, *Anna Karenina*, and *Les Miserables*. .

Awards. Mr. Scourby received the Certificate of Merit from the American Foundation for the Blind (1955).

SEAL, ELIZABETH. Actress, singer. b. Elizabeth Anne Seal, Aug. 28, 1933, Genoa, Italy, to Frederick and Rill Seal. Father, ship broker. Studied at Royal Acad. of Dancing. Married 1961 to Zack Matalon, actor, director, producer; one son, one daughter. Relatives in theatre; brother, Richard Seal, actor; brother-in-law, Vivian Matalon, director. Member of AEA; AFTRA. Address: c/o Stanley Weiss, 401 Broadway, New York, NY 10013, tel. (212) WA 5-3886.

Theatre. Miss Seal made her first professional appearance as a dancer in the chorus of *Gay's the Word* (Saville, London, England, Feb. 16, 1951); subsequently, danced in the chorus of *The Glorious Days* (Palace, Feb. 28, 1953); danced and sang in *The Joys* (Players Th.); played Gladys in *The Pajama Game* (Coliseum, Oct. 13, 1955); Esmeralda in *Camino Real* (Phoenix, Apr. 8, 1957); Lola in *Damn Yankees* (Coliseum, Mar. 28, 1957); and Irma in *Irma La Douce* (Lyric, July 17, 1958), also making her N.Y.C. debut in it (Plymouth, Sept. 29, 1960).

She appeared as Josefa in the national touring company of *A Shot in the Dark* (opened Playhouse, Wilmington, Del., Oct. 17, 1962; closed Studebaker, Chicago, Ill., May 25, 1963); appeared in *Exiles* (Cleveland Play House, Ohio, 1964); appeared with her husband in *Have Bird, Will Travel* (Edinburgh, Scotland; on tour in England; Arts Th., Cambridge, England, Aug. 1965); replaced (Dec. 2, 1968) Judi Dench as Sally Bowles in *Cabaret* (Palace, London, Feb. 28, 1968); was Lucette in *Cat Among the Pigeons* (Prince of Wales Th., London, Apr. 15, 1969); and Kate Hardcastle in *Liberty Ranch!* (Greenwich, London, July 1972).

Films. Miss Seal has appeared in *Town on Trial* (Col., 1957); and *Cone of Silence.*

Television. She has appeared on the Perry Como Show (NBC, 1961); the Mike Wallace Show and Route 66 (CBS).

Night Clubs. With her husband, Zack Matalon, Miss Seal sang and danced at the Shoreham Hotel (Washington, D.C., 1963).

Awards. She received the Variety Club Award as most promising newcomer for her performance as Gladys in *The Pajama Game* (1957), and as best actress for her performance as Irma in *Irma La Douce* (1959); and the Antoinette Perry (Tony) Award for *Irma La Douce* (1961).

SEALE, DOUGLAS. Director, actor, scenic designer, educator. b. Douglas Robert Seale, Oct. 28, 1913, London, England, to Robert Henry and Margaret (Law) Seale. Father, engineer. Grad. from Rutlish, London, England, 1924–32; attended RADA, 1932–34. Served British Army, 1940–46.

Theatre. Mr. Seale first performed as the Duke of Plaza Toro in a Rutlish sch. production of *The Gondoliers* (1928); made his professional debut in London, playing Starling in *The Drums Begin* (Embassy, Apr. 1934); subsequently played D'Amville in *Queen of Scots* (New, June 8, 1934); and acted in repertory in England and Scotland (1934–40).

He joined (1946) the Shakespeare Memorial Th. (Stratford-upon-Avon), playing Bardolph and Erpingham in *Henry V*, Antonio in *Twelfth Night*, the Doctor in *Macbeth*, and the old Man in *Faustus;* appeared as Flute in *The Fairy Queen* (Royal Opera House, Covent Garden, London, Dec. 12, 1946).

Mr. Seale directed his first plays *While the Sun Shines*, and *Jupiter Laughs* (Perth, Scot. 1957); acted with the Shakespeare Memorial Th. (Stratford-upon-Avon, 1947), playing the Duke of York in *Richard II*, Trinculo in *The Tempest*, Escalus in *Measure for Measure*, and the Apothecary in *Romeo and Juliet;* subsequently appeared as Mr. Ireland in *The Hidden Years* (Fortune, London, Jan. 23, 1948); and directed *The Comedy of Errors* (Repertory Th., Birmingham, 1948).

He directed at the Bedford Th. (Camden Town, England, 1949) *Candide, Arms and the Man, Pygmalion, Mrs. Warren's Profession, Major Barbara*, and *The Inca of Jerusalem;* directed *The Romantic Young Lady* for the Birmingham Repertory Co. (1949); served as director of productions there *Uncle Vanya, A Month in the Country*, (Jan. 1950–55), staging such plays as *The Wild Duck, Henry V, Pericles*, and *Henry VI, Part 3;* directed *Henry VI, Part 3* (Old Vic, London, July 21, 1952); directed *Henry VI, Part 1, Henry VI, Part 2*, and *Henry VI, Part 3* (Repertory Th., Birmingham, June 1953; Old Vic, London, July 13–15, 1953).

He directed a Dutch-language production of *Saint Joan* (Amsterdam State Th., Netherlands, 1954); directed at the Old Vic, London, *Henry IV, Part 1* (Apr. 27, 1955); *Henry IV, Part 2* (Apr. 28, 1955); and *The Merry Wives of Windsor* (Sept. 27, 1955); directed his first opera, *The Marriage of Figaro* (Sadler's Wells Opera House, 1955); directed *Henry V* (Cambridge Drama Festival, Sander's Th., Mass., July 5, 1955); and directed the opera, *Fidelio* (Sadler's Wells Opera House, London, 1956).

His production of *Caesar and Cleopatra* was presented at the Th. des Nations (Paris, France, 1956), under the auspices of the Birmingham Repertory Co., subsequently it played in London (Old Vic, July 30, 1956). He directed *Fanny's First Play* for the Edinburgh (Scotland) Festival (Lyceum, 1956), and for the Berlin (Germany) Festival (1956).

For the Shakespeare Memorial Th., Mr. Seale directed *King John* (Stratford-upon-Avon, Apr. 16, 1957); and in London, for the Old Vic, directed *Richard III* (May 29, 1957), *Henry VI, Part 1* and *Henry VI, Part 2* (Oct. 16, 1957), *Henry VI, Part 3* (Oct. 17, 1957), and *King Lear* (Feb. 18, 1958); subsequently directed *School*, a musical (Prince's, London, Mar. 4, 1958); at the Shakespeare Memorial Th., *Much Ado About Nothing* (Stratford-upon-Avon, Aug. 26, 1958); a Dutch-language production of *Richard II* (State Th., Amsterdam, The Netherlands, 1958); and *The World of the Wonderful Dark* (Vancouver Festival, B.C., Canada, 1958).

He was appointed associate director of the Old Vic (Apr. 1958–July 1959), during which time he directed *Julius Caesar* (Oct. 8, 1958), *Macbeth* (Dec. 17, 1958), *Tartuffe* (Feb. 11, 1959), *The Magistrate* (Mar. 19, 1959), and the opera, *The Tempest or the Enchanted Island* (June 9, 1959); at the Old Vic (London), he directed *Saint Joan* (Feb. 9, 1960), and *She Stoops to Conquer* (Nov. 8, 1960); and at the Dublin (Ireland) Festival, directed *Landscape with Figures* (Olympic, 1959).

Mr. Seale made his N.Y.C. debut as a director with the production of *One Way Pendulum* (E. 74 St. Th., Sept. 18, 1961); and directed the Old Vic production of *Saint Joan* (NY City Ctr., Feb. 20, 1962).

For the American Shakespeare Festival, he directed *Henry IV, Part 1* (Stratford, Conn., June 17, 1962); directed *The Importance of Being Earnest* (Madison Ave. Playhouse, N.Y.C., Feb. 25, 1963); at the American Shakespeare Festival directed *Henry V* (June 12, 1963) and *The Comedy of Errors* (June 11, 1963); directed *Riverside Drive* (Th. de Lys, N.Y.C., Feb. 4, 1964); and played Mr. Hardcastle in *She Stoops to Conquer* (Playhouse in the Park, Cincinnati, Ohio, June 30, 1965).

In 1965, Mr. Seale was appointed artistic director of Center Stage, Baltimore, Md., where he directed *Caesar and Cleopatra*, in which he also played Caesar (Oct. 28, 1965); *Ardele* (Jan. 6, 1966), in which he also performed; *The Days Between* (Mar. 17, 1966); *The Chinese Wall* (Apr. 21, 1966), which he had also adapted; and *As You Like It* (May 26, 1966). During the 1966–67 season he played Harpagon in *The Miser* (Sept. 22, 1966); directed *Lady Audley's Secret* (Dec. 1, 1966), which he had also adapted; and for the 1967–68 season he directed and designed scenery for *Waiting for Godot* (Sept. 29, 1967), *The Member of the Wedding* (Oct. 6, 1967), *Hamlet* (Nov. 24, 1967), *The Devil's Disciple* (Jan. 12, 1968), and *The Royal Family* (Mar. 22, 1968); and he designed scenery for *An Enemy of the People* (Feb. 16, 1968).

At the John Fernald Co., Rochester, Mich., he appeared in *The Apple Cart* (Oct. 24, 1968) and directed *The Magistrate* (Nov. 28, 1968) and *Amphitryon 38* (Mar. 13, 1969). He became co-producing director, Goodman Memorial Th., Chicago, Ill., in 1969, where he directed *Soldiers* (Oct. 24, 1969), *The Tempest* (Jan. 23, 1970), *The Man in the Glass Booth* (Apr. 17, 1970), *Heartbreak House* (May 29, 1970), *The Threepenny Opera* (Oct. 12, 1970), *Twelfth Night* (Nov. 30, 1970), *Marching Song* (Mar. 1, 1971), his own adaptation of *Lady Audley's Secret* (May 24, 1971), *The Importance of Being Earnest* (Dec. 20, 1971), and *The Royal Family* (Jan. 25, 1972).

At the Cleveland (Ohio) Play House, he directed *A Doll's House* (Oct. 15, 1971), and for Washington (D.C.) Theatre Club, he directed his adaptation of *Lady Audley's Secret* (May 31, 1972). He played Giovanni in *Emperor Henry IV* (Ethel Barrymore Th., N.Y.C., Mar. 28, 1973); directed and appeared in his adaptation of *Lady Audley's Secret* (Eastside Playhouse, Oct. 3, 1972); directed *Look Back in Anger* (Cleveland Play House, Dec. 21, 1973); *Getting Married* (Hartford Stage Co., Hartford, Conn., Nov. 9, 1973); and played Oliver Seaton in *A Family and a Fortune* (Seattle Repertory Th., Seattle, Wash., Jan. 16, 1974). As artistic director (1974–75) of the Philadelphia (Pa.) Drama Guild at Walnut St. Th., he presented *Misalliance* (Nov. 21, 1974); *Ardele* (Jan. 9, 1975), which he also directed; *Long Day's Journey into Night* (Feb. 27, 1975); and *The Importance of Being Earnest* (Mar. 1975), which he also directed.

Television. He directed *The Rules of the Game* (Eng., TWW, 1959); and appeared as Givet in *Thérèse Raquin* (TWW, 1959).

Other Activities. Mr. Seale was artist in residence, Univ. of California (1964–65); and, while with Center Stage, Baltimore, Md., he taught acting at Boston (Mass.) University and Towson (Md.) State College.

SEELEN, ARTHUR. Theatre bookseller and publisher, actor. b. Arthur Seelenfreund, Oct. 1, 1923, Brooklyn, N.Y., to Henry and Celia (Cohn) Seelenfreund. Grad. DeWitt Clinton H.S., Bronx, N.Y., 1940; Coll. of the City of N.Y., B.S. 1944; attended Ohio State Univ., graduate study, 1946. Studied with Ezra Stone, Alan Schneider, Arthur Penn and Michael Redgrave at Amer. Theatre Wing (1954–56). Relative in theatre: cousin, Jerry Seelen, lyricist and comedy writer. Member of AEA; SAG; AFTRA. Address: (home) 150 E. 182nd St., Bronx, NY 10451, tel. (212) CY 5-7196; (bus.) Drama Book Shop, 150 W. 52nd St., New York, NY 10019, tel. (212) JU 2-1037.

Pre-Theatre. Chemist.

Theatre. Mr. Seelen is vice-president of Drama Book Specialists, publishers, and president of the Drama Book Shop, Inc. in N.Y.C. Mr. Seelen first appeared on stage as Kurt Mueller in the Ohio State Univ. Th. production of *Watch on the Rhine* (1945); made his N.Y.C. debut as Sebastien Dubois in *Deputy of Paris* (Henry St. Playhouse, Mar. 21, 1947); subsequently appeared as Mr. Webb in *Own Town* (E. Strodsberg Drama Festival, Pa., July 1947); played Gen. Bridgeworth in the ELT production of *Getting Married* (N.Y.C., Oct. 1952); and Gasparo in *The White Devil* (Phoenix, Mar. 17, 21, 1955).

In stock, for the Barnstormers (Tamworth, N.H., 1951), he played Spencer Grant in *Here Today*, Bishop Gregory in *Velvet Glove*, Dr. Anderson in *First Year*, Mr. Brink in *On Borrowed Time*, Mr. Armstrong in *The Man;* at the Allenbury Playhouse (Pa., 1953) he appeared as Gus Kennedy in *Glad Tidings*, and Bishop Gregory in *Velvet Glove;* appeared as Lonzman in *Liliom* (Brattle, Mass., 1954); in Cragsmere (N.Y., 1955), played Norman in *The Wedding Breakfast*, and H. C. Curry in *The Rainmaker;* and at the Niagara Melody Fair (Buffalo, N.Y., 1959) Ivanov in *Silk Stockings*, and Arturo in *Happy Hunting*. He played the Policeman in the pre-Bway tryout of *The Circus of Dr. Lao* (The Edgewater Beach Hotel Th., Chicago, Ill., 1958); and Rappaport in *The Wall* (Billy Rose Th., N.Y.C., Oct. 11, 1960).

Television and Radio. Mr. Seelen made his debut as Dromio of Ephesus in *The Comedy of Errors* (CBS, 1948); played Larimer in *A Matter of Dollars and Roubles* (Lamp Unto My Feet, CBS, 1959), and has appeared in over 20 television shows, including Campbell Sound Stage (NBC), Studio One (CBS), Philco Playhouse (NBC), US Steel Hour (CBS), and Theatre Guild of the Air (CBS). He has performed on radio broadcasts, including Nora Drake (CBS), Wendy Warren (CBS), and Right to Happiness (CBS).

Other Activities. Between engagements he has worked as assistant manager of a foreign film house in N.Y.C.; as a N.Y.C. bus guide for tourists; as enumerator for Federal Business Census; and as a field worker for Nielsen Television Ratings.

Recreation. Hiking, hi-fi, photography.

SEFF, RICHARD. Playwright, actor. b. Richard Philip Seff, Sept. 23, 1927, New York City, to Chester and Henrietta (Levy) Seff. Grad. DeWitt Clinton H.S., N.Y.C., 1943; New York Univ., B.A. 1947. Studied acting with Stella Adler, N.Y.C., 1949–50. Member of AEA; SAG; AFTRA. Address: 201 E. 79th St., New York, NY 10021.

Mr. Seff was a partner in the firm Hesseltine, Bookman & Seff (H.B.S.) Ltd., talent representatives, with offices in New York City (1962–69). He was assistant to Bertha Case at the Darrow Agency (1952); originated the Program Development Dept. for Robert Lawrence Productions (1952–53); was head of the Television Dept. at Liebling-Wood Agency (1953–54); associate director of the Legitimate Musical Theatre Dept. at MCA (1954–62); and vice-president of Creative Management Associates, representing writers and directors in the theatre (1969–73).

Theatre. Mr. Seff first appeared on stage in stock in *What a Life* (Newport Casino Th., R.I., July 1946), as a member of the resident company. He was assistant to Lucille Lortel for the first two seasons of her White Barn Th., Westport, Conn. (1948–49); appeared as Joseph Keefer "302" in *Darkness at Noon* (Alvin, N.Y.C., Jan. 13, 1951), and on tour (opened McCarter, Princeton, N.J., Sept. 28, 1951; closed Cox, Cincinnati, Apr. 26, 1952).

He is the author of *The Whole Ninth Floor* (Playhouse-on-the-Mall, Paramus, N.J., Feb. 1966); *Paris Is Out* (Brooks Atkinson Th., N.Y.C., Jan. 19, 1970); and *Consenting Adults* (Philadelphia, Pa., Summer 1974).

Films. He appeared in the feature film *Have A Nice Weekend* (Seva Prods. 1973).

Other Activities. He has acted in an advisory capacity with two theatrical investment syndicates.

Awards. Mr. Seff was nominated for the Donaldson Award for his performance as Joseph Keefer in *Darkness at Noon* (1950–51). He was valedictorian, P.S. 139, Brooklyn, N.Y. (1939).

Recreation. Photography, theatrical financing.

SEGAL, ALEX. Director, educator. b. Alexander Elias Segal, July 1, 1915, Brooklyn, N.Y., to Morris and Mary (Pappin) Segal. Father, delicatessen store owner. Attended Trenton (N.J.) H.S.; grad. Carnegie Inst. of Tech., B.A., 1940; M.A., 1942. Married Mar. 10, 1945, to Ruth Storm; one son, one daughter. Member of DGA (natl. council, 1960–63); SSD&C.

Theatre. Mr. Segal acted and directed at Wharf Th., Provincetown, Mass. (1940); directed at the Woodstock Playhouse (N.Y., Summer 1945) and the Ogunquit Playhouse, Me. (Summer 1947); directed *Compulsion* (Ambassador, Oct. 24, 1957); *Who Was That Lady I Saw You With?* (Martin Beck Th., Mar. 3, 1958); *Jolly's Progress* (Longacre, Dec. 5, 1959); the pre-Bway tryout of *We Take the Town* (opened Shubert, New Haven, Conn., Feb. 19, 1962; closed Shubert, Philadelphia, Pa., Mar. 17, 1962); and *One Flew Over the Cuckoo's Nest* (Cort, N.Y.C., Nov. 13, 1963).

Mr. Segal is chairman, Dept. of Drama, Univ. of Southern California.

Films. He directed *Ransom* (MGM, 1956); *All the Way Home* (Par., 1964); and *Joy in the Morning* (MGM, 1965).

Television. Mr. Segal was director at ABC of Actors' Studio (1949); the Boris Karloff Show (1949); Hollywood Screen Test (1950); Pulitzer Prize Playhouse (1950–51); Celanese Th. (ABC, 1951–52); directed and produced the Henry Aldrich Show (NBC, 1952); and US Steel Hour (ABC, 1953–55).

He directed *Trial of Anne Boleyn* (Omnibus, CBS, 1953); *Trial of Ben Johnson* (Omnibus, CBS, 1953); Seminar (ABC, 1953); *Dodsworth* (Producers Showcase, NBC, 1956); *Bloomer Girl* (Producers Showcase, NBC, 1956); *Happy Birthday* (Producers Showcase, NBC, 1956); *Angry Harvest* (Alcoa Hour, NBC, 1957); *Ride the Wild Mare* (Alcoa Hour, NBC, 1957); *The Winslow Boy* (Alcoa Hour, NBC, 1957); *A Marriage of Strangers* (Playhouse 90, CBS, 1959); *A Quiet Game of Cards* (Playhouse 90, CBS, 1959); *Divided We Stand* (American Heritage, CBS, 1959); *Not without Honor* (American Heritage, CBS, 1959); *John Honeyman* (American Heritage, CBS, 1959); for the Dupont Show of the Month (CBS, 1960), directed *Arrowsmith, Ethan Frome, Years Ago* and *The Lincoln Murder Case.*

He directed *People Need People* (Alcoa Premiere, ABC, 1961); the special, *Hedda Gabler* (CBS, 1963); *A Killing at Sundial* (Bob Hope Chrysler Show, NBC, 1963); *Death of a Salesman* (CBS, 1966); *The Crucible* (CBS, 1967); *The Diary of Anne Frank* (ABC, 1967); and *The Lie* (Playhouse 90, CBS, 1973).

Awards. Mr. Segal received the Peabody Awards for his directing at Actors' Studio (1949); and Celanese Theatre (1952); *TV Guide* Awards for Pulitzer Prize Playhouse (1950) and US Steel Hour (1953–54); NATAS (Emmy) Awards for Celanese Theatre (1952) and US Steel Hour (1953); *Look* Magazine Award as television director (1952); *Variety* Show Management Award as television director (1953–54); Christopher Award for his direction of *P.O.W.* on US Steel Hour (1954); an Award of Excellence from *Modern Photoplay* Magazine for US Steel Hour (1955); and Directors Guild of America awards for *The Diary of Anne Frank* and *Death of a Salesman.*

SEGAL, BEN. Producer, theatre owner. b. Benjamin Harris Segal, May 9, 1919, Boston, Mass., to Frank D. and Rebecca (Molstein) Segal. Father, restaurateur. Grad. Hamden (Conn.) H.S., 1941. Married Jan. 23, 1948 to Clarice E. Cumbly; two sons, one daughter. Relative in theatre: cousin, Maurice H. Bailey, theatre owner. Served US Army, 1941–43; rank, Sgt. Member of Theatre Consultants, N.Y.C. (dir. and vice-pres., 1959); MATA (dir., 1960–to date); AMBA/Oakdale Development Corp. (partner). Address: Rose Farm, 26 Mansion Road, Wallingford, CT 06492.

Theatre. Mr. Segal was general manager for approximately seven years of Anthony Brady Farrell productions (1949–54); and was production associate for Mr. Farrell's presentation of *Billy Budd* (Biltmore Th., N.Y.C., Feb. 10, 1951); with Chandler Cowles, produced *Fancy Meeting You Again* (Royale, Jan. 14, 1952); and the revival of *Of Thee I Sing* (Ziegfield, May 5, 1952); and was manager-director of the Shubert Th. (New Haven, Conn., 1943–54).

Mr. Segal is co-founder, president, and director of the Oakdale Musical Th., Wallingford, Conn. (1954–to date); and director of the Melody Fair Th., North Tonawanda, N.Y. (1959–to date). He is a partner in the Sunrise Th., Sunrise, Fla.

Recreation. Theatre.

SEGAL, DAVID F. Scenic and lighting designer. b. June 2, 1943, New York City, to Samuel Michael and Cynthia Shapiro (Zeger) Segal. Father, rabbi. Relative in theatre: Erich Segal, scenarist, educator. Educ. New Lincoln School, N.Y.C.; Univ. of Pennsylvania; NY Univ. Professional training at Studio and Forum of Stage Design (Tharon Musser). Married July 22, 1972, in Woodstock, N.Y., to Greer Goldman. Member of United Scenic Artists, Local 829; Allied Bd. of Trade. Address: 26 E. 10th St., New York, NY 10003, tel. (212) 478-4846.

Pre-Theatre. Mr. Segal was an interior and lighting designer for homes and offices and a theatre consultant.

Theatre. Mr. Segal was scenic and lighting designer, Bedford Springs (Pa.) Playhouse (Summer 1964); in N.Y.C., his first work was scene and lighting designs for the off-Bway productions *Say Nothing* (Jan Hus Playhouse, Jan. 27, 1965) and the double-bill *Ludlow Fair* and *The Madness of Lady Bright* (Th. East, Mar. 22, 1966). For the Seattle (Wash.) Repertory Th., he did lighting for *Henry IV, Part 1* (Nov. 1, 1967), *The Rehearsal* (Nov. 8, 1967), *You Can't Take It with You* (Dec. 13, 1967), *The Rivals* (Jan. 24, 1968), and *The Father* (Feb. 7, 1968).

Mr. Segal also did lighting for *Private Lives* (Th. de Lys, N.Y.C., May 19, 1968); scenery and lighting for the double bill *Lemonade* and *The Autograph Hound* (Jan Hus Playhouse, N.Y.C., Dec. 13, 1968); *Frank Gagliano's City* (Fortune, Mar. 10, 1969); lighting for *A Home Away From* (Village South Th., Apr. 28, 1969); and scenery for *The World's a Stage* (Lyceum, May 12, 1969). He did lighting for *Oh, Calcutta!* (Eden Th., June 17, 1969; tr. to Belasco Th., Feb. 26, 1971); scenery and lighting for *Pequod* (Mercury Th., June 26, 1969); lighting for *A Scent of Flowers* (Martinique, Oct. 29, 1969); for *Summertree* (Players Th., Dec. 9, 1969); for *Seven Days of Mourning* (Circle in the Square, Dec. 16, 1969); for *The Last Sweet Days of Isaac* (East Side Playhouse, Jan. 26, 1970); *The White House Murder Case* (Circle in the Square, Feb. 18, 1970); *Billy-No-Name* (Truck and Warehouse Th., Mar. 2, 1970); setting and lighting for *The House of Leather* (Ellen Stewart Th., Mar. 18, 1970); and the original design for scenery for *Spoon River Anthology* (Long Wharf Th., New Haven, Conn., Apr. 3, 1970).

He did the setting and lighting for *Whispers on the Wind* (Th. de Lys, N.Y.C., June 3, 1970); lighting for *Boesman and Lena* (Circle in the Square, June 22, 1970); setting and lighting for *A Dream Out of Time* (Promenade Th., Nov. 8, 1970); lighting for *Happy Birthday, Wanda June* (Th. de Lys, Oct. 7–Nov. 15, 1970; transferred to Edison Th., Dec. 22, 1970). He did lighting for *The Last Sweet Days of Isaac* (Shelterhouse Th., Playhouse in the Park, Cincinnati, Ohio, June 1, 1971); lighting for *Twigs* (Broadhurst, N.Y.C., Nov. 14, 1971); setting and lighting for *JFK* (Circle in the Square, Nov. 21, 1971); lighting for *The Soft Core Pornographer* (Stage 73, Apr. 11, 1972); setting and lighting for *That's Entertainment* (Edison Th., Apr. 14, 1972); lighting for *Shelter* (Playhouse in the Park, Cincinnati, Ohio, June 1, 1972); for *Pygmalion* (Queens Playhouse, Oct. 30, 1972); setting and lighting for *Green Julia* (Sheridan Square Playhouse, N.Y.C., Nov. 16, 1972); and lighting for *Dear Oscar* (Playhouse, Nov. 16, 1972).

He did scenic and lighting design for *Ring-a-Levio* (Studio Arena, Buffalo, N.Y., Jan. 4, 1973); lighting for *Irene* (Minskoff Th., N.Y.C., Mar. 13, 1973); for *A Phantasmagoria Historia of D. Johann Fausten Magister, PhD, MD, DD, DL, Etc.* (Truck and Warehouse Th., Apr. 24, 1973); for *Alpha Beta* (Eastside Playhouse, May 3, 1973); scenery and lighting for *Funny Face* (Studio Arena, Buffalo, N.Y., Dec. 6, 1973; Ford's Th., Washington, D.C., Jan. 2, 1974); lighting for the Marlene Dietrich national tour (Mar. 1974); and he was lighting designer for City Ctr. Acting Co. (Saratoga, N.Y., July–Aug. 1974 and national tour).

He was lighting designer for *Beyond the Horizon* (McCarter Th., Princeton, N.J., Nov. 1974); for national tour of *Irene* (opened Denver, Colo., Dec. 1974); for the opera *Die Walküre* (Kennedy Ctr., Washington, D.C., Dec. 1974); for *Linda Hopkins Sings Bessie Smith* (Ford's Th., Washington, D.C., Dec. 1974); for national tour of Marlene Dietrich (Apr. 1975); for *Meeting Place* (Playhouse II, N.Y.C., Apr. 1975); and for The Acting Co. (formerly City Ctr. Acting Co.) Saratoga, N.Y., engagement (July 1975), tour, and N.Y.C. presentations (Harkness Th.) of *The Robber Bridegroom* (Oct. 7, 1975), *Edward II* (Oct. 21, 1975), and *The Time of Your Life* (Oct. 28, 1975).

SEGAL, VIVIENNE. Actress, singer. b. Vivienne Sonia Segal, Apr. 19, 1897, Philadelphia, Pa., to Bernhard and Paula (Hahn) Segal. Father, physician. Attended Sisters of Mercy Acad., Philadelphia. Studied singing with Eleanor McLellan, N.Y.C.; Mrs. Phillips-Jenkins, Philadelphia; William S. Brady, N.Y.C.; Estelle Liebling, N.Y.C.; Pietro Cimini, Los Angeles, Calif. Married June 1923 to Robert Downing Ames, actor (marr. dis. July 1926); married Dec. 16, 1950, to Hubbell Robinson, Jr., television executive. Member of AEA; SAG; AFTRA.

Theatre. Miss Segal made her debut singing the title role of *Carmen* and Siebel in *Faust* (Acad. of Music, Philadelphia, 1914); made her N.Y.C. debut as Mizzi and Gaby in *The Blue Paradise* (Casino, Aug. 5, 1915), and toured in it (1916–17); played Elly in *My Lady's Glove* (Lyric, June 18, 1917); appeared in the revue *Miss 1917* (Century, Nov. 5, 1917); played Mollie Farrington in *Oh, Lady! Lady!* (Princess, Feb. 1, 1918); Kitty Wentworth in *The*

Little Whopper (Casino, Oct. 13, 1919); appeared in *The Three Kisses* (Springfield, Mass., Jan. 1921), *Tangerine* (Atlantic City, N.J., Feb. 1921); played Odette Darimonde in *The Yankee Princess* (Knickerbocker, N.Y.C., Oct. 2, 1922); the title role in *Adrienne* (George M. Cohan Th., May 28, 1923); and appeared in the *Ziegfeld Follies* (New Amsterdam, June 24, 1924).

Miss Segal played Daphne in *Florida Girl* (Lyric, Nov. 2, 1925); Evelyne Devine in *Castles in the Air* (Selwyn, Sept. 6, 1926); Margot Bonvalet in *The Desert Song* (Casino, Nov. 30, 1926); Constance Bonacieux in *The Three Musketeers* (Lyric, Mar. 13, 1928); Nadina in *The Chocolate Soldier* (Erlanger's, Sept. 21, 1931), and on tour (1932); played Frieda Hatfield in *Music in the Air* (Los Angeles, Calif., June 1933); Constance Bonacieux in *The Three Musketeers* and Nanette in *No! No! Nanette!* (St. Louis, Mo., June 1936); Countess Peggy Palaffi in *I Married an Angel* (Shubert, N.Y.C., May 11, 1938); Vera Simpson in *Pal Joey* (Ethel Barrymore Th., Dec. 25, 1940); Fay Merrill and Queen Morgan Le Fay in *A Connecticut Yankee* (Martin Beck Th., Nov. 17, 1943); Viola Gregory in the pre-Bway tryout of *Forever Is Now* (opened Playhouse, Wilmington, Del., Sept. 7, 1945; closed Shubert, Philadelphia, Sept. 15, 1945); Tatiana Kerskaya in *Music in My Heart* (Adelphi, N.Y.C., Oct. 2, 1947); Leslie Butterfield in *Great To Be Alive!* (Winter Garden, Mar. 23, 1950); and repeated the role of Vera Simpson in the revival of *Pal Joey* (Broadhurst, Jan. 3, 1952).

Films. Miss Segal made her debut in an early sound short film, singing excerpts from *Sweethearts* and *Maytime* (WB, 1927); and appeared in *Song of the West* (WB, 1930); *Golden Dawn* (WB, 1930); *Bride of the Regiment* (1st Natl., 1930); *Viennese Nights* (WB, 1930); and *Cat and the Fiddle* (MGM, 1934).

Television and Radio. She was soloist on the radio programs Album of Familiar Music (NBC, 1930); Waltz Time (NBC, 1930); and Phillips (CBS, 1930).

For television, she has appeared on Studio One (CBS), and Alfred Hitchcock Presents (CBS, 1960, 1961).

Awards. Miss Segal won the *Variety* N.Y. Drama Critics Poll and won the Donaldson Award for her performance as Vera Simpson in *Pal Joey* (1952).

Recreation. Gardening, modelling in clay.

SEIDMAN, J. S.

SEIDMAN, J. S. Theatrical investor, certified public accountant. b. Jacob Stewart Seidman, Sept. 8, 1901, Brooklyn, N.Y., to Louis and Fanny (Goldfarb) Seidman. Father, teacher. Grad. Eastern District H.S., Brooklyn, 1918; New York Univ. Sch. of Commerce, B.C.S. (magna cum laude) 1921; Fordham Univ. Sch. of Law, LL.B. (cum laude) 1924; St. Lawrence Univ., LL.M. (cum laude) 1925; New York Univ., B.S. (cum laude) 1928. Married Dec. 29, 1950, to Jan Sherman. Served USNR, special financial assignments for Secy. of Navy Forrestal, 1942–45; rank, Capt. Member of NYU Board of Trustees; ANTA (dir., NY chapter); New Dramatists Committee (dir.); Bd. of Standards & Planning for the Living Th. (chmn., comm. on economics); Actors Studio; Alpha Epsilon Pi; Beta Gamma Sigma (hon.); Alpha Beta Psi (hon.); Delta Mu Delta (hon.); Sphinx Club (hon.); Arch & Square (hon.); New York Univ. Club (dir.); Economic Club; Accountants Club of Amer.; Amer. Inst. of CPAs (pres., 1959); NY State Society of CPAs (pres., 1954); Amer. Accounting Assn. (vice-pres., 1946); Natl. Assn. of Cost Accountants (dir., 1947); Society of Business Advisory Professions; New York Univ. Commerce Alumni Assn. (pres., 1958); New York Univ. Alumni Federation (vice-pres., 1963); New York Univ. Finance Club (pres., 1961); Hospital for Joint Diseases (trustee); NY Bd. of Trade (exec. comm., 1960–63). Address: (home) 2 E. 67th St., New York, NY 10021, tel. (212) TR 9-3633; (bus.) Seidman & Seidman, 15 Columbus Circle, New York, NY 10023, tel. (212) 765-7500.

Mr. Seidman has been a managing partner of Seidman & Seidman, certified public accountants, with offices throughout the U.S.

Theatre. He has invested in 67 N.Y.C. productions, including *Brigadoon, Wonderful Town, Top Banana, Paint Your Wagon, The Best Man, The Rose Tattoo, Seidman & Son, Come Back Little Sheba,* and *Oh, Men! Oh, Women!*

Published Works. He wrote *Seidman's Legislative History of Federal Income Tax Laws: 1938–1961* (5 vols., 1939, 1947, 1954); has been editor of the Tax Clinic for the *Journal of Accountancy;* was tax columnist for the NY *Herald Tribune* (1937–57); and his articles on financial matters have appeared in the NY *Times, Reader's Digest, Tax Magazine, Commercial and Financial Chronicle, Barron's, America's Banking,* and others.

His articles on the theatre and investment have appeared in *Variety, Theatre Arts, Fortune,* and *Harvard Club* magazine.

Recreation. Theatre, travel.

SEIGER, MARVIN L.

SEIGER, MARVIN L. Educator, director, playwright. b. Marvin Leon Seiger, Apr. 14, 1924, Brooklyn, N.Y., to Abraham and Sarah (Weintraub) Seiger. Father, machinist. Grad. New Utrecht H.S., 1941; attended Brooklyn Coll., 1941–43; Virginia Polytech. Inst., 1944; grad. Univ. of California at Los Angeles, B.A. 1948. M.A. 1950; Indiana Univ., Ph.D. 1960. Married Sept. 5, 1954 to Barbara D. Singer; one son. Served US Army, ETO; 1943–45; rank, Cpl. Member of DGA, SAA, USITT, AETA (member exec. board, 1961–64), Theta Alpha Phi, Kap and Bells. Address: (home) 915 West End Ave., New York, NY 10025, tel. (212) UN 6-3394; (bus.) c/o Hunter Coll., 695 Park Ave., New York, NY 10021, tel. (212) TR 9-2100.

Since 1960, Mr. Seiger has been director of the Th. Workshop at Hunter Coll., where he has been a member of the faculty since 1955 (instructor, 1955–57; assistant professor, 1959–1970; assoc. provost, 1971–to date). He has held academic positions at the Univ. of California at Los Angeles (teaching assistant, theatre arts, 1948–49), and Indiana Univ. (teaching assistant, 1951–53; teaching associate, 1953–54; instructor, 1954–55). He was production assistant to John Houseman at the Amer. Shakespeare Festival (1957); and has been managing editor of *Educational Theatre Journal* (1962–65).

Theatre. Mr. Seiger wrote *Blue Concerto* (Players Ring Th., Los Angeles, Aug. 1952), which has received more than 150 productions throughout the world, including a production in Hebrew by the Habimah Players (Israel, 1961). The musical, *Beg, Borrow or Steal,* was based upon an original story by Mr. Seiger (Martin Beck Th., N.Y.C., Feb. 10, 1960).

Television. For WTTV, Bloomington, Ind., he wrote *Willy Bay* (1952), and *Letters from Fontainebleau* (1953).

Published Works. He has contributed articles to *Players Magazine, Speech Teacher, Jewish Historical Quarterly,* and *Quarterly Journal of Speech.* .

Awards. He received first prize in a Washington, D.C., play contest for *Blue Concerto* (1957), and *Willy Bay* (1958); and was awarded a Shuster faculty fellowship at Hunter Coll. (1961).

Recreation. Deep sea fishing, reading, family.

SEITZ, DRAN.

SEITZ, DRAN. Actress, director, producer, singer. b. Carolyn Jane Seitz, Sept. 27, 1928, Chicago, Ill. Father, State Dept. employee. Grad. Decatur (Ill.) H.S., 1947; Pasadena Playhouse, Coll. of Th. Arts, B.T.A. 1949; attended John Muir Jr. Coll., Pasadena, Calif., 1949–50; San Francisco State Coll., 1950–51; City Coll., San Francisco, 1950–51. Studied voice with Jean Ernest, 1959–63. Relative in theatre: twin sister, Tani Seitz, actress. Member of AEA; SAG; AFTRA.

Theatre. Miss Seitz made her professional debut as Linda in *Accent on Youth* (Eagle Rock Little Th., Calif., Oct. 21, 1949); subsequently directed a production of *Enchanted Stage* at the latter theatre; produced *Moon in Capricorn* (Village Th., Calif., Aug. 1, 1950); and wrote and produced *Vittorio* (Village Th., Sept. 1, 1950); appeared at the Muni Th., San Francisco, Calif., as Peggy McNab in *Father Malachy's Miracle* (Nov. 1950), and as Elizabeth in *Crime and Punishment* (Dec. 1950).

She appeared at the Straight Wharf Th., Nantucket, Mass. (Summer 1951) as Bertha in *Bertha, the Sewing Machine Girl,* performed in and directed *The Blue Vase,* played the Actress in *The Butter and Egg Man,* Miss Kirby in *Thunder Rock,* Julie Cavendish in *The Royal Family,* Anne in *The Double Door,* and Nora Fintry in *The White Steed.* During 1951–52, she owned and operated the Dobbs Ferry (N.Y.) Th., together with her sister, Tani Seitz, and Val Forslund, where they organized the Touchstone Players. There, Miss Seitz played Elmire in *Tartuffe,* which she also directed; appeared in and directed *Murder without Crime;* played Mrs. Antrobus in *The Skin of Our Teeth;* portrayed Linda and directed *Holiday;* appeared as the Wife and directed *The Adding Machine;* played Abbey in *Arsenic and Old Lace;* and staged *Elves and the Shoemaker* and *The Long Christmas Dinner.*

For summers 1952–53, again with Tani Seitz and Val Forslund, she operated the Blythewood Summer Th. at Chestertown, N.Y., where she directed, produced, or appeared in Bertha, the Sewing Machine Girl; Candlelight; Peg o' My Heart; The Father; Camille; Saint Joan; Bell, Book and Candle; Star Fish; Miss Julie; For Men Only; Scrap of Paper; and *Love and Let Love.*

Miss Seitz made her N.Y.C. debut as an ondine in Ondine (46 St. Th., Feb. 18, 1954); subsequently played Claud in *Fanny* (Majestic, Nov. 4, 1954); joined as Hilda in *Plain and Fancy* (Mark Hellinger Th., Jan. 27, 1955), which she repeated on tour (opened Forrest, Philadelphia, Pa., Mar. 6, 1956), and in summer theatre productions at Allentown, Pa.; Kansas City, Kan.; Louisville, Ky.; Camden, N.J.; Westbury, L.I., N.Y.; Valley Forge Music Fair, Devon, Pa.; and Atlanta, Ga. (1956–57).

She played Suzy in *Pipe Dream* and Sharon in *Finian's Rainbow* (Valley Forge Music Fair, 1956–57); went to Gaza, Egypt, where she appeared and sang in a UN Christmas production (1957); during the summer 1957 played Carrie in *Carousel* (Atlanta, Ga.); Julie in the same musical (Hyannis, Mass.); and Gloria in *Damn Yankees* (St. Louis, Municipal Opera Th., Mo.). She directed *Mandranola* (4th St. Th., N.Y.C., 1958); played Blanche Sartoris in *Widower's Houses* (Downtown Th., 1959); the Salvation Army Girl in *Guys and Dolls* (Warwick, R.I., 1959); Ariane in *Moonbirds* (Cort, N.Y.C., Oct. 9, 1959); Celimene in *Le Misanthrope* (IASTA, 1960); Lady Milford in *Love and Intrigue* (IASTA, 1960); Lady Mortimer in *Henry IV, Part I* (Phoenix, Mar. 1, 1960); and Lady Northumberland in *Henry IV, Part 2* (Cambridge Drama Festival, Mass., 1960).

Miss Seitz played Nellie Forbush in *South Pacific* (Beverly, Mass., 1960); Gwendolen in *Becket* (St. James, N.Y.C. Oct. 5, 1960); Lysistrata in *The Happiest Girl in the World* (Martin Beck Th., Apr. 3, 1961); toured South America as Annie Sullivan in a Theatre Guild and ANTA production of *The Miracle Worker* (1961); played Connie Dayton in *Come Blow Your Horn* (Detroit, Mich.; Washington, D.C.; Philadelphia, Pa., 1962); Leonore in *The Knight of Olmedo* (IASTA, N.Y.C.; Library of Congress, Washington, D.C., 1962); and was standby for Florence Henderson in *The Girl Who Came to Supper* (Bway Th., N.Y.C., Dec. 8, 1963). With her sister, Miss Seitz adapted, wrote lyrics for, and appeared in a musical version of *As You Like It* (White Barn Th., Westport, Conn., Sept. 6, 1964; ANTA Matinee Th. Series, Th. de Lys, N.Y.C., Oct. 27, 1964); and she appeared in *I Do, I Do* (Paper Mill Playhouse, Millburn, N.J., Dec. 1968).

Films. Miss Seitz appeared in *I, the Jury* (UA, 1953).

Television. She made her debut in *Cinderella* (KTTV, Los Angeles, Calif., Dec. 1949); and subsequently played Lady Mortimer in *Henry IV, Part 1* (Play of the Week, WNTA, 1960).

Night Clubs. She appeared as a singer at Number One Fifth Avenue (N.Y.C., 1959).

Recreation. Clothes designing, writing.

SEITZ, TANI. Actress. b. Sept. 27, 1928, Chicago, Ill. Father, State Dept. employee. Grad. Decatur (Ill.) H.S., 1946; Pasadena (Calif.) Playhouse, Coll. of Th. Arts, B.T.A. 1948; San Francisco State Coll., B.L.A. 1950. Studied voice with Jean Ernest, N.Y.C., 1961–63; dance with Ruth St. Denis, Hollywood, Calif. Relative in theatre: twin sister, Dran Seitz, actress. Member of AEA; AFTRA; SAG.

Theatre. Miss Seitz played the First Page in a stock production of *As You Like It* (Pasadena Playhouse, Calif., Apr. 23, 1947); Marie in the Calif. State Th. touring production of *Candlelight* (1949); Miss Haver in a stock production of *Evening Star* (Pasadena Playhouse, June 5, 1949); Tia in *Bird of Paradise* (Pasadena Playhouse, July 24, 1949); Sussette in *Bright Champagne* (Pasadena Playhouse, July 28, 1949); Sabina in *The Skin of Our Teeth* (Pasadena Playhouse, Dec. 1949); Genevieve in *Accent on Youth* (Eagle Rock Th., Calif., Oct. 21, 1949); Joanne Wilkes in *Moon in Capricorn* (Village Th., Calif., Aug. 1, 1950); Anna in *Vittorio* (Village Th., Calif., Sept. 1, 1950); The Queen in *The Eagle Has Two Heads* (Muni Th., San Francisco, Calif., Dec. 17, 1950); and Antiope in *The Warrior's Husband* (Muni Th., Apr. 18, 1951).

She joined the Norwich Summer Stock Th. (Summer 1951), appearing as Lorna in *Alice in Wonderland*, Susan Charmichel in *Detective Story*, Unice in *Streetcar Named Desire*, Jeannie in *Brigadoon*, M. E. Dodge Norton in *See Naples and Die*, Marie in *Come Back, Little Sheba*, Forsythe in *Told to Children*, in *Death of a Salesman*; and as a Dancer in *Lend an Ear*. She performed in *Thunder Rock*, and as Mrs. Cavendish in *Royal Family* (Touchstone Players, Mt. Vernon, N.Y., Sept. 1951).

As owner and operator, with her sister, Dran Seitz, and Val Forslund, of the Dobbs Ferry (N.Y.) Playhouse, she appeared in *The Adding Machine*, as Dorine in *Tartuffe*, Martha in *Arsenic and Old Lace*, Jan in *Murder without Crime*, and Julie in *Holiday* (Winter 1951–52).

At the Blythewood Summer Th., Loon Lake, N.Y., which she operated, with Dran Seitz and Val Forslund, she played Camille in *La dame aux camélias*; Jeanne Wilkes in *Moon in Capricorn*, Lisette Graham in *Bertha, the Sewing Machine Girl*, Marie in *Candlelight*, Dorine in *Tartuffe*, Peg in *Peg o' My Heart*, and directed *The Father* (Summer 1952). Again with the Blythewood Summer Th., she played Gillian in *Bell, Book and Candle*, performed in *Miss Julie*, as Jean in *Starfish*, Valerie in *Love and Let Love*, Marie in *Candlelight*, Louise in *Scrap of Paper*, and Tilly in *For Men Only* (Summer 1953).

Miss Seitz repeated the role of Jeanne Wilkes in *Moon in Capricorn* (Th. de Lys. N.Y.C., Oct. 28, 1953); portrayed an Ondine in *Ondine* (46 St. Th., Feb. 18, 1954); Claudine in *Fanny* (Majestic, Nov. 4, 1954); Silvia in *Island of Goats* (Fulton, Oct. 4, 1955); Ismene in *Antigone* (Carnegie Hall Playhouse, Apr. 3, 1956); Inez in *No Exit* (Th. East, Aug. 14, 1956); Anne Boleyn in *Royal Gambit* (Sullivan Playhouse, Mar. 4, 1959); Mrs. Davis in *The Confederates* (Th. Marquee, Sept. 28, 1959); Jan in *The Nervous Set* (Henry Miller's Th. May 12, 1959); Clytemnestra in *The Prodigal* (Downtown Th., Feb. 11, 1960); and appeared in *Le Misanthrope* (IASTA, Apr. 1960). She succeeded Juliet Randall as Lady Mortimer in *Henry IV, Part 1* (Phoenix, Mar. 1, 1960); followed Alice Drummond as Lady Northumberland in *Henry IV, Part 2* (Phoenix, Apr. 18, 1960); succeeded (Oct. 12, 1960) Juliet Randall in the role of Natasha Filippovna in *The Idiot* (Gate Repertory Th., Sept. 25, 1960); played Yse in *Noontide* (Th. Marquee, June 1, 1961); succeeded (Aug. 2, 1962) Madeleine Sherwood as Morgan Le Fey in *Camelot* (Majestic, Dec. 3, 1960); was Inez in *The Knight of Olmedo* (IASTA, Nov. 3, 1962); was in *As You Like It*, which, with Dran Seitz, she adapted and wrote lyrics for (White Barn Th., Westport, Conn., Sept. 6, 1964; ANTA Matinee Series, Th. de Lys., N.Y.C., Oct. 27, 1964); and appeared at Arena Stage, Washington, D.C., in *The Rehearsal* (Dec. 3, 1964) and *Heartbreak House* (Feb. 11, 1965).

Films. She appeared in *I, the Jury* (UA, 1953); and as Anne in *The Greenwich Village Story* (Shawn, 1963).

Television. Miss Seitz played the title role in *Cinderella* (KTTV, Los Angeles, Calif., Dec. 1949); and Anne Boleyn in *Royal Gambit* (CBS, Canada, Aug. 1961).

SEITZ, WAYNE T. Costume designer, executive. b. Wayne Thomas Seitz, Aug. 14, 1932, Alameda, Calif., to Wayne Carter and Beatrice Elizabeth (Thomas) Seitz. Father, office manager. Grad. San Leandro H.S., 1950; attended Univ. of Denver, 1951–53. Served US Army, 1954–56; rank, Pfc. Address: (home) 317 E. 83rd St., New York, NY 10028; (bus.) The American Costume Co., Inc., 810 Broadway, New York, NY 10003, tel. (212) GR 5-2587.

Pre-Theatre. Cannery worker, warehouse worker, book clerk, grocery clerk.

Theatre. Since 1960, Mr. Seitz has been president of The American Costume Co. He previously worked in a N.Y.C. costume company (1955–1960), and designed costumes at the Univ. of Denver (1952–53).

Mr. Seitz also designed costumes for *Streets of New York* (Maidman Th., Oct. 29, 1963).

SELDEN, ALBERT. Producer, composer, lyricist. b. Albert Wiggin Seldon, Oct. 20, 1922, New York City, to Lynde and Muriel (Wiggin) Seldon. Father, financier, Grad. Hotchkiss H.S., Lakeville, Conn., 1940; Yale Coll., B.A., 1943. Studied composition with Otto Luening, Columbia Univ. 1942–43; orchestration with Ted Royal, Stamford, Conn., 1950–52. Married Dec. 22, 1942, to Jean Beaven (marr. dis., Feb. 20, 1960); three sons, two daughters; married Feb. 27, 1960, to Carlye Rogerson; two sons, two daughters. Served US Army, 1942–45; rank, 1st Lt.; awarded Bronze Star. Member of Dramatists Guild, ASCAP, League of NY Theatres, SPA. Address: (home) Hadlyme, CT 06439; (bus.) Goodspeed Opera House, East Haddam, CT tel. (203) TR 3-8664.

Theatre. Mr. Selden's first Bway production was *Small Wonder* (Coronet, Sept. 15, 1948), for which he wrote the music with Baldwin Bergersen; subsequently wrote the music for the pre-Bway tryout of *A Month of Sundays* (opened Shubert, Boston, Mass., Dec. 25, 1951; closed Forrest, Philadelphia, Pa., Jan. 26, 1952); produced *The Grey-Eyed People* (Martin Beck Th., N.Y.C., Dec. 17, 1952); and presented touring productions of *Arms and the Man* (July–Aug. 1953); a summer-tryout production of *A Better Mouse Trap* (Bucks County Playhouse, New Hope, Pa., July 1954); and a tour of *A Palm Tree in a Rose Garden* (July–Aug. 1955).

With Morton Gottlieb, Mr. Selden produced *His and Hers* (48 St. Th., N.Y.C., Jan. 7, 1954); produced *Waiting for Gillian* (St. James's Th., London, Apr. 21, 1954); with Morton Gottlieb, produced the pre-Bway tryout of *The Amazing Adele*, for which he wrote the music and lyrics (opened Shubert, Philadelphia, Pa., Dec. 26, 1955; closed Shubert, Boston, Mass., Jan. 21, 1956); with Richard Kollmar, produced *The Body Beautiful* (Bway Th., N.Y.C., Jan. 23, 1958); produced *The Girls Against the Boys* (Alvin, Nov. 2, 1959); and has been producer and managing director of the Goodspeed Opera House (East Haddam, Conn., 1962–to date).

Mr. Selden presented the Albert Marre production of *Man of La Mancha* (Goodspeed Opera House, East Haddam, Conn., June 24, 1965); subsequently co-producing, with Hal James, the N.Y.C. production (ANTA Washington Square, Nov. 22, 1965). At the Goodspeed Opera House (East Haddam, Conn.), he presented a musical version of *Purple Dust* (July 22, 1965) and became managing director of the Goodspeed Opera Foundation, Inc., which presented *Mr. Gilbert, Mr. Sullivan and Mr. Green* (Aug. 19, 1965), *Beyond the Fringe* (June 27, 1966), *Engaged, or Cheviot's Choice* (July 18, 1966), *New Faces of 1966* (Aug. 1, 1966), and *What Every Woman Knows* (Aug. 22, 1966), for which he wrote the incidental music. He presented the pre-Bway tryout production of *What Do You Really Know About Your Husband?* (opened Shubert Th., New Haven, Conn., Mar. 9, 1967; closed there Mar. 11, 1967); was one of the producers of *Hallelujah, Baby!* (Martin Beck Th., N.Y.C., Apr. 26, 1967); co-produced *Portrait of a Queen* (Henry Miller's Th., Feb. 28, 1967); *Come Summer* (Lunt-Fontanne, Mar. 18, 1969); a revival of *Man of La Mancha* (Vivian Beaumont Th., Lincoln Ctr., June 22, 1972); *The Lincoln Mask* (Plymouth Th., Oct. 30, 1972); and *Irene* (Minskoff, Mar. 13, 1973).

Television. Mr. Selden composed the music for *54th Street Revue* (CBS, Jan. 1949); was the producer of *Little Women* (CBS, Oct. 1958); and *Gift of the Magi* (CBS, 1958).

Awards. Mr. Selden and Hal James won an Antoinette Perry (Tony) Award for their production of *Man of La Mancha* (1965–66).

Recreation. Tennis, collecting clocks, wine tasting.

SELDEN, SAMUEL. Educator, writer, director. b. Jan. 2, 1899, Canton, China, to Charles Card and Gertrude (Thwing) Selden. Father, missionary. Grad. Yale Univ., B.A. 1922; Illinois Coll., Litt.D. 1952. Married July 1936 to Wautell Gray Lambeth (dec. 1948); one son, one daughter; married Oct. 25, 1951, to Emily Crow. Served US Army, Medical Corps, 1918; rank, PFC. Member of ANTA; NTC; AETA (pres., 1959–60); SETC (pres., 1953–1955). Address: (home) 1817 South Lakeshore Drive, Chapel Hill, NC 27514; (bus.) Department of Dramatic Art, Univ. of N.C., Chapel Hill, NC 27514, tel. (919) 933-1133.

Since 1959, Mr. Selden has been chairman of the Dept. of Theatre Arts at the Univ. of California. He has held academic positions at the Univ. of North Carolina (instructor in English, 1927–36; assistant professor of dramatic art, 1936–44; professor and chairman of the Dept. of Dramatic Art, 1944–59).

He was appointed to the staff of the Carolina Playmakers (1927), and became director (1944), supervising experimental and public productions.

Mr. Selden was assistant technical director, stage manager, and resident actor at the Provincetown Playhouse (N.Y.C., 1922–27), where he played minor roles in *In the Zone*, and *Desire Under the Elms* (Greenwich Village Th., Nov. 11, 1924); was stage manager for the Greenwich Village Th. (1925–26); Intimate Opera Co. (1926); for the Gladys Klark Players (1922–27); and the Cape Playhouse (Dennis, Mass., 1927, 1928).

He has directed outdoor historical plays, including four by Paul Green: *The Lost Colony* (Waterside Th., Roanoke Island, N.C., 1937–41; 1946–52), *Wilderness Road* (Indian Fort Th., Berea, Ky., 1955–57), *The Confederacy* (Virginia Beach, Va., 1958), and *The Steven Foster Story* (J. Dan Talbott Amphitheatre, Bardstown, Ky., 1959, 1963); also, Kermit Hunter's *Forever This Land* (Kelso Hollow Th., New Salem State Park, Ill., 1951); and Robert Emmett McDowell's *Home Is the Hunter* (Fort Harrod Amphitheatre, Harrodsburg, Ky., 1963, 1964).

He is currently a member of the Administrative Committee of the Institute of Outdoor Drama, Chapel Hill, N.C.

Other Activities. Mr. Selden was an editor of *The Carolina Play-Book* (1928–1944); *Theatre Annual* (1944–1947), *La Revue Internationale de Theatre* (1947), and *Educational Theatre Journal* (1955–57).

Published Works. He wrote with Hunton Sellman, *Stage Scenery And Lighting* (1930); with Hubert Heffner and Hunton Sellman, *Modern Theatre Practice* (1935); wrote *A Player's Handbook* (1934); *The Stage in Action* (1942); *First Steps in Acting* (1947); *An Introduction to Playwriting* (1947); wrote with Mary T. Sphangos, *Frederick Henry Koch: Pioneer Playmaker; Man in His Theatre; Theatre Double Game;* and, with Tom Rezzuto, *Essentials of Stage Scenery.*

Mr. Selden edited the books *A Players Handbook of Short Scenes by William Shakespeare* (1960); for AETA, *Research in Drama and the Theatre in the Universities and Colleges of the United States, 1937–42* (1944); *Organizing a Community Theatre* (1945); *International Folk Plays* (1949); and has written more than seventy articles on the theatre for national and foreign theatre periodicals.

Awards. He received a Guggenheim Fellowship for study of European theatres (1938–39); the AETA Award of Merit (1962); and the SETC Award for Distinguished Career (1963).

SELDES, MARIAN. Actress. b. Marian Hall Seldes, Aug. 23, 1928, New York City, to Gilbert and Alice (Hall) Seldes. Father, author, critic. Grad. Dalton Sch., N.Y.C., 1945. Studied at Sch. of Amer. Ballet, N.Y.C., 1941–44; grad. Neighborhood Playhouse Sch. of the Th., 1947. Married Nov. 3, 1953, to Julian Arnold Claman (marr. dis. Aug. 17, 1961); one daughter. Member of AEA; AFTRA; SAG. Address: 125 E. 57th St., New York, NY 10022, tel. (212) PL 3-4595.

Theatre. Miss Seldes made her debut as a dancer in a Ballet Th. production of *Petroushka* (Metropolitan Opera House, N.Y.C., Oct. 12, 1942); subsequently played Tiger Lilly in *Alice in Wonderland* (Brattle, Cambridge, Mass., Summer 1945); and Nurse Libby in *Night Must Fall* and Agnes in *The Late George Apley* (Brattle, Cambridge, Mass., 1946).

For the Burlington (Vt.) Summer Th., she appeared as Ethel in *Peg o' My Heart*, Nancy in *Angel Street*, and Alexandra in *The Little Foxes* (St. Michael's Playhouse, 1947); followed by an Attendant in *Medea* (National, N.Y.C., Oct. 20, 1947); Dounia in *Crime and Punishment* (National, Dec. 22, 1947); rejoined the cast of *Medea* (Royale, Mar. 15, 1948), also touring as the Second Woman of Corinth in this production (opened Lobero Th., Santa Barbara, Calif., Sept. 3, 1948).

At St. Michael's Playhouse, Burlington, Vt., she played Laura in *The Glass Menagerie*, Christina in *The Silver Cord*, and Mrs. Manningham in *Angel Street* (1948); at the Kennebunkport (Me.) Playhouse, she played Gwendolyn in *The Importance of Being Earnest*, Alkmena in *Amphitryon '38*, Olive in *The Voice of the Turtle*, and Eliza Doolittle in *Pygmalion* (Summers 1949–50); and at St. Michael's Playhouse appeared in the title role of *Medea* (1950).

She played Anichu in *That Lady* (Martin Beck Th., N.Y.C., Nov. 22, 1949); Electra in *The Tower Beyond Tragedy* (ANTA, Sept. 22, 1950); and Nurse Phillips in *The High Ground* (48 St. Th., Feb. 20, 1951).

At the Corning (N.Y.) Summer Th., she played Julie in *Show Boat*, and appeared in *Dream Girl* (1951); played the First Woman of Corinth in an ANTA production of *Medea* (Hebbel, Berlin, Ger., Sept. 13, 1951); a Close Friend in *Come of Age* (NY City Ctr., Jan. 23, 1952); and at the Bermuda (B.W.I.) Th., played Birdie in *The Little Foxes*, and Julia in *Springtime for Henry* (Mar. 18–May 10, 1952).

At the Ivoryton (Conn.) Playhouse, she appeared as Anne in *Goodbye, Again* (Summer 1952); at Elitch Gardens (Denver, Colo.), as Queenie in *Bell, Book and Candle*, Alwyn in *Dangerous Corner*, and Jessica in *Point of No Return* (Summer 1953); played Bertha in *Ondine* (48 St. Th., N.Y.C., Feb. 18, 1954); and was an artist-in-resident at Stanford Univ. (Palo Alto, Calif.), playing Phedre in *The Cretan Women*, and the title role in her father's version of *Lysistrata* (Summer 1955).

She played Olivia in *The Chalk Garden* (Ethel Barrymore Th., N.Y.C., Oct. 26, 1955); Rachel in *The Flowering Peach* (Carthay Circle Th., Los Angeles, Calif., Summer 1956); Sara Callifer in *The Potting Shed* (La Jolla Playhouse, Calif., Sept. 1958); Romaine in *Witness for the Prosecution* (Players Ring Th., Los Angeles, Dec. 1958); Antoinette in *A Piece of Blue Sky* (Fort Lee Playhouse, N.J., May 1959); Symka in *The Wall*, and succeeded (Dec. 5, 1960) Yvonne Mitchell as Rachel (Billy Rose Th., N.Y.C., Oct. 11, 1960); played Mag in *The Long Voyage Home* and Emma Crosby in *Diff'rent*, a double bill (Mermaid, Oct. 17, 1961); and took over Claudia Morgan's role of Mrs. Patrick Campbell during the run of *A Fig Leaf in Her Bonnet* (Gramercy Arts, June 14, 1961).

She played Susan Loring in *A Gift of Time* (Ethel Barrymore Th., Feb. 22, 1962); Miss Frost in *The Ginger Man* (Orpheum, Nov. 21, 1963); Blackie in *The Milk Train Doesn't Stop Here Anymore* (Brooks Atkinson Th., Jan. 1, 1964); Regina in *All Women Are One* (Gate Th., Jan. 7, 1965); replaced (Apr. 1965) Irene Worth as Miss Alice in *Tiny Alice* (Billy Rose Th., Dec. 29, 1964); played Juana in *Juana La Loca* (American Place Th., May 12, 1965); the Nurse in *Medea* (Valley Music Th., Calif., Oct. 1965); Julia in *A Delicate Balance* (Martin Beck Th., N.Y.C., Sept. 22, 1966); Sylvia in *Before You Go* (Henry Miller's Th., Jan. 11, 1968); toured in *Who's Happy Now?* (Aug. 1968); appeared in *An Evening with James Agee* (Th. de Lys, N.Y.C., Feb. 10, 1969); was Olga in *The Three Sisters* (American Shakespeare Festival, Stratford, Conn., July 23, 1969); Daisy in *Mercy Street* (American Place Th., N.Y.C., Oct. 11, 1969); appeared in *Other People* (Berkshire Playhouse, Stockbridge, Mass., July 1970); was Marian in *Father's Day* (Golden Th., N.Y.C., Mar. 16, 1971); appeared in *The Celebration* (Hedgerow Th., Aug. 1971); toured in *Remember Me* (Summer 1972); was the Witness in Martha Graham's *Mendicants at Evening* (Alvin Th., N.Y.C., May 1973); played Charlotte in *For the Use of the Hall* (Trinity Repertory Th., Providence, R.I., Jan. 2, 1974); and directed *Next Time I'll Sing to You* (City Ctr. Acting Co., Billy Rose Th., Jan. 2, 1974).

Films. Miss Seldes made her debut as Caroline in *The Lonely Night* (Affiliated, 1951); and has appeared in *Mr. Lincoln* (de Rochemont, 1952); *The True Story of Jesse James* (20th-Fox, 1957); *The Light in the Forest* (Buena Vista, 1958); *Crime and Punishment USA* (Allied, 1959); *The Big Fisherman* (Buena Vista, 1959); and *The Greatest Story Ever Told* (UA, 1964).

Television. Miss Seldes made her debut as the Gentlewoman in the sleepwalking scene of *Macbeth* (ANTA Album, Sept. 29, 1950); and since then has appeared on various live and filmed dramatic programs, including frequent appearances on Today (NBC) as a reader of poetry.

Other Activities. In Feb. 1969, Miss Seldes became a member of the staff of the Drama Division, Juilliard School, N.Y.C.

Awards. Miss Seldes received a *Village Voice* off-Bway (Obie) Award in 1964 for her performance as Miss Frost in *The Ginger Man;* an Antoinette Perry (Tony) Award (Mar. 1967) for her portrayal of Julia in *A Delicate Balance;* the Drama Desk Award and a nomination for a Tony for playing Marian in *Father's Day* (1971).

SELLMAN, HUNTON D. Educator. b. May 20, 1900, Kemptown, Md., to John P. and Elizabeth (Young) Sellman. Father, physician; mother, nurse. Grad. Purdue Univ., B.S. 1922; Univ. of Arizona, M.S. 1925; attended Univ. of California at Berkeley, 1926; Univ. of North Carolina, 1928; Yale Univ., 1929–30. Studied at Actors' Studio, N.Y.C. (observer, 1953–54). Married July 22, 1933, to Priscilla Morrison, actress; two daughters. Served WW I, US Army; rank, Pvt. Member of ANTA; (natl. board, 1947–51; natl. tech; ATA comm., 1959–to date); Illuminating Engineering Society (natl. comm. for stage & television lighting, 1956–to date); NTC (hon.). Address: (home) 5015 Campanile Dr., San Diego, CA 92115, tel. (714) JU 2-2427; (bus.) c/o San Diego State Univ., San Diego, CA 92115, tel. (714) JU 2-4411.

From 1946 to 1971, when he retired as professor emeritus of drama, Mr. Sellman was professor in charge of theatre and director of theatre at San Diego State Univ. He directed approximately 30 student productions, and designed and supervised the lighting for more than 75 productions. He was a member of the faculty at the State Univ. of Iowa (1930–46), where he directed approximately 35 plays, including the premiere of *Dark of the Moon* (July 1944), and designed and supervised lighting for more than 150 student productions.

He was lighting and theatre consultant for numerous theatre buildings including three at the Univ. of Iowa, and at Iowa City H.S.; Univ. of Oregon; Ventura City Coll.; Sherwood Hall, La Jolla, Calif.; and two theatres for San Diego State Coll.

Pre-Theatre. Mechanical and electrical engineer.

Published Works. Mr. Sellman wrote, with Samuel Selden, *Stage Scenery and Lighting* (1930; rev. ed. 1936; 3d ed. 1959); with Samuel Selden and Hubert Heffner, *Modern Theatre Practice* (1935; 2d ed. 1939; 3d ed. 1973); and he wrote *Essentials of Stage Lighting* (1972).

Recreation. Fencing, photography.

SELWART, TONIO. Actor. b. Antonio Franz Thaeus Selmair-Selwart, June 9, 1896, Wartenberg, Bavaria, Germany, to Anton and Laura (Pleti) Selmair-Selwart. Father, physician. Grad. Gymnasium, Munich, Germany, 1916; attended Univ. of Munich, 1919–22. Studied at Falkenberg Dramatic Sch., Munich, 1925–26; Munich Sch. for Dramatic Art, 1926–27; with Mara Feldern-Foerster, Vienna, Austria, 1927; Francis Robinson Duff, N.Y.C., 1935–36; Benno Schneider, N.Y.C., 1937; Lee Strasberg, N.Y.C., 1938, 1940; Michael Chekhov, Los Angeles, Calif., 1951. Married Apr. 15, 1919, to Claire Volkhart, sculptress (dec. Feb. 11, 1935). Served WW I, German Armed Forces, Cavalry; rank, Lt. Member of AEA; AFTRA; SAG. Address: 130 W. 57th St., New York, NY 10019, tel. (212) CI 7-8252.

Theatre. Mr. Selwart made his debut in Munich as the Young German Knight in *Elga*, in which he also played Oginski (Bayrische Landesbuehne Th., Oct. 1927); also at the Bayrische Landesbuehne Th., he played Kosinsky in *Raeuber*, Guildenstern in *Hamlet*, the title role in *Don Carlos*, Barthel in *Andreas Hofer*, Max in *Die Welt ohne Maenner*, Pepi Leisinger in *Leinen aus Irland*, Giselher in *Nibelungen* (1928), Clemens in *Literatur*, Anatol in *Abschiedssouper*, the Young Lord in *Maerchen*, which he also directed, Lutigar in *Hermannsschlacht*, Lammspeter in *Meier Helmbrecht*, Pylades in *Iphigenie auf Tauris*, Fabrizio in *Mirandolina (Mistress of the Inn)*, Raleigh in *Journey's End* (1929), Zarewitz Alexander in *Der Patriot*, and the title role in *Prinz of Homburg* (1930).

At the St. Gallen (Switzerland) Th., he played Max Andermann in *Schelmeninsel*, Charles Murdock in *Ghost Train* (Jan. 1931), Georg Schilling in *Unter Geschaeftsaufsicht*, Fritz Appel in *Hulla di Bulla*, the Young Man in *Peripherie* (Feb. 1931), Melchior in *Spring's Awakening* (Mar. 1931), and Burdach in *Sturm in Wasserglass* (Apr. 1931).

He made his N.Y.C. debut with the Civic Repertory Th., playing the Second Mounted Policeman in *Liliom* (Oct. 26, 1932), followed by a Servant in *Camille* (Oct. 27, 1932), Nana in *Peter Pan* (Nov. 5, 1932), the Fish Footman in *Alice in Wonderland* (Dec. 12, 1932), and Melchior in *Spring's Awakening*, which he also directed (Mar. 1933).

He played Max Christman in *The Pursuit of Happiness* (Avon, Oct. 9, 1933), also in London (Vaudeville, May 30, 1934), toured the US in it (1934–35), and appeared in it in summer theatres (Casino, Newport, R.I., July 20, 1936; Suffern Th., N.Y., July 27, 1936).

Mr. Selwart played Rene Latour in *Laughing Woman* (John Golden Th., N.Y.C., Oct. 13, 1936), also at the Ann Arbor (Mich.) Drama Festival (Lydia Mendelssohn Th., May 27, 1937); Andreas Steiner in *Autumn Crocus* (Casino, Newport, Aug. 10, 1937); the title role in an Ann Arbor Drama Festival production of *Liliom* (Lydia Mendelssohn Th., May 24, 1938; Suffern Th., N.Y., July 1938; Plymouth, Conn., Aug. 13, 1938); Jacques Duval in *Cognac* (Casino, Newport, Aug. 30, 1938); Andreas Steiner in *Autumn Crocus* (Berkshire Playhouse, Stockbridge, Mass., Aug. 1938; Red Barn, Northport, N.Y., July 3, 1939); Lord Ivor Cream in *Serena Blandish* (Plymouth, Conn., Aug. 4, 1939); and at the Paper Mill Playhouse (Millburn, N.J.), played Max Christman in *The Pursuit of Happiness* (Aug. 14, 1939), and Rheinhardt in *Flight into China* (Sept. 12, 1939).

He played the Grand Duke Nikita in *Russian Bank* (St. James, N.Y.C., May 24, 1940); Baron Max von Alvensten in *Margin for Error* (Maplewood Th., N.J., July 20, 1940); Andreas Steiner in *Autumn Crocus* (Chapel Playhouse, Guilford, Conn., Aug. 12, 1940); Jeff Gordon in a French language production of *La Maison Cernée* (Arcade, Montreal, Canada, Mar. 16, 1941); Lt. Schoen in *Candle in the Wind* (Shubert, N.Y.C., Oct. 22, 1941); the title role in an ELT production of *The Affairs of Anatol* (Hudson Park Library, June 4, 1946); Erich Jaeger in *Temper the Wind* (Playhouse, Dec. 27, 1946); the title role in *Topaze* (Ithaca Th., N.Y., 1947); Stefan Jakubec in an ANTA-sponsored Invitational Series production of *Seeds in the Wind* (Lenox Hill Playhouse, Apr. 24, 1948; moved to Empire, May 25, 1948); Dr. Stockman in the pre-Bway tour of *The First Gentleman* (opened Shubert, New Haven, Conn., Mar. 1957; closed Walnut St. Th., Philadelphia, Pa., Apr. 1957); Gen. Otto von Kettler in *Hidden River* (Playhouse, N.Y.C., Jan. 23, 1957); Tsai, the Father, in *Lute Song* (NY City Ctr., Mar. 12, 1959); Monsignore Andrada in *And the Wind Blows* (St. Marks Playhouse, Aug. 28, 1959); and toured in *Brecht on Brecht* (opened Kresge Aud., Cambridge, Mass., Oct. 13, 1963).

Films. Mr. Selwart made his debut in *Edge of Darkness* (1943); followed by *The North Star* (RKO, 1943); *Hangmen Also Die* (UA, 1943); *The Cross of Lorraine* (MGM, 1943); *Wilson* (20th-Fox, 1944); *Strange Affair* (Col., 1944); *Tampico* (20th-Fox, 1944); *Hitler's Gang* (Par., 1944); *My Favorite Spy* (Par., 1944); *Il Lupo della Frontiera* (Safa-Palatino, 1951); *La Venus de l'Isle* (Luotto Films, 1953); *Senso* (Lux Films, 1954); *The Barefoot Contessa* (UA, 1954); *Il Visitatore* (Luotto Films, 1954); *Tradita* (Flora Films, 1954); *Vienna* (Thetis Films, 1955); *Helen of Troy* (WB, 1955); *Congo Crossing* (U, 1956); *The Naked Maja* (Titanus, 1958); *The Tempest* (Par., 1959); *The Nun's Story* (WB, 1959); *Romanoff and Juliet* (U, 1961); *The Reluctant Saint* (David-Royal Films, 1962); and *The Sign of Zorro* (Buena Vista, 1962); and *The Other Side of the Wind* (Orson Welles, 1974).

Television. He has appeared in *Riviera* (Studio One, CBS), as Ferdi in *Biography* (Prudential Hour), the Man in *Man and Wife* (Armstrong Circle Th., NBC), in *String of Pearls* (CBS), *The Bridge* (Elgin Th., ABC), on the Ken Murray Show (CBS), in *The American* (Philco Television Playhouse, NBC), *As Husbands Go* (Kraft Television Th., NBC), on The Defenders (CBS, 1963), and as the Commandant in *The Therezin Requiem* (Passover Special, CBS, Mar. 1964).

Recreation. Skiing, tennis, gymnastics, painting, piano, piano accordion, languages.

SELZNICK, IRENE MAYER. Producer. b. Irene Mayer, Apr. 2, 1910, Brooklyn, N.Y., to Louis B. and Margaret (Shenberg) Mayer. Father, film executive. Attended public schools in Brookline, Mass.; Hollywood (Calif.) Sch. for Girls. Married Apr. 29, 1930, to David O. Selznick, film executive (marr. dis. 1948); two sons. Member of League of NY Theatres (bd. of gov.); Assn. for Homemaker Service, Inc. (bd. of dir.); NY Citizen Council of the Natl. Council on Crime and Delinquency (bd. of dirs.). Address: (home) Hotel Pierre, 2 E. 61st St., New York, NY 10022; (bus.) 50 E. 58th St., New York, NY 10022, tel. (212) PL 8-3705.

Pre-Theatre. Juvenile probation officer for Los Angeles, Calif.

Theatre. Mrs. Selznick produced *Heartsong* (opened Shubert, New Haven, Conn., Feb. 27, 1947; closed Walnut St. Th., Philadelphia, Pa., Mar. 29, 1947); *A Streetcar Named Desire* (Ethel Barrymore Th., N.Y.C., Dec. 3, 1947; Aldwych, London, England, Oct. 11, 1949); *Bell, Book and Candle* (Ethel Barrymore Th., N.Y.C., Nov. 14, 1950; Phoenix, London, Oct. 5, 1954); *Flight into Egypt* (Music Box, N.Y.C., Mar. 13, 1952); with Irving Schneider, *The Chalk Garden* (Ethel Barrymore Th., Oct. 26, 1955; Haymarket, London, Apr. 12, 1956); and in association with H. M. Tennent Ltd., Donald Albery and F.E.S. Plays Ltd., *The Complaisant Lover* (Ethel Barrymore Th., N.Y.C., Nov. 1, 1961).

Films. Mrs. Selznick was an executive with the Selznick Intl. Pictures, Inc. (1936–40); and was associated with Vanguard Films (1941–49).

SEROFF, MUNI. Actor, director, singer. b. Munia Serebroff, Jan. 8, 1903, Kishinev, Russia, to Alexsander and Debora (Rothburd) Serebroff. Father, merchant. Grad. H.S. in Kishinev; received degree as Jurist, Faculty of Law, Univ. of Odessa, Russ. Studied at Odessa Art Sch., two years; Osarovski Branch of the Stanislavski Studio, Odessa; Member of AEA; Hebrew Actors Union; SAG; AFTRA.

Theatre. Mr. Seroff joined the Kiev (Russ.) Th. Grotesque repertory company (1920) and appeared at the Russki Th., Odessa. During the next five years, he appeared with various Russian repertory companies, his roles including Glukhovtsev in *The Days of Our Life* (Sheifers Th., Odessa), The Student in *The Cherry Orchard* and Vaska Tsyganok in *The Lower Depths* (Stamerovski Th., Odessa, 1922), Neschastlivtsev in *The Forest* and Raskolnikov in *Crime and Punishment* (Sibiriakov Th., 1922, 1923).

He joined (1924) the Yiddish Th. company of Molly Picon and her husband, Jacob Kalich, as leading man to Miss Picon, in Bucharest, Rumania. He toured Rumania, ending the season in Vienna, Aust.; continued to tour Europe in musical comedy roles (1924–26); and rejoined the Picon-Kalich company in N.Y.C. (1929).

Mr. Seroff made his English language debut as Boris Kolenkov in the Chicago company of *You Can't Take It with You* (Harris, Chicago, Ill., Feb. 7, 1937) and succeeded (May 1938) George Tobias in the role in the N.Y.C. production (Booth, Dec. 14, 1936).

He appeared with Maurice Schwartz' Yiddish Th. productions, playing such roles as Lorenzo in *Shylock* (Anderson, 1946–47) and the Russian Student in *The Grass Is Always Greener* (Anderson, 1947–48); and played Sidney in a Yiddish language production of *A Hole in the Head* (Anderson, 1958–59).

Mr. Seroff played Elias in *Between Two Thieves* (York Playhouse, Feb. 11, 1960); the Author-Narrator in *Shadow of Heroes* (York Playhouse, Dec. 5, 1961); the Foreman in *The Tenth Man* (Coconut Grove, Miami, Fla., Feb. 10, 1963); and President Vanan in *Corruption in the Palace of Justice* (Cherry Lane, N.Y.C., Oct. 8, 1963).

He was in *She Loves Me* (Charles Playhouse, Boston, Mass., Dec. 23, 1964); played Alexander Ratscin in *The Day the Whores Came Out to Play Tennis* (Players Th., N.Y.C., Mar. 15, 1965); was Marango in *The Kitchen* (New Th. Workshop, May 9, 1966; 81 St Th., June 13, 1966); Hirschman in *The Tenth Man* (NY City Ctr., Nov. 8, 1967); the Angel in *Gideon* (Th. of the Riverside Church, N.Y.C., 1968); the Sculptor in *Soldiers* (Billy Rose Th., May 1, 1968); Esdras in *Winterset* (Puerto Rican Traveling Th., N.Y.C. parks and playgrounds, Summer 1968); Klementi Radischev in *The End of All Things Natural* (Village South Th., Sept. 11, 1969); and Chief Joseph in *Indians* (Studio Arena, Buffalo, N.Y., May 6, 1971).

Films. Mr. Seroff has appeared in *Phantom of the Opera* (U, 1943); *Two Senoritas from Chicago* (Col., 1963); *Call of the Jungle* (Mono., 1944); *Copacabana* (UA, 1947); *Mr. Imperium* (MGM, 1951); and in the Sidney Toler *Charlie Chan* series (20th-Fox).

Television. During the 1961–62 season, Mr. Seroff appeared in episodes of such television series as Naked City (ABC); Route 66 (CBS); and The Defenders (CBS). He appeared as the Merchant in *Give Us Barrabas* (Hallmark Hall of Fame, NBC); Mr. Roth in *The Perfect Nurse* (The Nurses, CBS, 1963); Karl Eberhart in *The Takers* (Dupont Show of the Week, NBC, 1963–64 season); and the Music Critic in *Terezin Requiem* (Special, CBS, 1964).

Recreation. Painting.

SEYMOUR, ANNE. Actress. b. Anne Seymour Eckert, Sept. 11, 1909, New York City, to William Stanley and May Davenport (Seymour) Eckert. Father, copper expert; mother, May Davenport Seymour, actress, museum curator. Grad. Cathedral Sch. of St. Mary, Garden City, L.I., N.Y., 1926; attended Amer. Laboratory Theatre Sch., N.Y.C., 1927–28. Relatives in theatre: descended on the maternal side from great-great-great-grandfather, Jack Johnstone, Irish comedian; great-grandparents, Mr. and Mrs. (Fanny Vining) E. L. Davenport, American actor-manager and English actress; great-grandparents, Mr. and Mrs. (Lydia Eliza Griffith) James Seymour, Irish comedian and American actress; grandfather, William Seymour, actor, director, theatre-historian; grandmother, May Davenport, actress; great-aunt, Blanche Davenport (Bianca La Blanche), opera singer; great-uncle, Edgar L. Davenport, actor; great-aunt, Fanny Davenport, actress-manager; great-uncle, Harry Davenport, theatre and film actor; uncle, James Seymour, writer-director; aunt and uncle, Mr. and Mrs. (Abby Lewis) John D. Seymour, actor and actress. Member of AEA (Council, 1942); AFTRA (natl. bd., vice-pres. and secy., 1936–50; Chicago local, vice-pres, 1936; board, 1936–40; NY local bd., 1940–52); SAG; Amer. Theatre Wing (bd., 1959–62); Plays for Living (bd., 1961–to date); Veterans Hospital Radio and TV Guild (1st vice-pres.; 1961; board, Actors' Fund of Amer. (life mbr.); Episcopal Actors' Guild (council, 1961–to date; life mbr.).

Theatre. Miss Seymour made her professional debut touring outdoor theatres in New England and New York State with the Jitney Players, as Lady Sangazure in *The Sorcerer*, and the Nurse and Mrs. Couplet in *A Trip to Scarborough* (June 1928); followed by her first Bway assignment as a voice and general understudy in *Mr. Moneypenny* (Liberty, Oct. 16, 1928). With the Elverhoj Th. (Milton, N.Y.), she appeared as Miss Ashford in *The Private Secretary* (June 17, 1929), Sorel Bliss in *Hay Fever* (July 1, 1929), Lady Marden in *Mr. Pim Passes By* (July 8, 1929), Florrie Sands in *Saturday's Children* (July 15, 1929), Dona Barbarita in *The Romantic Young Lady* (July 22, 1929), Hannah Ferguson in *John Ferguson* (July 29, 1929), and Mrs. Ricketts in *Tweedles* (Aug. 5, 1929).

She played Natasha in *At the Bottom* (Waldorf, N.Y.C., Jan. 9, 1930); at the Millbrook (N.Y.) Th., played Miss Smith in *Enter Madam* (June 16, 1930), Lucy in *The Old Soak* (June 23, 1930), Madge Livingston in *Let Us Be Gay* (June 30, 1930); Lady Julia Marden in *Mr. Pim Passes By* (July 7, 1930), Betty Lee in *Coquette* (July 14, 1930), Dona Barbarita in *The Romantic Young Lady* (July 21, 1930), Mattie in *The Intimate Strangers* (July 28, 1930), the title role in *Miss Lulu Bett* (Aug. 4, 1930), Lady Minster in *The High Road* (Aug. 18, 1930), Mrs. Paul Ritter in *The Torchbearers* (Aug. 25, 1930), Grace Harrington in *The Patsy* (Sept. 1, 1930), and Lady Sangazure in *The Sorcerer* (Sept. 8, 1930).

Miss Seymour played Suzanne Carleton in *Puppet Show* (Belmont, N.Y.C., Oct. 28, 1930); was a member of the Copley Players (Boston, Mass., 1930–31), where she played Liz in *Rebound*, Kunegunde in *See Naples and Die*, Albine in *Her Cardboard Lover*, and Nora in *Heritage;* appeared in a small role in the Players Club production of *The Way of the World* (Guild, June 1, 1931); at the Westchester Playhouse (Mt. Kisco, N.Y.) and Millbrook (N.Y.) Th., appeared as Alice Montgomery in *Cock Robin*, Christina in *The Silver Cord* and Bertha in *The Fall Guy* (Summer 1931).

She played Maria in Ethel Barrymore's revival of *A School for Scandal* (Ethel Barrymore Th., N.Y.C., Nov. 10, 1931), and on national tour; and a small role in *Troilus and Cressida* (Bway Th., N.Y.C., June 6, 1932); in summer stock, portrayed Imogene in *Trelawney of the Wells* (Westchester Playhouse, Mt. Kisco, N.Y., 1934); Ann Hargraves in *The Wind and the Rain* (Ogunquit Playhouse, Me., 1936); Susan Haggett in *The Late Christopher Bean* (Ogunquit Playhouse, Me., 1937); Clara in *The Show-Off* (Cohasset Playhouse, Mass.; Silver Beach Th., Falmouth, Mass., 1937); Dona Barbarita in a Bucks County Playhouse production of *The Romantic Young Lady* (Philadelphia, Pa., 1942); Alicia Christie in *Black Chiffon* (Berkshire Playhouse, Stockbridge, Mass., 1953); Agnes Carol in *Time Out for Ginger* (Berkshire Playhouse, 1955); Clytemnestra in *Sacrifice to the Wind* (White Barn Th., Westport, Conn., July 9, 1955); and played Sara Delano Roosevelt in *Sunrise at Campobello* (Cort, N.Y.C., Jan. 30, 1958).

Films. She made her debut as Lucy Stark in *All the King's Men* (Col., 1949); subsequently appeared as Mary London in *The Whistle at Eaton Falls* (De Rochemont, 1951); Judge Randolph in *Man on Fire* (MGM, 1957); Eden's Mother in *Desire Under the Elms* (Par., 1958); Matilda Iler in *Handle with Care* (MGM, 1958); Amelia Tarbell in *Pollyanna* (Buena Vista, 1960); Miss McMasters in *Gift of Love* (20th-Fox, 1960); Sarah Halstead in *Home from the Hill* (MGM, 1960); Charlotte Percepied in *The Subterraneans* (MGM, 1960); Mrs. Bixby in *All the Fine Young Cannibals* (MGM, 1960); Grandma Beebe in *Misty* (20th-Fox, 1961); Irene in *Good Neighbor Sam* (Col., 1964); Dr. Sally Jennings in *Where Love Has Gone* (Par., 1964); and Myra Parker in *Stage to Thunder Rock* (Par., 1964).

Television and Radio. Miss Seymour first performed on radio as a leading lady in a radio stock company on WLW (Cincinnati, Ohio, Sept. 11, 1932). From 1933–40, she was in Chicago and during this period played in *Grand Hotel* (NBC, Sept. 1933); performed as Sally Gibbons and then the title role in The Story of Mary Marlin (NBC, 1934–36; CBS, 1936–40); performed on Cross Roads, Lights Out, Welcome Valley, Cameo, Then and Now, and Love Song; and directed the transcribed (recorded) series, Hope Alden's Romance (1937), Grandma Travels (1938), and Judy and Jane (1938).

From 1940–61, Miss Seymour acted on radio programs for all the major networks emanating from New York, such as Against the Storm (NBC, 1940; Mutual, 1949; ABC, 1953); played the title role in The Story of Mary Marlin (NBC, 1941); Prudence Dane in A Woman of America (NBC, 1943); Lily Boheme in *The Magnificent Montague* (NBC, 1950); and the Narrator in My Secret Story (NBC, 1951). Other radio programs that she appeared on were Mr. Keene, Tracer of Lost Persons, Mr. Chameleon, Hearthstone of the Death Squad, Bulldog Drummond, Ford Mystery Th. (NBC), The FBI in Peace and War (CBS), The Greatest Story Ever Told (ABC), The Th. Guild of the Air, Cavalcade, Philip Morris Playhouse, Inner Sanctum, Grand Central Station, Great Moments from Great Plays, Somerset Maugham Playhouse, Studio One, My True Story (ABC), Ave Maria, The Eternal Light, Light of the World, Dr. Brent, Lone Journey, Portia Faces Life, Mr. District Attorney, Our Gal Sunday, Helen Trent (CBS), Pepper Young's Family (NBC), Joyce Jordan (CBS), Miss Monitor on Monitor (NBC, 1954), and Armstrong Th. of Today (CBS). She has also written scripts for Armstrong Th. of Today.

Since 1952, she has performed in dramatic and comedy roles on television, appearing on Studio One (CBS), Robert Montgomery Presents (CBS), and Robert Montgomery Summer Th. (CBS), The Web (CBS), Kraft Television Th. (NBC), US Steel Hour (NBC), Lux Television Playhouse (CBS), Alcoa Presents (NBC), Armstrong Circle Th. (NBC), Climax! (CBS), the Jackie Gleason Show (CBS), the Martha Raye Show (NBC), the Arthur Godfrey Show (CBS), Steve Allen's Tonight Show (NBC), Mama (CBS), Follow Your Heart, The First Hundred Years, Schlitz Playhouse of Stars (CBS), Crunch and Des (NBC), Gunsmoke (CBS), Hawaiian Eye (ABC), Rawhide (CBS), The Defenders (CBS), The Nurses (CBS), Ben Casey (ABC), Naked City (ABC), Death Valley Days (ABC), My Three Sons (ABC), Eleventh Hour (NBC), Mr. Novak (NBC), Perry Mason (CBS), and appeared as Lucia Garrett on the Empire series (NBC, premiere Sept. 1962).

Recreation. Reading, writing, swimming, bridge, poker, tennis, gardening, driving, collecting "angels" and old pewter, walking, cooking.

SEYMOUR, JOHN D. Actor. b. John Russell Davenport Seymour, Oct. 24, 1897, Boston, Mass., to William and May (Davenport) Seymour. Father, actor, director, historian; mother, actress. Grad. DeWitt Clinton H.S., N.Y.C., 1916; attended Colgate Univ., 1916–18. Married 1921 to Joan Shaw, actress (dec. 1929); married 1929 to Frances Simpson, actress (marr. dis. 1951); one son, one daughter; married Apr. 22, 1951, to Abby Lewis, actress. Relatives in theatre: great-great-grandfather, Jack Johnstone, actor; maternal grandparents, E. L. Davenport and Fanny Vining, actors; paternal grandparents, James Seymour and Eliza Griffiths, actors; aunt, Fanny Davenport, actress; uncle, Edgar Davenport, actor; uncle, Harry Davenport, actor, director; aunt, Blanche Davenport, known as Bianca La Blanche, opera singer; sister, May Davenport Seymour, actress; niece, Anne Seymour, actress. Member of AEA; SAG; AFTRA; Delta Kappa Epsilon; Actors' Fund of Amer.; Episcopal Actors Guild; The Players (bd. of dir.). Address: 25 Minetta Lane, New York, NY 10012, tel. (212) AL 4-0485.

Theatre. Mr. Seymour made his debut as a wounded soldier in a 17-city Red Cross tour of *Out There*, for which he was also assistant stage manager (opened Natl. Th., Washington, D.C., May 13, 1918); and toured as a Waiter in *Happiness* (1918–19).

He made his N.Y.C. debut as a Wax Dummy in *A Young Man's Fancy* (Playhouse, Oct. 15, 1919); followed by Birra in *One Night in Rome* (Criterion, Dec. 2, 1919); a Messenger in John Barrymore's *Richard III* (Plymouth, Mar. 6, 1920); toured the South and Middle West in *Lightin'* (1920–22); played Monty Jones in *Thank You* (1922–23); and Jimmy in *The Clinging Vine* (1923–24).

He understudied Reinand Werrenrath as Sir Harry Bumper in The Players production of *The School for Scandal* (Lyceum, June 4, 1923); played five roles in the revue *Fashions of 1924* (Lyceum, July 18, 1923); Benjamin Franklin's grandson in *Poor Richard* (Forrest, Philadelphia, Pa., 1924); a Postillion in The Players production of *She Stoops to Conquer* (Empire, N.Y.C., June 9, 1924); Gregory Bradbroke in *Cape Smoke* (Martin Beck Th., Feb. 16, 1925); Mr. Denzil in The Player's production of *Trelawney of the Wells* (Knickerbocker, June 1, 1925); Frank Preston in *The Right to Love* (Wallack's, June 8, 1925); appeared in a tryout of *The School Mistress* (July, 1925); played Capt. Harry Tryon in *Dearest Enemy* (Knickerbocker, Sept. 18, 1925), and also toured in it (1926).

He appeared with the Vaughn Glaser Stock Co. (Toronto, Can., 1927); played a Passenger in *Blood Money* (Hudson, N.Y.C., Aug. 22, 1927); Neil Kent in *New York* (Mansfield, Nov. 14, 1927); Terry in *The Royal Family* (Newark, N.J., Nov. 1927); Manny Schiller in *57 Bowery* (Wallack's, N.Y.C., Jan. 26, 1928); and succeeded (Feb.–June 1928) Roger Pryor as Perry Stewart in *The Royal Family* (Selwyn, Dec. 28, 1927).

Mr. Seymour played Mat Muggins in *She Stoops to Conquer* (Erlanger's, May 14, 1928); Michael Morn in *Mr. Moneypenny* (Liberty, Oct. 16, 1928); Prince Hal in *Falstaff* (Coburn, Dec. 25, 1928); Terry Hamilton in *Flight* (Longacre, Feb. 18, 1929); appeared with the Jitney Players (Elvehoj, N.J.), as Sandy in *Spring Fever*, Willie in *Saturday's Children*, and the Author in *Romantic Young Lady;* played Sid Barnett in *Sweet Adeline* (Hammerstein's N.Y.C., Sept. 3, 1929); and Lieut. Ranelagh in *Becky Sharp* (Knickerbocker, June 3, 1929). With the Jitney Players, he appeared as the Author in *Romantic Young Lady*, and Michael in *Coquette* (Millbrook, N.Y., 1930); played Henry Bevan in *The Barretts of Wimpole Street* (Empire, N.Y.C., Feb. 9, 1931); and performed with the Jitney Players (Madison, Conn., 1931).

Mr. Seymour appeared as Christian de Neuvillette in Walter Hampden's *Cyrano de Bergerac* (New Amsterdam, N.Y.C., Dec. 26, 1932), also touring Southern and Western states (Feb.–June 1933; Oct. 1933–Mar. 1934); played George Harris in a three-week tour of *Uncle Tom's Cabin* (1933); toured (1933–34) in Walter Hampden's repertory productions of *Hamlet, Macbeth, Richelieu, The Servant in the House*, and *Richard III;* appeared with the company (44 St. Th., N.Y.C.) as Laertes in *Hamlet* (Dec. 25, 1934); de Mauprat in *Richelieu* (Dec. 26, 1934), Duke of Buckingham in *Richard III* (Dec. 27, 1934), and Malcolm in *Macbeth* (Dec. 29, 1934).

He played Mr. Wickham in *Pride and Prejudice* (Music Box, Nov. 5, 1935); David Cogswell in *Tide Rising* (Lyceum, Jan. 25, 1937); succeeded (Oct. 1937) Bigelow Sayre as Leeds in *Susan and God* (Plymouth, Oct. 7, 1937), also touring in it (1938–39); played John Marvin in *Lightin'* (Berkshire Playhouse, Stockbridge, Mass., 1938); and appeared there in eight plays (1939).

Mr. Seymour appeared in a preview of *No Code to Guide Her*, which closed before the scheduled opening (Cort, N.Y.C., Oct. 1939); performed at the Berkshire Playhouse in four productions (1940); toured as Spencer in *Here Today* (1940–41); played Ryland in *Solitaire* (Plymouth, N.Y.C., Jan. 27, 1942); Capt. Bentick in *The Moon Is Down* (Martin Beck, Apr. 7, 1942), in which he toured as Major Hunter (1942); toured Europe as Editor Webb in *Our Town* (1945); and the Far East and West Pacific as Sir James in *Petticoat Fever* (1946).

He played Thomas Wentworth Higginson in *Eastward in Eden* (Royale, N.Y.C., Nov. 18, 1947), Mr. Woods in *The Vigil* (Royale, May 21, 1948); a Shriner in *Light Up the Sky*, in which he occasionally substituted for Glenn Anders as Carlton Fitzgerald and Philip Ober as Owen Turner (Royale, Nov. 18, 1948).

He played Mr. Winslow in *The Winslow Boy* (North Shore Players, Marblehead, Mass., 1949); the Doctor in *The Father* (Cort, N.Y.C., Nov. 16, 1949); Dr. Harvester in *The Sacred Flame* (President, Oct. 6, 1952); appeared in the special Empire Th. Anniversary program, *Highlights of the Empire* (Empire, May 24, 1953); played, opposite his wife Abby Lewis, Joe Robinson in *Howie* (46 St. Th., Sept. 17, 1958); appeared as the Manager in a tryout of *Turn on the Night* (Playhouse-in-the-Park, Philadelphia, Pa., Aug. 1961); Mr. Wardsworth in the pre-Bway tryout of *Julia, Jake and Uncle Joe* (Theatre Playhouse, Wilmington, Del., Dec. 1960; Walnut St. Th., Philadelphia, 1961); Mr. Hoople in *Pal Joey* (NY City Ctr., May 29, 1963); Sir Edward in *The King and I* (NY City Ctr., June 10, 1963); appeared in *Life with Father* (NY City Ctr., 1967); and *Twelve Angry Men* (Queens Playhouse, Flushing, N.Y., Dec. 1972).

Films. Mr. Seymour has appeared in *Army Pictorial Patterns* (1955); *The Producers* (1967); and *The Sporting Club* (1969).

Television and Radio. Mr. Seymour has appeared on radio dramatic shows and serials (1933–to date); and on television dramatic programs (1947–to date).

Recreation. Swimming, sailing, pocket billiards.

SHAFFER, ANTHONY. Playwright. b. May 15, 1926, Liverpool, England, to Jack and Reka (Fredman) Shaffer. Grad. St. Paul's School, London; Trinity Coll., Cambridge, England, 1950. Married to Carolyn Soley; two daughters. Relative in theatre: twin brother, Peter Shaffer, playwright.

Pre-Theatre. Barrister, journalist, advertising man, television producer.

Theatre. Mr. Shaffer made his playwriting debut with *Savage Parade* (Globe, London, Mar. 17, 1963), followed by *Sleuth* (St. Martin's Th., London, Feb. 12, 1970 and Music Box, N.Y.C., Nov. 12, 1970), and *Murderer* (Garrick, London, Mar. 12, 1975).

Films. He has written the screenplays for *Frenzy* (U, 1973) and *Sleuth* (Palomar, 1973).

Television. He is the author of *Pig in the Middle*.

Published Works. Under the joint pseudonym Peter Anthony, Mr. Shaffer and his brother wrote the mystery novels *How Doth the Crocodile?* (1951), and *Woman in the Wardrobe* (1952), and under their own names, *Withered Murder* (1955).

Awards. For *Sleuth*, Mr. Shaffer was named most promising playwright (1969–70) by the Annual *Variety* Poll of London theatre critics, and received the Mystery Writer of America and the Antoinette Perry (Tony) awards (1971).

SHAFFER, PETER. Playwright. b. Peter Levin Shaffer, May 15, 1926, Liverpool, England, to Jack and Reka (Fredman) Shaffer. Father, realtor. Grad. St. Paul's Sch., London, Eng., 1944; Cambridge Univ., B.A. 1950. Served as conscript coal miner, England, 1944–47. Member of Dramatists Guild, Dramatists Club (London). Address: 18 Earls Terr., London W. 8, England.

Theatre. Mr. Shaffer wrote *Five Finger Exercise* (Comedy Th., London, England, July 16, 1958; Music Box, N.Y.C., Dec. 2, 1959; Globe, London, May 10, 1962); and two one-act plays, *The Private Ear* and *The Public Eye*(Morosco, N.Y.C., Oct. 9, 1963).

The National Th. opened its season at the Chichester (England) Festival with Mr. Shaffer's play *The Royal Hunt of the Sun* (July 7, 1964; ANTA Th., N.Y.C., Oct. 26, 1965); *Black Comedy* (Chichester Festival, July 27, 1965; Old Vic, London, Mar. 8, 1966), presented in N.Y.C. with *White Lies* (Ethel Barrymore Th., Feb. 12, 1967); *The Battle of Shrivings* (Lyric, London, England, Feb. 5, 1970); and *Equus* (Old Vic, July 26, 1973; Plymouth, N.Y.C., Oct. 24, 1974).

Films. Motion pictures of Mr. Shaffer's work include *Five Finger Exercise* (Col., 1962) and *The Pad . . . and How To Use It* (U, 1966), the film title for *The Private Ear.*

Television and Radio. He wrote the radio drama, *The Prodigal Father* (BBC, 1955).

For television, he wrote *The Salt Land* (ITV, 1955); and *Balcony of Terror* (BBC, 1957).

Other Activities. He was literary critic of *Truth* (1956–57) and a music critic for *Time and Tide* (1961–62).

Published Works. With his brother Anthony, Mr. Shaffer wrote two mystery novels, *How Doth the Little Crocodile?* (1952) and *Withered Murder* (1955).

Awards. Mr. Shaffer received the *Evening Standard* (Eng.) Drama Award (1958), and the NY Drama Critics Circle Award for Best Foreign Play for *Five Finger Exercise* (1960).

Recreation. Music, architecture, walking.

SHANK, THEODORE. Educator, writer, director. b. Theodore Junior Shank, Feb. 1, 1929, Brawley, Calif., to Theodore Benjamin and Anna (Kretz) Shank. Father, farmer. Grad. Brawley Union H.S., 1946; Univ. of California at Santa Barbara, B.A. 1950; Univ. of California at Los Angeles, M.A. 1952; Stanford Univ., Ph.D. 1956. Married Dec. 25, 1967, to Adele Edling; one son, one daughter from previous marriage. Served US Army, 1953–55; rank, Sgt. Member of ATA; Amer. Society for Th. Research, Northwest Drama Conference (bd. of dir., 1961–64); ANTA Regional Th. Council (bd. of gov., 1960–63; vice-pres., 1962). Address: (home) 1125 Bucknell Dr., Davis, CA 95616, tel. (916) 753-5678; (bus.) c/o Dept. of Dramatic Art, Univ. of California, Davis, CA 95616, tel. (916) 752-2147.

Since 1967, Mr. Shank has been professor in the Dept. of Dramatic Arts, Univ. of California at Davis (instructor, 1956–58); assistant professor, 1958–63; associate professor, 1963–67). He was department chairman (1961–69) and served as vice-chairman and then chairman of the faculty of the College of Letters and Science at Davis (1973–75). Before going to the Univ. of California, he had been a teaching assistant at Stanford Univ. (1952–53, 1956). He has lectured at the Universities of London, Exeter, Paris, at the California Institute of the Arts, and on television in London.

Theatre. At the Univ. of California at Davis, Mr. Shank has directed productions of *The Glass Menagerie* (Dec. 6, 1956), *The Doctor in Spite of Himself* (May 9, 1957), Anouilh's *Antigone* (Nov. 21, 1957), *An Italian Straw Hat* (May 8, 1958), *Hedda Gabler* (Dec. 11, 1958), *The Waltz of the Toreadors* (May 14, 1959), *Major Barbara* (Dec. 10, 1959), *As You Like It* (May 17, 1960), *The Cretan Woman* (Dec. 1, 1960); *The Rivals* (May 11, 1961), *Dido and Aeneas* (May 19, 1961), *The Madwoman of Chaillot* (July 20, 1961), *Macbeth* (Nov. 30, 1961), *The Threepenny Opera* (Oct. 25, 1962); *The Seagull* (Oct. 22, 1964), *Penny for a Song* (Oct. 21, 1965), *Stop It, Whoever You Are* (Nov. 30, 1966), a professional resident theatre production of *Schweyk in the Second World War* (Mar. 6, 1968), *The Past Sex Life of Samuel Norton* (July 18, 1969).

He has been co-author and director of the following collective theatre pieces: a professional resident theatre production of *Them, Inc.; An Entertainment with Music* (Mar. 12, 1969), *The Crimes and Trials of the Chicago 8-1+2* (June 2, 1971), *United Crates of America* (Mar. 29, 1972), and *Undead* (Mar. 6, 1973).

He has supervised the productions of approximately forty new plays written under his direction.

Published Works. Mr. Shank wrote *The Art of Dramatic Art* (1969; paperback ed., 1972) and "Theatre Collectives" in *Contemporary Dramatists* (1973). His articles have appeared in *Educational Theatre Journal, Theatre Survey, New Theatre, Entrétien, Yale French Studies, Teatroltre-Inventario,* and *The Drama Review.*

Awards. Mr. Shank received a Univ. of California Research Fellowship (1959), Univ. of California Humanities Institute Fellowships (1966 and 1973), and the Distinguished Teacher Award (1961) from the Univ. of California at Davis.

SHARAFF, IRENE. Costume designer. b. Boston, Mass. Attended NY Sch. of Fine and Applied Arts; The Arts Students League, N.Y.C.; Grande Chaumière, Paris. Member of United Scenic Artists of America; AMPAS; Costume Designers Guild. Address: c/o Gloria Safier, 667 Madison Ave., New York, NY 10021, tel. (212) TE 8-4868.

Theatre. Miss Sharaff's first N.Y.C. assignment was with Eva le Gallienne's Civic Repertory Th., as assistant to Aline Bernstein for set and costume designs for *L'Invitation au voyage* (Oct. 4, 1928), *The Cherry Orchard* (Oct. 15, 1928), *The Lady from Alfaqueque* (Jan. 14, 1929), *On the High Road* (Jan. 14, 1929), *A Sunny Morning* (April 13, 1929), *Mademoiselle Bourrat* (Oct. 7, 1929), *The Open Door* (Jan. 27, 1930), *The Women Have Their Way* (Jan. 27, 1930), *Romeo and Juliet* (April 21, 1930), and *The Green Cockatoo* (Oct. 9, 1930); designed with Miss Bernstein sets and costumes in *Siegfried* (Oct. 20, 1930) and *Alison's House* (Dec. 1, 1930); and designed sets and costumes (after Sir John Tenniel's drawings) for *Alice in Wonderland* (Dec. 12, 1932).

Miss Sharaff designed, with Varady and Pauline Lawrence, the costumes for *As Thousands Cheer* (Music Box, Sept. 30, 1933); designed costumes for the Ballet Russe de Monte Carlo's ballet drama, *Union Pacific* (St. James, April 25, 1934); was co-designer for *Life Begins at 8:40* (Winter Garden, Aug. 27, 1934); created sets for *Crime and Punishment* (Biltmore, Jan. 22, 1935); was designer with Constance Ripley, Billi Livingston, and Lee Simonson, for costumes in *Parade* (Guild, May 20, 1935); designed additional costumes for *The Great Waltz* (Center, Aug. 5, 1935); designed, with Connie DePinna, costumes for *Jubilee* (Imperial, Oct. 12, 1935); created sets and costumes for *Rosmersholm* (Shubert, Dec. 2, 1935); costumes for *Idiot's Delight* (Shubert, Mar. 24, 1936); *On Your Toes* (Imperial, Apr. 11, 1936); executed designs for modern dress in *White Horse Inn* (Center, Oct. 1, 1936); designed sets and costumes for the American Ballet production of *Jeu de Cartes* ("Card Party" or "Poker Game") (Metropolitan Opera House, world premiere April 27, 1937), employed again in the NY City Ballet production (premiere, NY City Ctr., Feb. 15, 1951).

Miss Sharaff designed costumes for *Virginia* (Center, Sept. 2, 1937); with John Hambleton, costumes for *I'd Rather Be Right* (Alvin, Nov. 2, 1937); created costumes for *The Boys from Syracuse* (Alvin, Nov. 23, 1938); *Gay New Orleans* (NY World's Fair, 1939); *The American Way* (Center, Jan. 21, 1939); *From Vienna* (Music Box, June 20, 1939); *Boys and Girls Together* (Broadhurst, Oct. 1, 1940); *All in Fun* (Majestic, Dec. 27, 1940); with Hattie Carnegie, costumes in *Lady in the Dark* (Alvin, Jan. 23, 1941) and the Revival (Bway Th., Feb. 27, 1943); created costumes for *The Land Is Bright* (Music Box, Oct. 28, 1941); *Sunny River* (St. James, Dec. 4, 1941); *Banjo Eyes* (Hollywood Th., Dec. 25, 1941); *By Jupiter* (Shubert, June 3, 1942); *Star and Garter* (Music Box, June 24, 1942); and *Count Me In* (Ethel Barrymore Th., Oct. 8, 1942).

She created costumes for the Ballet Theatre production of *Interplay* (premiere, Metropolitan Opera House, Oct. 17, 1945), worn again in the NY City Ballet production (premiere, NY City Ctr., Dec. 23, 1952); *Hamlet* (Columbus Circle Th., Dec. 13, 1945); *Billion Dollar Baby* (Alvin, Dec. 21, 1945); the pre-Bway tryout of *Bonanza Bound* (opened Shubert, Philadelphia, Pa., Dec. 26, 1947; closed there Jan. 3, 1948); *The Would-Be Gentleman* (Cort, Jan. 15, 1946); *Hamlet* (NY City Ctr., June 3, 1946); the Ballet Theatre production of *Facsimile* (premiere, Bway Th., Oct. 24, 1946); *Magdalena* (Ziegfeld, Sept. 30, 1948); *Montserrat* (Fulton, Oct. 29, 1949); *Dance Me a Song* (Royale, Jan. 20, 1950); NY City Ballet's *Age of Anxiety* (premiere, NY City Ctr., Feb. 26, 1950); Ballet Theatre's *Design with Strings* (premiere, Center, Apr. 25, 1950); *Michael Todd's Peep Show* (Winter Garden, June 28, 1950); *A Tree Grows in Brooklyn* (Alvin, Apr. 19, 1951), worn again in the national tour; Ballet Theatre's *Ensayo Sinfonico* (premiere, Metropolitan Opera House, N.Y.C., April 19, 1951).

She designed, with Pierre Balmain, gowns for *Palace Two-a-Day* (RKO Palace, Oct. 16, 1951); created costumes for *The King and I* (St. James, Mar. 29, 1952), worn later in national tours and two NY City Ctr. revivals (April 18, 1956; May 11, 1960); *Of Thee I Sing* (Ziegfeld, May 5, 1952); *Me and Juliet* (Majestic, May 28, 1953); *By the Beautiful Sea* (Majestic, Apr. 8, 1954); *On Your Toes* (46 St. Th., Oct. 11, 1954); *Shangri-La* (Winter Garden, June 13, 1956); *Candide* (Martin Beck Th., Dec. 1, 1956); *Happy Hunting* (Majestic, Dec. 6, 1956); *Small War on Murray Hill* (Ethel Barrymore Th., Jan. 3, 1957); *West Side Story* (Winter Garden, Sept. 26, 1957), worn again in national tours, the London production (Her Majesty's, Dec. 12, 1958), and in N.Y.C. (Winter Garden, Apr. 27, 1960); designed costumes for Jerome Robbins' *Ballets: U.S.A* (Alvin, Sept. 4, 1958); *Flower Drum Song* (St. James, Dec. 1, 1958); worn again on the national tour and in the London production (Palace, Mar. 24, 1960); created costumes for *Juno* (Winter Garden, N.Y.C., March 9, 1959); designed scenery and costumes for Judy Garland (Metropolitan Opera House, May 11, 1959); costumes for *Do Re Mi* (St. James, Dec. 26, 1960), worn later on national tour; for a revival of *The King and I* (NY City Ctr., June 12, 1963); *Jennie* (Majestic, Oct. 17, 1963); *The Boys from Syracuse* (Drury Lane, London, Nov. 7 1963); *The Girl Who Came to Supper* (Bway Th., N.Y.C., Dec. 8, 1964); and *Funny Girl* (Winter Garden, Mar. 26, 1964).

She designed costumes for a revival of *West Side Story* (NY City Ctr., Apr. 8, 1964); a revival of *The King and I* (State Th., July 6, 1964); for *Sweet Charity* (Palace, Jan. 29, 1966); for *Funny Girl* (Prince of Wales Th., London, England, Apr. 13, 1966); for *Hallelujah, Baby!* (Martin Beck Th., N.Y.C., Apr. 26, 1967); for *Sweet Charity* (Prince of Wales Th., London, Oct. 11, 1967); for a revival of *The King and I* (NY City Ctr., May 23, 1968); and for Debbie Reynolds in the title role of a revival of *Irene* (Minskoff Th., Mar. 13, 1973).

Films. Miss Sharaff designed costumes for *Madame Curie* (MGM, 1943); *Meet Me in St. Louis* (MGM, 1944); *Yolanda and the Thief* (MGM, 1945); *Ziegfeld Follies* (MGM, 1946); *The Best Years of Our Lives* (RKO, 1946); *The Secret Life of Walter Mitty* (RKO, 1947); *The Bishop's Wife* (RKO, 1947); *A Song Is Born* (RKO, 1948); *Every Girl Should Be Married* (RKO, 1948); *An American in Paris* (MGM, 1951); *Call Me Madam* (20th-Fox, 1953); *Brigadoon* (MGM, 1954); *A Star Is Born* (WB, 1954); *Guys and Dolls* (MGM, 1955); *The King and I* (20th-Fox, 1956); *Porgy and Bess* (Col., 1958); *Can-Can* (20th-Fox, 1958); *Flower Drum Song* (UI, 1961); *West Side Story* (UA, 1961); and Elizabeth Taylor's costumes for *Cleopatra* (20th-Fox, 1963); *The Sandpiper* (MGM, 1965); *Who's Afraid of Virginia Woolf?* (WB, 1966); and *The Taming of the Shrew* (Columbia/Royal, 1967); and costumes for Barbra Streisand in *Hello, Dolly!* (20th-Fox, 1969).

Television. Miss Sharaff designed clothes for Mary Martin, Ethel Merman, and the cast of the 1953 Ford Anniversary Telecast; Ethel Merman in

Panama Hattie (Best of Broadway, 1954); and *Aladdin* (Dupont Show of the Month, CBS, 1958).

Other Activities. She designed models for Rhea Mfg. Co.; for fashion shows in Hollywood, Calif., and N.Y.C.; drawings and jewelry for Paul Flato, N.Y.C., illustrations for *Vogue, Harper's Bazaar, Mademoiselle,* and *Seventeen* Magazines.

Awards. Miss Sharaff won Academy (Oscar) Awards for her costumes in *An American in Paris* (1951), *The King and I* (1956), *West Side Story* (1961), *Cleopatra* (1964), and *Who's Afraid of Virginia Woolf?* (1967); the Antoinette Perry (Tony) Award for *The King and I* (1952–53) and Tony nominations for *Sweet Charity* (1966) and *Hallelujah, Baby!* (1968).

SHARON, MURIEL. Children's theatre director, actress, playwright, educator. b. Muriel Betty Schochen, Dec. 24, 1920, Cleveland, Ohio, to Benjamin J. and Ella (Schwartz) Schochen. Father, realtor. Grad. Lakewood (Ohio) H.S., 1938; attended Ohio State Univ., 1938–40; grad. Western Reserve Univ., B.S. 1942; attended Bennington Coll., Summer 1944; Bristol (Eng.) Univ., 1952–53. In N.Y.C., studied acting with Sanford Meisner, 1949–50, and Lee Strasberg, 1954–55; dance with Martha Graham, 1945–48, American Sch. of Ballet, 1946–48; and mime with Etienne Decroux, 1950–60 and 1962. Married 1956, to Sidney Tillim, art critic and painter. Relative in theatre: sister, Seyril Schochen, playwright. Member of AETA (vice chairman, Reg. 14, 1958–61); CTC (chairman, Reg. 14, 1961–63). Address: (home) 166 E. 96th St., New York, NY 10028, tel. (212) FI 8-3840; (bus.) YM-YWHA, Lexington Ave. at 92nd St., New York, NY 10028, tel. (212) AT 9-2400.

Miss Sharon was director (1947–71) of the Children's Drama Dept. of the 92nd St. YM-YWHA (N.Y.C.); and she continues to teach and direct its Production Workshop; and has been artistic director of the Pocket Players, a professional touring company performing for children, initially organized by the YM-YWHA in 1955, but an independent operation since 1956. Productions she has directed for the Pocket Players include *Pierre Patelin, The Glass Slipper, Emil and the Detectives, The Tale of the Donkey,* and *Master of All Masters* (the latter two are of her own authorship).

She has directed, acted and taught, and, in some years, has combined all three activities. She was artistic director of the Jabberwocky Puppeteers (Cleveland, Ohio, 1940–42), which toured greater Cleveland with *The Firebird* and *Kintu.* The scenery and puppets for both plays were designed by Miss Sharon.

From 1942–44, she was instructor of dance and theatre at Ohio Univ. (Athens); she appeared at the Veteran's Th. (Duxbury, Mass., 1945) in roles that included Madame Arcati in *Blithe Spirit,* and Mrs. Terence in *Night Must Fall;* she appeared with the Nina Fonaroff Dance Co. (Apr. 1945) in *The Feast;* and for ELT in N.Y.C. (Hudson Park Branch Library, 1946), Ann Marie in *Thunder Rock* (1946), and Masha in *The Three Sisters* (May 14, 1947). She directed the Kurt List opera, *The Wise and the Foolish* (92nd St. YM-YWHA, 1951), which was the first atonal opera written for children and performed by adults who sang and children who spoke. She directed Stravinsky's *Histoire du soldat* (92nd St. YM-YWHA, 1954).

She was an instructor of creative dramatics and children's theatre at Cornell Univ. (Summers 1949–52; 1956–58); and directed the Jack-in-the-Green Players in children's plays which toured the playgrounds and parks of Westchester County (N.Y.) sponsored by the Westchester Recreation Association (Summers 1954–55); appeared as Miss Brooks in *Our Miss Brooks* (White Plains County Th., 1954); was production assistant for *Tiger at the Gate* (Plymouth, N.Y.C., Oct. 3, 1955), and the revue, *Joyce Grenfell Requests the Pleasure . .* (Bijou, Oct. 10, 1955); appeared as Lotte in *Emil and the Detectives,* which she also directed (Gramercy Arts, May 19, 1962); and was director of the Musical Theatre Acad. of New York Children's Sch. (1960–61). She was artistic director of the Saturday School of the Neighborhood Playhouse (N.Y.C., 1968–72).

Other Activities. Miss Sharon was consultant for the Creative Drama Center of the Children's Theatre Council (Binghamton, N.Y., 1951–52). She also has lectured on children's theatre and creative drama at Ithaca Coll. (1949), the British Drama League (1953) Sarah Lawrence Coll. (1957), Junior League of Brooklyn (1958), and Community Children's Theatre of Duchess County, N.Y. (1961). She presented a demonstration of creative dramatics on Wonder of Worlds (WNDT, 1962).

Miss Sharon studied psychodrama at the Moreno Inst. and Acad. (Beacon, N.Y., 1968–70). She is a certified director of psychodrama, has been a staff director at the Moreno Inst. in New York City; and has conducted sessions at Manhattan State Hosp., Putnam Memorial Hosp., Bennington, Vt., and elsewhere. She has also conducted sessions in creative dramatics, employing psychodramatic techniques.

Published Works. She has had articles published in such magazines as *American Educational Theatre Journal, Children's Theatre News,* and *Theatre-Enfance et Jeunesse.*

Awards. Miss Sharon received a Fulbright Scholarship (1952–53) to Great Britain to study style theatre and to investigate children's theatre. Her base of operations was the Univ. of Bristol.

Recreation. Painting, languages, hiking.

SHARP, WILLIAM. Educator, director. b. William Leslie Sharp, Sept. 3, 1924, Chicago, Ill., to Arthur E. and Alma (Melchior) Sharp. Father, mortgage banker. Grad. Andover Acad., 1942; Univ. of Chicago, B.A. 1943; M.A. 1949; Stanford Univ., Ph.D. 1953. Married Dec. 12, 1949, to Shirley Vanderwalker; one son, two daughters. Served US Army, 1943–46; rank, Cpl. Member of AETA (publications comm., 1960–62). Dept. of Dramatic Arts, Emerson College, Boston, MA 02116.

Since 1970, Mr. Sharp has been professor of dramatic arts and chairman of the dept. at Emerson College. he was visiting assoc. professor of speech and drama during 1964–66, and, later, assoc. professor (1966–70) at Stanford Univ.

Mr. Sharp was professor of drama at the Univ. of California at Riverside, where he was chairman of the dept. (1954–61) and there he directed and acted in numerous student productions, specializing in classical drama. He has also acted in productions at the Oregon Shakespeare Festival.

Published Works. Mr. Sharp is the author of *Language and Drama: Meanings for the Director and the Actor* (1970), and has contributed articles to *Educational Theatre Journal* "*Misalliance,* An Evaluation," 1956; "*Getting Married:* New Dramaturgy in Commedy," 1959; *Western Speech* "Meter and Oral Interpretation," 1958; *Tulane Drama Review* "W. B. Yeats: A Poet not in the Theatre," 1959; "A Play: Scenario or Poem," 1960; "An Unfashionable View of Tennessee Williams," 1962; and *Drama Survey* "Restoration Comedy: An Approach to Modern Production" (Winter 1968–69). He wrote the introduction to *School for Scandal,* edited by Robert Corrigan for Chandler Editions in Drama (1961).

SHATNER, WILLIAM. Actor. b. Montreal, Can., to Joseph and Anne Shatner. Father clothing manufacturer. Grad. West Hill H.S, Montreal; McGill Univ., B.A. 1952. Married Aug. 12, 1956, to Gloria Rand, actress (marr. dis. Mar. 1969); two daughters. Member of AEA; AFTRA; SAG; ACTA.

Theatre. Mr. Shatner made his debut at the Mountain Playhouse, Montreal (Summers 1952, 1953); and played juvenile roles at the Canadian Repertory Th., Ottawa, Can. (Winters 1952–53, 1953–54).

During 1954–56, at the Stratford Shakespeare Festival, Ontario, Can., he played Lucentio in *The Taming of the Shrew,* and juvenile roles in *The Merchant of Venice, Measure for Measure, Julius Caesar, Cymbeline, Oedipus Rex,* and *Henry V.*

Mr. Shatner played Usumcasane in Tamburlaine the Great (Winter Garden, N.Y.C., Jan. 19, 1956); Robert Lomax in *The World of Suzie Wong* (Broadhurst, Oct. 14, 1958); Paul Sevigne in *A Shot in the Dark* (Booth, Oct. 18, 1961); and Charlie Reader in *The Tender Trap* (Paper Mill Playhouse, Millburn, N.J., June 1970).

Films. He has appeared in *The Brothers Karamazov* (MGM, 1958); *The Explosive Generation* (UA, 1961); *Judgment at Nuremburg* (UA, 1961); *The Intruder* (CAD, 1962); and *The Outrage* (MGM, 1964).

Television. Mr. Shatner has appeared in many television dramas, including *All Summer Long* (Goodyear Playhouse, NBC, Oct. 1956); Omnibus (ABC) in *School for Wives* (Nov. 1956) and *Oedipus Rex* (Jan. 1957); Studio One (CBS) in *The Defenders, The Deaf Heart,* and *No Deadly Medicine* (all 1957); Alfred Hitchcock Presents (CBS) in *The Glass Eye* (1957) and *Mother, May I Go Out to Swim?* (1960); the US Steel Hour (CBS) in *Walk with a Stranger, A Man in Hiding,* and *Old Marshals Never Die* (all 1958); in *The Scarlet Pimpernel* (Family Classics, CBS, 1960); on Alcoa Premiere (ABC) in *The Promise* (1960) and *Million Dollar Hospital* (1963); and in *The Andersonville Trial* (Hollywood Television Th., NET, May 1970).

He also appeared in episodes of such series as Twilight Zone (CBS, 1960, 1963); Dr. Kildare (NBC, 1961, 1966); Naked City (ABC, 1962); The Defenders (CBS, 1962, 1963, 1965); The Nurses (CBS, 1963); 77 Sunset Strip (ABC, 1963); The Man from U.N.C.L.E. (NBC, 1964); The Virginian (NBC, 1965, 1969); Star Trek (NBC, 1966–68); Name of the Game (NBC, 1970); Ironside (NBC, 1970); Mission Impossible (CBS, 1971, 1972); Owen Marshall (ABC, 1971, 1972); Hawaii Five-O (CBS, 1972); and Marcus Welby (ABC, 1972).

Awards. Mr. Shatner received the Tyrone Guthrie Award as most promising actor (1956); and the *Theatre World* Award (1958).

Recreation. Riding, fencing, swimming, photography, archery, breeding Doberman Pinschers.

SHAVER, C. L. Educator. b. Claude L. Shaver, May 16, 1905, Kirksville, Mo., to David and Lucy (Cope) Shaver. Grad. Northeast Missouri State Teachers Coll., B.S. 1926; State Univ. of Iowa, M.A. 1929; Univ. of Wisconsin, Ph.D. 1937; post-doctoral studies: Univ. of California at Berkeley, Fall 1955; Univ. of Michigan, Summer 1957. Married 1928 to Ruth E. Dod; one daughter. Member of AETA (charter mbr.); ANTA (former mbr. of bd.); NTC; SWTC; ASTR; Speech Assn. of Amer.; Linguistic Society of Amer.; Amer. Dialect Society; Southern Speech Assn. Address: (home) 4782 Tulane Dr., Baton Rouge, LA 70808; (bus.) c/o Dept. of Speech, Louisiana State Univ., Baton Rouge, LA 70803.

As director of the Univ. Th. at Louisiana State Univ. he has staged more than 150 classical and contemporary works.

Other Activities. He was editor of *Southern Speech Journal* (1944–48); associate editor for drama and theatre, *Quarterly Journal of Speech* (1955–59); associate editor, speech for foreign and bi-lingual students, *The Speech Teacher* (1960–to date).

Published Works. Mr. Shaver wrote two one-acts plays: *In the Middle of the Road* (1928), and *Fantasia* (1931). He wrote "Goethe as a Theatre Director," in *Goethe After Two Centuries* (1925); "Steele MacKaye and the Delsarte Tradition," in *History of Speech Education in America* 1954); "The Minstrel Show," in *Encyclopedia Britannica* (1958); "Teaching Drama," and with Francine Merritt, "Teaching Voice and Diction," in *Speech Methods and Resources* (1961).

SHAW, GLEN BYAM. Director, actor. b. Glencairn Alexander Byam Shaw, Dec. 13, 1904, London, England, to John Liston Byam and Evelyn (Pyke-Nott) Shaw. Father and mother, painters. Attended Westminster Sch., London, 1918–22. Married July 8, 1929, to Angela Baddeley, actress; one son, one daughter. Served WW II, Royal Scots; rank, Maj. Member of AEA; Royal Shakespeare Th. (1960–to date). Address: (home) 169 Ashley Gardens, London, S.W. 1, England tel. Tate Gallery 9165; (bus.) c/o The English National Opera Company, The London Coliseum, St Martin's Lane, London W.C.2, England tel. 836.0111.

Theatre. Since 1962 Mr. Shaw has directed operas at the Sadler's Wells Th. and at the London Coliseum; was director of the Old Vic Th. Sch. and co-director, with Michel Saint Denis and George Devine, of the Old Vic Th. Centre (1947–51); director, with Anthony Quayle, of the Shakespeare Memorial Th. (1952–57), and sole director (1957–60).

Mr. Shaw made his stage debut as Colin Langford in *At Mrs. Beams* (Pavilion Th., Torquay, England, Aug. 1, 1923); followed by Yasha in *The Cherry Orchard* (Lyric, Hammersmith, London, May 25, 1925); appeared in repertory at J. B. Fagan's Oxford Playhouse (1926); played Tim Wakely in *Down Hill* (Queen's, London, June 1926); and the Student in *The Spook Sonata* (Oxford Th., June 1927).

He made his N.Y.C. debut as Pelham Humfrey in *And So to Bed* (Shubert, Nov. 9, 1927); played Peter Trophimof in *The Cherry Orchard* (Bijou, Mar. 5, 1928); Lord Straffield in *The Truth Game* (Globe, London, Oct. 5, 1928); Lyngstrand in *The Lady from the Sea* (Apollo, Nov. 4, 1928); appeared in productions with the Masque Th. company (Edinburgh, Scotland, 1928–29); played Lionel and Anthony Bramber in *Portrait of a Lady* ("Q", London, Aug. 1929); Charles in *The Hell Within* (Arts, July 1929); Trepley in *The Seagull* (Fortune, Sept. 25, 1929); Baron Tusenbach in *The Three Sisters* (Fortune, Oct. 23, 1929); Leonidas in *Marriage a la Mode* (*Lyric*, Hammersmith, Oct. 9, 1930); toured South Africa in *Marigold*, *Autumn Crocus*, and *The Truth Game* (1931); played the Young Actor in *Punchinello* (Globe, London, Feb. 1932); the Cripple and the King's Son in *The Miracle* (Lyceum, Apr. 9, 1932); Percinet in *The Fantasticks* (Lyric, Hammersmith, June 21, 1933); Alfredo in *As You Desire Me* (Gate, Sept. 1933); Earl of Southampton in *This Side Idolatry* (Lyric, Oct. 1933); succeeded (Nov. 1933) John Gielgud as Richard in *Richard of Bordeaux* (New, Feb. 2, 1933); played Darnley in *Queen of Scots* (New, June 8, 1934); Laertes in *Hamlet* (New, Nov. 14, 1934); Oswald in *Ghosts* (Duke of York's, July 30, 1935); Benvolio in *Romeo and Juliet* (New, Oct. 17, 1935); Captain O'Shea in *Parnell* (New, Nov. 4, 1936); toured as D'Arcy in *Pride and Prejudice* (Feb. 1937); played Lewis Dell in *He Was Born Gay* (Queen's, London, May 1937); and in repertory at the Queen's Th., appeared as the Duke of Norfolk and Sir Stephen Scroop in *Richard II*, Sir Benjamin Backbite in *The School for Scandal*, Solyony in *The Three Sisters*, and Gratiano in *The Merchant of Venice* (Sept. 1937–June 1938).

Mr. Shaw played Studsinsky in *The White Guard* (Phoenix, Oct. 6, 1938); Horatio in *Hamlet* (Lyceum, June 28, 1939), and repeated this role at Kronborg Castle, Elsinore, Denmark, directed, with Sir John Gielgud, *Richard II*, for the Oxford Univ. Dramatic Society (1935); directed *The Island* (Comedy, Feb. 10, 1938); with Sir John Gielgud, *The Merchant of Venice* (Queen's, Apr. 21, 1938); staged *Dear Octopus* (Queen's, London, Sept. 14, 1938; Broadhurst, N.Y.C., Jan. 11, 1939); *Rhondda Roundabout* (Globe, London, May 31, 1939); *The Winslow Boy* (Lyric, May 23, 1946; Empire, N.Y.C., Oct. 29, 1947); *Antony and Cleopatra* (Piccadilly, London, Dec. 20, 1946); *As You Like It* (Young Vic, Jan. 3, 1949); *Accolade* (Aldwych, Sept. 7, 1950); *The Merchant of Venice* (Young Vic, Sept. 25, 1950); and *Henry V* (Old Vic, Jan. 30, 1951).

At the Shakespeare Memorial Th. (Stratford-upon-Avon), Mr. Shaw directed *Coriolanus*, and *As You Like It* (1952), *Richard III*, and *Antony and Cleopatra* (1953), *Romeo and Juliet*, and *Troilus and Cressida* (1954), *Macbeth*, and *The Merry Wives of Windsor* (1955), *Othello* (1956), *As You Like It*, and *Julius Caesar* (1957), *Romeo and Juliet* and *Hamlet* (1958), and *King Lear* (1959).

He directed *Ross* (Haymarket, London, May 12, 1960); *The Last Joke* (Phoenix, Sept. 28, 1960); *The Complaisant Lover* (Ethel Barrymore Th., N.Y.C., Nov. 1, 1961); *Ross* (Eugene O'Neill Th., Dec. 26, 1961); the operas *The Rake's Progress* (Sadler's Wells, London, Feb. 2, 1962), and *Idomeneo* (Sadler's Wells, Oct. 11, 1962); *The Tulip Tree* (Haymarket, Nov. 29, 1962); the opera, *Cosi fan Tutte* (Sadler's Wells, Mar. 22, 1963); *Where Angels Fear to Tread* (St. Martin's, July 9, 1963); the operas, *Der Freischutz* (Sadler's Wells, Sept. 12, 1963), and *Hansel and Gretel* (Sadler's Wells, Dec. 19, 1963); *The Right Honourable Gentleman* (Her Majesty's Th., May 28, 1964); *You Never Can Tell* (1965); *The Rivals* (1966); *The Dance of Death* (National Theatre and Canadian tour); *The Merchant of Venice* (1967); *The Wild Duck* (1970), and the operas *Faust* (1964), *A Masked Ball* (1965), and *Die Fledermaus* (1966).

Awards. Mr. Shaw was C.B.E. (Commander of the British Empire, 1954). He received an honorary D. Litt. from Birmingham (England) Univ. (1959).

SHAW, HARLAN. Educational theatre, actor, director, costume designer, scenic designer. b. William Harlan Shaw, Apr. 3, 1922, near Tulia, Tex., to William Sample and Delia Cates (Harlan) Shaw. Father, carpenter. Grad. Abilene (Tex.) H.S., 1939; Hardin-Simmons Univ., B.A. 1943, M.A. 1949; Louisiana State Univ., Ph.D. 1955. Married Nov. 1, 1945, to Marjorie L. McQuade; two daughters. Served U.S. Navy Reserve (1943-46); participated in invasion of Iwo Jima, Okinawa, and the landing of occupational forces on Japan; rank, Lt. (j.g.). Member of AEA; SETC; SWTC; Theatres of Louisiana. Address: (home) 7450 Fieldston Rd., New Orleans, LA 70126, tel. (504) 242-0715; (bus.) Dept. of Drama and Communications, Univ. of New Orleans, New Orleans, LA 70122, tel. (504) 288-3161, ext. 317.

Theatre. Mr. Shaw made his acting debut with the University Baptist Church (Abilene, Tex., 1928); subsequently played major roles in seventeen productions in university theatres, summer stock, and with the Eddie Dowling Foundation. For various university theatres, he has directed twenty-six plays and operas; and designed sets for seventy-seven plays, operas, and musicals. He has served as costume designer for sixty-one plays, operas, and musicals for university theatres; seven plays for the Eddie Dowling Foundation; and twenty-seven operas and plays, beginning with *The Way of the World* (July 1962) for the Asolo Theatre (Sarasota, Fla.).

Published Works. He is the co-author of *Introduction to Theatrical Arts* (Kendall-Hunt, 1971, 1973); and wrote *Basic Pattern Drafting for the Theatrical Costume Designer* (Drama Book Specialists-Publishers, 1974). His costume designs have been published in various periodicals and textbooks.

Awards. Mr. Shaw received the National Opera Guild award for his scenic designs for *Ariadne auf Naxos* (1957); a Florida Development Commission award for his "generous contribution to the promotion of Florida, 1961–64"; a Florida State Univ. Research Council grant (1967); and a Univ. of New Orleans Liberal Arts research grant (1970–71) for work on *History of Men's Wear Since the Civil War.*

Recreation. Painting and sculpture.

SHAW, IRWIN. Playwright, producer, author. b. Feb. 27, 1913, New York City, to William and Rose (Tompkins) Shaw. Grad. James Madison H.S., Brooklyn, N.Y., 1929; Brooklyn Coll., B.A. 1934. Married Oct. 13, 1939, to Marian Edwards; one son. Relative in theatre: brother, David Shaw, playwright, television writer, and editor. Served US Army, Signal Corps, 1942–45; rank, Warrant Officer (j.g.).

Theatre. Mr. Shaw wrote *Bury the Dead* (Ethel Barrymore Th., N.Y.C., Apr. 18, 1936); *Siege* (Longacre, Dec. 8, 1937); *The Gentle People* (Belasco, Jan. 5, 1939), which was presented in France as *Phillippe et Jonas* (1952–56); *Retreat to Pleasure* (Belasco, N.Y.C., Dec. 17, 1941); *Sons and Soldiers* (Morosco, May 4, 1943); and *The Assassin* (Savoy, London, 1945; National, N.Y.C., Oct. 17, 1945).

He wrote, with Peter Viertel, *The Survivors* (Playhouse, N.Y.C., Jan. 19, 1948); adapted Marcel Archard's *Patate* (Henry Miller's Th., Oct. 28, 1958); and wrote *Children from Their Games* (Morosco, Apr. 11, 1963). The play *Lucy Crown* was adapted from his novel of the same title (Paris, France; Madrid, Spain, 1958); and *Step Lively, Boy* (Urban Arts Corps, N.Y.C., Jan. 31, 1973) was adapted by Vinnette Carroll, with music and lyrics by Micki Grant, from Mr. Shaw's *Bury the Dead*. .

Films. He wrote and produced *In the French Style* (Col., 1963).

Radio. He wrote radio serials (1934–36).

Other Activities. Drama critic for *The New Republic* (1947).

Published Works. He wrote *The Young Lions* (1950); *Mixed Company, Collected Stories* (1950); *Lucy Crown* (1956); *Tip on a Dead Jockey and Other Stories* (1957); *Two Weeks in Another Town* (1960); *The Troubled Air, Love on a Dark Street, Voices of a Summer Day*, and *In the Company of Dolphins* (1964); and *Rich Man, Poor Man* (1970).

He has written such stories as "Act of Faith," "The Eighty Yard Run," "Sailor Off the Bremen," and "Welcome to the City.".

Recreation. Skiing, tennis, traveling.

SHAW, ROBERT. Actor, playwright, novelist. b. Aug. 9, 1927, Westhoughton, Lancastershire, England, to Thomas and Doreen (Avery) Shaw. Father, physician. Attended schools in Truro and Cornwall, England. Studied theatre at RADA, London. Married 1952, to Jennifer Bourke, actress (marr. dis.); four daughters; married Apr. 13, 1963, to Mary Ure, actress (dec. Apr. 3, 1975); two daughters, two sons.

Theatre. Mr. Shaw made his stage debut (Summer 1949) at the Shakespeare Memorial Th. (Stratford-upon-Avon, England), playing Angus in *Macbeth*, Jupiter in *Cymbeline*, and Suffolk in *Henry VIII;* toured Australia with the company (Oct. 1949–Feb. 1950), and returned to Stratford to play Suffolk again in *Henry VIII*, the Second Gentleman in *Measure for Measure*, the Messenger in *Julius Caesar* (May 2, 1950), Conrade in *Much Ado About Nothing* (1950), and Burgundy in *King Lear* (July 18, 1950).

He made his London debut as Rosencrantz in Alec Guinness' *Hamlet* (New, May 17, 1951); joined the Old Vic Co. (1951–52), playing Cassio in *Othello*, and Lysander in *A Midsummer Night's Dream* and toured South Africa with the company, playing the same parts, as well as Malcolm in *Macbeth* (1952).

He played George Lamb in the London production of *Caro William* (Embassy, Oct. 22, 1952); and, at the Shakespeare Memorial Th., (Stratford-upon-Avon), appeared as Gratiano in *The Merchant of Venice* (Mar. 17, 1953), Dolabella in *Antony and Cleopatra* (Apr. 28, 1953), Tranio in *The Taming of the Shrew* (June 9, 1953), and Edmund in *King Lear* (July 14, 1953).

Mr. Shaw repeated his role as Dolabella in a London presentation of *Antony and Cleopatra* (Prince's, Nov. 4, 1953); played Topman in *Tiger at the Gates* (Apollo, June 2, 1955); and Lazlo Rimini in *Off the Mainland*, which he also wrote (Arts, May 30, 1956).

He played Sewell in *One More River* (New Shakespeare Th., Liverpool, May 1958), and in London (Duke of York's, Oct. 6, 1959); Blackmouth in *Live Like Pigs* (Royal Court, Sept. 30, 1958); succeeded (Nov. 1958) Mogens Wieth as Lazlo Rajk in *Shadow of Heroes* (Piccadilly, Oct. 7, 1958); played Sergeant Mitchem in *The Long and the Short and the Tall* (Royal Court, Jan. 7, 1959); Watson in *A Lodging for a Bride* (Westminster, Apr. 18, 1960); and De Flores in *The Changeling* (Royal Court, Feb. 21, 1961).

Mr. Shaw made his N.Y.C. debut as Aston in *The Caretaker* (Lyceum, Oct. 4, 1961); played Johann Wilhelm Mobius in *The Physicists* (Martin Beck Th., Oct. 13, 1964); wrote, based on his own novel, *The Man in the Glass Booth* (St. Martin's, London, July 27, 1967; Royale N.Y.C., Sept. 26, 1968); played the title role in the musical, *Gantry* (George Abbott Th., Feb 14, 1970); wrote *Cato Street* (Young Vic, London, Nov. 15, 1971); played Deeley in *Old Times* (Billy Rose Th., N.Y.C., Nov. 16, 1971; and on tour); and Edgar (The Captain) in *Dance of Death* (Vivian Beaumont Th., N.Y.C., Apr. 4, 1974).

Films. Mr. Shaw appeared in *The Lavender Hill*

Mob (U, 1951); *The Dambusters* (WB, 1955); *A Hill in Korea* (Br. Lion, 1956; US, *Hell in Korea); Sea Fury* (Rank, 1958); *Libel* (MGM, 1959); *THe Valiant* (Euro. Intl., 1962); *Tomorrow at Ten* (Blakely's, 1962; Governor, 1964); the film version of *The Caretaker*, entitled *The Guest* (Janus, 1964); the title role in *The Luck of Ginger Coffey* (Cont., 1964); *From Russia, With Love* (UA, 1964); *THe Battle of the Bulge* (WB, 1965); Henry VIII in *A Man for All Seasons* (Col., 1966); Gen. George Custer in *Custer of the West* (Cinerama, 1968); Stanley in *The Birthday Party* (Cont., 1968); *The Battle of Britain* (UA, 1969); Pizarro in *The Royal Hunt of the Sun* (Natl. Gen., 1969); *A Town Called Hell* (Scotia Intl., 1971); *Figures in a Landscape* (Natl. Gen., 1971); Lord Churchill in *Young Churchill* (Col., 1972); *The Hireling* (Col., 1973); *The Sting* (U, 1973); *A Reflection of Fear* (Col., 1973); *The Taking of Pelham One Two Three* (UA, 1974); and *Jaws* (U, 1975).

Television. He made his debut on British television in 1953, and has played in *Rupert of Hentzau; Hindle Wakes;* as Leontes in *The Winter's Tale;* in *The Florentine Tragedy;* as Claudius to Christopher Plummer's *Hamlet at Elsinore* (BBC, 1964; also seen in US); etc. His novel, *The Hiding Place*, was adapted and shown by the BBC.

In the US, he starred as Capt. Dan Tempest on the series The Buccaneers (CBS, 1957); played the Ghost of Christmas Future in *A Carol for Another Christmas* (UN special, ABC, Dec. 28, 1964); and played the title role in *Luther* (ABC, Jan. 29, 1968). His novel, *The Hiding Place*, was adapted for Playhouse 90 (CBS, Mar. 22, 1960).

Published Works. In addition to the above-mentioned plays, Mr. Shaw has written the novels, *The Hiding Place* (1959), *The Sun Doctor* (1961), *The Flag* (1965), *The Man in the Glass Booth* (1967), and *A Card from Morocco* (1969). He has written many book reviews and articles.

Awards. He received an Academy (Oscar) Award nomination (1967) as best supporting actor for his role in *A Man for All Seasons*.

For his novel, *The Sun Doctor*, he received the Hawthornden Prize (1962).

Recreation. Sports, reading.

SHAWHAN, APRIL. Actress, singer, dancer. b. Apr. 10, 1940, Chicago, Ill., to Mr. and Mrs. Paul Shawhan. Father, horse breeder. Attended Amer. Academy of Dramatic Arts. Member of AEA; AFTRA; SAG.

Theatre. Miss Shawhan played Sigrid in *The Song of Norway* (Philharmonic Aud., Los Angeles, Apr. 23, 1962); subsequently played Amy in *Jo* (Orpheum, N.Y.C., Feb. 12, 1964); Bernstein in *A Race of Hairy Men* (Henry Miller's Th., Apr. 29, 1965); Angela in *Three Bags Full* (Henry Miller's Th., Mar. 6, 1966); appeared in *Oh, What a Lovely War* (Alley Th., Houston, June 2, 1967); played Dora in *Dinner at Eight* (Alvin, N.Y.C., Sept. 27, 1968); with the NY Shakespeare Festival, played Ophelia in *Hamlet* (Anspacher Th., Dec. 26, 1967); played Nell Schmedt in *Home Fires*, part of a double-bill entitled *Cop-Out* (Cort Th., Apr. 7, 1969); Ado Annie in *Oklahoma* (NY State Th., June 23, 1969); with the NY Shakespeare Festival, Donna in *Mod Donna* (Public Th., May 3, 1970), and Hero in *Much Ado About Nothing* (Delacorte, Aug. 17, 1972; and Winter Garden, Nov. 11, 1972); and appeared as June in *Over Here* (Shubert, Mar. 6, 1974).

Awards. Miss Shawhan received the Theatre World Award (1965–66) for her performance in *Three Bags Full*.

SHEAFFER, LOUIS. Biographer, critic, press agent. b. Oct. 18, 1912, Louisville, Ky. Attended Univ. of North Carolina. Member of ATPAM.

Mr. Sheaffer is the author of a two-volume biography of Eugene O'Neill entitled *O'Neill, Son and Playwright* (1968), and *O'Neill, Son and Artist* (1973).

He was the drama critic for the Brooklyn *Eagle* from 1950 until the paper's demise in 1955, having served there as copy boy (1934), reporter, and film critic.

From 1956 to 1958, he was press agent for the Berkshire Playhouse, and Circle in the Square.

Awards. During his work on the O'Neill biography, Mr. Sheaffer received Guggenheim Fellowships in 1959, 1962, and 1969; and two grants-in-aid from the Amer. Council of Learned Societies. He is the recipient of the George Freedley Memorial Award (1968); and the Pulitzer Prize (1974).

SHEEN, MARTIN. Actor. b. Ramon Estevez, Aug. 3, 1940, Dayton, Ohio, to Francisco and Mary Ann (Phelan) Estevez. Attended Holy Trinity Grammar Sch. and Chaminade H.S., Dayton. Married Dec. 23, 1960, to Janet; four children.

Theatre. Mr. Sheen made his New York debut as a replacement in the role of Ernie in *The Connection* (The Living Th., N.Y.C., and European tour, 1959); again with The Living Th., played Hyllos in *Women of Trachis*, and the Third Soldier in *Cavalry* (1960), Horace in *Many Loves*, and The Man with the Turned-Up Nose in *In the Jungle of Cities* (1961); subsequently played Mike in *Never Live Over a Pretzel Factory* (Eugene O'Neill Th., Mar. 28, 1964); Timmy Cleary in *The Subject Was Roses* (Royale, May 25, 1964; and on tour, 1965–66); Vasco in *The Wicked Cooks* (Orpheum, N.Y.C., Jan. 23, 1967); appeared in a staged reading of *Drums in the Night* (Circle in the Square, three Monday evenings, Mar. 1967); played the title role in *Hamlet* (Public/Anspacher, Dec. 26, 1967); Romeo in *Romeo and Juliet* (Delacorte, Aug. 7, 1968); Johnny in *Hello and Goodbye* (Sheridan Sq. Playhouse, Sept. 18, 1969); Reese in *The Happiness Cage* (Public/Other, Feb. 1970); and replaced Harvey Keitel (Aug. 5, 1975) as Happy in *Death of a Salesman* (Circle in the Square/-Joseph E. Levine Th.).

Under the name Ramon G. Estevez, he wrote *Down the Morning Line* (Public/Other, Mar. 1969).

Films. Mr. Sheen made his film debut repeating his stage performance as Timmy Cleary in *The Subject Was Roses* (MGM, 1968); and has subsequently appeared in *The Incident* (20th-Fox, 1968); *Catch 22* (Par., 1970); *No Drums, No Bugles* (Cinerama, 1971); *Pickup on 101* (AI, 1972); *Rage* (WB, 1972); and *Badlands* (WB, 1974).

Television. Mr. Sheen's extensive television activity includes appearances on The Defenders (CBS, 1961); Armstrong Circle Th. (CBS); US Steel Hour (CBS); Outer Limits (ABC); East Side/West Side (CBS); *Ten Blocks on the Camino Real* (NET Playhouse, PBS); As the World Turns (CBS); The F.B.I. (ABC); N.Y.P.D. (ABC); Mission: Impossible (CBS); Hawaii Five-O (CBS); Medical Center (CBS); *The Andersonville Trials* (Hollywood Television Th., PBS); Ironside (NBC); *Montserrat* (Hollywood Television Th., PBS); Cannon (CBS); and Mannix (CBS); and the made-for-television films *Then Came Bronson* (NBC); *Mongo's Back in Town* (CBS); *Welcome Home, Johnny Bristol* (CBS); *That Certain Summer* (ABC); *Pursuit* (ABC); *The Execution of Private Slovik* (NBC); *The Story of Pretty Boy Floyd* (ABC); *The Last Survivor's* (NBC); *The California Kid* (ABC); *The Missiles of October* (CBS); *Catholics* (CBS); and *Sweet Hostage*.

SHELLEY, CAROLE. Actress. b. Aug. 16, 1939, London, England, to Curtis and Deborah (Bloomstein) Shelley. Father, composer; mother, singer. Grad. Arts Educational Sch., London; Royal Academy of Dramatic Arts, London. Studied Shakespeare with Eileen Thorndike, Iris Warren. Married 1967 to Al Woods (dec., 1971). Member of AEA; SAG; AFTRA.

Theatre. Miss Shelley made her stage debut as Little Nell in *The Old Curiosity Shop* (Southwark, England, 1950); and her London debut as Mabel in *Simon and Laura* (Apollo, 1955); subsequently appeared in the revues, *For Adults Only* (1958), *New Cranks* (Lyric, Hammersmith, England, 1959), and *The Art of Living* (Criterion, London, Aug. 18, 1960); played Jane in *Boeing-Boeing* (Apollo, Feb. 20, 1962); and replaced Maggie Smith (Dec. 1, 1963) as Mary McKellaway in *Mary, Mary* (Globe, London, Feb. 27, 1963), and subsequently toured in that role.

She made her American debut as Gwendolyn Pigeon in *The Odd Couple* (Plymouth, N.Y.C., Mar. 10, 1965); played Barbara in *The Astrakan Coat* (Helen Hayes Th., Jan. 12, 1967); Fay in *Loot* (Biltmore, Mar. 18, 1968); appeared in the revue, *Nöel Coward's Sweet Potato* (Ethel Barrymore Th., Sept. 29, 1968; moved to Booth, Nov. 1, 1968); replaced Linda Lavin (Mar. 25, 1969) as Patsy Newquist in *The Little Murders* (Circle in the Square, Jan. 5, 1969); and played Jacqueline Coryton in *Hay Fever* (Helen Hayes Th., Nov. 9, 1970).

She appeared in the Shaw Festival's production of *Tonight at 8:30* (Niagara-on-the-Lake, Ontario, Canada, Summer 1971); with the Stratford Festival of (Ontario) Canada, played Rosalind in *As You Like It* (June 5, 1972), Regan in *King Lear* (June 7, 1972), and Constance Neville in *She Stoops To Conquer* (July 25, 1972); toured with that company (Winter 1972) to Denmark, Holland, Poland and Russia, playing Regan in *King Lear* and Bianca in *The Taming of the Shrew;* subsequently, with the American Shakespeare Festival (Stratford, Conn.) played Mrs. Margery Pinchwife in *The Country Wife* (June 1, 1973), and The First Witch in *Macbeth* (July 6, 1973); played Nora in *A Doll's House* (Goodman Memorial Th., Chicago, Nov. 20, 1973); again at the American Shakespeare Festival (Stratford, Conn.), played Viola in *Twelfth Night* (June 15, 1974), and Lady Capulet in *Romeo and Juliet* (June 16, 1974); Jane in *Absurd Person Singular* (Music Box, N.Y.C., Oct. 8, 1974); and Ruth in the trilogy entitled *The Norman Conquests* (Morosco, Dec. 7, 1975) which included *Table Manners, Living Together*, and *Round and Round the Garden*.

Films. She made her performing debut at age three in *The Man from Morocco* (English Films, 1944); subsequently appearing in *Cure for Love* (British Lion, 1949); *It's Great To Be Young* (Fine Arts, 1957); *Give Us this Day; Carry On Regardless* (Governor, 1963); *Carry on Cabby* (1963); *No, My Darling Daughter* (Zenith International, 1964); *The Boston Strangler* (20th-Fox, 1968); and *The Odd Couple* (Par., 1969). She provided voices for the animated films, *The Aristocats* (BV, 1971); and *Robin Hood* (BV, 1974).

Television. Miss Shelley appeared on British television in many of the Brian Rix farces, The Dickie Henderson Show, and The Avengers. In the US, she has played Gwendolyn Pigeon in The Odd Couple series (ABC); and appeared in *A Salute to Noel Coward* (Camera Three, CBS).

SHELLEY, JOSHUA. Producer, actor, director. b. New York City. Grad. New York Univ., B.A., 1941. Married Dec. 21, 1959, to Molly McCarthy, actress. Member of AEA; SAG; AFTRA.

Theatre. Mr. Shelley appeared in *One Touch of Venus* (Imperial Th., N.Y.C., Oct. 7, 1943); took over for Adolph Green as Ozzie during the run of *On the Town* (Adelphi, Dec. 28, 1944); appeared in *Tid Bits of 1946* (Plymouth, July 8, 1946); played Joe Wollinski in *Tenting Tonight* (Booth, Apr. 2, 1947); took over for Red Buttons as Shyster Fisl during the run of *Barefoot Boy with Cheek* (Martin Beck Th., Apr. 3, 1947); appeared in the revue *Make Mine Manhattan* (Broadhurst, Jan. 14, 1948); played Arlecchino in *The Liar* (Broadhurst, May 18, 1950); Mischa Cogn in *Four Twelves Are 48* (48 St. Th., Jan. 17, 1951); Boris in *The Girl in Pink Tights* (Mark Hellinger Th., Mar. 5, 1954); Sidney Cohn in *On Your Toes* (46 St. Th., Oct. 11, 1954); and appeared in the revue *Phoenix '55* (Phoenix, Apr. 23, 1955).

He directed *Simply Heavenly* (85 St. Playhouse, May 21, 1957; moved to Playhouse, Aug. 20, 1957); played Colonel Yeast in *I Want You* (Maidman Playhouse, Sept. 15, 1961); directed *Come Live with Me* (Billy Rose Th., Jan. 26, 1967); and *The Ballad of Johnny Pot* (Th. Four, Apr. 26, 1971).

Films. Mr. Shelley appeared in *City Across the River* (U, 1949) and *Yes Sir, That's My Baby* (U, 1949).

Television and Radio. He wrote and directed the radio program Let's Playwright (1941); and performed in It Happened to Me, America Goes to Press, Dick Tracy, This Is Your Counterspy (NBC,

1947); Front Page Farrell (CBS, 1949–51); and The F.B.I. (NBC, 1950–52). He was a disc jockey on WINS (1948–49).

On television, he directed Star Time (Dumont, 1950); was Master of Ceremonies on To Tell The Truth (NBC, 1945). He performed in Philco Television Playhouse (NBC, 1949); Treasury Men in Action (NBC, 1949); Studio One (CBS, 1949, 1950, 1951); Man Behind the Badge (1949–51); Hallmark Hall of Fame (NBC, 1950); Silver Th. (NBC, 1950–51); Starlight Th. (1950); Big Story (NBC, 1950–51); Faye Emerson Show (1950); Danger (CBS, 1950, 1951, 1952); Suspense (CBS, 1950–51); We the People (1951–52); Holiday Hotel (ABC, 1951); The Defenders (CBS, 1961); and East Side/West Side (CBS, 1964). He produced and directed the Shari Lewis Show (NBC, 1962), and directed the Laughmakers with Woody Allen (ABC, 1962).

Other Activities. Mr. Shelley has been producing and developing properties at Talent Associates-Paramount, Ltd. He began operating his own acting school in 1955.

SHEPARD, SAM. Playwright. b. Samuel Shepard Rogers, Jr., Nov. 5, 1942, Fort Sheridan, Ill., to Samuel Shepard and Jane Elaine (Schook) Rogers. Educated Duarte (Calif.) H.S.; Mt. San Antonio Jr. Coll., Walnut, Calif., 1961–62; Yale Univ. Married Nov. 9, 1969, to O-Lan Johnson Dark, actress; one son. Address: c/o Toby Cole, 234 W. 44th St., New York, NY 10036.

Pre-Theatre. Race track hot-walker, stable hand, sheep shearer, herdsman, orange picker, car wrecker, busboy, waiter, musician.

Theatre. Mr. Shepard is the author of over thirty plays, many of which no longer exist, and most of which have never received commercial production, but have been widely performed by experimental theatres in the US and abroad. His produced plays include *Cowboys* (Th. Genesis, N.Y.C., Oct. 16, 1964); *Rock Garden* (Th. Genesis, Oct. 16, 1964), which was adapted and included in *Oh! Calcutta* (Eden, June 17, 1967); *Up to Thursday* (Cherry Lane Th., Feb. 10, 1965); *Dog* and *Rocking Chair* (La Mama ETC, Feb. 10, 1965); *Chicago* (Th. Genesis, Apr. 16, 1965), and *Melodrama Play* (La Mama ETC, May 18, 1967), which were included in *Six from La Mama* (Martinique, Apr. 12, 1966; and Mercury, London, Sept. 1967); *Icarus's Mother* (Caffe Cino, N.Y.C., Nov. 16, 1965; and Open Space, London, Spring 1971); *4-H Club* (Cherry Lane Th., N.Y.C., 1965), *Fourteen Hundred Thousand* (Firehouse Th., Minneapolis, Minn., 1966); *Red Cross* (Judson Poet's Th., N.Y.C., Provincetown Playhouse, Apr. 28, 1968; and Kings Head, London, Aug. 15, 1972); *La Turista* (Amer. Place Th., N.Y.C., Mar. 4, 1967; and Th. Upstairs (Royal Court), London, Mar. 19, 1969); *Cowboys #2* (Old Reliable, N.Y.C., Aug. 12, 1967; and Mark Taper Forum, Los Angeles, Nov. 1967); *Forensic and the Navigators* (Th. Genesis, N.Y.C., Dec. 29, 1967; and Astor Place Th., Apr. 1, 1970); *The Holy Ghostly* (La Mama New Troup, tour, 1969; and Kings Head, London, July 3, 1973); *The Unseen Hand* (La Mama ETC, N.Y.C., Dec. 26, 1969; Astor Place Th., Apr. 1, 1970; and Th. Upstairs, London, Mar. 12, 1973); *Operation Sidewinder* (Vivian Beaumont Th., N.Y.C., Mar. 12, 1970); *Shaved Splits* (La Mama ETC, July 20, 1970); *Mad Dog Blues* (Th. Genesis, Mar. 4, 1971); *Cowboy Mouth* (Transverse Th., Edinburgh, Scotland, Apr. 2, 1971), which appeared on a bill with *Black Dog Beast Bait* (American Place Th., Apr. 29, 1971); *The Tooth of Crime*, for which he also wrote lyrics (Open Space, London, July 17, 1972; Performing Garage, N.Y.C., Mar. 7, 1973; and Royal Court, London, June 5, 1974); *Geography of a Horse Dreamer*, which he also directed (Th. Upstairs (Royal Court), London, Feb. 2, 1974); *Little Ocean* (Hampstead Th. Club, Mar. 25, 1974); and *Action* and *Killer's Head* (San Francisco Magic Th., 1975; Amer. Place Th., N.Y.C., Apr. 4, 1975; and Royal Court, London, 1975).

In addition, he contributed material to the Open Th.'s (N.Y.C.) productions entitled *Terminal* (1971–72 season), and *Nightwalk* (1973).

Films. He co-authored the screenplays for *Me and My Brother* (New Yorker Films, 1967); *Zabriski Point* (MGM, 1970); and *Ringaleevio* (1971). He appeared in *Brand X* (CMB, 1970).

Awards. Mr. Shepard has received grants from the Guggenheim Foundation (1968); the Rockefeller Foundation (1967); and the Office for Advanced Drama Research; fellowships from Yale Univ., and the Univ. of Minnesota; and the Brandeis Univ. Creative Arts Medal (1976). He has received Off-Bway (Obie) awards for *La Turista* (1966–67), *Forensic and the Navigator* and *Melodrama Play* (1967–68), and *Action* (1974–75).

SHERIN, EDWIN. Director, actor. b. Jan. 15, Danville, Pa. Grad. Brown Univ., A.B. 1952. Studied at Paul Mann's Actors' Workshop; Amer. Shakespeare Festival Academy; Fanny Bradshaw. Served U.S. Navy, 1952–56; Lt. (jg). Married Mar. 29, 1975, to Jane Alexander, actress. Member of AEA; SAG; AFTRA; SSD & C; Actors Studio (directors unit).

Theatre. Mr. Sherin made his professional acting debut in *Measure for Measure* (Phoenix, N.Y.C., Jan. 22, 1957); with the NY Shakespeare Fest. (Belvedere Lake Th., Summer 1957); played Tybalt in *Romeo and Juliet*, and Malcolm in *Macbeth;* appeared as the Soldier in *L'Histoire du Soldat* (YM-YWHA, 1957); was an understudy for the Bway production of *Miss Lonelyhearts* (Music Box, Oct. 3, 1957); again appeared with the NY Shakespeare Fest. playing Hyman in *As You Like It;* (Heckscher Th., Jan. 20, 1958), and (Belvedere Lake Th., Summer 1958) Cassio in *Othello*, Sebastian in *Twelfth Night*, Touchstone in *As You Like It;* and Octavius Caesar in *Anthony and Cleopatra*. He understudied Paul Roebling in *Desert Incident* (John Golden Th., Mar. 24, 1959); with the Phoenix Th. (1960) played Prince Hal in *Henry IV, Parts 1 and 2*, and appeared in *Peer Gynt* and *Lysistrata;* played Jonathan Spring and was the understudy to Jack Lemmon in *Face of a Hero* (Eugene O'Neill Th., Oct. 20, 1960); was standby for Hal March in *Come Blow Your Horn* (Brooks Atkinson Th., Feb. 22, 1961); played Theodoric in *Romulus* (Music Box, Jan. 10, 1962); and appeared in off-Bway productions of *Dr. Willy Nilly* (Barbizon-Plaza Th., June 4, 1959); *Dif'rent* (Mermaid, Oct. 17, 1961); and *Night of the Auk* (Cricket, May 21, 1963).

He also appeared in stock productions with the Fred Miller Th., the Cambridge (Mass.) Drama Festival, Gladiators Arena Th., Linden Circle Th., the Hyde Park Playhouse, and Woodstock Summer Th.

Mr. Sherin's early directing credits include *Tristram* (Kaufmann Aud.); *Major Barbara* (Fred Miller Th.); an off-Bway production of *Diedre of the Sorrows* (Gate, N.Y.C., Oct. 14, 1959); Equity Library Theatre productions (Lennox Hill Playhouse) of *Joan of Lorraine* (Feb. 21, 1960), and *Mister Roberts;* several seasons of stock at the Wickford Summer Th. and the Center Players (Fairlawn, N.J.); and various industrial shows.

In 1964, he became assistant producing director at the Arena Stage (Washington, D.C.) where he staged *The Wall* (Jan. 29, 1964); *Dark of the Moon* (May 27, 1964); *Galileo* (Oct. 29, 1964); *Billy Budd* (Jan 7, 1965); *He Who Gets Slapped* (Mar. 18, 1965); a double-bill of *The Lonesome Train* and *Hard Travelin'* (May 27, 1965); *Project Immortality* (Feb. 1966); *Macbeth* (Oct. 25, 1966); *The Inspector General* (Feb. 23, 1967); *The Andersonville Trial* (May 23, 1967); *Major Barbara* (Sept. 26, 1967); *The Great White Hope* (world premiere, Dec. 12, 1967); *The Iceman Cometh* (Mar. 26, 1968); and *King Lear* (Jan. 21, 1969).

He made his Bway directing debut with *The Great White Hope* (Alvin, N.Y.C., Oct. 3, 1968); subsequently staging *Glory! Hallelujah!* (world premiere, American Conservatory Th., San Francisco, May 21, 1969); *The Pastime of Monsieur Robert* (Center Th. Group, Mark Taper Forum, Los Angeles, Nov. 5, 1970); *The Time of Your Life* (Kennedy Ctr., Washington, D.C., Jan. 15, 1972); *An Evening with Richard Nixon and . .* (Sam S. Shubert Th., N.Y.C., Apr. 30, 1972); for the American Shakespeare Festival, *Major Barbara* (Festival Th., Stratford, Conn., June 27, 1972); *6 Rms Riv Vu* (Helen Hayes Th., N.Y.C., Oct. 17, 1972); *Baba Goya* (American Place Th., May 9, 1973) which was retitled *Nourish the Beast* and re-opened (Cherry Lane Th., Oct. 3, 1973); for The NY Shakespeare Fest., *King Lear* (Delacorte, July 26, 1973); *Find Your Way Home* (Brooks Atkinson Th., Jan. 2, 1974); made his London debut directing *A Streetcar Named Desire* (Piccadilly Th., Mar. 14, 1974); subsequently staging *Of Mice and Men* (Brooks Atkinson Th., Feb. 9, 1975); the pre-Bway tryout of *The Red Devil Battery Sign* (opened Shubert, Boston, June 18, 1975; closed there June 28, 1975); *Sweet Bird of Youth* (Kennedy Ctr., Washington, D.C., Nov. 1975; Brooklyn Academy of Music, N.Y.C., Dec. 3, 1975; and Harkness, Dec. 28, 1975); and *Rex* (Lunt-Fontanne, Apr. 25, 1976).

Films. Mr. Sherin wrote the screenplay for *Over the Bridge;* wrote and was associate producer for *Obediah;* and directed *Valdez Is Coming* (UA, 1971); and *My Old Man's Place* (Cinerama, 1972).

Television. Mr. Sherin appeared as an actor on over seventy-five television dramas including The Nurses and Omnibus.

Awards. He received the Drama Desk, Outer Circle, and *Variety* Poll of NY Drama Critics awards (1968–69) for his direction of *The Great White Hope.*

SHEVELOVE, BURT. Playwright, director. b. Burton George Shevelove, Sept. 19, 1915, Newark, N.J., to Jacob J. and Betty (Lessner) Shevelove. Father, flour broker. Grad. Newark (N.J.) Acad., 1933; Brown Univ., A.B. 1937; attended Yale Univ., 1937–39. Served as ambulance driver for Amer. Field Service, 1942–44. Member of DGA; SSD&C; WGA; Dramatists Guild; The Players. Address: One Hyde Park St., London W2, England tel. 01-723-8828.

Theatre. Mr. Shevelove, billed as Billings Brown, first wrote for the stage for the revue *Small Wonder*, which he also directed (Coronet, N.Y.C., Sept. 15, 1948). Billed as Burt Shevelove, he subsequently directed *Kiss Me, Kate* (NY City Ctr., May 9, 1956); was librettist, with Larry Gelbart, of *A Funny Thing Happened on the Way to the Forum* (Alvin, N.Y.C., May 8, 1962); adapted and directed William Gillette's farce, *Too Much Johnson* (Phoenix, N.Y.C., Jan. 16, 1964); *Hallelujah, Baby* (Martin Beck Th., N.Y.C., Apr. 26, 1967); *No, No, Nannette* (46 St. Th., N.Y.C., Jan. 19, 1971); and the revival of *A Funny Thing Happened on the Way to the Forum* (Lunt-Fontanne, N.Y.C., Mar. 30, 1972).

Films. Mr. Shevelove was co-author and associate producer of *The Wrong Box* (Col., 1966).

Television. Mr. Shevelove has directed and/or produced *Art Carney Meets Peter and the Wolf* (ABC, Nov. 30, 1958); *Art Carney Meets the Sorcerer's Apprentice* (ABC, Apr. 5, 1959); Art Carney Specials (NBC, 1950–60); Chevrolet Golden Anniversary Show (NBC, Nov. 13, 1961); *The Opening Night* (CBS, Sept. 24, 1962); The Judy Garland Show (CBS, Mar. 19, 1963); The Bell Telephone Hour (NBC, 1960–64); The Red Buttons Show (CBS); The Jack Paar show (CBS); The Bill Baird Show (CBS); *An Evening with Richard Rodgers* (CBS); and The Victor Borge Show (NBC); and adapted and directed *June Moon* (NET).

Awards. Mr. Shevelove received an Antoinette Perry (Tony) Award (1963) for the libretto of *A Funny Thing Happened on the Way to the Forum;* a Christopher Award (1959) as producer of *Art Carney Meets Peter and the Wolf;* and a NATAS (Emmy) Award as director of *V.I.P.*

SHIPLEY, JOSEPH T. Drama critic, writer, teacher. b. Aug. 19, 1893, to Jay R. and Jennie (Fragner) Shipley. Father, lawbook salesman; mother, probation officer. Grad. City Coll. of N.Y., B.A. 1912; Columbia Univ., M.A. 1914; Ph.D. 1931. Two marriages; three sons, one daughter. Member of NY Drama Critics Circle (pres.,

1952–54; secy., 1968–to date); PEN; Phi Beta Kappa. Address: 29 W. 46th St., New York, NY 10036, tel. (212) 246-4314; (May-Oct.); 13 Gledhow Gardens, London, S.W. 50 AY, England tel. (01) 370-3521.

Mr. Shipley was drama critic for *The New Leader* (previously named *The Call*, and *The Leader*) 1918–1962. Abroad, he covered the NY theatre for *The Guardian* (England, 1961–63) for which he wrote occasional reports; and for *Theatre* (Paris, 1954–63), to which he contributed a monthly letter.

For Erwin Piscator's dramatic workshop, he conducted a seminar for professional playwrights (1953); and served as dean (1954–56).

Television and Radio. In his capacity as drama critic, he has appeared on Footlights Forum (WOR, 1938–39); and First Nights (WEVD, 1940–to date). He wrote *Mme. Sans Gene* which was produced on the Ford Hour (NBC).

Other Activities. Mr. Shipley has been associate professor and head of the department of English at Yeshiva Coll. (now Yeshiva Univ., 1928–42); and lecturer on literary and dramatic criticism for the graduate division of the City Coll. of N.Y. (1926–48). As the guest of fourteen governments, he spent a year traveling around the world lecturing on American life as shown in the theatre (1957–58).

Published Works. He is the author of *Guide to Great Plays* (1956), in which 670 plays, from Aeschylus to Tennessee Williams, are summarized, analyzed, and presented with a stage history and the comments of other critics; *Five Major Plays of Ibsen* (1965); *The Art of Eugene O'Neill* (1928); *The Quest for Literature* (1931); *Trends in Literature* (1949); *A Dictionary of World Literary Terms* (3rd ed., completely revised, 1970); over fifteen individual study guides to the plays of Shakespeare (1963–66); and numerous other books dealing with non-theatre subjects. He has written critical articles and reviews in the NY *Times*, *The Tribune; The Nation; Stage; The Saturday Review of Literature;* and *Poet Love*, among others; and contributed an article entitled "Word and Letter Games" to the *Encyclopedia Britannica* (15th edition).

Awards. Mr. Shipley is an honorary overseas member of The Critics Circle (London); and received the 1975 Townsend Harris Medal for distinguished contributions in his field from the City College of New York.

Recreation. Tennis, walking, chess, contemplation, word games.

SHOEMAKER, ANN. Actress. b. Ann Dorothea Shoemaker, Jan. 10, 1891, Brooklyn, N.Y., to Charles Frederick and Rita (Miller) Shoemaker. Father, chief of US Revenue Cutter Service (US Coast Guard). Attended Fairmount Seminary, Washington, D.C. Married 1923 to Henry Stephenson, actor (dec. 1956). Member of AEA; SAG; AFTRA; Episcopal Actors Guild; Actors Fund.

Theatre. Miss Shoemaker made her debut in production with the Chestnut St. Th. Stock Co. (Philadelphia, Pa., 1909); her N.Y.C. debut as Fanny Owens in *Nobody's Widow* (Hudson, Nov. 15, 1910); subsequently appeared in productions with the Albee Stock Co. (Providence, R.I., 1910–11); the Baker Stock Co. (Portland, Ore., 1914); the Keith Co. (Brooklyn, 1916); in vaudeville (1916–18); and appeared with the Union Hill (N.J.) Co. (1917–18).

She toured in *The Fool* (Chicago, Ill., 1923–24); played Sybil in *The Great God Brown* (Greenwich Village Th., N.Y.C., Jan. 23, 1926); Stella Bancroft in *The Noose* (Hudson, Oct. 20, 1926); succeeded Antoinette Perry as Margaret Newell in *The Ladder* (Mansfield, Oct. 22, 1926); played Pauline Chester in *We All Do* (Bijou, Feb. 28, 1927); "Min" Denton in *Speakeasy* (Mansfield, Sept. 26, 1927); Emily Sanford in *Whispering Friends* (Hudson, Feb. 28, 1928); Alice Keith in *Tonight at Twelve* (Hudson, Nov. 15, 1928); Mrs. Patience Boynton-Woodhouse in *Button, Button* (Bijou, Oct. 22, 1929); Isabella in *The Novice and the Duke* (Assembly, Dec. 9, 1929); and Lady Howard in *The Silent Witness* (Morosco, Mar. 23, 1931).

She appeared in productions in Newport, R.I. (1931); succeeded Merle Maddern as Lillian Garfield in *The Left Bank* (Little, N.Y.C., Oct. 5, 1931); played Helena Abercrombie in *Black Sheep* (Morosco, Oct. 13, 1932); Rosalind in *As You Like It* (Shakespeare Th., Nov. 26, 1932); Cap in *Proof Through the Night* (Morosco, Dec. 25, 1942); Miss McQuillan in *The Rich Full Life* (John Golden Th., Nov. 9, 1945); Lizzie Southworth in *Woman Bites Dog* (Belasco Th., Apr. 17, 1946); and Mrs. Brewster in *Twilight Walk* (Fulton, Sept. 24, 1951).

She appeared as Serena in the pre-Bway tryout of *The Intruder* (opened Locust St. Th., Philadelphia, Pa., Dec. 4, 1952; closed Northampton, Mass., Jan. 12, 1953); Helen Brown in *The Living Room* (Henry Miller's Th., N.Y.C., Nov. 17, 1954); toured as Monica Breedlove in the national company of *The Bad Seed* (opened Playhouse, Wilmington, Del., Dec. 1, 1955; closed Harris, Chicago, Ill., June 30, 1956); Mrs. Railton-Bell in the national company of the double bill *Separate Tables* (opened Locust St. Th., Philadelphia, Pa., Sept. 30, 1957; closed Blackstone, Chicago, Ill., Feb. 1, 1958); took over the role of Sara Delano Roosevelt in *Sunrise at Campobello* (Cort, N.Y.C., Jan. 30, 1958), also playing this role in its national tour (opened Blackstone, Chicago, Ill., Sept. 21, 1959; closed Tower Th., Atlanta, Ga., Jan. 30, 1960); played Lady Bracknell in *The Importance of Being Earnest* (Madison Ave. Playhouse, N.Y.C., Feb. 25, 1963); and was Mrs. Walsingham in *Half a Sixpence* (Broadhurst, Apr. 25, 1965).

Films. Miss Shoemaker appeared in *Alice Adams* (RKO, 1935); *Babes in Arms* (MGM, 1939); *Strike Up the Band* (MGM, 1940); *My Favorite Wife* (RKO, 1940); *Seventeen* (Par., 1940); *Magic Town* (RKO, 1947); and *Sunrise at Campobello* (WB, 1960).

Television. Between 1949 and 1956, she appeared on Omnibus (CBS), Studio One (CBS), Robert Montgomery Presents (NBC), Philco Television Playhouse (NBC), and Armstrong Circle Th. (CBS).

She also appeared on Dr. Kildare (NBC, 1962), Route 66 (CBS, 1962), and Mr. Novak (NBC, 1963).

SHORT, SYLVIA. Actress, singer. b. Sylvia Wheeler Short, Oct. 22, 1927, Concord, Mass., to Seabury T. and Eleanor (Ballou) Short. Father, sugar refiner; mother, singer. Grad. Concord Acad., 1945; Smith Coll., B.A. (Phi Beta Kappa) 1949. Studied acting at Old Vic Th. Sch., London, England, 1949–51; at Herbert Berghof (H B) Studio, N.Y.C., 1953–54; singing with Earl Rogers, N.Y.C., two years; Henry Jacoby, N.Y.C., four years. Married Feb. 7, 1953, to Fritz Weaver, actor; one son, one daughter. Member of AEA; AFTRA.

Theatre. Miss Short made her debut at age six as the daughter in a Concord (Mass.) Players' production of *Rip Van Winkle* (1933). Her professional debut was as Maria in *On Approval* (Dorset Playhouse, Vt., Summer 1947); followed by an engagement as contralto soloist in Mozart's "Requiem" (Smith Coll., 1948). She appeared with the Group 20 Players (Wellesley, Mass., Summers 1948–53); played the Whore in *Desire Caught by the Tail* (Living Th., N.Y.C., Jan. 1952); Portia in *The Merchant of Venice* (Barter Th., Abingdon, Va., Summer 1952); the title role in *Joan of Lorraine* (Bermudiana Th., Bermuda, Nov. 1953); and Kate in *The Taming of the Shrew* and the title role in *Saint Joan* (San Juan, P.R., Feb. 1954).

Miss Short played Miss Sterling in *The Clandestine Marriage* (Provincetown Playhouse, N.Y.C., Oct. 3, 1954); appeared in *The Passion of Gross* (Th. de Lys, Nov. 1955); and played Regan in Orson Welles' *King Lear* (NY City Ctr., Jan. 12, 1956). With the American Shakespeare Festival (Stratford, Conn.), she played Mariana in *Measure for Measure* (June 27, 1956); and at the Phoenix Th. (N.Y.C.), played Mary in *Family Reunion* (Oct. 20, 1958) and Lady Bountiful in *The Beaux' Stratagem* (Feb. 24, 1959); and played Mrs. Juniper in *The Golden Apple* (York, Feb. 12, 1962).

Television. Miss Short played Violet in *Man and Superman* (Hallmark Hall of Fame, NBC, 1957); has appeared on the US Steel Hour (NBC, 1959); and The Nurses (CBS, 1962).

Awards. Miss Short received a Fulbright Fellowship to study at the Old Vic Th. Sch. (1949–51); and the Barter Theatre Audition (1952).

Recreation. Skin-diving, sailing, marine biology, block-flute or recorder playing.

SHULL, LEO. Publisher, producer, columnist. b. Feb. 8, 1913, Milwaukee, Wis. Grad. Univ. of Pennsylvania, B.S. 1934; Temple Univ., M.A. 1936; attended New Sch. for Social Research, 1939–40. Married 1948, to Claire Klar; one son, one daughter. Member of Dramatists Guild; The Drama Desk; AGVA. 136 W. 44th St., New York, NY 10036, tel. (212) JU 6-6900.

Pre-Theatre. Journalism.

Theatre. Mr. Shull has been publisher of the weekly theatrical trade paper, *Show Business*, and publisher and writer for *Show Business Syndicate; Show Guide; Summer Theatres; Model's Guide; Who's Where; Angels; Production Directory; Dancer's Guide; Casting Guide;* and *Playwrighting for Broadway* (1941–to date).

Mr. Shull produced *Genius, Inc.* (St. James Th., N.Y.C., Jan. 4, 1943); *Norman Corwin Plays* (45 St. Th., 1943); *Political Revue* (Belasco, Oct. 1946); and, in association with Mary Learson and Anne Eisen, the double bill, *The Virtuous Island* and *The Apollo of Bellac* (Carnegie Hall Playhouse, Apr. 9, 1957).

Radio. Mr. Shull produced Show Business (WNEW, 1952).

SHULMAN, MAX. Novelist, playwright. b. Mar. 14, 1919, St. Paul, Minn., to Abraham and Bessie (Karchmer) Shulman. Grad. Univ. of Minnesota, B.A. 1942. Married Dec. 21, 1941, to Carol Rees (dec. May 17, 1963); three sons, one daughter; married June 14, 1964, to Mary Gordon Bryant, actress. Member of ALA; Dramatists Guild; WGA.

Theatre. Mr. Shulman adapted his novel, *Barefoot Boy with Cheek*, into a musical for the N.Y.C. stage (Martin Beck Th., Apr. 3, 1947); wrote, with Robert Paul Smith, *The Tender Trap* (Longacre, Oct. 13, 1954); and was librettist for *How Now, Dow Jones* (Lunt-Fontanne Th., Dec. 7, 1967).

Films. He wrote the screenplay for The Affairs of Dobie Gillis (MGM, 1953); his novel, *Rally Round the Flag Boys* was adapted for a movie (20th-Fox, 1958).

Television. He is the creator and writer of the television series Dobie Gillis (CBS, 1959–63); and has been a creative supervisor of comedy program development for MCA Revue Studios' Universal-TV. He has also appeared as a guest on Book Beat (NET, 1965).

Published Works. Mr. Shulman is the author of *Barefoot Boy with Cheek* (1943); *The Feather Merchants* (1944); *The Zebra Derby* (1946); *Sleep Till Noon* (1950); *The Many Loves of Dobie Gillis* (1953); *Max Shulman's Guided Tour of Campus Humor* (1955); *Rally Round the Flag Boys* (1957); *Anyone Got a Match* (1964).

He has also written short stories and articles for magazines, including an article entitled "Is It Ready?" for *TV Guide* (1965).

SHUMAN, MORT. Playwright, composer, singer. Member of AEA.

With Eric Blau, Mr. Shuman conceived the idea for *Jacques Brel Is Alive and Well and Living in Paris* (Village Gate, N.Y.C., Jan. 22, 1968), for which he wrote additional material, and in which he sometimes appeared; and wrote the music for *How To Get Rid of It* (Astor Place Th., Nov. 17, 1974).

SHUMLIN, HERMAN. Producer, director. b. Dec. 6, 1898, Atwood, Colo., to George and Rebecca (Slavin) Shumlin. Father, retail merchant, rancher. Attended Barringer Sch. Newark, N.J. Married 1968 to Diana Green Krasny. Address: 150 E. 77th St., New York, NY 10021, tel. (212) 737-8884.

Theatre. Mr. Shumlin was a reporter for the theatrical weekly. *The New York Clipper* (1924–25); motion picture editor for *Billboard* (1924–25); press representative for Schwab and Mandel (1926); and manager for Jed Harris (1927).

Mr. Shumlin produced, with Paul Streger, *Celebrity* (Lyceum, Dec. 26, 1927); *The Command Performance* (Klaw Th., Oct. 3, 1928); *Tonight at Twelve* (Hudson Th., Nov. 15, 1928); directed *Wine of Choice* (Guild Th., Feb. 21, 1938); produced, with George Haight and H. C. Potter, *Button, Button* (Bijou, Oct. 22, 1929); *The Last Mile* (Sam H. Harris Th., Feb. 13, 1930); with Harry Moses, *Grand Hotel* (National, Nov. 13, 1930); *Clear All Wires* (Times Sq. Th., Sept. 14, 1932); with Gilbert Miller, *The Bride of Torozko* (Henry Miller's Th., Sept. 13, 1934); *The Children's Hour* (Maxine Elliott's Th., Nov. 20, 1934); *Sweet Mystery of Life* (Shubert Th., Oct. 11, 1935); *Days to Come* (Vanderbilt Th., Dec. 15, 1936); *The Merchant of Yonkers* (Guild Th., Dec. 28, 1938); *The Little Foxes* (National, Feb. 15, 1939); *The Male Animal* (Cort, Jan. 9, 1940); and *The Corn Is Green* (National, Nov. 26, 1940).

He also produced *Watch on the Rhine* (Martin Beck Th., Apr. 1, 1941); *The Great Big Doorstep* (Morosco, Nov. 26, 1942); *The Searching Wind* (Fulton Th., Apr. 12, 1944); *The Visitor* (Henry Miller's Th., Oct. 17, 1944); directed *Kiss Them for Me* (Belasco Th., Mar. 20, 1945); produced *Jeb* (Martin Beck Th., Feb. 21, 1946); directed *The Biggest Thief in Town* (Mansfield Th., Mar. 30, 1949); produced, with Leland Hayward, *Daphne Laureola* (Music Box, Sept. 18, 1950); directed *The High Ground* (48 St. Th., Feb. 20, 1951); produced *Lace on Her Petticoat* (Booth Th., Sept. 4, 1951); *To Dorothy, a Son* (John Golden Th., Nov. 19, 1951); *Gertie* (Plymouth, Jan. 30, 1952); directed *Candida* (National, Apr. 22, 1952); *The Gambler* (Lyceum, Oct. 13, 1952); a revival of *Regina* (NY City Ctr., Apr. 4, 1953); *Wedding Breakfast* (48 St. Th., Nov. 20, 1954); produced, with Margo Jones, *Inherit the Wind* (National, Apr. 21, 1955); directed *Tall Story* (Belasco Th., Jan. 29, 1959); *Little Moon of Alban* (Longacre, Dec. 1, 1960); *Dear Me, the Sky Is Falling* (Music Box, Mar. 2, 1963); produced, with Roger L. Stevens, *Bicycle Ride to Nevada* (Cort, Sept. 24, 1963); *The Deputy* (Brooks Atkinson Th., Feb. 26, 1964); directed *Spofford,* which he also wrote (ANTA Th., Dec. 14, 1967); produced *Soldiers* (Billy Rose Th., May 1, 1968); and, with Diana Shumlin, *Transfers* (Village South Th., Jan. 22, 1970).

Films. Mr. Shumlin was assistant producer to Samuel Goldwyn (1931); and directed documentary films for the Office of War Information (1942–43).

He directed *Watch on the Rhine* (WB, 1943); and *The Confidential Agent* (WB, 1945).

SHURTLEFF, MICHAEL. Playwright, casting director. b. Charles Gordon Michael Shurtleff, July 3, Oslo, Norway, to Charles Joseph and Ruth (Matheson) Shurtleff. Grad. Austin H.S., Chicago, Ill.; Lawrence Coll. B.A.; Yale Univ. Sch. of Drama, M.F.A. Served WW II, US Army, editor of camp newspaper service, PTO. Member of Dramatists Guild; WGA; New Dramatists Comm.; Sigma Phi Epsilon. Address: 22 W. 24th St., New York, NY 10010, tel. (212) CH 3-5689.

Pre-Theatre. Teacher, court reporter.

Theatre. Since 1963, Mr. Shurtleff has been president of Casting Consultants, a central casting organization in N.Y.C. His firm has cast for *Here's Love* (Shubert Th., N.Y.C., Oct. 3, 1963), *Dylan* (Plymouth, Jan. 18, 1963), *Any Wednesday* (Music Box, Feb. 18, 1964), and *Anyone Can Whistle* (Majestic, Apr. 4, 1964).

He wrote *Call Me by My Rightful Name* (One Sheridan Sq., Jan. 31, 1961); *Come to the Palace of Sin* (Th. de Lys, Dec. 10, 1963); *I Hate to See a Party End; Four of Them* (Friday Th., N.Y.C., 1971); *I Want to Be With You* (NY Theatre Ensemble, N.Y.C., July 10, 1974); and *Take Very Good Care of Yourself* (Friday Th., Dec. 1, 1972).

Mr. Shurtleff started in the theatre as casting director and production assistant to William Hammerstein for musical plays at NY City Ctr. (1957–60). For David Merrick Productions, he was casting director for *The World of Suzie Wong* (Broadhurst, Oct. 14, 1958), *Gypsy* (Bway. Th., May 21, 1959), *The Good Soup* (Plymouth, Mar. 2, 1960), *Irma La Douce* (Plymouth, Sept. 29, 1960), *A Taste of Honey* (Lyceum, Oct. 4, 1960), *Becket* (St. James, Oct. 5, 1960), *Do Re Me* (St. James, Dec. 26, 1960), *Carnival!* (Imperial, Apr. 13, 1961), *Stop the World I Want to Get Off* (Shubert, Oct. 3, 1962), *Oliver!* (Imperial, Jan. 6, 1963); *1776* (46 St. Th., Mar. 16, 1969); *Jesus Christ, Superstar* (Mark Hellinger Th., Oct. 12, 1971); *Pippin* (Imperial, Oct. 23, 1972); *Miss Moffat* (pre-Bway tour, 1974); and *Chicago* (46 St. Th., May 12, 1975).

Films. He was casting director for *All the Way Home* (Par., 1963); *Andy* (U, 1964); *The Sound of Music* (20th-Fox), *The Sand Pebbles* (20th-Fox), wrote the screenplay for *Roar Like a Dove* (Col.); wrote the screenplay and directed *Call Me by My Rightful Name* (Don Murray Prods., 1973); and was casting director for *1776* (Col., 1972); and *Jesus Christ, Superstar* (U, 1973).

Television. He wrote the television play, *But If I Wait All the Best Boys Will Be Gone,* and was casting director for the series, East Side/West Side (CBS, Sept. 1963).

Recreation. Swimming, beachcombing, frisbee, badminton, dancing and bridge.

SHWARTZ, MARTIN. Press representative. b. Sept. 30, 1923, Boston, Mass., to Isadore and Bella (Smilow) Shwartz. Grad. Boston Latin Sch., 1940; Harvard Univ., B.A. 1944. Served USN, 1944–46; rank, Lt. (jg). Member of ATPAM. Address: (home) 2866 Belden Drive, Los Angeles, CA 90068, tel. (213) 469-0827; (bus.) LACLO, 135 N. Grand Ave., Los Angeles, CA 90012, tel. (213) 620-1280.

Pre-Theatre. Instructor of mathematics, Tufts Coll. (1943–44); civilian mathematician, US Office of Naval Research (1946–47).

Theatre. Since 1948, Mr. Shwartz has been a press representative for approximately 90 Bway productions including *My Fair Lady, Camelot, Mr. President, Do I Hear A Waltz?, Funny Girl, George M!, The Great White Hope,* the musical *Gigi, The Devil's Advocate, At the Drop of a Hat, Tovarich, The Hollow Crown, Auntie Mame, An Evening with Yves Montand, Kismet, I Am a Camera, Mrs. McThing, The Member of the Wedding,* The Royal Shakespeare Co., and the Music Th. of Lincoln Center. In 1972, he joined the Los Angeles Civic Light Opera Association as General Press Representative.

Films. Mr. Shwartz was a press representative for *Around the World in Eighty Days* (UA, 1956).

SHYRE, PAUL. Playwright, actor, director, producer. Grad. Miami (Fla.) H.S., 1945; attended Univ. of Florida, 1945–46; grad. AADA, 1947. Studied for the theatre with Harold Clurman, 1953–55. Served US Army, 1944–45; rank, Pvt. Member of AEA; AFTRA; SAG; The Players; Dramatist's League; Directors' Guild; SSDC. Address: 162 W. 56th St., New York, NY 10019, tel. (212) JU 2-5379.

Theatre. Mr. Shyre adapted and appeared in *Pictures in the Hallway* (48 St. Th., N.Y.C., Sept. 16, 1956), and *I Knock at the Door* (Belasco, Sept. 29, 1957), both of which he produced with Lucille Lortel and Howard Gottfried. He produced with Noel Behn, Howard Gottfried, and Lewis Manilow, *Purple Dust,* in which he played Basil Stoke (Cherry Lane, Dec. 27, 1956); played Shanaar in *Cock-a-Doodle Dandy,* which he produced in association with Lucille Lortel and Howard Gottfried (Carnegie Hall Playhouse, Nov. 12, 1958); adapted and directed *U.S.A.* (Martinique, Oct. 28, 1959); and *Drums Under the Windows,* which he also produced (Cherry Lane, Oct. 13, 1960); directed a double-bill of *Diff'rent* and *The Long Voyage Home* (Mermaid, Oct. 17, 1961); and adapted and directed *Creditors* (Mermaid, Jan. 25, 1962). For the Theatre Group, Univ. of California at Los Angeles, he adapted and directed *The Child Buyer* (Humanities Th., May 14, 1962). He was artistic director for the Fred Miller Th. (Milwaukee, Wis., 1962–63). Adapted and directed *A Whitman Portrait* (Gramercy Arts Th., N.Y.C., Oct. 11, 1966; and Open Space Th., London, 1967); adapted and directed *Will Rogers' U.S.A.* (pre-Bway tour, 1970; and Helen Hayes Th., N.Y.C., May 6, 1974); appeared in a revival of *Pictures in the Hallway* (Forum, N.Y.C., Apr. 29, 1971); and *An Unpleasant Evening with H. L. Mencken* (Ford's Th., Washington, D.C., Mar. 8, 1972; and Cherry Lane Th., N.Y.C., Jan. 16, 1975).

Awards. Mr. Shyre received a special *Village Voice* Off-Bway (Obie) Award (1957); has received the Vernon Rice Award (1958); and the Brandeis Univ. Creative Arts Award (1958). In 1965, Boston Univ. honored Mr. Shyre by establishing a collection of papers in his name.

Recreation. Music, collecting clocks, swimming, walking.

SIDNEY, SYLVIA. Actress. b. Sopia Kosow, Aug. 10, 1910, Bronx, N.Y., to Victor and Rebecca (Saperstein) Kosow. Attended N.Y.C. schools; Theatre Guild Sch., 1926. Studied with Rouben Mamoulian; Alfred Lunt and Lynn Fontanne; the Langners. Married Oct. 1935, to Bennett Cerf, publisher (marr. dis. 1936); married 1938, to Luther Adler, actor (marr. dis. 1946); one son; married 1947 to Carlton Alsop (marr. dis. 1951). Member of AEA; SAG; AFTRA. Address: South St., Roxbury, CT 06783, tel. (203) 354-0883.

Theatre. Miss Sidney played the title role in *Prunella,* her Th. Guild Sch. graduation play (Garrick, N.Y.C., June 15, 1926); made her professional debut in *The Challenge of Youth* (Poli's Th., Wash., D.C., Oct 11, 1926); her Bway debut succeeding (Jan. 3, 1927); Grace Durkin as Anita in *The Squall* (48 St. Th., Nov. 11, 1926); played Annabelle Porter in *Crime* (Eltinge, Feb. 22, 1927); Mary Norton in *Mirrors* (Forrest, Jan. 18, 1928); Amy in *The Breaks* (Klaw, Apr. 16, 1928); Rosalie in *Gods of the Lightning* (Little, Oct. 24, 1928); Elizabeth Girard in *Nice Women* (Longacre, June 10, 1929); and Patricia in *Cross Roads* (Morosco, Nov. 11, 1929).

She appeared as Patsy Coster in *Many a Slip* (Little, Feb. 3, 1930); Dot in *Bad Girl* (Hudson, Oct. 2, 1930); Lola Hobbs in *To Quito and Back* (Guild, Oct. 6, 1937); toured as Eliza in *Pygmalion* and in *Tonight at 8:30* (Summer 1938); and played Stella Goodman in the Group Th. production of *The Gentle People* (Belasco, N.Y.C., Jan. 5, 1939). She toured the US as Linda Brown in *Accent on Youth* (1941); Mrs. Manningham in *Angel Street* (opened Baltimore, Feb. 9, 1942); again as Eliza in *Pygmalion* (1942–43); and in the title role in *Jane Eyre* (1943); appeared in the pageant, *We Will Never Die* (Madison Square Garden, N.Y.C., 1943); and toured in *Joan of Lorraine* (1947), *Kind Lady* (1948), *O Mistress Mine* (1948–49), *The Two Mrs. Carrolls* (1949), *Pygmalion* (1949), *Goodbye, My Fancy* (1950), *Anne of the Thousand Days* (1950), and *The Innocents* (1950–51).

She played Alicia Christie in the pre-Bway tryout of *Black Chiffon* (opened Hartman, Columbus, Ohio, Oct. 8, 1951; closed Locust St. Th., Philadelphia, Nov. 3, 1951); Fanny Benton in the summer tryout of *The Gypsies Wore High Hats* (Falmouth Playhouse Coonamessett, Mass., Aug. 4, 1952); succeeded (John Golden Th., N.Y.C., Dec. 1952) Betty Field as Agnes in *The Fourposter* (Ethel Barrymore Th., Oct. 24, 1951); and played Anna in *A Very Special Baby* (Playhouse, Nov. 14, 1956). In 1958–59, she toured the US in the title role in *Auntie Mame,* including a N.Y.C. revival (NY City Ctr., Aug. 11, 1958); played Cora Flood in a stock tour of *The Dark at the Top of the Stairs* (Summer 1960); and Mrs. Kolowitz in *Enter Laughing* (Henry Miller's Th., N.Y.C., Mar. 13, 1963).

Miss Sidney played Beatrice Wright in "Damn You, Scarlett O'Hara" and Leslie Ross in "All My Pretty Little Ones," a double-bill entitled *Riverside Drive* (Th. de Lys, Feb. 4, 1964); toured as Mrs. Manningham in *Angel Street* (Summer 1964), in *The Silver Cord,* and in *Kind Lady;* toured with the National Repertory Th. (opened Nov. 8, 1965; closed Los Angeles, Mar 26, 1966), as Mrs. Malaprop in *The Rivals* and Constance, the Madwoman of Passy, in *The Madwoman of Chaillot;* played Regina in *The Little Foxes* (Summer, 1966); Mrs. Banks in a national tour of *Barefoot in the Park* (opened Playhouse, Wilmington, Del., Oct. 13, 1966; closed Endicott, N.Y., Dec. 10, 1966); Lady Bracknell in *The Importance of Being Earnest* (Oakland, Calif., Rep. Th., Dec. 1966); succeeded (Apr. 4, 1967) Ilka Chase as Mrs. Banks in the Bway company of *Barefoot in the Park* (Biltmore, Oct. 23, 1963); for the National Rep. Th., played Mrs. Hardcastle in *She Stoops to Conquer* (Ford's Th., Washington, D.C., Mar. 26, 1968); toured the US and Canada as Mrs. Baker in *Come Blow Your Horn* (opened Royal Alexandra Th., Toronto, Canada, Dec. 26, 1968); played Fräulein Schneider in a stock production of *Cabaret* (Wallingford, Conn., Summer 1970); Mrs. Baker in *Butterflies Are Free* (St. Louis, Mo., Summer 1972); Mrs. Venable in *Suddenly, Last Summer* (Ivanhoe Chicago, Jan. 1973); and Matty Seaton in the American premiere of *A Family and a Fortune* (Seattle, Wash., Rep. Th., Jan. 16, 1974).

Films. Since her debut in *Through Different Eyes* (Fox, 1929), Miss Sidney has appeared in *An American Tragedy* (Par., 1931); *City Streets* (Par., 1931); *Many a Slip* (U, 1931); *Confessions of a Co-Ed* (Par., 1931); *Street Scene* (UA, 1931); *The Miracle Man* (Par., 1932); *Ladies of the Big House* (Par., 1932); *Merrily We Go to Hell* (Par., 1932); *Madame Butterfly* (Par., 1932); *Nice Women* (U, 1932); *Make Me a Star* (Par., 1932); *Pick Up* (Par., 1933); *Jennie Gerhardt* (Par., 1933); *Good Dame* (Par., 1934); *Thirty Day Princess* (Par., 1934); *Behold My Wife* (Par., 1935); *Accent on Youth* (Par., 1935); *Mary Burns, Fugitive* (Par., 1935); *Trail of the Lonesome Pine* (Par., 1936); *Fury* (MGM, 1936); *Woman Alone* Gaumont-British, 1937; US *Sabotage*); *You Only Live Once* (UA, 1937); *Dead End* (UA, 1937); *You and Me* (Par., 1938); *City Streets* (Col., 1938); *One Third of a Nation* (Par., 1939); *The Wagons Roll at Night* (WB, 1941); *Blood on the Sun* (UA, 1945); *The Searching Wind* (Par., 1946); *Mr. Ace* (UA, 1946); *Love from a Stranger* (Eagle-Lion, 1947); *Les Miserables* (20th-Fox, 1952)); *Violent Saturday* (20th-Fox, 1955); *Behind the High Wall* (U, 1956); and *Summer Wishes, Winter Dreams* (Col., 1973).

Television. Miss Sidney has appeared on Schlitz Playhouse of Stars (CBS); Tales of Tomorrow (ABC); Lux Video Th. (CBS); Broadway TV Th. (Ind.) in *Theatre* (Sept. 29, 1952), *The Letter* (Nov. 3, 1952), *Climax* (May 18, 1953), *Dark Victory* (Nov. 16, 1953), *Kind Lady* (Nov. 30, 1953), and *Angel Street* (Dec. 21, 1953); on Ford Th. (NBC); Philco Playhouse (NBC); Kraft Th. (NBC); Climax (CBS); Star Stage (NBC); Playwrights '56 (NBC); 20th Century-Fox Hour (CBS); in *The Helen Morgan Story* (Playhouse 90, CBS, May 16, 1957); GE Th. (CBS); The June Allyson Show (CBS); Naked City (ABC); Route 66 (CBS); The Defenders (CBS); The Eleventh Hour (NBC); *In the Last Place* (Yom Kippur Special, CBS, Sept. 29, 1963); The Nurses (CBS); My Three Sons (ABC); *Do Not Fold, Spindle or Mutilate* (ABC Movie of the Week, Nov. 9, 1971); and played sister Mary Joel on the serial Ryan's Hope (ABC, Sept. 11–12, 1975).

Published Works. She wrote the *Sylvia Sidney Needlepoint Book* (1968).

Awards. For her performance in *Summer Wishes, Winter Dreams*, Miss Sidney won (1974) the Natl. Board of Review Award as best supporting actress, and was nominated for an Academy (Oscar) Award as best supporting actress.

SIEGEL, ARTHUR. Composer, actor, pianist. b. Dec. 31, 1923, Lakewood, N.J., to Nathan and Fanny (Kahn) Siegel. Father, produce wholesaler. Grad. Asbury Park H.S., N.J., 1940; AADA, 1942. Studied harmony and counterpoint at Juilliard Sch. of Music; N.Y.C. Member of Dramatists' Guild; AFM, Local 802; ASCAP; AGAC. Address: 29 W. 65th St., New York, NY 10023, tel. (212) EN 2-2989.

Theatre. Mr. Siegel started as musical director and performer at the Stamford (Conn.) Playhouse (1943–44); and composed music for a revue, *Wish You Were Here* (Greenwich Playhouse, Conn., Summer 1945).

He composed the music with Jeff Bailey and performed in *Lovely Me* (Adelphi Th., N.Y.C., Dec. 25, 1946); composed music for the pre-Bway tryout of *Curtain Going Up* (opened Forrest, Philadelphia, Pa., Feb. 15, 1952; closed there Apr. 1, 1952); *New Faces of 1952* (Royale, N.Y.C., May 16, 1952); *Shoestring Revue* (President, Feb. 28, 1955); and *New Faces of 1956* (Ethel Barrymore Th., June 14, 1956).

He composed music and was pianist for *Mask and Gown* (John Golden Th., Sept. 10, 1957); pianist for *Laughs and Other Events* (Ethel Barrymore Th., Oct. 10, 1960); composed music for *New Faces of 1962* (Alvin, Feb. 1, 1962); *Not While I'm Eating* (Madison Ave. Playhouse, Dec. 19, 1961), composed incidental music for the revival of *Hay Fever* (Helen Hayes Th., Nov. 9, 1970); and *The American Hamburger League* (the New Th., Sept. 16, 1969); and composed music for *New Faces of 1968* (Booth, N.Y.C., May 2, 1968); and *A Quarter for the Ladies Room* (Village Gate, N.Y.C., Nov. 1972).

He was pianist and arranger for Eddie Cantor's one-man show (Carnegie Hall, Mar. 21, 1950), and has also written music and special material for Imogene Coca, Hermione Gingold, and others.

Films. He contributed songs to the film *New Faces* (20th-Fox, 1954).

Television and Radio. He composed music for the radio revue, *New Faces* (NBC, June–Sept. 1948) and wrote a song for the television remake of *Miracle on Thirty-fourth Street* (MGM, 1973).

Night Clubs. Mr. Siegel composed music and was pianist for the revue, *New Faces* (Persian Room, Plaza Hotel, N.Y.C., 1948); and composed music for the revue, *Come As You Are* (Versailles Restaurant, N.Y.C., Mar. 1955). He is the musical director for Kaye Ballard's night club and television guest appearances.

Discography. With Kaye Ballard, he recorded readings from the comic strip, *Peanuts* (1962); composed the music for the children's record, *Learn to Tell Time* (1963); and performed as a singer in *Rodgers and Hart Revisited* (1964).

Recreation. Collecting phonograph records, books, theatre programs, and old sheet music and old magazines.

SIEGMEISTER, ELIE. Composer, musical director, educator, writer. b. Jan. 15, 1909, New York City, to William and Bessie (Gitler) Siegmeister. Father, physician. Grad. Boy's H.S., Brooklyn, N.Y., 1924; Columbia Univ., B.A. (Phi Beta Kappa) 1927; Ecole Normale de Musique, Paris, France, 1931; attended Juilliard Sch. of Music (fellow) 1935–38. Studied with Emil Friedberger, N.Y.C., 1924–27; Wallingford Riegger, 1926; Nadia Boulanger, Paris, 1927–32. Married Jan. 15, 1930, to Hannah Mersel; two daughters. Served as consultant to War Dept., 1945. Member of AFM, Local 802; Composers and Lyricists Guild of Amer. (vice-pres., 1961–62), Amer. Music Ctr. (vice-pres., 1961–63, 69), US Govt. Information Agency for Music, ASCAP, AGAC. Chairman, Council Creative Artists, Libraries, Museums, 1972–. Address: (home) 56 Fairview Ave., Great Neck, NY tel. (516) HU 2-6861; (bus.) c/o Hofstra University, Hempstead, NY tel. (516) IV 9-7000.

Theatre. In 1939, Mr. Siegmeister organized the Amer. Ballad Singers, and directed their Town Hall (N.Y.C.) concerts and national tours (1939–47).

He composed the music for the children's show, *Doodle Dandy of the U.S.A.* (Broadhurst Th., N.Y.C., 1942), which toured the US (1942–45); he arranged folk music, composed special music and was musical director for *Sing Out, Sweet Land* (Intl., Dec. 27, 1944); was choral arranger and composed dance music for *Carnival in Flanders* (New Century, Sept. 8, 1953); and composed the ballet and incidental music for *Kean* (Bway Th., Nov. 2, 1961).

His four operas, *Darling Corie* (1951), *Miranda and the Dark Young Man* (1955), *The Mermaid in Lock No. 7* (1958), and *The Plough and the Stars* (1963–69) have been performed by opera companies in the US Canada, France, and Belgium.

Mr. Siegmeister's *Western Suite* was premiered by the NBC Symphony Orchestra under the direction of Arturo Toscanini, his First Symphony by the NY Philharmonic under Leopold Stokowski, and his Fourth Symphony by the Cleveland Orchestra under Lorin Maazel. His major compositions have been performed by the NY Philharmonic, the Cleveland (Ohio) Orchestra, Detroit (Mich.) Symphony, St. Louis (Mo.) Symphony, Los Angeles (Calif.) Philharmonic, Vienna (Austria) Philharmonic, Oslo (Norway) Philharmonic, Hamburg (Germany) Philharmonic, the Scarlatti Orchestra of Naples (Italy), the Moscow (USSR) State Symphony, the BBC Symphony and London Symphony, London, England, and others.

Films. Mr. Siegmeister composed the score for *They Came to Cordura* (Col., 1959).

Other Activities. Mr. Siegmeister has been professor of music and composer-in-residence at Hofstra Univ. In 1948, he was visiting lecturer at the Univ. of Minnesota and in 1968 composer-in-residence at Haverford Coll.

Published Works. Mr. Siegmeister wrote with Olin Downes. *A Treasury of American Song* (1940); wrote *The Music Lover's Handbook* (1943), revised as *The New Music Lover's Handbook* (1973); *Work and Sing* (1944); *Invitation to Music* (1961); and *Harmony and Melody* (2 vols.)(1965–66). He has also contributed articles to the *Encyclopedia Americana, Musical America*, and NY *Times*.

Discography. The following works of Mr. Siegmeister have been recorded: *Ozark Set* (1943); *Sing Out, Sweet Land* (1944); *Sunday in Brooklyn* (1946); Symphony No. 3 (1957); String Quartet No. 2 (1960); Sextet for Brass and Percussion (1965); Piano Sonata No. 2 (1964); Violin-Piano Sonata No. 2 (1965 and 1970); No. 3 (1965); and No. 4 (1971); *Fantasy and Soliloquy* for solo cello (1964); and *On This Ground* for piano (1971).

SIKS, GERALDINE B. Educator, writer, director. b. Geraldine Mabel Brain, Feb. 11, 1912, Thorp, Wash., to George and Alice Pearl (Ellison) Brain. Father, farmer. Grad. Thorp H.S., 1929; Central Washington Coll. of Education, A.B. 1935; Northwestern Univ., M.A. 1941. Married July 26, 1941, to Charles J. Siks, translator; two sons. Relatives in theatre: sister, Hazel Dunnington, educator; brother, Dr. George Brain, educator. Member of ATA (board member, member of exec. council, 1961–63); CTC (chmn., comm. on children's drama in the college curriculum, 1960–63); Zeta Phi Eta (Beta); Delta Kappa Gamma (hon. member). Address: (home) 1754 N.E. 90th St., Seattle, WA 98115, tel. (206) LA 5-9606; (bus.) Drama TV-102, Univ. of Washington, Seattle, WA 98105.

Mrs. Siks is professor of drama (1965–to date) at the Univ. of Washington, where she has been a member of the faculty since 1949, serving as instructor (1951–55); assistant professor (1956–60); and associate professor (1960–65).

She was the recipient of a USOE contract in 1965–66 to research theatre arts materials for use in children's drama in seventeen European countries during a nine-month period. She presented a paper to the Fourth International Assembly of ASSITEJ (International Assn. of Th. for Children and Youth) at Albany, N.Y. (1972).

She was associate director of the Children's Th. (Evanston, Ill., 1937–41); children's theatre editor, western states, for *Players* Magazine (1954–55); children's drama editor for the *Educational Theatre Journal* (1955–57); and editor of the Children's Th. *Newsletter* of the Children's Th. Conference, Region Three (1957–59).

Published Works. Mrs. Siks wrote the following plays published by the Children's Th. Press: *Marco Polo* (1941), *Prince Fairyfoot* (1947), *The Sandlewood Box* (1954), and *The Nuremburg Stove* (1956).

She wrote, with Ruth Lease, *Creative Dramatics in the Home, School and Community* (1952); and wrote *Creative Dramatics: an Art for Children* (1958) and the preface for the Japanese edition (1974); Theatre Arts Materials Research (U.S. Office of Education-Eric, 1966); "A View of Current European Theatres for Children," Educational Th. Journal (May 1967); "On Teaching Drama," *On Teaching Speech in Elementary and Junior High Schools* (Indiana Univ. Press, 1971); and "The Elementary Program," *Drama Education Guidelines* (Wash. State Pub. Instruction Office, 1972).

She was editor-in-chief, with her sister, Hazel Brain Dunnington, of *Children's Theatre and Creative Dramatics in the United States: A Monograph* (1961); and editor of *Children's Literature for Dramatization: An Anthology* (1964).

Awards. Mrs. Siks was awarded firstplace (tie) in the Seattle Junior Program's Natl. Playwriting Contest for *The Nuremburg Stove* (1954); was elected to *Blue Book of Awards* (1955); received the ATA Junior Eaves Award (1962), and their Citation for Distinguished Work in Children's Drama in the US. She received the Distinguished Service Award of Zeta Phi Eta, National Speech Arts Fraternity for Women (1967); Diploma for Distinguished Achievement; and is the subject of commendation in The World Who's Who of Women, Cambridge, England (1973).

Recreation. Writing, fishing.

SILLMAN, LEONARD. Producer, director, author. b. Leonard Dexter Sillman, May 9, 1908, Detroit, Mich., to Morton and May (Grosslight) Sillman. Father, jeweler. Attended Northern H.S., Detroit, Mich. Relatives in theatre: June Carroll, sister, actress, singer, lyricist; Sidney Carroll, brother-in-law, author. Member of AEA; AGVA. Address: (home) 17 E. 79th St., New York, NY 10021, tel. (212) UN 1-5968; (bus.) tel. (212) TR 9-1380.

Theatre. Mr. Sillman performed in an act with Lew Fields (N.J., 1924); appeared in the vaudeville act, "Sillman and Coca" (Palace, N.Y.C., 1926); which toured the Kieth Circuit (1925–27). His first role was as Dick Trevor in the national tour of *Lady Be Good* (1926); followed by an appearance in the tour of *The Greenwich Village Follies* (1927).

He played Josephus in *Loud Speaker* (52 St. Th., N.Y.C., Mar. 7, 1927); appeared in *Merry-Go-Round* (Klaw, May 31, 1927); and *Temptations of 1930* (Mayan, Los Angeles, Calif., 1930); produced, directed, and appeared in *11:15 Revue* (Hollywood, Calif., 1930); appeared in *Hullaballoo* (Pasadena Community Playhouse, Calif., 1931), where he also produced and appeared in *Low and Behold* (July 3, 1933), later taking the revue to the Music Box Th. (Hollywood, July 1933).

He assembled cast and material for *New Faces* (Fulton, N.Y.C., Mar. 15, 1934); directed and appeared in *Fools Rush In* (Playhouse, Dec. 25, 1934); in stock, directed and appeared in *Calling All Men* (Cape Playhouse, Dennis, Mass., Summer 1935); produced and directed *New Faces of 1936* (Vanderbilt, N.Y.C., May 19, 1936); directed and appeared in *Up to the Stars* (Lydia Mendelssohn Th., Ann Arbor, Mich., May–June, 1936); and *Periphery* (Pasadena Community Playhouse, Calif., April 5, 1937); and assembled, staged, and contributed sketches to the revue *Who's Who* (Hudson, N.Y.C., Mar. 1, 1938).

Subsequently at the NY Drama Festival (Empire Th.), produced and directed *Journey's End* (Sept. 18, 1939); produced *They Knew What They Wanted* (Oct. 2, 1939); produced and directed *All in Fun* (Majestic, Dec. 27, 1940); produced, directed, and appeared in *New Faces of 1943* (Ritz, Dec. 22, 1942); and appeared in *The Petrified Forest* (Pasadena Community Playhouse, Calif., May 1944).

He produced *If the Shoe Fits* (Century, N.Y.C., Dec. 5, 1946); *Happy as Larry* (Coronet, Jan. 6, 1950); *New Faces of 1952* (Royale, May 16, 1952), which toured (opened Shubert, Boston, Mass., Apr. 1953; closed Cass, Detroit, Mich., Apr. 3, 1954); *Mrs. Patterson* (National, N.Y.C., Dec. 1, 1954); and *New Faces of 1956* (Ethel Barrymore Th., June 14, 1956). With Bryant Halliday, he produced *Mask and Gown* (John Golden Th., Sept. 10, 1957) and on tour (opened Curran Th., San Francisco, Calif., July 21, 1958; closed Great Northern, Chicago, Ill., Oct. 4, 1958); with John Roberts, produced *Miss Isobel* (Royale, N.Y.C., Dec. 26, 1957); presented, with Carroll and Harris Masterson, *A Second String* (Eugene O'Neill Th., Apr. 13, 1960); and directed *New Faces of 1962* (Alvin, Feb. 1, 1962).

Mr. Sillman produced *The Family Way* (Lyceum, N.Y.C., Jan. 13, 1965); and *New Faces of 1966* (tour, Summer 1966); produced and staged *New Faces of 1968* (Booth, N.Y.C., May 2, 1968); with Orin Lehman, produced *The American Hamburger League* (New Th., N.Y.C., Sept. 16, 1969); acted in a revival of *The Madwoman of Chaillot* (Sokol Th., N.Y.C., Mar. 22, 1970); and produced a revival of *Hay Fever* (Helen Hayes Th., N.Y.C., Nov. 9, 1970).

Films. Mr. Sillman appeared in *Goldie Gets Along* (RKO, 1933); *Whistling in the Dark* (MGM, 1933); and *Bombshell* (MGM, 1933); produced *Angel Comes to Brooklyn* (Rep., 1945); and *New Faces* (20th-Fox, 1954).

Television and Radio. He produced the radio program, New Faces on the Air (NBC, 1948); and produced and directed the television program, Best of New Faces (WNTA, Nov. 1960); made guest appearances on the Jack Paar Show (NBC); the Dick Cavett Show (ABC), and ABC News.

Night Clubs. Mr. Sillman produced the revue, *Come As You Are* (Versailles, N.Y.C., 1956).

Published Works. His autobiography, *Here Lies Leonard Sillman, Straightened Out at Last*, was published in 1961.

Recreation. Collecting theatrical memorabilia.

SILLS, PAUL. Director. b. Chicago, Ill. Grad. Francis W. Parker Sch.; Univ. of Chicago; Univ. of Bristol (England). Studied children's improvisational theatre with his mother, Viola Spolin. Three marriages; one son, three daughters.

Theatre. With David Shepherd, Mr. Sills cofounded (circa 1953) and directed the Improvisational Playwrights Th. Club (Chicago) which evolved into The Compass Players, subsequently becoming The Second City (1957), which was permanently established in Chicago in a complex housing a cabaret, an improvisational theatre, a children's improvisational school, and living quarters for performers and staff. In 1970, Mr. Sills formed The Body Politic, which he also directed.

In N.Y.C., he directed *From the Second City* (Royale, Sept. 26, 1961; and Sq. East, Dec. 23, 1961); subsequently, at Square East, with Bernard Sahlins and Howard Alk, co-produced, and, with Alan Arkin, co-directed *Seacoast of Bohemia* (Jan. 1962); and with Mr. Sahlins and Mr. Alk, presented *Alarums and Excursions* (May 29, 1962), for which he was supervising director; and *To the Water Tower* (Apr. 4, 1963), which he directed. He directed and, with Bernard Sahlins, co-produced *When the Owl Screams* (Sept. 12, 1963); and *Open Season at the Second City* (Jan. 13, 1964). With Arnold Weinstein, he co-directed *Dynamite Tonight* (York Playhouse, Mar. 15, 1964); directed the revival of that productions (Martinique, Mar. 15, 1967); conceived, from Ovid, *Metamorphoses* (Yale Repertory Th., New Haven, Nov. 27, 1969); devised, based upon Grimm, *Story Theatre* (Mark Taper Forum, Los Angeles, June 18, 1970; directed *Metamorphoses* (Mark Taper Forum, Feb. 4, 1971); directed *Paul Sills Story Theatre* (Ambassador, N.Y.C.), which included *Story Theatre* (Oct. 27, 1970), and *Ovid's Metamorphoses* (Apr. 22, 1971); created, co-authored, with Arnold Weinstein, and directed *The American Revolution, Part I* (Ford's, Washington, D.C., Sept. 27, 1973); and directed *Sweet Bloody Liberty* (Victory Gardens Th., May 1975).

Other Activities. While a student in England, he taught improvisational theatre at the Bristol Old Vic.

Awards. Mr. Sills received a Fulbright scholarship for study at the Univ. of Bristol. For *Paul Sills' Story Theatre*, (1970–71) he received the Antoinette Perry (Tony) Award for direction; The Outer Circle Award for Outstanding Achievement; and the Drama Desk Award for outstanding direction.

SILVER, JOE. Actor. b. Joseph Silver, Sept. 28, 1922, Chicago, Ill., to Morris and Sonja Silver. Father, salesman; mother, saleslady. Grad. East H.S., Green Bay, Wis., 1940; attended Univ. of Wisconsin, 1940–42. Studied at Amer. Th. Wing, N.Y.C., 1946–47. Married Jan. 8, 1950, to Chevi Colton, actress; one son, one daughter. Served US Army Signal Corps, 1944–46, high speed code operator intercepting Japanese messages; rank, S/Sgt. Member of AEA; SAG; AFTRA. Address: 46 Willow St., Brooklyn, NY 11201, tel. (212) UL 8-5739; tel. (212) SU 7-5400.

Pre-Theatre. Shoe salesman and hospital orderly.

Theatre. Mr. Silver made his NYC debut as Lov Bensey in *Tobacco Road* (Forrest Th., Sept. 5, 1942); subsequently appeared in *See My Lawyer* and *Boy Meets Girl* (Adams Th., Newark, N.J., July 1943); *The Goldfish Bowl* (Th. Showcase, N.Y.C., Aug. 1943); and played the Bell Boy in the national company of *The Doughgirls* (opened Sept. 1943).

He appeared in *The Octoroon* (Putnam County Playhouse, Lake Mahopac, N.Y., June 1946); played Burton Snead in *Heads or Tails* (Cort, N.Y.C., May 2, 1947); appeared in *The Terrorists* (Carnegie Hall, 1948); played the Waiter in *Nature's Way* (Coronet, Oct. 16, 1957); Weber in *Gypsy* (Bway Th., May 21, 1959); Squire Hardcastle in *O Marry Me!* (Gate, Oct. 27, 1961); Phil Barr in *The Heroine* (Lyceum, Feb. 19, 1963); the Producer in *You Know I Can't Hear You When the Water's Running* (Ambassador, Mar. 13, 1967); appeared in *The Shrinking Bride* (Mercury, Jan. 17, 1971); and played eight roles in *Lenny* (Brooks Atkinson Th., May 26, 1972).

Films. He played Charlie in *Diary of a Bachelor* (Homer Productions, 1963); appeared in *Move* (20th-Fox, 1970); *Rhinoceros* (A.F.T., 1972); and *The Apprenticeship of Duddy Kravitz* (Par., 1974).

Television. Mr. Silver made his first television appearance as a panelist on What's It Worth? (CBS, 1947); and has since appeared on 800 dramatic and comedy shows including: 54th Street Revue (CBS, 1949); Studio One (CBS, 1949); and the Red Buttons Show (CBS, 1953–55); and has performed on his own programs: Winston Telefinds (CBS, 1949); Captain Jet (CBS, 1954); and Space Funnies (CBS, 1959–60); Love, American Style (ABC, 1972); Gunsmoke (CBS, 1972); and is currently appearing in Love of Life (CBS).

He has also supplied the voices for over a thousand television and radio commercials (1950–to date).

Night Clubs. He appeared as a member of a comedy trio, "The Wry Guys" (Embassy Club, N.Y.C., 1946).

Recreation. Antique furniture refinishing, electrifying antique lamps, gardening, fishing, gourmet cooking.

SILVER, MONTY. Talent representative. b. Monroe Burton Silver, Aug. 7, 1933, Brooklyn, N.Y., to Irving and Lillian (Rock) Silver. Grad. Brooklyn Coll., B.A. 1957; attended State Univ. of Iowa, 1957–58. Married 1965 to Pamela Burrell, actress; two daughters. Served US Army, 1952–54; rank, Pfc. Member of AEA; SAG; AFTRA; TARA (director). Musical Arena Theatres Assn. Address: 850 Seventh Ave., New York, NY 10019, tel. (212) 765-4040.

Since 1960, Mr. Silver has been a talent representative with offices in N.Y.C. He was production associate for *Interlock* (ANTA Th., N.Y.C., Feb. 6, 1958); business manager for the South Shore Music Circus (Cohasset, Mass., Summer 1958); production stage manager for *Mistresses and Maidens at Home and in the Zoo*, and *Song of Songs* (Orpheum, Jan. 21, 1959); company manager for the Music Circus (Lambertville, N.J., Summer 1959); and an associate at Hillard Elkins, Inc., N.Y.C. (Fall 1959).

SILVERMAN, SYD. Newspaper publisher. b. Jan. 23, 1932, New York City, to Sidne L. and Marie (Saxon) Silverman. Father, newspaper publisher. Grad. The Manlius School, 1950; Princeton Univ., A.B. 1954. Married June 26, 1954 to Jan

McNally; two sons, one daughter. Served US Army, 1956; rank, 1st Lt.

In 1956, Mr. Silverman became president of Variety, Inc., and publisher of the weekly newspaper *Variety*, of which he became executive editor in 1973. Since 1956, he has also been president of Daily Variety, Ltd., and publisher of *Daily Variety* in Hollywood, Calif. Address: 154 W. 46th St., New York, NY 10036, tel. (212) 582-2700.

SILVERS, PHIL. Actor. b. May 11, 1911, Brooklyn, N.Y., to Saul and Sarah Silver. Father, sheet metal worker. Grad. P.S. 149, Bklyn., 1925; attended New Utrecht H.S., Bklyn., 1926. Married 1945 to Jo Carroll Dennison (marr. dis. 1950); married 1956 to Evelyn Patrick (marr. dis. 1966); five daughters. Member of AEA; AFTRA; AGVA; SAG; The Friars Club, Calif.

Pre-Theatre. Sports announcer, reporter.

Theatre. Mr. Silvers first performed as a singer in amateur "kiddie shows" (Apr. 1922); made his professional debut as a singer with the Gus Edwards Revue (Earle Th., Philadelphia, Pa., July 1925); and subsequently toured in vaudeville with Morris and Campbell and with the Minsky Burlesque Troupe (1934–39).

He first appeared on Bway as "Punko" Parks in *Yokel Boy* (Majestic, July 6, 1939); toured with the USO in the Mediterranean (WW II); played Harrison Floy in *High Button Shoes* (Century, N.Y.C., Oct. 9, 1947); Jerry Biff in *Top Banana* (Winter Garden, Nov. 1, 1951); Hubert Cram in *Do Re Mi* (St. James, Dec. 26, 1960); Frank Foster in *How the Other Half Loves* (Royale, Mar. 29, 1971); and Prologus and Pseudolus in a revival of *A Funny Thing Happened on the Way to the Forum* (Ahmanson Th., Los Angeles, Calif., Oct. 12, 1971; Lunt-Fontanne Th., N.Y.c., Mar. 30, 1972).

Films. He made his debut in *Hit Parade of 1941* (Rep., 1940); followed by roles in *All Through the Night* (WB, 1942); *You're in the Army Now* (WB, 1941); *Roxie Hart* (20th-Fox, 1942); *My Gal Sal* (20th-Fox, 1942); *Footlight Serenade* (20th-Fox, 1942); *Just Off Broadway* (20th-Fox, 1942); *Coney Island* (20th-Fox, 1943); *A Lady Takes a Chance* (RKO, 1943); *Four Jills in a Jeep* (20th-Fox, 1944); *Something for the Boys* (20th-Fox, 1944); *Take It or Leave It* (20th-Fox, 1944); *Diamond Horseshoe* (20th-Fox, 1945); *A Thousand and One Nights* (Col., 1945); *Cover Girl* (Col., 1944); *Don Juan Quilligan* (20th-Fox, 1945); *If I'm Lucky* (20th-Fox, 1946); *Summer Stock* (MGM, 1959); *Top Banana* (UA, 1954); *Lucky Me* (WB, 1954); *40 Pounds of Trouble* (U, 1962); *It's a Mad Mad Mad Mad World* (UA, 1963); *A Guide for the Married Man* (20th-Fox, 1967); *Boatniks* (Buena Vista, 1970); and *The Strongest Man in the World* (Buena Vista, 1975).

Television. Mr. Silvers first appeared as a comedian on the Arrow Comedy Show (NBC); subsequently appeared as Sgt. Bilko in the Phil Silvers Show (CBS, 1955–58); and on The New Phil Silvers Show (CBS, 1963); in *The Ballad of Louie the Louse* (CBS, Oct. 1959); *The Slowest Gun in the West* (CBS, Apr. 1960); *Damn Yankees* (NBC, Apr. 1967); and on Beverly Hillbillies (CBS, 1969, 1970).

Night Clubs. He made his night club debut as a comedian at the Copacabana, N.Y.C.

Published Works. Mr. Silvers wrote *The Laugh Is on Me* (1974).

Awards. For his performance as Jerry Biff in *Top Banana*, he received the Donaldson Award, the Antoinette Perry (Tony) Award and the *Variety* NY Drama Critics Poll (1951); for his television program, The Phil Silvers Show, he received three NATAS (Emmy) awards in 1956 and two in 1957. He won the Television Showman Award (best performer, best star, 1956). For his performance in the revival of *A Funny Thing Happened on the Way to the Forum*, Mr. Silvers received an Antoinette Perry (Tony) Award (1971–72) and was named in the *Variety* NY Drama Critics Poll (1971–72) as best actor in a musical.

Recreation. Sports of all kinds.

SILVERSTONE, JONAS T. Theatrical attorney, producer. b. Thomas Silverstone, Nov. 20, 1906, Brooklyn, N.Y., to Harry and Mary (Thomashefsky) Silverstone. Grad. Commercial H.S., Brooklyn, 1923; St. John's Coll. Sch. of Law, LL.B. 1928. Married 1939, to Beatrice Schleifman; one son, one daughter. Served WW II, US Army; rank, T/Sgt. Member of TVA, Jewish Theatrical Guild of America, The Players. Address: (home) 7 Blackstone Pl, Bronx, NY 10471, tel. (212) KI6-8196; (bus.) 230 Park Ave., New York, NY 10017, tel. (212) 616-8030.

Theatre. He participated in *Out of a Blue Sky* (Booth Th., N.Y.C., Feb. 8, 1930); *Birthright* (49 St. Th., Nov. 21, 1932); *Fly by Night* (Belmont, June 2, 1933); and produced *Entre Nous* (Provincetown Playhouse, 1937).

Recreation. Reading, fishing, farming.

SIMMS, HILDA. Actress. b. Hilda Theresa Moses, Minneapolis, Minn., to Emil and Lydia Marie (Webber) Moses. Father, engineer. Grad. St. Margaret's Acad., Minneapolis; attended Univ. of Minn., three years; grad. Hampton Inst., B.S.; attended Univ. of Paris (de la Sorbonne), 1950–52. Studied for the theatre at AADA, 1958–59; Carnegie Hall Drama Sch., 1959–60; acting with Robert J. Sailstad, Univ. of Minnesota; Etienne Decroux, Paris; Abbe Mitchell, Betty Cashman, Ezra Stone, and Harry Wagstaff Gribble, N.Y.C. Married Sept. 20, 1948, to Richard Angarola (marr. dis. 1963). Member of AEA; SAG; AFTRA.

Pre-Theatre. Waitress, domestic, recreation assistant, English literature teacher, speech therapist, artists' model, publicity.

Theatre. Miss Simms made her stage debut as Cathy in a college production of *Wuthering Heights* (Hampton Inst., 1942). With the American Negro Th., she played in *Three's a Family* (Lafayette Th., June 1943); and the title role in *Anna Lucasta* (NY Public Library, W. 135 St., June 8, 1944), in which she subsequently made her Bway debut (Mansfield, Aug. 30, 1944). She toured in *Anna Lucasta* (opened Civic, Chicago, Ill., Sept. 1945; His Majesty's, London, Oct. 29, 1947); appeared in *Desire Caught by the Tail* (Rudolph Steiner Hall, London, Feb. 1950); Stella Goodman in *The Gentle People* (Embassy, Apr. 1950); and Pervaneh in *Hassan* (Cambridge, May 9, 1951).

Miss Simms played Miss Dewpont in *The Cool World* (Eugene O'Neill Th., N.Y.C., Feb. 22, 1960). At the Red Barn Th. (Northport, N.Y.), she played in *The Captain's Paradise* and *Black Monday* (Summer 1961); and portrayed Laura Wright Reed in *Tambourines to Glory* (Little, N.Y.C., Nov. 2, 1963).

She toured in a one-woman show, *Love Letters of Famous Courtesans* (opened New Sch. for Social Research, 1961).

Films. Miss Simms made her debut in *The Joe Louis Story* (UA, 1953); and appeared in *Black Widow* (20th-Fox, 1954).

Television and Radio. From 1954–57, Miss Simms had her own radio program, Ladies Day with Hilda Simms. On television, she appeared in *A Man Is Ten Feet Tall* (Philco Television Playhouse, NBC, 1955); *Profiles in Courage* (Kraft Television Th., CBS, 1956); *Black Monday* (Play of the Week, WNTA, 1960); and The Nurses (CBS, 1962).

Awards. Miss Simms received awards from the Allied Forces, Central Europe (1951); the Minneapolis (Minn.) Urban League (1953); YMCA of the City of NY (1954); Hampton Alumni Assn. (1955); Harlem Hospital Sch. of Nursing (1956); Vocational Guidance and Workshop Center (1956); Abyssinian Baptist Church (1956); Natl. Council of Negro Women (1956); St. Augustine's Chapel (1957); Boy Scouts of America, Harlem (1957).

SIMON, BERNARD. Press representative, supplier of theatrical publicity materials, publisher. b. Bernard Aaron Simon, June 19, 1904, Pine Bluff, Ark., to Jacques B. and Carrie (Katzenstein) Simon. Father, motion picture exhibitor. Grad. Pine Bluff H.S., 1921; Columbia Univ., B.A., 1925. Married July 22, 1930, to Frances Kehrlein (marr. dis. 1953); one son; married Feb. 26, 1956, to Avivah Finkelman; one daughter. Member of ATPAM (bd. of gov., 1952–54); ATA; USITT; NETC; and SETC. Address: (home) 255 W. 88th St., New York, NY 10024, tel. (212) 352-1072; (bus.) c/o Package Publicity Service, Inc., 1564 Broadway, New York, NY 10036, tel. (212) CO 5-4188.

Theatre. Mr. Simon, while a student at Columbia Coll., was a Beggar and stage manager for *The Spook Sonata* (Provincetown Playhouse, N.Y.C., Jan. 5, 1924); subsequently was stage manager, and succeeded (Mar. 31, 1924) Harold McGee as Augustus Fogg in *Fashion* (Provincetown Playhouse, Feb. 2, 1924; moved Greenwich Village Th., Mar. 31, 1924; moved Cort, Apr. 14, 1924). He was drama reporter and critic for the NY *Morning Telegraph* (Sept. 1925–Mar. 1926), and assistant drama editor for the NY *Herald-Tribune* (1926–1927).

He was press representative in N.Y.C. for *The Wild Man of Borneo* (1927); *The 5 O'Clock Girl* (1927); the national tours of *Marco Millions* and *Strange Interlude* (1928–29); and in N.Y.C., *Children of Darkness* (1930); *Twelfth Night* (1930); *Art and Mrs. Bottle* (1930); *Overture* (1930); *Anatol* (1931); *Springtime for Henry* (1931); *Carrie Nation* (1932); *Goodbye Again* (1932); *Men in White* (1933); *Three-Cornered Moon* (1933); *Another Language* (1933); *Petticoat Fever* (1935); *There's Wisdom in Women* (1935); *Tovarich* (1935); *Promise* (1936); *The Country Wife* (1936); *Yes, My Darling Daughter* (1937); *The Amazing Dr. Clitterhouse* (1937); *Once Is Enough* (1938); and *Victoria Regina* (1936).

Mr. Simon was director of publicity and advertising for the NY Federal Theatre Project (1939); and was press representative for N.Y.C. productions of *Morning Star* (1940); *Claudia* (1941); *Counsellor-at-Law* (1942); *Three's a Family* (1943); *The Army Play-by-Play* (1943); *Are You with It?* (1945); *Live Life Again* (1945); *Made in Heaven* (1946); *Call Me Mister* (1946); *The Red Mill* (1946); *On Whitman Avenue* (1946); the pre-Bway tryout of *Windy City* (1946); in N.Y.C., *The Front Page* (1946); *A Young Man's Fancy* (1947); *Open House* (1947); *Trial Honeymoon* (1947); *Strange Bedfellows* (1948); *The Madwoman of Chaillot* (1948); tour of *Music in My Heart* (1948); in N.Y.C., *They Knew What They Wanted* (1949); *That Lady* (1949), and the tour; *Second Threshold* (1951); *Angels Kiss Me* (1951); *Lace on Her Petticoat* (1951); tours of *Die Fledermaus* (Metropolitan Opera tour, 1951), and *A Tree Grows in Brooklyn* (1952); and *The Fifth Season*, in N.Y.C. and on tour (1953).

He was a producer of the touring production of the *The Tender Trap* (opened McCarter, Princeton, N.J., Jan. 21, 1955); press representative in N.Y.C. for *Once Upon a Tailor* (1955); and for the touring production of *Can-Can* (1955–56); in N.Y.C. was associate press representative for *The Apple Cart* (1956); *Li'l Abner* (1956); the pre-Bway tryout of *The Joker* (1957); in N.Y.C., *Romanoff and Juliet* (1957); *The Dark at the Top of the Stairs* (1957); *A Shadow of My Enemy* (1957); *Oh! Captain* (1958); and *Interlock* (1958).

He was press representative in N.Y.C. for *Back to Methuselah* (1958); *Mrs. Warren's Profession* (1958); *Heloïse* (1958); *U.S.A.* (1959); *Vincent* (1959); *Deirdre of the Sorrows* (1959); *No Trifling with Love* (1959); and *Dinny and the Witches* (1959); associate press representative for *The Andersonville Trial* (1959); *Roman Candle* (1960); *One More River* (1960); *Caligula* (1960); and *Christine* (1960); press representative for *Machinal* (1960); *A Country Scandal* (1960); *The Idiot* (1960); *Man and Superman* (1960); *Emmanuel* (1960); *The 49th Cousin* (1960); *Montserrat* (1961); *The Moon in the Yellow River* (1961); *Five Posts in the Market Place* (1961); *O Marry Me* (1961); *One Way Pendulum* (1961); associate press representative for *From the Second City* (1961); *A Shot in the Dark* (1961); *Daughter of Silence* (1961); *The Night of the Iguana* (1961); press representative for *Rhinoceros* (1961); *Do You Know the Milky Way?* (1963); and for the tour of *Irma La Douce* (1962).

Films. He was press representative for *The House of Rothschild* (UA, 1934).

Other Activities. Since 1948, Mr. Simon has operated Package Publicity Service, Inc., of which he is founder and president, and which supplies publicity and advertising materials to resident, stock, community and educational theatres. He is also the publisher and editor of *Simon's Directory of Theatrical Materials, Services and Information,* and author of *Publicity Releases—How to Prepare and Submit Them.*

He was assistant editor of *Theatre* Magazine (1940), a reporter for the Rochester *Democrat and Chronicle* (June–Sept. 1925), and secretary to Sinclair Lewis (Mar.–Sept. 1926).

Recreation. Badminton, gardening, carpentry.

SIMON, JOHN. Critic. b. Jovan Ivan Simon, May 12, 1925, Subotica, Yugoslavia, to Joseph and Margaret (Revesz) Simon. Attended schools in Yugoslavia, England and US; grad. Harvard Univ., A.B. (English) 1946; A.M. (Comparative Lit.) 1948; Ph.D. (Comparative Lit.) 1959; attended Univ. of Paris, France, 1949–50. Served USAAF, 1944–45; rank Pfc. Member P.E.N.; Amer. Soc. of Cinematologists; Soc. of Film Critics. Address: 200 E. 36th St., New York, NY 10016, tel. (212) MU 5-8413.

Since 1960, Mr. Simon has been drama critic for *The Hudson Review* and since 1962, film critic for *The New Leader.* He has also been theatre critic for *Commonweal* (began 1967) and for *New York* magazine, where he later was a contributing editor and then film critic (began 1975); he was film critic for *Esquire* (1973–75); and he writes on theatre for the *New York Times.* He was theatre critic for N.Y.C. educational television station WNDT for a time before Nov. 1968.

Other Activities. Mr. Simon was a teaching fellow in English and the humanities at Harvard (1950–53); an instructor in humanities and classical literature, Univ. of Washington at Seattle (1953–54); instructor in humanities, Massachusetts Institute of Technology (1954–55); and assistant professor of literature, Bard Coll. (1957–59). He was associate editor of the Mid-Century Book Society (1959–61).

Published Works. Mr. Simon's critical essays have been collected in several volumes: *Acid Test* (1963); *Private Screenings* (1967); *Movies into Film: Film Criticism 1967–1970* (1971); *Singularities, Essays on the Theater 1964–1974* (1976); and *Uneasy Stages* (1976). He also wrote *Ingmar Bergman Directs* (1972) and edited, with Richard Schickel, *Film 67/68* (1968).

Awards. Mr. Simon received a Fulbright Fellowship (1949–50), a Rockefeller Foundation grant (1964–64), and the George Jean Nathan Award (1970–71) for criticism.

SIMON, LOUIS M. Director, administrator. b. Louis Mortimer Simon, Oct. 25, 1906, Salt Lake City, Utah, to Adolph and Stella (Furchgott) Simon. Father, merchant; mother, photographer. Attended Salt Lake City public schools; Culver Mil. Academy; Potter Sch. (San Francisco); Univ. of Pennsylvania (1923–24); Harvard Univ. (1924–25); Yale Univ. (1925–27). Trained with George Pierce Baker (1925–27); Max Reinhardt (Berlin and Salzburg, 1927–28). Married Oct. 23, 1941, to Edith Morrissey; one son. Served US Army, Ordnance Dept., 1941–45; theatre officer 1944–45; entered as Pvt., attained rank of Major. Member of AEA (1929–to date); Actors' Fund; Assoc. of Actors and Artistes of Amer. (international exec. secy., 1949–52); Amer. Th. Wing (bd. of dir., 1949–59); ANTA (bd. of dir., 1950–63). Address: (home) 444 Central Park W., New York, NY 10025, tel. (212) RI 9-6340; (bus.) Actors' Fund of America, 1501 Broadway, New York, NY 10036, tel. (212) 221-7300.

Theatre. Mr. Simon made his debut as The Poet in *The Lost Silk Hat* (Potter Sch. Aud., San Francisco, Mar. 1923); subsequently stage managed *The Pirate* (Lo Bero Th., Santa Barbara, Calif., Feb. 1929, and Belasco Th., Los Angeles, Mar. 1929); made his Bway debut as stage manager for *Red Dust* (Martin Beck Th., N.Y.C., Dec. 9, 1929); was costume designer and production stage manager for *Garrick Gaieties* (Guild, N.Y.C., Apr. 1930); stage manager for Midnight (Guild, N.Y.C., Dec. 29, 1930); technical director for *Oedipus Rex* and *Les Pas d'Acier* Metropolitan Opera, N.Y.C., Apr. 1931); assistant to the scenic designer for *The Cat and the Fiddle* (Globe, N.Y.C., Oct. 15, 1931); stage manager for *The Jewel Robbery* (Booth, N.Y.C., Jan. 13, 1932); director of *Thy People* (Red Barn Th., Locust Valley, N.Y., July 1932); and stage manager for *Rendezvous* (Broadhurst, N.Y.C., Oct. 12, 1932).

He co-directed *Run Lil' Chillun* (Lyric, N.Y.C., Mar. 1, 1933); stage managed *The World Waits* (Little Th., N.Y.C., Oct. 25, 1933), *False Dreams Farewell* (Little Th., N.Y.C., Jan. 15, 1934), *Bright Star* (Castle Sq. Th., Springfield, Dec. 1934), and *Prisoners of War* (Ritz, N.Y.C., Jan. 28, 1935); directed *Good Men and True* (Biltmore, N.Y.C., Oct. 25, 1935), *Honor Bright* (Shubert, New Haven, Conn., Sept. 1937); and *June Night* (Erlanger, Philadelphia, Jan. 1938); co-directed *Another Sun* (National, N.Y.C., Feb. 23, 1940); and was producing director of a repertory season (Mineola, N.Y., Th., Oct.–Nov. 1959).

Mr. Simon served as state director of the Federal Theatre Project in New Jersey (1936–37) and New York (1938–39); executive secretary of Actors Equity Assn. (1949–52); director of the professional training program of the American Theatre Wing (N.Y.C., 1952–58); and director of public relations for the Actors' Fund (1965–to date).

Films. Mr. Simon was secretary and interpreter to Max Reinhardt during preparation of an untitled film to star Lillian Gish (UA, Nov. 1928–Feb. 1929); and was a play reader at Metro-Goldwyn-Mayer (May–Sept. 1929).

Other Activities. Mr. Simon was executive secretary of the Pennsylvania Commission for the Gettysburg Centennial (Dec. 1961–Dec. 1963).

Published Works. Mr. Simon is the author of *Gettysburg* (Commonwealth of Pennsylvania, Dec. 1964); *A History of the Actors' Fund of America* (Theatre Arts Books, Dec. 1972); and stories and articles published in *The New Yorker,* The New York *Times, The New Republic* and *Theatre Arts* magazine.

Recreation. Carpentry and gardening.

SIMON, NEIL. Playwright, librettist, screenwriter. b. Marvin Neil Simon, July 4, 1927, Bronx, N.Y., to Irving and Mamie Simon. Father, salesman. Grad. DeWitt Clinton H.S., N.Y.C., 1943; attended N.Y. Univ., 1946. Married Sept. 30, 1953, to Joan Baim, dancer (dec. July 11, 1973); two daughters; married Oct. 25, 1973, to Marsha Mason, actress. Served USAAF, 1945–46; rank, Cpl. Relative in theatre: brother, Daniel (Danny) Simon, television writer and director. Member of Dramatists Guild; WGA, East.

Theatre. Mr. Simon's first writing for the theatre was for the "Camp Tamiment" (Pa.) revues (1952–53); with his brother, Danny, he wrote sketches for *Catch a Star* (Plymouth, N.Y.C., Nov. 6, 1955) and *New Faces of '56* (Ethel Barrymore Th., June 14, 1956); wrote *Come Blow Your Horn* (Brooks Atkinson Th., Feb. 22, 1961); the book for the musical *Little Me* (Lunt-Fontanne, Nov. 17, 1962); *Barefoot in the Park* (Biltmore, Oct. 23, 1963); *The Odd Couple* (Plymouth, Mar. 10, 1965); the book for the musical, *Sweet Charity* (Palace, Jan. 29, 1966); *The Star-Spangled Girl* (Plymouth, Dec. 21, 1966); *Plaza Suite,* three one-act plays entitled "Visitor from Mamaroneck," "Visitor from Hollywood," and "Visitor from Forest Hills" (Plymouth, Feb. 14, 1968); the book for the musical, *Promises, Promises* (Shubert, Dec. 1, 1968); *Last of the Red Hot Lovers* (Eugene O'Neill Th., Dec. 28, 1969); *The Gingerbread Lady* (Plymouth, Dec. 13, 1970); *The Prisoner of Second Avenue* (Eugene O'Neill, Nov. 11, 1971); *The Sunshine Boys* (Broadhurst, Dec. 20, 1972); *The Good Doctor* (Eugene O'Neill, Nov. 27, 1973); and *God's Favorite* (Eugene O'Neill, Dec. 11, 1974).

Films. Mr. Simon wrote the screenplays, adapted from his Bway plays, for *Barefoot in the Park* (Par., 1967), for which he was also assoc. producer; for *The Odd Couple* (Par., 1968); *Plaza Suite* (Par., 1971); *Last of the Red Hot Lovers* (Par., 1972); *The Prisoner of Second Avenue* (WB, 1975); and *The Sunshine Boys* (MGM, 1975). He also wrote the screenplays for *After the Fox* (UA, 1966); *The Out-of-Towners* (Par., 1970); *The Heartbreak Kid* (20th-Fox, 1972); and *Murder by Death* (Col., 1976). In addition, films were made, based on his plays, of *Come Blow Your Horn* (Par., 1963); *Sweet Charity* (U, 1969); and *Star-Spangled Girl* (Par., 1971).

Television. He has written for the Phil Silvers Arrow Show (NBC, 1948); the Tallulah Bankhead Show (NBC, 1951); the Sid Caesar Show (NBC, 1956–57); the Phil Silvers Show (CBS, 1958–59); the Garry Moore Show (CBS, 1959–60); and a number of NBC Specials, including *The Trouble with People* (NBC, Nov. 12, 1972).

Other Activities. Mr. Simon is owner of the Eugene O'Neill Th., N.Y.C.

Awards. Mr. Simon received the Antoinette Perry (Tony) Award in 1965, as author of *The Odd Couple,* after receiving nominations for *Little Me* (1963) and *Barefoot in the Park* (1964).

For the film of *The Odd Couple,* he received a Writers Guild Award and an Academy (Oscar) Award nomination (1969).

He received NATAS (Emmy) Award nominations for the Sid Caesar Show (1956–57) and for the Phil Silvers Show (1958–59); the Sam S. Shubert Foundation Award "in recognition of outstanding contribution to the American theater" (1968); *Cue* Magazine's Entertainer of the Year Award (Jan. 14, 1972); and a special Antoinette Perry (Tony) Award "for his over-all contribution to the theater" (1975).

Recreation. Golf, "rewriting.".

SIMON, ROGER HENDRICKS. Director, actor, teacher. b. Oct. 21, 1942, New York City, to Harold K. and Mildred K. Simon. Grad. Middlebury (Vt.) Coll., B.A. 1964; Yale School of Drama (Nikos Psacharopoulos, Constance Welch), M.F.A. 1967. Studied at NY Univ. Television and Film Workshop (honors certificate, 1965).

Theatre. Mr. Simon began his theatrical career as director of the Scarsdale (N.Y.) Summer Th. (1962–63). He was then assistant director, Williamstown (Mass.) Summer Th. (1965); director of the Pierson Coll. Drama Club, Yale Univ., New Haven, Conn. (1965–66); an actor with the Mobile Theatre Unit, NY Shakespeare Festival (1967); and stage manager and actor with Yale Repertory, New Haven, Conn. (1967–68).

On the professional stage, he directed *Keep Tightly Closed in a Cool Dry Place* (Traverse, Edinburgh Th. Festival, Scotland, and Open Space, London, England, Aug. 1968; Abbey Th., Dublin Th. Festival, Sept. 1968; Mickery, Amsterdam, The Netherlands, Oct. 1968); *War* (Open Space, London, Feb. 1969); *La Turista* (Royal Court, Mar. 1969; World Th. Festival, Nancy, France, Apr. 1969); *Package I,* a group of off-Bway plays (Open Space, London, Sept. 1969; Traverse, Edinburgh, Oct. 1969; Mickery, Amsterdam, The Netherlands, Oct. 1969); and (all at the Nieuw Rotterdam Toneel, Rotterdam, The Netherlands) *Little Malcolm and His Struggle Against the Eunuchs* (Oct. 1969), *The Devils* (Nov. 1969), and *War* (Dec. 1969).

He directed *War* and *Muzeeka* (Traverse, Edinburgh, Scotland, Nov. 1969); a revival of *Keep Tightly Closed in a Cool Dry Place* (Roundhouse, London, 1970); *Slag* (world premiere, Hampstead Th., London, Apr. 1970); *Bloomers* (Gardner Centre for the Arts, Brighton, England, Aug. 1970); *Cancer,* original title of *Moonchildren* (world premiere, Royal Court, London, Sept. 1970); and *Package II,* another program of off-Bway plays (American Embassy Th., London, 1970; Mickery, Amsterdam, The Netherlands, Oct. 1970; Boldhus Teatret, Copenhagen, Denmark, 1970).

He also directed *Slag* (Public, N.Y.C., Feb. 21, 1971); *The Last Sweet Days of Isaac* (Nieuw Rotterdam Toneel, The Netherlands, Sept. 1971); *Now There's Just the Three of Us* (Chelsea Th. Ctr., Brooklyn Acad. of Music, Oct. 19, 1971); *Tall and Rex* (Chelsea Th. Ctr., Oct. 26, 1971); *Dudes* (New Dramatists, Dec. 1971); *I Married You for the Fun of It*

(Yale Rep. Th., New Haven, Conn., Feb. 1972); *Suggs* (Forum, N.Y.C., Apr. 1972); *The Best Is Yet to Be* (Manhattan Th. Club, July 20, 1972); *Dudes* (John Drew Th., Easthampton, N.Y., Sept. 1972); *Artists for the Revolution* (Eugene O'Neill Playwrights Conference, 2nd Step Program, Drake Univ., Des Moines, Iowa, Oct. 1972); *Tonight We Kill Molly Bloom* (New Dramatists, N.Y.C., Nov. 30, 1972); and *Atheist in a Fox Hole* (New Dramatists, Dec. 1972).

Also *In the Summer House* (Juilliard Drama Div., N.Y.C., Mar. 1973); *The Complaint Department Closes at Five* (Manhattan Th. Club, Apr. 12, 1973); *Union Street* (NYC Parks Dept.–Joseph Papp Street Th., May 1973); *Moonchildren,* called *Cancer* in England (Chimera Th., St. Paul, Minn., June 1973); *Sex and the Single Dog* (Vineyard Players, Martha's Vineyard, Mass., Aug. 1973); *Bloomers* (Equity Library Th., Apr. 18, 1974); and *A Funny Thing Happened on the Way to the Forum* (Chimera Th., St. Paul, Minn., Sept. 1974). Mr. Simon also directed *Slag* (Toneelgroep Th., Arnhem, The Netherlands, Nov. 1974); *Madam Senator* (La Mama ETC, N.Y.C., Mar. 20, 1975); *The Rebirth Celebration of the Human Race at Artie Zabala's Off-Broadway Theater* (Shirtsleeve Th., July 10, 1975); *Bloomers* and *The Snob* (Toneelraad, Rotterdam, The Netherlands, Sept. 1975); and *Hot L Baltimore* (Belgian National Th., Jan. 1976. He also toured Nigeria, South Africa, and Iran as director of a special program on new American theatre for the US State Dept. (Jan.–Feb. 1976), and he directed *Cat on a Hot Tin Roof* (Chimera, St. Paul, Minn., Apr. 1976).

Other Activities. Mr. Simon was an instructor of acting and directing, American Dramatic Institute Abroad, London (Eng.) Univ. (1968); guest instructor, Regent Polytechnical Institute, London (1969); director, lecturer, and co-producer of the symposium on new American theatre, American Embassy, London (1969); and director, lecturer, and instructor for the workshop and performance tour of English universities sponsored by the American Embassy, London, of *Keep Tightly Closed in a Cool Dry Place.*.

SIMPSON, N. F.

Playwright. b. Norman Frederick Simpson, Jan. 29, 1919, London, England, to George Frederick and Elizabeth (Rossiter) Simpson. Grad. Emanuel Sch., London, England, 1937; Univ. of London, England, B.A. (honors) 1954. Married Feb. 9, 1944, to Joyce Bartlett; one daughter. Served British Army, Royal Artillery, 1941–43; Intelligence Corps, 1943–46; rank, Sgt. Member of Society of Authors. Address: 46 York Mansions, Prince of Wales Dr., London, S.W. 11, England.

Theatre. Mr. Simpson's plays, which have been produced in London, are *A Resounding Tinkle* (Royal Court Th., Dec. 1, 1957); *The Hole,* presented as part of a double bill with *A Resounding Tinkle* (Royal Court Th., Apr. 2, 1958); *One Way Pendulum* (Royal Court Th., Dec. 22, 1959); *The Form* (Arts, 1961); *The Cresta Run* (Royal Court Th., London, Oct. 27, 1965); and *Was He Anyone?* (Th. Upstairs, London, July 5, 1972). *One Way Pendulum* was produced in N.Y.C. (E. 74 St. Th., Sept. 18, 1961). A number of Mr. Simpson's sketches have been performed in various London revues: "Gladly, Otherwise Can You Hear Me" in the revue, *One to Another* (Apollo, Aug. 19, 1959); "Take It Away" in *You, Me and the Gatepost* (Nottingham Playhouse, June 27, 1960); "One Blast and Have Done" in *On the Avenue* (Globe, June 19, 1961); and "Always or More" in the revue *One Over the Eight* (Duke of York's, 1961).

Published Works. Mr. Simpson has written articles and sketches for the British periodicals, *Vogue, The Queen,* and *About Town;* book reviews for *Spectator* and *Time and Tide;* and articles for the American magazines, *Harper's* and *Vogue.*

Awards. He was awarded third prize in the *Observer* Play Competition for *A Resounding Tinkle* (1957); and received the Encyclopaedia Britannica Award for *One Way Pendulum* (1962).

Recreation. Reading, walking.

SIRCOM, ARTHUR R.

Director, actor, teacher. b. Arthur Rowland Sircom, Dec. 15, 1899, Malden, Mass., to Frank Rowland and Caroline Alice (Kenerson) Sircom. Father, banker. Grad. Malden H.S., 1917; Phillips Academy, 1920; Yale Coll., B.A. 1924; studied at Richard Boleslavsky's American Laboratory Th., N.Y.C., 1924–26. Served USAAF, WW II, 1942–43; transferred to US Army, Special Services, Feb. 1943), rank, Cpl. Member of AEA, Zeta Psi, honorary member of the Snarks, Inc. Address: (home) 2700 Que St., N.W., Washington, DC 20007, tel. (202) HO 2-8698; (bus.) Actors Equity Assn., 165 W. 46th St., New York, NY 10036.

Theatre. Mr. Sircom made his first stage appearance as the Widow Quin in a Yale Coll. Dramatic Assn. production of *The Playboy of the Western World* (Feb. 1922); his first professional appearance with the Jitney (touring repertory) Players as the Talker in *Red Feathers* (June 28, 1923), in which he appeared the rest of the season (July–Aug. 1923); appeared with the Jitney Players as Dr. Daly in *Sorcerer* and Lord Foppington in *Trip to Scarborough* (July–Aug. 1924); made his Bway debut as a farmhand in *They Knew What They Wanted* (Garrick, Nov. 24, 1924); appeared in walk-on parts in *Processional* (Garrick, Jan. 12, 1925); and returned for two seasons with the Jitney Players as Antonio in *The Duenna* (July–Aug. 1925), and as director of *Paolo and Francesca,* and *Love Is the Best Doctor,* in which he also appeared (July–Aug. 1926); with the American Laboratory Th., played Gillette Rapide in *The Straw Hat* (Amer. Lab. Th., N.Y.C., Oct. 24, 1925), and using the name Rowland Coombs, joined (Feb. 28, 1926) the cast as A Clergyman in *Granite* (Feb. 11, 1926).

He directed the Jitney Players in *Haste to the Wedding* and *Murderer in the Old Red Barn* (July–Aug. 1926); played Keeter in *The Trumpet Shall Sound* (Amer. Lab. Th., N.Y.C., Dec. 10, 1926); again directed the Jitney Players (July–Aug. 1927); appeared for two seasons with Henry Jewett's Boston Repertory Th. (Oct. 1927–May 1928); directed a season of summer stock at the Eiverhoj Th. (Milton-on-Hudson, N.Y., July–Aug. 1929); appeared in a coast-to-coast tour of Sir Philip Ben Greet's Shakespearean company in *Hamlet, Everyman, Much Ado About Nothing* and *Twelfth Night* (Nov. 1929–Apr. 1930); directed and appeared in a season of stock at the Millbrook (N.Y.) Th., of which he was co-producer (July–Aug. 1930); directed and appeared with the Jitney Players on tour in the East (Sept. 1930–May 1931); and returned to the Millbrook (N.Y.) Th. as director-producer (July–Aug. 1931).

Mr. Sircom directed *Springtime for Henry* (Bijou, N.Y.C., Dec. 9, 1931), which was produced by Kenneth Macgowan and Joseph Verner Reed in association with Mr. Sircom; *Money in the Air* (Ritz, Mar. 7, 1932); summer stock at the Westchester (Mt. Kisco, N.Y.) Country Playhouse and the Millbrook (N.Y.) Playhouse (July–Aug. 1932); *Men Must Fight* (Lyceum, N.Y.C., Oct. 14, 1932); *A Good Woman—Poor Thing* (Avon, Jan. 9, 1933); then a season of summer stock at the Griswold Th. (New London, Conn., June–Aug. 1933); directed, with the author, Kenyon Nicholson, *Sailor, Beware!* (Lyceum, N.Y.C., Sept. 28, 1933); directed *Give Us This Day* (Booth, Oct. 27, 1933); *All Good Americans* (Henry Miller's Th., Dec. 5, 1933); *Whatever Possessed Her* (Mansfield, Jan. 25, 1934); *Battleship Gertie* (Lyceum, Jan. 18, 1935); and seasons of summer stock at Bar Harbor (Me.) Th. (July 1935); and Locust Valley (N.Y.) Th. (Aug. 1935). He directed *Whatever Goes Up* (Biltmore, N.Y.C., Nov. 25, 1935); and *I Want a Policeman!* (Lyceum, Jan. 14, 1936); a season of summer stock at the Locust Valley (N.Y.) Th. (July–Aug. 1936); *Seen But Not Heard* (Henry Miller's Th., N.Y.C., Sept. 17, 1936); *Tide Rising* (Lyceum, Jan. 25, 1937); *Penny Wise* (Morosco, Apr. 19, 1937); a season of stock at the Cape Playhouse (Dennis, Mass., June–Aug. 1937), with which he was associated for more than ten seasons.

He staged *Tell Me, Pretty Maiden* (Mansfield, N.Y.C., Dec. 16, 1937); stock at the Maryland Th. (Baltimore, Md., May 1938); a season at the Cape Playhouse (July–Aug. 1938); *Window Shopping* (Longacre, N.Y.C., Dec. 23, 1938); *Day in the Sun* (Biltmore, May 16, 1939); another season at the Cape Playhouse (July–Aug. 1939); *A Case of Youth* (National, N.Y.C., Mar. 23, 1940); *The Romantic Mr. Dickens* (Playhouse, Dec. 2, 1940); directed productions at the Cape Playhouse (July–Aug. 1941); *All the Comforts of Home* (Longacre, N.Y.C., May 25, 1942); stock in Milwaukee, Wis. (Pabst, May 1942), in Philadelphia, Pa. (Bellevue-Stratford Hotel, July 1942); and at the Casino Th. (Newport, R.I., July 1943); staged *Ramshackle Inn* (Royale, N.Y.C., Jan. 5, 1944); with Elliott Nugent, directed *Mrs. January and Mr. X* (Belasco, Mar. 31, 1944); directed another season of stock at Cape Playhouse (July–Aug. 1944); and *The Odds on Mrs. Oakley* (Cort, N.Y.C., Oct. 2, 1944).

He was managing director of the Minneapolis (Minn.) Civic Th. (Winters 1946–48), where he staged eight productions; director at Cape Playhouse (Summers 1945–48); managing director of the Youngstown (Ohio) Playhouse, where he directed eighteen plays (1948–50); directed at Cape Playhouse (Summers 1948–50); directed productions at the Sombrero Th. (Phoenix, Ariz., Jan.–Mar. 1951); returned to Cape Playhouse (July–Aug. 1951); and returned again as managing director of the Youngstown (Ohio) Playhouse where he staged 12 productions (1952–53).

He directed summer theatre musical productions at Carter-Barron Amphitheatre (Washington, D.C., July–Aug. 1953); a touring production of *Sailor's Delight* (opened Huntington Hartford Th., Hollywood, Calif., Nov. 22, 1954; closed Lyceum, Minneapolis, Minn., Jan. 15, 1955); staged musical productions at the Iroquois Amphitheatre (Louisville, Ky., July–Aug. 1955); was managing director of the Honolulu (Hawaii) Community Th. (Sept. 6, 1955–Dec. 9, 1956); and director of the Williamsburg (Va.) Community Th. (Winter 1957).

He also directed a touring production of *House on the Rocks* (opened Shrine Aud., Harrisburg, Pa., June 21, 1958; closed Kenley Playhouse, Warren, Ohio, Aug. 9, 1958); and two seasons of stock at the Elitch Gardens Th. (Denver, Colo., Summers 1959, 1960).

He also directed summer-theatre productions in Worcester, Mass. (June 10, 1939), Falmouth, Mass. (1940), Olney, Md. (1940), Marblehead, Mass. (Aug. 19, 1941), Stamford, Conn. (Aug. 1942), Country Playhouse (Westport, Conn., July 1950), Fitchburg, Mass. (1952), Matunuck, R.I. (1952), Hinsdale, Ill. (1952), Ann Arbor, Mich. (1952), Princeton, N.J. (1953), Somerset, Mass. (1954), Bucks County Playhouse, New Hope, Pa. (1957–58).

Films. Mr. Sircom has directed *Notorious Sophie Lang* (Par., 1934); *Limehouse Blues* (Par., 1934); *Dangerous Corner* (RKO, 1934); and *One-Third of a Nation* (Par., 1939).

Other Activities. Mr. Sircom was lecturer on drama at the Yale Univ. Sch. of Drama (Jan. 1, 1940–Apr. 1941); head of the drama dept. at MacPhail Coll. of Music and Drama (winter sessions, 1946–48). Since 1933, he has directed three productions for the New York Amateur Comedy Club and eight for the Snarks (a women's theatre society) in N.Y.C.

Awards. Mr. Sircom received an award from the mayor of Minneapolis, Minn., for "outstanding service performed in Minneapolis' first Civic Theatre" (1947).

Since 1962, the annual awards given by the Youngstown Playhouse to those doing the best work in each phase of theatre work, have been named the Arthurs for Mr. Sircom who was director there in winters from 1948 through 1953.

Recreation. Music, writing, playing bridge.

SKELLY, MADGE. Actress, director, producer, educator. b. Madeleine Skelly, May 9, 1904, Pittsburgh, Pa., to Charles and Julia (Purcell) Skelly. Father, actor; mother, actress. Grad. Fifth Ave. H.S., Pittsburgh, 1920; Seton Hill Coll., B.A. 1924; Duquesne Univ., M.A. 1928; Univ. of Arizona (speech correction certificate) 1957; St. Louis Univ., Ph.D. 1961. Studied at AADA, N.Y.C., 1924–25. Married Dec. 8, 1928, to Richard Foust (dec. Apr. 6, 1963). During World War II, directed USO productions (1941–44); entertainment director at Nyack, N.Y., at POE (1944). Relatives in theatre: cousin, Hal Skelly, actor; uncle, Charles Purcell, actor; aunt, Irene Purcell, actress. Member of AEA; AFTRA; AFRA; Actors Fund (life mbr.); Council of Resident Stock Theatres (bd. of dir., 1959–61).

Miss Skelly was associate director of the Speech Clinic at Fontbonne Coll., St. Louis, and director of Speech Pathology Services at the V.A. Hospital and Shriners Hospital for Crippled Children.

Theatre. She made her debut touring with her mother at Little Willie in *East Lynne*, and one of the Kids in *Mrs. Wiggs of the Cabbage Patch* (Pennsylvania, West Virginia, Ohio, 1917); and performed in vaudeville productions (1918–19).

She made her N.Y.C. debut as Mrs. Lansing in *Lady Behave* (Cort, Nov. 16, 1943); toured New England as Penny in *You Can't Take It with You* (Summer 1944); directed productions at the Brattle Th. (Cambridge, Mass., Winters 1945–50); toured New England as Abby in *Arsenic and Old Lace* (Summer 1946); and was a member of the production staff of *A Young Man's Fancy* (Plymouth, N.Y.C., Apr. 29, 1947).

Miss Skelly was producer-manager and director at the Ramsdell Opera House, Manistee (Mich.) Summer Th. (1951–62); at the Drury Lane Th. (Chicago, Ill.), she played Penny in *You Can't Take It with You* (July–Aug. 1961), appeared in *The Man* (June–July 1962), and played Mabel Crosswaithe in *The Reluctant Debutante* (Aug. 1962).

Television. She appeared on You Be the Judge (CBS, 1945).

Other Activities. Miss Skelly taught theatre and speech at Duquesne Univ. (1936–40); Temple Univ. (1944–48); Univ. of Ariz. (1955–57); Maryville Coll. (1957–63); and St. Louis Univ. (1961–63).

Awards. She was selected by the Pittsburgh (Pa.) newspapers as the outstanding woman of the theatre (1937); received an Upjohn Fellowship to England (1951), and a citation from the Actors Fund for her service to regional professional theatres (1959).

SKINNER, CORNELIA OTIS. Actress, author. b. May 30, 1901, Chicago, Ill., to Otis and Maud (Durban) Skinner. Father, actor; mother, actress. Grad. Baldwin Sch., Bryn Mawr, Pa., 1918; Bryn Mawr Coll.; attended the Univ. of Paris (de la Sorbonne). Studied for the theatre at Jacques Copeau Sch., Paris; studied acting with Emile Dehelly, Paris. Married Oct. 2, 1928, to Alden Sanford Blodgett; one son. Member of AEA (2nd vice-pres., 1941); the Cosmopolitan Club; the Colony Club. Address: 131 E. 66th St., New York, NY 10022.

Theatre. Miss Skinner made her stage debut as Lady Macbeth in a student production of *Macbeth* (Bryn Mawr Coll.). She made her N.Y.C. debut as Dona Sarasate in her father's production of *Blood and Sand* (Empire Th., Sept. 20, 1921); subsequently played the Maid of Honor in *Will Shakespeare* (National, Jan. 1, 1923); Mrs. Ricketts in *Tweedles* (Frazee, Aug. 13, 1923); Geraldine Fairmont in *The Wild Westcotts* (Frazee, Dec. 24, 1923); Frances Bedell in *In His Arms* (Fulton, Oct. 13, 1924); and Sally Van Luyn in *White Collars* (Cort, Feb. 23, 1925).

Miss Skinner toured the US in a one-woman presentation of short character sketches of her own authorship, the first of similar programs (1925–28), in which she made her London debut (St. James's, June 1929). She appeared in the one-woman presentations of *The Wives of Henry VIII* (Avon, N.Y.C., Nov. 15, 1931), *The Empress Eugenie* (Lyceum, Nov. 22, 1932), *The Loves of Charles II* (48 St. Th., Dec. 27, 1933), and *Mansion on the Hudson* (Booth, Apr. 2, 1935).

She appeared in the title role in *Candida* (White Plains Playhouse, N.Y., Aug., 1935); appeared in her solo program (Little, London, Apr. 1937); appeared in a series of monologues entitled *Edna His Wife* (Little, N.Y.C., Dec. 7, 1937), which subsequently toured (1938). She toured in summer theatres as Cavallini in *Romance* (1938), the title role in *Candida* (1939), and Marion Froude in *Biography* (1940); played Angelica in *Love for Love* (Hudson, N.Y.C., June 3, 1940); Julie Lambert in *Theatre* (Hudson, Nov. 12, 1941), and on tour (1942); Emily Hazen in *The Searching Wind* (Fulton, N.Y.C., Apr. 12, 1944), and on its national tour (1944–45); and Mrs. Erlynne in *Lady Windermere's Fan* (Cort, N.Y.C., Oct. 14, 1946).

She performed in a program of her own character sketches (St. James's, London, June 28, 1949); and presented her one-woman program of *Paris '90* (Booth, N.Y.C., Mar. 4, 1952), in which she toured the US (1952–53), and also in London (St. Martin's, Feb. 22, 1954). She was Mistress of Ceremonies for the special *Highlights of the Empire* (Empire, N.Y.C., May 24, 1953); played Lady Britomart in *Major Barbara* (Martin Beck Th., Oct. 30, 1956); appeared in *Fun and Magic* (Shubert, Dec. 29, 1957); with Samuel Taylor, wrote and also played Katherine Dougherty in *The Pleasure of His Company* (Longacre, Oct. 22, 1958), and on tour (1959–60). She performed in *An Evening of Modern Character Sketches* (Paper Mill Playhouse, Millburn, N.J., May 1961); and appeared in the national company of *The Irregular Verb To Love* (1963–64).

Films. Miss Skinner appeared in *Kismet* (MGM, 1944) and *The Uninvited* (Par., 1944).

Television. She appeared in *Dearest Enemy* (NBC, Nov. 1955); *Merry Christmas, Mr. Baxter* (Alcoa Hour, NBC, Dec. 1956); on the Arthur Murray Show (NBC, July 15, 1957); was narrator for both Debutante '62 (NBC, Feb. 9, 1962) and *The Littlest Angel* (Exploring, NBC, Dec. 25, 1962); was in *Irregular Verb To Love* (NET, Nov. 1965); and *They* (NET Playhouse, Apr. 1970).

Published Works. Miss Skinner wrote the play, *Captain Fury* (1925); *Tiny Garments* (1932); *Excuse It, Please!* (1936); *Dithers and Jitters* (1938); *Soap Behind the Ears* (1941); with Emily Kimbrough, *Our Hearts Were Young and Gay* (1942); *Bottoms Up!* (1955); *Family Circle* (1948); *That's Me All Over* (1948), published in England as *Happy Family; The Ape in Me* (1959); and *Elegant Wits and Grand Horizontals* (1962).

She is also a regular contributor of stories and sketches to magazines, including *Vogue, Harper's Bazaar,* and *The New Yorker.*

Awards. Miss Skinner received the Barter Theatre Award for outstanding acting on the Broadway Stage (1952); the honorary degree of D.F.A. from Clark Univ., honorary L.H.D. and Phi Beta Kappa from the Univ. of Pennsylvania (June 1938); Honorary Doctor of Humanities degrees from St. Lawrence Univ., New York Univ., Univ. of Rochester, and Temple Univ. She has also received honorary degrees from Mills Coll. and Hofstra Coll. She is an Officier of the Academie Francaise (1954).

SKINNER, EDITH WARMAN. Educator, acting coach, voice, speech, and dialect coach. b. Edith Warman, Sept. 22, Moncton, New Brunswick, Canada, to Herbert Havelock and Agnes Lynn (Orr) Warman. Father, businessman; mother, teacher. Grad. Edith Cavell H.S., 1920; Leland Powers Sch., 1923; Columbia Univ., B.S. 1930, M.A. 1934. Studied speech (Summer 1925, 1926); and participated in Specialist class (1931–34) at Columbia with William Tilly; also studied with, and assistant to, Margaret Prendergast McLean. Married June 12, 1934, to Neil McFee Skinner, actor (marr. dis. 1939). Relatives in theatre: sister, Margaret Hewes Gosling, producer; nephew, Henry Hewes, drama critic for *Saturday Review/World.* Member of ATA. Address: (home) 1723 Wightman St., Pittsburgh, PA 15217; (bus.) c/o Carnegie-Mellon University Drama Dept., Pittsburgh, PA 15213.

Mrs. Skinner has been on the faculty of Carnegie-Mellon Univ. since 1937, serving as an Andrew Mellon Professor (1968–72); and visiting Andrew Mellon Professor (1972–74); and she is on the drama faculty of the Juilliard Sch. Division of Drama (1968–to date).

Theatre. Her productions at The Wharf Th. (Provincetown, Mass.) included *Ah, Wilderness,* starring Sinclair Lewis (1939). She was speech consultant for Siobhan McKenna's *Hamlet* (Th. de Lys, N.Y.C., Jan. 28, 1957); and speech coach for the Tyrone Guthrie Th. (Minneapolis, Minn., Spring 1964); the Amer. Conservatory Th. (William Ball, artistic dir., 1964–65); the Dana Andrews production of *Our Town* (1972); and the APA-Phoenix Repertory Co. (1966–68).

Published Works. She is the author of *Speak with Distinction,* and *Dialects for the Theatre.*

Awards. Mrs. Skinner was selected by the Pittsburgh *Gazette* as the outstanding woman in her field for her contribution to the community (Dec. 31, 1969).

SKINNER, TED. Educator. b. Donald Theodore Skinner, Apr. 5, 1911, Beverly, Kans., to Everton Thomas and Myrtle (Blount) Skinner. Father, banker, farm realtor. Grad. Manhattan (Kans.) H.S., 1929; attended Kansas State Univ., 1929–32; grad. Northwestern Univ., B.S. 1934; Colorado State Coll., M.A. 1938; Northwestern Univ., Ph.D. 1948. Married Dec. 25, 1936, to Mary French, teacher (marr. dis. Sept. 8, 1948); two sons, one daughter; married Jan. 22, 1950, to Mary Evelyn Goodman; one son, two daughters. Member of AETA; CTC; SAA; Southern Speech Assn.; Texas Speech Assn. (secy., 1955–58; vice-pres., 1963–64); Delta Tau Delta; Alpha Psi Omega; Pi Kappa Delta.

Since 1955, Mr. Skinner has been head of the Speech Dept. at Lamar State Coll. of Technology and Dean of the Sch. of Fine Arts. He has also directed student productions.

He was director of theatre at Valley Falls (Kan.) H.S. (1935–36); Manhattan (Kan.) H.S. (1936–38); Boulder (Colo.) H.S. (1938–43); Kansas State Teachers Coll. (1944–46); Southern Illinois Univ. (1947); and Texas Coll. of Arts & Industries (1947–55). He was a member of the directing staff at Northwestern University Th. (Summer 1943, 1944).

Since Sept. 1969, Mr. Skinner has served as director of theatre at the United States International Univ., San Diego, Calif., where he directed undergraduate theatre and Readers Theatre productions from 1969–73. He has been on a leave-of-absence since Sept. 1973. Address: 4785 Cobb Dr., San Diego, CA 92117.

Published Works. Mr. Skinner has contributed articles to *Dramatics Magazine, Quarterly Journal of Speech,* and *The Speech Teacher.*

Recreation. Tennis, golf, traveling, camping, and jogging.

SKIRPAN, STEPHEN J. Theatre equipment designer, lighting control consultant, inventor, writer; board chairman, President and major shareholder of Skirpan Lighting Control Corporation. b. Stephen James Skirpan, Aug. 13, 1930, Monessen, Pa., to John M. and Emma H. (Hudock) Skirpan. Father, physician. Grad. St. Vincent Coll. Prep. Sch., Latrobe, Pa., 1947; Univ. of Pittsburgh B.A. 1953; Yale Univ. Sch. of Drama, M.F.A. 1956. Married 1959, to Ann Beamon; one son, one daughter. Member of IATSE Local 3; AETA; ANTA; SMPTE; IES; USITT. Address: (home) 340 E. 80th St., New York, NY 10021, tel. (212) 988-0797; (bus.) c/o Skirpan Lighting Control Corp., 61-03 32nd Ave., Woodside, NY 11377, tel. (212) 274-7222.

Theatre. Mr. Skirpan was property master for the Civic Light Opera Assn. (Pittsburgh, Pa., Summer 1954); and worked as electrician at the Casino Th. (Pittsburgh, Pa., 1950–52); Shubert Th. (New Haven, Conn., 1953–56); and the Metropolitan Opera House (N.Y.C., 1959).

He was lighting control consultant for the new Metropolitan Opera House at Lincoln Center, New York, 1964, and lighting control consultant to the CBS Television, 1973.

Mr. Skirpan holds the following U.S. Patents on Theatre Dimmers and Control Systems: Patent 2,994,804, Aug. 1, 1961, *Lighting Control System;* Patent 3,049,645, Aug. 14, 1962, *Preset Lighting Control System;* Patent 3,193,725, July 6, 1965, *Control System for Solid Stage Controlled Rectifiers;* Patent 3,193,728, July 6, 1965, *Silicon Controlled Rectifier Dimmer;* Patent 3,397,344, August 13, 1968, *Lighting Control Apparatus;* Patent 3,534,224, October 13, 1970, *Control Apparatus for Electronic Dimmers;* Patent 3,534,242, Oct. 13, 1970, *Modular Control Units for Light Intensity Control Systems;* Patent 3,816,797, *Solid State Electronic Dimmer.*

Mr. Skirpan received a patent for the first system with infinite presetting for stage lighting control.

Other Activities. Mr. Skirpan was manager of the Stage Lighting Division of Metropolitan Electric Manufacturing Company, Long Island City, N.Y., 1956–59; manager of the Stage Lighting Division of Ward Leonard Electric Company, Mount Vernon, N.Y., 1959–64. In 1965 he organized Skirpan Lighting Control Corporation which designs and manufactures stage and studio lighting control systems. The company has produced thousands of dimmer systems for theatres and television studios throughout North America.

Published Works. He wrote *Electronic Lighting Control For Theatre and Television,* Official Bulletin of the IATSE, Winter 1957–58, No. 414; *Dimmer Systems for Theatrical Control,* distributed by USITT, November 1961; *Something New In Dimmers,* Official Bulletin of the IATSE, Part I–Winter 1961–62, Part II–Spring 1962, and *Professional Lighting Control,* 1968.

Awards. He received the Theatron Award for Stage Lighting (1952).

Recreation. Mr. Skirpan is a private pilot, skeet shooter and star gazer.

SKLAR, GEORGE. Playwright, novelist. b. May 31, 1908, Meriden, Conn., to Ezak and Bertha (Marshak) Sklar. Parents, sporting goods store owners. Grad. Meriden H.S., 1925; Yale Univ., B.A. (Phi Beta Kappa) 1929. Married Aug. 21, 1935, to Miriam Blecher, dancer, choreographer, teacher of modern dance; two sons, one daughter. Member of Dramatists Guild (exec. council, 1936–40), ALA, ELT (vice-pres. for Dramatists Guild, 1940–41). Address: 530 N. Fuller Ave., Los Angeles, CA 90036.

Theatre. Mr. Sklar wrote with Albert Maltz, *Merry-Go-Round* (Provincetown Playhouse, N.Y.C., Apr. 22, 1932), and *Peace on Earth* (Civic Repertory Th., Nov. 29, 1933).

With Paul Peters, he wrote *Stevedore* (Civic Repertory Th., Apr. 18, 1934, revived Oct. 1, 1934; Embassy, London, England, May 7, 1934); was a co-author of the revue *Parade* (Guild, May 20, 1935); and wrote *Life and Death of an American* (Maxine Elliott's Th., May 19, 1939).

Mr. Sklar and Vera Caspary adapted *Laura,* from Miss Caspary's novel of the same title ("Q," London, Jan. 30, 1945; Cort, N.Y.C., June 26, 1947).

He wrote *And People All Around* (Tufts Arena Th. July 15, 1966; followed by 40 productions in regional, community and university theatres; also produced by Bristol Old Vic, London, England, Oct. 30, 1967 and in Moscow, May 27, 1972); and wrote *Brown Pelican* (Alliance Th., Atlanta, Ga., Feb. 17, 1972).

Films. He wrote the screenplay for *Afraid to Talk* (U, 1932). He was a contract screenwriter for Columbia and Warner Brothers studios (1940–45), where he wrote or collaborated on the screenplays for *City without Men* (1943); and *First Comes Courage* (1943).

Published Works. Mr. Sklar wrote *Merry Go Round* (1932); *Peace on Earth* (1933); *Stevedore* (1934); *Parade* (1935); *Life and Death of an American* (1942); *Laura* (1947); *The Two Worlds of Johnny* (1947); *The Promising Young Men* (1951); *The House-warming* (1953); *The Identity of Dr. Frazier* (1961); *And People All Around* (1967 and 1968); and *Brown Pelican* (1974).

Awards. Mr. Sklar received a John Golden Fellowship in Playwriting (1939); and his play *And People All Around* was the 1966–67 selection of the American Playwrights Theatre.

SLEEPER, MARTHA. Actress. b. Martha Marie Sleeper, June 24, 1910, Lake Bluff, Ill., to William Bancroft and Minnie (Akass) Sleeper. Attended public schools in N.Y.C. and Los Angeles, Calif. Studied dance with Edward Chalif, five years. Married Apr. 7, 1934, to Hardie Albright, actor (marr. dis. Apr. 1940); married Feb. 14, 1941, to Harry Dresser Deutchbein, construction engineer. Member of AEA; SAG. Address: 106 Fortaleza, San Juan, Puerto Rico 00901.

Theatre. Miss Sleeper made her N.Y.C. debut as Madge Horton in *Stepping Out* (Fulton Th., May 20, 1929); subsequently played Paula in *Dinner at Eight* (Belasco, Los Angeles, Calif., 1933); appeared in *Double Door* (Mayan, Los Angeles, Feb. 19, 1934); played Mary Thorpe in *Good Men and True* (Biltmore, N.Y.C., Oct. 25, 1935); Kay Rowley in *Russet Mantle* (Masque, Jan. 16, 1936); and Princess Helene in *Save Me the Waltz* (Martin Beck Th., Feb. 28, 1938).

She appeared in *No More Ladies* (Th.-by-the-Sea, Matunuck, R.I., Aug. 1938; Red Barn, Locust Valley, N.Y., July 24, 1939); played Birdie Carrin in *I Must Love Someone* (Longacre, N.Y.C., Feb. 7, 1939); Julie in *The Cream in the Well* (Booth, Jan. 20, 1941); Tana Kincaid in *The Land Is Bright* (Music Box, Oct. 28, 1941); Gloria Endicott in *The Perfect Marriage* (Ethel Barrymore Th., Oct. 26, 1944); Harriet Vinion in *The Rugged Path* (Plymouth, Nov. 10, 1945); and Mrs. Blake in *Christopher Blake* (Music Box, Nov. 30, 1946).

Films. Miss Sleeper has appeared in *The Mailman* (FBO, 1923); *Skinner's Big Idea* (FBO, 1928); *Danger Street* (FBO, 1928); *The Air Legion* (RKO, 1928); *Taxi Thirteen* (FBO, 1929); *Voice of the Storm* (RKO, 1929); *Our Blushing Brides* (MGM, 1930); *War Nurse* (MGM, 1930); *Confessions of a Co-Ed* (Par., 1931); *Huddle* (MGM, 1932); *Rasputin and the Empress* (MGM, 1932); *Midnight Mary* (MGM, 1933); *Penthouse* (MGM, 1933); *Broken Dreams* (Mono., 1933); *Spitfire* (RKO, 1934); *West of the Pecos* (RKO, 1934); *Great God Gold* (Mono., 1935); *The Scoundrel* (Par., 1935); *Two Sinners* (Rep., 1935); *Tomorrow's Youth* (Mono., 1935); *Rhythm on the Range* (Par., 1936); *Four Days' Wonder* (U, 1937); and *The Bells of St. Mary's* (RKO, 1945).

SLEZAK, WALTER. Actor, singer, writer. b. Walter Leo Slezak, May 3, 1902, Vienna, Austria, to Leo and Elsa (Wertheim) Slezak. Father, opera singer, writer, comedian. Attended Theresianum, Vienna; Maximilians Gymnasium, Munich; Piaristen Convict, Vienna; and the Univ. of Vienna. Married Oct. 10, 1943, to Johanna Van Rijn, one son, two daughters. Member of SAG; AEA; AGMA; AFTRA.

Pre-Theatre. Medical student, bank clerk.

Theatre. Mr. Slezak made his N.Y.C. debut as Eric Molinar in *Meet My Sister* (Shubert Th., Dec. 30, 1930); subsequently appeared as Karl Reder in *Music in the Air* (Alvin, Nov. 8, 1932); Arno in the Philadelphia (Pa.) production of the pre-Bway tour of *Love! Out of the Window* (opened Erlanger, Oct. 1934); the Policeman in *Ode to Liberty* (Lyceum, N.Y.C., Dec. 21, 1934); Prof. Johann Volk in *May Wine* (St. James, Dec. 5, 1935); Thorvald Helmer in *A Doll's House* (Central City, Colo., July 1937); Harry Mischka Szigetti in *I Married an Angel* (Shubert, N.Y.C., May 11, 1938); and Emil Onzain in *Little Dark Horse* (John Golden Th., Nov. 16, 1941).

He played Joseph in *My Three Angels* (Morosco, Apr. 11, 1953); played Panisse in *Fanny* (Majestic, Nov. 4, 1954); the Prince Regent of England in *The First Gentleman* (Belasco, Apr. 15, 1957); Elliott Nash in *The Gazebo* (Lyceum, Dec. 12, 1958); made his opera debut as Szupan in *The Gypsy Baron* (Metropolitan Opera House, Nov. 25, 1959); was Fagin in *Oliver!* (Westbury Music Fair, N.Y., July 12, 1966); toured as Henry II in *The Lion in Winter* (Jan.–May 1968); and appeared as Frosch in *Die Fledermaus* (San Francisco Opera, Calif., Fall 1973).

Films. Since his debut in *Once Upon a Honeymoon* (RKO, 1942), Mr. Slezak has appeared in *This Land Is Mine* (RKO, 1943); *The Fallen Sparrow* (RKO, 1943); *And Now Tomorrow* (Par., 1944); *Lifeboat* (20th-Fox, 1944); *Till We Meet Again* (Par., 1944); *The Princess and the Pirate* (RKO, 1944); *The Spanish Main* (RKO, 1945); *Cornered* (RKO, 1945); *Salome Where She Danced* (U, 1945); *Born To Kill* (RKO, 1947); *Riffraff* (RKO, 1947); *Sinbad the Sailor* (RKO, 1947); *The Pirate* (MGM, 1948); *The Inspector General* (WB, 1949); *Yellow Cab Man* (MGM, 1950); *Bedtime for Bonzo* (U, 1951); *People Will Talk* (20th-Fox, 1951); *Confidentially Connie* (MGM, 1953); *Call Me Madam* (20th-Fox, 1953); *White Witch Doctor* (20th-Fox, 1953); *The Steel Cage* (UA, 1954); *Ten Thousand Bedrooms* (MGM, 1957); *Deadlier Than the Male* (Cont. 1957); *The Miracle* (WB, 1959); *The Gazebo* (MGM, 1960); *Come September* (U, 1961); *The Wonderful World of the Brothers Grimm* (MGM, 1962); *Emil and the Detectives* (Buena Vista, 1963); *Wonderful Life* (1964); *Swinger's Paradise* (Amer. Intl., 1965); *Dr. Coppelius* (Childhood, 1968); and *Black Beauty* (Par., 1971).

Television and Radio. Mr. Slezak played on more than two hundred dramatic radio programs; and has been a guest panelist on the opera quiz (Metropolitan Opera Broadcast).

On television, Mr. Slezak was in Studio One (CBS) productions on *Collector's Item, The Innocence of Pastor Muller* (both 1951), and *Portrait of a Citizen* (1956); in *Arms and the Man* (Omnibus, CBS, May 1953); *The Good Fairy* (Hallmark Hall of Fame, NBC, Feb. 1956); *Honored Guest* (Robert Montgomery Presents, NBC, June 1956); *The Best Wine* (Goodyear Playhouse, NBC, Sept. 1957); *Pinocchio* (NBC, Oct. 1957); *The Slightly Fallen Angel* (Alcoa Th., NBC, May 1959); *My Three Angels* (Ford Startime, NBC, Dec. 1959); on Great Mysteries (NBC) in *The Woman in White* (May 1960) and *The Inspector Vanishes* (Aug. 1960); in *A Cry of Angels* (Hallmark Hall of Fame, NBC, Dec. 1963); and *Heidi* (NBC, Nov. 1968). He appeared also in such series as Rawhide (CBS, 1963); 77 Sunset Strip (ABC, 1963); Dr. Kildare (NBC, 1964); Batman (ABC, 1966); and One Life to Live (ABC, 1974).

Published Works. He is author of *What Time's the Next Swan?* (1962).

Awards. Mr. Slezak received the Antoinette Perry (Tony) Award for the best leading actor in a musical, and won the critics award for his performance as Panisse in *Fanny.* .

Recreation. Scuba diving, chess, aviation, riding, golf, cooking, eating, thinking.

SMALLEY, WEBSTER. Playwright, producer, teacher. b. Webster Leroy Croxdale Smalley, Feb. 23, 1921, Walla Walla, Wash., to Earl T. and Zoa (Smalley) Croxdale. Attended Bellingham (Wash.) H.S.; Univ. of Washington, B.A. 1946; Columbia Univ., M.A. 1948; Stanford Univ., Ph.D. 1960. Married Oct. 1946 to Pernella Allen; two daughters, one son. Served 330th Inf., 83rd Div., Eur. Th., US Army, WW II; rank, 1st Sgt.; Bronze Star. Member of ATA, Na'l. Th. Conference; Speech Communication Assn. Address: (home) 903 W. 31st St., Austin, TX 78709, tel. (512) 452-5416; (bus.) Dept. of Drama, Univ. of Texas, Austin, TX 78712.

Mr. Smalley is chairman of the Dept. of Drama, Univ. of Texas, (1972–to date) and professor of playwriting (1969–to date). He was an instructor of playwriting, Univ. of Illinois (1950–51) and Univ. of Missouri (1952–53), and associate professor of theatre, Univ. of Illinois at Urbana (1955–69).

He is artistic director of the Conkel Workshop for Playwrights (Univ. of Texas at Austin, Summers 1970–to date) and chairman of the Playwrights Project, Univ. Resident Theatre Assn. (1972–to date). In 1949–50 he headed the script department of ANTA and Experimental Th. Inc. (N.Y.C.).

His play *Fragment* was produced off-Bway, N.Y.C., 1949.

Published Works. Mr. Smalley edited and wrote the introduction for *Five Plays* by Langston Hughes (1963) and wrote "The Man with the Oboe" (*Players*, Apr. 1963) and *Taste for Violence* (commissioned for the Illinois Sesquicentennial).

Awards. He received the New Play of the Year Award from the Southeast Theatre Conference in 1963.

SMITH, DODIE. Playwright, actress, author. b. May 3, Whitefield, Lancaster, England, to Ernest and Ella (Furber) Smith. Attended Whalley Range High School, Manchester and St. Paul's Girls' Sch., London, England. Studied acting at RADA, 1914–15. Married 1939 to Alec Macbeth Beesley. Member of Dramatists Guild, Society of Authors. Address: The Barretts, Finchingfield, Essex, England.

Theatre. Miss Smith wrote *Autumn Crocus* (Morosco, N.Y.C., Nov. 19, 1932); *Call It a Day* (Morosco, Jan. 28, 1936); *Dear Octopus* (Broadhurst, Jan. 11, 1939); and *Lovers and Friends* (Plymouth, Nov. 29, 1943). Until 1935 she wrote her plays under the pseudonym of C. L. Anthony.

In England she appeared in the sketch *Playgoers* (Tottenham Palace, 1915); toured in *Kitty Grey*, and *Mr. Wu* (1915); *Ye Gods, Jane*, and *Niobe* (1916–17); and appeared in *When Knights Were Bold* (Kingsway, Nov. 17, 1917). During 1918 she played in several music-hall sketches, appeared in various roles with the Portsmouth Repertory Co., and went to Dieppe, France, with a Lena Ashwell Concert Party. In England, she toured as Claudine in *Telling the Tale* (1919–20), and in *French Leave* (1921); appeared in *The Showing Up of Blanco Posnet* (Queen's Th., London, July 20, 1921); and played with the Everyman Company (Zurich, Switzerland, 1922).

Miss Smith wrote *British Talent* (Three Arts Club, London, 1924); *Autumn Crocus* (Lyric, Apr. 6, 1931); *Service* (Wyndham's, Oct. 12, 1932); *Touch Wood* (Haymarket, May 16, 1934); *Call It a Day* (Globe, Oct. 30, 1935); *Bonnet Over the Windmill* (New, Sept. 8, 1937); *Dear Octopus* (Queen's Th., Sept. 14, 1938 revived Haymarket, 1967); *Letter from Paris* adapted from Henry James' "The Reverberator" (Aldwych, Oct. 10, 1952); *I Capture the Castle* adapted from her novel of the same title (Aldwych, Mar. 4, 1954); and *These People, Those Books* which had a pre-London tryout (opened Grand Th., Leeds, Sept. 29, 1958).

Films. While at RADA, Miss Smith wrote a screenplay *Schoolgirl Rebels*, under the pen-name, Charles Henry Percy. She was associated with MGM (Hollywood, Calif., 1939); and Paramount (Hollywood, 1942; 1949).

The following motion pictures were adapted from her books and plays: *Looking Forward* adapted from her play *Service* (MGM, 1944); *Autumn Crocus* (Eng., 1934); *Call It a Day* (WB, 1937); *Dear Octopus* (Eng., 1945); and *The Hundred and One Dalmatians* adapted from her children's book of that name (Buena Vista, 1961).

Published Works. Miss Smith wrote the novels *I Capture the Castle* (1948); *The New Moon with the Old* (1963); *The Town in Bloom* (1965); *It Ends with Revelations* (1967); and *A Tale of Two Families* (1970). She also wrote the children's books *The Hundred and One Dalmatians* (1957); *The Starlight Barking* (1967); and the autobiography, *Look Back with Love* (1974).

Recreation. Reading, music, television, dogs.

SMITH, DOYLE R. Producer, actor, director, educator. b. Doyle Raymond Smith, May 25, 1924, Lima, Ohio, to Raymond Paul and Mary M. (Purnell) Smith. Father, jurist; mother, teacher. Grad. Lima Central H.S., 1942; attended Ohio Northern Univ. Law School, 1947–48; Drake Univ., 1948–49; grad. Univ. of Texas, M.F.A. 1951; attended Univ. of Oregon at Eugene Graduate School (1967–69). Married June 12, 1948, to Sara L. Schwab; two daughters. Served USAAF, Bomber Pilot, 1943–45; USAF Res. (ret.); rank, Capt. Member of AETA; ANTA; European Recreation Society, Toastmasters Intl., Bremerhaven Chapter (2nd vice-pres., pres., 1963; pres., 1964), Theta Alpha Phi, Pi Kappa Alpha; B.P.O.E. #174; Board of Deacons of First Congregational Church, Tacoma, Washington. Address: 3719 N. 36th St., Tacoma, WA 98407, tel. (206) 752-5068.

From 1955–60, Mr. Smith was assistant professor and director of theatre at Ohio Northern Univ., where he inaugurated the curricular program for a major in theatre. Since 1960 he has been employed as Entertainment Director, Army Special Services, Europe, stationed in France and Germany.

In addition to roles in university theatre, he has appeared professionally as Gratiano in *Othello* (Jan Hus House, N.Y.C., Jan.–Feb. 1954); Preston Mitchell in *For Love or Money*, John in *The Constant Wife*, the Hero in *Love Rides the Rails*, and Victor in *Private Lives* (Hutchinson Summer Th., Raymond, N.H., June–Aug. 1954); played Uncle Ben in *Death of a Salesman;* and Howard Bevins in *Picnic* (Malden Bridge Playhouse, N.Y., Aug.–Sept. 1957); Captain McLean in *The Teahouse of the August Moon*, Mr. Stratton in *Separate Tables*, Horace Vandergelder in *The Matchmaker*, Bud Walters in *Anniversary Waltz*, and Percival Browne in *The Boy Friend* (Weston Playhouse, Vt., July–Sept. 1958); and A. T. Packard in *Old Four Eyes*, an historical drama (Burning Hills Amphitheatre, Medora, N.D., Summer 1959).

As an Army Special Services Entertainment Director in France, he directed and produced *Born Yesterday* (Oct. 1960), and *Stalag 17* (Oct. 1961); at the Green Room Th., Bremerhaven, Germany, he produced *See How They Run* (Feb. 1962); directed and produced *The Boy Friend* (May 1962); produced *Muletail Prime* (July 1962); *Hello, Out There* (July 1962); *Fumed Oak* (July 1962); and *Death of a Salesman* (Nov.–Dec. 1962; moved to Bremerhaven Stadttheater, Dec. 1962); directed and produced *The Teahouse of the August Moon* (Feb. 1963; moved to Bremerhaven Stadttheater, Feb. 1963); directed and produced *Roman Candle* (Oct. 1963); produced Dickens' *Christmas Carol* (Dec. 1963); *Mrs. McThing* (Feb. 1964); produced and directed *Someone Waiting* (May 1964); and produced *Mind of a Killer* and *American Dream* (June 1964).

He produced and directed *A Sleep of Prisoners* (Apr. 1965), *Arsenic and Old Lace* (Oct. 1966), *Down in the Valley* and *Carousel* (May 1967) in the Green Room Th. and Bremerhaven Stadttheater, Bremerhaven, Germany; and toured Amerika Haus facilities through West Germany with American one-act plays under the auspices of USIS, American Embassy, Bonn (Jan.–Mar. 1967). He returned to the US in 1967 to attend the Univ. of Oregon at Eugene, where he was staging director for the Opera Workshop, School of Music. He sang Gherardo in *Gianni Schichi* and Monastoatos in *Die Zauberflute* for the Opera Workshop; the Balladeer in *Apple Tree* for the University Th.; and Dr. Falke in *Die Fledermaus* with the Eugene Symphony.

At the Tacoma Little Th., Tacoma, Wash., he directed *The Odd Couple, Night of the Iquana, Don't Drink the Water, Time of the Cuckoo, Waltz of the Toreadors, The Reluctant Debutante;* and was staging and musical director for *The King and I* (1969–70 season).

From 1970–to date, he was drama and music theatre critic for the *Tacoma Review* and free-lance critic for the *Tacoma News Tribune*, covering the Seattle Opera, the Seattle Repertory Th., and local university and community theatre productions. He is part-time professor of theatre and speech at Fort Steilacoom Community Coll., where he designed *Butterflies Are Free;* and was staging and musical director for *Guys and Dolls*. He played Mortimer in *Arsenic and Old Lace* for the Lakewood Players; was founding director/producer of Vagabond Theatres; and produced and directed *Diary of Adam and Eve*, which toured local schools.

Radio. He directed a thirteen-week series of original dramatic radio scripts for AFN, Europe; served as casting consultant and actor for English-language radio shows with Radio Bremen and Deutsche Rundfunk, Hamburg (Germany); and was guest emcee for the local radio talk show, Personal Choice, over Radio KTNT.

Awards. He received the 1962 USAREUR Tournament of Plays Best Play Award for his production of *Death of a Salesman* (Bremerhaven, Germany, Nov. 1962). His production of *The Teahouse of the August Moon* was invited to perform at the *Grosseshaus* (large house) in the Bremerhaven Stadttheater, the first time an American amateur community theatre group was invited to give a performance in a German professional theatre (1963).

SMITH, KENT. Actor. b. Frank Kent Smith, Mar. 19, 1907, New York City, to James E. and Charlotte L. Smith. Father, hotel owner and manager; mother, singer. Grad. Phillip's Exeter Acad., N.H., 1925; attended Harvard Univ., 1930. Married Jan. 15, 1937, to Elizabeth V. Gillette (marr. dis. 1954); one daughter; married Mar. 10, 1962, to Edith Atwater, actress. Served USAAF, 1943–45; rank, Pfc. Member of AEA (councillor, 1937–39; 1949–54); SAG; AFTRA.

Theatre. Mr. Smith first appeared on the stage assisting Blackstone, the Magician, from the audience (Gaiety Th., N.Y.C., Aug. 28, 1917); subsequently was a co-founder of the Univ. Players Guild (West Falmouth, Mass.), appearing with them as a leading man (Summers 1928–32), and appeared in Winter stock at the Maryland Th. (Baltimore, Md., 1932).

He appeared in productions at the Wardman Park Hotel Childrens Th. (Washington, D.C., 1929); played a juvenile in the pre-Bway tryout of *Blind Window*, which closed out of town (opened Ford's, Baltimore, Aug. 15, 1929) and appeared in juvenile roles (Goodman Memorial Th., Chicago, Ill., 1930; Univ. Players Guild, Maryland Th., Baltimore, 1931).

He played Lt. Chase in *Men Must Fight* (Lyceum, N.Y.C., Oct. 14, 1932); appeared in *Heat Lightning* (Booth, Sept. 15, 1933); *Spring in Autumn* (Henry Miller's Th., Oct. 24, 1933); as Karl Hoffman in *Drums Begin* (Shubert, Nov. 24, 1933); and Kurt von Obersdorf in *Dodsworth* (Shubert, Feb. 24, 1934).

He played Apollodoros in *Caesar and Cleopatra* (Suffern Playhouse, N.Y., June 10, 1935); Dunois in Katharine Cornell's *Saint Joan* (Martin Beck Th., N.Y.C., Mar. 9, 1936); Bob Winthrop in *Seen But Not Heard* (Henry Miller's Th., Sept. 17, 1936); Phineas McQuestion in *Wingless Victory* (Empire, Dec. 23, 1936); James Morell in *Candida* (Empire, Mar. 10, 1937); was leading man at Elitch Gardens (Denver, Colo., Summer 1937); played Duffy in *The Star-Wagon* (Empire, N.Y.C., Sept. 29, 1937); Matt Grogan in *How to Get Tough About It* (Martin Beck Th., Feb. 8, 1938); succeeded (Mar. 1938) Dennis King as Torvald Helmer in *A Doll's House* (Morosco, Dec. 27, 1937); and appeared in the pre-Bway tryout of *Herod and Marianne*, which closed out of town (opened Washington, D.C., Sept. 27, 1938).

Mr. Smith played the title role in *Jeremiah* (Guild, N.Y.C., Feb. 3, 1939); appeared in *Beaux' Stratagem* (Dock St. Th., Charleston, S.C., Mar. 29, 1939); as Peter Tor in *Christmas Eve* (Henry Miller's Th., N.Y.C., Dec. 27, 1939); "Hank" Rogers in *International Incident* (Ethel Barrymore Th., Apr. 2, 1940); appeared as the Actor and Guardian in a summer tour of *The Guardsman* (1940); played Rudd Kendall in *Old Acquaintance* (Morosco, N.Y.C., Dec. 23, 1940); and for the Actors Lab. Th. (Hollywood, Calif.), played Major Joppolo in *A Bell for Adano* (c. Sept. 1946).

He played Reverdy Johnson in *The Story of Mary Surratt* (Henry Miller's Th., N.Y.C., Jan. 20, 1947); Enobarbus in *Antony and Cleopatra* (Martin Beck Th., Nov. 28, 1947); Joe Saul in *Burning Bright* (Broadhurst, Nov. 19, 1948); Bolingbroke in *Richard II* (NY City Ctr., Feb. 10, 1949); Yancey in *The Wisteria Trees* (Martin Beck Th., Sept. 22, 1950); Edward Crossman in *The Autumn Garden* (Coronet, Mar. 7, 1951); toured as Cosmo Constantine in *Call Me Madam* (opened National, Washington, D.C., May 5, 1952; closed Shubert, Chicago, Ill., Apr. 18, 1953); appeared in *Paint Your Wagon* (Dallas State Fair, Tex., Summer 1953); played Colonel Sir Francis Chesney in *Charley's Aunt* (NY City Ctr., Dec.

22, 1953); John Shend in *What Every Woman Knows* (NY City Ctr., Dec. 22, 1954), also touring in it; Angelo in *Measure for Measure* (Amer. Shakespeare Festival, Stratford, Conn., Summer 1954); took over for Anthony Ross as the Professor during the run of *Bus Stop* (Music Box, N.Y.C., Mar. 2, 1955); played Warwick in Siobhan McKenna's *Saint Joan* (Phoenix, Sept. 11, 1956); Jamie Garland in the pre-Bway tryout of *Sweet Love Remembered* (opened Shubert, New Haven, Conn., Dec. 28, 1959; closed there, Dec. 31, 1959); succeeded (Chicago, Nov. 1961) Melvyn Douglas as William Russell in the national company tour of *The Best Man* (opened Hanna, Cleveland, Ohio, Sept. 16, 1961; closed Forrest, Philadelphia, Pa., Feb. 3, 1962); and appeared in a revival of *Ah, Wilderness!* (Pasadena Playhouse, Calif., 1966).

Films. Mr. Smith made his film debut in *Cat People* (RKO, 1942); followed by *Forever and a Day* (RKO, 1943); *Hitler's Children* (RKO, 1943); *Youth Runs Wild* (RKO, 1944); *The Spiral Staircase* (RKO, 1946); *The Voice of the Turtle* (WB, 1947); *Magic Town* (RKO, 1947); *Nora Prentiss* (WB, 1947); *The Fountainhead* (WB, 1949); *My Foolish Heart* (RKO, 1949); *The Damned Don't Cry* (WB, 1950); *Paula* (Col., 1952); *Comanche* (UA, 1956); *Sayonara* (WB, 1957); *Imitation General* (MGM, 1958); *The Badlanders* (MGM, 1958); *The Balcony* (Continental, 1963); *Covenant with Death* (WB, 1967); *Games* (U, 1967); *Kona Coast* (WB, 1968); *Assignment to Kill* (WB, 1968); *Pete 'n' Tillie* (U, 1972); and *Cops and Robbers* (UA, 1973).

Television. Mr. Smith played Death in *Death Takes a Holiday* (closed circuit, NBC, Sept. 16, 1939); was in many dramas on such programs as Philco Playhouse (NBC, 1950, 1951); Robert Montgomery Presents (NBC, 1951, 1953, 1957); Armstrong Circle Th. (NBC, 1951, 1957); Studio One (CBS, 1952); and Pulitzer Prize Playhouse (ABC, 1952). He appeared in *Richard II* (Hallmark Hall of Fame, NBC, Jan. 24, 1954); *Dark Victory* (Front Row Center, CBS, July 27, 1955); *Last Town Car* (GE Th., CBS, Feb. 1958); *The Night Stalker* (ABC, Jan. 1972); *Probe* (NBC, Feb. 1972); and *Another Part of the Forest* (Hollywood Television Th., PBS, Oct. 1972).

He also appeared on episodes of many series, including Have Gun, Will Travel (CBS, 1957, 1961, 1962); Wagon Train (NBC, 1960); Perry Mason (CBS, 1961, 1963); Gunsmoke (CBS, 1963, 1964); Great Adventure (CBS, 1964); Peyton Place (ABC, 1964); Beverly Hillbillies (CBS, 1965); Mission Impossible (CBS, 1967); Invaders (ABC, 1967); The F.B.I. (ABC, 1967, 1969); The Governor and J.J. (CBS, 1969, 1970); Night Gallery (NBC, 1972); Delphi Bureau (ABC, 1972); and Owen Marshall (ABC, 1972).

Recreation. Croquet, music.

SMITH, LOIS. Actress. b. Lois Arlene Humbert, Nov. 3, 1930, Topeka, Kans., to William O. and Carrie (Gottshalk) Humbert. Father, telephone company employee. Grad. Lincoln H.S., Seattle, Wash., 1948; studied at Univ. of Washington, 1948–51; Actors Studio, N.Y.C. (1955–to date). Married Nov. 5, 1948, to Wesley D. Smith, educator; one daughter. Member of AEA; SAG; AFTRA; Actors Studio; Ensemble Studio Theater Workshop. Address: c/o William McCaffrey Agency, 501 Madison Ave., New York, NY 10022, tel. (212) EL 5-1076.

Theatre. Miss Smith appeared as Jeannie in *Time Out for Ginger* (Lyceum Th., N.Y.C., Nov. 26, 1952); Antoinette in *The Wisteria Trees* (NY City Ctr., Feb. 2, 1955); Josephine in *The Young and Beautiful* (Longacre, Oct. 1, 1955; Arts, London, Eng., Aug. 15, 1956); Laura in *The Glass Menagerie* (NY City Ctr., Nov. 21, 1956); Carol Cutrere in *Orpheus Descending* (Martin Beck Th., Mar. 21, 1957); Mary Devlin in *Edwin Booth* (46 St. Th., Nov. 24, 1958); Alley in *Ding Dong Bell* (Westport Country Playhouse, Conn., Summer 1961); Sheila Knight in *Time of Hope* (Playhouse-in-the-Park, Philadelphia, Pa., Summer 1963); and Lucha Moreno in *Bicycle Ride to Nevada* (Cort, N.Y.C., Sept. 21, 1963).

At the Theatre of the Living Arts, Philadelphia, Pa., Miss Smith appeared as Virginia in *Galileo* (Jan. 6, 1965), Andromache in *Tiger at the Gates* (Feb. 9, 1965), Célimène in *The Misanthrope* (Mar. 16, 1965), Elena in *Uncle Vanya* (Nov. 16, 1965), Julie in *Miss Julie* (Mar. 22, 1966), and Pamela in *The Last Analysis* (May 3, 1966). She was also in the company's presentation of *A Dream of Love* (Sept. 13, 1966) and played the Preacher Woman in TLA's production of *Bechlch* (Dec. 20, 1966). She played Sonya in *Uncle Vanya* (Mark Taper Forum, Los Angeles, Calif., Aug. 21, 1969); Mary in *Sunday Dinner* (American Place Th. at St. Clement's Church, N.Y.C., Oct. 16, 1970); appeared in the four one-act plays comprising *Present Tense* (Sheridan Square Playhouse, July 18, 1972)—as Louise in *Come Next Tuesday,* as Judith in *Twas Brillig,* as the Woman in *So Please Be Kind,* as the Mother in *Present Tense;* and she played Cora in a revival of *The Iceman Cometh* (Circle in the Square/Joseph E. Levine Th., Dec. 13, 1973).

Films. She played Ann in *East of Eden* (WB, 1955); Spurs in *Strange Lady in Town* (WB, 1955); and appeared in *The Way We Live Now* (UA, 1970); *Five Easy Pieces* (Col., 1970); and *Up the Sandbox* (Natl. Gen., 1972).

Television. Miss Smith made her debut as Megan in *The Apple Tree* (Kraft Television Th., NBC, 1953); was in *Cindy's Fella* (Ford Startime, NBC, Dec. 15, 1959); played Julie in *Miss Julie* (Play of the Week, WNTA, 1960); Hilda in *The Master Builder* (Play of the Week, WNTA, 1961); was in *Do Not Go Gentle Into That Good Night* (CBS Playhouse, Oct. 17, 1967); *Talk to Me Like the Rain and Let Me Listen* (WNET, Dec. 3, 1970); and *Particular Men* (WNET); and has appeared on Robert Montgomery Presents (NBC), Studio One (CBS), Matinee Th. (NBC), Justice (NBC), Star Tonight (ABC), US Steel Hour (CBS), Loretta Young Show (NBC), The Defenders (CBS), The Naked City (ABC), Dr. Kildare (NBC), Route 66 (CBS), and others.

SMITH, LORING. Actor. b. Loring Burn Smith, Nov. 18, 1895, Stratford, Conn., to Mason M. and Nellie (Garlick) Smith. Father, exec. with Saks Fifth Ave., N.Y.C. Attended Lafayette H.S., Buffalo, N.Y., 1915–16; Stamford (Conn.) H.S., 1916–17. Married May 26, 1919, to Peggy Parker (marr. dis. June 6, 1921); married Jan. 6, 1922 to Natalie Sawyer; one daughter. Served with US Army, 1917–19; rank, Sgt. Member of AEA (council, 1948–53); AFTRA; SAG; The Lambs (vice-pres., 1956–60). Address: (home) 141 Main St., Norwalk, CT 06851, tel. (203) VI 7-1407; (bus.) c/o The Lambs, 130 W. 44th St., New York, NY 10036, tel. (212) JU 2-1515.

Theatre. Mr. Smith made his professional debut as Ollie in *Leave It to Jane* (LaSalle, Chicago, Ill., Feb. 1917); subsequently appeared in a vaudeville skit, *Smith and Sawyer* (1919), which he performed on the Keith-Orpheum and Pantages circuits (1919–39); appeared in *Tweekie* (Empire, Sydney, Australia, 1927); *Kiss the Boys Goodbye* (Harris, Chicago, Ill., 1939); toured in *Kiss the Boys Goodbye* (Summers 1939–40); and appeared in *George Washington Slept Here* (Cape Playhouse, Dennis, Mass., Summer 1941).

Mr. Smith made his N.Y.C. debut as Horace Moultrie in *The Life of Riley* (Broadhurst, Apr. 29, 1942); subsequently played in stock (Erlanger, Buffalo, N.Y., Summer 1942); in *Junior Miss* (Harris, Chicago, Ill., 1942); played Thomas W. Craig in *All for All* (Bijou, N.Y.C., Sept. 29, 1943); Robert Drexel Gow in *Over 21* (Music Box, Jan. 3, 1944), in which he subsequently toured (1944–45); appeared in a season of stock (Montclair Playhouse, N.J., Summer 1945); as Harrison Eames in *A Joy Forever* (Biltmore, N.Y.C., Jan. 7, 1946); toured in *Windy City* (Mar. 19, 1946–June 8, 1946); appeared in stock (Martha's Vineyard, Mass., Summer 1946).

He played Senator James McKinley in *John Loves Mary* (Booth, Feb. 4, 1947); Robert Vale-Waterhouse in the pre-Bway tryout of *That's the Ticket* (opened Shubert, Philadelphia, Pa., Sept. 24, 1948; closed there Oct. 2, 1948); Morton Graves in *The Happiest Years* (Lyceum, Apr. 25, 1949); Harvey Small in *Texas, Li'l Darlin'* (Mark Hellinger Th., Nov. 25, 1949); Captain Hamlin Kearney in *Captain Brassbound's Conversation* (NY City Ctr., Dec. 27, 1950); Harvey Small in *Texas, Li'l Darlin'* (State Fair, Dallas, Tex., 1951); Matthew Arnold Fulton in *Of Thee I Sing* (Ziegfeld, N.Y.C., May 5, 1952); Archibald K. Holly in *Be Your Age* (48 St. Th., Jan. 14, 1953); Edward L. McKeever in *The Solid Gold Cadillac* (Belasco, Nov. 5, 1953); and Horace Vandergelder in *The Matchmaker* (Royale, Dec. 5, 1955), with which he subsequently toured (opened Shubert, Detroit, Feb. 4, 1957).

He appeared in *The Soft Touch* (Coconut Grove Playhouse, Miami, Fla., 1957); in *Cradle and All* (Bucks County Playhouse, New Hope, Pa., Summer, 1959); and with the American Shakespeare Festival (Stratford, Conn.), played Sir Toby Belch in *Twelfth Night* (June 8, 1960), and Alonzo, King of Naples, in *The Tempest* (June 19, 1960). Mr. Smith appeared as Herr Brandel in *The Gay Life* (Shubert, N.Y.C., Nov. 18, 1961); toured in *The Mackerel Plaza* (June–Aug., 1963); played the Mayor in *A Murderer Among Us* (Morosco, Mar. 25, 1964).

Films. He has appeared in *Shadow of the Thin Man* (MGM, 1941); *Keep 'Em Flying* (U, 1941); *Close-up* (Eagle-Lion 1948); *Pat and Mike* (MGM, 1952); *The Clown* (MGM, 1953); *Ma and Pa Kettle at Waikiki* (U, 1955); *Happy Anniversary* (UA, 1959); *The Cardinal* (Col., 1963); and *Hurry Sundown* (Par., 1967).

Television. Mr. Smith has appeared on *Pride's Castle* (1949); Martin Kane (1951); Hallmark Hall of Fame (NBC, 1951); Armstrong Circle Th. (NBC, 1951); Mr. Peepers (NBC, 1952); Omnibus (NBC, 1952); Robert Montgomery Presents (NBC, 1953); I Remember Mama (CBS, 1953); Ed Sullivan Show (CBS, 1956); *Harvey* (Playhouse 90, CBS, 1958); Ansel Gibbs (1958); *The Miracle on Thirty-Fourth Street* (NBC, 1959); *Captain Brassbound's Conversion* (Hallmark Hall of Fame, NBC, 1960); *The Right Man* (1960); The Twilight Zone (CBS, 1960); *He Who Gets Slapped* (Play of the Week, WNTA, 1961); The Defenders (CBS, 1961); *Seven Keys to Baldpate* (1962); Profiles in Courage (NBC, 1963); and *Certain Honorable Men* (Prudential's On Stage, NBC, Sept. 12, 1968).

Recreation. Golf and all other outdoor sports.

SMITH, MILTON. Educator, director. b. Oct. 28, 1890, Springfield, Mass., to Henry Joseph and Jeanette (Machol) Smith. Father, superintendent, US Armory. Grad. Technical H.S., Springfield, 1909; Clark Univ., A.B. 1912; attended Harvard Univ., graduate studies, 1915–16; grad. Columbia Univ., M.A. 1919, Ph.D. 1930. Married June 18, 1921, to Mary Noble (marr. dis. 1929); one son; married May 22, 1941, to Helen Claire, actress. During WW I, served as govt. munitions inspector. Member of Amer. Assn. of Teachers of Speech; ATA.

Mr. Smith is director emeritus of the Sch. of Dramatic Arts (Columbia Univ.), where he was director (1952–59). Previously, he had been instructor (1920–30), and associate professor in the Teachers Coll. (1930–48).

His teaching of dramatic arts in the Extension Division of the University (1926) led to the establishment of the Sch. of Dramatic Arts. The Extension Division became the Sch. of General Studies, in which he was associate professor of dramatic arts (1935–48) and professor (1948–59). He was associate director of the Sch. of Dramatic Arts (1948–52).

Also, Mr. Smith taught English at the Allen Sch. (West Newton, Mass., 1912–15), and the Swarthmore (Pa.) Preparatory Sch. (1915–16); and was head of the English department in the Horace Mann Sch. for Boys (N.Y.C., 1916–28).

As director of the Sch. of Dramatic Arts (Columbia Univ.), Mr. Smith produced and directed more than 200 works, including new plays, new operas, and revivals. These included the premieres of *The New Freedom* by Marjorie Paradis (1930), for which he designed the settings and directed, with Elizabeth Van Nardroff; and *If Booth Had Missed* by Arthur Goodman (1931). Both of these plays won first prize in their respective years of production in the National Long Play Tournament at the Belasco Th. (N.Y.C.). Mr. Smith directed the Goodman work in its Bway production (Maxine Elliott's Th., Feb. 4, 1932). He also directed *The Fields Beyond* (Mansfield, Mar. 6, 1936).

Other premieres he produced and/or directed at Columbia Univ. include *Paul Bunyan,* the first opera by W. H. Auden and Chester Kallman who wrote the book, and Benjamin Britten, who wrote the music (Brander Matthews Th., May 5, 1941); *The Burglar's Opera,* libretto by Edward Eager and Alfred Drake, music by John Mindy (1942); he produced Gian-Carlo Menotti's *The Medium* (Brander Matthews Th., May 8, 1946); *The Mother of Us All,* text by Gertrude Stein, music by Virgil Thomson (May 1947); *The Barrier,* libretto by Langston Hughes, music by Jan Meyerowitz (1950), produced on Bway (Broadhurst Th., Nov. 2, 1950); and *Giants in the Earth,* libretto by Arnold Sundgaard, music by Douglas Moore (April 1951).

Mr. Smith directed *Prologue to Freedom* for the quadricentennial celebration of the first attempt to make a permanent settlement on this continent (Beaufort, S.C., Mar. 24–31, 1962).

Other Activities. Because of his interest in the revival of classics, especially of the eighteenth century, the following plays were produced at the double bicentennial at Columbia Univ. (Spring 1954), *The Beaux' Stratagem, The Conscious Lovers, The Beggar's Opera,* and *The Suspicious Husband.* The bicentennial commemorated the founding of the university and the 200th anniversary of the N.Y.C. real professional theatre. These plays were produced in the 1753–54 season, by Lewis Hallam and his "Company of English Comedians from London" at N.Y.C.'s first real theatre, the Nassau St. Th., which he had just built.

Published Works. Mr. Smith wrote *Magic in the Making* (1922), *Play Production* (1926; rev. 1948), and *Guide to Play Selection* (1936). He has also edited *Short Plays of Various Types, Julius Caesar, The Tempest,* and other Shakespearean texts.

SMITH, MURIEL. Actress, singer. b. Feb. 23, 1923, New York City, Grad. Roosevelt H.S., N.Y.C.; Curtis Inst., Philadelphia, Pa.; attended Columbia Univ. Studied with Westmoreland, Elizabeth Schuman, Gian Cario Menotti, Alfred Martino. Member of AEA; British AEA; SAG.

Theatre. Miss Smith made her N.Y.C. debut in the title role in *Carmen Jones* (Bway Th., Dec. 2, 1943), in which she subsequently toured, and repeated in N.Y.C. (NY City Ctr., Apr. 7, 1946). She played Dephine in *Our Lan'* (Henry St. Playhouse, Apr. 18, 1947; moved Royale, Sept. 27, 1947); Ella Hammer in *The Cradle Will Rock* (Mansfield, Dec. 26, 1947); Phaedra in *Hippolytus* (Lenox Hill Playhouse, Nov. 20, 1948); Bella in *Sojourner Truth* (Kaufmann Aud., YMHA, Apr. 21, 1948); and sang the title role in the opera, *Carmen* (Triborough Stadium, N.Y.C., July 16, 1948).

She appeared in the revue *Sauce Tartar* (Cambridge, London, May 18, 1949); the revue, *Sauce Piquante* (Cambridge, Apr. 27, 1950); as Bloody Mary in *South Pacific* (Drury Lane, Nov. 1, 1950); Lady Thiang in *The King and I* (Drury Lane, Oct. 8, 1953; NY City Ctr., Apr. 8, 1956); the title role in *Carmen Jones* (NY City Ctr., May 31, 1956); sang the title role in the opera, *Carmen* (Covent Garden, London, Dec. 17, 1956); appeared in the Moral Rearmament production of *The Crowning Experiment* (1958); and as Candida in *High Diplomacy* (Westminster Th., London, June 5, 1969). She also did a concert tour of Brazil (1965).

Films. Miss Smith appeared as Aicha in *Moulin Rouge* (UA, 1952); and as Mary in *The Voice of the Hurricane* (Selected Pictures, 1964).

Recreation. Swimming, walking, poetry.

SMITH, NORWOOD. Actor, singer. b. Francis Norwood Smith, Jr., Apr. 18, 1915, San Francisco, Calif., to Frank N. and Mary (Hague) Smith. Father, salesman. Grad. Los Angeles, (Calif.) H.S., 1932; Univ. of Calif., Los Angeles, 1936. Married Sept. 24, 1944, to Gloria Wolff (marr. dis. Nov. 1955); two daughters; married July 30, 1956, to Marilynn Bradley, singer (marr. dis. Aug. 1960); married Aug. 12, 1961, to Barbara Lang, known as Anne Lang, actress, singer. Served WW II, US Army, Transportation Corps; rank, Maj. Member of AEA; AFTRA; SAG; AGVA; Phi Gamma Delta (pres., Lambda Alpha chapter, UCLA). Address: 400 West End Ave., New York, NY 10024.

Pre-Theatre. Gas station attendant.

Theatre. Mr. Smith made his debut as Lothario in the opera *Mignon* (American Music Th., Los Angeles, 1941); subsequently appeared as Gaylor Ravenal in the national tour of *Show Boat* (Hartford Aud., Conn., Oct. 1947; closed Hartford, Columbus, Ohio, Apr. 1949); was a singer at the Orpheum Th. (Los Angeles, Calif., Oct. 1949); in stock, as Robert in *New Moon* (South Shore Music Circus, Cohasset, Mass., Summer 1951); as Dr. Engel in *The Student Prince* (Cape Cod Melody Tent, Hyannis, Mass., Summer 1951); at the Roxy Th., N.Y.C. (Oct. 1951); and played Caramello in *A Night in Venice* (Marine Th., Jones Beach, L.I., N.Y., Summer 1952).

Mr. Smith succeeded (Sept. 22, 1952) Robert Alda as Sky Masterson in *Guys and Dolls* (46 St. Th., N.Y.C., Nov. 24, 1950); succeeded (June 1954) Peter Cookson as Aristide Forestier in *Can-Can* (Shubert, May 7, 1953); played Sky Masterson in *Guys and Dolls* (Royal Nevada Hotel, Las Vegas, Nev., Oct. 1955); succeeded (Jan. 1956) Don Ameche, as Steve Canfield in *Silk Stockings* (Imperial, N.Y.C., Feb. 24, 1955); joined (Jan. 1959) *The Music Man* (Majestic, Dec. 19, 1957) as standby for Robert Preston as Prof. Harold Hill and played the role during Mr. Preston's vacation; and toured in the Oldsmobile Industrial Show (Summer 1960).

Mr. Smith appeared in stock (1955–64) in several of the above roles as well as Hajj in *Kismet;* Tommy in *Brigadoon;* the King in *The King and I;* Petruchio in *Kiss Me Kate;* Frank Butler in *Annie Get Your Gun;* Wild Bill Hickok in *Calamity Jane;* Herbie in *Gypsy;* Emile De Becque in *South Pacific;* and Cesar in *Fanny.* He played Mark Parker in *Ari* (Mark Hellinger Th., N.Y.C., Jan. 15, 1971); toured as Howard Benedict in the natl. co. of *Applause* (1971–73); and toured as Nat Miller in *Take Me Along* (Summer 1974).

Films. Mr. Smith has appeared in industrial motion pictures produced by Jam Handy (Detroit, Mich.); F. K. Rockett Prods. (Los Angeles, Calif.); USN; Kerbany-MPO (Detroit, Mich., 1958–to date); and has been narrator for industrial films.

Television and Radio. Mr. Smith had his own show, Norwood Smith Sings (Hollywood, Calif., two months, KNX, CBS, 1946; KECA, ABC, 1946–50); appeared on American Rhapsody (CBS, 1949–50); participated as a singer in NBC television color tests (1951); and has made many television commercials.

During the 1960s and 1970s, he appeared in such television serials as Edge of Night (CBS); As the World Turns (CBS); Search for Tomorrow (CBS); All My Children (ABC); Secret Storm (CBS); and Love of Life (CBS). He was also an announcer on WEVD.

SMITH, OLIVER. Designer, producer. b. Oliver Lemuel Smith, Feb. 13, 1918, Wawpawn, Wis., to Larue Free and Nina (Kincaid) Smith, Father, H.S. Principal. Grad. Penn State Univ., B.A. 1939. Member of Acacia; The Players; United Scenic Artists Union (Local 802). Address: 70 Willow St., Brooklyn, NY 11201.

Theatre. Mr. Smith designed the settings for the Ballet Russe de Monte Carlo productions of *Saratoga* (Metropolitan Opera House, N.Y.C., 1941) and *Rodeo* (Metropolitan, Oct. 26, 1942); the New Opera Company's production of *Rosalinda* (44 St. Th., Oct. 28, 1942); the Ballet Theatre's *Fancy Free* (Metropolitan, 1944); and the Cuevas Intl. Ballet production of *Sebastian* (1944). He designed, and with Paul Feigay, produced *On the Town* (Adelphi, Dec. 28, 1944); designed *Billion Dollar Baby* (Alvin, Dec. 21, 1945); for the Ballet Th., he designed *On Stage, Interplay,* and *Waltz Academy* (Metropolitan, 1945); designed and produced, with Herman Levin, *No Exit* (Biltmore, Nov. 26, 1946); and designed *Beggar's Holiday* (Bway Th., Dec. 26, 1946).

Since 1947, Mr. Smith has been director, with Lucia Chase of the Ballet Th.

He designed *Brigadoon* (Ziegfeld, Mar. 13, 1947); *High Button Shoes* (Century, Oct. 9, 1947); *Look, Ma, I'm Dancin'* (Adelphi, Jan. 29, 1948); for the Ballet Th., designed *Fall River Legend* (Metropolitan, Apr. 22, 1948); then designed *Miss Liberty* (Imperial, July 15, 1949); *Gentlemen Prefer Blondes,* which he produced with Herman Levin. (Ziegfeld, Dec. 8, 1949); *Pal Joey* (Broadhurst, Jan. 3, 1952); *Carnival in Flanders* (New Century, Sept. 8, 1953); *At Home with Ethel Waters* (48 St. Th., Sept. 22, 1953); *In the Summer House,* which he produced with The Playwright's Co., (Playhouse, Dec. 29, 1953); *The Burning Glass* (Longacre, Mar. 4, 1954); *Carousel* (NY City Ctr., June 2, 1954); the revival of *On Your Toes* (46 St. Th., Oct. 11, 1954); and *Will Success Spoil Rock Hunter?* (Belasco, Oct. 13, 1955).

Mr. Smith designed *My Fair Lady* (Mark Hellinger Th., Mar. 15, 1956); *Mr. Wonderful* (Bway Th., Mar. 22, 1956); *Auntie Mame* (Broadhurst, Oct. 31, 1956); *Candide* (Martin Beck Th., Dec. 1, 1956); and *A Clearing in the Woods,* which he produced in association with Roger L. Stevens (Belasco, Jan. 10, 1957). He was scenic designer for *Eugenia* (Ambassador, Jan. 30, 1957); *A Visit to a Small Planet* (Booth, Feb. 7, 1957); the revivals of *Brigadoon* (NY City Ctr., Mar. 27, 1957; Jan. 30, 1963); *West Side Story* (Winter Garden, Sept. 26, 1957); *Jamaica* (Imperial, Oct. 31, 1957); *Time Remembered* (Morosco, Nov. 12, 1957); *The Flower Drum Song* (St. James, Dec. 1, 1958); *Say, Darling* (Broadhurst, Apr. 3, 1958); *Destry Rides Again* (Imperial, Apr. 23, 1959); *Take Me Along* (Shubert, Oct. 12, 1959); *The Sound of Music* (Lunt-Fontanne Th., Nov. 16, 1959); *Five Finger Exercise* (Morosco, Dec. 2, 1959); *A Taste of Honey* (Lyceum, Oct. 4, 1960); *Becket* (St. James, Oct. 5, 1960); and *Camelot* (Majestic, Dec. 3, 1960).

For the 1960 Metropolitan Opera Co. season, he designed new productions of *La Traviata* and *Martha.* With James A. Doolittle and Charles Lowe, he produced and designed *Show Girl* (Eugene O'Neill Th., Jan. 12, 1961); designed *Mary, Mary* (Helen Hayes Th., Mar. 8, 1961); *The Gay Life* (Shubert, Nov. 18, 1961); *The Night of the Iguana* (Royale, Dec. 28, 1961); *Eddie Fisher at the Winter Garden* (Oct. 2, 1962); *Come On Strong* (Morosco, Oct. 4, 1962); and *Lord Pengo* (Royale, Nov. 19, 1962).

Mr. Smith produced, with Roger L. Stevens, and designed *Tiger, Tiger, Burning Bright* (Booth, Dec. 2, 1962); designed, and produced in association with Manuel Seff, *Natural Affection* (Booth, Jan. 31, 1963); designed *Children from Their Games* (Morosco, Apr. 11, 1963); *Barefoot in the Park* (Biltmore, Oct. 23, 1963); *110 in the Shade* (Broadhurst, Oct. 24, 1963); and designed the scenery for *Hello, Dolly!* (St. James, Jan. 16, 1964); and *Dylan* (Plymouth, Jan. 18, 1964).

Mr. Smith designed the sets for *Baker Street* (Bway Th., N.Y.C., Feb. 16, 1965); *The Odd Couple* (Plymouth, N.Y.C., Mar. 10, 1965); *Star Spangled Girl* (Plymouth, N.Y.C., Dec. 21, 1966); *Plaza Suite* (Plymouth, N.Y.C., Feb. 14, 1968); co-produced and designed the sets for *Indians* (Brooks Atkinson Th., N.Y.C., Oct. 13, 1969); designed the sets for *The Last of the Red Hot Lovers* (Eugene O'Neill Th., N.Y.C., Dec. 28, 1969); *Lovely Ladies, Kind Gentlemen* (Majestic, N.Y.C., Dec. 28, 1970); *The Patriots* (American Place Th., N.Y.C., Jan. 16, 1971); the Leonard Bernstein *Mass,* for the opening of the Kennedy Center for the Performing Arts (Washington, D.C., Sept. 10, 1971); *Lost in the Stars* (Imperial, N.Y.C., Apr. 18, 1972); and *Gigi* (Uris, Nov. 13, 1973).

For the American Ballet Theatre, he designed *Swan Lake* (1965); designed sets for the Boston Opera Co.'s production of *Moses and Aaron* (1965); *Carmen* and *Falstaff* for the National Opera Co. (1969); *Don Giovanni* (1969) for the Boston Opera Co., and the San Francisco Opera Co.; and *Giselle* (1970), and *Sleeping Beauty* (1974) for the American

Ballet Th.

Films. Mr. Smith was designer for *The Band Wagon* (MGM, 1953); *Oklahoma!* (MTC, 1955); *Guys and Dolls* (MGM, 1955); and *Porgy and Bess* (Col., 1959).

Other Activities. Mr. Smith designed the Ballroom and Peacock Alley (Waldorf-Astoria Hotel, N.Y.C.); The Columns (Savoy Hilton Hotel, N.Y.C.); the interiors of all the Longchamps Restaurants in N.Y.C.; The River Boat; the Star Lit Roof of the Waldorf Astoria; and the Tarrytown (N.Y.) Hilton Inn.

Awards. Mr. Smith has received Antoinette Perry (Tony) Awards for his settings for *My Fair Lady* (1957); *West Side Story* (1958); *The Sound of Music* (1960); *Becket* (1961); *Camelot* (1961); *Hello Dolly* (1962); and *Baker Street* (1965). Mr. Smith has won the *Variety* NY Drama Critics' Poll four times: for *My Fair Lady* (1956), when he tied with Jo Mielziner; for *Candide* (1957), when he tied with Rouben Ter-Arutuenian; and for *Destry Rides Again* (1959), when he tied with Oliver Messel; and for *Camelot* (1961). His designs for the film *Guys and Dolls* were nominated for an Academy (Oscar) Award (1956). In 1960, he received the Sam Shubert Award for the year's greatest contribution to the theatre. Mr. Smith was appointed by President John F. Kennedy to the committee for the Cultural Arts Center, Washington, D.C.

He is the recipient of the Distinguished Alumni Award (1961) of Penn. State Univ.; was appointed to the National Council of the Arts (1965–70) by President Lyndon B. Johnson; was named honorary Doctor of Literature by Bucknell Univ. (1973); and was declared Master Teacher of Scenic Design by New York Univ.

Recreation. Travel, painting.

SMITH, PATRICIA. Actress. b. Patricia Harlan Smith, Feb. 20, 1930, New Haven, Conn., to E. Allen Smith, Jr., and Virginia (Flint) Smith. Father, manufacturer; mother, antique dealer. Grad. Buxton Sch., Short Hills, N.J., 1947; attended Skidmore Coll., 1947–49. Studied at Neighborhood Playhouse Sch. of the Th., N.Y.C., 1949–51; Actors' Studio, N.Y.C., (mbr. 1952–to date). Member of AEA; SAG; AFTRA.

Theatre. Miss Smith made her debut as Tessie Tracy in *Sconset Heyday,* for which she was also choreographer (Straight Wharf Th., Nantucket, Mass., June 25, 1950); also at this theatre, played Sally in *The Voice of the Turtle,* and ingenue roles in *The Bat, Present Laughter,* and *Maria Mitchell,* and toured in *The Silver Whistle* (June–Aug. 1951).

She made her N.Y.C. debut as Jessica Lovell in *Point of No Return* (Alvin, Dec. 13, 1951); also touring in it (opened Ford's, Baltimore, Md., Nov. 24, 1952; closed Biltmore, Los Angeles, Calif., May 23, 1953); followed by Katie in *Maybe Tuesday* (Playhouse, N.Y.C., Jan. 29, 1958); Barbara Dickerson in *Howie* (46 St. Th., Sept. 17, 1958); Mary McKellaway in a national company tour of *Mary, Mary* (opened Central City Opera House, Colo., Aug. 6, 1962); and succeeded (July 1, 1963) Diana Lynn as Mary McKellaway in *Mary, Mary* (Helen Hayes Th., N.Y.C., Mar. 8, 1961).

Films. Miss Smith was in *The Spirit of St. Louis* (WB, 1957) and *The Bachelor Party* (UA, 1957).

Awards. Miss Smith received the Vernon Rice Summer Th. Honor Roll Award for her performance as Tessie Tracy in *Sconset Heyday* (1950).

Recreation. Swimming, piano, knitting.

SMITH, ROBERT PAUL. Playwright, novelist, poet. b. Apr. 16, 1915, Brooklyn, N.Y., to Joseph Elkin and Esther (Breckstone) Smith. Father, manufacturer. Grad. Horace Mann Sch., N.Y.C., 1932; Columbia Univ., B.A. 1936. Married Feb. 7, 1940, to Elinor Jane Goulding, artist, writer; two sons. Member of ALA; Dramatists Guild.

Theatre. Mr. Smith wrote with Max Shulman, *The Tender Trap* (Longacre Th., N.Y.C., Oct. 13, 1954; Saville, London, England, May 3, 1955).

Television and Radio. He was a continuity writer for CBS radio; and for television wrote The Chevy Showroom (ABC, July 3, 1958).

Published Works. Mr. Smith wrote *So It Doesn't Whistle* (1941); *The Journey* (1943); *Because of My Love* (1946); *The Time and the Place* (1951); *Where Did You Go? Out. What Did You Do? Nothing.* (1957); *Translations from the English* (1958); *How To Do Nothing with Nobody All Alone by Yourself* (1958); *Crank* (1962); *How To Grow Up in One Piece* (1963); *Nothingatall, Nothingatall, Nothingatall* (1965); *Got To Stop Draggin' That Little Red Wagon Around* (1969); and *Robert Paul Smith's Lost and Found* (1973). *Where He Went* (1958) is a volume of three previously published novels and . . . *and Another Thing* (1959) is a collection of poems.

Recreation. Building musical instruments, reading.

SMITH, WALLACE. Educator, director. b. Wallace Paul Smith, July 10, 1923, Cleveland, Ohio, to Paul C. and Helen L. (Poland) Smith. Father, trucking contractor; mother, nurse. Grad. Berea (Ohio) H.S., 1941; Baldwin-Wallace Coll., A.B. 1948; Northwestern Univ., M.A. 1952. Served US Army, 1943–45, PTO; rank, Cpl. Member of AETA (exec. comm., 1957–59; bd. of dir., 1964; 2nd vice-pres., 1968–69; 1st vice-pres., 1969–70; pres., 1971); SSTC; CTC; ACTA; NEA; SAA; CSSA; Ill. Speech Assn.; Ill. Ed. Assn.; ANTA; Alpha Sigma Phi; Theta Alpha Phi. Address: (home) 655 Irving Park Rd., Chicago, IL 60613, tel. (312) 472-6172; (bus.) c/o Evanston Township H.S., Evanston, IL tel. (312) 492-3809.

Since 1963, Mr. Smith has been director of the Secondary Sch. Th. Conference (assistant director, 1961–63; directing committee—course of study in theatre, 1963).

He served as advisor-consultant to the Education Laboratory Th. Project of USOE (1968–72); specialist in theatre to the Aesthetic Education Curriculum Project (1968–to date); evaluator to Project IMPACT, NDEA (1971–72); as trustee to the Amer. Council on Arts Education (1974); was a panel member on Artists-in-the-Schools for National Endowment for the Arts (1974); and has been evaluator and curriculum consultant to arts programs in school systems across the country.

At Evanston Township H.S., where he has been an instructor since 1957, Mr. Smith has been director of the State Demonstration Ctr. for Gifted Fine Arts Students (1967–71); director of the materials development project for gifted theatre students (1971–73); and coordinator of curriculum (1973–75). He was acting coach and director (1956–62) for the National H.S. Institute at Northwestern Univ.; and director of drama (1964) at the Governor's Honor Program for the State of Georgia.

SOBOLOFF, ARNOLD. Actor, singer. b. Arnold Steven Soboloff, Nov. 11, 1930, New York City, to Morris and Sarah (Artmann) Soboloff. Father, lingerie designer. Grad. H.S. of Music and Art, N.Y.C., 1948; Cooper Union, Certificate, 1951; studied acting at Herbert Berghof Sch., 1 yr.; with Harold Clurman, four months; and with Mira Rostova, four years. Married Aug. 2, 1960, to Suzanne Kauffman. Served USAF, 1951–54; rank, Airman 1/c. Member of AEA; AFTRA; SAG. Address: 145 W. 55th St., New York, NY 10019, tel. (212) JU 6-6300.

Pre-Theatre. Commercial art.

Theatre. Mr. Soboloff made his first stage appearance in the title role of a school production of *Aladdin* (P.S. 94, N.Y.C., Apr. 1940); later was stage manager for the double-bill of *The Lesson* and *Escurial,* the latter in which he made his first professional appearance as the Monk (Tempo Playhouse, Apr. 1956); joined (May 1957) as the Policeman in *The Threepenny Opera* (Th. de Lys, Sept. 20, 1955); succeeded (May 1957) Dick Stahl as Jack Goldman in *Career* (Seventh Ave. So., Apr. 30, 1957); played Perhotin and the Foreman in *The Brothers Karamazov* (Gate Th., Dec. 6, 1957); in stock, he was social director of the theater staff at Tamiment (Pa., Summer 1958); played Dr. Gachet in *Vincent* (Cricket, N.Y.C., Sept. 30, 1959); Dr. Kitchell in a touring production of *Bells Are Ringing* (June–Aug. 1959); the Clothes Moth in *The Clothes Moth and the Luna Moth* (Talent '60, Imperial, Apr. 1960); played eight roles in various plays in the USO tour of *B'way U.S.A.* (France, Italy, Germany, Spain, Sept. 1960–Jan. 1961).

He appeared as Neri, the Frenchman, in *Mandingo* (Lyceum, N.Y.C., May 22, 1961); appeared in stock as Leonard Lyons in *Venus at Large* (Westport Playhouse, Conn., July 1961); played four roles in *The Egg* (Cort, Jan. 8, 1962); Moscolito in *Bravo Giovanni* (Broadhurst, May 19, 1962); four roles in *The Beauty Part* (Music Box, Dec. 26, 1962); toured as Boris in *Can-Can* (Guber-Ford-Gross Circuit, July–Aug. 1963); Ellis in *One Flew Over the Cuckoo's Nest* (Cort, N.Y.C., Nov. 13, 1963); Treasurer Cooley in *Anyone Can Whistle* (Majestic, Apr. 4, 1964); and Count de la Ferrontière in *Gogo Loves You* (Th. de Lys, Oct. 9, 1964).

He played Big Daddy in *Sweet Charity* (Palace, Jan. 29, 1966); Patsy in *Mike Downstairs* (Hudson, Apr. 18, 1968); Ripe Banana in *Bananas* (The Forum, Lincoln Ctr., Dec. 4, 1968); the title role in the American Place Theater's *Papp* (St. Clement's Ch., Apr. 17, 1969); and appeared at the Stratford (Ontario, Canada) Festival in a musical version of *The Satyricon* (July 4, 1969). He was Nursie in *Camino Real* (Vivian Beaumont Th., N.Y.C., Jan. 8, 1970); Aaron in *Show Me Where the Good Times Are* (Edison Th., Mar. 5, 1970); appeared again at the Stratford Festival (Avon Th.), as The Architect in *The Architect and the Emperor* (July 20, 1970) and Mr. Bat in *Vatzlav* (Aug. 11, 1970); played in *Cyrano,* as Ligniere (Guthrie Th., Minneapolis, Minn., Jan. 23, 1973) and as Ragueneau (Palace, N.Y.C., May 13, 1973); was Lionel Stander in *Are You Now or Have You Ever Been?* (Th. of the Riverside Ch., Nov. 27, 1973); appeared in *Music! Music!* (NY City Ctr., Apr. 11, 1974); played Evens in *The Sea* (Manhattan Th. Club, Mar. 12, 1975); and was a replacement (Apr. 1975) in the cast of *Scapino* (Ambassador Th. and on tour).

Films. Mr. Soboloff appeared in *The Detective* (Col., 1968) and *Popi* (UA, 1969).

Television. Mr. Soboloff appeared in *The Day the Earth Stood Still* (Studio One, CBS, 1957); *The Deaf Heart* (Studio One, CBS, 1957); *No Deadly Medicine* (Studio One, CBS, 1958); the Sgt. Bilko series (CBS, 1958); Omnibus (NBC, 1958); Brenner (CBS, 1958; 1959); My True Story (CBS, 1959; 1961); Armstrong Circle Th. (CBS, 1959; 1961); House on High Street (ABC, 1959); in *Ninotchka* (ABC, Dec. 1959); on Naked City (CBS, 1961; 1962); Route 66 (CBS, 1961; 1963); The Defenders (CBS, 1962; 1963); The Nurses (CBS, 1963); in *More, More, More* (Dupont Show of the Week, NBC, May 31, 1964); in thirteen episodes of Masquerade (PBS, 1971–72); and in segments of Kojak (CBS, 1974). Mr. Soboloff made the television pilot films *Mr. Inside/Mr. Outside* (NBC Wednesday Mystery Movie, Mar. 14, 1973); and *Strike Force* (1975).

SOKOLOW, ANNA. Choreographer, dancer. b. 1912, Hartford, Conn. Studied for the theatre at the Neighborhood Playhouse Sch. of the Th.; dancing with Martha Graham, N.Y.C. Member of SSD&C. Address: 71 W. 55th St., New York, NY 10019.

Theatre. Miss Sokolow was choreographer of *The Great Campaign* (Princess Th., N.Y.C., Mar. 30, 1947). She designed the choreography for *Street Scene* (Adelphi, Jan. 9, 1947); *Sleepy Hollow* (St. James, June 3, 1948); *Regina* (46 St. Th., Oct. 31, 1949); and *Happy as Larry* (Coronet, Jan. 6, 1950). For the Studio Th. (N.Y.C.), she choreographed *The Dybbuk* (Mar. 17, 1951); assisted Elia Kazan with the direction of *Camino Real* (National Mar. 19, 1953); provided the dances for *Madam, Will You Walk* (Phoenix, Dec. 1, 1953); choreographed *Session for Eight* and *L'Histoire du soldat* (both Kaufmann Aud., 92 St. YM-YWHA, Dec. 18, 1954); *Rooms* (Anna Sokolow Co., 92 St. YM-YWHA, Feb. 24, 1955); and *Red Roses for Me* (Booth, Dec. 28, 1955).

Miss Sokolow designed the choreography for NY City Opera Co. productions of *La Traviata, Carmen, Die Fledermaus, The Tempest, Susannah, Orpheus in the Underworld,* and directed their production of Carl Orff's *The Moon* (NY City Ctr., Oct. 16, 1956). She choreographed *Copper and Brass* (Martin Beck Th., Oct. 17, 1957); and directed *Bugs* and *Veronica* (Pocket Th., Nov. 18, 1965). The Rep. Th. of Lincoln Ctr. production *Bananas* (Forum, Dec. 5, 1968) was based on an idea of hers; she created the movement for the American Place Theatre's *Pinkville* (St. Clement's Ch., Feb. 22, 1971); choreography for the American Shakespeare production of *The Merry Wives of Windsor* (Stratford, Conn., June 12, 1971); and her Players Project presented *Metamorphosis* in an adaptation by John White (Loeb Experimental Th., Harvard Univ., Cambridge, Mass., Summer 1971).

Among many other works created by Miss Sokolow for the theatre of the dance are: (with the Dance Unit) *Strange American Funeral* (N.Y.C., June 1935); *Slaughter of the Innocents* (Guild Th., Nov. 1937); and *Opening Dance* (Guild Th., Dec. 1937). Also *Ballad in a Popular Style* (Alvin Th., Feb. 26, 1939); *A Short Lecture and Demonstration on the Evolution of Ragtime as Presented by Jelly Roll Morton* (Danny Daniels and Group, 92 St. YM-YWHA, Dec. 21, 1952); *Lyric Suite* (New Dance Group, 92 St. YM-YWHA, Mar. 30, 1954); *Poem* (Anna Sokolow Th. Dance Co., Brooklyn Acad. of Music, Feb. 12, 1956); *Le grand spectacle* (Phoenix Th., May 13, 1957); and *Session '58* (Juilliard Dance Ensemble, Juilliard Concert Hall, Apr. 11, 1958).

Also *Dreams* (92 St. YM-YWHA, May 8, 1961); *Suite No. 5 in C Minor* (New Dance Group, 92 St. YM-YWHA, Mar. 9, 1963); *Opus '63* (Juilliard Dance Ensemble, Juilliard Concert Hall, May 10, 1963); *The Question* (Juilliard Dance Ensemble, Juilliard Concert Hall, Apr. 17, 1964); *Forms* (Anna Sokolow Dance Co., 92 St. YM-YWHA, Apr. 26, 1964); *Odes* and *Ballade* (both Juilliard Dance Ensemble, Juilliard Concert Hall, Feb. 12, 1965); *Opus '65* (Robert Joffrey Ballet, Delacorte Th., Sept. 11, 1965); *Time+6* (Boston Ballet, Back Bay Th., Boston, Mass., Jan. 17, 1966); *Night* (Juilliard Dance Ensemble, Juilliard Concert Hall, N.Y.C., May 6, 1966); *Déserts* (Anna Sokolow Dance Co., Hunter Coll. Playhouse, Mar. 11, 1967); *Memories* (Juilliard Dance Ensemble, Juilliard Concert Hall, Apr. 20, 1967); *Time+7* (Anna Sokolow Dance Co., Brooklyn Coll., Feb. 10, 1968); *Steps of Silence* (Rep. Dance Th. Co., Univ. of Utah, Salt Lake City, Utah, Oct. 26, 1968); Anna Sokolow Dance Co., Brooklyn Acad. of Music, N.Y.C., Nov. 13, 1968); and *Tribute* (Anna Sokolow Dance Co., Brooklyn Acad. of Music, Nov. 13, 1968).

Also *Echoes* (Juilliard Dance Ensemble, Juilliard Concert Hall, Mar. 20, 1969); *Magritte Magritte* and *Act without Words No. 1* (Lyric Th. Co. of Anna Sokolow, Edison Th., Apr. 13, 1970); *The Dove* (Juilliard Dance Ensemble, Juilliard Th., May 26, 1970); *Scenes from the Music of Charles Ives* (Dance Dept., Juilliard Sch. of Music, Juilliard Th., May 5, 1971); *Three Poems* (Juilliard Dance Ensemble, Juilliard Concert Hall, May 23, 1973); *Homage to Federico García Lorca* (José Limón Dance Co., Feb. 22, 1974); *Come, Come Travel with Dreams* (Juilliard Dance Ensemble, Juilliard Th., Apr. 5, 1974); *Ecuatorial* (Paul Sanasardo Dance Co., Brooklyn Acad. of Music, May 18, 1974); and *A Cycle of Cities* (Wolf Trap Farm Park, Vienna, Va., Aug. 8, 1974).

Television. Miss Sokolow was choreographer for *Esther the Queen* (Lamp Unto My Feet, CBS, Mar. 1960).

SOLEM, DELMAR E. Educator. b. Delmar Everett Solem, Jan. 13, 1915, Volin, S.D., to Martin and Anna (Rockne) Solem. Father, farmer. Grad. Volin H.S., 1933; Yankton Coll., B.A. 1937; Northwestern Univ., M.A. (theatre) 1947; Ph.D. (theatre) 1952. Married June 19, 1948, to Jane Robertson; three daughters. Served USN, WW II; rank, Ensign. Member of ANTA; AETA (bd. of dir., 1956–62; chairman, coll. curriculum project, 1954–55; admin. vice-pres., 1956–60); STC (div. dir., 1958; exec. council, 1959–60; vice-pres., 1959; pres., 1960); SSSA: Florida TC (hon. mbr.); Theatre Arts League of Greater Miami and Miami Beach Music and Arts League (hon. member). Address: (home) 9390 S.W. 181st St., Miami, FL 33157; (bus.) Univ. of Miami, Coral Gables, FL 33146, tel. (305) 284-3354.

Mr. Solem was visiting professor and coordinator of graduate studies at the Univ. of Georgia (1968–70); U.S. Dept. of State Theatre Specialist to British Honduras (1967–71); consultant and adjudicator for the Ministry of Education in the Bahama Islands (1968–71); consultant to and founder of the Univ. of the West Indies Drama Workshop in Nassau (1963–67).

From 1956–68, he was chairman of the Dept. of Drama at the Univ. of Miami. He held academic positions at Geddess (S.D.) H.S. (instructor of English and dramatics, 1937–39); Tracy H.S. (instructor and director of speech and theatre, 1947–48); Johns Hopkins Univ. (instructor and director in theatre, 1948–49); Northwestern Univ. (teaching fellow, 1949–52; visiting professor, Summer 1956); Univ. of Colorado (visiting professor, Summers 1952–53); Knox Coll. (chairman of the Dept. of Speech and Theatre, 1952–56).

Mr. Solem has been director and stage director of the Ring Th. at the Univ. of Miami since 1956; and is also the executive director of the Southern Shakespeare Repertory Th., which he founded in 1961.

He has acted in plays presented by Northwestern Univ.; at the San Francisco, Calif., World's Fair (1938–39); Oregon Shakespeare Festival Assn. (1938–39); Vagabond Th. (Baltimore, Md., 1941–43); the John Hopkins Playshop (1941–43); Lafayette (Ind.) Community Players (1946); and Hilltop Th. (Baltimore, Md., 1948).

Published Works. Mr. Solem has contributed articles on theatre to *The Hopkins Review* (1949); *Educational Theatre Journal* (1954); *Southern Speech Journal* (1959); *Equity Magazine* (1961); and *Southern Speech Journal* (1962). He was editor of the "Projects Page" of *Educational Theatre Journal* (1956–59); editor of "Projects Progress Newsletter" for AETA (1957–59); has written book reviews for *Theatre Arts* Magazine and *Educational Theatre Journal;* and was consultant to the editor of Southern Speech Journal (1968–70).

Awards. From AETA, Mr. Solem received three citations: in 1959, for achievement as administrative vice-president of AETA; in 1960, for contribution to AETA's Intercultural Exchange; and again in 1960, for his contribution to the Secondary Schools Division of AETA. From the SETC, he received a citation for administrative effectiveness for 1961.

Mr. Solem was the recipient of a research grant (1967) to study myth in Ibsen's *Peer Gynt* at the Univ. of Oslo (Norway).

Recreation. Woodworking, lapidary.

SOMMER, EDITH. Playwright. Married to Robert Soderbert.

Theatre. Miss Sommers wrote the play *A Roomful of Roses* (Playhouse, N.Y.C., Oct. 17, 1955; Cleveland Play House, Ohio, 1955–56).

Awards. She received a Barter Th. Scholarship (1939).

SONDERGAARD, GALE. Actress. b. Edith Holm Sondergaard, Litchfield, Minn., to Hans T. and Kirstine (Holm) Sondergaard. Father, educator, dairy expert; mother, piano teacher. Grad. Central H.S., Minneapolis, Minn., 1917; Univ. of Minnesota B.A. (English and public speaking) 1921; grad. Minneapolis Sch. of Dramatic Arts, 1921. Married 1922 to Neill O'Malley (marr. dis. 1930); married 1930 to Herbert Biberman, director; one son, one daughter. Relative in theatre: sister, Hester Sondergaard, actress. Member of AEA; SAG; AMPAS.

Theatre. Miss Sondergaard made her stage debut as an Old Lady in a Rocking Chair in a high-school production in Minneapolis (1916); and her first semi-professional appearance as an ingenue touring one-night stands in a summer Chautauqua circuit (1920).

As a member of the John Keller Shakespeare Co., she toured the US and Canada as Queen Gertrude in *Hamlet,* Jessica in *The Merchant of Venice,* Calpurnia in *Julius Caesar,* and a Witch in *Macbeth* (1921–22); played a season of stock in Milwaukee, Wis. (1922–23); was understudy in a touring production of *Seventh Heaven* (1924–25); subsequently played with the Jessie Bonstelle Stock Co. (Detroit, Mich., 1925–26; 1926–27).

She made her N.Y.C. debut succeeding (Nov. 1923) Isabelle Leighton as Edith Somers in *What's Your Wife Doing?* (49 St. Th., Oct. 1, 1923); subsequently played the Witch in *Faust* (Guild, Oct. 8, 1928); Sarah Undershaft in *Major Barbara* (Guild, Nov. 19, 1928); substituted for and later succeeded Judith Anderson (Dec. 1928) as Nina Leeds in *Strange Interlude* (John Golden Th., Jan. 30, 1928); appeared as Marie in *Karl and Anna* (Guild, Oct. 7, 1929); Nina in *Red Dust* (Martin Beck Th., Dec. 17, 1929); succeeded (May 1931) Eva Le Gallienne as Elsa in *Alison's House* (Civic Repertory Th., Dec. 1, 1930); Lydia Kimball and Gail Pingree in *American Dream* (Guild, Feb. 21, 1933); Anna in *Doctor Monica* (Playhouse, Nov. 6, 1933); played in summer theatre productions at Sharon, Conn. (1932), and Newport, R.I. (1933); played Lorinda Channing in *Invitation to a Murder* (Masque, N.Y.C., May 17, 1934); and subsequently played Frances Chapman in *Cue for Passion* (Royale, Dec. 19, 1940). She appeared in stock productions of *No Time for Comedy* (Newport, Calif., Summer 1948); *The Corn Is Green* (Norwich, Conn.; Fairhaven, Mass., 1948); *Ladies in Retirement* (Chicago, 1950); *Henry IV* (Seacliff, L.I., 1950); and played the Empress in *Anastasia* (Playhouse-in-the-Park, Philadelphia, Pa., 1956).

She toured in a one-woman show of dramatic readings entitled *Woman* (11 St. Th., Chicago, Ill.; Assistance League Playhouse, Hollywood, Calif.; Ogden State Coll., Ogden, Utah; Salt Lake City Arts Club, Salt Lake City, Utah; Woman's Club, Louisville, Ky., 1955–58), which she later presented in N.Y.C. (Gramercy Arts Th., Oct. 20, 1965); was Mrs. Kane in *Kicking the Castle Down* (Gramercy Arts Th., Jan. 18, 1967); appeared with the Minnesota Th. Co. as Claire Zacharassian in *The Visit* (Tyrone Guthrie Th., Minneapolis, Minn., Sept. 11, 1967) and (both Crawford Livingston Th., St. Paul, Minn.) in *Tango* (Dec. 29, 1967) and *Enrico IV* (Feb. 16, 1968); was in *The Crucible* (Ahmanson Th., Los Angeles, Calif., Dec. 5, 1972); and played Blanche in *A Family and a Fortune* (Seattle Repertory Th., Seattle, Wash., Jan. 16, 1974).

Films. Since her screen debut as Faith in *Anthony Adverse* (WB, 1936); Miss Sondergaard has appeared in *Maid of Salem* (Par., 1937); *Seventh Heaven* (20th-Fox, 1937); as Mrs. Dreyfus in *The Life of Emile Zola* (WB, 1937); *Lord Jeff* (MGM, 1938); *Dramatic School* (MGM, 1938); *The Cat and the Canary* (Par., 1939); *The Llano Kid* (Par., 1939); *The Life of Hjam Solomon* (WB, 1939); *Juarez* (WB, 1939); *Never Say Die* (Par., 1939); *The Blue Bird* (20th-Fox, 1940); *The Mark of Zorro* (20th-Fox, 1940); *The Letter* (WB, 1940); *The Black Cat* (U, 1941); *My Favorite Blonde* (Par., 1941); *Paris Calling* (U, 1941); *Appointment in Berlin* (Col., 1942); *A Night To Remember* (Col., 1942); *Isle of Forgotten Sins* (Col., 1942); *The Spider Woman* (U, 1943); *The Strange Death of Adolf Hitler* (U, 1943); *Gypsy Wildcat* (U, 1944); *Christmas Holiday* (U, 1944); *Enter Arsene Lupin* (U, 1944); *The Climax* (U, 1945); *A Night in Paradise* (U, 1945); *Time of Their Lives* (U, 1946); *The Spider Woman Strikes Back* (U, 1946); *Anna and the King of Siam* (20th-Fox, 1946); *The Road to Rio* (Par., 1947); *The Pirates of Monterey* (U, 1947); *East Side/West Side* (MGM, 1949); *Slaves* (Cont., 1969); and *The Return of a Man Called Horse* (UA, 1976).

Television. Miss Sondergaard's television appearances include It Takes a Thief (ABC, 1969); Get Smart (CBS, 1970); The Best of Everything (ABC, 1971); The Bold Ones (NBC, 1971); *The Cat Creature* (ABC, Dec. 1973); and Ryan's Hope (ABC, 1976).

Awards. Miss Sondergaard received the Academy (Oscar) Award for her performance as Faith in *An-*

thony Adverse (1936) and was nominated for the Academy (Oscar) Award for her performance as Lady Thiang in *Anna and the King of Siam* (1946). In 1968, she received the Univ. of Minnesota outstanding achievement award.

Recreation. Swimming, tennis, walking, skating.

SONDHEIM, STEPHEN. Composer, lyricist. b. Stephen Joshua Sondheim, Mar. 22, 1930, New York City, to Herbert and Janet (Fox) Sondheim. Father, manufacturer; mother, fashion designer. Grad. George Sch., Newton, Pa., 1946; Williams Coll., B.A. 1950. Studied composition with Milton Babbitt. Member of Dramatists Guild (pres., 1972–73); ALA; ASCAP; WGA.

Theatre. Mr. Sondheim made his N.Y.C. debut as composer of the incidental music for *The Girls of Summer* (Longacre Th., Nov. 19, 1956). He wrote the lyrics for *West Side Story* (Winter Garden, Sept. 26, 1957; returned Apr. 27, 1960); the lyrics for *Gypsy* (Bway Th., May 21, 1959); the incidental music for *Invitation to a March* (Music Box, Oct. 29, 1960); the music and lyrics for *A Funny Thing Happened on the Way to the Forum* (Alvin, May 8, 1962); and the music and lyrics for *Anyone Can Whistle* (Majestic, Apr. 4, 1964).

He also wrote lyrics for *Do I Hear a Waltz?* (46 St. Th., Mar. 18, 1965); music and lyrics for *Company* (Alvin, Apr. 26, 1970); for *Follies* (Winter Garden, Apr. 4, 1971); *A Little Night Music* (Shubert Th., Feb. 25, 1973); incidental music for *The Enclave* (Th. Four, Nov. 15, 1973); additional lyrics, with John Latouche, for a revival of *Candide* (Chelsea Th. Ctr. of Brooklyn, Brooklyn Acad. of Music, Dec. 11, 1973; transferred to Bway Th., Mar. 10, 1974); his lyrics were included in *By Bernstein* (Chelsea Th. Ctr. of Brooklyn, Westside Th., Nov. 23, 1975); and he wrote music and lyrics for *Pacific Overtures* (Winter Garden, Jan. 11, 1976).

Films. With Anthony Perkins, Mr. Sondheim wrote the screenplay for *The Last of Sheila* (WB, 1973).

Television. Mr. Sondheim wrote segments of the Topper series (NBC, 1953) and scripts for The Last Word (CBS).

Discography. *Sondheim/A Musical Tribute* (WB, 1973) is a recording containing most of the AMDA/Hemophilia Fdtn. tribute. Original cast albums were published for *Do I Hear a Waltz?* (Col., 1965); *Company* (Col., 1970); *Follies* (Capitol, 1971); *A Little Night Music* (Col., 1973).

Awards. For *Company*, Mr. Sondheim was named outstanding composer (1969–70) by the Drama Desk, was named in the *Variety* NY Drama Critics poll (1969–70) as best composer, and *Company* won the NY Drama Critics' Circle Award as best musical. In the 1970–71 Antoinette Perry (Tony) Award selections, *Company* was named best musical, and Mr. Sondheim received a Tony for composing the best musical score and a second Tony as best lyricist. For *Follies*, he was named in the 1970–71 *Variety* poll of NY Drama Critics as best composer and best lyricist; received a Tony Award (1971–72) for composing the best score; and *Follies* received a Tony nomination as best musical. *A Little Night Music* received a Tony (1972–73) as best musical, and Mr. Sondheim received a Tony for composing the best score, Drama Desk awards as outstanding composer and outstanding lyricist, and the Los Angeles Drama Critics Circle Award (1974–75) for music and lyrics; and *Pacific Overtures* was named by the NY Drama Critics as best musical (1976). Mr. Sondheim was also honored by the American Musical and Dramatic Academy (AMDA) and the Natl. Hemophilia Fdtn. jointly with a musical salute to him and his work (Shubert Th., Mar. 11, 1973).

SONDHEIMER, HANS. Production stage manager, technical director, lighting director. b. Dec. 6, 1901, Glenhausen, Germany, to Elkan and Gertrud (Rapp) Sondheimer. Father, attorney. Grad. Inst. of Technology, Munich, Bavaria. Dipl. Ing., 1925. Studied with Prof. Adolph Linnebach, Munich, Germany, 1921–27. Married June 1945, to Doris Einstein, stage manager, lighting director (marr. dis. 1953); married June 17, 1957, to Jane Rosett, traffic manager. Member of AEA; AGMA; USITT (bd. of dir.; chairman, comm. on theatre engineering, 1960–to date). Address: 30 W. 60th St., New York, NY 10023, tel. (212) JU 2-6919.

Theatre. Mr. Sondheimer was technical assistant for the production of the opera, *Die Konigs Kinder* (State Th., Munich, Germany, Apr. 1925); supervised the building of the Hamburg (Germany) Opera House (1925–27); and was technical director for the State Theatre Darmstadt (1927–29); for the Berliner, German Art, Renaissance, Lessing and Schiller theatres (1929–33); and for the Berliner Th. in Kommandantern St., Berlin (1933–39).

In N.Y.C., Mr. Sondheimer worked with Erwin Piscator at the New Sch. for Social Research as an instructor in stagecraft and production (1939–51), and as technical director for their productions (1940–50).

He was technical director for *St. Joan* (Civic Th., Washington, D.C., 1940); for the North Shore Playhouse (Marblehead, Mass., Summer 1940); projection consultant for the Second Sound Show at Stevens Inst. (Hoboken, N.J., 1941); technical director for *Children's Christmas Story* (NY City Ctr., 1943); and *St. Matthew Passion* (Metropolitan Opera, 1943).

Mr. Sondheimer was lighting director for the Theatre Guild production of *Innocent Voyage* (Belasco, N.Y.C., Nov. 15, 1943); lighting consultant for *South Pacific* (Cort, Jan. 29, 1943); lighting director for *Jacobowsky and the Colonel* (Martin Beck Th., Mar. 14, 1944).

He was executive stage manager for the NY City Opera Co. (NY City Ctr. 1944–to date); technical director for the American Opera Co. (Academy of Music, Philadelphia, Pa., 1945–51); designed and supervised the building of the Lenox (Mass.) Theatre (July 1946) and was technical designer there (Summer 1946); was theatrical consultant for the White Barn Th. (Westport, Conn., 1949).

He was production stage manager for *Peer Gynt* (ANTA, N.Y.C., Jan. 28, 1951); production manager for a tour of *Die Fledermaus* (1951); technical director for *La Bohème* and *The Marriage of Figaro* (Central City Opera Co., Colo., Summer 1951); and production designer and lighting director for *The Abduction of Seraglio* (Katonah, N.Y., June 1953).

From 1952 to 1960, Mr. Sondheimer was production manager and technical director for touring industrial shows. He was production coordinator of the Deutsches Schauspielhaus (Hamburg, Germany) production of *Faust* (NY City Ctr., Feb. 1961). He was vice-president in charge of operations, production manager, and technical director for Marketing Concepts, Inc., a producer of industrial shows (1963–65); production coordinator for the Bavarian State Th. (NY City Ctr., April 1966); technical advisor for the Hamburg State Opera (US tour, 1967); technical director of the Vienna Burgtheatre (US tour, 1968); and has served as consultant to the John F. Kennedy Center for the Performing Arts, Washington, D.C. (1968–71); the Astor Th., N.Y.C., (1968); the Cincinnati (Ohio) Music Hall (1968–71); the National Parks Service's Filene Center, Wolf Trap Farm Park, Vianna, Wa. (1968–71); the Patricia Corbett Pavilion, College Conservatory of Music, Univ. of Cincinnati (Ohio) (1969); and to the Performing Arts Center, State Univ. of NY, at Purchase (1969).

Other Activities. Mr. Sondheimer has lectured at City Coll. of N.Y., the N.Y. Public Library and Cooper Union, N.Y.C., on theatrical technique.

He was a member of the US delegation to the Prague (Czechoslovakia) Quadrenniale (1970), and to the Third Congress (Avignon, France, 1973) of O.I.S.T.T.

Recreation. Horseback riding, photography, stamp collecting, travel.

SOPER, PAUL. Educator. b. Paul Leon Soper, Feb. 6, 1906, Bemidji, Minn., to Marcus A. and Elsie (Aleshire) Soper. Father, clergyman. Grad. Yakima H.S., Wash., 1923; attended Cheney Normal Sch., Wash., 1924–25; Coll. of Puget Sound, 1925–26; Univ. of Washington, A.B. 1930, M.A. 1932; Cornell Univ., Ph.D. 1941. Married Dec. 17, 1933, to Helen Knowles, theatrical costumer; two sons. Member of SCAA (member of legis. assembly, 1964); Southern Speech Assn. (pres., 1943–44); SETC; Phi Kappa Phi. Address: (home) 8017 Chesterfield Dr., Knoxville, TN 37919, tel. (615) 524-2981; (bus.) Univ. of Tennessee, Knoxville, TN tel. (615) 524-2981.

From 1945 to 1972, Mr. Soper was chairman of the Speech and Theatre Division at the Univ. of Tennessee and executive director of the Carousel Th. and of the Univ. of Tennessee Th. where he had taught since 1936 (instructor of English, 1936–41; assist. prof., 1941–44; assoc. prof., 1944–47; prof., 1947–to date). He retired from dept. headship and theatre work in 1972 to return to full-time teaching.

He held academic positions at Western State College (director of speech and drama, 1931–36); the Univ. of Washington (teaching fellow, 1930–31); and has been executive director of the Carousel Th., a university-community theatre, since its inception in 1951.

He has contributed articles on speech and theatre to *Quarterly Journal of Speech, Southern Speech Journal* and *Tennessee Studies*.

Published Works. Mr. Soper wrote the college textbook, *Basic Public Speaking* (1949, rev. 1956, 1963).

Awards. He was awarded an honorary Doctorate of Humane Letters by Findlay College (Dec. 5, 1962).

SOREL, GUY. Actor, announcer. b. August 12, 1914, Paris, France, to Jules and Denise Sorel. Father, Merchant; mother, fashion designer. Attended Ethical Culture Sch. (N.Y.C.); McBurney Sch. (N.Y.C.); and Lycee Carnot (Paris). He trained for the theatre at the American Academy of Dramatic Arts (N.Y.C.). Married Jan. 13, 1945, to Mary Jane Higby. Member of AEA; AFTRA (twice delegate to national conventions and member of the board); The Players. Address: (home) 152 E. 94th St., New York, NY 10028, tel. (212) 289-6455; (bus.) tel. (212) SU 7-5400.

Pre-Theatre. Mr. Sorel worked for a cigarette paper manufacturing firm in England (1934–36), and was in retailing in New York and Philadelphia (1936–39).

Theatre. Mr. Sorel made his amateur debut as Paul Duhamel in *The Wind and the Rain* (Plays and Players Th., Philadelphia, 1939); debuted professionally as the Examiner in *Outward Bound* (Cape May, N.J., Playhouse, Summer 1941), and on Bway as Clemenceau in *In Time to Come* (Mansfield, Dec. 28, 1941). He subsequently played Stefan in *Winter Soldiers* (New School Experimental Th., N.Y.C., Nov. 30, 1942); William Beecher in *Harriet* (Henry Miller's Th., N.Y.C., Mar. 4, 1943); Alexander Hamilton in *The Patriots* (NY City Ctr. Th., N.Y.C., Dec. 21, 1943, and on national tour, 1943–44); Lucien Gerard in *The Assassin* (National, N.Y.C., Oct. 18, 1945); Andre in *Monique* (John Golden Th., N.Y.C., Oct. 23, 1957); Roy Litchfield in *Face of a Hero* (Eugene O'Neill Th., N.Y.C., Oct. 21, 1960); Dr. Cartier in *A Gift of Time* (Ethel Barrymore Th., N.Y.C., Feb. 23, 1962); Gomez in the US premiere of T. S. Eliot's *The Elder Statesman* (Fred Miller Th., Milwaukee, Feb.–Mar. 1963); the Bishop of Limoux in *The Burning of the Lepers* (York, N.Y.C., Dec. 4, 1963); and was a replacement in the role of Buderus in *The Rothschilds* (Lunt-Fontanne, N.Y.C., July 1971).

Films. Mr. Sorel was seen as Robert Hélier in *The Thirteenth Letter* (20th-Fox, 1951); and appeared in *Tell Me That You Love Me, Junie Moon* (Par., 1970).

Television and Radio. Mr. Sorel appeared in The Standard Brands Hour Glass (NBC, 1946). He has been an announcer on radio and TV.

Recreation. Bridge, and "visiting England as often as possible.".

SOULE, ROBERT. Scenic and costume designer. b. Robert Donald Soule, Nov. 4, 1926, Bushnell, Ill., to Phil M. and Veda (Houston) Soule. Attended Western Univ., 1944–45; Pasadena Playhouse Coll. of Theatre Arts, 1947–49. Served USN, 1945–46. Member of United Scenic Artists. Address: 9 Thomas St., Providence, RI 02903, tel. (401) 331-0276.

Theatre. Mr. Soule first designed sets and costumes for a Pasadena (Calif.) Playhouse production of *The Alchemist* (1948). His first professional assignment was as designer for the Sombrero Playhouse (Phoenix, Ariz., Winters 1949–51), where his first production was *Born Yesterday.* During these years, he was also designer for El Teatro de Santa Fe in New Mexico (Summers). He was set designer for the Omaha (Neb.) Community Theatre (1951); and the Bar Harbor (Me.) Playhouse (1952). In New York, he designed the sets for the ELT production of *The Glass Menagerie* (Lenox Hill Playhouse, Nov. 19, 1952); *The Time of Storm* (Greenwich Mews, Feb. 26, 1954).

He was set designer for the following summer theatres: Seacliff (L.I.) Summer Theatre (1953); Theatre-by-the-Sea (Matunuck, R.I., 1954); North Shore Music Theatre (Beverly, Mass., 1955); Valley Forge Music Fair (Devon, Pa., 1956); and Playhouse-in-the-Park (Philadelphia, Pa., 1957); designed the settings for *Garden District* (York, N.Y.C., Jan. 7, 1958); settings and costumes for *The Long Gallery* (RNA Th., Mar. 6, 1958); *The Enchanted* (Renata, Apr. 22, 1958); the settings for *The Golden Six* (York, Oct. 25, 1958); was designer for the Coconut Grove Playhouse (Miami, Fla., 1958); designed the settings and costumes for *A Trip to Bountiful* (Theatre East, N.Y.C., Feb. 26, 1959); the sets for *Widowers' Houses* (Downtown, Mar. 2, 1959); and the settings for the touring company of *Garden District* (opened Warren, Atlantic City, N.J., Mar. 11, 1959).

He designed the settings for *Chic* (Orpheum, N.Y.C., May 19, 1959); was designer for the Phoenicia (N.Y.) Playhouse (Summer 1959); designed the set and costumes for *Orpheus Descending* (Gramercy Arts, N.Y.C., Oct. 5, 1959); and was set designer for three summers for Casa Manaña (Fort Worth, Tex., Summers 1960–63); designed the sets for *The Pretenders* (Cherry Lane Th., N.Y.C., May 24, 1960); *Greenwich Village, USA* (One Sheridan Square Th., N.Y.C., Sept. 28, 1960); *Donogoo* (Greenwich Mews, Jan. 18, 1961); was assistant designer for *How To Make a Man* (Brooks Atkinson Th., Feb. 2, 1961); the settings and lighting for *"Elsa Lanchester—Herself"* (41 St. Th., Feb. 4, 1961); the settings for *The Tiger Rag* (Cherry Lane, Feb. 16, 1961), *The Tattooed Countess* (Barbizon-Plaza, Apr. 3, 1961), and *Red Roses for Me* (Greenwich Mews, Nov. 27, 1961); the sets and costumes for *Fly, Blackbird* (Mayfair, Feb. 5, 1962); the sets for *A Pair of Pairs* (Van Dam, Apr. 24, 1962); the sets and costumes for *Riverwind* (Actors Playhouse, Dec. 12, 1962); and designed a revised version of *The Milk Train Doesn't Stop Here Anymore* (Barter Th., Abingdon, Va., Sept. 16, 1963).

Mr. Soule was resident designer for the Milwaukee (Wisc.) Repertory Th. (1965–66) where productions included *The Tempest, Oh Dad, Poor Dad, . . ., Once Upon a Mattress, Uncle Vanya,* and *Pantagalles.* At the Actors Theatre (Louisville, Ky.), he designed productions of *The Importance of Being Earnest, No Exit, A Flea in Her Ear, Waiting for Godot, A School for Scandal, Private Lives, Death of a Salesman, Charlie's Aunt,* and *The Tavern.* For the Trinity Square Repertory Co. (Providence, R.I., 1968–to date), he has designed productions of *Red Roses for Me, Adaptation/Next, Little Murders, Harvey, Love for Love, The Price, A School for Wives, Lady Audley's Secret, Sherlock Holmes, For the Use of the Hall, Alfred the Great, Jumpers, Emperor Henry,* and *Tooth of Crime.*

He has designed numerous productions for The Barter Th. (Abingdon, Va., 1964); Westport (Conn.) Playhouse (1967); Little Theatre on the Square (Sullivan, Ill., 1967–75); and The Embers Dinner Th., (Louisiana, 1971).

Films. Mr. Soule was art director for *Turnabout,* produced independently by the Rockefeller Foundation (1949).

Television. He was set designer for Truth or Consequences (NBC, 1950–51); The Billy Burke Show; You Asked for It; This Is Your Life; and the WJAR-TV News.

Night Clubs. Mr. Soule designed Charles Pearce's Moppets, (Red Carpet Club, Miami, Fla., Feb. 1, 1962); and sets for one-man shows with Louis Armstrong, Paul Whiteman, Dave Brubeck, Sophie Tucker, George Jessel, Carol Channing, Phyllis Diller and Ted Lewis.

Other Activities. Mr. Soule was staff display designer for Kentucky Scenic Studio (Louisville, Ky., 1966); and has been designer-in-residence at Mount Holyoke (Mass.) Coll. (Fall 1974), and Rhode Island Coll. (Providence, R.I., Fall 1975).

His industrial design credits include work for Royal Crown Cola, Supermarkets of America, American Motel-Hotel Association, Brown-Forman Liquors (Centennial Exhibit), General Electric, Johnson and Johnson, and Congoleum.

Mr. Soule was co-owner and co-designer of a window display corporation called Display Service (N.Y.C.).

In addition, he designed the Leonadorff "Wonderama" at the 1964 New York World's Fair.

SPALDING, GRAYDON. Actor. b. July 4, 1911, Windsor, Vt., to Charles Daniel G. and Elizabeth G. (Hanaford) Spalding. Father, engineer and carpenter, Pasadena (Calif.) Playhouse. Relative in theatre, brother, C. Gordon Spaulding, box office manager and stage photographer, Pasadena Playhouse. Educ. public schools and junior college, Pasadena, Calif. Served US Army, 1942–45. Member of AEA; Pasadena Playhouse Alumni & Associates; Delta Psi Omega (past); Fine Arts Club, Pasadena (pres., 1966–67, 1974–75; vice-pres., 1970–72); Rounce & Coffin Club, Los Angeles; International Platform Assoc. Address: 2299 Francisco Dr., Newport Beach, CA 92660, tel. (714) 548-2543.

Theatre. From 1928 to 1968, Mr. Spalding appeared in many productions during regular seasons and annual summer festivals at pasadena (Calif.) Playhouse, where his parts included a Senator and Nazarene in *Lazarus Laughed* (Apr.–May 1928); a Cowcadden in *What Every Woman Knows* (Feb. 1931); Porter's Man in *Henry VIII* (Nov.–Dec. 1932); various parts in *Richard II; Henry IV, Part 2; Henry VI, Part 2* (Summer 1935); Silver Tosh in *The Little Minister* (Summer 1940); Mr. Pincus in *The Front Page* (Apr. 1941); Muche in *Topaze* (Apr.–May 1941); William Gosling in *Good Gracious, Annabelle* (July 1942); Johann Breitstein in *Counsellor-at-Law* (Aug. 1945); Wilson in *The Late George Apley* (Feb. 1947); and Rev. Dr. Lloyd in *Life with Father* (Dec. 1948–Jan. 1949). Also Vincent Kilpatrick in *The Gentleman from Athens* (Feb. 1949); Lyman Beecher in *Harriet* (Aug. 1952); Dr. Harper in *Arsenic and Old Lace* (Mar. 1954); James Telfer in *Trelawny of the Wells* (Dec. 1954–Jan. 1955); Kit Carson in *The Time of Your Life* (Mar.–Apr. 1959); Sen. Robert E. Lyons in *Of Thee I Sing* (Apr.–June 1960); the Bishop of York in *Becket* (Apr.–May 1962); and Grandpa Vanderhoff in *You Can't Take it with You* (Nov.–Dec. 1968).

In addition to his work at Pasadena Playhouse (1928–68), Mr. Spalding appeared in various other California theatres: Brown's Playbox; Santa Ana Playhouse; Patio Theatre; Lobero Th., Santa Barbara; Padua Hills Th. He was also active with such organizations as 18 Actors, Inc., Montrose, Calif. (1956–58) and Spectrum Productions (California Institute of Technology, Pasadena, 1972–to date). He made his professional debut with 18 Actors, Inc., as Mr. Gill in *The Show-Off* (Elk's Club, Pasadena, Feb. 4–19, 1951) and with the same organization later played Old Man Nelson in *Hope Is the Thing with Feathers* (Apr. 15–30, 1951), Winchell in *Family Reunion* (Feb. 28–Mar. 17, 1952), Rev. Williams in *The Old Lady Shows Her Medals* (Mar. 30–Apr. 20, 1952), Mr. Wadhurst in *Hands Across the Sea* (Mar. 7–22, 1953), and repeated his performance in *Hope Is the Thing with Feathers,* (May 5–28, 1955).

Films. Mr. Spalding is in the Pasadena, Calif., centennial film (1974).

Television and Radio. Mr. Spalding made his radio debut as Balthasar in *The Lost Star* (KGER, Long Beach, Calif., 1931) and was in many later broadcasts, including a 13-week drama series (KPPC, Pasadena, Sept. 1937–Feb. 1938); and special Easter, Lincoln's Birthday, and Washington's Birthday broadcasts (KWKW, Pasadena). On television, he appeared on *Research at the Huntington Library* (Citywatchers, PBS, 1973, 1974).

Other Activities. From 1945 to 1975, Mr. Spalding was at the Henry E. Huntington Library, Art Gallery and Botanical Gardens, San Marino, Calif., where he was assistant supervisor for twelve years and supervisor for eighteen years of the rare book vaults.

Recreation. Typesetting and operating hand press; collecting rare early Vermont imprints.

SPARER, PAUL. Actor. b. Boston, Mass. Grad. magna cum laude, Psychology, Harvard Univ. Served as fighter pilot, US Air Force, W.W. II; rank, Capt. Married Nancy Marchand, actress; one son, two daughters. Member of AEA; AFTRA. Address: 205 W. 89th St., New York, NY 10024, tel. (212) TR 3-7889.

Theatre. Mr. Sparer made his acting debut in a small part in Pirandello's *Henry IV* (Brattle Th., Cambridge, Mass.) where he subsequently played in over forty productions. He made his New York debut with that company at NY City Ctr., playing Dumain in *Love's Labour's Lost* (Feb. 4, 1953); subsequently playing Salanio in *The Merchant of Venice* (Mar. 4, 1953); Cassio in *Othello* (Sept. 7, 1955); and Owen Glendower in *Henry IV, Part 1* (Sept. 21, 1955). He played Gilles de Rais in *Saint Joan* (Phoenix Th., Sept. 11, 1956); Earl of Gloucester in *King Lear* (Players' Th., Jan. 2, 1959); Heracles in *Two Philoctetes* (ANTA Matinee Series, Jan. 13, 1959); appeared in various roles with The Antioch (Ohio) Shakespeare Fest. (Summer 1959); played Borachio in *Much Ado About Nothing* (Lunt-Fontanne, N.Y.C., Sept. 17, 1959); John Brown in *Cut of the Axe* (Ambassador, N.Y.C., Feb. 1, 1960); returned to the Antioch (Ohio) Shakespeare Fest. (Summer 1960); played Leone Gala in *The Rules of the Game* (Gramercy Arts Th., N.Y.C., Dec. 19, 1960); as a founding member (1960) and associate artistic director of the Association of Producing Artists (APA), played Boris Trigorin in *The Sea Gull* (Folksbiene Playhouse, Mar. 21, 1961); and Tom Allen in *The Tavern* (Folksbiene Playhouse, Apr. 4, 1961); at the American Shakespeare Fest., Stratford, Conn., he played Corin in *As You Like It* (June 27, 1961), Lennox in *Macbeth* (June 28, 1961), and Ulysses in *Troilus and Cressida* (July 23, 1961); played the Prosecuting Captain in *A Cook for Mr. General* (The Playhouse, N.Y.C., Oct. 19, 1961); Auba Abu Tayi in *Ross* (Eugene O'Neill Th., Dec. 26, 1961); again for APA at the Phoenix Th., played Lamberto Laudisi in *Right You Are If You Think You Are,* Tom Allen in *The Tavern,* Moliere in *Impromptu at Versailles,* and Satin in *The Lower Depths* (season opened Mar. 4, 1961); and Mendoza in *Man and Superman* (Dec. 6, 1964), Dolokhov in *War and Peace* (Jan. 11, 1965), and Holofernes in *Judith* (Mar. 24, 1965); in a triple-bill entitled *The World of Ray Bradbury,* played Mead in *The Pedestrian,* The Stranger in *To The Chicago Abyss,* and David MacLean in *The Veldt* (Orpheum, Oct. 8, 1965); at the Amer. Shakespeare Fest., Stratford, Conn., played Robert Shallow in *Falstaff (Henry IV, Part 2)* (June 18, 1966), Sir Reginald Fitz Urse in *Murder in the Cathedral* (June 19, 1966), and Cassius in *Julius Caesar,* which he also directed (June 22, 1966); appeared in *Andorra* (Winnipeg, Canada, Winter 1966); played the Lecturer in *After the Rain* (John Golden Th., N.Y.C., Oct. 9, 1967); was standby to Arthur Kennedy in the role of Walter Fanz in *The Price* (Morosco, Feb. 7, 1968); played Disley in *Teaparty* on a double-bill with *The Basement* (Eastside Playhouse, Oct. 15, 1968); the title role in *In the Matter of J. Robert Oppenheimer* (revival Vivian Beaumont Th., June 26, 1969); Richard Plantagenet in *Henry VI, Part 1* (Delacorte, June 23, 1970); Richard Duke of York in *Henry VI, Part 2* (Delacorte, June 24, 1970); the General in *The Happiness Cage* (Newman/Public, Oct. 4, 1970); Halvard Solness in *The Master Builder* (Roundabout, Oct. 17, 1971); Albert Valpor in *The Water Hen* (Brooklyn Acad. of Music, May 9, 1972); succeeded Mark Hammer as Leonato in *Much Ado About Nothing* (Winter Garden, Nov. 11, 1972); appeared with the Hartford (Conn.) Stage Co. (1973–74 season); played Giovanni in *The Burnt Flower Bed* (Roundabout/Stage 2, N.Y.C., July 2, 1974); was standby to Rex Harrison and Martin Gabel in *In Praise of Love* (Morosco, Dec. 10, 1974); and appeared in *Duck Variations* (St. Clement's Church, Dec. 1975).

Films. Mr. Sparer has appeared in *A Doll's House* for *Encyclopaedia Britannica*.

Television. Mr. Sparer's appearances include Hallmark Hall of Fame (NBC); US Steel Hour; Armstrong Th.; The Modern World of William Shakespeare (NBC); and the daytime dramas Edge of Night (CBS) and Somerset (NBC).

Recreation. Photography.

"SPELVIN, GEORGE." Actor. Reputedly born c. 1886, New York City. Relatives in theatre: "George Spelvin, Jr.," "Georgette Spelvin," "Georgiana Spelvin"; the English branch of the family includes "Walter Plinge," "Mr. Bart," and "Mr. F. Anney.".

Theatre. "George Spelvin" was, according to existing records, discovered by Edward Abeles and first played a minor role in the Bway production of *Karl the Peddler* (1886). He then appeared in *Brewster's Millions* (New Amsterdam Th., Dec. 31, 1906), becoming co-author Winchell Smith's favorite actor and superstition, and appearing in most of Mr. Smith's subsequent productions.

"George Spelvin" appeared in minor roles in *Polly of the Circus* (Liberty, Dec. 23, 1907); the pre-Bway tryout of *That Little Affair at the Boyd's* (closed Washington, D.C., June 16, 1908); Maude Adams' productions of *Joan of Arc, As You Like It,* and *What Every Woman Knows, The Fortune Teller* (Gaiety, N.Y.C., Sept. 4, 1909); *Officer 666* (Gaiety, Jan. 29, 1912); and *Seven Keys to Baldpate* (Astor, Sept. 22, 1913).

He played Moses in *Turn to the Right* (Gaiety, Aug. 18, 1916); Zeb Crothers in *Lightnin'* (Gaiety, Aug. 26, 1918); the Policeman in *Three Wise Fools* (Criterion, Oct. 31, 1918); appeared in *The First Year* (Little, Oct. 20, 1920); *Seventh Heaven* (Booth, Oct. 30, 1922); played Mr. X in *Polly Preferred* (Little, Jan. 11, 1923); Ramirez in *Spring in Autumn* (Henry Miller's Th., Oct. 24, 1933); a Betting Man in *High Button Shoes* (Shubert, Oct. 9, 1947); toured as a Policeman in *Sailor's Delight* (opened Huntington Hartford Th., Los Angeles, Calif., Nov. 22, 1954); and played Colonel Dent in *Jane Eyre* (Belasco, N.Y.C., May 1, 1958).

He appeared as one of the people in the River Camp in *John Turner Davis* (Sheridan Sq. Playhouse, July 1, 1958); Franklin Basuto in the pre-Bway tryout of *Goodwill Ambassador* (opened Shubert, New Haven, Conn., Mar. 16, 1960; closed Wilbur, Boston, Mass., Mar. 26, 1960); was an understudy in the national touring company of *Milk and Honey* (opened Shubert, Philadelphia, Pa., Jan. 29, 1963; closed Biltmore, Los Angeles, Calif., Sept. 7, 1963); played Mr. Morton in *The Purple Canary* (Midway, N.Y.C., Apr. 22, 1963); and the Voice in *The Chief Thing* (Greenwich Mews, Apr., 29, 1963).

He was a dancer in *Mardi Gras!* (Marine Th., Jones Beach, N.Y., Summer 1966); an understudy for *The End of All Things Natural* (Village South Th., Sept. 11, 1969); and toured with members of his family in *Six Characters in Search of an Author* (Summer 1970–to date).

Films. "George Spelvin" was in a number of D. W. Griffith motion pictures, notably as a Union Soldier in *Birth of a Nation* (UA, 1915), a Villager in *Hearts of the World* (Comstock-World, 1918), and a Country Dancer in *Way Down East* (UA, 1920). Later films include *The Ghost Goes West* (UA, 1936); *The Invisible Man Returns* (U, 1940); *Nobody Lives Forever* (WB, 1946); *From Here to Eternity* (Col., 1953); *The Unearthly* (Rep., 1957); and *The Dream Maker* (U, 1964).

Television. "Mr. Spelvin" made his television debut on The Fugitive (ABC); and has appeared on such programs as The Eternal Light (NBC); Everlasting Road (ABC); The Guiding Light (CBS); The Untouchables (ABC); Edge of Night (CBS); Night Gallery (NBC); Wanted Dead or Alive (CBS); and The Invisible Man (NBC).

SPEWACK, BELLA. Playwright. b. Bella Cohen, Mar. 25, 1899, Bucharest, Romania, to Adolph and Fanny (Lang) Cohen. Grad. Washington Irving H.S., N.Y.C., 1917. Married Mar. 25, 1922, to Samuel Spewack, playwright (dec. Oct. 14, 1971). Member of Dramatists Guild; WGA, East. Address: 171 W. 57th St., New York, NY 10019, tel. (212) PL 7-5286.

Pre-Theatre. Reporter, foreign correspondent.

Theatre. Mrs. Spewack wrote with her husband, Samuel Spewack, *The War Song* (National, N.Y.C., Sept. 24, 1928); *Poppa* (Biltmore, Dec. 24, 1928); *Clear All Wires* (Times Square Th., Sept. 14, 1932); *Spring Song* (Morosco, Oct. 1, 1934); *Boy Meets Girl* (Cort, Nov. 27, 1935; revived Windsor, June 22, 1943); the book for the musical, *Leave It to Me* (Imperial, Nov. 9, 1938; return engagement Sept. 4, 1939); *Miss Swan Expects* (Cort, Feb. 20, 1939); *Woman Bites Dog* (Belasco, Apr. 17, 1946); the book for the musical, *Kiss Me, Kate* (New Century, Dec. 30, 1948; return engagement Bway Th., Jan. 8, 1952; revived NY City Ctr., May 9, 1956); *My 3 Angels* (Morosco, Mar. 11, 1953); and *The Festival* (Longacre, Jan. 18, 1955). She produced her husband's play, *Golden State* (Fulton, Nov. 25, 1950).

Films. The Spewacks collaborated on the screenplays for 20 films, including *Clear All Wires* (MGM, 1933); *When Ladies Meet* (MGM, 1933); *Should Ladies Behave?* (MGM, 1933); *The Nuisance* (MGM, 1933); *The Cat and the Fiddle* (MGM, 1934); *Rendezvous* (MGM, 1935); *Vogues of 1938* (UA, 1937); *Boy Meets Girl* (WB, 1938); *Three Loves Has Nancy* (MGM, 1938); *My Favorite Wife,* for which they also wrote the original story (RKO, 1940); and *Weekend at the Waldorf* (MGM, 1945).

Television. They wrote adaptations of *Kiss Me, Kate* (NBC, 1959), and *My Three Angels* (NBC, 1960); and the original teleplay *Enchanted Nutcracker* (ABC, 1963).

Awards. Mrs. Spewack and her husband received the Roi Cooper Megrue Prize (1936) for *Boy Meets Girl,* and the Antoinette Perry (Tony) Award (1948) for *Kiss Me, Kate.*.

SPIGELGASS, LEONARD. Playwright, writer. b. Brooklyn, N.Y., to Abraham and Rebecca (Ratner) Spigelgass. Father, attorney. Grad. New York Univ., B.A. 1929. Served WW II, US Army; rank, Lt. Col. Member of Dramatists Guild; WGA; ALA. Address: c/o Writers Guild of America, West, 8955 Beverly Blvd., Los Angeles, CA 90048.

Theatre. Mr. Spigelgass wrote *A Majority of One* (Shubert Th., Feb. 16, 1958) and *Dear Me the Sky Is Falling* (Music Box, Mar. 2, 1963), based on a story by Gertrude Berg and James Yaffe; *Wrong Way Light Bulb* (Golden Th., Mar. 4, 1969); *Look to the Lilies* (Lunt-Fontanne, Mar. 29, 1970), which was the basis of *Mack and Mabel* (Majestic, Oct. 5, 1974).

Films. Initially a reader and story editor, Mr. Spigelgass has written the screenplays for *Princess O'Hara* which he also produced (U, 1935); *The Boys from Syracuse* (U, 1940); *Tight Shoes* (U, 1941); *All Through the Night* (WB, 1942); *Butch Minds the Baby* (U, 1942); *Big Street* (RKO, 1942); *The Perfect Marriage* (Par., 1946); *I Was a Male War Bride* (20th-Fox, 1949); *Because You're Mine* (MGM, 1952); *Deep in My Heart* (MGM, 1954); *Silk Stockings* (MGM, 1957); *Pepe* (Col., 1960); *A Majority of One* (WB, 1961); and *Gypsy* (WB, 1962).

Television. Mr. Spigelgass wrote *Eloise* (Playhouse 90, CBS, 1956) *The Helen Morgan Story* (Playhouse 90, CBS, 1957) and has written for–Wide World of Entertainment (ABC); 20th Century-Fox Presents (1974); and Entertainment Hall of Fame (1974).

Published Works. He wrote *The Scuttle Under the Bonnet* (1962), and *Fed to the Teeth* (1964); and was co-author with Edward G. Robinson, of *All My Yesterdays* (1973).

SPRIGGE, ELIZABETH. Novelist, biographer, lecturer, director, producer, translator. b. Elizabeth Miriam Squire Sprigge, June 19, 1900, London, England, to Sir Squire and Mary Ada (Moss) Sprigge. Father, editor of *The Lancet.* Grad. St. Paul's Girls Sch.; Havergal Coll., Toronto, Can.; Bedford Coll., London. Married July 23, 1921, to Mark Napier (marr. dis. 1946); two daughters. Relative in theatre: brother-in-law, Alan Napier, actor. Address: 75 Ladbroke Grove, London W.11, 2 PD, England tel. 01-727-9630.

In 1930, Miss Sprigge translated August Strindberg's *The Bond,* with Claude Napier; wrote, with Katriona Sprigge, *Elizabeth of Austria* (Garrick Th., London, Nov. 3, 1938); was the co-founder of "48 Theatre" which produced, among other plays, Gertrude Stein's *Yes Is for a Very Young Man* and led to a commission to write Miss Stein's biography (1948).

She co-founded The Watergate Th. (London) and directed productions there, including her own translation of Strindberg's *The Great Highway* (1949–52); and translated Bjrnsterne Bjrnson *Mary Stuart in Scotland* for the Edinburgh (Scotland) Intl. Festival (Gateway Th., 1960).

Published Works. Her translations include *Six Plays of Strindberg* (1955); *Five Plays of Strindberg* (1960); *Twelve Plays of Strindberg* (1962); *August Strindberg, Plays* (1963); *The Difficulty of Being* by Jean Cocteau (1966); and *The Red Room* by Strindberg (1967). Her novels are *A Shadowy Third* (1929), *Faint Amorist* (1930), *The Old Man Dies* (1933), *Castle in Andalusia* (1935), *The Son of the House* (1937), *The Raven's Wing* (1940); and her children's books include *Children Alone* (1935), *Pony Tracks* (1936), and *Two Lost on Dartmoor* (1940). Her biographies include *The Strange Life of August Strindberg* (1949); *The Life and Work of Gertrude Stein* (1957), (with Jean-Jacques Kihm) *Jean Cocteau: The Man and the Mirror* (1968); *Sybil Thorndike Casson* (1971); and *The Life of Ivy Compton-Burnett* (1973).

Recreation. Travel, country living.

SQUIBB, JUNE. Actress. b. June Louise Squibb, Nov. 6, 1935, Vandalia, Ill., to Lewis C. and Joybelle Squibb. Father, insurance agent. Grad. Vandalia Community H.S.; attended Eastern Illinois State Coll.; and Patricia Stevens Modeling Sch. Studied at Cleveland (Ohio) Play House with Benno Frank, three years; in N.Y.C. studied voice with Jack Lee and Bob Gorman, dance with Frank Wagner, musical theatre with Ken McMillan (HB Studio), and acting with Charles Kakatsakis. Married May 18, 1953, to Edward Sostek, stage manager (marr. dis. Dec. 1959); married Sept. 1, 1967, to Charles Kakatsakis, director, teacher; one son. Member of AEA; AFTRA; SAG; AGVA. Address: 885 West End Ave., Apt. 6C, New York, NY 10025, tel. (212) 866-2446 or (212) LT 1-6470.

Theatre. Miss Squibb acted at the Cleveland (Ohio) Play House (1953–55), appearing as the Physical Education Major in *Goodbye My Fancy* (1953); Ismene in *Antigone* (1953); Lucy in *Ladies in Retirement* (1953); Daisy in *Bloomer Girl* (1954); Abigail in *The Crucible* (1954); Titania in *A Midsummer Night's Dream* (1954); the Blind Date in *Best Foot Forward* (1954); the Wicked Witch in *The Wizard of Oz* (1954); Mrs. Spofford in *Gentlemen Prefer Blondes* (1954); and the Cockney Maid in *Night Must Fall* (1955).

At the Hilltop Th. (Biltmore, Md., 1955), she played the ingenue in *Here Today* (June); appeared in *The Remarkable Mr. Pennypacker* (July), and *My 3 Angels* (July), played the Blonde in *Happy Birthday* (Aug.), the Wife in *Lullaby* (Aug.), and Doris in *What Ever Happened* (Sept.).

She played Miss Delaware Water Gap in the ELT production of *Best Foot Forward* (Lenox Hill Playhouse, N.Y.C., Feb. 22, 1956); Ardis in *Sable Brush* (Royal, Apr. 1956); Marie What-Ever-Her-Name-Was in *The Seven Year Itch* (Allenberry Playhouse, Boiling Springs, Pa., July 1956); Winnie in the ELT production of *Annie Get Your Gun* (Lenox Hill Playhouse, N.Y.C., Feb. 26, 1957); and again at the Stamford Playhouse (Conn., Mar. 1957); and Dulcie in a summer tour of *The Boy Friend* (June 1957), a role she repeated in N.Y.C. (Downtown, Jan. 25, 1958).

Miss Squibb played Ellie in *Show Boat* (Rye Music Th., N.Y., June 1958); Dulcie in *The Boy Friend* (Ivar Th., Hollywood, Calif., Jan. 1959); Irene in *Say, Darling* (Cape May Playhouse, N.J., June 1959); Hilda in *Plain and Fancy* (Mt. Gretna Playhouse, Pa., July 1959); toured as a comedienne in *Lend an Ear* (July 1959), and appeared in it in N.Y.C. (Renata Th., Sept. 24, 1959). She took part in a USO-sponsored revue in Thule, Greenland (Dec. 1959).

She appeared as Eva Tanguay in the revue *Turn Back the Clock* (The Meadows, Framingham, Mass., May 1960); succeeded (Aug. 1960) Chatzi Foley as Electra in *Gypsy* (Bway Th., May 21, 1959), and toured in it (opened Rochester Aud., N.Y., Mar. 29, 1961; closed American, St. Louis, Mo., Dec. 9, 1961).

She played Janice Dayton in *Silk Stockings* (Westchester Dinner Th., N.Y.; St. Louis Dinner Th., Mo., May 1962); Gladys in *The Pajama Game* (Charlotte Summer Th., Charlotte, N.C., June 1962); Tessie Tura in *Gypsy* (Charlotte Summer Th., July 1962); and toured as Electra in *Gypsy* (July 1962). She repeated her performance as Electra (Meadowbrook Dinner Th., Cedar Grove, N.J., Dec. 1964) and as Tessie Tura (Coconut Grove Playhouse, Miami Beach, Fla., Mar. 1965); played Susan in *Desert Song* (Lambertville Music Tent, Lambertville, N.J., July 1965); and repeated her role as Ellie in *Show Boat* (Starlite Th., Indianapolis, Ind., Aug. 1965).

Miss Squibb performed as a comedienne in a USO revue touring the Pacific islands and in Asia (Jan.–Mar. 1966); she played Hedy in *How to Succeed in Business Without Really Trying* (Cecilwood Th., Fishkill, N.Y., June 1966); Gloria Rasputin in *Bye Bye Birdie* (Municipal Opera, St. Louis, Mo., July 1966); Billie Dawn in *Born Yesterday* and the Countess in *You Never Know* (both Cecilwood Th., Fishkill, N.Y., Aug. 1966); Ellen in *Luv* (Cecilwood Th., June 1967); Daisy Gamble in *On a Clear Day You Can See Forever* (Cecilwood Th., July 1967); and repeated her performance as Tessie Tura in *Gypsy* (Starlite Th., Indianapolis, Ind., July 1967).

Miss Squibb played Felice Bonnard in *The Happy Time* (Ahmanson Th., Los Angeles, Calif., Nov. 1967; Broadway Th., N.Y.C., Jan. 18, 1968); was in *U.S.A.* and *Spoon River Anthology* (Theatre Co. on the Hudson, Bard Coll., Annandale-on-the-Hudson, N.Y., Aug. 1970); was in *Division Street* (Th. of Riverside Ch., N.Y.C., Mar. 1972); played Mrs. Box in *Sitting* and Miss Rackley in *The Saving Grace* (Studio Arena, Buffalo, N.Y., Nov. 9, 1972); was the Wife in *A Delicate Balance* by Frank Duane, one of three plays on the program *An Evening with the Bourgeoisie* (AMAS Rep. Th., N.Y.C., Jan. 1973); was Martha Foley in *Run from the Hunter* (Lambs Club, Feb. 1973); Olga in *The Three Sisters* (AMAS Rep. Th., Mar. 1973); appeared at the Alhambra Dinner Th., Jacksonville, Fla., as Alice Pepper in *Tunnel of Love* (Sept.–Oct. 1973) and Ann in *The Perfect Set-Up* (Nov.–Dec. 1973); was Saunders in *Fallen Angels* (Beverly Barn, Shreveport, La., and Beverly Dinner Th., New Orleans, La., Jan.–Mar. 1974); and Juliet in *Wake Up Darling* (Alhambra Dinner Th., Jacksonville, Fla., Aug.–Sept. 1974).

Television. Miss Squibb was on Show Street (ABC, Sept.–Nov. 1964) and in As the World Turns (CBS, Sept. 1971).

Night Clubs. Miss Squibb appeared as a comedienne in *No Shoe Strings* (Upstairs at the Downstairs, N.Y.C., Aug. 1962); in *Beyond the Binge* (Madeira Club, Provincetown, Mass., July 1963); on the cruise ship SS Atlantic in *Best of Everything* (Dec. 1963–Jan. 1964); and in *Up the Ante* (Madeira Club, Provincetown, Mass., July 1964). She and Barry Dennen formed a comedy team playing at Upstairs at the Duplex (Feb. 1965), where she was also in the revue *The Third World War* (May 1965); and she appeared again on the SS Atlantic in *Best of Everything* (Fall 1965).

Recreation. Swimming and reading.

SQUIRE, KATHERINE. Actress. b. Mar. 9, Defiance, Ohio, to Virgil and Mary (Haag) Squire. Father, banker. Grad. Defiance (Ohio) H.S., 1921; Ohio Wesleyan Univ., B.A. (Phi Beta Kappa) 1925. Studied acting at Amer. Laboratory Th., N.Y.C., 1927–29; Cleveland (Ohio) Play House, 1929–30; with Benno Schneyder, 1936–37; at Actors' Studio, N.Y.C. (mbr., 1953–to date). Married 1928 to Byron McGrath, actor (marr. dis. 1936); married Aug. 10, 1940, to George Mitchell, actor, writer. Member of AEA; AFTRA; SAG.

Theatre. Miss Squire made her debut as Viola in *Twelfth Night* (Ohio Wesleyan Univ., 1925); subsequently, for the American Laboratory Th., appeared as one of the Watches in *Much Ado About Nothing* (Nov. 18, 1927) and as Nathalia Hovind in *At the Gate of the Kingdom* (Dec. 8, 1927); at the Cleveland (Ohio) Playhouse, played Maria in *Twelfth Night*, Tessa in *The Constant Nymph*, the title role in *Serena Blandish*, and Hedvig in *The Wild Duck* (1927–29); later appeared in productions at the Woodstock (N.Y.) Playhouse (1928) and the University Playhouse, Falmouth, Mass. (1929).

She played Mona in *Black Tower* (Sam H. Harris Th., N.Y.C., Jan. 11, 1932); Julia Wilson in *Goodbye Again* (Masque, Dec. 28, 1932); Helen Tyson in *Hipper's Holiday* (Maxine Elliott's Th., Oct. 18, 1934); Winifred Shaw in *Lady of Letters* (Mansfield, Mar. 28, 1935); Hannah Priest in *Life's Too Short* (Broadhurst, Sept. 10, 1935); understudied Ruth Gordon as Mattie Silver in *Ethan Frome* (National, Jan. 21, 1936); succeeded (May 1937) Peggy Ashcroft as Lise in *High Tor* (Martin Beck Th., Jan. 8, 1937); appeared as Mrs. Roberts in *Many Mansions* (Biltmore, Oct. 27, 1937); and succeeded (1938) Joyce Arling as Miss Wheeler in *What a Life* (Biltmore, Apr. 13, 1938).

Miss Squire was a member of the Shakespeare Repertory company performing at the Globe Theatre (NY World's Fair, 1939); toured as Thea Elvsted in the Eva Le Gallienne production of *Hedda Gabler* (1940); played Nurse Cotton in *Liberty Jones* (Shubert, N.Y.C., Feb. 5, 1941); appeared at the Bucks County Playhouse, New Hope, Pa. (1942); the Chapel Theatre, Guilford, Conn. (1942); played Anna Petrovna Chernov in *The Family* (Windsor, N.Y.C., Mar. 30, 1943); Mrs. Lynch (Miss Sally) in *Chicken Every Sunday* (Henry Miller's Th., Apr. 5, 1944); for the USO (WW II) toured Europe in *Ten Little Indians* (1944–45) and the Pacific Theatre of Operations as Madam Arcati in *Blithe Spirit* (1945–46); played Bernice Desos in the pre-Bway tryout of *Three Indelicate Ladies* (opened, Shubert, New Haven, Conn., Apr. 10, 1947; closed, Wilbur, Boston, Mass., Apr. 19, 1947); at the Margo Jones Th., Dallas, Tex., Kate in *The Taming of the Shrew* and the Madonna in *Portrait of a Madonna* (1947–48); and played Mom in the ANTA Experimental Theatre's production of *Cock-a-Doodle-Doo* (Lenox Hill Playhouse, N.Y.C., Feb. 26, 1949).

She appeared in productions at the Seacliff (N.Y.) Summer Th. (1950, 1951, 1952); Westport (Conn.) Country Playhouse (1951, 1953, 1961); Cape Playhouse, Dennis, Mass. (1951); and the Pocono Playhouse, Mountainhome, Pa. (1954); played Sitter Mavis in *The Traveling Lady* (Playhouse, N.Y.C., Oct. 27, 1954); the Mother in *Six Characters in Search of an Author* (Phoenix, Dec. 11, 1955); Brigid Muldoon in *The Sin of Pat Muldoon* (Cort, Mar. 13, 1957); Mrs. Grigson in *The Shadow of a Gunman* (Bijou, Nov. 19, 1958); the Queen in *The Cave Dwellers* (Dahl Th., Hollywood, Calif., May–July 1958); appeared in productions at the Sombrero Playhouse, Phoenix, Ariz. (1958); was Mrs. Bryant in *Roots* (Mayfair, N.Y.C., Mar. 6, 1961); played at the Charles Playhouse, Boston, Mass., in *A Touch of the Poet* (Sept. 29, 1964) and *The Rivals* (Nov. 11, 1964); was Julie in *This Here Nice Place* (Th. 80 St. Mark's, N.Y.C., Nov. 1, 1966); appeared at the Tyrone Guthrie Th., Minneapolis, Minn., in *Thieves' Carnival* (June 2, 1967), *Harpers Ferry* (June 3, 1967), and *The Visit* (Sept. 11, 1967); was Stella in *Boy on the Straight-Back Chair* (American Place Th., N.Y.C., Feb. 14, 1969); and was in *Right You Are If You Think You Are* (Meadow Brook Th., Rochester, Mich., Feb. 1, 1973).

Films. Miss Squire appeared in *The Story on Page One* (20th-Fox, 1959); *Song without End* (Col., 1960); and *Studs Lonigan* (UA, 1960).

Television. She made her debut on Studio One (CBS, 1949); and has appeared on Playhouse 90 (CBS); Philco Television Playhouse (NBC); Kraft Television Th. (NBC); Alcoa Presents (NBC); Alcoa Premiere (ABC); Armstrong Circle Th. (CBS); Matinee Th. (NBC); Alfred Hitchcock Presents (CBS); Twilight Zone (CBS); Thriller; Bus Stop; The Texan; Dr. Kildare (NBC); and the Loretta Young Show (NBC).

Recreation. Photography, writing.

SQUIRE, WILLIAM. Actor. b. Apr. 29, 1920, Neath, Wales, to William and Martha (Bridgeman) Squire. Studied at RADA, London (L.C.C. Scholar). Married to Elizabeth Dixon. Member of AEA; British AEA.

Theatre. Mr. Squire made his N.Y.C. debut with the Old Vic Co. on their American tour as a Traveler in *Henry IV, Part 1* (Century Th., May 6, 1946). He succeeded (Sept. 1961) Richard Burton as King Arthur in the musical, *Camelot* (Majestic, Dec. 3, 1960).

He made his stage debut with the Old Vic Co. (Sept. 1945); with the same company, appeared as Lord Mowbray in *Henry IV, Part 2* (May 7, 1946); and as one of the Chorus of Theban Elders in *Oedipus* (May 20, 1946). He played Benvolio in *Romeo and Juliet* (Bolton's, London, Aug. 7, 1947); Dick in *The Patch Cloak* (Bolton's, Nov. 26, 1947); the Knave in *The Dragon and the Dove* (Mercury, Jan. 12, 1948); and, at the Royal Shakespeare Th., Ratty in *Toad of Toad Hall* (Stratford-upon-Avon, Dec. 1948).

He was a member of the Royal Shakespeare Co. appearing the first year as the Citizen in *King John*, Laertes in *Hamlet*, Time in *The Winter's Tale*, Ulysses in *Troilus and Cressida*, and the Duke in *Othello* (1948); and Verges in *Much Ado About Nothing*, Oberon in *A Midsummer Night's Dream*, Cloten in *Cymbeline*, and the Lord Chamberlain in *Henry VIII* (1949). He appeared with the Birmingham Rep. Th. (1950) as Dawlish in *Summer Day's Dream*, Tommy Turner in *The Male Animal*, and Cat in *The Blue Bird*. He rejoined (1951) the Royal Shakespeare Co., playing Exton in *Richard II*, Rumour and Silence in *Henry IV, Part 2*, The Chorus in *Henry V*, Sebastian in *The Tempest*, and the First Witch in *Macbeth*, and Ratty in *Toad of Toad Hall* (Royal Shakespeare Th., Dec. 1951).

With the Bristol Old Vic Co., Mr. Squire played the Duke in *Two Gentlemen of Verona*, Vezinet in *The Italian Straw Hat*, the Wicked Fairy in *The Love of Four Colonels*, Timothy in *A Penny for a Song*, and Banquo in *Macbeth* (1952); with the London Old Vic Co., appeared as Benvolio in *Romeo and Juliet* (Sept. 15, 1952), Vezinet in *An Italian Straw Hat* (Nov. 18, 1952), Gratiano in *The Merchant of Venice* (Jan. 6, 1953), Casca in *Julius Caesar* (Feb. 24, 1953), Cranmer in *Henry VIII* (May 6, 1953), Horatio in *Hamlet* (Sept. 14, 1953), Lafeu in *All's Well That Ends Well* (Sept. 15, 1953), the King of France in *King John* (Oct. 27, 1953), Sir Andrew Aguecheek in *Twelfth Night* (Jan. 6, 1954), and Menenius in *Coriolanus* (Feb. 23, 1954).

He again played Ratty in *Toad of Toad Hall* (Prince's, London, Dec. 23, 1954); succeeded (Sept. 1955) Paul Daneman in the role of Vladimir in *Waiting for Godot* (Arts Th. Club, Aug. 3, 1955); Captain Cat in *Under Milk Wood* (New, Sept. 1956); Federico Gomez in *The Elder Statesman* (Cambridge, Sept. 25, 1958); and the Narrator in *Cider with Rosie* (Hampstead Th. Club, London, Sept.

1963; transferred to Garrick Th., Oct. 1963).

With the Royal Shakespeare Th., Stratford on Avon, England, Mr. Squire played Mowbray in *Richard II* (Apr. 15, 1964), Glendower in *Henry IV, Part 1* (Apr. 16, 1964), and Charles VI in *Henry V* (June 3, 1964); in *The Wars of the Roses* was William de la Pole in *Henry VI* (July 29, 1964), the Duke of Buckingham in *Edward IV*, and Buckingham in *Richard III;* and he appeared as Antonio in *The Merchant of Venice* (Apr. 15, 1965), Don Adriano in *Love's Labour's Lost* (Apr. 7, 1965), and the Player King in *Hamlet* (Aug. 19, 1965).

Mr. Squire also played Teddy Lloyd in *The Prime of Miss Jean Brodie* (Wyndham's, London, May 5, 1966); Sebastian in *The Tempest* (Old Vic, London, Mar. 5, 1974); and Headmaster Sunstroke in *Spring Awakening* (Old Vic, May 28, 1974).

Films. He appeared in *The Man Who Never Was* (20th-Fox, 1956); *Alexander, the Great* (UA, 1956); *Pursuit of the Grat Spee* (Rank, 1957); *Where Eagles Dare* (MGM, 1969); and *Anne of the Thousand Days* (U, 1970).

Television. Mr. Squire first appeared on television in 1954 and since that time has been on many programs.

STADLEN, LEWIS J. Actor. b. Lewis Joseph Stadlen, Mar. 7, 1947, Brooklyn, N.Y., to Allen Swift and Vivienne (Schwartz) Stadlen. Father, actor; mother, teacher. Educ. Highland Preparatory School. Professional training at Stella Adler Theatre Studio. Member of AEA; SAG; AFTRA. Address: 15 W. 75th St., New York, NY 10023, tel. (212) 799-7159.

Pre-Theatre. Waiter.

Theatre. Mr. Stadlen made his stage debut as Mendel in *Fiddler on the Roof* (McVicker Th., Chicago, Ill., Feb. 25, 1967), touring with the company until Aug. 30, 1969. He made his N.Y.C. debut as Groucho Marx in *Minnie's Boys* (Imperial, Mar. 26, 1970), and first appeared off-Bway as Reese in *The Happiness Cage* (Public Th., Sept. 10, 1970). He was Isaac in *The Last Sweet Days of Isaac* (Happy Medium Th., Chicago, Ill., July 20, 1971); toured (starting Nov. 21, 1971) as Harry the Hoofer in *The Time of Your Life;* repeated his role as Groucho in *Minnie's Boys* (Pittsburgh Civic Light Opera, Pittsburgh, Pa., July 5, 1972); was Allen Felix in *Play It Again, Sam* (Bucks County Playhouse, New Hope, Pa., July 15, 1972); Ben Silverman in *The Sunshine Boys* (Broadhurst, N.Y.C., Dec. 20, 1972); appeared again as Groucho in *Minnie's Boys* (Playhouse-in-the-Park, Philadelphia, Pa., Aug. 25, 1973); and was Voltaire, Dr. Pangloss, the Governor, the Host, and the Sage in the revival of *Candide* (Brooklyn Acad. of Music, N.Y.C., Dec. 11, 1973–Jan. 20, 1974; re-opened Broadway Th., Mar. 10, 1974).

Films. Mr. Stadlen was Irwin Potowski in *Parades* (Cinerama, 1972); Julian Branch in *Savages* (Angelika Productions, 1972); Arnie Handel in *Portnoy's Complaint* (WB, 1972); and Jerry Berman in *Serpico* (Par., 1973).

Television. Mr. Stadlen played the role of the Stage Manager in *George M!*

Awards. For his performance as Groucho in *Minnie's Boys*, Mr. Stadlen received the Outer Circle, *Theater World*, and Drama Desk awards (all 1970), and he received a nomination for an Antoinette Perry (Tony) Award as best actor in a musical for his performance in *Candide* (1974).

STAHL, HERBERT M. Educator, director. b. Aug. 23, 1914, Freeman, S.D., to George P. and Katherine (Hofer) Stahl. Father, farmer. Grad. Huron (S.D.) H.S., 1932; Huron Coll., B.A. 1936; Colorado State Coll., M.A. 1938; Univ. of Washington, Ph.D. 1949. Married Dec. 29, 1944, to Helen Rae Carson; four sons. Served USNR, 1942–46; rank, Lt. Member of AETA (exec. vice-pres., 1963–64; pres., 1964–65, S. Calif. Dist.); ANTA; AAUP; Calif. Teachers Assn.; NCP; Theta Alpha Phi; Faculty Club of Univ. of S. California. Address: (home) 27520 Elmbridge Dr., Rancho Palos Verdes, CA 90274, tel. (213) 541-2247; (bus.) Univ. of Southern California, University Park, Los Angeles, CA 90007, tel. (213) RI 8-2311, ext. 6099.

Mr. Stahl has been acting chairman of the Department of Drama at the Univ. of Southern California at Los Angeles, where he has been a member of the faculty since 1950, and has directed approximately thirty major productions including *The Gentleman from Olmedo*, a new adaptation of Lope de Vega's play, *El Caballero de Olmedo*, by Everett W. Hesse and Mr. Stahl.

He was previously head of the Department of Drama at Huron Coll., S.D. (1936–37); taught in the Tulsa (Okla.) Public School System (1938–41); and was a member of the Dept. of English at the Univ. of Washington (1946–49).

Mr. Stahl currently directs research and supervises doctoral studies at the Univ. of Southern California at Los Angeles.

Published Works. In collaboration with Dr. George Knox, he has contributed *Dos Passos and "The Revolting Playwrights"* to *Essays and Studies on American Language and Literature* (1964). Dr. Stahl, in collaboration with Dr. Everett W. Hesse, contributed new translations of Lope de Vega's plays *Fuente Ovejuna (The Pride and the Fury)* and *El Caballero de Olmedo (The Gentleman from Olmedo)* to *Literary Discoveries;* and he has written articles for the *Educational Theatre News*. .

Recreation. Hunting, fishing, and golf.

STAIGER, LIBI. Actress, singer. b. Elizabeth Anne Staiger, Jan. 10, 1928, Harrisburg, Ill., to J. Roy and Mae (Ament) Staiger. Father, jewelry store proprietor; mother, social worker. Grad. Harrisburg Township H.S., 1945; attended Univ. of Illinois, 1945–48. Married June 19, 1953, to Jerome Eskow, director and drama chairman—High School of Performing Arts (N.Y.C.); one daughter. Relative in theatre: sister, Dorothy Staiger, singer. Member AEA; SAG; AGVA; AFTRA. Address: 890 West End Ave., New York, NY 10025, tel. (212) AC 2-8633.

Theatre. Miss Staiger first appeared with the Hilltop Lodge Stock Co., as Lady Bracknell in *The Importance of Being Earnest* (Pawling, N.Y., June 1951); and played Lois (Bianca) in a stock production of *Kiss Me, Kate* (Summer 1952). She made her N.Y.C. debut as assistant stage manager and chorus member of *Wonderful Town* (Winter Garden, Feb. 25, 1953); subsequently played Melba (for the Chicago, Ill., run) in the national company of *Pal Joey* (opened Shubert, Washington, D.C., Apr. 20, 1953).

She played Cora Belmont in *By the Beautiful Sea* (Majestic, N.Y.C., Apr. 8, 1954); Ruth in a stock production of *Wonderful Town* (Cape Cod Melody Top, Hyannis, Mass.; South Shore Music Circus, Cohasset, Mass., 1955); at the Musicarnival (Cleveland, Ohio, 1956), appeared as Ruth in *Plain and Fancy* and Sally in *Call Me Madam;* at the Melody Fair (Buffalo, N.Y.), played Lalume in *Kismet* (1956), Babe in *Pajama Game* (1957), and Pistache in *Can-Can* (1957); at the Musicarnival (Cleveland, Ohio), portrayed Ninotchka in *Silk Stockings* (1957), and Annie in *Annie Get Your Gun* (1958); played the lead (1958) in an industrial show for Milliken Fabrics, and for Buick cars (Samlen Productions).

In N.Y.C., she played Chloe in *Destry Rides Again* (Imperial, Apr. 23, 1959); Cleo in *The Most Happy Fella* (NY City Ctr., Feb. 10, 1959), repeating the role in the London production (Coliseum, Apr. 21, 1960); at summer theatres appeared as Frenchy in *Destry Rides Again* (1961), and Babe in *The Pajama Game* (1962); and appeared in the title role in *Sophie* (Winter Garden, N.Y.C., Apr. 15, 1963).

Films. Miss Staiger appeared as a Night Club Singer in *Undersea Girl* (Allied, 1957).

Television. She was a guest on the Steve Allen Show (NBC, 1962); and has done approximately 300 television commercials.

Night Clubs. Miss Staiger co-starred at Mister Kelly's (Chicago, Ill., 1962).

Recreation. Needlepoint, cooking, bridge, interior decorating, playing the cello.

STANDER, LIONEL. Actor, producer. b. Lionel Jay Stander, Jan. 11, 1908, New York City, to Louis E. and Bella Stander. Father, accountant. Grad. Mt. Vernon (N.Y.) H.S., 1926; attended Univ. of North Carolina, 1927–28. Married 1928 to Lucy Dietz, artist (marr. dis. 1936); one daughter; married 1938 to Alice Twitchell, artist (marr. dis. 1942); married Oct. 5, 1945, to Vahanne Havens Monteagle (marr. dis. Sept. 10, 1950); two daughters; married Sept. 17, 1953, to Diana Radbec, singer (marr. dis. Nov. 11, 1963); one daughter; married Jan. 21, 1964, to Maria Penn, artist (marr. dis.); married 1971 to Stephanie Van Hennik; one daughter. Served USAAF, 1942–45. Member of AEA; SAG; AFTRA; AGVA.

Pre-Theatre. Newspaper reporter.

Theatre. Mr. Stander made his N.Y.C. debut with the Provincetown Players as a Cop, and the First Fairy in *him* (Provincetown Playhouse, Apr. 18, 1928); played Yank in the Company's production of *S. S. Glencairn* (Jan. 9, 1929); Chock in *Little Ol' Boy* (Playhouse, Apr. 24, 1933); Stephen in *The Bride of Torozko* (Henry Miller's Th., Sept. 13, 1934); and Feodor Dobinsky in *The Drums Begin* (Shubert, Nov. 24, 1933). With Bern Bernard, he produced *Brooklyn, U.S.A.* (Forrest, Dec. 2, 1941).

He played Lowell Ludlow in *Pal Joey* (Broadhurst, Jan. 2, 1952; and on tour opened Shubert, Washington, D.C., Apr. 20, 1953); Sgt. Murdock in *The Conquering Hero* (ANTA, Jan. 16, 1961); the Commissioner of Police in *The Policemen* (Phoenix, Nov. 21, 1961), which appeared on a double-bill with *Androcles and the Lion;* succeeded Peter Bull as Tetzel in *Luther* (St. James, Sept. 25, 1963); and was J. Pierpont Mauler in *Saint Joan of the Stockyards* (Queens, London, June 11, 1964).

Films. Mr. Stander appeared in *Page Miss Glory* (WB, 1935); *The Gay Deception* (Col., 1935); *The Scoundrel* (Par., 1935); *Mr. Deeds Goes to Town* (Col., 1936); *The Music Goes 'Round* (Col., 1936); *Meet Nero Wolfe* (Col., 1936); *Guadalcanal Diary* (20th-Fox, 1943); *The Big Show-Off* (Rep., 1945); *In Old Sacramento* (Rep., 1946); *The Kid from Brooklyn* (RKO, 1946); *Gentleman Joe Palooka* (Mono., 1946); *Specter of the Rose* (Rep., 1946); *Mad Wednesday* (UA, 1947); *Call Northside 777* (20th-Fox, 1948); *Unfaithfully Yours* (20th-Fox, 1948); *Trouble Makers* (Mono., 1948); *Two Gals and a Guy* (UA, 1951); *St. Benny the Dip* (UA, 1951); *A Star Is Born* (WB, 1954); *Pal Joey* (Col., 1957); *The Loved One* (MGM, 1965); *Cul de Sac* (Sigma III, 1966); *Beyond the Law* (Grove, 1967); *A Dandy in Aspic* (Col., 1968); *The Gang That Couldn't Shoot Straight* (MGM, 1971); *Pulp* (UA, 1972); and *The Black Bird* (Col., 1975).

Beginning in 1966, Mr. Stander also made many films in Italy, notably *Per Grazia Ricevuta* (1970).

Television and Radio. Mr. Stander performed on the Fred Allen Show, the Eddie Cantor Show, the Rudy Vallee Show, and the Kraft Music Hall. On Italian television, he was in The Adventures of Pinocchio (RAI-TV).

STANLEY, KIM. Actress. b. Patricia Kimberly Reid, Feb. 11, 1925, Tularosa, N. Mex., to J. T. and Ann (Miller) Reid. Father, professor of philosophy; mother, painter, decorator. Attended Univ. of New Mexico; grad. Univ. of Texas, B.A. (Psychology) 1945. Studied acting at Pasadena Playhouse, Calif., 1945–46; Actors' Studio, N.Y.C. Married 1948 to Bruce Franklin Hall, actor (marr. dis.); married to Curt Conway, director (marr. dis. 1956); one son, one daughter; married Aug. 1958 to Alfred Ryder, actor, director; one daughter. Member of AEA; SAG; AFTRA.

Pre-Theatre. Model, waitress.

Theatre. Miss Stanley made her first stage appearance in *Thunder Rock* (Univ. of New Mexico, 1942); in stock, appeared as the Manicurist in *Boy Meets Girl* (Louisville, Ky., Winter 1946); Corliss Archer in *Kiss and Tell*, and Prudence in *The Pursuit of Happiness* (Pompton Lakes, N.J., Summer 1947).

She appeared as Iris in *The Dog Beneath the Skin* (Carnegie Recital Hall, N.Y.C., Dec. 25, 1948); performed in *him* (Provincetown Playhouse, 1949);

played Denise in *Yes Is for a Very Young Man* (Cherry Lane Th., 1949); and played the title role in the ELT production of *St. Joan* (Nov. 5, 1949).

She succeeded Julie Harris (Dec. 1949) as Felisa in *Monserrat* (Fulton, Oct. 29, 1949); appeared as Adela in *The House of Bernarda Alba* (ANTA, Jan. 7, 1951); Anna Revers in *The Chase* (Playhouse, Apr. 15, 1952); Millie Owens in *Picnic* (Music Box, Feb. 19, 1953); Georgette Thomas in *The Traveling Lady* (Playhouse, Oct. 27, 1954); Cherie in *Bus Stop* (Music Box, Mar. 2, 1955); and Virginia in *A Clearing in the Woods* (Belasco, Jan. 10, 1957).

Miss Stanley made her London debut as Maggie in *Cat on a Hot Tin Roof* (Comedy, Jan. 30, 1958); played Sara Melody in *A Touch of the Poet* (Helen Hayes Th., N.Y.C., Oct. 2, 1958); Lea de Lonval in *Cheri* (Morosco, Oct. 12, 1959); Elizabeth von Ritter in *A Far Country* (Music Box, Apr. 4, 1961); Sue Barker in *Natural Affection* (Booth, Jan. 31, 1963) and Masha in *The Three Sisters* (Morosco, June 22, 1964).

Films. She made her debut in *The Goddess* (Col., 1958); and subsequently appeared in *Seance on a Wet Afternoon* (Artixo, 1964).

Television. She appeared on You Are There (CBS); *Joey* (Goodyear Playhouse, NBC, Mar. 25, 1956); *The Bridge* (ABC, Jan. 11, 1955); *Flight* (NBC, Feb. 28, 1956); repeated the role of Georgette Thomas in *The Traveling Lady* (Studio One, CBS, Apr. 22, 1957); appeared in *Clash by Night* (Playhouse 90, CBS, June 13, 1957); *That's Where the Town's Going* (CBS, Apr. 17, 1962); *Flesh and Blood* (NBC, Jan. 26, 1968); *U.M.C.* (CBS, Apr. 17, 1969); and *I Can't Imagine Tomorrow* (NET Playhouse, Jan. 9, 1971); and was on Ben Casey (ABC, 1963); Eleventh Hour (NBC, 1964); Name of the Game (NBC, 1971); Medical Center (CBS, 1971); and Night Gallery (NBC, 1972).

Other Activities. Miss Stanley has taught retarded children and been a teacher of acting at the College of Santa Fe, N.M. (1975–).

Awards. For her performance as Cherie in *Bus Stop*, Miss Stanley received the Donaldson Award (1955), and won the *Variety* NY Drama Critics' Poll (1955). She was nominated for an Academy (Oscar) Award (1959) for her performance in *The Goddess*; received the ANTA Award (1959) for outstanding contribution to the art of the living theatre; and the NATAS (Emmy) Award (1963) for her performance in *A Cardinal Act of Mercy*..

STANLEY, PAT. Actress, singer, dancer. b. Patricia Stanley, Apr. 12, 1931, Cincinnati, Ohio, to Richard Mulford and Catherine (Leman) Stanley. Father, bus distributor. Grad. Principia Upper Sch., St. Louis, Mo., 1949; William Woods Coll. A.A. 1951. Married Feb. 19, 1962, to William Hanley, playwright. Relative in theatre: sister-in-law, Ellen Hanley, actress, singer. Member of AEA; AFTRA; SAG.

Theatre. Miss Stanley made her N.Y.C. debut as a dancer in the chorus of *Of Thee I Sing* (Ziegfeld Th., May 5, 1952); was principal dancer and played Sally in *Touch of Venus* (Summer 1952); was principal dancer and played Sally in the natl. tour of *A Tree Grows in Brooklyn* (opened Klein Memorial Aud., Bridgeport, Conn., Oct. 10, 1952; closed Shubert, Chicago, Ill., Nov. 29, 1952); at the Palm Beach Playhouse, Fla., appeared as Jeannie in *Brigadoon*, and in the revue *Lend an Ear* (Summer 1953); played Siska in *Carnival in Flanders* (New Century, N.Y.C., Sept. 8, 1953); toured as Gladys in the national company of *Pajama Game* (opened Shubert, New Haven, Conn., Jan. 29, 1955), and played the same role in N.Y.C. (NY City Ctr., May 15, 1957).

Miss Stanley appeared as Carrie Pipperidge in *Carousel* (NY City Ctr., Sept. 11, 1957); Lillian Barley in *Blue Denim* (Playhouse, Feb. 27, 1958); Lois Lee in *Goldilocks* (Lunt-Fontanne Th., Oct. 11, 1958); Gladys in *Pajama Game* (State Fair Music Hall, Dallas Summer Musicals, Tex., Summer 1959); Dora in *Fiorello!* (Broadhurst, N.Y.C., Nov. 23, 1959); Eileen Taylor in *Sunday in New York* (Cort, Nov. 29, 1961); and Carrie Pipperidge in *Carousel* for the Los Angeles Civic Light Opera Assn. (opened Curran, San Francisco, Calif., Apr. 22, 1963).

Films. Miss Stanley made her screen debut in *Ladies Man* (Par., 1961).

Night Clubs. Miss Stanley appeared in *Graham Crackers* at the Upstairs at the Downstairs, N.Y.C. (Feb. 1963).

Awards. For her performance as Lois Lee in *Goldilocks*, Miss Stanley received the Antoinette Perry (Tony) Award as best supporting actress in a musical (1959).

Recreation. Painting.

STAPLETON, JEAN. Actress. b. Jeanne Murray, Jan. 19, 1923, New York City, to Joseph E. and Marie (Stapleton) Murray. Father, billboard advertising salesman; mother, singer. Grad. Wadleigh H.S., N.Y.C., 1939; attended Hunter Coll., N.Y.C. Studied acting with Carli Laklan, Amer. Apprentice Th., N.Y.C.; Jane Rose and William Hansen, Amer. Actors' Co.; Joseph Anthony and Peter Frye, Amer. Th. Wing, 1947–48; Harold Clurman, N.Y.C. Married Oct. 26, 1957, to William H. Putch, producer-/owner of the Totem Pole Playhouse, Fayetteville, Pa., director, writer; one son; one daughter. Relatives in theatre; uncle, Joseph E. Deming, vaudevillian; brother, Jack Stapleton, actor; cousin, Betty Jane Watson, singer, actress. Member of AEA (mbr. of council, 1958–63); SAG; AFTRA.

Theatre. Miss Stapleton first worked in the theatre as secretary for the Greenwood Playhouse, Peaks Island, Me. (Summer 1941); subsequently acted at the Peterborough (N.H.) Playhouse (Summer 1946); and in Whitefield, N.H., at the Chase Barn Playhouse (Summers 1947–48).

She made her N.Y.C. debut as Mrs. Watty in the ELT production of *The Corn is Green* (Feb. 4, 1948); toured as Myrtle Mae in *Harvey* (1948–49), and repeated the role (Coonamessett, Mass.; Falmouth Playhouse, Mass.; Atlantic City, N.J.; No. Shore Music Th., Mass.; Summer 1949), and again on tour (1949–50). She toured as Mrs. Coffman and understudied Shirley Booth in *Come Back, Little Sheba* (1950–51); and played this role among others in stock (Pocono Playhouse, Mountainhome, Pa., Summers 1951–53); appeared as Mother in *American Gothic* (Circle in the Square, N.Y.C., Nov. 1953).

She played Inez in *In the Summerhouse* (Playhouse, Dec. 29, 1953); subsequently appeared as Sister in *Damn Yankees* (46 St. Th., May 5, 1955); and Sue in *Bells Are Ringing* (Shubert, Nov. 29, 1956). In stock she appeared in *A Soft Touch* (Coconut Grove Playhouse, Miami, Fla., Feb. 1957); played Woody in *Goodbye, My Fancy*, Miss Cooper in *Separate Tables*, Mother in *Charm*, Grace in *Bus Stop*, and Mme. St.-Pe in *The Waltz of the Toreadors* (Totem Pole Playhouse, Fayetteville, Pa., Summer 1958); played Swart Petry in the pre-Bway tryout of *A Swim in the Sea* (opened Walnut St. Th., Philadelphia, Pa., Sept. 15, 1958; closed there Sept. 27, 1958); played Maisie Madigan in *Juno* (Winter Garden, N.Y.C., Mar. 9, 1959); at the Totem Pole Playhouse (Fayetteville, Pa.), played Sally Adams in *Call Me Madam* (Summer 1959); and Mrs. Laura Partridge in *The Solid Gold Cadillac* (Summer 1960). She played Mrs. Ochs in *Rhinoceros* (Longacre, N.Y.C., Jan. 9, 1961), and on tour (opened Alcazar, San Francisco, Calif., Oct. 3, 1961; closed Huntington Hartford, Los Angeles, Calif., Nov. 11, 1961).

Miss Stapleton returned to the Totem Pole Playhouse (Fayetteville, Pa.), to play Mrs. Keller in *The Miracle Worker*, Emma in *Apple in the Attic*, various roles in *A Thurber Carnival*, Opal in *Everybody Loves Opal*, and Aunt Eller in *Oklahoma!* (Summer 1962); appeared as Mrs. Baker in *Come Blow Your Horn*, Mrs. Spofford in *Gentlemen Prefer Blondes*, and Nannie in *All for Mary* (Summer 1963). She played Mrs. Strakosh in *Funny Girl* (Winter Garden, N.Y.C., Mar. 24, 1964); spent another season at the Totem Pole Playhouse, playing Brewster in *A Rainy Day in Newark*, Rosemary in *Picnic*, Annabelle in *George Washington Slept Here*, Mrs. Walworth in *Speaking of Murder*, Mrs. Pearce in *My Fair Lady*, Mrs. Yoder in *Papa Is All*, and the Mother Abbess in *The Sound of Music* (Summer 1964).

She played Miss Skillon in *See How They Run*, Veta Louise Simmons in *Harvey*, Abby Brewster in *Arsenic and Old Lace*, Grace Kimbrough in *Never Too Late*, the Mother in *Enter Laughing*, Anne Michaelson in *Take Her, She's Mine*, and Anna Leonowens in *The King and I* (Totem Pole Playhouse, Summer 1965); Miss Holroyd in *Bell, Book and Candle*, Mrs. Deazy in *Jenny Kissed Me*, Aunt Kate Barnaby in *How Far Is the Barn?* Nettie Fowler in *Carousel*, and Dorothy in *Any Wednesday* (Totem Pole Playhouse, Summer 1966). Her subsequent Totem Pole Playhouse appearances include *Southwest Corner* and *Hello, Dolly!* (Summer 1971); *Come Back, Little Sheba, Everybody Loves Opal*, and *Butterflies Are Free* (Summer, 1972); *The Time of the Cuckoo* (Summer 1973; repeated at the Ahmanson Th., Los Angeles, Apr. 2, 1974); *Lullaby* and *The Vinegar Tree* (Summer 1974); and *The Secret Affairs of Mildred Wild* (Summer 1975).

Films. Miss Stapleton made her debut as Sister in *Damn Yankees* (WB, 1958); played Sue in *Bells Are Ringing* (MGM, 1960); and appeared in *Something Wild* (UA, 1961); *Up the Down Staircase* (WB, 1967); *Cold Turkey* (UA, 1971); and *Klute* (WB, 1971).

Television. Miss Stapleton has played the role of Edith Bunker on the All in the Family series (CBS, premiere Jan. 12, 1971–to date. She previously appeared on Camera Three (CBS); Danger (CBS); Studio One (CBS); Philco Television Playhouse (NBC); Omnibus (CBS); Woman with a Past (CBS); Today Is Ours (NBC); Naked City (ABC); Armstrong Circle Th. (NBC); The Defenders (CBS); The Nurses (CBS); Eleventh Hour (NBC); Dr. Kildare (NBC); Dennis the Menace (CBS); the Jackie Gleason Show (CBS); Car 54, Where Are You? (NBC); True Story (NBC); and The Patty Duke Show (ABC).

Awards. Miss Stapleton received two NATAS (Emmy) Awards for her role on All in the Family, as "best actress in a comedy series" (1971, 1972).

STAPLETON, MAUREEN. Actress. b. Lois Maureen Stapleton, June 21, 1925, Troy, N.Y., to John P. and Irene (Walsh) Stapleton. Grad. Catholic Central (Troy) H.S., 1942. Studied acting at the H B (Herbert Berghof) Studio, N.Y.C., two years. Married July 1949 to Max Allentuck, business mgr. (marr. dis. Feb. 1959); one son, one daughter; married July 1963 to David Rayfiel, playwright (marr. dis.). Member of AEA; SAG; AFTRA.

Theatre. Miss Stapleton made her N.Y.C. debut as Sara Tansey in *Playboy of the Western World* (Booth, Oct. 26, 1946); subsequently toured as Wilson in *Barretts of Wimpole Street* (1947–48); appeared as Iris in *Antony and Cleopatra* (Martin Beck Th., N.Y.C. Nov. 26, 1947); Miss Hatch in *Detective Story* (Hudson, Mar. 23, 1949); Emilie in *The Bird Cage* (Coronet, Feb. 22, 1950); and Serafina in *The Rose Tattoo* (Martin Beck Th., Feb. 3, 1951), and on tour (opened His Majesty's, Montreal, Canada, Oct. 29, 1951; closed Curran, San Francisco, Calif., Apr. 5, 1952).

She played Bella in *The Emperor's Clothes* (Ethel Barrymore Th., N.Y.C., Feb. 9, 1953); succeeded Beatrice Straight in the role of Elizabeth Proctor in *The Crucible* (Martin Beck Th., Jan. 22, 1953); played Lady Anne in *Richard III* (NY City Ctr., Dec. 9, 1953); Masha in *The Seagull* (Phoenix, May 11, 1954); Flora Meighan in *27 Wagons Full of Cotton*, presented on a double bill with *All in One* (Playhouse, Apr. 19, 1955); Lady Torrance in *Orpheus Descending* (Martin Beck Th., Mar. 21, 1957); Aunt Ida in *Cold Wind and the Warm* (Morosco, Dec. 8, 1958); and Carrie Berniers in *Toys in the Attic* (Hudson, Feb. 25, 1960).

She was Amanda Wingfield in a revival of *The Glass Menagerie* (Brooks Atkinson Th., May 4, 1965); repeated her performance as Serafina in a revival of *The Rose Tattoo* (NY City Ctr., Oct. 20, 1966); played the roles of Karen Nash, Muriel Tate, and Norma Hubley in *Plaza Suite* (Plymouth, Feb. 14, 1968); was Beatrice Chambers in *Norman, Is That You?* (Lyceum, Feb. 19, 1970); Evy Meara in *The Gingerbread Lady* (Plymouth, Dec. 13, 1970);

Georgie Elgin in a revival of *The Country Girl* (Eisenhower Th., John F. Kennedy Ctr., Washington, D.C., Nov. 16, 1971; Billy Rose Th., N.Y.C., Mar. 15, 1972); Mildred Wild in *The Secret Affairs of Mildred Wild* (Ambassador, Nov. 14, 1972); Juno in *Juno and the Paycock* (Mark Taper Forum, Los Angeles, Calif., Nov. 7, 1974); and again played Amanda Wingfield in a revival of *The Glass Menagerie* (Circle in the Square, Dec. 18, 1975).

Films. Miss Stapleton appeared in *Lonelyhearts* (UA, 1958); *The Fugitive Kind* (UA, 1960); *A View from the Bridge* (Cont., 1962); *Bye Bye Birdie* (Col., 1962); *Trilogy* (Allied Artists, 1969); *Airport* (U, 1970); and *Plaza Suite* (Par., 1971).

Television. Miss Stapleton appeared on many television programs, including Goodyear Playhouse (NBC, 1953); Philco Playhouse (NBC, 1954, 1955); Armstrong Circle Th. (NBC, 1955, 1956); *All the King's Men* (Kraft Th., NBC, May 1958); *For Whom the Bell Tolls* (Playhouse 90, CBS, Mar. 1959); Naked City (ABC, 1961, 1962); East Side/West Side (CBS, 1964); *Save Me a Place at Forest Lawn* (NY Television Th., NET, Mar. 1966); *Among the Paths to Eden* (Xerox Special Event, ABC, Dec. 1967); *Mirror, Mirror Off the Wall* (On Stage, NBC, Nov. 1969); *Tell Me Where It Hurts* (General Electric Th., CBS, Mar. 1974); and *Queen of the Stardust Ballroom* (CBS, 1975).

Awards. For her performance as Serafina in *The Rose Tattoo*, she received the Antoinette Perry (Tony) Award (1951) and the Peabody Award (1951); for her performance in *Plaza Suite*, she received a Tony nomination (1968); for her performance in *The Gingerbread Lady*, she received Tony and Drama Desk awards and was a winner in the *Variety* NY Drama Critics Poll (all 1971); she received a NATAS (Emmy) Award (1968) for her performance in *Among the Paths to Eden*; and in 1969 she received a National Institute of Arts and Letters Award.

Recreation. Poker.

STARBUCK, JAMES. Choreographer, actor, director, dancer. b. Albuquerque, N.M. Grad. Fremont H.S., Oakland, Calif.; attended Coll. of the Pacific. Studied acting with Robert Warwick, Calif., one year; make-up with Norman Fields. Performed in USO productions, WW II. Member of AGMA; AFTRA; ATAS; DGA.

Theatre. Mr. Starbuck made his debut in California, appearing in juvenile roles with the Merrit Players and the William Fariss Players (1932); and danced in the Ballet Moderne production of *Salome* (Greek Th., Berkeley, Calif., 1934).

During 1935–38, he danced with the San Francisco Opera Ballet; during 1939–44, he toured with the Ballet Russe de Monte Carlo, dancing such roles as Algernon Swinburne in *Ghost Town*, the Peruvian in *Gaieté Parisienne*, the Governor in *The Three-Cornered Hat*, the American Sailor in *The Red Poppy*, the Champion Roper in *Rodeo*, the Tartar Chief in *Ancient Russia*, Pierrot in *Carnival*, Eustace Telly in *The New Yorker*, the Shah's Brother in *Scheherazade*, and also appeared in *Chopin Concerto*, *The Snow Maiden*, *St. Francis*, *Seventh Symphony*, *Rouge et Noir*, and *The Nutcracker*.

He made his first Bway appearance as the premiere danseur in *The Merry Widow* (Majestic, Aug. 4, 1943); danced in *Song of Norway* (Imperial, Aug. 21, 1944); appeared as the Champion Roper in *Rodeo* (NY City Ctr., Sept. 1944); and toured in *Early to Bed* (June–Aug. 1944).

Mr. Starbuck played a juvenile in *The O'Brien Girl* (St. Louis Municipal Opera, Mo., June 1945); choreographed the pre-Bway tour of *Fanny* (opened Shubert, Boston, Mass., Sept. 20, 1945); during Summers 1945, 1946 and 1948, he danced in and choreographed productions at the Camp Tamiment (Pa.) Th.; played the Dancing Ram in *The Winter's Tale* (Cort, N.Y.C., Jan. 15, 1946); and choreographed the ELT production of *Tonight at 8:30* (USO Workshop Th., N.Y.C., Feb. 1946).

He appeared in stock productions of *The Three Musketeers* and *The Great Waltz* (Pitt Stadium, Pittsburgh, Pa., July 1947); danced in *Music in My Heart* (Adelphi, N.Y.C., Oct. 2, 1947); played Walt in *Sleepy Hollow* (St. James, June 3, 1948); danced in Orchestral Concerts for Young People (Hunter Coll. Playhouse, N.Y.C.; Mosque Th., Newark, N.J., Nov. 1948); and directed and appeared in a pageant for the Natl. Conference of Christians and Jews (Waldorf Astoria Hotel, N.Y.C., Nov. 1948).

He danced in *Song of Norway* (Masonic Temple Aud., Detroit, Mich., Dec. 1948; Pittsburgh, Pa., June 1949); directed the musical numbers for *Peep Show* (Winter Garden, N.Y.C., June 28, 1950); directed and choreographed the musical production numbers for the pre-Bway tryout of *Strip for Action* (opened Shubert, New Haven, Conn., Mar. 17, 1956); choreographed Alexandra Danilova's Concert Ballet Co. production of *Manhattan Moods* (S. Afr., Summer 1956); directed the musical numbers for *Oh, Captain!* (Alvin, N.Y.C., Feb. 4, 1958); directed and appeared in the Bell Telephone industrial show, *What's Popping in Shopping* (Statler Hotel, Jan. 14, 1959); directed and choreographed *The Buick Show* (Flint, Mich., Aug. 1959), also its tour (Aug.–Nov. 1959); served as associate director for *A Thurber Carnival* (ANTA, N.Y.C., Feb. 26, 1960); and for the Little Orchestra Society "Orchestral Concerts for Young People," he staged the ballet, *The Comedians* (Carnegie Hall, Dec. 8, 1962).

Mr. Starbuck staged and directed the entire production of *Sing Along with Mitch* personal appearance tour (opened Steel Pier, Atlantic City, N.J., July 2, 1964; closed Latin Casino, Camden, N.J., Oct. 11, 1964).

Films. Mr. Starbuck danced in two short films: *Gaieté Parisienne* and *Capriccio Espagnol* (WB, 1942); and was choreographer for *The Court Jester* (Par., 1956).

Television. He danced in and choreographed Variety Showcase (CBS, 1946); a closed circuit experimental show (NBC, 1947); Admiral Broadway Revue (NBC, Jan.–June 1949); Inside USA with Chevrolet (CBS, Nov. 1949–Jan. 1950); choreographed and directed musical numbers for Your Show of Shows (NBC, 1950–54); a Bob Hope Special (NBC, 1950); directed musical numbers for Shower of Stars (CBS, 1955); and danced in and choreographed Frankie Laine Time (CBS, July–Sept. 1955).

He directed dances and musical numbers for the specials, *Heidi* (NBC, Oct. 1, 1955); *The Great Waltz* (NBC, Nov. 5, 1955), *Dearest Enemy* (NBC, Nov. 26, 1955), Maurice Chevalier Show (NBC, 1955), *Panorama* (NBC, Feb. 26, 1956), *Heaven Will Protect the Working Girl* (NBC, Mar. 20, 1956), and *Marco Polo* (NBC, Apr. 14, 1956); choreographed *The Big Record* (CBS, 1957–58); and directed musical numbers and appeared on the Arthur Murray Party (NBC, 1958–60).

He directed and choreographed numbers for the Oldsmobile Music Th., (CBS, 1959); Bell Telephone Hour (NBC, 1959–60); staged and appeared on *A Toast to Bob Hope* (NBC, 1960); staged and choreographed musical numbers for *Hollywood Sings* (Sunday Showcase, NBC, 1960); the Jack Paar Special (NBC, 1960); Sing Along with Mitch (NBC, 1960–64), on which he performed, and also served as co-director (1963–64); and was associate producer and director of Great Music from Chicago (Nov. 1962).

Night Clubs. Mr. Starbuck directed the acts for Lisa Kirk at the Persian Room (Plaza Hotel, N.Y.C., 1954); Dorothy Dandridge at the Waldorf Astoria Hotel (N.Y.C., 1955); in 1955, Maurice Chevalier at the Dunes (Las Vegas, Nev.) and Waldorf Astoria Hotel (N.Y.C.); and in 1958, Marguerite Piazza at The Sands (Las Vegas, Nev.) and the Persian Room (Plaza Hotel, N.Y.C.).

Awards. Mr. Starbuck received USO citations during WW II; a plaque from the Dance Educators of America for "distinctive contribution to the dance" (1950); and a citation from *Variety* Magazine for his choreography for Your Show of Shows (1950).

Recreation. Languages, music.

STAUB, AUGUST W. Director, actor, playwright, theatre historian, filmmaker. b. August William Staub, Oct. 9, 1931, New Orleans, La., to August Harry and Laurel (Elfer) Staub. Father, accountant. Educ. Jesuit H.S., New Orleans; grad. Louisiana State Univ., B.A. 1952; M.A. 1956; Ph.D. 1960. Married Nov. 22, 1952, to Patricia Kay Gebhardt; one daughter. Served in US Army; Korea, 1952–54; highest rank, 1st Lt. Member of ATA (bd. of dir., 1973–75); SWTC (vice-pres., 1972; pres. 1973); SCA. Address: (home) 5551 Pratt Dr., New Orleans, LA 70122, tel. (504) 283-5218; (bus.) Dept. of Drama and Communications, Univ. of New Orleans, Lake Front, New Orleans, LA 70122.

Mr. Staub became chairman of the Dept. of Drama and Communications, Louisiana State Univ. (LSU), New Orleans, in 1966. He joined the staff of the university in 1955 as an instructor and technical director of University Theatre; was then (1956–58) an instructor and scene designer, Eastern Michigan Univ.; assistant professor and associate director, University Th., University of Florida (1960–64); and returned to LSU, New Orleans, as associate professor (1964–66).

Theatre. At Louisiana State Univ. Th., Mr. Staub played Luigi in *Darkness at Noon* and appeared in productions of *The Torchbearers* (1952); as He in *He Who Gets Slapped* and Judge Hathorne in *The Crucible* (both 1954); Anton Schill in *The Visit* and Stanley Kowalski in *A Streetcar Named Desire* (both 1956); and as Ajax in *One for Love* (1957). As associate director, Dunes Summer Th., Michigan City, Ind. (Summers 1956–59), he directed *The Little Hut* (June 1956), *Anastasia* (July 1956), *The Male Animal* (Aug. 1956), *Champagne Complex* (June 1957), *The Tunnel of Love* (July 1957), *King of Hearts* (Aug. 1957), *Gigi* (June 1958), and played General St. Pé in *The Waltz of the Toreadors* (July 1958).

At Eastern Michigan Univ., he directed *The Glass Menagerie* (Apr. 1957) and *Androcles and the Lion* (Apr. 1958); and at the Univ. of Florida, *Pantagleize* (Apr. 1961), *The Rainmaker* (Aug. 1961), *Oedipus* (Mar. 1962), *The Madwoman of Chaillot* (Jan. 1963), *The Threepenny Opera* (Mar. 1964), and *Summer and Smoke* (June 1964). Mr. Staub has directed over thirty plays for the Univ. of New Orleans (1964–to date); also directed *Bull*, a theatrical revue, which he also created (Fatted Calf, New Orleans, 1969); and did his own adaptation of *Lysistrata* (Agnes Scott Th., Fort Worth, Tex.).

Films. Mr. Staub wrote and directed his version of *Agamemnon*.

Published Works. Mr. Staub wrote *A Small Bare Space* (1970); *Introduction to Theatrical Arts* (1971); *Creating Theatre: The Art of Theatrical Directing* (1973); *Media and the Small Budget* (1973); and over twenty periodical articles.

Awards. Mr. Staub was awarded a Louisiana State Univ. Distinguished Faculty Fellowship (1972) and an NEA Filmmaker-in-the-Schools Grant (1973).

Recreation. Bicycling, boating.

STAVIS, BARRIE. Playwright. b. June 16, 1906, New York City, to Abraham and Fanny (Garfinkel) Stavis. Father, wholesale merchant. Grad. New Utrecht H.S., Brooklyn, N.Y., 1924; Columbia Univ. 1924–27. Married May 17, 1950, to Bernice Coe; one son, one daughter. Served US Army, Signal Corps, 1942–45; rank T/Sgt. Member of Dramatists Guild; Authors Guild; ASCAP; P.E.N.; USITT (founding mbr.; bd. of dir., 1961–64; 1969–71); ATA; ANTA. Address: 70 E. 96th St., New York, NY 10028, tel. (212) 831-5355.

Theatre. Mr. Stavis wrote *The Sun and I*, which was first produced by the Columbia Univ. drama department (1933); and was revised for Bway presentation (Adelphi Th., Feb. 26, 1937) under the sponsorship of the Federal Th. (WPA) project.

Mr. Stavis was one of a group of actors, directors, technicians, scenic artists, and playwrights, who formed a producing group called New Stages; their first production was Mr. Stavis' *Lamp at Midnight* (New Stages Th., Dec. 21, 1947); which has also been performed at the Bristol Old Vic with Peter O'Toole (Nov. 11, 1956). New Stages subsequently revived *The Sun and I*(New Stages, Mar. 20, 1949). Mr. Stavis also wrote *The Man Who Never Died*(Jan Hus House, Nov. 21, 1958); *Coat of Many Colors* (Pardoe Th., Provo, Utah, Apr. 20, 1966); and *Harpers Ferry*(world premiere: Tyrone Guthrie Th., Minneapolis, Minn., June 3, 1967), which was the first new play produced at the Guthrie.

The Man Who Never Died was made into an opera with music by Alan Bush (premiere, Staatsoper, Berlin, Germany, Sept. 29, 1970); *Lamp at Midnight* was presented in a one-hour abridgment (Chicago Museum of Science and Industry, Nov. 6, 1972) and, under the title *Galileo Galilei*, as an oratorio with music by Lee Hoiby (Von Braun Civic Ctr., Huntsville, Ala., Mar. 15, 1975).

Television. Mr. Stavis's *Lamp at Midnight* was televised (Hallmark Hall of Fame, NBC, Apr. 27, 1966).

Other Activities. Mr. Stavis has lectured and/or conducted seminars in playwriting at Columbia Univ., Southern Illinois Univ., Univ. of Minnesota, Syracuse Univ., Univ. of South Florida, Univ. of Utah, Univ. of Delaware, Univ. of Kansas, Pennsylvania State Univ., Brigham Young Univ., Millikin Univ., Evansville Univ., Hamlin Univ., The Menninger Foundation, and other institutions.

Published Works. In addition to his plays, Mr. Stavis wrote a novella, *The Chain of Command* (1945); a novel, *Home, Sweet Home!* (1949); and a history, *John Brown: The Sword and the Word*(1970). He edited, in collaboration with Frank Harmon, *The Songs of Joe Hill*(1955); and he has contributed articles to *The Saturday Evening Post, Life, Collier's, Ladies Home Journal, Folk Music, Tomorrow,* and *This Week* magazines.

Discography. Mr. Stavis's *Joe Hill: Poet/Organizer,* Parts 1 and 2, was released by Folk Music (1964).

Awards. He received a Yaddo Residence Fellowship (1939) and two awards from the National Th. Conference (1948, 1949).

His play *Banners of Steel* was one of two plays selected in the first annual American Playwrights Th. competition (Apr. 1964). He was a Visiting Fellow at the Institute for the Arts and Humanistic Studies, Pennsylvania State University (1971).

Recreation. Sailing, swimming, fishing.

STEIN, JOSEPH. Playwright, librettist. b. May 30, 1912, New York City, to Charles and Emma (Rosenblum) Stein. Grad. James Monroe H.S., Bronx, N.Y., 1928; City Coll. of New York, B.S.S. 1934; attended Sch. of Social Research, Columbia Univ., 1935–37. Married to Sadie Singer; three sons. Member of ALA; Dramatists Guild; WGA; Acad. of TV Arts & Sciences. Address: 330 W. 58th St., New York, NY 10019, tel. (212) 246-9709.

Pre-Theatre. Social worker.

Theatre. In collaboration with Will Glickman, Mr. Stein contributed sketches to the revue, *Inside U.S.A.* (Century Th., N.Y.C., Apr. 30, 1948); the revue, *Lend An Ear*(Natl., Dec. 16, 1948); the play *Mrs. Gibbons Boys*(Music Box, May 4, 1949; Westminster, London, Dec. 11, 1956); sketches for *Alive and Kicking* (Winter Garden, N.Y.C., Jan. 17, 1950); the book for *Plain and Fancy*(Mark Hellinger Th., Jan. 27, 1955; Drury Lane, London, Jan. 25, 1956); the book for *Mr. Wonderful* (Bway Th., N.Y.C., Mar. 22, 1956); and the book for *The Body Beautiful*(Bway Th., Jan. 23, 1958). He was the sole author of the book for *Juno*(Winter Garden, Mar. 9, 1959); wrote, with Robert Russell, the book for *Take Me Along* (Shubert, Oct. 22, 1959); wrote the comedy, *Enter Laughing* (Henry Miller's Th., Mar. 13, 1963); the book for *Fiddler on the Roof*(Imperial, Sept. 22, 1964; Alhambra Th., Tel Aviv, Israel, June 7, 1965; Her Majesty's Th., London, Feb. 16, 1967); and the book for *Zorba*(Imperial, N.Y.C., Nov. 17, 1968). He was one of several contributors to the book of *Irene*(Minskoff Th., Mar. 13, 1973).

Mr. Stein co-produced *We Bombed in New Haven* (Ambassador, Oct. 16, 1968).

Films. He wrote, with Carl Reiner, the screenplay, and produced *Enter Laughing*(Col., 1967), based on Mr. Stein's play, which was in turn based on Mr. Reiner's novel of the same name. He also wrote the screenplay for *Fiddler on the Roof*(UA, 1971).

Television and Radio. On radio, he wrote scripts for Lower Basin Street (1944); Raleigh Room (NBC, 1944–47); and the Henry Morgan Show (ABC, 1946–49). For television, he wrote material for the NBC All-Star Show (NBC, 1950–51); Your Show of Shows (NBC, 1952–53); the Sid Caesar Show (CBS, 1953–54); and several "specials" for Phil Silvers, Debbie Reynolds, and others (1955–62).

Awards. For *Fiddler on the Roof,* he received two Antoinette Perry (Tony) Awards (1965); the New York Drama Critics' Circle Award (1964–65); and the B'nai B'rith Music and Performing Award for "exceptional creative achievement" (June 16, 1965).

STELOFF, FRANCES. Bookseller. b. Dec. 31, 1887, Saratoga Springs, N.Y., to Simon Abraham and Tobe (Metzner) Steloff. Father, farmer. Attended Roxbury (Mass.) Evening H.S. Married June 17, 1923, to David Moss, bookseller (marr. dis. 1929). Member of ABA. Address: Gotham Book Mart, 41 W. 47th St., New York, NY 10036, tel. (212) PL 7-0367.

Since Jan. 2, 1920, Miss Steloff has been owner of the Gotham Book Mart, a bookstore emphasizing books on the theatre and related subjects, located in N.Y.C. A biography of Miss Steloff, and the story of the Gotham Book Mart, entitled *Wise Men Fish Here,* was written by W. G. Rogers (1965).

STERLING, JAN. Actress. b. Jane Sterling Adriance, Apr. 3, 1923, New York City, to William Allen Ardiance. Attended Fay Compton's Dramatic Sch., London, England. Married to John Merivale (marr. dis.); married May 12, 1950, to Paul Douglas (dec. 1959); one son. Member of AEA; SAG; AFTRA.

Theatre. Miss Sterling made her Bway debut as Christ Faringdon in *Bachelor Born* (Morosco, Jan. 25, 1938); followed by the role of Nancy Holmes in *When We Are Married* (Lyceum, Dec. 25, 1939); Judith Weaver in *Grey Farm* (Hudson, May 3, 1940); succeeded Virginia Field in *Panama Hattie* (46 St. Th., Oct. 30, 1940); understudied for *The Three Sisters*(Ethel Barrymore Th., Dec. 21, 1942); played Margaret Stanley in *This Rock* (Longacre, Feb. 18, 1943); succeeded Beatrice Pearson as Jan Lupton in *Over 21*(Music Box, Jan. 3, 1944); played Edith Bowsmith in *The Rugged Path* (Plymouth, Nov. 10, 1945); Zelda Rainier in *Dunnigan's Daughter*(John Golden Th., Dec. 26, 1945); Janet Alexander in *This, Too, Shall Pass*(Belasco, Apr. 30, 1946); and Daphne Stillington in *Present Laughter* (Plymouth, Oct. 29, 1946).

She toured as Billie Dawn in *Born Yesterday* (opened Erlanger, Chicago, Ill., 1947), and succeeded (May 25, 1949) Judy Holliday in the role in the N.Y.C. company (Lyceum, Feb. 4, 1946); toured (1948) as Mary in *John Loves Mary;* played Karen Norwood in *Two Blind Mice* (Cort, N.Y.C., Mar. 2, 1949); Mary Murray in *Small War on Murray Hill* (Ethel Barrymore Th., Jan. 3, 1957); appeared in *The Spider's Web* (Chicago, Ill., Aug. 1958); toured as Nell Nash in *The Gazebo* (1959); played Ann in *The Perfect Setup*(Cort, N.Y.C., Oct. 24, 1962); and Madelaine Robbins in *Once for the Asking*(Booth, Nov. 20, 1963).

She was Terry in *The River* and Mary in *Mary Agnes Is Thirty-Five,* two plays on the program billed as *Friday Night*(Pocket Th., Feb. 8, 1965); toured in *Black Comedy* (Feb.–Apr. 1969); was a member of the company at the New Theatre for Now Workshop, Mark Taper Forum, Los Angeles, Calif. (June 1969); succeeded (Jan. 1970) Peggy Cass as Mollie Malloy in a revival of *The Front Page*(Ethel Barrymore Th., N.Y.C., Oct. 18, 1969); toured in *Butterflies Are Free* (Oct. 1971–Mar. 1972); and played Lola in *Come Back, Little Sheba*(Queens Playhouse, Flushing, N.Y., Aug. 22, 1974; Studio Arena Th., Buffalo, N.Y., Oct. 31, 1974).

Films. Miss Sterling made her first appearance in *Johnny Belinda*(WB, 1948); followed by *Union Station* (Par., 1950); *Caged* (WB, 1950); *The Skipper Surprised His Wife*(MGM, 1950); *The Mating Season* (Par., 1951); *The Big Carnival*(Par., 1951); *Rhubarb* (Par., 1951); *Appointment with Danger*(Par., 1951); *Sky Full of Moon*(MGM, 1952); *Flesh and Fury*(U, 1952); *Pony Express* (Par., 1953); *The Vanquished* (Par., 1953); *Split Second*(RKO, 1953); *Alaska Seas* (Par., 1954); *The High and the Mighty*(WB, 1954); *Return from the Sea*(Allied, 1954); *The Human Jungle*(Allied, 1954); *Women's Prison*(Col., 1955); *Female on the Beach*(U, 1955); *Man with the Gun*(UA, 1955); *1984*(Col., 1956); *The Harder They Fall*(Col., 1956); *Slaughter on Tenth Avenue* (U, 1957); *High School Confidential* (MGM, 1958); *Love in a Gold Fish Bowl* (Par., 1961); *The Incident* (20th-Fox, 1967); and *The Minx*(Cambist, 1969).

Television. Miss Sterling has appeared in many television plays, including *The Book Overdue* (Medallion Th., CBS, Jan. 1954); *Trip Around the Block* (Ford Th., NBC, Oct. 1954); presentations of Rheingold Th. (NBC, 1955); Lux Video Th. (NBC, 1956, 1957); in Playhouse 90's *Requiem for a Heavyweight*(CBS, Oct. 1956) and *Clipper Ship*(CBS, Apr. 1957); on Climax (CBS, 1956, 1957); Kraft Th. (NBC, 1958); Alfred Hitchcock Presents (CBS, 1958); Alcoa Th. (NBC, 1960); GE Th. (CBS, 1960); Dick Powell Th. (NBC, 1961, 1963); and Alfred Hitchcock Th. (CBS, 1962).

She appeared also on episodes of many serials, including Wagon Train (NBC, 1959, 1961); Untouchables (ABC, 1960); Bonanza (NBC, 1960); Naked City (ABC, 1961); Burke's Law (ABC, 1963, 1965); Mannix (CBS, 1968); Name of the Game (NBC, 1969); The Guiding Light (CBS, 1970); and Medical Center (CBS, 1971).

STERN, EDWARD J. Director. b. Edward Jules Stern, June 10, 1946, New York City, to Jack and Syd Stern. Father, manufacturer. Educ. Riverdale School, McBurney School, both in N.Y.C.; grad. Univ. of Virginia (Phi Beta Kappa), B.A.; Indiana Univ., M.A. Married Dec. 23, 1968, to Annie Kate Ward. Address: (home) 3726 Totem Lane, Indianapolis, IN 46208, tel. (317) 926-5859; (bus.) 411 E. Michigan St., Indianapolis, IN 46204, tel. (317) 635-5277.

Pre-Theatre. Mr. Stern was an instructor of acting at Indiana Univ., Bloomington, Ind.

Theatre. Mr. Stern directed a production of *Spoon River Anthology* (Univ. of Virginia, Charlottesville, Va., 1964) and was managing director, Rockbridge Players, Lexington, Va. (Summer 1967). In 1971 he was a co-founder (with Benjamin Mordecai and Gregory Poggi) of the Indiana Repertory Theatre in Indianapolis. He became artistic director of the company in Nov. 1972, responsible for play selection, casting, and supervision.

Productions presented by Indiana Repertory Th. under Mr. Stern's direction include *Charley's Aunt* (Sept. 1972), *Fables Here and Then*(Oct. 1972), *The Glass Menagerie* (Feb. 1973), *What the Butler Saw* (Oct. 1973), *Of Mice and Men* (Nov. 1973), and *Sherlock Holmes*(Mar. 1974). He was artistic director for *Scapin* and *Shakespeare Alive* (both Nov. 1972), *House of Blue Leaves* (Jan. 1973), *Count Dracula*(Mar. 1973), *Our Town*(Oct. 1973), *Jacques Brel Is Alive and Well and Living in Paris, The Servant of Two Masters,* and *Comedy Kaleidoscope* (all Jan. 1974).

STERNE, MORGAN. Actor. b. Albert Morganstern, May 9, 1926, Cleveland, Ohio, to Aaron and Bessie Morgenstern. Father, electrician. Grad. Taft H.S., N.Y.C., 1943; attended Rutgers Univ.; Carnegie Inst. of Tech., 1946; Mexico City (Mex.) Coll., 1948–49. Studied acting with Lee Strasberg, N.Y.C.; Joe Bromberg; Seki Sano. Married June 17, 1947, to Lois Marie Eicher; two sons, one daughter. Served WW II, US Army Inf., PTO. Member of AEA; SAG; AFTRA.

Theatre. Mr. Sterne first performed with Spur Repertory Th. (Cherry Lane Th., N.Y.C., 1946), playing Jerry Devine in *Juno and the Paycock,* Moe Axelrod in *Awake and Sing,* and Mr. Dearth in *Dear Brutus;* he played Pvt. Dino Callucci in *A Sound of Hunting* (Cherry Lane, May 1954); joined (Aug. 1957) as Edmund Tyrone in *Long Day's Journey into*

Night (Helen Hayes Th., July 7, 1956); played Jade in *Night Circus* (John Golden Th., Feb. 2, 1958); toured as Joe Varga in *A Piece of Blue Sky* (1959); appeared as Roger in *The Good Soup* (Plymouth, N.Y.C., Mar. 2, 1960); Rev. Shannon in a pre-Bway tryout of *The Night of the Iguana* (Coconut Grove, Fla., 1960); toured South America with the Actors Studio (1961); played Alex in *The Garden of Sweets* (ANTA, N.Y.C., Oct. 31, 1961); was standby for Jason Robards, Jr., in *A Thousand Clowns* (Eugene O'Neill Th., Apr. 5, 1962); played Larry Kogen in *Seidman and Son* (Belasco, Oct. 15, 1962); and appeared in *Cages* (York, June 13, 1963); replaced (Oct. 16, 1963) Jack Warden in *Cages* (York, June 13, 1963); played Antony in *Antony and Cleopatra* (Oct. 19, 1966) and was in *The Cherry Orchard* (Mar. 1, 1967), both with Stanford (Calif.) Repertory; appeared at Pasadena (Calif.) Playhouse in *Hey You, Light Man* (1968); and directed *Click* (Mark Taper Forum, Los Angeles, Oct. 28, 1968).

Films. Mr. Sterne appeared in *Nine Miles to Noon* (1960); and played Garcin in *No Exit* (ZEN, 1962).

Television. He made his first appearance on Kraft Television Th. (NBC, 1959); played Joe Varga in *A Piece of Blue Sky* (Play of the Week, WNTA, 1960); Bezano in *He Who Gets Slapped* (Play of the Week, WNTA, 1961); appeared on The Nurses (CBS, 1963); and The Defenders (CBS, 1963).

Recreation. Speed ice skating, photography.

STERNHAGEN, FRANCES. Actress. b. Frances Hussey Sternhagen, Jan. 13, 1930, Washington, D.C., to John M. and Gertrude S. (Wyckoff) Sternhagen. Father, judge, US tax court. Grad. Madeira Sch., Fairfax Co., Va., 1947; Vassar Coll., B.A. 1951; attended Catholic Univ., 1952. Studied acting with Sanford Meisner. Married Feb. 13, 1956, to Thomas A. Carlin, actor; six children. Member of AEA; AFTRA; SAG. Address: 152 Sutton Manor Rd., New Rochelle, NY 10805, tel. (914) NE 2-5696.

Theatre. Miss Sternhagen first appeared as the Easter Rabbit in a fourth grade sch. play (Potomac Sch. Gym., Washington, D.C., 1939); was elected head of drama clubs in H.S. and Coll., and directed several plays, which led to a year of teaching dramatics at Milton Acad., Milton, Mass., 1952.

Her professional appearance began at the Bryn Mawr (Pa.) Summer Theatre (1948), where she played Laura in *The Glass Menagerie,* and Mrs. Manningham in *Angel Street;* at the Arena Stage, Washington, D.C., she appeared as Mrs. Margery Pinchwife in *The Country Wife* (Jan. 1953), Mrs. Webb in *Our Town* (Feb. 1953), Nancy Stoddard in *The Country Girl* (May 1953); Phyllis Carmichael in *My Heart's in the Highlands* (Sept. 1953), Juliette in *Thieves' Carnival* (Oct. 1953), Doto in *A Phoenix Too Frequent,* Ma Kirby in *The Happy Journey from Trenton to Camden* (Nov. 1953), Muriel McComber in *Ah, Wilderness!* (Jan. 1954), and Elvira in *Blithe Spirit* (Apr. 1954); at the Olney (Md.) Theatre, played Lavinia Chamberlayne in *The Cocktail Party* (July 1954), Ann in *Outward Bound* (July 1954), Georgie Elgin in *The Country Girl* (Aug. 1954), and Lady Ariadne Utterwood in *Heartbreak House* (Aug. 1954).

Miss Sternhagen made her N.Y.C. debut as Eva in *Thieves' Carnival* (Cherry Lane, Feb. 1, 1955); appeared as Miss T. Muse and understudied Helen Hayes as Mrs. Antrobus and Mary Martin as Sabina in the ANTA Salute to France production of *The Skin of Our Teeth* (Th. Sarah Bernhardt, Paris, France, June 1955); and on tour in the US (Washington, D.C.; Chicago, Ill., July 1955) and (ANTA Th., N.Y.C., Aug. 17, 1955); played one of the Widows Yang in *The Carefree Tree* (Phoenix Th., Oct. 11, 1955); Lydia Carew in *The Admirable Bashville* (Cherry Lane Th., Feb. 20, 1956); Gretchen in a stock production of *Faust* (Theatre-on-the-Green, Wellesley, Mass., July 1956); Mrs. Margery Pinchwife in *The Country Wife* (Renata, N.Y.C., June 26, 1957); toured summer theatres as Opal in *The Isle of Cipango* and the Postmistress in *Pound on Demand* as part of the bill, *Triple Play* (1958); succeeded (Sept. 1958) Anne Meara as the Nymph in *Ulysses in Nighttown* (Rooftop, June 5, 1958); played the title role in *The Saintliness of Margery Kempe* (York, Feb. 21, 1959).

She appeared as Dee Jones in *Viva Madison Avenue!* (Longacre, N.Y.C., Apr. 6, 1960); as Miss Madrigal in a stock tour of *The Chalk Garden* (July 1960); succeeded (July 1960) Jane Romano as Selma Chargesse in *Red Eye of Love* (Provincetown Playhouse, June 12, 1960); played Gwendolyn in *The Importance of Being Earnest* (McCarter Th., Princeton, N.J., Nov. 10, 1960); Hypatia Tarleton in *Misalliance* (Sheridan Sq. Th., N.Y.C. Sept. 25, 1961); and Alice McAnany in *Great Day in the Morning* (Henry Miller's Th., Mar. 28, 1962). She subsequently appeared in stock productions as Mrs. Levi in *The Matchmaker* (Olney Th., Md., Aug. 1962); and Sabina in *The Skin of Our Teeth* (Brandeis Forum Th., Waltham, Mass., June 1963); played Lois in *A Matter of Like Life and Death* as part of the bill with *Opening Night* (East End Th., N.Y.C., Oct. 2, 1963); and "W2" in Samuel Beckett's *Play* (Cherry Lane, Jan. 4, 1964).

She played Rose in "The Room" and Flora in "A Slight Ache," in *The New Pinter Plays* (Writers Stage Th., Dec. 9, 1964); Susan Throssel in *Quality Street* (Bucks County Playhouse, New Hope, Pa., Aug. 23, 1965); Mrs. Ashton Dilke in *The Right Honorable Gentleman* (Billy Rose Th., N.Y.C., Oct. 19, 1965); Mrs. Hopewell in *The Displaced Person* (Amer. Place Th., Dec. 16, 1966); was standby for Eileen Heckart in several roles in *You Know I Can't Hear You When the Water's Running* (Ambassador, Mar. 13, 1967); played Lavinia Chamberlayne in *The Cocktail Party* (Oct. 7, 1968) and Loreleen in *Cock-a-Doodle Dandy* (Jan. 20, 1969) for the APA-Phoenix Co. (Lyceum Th.); was standby for Jeanie Carson in several roles in *Blood Red Roses* (John Golden Th., Mar. 22, 1970); played the Widow Quin in *The Playboy of the Western World* (Vivian Beaumont Th., Jan. 7, 1971); was standby for Madeleine Sherwood (the Daughter) and Colleen Dewhurst (the Mistress) in *All Over* (Martin Beck Th., Mar. 27, 1971); standby for Nancy Marchand (Elizabeth) and Salome Jens (Mary) in *Mary Stuart* (Vivian Beaumont Th., Nov. 1, 1971); played Mavis Parodus Bryson in the revival of *The Sign in Sidney Brustein's Window* (Longacre, Jan. 26, 1972); Pauline in *Enemies* (Vivian Beaumont Th., Nov. 9, 1972); several roles in *The Good Doctor* (Eugene O'Neill Th., Nov. 27, 1973); and Dora Strang in *Equus* (Plymouth, Oct. 24, 1975).

Films. Miss Sternhagen played a social worker in a Family Service Association film for Mental Health (1954); Charlotte Wolf in *Up the Down Staircase* (WB, 1967); lady on bus in *The Tiger Makes Out* (Col., 1967); and Mrs. McCluskey in *Two People* (U, 1973).

Television. She first appeared as Nellie in *The Great Bank Robbery* (Omnibus, CBS, 1955); recreated the role of Eva in *Thieves' Carnival* and played Miss Mabee in *In a Garden* (Play of the Week, WNTA, 1961); and has performed on Camera Three (CBS); Lamp Unto My Feet (CBS); The Nurses (CBS); The Defenders (CBS); Robert Montgomery Presents (NBC); Alcoa Hour (NBC); Studio One (CBS); Profiles in Courage (NBC); *How He Lied to Her Husband* (Rep. Th., Ind., Feb. 17, 1965); *T. S. Eliot—The Wasteland* (Educ., Mar. 1, 1965); For the People (CBS); Look Up and Live (CBS); Directions (ABC); played Toni on the Love of Life serial (CBS, June 1967 through 1968); and Phyllis Corrigan on The Doctors serial (NBC, 1970).

Awards. She received *Village Voice* Off-Bway (Obie) Awards for her performances in *The Admirable Bashville* (1956), *The Country Wife* (1957), and *The New Pinter Plays* (1965); the Clarence Derwent Award for *The Admirable Bashville* (1956) and *The Country Wife* (1957); and the Antoinette Perry (Tony) Award for *The Good Doctor* (best actress in a supporting role in a play, 1974).

Recreation. Singing, painting, swimming, sailing.

STEVENS, CLIFFORD. Talent representative, production assistant. b. Clifford Stevens Weisse, Nov. 1, 1936, New York City, to Charles and Frieda Weisse. Father, salesman. Grad. George Washington H.S., N.Y.C., 1953; New York Univ., B.A. 1956. Member of Sociét é des Auteurs et Compositeurs (Paris, France).

Theatre. Mr. Stevens was assistant to the producers, Carmen Capalbo and Stanley Chase, for *The Threepenny Opera* (Th. de Lys, Sept. 20, 1955); was a production assistant at the Woodstock (N.Y.) Summer Playhouse (1956); subsequently was assistant to Joseph Papp for the New York Shakespeare Festival on *Titus Andronicus* (Shakespeare Th. Workshop, Nov. 27, 1956); during 1957 served as publicity director for Equity Library Th.; and was production assistant for the following shows at the Bijou: *The Potting Shed* (Jan. 29, 1957); *A Moon for the Misbegotten* (May 2, 1957); and *The Cave Dwellers* (Oct. 19, 1957).

During 1957, he was production assistant for the ANTA Matinee Series (Th. de Lys); produced and directed staged readings of *The Importance of Being Earnest* and *The Confidential Clerk* (Guild for the Blind, N.Y.C.); was company manager for *The Saturday Night Kid* (Provincetown Playhouse, May 15, 1958); assistant to Stanley Chase for the European tour of *Free and Easy* (1958–60); was production assistant for *The Pretender* (Cherry Lane, N.Y.C., May 24, 1960); and was production associate for *Fiesta in Madrid* (NY City Ctr., May 28, 1969).

STEVENS, LESLIE. Playwright, director, producer. b. Feb. 3, 1924, Washington, D.C., to Leslie C. and Nell (Millikin) Stevens. Father, vice admiral; mother, lecturer. Grad. Westminster Abbey, London, Eng., B.A. 1940; Yale Univ., Sch. of Drama, M.F.A. 1947. Studied playwriting at Amer. Th. Wing with Moss Hart, Howard Lindsay, 1948–50; with Robert Anderson. Served USAAF, Iceland, 1943–45; married Ramse Carroll (marr. dis. 1955; married 1958 to Kate Manx (marr. dis. 1963); one son. Served USAAF, Iceland, 1943–45; rank, Capt. Member of Dramatists Guild; WGA, West; DGA; Producer's Guild; MPAA; Antenna Panel (pres., 1963–64). Address: (home) 8560 Hedges Place, Hollywood, CA 90069; (bus.) Daystar Productions and Leslie Stevens Productions, 9200 Sunset Blvd., Hollywood, CA 90069.

Theatre. Mr. Stevens wrote *Bullfight* (Th. de Lys, N.Y.C., Jan. 12, 1954); *Champagne Complex* (Cort Th., Apr. 12, 1955); *The Lovers* (Martin Beck Th., May 10, 1956); *Marriage-Go-Round* (Plymouth, Oct. 29, 1958); and the book for *The Pink Jungle* (opened Alcazar, San Francisco, Calif., Oct. 14, 1959; closed Shubert, Boston, Mass., Dec. 12, 1959).

He also wrote the plays, *Marlowe* (1956), *Wonderful, Wonderful World* (1964), *The Mother Image* (1964), *Bloodline* (1973), and *Love Life* (1974).

Films. He wrote the screenplay for *The Left Handed Gun* (WB, 1958); *Marriage-Go-Round* (20th-Fox, 1960); wrote the screenplay and directed *Private Property* (Citation, 1960); and produced, directed, and wrote the screenplay for *Hero's Island* (UA, 1962).

Television. He was the chief writer of Paul Gregory's Crescendo (CBS, 1956); chief writer on 75th Anniversary of Standard Oil (NBC, 1956); wrote six teleplays for Playhouse 90; *Invitation to a Gunfighter, Charley's Aunt, Rumors of Evening, Violent Heart, Portrait of a Murderer,* and *The Second Man* (CBS, 1957); and adapted *Bloomer Girl* (Producers Showcase, NBC, 1958). He was also the creator, producer, writer, and director for the series, Stoney Burke (ABC); Outer Limits (ABC, 1963–64); the pilot for It Takes a Thief (ABC, 1968); The Name of the Game (NBC); McCloud (NBC); and the feature television film *Fer de Lance* (1974). Mr. Stevens has also been an executive producer for television productions of Warner Bros. and Universal Studios.

Recreation. Helicopter pilot, languages.

STEVENS, ONSLOW. Actor, director. b. Onslow Ford Stevenson, Mar. 29, 1906, Los Angeles, Calif., to Houseley and Marguerite (Behrens) Stevenson. Father, actor. Grad. Annandale Grammar Sch., Eagle Rock, Calif., 1920; grad. Pasadena (Calif.) Playhouse Coll. of Th. Arts, M.A. 1931. Married Mar. 4, 1936, to Anne Arthur (marr. dis. 1942); one son; married Apr. 15, 1943, to Vanessa Clark (marr. dis. 1945); one daughter; married Oct. 21, 1961, to Rose Marsel. Relatives in theatre: brothers, Houseley Stevenson, Jr., television producer, and Bob Stevenson, actor. Member of SAG; AEA; AFTRA.

Theatre. Mr. Stevens made his professional debut as Antony in *Julius Caesar* (Pasadena Playhouse, Calif., 1931). Since then, he has played in and directed more than fifty productions at the Pasadena (Calif.) Playhouse, returning there from time to time from his engagements in New York. Among the productions with which he was associated at Pasadena are: *Richard III, The Time of Your Life, They Knew What They Wanted, The Cherry Orchard, Thought, Le bourgeois gentilhomme,* the chronicle plays of Shakespeare, *Outward Bound, The Armored Train, The Dybbuk, Mourning Becomes Electra, Counsellor-at-Law,* and *The Seagull.*

Mr. Stevens first appeared in N.Y.C. as David Kingsley in *Stage Door* (Music Box, Oct. 22, 1936); and subsequently played in summer-stock productions of *Suzanna and the Elders* and *Dame Nature* (Westport Country Playhouse, Conn., 1938). He toured in the role of Rev. Morell with Cornelia Otis Skinner in *Candida* (1939); played Geoffrey in *The Two Mrs. Carrolls* (Booth, N.Y.C., Aug. 3, 1943); Dr. Charles Wadsworth in *Eastward in Eden* (Royale, Nov. 18, 1947); and Barney in *A Clearing in the Woods* (Belasco, Jan. 10, 1957).

Films. Mr. Stevens's films include *Heroes of the West* (U, 1932); *Once in a Lifetime* (U, 1932); *Peg o' My Heart* (MGM, 1933); *Counsellor-at-Law* (U, 1933); *Only Yesterday* (U, 1933); *This Side of Heaven* (MGM, 1934); *The Three Musketeers* (RKO, 1935); *Under Two Flags* (20th-Fox, 1936); *House of Dracula* (U, 1945); *Angel on My Shoulder* (UA, 1946); *Canyon Passage* (U, 1946); *O.S.S.* (Par., 1946); *Night Has a Thousand Eyes* (Par., 1948); *Walk a Crooked Mile* (Col., 1948); *Red, Hot and Blue* (Par., 1949); *Lonely Hearts Bandits* (Rep., 1950); *Lorna Doone* (Col., 1951); *Sealed Cargo* (RKO, 1951); *San Francisco Story* (WB, 1952); *Charge at Feather River* (WB, 1953); *Lion Is in the Streets* (WB, 1953); *Them* (WB, 1954); *They Rode West* (Col., 1954); *New York Confidential* (WB, 1955); *Tribute to a Bad Man* (MGM, 1956); *Outside the Law* (U, 1956); *Kelly and Me* (U, 1957); and *All the Fine Young Cannibals* (MGM, 1960).

Television. He has appeared on Wagon Train (NBC), Restless Gun (NBC), and the Outlaws (NBC, 1952–to date).

STEVENS, PAUL. Actor. b. Paul Steven Gattoni, June 17, 1924, Los Angeles, Calif., to Joseph and Josephine (Fanquini) Gattoni. Father, laborer. Grad. Abraham Lincoln H.S., Los Angeles, Calif., 1943; attended Univ. of California at Los Angeles, 1944; grad. Pasadena (Calif.) Playhouse, 1945; Geller Th., Hollywood, Calif., 1950. Married Sept. 27, 1951, to Carol Southard, actress. Served USAAF, 1947; rank, Staff Sgt. Member of AEA; AFTRA; SAG. Address: 205 W. 89th St., New York, NY 10024, tel. (212) SU 7-5728.

Theatre. Mr. Stevens made his N.Y.C. debut as Bassanio in *The Merchant of Venice* (NY City Ctr., Mar. 4, 1953); subsequently appeared as Chitling in *Oliver Twist,* which was included in the program, *Highlights of the Empire* (Empire, May 24, 1953); as Orlando in *As You Like It* (Oct. 1955) and Romeo in *Romeo and Juliet* (Dec. 1955) at the Shakespearean Theatre Workshop (later known as NY Shakespeare Festival) (Emmanuel Presbyterian Church).

Mr. Stevens appeared as Assistant Prosecutor Padua in *Compulsion* (Ambassador, Oct. 24, 1957); Proteus in *Two Gentlemen from Verona* (NY Shakespeare Festival, Belvedere Lake Th., July 1957); succeeded Ford Rainey (Mar. 11, 1958) as Deputy Governor Danforth in *The Crucible* (Martinique, Mar. 11, 1958); appeared in the title role in *Ivanov* (Renata, Oct. 7, 1958); as Lucien in *Jeanette* (Maidman Playhouse, Mar. 24, 1960); Captain Thibaudeau in *General Seeger* (Lyceum, Feb. 28, 1962); Prospero in *The Tempest* (NY Shakespeare Festival, Delacorte Th., July 16, 1962); as the Priest in *Andorra* (Biltmore, Feb. 9, 1963); and as Giovanni Bertelli in *The Advocate* (ANTA, Oct. 14, 1963). At the NY Shakespeare Festival (Delacorte Th.) he played Don Adriano de Armado in *Love's Labour's Lost* (June 9, 1965) and Hector in *Troilus and Cressida* (Aug. 4, 1965). He was the Duke of Brachiano in *The White Devil* (Circle in the Square, Dec. 6, 1965); played in *The Sorrows of Frederick* (Center Th. Group, Los Angeles, Calif., June 23, 1967); and was Josef Gross in *The Memorandum* (Public Th., N.Y.C., May 5, 1968).

Films. Mr. Stevens has appeared in *Exodus* (UA, 1960); *The Mask* (WB, 1961); and *Advise and Consent* (Col., 1962).

Recreation. "A complete do-it-yourself addict.".

STEVENS, ROGER L. Producer. b. Mar. 12, 1910, Detroit, Mich., to Stanley G. and Florence (Jackson) Stevens. Grad. Choate Sch., Wallingford, Conn., 1928; attended Univ. of Mich., 1928–30. Married Jan. 1, 1938, to Christine Gesell; one daughter. Served USNR, 1943–46; rank, Lt. Member of Producers Th. (pres., 1954–60); Phoenix Th. (past pres., from 1955; ANTA (treas., 1952–65); Metropolitan Opera Co. (bd. mem., 1958–to date); Actors Studio Th. (genl. admin., 1963–66); American Shakespeare Fest. and Acad. (co-founder; trustee; mbr. of exec. comm., 1954–to date); New Dramatists Comm. (pres., 1957–59); John F. Kennedy Center for the Performing Arts (chmn., bd. of trustees, 1961–to date); Special Asst. to Pres. Lyndon Johnson, on the Arts 1964–68); Natl. Council on the Arts (chmn., 1964–69); Natl. Endowment for the Arts 1965–69); Amer. Film Inst. (trustee; chmn. of bd., 1969–72); Natl. Opera Inst. (pres., to date); Racket and Tennis Club, N.Y.C.; Century Assn., N.Y.C.; Pilgrims of the US; Bohemian, San Francisco, Detroit (Mich.) Athletic Club; Phi Gamma Delta. John F. Kennedy Center, Washington, DC 20566.

Theatre. Mr. Stevens produced *Twelfth Night* (Empire Th., Oct. 3, 1949); followed by *Peter Pan* (Imperial, Apr. 24, 1950); produced, with George Freedley, *The Cellar and the Well* (ANTA, Dec. 10, 1950); and Cheryl Crawford, in association with Mr. Stevens, produced *Peer Gynt* (ANTA, Jan. 28, 1951).

In 1951, Mr. Stevens became a member of the Playwrights Co., and remained with the organization until its dissolution in 1960. During that period the company produced or co-produced 38 Bway productions, beginning with *The Fourposter* (Ethel Barrymore Th., Oct. 24, 1951); *Barefoot in Athens* (Martin Beck Th., Oct. 31, 1951); and *The Grand Tour* (Martin Beck Th., Dec. 10, 1951).

The company produced *Mr. Pickwick* (Plymouth, Sept. 17, 1952); produced, with Robert Whitehead, *The Emperor's Clothes* (Ethel Barrymore Th., Feb. 9, 1953); produced *Tea and Sympathy* (Ethel Barrymore Th., Sept. 30, 1953); *Sabrina Fair* (National, Nov. 11, 1953); *The Winner* (Playhouse, Feb. 17, 1954); *Ondine* (46 St. Th., Feb. 18, 1954); and produced, with Oliver Smith, *In the Summer House* (Playhouse, Dec. 29, 1953).

Producers Theatre, of which Mr. Stevens is president, was formed in 1954. Its initial presentation was *The Confidential Clerk,* which was produced with Henry Sherek (Morosco, Feb. 11, 1954). Independently, Mr. Stevens produced with Alfred de Liagre, Jr., *Escapade* (48 St. Th., Nov. 18, 1953); with Robert Whitehead, *The Remarkable Mr. Pennypacker* (Coronet, Dec. 30, 1953); and, with Alfred de Liagre, Jr., T. Edward Hambleton, and Norris Houghton, *The Golden Apple* (Phoenix, Mar. 11, 1954; Alvin, Apr. 20, 1954).

The Playwrights Co. produced *All Summer Long* (Coronet, Sept. 23, 1954); *The Traveling Lady* (Playhouse, Oct. 27, 1954); *The Bad Seed* (46 St. Th., Dec. 8, 1954); and *Cat on a Hot Tin Roof* (Morosco, Mar. 24, 1955); and produced with George Boroff, *Once Upon a Tailor* (Cort, May 23, 1955). Producers Th. presented *The Flowering Peach* (Belasco, Dec. 28, 1954). Independently, Mr. Stevens produced, with Katherine Cornell, *The Dark Is Light Enough* (ANTA, Feb. 23, 1955); with Robert Whitehead, *Bus Stop* (Music Box, Mar. 2, 1955); with Kermit Bloomgarten and Mr. Whitehead, the double-bill of *A View from the Bridge* and *A Memory of Two Mondays* (Coronet, Sept. 29, 1955); and, with Hardy Smith, Ltd., *Island of Goats* (Fulton, Oct. 4, 1955).

Producers Th. presented *Joyce Grenfell Requests the Pleasure. . .* (Bijou, Oct. 10, 1955); and in association with Stratford (Ontario, Canada) Shakespeare Festival, *Tamburlaine the Great* (Winter Garden, Jan. 19, 1956). The Playwrights Co. produced, with Henry W. Margolis, *Tiger at the Gates* (Plymouth, Oct. 3, 1955); produced *The Ponder Heart* (Music Box, Feb. 16, 1956); and produced, with Gayle Stine, *The Lovers* (Martin Beck Th., May 10, 1956). Producers Th. presented, in association with Hecht-Lancaster, *Separate Tables* (Music Box, Oct. 25, 1956); produced, with Robert L. Joseph, *Major Barbara* (Martin Beck Th., Oct. 30, 1956); produced, with Gilbert Miller, *The Sleeping Prince* (Coronet, Nov. 1, 1956); and produced *Waltz of the Toreadors* (Coronet, Jan. 17, 1957); *A Hole in the Head* (Plymouth, Feb. 28, 1957); and *Orpheus Descending* (Martin Beck Th., Mar. 21, 1957); The Playwrights Co. produced, *A Small War on Murray Hill* (Ethel Barrymore Th., Jan. 3, 1957). Independently, Mr. Stevens produced, with Oliver Smith, *A Clearing in the Woods* (Belasco, Jan. 10, 1957); and, with Richard Adler, *The Sin of Pat Muldoon* (Cort, Mar. 13, 1957).

Robert E. Griffith and Harold S. Prince produced, by arrangement with Mr. Stevens, *West Side Story* (Winter Garden, Sept. 26, 1957); and Sol Hurok, in association with Mr. Stevens, presented Emlyn Williams in the latter's *A Boy Growing Up* (Longacre, Oct. 7, 1957). Mr. Stevens produced, with Gilbert Miller and Henry Sherek, *Under Milk Wood* (Henry Miller's Th., Oct. 15, 1957); with Laurier Lister, *Joyce Grenfell Presents* (Lyceum, Apr. 7, 1958); and, with Katharine Cornell, *The Firstborn* (Coronet, Apr. 30, 1958).

The Playwrights Co. produced, in association with Milton Sperling, *Time Remembered* (Morosco, Nov. 12, 1957); produced with Lance Hamilton and Charles Russell, *Nude with Violin* (Belasco, Nov. 14, 1957); with Gilbert Miller, *The Rope Dancers* (Cort, Nov. 20, 1957); with Malcolm Wells and Daniel Blum, *The Country Wife* (Adelphi, Nov. 27, 1957); with the Th. Guild, *The Summer of the 17th Doll* (Coronet, Jan. 22, 1958); and, with Lance Hamilton and Charles Russell, *Present Laughter* (Belasco, Jan. 31, 1958). Producers Th. presented the Lunts in *The Visit* (Lunt-Fontanne, May 5, 1958).

The Playwrights Co. produced, with James M. Slevin and John Gerstad, *Howie* (46 St. Th., Sept. 17, 1958); with David Susskind, *Handful of Fire* (Martin Beck Th., Oct. 1, 1958); with Frederick Brisson, *The Pleasure of His Company* (Longacre, Oct. 22, 1958); with José Ferrer, *Edwin Booth* (46 St. Th., Nov. 24, 1958); with Franchot Productions, *Cue for Passion* (Henry Miller's Th., Nov. 25, 1958); with Frederick Brisson, *The Gazebo* (Lyceum, Dec. 12, 1958); with Gilbert Miller, Lance Hamilton, and Charles Russell, *Look After Lulu* (Henry Miller's Th., Mar. 3, 1959); and, with Oliver Smith and Oliver Rea, *Juno* (Winter Garden, Mar. 9, 1959). Producers Th. presented *A Touch of the Poet* (Helen Hayes Th., Oct. 2, 1958); *Goldilocks* (Lunt-Fontanne, Oct. 11, 1958); *The Man in the Dog Suit* (Coronet, Oct. 30, 1958); and *The Cold Wind and the Warm* (Morosco, Dec. 8, 1958).

By arrangement with Producers Th., the Cambridge Drama Festival presented *Much Ado About Nothing* (Lunt-Fontanne, Sept. 17, 1959). The Playwrights Co. produced, with Robert Lewis, *Chéri* (Morosco, Oct. 12, 1959); with Don Herbert, *The Flowering Cherry* (Lyceum, Oct. 21, 1959); with Frederick Brisson, *Five Finger Exercise* (Music Box, Dec. 2, 1959) and produced *Silent Night, Lonely Night* (Morosco, Dec. 3, 1959), and *The Best Man*

(Morosco, Mar. 31, 1960). Independently, Mr. Stevens produced with Alfred de Liagre, Jr., in association with Laurence Olivier, *The Tumbler* (Helen Hayes Th., Feb. 24, 1960); and produced, with Sol Hurok, *Duel of Angels* (Helen Hayes Th., Apr. 19, 1960).

The following season he produced *Rosemary and The Alligators*(York Playhouse, Nov. 14, 1960); produced, with Frederick Brisson, *Under the Yum-Yum Tree*(Henry Miller's Th., Nov. 16, 1960); with Robert Whitehead, *Conquering Hero* (ANTA, Jan. 16, 1961); with John Shubert, in association with S. S. Krellberg, *Julia, Jake and Uncle Joe*(Booth, Jan. 28, 1961); with Robert Whitehead, in association with Alfred R. Glancy, Jr., *Midgie Purvis* (Martin Beck Th., Feb. 1, 1961); produced *Mary, Mary* (Helen Hayes Th., Mar. 8, 1961; Queen's, London, Feb. 27, 1963); produced, with Sol Hurok, in association with Michael Redgrave and Fred Sadoff, *The Importance of Being Oscar*(Lyceum, Mar. 14, 1961); and, with Joel Schenker, *A Far Country*(Music Box, Apr. 4, 1961).

During the 1961–62 season, Mr. Stevens produced, with Frederick Brisson and Gilbert Miller, *The Caretaker* (Lyceum, Oct. 4, 1961); with Fields Productions, *Blood, Sweat and Stanley Poole* (Morosco, Oct. 5, 1961); produced, in association with Seven Arts, *Everybody Loves Opal* (Longacre, Oct. 11, 1961); produced, with Robert Whitehead, *A Man for All Seasons*(ANTA, Nov. 22, 1961); with Frederick Brisson, in association with Samuel Taylor, *First Love*(Morosco, Dec. 25, 1961); produced, in association with Henry Guettel, *Romulus*(Music Box, Jan. 10, 1962); the Phoenix Th., by arrangement with Mr. Stevens, produced *Oh Dad, Poor Dad, Mama's Hung You in the Closet and I'm Feelin' So Sad* (Phoenix, Feb. 26, 1962).

Mr. Stevens produced a stock tryout of *Tender Loving Care* (Coconut Grove Playhouse, Miami, Fla., Spring 1962); after appearances at the Seattle World's Fair, presented the Royal Dramatic Th. of Sweden in rep. performances of *Miss Julie, The Father,* and *Long Day's Journey into Night* (Cort, N.Y.C., May 14, 1962); and in London, presented *Judith* (Her Majesty's s, June 20, 1962).

With Robert Whitehead, Mr. Stevens produced the pre-Bway tryout of *Banderol* (opened Forrest, Philadelphia, Sept. 17, 1962; closed there, Sept. 22, 1962); produced, with Herbert Swope, Jr., *Step on a Crack* (Ethel Barrymore Th., N.Y.C., OCt. 17, 1962); with Howard Erskine and Joseph Hayes, *Calculated Risk*(Ambassador, Oct. 31, 1962); with Oliver Smith, *Tiger, Tiger Burning Bright* (Both, Dec. 22, 1962); produced *The Milk Train Doesn't Stop Here Anymore*(Morosco, Jan. 16, 1963); produced, with Cheryl Crawford, *Andorra* (Biltmore, Feb. 9, 1963); and, with Sam Wanamaker, *Children from Their Games*(Morosco, Apr. 11, 1963). During the 1963–64 season, Mr. Stevens produced with T. Edward Hambleton, by arrangement with the Phoenix Th., *Oh Dad, Poor Dad, Mama's Hung You in the Closet and I'm Feelin' So Sad* (Morosco, Aug. 27, 1963); produced, with Herman Shumlin in assoc. with Nelson Morris and Randolph Hale, *Bicycle Ride to Nevada*(Cort, Sept. 24, 1963); produced *The Private Ear* and *The Public Eye* (Morosco, Oct. 9, 1963); produced, with Joel Schenker, *A Case of Libel* (Longacre, Oct. 10, 1963); produced, with Frederick Brisson and Donald Alberry, the pre-Bway tryout of *Time of the Barracudas* (opened Curran, San Francisco, Oct. 21, 1963; closed Huntington Hartford Th., Los Angeles, Nov. 23, 1963); produced *A Rainy Day in Newark* (Belasco, N.Y.C., Oct. 22, 1963); *The Chinese Prime Minister* (Royale, Jan. 2, 1964; Globe, London, May 20, 1965); and with Cheryl Crawford, produced a double-bill of "The Dirty Old Man" and "Sarah and the Sax" entitled *Doubletalk* (Th. de Lys, N.Y.C., May 4, 1964).

Stevens Productions, Inc., presented, with Bonfils-Seawell Enterprises and David Oppenheim, *The Last Analysis* (Belasco, Oct. 1, 1964); presented, with Samuel Taylor and Bonfils-Seawell Enterprises, *Beekman Place*(Morosco, Oct. 7, 1964); presented, with Allen-Hodgdon Inc., *The Physicists* (Martin Beck Th., Oct. 13, 1964); supervised the production of *Hang Down Your Head and Die*(Mayfair, Oct. 18, 1964); presented, with Hume Cronyn, Allen-Hodgdon Inc., and Bonfils-Seawell Enterprises, Inc., *Slow Dance on the Killing Ground*(Plymouth, Nov. 30, 1964); presented *Poor Richard* (Helen Hayes Th., Dec. 2, 1964); Gilbert Miller presented, in assoc. with Stevens Productions Inc., *Diamond Orchid*(Henry Miller's Th., Feb. 10, 1965); and Allen-Hodgdon, Inc. presented, with Stevens Productions, Inc., and Harold Fielding, *Half a Sixpence* (Broadhurst, Apr. 25, 1965).

Mr. Stevens presented, with Lyn Austin, Oliver Smith, and Joel Schenker, *Indians*(Brooks Atkinson Th., Oct. 13, 1969); with Robert Whitehead and Robert W. Dowling, *Sheep on the Runway* (Helen Hayes Th., Jan. 31, 1970); with Donald Alberry, *COnduct Unbecoming* (Ethel Barrymore Th., Oct. 12, 1970); in assoc. with the Royal Shakespeare Co. *Old Times*(Billy Rose Th., Nov. 16, 1971); with Mr. Whitehead, *Finishing Touches* (Plymouth, Feb. 8, 1973); and with James M. Nederlander and Eddie Kulukundis, The Royal Shakespeare Co. production of *London Assurance* (Palace, Dec. 5, 1974).

As head of the John F. Kennedy Center for the Performing Arts (Washington, D.C.), Mr. Stevens has booked all attractions into the Center's three auditoriums (Eisenhower Th., Opera House and Concert Hall), since their openings (Fall 1971). He has also presented some thirty productions mounted specifically for the Center or presented with the Center's participation, which have subsequently played elsewhere. These include: in association with Hugh O'Brian, a revival of *The Country Girl* (Eisenhower Th., Washington, D.C., Nov. 16, 1971; Billy Rose Th., N.Y.C., Mar. 15, 1972); with Diana Shumlin, a revival of *Lost in the Stars*(Opera House, Washington, D.C., Feb. 19, 1972; Imperial, N.Y.C., Apr. 18, 1972); with Arthur Cantor, by arrangement with H. M. Tennent Ltd., a revival of *Captain Brassbound's Conversion* (Opera House, Washington, D.C., Mar. 13, 1972; Ethel Barrymore Th., N.Y.C., Apr. 17, 1972, and on tour); with J. Charles Gilbert a tour of *The Pleasure of His Company* (opened Eisenhower Th. Washington, D.C., July 10, 1972; closed Huntington Hartford Th., Los Angeles, Sept. 9, 1972); with J. Charles Gilbert in association with Moe Septee, *The Jockey Club Stakes* (Eisenhower Th., Fall 1972; Cort, N.Y.C., Jan. 24, 1973; and on tour); Otto Preminger, with Kennedy Center Productions, presented *Full Circle* (Eisenhower Th., Fall 1973; ANTA, N.Y.C., Nov. 7, 1973); Konrad Matthaei, in association with Mr. Stevens and Richmond Crinkley (for Kennedy Center Productions), presented, with Hale Matthews, by arrangement with the Goodman Th. Ctr., Chicago, *The Freedom of the City* (Eisenhower Th., Dec. 1973; Alvin, N.Y.C., Feb. 17, 1974); Kennedy Center Productions, with Frederick Brisson, presented *Jumpers* (Eisenhower Th., Feb. 18, 1974; Billy Rose Th., N.Y.C., Apr. 22, 1974); and presented, with Martin Feinstein and Alexander Morr, *Odyssey* (Opera House, Washington D.C., Dec. 29, 1974) which toured for a year and opened in N.Y.C. as *Home, Sweet Homer* (Palace, Dec 30, 1975). During the 1975–76 season, a series of revivals of American plays was presented by the Kennedy Center and Xerox Corp. Amer. Bicentennial Th., some of which went on to N.Y.C., including *Skin of Our Teeth,* presented in association with Ken Marsolais (Eisenhower Th., Washington, D.C., July 16, 1975; Mark Hellinger Th., N.Y.C., Sept. 9, 1975); a revised version of *Picnic,* entitled *Summer Brave* (Eisenhower Th., Fall 1975; presented in N.Y.C., by Fritz Holt, Barry Brown, Burry Fredrik at the ANTA, Oct. 26, 1975); *Sweet Bird of Youth* (Eisenhower Th., Fall 1975; presented in N.Y.C., by Michael Harvey and Harvey Frand at the Harkness Th., Dec. 1975); and *The Royal Family* (Eisenhower Th., Nov. 12, 1975; presented in N.Y.C. by Barry M. Brown, Burry Fredrik, Fritz Holt and Sally Sears at the Helen Hayes Th., Dec. 30, 1975).

Other Activities. Real estate.

Awards. Mr. Stevens holds the honorary degrees of D. Hum., Wayne State Univ., (1960); L.H.D., Tulane Univ. (1960); D. Humane Letters, Univ. of Michigan (1964); LL.D. Amherst Coll. (1968); and honorary degrees from Skidmore Coll. (1969), Univ. of Illinois (1970), and Boston Univ. (1970). He received the Sam H. Shubert Foundation Award (1957) as outstanding Bway producer, and a special Antoinette Perry (Tony) Award (1971).

Among the plays which Mr. Stevens, the Playwrights Co., and Producers Th. have produced or co-produced that have won the NY Drama Critics Circle Award are *Ondine* (best play, 1954); *The Golden Apple*(best musical, 1954); *Cat on a Hot Tin Roof* (best play, 1955); *Tiger at the Gates* (best foreign play, 1956); *The Waltz of the Toreadors* (best foreign play, 1957); *The Visit*(best foreign play, 1959); *Five Finger Exercise*(best foreign play, 1960); and *A Man for All Seasons* (best foreign play, 1962).

The Antoinette Perry (Tony) Award was won by *The Fourposter*(best play, 1952) and by *A Man for All Seasons* (best play, 1962).

The Outer Circle Award was won by *The Visit* (best play, 1959) and by *Oh Dad, Poor Dad, Mama's Hung You in the Closet and I'm Feelin' So Sad* (most original play, 1962).

STEVENSON, MARGOT. Actress. b. New York City, Feb. 8, 1918, to Charles Alexander and Frances (Riley) Stevenson. Father, actor. Grad. The Brearley Sch., N.Y.C., 1935. Studied acting with Laura Eliot, N.Y.C., 1936–39; Mary Tarcai, N.Y.C., 1937; and Don Richardson, N.Y.C., 1948. Married July 6, 1943, to Robert W. Russell, author (marr. dis. 1950); married Apr. 20, 1953, to Val Avery, actor; one daughter. Member of AEA (council, 1957–62); British AEA; AFTRA; SAG. Address: 84 Grove St., New York, NY 10014, tel. (212) CH 3-2378, CH 3-6321.

Theatre. Miss Stevenson made her first stage appearance as Juliet in The Brearley Sch. production of *Romeo and Juliet*(1932); her Bway debut as Alice Incze in *Firebird*(Empire Th., Nov. 21, 1932); subsequently appeared as a Guest in *Evensong*(Selwyn, Jan. 1, 1933); and Lady Bay-Clender (Rosie) in *A Party*(Playhouse, Aug. 23, 1933).

On Katharine Cornell's cross-country tour, she played a small role in *Romeo and Juliet* and Bella Hedley in *The Barretts of Wimpole Street* (1933–34), which she repeated in the Bway production (Martin Beck, Th., Feb. 25, 1935); appeared as Estelle Joyce in *Symphony*(Cort, Apr. 26, 1935); Berna Bowen in *Truly Valiant* (49 St. Th., Jan. 9, 1936); succeeded (June 1936) Valerie Cossart as Vera in *Call It a Day* (Morosco, Jan. 28, 1936); understudied Margaret Sullivan as Terry and played Kendall Adams in *Stage Door*(Music Box, Oct. 22, 1936); appeared as Alice Sycamore in *You Can't Take It with You* (Booth, Dec. 14, 1936); played in the pre-Bway tryout of *Easy Does It* (San Diego, Calif., 1940); and appeared as Ellen Turner in a stock production of *The Male Animal*(Ivoryton Playhouse, Conn., Summer 1940).

Miss Stevenson played Pam in *Golden Wings* (Cort, N.Y.C., Dec. 8, 1941); Meg in *Little Women* (NY City Ctr., Dec. 30, 1944); succeeded Jan Sterling as Edith Bowsmith in *The Rugged Path* (Plymouth, Nov. 10, 1945); played Maudie in *The Leading Lady*(National, Oct. 18, 1948); was understudy to Lilli Palmer as Perpetua in *Venus Observed* (New Century, Feb. 13, 1952), later playing the role of Jessie Dill (Lydia Mendelsohn Th., Ann Arbor, Mich., early June 1952); appeared at Elitch Gardens (Denver, Colo., late June 1952); made her London debut as Marianne Ames in *Sweet Peril*(St. James's, Dec. 3, 1952); followed by Helen Sherman in *The Seven Year Itch* (Aldwych, May 14, 1953); appeared again at Elitch Gardens (Summer 1954).

She played Mrs. Perry in *The Young and the Beautiful* (Longacre, N.Y.C., Oct. 1, 1955); succeeded (Feb. 18, 1957) Claudia Morgan as Amanda, Postmistress General, in *The Apple Cart*(Plymouth, Oct. 18, 1956), which she repeated on tour (opened National, Washington, D.C., Mar. 4, 1957); toured as Mrs. Biddle in *The Happiest Millionaire*(opened Dupont Th., Wilmington, Del., Oct. 2, 1957); played the Nurse in *Portrait of a Madonna,* and a Girl in Charge in *A Pound on Demand,* in the triple-bill called *Triple Play* (Playhouse, N.Y.C., Apr. 15, 1959); and was understudy to Ruth White as Edith

Maitland, and to Elizabeth Wilson as Hilda Rose in *Big Fish, Little Fish* (ANTA, Mar. 15, 1961).

With the APA, she toured as Mrs. Candour in *The School for Scandal*, the Woman in *The Tavern*, and Paulina in *The Seagull* (Boston, Falmouth, Mass.; East Hampton, N.Y., Summer 1961; Bucks County Playhouse, New Hope, Pa., July 24–Aug. 5, 1961); succeeded Agnes Morehead as Miss Swanson in *Lord Pengo* (Royale, Nov. 19, 1962); appeared as Lady Bracknell in a stock production of *The Importance of Being Earnest* (Greenhills, Reading, Pa., July 1963); played in *Kind Sir* (Avondale Playhouse, Indianapolis, Ind., June 23, 1964; Northland Playhouse, Detroit, Mich., June 30, 1964); was head dramatic coach at the Camp for the Performing Arts (Rambler, N.Y., July–Aug. 1964); appeared as Mrs. Gibbs in *Our Town* (Bucks County Playhouse, Sept. 7, 1964); Grace Sample in *One by One* (Belasco Th., N.Y.C., Dec. 1, 1964); and Lady Gregory in *Hostile Witness* (Music Box, Feb. 17, 1966).

Films. Miss Stevenson appeared in *Smashing the Money Ring* (WB, 1939); *Calling Philo Vance* (WB, 1940); *Granny Get Your Gun* (WB, 1940); *Invisible Stripes* (WB, 1940); and *Castle on the Hudson* (WB, 1940).

Television and Radio. She has performed on radio in Aunt Jenny's Real Life Stories (CBS); My True Story (ABC); Stella Dallas (NBC); Grand Central Station (CBS); The Shadow; Mystery Rogue's Gallery; The Fat Man; Screen Guild on the Air; Front Page Farrell; and Life Can Be Beautiful.

She has appeared on such television programs as The Nurses (CBS); The Defenders (CBS); Philco Television Playhouse (ABC); Mama (CBS); and Th. Guild on the Air.

STEWART, DONALD OGDEN.

Playwright, actor, author. b. Nov. 30, 1894, Columbus, Ohio, to Gilbert Holland and Clara (Ogden) Stewart. Father, attorney. Grad. Phillips Exeter Acad., 1912; Yale Univ., A.B. 1916. Married July 24, 1926, to Beatrice Ames (marr. dis. Oct. 1937); two sons; married Mar. 4, 1939, to Ella Winter. Served USNRF, 1917–19; rank, Chief Quartermaster. Member of Saville Club, London; Delta Kappa Epsilon.

Pre-Theatre. Author.

Theatre. Mr. Stewart made his N.Y.C. debut in the role of Nick Potter in *Holiday* (Plymouth Th., Nov. 26, 1928); subsequently wrote and also appeared as Les Crawford in *Rebound* (Plymouth, Feb. 3, 1930); wrote the book for the musical, *Fine and Dandy* (Erlanger, Sept. 23, 1930); and wrote *How I Wonder* (Hudson, Sept. 30, 1947).

He wrote *The Kidders* (Arts, London, Nov. 12, 1957); and *Honour Bright* (Lyric, Hammersmith, June 17, 1958).

Films. Mr. Stewart appeared as Van Dyck in *Not So Dumb* (MGM, 1930). From 1930–50 Mr. Stewart either wrote or collaborated on the screenplays for *Laughter* (Par., 1930); *Smilin' Through* (MGM, 1932); *White Sister* (MGM, 1933); *Going Hollywood* (MGM, 1933); *Dinner at Eight* (MGM, 1933); *The Barretts of Wimpole Street* (MGM, 1934); *Another Language* (MGM, 1935); *No More Ladies* (MGM, 1935); *Prisoner of Zenda* (UA, 1937); *Holiday* (Col., 1938); *Marie Antoinette* (MGM, 1938); *Love Affair* (RKO, 1939); *Kitty Foyle* (RKO, 1940); *The Philadelphia Story* (MGM, 1940); *That Uncertain Feeling* (UA, 1941); *A Woman's Face* (MGM, 1941); *Tales of Manhattan* (20th-Fox, 1942); *Keeper of the Flame* (MGM, 1942); *Without Love* (MGM, 1945); *Life with Father* (WB, 1947); *Cass Timberlaine* (MGM, 1947); and *Edward, My Son* (MGM, 1949).

Published Works. Mr. Stewart wrote *A Parody Outline of History* (1921); *Perfect Behavior* (1922); *Aunt Polly's Story of Mankind* (1923); *Mr. and Mrs. Haddock Abroad* (1924); *The Crazy Fool* (1925); *Mr. and Mrs. Haddock in Paris, France* (1926); *Father William* (1928); and *By a Stroke of Luck!* (1975).

Awards. Mr. Stewart won the Academy (Oscar) Award (1940) for best screenplay for the film version of *The Philadelphia Story*.

Recreation. Life.

STEWART, ELLEN.

Producer. b. Alexandria, La. Attended Arkansas State Univ. Address: La Mama Experimental Theatre Club, 74-A E. 4th St., New York, NY 10003.

Pre-Theatre. Designer of women's fashions.

Theatre. Miss Stewart is the founder (1962) and executive director of La Mama Experimental Theatre Club (N.Y.C.), one of the first of the off-off Bway groups, providing a testing ground for new plays and playwrights, as well as directors and actors. Over five hundred plays by nearly two hundred playwrights have been presented during the group's history as a private nonprofit organization. The first La Mama ETC presentation was an adaptation of Tennessee Williams' story, *One Arm* (July 1962). The first original play was *In a Corner of the Morning* (Aug. 1962) by Michael Locasio. The works of Harold Pinter were introduced to the US in Miss Stewart's production of *The Room* (Nov. 1962). Other playwrights of note who have had their works produced at La Mama ETC include Paul Foster; Leonard Melfi; Lanford Wilson (*The Rimers of Eldritch*); Israel Horovitz; Tom Eyen; Sam Shepard; Megan Terry (*Viet Rock*); Jean-Claude van Itallie (*America Hurrah*); Rochelle Owens; and Adrienne Kennedy.

Tom O'Horgan joined Miss Stewart's group in 1964, directing *Futz!* and *Tom Paine*, which were later produced successfully in the commercial theatre. He later directed the first European tour (1965) of plays from La Mama, which consisted of twenty-one works, including Sam Shepard's *Chicago*. The European tours have become an integral part of the theatre's activity, and Cafes La Mama now operate in London, Paris, Vancouver, South America, Australia, Indonesia, the Soviet Union, Lebanon, and Israel, all with the guidance and financial support of Miss Stewart.

The New York operation is currently housed in a six-story building containing two separate playing areas, and has additional space in an annex acquired in 1973, and consists of: The Troupe, which tours with completed works; The Ensemble, concentrating on new productions; and The Plexus, a training and performing company experimenting in new theatrical forms.

The facility also serves as a base for John Vaccaro's Play-House of the Ridiculous, several bilingual troupes and the Jarboro Co., composed of black actors. Miss Stewart also provides space and advisory services to The Native Amer. Th. Ensemble, presenting plays with, by, and for American Indians; and The Third World Institute of the Arts.

Other Activities. Until 1971, Miss Stewart supported her theatre activities by her work as a clothing designer. Early in La Mama's history, she operated a boutique as part of the theatre, where she sold her designs.

Awards. Miss Stewart, in behalf of La Mama ETC, has received grants from the Rockefeller, Ford and Kaplan foundations, and from the National Foundation for the Arts. She is the recipient of the Brandeis Award (1967); the Margo Jones Award (1968–69) for encouraging production of new playwrights; the NY State Council on the Arts Award (1973); the Fiorello La Guardia Award (1973) of the Center for NYC Affairs; a special Off-Bway (Obie) Award (1974–75) for off-off Bway achievement; and an honorary D.H.L. degree from Bard College (1975).

STEWART, MICHAEL.

Playwright. b. Aug. 1, 1929, New York City, to William E. and Kate (Dunitz) Rubin. Grad. Yale Univ., M.F.A. 1953. Member of Dramatists Guild. Address: c/o Linden & Deutsch, 110 E. 59th St., New York, NY 10022.

Theatre. Mr. Stewart has contributed sketches to *Shoestring Revue* (President Th., N.Y.C., Feb. 28, 1955); *Shoestring '57* (Barbizon-Plaza, Nov. 5, 1956); and *The Littlest Revue* (Phoenix, May 22, 1956).

He wrote the book for *Bye Bye Birdie* (Martin Beck Th., Apr. 14, 1960); *Carnival!* (Imperial, Apr. 13, 1961); *Hello, Dolly!* (St. James Th., Jan. 16, 1964); wrote the play *Those That Play the Clowns* (ANTA Th., Nov. 24, 1966); and the book for *George M!* (Palace, Apr. 10, 1968).

Television. Mr. Stewart wrote material for Caesar's Hour (NBC, 1955–59).

STEWART, PAULA.

Actress, singer. b. Dorothy Paula Zurndorfer, Apr. 9, 1933, Chicago, Ill., to Walter and Esther (Morris) Zurndorfer. Father, physician and surgeon; mother, actress, singer. Grad. Frances Shimer Girls Sch., Mt. Carroll, Ill., studied drama and music at Northwestern Univ., two years; voice with Helen Cahoon, N.Y.C., four years; acting with Sanford Meisner, Neighborhood Playhouse School of the Th., two years. Married Dec. 22, 1953, to Burt F. Bacharach, conductor and composer (marr. dis. May 9, 1958); married Mar. 30, 1961, to Jack Carter, entertainer (marr. dis. Feb. 1970); one son. Member of AEA; SAG; AFTRA; AGVA; Gamma Phi Beta sorority at Northwestern Univ.

Theatre. Miss Stewart was understudy for the role of Fiona in the national company of *Brigadoon* (opened Curran, San Francisco, Calif., Aug. 8, 1949); appeared as Julie Jordan in *Carousel* (State Fair Music Hall, Dallas, Tex., Summer 1955); sang Mimi in *La Bohème* (3 St. Settlement, N.Y.C., 1956); played Magnolia in *Show Boat*, and Marsinah in *Kismet* (Detroit, Mich., Summer 1956); Kathy in *The Student Prince*, appeared in *Hit the Deck*, and played Sarah in *Guys and Dolls* (St. Louis Municipal Opera, Mo., Summer 1956); joined (Sept. 4, 1957) the cast as Polly Peachum in *The Threepenny Opera* (Th. de Lys, N.Y.C., Sept. 20, 1955); played Rosabella in *The Most Happy Fella* (NY City Ctr., Feb. 10, 1959); and was a principal in the revue, *From A to Z* (Plymouth, Apr. 20, 1960).

She played the Lieutenant in *Operation Madball* (Bucks County Playhouse, New Hope, Pa., Summer 1960); Jane Jackson in *Wildcat* (Alvin, N.Y.C., Dec. 16, 1960); Audrey in *Let It Ride!* (Eugene O'Neill Th., Oct. 12, 1961); Angela Ballantine in *Critic's Choice* (Playhouse-in-the-Park, Philadelphia, Pa., Summer 1963); Belle and Baby in a tour of *Little Me* (Summer 1964); replaced (1965) Bernice Massi as Laurette Harrington in *What Makes Sammy Run?* (54 St. Th., N.Y.C., Feb. 27, 1964); and again played Belle and Baby in *Little Me* (Las Vegas, Mar. 1968).

Films. She played Carlotta in *Dairy of a Bachelor* (1963).

Television. She has performed as both singer and actress on the Ed Sullivan Show (CBS); Omnibus (NBC); the Jack Paar Show (NBC); *Bloomer Girl* (NBC); Route 66 (CBS); Diagnosis Unknown (CBS); Car 54, Where Are You? (NBC); the Joey Bishop Show (NBC); the Rudy Vallee Show (CBS); the Perry Mason series (CBS); Love, American Style (ABC); the Jackie Gleason Show (CBS); the Merv Griffin Show (CBS); appeared on *Love and Laughs: Three Comedians and Their Wives* (Open End, Ind., 1965); was a guest on the Alumni Fun series (CBS); On Broadway Tonight (CBS); Girl Talk (ABC); was a co-host of the *Miss American Teenager Contest* (Ind., Sept. 12, 1965); and appeared on the Lucy Show (CBS, 1970).

Night Clubs. She has appeared at the Versailles in *Nice to See You* (N.Y.C., 1953); at the Eden Roc (Miami, Fla., 1960); and the Fontainebleau (Miami, 1960); and at El Rancho (Las Vegas, Nev., 1960).

Discography. Miss Stewart recorded an album entitled The Gershwin Years (Decca, 1960).

Recreation. Flying, riding, motorcycling, water skiing, designing and sewing, decorating.

STICKNEY, DOROTHY.

Actress. b. Dorothy Hayes Stickney, June 21, 1900, Dickinson, N.D., to Victor Hugo and Margaret (Hayes) Stickney. Father, physician. Attended St. Catherine's Coll., 1919–20; grad. Northwestern Dramatic Sch., Minneapolis, Minn., 1921. Studied acting with Christine Brooks (two years). Married Aug. 13, 1927, to Howard Lindsay, playwright, actor, producer. Member of AEA; AFTRA; SAG; Actors' Fund; Cosmopolitan Club; theatre representative for Zonta International. Address: 13 E. 94th St.,

New York, NY 10028, tel. (212) SA 2-4428.

Pre-Theatre. Dance teacher.

Theatre. Miss Stickney made her debut as an actress-singer-dancer-musician in a quartet known as "The Southern Belles" (Summer 1921).

She made her N.Y.C. debut as Anita in *The Squall* (48 St. Th., Nov. 11, 1926); played Liz in *Chicago* (Music Box, Dec. 30, 1926); Claudia Kitts in *March Hares* (Little, Apr. 2, 1928); Cherry in *The Beaux' Stratagem* (Hampden's Th., June 4, 1928); Mollie Molloy in *The Front Page* (Times Square Th., Aug. 14, 1928); Rose Sibley in *Milestones* (Empire, June 2, 1930); Miss Krail in *Philip Goes Forth* (Biltmore, Jan. 12, 1931); Mincing in *The Way of the World* (Guild, June 1, 1931); Stella Hallam in *Another Language* (Booth, Apr. 25, 1932); Lorena Watkins in *The County Chairman* (Natl., May 25, 1936); and Granny in *On Borrowed Time* (Longacre, Feb. 3, 1938).

She played Vinnie in *Life with Father*, in which her husband played Clare (Empire, Nov. 8, 1939); Vinnie in *Life with Mother* (Empire, Oct. 20, 1948); Laura Mitchell in *The Small Hours* (Natl., Feb. 15, 1951); Dolly in *To Be Continued* (Booth, Apr. 23, 1952); Margaret Munson in *Kind Sir* (Alvin, Nov. 4, 1952); and Maggie in *The Honeys* (Longacre, Apr. 28, 1955).

Her one-woman show, *A Lovely Light*, premiered at the Barter Th. (Abingdon, Va., Sept. 1958), was presented in N.Y. (Hudson, Feb. 8, 1960), in London (Globe, June 9, 1960), toured the US (1960–62), and was revived in N.Y. (Mayfair, Jan. 6, 1964).

She played Katie Delaney in *The Riot Act* (Cort, Mar. 7, 1963); appeared in the revival of *Life with Father* (NY City Ctr., Oct. 1967); as Mrs. Ryan in *The Mundy Scheme* (Royale Th. Oct. 1969); and as Berthé in *Pippin* (Imperial Th., June 1973).

Films. Miss Stickney has appeared in *Working Girls* (Par., 1931); *The Little Minister* (RKO, 1934); *Murder at the Vanities* (Par., 1934); *I Met My Love Again* (UA, 1938); *What a Life* (Par., 1939); *The Uninvited* (Par., 1944); *The Catered Affair* (MGM, 1956); *The Remarkable Mr. Pennypacker* (20th-Fox, 1959); *I Never Sang for My Father* (Col., 1970), and others.

Television. She played Abbey in *Arsenic and Old Lace*, the Queen Mother in Rodgers and Hammerstein's *Cinderella*, in which her husband played the King, and appeared on Camera Three (CBS).

Her one-woman show, *A Lovely Light*, was presented on WNEW for The Festival of the Performing Arts (Apr. 17, Apr. 22, 1962).

She also appeared in *Certain Honorable Men* (NBC); *Bingo Twice a Week* (Norman Corwin Presents, Sept. 1971); and *The Homecoming* (CBS).

Published Works. Miss Stickney has published six poems: "You're Not the Type," "My Dressing Room," "My Love and I in a Hansom Cab," "My Little Room," "My Someday House," and "Blue Paradise.".

Awards. She received the Barter Th. Award and the NY Drama League Medal for her performance as Vinnie in *Life with Father* (1940); an honorary M.A. from Bowdoin Coll. (1951); the March of Dimes Award, 1968; and an M.A. degree from Dickinson State Coll., N.D. (1968).

Recreation. Collecting music boxes, fairy lights, gardening.

STIEFEL, MILTON. Director, actor, producer. b. May 15, 1900, New York City, to Adolph and Bertha Stiefel. Father, singer. Attended DeWitt Clinton H.S., N.Y.C. Relative in theatre: brother, H. Irving Stiefel, business manager. Member of COST (bd. of dir., 1962–to date, pres., 1929–52 when it was the Summer Stock Th. Assn.); AEA; ATPAM. Address: (home) Wellington Hotel, Seventh Ave. and 55th St., New York, NY 10019, tel. (212) CI 7-3900; (bus.) The Ivoryton Playhouse, Ivoryton, CT 06442, tel. (203) SO 7-8250.

Theatre. Mr. Stiefel was assistant stage manager for *Chu Chin Chow* (Manhattan Opera House, Oct. 22, 1917), and on tour was stage manager and played the Lover (1919); then was director, and played the Lover and the Cobbler (1920–1923).

He joined the E. H. Sothern and Julia Marlowe Shakespearean (repertory) Co., and at the Jolson Th., N.Y.C., his roles included a Servant to Petruchio in *The Taming of the Shrew* (Oct. 15, 1923); the Second Gravedigger in *Hamlet* (Oct. 15, 1923); a Serenade Singer in *The Merchant of Venice* (Nov. 5, 1923); and Gregory in *Romeo and Juliet* (Nov. 12, 1923). He was stage manager for and appeared with the Jessie Bonstelle Stock Co. (Detroit, Mich., 1924–25); was stage manager for *Accused* (Belasco, N.Y.C., Sept. 29, 1925); and *What Never Dies* (Lyceum, Dec. 28, 1926); directed the Margaret Anglin production of *Electra* (Gallo, Dec. 1, 1927); was company manager for the *Russian Royal Choir* (N.Y.C., 1928); and *The Passion Play* (NY Hippodrome, 1928); and was general manager for the touring company of *The Miracle* (1928–1929).

Mr. Stiefel founded the summer stock theatre, The Ivoryton Playhouse, Conn., where he is director and producer (1930–to date). Katharine Hepburn started her career here under Mr. Stiefel's direction in 1931.

He directed *First Night* (Eltinge, N.Y.C., Nov. 26, 1930); and *Unexpected Husband* (48 St. Th., June 2, 1931); in stock, directed at the Cedarhurst Th., N.Y. (1931); directed *Her Tin Soldier* (Playhouse, N.Y.C., Apr. 6, 1933); produced, with Frank Lewis, *Another Love*, which he also directed (Vanderbilt, Mar. 19, 1934); directed *I Must Love Someone* (Longacre Th., Feb. 7, 1939); and *Horse Fever* (Mansfield, Nov. 23, 1940).

He was affiliated with the USO as emcee and manager for the play *You Can't Take It with You* (1942), and as manager for the *USO Show* (1946). He was producer-director at the Capitol Th. (St. Petersburg, Fla., Winter 1953); and director at the Margo Jones Th. (Dallas, Tex., Winter 1959).

Films. Mr. Stiefel was dialogue and test director on *Curly* (Col., 1943), and *Mr. Winkle Goes to War* (Col., 1944); and appeared in *Whiplash* (WB, 1948).

Awards. He received a citation from US Navy for "cooperation in entertainment field during WW II.".

Recreation. Photography, boating.

STINE, LAWRENCE. Educator. b. Lawrence Carl Stine, May 16, 1912, near Shelbyville, Indiana, to Carl W. and Dosie (Spellman) Stine. Father, timber buyer. Grad. Edinburg (Ind.) H.S., 1930; Indiana Bus. Coll., 1941; attended Indiana Univ., 1944–45; grad. Butler Univ., B.A. 1947; State Univ. of Iowa, M.A. 1951, Ph.D. 1962. Served US Army, 1942–43; rank, T/5. Member of ATA; SAA; CSSA; SDSA; Alpha Psi Omega (advisor for Lambda Sigma Chap.); Tau Kappa Alpha; Phi Kappa Phi; Pi Gamma Mu; Omega Tau Alpha. Address: (home) West 18th St., Brookings, SD 57006, tel. (605) 692-5488; (bus.) c/o College of Arts and Science, South Dakota State Univ., Brookings, SD 57006, tel. (605) 688-4723.

Mr. Stine became associate dean of the College of Arts and Science at South Dakota State Univ. in 1969. He became director of theatre there in 1952, when he joined the university faculty as instructor, subsequently holding the posts of assistant professor (1953–61), associate professor (1961–63), and professor and head of the department of speech (1963–69).

Theatre. He directed and appeared in his own play, *Magdala Speaks*, which was produced in Edinburg, Ind.

Awards. He received a Certificate of Outstanding Teaching from South Dakota State Univ. (1958–59).

Recreation. Music, reading drama literature, attending theatre "from local high school productions to the foremost professional productions in the country.".

STITT, MILAN. Playwright, producer, theatre administrator. b. Detroit, Mich., Feb. 9, 1941, to Howard Milan and Audrien (Prindle) Stitt. Father, educator. Grad. Univ. of Michigan, B.A. 1963; Yale Univ. Drama School, M.F.A. 1966. Studied playwriting with Kenneth Rowe and John Gassner. Married 1962 to Lenore Richars (marr. dis. 1965). Member of Dramatists Guild; Off-Off Broadway Alliance. Address: 412 W. 20th St., New York, NY 10011.

Theatre. While studying at the Univ. of Michigan, Mr. Stitt played the role of George in *Our Town* (tour, Switzerland, Experiment in International Living, Summer 1961). Later he worked as drama critic for the *Detroit Free Press*, 1961–63; was assistant press representative for the American Shakespeare Festival, Summer 1965; projects director for the Long Wharf Th., 1965–66; special projects director for the American Shakespeare Festival, 1967–68; and development co-ordinator for the American Place Th., 1968–70.

On off-Bway, he co-produced *Kiss Now* (Martinique Th., N.Y.C., 1970); and on off-off Bway, for the Triad Playwrights Co., of which he was a founder and executive director, he produced four plays: *The Girl Who Loved the Beatles* (Lincoln Center Library Auditorium, Summer 1974); *Triad Singles* (Stage One, Summer 1975); *When I Lived in Baton Rouge* (Direct Th., Oct. 1975); and *Coconut Beach* (Direct Th., Feb. 1976).

With Victor Miller, Mr. Stitt wrote *In the Pursuit* (Hofbrau Haus, N.Y.C., Fall 1967). He is also the author of *Edie's Home*, which was produced by Triad Playwrights Co. (Stage One, N.Y.C., Aug. 1975) and on radio (WBAI, N.Y.C., Dec. 1975).

His play *The Runner Stumbles* was first developed in the Boston Univ. Playwrights Workshop at the Berkshire Th. Festival (Aug. 1970) and was further developed in a showcase production (Manhattan Th. Club, N.Y.C., Dec. 1974). It had its world premiere at the Hartman Th. Company (Stamford, Conn., Dec. 30, 1975) and was produced on Bway (Little Th., N.Y.C., May 18, 1976).

Published Works. *The Runner Stumbles* was published in 1976.

Awards. He has received the Avery Hopwood Playwriting Award (1962; 1963); and *The Runner Stumbles* was included in *Best Plays of 1975–76*..

Recreation. Cooking, plants.

STIX, JOHN. Director. b. John Morris Stix, Nov. 14, 1920, St. Louis, Mo., to Ernest W. and Erma (Kingsbacher) Stix. Father, manufacturer. Grad. John Burroughs School, St. Louis, 1938; Black Mountain Coll., 1942; Yale Univ., M.F.A., 1949. Served US Army Signal Corps, ETO, 1942–45. Member of Actors Studio; AEA; SSD&C; Natl. Th. Conf. Address: Route 9W, Nyack, NY 10960.

Theatre. Mr. Stix first appeared on stage as the Son in a St. Louis (Mo.) Community Th. production of *The Little Clay Cart* (1928); and appeared as a walk-on in *The Drunkard* (Milford Playhouse, Conn., 1939). He stage managed an Actors Laboratory production of *Home of the Brave* (Las Palmas Th., Los Angeles, Calif., July 22, 1946), and was a member of the resident company at the Ridgefield (Conn.) Summer Th. (June–Aug. 1947).

He directed *The Shoemaker's Prodigious Wife* (Provincetown Playhouse, N.Y.C., June 1949), where he also directed *The Father* (July 1949), and *Earth Spirit* (June 1950); directed *Mary Rose* (ANTA, Mar. 4, 1951); *The Animal Kingdom* (Westport Country Playhouse, Conn., June 1951); *Jane* (Maplewood Playhouse, N.J., July 1952); *In the Summer House* for the Ann Arbor (Mich.) Drama Festival (Lydia Mendelssohn Th., Apr. 1953); *Take a Giant Step* (Lyceum, N.Y.C., Sept. 24, 1953); at the Falmouth (Mass.) Playhouse, the Helen Hayes Festival of Plays, including: *What Every Woman Knows*, *Mrs. McThing*, *Mary of Scotland*, and *The Wisteria Trees* (Summer 1954); *What Every Woman Knows* (Huntington Hartford Th., Los Angeles, Sept. 1954; NY City Ctr., Dec. 22, 1954); and at the NY City Ctr., directed *The Wisteria Trees* (Feb. 2, 1955), and William Marshall's *Othello* (Sept. 7, 1955).

He directed *Othello* (Brattle Th., Cambridge, Mass., 1956); *Too Late the Phalarope* (Belasco, N.Y.C., Oct. 11, 1956); summer tours of *Caesar and Cleopatra*, and *An Epitaph for George Dillon* (1950);

and the pre-Bway tryout of *There Must Be a Pony* (opened Paper Mill Playhouse, Millburn, N.J., July 16, 1962). Served as artistic director, Baltimore Center Stage (1969–74) where he directed *Journey of the Fifth Horse, A Doll's House, A Cry of Players, Park, The Trial of the Catonsville Nine, Fire in the Mindhouse, Slow Dance on the Killing Ground, Andorra, Hot L Baltimore,* and *Who's Afraid of Virginia Woolf?*. The production of *Slow Dance* was transferred to the Sheridan Sq. Playhouse (N.Y.C., May 1971).

Films. He was assistant director to Hans Richter for *Dreams That Money Can Buy* (1948); and, with Charles Guggenheim, directed *St. Louis Bank Robbery* (Guggenheim Associates, 1957). Mr. Stix is co-author of the screen adaptation of Elia Kazan's *The Assassins.*.

Television. Mr. Stix directed ten Omnibus (NBC) productions, including; *Duchess and the Smugs* (1953); *Hilde and the Turnpike* (1953); and *Birth of Modern Times* (1956); and directed *The Master Builder* (Play of the Week, WNTA, 1960).

Other Activities. He was visiting lecturer at Yale and Columbia universities, Brooklyn and Goucher colleges; artistic administrator of the Lee Strasberg Th. Institute (1969–70); and a member of the faculty at Juilliard Drama Division (1975–to date).

Recreation. Riding, tennis, photography.

STODDARD, HAILA. Actress, director, producer. b. Nov. 14, 1913, Great Falls, Montana, to George Ogden and Ivy (Leavitt) Stoddard. Father, efficiency expert. Grad. Los Angeles (Calif.) H.S., 1930; Univ. of Southern Calif., B.S. 1934. Married 1930 (marr. dis. 1934); married Apr. 3, 1938, to Jack Kirkland, playwright (marr. dis. 1947); one son, one daughter; married 1948 to Harold Bromley, State Dept. official (marr. dis. 1954); one son; married 1956 to Whitfield Connor, actor. Member of AEA; AFTRA; SAG; Pi Beta Phi; Zetz Phi Eta. Address: Ladder Hill South, Weston, CT 06880, tel. (203) 277-8227.

Theatre. Miss Stoddard was understudy to the ingenue role in *Merrily We Roll Along* (Belasco Th., Los Angeles, 1934); subsequently played Pearl in a cross-country tour of *Tobacco Road* (1935–36); and at the Ivoryton (Conn.) Playhouse, appeared in ten productions (Summers 1936–37), including *Jazz Age, Idiot's Delight, The Old Maid* and *Sailor Beware.*

She succeeded (Sept. 1937) Peggy Conklin as Ellen Murray in *Yes, My Darling Daughter* (Playhouse, N.Y.C., Feb. 9, 1937); played Nina in *A Woman's a Fool— To Be Clever* (Natl., Oct. 18, 1938); Rita in *I Know What I Like* (Hudson, Nov. 24, 1939); Agnes Keefe in *Kindred* (Maxine Elliott's Th., Dec. 26, 1939); and Sister Suzanna Leeds in *Suzanna and the Elders* (Morosco, Oct. 29, 1940). During this period, she played three seasons of stock at the Bucks County Playhouse (New Hope, Pa., Summers 1939–41), including roles in *The Philadelphia Story, Petticoat Fever, Our Betters, Skylark, The Play's the Thing, Golden Boy, Mr. and Mrs. North,* and *Biography.*

She played Lydia Languish in *The Rivals* (Shubert, Jan. 14, 1942), and on tour; Mariah Meade in *The Moon Vine* (Morosco, N.Y.C., Feb. 11, 1943); Elvira in *Blithe Spirit* (Morosco, Sept. 16, 1943), and on tour; toured the South Pacific as Lorraine Sheldon in a USO production of *The Man Who Came to Dinner* (1944–45); and produced *Clover Ring* (Plymouth Th., Boston, Feb. 5–10, 1945); produced, with Joseph M. Hyman and Bernard Hart, *The Secret Room* (Royale, N.Y.C., Nov. 7, 1945); and with Jack Kirkland, Mr. Kirkland's play, *Georgia Boy* (Copley Th., Boston, Dec. 29, 1945–Jan. 5, 1946).

Miss Stoddard succeeded (1946) Betty Field as Georgina Allerton in *Dream Girl* (Coronet, N.Y.C., Dec. 14, 1945); and toured in the role (1947); played Katie in *Rip Van Winkle* (NY City Ctr., July 15, 1947); toured as Joan in *Joan of Lorraine* (1947), in *The Trial of Mary Dugan* (1947), and as Sally in *The Voice of the Turtle* (1947); played Lee Manning in *Doctor Social* (Booth, N.Y.C., Feb. 11, 1948); re-created her roles in stock productions of *Dream Girl* (1948) and *The Voice of the Turtle* (1948); and played in stock tours of *Goodbye, My Fancy* (Summer 1949) and as Simone in *Her Cardboard Lover* (Summer 1949).

She played Mrs. Jelliwell in *Springtime for Henry* (John Golden Th., N.Y.C., Mar. 14, 1951, and on tour); Ethel Nash in *Glad Tidings* (Lyceum, N.Y.C., Oct. 11, 1951, and on tour); and succeeded (early 1952) Celeste Holm as Irene Elliott in *Affairs of State* (Royale, N.Y.C., Sept. 25, 1950, and on tour); played Lily Garland in a stock tour of *Twentieth Century* (Summer 1952); at the Memphis, Tenn., Arena Th., played Maud Abbott in *Glad Tidings* (Nov. 18, 1952) and Marion Froude in *Biography* (Nov. 25, 1952); appeared in 10 productions at Elitch Gardens (Denver, Colo., 1953).

She played Kay Allen in *The Frogs of Spring* (Broadhurst, N.Y.C., Oct. 20, 1953); produced, with Harold Bromley, *Dead Pigeon* (Vanderbilt, Dec. 23, 1953); appeared in three plays at the British Colonial Th. (1954); produced *One Eye Closed* (Bijou, N.Y.C., Nov. 24, 1954), taking over the role played by Constance Ford on opening night, due to Miss Ford's illness; succeeded (Apr. 25, 1955) Mary Anderson as Marian Harrison in *Lunatics and Lovers* (Broadhurst, Dec. 13, 1954), and later directed the touring production (1955); was standby for the title role in *Auntie Mame* (Broadhurst, N.Y.C., Oct. 3, 1956), eventually playing the role (June 1958) during Greer Garson's illness; with her husband, Whitfield Connor, played Helen in *Ever Since Paradise* (Carnegie Recital Hall, July 11, 1957); played Edith Rollo in *Patate* (Henry Miller's Th., Oct. 28, 1958); and adapted (with Tamara Geva) and produced (with Michael Davis and Helen Bonfils) *Come Play with Me* (York, Apr. 30, 1959), based on Marcel Achard's play, *Voulez-vous jouer avec moi?*

Miss Stoddard produced, with Helen Bonfils and Michael Davis, *A Thurber Carnival* (ANTA, Feb. 26, 1960), its national tour, and the London production (Savoy, Apr. 11, 1962).

With Miss Bonfils, she formed Bonard Productions, which produced, in association with Charles Russell, *Sail Away* (Broadhurst, N.Y.C., Oct. 3, 1961), its national tour, and the London production (Savoy, June 21, 1962); Bonard produced, with Henry Sherek, *The Affair* (Henry Miller's Th., N.Y.C., Sept. 20, 1962); *The Hollow Crown* (Henry Miller's Th., Jan. 29, 1963); *The Beast in Me* (Plymouth, May 16, 1963), which Miss Stoddard conceived; Miss Stoddard succeeded (Sept. 18, 1963) Elaine Stritch as Martha in the matinee company of *Who's Afraid of Virginia Woolf?* (Billy Rose Th., Oct. 13, 1962); Bonard presented a tour of *The Hollow Crown* (opened McCarter Th., Princeton, N.J., Dec. 30, 1963; closed Univ. of Md., College Park, Md., Apr. 25, 1964); presented, in association with Howard Atlee, a double-bill of *Dark Corners* (in which Miss Stoddard played Charlotte) and *Mr. Grossman* (Actors Playhouse, N.Y.C., May 5, 1964); presented, with Donald Seawell, The Royal Shakespeare Co. in *King Lear* (May 18, 1964) and *The Comedy of Errors* (May 20, 1964) at the NY State Th.; and presented, in association with Kathleen and Justin Sturm, *That Hat!* (Th. Four, Sept. 23, 1964).

Miss Stoddard presented, with Mark Wright and Leonard S. Field, *The Birthday Party* (Booth, Oct. 3, 1967); with Mr. Wright and Duane Wilder, *Private Lives* (Th. de Lys, May 19, 1968); with Messrs. Wright and Wilder, *The Gingham Dog* (John Golden Th., Apr. 23, 1969); with Messrs. Wright and Wilder, *The Last Sweet Days of Isaac* (Eastside Playhouse, Jan. 26, 1970); with Messrs. Wright and Wilder, *Lemon Sky* (Playhouse, May 17, 1970); she presented, with Neal Du Brock, *The Survival of Saint Joan* (Anderson, Feb. 28, 1971); and, with Arnold H. Levy, *Lady Audley's Secret* (Eastside Playhouse, Oct. 3, 1972).

Miss Stoddard adapted, with William Teitel, from the works of Ring Lardner, *A Round with Ring* (ANTA Matinee Series, Th. de Lys, Oct. 27, 1969), which she co-directed with Darwin Knight.

Television and Radio. Miss Stoddard played Sue Evans Miller, the little sister, on the radio serial Big Sister (CBS, 1937–39).

For sixteen years, she appeared as Pauline on the television serial The Secret Storm (CBS, premiere Feb. 1, 1954); as well as performing on Studio One (CBS, 1950); Philco Playhouse (NBC); Prudential Playhouse (CBS); Goodyear Playhouse (NBC); Kraft Th. (NBC); The Web (CBS); US Steel Hour (CBS); and Robert Montgomery Presents (NBC).

Recreation. Cooking ("expert in any language").

STOLZ, DON. Producer, director. b. Donald Dixon Stolz, July 12, 1919, Castleton, Kans., to Fred and Dorothy (Cooper) Stolz. Father, clergyman. Attended Waynoka (Okla.) H.S., 1930–31; grad. Guthrie (Okla.) H.S., 1932; grad. Oklahoma City Univ., B.A., B.F.A. 1938; Northwestern Univ., M.A. (theatre) 1940. Served WW II. USN, PTO; rank, Lt. Married June, 1944, to Joan Fuller; five sons; one daughter (dec. 1955). Relatives in theatre: sons, Peter, Thomas, Donald, Tim, and John Stolz, actors. Member of AEA; AFTRA (bd. member, Twin City, Minn. local, 1958–59; pres., 1960); Rotary Club; Blue Key; Lambda Chi Alpha; National Collegiate Players. Address: Old Log Theatre, Box 250, Excelsior, MN 55331, tel. (612) GR 4-5951.

Theatre. Mr. Stolz first appeared as the Christ Child in a religious play presented at his father's church (1921); subsequently performed with several tent shows; and played the Juvenile in a production of *Down East* (July 1935).

He joined the Old Log Theatre, Excelsior, Minn., as director and actor (1940). The first play he directed there was *Ned McCobb's Daughter.* He purchased the theatre (1946), designed scenery, acted in almost every play, managed the theatre, and directed every play (approximately 300 plays, 1946–60). He built a new theatre (1960), which is currently in year-round operation.

Other Activities. Mr. Stolz has been a speech teacher, a writer, and producer, and a director of sales meetings and industrial shows.

Recreation. Painting, tennis, swimming.

STONE, EZRA. Director, actor, producer, writer, teacher, farmer. b. Ezra Chaim Feinstone, Dec. 2, 1917, New Bedford, Mass., to Solomon and Rose (Meadow) Feinstone. Father, chemist, teacher. Grad. Oak Lane Country Day Sch. of Temple Univ., Philadelphia, Pa., 1934; and AADA, 1935; extension courses at Columbia Univ., 1935–38; City Coll. of New York, 1936–38. Married Oct. 5, 1942, to Sara Seegar, actress; one son, one daughter. Relatives in theatre: sisters-in-law, Dorothy Seegar, singer, actress; Miriam Seegar, actress; brother-in-law, Tim Whelan, producer-director, writer; nephew, Tim Whelan, Jr. producer, director, screenwriter. Served US Army, Special Services, 1940–43; rank, Staff Sgt.; USAAF, 1943–46; rank, M/Sgt. Director of USO Camp shows, 1948. Member of AEA; SAG; AGVA; WGA, East; WGA, West; AFTRA; Radio and TV Directors' Guild; SDG; SDIG; AADA; SSD&C (secy., 1960); TV Producers' Guild; Dramatists Guild; ANTA; Acad. TV Arts & Sciences; Actors' Fund of America; Radio Pioneers of America; Amer. Legion; Amer. Veterans' Committee; Air Force Society; Pennsylvania Assn. of Rescue Squads; Newton Reliance Co.; Ayrshire Breeders' Assn.; Dairy Herd Improvement Assn.; Sacred Order of Old Bastards, Ft. Lauderdale, Fla.; Committee on Economic Development (Radio & TV comm. 1955); Amer. Assn. for the UN. Address: (home) 2100 Castilian Dr., Hollywood, CA 90028, tel. (213) HO 7-9777; Stone Meadows Farm, Newton, Bucks Co., PA 18940, tel. (215) WO 8-3709; (bus.) c/o Peter Witt Assoc., Inc., 37 W. 57th St., New York, NY 10019; General Artists Corp., c/o Irving Salkow, 1801 Ave. of the Stars, Beverly Hills, CA 90212.

Theatre. Mr. Stone first appeared on stage at age seven as a Young Child in both *Phosphorus* and *Suppressed Desires* (YMHA Players, Philadelphia, 1924); made his professional debut with the repertory company, the Natl. Junior Th. of Washington, D.C., touring the East Coast (1924–31) in such roles as Incas the Younger in *The Last of the Mohicans,*

Georgie in *Quality Street,* Sid Sawyer in *Tom Sawyer* (Alvin, N.Y.C., Dec. 25, 1931), and Jim Hawkins in *Treasure Island* (Alvin, Jan. 5, Jan. 7, 1932); performed in a Plays and Players Club production of *The Flower Seller* (Philadelphia, Pa., 1929); and toured in a vaudeville act (Steel Pier, Atlantic City, N.J.; Keith's Th., Wilmington, Del., 1932).

He made his Bway debut in seven roles in the revue, *Parade* (Guild, May 20, 1935); subsequently appeared as Abie Applebaum in the pre-Bway tryout of *Room Service* (closed Philadelphia, Pa., 1935); Studio Messenger in a touring production of *Ah, Wilderness!* (Sept. 1935); played Ed in *Oh Evening Star!* (Empire, N.Y.C., Jan. 8, 1936); succeeded (June 1936) Hayden Rorke as Al in *Three Men on a Horse* (Playhouse, N.Y.C., Jan. 30, 1935); played "Mistol" Bottome in *Brother Rat* (Biltmore, Dec. 16, 1936), and directed the touring productions; succeeded William Mendrek as the Bank Messenger in *Room Service* (Cort, N.Y.C., May 19, 1937), which he directed on tour; Henry Aldrich in *What a Life* (Biltmore, N.Y.C., Apr. 13, 1938), later directing the touring company; and joined the Castas Dromio during the run of *The Boys From Syracuse* (Alvin, N.Y.C., Nov. 23, 1938).

He directed *See My Lawyer* (Biltmore, Sept. 27, 1939), in which he succeeded (Feb. 1940) Milton Berle as Arthur Lee; directed with Herbert Berghof, the revue *Reunion in New York* (Little, Feb. 21, 1940); and directed a summer tryout of *Your Loving Son,* in which he appeared as Joshua Winslow, Jr. (Brattle, Cambridge, Mass., 1940).

Mr. Stone directed and appeared in US Army Special Services touring productions of *We're Ready, First Year, Brother Rat, Three Men on a Horse,* and *Six Jerks in a Jeep;* directed *This Is the Army* (Bway Th., N.Y.C., July 4, 1942) and on tour; directed *Salvo* (Metropolitan Opera House, N.Y.C., 1943); the tours of the Air Force revues, *Bonds Away* (1943), *At Your Service* (1943), and *You Bet Your Life* (1943); *January Thaw* (John Golden Th., N.Y.C., Feb. 4, 1946); *Me and Molly* (Belasco, Feb. 26, 1948); *To Tell You the Truth* (New Stages Th., Apr. 18, 1948); played Sir Epicure Mammon in *The Alchemist* (NY City Ctr., May 6, 1948); directed *At War with the Army* (Booth, Mar. 8, 1949); and appeared as Tony Lumpkin in *She Stoops to Conquer* (NY City Ctr., Dec. 29, 1949).

He directed the pre-Bway tryouts of *The Man That Corrupted Hadleyburg* (opened Erlanger, Philadelphia, Pa., Apr. 1951; closed there Apr. 1951); *Count Your Blessings* (Bucks County Playhouse, New Hope, Pa., Summer 1952); *Blue Danube* (Bucks County Playhouse, Summer 1952); staged *The Pink Elephant* (Playhouse, N.Y.C., Apr. 22, 1953); directed the summer touring companies of *Loco* (1953); and *The Play's the Thing* (1953); directed the pre-Bway tryout of the Theatre Guild production of *Comin' Thru the Rye* (Olney Th., Md., Summer 1953); at the Bucks County Playhouse (New Hope, Pa.), directed *Blithe Spirit* (Summer 1954); and *Mrs. Gibbon's Boys* (Summer 1955); directed the tent ice show version of *On the Town* adapted from the musical (opened Asbury Park, N.J., 1956; closed Lambertville, N.J., 1956); and staged *Wake Up Darling* (Ethel Barrymore Th., N.Y.C., May 2, 1956).

Mr. Stone directed the pre-Bway tryout of the musical, *The Mistress of the Inn,* based on the play of the same name (Bucks County Playhouse, New Hope, Pa., Summer 1956); directed a stock production of *Season in the Sun* (Bucks County Playhouse, Summer 1957); staged a summer tryout of *Half in Earnest* (Bucks County Playhouse, June 17, 1957); appeared as the Son-in-Law in a stock production of *The Middle of the Night* (Bucks County Playhouse, Summer 1958); directed Ethel Barrymore Colt in a one-woman show, *Curtains Up!* (ANTA matinee theatre series, Th. de Lys, Dec. 16, 1958); played Banjo in *The Man Who Came to Dinner* and Maxwell Archer in *Once More, With Feeling* (Bucks County Playhouse, Summer 1959); and directed *Curtains Up!* (East 74 St. Th., Nov. 2, 1959).

He was director of the West Coast tryout of *Only Game in Town* (opened Ivar Th., Hollywood, Calif. closed there 1960); appeared as Capt. Andy in *Show Boat* (Cape Cod Melody Tent, Hyannis, Mass., Summer 1960); at the Sombrero Playhouse (Phoenix, Ariz.), directed *Dear Ruth* (Feb. 1962) and *Come Blow Your Horn* (Feb. 1963); staged and produced the IBM industrial show entitled *100 Percent Club* (San Francisco, Calif., Mar. 1963; N.Y.C., July 1964); directed a benefit performance of *Tunnel of Love* (Biltmore, Los Angeles, Calif., Mar. 1963); a summer tryout of *God Bless Our Bank* (opened Charlotte, N.C., June 1963; closed Westport Country Playhouse, Conn.); and a stock production of *Fallen Angels* (La Jolla Playhouse, Calif., Aug. 1963).

Films. Mr. Stone played Ally Bangs in *Those Were the Days* (Par., 1940); appeared in *This Is the Army* (WB, 1943); did the live-action staging for *The Daydreamer* (Embassy, 1966); and was one of the directors of *Tammy and the Millionaire* (U, 1967).

Television and Radio. Mr. Stone first did commercials in Philadelphia (1932–34) for *Children's Hour* (WPEN), Young America (WCAU 1932–34), and for the Tasty Yeast Program (NBC-Red Network, N.Y.C., 1934–35). From 1938–40, he appeared on the Rudy Vallee Show (NBC), Kate Smith Show (CBS), Eddie Cantor Show (NBC), Fred Allen Show (NBC), Walter O'Keefe Show (NBC), Jack Benny Show (NBC), Norman Corwin Show (CBS), Kay Kayser Show (NBC), Stoopnagle and Bud (CBS), We the People (CBS), Hobby Lobby (CBS), Edgar Bergen Show (NBC), and Lux Radio Th. (CBS). He created and played Henry on The Aldrich Family series (NBC, 1938–41; CBS, 1945–51); and performed on The Eternal Light series (NBC, 1951–to date).

He first appeared on television in an FCC demonstration, as Henry in The Aldrich Family (NBC, 1940); subsequently was producer and/or director of the Olsen and Johnson Buick Show (NBC, 1948–49), for which he also wrote sketches: Li'l Abner (ABC, 1948); The Aldrich Family (NBC, 1949); Danny Thomas Show (NBC, 1950–51); Martha Raye Show (NBC, 1950–51); Fred Allen Show, for which he wrote sketches (NBC, 1950–51); Ed Wynn Show (NBC, 1950–51); Colgate Comedy Hour with Herb Shriner (NBC, 1950–51); Ezio Pinza Show, for which he wrote sketches (NBC, 1950–51); Life with Father (CBS, 1952); Love That Guy (CBS, 1953); Auto Light Easter Parade (CBS, 1953); I Married Joan (NBC, 1954–55); Joe and Mabel (CBS, 1955–56); Caesar's Hour, for which he was also sketch editor (NBC, 1956); a special, *Command Performance* with Ed Wynn, for which Mr. Stone wrote, with Larry Gelbhardt, the script (NBC, 1957); a special, *Command Performance* with Ethel Barrymore (NBC, 1958); *4 and 20 Buddahs* (Coronado 9, Syndicated, 1959); *Kelly and the College Man* (Bachelor Father, NBC, 1959); and Angel (CBS, 1960).

He directed *Affairs of Anatol* (CBS, 1961); produced and directed The Hathaways (ABC, 1961), for which he wrote, with Rick Dorio, the episodes, *Swami Chimp* and *A Man for Amanda* (1961); produced the Shari Lewis Show (NBC, 1962); and produced and directed the Shari Lewis Show (NBC, May 1963); and directed the IBM industrials "*. . . a better way*" (1963) and *Area for Action* (1963). He directed *Wake Up Darling* and *Time for Elizabeth* (Bob Hope Presents, NBC, Feb.–Mar. 1964); and the series, My Living Doll (CBS, 1964–65). He produced and directed *Take Five* (July 1964); and *The Know How People* (Oct. 1964), for IBM Processing Div.

Mr. Stone has appeared in *Deuteronomy Katz* (NBC, 1952); *Tvye* (NBC, 1953); on the Faye Emerson Show (CBS, 1954); as Urial in *Trial of Urial* (NBC, 1959); Rabbitt in *Kim Quixote* (Hawaiian Eye, ABC, 1960); and in *Flashback* (CBS, Can., 1963).

He has also been a consultant for WUNC-TV (Chapel Hill, N.C., 1955), WHYY-TV (Philadelphia, 1958), and the Educational Radio and TV Center, Ann Arbor, Mich. (1958); and serves as chairman of the Advisory Council of the Radio and TV Dept. of the Univ. of Judaism, Hollywood, Calif. (1962–to date).

In addition, Mr. Stone served as writer-director for Petticoat Junction (CBS); The Phyllis Diller Show (ABC); Lost in Space (CBS); Please Don't Eat the Daisies (NBC); Julia (NBC); The Flying Nun (ABC); The Debbie Reynolds Show (NBC); The Jimmy Stewart Show (NBC); and The Sandy Duncan Show.

Night Clubs. Mr. Stone directed the revue, *The Roaring Twenties* (Blackhawk, Chicago, Ill., 1951).

Other Activities. He has taught at AADA (1956–59), in 1956, he founded and was executive director of the postgraduate professional center of AADA. Since 1959, he has been associate director of AADA. He also taught at the Amer. Wing, Professional Training Program (1946–58).

Since 1945, he has directed student productions and/or lectured at the Univ. of Virginia, Temple Univ., Univ. of Pennsylvania, Michigan State Univ., Adelphi, Brooklyn Coll., Boston Univ., the New Sch., Yale Univ., and Univ. of North Carolina.

He served as special projects consultant to the Secretary of Commerce of the Commonwealth of Pa. (1952); was consultant for the Fred Miller Th. (Milwaukee, Wis., 1956); the Ford Foundation's Humanities Program (1958); and Fresno (Calif.) Community Th. (1960), and raises purebred dairy cattle.

Published Works. Mr. Stone wrote, with Weldon Nelick, *Coming Major* (1945); and has contributed articles to magazines and newspapers; and since Nov. 1962, has written a monthly humor column, "Actors' Glossary," for *Equity* magazine.

Awards. Mr. Stone has won the following awards: National Visuals, Cris, N.A.M., and Gold Eagle.

STONE, HAROLD. Director. Grad. Howard Univ., 1953.

Mr. Stone began his career as a stage manager for David Merrick's production of *La Plume de Ma Tante* (Royale, N.Y.C., Nov. 11, 1958); and made his N.Y.C. directing debut with the off-Bway musical *Ernest in Love* (Gramercy Arts, May 4, 1960); subsequently staging *In White America* (Sheridan Square Playhouse, Oct. 31, 1963; re-opened, Players, May 18, 1965); and *Abraham Cochran* (Belasco, Feb. 17, 1964). For American Conservatory Th. (San Francisco), he directed *In White America* (Aug. 31, 1965); and *The Devil's Disciple* (Oct. 9, 1965); staged a revival of *Room Service* (Th. of the Living Arts, Philadelphia, Nov. 1, 1966); and returned to ACT to direct *The Time of Your Life* (Feb. 7, 1967), and *U.S.A.* (Mar. 28, 1967).

He subsequently directed *Poor Bitos* (Arena Stage, Washington, D.C., Sept. 27, 1967); *An Ordinary Man* (Cherry Lane Th., N.Y.C., Sept. 9, 1968); *A Way of Life* (ANTA, Jan. 18, 1969); *The Memory Bank* (Tambellini's Gate, Jan. 11, 1970); *Room Service* (Edison, May 12, 1970); *Charley's Aunt* (Brooks Atkinson Th., July 4, 1970); *Ring 'Round the Bathtub* (Martin Beck Th., Apr. 29, 1972); *Scenes from American Life* (Goodman Th. Center, Chicago, Nov. 26, 1972); for the National Th. of the Deaf, *Optimism or the Misadventures of Candide* (world premiere, Eugene O'Neill Memorial Th. Ctr., Waterford, Conn., Sept. 1973), which he conceived and adapted from the Voltaire novel; *I Got a Song* (world premiere, Studio Arena, Buffalo, N.Y., Sept. 24, 1974); and *Dream of a Blacklisted Actor* (Ensemble Studio Th., May 1, 1975).

STONE, PAULA. Producer, actress. b. Jan. 20, 1916, New York City, to Fred and Allene (Crater) Stone. Parents, vaudeville performers. Attended Kew-Forrest Sch. Married 1939 to Duke Daley (dec. 1943); married Jan. 30, 1946, to Michael Sloane, producer; one son. Relatives in theatre: sister, Dorothy, dancer; family: Fred, Allene, Paula, and Dorothy, known as The Stepping Stones in vaudeville. Member of AEA; SAG; AFTRA.

Theatre. Miss Stone made her stage debut as a dancer in *Ripples* (New Amsterdam Th., N.Y.C., Feb. 11, 1930); subsequently appeared in *Smiling Faces* (Shubert, Aug. 30, 1932); played Olly Frey in *A Church Mouse* (Mansfield, June 26, 1933); and appeared in *White Horse Inn* (Center, Oct. 1, 1936).

She produced, with Hunt Stromberg, Jr., *The Red Mill* (Ziegfeld, Oct. 16, 1945); produced, with her husband, Michael Sloane, *Sweethearts* (Shubert, Jan. 21, 1947); participated in the production of *The Country Girl* (Lyceum, Nov. 10, 1950); produced, with Michael Sloane, *Top Banana* (Winter Garden, Nov. 1, 1951); and produced, with Michael Sloane, Johnny Burke, and Jimmy Van Heusen, *Carnival in Flanders* (Century, Sept. 8, 1953).

With John Gregor and Desmond Ainsworth, she acquired rights to The Lyric, Hammersmith (England), which they re-opened as the New Lyric Th. (June 19, 1964).

Films. Miss Stone first appeared in *Slide, Kelly, Slide* (MGM, 1927); subsequently *Two Against the World* (WB); *Hop-a-long Cassidy* (Par., 1935); *Colleen* (WB, 1936); *The Singing Kid* (1st Natl., 1936); *Treachery Rides the Range* (WB, 1936); and *Idiot's Delight* (MGM, 1939).

Television and Radio. Miss Stone performed on her own radio program, the Paula Stone Show (MBS), for which she was also writer-producer.

For television, she appeared on Angel Audition (ABC).

Recreation. Children.

STONE, PETER. Playwright, scenarist. b. Peter Hess Stone, Feb. 27, 1930, Los Angeles, Calif., to John and Hilda (Hess) Stone. Father, film producer; mother, film writer. Grad. Univ. H.S., 1947; Bard Coll., B.A. 1951; Yale Univ., M.F.A. 1953. Married Feb. 17, 1961, to Mary O'Hanley. Member of WGA, Dramatists Guild (exec. council); Authors League (exec. council). Address: 160 E. 71st St., New York, NY 10021, tel. (212) BU 8-1099.

Theatre. Mr. Stone wrote *Friend of the Family* (Crystal Palace, St. Louis, Mo., Dec. 9, 1948); books for the musicals *Kean* (Broadway Th., N.Y.C., Nov. 2, 1961); *Skyscraper* (Lunt-Fontanne Th., N.Y.C., Nov. 13, 1965); *1776* (46 St. Th., Mar. 16, 1969); *Two by Two* (Imperial, Nov. 10, 1970); *Sugar* (Majestic, Apr. 9, 1972); and the play *Full Circle* (ANTA Th., Nov. 7, 1973).

Films. Mr. Stone was both author and scenarist of *Charade* (U, 1963); scenarist of *Father Goose* (U, 1964); *Mirage* (U, 1965); *Arabesque* (U, 1966); *The Secret War of Harry Frigg* (U, 1968); *Sweet Charity* (U, 1970); *1776* (Col., 1973); *Skin Game* (WB, 1972); and *The Taking of Pelham 1-2-3* (UA, 1974).

Television. Mr. Stone has written for Studio One (CBS, 1956); Brenner (CBS, 1959); Witness (CBS, 1961); Asphalt Jungle (ABC, 1961); Defenders (CBS, 1961–62); Espionage (NBC, 1963); and Adam's Rib (ABC, 1973–74). He wrote the book for the musical special *Androcles and the Lion* (NBC, 1969).

Awards. Mr. Stone received the NATAS (Emmy) Award for The Defenders (1962); the WGA Award for writing achievement for his television play, *The Benefactors* (1962); the WGA Award for Best Comedy Film; the Mystery Writers of America Award for Best Mystery Film for *Charade* (1964); the Academy (Oscar) Award for *Father Goose* (1964); Antoinette Perry (Tony), NY Drama Critics Circle, and Drama Desk awards for *1776* (all 1969); and the Christopher Award for the script of the film *1776* (1973). Mr. Stone received the honorary degree of D.Litt. from Bard College in 1961.

STOPPARD, TOM. Playwright. b. Thomas Straussler, July 3, 1937, Zlin, Czechoslovakia, to Dr. and Mrs. Eugene Straussler. Educated Dolphin Sch., Nottinghamshire, England; Pocklington Sch., Yorkshire, England. Married 1965 to Jose Ingle (marr. dis., 1972); two sons; married 1972 to Dr. Miriam Moore-Robinson, one son. Address: c/o Fraser and Dunlop Scripts, Ltd., 91 Regent St., London W1R8RU, England.

Pre-Theatre. Reporter and critic (1954–58), *Western Daily Press*, Bristol, England; Bristol *Evening World* (1958–60); reviewer for *Scene* Magazine (1962); freelance reporter (1960–63).

Theatre. Mr. Stoppard's first play to receive production was *The Gamblers* (Bristol, England, 1965); followed by *Rosencrantz and Guildenstern are Dead* (Edinburgh Festival, 1966), a revised version of which was presented by the National Th. Co. (Old Vic Th., London, Apr. 12, 1967; and Alvin, N.Y.C., Oct. 16, 1967). Based upon an earlier television play entitled *A Walk on the Water*, he wrote *Enter a Free Man* (St. Martin's Th., London, Mar. 28, 1968), which made its N.Y.C. debut in an off-Bway production (St. Clements Th., Dec. 17, 1974); an adaptation of *Tango* (Aldwych, London, May 25, 1968); *The Real Inspector Hound* (Criterion, London, June 17, 1968); and *After Magritte* (Almost Free Th., Dec. 1971), which played as an off-Bway double-bill in N.Y.C. (Th. Four, Apr. 23, 1972); *Albert's Bridge* (Oxford Th. Group, Edinburgh Festival, 1969), a revised version of an earlier radio play of the same title; *Dogg's Our Pet* (London, 1971); *Jumpers* (National Th. Co., Old Vic 1972; Kennedy Ctr., Washington, D.C., Feb. 18, 1974; and Billy Rose Th., N.Y.C., Apr. 22, 1974); an adaptation of Garcia Lorca's *The House of Bernarda Alba* (Greenwich, London, March 1973); and *Travesties* (Aldwych, June 10, 1974; and Ethel Barrymore Th., N.Y.C., Oct. 30, 1974).

Mr. Stoppard directed a production of *Born Yesterday* (Greenwich, London, Spring 1973).

Films. He co-authored the screenplay for *The Romantic Englishwoman* (New World Pictures, 1975).

Television and Radio. Mr. Stoppard's radio plays include *The Dissolution of Dominic Boot* (BBC, 1964); *M Is for Moon Among Other Things* (BBC, 1964); *If You're Glad I'll Be Frank* (BBC, 1965); *Albert's Bridge* (BBC, 1967); *Where Are They Now?* (BBC, 1970); and *Artist Descending a Staircase* (BBC, 1972).

His television scripts include *A Walk on the Water* (BBC, 1963), which was revised and retitled *The Preservation of George Riley* (BBC, 1964), *A Separate Peace* (BBC, 1966); *Teeth* (BBC, 1967); *Another Moon Called Earth* (BBC, 1967); *Neutral Ground* (BBC, 1968); *The Engagement* (Experiment in Television, NBC, 1970); a documentary, *One Pair of Eyes* (BBC, 1972); and *Eleventh House* (BBC, 1975), written with Clive Exton.

Published Works. Mr. Stoppard is the author of a novel, *Lord Malquist and Mr. Moon* (1968). His short stories, with others, appear in *Introduction 2* (1964).

Awards. Mr. Stoppard was the recipient of a Ford Foundation grant (1964); the John Whiting Award (1967); the *Evening Standard* Award (1967, 1973); Prix Italia (1968); and the NY Drama Critics Circle and Antoinette Perry (Tony) awards (1967–68) for *Rosencrantz and Guildenstern Are Dead*.

STORCH, ARTHUR. Actor, director, educator. b. June 29, 1925, Brooklyn, N.Y., to Sam and Bessie Storch. Father, baker. Grad. Thos. Jefferson H.S., 1942; attended Brooklyn Coll., 1943; grad. New Sch. for Social Research, B.A. 1949. Studied at Actors' Studio, N.Y.C. (mbr., 1952–to date). Served US Army, Anti-Aircraft, ETO, 1943–46; awarded 3 Battle Stars. Member of AEA; SAG; AFTRA; SSD&C. Address: Syracuse Stage, 820 E. Genesee St., Syracuse, NY 13210.

Mr. Storch is artistic director of Syracuse Stage, and chairman of the Dept. of Drama of Syracuse Univ. (1974–to date).

Theatre. Mr. Storch first performed in stock productions at Deertrees, Me. (Summer 1951); subsequently appeared at the Allenberry Playhouse, Boiling Springs, Pa. (1952); played Maurice Maynall Simmons in *End as a Man* (Theatre de Lys, N.Y.C., Sept. 15, 1953; moved to Vanderbilt, Oct. 14, 1953); appeared in productions at the Woodstock (N.Y.) Playhouse (Summer 1954); played Lt. Mike Livingston in *Time Limit!* (Booth, N.Y.C., Jan. 14, 1956); Gene Mitchell in *Girls of Summer* (Longacre, Nov. 19, 1956); Luke Gant in *Look Homeward, Angel* (Ethel Barrymore Th., Nov. 28, 1957); the Businessman in *Night Circus* (John Golden Th., Dec. 2, 1958); Mr. McWilliams in *The Long Dream* (Ambassador, Feb. 17, 1960); and was understudy to Frank Lovejoy as Joseph Cantwell in *The Best Man* (Morosco, Mar. 31, 1960).

He directed *Talking to You* and *Across the Board on Tomorrow Morning (two by Saroyan)* (East End Th., Oct. 22, 1961); *The Twenty-Five Cent White Cap* and *George Washington Crossing the Delaware (Three by Three)* (Maidman Playhouse, Feb. 1962); *The Typist and the Tiger* (Orpheum, Feb. 4, 1963); *Talking to You* (Duke of York Th., London, 1963); *The Owl and the Pussycat* (ANTA, N.Y.C., Nov. 19, 1964); *The Impossible Years* (Playhouse, N.Y.C., Oct. 13, 1965); *Under the Weather* (Festival of Two Worlds, Spoleto, Italy, 1966; and Cort, N.Y.C., Oct. 27, 1966); *Golden Rainbow* (Shubert, N.Y.C., Feb. 4, 1968); *The Local Stigmatic* (Actors Playhouse, N.Y.C., Nov. 3, 1969); and *The Chinese and Dr. Fish* (Ethel Barrymore Th., N.Y.C., Mar. 10, 1970).

Films. Mr. Storch made his debut as Simmons in *The Strange One* (Col., 1957); and subsequently appeared in *The Mugger* (UA, 1958); and in *Girl of the Night* (WB, 1960); and directed *Holding On* (1972).

STORCH, LARRY. Actor, comedian. b. Lawrence Samuel Storch, Jan. 8, 1923, New York City, to Alfred and Sally (Kupperman) Storch. Father, realtor; mother, telephone operator. Attended DeWitt Clinton H.S., N.Y.C., 1936–38. Married July 10, 1961, to Norma Catherine Greve. Served USN, PTO, 1942–46; rank, Musician 2nd Class. Relatives in theatre: brother, Jay Lawrence, comedian. Member of AEA; SAG; AGVA; AFTRA.

Theatre. Mr. Storch appeared in *The Littlest Revue* (Phoenix, N.Y.C., May 22, 1956); and as Orlov in *Who Was That Lady I Saw You With?* (Martin Beck Th., Mar. 3, 1958).

Films. He has appeared in *Gun Fever* (WB, 1958); *The Last Blitzkrieg* (Col., 1958); *Who Was That Lady I Saw You With?* (Col., 1960); *40 Pounds of Trouble* (U, 1962); *Wild and Wonderful* (U, 1963); *Captain Newman, M.D.* (U, 1964); and *Sex and the Single Girl* (WB, 1964).

Television. He made his debut on The Shower of Stars (Dumont, 1948); was a summer replacement (1953) for Jackie Gleason; was in the series F Troop (CBS, 1974); and in the children's show *The Ghost Busters* (CBS, 1975).

Night Clubs. He has frequently appeared as a comedian in such night clubs as Copacabana, N.Y.C.; Ciro's in Hollywood; and many others; he was at one time co-owner of the Crystal Room, N.Y.C.

Recreation. Swimming, skin diving, playing saxophone.

STOREY, DAVID. Playwright, novelist. b. July 13, 1933, Wakefield, Yorkshire, England. Grad. Queen Elizabeth Grammar Sch., Wakefield, 1951; Wakefield Art Sch., 1953; Slade Sch. of Fine Art, London, 1956.

Theatre. Mr. Storey made his playwriting debut with *The Restoration of Arnold Middleton* (Edinburgh, 1966; and Royal Court, London, July 5, 1967); subsequently wrote *In Celebration* (Royal Court, Apr. 22, 1969); *The Contractor* (Royal Court, Oct. 20, 1969; and Long Wharf Th., New Haven, Conn., Dec. 1971); *Home* (Royal Court, London, June 17, 1970; and Morosco, N.Y.C., Nov. 17, 1970); *The Changing Room* (Royal Court, London, 1971; and Long Wharf, New Haven, Conn., Nov. 17, 1972; moved to Morosco, N.Y.C., Mar. 6, 1973); *Cromwell* (Royal Court, London, 1973); and *The Farm* (Royal Court, 1973).

Films. He wrote the screenplay for *This Sporting Life* (Walter-Reade-Sterling, 1963).

Other Activities. Mr. Storey was a professional player with the Leeds Rugby League Club (1952–56).

Published Works. Mr. Storey is the author of *This Sporting Life* (1960); *Flight into Camden* (1960); *Radcliffe* (1964); *Pasmore* (London, 1972); and *A Temporary Life* (London, 1973).

Awards. He has received the Macmillan Fiction Award (1959); the Rhys Memorial Award (1961); The Maugham Award (1963); the Evening Standard Award (1967, 1970); the Variety Club of Great Britain Writer of the Year Award (1971), for *The Contractor;* and the NY Drama Critics Circle and the Antoinette Perry (Tony) awards for *Home* (1970–71); and *The Changing Room* (1972–73).

STRAIGHT, BEATRICE. Actress, producer. b. Beatrice Whitney Straight, Aug. 2, Old Westbury, L.I., N.Y., to Major Willard Dickerman and Dorothy (Whitney) Straight. Father, businessman, diplomat. Attended Lincoln Sch., N.Y.C., Dartington Hall, Totnes, Devon, England; Cornish Sch., Seattle, Wash. Studied acting with Tamara Daykarhanova; with Michael Chekhov at the Chekhov Th. Sch., N.Y.C. Married June 2, 1949, to Peter Cookson; two sons. Member of AEA; AFTRA; SAG. Address: (home) R.F.D., Canaan, CT 06018, tel. Sheffield, MA; (bus.) c/o Kaplan-Veidt, 667 Madison Ave., New York, NY 10021, tel. (212) PL 5-2214.

Pre-Theatre. Painting, dancing.

Theatre. Miss Straight has appeared on Bway as a Spinning Girl in *Bitter Oleander* (Lyceum, Feb. 11, 1935); Lisa in *The Possessed* (Lyceum, Oct. 24, 1939); Viola in *Twelfth Night* (Little, Dec. 2, 1941); Angela in *Land of Fame* (Belasco, Sept. 21, 1943); Felina in *The Wanhope Building* (Princess, Feb. 9, 1947); Emily Dickinson in *Eastward in Eden* (Royale, Nov. 18, 1947); and Lady Macduff in *Macbeth* (National, Mar. 31, 1948). She succeeded Wendy Hiller (Summer 1948) as Catherine Sloper in *The Heiress* (Biltmore, Sept. 29, 1948), in which she later toured (commencing Oct. 1948); appeared as Miss Giddens in *The Innocents* (Playhouse, Feb. 1, 1950); Elizabeth Proctor in *The Crucible* (Martin Beck Th., Jan. 22, 1953); and as Marie Chassaigne in *The River Line* (Carnegie Hall Playhouse, Jan. 2, 1957); and with Michael Chekhov's Dartington Hall Players, toured as Viola in *Twelfth Night* and as Goneril in *King Lear*.

She is one of the founders of the producing organization, Theatre, Inc., which revived *Pygmalion* (Ethel Barrymore Th., Dec. 26, 1945); and *Playboy of the Western World* (Booth Th., Oct. 26, 1946); and which first presented the Old Vic Th. Co. in the US (Century, N.Y.C.); this program included *Henry IV, Part 1* (May 6, 1946); *Henry IV, Part 2* (May 7, 1946); *Uncle Vanya* (May 13, 1946); and a double bill of *Oedipus* and *The Critic* (May 20, 1946).

She appeared in the title role of the IASTA production of *Phèdre* (Greenwich Mews Th., Feb. 10, 1966), repeating her performance at the Festival of American Arts and Humanities, American Embassy Th., London, England (June 15–19, 1966), followed by an additional week at Dartington Hall, Totnes, Devonshire; played Blanche in *A Streetcar Named Desire* (Berkshire Th. Festival, Stockbridge, Mass., July 11–22, 1967); Mrs. Toothe in *Everything in the Garden* (Plymouth, N.Y.C., Nov. 29, 1967); again played Blanche in *A Streetcar Named Desire* (City Island Th., N.Y., May 13, 1969; Las Palmas Th., Hollywood, Calif., Jan. 2, 1970); was the Mother in *The Palace at 4 A.M.* (John Drew Th., East Hampton, N.Y., Aug. 9–19, 1972); Mrs. Alving in a revival of *Ghosts* (Roundabout Th., Mar. 13, 1973); and Kate Keller in a revival of *All My Sons* (Roundabout Th., Oct. 28, 1974). Miss Straight also operates Young World Foundation, a company which produces plays for children, notably *Who Am I?* (1971–72–73), directed by Miss Straight.

Films. Miss Straight has appeared in *Phone Call from a Stranger* (20th-Fox, 1952); *Patterns* (UA, 1956); *The Silken Affair* (DCA, 1957); *The Nun's Story* (WB, 1959); and *The Young Lovers* (MGM).

Television and Radio. Miss Straight was in *The Magnificent Failure* (Hallmark Hall of Fame, NBC, May 25, 1952); *Where Have You Been, Lord Randall, My Son?* (Eleventh Hour, NBC, Jan. 9, 1963); and appeared on Mission Impossible (CBS, Nov. 26, 1966); Felony Squad (ABC, Nov. 20, 1967); and Matt Lincoln (ABC, Nov. 12, 1970). She has appeared also on Playhouse 90 (CBS); Kraft Television Th. (NBC); Studio One (CBS); Ben Casey (ABC); Dr. Kildare (NBC); The Nurses (CBS); and Lamp Unto My Feet (CBS).

During WW II, Miss Straight had her own radio program on WMCA (N.Y.C.), which broadcast dramatic stories of the underground.

Awards. She received the Antoinette Perry (Tony) Award (1952–53) for her performance as Elizabeth Proctor in *The Crucible*.

STRASBERG, LEE. Acting teacher, actor, director. b. Nov. 17, 1901, Budanov, Austria-Hungary, to Baruch Meyer and Ida (Diner) Strasberg. Emigrated to US, 1909; naturalized, 1936. Studied for the stage with Richard Boleslavski and Maria Ouspenskaya at the American Laboratory Th., N.Y.C. Married Nora Z. Krecaun (dec. 1929); married Mar. 11, 1935, to Paula Miller, actress, coach (dec. Dec. 29, 1966); one daughter, Susan, actress; one son, John, actor; married Jan. 7, 1968, to Anna Mizrahi; two sons. Address: (home) 135 Central Park West, New York, NY 10023, tel. (212) TR 7-2469; (bus.) c/o Actors Studio, 432 W. 44 St., New York, NY 10036, tel. (212) PL 7-0870.

In 1947, Mr. Strasberg was asked to join the Actors Studio, N.Y.C., founded earlier that year by Elia Kazan, Cheryl Crawford, and Robert Lewis; he has been Director of the Studio from 1948 to date; and also teaches privately at his own acting schools, the Lee Strasberg Theater Institutes, Inc. (34 W. 13th St., New York, NY 10011; and 6757 Hollywood Blvd., Hollywood, Calif., 90028), both established in 1969. He conducted, with his wife, Paula, an acting seminar at the Fest. of Two Worlds (Spoleto, Italy, Summer 1962); conducted an acting seminar and participated in the Hall of Education program at the NY World's Fair (1964–65); lectured on Stanislavsky in Paris (Th. National Populaire, Sept. 1967); and has lectured at Harvard, Brown, Brandeis, and Northwestern Universities.

Theatre. Mr. Strasberg was assistant stage manager for *The Guardsman* (Garrick Th., N.Y.C., Oct. 13, 1924); actor-director with the Chrystie St. Settlement House (N.Y.C., 1925); played the First Soldier in *Processional* (Garrick, Jan. 12, 1925); and appeared in *The Garrick Gaieties* (Garrick, June 3, 1925). He appeared in walk-on roles in *Goat Song* (Guild, Jan. 25, 1926) and *The Chief Thing* (Guild, Mar. 22, 1926); and was stage manager for the second edition of *The Garrick Gaieties* (Garrick, May 10, 1926). He played Nick in *Four Walls* (John Golden Th., Sept. 19, 1927); Pimples in *Red Rust* (Martin Beck Th., Dec. 17, 1929); joined (Sept. 1930) the cast of *The Garrick Gaieties* (Guild, June 4, 1930); and played Ali Hakim in *Green Grow the Lilacs* (Guild, Jan. 26, 1931).

In the summer of 1931, Mr. Strasberg (with Harold Clurman and Cheryl Crawford) formed the Group Theater, renting a barn and several bungalows in Brookfield Center, Conn., to rehearse plays with approx. 28 actors. For the Group Th., he directed, with Cheryl Crawford, *The House of Connelly* (Martin Beck Th., N.Y.C., Sept. 28, 1931); and directed *1931* (Mansfield, Oct. 10, 1931), *Night Over Taos* (48 St. Th., Mar. 9, 1932), and *Success Story* (Maxine Elliott's Th., Sept. 26, 1932). Apart from the Group Th., he directed *Hilda Cassidy* (Martin Beck Th., May 4, 1933); and for the Group Th., *Men in White* (Broadhurst, Sept. 26, 1933), *Gentlewoman* (Cort, Mar. 22, 1934), *Gold* (Morosco, Nov. 28, 1934), acted in *Till the Day I Die* (Longacre, Mar. 26, 1935), on a double bill with *Waiting for Lefty;* directed *The Case of Clyde Griffiths* (Ethel Barrymore Th., Mar. 13, 1936), *Johnny Johnson* (44 St. Th., Nov. 19, 1936), and *Many Mansions* (Biltmore, Oct. 27, 1937), following which he resigned from the Group Th.

Mr. Strasberg staged *Roosty* (Lyceum, Feb. 14, 1938); *All the Living* (Fulton, Mar. 24, 1938); *Dance Night* (Belasco, Oct. 14, 1938); *Summer Night* (St. James, Nov. 2, 1939); *The Fifth Column* (Alvin, Mar. 6, 1940); *Clash by Night* (Belasco, Dec. 27, 1941); *R.U.R.* (Ethel Barrymore Th., Dec. 3, 1942); *Apology,* which he also produced (Mansfield, Mar. 22, 1943); the drama *South Pacific* (Cort, Dec. 29, 1943); *Skipper Next to God* (Maxine Elliott's Th., Jan. 4, 1948); *The Big Knife* (Natl., Feb. 24, 1949); *The Closing Door* (Empire, Dec. 1, 1949); and *Peer Gynt* (ANTA, Jan. 28, 1951).

As Dir. of the Actors Studio Th. (1962–66), he supervised their production of *Marathon '33* (ANTA, Dec. 22, 1963) and directed *The Three Sisters* (Morosco, June 22, 1964; and at the World Th. Season, Aldwych Th., London, May 12, 1965, his London directing debut). He supervised a revival of *The Country Girl* (NY City Ctr., Sept. 29, 1966).

Films. He played Hyman Roth in *The Godfather, Part II* (Par., 1974).

Published Works. Mr. Strasberg's tape-recorded teaching sessions at the Actors Studio were edited for publication by Robert H. Hethmon, as *Strasberg at the Actors Studio* (1965).

Awards. He was nominated (1975) for an Academy (Oscar) Award as best supporting actor for his role in *The Godfather, Part II.* He received the Kelcey Allen Award (N.Y.C., 1961); and the Centennial Gold Medal Award for excellence in dramatic arts (Boston Coll., 1963).

Recreation. Music, reading, collecting rare books.

STRASBERG, SUSAN. Actress. b. Susan Elizabeth Strasberg, May 22, 1938, New York City, to Lee and Paula (Miller) Strasberg. Father, head of Actors' Studio, teacher; mother, actress, teacher. Attended H.S. of Music and Arts; H.S. of Performing Arts; Professional Sch. Studied acting at Actors' Studio (mbr., 1961–to date). Married Sept. 25, 1965, to Chris Jones. Relative in theatre: brother, John Strasberg, actor, director. Member of AEA; SAG; AFTRA. Address: 135 Central Park West, New York, NY 10023.

Theatre. Miss Strasberg made her debut in *Maya* (Th. de Lys, N.Y.C., June 9, 1953); subsequently appeared as Anne in *The Diary of Anne Frank* (Cort Th., Oct. 5, 1955); Amanda in *Time Remembered* (Morosco, Nov. 12, 1957); Minnie Parnell in *Shadow of a Gunman* (Bijou, Nov. 20, 1958); with NY City Ctr., *The Time of Your Life* (Brussels World's Fair, Belgium, Nov. 1958); in stock, toured in *Caesar and Cleopatra* (Summer 1959); and played Marguerite Gautier in *The Lady of the Camellias* (Winter Garden, N.Y.C., Mar. 23, 1963).

Films. She has appeared in *Cobweb* (MGM, 1955); *Picnic* (Col., 1955); *Stage Struck* (Buena Vista, 1958); *Kapo* (Independent, 1960); *Scream of Fear* (Col., 1961); *Adventures of a Young Man* (20th-Fox, 1962); *The Disorder* (Italy, 1964); *The High Bright Sun* (Rank, 1964); *The Trip* (Amer. Intl., 1967); *Psych-Out* (Amer. Intl., 1968); and *The Name of the Game Is Kill* (Fanfare, 1968).

Television. Miss Strasberg appeared in *Catch a Falling Star* (Goodyear Playhouse, NBC, June 1953); *Romeo and Juliet* (Kraft Th., NBC, June 1954); *Dear Brutus* (Omnibus, CBS, Jan. 1956); *The Cherry Orchard* (Play of the Week, NET, Dec. 1959); *Four Kings* (Bob Hope Chrysler Th., NBC, Nov. 1963); *The Experiment* (CBS Playhouse, 1969); and other plays. She has also appeared on such series as The Marriage (NBC, 1954); Dr. Kildare (NBC, 1963); Burke's Law (ABC, 1964); The Virginian (NBC, 1966); The F.B.I. (ABC, 1967, 1968); Name of the Game (NBC, 1968); Marcus Welby, M.D. (ABC, 1969); Men from Shiloh (NBC, 1970); Alias Smith and Jones (ABC, 1971); McCloud (CBS, 1971); Night Gallery (NBC, 1971); Medical Center (CBS, 1971); and Owen Marshall (ABC, 1972).

Recreation. Painting, fashion design.

STRAUSS, JOHN. Composer, conductor, musician, arranger. b. John Leonard Strauss, April 28, 1920, New York City, to Maurice Henry and Marie (Haberman) Strauss. Grad. Columbia Grammar H.S., N.Y.C., 1942; Yale Univ. Sch. of Music, M.A. 1951. Studied piano with Clarence Adler, Ethel Chasins; harpsichord with Ralph Kirkpatrick; conducting with Paul Boepple; composition with Israel Citkowitz, Quincy Porter, Paul Hindemith. Married Nov. 4, 1951, to Charlotte Rae, actress, singer; two sons. Served US Army 1943–45, ETO; rank, T4 Sgt. Member of AFM, Local 802; Amer. Soc. of Musical Arrangers; ASCAP; Motion Picture Editors, Local 771.

Theatre. Mr. Strauss' *Night Music* was first performed at the Modern Art Museum Aud., N.Y.C. (Apr. 1952). He composed the music for Robert Joffrey's works *Scaramouche* and *Umpateedle*

(YMHA, N.Y.C.; Jacob's Pillow Dance Festival, Lee, Mass., July 1953).

He composed the incidental music for *Thieves' Carnival*(Kaufmann Aud., N.Y.C., April 1954); was orchestrator of and contributed songs to *The Littlest Revue* (Phoenix, May 22, 1956); composed *Three Dramatic Monologues* (Lorca) (Circle in the Square, Mar. 24, 1958); was musical director for *Morning Sun* (Phoenix, Oct. 6, 1963).

Films. He composed the score for the documentary short subject *New York in 10 Hours* and has selected and supervised music preparation for many industrial and documentary films.

Television. He was composer-conductor for the Phil Silvers Show (CBS, 1955–59); for *Death Takes a Holiday*(ABC, Dec. 1952); composed *The Accused*, an operatic monologue performed by Patricia Neway (CBS, May 1961); and was composer-conductor of the series Car 54, Where Are You? (NBC, 1961–63); the series Brenner (CBS); and for Rheingold Th. (NBC). He composed the original score for *The Stamp of Steinberg*(CBS, Camera 3). Mr. Strauss has also chosen and supervised music preparation for many spot commercials.

Night Clubs. Mr. Strauss has prepared special material and arrangements for his wife, Charlotte Rae.

Discography. Mr. Strauss arranged and conducted the accompaniments for his wife on the recording *Songs I Taught My Mother*(Vanguard, 1955) and has done arrangements and orchestrations for Capitol Records' Jewish Folk Music series (1964).

Awards. *New York in 10 Hours*received Honorable Mention at the Bergamo Film Festival (1963).

STREISAND, BARBRA. Actress, singer. b. Barbara Streisand, Apr. 24, 1942, Brooklyn, N.Y., to Emanuel and Diana (Rosen) Streisand. Father, English teacher; mother, school clerk. Grad. Erasmus Hall H.S, 1958. Married Mar. 21, 1963, to Elliott Gould, actor (marr. dis. 1971); one son. Member of AEA; AFTRA; AGVA;.

Theatre. Miss Streisand made her stage debut in the revue, *Another Evening with Harry Stoones* (Gramercy Arts, Oct. 21, 1961); subsequently appeared as Miss Marmelstein in *I Can Get It for You Wholesale*(Shubert, Mar. 22, 1962); appeared in a concert with Sammy Davis, Jr. (Hollywood Bowl, Calif., Oct. 5, 1963); and played Fanny Brice in *Funny Girl* (Winter Garden, Mar. 26, 1964; Prince of Wales Th., London, England, Apr. 13, 1966).

Films. Miss Streisand's motion pictures include *Funny Girl* (Col., 1968); *Hello, Dolly!* (20th-Fox, 1969); *On a Clear Day You Can See Forever* (Par., 1970); *The Owl and the Pussycat* (Col., 1970); *What's Up, Doc?* (WB, 1972); *Up the Sandbox* (Natl. Gen., 1972); *The Way We Were* (Col., 1973); *For Pete's Sake* (Col., 1974); and *Funny Lady* (Col., 1975).

Television. Miss Streisand has appeared on PM East (WNEW-TV, 1961); the Judy Garland Show (CBS, 1963); Ed Sullivan Show (CBS, 1962, 1963); Dinah Shore Show (NBC, 1962); Bob Hope Show (NBC, 1963); and the Tonight Show (NBC).

Television specials in which she starred include *My Name Is Barbra* (CBS, 1965); *Color Me Barbra* (CBS, 1966); *Belle of 14th Street* (CBS, 1967); *Barbra S-and Other Musical Instruments* (Col., 1973); and *From Funny Girl to Funny Lady* (ABC, 1974). *Barbra Streisand: A Happening in Central Park* (CBS, 1968) was a tape of Miss Steisand's June 1967 Sheep Meadow, Central Park, N.Y.C., concert.

Night Clubs. Miss Streisand made her night club debut at Bon Soir (N.Y.C., Sept. 1960); subsequently appeared at the Blue Angel (N.Y.C.); Basin St. East (N.Y.C., May 1963); Mr. Kelly's (Chicago, Ill.); the hungry i (San Francisco, Calif.); Crystal Palace (St. Louis, Mo.); Caucus Club (Detroit, Mich.); Riviera Hotel (Las Vegas, Nev., July 1963); Coconut Grove (Los Angeles, Calif., 1963); and Harrah's Club (Lake Tahoe, Nev.).

Discography. Miss Streisand has made the following recordings: *Pins and Needles*(Col., 1962); *The Barbra Streisand Album* (Col., May 1963); *The Second Barbra Streisand Album*(Col., Oct. 1963); *Barbra Streisand, The Third Album* (Col., 1964); and *People* (Col., 1964); and the original cast recordings of *I Can Get It for You Wholesale* (Col., June 1962); and *Funny Girl* (Col., 1964).

Awards. For her performance as Miss Marmelstein in *I Can Get It for You Wholesale,* Miss Streisand was co-winner, with Sandy Dennis, of the *Variety* NY Drama Critics Poll, and received an Antoinette Perry (Tony) Award nomination (1962). She won the *Cue* Magazine Entertainer of the Year Award (1963).

For her performance as Fanny Brice in *Funny Girl,* she received an Antoinette Perry (Tony) Award nomination for best actress in a musical comedy (1964), and in 1968 she was a co-winner of the best actress Academy (Oscar) Award for her recreation of the role on film. She also received a NATAS (Emmy) Award nomination for her performance on the Judy Garland Show (1963) and an Emmy Award for her special *My Name Is Barbra* (1965) and two NARAS (Grammy) Awards for best album (The Barbara Streisand Album) and best female performer of the year (1963).

STRICKLER, JERRY. Actor. b. William Jerry Strickler, Dec. 4, 1939, Goose Creek, Tex., to William Jules and Lucille (Newman) Strickler. Mother and father, teachers. Grad. Robert E. Lee H.S., Baytown, Tex., 1958; attended Southwestern Univ. (Texas), 1958–60. Studied with Herbert Machiz at Amer. Theatre Wing, N.Y.C., 1960–61. Married Oct. 13, 1961, to Alberta Grant, actress (marr. dis. Mar. 8, 1969). Member of AEA; SAG; AFTRA; National Academy of Television Arts & Sciences; The Players; The Masquers. Address: c/o The Masquers, 1765 N. Sycamore Ave., Hollywood, CA 90028, tel. (213) 874-0840.

Theatre. Mr. Strickler first appeared on stage singing "April Showers" (Ivywild Elementary School, Colorado Springs, Colo., Apr. 1947); as a student at Southwestern Univ. appeared in *You Never Can Tell, The Skin of Our Teeth, Liliom,* and *The Shewing-Up of Blanco Posnet.*

He made his professional debut as Prince Charming in *Sleeping Beauty* (Alley Th., Houston, Tex., July 1959); subsequently at the Alley Th., appeared in *Once More, With Feeling* (1959), played Payne in *Mister Roberts*(1960); the Tin Woodman in *The Wizard of Oz*(1960), Corporal Reeves in *Make a Million* (1960), and Daley in *Sunrise at Campobello* (1960). At the Amer. Theatre Wing, he played Jimmy in *The Rainmaker* (1960), and Richard in *Ah, Wilderness!* (1961); played Freddie in the national tour of *Bye Bye Birdie* (opened Curran, San Francisco, Calif., Apr. 24, 1961); closed Orpheum, Minneapolis, Minn., Mar. 17, 1962); Orlando in the Amer. Theatre Wing tour of *As You Like It*(1961); Dick in a stock presentation of *Tender Loving Care*(Coconut Grove, Fla., Apr. 1962); appeared in *Mr. President* (Kansas City Starlight Opera and St. Louis Municipal Opera, Summer 1964); *The Sound of Music*(Cape Cod Melody Tent, Hyannis, Mass.; South Shore Music Circus, Cohasset, Mass.; and North Shore Music Circus, Beverly, Mass.; all Summer 1965); *110 in the Shade*(Kansas City Starlight Opera, Summer 1966); *How to Succeed in Business Without Really Trying* (Mill Mountain, Va., Playhouse, Summer 1966); and *Wait Until Dark*(Corning, N.Y., Summer Th., 1968). For The Masquers Th., Hollywood, he appeared in *The Rainmaker* (1969), *Tom Jones* (1970), *An Affair of Honour* (1971), *Ten Nights in a Barroom* (1971), and *Lie a Little* (1972). He currently appears in a one-man show, *David Crockett, Storyteller, Congressman, Defender of the Alamo*(tour, 1975–76).

Mr. Strickler made his N.Y.C. debut as Larry in *Mr. President*(St. James, Oct. 20, 1962); appeared in *Love and Kisses* (Music Box, Dec. 18, 1963); *Rate of Exchange* (Players Th., Apr. 1, 1968); and *Venus Is* (Billy Rose Th., closed Apr. 9, 1969, prior to opening).

Films. Mr. Strickler appeared in *House of Seven Corpses* (Philip Yordan Prods., 1973).

Television. Mr. Strickler has appeared on Police Story (NBC); Mannix (CBS); Cannon (CBS); The Magician (NBC); Night Gallery (NBC); Mod Squad (ABC); The Smith Family (ABC); San Francisco International (NBC); Lancer (CBS); and The New People (ABC).

Recreation. Tennis, swimming, reading.

STRIESFIELD, HERB. Press agent. b. Herbert Arthur Striesfield, Oct. 6, 1946, Amesbury, Mass., to Louis and Sadie Striesfield. Father, owner of a retail store; mother civil servant. Educ. Haverhill (Mass.) public schools; Tilton (N.H.) School; School of Public Communication, Boston Univ. Professional training as apprentice to Robert Ganshaw (1969–70) on *No Place to Be Somebody* and to Dorothy Rose (1970–73) on *Sleuth.* Member of ATPAM. Address: 230 Riverside Dr., New York, NY 10025, tel. (212) 749-4864.

Pre-Theatre. Before going into theatrical work, Mr. Striesfield did public relations for Communications Planners, Inc., and advertising for Woolco/Woolworth Corp.

Theatre. Mr. Striesfield's first work in the theatre was as assistant to Robert Ganshaw for the off-Bway production of *No Place To Be Somebody* (1969–70). He worked with Dorothy Ross as press representative on *Sleuth* (1970–73) and *Please Don't Cry and Say No* (1972); was press agent for Circle Repertory Co., N.Y.C., from 1972 to 1975, representing *The Hot l Baltimore* and *When You Comin' Back, Red Ryder?* (1973), *The Sea Horse* (1974), and *The Mound Builders* (1975). Mr. Striesfield was also press agent for the off-Bway revival of *Women Behind Bars* (1975) and for *Grass Widows* (1976). In 1975, he became press agent for the South St. Seaport Th., South St. (N.Y.C.). Museum.

Recreation. Travel, collecting stage and film memorabilia.

STRITCH, ELAINE. Actress, singer. b. Feb. 2, 1925, Detroit, Mich., to George J. and Mildred (Tobe) Stritch. Father, rubber company exec. Grad. Sacred Heart Convent, Detroit; Deuchesne Residence Finishing Sch. Studied acting at the Dramatic Workshop of the New Sch. for Social Research, N.Y.C. 1944; singing with Burt Knapp, 1948–58. Married Feb. 2, 1973, to John M. Bay, actor. Member of AEA; SAG; AGVA; AFTRA.

Theatre. Miss Stritch played a Tiger and the Cow in *Bobino,* a children's show sponsored by the New Sch. for Social Research (Adelphi, Apr. 1944); for the Th. of All Nations, appeared as the Parlor Maid in *The Private Life of the Master Race* (CCNY Aud., June 11, 1945); played Betty Lord in the pre-Bway tryout of *Woman Bites Dog* (opened Walnut St. Th., Philadelphia, Pa., Apr. 1, 1946); Lady Sybil in *What Every Woman Knows* (Westport Country Playhouse, Conn., Summer 1946); made her Bway debut as Pamela Brewster in *Loco* (Biltmore, Oct. 16, 1946); succeeded (Feb. 1947) Jane Middleton as Miss Crowder in *Made in Heaven* (Henry Miller's Th., Oct. 24, 1946); and played Roberts in the pre-Bway tryout of *Three Indelicate Ladies* (opened Shubert, New Haven, Conn., Apr. 10, 1947).

She appeared in the revue *The Shape of Things* (John Drew Th., Easthampton, N.Y., July 26, 1947); played Regina Giddens in *The Little Foxes* (Rooftop, Oct. 23, 1947); appeared in the revue *Angel in the Wings* (Coronet, Dec. 11, 1947); played Dallas Smith in the summer tryout of *Texas Li'l Darlin'* (Westport Country Playhouse, Conn., Aug. 29, 1949); June Farrell in *Yes, M'Lord* (Booth, N.Y.C., Oct. 4, 1949); understudied Ethel Merman as Sally Adams in *Call Me Madam* (Imperial, Oct. 12, 1950), toured in the role (opened National, Washington, D.C., May 5, 1952); closed Shubert, Chicago, Ill., Apr. 18, 1953); played Melba Snyder in the revival of *Pal Joey* (Broadhurst, Jan. 3, 1952); Carol Frazer in the summer tryout of *Once Married, Twice Shy* (Westport Country Playhouse, Conn., July 27, 1953); and Hattie in *Panama Hattie* (Iroquois Amphitheatre, Louisville, Ky., July 12, 1954).

She played Peggy Porterfield in *On Your Toes* (46 St. Th., Oct. 11, 1954); Grace in *Bus Stop* (Music Box, Mar. 2, 1955); Gertrude Muldoon in *The Sin of Pat Muldoon* (Cort, Mar. 13, 1957); Maggie Harris in *Goldilocks* (Lunt-Fontanne Th., Oct. 11, 1958); Leona Samish in *The Time of the Cuckoo* (Hunterdon

Hills Playhouse, Jutland, N.J., June 3, 1959); Mimi Paragon in *Sail Away* (Broadhurst, N.Y.C., Oct. 3, 1961; Savoy, London, June 21, 1962); succeeded (Apr. 24, 1963) Kate Reid as Martha in the matinee company of *Who's Afraid of Virginia Woolf?* (Billy Rose Th., Oct. 13, 1962); and appeared in the pre-Bway tryout of *Time of the Barracudas* (opened Curran, San Francisco, Calif., Oct. 21, 1963; closed Huntington Hartford Th., Los Angeles, Calif., Nov. 23, 1963).

Miss Stritch played Martha in a touring stock production of *Who's Afraid of Virginia Woolf?* (Summer 1965); Anna Leonowens in a tour of *The King and I* (1965); again played Martha in *Who's Afraid of Virginia Woolf?* (tour, opened Kennebunkport, Me., Playhouse, June 27, 1966); Babylove Dallas in a musical version of *The Grass Harp* (Trinity Square Repertory Co., Providence, R.I., Dec. 26, 1966); Ruth in *Wonderful Town* (revival NY Ctr., May 17, 1967); Dorothy Cleves in a stock tour of *Any Wednesday* (Summer 1967); Amanda Prynne in *Private Lives* (Th. de Lys, N.Y.C., May 19, 1968); toured as Vera Charles in *Mame* later playing the title role (1967); and played Joanne in *Company* (Alvin, N.Y.C., Apr. 26, 1970; and national tour, opened Ahmanson, Los Angeles, May 20, 1971).

In her London debut, Miss Stritch again played Joanne in *Company* (Her Majesty's Th., Jan. 18, 1972); and appeared in *Small Craft Warnings;* and *The Gingerbread Lady.*.

Films. Miss Stritch appeared in *The Scarlet Hour* (Par., 1956); *Three Violent People* (Par., 1956); *A Farewell to Arms* (20th-Fox, 1957); *The Perfect Furlough* (UI, 1958); *Who Killed Teddy Bear?* (Magna, 1965); and *The Sidelong Glances of a Pigeon Kicker* (MGM, 1970), and re-released under the title *Pigeons* (Plaza, 1971).

Television and Radio. She has performed on radio on Inner Sanctum, Young Widder Brown and Real Life Stories.

Miss Stritch made her television debut on the Growing Paynes series (1949); subsequently appeared in *Full Moon Over Brooklyn;* on Pantomine Quiz (1955); Mr. Peepers (NBC, 1955); played Ruth in the My Sister Eileen series (CBS); *Washington Square* (NBC); *The Red Mill* and *Red Peppers* on Studio One (CBS); Climax! (CBS); Alcoa Hour (NBC); Wagon Train (NBC); The Ed Sullivan Show (CBS); The Milton Berle Show (NBC); The Nurses (CBS); played Tracy Sadler on The Trailmaster series (ABC); Miss G. on The Trials of O'Brien series (CBS); Anna in *The Wedding* (Esso Repertory Th., 1965); and appeared in the documentary dealing with the production of the *Company* cast album (ABC).

STROOCK, BIANCA. Costume designer. b. Nov. 11, 1896, Bianca B. Hershfield, New York City, to Reuben and Sarah (Samuels) Hershfield. Father, clothing manufacturer. Married June 16, 1915, to James E. Stroock, pres. of Brooks Costume Co., two daughters, Geraldine Brooks and Gloria Stroock Stern, actresses. Relatives in theatre: son-in-law, Budd Schulberg, playwright, novelist; son-in-law, Leonard Stern, television producer. Member United Scenic Artists, local 829. Address: 785 Park Ave., New York, NY 10021, tel. (212) BU 8-6420.

Theatre. Mrs. Stroock designed costumes for *The Gay Divorce* (Ethel Barrymore Th., Nov. 29, 1932); *She Loves Me Not* (46 St. Th., Nov. 20, 1933); *The Children's Hour* (Maxine Elliott's Th., Nov. 20, 1934); *The Philadelphia Story* (Shubert, Mar. 28, 1939); *Junior Miss* (Lyceum, Nov. 18, 1941); *Claudia* (Booth, Dec. 12, 1941); *Counsellor-at-Law* (Royale, Nov. 24, 1942); *The Dough Girls* (Lyceum, N.Y.C., Dec. 30, 1942); *The Voice of the Turtle* (Morosco, Dec. 8, 1943); *Soldier's Wife* (John Golden Th., Oct. 4, 1944); *Dear Ruth* (Henry Miller's Th., Dec. 13, 1944); *Christopher Blake* (Music Box, Nov. 30, 1946); and *Sabrina Fair* (Natl., Nov. 11, 1953).

Mrs. Stroock also designed fashions for the personal wardrobes of Florenz Ziegfeld, his wife, and his daughter.

Other Activities. Mrs. Stroock has been a member of the Columbia Univ. *Law Journal* staff; the Entertainment Committee of the Stage Door Canteen; director of the Federation Thrift Shop and is a member of *The Woman Pays* Club. During WW II, she designed costumes for use in USO shows abroad.

Recreation. Painting in oils.

STROOCK, JAMES E. Business executive. b. Sept. 4, 1891, Boston, Mass., to Ely and Joan (Oliver) Stroock. Father, clothing manufacturer. Grad. H.S. of Commerce, N.Y.C., 1908. Married June 16, 1915, to Bianca Hershfield, costume designer; two daughters, Geraldine Brooks, actress, and Gloria Stroock Stern, actress. Served WW II, head of entertainment committee, Stage Door Canteen, N.Y.C. Relatives in theatre: son-in-law, Budd Schulberg, playwright, writer; son-in-law, Leonard Stern, television producer. Member of City Athletic Club. Address: (home) 785 Park Ave., New York, NY 10021, tel. (212) BU 8-6420; Seaview, Fire Island, NY 11782, tel. (212) JU 3-5872; (bus.) Brooks-Van Horn Costume Co., 16 W. 61st St., New York, NY 10023, tel. (212) PL 7-5800; Brooks Uniform Co., 75 W. 45th St., New York, NY 10036, tel. (212) JU 6-0010.

Pre-Theatre. Automobile and Wall Street columnist for NY *Evening Globe* (1909–13), and fashion editor for *Vaudeville* (1912).

Theatre. Mr. Stroock has been executive consultant and director of Brooks-Van Horn Costume Co., and during the past 50 years has executed costumes for legitimate theatre, television, motion pictures, ice shows and industrial shows.

STROUSE, CHARLES. Composer. b. Charles Louis Strouse, June 7, 1928, New York City, to Ira and Ethel (Newman) Strouse. Father, businessman. Grad. DeWitt Clinton H.S., N.Y.C., 1944; Eastman Sch. of Music, B.M. 1947. Studied composition with David Diamond, Arthur Berger, Nadia Boulanger, Aaron Copland, and Israel Citkowitz. Married Sept. 23, 1962, to Barbara Siman. Member of AFM, Local 802; ASCAP; AGAC; Dramatists Guild. Address: 171 W. 57th St., New York, NY 10019.

Theatre. Mr. Strouse wrote music for stock productions at Green Mansions Th. (Warrensburg, N.Y., 1952–55); contributed songs and was musical director for *Shoestring Review* (President, N.Y.C., Feb. 28, 1955); contributed songs to *Shoestring '57* (Barbizon-Plaza, Nov. 5, 1956); wrote music for *Pound in Your Pocket* (Royal Poinciana, Palm Beach, Fla., Summers 1956–57); *Bye Bye Birdie* (Martin Beck Th., N.Y.C., Apr. 14, 1960); *All American* (Winter Garden, Mar. 19, 1962); *Golden Boy* (Majestic, Oct. 20, 1964); *It's a Bird It's a Plane It's SUPERMAN* (Alvin Th., Mar. 29, 1966); and *Applause* (Palace, Mar. 30, 1970).

Films. Mr. Strouse wrote music for *The Mating Game* (MGM, 1959); and his music for *Bye Bye Birdie* was used in the screen version (Col., 1963). Other films for which he wrote music include *Bonnie and Clyde* (WB, 1967) and *The Night They Raided Minsky's* (UA, 1968).

Awards. Antoinette Perry (Tony) awards for best musical play were received by *Bye Bye Birdie* (1961) and *Applause* (1970).

STRUDWICK, SHEPPERD. Actor. b. Sept. 22, 1907, Hillsboro, N.C., to Shepperd and Susan (Read) Strudwick. Father, sculptor; mother, musician. Grad. Virginia Episcopal Sch., Lynchburg, 1925; Univ. of North Carolina, A.B. (Phi Beta Kappa, and Order of the Golden Fleece) 1928. Studied acting with Leo Bulgakow, N.Y.C., one year; Samuel Rosen, N.Y.C., four years; Lee Strasberg, N.Y.C., three years; Actors' Studio, N.Y.C. (mbr., 1962–to date). Married May 10, 1936, to Helen Wynn, writer (marr. dis. 1946); one son; married Sept. 3, 1946, to Jane Straub, public relations exec. (marr. dis. 1959); married Aug. 27, 1960, to Margaret O'Neill, actress (marr. dis. 1973). Served WW II, USN; rank, Lt. (s.g.). Relative in theatre: Lucille Strudwick, actress. Member of AEA; SAG; AFTRA; Amer. Veterans Committee (Calif. state chmn., 1946); Delta Kappa Epsilon. Address: International Famous Agency, 1301 Ave. of the Americas, New York, NY 10019, tel. (212) 556-5600.

Theatre. Mr. Strudwick made his first appearance on a stage in a college production of *Pierrot* (1925); and his N.Y.C. debut as Wu-Hu-Git in *Yellow Jacket* (Coburn Th., Nov. 7, 1928).

He toured stock theatres in juvenile roles (1929); appeared in productions with the Jitney Players (Madison, Conn., 1930); played Alan McClain in *Both Your Houses* (Royale, N.Y.C., Mar., 6, 1933); Richard Kurt in *Biography* (Ethel Barrymore Th., Feb. 5, 1934); John McClure in *Let Freedom Ring* (Broadhurst, Nov. 6, 1935); Will Dexter in *The End of Summer* (Guild, Feb. 17, 1936);, also touring in it (1936–37); Orlando in *As You Like It* (Ritz, N.Y.C., Oct. 30, 1937); appeared in and co-produced plays at the Surry (Me.) Th. (1937–39); and played Vershinin in *The Three Sisters* (Longacre, N.Y.C., Oct. 14, 1939).

Also, Mr. Blake in *Christopher Blake* (Music Box, Nov. 31, 1946); George Henderson in *Affairs of State* (Royale, Sept. 25, 1950); Charley Nichols in *The Ladies of the Corridor* (Longacre, Oct. 21, 1953); Sir Colenso Ridgeon in *The Doctor's Dilemma* (Phoenix, Jan. 11, 1955); Aegeus in *The Medea* at the International Drama Festival (Sara Bernhardt Th., Paris, France, July 1955); Trigorin in *The Seagull* (Fourth St. Th., N.Y.C., Oct. 22, 1956); the Father in *Night Circus* (John Golden Th., Dec. 2, 1958); Lucius Whitmore in *Only in America* (Cort, Nov. 19, 1959); toured in the title role of *J. B.* (opened Playhouse, Wilmington, Del., Oct. 19, 1960; closed Camp Th., Lejeune, N.C., Apr. 15, 1961); succeeded (Nov. 14, 1961) Staats Cotsworth as Manders in *Ghosts* (Fourth St. Th., N.Y.C., Sept. 21, 1961); played George in the matinee company of *Who's Afraid of Virginia Woolf?* (Billy Rose Th., Oct. 13, 1962), later taking over (Aug. 1963) this role in the evening company, and also toured in it (opened Colonial, Boston, Mass., Sept. 2, 1963).

He played Abraham Lincoln in *The Last Days of Lincoln* (Actors Studio at the Library of Congress, Washington, D.C., Apr. 12, 1965; and Th. de Lys, N.Y.C., Apr. 20, 1965); the Archbishop in *The Devils* (Broadway Th., Nov. 16, 1965); the Duke in *Measure for Measure* (NY Shakespeare Festival, Delacorte Th., July 13, 1966); the Cardinal Inquisitor in *Galileo* (Vivian Beaumont Th., Lincoln Ctr., Apr. 13, 1967); John Lansdale in *In the Matter of J. Robert Oppenheimer* (Vivian Beaumont Th., Lincoln Ctr., Summer 1969); replaced Arthur Kennedy as Walter Franz in *The Price* (Morosco, Oct. 28, 1968; The Duke of York Th., London, Mar. 4, 1969; and national tour, Sept. 1969–May 1970); played Commander Bucher in *Pueblo* (Arena Stage, Washington, D.C., Feb. 26, 1971); played the title role in *Timon of Athens* (Delacorte Th., N.Y.C., Summer 1971); and played Reverdy Johnson in *Assassination 1865* (Goodman Th., Chicago, Ill., Oct. 27, 1971).

As artist in residence at the Univ. of Michigan, (Jan.–Mar. 1972) he appeared as Prospero in *The Tempest,* and Dobbs in *Child's Play;* subsequently played Herbert Dean in *The Royal Family* (Shaw Festival, Niagara-on-the-Lake, June 12, 1972); Associate Justice Jacob Balding in *Conflict of Interest* (Arizona Civic Th., Tucson, Ariz., Oct. 12, 1972); Willy Loman in *Death of a Salesman* (artist-in-residence, Univ. of No. Carolina, Greensboro, N.C., Nov. 8, 1972); the Public Prosecutor in *A Public Prosecutor Is Sick of It All* (Arena Stage, Washington, D.C., Jan. 31, 1973); and General Birabeau in *The Desert Song* (on tour, Summer 1973; and Uris, N.Y.C., Sept. 4, 1973).

Films. Since making his debut in *That Mothers Might Live* (MGM, 1938), Mr. Strudwick has appeared in over fifty films, including *Flight Command* (MGM, 1940); *Dr. Kildare's Strange Case* (MGM, 1940); *Belle Starr* (20th-Fox, 1941); *Men in Her Life* (Col., 1941); *Remember the Day* (20th-Fox, 1941); *Ten Gentlemen from West Point* (20th-Fox, 1942); *Loves of Edgar Allen Poe* (20th-Fox, 1942); *The Chetniks* (20th-Fox, 1943); *Enchantment* (RKO, 1947); *Joan of Arc* (RKO, 1948); *The Red Pony* (Rep.,

1949); *All the King's Men* (Col., 1949); *A Place in the Sun* (Par., 1951); *The Eddie Duchin Story* (Col., 1956); *Psychomania* (UA, 1962); *Operation Rescue* (Par., 1967); *The Monitors* (UA, 1968); *The Slaves* (Th. Guild, 1969); and *Cops and Robbers* (UA, 1973).

In the films he appeared in for 20th Century-Fox, he was billed as John Shepperd.

Television. Mr. Strudwick played Professor Ashley in *The Last Thing I Do* (Studio One, CBS); Senator Greet in *Little Men, Big World* (Studio One, CBS); the Teacher-Father in *The Fathers* (Studio One); the Reporter in *Portrait of Smoke* (Philco Television Playhouse, NBC); Benedict Arnold in *Pride's Way* (Philco Television Playhouse, NBC); Arthur Collins in *Catch A Falling Star* (Goodyear Television Playhouse, NBC); Eilert Lovborg in *Hilda McKay*, which was based on *Hedda Gabler* (Kraft Television Th., NBC); the City Editor in *City Editor* (Armstrong Circle Th., NBC); Alvin Boyle in *The Lady Looks Ahead* (Gulf Oil Co., CBS); the Lawyer-Husband in *The Visitor* (Armstrong Circle Th., CBS); Alexander Hamilton in *Hamilton-Burr Duel* (You Are There, CBS); Gov. Brad Duncan in *Squeeze Play* (Danger, CBS); John Andros in *The Party* (Revlon Mirror Th. CBS); George in *Daisy Mayme* (Pulitzer Prize Playhouse, ABC); the Psychopathic Doctor in *The Season of Divorce* (Curtain Call, NBC); the Lawyer in *The Fatal Hour* (Inner Sanctum, NBC); the Judge in *Double Negative* (The Doctors, CBS); served as Narrator for The Passerby; and Man's Heritage.

During 1954–55, he appeared in the following roles on You Are There (CBS); Dr. Semmelweis in *The Tragic Hour of Dr. S.;* Crito in *The Death of Socrates;* King Solomon in *The Plot Against King Solomon;* President Andrew Jackson in *Cabinet Crisis—Peggy Eaton;* and General Andrew Jackson in *Jackson and LaFitte at New Orleans.*

Also during 1954–55, he played Dr. Hudson in Dr. Hudson's Maine Case (Frontiers of Faith, CBS); the Psychiatrist in *Lady in the Dark* (Max Leibman Presents, NBC); Tyriesius in *Antigone* (Omnibus, CBS); the Hollywood Star in *The Ghost Writer* (Philco Television Playhouse, NBC); Cassius in *Julius Caesar* (Studio One, CBS); and Lycon in *Barefoot in Athens* (Hallmark Hall of Fame, NBC).

Mr. Strudwick has also appeared on The Defenders (CBS); The Nurses (CBS); Westinghouse Special (CBS); US Steel Hour (CBS); Playhouse 90 (CBS); Climax! (CBS); Look Up and Live (CBS); The Verdict Is Yours (CBS); Perry Mason (CBS); The Californians; Harbor Master; and Wagon Train (NBC); MacMillan and Wife (NBC); and The Name of the Game (NBC).

He played Dr. Field in As the World Turns (CBS, 1964–65); Jim Matthews in Another World (NBC, 1965–68); and Mr. Gibson in One Life to Live (ABC, 1972).

Awards. Mr. Strudwick received a citation from the governor of North Carolina for "excellence in the performing arts" (1963).

Recreation. Tennis, swimming, riding, gardening, carpentry, reading, music.

STYNE, JULE. Composer, producer, music publisher. b. Julius Kerwin Stein, Dec. 31, 1905, London, England, to Isadore and Anna (Kertman) Stein. Father, produce merchant. Attended Chicago (Ill.) Coll. of Music, 1914–24; Northwestern Univ. 1927. Married Aug. 9, 1926, to Ethel Rubenstein (marr. dis. 1951); two sons; married June 4, 1962, to Margaret Brown, actress, model. Relative in theatre; son, Stanley Styne, lyricist. Member of Dramatists Guild; SSD&C; AFM; ASCAP (board member, 25 yrs.; board of review, 1963–64); AMPAS, League of NY Theatres; The Friars.

Theatre. Mr. Styne composed the music for *High Button Shoes* (Century Th., N.Y.C., Oct. 9, 1947); *Gentlemen Prefer Blondes* (Ziegfeld Th., Dec. 8, 1949); produced with Harry Rigby and Alexander H. Cohen, *Make a Wish* (Winter Garden, Apr. 18, 1951); composed music for the revue, *Two on the Aisle* (Mark Hellinger Th., July 19, 1951); produced with Leonard Key and Anthony B. Farrell, *Pal Joey* (Broadhurst, Jan. 3, 1952); and with George Abbott, *In Any Language* (Cort, Oct. 7, 1952).

He composed the music for *Hazel Flagg*, which he also produced with Anthony B. Farrell (Mark Hellinger Th., Feb. 11, 1953); composed additional music for Mary Martin's *Peter Pan* (Winter Garden, Oct. 20, 1954); produced *Will Success Spoil Rock Hunter?* (Belasco, Oct. 13, 1955); produced with George Gilbert and Lester Osterman, *Mr. Wonderful* (Bway Th., Mar. 22, 1956); composed the music for *Bells Are Ringing* (Shubert, Nov. 29, 1956); *Say, Darling*, which he also produced with Lester Osterman (ANTA, Apr. 3, 1958); *Gypsy* (Bway Th., May 21, 1959); *Do Re Mi* (St. James, Dec. 26, 1960); *Subways Are for Sleeping* (St. James, Dec. 27, 1962); *Arturo Ui* (Lunt-Fontanne Th., Nov. 11, 1963); and *Funny Girl* (Winter Garden, Mar. 26, 1964; moved to Majestic, Mar. 14, 1966; moved to Broadway Th., Nov. 28, 1966; and produced in London at the Prince of Wales' Th., Apr. 13, 1966).

On Stage Productions, co-founded (1962), by Mr. Styne and Lester Osterman, produced *High Spirits* (Alvin, Apr. 7, 1964); *Fade Out—Fade In* (Mark Hellinger Th., May 26, 1964), for which Mr. Styne composed the music; and *Something More* (Eugene O'Neill Th., Nov. 10, 1964), which Mr. Styne also directed.

He wrote the music for the Ford industrial show, *Thrill of a Lifetime* (Mark Hellinger Th., Aug. 27, 1965); *Hallelujah, Baby!* (Martin Beck Th., Apr. 26, 1967); *Darling of the Day* (George Abbott Th., Jan. 27, 1968); *Look to the Lilies* (Lunt-Fontanne, Mar. 29, 1970); the pre-Bway tryout of *Prettybelle* (opened Shubert, Boston, Feb. 1, 1971; closed there Mar. 6, 1971); *Sugar* (Majestic, N.Y.C., Apr. 9, 1972); *Lorelei*, based upon his earlier *Gentlemen Prefer Blondes* (pre-Bway tour opened Civic Ctr. Music Hall, Oklahoma City, Feb. 26, 1973), later revised and re-titled *Lorelei* or "Gentlemen Still Prefer Blondes" (Palace Th., N.Y.C., Jan. 27, 1974); and a revival of *Gypsy* (pre-Bway tour opened Royal Alexandra Th., Toronto, Mar. 25, 1974), and opened on Bway (Winter Garden, N.Y.C., Sept. 23, 1974).

Films. He collaborated on songs or film scores for *Sailors on Leave* (Rep., 1941); *Sweater Girl* (Par., 1942); *Priorities on Parade* (Par., 1942); *Youth on Parade* (Rep., 1942); *Hit Parade of 1943* (Rep., 1943); *Carolina Blues* (Col., 1944); *Follow the Boys* (U, 1944); *Anchors Aweigh* (MGM, 1945); *Tonight and Every Night* (Col., 1945); *Don't Fence Me In* (Rep., 1945); *Stork Club* (Par., 1945); *The Kid from Brooklyn* (RKO, 1946); *Tars and Spars* (Col., 1946); *Sweetheart of Sigma Chi* (Mono., 1946); *Earl Carroll Sketch Book* (Rep., 1946); *It Happened in Brooklyn* (MGM, 1947); *Ladies' Man* (Par., 1947); *Two Guys from Texas* (WB, 1948); *It's a Great Feeling* (WB, 1949); *The West Point Story* (WB, 1950); *Double Dynamite (It's Only Money)* (RKO, 1951); *Two Tickets to Broadway* (RKO, 1951); *Meet Me After the Show* (20th-Fox, 1951); *Macao* (RKO, 1952); *Gentlemen Prefer Blondes* (20th-Fox, 1953); *Three Coins in the Fountain* (20th-Fox, 1954); *Living It Up*, based upon his earlier *Hazel Flagg* (Par., 1954); *My Sister Eileen* (Col., 1955); *How to be Very, Very Popular* (20th-Fox, 1955); *Bells Are Ringing* (MGM, 1960); *Gypsy* (WB, 1962); *What A Way to Go* (20th-Fox, 1964); and *Funny Girl* (Col., 1968).

Television. He composed the music for *Ruggles of Red Gap* (1957); *Mr. Magoo's Christmas Carol* (NBC, 1962); wrote the songs for *Peter Pan* (NBC, 1960); produced *Anything Goes* (1957); *Panama Hattie* (1967); *The Best of Broadway* (1957); and the Eddie Fisher Show (NBC, 1959); appeared as himself on Bilko (ABC, 1964); wrote, with Bob Merrill, the score for *The Dangerous Christmas of Red Riding Hood* or "Oh Wolf, Poor Wolf" (ABC, 1965), of which they were executive producers; appeared on *A Funny Girl Happened to Me on the Way to the Piano* (London, 1966). His *High Button Shoes* was adapted for television (CBS, 1966), for which, with Sammy Cahn, he wrote the songs; appeared on the Today Show (NBC, 1966–67); wrote the music for *I'm Getting Married* (Stage 67, ABC, 1967); and, with Sammy Cahn, wrote the music for *The Night the Animals Talked* (ABC, 1970).

Other Activities. Mr. Styne was voice coach to Alice Faye and Shirley Temple, among others, during the late 1930's; and was named Entertainment Consultant, Vice President, and member of the board of Caesar's Palace (Las Vegas, 1966).

Awards. He received the Academy (Oscar) Award for the title song from *Three Coins in the Fountain* (1954).

He received Academy (Oscar) Award nominations for "It Seems I Heard That Song Before" from *Youth on Parade* (1942); "A Change of Heart" from *Hit Parade of 1943;* "Anywhere" from *Follow the Boys* (1944); "I'll Walk Alone " from *Tonight and Every Night* (1945); "I Fall in Love too Easily" from *Anchors Aweigh* (1945); "It's Magic" from *Romance on the High Seas* (1948); and the title songs from *It's a Great Feeling* (1948); and *Funny Girl* (1968). Mr. Styne received tribute in the Congressional Record of Aug. 10, 1964, noting his twenty-fifth anniversary in show business; received (June 3, 1966) one of the first Anglo-American Awards for "outstanding contribution to British theatre" for *Funny Girl;* was honored by "Jule Styne Day," proclaimed Oct. 19, 1967, by the U.S. Pavilion, Expo '67, Montreal; received an Antoinette Perry (Tony) Award for *Hallelujah, Baby!* (1967); and was honored by *Jule's Friends at the Palace* (Palace Th., N.Y.C., May 19, 1974), a gala benefit for the Metropolitan Chapter of the National Hemophilia Foundation and the American Musical and Dramatic Academy.

Recreation. Golf, song writing.

SUGRUE, FRANK. Producer. b. Francis Patrick Sugrue, Jan. 6, 1927, Boston, Mass., to Denis J. and Margaret T. (Downing) Sugrue. Father, locksmith. Grad. Dorchester (Mass.) H.S., 1944; Newman Prep. Sch., 1947; Boston Univ., B.S. 1952; Northeastern Law Sch., LL.B. 1956. Married June 1953 to Eleanor Desmond, editor (marr. dis. Feb. 1964). Served USMC, PTO, 1944–46; rank, Cpl. Member of NETC (vice-pres., 1961–62; adv. bd., 1963–64); Dance Circle of Boston (adv. bd., 1963–64). Address: (home) 63 Mt. Vernon St., Boston, MA 02108, tel. (617) 542-2111; (bus.) The Charles Playhouse, 76 Warrenton St., Boston, MA 02116, tel. (617) 542-1740.

Theatre. In 1958, Mr. Sugrue and Michael Murray founded the Charles Playhouse, a resident professional theatre in Boston; as producer and managing director, he has presented some one hundred fifty plays.

He first produced at the Stateside Th. (Tientsin, China), which he founded (1946) while serving with the USMC; later, produced *The Moon Is Blue* (Town Hall, Edgartown, Martha's Vineyard, Mass., Sept. 1959); and with Jerome Rosenfeld and Natl. Productions, *Two for the Seesaw* (Wilbur Th., Boston, Mass., Apr. 1961).

Recreation. Reading, skiing, sailing, golf, travel, art, jazz, and theatre.

SULKA, ELAINE. Actress, producer, theatre manager. b. New York City, to Michael and Anna (Chehovich) Sulka; father, grocer, butcher. Grad. Queens College, Phi Beta Kappa, B.A. in Sociology; Brown Univ., M.A. in Sociology. Attended Univ. of Wisconsin. Trained for the stage at San Francisco Actors Workshop, 1957–60; American Shakespeare Festival and Academy, 1963. Married June 1967 to Philip Meister, producer, director; one daughter. Member of AEA. Address: Cubiculo Th., 414 W. 51st St., New York, NY 10019, tel. (212) 265-2139.

Pre-Theatre. Probation officer; criminologist.

Theatre. Miss Sulka made her acting debut playing small parts in various productions at the San Francisco Actors Workshop (1957–60); subsequently appeared with the San Diego Globe Th. Co. (1961); and (1963) the American Shakespeare Festival (Stratford, Conn.), understudying Rosemary Murphy in the roles of The Courtesan in *The Comedy of Errors* and Goneril in *King Lear* (replacing her (Fall 1963) in the latter part). She has appeared in approximately thirty productions with the National Shakespeare Co. (1963–to date) and at the Cubiculo

Th. (1968–to date), including many of the roles in the classical canon. Elsewhere, she has appeared in *Brotherhood* (St. Mark's Playhouse, N.Y.C., Jan. 1971); played Marylou in *Brothers* (Th. Four, Jan. 1972); and understudied Irene Papas in the title role of *Medea* (Circle in the Square/Joseph E. Levine Th., Jan. 17, 1973), performing the role on six occasions.

She is managing director, and, with her husband, co-founder of the National Shakespeare Co. (1963–to date), which has produced and toured thirty-nine abbreviated and full length Shakespearian productions throughout the educational community; The Cubiculo Th. (1968–to date), an experimental art center (a complex of 2 performing and several rehearsal spaces), devoted to showcasing new talent in dance, music, poetry, acting, playwriting, and directing, where some two hundred-fifty presentations have been staged; and the New York Theatre Co. (1974–to date) which produces and tours revivals of Bway musicals.

Published Works. Her short stories have appeared in the periodicals *Woman* and *Aphra*. .

Awards. Miss Sulka was the recipient of scholarships and fellowships to Brown Univ. and the Univ. of Wisconsin.

Recreation. Writing; her play, *Clytemnestra*, was produced at the Cubiculo Th. in May 1976.

SULLIVAN, BARRY. Actor. b. Patrick Barry Sullivan, Aug. 12, 1912, Bronx, N.Y., to Cornelius Daniel and Ellen Sullivan. Father, realtor. Attended St. Regis Prep. Sch., 1927; New York Univ., 1931; Temple Univ., 1932–34. Married Aug. 13, 1937, to Marie Brown, actress (marr. dis. June 25, 1957); married July 25, 1958, to Brigitta Hall, known as Gita Hall, actress (marr. dis. 1960); married Aug. 5, 1962, to Desiree Sumara, actress. Member of AEA; SAG; AFTRA.

Theatre. Mr. Sullivan made his first appearance on a stage as Johnny Case in *Holiday* (Temple Univ., 1933); and his N.Y.C. debut as Capt. Lynch in *I Want a Policeman* (Lyceum Th., Jan. 14, 1936).

He appeared as a walk-on in *Idiot's Delight* (Shubert, Aug. 31, 1936); St. Denis in *St. Helena* (Lyceum, Oct. 6, 1936); succeeded (Apr. 21, 1937) Eddie Albert as Bing Edwards in *Brother Rat* (Biltmore, Dec. 16, 1936); played Atwood Post in *All That Glitters* (Biltmore, Jan. 19, 1938); and Roger Sanford in *Eye on the Sparrow* (Vanderbilt, May 3, 1938).

In stock, he appeared in *7-11* (Cohasset, Mass., Aug. 1938); played Dr. Ellis Plum in the pre-Bway tryout of *Angela Is 22* (opened Cass, Detroit, Mich., Feb. 20, 1939; closed Selwyn, Chicago, Ill., Mar. 12, 1939); David in the pre-Bway tryout of *Yankee Fable* (opened Colonial, Boston, Mass., Oct. 1938; closed there Nov. 5, 1938); Bert Jefferson in the national tour of *The Man Who Came to Dinner* (opened Cass, Detroit, Mich., Sept. 15, 1940), and succeeded (Apr. 20, 1941) Joseph Allen, Jr., in the latter role in N.Y.C. (Music Box, Oct. 16, 1939).

He played Eric Reynolds in *Mr. Big* (Lyceum, Sept. 30, 1941); Andy Blayne in *Ring Around Elizabeth* (Playhouse, Nov. 17, 1941); temporarily replaced (Nov. 27, 1941) Hugh Marlowe as Wayne Kincaid in *The Land Is Bright* (Music Box, Oct. 28, 1941); appeared as Coaly Lewis in *Johnny 2 × 4* (Longacre, Mar. 16, 1942); appeared in *Biography* (La Jolla Playhouse, Calif., Summer 1947); played Shepherd Henderson in a tour of *Bell, Book and Candle* (Somerset, Mass., June 29, 1953); succeeded (May 31, 1954) Henry Fonda as Lt. Barney Greenwald in *The Caine Mutiny Court-Martial* (Plymouth, N.Y.C., Jan. 20, 1954); played Lt. Peter Van Vaanderen in *Too Late the Phalarope* (Belasco, Oct. 11, 1956); Max Grady in the pre-Bway tour of *Goldilocks* (Fall 1958); and substituted (Atlanta, Ga., Jan. 19, 1960; Chattanooga, Tenn., Feb. 19, 1960) for Gary Merrill during the tour of *The World of Carl Sandburg*. .

Films. Mr. Sullivan has appeared in *We Refuse to Die* (Par., 1942); *The Woman of the Town* (UA, 1943); *Rainbow Island* (Par., 1944); *And Now Tomorrow* (Par., 1944); *Lady in the Dark* (Par., 1944); *Duffy's Tavern* (Par., 1945); *Two Years Before the Mast* (Par., 1946); *Suspense* (Mono., 1946); *The Gangster* (AA, 1947); *A Life of Her Own* (MGM, 1950); *Nancy Goes to Rio* (MGM, 1950); *Grounds for Marriage* (MGM, 1950); *Mr. Imperium* (MGM, 1951); *Unknown Man* (MGM, 1951); *No Questions Asked* (MGM, 1951); *Cause for Alarm* (MGM, 1951); *Payment on Demand* (RKO, 1951); *Three Guys Named Mike* (MGM, 1951); *The Bad and the Beautiful* (MGM, 1952); *Skirts Ahoy!* (MGM, 1952); *China Venture* (Col., 1953); *Cry of the Hunted* (MGM, 1953); *Jeopardy* (MGM, 1953); *Her 12 Men* (MGM, 1954); *Playgirl* (U, 1954); *The Miami Story* (Col., 1954); *Loophole* (AA, 1954); *Strategic Air Command* (Par., 1955); *Queen Bee* (Col., 1955); *Texas Lady* (RKO, 1955); *The Maverick Queen* (Rep., 1956); *Julie* (MGM, 1956); *Dragoon Wells Massacre* (AA, 1957); *Forty Guns* (20th-Fox, 1957); *The Way to the Gold* (20th-Fox, 1957); *Another Time, Another Place* (Par., 1958); *Wolf Larsen* (AA, 1958); *The Purple Gang* (AA, 1960); *Seven Ways from Sundown* (U, 1960); *Light in the Piazza* (MGM, 1962); *Gathering of Eagles* (U, 1963); *Pyro* (AMI, 1963); Stage to Thunder Rock (Par., 1964); *Buckskin* (Par., 1968); and *Tell Them Willie Boy Is Here* (U, 1970).

Television. Mr. Sullivan appeared in Ford Th. (NBC) productions of *As the Flame Dies* (Nov. 1953) and *The Fugitives* (Jan. 1954); in *The Merry Widow* (NBC, Apr. 1955); in Ford Star Jubilee (CBS) productions of *The Caine Mutiny Court-Martial* (Nov. 1955) and *A Bell for Adano* (June 1956); on Playhouse 90 (CBS) in *Snow Shoes* (Jan. 1957), *Ain't No Time for Glory* (June 1957), *Nightmare at Ground Zero* (May 1958), *A Quiet Game of Cards* (Jan. 1959), and *Dark December* (Apr. 1959); and on Zane Grey Th. (CBS) in *Shadow of a Dead Man* (Apr. 1958), *Bury Me Dead* (Dec. 1958), and *The Lonely Gun* (Oct. 1959). Also on the US Steel Hour (CBS) in *Operation Northstar* (Dec. 1960) and *Night of the Fourth* (July 1962); Wagon Train (ABC, 1962); *Day of Reckoning* (Alfred Hitchcock Th., CBS, Nov. 1962); *Crazy Sunday* (Dick Powell Th., NBC, Dec. 1962); Route 66 (CBS, 1963); The Virginian (NBC, 1963, 1969); and Ben Casey (ABC, 1963).

Other programs on which he appeared include Slattery's People (CBS, 1964); Twelve O'Clock High (ABC, 1965); The Road West (NBC, 1966); Bonanza (NBC, 1967); The Man from U.N.C.L.E. (NBC, 1968); Name of the Game (NBC, 1969, 1971); It Takes a Thief (ABC, 1969, 1970); High Chaparral (CBS, 1970); Medical Center (CBS, 1970); *The Price* (Hallmark Hall of Fame, NBC, Feb. 1971); Marcus Welby, M.D. (ABC, 1971); Mannix (ABC, 1972); and *Another Part of the Forest* (Hollywood Television Th., PBS, Oct. 1972).

SULLIVAN, JO. Actress, singer, executive. b. Elizabeth Josephine Sullivan, Aug. 28, Mound City, Ill., to Hessie and Eileen (Woods) Sullivan. Grad. Mounds H.S., Mound City, Ill., 1945; attended Columbia Univ. 1947–48. Studied singing with Alba Clawson, Colin Romoff; acting with Lee Strasberg. Married 1952 to Donald Jacobs (marr. dis. 1957); married 1959 to Frank Loesser, composer (dec. 1969). Two daughters. Married Dec. 21, 1973, to John Osborn. Member of AEA; AGVA; SAG. Address: 161 E. 70th St., New York, NY 10021, tel. (212) 249-0911.

Miss Sullivan is president of Frank Music, Inc.

Theatre. She made her N.Y.C. debut as Juliet in *Let's Make an Opera* (John Golden Th., Dec. 13, 1950); subsequently played Julie in *Carousel* (NY City Ctr., June 2, 1954); Polly Peachum in *The Threepenny Opera* (Th. de Lys, Mar. 10, 1954); Rosabella in *The Most Happy Fella*, for which Frank Loesser adapted the book and wrote the music and lyrics (Imperial, May 3, 1956), also touring in it (opened Riviera, Detroit, Mich., Dec. 23, 1957; closed Philharmonic Aud., Los Angeles, Calif., June 28, 1958); Eileen in *Wonderful Town* (NY City Ctr., Mar. 5, 1958); and Magnolia in *Show Boat* (NY City Ctr., Apr. 12, 1961).

She has appeared in stock as Dorothy in *The Wizard of Oz*; Sharon McLonergan in *Finian's Rainbow* (Starlight Theatre, Kansas City, Mo.); Kathie in *The Student Prince*, Kitty Verdun in *Where's Charley?* and Adele in *Die Fledermaus* (Lambertville Music Circus, N.J.).

Television. Miss Sullivan has sung in Respighi's opera, *The Sleeping Beauty*, and Alec Wilder's opera, *Chicken Little* (Omnibus, CBS, 1951–52); and on the Ed Sullivan Show (CBS, 1956, 1957).

SUNDBERG, CLINTON. Actor. b. Dec. 7, 1906, Vienna, S.D., to C. H. and Grace (Coffey) Sundberg. Father, auditor. Grad. Appleton (Minn.) H.S., 1922; Hamline Univ., B.A. 1926. Married Jan. 18, 1942, to Margaret Joyce; one son, one daughter. Member of AEA; SAG; AFTRA; The Players. Address: (home) 827 21st St., Santa Monica, CA 90403, tel. (213) EX 5-3413; (bus.) c/o Cunningham and Associates, 5900 Wilshire Blvd., Los Angeles, CA 90036; c/o The Players Club, 16 Gramercy Park, New York, NY 10003, tel. (212) GR 5-3166.

Pre-Theatre. High school English teacher.

Theatre. Mr. Sundberg made his stage debut appearing in stock (Manchester, N.H., 1929); subsequently at Jefferson Th. (Portland, Me., 1929); toured as David in *Michael and Mary* (1931); Fred in *Silent Witness* (1932); made his N.Y.C. debut as Martin Lodge in *Nine Pine Street* (Longacre Th., Apr. 27, 1933); appeared as Laval in *She Loves Me Not* (Adelphi Th., London, Apr. 8, 1934); succeeded (Ethel Barrymore Th., Mar. 5, 1935) Bretaigne Windust as Roland in *The Distaff Side* (Booth, N.Y.C., Sept. 25, 1934); and played Charles Talbot in *I Want a Policeman* (Lyceum, Jan. 14, 1936).

He appeared as Robi Law in *Boy Meets Girl* (Shaftsbury Th., London, Mar. 8, 1936); toured the US as Davis in *Room Service* (1937); played Wilder in *Stars in Your Eyes* (Majestic, N.Y.C., Feb. 9, 1939); toured as Mortimer in *Arsenic and Old Lace* (1941); succeeded (1942) Allyn Joslyn as Mortimer in *Arsenic and Old Lace* (Fulton, N.Y.C., Jan. 10, 1941), and toured in the production (1942).

Mr. Sundberg toured as Max in *Over 21* (1943–44); played George Bowsmith in *The Rugged Path* (Plymouth, N.Y.C., Nov. 10, 1945); Mr. Kraler in *The Diary of Anne Frank* (Cort, Oct. 5, 1955); Stewart Stoddard in *The Man in the Dog Suit* (Coronet, Oct. 30, 1958); Dr. Monroe Sidensticker in *Midgie Purvis* (Martin Beck Th., Feb. 1, 1961); toured as Oscar Nelson in a national company of *Mary, Mary* (opened Central City Opera House, Colo., Aug. 6, 1962), and succeeded (Mar. 14, 1964) Alan Bunce as Oscar Nelson in the Bway company (Helen Hayes Th., Mar. 8, 1961).

Films. Mr. Sundberg appeared in *Undercurrent* (MGM, 1946); *Undercover Maisie* (MGM, 1947); *Living in a Big Way* (MGM, 1947); *Song of Love* (MGM, 1947); *The Hucksters* (MGM, 1947); *The Kissing Bandit* (MGM, 1948); *Easter Parade* (MGM, 1948); *Good Sam* (RKO, 1948); *A Date with Judy* (MGM, 1948); *Words and Music* (MGM, 1948); *Command Decision* (MGM, 1948); *In the Good Old Summertime* (MGM, 1949); *Key to the City* (MGM, 1950); *Annie Get Your Gun* (MGM, 1950); *The Toast of New Orleans* (MGM, 1950); *The Fat Man* (U, 1951); *As Young as You Feel* (20th-Fox, 1951); *The Belle of New York* (MGM, 1952); *The Girl Next Door* (20th-Fox, 1953); *Main Street to Broadway* (MGM, 1953); *The Caddy* (Par., 1953); *The Birds and the Bees* (Par., 1956); *Bachelor in Paradise* (MGM, 1961); *The Wonderful World of the Brothers Grimm* (MGM, 1962); *How the West Was Won* (MGM, 1962); and *Hotel* (WB, 1968).

Television. Mr. Sundberg has appeared in many programs such as *Studio I* (CBS), etc.

Recreation. Photography.

SUNDGAARD, ARNOLD. Playwright, librettist. b. Arnold Olaf Sundgaard, Oct. 31, 1909, St. Paul, Minn., to Olaf Johannes and Borghild Marie (Pehrson) Sundgaard. Father, machinist. Grad. Johnson H.S., St. Paul, 1927; Univ. of Wisconsin, B.A. 1935; attended Yale Univ., 1932–34, 1935–36. Married Jan. 3, 1929, to Margaret Christensen (marr. dis. 1940); one son, two daughters; married Jan. 17, 1940, to Marge Kane; two sons. Member of Dramatists Guild; ASCAP; Theatre, Inc. (member, board of dir., 1945–47). Address: Bungtown Rd.,

Cold Spring Harbor, L.I., NY tel. (516) Myrtle 2-2824.

Theatre. Mr. Sundgaard wrote *Spirochete*, a "Living Newspaper" for the Federal Th. (WPA) Project (Blackstone Th., Chicago, Ill., 1938); subsequently, with Marc Connelly, wrote *Everywhere I Roam* (Natl., N.Y.C., Dec. 29, 1938); wrote *The First Crocus* (Longacre, Jan. 2, 1942); wrote the book for a musical, *Rhapsody* (Century, Nov. 22, 1944); and the Labor Stage production of *The Great Campaign* (Princess, Mar. 30, 1947).

He wrote *Promised Valley*, a musical drama (Utah Centennial, 1947); the libretto (music by Kurt Weill) for *Down in the Valley*, a folk opera (Lemonade Opera Co., N.Y.C., July 7, 1948); the libretto (music by Douglas Moore) for *Giants in the Earth* (Columbia Univ. Opera Workshop, Mar. 28, 1951); and for the musical play *The Wind Blows Free* (Ramapo Lyric Festival, N.Y., 1950).

He wrote the libretto (music by Alec Wilder) for the folk opera, *The Lowland Sea* (N.J. State Teachers Coll., Montclair, Apr. 28, 1953); wrote the play, *The Kilgo Run* (Bucks County Playhouse, New Hope, Pa., 1955; Century City Playhouse, Los Angeles, Calif., June 5, 1964); the librettos for the one-act operas, *Sunday Excursion*, with music by Alec Wilder (Grass Roots Opera Co., Raleigh, N.C., 1955) and *Gallantry* with music by Douglas Moore (Columbia Univ. Opera Workshop, N.Y.C., Mar. 19, 1958); and the book and lyrics for *Kittiwake Island* (Martinique, Oct. 15, 1960). He wrote the cantata *The Greenfield Christmas Tree* (Hartford Symphony and Chorus, Conn., Dec. 8, 1962); a play, *Forests of the Night* (Actors' Studio, N.Y.C., Feb. 5, 1963); and a play, *Of Love Remembered* (ANTA Th., Feb. 18, 1967).

Films. Mr. Sundgaard wrote the documentary *The World We Live In* (Transfilm, 1958).

Television and Radio. He wrote the radio series Report on the Underground (WMCA, N.Y.C., 1943–44).

For television, he wrote the following four programs for Omnibus (CBS): *Village Incident: India* (1954); *Beethoven's Fifth Symphony* (1955); *Four Flags of the Confederacy* (1956); and *Jack Be Normal* (1957). He also wrote *Gallantry* (CBS, 1962).

Other Activities. Playwright in residence (Univ. of Texas, 1945); lecturer (Columbia Univ., 1945–49); associate professor (Univ. of Illinois, 1949); head of the drama dept. (Bennington Coll., 1949–51); and instructor (Berkshire Music Festival, Tanglewood, Mass., 1951).

Published Works. He is the author of a novella, *What'll I Say to Her Now* (1938); *Spirochete, a Living Newspaper* (1938); the play, *Virginia Overture* (1941); one-act plays for *The Best One-Act Plays* of 1941, 1943, 1944; and a short story, *Ken* (1959).

Awards. He received a Rockefeller Fellowship for graduate study at Yale Univ. (1935–36); a Dramatists Guild Fellowship (1939); and a Guggenheim Fellowship in creative writing (1951); and was a US exchange lecturer (Trinity Coll., Dublin, Ire., 1958–59).

SUNDSTROM, FLORENCE. Actress. b. Florence E. Sundstrom, Feb. 9, 1918, New York City, to E. W. and Jetta M. (Osmundsen) Sundstrom. Father, Capt. USN, US Maritime Service. Attended Great Neck H.S., N.Y., 1932. Studied acting with Alma Pierce Power Waters, Bayside, N.Y., six years, music with Dorothy Brown, eight years, dance with Vida Godwin, Galveston, Tex., eight years. Married Dec. 20, 1940, to Ronald Graham (dec. July 4, 1950). Member of AEA; SAG; AFTRA.

Pre-Theatre. Modeled for John Robert Powers.

Theatre. Miss Sundstrom made her first appearance on a stage in a recital (Ursuline Convent, Galveston, Tex., Dec. 1922).

She made her N.Y.C. debut taking over Ruth Yorke's role as Phyllis during the run of *Parnell* (Ethel Barrymore Th., Nov. 11, 1935); subsequently played Snow Bird in *Petticoat Fever* (New Rochelle Playhouse, N.Y., 1936); Vivian Caldwell in *Bright Honor* (48 St. Th., N.Y.C., Sept. 27, 1936); toured as Joyce in *Brother Rat* (1937) succeeding Marion Kate (Natl. Th., Mar. 1938) as Kate Rue Wynn Cahoon in the N.Y.C. company (Biltmore, Dec. 16, 1936); played Rose in *The Good* (Windsor, Oct. 5, 1938); took over the role of Marge during the run of *I Must Love Someone* (Longacre, Feb. 7, 1939); and took over Vivian Vance's role as Mrs. Valentine during the run of *Skylark* (Morosco, Oct. 11, 1939).

She played Nancy in *Gas Light (Angel Street)* (Saratoga, N.Y., 1940; Newport Playhouse, R.I., 1940); appeared in *Johnny Belinda* (Garden Pier, Atlantic City, N.J., 1940); played the German Maid in *Margin for Error* (Maplewood Th., N.J., 1940); Lenore in *Retreat to Pleasure* (Belasco, N.Y.C., Dec. 17, 1940); Mrs. Valentine in *Skylark* (Bucks County Playhouse, New Hope, Pa., 1941); Barbara in *Johnny on a Spot* (Plymouth, N.Y.C., Jan. 8, 1942); Vivian in *They Should Have Stood in Bed* (Mansfield, Feb. 13, 1942); Dinky Higgens in *The Rich Get Richer* (Scarsdale, N.Y., 1942); Karyl in *The Sun Field* (Biltmore, N.Y.C., Dec. 9, 1942); and Billie La Tour in the pre-Bway tryout of *Franklin Street* (National, Washington, D.C., 1943).

Also Pepi in *Mr. Strauss Goes to Boston* (Century, N.Y.C., Sept. 6, 1945); Lily in *Marriage Is for Single People* (Cort, Nov. 21, 1945); Hessie in the pre-Bway tour of *Dearly Beloved* (opened Newark Opera Playhouse, N.J., Feb. 14, 1946; closed Locust, Philadelphia, Pa., Feb. 23, 1946); Bella in *Happy Birthday* (Broadhurst, N.Y.C., Oct. 31, 1946); Miriam in *Guest in the House* (Mountain Park Casino, Holyoke, Mass., 1948); Vivian in *For Love or Money* (Ogunquit Playhouse, Me., 1948); succeeded (July 7, 1949) Dortha Duckworth as Ellen Griswold in *Goodbye My Fancy* (Morosco, N.Y.C., Nov. 17, 1948), repeating this role on a N.Y.C. Subway circuit tour (1950); played Bessie in *The Rose Tattoo* (Martin Beck Th., Feb. 3, 1951); Gracie in *Faithfully Yours* (Coronet, Oct, 18, 1951); and Signora Serelli in *Right You Are, If You Think You Are* and Mabel in *The Tin Wedding* (Westport Country Playhouse, Conn., 1952).

Also, Mrs. Meeker in *See the Jaguar* (Cort, N.Y.C., Dec. 3, 1952); Tabitha in *Darling Darling* (Westport Country Playhouse, 1953); "Fatty" Pert in *Look Homeward, Angel* (Ethel Barrymore Th., N.Y.C., Nov. 28, 1957), also touring in it (opened Playhouse, Wilmington, Del., May 31, 1960); Mistress Overdone in a Univ. of Calif. at Los Angeles Th. Group production of *Measure for Measure* (1962); appeared in the pre-London tryout of *The Country Boy* (Oct. 1963); and took over (Apr. 17, 1964) for Vickie Vale, alternating in *Anything Goes* and *High Button Shoes* (Thunderbird Hotel, Las Vegas, Nev.).

Films. Miss Sundstrom made her debut in short subjects at Warner Bros. Studios, Brooklyn, N.Y. (1932); subsequently appeared in *The Rose Tattoo* (Par., 1955); *The Vagabond King* (Par., 1956); *Spring Reunion* (UA, 1957); and *Bachelor in Paradise* (MGM, 1961).

Television. She made her first appearance as the Secretary in *The Butter and Egg Man* (NBC, 1936); appeared in *The Show-Off* (NBC, 1936); and during 1947–48, performed on the following programs: Kraft Television Th. (NBC), Philco Television Playhouse (NBC), Armstrong Circle Th. (CBS), Studio One (CBS), Climax! (CBS), Th. Guild (CBS), Lamp Unto My Feet (CBS), Bonino (CBS), Mr. Peepers (NBC), Jamie (NBC), and Alcoa Premiere (ABC).

She played Belle Dudley on The Life of Riley (NBC, 1955); appeared on Playhouse 90 (CBS, 1956); David Niven (ABC, 1956); Medic (NBC, 1956); Climax! (CBS, 1956); My Favorite Husband (NBC, 1956); Malibu Run (ABC, 1961); played Flo on Hazel (NBC, 1961–64); appeared on The Verdict Is Yours (CBS, 1962); The Real McCoys (NBC, 1962); Bonanza (NBC, 1963); and Day in Court (ABC, 1963–64).

Recreation. Portrait painting, sailing, swimming, gardening.

SUSSKIND, DAVID. Producer. b. Dec. 21, 1920, Brookline, Mass., to Benjamin and Frances (Lear) Susskind. Father, insurance executive. Attended Univ. of Wisconsin, 1938–40; grad. Harvard Univ., B.S. 1942. Served USN, 1942–46. Married Aug. 23, 1939, to Phyllis Briskin (marr. dis.); one son, two daughters; married Apr. 22, 1966, to Joyce Davidson; one daughter. Member of AFTRA; NATAS (vice-pres., bd. of gov.); Screen Producers Guild.

Theatre. Mr. Susskind produced *A Very Special Baby* (Playhouse, N.Y.C., Nov. 14, 1956); *A Handful of Fire* (Martin Beck Th., Oct. 1, 1958); with Hardy Smith, *Rashomon* (Music Box, Jan. 27, 1959); with Daniel Melnick, in association with Joseph E. Levine, *Kelly* (Broadhurst, Feb. 6, 1965); with Messrs. Melnick and Levine, in association with John and Roy Boulting, *All in Good Time* (Royale, Feb. 18, 1965); and, with Daniel Melnick, *Brief Lives* (John Golden Th., Dec. 18, 1967).

Films. He produced *Edge of the City* (MGM, 1957); *A Raisin in the Sun* (Col., 1961); *Requiem for a Heavyweight* (Col., 1962); *All the Way Home* (Par., 1963); *Lovers and Other Strangers* (1970); and *The Pursuit of Happiness* (1971).

Television. From 1958–67, he produced and served as moderator of the discussion program, Open End, which has appeared on various networks. He later served in the same capacity on The David Susskind Show (1967–to date).

His production firm has produced for the following: Philco-Goodyear Playhouse (NBC, 1948–55); Mr. Peepers (NBC, 1951–55); Armstrong Circle Th. (NBC, 1955–57; CBS, 1957–63); Kaiser Aluminum Hour (NBC, 1957); Rexall Specials (NBC, 1957–60); Dupont Show of the Month (CBS, 1957–61); Kraft Television Th. (NBC, 1959); Play of the Week (WNTA, 1959–61); Festival of Performing Arts (1961–62; 1962–63); East Side/West Side (CBS, 1963–64); Dupont Show of the Week (NBC, 1963–64); and Hallmark Hall of Fame (1971).

Awards. Mr. Susskind has received seven NATAS (Emmy) Awards, two Peabody Awards, two Intl. Television Film Festival (Monaco) Awards; two Newspaper Guild Awards; eight Sylvania Television Awards; two *TV Film Daily* Awards as producer of the year, and four for program of the year; two awards from NATAS; a Screen Producers Guild Award; three B'nai Brith Awards; a Catholic Th. Award; a Protestant Council Award; and the Robert Sherwood Award.

SVOBODA, JOSEF. Scenic designer. b. May 10, 1920, Caslav, Czechoslovakia. Grad. Sch. of Applied Arts, Prague, Czechoslovakia.

Theatre. Mr. Svoboda has pioneered multi-media, multi-screen, and modern technical approaches in scenic design. His first works, executed for a provisional theatre at the Smetana Museum (1943), included *Fragments from Empedocles, The Bridal Crown, Foxtrap,* and *Songs of the Fair.* In 1948, he made his professional debut as chief designer of the May 5 Opera House (Prague); subsequently joining the National Theatre of Prague as chief designer and technical director (1951–to date). There, he heads a staff of three hundred and designs approximately thirty productions per year, including drama, ballet, opera, and symphonic concerts.

In the US, he designed the settings for the opera *Intolleranza* (Boston Opera Co.); and *Carmen* (Metropolitan Opera Co., N.Y.C., 1972); and the American production of *Jumpers* (Kennedy Ctr., Washington, D.C., Feb. 18, 1974; and Billy Rose Th., N.Y.C., Apr. 22, 1974).

Mr. Svoboda has designed productions for major opera, ballet and theatre companies all over the world, including the Old Vic, the Vienna State Opera, La Scala, Covent Garden, the Royal Opera of Stockholm and the Bayreuth Festival.

Films. Mr. Svoboda designed *Three Sisters* (Amer. Film Th., 1974).

Other Activities. Exhibitions of photographs, drawings and working models of his designs have been shown by the Royal Institute of British Architects (London, 1967), and Denison Univ. (Granville, Ohio, Spring 1975).

Mr. Svoboda was co-creator of "Laterna Magica" at the Brussels Expo (1958), and designed the Czechoslovakian Exposition at Montreal Expo '67.

Awards. From the Czechoslovakian government, Mr. Svoboda has received the State Prize; the Order of Labour (1963); and the titles of Honoured Artist (1966), and National Artist (1968). From the Brazilian government, he received the 1961 Gold Medal at the São Paulo Biennial.

SWANN, DONALD. Composer, singer, pianist. b. Donald Ibrahim Swann, Sept. 30, 1923, Llanelly, Wales, to Herbert William and Naguime (Sultan) Swann. Father, physician. Grad. Westminster Sch., London, England, 1941; Oxford Univ., M.A. (with honors) 1948. Married Aug. 7, 1955, to Janet Mary Oxborrow; two daughters. Served WW II as conscientious objector with Friends (Quaker) Ambulance Unit, Middle East and Greece, and with UNRRA. Member of British Musicians' Union; AEA; Composers Guild of Gr. Britain. Address: 13 Albert Bridge Rd., London S.W.11, 4PX, England tel. (01) 622-4281.

Theatre. Mr. Swann's first assignments were composing songs for revues in London, often with lyrics by Michael Flanders, notably *Airs on a Shoestring* (Royal Court Th., Apr. 22, 1953), subsequently wrote art songs, including settings of poems by John Betjeman, and musical plays, including *Wild Thyme* (Duke of York's, July 4, 1955); composed the music and appeared with Mr. Flanders in their revue *At the Drop of a Hat* (New Lindsey, Dec. 31, 1956), which they brought to N.Y.C. (John Golden Th., Oct. 8, 1959, and 1967) and toured the US and Canada (opened Playhouse, Wilmington, Del., Oct. 26, 1960; closed O'Keefe Center, Toronto, Canada, Mar. 11, 1961) and Great Britain and Ireland (1961–62); appeared with Mr. Flanders in a second edition of *At the Drop of Another Hat* (Haymarket, London, Oct. 2, 1963), in which they toured Australia and New Zealand (Sept.–Dec. 1964); composed the opera, *Perelandra*, based on a story by C. S. Lewis (Mermaid, London, June 21, 1964); toured the US and Canada with *At the Drop of Another Hat* (Booth, N.Y.C., Dec. 27, 1966); and currently presents concerts of his works under the title *Between the Bars*. .

Television and Radio. For radio, Mr. Swann composed (under the pseudonym Hilda Tablet) satirical music for the Third Programme series (1950's); broadcast his own series of four talks entitled Swann Alone (1961–62); on TV, performed in *At the Drop of a Hat* on David Susskind's Festival of Performing Arts (1962); and, during the American engagement of the revue, appeared on the Jack Paar Show (NBC), Ed Sullivan Show (CBS), and the Dave Garroway Show (NBC).

He contributed an original score to *The Great Glass Hive* for Omnibus (BBC).

Other Activities. Since 1958, he has composed sacred music and carols, most of which were published and recorded, including *Festival Matins*.

He has written a book of autobiographical reflections entitled *The Space Between the Bars;* and has another work in progress. His involvement with peace-seeking organizations has taken him to the Middle East and Northern Ireland with the concert "A Crack in Time." .

SWANN, FRANCIS. director, Playwright, novelist, 8. b. Francis Edward Swann, July 16, 1913, Annapolis, Md., to S. Donovan and Rita (Harrell) Swann. Father, artist; mother, newspaper reporter, editor. Grad. Gilman Sch., Baltimore, Md., 1931; attended Princeton Univ. and Johns Hopkins Univ. Married Jan. 15, 1944, to Jean Phillips, one son. Relatives in theatre: brother, Don Swann, Jr., producer; sister, Lyn Swann, actress, producer. Served USNR, 1943–46; rank, Lt. (jg). Member of Dramatists Guild; WGA, East; Authors League of America.

Pre-Theatre. Press representative, newspaper reporter.

Theatre. Mr. Swann first appeared as an actor, playing a Germ in *Pandora's Box* (Lyceum Th., Baltimore, Md., Oct. 1919); subsequently appeared as Ham in *Post Road* (Oak Bluffs, Martha's Vineyard, Mass., Aug. 1934); made his N.Y.C. debut playing a Hero in *Too Many Heros* (Hudson, Nov. 15, 1937); followed by the role of a Tavern Singer in *Gloriana* (Little, Nov. 25, 1938); and Harrington and Dr. Millengen in *Bright Rebel* (Lyceum, Dec. 27, 1938).

Mr. Swann wrote *Out of the Frying Pan*, which received a tryout under his direction at the Hilltop Th. (Baltimore, Md., Sept. 1940), and was produced in N.Y.C. (Windsor, Feb. 11, 1941). He wrote and produced with Zion Myers the pre-Bway tryout of *It's in the Air* (Belasco, Los Angeles, Calif., Aug. 1945), which closed after eight weeks; wrote, with Victor Clement, *Bad Angel* (Phoenix, West Los Angeles, 1949); *Whatever Happened* (Hilltop, Baltimore, Md., Sept. 1956); *Prior to Broadway* (Hilltop, Baltimore, Md., Sept. 1958); contributed special material to *The Follies of 1910* (Carnegie Playhouse, N.Y.C., Jan. 12, 1960); wrote *Into the Fire* (Gateway, Somers Point, N.J., Aug. 1961); with Robert Simon wrote the libretto for the opera *Rehearsal Call* (Juilliard Sch. of Music, N.Y.C., Feb. 11, 1962); and wrote the book for *Paradise Island*, which he also directed (Marine Th., Jones Beach, N.Y., Summers 1961, 1962).

Films. Mr. Swann wrote the story for *Young and Willing* (UA, 1943), based on his play *Out of the Frying Pan;* and wrote or collaborated on the screenplays for *Shine on Harvest Moon* (WB, 1944); *Make Your Own Bed* (WB, 1944); *A Very Rich Man* (WB, 1944); *The Time, the Place, and the Girl* (WB, 1946); *Love and Learn* (WB, 1947); *The Gay Intruders* (20th-Fox, 1948); *Jungle Patrol* (20th-Fox, 1948); *Roy Rogers* (Rep., 1949); *Miss Grant Takes Richmond* (Col., 1949); *Cover Up* (UA, 1949); *Mrs. Mike* (UA, 1949); *711 Ocean Drive* (Col., 1950); *The Barefoot Mailman* (Col., 1951); *Adventures of Haji Baba* (Walter Wanger, 1952); *One Big Affair* (UA, 1962); *Force of Impulse* (Sutton, 1961); and was co-author of the story and screenplay for *Instant Love*. .

Television. Mr. Swann wrote for Racket Squad (1948).

Published Works. He wrote the suspense novel *The Brass Key* (1964).

Recreation. Fishing.

SWEET, BLANCHE. Actress. b. Sarah Blanche Sweet, June 18, 1896, Chicago, Ill., to Pearl Alexander Sweet. Mother, dancer. Attended boarding school, Berkeley, Calif., 1905–07, 1908–09. Married June 7, 1922, to Marshall Neilan, film director (marr. dis. 1929); married Oct. 9, 1935, to Raymond Hackett, actor (dec. July 7, 1958). Member of AEA; SAG; AFTRA.

Theatre. Miss Sweet made her debut prior to her first birthday in a stock production of *Blue Jeans* (Cincinnati, Ohio, 1897); subsequently, as a child actress, appeared with such performers as Maurice Barrymore, Holbrook Blynn, Chauncey Olcott, Gertrude Hoffman and Fiske O'Hara.

She played Blanche Alexander Guilbert in *The Battle of the Strong* (Macauley's, Louisville, Ky., Nov. 29, 1901); later, appeared in a vaudeville show (Fox, Brooklyn, N.Y., June 16, 1934); played Mrs. Chisholm in *The Petrified Forest* (Broadhurst, N.Y.C., Jan. 7, 1935); appeared in a tour of *The Party's Over* (opened Erlanger, Philadelphia, Pa., 1934); played Carrie Hammond in *There's Always a Breeze* (Windsor, N.Y.C., Mar. 2, 1938); Martha Wood Baugh in *Aries Is Rising* (John Golden Th., Nov. 21, 1939); and Mrs. Brandt in *Those Endearing Young Charms* (Booth, June 16, 1943).

Films. Miss Sweet made her debut in *The Pit* (1909); subsequently she appeared in *Quirk of Fate* (1909); *Judith of Bethulia* (1914); *Home Sweet Home* (Mutual, 1914); *The Avenging Conscience* (Griffith-Mutual, 1914); *The Second Mrs. Roebuck* (Majestic, 1914); *The Little Country Mouse* (Majestic, 1914); *The Clew* (Lasky-Par., 1915); *A Corner in Wheat* (Biograph, 1915); *The Lonedale Operator* (Griffith, 1915); *How She Triumphed* (1915); *The Long Road* (1915); *Stolen Goods* (Lasky-Par., 1915); *The Coming of Angelo* (Biograph, 1915); *The Secret Sin* (Par., 1915); *The God Within* (Biograph, 1915); *The Battle* (Biograph, 1915); *The Painted Lady* (Biograph, 1915); *Golden Chance* (Par., 1915); *The Secret Orchard* (Lasky-Par., 1915); *The Captive* (Lasky-Par., 1915); *Unprotected* (Par., 1916); *Ragamuffin* (Par., 1916); *Sowers* (Par., 1916); *Three Friends* (Biograph, 1916); *Thousand Dollar Husband* (Par., 1916); *Dupe* (Par., 1916); *Public Opinion* (Par., 1916); *The Odalisque* (Majestic, 1916); *Evil Eye* (Par., 1917); *Tides of Barnegat* (Par., 1917); *Silent Partner* (Par., 1917); *Those without Sin* (Par., 1917); *The Woman* (HWF, 1918); *Hushed Hour* (Gar., 1919); *Fighting Cressy* (RKO Pathé, 1919); *A Woman of Pleasure* (RKO Pathé, 1919); *Deadlier Sex* (RKO Pathé, 1920); *The Unpardonable Sin* (Gar., 1920); *Simple Souls* (RKO Pathé, 1920); *Girl in the Web* (RKO Pathé, 1920); *That Girl Montana* (RKO Pathé, 1921); *The Meanest Man in the World* (1st Natl., 1923); *Anna Christie* (1st Natl., 1923); *In the Palace of the Kings* (Goldwyn, 1923); *The Painted Lady* (20th-Fox, 1924); *Tess of the D'Ubervilles* (MGM, 1924); *Men and Women* (Par., 1925); *Sporting Venus* (MGM, 1925); *Far Cry* (1st Natl., 1926); *Bluebeard's Seven Wives* (1st Natl., 1926); *The Lady from Hell* (Associated Exhibitors, 1926); *Diplomacy* (Par., 1926); *Singed* (20th-Fox, 1927); *The Woman in White* (World Wide, 1929); *The Woman Racket* (MGM, 1930); *Show Girl in Hollywood* (1st Natl., 1930); *The Silver Horde* (RKO, 1930); *The Battle* (Leon Garganoff, 1934); and *The Five Pennies* (Par., 1959).

Television and Radio. Miss Sweet performed on the radio series Beauty Talk (WABC, 1935) and Rich Man's Darling (WABC, 1936).

On television, she has appeared on such shows as Climax! (CBS, 1958); The Thin Man series (NBC, 1958); and Dobie Gillis (CBS, 1960).

SWEET, DOLPH. Actor, director, teacher. b. Adolphus Jean Sweet, July 18, 1920, New York City, to John Walter and Louise (Brasser) Sweet. Father, mechanic. Grad. Northport (N.Y.) H.S., 1938; attended Univ. of Alabama, 1939–40, 1942–43; grad. Columbia Coll., A.B. (Phi Beta Kappa) 1947; Columbia Univ., M.A. 1949. Studied voice with Peyton Hibbett, N.Y.C., 1951–52; with Elizabeth Howell, N.Y.C., 1971–73; acting with Tamara Daykarhanova and Joseph Anthony at the Daykarhanova Sch. for the Stage, N.Y.C., 1958–70. Married Oct. 24, 1945, to Reba Gillespie, dietician (marr. dis. 1970); one son; Oct. 5, 1974, to Iris Braun, actress. Served WW II, USAAF, ETO; awarded Purple Heart, Distinguished Flying Cross; USAF Res. (ret.), rank lt.-col. Member of AEA; SAG. Address: (home) 159-00 Riverside Dr. West, New York, NY 10032, tel. (212) 781-9601; (bus.) c/o Sallee Held, Ltd. (Richard Dickens), 5 E. 57th St., New York, NY 10022, tel. (212) 371-9754.

Pre-Theatre. Textile foreman, truck driver, educator.

Theatre. Mr. Sweet first appeared on stage while a prisoner of war, playing Mrs. White in *The Monkey's Paw* (Stalag Luft III, Sagan, Ger., Mar. 1944); subsequently was head, Drama Division, English Dept., and director of the Barnard Coll. Th., N.Y.C. (1949–61); played Wilson in *Harvey* (Lakes Region Playhouse, N.H., July 3, 1950), where he also appeared as C. K. Dexter Haven in *The Philadelphia Story* (July 10, 1950). Paul Verrall in *Born Yesterday* (July 17, 1950), Wilbur in *For Love or Money* (July 31, 1950), Van Rensselaer in *Knickerbocker Holiday* (Aug. 12, 1950), Larry in the world premiere of *The Country Girl* (Aug. 14, 1950), a Sharecropper in *Finian's Rainbow* (Aug. 21, 1950), and played several roles in *On the Town* (Aug. 28, 1950).

Again at the Lakes Region Playhouse, he played Archie Beaton in *Brigadoon* (July 2, 1951), Lov Bensey in *Tobacco Road* (July 16, 1951), Mitch in *A Streetcar Named Desire* (July 30, 1951), Matt in *Post Road* (Aug. 6, 1951), and Mike Coldpack in *So Help Me, Jackson* (Aug. 20, 1951). At the Chautauqua (N.Y.) Opera Assn., he appeared in the chorus of *The Gondoliers* (July 11, 1952), *La Traviata* (July 18, 1952), *Martha* (July 25, 1952), *Lucia di Lammer-*

moor (Aug. 1, 1952), played the Page in *Amahl and the Night Visitors* (Aug. 8, 1952), and appeared in *Carmen* (Aug. 15, 1952).

Mr. Sweet directed *The Penguin* (Current Stages, N.Y.C., June 15, 1953); the premiere of *Don Juan in the Russian Manner* (Barnard Coll. Th., Apr. 21, 1954); at the Cherry County Playhouse (Traverse City, Mich.), played Lord Allen Frobisher in *Jane* (July 3, 1956), Mr. Carver in *Three Men on a Horse* (July 24, 1956), Ed Hoffman in *Time Out for Ginger* (July 31, 1956), the Psychiatrist in *Ten Little Indians* (Aug. 7, 1956), Richard Greatham in *Hay Fever* (Aug. 21, 1956), and Sam Jackson in *White Sheep of the Family* (Aug. 28, 1956). At the Barter Th. (Abingdon, Va., June 6–Sept. 6, 1958), he played General Powers in *Visit to a Small Planet*, Sgt. King in *No Time for Sergeants*, Matthew Harrison Brady in *Inherit the Wind*, the Director in *Six Characters in Search of an Author*, and Sandor Turai in *The Play's the Thing*.

He produced, with Mildred Dunnock, the premiere of a short version of *The Fantasticks* (Barnard Coll. Th., N.Y.C., Aug. 4, 1959); played Vincent in *Legend of Lovers* (41 St. Th., Oct. 27, 1959); the Grocer and the Fireman in *Rhinoceros* (Longacre, Jan. 9, 1961), in which he was also understudy to Zero Mostel as John and later succeeded (Sept. 18, 1961) Morris Carnovsky as the Logician, a role he repeated on tour (opened Alcazar, San Francisco, Calif., Oct. 3, 1961; closed Huntington Hartford Th., Los Angeles, Calif., Nov. 11, 1962).

He appeared as the Chef in *Romulus* (Music Box, N.Y.C., Jan. 10, 1962); was standby for Sandor Szabo as Commodore Roseabove in *Oh, Dad, Poor Dad, Mama's Hung You in the Closet and I'm Feelin' So Sad* (Phoenix, Feb. 26, 1962); played the title role in *The Dragon* (Phoenix, Apr. 9, 1963); toured as Shamus Tobin in *The Unsinkable Molly Brown* (opened Valley Forge Music Fair, Pa., May 27, 1963; closed Painters Mill Music Fair, Baltimore, Md., Aug. 11, 1963); played Sacco in *The Advocate* (ANTA, N.Y.C., Oct. 14, 1963); Johnson in *Too Much Johnson* (Phoenix, Jan. 15, 1964); and Max in *The Sign in Sidney Brustein's Window* (Longacre, Oct. 15, 1964).

He played the role of Bonnie Doon in *The Great Indoors* (Eugene O'Neill Th., Feb. 1, 1966); was Max, the cafe owner, in *Berlin Is Mine* (Forum, Lincoln Ctr., Apr. 3, 1966); replaced (May 1966) David Doyle as Bludgeon, a Bargee, in *Serjeant Musgrave's Dance* (Th. de Lys, Mar. 8, 1966); replaced (Dec. 1, 1966) Tom Ahearne as Edward Quinn in *Hogan's Goat* (American Place Th., St. Clements Ch., Nov. 11, 1965); played Stever Kenny in *The Natural Look* (Longacre, Mar. 11, 1967); was Sussex in *The Ceremony of Innocence* (American Place Th., St. Clements Ch., Jan. 1, 1968); Whiskers in *Billy* (Billy Rose Th., Mar. 22, 1969); Frank Bishop in *The Penny Wars* (Royale, Oct. 15, 1969); was the King in *Exit the King* (Marymount Th., Tarrytown, N.Y., 1970); repeated his performance as Max in a revival of *The Sign in Sidney Brustein's Window* (Longacre, Jan. 26, 1972); played the title role in *Agamemnon* (McCarter Th., Princeton, N.J., Oct. 26, 1972); and Stanley in *Bread* (American Place Th., Jan. 12, 1974).

Films. Mr. Sweet appeared in *You're a Big Boy Now* (7 Arts, 1967); *The Swimmer* (Col., 1968); *Finian's Rainbow* (WB, 1968); *A Lovely Way to Die* (U, 1968); *The April Fools* (Natl. Gen., 1969); *The Lost Man* (U, 1969); *The Out-of-Towners* (Par., 1970); *Colossus: The Forbin Project* (U, 1970); *The New Centurions* (Col., 1972); *Cops and Robbers* (UA, 1973); *Fear Is the Key* (Par., 1973); and *The Amazing Grace* (UA, 1974).

Television. Mr. Sweet made his first television appearances on The Defenders (CBS, 1961–63) and also played on The Nurses (CBS, 1963) and East Side/West Side (CBS, 1963). He played the title role in the television version of *The Dragon* (Dupont Show of the Week, NBC, 1963); Sacco in *The Advocate* (Opening Night on Broadway, Oct. 15, 1963); Sgt. Garrison on The Trials of O'Brien (CBS, Sept. 1965–Feb. 1966); Harry Constable on The Edge of Night (CBS, 1967); Sheriff Jesse Bard in *The Desperate Hours* (ABC, Dec. 13, 1967); Morgan in *To Confuse the Angel* (Prudential's Onstage, NBC, Mar. 15, 1970); the General in *Between Time and Timbuktu* (NET Playhouse, PBS, Mar. 1972); Henry Peterson in *The Watergate Tapes*; the Sheriff in *The Migrants*; and Gil McGowan on Another World (NBC, 1974–75).

Other Activities. In addition to his stage, screen, and television activities, Mr. Sweet is executive director of Daykarhanova Actors, Inc., a nonprofit theatre group dedicated to improving the creative conditions surrounding the actor.

Recreation. Swimming, reading, cooking, eating, drinking.

SWENSON, INGA. Actress. b. Dec. 29, Omaha, Neb., to A. C. R. and Geneva (Seeger) Swenson. Father, attorney, Swedish consul. Grad. Central H.S., Omaha, 1950; studied acting with Alvina Krause, Northwestern Univ., 1950–54; with Uta Hagen, HB (Herbert Berghof) Studio, N.Y.C., 1954; with Lee Strasberg, Actors' Studio, 1958–to date. Married Feb. 21, 1953, to Lowell M. Harris, actor, singer; two sons. Member of AEA; AFTRA; SAG; AGVA.

Theatre. Miss Swenson made her stage debut as Maid Marian in the Omaha Central H.S. production of *Robin Hood* (Dec. 1948); her professional debut as the Maid in *Peg O' My Heart* (Berkshire Playouse, Stockbridge, Mass., Summer 1949); subsequently at The Playhouse (Eaglesmere, Pa.), played Princess Alexandria in *The Swan*, Minnie Fay in *The Merchant of Yonkers*, was a singer in *Sing Out, Sweet Land*, and an extra in *Othello* (Summer 1952); Aunt Anna Rose in *Treasure Hunt*, Monica in *The Medium* and Lucy in *The Telephone*, Dunyasha in *The Cherry Orchard*, Alizon Elliot in *The Lady's Not for Burning*, Isabelle in *Ring Around the Moon* (Summer 1953); Georgie Elgin in *The Country Girl*, Celia Copplestone in *The Cocktail Party*, Mrs. Larue in *Mrs. McThing*, Countess Aurelia in *The Madwoman of Chaillot*, Angelique in *The Imaginary Invalid* (Summer 1954).

She portrayed Olivia in *Twelfth Night* (Shakespearewrights, Jan Hus House, N.Y.C., Nov. 9, 1954); appeared as a singer in *New Faces of '56* (Ethel Barrymore Th., June 14, 1956); played Princess Charlotte in *The First Gentleman* (Belasco, Apr. 25, 1957); toured (Summer 1957) as Marie Louise in a stock production of *My Three Angels* (Falmouth Playhouse, Mass.; Playhouse-in-the-Park, Philadelphia, Pa.; Edgewater Beach Playhouse, Chicago, Ill.; Oakdale Music Th., Wallingford, Conn.); appeared at the Royal Poinciana Playhouse (Palm Beach, Fla.), as Madge in *Picnic* and Amy Kittridge in *A Swim in the Sea* (Spring, 1958).

She performed with the American Shakespeare Stratford Fest. (Stratford, Conn.), as Ophelia in *Hamlet* (June 19, 1958), Helena in *A Midsummer Night's Dream* (June 20, 1958); and Perdita in *The Winter's Tale* (July 20, 1958); played Amy Kittridge in the pre-Bway tryout of *A Swim in the Sea* (opened Walnut St. Th., Philadelphia, Pa., Sept. 15, 1958; closed there Sept. 27, 1958); and with the American Shakespeare Fest. (Stratford, Conn.), she appeared as Juliet in *Romeo and Juliet* (June 12, 1959).

Miss Swenson played Solveig in *Peer Gynt* (Phoenix, N.Y.C., Jan. 12, 1960); Julie Jordan in *Carousel* (Wallingford, Conn.; Framingham, Mass.; Warwick, R.I., 1960); was Julie Andrews' standby as Guenevere in *Camelot* (Majestic, N.Y.C., Dec. 3, 1960); played Julie Jordan in *Carousel* (Melody Top Th., Hillside, Ill., June 1962); Gillian in *Bell, Book and Candle* (Kiamesha Playhouse, Kiamesha Lake, N.Y., July 1962); Desdemona in *Othello* (Arena Stage, Washington, D.C., Spring 1963); Magnolia in a summer-theatre production of *Show Boat* (Warren, Ohio; Columbus, Ohio, Summer 1963); Lizzie in *110 in the Shade* (Broadhurst, N.Y.C, Oct. 24, 1963), which she repeated on the West Coast (Curran, San Francisco, Calif.; Philharmonic Aud., Los Angeles, Calif., Aug. 10–Nov. 22, 1964). She was Irene Adler in *Baker Street* (Bway Th., N.Y.C., Feb. 10, 1965); repeated her performance as Lizzie in *110 in the Shade* (Palace, London, England, Feb. 8, 1967); played Eliza Doolittle in the City Ctr. Light Opera Co. revival of *My Fair Lady* (NY City Ctr., June 13, 1968); and appeared in a production of *The Crucible* (Ahmanson Th., Los Angeles, Calif., Dec. 5, 1972).

Films. She played Mrs. Keller in *The Miracle Worker* (UA, 1962); and Mrs. Brig Anderson in *Advise and Consent* (Col., 1962).

Television. Miss Swenson made her television debut in Canada as a singer on the Chrysler Special (CBC, Jan. 1957) and played Kate in *The Gay Deceivers* (CBC, 1957); Liza in *The Best Wine* (Goodyear Playhouse, (US, NBC, 1957); Marjorie in *The World of Nick Adams* (Seven Lively Arts, CBS, 1957); Maria in *Heart of Darkness* and Milly Theale in *Wings of the Dove* (Playhouse 90, CBS, 1958); Vera in *Goodbye, But It Doesn't Go Away* (US Steel Hour, CBS, 1958); Rose Maylie in *Oliver Twist* (Dupont Show of the Month, CBS, 1959); and Lady Jane in *Victoria Regina* (Hallmark Hall of Fame, NBC, 1961).

She appeared in episodes of The Defenders (CBS, 1961, 1962); Bonanza (NBC, 1962, 1963); Dr. Kildare (NBC, 1962); The Nurses (CBS, 1963); performed three times on American Musical Th. (CBS, 1964); was a guest on the Tonight Show (NBC, May 1964); appeared in *My Father and My Mother* (CBS Playhouse, Feb. 1968); in episodes of Medical Center (CBS, 1970, 1971); in *The Tape Recorder* (NET Playhouse, PBS, 1970); and *Earth II* (NBC, 1971).

Night Clubs. She appeared as a featured singer and dancer in *Come As You Are* (Versailles Club, N.Y.C., 1955).

Other Activities. Miss Swenson has appeared as a soloist with the Boston Symphony Orchestra and the Omaha Symphony.

Awards. Miss Swenson received the Aegis Theatre Award (1956) for her performance in *New Faces of '56*; the *Theatre World* Award, the Outer Circle Critics Award and won the *Variety* NY Drama Critics Poll (1957) for her performance as Princess Charlotte in *The First Gentleman*; and the Outer Circle Critics Award and a nomination for the Antoinette Perry (Tony) Award (1964) for her performance as Lizzie in *110 in the Shade*.

Recreation. Reading, music.

SWENSON, SWEN. Actor, singer, dancer. b. Jan. 23, 1934, Inwood, Iowa, to Swen and Myrtle (Knutson) Swenson. Father, farmer. Grad. Washington H.S., Sioux Falls, S.D. Studied for the theatre at Jacob's Pillow, Lee, Mass.; acting with Mira Rostova; voice with Keith Davis; ballet with Robert Joffrey, N.Y.C.; Mme. Roseanna, Paris, France; Valerie Bettis, Nanette Charisse, Amer. Ballet Sch. Served USN. Member of AEA; AFTRA; AGMA; AGVA; SAG; English Equity; SSDC. Address: 16 Minetta Lane, New York, NY 10012, tel. (212) SP 7-1131; 9837 Enston Dr., Beverly Hills, CA 90210.

Pre-Theatre. Farming, elevator operator, shoe salesman, clothing salesman, assistant manager of motion picture house, art teacher, law clerk, bank clerk, model.

Theatre. Mr. Swenson made his N.Y.C. debut in the chorus of *Great To Be Alive!* (Winter Garden Th., Mar. 23, 1950); subsequently was an understudy and appeared in the chorus of *Bless You All* (Mark Hellinger Th., Dec. 14, 1950); played Jewel in *As I Lay Dying* (ANTA), and toured as a pantomimist with the Mata and Hari Company.

He appeared as a soloist in summer productions of *Annie Get Your Gun* and *Plain and Fancy* (Starlight Th., Kansas City, Mo.), played Don Juan in *Me and Juliet* (Civic Light Opera Assn., Pittsburgh, Pa.), Rusty Charlie in *Guys and Dolls* (Lambertville Music Circus, Pa.), and Bill Calhoun in *Kiss Me, Kate* (Flint, Mich.). Mr. Swenson played Blazes Boylan in *Ulysses in Nighttown* (Rooftop, N.Y.C., June 5, 1958); the Poet in the world premiere of Menotti's *Unicorn, Mantagor and Gorgon* (Library of Congress, Washington, D.C.); Bugs Watson in *Destry Rides Again* (Imperial, N.Y.C., Apr. 23, 1959); Oney Tate in *Wildcat* (Alvin, Dec. 16, 1960); Mayor Hector in *The Golden Apple* (York, Feb. 12, 1962); and George Musgrove in *Little Me* (Lunt-Fontanne Th., Nov.

17, 1962; on tour, opened Rochester (N.Y.) Aud., Jan. 30, 1964, closed Civic Aud., Pasadena, Calif., Aug. 1, 1964; and Cambridge Th., London, 1964–65).

He toured summer theatres as Joey in *Pal Joey* (1963); appeared as a solo dancer at the Radio City Music Hall, N.Y.C. (1963); played Tony in summer stock productions of *The Boy Friend* (Los Angeles, San Francisco, Milwaukee); played Bliss Stanley in *A Joyful Noise* (Mark Hellinger Th., N.Y.C., Dec. 15, 1966); Folial in *Escurial* (East 74 St. Playhouse, N.Y.C., Mar. 5, 1968); and The Devil in *The Apple Tree* ( ); produced *And Puppy Dog Tails* (previewed Astor Place Th., N.Y.C., Sept. 18, 1969; opened Bouwerie Lane Th., N.Y.C., Oct. 19, 1969); played Billie Early in the national tour of *No, No, Nanette* (opened Music Hall, Dallas, Tex., Oct. 6, 1972; closed Garden State Arts Ctr., Woodbridge, N.J., Aug. 4, 1973); Michael Stone in *Molly* (Alvin, N.Y.C., Nov. 1, 1973); and Bella-Bello in *Ulysses in Nighttown* (Winter Garden, N.Y.C., Mar. 10, 1974).

Films. He has appeared in the French film, *Nez de Cuir*, and the English film, *Monte Carlo Baby*, and the American film, *What's the Matter with Helen?* (UA, 1971).

Television. Mr. Swenson has appeared on the Ed Sullivan Show (CBS), the Milton Berle Show (NBC), Your Show of Shows (NBC), the Patti Page Show, the Martha Raye Show (NBC), the Andy Williams Show (NBC), the Perry Como Show (NBC), Your Hit Parade, and the Keefe Brasselle Show (Summer 1963); the "Special", *Fol de Rol* (ABC, Jan. 1972); The Merv Griffin Show (Metro-Media, 1969); and The Tonight Show, starring Johnny Carson (NBC, 1969).

Night Clubs. He performed for one year at the Lido in Paris; played The Desert Inn Hotel in Las Vegas; and The Playboy Resort, Lake Geneva, Wisc., 1969.

Awards. He received the *Theatre World* Award and a nomination for the Antoinette Perry (Tony) Award for his performance as George Musgrove in *Little Me* (1962–63); received the Year of the Negev Award (June 24, 1962); and the *Theatre World* Award for his performance in *A Joyful Noise* (1966).

Recreation. Horses, motorcycles, swimming, water-skiing, painting, Yorkshire and Italian Greyhound breeding, collecting giant wood carvings, cigar store Indians, ship figureheads, and carousel animals.

SWERLING, JO. Screenwriter, playwright, sketch writer. b. Joseph Swerling, Apr. 8, 1897, Russia. Married; two sons. Member of SWG; Dramatists Guild.

Theatre. Mr. Swerling first wrote sketches for vaudeville; subsequently wrote *One of Us* (Bijou Th., N.Y.C., Sept. 9, 1918); *The New Yorkers* (Edith Totten Th., Mar. 10, 1927); and *Kibitzer* (Royal, Feb. 18, 1929).

He wrote, with Abe Burrows, the book for the musical, *Guys and Dolls* (46 St. Th., Nov. 24, 1950; Coliseum, London, May 28, 1953).

Films. Mr. Swerling wrote for *Ladies of Leisure* (Col., 1930); *Around the Corner* (Col., 1930); with Dorothy Howell, wrote the dialogue and continuity for *Rain and Shine* (Col., 1930); *Sisters* (Col., 1930); *Madonna of the Streets* (Col., 1930); the dialogue and continuity for *Hell's Island* (Col., 1930); *The Miracle Woman* (Col., 1931); *Ten Cents a Dance* (Col., 1931); *Good Bad Girl* (Col., 1931); and the adaptation for *Platinum Blonde* (Col., 1931).

Among Mr. Swerling's many other screenplays, on some of which he had a collaborator, are *Dirigible* (Col., 1931); *Washington Merry-Go-Round* (Col., 1932); *Man's Castle* (Col., 1933); *No Greater Glory* (Col., 1934); *Sisters Under the Skin* (Col., 1934); with Robert Riskin, *The Whole Town's Talking* (Col., 1935); *Pennies from Heaven* (Col., 1936); *Double Wedding* (MGM, 1937); *Made for Each Other* (Selznick, 1939); with Niven Busch, *The Westerner* (UA, 1940); *Confirm or Deny* (20th-Fox, 1941); *Blood and Sand* (20th-Fox, 1941); with Herman J. Mankiewicz, *The Pride of the Yankees* (RKO, 1942); the story for *A Lady Takes a Chance* (RKO, 1943); *Crash Dive* (20th-Fox, 1943); *Lifeboat* (20th-Fox, 1944); *Leave Her to Heaven* (20th-Fox, 1945); and *Thunder in the East* (Par., 1953).

Television. He collaborated with Hal Stanley on the book for *The Lord Don't Play Favorites* (Producers' Showcase, NBC, Sept. 17, 1956).

SWOPE, HERBERT BAYARD, JR. Director, producer, theatre executive. b. New York City, to Herbert Bayard and Margaret (Powell) Swope. Father, journalist. Attended Horace Mann Sch., N.Y.C.; Princeton Univ. Married 1947 to Margaret Hayes, actress; one son, one daughter. Relative in theatre: cousin (by marriage), Dorothy McGuire, actress. Served USN, 1941–46; rank, Lt. Member of DGA, Screen Producers Guild, The Lambs, Princeton Club.

Pre-Theatre. Reporter for NY *Herald Tribune* (1938); trade news editor, copywriter, CBS (1939–41).

Theatre. Mr. Swope was producer with Bruce Powell, at the Chapel Th. (Great Neck, L.I., N.Y., Summer 1939).

He directed *Fragile Fox* (Belasco Th., N.Y.C., Oct. 2, 1954); produced with Roger L. Stevens, *Step on a Crack*, which he also directed (Ethel Barrymore Th., Oct. 17, 1962); and produced in association with Messrs. Bufman and Seiden, *Fair Game for Lovers* (Cort, Feb. 10, 1964).

In 1969, Mr. Swope and The Producing Managers Co. began operating theatres at Pennsylvania and New Jersey Shopping Centers. In 1973–74, Mr. Swope was a vice-president of the Walter Reade Organization, Inc.

Films. Mr. Swope produced *Hilda Crane* (20th-Fox, 1956); *True Story of Jesse James* (20th-Fox, 1957); *Three Brave Men* (20th-Fox, 1957); *The Bravados* (20th-Fox, 1958); and *Fiend Who Walked the West* (20th-Fox, 1958).

Television. He was a director for CBS, becoming Mobile Unit Director, directing sports events from Madison Square Garden, Forest Hills, Belmont Park and Baker Field (1946–48). He directed the series Broadway Spotlight (NBC, 1949); The Black Robe (NBC, 1949–50); The Band of America (NBC, 1950); produced The Clock (NBC, 1950–51); produced and directed Lights Out (NBC, 1950–52); directed Robert Montgomery Presents (NBC, 1952–53); produced and directed *K-2-The Savage Mountain* (NBC, 1954); directed for the Armstrong Circle Th. (NBC, 1955); and was executive producer for Wide, Wide World (NBC, 1954–55). Mr. Swope produced and directed the original production tests and first public exhibition of color video tape from the Sarnoff Research Ctr., Princeton, N.J. Miss Hayes was the subject (1953). He directed *Arsenic and Old Lace* (Best of Broadway, CBS, 1955); directed and produced the spectacular *Remember. . . 1938* (NBC, 1955); directed the Climax! series (CBS, 1955); and was executive producer for 20th-Century-Fox TV-Martin Mambo Productions. He was executive producer for the Dobie Gillis pilot film (CBS, 1959); the Five Fingers series, which he also produced (NBC, 1960); and directed *"The Abe Reles Story"* (The Witness, CBS, Dec. 1961).

Other Activities. Mr. Swope was an executive in N.Y.C. with Off-Track Betting (OTB) Corp. (1970–72).

Awards. Robert Montgomery Presents (NBC, 1952–53 season), which Mr. Swope directed, won the Sylvania Award for outstanding achievement in creative directorial technique, the *Look* Magazine Award, Radio and TV Editors Award and the *TV Guide* Award.

Recreation. Croquet, horseracing, poker, traffic safety and control, fire prevention, working as a member, board of trustees, Freedom House.

SYDOW, JACK. Director, playwright. b. John David Sydow, Jr., Oct. 7, 1921, Rockford, Ill., to John David and Ida Beulah (Hoover) Sydow. Father, corporate manager, photo-engraver. Grad. Rockford H.S., 1939; Univ. of Illinois, B.S. 1947; Yale Univ. Sch. of Drama, M.F.A. 1950. Served USAAF, 1942–45. Member of SSD&C; AEA; AFTRA; AGMA.

Theatre. Mr. Sydow was co-director of a revue for the Air Transport Command (Bamboo Music Hall, Chabua, India, June 1943), which later toured India, Africa, Arabia, and Egypt (1943–44); and was staff director for the ATC Entertainment Production Unit in Calcutta, India (Sept. 1944–Sept. 1945).

He directed *Ladies in Retirement* (The Little Th., Rockford, Ill., Jan. 1946). At the Town Hall Th. (Sturbridge, Mass.), he directed *Outward Bound, Arsenic and Old Lace*, and *East Lynne* (Summer 1948); *John Loves Mary, Blithe Spirit, My Sister Eileen, The Man Who Came to Dinner, The Philadelphia Story, The Glass Menagerie, You Can't Take It with You, Peg o' My Heart*, and *The Late Christopher Bean* (Summer 1949).

He directed *Come What May* (Weidman Studio, N.Y.C., Apr. 1950); at the Woodstock Playhouse (N.Y.), *The Enchanted* (July, 1951) and *The Respectful Prostitute* (Aug. 1951); at the Hunter Coll. Playhouse (N.Y.C.), *Trial by Jury* (Dec. 1951), *Ruddigore* (Mar. 1952), and *The Gondoliers* (Mar. 1953).

He was production stage manager for the Lemonade Opera production of *Les Mamelles de Tiresias* (Brandeis Univ. Th. Festival, Waltham, Mass., Summer 1953); assistant stage director for *Babar, the Elephant, Ariadne auf Naxos, Hansel and Gretel*, and *L'Enfant et les sortilèges* (Little Orchestra Society, N.Y.C., 1953–55); and directed *Two for Fun* (Greenwich Mews, June 1955).

He directed at the Tamiment (Pa.) Playhouse an original musical revue each week (Summers 1957; 1958), as well as two pre-Bway musicals: *The Emperor's New Clothes* (1957), and *Once Upon a Mattress* (1958). With Boris Tumarin, Mr. Sydow adapted *The Brothers Karamazov* (Gate, N.Y.C., Dec. 6, 1957); was assistant director to George Abbott for *Once Upon a Mattress* (Phoenix, May 11, 1959), also serving as stage manager and assistant director for this production (Alvin, Nov. 25, 1959), and directed the national touring company (1960–61).

With Boris Tumarin, he adapted *The Idiot* (Gate, N.Y.C., Sept. 25, 1960); directed a bus and truck tour of *Once Upon a Mattress* (Oct. 1960); and staged *The Sudden End of Anne Cinquefoil* (East End Th., N.Y.C., Jan. 10, 1961). For the Amer. Festival at the Boston Arts Ctr., he directed the American premiere of the opera *The Turn of the Screw* (June 1961), choreographed *Anatol* (July 1961), and directed *Elizabeth the Queen* (Aug. 1961).

In 1961, Mr. Sydow, with Eva Le Gallienne, was a founding director of the National Repertory Th. (NRT), and he directed *Mary Stuart* and *Elizabeth the Queen* for NRT's first cross-country tour (Oct. 1961–Apr. 1962). He also directed stock productions (Royal Poinciana Playhouse, Palm Beach, Fla.) of *Chrysanthemum* (Jan. 1962) and *Brigadoon* (Mar. 1962); touring productions of *Here Today* (June 1962), *Kismet* (July 1962), and *Kiss Me, Kate* (Aug. 1962); and stock productions (Sombrero Playhouse, Phoenix, Ariz.) of *Here Today* (Jan. 1963), *Ring 'Round the Moon* (Feb. 1963), and *The Miracle Worker* (Feb. 1963). Mr. Sydow directed *The Matchmaker* (Royal Poinciana Playhouse, Palm Beach, Fla., Mar. 1963); was replacement director for *Sophie* (Winter Garden, N.Y.C., Apr. 15, 1963); and a summer tour of *Call Me Madam* (July 1963). In Oct. 1963, NRT began its second tour for which Mr. Sydow directed *Ring 'Round the Moon* and *The Crucible*, the latter of which also played in N.Y.C. (Belasco, Apr. 6, 1964). He also directed *The Amorous Flea* (E. 78 St. Playhouse, Feb. 17, 1964); directed the NY Shakespeare Festival mobile production of *A Midsummer Night's Dream* (five-borough tour in N.Y.C.: June 26–Aug. 29, 1964). In 1965, he directed *The Rivals* for NRT; a touring package of *The Music Man*; and *Major Barbara* and *Misalliance* (Westport Country Playhouse, Conn.); and in 1966 a revival of *Annie Get Your Gun* (State Th., May 31, 1966; reopened Bway Th., Sept. 21, 1966). For NRT's 1966 tour, he directed productions that later played in N.Y.C. (all ANTA Th.) of *The Imaginary Invalid* (May 1, 1967), *A Touch of the*

Poet(May 2, 1966), and *Still Life*(May 3, 1967); also directed stock and package tours of *Luv* and *On a Clear Day You Can See Forever*(both 1967); the NRT production of *John Brown's Body*(Ford's Th., Washington, D.C., Feb. 12, 1968); and he directed *Sganarelle* for the National Th. of the Deaf (ANTA Th., Jan. 12, 1970).

Awards. As adapter with Boris Tumarin of *The Brothers Karamazov*, Mr. Sydow received *The Village Voice* Off-Bway (Obie) Award for Best Play (1957–58), and received a King Gustave V Fellowship from the American Scandinavian Foundation to study theatre in Sweden (July 1950–Apr. 1951). He was nominated for an Antoinette Perry (Tony) Award (1967) as best director of a musical play for *Annie Get Your Gun.*

SYMONDS, ROBERT. Actor, director, teacher. Robert Barry Symonds, Dec. 1, 1926, Bristow, Okla., to Walter Stout and Nellie (Barry) Symonds. Father, member of Christian Science Board of Lectureship; mother, Christian Science practitioner. Grad. Alamo Hts. H.S., San Antonio, Tex., 1943; attended Univ. of Texas, 1943–44, 1948–54; Univ. of Missouri, 1944–45; studied with B. Iden Payne, Univ. of Texas, San Antonio. Married Sept. 15, 1952, to Jan Kaderli; one son, two daughters. Served US Army, May 1945–Dec. 1946; rank, Staff Sgt. Member of AEA; SAG; AFTRA.

Theatre. From 1954 to 1965, Mr. Symonds was an actor and director at the Actor's Workshop, San Francisco, Calif., for which he played Estragon in *Waiting for Godot* (Marines' Th., San Francisco, Mar. 1, 1957; York, N.Y.C., Aug. 1958–Sept. 1958; Brussels World's Fair, Belgium, Sept. 1958; Seattle World's Fair, Wash., July 1962); Archie Rice in *The Entertainer* (Marines' Th., San Francisco, Feb. 6, 1959); Hamm in *Endgame* (Encore Th., May 10, 1959); Major-Domo in *Ariadne auf Naxos*(War Memorial Opera House, Oct. 13, 1959); Krapp in *Krapp's Last Tape* (Encore, Feb. 7, 1961); at the Marines' Th., directed *The Maids* (Mar. 1, 1961), played the title role in *Galileo* (Dec. 14, 1962), directed and played the title role in *Volpone* (Feb. 22, 1963), directed *The Taming of the Shrew* (Oct. 4, 1963); played Davies in *The Caretaker* (Nov. 15, 1963); and directed *The Night of the Iguana* (Apr. 3, 1964), again directed and played the title role in *Volpone* (Aug. 5, 1964), and directed *The Country Wife* (Nov. 27, 1964).

From 1965 to 1973, he was an actor and stage director at the Repertory Theatre of Lincoln Center, N.Y.C., where, at the Vivian Beaumont Th., he played Robespierre in *Danton's Death* (Oct. 21, 1965), again directed and played Mr. Sparkish in *The Country Wife* (Dec. 9, 1965), and played the Judge and Adzak in *The Caucasian Chalk Circle* (Mar. 24, 1966). He became associate director of the Repertory Th. of Lincoln Ctr. in 1966; and, at the Vivian Beaumont Th., was Jeremy Butler in *The Alchemist* (Oct. 13, 1966), directed *The East Wind* (Feb. 9, 1967) and replaced (Feb. 23) Michael Granger as *Zauber* in the same play, played Federzoni in *Galileo* (Apr. 13, 1967), Chaplain de Stogumber in *Saint Joan* (Jan. 4, 1968), and Kemp in *A Cry of Players* (Nov. 14, 1968).

At the Forum Th., Lincoln Ctr., he directed *Bananas*(Dec. 5, 1968) and played Dominic Christian in *The Inner Journey* (Mar. 20, 1969); and at the Vivian Beaumont Th., was Harpagon in *The Miser* (May 8, 1969), Ward V. Evans in a return engagement of *In the Matter of J. Robert Oppenheimer* (June 26, 1969), Kit Carson in *The Time of Your Life*(Nov. 6, 1969), and Lord Mulligan in *Camino Real*(Jan. 8, 1970). At the Forum, he was Mendacious Porpentine in *The Disintegration of James Cherry* (Jan. 29, 1970), appeared on a double-bill as Duff in *Landscape* and Rumsey in *Silence* (Apr. 2, 1970), and directed *Amphitryon* (May 28, 1970). He directed *The Good Woman of Setzuan* (Vivian Beaumont Th., Nov. 5, 1970); at the Forum, played Goldberg in *The Birthday Party* (Feb. 5, 1971), repeated his roles in *Landscape* and *Silence* (Feb. 9, 1971), appeared in *Scenes From American Life* (Mar. 25, 1971), and was Edgar in *Play Strindberg* (June 3, 1971); and at the Vivian Beaumont Th., was Sir Amias Paulet in *Mary Stuart* (Nov. 11, 1971) and Basho in *Narrow Road to the Deep North* (Jan. 6, 1972).

In the Lincoln Ctr. production of *Play Strindberg*, he repeated his performance as Edgar (Studio Arena, Buffalo, N.Y., Apr. 6, 1972; Olney Th., Olney, Md., May 30, 1972); played Fintan Kinnore in *Patrick Pearse Motel* (Olney Th., Aug. 22, 1972); was Zahkar Bardin in *Enemies* (Vivian Beaumont Th., Nov. 9, 1972); Steve Hubbell in a revival of *A Streetcar Named Desire* (Vivian Beaumont Th., Apr. 26, 1973); the Prime Minister in a revival of *The Student Prince* (pre-Bway, opened Acad. of Music, Philadelphia, Pa., June 5, 1973; closed State Fair, Dallas, Tex., Oct. 21, 1973); repeated his performance as Steve Hubbell in a return engagement of the revival of *A Streetcar Named Desire* (St. James Th., N.Y.C., Oct. 4, 1973); played Edgar in and directed *Comedy of Marriage*, formerly titled *Play Strindberg* (Alley Th., Houston, Tex., Feb. 28, 1974); and was the Reverend, the President, a Man, and the Sheriff in *The Death and Life of Jesse James* (Mark Taper Forum, Los Angeles, Calif., July 19, 1974).

Other Activities. Mr. Symonds was a member of the faculty at the Univ. of California Extension (1964–65).

SYPHER, WYLIE. Educator. b. Dec. 12, 1905, Mt. Kisco, N.Y., to Harry and Martha (Berry) Sypher. Grad. Amherst Coll., B.A. (Phi Beta Kappa) 1928; Tufts Univ., M.A. 1929; Harvard Univ., Ph.D. 1932, Litt.D., Middlebury, 1969; L.H.D., Simmons, 1973. Married Aug. 31, 1929, to Lucy Johnston, one son, one daughter. Member of P.E.N.; Dante Society. Address: (home) 60 Williston Rd., Auburndale, MA 02166, tel. (617) 527-2604; (bus.) c/o Simmons Coll., Boston, MA 02115, tel. (617) 738-2143.

Since 1950, Mr. Sypher has been dean of the Graduate Division of Simmons Coll., where he has been a member of the faculty since 1929; (instructor of English 1929–36; assistant professor, 1936–41; associate professor, 1941–45; professor and chairman, Dept. of English, 1945–71, and alumnae professor, 1966–72). Previously, he was a fellow in English at Tufts Univ. (1927–29). He has given summer lectures at the Univ. of Minnesota (1945); Univ. of Wisconsin (1948, 1951); the Bread Loaf Sch. of English (1957–74); and was lecturer in English and coordinator of graduate programs in English, Simmons Coll. (1972–to date). He was named Robert Frost Professor of Literature, Bread Loaf Sch. of English, in 1968.

Published Works. He wrote *Guinea's Captive Kings* (1942); *Enlightened England* (1947); *Four Stages of Renaissance Style* (1955); *Comedy* (1956); *Rococo to Cubism in Art and Literature* (1960); *Loss of the Self* (1962); *Art History* (1963), and *Literature and Technology*, (1968).

Awards. Mr. Sypher received Guggenheim Fellowships for research in the theory of fine arts and literature (1950–51; 1959–60).

SYSE, GLENNA. Drama critic. b. Glenna Marie Lowes, Oct. 5, 1927, Weyburn, Saskatchewan, Canada, to Norman John and Marie Wallace (Cunningham) Lowes. Grad. Univ. of Manitoba, Winnipeg, Canada, B.A. 1949; Royal Conservatory of Music, Toronto, A.C.T.M. 1946; graduate study at Univ. of Minnesota, 1949–50. Married July 10, 1954, to Norman Douglas Syse. Member of Amer. Newspaper Guild. Address: (home) 6826 N. Oakley, Chicago, IL 60601, tel. (312) SH 3-4866; (bus.) Chicago *Sun-Times*, 401 N. Wabash, Chicago, IL 60601, tel. (312) 321-2669.

Since August 1958, Mrs. Syse has been drama and ballet critic for the Chicago *Sun-Times*. She was first associated with the newspaper as a reviewer of the arts (Oct. 1954).

SZABO, SANDOR. Actor. b. Sandor Bela Szabo, Apr. 25, 1915, Budapest, Hungary, to Erno and Katalin (Paliffy) Szabo. Grad. H.S. in Budapest, 1934; Acad. of Th., Budapest, diploma 1938. Married 1940 to Kato Barczy; two sons. Member of AEA; AFTRA; SAG.

Theatre. Mr. Szabo made his debut as Lysander in *A Midsummer Night's Dream* (Natl. Th., Budapest, 1940). He was a member of the Natl. Th. (1940–49), playing Laertes in *Hamlet*, Ferdinand in *The Storm*, the title role in *Don Carlos*, Mark Antony in *Julius Caesar*, the title role in *Macbeth*, Mat in *Anna Christie*, the title role in *Tartuffe*, and others. He was a member of the Vig Th. Co. (1949–53), playing the Negro in *Deep Are the Roots*, Trigorin in *The Seagull*, the title role in *Cyrano de Bergerac*, and others.

He toured the U.S. in *Royal Enclosure* (Summer 1959); played Vershinin in *The Three Sisters* (4th St. Th., N.Y.C., Sept. 29, 1959); took over Frank Overton's role as Paul Stumpfig during the run of *Big Fish, Little Fish* (ANTA, Mar. 15, 1961); played Ivan Malekhine in *First Love* (Morosco, Dec. 25, 1961); Commodore Roseabove in *Oh Dad, Poor Dad, Mamma's Hung You in the Closet and I'm Feelin' So Sad* (Phoenix, Feb. 26, 1962; moved to Morosco, Aug. 27, 1963); Zoltan Karpathy in *My Fair Lady* (NY City Ctr., May 20, 1964); and substituted (June 28, 1964) for Kurt Kasznar for three weeks as Victor Velasco in *Barefoot in the Park* (Biltmore, Oct. 23, 1963), then touring in the part. He was Hans Bethe in *In the Matter of J. Robert Oppenheimer* (Vivian Beaumont Th., N.Y.C., June 26, 1969) and appeared at the Guthrie Th., Minneapolis, Minn., as Lieutenant Ovchukhov in *A Play by Aleksandr Solzhenitsyn* (Oct. 13, 1970) and in *The Diary of a Scoundrel* (Nov. 9, 1971).

Films. He has appeared in 25 Hungarian films.

Television. Mr. Szabo has appeared on Dr. Kildare (CBS), Sea Hunt (CBS), and Naked City (ABC).

Awards. Mr. Szabo received three gold medals from the Hungarian government for outstanding acting, and a Rockefeller Scholarship to study English through ANTA.

Recreation. Skiing, tennis.

T

TABORI, GEORGE. Playwright, novelist. b. May 24, 1914, Budapest, Hungary, to Cornelius and Elsa (Ziffer) Tabori. Father, historian, journalist. Grad. Zrinyi Gymnasium, 1932. Married July 4, 1954, to Viveca Lindfors, actress (marr. dis.); two sons, one daughter. Served British Army, 1941–43; as Intelligence officer and broadcaster. Member of Dramatists Guild, ALA; SWG. Address: Schweinfurtstrasse 60, 1 Berlin 33, West Germany tel. 823-1066.

Pre-Theatre. Waiter, cook, tourist guide, foreign correspondent, novelist, translator.

Theatre. Mr. Tabori wrote *Flight into Egypt* (Music Box, N.Y.C., Mar. 18, 1952); *The Emperor's Clothes* (Ethel Barrymore Th., Feb. 9, 1953); adapted Strindberg's *Miss Julie* (Phoenix, Feb. 21, 1956); wrote *Brouhaha* (Aldwych, London, Aug. 27, 1958; 175 E. Bway Playhouse, N.Y.C., Apr. 26, 1960); adapted and arranged writings of Bertholt Brecht, entitled *Brecht on Brecht* (Th. de Lys, Jan. 3, 1962; Royal Court Th., London, England, and Lilla Theatern, Stockholm, Sweden, 1962–63). He adapted Max Frisch's *Andorra* (Biltmore, N.Y.C., Feb. 9, 1963); and Brecht's *Arturo Ui* (Lunt-Fontanne, Nov. 11, 1963); wrote *The Niggerlovers* (Orpheum, N.Y.C., Sept. 26, 1968; and Th. des Nations, Paris, France, 1974); wrote and directed *The Cannibals* (Amer. Place Th., N.Y.C., Oct. 17, 1968; and Schiller Th., Berlin, Germany, 1971); *Pinkville* (Amer. Place Th., N.Y.C., Mar. 17, 1971); and *Clowns* (Tubingen, Sweden, 1972); and directed *Kohlhaas* (Bonn, Germany, 1974); and *Afore Night Comes* and *Knots* (Bremen, Germany, 1975).

Films. The motion picture *Crisis* (MGM, 1950) was based on a novel by Mr. Tabori. He wrote the original story and screenplay for *Young Lovers* (Rank, 1952); the screenplay for *I Confess* (WB, 1953); the story and screenplay for *The Journey* (MGM, 1959); and the screenplays for *No Exit* (ZEN, 1962); and

Secret Ceremony (U, 1969).

Television. Mr. Tabori wrote *Insomnia* (Berlin, 1975).

Published Works. Mr. Tabori wrote the novels *Beneath the Stone, Companions of the Left Hand, Original Sin, The Caravan Passes,* and *The Good One.*

Awards. For *Young Lovers,* Mr. Tabori received the Academy Award (London, Eng., 1953).

Recreation. Chess.

TABORI, KRISTOFFER. Actor. b. Christopher Donald Siegel, Aug. 4, Malibu, Calif., to Viveca Lindfors, actress, and Don Siegel, film director; stepson of George Tabori, playwright. Relative in theatre: brother-in-law, Martin Fried, stage director. Educ. Dalton Sch., N.Y.C.; Riverdale Country Day School, N.Y.C.; P.S. 198 and J.H.S. 167 (both N.Y.C.); H.S. of Performing Arts, N.Y.C.; New Lincoln School, N.Y.C. Professional training with Ada Mather and Diana Maddox, coaches; Viveca and George Tabori; Gui Andrisano, dance; Joseph Scott, voice; Vincent Gugleotti, acrobatics; Bob Harrison, voice. Member of AEA; SAG; AFTRA. Address: 172 E. 95th St., New York, NY 10028, tel. (212) 427-8412.

Theatre. Mr. Tabori made his first appearance on stage as Thisbe in a production of *A Midsummer Night's Dream* (YMHA, N.Y.C.), and his first professional engagements were at the Berkshire Th. Festival, Stockbridge, Mass., where he played Balthassar in *The Merchant of Venice* (July 19, 1966); was in *Waiting for Godot* (Aug. 2, 1966); *The Threepenny Opera;* and *A Funny Thing Happened on the Way to the Forum.* He was in *Three Boards and a Passion* (Royal Alexandra Th., Toronto, Ontario, Canada, 1966); made his off-Bway debut in *Little Emil and the Detectives;* played Jose in *The Guns of Carrar* (ANTA Matinee Series, Th. de Lys., Dec. 9 and 10, 1968); was the Player Queen and the Second Gravedigger in *Hamlet* (American Shakespeare Festival, Stratford, Conn., June 18, 1969); appeared in *Three Boards and a Passion;* made his Bway debut as Tyler Bishop in *The Penny Wars* (Royale, Oct. 15, 1969); played the Boy, Davy in *Henry V* (ANTA, Nov. 10, 1969); Joe Morris in *Dream of a Blacklisted Actor* (ANTA Matinee Series, Th. de Lys, Dec. 15, 1969); and was Charley Gordon in *How Much, How Much?* (Provincetown Playhouse, May 17, 1970).

Mr. Tabori also played Romeo in *Romeo and Juliet* (Studio Arena, Buffalo, N.Y., Mar. 2, 1972); Prince Hal in *Henry IV, Part 1* (Mark Taper Forum, Los Angeles, Calif., Oct. 26, 1972); Orlando in *As You Like It* (Los Angeles Shakespeare Festival, Pilgrimage Th., Sept. 3, 1973); was in *The Rose Tattoo* (Walnut St. Playhouse, Philadelphia, Pa., Nov. 27, 1973); and played Leeds in *The Wager* (Eastside Playhouse, N.Y.C., Oct. 21, 1974).

Films. Mr. Tabori made his motion picture debut in *Weddings and Babies;* and he appeared in *John and Mary* (1969); *Sweet Charity* (1969); *Making It* (20th-Fox, 1971); and *Journey through Rosebud* (Cinerama, 1972).

Television and Radio. Mr. Tabori has been on Radio Mystery Th., and he first appeared on television in *Neither Are We Enemies* (Hallmark Hall of Fame, Mar. 13, 1970). Other television films and specials in which he appeared include *A Memory of Two Mondays* (NET Playhouse, PBS, Jan. 28, 1971); *The Glass House* (Feb. 4, 1972); *Family Flight* (ABC, Oct. 25, 1972); *Terror on the Beach; The Lady's Not for Burning; QB VII* (ABC, Apr. 29 and 30, 1974); and *Ben Franklin: The Statesman* (CBS, Jan. 28, 1975). Mr. Tabori also appeared on *The One-Eyed Mule's Time Has Come* (James Garner Show, NBC, Nov. 23, 1971); and on episodes of The Young Lawyers; Medical Center (CBS, Sept., Oct. 1972); Marcus Welby, M.D. (ABC); The Rookies (ABC); Toma; and Cannon (CBS).

Awards. Mr. Tabori received a *Theatre World* Award for his performance in *How Much, How Much?.*

TACKNEY, STANLEY. Actor, director, producer. b. Stanley James Tackney, July 2, 1909, New York City, to James Henry and Elizabeth (Mohan) Tackney. Father, real estate developer. Grad. Manhattan Prep Sch., Riverdale, N.Y., 1927; Manhattan Coll., B.B.A. 1931. Studied drama with Milton Smith at Columbia Univ., 1931–33. Member of AEA (council, 1957–67); SAG; AFTRA; Beta Sigma.

Pre-Theatre. Accountant, real estate broker, registered representative in stock brokerage house.

Theatre. Mr. Tackney first appeared on stage as Digger in a touring company of *The Hasty Heart* (opened Playhouse, Wilmington, Del.; closed Savannah, Ga., 1946); made his N.Y.C. debut as Ninian in a one-act play, *Afternoon Storm,* which was part of a triple-bill with *Celebration* and *Hope Is the Thing with Feathers* (Maxine Elliott's Th., Apr. 11, 1948); subsequently played the First Clerk in *Point of No Return* (Alvin, Dec. 13, 1951); Russell Lawson in *High Named Today* (Th. de Lys, Dec. 10, 1954); produced two seasons of stock at the Williamsport Summer Th., Pa. (1955–56); and played Heffernan in the pre-Bway tryout of *Build with One Hand* (opened Shubert, New Haven, Conn., Nov. 7, 1956; closed Ford's Th., Baltimore, Md., Nov. 27, 1956).

Mr. Tackney was resident director at the Thousand Island Playhouse (Alexandria Bay, N.Y., Summer 1957); at the Cincinnati (Ohio) Summer Playhouse (1958–59); and at the Atlanta (Ga.) Summer Th. (1960–61); played General Lew Wallace in the bus-and-truck tour of *The Andersonville Trial* (opened Center, Norfolk, Va., Sept. 28, 1960; closed Community Ctr., Hershey, Pa., Apr. 15, 1961); and joined the national tour of *My Fair Lady* (opened Auditorium, Rochester, N.Y., Mar. 18, 1957; closed O'Keefe Ctr., Toronto, Ontario, Canada, Dec. 15, 1963).

Television. He has appeared on Robert Montgomery Presents (NBC); Big Town (CBS); the Burns and Allen Show (CBS); Inner Sanctum (NBC); the Bob Hope Show (NBC); and The Defenders (CBS).

Recreation. Photography.

TALBOT, LYLE. Actor, director. b. Lyle Henderson Talbot, Feb. 8, 1902, Pittsburgh, Pa., to J. Edward and Florence (Talbot) Henderson. Father, actor; mother, actress. Grad. Tech. H.S., Omaha, Nebr., 1918; attended Univ. of Nebraska, 1918. Married June 19, 1947, to Margaret Abbot, actress; two sons, two daughters. Served USAAF, Special Services, 2 1/2 years; rank, S/Sgt. Relative in theatre: son, Stephen, actor. Member of AEA; AFTRA (natl. bd., 1959–to date); SAG (fdr.; bd. of dir.); Masons; Shriners. Address: 3942 Goodland Ave., Studio City, CA 91604, tel. (213) PO 1-9920.

Theatre. Mr. Talbot made his stage debut with MacKnight, the Hypnotist (1921); toured the Midwest with the Chase-Lister Rep. Co. (1923–25); appeared in Toby (tent repertory) shows, and played in stock theatres throughout the US, including a tour as the Villain in *St. Elmo,* with the Whetten Rep. Co., Colo.

He played Don Stackhouse in *Separate Rooms* (Maxine Elliott's Th., N.Y.C., Mar. 23, 1940); toured as Krogstad in *A Doll's House* (1945); as Dawson Kennedy in the pre-Bway tryout of *The Legend of Lou* (opened Cass, Detroit, Mich., Sept. 2, 1946; closed there Sept. 14, 1946); and has owned and directed his own stock company (Lyceum Th., Memphis, Tenn., 1928–to date). He has also toured with the National Theatre production of *Never Too Late* (1966); appeared in Richard Rodgers' revival production of *South Pacific* (Lincoln Ctr., N.Y.C., 1969); and starred in road tour companies of *The Odd Couple* and *There's a Girl in My Soup.* .

Films. Mr. Talbot made his screen debut in *Love Is a Racket* (1st Natl., 1932); subsequently appeared in *No More Orchids* (Col., 1932); *20,000 Years in Sing Sing* (1st Natl., 1933); *One Night of Love* (Col., 1934); *Oil for the Lamps of China* (WB, 1935); *Sunrise at Campobello* (WB, 1960); and over 150 feature films.

Television. Mr. Talbot played Joe Randolph on the Adventures of Ozzie and Harriet (ABC, 1955–64); appeared on Climax! (CBS); Lux Video Th. (NBC); Matinee Th. (NBC); Arrest and Trial (ABC); The Lucy Show (CBS); The Red Skelton Show (CBS); Burns and Allen (NBC); the Robert Cummings Show (NBC); Wagon Train (NBC); The Danny Thomas Show (ABC); and 77 Sunset Strip (NBC).

Awards. As one of the founders of SAG, he received a Gold Life Membership Card (1960); and is honorary Mayor of Studio City, Calif.

TALIAFERRO, MABEL. Actress. b. Maybelle Evelyn Taliaferro, May 21, 1887, New York City, to Robert and Anna (Barriscale) Taliaferro. Mother, theatrical manager, talent representative, actress. Attended Holy Angels Convent, Fort Lee, N.J., 1896–98; MacDuffie's Sch. for Young Ladies, Springfield, Mass., 1901–02. Married Oct. 31, 1906, to Frederick W. Thompson, producer, director, theatrical manager (marr. dis. Mar. 15, 1912); married June 1, 1913, to Thomas J. Carrigan, actor (marr. dis. May 1919), one son; married Jan. 11, 1920, to Joseph P. O'Brien, sculptor (marr. dis. June 15, 1929); married 1930 to Robert Ober, playwright, actor (dec. Dec. 7, 1950). Relatives in theatre: sister, Edith Taliaferro, actress; cousin, Bessie Barriscale, actress. Member of AEA; SAG.

Theatre. Miss Taliaferro made her stage debut as a child actress in the role of Baby Bascombe in *Blue Jeans* (New Natl. Th., Washington, D.C., Dec. 5, 1892); joined the company of *Shore Acres* (Daly's, N.Y.C., Dec. 25, 1893); subsequently appeared in *A Ride for Life* (People's, Oct. 15, 1894); *Patent Applied For* (People's, Dec. 25, 1894); and *Logan's Luck,* later called *Human Heart* (People's, June 3, 1895); played the Malone Child in *The Minstrel of Clare* (14 St. Th., Mar. 2, 1896); Julian Desmond in *For Fair Virginia* (Columbus, Dec. 14, 1896); appeared in *Mavourneen* (14 St. Th., May 10, 1897); played Gertrude Thornton in *Truth* (Park, Boston, Mass., Apr. 18, 1898); and appeared in *The Banker's Daughter* (Columbus, N.Y.C., May 30, 1898).

She played Esther Ansell in *The Children of the Ghetto* (Herald Square Th., Oct. 16, 1899), which she repeated in London (Adelphi, Dec. 11, 1899); Angie Vollmer in *Lost River* (14 St. Th., N.Y.C., Oct. 3, 1900); Mary Vine in *The Price of Peace* (Bway Th., Mar. 21, 1901); subsequently appeared in *An American Invasion* (Bijou, Oct. 20, 1902); *The Little Princess* (Criterion, Jan. 14, 1903); and *The Land of Heart's Desire* (Carnegie Lyceum, June 3, 1903); played Lovey Mary in *Mrs. Wiggs of the Cabbage Patch* (Savoy, Sept. 3, 1904); Dolly Clandon in *You Never Can Tell* (Garrick, Jan. 7, 1905); toured as Ann in *In the Bishop's Carriage* (1905); appeared in vaudeville (Proctor's 23 St. Th., Apr. 2, 1906); with William Collier, toured Australia as Agnes Colt in *On the Quiet* and appeared in *The Dictator* (Summer 1906); and repeated the role of Agnes in *On the Quiet* (Beck's, Bellingham, Washington, D.C., Sept. 26, 1906).

Miss Taliaferro played in *Pippa Passes* (Majestic, N.Y.C., Nov. 12, 1906); Polly in *Polly of the Circus* (Liberty, Dec. 23, 1907); billed as "Nell," she played Madeleine in *Springtime* (Liberty, Oct. 19, 1909); resuming her own name, played Parthenia in *Ingomar* (Liberty, Dec. 1909); appeared in *The Land of Heart's Desire* (Washington, D.C., Feb. 1910); played Rosalie in *The Call of the Cricket* (Belasco, N.Y.C., Apr. 19, 1910); and Edith in *My Man* (Grand Opera House, Aug. 26, 1910).

She toured in vaudeville in *Taken on Credit* and *The Return of Tori San,* which she had written herself (1912); played the title role in *Sunday* (Suburban Garden, St. Louis, Mo., July 1913); Victoria Claffenden in *Young Wisdom* (Criterion, N.Y.C., Jan. 5, 1914); appeared in *The New Henrietta* (Cort, Chicago, Ill., Dec. 1914); and *The Banker's Wife* (Chicago, 1915); played Mary O'Neill in *The Woman Thou Gavest Me* (Shubert, Boston, Apr. 1917); Annabel Lee in *Luck in Pawn* (48 St. Th., N.Y.C., Mar. 24, 1919); Barbara in the Shakespeare Playhouse production of *The Piper* (Fulton, Mar. 19, 1920); the title role in *Alice in Wonderland* (Little, Apr. 1920); and toured the vaudeville circuits in *Connie* (Feb. 1921).

Miss Taliaferro played Sally Newton in Robert Ober's play, *Back Fire* (Vanderbilt, N.Y.C., June 13, 1932); Ann in *Ann Adams, Spinster* (Sutton, Chicago, Mar. 1933); appeared in *The Cradle Song* (Ogunquit Playhouse, Me., Aug. 1933); played Fanny Grey in *Autumn Crocus* (Hollis St. Th., Boston, Mass., Mar. 1934); and toured as Leonora Perrycoste in *There's Always Juliet* (commencing May, 1934).

With Clare Tree Major's children's theatre troupe, she played Princess Isabel in *The Prince's Secret* (Barbizon-Plaza Th., N.Y.C., Apr. 27, 1935); subsequently toured the N.Y.C. Subway Circuit as Delia Lovell in *The Old Maid* (opened Jamaica, L.I., June 1936); appeared in summer stock as Karen Wright in *The Children's Hour* (Centerville, Mass., July 1937); Ellen in *Grandpa* (Newport, R.I., Aug. 1938); and toured as Harriet Stanley in *The Man Who Came to Dinner* (1940); played Mrs. Douglas in *George Washington Slept Here* (Lyceum, N.Y.C., Oct. 18, 1940); toured as Mrs. Brown in *Claudia* (1941); played Mrs. Grace Stewart in *Victory Belles* (Mansfield, N.Y.C., Oct. 26, 1943); Serena in *Bloomer Girl* (Shubert, Oct. 5, 1944), toured in that role and repeated it in the NY City Ctr. revival (Jan. 6, 1947); Mrs. Anders in *Springtime Folly* (John Golden Th., Feb. 26, 1951); and Mary Richards in the pre-Bway tryout of *The Man that Corrupted Hadleyburg* (Erlanger, Philadelphia, Pa., Apr. 14, 1951).

Films. Miss Taliaferro appeared in *Cinderella* (Par., 1914); *The Three of Us* (1914); *The Dawn of Love* (Metro, 1916); *God's Half Acre* (Metro, 1916); *The Snowbird* (Metro, 1916); *Her Great Price* (Metro, 1916); *The Sunbeam* (Metro, 1916); *The Jury of Fate* (Metro, 1917); *A Magdalen of the Hills* (Metro, 1917); *A Wife by Proxy* (Metro, 1917); *Peggy Leads the Way* (Amer. Mutual, 1917); *The Barricade* (Metro, 1917); *Draft 258* (Metro, 1918); *The Battle for Billions* (1919); and *Sentimental Tommy* (Par., 1921).

Other Activities. Antique dealer.

Published Works. Miss Taliaferro wrote a book of verse entitled *Lights and Highlights;* and various monologues and short stories.

TALLMER, JERRY. Newspaperman, critic, writer, editor. b. Dec. 9, 1920, New York City, to Albert F. and Ilona (Loewenthal) Tallmer Müller-Munk. Father, businessman. Grad. Lincoln Sch. of Teachers' Coll., N.Y.C., 1938; Dartmouth Coll., B.A. 1946. Married June 19, 1949, to Margaret Ann Muendel (marr. dis. 1955); married April 15, 1959, to Louise Tillis (marr. dis.); married July 12, 1964, to Marcia Ann Levant; one son, one daughter. Served USAAF, 1941–45; rank T/Sgt. Member of NY Newspaper Guild; NY Drama Desk (Vernon Rice Awards Comm.). Address: 359 W. 18th St., New York, NY 10011.

From 1955–62, Mr. Tallmer was associate editor and drama critic of *The Village Voice,* of which he was a founder and where he originated the Off-Bway (Obie) Awards.

From 1962 to 1974, he was drama editor and off-Bway drama critic for the NY *Post,* for which he also wrote jazz, television, movie and art criticism. He has contributed articles to *Playboy, Cavalier, Evergreen Review, Encore, Show Business Illustrated, Pageant, Dissent,* the Montreal *Star* and other publications.

Television. Mr. Tallmer appeared on *Whatever Happened to Off-Broadway?* (U.S.A.—Theatre, Educ., Dec. 23, 1965).

Awards. Mr. Tallmer received the George Jean Nathan Award in Drama Criticism for his reviews in *The Village Voice* (1962), and a Ford Foundation grant (1964).

TANDY, JESSICA. Actress. b. June 7, 1909, London, England, to Harry and Jessie Helen (Horspool) Tandy. Attended Dame Alice Owen's Girls' School, London, 1919–24; Ben Greet Acad. of Acting, London, 1924–27. Married 1932 to Jack Hawkins, actor (marr. dis.); one daughter; married Sept. 27, 1942, to Hume Cronyn, actor; one son; one daughter. Member of AEA; SAG; AFTRA. Address: Box 85A, Route 137, Pound Ridge, NY 10576.

Theatre. Miss Tandy made her professional debut as Sara Manderson in *The Manderson Girls* (Playroom Six, London, Nov. 22, 1927); subsequently joined (1928) the Birmingham (England) Repertory Co., appearing as Gladys in *The Comedy of Good and Evil* and Ginevra in *Alice Sit-by-the-Fire;* played Lydia Blake in a touring production of *Yellow Sands* (1928); appeared as Lena Jackson in *The Rumour* (Court, London, Feb. 21, 1929); the Typist in *The Theatre of Life* (Arts, Apr. 5, 1929); Maggie in *Water* (Little, June 25, 1929); and Aude in *The Unknown Warrior* (Haymarket, Nov. 1929).

She made her Bway debut as Toni Rakonitz in *The Matriarch* (Longacre, Mar. 18, 1930); played Olivia in *Twelfth Night* for the Oxford Univ. Dramatic Society (Oxford, England, Summer 1930); Cynthia Perry in *The Last Enemy* (Shubert, N.Y.C., Oct. 30, 1930); Fay in *The Man Who Pays the Piper* (St. Martin's, London, Feb. 10, 1931); Audrey in *Autumn Crocus* (Lyric, Apr. 6, 1931); Ruth Blair in *Port Said* (Wyndham's, Nov. 1, 1931); Anna in *Musical Chairs* (Arts, Nov. 15, 1931); *Below the Surface* (Repertory Players, Jan. 1932); *Juarez and Maximilian* (Phoenix, Feb. 1932); appeared at the Cambridge Festival Th. in *Troilus and Cressida, See Naples and Die, The Witch, Rose without a Thorn, The Inspector General,* and *The Servant of Two Masters* (Apr.–June 1932).

Miss Tandy played Carlotta in *Mutual Benefit* (St. Martin's, London, July 10, 1932); Manuela in *Children in Uniform* (Duchess, Oct. 7, 1932); Alicia in *Lady Audley's Secret* (Arts, Jan. 22, 1933); Marikke in *Midsummer Fires* (Embassy, May 21, 1933); Titania in *A Midsummer Night's Dream* (Open Air Th., Regents Park, July 5, 1933); succeeded (Nov. 1933) Maisie Darrell as Betty in *Ten Minute Alibi* (Haymarket, Jan. 2, 1933); appeared in *The Romantic Young Lady* (Fulham Shilling Th., Jan. 1934); as Rosamund in *Birthday* (Cambridge, Feb. 2, 1934); Viola in *Twelfth Night* and Anne Page in *The Merry Wives of Windsor* (Manchester Hippodrome, Apr.–May 1934); and Eva Whiston in *Line Engaged* (Duke of York's Th., London, Oct. 24, 1934).

She played Ophelia in John Gielgud's *Hamlet* (New, Nov. 14, 1934); Ada in *Noah* (New, July 2, 1935); Anna Penn in *Anthony and Anna* (Whitehall, Nov. 8, 1935); Marie Rose in *The Ante-Room* (Queen's, Aug. 14, 1936); Jacqueline in *French without Tears* (Criterion, Nov. 6, 1936); Pamela in *Honour Thy Father* (Arts, Dec. 6, 1936); with the Old Vic Co., Viola and Sebastian in *Twelfth Night* (Feb. 23, 1937), Katherine in *Henry V* (Apr. 6, 1937); and appeared as Ellen Murray in *Yes, My Darling Daughter* (St. James's, June 3, 1937).

She appeared as Kay in *Time and the Conways* (Ritz, Jan. 3, 1938); Leda in *Glorious Morning* (Duchess, May 28, 1938); Nora in *The White Steed* (Cort, N.Y.C., Jan. 10, 1939); Viola in *Twelfth Night* (Open Air Th., Regents Park, London, July 31, 1939); with a repertory company, toured Canada in *Charles, the King, Geneva* and *Tobias and the Angel* (1939); played the Deaconess in *Geneva* (Henry Miller's Th., N.Y.C., Jan. 30, 1940); appeared with the Old Vic Co. as Cordelia in John Gielgud's *King Lear,* directed by Harley Granville Barker (Apr. 15, 1940), and Miranda in *The Tempest* (May 29, 1940).

Miss Tandy appeared as Dr. Mary Murray in *Jupiter Laughs* (Biltmore, N.Y.C., Sept. 9, 1940); Abigail Hill in *Anne of England* (St. James, Oct. 7, 1941); Cattrin in *Yesterday's Magic* (Guild, Apr. 14, 1942); Lucretia Collins in an Actor's Laboratory Th. production of *Portrait of a Madonna,* directed by her husband, Hume Cronyn (Las Palmas Th., Los Angeles, Calif., Summer 1946); and played Blanche du Bois in *A Streetcar Named Desire* (Ethel Barrymore Th., N.Y.C., Dec. 3, 1947).

She played in *Now I Lay Me Down To Sleep,* staged by Mr. Cronyn at Stanford Univ. (Palo Alto, Calif., July 1949); appeared with Mr. Cronyn in *The Little Blue Light* (Brattle Th., Cambridge, Mass., Aug. 14, 1950); played the title role in *Hilda Crane* (Coronet, N.Y.C., Nov. 1, 1950), which Mr. Cronyn directed; Agnes in *The Fourposter* (Ethel Barrymore Th., Oct. 24, 1951); Mary Doyle in the first production of the Phoenix Th., *Madam, Will You Walk* (Phoenix, Dec. 1, 1953); toured with Mr. Cronyn in concert readings, *Face to Face* (Sept.–Dec. 1954); played Agnes in *The Fourposter* (NY City Ctr., Jan. 5, 1955); Mary Honey in *The Honeys* (Longacre, Apr. 28, 1955); and Frances Farrar in *A Day by the Sea* (ANTA, Sept. 26, 1955).

Miss Tandy and Mr. Cronyn toured in a stock production of *The Man in the Dog Suit,* in which she played Martha Walling (Summer 1957); toured in *Triple Play,* a bill of three one-act works and a monologue, in which she played Lucretia Collins in *Portrait of a Madonna,* The Public in *A Pound on Demand,* and Angela Nightingale in *Bedtime Story* (Summer 1958); played Martha Walling in *The Man in the Dog Suit* (Coronet, N.Y.C., Oct. 30, 1958); repeated her roles in *Triple Bill* (Playhouse, Apr. 15, 1959); played Louise Harrington in *Five Finger Exercise* (Music Box, Dec. 2, 1959), and on tour (1960–61).

Miss Tandy appeared at the American Shakespeare Festival (Stratford, Conn.), as Lady Macbeth in *Macbeth* (June 28, 1961) and Cassandra in *Troilus and Cressida* (July 23, 1961); played Edith Maitland in *Big Fish, Little Fish* (Duke of York's Th., London, Sept. 18, 1962); appeared with the Minnesota Theatre Co. (Tyrone Guthrie Th., Minneapolis, Minn.) in its first season, as Gertrude in *Hamlet* (May 7, 1963), Olga in *The Three Sisters* (June 18, 1963), and Linda in *Death of a Salesman* (July 16, 1963).

She played Fraulein Doktor Mathilde von Zahnd in *The Physicists* (Martin Beck Th., Oct. 14, 1964); performed with her husband in *Hear America Speaking* at the White House, Washington, D.C., at the request of President and Mrs. Lyndon B. Johnson (Feb. 2, 1965); appeared as Lady Wishfort in *The Way of the World,* Madame Ranevskaya in *The Cherry Orchard,* and the Mother-in-Law in *The Caucasian Chalk Circle* (Tyrone Guthrie Th., Minneapolis, Minn., May–Dec. 1965); appeared as Agnes in *A Delicate Balance* (Martin Beck Th., N.Y.C., Sept. 22, 1966; and on tour of US through June 1967); played Froisine in *The Miser* (Mark Taper Forum for the Center Th. Group, Los Angeles, March, 1968); Hesione Hushabye in *Heartbreak House* (Shaw Festival, Niagara-on-the-Lake, Ontario, Canada, June 1968); Pamela Pew-Pickett in *Tchin-Tchin* (Ivanhoe Th., Chicago, Oct. 1969); Marguerite Gautier in *Camino Real* (Lincoln Center, N.Y.C., Jan. 1970); Marjorie in *Home* (Morosco, Nov. 17, 1970); the Wife in *All Over* (Martin Beck Th., Mar. 27, 1971); appeared in *Promenade All* (tour, Summer 1972–Winter 1973); appeared as Winnie in *Happy Days* (Nov. 20, 1972), and as The Mouth in *Not I* (world premiere, Nov. 22, 1972) as part of a Samuel Beckett Festival (Lincoln Center, N.Y.C.). She toured the East Coast in *Not I* (1973); and appeared as Anna-Mary Conklin in *Come into the Garden, Maud,* and as Hilde Latymer in *A Song at Twilight,* billed as *Noel Coward in Two Keys* (Ethel Barrymore Th., N.Y.C., Feb. 28, 1974).

Films. Miss Tandy made her debut in England in *The Indiscretions of Eve;* followed by her first American film, *Murder in the Family* (1938); *The Seventh Cross* (MGM, 1944); *The Valley of Decision* (MGM, 1945); *Dragonwyck* (20th-Fox, 1946); *The Green Years* (MGM, 1946); *Forever Amber* (20th-Fox, 1947); *A Woman's Vengeance* (U, 1947); *September Affair* (Par., 1950); *The Desert Fox* (20th-Fox, 1951); *The Light in the Forest* (Buena Vista, 1958); *Adventures of a Young Man* (20th-Fox, 1962); and *The Birds* (U, 1963); and she appeared as Edna in *Butley* (Ely Landau Prods., 1973).

Television and Radio. Miss Tandy has appeared on television in England (1939), and in America (1948–to date). With her husband, she performed in their series, The Marriage, on radio and television (NBC, 1953–54); appeared in *Christmas 'til Closing* (NBC, Dec. 18, 1955); *The Moon and Sixpence* (NBC, 1959); the Alfred Hitchcock Hour (CBS); the Hallmark Hall of Fame (NBC); The Fallen Idol (NBC); the Dupont Show of the Month (CBS, 1959); and *Tennessee Williams' South* (CBS, 1973).

Discography. She has performed in *The Wind and the Willows,* with her husband; as Volumnia in *Cori-*

olanus, with Richard Burton; and as Amanda in *The Glass Menagerie.*

Awards. Miss Tandy won the Antoinette Perry (Tony) and the Twelfth Night Club awards for her performance as Blanche du Bois in *A Streetcar Named Desire* (1948); with her husband, Hume Cronyn, received the Comoedia Matinee Club's Award for their performances in *The Fourposter* (1952); received the Delia Austrian Award from the NY Drama League for her performance as Louise Harrington in *Five Finger Exercise* (1960); received the Village Voice Off-Broadway (Obie) Award (1972–73) for her performance in *Not I;* and the Drama Desk Award (1973) for her performances in *Happy Days* and *Not I.*

TANSWELL, BERTRAM. Director, actor. b. Albert Henry Silas Russell Tanswell, Sept. 1, 1908, Blandford Eng., to William and Alice Catherine (Eyers) Tanswell. Father, stable and garage business. Attended Blandford Boys' Sch., 1917–22; grad. Iowa City (Iowa) H.S., 1927; Univ. of Iowa, B.A. 1932. Member of AEA; AFTRA; SAG. Address: 512 N. Sycamore Ave., Hollywood, CA 90036, tel. (213) 934-7744.

Theatre. Mr. Tanswell has been director of the Kalamazoo (Mich.) Civic Players since 1963.

He made his debut as a page boy in a town pageant (Blandford, England, Dec. 1911); subsequently appeared with the Old Globe Players (Chicago, Ill.) in Shakespearean plays at the Chicago World's Fair; San Diego (Calif.) Exposition; Dallas (Tex.) Centennial; and tours in between (1934–37); played Puck in *A Midsummer Night's Dream* and Gremio in *The Taming of the Shrew* in the Margaret Webster World's Fair Shakespeare Co. (N.Y., 1939); made his Bway debut as "Old Crump" in *Bachelor Born* (Morosco, Jan. 25, 1938); followed by appearances as Second Pilot Officer in *Heart of a City* (Henry Miller's Th., Feb. 12, 1942); Detective Raines in *I Killed the Count* (Cort, Aug. 31, 1942); Scrivener in *Richard III* (Forrest, Mar. 24, 1943); and Corp. Ticker in *Storm Operation* (Belasco, Jan. 11, 1944).

He was understudy to Jack Manning (Apr. 18, 1944) as Roderigo in *Othello* (Shubert, Oct. 19, 1943); played Johnny in *Harlequinade,* part of the double-bill with *The Browning Version* (Coronet, Oct. 12, 1949); Jackson, Maintopman, in *Billy Budd* (Biltmore, Feb. 10, 1951); and succeeded William Hansen (Mar. 12, 1956) in the role of Mr. Oshira in *The Teahouse of the August Moon* (Martin Beck Th., Oct. 15, 1953).

In summer stock, he appeared with the Valley Players (Holyoke, Mass., Summers 1942–59); at the Paper Mill Playhouse (Millburn, N.J., Summers, 1940, 1943, 1953); at the Phoenix Th., Ariz., Summer 1950); and at the Casa Mañana Th. (Fort Worth, Tex., Summer 1961).

He has been a guest director and teacher at Denison Univ. (1946–63); and in association with the university has directed and co-managed five overseas tours for the US Army. From 1956 to 1963, Mr. Tanswell performed and directed at the Cleveland (Ohio) Play House.

Mr. Tanswell served on the staff of the Cleveland Playhouse as director and actor (1956–63); served as artistic director of the Civic Players, Kalamazoo, Mich. (1963–68); and is currently free-lance director of the Community Players (Long Beach) and Laguna-Moulton Th. (Laguna Beach, Calif.).

He was guest director of the Cleveland Playhouse (1971–72); the Court Th. Beloit, Wis. (1972–74); and the Old Globe Th., San Diego, Calif. (1973–74).

TARANOW, GERDA. Theatre historian, educator. b. New York, City, to Samuel and Sabina (Ostro) Taranow. Grad. NY Univ., B.A. 1952; M.A. 1955; Yale Univ., Ph.D. 1961 (post-doctoral fellowship). Member of IFTR; La Société du Théâtre; ASTR; Association of Recorded Sound Collections; TLA; MLA. Address: (home) 292 Pequot Ave., New London, CT 06320, tel. (203) 442-1078; (bus.) Connecticut Coll., New London, CT 06320, tel. (203) 442-5391.

Miss Taranow became associate professor of English at Connecticut Coll. in 1970; she had been assistant professor from 1967 to 1970. Previously, she had been in the Dept. of English, Univ. of Kentucky, as instructor (1963–65) and assistant professor (1965–66) and in the Dept. of English, Syracuse (N.Y.) Univ., as assistant professor (1966–67).

Published Works. Miss Taranow is author of *Sarah Bernhardt: The Art Within the Legend* (1972).

Recreation. Opera, dance.

TARRANT, L. NEWELL. Director, actor, manager. b. Levi Newell Tarrant, Jr., Feb. 28, 1911, Brownwood, Tex., to Levi Newell Tarrant, Sr. and Katie (Smith) Tarrant. Father, coffee importer and manufacturer. Grad. Breckenridge (Tex.) H.S., 1928; Baylor Univ., B.A. 1933; Northwestern Univ., M.A. 1937. Married Sept. 22, 1940, to Jean Lob, actress; three sons. Relative in theatre: son, Newell, III, actor. Served USNR, ETO, 1942–45; rank, Lt. Cmdr. Member of AEA; AETA (board of dir., 1959–61); NTC (bd. of trustees, 1948–51); ANTA (bd. of dir., exec. committee, 1955–59); ACTA (bd. of governors, 1961–64); TCG (advisory bd., 1961–63); USITT. Honolulu Community Theatre, Alohea at Makapuu, Honolulu, Hawaii 96816, tel. 740274.

Pre-Theatre. Men's wear merchandising, Hub Clothiers, Breckenridge, Tex. (1927–29).

Theatre. Since 1966, Mr. Tarrant has been artistic director of the Honolulu Community Theatre, where he stages approximately seven plays each season, including at least one original script. Mr. Tarrant was managing director of the theatre from 1963 to 1966.

He made his debut in a school production of *Oh, Kay!* (1928); was director of the Temple (Tex.) Little Theatre (Sept. 1933), where he remained for one season; director of the Fort Wayne (Ind.) Civic Th. (Sept. 1937–June 1940); producer, director and actor at the Th. of the Dunes (Beverly Shore, Ind., 1939–42), where he made his professional debut as Alan Squier in *The Petrified Forest* (July 1939); was director of the Tulsa (Okla.) Little Th. (1940–41); the Springfield (Ohio) Civic Theatre (1942); an ELT production of *Ladies in Retirement* (Lenox Hill Playhouse, N.Y.C., 1944); directed a season at the Raleigh (N.C.) Little Th. (1945); and a season at the Cain Park Th. (Cleveland Heights, Ohio, 1946).

He became managing director of The Playhouse, a professional theatre company (Erie, Pa., Sept. 1, 1946), a position he held for 15 years, presenting the original plays *Anything Can Happen, Holiday for Players, The Cellar and the Well, The Golden Age, The Fickle Prince, The Beast of the Bush, Double Header, Inside Emily Payne, Three Needles in a Haystack;* was actor-director at the Penn Playhouse (Meadville, Pa., Summers 1949–50); and managing director for the Peninsula Playhouse (Erie, Pa., 1956–61).

Television. He appeared on local dramatic programs as actor and director in Erie, Pa. (WICU, 1949).

Other Activities. Mr. Tarrant taught play production at Northwestern Univ. (1935–37); speech acting, genl. theatre practice at Fort Wayne Extension Center of Indiana Univ. (1937–40); and at the Student Th. School of the Erie Playhouse where he was managing director (1946–62). At Honolulu Community Th., he teaches classes in acting and stagecraft.

Recreation. Tennis, music, writing, all spectator sports.

TAUBMAN, HOWARD. Drama and music critic, writer. b. July 4, 1907, New York City, to Max and Etta (Shubert) Taubman. Grad. De Witt Clinton H.S., N.Y.C. 1925; Cornell Univ., A.B. (Phi Beta Kappa) 1929. Married July 3, 1934, to Nora Stern; two sons. Member of Dutch Treat Club, NY Drama Critics' Circle (pres., 1962–to date).

From 1966 until his retirement in 1972, Mr. Taubman was critic at large in the NY *Times,* where he had been a member of the staff since 1929 (music editor, 1935–55; music critic, 1955–60; drama critic, 1960–66).

Published Works. Mr. Taubman has written *Opera Front and Back* (1938); *Music as a Profession* (1939); *Music on My Beat* (1943); *The Maestro: The Life of Arturo Toscanini* (1951); *How To Build a Record Library* (1955); *How To Bring Up Your Child to Enjoy Music* (1957); *The Making of the American Theatre* (1965); and *The NY Times Guide to Listening Pleasure* (1969). He has contributed articles to the *Times* Magazine and Book Review; and to many other leading magazines.

Awards. Mr. Taubman has been given honorary Doctor of Music degrees from Oberlin Coll. (1959), Temple Univ. (1958), and the Philadelphia Acad. of Music (1959).

TAVEL, RONALD. Playwright, actor, director, scenarist, film maker. b. Ronald S. Tavel, Brooklyn, N.Y., May 17, 1941, to George and Florence (Sterns) Tavel. Father, craftsman, ring designer; mother, legal secretary. Relative in theatre: Harvey Tavel, director, actor. Grad. Brooklyn Coll., B.A., 1960; Univ. of Wyoming, M.A. 1961. Member of NY Theatre Strategy (founding member, 1972–to date). Address: (home) 438 W. Broadway, New York, NY 10013, tel. (212) 226-4725; (bus.) Helen Merrill, Barber and Merrill, 337 W. 22nd St., New York, NY 10011, tel. (212) 924-6314.

Theatre. Mr. Tavel began his theatrical career as an off-Bway performer with his portrayal of Aneximander in *Aegean Fable* (Originals Only Co., N.Y.C., 1952). He later appeared on stage as El Director in *The Life of Juanita Castro,* which he also wrote (Playhouse of the Ridiculous, N.Y.C., Jan.–Feb. 1967); Enigma in *In Search of the Cobra Jewels* (Playwrights' Workshop Club, Bastiano's, Oct. 4, 1972); and St. John the Divine in *Infinity* (St. Peter's Church, May 1974).

Plays written by Mr. Tavel and their first performances include *The Life of Juanita Castro* and *Shower* (Coda Galleries, N.Y.C., July 1965); *Tarzan of the Flicks* (Goddard Coll., Plainfield, Vt., Dec. 1965); *The Life of Lady Godiva* (Playhouse of the Ridiculous, Apr. 1966); *Screen Test* and *Indira Gandhi's Daring Device* (Playhouse of the Ridiculous, Sept. 1966); *Kitchenette* (Playhouse of the Ridiculous, Jan. 1967); *Gorilla Queen* (Judson Memorial Ch., Mar. 10, 1967); *Vinyl* (Caffe Cino, Oct. 1967); *Canticle of the Nightingale* (Stockholm, Swed., 1968); *Cleobis and Bito* (The Extension, N.Y.C., Spring 1968); *Arenas of Lutetia* (Judson Memorial Church, Nov. 1968); *Boy on the Straight-Back Chair* (American Place Th., Feb. 14, 1969); *Vinyl Visits an FM Station* (The Playwrights Unit, May 1970); *Bigfoot* (Th. Genesis, Nov. 9, 1972); *Secrets of the Citizens Correction Committee* (Theatre at St. Clements, Oct. 17, 1973); *How Jacqueline Kennedy Became Queen of Greece* (Th. Genesis, Nov. 2, 1973).

Mr. Tavel was appointed first resident playwright at The Actors Studio, N.Y.C., in 1972. He has also been an advisor-contributor to the Subplot Theatre (part of The American Place) and playwright-in-residence, The Theatre of The Lost Continent, N.Y.C.

Films. As scenarist for Andy Warhol Films, Inc. (1964–66), Mr. Tavel wrote *Harlot,* for which he was also a narrator (1964) and *Space* (1965); he wrote and directed *Screen Test* and *Philip's Screen Test,* in both of which he was the Inquisitor; *Suicide,* in which he played Flowerman; *The Life of Juanita Castro,* in which he played El Director; *Horse,* in which he was the Instructor; *Vinyl;* and *Kitchen,* in which he played the Promptor (all 1965); *Hedy,* in which he played the Promptor; and *Withering Sights,* in which he played the Inquisitor (both 1966); and he wrote the "Hanoi Hanna, Radio Star" and "Silent Witnesses" sequences of *The Chelsea Girls* (1966).

Television and Radio. Mr. Tavel played the Horseman in *Firescape: Suicide Notations* (Rudy Stern Telefilms, 1972). Several of his poems were written for and broadcast by WRVR Anthology of the Air.

Other Activities. Mr. Tavel has been a lecturer for the NY State Council on the Arts, and he was literary advisory for *Scripts* magazine 1971–72).

Published Works. Mr. Tavel wrote the novel

Street of Stairs (1968) and *Christina's World*, a three-act play in verse (*Chicago Review*, vol. 16, no. 1, 1963). His essays have appeared in such periodicals as *Graffiti; Tri-Quarterly; Aspen; Film Culture; Filmwise; Inter/View;* and in the book *The New American Cinema* (1967); and his poetry has been published in *The Lyric; Writing at Wyoming; Chicago Review; Wormwood; Tri-Quarterly; Graffiti; — You;* and *Poets at Le Metro.*

Awards. Mr. Tavel received *Village Voice* off-Bway (Obey) awards for playwriting for *Boy on the Straight-Back Chair* (1968–69) and *Bigfoot* (1972–73). He received the American Place Theatre grant in playwriting (1970); Creative Artists Public Service Program grants (1971, 1974); the Rockefeller Foundation Stipend in playwriting (1972); and a Guggenheim Memorial Foundation fellowship (1973–74).

TAYLOR, DWIGHT. Playwright, novelist. b. Jan. 1, 1902, New York City, to Charles A. and Laurette (Cooney) Taylor. Father, playwright; mother, actress. Attended Downside Sch., England, 1914–15; Lawrenceville Sch., N.J., 1916–20; Natl. Acad. of Design, N.Y.C., 1921; Art Students League, N.Y.C., 1922. Married 1930 to Marigold L. Langworthy (dec.); two sons, one daughter; married 1945 to Natalie Visart, costume designer; one son, one daughter. Member of ALA; Dramatists Guild; WGA, West (on board, from inception; chairman of first television comm., 1948; secy., 1936). Address: 60 Coggeshall Ave., Newport, RI 02840, tel. (401) 846-9894.

Pre-Theatre. Artist.

Theatre. Mr. Taylor wrote the pre-Bway tryout of *Don't Tell George* (opened Wilmington, Del., 1928; closed Washington, D.C., 1928); *Lipstick*, which also closed during its pre-Bway tryout (Scarborough, N.Y., 1929); the book for the musical *The Gay Divorce* (Ethel Barrymore Th., N.Y.C., Nov. 29, 1932; Palace, London, Nov. 2, 1933); produced, with Oscar Hammerstein, *Where Do We Go from Here?* (Vanderbilt, N.Y.C., Nov. 15, 1938); and wrote, with Reginald Lawrence, the book for the musical *Out of This World* (Century, Dec. 21, 1950; Actors' Playhouse, Oct. 30, 1957).

Films. He wrote the original story for *Numbered Men* (1st Natl., 1930); the screenplay for *Secrets of a Secretary* (Par., 1931); *Are You Listening?* (MGM, 1932); *To-Day We Live* (MGM, 1933); *If I Were Free* (RKO, 1933); the original story for *The Gay Divorcee* (RKO, 1934); the original story and collaborated on the screenplay for *Top Hat* (RKO, 1935); the original story for *Paris in the Spring* (Par., 1935); collaborated on the screenplay for *Follow the Fleet* (RKO, 1936); adapted *The Awful Truth* (Col., 1937); wrote the screenplay for *Head Over Heels* (Gaumont-British, 1938); the original story for *Gangway!;* collaborated on the screenplay for *The Amazing Mr. Williams* (Col., 1939); wrote the screenplay for *When Tomorrow Comes* (U, 1939); adapted *East Side of Heaven* (U, 1939); wrote the screenplay for *Rhythm on the River* (Par., 1940); collaborated on the screenplay for *Kiss the Boys Goodbye* (Par., 1940); wrote the screenplay for *I Wake Up Screaming* (20th-Fox, 1941); *Nightmare* (U, 1942); collaborated on the screenplay for *The Thin Man Goes Home* (MGM, 1945); wrote the screenplay for *Conflict* (WB, 1945); adapted *The Foxes of Harrow* (20th-Fox, 1947); wrote the original story and screenplay for *Something To Live For* (Liberty, 1952); adapted *We're Not Married* (20th-Fox, 1952); wrote the screenplay for *Vicki* (20th-Fox, 1953) the original story for *Pick Up on South Street* (20th-Fox, 1953); collaborated on the screenplays for *Special Delivery* (TransRhine, 1955); *Interlude* (U, 1956); and *Boy on a Dolphin* (20th-Fox, 1957).

Television. Mr. Taylor wrote the original story for *The Pink Cloud* (1958); the teleplay for *The Girl on the Grass* (1959); *For Better or Worse* (1959); and, for The Thin Man series, the original story and teleplay for *Show Biz* (1959), and collaborated on the teleplay for *The Fatal Cliché* (1960) and *Angels in Paradise* (1960). He also wrote the original story and teleplay for the pilot for the original Loretta Young Show, entitled *Trial Run* (1953).

Published Works. He wrote his memoirs, *Joy Ride* (1959); a biography of his father, *Blood and Thunder* (1963), and *What Sank the Dreamboat?* (1964).

Awards. He has received two Box Office Blue Ribbon Awards, for *Top Hat* (1935) and *Boy on a Dolphin* (1957); the Golden Lion Award (1953) for *Pick Up on South Street* at the Venice Film Festival; and was made Knight of George I by the King of Greece (1957) for *Boy on a Dolphin.*

Recreation. Drawing, painting.

TAYLOR, HELEN MARIE. Actress, director, educator, theatre consultant. b. Waco, Tex., to Howell Lewis and Marie (Chumley) Taylor. Father, attorney. Attended Oxford Univ., London, England, 1949–50; grad. London Univ., 1952. Studied for the theatre at AADA, N.Y.C., 1949; RADA, London, 1950–52 (diploma with special acting honors); Amer. Th. Wing Sch., N.Y.C., 1954; IASTA, N.Y.C., 1961–63; MATA, N.Y.C., 1963. Married June 22, 1945, to George Barber Munroe, vice-pres., Phelps-Dodge Copper Corp. Member of AEA; AFTRA; SAG; Filson Club Historical Society; English Speaking Union; RADA, London (bd. of gov., assoc. mbr., 1961, Amer. auditions bd. mbr.); Natl. Council on the Arts in Gov.; Lincoln Square Community Council; APA (promotions dir., 1960–62); N.Y. Citizens Comm. for Free Shakespeare in Central Park (co-chairman, 1959); Poetry and Drama Ensemble (dir., 1961); Prospect Park Summer Th. Comm., Inc., N.Y.C., (founding mbr.); ASFTA (fdr., 1955); Godesburg Th., Bonn, Germany (bd. of dir., 1952); Dallas, (Tex.) Th. Ctr. (adv. bd., 1959–60); Amanda Steel Scholarship Fund for RADA (founders comm.); Th. Louisville, Inc., Ky. (fdr., exec. comm., bd. of dir., 1963–64). Address: Meadow Farm, Orange, VA 22960. been executive director of the Amer. Assn. of RADA, which she founded; and has served on the advisory committee, Clark Ctr. for the Performing Arts, N.Y.C.

Pre-Theatre. Model.

Theatre. Miss Taylor made her Bway debut succeeding (1944) Pamela Gillespie as Mary Skinner in *Life with Father* (Empire, Nov. 8, 1939), then toured cross-country in this role (closed 1945); in stock, she played Elizabeth Clochessy in *Goodbye Again* (Brattle, Cambridge, Mass., Summer 1947); in England, was assistant director of the New Coll. Gardens Festival productions of *A Midsummer Night's Dream* (Oxford, 1950), and played a Fairy. She made her London debut as Mrs. Bramson in a GI production of *Night Must Fall* (Vanbrugh Th., 1951); appeared as Kate Hardcastle in *She Stoops to Conquer* (1952), Mrs. Danvers in *Rebecca* (1952), and directed *A Midsummer Night's Dream* (1953) at the American Th. (Bonn, Germany, where she also taught acting and lectured.

During 1954–55, Miss Taylor was instructor in Shakespeare and Acting Styles at AADA, N.Y.C. She appeared in *The Ridiculous Young Ladies* (Lenox Hill Playhouse, 1955); and played Ophelia in *Hamlet* (Shakespearewrights Th., Oct. 27, 1956). At the Dallas Th. Ctr., Tex., Miss Taylor served as acting instructor and played in *Of Time and the River* (1959); and *Cross-Eyed Bear* (1960). During this period she lectured on the theatre at colleges and universities in Texas.

With APA, during the 1960–61 season, Miss Taylor played Alison in *The Lady's Not for Burning*, Virginia in *The Tavern*, and Hiacenta in *Scapin* (McCarter Th., Princeton, N.J.). As promotion director for APA, she was responsible for the negotiations leading to the establishment of a professional repertory company in residence at a major university on a continuing basis (APA-Univ. of Michigan, Ann Arbor, 1962–to date). In N.Y.C., she played the Leader of the Chorus in the IASTA production of *Electra* (1961); and directed a stage reading called *Love Poetry Through the Ages*, which toured N.Y. Public Libraries. Following this, she toured as Kate Keller in *The Miracle Worker* (1962).

Films. Miss Taylor dubbed the voice of the leading lady in *Entrée des Artistes* (Spectra, 1953); and *Toxie* (Spectra, 1953).

Television. Miss Taylor has appeared on Studio One (CBS, 1957); Lamp Unto My Feet (CBS); and has made a number of commercials.

Awards. Miss Taylor received the L.U.D. Board of Regents Award (RADA, 1952). For her performance in *Hamlet* (1956), she was recipient of the Brandeis Award (1957), and for her direction of *Love Poetry Through the Ages*, she won the Public Library Award (1961).

Recreation. Genealogy, American history, metaphysics, para-psychology.

TAYLOR, JUNE. Choreographer. b. 1918, Chicago, Ill. Studied with Merriel Abbott. Married 1941 to Sol Lerner.

Theatre. Miss Taylor made her debut as a chorus dancer in *George White's Scandals* (Chicago, Ill., 1931); subsequently danced at the Palace (N.Y.C., 1938); was a "glamor girl" in the vaudeville-burlesque show *52nd St. Follies* (Continental, Feb. 18, 1939); and *Spring Time Follies* (Star, Bklyn., May 1941).

Miss Taylor was choreographer of *Pleasure Island* (Marine Th., Jones Beach, L.I., N.Y., 1961); *Around the World in 80 Days* (Marine Th., June 22, 1963); and *Mardi Gras!* (Marine Th., June 26, 1965).

Television. Miss Taylor has been choreographer of the June Taylor Dancers (Ed Sullivan Show, CBS); has been choreographer for the Jackie Gleason Show (1950) and for Broadway Spotlight.

Night Clubs. She danced at the Dorchester Cabaret (London, 1938); with the Chez Paree Adorables (Chez Paree, Chicago, Ill.); and at the Palmer House (Chicago).

TAYLOR, NOEL. Costume designer. b. Jan. 17, 1913, Youngstown, Ohio, to Harold A. and Margery (Clark) Taylor. Father, financier, broker; mother, artist. Studied costume design in Paris, Fr. Served WW II, USCG. Member of United Scenic Artists.

Theatre. Mr. Taylor began his career in the theatre as an actor and playwright. He made his Bway debut as a bellboy in *Reunion in Vienna* (revived, Martin Beck Th., N.Y.C., Nov. 16, 1931), and played in various stock productions and tours, including a season of stock at Litchfield, Conn. (Summer 1933). He played Peter in his own play, *Cross Ruff* (Masque, N.Y.C., Feb. 19, 1935).

He designed the costumes for *Alice in Wonderland* (Intl. Th., N.Y.C., Apr. 5, 1947); *Twentieth Century* (ANTA, Dec. 24, 1950); *Stalag 17* (48 St. Th., May 8, 1951); *The Wild Duck* (NY City Ctr., Dec. 26, 1951); *Come of Age* (revived, NY City Ctr., Jan. 23, 1952); *One Bright Day* (Royale, Mar. 19, 1952); *The Male Animal* (revived, NY City Ctr., Apr. 30, 1952; moved to Music Box, May 15, 1952); *Tovarich* (revived, NY City Ctr., May 14, 1952); *First Lady* (revived, NY City Ctr., May 28, 1952); *Bernadine* (Playhouse, Oct. 16, 1952); *Dial 'M' for Murder* (Plymouth, Oct. 29, 1952); *The Grey-Eyed People* (Martin Beck Th., Dec. 17, 1952); *The Teahouse of the August Moon* (Martin Beck Th., Oct. 15, 1953; NY City Ctr., Nov. 8, 1956); *The Ladies of the Corridor* (Longacre, Oct. 21, 1953); *In the Summer House* (Playhouse, Dec. 29, 1953); *The Burning Glass* (Longacre, Mar. 4, 1954); and for the London production of *The Teahouse of the August Moon* (Her Majesty's Th., Apr. 22, 1954).

He designed the costumes for *Festival* (Longacre, N.Y.C., Jan. 18, 1955); *No Time for Sergeants* (Alvin, Oct. 20, 1955); *Time Limit!* (Booth, Jan. 24, 1956); *The Apple Cart* (Plymouth, Oct. 18, 1956); and all costumes except Rosalind Russell's, for *Auntie Mame* (Broadhurst, Oct. 31, 1956); designed the costumes for *Good as Gold* (Belasco, Mar. 7, 1957); *The Square Root of Wonderful* (National, Oct. 30, 1957); *The Body Beautiful* (Bway Th., Jan. 23, 1958); *Comes a Day* (Ambassador, Nov. 6, 1958); *Tall Story* (Belasco, Jan. 29, 1959); *The Wall* (Billy Rose Th., Oct. 11, 1960); *Little Moon of Alban* (Longacre, Dec. 1, 1960); *Everybody Loves Opal* (Longacre, Oct. 11, 1961); *A Shot in the Dark* (Booth, Oct. 18, 1961);

Write Me a Murder (Belasco, Oct. 26, 1961); *The Night of the Iguana* (Royale, Dec. 28, 1961); *General Seeger* (Lyceum, Feb. 28, 1962); *Great Day in the Morning* (Henry Miller's Th., Mar. 28, 1962); *Pullmann Car Hiawatha* (Circle in the Square, Dec. 3, 1962) *Desire Under the Elms* (Circle in the Square, Jan. 8, 1963); *The Riot Act* (Cort, Mar. 7, 1963); *Strange Interlude* (Hudson, Mar. 11, 1963); *One Flew Over the Cuckoo's Nest* (Cort, Nov. 13, 1963); *Marathon '33* (ANTA, Dec. 22, 1963); and *What Makes Sammy Run?* (54 St. Th., Feb. 27, 1964).

Also *Hughie* (revived, Royale, Dec. 22, 1964); *Matty and the Moron and Madonna* (Orpheum, Mar. 29, 1965); *And Things That Go Bump in the Night* (Royale, Apr. 26, 1965); *Baal* (Martinique, May 6, 1965); *Play That on Your Old Piano* (Renata, Oct. 14, 1965); *The White Devil* (Circle in the Square, Dec. 6, 1965); *The Great Indoors* (Eugene O'Neill Th., Feb. 1, 1966); *Slapstick Tragedy* (Longacre, Feb. 22, 1966); *The Loves of Cass McGuire* (Helen Hayes Th., Oct. 6, 1966); *We Have Always Lived in the Castle* (Ethel Barrymore Th., Oct. 19, 1966); *Dr. Cook's Garden* (Belasco, Sept. 25, 1967); *Song of the Grasshopper* (ANTA, Sept. 28, 1967); *Lovers* (Vivian Beaumont Th., July 25, 1968); *We Bombed in New Haven* (Ambassador, Oct. 16, 1968); *Possibilities* (Players, Dec. 4, 1968); *The Mundy Scheme* (Royale, Dec. 11, 1969); and *Brightower* (John Golden Th., Jan. 28, 1970).

Mr. Taylor designed the Story Theater production of *Ovid's Metamorphosis* (Mark Taper Forum, Los Angeles, Feb. 4, 1971; Ambassador, N.Y.C., Apr. 22, 1971); *Major Barbara* (Mark Taper Forum, Los Angeles, Aug. 26, 1971); *A Funny Thing Happened on the Way to the Forum* (revived, Ahmanson, Oct. 12, 1971; moved to Lunt-Fontanne, N.Y.C., Mar. 30, 1972); *The Caine Mutiny Court-Martial* (revived, Ahmanson, Los Angeles, Nov. 30, 1971); *Volpone* (Mark Taper Forum, Mar. 9, 1972); *Don't Bother Me I Can't Cope* (Mark Taper Forum, Aug. 10, 1972; ACT, San Francisco, July 21, 1973; and Ford's Th., Washington, D.C., Apr. 23, 1974); the Story Th. production of *The American Revolution, Part I* (Ford's Th., Washington, D.C., Fall 1973); *Mourning Becomes Electra* (Circle in the Square/Joseph E. Levine Th., N.Y.C., Nov. 15, 1972); *The Crucible* (Ahmanson, Los Angeles, Dec. 5, 1972); *The Last of Mrs. Lincoln* (ANTA Th., N.Y.C., Dec. 12, 1972); *The Mind with the Dirty Man* (Mark Taper Forum, Los Angeles, Mar. 15, 1973); *The Hot l Baltimore* (Mark Taper Forum, Aug. 2, 1973); *Hamlet* (Mark Taper Forum, Mar. 14, 1974); and *The Norman Conquests* (Morosco, N.Y.C., Dec. 7, 1975).

Films. Mr. Taylor designed the costumes for *Generation* (AVCO-Embassy, 1969); *Mrs. Pollifax-Spy* (UA, 1971); and *Rhinoceros* (Amer. Film Th., 1974).

Television. He has designed costumes for more than 60 productions for Hallmark Hall of Fame (NBC, 1952–65), including *Green Pastures, Little Moon of Alban, Macbeth, The Holy Terror, Victoria Regina,* and *The Magnificent Yankee;* has designed the costumes for Menotti's opera *The Labyrinth* (NBC, 1962) and other NCB Opera Co. productions; for Dupont Show of the Month (NBC); *The Turn of the Screw* (Ford Startime, NBC, Oct. 20, 1959); *Boswell's Life of Johnson;* and others, and has supervised the costumes for the daytime series A World Apart (ABC, Mar. 1970–June 1971).

Awards. For his costumes for *Slapstick Tragedy,* Mr. Taylor won (1966) the Joseph Maharam Award, and was nominated for an Antoinette Perry (Tony) Award.

TAYLOR, RENEE. Actress, playwright. b. New York City, to Charles and Frieda Wexler. Professional training at American Acad., N.Y.C. (acting). Married Sept. 1965 to Joseph Bologna, director, playwright, actor.

Theatre. Miss Taylor played Bubbles in *Dinny and the Witches* (Cherry Lane Th., N.Y.C., Dec. 9, 1959); the Telephone Operator in *Machinal* (Gate Th., Apr. 7, 1960); appeared in the revue *The Third Ear* (Premise Th., May 28, 1964); understudied Anne Jackson as Ellen in *Luv* (Booth Th., Nov. 11, 1964); played Sheila in *Agatha Sue I love you* (Henry Miller's Th., Dec. 14, 1966); various roles in *Willie Doesn't Live Here Anymore* (Th. de Lys, Feb. 6, 1967); and, with Joseph Bologna, wrote *Lovers and Other Strangers,* in which she also played Wilma (Brooks Atkinson Th., Sept. 18, 1968).

Films. Miss Taylor and Joseph Bologna collaborated on the short *2;* they collaborated with David Z. Goodman on the filmscript for *Lovers and Other Strangers* (Cinerama, 1970); and Miss Taylor and Mr. Bologna were co-authors of and appeared in *Made for Each Other* (20th-Fox, 1971).

Television. With her husband, Joseph Bologna, she wrote *Acts of Love and Other Comedies* (CBS, Mar. 1973), and was a creator of and wrote some of the scripts for Calucci's Department (CBS, 1973). She was also co-author of and appeared in *Paradise* (CBS, Mar. 1974); and was co-author of *Three for Two* (CBS, Sept. 1975).

Awards. Miss Taylor and Joseph Bologna received a NATAS (Emmy) Award for the script of *Acts of Love and Other Comedies* (1973).

TAYLOR, ROBERT U. Setting and lighting designer, costume designer. b. Robert Umholtz Taylor, July 21, 1941, Lexington, Va., to John Robert and Helen (Dold) Taylor. Father, chemist; exec. vice-pres. American Viscose Corp. Attended public schools Roanoke, Va.; Univ. of Pennsylvania; Pennsylvania Acad. of the Fine Arts; Yale Drama School (studied design under Donald Oenslager, Charles Elson). Married June 1963 to Jane Shure (marr. dis. 1965); July 31, 1971, to Margaret Karagias. Member United Scenic Artists, Local 829. Address: 235 W. 71st St., New York, NY 10023, tel. (212) 787-0545.

Theatre. Mr. Taylor's first set designs were done for the Summer Th. of Roanoke, Va. (June 1959). He designed numerous productions through the 1960s and into the 1970s for ten college theatres, including twelve for the Univ. of Pennsylvania (1960–63), nine for St. Cloud Coll. (1963–65), and eight for Hunter Coll. (1971–74).

His first professional work (Summer 1964) consisted of designs for sets and costumes for six productions by the Peterborough (N.H.) Players and four productions for the Westchester (N.Y.) Th. He designed sets for the New Haven (Conn.) Opera Society's *Hansel and Gretel* (May 1965); for *Under Milk Wood* (Guthrie Experimental Th., Minneapolis, Minn., May 1966); sets and costumes for *The Bacchae* (Yale School of Drama, New Haven, Conn., May 1966); sets for Yale Repertory Theatre's 1967 productions (New Haven, Conn.) of *Enrico IV* and *We Bombed in New Haven* (Dec. 4, 1967); and scenery for *The Bench* (Gramercy Arts, N.Y.C., Mar. 4, 1968).

He designed sets and costumes for *The Balcony* (June 1968) and *Troilus and Cressida* (July 1968), both at the Loeb Rep. Th., Harvard Univ., Cambridge, Mass.; sets for *The Judas Applause* (Chelsea Th. Ctr., Brooklyn Acad. of Music, N.Y.C., May 9, 10, 16, 17, 1969); *A Streetcar Named Desire* (City Island Th., N.Y.C., Dec. 1969); *But Most of Us Cry in Movies* (La Mama E.T.C., N.Y.C., Jan. 28, 1970); *The Nest* (Mercury Th., Apr. 9, 1970); *Ardele* (Playhouse in the Park, Cincinnati, Ohio, May 1970); *More War in Store* (Old Reliable Th., N.Y.C., Sept. 14, 1970); *Touch* (Village Arena Th., Nov. 8, 1970); *Coocooshay* (Public Th., Dec. 16, 1970); and *Istanboul* (Actors Playhouse, Feb. 8, 1971).

He also did sets and lighting for *Catch 22* and four other productions (John Drew Th., East Hampton, Long Island, N.Y., May–July 1971); sets for *Unlikely Heroes* (Plymouth, N.Y.C., Oct. 26, 1971); *The Beggar's Opera* (Chelsea Th. Ctr., Brooklyn Acad. of Music, Mar. 21, 1972); *Saved* (Cherry Lane, Apr. 1972); for a revival of *We Bombed in New Haven* (Circle in the Square, Sept. 14, 1972); *Lady Day* (Chelsea Th. Ctr., Brooklyn Acad. of Music, Oct. 17, 1972); and sets for *The Foursome* (Arena Stage, Washington, D.C., Nov. 3, 1972). He did sets and visuals for *In the Matter of J. Robert Oppenheimer* (Goodman Th., Chicago, Ill., Jan. 7, 1973); sets (at Arena Stage, Washington, D.C.) for *A Look at the Fifties* (Feb. 14, 1973), *Enemies* (Mar. 21, 1973), and *Raisin* (May 23, 1973; also 46th St. Th., N.Y.C., Oct. 18, 1973); and sets for *Sisters of Mercy* (Shaw Festival, Niagara on the Lake, Ontario, Can., June 1973; Th. de Lys, N.Y.C., Sept. 25, 1973); and, at the McCarter Th., Princeton, N.J., scenery for *The Seagull* (Oct. 4, 1973), *The Entertainer* (Nov. 15, 1973), *The Daughter-in-Law* (Mar. 7, 1974), and *You Never Can Tell* (Mar. 28, 1974); and he did the set for *Fashion* (McAlpin Th., N.Y.C., Feb. 18, 1974).

Television. Since 1970, Mr. Taylor has done sets for television commercials.

Other Activities. In addition to his theatrical work, Mr. Taylor is a painter in oils and watercolors; has had three one-man shows; and his work is hung in six US galleries. He has also designed several restaurants and nightclubs; is a consultant to architects on theatre projects; has designed publicity campaigns and been art director for several advertising agencies. He helped found the Colonnades Th. Lab, N.Y.C., and has taught at Hunter Coll. Theatre Dept. and Princeton Univ.

Awards. In 1969, Mr. Taylor was a guest of the West German government to attend and discuss the theatre of Germany. He received the Maharam and Drama Desk awards for his scenery for *The Beggar's Opera* (1972).

Recreation. Painting, playing piano, organ, flute, sitar, guitar, and bagpipes. Mr. Taylor also lists as his "more contemplative and collective" hobbies, the "American super-hero comic book and its artists; and the study of ritual magic.".

TAYLOR, SAMUEL. Playwright. b. June 13, 1912, Chicago, Ill. Married to Suzanne Combes Taylor, author and translator; two sons. Member of the Dramatists Play Service (pres.). Address: East Blue Hill, ME 04629.

Theatre. Mr. Taylor wrote *The Happy Time,* based on the book by Robert Fontaine (Plymouth Th., Jan. 24, 1950); *Sabrina Fair* (National Th., Nov. 11, 1953); with Cornelia Otis Skinner, *The Pleasure of His Company* (Longacre Th., Oct. 22, 1958); *First Love,* based on the Romain Gary memoir; *Promise at Dawn* (Morosco Th., Dec. 25, 1961); with Richard Rodgers, *No Strings* (54 St. Th., Mar. 15, 1962); *Beekman Place* (Morosco Th., Oct. 7, 1964); and *Avanti!* (Booth Th., Jan. 31, 1968).

TAYLOR, WILLIAM S. Stage manager, director, general manager. b. Dec. 2, 1925, Dillon, S.C., to Linwood K. and Ethel (Kennedy) Taylor. Father, retired lumberman. Grad. Lower Richland H.S., Lykesland, S.C., 1941; attended Univ. of South Carolina, 1941–42; North Carolina State Coll., 1942–43; Catawba Coll., 1946–47. Studied drama at the Dock St. Sch. of the Theatre, Charleston, S.C. 1947–50. Served USAAF, 1943–46; rank, 2nd Lt. Member of AEA; AGMA.

Theatre. Mr. Taylor was assistant director at the Dock St. Th. (Charleston, S.C., 1950–51); casting director for the US Army Signal Corps Studios director (Long Island City, N.Y., 1953–56); stage manager for the Lakewood Playhouse (Barnesville, Pa., Summer 1956); directed stock production of *Will Success Spoil Rock Hunter?* and *Uncle Willie* and others (Premier Productions, Ltd., Toronto, Ont., Canada, Winters 1956, 1957); and was stage manager and co-director at the Daytona Beach (Fla.) Playhouse (Peabody Aud., 1957).

He was also stage manager and co-director for Shanta Rao and her Dancers of India (ANTA, N.Y.C., 1957), and its subsequent tours of the US and Israel (1957–58); consultant for the Ford Foundation's Program for Playwrights (May 1958–May 1960); and assistant executive director of ANTA (May 1960–May 1962). He was executive director of the American Dance Festival sponsored by Connecticut Coll. (New London, June 1962); stage manager for the Asia Society Performing Arts Program national tours of *Sangeeta Madras, Music of South India* (Fall 1962), and the *Bharatiya Kala Kendra Dancers of India* (Spring 1963). He was appointed exec. dir. of the Seattle (Wash.) Repertory

Th. (1963); and subsequently became gen. manager of the Front Street Th. (June 1965).

Recreation. Fencing, photography, chess.

TEER, BARBARA ANN. Director, actress, dancer. b. East St. Louis, Ill. Attended Univ. of Illinois, B.S.; Univ. of Wisconsin; Connecticut Coll. for Women. Studied acting with Sanford Meisner; Paul Mann; Lloyd Richards. Address: c/o National Black Th., 9 E. 125th St., New York, NY 10027.

Theatre. Miss Teer is the founder (1968) and director (1967–to date) of the National Black Theatre, a group organized to evolve a theatre which eschews traditional forms and values, concerning itself with "the ritual celebration of Black spirituality." The theatre is referred to as "The Temple of Liberation"; the acting troupe as "The Liberators." The company's premiere production was *Ritual* (NBT, 1971); followed by *Change! Love Together! Organize! A Revival* (NBT, July 1, 1972); and *A Soul Journey into Truth* (NBT, Fall, 1974).

Under the auspices of NBT, lectures and workshops dealing with both the arts and problems of daily life are presented regularly, as well as concerts, poetry readings, and films.

Previously, Miss Teer appeared as a dancer in *Kwamina* (54 St. Th., N.Y.C., Oct. 23, 1961); played Bella Belafunky in *Raisin' Hell in the Son* (Provincetown Playhouse, July 2, 1962); was a replacement in the revue *The Living Premise* (Premise Th., June 13, 1963); played Violet in *Home Movies* (Provincetown Playhouse, N.Y.C., May 11, 1964); appeared in *Funnyhouse of a Negro* (Th. Co. of Boston, Mar. 11, 1965); was a replacement in *Prodigal Son* (Greenwich Mews Th., May 20, 1965); on a double-bill with *Happy Ending*, played Mary in *Day of Absence* (St. Mark's Playhouse, Nov. 15, 1965); Clara in *Who's Got His Own* (Amer. Place Th. at St. Clement's, Oct. 12, 1966); Jean Biggs in *The Experiment* (Orpheum, May 8, 1967); and directed *The Believers* (Garrick, May 9, 1968); and *Five on the Black Hand Side* (Amer. Place Th. at St. Clement's, Jan. 1, 1970).

Miss Teer taught with Robert Hooks Group Th. Workshop (1965); was a dancer with the Henry St. Playhouse Dance Co., and the Alvin Ailey Dance Co.; and appeared with Pearl Bailey in Las Vegas, and with the Newport Jazz Festival (74 St. Th., 1962).

Films. Miss Teer appeared in *Gone Are the Days* (Hammer Bros., 1964), which was the film version of *Purlie Victorious; The Pawnbroker* (Landau, 1965); *The Group* (UA, 1966); and *The Slaves* (Th. Guild, 1969).

Television. She has appeared on *A Carol for Another Christmas* (ABC); Camera Three (CBS); Kaleidoscope (NBC); The Ed Sullivan Show (CBS); and Black Journal (WNET, 1972).

Published Works. Articles by Miss Teer entitled "The Black Woman: She Does Exist" (May 14, 1967), and "We Can Be What We Were Born To Be" (July 7, 1968) have appeared in the NY *Times*.

Awards. Miss Teer received the Vernon Rice Award (1965) for her performance in *Home Movies*.

TEICHMANN, HOWARD. Playwright, educator. b. Howard Miles Teichmann, Jan. 22, 1916, Chicago, Ill., to Jack and Rose Teichmann. Father, businessman (ret.). Grad. Univ. of Wisconsin, B.A. 1938. Married Apr. 2, 1939, to Evelyn; one daughter. Served WW II, Senior Editor, OWI, Overseas Branch; expert consultant in radio, US Army on staff of Lt. Gen. Brehon Somerrell. Member of Dramatists Guild; The Authors Guild; Sigma Delta Chi; Zeta Beta Tau. Address: 863 Park Ave., New York, NY 10021, tel. (212) RH 4-0474.

Mr. Teichmann is a professor of English at Barnard Coll., Columbia Univ.

Mr. Teichmann began work in the professional theatre as an assistant stage manager for Orson Wells' Mercury Th. (1938); subsequently became stage manager and assistant to the pres. of the Mercury Th. He wrote, with George S. Kaufman, *The Solid Gold Cadillac* (1953); and wrote *Miss Lonelyhearts* (1957); *The Girls in 509* (1959); *Julia, Jake and Uncle Joe* (1961); and *A Rainy Day in Newark* (1963). From 1962 to 1972, he was the administrator of the Sam S. Shubert Foundation.

Television and Radio. He wrote material for and produced the Mercury Th. of the Air; subsequently wrote for the Campbell Playhouse; the Helen Hayes Th.; Texaco Star Th.; CBS Workshop; Cavalcade of America; the Gertrude Lawrence Revue; They Live Forever; the Ford Th. of the Air; and many others.

For television, he wrote *A Day in the Life of a Chorus Girl;* wrote for Theatre USA; Showtime USA; USA Canteen; the Ford Fiftieth Anniversary Show; and others.

Published Works. In 1972, he wrote the biography *George S. Kaufman: An Intimate Portrait*, and in 1976 published *Smart Aleck – The Wit, World and Life of Alexander Woollcott*. .

Awards. He received a Distinguished Service Award (1959) from the Univ. of Wisconsin and the Declaration of Esteem and Appreciation (1972) from the Broadway Association.

TEITEL, CAROL. Actress. b. Carolyn Sally Kahn, Aug. 1, 1929, Brooklyn, N.Y., to Henry and Blanche Kahn. Father, electrical engineer. Grad. Girls H.S., Brooklyn, 1945. Studied acting with Leo Bulgakov at Master Inst., N.Y.C., 1942; William Hansen, Lee Strasberg, and Edward Greer at Amer. Th. Wing, N.Y.C., 1950–52. Married Aug. 10, 1949, to Nathan R. Teitel, playwright, educator. Member of AEA; AFTRA; SAG. Address: 365 W. 25th St., New York, NY 10001, tel. (212) AL 5-9376, (212) JU 6-6300.

Pre-Theatre. Sales clerk, worked for newspaper.

Theatre. Miss Teitel made her first stage appearance as Anyutka in *Power of Darkness* (Master Inst. Th., N.Y.C., 1942); toured colleges with *Theatre As You Like It*, performing scenes from plays by Shakespeare and Tennessee Williams; appeared in *Billy the Kid* (Carnegie Hall, N.Y.C., Dec. 1952); subsequently succeeded (Oct. 1954) Jo Rabb as Foible in *The Way of the World* (Cherry Lane, Oct. 2, 1954); played Beatrice in *The Anatomist* (Royale, Mar. 1957); and Laura in *The Glass Menagerie* (Strand, Long Beach, N.J., Aug. 1957).

She was general understudy in *The Country Wife* (Adelphi, N.Y.C., Nov. 27, 1957); standby for Joan Plowright in the role of Jean Rice in *The Entertainer* (Royale, Feb. 12, 1958); played Princess Pavlikov in a stock production of *Nude with Violin* (White Barn, Irwin, Pa., June 1958); Lady Angatell in *The Hollow* (Arena Stage, Washington, D.C., Dec. 1958); appeared in *Harvey* (Bristol Playhouse, Pa., 1959); and at the Provincetown Playhouse (N.Y.C., Mar.–Sept. 1959), played Leo in *Getting Married*, the title role in *Dark Lady of the Sonnets*, appeared in *Poison, Passion and Putrefaction*, and in *Blanco Posnet*, in repertory.

She played Alexandra Ivanovna Platunov in *A Country Scandal* (Greenwich Mews, May 5, 1960); Arinoe in *Le Misanthrope* (IASTA, Mar. 1960); was standby for Patricia Jessel in the role of Mrs. Julia Stewart in the pre-Bway tryout of *Catstick* (opened Shubert, New Haven, Conn., Jan. 4, 1961; closed Wilbur, Boston, Mass., Jan. 14, 1961); appeared as Mrs. Ogmore-Pritchard, Mary Anne Sailors, Mrs. Benyon, and Mrs. Dai Breadtwo in *Under Milk Wood* (Circle in the Square, Mar. 29, 1961); played She in a stock production of *Objective Case* (White Barn, Westport, Conn., 1961); the Nurse and was standby for Joan Hackett as Katherine in *Journey to the Day* (Westport Country Playhouse, Conn., 1961); played Claire in *The Maids* (Charles Playhouse, Boston, Mass., Nov.–Dec. 1961); Dame Pliant in *The Alchemist* and Jessica in *The Merchant of Venice* (McCarter Th., Princeton, N.J., 1962); Miss Myfanwy Price, Lily Smalls, the Child, and Mrs. Organ Morgan in *Under Milk Wood* (Circle in the Square, N.Y.C., Dec. 3, 1962) in a double bill with *Pullman Car Hiawatha*, in which she played A Maiden Lady, and in which she also toured colleges (Oct. 1961; Oct. 1962). She appeared in a concert production of *An Evening with Ring Lardner* (YMHA, N.Y.C., Dec. 1962); played Nicole in *Le Bourgoise Gentilhomme* and Virginia in *Galileo* (McCarter Th., Princeton, N.J., 1963).

Miss Teitel played Hero in *Much Ado About Nothing*, Margery Pinchwife in *The Country Wife*, and Ann Whitefield in *Man and Superman* (Hopkins Center, Dartmouth Coll., Hanover, N.H., 1963); a Lady-In-Waiting and was standby for Eileen Herlie in the role of Gertrude in Richard Burton's *Hamlet* (Lunt-Fontanne, N.Y.C., Apr. 9, 1964); appeared in *Juana La Loca* (American Place Th., June 9, 1964); appeared with the Association of Producing Artists (APA), Ann Arbor, Mich., as Violet in *Man and Superman* (Sept. 30, 1964) and as Susannah in *Judith* (Oct. 28, 1964); and played the title role in *Colombe* (Garrick Th., N.Y.C., Feb. 23, 1965).

Miss Teitel was a founding member of the American Conservatory Th. (ACT) in 1965, appearing in productions of the initial Pittsburgh, Pa., season; then at Westport, Conn.; the Ravinia (Ill.) Festival; and the Stanford Festival, Palo Alto, Calif. She was standby for Verna Bloom as Charlotte Corday and played a patient in *Marat/Sade* (Majestic, N.Y.C., Jan. 3, 1967); and appeared with American Conservatory Th. at the Geary Th., San Francisco, Calif., where she repeated her roles in *Under Milk Wood* (Nov. 21, 1967) and played Linda Loman in *Death of a Salesman* and Mrs. Webb in *Our Town* (Jan. 25, 1968). She was Bettina in *The Bench* (Gramercy Arts, N.Y.C., Mar. 4, 1968); and, again with ACT (Geary Th., San Francisco), Yvonne in *A Flea in Her Ear* (Dec. 10, 1968), Sonya in *Uncle Vanya*, Abby in *Arsenic and Old Lace*, Lena in *Misalliance*, Mrs. Noah in *Noah*, the White Woman in *In White America*, the Mother in *Six Characters in Search of an Author*, and Miss Gilchrist in *The Hostage*. When American Conservatory Th. visited N.Y.C. in 1969, she repeated her performance as Yvonne in *A Flea in Her Ear* (ANTA Th., Oct. 3, 1969).

She was Mrs. Charpolsky in *Seven Days of Mourning* (Circle in the Square, Dec. 16, 1969); played Diana in *The Initiation* (Off Center Th., Seattle Repertory Th., Seattle, Wash., Feb. 24, 1970); was standby for Shirley Booth as Judith Bliss in *Hay Fever* (Helen Hayes Th., N.Y.C., Nov. 9, 1970); Aksinya in *Yegor Bulichov* (Long Wharf Th., New Haven, Conn., Dec. 18, 1970); replaced (July 20, 1971) Geraldine Fitzgerald as Mary Tyrone in *Long Day's Journey into Night* (Promenade Th., N.Y.C., Apr. 21, 1971); played Olga in *You Can't Take It with You* (Long Wharf Th., New Haven, Conn., Oct. 22, 1971); Mrs. Ewbank in *The Contractor* (Long Wharf Th., Nov. 19, 1971); Elizabeth in Schiller's *Mary Stuart* (Williamstown Th., Williamstown, Mass., 1972); Yvonne Chandel in *The Happy Hunter* (Kalita Humphreys Th., Dallas, Tex., Oct. 24, 1972); Lady Macbeth in *Macbeth* (Actors Th. of Louisville, Ky., Mar. 22, 1973); was standby for Eileen Herlie as Queen Mary in *Crown Matrimonial* (Helen Hayes Th., N.Y.C., Oct. 2, 1973); and appeared in two one-act plays by her husband, Nathan Teitel: *Duet* and *Trio* (Th. at St. Clements, Mar. 28, 1974).

Television. Miss Teitel has appeared on The Verdict Is Yours (ABC, 1959); Lamp Unto My Feet (CBS, 1959); The Catholic Hour (NBC, 1960–62), including its production of *The Little Moon of Alban* (May 1961); and on The Eternal Light (NBC, 1961–64). She appeared on NET Playhouse, repeating her stage roles in *Under Milk Wood*, played Lina in *Misalliance*, and was in Ch. 13's *An American Christmas* (1971–72–73). She played Mrs. Ulysses S. Grant in *Surrender at Appomattox* (CBS); created the role of Celia Burns on Edge of Night (CBS); and was on The Guiding Light (CBS) as Lady Kemble (1970) and as Victoria Ballinger (1973–74).

TELFORD, ROBERT S. Director. b. Robert Sheldon Telford, Aug. 12, 1923, Staten Island, N.Y., to Harold George Telford and Edna (Alderman) Telford. Grad. Shaker Heights (Ohio) H.S., 1940; attended Kent State Univ., 1940–43; grad. Pasadena Playhouse Sch. of the Th., B.T.A. 1948; Yale Univ. Sch. of Drama, M.F.A. 1955. Married Jan. 28, 1951, to Joanne Johnson; one son, one daughter. Served US Army, 1943–46, 1950–52; rank, 1st Lt. Member of ANTA (executive committee 1961–64); ACTA (co-fdr., 1958; asst. dir., 1959–61; dir., 1961–62); AETA; NTC; SETC (chmn., Community Th. Div., 1956–57; chmn., Community Th. Directory committee, 1957–64).

In 1970, Mr. Telford became managing director of the Tulsa (Okla.) Little Th. Previously, he directed at the Stamford (Conn.) Summer Th. (Summer 1950); Indiana (Pa.) Summer Th. (Summers 1953–54); Woodbridge (Conn.) Community Th. (1954); and Town Th. (Columbia, S.C., 1955–58). He was producer-director of the Virginia Museum Th. (1958–67) and artistic director and general manager of "STARCO" (William Erdington Scott Th., Ft. Worth, Texas, 1967–69).

Television. Mr. Telford appeared on the Ken Murray Show (NBC, 1950).

Other Activities. Mr. Telford was moderator of the West Texas Th. Festival (Th. Center, Midland, Texas, Apr. 15, 1967).

Recreation. Opera.

TER-ARUTUNIAN, ROUBEN. Scenic designer, costume designer. b. July 24, 1920, Tiflis, USSR, to Guegam and Anaida (Seylanian) Ter-Arutunian. Father, lawyer, Grad. Hohenzollern Oberreal Schule, Berlin, Germany, 1938; studied concert piano, 1938; attended Reimann Art Sch., Berlin, 1939–41; Music Hochschule, Berlin, 1941–42; Friedrich-Wilhelm Univ., Berlin, 1941–43; Univ. of Vienna, Austria, 1944–45; Ecole des Beaux Arts, Paris, France, 1947–50. Immigrated to US, 1951; naturalized, 1957. Member of United Scenic Artists, Local 829. Address: 360 E. 55th St., New York, NY 10022, tel. (212) PL 5-4619.

Theatre. Mr. Ter-Arutunian designed costumes for soloists of the Berlin State Opera Ballet (1941); the Dresden Opera House production of *The Bartered Bride* (1942); the Vera Mahlke Ballet Company's *Getanzte Malerei* (Dresden and Berlin, Ger., 1942); a special performance of Strauss' *Salomé* at the Vienna Opera House, honoring the composer's eightieth birthday (1944); and designed scenery and costumes for the Paris Opéra Comique production of the ballet *Concerto* (1950).

He designed sets and costumes for the NY City Opera Co. productions of *Bluebeard's Castle* and *L'Heure Espagnole* (1952), and of *La Cenerentola, The Trial,* and *Hansel and Gretel* (1953); all five presented at NY City Ctr. In 1955, he designed the scenery and costumes for the NY City Ballet's *Souvenirs* (NY City Ctr.).

In 1956, Mr. Ter-Arutunian was commissioned by the American Shakespeare Festival and Acad. (Stratford, Conn.) to design a new stage, which was retained until 1960. He designed the scenery and costumes for the Festival's productions of *King John* and *Measure for Measure* (1956), which were used when the latter production was repeated at the Phoenix Th. (N.Y.C., Jan. 22, 1957), *Othello,* and *Much Ado About Nothing* (1957), and scenery for *The Merchant of Venice* (1957).

He designed scenery and costumes for *New Girl in Town* (46 St. Th., May 14, 1957); scenery for *Who Was That Lady I Saw You With?* (Martin Beck Th., Mar. 3, 1958); and for the Los Angeles (Calif.) Civic Light Opera Assn. production of *At the Grand* (Philharmonic Aud., July 7, 1958).

During 1958, he also designed the sets and costumes for NY City Ballet's *The Seven Deadly Sins* (NY City Ctr.); the John Butler Dance Th. production of *Masque of the Wild Man,* and for the premiere of the opera, *The Scarf,* both presented at the Festival of Two Worlds (Spoleto, It.); and sets for the opera, *Maria Golovin* (Brussels World's Fair, Belg., 1958; Martin Beck Th., N.Y.C., Nov. 5, 1958; La Scala, Milan, It.; NY City Ctr., Summer 1959).

He designed the scenery and costumes for *Redhead* (46 St. Th., Feb. 5, 1959); worked on three productions (1959) for the NY City Opera Co., *Maria Golovin* (scenery), *The Scarf* and *The Devil and Daniel Webster* (scenery and costumes); and designed the scenery for *Advise and Consent* (Cort, Nov. 17, 1960).

He designed a new stage (1960) for the American Shakespeare Festival and Academy, and the sets and costumes for their productions of *Twelfth Night* and *Antony and Cleopatra;* and the sets and costumes for Paul Taylor's ballet, *Fibres* (1960); scenery and costumes for *Donnybrook* (46 St. Th., May 18, 1961); the NY City Opera Co. production of *Il Trittico* (NY City Ctr., 1961); *Blood Moon* (San Francisco War Memorial Opera House, 1961); scenery only for the Los Angeles Civic Light Opera Assn. production of *The Merry Widow* (1961), and for Martha Graham's Visionary Recital, later retitled *Samson Agonistes* (1961); sets and costumes for *A Passage to India* (Ambassador, N.Y.C., Jan. 31, 1962); scenery for the pre-Bway tryout of *The Umbrella* (opened New Locust, Philadelphia, Pa., Jan. 18, 1962; closed there Jan. 27, 1962); scenery and costumes for the San Francisco Ballet's production of *Swan Lake* and Glenn Tetley's ballet, *Pierrot Lunaire* (both 1962).

He designed sets and costumes for *Hot Spot* (Majestic, N.Y.C., Apr. 19, 1963); *Save Me a Place at Forest Lawn* and *The Last Minstrel* (Pocket Th., May 8, 1963); *Arturo Ui* (Lunt-Fontanne Th., Nov. 11, 1963); for the Hamburg (Germany) State Opera's *Orpheus and Eurydice* (Nov. 16, 1963); for the NY Pro Musica and Metropolitan Museum of Art's production of *The Play of Herod* (The Cloisters, N.Y.C., 1963); for the Joffrey Ballet's *Time Out of Mind* (1963) and the Cologne (Germany) Opera's production of the ballet *Souvenirs;* and *The Milk Train Doesn't Stop Here Any More* (Brooks Atkinson Th., Jan. 1, 1964); and settings for *The Deputy* (Brooks Atkinson Th., Feb. 26, 1964).

For NY City Ballet, he designed scenery and costumes for *Swan Lake,* scenery for *Ballet Imperial* and *The Nutcracker,* and he designed scenery and costumes for Netherlands Dance Theatre's *Pierrot Lunaire* (all 1964). He designed scenery and costumes for American Ballet Theatre's *Sargasso,* NY City Ballet's *Harlequinade,* San Francisco Ballet's *Lucifer,* the Paul Taylor Dance Company's *Nine Dances with Music by Corelli,* the Netherlands Dance Theatre's *Fieldmass,* and scenery for the Cologne (Germany) Opera's *The Nutcracker* (all 1965).

He designed scenery for *The Devils* (Broadway Th., N.Y.C., Nov. 16, 1965); scenery and costumes for *Ivanov* (London 1965; Sam S. Shubert Th., N.Y.C., May 3, 1966); for *Pelleas and Melisande* (Festival of Two Worlds, Spoleto, Italy, 1966); for *Medea* (Rome 1966); for *Eh!* (Circle in the Square, N.Y.C., Oct. 16, 1966); for American Ballet Theatre's *Ricercare* and Pennsylvania Ballet's *Villon* (both 1966); designed the production for *The Party on Greenwich Avenue* (Cherry Lane, May 10, 1967); designed scenery and costumes for the American Shakespeare Festival's *Macbeth* (Stratford, Conn., July 30, 1967); and designed Ballet Rambert's *Pierrot Lunaire* and *Ricercare,* Pennsylvania Ballet's *Gala Dix,* and the Harkness Ballet's *Firebird, After Eden,* and *A Season in Hell* (all 1967).

He designed scenery for *Exit the King* (Lyceum, N.Y.C., Jan. 9, 1968); *I'm Solomon* (Mark Hellinger Th., Apr. 23, 1968); scenery and costumes for the Santa Fe (N.M.) Opera's *Madame Butterfly* and scenery for its production of *The Bassarids* (both 1968); and (all 1968) scenery and costumes for the Pennsylvania Ballet's *Ceremony,* for the NY City Ballet's *Requiem Canticle,* for the Royal Danish Ballet's *Pierrot Lunaire,* scenery for the Martha Graham Company's *A Time of Snow,* for the Berlin (Germany) Deutsche Oper's *Ballet Imperial,* and scenery and costumes for productions of *Souvenirs* (Theater an der Wien, Vienna, Austria; Harkness Ballet, Monte Carlo). He designed scenery and costumes for the Santa Fe (N.M.) Opera's *The Devils of Loudon* (1969); designed the production *The Dozens* (Booth Th., N.Y.C., Mar. 13, 1969); designed scenery for *Promenade* (Promenade Th., June 4, 1969); for American Ballet Company's *Harbinger* (Festival of Two Worlds, Spoleto, Italy, 1969); and designed scenery and costumes for the ballets *Transitions* (Cologne Opera, Ger., 1969); *Souvenirs* (Malmo, Sweden, 1970); the Royal Swedish Ballet's *Ricercare* (1970); the Boston (Mass.) Ballet's *The Minotaur* (1970); and *The Unicorn, the Gorgon, and the Manticore* (Festival of Two Worlds, Spoleto, Italy, 1970).

He designed scenery and costumes for *All Over* (Martin Beck Th., N.Y.C., May 1, 1971); for the Hamburg (Germany) State Opera ballet *Chronochromie* (1971); for *Liebelei* (Akademie Th., Vienna, Austria, 1972); for the Cincinnati (Ohio) Symphony and Ballet production of *The Unicorn, the Gorgon, and the Manticore* (1972); for the NY City Ballet's Stravinsky Festival (1972) productions of *Concerto for Piano and Wind Instruments, The Song of the Nightingale, Choral Variations—von Himmel hoch,* and *Symphony of Psalms;* for American Ballet Theatre's *Some Times* (1972); the Royal Ballet's *Laborintus* (Royal Opera House, Covent Garden, London, England, 1972); the Alvin Ailey American Dance Theatre's *According to Eve* (1972); the Bavarian State Opera Ballet's *Pierrot Lunaire* (Munich, Germany, 1972); NY City Ballet's *Symphony in Three Movements, Cortège Hongrois,* and *An Evening's Waltzes* (all 1973); Pennsylvania Ballet's *Black Angel* (1973); City Center Joffrey Ballet's *Remembrances* (1973); Stuttgart (Ger.) Ballet's *Voluntaries* 1973); *Celebration* and *The Art of the Pas-de-Deux* (both Festival of Two Worlds, Spoleto, Italy, 1973); *Pelleas and Melisande* (La Scala, Milan, and Teatro La Fenice, Venice, Italy; both 1973); NY City Ballet's *Variations pour une Porte et un Soupir* (1974); San Francisco Ballet's *La Sonnambula* (1974); and he designed settings for *Goodtime Charley* (Palace Th., N.Y.C., Mar. 3, 1975).

Films. Mr. Ter-Arutunian did the production design and costumes for *The Loved One* (MGM, 1965) and production design and scenery for *Such Good Friends* (Par., 1971).

Television. Mr. Ter-Arutunian was a staff designer for CBS (1951–53), ABC (1953), and NBC (1954–57). He designed sets for the Burt Parks Show and This Is Show Business (both CBS, 1951), The Toast of the Town (CBS, 1952), and Studio One (CBS, 1952–53); designed costumes and scenery for NBC Opera productions of *The Abduction from the Seraglio* (1954), *The Would-Be Gentleman* and *Ariadne auf Naxos* (both 1955), *The Magic Flute* (1956), and sets for *Maria Golovin* (1959). He designed sets for *Reunion in Vienna* (Producer's Showcase, NBC, 1955); scenery and costumes for *Antigone* (NBC, 1956); for Hallmark Hall of Fame (NBC) presentations of *The Taming of the Shrew* (1956), *Twelfth Night* (1957), and *The Tempest* (1959); sets and costumes for the Bell Telephone Hour (NBC, 1958); *Swing into Spring* (CBS, 1958); sets for *A Musical Bouquet for Maurice Chevalier* (CBS, 1960); sets and costumes for *The Flood* (CBS, 1962); for *The Art of the Prima Donna* (Bell Telephone Hour, NBC, 1966); sets for the Marlene Dietrich Special *I Wish You Love* (BBC, CBS, 1973); and sets and costumes for *Rachel, La Cubana* (NET Opera Th., PBS, 1973).

Other Activities. Mr. Ter-Arutunian designed scenery, costumes, and club interiors for US Third Army Special Services in West Germany (1945–47). His work is represented in the collection of the Museum of Modern Art, N.Y.C.; the Theatre Collection, Houghton Library, Harvard Univ., Cambridge, Mass.; and the Theatre and Dance collections, Library and Museum of the Performing Arts (LMPA), Lincoln Ctr., N.Y.C. In 1968, the Vincent Astor Gallery, LMPA; the Canyon Road Art Gallery, Santa Fe, N.M.; and the Wright-Hepburn-Webster Gallery, N.Y.C., held exhibitions of Mr. Ter-Arutunian's theatre designs.

Published Works. Mr. Ter-Arutunian wrote "In Search of Design" in *Dance Perspectives* 28 (1966).

Awards. Mr. Ter-Arutunian received the NATAS (Emmy) Television Award for best art direction for *Twelfth Night* (1957); the Outer Circle Award for best scenic designs for *Who Was That Lady I Saw You With?* (1958); and the Antoinette Perry (Tony) Award for best costume designs for *Redhead* (1959).

TERRELL, ST. JOHN. Theatre owner, actor, producer. b. George Clinton Eccles, Dec. 12, 1916, Chicago, Ill., to George Clinton and Reta (Terrell) Eccles. Father, lumber broker; mother, editor. Attended Columbia Univ., 1934–37; New York Univ., 1937; York Collegiate Inst., 1942–43; Washington and Lee Univ., 1943–44; Northwestern Univ., 1946–47. Married Sept. 12, 1952, to Elrita Batholomew; one son (marr. dis. 1974); married 1974 to Mary Irine Gallagher. Served USAAF, 1942–45; rank, Flight Officer. Member of AEA; SAG; Music Circus of America (pres., 1951); MATA (pres., 1955–57; honorary pres., 1958–63); The Players (bd. of dir., 1962). Address: (home) "Chez Nous," 248 W. Upper Ferry Rd., Ewing Township, NJ 08628, tel. (609) 882-4569; (bus.) 286 W. 11th St., New York, NY 10014, tel. (212) AL 5-6310.

Mr. Terrell was the founder and proprietor of the Music Circus in Lambertville, N.J. until 1973.

Theatre. He made his debut as Will in *The Thirteenth Chair* with Mrs. Patrick Campbell (Guilford, Conn., 1937); his Bway debut as Lubin in *Judgement Day* (Belasco, Sept. 12, 1934); toured with the Walter Hampden Repertory Company as Tyrell in *Richard III*, Rosencrantz in *Hamlet* and Ross in *Macbeth* (1934–35); played the Sailor and understudied Burgess Meredith as Mio in *Winterset* (Martin Beck Th., N.Y.C., Sept. 25, 1935); and appeared in stock productions at the Starlight Th., Pauling, N.Y. (Summers 1935–36).

He produced *Three by Thurber*, which he adapted with Paul Ellwood (Th. de Lys, N.Y.C., Mar. 7, 1955).

Television and Radio. During 1933–41, he performed on such CBS radio programs as *Jack Armstrong, Little Orphan Annie* and *The First Nighters*. He adapted James Thurber's works for Robert Montgomery's television productions.

Other Activities. He is co-owner and general manager of Reta Terrell Perfumes, Inc., and president of the Hunterdon Development Corp. He produces the annual commemorative pageant of *Washington Crossing the Delaware*, depicting the title role (1953–to date). Mr. Terrell was appointed by President John F. Kennedy as Federal Chairman of the New Jersey Tercentenary Celebration Commission; appointed by Governor Hughes (N.J.) cochairman of President Johnson's Birthday Celebration (Aug. 27, 1964); was chairman of the Performing Arts Feasibility Study for the New Jersey State Council on the Arts (1965); and was a member of the Council of the Arts, New Jersey (1966–72).

Recreation. Astronomy, light plane flying, tennis, and blue water sailing.

TERRY, MEGAN. Playwright, director. b. July 22, 1932, Seattle, Wash. Attended Banff Sch. of Fine Arts, Summers 1950–52, 1956; Univ. of Alberta (Canada), 1952–53; Univ. of Washington (Seattle), B.Ed., 1956; writer-in-residence, Yale Univ. Drama Sch., 1966–67. Member of NY Theatre Strategy (founding mbr.; treas., 1971); Women's Theatre Council (founding mbr., 1971).

Theatre. Miss Terry wrote and directed *Viet Rock* (Martinique, N.Y.C., Nov. 10, 1966), originally entitled *Viet Rock; A Folk War Movie*. Previously, with the Cornish Players (Seattle, Wash., 1955) she wrote and directed *Beach Grass, Seascape*, and *Go Out and Move the Car*. off-off-Bway, she directed with the Open Theatre's Playwrights Workshop (1962–68); and in Los Angeles (1970), directed her play, *The Tommy Allen Show*.

Other works by Miss Terry that have presented in off-off-Bway and experimental productions include *New York Comedy: Two* (Saratoga, N.Y., 1961); *Ex-Miss Copper Queen on a Set of Pills* (N.Y.C., 1963); *When My Girlhood Was Still All Flowers* (N.Y.C., 1963); *Eat at Joe's* (N.Y.C., 1964); *Calm Down Mother* (N.Y.C., 1965; and London, 1969); *Keep Tightly Closed in a Cool Dry Place* (N.Y.C., 1965; and Company Th., Los Angeles, 1967–68 season); *The Magic Realists* (N.Y.C., 1966); *Comings and Goings* (N.Y.C., 1966; and Edinburgh, 1968); *The Gloaming, Oh My Darling* (Minneapolis, Minn., 1966; and Company Th., Los Angeles, Jan. 13, 1972); *The Key Is on the Bottom* (Los Angeles, 1967); *Changes* (La Mama ETC, Jan. 4, 1968); *The People vs. Ranchman* (Fortune, N.Y.C., Oct. 27, 1968); *Jack-Jack* (Minneapolis, 1968); *Massachusetts Trust* (Waltham, Mass., 1968); *Approaching Simone* (Boston and N.Y.C., 1970); *Grooving* (N.Y.C., 1972); *Choose a Spot on the Floor* (Omaha, Neb., 1972), with Jo Ann Schmidman; *Nightwalk* (Open Th., London; and Th. of St. Clements, N.Y.C., Sept. 8, 1973), a work in progress devised with Jean-Claude van Itallie, Sam Shepard, and others; *Susan Peretz at the Manhattan Theatre Club* (Manhattan Th. Club, N.Y.C., May 24, 1973); *All Them Women* (Westbeth Playwright's Feminist Cooperative, Jan. 11, 1974), written with Patricia Haron, Sally Ordway, Delores Walker and others; and *The Pioneer* and *Pro Game* (Th. Genesis, Nov. 1974).

In addition, Miss Terry, with Jose Tapla, contributed additional lyrics to *Thoughts*, a musical by Lamar Alford (Th. de Lys, N.Y.C., Mar. 19, 1973).

Television and Radio. For radio, Miss Terry wrote *Sanibel and Captiva* (1968); and *American Wedding Ritual Monitored/Transmitted by the Planet Jupiter* (1972). Her televised plays include *The Dirt Boat*, which she directed (1955); *Home* (WNET, 1968); *One More Little Drinkie* (1969); and *Brazil Fado; You're Always with Me* (1972).

Published Works. Her critical study "Who Says Only Words Make Great Drama," appeared in the NY *Times* (Nov. 10, 1968).

Awards. Miss Terry was the recipient of the Stanley Drama Award (1965); the Office of Advanced Drama Research Award (1965); an ABC-Yale Univ. Fellowship (1966); and a Rockefeller Foundation grant (1968).

TETZEL, JOAN. Actress. b. Joan Margaret Tetzel, June 21, 1921, New York City, to George James and Sara (MacPhee) Tetzel. Father, artist. Attended Professional Children's Sch., N.Y.C. Married May 27, 1949, to Oscar Homolka, actor. Member of AEA; AFTRA; SAG.

Theatre. Miss Tetzel made her N.Y.C. debut as Renie in *Lorelei* (Longacre Th., Nov. 29, 1938). She was an understudy in the role of Alexandra in *The Little Foxes* (Natl., Feb. 15, 1939); played Louise in *Liliom* (44 St. Th., Mar. 25, 1940); Pernette Faber in *The Happy Days* (Henry Miller's Th., May 13, 1941); Daphne Randall in *The Damask Cheek* (Playhouse, Oct. 22, 1942); Georgie Stowe in *Harriet* (Henry Miller's Th., Mar. 3, 1943); Jessica in *Peepshow* (Fulton, Feb. 3, 1944); Dora in *Pretty Little Parlor* (Natl., Apr. 17, 1944); Katrin in *I Remember Mama* (Music Box, Oct. 19, 1944); Clarissa Blynn Cromwell in *Strange Bedfellows* (Morosco, Jan. 14, 1948); and Jessica in *Red Gloves* (Mansfield, Dec. 4, 1948).

She played Susan in *The Little Hut* (Lyric, London, Aug. 23, 1950); Eva Harold in *The Winner* (Playhouse, N.Y.C., Feb. 17, 1954); Hilda Wangel in *The Master Builder* (Phoenix, Mar. 1, 1955); Nurse Ratched in *One Flew Over the Cuckoo's Nest* (Cort, Nov. 13, 1963); the Wife in *The Dance of Death* (Yvonne Arnaud Th., Guildford, England, June 26, 1966); and Fiona Foster in *How the Other Half Loves* (Lyric, London, Aug. 1970).

Films. Miss Tetzel has appeared in *Duel in the Sun* (Selznick, 1946); *The Paradine Case* (Selznick, 1948); *File on Thelma Jordan* (Par., 1949); and *Hell Below Zero* (Col., 1954); and *Joy in the Morning* (MGM, 1965).

Television. Miss Tetzel has appeared on segments of Thriller (Ind., 1964); Gunsmoke (CBS, 1966); and Alfred Hitchcock Presents (Ind., 1967).

Recreation. Collecting records, walking, reading.

THATCHER, TORIN. Actor. b. Torin Herbert Erskine Thatcher, Jan. 15, 1905, Bombay, India, to Torin James Blair and Edith Rachel (Batty) Thatcher. Father, member of the Indian police; mother, voice and piano teacher. Attended Bedford Sch., Eng., 1913–22; studied acting at Maddermarket Th., Norwich, Eng., 1923–24; RADA, 1925–26. Served British Territorial Army, 1924–27; Royal Artillery, British Army, 1940–45, rank, Lt. Col. Married July 16, 1940, to Rita Daniel, actress (dec. 1951); married June 12, 1952, to Anna Marie Leborgne. Member of AEA; SAG; British AEA; AFTRA; Canadian AEA; NATAS.

Pre-Theatre. Teacher.

Theatre. Mr. Thatcher made his London debut as Morgan James in *The Snowstorm* ("Q" Th., Apr. 12, 1926); followed by a season of plays at Oxford Playhouse, and later at A.D.C. Th., Cambridge. His roles included Schaaf in *A Month in the Country, Marriage*, Li Lao in *The Veil of Happiness*, and the Lover in *The Triumph of Death* (Summer 1926); played Mr. Jarvis in *Grumpy* (Budleigh, Salterton, Aug. 1926), and on tour.

From Oct. 1926–June 1927, he appeared in the following plays at the Festival Th., Cambridge: *Magic; The New Morality;* played Guido Colonna in *Monna Vanna;* Aegisthus in *The Oresteia;* Torino in *The Rumour;* the Tramp in *The Insect Play;* Septimus in *The Player Queen;* Conochar in *On Baille's Strand;* Sir Soloman Raub in *The Man Who Ate Poppomack;* Nicetas in *Heraclius;* Bill in *The Glittering Gate;* appeared in *Love for Love; Red Nights of the Tcheka; And in the Tomb Were Found;* played the Actor in *The Pleasure Garden;* the Agitator in *Don Juan;* Ferrovius in *Androcles and the Lion;* the Boss in *The Adding Machine;* and Col. Jeffries in *Sweeney Todd, Demon Barber of Fleet Street*.

With the Old Vic (London, Sept. 1927–June 1929), he played Tranio in *The Taming of the Shrew;* Solanio in *The Merchant of Venice;* Borachio in *Much Ado About Nothing;* Bassanio in *The Merchant of Venice;* the Ghost in *Hamlet;* Oliver in *As You Like It;* Mountjoy in *The Merry Wives of Windsor;* Benvolio in *Romeo and Juliet;* and Ross in *Macbeth;* Summer 1928, toured in repertory with the company in *Macbeth, As You Like It, The Merchant of Venice*, and *Hamlet;* returned for second season to play Horatio in *Hamlet*, Cornwall in *King Lear*, Longaville in *Love's Labour's Lost*, Herald in *The Two Nobel Kinsmen*, the Voice of Christ in *Mary Magdalen*, the Voice of God in *Everyman*, the Speaker in *Adam's Opera;* Snake in *The School for Scandal*, Faulkland in *The Rivals;* and Sebald in *Pippa Passes*, which he also directed.

During this period, he also played Diarmuid in *Diarmuid and Grainne* (Tottenham Ct. Road, London, 1928); Antonio in *The Duchess of Malfi* and Stephen Rolf in *Comic Artists* (Players, 1928); the Second Stranger in *The Skin Game* (Wyndham's, July 30, 1929); Basil Gullhoppity in *Veronica* (Arts, Sept. 18, 1929); Inspector Enderby in *Michael and Mary* (St. James's, Feb. 1, 1930); and appeared in *Fratricide Punished* (Scala, c. 1930).

During 1930–31, he was a member of the Macdona Players, a repertory company, playing Hector Malone, Jr., in *Man and Superman* (Court, London, Jan. 6, 1930); and touring for ten months as Dubedat in *The Doctor's Dilemma;* Hector Malone, Jr., in *Man and Superman;* Mr. Vanhattan in *The Apple Cart;* Sergius Saranof in *Arms and the Man;* Bohun K.C. in *You Never Can Tell;* Sinjon Hotchkiss in *Getting Married;* Joseph Perceval in *Misalliance;* Duvallet in *Fanny's First Play;* and Praed in *Mrs. Warren's Profession*.

Mr. Thatcher played a season at the Embassy Th. (London), appearing as Hodges in *This Woman's Business* (May 16, 1932), Paul Travers in *The Twelfth Hour* (June 13, 1932), Denis in *Dance with No Music* (June 27, 1932), the Professor in *The Scion* (July 11, 1932), David in *The Silver Cord* (July 25, 1932), and the Burglar in *Behind the Blinds*. He played Eben in *Alison's House* (Little, Oct. 11, 1932); William in *Doctor's Orders* (Globe, Jan. 31, 1933); Nicholas May in *Tomorrow and Tomorrow* (St. Martin's, Mar. 19, 1933); Major Zimoff in *Command Performance* (Saville, Oct. 17, 1933); Sir Francis Chesney in *Charley's Aunt* (Gaiety, Dec. 23, 1933); Karl Hoffman in *The Drums Begin* (Embassy, Apr. 2, 1934); Rassendyland, Prince of Ruritania, in *The Prisoner of Zenda* (Th. Royal, Windsor, 1934); the Old Emperor in *Aureng-Lebe* (Westminster, London, May 30, 1934); Edward Rochester in *The Master of Thornfield* (King's Hammersmith, Aug. 20, 1934); Lion in *Ding and Co.* (Embassy, Nov. 19, 1934); appeared in *Invitation to a Murder* (Globe, Nov. 1934); played Antonio in *The Duchess of Malfi;* Michael Verner in *Valkyrie* (Westminster, Apr. 23, 1935); Alcibiades in *Timon of Athens* (Westminster, Nov. 19, 1935); Count Feria in *Mary Tudor* (Playhouse, Dec. 12, 1935); Edgar Fraser in *Green Waters*

(Vaudeville, May 25, 1936); Constant in *The Provoked Wife* (Embassy, Oct. 5, 1936); the Ghost and Claudius in *Hamlet* (Old Vic, Jan. 5, 1937), which he later repeated at Elsinore, Denmark; Ned Marshall in *The Constant Sinner* ("Q", London, Apr. 5, 1937); Claudius in *Hamlet* (Westminster, July 9, 1937); and Peter Boyne in *People at Sea* (Apollo, Nov. 24, 1937).

Mr. Thatcher played Galileo in *The Painted Smile* (New, Mar. 31, 1938) and the Minister of Propaganda in *The Power and the Glory* (Savoy, Apr. 8, 1938), both of which were running simultaneously, necessitating Mr. Thatcher to leave the New Th. following Act I of *The Painted Smile* in order to arrive at the Savoy Th. in time to appear in Acts II and III of *The Power and the Glory.*

He played David Shiel in *Music at Night* (Embassy, 1938); George Simon in *Counsellor-at-Law* ("Q", 1939); and Henry Higgins in *Pygmalion* (Intimate Th., Palmers Green, 1940).

During WW II, while stationed in Egypt, he played Claudius in *Hamlet* (Opera House, Cairo, 1944); Group Captain in *How Are They at Home,* and Ferovius in *Androcles and the Lion* (Garrison Th., Cairo, 1944).

He was a founder (1945), with William Fox and Michael Narriott, of Reunion Theatre Assn., which was formed for the purpose of rehabilitating ex-servicemen and women in all branches of the theatre. In London, he appeared as the Earl of Bothwell in *Golden Eagle* (Westminster, Jan. 29, 1946); under the pseudonym "T. Atkinson," was author, with Peter Powell, William Fox, Alec Clunes, and W. P. Templeton, and also played the role of Joe Rock in *Exercise Bowler* (Arts, Apr. 18, 1946); appeared as Kim Barrie in *In the Palm of Your Hand* ("Q", Dec. 10, 1946); Dan Bradbourne in *Deep as a Well* ("Q", May 6, 1947); Sir Richard Hickory in *Portrait of Hickory* (Embassy, Apr. 20, 1948); and Uriah in *Jonathan* (Aldwych, July 29, 1948).

Mr. Thatcher made his Bway debut as Harry Soames in *Edward, My Son* (Martin Beck Th., Sept. 30, 1948); followed by the role of Antonio Perez in *That Lady* (Martin Beck Th., Nov. 22, 1949); John Claggart, Master-at-Arms, in *Billy Budd* (Biltmore, Feb. 10, 1951); Seti the Second in *The Firstborn* (Coronet, April 29, 1958); Captain Keller in *The Miracle Worker* (Playhouse, Oct. 19, 1959); Charles Sturrock in *Write Me a Murder* (Belasco, Oct. 26, 1961); and Dr. Philip Burton in *Hidden Stranger* (Longacre, Jan. 8, 1963).

Films. Mr. Thatcher made his debut in *General John Regan* (Brit. Intl., 1934); followed by roles in *Drake of England; School for Stars; The Red Wagon* (Alliance, 1935); *The Man Who Could Work Miracles* (UA, 1937); *Young and Innocent; Climbing High* (20th-Fox, 1939); *Let George Do It* (FIA, 1940); *Last Train to Munich; Law and Disorder; Case of the Frightened Lady; Barrabas; The Common Round and the Proconsul; Old Mother Riley M.P.; Major Barbara* (UA, 1941); *Saboteur* (U, 1942); *The Captive Heart* (U, 1947); *I See a Dark Stranger; Great Expectations* (U, 1947); *When the Bough Breaks; Jassy* (U, 1948); *The End of the River* (U, 1948); *Bonnie Prince Charlie; The Fallen Idol* (Selznick, 1949); *The Black Rose* (20th-Fox, 1950); *The Crimson Pirate* (WB, 1952); *Affair in Trinidad* (Col., 1952); *The Snows of Kilimanjaro* (20th-Fox, 1952); *Blackbeard, the Pirate* (RKO, 1952); *The Desert Rats* (20th-Fox, 1953); *Houdini* (Par., 1953); *The Robe* (20th-Fox, 1953); *Knock on Wood* (Par., 1954); *The Black Shield of Falworth* (U, 1954); *Bengal Brigade* (U, 1954); *Helen of Troy* (WB, 1955); *Lady Godiva* (U, 1955); *Diane* (MGM, 1955); *Love Is a Many-Splendored Thing* (20th-Fox, 1955); *Istanbul* (U, 1957); *Band of Angels* (WB, 1957); *Darby's Rangers* (WB, 1957); *Witness for the Prosecution* (UA, 1957); *The Canadians* (20th-Fox, 1961); *Jack the Giant Killer* (UA, 1962); *The Sweet and the Bitter* (Hollyburn Prod., Can., 1962); *Music at Midnight* (MRA, 1963); *From Hell to Borneo* (Mont Prods., Philippines, 1964); *Mutiny on the Bounty* (1961); *The Sandpiper* (Film Way); *Hawaii* (Mirisch Bros.); and *The Kings Pirate* (UI).

Television and Radio. Mr. Thatcher made his radio debut in London (c.1927), and subsequently performed regularly for the BBC in serials and dramatic programs. He made his television debut at the Alexander Palace, London (BBC, c.1937–38), appearing approximately 8 or 9 times in dramatic works prior to WW II, including *The Duchess of Malfi* and *Broadway.*

In the US, he has performed frequently on dramatic radio and television programs, including You Are There (CBS); GE Th. (CBS); US Steel Hour (CBS); Suspense (CBS); The Trap; The Web (CBS); Climax! (CBS); Playhouse 90 (CBS); Somerset Maugham Th. (ABC); Zane Grey Th., (NBC); Wagon Train (NBC); Hazel (NBC); Bob Hope Th. (NBC); Profiles in Courage; Great Adventure; The Defenders (CBS); Slattery's People (CBS); My Three Sons (ABC); Hitchcock Presents (CBS); and twice played the title role in *Othello* (Philco Television Playhouse, NBC, 1951, 1953). He has also appeared on Voyage to the Bottom of the Sea; Lost in Space; Time Tunnel; Land of the Giants; Star Trek; Search; Mission: Impossible; Night Gallery; Dupont Show of the Month; Hallmark Hall of Fame; Bonanza; Perry Mason; The Real McCoys; Petrocelli; East Side, West Side; and The Untouchables.

Awards. Mr. Thatcher received the Sylvania Award for his performance in the television play, *Beyond This Place* (1957).

Recreation. Reading, gardening, swimming, travel.

THAXTER, PHYLLIS. Actress. b. Phyllis St. Felix Thaxter, Nov. 20, Portland, Me., to Sydney St. Felix and Marie Phyllis (Schuyler) Thaxter. Father, supreme court judge; mother, actress. Grad. Deering (Me.) H.S., 1937; attended St. Genevieve Sch., Montreal, Can., 1937–38; studied acting with Montreal Repertory Th., 1937–38. Married Nov. 16, 1944, to James T. Aubrey, Jr. (marr. dis. 1962); one son, one daughter, Skye Aubrey, actress; married Dec. 27, 1962, to Gilbert Lea. Member of AEA; SAG; AMPAS; AFTRA, NATAS. Address: 1125 Park Ave., New York, NY 10028, tel. LE 4-5678.

Theatre. Miss Thaxter made her debut as Daphne, with Laurette Taylor, in Miss Taylor's play, *At the Theatre* (Ogunquit Playhouse, Me., Summer 1938); her Bway debut succeeding (Fall 1938) one of the students in *What a Life* (Biltmore, Apr. 13, 1938); subsequently played Lempi and understudied in *There Shall Be No Night* (Alvin, Apr. 29, 1940); played the title role in *Claudia* (Selwyn, Chicago, Ill., 1941); and succeeded Dorothy McGuire in this role in N.Y.C. production (Booth, Feb. 12, 1941). She succeeded Kay Stewart as Kate Bannion in the pre-Bway tryout of *Heartsong* (opened Shubert, New Haven, Conn., Feb. 27, 1947; closed Walnut St. Th., Philadelphia, Pa., Mar. 29, 1947); played Nancy in *Sundown Beach* (Belasco, N.Y.C., Sept. 7, 1948); Anne Michaelson in *Take Her, She's Mine* (Biltmore, Dec. 21, 1961); Agnes Carol in *Time Out for Ginger* (Ogunquit, Me., Playhouse; Cape Playhouse, Dennis, Mass., Summer 1963); Mary (Mrs. Stephen) Haines in *The Women* (Paper Mill Playhouse, Millburn, N.J., Mar. 22, 1966); and Alice Kingsley in *The Impossible Years* (Royal Poinciana Playhouse, Palm Beach, Fla., Jan. 1967).

Films. She has appeared in *Thirty Seconds Over Tokyo* (MGM, 1944); *Bewitched* (MGM, 1945); *Weekend at the Waldorf* (MGM, 1945); *Living in a Big Way* (MGM, 1947); *Sea of Grass* (MGM, 1948); *Act of Violence* (MGM, 1948); *Sign of the Ram* (Col., 1948); *Blood on the Moon* (RKO, 1948); *No Man of Her Own* (Par., 1950); *Breaking Point* (WB, 1950); *Jim Thorpe-All American* (WB, 1951); *Fort Worth* (WB, 1951); *Come Fill the Cup* (WB, 1951); *Springfield Rifle* (WB, 1952); *She's Working Her Way Through College* (WB, 1952); *Operation Secret* (WB, 1952); *Women's Prison* (Col., 1955); *Man Afraid* (U, 1957); and *The World of Henry Orient* (UA, 1964).

Television. Miss Thaxter made her debut in *Miracle in the Rain* (Tales of the City, CBS, Aug. 20, 1953) and has since appeared on US Steel Hour (CBS); Ford Th. (NBC); Robt Montgomery Presents (NBC); Video Th. (CBS); Lux Video Th. (NBC); Schlitz Playhouse of Stars (CBS); Shower of Stars (CBS); Climax (CBS); Loretta Young Show (NBC); Stage 7 (CBS); Fireside Th. (NBC); Alfred Hitchcock Presents (CBS); Studio 57 (CBS); Studio One (CBS); Frank Sinatra Show (ABC); Wagon Train (NBC); Lux Playhouse (CBS); G.E. Th. (CBS); Playhouse 90 (CBS); The Outlaws (NBC); Thriller (NBC); Rawhide (CBS); Twilight Zone (CBS); Kraft Th. (NBC); The Defenders (CBS); The FBI (ABC); Coronet Blue (CBS); The Invaders (ABC); Lancer (CBS); Bonanza (NBC); Medical Center (CBS); *Incident in San Francisco* (ABC telefilm, Feb. 28, 1971); *The Longest Night* (ABC telefilm, Sept. 12, 1972); and Cannon (CBS).

Recreation. Tennis, riding, needlepoint, antiques, "taking care of my husband.".

THIRKIELD, ROB. Actor, director, producer, set designer, teacher. b. Robert Leeming Thirkield, July 29, 1936, Glen Cove, L.I., N.Y., to Gilbert Haven and Helen (Leeming) Thirkield. Father, banker. Relative in theatre: cousin, Esther Leeming, actress. Educ. Berkeley Institute, Brooklyn; Poly Prep; Choate School, Wallingford, Conn. Grad. Wesleyan Univ., Middletown, Conn., B.A.; Northwestern Univ., Evanston, Ill. Professional training with Ralph Pendleton at Wesleyan; Alvina Krause at Northwestern; James Tuttle, Eugenio Barba, Blanche Evan (dance), Gerard Russak (voice). Served in US Army, 1960–62. Married June 30, 1969, to Tanya Berezin; one son, one daughter. Member of AEA; SAG. Circle Repertory Th., 2307 Broadway, New York, NY 10024, tel. (212) 874-1080; 101 Central Park West, New York, NY 10023, tel. (212) EN 2-9026.

Theatre. Mr. Thirkield first appeared on stage at Berkeley Institute as a Customer in a student production of *The Shoemaker and the Elves* (1945). In 1957, he was in summer stock at Eagles Mere Playhouse, Pa., as Serensky in *Anastasia* (July) and as Laertes in *Hamlet* (Aug. 14); at Wesleyan, he played Trofimoff in *The Cherry Orchard* (Nov. 20, 1957) and directed *The Bald Soprano* (Feb. 1958); and at Northwestern, he played Fiers in *The Cherry Orchard* (Jan. 30, 1959), Tiresias in *Oedipus* (July 1959), and Caesar in *Caesar and Cleopatra* (Nov. 20, 1959). He appeared as Mr. Fowler in *Separate Tables* (Little Th., Niagara Falls, N.Y., Jan. 1961); made his off-off-Bway debut in N.Y.C. as Jason in *Medea* (Caffe Cino, Nov. 25, 1962) and his off-Bway debut as Allmers in *Little Eyolf* (Actors' Playhouse, Apr. 1, 1964).

He appeared also as the Stranger and Fick in *Balm in Gilead* (La Mama ETC, Jan. 26, 1965); Peter in *A Taste of Honey* (Broadway Th. Co., Fallsburg, N.Y., July 1965); in the title role in *Christopher Columbus* (Spencer Memorial Ch., Brooklyn, N.Y., Oct. 23, 1965); in *Krapp's Last Tape* (Actors' Studio, Nov. 1965); as Shakespeare in *The Owl Answers* (Th. de Lys, Dec. 14, 1965); and with La Mama ETC as Skelly in *The Rimers of Eldritch* (N.Y.C., July 13, 1966), Gelderen in *Homo* (Zagreb, Yugoslavia, Sept. 1966), Satz in *Futz* (N.Y.C., Mar. 1, 1967), and Louis XVI in *Tom Paine* (N.Y.C., May 1967; Spoleto, Italy, July 1967; Church Hill Th., Edinburgh Festival, Scotland, Sept. 1967; Vaudeville Th., London, England, Oct. 1967); as Rob in *Untitled Play* (Judson Ch., N.Y.C., Jan. 26, 1968); and in the title role in *Tom Paine* (Th. 74, June 1968).

In July 1969, Mr. Thirkield was co-founder (with Marshall Mason) of the Circle Repertory Co., N.Y.C., and for Circle Th. he directed *A Practical Ritual* (Mar. 27, 1970); played Chebutykin in *The Three Sisters* (Jan. 11, 1970); directed *The Ghost Sonata* (Mar. 1970; Nov. 26, 1971); played Graham in *3 by Lanford Wilson* (May 21, 1972); played Mr. Morse in *Hot l Baltimore* (Feb. 4, 1973) and at Circle in the Square (Mar. 22, 1973); directed *The Persians* (May 19, 1974); and played Dr. August Howe in *The Mound Builders* (Feb. 2, 1975).

Films. Mr. Thirkield repeated his performance as Satz in the motion picture version of *Futz* (Guvnor Prod., 1969).

Recreation. Opera records, photography, singing, jogging.

THOMAS, FRANK, JR. Actor, director, producer, writer. b. Apr. 9, 1926, New York City, to Frank M. and Mona (Bruns) Thomas. Father, actor; mother, actress. Grad. Hollywood (Calif.) H.S., 1941; Kings Point Maritime Acad., Ensign, 1943. Served USNR and US Maritime Service, 1941–46; rank (Navy) Lt. (j.g.); (Maritime Service) Lt. Commander. Relatives in theatre: uncle, Calvin Thomas, actor; aunt, Margaret Mosier Thomas, actress. Member of AEA; AFTRA (local board, 1950–54; natl. bd., 1950–64); SAG (mbr. of council, 1952–60); WGA; The Lambs (recording secy., 1958–64); The Circumnavigators Club.

Theatre. Mr. Thomas made his Bway debut as a Newsboy in *Carrie Nation* (Biltmore, Oct. 29, 1932); subsequently played Possum in *Little Ol' Boy* (Playhouse, Apr. 24, 1933); Martin in *Thunder on the Left* (Maxine Elliott's Th., Oct. 31, 1933); Bobbie Phillips in *Wednesday's Child* (Longacre, Jan. 16, 1934); Jimmy Magee in *The First Legion* (46 St. Th., Oct. 1, 1934); Dewey Roberts in *Remember the Day* in which his father played Mr. Roberts (National, Sept. 25, 1935); Duke Winthrop in *Seen But Not Heard* (Henry Miller's Th., Sept. 17, 1936); and Joshua Winslow, Jr., in *Your Loving Son* (Little, Apr. 4, 1941).

He appeared in stock productions at the Lakewood Th., Skowhegan, Me. (Summer 1947); in *Rear Echelon* (Master Inst., N.Y.C., Nov. 1953), which closed during previews; appeared in *King of Hearts* (Paper Mill Playhouse, Millburn, N.J., Summer 1955); was a resident actor at Elitch's Gardens, Denver, Colo. (Summer 1956); directed *The Mousetrap* (16 St. Th., Sept. 4, 1959); for The Lambs, directed *The White Sheep of the Family* (1963); and produced *The Lambs Gambol* honoring John Wayne (Waldorf-Astoria Hotel, N.Y.C., 1963).

Films. Mr. Thomas made his debut as Bobbie Phillips in *Wednesday's Child* (RKO, 1934); subsequently appeared in *A Dog of Flanders* (RKO, 1935); *Tim Tyler* (U, 1937); *Boy's Town* (MGM, 1938); *Angels Wash Their Faces* (WB, 1939); *On Dress Parade* (WB, 1939); *Code of the Streets* (U, 1939); eight Nancy Drew films (WB, 1939–41); *Invisible Stripes* (WB, 1940); *Flying Cadets* (U, 1941); *One Foot in Heaven* (WB, 1941); *The Major and the Minor* (Par., 1942); *Always in My Heart* (WB, 1942); *In Society* (U, 1942); *The Battle of City Hall* (WB, 1942); wrote the screenplays of *Mega-Monster* (Olympiad Films) and *Five Keys to Death*.

Television and Radio. From 1956 to 1960, Mr. Thomas performed on many radio shows, including This Is Your F.B.I., Mr. Keen, Quiet Please, Stella Dallas, Our Gal Sunday, Backstage Wife, Helen Trent, My True Story, Whispering Street; wrote additional dialogue for Quiet Please (WOR, 1948–50); commercials for Tetley Tea (1957–63); was radio spokesman for Bengay (1959–60).

He appeared in and served as writer and associate producer for the first daily television serial Women to Remember (Dumont, 1948); wrote commercials for the Arthur Murray Show (ABC, 1949); scripts for Volume One (ABC, 1948); Escape (CBS, 1949); appeared in the title role of Tom Corbett, Space Cadet (CBS, 1950; ABC, 1951–52; Dumont, 1953–54; NBC, 1955); wrote scripts and performed in commercials for the sponsors of the program.

Mr. Thomas has appeared on Danger (CBS); Crime Syndicated (CBS); Armstrong Circle Theatre (NBC); Young Love (NBC, 1956); The Guiding Light (CBS, 1957); As the World Turns (CBS, 1958–59); and Love of Life (CBS, 1958); wrote (1958–60) scripts for True Story (NBC), including *Mordecai's Mark*, *The Inheritance*, *That's Uncle Wyllis*, *The Perfect Pigeon*, and *The Three Hats*; and was executive producer of Four Star Television's series, Josie and Joe (synd., 1960–62).

Recreation. Golf, tennis, sailing.

THOMPSON, JAY. Playwright, composer, lyricist. b. Jennings Lewis Thompson, Jr., Dec. 27, 1927, Spartanburg, S.C., to Jennings Lewis Thompson, Sr., and Elizabeth (Lake) Thompson. Father, attorney. Grad. Spartanburg H.S., 1945; attended Wofford Coll. 1945–46; studied with Hans Conradi at Peabody Conservatory, Baltimore, Md., 1948–49; grad. Converse Coll. (Pi Kappa Lamda Award for highest school achievement, 1953), B. Mus. 1953; studied with Gustave Reese and Curt Sachs at New York Univ., 1953–55. Member of AEA; Dramatists Guild; AFM; ASCAP; Pi Kappa Lambda; Mu Sigma.

Theatre. Mr. Thompson was musical director for summer-theatre productions at Hilltop Th. (Baltimore, Md., Summer 1955); and Mill Playhouse (Hammonton, N.Y., Summer 1955); and for a summer touring production of *Where's Charley?* (1956); an ELT production of *Annie Get Your Gun* (Lenox Hill Playhouse, N.Y.C., Feb. 26, 1957); returned as musical director to Mill Playhouse (Hammonton, N.J., Summer 1957), where a revue entitled *Grist for the Mill*, written in collaboration with Bobby Herget and Tom Hansen, and a musical adaptation of *The Drunkard*, written with Mr. Hansen, were staged. Another revue, *Extracurricular*, which he also wrote with Mr. Hansen, was presented at Finch Coll., N.Y.C. (Spring 1958).

Mr. Thompson wrote songs and sketches for revues presented at Tamiment Th., Pa. While there, he and Marshall Barer wrote the book and lyrics for a musical entitled *The Princess and the Pea* (Aug. 1958). Alone, he wrote the short work *Fugue for Three Marys* (Chapel Players, Bway Congregational Church, N.Y.C., Mar. 22, 1959).

The Princess and the Pea was expanded by the authors and Dean Fuller and retitled *Once Upon a Mattress* (Phoenix, May 11, 1959; moved Alvin, Nov. 25, 1959). He wrote the one-act musical, *The Bible Salesman* (Chapel Players, Bway Congregational Church, Feb. 21, 1960); wrote the music and lyrics for the sketch "Pill Parade" included in the revue *From A to Z* (Plymouth, Apr. 20, 1960); wrote book, lyrics, and music for *The Oldest Trick in the World*, which was presented with *The Bible Salesman* under the title *Double Entry* (Martinique, Feb. 20, 1961; Croydon Th., London, 1961).

He wrote, with David Axelrod, Portia Nelson, and others, *Three Cheers for the Tired Businessman*, for which he also did musical supervision and arrangements (Happy Medium Th., Chicago, Ill., Dec. 26, 1963); wrote, with Nina Savo, the book for *Royal Flush*, for which he also wrote the music and lyrics (pre-Bway: opened Shubert Th., New Haven, Conn., Dec. 31, 1964; closed Shubert Th., Philadelphia, Pa., Jan. 20, 1965); and did dance music arrangements for *Lorelei* (Palace, N.Y.C., Jan. 27, 1974).

Television. Mr. Thompson was musical director for WAAM-TV (Baltimore, Md., 1949–51). *Once Upon a Mattress* was presented as a CBS Special (June 3, 1964), with dance music and background music composed by Mr. Thompson.

Night Clubs. He has contributed material to Julius Monk's *Demi-Dozen* (N.Y.C., Sept. 1958); and has written special material for such night club performers as Dorothy Loudon and Jaye P. Morgan.

Recreation. Magic, mathematics, reading murder mysteries.

THOMPSON, SADA. Actress. b. Sada Carolyn Thompson, Sept. 27, Des Moines, Iowa, to Hugh Woodruff and Corlyss Elizabeth (Gibson) Thompson. Grad. Scotch Plains (N.J.) H.S.; Carnegie Inst. of Technology, B.F.A. Married Dec. 18, 1949, to Donald E. Stewart; one daughter, Liza, costume designer. Member of AEA (former council mbr.); AFTRA; SAG. Address: 35-64 80th St., Jackson Heights, NY 11372.

Theatre. Miss Thompson made her stage debut at the Carnegie Inst. of Technology as Nick's Ma in *The Time of Your Life* (1945); and first appeared on the professional stage as Harmony Blueblossom in *The Beautiful People* (University Playhouse, Mashpee, Mass., June 30, 1947), where she also appeared as Lady Bracknell in *The Importance of Being Earnest* (July 7, 1947), the title role in *Peg o' My Heart* (July 14, 1947), and Adamina Wood in *Dawn from an Unknown Ocean* (Aug. 25, 1947); Eileen in *Where Stars Walk* (July 12, 1948), Leda in *Amphitryon 38* (July 26, 1948), Nina in *The Seagull* (Aug. 9, 1948), and Ruth in *Thunder on the Left* (Aug. 30, 1948).

She played the title role in *Joan of Lorraine* (Pittsburgh Playhouse, Pa., Oct. 7, 1948); Mrs. Phelps in *The Silver Cord* (Morris Kaufmann Memorial Th., Pittsburgh, Mar. 29, 1949); and in stock at the Henrietta Hayloft (Th.), Rochester, N.Y. (Summer 1949), played Mrs. Higgins in *Pygmalion* (June 30), Emily Creed in *Ladies in Retirement* (July 6), Peg in *Peg o' My Heart* (July 13), the title role in *Jenny Kissed Me* (Aug. 3), Mrs. Montgomery in *The Heiress* (Aug. 17), Emily Webb in *Our Town* (Aug. 24), Raina Petkoff in *Arms and the Man* (Aug. 31), and Madame Arcati in *Blithe Spirit* (Sept. 4).

She appeared as Gail in *Happy Birthday* (Playhouse, Erie, Pa., Oct. 18, 1949); with the Children's Touring Th., Pittsburgh, played in *Indian Captive* (Mar. 7, 1950) and *Alice in Wonderland* (Apr. 26, 1950).

At the Hayloft Th. (Summer 1950), she played Billie Dawn in *Born Yesterday* (July 4), Muriel in *Ah, Wilderness!* (July 11), Annie Marble in *Payment Deferred* (July 18), Jackie Coryton in *Hay Fever* (July 25), Birdie Hubbard in *The Little Foxes* (Aug. 8), Bette Logan in *Heaven Can Wait* (Aug. 15), Frances Black in *Light Up the Sky* (Aug. 22), Hilda Manney in *Room Service* (Sept. 5), and Donna Lucia D'Alvadorez in *Charley's Aunt* (Sept. 12). She played Isabel in a reading of *The Enchanted* (Pittsburgh Playhouse, Pa., Nov. 26, 1950); Carmella in *Halloween Bride* (Arena Th., Rochester, N.Y., Sept. 6, 1951); Peg in *Peg o' My Heart* (Pittsburgh Playhouse, Feb. 23, 1952); and understudied Ruth Warrick in the pre-Bway tryout of *A Certain Joy* (opened Playhouse, Wilmington, Del., Feb. 12, 1953; closed Locust, Philadelphia, Feb. 21, 1953).

She made her N.Y.C. debut in a reading of *Under Milk Wood* (Kaufmann Aud., May 14, 1953), playing several parts; played in a tryout of Dos Passos' *U.S.A.* (White Barn Th., Westport, Conn., Aug. 8, 1953); and played Patty in *The Moon Is Blue* (Niagara Falls, Summer Th., Ontario, Sept. 7, 1953). At the Totem Pole Playhouse, Fayetteville, Pa. (Summer 1954), she again played Peg in *Peg o' My Heart* (July 5, 1954), Nita Havemeyer in *For Love or Money* (July 12), and Leona Samish in *The Time of the Cuckoo* (July 19).

She played Mrs. Heidelberg in *The Clandestine Marriage* (Provincetown, N.Y.C., Oct. 2, 1954); took part in a reading of *Murder in the Cathedral* (Kaufmann Aud., Dec. 12, 1954); was understudy to Betty Field as Sally Ann Peters in *Festival* (Longacre, Jan. 18, 1955); appeared as Cornelia in *The White Devil* (Phoenix, Mar. 14, 1955); played Lavinia Chamberlayne in *The Cocktail Party* (Barter Th., Abingdon, Va., July 4, 1955); Feng Nan in *The Carefree Tree* (Phoenix, N.Y.C., Oct. 11, 1955); and appeared as Laura in *The Glass Menagerie* (Inst. for the Blind, NYC, Nov. 30, 1955). At the Totem Pole Playhouse (Summer 1956), she played Lizzie Curry in *The Rainmaker* (July 23, 1956), and the title role in *Anastasia* (July 30, 1956); gave a reading from the poems of Dylan Thomas (Donnell Memorial Library Th., N.Y.C., Oct. 1956); played Eliante in *The Misanthrope* (Th. East, Nov. 12, 1956); Isadora Duncan and Eleanor Stoddard in *U.S.A.* (ANTA Matinee Series, Th. de Lys, Dec. 18, 1956); appeared as Valerie Barton in *The River Line* (Carnegie Hall Playhouse, Jan. 2, 1957); and Masha in *The Three Sisters* (Arena Stage, Washington, D.C., Apr. 9, 1957). At the Amer. Shakespeare Festival, Stratford, Conn. (Summer 1957), she played Emilia in *Othello* (June 22) and Margaret in *Much Ado About Nothing* (Aug. 3); played the latter part in the touring production of the play (opened Locust Th., Philadelphia, Dec. 30, 1957; closed Shubert, Boston, Feb. 17, 1958); appeared as Babakina in *Ivanov* (Renata, N.Y.C., Oct. 7, 1958); Mrs. Coyne in the musical *Juno* (Winter Garden, Mar. 9, 1959); and Nastasya Filippovna in a reading of *The Idiot* (Masters Inst., Oct. 1959). At the Amer. Shakespeare Festival, she played Mistress Quickly in *The Merry Wives of Windsor* (July 8, 1959) and a Widow of Florence in *All's Well That Ends Well* (July 29, 1959); played her original roles in *U.S.A.* (Royal Poinciana Playhouse, Palm Beach, Fla., Nov. 29, 1959); and at the Amer. Shakespeare Festival, played Maria in *Twelfth Night* (June 3, 1960), Juno in *The Tempest* (June 14, 1960), and Octavia in *Antony and Cleopatra* (July 22, 1960).

She appeared as Nastasya Filippovna in *The Idiot* (Chrysler Aud., Rye, N.Y., Nov. 20, 1960); played several parts in the revival of *Under Milk Wood* (Circle in the Square, Mar. 29, 1961); Emma Crosby in *Diff'rent* (NY Playhouse, Hyde Park, July 1961); at the Amer. Shakespeare Festival, appeared as the Duchess of York in *Richard II* (June 17, 1962), and Lady Percy in *Henry IV, Part 1* (June 18, 1962); played Mrs. Molloy in a touring production of *The Matchmaker* (NY State Th., Oct. 8–Nov. 22, 1962); Mrs. Rhythm in *The Last Minstrel* (Pocket, May 8, 1963); appeared in a tryout of *The Wind of Heaven* (Westport Country Playhouse, Conn., Oct. 22, 1963); *Long Day's Journey into Night* (Fred Miller Th., Milwaukee, Wis., Mar. 11, 1964); played Emilia in *Othello* (Delacorte, N.Y.C., July 14, 1964); Dorine in *Tartuffe* (ANTA-Washington Sq. Th., Jan. 14, 1965); repeated her role in *Tartuffe* (Amer. Conservatory Th., San Francisco, Calif., Jan. 21, 1966); appeared in *Dear Liar* (ACT, San Francisco, 1966 season); played Amanda in *The Glass Menagerie* (Milwaukee Repertory Th., Mar. 17, 1966); Florence Edwards in *Johnny No-Trump* (Cort Th., N.Y.C., Oct. 8, 1967); appeared in *A Delicate Balance* (Studio Arena, Buffalo, Feb. 8, 1968); in repertory at Studio Arena, Buffalo, played Mommy in *The American Dream* on a double-bill with *The Death of Bessie Smith* (Sept. 10, 1968) and Winnie in *Happy Days* (Sept. 20, 1968); this repertory was then transferred to the Billy Rose Th., N.Y.C., the double-bill opening Oct. 2, and *Happy Days* opening Oct. 12, 1968; played Mrs. Darlene Finch in *An Evening for Merlin Finch* on a double-bill with *A Great Career* (Forum Th., Lincoln Center, Dec. 29, 1968); Lady Macbeth in *Macbeth* (APA at the Univ. of Michigan, Sept. 16, 1969); Beatrice in *The Effects of Gamma Rays on Man-in-the-Moon Marigolds* (Mercer-O'Casey Th., N.Y.C., Apr. 7, 1970); Christine Mannon in *Mourning Becomes Electra* (Amer. Shakespeare Festival Th., Stratford, Conn., June 16, 1971); the title roles in *Emily, Celia, Dorothy,* and *Ma,* presented under the collective title *Twigs* (Broadhurst, N.Y.C., Nov. 14, 1971; and on tour, 1972); appeared in *The Cherry Orchard* (Geary Th., San Francisco, Mar. 19, 1974); and played Rosa in *Saturday Sunday Monday* (Martin Beck Th., N.Y.C., Nov. 21, 1974).

Films. Miss Thompson appeared as Margaret in *You Are Not Alone* (Himan Brown, 1961); *The Pursuit of Happiness* (Col., 1971); and *Desparate Characters* (ITC, 1971).

Television and Radio. She was on CBS radio as Jane Stewart, Your Shopping Reporter (June 5, 1955). On television she has appeared on the Goodyear Playhouse (NBC, 1954); Rocky King, Detective (Dumont); Robert Montgomery Presents (NBC); Kraft Th. (NBC); Camera Three (CBS); Big Story (NBC); Lamp Unto My Feet (CBS); The Everlasting Road (ABC); DuPont Show of the Month (NBC); The Nurses (CBS); Owen Marshall (ABC); Love Story (ABC); *Carl Sandburg's Lincoln;* and Family (CBS); as well as the major talk shows.

Awards. She received the Drama Desk's Vernon Rice Award for her performance in *The River Line,* and *The Misanthrope* (1957); and the *Village Voice* Off-Bway (Obie) Award, 1964–65, for her performance in *Tartuffe.* For her performance in *The Effects of Gamma Rays on Man-in-the-Moon Marigolds,* she received the Drama Desk, Off-Bway (Obie), and *Variety's* Poll of Off-Bway Critics awards, and *Best Plays* citation as Best Actress (1969–70); and for *Twigs,* the Sarah Siddons, Drama Desk, *Best Plays, Variety's* Poll of NY Drama Critics, and Antoinette Perry (Tony) awards (1971–72).

Recreation. Reading.

THOMSON, VIRGIL. Composer, music critic, musical director. b. Virgil Garnett Thomson, Nov. 25, 1896, Kansas City, Mo., to Quincy Alfred and May (Gaines) Thomson. Father, postal clerk. Grad. Central H.S., Kansas City, 1914; Kansas City Junior Coll., A.A. 1919; Harvard Coll., B.A. 1922; Syracuse Univ., D.F.A. 1946. Studied piano with H. Gebhard, organ with W. Goodrich, Boston, Mass., composition with Rosario Scalero, N.Y.C., Nadia Boulanger, Paris. Served WW I, US Army, field artillery and aviation; rank, 2nd Lt. Member of AGAC (member of board, 1957–to date); ASCAP (board of review, 1959–to date); AFM, Local 802; AGMA; Newspaper Guild; Fellow of American Academy of Arts and Sciences; American Academy of Arts and Letters; Honorable Order of Kentucky Colonels; Legion d' Honneur (officer). Address: 222 W. 23rd St., New York, NY 10011, tel. (212) CH 3-3700..

Theatre. Mr. Thomson wrote the opera *Four Saints in Three Acts* (Avery Memorial Th., Hartford, Conn., Feb. 8, 1934; 44 St. Th., N.Y.C., Feb. 20, 1934); composed incidental music for *A Bride for the Unicorn* (Brattle Th., Cambridge, Mass., 1935); *Macbeth* (Lafayette, N.Y.C., Apr. 9, 1936); *Injunction Granted* (Vanderbilt, July 24, 1936); Leslie Howard's *Hamlet* (Imperial, Nov. 10, 1936); composed the ballet *Filling Station* (Ballet Caravan, Avery Memorial Th., Jan. 6, 1937); incidental music for *Antony and Cleopatra* (Mansfield, Nov. 10, 1937); and was librettist, composer, and musical director for the opera *The Mother of Us All* (Brander Matthews Th., May 1947).

He composed incidental music for *Ondine* (46 St. Th., Feb. 18, 1954); composed the ballet *The Harvest According* (Metropolitan Opera House, Oct. 1954); and *Bayou* (NY City Ctr., 1956).

For the American Shakespeare Festival, Stratford, Conn., Mr. Thomson wrote incidental music for *King John* (June 26, 1956); *Measure for Measure* (June 27, 1956); *Othello* (June 22, 1957); *The Merchant of Venice* (July 10, 1957); and *Much Ado About Nothing* (Aug. 3, 1957); and composed incidental music for *Bertha* (Cherry Lane, Feb. 11, 1962).

Films. Mr. Thomson composed the scores for *The Plow That Broke the Plains* (1936); *The River* (1937); *The Spanish Earth* (1937); *Tuesday in November* (1945); *Louisiana Story* (Lopert, 1948); *Power Among Men* (United Nations, 1958); and *The Goddess* (Col., 1958).

He also wrote the music for *Journey to America* (US Pavillion, NY World's Fair, Apr. 1964).

Television. He composed music for and was musical director of *King Lear* (Omnibus, CBS, 1955).

Other Activities. He was music critic for the NY *Herald Tribune* (1940–54).

Published Works. He wrote *The State of Music* (1939 2nd ed. 1961); *The Musical Scene* (1945); *The Art of Judging Music* (1948); *Music Right and Left* (1951); *Music Reviewed: 1940–1954* (1966); *Virgil Thomson* (1966); and *American Music Since 1910* (1971).

Awards. Mr. Thomson received the David Bispham Medal for American Opera (1934); the Pulitzer Prize in Music for his score for the film *Louisiana Story* (1948); honorary Litt.D. degrees from Rutgers Univ. (1956), Park Coll. (1966), and Roosevelt Univ. (1968); and honorary Mus. Doc. degrees from Fairfield Univ. (1968) and New York Univ. (1971).

He received the Academic Medal from New York Univ. (1961); the Gold Medal for Music from the National Institute of Arts and Letters (1966); and the Brandeis Univ. Award (1961).

THRASHER, ETHELYN. Producer. b. Ethelyn Reid, June 28, 1912, Philadelphia, Pa., to Jackson G. and Delfa J. (Packard) Reid. Father, insurance appraiser; mother, Federal Court bailiff. Grad. Upper Darby (Pa.) H.S., 1930; studied cost accounting, Philadelphia Bus. Sch., 1931. Married Aug. 19, 1933, to Robert R. Thrasher; one son. Member of ATPAM.

Pre-Theatre. In charge of school funds for the Upper Darby (Pa.) School System.

Theatre. At the Colonial Playhouse (Aldan, Pa., 1940–45), Mrs. Thrasher was director-manager and played the title role in *Anna Christie,* Sadie Thompson in *Rain,* Mabel in *Three Men on a Horse,* Connie in *The Barker,* Miriam in *Guest in the House,* Mrs. Bramson in *Night Must Fall* Mama in *Papa Is All,* Aunt Hestor in *Bill of Divorcement,* Ellen in *Ladies in Retirement,* Mrs. Crochett in *The Great Big Doorstep,* Mme. Arcati in *Blithe Spirit,* Julia in *Theatre,* Julia in *Springtime for Henry,* Grace in *The Show-Off,* Connie in *Yes, My Darling Daughter,* Mrs. Pratt in *Ladies of the Jury,* Nancy in *Angel Street,* Mrs. Phelps in *The Silver Cord,* Connie in *Nine Pine Street,* Grace in *The Patsy,* and Millie in *Old Acquaintance.*

She was production manager for the Bucks County Playhouse (New Hope, Pa., Summer 1944); production manager (1952), manager (1952–1960), and in 1960 became producer for the Playhouse-in-the-Park (Philadelphia, Pa.), where she presented *Turn on the Night* (1961), *Garden in the Sea* (1962), *Winterkill* (1962), *Time of Hope,* adapted from C. P. Snow's novel of the same name (1963), and *Madly in Love* (1963). In N.Y.C., she was co-producer of *Me and Thee* (John Golden Th., Dec. 7, 1965).

Mrs. Thrasher was director and teacher of theatre and music at the Karay Studios (Philadelphia, Pa., 1948–49); and, in conjunction with the Playhouse-in-the-Park, Philadelphia, Pa., formed a professional children's theatre, running an annual national contest and producing new and original children's plays with music (1961–to date).

Television. Mrs. Thrasher taped nine one-hour children's shows (WFIL, 1962–63).

Recreation. Dancing, acting, reading, writing.

TICHENOR, TOM. Puppeteer, actor, director, playwright, designer, composer. b. Thomas Hager Tichenor, Feb. 10, 1923, Decatur, Ala., to Jacob Marshall and Emma (Moore) Tichenor. Father, educator; mother, dressmaker. Grad. Hume-Gogg, H.S., Nashville, Tenn., 1940; attended George Peabody Coll., 1946–48. Served US Army, 1943–45, ETO, Special Services; rank, Cpl. Member of AEA; AFTRA; SAG; Puppeteers of America.

Theatre. Mr. Tichenor first appeared, with his own marionettes, in *Puss in Boots* (Nashville, Tenn., Public Library, Nov. 1938); subsequently appeared with the Nashville Children's Theatre in *The Ghost of Mr. Penny* (Oct. 1939).

From 1947 to 1960, he was general consultant and director of children's entertainment for the Nashville Public Library, where he produced, directed, and appeared in weekly marionette shows. He designed costumes and wrote for *Night of the Full Moon* (Nashville Circle Th., May 1957); designed costumes for *The Tempest* (Memphis Shakespearean Festival, Tenn., Apr. 20, 1960) and designed costumes and wrote *The Dancing Princesses* (Nashville Children's Th., Dec. 10, 1960).

Mr. Tichenor created and supervised the puppets for *Carnival!* (Imperial Th., N.Y.C., Mar. 13, 1961), and for its subsequent national tours, as well as productions in England, Australia and South America. He wrote, produced, appeared in, and created puppets for *The Bremen Town Musicians* (Jan Hus House, N.Y.C., four weekends, commencing May 5, 1962). His adaptation of the Chinese folk tale *The Moon Maiden* was performed at the Museum of the City of New York's Puppet Exhibition (May 22, 1962); and at special Christmas programs at Museum of Contemporary Crafts (Dec. 15, 1962; Dec. 14, 1963).

He wrote *Trip to the Moon* (Jan. 1958); *Seven at One Blow* (Oct. 1959); *The Three Spinners* (Dec. 1959), children's plays which have been performed throughout the US.

Films. Mr. Tichenor made his debut as a Congressman in *Davey Crockett, King of the Wild Frontier* (Buena Vista, 1955). For The Festival of Gas Pavilion (NY World's Fair), he created puppets, produced, and appeared in *The Tale of Truthful George* (1964–65).

Television and Radio. From 1938 to 1942, Mr. Tichenor performed on weekly dramatic shows for WSIX (Nashville, Tenn.). In 1941–42, he wrote, directed, and performed on his own show, *Jerome, the Gnome* (WSIX); wrote and performed in *Wormwood Forest* (WSM, Nashville, 1947–49), *Bozo the Clown* (WSM, 1959–60); and *Tree House* (WKNO, 1960).

In N.Y.C., he has made guest appearances on *Memory Lane* (ABC, 1961); *Kraft Music Hall* (NBC, 1961); *Wonderama* (WNEW, 1962); *The Family Show* (NBC, 1962); the Today Show (NBC, 1962); *Funny Company* (WOR, 1964); and *Birthday House* (WNBC, 1964).

Other Activities. Mr. Tichenor designed stuffed animal toys for Bantam, adapted from puppets used in movie, *Tale of Truthful George.* He was artistic advisor for the Children's Department of the new Nashville (Tenn.) Public Library Building (1964); has been a dress designer and commercial artist. During the 1963 holiday season, he produced two puppet shows which were performed in Macy's (N.Y.C.) window.

Discography. Mr. Tichenor composed the music and wrote the lyrics for *Little Pioneer* (Col., 1955).

Awards. For *Wormwood Forest* (WSM, Nashville), Mr. Tichenor received the *Variety* Local Radio Programming Award (1948).

Recreation. Swimming, painting, furniture designing, building.

TILTON, JAMES F. Scenic designer, art director. b. James Floyd Tilton, July 30, 1937, Rochelle, Ill., to Norval B. and Magdeline Ripplinger (Marelli) Tilton. Father, photoengraver. Grad. West H.S., Rockford, Ill.; State Univ. of Iowa, B.A. 1959. Studied at Lester Polakov Studio of Stage Design, 1963. Served in US Army, Oct. 1959–Oct. 1962. Married Dec. 26, 1962, to Helga Strang. Member United Scenic Artists, Local 829. Address: 165 West 93rd St., New York, NY 10025, tel. (212) 222-5522.

Theatre. Mr. Tilton made his debut in the theatre playing the role of Ted in *Our Miss Brooks* at Rochelle (Ill.) Central School in 1951. While serving in the Army, he was resident designer, Frankfurt (Germany) Playhouse, where he did settings and lighting for *Silk Stockings* (June 1960); his first work for the professional stage was as set and lighting designer for a summer theatre production of *Finian's Rainbow* (John Drew Th., East Hampton, N.Y., July 1963).

He has since been active both on and off Bway and in regional theatres. He was principal designer (1963–70) for the Association of producing Artists (APA) Repertory productions in N.Y.C. and at Lydia Mendelssohn Th., Ann Arbor, Mich., where APA participated in the Univ. of Michigan Professional Theatre Program (PTP). He designed sets for *Much Ado About Nothing* (PTP, Ann Arbor, Oct. 8, 1963); *Scapin* and *Impromptu at Versailles* (Phoenix, N.Y.C., Mar. 9, 1964); and *The Lower Depths* (Phoenix, Mar. 30, 1964). Mr. Tilton did sets for Front St. Th., Memphis, Tenn., productions, in 1964, of *My Three Angels, Misalliance, The Taming of the Shrew, The Little Hut, The Sound of Music* (June 9), *The Country Wife* (July 22), *Damn Yankees* (Aug. 10), *My Fair Lady* (Sept. 20), *The Seven-Year Itch* (Oct. 22), and *Ah! Wilderness* (Nov. 19); and, in 1965, of *Roberta* (Jan. 14), *The Music Man* (Feb. 11), and *A Midsummer Night's Dream* (Apr. 8). He did settings and lighting for *Herakles* (PTP, Ann Arbor, Oct. 27, 1965); *You Can't Take It With You* (APA Rep. Co., Lyceum, N.Y.C., Nov. 23, 1965); *The Tavern* (Front St. Th., Memphis, Tenn., Dec. 23, 1965); scenery for *Guys and Dolls* (Front St. Th., Feb. 17, 1966); scenery for *Sweet of You to Say So, The Cat and the Moon,* and *Escurial* (all PTP, Ann Arbor, Sept. 27, 1966); and *The Flies* (Ann Arbor, Oct. 25, 1966).

He designed scenery for APA Repertory Co. (Lyceum, N.Y.C.) productions of *The School for Scandal* (Nov. 21, 1966), *Right You Are* (Nov. 22, 1966), *We Comrades Three* (Dec. 20, 1966), *The Wild Duck* (Jan. 11, 1967), *War and Peace* (Mar. 21, 1967), scenery and lighting for *Pantagleize* (Nov. 30, 1967) and *The Show-Off* (Dec. 5, 1967), lighting for *Exit the King* (Jan. 9, 1968), and scenery and lighting for *The Cherry Orchard* (Mar. 19, 1968). He designed the West Coast production of *The Latent Heterosexual* (Huntington Hartford Th., Los Angeles, Calif., May 2, 1968); designed scenery and lighting for APA Repertory Co. (Lyceum, N.Y.C.) productions of *The Cocktail Party* (Oct. 7, 1968) and *The Misanthrope* (Oct. 9, 1968); designed scenery and lighting for *Ballad for a Firing Squad* (Th. de Lys, Dec. 13, 1968); *Cock-a-Doodle Dandy* (APA Rep. Co., Lyceum, Jan. 20, 1969); *Hamlet* (APA Rep. Co., Lyceum, Mar. 3, 1969); scenery for *Oh! Calcutta!* (Eden Th., N.Y.C., June 17, 1969); scenery and lighting for *The Doctor's Dilemma* (Shaw Festival, Niagara-on-the-Lake, Ontario, Can., Summer 1969); *Macbeth* (PTP, Ann Arbor, Mich., Sept. 16, 1969); *Play* and *The Chronicles of Hell* (PTP, Ann Arbor, Sept. 1969); *Private Lives* (Billy Rose Th., N.Y.C., Dec. 4, 1969); *The Criminals* (PTP, Ann Arbor, Jan. 26, 1970; Sheridan Sq. Th., N.Y.C., Feb. 25, 1970); and *Harvey* (ANTA, N.Y.C., Feb. 24, 1970).

He designed *Love-In* (Kansas City Opera, Municipal Auditorium, May 1970); scenery, lighting, and projections for *The Merchant of Venice* (American Conservatory Th., San Francisco, Calif., Nov. 14, 1970); scenery and lighting for *The School for Wives* (Lyceum, N.Y.C., Feb. 16, 1971); scenery for the Bway engagement of *Oh! Calcutta!* (Martin Beck Th., Feb. 26, 1971); and he designed *Siamese Connections* (PTP, Ann Arbor, Mar. 16, 1971). He designed scenery, lighting, and projections for *The Selling of the President* (American Conservatory Th., San Francisco, Calif., Mar. 30, 1971); scenery for *Charley's Aunt* (Asolo Th., Sarasota, Fla., May 21, 1971); scenery for American Conservatory Th., San Francisco, Calif., productions of *Caesar and Cleopatra* (Oct. 30, 1971) and *Antony and Cleopatra* (Nov. 2, 1971); scenery for *The Grass Harp* (Martin Beck Th., N.Y.C., Nov. 2, 1971); scenery for *The Matchmaker* (Asolo Th., Sarasota, Fla., May 5, 1972); scenery and lighting for summer stock (John Drew Th., East Hampton, N.Y., Summer 1972); and scenery and lighting for *Rainbow* (Orpheum, N.Y.C., Dec. 18, 1972).

He designed scenery, lighting, and projections for *The Merchant of Venice* (Vivian Beaumont Th., Mar. 1, 1973); visual conception for *The Inspector General* (Edison Th., Jan. 28 & 29, 1973); scenery and lighting for *The Seagull* (Astor Place Th., Apr. 1973); *Miracle Play* (Playhouse II, Dec. 30, 1973); and for Studio Arena Th., Buffalo, N.Y., productions of *That Championship Season* (Jan. 3, 1974) and *Flint* (Jan. 31, 1974); scenery and lighting for *Seascape* (Sam S. Shubert Th., N.Y.C., Jan. 26, 1975); setting, lighting, and costumes for *The Marriage of Figaro* (Hancher Auditorium, Univ. of Iowa, Iowa City, Apr. 1975); and designed *Macrun's Guevara* (Playhouse II, N.Y.C., May 8, 1975). He has also designed industrial shows for Avon (Dec. 1973; 1974) and for Seagram and Seven-Up (both 1974).

Films. Mr. Tilton was art director for *Dear Dead Delilah* (Southern Star Productions, 1972).

Awards. For his lighting of *Seascape,* Mr. Tilton won an Antoinette Perry (Tony) Award in 1975 as best lighting designer.

TOBIAS, GEORGE. Actor. b. 1905, New York City. Father, actor; mother, actress. Member of AEA; SAG; AFTRA.

Pre-Theatre. Seaman, factory worker, odd jobs.

Theatre. Mr. Tobias played One of the Mob in *The Mob* (Neighborhood Playhouse, N.Y.C., Oct. 9, 1920); subsequently appeared in *The Fool* (Times Square Th., Oct. 3, 1922); played Corporal Lipinsky in *What Price Glory?* (Plymouth, Sept. 3, 1924); Carthalo in *The Road to Rome* (Playhouse, Jan. 31, 1927); the Sergeant of the Guard in *The Gray Fox* (Playhouse, Oct. 22, 1928); Ivan in *S.S. Glencairn* (Provincetown Playhouse, Jan. 9, 1929); Santiago in *Fiesta* (Provincetown Playhouse, Sept. 17, 1929); and appeared in *Elizabeth the Queen* (Guild, Nov, 3, 1930).

He played Alois in *Sailors of Cattaro* (Civic Repertory Th., Dec. 10, 1934); Bakovchen in *Black Pit* (Civic Repertory Th., Mar. 20, 1935); Meyer in *Paths of Glory* (Plymouth, Sept. 25, 1935); Ace in *Hell Freezes Over* (Ritz, Dec. 28, 1935); Pellegrino in the pre-Bway tryout of *Name Your Poison* (opened Shubert, Newark, N.J., Jan. 20, 1936); Gregory Smith in *Star Spangled* (John Golden Th., N.Y.C., Mar. 10, 1936); Harry Smithers in a stock production of *The Emperor Jones;* appeared in *What Price Glory?* (Suffern, N.Y., July 1936); played Boris Kolenkhov in *You Can't Take It with You* (Booth, N.Y.C., Dec. 14, 1936); and Hank Russo in *Good Hunting* (Hudson, Nov. 21, 1938).

He succeeded Harold Stone as Stosh in *Stalag 17* (48 St. Th., May 8, 1951), also touring in this role (opened Biltmore, Los Angeles, Calif., June 27, 1952); played Commissar Markovitch in *Silk Stockings* (Imperial, N.Y.C., Feb. 24, 1955); Appopolous in *Wonderful Town* (American Pavilion Th., Brussels World's Fair, Belgium, 1958); and succeeded Henry Corden as Maxwell Archer in *Once More with Feeling* (Alcazar, San Francisco, Calif., June 8, 1959).

Films. Mr. Tobias made his debut in *Maisie* (MGM, 1939); and has appeared in *Ninotchka* (MGM, 1939); *The Hunchback of Notre Dame* (RKO, 1939); *They All Come Out* (MGM, 1939); *Balalaika* (MGM, 1939); *City for Conquest* (WB, 1940); *South of Suez* (WB, 1940); *Music in My Heart* (Col., 1940); *East of the River* (WB, 1940); *River's End* (WB, 1940); *They Drive by Night* (WB, 1940); *The Man Who Talked Too Much* (WB, 1940); *Torrid Zone* (WB, 1940); *Saturday's Children* (WB, 1940); *Affectionately Yours* (WB, 1941); *The Strawberry Blonde* (WB, 1941); *Sergeant York* (WB, 1941); *Out of the Fog* (WB, 1941); *Captains of the Clouds* (WB, 1942); *Wings of the Eagle* (WB, 1942); *My Sister Eileen* (Col., 1942); *This Is the Army* (WB, 1943); *You're in the Army Now* (WB, 1941); *Air Force* (WB, 1943); *The Mask of Dimitrios* (WB, 1944); *Between Two Worlds* (WB, 1944); *Objective, Burma!* (WB, 1945); *Her Kind of Man* (WB, 1946); *Nobody Lives Forever* (WB, 1946); *My Wild Irish Rose* (WB, 1947); *Sinbad the Sailor* (RKO, 1947); *The Set-Up* (RKO, 1949); *Everybody Does It* (20th-Fox, 1949); *The Judge Steps Out* (RKO, 1949); *Southside 1000* (Allied, 1950); *Mark of the Renegade* (U, 1951); *Magic Carpet* (Col., 1951); *Ten Tall Men* (Col., 1951); *Rawhide* (20th-Fox, 1951); *The Tanks Are Coming* (WB, 1951); *Desert Pursuit* (Mono., 1952); *The Glenn Miller Story* (U, 1954); *The Tall Men* (20th-Fox, 1955); *The Seven Little Foxes* (Par., 1955); *Silk Stockings* (MGM, 1957); *The Tattered Dress* (U, 1957); *Marjorie Morningstar* (WB, 1958); *Bullet for a Badman* (U, 1964); *Nightmare in the Sun* (Zodiac, 1965); *The Glass Bottom Boat* (MGM, 1966); and *The Phynx* (WB, 1970).

Television and Radio. Mr. Tobias performed in the radio play *Schoolhouse at the Front* (Cavalcade of America, NBC, July 19, 1943).

For television he appeared in *Here Lies François Gold* (Telephone Time, ABC, Sept. 17, 1957); *To Walk the Night* (Climax! CBS, Dec. 19, 1959); The Deputy (ABC, 1964); Sam Benedict (Ind., 1964); The Loretta Young Show (NBC, 1964); Bob Hope Presents (NBC, 1964); The Joey Bishop Show (CBS, 1964); Bewitched (ABC, 1965–67); 77 Sunset Strip (Ind., 1965); The Untouchables (Ind., 1966); and The Man from U.N.C.L.E. (NBC, 1967).

Recreation. Baseball, music, record collecting.

TOLAN, MICHAEL. Actor. b. Detroit, Mich., to Morris and Gertrude (Gold) Tuchow. Grad. Central H.S., Detroit, Mich., 1943; Wayne Univ., B.A. 1947. Studied with Stella Adler, N.Y.C., 1950–54. Married June 28, 1966, to Rosemary Forsyth, actress. Member of SAG; AFTRA; AEA (mbr., gov. council, 1961–to date).

Theatre. Mr. Tolan was founder of The Actors' Co., Detroit, Mich. (1947), where he appeared in repertory productions as Dr. Astrov in *Uncle Vanya,* Rev. Morell in *Candida,* John Worthing in *The Importance of Being Earnest,* and the title role in *Oedipus* (1947–49).

He played a Senatorial Messenger and First Sentinel in *Coriolanus* (Phoenix, N.Y.C., Jan. 19, 1954); a Chauffeur in *Will Success Spoil Rock Hunter?* (Belasco, Oct. 13, 1955), later replacing (Apr. 16, 1956) Walter Matthau as Michael Freeman; Mother in *A Hatful of Rain* (Lyceum, Nov. 9, 1955); John Rivers in *The Genius and the Goddess* (Henry Miller's Th., Dec. 9, 1957); succeeded (Jan. 10, 1958) Gerald Sarracini as Igor Romanoff in *Romanoff and Juliet* (Plymouth, Oct. 10, 1957); performed at the YMHA Poetry Series in *Murder in the Cathedral* and

Tower Beyond Tragedy (Kaufmann Concert Hall, N.Y.C., 1956) repeating the performance at the Library of Congress, Washington, D.C., with the Vox Poetica group (1958); and was guest reader for the Poetry Society of America (N.Y.C., 1958, 1964).

He played Jerome Black in *A Majority of One* (Shubert, Feb. 16, 1959); Freud in *A Far Country* (Music Box, Apr. 5, 1961; Huntington Hartford, Hollywood, Calif., Nov. 1961; Geary, San Francisco; Dec. 1961); appeared in winter stock as Rudd Kendall in *Old Acquaintance* (Royal Poinciana Playhouse, Palm Beach, Fla., 1961); played Ralph Granger in the pre-Bway tryout of *Banderol* (opened Forrest, Philadelphia, Pa., Sept. 17, 1962; closed there Sept. 22, 1962).

Mr. Tolan is one of the founders and a member of the board of trustees of the American Place Th., N.Y.C., a theatre for works-in-progress and readings of new American plays, which was incorporated in 1962 and received nonprofit corporation status in 1964.

During its first year of operation, American Place Th. presented readings of plays by William Goven, Robert Lowell, Niccolo Tucci, and Mary Lee Settle. Originally based at St. Clement's Church, the theatre moved into its own new quarters in the Bway area in 1970.

As associate artistic supervisor of the American Place Th. (1964–71), Mr. Tolan produced *The Old Glory* (St. Clement's Church, Nov. 1, 1964; moved to Th. de Lys, N.Y.C., Jan. 14, 1965); and subsequently at St. Clement's, *The Outside Man* (Dec. 16, 1964); *Lower Than the Angels* (Jan. 30, 1965); *Harry, Noon and Night* (Mar. 12, 1965); and *Juana La Loca* (May 12, 1965); was an associate director for *Brother to Dragons* (June 2, 1965), in which he played Lilburn Lewis; *A Step Away from War* (June 21, 1965); *Jonah* (Feb. 15, 1966); *The Journey of the Fifth Horse* (Apr. 21, 1966), in which he played Nikolai Alexeevich Chulkaturin; *Who's Got His Own* (Sept. 30, 1966); *Mercy Street* (Oct. 2, 1969); *Five on the Black Hand Side* (Jan. 1, 1970); *Two Times One* (Mar. 9, 1970); *The Pig Pen* (May 20, 1970); *Sunday Dinner* (Nov. 2, 1970); the first production in the new theatre, *The Carpenters* (American Place Th., Dec. 21, 1970); *Pinkville* (St. Clement's, Mar. 17, 1971); *Bog Bay Beast Bait* (Amer. Place Th., Apr. 29, 1971). He played Eli in *Eli the Fanatic*, part of a triple bill by Philip Roth entitled *Unlikely Heroes*, which also included *Defender of the Faith* and *Epstein* (Plymouth, Oct. 26, 1971).

Films. Mr. Tolan appeared as Duke Malloy in *The Enforcer* (WB, 1951); and played Lazarus in *The Greatest Story Ever Told* (UA, 1964).

With Albert Rubin, he formed Alto Productions to produce feature motion pictures and television series (Oct. 1965).

Television and Radio. On radio, he performed on The Lone Ranger, The Green Hornet, and Challenge of the Yukon (ABC, Detroit, Mich., 1945).

Mr. Tolan has appeared on television on the Eleventh Hour (NBC); The Nurses (CBS); Dupont Show of the Week (CBS); Route 66 (CBS); and the US Steel Hour (NBC); in *The Dybbuk, Volpone, Lament for a Bullfighter,* and *Wingless Victory* (Play of the Week series, WNTA-TV, 1960–61); as Dr. "Ski" Tazinski on the series The Nurses (CBS).

He has also appeared on Espionage (NBC); Ladies' Man (CBS); Naked City (Ind.); Eleventh Hour (Ind.); Play of the Week (NET); *The Journey of the Fifth Horse* (NET); Bob Hope Presents (NBC); Felony Squad (ABC); *Wallace Stevens: A Poet's Season* (NET); The Bell Telephone Hour (NBC); *Stage for Protest* (NET); Tarzan (NBC); Rat Patrol (ABC); The Invaders (ABC); Mannix (CBS); The F.B.I. (ABC); Mission: Impossible (CBS); Journey to the Unknown (ABC); Dan August (ABC); Owen Marshall (ABC); Nichols (NBC); Medical Center (CBS); Cannon (CBS); and Ghost Story (NBC).

Awards. He won the professional acting artist in residence fellowship to Stanford Univ., Calif., 1950; was nominated for the Sylvania Award for best television performance in a starring role for *Teddy Bear* (Kraft Th., NBC, 1957); and won the Broadway Show League's Most Valuable (baseball) Player Award (1959).

Recreation. Baseball, tennis.

TOMS, CARL. Designer. b. Kirkby-in-Ashfield, Nottinghamshire, England, May 29, 1927, to Bernard and Edith Toms. Mother, tailor. Educ. High Oakham School, Nottingham; Mansfield Coll. of Art. Professional training at Royal Coll. of Art; Old Vic School. Served in Royal Army Ordinance Corps, 1945–48. Member of United Scenic Artists; Association of Cinematograph Television and Allied Technicians. Address: (home) 49 Noel Rd., London, N.1, England tel. 836-4283; (bus.) c/o Trafalgar Perry Ltd., 12A Goodwin's Court, St. Martin's Lane, London, W.C.2, England tel. 240-3804.

Theatre. His first professional work as theatrical designer was for a production of *Apollo de Bellac* (Royal Court Th., London, May 14, 1957); followed by *Beth* (Apollo Th., Mar. 20, 1958); *Something To Hide* (St. Martin's Th., Apr. 29, 1958); *Susanna's Secret* (Glyndebourne Opera House, Sussex, July 18, 1958); the ballet *La Reja* (Ballet Rambert, Sadler's Wells Th., June 1, 1959); *The Complaisant Lover* (Globe, London, June 18, 1959); *The Seashell* (Edinburgh, Scotland, 1959); *No Bed for Bacon* (Bristol Old Vic, England, July 1959); the ballet *Pièce d'Occasion* (Festival Ballet, Festival Hall, London, 1959); *La Cenerentola* (Sadlers Wells Th., Oct. 29, 1959); *The Merry Wives of Windsor* (Old Vic, 1959); *New Cranks* (Lyric Th., Hammersmith, Apr. 1960); *Radamisto* (Sadler's Wells Th., 1960); and, with John Piper, *A Midsummer Night's Dream* (world premiere, Aldeburgh Festival, Suffolk, June 1960); *Susanna's Secret* (Edinburgh Festival, Scotland, Aug. 1960); *The Barber of Seville* (Sadler's Wells Th., London, 1960); *A Midsummer Night's Dream* (Old Vic, Dec. 1960); and *Camille* (Old Vic, July 1961, and world tour).

Also, *Alas, Poor Fred* (Rosehill Th., Cumberland, Oct. 1961); *Iphigenie en Tauride* (Edinburgh Festival, Aug. 1961; Royal Opera House, London, Sept. 1961); *Write Me a Murder* (Lyric, Mar. 1962); *A Time To Laugh* (Piccadilly Th., Apr. 1962); *Who'll Save the Plowboy?* (Haymarket, Apr. 2, 1963); *Our Man in Havana* (Sadler's Wells Th., London, July 2, 1963); *Midsummer Mink* (Th. Royal, Windsor, July 30, 1963); *Ballet Imperial* (Royal Opera House, London, Oct. 18, 1963); *Swan Lake* (Royal Opera House, Covent Garden, Dec. 12, 1963); *The Importance of Being Earnest* (Nottingham Playhouse, Nottingham, England, Dec. 18, 1963) and two productions previewed in Brighton before Latin American and Western European tours: *The Merchant of Venice* (Mar. 3, 1964) and *A Midsummer Night's Dream* (Mar. 4, 1964).

He also designed *A Singular Man* (Comedy Th., London, Oct. 21, 1964); *Public Mischief* (St. Martin's Th., May 12, 1965); the 1966 Edinburgh Festival's *The Trojan Women* (Aug.) and *The Winter's Tale* (Aug.; later presented in London at the Cambridge Th., Sept. 30, 1966); *She Stoops To Conquer* (Nottingham Playhouse, Dec. 7, 1966); *The Burglar* (Vaudeville Th., London, Feb. 22, 1967); *Fallen Angels* (Vaudeville Th., Apr. 4, 1967); the opera *Die Frau ohne Schatten* (Royal Opera House, Covent Garden, June 14, 1967); and the 1967 Edinburgh Festival's *A Midsummer Night's Dream* (Aug. 21; later presented in London at the Saville Th., Sept. 27, 1967), *The Tricks of Scapin* (Aug. 30), and *The Soldier's Tale* (Sept. 4). He designed for London's National Th. *Edward II* (Apr. 30, 1968) and *Love's Labour's Lost* (Dec. 1968); for the 1969 Chichester Festival *The Magistrate* (May 21; later presented in London at the Cambridge Th., Sept. 18, 1969) and *Antony and Cleopatra* (July 23); and he designed a production of the opera *Falstaff* (Welsh National Opera, Sept. 1969). He designed *Sleuth* (St. Martins Th., London, Feb. 12, 1970); *The Girl Friend* (Apollo Th., Feb. 17, 1970); and the 1970 Chichester Festival's *The Alchemist* (May 20) and *Vivat! Vivat Regina!* (May 20), the latter transferring to London (Piccadilly Th., Oct. 8, 1970).

In Aug. 1970, Mr. Toms was appointed head of design for the Young Vic Company. Productions he has designed since that time include, for the Young Vic, *Scapin* (Sept. 11, 1970) and *The Soldier's Tale* (Sept. 18, 1970); *Cyrano de Bergerac* (National, Oct. 20, 1970); the American production of *Sleuth* (Music Box, N.Y.C., Nov. 12, 1970); three more Young Vic productions: *The Taming of the Shrew* (Nov. 18, 1970), *The Wakefield Mystery Plays* (Dec. 5, 1970), and *King Stag* (Dec. 22, 1970); and a French production of *Sleuth* (Th. de la Michodière, Dec. 16, 1970).

For the 1971 Chichester Festival, he designed *The Rivals* (May 5), *Caesar and Cleopatra* (July 7), and *Reunion in Vienna* (July 21); he designed an American production of *Vivat! Vivat Regina!* (Broadhurst, N.Y.C., Jan. 20, 1972); designed *She Stoops To Conquer* (Young Vic, London, Feb. 3, 1972); another production of *Reunion in Vienna* (Piccadilly Th., Feb. 17, 1972); *The Beheading* (Apollo Th., Feb. 24, 1972); *Vivat! Vivat Regina!* (Birmingham Rep. Th., Birmingham, England, Mar. 2, 1972); for the Young Vic, *Deathwatch* and *The Maids* (Apr. 1972); designed costumes for two productions of the Guthrie Th., Minneapolis, Minn.: *A Midsummer Night's Dream* (July 7, 1972) and *The Relapse* (July 12, 1972); and he designed the San Francisco (Calif.) Opera production of *Lucia di Lammermoor* (Nov. 8, 1972). He designed *Fanfare for Europe* (Royal Opera House, Covent Garden, London, Jan. 1973); *Dear Love* (Comedy Th., London, May 16, 1973); *French without Tears* (Young Vic, July 27, 1973); *Much Ado About Nothing* (Europalia, Brussels, Belgium, Oct. 9, 1973; Young Vic, London, England, Oct. 19, 1973); *Section 9* (Royal Shakespeare Co., Place Th., London, Oct. 1973); the opera *Peter Grimes* (San Francisco Opera, Oct. 27, 1973); and the opera *I Puritani* (NY City Opera, Los Angeles, Calif., Nov. 28, 1973, and NY State Th., Lincoln Ctr., N.Y.C., Feb. 1974).

Mr. Toms also designed *Sherlock Holmes* (Aldwych Th., London, Dec. 22, 1973; Broadhurst, N.Y.C., Nov. 13, 1974); *The Waltz of the Toreadors* (Haymarket, London, Feb. 14, 1974); three productions for the 1974 American engagement of the Young Vic Co. at the Brooklyn Acad. of Music, N.Y.C.: *The Taming of the Shrew* (Mar. 7), *Scapino* (Mar. 13), and *French without Tears* (Mar. 15); *Travesties* (Royal Shakespeare Co., Aldwych Th., London, England, July 10, 1974); and, for Der Nederlandse Operastichting, Amsterdam, The Netherlands, a production of the opera *Un Ballo in Maschera* (Oct. 1974).

Films. Mr. Toms designed costumes for the films *She* (Hammer, 1965); *The Quiller Memorandum* (20th-Fox, 1966); *One Million Years B.C.* (20th-Fox, 1967); *Prehistoric Women* (1967); *Rocket to the Moon* (1967); *The Winter's Tale* (WB, 1968); *When Dinosaurs Ruled the Earth* (1970); and *Moon Zero Two* (1970).

Television. Mr. Toms began designing for television with *Nude With Violin* (ATV Globe, 1959), continuing with *Clutterbuck* (1959), *Autumn Garden* (1959), *Boule de Suif* (June 1961), and *The Sandcastle* (Mar. 21, 1963), all for ATV Globe, and *Twelfth Night* (ATV Network Ltd., Mar. 18, 1968).

Other Activities. Mr. Toms designed bridesmaids' dresses for the wedding of Her Royal Highness, The Princess Margaret (Westminster Abbey, May 1960); designed the gala performance for the state visit of the King and Queen of Nepal (Royal Opera House, Covent Garden, Oct. 1960); and was design consultant for the investiture of His Royal Highness, The Prince of Wales (Caernarvon Castle, Wales, July 1, 1969). He designed the gown worn by Raquel Welch for her presentation to Her Majesty, Queen Elizabeth, at the Royal Film Performance (Mar. 14, 1966); designed the program cover for the 1961 Glyndebourne Opera Season; the presentation gift voucher for the Royal Opera House, Covent Garden (Dec. 1961); the 1961 Christmas card for the Sunshine Charity Fund for the Blind Babies and the 1962 Christmas Card for the Girls' Guildry Charity; and designed the show cards for the opening of the Regency exhibitions, Royal Pavilion, Brighton (July 1962, 1963, 1964).

Mr. Toms also designed decorations for the Terrace Room, Dorchester Hotel, Park Lane, London (1961); the exhibition of Sekers Furnishing Fabrics at Woollands of Knightsbridge for West Cumberland and Silk Mills (Feb. 1961); decorated Nicolas Sekers' London House (1961); designed decorations for Quaglino's Restaurant, Bury St. Edmunds (Oct. 1961); completed decoration and structural alterations of the bar and restaurant, Barrie Room, Kensington Palace Hotel, London (Sept. 1962); painted the murals in the London home of Lady Rupert Nevill (1962); decorated the American Bar, Kensington Palace Hotel (June 1963); completed decoration and structural alterations of the entire Osbourne Hotel, Mumbles, Wales (Aug. 1963); and completed the re-designing of the Theatre Royal, Windsor (1965). Mr. Toms was also design consultant for the structural and interior work for the apartments of Her Royal Highness, The Princess Margaret, Countess of Snowden, in Kensington Palace.

Awards. Mr. Toms was made an Officer of the British Empire (O.B.E.), receiving the Order in the Prince of Wales' Investiture Honours (July 1969). He won an Antoinette Perry (Tony) Award in 1975 as best scenic designer for his *Sherlock Holmes* settings.

Recreation. Parrots, gardening, travel.

TOPAZ, MURIEL. Dance notator, administrator, choreographer, dancer. b. Muriel Helen Topaz, May 7, 1932, Philadelphia, Pa., to Joseph and Rhea (Rosenblum) Topaz. Father, manager. Grad. Olney H.S., 1950; attended New York Univ., 1950–51; Juilliard Sch. of Music, 1951–54; Dance Notation Bureau, teaching certification, 1954, professional notator certification 1962. Studied dance with Anthony Tudor, Martha Graham; Labanotation with Ann Hutchinson, N.Y.C., 1951–54; Lucy Venable, N.Y.C., 1954–56. Married June 5, 1954, to Jacob Druckman, composer, one son, one daughter. Member of Dance Notation Bureau (vice-pres., 1959–61; chmn., bd. of dir., 1961). Address: (home) 780 Riverside Dr., New York, NY 10032; (bus.) Dance Notation Bureau, 19 Union Sq. W., New York, NY 10003, tel. (212) 989-5535.

Theatre. Miss Topaz made her debut as a dancer in the role of Euridice in the ballet *Orfeo* (Neighborhood Playhouse, Philadelphia, Pa., 1948); danced in concert at the Academy of Music, Philadelphia, Pa. (1948); Plays and Players Th., Philadelphia, Pa. (1949); gave solo dance recitals at the Neighborhood Playhouse, Philadelphia, Pa.; danced in the opera, *Acres of Sky* (Brander Mathews Th., Columbia Univ., N.Y.C., 1952); in the ballets *Desert Gods* and *Brittania Triumphus* (Juilliard Sch. of Music, 1953); danced in and was notator of *With My Red Fires* (Juilliard Sch. of Music, 1954); danced in and choreographed for *Danses Roses et Noires* (Salle D'Iena, Paris, 1955); danced in and choreographed a concert at Arts du Mouvement (Paris, 1955); was choreographer of a dance concert at Henry St. Playhouse (N.Y.C., 1956); notator of sections of *Dawn in N.Y.* (Juilliard Sch. of Music, 1956); *Agon* (NY City Ctr., 1959); *Episodes* (NY City Ctr., 1960); *Day on Earth* (Connecticut Coll., 1960); the musical *Bye Bye Birdie* (Martin Beck Th., N.Y.C., Apr. 14, 1960); choreographer for King's-Town Playhouse, Bordentown, N.J. (1962); and Rider Coll., Trenton, N.J. (1963).

She has taught dance at her own private studio (Philadelphia, Pa., 1948–50); YWHA (Jersey City, N.J., 1951); Société de la Danse (Paris, 1955); her own studio in N.Y.C. (1956–59); has taught dance notation at Juilliard Sch. of Music (1959–70); the Dance Notation Bureau (1961–to date); and Jacob's Pillow, Lee, Mass. (1961).

Miss Topaz supervised the training of professional notators under a Rockefeller grant (1964) and is a Fellow of the International Council of Kinetography Laban (ICKL) (1963–to date). Miss Topaz was rehearsal director of the Juilliard Dance Ensemble (1966–68), acting as assistant to Jose Limon and Anna Sokolow. She has acted as dance coordinator for the Research Personel Program at Lincoln Center (1967–68) and is currently director of Labanotation at the Dance Notation Bureau.

Miss Topaz was notator of the Joffrey Ballet's production of Jerome Robbins' *Interplay;* American Ballet Theatre's production of Jerome Robbins' *Les Noces;* Paul Taylor's *Three Epitaphs;* Juilliard Sch. of Music's production of Anna Sokolow's *Odes Duet;* Anthony Tudor's *Jardin aux Lilas;* and José Limon's *The Moor's Pavane.*.

TORN, RIP. Actor, director. b. Elmore Rual Torn, Feb 6, 1931, Temple, Tex., to Elmore Rual and Thelma (Spacek) Torn. Father, economist. Attended Longview (Tex.) H.S., 1944–47; grad. Taylor (Tex.) H.S., 1948; attended Texas A&M Coll., 1948–50; grad. Univ. of Texas, B.S. (Fine Arts) 1953. Studied diction with Alice Hermes, N.Y.C., eight years; voice with Simon Mitchnecic, N.Y.C., four years; singing with Al Malver, six years; acting with Sanford Meisner, N.Y.C., five months; and with Lee Strasberg, N.Y.C.; with Barucia Lumet, Dallas, Tex., six months; at the Martha Graham Sch. of Dance, N.Y.C., six months. Married Jan. 15, 1955, to Ann Wedgeworth, actress (marr. dis. June 1961); one daughter; married to Geraldine Page, actress. Served in the National Guard, eight years; rank, 1st Lt. Member of AEA; AFTRA; SAG; Actors' Studio (bd. of dir., prod. bd.; 1st chairman, founding comm.); Sigma Chi.

Pre-Theatre. Oilfield and pipeline roustabout, qualified architectural draftsman.

Theatre. Mr. Torn made his N.Y.C. debut succeeding (June 1956) Alex Nicol as Brick in *Cat on a Hot Tin Roof* (Morosco Th., Mar. 24, 1955); subsequently appeared as Val in a stock production of *Orpheus Descending* (Coconut Grove Playhouse, Miami, Fla., Mar. 1958); Bubba John in *Chaparral* (Sheridan Sq. Playhouse, N.Y.C., Sept. 9, 1958); Tom Junior in *Sweet Bird of Youth* (Martin Beck Th., Mar. 10, 1959), and succeeded (Jan. 1960) Paul Newman as Chance Wayne in the latter play, touring in it later that year.

He played Carlo in *Daughter of Silence* (Music Box, N.Y.C., Nov. 30, 1961); the title role in *Macbeth* (Univ. of Texas, Austin, Apr. 1962); Eben Cabot in *Desire Under the Elms* (Circle in the Sq., N.Y.C., Jan 8, 1963); succeeded (May 15, 1963) Ben Gazzara as Edmund Darrell in *Strange Interlude* (Hudson, Mar. 11, 1963); and played Lyle in *Blues for Mr. Charley* (ANTA, Apr. 23, 1964).

Mr. Torn also played Peter in *The Kitchen* (81 St. Th., June 13, 1966); Bernie Dodd in *The Country Girl* (NY City Ctr., Sept. 29, 1966); Marion Faye in *The Deer Park* (Th. de Lys, Jan. 31, 1967); and directed *The Beard* (Evergreen, Oct. 24, 1967). He was Roberto in *The Cuban Thing* (Henry Miller's Th., Sept. 24, 1968); directed the London, Eng., production of *The Beard* (Royal Court, Nov. 1968); directed *The Honest-to-God Schnozzola* (Gramercy Arts, N.Y.C., Apr. 21, 1969); and played Edward Morris in *Dream of a Blacklisted Actor* (Th. de Lys, Dec. 15, 1969). He was Edgar in *The Dance of Death* (Arena Stage, Washington, D.C., Apr. 16, 1970; Ritz Th., N.Y.C., Apr. 28, 1971); directed *Look Away* (Playhouse Th., Jan. 7, 1973); was William McLeod in *Barbary Shore* (Florence S. Anspacher Th., Dec. 18, 1973); the Captain in *The Father* (Yale Repertory Th., New Haven, Conn., Feb. 21, 1975); and Tom, Son in *The Glass Menagerie* (Circle in the Square, N.Y.C., Dec. 19, 1975).

Films. Mr. Torn made his motion picture debut as Brick in *Baby Doll* (WB, 1956). His later films include *Time Limit* (UA, 1957); *King of Kings* (MGM, 1961); *Hero's Island* (UA, 1962); *Sweet Bird of Youth* (MGM, 1962); *One Spy Too Many* (MGM, 1966); *Beach Red* (UA, 1967); *Beyond the Law* (Grove, 1968); *Sol Madrid* (MGM, 1968); *Coming Apart* (1969); *Tropic of Cancer* (Par., 1970); *Payday* (Cinerama, 1973); and *Crazy Joe* (Col., 1974).

Television. Mr. Torn has appeared on many television programs, including *Murder of a Sandflea* (Kraft Television Th., NBC, Sept. 1956); *The Blue Hotel* (Omnibus, ABC, Nov. 1956); *Wetback Run* (US Steel Hour, CBS, 1956); *So Short a Season* (Kaiser Aluminum Hour, NBC, Feb. 1957); *Number 22* (Alfred Hitchcock Presents, CBS, Feb. 1957); *The Big Wave* (Alcoa Presents, NBC, 1957); *The Little Bullfighter* (US Steel Hour, CBS, June 1957); *Hostages to Fortune* (Alcoa Hour, NBC, July 1957); *The Killer Instinct* (Kraft Th., NBC, Sept. 1957); *Bomber's Moon* (Playhouse 90, CBS, May 1958); *Johnny Belinda* (Hallmark Hall of Fame, NBC, Oct. 1958); *Murder and the Android* (Producers Showcase, NBC, Nov. 1959); *Face of a Hero* (Playhouse 90, CBS, Jan. 1959); *The Tunnel* (Playhouse 90, CBS, Dec. 1959); *Twenty-Four Hours in a Woman's Life* (CBS, Mar. 1961); The Untouchables (ABC, 1961, 1963); Frontier Circus (CBS, 1961); *Crazy Sunday* (Dick Powell Th., NBC, Dec. 1962); Naked City (ABC, 1962); Dr. Kildare (NBC, 1962, 1964); Route 66 (CBS, 1963); Channing (ABC, 1963); Eleventh Hour (NBC, 1964); Ben Casey (ABC, 1964); The Man from U.N.C.L.E. (NBC, 1965); *Monserrat* (Hollywood Television Th., WNET, Mar. 1971); Bonanza (NBC, 1971); Mannix (CBS, 1972); and he portrayed Walt Whitman in *Song of Myself* (PBC, Mar. 9, 1976).

Awards. Mr. Torn received the *Theatre World* Award (1959) for his portrayal of Bubba John in *Chaparral* and *Village Voice* Off-Bway (Obie) Awards in 1967, for his distinguished performance in *The Deer Park,* and in 1968, for his distinguished direction of *The Beard.*.

Recreation. Hunting, fishing, skin-diving, swimming, drawing, writing.

TOSER, DAVID. Costume designer. b. David Franz Toser, Milwaukee, Wis., to Franz Carl and Janet (Young) Toser. Father, retired business executive; mother, social activist. Grad. Milwaukee (Wisc.) Univ. Sch.; Brown Univ., B.A.; Yale Univ., M.F.A.; attended Parsons Sch. of Design, N.Y.C.; Art Students League, N.Y.C. Member of United Scenic Artists of America, Local 829. Address: 253 E. 77th St., New York, NY 10021, tel. (212) 734-4029.

Theatre. Mr. Toser made his debut as costume designer for *Christopher Fish,* a children's musical, presented off-Bway in 1962. He subsequently designed the costumes for the world premiere production of *After You, Mr. Hyde* (Goodspeed Opera House, East Haddam, Conn., June 24, 1968); for *Noel Coward's Sweet Potato* (Ethel Barrymore Th., N.Y.C., Sept. 29, 1968); *The Great White Hope* (Alvin, N.Y.C., Oct. 3, 1968); *Shoot Anything with Hair That Moves* (Provincetown Playhouse, N.Y.C., Feb. 2, 1969); *Does a Tiger Wear a Necktie?* (Belasco, N.Y.C., Feb. 25, 1969); *Our Town* (ANTA Th., N.Y.C., Nov. 27, 1969); *Any Resemblance to Persons Living* (Gate Th., N.Y.C., May 24, 1971); *Status Quo Vadis* (Brooks Atkinson Th., N.Y.C., Feb. 18, 1973); the world premiere of *Shenandoah* (Goodspeed Opera House, East Haddam, Conn., Aug. 12, 1974); and the U.S. premiere of *The Old Ones* (Th. at the Lambs, N.Y.C., Dec. 6, 1974). He was the costume supervisor for the London productions of *No, No, Nanette* and *Gypsy,* and has designed the costumes for several industrial shows.

Awards. Mr. Toser was the recipient of the Ethel Frankau Scholarship in Costume Design (Yale Drama Sch., 1963–64).

Recreation. Travel, reading, gardening, swimming, cooking.

TOWNES, HARRY. Actor. b. Sept. 18, Huntsville, Ala. Member of AEA; AFTRA; SAG.

Theatre. Mr. Townes appeared in a revival of *Tobacco Road;* and *Strip for Action* (Natl., N.Y.C., Sept. 30, 1942); played Tom Burton in *Mr. Sycamore* (Guild, Nov. 13, 1942); replaced David Wayne (Feb. 1948) as Og in *Finian's Rainbow* (46 St. Th., Jan. 10, 1947); played Feste in *Twelfth Night* (Empire, Oct. 3, 1949); Irv in *Gramercy Ghost* (Morosco, Apr. 26, 1951); Gordon Gray in *In the Matter of J. Robert Oppenheimer* (Mark Taper Forum, Los Angeles, 1967–68 season); appeared in *Red Roses for Me* (Goodman, Chicago, Jan. 3, 1969); again played Gordon Gray in *In the Matter of J. Robert Oppenheimer* (Vivian Beaumont Th., N.Y.C., Mar. 6, 1969); and appeared in *Ah, Wilderness* (Alley Th., Houston, Nov. 29, 1973).

Films. Mr. Townes' appearances include *Operation*

Manhunt (UA, 1954); *The Mountain* (Par., 1956); *The Brothers Karamazov* (MGM, 1958); *Cry Tough* (UA, 1959); and *Fitzwilly* (UA, 1967).

Television. He has performed extensively on all the major networks, his appearances including Bob Cratchitt in *A Christmas Carol* (Kraft Television Th., ABC, 1953); *The Andersonville Trial* (Climax, CBS, 1957); Judd for the Defense (ABC, 1968); and *Elizabeth the Queen* (1968).

TRASK, FRANKLIN. Producer, actor, educator. b. A. Franklin Trask, Aug. 17, 1907, Boston, Mass., to Albert M. and Bertha (Huntington) Trask. Father, railroad dispatcher. Grad. Dorchester (Mass.) H.S., 1926; Boston Univ., B.S. 1930; attended Harvard Univ., 1936–37; grad. New York Univ., M. Ed. 1938; Columbia Univ., A.M. 1939; Boston Univ., Ed. M. 1940; Staley Coll., Ph.D. 1943. Married 1938 to Alison Hawley. Member of National Assn. of Dramatics (pres., 1933–to date); Rotary International. Address: (home) Center Hill Rd., Plymouth, MA 02360, tel. (617) 224-3697; (bus.) c/o Priscilla Beach Theatre, Plymouth, MA 02360, tel. (617) 224-3886.

Theatre. Dr. Trask is the producer of the Cape Cod Th. (Yarmouth, Mass., 1933–to date). He has been producer at the Lake Shore Playhouse (Westford, Mass., 1933–36); presented two hundred plays at the Brattle Th. (Harvard Sq., Cambridge, Mass., 1944–49); and was producer of a circuit of twelve summer theatres presenting legitimate productions in resort cities in Massachusetts (1958–62). For thirty-five years, he operated a theatre school for actors in Plymouth, Mass.

Dr. Trask appeared as Dr. Haggert in a touring production of *The Late Christopher Bean* (Florida, 1937).

Other Activities. Dr. Trask is a former speech teacher for the Dale Carnegie Institute. His Franklin Trask Foundation is responsible for the yearly disposition of theatre scholarships to schools and little theatres.

Recreation. Living theatre, and is engaged in real estate investing and philanthropy.

TRAUBE, SHEPARD. Director, producer, writer. b. Feb. 27, 1907, Malden, Mass., to William and Helen Traube. Father, editor. Grad. DeWitt Clinton H.S., N.Y.C., 1925; attended Univ. of Pennsylvania, 1925–26; grad. New York Univ., B.S. (drama) 1929. Studied with Jasper Deeter (Hedgerow Th.), 1929. Married June 29, 1935, to Mildred Gilbert, director of the Balin-Traube Art Gallery; two daughters. Relatives in theatre: brother, Lenny L. Traube, talent representative; sister-in-law, Beverly Anderson Traube, talent representative. Served US Army, Signal Corps, 1942–45; rank, Maj.; received Meritorious Unit Citation and Mayor Fiorello La Guardia's Medal for Distinguished War Entertainment (1942). Member of SSD&C (founding pres., 1959–62); SDIG (exec. board, 1960–62); Intl. Inst. of Arts and Letters (fellow); Pi Lamda Phi. Address: 168 W. 86th St., New York, NY 10024, tel. (212) TR 3-1579.

Theatre. Mr. Traube was assistant stage manager for *Twelfth Night* (Maxine Elliot's Th., N.Y.C., Oct. 15, 1930); produced, with Sidney Harmon and Walter Holt *Precedent* (Provincetown Playhouse, Apr. 14, 1931); directed and produced, with Max Sonino, *No More Frontier* (Provincetown Playhouse, Oct. 21, 1931); and directed *A Thousand Summers*, presented by Arch Selwyn, by arrangement with Shepard Traube (Selwyn, May 24, 1932).

He produced and directed *The Sophisticrats* (Bijou, Feb. 13, 1933); *But Not for Love* (Empire, Nov. 26, 1934); *Angel Street* (John Golden Th., Dec. 5, 1941); directed *Winter Soldiers* (Studio Th., New Sch. for Social Research, Nov. 29, 1942); produced and directed *The Stranger* (Playhouse, Feb. 12, 1945); *The Gioconda Smile* (Lyceum, Oct. 7, 1950); and *The Green Bay Tree* (John Golden Th., Feb. 1, 1951).

He produced the national tour of *Bell, Book, and Candle*, by arrangement with Irene Selznick (opened Playhouse, Wilmington, Del., Dec. 21, 1951; closed Locust, Philadelphia, Pa., Mar. 14, 1953); directed *Time Out for Ginger*, which he produced with Gordon Pollock, in association with Don Hershey (Lyceum, N.Y.C., Nov. 26, 1952); directed *The Girl in the Pink Tights*, which he produced in association with Anthony B. Farrell (Mark Hellinger Th., Mar. 5, 1954); produced and directed *The Grand Prize* (Plymouth, Jan. 26, 1955); directed *Goodbye Again*, which he revived with J. H. Del Bondio (Helen Hayes Th., Apr. 24, 1956); and produced and directed *Holiday for Lovers* (Longacre, Feb. 14, 1957).

Mr. Traube directed *Monique*, which he produced in association with Stephen E. Sharmat (John Golden Th., Oct. 22, 1957); directed the national tour of *The Tunnel of Love* (opened Veterans War Memorial Aud., Columbus, Ohio, Oct. 4, 1958; closed Coliseum, Evanston, Ind., Dec. 6, 1958); directed the pre-Bway tour of *The Gay Felons* (opened Wilmington, Del., Feb. 12, 1959; closed Ford's, Baltimore, Md., Mar. 14, 1959); the pre-Bway tour of *Memo*, which he produced with Glenn Rose (opened Shubert, New Haven, Conn., Feb. 27, 1963; closed Wilbur, Boston, Mass., Mar. 9, 1963); directed and produced *Keep Off the Grass* (opened Mechanic Th., Baltimore, Md., April 3, 1972; closed Hanna Th., Cleveland, Ohio, Apr. 22, 1972); directed and produced, with Buff Cobb, *Children of the Wind* (opened Studebaker Th., Chicago, Ill., Sept. 26, 1973; closed Belasco Th., N.Y.C., Sept. 29, 1973).

Films. He directed and produced *Goose Step* (PRC, 1939); *Street of Memories* (20th-Fox, 1940); *For Beauty's Sake* (20th-Fox, 1941); *The Bride Wore Crutches* (20th-Fox, 1941); and *Once Upon a Coffee House*. .

Published Works. He wrote *So You Want to Go into the Theatre* (1936); the novel *Glory Road* (1935), and many articles published in such magazines as *Theatre Arts*. .

Awards. Mr. Traube was voted Best Director for *Angel Street* by the *Variety* Drama Critics Poll (1941–42). He directed *The Patriots*, which was voted Best Play of 1942–43 by the NY Drama Critics' Circle, and *The Winter Soldiers*, which was awarded the Sidney Howard Prize (1942).

Recreation. Photography, tennis.

TRAVERS, BEN. Playwright, novelist. b. Dec. 11, 1886, Hendon, Middlesex, England, to Walter Francis and Margaret (Burges) Travers. Attended Charterhouse, Surrey, England. Married Apr. 29, 1916, to Violet Mouncey (dec. 1951). Served WW I RNAS; rank, Maj.; WW II RAF (1939–43); rank, Squadron Leader; decorated with Air Force Cross. Member of Dramatists' Club, London (pres., 1956–60); Garrick Club, London.

Pre-Theatre. Publisher, with John Lane, of *The Bodley Head* (London, 1911–14).

Theatre. Mr. Travers adapted from his novel of the same name, *The Dippers* (Criterion, London, Aug. 22, 1922); and adapted from the Viennese, *The Three Graces*, with music by Franz Lehar (Empire, Jan. 26, 1924). He wrote a series of plays which were known as "The Aldwych Farces," because most had been produced at the same theatre with essentially the same cast. They were *A Cuckoo in the Nest* (Aldwych, July 22, 1925; revived by English Stage Co., Royal Court Th., Oct. 22, 1964); *Rookery Nook* (Aldwych, June 30, 1926; revived St. Martin's, May 23, 1942); *Thark* (Aldwych, July 4, 1927); *Plunder* (Aldwych, June 26, 1928); *Mischief* (Fortune, 1928); *A Cup of Kindness* (Aldwych, May 7, 1929); *A Night Like This* (Aldwych, Feb. 18, 1930); *Turkey Time* (Aldwych, May 26, 1931); *Dirty Work* (Aldwych, May 7, 1932); and *A Bit of a Test* (Aldwych, Jan. 30, 1933).

He also wrote *Chastity, My Brother* (Embassy, 1936); *O Mistress Mine* (St. James's, 1936); *Banana Ridge* (Strand, Oct. 15, 1938); *Spotted Dick* (Strand, Aug. 23, 1939); *She Follows Me About* (Garrick, Oct. 15, 1943); *Outrageous Fortune* (Winter Garden, Nov. 13, 1947); *Wild Horses* (Aldwych, Nov. 6, 1952); a revised version of *O Mistress Mine*, entitled *Nun's Veiling* (Bromley Repertory, 1953); *Corker's End* (1968); and *Rookery Nook* was the basis for the musical *Popkiss* (Cambridge Arts, May 16, 1972).

Films. Mr. Travers wrote screenplays for the following Gaumont-British productions, *Fighting Stock, Stormy Weather, Foreign Affairs, Lady in Danger, Dishonour Bright, Pot Luck, For Valour, Old Iron, Second Best Bed, Just My Luck*, and *The Chance of a Night-Time*, adapted from his novel *The Dippers;* also for British-Gaumont, wrote adaptations of the Aldwych Farces, *Rookery Nook, Mischief, A Cuckoo in the Nest, Thark, Plunder, A Cup of Kindness, A Night Like This*, and *Turkey Time*.

Television. *Rookery Nook, Thark, Plunder, A Cuckoo in the Nest*, and *A Cup of Kindness* have been presented on BBC (London). Mr. Travers also wrote *Potter* (BBC).

Published Works. He wrote the novels *The Dippers* (1921), *A Cuckoo in the Nest* (1922), *Rookery Nook* (1923), *Mischief* (1925), *Hyde Side Up* (1933); an anthology, *The Leacock Book* (1930); short stories, *The Collection To-Day* (1932); and an autobiography, *Vale of Laughter* (1957).

TRAVIS, MICHAEL. Costume designer. b. Louis Torakis, Apr. 13, 1928, Detroit, Mich., to Manos and Argero (Mbrokalakis) Torakis. Father, carpenter. Grad. Eastern H.S., Detroit, 1945; attended Ecole Guerre LaVigne, Paris, 1948–49; Sorbonne Univ., 1949–50. Served US Army, ETO, 1946–48; rank, S/Sgt. Member of United Scenic Artists, Local 829.

Theatre. Mr. Travis designed costumes for productions at the Music Fair, Camden, N.J., the Valley Forge Music Fair, Devon, Pa., and the Westbury (N.Y.) Music Fair (Summers 1955–58); for *Show Boat* at the Marine Theatre, Jones Beach, N.Y. (Summers 1956–57); *The King and I* and *Kismet* at the Paper Mill Playhouse (Millburn, N.J., 1956); and *The Golden Egg* at Ivoryton (Conn.) Playhouse (1957).

Also, for *Judy Garland at the Palace* (N.Y.C., May 1957); *Song of Norway* (Marine Th., Jones Beach, Summers (1958–59); for productions at the St. Louis (Mo.) Municipal Opera (1958); Eve Arden's *Auntie Mame* (Biltmore, Los Angeles, Calif., Sept. 8, 1958); *Once More with Feeling* (Natl., N.Y.C., Oct. 21, 1958); *Third Best Sport* (Ambassador, Dec. 30, 1958); *Happy Town* (54 St. Th., Oct. 7, 1959); *Hit the Deck* (Marine Th., Jones Beach, Summer 1960); *The Rape of the Belt* (Martin Beck Th., Nov. 5, 1960); *Rhinoceros* (Longacre, Jan. 9, 1961); the pre-Bway tryout of *High Fidelity* (opened Walnut, Philadelphia, Pa., Sept. 14, 1961; closed there Sept. 16, 1961); *Blood, Sweat and Stanley Poole* (Morosco, N.Y.C., Oct. 5, 1961); *A Cook for Mr. General* (Playhouse, Oct. 19, 1961); *Come on Strong* (Morosco, Oct. 14, 1962); *The Advocate* (ANTA, Oct. 14, 1963); *Conversations in the Dark* (opened Walnut, Philadelphia, Pa., Dec. 23, 1963; closed there Jan. 4, 1964); and *Roar Like a Dove* (Booth, May 21, 1964); *I Was Dancing* (Lyceum, Nov. 8, 1964); *Robert Frost: Promises to Keep* (Th. Group–UCLA, Los Angeles, Calif., July 7, 1965); and for the pre-Bway tryout of *The Hemingway Hero* (opened Shubert Th., New Haven, Conn., Feb. 21, 1967; closed Wilbur Th., Boston, Mass., Mar. 4, 1967).

Television. Mr. Travis was costume designer for *The Voice of Firestone* (ABC, 1957–59; 1961–63); Music for a Summer's Night (ABC, 1959); 26 shows on The Play of the Week (WNTA, 1959–60), including: *Medea, The Waltz of the Toreadors, The Cherry Orchard, The Emperor's Clothes, A Month in the Country, The White Steed, Don Juan in Hell, Juno and the Paycock, A Very Special Baby, Lullaby, The Climate of Eden, The Grass Harp, Volpone, Tiger at the Gates*, and *Thieves' Carnival;* the Frank Sinatra Special (ABC, 1960); Highways of Melody (NBC, 1961); and the Bell Telephone Hour (NBC, 1961–63). He was also costume designer for Rowan & Martin's Laugh-In (NBC, 1966–73) and for *The Andersonville Trial* (Hollywood Television Th., PBC, May 17, 1970).

Night Clubs. He designed costumes for a revised version of the revue *Meet the People* (Billy Rose's Diamond Horseshoe, N.Y.C., Apr. 13, 1955); for Lilo at the Persian Room of the Plaza Hotel

(N.Y.C., Oct. 1957); Los Chavalos de España at the Empire Room (Waldorf-Astoria Hotel, N.Y.C., 1957); Eartha Kitt in Las Vegas, Nev. (1957, 1958); Genevieve at the Empire Room (Waldorf-Astoria Hotel, 1961); Dolores Gray at the Empire Room (Waldorf-Astoria Hotel, 1962); and for the night club act of Dionne Warwick.

TROTMAN, WILLIAM C. Actor, director, designer. b. William Cecil Trotman, Oct. 19, 1930, Winston-Salem, N.C., to John Cecil and Maude (Bohannon) Trotman. Father, tobacco manufacturer. Grad. Reynolds H.S., Winston-Salem, N.C., 1949; attended Davidson Coll., 1949–52; grad. Univ. of North Carolina, A.B. 1954, M.A. 1955. Studied acting at the Amer. Th. Wing, 1955, Stella Adler Th. Studio, 1955. Served US Army, 1956–57; rank, Sp. 3; received Commendation Medal, 1957. Member of AEA. Address: (home) 3128 Bonhurst Dr., Winston-Salem, NC 27106, tel. (919) 725-2493; (bus.) Alley Theatre, 615 Texas Ave., Houston, TX 77002, tel. (713) 228-9341.

Theatre. Mr. Trotman is currently staff director, head of design and resident actor at the Alley Theatre (Houston, Tex.). He was director and general manager of *Sword of Gideon* (Kings Mountain, N.C., June 1954); appeared in stock productions at the Barn Th. (Augusta, Mich., May, 1955); was resident actor and scenic designer at the Erie Playhouse (Erie, Pa., 1955, 1957, 1959); at the Alley Th. (Houston, Tex., 1959–to date); performed in the outdoor drama, *Unto These Hills* (Cherokee, N.C., 1958, 1960, 1961, 1963); was director of drama, Governor's Sch. of N.C. (Summer 1964–65); dean of drama, N.C. Sch. of the Arts (1965–66); resident designer of Attco, Inc. (Honolulu, Hawaii, 1966–70); designer for the Honolulu (Hawaii) Civic Light Opera (Summers 1966–70); resident actor and designer for Symposium I and II, (Canadian tour, 1967–68); acted in *Red, White, and Maddox* (Cort, N.Y.C., Jan. 26, 1969); and was actor and designer for the Charles Playhouse (Boston, 1969–70).

Films. Mr. Trotman was an assistant producer with Gordon Kay Associates, Hollywood, Calif. (1958).

Awards. He received Carolina Playmakers Alumnal Award (Univ. of North Carolina, 1969).

TROY, LOUISE. Actress, singer. b. Louise J. Troy, Nov. 9, New York City. Attended Friends Seminary, N.Y.C. Studied acting at AADA; with Lee Strasberg, Stella Adler, N.Y.C. Member of AEA; AFTRA; SAG. Address: One University Place, New York, NY 10003; 8358 Sunset Blvd., Los Angeles, CA 90069.

Theatre. Miss Troy first appeared on stage as the Sphinx in *The Infernal Machine* (The Club Th., N.Y.C.), subsequently played Jessica in their production of *The Merchant of Venice* (Jan. 7, 1955); Marjorie in *Pipe Dream* (Shubert Th., Nov. 30, 1955); Sophie Otford in *Conversation Piece* (Barbizon-Plaza Th., Nov. 18, 1957); joined the cast of the revue *Salad Days* (Barbizon-Plaza Th., Nov. 10, 1958); played the Exiled Queen Natasha in a stock tour of *Royal Enclosure* (Summer 1960); appeared in the revue *O, Oysters!!!* (Village Gate, Jan. 26, 1961); and played Annie in *Anatol* (Cambridge Art Center, Mass., Summer 1961).

She played Dominique in *A Shot in the Dark* (Booth, Oct. 18, 1961); Mrs. Kristine Linde in *A Doll's House* (Th. Four, Feb. 2, 1963); Natalia Mayovskaya in *Tovarich* (Bway Th., Mar. 18, 1963); Ruth in *High Spirits* (Alvin, Apr. 7, 1964); Maggie Hobson in *Walking Happy* (Lunt-Fontanne Th., 1966–67 season); appeared in *Last Analysis* (Circle in the Square, 1971); in *Judy and Jane* (Bijou, 1972); and in *Waltz of the Toreadors* (Walnut Th., Philadelphia, 1973).

Television. Miss Troy appeared as Gwendolen in *Who's Ernest?* (US Steel Hour, CBS); on the Salad Days Special (CBC, Toronto, Canada); in East Side, West Side; Run for Your Life; Hogan's Heroes; Cannon; Barnaby Jones; Toma; and the serials Eternal Light and Love of Life (CBS).

Awards. For her performance in *The Infernal Machine,* Miss Troy received the *Show Business* off-Bway Award. She was nominated for Antoinette Perry (Tony) Awards for her performance in *Tovarich* (1963), *High Spirits* (1964), and *Walking Happy* (1966–67).

TRUEMAN, PAULA. Actress. b. Apr. 25, 1907, New York City, to Joseph and Eva Trueman. Father, bookkeeper. Grad. Girls H.S., Brooklyn, N.Y.; Hunter Coll., A.B. Studied acting at the Neighborhood Playhouse Sch. of the Th. (fellowship). Married Nov. 17, 1936, to Harold Sterner, architect. Member of AEA; SAG; AFTRA.

Theatre. Miss Trueman was a dancer in the Fokine Ballet troupe production of *Thunderbird* (Hippodrome Th., N.Y.C., 1922); at the Neighborhood Playhouse, played Madanika in *The Little Clay Cart* (Dec. 5, 1924), appeared in *The Grand Street Follies (Second Edition)* (May 20, 1924), played the Hostess in *The Legend of the Dance* (Mar. 31, 1925), a Near Relative and one of the Thames' Banks in *The Critic, or A Tragedy Rehearsed* (May 8, 1925), appeared in *The Grand Street Follies (Third Edition)* (June 18, 1925), played Gitl in *The Dybbuk* (Dec. 15, 1925), the Princess in *A Burmese Pwe* and Too Fei in *Kuan Yin* (Mar. 16, 1926), Irene in *The Romantic Young Lady* (May 4, 1926), appeared in *The Grand Street Follies (Fourth Edition)* (June 15, 1926), played Madanika in *The Little Clay Cart* (Nov. 4, 1926), Gitl in *The Dybbuk* (Dec. 16, 1926), the Lady Friend in *Pinwheel* (Feb. 3, 1927), Columbina in *Commedia dell' Arte* (Apr. 5, 1927), and appeared in *The Grand Street Follies (Fifth Edition)* (May 19, 1927; Little Th., May 31, 1927). She played Valeria in a series of special matinee performances of *Lovers and Enemies* (Little, Sept. 20, 1927); Liza in *if* (Little, Oct. 25, 1927); Maureen Milton, a critic in *The Love Nest* (Comedy, Dec. 22, 1927); Hermance in *Maya* (Comedy, Feb. 21, 1928); appeared in *The Grand Street Follies of 1928* (Booth, May 28, 1928); *The Grand Street Follies of 1929* (Booth, May 1, 1929); and *Sweet and Low* Chanin's 44 St. Th., Nov. 17, 1930); toured in *Grand Hotel* (1930); Tessie Wede in *Ladies of Creation* (Cort, N.Y.C., Sept. 8, 1931); at the Shakespeare Th., Puck in *A Midsummer Night's Dream* (Nov. 17, 1932), Jessica in *The Merchant of Venice* (Nov. 23, 1932), and Margaret in *Much Ado About Nothing* (Dec. 3, 1932); played a Woman in *Panic* (Imperial, Mar. 14, 1935); Essie in *You Can't Take It with You* (Booth, Dec. 14, 1936); Hester in *George Washington Slept Here* (Lyceum, Oct. 18, 1940); Mary Franklin in *Kiss and Tell* (Biltmore, Mar. 17, 1943); Phoebe Fuller in *Feathers in a Gale* (Music Box, Dec. 21, 1943); and Esther in *Violet* (Belasco, Oct. 24, 1944). During WW II, she toured in the USO production of *The Man Who Came to Dinner* (PTO). Miss Trueman performed as Gertrude Adams in the pre-Bway tryout of *Laughing Water* (opened Shubert, New Haven, Conn., Nov. 16, 1944; closed Plymouth Th., Boston, Mass., Nov. 25, 1945); and Mrs. Esterhazy in the pre-Bway tryout of *Accidentally Yours* (opened Junior College Aud., Sacramento, Calif., Mar. 15, 1947; closed Selwyn, Chicago, Ill., June 14, 1917). She played Mrs. Tremaine in *For Love or Money* (Henry Miller's Th., N.Y.C., Nov. 4, 1947); at the Olney (Md.) Playhouse, appeared in stock presentations of *The Heiress* and *The Book of Charm* (Summer 1948); appeared in *Gentlemen Prefer Blondes* (Ziegfeld, N.Y.C., Dec. 8, 1949); played Sybil in *Mrs. McThing* (ANTA, Feb. 20, 1952), and on tour (opened Colonial, Boston, Mass., Jan. 13, 1953; closed Nixon, Pittsburgh, Pa., May 30, 1953); and understudied Josephine Hull as Mrs. Laura Partridge in *The Solid Gold Cadillac* (Belasco, N.Y.C., Nov. 5, 1953). At the Berkshire Playhouse (Stockbridge, Mass.) she appeared in stock productions of *The Solid Gold Cadillac* (Summer 1954) and *The Book of Charm* (Summer 1955). She played Juliet in *Wake Up, Darling* (Ethel Barrymore Th., N.Y.C., May 2, 1956); and appeared in a stock production of *Through the Eye of the Needle* (Hampton Playhouse, N.H., Summer 1956). She played Mrs. Forsythe in *A Family Affair* (Billy Rose Th., N.Y.C., Jan. 27, 1962); Mrs. Wade in *Wonderful Town* (NY City Ctr., Feb. 13, 1963); Little Mother in *Like Other People* (Village South Th., Mar. 29, 1963); and appeared in *The Sunday Man* (Morosco, May 12, 1964).

Miss Trueman played Mrs. Squire in *The Music Man* (NY City Ctr., N.Y.C., June 16, 1965); Mrs. Potts in the pre-Bway tryout of *Hot September* (opened Shubert, Boston, Sept. 14, 1965; closed there Oct. 9, 1965); in a bill entitled *Three by Thornton Wilder* (Cherry Lane Th., Sept. 6, 1966), played Mother Bayard in *The Long Christmas Dinner,* Mme. Pugeot in *Queens of France,* and Ma Kirby in *The Happy Journey to Trenton and Camden;* Harriet Stanley in *Sherry!* (Alvin, Mar. 28, 1967); for the ANTA Matinee Series, appeared as Margaret in *Postcards* (Th. de Lys, Dec. 4–5, 1967); and played Mrs. Fish in *The Chinese and Dr. Fish* (Ethel Barrymore Th., Mar. 10, 1970).

Films. Miss Trueman played Mrs. Fenty in *Paint Your Wagon* (Par., 1969); the Nurse in *The Anderson Tapes* (Col., 1970); and Mattie in *Homebodies* (Avco-Embassy, 1974).

Recreation. Sailing, walking, gardening.

TUDOR, ROWAN. Actor, director, singer. b. Cornelius Koster, Nov. 4, 1905, San Francisco, Calif., to Henry and Anita (Radoszewski) Koster. Father, architect; mother, translator, inventor. Grad. George Washington H.S., N.Y.C., 1921; Eastman Sch. of Music, Rochester, N.Y., 1923. Studied voice with Mme. Aida Grass Morris, Mischa Ferenzo, Mme. Whilemina Kerr, and Enzo del Orefice. Married June 15, 1934, to Edna V. Brush, financial secretary. Member of AEA (on council, 1959–69); AFTRA; SAG; AGVA; Episcopal Actor's Guild (on council, treas., 1973). Address: 670 Riverside Dr., New York, NY 10031, tel. (212) WA 6-9738.

Pre-Theatre. Hotel auditor.

Theatre. Mr. Tudor made his debut in vaudeville as Silvio in a touring production of *Pagliacci* (1925); subsequently appeared in Amer. Opera Co. productions as Figaro in *The Marriage of Figaro,* Silvio in *Pagliacci,* and Valentine in *Faust* (Alvin, N.Y.C., 1928).

He played Lt. Rene LeMotte in *Mademoiselle Modiste* (Al Jolson's Th., Oct. 7, 1929), also touring in it (1929–30); understudied Joseph Macauley as Alonzo in *Revenge with Music* (New Amsterdam, Nov. 28, 1934); played Jack Thurston in *The Firefly,* and Viscount Rebeau in *The New Moon* (Toledo Civic Opera, Ohio, 1939); Jack Thurston in *The Firefly* (Paper Mill Playhouse, Millburn, N.J., 1941); appeared in productions at the Louisville (Ky.) Amphitheatre (1943); Grand Rapids (Mich.) Municipal Opera (1944); played Mayor A. Oakey Hall in *Up in Central Park* (Century, N.Y.C., Jan. 27, 1945), also touring in it (1946–47); performed at the St. Louis (Mo.) Municipal Opera (1948); played Herald Reader and took over Don MacClelland's role as the Mayor during the run of *Miss Liberty* (Majestic, N.Y.C., July 15, 1949), and played this latter role on tour (1950); appeared as Clayfoot Trowbridge and Evans in *Flahooley* (Broadhurst, N.Y.C., May 15, 1951); performed in stock at Lambertville, N.J., Neptune, N.J., and Miami, Fla. (1950); appeared in *Oklahoma!* and *The New Moon* at the Cleveland (Ohio) Musicarnival (1954); appeared and directed at Detroit (Mich.) Melody Circus (1955–56); performed at Starlight Musicals (Indianapolis, Ind., 1957–58, 1962); Highland Park (Ill.) Music Th. (1960); Cohasset (Mass.) Music Circus (1961); at the Meadowbrook (N.J.) Dinner Th., appeared in *Annie Get Your Gun, Song of Norway,* and *Plain and Fancy;* appeared in productions at the Cohasset (Mass.) Music Circus (1963), Meadowbrook (N.J.) Dinner Th. (1963); and played Buffalo Bill in *Annie Get Your Gun* (McKeesport Dinner Th., Pa.; Westchester Dinner Th., Yonkers, N.Y.).

Mr. Tudor appeared as Colonel Pickering in *My Fair Lady* (summer th. tour, 1964); played the Prime Minister in *The King and I* (summer th. tour, 1965); as Sir Henry Beekman in *Gentlemen Prefer Blondes* (Meadowbrook Dinner Th., 1965); as Colonel Bullmoose in *Li'l Abner* (Casa Mañana, Fort Worth, Tex., 1966); Sidney Fineman in *What Makes Sammy Run?* (Casa Mañana, 1966); Wang Chi Yang in

Flower Drum Song (Casa Mañana, 1966); played Conrad Fuller in *On a Clear Day You Can See Forever* in the national tour (1966 and 1967) and at the St. Paul Civic Opera (1968); played Father Nordrak in *Song of Norway*(St. Paul Civic Opera, 1968) Buffalo Bill in *Annie Get Your Gun* (St. Louis Municipal Opera, 1968; and Kansas City Starlight Opera Co., 1968); Nova Kovic in *The Merry Widow* (St. Louis Municipal Opera, 1968); directed *On a Clear Day You Can See Forever* (Miami Univ. and Oxford, Ohio, 1969); Papa Yoder in *Plain and Fancy*(Kenley Players, Warren, Dayton, and Columbus, Ohio, 1970); and the Governor/Innkeeper in *Man of La Mancha*(Kenley Players, 1970; summer tours, Denver, Colorado Springs, Colo., 1971; national tour, 1971; Cambridge Dinner Th., Mass., 1972; Orpheum Th., San Francisco, Calif., 1972; and Thunderbird Dinner Th., Jacksonville, Fla., 1973).

Television. He played John Wanamaker on Frontiers of Faith (NBC, 1950).

Night Clubs. Mr. Tudor has appeared as emcee and singer at the Chez Maurice (Montreal, Canada, 1940).

Discography. He sang Lockit in *The Beggar's Opera* (1954).

Recreation. Photography.

TUMARIN, BORIS. Actor, director, teacher. b. Boris Tumarinson, Apr. 4, 1910, Riga, Latvia, to Joseph and Hanna (Lifshitz) Tumarinson. Father, businessman. Grad. Gymnasium Riga, Latvia, 1928; attended Acad. of Arts, Riga, 1926–31; Acad. of Arts, Berlin, Ger., 1931–32. Studied acting at Drama Studio, Riga, 1926–31; Michael Chekhov Seminar, Riga, 1930–31; Max Reinhardt Seminar, Berlin, 1931–32; Daykarhanova Sch. for the Stage, N.Y.C., 1939–40; Jilinsky Actors Workshop, N.Y.C., 1940–42. Married Mar. 27, 1936, to Bertha Weinberg, psychoanalyst; one son. Served Latvian Army, 1933; WW II, US Army; rank, S/Sgt. Relatives in theatre: brother, Paul, actor; sister, Lena, actress; sister, Sonya, singer. Member of AEA; AFTRA; SAG; SSD&C; Workmen's Circle Fraternal Organization. Address: 118 W. 79th St., New York, NY 10024, tel. (212) SC 4-2305.

Theatre. Mr. Tumarin made his first appearance as Eli in a school production of Sholom Aleichem's *Mottell* (Riga, Latvia, 1924); and his professional debut as the Pastor in *The Father* (Kaunas, Lithuania, 1928). His other European engagements include: directing and performing with the Jewish Labor Th. (1932–34); appearances with the Jewish Repertory Th. (1934–35); and touring as a one-man show (Baltic countries and Poland, 1934–37).

He directed and played Ole in *The Emperor's New Clothes*(Heckscher Th., N.Y.C., Dec. 1941); played Karel in Irwin Piscator's production of *Winter Soldiers* (Studio Th., New Sch. for Social Research, Nov. 29, 1942); Dr. Isaacs in *The Family*(Windsor, Mar. 30, 1943); and directed and appeared in an ELT production of *A Chekhov Carnival* (Mar. 18, 1946).

He played the Captain in *You Touched Me,* and Nick in *The Time of Your Life* (Westchester Playhouse, Mt. Kisco, N.Y., Summer 1946); General Assolant in an ELT production of *Paths of Glory* (Feb. 1947); Cradeau in a summer theatre production of *No Exit* (Kingsmith Th., Washington, D.C., Summer 1947); directed *Lamp at Midnight* (New Stages, N.Y.C., Dec. 21, 1947); *The Criminals* (Smithtown Th., N.Y., Summer 1948); played Canoris in *The Victors* (New Stages, N.Y.C., Dec. 26, 1948); directed *Blood Wedding* (New Stages, Feb. 6, 1949); and *The Sun and I*(New Stages, Mar. 20, 1949).

He directed *The House of Bernarda Alba* (ANTA, N.Y.C., Jan. 7, 1951); played Miroslav Babicka in *The Prescott Proposals* (Broadhurst, Dec. 16, 1953); Melchior Feydak in *Biography* (Pocono Playhouse, Mountainhome, Pa., Summer 1954); directed *Sands of the Negev* (President, N.Y.C., Oct. 19, 1954); played Chernov in *Anastasia* (Lyceum, Dec. 29, 1954); George Mainzer in *The Innkeepers* (John Golden Th., Feb. 2, 1956); directed and played Chernov in a tour of *Anastasia* (Summer 1956); directed *Desire Under the Elms* (Studebaker Th., Chicago, Ill., Winter 1956); directed and, with Jack Sydow, adapted *The Brothers Karamozov* (Gate, N.Y.C., Dec. 6, 1957); toured summer theatres as Mancini in *He Who Gets Slapped* (Summer 1958); and appeared as Vassily Solyony in *The Three Sisters* (4th St. Th., N.Y.C., Sept. 21, 1959).

Mr. Tumarin played Juror 11 in *Twelve Angry Men* (Bucks County Playhouse, New Hope, Pa., Summer 1960); directed and, with Jack Sydow, adapted *The Idiot* (Gate, N.Y.C., Sept. 25, 1960); directed *Montserrat* (Gate, Jan. 8, 1961); appeared as Cardinal Marotta in *The Devil's Advocate* (Billy Rose Th., Mar. 9, 1961); Father Anastasios in *The Garden of Sweets* (ANTA, Oct. 31, 1961); directed and played Shylock in *The Merchant of Venice*(Gate, Feb. 2, 1962); appeared as Mr. Kronheim in *Venus at Large* (Morosco, Apr. 12, 1962); Max in *Whisper into My Good Ear,* part of a double bill with *Mrs. Dally Has a Lover*(Cherry Lane, Oct. 1, 1962); Gottlieb Biedermann in *The Firebugs*(Maidman, Feb. 11, 1963); succeeded (June 21, 1963) David Hurst as Shpigelsky in *A Month in the Country* (Maidman, May 28, 1963); and played M. Huspar in *Traveller without Luggage* (ANTA, Sept. 17, 1964).

Mr. Tumarin appeared as King Ambrose in *The Giant's Dance* (Cherry Lane, Nov. 16, 1964); as Aleko Bereshvili in the Repertory Th. of Lincoln Center's production of *The Caucasian Chalk Circle* (Vivian Beaumont, March 24, 1966); starred as Alper in the City Center revival of *The Tenth Man*(NY City Ctr., Nov. 8, 1967). He appeared as Shylock in the Milwaukee Repertory Th. production of *The Merchant of Venice* (Jan. 26, 1967); as The Presiding Judge in *The Man In the Glass Booth* (Royale, Sept. 26, 1968).

Mr. Tumarin directed the Milwaukee Repertory Th. production of *The Three Sisters* (Jan. 31, 1969); directed the production of *A Midsummer Night's Dream* (Todd Wehr Th., Oct. 2, 1969); appeared as Ephraim Davidoff in *The Head of Hair* (New Th. Workshop, Jan. 31, 1970); directed *The Lower Depths* for the City Center Acting Co. (Good Shepherd-Faith Church, Oct. 24, 1972); directed Sir William Walton's opera *The Bear* for the Juilliard American Opera Center (Juilliard Th., Mar. 29, 1973); and directed *The Three Sisters* for the City Center Acting Co. (Billy Rose Th., Dec. 8, 1973).

Television. He has performed in *The Great Sebastians* (1957); *Don Quixote* (Nov. 9, 1959); *Ninotchka* (Apr. 26, 1960); on The Defenders (CBS); Naked City (ABC); The Nurses (CBS); The Eternal Light (NBC); Directions (ABC); and appeared as Dr. Geller in the daytime serial The Doctors (NBC).

Other Activities. Mr. Tumarin has taught acting at the Amer. Th. Wing (1949–51); Irwin Piscator's Dramatic Workshop (1949–50); and the Actor's Workshop, which he directed (1951–52).

In 1970 he joined the faculty of the Drama Division of the Juilliard School where he is teaching technique of acting and directing.

Awards. For their adaptation of *The Brothers Karamozov,* Messrs. Tumarin and Sydow received *The Village Voice* Off-Bway (Obie) Award (1958).

Mr. Tumarin received the Vernon Rice Award for his participation in the founding of the Gate Repertory Co. (1961).

TURNEY, CATHERINE. Playwright. b. Dec. 26, 1906, Chicago, Ill., to George and Elizabeth (Blamer) Turney. Father, business executive. Attended Bishop Sch., La Jolla, Calif., 1922–24. Studied at Pasadena (Calif.) Playhouse Sch. of the Th., 1928–30. Married 1931 to Cyril Armbrister, radio director (marr. dis. 1938); married Feb. 18, 1940, to George Reynolds, actor (marr. dis. 1948). Member of Dramatists Guild. Address: Dramatists Guild, 234 W. 44th St., New York, NY 10036, tel. (212) 563-2233.

Theatre. Miss Turney wrote *Bitter Harvest* (Arts Th., London, Eng., Jan. 29, 1936); and wrote, with Jerry Horwin, *My Dear Children* (Belasco, N.Y.C., Jan. 31, 1940).

Films. She was a contract writer for MGM (1936–37) and Warner Bros. (1943–48).

Television and Radio. She wrote radio scripts for Strange As It Seems (1934–35), and Don Lee Broadcasting System (CBS, 1940); and has written for television (1950–to date).

TUTIN, DOROTHY. Actress. b. April 8, 1930, London, England, to Dr. John Tutin and Adie (Fryers) Tutin. Father, scientist. Attended St. Catherine's Sch., Bramley, Guildford, England, 1939–45. Member of British AEA; Variety Club. Studied for stage at PARADA and RADA, London, 1947–49. Address: 8 Chester Close, Queen's Ride, Barnes, London S.W. 13, England.

Theatre. Miss Tutin made her stage debut in London as Princess Margaret in *The Thistle and the Rose* (Bolton's Th., Sept. 6, 1949); subsequently she joined the Bristol Old Vic Co., where she appeared as Phoebe in *As You Like It* (Royal Th., Jan. 1950), Anni in *Captain Carvallo* (1950), and Belinda in *The Provoked Wife* (1950); appeared with the London Old Vic Co. as Win-the-Fight Littlewit in *Bartholomew Fair* (Dec. 18, 1950), Princess Katherine in *Henry V* (Jan. 30, 1951), and Anne Page in *The Merry Wives of Windsor* (May 31, 1951).

She played Martina in *Thor, with Angels* (Lyric, Hammersmith, Sept. 27, 1951); Hero in *Much Ado About Nothing* (Phoenix, Jan. 11, 1952); Rose Pemberton in *The Living Room* (Wyndham's, Apr. 16, 1953); Sally Bowles in *I Am a Camera* (New, March 12, 1954); Joan of Arc in *The Lark* (Lyric, Hammersmith, May 11, 1955); Hedvig in *The Wild Duck* (Saville, Dec. 21, 1955); toured as Caroline Treherne in *The Gates of Summer* (1956–57); and appeared as Jean Rice in *The Entertainer*(Royal Court, London, April 10, 1957).

In 1958 she appeared with the Shakespeare Memorial Th. (Stratford-upon-Avon), as Juliet in *Romeo and Juliet* (Apr. 8), Viola in *Twelfth Night* (Apr. 28), and as Ophelia in *Hamlet* (June 3), and toured the USSR in these roles; played Dolly in *Once More, with Feeling* (New, London, July 9, 1950); in 1960, with the Shakespeare Memorial Th. (Stratford-upon-Avon), played Portia in *The Merchant of Venice* (Apr. 12), Viola in *Twelfth Night* (May 17), Cressida in *Troilus and Cressida* (July 26). She appeared as Sister Jeanne of the Angels in *The Devils* (Royal Shakespeare Th., Stratford-upon-Avon; Edinburgh Festival, Scotland, Summer 1962; Aldwych, London, Feb. 20, 1961; Nov. 18, 1962); and played Cressida in *Troilus and Cressida* (Aldwych, Oct. 15, 1962).

Miss Tutin made her N.Y.C. debut in *The Hollow Crown* (Henry Miller's Th., Jan. 29, 1963); played Polly Peachum in *The Beggar's Opera* (Aldwych, London, July 1963); Queen Victoria in *Portrait of a Queen* for the Bristol Old Vic Co. (Th. Royal, Bristol, Mar. 2, 1965; and Henry Miller's Th., N.Y.C., Feb. 28, 1968); Rosalind in *As You Like It* (Stratford-upon-Avon, 1967; and Los Angeles, 1968); appeared in *Play on Love* (St. Martin's Th., London, Jan. 14, 1970); The Royal Shakespeare Co.'s *Old Times* (Aldwych, London, June 1, 1971); played the title role in *Peter Pan* (Coliseum, London, Dec. 27, 1971); and Maggie Wylie in *What Every Woman Knows* (Abbey Th., London, Nov. 28, 1973).

Films. Miss Tutin appeared as Manette in *A Tale of Two Cities* (Rank, 1958); Polly Peachum in *The Beggar's Opera* (Wilcox-Neagle, 1949); and Cecily in *The Importance of Being Earnest* (U, 1952).

Television. Miss Tutin appeared on British television in *The Wild Duck* (K&JC Lt., 1956); *The Living Room* (H. M. Tennent, 1956); *Rebecca* (H. M. Tennent, 1956); *Victoria Regina* (H. M. Tennent, 1957); *Invitation to a Voyage* (H. M. Tennent, 1957); *Antigone* (BBC, 1959); *Colombe* (BBC, 1959); *Carrington V.C.* (Anglia, 1959); *The Cherry Orchard* (BBC, 1962); and in the US in *Scent of Fear* (ABC, 1959); played Queen Henrietta Maria in *Cromwell* (Col. 1970); and Sophie Breska in *The Savage Messiah* (MGM, 1972).

Miss Tutin appeared in *The Six Wives of Henry VIII* (BBC and NET); and *Vienna 1900* (BBC and NET).

Awards. The Variety Club of Great Britain cited Miss Tutin for her acting (1953); for her performance as Viola in *Twelfth Night*, she received the London *Evening Standard* Award (1960); and the Variety Club Film Award for her performance as Sophie Breska in *The Savage Messiah* (1972).

Recreation. Music.

TUTTLE, DAY. Director, actor, playwright, educator. b. Frank Day Tuttle, Jr., June 9, 1902, Brooklyn, N.Y., to Frank Day and Florence (Guertin) Tuttle. Father, coal merchant; mother, writer, philanthropic worker. Attended Hotchkiss Sch., Lakeville, Conn., 1916–20; grad. Yale Univ., B.A. 1924; attended Graduate Sch. of Business Administration, New York Univ., 1931–32; grad. Yale Univ. Sch. of Drama, M.F.A. 1936. Studied Shakespeare and Anglo-American stage speech with Margaret Carrington, Santa Barbara, Calif., and N.Y.C., 1929–32. Married Nov. 26, 1927, to Lauralee Skinner, educator; two sons, two daughters. Relative in theatre: great-uncle, Hiram Henry, minstrel performer and impressario. Member of AEA; Dramatists Guild; SSD&C; League of Off-Bway Theatres; ATA; ANTA; Coffee House Club. Address: 3 Country Club Road, Bellport, NY 11713, tel. (516) 286-1561.

Pre-Theatre. Instructor at Yale Univ. (1924–25).

Theatre. Mr. Tuttle first appeared in productions for the Yale Dramatic Assn., including the role of the Fool in *King Lear*, which was directed by Monty Woolley.

He made his N.Y.C. debut as a walk-on in *The Glass Slipper* (Guild, Oct. 19, 1925); subsequently played a Page and a Spectator in Walter Hampden's *The Merchant of Venice* (Hampden's Th., Dec. 26, 1925); a Soldier in a special matinee performance of Walter Hampden's *Hamlet* (Hampden's Th., Jan. 1, 1926); and appeared in the revue, *Bad Habits of 1926* (Greenwich Village Th., Apr. 30, 1926).

At the Lobero Th. (Santa Barbara, Calif.), he played Bepe in *The Romantic Young Lady* (July 1926), Apollodorus in *Caesar and Cleopatra* (Sept. 1926), Simon in *Hay Fever* (Oct. 1926), the Captain in *Androcles and the Lion* (Mar. 1928), Woodley in *Young Woodley* (Mar. 1929), Lightfoot in *Wings Over Europe* (Mar. 1930), Kublai, the Great Kaan, in *Marco Millions* (Apr. 1930), the Dauphin in *Saint Joan* (June 1930), and Gaston de Raousset in *Emperatriz*, which he also wrote (Aug. 1930).

At the Westchester Playhouse (Mt. Kisco, N.Y.), he appeared as Ned Seton in *Holiday*, a Reporter in *The Great Adventure*, a Priest in *Night at the Inn*, and a Soldier in *The Critic* (June–July 1931).

He played Frank Oakes in *In Love with Love*, Barry Wall in *A Night in June*, the title role in *The Faun*, and Robert Seward in *Men Must Fight* (Westchester Playhouse; Millbrook Summer Th., N.Y. June–July 1932).

From 1932–40, with Richard Skinner, Mr. Tuttle produced one hundred and four summer productions at the Westchester Playhouse, Tuttle directing sixty of these productions, and playing such roles as Lt. Raleigh in *Journey's End* (June 1933), Marchbanks in *Candida* (July 1933), Richard Kurt in *Biography* (1934), Simon in *Hayfever*, and John Carteret in *Smilin' Thru* (July 1935).

Also during this period, at the Westchester Playhouse, he presented Margaret Anglin in *Retreat from Folly* (June–July 1937), Henry Fonda in *The Virginian* (July–Aug. 1937), Frances Farmer and Phillips Holmes in *The Petrified Forest* (Aug.–Sept. 1937), Laurette Taylor in the title role of *Candida*, in which he repeated his role as Marchbanks (Aug.–Sept. 1938), and Jose Ferrer in *Charley's Aunt* (Aug. 1940).

He wrote *No Answer*, which premiered at the Yale Univ. Th. (May 1936), and was produced by The Stagers in N.Y.C. (Nora Bayes Th., Mar. 1938).

At the Washington (D.C.) Civic Th., he directed *Caesar and Cleopatra* (Oct. 1936), *Kind Lady* (Nov. 1936), *The Petrified Forest* (Dec. 1936), *It Can't Happen Here* (Jan. 1937), *The Front Page*, (Mar. 1937), and *Lysistrata* (May 1937).

In association with Richard Skinner and Cheryl Crawford, he produced *Family Portrait* (Morosco, N.Y.C., Mar. 8, 1939), and at the Washington Civic Th., directed such productions as *Merrily We Roll Along* (Oct. 1939), *Criminal-at-Large* (Nov. 1939), *The Devil and Daniel Webster* (Jan. 1940), *The Fall of the City* (Jan. 1940), *At Mrs. Beam's* (Apr. 1940), and a bill of Nöel Coward one-acts, including *Ways and Means*, *Fumed Oak* and *Hands Across the Sea*. In the first of this trio, he played Toby (May, 1940).

With Erwin Piscator, he directed a Washington Civic Th. production of Louise Rainer's *Saint Joan* (Belasco, Washington, D.C., 1940); played Max Jacobs in a summer production of *Twentieth Century* (Westchester Playhouse, 1940); with Richard Skinner produced a revival of *Charley's Aunt* (Cort, N.Y.C., Oct. 17, 1940); and with Harold Bromley, *The Life of Reilly* (Broadhurst, Apr. 29, 1942).

Mr. Tuttle directed productions at the Sayville (N.Y.) Summer Th. (June–July 1942); an ELT production of *Our Town* (NY Public Library, Hudson Branch, Dec. 1946); and *The Deputy of Paris* (Henry Street Playhouse, Mar. 21, 1947).

In collaboration with Hallie Flanagan Davis and Sylvia Gassel, he wrote *$e = mc_2$, Living Newspaper of the Atomic Age*, which premiered at the Smith Coll. Th. (Oct. 1947).

He directed six summer productions at the Strand Th. (Wilmington, Del., 1954); played William Marble in the Northampton (Mass.) Players production of *Payment Deferred* (May 1955); directed *In Good King Charles's Golden Days* (Downtown Th., N.Y.C., Jan. 24, 1957); and an opera, *Gallantry* (Brander Matthews Th., N.Y.C., Mar. 28, 1958).

During 1958–59, he remodeled a N.Y.C. motion picture house, naming it the East 74 Street Th., where he produced and directed *Lysistrata* (May 1959). In Fall 1961, he leased it to T. Edward Hambleton and Norris Houghton, managing directors of the Phoenix Th., who renamed it The Phoenix Th., and, until 1964, produced their plays in it.

Mr. Tuttle directed summer productions at the Gateway Th. (Bellport, N.Y., June–Aug. 1958); produced *The Book of Job* (Christ Church Methodist, N.Y.C., Feb. 9, 1962), directed *The Threepenny Opera* (Gateway Th., Bellport, June 1962); played Francis Bacon in an ELT production of *Elizabeth the Queen* (Master Inst., Nov. 9, 1962), and Father in *Life with Father* (Gateway Th., Bellport, Aug. 1963).

Radio. He directed The March of Time (NBC, 1942–43); The Aldrich Family (NBC, 1943); Mystery Th. (NBC, 1943–44); William and Mary (CBS, 1943–44); and Bright Horizon (1943–45).

Other Activities. Mr. Tuttle was assistant professor of English at the Coll. of the City of New York, where he taught radio writing and playwriting (1944–47); was associate professor of theatre at Smith Coll. (1947–54), Bard Coll. (1954–55); and lectured on dramatic writing at the Berkshire Writers Conference (Lenox, Mass., Summer 1963). In the winter of 1964–65, he taught English Composition at the State Univ. of N.Y. at New Paltz, a course in Shakespeare at Douglass College, N.J., and a graduate seminar in play production at Brooklyn College. He was associate professor in the Dept. of Theatre and Speech at Briarcliff Coll. (1965–68); and taught English composition, Shakespeare, creative writing, and remedial writing at the Borough of Manhattan Community Coll. (Winter 1968–Spring 1970).

Published Works. He has published articles in *Theatre Arts*, and *Collier's Encyclopedia*. He is the author, with Dorothy Olney, of *G.B. eSsence of Women*, adaptations of scenes from the plays of George Bernard Shaw (The Dramatic Publishing Co., Chicago, 1974).

Recreation. Gardening, sailing, swimming.

TWAIN, NORMAN. Producer, director. b. Norman Louis Twain, Sept. 13, 1930, Atlantic City, N.J., to Charles and Doris (Ager) Twain. Father and mother, merchants. Grad. Sarasota (Fla). H.S.; Columbia Coll., A.B., 1952; M.A. (English) 1953. Married Nov. 1964 to Sandra Church, actress. Served US Army, 1953–55. Member of SDG; League of NY Theatres. Address: 119 W. 57th St., New York, NY 10019, tel. (212) 582-0777.

Theatre. Mr. Twain produced with Warner Le Roy, *The Golden Six* (York Playhouse, Oct. 25, 1958); with Bernard Miller, *Epitaph for George Dillon* (Henry Miller's Th., Jan. 12, 1959); produced and directed *A Distant Bell* (Eugene O'Neill Th., Jan. 13, 1960); produced by arrangement with the English Stage Co., Ltd., *Roots* (Mayfair, Mar. 6, 1961); produced, with Carroll and Harris Masterson, *The Lady of the Camellias* (Winter Garden, Mar. 20, 1963); produced, in association with Carroll and Harris Masterson, *Traveller without Luggage* (ANTA, Sept. 17, 1964); and in association with Edward Padula and Carroll and Harris Masterson, *Bajour* (Shubert, Nov. 23, 1964).

He produced *Gilbert Becaud on Broadway* (Longacre, Oct. 31, 1966); produced, with Carroll and Harris Masterson, *The Apparition Theater of Prague* (Cort, Nov. 16, 1966); with Edward Specter Productions, *Henry, Sweet Henry* (Palace, Oct. 23, 1967); with Marcel Akselrod by arrangement with Feliz Marouani, *Gilbert Becaud Sings Love* (Cort, Oct. 6, 1968); in association with Albert I. Fill, *Charles Aznavour* (Music Box, Feb. 4, 1970); produced *Lolita, My Love* (pre-Bway: opened Shubert Th., Boston, Mass., Mar. 18, 1971; closed there Mar. 27, 1971); *Nicol Williamson's Late Show* (Eastside Playhouse, June 26, 1973); and, in association with Michael Liebert, *The World of Lenny Bruce* (Players Th., June 11, 1974).

TYNAN, KENNETH. Drama critic, journalist. b. Kenneth Peacock Tynan, Apr. 2, 1927, Birmingham, England, to Sir Peter Peacock and Letitia (Rose) Tynan. Father, chain store owner. Grad. King Edward Sch., Birmingham, England, 1945; Oxford Univ., B.A. 1949. Married Jan. 25, 1951, to Elaine Dundy, novelist (marr. dis. May 1964); one daughter; married June 1967 to Kathleen Halton; one daughter, one son. Address: 20 Thurloe Square, London S.W. 7, England.

He was drama critic for *The Spectator* (1951–52); *The Evening Standard* (1952–53); *The Daily Sketch* (1953–54); *The Observer* (1954–58); (1960–63); and *The New Yorker* (1958–60).

He joined the Lichfield Repertory Co. (1949); directed *Man of the World* (Lyric, Hammersmith Th., London 1950); an Arts Council tour of *Othello* (1950); and appeared as the Player King in Alec Guinness' *Hamlet* (New, May 17, 1951).

From 1963 to 1973, he was literary manager of the National Th.; advisor and co-author of the revue *Oh! Calcutta!* (N.Y., 1969; London, 1970); co-producer of *Soldiers* (London, 1968).

Films. He was script editor for Ealing Films (England, 1956–58).

He was also film critic of *The Observer* (1964–66).

Television and Radio. Mr. Tynan was co-author of the radio feature, The Quest for Corbett (BBC, 1956); and produced the Television Arts series, Tempo (ABC, 1961–62). He also wrote the script for the ABC documentary *The Actor* (1968).

Published Works. Mr. Tynan wrote *He That Plays the King* (1950); *Persona Grata* (1953); *Bull Fever* (1955); *Alec Guinness* (1961); *Curtains* (1961); and *Tynan Right and Left* (1967).

Recreation. Food and wine, watching bullfights.

TYSON, CICELY. Actress. b. Dec. 19, New York City, to William and Fredricka Tyson. Grad. P.S. 121; Margaret Knox Jr. H.S.; Charles Evans Hughes H.S.. Studied acting with Vinette Carroll; Paul Mann; Lloyd Richards; Actors Studio. Member of AEA; SAG; AFTRA; Actors Studio.

Pre-Theatre. Model, secretary, band singer.

Theatre. Miss Tyson gained her early theatre experience with The Amer. Conservatory Th.; made her first N.Y.C. appearance playing Barbara Allen in *Dark of the Moon* (Harlem YMCA, 1958); appeared in *Talent '59* (St. James, May 1959); understudied Eartha Kitt in *Jolly's Progress* (Longacre, Dec. 5, 1959); appeared in *The Cool World* (Eugene O'Neill Th., Feb. 22, 1960); played Virtue in The Negro Ensemble Co. production of *The Blacks* (St. Mark's Playhouse, May 4, 1961), a role she repeated at the Berlin and Venice Festivals; played

Mavis in *Moon on a Rainbow Shawl* (11 St. Th., N.Y.C., Jan. 15, 1962); Celeste in *Tiger, Tiger, Burning Bright* (Booth, Dec. 22, 1962); Joan in *The Blue Boy in Black* (Masque, Apr. 30, 1963); was a summer replacement in *The Last Minstrel* (Pocket Th., May 8, 1963); played Rev. Marion Alexander in *Trumpets of the Lord* (Astor Place Th., Dec. 21, 1963); was featured in *An Evening of Negro Poetry and Folk Music*, Delacorte, Aug. 15, 1966); with the Amer. Conservatory Th., appeared in *In White America*, *Tartuffe*, *A Servant of Two Masters*, and *The Apollo of Bellac;* appeared in *A Hand Is On the Gate* (Longacre, N.Y.C., Sept. 21, 1966); played Myrna Jersey in *Carry Me Back to Morningside Heights* (John Golden Th., Feb. 27, 1968); appeared in *To Be Young, Gifted, and Black* (Cherry Lane Th., Jan. 2, 1969); again played Rev. Marion Alexander in *Trumpets of the Lord* (Brooks Atkinson Th., Apr. 29, 1969); played Eliza Dolittle in *Pygmalion* (Playhouse in the Park, Cincinnati, Ohio, Apr. 9, 1970); and Abbie Putnam in *Desire Under the Elms* (Academy Festival Th., Lake Forrest, Ill., June 1974).

Films. She has appeared in *Twelve Angry Men* (UA, 1957); *Caribe Gold* (Premiere Pictures, 1957); *The Last Angry Man* (Col., 1959); *Odds Against Tomorrow* (UA, 1959); *A Matter of Conviction; Who Was That Lady?* (Col., 1960); *A Man Called Adam* (Embassy, 1966); *The Comedian* (MGM, 1967); *The Heart Is a Lonely Hunter* (WB-Seven Arts, 1968); *Sounder* (20th-Fox, 1972); *The River Niger* (Cine Artists, 1976); and *The Blue Bird* (20th-Fox, 1976).

Television. Miss Tyson's appearances include Frontiers of Faith; Directions '61; *Brown Girl, Brown Stones;* The Bill Cosby Show; East Side/West Side (CBS); Slattery's People (CBS); I Spy (NBC); The Guiding Light (CBS); Cowboys in Africa (ABC); The F.B.I. (ABC); Medical Center (CBS); On Being Black; Courtship of Eddie's Father (ABC); Here Come the Brides (ABC); Mission: Impossible (CBS); Gunsmoke (CBS); *Marriage: Year One* (NBC); Emergency (NBC); Wednesday Night Pout (NBC); Camera Three (CBS); The Nurses; CBS-TV Workshop; *The Autobiography of Miss Jane Pittman* (CBS, 1974); and *Just An Old Sweet Song* (CBS, 1976).

Other Activities. With Arthur Mitchell, she organized the Dance Th. of Harlem (1968). She served on the board of directors of Urban Gateway, an organization devoted to exposing children to the arts; and serves as trustee to the Amer. Film Institute, and the Human Family Institute.

Awards. Miss Tyson received a Nina Jacobson scholarship from ACT; the Vernon Rice Award (1961–62) for her performances in *The Blacks* and *Moon on a Rainbow Shawl;* The Capitol Press Club Award for East Side/West Side; the Best Actress awards of the Atlanta (Ga.) Film Festival (1972) and of the National Society of Film Critics, an Academy (Oscar) Award nomination, and Screen World's Most Promising Personality Award (1972) for *Sounder;* and the NATAS (Emmy) Award (1974) for *The Autobiography of Miss Jane Pittman.*

She has received awards from the NAACP, and the National Council of Negro Women; honorary doctorates from Atlanta, Loyola, and Lincoln universities; and Harvard Univ. honored her with "Cicely Tyson Day" (Apr. 18, 1974).

U

UGGAMS, LESLIE. Singer, actress. b. May 25, 1943, New York City, to Harold and Juanita (Smith) Uggams. Father, elevator operator and maintenance man, formerly with Hall Johnson Choir; mother, former Cotton Club chorus girl. Attended Professional Children's School (N.Y.C.); Juilliard Sch. of Music. Studied with Robert Lewis. Married Oct. 16, 1965, to Grahame Pratt, theatrical manager, television script writer; one daughter. Relatives in theatre; aunt, Eloise Uggams, singer, actress; uncle, John M. Smith, musician. Member of AEA; SAG; AFTRA; AGVA; AGMA.

Theatre. Miss Uggams appeared in *The Boy Friend* (Berkeley, Calif., Summer 1966); subsequently made her Bway debut as Georgina in *Hallelujah, Baby!* (Martin Beck Th., N.Y.C., Apr. 26, 1967); played Cleopatra in *Her First Roman* (Lunt-Fontanne Th., Oct. 20, 1967); and Sally Bowles in *Cabaret* (Westbury, Long Island, N.Y. Music Fair, July 28, 1970). Prior appearances as a singer include The Apollo Th. (N.Y.C., 1952); Radio City Music Hall (N.Y.C., 1960); and the Portland (Ore.) Auto Show (Nov. 1964).

Films. Miss Uggams sang the theme song for the sound track of *Inherit the Wind* (UA, 1960); and has appeared in *Two Weeks in Another Town* (MGM, 1962); *Black Girl* (Cinerama, 1972); and *Skyjacked* (MGM, 1972).

Television. Miss Uggams made her professional debut at age six on Beulah (ABC, 1950). Subsequent appearances include Sing Along with Mitch (NBC, 1961–64); The Leslie Uggams Show (CBS); *Hallelujah, Leslie!* (ABC); *'S Wonderful, 'S Marvelous, 'S Gershwin;* I Spy (NBC); The Girl from U.N.C.L.E. (NBC); The Mod Squad (ABC); and most major variety shows on all networks.

Night Clubs. Miss Uggams' appearances include The Persian Room (Plaza Hotel, N.Y.C.); the Copacabana (N.Y.C.); The Sands Hotel (Las Vegas); El San Juan Hotel (Puerto Rico); The Royal Box (Americana Hotel, N.Y.C.); The Chequers (Sydney, Australia); the Chevron-Hilton Hotel (Sydney, Australia); the Flamingo Hotel (Las Vegas); the Deauville Hotel (Miami Beach); Coconut Grove (Hollywood); the Empire Room (Waldorf-Astoria Hotel, N.Y.C.); and the Elmwood Casino (Windsor, Ontario, Canada).

Other Activities. Miss Uggams appeared at the White House (Washington, D.C.) by the request of Pres. and Mrs. Lyndon B. Johnson.

Published Works. With Marie Fenton, she wrote *The Leslie Uggams Beauty Book* (1966).

Discography. Discovered by Mitch Miller, who was then an Artist and Repertoire man, Miss Uggams first recorded on the Columbia label (1961), which subsequently issued the album for *Hallelujah, Baby!* (1968). Other recordings include *'S Wonderful, 'S Marvelous, 'S Gershwin* (Daybreak); and numerous solo popular music albums (Atlantic, 1967; and Motown).

Awards. Miss Uggams was named Most Promising Personality by *Theatre World* (1966–67); Most Promising New Bway Actress (1966–67) by the Annual *Variety* New York Drama Critics Poll; and received the Antoinette Perry (Tony) Award (1967–68) for *Hallelujah, Baby!.*

USTINOV, PETER. Actor, director, playwright, author. b. Peter Alexander Ustinov, Apr. 16, 1921, London, England, to Iona and Nadia (Benois) Ustinov. Father, journalist; mother, painter. Attended Westminster Sch., London. Studied for the theatre at London Theatre Sch. with Michel Saint-Denis. Married 1940 to Isolde Denham (marr. dis. 1950); one daughter; married 1953 to Suzanne Cloutier, actress (marr. dis. 1971); married 1972 to Helene du Lau d'Allemans; one son, two daughters. Served British Army, Royal Sussex Regiment (1942–46). Member of British AEA; Arts Theatre; R.A.C.; Garrick Club. Address: c/o Christopher Mann Ltd, 140 Park Lane, W1.

Theatre. Mr. Ustinov wrote *The Love of Four Colonels* (Shubert Th., N.Y.C., Jan. 15, 1953), in which he had appeared in London (see below). His first N.Y.C. appearance was as the General in his play, *Romanoff and Juliet* (Plymouth, Oct. 10, 1957), in which he toured (opened Royal Alexandra Th., Toronto, Ont., Can., Sept. 15, 1958; closed Blackstone, Chicago, Ill., Jan. 3, 1959). He appeared as Sam Old in his play, *Photo Finish* (Brooks Atkinson Th., N.Y.C., Feb. 12, 1963). Both of these works had been staged previously in London.

Mr. Ustinov made his professional debut as Waffles in a production of *The Wood Demon* (Barn Th., Shere, England, July 18, 1938), made his London debut in a sketch, which he had written, *The Bishop of Limpopoland* (Players' Th. Club, Aug. 30, 1939); later joined the Aylesbury Repertory Co. and played in *White Cargo*, *Laburnam Grove*, and *Rookery Nook* (Oct.–Dec. 1939); appeared as the Rev. Alroy Whittingstall in *First Night* (Richmond, London, Jan. 29, 1940); performed in a revue, *Swinging the Gate* (Ambassadors', May 22, 1940); played M. Lescure in *Fishing for Shadows*, which he adapted from the French (Threshold, Oct. 10, 1940); appeared in a revue, *Diversion* (Wyndham's, Oct. 28, 1940); and *Diversion No. 2* (Wyndham's, Jan. 2, 1941), in both of which he wrote his own sketches.

He directed his first production, *Squaring the Circle* (Vaudeville, Aug. 27, 1941); appeared as Petrovitch in *Crime and Punishment* (Wimbledon, London, June 18, 1946); appeared as Caligula in *Frenzy*, a play he adapted from Ingmar Bergman (St. Martin's, Apr. 21, 1948); as Sgt. Dohda in *Love in Albania*, which he also directed (Lyric, Hammersmith, June 7, 1949); and his play, *The Man in the Raincoat* was produced at the Edinburgh (Scot.) Festival (Summer 1950).

In his play, *The Love of Four Colonels*, he played a Miserable Immortal (Streatham Hill, London, Apr. 9, 1951), and when the play moved to Wyndham's Th. (May 28, 1951), the name of the character he had been playing was changed to Carabosse. At Brighton, he directed a production of *A Fiddle at the Wedding* (Royal, Oct. 1952); in London, he directed his own play *No Sign of the Dove* (Savoy, Dec. 3, 1953); in his play, *Romanoff and Juliet*, he appeared as the General (Piccadilly, May 17, 1956), subsequently making his N.Y.C. debut in it (see above). He toured with the Old Vic Co. to the USSR and repeated his role in *Romanoff and Juliet* there; played Sam Old and directed, with the assistance of Nicholas Garland, his own play, *Photo Finish* (London, Apr. 1962); and directed three one-act operas, *L'Heure Espagnole*, *Erwartung*, and *Gianni Schicchi* (Covent Garden, June 16, 1962).

Mr. Ustinov wrote and directed *Halfway Up the Tree* (Brooks Atkinson Th., N.Y.C., Nov. 7, 1967); and wrote and starred in *The Unknown Soldier and His Wife* (Vivian Beaumont Th., Lincoln Center, N.Y.C., July 6, 1967, and George Abbott Th., N.Y.C., Sept. 18, 1967). Other productions of the latter were staged at the Chichester (England) Festival (1968), and at the New London (England) Th. (1973).

Mr. Ustinov directed his first opera, Mozart's *The Magic Flute*, for the Hamburg (Germany) Opera in 1968. In 1973, he directed and designed scenery and costumes for *Don Giovanni* at the Edinburgh (Scotland) Festival, and produced, directed and designed the sets and costumes for Massenet's *Don Quichotte* for the Paris Opera.

Films. Mr. Ustinov made his debut in *Mein Kampf* (1941); subsequently, appeared in *The Way Ahead* (20th-Fox, 1945); was producer, director, and scenarist for a British Air Ministry documentary, *School for Secrets* (1946); appeared in *Odette* (Lopert, 1951); *Hotel Sahara* (UA, 1951); played Nero in *Quo Vadis* (MGM, 1951); appeared in *Beau Brummel* (MGM, 1954); *The Egyptian* (20th-Fox, 1954); played Joseph in *We're No Angels* (Par., 1955); *Spartacus* (U, 1960); *The Sundowners* (WB, 1960); produced, directed and repeated his stage role of the General in the film version of *Romanoff and Juliet* (U, 1961); and produced, directed, appeared in *Billy Budd* (Allied, 1962); *Topkapi* (UA, 1964); *John Goldfarb, Please Come Home* (20th-Fox, 1965); *The Comedians* (MGM, 1967); *Blackbeard's Ghost* (Buena Vista, 1968); *Hot Millions* (MGM, 1968); *Viva Max* (Commonwealth United, 1969); *Big Truck and Poor Clare* (Kastner-Judd-Kanter, 1971); and *Hammersmith Is Out* (Cinerama, 1972).

Television. Mr. Ustinov wrote the script for *Crescendo* (CBS); appeared in *Peer Gynt* (BBC); wrote the script for *Moment of Truth*, in which he also appeared (Omnibus, NBC, Feb. 23, 1958); played the title role in *The Life of Samuel Johnson;* wrote the script for *The Empty Chair*, in which he played Danton (NBC, Dec. 8, 1958); narrated *The Countdown* (CBS, Apr. 5, 1958); in London, he appeared in Ustinov in Orbit (ATV, 1962). He starred in *Bare-*

foot in Athens on Omnibus (CBS, 1966); and *Storm in Summer* for Hallmark Hall of Fame (NBC, 1970). He has appeared as a guest on many variety and talk shows with such hosts as Jack Paar, Perry Como, Steve Allen and David Frost.

Published Works. His published plays include *House of Regrets* (1942), *Beyond* (1943), *Blow Your Own Trumpet* (1943), *The Banbury Nose* (1944), *The Tragedy of Good Intentions* (1945), *The Indifferent Shepherd* (1948), *High Balcony* (1952), and *Paris, Not So Gay* (1958).

His books include *Add a Dash of Pity* (1959), *Ustinov's Diplomats* (1960), *The Loser* (1960), *We Were Only Human* (1961), *Frontiers of the Sea* (1966) and *Krumnagel* (1971).

Discography. Mr. Ustinov has recorded *Peter and the Wolf, Mock Mozart, Grand Prix of Gibraltar, The Nutcracker Suite, The Soldier's Tale, Hary Janos,* and *The Little Prince.*.

Awards. For his play, *The Love of Four Colonels,* Mr. Ustinov received the NY Drama Critics' Circle Award for "the best foreign play" of the season, and the Donaldson Award (1953). He received the London *Evening Standard* Drama Award for the "best new play," *Romanoff and Juliet* (1957); the Benjamin Franklin Award (1957) from the Royal Society of Arts; a NATAS (Emmy) Award for his performance in *The Life of Samuel Johnson;* a Golden Globe Award (Foreign Press, Hollywood) for his performance in *Quo Vadis;* an Academy (Oscar) Award as best supporting actor for *Spartacus* (1960); and a NARAS (Grammy) Award for his recording of *Peter and the Wolf.*

Mr. Ustinov received the Academy Award for best supporting actor for his performance in *Topkapi* (1964). He received the NATAS (Emmy) Award as outstanding single performance in a leading role for his performances in *Barefoot in Athens* (1966), and in *Storm in Summer* (1970).

He has received the following honorary doctorate degrees: Music (Cleveland Inst. of Music, 1967); Laws (Univ. of Dundee, 1969); Laws (La Salle College of Philadelphia, 1971); and the Arts (Univ. of Lancaster, 1972). In 1968, Mr. Ustinov was made a rector of the Univ. of Dundee (Scotland) and was reinstated in that post in 1971.

Recreation. Squash, tennis, music.

V

VACCARO, BRENDA. Actress. b. Brenda Buell Vaccaro, Nov. 18, 1939, Brooklyn, N.Y., to Mario A. and Christina (Pavia) Vaccaro. Father, lawyer, restaurateur; mother, restaurateur. Grad. Thomas Jefferson H.S., Dallas, Tex., 1958; Neighborhood Playhouse Sch. of the Th., N.Y.C., 1960. Member of AEA; SAG; AFTRA.

Theatre. Miss Vaccaro first performed as an Old Woman in a school production of *The Land of Dreams Come True* (Ursuline Acad., Dallas, Tex., Apr. 1946).

She made her professional debut as Angelina in *The Willow Tree* (Margo Jones Th., Dallas, 1951); subsequently played Gloria Gulock in *Everybody Loves Opal* (Longacre, N.Y.C., Oct. 11, 1961); Miss Novick in *Tunnel of Love* (Westbury Music Fair, N.Y., June 1, 1962); Laura Howard in *The Affair* (Henry Miller's Th., N.Y.C., Sept. 20, 1952); and Melissa Peabody in *Children from Their Games* (Morosco, Apr. 11, 1963).

She played Toni in *Cactus Flower* (Royale, Dec. 8, 1965); Reedy Harris in *The Natural Look* (Longacre, Mar. 11, 1967); Cynthia in *How Now, Dow Jones* (Lunt-Fontanne Th., Dec. 7, 1967); Nancy Scott in *The Goodbye People* (Ethel Barrymore Th., Dec. 3, 1968); and Louise in *Father's Day* (John Golden Th., Mar. 16, 1971).

Films. Miss Vaccaro appeared in *I Love My Wife* (U, 1970) and *Once Is Not Enough* (1975).

Television. She appeared in The Greatest Show on Earth (ABC, July 9, 1963); The Fugitive (ABC, Aug. 23, 1963); The Defenders (CBS, June 29, 1964); Mar. 25, 1965); The F.B.I. (ABC, Nov. 23, 1969); The Name of the Game (NBC, Feb. 26, 1971); Marcus Welby (ABC, Oct. 10, 1972); Banacek (NBC, Nov. 15, 1972); McCloud (NBC, Dec. 24, 1972); *Sunshine* (CBS, Nov. 9, 1973); *The Trial of Julius and Ethel Rosenberg* (ABC, Jan. 28, 1974); and her own series, *Sara* (1976).

Awards. She received the *Theatre World* Award for her performance as Gloria Gulock in *Everybody Loves Opal* (1961) and was nominated for Antoinette Perry (Tony) awards, for 1965–66 in the supporting actress category for her performance in *Cactus Flower* and for 1967–68 in the female musical star for her performance in *How Now, Dow Jones.*.

VALE, MARTIN. Playwright. b. Marguerite Vale. Married 1922 to Bayard Veiller, playwright, press representative (dec. June 16, 1943).

Theatre. Miss Vale wrote *The Two Mrs. Carrolls* (St. Martin's Th., London, June 12, 1935), which was subsequently presented in a pre-Bway tour (National, Washington, D.C., Dec. 28, 1936; closed out of town), and in N.Y.C. (Booth, Aug. 3, 1943). She wrote, with her husband, Bayard Veiller, *'Twill Freeze Your Blood.*

Films. *The Two Mrs. Carrolls* was filmed (WB, 1947).

Television. *The Two Mrs. Carrolls* was presented on television (1961).

VALENCY, MAURICE. Educator, playwright. b. Maurice Jacques Valency, Mar. 22, 1903, New York City, to Jacques and Mathilde (Solesme) Valency. Grad. Townsend Harris Hall H.S., N.Y.C., 1919; City Coll. of New York, A.B. 1923. Columbia Univ., A.M. 1924; LL.B. 1927; Ph.D. 1939. Married Dec. 25, 1936, to Janet Cornell. Member of ASCAP; WGA, East: Dramatists Guild (on council, 1950–72; vice-pres., Dramatists Guild Fund, 1962–to date; bd. of dir., Dramatists Play Service, 1958–68); Renaissance Soc. of Amer.; Amer. Comparative Literature Assn. (adv. bd.); MLA; Dante Soc.; Chinese Art Soc.; Authors League (secy. 1966–to date; bd. of dir., Authors League Fund, 1966–to date); Pulitzer Prize Drama Jury (chmn., bd. of dir. 1952–68); National Book Award Jury (1969, 1971); Asian Soc. Address: (home) 404 Riverside Dr., New York, NY 10025, tel. (212) RI 9-5181; (bus.) The Julliard School, Lincoln Center, New York, NY 10023, tel. (212) 799-5000.

Mr. Valency is director of Academic Studies at the Juilliard Sch. (1971–to date). He is professor emeritus (1971) at Columbia Univ., where he had previously served as Brander Matthews professor of dramatic literature (1968–71); professor of comparative literature (1954–68); and associate professor (1946–54). He previously held academic positions at City Coll. of New York (instructor in philosophy, 1931–33); and Brooklyn Coll. (instructor in English, 1933–42; assistant professor, 1942–46).

Theatre. Mr. Valency wrote *Whirlpool* (Hedgerow Th., Moylan, Pa., 1928); *The Thracian Horses* (Cleveland Play House, Ohio, 1941; Brandeis Festival, Brandeis Univ., Waltham, Mass., 1956; Lyric, Hammersmith, London, May 8, 1946; Rome, October 15, 1950; Orpheum, N.Y.C., Sept. 27, 1961); *The Reluctant Virgin* (Cain Park, Cleveland, Ohio, 1947); and *The Long Night* (Florida State Univ., 1963).

He wrote the English adaptation of Giraudoux's *The Madwoman of Chaillot* (Belasco, N.Y.C., Dec. 27, 1948); *The Enchanted* (Lyceum, Jan. 18, 1950); *Ondine* (46 St. Th., Feb. 18, 1954); and a double-bill *The Virtuous Island* and *The Apollo of Bellac* (Carnegie Hall Playhouse, Apr. 9, 1957).

Mr. Valency adapted Duerrenmatt's play *The Visit* (Lunt-Fontanne Th., May 5, 1958); for the Metropolitan Opera Co., adapted the librettos for *La Perichole* (November 25, 1958), and *The Gypsy Baron* (Dec. 15, 1960); and, for the American Opera Center, adapted Chabrier's *Le Roi Malgre Lui* (Juilliard Sch. of Music, 1974).

Television. Mr. Valency wrote *Battleship Bismarck* (CBS, 1951); for Omnibus, wrote *Toine* (1953); *The Man without A Country* (1953); *The Apollo of Bellac* (1954); *She Stoops To Conquer* (1955); and *The Virtuous Island* (1956); for GE Th. (CBS), *The Second Stranger* (1957), and *Feathertop* (1957). Among his other television credits are plays for Alcoa (ABC) and The Hallmark Hall of Fame (NBC).

Other Activities. Mr. Valency serves as Humanities advisor to the Text-Film Division of McGraw Hill, and is Humanities advisory editor for the Encyclopedia Americana.

Published Works. Mr. Valency has published *The Tragedies of Herod* (1939); *In Praise of Love* (1959); *The Palace of Pleasure* (1960); *The Flower and the Castle* (1963); *The Breaking String* (1966); and *The Cart and the Trumpet* (1973). He has also written numerous articles and reviews.

Awards. He received a Ford Foundation research grant (1958); two Guggenheim Fellowships (1961, 1963); and his adaptations of *The Madwoman of Chaillot* (1948), *Ondine* (1954), and *The Visit* (1959) won the NY Drama Critics Awards for foreign plays. Mr. Valency has received several ASCAP Awards (Standard, 1965–to date).

VALENTINE, PAUL. Actor, choreographer, dancer. b. William Wolf Daixel, Mar. 23, 1919, New York City. Grad. Commercial H.S. Married to Lili St. Cyr, performer (marr. dis. 1949); married May 6, 1952, to Princess Flavine Sultana Bashi Abdul Alikhan. Member of AEA; SAG; AGVA; AGMA; AFTRA.

Theatre. Mr. Valentine began as a dancer at age fourteen, with the Ballet Russe de Monte Carlo; subsequently danced with the Fokine Ballet, and the Mordkin Ballet. Billed as Valia Valentinoff, he made his N.Y.C. debut as the Premier Dancer of Drury Lane in *Virginia* (Center Th., Sept. 2, 1937); billed as Valentinoff, appeared in the revue, *Sons o' Fun* (Winter Garden, Dec. 1, 1941); played Francois Robert in the pre-Bway tryout of *Marianne* (opened National, Washington, D.C., Jan. 10, 1944); and billed as Val Valentinoff played Felix Charrel and Sailor Val in *Follow the Girls* (Century, N.Y.C., Apr. 8, 1944). Billed as Paul Valentine, he appeared as Pinky Harris in *Wish You Were Here* (Imperial, June 25, 1952); Clayton Harrison in *Hit the Trail* (Mark Hellinger Th., Dec. 2, 1954); Frank Butler in a stock production of *Annie Get Your Gun* (Capri, Atlantic Beach, N.J., June 25, 1956); and a Spaniard in *Oh, Captain!* (Alvin, N.Y.C., Feb. 2, 1958).

For Lili St. Cyr, Mr. Valentine has choreographed, directed and produced *The Lively Arts; French Postcard Revue; Life Is a Circus,* and other routines.

In summer stock, Mr. Valentine played Prince Danilo in *The Merry Widow* (Greek Th., Los Angeles, Calif.), and has appeared in *Golden Boy, Rain, The Little Foxes,* and *Personal Appearance.*.

Films. Mr. Valentine appeared in *Out of the Past* (RKO, 1947); *House of Strangers* (20th-Fox, 1949); *Love Happy* (UA, 1949); *Special Agent* (Par., 1949); *Something to Live For* (Par., 1952); and *Love Island* (Astor, 1953).

Television and Radio. On radio, Mr. Valentine performed on True Confessions, National Hour, and Best Sellers. On television, he appeared in Martin Kane (CBS); Danger (CBS); Lights Out! (NBC); and the Paul Winchell Show.

Night Clubs. Mr. Valentine has performed at Leon and Eddie's (N.Y.C., 1952); Stage Coach Inn (Hackensack, N.J., 1954, 1955); The Elegante (Brooklyn, N.Y., 1955); and at the Midwood Terrace (Brooklyn, N.Y., 1957).

VAN, BOBBY. Actor, director, singer, dancer. b. Robert Van Stein, Dec. 6, 1935, to Harry King and Minna Ann Van Stein. Father, actor, dancer. Educ. N.Y.C. public schools, Metropolitan Vocational High School; NY Coll. of Music. Professional training with Joe Costello (trumpet); Juan Hernandez (acting). Married May 1, 1968, to Elaine Joyce. Member of SAG; AFTRA; AEA; AGUA. Address: (home) 724 No. Roxbury Dr., Beverly

Hills, CA 90210, tel. (213) 271-8500; (bus.) William Morris Agency, 1350 Ave. of the Americas, New York, NY 10019, tel. (212) 586-5100.

Theatre. Mr. Van's first stage appearances were in USO vaudeville shows at Seamens Institute, N.Y.C., and at Forts Dix and Monmouth, N.J. (all 1946). His professional debut in vaudeville (Lyric Th., Fitchburg, Mass., 1947) was followed by engagements in Miami, Fla. (Olympia Th., 1948) and N.Y.C. (Strand Th., 1949; Paramount Th., 1950). His first Bway show was *Alive and Kicking* (Winter Garden Th., Jan. 17, 1950); he toured in the American Legion revue *Red, White and Blue* (opened Paramount, Los Angeles, Oct. 7, 1950; closed Opera House, Chicago, Jan. 20, 1951); played Junior in a revival of *On Your Toes* (46 St. Th., N.Y.C., Oct. 11, 1954); made his London debut at the Palladium (1958); appeared in a summer stock production of *Pal Joey* (Circle Th., San Diego, Cal., 1960); played Billy Early in a revival of *No, No, Nanette* (46 St. Th., Jan. 17, 1971); and Steve Anderson in *Doctor Jazz* (Winter Garden, Mar. 19, 1975).

Films. Mr. Van's first film, *Because You're Mine* (MGM, 1952), was followed by *Skirts Ahoy!* (MGM, 1952); *Small Town Girl* (MGM, 1953); *The Affairs of Dobie Gillis* (MGM, 1953); *Kiss Me Kate* (MGM, 1954); *Lost Flight* (U, 1968); and *Lost Horizon* (Col., 1973).

Television. Mr. Van's first television appearance was on the Admiral Broadway Revue (1950). He was on the Milton Berle Show (NBC, 1951) and was in *The Time of Your Life* (Playhouse 90, CBS, Sept. 1958).

Night Clubs. Mr. Van appeared at Chez Ami, Buffalo, N.Y. (1948) and Copacabana, N.Y.C. (May 1955).

Awards. Mr. Van received an Antoinette Perry (Tony) Award nomination as best actor in a musical (1970–71) for his performance in *No, No, Nanette.*

VANCE, NINA. Producer, director. b. Nina Eloise Whittington, Oct. 22, Yoakum, Tex., to Calvin Perry and Minerva (De Witt) Whittington. Father, cotton broker. Grad. Yoakum (Tex.) H.S., 1930. Texas Christian Univ., A.B. 1935; attended Univ. of Southern California, 1936; Columbia Univ., 1937. Member of AEA; ANTA; Theatre Communications Group. Address: (home) 1400 Hermann Dr., Houston, TX 77004; (bus.) Alley Theatre, 615 Texas Ave., Houston, TX 77002, tel. (713) 228-9341.

Pre-Theatre. English and drama teacher.

Theatre. Miss Vance has been producer and director of the Alley Th., Houston, Tex., since its inception in 1947.

For the Alley Th., she has directed the following productions: *A Sound of Hunting* (Nov. 18, 1947); *Payment Deferred* (Feb. 3, 1948); *Another Part of the Forest* (Apr. 6, 1948); *Caroline* (May 9, 1948); *Clash By Night* (Oct. 5, 1948); *John Loves Mary* (Nov. 30, 1948); *The Children's Hour* (Feb. 8, 1949); *Another Language* (Apr. 5, 1949); *Desire Under the Elms* (July 12, 1949); *The Gentle People* (Oct. 25, 1949); *No Exit* (Dec. 7, 1949); *Season with Ginger* (Feb. 7, 1950); *Light Up the Sky* (Apr. 25, 1950); *Wingless Victory* (June 20, 1950); *Joshua Beene and God* (Nov. 1, 1950); *The Magic Fallacy* (Dec. 31, 1950); *Golden Boy* (Feb. 13, 1951); *Angelica* (June 5, 1951); *The Hasty Heart* (July 21, 1951); *The Enchanted* (Aug. 23, 1951); *Goodbye, My Fancy* (Sept. 27, 1951); *Thunder Rock* (Nov. 15, 1951); *The Man* (Dec. 31, 1951); *Miss Julie* (Feb. 12, 1952); *Life with Mother* (Apr. 24, 1952); *Home of the Brave* (June 26, 1952); *The Barretts of Wimpole Street* (July 21, 1952); *The Skin of Our Teeth* (Nov. 6, 1952); *Burlesque* (Dec. 25, 1952); *Stalag 17* (1952); *Rose Tattoo* (Feb. 5, 1953); *My Dear Delinquents* (Apr. 21, 1953); *Elizabeth the Queen* (June 23, 1953); *I Am a Camera* (Aug. 6, 1953); *Miranda* (Oct. 1, 1953); *The Play's the Thing* (1953); *Death of a Salesman* (Feb. 23, 1954); *Mrs. McThing* (Apr. 22, 1954); *The Shrike* (May 27, 1954); *Affairs of State* (July 1, 1954); *Open House* (Sept. 14, 1954); *Picnic* (Oct. 19, 1954); *My Three Angels* (Dec. 16, 1954); *All My Sons* (Dec. 25, 1954); *Dial 'M' for Murder* (Mar. 1, 1955); *The Lady's not for Burning* (Apr. 15, 1955); *Light Up the Sky* (May 17, 1955); *The Remarkable Mr. Pennypacker* (July 12, 1955); *The Rainmaker* (Sept. 13, 1955); *The Glass Menagerie* (Oct. 25, 1955); *The Tender Trap* (Dec. 25, 1955); *Hedda Gabler* (Feb. 25, 1956); *Fifth Season* (Mar. 20, 1956); *Room Full of Roses* (May 29, 1956); *Detective Story* (July 17, 1956); *Career* (Aug. 28, 1956); *Sabrina Fair* (Sept. 25, 1956); *Anastasia* (Nov. 8, 1956); *Anniversary Waltz* (Dec. 25, 1956); *A View From the Bridge* (Feb. 13, 1957); *The Lark* (Apr. 24, 1957); *Wedding Breakfast* (May 23, 1957); *Time Limit* (June 27, 1957); *Time Out for Ginger* (Aug. 8, 1957); *The Chalk Garden* (Oct. 3, 1957); *Will Success Spoil Rock Hunter?* (Nov. 7, 1957); *The Matchmaker* (Dec. 26, 1957); *The Reluctant Debutante* (Feb. 6, 1958); *Three Love Affairs,* a triple-bill (Oct. 3, 1958); *Julius Caesar* (Apr. 17, 1958); *Middle of the Night* (May 15, 1958); *Champagne Complex* (June 19, 1958); *The Remarkable Mr. Pennypacker* (July 24, 1958); *Gigi* (Sept. 4, 1958); *The Madwoman of Chaillot* (Oct. 9, 1958); *Spider's Web* (Nov. 12, 1958); *The Wonderful Cure* (Nov. 27, 1958); *Tunnel of Love* (Dec. 23, 1958); *The Crucible* (Feb. 5, 1959); *Orpheus Descending* (May 7, 1959); *The Iceman Cometh* (July 8, 1959); *Rashomon* (Nov. 11, 1959); *Waltz of the Toreadors* (Dec. 10, 1959); *Moon for the Misbegotten* (Apr. 13, 1960); *Mister Roberts* (July 20, 1960); *The Library Raid* (Oct. 12, 1960); *Jane* (Nov. 9, 1960); *Ondine* (Dec. 14, 1960); *An Enemy of the People* (Feb. 22, 1961); *Six Characters in Search of an Author* (Apr. 19, 1961); with John Wylie, a bill composed of *The Proposal, In the Zone, Bound East for Cardiff, The End of the Beginning,* collectively entitled *Friends and Lovers* (May 10, 1961); *Misalliance* (Oct. 17, 1961); *Volpone* (Dec. 12, 1961); the premiere of *Garden Spot U.S.A.* (Apr. 25, 1962); *One Woman Show* (May 10, 1962); *The Miracle Worker* (May 16, 1962); *Becket* (Oct. 24, 1962); *Long Day's Journey into Night* (May 22, 1963); *The Queen and the Rebels* (Oct. 23, 1963); *The Three Sisters* (Feb. 26, 1964); *The Trojan Women* (Nov. 25, 1964); *The Tenth Man* (Jan. 6, 1965); *The Effect of Gamma Rays on Man in the Moon Marigolds* (world premiere, May 12, 1965); *Right You Are If You Think You Are* (Jan. 5, 1966); *Duel of Angels* (Mar. 30, 1966); *The Sea Gull* (Feb. 22, 1967); *The Caretaker* (July 18, 1967); *Galileo* (Nov. 26, 1968); *The Rose Tattoo* (Oct. 16, 1969); *Mourning Becomes Electra* (Oct. 22, 1970); *Camino Real* (October 21, 1971); *Pantagleize* (Oct. 1972); *All over* (1973) and *The Purification* (1973).

She has also staged productions of *The Matchmaker* (Playhouse-in-the-Park, Philadelphia, Pa., June 1960); *The Crucible* (Playhouse-in-the-Park, Philadelphia, Pa., June 1961); and *Volpone* (Arena Stage, Washington, D.C., Dec. 1962).

Other Activities. Miss Vance was invited by President John F. Kennedy to serve on the Advisory Committee of the proposed Natl. Cultural Ctr. (1961); and was appointed by the Secretary of State to the Advisory Committee on the Arts of the US Advisory Commission in Education and Cultural Affairs (1961).

Awards. She received a grant from the English Speaking Union (1958) to observe and report on theatre conditions in Eng.; a $10,000 personal director's grant from the Ford Foundation for travel and study (1959); and the Matrix Award (1960) from Theta Sigma Phi in recognition for her outstanding contribution to the field of fine arts.

In 1962, the Alley Th. received a $2.1 million Grant from the Ford Foundation to construct a new building in downtown Houston on a site given the Alley by Houston Endowment, Inc., totaling 5/6ths of a square block. The New Alley Theatre opened in December 1968.

In May 1969, Miss Vance was given an honorary D.Litt. degree from the Univ. of St. Thomas, Houston, Tex.

VAN CLEVE, EDITH. Talent representative, actress, director. b. Edith Livingston Van Cleve, Oct. 11, 1903, Cleveland, Ohio, to Herman Baker and Adele (Battershall) Van Cleve. Father, industrialist. Grad. Montclair (N.J.) H.S., 1920. Studied at AADA, N.Y.C., 1921; with Theodora Ursula Irvine, Montclair, N.J. and N.Y.C., 1921; Charles Jehlinger, N.Y.C., 1921. Member of AEA (on council, 1937–42), AFTRA, SAG, Amer. Horse Shows Assn., Eastern Saddle Horse Breeders Assn., US Equestrian Team, American Saddle Horse Breeder's Assoc., The Fund for Animals and Animal Rights, Inc., Common Cause, Friends of the Earth, Environmental Defense Fund, Animal Welfare Inst. Address: (home) Plaza Hotel, Fifth Ave. at 59th St., New York, NY 10019, tel. (212) PL 9-3000; (bus.) Bret Adams, Ltd., 36 E. 61st St., New York, NY 10021, tel. (212) PL 2-7864.

Since 1941, Miss Van Cleve has been an artists representative, and currently is associated with Bret Adams, Ltd.

Theatre. She made her first appearance as a Wedding Guest and understudied Jane Cowl in a touring production of *Smilin' Through* (1921); subsequently made her N.Y.C. debut as Sister Carmen in *Malvaloca* (48 St. Th., Oct. 2, 1922); played Rosaline and understudied Jane Cowl as Juliet in *Romeo and Juliet* (Henry Miller's Th., Jan. 24, 1923); appeared as a Maid in *Pelleas and Melisande* (Times Sq., Dec. 4, 1923); Octavia in *Antony and Cleopatra* (Lyceum, Feb. 19, 1924); Baby in the pre-Bway tour of *The Butter and Egg Man* (Natl., Wash., D.C., 1924); and Gusti in *The Depths* (Broadhurst, N.Y.C., Jan. 27, 1925).

She played Mary in *The New Gallantry* (Cort, Sept. 14, 1925); appeared in the pre-Bway tour of *One of the Family* (Chicago, Ill., 1925); played Ruby in *Broadway* (Broadhurst, N.Y.C., Sept. 16, 1926); understudied Katherine Alexander as Isabel Drury, and succeeded (Nov. 1928) Katherine Carrington as Lucinda Overbeck in *Little Accident* (Morosco, Oct. 9, 1928); played Mademoiselle Elise de Mallet in *The Channel Road* (Plymouth, Oct. 17, 1929); toured as Lucille in *June Moon* (1930–31); and appeared in the pre-Bway tour of *Eldorado* (Newark, N.J., 1931).

Miss Van Cleve appeared as Miss Croft in *Wild Waves* (Times Sq. Th., N.Y.C., Feb. 19, 1932); Beth Harkness in *American Dream* (Guild, Feb. 21, 1933); Lucille in *June Moon* (Ambassador, May 15, 1933); Doris Grey in *Three and One* (Longacre, Oct. 25, 1933); Gloria in *Three Men on a Horse* (Playhouse, Jan. 30, 1935); succeeded (May 1936) Julie Lawrence as Peggy in *Boy Meets Girl* (Cort, Nov. 27, 1935); directed five touring-company productions of *Three Men on a Horse* (1935–36); played Lucy Powell in *Angel Island* (Natl., Oct. 20, 1937); Frances Fellowes in *All That Glitters* (Biltmore, Jan. 19, 1938); Miss Pike in *What a Life* (Biltmore, Apr. 13, 1938); Maggie Brown in *Ring Two* (Henry Miller's Th., Nov. 22, 1939); Maude in *Goodbye in the Night* (Biltmore, Mar. 18, 1940); appeared in the pre-Bway tour of *White-Haired Boy* (Wilbur, Boston, Mass., 1940); and was resident director of the Amherst Summer Th. (Mt. Kisco, N.Y.), appearing as the Wife in *Springtime for Henry,* and in *Paris Bound.*

Films. She appeared in *Hat, Coat, and Glove* (RKO, 1934); and the *The Age of Innocence* (RKO, 1934).

Recreation. Riding, driving, raising and showing American saddlebred horses, bridge, country living.

VANDERBILT, GLORIA. Actress, writer, painter. b. Gloria Laura Morgan Vanderbilt, Feb. 20, 1924, New York City, to Reginald and Gloria (Morgan) Vanderbilt. Father, financier. Grad. Mary C. Wheeler H.S., Providence, R.I., 1941. Studied acting at Neighborhood Playhouse Sch. of the Th., N.Y.C., 1955–58. Married Apr. 21, 1945, to Leopold Stokowski, conductor (marr. dis. 1955); two sons; married Aug. 27, 1956, to Sidney Lumet, director (marr. dis. 1963); married Dec. 24, 1963, to Wyatt Cooper, writer. Member of AEA; AFTRA; SAG; Dramatists Guild.

Theatre. Miss Vanderbilt made her debut touring stock theatres as Alexandra in *The Swan* (opened Pocono Playhouse, Pa., Aug. 1954); in N.Y.C. she subsequently played Elsie in *The Time of Your Life* (NY City Ctr., Jan. 19, 1955); Madge in *Picnic* (Ivoryton, Playhouse, Conn.; Falmouth Playhouse, Mass., Summer 1955); Olympia in *The Spa* (Paper Mill Playhouse, Millburn, N.J.; Hyde Park Playhouse, N.Y.; Cape Playhouse, Dennis, Mass., Summer 1956); Wilma in *The Minotaur*(Westport Country Playhouse, Conn., Sept. 2, 1957); the title role in *Peter Pan* (Andover Playhouse, Mass., Aug. 4, 1958); and Rosa in *The Burnt Flower Bed*(Westport Country Playhouse, Aug. 15, 1960).

Television. Miss Vanderbilt appeared on Kraft Th. (NBC, 1958); the Art Carney Special (Dupont Show of the Month, NBC, Nov. 4, 1959). She has also been on Studio One (CBS), US Steel Hour (CBS) Four Star Playhouse (CBS), and Adventures in Paradise (ABC).

Other Activities. Her paintings were exhibited at the Bertha Schaefer Gallery (N.Y.C., 1953) and the Juster Gallery (N.Y.C., 1957).

Published Works. She wrote short stories for *Cosmopolitan* (Aug. 1962; Aug. 1963); her book reviews have appeared in *Cosmopolitan, The Saturday Review of Literature,* and the New York *Times;* and she published *Love Poems* (1955).

Awards. Miss Vanderbilt received the Sylvania Award for her performance on the Art Carney Special (1959).

Recreation. Reading, bowling, going to the movies.

VAN der VLIS, DIANA. Actress. b. June 9, 1935, Toronto, Canada, to Adrian J. and Ann M. Van der Vlis. Father, store planner, interior decorator. Attended RADA, London, Eng., 1953–54; studied privately with Sanford Meisner at the Neighborhood Playhouse Sch. of the Th., N.Y.C., 2 1/2 years. Married June 6, 1960, to Roger T. Donald, publisher; one son, one daughter. Member of AEA; SAG; AFTRA.

Theatre. Miss Van der Vlis made her debut as June Stanley in *The Man Who Came to Dinner*(Little Th., Winnipeg, Canada, 1950); and her first professional appearance as Sorel Bliss in *Hay Fever* (Crest Th., Toronto, May 1955).

During 1955–56 at the Crest Th., she played Desdemona in *Othello,* Maria in *The School for Scandal,* Gloria in *You Never Can Tell,* Ismeme in *Antigone,* Raina Petkoff in *Arms and the Man,* and Sybil in *An Inspector Calls.*

She made her N.Y.C. debut as Cordelia Biddle in *The Happiest Millionaire* (Lyceum, Nov. 20, 1956); took over for Sarah Marshall as Ellen Spelding during the run of *Visit to a Small Planet* (Booth, Feb. 7, 1957), also touring in its (opened Playhouse, Wilmington, Del., Feb. 5, 1958; closed Geary, San Francisco, Calif., June 28, 1958); played Caroline Lawton in *Comes a Day*(Ambassador, N.Y.C., Nov. 6, 1958); Jennifer Grant in *A Mighty Man Is He* (Cort, Jan. 6, 1960); Antoinette Sevigne in *A Shot in the Dark* (Booth, Oct. 18, 1961); and Jane Escobar in *On an Open Roof* (Cort, Jan. 28, 1963).

She appeared at the 1968 American Shakespeare Festival, Stratford, Conn., as Rosalind in *As You Like It* (June 23) and in *Love's Labour's Lost* (June 26); was Mlle. de Ste. Euverte in *The Waltz of the Toreadors* (Eisenhower Th., John F. Kennedy Ctr., Washington, D.C., June 19, 1973; Circle in the Square/Joseph E. Levine Th., N.Y.C., Sept. 13, 1973); and was in a revival of *Present Laughter* (Eisenhower Th., John F. Kennedy Ctr., Apr. 29, 1975).

Films. She played Dr. Fairfax in *The Man with the X-Ray Eyes* (1963).

Television. She has appeared on Alfred Hitchcock Presents (CBS); Checkmate (CBS, 1960); East Side West Side (CBS, 1963); Dupont Show of the Week (NBC, 1963); The Fugitive (ABC, 1963); Route 66 (CBS, 1963); Doctor Kildare (NBC, 1964); and The Defenders (CBS, 1964).

VAN FLEET, JO. Actress. b. Oakland, Calif., to Roy H. and Elizabeth (Gardner) Van Fleet. Grad. Col. of the Pacific, B.A.; attended Neighborhood Playhouse Sch. of the Th. Studied acting with De Marcus Brown, Coll. of the Pacific; Sanford Meisner, Neighborhood Playhouse Sch. of the Th.; Elia Kazan, Lee Strasberg, Actors' Studio. Married to William Bales, teacher of modern dance; one son. Member of AEA; AFTRA; SAG. Address: c/o Maurice Greenbaum, 437 Madison Ave., New York, NY 10022, tel. (212) 758-4010.

Theatre. Miss Van Fleet made her theatrical debut as Miss Phipps in a touring production of *Uncle Harry*(1945). She made her N.Y.C. debut as Dorcas in *The Winter's Tale*(Cort Th., Jan. 15, 1946); subsequently appeared as Major Orlov in *The Whole World Over* (Biltmore, Mar. 27, 1947); Connie in *The Closing Door* (Empire, Dec. 1, 1949); Regan in *King Lear*(National, Dec. 25, 1950); Miss Foster in *Flight Into Egypt* (Music Box, Mar. 18, 1952); Marguerite Gautier in *Camino Real*(National, Mar. 19, 1953); and Jessie Mae Watts in *The Trip to Bountiful* (Henry Miller's Th., Nov. 3, 1953). She played Daisy in *My Aunt Daisy* (Westport Country Playhouse, Conn., Summer 1954); Eliza Gant in *Look Homeward, Angel* (Ethel Barrymore Th., N.Y.C., Nov. 28, 1957); Amanda Wingfield in *The Glass Menagerie* (Westport Country Playhouse, Conn., Summer 1959); Frances in *Rosemary*and Mrs. Kittel in *The Alligators*(York Playhouse, N.Y.C., Nov. 14, 1960); Claire Zachanassian in *The Visit* (Playhouse-in-the-Park, Philadelphia, Pa., Summer 1961); and Frieda in *I Rise in Flames Cried the Phoenix,* and the title role in *The Lady from Larkspur Lotion*(Festival of Two Worlds, Spoleto, Italy, Summer, 1961). She played Madame Rosepettle in *Oh Dad, Poor Dad, Mama's Hung You in the Closet and I'm Feelin' So Sad*(Phoenix, N.Y.C., Feb. 26, 1962); and appeared in *The Effect of Gamma Rays on Man-In-The-Moon Marigolds* and *The Gingerbread Lady* (Arena Th., Buffalo, N.Y.).

Films. Miss Van Fleet appeared in *East of Eden* (WB, 1955); *The Rose Tattoo* (Par., 1955); *I'll Cry Tomorrow*(MGM, 1955); *Gunfight at the O.K. Corral* (Par., 1956); *The King and Four Queens*(UA, 1956); *This Angry Age* (Col., 1957); and *Wild River* (Col., 1960). She has also appeared in *I Love You, Alice B. Toklas; 80 Steps to Jonah;*and *The Gang Who Couldn't Shoot Straight.*

Awards. For her performance as Jessie Mae Watts in *The Trip to Bountiful,* Miss Van Fleet received the Donaldson Award, the Antoinette Perry (Tony) Award, and a *Show Business* Award (1954). She received the *Look* Magazine Award, the *Film Daily* Award, and the Motion Picture Exhibitors Award for her performance in *I'll Cry Tomorrow*(1955). She also received the Academy (Oscar) Award for her performance in *East of Eden* (1955); won the *Variety* NY Drama Critics Poll Award (1958) for her performance as Eliza Gant in *Look Homeward, Angel.* From the Coll. of the Pacific, she was awarded an honorary degree of D.F.A.

van GRIETHUYSEN, TED. Actor, director, costume designer. b. Theodore Andre van Griethuysen, Jr., Nov. 7, 1934, Ponca City, Okla., to Theodore Andre and Treva Jane (Ogan) van Griethuysen. Father, oil company employee. Grad. Lamar H.S., Houston, Tex., 1952; Univ. of Texas, B.F.A. (summa cum laude) 1956); attended Yale Univ. Sch. of Drama, 1957–58. Studied acting with B. Iden Payne, Austin, Tex., (1952–56); at LAMDA, London, Eng., 1956–57; with William Hickey, N.Y.C., 1959–60; with Michael Howard, N.Y.C., 1960–61; Aesthetic Realism with Eli Siegel. Married May 26, 1962, to Rebecca Thompson, actress. Member of AEA; SAG; AFTRA; United Scenic Artists (assoc. mem. in costume design, 1959–to date). Address: 110 Bank St., New York, NY 10014, tel. (212) YU 9-0845.

Theatre. Mr. van Griethuysen made his debut as the Lion in *Androcles and the Lion* (Four Arts Th., Houston, Tex., Oct. 24, 1951); subsequently appeared there as Sebastian in *Twelfth Night* (Jan. 31, 1952); Michael Brown in *O Mistress Mine*(Little Th., Apr. 23, 1952); Rudy Gibbons in *My Dear Delinquents* (Alley Th., June 23, 1953); Orestes in *The Flies* (Alley Th., Jan. 18, 1955); in 1955, appeared at the San Diego (Calif.) Shakespeare Festival as Claudio in *Measure for Measure,* Gremio in *The Taming of the Shrew,* and Laertes in *Hamlet;* in 1956, at the Oregon Shakespeare Festival as Romeo in *Romeo and Juliet;* Clarence in *Richard III;* Guiderius in *Cymbeline;* and the King of Navarre in *Love's Labour's Lost.*

He appeared (1957), in LAMDA (London) productions as Rameses in *The Firstborn;* in the title role of *Richard III;* as Iago in *Othello;* and was production assistant to Peter Brook for the London production of *The Tempest* (Drury Lane, Dec. 5, 1957).

At the Williamstown (Mass.) Summer Th. (1958), Mr. van Griethuysen played Pierre in *The Madwoman of Chaillot* and the Prince in *Time Remembered;* appeared as the Rake in *The Failures* (Fourth St. Th., N.Y.C., Jan. 5, 1959); Li-Wang in a revival of *Lute Song*(NY City Ctr., Mar. 12, 1959); the Prince in *Time Remembered* (Stockbridge Summer Th., Mass. 1959), where he also appeared as Octavius in *Man and Superman;* Judd Steiner in *Compulsion;* John Worthing in *The Importance of Being Earnest;* Thomas Mendip in the *Lady's Not for Burning;* and Lord Brockhurst in *The Boyfriend.* He played Tom Lee in the ELT showcase production of *Tea and Sympathy* (Majestic, N.Y.C., Apr. 20, 1959); the Son in the ANTA Matinee Series' production of *The Purification* (Th. de Lys, Dec. 8, 1959); was costume designer for *The Crystal Heart* (E. 74 St. Th., Feb. 15, 1960); played Ferdinand in *Love and Intrigue*(IASTA, Feb. 1960); and appeared in a concert reading of Eli Siegel's *Hamlet: Revisited* (Terrain Gallery, Dec. 8, 1960).

At the American Shakespeare Festival, Stratford, Conn., he played Florizel in *The Winter's Tale*(April 25, 1960); Adrian in *The Tempest* (June 19, 1960); and the Egyptian Messenger in *Antony and Cleopatra* (July 31, 1960); at the Phoenix Th., N.Y.C., played Mr. Hastings in *She Stoops to Conquer* (Nov. 1, 1960); Sgt. Tinley in *The Plough and the Stars* (Dec. 6, 1960); Jules Thibodeaux in *The Octoroon* (Jan. 27, 1961); and Laertes in *Hamlet* (Mar. 16, 1961).

At the American Shakespeare Festival Theatre, Stratford, Conn., he played M. Le Beau in *As You Like It*(June 15, 1961); Donalbain in *Macbeth* (June 16, 1961); and Troilus in *Troilus and Cressida* (July 23, 1961), which was later presented at the White House in a program of scenes from Shakespeare (Oct. 5, 1961); appeared as Young Marlow in *O Marry Me!*(Gate, N.Y.C., Oct. 27, 1961); Ayamonn in *Red Roses for Me* (Greenwich Mews, Nov. 27, 1961); made his Bway debut as Aemilian in *Romulus* (Music Box, Jan. 10, 1962); played Oliver Brown in *The Moon Beseiged*(Lyceum, Dec. 5, 1962); directed and appeared in a return engagement of *Hamlet: Revisited*(Terrain Gallery, Jan. 20, 1963); appeared in *The Reality Comic Show* (Terrain Gallery, July 4, 1963); played Richard III in *The White Rose and the Red* (Stage 73, Mar. 16, 1964); and Oberon in the NY Shakespeare Festival's traveling production of *A Midsummer Night's Dream* (June 27, 1964); played Jones/Maples in *Inadmissible Evidence* (Belasco, N.Y.C., Nov. 30, 1965); designed costumes for *Javelin* (Actors' Playhouse, Nov. 10, 1966); played Cardinal Bellarmine in *Galileo* (Vivian Beaumont Th., Apr. 13, 1967); associate in acting, Sch. of Arts (Columbia Univ., 1967–68); played Tim Law in *Basement* (Eastside Playhouse, Oct., 1968).

Mr. van Griethuysen founded the Opposites Company and is the artistic director (1968–to date). He played Joseph Surface in *School for Scandal*(Terrain Gallery, Summer, 1969); Mr. Horner in *The Country Wife* (Terrain Gallery, Summer, 1969); Orestes in *Andromache* (Terrain Gallery, Summer, 1969); directed and played the role of Eilert Lovborg in *Hedda Gabler* (Terrain Gallery, Dec. 6, 1969); re-opened Actors' Playhouse (Jan. 16, 1970); directed and played *Othello* (Terrain Gallery, June, 1972); and played Rip Van Winkle/Richard III in *Goodbye Profit System*(Terrain Gallery, Aug., 1972).

Television. He appeared as Mortimer in *Henry IV, Part I* (Play of the week, WNTA, 1960); the Son in *The Avenger* (The Defenders, CBS, 1962); the Young Sailor in *The Thunder of Ernie Bass* (The Nurses, CBS, 1962); Mr. Fenno in *The Patriot*(Hallmark Hall of Fame, NBC, 1963); and the title role in Mary Shelley's *Frankenstein* (The Human Stage, WOR); Little Fox in *The Pit* (Lamp Unto My Feet, CBS, 1965); Milton in *Lamp at Midnight* (Hallmark Hall of Fame, NBC, 1966); Gilles de Rais in *St. Joan* (Hallmark Hall of Fame, NBC, 1967); and Hansen in *Everybody Loved Him* (NYPD, ABC, 1969).

VAN HEUSEN, JAMES. Composer, producer. b. Edward Chester Babcock, Jan. 26, 1913, Syracuse, N.Y., to Arthur E. and Ida May (Williams) Babcock. Father, building contractor. Attended Central H.S., Syracuse, 1927–28; Cazenovia (N.Y.) Seminary, 1929. Studied in Syracuse with Prof. Colburn; voice with Dr. Howard Lyman; attended Syracuse Univ., 1930–32. Member of Composers & Lyricists Guild; AGAC; ALA; ASCAP; The Manuscript Society; Elks Club (Palm Springs, Calif.); Thunderbird Golf Club (Palm Springs, Calif.); Racquet Club and Press Club (Palm Springs, Calif.).

Pre-Theatre. Elevator operator.

Theatre. Mr. Van Heusen's first published song, "Harlem Hospitality," was performed in the *Cotton Club Revue* (Harlem, N.Y.C., Oct. 1933). He composed the scores for *Swingin' the Dream* (Center Th., Nov. 29, 1939); Billy Rose's Aquacade (NY World Fair, 1940); *Nellie Bly* (Adelphi, N.Y.C., Jan. 21, 1946); *Carnival in Flanders*, which he produced with Paula Stone, Mike Sloane, and Johnny Burke (New Century, Sept. 8, 1953); *Skyscraper* (Lunt-Fontanne Th., Nov. 13, 1965); and *Walking Happy* (Lunt-Fontanne Th., Nov. 26, 1966).

Films. Mr. Van Heusen wrote, with lyricist Johnny Burke and later with lyricist Sammy Cahn, scores or songs for *Love Thy Neighbor* (Par., 1940); *The Road to Zanzibar* (Par., 1941); *Playmates* (RKO, 1941); *Road to Morocco* (Par., 1942); *Dixie* (Par. 1943); *Lady in the Dark* (Par., 1944); *Going My Way* (Par., 1944); *Belle of the Yukon* (RKO, 1944); *Road to Utopia* (Par., 1945); *The Bells of St. Mary's* (RKO, 1945); *Welcome Stranger* (Par., 1947); *The Road to Rio* (Par., 1947); *A Connecticut Yankee in King Arthur's Court* (Par., 1949); and *Top o' the Morning* (Par., 1949).

Also, *Riding High* (Par., 1950); *Mr. Music* (Par., 1950); *You Can Change the World*, in which he also appeared (Goldwyn, 1951); *Road to Bali* (Par., 1952); *Little Boy Lost* (Par. 1953); *My Heart Goes Crazy* (UA, 1953); *Not as a Stranger* (UA, 1955); *Young at Heart* (WB, 1954); *Tender Trap* (MGM, 1955); *Anything Goes* (Par., 1956); *Pardners* (Par., 1956); *The Joker Is Wild* (Par., 1957); *Paris Holiday* (UA, 1958); *Some Came Running* (MGM, 1958); *Say One for Me* (20th-Fox, 1959); *A Hole in the Head* (UA, 1959); *Journey to the Center of the Earth* (20th-Fox, 1959); *Career* (Par., 1959); *This Earth Is Mine* (U, 1959); *Night of the Quarter Moon* (MGM, 1959); *Let's Make Love* (20th-Fox, 1960); *High Time* (20th-Fox, 1960); *Ocean's Eleven* (WB, 1960); *Who Was That Lady?* (Par., 1960); *Wake Me When It's Over* (20th-Fox, 1960); *The World of Suzie Wong* (Par., 1960); *Surprise Package* (Col., 1960); *The Road to Hong Kong* (UA., 1962); *Walk on the Wild Side* (Col., 1962); *Boys' Night Out* (MGM, 1962); *Papa's Delicate Condition* (Par., 1963); *Thoroughly Modern Millie* (U, 1967); and *Love and Marriage* (Embassy, 1969).

Television and Radio. Mr. Van Heusen composed the score for the musical version of Thornton Wilder's play *Our Town* (Producers Showcase, NBC, Sept. 19, 1955). With Sammy Cahn, he produced four spectaculars called the Frank Sinatra Show (1959–60). He composed the title song for the series Hazel (CBS).

Other Activities. He is a pilot with 8,000 flying hours to his record. During WW II, he worked with Lockheed Aircraft as production test pilot.

Published Works. He has composed music for such popular songs as "It's the Dreamer in Me" (1938); "All This and Heaven Too" 1939); "Darn That Dream" (1939); "Imagination" (1940); "Moonlight Becomes You" (1942); "Swinging on a Star" (1944); "But Beautiful" (1947) "Love and Marriage" (1955); "All the Way" (1957); "To Love and Be Loved" (1958); "High Hopes" (1959); "The Second Time Around" (1960); and "Call Me Irresponsible" (1963).

In Jan. 1944, Mr. Van Heusen and Johnny Burke formed their own music publishing firm, Burke-Van Heusen, Inc., and in 1950 they formed a second firm called Burvan. Both firms published other composers' works, as well as Messrs. Van Heusen and Burke's songs. Mr. Van Heusen is president of Burke-Van Heusen, Inc. and St. James Music Corp., and vice-president of Maraville Music Corp.

Awards. Messrs. Van Heusen and Burke received an Academy (Oscar) Award for their song "Swinging on a Star" (*Going My Way*, 1944); as well as nominations the same year for "Aren't You Glad You're You" from the same film, and "Sleighride in July" (*Belle of the Yukon)*. Messrs. Van Heusen and Cahn received Academy (Oscar) awards for their songs "All the Way" (*The Joker Is Wild*, 1957), and "High Hopes" (*Hole in the Head*, 1959); and nominations for "Love Is the Tender Trap" (*The Tender Trap*, 1955), "To Love and Be Loved" (*Some Came Running*, 1958), and "The Second Time Around" (*High Time*, 1960). They received an Academy (Oscar) Award for their song "Call Me Irresponsible" (*Papa's Delicate Condition*, 1964). "All the Way" received the Cash Box Award (1957) for most programmed record on radio.

His score for the television musical *Our Town* was nominated for a NATAS (Emmy) Award (1956), and the song "Love and Marriage" from the same show won the NATAS (Emmy) Award for best song of the year. Mr. Van Heusen and Sammy Cahn were nominated for a Tony Award (1967) as best composer and lyricist for *Walking Happy*.

He received a citation and plaque from US Secretary of the Treasury, Fred M. Vinson, for services rendered in behalf of the War Finance Program (Dec. 31, 1945); a silver medal from the US Treasury Dept. for services to the Treasury in behalf of war and victory loan campaigns (Apr. 3, 1946); a scroll from the officers and men of the 86th Infantry Regiment of the US Army for his song "The 86th! The 86th!; a commission as honorary Texas citizen from Gov. Price Daniel (Mar. 31, 1958); a plaque from the Los Angeles, Calif., City Council commending him for promoting better understanding through the international language of American song (1958); a Halo plaque from the Saints & Sinners organization of Los Angeles for distinguished service to help promote the program of providing milk for underprivileged children in Los Angeles city schools and giving financial aid to other worthy causes of the community in the field of humanitarianism (1958); and a Distinguished Alumnus Award from Cazenovia Seminary (June 1961).

VAN ITALLIE, JEAN-CLAUDE. Playwright, director, producer, teacher. b. May 25, 1936, Brussels, Belgium, to Hugo F. and Marthe M. van Itallie. Father, investment adviser. Att. Great Neck (N.Y.) H.S.; Deerfield (Mass.) Acad.; Harvard, B.A. 1958; studied acting at The Neighborhood Playhouse, Summer 1958. Member of Writers Guild of Amer. Address: 463 West St., New York, NY 10014.

Theatre. Mr. van Itallie debuted as a writer with *War* (Barr-Albee-Wilder Playwrights Workshop, N.Y.C., Dec. 22, 1963); subsequently, *Almost Like Being, I'm Really Here* and *Hunter and Bird* were presented at The Open Theatre (N.Y.C., 1963), where he was playwright-in-residence (1963–68). He wrote *Motel* and *Pavanne* (Cafe La Mama, N.Y.C., 1965); *American Hurrah* (Pocket Th., N.Y.C., Jan. 6, 1966; and Royal Cort Th., London, 1967); *The Serpent* (Teatro degil Arti, Rome, 1968; and Open Th., N.Y.C., Feb. 20, 1969); wrote and directed *King of the U.S.* (Th. for the New City, N.Y.C., May 15, 1972); and wrote *Mystery Play* (Cherry Lane Th., N.Y.C., Jan. 3, 1973). While playwright-in-residence at McCarter Th. (Princeton, N.J., 1973–74), he wrote a new version of *The Seagull* (McCarter Th., 1973; and Manhattan Th. Club, N.Y.C., Jan. 21, 1975).

Television. Mr. van Itallie wrote *The Stepinac Case* for Look Up and Live (CBS, 1963); and his *Pavanne* was presented on NET, 1965.

VAN NOSTRAND, MORRIS ABBOTT. Publisher, literary representative. b. Morris Abbott Van Nostrand, Jr., Nov. 24, 1911, New York City, to Morris Abbott and Margaret Adrianna (Edwards) Van Nostrand. Father, importer. Grad. St. Paul's Sch., Garden City, N.Y., 1930; Amherst Coll., B.A. 1934. Married Dec. 28, 1934, to Jane Alexander (dec. 1944); two daughters; married July 3, 1953, to Julia de La Roche Eaton, model; two daughters. Relative in theatre: uncle, Wally Van, silent film actor. Member of ANTA (dir.); New Dramatists Comm. (dir.); The Lambs; Nassau Country Club; Glen Cove, N.Y.; Chi Phi; Amherst Club. Address: (home) 115 Greenway North, Forest Hills, NY 11375, tel. (212) BO 8-1822; (bus.) c/o Samuel French, Inc., 25 W. 45th St., New York, NY 10036, tel. (212) JU 2-4700.

Since 1952, Mr. Van Nostrand has been president of Samuel French, Inc., and has been a member of the firm since 1934. He has also been president of Samuel French, Ltd., Canada (1952–to date), and president of Walter H. Baker Co., Boston, Mass. (1953–date).

Recreation. Golf, bowling, collecting old published plays.

VAN PATTEN, DICK. Actor. b. Richard Vincent Van Patten, Dec 9, 1928, Kew Gardens, N.Y., to Richard and Josephine (Acerno) Van Patten. Father, interior decorator; mother, advertising. Grad. Richmond Hills H.S., Richmond Hill, L.I., N.Y., 1948. Member of AEA; SAG; AFTRA. Married April 25, 1954, to Patricia Poole, dancer; three sons. Relative in theatre: sister, Joyce Van Patten, actress.

Theatre. Mr. Van Patten made his first appearance on a stage at the age of six, with a recitation in an MGM screen and voice contest, which he won (Loew's State Th., N.Y.C., Oct. 1934).

He made his Bway debut as the Child in *Tapestry in Gray* (Shubert, Dec. 27, 1935); played Henry Wadsworth Benson in the pre-Bway tryout of *Home Sweet Home* (opened Greenwich Guild Th., Conn., June 29, 1936; closed Copley, Boston, Mass.); appeared as Isaac in *The Eternal Road* (Manhattan Opera House, N.Y.C., Jan. 7, 1937), billed as Dickie Van Patten, which he used subsequently. He played Theodore in *Goodbye Again* (Pine Brook Country Club, Nichols, Conn., Aug. 25, 1937); a Boy in *On Borrowed Time* (Longacre, N.Y.C., Feb. 3, 1938); Nine in *Run, Sheep, Run* (Windsor, Nov. 3, 1938); Karl Gunther in *The American Way* (Center, Jan. 21, 1939); at the Wharf Th. (Provincetown, Mass.), played Pete Brown in *The Woman Brown* (Aug. 14, 1939); and Tommy in *Ah, Wilderness!* (Aug. 21, 1939); repeated his role in *The Woman Brown* (Biltmore, N.Y.C., Dec. 8, 1939); again played Tommy in *Ah, Wilderness!* (Maplewood Th., N.J., June 24, 1940); appeared as Jessie in summer theatre tryouts of *Our Girls* (Starlight Th., Pawling, N.Y., July 9, 1940); Moses in *Something About a Soldier* (Bucks County Playhouse, New Hope, Pa., Sept. 2, 1940); and Toby in *Carriage Trade* (Stamford Playhouse, Conn., 1940); Roger in *The Lady Who Came To Stay* (Maxine Elliott's Th., N.Y.C., Jan. 2, 1941); Timothy Kincaid in *The Land Is Bright* (Music Box, Oct. 28, 1941); Bodo in *Watch on the Rhine* (Majestic, Boston, June 22, 1942); in a summer-theatre tryout production as "Short Pants" Houlihan in *Evening Rise* (Woodstock Playhouse, N.Y., Aug. 13, 1942); as the Telegraph Boy in *The Skin of Our Teeth* (Plymouth, N.Y.C., Nov. 18, 1942); Elwood in *The Snark Was a Boojum* (48 St. Th., Sept. 1, 1943); Felix in *Decision* (Belasco, Feb. 2, 1944); succeeded (May 30, 1944) Robert White in the part of Dexter Franklin in *Kiss and Tell* (Biltmore, Mar. 17, 1943); played Sgt. Walter Burrows in *Too Hot for Maneuvers* (Broadhurst, May 2, 1945); and Ernie Sheffield in *The Wind Is Ninety* (Booth, June 21, 1945).

Billed as Dick Van Patten, he appeared as Michael Brown in *O Mistress Mine* (Empire, Jan. 23, 1946), in summer-theatre productions in Montclair, N.J., Th. Aug. 23, 1948) and Long Beach, N.Y. (Crest Th., Aug. 30, 1948); and in the national (touring) production of *O Mistress Mine* (opened Locust, Philadelphia, Pa., Dec. 6, 1948); played Toto in the pre-Bway tryout tour of *Cry of the Peacock* (opened Locust, Philadelphia, Mar. 27, 1950); succeeded (May 29, 1950) Murray Hamilton in the role of Ensign Pulver in *Mister Roberts* (Alvin, N.Y.C., Feb. 18, 1948), which he also played in a summer-theatre production (Quarterdeck Th., Atlantic City, N.J., July 20, 1951).

He appeared as Nels in *Here's Mama* at the Ogunquit (Me.) Playhouse (July 14, 1952), and at Cape Playhouse (Dennis, Mass., July 21, 1952); succeeded (Sept. 22, 1952) John Gerstad as Michael Barnes in *The Male Animal* (Music Box, May 15, 1952), which he repeated in stock at the Jamaica (N.Y.) Th. (July 21, 1953), and the Brighton Th. (Brooklyn, N.Y., July 28, 1953); repeated the role of Ensign Pulver in *Mister Roberts* (Summers 1953, 1954); at the Pocono Playhouse (Mountainhome, Pa.), played Charlie Reader in *The Tender Trap* (July 25, 1955), and Grant Cobbler in *Oh, Men! Oh, Women!* (Aug. 1, 1955); at Long Beach (N.Y.) Playhouse, appeared as Happy in *Death of a Salesman* (Aug. 16, 1955), and at the Avondale Playhouse (Indianapolis, Ind.) as Francis X. Dignan in *King of Hearts* (Aug. 1956).

He appeared as George Macauley in a tour of *Will Success Spoil Rock Hunter?* (1957); played Ensign Beau Gilliam in *Golden Fleecing* on tour (Summer 1960); Ruby Pulaski in *Have I Got a Girl for You* (Music Box, N.Y.C., Dec. 2, 1963); and Henry Greene in a summer package tour of *Strictly Dishonorable* (Mt. Tom Playhouse, Holyoke, Mass.; Vineland, Toronto, Can.; Tappen Zee Playhouse, N.Y.; Elitch Gardens, Denver, Colo.; Summer 1964); was standby to Orson Bean as Tom Considine and to David Doyle as Billy Ryan in *I Was Dancing* (Lyceum, N.Y.C., Nov. 8, 1964); played Henry Green in *Strictly Dishonorable* (tour, summer 1965); was general understudy and stage manager for *A Very Rich Woman* (Belasco, N.Y.C., Sept. 30, 1965); played Mr. Hollender in *Don't Drink the Water* (Coconut Grove Playhouse, Miami, 1967–68 season); played the Hon. Newton Prince in *But, Seriously . . .* (Henry Miller's Th., N.Y.C., Feb. 27, 1969); succeeded James Coco (Sept. 22, 1969) in the role of Marion Cheever in *Next* on a double-bill with *Adaptation* (Greenwich Mews Th., Feb. 10, 1969); and later replaced Mr. Coco in the Los Angeles company of that bill (Mark Taper Forum, Oct. 23, 1969).

Films. Mr. Van Patten has appeared as Jimmy Dugan in *Reg'lar Fellers* (Producers Releasing Corp., 1941); and Edgar Palmer in *Psychomania* (1964), Victoria Films; appeared in *Charly* (Cinerama, 1968); *Zacharia* (Cinerama, 1971); *Making It* (20th-Fox, 1971); *Joe Kid* (U, 1972); *Dirty Little Billy* (Col., 1972); *Snowball Express* (BV, 1972); *Westworld* (MGM, 1973); and *Soylent Green* (MGM, 1973); and *Superdad* (BV, 1974).

Television and Radio. Mr. Van Patten made his radio debut as Mark Brown in the series Young Widder Brown (NBC, 1941), playing the role for five years; played Hartzell in One Foot in Heaven (CBS); Teddy Thompson in Miss Hatty (NBC); Wilfred in Duffy's Tavern (CBS); Toby Smith in Henry Aldrich (NBC); Ray in David Harum (NBC); Teddy in Right to Happiness (NBC); Jimmy Dugan in Reg'lar Fellers (WEAF, N.Y.C.); performed on March of Time (WEAF, Aug. 6, 1942), on Th. Guild on the Air, played Dexter Franklin in *Kiss and Tell* (Sept. 14, 1947); Chic in *Wednesday's Child* (May 23, 1948); Michael Brown in *O Mistress Mine* (Jan. 9, 1949); Roger in *Theatre* (Nov. 26, 1950); Wayne in *State Fair* (Dec. 31, 1950; Jan. 4, 1953); Ben Banks in *Father of the Bride* (Feb. 25, 1951); Nick Kane in *Elmer the Great* (May 27, 1951); Cadet Osborne in *The Major and the Minor* (Oct. 14, 1951); and Nat Kahn in *Good Housekeeping* (Dec. 2, 1951).

He made his television debut as a child on Story Hour (Dumont, 1936); played Nels in the series *Mama* (CBS, 1949–58); appeared in *Final Ingredient* (ABC, Apr. 1959); played Larry Renfrew on Young Dr. Malone (NBC, Jan. 1961–Mar. 1963); and, since 1958, has appeared frequently on dramatic series, including Kraft Television Th. (NBC), The Nurses (CBS), The Verdict Is Yours (CBS), Mike Hammer, Silent Service, Rawhide (CBS), *Men in White* (Dupont Show of the Month, CBS, Sept. 30, 1960), and others. He also appeared in commercials (1961–63).

Recreation. Tennis, swimming, horseback riding.

VAN PATTEN, JOYCE.

Actress. b. Joyce Benigna Van Patten, Mar. 9, 1934, New York City, to Richard and Josephine (Acerno) Van Patten. Father, interior decorator; mother, adv. dept. of *U.S. News and World Report.* Attended Lodge Sch., N.Y.C. Relative in theatre: brother, Dick Van Patten, actor. Member of AEA; SAG; AFTRA.

Pre-Theatre. Model.

Theatre. Miss Van Patten made her first stage appearance at age two as the winner of a Shirley Temple resemblance contest (RKO Th., Richmond Hill, L.I., July 29, 1936); made her Bway debut at age six, succeeding Eleanor Drexler as Mae Yearling in *Love's Old Sweet Song* (Plymouth, May 2, 1940), with which she toured (opened Ford's, Baltimore, Md., 1940); subsequently played Marie Antoinette Benson in *Popsy* (48 St. Playhouse, N.Y.C., Feb. 10, 1941); Zoey in a summer theatre production of *Family Honeymoon* (Lakewood Th., Skowhegan, Me., July 14, 1941); Mary in *This Rock* (Longacre, N.Y.C., Feb. 18, 1943); alternated with Nancy Nugent in the role of Patricia Frame in *Tomorrow the World* (Ethel Barrymore Th., Apr. 14, 1943), repeating the role at Elitch Gardens (Denver, Colo., July 1944); played Helen Williams in *The Perfect Marriage* (Ethel Barrymore Th., N.Y.C., Oct. 26, 1944); Joan in *The Wind Is Ninety* (Booth, June 21, 1945); Judy in a summer theatre tour of *Junior Miss* (1946); and Ilka Morgan in *The Bees and the Flowers* (Cort, Sept. 26, 1946).

She appeared as Miriam in summer theatre tours of *Dear Ruth* (1947), and as Monica in *The Second Man* (1948); and played a season of stock at Elitch Gardens (Summer 1949); was stand-by for Peggy Anne Garner in the role of Ruth in *The Man* (Fulton, N.Y.C., Jan. 19, 1950); appeared as Judy in *Junior Miss* at the Lake Whalom (Mass.) Playhouse (June 1950); in *Good Housekeeping* (Casino in the Park, Holyoke, Mass., June 18, 1951); as Pat in a summer theatre tour of *The Male Animal* (1953); played the role of Joyce Reid in the pre-Bway tryout of *Put Them All Together* (opened Shubert, New Haven, Conn., Dec. 29, 1954; closed Plymouth, Boston, Mass., Jan. 15, 1955); and appeared in a touring production of *Spice of Life* (Spring 1955).

Miss Van Patten played Julie Gillis in *The Tender Trap* and Myra Hagerman in *Oh, Men! Oh, Women!* at the Pocono Playhouse (Mountainhome, Pa., July 25, and Aug. 1, 1955); Elsa in *The Desk Set* (Broadhurst, N.Y.C., Oct. 24, 1955); and Shirl in *A Hole in the Head* (Plymouth, Feb. 28, 1957); Mary Magdalene in *Between Two Thieves* (York, Feb. 11, 1960), and repeated the role with Theatre West (of which she is a founder) at U.C.L.A. (Calif., Oct., 1961); later appeared at U.C.L.A. in several roles in *Spoon River Anthology* (May 1, 1963); and subsequently returned to New York with the production, retitled *Spoon River* (Booth, Sept. 29, 1963).

She played Sarah in *The Lover* on a triple-bill with *I Rise in Flame, Cried the Phoenix* and *Windows* (The Th. Group, U.C.L.A., June 4, 1965); appeared in *Who Wants To Be the Lone Ranger?* (Center Th. Group, New Th. for Now Workshop, Los Angeles, 1970–71 season); played Canina in *Volpone* (Center Th. Group, Mark Taper Forum, Los Angeles, Mar. 9, 1972); appeared in *Spoon River* (Th. West, Los Angeles, May 19, 1972); played Gloria in *Twenty-three Years Later* (Ctr. Th. Group Mark Taper Forum, New Th. for Now, Sept. 26, 1973); and succeeded Ellen Burstyn (Nov. 1975) in *Same Time Next Year* (Brooks Atkinson Th., Mar. 13, 1975); subsequently touring in that role (opened Royal Alexandra Th., Toronto, Dec. 1, 1975).

Films. Miss Van Patten made her debut as Mae in *Reg'lar Fellers* (PRC Pictures, 1941); and has appeared in *14 Hours* (20th-Fox, 1951); *The Goddess* (Col., 1958); *I Love You, Alice B. Toklas* (WB-Seven Arts, 1968); *The Trouble with Girls* (MGM, 1968); *Pussycat, Pussycat, I Love You* (UA, 1970); *Making It* (20th-Fox, 1971); *Something Big* (Natl. Gen., 1971); *Thumb-Tripping* (Avco-Embassy, 1972); *Bone* (Jack Harris Enterprises, 1972); and *Mame* (WB, 1974).

Television and Radio. She made her radio debut on Nila Mack's Let's Pretend (CBS, 1941); and performed on the program Reg'lar Fellers (June–Aug. 1941); played the title role on the Penny radio series (1946); performed on the Th. Guild of the Air (1950–55); Grand Central Station and Wendy Warren; and regularly on My True Story (ABC, 1957). On television she has appeared on the Hour Glass (NBC, May 23, 1946); in *The Flattering Word* (NBC, June 2, 1946); *Dinner at Eight* (NBC, Oct. 1948); on Hollywood Screen Test (WJS-TV, Mar. 27, 1949); Martin Kane, Private Eye (CBS, 1949); and *Brief Music* (Kraft Television Th., NBC, Apr. 25, 1951).

Also, Philco Television Playhouse (NBC); Kraft Television Playhouse (NBC); and Armstrong Circle Th. (NBC); played Sally in *Charm Boy;* Fanny in Hemingway's *The Killers* (Buick Show, CBS, Nov. 19, 1959); Nurse Clara on Young Dr. Malone (NBC, 1959–60); appeared on Armstrong Circle Th. (NBC, Mar. 2, 1960); the Wendy Barrie Show (WNTA, May 28, 1960); appeared on The Law and Mr. Jones (ABC, 1960); the series Brighter Day (CBS, 1961); Ben Casey (ABC, 1961); The Verdict Is Yours (CBS, Mar. 28–Apr. 6, 1961); Dobie Gillis (CBS, 1962); Bus Stop (ABC, 1962); Target: The Corruptors (ABC, 1962); Checkmate (CBS, 1962); The Detectives (NBC, 1962); in Dr. Kildare (NBC, 1962); the Loretta Young Show (CBS, 1962); appared in one of her original sketches on George Gobel Presents (Alcoa Hour, ABC, Jan. 31, 1963); Perry Mason, (CBS, 1963); the Lloyd Bridges Show, (CBS, 1963); Alfred Hitchcock (CBS, 1963); Gunsmoke (CBS, 1963); Stoney Burke (ABC, 1963); The Untouchables (ABC, 1963); and Wide Country (NBC, 1963). She also appeared in episodes of Twilight Zone (CBS, 1963); The Defenders (CBS, 1963); Outer Limits (ABC, 1963); Dr. Kildare (NBC, 1963); the Theatre West Production of *Feiffer Sketches on Steve Allen Show* (NBC); and the Danny Kaye Show (CBS).

Night Clubs. Miss Van Patten appeared in a musical revue *Wild Wicked World,* for which she wrote the sketches (Interlude Club, Hollywood, Calif., Nov. 1962).

Awards. She received a Donaldson Award for her performance in *Tomorrow the World* (1944).

Recreation. Swimming, painting, embroidery, and cooking.

VAN PEEBLES, MELVIN.

Playwright, actor, director, producer, composer, lyricist. b. Aug. 21, 1932, Chicago, Ill. Attended West Virginia State Coll.; Grad. Ohio Wesleyan Univ., B.A. 1953; attended Univ. of Amsterdam, Holland. Served U.S. Air Force.

Pre-Theatre. San Francisco cable car grip-man.

Theatre. For a time, Mr. Van Peebles was an actor with the Dutch National Theatre, touring in *The Hostage.*

He made his American theatrical debut as the author, composer and lyricist of *Ain't Supposed To Die a Natural Death* (Ethel Barrymore Th., N.Y.C., Oct. 20, 1971); and wrote the book, music and lyrics, and produced *Don't Play Us Cheap* (Ethel Barrymore Th., May 16, 1972). In *Out There by Your Lonesome* (Philharmonic Hall, N.Y.C., Feb. 26, 1973, and on tour), Mr. Van Peebles performed songs and comedy material of his own devising in a one-man show.

Films. He wrote and directed *The Story of a Three-Day Pass* (Sigma III, 1967) which was based upon his novel *La Permission,* and released in France under that title; directed *Watermelon Man* (Col., 1970); and wrote, directed, produced, and played the title role in *Sweet Sweetback's Baadasssss Song* (Cinemation Industries, 1971).

Night Clubs. Mr. Van Peebles has performed his own material at The Bottom Line (N.Y.C., June 1974).

Published Works. Mr. Van Peebles first work was his photo-essay, *The Big Heart* (1967). He subsequently wrote *Un Ours pour le F.B.I. (A Bear for the F.B.I.,* 1964); *Un Americain en Enfer* (1965); *Le Chinôis du 14eme* (1966); *Fête d' Harlem* (Party in Harlem, 1967); and *La Permission* (1967).

Discography. His recordings of his own works include *Br'er Soul* (1969); *Ain't Supposed To Die a Natural Death; As Serious as a Heart-Attack* (A & M,

1971); and *What the . . You Mean I Can't Sing* (A & M, 1974).

VAN ZANDT, PORTER. Stage manager, actor, director. b. Porter Wisner Van Zandt, Jr., May 18, 1923, Rochester, N.Y., to Porter Wisner and Carol (Dalrymple) Van Zandt. Father, probation officer. Grad. West H.S., Rochester, 1941; Univ. of North Carolina, A.B., 1948. Married Sept. 25, 1948, to Betty Lou Cypert; one son, one daughter. Served USN 1942–46; rank, Lt. (j.g.). Member of AEA; AFTRA; SAG. Address: 118 W. 79th St., New York, NY 10024, tel. (212) TR 7-7202.

Since Feb. 1973, Mr. Van Zandt has been the executive director of the City Center Acting Company.

Theatre. Mr. Van Zandt first appeared in stock presentations at the Olney (Md.) Th. (1949, 1950); subsequently played Uncle Willy in a touring production of *The Devil's Disciple* (1950); was assistant stage manager and played Thompson in *Dial 'M' for Murder* (Plymouth Th., N.Y.C., Oct. 29, 1952); appeared in *Richard III* (NY City Ctr., Dec. 9, 1953; was stage manager for *The Bad Seed* (46 St. Th., Dec. 8, 1954), also touring in it (opened Playhouse, Wilmington, Del., Dec. 1, 1955; closed Harris, Chicago, Ill., June 30, 1956); was assistant stage manager for *Small War on Murray Hill* (Ethel Barrymore Th., N.Y.C., Jan. 3, 1957); became assistant stage manager (May 1957) for *A Hole in the Head* (Plymouth, Feb. 28, 1957); was stage manager for *The Egg Head* (Ethel Barrymore Th., Oct. 9, 1957); *Two for the See Saw* (Booth, Jan. 16, 1958); *The Miracle Worker* (Playhouse, Oct. 19, 1959); and for *All the Way Home* (Belasco, Nov. 30, 1960).

He directed *The Miracle Worker* for an Amer. Repertory Th. Guild tour of Europe and South America (1961); was stage manager for *Gideon* (Plymouth, N.Y.C., Nov. 9, 1961); and *A Thousand Clowns* (Eugene O'Neill Th., Apr. 5, 1962).

He directed the Australian production of *The Miracle Worker* (1962); was stage manager for *Mother Courage and Her Children* (Martin Beck Th., N.Y.C., Mar. 28, 1963); and directed the national tour of *A Thousand Clowns* (opened Providence, R.I., Sept. 30, 1963; closed Rochester, N.Y., Feb. 8, 1964).

VAUGHAN, GLADYS. Director. b. Gladys Regier, Feb. 23, Wayland, Iowa, to P. K. and Marie (Staufer) Regier. Father, clergyman. Attended Bethel Coll.; grad. Kansas State Teachers Coll., B.A. 1944; attended Stanford Univ., 1946–48. Married Aug. 26, 1948, to Stuart Vaughan, director (marr. dis. 1960). Member of AEA; SSD&C; Actors' Studio (directors unit).

Theatre. Miss Vaughan was assistant to the director of the St. Augustine (Fla.) Civic Th. (1948–49); subsequently under a Fulbright Grant, visited and studied 20 British repertory theatres (1949–50); assisted the director at the Conneaut (Ohio) Community Th. (1952); was assistant stage manager at the Bahama Playhouse (Nassau, Jan.–Apr., 1953); assistant to the director of the Amer. Shakespeare Festival Th. and Acad. (1954); and stage manager at the Mountain Playhouse (Braddock Hts., Md., Summer 1954).

She was assistant to the director of *Pictures in the Hallway* (Playhouse, N.Y.C., Sept. 16, 1956); *I Knock at the Door* (Belasco, Sept. 29, 1957); and was director of Community Plays for the Amer. Th. Wing (1959).

Miss Vaughan, whose association with the NY Shakespeare Festival began in 1955, served until 1961 as assistant director to Joseph Papp, Gerald Freedman, and Stuart Vaughan. For this company she was associate producer to Joseph Papp, for *Much Ado About Nothing* (Wollman Rink, Central Park, N.Y.C., July 5, 1961); directed *Richard II* (Wollman Rink, Aug. 24, 1961); directed with Mr. Papp, *The Merchant of Venice* (Delacorte Th., June 19, 1962), *King Lear* (Delacorte Th., Aug. 13, 1962); and directed *Macbeth* (Heckscher, Nov. 11, 1962), which also toured N.Y.C. schools.

For the Memphis (Tenn.) Shakespeare Festival, she directed *Much Ado About Nothing* (Apr. 1962), and *Henry V* (Feb. 1963); and, for the NY Shakespeare Festival directed *The Winter's Tale* (Delacorte, Aug. 14, 1963).

She directed *Baal* (Martinique, N.Y.C., May 6, 1964), and *Othello* (Delacorte, July 8, 1964), re-staging these productions when they were opened in repertory (Martinique, Oct. 12, 1964) off-Bway; directed *Othello* for Playhouse-in-the-Park (Philadelphia, Aug. 17, 1964); *Coriolanus* (Delacorte, N.Y.C., July 7, 1965); and the NY Shakespeare Festival's Mobile Th. production of *Macbeth* (June 28, 1966); was associate director for *Measure for Measure* (Delacorte, July 12, 1966); and *King Richard III* (Delacorte, Aug. 9, 1966); directed staged readings of *Drums in the Night* (Circle in the Sq., Mar. 1967), and *Afore Night Come* (Circle in the Square, Apr. 1967); directed *The Blood Knot* (Arena Stage, Washington, D.C., Jan. 16, 1968); and, for the Chelsea Th. Ctr.'s Playwright's Forum, *Thunder in the Index* (Brooklyn Acad. of Music (1968–69 season).

She wrote *Legend of Suzanne*, a one-act play (Stanford Univ., 1947); Terre Haute State Teachers Coll. (1948); and *The Strange One* (Emporia State Teachers Coll., and high schools throughout the US).

Television and Radio. She was women's editor for radio station WIKK (Erie, Pa., 1950–51); women's editor and commentator for WICU-TV (Erie, Pa., 1951–52); and for WHAM (Rochester, N.Y., 1952).

Other Activities. Miss Vaughan did publicity and was a promotion writer for NY Antiques Fair (1953, 1954).

VAUGHAN, STUART. Director, actor, playwright. b. John Walker Vaughan, Aug. 23, 1925, Terre Haute, Ind., to John Harwood and Pauletta (Walker) Vaughan. Father, Capt., Air Corps; mother, U.S. Civil Service. Grad. Garfield H.S., Terre Haute, 1942; Indiana State Coll., B.A. 1945; Indiana Univ., M.A. 1946. Studied acting with Harold Clurman, 1954–56. Married 1948 to Gladys Regier, director (marr. dis. 1960); married Aug. 22, 1960, to Helen Quarrier, actress (dec. Dec. 25, 1963); married Apr. 14, 1965, to Anne Thompson, actress. Member of AEA; SSDC; Dramatists Guild; New Dramatists. Address: 261 St. John's Ave., Yonkers, NY 10704, tel. (914) 423-3363.

Theatre. Mr. Vaughan made his professional debut playing Stewart Kennedy in a touring company of *Her Unborn Child* (1946); subsequently directed at the Little Th. (St. Augustine, Fla., 1948–49), and the Belfry Th. (Williams Bay, Wis.); appeared in stock at the Erie Playhouse (Erie, Pa., 1950–52); the Rochester Arena Th. (N.Y., Spring 1952); directed and appeared at the British Colonial Th. (Nassau, Bahamas, Spring 1953); The Playhouse (Old Orchard Beach, Me., Summer 1953); played the Sergeant of the Guard and was assistant stage manager of *The Strong Are Lonely* (Broadhurst N.Y.C., Sept. 29, 1953); was understudy and assistant stage manager for *The Confidential Clerk* (Morosco, Feb. 11, 1954); played Mr. Lovewell in *The Clandestine Marriage* (Players, Oct. 2, 1954); Hector in *Thieves' Carnival* (Cherry Lane, Feb. 1, 1955); and was stage manager for *The Chalk Garden* (Ethel Barrymore Th., Oct. 26, 1955).

Mr. Vaughan directed *I Knock at the Door* and *Pictures in the Hallway* (Kaufmann Aud., YMHA, 1956); *The Taming of the Shrew* and *Julius Caesar* for the NY Shakespeare Festival (East Side Amphitheatre, Summer 1956); *Pictures in the Hallway* (Playhouse, Sept. 16, 1956); *The River Line* (Carnegie Hall Playhouse, Jan. 2, 1957); *Romeo and Juliet, The Two Gentlemen of Verona*, and *Macbeth* for the NY Shakespeare Festival (Belvedere Lake Th., Summer 1957); *I Knock at the Door* (Belasco, Sept. 29, 1957); for the NY Shakespeare Festival, *Richard III* (Heckscher Th., Nov. 25, 1957), *As You Like It*, (Heckscher Th., Jan. 20, 1958), and *Othello* (Belvedere Lake Th., Aug. 6, 1958).

Mr. Vaughan became artistic director of the Phoenix Th. (1958), where he directed *The Family Reunion* (Oct. 20, 1958); *The Power and the Glory* (Dec. 10, 1958); and *The Beaux' Strategem* (Feb. 24, 1959); staged *Julius Caesar* for the NY Shakespeare Festival (Belvedere Lake Th., Aug. 3, 1959); for the Phoenix Co., directed *The Great God Brown* (Coronet, Oct. 6, 1959); and at the Phoenix Th., *Pictures in the Hallway* (Dec. 26, 1959); *I Knock at the Door; Peer Gynt* (Jan. 12, 1960); and *Henry IV, Part 1* (March 1, 1960); in 1960–61 at the Phoenix Th. directed *She Stoops to Conquer* (Nov. 1, 1960); *The Plough and the Stars* (Dec. 6, 1960); *The Octoroon* (Jan. 27, 1961); and *Hamlet* (Mar. 16, 1961); played Algernon in, and directed, *The Importance of Being Earnest* and directed *Medea* (Antioch Area Th., Yellow Springs, Ohio, Summer 1962); staged *The Good Woman of Setzuan* for the Studio Th. (Buffalo, N.Y., Nov. 1962); for the Phoenix Th. directed *Abe Lincoln in Illinois* (Anderson, Jan. 21, 1963) and *The Taming of the Shrew* (Anderson, Mar. 6, 1963).

As artistic director of the Seattle (Wash.) Repertory Th. (1963–66), Mr. Vaughan staged *King Lear* (Seattle Center Playhouse Nov. 13, 1963); supervised the direction of *The Firebugs* (Nov. 14, 1963); directed *The Lady's Not For Burning* (Jan. 1, 1964); supervised the direction of *Death of a Salesman* (Feb. 12, 1964); and directed *Shadows of Heroes* (April 1, 1964); during 1964–65, co-directed and played Tanner in *Man and Superman;* directed *Twelfth Night;* produced *Ah! Wilderness*, and *The Cherry Orchard;* and directed *Hamlet;* directed *The Taming of the Shrew* (Seattle and King County (Wash.) parks, Summer 1965); during 1965–66, directed *The Importance of Being Earnest*, in which he played Algernon; directed *Heartbreak House;* and produced *Long Day's Journey Into Night;* subsequently serving as artist-in-residence at Reed Coll. (Portland, Ore., Jan.–Apr. 1967).

Mr. Vaughan was founder and producer-director (1966–69) of the Repertory Theatre of New Orleans (La.) where he presented *Charley's Aunt, Romeo and Juliet, Our Town*, and *The Rivals* (1966–67); *The Crucible, St. Joan, A Midsummer Night's Dream*, and *Tartuffe* (1967–68); *Arms and the Man, Twelfth Night, An Enemy of the People*, Ionesco's *The Chairs* and *The Bald Soprano*, and *Private Lives* (1968–69).

For the NY Shakespeare Festival (Summer 1969) he adapted and directed *The War of the Roses*, which included *Henry VI*, Parts 1, 2, and 3, and *Richard III* in repertory. Mr. Vaughan wrote and directed *Assassination 1865* (Goodman Th., Chicago, 1971); and *Ghost Dance* (Trinity Sq. Repertory Co., Providence, R.I., 1973).

With Anne Thompson, he has adapted *The Servant of Two Masters* (Calif. Actors Th., 1975); and Porte-Riche's *Amoreuse* (1975).

Television. Mr. Vaughan directed *The Lady's Not For Burning* (Omnibus, CBS, 1968).

Other Activities. Mr. Vaughan has been an instructor, Indiana State Univ. (1947–48); adjunct professor, Brooklyn Coll. (1960); visiting professor, Loyola Univ. of the South (1968); adjunct professor, C. W. Post Coll. (1971); and visiting professor, Harvard Univ. (1971), Univ. of Kansas (Summers 1971–72), Ohio State Univ. (1974). and Univ. of Georgia (1975).

Published Works. He is the author of *The Royal Game* (Dramatic Publishing Co., 1974); and is co-editor of *The Bantam Shakespeare*, nineteen single volumes of Shakespeare's plays in paperback (1960–64).

Awards. Mr. Vaughan received the Vernon Rice Award and *The Village Voice* Off-Bway (Obie) Award for his direction of the NY Shakespeare Co. (1958); a Rockefeller artist in residence grant, Stanford Univ. (1947); Fulbright grant for study of British repertory theatres (1949–50); and a Ford Foundation directors grant for European travel and study (1961–62).

Recreation. Fencing, American Indian songs and dances.

VEGA, JOSE. Production manager, director, producer. b. Nord Jose Vega, Nov. 7, 1920, New York City, to Manuel and Pilar Cagancho Vega. Married Dec. 21, 1943, to Victoria Vandyke; one daughter. Member of AEA; SAG; NATAS. Address: 32 King St., New York, NY 10014, tel. (212) WA 4-8947.

Theatre. Mr. Vega made his debut as a dancer in the opera *Prince Igor* (Brooklyn Acad. of Music, N.Y., 1937); subsequently performed as a flamenco dancer in the opera *Carmen* (Mecca Temple, N.Y.C., Apr. 13, 1940); a flamenco soloist in the Senia Russakof Ballet (Jordan Hall, Boston, Mass., May 15, 1940); and toured the US as Jose Vega and His Spanish Ensemble (1939–42).

He made his debut in a speaking role as a Detective in *Mr. and Mrs. North*, which toured (Catskills, N.Y., June 1942); appeared at the Peaks Island Playhouse (Peaks Island, Me., June 1943); in *My Sister Eileen*, touring as a Sailor and understudy to Joseph Kallini in the role of the Consul (Nov. 1943); played the Consul and a Sailor for a tour of summer theatres (June 1944) and the NY Co. Subway Circuit (Sept. 1944); appeared as Gurdensteen in *Hamlet* (Bridgeport Summer Th., Conn., Spring 1945); Croupier in *Her Cardboard Lover* (Montclair Playhouse, N.J., June 1945); and at the Martha's Vineyard Playhouse, Oak Bluffs, Mass., as Count Giolio Dórse in *Within This Hour* (Aug. 1945), and Corporal Resnick in *Return to Eden* (Sept. 1945).

His first Bway assignment was stage manager and understudy for the role of Property Man in *Lute Song* (Plymouth Th., Feb. 6, 1946); performed in and was stage manager at Martha's Vineyard Playhouse, Oak Bluffs, Mass. (June 1946); assistant stage manager and general understudy for *Another Part of the Forest* (Fulton, N.Y.C., Nov. 20, 1946); performed and was stage manager at Falmouth (Mass.) Playhouse and Martha's Vineyard Playhouse, Oak Bluffs, Mass. (June 1947); was stage manager for the Chicago, Ill., production of *Another Part of the Forest* (Erlanger Th., Sept. 1947); stage manager and assistant to the producer at Falmouth (Mass.) Playhouse and Martha's Vineyard Playhouse, Oak Bluffs, Mass. (June 1948); and stage manager of the industrial show *Ford 49'er* (Waldorf-Astoria, N.Y.C., Fall 1948).

Mr. Vega was assistant stage manager and understudy to Nick Dennis and Rudy Bond as Pablo and Steve in *A Streetcar Named Desire* (Ethel Barrymore Th., Dec. 3, 1947), and for its US tour, revival at the NY City Ctr. (May 23, 1950), and tour of the N.Y.C. Subway Circuit (June 1950); production stage manager for *Bell, Book and Candle* (Ethel Barrymore Th., Nov. 14, 1950); director of a stock production of *A Streetcar Named Desire* (Princeton Summer Th., N.J., June 1951); and producer-director at the Roosevelt Playhouse (Miami Beach, Fla., July 1951).

He was production stage manager for *I Am a Camera* (Empire, N.Y.C., Nov. 28, 1951); *Flight into Egypt* (Music Box, Mar. 18, 1952); producer-director of a season of stock at the Astor Th. (Syracuse, N.Y., June 1952); production stage manager for a revival of *The Children's Hour* (Coronet, N.Y.C., Dec. 18, 1952); director of a summer tour of *Bell, Book and Candle* (June 1953); production stage manager for *The Seven Year Itch* (Fulton, Mar. 28, 1955); appeared in and directed productions at the Lakewood Th. (Barnsville, Pa., June 1955); was production stage manager for *The Chalk Garden* Ethel Barrymore Th., Oct. 26, 1955); director of the summer tour of *The Bad Seed* (June 1956); director of summer stock productions at Joy Thomson's Tent Theatre (Mt. Gabriel, Can., July 1956); production stage manager for *A Very Special Baby* (Playhouse, N.Y.C., Nov. 14, 1956); and *Anniversary Waltz* (Blackstone Th., Chicago, Ill., Dec. 1956).

Mr. Vega was production stage manager for *The Genius and the Goddess* (Henry Miller's Th., N.Y.C., Dec. 9, 1957); stage manager for a tour of *Jane Eyre* (Feb. 13, 1958); production manager of *Handful of Fire* (Martin Beck Th., N.Y.C., Oct. 1, 1958), and *Rashomon* (Music Box, Jan. 27, 1959); directed the summer tour of *Show Girl* (June 1961); was production manager for industrial shows for Lincoln-Mercury (Western tour, Aug. 1961) and Plymouth (Western tour, Sept. 1961); production for *The Aspern Papers* (Playhouse, N.Y.C., Feb. 7, 1962); *Night Life* (Brooks Atkinson Th., Oct. 23, 1962); the tour of *Mark Twain Tonight* (Mar. 1963); joined (May 11, 1963) as production manager, *The Boys from Syracuse* (Theatre Four, N.Y.C., Apr. 15, 1963); was production manager for *Semi-Detached* (Music Box, Oct. 7, 1963); and production stage manager for *High Spirits* (Alvin, Mar. 31, 1964).

He was production manager of *Something More* (Eugene O'Neill Th., N.Y.C., Nov. 11, 1964); *Oliver* (National tour, 1964); *Hello, Dolly* (Las Vegas, Nev., and international company, 1965); *The Impossible Years* (N.Y.C., Oct. 13, 1965); *The Lion in Winter* (Ambassador, N.Y.C., Mar. 3, 1966); the Eugene O'Neill Fdtn. Playwright's Conference (Summer 1966); *Those that Play the Clowns* (ANTA, N.Y.C., Nov. 24, 1966); production manager for *The Natural Look* (Longacre, N.Y.C., Mar. 11, 1967); general manager of *To Clothe the Naked* (Sheridan Sq. Th., N.Y.C., Apr. 27, 1967); production manager for *Something Different* (Cort, N.Y.C., Nov. 28, 1967); *George M!* (Palace, N.Y.C., Apr. 10, 1967); and *Fire* (Longacre, N.Y.C., Jan. 28, 1969); general manager for *Salvation* (Jan Hus Th., N.Y.C., Sept. 24, 1969); *Paris Is Out* (Brooks Atkinson Th., N.Y.C., Jan. 19, 1970); *W.C.* (pre-Bway tryout, Summer 1970); *The Earl of Rustin* (Billy Rose Th., N.Y.C., May 5, 1971); *The Me Nobody Knows* (Orpheum, N.Y.C., May 18, 1970); *A Dream Out of Time* (Promenade, N.Y.C., Nov. 8, 1970); company manager of *A Doll's House* (tour, 1971); *JFK* (Circle in the Square, N.Y.C., Nov. 21, 1971); *Oh, Calcutta* (Eden, N.Y.C., Jan. 17, 1969); company and production manager for *A Funny Thing Happened on the Way to the Forum* (Lunt-Fontanne Th., N.Y.C., Mar. 30, 1972); production and company manager for *The Rothschilds* (national co., 1971); general and company manager for *The Sunshine Boys* (Broadhurst, N.Y.C., Dec. 20, 1972); company manager for *Two Gentlemen of Verona* (Delacorte, N.Y.C., July 27, 1971); and St. James Th., N.Y.C., Dec. 1, 1971); and general and company manager for *The Good Doctor* (Eugene O'Neill Th., N.Y.C., Nov. 27, 1973); general manager for *Miss Moffat* (pre-Bway tryout, 1974); and general and company manager for *The Wiz* (Majestic, N.Y.C., Jan. 5, 1975).

Night Clubs. Mr. Vega danced at El Patio (Mexico City, Mexico, Jan.–Feb. 1943).

Awards. The television program Open End, which Mr. Vega produced, received a NATAS (Emmy) NY Area Award (1958–59); and the Art Carney Special, *V.I.P.*, for which Mr. Vega was associate producer, received a NATAS (Emmy) Award (1959–60).

VEIDT, LILY. Talent representative. b. Lily Ilona Barta, July 25, Miskolc, Hungary, to Eugen and Hermion Barta. Attended high school in Vienna, Aust.; finishing school in Lausanne, Switz. Married June 24, 1924, to Paul Preger (marr. dis. 1932); married Mar. 30, 1933, to Conrad Veidt (dec. Apr. 3, 1943). Member of TARA. Address: (home) 176 E. 71st St., New York, NY 10021; (bus.) 667 Madison Ave., New York, NY 10021, tel. (212) 421-7370.

Miss Veidt has been a partner of Harriet Kaplan-Lily Veidt, Inc., a franchised talent agency, representing artists in the theatre.

VENORA, LEE. Singer, actress. b. Elena Sinaguglia, Feb. 16, 1932, Bridgeport, Conn., to Joseph and Angela (Lazzara) Sinaguglia. Father, construction worker; mother, seamstress. Grad. Warren Harding H.S., Bridgeport, Conn., 1949; Julius Hartt Sch. of Music, Hartford, Conn., 1953. Studied voice with Maurice Jampol, N.Y.C., 1953–63; Otto Guth, N.Y.C., 1959–63; Rosalie Snyder, N.Y.C., 1962–63; Clytie Mundy, Wilton, Conn., 1962–63. Married Sept. 4, 1954, to Louis R. Venora (marr. dis. July, 1959). Member of AEA; AGMA; AFTRA.

Theatre. Miss Venora made her stage debut as the French Maid in the operetta *Sari* (Warren Harding H.S., Feb. 1947); her professional debut in the chorus of a production of *South Pacific* (Paper Mill Playhouse, Millburn, N.J., Mar. 1955); at the same theatre, appeared in the chorus of *Guys and Dolls* (May 1955); was in the chorus of an industrial production, *Buick Show*, which toured the US (Sept. 1955); played Tuptim in a production of *The King and I* (Paper Mill Playhouse, Millburn, N.J., Mar. 1956); repeated the role at the Westbury (N.Y.) Music Fair (July 1956); played Marsinah in *Kismet* (South Shore Music Circus, Cohasset, Mass., Aug. 1956); Jennifer in *Paint Your Wagon* (Cape Cod Melody Tent, Hyannis, Mass., 1956); Tuptim in *The King and I* (South Shore Music Circus, Cohasset, Mass., Aug. 1956); Marsinah in *Kismet* (Flint Musical Th., Mich., Aug.–Sept. 1956); Cleo in *Out of This World* (Bucks County Playhouse, New Hope, Pa., May, 1957); Dorothy in *The Wizard of Oz* (Th. Under the Stars, Atlanta, Ga., July 1957); Fiona in *Brigadoon* (South Shore Music Circus, Cohasset, Mass., July 1957); was soprano soloist in an industrial touring show, *Chevrolet Show* (Aug. 1957); and played Tuptim in *The King and I* (Miami Music Th., Fla., Jan. 1958).

Miss Venora made her operatic debut with the NY City Opera Co. (NY City Ctr.) as the Scotch Girl in the N.Y.C. premiere of *Tale for a Deaf Ear* (Apr. 6, 1958); sang Laetitia in *The Old Maid and the Thief* and Monica in *The Medium* (Apr. 1958); and made her European debut in the title role in *Susannah*, which the NY City Opera Co. presented at the Brussels World's Fair (Belgium, June 1958).

She played the title role in *Fanny* (Oakdale Musical Th., Wallingford, Conn., July 1958); Kathy in *The Student Prince* (Warwick, R.I., Musical Th., Aug. 1958); with the NY City Opera Co., appeared as Micaëla in *Carmen* (Sept. 1958); Lucia in *The Rape of Lucretia* (Oct. 23, 1958); the title role in *Susannah* (Oct. 1958); Consuelo in *He Who Gets Slapped* (Apr. 12, 1959); St. Joan in *The Triumph of St. Joan* (Apr. 16, 1959); and the title role in *Susannah* (Apr. 1959); in stock, appeared as Nina in *Song of Norway* (St. Louis Municipal Opera, Mo., June 1959); Lady Katherine in *Vagabond King* (Dallas State Fair, Tex., July 1959); and Micaëla in *Carmen* (St. Louis Municipal Opera, Mo., Aug. 1959).

Miss Venora played Molly Bixby in *Happy Town* (54 St. Th., N.Y.C., Oct. 7, 1959); was soprano soloist with the NY Philharmonic in Bach's *Magnificat in D* (Carnegie Hall, N.Y.C., Dec. 1959); sang the title role in *Manon* (Vienna Volksoper, Austria, Mar. 1960); with the NY Philharmonic, was soprano soloist in Hindemith's *Mathis der Mahler* (Carnegie Hall, N.Y.C., May 1960); in stock appeared as Natalie in *The Merry Widow* (Starlight Th., Kansas City, Mo., July 1960); toured as Maria in *West Side Story* (opened Starlight Th., Kansas City, Mo., July 1960); sang Mimi in *La Bohème* (Ft. Worth Opera Assn., Tex., Oct. 1960); Mistress Ford in *Falstaff* (Mobile Opera Assn., Ala., Mar. 1961); the title role in *Susannah* (Baltimore, Md., Apr. 1961) and Mimi in *La Bohème* (San Francisco Opera, Calif., May 1961).

She sang Juliet in *Romeo and Juliet* (San Francisco Opera, Calif., May 1961); at the Boston (Mass.) Arts Festival, Mary Stone in *The Devil and Daniel Webster* and Miriam in *The Scarf* (May 1961); the Composer in *Ariadne auf Naxos* (Cincinnati Summer Opera, Ohio, June 1961); Mimi in *La Bohème* (Cincinnati Summer Opera, Ohio, June 1961); Leila in *The Pearlfishers* (Empire State Music Festival, Bear Mountain, N.Y., July, 1961); played Anna Danby in *Kean* (Bway Th., N.Y.C., Nov. 2, 1961); sang Cio-Cio San in *Madama Butterfly* (Ft. Worth Opera Assn., Tex., Jan. 1962); with the NY City Opera Co., appeared as Deborah in the world premiere of *The Golem* (NY City Ctr., Mar. 22, 1962); sang the title role in *Manon* and Leila in *The Pearlfishers* (San Francisco Opera, Calif., May 1962); and in stock, played Marsinah in *Kismet* (Los Angeles Civic Light Opera Assn., Calif., July 1962). She sang Susanna in *The Marriage of Figaro* (Tulsa Opera Assn., Okla., Mar. 1963); Mimi in *La Bohème* (Mobile Opera Assn., Ala., Mar. 1963); Monica in *The Medium* and the title role in *Susannah* (NY City Ctr., May, 1963); Norina in *Don Pasquale* (San Francisco Opera, Calif., May 1963); Concepcion in

L'Heure Espagnol (San Francisco Opera, Calif., June 1963); the title role in *Manon* (Salt Lake City Opera, Utah, June 1963). In stock, appeared as Lili in *Carnival* (Starlight Th., Kansas City, Mo., 1963); was soprano soloist in Bach's *B Minor Mass* at the Midsummer's Eve Festival (Philharmonic Hall, N.Y.C., Aug. 8, 1963); in stock, appeared as Maria in *West Side Story* (St. Louis Municipal Opera, Mo., Aug. 1963); was soprano soloist with the NY Philharmonic in Mahler's *Symphony No. 2* (Philharmonic Hall, Sept. 1963); sang Blanche in *Dialogues of the Carmelites* and Mimi in *La Bohème* (San Francisco Opera, Calif., Oct.–Nov. 1963); Cio-Cio San in *Madama Butterfly* (Klein Memorial Th., Bridgeport, Conn., Nov. 1963); and Mimi in *La Bohème* (Houston, Grand Opera, Tex., Dec. 1963).

At the San Francisco Opera (1964), she sang in *Parsifal; Die Frau ohne Schatten;* was Cherubino in *The Marriage of Figaro;* Marzellina in *Fidelio;* Micaela in *Carmen;* Lauretta in *Gianni Schicchi;* and Esmerelda in *The Bartered Bride.* Miss Venora was a member of the City Ctr. (N.Y.C.) Gilbert and Sullivan Co. (City Ctr., Mar. 18–Apr. 5, 1964); sang at the Marc Blitzstein Memorial Concert (Philharmonic Hall, Lincoln Ctr., N.Y.C., Apr. 19, 1964); and was Tuptim in a revival of *The King and I* (NY State Th., Lincoln Ctr., July 6, 1964). During the 1964–65 season she sang in concert with the Montreal (Quebec, Canada) Symphony; was Gretel in *Hansel and Gretel* (Tulsa Opera, Okla.); Mimi in *La Bohème* (Syracuse Opera, N.Y.); Juliette in *Romeo et Juliette* (Houston Grand Opera, Tex., Feb. 4–6, 1965); and Vera in *Natalia Petrovna* (Washington Opera Soc., Washington, D.C.). She repeated her performance as Tuptim in *The King and I* (Dorothy Chandler Pavilion, Los Angeles, Calif., May 1965) and repeated her performance as Marsinah in *Kismet* (NY State Th., June 22, 1965); appeared with the West Berlin (Germany) State Opera (1965–66) as Cio-Cio San in *Madama Butterfly* and Mélisande in *Pélleas et Mélisande;* and was Zdenka in *Arabella* (Stuttgart Opera, Germany, Jan. 1967).

Television. Miss Venora has made many appearances on the Bell Telephone Hour (NBC) and NBC Television Opera Th.; has appeared in *Der Rosenkavalier* (Lincoln Presents Leonard Bernstein, CBS, Feb. 1959); *The Medium* (Omnibus, NBC, Feb. 1959); Bach's *Magnificat in D* (Ford Startime, NBC, Dec. 1959); and *The Drama of Carmen* (CBS). She was in *The Thirteen Clocks* (CBC) and played the role of Young Rachel in *Rachel, La Cubana* (WNET Opera Th., PBS, Mar. 4, 1974).

Discography. Miss Venora's recordings include Bach's *Magnificat in D* (Col.); *Carousel* (Command); Mahler's *Symphony No. 2* (Col.); *The King and I* (RCA-Victor); and *Kean* (Col.).

Recreation. Waterskiing, antique hunting, cooking, scrabble, poker, Mah-Jongg, bridge.

VENUTA, BENAY. Actress, singer. b. Venuta Rose Crooke, Jan. 27, 1912, San Francisco, Calif., to Ernest and Frances (Scalmanini) Crooke. Grad. Palo Alto (Calif.) H.S.; Beaupré, Geneva, Switzerland, 1930. Married Oct. 22, 1936, to Kenneth Kelly, physician (marr. dis. 1938); married Jan. 18, 1939, to Armand S. Deutsch (marr. dis. 1950); two daughters; married Feb. 15, 1951, to Fred Clark, actor (marr. dis. 1963). Member of AEA; AFTRA; SAG. Address: 50 E. 79th St., New York, NY 10021, tel. (212) BU 8-3786.

Theatre. Miss Venuta first appeared as a dancer in *The Big Parade* (Grauman's Egyptian Th., Hollywood, Calif., 1928); subsequently toured as a dancer in *Tip Toes* (Los Angeles and San Francisco, Calif.); and made vaudeville appearances on the Fanchon and Marco Circuit. She made her N.Y.C. debut, succeeding (July 22, 1935) Ethel Merman as Reno Sweeny in *Anything Goes* (Alvin, Nov. 21, 1934), with which she also toured. She subsequently played Lillian Mahoney in *Orchids Preferred* (Imperial Th., N.Y.C., May 11, 1937); Myra Stanhope in *Kiss the Boys Goodbye* (Henry Miller's Th., Sept. 28, 1938); Hippolyta in *By Jupiter* (Shubert, June 3, 1942); and Battle Annie in *Nellie Bly* (Adelphi, Jan. 21, 1946). In stock, she appeared in *The Philadelphia Story, Personal Appearance, My Sister Eileen,* and *Girl Crazy* (Los Angeles, Calif., 1947–50); and played Frances in *Light Up the Sky* (Las Palmas, Hollywood, Calif., 1950).

She played Laura Carew in *Hazel Flagg* (Mark Hellinger Th., N.Y.C., Feb. 11, 1953); in stock, appeared in *Liliom, Bus Stop,* and *Time of the Cuckoo* (La Jolla Playhouse, Calif.); played Estelle O'Shea in *Copper and Brass* (Martin Beck Th., N.Y.C., Oct. 17, 1957); Vera Simpson in *Pal Joey* (Civic Playhouse, Hollywood, Calif., 1958); Vera Charles in *Auntie Mame* (opened Russ Aud., San Diego, Calif., Aug. 4, 1958; closed Geary, San Francisco, Calif., Dec. 13, 1958); Rose in *Gypsy* (Riviera, Las Vegas, Nev., July 3, 1960); Mrs. Baker in the tour of *Come Blow Your Horn* (opened Fisher, Detroit, Mich., July 3, 1962); toured as Belle Poitrine, Today, in a stock production of *Little Me* (Guber-Ford-Gross Circuit, Summer 1963); and temporarily replaced (Apr. 23, 1964) Tresa Hughes as Mildred in the Theatre Guild production of *Dear Me, The Sky Is Falling* (Music Box, N.Y.C., Mar. 2, 1963).

She appeared as Mrs. Mullins in the revival of *Carousel* (NY State Th., Lincoln Ctr., Aug. 11, 1965); Dolly in *Annie Get Your Gun* (NY State Th., Lincoln Ctr., May 31, 1966); and Pearl in *The Prisoner of Second Avenue* (Royal Poinciana Playhouse, Palm Beach, Fla., 1972).

Films. Miss Venuta has appeared in *Trail of 98* (MGM, 1928); *Kiki* (UA, 1931); *Repeat Performance* (Eagle Lion, 1947); *I, Jane Doe* (Rep., 1948); *Annie Get Your Gun* (MGM, 1950); *Call Me Mister* (20th-Fox, 1951); *Ricochet Romance* (U, 1954); and *The Fuzzy Pink Nightgown* (U, 1957).

Night Clubs. Miss Venuta sang at Billy Rose's Casa Mañana (N.Y.C., 1938); the Clover Club (Hollywood, 1938); the Riviera (N.J., 1939); Flamingo Hotel (Las Vegas, 1950); Mocambo (Hollywood, 1956); Bimbo's (San Francisco, 1956–57); the Plaza (N.Y.C., 1963); and the Roosevelt Grill (New Orleans, 1963).

VERDON, GWEN. Actress. b. Gwyneth Evelyn Verdon, Jan. 13, 1926, Culver City, Calif., to Joseph W. and Gertrude Verdon. Father, electrician; mother, dancer. Grad. Hamilton H.S., 1938–42. Studied dancing with E. Belcher, Los Angeles, Calif.; Gertrude Verdon; Carmelita Marrachi; and Jack Cole. Married Apr. 3, 1960, to Bob Fosse, director, choreographer; one daughter; one son, Jim Henaghean, actor. Member of AEA; AGVA; SAG; AFTRA; Post Graduate Center for Mental Health (bd. of dir.). Address: (home) 91 Central Park West, New York, NY 10023, tel. (212) 787-8308; (bus.) c/o Aaron Shapiro, 1180 Ave. of the Americas, New York, NY 10036, tel. (212) 575-1313.

Theatre. Miss Verdon made her debut as the Gambling Dancer in the pre-Bway tryout of *Bonanza Bound* (opened Shubert Th., Philadelphia, Pa., Dec. 26, 1947; closed there Jan. 3, 1948); was assistant choreographer to Jack Cole for *Magdalena* (Ziegfeld, N.Y.C., Sept. 20, 1948); Mr. Cole's assistant and a dancer in *Alive and Kicking* (Winter Garden, Jan. 17, 1950); played Claudine in *Can-Can* (Shubert, May 7, 1953); Lola in *Damn Yankees* (46 St. Th., May 5, 1955); Anna Christie in *New Girl in Town* (46 St. Th., May 14, 1957); and Essie Whimpole in *Redhead* (46 St. Th., Feb. 5, 1959).

Films. Miss Verdon was assistant choreographer to Jack Cole and danced in *On the Riviera* (20th-Fox, 1951); *David and Bathsheba* (20th-Fox, 1951); *Meet Me After the Show* (20th-Fox, 1951); *The Farmer Takes a Wife* (20th-Fox, 1953); and played Lola in *Damn Yankees* (WB, 1958).

Awards. Miss Verdon has received two Donaldson Awards and the Antoinette Perry (Tony) Award for her performance as Claudine in *Can-Can* (1953) and the *Theatre World* Award (1953). She received the D.E.A. Award (1955) and The Lambs Award (1956).

She won Antoinette Perry (Tony) awards for her performances as Lola in *Damn Yankees* (1956), Anna Christie in *New Girl in Town* (1957), and Essie Whimpole in *Redhead* (1959). She has also received the Film Daily Award (1959), the Laurel Award (1959) and the Dance Magazine Award (1962).

VEREEN, BEN. Actor, dancer. b. Benjamin Augustus Vereen, Oct. 10, 1946, Miami, Fla. Grad. H.S. of Performing Arts, N.Y.C. Married; one son.

Theatre. Mr. Vereen appeared as Brother Ben in a touring company of *Sweet Charity* (Caesar's Palace, Las Vegas, Nev., Dec. 29, 1966); as the Fight Announcer in a touring company of *Golden Boy* (Auditorium Th., Chicago, Ill., Apr. 23, 1968); and succeeded Barry McGuire as Claude in *Hair* (Biltmore, N.Y.C., Apr. 29, 1968), later touring as Hud in the same show (Aquarius Th., Los Angeles, Calif., Nov. 28, 1968). He played Judas Iscariot in *Jesus Christ Superstar* (Mark Hellinger Th., N.Y.C., Oct. 12, 1971); and was the Leading Player in *Pippin* (Imperial, Oct. 23, 1972).

Films. Mr. Vereen appeared in *Funny Lady* (Col., 1975).

Television. Mr. Vereen had his own variety show, Comin' at Ya (NBC, 1975) and appeared as Louis Armstrong in the television film *Louis Armstrong—Chicago Style* (ABC, Jan. 25, 1976).

Night Clubs. Mr. Vereen appeared at the Empire Room (Waldorf-Astoria, N.Y.C., Apr. 1975) and the Persian Room (Plaza Hotel, N.Y.C., Mar. 16–Apr. 3, 1976).

Discography. Mr. Vereen is on the recording of *Jesus Christ Superstar* (Decca) and *Pippin* (Motown) and has also recorded *High Steppin' Mama*. .

Awards. For his performance in *Jesus Christ Superstar,* Mr. Vereen was nominated for an Antoinette Perry (Tony) Award (1972) as best supporting actor in a musical and won the *Variety* NY Drama Critics Poll as best supporting actor; for his performance in *Pippin,* he was awarded a Tony (1973) as best actor in a musical and received a Drama Desk Award. In 1975, he received AGVA's "Entertainer of the Year" Award.

VICTOR, LUCIA. Production stage manager, director, playwright. b. Lucia Adelaide Victor Baker, Jan. 8, Keokuk, Iowa, to Jesse Edgar and Adelaide (La Taste) Baker. Father, opera impresario. Grad. Francis Parker H.S., Chicago, Ill.; Univ. of Chicago. Married Milton Chalifoux, musician (marr. dis.); married Sidney Breeze, actor (marr. dis.); married Frank Dudley, actor, stage manager. Member of SSD&C (dir., 1971–73); AEA (council, 1954–64); AGMA; Dramatists Guild. Address: Farmers Mill Road, Carmel, NY 10512, tel. (914) 225-7470.

Theatre. Miss Victor was assistant stage manager for the double-bill, *Magic* and *Hello Out There* (Belasco Th., Sept. 29, 1942); and for the CIO's production of *Marching with Johnny* (1943); stage manager for *This Rock* (Longacre, Feb. 18, 1943); asst. stage manager for *The Searching Wind* (Fulton, Apr. 12, 1944); stage manager for *Hope for the Best* (Fulton, Feb. 7, 1945); and *Kiss Them for Me* (Belasco, Mar. 20, 1945). She directed at Cecilwood Th., Fishkill, N.Y. (Summer 1948); at the Woodstock Th., N.Y., and at the Margaret Webster Drama Sch., Woodstock (Summer 1950).

She was lighting stage manager for *King Lear* (National, N.Y.C, Dec. 25, 1950); production stage manager for *Mary Rose* (ANTA, Mar. 4, 1951); general stage manager for *To Dorothy, a Son* (John Golden Th., Nov. 19, 1951); stage manager for *Gertie* (Plymouth, Jan. 30, 1952); advance director for a stock touring production of *Kiss Me, Kate* (Summer 1952); production stage manager for *The Gambler* Oct. 13, 1952); and *Touchstone* (Music Box, Feb. 3, 1953); stage manager for *The American Dance* (Alvin, May 1953); advance director for a stock touring production of *Gentlemen Prefer Blondes* (Summer 1953).

At NY City Ctr., she was lighting stage manager for *Cyrano de Bergerac* (Nov. 11, 1953), *The Shrike* (Nov. 25, 1953), and *Richard III* (Dec. 9, 1953); was production stage manager for *The Immoralist* (Royale, Feb. 8, 1954); the pre-Bway tour of *Paradise Question* which closed out of town; and Martha Graham's dance program (54 St. Th., N.Y.C.,

1954); stage manager for *King of Hearts* (Lyceum, Apr. 1, 1954); at NY City Ctr., was production stage manager for *Show Boat* (May 5, 1954), *Die Fledermaus* (May 19, 1954), and *Carousel* (June 2, 1954); for *Second American Dance* (ANTA, 1954); and for *House of Flowers* (Alvin, Dec. 30, 1954).

She was production stage manager for the NY City Ballet's Co.'s European tour (1955); stage manager (Sept. 1955) for *Inherit the Wind* when it reopened (National, Apr. 21, 1955), and later assistant to the director with the national touring company (opened Blackstone, Chicago, Feb. 8, 1956; closed Ford's, Baltimore, Md., Jan. 19, 1957); production stage manager for *The Rope Dancers* (Cort, N.Y.C., Nov. 20, 1957); and for Martha Graham's dance program (54 St. Th., 1958). She wrote the play *Detour After Dark* (Fortune, London, England, June 8, 1959); was production stage manager for *Take Me Along* (Shubert Th., N.Y.C., Oct. 22, 1959); *Becket* (St. James, Oct. 5, 1960); and succeeded (June 1, 1961) Neil Hartley as production stage manager for *Carnival!* (Imperial, Apr. 13, 1961), on its national tour she was assistant director, and director when the show played in London, England, and Melbourne, Australia (1962).

She directed *Carnival!* (Paramus Playhouse, N.J., Summer 1963), and on tour the same season; took over (Mar. 1963) as stage manager for *Tchin-Tchin* (Plymouth, Oct. 18, 1963); was production stage manager for Martha Graham in London, and at the Edinburgh (Scotland) Festival (1963); *The Rehearsal* (Royale, N.Y.C., Sept. 23, 1963); assistant to the director and production stage manager for *Hello Dolly!* (St. James, Jan. 16, 1964); assistant to the director of *I Do! I Do!* (46 St. Th., Dec. 5, 1966); directed additional productions of *I Do! I Do!* (Palm Beach, Fla., Jan. 1969; bus-and-truck touring company, 1969–70); Phyllis Diller to play (Dec. 26, 1969) Dolly Gallagher Levi in *Hello, Dolly!*; directed *Billy Noname* (Truck & Warehouse Th., N.Y.C., Mar. 2, 1970); Ethel Merman to play (Mar. 28, 1970) Dolly Gallagher Levi in *Hello, Dolly!*; Pearl Bailey to tour as Dolly Gallagher Levi (1971); directed *Ari* (Mark Hellinger Th., N.Y.C., June 15, 1971); directed a touring production of *The Sound of Music* (Summer 1971); a road company of *The Fantasticks* (Boston, Mass., Oct. 3, 1971); and directed *Heathen!* (Billy Rose Th., N.Y.C., May 21, 1972).

Miss Victor joined the office of David Merrick as head of production in 1972; subsequently was production head on *Out Cry* (Lyceum, Mar. 1, 1973); *The One-Night Stand* (pre-Bway: opened Fisher Th., Detroit, Mich., Aug. 6, 1973; closed Forrest Th., Philadelphia, Pa., Sept. 22, 1973); *Mack & Mabel* (Majestic, N.Y.C., Oct. 6, 1974); and for the National Th. from Great Britain revival of *The Misanthrope* (St. James, Mar. 13, 1975). Miss Victor also directed Pearl Bailey as Dolly Gallagher Levi for a farewell tour of *Hello, Dolly!* (1975); a touring production of *Forty Carats* (Summer 1975); and adapted lyrics for songs in *Dear Piaf* (Mama Gail's, N.Y.C., Dec. 19, 1975).

Other Activities. Miss Victor gave tutorials in playwriting and directing at Bennington (Vt.) Coll. in 1975.

Recreation. Travel, reading, food, home gardening.

VIDAL, GORE. Playwright, novelist. b. Oct. 3, 1925, West Point, N.Y., to Eugene L. and Nina (Gore) Vidal. Grad. Phillips Exeter Acad., N.H., 1943. Served US Army, 1943–46; rank, WO (jg). Member of Dramatists Guild, NY Athletic Club. Address: 360 E. 55th St., New York, NY 10022.

Theatre. Mr. Vidal wrote *Visit to a Small Planet* (Booth Th., N.Y.C., Feb. 2, 1957); *The Best Man* (Morosco, Mar. 31, 1960); adapted Friedrich Duerrenmatt's play, *Romulus* (Music Box, Jan. 10, 1962); wrote *Weekend* (Broadhurst, Mar. 13, 1968); and *An Evening with Richard Nixon and . . .* (Shubert, Apr. 30, 1972).

Films. He wrote the screenplays for *The Catered Affair* (MGM, 1956); *I Accuse!* (MGM, 1958); *The Scapegoat* (MGM, 1959); wrote, with Tennessee Williams, the screenplay for *Suddenly, Last Summer* Col., 1959); participated in the writing of *Ben-Hur* (MGM, 1959); adapted his play, *The Best Man* (UA, 1964); wrote, with Francis Ford Coppola, *Is Paris Burning?* (Par., 1966); and wrote the screenplay for *Last of the Mobile Hot-Shots* (WB, 1969).

Adapted to the screen by others were his teleplay *The Death of Billy the Kid*, released as *The Left Handed Gun* (WB, 1958); his play *Visit to a Small Planet* (Par., 1960); and his novel *Myra Breckinridge* (20th-Fox, 1970).

He appeared briefly in *Fellini's Roma* (UA, 1972).

Television. Mr. Vidal wrote *Dark Possession* (Studio One, CBS, Feb. 15, 1954); *A Sense of Justice* (Philco Playhouse, NBC, Feb. 6, 1955); *The Death of Billy the Kid* (Philco Playhouse, NBC, July 24, 1955); *Visit to a Small Planet* (Goodyear Playhouse, NBC, May 8, 1955); *Honor* (Playwrights '56, NBC, 1956); *The Indestructible Mr. Gore* (NBC, Dec. 13, 1959) which he narrated, and wrote about his grandfather; adaptations of *Dr. Jekyll and Mr. Hyde, Smoke, Barn Burning, The Turn of the Screw, A Farewell to Arms,* and *Stage Door;* as well as many other scripts for such shows as Suspense (CBS), Danger (CBS), Climax, and Omnibus (NBC).

He was host for the Hot Line series (WPIX, N.Y.C., from Fall 1964 to Dec. 30, 1964); and has been a frequent guest on talk shows including Editorial Page (Ind., 1964–65); the Today Show (NBC, 1964–67); the Art of Film series (Educ., 1964–65); the Steve Allen Show (Ind., 1964–65); Open End (Ind., 1965–66); *The Homosexual* special (CBS Reports, CBS, Mar. 7, 1967); and Face to Face (WNEW, N.Y.C., June 11, 1967).

He provided (with William F. Buckley, Jr.) commentary for the ABC coverage of the Democratic and Republican National Presidential Conventions (Summer 1968).

Other Activities. Mr. Vidal was the Democratic/Liberal candidate for US Congress from New York's 29th District (1960); founder of the newspaper *The Hyde Park Townsman* (1960); mbr., Democratic Natl. Convention Platform Comm. (1960); mbr., President's Adv. Comm. on the Arts (1961–63); a Natl. Book Award judge for fiction (1963); and co-chmn. of the New Party (1970–71).

Published Works. Mr. Vidal wrote *Williwaw* (1946); *In a Yellow Wood* (1946); *The City and the Pillar* (1948); *The Season of Comfort* (1949); *A Search for the King* (1950); *Dark Green, Bright Red* (1950); *The Judgment of Paris* (1952); *Messiah* (1954); a collection of short stories, *A Thirsty Evil* (1956); *Visit to a Small Planet and Other TV Plays* (1956); edited *Best TV Plays* (1956); wrote a book of essays, *Rocking the Boat* (1962); *Julian* (1964); *The City and the Pillar Revised* (1965); *Washington, D.C.* (1967); *Sex, Death and Money* (1968); *Myra Breckinridge* (1968); a book of essays, *Reflections Upon a Sinking Ship* (1969); *Two Sisters: A Novel in the Form of a Memoir* (1970); *Burr* (1973); and *Myron* (1974).

He was drama critic for *The Reporter* (1959) and has contributed frequently to *Partisan Review;* the New York *Herald Tribune; Esquire;* and other periodicals.

Awards. Mr. Vidal was nominated for a Screen Writers Annual Award for *The Best Man* (1964).

VOLKERT, ERIE T. Educator, director. b. Erie Theodore Volkert, Jan. 5, 1913, Racine, Wis., to Theodore and Gertrude (Hoelter) Volkert. Father, minister. Grad. Washington Park H.S., Racine, 1929; Lawrence Coll., A.B. 1935; Northwestern Univ., M.A. 1939. Married Sept. 2, 1939, to Mary Voecks; two sons, two daughters. Member of ANTA; AETA; NCP; Phi Delta Theta; New Eng. Th. Conference; Vermont Historical Society (advisory bd.); Lions Club (pres. 1955). Address: (home) 54 N. Pleasant St., Middlebury, VT 05753, tel. (802) DU 8-2085; (bus.) c/o Wright Memorial Th., Middlebury Coll., Middlebury, VT 05753, tel. (802) DU 8-2665.

Since 1941, Mr. Volkert has been director of the Wright Memorial Th., at Middlebury Coll., where he also teaches drama.

He was teacher-director of theatre at Lawrence Coll., Appleton, Wis. (1936–38); at Huron Coll., Huron, So. Dakota (1939–40); at Randolph Macon Women's Coll., Lynchburg, Va. (1940–41); and at the Bread Loaf Graduate Sch. of Eng., Middlebury, Vt. (1946–1968). He is on the board of directors for the Middlebury Community Th., the Middlebury Children's Th. and the Th. Group Limit-Vermont (summer touring th.).

VOLLAND, VIRGINIA. Costume designer. b. Dorothy Virginia Volland, Aug. 2, 1909, Chicago, Ill., to Paul Frederick and Gladys Sydney (Crouch) Volland. Father, publisher. Grad. Los Angeles H.S., 1925; Stanford Univ., B.A. 1929. Married Aug. 2, 1931, to Mervyn Clark Williams, actor (marr. dis. 1940); one daughter; married Aug. 3, 1940, to Frederick Cameron Skillman, Col. (ret.), US Army (marr. dis. 1946); married 1947 to Felix Jacoves, film director (marr. dis. 1947). Member of United Scenic Artists, local 829 (exec. bd., 1955); WGA, East.

Pre-Theatre. Dress designing.

Theatre. Miss Volland performed as a showgirl in *The Wonder Bar* (Nora Bayes Th., N.Y.C., Mar. 17, 1931). She first designed costumes for the Play Room Club's production of *The Infernal Machine,* which she also co-produced (W. 20 St. Th., Oct. 14, 1937); subsequently designed costumes for *Time Out for Ginger* (Lyceum, Nov. 26, 1952); *Gently Does It* (Playhouse, Oct. 28, 1953); *Sweet Peril* (St. James's, London, Dec. 3, 1952); *Down Came a Blackbird* ("Q" Th., London, Sept. 1, 1953); the national US tour of *Two's Company* (1953); *The Paradise Question* (1953); *One Eye Closed* (Bijou, N.Y.C., Nov. 24, 1954); *The Bad Seed* (46 St. Th., Dec. 8, 1954); *The Grand Prize* (Plymouth, Jan. 26, 1955); *The Hot Corner* (John Golden Th., Jan. 25, 1956); *The Tunnel of Love* (Royale, Feb. 13, 1957); *Hide and Seek* (Ethel Barrymore Th., Apr. 2, 1957); *The Genius and the Goddess* (Henry Miller's Th., Dec. 10, 1957); *Two for the Seesaw* (Booth, Jan. 16, 1958); *Sunrise at Campobello* (Cort, Jan. 30, 1958); *The Gazebo* (Lyceum, Dec. 12, 1958); *A Raisin in the Sun* (Ethel Barrymore Th., Mar. 11, 1959); *Integration Showcase* (Majestic, Apr. 20, 1959); and *A Mighty Man Is He* (Cort, Jan. 6, 1960).

Published Works. Miss Volland wrote *Designing Woman; The Art and Practice of Theatrical Costume Design* (1966).

Recreation. Swimming, fencing, horseback riding, and archery.

von FURSTENBERG, BETSY. actress. b. Elizabeth Caroline Maria Agatha Felicitas Therese von Furstenberg-Hedringen, Aug. 16, Neiheim Heusen, Ger., to Count Franz-Egon and Elizabeth (Johnson) von Furstenberg. Attended Miss Hewitt's Classes, N.Y.C.; grad. N.Y. Tutoring Sch., N.Y.C. Studied acting with Sanford Meisner. Married June 16, 1954, to Guy Vincent de la Maisoneuve, mining engineer; one son, one daughter. Member of AEA; SAG; AFTRA. Address: 106 E. 85th St., New York, NY 10028.

Theatre. Miss von Furstenberg made her N.Y.C. debut as Thankful Mather in *Second Threshold* (Morosco Th., Jan. 2, 1951); in stock, appeared in *For Love of Money* (Westport Country Playhouse, Conn., 1951); played Lorraine in *Dear Barbarians* (Royale, N.Y.C., Feb. 21, 1952); toured as Gabby in *The Petrified Forest,* as Lisa in *Jason,* and appeared in *Second Man* (Summer 1952); appeared as Josephine Perry in the pre-Bway tryout of *Josephine* (opened Playhouse, Wilmington, Del., Jan. 8, 1953; closed Selwyn, Chicago, Ill., Feb. 7, 1953); Myra Hagerman in *Oh, Men! Oh, Women!* (Henry Miller's Th., N.Y.C., Dec. 17, 1953); Lady Sybil Tenterden in *What Every Woman Knows* (NY City Ctr., Dec. 22, 1954); repeated her role in *Oh, Men! Oh, Women!* on tour (Summer 1955); and played Laurel in *The Chalk Garden* (Ethel Barrymore Th., Oct. 26, 1955).

She played Kate in *Child of Fortune* (Royale, N.Y.C., Nov. 11, 1956); Maggie Turk in *Nature's Way* (Coronet, Oct. 16, 1957); Elizabeth Compton in *The Making of Moo* (Rita Allen Th., June 11,

1958); Frankie Jordan in *Say, Darling* (revived NY City Ctr., Feb. 25, 1959); Helen in *Wonderful Town* (revived NY City Ctr., Mar. 5, 1959); Cassandra Redwine in *Season of Choice* (Barbizon-Plaza, Apr. 13, 1959); Margaret in *Much Ado About Nothing* (Lunt-Fontanne Th., Sept. 17, 1959); and Tiffany Richards in *Mary, Mary* (Helen Hayes Th., Mar. 8, 1961).

Miss von Furstenberg played Sylvia Greer in *The Paisley Convertible* (Henry Miller's Th., Feb. 11, 1967); Helen in *Wonderful Town* (revived NY City Ctr., May 17, 1967); Cecile Jeanrenaud in *Beyond Desire* (Th. Four, Oct. 10, 1967); Helen Claiborne in *Avanti!* (Booth, Jan. 31, 1968); Sybil Chase in a revival of *Private Lives* (Th. de Lys, May 19, 1968); Toby Landau in *The Gingerbread Lady* (Plymouth, Dec. 13, 1970), and on tour (opened Huntington Hartford, Los Angeles, Oct. 22, 1971; closed Playhouse, Wilmington, Del., May 6, 1972); and Eva in the national tour of *Absurd Person Singular* (opened Shubert, Chicago, Oct. 28, 1975), playing the role in the N.Y.C. production for a week (Jan. 12, 1976) during Sandy Dennis' absence.

Films. She made her debut in *Women without Names* (Lopert, 1951).

Television. Miss von Furstenberg re-created her Bway role of Thankful Mather in *Second Threshold* (Pulitzer Prize Playhouse, ABC, Apr. 27, 1951), and has appeared on Armstrong Circle Th. (NBC); TV Sound Stage (NBC); Medallion Th. (CBS); Omnibus (CBS); Appointment with Adventure (CBS); Robt. Montgomery Presents (NBC); Kraft Th. (NBC); Have Gun, Will Travel (CBS); Alfred Hitchcock Presents (ABC); *Crime of Passion* (Play of the Week, WNTA, Nov. 30, 1959); *The Fifth Column* (CBS, Jan. 29, 1960); Adventures in Paradise (ABC); *Tonight in Samarkand* (Golden Show, CBS, Mar. 24, 1962); The Defenders (CBS); *Your Money or Your Wife* (CBS telefilm, Dec. 19, 1972); etc.

von REINHOLD, CALVIN. Dancer, actor, choreographer, singer. b. Calvin Jack von Reinhold Lutz, Jan. 17, 1927, Regina, Canada, to Fridolin and Laura (Miller) von Reinhold Lutz. Father, engineer. Grad. John Oliver H.S., Vancouver, B.C., 1947; John Oliver Business Sch., Vancouver, 1949. Studied ballet and Spanish dancing at Kay Armstrong Ballet Sch., Vancouver, 1947–50; Russian Ballet with George Goncharov, London, England, 1951–54; ballet with Anna Northgate, London, 1951–54; Indian dance with Ram Gopal, London, 1952–54; jazz with John Gregory, N.Y.C., 1957–58; and Matt Mattox, N.Y.C., 1957–63. Member of AEA; AFTRA; AGVA.

Pre-Theatre. Secretary, paymaster.

Theatre. Mr. von Reinhold made his debut as a dancer in *Call Me Madam* (Coliseum, London, Eng., Mar. 15, 1952); danced in *Wish You Were Here* (Casino, Oct. 10, 1953); and *Pal Joey* (Prince's Th., Mar. 31, 1954); made his N.Y.C. debut as a dancer in *Say, Darling* (ANTA, Mar. 3, 1958); was choreographer at the Cape Cod Melody Tent (Hyannis, Mass., Summers 1959–61), where he also played Harry Beatin in *Brigadoon.*

He appeared with Beatrice Kraft at the Radio City Music Hall (N.Y.C., 1961); danced in *No Strings* (54 St. Th., Mar. 15, 1962); at the Circle Arts Th. (San Diego, Calif., Summers 1962–64), played Harry Beaton in *Brigadoon,* Curly in *Oklahoma!,* and Mambo Joe in *Damn Yankees;* and choreographed and staged the musical numbers for *The Sound of Music* (June 11, 1964), *Li'l Abner* (June 30, 1964), *The Music Man* (July 14, 1964), *Gentlemen Prefer Blondes* (July 28, 1964), *The King and I* (Aug. 11, 1964), and *My Fair Lady* (Aug. 25, 1964). He also choreographed *High Spirits* (Princess Th., Melbourne, Australia, Mar. 19, 1965).

Films. He danced in *Gentlemen Marry Brunettes* (UA, 1955); and *The King's Rhapsody.*

Television. He appeared in London as choreographer and dancer on the Vera Lynn Show (Associated Rediffusion Ltd., 1956); and on Youth Takes a Bow (Associated Rediffusion Ltd., 1956).

In the U.S., he danced in *Swing into Spring* (1961); *Huck Finn* (1961); on the Ed Sullivan Show (CBS, 1962, 1963); and The Bell Telephone Hour (NBC, 1964–65).

Night Clubs. He has performed at the Embassy Club (London, 1955); Flamingo Hotel (Las Vegas, Nev. 1958); Chateau Madrid (N.Y.C., 1960); and the Latin Quarter (N.Y.C., 1962).

Other Activities. Teaches dancing.

Recreation. Collecting Indian bronze statues and antique keys.

VOSKOVEC, GEORGE. Actor, director, playwright. b. Jiri (George) Voskovec, June 19, 1905, Sazava, Czechoslovakia, to Vaclav and Jirina (Pinkas) Voskovec. Father, Col., military band leader; mother, teacher. Grad., Lycée Carnot, Dijon, France, 1924; Univ. of Dijon, France, B.A. 1924; studied law and philosophy, Charles Univ., Prague, Czechoslovakia 1924–27. Married July 25, 1946, to Anne Gerlette (dec. May 27, 1958); two daughters; married Sept. 16, 1961, to Christine McKeown, theatre public relations, producer. Member of AEA; AFTRA; SAG; Coffee House Club (N.Y.C.). Address: c/o AEA, 165 W. 46th, New York, NY 10036.

Pre-Theatre. Poetry and editorial writing in periodicals on cultural subjects (Czechoslovakia and France).

Theatre. Mr. Voskovec made his stage debut as Publius in *Vest Pocket Revue,* which he also wrote with Jan Werich ("Liberated Th.," Prague, Apr. 19, 1927). Together with Jan Werich, he was associated with this theatre, later known as the V&W Th., as co-author of twenty-six plays, actor, producer, director, and stage designer until his arrival in the US (Jan. 1939).

He wrote, with Mr. Werich, *Heavy Barbara,* in which he played the First Soldier (Cleveland Play House, Ohio, Mar. 1940); and *The Ass and the Shadow,* in which he played Taxidermes (Cleveland Play House, Nov. 1940); made his N.Y.C. debut as Trinculo in *The Tempest* (Alvin, Jan. 25, 1945); directed three stage comedies for the USO camp shows, which toured the PTO (1945); was co-producer, and played Banjo, in Jan Werich's adaptation of *The Man Who Came to Dinner* (V&W Th., Prague, Czechoslovakia, 1946), where he also was co-author of the book and lyrics, co-producer, and director of *Fist in the Eye* (1947–48). He wrote the Czech adaptations, and directed both *The Skin of Our Teeth* (National Th. of Prague, June 1947), and *Finian's Rainbow* (V&W Th., Mar. 1948), which he produced with Jan Werich, co-author of book and lyrics of the latter musical adaptation.

In 1949 he founded the American Th. of Paris (France) where he produced six plays; *Three in One, Four in One, No Exit, Curly, Our Town* and *Knickerbocker Holiday;* directed *Four in One,* and designed *Knickerbocker Holiday* (1949–51). He appeared as Colonel Aime Frappot in *The Love of Four Colonels* (Shubert, N.Y.C., Jan. 15, 1953); Dr. Marek in *His and Hers* (46 St. Th., Jan. 7, 1954); Sasha in *Festival* (Longacre, Jan. 18, 1954); and Dr. Dorn in *The Seagull* (Phoenix, May 11, 1954); toured summer theatres as Herr Steiner in *Autumn Crocus,* opposite Margaret Truman (1956); played the title role in *Uncle Vanya* (Fourth St. Th., Jan. 31, 1956); and Mr. Frank in *The Diary of Anne Frank* (Phoenix, London, Nov. 29, 1956).

He toured summer theatres in *Janus* (1957); appeared as the Manufacturer in *Middle of the Night* (Bucks County Playhouse, New Hope, Pa., Summer, 1958); Alper in *The Tenth Man* (Booth, N.Y.C., Nov. 5, 1959); Paul Stumpfig in *Big Fish, Little Fish* (ANTA, Mar. 15, 1961); the title role in *A Call on Kuprin* (Broadhurst, May 25, 1961); the Doctor in *Do You Know the Milky Way?* (Billy Rose Th., Oct. 16, 1961); appeared in *Brecht on Brecht* (Th. de Lys, Jan. 3, 1962); played Kurt Pastor in the pre-Bway tryout of *Banderol* (opened Forrest, Philadelphia, Pa., Sept. 17, 1962; closed there Sept. 22, 1962); appeared as Charnak in *Nobody Loves Me* (Bucks County Playhouse, Summer 1963); Caesar in the American Shakespeare Festival production of *Caesar and Cleopatra* (Stratford, Conn., July 30, 1963); the Player King in *Hamlet* (Lunt-Fontanne, N.Y.C., Apr. 9, 1964); and Ernst Heinrich Ernesti (Einstein) in *The Physicists* (Martin Beck Th., Oct. 13, 1964).

As a member of the Repertory Th. of Lincoln Center (1966–67), he played Sir Epicure Mammon in *The Alchemist;* Konarsky in *East Wind,* and Pope Urban VIII in *Galileo.* In collaboration with Christine McKeown, he adapted into English two plays by Czech playwright J. Topol, which he directed under the title of *Two from Prague,* at the Drama School of the Univ. of Oklahoma (1968). He was Herr Schultz in the musical *Cabaret* (Imperial, N.Y.C., 1968–69); Dr. Axelrod in *The Penny Wars* (Royale, 1966); played Dag Hammarskjold in *Murderous Angels* (Mark Taper Forum, Los Angeles, 1970); Mr. Glas in *Slow Dance on the Killing Ground* (Actors' Playhouse, N.Y.C., 1970); the Best Friend in *All Over* (Martin Beck Th., 1971); Otto Beethoven in *The Killdeer* (Public Th., 1974); and Arthur Freeling in *The Headhunters* (Kennedy Ctr., Washington, D.C., 1974).

Films. Mr. Voskovec made his debut in the Czech film, *A Tale of May* (Electa, 1926); subsequently appeared in *Kate, the Mart Girl* (Electa, 1927); with Mr. Werich, wrote the screenplay for *Powder and Gas* (VAW, 1930), in which he also appeared; *Your Money or Your Life* (AB, 1932); *Hej-Rup* (Meisner Films, 1934); the original story upon which was based the film, *The Golem* (AB, 1935); and *The World Is Ours* (AB, 1936), in which he also appeared. He wrote and directed a documentary movie for the Intl. Refugee Organization (a U.N. Specialized Agency) about displaced persons camps in Italy (1950).

In the US, he appeared in *Anything Can Happen* (Par., 1952); *Affair in Trinidad* (Col., 1952); *The Iron Mistress* (WB, 1952); played Juror No. 11 in *Twelve Angry Men* (UA, 1957); Mr. Herman in *Wind Across the Everglades* (WB, 1958); Stieglitz in *The Bravados* (20th-Fox, 1958); the Psychiatrist in *Butterfield 8* (MGM, 1960); appeared in *The Spy Who Came in from the Cold* (WB, 1965); *Mr. Buddwing* (Par., 1965); was Peter Hurkos in *The Boston Strangler* (20th-Fox, 1968); the General in *The Iceman Cometh* (Amer. Film Th., 1973); and the ESP Professor in *Man on the Swing* (Par., 1973).

Television and Radio. With Jan Werich he wrote 2,000 special feature war information and political satire programs broadcast to Czechoslovakia during WW II by the US Office of War Information (1942–46). As program specialist at UNESCO's Mass Comm. Dept. in Paris (1948–50), he organized their Radio News Letter, and participated in international mass communications conferences.

He made his television debut in *A Certain Feeling* (Studio One, CBS, Dec. 1951); and has appeared (1952–to date) on Playhouse 90, Studio One, Hallmark Hall of Fame, and Naked City as well as on Mannix, Mission: Impossible, Streets of San Francisco, Hawaii Five-O, and the NET Television Playhouse.

In England, he appeared in the title role of *Uncle Vanya,* and as Judge Brock in *Hedda Gabler* (both BBC, London, 1957).

He also appeared in the role of Albert Einstein in *The Particular Men* (Net, 1972), and in *Dr. Einstein Before Lunch* (NBC, 1973).

Published Works. Mr. Voskovec wrote a book of verse and essays, *A Hat in the Brush,* in Czechoslovakian, published in Prague in 1965 and 1966 in two successive editions.

Awards. He received the *Village Voice* Off-Bway (Obie) Award for his performance in the title role in *Uncle Vanya* (1956).

VROOM, PAUL. Producer, general manager, company manager, theatre manager, press representative. b. Paul O'Sullivan, Feb. 17, 1917, New York City. Legally adopted by uncle, Lodewick Vroom, producer and manager, and aunt, Florence Vroom, actress. Grad. St. Ann's Acad., N.Y.C., 1934; attended Columbia Univ., 1934–37. Married July 28, 1943, to Lorraine. Served WW II; US Army, Infantry, Spec. Svcs. and Air Force; rank,

Sgt. Member of ATPAM. Address: (home) 325 E. 41st St., New York, NY 10016, tel. (212) Yukon 6-2973; (bus.) Palace Theatre, 1564 Broadway, New York, NY 10036, tel. (212) PL 7-2626.

Theatre. Mr. Vroom was assistant to the producer for the Civic Light Opera Co. presentations of Gilbert and Sullivan in N.Y.C. (Summer 1935); while a college student, assisted his father, Lodewick Vroom, who served as staff associate for *Tovarich* (Plymouth, N.Y.C., Oct. 15, 1936); *Around the Corner* (48 St. Th., Dec. 28, 1936); *The Amazing Doctor Clitterhouse* (Hudson, Mar. 2, 1937); and *The Philadelphia Story* (Shubert, Mar. 28, 1939); was press representative for Ruth Draper in her repertory of dramatic sketches (Booth, Jan. 19, 1936); and *30 Days Hath September* (Hudson, Sept. 30, 1938).

Mr. Vroom was press representative for the Lyric Opera Co. presentation of Gilbert and Sullivan in N.Y.C. (1940); produced a season of stock at the Glen Rock (N.J.) Playhouse (Summer 1941); during WW II, was house manager for *This Is the Army* (Bway Th., July 4, 1942); and *Winged Victory* (44 St. Th., Nov. 20, 1943); company manager for the pre-Bway tryout of *Salute to Murder* (opened Shubert-Lafayette, Detroit, Mich., Mar. 24, 1946; closed out of town); *The Magnificent Heel* (opened Erlanger, Buffalo, N.Y., Sept. 4, 1946; closed out of town); general manager for *Craig's Wife* (Playhouse, Feb. 12, 1947); *The First Mrs. Fraser* (Shubert, Nov. 5, 1947); *Forward the Heart* (48 St. Th., Jan. 28, 1949); business manager for *Bruno and Sidney* (New Stages Th., N.Y.C., May 3, 1949); and general manager for *The Respectful Prostitute* (Chicago, Spring 1949).

He was general manager for *The Father* (Cort, N.Y.C., Nov. 16, 1949); *Affairs of State* (Royale, Sept. 25, 1950); Louis Calhern's *King Lear* (Natl., Dec. 25, 1950); *The King of Friday's Men* (Playhouse, Feb. 21, 1951); *Twilight Walk* (Fulton Sept. 24, 1951); *Faithfully Yours* (Coronet, Oct. 18, 1951); with Irving Cooper, produced *The Number* (Biltmore, Oct. 30, 1951); was business manager and associate producer for *My Darlin' Aida* (Winter Garden, Oct. 27, 1952); general manager for *On Borrowed Time* (48 St. Th., Feb. 10, 1953); company manager for the Bway presentation of *End As a Man* (opened Th. de Lys, Sept. 15, 1953; moved to Vanderbilt, Oct. 14, 1953); and the Bway presentation of *The Girl on the Via Flaminia* (opened Circle in the Square, Feb. 9, 1954; moved to 48 St. Th., Apr. 1, 1954).

In association with Bernard Straus, Mr. Vroom produced *Fragile Fox* (Belasco, Oct. 12, 1954); was general manager for *A Day by the Sea* (ANTA, Sept. 26, 1955); managed the Lunt-Fontanne, ANTA and 46 St. theatres (1956–61); produced, with Barnard Straus and Adna Karns, *Double in Hearts* (John Golden Th., Oct. 16, 1956); was general manager for Th. Under the Stars (Central Park, N.Y.C., Summer 1957); *Make a Million* (Playhouse, Oct. 23, 1958); produced, with Harriet Parsons, Charles Hollirith, Jr., and William Dean, *Rape of the Belt* (Martin Beck Th., Nov. 5, 1960); was company manager for *Midgie Purvis* (Martin Beck Th., Feb. 1, 1961); general manager for *Let It Ride!* (Eugene O'Neill Th., Oct. 12, 1961); with Buff Cobb and Burry Fredrik, produced *Too True to Be Good*, for which he was also general manager (54 St. Th., Mar. 12, 1963); with Buff Cobb and Albert Marré, produced *Never Live Over a Pretzel Factory*, for which he was general manager (Eugene O'Neill Th., Mar. 28, 1963); and was general manager for *Dear Love* (1970–71). From 1966–to date Mr. Vroom has been general manager of the Palace Th.; and from 1972–to date he has been general manager of the Uris Th.

Films. He was company manager for the film version of Shakespeare's *Henry V* (UA, 1946).

Awards. Mr. Vroom was nominated for the Antoinette Perry (Tony) Award for his production of *Too True to Be Good* (1963).

Recreation. Baseball, football, tennis, basketball, stamp collecting.

W

WADDINGTON, PATRICK. Actor, singer. b. Patrick William Simpson Waddington, Aug. 19, 1901, York, England, to William Henry and Mary Louisa (Simpson) Waddington. Father, former lessee of Th. Royal (York), builder of Londesborough Th. (Scarborough), piano manufacturer; mother, actress. Grad. Gresham's Sch., Holt, England, 1919; St. John's Coll., Oxford Univ., M.A. 1923. Studied voice with Raymond Von Meuhlen. Served London Fire Brigade, 1937–39; R.A.F. 1940–45; rank, Squadron Leader; Reserve, 1946–56; rank, Squadron Leader. Member of AEA; British AEA; AFTRA; IASTA; Oxford Univ. Drama Society (secy., 1922–23); York Civic Trust (England); English Speaking Union; Merchant Adventurers Co. of the City of York; Oxford Society; York Georgian Society; Green Room Club (London).

Theatre. Mr. Waddington first performed as Peter in Ibsen's *The Pretenders* (New Th., Oxford, England, Mar. 1920); subsequently toured Scandinavia with the Oxford Univ. Drama Society in *Loyalties* (1922–23), which was directed by the author, John Galsworthy; and made his first professional appearance as Valentine in *Two Gentlemen of Verona* (Birmingham Repertory Th., Nov. 22, 1924).

He sang as Don Antonio in Sheridan's operetta, *The Duenna* (Birmingham Repertory Th., Dec. 1924); made his London debut as Rosencrantz in the first modern dress production of *Hamlet* (Kingsway, Aug. 25, 1925); played Freddie in *The Master* (Queen's, Mar. 1, 1926; Fomin in *Katerina* (Barnes, Mar. 30, 1926); toured as Geoffrey in *Mary, Mary, Quite Contrary* (Aug. 1926); played Smith in *A House of Cards* (Little, Nov. 18, 1926); toured as John Whittaker in *Easy Virtue* (Feb. 1927); appeared as Lundberg in *Samson and Delilah* (Arts, July 17, 1927); Jerry Budd in *The Golden Calf* (Globe, Sept. 14, 1927); toured as Lord Vail in *Luck of the Vails* (Jan. 1928); and played Sydney in *Holding Out the Apple* (Globe, London, June 16, 1928).

He appeared as Walter How in *Justice* (Wyndham's, July 4, 1928), and Charles Windsor in *Loyalties* (Wyndham's Aug. 9, 1928), having appeared in both roles at the First International Drama Festival (Th. de L'Odéon, Paris, July 1928); Pierrot in *The Theatre of Life* (Arts, London, Apr. 15, 1929); Kenneth Raglan in *Rope* (Ambassadors', Apr. 25, 1929); Nicholas Fayne in *Heat Wave* (St. James's, Oct. 15, 1929); Guildenstern in Henry Ainley's *Hamlet* (Haymarket, Apr. 22, 1930); and appeared in the revue *Charlot's Masquerade* (Cambridge, Sept. 4, 1930); played Harry Bronson in *The Belle of New York* (Daly's, Apr. 2, 1931); sang Lancelot in the operetta *La Poupée* (Daly's, Dec. 1931); and toured variety theatres Spring 1932).

He sang Captain Gustl Von Ploetz in the opera *The Land of Smiles* (Dominion, May 31, 1932); played Duke of Brixham in *Tomorrow Will Be Friday* (Haymarket, Aug. 23, 1932); sang in the light opera *Prudence* (Opera House, Leicester, Dec. 1932); played John Carslake in *For Better, for Worse* (Arts, London, Apr. 27, 1933); appeared in the revue *On with the Show* (Prince's, Dec. 20, 1933); played David Lister in *First Episode* ("Q," Sept. 11, 1933); and Toni Silver in *No Way Back* (Whitehall, May 17, 1934).

He made his N.Y.C. debut as David Lister in *First Episode* (Ritz, Sept. 17, 1934); played Prince Hal in *Henry IV, Part I* (His Majesty's, London, Feb. 28, 1935); appeared in *Sleeping Beauty: or What a Witch* (Vaudeville, Dec. 14, 1935); played Dr. Cecil Macrae in *Glass Houses* (Royalty, Apr. 15, 1936); toured as Elyot Chase in *Private Lives*, and Raymond Dabney in *The Man in Possession* (Fall 1936); appeared in *What Should a Husband Do?* (Th. Royal, Brighton, Mar. 1937); *Follies of 1938* (Saville, May 5, 1938); played Gerald Millett in *Weights and Measures* (Richmond, Nov. 21, 1938); appeared in *Good and Proper* (Kings, Glasgow, Scot., Apr. 1939); played George Osborne in *Vanity Fair* (Queen's, London, May 14, 1946), also touring in it (Winter 1946–47); Sir John Mannering in *Said the Spider* (Wimbledon, Oct. 27, 1947; moved Embassy, Nov. 11, 1947); in Fool's Paradise (Arts, Ipswich, Apr. 1948); Geoffrey Temple in *Miss Turner's Husband* (St. Martin's, London, May 6, 1949); Mr. Baxter in *The Mollusc* (Arts, June 21, 1949); Dr. Jack Davidson in *Johnny Belinda* (Th. Royal, Brighton, Feb. 1950); Richard Wyndham in *The Holly and the Ivy* (Lyric, Hammersmith, Mar. 28, 1950); and Roderick Glyde in *The Navy at Sea* (Comedy, Feb. 26, 1952).

He served as assistant director of a pageant, *International Military Tattoo* (Empire Stadium, Vancouver, B.C., Canada, June 1958); was standby for Cyril Ritchard as Biddeford Poole in *The Pleasure of His Company* (Longacre, N.Y.C., Oct. 22, 1958); toured as the Earl of Leicester in *Mary Stuart* (opened Sacramento H.S. Aud., Calif., Oct. 2, 1959); played Mr. Welland Strong in an ELT production of *A Trip to Chinatown* (Lenox Hill Playhouse, N.Y.C., Mar. 7, 1961); Louis Compass in *The Magnificent Hugo* (Comedy, Apr. 7, 1961); Sir Frances Chesney in a stock production of *Where's Charley?* (Oakdale Musical Th., Wallingford, Conn., June 1961); Count de Koeberg in *Kean* (Bway Th., N.Y.C., Nov. 2, 1961); Professor Kroll in *Rosmersholm* (Fourth St. Th., Apr. 11, 1962); Alex Nightingale in *The Affair* (Henry Miller's Th., Sept. 20, 1962); Don Pedro in the IASTA production of *Knight from Olmedo* (Coolidge Aud., Washington, D.C., Nov. 25, 1962); Jean de Malestroit in *Darker Flower* (Pocket, N.Y.C., Mar. 8, 1963); the First God in the IASTA production of *The Good Woman of Setzuan* (Drama Inst., N.Y.C., Mar. 10, 1963); Sir Edward Ramsey in *The King and I* (Mineola Playhouse, L.I., N.Y., Apr. 1, 1963); Bulteel in the ELT production of *Mister Johnson* (Master Inst., N.Y.C., Oct. 5, 1963); Colonel Pickering in *Pygmalion* (Manitoba Center, Canada, Oct. 1963); toured as Colonel Pickering in *My Fair Lady* (opened Hippodrome, Bristol, England, Mar. 1964; closed Hippodrome, Birmingham, England, Aug. 24, 1964); and was Gen. Sir Alan Brooke in *Soldiers* (New, London, Feb. 1969).

Films. Mr. Waddington appeared in *Loyalties* (Auten, 1934); *The Black Tulip* (Fox, 1934); *I Give My Heart* (Elstree, 1935); *Journey Together* (England, 1946); *School for Secrets* (Rank, 1946); *Esther Waters* (Rank, 1946); *The Clouded Crystal* (Rank, 1947); *It's Not Cricket* (Rank, 1947); *That Dangerous Age* (Rank, 1948); *The Wooden Horse* (Korda, 1949); *The Moonraker* (British Lion, 1957); *Family Doctor* (Fox, 1957); and *A Night To Remember* (Rank, 1958).

Television. He made his debut in experimental appearances in Baird's Laboratory (Long Acre, London, June 1933); played the General in *Getting Married* (BBC, 1957); Lord Innspond in *The Calendar* (BBC, 1957); the General in *His Excellency* (BBC, 1957); the Group Captain in the series Escape (BBC, 1957); and Mr. Sydney Male in the series Wideawake (BBC, 1958).

He made his first appearance on US television as the Judge in *Verdict of Three* (Playhouse 90, CBS, 1958); subsequently appeared as the Earl of Leicester in *Mary Stuart* (Play of the Week, WNTA, 1960); Colonel Fielding in *The Case of the Missing Wife* (US Steel Hour, CBS, 1960); Ames in *Heaven Can Wait* (Dupont Show of the Month, NBC, 1960); and Major Smith in *The Immortal Piano* (Armstrong Circle Th., NBC, 1960).

Night Clubs. He performed in *That Certain Trio* (Cafeé de Paris, London, 1930) and appeared in London in revivals of this show at the Dorchester, Savoy, and Berkeley hotels (1937–40).

Other Activities. He was administrator of the Actors' Orphanage Fund (1952–56).

Recreation. Horseback riding, sailing, collecting paintings, encouraging painters, directing drama.

WAGER, MICHAEL. Actor, director, writer. b. Emanuel Weisgal, Apr. 29, 1925, New York City, to Meyer W. and Shirley (Hirshfeld) Weisgal. Father, chairman of board, Weizmann Inst. of Science, Rehovoth, Isr. Grad. DeWitt Clinton H.S., N.Y.C., 1941; Harvard Univ., B.A. 1945; M.A. 1948. Studied at Actors' Studio, N.Y.C.; H B (H. Berghof) Studio, N.Y.C., one year; with Stella

Adler, N.Y.C., two years; with Uta Hagen, N.Y.C., one year. Married Dec. 21, 1948, to Mary Jo Van Ingen (marr. dis. 1955); one daughter; married Oct. 9, 1962, to Susan Blanchard Fonda; one son. Served US Army, Chinese language interpreter, 1943–45; rank, T/5. Member of AEA; AFTRA; SAG; Actors' Studio Theatre; Signet Society.

Theatre. Mr. Wager made his debut as the Boy in a Harvard Dramatic Club production of *The Shoemaker's Prodigious Wife* (Brattle Th., Cambridge, Mass., 1940); at the Westport (Conn.) Country Playhouse, appeared as Castro in *The Girl of the Golden West* (Summer 1947), and Henry in *The Skin of Our Teeth* (Summer 1948); and was a founding member and director of the Brattle Th. (Cambridge, Mass.), where he played O'Connor in *Shadow and Substance* and Cusins in *Major Barbara* (Summer 1948).

He made his NY debut as Julian in an ELT production of *Martine* (Lenox Hill Playhouse, Mar. 12, 1949); succeeded (Dec. 1949) Wright King as a Young Collector in *A Streetcar Named Desire* (Ethel Barrymore Th., Dec. 3, 1947), also touring in it (opened Locust, Philadelphia, Pa., Jan. 1950); played Peter Mitchell in *The Small Hours* (National, N.Y.C., Feb. 15, 1951); Vernon Kinswood in *Bernardine* (Playhouse, Oct. 16, 1952); Lorenzo in *The Merchant of Venice* (NY City Ctr., Mar. 4, 1953); succeeded (Mar. 7, 1953) Roddy McDowall as Bentley Summerhays in *Misalliance* (NY City Ctr., Feb. 18, 1953; moved to Ethel Barrymore Th., Mar. 6, 1953); played Wilbur Fifield in *The Remarkable Mr. Pennypacker* (Coronet, Dec. 30, 1953); Roderigo in William Marshall's *Othello* (NY City Ctr., Sept. 7, 1955); Prince Hal in *Henry IV, Part 1* (NY City Ctr., Sept. 21, 1955); the Son in *Six Characters in Search of an Author* which he also adapted with Tyrone Guthrie (Phoenix, Dec. 11, 1955); the Dauphin in *Saint Joan* (Phoenix, Sept. 11, 1956; moved to Coronet, Dec. 25, 1956); and in Athens (Greece), played Hermes in *Prometheus Bound* (Th. of Herodus Atticus, Summer 1957).

Mr. Wager played Shendi in *The Firstborn* (Coronet, N.Y.C., Apr. 29, 1958), also in Tel Aviv, Israel (Habimah, May 1958); Nick in the pre-London tryout of *The Deserters*, which closed out of town (opened Th. Royal, Brighton, Sept. 1, 1958); at the Cambridge (Mass.) Drama Festival, appeared as Andrew Aguecheek in *Twelfth Night* and Malcolm in *Macbeth* (Summer 1959); played Sasha in *The Cradle Will Rock* (NY City Ctr., Feb. 11, 1960); Mesa in *Noontide* (Th. Marquee, June 1, 1961); and appeared in *Brecht on Brecht* (Th. de Lys, Jan. 3, 1962), also directing its Washington (D.C.) company (1963).

Mr. Wager participated in the Marc Blitzstein Memorial Concert (Philharmonic Hall, N.Y.C., Apr. 19, 1964); succeeded (Aug. 17, 1964) Gerald Hiken as Andrei in *The Three Sisters* (Morosco, June 22, 1964); produced *Where's Daddy?* (Billy Rose Th., Mar 2, 1966); played Benya Crick in *Sunset* (81 St. Th., May 12, 1966); Charles Bodie in *The Penny Friend* (Stage 73, Dec. 26, 1966); Carlos in *The Cuban Thing* (Henry Miller's Th., Sept. 24, 1968); directed *Nag's Head* (New, Mar. 1969); played Ferdinand Gadd in *Trelawney of the Wells* (Public, Oct. 11, 1970); and Petruchio in *The Taming of the Shrew* (Roundabout Th., Jan. 30, 1972).

Films. Mr. Wager made his debut as Allen Goodman in *Hill 24 Does Not Answer* (CMP, 1954), followed by David Ben Ami in *Exodus* (UA, 1960), and Thomas in *King of Kings* (MGM, 1961).

Television. He made his debut as the Blind Lover in *Mr. Om* (NBC, 1948).

WAGNER, ARTHUR. Educator. b. May 11, 1923, New York City, to Moe and Fanny Wagner. Father, tailor. Grad. Stuyvesant H.S., N.Y.C., 1940); Earlham Coll., Richmond, Ind., B.A. 1946; Smith Coll., Northampton, Mass., M.A. 1948; Stanford Univ., Palo Alto, Calif., Ph.D. 1962. Studied with Paul Mann, N.Y.C., 1954–56. Married June 16, 1956, to Molli Joan Mercer, pharmacist; one son, one daughter. Served US Army, 1943–46. Member ATA; Florida Th. Conf. (1st vice-pres.); and Univ. & Coll. Th. Assoc. (vice-pres., 1972). Address: (home) 1045 Cordevo Rd., Del Mar, CA 92014, tel. (714) 755-3329; (bus.) Dept. of Drama, Univ. of Calif., San Diego, La Jolla, CA 92037, tel. (714) 453-2000.

Since 1972, Mr. Wagner has been chairman, Dept. of Drama, Univ. of Calif., San Diego. He was director, AAFA of actor training program (Temple Univ., 1969–72; Ohio Univ., 1967–69; Tulane Univ., 1965–67); and head of the Theatre Arts Dept. (Rollins Coll., 1956–65). He is a full professor and is presently doing research on the application of theory of transactional analysis to actor training.

Awards. He received the Danforth Foundation Teacher Study Grant (1951–62).

WAGNER, FRANK. Choreographer, director, teacher. b. Franklin A. Wagner, Jan. 4, St. Marys, W.Va., to Homer Cecil and Mabel (Carpenter) Wagner. Father, dentist; mother, nurse. Grad. Ravenswood (W.Va.) H.S., 1939; attended Marietta Coll., 1939–41; Priscilla Beach Drama Festival, Plymouth, Mass., Summers 1940 and 1941; in N.Y.C., attended Irvine Sch. of Th., 1941–42; studied at the Amer. Th. Wing with Hanya Holm, Jose Limon, Mme. Platova, Mme. Daganova, and singing with Eleanor McClellan, 1945–49; studied with Mme. Anderson, 1949–59; at the Dunham Sch. of Dance and Th. with Kurt Cerf, Miriam Battista, and Kate Warriner (teacher's certificate). Married Jan. 1, 1956, to Marsha J. Reynolds, dancer, singer; one daughter. Relative in theatre: cousin, Alden Goodno, musician, theatre manager. Served US Army, 1942–45. Special Services, Gold Star Award, 5 Battle Stars; rank S/Sgt. Member of AEA; SAG; AFTRA; AGVA; Marietta Coll. Gold Key Society; Lambda Chi Alpha. Address: (home) 140 W. 55th St., New York, NY 10019, tel. (212) PL 7-3696; (bus.) c/o International Dance School, Carnegie Hall, New York, NY 10019, tel. (212) CI 7-6056.

Theatre. Mr. Wagner, billed as Frank Wagner, performed in concerts with Myra Kinch, Choreographer's Workshop, and Syvilla Fort's Dunham Experimental Group (1947–49); played Nick in *Sleepy Hollow* (St. James, June 3, 1948), billed as Franklin Wagner. His first work as choreographer was for the Pittsburgh (Pa.) Playhouse revue *Of All Things!* (May 1949).

He staged *Of All Things!* (Ogunquit Playhouse, Me., Aug. 8, 1949); staged dance and musical numbers for summer theatre productions of *Touch and Go, Sugar and Spice*, and *Too Many Girls* (Smithtown Th., L.I., N.Y.); at the Steuben Glass Th. (Corning, N.Y.), staged dances and musical numbers and also appeared in *Happy Birthday* (June 26, 1951), *Anything Goes* (July 2, 1951), and *Show Boat* (July 16, 1951); at the Pittsburgh Playhouse, he staged the dance and musical numbers for *Of All Things* (Apr. 30, 1949), *On Your Mark* (May 5, 1951), *Wonderful Good* (May 10, 1952), *Dance for Joy* (Nov. 13, 1952), *Best Foot Forward* (Feb. 7, 1953), *Three to One* (May 2, 1953). He staged *Between Friends* (Pittsburgh Playhouse, May 1, 1954); became choreographer of the Pittsburgh Civic Light Opera, where he staged the dances and musical numbers for *The Merry Widow, Oklahoma!, Student Prince*, and *Bitter Sweet* (Summer 1954); in N.Y.C., staged the dance and musical numbers for *I Feel Wonderful* (Th. de Lys, Oct. 18, 1954); *The Feminine Touch* (Baltimore, Md., 1955); at Green Mansions (Warrensburg, N.Y.), staged revues and operas, including *Cinderella* and *The Threepenny Opera* (Summer 1955); revues and a jazz opera, *Fat Tuesday* (Tamiment Playhouse, Pa., Summer 1956); dances for *Ziegfeld Follies* (Winter Garden, N.Y.C., Mar. 1, 1957); again at Tamiment, Pa., revues (Summer 1957); and revues at Green Mansions (Warrensburg, N.Y., Summer 1958); staged the Charleston dance for Judith Anderson in *Comes a Day* (Ambassador, N.Y.C., May 6, 1958); staged the dances and musical numbers for *Babes in Arms* (Palm Beach, Fla., Mar. 1959; toured summer theatres, 1959); for an industrial revue, Pontiac (Aug. 1959); and at South Shore Music Circus (Cohassett, Mass.), he staged dances and musical numbers for *Oklahoma!, Carousel, The Great Waltz*, and *Pajama Game* (July–Aug. 1960); for industrial revues, Chevrolet (Aug. 1961 & 1962) and N.Y. Telephone Co. (1962); and a summer-theatre production of *Music in the Air* (South Shore Music Circus, June 6, 1963). He staged and directed industrial shows for Con Edison, Magee Carpets, Schaefer's Beer, Coca-Cola, Kleinerts, Ship 'n Shore, and Dictaphone (1963–64); and directed and staged the Chrysler-Plymouth Presentation Show, *This Is the Year That Is!* (St. Paul, Minn., Oct. 3, 1964; Seattle, Wash., Oct. 10, 1964).

Subsequently, he directed and choreographed *New Faces of 1968* (Booth Th., May 1968); staged musical numbers for *How To Steal an Election* (Pocket Th., Oct. 1968); directed and staged N.Y. Telephone industrial shows for state fairs in N.Y., Ohio, and Texas (1969–71); directed and staged *The Great American Musical Comedy* (John Drew Th., East Hampton, N.Y., July 1973); and directed and choreographed the Eaton Truck Industrial (Chicago, 1972).

Television. Mr. Wagner has staged dance sequences for Suspense (CBS); numbers from musicals transferred to television on the Ed Sullivan Show (CBS); for Year in Review (CBS); and closed circuit commercials for Armstrong Linoleum Co. In addition, he has produced four TV specials in Cologne, Germany.

Night Clubs. He has staged and choreographed the night club revues, *Midnight in Paris* (Latin Quarter N.Y.C., July 3, 1955); *The Thousand and Second Night* (Versailles, Dec. 14, 1955); staged *Six Dressed to the Nines* (Upstairs at the Downstairs, Sept. 1960); *Tennish Anyone* (Downstairs at the Upstairs, Dec. 1960); *Seven Come Eleven* (Upstairs at the Downstairs, Oct. 1961); *Dime a Dozen* (Plaza Hotel, Oct. 18, 1962); *Struts and Frets* (Julius Monk's, Chicago, May 8, 1963); and *Baker's Dozen* (Plaza Hotel, N.Y.C., Jan. 10, 1964).

He has also staged an act for the Barry Sisters; and for Jean-Pierre Aumont and Marisa Pavan.

Other Activities. Mr. Wagner has taught modern jazz at the International Dance Sch., N.Y.C., and has taught at the Dunham Sch. of Dance and Th. and the Pittsburgh (Pa.) Playhouse; and during the summers 1967–70 he taught jazz dance at the International Dance Festival, Cologne, Germany.

Mr. Wagner has devised an exercise technique that is being taught by himself and trained instructors at Body Works, Bergdorf-Goodman, N.Y.C.

Published Works. Mr. Wagner is the author of an exercise book called *Body Works* (1975).

Recreation. Collecting antiques, tennis, swimming.

WAGNER, ROBIN. Scenic, lighting, and costume designer. b. Robin Samuel Anton Wagner, Aug. 31, 1933, San Francisco, Calif., to Jens Otto and Phyllis Catherine (Smith) Wagner. Father, engineer. Grad. Balboa H.S., San Francisco, 1952. Attended California Sch. of Fine Arts, 1952–54. Married Sept. 12, 1959, to Joyce Marie Workman (marr. dis. 1969); one son, two daughters; married Nov. 1971 to Paula Sue Kauffman, actress (known professionally as Paula Wagner). Member of United Scenic Artists. Address: (home) 49 Grove St., New York, NY 10014, tel. (212) 691-5706; (bus.) 34 W. 13th St., New York, NY 10014, tel. (212) 691-8529.

Theatre. Mr. Wagner designed the sets (1953) for the Golden Gate Opera Workshop productions of *Don Pasquale, Amahl and the Night Visitors*, and *Zanetto* (San Francisco, Calif.); the sets for presentations by the Contemporary Dancers (Theatre Arts Colony); subsequently designed the sets for the Theatre Arts Colony production of *Tea and Sympathy* (San Francisco, 1954).

He designed the sets for *The Immoralist* and *Dark of the Moon* (Encore Th., San Francisco, 1955). For the Actors Workshop (Marines Memorial Th., San Francisco); he designed scenery for *The Miser* (May 15, 1958), *The Ticklish Acrobat* (June 5, 1958), and *The Plaster Bambino* (Oct. 22, 1959); designed scenery and costumes for the San Francisco Ballet Co. production of *Filling Station;* and the scenery and lighting for the Sacramento (Calif.) Civic Theatre production of *The Guardsman* (1958).

He designed the set and lighting for the Actors Workshop production of *Waiting for Godot*(Marines Memorial Th., San Francisco, Feb. 1957), that played off-Bway (York, Aug. 1958), before being presented at the Brussels World's Fair (Belgium, 1958), and later (Feb. 1959) revived in San Francisco.

His first N.Y. assignment was designing the production of *And the Wind Blows* (St. Mark's Playhouse, Apr. 28, 1959); subsequently designed a season of musical productions presented at the Sacramento (Calif.) Music Circus (1959); designed the set and lighting for *The Prodigal* (Downtown, N.Y.C., Feb. 11, 1960); and *Between Two Thieves* (York, Feb. 11, 1960); was assistant to designer Ben Edwards for *A Second String* (Eugene O'Neill Th., Apr. 13, 1960); designed the set for the musical productions at the Meadowbrook (N.J.) Dinner Theatre (Feb.–Sept. 1960); was assistant to designer Ben Edwards for *Face of a Hero* (Eugene O'Neill Th., Oct. 20, 1960); and designed the set and lighting for *Borak* (Martinique, Dec. 13, 1960).

Mr. Wagner was again assistant to designer Ben Edwards for *Midgie Purvis*(Martin Beck Th., Feb. 1, 1961); and *Big Fish, Little Fish* (ANTA, Mar. 15, 1961); designed the set and lighting for *A Worm in Horseradish*(Maidman, Mar. 13, 1961); the sets and lighting for the musical productions at the Carousel Th. (Framingham, Mass.), the Oakdale Th. (Wallingford, Conn.), and the Warwick (R.I.) Th. (Summer 1961).

He was assistant to designer Ben Edwards for the Bway production of *The Aspern Papers* (Playhouse, Feb. 7, 1962); and designed the settings and lighting for *Entertain a Ghost* (Actors' Playhouse, Apr. 9, 1962), and for *The Days and Nights of Beebee Fenstermaker*(Sheridan Sq. Playhouse, Sept. 17, 1962); designed the settings, lighting and costumes for the Irish Players touring production of *The Playboy of the Western World*(Oct. 5, 1962–Dec. 3, 1962); and designed the set for *Cages*(York, June 13, 1963). He was assistant to designer Oliver Smith for *110 in the Shade*(Broadhurst, Oct. 24, 1963); he designed the set and lighting for *In White America* (Sheridan Sq. Playhouse, Oct. 31, 1963); and *The Burning*(York, Dec. 3, 1963); was assistant to designer Oliver Smith for *Hello, Dolly!* (St. James, Jan. 16, 1964); and designed the sets for *The White Rose and the Red* (Stage 73, Mar. 16, 1964).

As principal designer (1964–67) at Arena Stage, Washington, D.C., he designed sets for *Dark of the Moon* (May 27, 1964), *Galileo* (Oct. 29, 1964), *He Who Gets Slapped* (Mar. 18, 1965), the double-bill *Hard Travelin'*and *Lonesome Train* (May 27, 1965), *St. Joan*(Oct. 28, 1965), *The Skin of Our Teeth*(Dec. 2, 1965), *Project Immortality*(Jan. 6, 1966), *Serjeant Musgrave's Dance*(Mar. 17, 1966), *Oh, What a Lovely War!* (June 3, 1966), *Macbeth* (Oct. 25, 1966), *The Magistrate* (Dec. 6, 1966), *The Inspector General* (Feb. 23, 1967), *The Andersonville Trial* (May 23, 1967), *Major Barbara* (Sept. 26, 1967), and *Poor Bitos* (Sept. 27, 1967).

Mr. Wagner also designed scenery for *The Condemned of Altona* (Vivian Beaumont Th., N.Y.C., Feb. 3, 1966); *Galileo* (Vivian Beaumont Th., Apr. 13, 1967); *The Trial of Lee Harvey Oswald* (ANTA, Nov. 5, 1967); *A Certain Young Man* (Stage 73, Dec. 26, 1967); *Hair* (Biltmore, Apr. 29, 1968; London, England, 1969); *In Three Zones* (Forum, N.Y.C., 1968); *The Cuban Thing* (Henry Miller's Th., Sept. 24, 1968); *The Great White Hope* (Alvin Th., Oct. 3, 1968); *Love Match* (pre-Bway: opened Palace West, Phoenix, Ariz., Nov. 3, 1968; closed Ahmanson Th., Los Angeles, Calif., Jan. 4, 1969); *Lovers and Other Strangers*(Brooks Atkinson Th., N.Y.C., Nov. 16, 1968); *Promises, Promises* (Sam S. Shubert Th., Dec. 1, 1968; Prince of Wales Th., London, England, 1969).

He designed scenery for *The Watering Place*(Music Box, N.Y.C., Mar. 12, 1969); *My Daughter, Your Son* (Booth Th., May 13, 1969); *Edith Stein* (Arena Stage, Washington, D.C., Oct. 23, 1969); *Gantry* (George Abbott Th., N.Y.C., Feb. 14, 1970); *Mahagonny* (Anderson Th., Apr. 28, 1970); *The Engagement Baby*(Helen Hayes Th., May 21, 1970); *Lenny* (Brooks Atkinson Th., May 26, 1971); *Jesus Christ Superstar*(Mark Hellinger Th., Oct. 12, 1971); *Inner City* (Ethel Barrymore Th., Dec. 19, 1971); *Sugar* (Majestic, Apr. 9, 1972); for the National Opera Company touring *Lulu* (1972); and for American Shakespeare Festival (Stratford, Conn.) productions of *Julius Caesar* (June 22, 1972) and *Antony and Cleopatra* (June 23, 1972).

He designed scenery for the West Coast production of *Jesus Christ Superstar*(Universal Amphitheater, Los Angeles, Calif., June 26, 1972); for *Lysistrata* (Brooks Atkinson Th., N.Y.C., Nov. 13, 1972); for *Mary C. Brown and the Hollywood Sign* (closed during previews: Shubert Th., Los Angeles, Calif., Dec. 1972); *Seesaw* (Uris Th., N.Y.C., Mar. 18, 1973); *Full Circle* (ANTA, Nov. 7, 1973); and *Rachael Lily Rosenbloom and Don't You Ever Forget It* (closed during previews: Broadhurst, Nov. 26 –Dec. 1, 1973). He directed Jean Cocteau's *Orpheus* (Th. in Space, N.Y.C., Oct. 1973); designed scenery for *Mack and Mabel* (Majestic, Oct. 6, 1974); and conceived, adapted, and designed *Sgt. Pepper's Lonely Hearts Club Band on the Road* (Beacon, Nov. 17, 1974).

Films. Mr. Wagner designed *The Old Man's Place* (Cinerama, 1972).

Awards. Mr. Wagner received a Drama Desk Award for *Lenny*(1971); was nominated for an Antoinette Perry (Tony) Award for *Jesus Christ Superstar* (1972); received the Joseph Maharam Award for scenic design for *Seesaw*(1973); and was nominated for Los Angeles Drama Critics Circle awards for *Mack and Mabel* and *Seesaw.*

WAISSMAN, KENNETH. Producer. b. Kenneth Jay Waissman, Jan. 24, 1942, Baltimore, Md., to Charles William and Hilda (Shutz) Waissman. Father, jeweler. Grad. P.S. 69 and Forest Park High School (Baltimore); Univ. of Maryland (College Park); New York Univ. Married June 17, 1973, to Maxine Fox. Relative in theatre: wife, his co-producer. Member of League of N.Y. Theatres and Producers. Address: 1564 Broadway, New York, NY 10036, tel. (212) 246-0005.

Theatre. Mr. Waissman made his debut at the Johns Hopkins Children's Th., (Baltimore), in 1951. He subsequently served as an apprentice at the Hilltop Playhouse (Owings Mills, Md., June 1959). As a member of the Peace Corps (Aug. 1964–Aug. 1966), Mr. Waissman produced and directed cultural and educational television programs in South America. He gained experience in professional theatre as production assistant to Fryer, Carr and Harris, theatrical producers (1968–69), and as production assistant to George Abbott for *The Education of Hyman Kaplan* (Alvin, N.Y.C., Apr. 4, 1968). He produced *Fortune and Men's Eyes* (Stage 73, N.Y.C., Oct. 22, 1969). He subsequently co-produced with his wife, Maxine Fox, *And Miss Reardon Drinks a Little* (Morosco, N.Y.C., Feb. 25, 1971); produced *Grease* (Royale, N.Y.C., Feb. 14, 1972, and New London (England) Th., June 17, 1973); and *Over Here!*, starring the Andrews Sisters (Shubert, N.Y.C., Mar. 6, 1974).

Awards. Mr. Waissman was nominated for the Antoinette Perry (Tony) Award as producer, best musical, for *Grease* (1971–72), and *Over Here!* (1973–74). He is a member of the honorary journalism fraternity, Sigma Delta Chi.

Recreation. Swimming, painting, hiking.

WALKEN, CHRISTOPHER. Actor. b. Mar. 31, 1943, Astoria, N.Y., to Mr. and Mrs. Paul Walken. Father, baker. Attended Hofstra Univ. Studied with Wynn Handman; David Craig; Marion Rich, Jamie Rogers; Eve Collyer. Married. Member of AEA; SAG; AFTRA.

Pre-Theatre. Model, circus performer.

Theatre. Billed as Ronald Walken, he made his Bway debut as David in *J. B.* (ANTA, N.Y.C., Dec. 11, 1958); played Clayton "Dutch" Miller in *Best Foot Forward* (Stage 73, Apr. 2, 1963); appeared in a touring production of *West Side Story* with Anna Marie Alberghetti; and was a member of the chorus in *High Spirits* (Alvin, Apr. 17, 1964). As Christopher Walken, he played A Killer in *Baker Street* (Bway Th., Feb. 16, 1965); Philip, King of France in *The Lion in Winter* (Ambassador, Mar. 3, 1966); Claudio in *Measure for Measure*(Delacorte, July 12, 1966); Jack Hunter in *The Rose Tattoo* (NY City Ctr., Oct. 20, 1966; and Billy Rose Th., Nov. 9, 1966); The Unknown Soldier in *The Unknown Soldier and His Wife* (Vivian Beaumont Th., July 6, 1967); and Achilles in *Iphigenia in Aulis* (Circle in the Square, Nov. 21, 1967).

With the American Shakespeare Festival (Festival Th., Stratford, Conn., June 10–Oct. 12, 1968), he played Romeo in *Romeo and Juliet*, Lysander in *A Midsummer Night's Dream*, and Felton in *The Three Musketeers;* subsequently played Rosencrantz in *Rosencrantz and Guildenstern Are Dead* (Parker Playhouse, Fort Lauderdale, Fla., Feb. 10, 1969); appeared in *Julius Caesar*, and *A Comedy of Errors* with the San Diego National Shakespeare Festival (June 10–Sept. 14, 1969); played Alan in *Lemon Sky* (Playhouse Th., N.Y.C., May 17, 1970); Henry in *The Night Thoreau Spent in Jail*(Goodman Memorial Th., Chicago, Jan. 18, 1971); appeared in *Scenes from American Life*(Forum, N.Y.C., Mar. 25, 1971); played Posthumus Leonatus in *The Tale of Cymbeline*(Delacorte, Aug. 12, 1971); the title role in *Caligula* (Yale Repertory Th., New Haven, Conn., Nov. 25, 1971); in a bill of plays entitled *Metamorphosis*(American Place Th., N.Y.C., Apr. 8, 1972), played Georg in *The Judgment;* subsequently played Sintsov in *Enemies* (Vivian Beaumont Th., Nov. 9, 1972); Jack Clitheroe in *The Plough and the Stars* (Vivian Beaumont Th., Jan. 4, 1973); and Bassanio in *The Merchant of Venice* (Vivian Beaumont Th., Mar. 1, 1973); appeared in a double-bill of *Dance of Death* and *Miss Julie*(Long Wharf Th., New Haven, Conn., May 11, 1973); with the Lincoln Ctr. Repertory Theatre (Mitzi E. Newhouse Th.), played Achilles in *Troilus and Cressida* (Dec. 2, 1973), Antonio in *The Tempest* (Feb. 10, 1974), and the title role in *Macbeth* (Apr. 13, 1974). He played the title role in *Hamlet* (Seattle, Wash., Center Playhouse, Oct. 16, 1974); and Chance Wayne in *Sweet Bird of Youth*(Brooklyn Acad. of Music, Dec. 3, 1974; and Harkness, N.Y.C., Dec. 29, 1975).

Films. He has appeared in *The Anderson Tapes* (Col., 1971); *The Happiness Cage* (Cinerama, 1972); and *Next Stop, Greenwich Village* (20th-Fox, 1976).

Television. Mr. Walken's appearances include Hallmark Hall of Fame (NBC); Armstrong Circle Th. (NBC); Studio One (CBS); The Naked City (Ind.); and the Bell Telephone Hour (NBC).

Awards. Mr. Walken received the Clarence Derwent Award (1966) for his performance in *The Lion in Winter;* was named *Theater World's* Most Promising Personality (1966–67) for *The Rose Tattoo;* and received the Joseph Jefferson Award (1970–71 for his performance in *The Night Thoreau Spent in Jail.*

WALKER, DON. Composer, arranger, orchestrator, conductor. b. Donald John Walker, Oct. 28, 1907, Lambertville, N.J., to Thomas John and Blanche Stevenson (Basford) Walker. Father, grocer and butcher; mother, ceramic artist. Grad. Lambertville (N.J.) H.S., 1922; Rider Coll., B.C.S. and B.S. in Accountancy, 1925; Wharton Sch. of Business, B.S. (Economics), 1929. Studied music with Mary Gillingham Brown, Lambertville, N.J.; piano, pipe organ, drums, flute, clarinet, trombone and saxophone, 1916–23. Married Mar. 14, 1931, to Audrey Irene Langrill-Simpson; one son, one daughter. Relative in theatre: daughter, Ann (Walker) Liebgold, dancing teacher. Member of AFM, Local 802; Dramatists Guild; ASCAP; Beta Sigma Gamma; New Hope Historical Soc.; All-American Gladiolus Selections (dir. and judge). Address: (home) 323 Aquetong Rd., New Hope, PA 18938; (bus.) c/o The Chelsea Music Service, 1841 Broadway, New York, NY 10023.

Theatre. Mr. Walker was conductor and orchestrator of the Univ. of Pennsylvania's Mask and Wig production, *Ruff-Neck* (Garrick Th., Philadelphia, 1932); since then he has orchestrated the music for more than one hundred Bway shows.

He composed and orchestrated the score of *Allah Be Praised* (1942), with the exception of three songs written by Baldwin Bergerson; collaborated with Clay Warnick on the entire score, music, and lyrics for *Memphis Bound*, which he also orchestrated (1945); wrote and orchestrated the entire score of *Courtin' Time* (1951); *Sweet Mistress* (originally *Mistress of the Inn*) in collaboration with Ira Wallach, which received a tryout production at the Bucks County Playhouse (1957); and the incidental music for *Beauty Part* (1962).

He orchestrated his first Bway score in 1935, Sigmund Romberg's *Maywine;* for Bway, he has also orchestrated Cole Porter's *Leave It to Me* (1938); Richard Rodgers' *By Jupiter* (1942); Johnny Green's *Beat the Band* (1942); and Richard Rodgers' *Carousel* (1945). In 1945, he orchestrated a series of Sigmund Romberg concerts for Robin Hood Dell (Philadelphia, Pa.); he orchestrated Sigmund Romberg's *Up in Central Park* (1947); collaborated with Robert Russell Bennett on the orchestrations for Burton Lane's *Finians' Rainbow* (1947); and Cole Porter's *Kiss Me, Kate* (1948).

Mr. Walker orchestrated the music for Hugh Martin's *Look Ma, I'm Dancing;* Jay Gorney's *Touch and Go* (1949); Jule Styne's *Gentlemen Prefer Blondes* (1949); Irving Berlin's *Miss Liberty* (1949); Harold Rome's *Bless You All* (1950); the revival of George Gershwin's *Of Thee I Sing* (1950); Irving Berlin's *Call Me Madam* (1950); Johnny Mercer's *Top Banana* (1951); the revival of Richard Rodgers' *Pal Joey* (1951); Harold Rome's *Wish You Were Here* (1952); William Roy's *Maggie* (1953); Jule Styne's *Hazel Flagg* (1953); James Van Heusen's *Carnival in Flanders* (1953); Leonard Bernstein's *Wonderful Town* (1953); and Richard Rodgers' *Me and Juliet* (1953).

He developed and orchestrated Sigmund Romberg's partly finished music for *The Girl in Pink Tights* (1954); orchestrated Richard Adler and Jerry Ross' *The Pajama Game* (1954); Cole Porter's *Silk Stockings* (1955), Richard Adler and Jerry Ross' *Damn Yankees* (1955); Frank Loesser's *The Most Happy Fella* (1956; London, 1958); Robert Goldman, Glenn Paxton and George Weiss' *First Impressions* (1959); Frank Loesser's *Greenwillow* (1960); Meredith Wilson's *The Unsinkable Molly Brown* (1960); Arthur Schwartz's *The Gay Life* (1961); Jerry Bock and Sheldon Harnick's *She Loves Me!* (1963); Meredith Wilson's *Here's Love* (1963); Ervin Drake's *What Makes Sammy Run?* (1964); Jerry Bock and Sheldon Harnick's *Fiddler on the Roof* (1964); John Kander and Fred Ebb's *Flora, the Red Menace* (1964); *Cabaret* (1965), *The Happy Time* (1967), and *Zorba* (1969); Ervin Drake's *Her First Roman* (1970); Jerry Bock and Sheldon Harnick's *The Rothschilds* (1971); John Kander and Fred Ebb's *70 Girls 70* (1972); and Peter Udell and Gary Geld's *Shenandoah* (1974).

Mr. Walker has provided arrangements for vocal choirs, including Fred Waring's Pennsylvanian's and The Cities Service Chorus. He is currently involved in a project, sponsored by Music Theatre International, that is designed to make grand opera productions in English feasible for high schools, colleges, and amateur groups. The program has resulted thus far in completed and tested versions of *La Bohème* (Nov. 1973); and *Carmen* (Dec. 1974); and a work-in-progress, *Barber of Seville.*

Films. Mr. Walker adapted and arranged the score for *A Thousand Clowns* (UA, 1966) for which he received an Academy Award nomination (1967).

Television and Radio. Mr. Walker was orchestrator for Fred Waring (Old Gold Show, 1926–33); Al Goodman (Lucky Strike, Good Gulf, 1934–35); Sigmund Romberg (Swift-Raleigh, 1935–36; 1946–47); assistant to Frank Black (NBC, 1938–43); conductor and orchestrator for *Only Yesterday* (CBS, 1944); orchestrator for Max Liebman's Show of Shows (1950–51); and conductor for Your Hit Parade (NBC, 1957).

Other Activities. Mr. Walker was a lecturer at the Hunter Coll. Sch. of Adult Education (1957–59). He is president and director of Donald Music, Inc., and vice-president of Cryers, Inc.

He owns and operates a commercial farm which hybridizes and grows gladiolus under the name of Harmony Hill Glads, having produced a number of important new exhibition and commercial varieties.

Published Works. He is the composer of the following popular songs: "The Way of Dreams" (1928); "The Magic Highway" (1931); "The Land and My Music" (1933); "Let's Go Too Far" (1942); "Growin' Pains" (1945); and "The Nightingale, the Moon and I" (1945).

His published scores include *Courtin' Time* (1951); *Sweet Mistress* (1957); and *The Beauty Part* (1962).

Recreation. Tennis, golf.

WALKER, JOSEPH A. Playwright, actor, director. b. Feb. 23, 1935, Washington, D.C., to Joseph and Florine Walker. Father, housepainter. Grad. Dunbar H.S. (Washington, D.C.), 1952; Howard Univ., B.A., Catholic Univ. M.F.A. 1970. Served USAF; rank, 2nd Lt. Married to Barbara Brown (marr. dis. 1965), two sons; married Feb. 24, 1970, to Dorothy Dinroe, composer, one daughter.

Pre-Theatre. Cab driver, postal employee, high school teacher.

Theatre. Mr. Walker was co-author of the book and lyrics, and played The Narrator in *The Believers* (Garrick, N.Y.C., May 9, 1968); played Chaucer and understudied and eventually replaced Moses Gunn in various roles in *Cities in Bezique* (Public, Jan. 4, 1969); wrote *The Harangues* (St. Mark's Playhouse, Jan. 13, 1970); wrote, directed and contributed to the choreography of *Ododo* (St. Mark's Playhouse, Nov. 17, 1970); and wrote *The River Niger* (St. Mark's Playhouse, Dec. 5, 1972; and Brooks Atkinson Th., Mar. 27, 1973).

Previously, he was an actor with the Olney (Md.) Theatre and Arena Stage (Washington, D.C.); and while in graduate school (Catholic Univ., Washington, D.C.), played leads in *Prometheus Bound* and *Requiem for a Heavyweight.*

Mr. Walker is co-founder (1973) and artistic director of The Demi-Gods, a musical, dance, theatre repertory company for which he has written and directed *Yin Yang* (Oct. 1973); and *Antigone Africanus* (Mar. 1975).

Films. He wrote the screenplay for *The River Niger* (1976); and appeared in *April Fools* (Natl. Gen. 1969); and *Bananas* (UA, 1971).

Television. Mr. Walker's television appearances include NYPD (ABC); and A Man Called Adam.

WALKER, NANCY. Actress. b. Anna Myrtle Swoyer, May 10, 1922, Philadelphia, Pa., to Dewey Stewart and Myrtle (Lawler) Swoyer. Father, comedian, known as Dewey Barto. Grad. Bentley Sch., N.Y.C., 1929; Professional Children's Sch., N.Y.C., 1930–40. Married Jan. 29, 1951, to David Craig, coach; one daughter. Member of AEA; AFTRA; SAG.

Theatre. Miss Walker made her N.Y.C. debut as the Blind Date in *Best Foot Forward* (Ethel Barrymore Th., Oct. 1, 1941); subsequently appeared as Hildy in *On the Town* (Adelphi, Dec. 28, 1944); Yetta Samovar in *Barefoot Boy with Cheek* (Martin Beck Th., Apr. 3, 1947); Lily Malloy in *Look, Ma, I'm Dancin'* (Adelphi, Jan. 29, 1948); appeared in *Along Fifth Avenue* (Broadhurst, Jan. 13, 1949); played Madge in the pre-Bway tryout of *Waltz Me Around Again* (opened Brighton, Brighton Beach, L.I., N.Y., Sept. 14, 1948; closed there Sept. 18, 1948); Shirley Harris in the pre-Bway tryout of *A Month of Sundays* (opened Shubert, Boston, Mass., Dec. 25, 1951; closed Forrest, Philadelphia, Pa., Jan. 26, 1952); joined (Oct. 1953) as Gladys in *Pal Joey* (Broadhurst, N.Y.C., Jan. 3, 1952); appeared in the revue *Phoenix '55* (Phoenix, Apr. 23, 1955); played Julia Starbuck in *Fallen Angels* (Playhouse, Jan. 17, 1956); Katey O'Shea in *Copper and Brass* (Martin Beck Th., Oct. 17, 1957); Ruth in *Wonderful Town* (NY City Ctr., Mar. 5, 1958); appeared in *The Girls Against the Boys* (Alvin, Nov. 2, 1959); and played Kay Cram in *Do Re Mi* (St. James, Dec. 26, 1960, and on tour, 1962).

She directed *UTBU* (Helen Hayes Th., Jan. 4, 1966); appeared in stock as Libby Hirsch in *Dear Me, the Sky Is Falling* and as Julia Starbuck in *Fallen Angels*, which she also directed (Summer 1966); toured as Ellen Manville in *Luv* (Oct.–Dec. 1966); appeared with APA Repertory (Lyceum, N.Y.C.) as Charlotta Ivanovna in *The Cherry Orchard* (Mar. 19, 1968) and Julia in *The Cocktail Party* (Oct. 7, 1968); substituted (June 20–Sept. 12, 1968) for Helen Hayes as Mrs. Fischer in an APA revival of *The Show-Off* (Lyceum, Dec. 5, 1967); played Domina in *A Funny Thing Happened on the Way to the Forum* (Ahmanson Th., Los Angeles, Calif., Oct. 12, 1971); and appeared in the "Tribute to Stephen Sondheim" (Philharmonic Hall, N.Y.C., Mar. 1972).

Films. Miss Walker made her debut in *Best Foot Forward* (1943); subsequently appeared in *Girl Crazy* (1943); *Broadway Rhythm* (1944); and *Lucky Me* (WB, 1954).

Television. She has appeared on the Ed Sullivan Show (CBS) and the Garry Moore Show (CBS); was on Love, American Style (ABC, 1971); has appeared as the housekeeper on McMillan and Wife (NBC, 1971–to date); on the Mary Tyler Moore Show (CBS, 1971, 1972), some episodes of which she directed; was on Medical Center (CBS, 1972); Bridget Loves Bernie (CBS, 1972); the pilot *Keep the Faith* (CBS, 1972); *Every Man Needs One* (ABC, 1972); and played Rhoda's mother on Rhoda (CBS, 1974–to date). In 1970, Miss Walker began appearing regularly as Rosie in Bounty paper towels commercials.

Awards. Miss Walker received the Geminii Award (Apr. 1975) from American Women in Radio and TV.

WALLACE, GEORGE. Actor, singer. b. George Dewey Wallace, June 8, 1924, New York City, to George and Helen (Dewey) Wallace. Father, swimming instructor; mother, fashion model. Grad. Far Rockaway H.S., 1941. Studied singing with Lillian Sloane, Hollywood, Calif., four years; acting with Ben Bard, Hollywood, Calif., two years. Married 1942 to Lydia Robles (marr. dis. 1949); one daughter; married 1956, to Sandra Devlin, dancer (marr. dis. 1960). Served USN, ETO, PTO, 7 1/2 yrs. Member of AEA; SAG; AFTRA; AGVA.

Pre-Theatre. Lumberjack, tree surgeon, bartender.

Theatre. Mr. Wallace made his N.Y.C. debut as Mac in *Pipe Dream* (Shubert Th., Nov. 30, 1955); subsequently succeeded (1957) John Raitt as Sid Sorokin in *The Pajama Game* (St. James, May 13, 1954); played Matt in *New Girl in Town* (46 St. Th., May 14, 1947); appeared in stock productions as Matt in *New Girl in Town* (Warwick Musical Th., R.I.; Carousel, Framingham, Mass.; Oakdale Musical Th., Wallingford, Conn., Summer 1958); Frank Butler in *Annie Get Your Gun* (Carousel, Framingham, Mass., Summer 1958); Fred Graham in *Kiss Me, Kate* (Sacramento Music Circus, Calif., Summer 1958); Frank Butler in *Annie Get Your Gun* (Casa Mañana Th., Fort Worth, Tex., Summer 1959); Billy Bigelow in *Carousel* (Musicarnival, Cleveland, Ohio, Summer 1959); Joe Dynamite in *Wildcat* (State Fair Music Hall, Dallas, Tex.; Buffalo, N.Y., Summer 1960); Frank Butler in *Annie Get Your Gun* (Carousel, Framingham, Mass., Summer 1961); Johnny Brown in *The Unsinkable Molly Brown* (State Fair Music Hall, Dallas, Tex., Summer 1963); and Joe Dynamite in *Wildcat* (Theatre-under-the-Stars, Atlanta, Ga.; Starlight Th., Kansas City, Mo., Summer 1963).

He played Randolph of the Royal Mounted, James O'Connor, and Omar in *Jennie* (Majestic, N.Y.C., Oct. 17, 1963); succeeded Louis Hayward (Colonial Th., Boston, Mass., Mar. 1964) as King Arthur in a national tour of *Camelot;* replaced (Oct. 16, 1968–Oct. 14, 1969) Earle MacVeigh as the Innkeeper in the national company of *Man of La Mancha* (opened Shubert Th., New Haven, Conn., Sept. 24, 1966); replaced (May 13–Oct. 25, 1971) Charles Braswell as David in *Company* (Alvin, N.Y.C., Apr. 26, 1970); and replaced (Oct. 25, 1971) Lee Goodman as David in the national company of *Company* (Ahmanson Th., Los Angeles, Calif., May 20, 1971).

Films. He appeared in *Forbidden Planet* (MGM, 1956); and *Six Black Horses* (U, 1962).

Television. Mr. Wallace performed on the Ed Sullivan Show (CBS); Armstrong Circle Th. (CBS); Lux Video Th. (CBS); played in *International Incident* (Fireside Th. (NBC); and has appeared in episodes of such series as Gunsmoke (CBS); Maverick (ABC); and Rawhide (CBS).

Awards. Mr. Wallace, while in the USN, won the Pacific Fleet light heavyweight Boxing Championship; and the Pacific Fleet Athletic Award as outstanding athlete of the year.

For his performance on television in *International Incident*, he received a Sylvania Award (1951); and was nominated for the NY Drama Critics' Circle Award for his performance as Matt in *New Girl in Town* (1957).

WALLACE, PAUL. Actor, singer, dancer. b. Paul Norton Willens, May 26, 1938, Los Angeles, Calif., to Samuel and Ann (Goldstein) Willens. Father, dry cleaning business. Attended Washington H.S., 1955–56; attended Van Nuys (Calif.) H.S., 1956–57. Studied in Hollywood, Calif., at Players Ring Theatre Sch., one year; Geller Theatre Sch., two years; studied acting with Blair Cutting, three years; tap dance with Louis Da Pron, ten years; modern jazz with Deloris Blacker, six years; ballet with Michael Brigante, ten years. Studied singing with Keith Davis, N.Y.C., three years; drama and dance in Europe. Relative in theatre: brother, Marvin Willens, stunt man in films and television. Member of SAG; AEA; AFTRA. Address: (home) 17720 Marcello Pl., Encino, CA 91316; (bus.) tel. (213) 344-6094.

Theatre. Mr. Wallace made his stage debut as Dutch Miller in *Best Foot Forward* (Civic Playhouse, Los Angeles, Calif., Sept. 1954); subsequently appeared in stock as Bill Calhoun in *Kiss Me, Kate* (Th.-Under-the-Stars, Vancouver, B.C., Canada, 1956); Steam Heat Boy in *Damn Yankees* (Th.-under-the-Stars, 1957); Hans Schmidt in *Letters to Lucerne* (Players Ring Th., Hollywood, Calif., 1958); made his Bway debut as Tulsa in *Gypsy* (Bway Th., May 21, 1959); toured Australia as Billy Early in *No, No, Nanette* (1973); and toured in his one-man show, *Paul Wallace in Concert* (1974–to date).

Films. Mr. Wallace made his debut in *Crime in the Streets* (Allied, 1956); appeared in *The Young Stranger* (U, 1957); *Johnny Trouble* (WB, 1957); and played Tulsa in *Gypsy* (WB, 1962).

Television. He made his television debut as dancer and singer on the Colgate Comedy Hour (NBC, June 1952); subsequently appeared as Kippy in Father Knows Best (CBS, Sept. 1954); a Young Soldier in Navy Log (ABC, 1957); Roger in *Rebel* (Matinee Th., NBC, 1957); on Ford Startime (CBS, Feb. 23, 1960); and the Arthur Murray Dance Party (NBC, 1961).

Awards. Mr. Wallace was cited by the Hollywood Foreign Press for his performance as Tulsa in the film version of *Gypsy* (1963).

Recreation. Swimming, reading, "collecting bios of theatre and film people," reading scripts, rehearsing, sunbathing, driving his car, travel.

WALLACH, ELI. Actor. b. Dec. 7, 1915, Brooklyn, N.Y., to Abraham and Bertha (Schorr) Wallach. Father, stationery store owner. Grad of Erasmus Hall H.S., Brooklyn, N.Y., 1932; Univ. of Texas, B.A. 1936; City Coll. of New York, M.S. (Education) 1938; studied acting with Sanford Meisner, Neighborhood Playhouse Sch. of the Th., N.Y.C., 1938–40; and Lee Strasberg, Actors' Studio (charter member, 1947–to date). Married Mar. 5, 1948, to Anne Jackson, actress; one son, two daughters. Served with US Army, 1941–45. PTO, ETO; rank, Capt. Member of AEA; SAG; AFTRA.

Pre-Theatre. Playground director, camp counselor, hospital registrar.

Theatre. Mr. Wallach first appeared on the stage as an Old Man in a Brooklyn Boys Club production of *Fiat Lux;* played the title role in *Liliom* (Curtain Club, Univ. of Texas, 1936); and appeared in *The Bo Tree* (Locust Valley, L.I., N.Y., 1939).

Mr. Wallach made his N.Y.C. debut as the crew chief in *Skydrift* (Belasco, Th., Nov. 13, 1945); toured with the American Repertory Th. and appeared during its Bway season at the Intl. Th., as Cromwell in *Henry VIII* (Nov. 6, 1946), as Busch in *Yellow Jack* (Feb. 27, 1947) and as the 2 of Spades and Leg of Mutton in *Alice in Wonderland* (Apr. 5, 1947); played Diomedes in *Antony and Cleopatra* (Martin Beck Th., Nov. 26, 1947); joined the company as Stefanowski in *Mr. Roberts* (Alvin, Feb. 18, 1948); played Alvar Mangiacavallo in *The Rose Tattoo* (Martin Beck Th., Mar. 3, 1951); Kilroy in *Camino Real* (Natl., Mar. 19, 1953); and Julien in *Mademoiselle Colombe* (Longacre, Jan. 6, 1954).

In London, Mr. Wallach appeared as Sakini in *The Teahouse of the August Moon* (Her Majesty's Th., Apr. 22, 1954), succeeded (Feb. 1955) David Wayne in the role in the N.Y.C. production (Martin Beck Th., Oct. 15, 1953), and toured with the Bway company (opened Colonial, Boston, Mass., Apr. 2, 1956; closed Natl., Washington, D.C., July 7, 1956).

He played Bill Walker in *Major Barbara* (Martin Beck Th., Oct. 30, 1956); Willie in *The Cold Wind and the Warm* (Morosco, Dec. 8, 1958); Berenger in *Rhinoceros* (Longacre, Jan. 9, 1961); and appeared with his wife, Anne Jackson, in *The Typists* and *The Tiger* (Orpheum, Feb. 4, 1963); subsequently appeared in the London production (Globe, May 25, 1964); and with her, appeared in *Luv* (Booth, Nov. 11, 1964); in *Promenade, All!* (Alvin Th., Apr. 16, 1972); and as Gen. St. Pé. in a revival of *The Waltz of the Toreadors*, again with his wife (Circle in the Square-Joseph E. Levine Th., Sept. 13, 1973) and on tour (1974).

Films. Mr. Wallach made his film debut as Silva Vaccaro in *Baby Doll* (WB, 1956); followed by appearances in *The Lineup* (Col., 1958); as the Bandit Chief in *The Magnificent Seven* (UA, 1960); Guido in *The Misfits* (UA, 1961); Charlie Gant in *How the West Was Won* (MGM, 1962); the Corporal in *Adventures of a Young Man* (20th-Fox, 1962); General in *Lord Jim;* and Stratos in *Moon Spinners* (Buena Vista, 1964). Among his later films are *The Tiger Makes Out* (Col., 1967); *The Good, the Bad, the Ugly* (UA, 1968); *The Angel Levine* (UA, 1970); and *Cinderella Liberty* (20th-Fox, 1973).

Television and Radio. He performed in radio plays (WLID, Bklyn., N.Y. 1936–38). His numerous television appearances include performances on Philco Playhouse (NBC) in *The Baby* (Sept. 13, 1953), *Shadow of the Champ* (Mar. 20, 1955), and *The Outsiders* (Sept. 18, 1955); in *The Lark* (Hallmark Hall of Fame, NBC, Feb. 10, 1957); *Albert Anastasia* (Climax, CBS, Feb. 27, 1958); on Playhouse 90 (CBS) in *The Plot to Kill Stalin* (Sept. 25, 1958) and *For Whom the Bell Tolls* (Mar. 12, 19, 1959); *Hope Is The Thing with Feathers* (Robert Herridge Th., CBS, Sept. 22, 1960); *Tomorrow the Man* (Dick Powell Th., NBC, Oct. 2, 1962); and *The Typists* (Hollywood Television Th., PBS, Oct. 10, 1971).

Awards. For his performance in *The Rose Tattoo*, Mr. Wallach won the Donaldson Award, *Variety* NY Drama Critics Poll, Antoinette Perry (Tony) Award; and the *Theatre World* Award for promising personalities (1951); and he received the British Academy Award for his performance in the film *Baby Doll*.

Recreation. Watercoloring, photography, dance swimming, and tennis.

WALLACH, IRA. Playwright, lyricist, novelist. b. Jan. 22, 1913, N.Y.C., to Morris David and Rose (Sims) Wallach. Father, dentist. Grad. New Rochelle (N.Y.) H.S., 1927; attended Cornell Univ., 1927–28. Married Jan. 25, 1941, to Devera Sievers (marr. dis.); married June 4, 1970, to Lillian Opatoshu; one daughter. Served US Army, PTO, Medical Corps, 2½ yrs. Member of SWG; WAG, West; Dramatists Guild; Aircraft Owners and Pilots Assn. Address: 345 W. 58 St., New York, NY 10019, tel. (212) 247-3479.

Theatre. Mr. Wallach wrote the book for the musical, *Horatio* (Margo Jones Th., Dallas, Tex., Mar. 8, 1954); subsequently wrote the sketches for the revue, *Phoenix '55* (Phoenix, N.Y.C., Apr. 23, 1955); wrote a sketch for *Surprise Party* (a one-night benefit performance, Phoenix, 1957); lyrics for the revue, *Sticks and Stones* (Bucks County Playhouse, New Hope, Pa., Summer 1956); lyrics and book for the musical adaptation of *Mistress of the Inn* (Bucks County Playhouse, Summer 1957); and collaborated with A. S. Ginnes in writing *Drink to Me Only* (54 St. Th., N.Y.C., Oct. 8, 1958).

He wrote the sketches and lyrics for *Dig We Must* (John Drew Th., East Hampton, L.I., N.Y., July 4, 1959); lyrics for the musical adaptation of *Petticoat Fever* (Bucks County Playhouse, New Hope, Pa., Summer 1960); adapted the book for a revival of *Hit the Deck* (Marine Th., Jones Beach, L.I., N.Y., Summer 1960); wrote the book for the musical, *Smiling, the Boy Fell Dead* (Cherry Lane, N.Y.C., Apr. 9, 1961); and for *The Absence of a Cello* (Bucks County Playhouse, New Hope, Pa., Summer 1963; Ambassador, N.Y.C., Sept. 21, 1964); wrote the book and lyrics for *Kaboom* (The Bottom Line, N.Y.C., May 1, 1974).

Films. Mr. Wallach has written the screenplays for the following films, produced by Filmways with MGM: *Boys Night Out* (1962), *The Wheeler Dealers*, which he wrote with George Goodman (1963); and *Hot Millions* (1964).

Published Works. He has written the novels, *The Horn and the Roses* (1947); *How to Be Deliriously Happy* (1950); *Hopalong-Freud* (1951); *Hopalong-Freud Rides Again* (1952); *Gutenberg's Folly* (1954); *How to Pick a Wedlock* (1956); *Muscle Beach* (1959); and *The Absence of a Cello* (1960).

Awards. The film *Hot Millions* was nominated for an Academy Award and was named the best comedy screenplay of 1964 by the Writers Guild of Great Britain.

Recreation. Tennis, light plane flying.

WALLMAN, LAWRENCE A. Educator. b. Lawrence Albert Wallman, June 18, 1902, Elkins, W.Va., to Herman C. and Mary Elizabeth (Dougherty) Wallman. Father, accountant. Grad. Fairmont (W.Va.) H.S., 1921; attended Fairmont Normal Sch., 1921–23; grad. West Virginia Univ., B.A. 1927, M.A. 1929; attended Northwestern Univ., summer, 1932; Univ. of Pittsburgh, summers 1949–50. Married Aug. 4, 1934, to Louise Heim; two sons. Member of SAA; AETA; West Virginia Intercollegiate Speech Assn. (pres., exec. secy., 1935–64); State Speech Assn.; Alpha Psi Omega; Phi Kappa Sigma; Tau Beta Iota. Address: (home) 1324 College Pk., Fairmont, WV 26554, tel. (304) 366-3338; (bus.) Fairmont State Coll., Fairmont, WV 26554, tel. (304) 363-4000.

Mr. Wallman was chairman of the Speech Dept. at Fairmont State Coll., where he was a member of the faculty from 1929 until his retirement in 1970. He founded the West Virginia State Collegiate One-Act Play Contest Festival (1929); and the West Virginia State High School Thespian One-Act Play Contest (1950). He has directed more than 100 student productions, and founded the Masquer's Town and Gown Summer Th. (1960), the first collegiate summer repertory theatre in the state, now in it's fourteenth season, and has acted in many of the recent performances.

In 1963, he was chief of the drama division for the West Virginia Centennial Showboat "Rhododendron.".

Pre-Theatre. Reporter, salesman.

Recreation. Theatre, tennis, spectator sports, dancing.

WALLOP, DOUGLASS. Playwright, novelist. b. John Douglass Wallop, III, Mar. 8, 1920, Washington, D.C., to John Douglass and Marjorie E. (Ellis) Wallop. Father, insurance agent. Grad. Central H.S., 1937; Univ. of Maryland, B.A. (commerce) 1942. Married Jan. 6, 1949, to Lucille Fletcher, writer. Member of Dramatists Guild; ALA; WGA, East. Address: 3435 S. 8th St., Arlington, VA 22204.

. Journalist for AP and UP.

. Mr. Wallop wrote, with George Abbott, ɔook for the musical *Damn Yankees* (46 St. Th., May 5, 1955) which was based on Mr. Wallop's novel entitled *The Year the Yankees Lost the Pennant.*

Published Works. He has written the following novels: *Night Light* (1953); *The Year the Yankees Lost the Pennant* (1954); *The Sunken Garden* (1956); *What Has Four Wheels and Flies?* (1959); *Ocean Front* (1963); *So This Is What Happened to Charlie Moe* (1966); *The Mermaid in the Swimming Pool* (1968); *Baseball—An Informal History* (1969); *The Good Life* (1969); *Stone* (1971); and *Howard's Bag* (1973).

Awards. Mr. Wallop, and Mr. Abbott, received the Antoinette Perry (Tony) Award for *Damn Yankees* (1956).

WALSH, FREDERICK G. Educator, director, playwright. b. Frederick George Walsh, May 31, 1915, New Bedford, Mass., to Frederick and Mary Ellen (Farmworth) Walsh. Father, textile worker. Grad. New Bedford H.S., 1932; North Carolina State Coll., B.S. 1936, M.S. 1938; Univ. of North Carolina, M.A. (playwriting fellowship) 1940; Western Reserve Univ., M.F.A. 1951, Ph.D. 1952. Married June 6, 1945, to Jennie L. Norman; two sons. Served USNR, 1942–45; rank, Lt.; awarded Bronze Star with Combat V. Member of AETA; NTC; Lions International (Dist. Gov., Internatl. Counselor). Address: (home) 515 30th Ave., N. Fargo, ND 58101, tel. (701) AD 5-5924; (bus.) Dept. of Speech and Drama, North Dakota State Univ., Fargo, ND 58101, tel. (701) AD 5-6411.

In 1949, he founded the Huron (Ohio) Playhouse, and directed there (1945–50); was consulting designer of the Williston High School Aud.; designed the Burning Hills Amphitheatre, Medora, N.D.; where he directed *Old Four Eyes* (Summers 1958–59–60); designed the Custer Memorial Amphitheatre, Mandan, N.D., where his play *Trail West,* written in collaboration with W. T. Chicester, was produced (1959–60–61). In 1963 he wrote *The Trial of Louis Riel,* which he also directed at the Little Country Th., Fargo, N.D. He was selected to give annual faculty lectures at North Dakota State Univ. (1964).

He was also consulting designer of Askanase Hall (New Theatre), 1968; made a lecture tour of New Zealand, Ceylon, Pakistan, Afghanistan, Iran, Turkey, Lebanon, and Jordan in 1971; founded the Prairie Stage, a touring company which gave 80 performances each season during the Summers 1972–74; and was acting chairman of the Dept. of Art (1971–73) and acting director of athletics (1973) at North Dakota State University.

Published Works. Mr. Walsh wrote *Out from New Bedford* (1948); *In-Laws Out* (1948); *It Belongs to Me* (1949); and *The Trial of Louis Riel* (1965).

Awards. Mr. Walsh received the Blue Key "Doctor of Service" Award (1965).

Recreation. Golf, bridge, philately.

WALSTON, RAY. Actor, director. b. Nov. 2, 1918, New Orleans, La., to Harry and Mittie (Kimball) Walston. Father, lumber man. Married Nov. 3, 1943, to Ruth Calvert; one daughter. Member of AEA; SAG; AFTRA; The Lambs; The Players; Magic Club.

Pre-Theatre. Printer and reporter.

Theatre. Mr. Walston first appeared as Buddy in *High Tor* (Community Players, Houston, Tex., Sept. 1938); made his professional debut as Hadrian in the first tryout production of *You Touched Me* (Cleveland Play House, Ohio, Sept. 1943); his Bway debut as a walk-on and as understudy to Morton DaCosta as Osric in Maurice Evans' *Hamlet* (Columbus Circle, Dec. 13, 1945); played Schwartz in *The Front Page* (Royale, Sept. 4, 1946); in summer stock, played Mississip' in *Kiss Them for Me* (Clinton Playhouse, Conn., 1947); played Sam Phelps in the pre-Bway tryout of *Three Indelicate Ladies* (opened Shubert, New Haven, Conn., Apr. 10, 1947; closed Wilbur, Boston, Mass., Apr. 19, 1947); and appeared in a walk-on role in *The Survivors* (Playhouse, N.Y.C., Jan. 19, 1948).

He played the Traveling Salesman, Mr. Kramer, in Margo Jones' production of *Summer and Smoke* (Music Box, Oct. 6, 1948); Ratcliff in *Richard III* (Booth, Feb. 8, 1949); Rodla in *Mrs. Gibbon's Boys* (Music Box, May 4, 1949); the Telephone Man in *The Rat Race* (Ethel Barrymore Th., Dec. 22, 1949); toured ten cities and played a year in Chicago as Luther Billis in *South Pacific* (1950), and made his London debut in this role (Drury Lane, Nov. 1, 1951).

He appeared as Mac in *Me and Juliet* (Majestic, N.Y.C., May 28, 1953); Capt. Jonas in *House of Flowers* (Alvin, Dec. 30, 1954); Mr. Applegate in *Damn Yankees* (46 St. Th., May 5, 1955), and temporarily replaced Bobby Clark in the role on tour (1956–57); played Michael Haney in *Who Was That Lady I Saw You With?* (Martin Beck Th., March 3, 1958); was Eddie in *Agatha Sue I love you* (Henry Miller's Th., Dec. 14, 1966); toured as the Steward in *The Canterbury Tales* (Dec. 1969–Apr. 1970); and replaced George Rose as Lutz in the pre-Bway tryout of a revival of *The Student Prince* (opened Acad. of Music, Philadelphia, Pa., June 5, 1973; closed State Fair, Dallas, Tex., Oct. 21, 1973).

Films. Mr. Walston appeared in *Kiss Them for Me* (20th-Fox, 1957); *South Pacific* (Magna, 1958); *Damn Yankees* (WB, 1958); *Say One for Me* (20th-Fox, 1959); *Tall Story* (WB, 1960); *The Apartment* (UA, 1960); *Portrait in Black* (U, 1960); *Convicts Four* (AA, 1962); *Wives and Lovers* (Par., 1963); *Who's Minding the Store?* (Par., 1963); *Caprice* (20th-Fox, 1967); *Paint Your Wagon* (Par., 1969); and *The Sting* (U, 1973).

Television. Mr. Walston made his debut on Suspense (CBS, 1950) and has since appeared in *There Shall Be No Night* (Hallmark Hall of Fame, NBC, Mar. 17, 1957); *The Killers* (CBS, Nov. 19, 1959); and *Uncle Harry* (Play of the Week, Ind., Dec. 5, 1960); and on such programs as Studio One (CBS), Playhouse 90 (CBS), You Are There (CBS), and Producers Showcase (NBC) on which he played Ernie Pyle in a special tribute written by Robert E. Sherwood; and has sung and danced on such programs as the Ed Sullivan Show (CBS), Perry Como Show (NBC), and Arthur Godfrey Show. He appeared as Uncle Martin in the series My Favorite Martian (CBS).

Awards. He received the Clarence Derwent Award and won the *Variety* NY Drama Critics' Poll for his performance as Mr. Kramer in *Summer and Smoke* (1949). He also received an Antoinette Perry (Tony) Award for his performance as Mr. Applegate in *Damn Yankees* (1955).

Recreation. Polo, riding, shooting, bicycling, photography, chess, and cooking.

WALTER-BRIANT, FREDDA. Wardrobe supervisor. b. Freda Pearl Smith, July 25, 1912, Oklahoma City, Olka., to Fred A. and Pearl (Haught) Smith. Father, plasterer; mother, wardrobe supervisor. Grad. Carl Schurz H.S., Chicago, Ill., 1930. Married July 22, 1936, to August Walter-Briant, pantominist (dec. 1969); one daughter. Relative in theatre: step-father, James N. Zachry, stage carpenter. Member of Theatrical Wardrobe Attendants Union, Local 764; IATSE (trustee of exec. bd., vice-pres. of union, trustee on bd. of trustees for Union Pension and Welfare Fund, 1963–to date; bus. rep. of the union, 1972–to date). Address: 6515 Boulevard East, West New York, NJ 07093, tel. (201) 864-1888.

Pre-Theatre. Secretary, seamstress.

Theatre. Mrs. Walter-Briant first performed as a dancer, with the Pavley-Oukrainsky Ballet Co. (Chicago, Ill., 1930–33). Her first N.Y.C. assignment was as dresser (Mar. 1952) for *Guys and Dolls* (46 St. Th., Nov. 24, 1950).

She became wardrobe supervisor for *In the Summer House* (Playhouse, Dec. 29, 1953); was wardrobe assistant for *Ondine* (46 St. Th., Feb. 18, 1954); and wardrobe supervisor for *The Rainmaker* (Cort, Feb. 28, 1954); *Cat on a Hot Tin Roof* (Morosco, Mar. 24, 1955); *Protective Custody* (Ambassador, Dec. 28, 1956); *Ziegfeld Follies* (Winter Garden, Mar. 1, 1957); *Time Remembered* (Morosco, Nov. 12, 1957); *J. B.* (ANTA, Dec. 11, 1958); *The Sound of Music* (Lunt-Fontanne, Nov. 16, 1959); *Jennie* (Majestic, Oct. 17, 1963); and for *Fade Out—Fade In* (Mark Hellinger Th., May 26, 1964). She was wardrobe supervisor for *On a Clear Day* (Mark Hellinger Th., 1965); *How Now Dow Jones* (Lunt-Fontanne Th., 1966); *The Great White Hope* (Alvin Th., 1967); *Butterflies are Free* (Booth, 1968); *Mother Earth* (Belasco Th., 1972); Milliken Breakfast Show (Waldorf Astoria, 1965–1972); Ford Automobile Show (1967); General Electric Management Show (1967); Pontiac Management Show (1972); and the Buick Announcement Show (1972).

She was also consultant for the wardrobe and dressing room accommodations for the Repertory Th. of Lincoln Ctr. (ANTA–Washington Square, N.Y.C.).

Television. She was wardrobe supervisor for the series, You Are There (CBS, 1954).

WALTERS, WALTER H. Educator, administrator. b. Walter Henry Walters, Dec. 19, 1917, Troy, Ala., to Walter H. and Julia (Coleman) Walters. Father, pharmacist. Grad. Troy (Ala.) H.S., 1935; Troy State Univ., B.S. 1939; Univ. of Wisconsin, Ph.M. 1947; Western Reserve Univ., M.F.A. 1949, Ph.D. 1950; attended Louisiana State Univ., Summer 1941. Married Sept. 18, 1947, to Geraldine Ross; two sons, one daughter. Served USNR; rank, Lt.; citation for Meritorious Service by Chief of Naval Operations. Member of Intl. Council of Fine Arts Deans (vice-chmn., 1973, chmn., 1973–74); US Inst. for Th. Tech. (1st vice-pres., 1970–71, pres., 1971–72); Univ. & Coll. Th. Assn., Am. Th. Assoc. (dir., 1970–71); Th. Assoc. of Pa.; Comm. of Pa. Council on the Arts (1969–71); Arts in Society (bd. of adv. editors); Pa. Council on the Arts (chmn., th. adv. panel, 1972–73). Address: (home) 526 Glenn Road, State College, PA 16801, tel. (814) 237-7047; (bus.) Pennsylvania State Univ., 111 Arts Bldg., University Park, PA 16802, tel. (814) 865-2591.

Mr. Walters is currently dean of the College of Arts and Architecture and director of University Arts Services at Pennsylvania State Univ. Formerly he had been head of the Dept. of Theatre and Film (1954–66); producer of the University Th.; and founder and producer of the Pennsylvania State Festival Th., all at Pennsylvania State Univ. Previously he taught in the public school system of Alabama (1939–42); and served as a graduate asst. at the Univ. of Wisconsin (1946–48) and at Pennsylvania State Univ.

Recreation. Swimming, tennis, cooking.

WALTON, TONY. Scenic and costume designer. b. Anthony John Walton, Oct. 24, 1934, Walton-on-Thames, Surrey, England, to Lancelot Henry Frederick and Hilda Betty (Drew) Walton. Father, orthopedic surgeon. Attended Radley Coll., Oxford, 1948–1952; City of Oxford Sch. of Technology, Art and Commerce, 1949–52; Slade Sch. of Art, London, 1954–55. Married May 10, 1959, to Julie Andrews, actress, singer (marr. dis. 1967); one daughter. Served RAF (1952–54); rank, pilot officer. Member of United Scenic Artists. Address: c/o Sterling Lord, 660 Madison Ave., New York, NY 10021, tel. (212) PL 1-2533; c/o Theatre Projects, 10 Long Acre, London, W.C.2, England tel. 836-7877.

Pre-Theatre. Mr. Walton worked as a commercial artist for an advertising firm (1952); and did art work (caricatures, drawings, and paintings) for book publishers and for publications including *Playbill, Theatre Arts, Vogue, Harper's* and *The Observer* (1956–59).

Theatre. Mr. Walton's first theatre assignment in N.Y.C. was as the designer of settings and lighting for *Conversation Piece* (Barbizon-Plaza, Nov. 18, 1957); from 1958 to 1960, he was director, with Philip Wiseman, of Spur Productions, Ltd., London, which presented *The Ginger Man* (Fortune Th., Sept. 15, 1959); *New Cranks* (Lyric, Hammersmith, Apr. 12, 1960), and *Fairy Tales of New York* (Comedy,

Jan. 24, 1961). He designed the settings and costumes for *Valmouth* (York, N.Y.C., Oct. 6, 1960), for which he had also designed the London production (see below); designed settings and costumes for *Once There Was a Russian* (Music Box, N.Y.C., Feb. 18, 1961); for *A Funny Thing Happened on the Way to the Forum* (Alvin, May 3, 1962); the costumes for *The Rehearsal* (Royal, Sept. 23, 1963). In 1963, he became a partner, with Harold Prince and Richard Pilbrow, in Forum Ventures, a London-based producing company that presented *A Funny Thing Happened on the Way to the Forum* (Strand, Oct. 3, 1963) and *She Loves Me* (Lyric, Apr. 29, 1964). He designed sets, costumes, and projections for *Golden Boy* (Majestic, N.Y.C., Oct. 20, 1964); sets and costumes for *The Apple Tree* (Sam S. Shubert Th., Oct. 18, 1966); sets for *Pippin* (Imperial, Oct. 23, 1972); sets, costumes, and projections for *Shelter* (John Golden Th., Feb. 6, 1963); settings and costumes for *Uncle Vanya* (Circle in the Square/Joseph E. Levine Th., June 4, 1973); settings for the San Francisco Ballet's *Harp Concerto* (June 13, 1973); settings and costumes for *The Good Doctor* (Eugene O'Neill Th., Nov. 27, 1973); sets and costumes for the San Francisco Ballet's *Mother Blues* (Jan. 19, 1974); settings and costumes for *Clams on the Half Shell Revue* (Minskov Th., N.Y.C., Apr. 17, 1975); settings for *Chicago* (46 St. Th., June 3, 1975); and sets and costumes for the Santa Fe (N.M.) Opera Company's *The Cunning Little Vixen* (Opera House, Santa Fe, N.M., July 29, 1975).

Mr. Walton's first assignment in the theatre was with the Wimbledon (England) Repertory Co. as assistant designer of *Lady Audley's Secret;* subsequently he was designer for repertory productions of *Worm's Eye View* and *The Moon Is Blue* (Wimbledon Th., England, June 1955). The first London production for which he designed settings and costumes was *Valmouth* (Lyric, Hammersmith, Oct. 2, 1958); subsequently designed the settings and costumes for the London production of *Fool's Paradise* (Apollo, Apr. 1, 1959); the setting for *The Pleasure of His Company* (Haymarket, Apr. 23, 1959); settings and costumes for *The Ginger Man* (Fortune, Sept. 15, 1959); *Pieces of Eight* (Apollo, Sept. 23, 1959); *The Most Happy Fella* (Coliseum, Apr. 21, 1960); *One Over the Eight* (Duke of York's, Apr. 5, 1961); *A Wreath for Udomo* (Lyric, Hammersmith, Nov. 9, 1961); *Cindy-Ella* (Garrick Th., Dec. 17, 1962; Arts, Dec. 24, 1963); the opera, *The Love of Three Oranges* (Sadler's Wells Th., Apr. 24, 1963); for the Edinburgh (Scotland) Festival, the opera *The Rape of Lucretia* (King's, Aug. 19, 1963 and on international tour; settings and costumes for *A Funny Thing Happened on the Way to the Forum* (Strand, London, Oct. 3, 1963); *Caligula* (Phoenix, Apr. 6, 1964); settings, costumes, and film projections for the opera *Otello* (Spoleto Festival, Teatro Nuovo, Spoleto, Italy, June 24, 1965); settings and costumes for the opera *Midsummer Marriage* (Royal Opera House, Covent Garden, London, Apr. 10, 1968); sets, costumes, and projections for *Golden Boy* (Palladium, June 4, 1968); sets and costumes for *Triple Bill* (National Th., Old Vic, June 18, 1968); sets, costumes, and projections for *The Travails of Sancho Panza* (National Th., Old Vic, Dec. 18, 1969); sets and costumes for *Once Upon a Time* (Duke of York's, Dec. 22, 1972); sets for *Pippin* (Her Majesty's, Oct. 29, 1973; also Theater an der Wien, Vienna, Austria, Feb. 10, 1974; Her Majesty's, Melbourne, Australia, Apr. 10, 1974; Her Majesty's, Adelaide, Australia, June 1974; Her Majesty's, Sydney, Australia, Aug. 10, 1974).

Films. Mr. Walton was costume designer and production design consultant for *Mary Poppins* (Buena Vista, 1965); costume and production designer for *A Funny Thing Happened on the Way to the Forum* (UA, 1966); costume designer and production design consultant for *Fahrenheit 451* (U, 1967); production and costume designer for *Petulia* (WB-7 Arts, 1968); for *The Sea Gull* (WB-7 Arts, 1968); production designer for *The Boy Friend* (EMI-MGM, 1971); and production and costume designer for *Murder on the Orient Express* (EMI-Par., 1974).

Television. He designed three productions of the Julie Andrews Show (BBC, Nov.–Dec. 1959) and was set designer for Marlo Thomas and Friends in *Free To Be You and Me* (ABC, Mar. 11, 1974).

Other Activities. Since 1959, Mr. Walton has been director of Theatre Projects, Ltd., a London firm which services all the technical departments of theatre, specializing in lighting (design and equipment), sound (effects and equipment), and general design services. Each of these is a subsidiary company in itself, such as Theatre Projects Lighting and Theatre Projects Sound.

He had a one-man exhibition of theatre caricatures and designs at the NY Circulating Library of Paintings (Feb. 4, 1957); and one-man exhibitions of paintings and theatre designs at the Hazlitt Gallery, London (Mar. 3, 1959); Wright-Hepburn Gallery, London (Oct. 2, 1967); and the Wright-Hepburn-Webster Gallery, N.Y.C. (Nov. 12, 1968); and he also participated in group shows at the last two.

He designed and painted the murals on theatre themes at the Seven Arts Ctr. (N.Y.C., Apr. 1958).

Mr. Walton has done occasional illustrative assignments for book jackets, as well as caricatures, magazine illustrations, and theatre posters. Among books he has illustrated are *Peacocks and Avarice* (N.Y.C., 1957); *Cindy-Ella* (London, 1962); *God Is a Good Friend To Have* (N.Y.C., 1969); *Witches' Holiday* (N.Y.C., 1971); *Pop Corn* (N.Y.C., 1972); and, for the Limited Editions Club, *The Importance of Being Earnest* and *Lady Windermere's Fan* (N.Y.C., 1973).

Awards. Mr. Walton received an Antoinette Perry (Tony) Award (1973) for *Pippin;* a Drama Desk Award (1973) for *Pippin* and *Shelter;* and a NATAS (Emmy) Award for *Free To Be You and Me* (1974). He was nominated for a Tony (1967) for *The Apple Tree* and for AMPAS (Oscar) awards for *Mary Poppins* and *Murder on the Orient Express.*.

Recreation. Painting, photography, music, tennis, music-hall and vaudeville, films, and writing doggerel verse.

WANAMAKER, SAM. Actor, director, producer. b. June 14, 1919, Chicago, Ill., to Morris and Molly (Bobele) Wanamaker. Attended Drake Univ., 1935–36; Goodman Th., Chicago, 1936–39. Married May 26, 1940, to Charlotte Holland; three daughters. Served US Army, 1943–46; rank, Pfc. Member of AEA; SAG; AFTRA. Address: (home) London, England; (bus.) International Famous Agency, 1301 Ave. of the Americas, New York, NY 10019, tel. (212) 556-5600.

Theatre. Mr. Wanamaker appeared as Medvedev in *The Lower Depths* (Goodman Memorial Th., Chicago, Ill., Jan. 11, 1937); Mr. Zero in *The Adding Machine* (Goodman Memorial Th., 1938); Edgar in *King Lear* (Goodman Memorial Th.); acted and directed in Chicago summer theatres (Woodstock, Ill.; Fishcreek, Wis., 1936–39); appeared with the Globe Shakespearean Th. (Cleveland World's Fair, Ohio, 1936); the Chicago (Ill.) Civic Repertory Th. (1938); and directed *The Gentle People* (Jewish People's Inst. Th., Chicago, Feb. 1940).

He made his N.Y.C. debut as Lester Freed in *Cafe Crown* (Cort, Jan. 23, 1942); subsequently appeared as Kirichenko in *Counterattack* (Windsor, Feb. 3, 1943); Mac Sorrell in *This, Too, Shall Pass* (Belasco, Apr. 30, 1946); Jimmy Masters in *Joan of Lorraine* (Alvin, Nov. 18, 1946); directed and appeared as Matt Cole in *Goodbye, My Fancy* (Morosco, Nov. 17, 1948); and directed George Bernard Shaw's *Caesar and Cleopatra* (Natl. Th., Dec. 21, 1949).

For his London debut, he coproduced, directed and appeared as Bernie Dodd in *Winter Journey* (St. James's, Apr. 3, 1952); produced, with Jack Hylton, and played Jim Downs in *The Shrike* (Prince's, Feb. 13, 1953); directed *Purple Dust* (Royal, Glasgow, Scot., Apr. 29, 1953); and *Foreign Field* (Royal, Birmingham, Eng., Sept. 15, 1953); produced, with Ralph Birch, directed, and played Charles Castle in *The Big Knife* (Duke of York's, London, Jan. 1, 1954); directed *The Soldier and the Lady* (Wimbledon, May 31, 1954); and *The World of Sholom Aleichem* (Embassy, London, Jan. 11, 1955); produced, with Jack de Leon, directed, and appeared as Laurent in *The Lovers* (Winter Garden, May 6, 1955); directed *The Threepenny Opera* (Royal Court, Feb. 9, 1956); directed, with Jack Minster, and played Bill Starbuck in *The Rainmaker* (Golders Green, Apr. 9, 1956); directed and appeared as Polo Pope in *A Hatful of Rain* (Prince's, Mar. 7, 1957).

Mr. Wanamaker was artistic director, New Shakespeare Th., Liverpool, Eng. (1957–59), where he produced, and/or directed, and/or acted in the following productions: *A View From the Bridge* (Oct. 1957); *Tea and Sympathy* (Nov. 1957); *Finian's Rainbow* (Dec. 1957); *One More River* (Mar. 1958); *Cat on a Hot Tin Roof* (Apr. 1958); *The Potting Shed* (May 1958); *Reclining Figure* (June 1958); *King of Hearts* (July 1958); and *Bus Stop* (Aug. 1958). He played Alvaro Mangiacavallo in *The Rose Tattoo* (New, London, Jan. 15, 1959); Iago in *Othello* (Shakespeare Memorial Th., Stratford-upon-Avon, Apr. 7, 1959); Dr. Joseph Breuer in *A Far Country* (Music Box, N.Y.C., Apr. 4, 1961); Henry VIII in *Royal Gambit* (Goodman Memorial Th., Chicago, Ill., Jan. 13, 1961); directed a stock production of *Ding Dong Bell* (Westport Country Playhouse, Conn., Sept. 4, 1961); and directed the operas *King Priam* (Coventry Festival, England, May 29, 1962; Covent Garden, London, June 1962) and *La Forza del Destino* (Covent Garden, Sept. 28, 1963).

He produced, with Roger L. Stevens, and directed *Children from Their Games* (Morosco, N.Y.C., Apr. 11, 1963); directed *A Case of Libel* (Longacre, Oct. 10, 1963); *A Murderer Among Us* (Morosco, Mar. 25, 1964); and directed and played the title role in *Macbeth* (Goodman Memorial Th., Chicago, Ill., Nov. 27, 1964).

In 1970–71, Mr. Wanamaker founded and became executive director of the Globe Playhouse Trust and World Centre for Shakespeare Studies and the Bankside Globe Cinema in London, England; under the sponsorship of John Player, Mr. Wanamaker's first season of Shakespearean theatre was launched at the Globe in 1972–73. In 1973, Mr. Wanamaker also directed the opening production of the Sydney (Australia) Opera House, *War and Peace;* and he played Pres. Richard M. Nixon in the reading of the White House tape transcripts (Royal Court, London, England, June 16, 1974).

Films. He appeared in *Give Us This Day* (Eagle Lion, 1949); played Filipenko in *Taras Bulba* (UA, 1962); performed in *Man in the Middle* (20th-Fox, 1964); *Those Magnificent Men in Their Flying Machines* (20th-Fox, 1964); *The Spy Who Came in from the Cold* (Par., 1965); *Warning Shot* (Par., 1967); *The Day the Fish Came Out* (Internat'l. Classics, 1967); and *The Sellout* (WB, 1975). He directed *The File of the Golden Goose* (UA, 1968); *The Executioner* (Col., 1970); *Catlow* (UA, 1971); and *Sinbad III* (Col., 1975).

Television. He appeared in *The Big Wheel* (ABC, Eng., June 1960); on the special *Russians: Self Impressions* (CBS, Jan. 1963); on Outer Limits (ABC, 1963); Espionage (NBC, 1964). He also appeared in or directed episodes of many other television programs, including The Defenders (CBS, 1964); For the People (CBS, 1965); Gunsmoke (CBS); The Hawk (ABC, 1966); Court Martial (ABC, 1966); Custer (ABC, 1967); Cimarron Strip (CBS, 1967); and The Champions (NBC, 1968). He directed Lancer (CBS, 1968); and appeared in *Arturo Ui* (BBC, 1973) and *The Law* (NBC, Oct. 22, 1974).

WARD, DOUGLAS TURNER. Director, actor, playwright. b. May 5, 1930, Burnside, La. Educ. Wilberforce (Ohio) Univ.; Univ. of Michigan.

Theatre. As an actor, Mr. Ward used the name Douglas Turner until 1972; his writing and directing and, since 1972, his acting have been under his full name. He appeared in N.Y.C. as Joe Mott in *The Iceman Cometh* (Circle in the Square, May 8, 1956), assuming that part after the play had opened; was the Moving Man in *A Raisin in the Sun* (Ethel Barrymore Th., Mar. 11, 1959), also understudying Sidney Poitier as Walter Lee Younger and subsequently touring with the play in that part. He replaced (Sept. 1961) Roscoe Lee Browne as Archibald Wellington in *The Blacks*(St. Marks Playhouse, May 4, 1961); was a Porter in *Pullman Car Hiawatha* (Circle in the Square, Dec. 3, 1962); replaced James Earl Jones as Zachariah Pieterson in *The Blood Knot* (Cricket Th., Mar. 1, 1963); played Fitzroy in *Rich Little Rich Girl* (pre-Bway tryout: Walnut St. Th., Philadelphia, Pa., Oct. 26–Nov. 7, 1964); the 3rd Roman Citizen in *Coriolanus* (Delacorte Th., N.Y.C., July 7, 1965); and he wrote *Happy Ending*, in which he played Arthur, and *Day of Absence*, in which he played the Mayor and Clan (St. Marks Playhouse, Nov. 15, 1965), later touring with the plays.

In March 1967, Mr. Ward with Robert Hooks and Gerald S. Krone founded the Negro Ensemble Company (NEC), aided by $434,000 from the Ford Foundation, and Mr. Ward has since served as artistic director of the organization. He also appeared in or directed some NEC productions (all at St. Mark's Playhouse, N.Y.C.), playing Oba Danlola in *Kongi's Harvest* (Apr. 14, 1968), Thomas in *Daddy Goodness* (June 4, 1968), which he also directed; Russell B. Parker in *Ceremonies in Dark Old Men* (Feb. 4, 1969); and directing *Contribution* on the program *An Evening of One Acts* (Mar. 25, 1969) and *Man Better Man* (July 2, 1969). He also wrote *The Reckoning* (not a NEC production), in which he played Scar (St. Mark's Playhouse, Sept. 4, 1969).

For NEC, he was one of the Black Men in *Tribal Harangue Two* and *Asura in Harangue*, two of the four plays on the program *The Harangues* (St. Mark's Playhouse, Dec. 30, 1969); and he directed a double-bill of his own plays *Brotherhood* and *Day of Absence* (Mar. 10, 1970); directed *Perry's Mission* (Jan. 12, 1971); *Ride a Black Horse* (May 25, 1971); and *A Ballet Behind the Bridge* (Mar. 7, 1962). Using his full name, Mr. Ward appeared as Frederick Douglass in *Frederick Douglass. . . Through His Own Words* (May 9, 1972); Johnny Williams in *The River Niger*, which he also directed (St. Mark's Playhouse, Dec. 5, 1972; reopened at Brooks Atkinson Th., Mar. 27, 1973), in which he also toured (1973). He directed *The Great Macdaddy* (St. Mark's Playhouse, Feb. 12, 1974); *The First Breeze of Summer*, in which he also played Harper Edwards (St. Mark's Playhouse, Mar. 2, 1975); and *Waiting for Mongo* (May 18, 1975).

Television. Mr. Ward recreated the role of Russell B. Parker in *Ceremonies in Dark Old Men* (PBS, Jan. 6, 1975), and he has appeared on East Side/West Side (CBS); Edge of Night (CBS); Dupont Show of the Month (NBC); and other programs.

Awards. In 1973, Mr. Ward and the Negro Ensemble Company received the Margo Jones Award for contributing to the theatre by producing new plays on a continuing basis. Mr. Ward has twice been cited by the *Village Voice* off-Bway (Obie) Award committee for distinguished performances: in 1966 for playing the Mayor in *Day of Absence* and in 1973 for playing Johnny Williams in *The River Niger*. In addition, he received a Vernon Rice-Drama Desk Award (1966) for writing *Day of Absence* and *Happy Ending*, and in 1974 was nominated for a Tony as best supporting actor for his performance in *The River Niger*.

WARD, JANET. Actress. b. Janet Anne Werner, Feb. 19, New York City, to Gene and Edna (Quinn) Werner. Father, motion picutre company employee. Grad. Newtown H.S., Jackson Heights, N.Y.; studied at Actors' Studio (member 1952–to date). Member of AEA; AFTRA; SAG.

Theatre. Miss Ward made her professional debut as Kate Hereford in a touring production of *Snafu* (1945); subsequently played Claire Blakeley in the national touring production of *Dream Girl* (opened Selwyn, Chicago, Nov. 1946), succeeded Judith Parrish as Georgiana Allerton, and repeated the part of Claire Blakeley in the N.Y.C. production. With the Margaret Webster Shakespeare Co., she played the Second Witch in *Macbeth*, and the Second Player (Player Queen) in *Hamlet* (opened Buffalo, N.Y., Sept. 28, 1948; closed Philadelphia, Pa., Apr. 26, 1949); in N.Y.C., succeeded (June 14, 1949) Louise Platt as Mady Boleyn in *Anne of the Thousand Days* (Shubert, Dec. 8, 1948); succeeded (June 23, 1949) Maureen Stapleton as Miss Hatch and later succeeded (Mar. 1950) Anne Burr as Mary McLeod in *Detective Story* (Hudson, Mar. 23, 1949); and understudied Barbara Bel Geddes as Mordeen in *Burning Bright* (Broadhurst, Oct. 18, 1950).

She played Maura Pender in *The King of Friday's Men* (Playhouse, Feb. 21, 1951); understudied Bette Grayson as Lorna in *Golden Boy* (ANTA, Mar. 12, 1952); played the Friend in *Middle of the Night* (ANTA, Feb. 8, 1956); Canina in *Volpone* (Rooftop, Jan. 7, 1957); Fay Doyle in *Miss Lonelyhearts* (Music Box, Oct. 3, 1957); Katie in *Chaparral* (Sheridan Square Playhouse, Sept. 9, 1958); the Girl in *J. B.* (ANTA, Dec. 11, 1958), and later succeeded (Sept. 28, 1959) Nan Martin as Sarah. She succeeded Edith King as Charlotte Peloux in *Cheri* (Morosco, Oct. 12, 1959); played Alice Langdon in *Deep Are the Roots* (St. Marks, Playhouse, Oct. 3, 1960); Lola in an ANTA-sponsored production of *Come Back, Little Sheba* (Flint Jr. Coll., May 11, 1960); Jenny Beales in *Roots* (Mayfair, N.Y.C., Mar. 6, 1961); Rose and a Woman in the Cafe in *The Egg* (Cort, Jan. 8, 1962); Cheri in an ANTA-sponsored production of *Bus Stop* (Eastern New Mexico Univ., July 17, 1962); succeeded (July 2, 1963) Anne Jackson as Gloria and Sylvia, respectively, in the double bill, *The Typists and The Tiger* (Orpheum, N.Y.C., Feb. 4, 1963); played Sophie Seidman in a touring production of *Seidman and Son* (opened Tappan Zee Playhouse, Nyack, N.Y., Sept. 7, 1963; closed Geary, San Francisco, Calif., Feb. 22, 1964); played Doris Lessing in *Play with a Tiger* (Renata, N.Y.C., Dec. 30, 1964); played opposite Alan King in *The Impossible Years* (Playhouse, N.Y.C., Oct. 13, 1965); played Hazel in *Of Love Remembered* (ANTA, N.Y.C., Feb. 18, 1967); Nurse Rotched in *One Flew Over the Cuckoo's Nest* (Mercer-Hansberry, Mar. 23, 1971); played the Mother in *Summertree* (Players, N.Y.C., Dec. 9, 1969); and appeared with the Yale Repertory Theatre.

Films. Miss Ward has appeared in *Fail Safe* (Col., 1964): *The Anderson Tapes* (Col., 1971); and *Night Moves* (WB, 1975).

Television. Miss Ward has appeared on You Are There (CBS); Philco Television Playhouse (NBC); Studio One (CBS); Danger (CBS); Alfred Hitchcock Presents (CBS); US Steel Hour (CBS); The Defenders (CBS); Perry Mason (CBS); in *Emmanuel* (Play of the Week, WNTA); on Love of Life (CBS); and Another World (NBC); and co-starred with Lee J. Cobb in a pilot for the series *Dr. Max* (CBS).

Awards. Miss Ward was nominated for the Sarah Siddons Award for her performance in *The Egg* in the pre-Bway tryout production (Chicago, Ill., 1961).

Recreation. Painting, reading, good discussions, politics.

WARDEN, JACK. Actor. b. Sept. 18, 1920, Newark, N.J., to John W. Lebzelter and Laura (Vickers) Warden. Attended Barringer H.S., Newark, 1935; Our Lady of Good Counsels, Newark, 1936; grad. DuPont Manual H.S., Louisville, Ky., 1938. Married Oct. 11, 1958, to Wanda Dupree, actress; one son. Served USN, China, 1938–41; US Maritime Service, 1941–42; US Army, Paratroopers, 1941–46; rank, S/Sgt. Member of AFTRA; SAG; AEA; Natl. Maritime Union.

Theatre. Mr. Warden made his debut touring in *There Is Always Juliet* (Th. of the Open Road, New England); subsequently joined the Margo Jones Th. Co. (Dallas, Tex., 1947), playing Sir Toby Belch in *Twelfth Night*, Algernon Moncrieff in *The Importance of Being Earnest*, Tony Lumpkin in *She Stoops to Conquer*, Trisotin in *The Learned Ladies*, Gremio in *The Taming of the Shrew*, and Yasha in *The Cherry Orchard*, and appeared in the premieres of *Front Porch* (retitled *Picnic*), *Summer and Smoke*, *Leaf and Bough* 1947–51).

He made his N.Y.C. debut as Mickey in *Golden Boy* (ANTA, Mar. 12, 1952); played Johnny in *Lullaby* (Lyceum, Feb. 3, 1954); Mike Hertzog in *Sing Me No Lullaby* (Phoenix, Oct. 14, 1954); Marco in *A View from the Bridge* (Coronet, Sept. 29, 1955); Joey in *A Very Special Baby* (Playhouse, Nov. 14, 1956); Dave in *The Body Beautiful* (Bway Th., Jan. 23, 1958); appeared in the double-bill *Cages* (York, June 13, 1963); the pre-Bway tryout of *Conversations in the Dark* (opened Walnut Th., Philadelphia, Pa., Dec. 23, 1963; closed Jan. 4, 1964); *A Wen* and *Orange Souffle*, presented under the title *Under the Weather* (Festival of Two Worlds, Spoleto, Italy, Summer 1966); and *The Man in the Glass Booth* (Royale, N.Y.C., Apr. 1, 1969).

Films. Mr. Warden has appeared in *The Asphalt Jungle* (MGM, 1950); *Bachelor Party* (UA, 1957); *Twelve Angry Men* (UA, 1957); *Edge of the City* (MGM, 1957); *Darby's Rangers* (WB, 1958); *Run Silent, Run Deep* (UA, 1958); *The Sound and the Fury* (20th-Fox, 1959); *That Kind of Woman* (Par., 1959); *Wake Me When It's Over* (20th-Fox, 1960); *Escape from Zahrain* (Par., 1962); *Donovan's Reef* (Par. 1962); *The Thin Red Line* (UA, 1964); *Blindfold* (U, 1966); *Summertree* (Col., 1971); *Who Is Harry Kellerman?* (Natl. Gen., 1971); *The Sporting Club* (Avco-Embassy, 1971); *Welcome to the Club* (Col., 1971); *Billy Two Hats* (UA, 1974); *The Apprenticeship of Duddy Kravitz* (Par., 1974); and *Shampoo* (Col., 1975).

Television. Mr. Warden first appeared on television as Arthur Clary in *Ann Rutledge* (Philco Television Playhouse, NBC, Feb. 12, 1950); subsequently played Gorman in *Retaliation* (Cavalier Th., NBC, Dec. 12, 1951); the title role in *The Champ* (Assignment: Man Hunt NBC, Aug. 16, 1952); Lefty in *Snookie* (Kraft Television Th., NBC, Feb. 18, 1953); Teddy Merrill in *Chester Potter of the Pittsburgh Press* (The Big Story, NBC, Mar. 6, 1953); Jerry French in *Comeback* (Gulf Playhouse; First Person, NBC, July 24, 1953); and appeared in *Old MacDonald Had a Curve* (Kraft Television Th., NBC, Aug. 5, 1953). He played Brick Nelson in *The Promise* (Campbell Soundstage, NBC, Sept. 11, 1953); Frank T. Whip on the Mister Peepers Show (NBC, Nov. 8, 1953; June 12, 1955); the Taxi Driver in *Dream House* (Kraft Television Th., NBC, Nov. 4, 1953); Blik in *Train to Trouble* (Goodyear Television Playhouse, NBC, Nov. 8, 1953); Dr. Max in *Native Dancer* (Goodyear Television Playhouse, NBC, Mar. 28, 1954); Pete in *Jean Barrett of the Philadelphia Evening Bulletin* (The Big Story, NBC, Apr. 16, 1954); Sheriff Bass in *Dr. Rainwater Goes A-Courtin'* (Kraft Television Th., NBC, Apr. 28, 1954); Stamper in *The Worried Ban Blues* (Kraft Television Th., NBC, Aug. 18, 1954); and appeared on the Imogene Coca Show (NBC, Nov. 27, 1954). He played Hal in *Class of '58* (Goodyear Television Playhouse, NBC, Dec. 19, 1954); Bill Foley in *Roger Dove*, Hartford (Conn.) *Courant* (The Big Story, NBC, Dec. 31, 1954); Lt. Earl Floyd in *Save Me Now* (Justice, NBC, Jan. 13, 1955); Ted Link in *Ted Link of the St. Louis Post Dispatch* (The Big Story, NBC, Mar. 4, 1955); Buzz Calderone in *Shadow of the Champ* (Philco Television Playhouse, NBC, Mar. 20, 1955); Boze in *The Petrified Forest* (Producers' Showcase, NBC, May 30, 1955); Alex Hamner in *Flight from Fear* (Justice, NBC, Oct. 16, 1955); Harry Pomeroy in *The Mechanical Heart* (Goodyear Television Playhouse, NBC, Nov. 6, 1955); Frank Doran in *Tragedy in a Temporary Town* (Alcoa Hour, NBC, Feb. 19, 1956); and appeared in *A Very Special Baby* (Home Show, NBC, Oct. 25, 1956).

Also, Sgt. Debb in *A Real Fine Cutting Edge* (Kaiser Aluminum Hour, NBC, Jan. 15, 1957); Robert de Beaudrincourt in *The Lark* (Hallmark Hall of Fame, NBC, Feb. 10, 1957); a Newspaperman in *The Flight* (Suspicion, NBC, Nov. 25, 1957); Jack Armstrong in *Abraham Lincoln; The Early Years* (Omnibus, NBC, Feb. 1, 1959); Mike Wilson in *The Paiute War* (Bonanza, NBC, Oct. 3, 1959); Emmet Fitzgerald in *The Moment of Truth* (Five Fingers, NBC, Oct. 17, 1959); Ollie in *Starfall* (The Outlaws, NBC, Nov. 24–Dec. 1, 1960); Martin in *The Martin Onyx Story* (Wagon Train, NBC, Jan. 3, 1962); Axton in *The Traveler* (Tales of Wells Fargo, NBC, Feb. 24, 1962); and Jubal Tatum in *Throw a Long Rope* (The Virginian, NBC, Oct. 3, 1962).

He has subsequently appeared in sequences on all major networks shows, including: The Trailmaster (ABC); Walt Disney's World (NBC), Dr. Kildare (NBC); Naked City (ABC); Bob Hope Presents (NBC); Slattery's People (CBS); Bus Stop (Ind.); Great Adventure (CBS); The Untouchables (ABC); Desilu Playhouse (NBC); The Breaking Point (Ind.); The Wackiest Ship in the Army (NBC); Twilight Zone (CBS); Route 66 (CBS); Ben Casey (ABC); The Fugitive (ABC); The Invaders (ABC); and in his own series, N.Y.P.D. (ABC).

Recreation. Tennis, swimming.

WARFIELD, WILLIAM. Singer, actor. b. Jan. 22, 1920, West Helena, Ark., to Robert E. and Bertha (McCamery) Warfield. Attended Eastman Sch. of Music, 1938–42. Studied with Elsa Miller, 1935–38; Arthur Kraft, 1938–42; at American Th. Wing, 1948–50; with Otto Herz, 1948–50; Yves Tinayre, 1948–55; Rosa Ponselle, 1958–to date. Married Aug. 31, 1952, to Leontyne Price (marr. dis., Dec. 1972). Served US Army 1942–46, Intelligence; rank, Sgt. Member of AEA; SAG; AFTRA; AGMA; NAACP (life mbr.). Address: c/o Larney Goodkind, 30 E. 60th St., New York, NY 10022, tel. (212) EL 5-6560.

Theatre. Mr. Warfield toured the US and Canada in the revue, *Call Me Mister* (1947–48); made his N.Y.C. debut as Aneas in *Set My People Free* (Hudson Th., N.Y.C., Nov. 3, 1948); followed by Cal, the Butler, in *Regina* (46 St. Th., Oct. 31, 1949); and performed at Town Hall (Mar. 19, 1950; Jan. 28, 1951; Nov. 3, 1957).

He played Porgy in *Porgy and Bess* (State Fair Music Hall, Dallas, Tex., June 9, 1952; Chicago, Ill., June 25, 1952; Pittsburgh, Pa., July 22, 1952; Washington, D.C., Aug. 5, 1952), and appeared in it in Europe (Volksoper, Vienna, Austria, Sept. 7, 1952; Opera, Berlin, Germany, Sept. 17, 1952; Stoll, London, Oct. 9, 1952).

Since 1950, he has toured the US and abroad in concert and as soloist with major symphonic orchestras, including foreign "good will" tours for the US State Department. He toured Australia (1950, 1958); was soloist with the Philadelphia (Pa.) Orchestra under Eugene Ormandy on its first European tour (1956); toured Africa and the Middle East (Liberia, Ghana, Nigeria, So. Rhodesia, Tanganyika, Kenya, Uganda, Ethiopia, Israel, Lebanon, Turkey, Greece, Yugoslavia, 1956); Western Europe (1956, 1963); Asia (Iran, Pakistan, India, Burma, Malaya, Vietnam, Thailand, Hong Kong, Formosa, Cambodia, The Philippines, 1958); two world tours (1958), including a recital at the Amer. Th. (US Pavilion, Brussels World's Fair, Belgium, Sept. 1, 1958); Cuba (1959), where he participated in the dedication of Casa de Estados Unidos; was soloist at Casals Festival (Puerto Rico, 1962, 1963); Arts Festival (Rio de Janeiro and Sao Paolo, Brazil, 1963); and toured Germany with Pablo Casals (1963).

Mr. Warfield has performed frequently in oratorios, including Handel's *Messiah*, Bach's *St. Matthew's Passion*, Mendelsshons's *Elijah*, Mozart's *Requiem*, Brahms' *Requiem*, Verdi's *Requiem*, Casals' *El Pesebre*, Bloch's *Hebrew Service*, Menotti's *Death of the Archbishop of Brindisi;* Beethoven's *Missa Solemnis*, Wm. Walton's *Belshazar's Feast*, and Berlioz' *Damnation of Faust*.

He was featured in the role of Joe in Richard Rodgers' revival of *Showboat* (NY State Th., Lincoln Ctr., N.Y.C., 1966); repeated the role abroad (Vienna, Austria, Volksoper, 1971–72); and sang the title role in Puccini's *Gianni Schicchi* (Central City, Colo., Opera House).

Films. He played Joe in *Show Boat* (MGM, 1951); and, with Orson Welles, narrated *Masters of the Congo Jungle* (20th-Fox, 1959) for the Belgian government.

Television. He appeared as De Lawd in *The Green Pastures* (Hallmark Hall of Fame, NBC, Oct. 17, 1952), and others.

Other Activities. Mr. Warfield is a professor in the School of Music at the Univ. of Illinois (1974–to date); a member of the board of the Duke Ellington Fellowship program at Yale Univ. (1973–to date); and served as trustee (1965–72) for the N.Y. Coll. of Music before its merger with N.Y.U.

Discography. Mr. Warfield is a recording artist for RCA Victor, Columbia, Capitol, and MGM records.

Awards. Mr. Warfield received an honorary Dr. of Laws degree from the Univ. of Arkansas (1972), and is an honorary life member of Alpha Iota Sinfonia fraternity.

WARING, RICHARD. Actor. b. Richard Waring Stephens, May 27, 1914, Chalfont, Buckinghamshire, England, to Thomas E. and Evelyn M. (Waring) Stephens. Father, portrait painter. Attended University College Sch., London, 1923–29; Westminster Sch. of Art, London, 1929–30. Married 1934 to Florida Friebus, actress (marr. dis. 1952). Served WW II, US Army Intelligence. Member of AEA; SAG; AFTRA. Address: 57 W. 10th St., New York, NY 10011, tel. (212) AL 4-3825.

Theatre. Mr. Waring joined Eva Le Gallienne's Civic Repertory Co. as an apprentice in 1930, and made his first appearance in N.Y.C. as a Drummer Boy in *Romeo and Juliet* (Civic Repertory Th., Oct. 6, 1930); also appeared at the Civic Repertory Th. as a Servant in *Camille* (Jan. 26, 1931), the Second Policeman of the Beyond in *Liliom* (Oct. 26, 1932), the Crocodile in *Peter Pan* (Nov. 5, 1932), Henry Austen in *Dear Jane* (Nov. 14, 1932), and the White Rabbit and Goat in *Alice in Wonderland* (Dec. 12, 1932); played as Romeo in *Romeo and Juliet* (Colonial, Boston, 1933), and toured with the production; was Tiburce de Lorget in *L'Aiglon* (Broadhurst, N.Y.C., Nov. 3, 1934); Antonio in *The Cradle Song* (Broadhurst, Dec. 10, 1934); Armand in *Camille* (Shubert, Dec. 4, 1935); and Adolf Adalid in *The Women Have Their Way* (Shubert, Dec. 7, 1935).

He succeeded (July 1936) James MacColl in the role of Rodney Bevan in *Boy Meets Girl* (Cort, Nov. 27, 1935); appeared as Dr. Peter Willens in *Come Across* (Playhouse, Sept. 14, 1938); in Frank Fay's vaudeville show, played the Balcony Scene with Eva Le Gallienne, from *Romeo and Juliet* (44 St. Th., Mar. 1939), and toured with it; appeared as John Wilkes Booth in *The Man Who Killed Lincoln* (Longacre, N.Y.C., Jan. 17, 1940); Harold Fairfield in *At the Stroke of Eight* (Belasco, May 20, 1940); Morgan Evans in *The Corn Is Green* (National, Nov. 26, 1940), and on tour; and Mort Curruth in *Truckline Cafe* (Belasco, N.Y.C., Feb. 27, 1946).

Mr. Waring joined the American Repertory Th. (International Th.) and played the Duke of Buckingham in *Henry VIII* (Nov. 6, 1946), John Shand in *What Every Woman Knows* (Nov. 8, 1946), the Captain in *Androcles and the Lion* (Dec. 19, 1946), and the Mad Hatter in *Alice in Wonderland* (Apr. 5, 1947). He repeated the role of Morgan Evans in *The Corn Is Green* (NY City Ctr., Jan. 11, 1950); appeared as Nathaniel Coombs in *Gramercy Ghost* (Morosco, Apr. 26, 1951); Charudatta in *The Little Clay Cart* (Th. de Lys, June 30, 1953), and Angelo in *Measure for Measure* (Phoenix, Jan. 22, 1957).

At the American Shakespeare Festival (Stratford, Conn.), he played Cassio in *Othello* (June 22, 1957), Antonio in *The Merchant of Venice* (July 10, 1957), and Don John in *Much Ado About Nothing* (Aug. 3, 1957); portrayed John Wilkes Booth in *Edwin Booth* (46 St. Th., Nov. 24, 1958); at the American Shakespeare Festival, appeared as Fortinbras in *Hamlet* (June 19, 1958), Oberon in *A Midsummer Night's Dream* (June 20, 1958). Polixenes in *The Winter's Tale* (July 20, 1958), Oberon in *A Midsummer Night's Dream* (June 20, 1959), Sir Hugh Evans in *The Merry Wives of Windsor* (July 8, 1959), and Parolles in *All's Well That Ends Well* (Aug. 1, 1959).

Mr. Waring toured with the Arnold Moss Festival Players as Angelo in *Measure for Measure* (Oct.–Dec. 1959), and as Caliban in *The Tempest* (Oct.–Dec. 1959); at the American Shakespeare Festival, appeared as Malvolio in *Twelfth Night* (June 8, 1960), Antonio in *The Tempest* (June 19, 1960), and Soothsayer in *Antony and Cleopatra* (July 31, 1960); with the same company, toured as Oberon in *A Midsummer Night's Dream* (opened Colonial, Boston, Mass., Sept. 26, 1960; closed National, Washington, D.C., Feb. 25, 1961); at Stratford, Conn., appeared as Sir Oliver Martext in *As You Like It* (June 15, 1961), MacDuff in *Macbeth* (June 16, 1961), Aeneas in *Troilus and Cressida* (July 23, 1961), and Owen Glendower in *Henry IV, Part 1* (June 17, 1962).

He appeared as Lopahin in *The Cherry Orchard* (Th. Four, N.Y.C., Nov. 14, 1962); Dr. Rank in *A Doll's House* (Theatre Four, Feb. 2, 1963); Col. Vershinin in *The Three Sisters* (Goodman Memorial Th., Chicago, Ill., Nov. 29, 1963); Astolpho in the English-cast production of *La Vida Es Sueno* ("Life Is a Dream") (Astor Place Playhouse, Mar. 19, 1964); toured in *Love and Marriage* (June 29–Sept. 5, 1964); in *Dial M for Murder* (1966); and played King Leopold of Belgium and Viscount Palmerston in *Portrait of a Queen* (Henry Miller's Th., Feb. 28, 1968).

Films. Mr. Waring appeared in *Mr. Skeffington* (WB, 1944).

Television and Radio. He has performed on You Are There (CBS), Hallmark Hall of Fame (NBC), Alfred Hitchcock Presents (CBS), and the US Steel Hour (CBS).

Awards. He received the Delia Austrian Award (1941) from the Drama League for his performance as Morgan Evans in *The Corn Is Green.*.

WARNICK, CLAY. Composer, producer, musical director, arranger. b. Henry Clay Warnick, Jr., Dec. 14, 1915, Tacoma, Wash., to Henry Clay and Lillian (D'Arcy) Warnick. Father, civil engineer. Grad. West Orange (N.J.) H.S., 1931; Colgate Univ. B.A. (Phi Beta Kappa) 1935; attended Juilliard Sch. of Music, 1935–36. Studied composition and conducting with Tibor Serly, N.Y.C., 1936–40. Married Aug. 1, 1936, to Phyllis Saynor; two sons, two daughters. Member of ASCAP; AFM, Local 802; Delta Upsilon; Colgate Alumni Club of Northern N.J.

Theatre. Mr. Warnick first composed the music and lyrics and served as musical director for a Colgate Univ. varsity show, *Pardon My Passion* (Smalley's Th., Hamilton, N.Y., May 1935); subsequently was orchestrator and vocal arranger for *Ziegfeld Follies* (Th. on Treasure Island, San Francisco World's Fair, Calif., June 1939); musical director, orchestrator, and vocal arranger for the pre-Bway tryout of *Three After Three* (opened Shubert, Boston, Mass., Oct. 1939; closed Cass, Detroit, Mich., Mar. 1940); and at the Cass Th. (Detroit, Mich.), was musical director and arranger for *Blossom Time, Madame Du Barry, The Student Prince,* and *Too Many Girls* (1940–41).

He was vocal director and arranger for *High Kickers* (Broadhurst, N.Y.C., Oct. 31, 1941); *Banjo Eyes* (Hollywood, Dec. 21, 1941); *By Jupiter* (Shubert, June 3, 1942); *Count Me In* (Ethel Barrymore Th., Oct. 8, 1942); *Ziegfeld Follies* (Winter Garden, Apr. 1, 1943); the pre-Bway tryout of *Dancing in the Streets* (opened Shubert, Boston, Mass., Mar. 23, 1943; closed there Apr. 10, 1943); *Early to Bed* (Broadhurst, N.Y.C., June 17, 1943); *Bright Lights* (Forrest, Sept. 16, 1943); *Artists and Models* (Bway Th., Nov. 5, 1943); *A Connecticut Yankee* (Martin Beck Th., Nov. 17, 1943); and *Jackpot* (Alvin, Jan. 13, 1944).

He composed the music and was vocal director and arranger for *Dream with Music* (Majestic, May 18, 1944); musical director and vocal arranger for the pre-Bway tryout of *Glad to See You* (opened Shubert, Boston, Mass., Oct. 1944; closed Forrest, Philadelphia, Pa., Dec. 1944); collaborated with Don Walker on the music and lyrics for *Memphis Bound* (Bway Th., N.Y.C., May 24, 1945); was vocal director and arranger for *Are You with It?* (Century, Nov. 10, 1945); and *Spring in Brazil* (Great Northern, Chicago, Ill., Dec. 1945).

Mr. Warnick was vocal director and arranger for *The Duchess Misbehaves* (Adelphi, N.Y.C., Feb. 13, 1946); musical supervisor and vocal arranger for the pre-Bway tryout of *Windy City* (opened Shubert, Boston, Mass., Mar. 1946; closed Great Northern, Chicago, Ill., May 1946); vocal director and arranger for *Park Avenue* (Shubert, N.Y.C., Nov. 4, 1946); musical director and vocal arranger for *Hold It!* (National, May 5, 1948); and composed the music and lyrics, and toured as musical director for a stock production of *We Found Us an Angel* (Summer 1948).

He was musical director and vocal director for *Heaven on Earth* (New Century, Sept. 16, 1948); was musical director, vocal arranger and wrote additional numbers for *All for Love* (Mark Hellinger Th., N.Y.C., Jan. 22, 1949); musical director for *Aqua Show* (Aquacade, Flushing, N.Y., Summer 1949); contributed music and lyrics to *Tickets Please* (Coronet, Apr. 27, 1950); and was musical director and vocal arranger for the revue *Peep Show* (Winter Garden, June 28, 1950).

He was musical director for *Once Upon a Mattress* (Phoenix, Nov. 5, 1959; moved to Bway Th., Nov. 29, 1959); musical director and vocal arranger for *Donnybrook!* (46 St. Th., May 18, 1961); musical director for *Ice-Capades* (Madison Square Garden, N.Y.C., Aug. 28, 1961); and vocal director and arranger for *Little Me* (Lunt-Fontanne, Nov. 17, 1962).

Films. Mr. Warnick was vocal arranger and orchestrator for the theme song of *The Roosevelt Story* (Col., 1938).

Television and Radio. He was engaged in radio musical production for WOR (1936–39); WNBC (1940–42); and WCBS (1949–50).

For television, he was vocal director and vocal arranger for Elgin-American Thanksgiving Day Show (International Th., NBC, 1949); composed "Stars Over Broadway," the theme of Your Show of Shows (NBC, 1950–54); was choral director and vocal arranger for Your Show of Shows (NBC, 1951–54); composed the music and was vocal arranger for *Lady in the Dark* (NBC, Sept. 25, 1954); *Sunday in Town* (NBC, 1954); *Satins and Spurs* (NBC, Sept. 12, 1954); *Follies of Suzy* (NBC, Oct. 23, 1954); *Fanfare* (NBC, Nov. 2, 1954); *Best Foot Forward* (NBC, Nov. 20, 1954); *Spotlight* (NBC, Dec. 5, 1954); *Babes in Toyland* (NBC, Dec. 18, 1954; Dec. 18, 1955); *Heidi* (NBC, Oct. 1, 1955); vocal arranger and musical adaptor for *The Great Waltz* (NBC, Nov. 5, 1955); *Dearest Enemy* (NBC, Nov. 26, 1955); the Maurice Chevalier Show (NBC, Dec. 4, 1955; May 20, 1956); *Good Times* (NBC, Jan. 2, 1955); *Naughty Marietta* (NBC, Jan. 15, 1955); *Variety* (NBC, Jan. 30, 1955); *Big Time* (NBC, Feb. 27, 1955); *A Connecticut Yankee* (NBC, Mar. 12, 1955); *The Merry Widow* (NBC, Apr. 9, 1955); *Kaleidoscope* (NBC, Apr. 24, 1955); *The Desert Song* (NBC, May 7, 1955); *Promenade* (NBC, May 22, 1955); *The Chocolate Soldier* (NBC, June 4, 1955); *Paris in the Springtime* (NBC, Jan. 27, 1956); *Panorama* (NBC, Feb. 26, 1956); *Heaven Will Protect the Working Girl* (NBC, Mar. 20, 1956); composed the music for *Marco Polo* (NBC, Apr. 14, 1956); was musical adaptor and vocal arranger for *Music of Gershwin* (NBC, May 12, 1956); and composed the music for *Holiday* (NBC, June 9, 1956).

He was vocal director and arranger for Caesar's Hour (NBC, 1956–57); the Bob Crosby Show (NBC, 1957–58); Your Hit Parade (CBS, 1958–59); the Jimmy Rodgers Show (NBC, 1958–59); two US Steel Hour specials (CBS, 1959–60); Bell Telephone Hour Special (CBS, 1960); Big Party (CBS, 1960); and Private Eye (CBS, 1961).

Night Clubs. He was musical director, orchestrator, and vocal arranger for *Cross Country*, which was performed at the Latin Quarter (Boston, Mass., 1949).

Other Activities. He has been staff choral arranger for music publishers; taught composition at Trenton (N.J.) State Teachers Coll.

Awards. Mr. Warnick received Honorable Mention in the Donaldson Awards for *Memphis Bound* (1945).

Recreation. Golf, tennis, swimming, bowling, water skiing.

WARREN, BRETT. Director, teacher, writer. b. Louis Breitberg, July 6, 1910, New York City, to Joseph and Sophie (Rothstein) Breitberg. Father, merchant; mother, nurse. Grad. South Side H.S., Newark, N.J., 1927; attended Toledo Univ., 1927–29; Columbia Univ., 1930–31; 1956–57; 1962. Married Mar. 15, 1936, to Mildred Heiligman (marr. dis. 1954); married Sept. 29, 1955, to Ruth Socolov; one son. Served WW II, USAAF, PTO. Member of AEA. Address: (home) Rock Creek Terrace, Bldg. 14, Apt. 5, Englewood, NJ 07631, tel. (201) 569-7137; (bus.) Hotel Ansonia, 2109 Broadway, New York, NY 10023, tel. (212) TR 7-9140.

Theatre. Mr. Warren directed *Till the Day I Die* (Second Ave. Th., N.Y.C., Nov. 15, 1935); *Can You Hear Their Voices?* (Civic Rep. Th., Sept. 12, 1935), and a double bill *Pastry Baker* and *Human Nature* (Provincetown Playhouse, Mass., Nov. 1936).

For the Federal Th. (WPA) Project, he directed with Alfred Saxe, *The Great Catherine* (Experimental, N.Y.C., May 13, 1936); was assistant director of *Injunction Granted* (Biltmore, July 24, 1936); directed *Power* (Ritz, Feb. 23, 1937); and *Mississippi Rainbow* (49 St. Th., Mar. 1938).

He directed two pageants for the ILGWU and Fight for Freedom: *I Hear America Singing* (1940), and *Fun to Be Free* (Madison Square Garden, 1941), managed the national tour of *Deep Are the Roots* (1946–47); and the ANTA production of *The Wanhope Building* (Princess, Feb. 9, 1947).

During 1946–50, he taught acting at the Dramatic Workshop of the New School for Social Research and directed its productions at the President Th. of *Prologue to Glory* (1947), *Shadow of a Gunman* (1947), *Private Hicks* (1948), *The Little Foxes* (1949), and *The House in Berlin* (1950). He directed a season of stock at the Orange County (N.Y.) Playhouse (Summer 1948); and was director of the Southhold (N.Y.) Playhouse (Summers 1949–50).

In 1951, Mr. Warren organized the Actors Mobile Th. Acting Sch., of which he has been director.

Television. In 1953, Mr. Warren directed for the Actors Studio series (CBS); and in 1954, wrote scripts for the Lights Out series (NBC). His play, *The Devil in Scotland*, has been produced on NBC (1951).

Recreation. Gardening, photography.

WARREN, HARRY. Composer. b. Harry Salvatore Warren, Dec. 24, 1893, Brooklyn, N.Y., to Anthony and Rachel (De Luca) Warren. Father, factory worker. Grad. Commercial H.S., 1912. Married Dec. 19, 1917, to Josephine Wensler; one daughter. Served WW I, USN. Member of ASCAP (bd. of dir., 1929–33); AGAC; AMPAS (bd. of dir., 1947–50). Address: 9425 Sunset Blvd., Beverly Hills, CA 90210, tel. (213) CR 5-7233.

Theatre. Mr. Warren first performed playing the drums in a brass band for carnival shows; has been a stage hand, actor and assistant director for the Vitagraph motion picture company.

He contributed music to *Sweet and Low* (46 St. Th., N.Y.C., 1930); wrote the music for *The Laugh Parade* (Imperial, Nov. 2, 1931); and wrote five songs for Billy Rose's *Crazy Quilt* (44 St. Th., May 19, 1931). He wrote the score for *Shangri-La* (Winter Garden, June 13, 1956).

Films. He has written songs for *Spring Is Here* (1st Natl., 1930); *42nd Street* (WB, 1933); *Gold Diggers of 1933* (WB, 1933); *Roman Scandals* (UA, 1933); *Footlight Parade* (WB, 1933); *Moulin Rouge* (UA, 1934); *20 Million Sweethearts* (1st Natl., 1934); *Wonder Bar* (1st Natl., 1934); *Dames* (WB, 1934); *Gold Diggers of 1934* (WB, 1934); *Sweet Music* (WB, 1935); *Gold Diggers of 1935* (1st Natl., 1935); *Go Into Your Dance* (1st Natl., 1935); *Broadway Gondolier* (WB, 1935); *Stars Over Broadway* (WB, 1935); *Shipmates Forever* (1st Natl., 1935); *Living on Velvet* (1st Natl., 1935); *In Caliente* (1st Natl., 1935); *Page Miss Glory* (WB, 1935); *Cain and Mabel* (WB, 1936); *Hearts Divided* (1st Natl., 1936); *Colleen* (WB, 1936); *Gold Diggers of 1937* (1st Natl., 1936); *Sing Me a Love Song* (1st Natl., 1936); *Melody for Two* (WB, 1937); *Stolen Melody* (WB, 1937); *Mr. Dodd Takes the Air* (WB, 1937); and *The Singing Marine* (WB, 1937).

Mr. Warren has also written songs for *San Quentin* (1st Natl., 1937); *Gold Diggers in Paris* (WB, 1938); *Garden of the Moon* (WB, 1938); *Going Places* (WB, 1938); *Hard to Get* (WB, 1938); *Jezebel* (WB, 1938); *Cowboy from Brooklyn* (WB, 1938); *Naughty But Nice* (WB, 1939); *Honolulu* (MGM, 1939); *Tin Pan Alley* (20th-Fox, 1940); *Young People* (20th-Fox, 1940); *Down Argentine Way* (20th-Fox, 1940); *The Great American Broadcast* (20th-Fox, 1941); *Sun Valley Serenade* (20th-Fox, 1941); *Weekend in Havana* (20th-Fox, 1941); *That Night in Rio* (20th-Fox, 1941); *Iceland* (20th-Fox, 1942); *Springtime in the Rockies* (20th-Fox, 1942); *Orchestra Wives* (20th-Fox, 1942); *The Gang's All Here* (20th-Fox, 1943); *Sweet Rosie O'Grady* (20th-Fox, 1943); *Hello, Frisco, Hello* (20th-Fox, 1943); *Diamond Horseshoe* (20th-Fox, 1945); *Yolanda and the Thief* (MGM, 1945); *Ziegfeld Follies* (MGM, 1946); *Harvey Girls* (MGM, 1946); *Three Little Girls in Blue* (20th-Fox, 1946); *Summer Holiday* (MGM, 1948); *The Barkleys of Broadway* (MGM, 1949); *Take Me Out to the Ballgame* (MGM, 1949); *Summer Stock* (MGM, 1950); *Pagan Love Song* (MGM, 1950); *Texas Carnival* (MGM, 1951); *Skirts Ahoy* (MGM, 1952); *Belle of New York* (MGM, 1952); *Just for You* (Par., 1952); *The Caddy* (Par., 1953); *Artists and Models* (Par., 1955); *The Benny Goodman Story* (UI, 1955); *The Rose Tattoo* (Par., 1955); *The Birds and the Bees* (Par., 1956); *Rock-a-Bye-Baby* (20th-Fox, 1957); *An Affair To Remember* (20th-Fox, 1957); *Separate Tables* (UA, 1958); *These Thousand Hills* (20th-Fox, 1959); *CinderFella* (Par., 1960); *The Ladies' Man* (Par., 1961); and *Satan Never Sleeps* (20th-Fox, 1962).

Awards. Mr. Warren has received three Academy (Oscar) awards: for the song "Lullaby of Broadway" *(Gold Diggers of 1935)*; "You'll Never Know" (*Hello, Frisco, Hello*, 1943); and "On the Atchison, Topeka and the Santa Fe" (*Harvey Girls*, 1946). He received an award (1940) from the Amer. Federation of Music Clubs for "Down Argentine Way." The songs, "Don't Give Up the Ship," and "We're Shovin' Right Off" were adopted by the US Naval Academy and the US Marines, respectively.

Recreation. Golf.

WARREN, JEFF. Actor, director, singer. b. George Warren Jones, Jan. 21, 1921, Wagner, S.D., to Frank and Mary Frances (Strain) Jones. Parents, furniture dealers. Grad. Central H.S., Minneapolis, Minn., 1939; attended Univ. of Minnesota, 1939–42; studied voice with James French, Minneapolis, 1937–42; Dimitri Mitropolous, 1941–42; acting with Lee Strasberg, N.Y.C., 1947. Member of AEA (chorus exec. committee, 1947; chorus council, 1948–52; council, 1957, 1958–62, 1963–64); British AEA; Australian AEA; AGVA; AFTRA; Theta Chi. Address: 401 E. 63rd St., New York, NY 10021, tel. (212) TE 2-9319.

Theatre. Mr. Warren made his stage debut at age seven in a public school production of *The Gingerbread Man* (Ravinia, S.D., 1928); and his professional debut as a supernumerary, a spear carrier, in the Ballet Russe de Monte Carlo production of *Le Coq d'Or* (Northrop Aud., Minneapolis, Minn., 1940).

Using the professional name Warren Jones, he appeared as tenor soloist and member of the chorus in the national tour of *Lady in the Dark* (Forrest Th., Philadelphia, Pa., Sept. 28, 1942; Bway Th., N.Y.C., Feb. 27, 1943).

Thereafter under the name Jeffrey (or Jeff) Warren, he appeared in the chorus and was understudy to Kenny Baker as Rodney Hatch in *One Touch of Venus* (Imperial, Oct. 7, 1943), playing the role for one month (Nov. 1943); succeeded (44th St. Th., Oct. 16, 1944) John Battles as the Yokel Sailor and was understudy to Norman Lawrence as the juvenile lead in *Follow the Girls* (Century, April 8, 1944); was in the chorus and understudy to Gilbert Russell as Ralph Rackstraw in *Hollywood Pinafore* (Alvin, May 31, 1945); was a member of the chorus and understudy to Bill Johnson and Robert Field as Alex Martland and Harry Scott, respectively, in *The Day Before Spring* (National, Nov. 22, 1945); was in the chorus of *A Flag Is Born* (Bway Th., Sept. 14, 1946);

played Sandy Dean and understudied Lee Sullivan as Charlie Dalrymple in *Brigadoon* (Ziegfeld, Mar. 13, 1947), and in *Brigadoon* played Charlie Dalrymple in a USO tour of veterans hospitals in 47 states (opened Oct. 11, 1948); appeared as Tommy Albright in another USO tour of US zones in Germany, Paris, Tripoli, and the Azores (opened June 16, 1949); played Charlie Dalrymple in the national company tour (opened Curran, San Francisco, Calif., Aug. 8, 1949; NY City Ctr., May 2, 1950), and repeated the role at the State Fair Casino (Dallas, Tex., July 10, 1950).

He succeeded (May 28, 1951) William Kraeh as the French tenor and understudied Eric Brotherson as Henry Spofford in *Gentlemen Prefer Blondes* (Ziegfeld, Dec. 8, 1949); succeeded (Aug. 11, 1951) Russell Nype as Kenneth Gibson in *Call Me Madam* (Imperial, Oct. 12, 1950), repeating the role for the London production (Coliseum, Mar. 15, 1952); and played Paul Chandler in *Wedding in Paris* (Hippodrome, Apr. 3, 1954), in which he subsequently toured.

In stock, Mr. Warren played Charlie Dalrymple in *Brigadoon*, the Caliph in *Kismet* and Lt. Cable in *South Pacific* (Municipal Th., Atlanta, Ga., July–Aug. 1956); Lt. Cable in *South Pacific* (Niagara Melody Fair, Tonawanda, N.Y., Aug. 28, 1956); Tommy Keeler in *Annie Get Your Gun* (Stamford Playhouse, Conn., Apr. 7, 1957); Peter Reber in *Plain and Fancy* (Westchester Music Th., Rye, N.Y., June 25, 1957); Peter Reber in *Plain and Fancy*, Mr. Snow in *Carousel*, Jack Chesney in *Where's Charley?*, and the Tin Woodman in *The Wizard of Oz* (Municipal Th., Atlanta, Ga., June–July 1957); Julio in *Paint Your Wagon* (Municipal Th., Atlanta, Ga., July 15, 1958); and Herman in *The Most Happy Fella* (Miami Music Th., Fla., Aug. 12, 1958).

He has appeared in the following industrial shows: Chevrolet (Sept. 1957, two-month tour; Aug. 1958, six weeks; Coca-Cola (Jan. 1958, six weeks; Aug. 1958, St. Louis four weeks; Feb. 1960, six weeks); Hamm's Beer (Feb. 1959, St. Paul, two weeks).

In stock, Mr. Warren appeared as Kenneth Gibson in *Call Me Madam* (Meadowbrook Dinner Th., Cedar Grove, N.J., May 5, 1959); Charlie Dalrymple in *Brigadoon* (Paper Mill Playhouse, Millburn, N.J., June 23, 1959); a principal in a tour of *Lend an Ear* (Pocono Playhouse, Mountainhome, Pa., Aug. 17, 1959; Renata, N.Y.C., Sept. 24, 1959); and Sandy Stewart in *Happy Hunting* (Meadowbrook Dinner Th., Cedar Grove, N.J., Dec. 8, 1960).

Mr. Warren directed a season of stock at the Little Th. (Sullivan, Ill.) which included *South Pacific; Pal Joey; A Tree Grows in Brooklyn*, in which he played Johnny; *Li'l Abner; West Side Story; Carousel*, in which he played Mr. Snow; and *Redhead* (Summer 1960); became (Jan. 23, 1961) stage manager and understudy to Jules Munshin in the revue *Show Girl* (Eugene O'Neill Th., N.Y.C., Jan. 12, 1961); at the Little Th. (Sullivan, Ill.), directed *Take Me Along*, in which he played Nat; *Brigadoon*, in which he played Charlie Dalrymple; *Paint Your Wagon; Bloomer Girl; The Merry Widow*, for which he revised the book and played Danilo; *Anything Goes;* and *Flower Drum Song*, in which he appeared as Wang Ta (Summer 1961); directed *Down in the Valley* (Actors' Playhouse, N.Y.C., June 5, 1962); at the Little Th. (Sullivan, Ill., Summer 1962), staged *Tunnel of Love; The Glass Menagerie; The King and I*, in which he played the King; *Bye Bye Birdie; Oklahoma!; Gypsy;* and *The Music Man*, in which he appeared as Harold Hill; played Lt. Cable in *South Pacific* (Circle Arts, San Diego, Calif., Aug. 27, 1962); and directed a benefit production of the *Green Door Follies* (Ashtabula Playhouse, Ohio, Nov. 14, 1962).

Mr. Warren played the King in the Australian company of *The King and I* (Princess, Melbourne, Dec. 22, 1962; Tivoli, Sydney, July 17, 1963), and on tour in New Zealand (opened St. James, Wellington, Feb. 15, 1964).

Television. Mr. Warren made his debut as solo vocalist on a variety program (Dumont-Par., L.A., July 1943); subsequently appeared as Brack Weaver in *Down in the Valley* (BBC, London, May 6, 1955) and performed on more than 30 programs in the US, Europe, and Australia.

Night Clubs. He was soloist on the S.S. *Brazil* for a South American tour and made night club appearances in Rio de Janeiro and Buenos Aires (Aug.–Sept. 1948); appeared at Number One Fifth Avenue (Nov. 6, 1951, three mos.; Dec. 1953, eight wks.; Jan. 10, 1956, eight wks.); and at the Dorchester Hotel (London, July 5, 1954, four wks.).

Recreation. Swimming; still and movie photography; writing; collecting books, phonograph records, programs, music, scripts, vocal scores, and other theatrical memorabilia.

WARRICK, RUTH. Actress. Studied with Antoinette Perry and Brock Pemberton. Married 1938, to Erik Rolf, actor, radio announcer (marr. dis.); one daughter; married Apr. 23, 1950, to Carl Neubert (marr. dis.); married July 18, 1953, to Robert McNamara. Member of AEA; SAG; AFTRA.

Theatre. Miss Warrick played in stock at the Univ. of Kansas City (1933–36). In stock, she played Margo Wendice in *Dial 'M' for Murder* (Summer 1955); in *The Thorntons* (Provincetown Playhouse, Feb. 14, 1956); followed by the role of Mary Spain in *Miss Lonelyhearts* (Music Box, Oct. 3, 1957); Dolores Dixon in *Single Man at a Party* (Th. Marquee, N.Y.C., Apr. 21, 1959); was standby for Eileen Herlie in the role of Lily in *Take Me Along* (Shubert, Oct. 22, 1959), and later succeeded her.

In stock, she played Anna Leonowens in *The King and I* (Music Fair, Dixie Plaza, Toronto, Ontario, Canada, 1960); appeared in *Who's Afraid of Virginia Woolf?* (Los Angeles, 1967); and *Long Day's Journey into Night* (Los Angeles, 1967); presented her own one-woman show (Los Angeles, and on tour, 1968–69); and played Emmaline Marshall in the revival of *Irene* (Menskoff, N.Y.C., Mar. 13, 1973, and on tour, 1974–75).

Films. Her first appearance was as Mrs. Kane in *Citizen Kane* (RKO, 1941); subsequently played in *Obliging Young Lady* (RKO, 1941); *The Corsican Brothers* (UA, 1941); *Journey into Fear* (RKO, 1942); *Forever and a Day* (RKO, 1943); *The Iron Major* (RKO, 1943); *Secret Command* (Col., 1944); *Mr. Winkle Goes to War* (Col., 1944); *Guest in the House* (UA, 1944); *China Sky* (RKO, 1945); *Driftwood* (Rep., 1947); *Daisy Kenyon* (20th-Fox, 1947); *Arch of Triumph* (UA, 1948); *A Letter to Three Husbands* (20th-Fox, 1948); *The Great Dan Patch* (UA, 1949); *Make Believe Ballroom* (Col., 1949); *Let's Dance* (Par., 1950); *One Too Many* (Hallmark, 1950); *Roogies' Bump* (Rep., 1954); and *The Great Bank Robbery* (WB-Seven Arts, 1969).

Television and Radio. Miss Warrick's first radio performance was in *The Birds* (1937); subsequently performed on Mercury Th. on the Air (1939); and Grand Central Station (1940). On television, she has played in the series As the World Turns (CBS, 1956–to date); and Father of the Bride (ABC, 1961–62); and played Hannah Cord on Peyton Place (ABC, 1966–68).

Awards. Miss Warrick was "Miss Jubilesta" (Kansas City) in 1937.

WASHBURN, JACK. Singer, actor. b. Jack Charles Washburn, Dec. 4, 1927, Rockford, Ill., to Benjamin and Marguerite (Hocher) Washburn. Father, civil service employee. Grad. San Juan H.S., Sacramento, Calif. Studied voice with Easton Kent, San Francisco, 1946–1954; Raoul Querze, N.Y.C., 1954–59; acting at Warner Bros. Dramatic Sch., Hollywood, 1957. Married Aug. 15, 1953, to Diane Louise, fashion model; one son, one daughter. Served USN, 1945–46; US Army, 1950–52; rank Pfc. Member of AEA; AFTRA; SAG. Address: (home) Glen Gables, New Hope, PA 18938, tel. (215) 862-2179; (bus.) 1564 Broadway, New York, NY 10036.

Pre-Theatre. Retail merchandising.

Theatre. Mr. Washburn made his professional debut as Lt. Bumerli in production of *The Chocolate Soldier* (Lambertville Music Circus, N.J., June, 1954), where he also played Carl Van Dam in *The Red Mill*, and Jack Negley in *My Maryland*.

He made his N.Y.C. debut succeeding (Sept. 1955) William Tabbert as Marius in *Fanny* (Majestic, Nov. 4, 1954), also touring in this role with the national company (opened Shubert, Boston, Mass., Dec. 25, 1956; closed Hanna, Cleveland, Ohio, May 25, 1957), and the West Coast company (Civic Light Opera Assn.; San Francisco and Los Angeles, Calif., Summer 1957).

He played Woody in *Finian's Rainbow* (St. Louis Municipal Opera, Mo., Aug., 1958); Prince Danilo in *The Merry Widow* (Rye Music Th., N.Y.; Rosecroft Music Circus, Md.; Brandywine, Pa., Summer 1959); Ravenal in *Show Boat* (Rosecroft Music Circus, Rye Music Th., Summer 1959); Billy in *Carousel* and Tom Baxter in *Redhead* (Highland Park Music Th., Ill., Summer 1960); Tom Baxter in *Redhead* and Marius in *Fanny* (Starlight Musical Th., Indianapolis, Ind., Summer 1960); Larry Dodd in *Paradise Island* (Marine Th., Jones Beach, N.Y., Summer 1961); Lt. Bumerli in *The Chocolate Soldier* (Lambertville Music Circus), Prince Karl in *The Student Prince*, and Fred Graham in *Kiss Me, Kate* (Bradford Roof, Boston, Summer 1962); and Youssein Daver in *Mr. President* (St. James, N.Y.C., Oct. 20, 1962).

His later appearances have included co-starring roles with Patti Page in Dallas and Los Angeles; tours of *Sweet Charity* with Chita Rivera and *Brigadoon* with Doretta Morrow; roles in *The Fantasticks, Forty Carats, Come Blow Your Horn, Twelfth Night*, and *1776* at the Bucks County Playhouse; and a tour of *Forty Carats* with Joan Fontaine.

Films. Mr. Washburn played Tony in *Black Orchid* (Par., 1958).

Television. He made his debut on Talent Prospector (ABC, 1949); appeared on local and network programs in San Francisco, including Ruby's Traveline (KPIC Westinghouse), was a winning contestant on Arthur Godfrey's Talent Scouts (CBS), appeared on the Arthur Godfrey Show (CBS), the Ed Sullivan Show (CBS), the Steve Allen Show (NBC), the Arlene Francis Show (NBC), and others.

Other Activities. He appeared as guest soloist with the Memphis (Tenn.) Symphony, and the Kent (Ohio) Symphony (July, 1963).

Awards. He was voted best singer on television in San Francisco (1949, 1950, 1953).

Recreation. Tennis, collecting old and classical records, children, swimming, golf, horses.

WASSERMAN, DALE. Playwright. b. Nov. 2, 1917, Rhinelander, Wis., to Samuel and Hilda (Paykel) Wasserman. Father, motion picture theatre operator. Relatives in theatre: sister, Eve Wasserman, story editor; nephew, John L. Wasserman, columnist, *San Francisco Chronicle;* niece, Arlene Garber, newspaper television editor. Member of French Society of Authors and Composers; Spanish Society of Authors; WGA, East (chairman, censorship comm., 1958; credits arbitration comm., 1958; labor grievances comm., 1959; natl. council, 1960–64); Dramatists Guild; ALA. Address: (home) Malaga, Spain; (bus.) c/o D. W. Katz & Co., 10 E. 40th St., New York, NY 10016.

Theatre. With Bruce Geller, Mr. Wasserman wrote *Livin' the Life* (Phoenix Th., N.Y.C., Apr. 27, 1957); subsequently wrote *The Pencil of God* (Karamu Th., Cleveland, Ohio, 1961); *998* (Professional Th., Hollywood, Calif., 1962); and *One Flew Over the Cuckoo's Nest* (Cort, N.Y.C., Nov. 14, 1963).

Films. He wrote the screenplay for *World Strangers* (Fortuna, 1955); *The Vikings* (UA, 1958); *Two Faces to Go* (Italian-American, 1959); *Aboard the Flying Swan* (1962); and *Jangadeiro* (1962).

He wrote a script for *Cleopatra* (20th-Fox, 1963); the screenplay for *Quick Before It Melts* (MGM, 1964); and *Man of La Mancha* (UA, 1972).

Television. He has written the following scripts for Kraft Television Th. (NBC); *Elisha and the Long Knives* (1954), *Fiddlin' Man* (1954), *Boys Will Be Boys* (1955), *Drop on the Devil* (1955), *The Luck of Roaring Camp* (1956), *The Fool Killer* (1956), *Collision* (1956), *The Medallion* (1958), *The Gentle Grafter*

(1958), and *Look What's Going On* (1959).

He wrote *The Fog* (Climax, CBS, 1956); *The Time of the Draught* (Ponds' Th., ABC, 1957); *Long After Summer* (Alcoa Hour, NBC, 1957); *The Milwaukee Rocket* (Matinee Th., NBC, 1957); *The Bequest* (Four Star Th., NBC, 1957); *The Forger* (Ponds' Th., ABC); *The Man That Corrupted Hadleyburg* (Matinee Th., NBC, 1958); *American Primitive* (Studio One, CBS, 1959); *Brotherhood of the Bell* (Studio One, CBS, 1960); a pilot film, *The Blue Angels* (1960); *I, Don Quixote* (Dupont Show of the Month, NBC, 1960); *Engineer of Death: The Eichmann Story* (Armstrong Circle Th., CBS, 1961); *The Citadel* (Special Tonight, ABC, 1961); a pilot film, *Grand Deception* (1961); adapted *The Power and the Glory* (CBS, 1961); *The Lincoln Murder Case* (DuPont Show of the Month, NBC, 1962); *Circle of Death* (True, CBS, 1962); and *The Stranger* (Richard Boone Anthology, NBC, 1963).

Published Works. He has contributed short stories and articles to *Redbook, True, Argosy, Cavalier,* New York *Times,* and *Variety;* and has written *Man of La Mancha; One Flew Over the Cuckoo's Nest; Top TV Plays of the Year;* and is represented in the Viking Critical Library with scripts of *The Power and the Glory* and *One Flew Over the Cuckoo's Nest.*

Awards. Mr. Wasserman's *Elisha and the Long Knives* was voted the Top Television Play of the Year (1954).

He received the Writers Guild Award for *The Fog* (1957); was nominated for the NATAS (Emmy) Award and received the Writers Guild of Amer. Award for *I, Don Quixote* (1960); nominated for the NATAS (Emmy) Award and received the Writers Guild of Amer. Award for *The Lincoln Murder Case* (1961).

Man of La Mancha received the Antoinette Perry (Tony), New York Critics Circle, Outer Circle, Saturday Review citation, and Spanish Pavilion awards, and several others; and received the Joseph Jefferson Award for *One Flew Over the Cuckoo's Nest.*

WATERS, ETHEL. Actress, singer. b. Oct. 31, 1900, Chester, Pa., to John Wesley and Louise Tar (Anderson) Waters. Married 1914 to Merritt Purnsley (marr. dis.); married to Edward Mallory. Served WW II, Seventh Women's Ambulance Corps, and was honorary captain of the Calif. State Militia. Member of AFTRA; SAG; AEA (exec. council, 1942–43); Negro Actors Guild of Amer. (vice-pres., 1942–43); AGVA; AGMA.

Pre-Theatre. Domestic service.

Theatre. Miss Waters made her debut in vaudeville at the Lincoln Th. (Baltimore, Md., circa 1917); subsequently played Sweet Mama Stringbean and sang and danced with the "Hill Sisters Trio," playing the leading vaudeville circuits (1917–27).

She made her Bway debut in the revue, *Africana* (Daly's Th., N.Y.C., July 11, 1927); appeared in Lew Leslie's *Blackbirds of 1930* (Royale, Oct. 22, 1930); *Rhapsody in Black* (Sam H. Harris Th., May 4, 1931); *As Thousands Cheer* (Music Box, Sept. 30, 1933); *At Home Abroad* (Winter Garden, Sept. 19, 1935); in concert at Carnegie Hall (1938); and sang at the Roxy and the Palace theatres (N.Y.C.).

She appeared as Hagar in *Mamba's Daughters* (Empire, N.Y.C., Jan. 3, 1938); as Petunia Jackson in *Cabin in the Sky* (Martin Beck Th., Oct. 25, 1940); and in the revue, *Blue Holiday* (Belasco, May 21, 1945). In summer stock, she performed in *The Voice of Strangers* (Ivy Tower Playhouse, Spring Lake, N.J.).

She played Berenice Sadie Brown in *The Member of the Wedding* (Empire, N.Y.C., Jan. 5, 1950), with which she toured (opened Cass Th., Detroit, Mich., Sept. 3, 1951; closed Shubert, New Haven, Conn., May 3, 1952); performed in *At Home with Ethel Waters* (48 St. Th., N.Y.C., Sept. 22, 1953); appeared in the pre-Bway tryout of *Gentle Folk;* under the auspices of the US State Dept., repeated her role as Bernice in *The Member of the Wedding* (Congress Hall, Berlin, Sept. 20, 1957); performed in *An Evening with Ethel Waters* (Renata, N.C., Apr. 8, 1959); repeated her role as Berenice in *The Member of the Wedding* (Pasadena Playhouse, Calif., Feb. 7, 1964; and on tour, 1970). She has often devoted her time to sacred music and has appeared in Billy Graham's Youth for Christ rallies and the Ford Philpot Crusades.

During her career, Miss Waters has introduced such songs as "Dinah," "Am I Blue," "Stormy Weather," "Heat Wave," "Suppertime," "Happiness Is Just a Thing Called Joe," and "Takin' a Chance on Love." She was the first woman to sing "St. Louis Blues" professionally.

Films. She made her debut in *On with the Show* (WB, 1929); and has appeared in *The Cotton Club, New York* (1930); *Hot n' Bothered* (1934); *Tales of Manhattan* (20th-Fox, 1942); *Cairo* (MGM, 1942); *Stage Door Canteen* (UA, 1943); repeated her role as Petunia Jackson in the film version of *Cabin in the Sky* (MGM, 1943); appeared in *Pinky* (20th-Fox, 1949); *Carib Gold* (Par., 1952); repeated her role as Berenice Sadie Brown in the film version of *The Member of the Wedding* (Col., 1952); and played Dilsey in *The Sound and the Fury* (20th-Fox, 1959).

Television and Radio. She has performed on radio since 1934. On television, she has made daily appearances on the Tex and Jinx Show (NBC, 1954); played the role of Dilsey in *The Sound and the Fury* (NBC, 1955); appeared in the title role in *Mama Cooper* (Daniel Boone, NBC, 1970); and appeared on Johnny Carson's *Sun City Scandals '72* (The Tonight Show, NBC, 1972).

Night Clubs. She made her debut at Edmond's Cellar (N.Y.C.); and has sung at the Plantation Club and the Cotton Club, among others.

Published Works. *His Eye Is on the Sparrow* (1950) is Miss Waters' autobiography, written in collaboration with Charles Samuels. She subsequently wrote a sequel, *To Me It's Wonderful* (1972).

Discography. Her recordings include *Miss Ethel Waters* (Monmouth); *Ethel Waters* (Columbia); and *Ethel Waters' Greatest Years* (Columbia).

Awards. She has twice been nominated for the Academy (Oscar) Award, for her performances in *Pinky* (1949); and as Berenice Sadie Brown in *The Member of the Wedding* (1952). She was recipient of a plaque from the Negro Actors Guild of America for her role in *Pinky* (1949); a St. Genesius Medal (1951) by ANTA; and the Joseph Jefferson Award (Chicago, 1970) for her performance in *The Member of the Wedding.*.

WATERSTON, SAM. Actor. b. Samuel A. Waterston, Nov. 15, 1940, Cambridge, Mass., to George C. and Alicia A. Waterston. Father, teacher; mother, painter. Grad. Groton Acad.; Groton Acad.; Yale Univ., 1962. Studied with John Berry, Amer. Actor's Workshop, Paris; Frank Corsaro, N.Y.C. Married 1964 to Barbara Rutledge Johns (marr. dis.), one son; married 1976 to Lynn Woodruff. Member of AEA; SAG.

Theatre. Mr. Waterston made his stage debut as Creon's page in *Antigone* while at Brooks Sch. (North Andover, Mass.) and acted with various summer stock companies, including The Clifton (Conn.) Playhouse where he played Estragon in *Waiting for Godot* (Summer 1962). He played Lucky in *Waiting for Godot* (Yale Univ.); the Bill Collector in *A Streetcar Named Desire* (Group Twenty Th., Wellesley, Mass.); played Jonathan in a touring company of *Oh, Dad, Poor Dad, Mama's Hung You in the Closet and I'm Feeling So Sad* (Civic, Chicago, Apr. 2, 1963), a production which subsequently opened on Bway (Morosco, N.Y.C., Aug. 27, 1963); played Silvius in *As You Like It* (1963); appeared in *Thistle in My Bed* (Gramercy Arts, Nov. 19, 1963); succeeded Roddy Maude-Roxby (July 14, 1964) in the role of Colin in *The Knack* (New Th., May 27, 1964); played Woodfin in *Fitz,* on a double-bill with *Biscuit* (Circle in the Square, May 16, 1966); appeared in the American premiere of *Eh?* (Playhouse in the Park, Cincinnati, July 13, 1966); for the American Place Th. (St. Clement's, N.Y.C.), played Kent in *La Tourista* (Mar. 4, 1967), and appeared in *Posterity for Sale* (May 11, 1967), played Robert in *Halfway Up the Tree* (Brooks Atkinson Th., Nov. 7, 1967); Aslan in *Ergo* (Public/Anspacher, Mar. 3, 1968); on a double-bill played Jim in *Red Cross* and Jack Argue in *Muzeeka* (Provincetown Playhouse, Apr. 28, 1968); and for the NY Shakespeare Festival (Delacorte Th.) Prince Hal in *Henry IV, Part 1* (June 11, 1968), and *Part 2* (June 18, 1968).

He played Gary Rogers in *Spitting Image* (Th. de Lys, Mar. 2, 1969); John Grass in *Indians* (Brooks Atkinson Th., Oct. 13, 1969); Phanacles in *The Brass Butterfly* (Chelsea Th. Center, Jan. 28, 1970); Aaron in *And I Met a Man* (Lincoln Sq. Cabaret Th., Apr. 10, 1970); Simon Bliss in *Hay Fever* (Helen Hayes Th., Nov. 9, 1970); Thomas Lewis in *The Trial of the Catonsville Nine* (Good Shepherd Faith Church, Feb. 7, 1971; moved to Lyceum, June 2, 1971); with the Center Th. Group (Mark Taper Forum, Los Angeles), played Mosca in the musical comedy, *Volpone* (world premiere, Mar. 9, 1972); and Oliver in *A Meeting by the River* (Apr. 26, 1972); Laertes in *Hamlet* (Delacorte, June 20, 1972); Benedick in *Much Ado About Nothing* (Delacorte, N.Y.C., Aug. 16, 1972; moved to Winter Garden, Nov. 11, 1972); repeated the role of Oliver in *A Meeting by the River* (Edison, Dec. 18, 1972); played Prospero in *The Tempest* (Public/Mitzie E. Newhouse Th., Feb. 10, 1974); Torvald Helmer in *A Doll's House* (Vivian Beaumont Th., Mar. 5, 1975); and the title role in *Hamlet* (Delacorte, June 23, 1975; moved to Vivian Beaumont Th., Dec. 17, 1975).

Mr. Waterson was the narrator for a single performance of Honegger's *King David* (Church of Our Savior, N.Y.C., Jan. 19, 1976).

Films. Mr. Waterston has appeared in *Fitzwilly* (UA, 1967); *Generation* (Avco-Embassy, 1969); *Three* (UA, 1969); *Who Killed Whats'ername* (Cannon 1971); *Savages* (Angelikas Films, 1972); *The Great Gatsby* (Par., 1974); and *Rancho Deluxe* (UA, 1975). His unreleased film appearances include *The Plastic Dome of Norma Jean; Sidewalks of New York; Run, Shadow, Run; Journey into Fear;* and *Mahoney's Estate.*.

Television. He has appeared on Dr. Kildare; NYPD (ABC); and Hawk (ABC); played Tom Wingfield in *The Glass Menagerie* (ABC, 1973); and Benedick in the television version of the stage production of *Much Ado About Nothing* (CBS, 1973).

Awards. For his performance in *Much Ado About Nothing,* he received the Drama Desk, Drama Critics Circle, and Off-Bway (Obie) awards (1972–73).

Recreation. Skiing, sailing, tennis.

WATSON, BETTY JANE. Actress, singer. b. Elizabeth Jane Watson, Dec. 28, 1928, Bloomington, Ill., to James R. and Elizabeth Jane (Stapleton) Watson. Attended Lincoln Junior H.S., Rockford, Ill. Studied voice at Amer. Conservatory of Music, Chicago, Ill. Married Nov. 5, 1944, to Gerald L. Austensen (marr. dis. 1961); three daughters; married Oct. 6, 1962, to Salvatore Cantacroce. Relative in theatre: cousin, Jean Stapleton, actress. Member of AEA; AFTRA; AGVA. Address: Hudson Terrace, Piermont, NY 10968, tel. (212) 349-1806.

Theatre. Miss Watson made her N.Y.C. debut succeeding (1944) Joan Roberts as Laurey in *Oklahoma!* (St. James Th., Mar. 31, 1943), also toured in this role (1944–46), and played it in London (Drury Lane, Apr. 31, 1947).

She played a Girl in *Toplitsky of Notre Dame* (Century, N.Y.C., Dec. 26, 1946); Katrina Van Tassel in *Sleepy Hollow* (St. James, June 3, 1948); appeared in the revue *Hilarities* (Adelphi, Sept. 9, 1948); and played Kathy Robinson in *As the Girls Go* (Winter Garden, Nov. 13, 1948).

She took over Mary Hatcher's role as Dallas Smith during the run of *Texas, Li'l Darlin'* (Mark Hellinger Th., Nov. 25, 1949); took over Martha Raye's role as Annie during the run of *Annie Get Your Gun* (NY City Ctr., Feb. 19, 1958); in stock, played Nellie Forbush in *South Pacific* (Highland Park, Ill., 1955); at the Meadowbrook (N.J.) Dinner Th., played Babe Williams in *The Pajama Game* (1958), and Annie Oakley in *Annie Get Your Gun* (Sept.–Nov. 1961); substituted (May 1961) for Lucille Ball as Wildcat Jackson in *Wildcat* (Alvin, N.Y.C., Dec. 16, 1960), and later succeeded Miss

Ball in the same role; and appeared as Mamie Candijack in *Sail Away* (Broadhurst, Oct. 3, 1961).

Television. She has appeared on the Jack Paar Show (NBC), the Ed Sullivan Show (CBS), the Robert Alda Show (ABC), Suspense (CBS), the Mohawk Rug Show (ABC), and Mazda at Home Show (ABC).

Night Clubs. Miss Watson has performed at the Palmer House (Chicago, Ill.), Mayflower Hotel (Washington, D.C.). Hotel Pierre (N.Y.C.), and the Bismarck Hotel (Chicago).

Recreation. Swimming.

WATSON, DOUGLASS. Actor. b. Larkin Douglass Watson III, Feb. 24, 1921, Jackson, Ga., to Larkin Douglass, Jr., and Caroline (Smith) Watson. Father, teacher. Grad. Riverside Military Acad., Gainesville, Ga., 1938; Univ. of North Carolina, A.B. 1942. Studied acting with Maria Ouspenskaya, Hollywood, Calif., 1942–43. Married Nov. 28, 1942, to Harriett Eugenia Loaring-Clark; one son, two daughters. Served WW II, USAAF; awarded Distinguished Flying Cross, Air Medal with five Clusters, and Purple Heart (twice). Member of AEA; SAG; AGMA; AFTRA. Address: 11 Sagamore Rd., Island Park, NY 11558, tel. (516) GE 1-1105.

Theatre. Mr. Watson first performed as a dancer, with the Martha Graham Company, in *Letter to the World, Dark Meadow,* and other of Miss Graham's works, on Bway and on tour. He made his acting debut as Rugby (servant to Dr. Caius), and later as Fenton, in a tour of *The Merry Wives of Windsor,* starring Charles Coburn (opened Playhouse, Wilmington, Del., Mar. 15, 1946; closed His Majesty's, Montreal, Canada, Sept. 14, 1946); subsequently played the role of Don Parritt in the Bway co. of *The Iceman Cometh* (Martin Beck Th., Oct. 9, 1946) for one performance late in the run, before playing the role in the Th. Guild tour; followed by Eros in *Antony and Cleopatra* (Martin Beck, N.Y.C., Nov. 26, 1947). He succeeded (May 25, 1948) Arthur Franz as Capt. Jenks in *Command Decision* (Fulton, Oct. 1, 1947); played Eugene in *The Leading Lady* (National, Oct. 18, 1948); Dorset in *Richard III* (Booth, Feb. 8, 1949); Richard Johnson in *The Happiest Years* (Lyceum, Apr. 25, 1949); was standby for Richard Hart as Bert Warren in *Leaf and Bough* (Cort, Jan. 21, 1949); played Rodrigo in *That Lady* (Martin Beck Th., Nov. 22, 1949); Peter Whitfield in *The Wisteria Trees* (Martin Beck Th., Mar. 29, 1950); Romeo in *Romeo and Juliet* (Broadhurst, Mar. 10, 1951); Andre in a summer theatre tour of *Her Cardboard Lover* (commencing May 1, 1951); and a Messenger in Judith Anderson's *Medea* (Berlin Festival, Ger., Sept. 1, 1951).

Also, Eben Cabot in *Desire Under the Elms* (ANTA, N.Y.C., Jan. 16, 1952); Herbert Westman in *The Brass Ring* (Lyceum, Apr. 10. 1952); Mike Decker in *Sunday Breakfast* (Coronet, May 28, 1952); appeared in *Murder in the Family* (Berkshire Playhouse, Stockbridge, Mass., Summer 1952); succeeded (Jan. 1, 1953) John Ericson as Sefton in the national tour of *Stalag 17* (opened Biltmore, Los Angeles, June 26, 1952; closed Natl., Washington, D.C., May 16, 1953); played Lord Ravensbane in *The Scarecrow* (Th. de Lys, N.Y.C., June 16, 1953); and Don in *Time of the Cuckoo* (Central City Festival, Colo., Summer 1953).

At NY City Ctr. he appeared as Christian de Neuvillette in *Cyrano de Bergerac* (Nov. 11, 1953), and Henry, Earl of Richmond, in *Richard III* (Dec. 9, 1953); played Colby Simpkins in *The Confidential Clerk* (Morosco, Feb. 11, 1954); the Son in *This Happy Breed* (John Drew Th., East Hampton, N.Y., Summer 1954); Ralph Touchett in *Portrait of a Lady* (ANTA, N.Y.C., Dec. 21, 1954); Valere in *The Miser* (Downtown Natl. Th., Mar. 24, 1955); and as artist-in-residence at Stanford Univ., Hippolytos in *The Cretan Woman* and Kilroy in *Camino Real* (June 1955); played Anthony Harker in *The Young and Beautiful* (Longacre, Oct. 1, 1955); and Armand, Comte de Montfort, in *Little Glass Clock* (John Golden Th., Mar. 26, 1956); at the Cambridge (Mass.) Drama Festival, he played the title role in *Henry V* (Harvard Univ., Sanders Th., July 5, 1956); Valentine in *You Never Can Tell* (John Drew Th., East Hampton, N.Y., Summer 1956); and Gregor in *Metamorphosis,* and Golaud in *Pelleas and Melisande,* both of which productions he devised for the Kuriakos Th. (ANTA Matinee Series, Th. de Lys, N.Y.C., Feb. 19, 1957).

He was standby for Cliff Robertson as Val Xavier in *Orpheus Descending* (Martin Beck Th., Mar. 21, 1957); was narrator for the Kuriakos Th. production of *Pale Horse, Pale Rider* (White Barn, Westport, Conn., Sept. 15, 1957; Jan Hus Th., N.Y.C., Dec. 9, 1957); succeeded (Dec. 12, 1957) Richard Easton as Mr. Harcourt in *The Country Wife* (Adelphi, Nov. 27, 1957); succeeded (Mar. 1, 1958) Gerlad Metcalf as Brian O'Bannion in the national touring co. of *Auntie Mame* (opened Hanna, Cleveland, Ohio, Oct. 30, 1957; closed Erlanger, Chicago, Ill., Jan. 17, 1959); played Jason Redwine in *Season of Choice* (Barbizon-Plaza Th., N.Y.C., Apr. 13, 1959); and toured stock theatres as M. Redon-la Mur in *Nina* (Summer 1959).

At the Amer. Shakespeare Festival (Stratford, Conn.), he played Leontes in *The Winter's Tale* (Apr. 25, 1960), Canidius in *Antony and Cleopatra* (Aug. 1, 1960), and on national tour, in repertory, repeated his role in *The Winter's Tale,* and played Lysander in *A Midsummer Night's Dream* (opened Colonial, Boston, Sept. 26, 1960); closed National, Washington, D.C., Feb. 25, 1961); also, at the Amer. Shakespeare Festival, he played Orsino in *Twelfth Night* (Apr. 10, 1961). For the National Shakespeare Festival (San Diego, Calif.), he played the title role in *Richard III;* Antonio in *The Merchant of Venice;* and Orsino in *Twelfth Night* (Old Globe Th., Summer 1961).

He played Bassanio in *The Merchant of Venice* (Gate, N.Y.C., Feb. 2, 1961); was standby for Patrick O'Neal as Rev. T. Lawrence Shannon in *The Night of the Iguana* (Royale, Dec. 28, 1961); succeeded (June 25, 1962) Keith Baxter as King Henry VIII in *A Man for All Seasons* (ANTA, Nov. 22, 1961); at the American Shakespeare Festival, appeared as Edmund in *King Lear,* Antipholus in *The Comedy of Errors,* and the Dauphin in *Henry V* (Summer 1963). He played Brother Dominic in the opera, *Jeanne d'arc au bûcher (Joan at the Stake)* (NY City Ctr., Oct. 3, 1963), Tarver in *The Chinese Prime Minister* (Royale, Jan. 3, 1964); and at the Amer. Shakespeare Fest., played the title role in *Richard III,* and Don Pedro in *Much Ado About Nothing* (Summer 1964).

Mr. Watson played Prospero in *The Tempest* (Univ. of Southern Florida, Nov. 1964); succeeded (Dec. 1965) to a role in *The Right Honorable Gentleman* (Billy Rose Th., N.Y.C., Oct. 19, 1965); at the Amer. Shakespeare Fest., played Pistol in *Falstaff (Henry IV, Part II,* June 18, 1966), Sir Hugh de Morville in *Murder in the Cathedral* (June 19, 1966), and Brutus in *Julius Caesar* (June 22, 1966); played Wadsworth in *Come Slowly, Eden* (ANTA Matinee Series, Th. de Lys, N.Y.C., Dec. 5–6, 1966); the Herald in *Marat/Sade* (revived Majestic, Jan. 3, 1967); Sir Thomas More in *A Man For All Seasons* (Univ. of Wisconsin, Madison, Feb. 1967); at the National Shakespeare Fest. (San Diego, Calif.), played the title role in *Othello* (June 15, 1967) and Parolles in *All's Well That Ends Well* (June 16, 1967); and played Mr. Perry, and succeeded Roy Cooper as Teddy Lloyd in *The Prime of Miss Jean Brodie* (Helen Hayes Th., N.Y.C., Jan. 16, 1968).

He played Maj. Gen. Stanley in *The Pirates of Penzance* (NY City Ctr., Apr. 25, 1968); played the title role in a tour of *Dylan* (Spring 1969); Teddy Lloyd in a tour of *The Prime of Miss Jean Brodie* (Summer 1969); Vershinin in *The Three Sisters* (Seattle, Wash., Rep. Th., Nov. 19, 1969); toured as Victor Franz in *The Price* (opened Paper Mill Playhouse, Millburn, N.J., Jan. 13, 1970; closed Music Hall, Wichita, Kans., Apr. 23, 1970); played Jack in Mayo Simon's *L.A. under Siege* (New Th. for Now, Mark Taper Forum, Los Angeles, Aug. 2, 1970); at the Seattle, Wash., Rep. Th., played Buffalo Bill in *Indians* (Oct. 21, 1970) and John of Gaunt in *Richard II* (Mar. 6, 1971); played Father Phillip Berrigan in *The Trial of the Catonsville Nine* (Center Th. Group, Mark Taper Forum, Los Angeles, June 17, 1971); with the NY Shakespeare Fest., played the title role in *The Hunter* (Public Th. Annex, May 23, 1972), Don Pedro in *Much Ado About Nothing* (Delacorte, Aug. 16, 1972, and Winter Garden, Nov. 11, 1972), the Duke Senior in *As You Like It* (Delacorte, June 21, 1973) and Kent in *King Lear* (Delacorte, July 26, 1973); and played Norwin Spokesman in *Over Here* (Shubert, Mar. 6, 1974).

Films. Mr. Watson has appeared in *Julius Caesar* (MGM, 1953); *Sayonara* (WB, 1957); Father Phillip Berrigan in *The Trial of the Catonsville Nine* (Cinema V, 1972); and in *Ulzana's Raid* (U, 1972).

Television. Mr. Watson has appeared in *The Sire de Maletroit's Door* (Starlight Th., CBS, Apr. 30, 1950); *Richard III* (NBC, July 30, 1950); Kraft Television Th. (NBC); Robert Montgomery Presents (NBC); *The Dark Side of the Moon* (NBC, Aug. 18, 1957); Lamp Unto My Feet (CBS); etc. He has also been a regular performer on the daytime series, Moment of Truth (NBC); Search for Tomorrow (CBS); and as Mackenzie Cory on Another World (NBC, to date).

Awards. He received the *Theatre World* Award for his performance as Eros in *Antony and Cleopatra* (1948); the Clarence Derwent Award for his performances in *That Lady* and *The Wisteria Trees* (1950); the *Variety* Poll of NY Drama Critics for *The Wisteria Trees* (1950); and a Drama Desk Award for *Much Ado About Nothing* (1973).

WATSON, LEE. Lighting designer. b. Leland Hale Watson, Feb. 18, 1926, Charleston, Ill., to Dallas V. and Hazel (Emma) Watson. Father, railroad telegrapher; mother, politician. Grad. Eastern Illinois State Teachers Coll. H.S., Charleston, 1943; State Univ. of Iowa, B.A. (Phi Beta Kappa) 1948; Yale Univ., M.F.A. 1951. Served US Army, Infantry, 1945–46; rank, Pvt. Member of AEA; IATSA, Theatrical Protective Union, #1; United Scenic Artists, Local 829 (vice-pres., 1961–63; lighting trustee, 1973–to date); SAA; ATA; TLA; USITT; Phi Sigma Epsilon. Address: 40-04 215th Place, Bayside, NY 11361, tel. (212) 224-8611.

Pre-Theatre. Radio engineer.

Theatre. While in high school, Mr. Watson worked at first as technical director for the Eastern Ill. State Teachers Coll. productions of plays and variety shows (1940). He first worked as a professional lighting designer for *Earth Spirit* (Provincetown Playhouse, N.Y.C., June 1950); subsequently worked as lighting designer and technical director at the Norwich (Conn.) Summer Th. (1950); made his Bway debut as lighting designer for *The Traveling Lady* (Playhouse Th., Oct. 27, 1954); for the *ANTA Album* (Adelphi, 1954); *A View from the Bridge* (Coronet, Sept. 29, 1955); *The Diary of Anne Frank* (Cort, Oct. 5, 1955); for the pre-Bway tryout of *Dancing in the Chequered Shade* (opened McCarter Th., Princeton, N.J., Dec. 20, 1955; closed Wilbur, Boston, Mass., Dec. 31, 1955); was projection supervisor for *The Lovers* (Martin Beck Th., N.Y.C., May 10, 1956); was technical and lighting director for *The Teahouse of the August Moon* on a tour of the Caribbean and South America (1956); was lighting designer for *Harbor Lights* (Playhouse, N.Y.C., Oct. 4, 1956); *Girls of Summer* (Longacre, Nov. 19, 1956); *Protective Custody* (Ambassador, Dec. 28, 1956); *A Moon for the Misbegotten* (Bijou, May 2, 1957); *Mask and Gown* (John Golden Th., Sept. 10, 1957); *The Cave Dwellers* (Bijou, Oct. 19, 1957); *Miss Isobel* (Royale, Dec. 26, 1957); *Garden District* (York, Jan. 7, 1958); for the pre-Bway tryout of *This Is Goggle* (opened McCarter, Princeton, N.J., Jan. 23, 1958; closed Shubert, Washington, D.C., Feb. 1, 1958); and for *Portofino* (Adelphi, N.Y.C., Feb. 21, 1958).

He was scenic and lighting designer for *The Next President* (Bijou, Apr. 9, 1958); for the NY City Opera, was lighting designer for *Lost in the Stars* (NY City Ctr., Apr. 10, 1958) and *Good Soldier Schweik* (NY City Ctr., Apr. 23, 1958); for *Comic Strip* (Barbizon-Plaza, May 14, 1958); *Roberto Iglesias Ballet Español* (Bway, Oct. 7, 1958); scenic supervisor for *Theatre National Populaire* (Bway, Oct. 14, 1958); lighting designer for the NY City Opera's production of *The Rape of Lucretia* (NY

City Ctr., Oct. 23, 1958); for *The Golden Six* (York, Oct. 25, 1958); the *Beryozka Russian Dance Company* (Bway Th., Nov. 4, 1958); *The Night Circus* (John Golden Th., Dec. 2, 1958); *On the Town* (Carnegie Hall Playhouse, Jan. 15, 1959); for the pre-Bway tryout of *The Poker Game* (opened Shubert, Washington, D.C., Jan. 16, 1959; closed Forrest, Philadelphia, Pa., Jan. 31, 1959); *The Legend of Lizzie* (54 St. Th., N.Y.C., Feb. 9, 1959); for the touring production of *Garden District* (opened Warren, Atlantic City, N.J., Mar. 11, 1959; closed Civic Th., Chicago, Ill., May 30, 1959); for the NY City Opera, was lighting designer for *Maria Golovin* (NY City Ctr., Mar. 30, 1959), and for the double bill, *The Scarf* and *The Devil and Daniel Webster* (NY City Ctr., Apr. 5, 1959).

Mr. Watson was lighting designer for Dos Passos' *U.S.A.* Martinique, Oct. 28, 1959); the European production of *Free and Easy* (Carre Th., Amsterdam, Netherlands, Dec. 17, 1959); the Bolshoi Ballet tour of the US and Canada (commencing Apr. 18, 1959); the Bayanihan Phillipines Dance Co. (Winter Garden, N.Y.C., Oct. 13, 1959); scenery and lighting designer for *A Lovely Light* (Hudson, Feb. 8, 1960); lighting designer for *The Jackass* (Barbizon-Plaza, Mar. 23, 1960); *Port Royale* (Grace Church, Apr. 24, 1960); *The Pretenders* (Cherry Lane, May 24, 1960); *Machinal* (Gate, Apr. 7, 1960); *The Shoemaker and the Peddler* (E. 74 St. Th., Oct. 14, 1960); the Pontiac Show (Detroit, Mich., 1960); production designer for *The Importance of Being Oscar* (Lyceum, Mar. 14, 1961); production designer for *Moby Dick* (Madison Ave. Playhouse, Apr. 10, 1961); lighting designer for *The Blacks* (St. Mark's Playhouse, May 4, 1961); for *Men, Women and Angels, A Midsummer Night's Dream,* and *Do You Know the Milky Way?* (Vancouver Festival, B.C., Can., Summer 1961); for the pre-Bway tryout of *High Fidelity* (opened Walnut St. Th., Philadelphia, Pa., Sept. 14, 1961; closed there Sept. 16, 1961); *Do You Know the Milky Way?* (Billy Rose Th., N.Y.C., Oct. 16, 1961); the opera, *Second Hurricane* (Museum of Modern Art, Jan. 26, 1961); *Madame Aphrodite* (Orpheum, Dec. 29, 1961); the Chevrolet Show (Detroit, Mich., 1961); the Coca Cola Show (Miami, Fla., 1961); Century 21, Seattle (Wash.) World's Fair (1962); and the Chevrolet Show (Detroit, Mich., 1962).

Mr. Watson was also lighting designer for the Joske Fashion Show (Music Hall, Houston, Tex., 1968); Houston Jazz Ballet (Jones Hall, Houston, 1968); Houston Ballet Foundation's *Giselle* (Jones Hall, 1968) and the company's seven-state tour (1969). He designed lighting for Houston Grand Opera productions of *Madame Butterfly, Salomé, La Bohème, Tales of Hoffman, The Ballad of Baby Doe* (also sets and projections), *Cavalleria Rusticana, Gianni Schicchi, Turandot, Fledermaus, Aida,* Orff's *The Moon, Pagliacci,* and *Carmen* (all Jones Hall, Houston, 1968–72); for the Louise Nevelson Sculpture Show (Museum of Fine Arts, Houston, 1969); for *Iolanthe, H.M.S. Pinafore,* and *Trial by Jury* (Jones Hall, 1969–70); and for *The Boy Friend, Kismet, Once Upon a Mattress, Gypsy, Can-Can,* and *South Pacific* (all Theatre-under-the-Stars, Miller Th., Houston, 1969–72).

He designed lighting for the Dallas (Tex.) Civic Opera's *Rigoletto* (State Fair Music Hall, 1970); for the Missouri Rep. Th. productions in Kansas City, Mo., of *The Skin of Our Teeth* (July 2, 1970), *Harvey* (July 9, 1970), *Indians* (July 16, 1970), *Exit the King* (July 23, 1970), *The Tempest* (Aug. 6, 1970), and *Arms and the Man* (Aug. 13, 1970); for productions by Arena Stage, Washington, D.C., of *The Night Thoreau Spent in Jail* (Oct. 23, 1970), *Pueblo* (Feb. 26, 1971), and *Wipe-Out Games* (Apr. 9, 1971); for *A Midsummer Night's Dream* (Miller Th., Houston, Tex., 1971); for the ballet *Cinderella* (Margo Marshall Ballet, Jones Hall, Houston, 1971); and for the children's play *Bird Boy* (Jones Hall, 1971).

He also designed lighting for the Florentine Opera Company's *Madame Butterfly* (Uihlein Th., Milwaukee, Wis., 1972); for *Dear Janet Rosenberg, Dear Mr. Koening* (Cubiculo Th., N.Y.C., June 8, 1972); *A Quarter for the Ladies Room* (Village Gate, Nov. 12, 1972; the Baltimore (Md.) Opera's *Carmen* (1973); the *Pontiac Show* (Detroit, Mich., 1973); and for *The Little Foxes* (Walnut St. Th., Philadelphia, Pa., Apr. 11, 1974).

He was lighting designer for the NY City Opera for *The Turn of the Screw* (NY City Ctr., Mar. 25, 1962), and *Carmen* (NY City Ctr., Oct. 14, 1962); lighting designer and supervisor at the Seattle (Wash.) World's Fair, for the Swedish Royal Dramatic Th. productions of *The Father, Miss Julie,* and *Long Day's Journey into Night,* and lighting designer for the Ceylon Dancers (Summer 1962); was lighting designer for *The Cherry Orchard* (Theatre Four, N.Y.C., Nov. 14, 1962); and for the revue, *Lamb's Gambol* (Waldorf-Astoria Hotel, Apr. 6, 1963).

Television. From 1951 to 1955, Mr. Watson was lighting director at CBS for numerous programs, including Casey Crime Photographer; and was lighting director for the Arthur Murray Dance Party (Dumont, 1953); lighting director and scenic designer for *Get Set, Go* for the US Army Signal Corps (1956–57); lighting consultant for S. McKenna (UN TV, 1958); and was lighting director for commercials for Videotape Productions (1960–63), and for MGM Telestudios (1959–63).

Night Clubs. He was lighting designer for *Viva La Femme* (Latin Quarter, N.Y.C., 1960).

Other Activities. Mr. Watson was an instructor at Utah State Agricultural College, Logan, Utah 1948–49); and has taught at Brooklyn (N.Y.) College (1950, 1955); at Polakov Studio of Design, N.Y.C. (1958–62); the Univ. of Houston (1968–70); and C. W. Post College, Long Island Univ., Greenvale, N.Y., where he was appointed assistant professor in 1971.

Published Works. Mr. Watson wrote, with Joel E. Rubin, *Theatrical Lighting Practice* (1955) and is author of articles that have appeared in *World Theatre, Educational Theatre Journal, Nation's Schools, Player's* and the *American School Board Journal*.

Awards. *Machinal* (1960) won a *Village Voice* off-Bway (Obie) Award as best physical production of the year.

Recreation. Swimming, ballet, classical music.

WATSON, SUSAN. Actress, singer, dancer. b. Susan Elizabeth Watson, Dec. 17, 1938, Tulsa, Okla., to Robert J. and Gretchen (Warren) Watson. Father, geologist, geophysicist. Grad. Central H.S., Tulsa, 1957; attended Juilliard Sch. of Music, 1957–58. Studied dancing with Suzanne Aker, Tulsa, 1954–57; Hanya Holm, N.Y.C., 1955; Peter Gennaro, N.Y.C., 1958–62; acting with Uta Hagen at HB Studio, N.Y.C., 1959–62; singing with Tony Franco, N.Y.C., 1961; Karen Gustafson, N.Y.C., 1962. Married Oct. 30, 1959, to Roger LePage, actor (marr. dis. 1963); married Feb. 16, 1964, to Norton W. Wright, producer; one son. Address: c/o International Famous Agency, 1301 Ave. of the Americas, New York, NY 10019, tel. (212) 556-5600.

Theatre. Miss Watson made her first appearance on a stage as a dancer in her high school's production of *Green Grow the Lilacs* (Tulsa, 1954).

She made her professional debut as Baby Betsy in *By the Beautiful Sea* (Starlight Th., Kansas City, Mo., Summer 1957); subsequently appeared in the ensemble and played minor roles in *Silk Stockings,* and *Happy Hunting* (Toronto Music Tent, Canada, Summer 1958); played Velma and understudied Marlys Watters as Maria in *West Side Story* (Her Majesty's Th., London, Eng., Dec. 12, 1958); played the Girl in the premiere of *The Fantasticks* (Minor Latham Th., N.Y.C., 1959); and appeared in the revues, *Lend an Ear* (Renata, Sept. 24, 1959), and *Follies of 1910* (Carnegie Playhouse, Jan. 12, 1960).

She played Kim MacAfee in *Bye Bye Birdie* (Martin Beck Th., Apr. 14, 1960); toured as Lili in the national company of *Carnival!* (opened Rochester Aud., N.Y., Dec. 7, 1961), also taking over for Anna Marie Alberghetti as Lili during the N.Y.C. run (Imperial, Apr. 13, 1961); and played Louise in *Gypsy,* and Lili in *Carnival!* (St. Louis Municipal Opera, Mo., Summer 1963).

She was Janine Nicolet in *Ben Franklin in Paris* (Lunt-Fontanne Th., Oct. 27, 1964); Carrie in a revival of *Carousel* (NY State Th., Aug. 10, 1965); Laurey in a revival of *Oklahoma!* (NY City Ctr., Dec. 15, 1965); Amy in a revival of *Where's Charley?* (NY City Ctr., May 25, 1966); Jenny Lee in *A Joyful Noise* (Mark Hellinger Th., Dec. 15, 1966); Angel in *Celebration* (Ambassador, Jan. 22, 1969); Cynthia Mason in *Beggar on Horseback* (Vivian Beaumont Th., May 14, 1970); Nanette in a revival of *No, No, Nanette* (46 St. Th., Jan. 19, 1971); and appeared in a revival of *Funny Face* (Studio Arena, Buffalo, N.Y., Dec. 6, 1973; Ford's Th., Washington, D.C., Jan. 2, 1974).

She played the title role in *Gigi* at various theatres (Paper Mill Playhouse, Millburn, N.J.; Poinciana Playhouse, Palm Beach, Fla.; Westport Country Th., Westport, Conn.); was Fran Kubelik in *Promises, Promises* (Meadow Brook Th., Cedar Grove, N.J., 1972; Milwaukee Melody Top, Milwaukee, Wis., 1973); Marian in *Music Man* (Paper Mill Playhouse, Millburn, N.J.); and appeared at the Sylvan Th., Washington Shakespeare Festival in 1974 as Viola in *Twelfth Night* and Cecily in *The Importance of Being Earnest*.

Television. Miss Watson has appeared on American Musical Th. (CBS, 1962); the Dobie Gillis Show, (CBS, 1963); in the pilot film for *Trader Brown* (CBS, 1963); on the Bell Telephone Hour (NBC, 1964); in *The Fantasticks* (Hallmark Hall of Fame, NBC, 1964); and *Rodgers and Hart Revisited* (Studio 2, CBS, 1964); *Jerome Kern and the Princess* (Studio 2, CBS); *The Front Page* (Metromedia); Sesame Street (PBS, 1970); and the David Frost Show (1971).

Awards. She received the Tulsa Philharmonic Youth Concert Award (1955); the Tulsa Opera Dance Scholarship (1956); and was nominated for an Antoinette Perry (Tony) Award (1967) for best supporting actress in a musical for her performance in *A Joyful Noise*.

Recreation. Water sports, diving, skiing, traveling.

WATT, DOUGLAS. Drama critic, composer, writer. b. Jan. 20, 1914, New York City, to Benjamin and Agnes Watt. Father, structural engineer. Grad. P.S. 44, Bronx, N.Y.; Bogota (N.J.) H.S., 1930; Cornell Univ., 1934. Married Nov. 5, 1937, to Ray Mantel; two sons. Married Aug. 27, 1951, to Ethe Madsen; two daughters. Served U.S.A.A.F., WW II. Member of NY Drama Critics Circle (vice-pres., 1973–75; pres., 1975–77); ASCAP; AGAC; Newspaper Guild. Address: (home) 27 W. 86th St., New York, NY 10024, tel. (212) TR 7-2320; (bus.) 220 E. 42nd St., New York, NY 10017, tel. (212) MU 2-1234.

Mr. Watt is the drama critic for the NY *Daily News* (1971–to date).

Other Activities. Songs written by Mr. Watt that have been published and recorded include *There's Not a Moment To Spare* (1939); *After All These Years* (1940); *I'd Do It Again* (1941); *Man* (1945); and *Heaven Help Me* (1968).

Recreation. Reading, swimming, golfing.

WATTS, RICHARD. Drama critic. b. Stephen Richard Watts, Jr., Jan. 12, 1898, Parkersburg, W.Va., to Richard Watts Sr., and Katherine (Reed) Watts. Grad. Townsend Harris H.S.; attended Columbia Univ., N.Y.C., 1917–21. Served in Students Army Training Corps, 1917; OWI, 1942–44. Member of NY Drama Critics Circle; NY Newspaper Guild. c/o New York *Post,* 210 South St., New York, NY 10002, tel. (212) 349-5000.

Mr. Watts was a reporter for the Brooklyn *Times* (1922–23); asst. night editor, Herald Sun Syndicate (1923–24); film critic for the NY *Herald Tribune* (1924–36); drama critic for the NY *Herald Tribune* (1936–42); and since 1946, drama critic for the NY *Post,* from which position he retired in May 1974, but continued to write a Saturday drama column as well as occasional other pieces (to date).

Awards. He won the James R. Quirk Award in 1974.

WAYNE, DAVID. Actor. b. Wayne James McMeekan, Jan. 30, 1914, Traverse City, Mich., to David and Helen (Mason) McMeekan. Father, salesman. Grad. Bloomingdale (Mich.) H.S.; attended Western Michigan Univ., 1931–33. Married Dec. 21, 1941, to Jane Trix; one son, two daughters. Served Amer. Field Service, Egypt and Libya, 1941–43; rank, Lt.; US Army, 1944–46; rank, 1st Lt. Member of AEA (on council, 1948, 1957); AFTRA; SAG; The Lambs; The Players; The Friars; Weston Gun Club.

Pre-Theatre. Statistician.

Theatre. Mr. Wayne made his first professional appearance as Touchstone in a Cleveland (Ohio) Exposition production of *As You Like It* (Globe Th., June 1, 1936); and during Sept. 1936–June 1937, he toured Eastern and Southern states with the Tatterman Marionettes.

He made his N.Y.C. debut as a walk-on in *Escape This Night* (44 St. Th., Apr. 22, 1938); appeared in stock productions at the Chase Barn Th. (Whitefield, N.H., Summer 1938); played Harvey Bodine in *Dance Night* (Belasco, N.Y.C., Oct. 14, 1938); Karl Gunther in *The American Way* (Center, Jan. 1, 1939); toured as Michael in *The Male Animal* (1939); played Jimmy Hanley in *Scene of the Crime* (Fulton, Mar. 28, 1940); Nish in *The Merry Widow* (Majestic, Aug. 4, 1943); His Conscience in *Peep Show* (Fulton, Feb. 3, 1944); and Mrs. Meachem in *Park Avenue* (Shubert, Nov. 4, 1946).

Also, Og in *Finian's Rainbow* (46 St. Th., Jan. 10, 1947); Ensign Pulver in *Mr. Roberts* (Alvin, Feb. 18, 1948); Sakini in *The Teahouse of the August Moon* (Martin Beck Th., Oct. 15, 1953); Uncle Daniel Ponder in *The Ponder Heart* (Music Box, Feb. 16, 1956); Mr. Finnegan in *The Loud Red Patrick* (Ambassador, Oct. 3, 1956); Jack Jordan in *Say, Darling* (ANTA, April 3, 1958); Juniper in the pre-Bway tryout of *Juniper and the Pagans* (opened Colonial, Boston, Mass., Dec. 10, 1959; closed Forrest, Philadelphia, Pa., Dec. 26, 1959); George Kimball in *Send Me No Flowers* (Brooks Atkinson Th., N.Y.C., Dec. 5, 1960); Sonny Stone in *Venus at Large* (Morosco, Apr. 12, 1961); and Private Meek in *Too True To Be Good* (54 St. Th., Mar. 12, 1963).

In 1964, he joined the Lincoln Ctr. Repertory Co., and at the ANTA-Washington Sq. Th., played the Chairman in *After the Fall* (Jan. 23, 1964), Kublai, the Great Kaan, in *Marco Millions* (Feb. 20, 1964), Brock Dunnaway in *But for Whom Charlie* (Mar. 12, 1964), and Von Berg, a Prince, in *Incident at Vichy* (Dec. 3, 1964). He played Ezra Baxter in *The Yearling* (Alvin, Dec. 10, 1965); Captain Andy in *Show Boat* (NY State Th., July 19, 1966); Dr. Jack Kingsley in *The Impossible Years* (Playhouse-in-the-Park, Philadelphia, Pa., June 1966; and Royal Poinciana Playhouse, Palm Beach, Fla., Jan. 1967); Grandpere Bounard in *The Happy Time* (Bway Th., N.Y.C., Jan. 18, 1967); presented a solo evening entitled *An Unpleasant Evening with H. L. Mencken* (Ford's Th., Washington, D.C., 1971); and appeared with the Bucks County Playhouse (New Hope, Pa., Summer 1972).

Films. Mr. Wayne made his debut as Mitch in *Portrait of Jenny* (Selznick, 1948); subsequently appeared in *Adam's Rib* (MGM, 1949); *Reformer and the Red Head* (MGM, 1950); *My Blue Heaven* (20th-Fox, 1950); *Stella* (20th-Fox, 1950); *"M"* (Col., 1951); *Up Front* (U, 1951); *As Young As You Feel* (20th-Fox, 1951); *Wait Till the Sun Shines Nellie* (20th-Fox, 1951); *O. Henry's Full House* (20th-Fox, 1952); *We're Not Married* (1952); *With a Song in My Heart* (20th-Fox, 1952); *I Married a Millionaire* (20th-Fox, 1952); *Tonight We Sing* (20th-Fox, 1953); *The 'I Don't Care' Girl* (20th-Fox, 1953); *The Tender Trap* (MGM, 1955); *The Last Angry Man* (Col., 1959); *The Big Gamble* (20th-Fox, 1961); and *Huckleberry Finn* (UA, 1974).

Television. Mr. Wayne first appeared in an Actors' Studio production of *The Thousand Dollar Bill* (ABC, 1948). Subsequent appearances include Sam Benedict (Ind., 1965); The Trailmaster (ABC, 1964–65); *The Lincoln Center Day* special (CBS, 1964); Burke's Law (ABC, 1964); Wendy and Me (ABC, 1964–65); The Bing Crosby Show (ABC, 1964); Mr. Broadway (CBS, 1964); Naked City (Ind., 1965); Twilight Zone (Ind., 1965); Batman (ABC, 1966); Alumni Fun (CBS, 1965); Route 66 (Ind. 1966); Hallmark Hall of Fame (NBC, 1966); Bob Hope Presents (NBC, 1966); Alfred Hitchcock Presents (Ind., 1966); The American Sportsman (ABC, 1967); *The Legend of Mark Twain* (ABC, 1967); CBS Playhouse; *Arsenic and Old Lace* (ABC); The World of Disney (NBC); Matt Lincoln (ABC); Name of the Game (NBC); The Good Life (NBC); Men at Law (CBS); Cade's County (CBS); The Streets of San Francisco (ABC); Eye on New York (WCBS); and Ellery Queen (NBC).

Awards. For his performance as Og in *Finian's Rainbow*, Mr. Wayne received an Antoinette Perry (Tony) Award (1947), a Drama Guild Award (1948), and a Comoedia Club Award (1948). For his performance as Sakini in *The Teahouse of the August Moon*, he received an Antoinette Perry (Tony) Award, a Drama Guild Award, a Comoedia Club Award, and The Barter Th. Award (1954).

Recreation. Golf, shooting, fishing, boating.

WAYNE, PAULA. Actress, singer. b. Paula Watkins, Nov. 3, 1937, Hobart, Okla., to Ralph and Jewell Watkins. Father, rancher. Grad. high school. Mountain View, Okla., 1954; attended Oklahoma Coll. for Women, 1954–55 (scholarship); Married Oct. 24, 1956, to Robert I Myerson, stage manager, director, writer; one son, one daughter (marr. dis.); married to Robert Shelley. Member of AEA; AFTRA; SAG; Sigma Alpha Iota.

Pre-Theatre. Model.

Theatre. Miss Wayne first performed in the chorus on a tour of *Damn Yankees* (1956); made her N.Y.C. debut as Ziegfeldian in *Ziegfeld Follies* (Winter Garden Th., Mar. 1, 1957); subsequently played Violet in *Wonderful Town* (NY City Ctr., Mar. 5, 1958); Cheryl Merrill in *Say, Darling* (NY City Ctr., Feb. 25, 1959); Sheila in *Hi, Paisano!* (York Playhouse, Sept. 30, 1961); the Young Woman in *Night Life* (Brooks Atkinson Th., Oct. 23, 1962); performed in the ELT production of *Paint Your Wagon* (Master Inst., Feb. 24, 1962); as Gale Joy in *Best Foot Forward* (Stage 73, Apr. 2, 1963); and as Lorna Moon in *Golden Boy* (Majestic, Oct. 20, 1964). In summer stock, she has appeared in *Fiorello!, Oklahoma!, Roman Candle, Girl Crazy, Song of Norway, Meet Me in St. Louis*, and *Wish You Were Here*.

Films. She has dubbed voices in more than 50 foreign films for such performers as Gina Lollobrigida, Sophia Loren, and Claudia Cardinale.

Television and Radio. Miss Wayne has made frequent appearances on the radio show, Arthur Godfrey Time (CBS); and on television programs including The Tonight Show (NBC); The Verdict Is Yours (CBS); Our Five Daughters; Everglades; the Ethel Merman Chevy Special; the Sammy Davis Jr. Show (NBC); Memory Lane (Ind.); Girl Talk (ABC); the American Musical Th. series (CBS); Clay Cole Show (Ind.); Merv Griffin Show (Ind.); Upbeat (Ind.); Hawk (ABC); Mike Douglas Show (ABC); and the Swinging Sound Variety Special (Ind., 1967).

Night Clubs. Miss Wayne made her night club debut at the Flamingo (Las Vegas, Dec. 1965) and has subsequently played all over the country.

Awards. She received an operatic scholarship from Rose Bampton and Sir Wilfred Felletier (1955–56).

Recreation. Horseback riding, swimming, reading.

WEAVER, FRITZ. Actor. b. Jan. 19, 1926, Pittsburgh, Pa., to John C. and Elsa (Stringaro) Weaver. Grad. Peabody H.S., Pittsburgh, 1944; Univ. of Chicago, B.A., 1952. Studied at H B Studio, N.Y.C., 1955–56. Married Feb. 7, 1953, to Sylvia Short; one son, one daughter. Relative in theatre: sister, Mary Irene Weaver, television scenic designer. Member of AEA; SAG; AFTRA; AGMA. Address: (home) 161 W. 75th St., New York, NY 10023; (bus.) c/o Lucy Kroll Agency, 119 W. 57th St., New York, NY 10019, tel. (212) PL 7-4250.

Theatre. Mr. Weaver appeared in productions at the Barter Th. (Abingdon, Va.), and on their cross-country tours (1952–54). With the Group 20 Players (Wellesley, Mass.), he played Petruchio in *The Taming of the Shrew*, Sir Francis Chesney in *Charley's Aunt*, the Preacher in *Dark of the Moon*, Oberon in *A Midsummer Night's Dream*, Caesar in *Androcles and the Lion*, and Edward II in *Carnival King* (Summer 1953).

He made his N.Y.C. debut as Fainall in *The Way of the World* (Cherry Lane, Oct. 2, 1954); followed by a Secretary in *The Doctor's Dilemma* (Phoenix, Jan. 11, 1955); Flamineo in *The White Devil* (Phoenix, Mar. 17, 1955); and at the Amer. Shakespeare Festival (Stratford, Conn.) appeared as Casca in *Julius Caesar* (July 12, 1955), and Antonio in *The Tempest* (Aug. 1, 1955).

He played Maitland in *The Chalk Garden* (Ethel Barrymore Th., Oct. 26, 1955), at the Amer. Shakespeare Fest., Philip Faulconbridge in *King John* (June 26, 1956), and Gremio in *The Taming of the Shrew* (Aug. 5, 1956); Marc Bradley in *Protective Custody* (Ambassador, N.Y.C., Dec. 28, 1956); and the title role in *Miss Lonelyhearts* (Music Box, Oct. 3, 1957).

At the American Shakespeare Fest., Mr. Weaver played the title role in *Hamlet* (June 19, 1958); and appeared with the Phoenix Th. Co., (N.Y.C.), as Harry Lord Monchensey in *The Family Reunion* (Oct. 20, 1958), and the Priest in *The Power and the Glory* (Dec. 10, 1958); for the Cambridge (Mass.) Drama Festival, played Malvolio in *Twelfth Night* (June 1959); and for the Phoenix, Th. Co., Dion Anthony in *The Great God Brown* (Coronet, Oct. 6, 1959), the title role in *Peer Gynt* (Jan. 12, 1960), the title role in *Henry IV, Part 1* (Mar. 1, 1960); and the title role in *Henry IV, Part 2* (Apr. 18, 1960). He played the title role in *Henry IV, Parts 1 and 2* at the Cambridge Drama Festival (Summer 1960); and Mark in *Men, Women and Angels* at the Vancouver Festival (Queen Elizabeth Th., British Columbia, Canada Aug. 14, 1961).

He played Henderson in *All American* (Winter Garden, N.Y.C., Mar. 19, 1962); succeeded (Summer 1962) Walter Matthau as M. Beaurevers in *A Shot in the Dark* (Booth, Oct. 18, 1961); was Narrator, with the New York Philharmonic, of Debussy's *Martyrdom of St. Sebastian* (Philharmonic Hall, Sept. 30, 1962); played Van Miessen in *Lorenzo* (Plymouth, Feb. 14, 1963); Phileas Fogg in *Around the World in 80 Days* (Jones Beach Marine Th., N.Y., Summer 1963); and appeared in several roles in *The White House* (Henry Miller's Th., May 19, 1964).

Mr. Weaver played Sherlock Holmes in *Baker Street* (Broadway Th., N.Y.C., Feb. 16, 1965); Frederick the Great in *The Sorrows of Frederick* (Mark Taper Forum, Los Angeles, June 1967); Henry Higgins in *My Fair Lady* (NY City Cir., June 13, 1968); Jerome Malley in *Child's Play* (Royale, Feb. 17, 1970); the title role in *Macbeth* for the American Shakespeare Fest. (Stratford, Conn., 1973); and succeeded Richard Kiley (Mar. 7, 1975) in *Absurd Person Singular* (Music Box, N.Y.C.).

Films. Mr. Weaver narrated *The Crimson Curtain* (Rembrandt, 1955); appeared in *Fail-Safe* (Col., 1964); narrated *The Guns of August* (U, 1964); and appeared in *To Trap a Spy* (MGM, 1966); *The Maltese Bippy* (MGM, 1967); and *A Walk in the Spring Rain* (Col., 1970).

Television. He has appeared on Kraft Television Th. (NBC., Nov. 1955); Lamp Unto My Feet (CBS, Apr. 1955); *She Stoops to Conquer* (Omnibus, ABC, Nov. 1955); in *We Must Kill Tony* (US Steel Hour, CBS, Sept. 1956); *The Playwright and the Star* (Studio One, CBS; Apr. 1957); *The Deaf Heart* (Studio One, CBS, Oct. 1957); Armstrong Circle Th. (NBC, Feb. 1958); *A Moment of Truth* (Omnibus, NBC, Feb. 1958); *A Tale of Two Cities* (Dupont Show of the Month, NBC, Mar. 1958); *The Little Tin God* (US Steel Hour, CBS, Mar. 1959); *Out of the Dust* (Playhouse 90, CBS, Apr. 1959); in a scene from *The Crucible* (Salute to the American Theatre, CBS, Dec. 1959; Apr. 1960); and played Brutus in *Julius Caesar* (CBC, Canada, Oct. 1960).

He appeared in *The Potting Shed* (Play of the Week, WNTA, Jan. 1961); *The Devil Makes Sunday* (US Steel Hour CBS, Feb. 1961); *Jane Eyre* (Family

Classics, CBS, Apr. 1961); *The Power and the Glory* (NBC, Mar. 1961); *The Night of the Storm* (Dupont Show of the Month, NBC, Mar. 1961); on The Nurses (CBS, 1962); The Defenders (CBS, 1962); Dr. Kildare (NBC, 1963).

Mr. Weaver has appeared in numerous major network series and films, including Espionage (NBC); Great Adventures (CBS); The Man from U.N.C.L.E. (NBC); Rogues (NBC); 12 O'Clock High (ABC); Cain's Hundred (NBC); US Steel Hour (CBS); The Fugitive (ABC); Mission: Impossible (CBS); Combat (ABC); Experiment in Television (NBC); *The Crucible* (CBS); Room 222 (ABC); *The Borgia Stick* (NBC); The Invaders (ABC); The Big Valley (ABC); Gentle Ben (CBS); N.Y.P.D. (ABC); The F.B.I. (ABC); CBS Playhouse; Mannix (CBS); The Outcasts (ABC); Felony Squad (ABC); Ironside (NBC); *Berlin Affair* (NBC); Dan August (ABC); Cannon (CBS); Owen Marshall (ABC); *Heat of Anger* (CBS); Hunter (CBS); Banyon (NBC); and Mod Squad (ABC).

Awards. Mr. Weaver received the Clarence Derwent Award for his performance as Flamineo in *The White Devil* (1955); and a *Theatre World* Award for his performance as Maitland in *The Chalk Garden* (1956). He was nominated for the Antoinette Perry (Tony) Award for his performance as Maitland in *The Chalk Garden* (1955), and the title role in *Miss Lonelyhearts* (1957).

For his performance in *Child's Play* (1970), he received the *Variety* Critics Poll, the Outer Critics Circle, the Drama Desk and the Antoinette Perry (Tony) awards.

WEAVER, RICHARD A. Educator, playwright, designer, theatre manager. b. Richard Alden Weaver, Sept. 20, 1934, Okmulgee, Okla., to Alden Kirby and Winnie B. Weaver. Grad. Univ. of Oklahoma, B.F.A. 1959; M.F.A. 1964; Univ. of Missouri, Ph.D. 1973. Married 1952 to Jeane Steinert; three children (marr. dis. 1971); 1972 to Alice French, actress. Member of ATA (chmn., student playwriting awards for Southwest Region, ACTF, 1974–77; programs, 1974, 1975 conventions; state chmn., ACTF 1975–76); ANTA; SCA; SWTC; Texas Educ. Th. Assn.; Missouri Assn. of Jr. Coll. Speech Assn. (pres., 1969–71); Colorado State Speech Assn. (bd. of dir., 1965–67). Address: (home) 3829-A-51st, Lubbock, TX 79413, tel. (806) 797-2331; (bus.) Univ. Th., Texas Tech Univ., P.O. Box 4298, Lubbock, TX 79409, tel. (806) 742-2153.

Mr. Weaver became director of theatre and associate professor of theatre arts, Texas Tech Univ., in 1972. He had previously taught drama in high schools at Ellis, Kans. (1959–62), and Craig, Colo. (1962–64); had been designer/technical director and assistant professor of drama, Mesa Coll., Grand Junction, Colo. (1964–67); designer/technical director and assistant professor of theatre, Northwest Missouri State Coll., Maryville, Mo. (1967–69); and director of theatre, chairman of the Dept. of Speech and Drama, and assistant professor of speech at Columbia (Mo.) Coll. (1969–72).

Theatre. Mr. Weaver organized the Columbia (Mo.) Dinner Th. in 1970 and managed it until 1973, producing during that period *The Fantasticks*, *The Drunkard*, and *The Serpent* (all Summer 1970); *I Do! I Do!*, *Luv*, and *You Know I Can't Hear You When the Water's Running* (all Summer 1971). His own play *The Birds and Bees and Marti's Knees* received a Columbia Coll. Theatre Workshop production in 1970. Mr. Weaver was also stage manager of the Mummers Th., Oklahoma City, Okla. (Summer 1958), and technical director, Nodoway Community Th. Enterprises (1965–67).

Published Works. Mr. Weaver's articles have appeared in professional journals and in *Players Magazine*, and in 1973 he became editor of the Southwest Theatre Conference publication *Theatre Southwest*.

Awards. At the Univ. of Missouri, Mr. Weaver held the curator's fellowship (1968–72) and a graduate fellowship in speech and dramatic arts (1970). He was also awarded the university's Purple Mask and the Univ. of Oklahoma Buffalo Mask.

Recreation. Golf, writing, big game hunting.

WEBB, ALAN. Actor, director. b. Alan Norton Fletcher Webb, July 2, 1906, York, England, to Thomas Francis Albertoni and Lili E. (Fletcher) Webb. Father, insurance executive. Attended St. Olaves Sch., York, 1916–18; Branicote Sch., Scarborough, 1918–20; R.N. Coll. Osborne, 1920–22; R.N. Coll. Dartmouth, 1922–24. Served British Royal Navy, Artillery; 1940–45; rank, Capt. Member of AEA. Address: 41 Chesham St., London, S.W.1, England tel. BEL 8356.

Theatre. Mr. Webb made his acting debut with the Lena Ashwell Players (London), as Lawyer Hawkins in *The Devil's Disciple* (Century, Apr. 1924), appearing in productions with this company (1924–26); with the J. B. Fagan's Oxford Players (1926–28); and with the Masque Th. Co. (Edinburgh and Glasgow, Scotland, 1928).

He played Dr. Trewhawke in *Out of the Sea* (Strand, London, Nov. 1928); followed by Dr. Parpalaid in *Dr. Knock* (Strand, Dec. 6, 1928); and Ordulph in *The Mock Emperor* (Queen's, Jan. 29, 1929).

He appeared in productions with the Liverpool Repertory Co. (1929–31); Croydon Repertory Co. (1932–33); played Marvin Holland in *This One Man* (Embassy, London, Apr. 1933); the Rev. Arthur Bell Nicholls in *The Brontës* (Royalty, Apr. 20, 1933); Bruno Pieri in *As You Desire Me* (Gate, Sept. 1933); and with the Croydon Repertory Co., as Peter Mannoch in *The Mannoch Family*, and Edgar in *Wuthering Heights* (Oct.–Dec. 1933). He toured as the Earl of Oxford in *Richard of Bordeaux* (1934); and was a member of the Old Vic-Sadler's Wells Co. (London, 1934–35).

He played Felix Cotton in *Hervey House* (His Majesty's Th., May 1935); Major Sergius Saranoff in *Arms and the Man* (Embassy, July 1935); Charles Tritton in *The Wind and the Rain* (Queen's Th., Aug. 1935); appeared in a pre-London tour of *Tonight at 7:30* (Oct. 1935), and in London, where it was retitled *Tonight at 8:30* (Phoenix, Jan. 9, 1936).

Mr. Webb played Alan Crane in *Comedienne* (Haymarket, June 16, 1938); Dr. Evan Jones in *She, Too, Was Young* (Wyndham's, Aug. 16, 1938); Caleb Deecie in *Two Roses* (Savoy, Dec. 1938); and Ernest Friedman in *Design for Living* (Haymarket, Jan. 25, 1939). He succeeded (Nov. 25, 1945) Nicholas Phipps as Charles in *Blithe Spirit* (Piccadilly, July 2, 1941); and succeeded (Apr. 1946) Clive Brook as Michael Wentworth in *The Years Between* (Wyndham's, Jan. 10, 1945).

He directed *The Rossiters* (Lyric, Hammersmith, Mar. 4, 1947); and *Peace in Our Time* (Lyric, July 22, 1947); played Ryall in *Treasure Hunt* (Apollo, Sept. 14, 1949); Sir Timothy Bellboys in *A Penny for a Song* (Wimbledon, Feb. 12, 1951); Polonius in Alec Guinness' *Hamlet* (New, May 7, 1951); Henry Higgins in *Pygmalion* (Edinburgh Festival, Scotland, Aug. 1951); Henry Blessington in a touring production of *Adam's Apple* (1952); Eggerson in *The Confidential Clerk* (Edinburgh Festival, Aug. 1953; Lyric, London, Sept. 16, 1953); and Sir George Treherne in *Both Ends Meet* (Apollo, June 9, 1954).

Mr. Webb joined the Shakespeare Memorial Th. (Stratford-upon-Avon), where he played Sir Toby Belch in *Twelfth Night* (Apr. 12, 1955), the King of France in *All's Well That Ends Well* (Apr. 26, 1955), and Marcus Andronicus in *Titus Andronicus* (Aug. 16, 1955). He appeared as Lord Summerhayes in *Misalliance* (Lyric, Hammersmith, London, Feb. 8, 1956); Punalo Alani in *South Sea Bubble* (Lyric, Apr. 25, 1956); repeated his role as Marcus Andronicus in *Titus Andronicus* with the Shakespeare Memorial Th., on its European tour (1957), and in London (Stoll, July 1, 1957); played Inspector Davies in *Something to Hide* (St. Martin's, Apr. 29, 1958); Andrew Undershaft in *Major Barbara* (Royal Court, Aug. 28, 1958); and Janos Kadar in *Shadow of Heroes* (Piccadilly, Oct. 7, 1958).

He took over Wilfrid Hyde White's role of Andrew Bennet during the run of *Not in the Book* (Criterion, Apr. 2, 1958); played Duddard in *Rhinoceros* (Royal Court, Apr. 28, 1960); with the Royal Shakespeare Co., played Gloucester in *King Lear* (Stratford-upon-Avon, Nov. 1962), in London (Aldwych, Dec. 9, 1962), and at the Paris (France) Festival (May 1963); appeared as Ernst Heinrich Ernesti (Einstein) in *The Physicists* (Aldwych, 1963); and as Pope Pius XII in *The Representative* (Stratford-upon-Avon, Sept. 1963). He played Bent in *The Chinese Prime Minister* (Globe, London, May 20, 1965); and Chebutykin in *Three Sisters* (Royal Court, Apr. 18, 1967).

Mr. Webb made his N.Y.C. debut as Mr. Wadhurst in *Hands Across the Sea*, Sir Reginald French in *The Astonished Heart* and Mr. Edwards in *Red Peppers*, a part of the bill entitled *Tonight at 8:30* (National, Nov. 24, 1936); subsequently played Roger in *George and Margaret* (Morosco, Sept. 27, 1937); Arthur Winslow in *The Winslow Boy* (Empire, Oct. 29, 1947), also touring in it (May–Nov. 1948); Adolphe in *Nina* (Royale, Dec. 5, 1951); William Collyer in *The Deep Blue Sea* (Morosco, Nov. 5, 1952); Dr. Henry Maartens in *The Genius and the Goddess* (Henry Miller's Th., Dec. 10, 1957); Mazzini Dunn in *Heartbreak House* (Billy Rose Th., Oct. 18, 1959); Nonno (Jonathan Coffin) in *The Night of the Iguana* (Royale, Dec. 28, 1961); Bent in *The Chinese Prime Minister* (Royale, Jan. 2, 1964); William Uggims in *UTBU* (Helen Hayes Th., Jan. 4, 1966); Uncle Julian in *We Have Always Lived in the Castle* (Ethel Barrymore Th., Oct. 19, 1966); and Tom Garrison in *I Never Sang For My Father* (Longacre, Jan. 25, 1968).

Films. Mr. Webb appeared as Mr. Armitage in *The Pumpkin Eater* (Royal Intl., 1964); Alden Hoving in *The Third Secret* (20th-Fox, 1964); Colonel Brant in *King Rat* (Col., 1965); Shallow in *Chimes at Midnight* (Peppercorn-Wormster, 1966) subsequently titled *Falstaff;* Gremio in *The Taming of the Shrew* (Col., 1967); Thomas Crick in *Women in Love* (UA, 1970); Dada Kemp in *Entertaining Mr. Sloane* (Cont., 1970); and as Gloucester in *King Lear* (Filmways, 1971).

Television. Mr. Webb has appeared extensively on British television. His US television appearances include *The Holy Terror* (Hallmark Hall of Fame, NBC, 1965).

Recreation. Reading, music, gardening.

WEBB, RUTH. Talent representative, actress, singer. b. Ruth Thea Ford, Mar. 17, 1923, New York City, to Harry A. and Helen (Dentler) Ford. Father, manufacturer; mother, singer. Grad. St. Petersburg (Fla.) H.S., 1941; attended Greer Sch. for Girls, Birmingham, Pa., 1941–42; St. Petersburg Jr. Coll., 1942–43. Studied acting with Mary Ann Dentler, Lorna Carroll, St. Petersburg; singing with her mother, Helen Ford; in N.Y.C., with Thelma Gainsborough, 1961; Leon Rothier, 1942; Robert Kobin, 1962. Married Jan. 15, 1942, to John Cother Webb, actor (marr. dis. Jan. 29, 1948), one son; married July 1, 1948, to Richard Ober (marr. dis. Aug. 11, 1950); married Oct. 17, 1953, to Albert Benajam (marr. dis.), one son; married Dec. 31, 1963, to Robert Cosden, actor (marr. dis. July 1972). Relative in theatre: aunt, Mary Ann Dentler, actress, director. Member of AEA; SAG; AGVA. Address: (home) 7500 DeVista Drive, Hollywood, CA 90046, tel. (213) 274-4311; (bus.) Ruth Webb, Ltd., 9229 Sunset Blvd., Suite 509, Hollywood, CA 90069, tel. (213) 274-4311.

Theatre. Since May 1974, Miss Webb has been owner and president of Ruth Webb, Ltd., of Los Angeles, Calif., and N.Y.C., representing stage, screen, television, and variety talent. Previously she was a talent representative with the Laura Arnold Agency of N.Y.C., and from 1962 to 1964 she was head of the Ruth Webb Agency. From 1964 to 1974, she was sole owner of the Webb-Cosden Agency, N.Y.C.

Miss Webb's first stage appearance was as the White Rabbit in the Mirror Lake Grammar School's production of *Alice in Wonderland* (Mar. 1932); subsequently appeared in *Band Box Revue* (May 1935), and other productions of the Band Box Players (St. Petersburg, Fla., 1935); in stock, she was the ingenue with Band Box Players (Suffield, Conn., Summers 1936–37; and St. Petersburg, Fla., Winters 1936–37); toured as Billie in *Behind Red Lights* (opened Maryland Th., Baltimore, 1937; closed Music Hall, Miami Beach, Fla., 1938); in stock, was leading lady at Th. in the Dale (Marbledale, Conn., Summer 1939); Broadway Th. (North Bergen, N.J., Winter 1940); Harbor Playhouse (Marion, Mass., Summer 1940); played Bernice in *A Thousand to Boot* (Metropolitan Players, N.Y.C., Spring 1941); and returned as leading lady to Harbor Playhouse (Marion, Mass., Summer 1941).

Miss Webb, billed as Ruth Thea Ford, made her Broadway debut as Miss Marshall, and understudied Arlene Francis as Doris in *The Walking Gentlemen* (Belasco, May 7, 1942); then billed as Ruth Webb, played Opal, and understudied Muriel Angelus as Madame Rowena in *Early to Bed* (Broadhurst, June 17, 1943); toured in this show playing the role of Madame Rowena (opened Flatbush Th., Brooklyn, N.Y., June 6, 1944); played Nadine and understudied Luba Malina as Countess Landovska in *Marinka* (Winter Garden, N.Y.C., July 18, 1945); succeeded (Oct., 1945) Betty Comden as Claire de Loon in *On the Town* (Martin Beck Th., Dec. 28, 1944); replaced (Cass Th., Detroit, Mich., Mar. 15, 1946) Jacqueline Susann as Fudge in *Between Covers* (pre-Bway: opened Hanna Th., Cleveland, Ohio, Feb. 25, 1946; closed Great Northern, Chicago, Ill., Mar. 23, 1946); and played Lady Peaseley in the pre-Bway tryout of *Best of Friends* (opened Navy Recreation Park, Norfolk, Va., Apr. 15, 1947; closed there May 5, 1947).

In stock, Miss Webb appeared at Mt. Vernon (N.Y.) Summer Th. (Summer 1948); Crandall Th. (Chatham, N.Y.); Chapel Playhouse (Guilford, Conn.); and Meridian Park Th. (Washington, D.C.) during the summer of 1949. In the summer of 1950, she appeared at Paper Mill Playhouse (Millburn, N.J.); Marblehead Playhouse, Mass.; Lakes Region Playhouse (Gilford, N.M.); Spa Summer Th. (Saratoga Springs, N.Y.); Boston Summer Th., Mass., and Grist Mill Playhouse (Andover, N.J.); in 1951, she appeared at Musical Tent (St. Petersburg, Fla.), and Starlight Musical Th. (Indianapolis, Ind.); and toured as Kate in *Kiss Me, Kate* (opened Casino Th., Newport, R.I., June 23, 1952; closed Niagara Falls Summer Th., Ontario, Canada, Sept. 6, 1952). In 1953, she again appeared at Paper Mill Playhouse (Millburn, N.J.); in 1954, at Melody Circle Th. (Allentown, Pa.); in Summer 1956, toured as Mme. Baltin in *You Never Know* (opened Ogunquit Th., Me.; closed John Drew Memorial Th., East Hampton, N.Y.); in 1957, appeared at Music Circle Tent (Detroit, Mich.); and Musical Tent (Flint, Mich.); in 1958, returned to the latter two tents, and appeared at the Iroquois Amphitheatre (Louisville, Ky.). Miss Webb appeared at the Meadowbrook (N.J.) Dinner Th. as Donna Lucia in *Where's Charley?* (Feb. 28, 1960); as Madame Dubonnet in *The Boy Friend* (Mar. 18, 1960); played Ruth *Wonderful Town* and the title role in *Auntie Mame* (Gretna Playhouse, Mt. Gretna, Pa., Summer, 1960); returned to the Meadowbrook (N.J.) Dinner Th., to play Meg in *Damn Yankees* (Sept. 12, 1961); and repeated this role at Gretna Playhouse (Mt. Gretna, Pa., July 30, 1962); then repeated Meg in *Damn Yankees* at the Westchester Dinner Th. (Yonkers, N.Y., Sept. 5, 1962).

Television. Miss Webb has appeared on Recipe for Happiness (1945); the Virginia Graham Show (1945); and the Johnny Carson Show (1971).

Night Clubs. Miss Webb made her debut at the Deauville Casino (Paris, France, June 1939); and has performed at The Latin Quarter (N.Y.C., 1948); Night Cap Club (N.Y.C., 1949); Rainbow Room (Asbury Park, N.J., 1949); Park Ave. Restaurant and Penthouse Club (N.Y.C., 1950); Hotel Shelburne (N.Y.C., 1959); East Side Show Spot and Le Vouvray (N.Y.C., 1951); Tiger Lily, Cafe Society Downtown and Cafe Albert (N.Y.C., 1952); Georgia's Blue Room, Cafe James (N.Y.C., 1953); Casa Mia and Pygmalion (N.Y.C., 1954); Celebrity Room (N.Y.C., 1955); Fireside Lounge (Flint, Mich., 1956); York Inn (N.Y.C., 1957); Studio Club (Mt. Vernon, N.Y., 1958); and the Playroom Club (N.Y.C., 1958).

Awards. Miss Webb won the title of Princess in the Festival of States (St. Petersburg, Fla., 1939). She filled in at the last moment for the ailing Miss Wyoming, and represented that state, which she had never seen.

Recreation. Swimming, flower arranging.

WEBBER, ROBERT. Actor. b. Robert L. Webber, Santa Ana, Calif., to Robert and Alice Webber. Father, merchant seaman. Grad. Oakland (Calif.) Tech. H.S. 1942; attended Compton Jr. Coll., 1946. Married Oct. 1, 1953, to Miranda Jones (marr. dis. July 1958); married April 23, 1972 to Del Mertens. Served WW II, US Marine Corps. Member of AEA; SAG; AFTRA. Address: c/o Jay Julien, 9 E. 41st St., New York, NY 10017.

Theatre. Mr. Webber made his debut as Bill in a high school production of *A Night at an Inn* (Oakland, Calif., 1941); his professional debut as Wint Selby in a stock production of *Ah, Wilderness!* (Lake Whalom Playhouse, Fitchburg, Mass., Summer 1947); his Bway debut as the Marine Sgt. in *Two Blind Mice* (Cort Th., Mar. 2, 1949); succeeded Richard Hart as Matt Cole in *Goodbye, My Fancy* (Morosco, Nov. 7, 1949), in which he toured.

He played Perry Stewart in *The Royal Family* (NY City Ctr., Jan. 10, 1951); Irvin Blanchard in *No Time for Sergeants* (Alvin, Oct. 20, 1955); David Cutrere in *Orpheus Descending* (Martin Beck Th., Mar. 21, 1957); Harry Bohlan in *Fair Game* (Longacre, Nov. 2, 1957); and Chick Clark in *Wonderful Town* at the Brussels World's Fair (Belgium, Summer 1958).

He played Ricky Powers in *A Loss of Roses* (Eugene O'Neill Th., N.Y.C., Nov. 28, 1959); and George Haverstick in *Period of Adjustment* (Helen Hayes Th., Nov. 10, 1960).

Films. Mr. Webber made his debut in *Highway 301* (WB, 1950); subsequently appeared as the Advertising Man in *12 Angry Men* (UA, 1956); Ricky Powers in *The Stripper*, adopted from *A Loss of Roses* (20th-Fox, 1963); *Hysteria* (Hammer, 1964); *The Sandpiper* (MGM); *Harper* (WB); *The Silencers* (Col.); *Dead Heat on the Marry-Go-Round* (Col.); *Tequnica De Omicidio* (Italian); *Every Man is My Enemy* (Italian); *The Third Day* (WB); *Don't Make Waves* (Col.); *The Big Bounce* (WB); *Manon 70* (French); *Macedoine* (French); *The Dirty Dozen* (MGM); *Dollars* (Col.); *Bring Me the Head of Alfredo Garcia* (UA); and *The Great White Hope* (20th-Fox).

Television. Mr. Webber has appeared on about 400 programs, including Studio One (CBS); Playhouse 90 (CBS); Kraft Television Th. (NBC); Robert Montgomery Presents (NBC); The Dick Powell Th. (NBC); The Defenders (CBS); Ben Casey (ABC); The Nurses (CBS); The Greatest Show on Earth (ABC); Naked City (ABC); Route 66 (CBS); McCloud (NBC); Ironsides; Cannon; Double Indemnity; The Champions; The Bold Ones; Mannix (CBS); Hawkins on Murder; Streets of San Francisco (ABC); Kojak; Banacek; Outer Limits; Hitchcock Presents; and many others.

Recreation. Classical music, opera, reading, tennis, "avid sports fan and balletomane.".

WEIDMAN, JEROME. Librettist, novelist, short story writer, essayist, and television dramatist. b. Apr. 4, 1913, New York City, to Joseph and Annie (Falkovitz) Weidman. Father, pocket-maker. Grad. DeWitt Clinton H.S., 1930; attended New York Univ. 1931–34; New York Univ. Law Sch., 1934–37. Married Jan. 18, 1943, to Elizabeth Ann Payne; two sons. Member of Dramatists Guild; WGA, West; ALA. Address: 1390 S. Ocean Blvd., Pompano Beach, FL 33062.

Theatre. Mr. Weidman was librettist, with George Abbott, of the book for the musical, *Fiorello!* (Broadhurst, N.Y.C., Nov. 23, 1959; NY City Ctr., June 13, 1962); and with George Abbott, wrote the book for *Tenderloin* (46 St. Th., Oct. 17, 1960); wrote the book for the musical, *I Can Get It for You Wholesale* (Shubert, Mar. 22, 1962); and for the pre-Bway tryout of *Cool Off!* (opened Forrest, Philadelphia, Pa., Mar. 31, 1964; closed there Apr. 4, 1964).

Television. He created the weekly dramatic series, The Reporter (CBS).

Published Works. Mr. Weidman has written the novels *I Can Get It for You Wholesale* (1937); *What's in it for Me?* (1938); *I'll Never Go There Any More* (1940); *The Lights Around the Shore* (1941); *Too Early to Tell* (1946); *The Price Is Right* (1949); *The Hand of the Hunter* (1950); *Give Me Your Love* (1951); *The Third Angel* (1953); *Your Daughter Iris* (1955); *The Enemy Camp* (1958); *Before You Go* (1960); *The Sound of Bow Bells* (1962); *Word of Mouth* (1964); *Other People's Money* (1965); *The Center of the Action* (1969); *Fourth Street East* (1971); *Last Respects* (1972); and *Tiffany Street* (1974).

He has written the following collections of short stories: *The Horse that Could Whistle "Dixie"* (1939); *The Captain's Tiger* (1950); *A Dime a Throw* (1952); *My Father Sits in the Dark, and Other Selected Stories* (1961); *The Death of Dickie Draper* (1962); and *Nine Stories* (1964). He has written *Letter of Credit* (1940), a travel book; *Traveler's Cheque* (1951), a collection of essays; and with others, *First College Bowl Question Book* (1961); and *Back Talk* (1963).

Awards. Mr. Weidman and George Abbott received the Pulitzer Prize for Drama, the Antoinette Perry (Tony) Award, and the NY Drama Critics Circle Award (1960) for composing the book of *Fiorello!*.

WEIDNER, PAUL. Director, actor, producer. b. Paul Russell Weidner, Mar. 29, 1934, Charleston, S.C., to Paul Russell and Joanna (Powers) Weidner. Father, teacher. Grad. College of Charleston, B.A. 1955; postgraduate work, Univ. of Besançon, France, on Fulbright scholarship, 1955–56; Yale Drama School, M.F.A. in directing 1962. Studied acting with Michael Howard, N.Y.C., 1962–64. Served in US Army, 1956–58. Member of AEA; SSD&C; League of Resident Theatres; NTC. Address: (home) 17 Haynes St., Apt. 2, Hartford, CT 06103, tel. (203) 278-8289; (bus.) Hartford Stage Co., 65 Kinsley St., Hartford, CT 06103, tel. (203) 525-5601.

Pre-Theatre. Worked for French government tourist office, N.Y.C. (1959).

Theatre. Mr. Weidner made his stage debut playing the title role in *The Winslow Boy* (Footlight Players, Charleston, S.C., Jan. 1948); his professional debut in a N.Y.C. production of *Six Characters in Search of an Author* (Martinique Th., 1963); and appeared at the Asolo Th., Sarasota, Fla. (June–Aug. 1964) as Andrew Aguecheek in *Twelfth Night* and Argan in *The Imaginary Invalid*. With the Hartford (Conn.) Stage Co., he repeated Argan (Oct. 23, 1964), following with performances as Telyegin in *Uncle Vanya* (Feb. 12, 1965), Hastings in *She Stoops to Conquer* (Mar. 12, 1965), Vladimir in *Waiting for Godot* (Apr. 9, 1965), and Trinculo in *The Tempest* (May 7, 1965). He returned to Asolo Th., Sarasota, Fla. (June–Aug. 1965), where he played Polonius in *Hamlet*, Nano in *Volpone*, and Demokos in *Tiger at the Gates;* then rejoined Hartford Stage Co., directing *Tartuffe* (Nov. 19, 1965), playing Algernon in *The Importance of Being Earnest* (Feb. 11, 1966) and the General in *The Balcony* (Mar. 11, 1966), and directing *Twelfth Night* (Apr. 8, 1966). At Asolo Th. (June–Aug. 1966), he was Verges in *Much Ado About Nothing*, Harpagon in *The Miser*, and Mr. Smith in *The Bald Soprano*, returning then to Hartford Stage Co. and directing *Endgame* and *Act without Words* (Nov. 11, 1966), playing Chebutykin in *The Three Sisters* (Dec. 16, 1966), and directing *The Servant of Two Masters* (Mar. 31, 1967); at Asolo Th. (June–Aug. 1967) he played the Mute in *The Madwoman of Chaillot* and directed *The Farce of Scapin;* he also directed *Look Back in Anger* (Asolo Th., Mar. 11, 1968).

At the Hartford Stage Co., he produced *The Seagull* (Oct. 11, 1968), which he also directed; *The Rose Tattoo* (Nov. 22, 1968); *The Waltz Invention* (Jan. 3, 1969), which he also directed; *The Homecoming* (Feb. 14, 1969); *The Trial* (Mar. 28, 1969), which he also directed; *Life with Father* (May 9, 1969); *A Delicate Balance* (Oct. 17, 1969) and *The Farce of Scapin* (Nov. 28, 1969), both of which he also directed; *Joe Egg* (Jan. 9, 1970) and *Misalliance* (Feb. 20, 1970); *The Trial of A. Lincoln* (Apr. 3,

1970), which he directed; and *Anything Goes* (May 15, 1970). He directed *The Price* (Williamstown Summer Th., Williamstown, Mass., July 2, 1970); and for the Hartford Stage Co. produced *Rosencrantz and Guildenstern Are Dead* (Oct. 16, 1970), which he also directed; *Ring Round the Moon* (Nov. 27, 1970); *A Gun Play* (Jan. 8, 1971), which he also directed; *Long Day's Journey into Night* (Feb. 19, 1971), *Blithe Spirit* (Apr. 2, 1971); *The Boys in the Band* (May 14, 1971), which he also directed; and he directed *The Liar* (Milwaukee Rep. Th., Wisconsin, Mar. 12, 1971).

At the Hartford Stage Co., he produced *No Place To Be Somebody* (Oct. 15, 1971); *Henry V* (Nov. 26, 1971) and *Rooted* (Jan. 7, 1972), both of which he also directed; *Charley's Aunt* (Feb. 18, 1972); *Tiny Alice* (Mar. 31, 1972), which he also directed; *Loot* (May 12, 1972); *The Misanthrope* (Oct. 6, 1972), which he also directed; *A Streetcar Named Desire* (Nov. 24, 1972); *Nightlight* (Jan. 12, 1973), *You Can't Take It with You* (Feb. 23, 1973), and *Old Times* (Apr. 6, 1973), all of which he directed; *Juno and the Paycock* (May 18, 1973); *My Sister, My Sister* (Sept. 28, 1973), which he also directed; *Getting Married* (Nov. 9, 1973); *Ubu-Roi* (Dec. 21, 1973), which he also directed; *Arsenic and Old Lace* (Feb. 8, 1974); and *A Touch of the Poet* (Mar. 29, 1974) and *The School for Scandal* (May 17, 1974), both of which he also directed.

Recreation. Reading (history), skiing, travel (France, England).

WEILER, BERENICE. Producer, director, manager, stage manager. b. Berenice J. Weiler, July 3, 1927, New York City, to Sidney S. and Lillian (Hammer) Weiler. Father, manufacturer. Grad. Hunter Coll. H.S., N.Y.C.; Hunter Coll., B.A.; attended New Sch. for Social Research. Member of AEA; AFTRA; ATAS. Address: 900 West End Ave., New York, NY 10025, tel. (212) MO 3-4487.

Theatre. Miss Weiler toured as a general understudy in a USO production of *The Late Christopher Bean*, for which she was also stage manager (North Atlantic and Europe).

At the Bar Harbor (Me.) Playhouse, she appeared in and stage managed *The First Mrs. Fraser, Dream Girl*, and *Laura* (1948); and stage managed and directed *Biography, Hay Fever, The Hasty Heart*, and *The Bat* (1949).

She was stage manager for a UN production of *Dawn's Early Light* (N.Y.C., Spring 1950); directed summer productions at the Fairhaven (Mass.) Theatre (1950); was stage manager for productions at the Chevy Chase (Ill.) Theatre (1950); directed *Papa Is All*, which toured summer theatres (1951); and was stage manager for a tour of *Jezebel's Husband* (opened Pocono Playhouse, Pa., Summer 1952).

She was stage manager for *Highlights of the Empire* (Empire, N.Y.C., May 4, 1953); directed a tour of *What's the Rush* (Summer 1956); was stage manager for an industrial production, *Rheingold Beer Show* (Summer 1957); production assistant for the pre-Bway tryout of *The Saturday Night Kid* (Westport Country Playhouse, Conn., Sept. 9, 1957); and *The Egghead* (Ethel Barrymore Th., N.Y.C., Oct. 9, 1957).

For the Amer. Shakespeare Festival, (Stratford, Conn.), she served as production coordinator (1960, 1962), production manager and administrator (1963), assoc. producer (1964–67), and managing producer (1968–73).

Off Bway, she produced *Carving a Statue* (Gramercy Arts Th., N.Y.C., Apr. 30, 1968) and was company manager for *Kaboom!* (Bottom Line Th., May 1, 1974).

Films. Miss Weiler was production coordinator and director of *Ten Girls Ago*, which was presented at the Boston (Mass.) Arts Film Festival (June–July 1962).

Television. She was production assistant for the Colgate Comedy Hour (NBC, 1951); assistant to the director of What's My Name? (NBC, 1951); Cosmopolitan Th. (ABC, 1952); assistant to the producer of Omnibus (CBS, 1952); and associate producer of Comeback Story (NBC, 1953–54).

She was assistant to the producer of Caesar's Hour (NBC, 1954–57); Caesar Presents (NBC, 1955); associate producer of Sid Caesar Invited You (ABC, 1958; BBC, London, 1958); casting director of The Hallmark Hall of Fame (NBC, 1958); associate producer of Our American Heritage (NBC, 1959); and The Art of Seeing (WNDT, N.Y., 1962).

Recreation. Reading, traveling, swimming, riding.

WEINER, ROBERT. Producer. b. Robert Lester Weiner, Sept. 9, New York City. Grad. Cherry Lawn Sch., Darien, Conn.; Columbia Univ., B.A. Member of League of NY Theatres; NARAS; NATAS; Rock Writers of America. Address: 161 W. 54th St., Suite 403, New York, NY 10019, tel. (212) 245-8298.

Theatre. Mr. Weiner was, at first, copy boy for *Variety* (1950); and production assistant for the Show of the Month Club, Inc. (1950); subsequently press assistant to Arthur Cantor for approximately 25 shows produced in N.Y.C. and on television (1953–57); box office treasurer for the Newport (R.I.) Casino Th. (Summer 1955); production assistant for *The Desk Set* (Broadhurst Th., N.Y.C., Oct. 24, 1955); *Shangri-La* (Winter Garden, June 13, 1956); *Auntie Mame* (Broadhurst, Oct. 31, 1956); produced two company tours of *No Time for Sergeants* (1958); and produced, with Emmett Rogers, *Tall Story* (Belasco, Jan. 29, 1959).

He produced the musical revue, *Medium Rare* (Happy Medium, Chicago, Ill., June 29, 1960); was general manager for the musical, *Double Entry* (Martinique, N.Y.C., Feb. 20, 1961); produced the tryout of the musical revue, *Put It in Writing* (Royal Poinciana Playhouse, Palm Beach, Fla., Feb. 1962), and the Chicago production (Happy Medium, Chicago, June 28, 1962); was production supervisor and general manager for *Spoon River* (Booth, N.Y.C., Sept. 29, 1963); and *What Makes Sammy Run?* (54 St. Th., Feb. 27, 1964).

Mr. Weiner served as administrator of Jerome Robbins' American Theatre Laboratory (1966); was general manager for *A Day in the Death of Joe Egg* (Brooks Atkinson Th., Feb. 1, 1968); and general manager and production supervisor for *Her First Roman* (Lunt-Fontanne Th., Oct. 20, 1968); and *Gantry* (George Abbott Th., Feb. 14, 1970).

Films. He was production supervisor and casting director for *Who Killed Teddy Bear* (Magna, 1965); associate producer of *Bullitt* (WB-Seven Arts, 1968); technical advisor to the director for *John and Mary* (20th-Fox, 1969); producer of the cinema vèrité film *Groupies* (1970); production executive and casting supervisor for *The French Connection* (20th-Fox, 1971); and production executive and casting supervisor for *The Seven-Ups* (20th-Fox, 1973).

Television. Mr. Weiner was production supervisor for the Hartford, Conn., pay television production of *Spoon River* (Nov. 1963), and of *Electric Showcase* (ABC, 1965); associate producer for D'Antoni/Baer Television Productions (1965–66); associate producer of the *Comedy Tonight* series (CBS, 1970); and producer of the Christopher Award winning special, *Dylan Thomas' "A Child's Christmas in Wales,"* starring Sir Michael Redgrave and the National Theatre of the Deaf (CBS, 1973).

Other Activities. At the Yale Univ. School of Drama, Mr. Weiner served assistant to Dean Robert Brustein, managing director of theatre operations, executive producer, and liaison for the "Yale-ABC Writing for the Camera" grant (1966).

Published Works. He has been a contributor to Al Aronowitz' "Pop Scene" column in the New York *Post* (1972); a contributing editor to *Words and Music* Magazine (1972); a film reviewer and contributing editor to *Andy Warhol's Inter-View* Magazine (1970–73); and pop music columnist for *Tambourine* Magazine, and Kal Rudman's *Friday Morning Quarterback* (1972–74).

WEINSTEIN, ARNOLD. Playwright, director, lyricist, educator, poet. b. June 10, 1927, New York City, to Simon and Ada Weinstein. Father, hotel manager. Attended Univ. of London, 1949–50; grad. Hunter Coll., B.A. (Phi Beta Kappa) 1951; Harvard Univ., M.A. 1953. Served USN, 1944–46.

Pre-Theatre. Taught at New York Univ., Univ. of Southern California, Rutgers Univ.

Theatre. Mr. Weinstein wrote *Red Eye of Love* (Living Th., N.Y.C., June 12, 1961), which was also presented in Scandinavia, Canada, Italy, and in summer theatres in the US (1963).

He wrote the lyrics for *Fortuna*, which he also adapted (Maidman, N.Y.C., Jan. 3, 1962); and his one-act play, *The 25c White Cap*, was presented as part of a triple-bill, *Three by Three* (Maidman, Mar. 1963).

With Paul Sills, he directed *Open Season at Second City* (Second City, Jan. 22, 1964); he wrote the libretto for the Actors' Studio production of the opera, *Dynamite Tonight* (York, Mar. 15, 1964); translated and adapted for Story Theatre Ovid's *Metamorphoses* (Yale Repertory Th., New Haven, Conn., Nov. 27, 1969; Ambassador, N.Y.C., Apr. 22, 1971); wrote an English adaptation of *Mahagonny* (Anderson Th., May 3, 1970); and wrote, with Paul Sills, and played Col. Dalrymple in *The American Revolution, Part 1* (Ford's Th., Washington, D.C., Sept. 1973).

Television. His play, *Red Eye of Love*, was telecast twice in London (BBC, 1963).

Other Activities. Mr. Weinstein was head of the playwriting program, Yale Univ. School of Drama from 1966 to 1970.

Published Works. He wrote a volume of poetry, *Different Poems by the Same Author* (1960). His poems have been published in *Saturday Review, Harper's Bazaar, Encounter, Poetry* Magazine, and *New Directions.* .

Awards. Mr. Weinstein received the Univ. of London Poetry Prize (1950); and a Harvard Fellowship in Classics (1951).

WEISFELD, ZELMA H. Costume designer, educator. b. Zelma Hope Weisfeld, Oct. 9, 1931, Philadelphia, Pa., to Nathan and Stella Grace (Ritchie) Weisfeld. Father, neckwear manufacturer. Grad. Olney H.S., 1949; Temple Univ., A.B. 1953; Yale Univ. Sch. of Drama, M.F.A. 1956; attended Ann Chriss Sch. of Dance, Philadelphia, 1945–50. Member of ATA; ANTA; United Scenic Artists Union, Local 829; Women of the Faculty (Univ. of Michigan); ZONTA International; Speech Communication Assn.; Michigan Speech Assn.; USITT; Women's Research Club of Michigan; ACTA; Costume Society of Great Britain; and Zeta Phi Eta (hon.). Address: (home) 1716 Charlton, Ann Arbor, MI 48103, tel. (313) 665-7946; (bus.) Univ. Michigan, Dept. of Speech, Ann Arbor, MI 48103, tel. (313) 764-6303.

Her first assignment as a designer was at the Yale Sch. of Drama, where she designed the costumes for *Major Barbara* (1954); subsequently she designed costumes at Green Mansions (N.Y., Summer 1954); for *Coriolanus* (Yale Sch. of Drama, 1956); designed a production of *Madame Butterfly* (New Haven Experimental Opera Co., Conn., 1956); designed costumes for the ELT production of *The Love of Four Colonels* (Lenox Hill Playhouse, N.Y.C., Apr. 10, 1957); variety shows at Tamiment, Pa. (Summer 1957); and for 38 shows at the Pittsburgh (Pa.) Playhouse (1958–60); for KDKA-TV in Pittsburgh (1958); and for the Shakespeare Series and the Great Books Series on educational television (Univ. of Michigan Broadcasting, 1960–63).

Awards. Miss Weisfeld received the Lord Memorial Scholarship, Yale Sch. of Drama, as "outstanding second year woman" (1955); and was awarded a faculty research fellowship by the Univ. of Michigan (1965).

Recreation. Attending theatre; touring England.

WEISS, PETER. Playwright, author, filmmaker, painter. b. Nov. 8, 1916, Nowawes (near Berlin), Germany, to Eugene and Frieda (Hummel) Weiss. Educ. Art Acad., Prague, Czechoslovakia. Married 1964 to Gunilla Palmstierna, scene and costume designer. Address: c/o Surhkamp Verlag,

Frankfurt am Main, West Germany.

Pre-Theatre. Mr. Weiss left Germany in 1934, then living in England, Switzerland, and Czechoslovakia at different times before settling in Sweden in 1939 and becoming a citizen of that nation. He began his career making documentary and experimental films in Sweden (1952–58).

Theatre. The first of Mr. Weiss's plays to be produced was *Nacht mit Gästen (Night with Guests)* (Schiller Th., West Berlin, Ger., Oct. 1963). This was followed by *The Persecution and Assassination of Marat as Performed by the Inmates of the Asylum of Charenton under the Direction of the Marquis de Sade,* known as *Marat/Sade* (Schiller Th., Apr. 29, 1964; Royal Shakespeare Co., Aldwych, London, England, Aug. 20, 1964; Martin Beck Th., N.Y.C., Dec. 27, 1965).

Die Ermittlung (The Investigation) was premiered in more than a dozen productions throughout West and East Germany (Oct. 19, 1965) and was followed by *The Song of the Lusitanian Bogey* (Scala Th., Stockholm, Sweden, Jan. 20, 1967; St. Mark's Playhouse, N.Y.C., July 30, 1968); *How Mr. Mockinpott Was Cured of His Sufferings* (Hanover State Th., Germany, 1967; Greenwich Mews Th., N.Y.C., May 31, 1973); *Vietnam Discourse,* the short version of a much longer title (Frankfurt, Germany, 1968); *Trotsky in Exile* (Dusseldorf, Germany, Jan. 1970); *Hölderlin* (Staats Th., Stuttgart, Germany, Sept. 15, 1971); *The Tower,* originally written in 1948 (Actors' Experimental Unit, N.Y.C., Apr. 24, 1974); and Mr. Weiss's adaptation of Franz Kafka's *The Trial* (Bremen, Germany, 1974).

Films. Mr. Weiss wrote, directed, and helped film *Hallucinations* (1953), *Faces in the Shadow* (1956), both short subjects; *The Mirage* (1958); and *The Studio of Dr. Faust. Marat/Sade* was made into a motion picture (UA, 1967).

Television. *The Investigation* was televised (NBC, Apr. 1967).

Published Works. Mr. Weiss's novels include *Der Schatten des Körpers des Kutschers (The Shadow of the Coachman's Body,* 1960); *Abschied von dem Eltern* (1961); *The Leavetaking,* (1962); *Fluchtpunkt* (*Point of Escape,* 1962); *Das Gesprach der drei Gehenden* (*The Conversation of the Three Walkers,* 1963); and *Exile* (1968).

Awards. *Marat/Sade* was awarded a Tony and received the Drama Critics Circle Award as the best play of the 1965–66 season.

WEISSBERGER, L. ARNOLD.

Theatrical lawyer, author. b. Lenson Arnold Weissberger, Jan. 16, 1907, New York City, to Harry Arnold and Anna (Lenson) Weissberger. Grad. Ethical Culture Sch., N.Y.C., 1923; Harvard Univ., A.B. (magna cum laude) 1927; Harvard Univ. Law Sch., LL.B. (cum laude) 1930. Served US Army Signal Corps, 1942–43. Member of Bar Assn. of N.Y.C., Bronx House (dir. and vice-pres., 1936–50); Federation for Jewish Philanthropic Societies (trustee, 1940–50); Fountain House Foundation (dir.); American Inst. of Music (dir.); Harlem Eye and Ear Hosp. (trustee); John Golden Fund (dir.); New Dramatists (chmn.); Friends of the Theatre and Music Collection of the Museum of the City of New York (chmn.); Museum of the City of New York (trustee); Dance Notations Bureau (dir.); Bedside Network (advisor); Actor's Studio (dir., 1969–72); Jose Greco Foundation for Hispanic Dance (chmn. of the bd.); Martha Graham Center of Contemporary Dance (bd. mem. and secy.). Address: (home) 45 Sutton Place, South, New York, NY 10022, tel. (212) EN 2-9319; (bus.) 120 E. 56th St., New York, NY 10022, tel. (212) PL 8-0800.

Mr. Weissberger has practiced law in New York City with the firms of Guggenheimer & Untermeyer (1930–34); Reigelman, Hess and Hirsch (1935–39); subsequently formed his own firm (1939); and the partnerships of Weissberger and Frosch (1955–70); and Weissberger and Harris (1972–to date).

Published Works. "Influence of Machiavelli in Tudor England" appeared in *Political Science Quarterly* (1927) and "Federal Trial Judge: Comment on the Evidence" appeared in *Brooklyn Law Review* (1931). Mr. Weissberger is the author of *Famous Faces,* a photograph album of personal reminiscences containing 1500 photographs of celebrities, with a foreword by Sir Noel Coward, and commentaries by Orson Welles, Dame Rebecca West, Sir John Gielgud, Douglas Fairbanks, Jr., Anita Loos and Igor Stravinsky (1973).

WELCH, ELISABETH.

Actress, singer. b. Elisabeth Margaret Welch, Feb. 27, 1909, New York City, to John Wesley and Elisabeth (Kay) Welch. Father, gardener. Grad. Julia Richman H.S., N.Y.C., 1927. Member of AEA. Address: 4A Capener's Close, London, S.W.1, England.

Pre-Theatre. She was a child welfare worker with a branch of the Henry St. Settlement (N.Y.C., 1924–28).

Theatre. Miss Welch made her debut as a singer and understudied in *Blackbirds of 1928* (Liberty Th., N.Y.C., May 9, 1928), and accompanied the production to Paris (Moulin Rouge Th., June 1929); subsequently sang in *The New Yorkers* (Bway Th., N.Y.C., Dec. 8, 1930).

Since 1933, Miss Welch has appeared in British productions. She made her London debut as a singer in the revue, *Dark Doings* (Leicester Sq., June 1933); played Haidee Robinson in *Nymph Errant* (Adelphi, Oct. 6, 1933); sang the role of Cleo Wellington in *Glamorous Night* (Drury Lane, May 2, 1935); appeared in the revues, *Let's Raise the Curtain* (Victoria Palace, Sept. 1936), *It's in the Bag* (Saville, Nov. 1937), and *All the Best* (Opera House, Blackpool, June 1938); and played at variety theatres throughout the British Isles in her own singing act (Jan. 1939). She appeared as Clementine in *No Time for Comedy* (Haymarket, London, March 27, 1941); and in the revue, *Sky High* (Phoenix, June 4, 1942). She joined (Dec. 1942) the first ENSA group to leave England, appearing in the revue, *Christmas Party* with a company that included Edith Evans, John Gielgud, Beatrice Lillie, Michael Wilding and Jeanne de Casalis (Gibraltar and Malta, Jan. 1943); appeared in the revue, *We're All in It* (Opera House, Blackpool, May 1943); as Josie in *Arc de Triomphe* (Phoenix, London, Nov. 9, 1943); in the revues, *Happy and Glorious* (Palladium, Oct. 3, 1944), *Tuppence Coloured* (Lyric, Hammersmith, Sept. 4, 1947), *Oranges and Lemons* (Lyric, Hammersmith, Nov. 26, 1948), *Penny Plain* (St. Martin's, June 28, 1951), and *Pay the Piper* (Saville, Dec. 21, 1954); played Sweet Ginger in *The Crooked Mile* (Cambridge, Sept. 10, 1959); appeared in *Cindy Ella* (Garrick, Dec. 17, 1962; New Arts, Dec. 23, 1963); appeared in *Night Is for Delight* (Yvonne Arnaud Th., Oct. 1966); in a one-woman show, *Marvellous Party* (Hampstead Th., Dec. 1970); and *The Sweetest Sounds* (Yvonne Arnaud Th., Sept. 1971); and played Berthe in *Pippin* (Her Majesty's Th., Oct. 1973).

Films. Miss Welch appeared in *Big Fella* (British Lion, 1937); *Song of Freedom* (Treo, 1938); *Over the Moon* (UA, 1940); *Fiddler's Three* (Ealing, 1943); *Dead of Night* (U, 1946); and *Our Man in Havana* (Col., 1960).

Television and Radio. On radio, Miss Welch has performed in many musical programs, in Shaw's *Adventures of a Black Girl in Her Search for God* (BBC, June 1944); *Back to Methusula* (BBC, Dec. 1965); and *A Paul Robeson Celebration* (BBC, Apr. 1974). On television she appeared in *No Time for Comedy* (BBC, June 1956); *Miss Patterson* (BBC, June 1956); in her own series, *Music at Teatime* (BBC, Nov. 1957); *Me and the Night and the Music* (BBC, Nov. 1957); *The Grass Harp* (ITV, Dec. 1957); Somerset Maugham's *Facts of Life* (ITV, April 7, 1960); *Crane* (AR, Feb. 1964); *The Rise and Fall of Nellie Brown* (ATV, Dec. 1964); *The Long Cocktail Party* (BBC, July 1965); *Take a Sapphire* (BBC, Jan. 1966); *Going for a Song* (BBC, Feb.–Mar. 1966); *Cindy Ella* (BBC, Dec. 1966); *Before the Fringe* (BBC, Jan.–Feb. 1967); *The Moon and Sixpence* (BBC, Nov. 1967); various segments of the children's programs, *Playschool* and *Jackanory* (BBC, 1966–73); and *Looks Familiar* (Thames, 1973).

Night Clubs. Miss Welch toured Europe and N.Y.C. as a singer in a cabaret show (Apr. 1930–May 1933); had her own singing act (1949–51), appearing in London restaurants including Pigalle, Quaglino's and Allegro; in 1954, at Quaglino's, Allegro, and Café de Paris; at the Hotel Imperial (Tourguay, England, Aug. 1964), and, in Hong Kong, at the Hotel Mandarin (Mar.–Apr. 1967).

WELLES, ORSON.

Director, actor, producer, author. b. George Orson Welles, May 6, 1915, Kenosha, Wis., to Richard Head and Beatrice (Ives) Welles. Father, inventor, traveler; mother, pianist. Attended Todd Sch., Woodstock, Ill., 1925–30. Married Dec. 20, 1934, to Virginia Nicholson (marr. dis.), one daughter; married Sept. 7, 1942, to Rita Hayworth (marr. dis.); one daughter; married 1956 to Paola Mori, La Comtesse di Girafalco; one daughter. Member of AEA; SAG; Lotos Club. Address: Via Bordighere, 26, Fregene, Italy.

Pre-Theatre. Reporter, painter.

Theatre. Mr. Welles first performed at age nine, playing Peter Rabbit in Marshall Field's department store (Chicago, Ill.); while a student at the Todd Sch., directed and played the Soothsayer in *Julius Caesar* (Woodstock, Ill., 1927); made his professional acting debut in Dublin, Ire., as the Duke of Wurtemburg in *The Jew Süss* (Gate Th., Nov. 1931).

He joined Katharine Cornell's US touring company (1933–34), playing Mercutio in *Romeo and Juliet* (opened Erlanger, Buffalo, N.Y., Nov. 1933); Marchbanks in *Candida* (opened Metropolitan, Seattle, Wash., Dec. 1933); and Octavius Moulton-Barrett in *The Barretts of Wimpole Street.* He played the title role in a stock production of *Hamlet* (Woodstock, Ill., Summer, 1934); subsequently made his Bway debut as both Chorus and Tybalt in Miss Cornell's production of *Romeo and Juliet* (Martin Beck Th., Dec. 20, 1934); appeared as McGafferty in the Phoenix Th. production of *Panic* (Imperial, Mar. 14, 1935); Andre Pequot in *Ten Million Ghosts* (St. James, Oct. 23, 1936); directed for the Federal Th. (WPA) Project, the Negro People's Th. production of *Macbeth* (Lafayette, Apr. 9, 1936) and *Turpentine* (Lafayette, 1936); also for the WPA, directed *Horse Eats Hat* (Maxine Elliott's Th., c. Sept. 1936), and directed, designed, and appeared in the title role in *Dr. Faustus* (Maxine Elliott's Th., Jan. 8, 1937).

In 1937, he and John Houseman founded the Mercury Th., and with this group Mr. Welles directed a modern-dress production of *Julius Caesar* (Mercury, Nov. 11, 1937), in which he portrayed Marcus Brutus; directed *The Cradle Will Rock* (Mercury, Dec. 5, 1937); *The Shoemaker's Holiday* (Mercury, Jan. 1, 1938); and *Heartbreak House* (Mercury, Apr. 29, 1938), in which he appeared as Captain Shotover; directed a stock production of *The Importance of Being Earnest* (Cape Playhouse, Dennis, Mass., Aug. 1, 1938); and directed *Danton's Death* (Mercury, N.Y.C., Nov. 2, 1938), in which he played St. Just.

He directed his own adaptation of Shakespeare's histories, entitled *Five Kings* (Colonial, Boston, Feb. 1939), in which he portrayed Falstaff; directed and appeared as the Rajah in *The Green Goddess* (Pittsburgh, Pa., June 15, 1939); produced, with John Houseman, and directed *Native Son* (St. James, N.Y.C., Mar. 24, 1941); and adapted, directed and played Dick Fix in *Around the World in 80 Days* (Adelphi, May 31, 1946), produced by Mercury Productions.

In Paris, France, he participated in the production of his own play, *The Unthinking Lobster* (Th. Edouard VII, June 1950), in which he appeared as Jake; directed and played Dr. Faustus in his adaptation of *Faust,* entitled *Time Runs* (West German tour); later directed and played the title role in *Othello* (St. James's, London, England, Oct. 18, 1951); wrote the libretto for the ballet, *The Lady in the Ice* (Stoll, Sept. 7, 1943); and directed his adaptation of Melville's novel, *Moby Dick* (Duke of York's Th., June 16, 1955), in which he portrayed the role of the Actor Manager.

Mr. Welles directed and played the title role in *King Lear* (NY City Ctr., Jan. 12, 1956); adapted Shakespeare's *Henry IV, Parts 1 and 2* and *Henry V* for an Irish production entitled *Chimes at Midnight* (Gaiety, Dublin, Feb. 29, 1960), in which he played Falstaff; directed and designed a production of *Rhinoceros* (Royal Court, London, Apr. 28, 1960); and adapted Melville's novel, *Moby Dick* (Ethel Barrymore Th., N.Y.C., Nov. 28, 1962).

Films. He did the narration for *The Swiss Family Robinson* (RKO, 1940); wrote, with Herman J. Mankiewicz, produced, directed and played the title role in *Citizen Kane* (RKO, 1941); wrote, with Joseph Cotton, produced, directed, and appeared in *The Magnificent Ambersons* (RKO, 1942); wrote, with Joseph Cotton, produced and played Col. Haki in *Journey into Fear* (RKO, 1942); and wrote and produced the unreleased *It's All True* (1942). He appeared as Rochester in *Jane Eyre* (20th-Fox, 1944); played in *Follow the Boys* (U, 1944); and *Tomorrow Is Forever* (RKO, 1946); directed and performed in *The Stranger* (RKO, 1946); wrote the scenario for *Monsieur Verdoux* (UA, 1947); wrote, produced, directed, and appeared as Black Mike O'Hara in *The Lady from Shanghai* (Col., 1948); and produced, directed, and portrayed the title role in *Macbeth* (Rep., 1948).

He appeared as Cagliostro in *Black Magic* (UA, 1949); played in *Prince of Foxes* (20th-Fox, 1949); and *The Black Rose* (20th-Fox, 1950); portrayed Harry Lime in *The Third Man* (SRO, 1950); appeared in *Trent's Last Case* (Rep., 1953); *Trouble in the Glen* (Rep., 1954); portrayed Lord Mountdrago in *Three Cases of Murder* (Assoc. Artists, 1955); produced, directed, and played the title role in *Othello* (UA, 1955); appeared as Mapple in *Moby Dick* (WB, 1956); performed in *Man in the Shadow* (U, 1957); played Benjamin Franklin in *Royal Affairs in Versailles* (TFC, 1957); wrote, directed, and performed in *Touch of Evil* (U, 1958); appeared in *The Long Hot Summer* (20th-Fox, 1958); and *The Roots of Heaven* (20th-Fox, 1958); played the Defense Attorney in *Compulsion* (20th-Fox, 1959); appeared in *A Crack in the Mirror* (20th-Fox, 1960); produced, directed, and played the title role in *Othello* (U, 1960); appeared in *David and Goliath* (Allied, 1961); *Ferry to Hong Kong* (20th-Fox, 1961); *The Tartars* (MGM, 1962); wrote, produced, directed, and appeared in the title role in *Mr. Arkadin* (Cari, 1962); directed his adaptation of Kafka's novel, *The Trial* (GIB, 1963); appeared as Benjamin Franklin in *Lafayette* (1963); and produced *V.I.P.* (MGM, 1963).

Mr. Welles was narrator of *A King's Story* (Col., 1965); played Teacher in *The Fabulous Adventure of Marco Polo* (MGM, 1966); wrote, based on several Shakespeare plays, directed and played Falstaff in *Chimes at Midnight* (Peppercorn-Wormser, Inc., 1966), which was subsequently titled *Falstaff;* played Nordling in *Is Paris Burning?* (Par., 1966); Cardinal Wolsey in *A Man for All Seasons* (Col., 1966); Le Chiffre in *Casino Royale* (Col., 1967); Louis of Mozambique in *The Sailor from Gibraltar* (Lopert, 1967); appeared in *Oedipus the King* (U, 1968); and *I'll Never Forget What's His Name* (U, 1968); directed and acted in *The Immortal Story* (Altura Films, 1969); appeared in *House of Cards* (U, 1969); *The Southern Star* (Col., 1969); *Start the Revolution without Me* (1970); *The Kremlin Letter* (20th-Fox, 1970); *Catch-22* (Par., 1970); *A Safe Place* (Col., 1971); and *Necromancy* (Cinerama, 1972).

Television and Radio. Mr. Welles played Duke in a radio production of *Twelfth Night* (Aug. 20, 1937); and played Lamont Cranston in the radio series, The Shadow (1937). He was adaptor, narrator, and producer of a series which premiered with *Dracula* (July 11, 1938), followed by *Peter Ibbetson, Rebecca, Arrowsmith, 39 Steps, The Affairs of Anatole* (Aug. 22, 1938), *Abraham Lincoln, A Tale of Two Cities, Treasure Island, The March of Time, The Invasion from Mars* (Oct. 30, 1938), and ended with *Les Misérables.* He also performed in *Becky Sharp* (1940) and *A Passenger to Bali* (1946).

He played the title role in the telecast of *King Lear* (Omnibus, CBS, Oct. 18, 1953); appeared in *Twentieth Century* (Ford Star Jubilee, CBS, Apr. 8, 1956); was author, producer, narrator and director of *The Fountain of Youth* (Colgate Th., Sept. 16, 1958); and in England was the story teller for *An Arabian Night* (Associated Rediffusion, June 1960).

Mr. Welles was narrator for *Americans on Everest* (CBS); appeared on Shindig (ABC); narrated numerous National Geographic specials (CBS); played himself on a segment of I Love Lucy (CBS); appeared in *Life in the Balance* (NET); was the subject of his work on Camera Three (CBS); and appeared on The Dick Cavett Show (ABC).

Other Activities. At the California State Fair (Sacramento, Sept. 3, 1941), Mr. Welles performed as a magician.

Published Works. Mr. Welles was the editor for *Everybody's Shakespeare* (c. 1935); wrote the novel, *Mr. Arkadin* (1956); wrote a column for the NY *Post* entitled "Orson Welles' Almanac" (1945); and wrote *Moby Dick—Rehearsed* (1965).

Awards. He received the Claire M. Senie plaque (Drama Study Club, 1938); and, with Mr. Mankiewicz, an Academy (Oscar) Award for his film *Citizen Kane* (RKO, 1941); the Twentieth Anniversary Special Prize at the Cannes International Film Festival for *Chimes at Midnight* (1966); and the American Film Institute Award for Life Achievement (1974).

WELLES, VIOLET. Press representative. b. Violet Fidel, July 1, Brooklyn, N.Y., to Herman and Lenore B. Fidel. Father, sales engineer; mother, teacher. Grad. New Utrecht H.S., Brooklyn; Univ. of North Carolina, B.A. Married to Metro Welles, teacher. Member of ATPAM; New Dramatists Comm. Address: 174 W. 76th St., New York, NY 10023, tel. (212) TR 4-7472.

Pre-Theatre. Educator.

Theatre. Miss Welles was the author of *The Spring Affair* (Margo Jones Th., Dallas, Tex., 1956) and *Boy on the Beach* (Pennsylvania State Univ. Th., 1958); and press representative for *A Thousand Clowns, Miracle Worker, Spoon River, Journey to the Day, What Makes Sammy Run?, The Royal Hunt of the Sun,* and *Man of La Mancha.*

Television. She wrote the daytime series, Dark Shadows.

Awards. She received the Fred Koch Playwriting Fellowship and the John Golden Playwriting Fellowship.

WESKER, ARNOLD. Playwright. b. May 24, 1932, London, England, to Joseph and Leah (Perlmutter) Wesker. Father, tailor's machinist; mother, tailor's machinist, cook. Attended Upton House Central Sch., London, 1941–46; London Sch. of Film Technique, 1955–56. Married Nov. 14, 1958, to Doreen Cecile ("Dusty") Bicker; two sons, one daughter. Served RAF (1950–52). Address: 27 Bishops Rd., London, N.6, England; c/o Centre 42, 20 Fitzroy Sq., London, W.1, England tel. Euston 5994.

Pre-Theatre. Furniture-maker's apprentice, carpenter's mate, bookseller's asst., plumber's mate, farm laborer, kitchen porter, and pastry cook.

Theatre. Mr. Wesker wrote *Chicken Soup with Barley* (Belgrade Th., Coventry, England, July 7, 1958; Royal Court, London, July 14, 1958); *Roots* (Belgrade, May 25, 1959; Royal Court, June 30, 1959; Mayfair, N.Y.C., Mar. 6, 1961); *The Kitchen* (Royal Court, Sept. 6, 1959; 81 St. Th., N.Y.C., June 13, 1966); *I'm Talking about Jerusalem* (Belgrade, Mar. 28, 1960; Royal Court, July 27, 1960); *Chips with Everything* (Royal Court, Apr. 27, 1962; Plymouth, N.Y.C., Oct. 1, 1963); *The Nottingham Captain,* a moral for narrator, voices and orch. (Trades Union Festival, Centre 42, Wellingborough, Northants, England, 1962); *Four Seasons* (Saville, London, Sept. 21, 1965; Th. Four, N.Y.C., Mar. 14, 1968); *Their Very Own and Golden City* (Royal Court, May 19, 1966; previous European productions); *The Friends* (Roundhouse, Chalk Farm, May 19, 1970; directed this production); *The Old Ones* (Royal Court, Aug. 8, 1972; Th. at the Lambs Club, N.Y.C., Dec. 6, 1974); and *The Journalists* (Jackson's Lane Community Centre, Highgate, North London, July 1975).

Films. His play, *The Kitchen,* was filmed (Kingsley, 1961).

Television. Mr. Wesker's first television script was *Menace* (London, Dec. 1963). His three plays (*Chicken Soup with Barley, Roots,* and *I'm Talking about Jerusalem*) were presented as The Wesker Trilogy (BBC-2, final telecast Feb. 6, 1966). Mr. Wesker appeared on the Look of the Week series (BBC-1, Oct. 30, 1966).

Other Activities. He founded (in 1962) Centre 42, an organization of writers, actors, musicians, painters, and architects, which presents arts festivals in English industrial communities, at the request of any local spontaneously-formed festival committee.

He wrote for a month (1971) at The London *Sunday Times,* from which experience came the play, *The Journalists.* .

Published Works. Mr. Wesker has written a volume of essays and lectures, *Fears of Fragmentation* (1970); a long short story, *Six Sundays in January* (1971); and a volume of short stories, *Love Letters on Blue Paper* (1975).

Awards. For his play, *Chicken Soup with Barley,* Mr. Wesker received the Arts Council Bursary (1959) and the *Evening Standard* Award as Most Promising British Playwright (1960). He won a first prize from the *Encyclopaedia Brittanica* (1961); his play *Chips with Everything* was voted best play of the year in the *Variety* London Theatre Critics' Poll (1963). He won the 1964 Marzotto (Italy) Drama Award for the best unpublished play for *Their Very Own and Golden City.*

WEST, MAE. Actress, playwright, screenwriter. b. Aug. 17, 1892, Brooklyn, N.Y., to John Patrick and Matilda (Delker-Dolger) West. Attended public schools and tutored privately. Married 1911 to Frank Wallace (marr. dis. 1943). Member of AEA; AFTRA; SAG; AGVA; Order of Kentucky Colonels. Address: 514 Pacific Coast Highway, Santa Monica, CA 90406.

Theatre. Miss West first appeared professionally at age five in Hal Clarendon's Stock Co. (Gotham Th., Bklyn., 1897), where she played the title role in *Little Nell the Marchioness,* Lovey Mary in *Mrs. Wiggs of the Cabbage Patch,* the Angel Child in *Ten Nights in a Bar Room,* Willie Carlyle in *East Lynne,* and Jessie in *The Fatal Wedding* (1897–1903).

She made her N.Y.C. debut as Maggie O'Hara in *A la Broadway* (Follies Bergere Th., Sept. 22, 1911; followed by Mlle. Angélique in *Vera Violetta* (Winter Garden, Nov. 20, 1911); La Petite Daffy in *A Winsome Widow* (Moulin Rouge, Apr. 11, 1912); and Maria Tamburri in *Such Is Life* (San Francisco, Calif., July 1913). She toured for five years as "Vaudeville's Youngest Headliner" for the Keith Circuit; played Mayme Dean in *Sometime* (Shubert, N.Y.C., Oct. 4, 1918); and appeared in the revues, *Demi-Tasse* (Capitol, Nov. 1919), and *The Mimic World* (Century Promenade, Aug. 15, 1921); played Margie LaMont in *Sex* (Daly's, Apr. 26, 1926), which she also wrote, under the name of Jane Mast; wrote *The Drag* (1927), which toured but was banned from N.Y.C.; played Evelyn Carson in *The Wicked Age* (Daly's, Nov. 4, 1927); wrote and played the title role in *Diamond Lil* (Royale, Apr. 9, 1928); wrote *Pleasure Man* (Biltmore, Oct. 1, 1928); wrote and played Babe Gordon in *The Constant Sinner* (Royale, Sept. 14, 1931); wrote and played the title role in *Catherine Was Great* (Shubert, Aug. 2, 1944); and toured cross-country in *Ring Twice Tonight* (May 1946).

She performed in *Diamond Lil* (Prince of Wales's Th., London, England, Jan. 24, 1948; Coronet, N.Y.C., Feb. 5, 1949), toured in it (1949–50), and returned in it to N.Y.C. (Bway Th., Sept. 14, 1951). She toured summer theatres as Carliss Dale in *Come On Up . . Ring Twice!,* which she also adapted (1952); and appeared in *Sextet,* which she adapted from an idea by Charlotte Francis (Edgewater Beach Hotel, Chicago, Ill.; Northland Playhouse, Detroit, Mich.; Kenley Players, Warren and Columbus, Ohio; Coconut Grove Playhouse, Miami, Fla., 1961).

Films. Miss West appeared for Paramount Pictures: in *Night after Night* (1932); as Lady Lou in an adaptation of her play, *Diamond Lil*, entitled *She Done Him Wrong* (1933); in *I'm No Angel* (1933); as Ruby Carter in *Belle of the Nineties* (1934), for which she wrote the screenplay; as Cleo Borden in *Goin' to Town* (1935; wrote the screenplay); Frisco Doll in *Klondike Annie* (1936; wrote story and screenplay); as Mavis Arden in *Go West, Young Man* (1936; wrote screenplay); and as Peaches O'Day in *Every Day's a Holiday* (1938; story and screenplay). She wrote (with W. C. Fields) the story and screenplay, and played Flower Belle Lee, in *My Little Chickadee* (U, 1940); played Fay Laurence in *The Heat's On* (Col., 1943); was seen in the anthology film, *The Love Goddesses* (Walter Reade-Sterling, 1965); and played Leticia in *Myra Breckinridge* (20th-Fox, 1970).

Television. Miss West appeared twice on the *Mister Ed* series (NBC, 1964 and 1965).

Published Works. Miss West wrote her autobiography, *Goodness Had Nothing to Do With It* (1959; updated 1970) and the novel *Pleasure Man* (1975), based on her 1928 play.

Discography. She recorded an LP album, *The Naked Ape*.

WETMORE, JOAN. Actress. b. Joan Deery, Sydney, Australia, to Arthur and Agnes (Thorn) Deery. Father, lawyer; mother, actress. Attended Winsor Convent, Australia; Horace Mann H.S., N.Y.C.; George Washington H.S., N.Y.C. Married Feb. 21, 1941, to W. Palmer Dixon; two sons. Member of AEA; AFTRA. Address: 550 Park Ave., New York, NY 10021.

Theatre. Miss Wetmore made her N.Y.C. debut as Bella Manchester in *The Two Bouquets* (Windsor Th., May 31, 1938); subsequently played a Lady and a Lecturer in *Everywhere I Roam* (Natl., Dec. 29, 1938); Katherine Winthrop Holmes in *Two on an Island* (Broadhurst, Jan. 22, 1940); Phyllis Glenning in *Kind Lady* (Playhouse, Sept. 3, 1940); Cora Simon in *Counsellor-at-Law* (Royale, Nov. 24, 1942); Millicent Prince in *A New Life* (Royale, Sept. 15, 1943); Norma in *For Keeps* (Henry Miller's Th., June 14, 1944); Margaret Hicks Harwood in *Hope for the Best* (Fulton, Feb. 7, 1945); Condace Barrett in *The Small Hours* (Natl., Feb. 15, 1951); Natasha in *A Girl Can Tell* (Royale, Oct. 29, 1953); appeared in *Last Love of Don Juan* (Rooftop, Nov. 23, 1955); played Chrysothemis in *Electra*, and Muriel Palmer in *Harlequinade* in a double-bill (Rita Allen Th., Feb. 3, 1959); Mrs. Lunn in *Overruled*, Mrs. Secondborn in *Buoyant Billions*, and Lesbia Grantham in *Getting Married*, which were presented in a program entitled *A Shaw Festival* (Provincetown Playhouse, May 26, 1959); Claire Munson in *Advise and Consent* (Cort, Nov. 17, 1960); appeared in *A Very Rich Woman* (Belasco Th., Sept. 30, 1965); and in *The Great Indoors* (Ethel Barrymore Th., Feb. 1967).

Television. Miss Wetmore has appeared on Dupont Show of the Month (NBC); Studio One (CBS); The Defenders (CBS); Robert Montgomery Presents (NBC); Young Doctor Malone (NBC); US Steel Hour (CBS); Kraft Television Th. (CBS); The Doctors (NBC); Playhouse 90 (CBS); Philco Playhouse (NBC); *The Nurses* (CBS); and *The Guiding Light* (CBS).

Recreation. Golf, painting, reading.

WEXLER, PETER. Setting and lighting designer, costume designer, theatre and performing space designer. b. Peter John Wexler, Oct. 31, 1936, New York City, to S. David and Berda Wexler. Educ. N.Y.C. public schools. Grad. School of Architecture, Univ. of Michigan, B.S. in design, 1958; also attended Yale School of Drama, 1958. Mr. Wexler received additional professional training as a scene painter (1947–54) with the Cleveland Playhouse, Chautauqua, N.Y., and the Chautauqua (N.Y.) Opera Assn. Married Nov. 30, 1962, to Constance Ross. Member of United Scenic Artists, Local 829; Scenic Artists 816—IATSE; USITT. Address: 277 West End Ave., New York, NY 10023, tel. (212) 877-9494.

Theatre. Mr. Wexler designed scenery, lighting, and costumes for the NY Shakespeare Festival *Antony and Cleopatra* (Heckscher Th., Jan. 13, 1959); for *The Big Knife* (Seven Arts Playhouse, Nov. 12, 1959); designed scenery and lighting for *Brecht on Brecht* (Th. de Lys, Jan. 3, 1962); for *Portrait of the Artist as a Young Man* (Martinique, May 28, 1962); for *The Threepenny Opera* (Sacandaga Playhouse, Sacandaga, N.Y., Summer 1962); and he designed scenery and lighting for *Abe Lincoln in Illinois* (Phyllis Anderson Th., N.Y.C., Jan. 21, 1963). He designed scenery, lighting, and costumes for *The Taming of the Shrew* (Phyllis Anderson Th., Mar. 6, 1963); designed the Emily Frankel ballet *Dreams* (New York, May 1964); designed scenery and lighting for *Watch the Birdie* (Coconut Grove Playhouse, Miami, Fla., July 14, 1964); designed the stage installation for the Czechoslovakian projected scenery show *Laterna Magika* (Carnegie Hall, N.Y.C., Aug. 3, 1964); designed scenery and lighting for the Association of Producing Artists production of *War and Peace* (Ann Arbor, Mich., Sept. 30, 1964; Phoenix Th., N.Y.C., Jan. 11, 1965); for *Mystery of Elche* (New York, Winter 1964); and scenery, costumes, and lighting for the Robert Joffrey Ballet *Capers (Caprice)* on tour (Bolshoi Th., Moscow, USSR, Winter 1964).

He also designed scenery, lighting, and costumes for the Corpus Christi Symphony Orchestra production of *La Bohème* (New York, Mar. 1965); scenery and lighting for the opera *Lizzie Borden* (NY City Ctr. Opera Co., Spring 1965); scenery, lighting, and costumes for *The Deputy* (The Theatre Group, Los Angeles, Calif., Aug. 13, 1965) and national tour; and designed scenery and lighting for *The Burnt Flower Bed* (Th. Guild, N.Y., July 1965). He designed scenery for *The White Devil* (Circle in the Square, Dec. 6, 1965); scenery and lighting for *The Magic Flute* (Washington Opera Soc., Washington, D.C., Jan. 1966); scenery, lighting, and costumes for *Cosi fan tutte* (Corpus Christi Symphony Orchestra, Corpus Christi, Tex., Apr. 1966); for *Candide* (Center Theatre Group, Los Angeles, Calif., July 12, 1966); scenery and lighting for the tour of *On a Clear Day You Can See Forever* (1966); for *A Joyful Noise* (Mark Hellinger Th., N.Y.C., Dec. 15, 1966); and he designed scenery for *Possibilities* (scheduled Dec. 1966, but unproduced).

Mr. Wexler became principal designer, Center Theatre Group (formerly Theater Group), Mark Taper Forum, Los Angeles, Calif., in 1967 and has also been design advisor there (1968–to date), and he designed scenery, lighting, and costumes for that theatre's opening production, *The Devils* (Apr. 14, 1967) and for *The Marriage of Mr. Mississippi* (Aug. 25, 1967). He designed scenery for *The Happy Time* (Bway Th., N.Y.C., Jan. 18, 1968); scenery and, with Elinor Bunin, projections for *In the Matter of J. Robert Oppenheimer* (Mark Taper Forum, May 24, 1968); scenery and lighting for *Camino Real* (Mark Taper Forum, Aug. 21, 1968); scenery and, with Elinor Bunin, projections for *In the Matter of J. Robert Oppenheimer* (Vivian Beaumont Th., N.Y.C., Mar. 6, 1969); scenery for *Chemin de Fer* (Mark Taper Forum, June 5, 1969); scenery and costumes for *Uncle Vanya* (Mark Taper Forum, Aug. 21, 1969); and lighting for the NY Philharmonic presentation of Scriabin's *Prometheus* (Oct. 1969).

He designed scenery and costumes for *Camino Real* (Vivian Beaumont Th., Jan. 8, 1970); scenery for *Minnie's Boys* (Imperial, Mar. 26, 1970); for *Murderous Angels* (Mark Taper Forum, Feb. 5, 1970); costumes for Rosebloom (Mark Taper Forum, Oct. 5, 1970); scenery for the Phoenix Th. production of *The Trial of the Catonsville Nine* (Good Shepherd Faith Church, N.Y.C., Feb. 7, 1971; transferred to Lyceum, June 2, 1971); for *The Trial of A. Lincoln* (New York, Mar. 1971); scenery for the Center Th. Group production of *The Trial of the Catonsville Nine* (Mark Taper Forum, June 17, 1971); scenery and lighting for *The Gershwin Years* (Philharmonic Hall, N.Y.C., Oct. 1971); scenery for *Godspell* (Mark Taper Forum, Nov. 4, 1971); scenery for *Murderous Angels* (Playhouse, N.Y.C., Dec. 20, 1971); for *The Web and the Rock* (Th. de Lys, Mar. 19, 1972); and scenery and costumes for the Central City (Colo.) Opera House Assn. production of *Curlew River* (July 1972).

Mr. Wexler also designed scenery for *Mass* (Mark Taper Forum Los Angeles, Jan. 4, 1973); scenery, costumes, and visual effects (film) for the Metropolitan Opera production of *Les Troyens* (Metropolitan Opera House, N.Y.C., Oct. 22, 1973); scenery, lighting, and costumes for the Concert Artists Guild presentation of *Church Trilogy* (St. James Ch., N.Y.C., Nov. 1973); scenery and lighting for *Hamlet* (Mark Taper Forum, Los Angeles, Mar. 14, 1974); and for *Henry IV, Parts 1* and *2* (Goodman Th., Chicago, Ill., Mar. 29, 1974).

Films. Mr. Wexler designed scenery for *Andy* (U, 1965); was production designer for the film *The Trial of the Catonsville Nine* (U, 1973); and designed scenery and lighting and edited the New York Philharmonic Hall films *Happy Talk* (1972) and *Review of Reviews* (1973).

Television. Mr. Wexler designed scenery for *Say When* (1962); the Merv Griffin Show (NBC, May–Oct. 1965); and designed the 1971 Cleo Awards ceremony and, with Michael Bennett, the film title art for the ceremony (American Television Commercials Festival, N.Y., 1971).

Concerts. Mr. Wexler became associated with the annual NY Philharmonic Promenades concerts at Philharmonic Hall (later Avery Fisher Hall) in June 1965, when he designed the scenery and interior, performing the same function in June 1966; and since May 1967, he has designed scenery, lighting, interior, exterior, and graphics for the concerts. In addition he was responsible for the spatial conception, audience design, lighting, and graphics for the annual June Rug Concerts, also at Philharmonic Hall, in 1973 and 1974.

Other Activities. In addition to his theatre work, Mr. Wexler has taught and/or lectured at the Univ. of Michigan, the State Univ. of NY (Binghamton), and the Univ. of Arizona, Tucson. His designing commissions outside the theatre include the stage for use in the White House, Washington, D.C. (1961); lighting for the *Time* and *Life* dinner (Waldorf-Astoria Hotel, N.Y.C., 1963); for the *Scapino* ballet and "Eleanor Roosevelt Tribute" (Philharmonic Hall, N.Y.C., Winter 1964). Mr. Wexler designed the theatre complex Upper West, N.Y.C. (Aug. 1970); designed "A Sculpture Call Park," 17 Battery Place, N.Y.C. (June 1971); and was responsible for the spatial conception and design of the theatre at Stage B, 20th Century-Fox, Center Th. Group, Los Angeles, Calif. (Sept. 1973).

Published Works. Mr. Wexler's drawings for costumes and scenery have appeared in such publications as the *Saturday Review, Interiors, Theatre Design and Technology, Players Magazine, Theatre Crafts*, the Metropolitan Opera Association's *Opera News*, and the Metropolitan Opera *Souvenir Book* (1973). NY State Univ. (Binghamton) held a retrospective of his drawings (1966), and he had a one-man show at the Wright-Hepburn-Webster Gallery, N.Y.C., in Feb. 1969.

Awards. Mr. Wexler won the ANTA-ITI "War and Peace" competition (Spring 1965), and his model is on display at the Museum of Modern Art, Paris, France, and the Museum of Contemporary Crafts, N.Y.C. He was nominated for Drama Desk and Joseph Maharam awards as best designer (1966) for his scenery for *The White Devils;* won those awards (1968) as best designer of a musical for *The Happy Time* and was nominated for an Antoinette Perry (Tony) Award as best designer, also for *The Happy Time*. For *In the Matter of J. Robert Oppenheimer*, he was again a Drama Desk and Joseph Maharam Award nominee as best designer (1969). In 1971 and 1972, he won the Los Angeles Drama Critics Circle award for continued distinguished achievement in set design in the Los Angeles theatre.

WHARTON, BETTY. Theatre librarian and researcher, actress. b. Betty Ann Jenks, June 26, 1911, to Edward Dyer and Lila (Von Ache) Jenks. Father, businessman. Educ. Misses Janes' School, Hollywood, Calif.; Hollywood School for Girls. Professional training at Pasadena (Calif.) Playhouse Coll. of Theatre Arts (1929–31); School of Library Science, Columbia Univ., 1962–63. Married 1936 to Carl Edgar Fisher, theatrical manager (marr. dis.); one daughter; 1949 to John Franklin Wharton, lawyer. Member of TLA (exec. bd., 1973–77); ASTR; IFTR; AEA; AFTRA (honorable withdrawal). Address: (home) 141 E. 72nd St., New York, NY 10021, tel. (212) LE 5-8473; (bus.) Performing Arts Research Center, 111 Amsterdam Ave., New York, NY 10023, tel. (212) 799-2200.

In 1963, Mrs. Wharton became a member of the staff of the Theatre Collection, Performing Arts Research Center, Lincoln Center, N.Y.C.

Theatre. Known on the stage as Mary Mason, Mrs. Wharton made her debut as Marjorie Jones in *Penrod* (Egan Th., Los Angeles, Calif., 1918). As a member of the Smith-King Players (1920), Pasadena, Calif., she played roles in several productions and later (1929–32) appeared in twenty productions of the Pasadena Community Playhouse. She was Acacia in *The Passion Flower* (Olvera St. Th., Los Angeles, 1932) and made her Bway debut as Peggy in *The Sky's the Limit* (Fulton Th., Dec. 17, 1934), following with appearances as Maria in *The Field of Ermine* (Mansfield Th., Feb. 8, 1935); Joan Collett in *Call It a Day* (Morosco, Jan. 28, 1936); Claire Ramm in *Brother Rat* (Biltmore, Dec. 16, 1936); Carol Birth in *The Schoolhouse on the Lot* (Ritz Th., Mar. 22, 1938); and Mattie Kate Baugh in *Aries Is Rising* (John Golden Th., Nov. 21, 1939). She replaced Betty Field as Clare Wallace in *The Primrose Path* (Biltmore, Jan. 4, 1939); played Cece Sawyer in *Goodbye in the Night* (Biltmore, Mar. 18, 1940); Kitty Verdun in *Charley's Aunt* (Cort, Oct. 17, 1940); Norma Cole in *Cafe Crown* (Cort, Jan. 23, 1942); and toured Canada and the US as Sybil Chase in a revival of *Private Lives.*

Mrs. Wharton also played in summer stock, making her debut in *Trio* (White Plains, N.Y., 1934) and appearing from 1938 to 1943 in theatres in Maplewood and Montclair, N.J.; Newport, R.I.; Stockbridge, Mass.; Buck's County, Penna.; and at Elitch's Gardens, Denver, Colo.

Films. Mrs. Wharton became a contract player at RKO in 1932 and made her first film appearance in *The Age of Consent* (RKO) the same year. Her other motion pictures include *Walls of Gold* and *The Mad Game* (both 20th-Fox, 1933).

Television and Radio. Mrs. Wharton was active in radio (1939–45) on such programs as Maudie's Diary (WABC), The Aldrich Family (NBC), My Best Girls (WJZ), and FBI in Peace and War. Daytime serials in which she played were The Life and Loves of Dr. Susan, The Strange Romance of Evelyn Winters, and Betty and Bob. She made her television debut in Subway Express (1950).

Published Works. Mrs. Wharton wrote biographies of theatre personalities for the 1968 *Grolier Encyclopedia International;* selected photographs for John Wharton's *Life Among the Playwrights* (1974); and is author of *The Chamberlain and Lyman Brown Collection,* Performing Arts Resources, Vol. 1 (1975).

Recreation. Travel, collection of Eighteenth-century theatrical autograph manuscripts.

WHARTON, JOHN F. Lawyer, writer. b. John Franklin Wharton, July 28, 1894, Newark, N.J., to Charles A. and Lenna I. (Lyon) Wharton. Father, manufacturer. Grad. East Orange (N.J.) H.S., 1911; attended Williams Coll., 1911–1915; grad. Columbia Univ. Law Sch., B.A., LL.B. 1920. Married Dec. 6, 1924, to Carly Bumiller, producer (marr. dis.); two daughters; married, Aug. 30, 1949, to Betty A. (Mary Mason) Jenks, actress. Served WW I, US Naval Aviation; WW II, Board Economic Welfare. Member of Phi Beta Kappa, Theta Delta Chi. Address: (home) 141 E. 72nd St., New York, NY 10021, tel. (212) LE 5-8473; (bus.) 345 Park Ave., New York, NY 10022, tel. (212) 935-8620.

Mr. Wharton was a co-founder of the law firm of Paul, Weiss, Rifkind, Wharton & Garrison. He has been active in theatrical law since 1923. His practice includes playwrights, actors, directors, producers, theatre owners, scenic designers, builders, painters, and others in the theatrical field. He assisted in developing forms of contracts with play investors during the 1920's, and, in 1940, he worked out a form of limited partnership which has been used since. He also proposed a plan permitting authors to make pre-production sales to motion picture rights, and, with the late Jacob Wilk, developed a standard form for these sales, variations of which are still in use.

In 1938, Mr. Wharton became co-founder of The Playwrights Producing Co., Inc., acting as general counsel, president, and general business advisor for 22 years. He was general counsel for ANTA, 1938–48, aided in financing its first play series, and served as a director there for 15 years; was co-founder of the New Dramatists Committee, where he was general counsel and director (1951–60); has been chairman of the board of Theatre Inc. which sponsors the Phoenix Th.; was co-founder and chairman of the board of the Inst. for Advanced Studies in the Theatre (IASTA); director of the Amer. Academy of Dramatic Arts (AADA), Little Orchestra Society, Inc., Kurt Weill Foundation for Music, Theatre Development Fund (which he helped to organize), and Ballet Theatre Foundation. He is also Director-Consultant, Legitimate Theatre Exploratory Commission (1964–to date) and is sole trustee of Cole Porter's musical and literary works (1964–to date).

Films. He represented Selznick International Pictures during production in the first three-color process of *Gone With the Wind* and represented the inventor of the Cinerama process for films.

Television. He represented Philo T. Farnsworth, inventor of modern television; and Farnsworth Television and Radio Corp. (1928–49).

Published Works. His articles on the theatre have appeared in *Saturday Review,* the New York *Times,* and the Chicago *Daily News.* Mr. Wharton also wrote *This Road to Recovery* (1933), *Earning a Living* (1945); *The Explorations of George Burton* (1951), and *Life Among the Playwrights* (1974). He has also written extensively on world peace and various social and economic problems.

Awards. Mr. Wharton received the Kelcey Allen Award in 1965, was named by *Variety* as the man who did most for the theatre in 1966, and in 1974 received a special Antoinette Perry (Tony) Award and a special New Dramatists, Inc. Award.

Recreation. Bridge, gardening.

WHEELER, HUGH. Playwright. b. Hugh Callingham Wheeler, Mar. 19, 1916, London, England, to Harold and Florence (Scammell) Wheeler. Father, civil servant. Grad. Clayesmore Sch., 1932; Univ. of London 1936. Served WW II, US Army, Medical Corps. Naturalized, 1942. Member of Dramatists Guild; WGA. Address: Twin Hills Farm, Monterey, MA tel. (413) 528-0770.

Pre-Theatre. Novelist.

Theatre. Mr. Wheeler wrote *Big Fish, Little Fish* (ANTA Th., N.Y.C., Mar. 15, 1961; Duke of York's, London, Oct. 1962); and *Look: We've Come Through!* (Hudson, N.Y.C., Oct. 25, 1961; *We Have Always Lived in the Castle* (Ethel Barrymore Th., Oct. 19, 1966); wrote the book for *A Little Night Music* (Sam S. Shubert Th., Feb. 25, 1973); with Joseph Stein adapted the book for a revival of *Irene* (Minskoff Th., Mar. 13, 1973); and wrote the book for the revival of *Candide* (Broadway Th., Mar. 10, 1974).

Films. Mr. Wheeler wrote, with Peter Viertel, the screenplay for *Five Miles to Midnight* (UA, 1962); the screenplay for *Something for Everyone* (Natl. Gen., 1970); and, with Jay Presson Allen, *Travels with My Aunt* (MGM, 1973).

Published Works. Under the pseudonyms, Patrick Quentin, Q. Patrick, and Jonathan Stagge, he has written more than thirty novels, including *A Puzzle for Fools* (1938); *Black Widow* (1952); *My Son, the Murderer* (1954); *Man in the Net* (1955); *Man with Two Wives* (1955); and *Ordeal of Mrs. Snow* (1962).

Awards. In 1972, Mr. Wheeler received the Edgar Allen Poe Award and was nominated for the Screen Writers Award. In 1973, he received a Drama Desk Award as outstanding book writer for *A Little Night Music;* the show received two Antoinette Perry (Tony) awards—for best musical and best book of a musical; and the NY Drama Critics Circle chose it as best musical. In 1974, Mr. Wheeler again received the Drama Desk Award as outstanding book writer, this time for *Candide,* which also received a Tony for best book of a musical, and was chosen by the NY Drama Critics Circle and the Outer Circle as best musical.

Recreation. Music, travel.

WHEELER, LOIS. Actress. b. July 12, 1920, Stockton, Calif., to Raymond and Catherine Wheeler. Father, former mayor of Stockton. Grad. St. Mary's Convent, Stockton, 1939; Coll. of the Pacific, B.A. 1943. Studied at Actors' Studio, N.Y.C. (member 1949–to date); Neighborhood Playhouse Sch. of the Th., N.Y.C., 1941–43. Married May 23, 1949, to Edgar Snow; one son, one daughter. Member of AEA; SAG; AFTRA. Address: 9 W. 10th St., New York, NY 10011.

Theatre. Miss Wheeler made her N.Y.C. debut as Margaret in *The Innocent Voyage* (Belasco Th., Nov. 15, 1943); played Joan in *Pick-Up Girl* (48 St. Th., May 3, 1944); Janet Logan in *Trio* (Belasco, Dec. 29, 1944); and succeeded (June 1944) Augusta Dabney as Ruth Wilkins in *Dear Ruth* (Henry Miller's Th., Dec. 13, 1944), and on tour (six months).

She played Ann Deever in *All My Sons* (Coronet, N.Y.C., Jan. 29, 1947); Lee Baron in *The Young and Fair* (Fulton, Nov. 22, 1948); Paula in *Dinosaur Wharf* (National, Nov. 8, 1951); Miriam in *The Fifth Season* (Cort, Jan. 23, 1953); Clara Gerrity in *The Troublemakers* (President, Dec. 30, 1954); and Katerina Ivanovna in *The Trial of Dmitri Karamozov* (Jan Hus House, Jan. 27, 1958).

Films. She has appeared in *My Foolish Heart* (RKO, 1949); and *The Deep Well* (1951).

Television. Miss Wheeler has appeared on the series The Guiding Light (CBS, 1952–59); Ford Th. (CBS); and Armstrong Circle Th. (CBS).

WHITE, BRADFORD. Educator, director, designer. b. Taul Bradford White, Jr., Nov. 3, 1912, Rome, Ga., to Taul Bradford and Everett (McGuire) White, Sr. Father, salesman; mother, teacher. Grad. Darlington Sch. for Boys, Rome, Ga., 1930; Univ. of North Carolina, A.B. 1934; Yale Univ. Sch. of Drama, M.F.A. 1939; attended Univ. of Wisconsin, 1934–35. Married Sept. 1948 to Margaret Ashford; two sons. Served US Army, 1942–45; rank, Top Sgt. Relative in theatre: cousin, Louise Lamont, director, Lamont Children's Th., Chapel Hill, N.C. Member of AETA; STC; Tenn. Educ. Assn.; Phi Beta Kappa; Phi Delta Theta. Address: (home) 1160 Minor Cove, Memphis, TN 38111, tel. (901) FA 3-3725; (bus.) Speech and Drama Dept., Memphis State University, Memphis, TN 38111, tel. (901) 324-3601.

Since 1955, Mr. White has been professor of speech and drama at Memphis State Univ. where he has been a member of the faculty since 1948, and has directed and designed approximately 20 productions.

He was costume designer for the Drama Dept. of the Univ. of Texas (1939–40); and scene technician at the Lake Placid Summer Th. (1938).

Since 1969, he has been a stage director and a member of the Board of Directors for the Red Balloon Players, childrens' theatre company.

Awards. As director and producer of the Memphis Shakespeare Festival, he was cited for contributions on its 10th anniversary.

Recreation. Painting, swimming, cycling.

WHITE, GEORGE C. Theatre executive, actor, stage director, lighting designer, stage manager. b. George Cooke White, Aug. 16, 1935, New London, Conn., to Nelson C. and Aida (Rovetti)

White. Father, artist. Educ. Loomis School, Windsor, Conn.; grad. Yale Univ., 1957; Yale School of Drama, M.F.A., 1961; studied at Univ. of Paris (Sorbonne); Univ. of Birmingham, England, and Shakespeare Institute, Stratford-on-Avon, England. Served in 4th Armored Div., US Army, 1957–59. Married July 5, 1958, to Elizabeth Darling; two sons, one daughter. Member of the boards of American Playwrights Th.; ITI; Eastern Connecticut Symphony and Dance Arts Council; Rehearsal Club; Theater of Latin America; Manhattan Theatre Club; member Yale Drama Alumni (exec. comm.); Yale Alumni (dir.); Theatre Communications Group Experimental Theatre Panel; The Players Club. Address: (home) 123 E. 80th St., New York, NY 10021, tel. (212) BU 8-6108; (bus.) 1860 Broadway, New York, NY 10023, tel. (212) CI 6-1485.

Theatre. Mr. White is president of the Eugene O'Neill Memorial Theater Center, Inc., which he founded at Waterford, Conn., in 1964. His previous theatrical activities included management of the International Ballet Festival, Nervi, Italy (1954); being stage manager for the world tour of the Imperial Japanese Azuma Kabuki Co. (1955); and he played several roles in an off-Bway production of *John Brown's Body* (Martinique, N.Y.C., June 21, 1960).

Television. Mr. White played the role of Sgt. Bruce Bennett in *Citizen Soldier* (1958). He was production coordinator for the syndicated Festival of Performing Arts (1961–63) and for East Side, West Side (CBS, 1963).

Published Works. Mr. White's articles have appeared in *Theatre Quarterly, New England Theatre,* and *Southeastern Theatre Magazine.*

Discography. Mr. White has recorded spiritual rhythm and blues.

Awards. Mr. White received the Margo Jones Award (1968), special citations of the New England Theatre Conference (1968, 1974), and the Community Theater Council Award (1974).

Recreation. Fishing, sailing, tennis, fencing, squash, wine tasting.

WHITE, JANE. Actress. b. New York City, to Walter and Gladys (Powell) White. Father, exec. secy., N.A.A.C.P., author. Grad. Fieldston Ethical Culture Sch., N.Y.C.; Smith Coll., B.A. Studied acting with Herbert Berghof, 1945; Peter Frye, 1945–46; George Auerbach, 1948; Uta Hagen, 1950–52; voice with Anna Hamlin, William Laurence, Marjorie Schloss; dance with Hanya Holm. Married May 19, 1962, to Alfredo Viazzi, restaurant owner. Member of AEA (councillor, 1952–53; 1954–60; 1961–66); SAG (councillor, 1963); AFTRA. Address: 99 Bank St., New York, NY 10014, tel. (212) 929-1994.

Theatre. Miss White made her debut as Nonnie in *Strange Fruit* (Royale Th., N.Y.C., Nov. 29, 1945); subsequently appeared as Curley's Wife in *Of Mice and Men* (Dramatic Workshop, June 6, 1946); played the Woman in Green in the ELT production of *Peer Gynt* (Greenwich Mews Playhouse, Mar. 24, 1947); Muriel Broderick in *Almost Faithful* (Hayloft Th., Allentown, Pa., Aug. 18, 1947); Mrs. Lincoln in *The Washington Years* (Amer. Negro Th., Mar. 1948); a Butterfly and a Moth in *The Insect Comedy* (NY City Ctr., June 3, 1948); Elvira in *Blithe Spirit* (Hayloft, July 19, 1948); Anna Velasquez in *City of Kings* (Blackfriars Guild, Feb. 1949); played Katherine in *The Taming of the Shrew* (Hayloft, July 18, 1949); and Barbara Allen in *Dark of the Moon* (Hayloft, Sept. 12, 1949).

She appeared in *Come What May* (Weidman Studio, May 10, 1950); in *Razzle Dazzle* (Arena Th., Edison Hotel, Feb. 19, 1951); played Ellen in *The Climate of Eden* (Martin Beck Th., Nov. 13, 1952); and Carol in *Take a Giant Step* (Lyceum, Sept. 24, 1953).

She played Mercy Wellman in *Time of Storm* (Greenwich Mews, Feb. 25, 1954); the title role in *Hedda Gabler* (YMHA, Nov. 13, 1956); Florence in *The Real Me* (Sharon Playhouse, Conn., June 19, 1956); the title role in the ELT production of *Lysistrata* (Lenox Hill Playhouse, Dec. 12, 1956); Mrs. Muskat in *Liliom,* which she also directed (Peterborough Players, N.H., Aug. 27, 1957); the Mad Wife in *Jane Eyre* (Belasco, N.Y.C., May 1, 1958); Obregon's Wife in *The Power and the Glory* (Phoenix, Dec. 10, 1958); the Queen in *Once Upon a Mattress* (Phoenix, May 11, 1959; moved Alvin, Nov. 25, 1959); Katherine in the NY Shakespeare Festival production of *The Taming of the Shrew* (Belvedere Lake Th., N.Y.C., Aug. 18, 1960); Margaret in *Hop, Signor!* (Cricket, May 7, 1962); and Helen of Troy in *The Trojan Women* (Circle in the Square, Dec. 23, 1963).

She played the Princess of France in *Love's Labour's Lost,* Volumnia in *Coriolanus,* Helen of Troy in *Troilus and Cressida* (NY Shakespeare Festival, Central Park, Summer 1964); Madame Rosepettle in *Oh, Dad, Poor Dad, Momma's Hung You in the Closet, and I'm Feeling So Sad* (Rome, Italy, 1966); Reverend Marian Alexander in *Trumpets of the Lord* (Rome, Italy, Theatre Odeon, Paris, France, 1967); succeeded Irene Pappas as Clytemnestra in *Iphigenia in Aulis* (Circle in the Square, N.Y.C., Nov. 21, 1967); played Barbara in *The Cuban Thing* (Henry Miller's Th., Sept. 24, 1968); the Queen in *Cymbeline* (NY Shakespeare Festival, Central Park, Summer 1971); and Luisa in *The Burnt Flowerbed* (Roundabout, N.Y.C., July 2, 1974).

Films. Miss White played the madame, Janie Dale in *Klute* (WB, 1971). She was technical advisor for *Pinky* (20th-Fox, 1949); and script consultant for *Lost Boundaries* (FC, 1949).

Television. She made her television acting debut on Stage 13 (CBS, June 14, 1950); subsequently appeared on Kraft Television Th. (NBC, July 24, 1957); Alcoa Presents (NBC, Feb. 20, 1956); Studio One (CBS, June 24, 1957); Casey, Crime Photographer (CBS, Sept. 20, 1951); Lamp Unto My Feet (CBS, Oct. 14, 1956); The Shari Lewis Show (NBC, Jan. 6, 1962; June 29, 1963); and on *Car 54, Where Are You?* (CBS, Nov. 1, 1961); and the Queen in *Once Upon a Mattress* (CBS, June 3, 1964).

She played Nurse Lydia Holliday on *The Edge of Night* (CBS, 1968–69); appeared on *The Secret Storm* (CBS, 1971); *A World Apart* (ABC, 1971); and repeated her performance as the Queen in *Once Upon a Mattress* (CBS, Dec. 12, 1972).

Miss White was co-founder and vice-president of Torchlight Productions (1947–49), an independent packager of radio and television programs.

Other Activities. She formed Jane White's Classes, Inc., which offered professional theatrical training (1960–64).

Awards. Miss White received the 1965 *Village Voice* Off-Broadway (Obie) Award as best actress of the year.

WHITE, JESSE. Actor, comedian. b. Jesse Marc Weidenfeld, Jan. 3, 1919, Buffalo, N.Y., to Elias and Freda (Zwernbaum) Weidenfeld. Father, businessman. Grad. West H.S., Akron, Ohio, 1936. Married Jan. 18, 1942, to Simmy Conn; two daughters. Member of AEA; SAG; AFTRA. Address: 517 N. Rexford Dr., Beverly Hills, CA 90210, tel. (213) CR 4-8111.

Pre-Theatre. Beauty supply business; jewelry business; manufacturer of corsets and brassieres.

Theatre. Mr. White made his debut as the Court Jester in *Mary of Scotland* (Weathervane Playhouse, Akron, Ohio, 1934); toured as a Nazi Soldier in *The Moon Is Down* (1942); and made his first N.Y.C. appearance as the Vacuum Cleaner Salesman in *Sons and Soldiers* (Morosco, May 4, 1943).

He played Gus Wagner in *My Dear Public* (46 St. Th., Sept. 9, 1943); appeared in the pre-Bway tryout of *Unexpected Honeymoon* (Great Northern, Chicago, Ill., 1943); J. B. McGuire in *Mrs. Kimball Presents* (48 St. Th., Feb. 29, 1944); Ajax 1st in *Helen Goes to Troy* (Alvin, Apr. 24, 1944); Duane Wilson in *Harvey* (48 St. Th., Nov. 1, 1944); toured in *Goodnight Ladies* (1949); appeared in *A Month in the Country* (Westport Country Playhouse, Conn., 1948); played Marochek in *Red Gloves* (Mansfield, N.Y.C., Dec. 4, 1948); and succeeded (1949) Paul Douglas as Harry Brock in *Born Yesterday* (Lyceum, Feb. 4, 1946).

Mr. White has also appeared in the following stock productions: *Will Success Spoil Rock Hunter?* (Carthay Circle, Los Angeles, Calif., 1956); *A Hole in the Head* (Civic Th., Los Angeles, 1957); *Guys and Dolls* (Sacramento Music Circus, Calif., 1959); *Kiss Me, Kate* (Sacramento Music Circus, 1960); *Show Boat* (Melodyland, Berkeley, Calif., 1963); and *Born Yesterday* (Sombrero Playhouse, Phoenix, Ariz., 1963).

He played Ernie Hempel in *Stubborn Ernie* (Friars Club, Los Angeles, June 14, 1964); Stickpin Sidney Crane in *Kelly* (Broadhurst, N.Y.C., Feb. 6, 1965); First Man in *Kiss Me, Kate* (NY City Ctr., May 12, 1965); replaced (May 28, 1969) John McGiver as the Mayor in *The Front Page* (Ethel Barrymore Th., May 10, 1969); and played Duane Wilson in *Harvey* (ANTA Th., Feb. 24, 1970; Phoenix Th. tour opened in Central City, Colo., July 31, 1971; closed Studebaker Th., Chicago, Nov. 20, 1971).

Films. He made his debut in *Harvey* (UI, 1950); followed by *Katie Did It* (UI, 1950); *Bonzo* (UI, 1951); *Francis Goes to the Races* (UI, 1951); *Callaway Went That-Away* (MGM, 1951); *Death of a Salesman* (Col., 1951); *The Girl in White* (MGM, 1952); *Million Dollar Mermaid* (MGM, 1952); *Champ for a Day* (Rep., 1953); *Forever Female* (Par., 1953); *Gunsmoke* (UI, 1953); *Hell's Half Acre* (Rep., 1954); *Witness to Murder* (UA, 1954); *Not As a Stranger* (UA, 1955); *The Girl Rush* (Par., 1955); *The Come On* (AA, 1955); *The Bad Seed* (WB, 1956); *He Laughed Last* (Col., 1956); *Back From Eternity* (RKO, 1956); *Designing Woman* (MGM, 1957); *Johnny Trouble* (WB, 1957); *God Is My Partner* (20th-Fox, 1957); *Marjorie Morningstar* (WB, 1958); *Legs Diamond* (WB, 1958); *Country Music Holiday* (WB, 1959); *211 Grand Canal* (Allied, 1959); *Three Blonds in His Life* (Riley Jackson Films, 1960); *The Big Night* (Par., 1960); *Tomboy and the Champ* (UI, 1961); *On the Double* (Par., 1961); *The Right Approach* (20th-Fox, 1961); *Sail a Crooked Ship* (Col., 1961); *A Fever in the Blood* (WB, 1961); *It's Only Money* (Par., 1962); *Yellow Canary* (Col., 1962); *It's a Mad, Mad, Mad, Mad World* (UA, 1963); *Looking for Love* (MGM, 1964); *A House is Not a Home* (Par., 1964); *Erasmus with Freckles* (20th-Fox, 1964); *Pajama Party* (Amer. Int., 1964); *Dear Brigitte* (20th-Fox, 1965); *The Ghost in the Invisible Bikini* (Amer. Int., 1966); *The Reluctant Astronaut* (U, 1967); *The Spirit is Willing* (Par., 1967); *Togetherness* (Gen. Film Corp., 1970); and *Bless the Beasts and Children* (Col., 1971).

Television. Mr. White's earliest television appearances include Chevrolet Th. (NBC, 1945); Colgate Th. (NBC, 1945); and Ford Th. (CBS, 1947). He was a continuing character for five years on the Danny Thomas Show (CBS); six years on the Ann Southern Show (ABC, 1953–55; 1958–60); the Frank Sinatra Show (ABC, 1958); the Tammy Grimes Show (ABC); and has appeared frequently on numerous comedy, panel, dramatic and talk shows.

Recreation. Baseball, painting, playing an occasional night club date.

WHITE, JOAN. Producer, actress, director. b. Dec. 3, 1909, Alexandria, Egypt, to Henry William George and Kathleen Mabel (Beach) White. Father, businessman. Attended St. Helen's Sch., Northwood, Middlesex, England, 1922–27; grad. RADA, London, England, 1930; received first class certificate, London Sch. of Domestic Economy, 1927; studied speech and drama with Julie Huntsman, London, seven years; voice with Gwenn Knight, London, five years, and Don Brassington, N.Y.C., one year. Married Apr. 25, 1933, to John Vesey Beanes (marr. dis. 1936); married Jan. 21, 1937, to Archibald Patrick Moore (marr. dis. 1955); two daughters, one of whom is Judy White, actress; married May 23, 1958, to Robert Paine Grose, designer, director, producer (marr. dis. 1970). Member of British AEA; AFTRA; Assn. Canadian Radio and TV Artists; Girl Guides (Lt., 1922–29). Address: 171 W. 71st St., New York, NY 10023, tel. (212) SU 7-3189.

Pre-Theatre. Speech teacher.

Theatre. Miss White made her professional debut

playing Azorah in *Tobias and the Angel* and other roles in repertory at the Festival Th., where she also served as an apprentice (Cambridge, England, Sept.–Dec. 1930); made her London debut as the Nurse in *Betrayal* (Little Th., Jan. 7, 1931); subsequently played Kate in *A Knight Passed By* (Ambassadors', June 6, 1931); at the Westminster Th., played Janet in *The Anatomist* (Oct. 7, 1931), Azorah in *Tobias and the Angel* (Mar. 9, 1932), which she repeated at the Alhambra Th. (Edinburgh, Scotland); at the Westminster Th., portrayed Margarita in *The Kingdom of God* (June 1, 1932), Moth in *Love's Labour's Lost* (July 6, 1932), Laurie in *Follow Me* (Nov. 11, 1932); Assistant Stage Manager in *Six Characters in Search of an Author* (Nov. 1932), and Euodias in *Jonah and the Whale* (Dec. 12, 1932).

Miss White played Eve in *Synthetic Virgin* (Royalty, London, Feb. 19, 1933); Angela Knowle in *Vacant Possession* (Fortune, Oct. 2, 1933); Joan Buckland in *A Present from Margate* (Shaftesbury, Dec. 14, 1933); Mandanika in *The Golden Toy* (Coliseum, Feb. 28, 1934); Charlotte in *Charlotte's Progress* (Mercury, July 11, 1934); Bella Hedley in *The Barretts of Wimpole Street* (Piccadilly, Jan. 22, 1935). She directed stock productions of *Outward Bound* and *I'll Leave It to You* (Bexhill, Sussex, Summer 1935); appeared as Connie Windlestrow in *The Black Eye* (Shaftesbury, London, Oct. 11, 1935); Claudine in *The Luck of the Devil* (Arts, Jan. 12, 1936); Tonie in *Children to Bless You* (Ambassadors', Mar. 3, 1936); Button Faringdon in *Housemaster* (Apollo, Nov. 12, 1936); Cissy in a command performance of *Silver King* (Lyceum, Dec. 17, 1937); Susannah in *Susannah and the Elders* (Duke of York's, Sept. 31, 1937); Judy Bingley in *Little Ladyship* (Strand, Feb. 7, 1939); and Commere in an All Star Variety (Royal, Chester, 1940).

She played Judy Graves in *Junior Miss* (Saville, London, Mar. 24, 1943), and on tour; played Janey Jenkins in *The Cure for Love* (Westminster, London, July 12, 1945); toured as Tony in *This Desirable Residence* (1946); played Doto in *A Phoenix Too Frequent* (Arts, London, Nov. 20, 1946); directed *Flat Spin*, in which she played Lady Beatrice Willisder (His Majesty's, London, May 4, 1947); directed *The Young May Moon* (Piccadilly, June 22, 1947); played Tabitha in a try-out of *The Moon to Play With* (Royal Connaught Th., Worthing, Oct. 1947); Leah Barr in *Ten Shilling Doll* (Torch, London, Sept. 14, 1948).

With the Birmingham Repertory Co. (Jan.–June 1948), Miss White played the Duchess of York in *Richard III*, Madame Maniefa in *Diary of a Scoundrel*, the Chorus Girl in *A Cassilis Engagement*, a Spanish Dancer in *The Romantic Young Lady*, appeared in *The Marvellous History of St. Bernard*, and in *A Modern Everyman*. At the Arts Th. (Salisbury, Sept. 1949–June 1950), played Lady Kitty in *The Circle*, Mrs. Goldfinch in *A Pair of Spectacles*, Mrs. Malaprop in *The Rivals*, the Fairy Queen in *Aladdin*, and Penelope Toop in *See How They Run*. With the Bristol Old Vic (Sept. 1950–Apr. 1951), played Mistress Quickly in *The Merry Wives of Windsor*, Julia in *The Cocktail Party*, Margaret Devize in *The Lady's Not for Burning*, Mrs. Candour in *The School for Scandal*, and Mrs. Posket in *The Magistrate*.

She appeared as Gloria Cavendish in Storks Don't Talk (Comedy, London, July 11, 1951); Johanna in *Night of Masquerade* ("Q," Apr. 29, 1952); was assistant director and actress in *The Queen's Husband*, *The Beaver Coat*, and *The Hollow Crown* (Dundee, Scotland, Fall 1952); directed *The Miser* (Arts, Salisbury, 1953); played Lady Kitty in *The Circle* and Yvonne in *Les Parents Terribles* (both Playhouse, Manchester, Nov. 1953); appeared as Rosie and Maud Neville in *A London Actress* (Arts, London, Dec. 16, 1953); Miss Marcy in *I Capture the Castle* (Aldwych, Mar. 4, 1954); and directed *Quality Street*, *Angels in Love*, and *Ten Little Indians* (all Prince of Wales's Th., Cardiff, Wales, Summer 1956).

Miss White directed *Present Laughter* (Crest, Toronto, Canada, Mar. 1956); played the role of Miss Marple in *Murder at the Vicarage* (Crest, Toronto, May 1, 1956); was appointed director of the Trans Canada Th. Co. (Grand Th., London, Ontario, July–Sept. 1956) for such plays as *Dear Charles*, *The Seven Year Itch*, *Happiest Days of Your Life*, *Ten Little Indians*, *All For Mary*, *Sabrina Fair*, and *O Mistress Mine;* produced and directed plays at the Maple Leaf Th. (London, Ontario, Summer 1957); directed a musical production of *You Can't Take It with You* (Univ. of West Ontario, Nov. 1957); and played Sheila Broadbent in *The Reluctant Debutante* (Maple Leaf Th., London, Ontario, July 1959).

She made her US debut succeeding (Sept. 1958) Margery Maude as Mrs. Higgins in the national tour of *My Fair Lady* (opened Auditorium, Rochester, N.Y., Mar. 18, 1957; closed O'Keefe Ctr., Toronto, Ontario, Canada, Dec. 14, 1963).

From 1960 to 1964, she was producer, with her husband, Robert Paine Grose, of the Berkshire Playhouse (Stockbridge, Mass.). During the 1960 summer season, she directed productions of *Two for the Seesaw*, *Witness for the Prosecution*, *The Gazebo*, *Happiest Days of Your Life*, *Dear Miss Phoebe*, *Misalliance* and played the role of Madame St. Pe in *The Waltz of the Toreadors;* for the 1961 season, directed *The Marriage-Go-Round*, *Roar Like a Dove*, *Breath of Spring*, *Susannah and the Elders*, played Camille in *Invitation to a March*, and the Housekeeper in *Ten Little Indians;* for the 1962 season, directed *Critic's Choice*, *Send Me No Flowers*, *Under the Yum-Yum Tree*, *See How They Run*, played Miss Marple in *Murder at the Vicarage*, and the Countess in *You Never Know;* for the 1963 season, directed *Lady Audley's Secret* and played Miss Moffat in *The Corn Is Green;* and for the 1964 season, directed *Time of the Cuckoo*, *The Silver Cord*, *Journey to Bahia* (US premiere), *The Cradle Song*, and played Mrs. Higgins in *My Fair Lady*.

In addition to her work at the Berkshire Playhouse, Miss White appeared as Julia in *The Cocktail Party* (Charles Th., Boston, Mass., Mar. 1961); Mrs. Turton in *A Passage to India* (Ambassador, N.Y.C., Jan. 31, 1962); directed *Lady Audley's Secret or Who Pushed George* (NY World's Fair, 1964); and directed *The Foot on the Stairs* (Th. de Lys, N.Y.C., Nov. 10, 1964).

In 1965, with Robert Paine Grose, Miss White purchased the Yarmouth (Mass.) Th. on Cape Cod, where she directed *George Washington Slept Here*. She played Lady Insdale in *On a Clear Day You Can See Forever* (Colonial, Boston, Mass., Sept. 1965); Lady Britomart in *Major Barbara* (Charles Playhouse, Boston, Dec. 15, 1965); was in *Serjeant Musgrave's Dance* (Th. de Lys, N.Y.C., Mar. 8, 1966); directed *A Madrigal of Shakespeare* (White Barn Th., Westport, Conn., July 23, 1967); and played Mrs. Dedalus in *Stephen D* (East 74 St. Th., N.Y.C., Sept. 24, 1967) and Lady Bracknell in *The Importance of Being Earnest* (Trinity Square Rep., Providence, R.I., Dec. 28, 1967).

In 1968, she directed another production of *A Madrigal of Shakespeare* (Th. de Lys, N.Y.C., Feb. 12, 1968); was Mrs. Tarleton in *Misalliance* (Playhouse in the Park, Cincinnati, Ohio, Apr. 4, 1968); played Abby in *Arsenic and Old Lace* and Mrs. Banks in *Barefoot in the Park* (both Cecilwood Playhouse, Fishkill, N.Y.); and at the Edinburgh (Scotland) Festival co-presented *Years of the Locust*.

From Sept. 1968 to Feb. 1969, she was a member of the Nottingham (England) Playhouse where she played Elinor in *King John*, Mrs. Candour in *The School for Scandal*, and appeared in *The Ruling Class*. She was Grace in *Joe Egg* (Seattle Rep. Th., Seattle, Wash., Nov. 25, 1969); and in 1970 directed *The Seagull* and *Love's Labour's Lost* (both Univ. of Washington, Seattle); played Meg in *The Birthday Party* (A Contemporary Th., Seattle); directed *Every Number Wins* (Adeline Semee Th., England) and *The Merry Wives of Windsor* (Univ. of Washington); and played Frosine in *The Miser* (Seattle Rep. Th., Dec. 9, 1970).

In 1971, she played Mrs. Crow in *Hadrian VII* (A Contemporary Th., Seattle) and directed *The Corrupters* (Thorndike Th., Leatherhead, England) and *A Marriage Proposal* (Univ. of Washington); in 1972, she directed *Tobias and the Angel* (Thorndike Th. and Edinburgh Festival Fringe) and *The House of Bernarda Alba* (Univ. of Washington); and in 1973, she directed *Jonah and the Whale* (Thorndike Th. and Edinburgh Festival Fringe); *The Emperor's New Clothes* (Univ. of Washington); and she played Aunt Penniman in *The Heiress* (A Contemporary Th., Seattle, Washington, 1974).

Films. Miss White made her debut in England in 1931; subsequently appeared as the Child in *Admirals All* (RKO, 1936); the Post Mistress in *Second Bureau* (Film Alliance); Phoebe in *As You Like It* (Fox, 1936); Toni in *A Girl Must Live* (U, 1939); and a Companion in *The Last of the Mohicans* (Lon Chaney, Can., 1956).

Television and Radio. Miss White has read her own short stories for English radio. In addition, she played the Girl in *Badgers Green* (BBC, London, May 21, 1935); Cathy in *Wuthering Heights* (BBC, May 21, 1935); Sara in *Tobias and the Angel* (BBC, 1936); the Woman in *The Forest* (BBC, Sept. 1945); Babs in the serial, *The Vagueleys* (BBC, 1947–48). In Canada, she played the Leader of the Chorus in *Lysistrata* (CBC, Apr. 1956).

She appeared on British television as Janey in *Cure for Love* (BBC, Oct. 1954); Thirza Topper in *A Farmer's Wife* (BBC, Feb. 3, 1955); the Twin in *Yellow Sands* (BBC, Mar. 1955); and Mrs. Fishwick in *Truant in Park Lane* (BBC, Oct. 1955); for Canadian television, played the Concierge in *The Empty Frame* (CBC, 1956–1957); appeared on *To Live in Peace* (CBC, 1956–57); and played Madame Maniefa in *Diary of a Scoundrel* (CBC, 1956–57); for US television, played Mrs. Page in *The Citadel* (ABC, 1959); Jemima Pinkerton in *Vanity Fair* (ABC, 1960); Lucy in *Twenty-Four Hours in the Life of a Woman* (CBS, Feb. 1961); Mrs. Hopkins in *Pygmalion* (Hallmark Hall of Fame, NBC, Jan. 1963); Mrs. Gladstone in *The Invincible Mr. Disraeli* (Hallmark Hall of Fame, NBC, Mar. 1963); and Mrs. Bradman in *Blithe Spirit* (Hallmark Hall of Fame, NBC, Dec. 1966).

Night Clubs. She starred as Mrs. Wilson in *The Drunkard* (Stage Door, Toronto, Canada, 1958).

Other Activities. She taught acting at the Central Sch. of Speech Training and Dramatic Art, London (1947–55); at the Royal Acad. of Dramatic Art, London (1951–55); at the Ryerson Institute of Technology, Toronto, Ontario, Canada, where she was on the staff of the television arts dept. (1956–57); and she conducted her own speech and drama studio in N.Y.C. (1966–67). She held an appointment as lecturer in drama, Univ. of Washington, Seattle (1969–75), where in 1970, she inaugurated the English summer theatre school foreign study program and, in 1971, a television workshop, an interdisciplinary program with writers and technicians.

Awards. Miss White is an associate of RADA (London); and holds the (Junior and Senior) Gold Medal of the Poetry Society (London).

Recreation. Cooking, writing, swimming, car driving, theatre-going.

WHITE, MICHAEL. Producer. b. Jan. 16, 1936, to Victor and Doris (Cohen) White. Father, co-director. Educ. Lyceum Alpineum, Zuoz; Sorbonne, Paris. Married Jan. 15, 1965, to Sarah Hillsdon; two sons, one daughter. Member of Soc. of West End Managers; Royal Court Th. (council mbr.); Institute of Contemporary Arts (council mbr.); Turf Club. Address: 13 Duke St., St. James's, London, S.W.I. 6 YDB, England tel. 839-3971.

Theatre. Mr. White produced, with Peter Daubeny, *The Connection* (Duke of York's Th., London, Feb. 1961); and, all with Oscar Lewenstein at the Th. Royal, Stratford, Eng., *The Secret of the World* (Mar. 1962), *The Scatterin'* (Apr. 1962), *Jungle of the Cities* (June 1962), and *The Voice of Shem* (July 1962). He also produced *The Blood Knot* (Arts Th. Club, London, Feb. 1963); *Cambridge Circus* (Arts Th. Club; Lyric, July 1963); *The *** Show* (Phoenix, Sept. 1963); and, with William Donaldson, *Oscar Brown, Jr., Entertains* (Prince Charles Th., Aug. 1963).

He was producer for the Merce Cunningham Dance Co. (Sadler's Wells, June 1964; Aug. 1966); the Graceila Martinez Dance Co. (Comedy & Saville, June 1964); produced *Hamp* (Lyceum, Edinburgh, Scotland, Aug. 1964); *Son of Oblomov*

(Comedy, London, Dec. 1964); *Any Wednesday* (Apollo, Aug. 1965); was producer for the Yvonne Rainer Dance Co. (Comedy, Sept. 1965); produced, with Ed Swann, *Saturday Night and Sunday Morning* (Prince of Wales Th., Feb. 1966); with Philip Grout and Moray Watson, *How's the World Treating You?* (Comedy, June 1966); and, with Wolf Mankowitz, the tour of *Adam's Apple* (July 1966). He produced *The Trials of Brother Jero* (Hampstead, June 1966); *The Blood Knot*(Hampstead, June 1966); with Leonard Field, *Breakdown* (Gate, Dublin, Oct. 1966) and *Hogan's Goat* (Olympia, Dublin, Oct. 1966); was producer for *Yoko Ono—Music of the Mind*(Jeanette Cochrane Th., London, Nov. 1966); produced, with Memorial Enterprises, *The Burglar* (Vaudeville, Feb. 1967); and, with the English Stage Co., *America Hurrah* (Royal Court, Aug. 1967).

Mr. White also produced, with Oscar Lewenstein, *Philadelphia, Here I Come!* (Apollo, Sept. 1967); produced *Tom Paine* (Vaudeville, London, Oct. 1967); with Michael Codron, *Fanghorn* (Fortune, Nov. 1967); was producer for the *Paper Bag Players* (Royal Court, Dec. 1967); and produced, with Oscar Lewenstein, *Loot* (Criterion, 1967; Biltmore, N.Y.C., Mar. 18, 1968); and, in association with William Dorr, the N.Y.C. engagement of *Tom Paine* (Stage 73, Mar. 25, 1968). He produced *Summer* (Fortune, London, July 1968); with Leonard Field, *The Au Pair Man* (Duchess, Sept. 1968); *Fortune and Men's Eyes*(Comedy, Oct. 1968); *The Beard* (Royal Court, Nov. 1968); and, with Kenneth Tynan and Norman Granz, *Soldiers*(New, Dec. 1968).

He produced *Arturo Ui* (Saville, July 1969); *So What About Love* (Criterion, Sept. 1969); *Sleuth* (St. Martin's, Feb. 1970); with Memorial Enterprises, a revival of *Widowers' Houses* (Royal Court, Apr. 1970); with Robert Stigwood and Hillard Elkins, *Oh! Calcutta!* (Royalty, Duchess, July 1970); and, with Helen Bonfils and Morton Gottlieb, the N.Y.C. presentation of *Sleuth*(Music Box, Nov. 12, 1970). He produced *Hamlet*(Fortune, London, Apr. 1971); with Robert Stigwood and Bob Swash, *The Dirtiest Show in Town* (Duchess, May 1971); produced *As Time Goes By* (Th. Upstairs, Sept. 1971); *Friday* (Th. Upstairs, Nov. 1971); *The Threepenny Opera* (Prince of Wales, Feb. 1972); *Julius Caesar* (New, Mar. 1972); with Woodfall Productions, *I, Claudius* (Piccadilly, July 1972); with Robert Stigwood and Granada, *Joseph and the Amazing Technicolor Dreamcoat* (Roundhouse, Albery, Feb. 16, 1973); with the Royal Court Th., *A Sense of Detachment* (Royal Court, Dec. 4, 1972); with Bernard Delfont, *A Doll's House* (Criterion, Feb. 20, 1973); and he produced, with Robert Stigwood, *Two Gentlemen of Verona* (Phoenix, Apr. 1973).

Mr. White was also producer of *The Rocky Horror Show* (Classic, Kings Road, May 1973); *The Ride Across Lake Constance* (Hampstead & Mayfair, Nov. 1973); *Judies* (Comedy, Dec. 1973); *Snap* (Vaudeville, Feb. 1974); produced, with the Royal Court, the Athol Fugard Africa season (Ambassadors, Mar. 1974); and he produced *That Championship Season* (Garrick, May 1974).

WHITE, MILES. Costume designer. b. Miles Edgren White, July 27, 1920, Oakland, Calif., to Carlos G. and Verna (Edgren) White. Father, attorney. Attended Univ. of California; California Sch. of Fine Arts, San Francisco; California Sch. of Arts and Crafts, Oakland; Art Students League, N.Y.C. Member of United Scenic Artists, AMPAS, Costume Designers Guild. Address: 360 E. 55th St., New York, NY 10022, tel. (212) PL 3-3874.

Theatre. Mr. White at first designed costumes for *Right This Way* (46 St. Th., N.Y.C., Jan. 4, 1938); subsequently designed costumes for *Best Foot Forward*(Ethel Barrymore Th., Oct. 1, 1941); *The Pirate* (Martin Beck Th., Nov. 25, 1942); *Oklahoma!* (St. James, Mar. 31, 1943); *Ziegfeld Follies*(Winter Garden, Apr. 1, 1943); *Early to Bed* (Broadhurst, June 17, 1943); *Allah Be Praised!* (Adelphi, Apr. 20, 1944); *Dream with Music* (Majestic, May 18, 1944); *Bloomer Girl* (Shubert, Oct. 5, 1944); *Carousel* (Majestic, Apr. 19, 1945; *The Day Before Spring* (National, Nov. 22, 1945); *Gypsy Lady* (Century, Sept. 17, 1946); *The Duchess of Malfi* (Ethel Barrymore Th., Oct. 15, 1946); and *High Button Shoes*(Century, Oct. 9, 1947).

He created costumes for the Ballet Theatre production of *Fall River Legend* (Metropolitan Opera House, Apr. 22, 1948); *Gentlemen Prefer Blondes* Ziegfeld, Dec. 8, 1949); *Bless You All* (Mark Hellinger Th., Dec. 14, 1950); *Pal Joey* (Broadhurst, Jan. 3, 1952); *Three Wishes for Jamie* (Mark Hellinger Th., Mar. 21, 1952); *Two's Company*(Alvin, Dec. 15, 1952); *Hazel Flagg* (Mark Hellinger Th., Feb. 11, 1953); *The Girl in Pink Tights* (Mark Hellinger Th., Mar. 5, 1954); *Ankles Aweigh* (Mark Hellinger Th., Apr. 18, 1955); *Eugenia* (Ambassador, Jan. 30, 1957); *Jamaica* (Imperial, Oct. 31, 1957); *Time Remembered* (Morosco, Nov. 12, 1957); *Oh Captain!* (Alvin, Feb. 4, 1958); *Chéri* (Morosco, Oct. 12, 1959); *Take Me Along*(Shubert, Oct. 22, 1959); *Bye Bye Birdie* (Martin Beck Th., Apr. 14, 1960); *The Unsinkable Molly Brown* (Winter Garden, Nov. 3, 1960); *Show Girl* (Eugene O'Neill Th., Jan. 12, 1961); *Milk and Honey* (Martin Beck Th., Oct. 10, 1961); the Los Angeles Civic Light Opera Assn. production of *Song of Norway* (Philharmonic Aud., Los Angeles, Calif., Apr. 23, 1962; Curran, San Francisco, Calif., July 28, 1962); the pre-Bway tryout of *Zenda* (opened Curran, San Francisco, Aug. 5, 1963; closed Pasadena Civic Aud., Calif., Nov. 16, 1963); *Oklahoma!* (NY State Th., Lincoln Ctr., N.Y.C., June 23, 1969); *Candida* (Longacre, N.Y.C., Apr. 6, 1970); *A Day in the Life of Just About Anyone* (Bijou, N.Y.C., Mar. 9, 1971); *A Quarter for the Ladies Room* (Village Gate, N.Y.C., Nov. 12, 1972); *Tricks* (Alvin, N.Y.C., Jan. 8, 1973); and the Ballet Th.'s production of *Sleeping Beauty* (NY State Th., July 2, 1974).

In addition, he has designed ten productions for the Ringling Bros., and Barnum and Bailey Circus (beginning in 1944); the Seattle (Wash.) Worlds Fair theme production, *The Threshold and the Threat* (1962); *The Brightest Show on Earth* and *All About Elsie* for the NY World's Fair (1964–65); Festival U.S.A., a musical revue sponsored by the US Dept. of Agriculture for the Tokyo Worlds Fair (1968); and ten productions for the Ice Capades.

Films. Mr. White designed costumes for *Up in Arms* (RKO, 1944); *The Kid from Brooklyn* (RKO, 1946); *The Greatest Show on Earth* (Par., 1952); *There's No Business Like Show Business* (20th-Fox, 1954); and *Around the World in Eighty Days* (UA, 1956).

Television. He designed the costumes for a Hallmark Hall of Fame production of *Pinocchio* (NBC).

Night Clubs. He designed costumes for Tallulah Bankhead's appearance at the Cafe de Paris, London; and for revues at Billy Rose's Diamond Horseshoe, Bill Miller's Riviera, the Versailles, and the Copacabana.

Awards. He received Antoinette Perry (Tony) awards for his costume designs in *Bless You All* (1950) and *Hazel Flagg* (1953); Donaldson awards for *Bloomer Girl* (1945), *High Button Shoes* (1948), *Gentlemen Prefer Blondes* (1950), and *Pal Joey* (1952). He was nominated for Academy (Oscar) awards for his costumes in *The Greatest Show on Earth* (1952), *There's No Business Like Show Business* (1954), and *Around the World in 80 Days* (1956).

WHITE, ONNA. Choreographer. b. Nova Scotia. Married to Larry Douglas, actor, singer; one daughter. Member of SSD&C; AGMA; AEA. Address: 19 Hamilton Terr., New York, NY 10031.

Theatre. Miss White made her professional debut as a member of the corps de ballet with the San Francisco (Calif.) Opera Ballet Co.; subsequently danced in the chorus of *Finian's Rainbow* (46 St. Th., N.Y.C., Jan. 10, 1947), and assisted Michael Kidd, choreographer, for the London production (Palace, Oct. 21, 1947), and restaged the dances for a revival (NY City Ctr., May 18, 1955). She danced in the chorus of *Guys and Dolls* (46 St. Th., Nov. 24, 1950), assisted Mr. Kidd for the London production (Coliseum, May 28, 1953), and restaged the dances for a revival (NY City Ctr., Apr. 20, 1955); and danced in the chorus of *Silk Stockings* (Imperial, Feb. 24, 1955).

Miss White choreographed *Carmen Jones* (NY City Ctr., May 31, 1956); *The Music Man* (Majestic, Dec. 19, 1957), and two subsequent tours (opened Philharmonic Aud., Los Angeles, Calif., Aug. 18, 1958; closed Shubert, Boston, Mass., Mar. 17, 1962; opened Rajah, Reading, Pa., Sept. 18, 1961; closed Bushnell Aud., Hartford, Conn., Apr. 28, 1962).

She choreographed *Whoop-Up* (Shubert, N.Y.C., Dec. 22, 1958); *Take Me Along* (Shubert, Oct. 22, 1959); *Irma La Douce* (Plymouth, Sept. 29, 1960); *Let It Ride!* (Eugene O'Neill Th., Oct. 12, 1961); *I Had a Ball* (Martin Beck Th., Dec. 15, 1964); *Half a Sixpence* (Broadhurst, Apr. 25, 1965; also, national tour: opened Curran, San Francisco, July 26, 1966); *Mame* (Winter Garden, N.Y.C., May 24, 1966); *Illya Darling* (Mark Hellinger Th., Apr. 11, 1967); *A Mother's Kisses* (Pre-Bway tryout opened Shubert, New Haven, Sept. 23, 1968; closed Mechanic, Baltimore, Oct. 19, 1968); *1776* (46 St. Th., N.Y.C., Mar. 16, 1969); directed and choreographed *Gantry* (George Abbott Th., Feb. 14, 1970); choreographed *70, Girls, 70* (Broadhurst, Apr. 15, 1971); and *Gigi* (Uris Th., Nov. 13, 1973).

Films. Miss White choreographed *The Music Man* (WB, 1962); *Bye Bye Birdie* (Col., 1963); *Oliver!* (Col., 1968); *1776* (Col., 1972); *The Great Waltz* (MGM, 1972); and *Mame* (WB, 1974).

Awards. Miss White won a special Academy (Oscar) Award for her choreography for *Oliver!* (1968).

WHITEHEAD, ALLEN. Music publisher, producer. b. Allen B. Whitehead, July 17, 1921, Rocky Mount, N.C., to Howell and Lillie (Dunn) Whitehead. Grad. Rocky Mount H.S., 1937; attended Univ. of South Carolina, 1937–41. Married Jan. 23, 1964, to Rosemarie Aeschlimann. Served USN, 1942–45, as a recruiter. Address: (home) 320 E. 57th St., New York, NY 10022; (bus.) c/o Frank Productions Inc., 119 W. 57th St., New York, NY 10019, tel. (212) CO 5-3600.

Theatre. Mr. Whitehead has been president of Frank Productions, Inc., which was associated with the production of *The Music Man* (Majestic, N.Y.C., Dec. 19, 1957); *Greenwillow* (Alvin, Mar. 8, 1960); *The Most Happy Fella* (Coliseum, London, Apr. 21, 1960); *The Fantasticks* (Apollo, London, Aug. 1961); *How To Succeed in Business Without Really Trying* (46 St. Th., N.Y.C., Oct. 14, 1961); the pre-Bway tryout of *Pleasures and Places* (opened Fisher Th., Detroit, Mar. 11, 1965; closed there, Apr. 10, 1965); *Wait a Minim!* (Golden, N.Y.C., Mar. 7, 1966); and *Canterbury Tales* (Eugene O'Neill Th., Feb. 3, 1969).

Mr. Whitehead was General Manager for *Loot* (Biltmore, Mar. 18, 1968).

WHITEHEAD, PAXTON. Actor, director, writer. b. Francis Edward Paxton Whitehead, Oct. 17, 1937, Kent, England, to Charles Parkin and Louise (Hunt) Whitehead. Father, lawyer. Educ. Rugby School, England. Studied at Webber-Douglas School of Singing and Dramatic Art, London. Married Jan. 2, 1971, to Patricia Gage; one stepdaughter. Member of AEA; AFTRA; ACTRA; British Actors Equity. Address: (home) Box 774, Niagara-on-the-Lake, Ontario, Canada tel. (416) 468-2153; (bus.) c/o Barna Ostertag, 501 Fifth Ave., New York, NY 10017, tel. (212) OX 7-6339.

Theatre. Mr. Whitehead made his theatrical debut as the Kentish Colt in *The Epilogue* (The Old Stagers, Canterbury, England, Aug. 1949), and his professional debut as Alphonse in *All for Mary* (Devonshire Park Th., Eastbourne, Aug. 1956). In 1957, he toured in repertory with the Anew Macmaster Co. in Ireland and appeared in repertory at the Castle Th., Farnham, England. He was a member of the Shakespeare company, Stratford-on-Avon, in 1958 and toured with the group in the USSR as Francisco in *Hamlet* (Moscow, Leningrad, Dec. 1958–Jan. 1959), then touring in the United Kingdom as the lead in *The Grass Is Greener* (1959) and Freddy in *Pygmalion* (1960).

His first American appearances were off-Bway, first as the Prologue in *Gallows Humor* (Gramercy Arts, N.Y.C., Apr. 18, 1961), followed by the Prosecuting Counsel in *One Way Pendulum* (E. 74 St. Th.,

Sept. 18, 1961), and he made his Bway debut as Gilbert Dawson-Hill, Q.C., in *The Affair* (Henry Miller's Th., Sept. 20, 1962). He was Torvald Helmer in *A Doll's House* (Th. Four, Feb. 2, 1963); appeared at the American Shakespeare Festival, Stratford, Conn., as the King of France in *King Lear* (June 4, 1963) and Gower in *Henry V* (May 31, 1963); went on tour (Aug. 5, 1963) in *Beyond the Fringe* and appeared in *Beyond the Fringe 1964* (John Golden Th., N.Y.C., Jan. 8, 1964). He played at the Front St. Th., Memphis, Tenn., as Horner in *The Country Wife* (July 22, 1964) and Higgins in *My Fair Lady* (Sept. 20, 1964); was Jack in *The Rivals* (Charles Playhouse, Boston, Mass., Nov. 11, 1964); Archie Rice in *The Entertainer* (Hartford Stage Co., Hartford, Conn., Jan. 15, 1965); and Adolphus Cusins in *Major Barbara* (Playhouse in the Park, Cincinnati, Ohio, 1965). He played Randall Utterword in *Heartbreak House*, Christoforou in *The Public Eye*, and Algernon in *The Importance of Being Earnest* (all Manitoba Th. Ctr., Winnipeg, Canada, 1965); was John Worthing in *The Importance of Being Earnest* (Canadian Players, Toronto, Canada, Jan.–Apr. 1966); Lord Summerhays in *Misalliance* and Magnus in *The Apple Cart* (both Shaw Festival, Niagara-on-the-Lake, Ontario, Canada, May–Sept. 1966); and Fancourt in *Charley's Aunt* (Manitoba Th. Ctr., Winnipeg, Sept.–Dec. 1966).

In 1967, Mr. Whitehead became artistic director of the Shaw Festival, Niagara-on-the-Lake, where he played Sergius in *Arms and the Man*, Cusins in *Major Barbara*, and directed *The Circle* (all 1967); played Hector Hushabye in *Heartbreak House* and Coustouillu in *The Chemmy Circle*, which, with Suzanne Grossmann, he had also translated and adapted, and which he directed (both 1968). He also appeared in *Charley's Aunt* (Studio Arena Th., Buffalo, N.Y., Apr. 4, 1968); directed *A Flea in Her Ear* (Charles Playhouse, Boston, Mass., Feb. 4, 1969); was in *The Guardsman* and played Dubedat in *The Doctor's Dilemma* (both Shaw Festival, 1969); was in *Chemin de Fer*, which, with Suzanne Grossman, he had translated and adapted (Mark Taper Forum, Los Angeles, Calif., June 5, 1969); and in *Rondelay* (Hudson West Th., N.Y.C., Nov. 5, 1969). He played the Emperor in *The Brass Butterfly* (Chelsea Th. Ctr., Jan. 1970); appeared again in *The Chemmy Circle* (Arena Stage, Washington, D.C., Mar. 4, 1970); was the Rev. Alexander Mill in *Candida* (Longacre, N.Y.C., Apr. 11, 1970); Hector Hushabye in *Heartbreak House* (Goodman Memorial Th., Chicago, Ill., May 29, 1970); directed *The Secretary Bird* (Main Stage, Vancouver, British Columbia, Canada, Sept. 30, 1970); and directed and played Tempest in *Forty Years On* (Shaw Festival, 1970).

He was Charteris in *The Philanderer* and acted leads in *Tonight at 8:30* (both Shaw Festival, 1971); adapted, with Suzanne Grossmann, *There's One in Every Marriage* (Avon Th., Stratford Festival, Ontario, Canada, Aug. 6, 1971; Royale, N.Y.C., Jan. 3, 1972); directed, at Main Stage, Vancouver, British Columbia, *The Chemmy Circle* (Oct. 8, 1971) and *The Sorrows of Frederick* (Nov. 12, 1971); directed *Misalliance* and *Getting Married* (both Shaw Festival, 1972); directed *Misalliance* (John F. Kennedy Ctr., Washington, D.C., June 26, 1972); *Forty Years On* (Main Stage, Vancouver, British Columbia, Oct. 16, 1972); appeared in *The Philanderer* (John F. Kennedy Ctr., Jan. 2, 1973); directed *Arms and the Man* (Main Stage, Vancouver, British Columbia, Apr. 9, 1973); played Valentine in *You Never Can Tell* and Savoyard in *Fanny's First Play* (both Shaw Festival, 1973); directed and played Fancourt in *Charley's Aunt* (Shaw Festival, 1974) and toured with it; and directed *Misalliance* (Walnut St. Th., Philadelphia, Pa., Nov. 1974).

Television. Mr. Whitehead was Lord Darlington in *Lady Windermere's Fan* (CBC, 1966); the Doctor in *Wit and World of GBS* (BBC/CBC, 1971); Lord Dufferin in *The National Dream* (CBC, 1973); and Z in *Village Wooing* (CBC, 1974).

WHITEHEAD, ROBERT. Producer. b. Mar. 3, 1916, Montreal, Canada, to William Thomas and Lena Mary (Labatt) Whitehead. Attended Argyle Sch., Montreal 1925–26; Trinity Coll. Sch., 1929–34; Lower Canada Coll. 1927–29. Married Apr. 16, 1948, to Virginia Bolen, antique dealer (marr. dis.). Married May 8, 1968, to Zoe Caldwell, actress. Served with American Field US Army Service, 1942–46, Africa; as volunteer with British 8th Army, Africa-Italy; British 14th Army, Burma. Relative in theatre: cousin, Hume Cronyn, actor. Member of League of NY Theatres (past pres., bd. of gov., secy., 1967); American Shakespeare Festival, Stratford, Conn. (trustee); Neighborhood Playhouse (pres.). Address: (home) 120 East End Ave., New York, NY 10028; (bus.) 165 W. 46th St., New York, NY 10036, tel. (212) PL 7-5100.

Theatre. Since 1960, Mr. Whitehead has been director, with Elia Kazan, of the Repertory Th. of Lincoln Center for the Performing Arts, N.Y.C., which has produced *After the Fall* (Jan. 23, 1964); *Marco Millions* (Feb. 20, 1964); and *But for Whom Charlie* (Mar. 12, 1964), and during the 1964–65 season, *The Changeling, Incident at Vichy*, and *Tartuffe*, all at the ANTA Washington Square Th.

Mr. Whitehead produced *Medea* (Natl. Th., Oct. 20, 1947); followed by *Crime and Punishment* (Natl., Dec. 22, 1947); and *The Member of the Wedding* (Empire, Jan. 5, 1950). In 1951, he became managing director for ANTA, and produced *Desire Under the Elms* (ANTA, Jan. 16, 1952); *Mrs. McThing* (ANTA, Feb. 20, 1952); *Golden Boy* (ANTA, Mar. 12, 1952); *Four Saints in Three Acts* (Bway Th., Apr. 16, 1952); and *Sunday Breakfast* (Coronet, May 28, 1952); produced *The Time of the Cuckoo* (Empire, Oct. 15, 1952); as executive producer of the Producers Th., which he organized (1953) together with Robert W. Dowling and Roger L. Stevens, produced *The Emperor's Clothes* (Ethel Barrymore Th., Feb. 9, 1953) and produced, with Roger L. Stevens, *The Remarkable Mr. Pennypacker* (Coronet, Dec. 30, 1953); *The Confidential Clerk* (Morosco, Feb. 11, 1954); *The Flowering Peach* (Belasco, Dec. 28, 1954); and *The Skin of Our Teeth* (ANTA, Aug. 17, 1955). With Roger L. Stevens, he produced *Bus Stop* (Music Box, Mar. 2, 1955); with Roger L. Stevens and Kermit Bloomgarden, produced *A View from the Bridge* (Coronet, Sept. 29, 1955); and produced *Tamburlaine the Great* (Winter Garden, Jan. 19, 1956); *Separate Tables* (Music Box, Oct. 25, 1956); *Major Barbara* (Martin Beck Th., Oct. 30, 1956); and *The Sleeping Prince* (Coronet, Nov. 1, 1956).

With the Producers Th., he produced *The Waltz of the Toreadors* (Coronet, Jan. 17, 1957), and its return engagement (Coronet, Mar. 4, 1958); *A Hole in the Head* (Plymouth, Feb. 28, 1957); and *Orpheus Descending* (Martin Beck Th., Mar. 21, 1957).

He produced *The Day the Money Stopped* (Belasco, Feb. 20, 1958); *The Visit* (Lunt-Fontanne Th., May 5, 1958); *A Touch of the Poet* (Helen Hayes Th., Oct. 2, 1958); *Goldilocks* (Lunt-Fontanne, Oct. 11, 1958); *The Cold Wind and the Warm* (Morosco, Dec. 8, 1958); *Much Ado About Nothing* (Lunt-Fontanne, Sept. 17, 1959). With R. L. Stevens, he produced *The Conquering Hero* (ANTA, Jan. 16, 1961); *Midgie Purvis* (Martin Beck Th., Feb. 1, 1961), and *A Man For All Seasons* (ANTA, Nov. 22, 1961).

Mr. Whitehead and Elia Kazan were co-directors of the Repertory Theatre of Lincoln Center for the Performing Arts (ANTA—Washington Square Th., N.Y.C., 1964–65) which presented *The Changeling* (Oct. 29, 1964) and *Incident at Vichy* (Dec. 3, 1964).

Friedrich Durrenmatt's *The Physicists* was presented by arrangement with Mr. Whitehead (Martin Beck Th., Oct. 13, 1964); *Where's Daddy?* (Billy Rose Th., Mar. 2, 1966) which had previously been titled *Family Things—Etc.* (summer tryout touring production, 1965), was presented by Michael Wager by arrangement with Mr. Whitehead. By agreement with Whitehead-Stevens Productions, Inc., *The Prime of Miss Jean Brodie* was presented in England (Wyndham's, London, May 5, 1966), and with Robert W. Dowling as co-producer, on Bway (Helen Hayes Th., N.Y.C., Jan. 16, 1968). Messrs. Whitehead, Stevens and Dowling subsequently produced *Bequest to the Nation* (London, 1970); and *The Price* (Morosco, N.Y.C., Feb. 7, 1968). With Roger L. Stevens, Mr. Whitehead produced *The Creation of the World and Other Business* (Shubert, Nov. 30, 1972); and *Finishing Touches* (Plymouth, Feb. 8, 1973).

Television. Mr. Whitehead has appeared as a guest on Metropolitan Memo (Ind., 1964); *The Lincoln Center Day* special (CBS, 1964); The Today Show (NBC, 1964–65); and Directions (ABC, 1965).

Other Activities. He served on the permanent drama panel of the US State Department's cultural presentations program (1965).

Awards. The following of Mr. Whitehead's received the NY Drama Critics Circle Award as best play of the year: *The Member of the Wedding* (1950); *The Waltz of the Toreadors* (1957); *The Visit* (1958); and *A Man For All Seasons* (1961), which received five Antoinette Perry (Tony) Awards.

Mr. Whitehead has also received the Sam S. Shubert Foundation award (1973).

WHITING, FRANK M. Educator, writer, director. b. Dec. 6, 1907, Wallsburg, Utah, to John C. and Elizabeth (McCoard) Whiting. Father, rancher; mother, teacher. Grad. Brigham Young Univ., B.A. 1930; Univ. of Utah, M.A. 1932; Univ. of Minnesota, Ph.D. 1941. Studied acting with Maud Sheerer, N.Y.C., 1931. Served Natl. Guard, 1929–30. Member of NCTA (pres., 1951–52); ATA (pres., 1956; chairman, Overseas Touring Comm., 1957); ANTA; NTC; Speech Communication Association; CTC. Address: (home) 2036 Seabury Ave., Minneapolis, MN 55406, tel. (612) FE 5-6097; (bus.) 105 Shelvin Hall, Univ. of Minnesota, Minneapolis, MN 55414, tel. (612) 373-3461.

From 1943 to 1971, Mr. Whiting served as director of the University Th. (Univ. of Minnesota), where he was previously technical director of the theatre (1937–43). At the Univ. of Minnesota he was assistant and later associate professor of theatre arts, 1943–51, and professor from then until 1972. Since that time he has been vice-provost. He held academic positions at the Univ. of Utah (instructor, speech and theatre, 1934–37); Banff (Canada) Sch. of Fine Arts (technical director, Summer 1942; director, Summer 1952); Michigan State Univ. (guest director, Summer 1954).

Since 1958, he has been captain and director of the Minnesota Centennial Showboat.

Mr. Whiting was a member of the steering committee for the Tyrone Guthrie Th. (1960–62); and has been on the board of directors of the Minnesota Th. Co. (1962–to date).

Published Works. Mr. Whiting wrote *An Introduction to the Theatre* (1954; rev. eds., 1961, 1969); with Melvin White, *Playreaders Repertory* (1970); and a dramatization of *Huckleberry Finn* (1948, 1969).

Awards. Mr. Whiting received the Eaves Award (1961) for outstanding contribution to the American theatre, and the Univ. of Minnesota's theatre in Rarig Center is named for him.

WICKES, MARY. Actress. b. Mary Isabelle Wickenhauser, June 13, St. Louis, Mo., to Mr. and Mrs. Frank A. Wickenhauser. Father, banker. Grad. Washington Univ. (St. Louis), A.B.; attended Columbia Univ. Member of AEA; SAG; AFTRA.

Theatre. Miss Wicks gained her earliest theatrical experience with the St. Louis Little Th., and the Arthur Casey Stock Co. In 1934, she was engaged by the Berkshire Playhouse (Stockbridge, Mass.) where she subsequently appeared in more than eighty productions in eight summer seasons. She made her Bway debut as the understudy to Margaret Hamilton in *The Farmer Takes a Wife* (46 St. Th., N.Y.C., 1934); appeared in *One Good Year* (Lyceum, 1935); played Mildred in *Spring Dance* (Empire, 1936); Little Mary in *Stage Door* (Sam H. Harris Th., Oct. 22, 1936); appeared in *Swing Your Lady* (Booth, 1937); played Annie in *Father Malachy's Miracle* (Guild, Nov. 17, 1937); appeared in *Hitch Your Wagon* (1937); and *Too Much Johnson* (1938); played

Christine in *Danton's Death* (Mercury, Nov. 2, 1938); appeared in *Stars in Your Eyes*(Majestic, Feb. 9, 1939); played Miss Preen in *The Man Who Came to Dinner* (Music Box, Oct. 16, 1939); Annabelle Fuller in *George Washington Slept Here* (Bucks County Playhouse, New Hope, Pa., July 1941); Nancy Parker in *Jackpot* (Alvin, N.Y.C., Jan. 14, 1944; and national tour); Amelia in *Dark Hammock* (Forrest Th., N.Y.C., Dec. 11, 1944); Miss Hebe in *Hollywood Pinafore* (Alvin, May 31, 1945); Nina Stover in *Apple of His Eye* (Biltmore, Feb. 5, 1946); played the title role in *Elizabeth the Queen*(Berkshire Playhouse, Stockbridge, Mass., Summer 1946); Mrs. Betty Nelson in *Park Avenue*(Shubert, N.Y.C., Nov. 4, 1946); appeared in the pre-Bway tryout of *Hey Day* (opened Shubert, New Haven, Mar. 13, 1947; closed there Mar. 15, 1947); played Esther Murray in *Town House*(National, N.Y.C., Sept. 23, 1948); and, on tour, played Madame Arcati in *Blithe Spirit* (Summer 1966). With the American Conservatory Th. (San Diego), she appeared in *The Mystery Circle* (Dec. 5, 1972), *You Can't Take It with You* (Jan. 30, 1973), and *The Crucible*(Apr. 3, 1973); and was seen in *Juno and the Paycock* with the Center Th. Group (Mark Taper Forum, Los Angeles, Nov. 7, 1974).

Films. Among Miss Wickes' extensive appearances are *The Man Who Came to Dinner*(WB, 1941); *Now Voyager* (WB, 1942); *Happy Land* (20th-Fox, 1943); *June Bride* (WB, 1948); *The Petty Girl* (Col., 1950); *On Moonlight Bay*(WB, 1951); *I'll See You in My Dreams*(WB, 1952); *The Actress*(MGM, 1953); *White Christmas* (Par., 1954); *Destry* (UI, 1955); *Good Morning, Miss Dove*(20th-Fox, 1955); *Don't Go Near the Water* (MGM, 1956); *It Happened to Jane* (Col., 1959); *Cimarron* (MGM, 1961); *The Music Man* (WB, 1962); *Fate Is the Hunter* (20th-Fox, 1964); *Dear Heart*(WB, 1965); *The Trouble with Angels* (Col., 1966); *Where Angels Go, Trouble Follows* (Col., 1968); *The Spirit Is Willing*(Par., 1968); *Snowball Express*(BV, 1972); and *Napoleon and Samantha* (BV, 1972).

Television. Miss Wickes' extensive credits include The Gertrude Berg Show (CBS); Halls of Ivy; Dennis the Menace; Mrs. G. Goes to College (CBS); *The Catbird Seat* (NBC); *The Man Who Came to Dinner* (NBC); the Danny Thomas Show (ABC); and Doc (CBS).

WICKHAM, GLYNNE. Educator, director. b. Glynne W. G. Wickham, May 15, 1922, Capetown, South Africa. Attended Winchester Coll., England, 1935–40; grad. New Coll., Oxford Univ., B.A. 1946, M.A. 1947, Ph.D. 1952. Married May 1, 1954, to Marjorie Heseltine; two sons, one daughter. Served RAF, 1942–46; rank, Flight Lt. and Navigator. Member British Th. Museum (adv. comm., 1974–to date); Bankside Globe Th. Trust (exec. comm., 1970–to date). Address: (home) 6 College Rd., Clifton, Bristol 8, England tel. Bristol 34918; (bus.) Dept. of Drama, University of Bristol, Bristol, England tel. Bristol 24161.

Since 1955, Mr. Wickham has been head of the Drama Dept. at the Univ. of Bristol; was given the first chair of drama created in an English university (1960); was visiting professor of drama at the State Univ. of Iowa, where he directed a student production of *The White Devil* (Jan.–June 1960); and was visiting professor of theatre history, Yale University (1970).

Theatre. Mr. Wickham directed *The Birthday Party* (American premiere, Encore Th., San Francisco Actor's Workshop, Calif., July 15, 1960); and staged *The Play of Daniel* (Carmel Drama Festival, Calif., July 1960); and directed *Brother Jero's Metamorphosis* (Bristol Old Vic, Bristol, England, Mar. 1974).

Other Activities. He was adviser to the Finnish National Th. on the establishment of a drama department at the Univ. of Helsinki (Jan. 1963); was appointed to the board of governors of the Bristol Old Vic Trust, Ltd. (Apr. 1, 1963); and lectured on English medieval drama at the Intl. Federation of Societies for Th. Research (Venice, Italy, Sept. 1963); was a guest of State Univ. of NY (Binghamton) at a symposium on medieval drama in 1968; was chairman of a panel on Shakespeare's theatre at the 1st World Shakespeare Congress (Vancouver, B.C., Canada, 1971); and a panelist at "Shakespeare '74," City of New York and Centre for Performing Arts, Brooklyn Coll. (N.Y.C., Jan. 1974).

Published Works. Mr. Wickham wrote *Early English Stages* (3 vols., 1958–71); *Drama in a World of Science* (1961); *Shakespeare's Dramatic Heritage* (1969); and *The Medieval Theatre* (1974); and he edited *The Relations Between Universities and Radio and Films and Television* (1954).

Awards. He received a Rockefeller Fellowship for travel in the US (1953).

WIDDOES, KATHLEEN. Actress. b. Kathleen Effie Widdoes, Mar. 21, 1939, Wilmington, Del., to Eugene and Bernice Widdoes. Father, gypsy. Grad. Conrad H.S., 1956. Studied mime at Université au Théâtre des Nations, Paris, France, 1962. Married Jan. 22, 1963, to Richard Jordan, actor. Member of AEA; AFTRA; SAG. Address: 71 Horatio St., New York, NY 10014.

Theatre. Miss Widdoes made her debut as Alma in *Bus Stop*(Robin Hood Playhouse, Wilmington, Del., Aug. 1957); subsequently at the Robin Hood Playhouse, played Catherine in *A View from the Bridge* (Aug. 1957), and appeared in *The Primrose Path* (Sept. 1957). She toured Canada as Catherine in *A View from the Bridge* (Dec.–Jan. 1957); made her N.Y.C. debut as Teusret in *The Firstborn* (Coronet Th., Mar. 30, 1958), and played the role in Israel (Habimah, May 1958).

She played a Tourist and understudied France Nuyen as Suzie Wong in *The World of Suzie Wong* (Broadhurst, N.Y.C., Oct. 14, 1958); appeared as Irina in *The Three Sisters* (Fourth St. Th., Sept. 21, 1959); Sonja in *Notes from the Underground* (Th. de Lys, Nov. 1959); and toured Eastern states as Catherine in *A View from the Bridge* (Jan.–Feb. 1960).

At the NY Shakespeare Festival (Belvedere Lake), Miss Widdoes appeared as Katherine in *Henry V* (June 29, 1960) and Juliet in *Measure for Measure*(July 25, 1960); played Aglasia in *The Idiot* (Gate, Sept. 25, 1960); with the NY Shakespeare Festival (Wollman Rink), played Titania in *A Midsummer Night's Dream* (July 31, 1961) and the Queen in *Richard II*(Aug. 28, 1961); played Teresa del Castillo in the pre-Bway tryout of *We Take the Town*(opened Shubert, New Haven, Conn., Feb. 19, 1962; closed Shubert, Philadelphia, Pa., Mar. 17, 1962); Miranda in the NY Shakespeare Festival production of *The Tempest* (Delacorte, July 16, 1962); and Claire in *The Maids* (One Sheridan Square, Nov. 14, 1963).

She replaced Rosemary Harris as Alice in the APA-Phoenix production of *You Can't Take It with You*(Lyceum, N.Y.C., 1966); played Ersilia Drei in *To Clothe the Naked* (Sheridan Square Playhouse, Apr. 1967); as a member of the Yale Repertory Co. (New Haven, Conn., 1967–68), appeared in *The Three Sisters* and *'Tis a Pity She's a Whore;* played the Woman in *World War 2½* (Martinique, N.Y.C., Mar. 24, 1969); Mildred in *Willie*(The Other Stage, Oct. 1970); and Beatrice in the NY Shakespeare Festival production of *Much Ado About Nothing* (Winter Garden, N.Y.C., Nov. 11, 1972).

Films. She played Helena Davison in *The Group* (UA, 1966); Masha in *The Sea Gull* (WB-7 Arts, 1968); and appeared in *Savages*(New World, 1973).

Television. Miss Widdoes made her debut on Lamp Unto My Feet (CBS, 1957); subsequently played Jill on Young Dr. Malone (NBC, 1958); Emily in *Our Town* (NBC, 1959); the title role in *Colombe*(CBC, Can., 1960); the title role in *Ondine* (CBS, 1961); Joan in *The Lark* (CBC, 1962); and appeared on Ford Star Time (CBS), The Defenders (CBS, 1961, 1963, 1965), The Doctors (NBC, Sept. 1963), Dupont Show of the Month (CBS, 1960), Camera Three (CBS, 1960); The Doctors/The Nurses (CBS, 1965); Memory Lane (Ind., 1965–66); Twelve O'Clock High (ABC, 1966); and The Invaders (ABC, 1967); and played Beatrice in *Much Ado About Nothing* (CBS, 1973).

Awards. Miss Widdoes received a Fulbright Scholarship to study at the Université des Nations (1962).

WILBUR, RICHARD. Poet, translator, lyricist, teacher, critic. b. Richard Purdy Wilbur, Mar. 1, 1921, New York City, to Lawrence and Helen (Purdy) Wilbur. Father, portrait artist. Grad. Montclair (N.J.) H.S., 1938; Amherst Coll., A.B. 1942; Harvard Univ., M.A. 1947; Society of Fellows of Harvard Univ., 1947–50. Married June 20, 1942, to Charlotte Ward; three sons; one daughter. Served WW II, US Army, 36th Texas Inf. Div.; ETO; rank, T/3. Member of Dramatists Guild; NIAL; AAAS; AAAL. Address: (home) Cummington, MA 01026, tel. (413) 634-5420; (bus.) Wesleyan Univ., Middletown, CT 06457.

Since 1957, Mr. Wilbur has been a member of the faculty at Wesleyan Univ.; previously taught at Harvard Univ. 1950–54); and Wellesley Coll. (1954–57).

Mr. Wilbur translated from the French, Molière's *The Misanthrope*, which was produced by the Poet's Th. (Cambridge, Mass., Oct. 1955; Th. East, N.Y.C., Nov. 12, 1956); wrote the lyrics, with Dorothy Parker and John Latouche, for *Candide*(Martin Beck Th. Dec. 1, 1956); translated Moliere's *Tartuffe* (IASTA, Denver, Colo., July 1963), which was performed in repertory (Fred Miller Th., Milwaukee, Wis., Jan. 1964; the Repertory Th. of Lincoln Center, 1964–65 season) and later done in Stratford (Ontario) and London (England); and his translation of Moliere's *School for Wives* was done by the Phoenix Th. (Lyceum, N.Y.C., Feb. 16, 1971).

Published Works. Mr. Wilbur wrote *Beautiful Changes and Other Poems* (1948); *Ceremony and Other Poems* (1952); *Things of This World* (1956); *Advice to a Prophet* (1961); *Loudmouse* (1963); and edited the *Complete Poems of Edgar Allan Poe*(1961); a book of poems, *Walking to Sleep*(1969); and a book of poems and drawings, Opposites (1973); and edited *Poems of Shakespeare* (1966).

Awards. Mr. Wilbur received two Guggenheim Fellowships (1952, 1963); the Rome Prize (Amer. Acad. of Arts and Letters, 1954); the Pulitzer Prize in Poetry (1956); the Natl. Book Award (1956); the Millay Prize (1956); a Ford Fellow (1960); received an honorary L.H.D. from Lawrence Coll. (1960); the Cane Award (1961); was co-recipient of the Bollingen Translation Prize (1963); an honorary L.H.D. from Washington Univ. (1964); a D.Litt. from Amherst (1967); the Bollingen Prize for Poetry (1970); the Brandeis Creative Arts Award (1971); and the Shelley Memorial Prize (1973).

Recreation. Tennis, herb-gardening, boomeranging, late television shows.

WILCOX, COLLIN. Actress. b. Feb. 4, 1935, Highlands, N.C., to Jack H. and Virginia Randall (Bell) Wilcox. Father, farmer, professor of economics, artist, builder. Grad. West H.S., Knoxville, Tenn., 1952; Univ. of Tennessee, 1956; Goodman Memorial Th., 1955. Studied acting at Actors' Studio, N.Y.C. (mbr., 1961–to date). Married June 28, 1963, to Geoffrey Horne, actor. Relative in theatre: god-father, Watson Barrett, designer. Member of AEA; AFTRA; SAG. Address: 1730 LaLoma Ave., Berkeley, CA 94709.

Theatre. Miss Wilcox made her stage debut at age nine as a Dead Woman in *Our Town* (Highlands, N.C., 1944). She was resident ingenue at the Carousel Th. (1952–54, 1956); and in Chicago (Ill.), played Catherine in *A View from the Bridge* (Studebaker Th., Dec. 1956).

Miss Wilcox made her N.Y.C. debut as Ellen Wells in *The Day the Money Stopped* (Belasco, Feb. 20, 1958); subsequently played Dorrie in the pre-Bway tryout of *Crazy October* (opened Shubert, New Haven, Conn., Oct. 8, 1958; closed Shubert, Washington, D.C., Oct. 25, 1958; reopened Cass, Detroit, Mich., Nov. 10, 1958; closed Geary, San Francisco, Calif., Jan. 3, 1959).

She was standby for Diane Cilento in the role of Marie-Paule II in *The Good Soup* (Plymouth, N.Y.C., Mar. 2, 1960); played Esmeralda in *Camino Real* (St. Mark's Playhouse, May 16, 1960); was standby for Sandra Church as Robin Austin in *Under the Yum-Yum Tree*(Henry Miller's Th., Nov. 16, 1960); and later played the role (Coconut Grove

Playhouse, Miami, Fla., May 1961); played Chris in *Call Me By My Rightful Name* (Theatre O, Washington, D.C., Aug. 1961); played Belle Dort in *Look: We've Come Through* (Hudson, N.Y.C., Oct. 25, 1961); Isabel in *Period of Adjustment* (Stage Society, Los Angeles, Calif., Dec. 28, 1961), and repeated that role in the London production (Royal Court and Wyndham's Th., June 1962).

She played Madeline in the Actors' Studio production of *Strange Interlude* (Hudson, N.Y.C., Mar. 11, 1963), and during the run was married to Geoffrey Horne, another member of the cast, on stage at the Martin Beck Th., where the play was being presented at the time. In Dec. 1963, Miss Wilcox, played Nina in The Theatre Group production of *The Seagull* (Univ. of California at Los Angeles, Dec. 1963); and appeared in *The Family Way* (Lyceum, N.Y.C., Jan. 13, 1965).

Films. Miss Wilcox appeared in *To Kill a Mockingbird* (U, 1962); *The Name of the Game Is Kill* (Fanfare, 1968); *The Revolutionary,* with John Voight (U, 1969); *The Baby Maker* (Natl. Gen., 1970); *Catch 22* (Par., 1970); and *Jump* retitled *Fury on Wheels* (Cannon, 1971).

WILDER, CLINTON. Producer. b. Clinton Eugene Wilder, Jr., July 7, 1920, Irvine, Pa., to Clinton Eugene and Frances (Kornreich) Wilder, Sr. Father, engineer, manufacturer. Grad. Lawrenceville (N.J.) Sch. 1939; Princeton Univ., 1942. Served US Army, anti-aircraft artillery 1942–43; USAAF 1943–45, appeared in AAF production Winged Victory, 1943–44. Member of AEA; League of NY Theatres; League of Off-Bway Theatres; TDF (founding member and dir., 1968–74). Address: Quogue, NY 11959, tel. (212) RH 4-5082.

Theatre. Mr. Wilder was stage manager for *Heartsong* (tour 1947); and *Streetcar Named Desire* (Ethel Barrymore Th., Dec. 3, 1947); was subsequently associated with Cheryl Crawford in the production of *Regina* (46 St. Th., N.Y.C., Oct. 31, 1949); produced *The Tender Trap* (Longacre, Oct. 13, 1954); and Edward Hambleton and Norris Houghton, in association with Mr. Wilder, produced *Six Characters in Search of an Author* (Phoenix, Dec. 11, 1955). Mr. Wilder produced, with George Axelrod, *Visit to a Small Planet* (Booth, Feb. 7, 1957); and with Donald Albery, presented *The World of Suzie Wong* (Prince of Wales's, London, Nov. 17, 1959).

In 1961, Mr. Wilder and Richard Barr formed a producing unit called "Theatre 1961" to present experimental plays off-Bway. They presented the double bill, *The American Dream* and *Bartleby* (York, Jan. 21, 1961). *Bartleby* was dropped for *The Valerie Bettis Dance Theatre* (Feb. 7, 1961), which was replaced by *The Death of Bessie Smith* (Feb. 28, 1961). They next presented *Gallows Humor* (Gramercy Arts, Apr. 18, 1961). As "Theatre 1962," Messrs. Wilder and Barr produced *Happy Days* (Cherry Lane, Sept. 17, 1961); and a program of works in repertory, called *The Theatre of the Absurd* (Cherry Lane, Feb. 11, 1962), including *Endgame, Bertha, Gallows Humor, The Sandbox, Deathwatch, Picnic on the Battlefield, The American Dream, The Zoo Story,* and *The Killer.*

As "Theatre 1963," they presented the double bill, *Mrs. Dally Has a Lover* and *Whisper into My Good Ear* (Cherry Lane, Oct. 1, 1962); *Who's Afraid of Virginia Woolf?* (Billy Rose Th., Oct. 13, 1962); *Like Other People* (Village South, Mar. 29, 1963); and a revival of *The American Dream* and *The Zoo Story* (Cherry Lane, May 29, 1963).

Messrs. Wilder and Barr, together with Edward Albee, formed "Theatre 64," and leased the Cherry Lane Th. through June 1967. There, they have produced *Corruption in the Palace of Justice* (Oct. 8, 1963), and a double bill of Samuel Beckett's *Play* and, by arrangement with Michael Codron in association with David Hall, Harold Pinter's *The Lover* (Jan. 4, 1964). At the East End Th., they presented *Funnyhouse of a Negro* (Jan. 14, 1964). "Theatre 1964" has also established a Playwrights Unit and leased the Village So. Th. through Sept. 1965 for the presentation of workshop productions of the work of new American playwrights.

With Mr. Barr, he produced *Who's Afraid of Virginia Woolf?* (Piccadilly Th., London, 1964); with Messrs. Barr and Albee, produced *Two Executioners, Dutchman,* and *The Giants' Dance* (Cherry Lane Th., N.Y.C., Mar. 24, 1964); on Bway, with Mr. Barr, produced *Tiny Alice* (Billy Rose Th., Dec. 29, 1964); at the Cherry Lane, with Messrs. Barr and Albee, produced *Up to Thursday, Balls,* and *Home Free* (Feb. 10, 1965); *Pigeons* and *Conerico Is Here to Stay* (Mar. 9, 1965); *Lovely, Hunting the Jingo Bird* (Mar. 25, 1965); and *Do Not Pass Go* (Apr. 19, 1965). On Bway, with Mr. Barr, he produced *Malcolm* (Shubert, Jan. 11, 1966); at the Cherry Lane, with Messrs. Barr and Albee, produced a triple bill of Thornton Wilder plays entitled *The Long Christmas Dinner;* which also included *Queens of France* and *The Happy Journey from Trenton to Camden* (Sept. 6, 1966); and *The Butter and Egg Man* (Oct. 17, 1966); with Messrs. Barr, Albee and Michael Kasden, produced *Match Play* and *A Party for Divorce* (Provincetown Playhouse, N.Y.C., Oct. 11, 1966); with Mr. Barr, produced *A Delicate Balance* (Martin Beck Th., N.Y.C., Aug. 22, 1966); at the Cherry Lane, with Messrs. Barr and Albee, produced *Night of the Dance* (Dec. 28, 1966); *The Rimers of Eldritch* (Feb. 20, 1967); and *The Party on Greenwich Avenue* (May 10, 1967); with Messrs. Barr and Charles Woodward, produced *Johnny No-Trump* (Cort, N.Y.C., Oct. 3, 1967); with Mr. Barr, produced *Everything in the Garden* (Plymouth, N.Y.C., Nov. 29, 1967); *How Much, How Much?* (Provincetown Playhouse, N.Y.C., Apr. 20, 1970); with Alexander H. Cohen, produced *Home* (Morosco, N.Y.C., Nov. 17, 1970); with Messrs. Lansbury and Beruh, produced *Enclave* (Th. Four, N.Y.C., Nov. 15, 1973); and, with Messrs. Barr and Woodward, *Seascape* (Shubert, N.Y.C., Jan. 26, 1975).

Awards. Messrs. Wilder and Barr received the Vernon Rice Award (1962) for their "Theatre 1961" productions; and *Who's Afraid of Virginia Woolf?* received the Antoinette Perry (Tony) Award (1963); the NY Drama Critics' Circle Award (1963); and the Margo Jones Award (1965).

WILDER, GENE. Actor. b. Jerome Silberman, June 11, 1934, Milwaukee, Wis., to William J. and Jeanne (Baer) Silberman. Father, importer. Grad. Washington H.S., Milwaukee, 1951; State Univ. of Iowa, B.A. 1955. Studied acting with Herman Gottlieb, Milwaukee, 1946–51; Old Vic Theatre Sch., Bristol, England, 1955–56; Herbert Berghof (HB) Studio, N.Y.C., 1957–59; Actors' Studio (member, 1961–to date). Married July 22, 1960, to Mary Mercier, actress. Served US Army, 1956–58. Member of AEA; AFTRA. Address: (home) 157 E. 57th St., New York, NY 10022, tel. PL 5-7636; (bus.) c/o Kaplan and Veidt, 667 Madison Ave., New York, NY 10021, tel. (212) PL 5-2214.

Pre-Theatre. Chauffeur, toy salesman, fencing instructor.

Theatre. Mr. Wilder made his debut as Balthazar in *Romeo and Juliet* (Milwaukee Playhouse, Wis., Oct., 1948); and in stock, played Rosen in *The Late Christopher Bean* and appeared in *The Cat and the Canary* (Reginald Goode Th., Poughkeepsie, N.Y., July–Aug. 1949).

At the Tower Ranch Tenthouse Th. (Eagle River, Wis.), he appeared in *The Drunkard* (June 1951); played Vernon in *Summer and Smoke* (July 1951); Mansky in *The Play's the Thing* (July 1951); Mr. Weatherbee in *Arsenic and Old Lace* (Aug. 1951); Howard in *Death of a Salesman* (July 1952); Ed in *Come Back, Little Sheba* (July 1952); and the Principal in *The Happy Time* (Aug. 1952).

At the Cambridge (Mass.) Drama Festival (July 1959), he played the Second Officer and was fencing choreographer for *Twelfth Night* and *Macbeth.*

He made his N.Y.C. debut as Frankie Bryant in *Roots* (Mayfair Th., Mar. 6, 1961); subsequently played Andrew in *All the Way Home* (Playhouse-in-the-Park, Philadelphia, Pa., July 1961); the Hotel Valet in *The Complaisant Lover* (Ethel Barrymore Th., N.Y.C., Nov. 1, 1961); also touring in it (opened Sombrero Playhouse, Phoenix, Ariz., Mar. 12, 1962); the Captain in *Mother Courage and Her Children* (Martin Beck Th., N.Y.C., Mar. 28, 1963); toured as Julius Sagamore in the Theatre Guild production of *The Millionairess* (1963); and played Billie Bibbit in *One Flew Over the Cuckoo's Nest* (Cort, N.Y.C., Nov. 13, 1963).

He appeared as Smiley in *Dynamite Tonight* (York, Mar. 15, 1964); and in several roles in *The White House* (Henry Miller's Th., May 19, 1964), also touring summer theatres in it (July 13–Sept. 12, 1964).

Mr. Wilder was a standby for Alan Arkin, succeeding (June 13, 1966) Gabriel Dell in the role of Harry Berlin in *Luv* (Booth, N.Y.C., Nov. 11, 1964), having previously played the role at the Royal Poinciana Playhouse (Palm Beach, Fla., Jan. 17, 1966).

Films. He has appeared in *Bonnie and Clyde* (WB, 1967); *The Producers* (Embassy, 1968); *Start the Revolution Without Me* (WB, 1970); *Quacker Fortune Has an Uncle in the Bronx; Willie Wonka and the Chocolate Factory* (Par., 1971); *Everything You Always Wanted to Know About Sex, But Were Afraid to Ask* (UA, 1972); *Blazing Saddles* (WB, 1974); *Rhinoceros* (Amer. Film Th., 1974); *Young Frankenstein* (20th-Fox, 1974); and *The Little Prince* (Par., 1974).

Television. Mr. Wilder played Happy Penny in *Wingless Victory* (Play of the Week, WNTA, 1961); appeared on Armstrong Circle Th. (CBS, 1962); played Muller in *The Sound of Hunting* (Dupont Show of the Week, NBC, 1962); Wilson in *The Interrogators* (Dupont Show of the Week, NBC, 1962); the German Voice on 20th Century (CBS, 1962); the Head Waiter in *Reunion with Death* (The Defenders, CBS, 1962); the Reporter in *Windfall* (Dupont Show of the Week, NBC, 1962); Yonkel in *Home for Passover* (Eternal Light, NBC, 1966); Bernard in *Death of a Salesman* (CBS, 1966); and appeared in *Thursday's Game* (ABC, 1974).

Awards. He received the Clarence Derwent Award (1962) for his performance as the Hotel Valet in *The Complaisant Lover.* .

Recreation. Tennis, fencing, bridge.

WILLARD, HELEN D. Curator-librarian. b. Helen Delano Willard, Nov. 1, 1905, Chicago, Ill., to Henry Francis and Georgia (Vea) Willard. Father, educational administrator; mother, teacher. Attended Oberlin Coll., 1922–23; Univ. of Wisconsin, A.B. 1928; attended Columbia Univ., 1932–33. Address: 8 Chauncy St., Cambridge, MA 02138, tel. (617) KI 7-5546.

From 1960–72, Miss Willard was curator of the Harvard Theatre Collection; worked at the Fogg Art Museum, Harvard Univ. (1943–56), where she became assistant curator of drawings; and was on the staff of the Museum of Fine Arts (Boston, Mass.), in the Print Room.

She retired on June 30, 1972.

Other Activities. Miss Willard was previously a teacher of English, adult education, and editing and publishing, the latter mainly in the field of fine arts.

WILLIAMS, ANN. Actress. b. Ann Morgan Williams, May 18, 1935, Washington, D.C., to John Oscar and Alys (Gott) Williams. Father, agricultural scientist, animal husbandman. Grad. Washington-Lee H.S., Arlington, Va., 1953; George Washington Univ., A.A. 1956. Studied acting with Sanford Meisner at Neighborhood Playhouse Sch. of the Th., 1957; Wynn Handman, 1957–59; Lee Strasberg, 1962–63; voice with Margot Rebeil, 1958–63; Shakespeare with Douglas Seale, 1962, and Philip Burton, 1963. Married; one daughter. Member of AEA; AFTRA; SAG; Actors' Studio. Address: (home) 140 W. 79th St., New York, NY 10024, tel. (212) EN 2-8016; (bus.) c/o The Doctors, NBC, 30 Rockefeller Plaza, New York, NY 10020; c/o GAC, 640 Fifth Ave., New York, NY 10019.

Pre-Theatre. Part-time secretary at Pentagon; Federal Trade Commission.

Theatre. Miss Williams made her professional debut as a supernumerary in the ANTA touring production of *The Skin of Our Teeth* (Natl. Th., Washington, D.C., Sept. 1955); subsequently played

Miss Weston in the national tour of *Damn Yankees* (opened Shubert, New Haven, Conn., Jan. 21, 1956; closed Royal Alexandra, Toronto, Ontario, Canada, May 18, 1957); succeeded Beverly Dixon as Brenda and was understudy to Betty O'Neill in the role of Babe Williams in the national tour of *The Pajama Game*(opened Shubert, New Haven, Conn., Jan. 29, 1955; closed Civic Th., New Orleans, La., Feb. 16, 1957).

She made her N.Y.C. debut as Mrs. Dowling in *New Girl in Town* (46 St. Th., May 14, 1957) in which she also understudied Gwen Verdon in the role of Anna. She was understudy to Georgann Johnson as Vicky Remsen in *Drink to Me Only* (54 St. Th., Oct. 8, 1958); and to Phyllis Love, Patricia Roe, and Evans Evans as the three daughters, Barrett, Waverly, and Flagg Greer in *A Distant Bell* (Eugene O'Neill Th., Jan. 13, 1960); and appeared as Mary in *Between Two Thieves* (York, Feb. 11, 1960).

At the Alley Th., (Houston, Tex.), Miss Williams played Gerry LaMossa in *The Library Raid*(Oct. 12, 1960); Anne Tower in *Jane*(Nov. 9, 1960); the title role in *Ondine*(Dec. 14, 1960); Alexandra Giddens in *The Little Foxes* (Jan. 17, 1961); Petra in *An Enemy of the People*(Feb. 22, 1961); Mignonette in *The Happy Time* (Mar. 16, 1961); the Stepdaughter in *Six Characters in Search of an Author*(Apr. 19, 1961); and Catherine Winslow in *The Winslow Boy*(June 6, 1961).

She appeared as Frances Black in *The Milk Train Doesn't Stop Here Anymore* (Morosco, N.Y.C., Jan. 16, 1963), and as Karen Richards in *Applause* (Palace, Mar. 30, 1970).

Television. She appeared on *Last of the Belles* (Kraft Television Th., NBC, 1958); performed on Kraft Mystery Th. (NBC, 1958); played Emily Harker in *The Apple Orchard* (the Talk Back series, 1958); appeared on The Verdict Is Yours (CBS, 1958); in *The Head of a King* (CBS Workshop, 1959); on the Robert Herridge Th. (CBS, 1959); and in *Dead on the Field of Honor* (Naked City, ABC, 1961); played a running role, Erica Brandt, on Young Doctor Malone (NBC, Feb. 1962–Mar. 1963); Doctor Margaret Fielding on The Doctors (NBC, July 1963–1965); appeared on the Jesse James series (ABC, 1966); Hawk (ABC, 1966); and was a regular performer on Search for Tomorrow (CBS, 1972).

Awards. For her performance as Frances Black in *The Milk Train Doesn't Stop Here Anymore,* Miss Williams received the Fanny Kemble Award from the Charlotte Cushman Society (June 4, 1963) for best supporting actress, as voted by the Philadelphia (Pa.) drama critics.

Recreation. Horseback riding, polo, golf, skiing, painting, music, writing (poetry and children's stories).

WILLIAMS, CLARENCE III.

Actor. b. Aug. 21, 1939, New York City. Attended Clark Jr. H.S., Bronx; Frederick Dutton Jr. H.S., Harlem; Food Trades Vocational H.S., N.Y.C. Served US Army, parachutist, 101st Airborn Div. Married Nov. 1967 to Gloria Foster, actress.

Pre-Theatre. Cook, bartender, office worker.

Theatre. Mr. Williams made his first stage appearance in a YMCA production of *Dark of the Moon;* made his Bway debut as Chris in *The Long Dream* (Ambassador, Feb. 17, 1960); subsequently played Washington Roach in *Walk in Darkness*(Greenwich Mews Th., Oct 28, 1963); in a double-bill entitled *Double Talk* which included *The Dirty Old Man,* played The Sax in *Sarah and the Sax* (Th. de Lys, May 4, 1964); repeated that role in a summer stock production (Dobbs Ferry, N.Y., Summer 1964); played Randall in *Slow Dance on the Killing Ground* (Plymouth, N.Y.C., Nov. 30, 1964); Hector Case in *The Great Indoors* (Eugene O'Neill Th., Feb. 1, 1966); appeared in *Does a Tiger Wear a Necktie?* (Spingold Th., Brandeis Univ., Waltham, Mass., Feb. 2, 1967); and played Roosevelt in *The Party on Greenwich Avenue* (Cherry Lane Th., N.Y.C., May 10, 1967); and Hubert De Burgh in *King John*(Delacorte, July 5, 1967).

Films. He appeared in *The Cool World*(Cinema V, 1964).

Television. Mr. Williams' appearances include Daktari (CBS, 1967); the Danny Thomas Show (NBC, 1968); Tarzan; and the series The Mod Squad (ABC, 1968–72).

Awards. Mr. Williams was named a *Theatre World* Most Promising Personality (1964–65) for his performance in *Slow Dance on the Killing Ground*. .

WILLIAMS, EMLYN.

Actor, director, playwright. b. George Emlyn Williams, Nov. 26, 1905, Pen-y-Ffordd, Flintshire, North Wales, to Richard and Mary (Williams) Williams. Father, innkeeper. Studied at Holywell County Sch., N. Wales, 1916–23; St. Julien Sch., Haute Savoie, France; grad. Oxford Univ., M.A. 1927. Married July 1934 to Molly O'Shann; two sons. Relative in theatre: son, Brock Williams, actor. Member of AEA; SAG. Address: 123 Dovehouse St., London S.W.3, England tel. Flaxman 0208.

Theatre. Mr. Williams made his N.Y.C. debut as the Boy to Pepys in *And So to Bed* (Shubert Th., Nov. 9, 1927); followed by Lord Lebanon in *Criminal at Large* (Belasco, Oct. 10, 1932); Dan in *Night Must Fall,* which he also wrote (Ethel Barrymore Th., Sept. 28, 1936); Izquiredo in *Montserrat* (Fulton, Oct. 29, 1949); and gave a solo performance from Dickens' works in a program entitled, *Emyln Williams as Charles Dickens* (John Golden Th., Feb. 4, 1952), toured in it, and reopened in it in N.Y.C. (Bijou, Apr. 20, 1953).

He adapted *A Month in the Country* (Studebaker, Chicago, Ill., 1956); gave a solo performance from Dylan Thomas' *A Boy Growing Up* (Longacre, N.Y.C., Oct. 7, 1957), and on tour; played Ascolini in *Daughter of Silence* (Music Box, N.Y.C., Nov. 30, 1961); succeeded (July 1, 1962) Paul Scofield as Sir Thomas More in *A Man for All Seasons* (ANTA, Nov. 22, 1961); and played Pope Pius XII in *The Deputy* (Brooks Atkinson Th., Feb. 26, 1964).

Mr. Williams made his London debut as Pelling's Apprentice in *And So to Bed* (Savoy, Apr. 4, 1927); followed by the Rev. Yorke and Billy Saunders in *The Pocket-Money Husband* (Arts, Oct. 1928); Jack in *Glamour,* which he also wrote (Embassy, Dec. 1928); Beppo in *Mafro, Darling* and Berthold in *The Mock Emperor*(Queen's Th., Jan. 29, 1929); Camille in a French-language production of *Thérèse Raquin* (Wyndham's, Feb. 4, 1929); the Trumpeter in *The Silver Tassie* (Apollo, Oct. 11, 1929); Captain Sandys in *Tunnel Trench*(Duchess, Nov. 1929); and Jules Marnier in *French Leave* (Vaudeville, Jan. 7, 1930).

Also, Giovanni d'Amora in an Italian-language production of *La Piccola* (Arts, Mar. 1930); the Usher in *The Fire in the Opera House* (Everyman, Mar. 1930); Angelo in *On the Spot* (Wyndham's, Apr. 2, 1930); Adolphe in a French-language production of *Devant la porte* (Arts, Sept. 1930); Commissar Neufeld in *The Mouthpiece* (Wyndham's, Nov. 1930); the title role in *Etienne* (St. James's, Feb. 1931); Lord Lebanon in *The Case of the Frightened Lady*(Wyndham's, Aug. 18, 1931); Youssef el Tabah in *Port Said,* which he also wrote (Nov. 1931); the Young Frenchman in *The Man I Killed* (Apollo, Mar. 1932); Jack in *Man Overboard* (Garrick, May 1932); Bramwell Brontë in *Wild Decembers* (Apollo, May 1933); adapted Sydney Howard's *The Late Christopher Bean* (St. James's, May 16, 1933); and wrote *Spring 1600* (Shaftesbury, Jan. 31, 1934).

He appeared as Piers Gaveston in *Rose and Glove* (Westminster, Sept, 1934); Eugene Beauharnais in his adaptation of *Josephine* (His Majesty's, Sept. 1934); Dan in *Night Must Fall,* which he also wrote (Duchess, May 31, 1935); and Lambert in *He Was Born Gay,* which he also wrote (Queen's, May 1937).

He joined the Old Vic Co. at Buxton, playing Oswald in *Ghosts*(Aug. 1937); Angelo in *Measure for Measure* (Oct. 12, 1937); and the Duke of Gloucester in *Richard III* (Nov. 2, 1937). He appeared as Morgan Evans in *The Corn Is Green,* which he also wrote (Duchess, Sept. 20, 1938); Maddoc Thomas in *The Light of Heart,* which he also wrote (Apollo, Feb. 21, 1940); and Cliff Parrilow in *The Morning Star* (Globe, Dec. 10, 1941). He directed *Watch on the Rhine* (Aldwych, Apr. 22, 1942); and *The Little Foxes* (Piccadilly, Oct. 21, 1942).

He wrote *The Druid's Rest* (St. Martin's, Jan. 26, 1944); toured military bases in the Middle East in productions which included *Blithe Spirit, Flare Path,* and *Night Must Fall*(1944); played Ambrose Ellis in *The Wind of Heaven,* which he also wrote (St. James's, Apr. 12, 1945); Sir Robert Morton in *The Winslow Boy*(Lyric, May 23, 1946); Saviello in *Trespass,* which he also wrote (Globe, July 16, 1947); and Will Trenting in *Accolade,* which he also wrote (Aldwych, Sept. 7, 1950).

He gave a solo performance as Dickens (Lyric, Hammersmith, Oct. 1951), also touring internationally in it; gave another solo performance as Charles Dickens in a reading of *Bleak House* at the Edinburgh (Scotland) Festival (Aug. 1952), and in London (Ambassadors', Sept. 1952); and appeared as Dickens at the National Eisteddfodd (Wales, Aug. 1953).

He played Fenn in *Someone Waiting,* which he also wrote (Globe, London, Nov. 25, 1953); gave a solo performance entitled *Dylan Thomas Growing Up* (Globe, May 21, 1955); played Hjalmar Ekdal in *The Wild Duck* (Saville, Dec. 21, 1955); and at the Shakespeare Memorial Th. (Stratford-upon-Avon), played Shylock in *The Merchant of Venice* (Apr. 17, 1956), Iago in *Othello* (May 29, 1956), and Angelo in *Measure for Measure* (Aug. 14, 1956).

He directed *Beth,* which he also wrote (Apollo, London, Mar. 20, 1958); toured Australia and New Zealand in solo performances as Dickens and Dylan Thomas (1958); in London, appeared in a return engagement of *A Boy Growing Up* (Globe, Sept. 2, 1958); played the Author in *Shadow of Heroes* (Piccadilly, Oct. 7, 1958); appeared in *Three,* a triple-bill consisting of *Polesden Lacey, A Slight Ache,* and *Lunch Home* (Arts, Jan. 1961); and for the National Theatre, adapted Ibsen's *The Master Builder* (June 1964).

He appeared as Charles Dickens in a tour of eighty cities in the US and Canada, followed by a tour of the Far East, including Pakistan, India, and Japan (1965), and an engagement in London (Globe, Aug. 1965); played Ignaty Illyich in *A Month in the Country* (Cambridge, England, Sept. 1965); took over the role of the Headmaster in *Forty Years On* (Apollo, London, Sept. 1969); and appeared as Charles Dickens in the Dickens Centenary world tour (1970) that included Australia, Russia, and the US.

Films. He made his debut in *The Case of the Frightened Lady* (Beaconsfield, 1932); followed by *The Citadel* (MGM, 1938); *The Last Days of Dolwyn,* which he also wrote and directed (1940); *The Stars Look Down* (MGM, 1941); *Major Barbara* (UA, 1941); *Three Husbands* (UA, 1950); *The Scarf* (UA, 1951); *Another Man's Poison* (UA, 1952); *Ivanhoe* (MGM, 1952); *The Deep Blue Sea* (20th-Fox, 1955); *I Accuse* (MGM, 1958); *Beyond This Place* (Allied, 1959); *The Wreck of the Mary Deare* (MGM, 1959); and *The L-Shaped Room* (Col., 1963).

Television. Mr. Williams has been a guest on New York, New York (ABC, 1964); played Gerald Lawen in *Mend Over Murder* on The Defenders (CBS, 1965); did readings from Charles Dickens on The Emlyn Williams special (CBS, 1967), and appeared on the Hall of Kings special (ABC, 1967).

Published Works. He wrote the plays, *Vigil* (1928), *Full Moon* (1929), *A Murder Has Been Arranged* (1930), *Vessels Departing* (1933), and *Pen Don* (1943). He wrote his autobiography, *George* (1961); the novel, *Beyond Belief* (1967); and *Emlyn, An Early Autobiography 1927–35* (1974).

Awards. Mr. Williams' play, *The Corn Is Green,* won the NY Drama Critics' Circle Award (1941); and received an honorary LL.D. from Bangor Univ. (1949).

The Order of Commander of the British Empire (C.B.E.) was conferred upon him in 1962.

Recreation. Reading, walking, tennis.

WILLIAMS, HERSCHEL. Playwright, director. b. Herschel V. Williams, Jr., June 30, 1909, Savannah, Ga., to Herschel V. Williams, Sr., and Lillian (Strickland) Williams. Grad. Newman Sch., New Orleans, La., 1925; attended Tulane Univ., 1922–25; grad. Yale Univ., Ph. B. 1931; Yale Univ. Sch. of Drama, M.F.A. 1957; American Univ., Beirut, Lebanon, certificate 1951. Married Sept. 19, 1949; to Edna Christenson (marr. dis. 1956); married Mar. 29, 1973, to Mrs. Eppes Hawes Berdeau. Served USAAF and USAF, 1942–52; rank, Col.; Bronze Star, Air Medal with 2 clusters, Commendation Medal, and 7 campaign medals. Member of AADA (committee for annual benefit 1961–63); ANTA, NY Chapter (bd. of dir., 1963–65), ANTA (natl. bd. of dir., 1964); Playwrights Guild; ALA; Air Force Assn.; Zeta Psi; Yale Club of N.Y.C.; Seawanhaka Corinthian Yacht Club; New Haven Lawn; Elizabethan Club; Oglethorpe Club; Boston Club; 1925 F Street Club; American Legion Air Post 501.

Pre-Theatre. Advertising.

Theatre. Mr. Williams wrote, with Josephine Bentham, *Janie* (Henry Miller Th., N.Y.C., Sept. 10, 1942); wrote with Elisabeth Cobb, *The Men We Marry* (Mansfield Th., Jan. 16, 1948); and presented *John Brown's Body* (Player's Th., June 21, 1960).

Films. He was assistant to the director of *Maytime* (MGM, 1937); and co-author of *Janie* (WB, 1944); and *Janie Gets Married* (WB, 1946).

Radio. Mr. Williams was producer-director of Rose and Drums (NBC, 1932–36); Rudy Vallee Hour (1932); Burns & Allen (1932–34); Alexander Woollcott (1934–35); Romberg Hour (1934–35); Show Boat (1936–37); Palmolive Beauty Box Th. (1937); Big Sister (1937–42); and was director of commercial program development and sales of CBS (1946–47).

WILLIAMS, JOHN. Actor. b. Hugh Ernest Leo Williams, Apr. 15, 1903, Chalfont St. Giles, Bucks, England, to Col. Alfred Ernest and May (Roome) Williams. Father, aide-de-camp to George V, Edward VIII, and George VI of Eng. Attended St. Romans Prep. Sch., Worthing, Eng., 1911–15; Lancing Coll., Sussex, Eng., 1916–17. Married Oct. 9, 1927, to Beatrice Helen Blanchard. Served RAF, 1941–46; rank, Flying Officer. Member of AEA; SAG; AFTRA. Address: (home) 817 Coast Blvd., South La Jolla, CA 92037; (bus.) c/o Jane Broder, 35 Park Ave., New York, NY 10016, tel. (212) 697-8044.

Theatre. Mr. Williams first performed in London as John Darling in *Peter Pan* (New Th., Dec. 27, 1916); subsequently played Bill Le Bas in *The Law Divine* (Wyndham's, Aug. 29, 1918); Charles Daingerfield in *Come Out of the Kitchen* (Strand, Mar. 15, 1920); Jack Torrance in *The Ruined Lady* (Comedy, June 25, 1920); Bobby Coote in *The Romantic Age* (Comedy, Oct. 18, 1920); and toured in *Mr. Pim Passes By* (Aug., 1921).

He appeared as Bertie Errol in *The Knave of Diamonds* (Globe, Apr. 23, 1921); John Darling in *Peter Pan* (St. James, Dec. 15, 1921); John Fitzgerald in *Enter Madame* (Royalty, Feb. 15, 1922); Sir Richard Paynton in *The Card Players* (Savoy, Apr. 26, 1922); Denny Craddock in *The Happy Ending* (St. James's, Nov. 30, 1922); Arthur Mannock in *Success* (Haymarket, June 21, 1923); Sam Garden in *The Painted Lady* (Everyman, Jan. 12, 1924); succeeded (Apr. 1924) Francis Lister as Clifford Hope in *The Fake* (Apollo, London, Mar. 13, 1924; Hudson, N.Y.C., Oct. 6, 1924).

He appeared as Gerald Shannon in *Dark Angel* (Longacre, Feb. 10, 1925); Lucien in *A Kiss in a Taxi* (Ritz, Aug. 25, 1925); Charles Murdock in *The Ghost Train* (Eltinge, Aug. 25, 1926); Howell James in *Mixed Doubles* (Bijou, Apr. 26, 1927); James Depew in *Ten Per Cent* (George M. Cohan Th., Sept. 13, 1927); Douglas Helder in *Interference* (Empire, Oct. 18, 1927); the Burglar in *The Happy Husband* (Empire, May 7, 1928); Lord Teylesmore in *The High Road* (Fulton, Sept. 10, 1928); Anton Schuh in *One, Two, Three* (Henry Miller's Th., Sept. 29, 1930); Richard Chalfont in *Petticoat Influence* (Empire, Dec. 15, 1930); Felix in *I Love an Actress* (Times Sq. Th., Sept. 17, 1931); John in *A Good Woman, Poor Thing* (Avon, Jan. 9, 1933); Sergeant Brace in *Ten Minute Alibi* (Ethel Barrymore Th., Oct. 17, 1933); and Clyde Lockert in *Dodsworth* (Shubert, Feb. 24, 1934).

He played Archie Leadenhall in *Full House* (Haymarket, London, Aug. 21, 1935); succeeded (June, 1936) Lawrence Grossmith as Frank Haines in *Call It a Day* (Morosco, N.Y.C., Jan. 28, 1936); appeared as Jack Winterly in *White Christmas* (Red Barn Th., Locust Valley, N.Y., July 1936); Mr. Slope in *Barchester Towers* (Martin Beck Th., N.Y.C., Nov. 30, 1937); Eric Lindon in *Once Is Enough* (Henry Miller's Th., Feb. 15, 1938); General Sir William Howe in the pre-Bway tryout of *Yankee Fable* (opened Colonial, Boston, Mass., Oct. 19, 1938; closed there Nov. 5, 1938); Cunningham in *Miss Swan Expects* (Cort, N.Y.C., Feb. 20, 1939); Philo Smith in *No Time for Comedy* (Ethel Barrymore Th., Apr. 17, 1939); Jerry Seymour in *Claudia* (Booth, Feb. 12, 1941); succeeded (May 1946) Raymond Massey as Henry Higgins in *Pygmalion* (Ethel Barrymore Th., Dec. 26, 1945); and toured as Colonel Grey in *Alice Sit-By-the-Fire* (1946).

Mr. Williams played Walter Wallace in *A Family Affair* (Playhouse, N.Y.C., Nov. 27, 1946); Mark Kennicott in *The Men We Marry* (Mansfield, Jan. 16, 1948); the Duke of Norfolk in *Anne of the Thousand Days* (Shubert, Dec. 8, 1948); Bishop Gregory in *The Velvet Glove* (Booth, Dec. 26, 1949); General Burgoyne in a tour of *The Devil's Disciple* (1950); Herbert Reedbeck in *Venus Observed* (New Century, N.Y.C., Feb. 13, 1952); Inspector Hubbard in *Dial 'M' for Murder* (Plymouth, Oct. 29, 1952); Belmann in *The Dark Is Light Enough* (ANTA, Feb. 23, 1955); General Allenby in *Ross* (Eugene O'Neill Th., Dec. 26, 1961); and Sir Gregory in *The Chinese Prime Minister* (Royale, Jan. 2, 1964); *Hay Fever* (Helen Hayes Th., Oct. 29, 1970).

Films. He made his debut as Inspector Hubbard in the screen version of *Dial 'M' for Murder* (WB, 1954); subsequently appeared in *Sabrina* (Par., 1954); *To Catch a Thief* (Par., 1955); *Solid Gold Cadillac* (Col., 1956); *D-Day, the Sixth of June* (20th-Fox, 1956); *Island in the Sun* (20th-Fox, 1957); *Will Success Spoil Rock Hunter?* (20th-Fox, 1957); *Witness for the Prosecution* (UA, 1957); *The Young Philadelphians* (WB, 1959); *Midnight Lace* (U, 1960); *Erasmus with Freckles* (20th-Fox, 1964); *Flea in Her Ear* (20th-Fox, 1967); *The Secret War of Private Frigg* (U, 1967); *Lost in the Stars* (American Film Th., 1974).

Television. He appeared as Inspector Hubbard in *Dial 'M' for Murder* (Hallmark Hall of Fame, NBC, 1957–58); *Men in White* (Dupont Show of the Month, CBS, Sept. 30, 1960); appeared as Col. Pickering in *Pygmalion* (Hallmark Hall of Fame, NBC, Feb. 6, 1963); and Family Affair (CBS, 1966).

Awards. He received the Antoinette Perry (Tony) Award, the Donaldson Award, and the *Variety* N.Y. Drama Critics Poll for his performance as Inspector Hubbard in *Dial 'M' for Murder* (1952).

Recreation. Golf, trout fishing, gardening.

WILLIAMS, ROBERT N. Educator. b. Robert Neff Williams, Groton, S.D., to Joseph J. and Frances M. Williams. Grad. Univ. of South Dakota, B.A.; Columbia Univ., M.A. Married to Ruth McAlister; two daughters. Served US Army, 1943–46. Member of Speech Assn. of the Eastern States; Speech Assn. of Amer.; AAUP. Address: 39 Claremont Ave., New York, NY 10027.

Since 1970, Mr. Williams has been on the voice and speech faculty, Drama Division, The Julliard School, and in charge of speech at the School of General Studies, Columbia Univ.; from 1957–67, he was head of the speech dept. of the Neighborhood Playhouse School of the Theatre; and from 1966–72, he was in charge of voice and speech, Theatre Division, School of the Arts, Columbia Univ.

Television. Mr. Williams served as speech consultant to Compass Productions for Hallmark Hall of Fame television productions (1956–67).

Awards. Mr. Williams received a Folger Shakespeare Library Fellowship (1973) for work with Folger Theatre Group productions as voice and speech consultant.

WILLIAMS, SAMMY. Actor, dancer. b. Samuel Joseph Williams, Nov. 13, 1948, Trenton, N.J., to Joseph and Nona Williams. Father, factory worker; mother, hospital attendant. Educ. Steinert H.S., Trenton, N.J.; Rider Coll., Trenton, N.J. Professional training John Tucci Sch. of Dance; Frances Kiernan Sch. of Dance (scholarship); Luigi's, N.Y.C. (jazz dance); Jo Jo Smith; Wally Harper (voice). Member of AEA; AFTRA; SAG. 425 Lafayette St., New York, NY tel. (212) EN 2-7600; 230 Riverside Dr., New York, NY 10025, tel. (212) 662-3340.

Pre-Theatre. Mr. Williams worked for the NJ Dept. of Transportation.

Theatre. Mr. Williams made his professional debut in 1960 as Jerome in *South Pacific* (Lambertville, N.J., Music Circus). In high school, he appeared in productions of *The King and I* and *The Teahouse of the August Moon* (1964); *Guys and Dolls* and *Mr. Roberts* (1965); and *Camelot* (1966). He was a member of the chorus in summer stock productions of *Funny Girl* and *Sweet Charity* (Latham, Corning, East Rochester, N.Y., July 1967); made his Bway debut as the Swing Dancer in a revival of *The Happy Time* (Bway Th., Jan. 18, 1968); toured (Jan.–June 1969) in the national company of *Hello, Dolly!*; was a dancer in a bar in *Applause* (Palace, N.Y.C., Mar. 30, 1970) and on tour (Dec. 1972–June 1973); toured as a member of the chorus in the national company of *Seesaw* (Mar.–Aug. 1974); appeared in the chorus of a summer stock production of *No, No, Nanette* (Guber Circuit, Sept. 1974); and returned to Bway as Paul in *A Chorus Line* (Newman Th., May 22, 1975; transferred to Shubert Th., Oct. 19, 1975).

Television. Mr. Williams first appeared on television as a dancer on the Ed Sullivan Th. (CBS, Oct. 1968). He danced in the televising of the 1970 Antoinette Perry (Tony) Awards ceremonies (Mar. 1970); on the Fred Astaire Special (NBC, Aug. 1973); and appeared as Orange in a Tropicana orange juice commercial (Jan. 1973) and as Paul in a commercial for *A Chorus Line* (May 1975).

Discography. Mr. Williams is on recordings of *The Happy Time* (1969); *Applause* (ABC, 1970); and *A Chorus Line* (1975).

Recreation. Bicycling, ice skating, swimming, cookery, gardening.

WILLIAMS, TENNESSEE. Playwright, writer, poet. b. Thomas Lanier Williams, Mar. 26, 1911, Columbus, Miss., to Cornelius Coffin and Edwina (Dakin) Williams. Father, sales manager. Attended Univ. of Missouri, 1931–33; Washington Univ., 1936–37; grad. State Univ. of Iowa, B.A. 1938. Member of Dramatists Guild; ASCAP; Alpha Tau Omega. Address: 1431 Duncan St., Key West, FL 33040.

Pre-Theatre. Clerk in shoe factory, elevator operator, waiter, teletype operator, cashier, movie usher.

Theatre. Mr. Williams first worked with the St. Louis (Mo.) Mummers, for whom he wrote his first produced play, *Candles to the Sun*, presented as a curtain raiser to *Bury the Dead* (Wednesday Club Aud., St. Louis, 1936); subsequently wrote *The Fugitive Kind*, also produced by the Mummers (1937); *Spring Song*, presented at the Univ. of Iowa (1938); and *Not About Nightingales* (St. Louis, 1939).

His play, *Battle of the Angels*, was produced in a pre-Bway tryout by the Theatre Guild (opened Wilbur, Boston, Mass., Dec. 20, 1940; closed there Jan. 1, 1941); followed by *Stairs to the Roof* (Playbox, Pasadena, Calif. 1944–45).

His first work presented on Bway was *The Glass Menagerie* (Playhouse, Mar. 31, 1945), which had been presented at the Civic Th. (premiere Chicago, Ill., Dec. 26, 1944); with Donald Windham, he wrote *You Touched Me!* (Booth, N.Y.C., Sept. 25, 1945); a one-act play, *This Property Is Condemned*, presented by ELT (Hudson Park Th., Mar. 1946); and *Portrait of a Madonna*, by the Actor's Laboratory Th. (Las Palmas, Los Angeles, Calif., 1946–47); a full-length play, *Summer and Smoke*, was presented by Margo Jones (Th. '47, Dallas, Tex., July 11, 1947), and in N.Y.C. (Music Box, Oct. 6, 1948); followed by *A Streetcar Named Desire* (Ethel Barrymore Th., Dec. 3, 1947); *The Rose Tattoo* (Martin Beck Th., Feb. 3, 1951), which later toured (1951–52); *Camino Real* (National, N.Y.C., Mar. 19, 1953); and *Cat on a Hot Tin Roof* (Morosco, Mar. 24, 1955), which also toured (1956–58).

His one-act play, *27 Wagons Full of Cotton* was produced as part of a triple-bill, entitled *All in One* (Playhouse, N.Y.C., Apr. 19, 1955); he wrote *Three Players of a Summer Game* (White Barn Th., Westport, Conn., July 19, 1955); *Orpheus Descending* (Martin Beck Th., N.Y.C., Mar. 21, 1957); *This Property Is Condemned* and *Portrait of a Madonna* were presented in Germany (Congress Hall, Berlin, commencing Sept. 20, 1957); and *Garden District*, a double-bill consisting of the one-act plays, *Something Unspoken* and *Suddenly, Last Summer* (York Playhouse, Jan. 7, 1958), which toured (1959).

Mr. Williams wrote the one-act play, *Talk to Me Like the Rain* (White Barn Th., Westport, Conn., July 26, 1958); *Sweet Bird of Youth* (Martin Beck Th., N.Y.C., Mar. 10, 1959), which later toured (1960); *I Rise in Flame, Cried the Phoenix*, which was presented on a double-bill (Phoenix, Apr. 14, 1959); and *The Purification*, which was presented as part of the ANTA Matinee Th. Series (Th. de Lys, Dec. 8, 1959). His play, *Period of Adjustment* was presented (Coconut Grove Playhouse, Miami, Fla., premiere, 1959), and in N.Y.C. (Helen Hayes Th., Nov. 10, 1960); followed by *The Night of the Iguana* (Royale, Dec. 28, 1961). *The Milk Train Doesn't Stop Here Anymore* was presented at the Festival of Two Worlds (world premiere, Spoleto, Italy, June, 1962), and in N.Y.C. (Morosco, Jan. 16, 1963); a revised version of the same play was staged (Barter Th., Abingdon, Va., Fall 1963), and another version in N.Y.C. (Brooks Atkinson Th., Jan. 1, 1964).

The Mutilated and *Guadiges Fraulein* were presented under the title *Slapstick Tragedy* (Longacre, N.Y.C., Feb. 22, 1966). *The Two Character Play* was presented in London (Hampstead Th. Club, 1967); and retitled *Outcry* (Lyceum, N.Y.C., Mar. 1, 1973). He subsequently wrote *The Seven Descents of Myrtle* (Ethel Barrymore Th., Mar. 27, 1967); *In the Bar of a Tokyo Hotel* (Eastside Playhouse, May 11, 1969); and *Small Craft Warnings* (New Th., Apr. 2, 1972).

Films. The following are the film adaptations of Mr. Williams' works: *The Glass Menagerie* (WB, 1950); *A Streetcar Named Desire* (WB, 1951); *The Rose Tattoo* (Par., 1955); *Baby Doll* (WB, 1956); *Cat on a Hot Tin Roof* (MGM, 1958); *Suddenly, Last Summer* (Col., 1959); *The Fugitive Kind* (UA, 1960); *Summer and Smoke* (Par., 1961); *The Roman Spring of Mrs. Stone* (WB, 1961); *Period of Adjustment* (MGM, 1962); *Sweet Bird of Youth* (MGM, 1962); and *The Night of the Iguana* (MGM, 1964); *This Property is Condemned* (Par., 1966); and (based upon *The Milk Train Doesn't Stop Here Anymore*) *Boom* (U, 1968).

Television. Four of his one-act plays were presented on Play of the Week (WNTA, Feb. 6, 1961); *I Rise in Flame, Cried the Phoenix; The Purification; Hello from Bertha;* and *The Lady of Larkspur Lotion;* and scenes from *Camino Real* were presented on Look Up and Live (CBS, 1964). His televised plays include *Portrait of a Madonna* (BBC, 1965); *Ten Blocks on the Camino Real* (NET, 1966); and *The Glass Menagerie* (CBS, 1966). Mr. Williams has made personal appearances on the Today Show (NBC, 1964–65); and Tonight (BBC, 1965).

Published Works. His published full-length plays include: *A Streetcar Named Desire* (1947, 1952); *Baby Doll; Cat on a Hot Tin Roof* (1955); *The Fugitive Kind; The Glass Menagerie; In the Winter of Cities* (1955); *Orpheus Descending* (1957); *Suddenly, Last Summer* (1958); *Sweet Bird of Youth* (1959; 1962); *A Period of Adjustment* (1960); *The Night of the Iguana* (1961); *The Rose Tattoo;* and *Summer and Smoke.*

The following of his one-act plays have been published: Mooney's Kid Don't Cry, This Property Is Condemned, and *At Liberty* (1941); *The Lady of Larkspur Lotion* (1942); *The Last of My Solid Gold Watches* (1943); *27 Wagons Full of Cotton* (1945); *The Unsatisfactory Supper* (1946); *American Blues, The Dark Room, The Case of the Crushed Petunias, The Long Stay Cut Short, The Unsatisfactory Supper,* and *Ten Blocks on the Camino Real* (1948); *I Rise in Flame, Cried the Phoenix* (1950); and *Lord Byron's Love Letter* (1962).

Mr. Williams wrote a collection of poems, *The Summer Belvedere* (1944); *One Arm, and Other Stories* (1948); *The Roman Spring of Mrs. Stone* (1950); and *Hard Candy: A Book of Stories* (1954); *The Knightly Quest* (1967), a collection of four short stories and a novella; and *Dragon Country,* a book of plays (1970).

Awards. For *The Glass Menagerie,* he received the NY Drama Critics' Circle Award, the Sidney Howard Memorial Award, and the Fourth Annual Award from the magazine *Sign* (1945); for *A Streetcar Named Desire,* the NY Drama Critics Circle Award, the Donaldson Award, and the Pulitzer Prize (1948); for *Cat on a Hot Tin Roof,* the NY Drama Critics' Circle Award and the Pulitzer Prize (1955); and for *Night of the Iguana,* first place in the London Critics' Poll for Best New Foreign Play (1964–65). He has also received two Rockefeller fellowships; a grant from the Inst. of Arts and Letters; a Brandeis Univ. Creative Arts Award medal (1965); The National Institute of Arts and Letters Gold Medal for Drama (1969); and the Tennessee Williams' Center for Literary Arts (Key West, Fla.) was dedicated in his honor (1975).

WILLIAMSON, HUGH ROSS.

Playwright. b. Jan. 2, 1901, to Hugh Ross and Grace (Walker) Williamson. Grad. Brighton Grammar Sch.; London Univ., B.A. (history honors). Married Nov. 3, 1941, to Margaret Cox. Member of the Savage Club, London; Gold Medallist and Associate of London Acad. of Music; Fellow of the Royal Society of Literature. Address: 193 Sussex Gardens, London W.2, England.

Theatre. Mr. Williamson's first play, *The Adventurer,* was produced in the US (Le Petit Th. du Vieux Carré, New Orleans, La., 1927); his play, *Teresa of Avila,* previously produced in Dublin and London (see below), was presented at the Kentucky State Th. (July 23, 1964).

He wrote *In a Glass Darkly* (Festival Th., Cambridge, England, Feb. 29, 1932); *Rose and Glove* (Westminster, London, Sept. 8, 1934); *The Seven Deadly Virtues* (Gate Th. Studio, Feb. 13, 1935); *Monsieur Moi* (Ambassadors', 1935); *Various Heavens* (Gate Th. Studio, Feb. 12, 1936); *Mr. Gladstone* (Gate Th. Studio, 1937); *Remember the Sun* (Criterion, May 11, 1947); an adaptation of *The Pilgrim's Progress* (Royal Opera House, Covent Garden, July 19, 1948); *Fool's Paradise* (Ipswich Arts Th., Mar. 21, 1949); *Queen Elizabeth* (Arts, London, Oct. 10, 1950); *Gunpowder Treason and Plot* (Ipswich Arts Th., May 28, 1951); *His Eminence of England* (Canterbury Cathedral Festival Play, July 1953); *Diamond Cut Diamond* (Library Th., Manchester, Aug. 31, 1954); the book for the musical, *Wild Grows the Heather,* based on J. M. Barrie's *The Little Minister* (Hippodrome, London, May 3, 1956); the commentary for the first British "Son et Lumière" presentation (Greenwich Park, Aug. 1957); *The Mime of Bernadette* (Royal Albert Hall, London, Feb. 10, 1958); *Heart of Bruce* (Edinburgh Festival, 1959); and *Teresa of Avila* (Dublin Festival, Sept. 11, 1961; Vaudeville, London, Oct. 20, 1961).

He made his debut as an actor, billed as Ian Rossiter, in *Bernadette of Lourdes* (Edinburgh Festival, Scot., 1958); and wrote the one-act plays, *The Cardinal's Learning* (1949), *Conversation with a Ghost* (1950), and *King Claudius* (1952).

Television and Radio. Mr. Williamson wrote the four-hour radio play, *Paul, a Bond Slave* (BBC, Fall 1944); and has written five television plays including *The Killing of the King,* which was presented in the US (WNTA).

Other Activities. Before becoming a free-lance writer, Mr. Williamson was drama critic for the Yorkshire *Post* (1925–30); editor of *The Bookman* (1930–34); and acting editor of the *Strand* Magazine (1934).

Published Works. He has written 14 historical novels including *Captain Thomas Schofield, The Silver Bowl, James by the Grace of God, Guy Fawkes, The Butt of Malmsey, The Marriage Made in Blood, A Matter of Martyrdom, The Cardinal in England, The Florentine Women, The Last of the Valois, Paris Is Worth a Mass;* seven historical plays including *His Eminence of England, Queen Elizabeth, Teresa of Avila, Gunpowder, Treason and Plot;* seven historical biographies including *Kind Kit* (1972), *Catherine de Medici* (1973), and *Lorenzo the Magnificent* (1974); and a book of historical enigmas (1974).

His historical works include *The Gunpowder Plot,* (1952), *The Day Shakespeare Died* (1962), and *The Beginning of the English Reformation.*.

WILLIAMSON, NICOL.

Actor. b. Hamilton, Scotland, Sept. 14, 1938. Professional training at Birmingham (England) School of Speech Training and Dramatic Art, 1953–56. Married July 17, 1973, to Jill Townsend; one son.

Theatre. Mr. Williamson began his career as an actor at the Dundee (Scotland) Repertory Th. (1960–61). He first appeared in England as I-ti in *That's Us* (Arts, Cambridge, Oct. 1961) and made his London debut in the same role (Royal Court, Nov. 3, 1961). He toured as Black Will in *Arden of Faversham* (Nov. 1961); was Flute in *A Midsummer Night's Dream* (Royal Court, Jan. 24, 1962); Malvolio in *Twelfth Night* (Royal Court, Feb. 18, 1962); S.A.C. Albert Meakin in *Nil Carborundum* (New Arts, Apr. 12, 1962); Satin in *The Lower Depths* (New Arts, May 9, 1962); and Leantio in *Women, Beware Women* (New Arts, July 4, 1962). He appeared also as the Man at the End in *Spring Awakening* (Royal Court, Apr. 21, 1962); Kelly in *Kelly's Eye* (Royal Court, June 12, 1963); Sebastian Dangerfield in *The Ginger Man* (Ashcroft Th., Croydon, Nov. 1963; moved to Royal Court, London, Nov. 1963); Bill Maitland in *Inadmissible Evidence* (Royal Court, Sept. 9, 1964); Peter Wykeham in *A Cuckoo in the Nest* (Royal Court, Oct. 22, 1964); Vladimir in *Waiting for Godot* (Royal Court, Dec. 30, 1964); and again played Bill Maitland in *Inadmissible Evidence* Wyndham's, Mar. 17, 1965).

He appeared as Joe Johnson in *Miniatures* (Royal Court, Apr. 25, 1965); Sweeney in *Sweeney Agonistes* on a program honoring T. S. Eliot (Globe, June 1965); and made his Bway debut again playing Bill Maitland in *Inadmissible Evidence* (Belasco Th., N.Y.C., Nov. 30, 1965). He played Alexei Ivanovitch Poprichtchine in *Diary of a Madman* (Duchess, London, Mar. 13, 1967); and replaced (May 27, 1968) George C. Scott as Sam Nash, Jesse Kiplinger, and Roy Hubley in *Plaza Suite* (Plymouth, N.Y.C. Feb. 14, 1966) for six weeks during Mr. Scott's illness; played the title role in *Hamlet* (Round House, London, Mar. 1969; Lunt-Fontanne Th., N.Y.C., May 1, 1969), then touring the US in that part (opened Colonial, Boston, June 16, 1969); and gave a one-man performance at the White House, Washington, D.C. (Mar. 19, 1970).

He played Ivan Voinitsky in *Uncle Vanya* (Circle in the Square/Joseph E. Levine Th., N.Y.C., June 4, 1973); appeared in a one-man show billed as *Nicol Williamson's Late Show* (Eastside Playhouse, June 26, 1973); played the title role in *Coriolanus* (Aldwych, London, Oct. 22, 1973); appeared in a one-man poetry and music reading billed as *Midwinter Spring* (Aldwych, Dec. 1973–Jan. 1974); played Malvolio in *Twelfth Night* (Stratford-on-Avon, Eng., Aug. 1974); the title role in *Macbeth* (Aldwych, London, Mar. 1975); and was Henry VIII in *Rex* (Lunt-Fontanne Th., N.Y.C., Apr. 25, 1976).

Films. Mr. Williamson's films include *Inadmissible Evidence* (Par., 1968); *The Bofors Gun* (Regional Film Distributors, 1968); *Laughter in the Dark* (Lopert, 1969); *The Reckoning* (Col., 1969); *Hamlet* (Col., 1969); and *The Jerusalem File* (MGM, 1972).

Television. Mr. Williamson portrayed Richard M. Nixon in *I Know What I Meant* (Granada, 1974).

Discography. Mr. Williamson's recordings include *Nicol Williamson* (CBS, 1971).

Awards. For his performance as Bill Maitland in

Inadmissible Evidence, Mr. Williamson was named in the *Variety* NY Drama Critics Poll and was nominated for an Antoinette Perry (Tony) Award as best actor (1965–66).

WILLINGHAM, CALDER. Playwright, novelist. b. Calder Baynard Willingham, Jr., Dec. 23, 1922, Atlanta, Ga., to Calder Baynard Sr., and Eleanor (Willcox) Willingham. Attended Darlington Preparatory Sch., Rome, Ga., 1936–40; The Citadel, 1940–41; Univ. of Virginia, 1941–43. Married 1945 to Helene Rothenberg (marr. dis. 1950); one son; married Sept. 15, 1953, to Jane Bennett; three sons, two daughters. Member of ALA.

Theatre. Mr. Willingham wrote *End as a Man,* based on his novel of the same title (Th. de Lys, N.Y.C., Sept. 15, 1953) and *How Tall Is Toscanini?* (Schoenberg Hall, Univ. of California, Los Angeles, 1967).

Films. Mr. Willingham wrote the screenplay for *End as a Man,* which was released under the title *The Strange One* (Col., 1957). Among his other screenplays are *Paths of Glory* (UA, 1957); *The Vikings* (UA, 1958); *One-Eyed Jacks* (Par., 1961); *Little Big Man;* and *The Graduate.* .

Published Works. He wrote the novels *End as a Man* (1947); *Geraldine Bradshaw* (1950); *Reach to the Stars* (1952); *Natural Child* (1953); *To Eat a Peach* (1955); *Eternal Fire* (1962); and a collection of short stories entitled *The Gates of Hell* (1951).

WILLIS, JOHN. Editor, educator, actor. b. Oct. 16, 1916, Morristown, Tenn., to John Bradford and George Anne (Myers) Willis. Father, pharmacist. Educ. Morristown public schools; Milligan Coll.; Univ. of Tennessee; Indiana Univ.; Harvard Univ. Studied speech and drama at summer theatres. Married 1940 to Anne Sheldon (marr. dis. 1946); 1960 to Claire Olivier (marr. dis. 1965). Member of NY Drama Desk; Alpha Psi Omega. Address: 190 Riverside Dr., New York, NY 10024, tel. (212) 877-2154.

Pre-Theatre. Mr. Willis was a teacher at Whitesburg (Tenn.) Consolidated School (1938–39); an instructor at the Univ. of Tennessee, Knoxville (1939–41); and in N.Y.C. public high schools (1955–to date). He is dean of and a teacher at National Acad. of Theatre Arts, Chappaqua, N.Y.

Theatre. Mr. Willis was in many school productions. He first appeared on the professional stage at Priscilla Beach Playhouse, Plymouth, Mass., in 1936; filled summer stock engagements at Olney, Md.; Milford, Conn.; Lake Hopatcong, N.J.; Blauvelt, N.Y.; Gloucester, Mass.; and Cedarhurst, N.Y.; was in an Equity Library Th. production of *Saint Joan;* and toured with the Clare Tree Major Children's Theatre.

Published Works. Mr. Willis was assistant editor of the yearbooks *Theatre World* (1945–65) and *Screen World* (1949–64); he succeeded Daniel Blum as editor of both in 1965 and began editing *Dance World* in 1966. He also edited *Opera World* (1952–54); *Pictorial History of American Theatre* (1950, 1960, 1970); *Great Stars of the American Stage* (1952); *Pictorial History of the Silent Screen* (1953); *Pictorial History of Opera in America* (1954); *Pictorial History of the Talkies* (1958) and *Pictorial History of Television* (1959).

Recreation. Collecting theatre memorabilia.

WILLMAN, NOEL. Director, actor. b. Noel Bath Willman, Aug. 4, 1918, Londonderry, Northern Ireland, to Romain and Charlotte Ellis (O'Neil) Willman. Educated privately in Londonderry and Strasbourg. Studied acting with Michel Saint-Denis at London Th. Studio. Member of Directors Union; AEA; SAG; AFTRA. Address: 33 Elizabeth St., London S.W.1, England tel. Sloane 1706.

Theatre. Mr. Willman first performed as a walk-on in John Gielgud's *Hamlet* (Lyceum Th., London, June 28, 1939); subsequently appeared as the Player in *The Beggar's Opera* (Haymarket, Mar. 5, 1940); toured with the Old Vic Co. in *The Witch,* and *The Merchant of Venice.*

He performed in the revue, *Light and Shade* (Ambassadors', London, July 29, 1942); as Grigori Tansmann in *House of Regrets* (Arts, Oct. 6, 1942); Lorenzo in *The Merchant of Venice* (New, Feb. 16, 1943); was engaged as an actor-director with the Old Vic Co. (Playhouse, Liverpool, 1943–45); appeared in productions with the Bristol Old Vic Co. (1946); and directed *A Doll's House* (Winter Garden, London, Jan. 17, 1946).

Mr. Willman played Baron Foehn in *The Eagle Has Two Heads* (Lyric, Hammersmith, London, Sept. 14, 1946); served as director, with Beatrix Lehmann, of the Arts Th. (Oct. 1946–Mar. 1947), directing *A Phoenix Too Frequent, Back to Methuselah,* and *The Turn of the Screw;* and toured in productions in South Africa (Mar.–Dec. 1947).

At the Shakespeare Memorial Th. (Stratford-upon-Avon, 1948), he played Robert Falconbridge in *King John,* Antonio in *The Merchant of Venice,* Osric in *Hamlet,* Gremio in *The Taming of the Shrew,* and Pandarus in *Troilus and Cressida.*

He played Darius in *Adventure Story* (St. James's, London, Mar. 17, 1949); Sir Joseph Wrathie in *Shall We Join the Ladies?* (Lyric, Hammersmith, Jan. 19, 1950); Old Tawn in *The Bay with a Cart* (Lyric, Hammersmith, Jan. 1950); the Stylish Young Man and the Prison Chaplain in *The Trial* (Winter Garden, Apr. 12, 1950); and made his N.Y.C. debut as Monsieur Henri in *Legend of Lovers* (Plymouth, Dec. 26, 1951).

He appeared as Colonel Izquierdo and directed, with Nigel Green *Montserrat* (Lyric, Hammersmith, London, Apr. 8, 1952); directed *The White Carnation* (Globe, Mar. 20, 1953); *Someone Waiting* (Globe, Nov. 25, 1953); appeared as the Interrogator in *The Prisoner* (Globe, Apr. 14, 1954); and Brack in *Hedda Gabler* (Westminster, Nov. 29, 1954).

At the Shakespeare Memorial Th. (Stratford-upon-Avon), he directed *All's Well That Ends Well* (Apr. 26, 1955); appeared as General Burgoyne and directed *The Devil's Disciple* (Winter Garden, London, Nov. 8, 1956); directed *It's the Geography That Counts* (St. James's, June 12, 1957); appeared as the Husband in *Rashomon* (Music Box, N.Y.C., Jan. 27, 1959); directed *A Man for All Seasons* (Globe, London, July 1, 1960; ANTA, N.Y.C., Nov. 22, 1961); played Eugene Striden in *Isle of Children* (Cort, N.Y.C., Mar. 16, 1962); directed *The Beauty Part* (Music Box, Dec. 26, 1962); *The Lion in Winter* (Ambassador, N.Y.C., Mar. 3, 1966); *Othello; Beware of the Dog* (Nottingham, England, Playhouse, 1967); *Brother and Sister* (on tour, and St. Martin's Th., London, 1967); *Ring 'Round the Moon* (Haymarket Th., London, 1968); and *Darling of the Day* (George Abbott Th., N.Y.C., Jan. 27, 1968).

Films. Mr. Willman played the Chief of Police in *Across the Bridge* (Rank, 1957); and appeared in *The Cone of Silence;* and *Dr. Zhivago* (MGM, 1966).

Television. In England, he has appeared in *The Green Bay Tree; Strange Interlude; The Crucible;* and made his US debut in the title role in *The Count of Monte Cristo* (Dupont Show of the Month, CBS, 1958).

In England, he directed The Autumn Garden (1966).

Awards. Mr. Willman received the Clarence Derwent Award (1954) for his performance as the Interrogator in *The Prisoner.*

Recreation. Tennis, playing piano.

WILLSON, MEREDITH. Composer, playwright, lyricist, musical director, musician. b. Robert Reiniger Meredith Willson, May 18, 1902, Mason City, Iowa, to John David and Rosalie Reiniger. Father, lawyer. Grad. Mason City (Iowa) H.S. Studied at Damrosch Inst. of Musical Art, N.Y.C., 1919–22; with Henry Hadley, 1923–24; with Georges Barrere, 1920–29; with Julius Gold, 1932–35. Married Aug. 29, 1920, to Elizabeth Wilson (marr. dis. 1946); married Mar. 13, 1948, to Ralina Zarova, concert artist (dec. 1966); married Feb. 14, 1968, to Rosemary Sullivan. Served US Army, 1942–45; rank, Maj. Member of ASCAP; Dramatists Guild; The Friars; Big Brothers of Greater Los Angeles (pres., 1956–61; The Family. Address: (home) Brentwood, CA 94513; (bus.) c/o Rinimer Corp., 9171 Wilshire Blvd., Beverly Hills, CA 90210, tel. (213) CR 4-5405.

Theatre. Mr. Willson first performed as a flutist in the John Philip Sousa band (1921–23).

He has also performed as a flutist with the New York Philharmonic (1924–1929).

He wrote the book, lyrics, and music for *The Music Man* (Majestic Th., N.Y.C., Dec. 19, 1957); music and lyrics for *The Unsinkable Molly Brown* (Winter Garden, Nov. 3, 1960); and the book, lyrics, and music for *Here's Love* (Shubert, Oct. 3, 1963).

Films. He composed the score for *The Great Dictator* (UA, 1940); and *The Little Foxes* (RKO, 1941).

Television and Radio. He served as musical director for radio station FFRC, San Francisco, Calif. 1930–33); NBC's Western Division (1933–37); network radio (NBC, Hollywood, Calif., 1937–42); network radio and television programs including The Big Show (NBC) for which he wrote the song "May the Good Lord Bless and Keep You" for Tallulah Bankhead.

Published Works. Mr. Willson has written the autobiographies, *There I Stood with My Piccolo* (1948); *Eggs I Have Laid* (1952); *But He Doesn't Know the Territory* (1959); and a novel, *Who Did What to Fedalia* (1950).

Awards. He received an Antoinette Perry (Tony) Award, a NY Drama Critics' Circle Award, an Outer Circle Award, and the Thespians Theatre Award for his composition of the book, lyrics, and music for *The Music Man* (1957–58).

He also received the Natl. Big Brother Award (1962) which was presented to him by President John F. Kennedy; an honorary D. Mus. (1956) from Parson's Coll., and from Coe Coll. (1960); and an honorary D. Litt. (1963) from the Indiana Inst. of Technology.

The Academy (Oscar) Award for best score was presented to him for *The Music Man* (1962).

Additionally, he received the first Grammy in NARAS history for *The Music Man* original Bway cast album; the honorary degree from Indiana Inst. of Technology (1963); and an honorary (D.F.A.) degree from Regis College, Denver, Colo. (1973).

WILMETH, DON B. Theatre historian, actor, director, educator, writer. b. Dec. 15, 1939, Houston, Tex., to Perry Davis and Pauline (Goodrum) Wilmeth. Father, magazine editor. Educ. Tyler (Tex.) H.S.; grad. Abilene (Tex.) Christian Coll., B.A 1961; Univ. of Arkansas, M.A. 1962; Univ. of Illinois, Ph.D. 1964. Married June 10, 1963, to Judy Eslie Harsgen; one son. Member of ATA; ASTR; TLA; NETC; Soc. for Theatre Rsch. (England); IFTR; AAUP. Address: (home) 525 Hope St., Providence, RI 02906, tel. (401) 521-6293; (bus.) Theatre Arts, Box 1897, Brown Univ., Providence, RI 02912, tel. (401) 863-2181.

Dr. Wilmeth became associate professor English, executive officer of the Theatre Arts Program, and associate director of theatre, Brown Univ., Providence, R.I., in 1967. He had been (1964–67) head of the Drama Dept. and assistant professor of speech and drama, Eastern New Mexico Univ., Portales, N.M.

From 1960 to 1974, he directed more than thirty productions at Abilene Christian Coll.; Univ. of Arkansas; Univ. of Illinois; Eastern New Mexico Univ.; Corral Playhouse (Portales and Clovis, N.M.); Brown Univ.; St. Lawrence Univ. Summer Theatre; and Brown Summer Theatre, which he founded in 1970. Among plays he directed were *Much Ado About Nothing, Carousel, The Rivals, Rhinoceros, Orestes* (Euripides), *Arms and the Man, Danton's Death, The Beggar's Opera, The Night of the Iguana, The Devils, Too True To Be Good, Barefoot in the Park,* and *Twelfth Night.*

He has acted over forty roles in plays given at Abilene Christian Coll.; Margo Jones Th., Dallas, Tex.; the Colorado Shakespeare Festival; Univ. of Arkansas; Champlain Shakespeare Festival, Burlington, Vt.; Univ. of Illinois; Barker Playhouse,

Providence, R.I.; and Brown Summer Th. He played Antonio in *Twelfth Night*, Pompey in *Antony and Cleopatra*, and Prince John in *Henry IV, Part 1* (all Mary Rippon Th., Boulder, Colo., July–Aug. 1960); and Cinna in *Julius Caesar*, Antonio in *The Tempest*, Derby in *Richard III*, and Duke Vincentio in *Measure for Measure* (all Champlain Shakespeare Festival, Burlington, Vt., Summer 1962).

Other Activities. Since 1971, Dr. Wilmeth has been a member of the book award jury, George Freedley Theatre Book Award, and from 1972 to 1974 he was on the board of directors of Barker Playhouse in Providence, R.I.

Published Works. Dr. Wilmeth's articles and book reviews have been published in such periodicals as *Southern Speech Journal*, *Journal* of the Illinois State Historical Society, *New England Theatre Journal*, *Theatre Notebook*, *Theatre Documentation*, *Choice*, *Theatre Survey*, *Educational Theatre Journal*, *Quarterly Journal of Speech*, *Nineteenth Century Theatre Journal*, and Providence *Journal*. He became theatre editor in 1974 of *Intellect: The Magazine for Educational and Social Affairs*. .

Awards. Brown Univ. awarded Dr. Wilmeth an honorary M.A. *ad eundem* (1970), and he was made a member of the honorary theatre fraternities Alpha Psi Omega (1959), Alpha Chi (1960), Phi Kappa Phi (1974), and the National Collegiate Players (1962). In 1964, the Univ. of Illinois awarded him an academic fellowship, and Brown Univ. awarded him research grants in 1968, 1969, 1971, and 1974.

Recreation. Tennis, reading, collecting rare books and theatrical memorabilia.

WILSON, ELIZABETH. Actress. b. Elizabeth Welter Wilson, Apr. 4, 1921, Grand Rapids, Mich., to Henry Dunning and Marie Ethel (Welter) Wilson. Father, insurance agent. Educ. Fountain St. Grade School and Central H.S.; Marywood Acad., all Grand Rapids; Grand Rapids Jr. Coll. Professional training at NY Neighborhood Playhouse; Sanford Meisner; Martha Graham; Harold Clurman. Member of AEA; SAG; AFTRA; AGVA. Address: 2 W. 67th St., New York, NY 10023, tel. (212) 877-8972.

Theatre. Miss Wilson first appeared on stage as Elizabeth in a high-school production of *Pride and Prejudice* (Grand Rapids, 1940); performed in summer stock at Nantucket (Mass.) Playhouse (1940); made her first professional appearance at Cape May (N.J.) Playhouse (1943); appeared in repertory with the Barter Th., Abingdon, Va. (1946); and made her Bway debut as Christine in *Picnic* (Music Box, N.Y.C., Feb. 19, 1953). This was followed by appearances in *Desk Set* (Broadhurst, Oct. 24, 1955); as Mrs. McCracken in *The Tunnel of Love* (Royale, Feb. 13, 1957); as Hilda Rose in *Big Fish, Little Fish* (ANTA, Mar. 15, 1961); Constance in *Yes Is for a Very Young Man* (Players, Mar. 4, 1963); Mrs. Murray in *Eh?* (Circle in the Square, May 24, 1967); Marjorie Newquist in *Little Murders* (Circle in the Square, Jan. 5, 1969); Martha Wilkins in *Sheep on the Runway* (Helen Hayes Th., Jan. 31, 1970); Mrs. Shin in *The Good Woman of Setzuan* (Vivian Beaumont Th., Nov. 5, 1970); Harriet in *Sticks and Bones* (John Golden Th., Mar. 1, 1972); Helen Wild in *The Secret Affairs of Mildred Wild* (Ambassador, Nov. 14, 1972); and Sonia in *Uncle Vanya* (Circle in the Square/Joseph E. Levine Th., June 4, 1973).

Films. Miss Wilson made her motion picture debut as Christine in *Picnic* (Col., 1956), following this with appearances in *The Goddess* (Col., 1958); *The Tunnel of Love* (MGM, 1958); *Patterns* (UA, 1956); *Happy Anniversary* (UA, 1959); *The Birds* (U, 1963); *A Child Is Waiting* (UA, 1963); *The Tiger Makes Out* (UA, 1967); *The Graduate* (Embassy, 1967); *Catch-22* (Par., 1970); *Little Murders* (20th-Fox, 1971); *The Day of the Dolphin* (Avco Embassy, 1973); *The Prisoner of Second Avenue* (WB, 1973); and *Man on a Swing* (1974).

Television. Miss Wilson made her first television appearances on Dumont closed circuit television (Schenectady, N.Y., 1945). She played Marg in Patterns (NBC, 1955); was Hecky in East Side/West Side (CBS, 1962); and starred in Another April (CBS, 1973).

Awards. Out-of-town critics named Miss Wilson for her performance in *Big Fish, Little Fish*, and she received an Antoinette Perry (Tony) Award as best supporting actress, a *Village Voice* Off-Bway (Obie) Award for her distinguished performance, and was named in the *Variety* poll of Bway drama critics as best actress in a supporting role for her performance in *Sticks and Bones* (1972).

WILSON, GENE A. Educator, director, technical director. b. Gene Andrew Wilson, June 27, 1920, Streator, Ill., to F. Ewing and June (McClanahan) Wilson. Father, recreation commissioner. Grad. Newton (Mass.) H.S., 1939; Denison Univ., A.B. 1948; Yale Univ., M.F.A. 1951. Married Sept. 3, 1949, to Elizabeth Anne Eberhart; three daughters. Served WW II, US Army, PTO; rank, T/Sgt. Member of AETA; ANTA; AAUP; SAA; Southern Speech Assn.; Alabama Speech Assn.; Alabama Th. Conference; CTC; Southeastern Th. Conference (chairman, auditions comm., 1964); Lambda Chi Alpha. Address: Dept. of Theatre/Dance, Univ. of Wisconsin-Whitewater, 800 Main St., Whitewater, WI 53190.

Since 1965, Mr. Wilson has been associate professor of Theatre, and since 1971 chairman of The Department of Theatre/Dance at the Univ. of Wisconsin-Whitewater. Previously he had been assistant professor of speech at the Univ. of Alabama, where he was a member of the faculty (1952–65) and technical director of the University Th. and instructor of speech, 1952–55.

During the Summers 1949–50, he was lighting director at the Wellesley Coll. Summer Th.; subsequently was technical director at the Famous Artist's Country Playhouse (Watkins Glen, N.Y., Summer 1951); and was technical director for the Footlight Players (Charleston, S.C., 1951).

At the Daniel Boone Th. (Boone, N.C.), he was lighting director (1952–56); designer and technical director (1956–63); and production director at the same theatre (1963–64), for the outdoor historical drama, *Horn in the West*. .

WILSON, JOHN S. Music critic. b. John Steuart Wilson, Jan. 6, 1913, Elizabeth, N.J., to Wylie G. and Alice (Niven) Wilson. Father, mechanical engineer. Grad. Newark Acad. N.J., 1931; Wesleyan Univ., B.A. 1935; Columbia Univ. Grad. Sch. of Journalism, M.S. 1942. Married 1937 to Katharine Beecher (marr. dis. 1939); married Jan. 2, 1950, to Susan Barnes; two sons. Served US Army, 1942–46; rank, Staff Sgt. Member of AFTRA. Address: R.D. #1, Princeton, NJ 08540.

Since 1952, Mr. Wilson has reviewed jazz, nightclub entertainment, and musical shows for the NY *Times*, and for *High Fidelity* Magazine. He has been a contributing editor to *Theatre Arts* Magazine; drama editor of *PM* (1942; 1946–47) and drama critic (1948); and N.Y.C. editor for *Down Beat* (1949–50).

Television and Radio. From 1954–70, Mr. Wilson has conducted a weekly radio program on jazz, *The World of Jazz* (WQXR). Since 1971, he has conducted a similar program, *Jazz Today*, for the Voice of America.

Published Works. He has written *The Collector's Jazz: Traditional and Swing* (1958); *The Collector's Jazz: Modern* (1959); and *Jazz, The Transition Years, 1940–1960* (1966).

WILSON, LANFORD. Playwright, actor. b. Lanford Eugene Wilson, Apr. 13, 1937, Lebanon, Mo., to Ralph and Violette (Lenhard) Wilson. Educ. Ozark (Mo.) H.S.; Southwest Missouri State, Springfield, Mo.; San Diego (Calif.) State. Member of Dramatists Guild; Authors League; WGA. Address: (home) Sag Harbor, NY 11963; (bus.) c/o Circle Repertory Th., 2307 Bway, New York, NY 10024, tel. (212) 874-1080.

Theatre. Caffe Cino, N.Y.C., produced Mr. Wilson's *So Long at the Fair* (Aug. 22, 1963), following with the double bill *Home Free!* and *No Trespassing* (Jan. 16, 1964) and *The Madness of Lady Bright* (May 14, 1964). Subsequent productions of Mr. Wilson's work include *Balm in Gilead* (Cafe La Mama, Jan. 20, 1965); *Ludlow Fair* (Caffe Cino, Feb. 11, 1965); *This is the Rill Speaking* (Caffe Cino, July 29, 1965); *Sand Castle* (Cafe La Mama, Sept. 22, 1965); *Sex Is Between Two People* and *Days Ahead* (both Caffe Cino, Jan. 6, 1966); and *Wandering* (Caffe Cino, Apr. 7, 1966), later included with ten other one-act plays by various authors on the program *Collision Course* (Cafe au Go-Go, May 8, 1968). Mr. Wilson also wrote *The Rimers of Eldritch* (Cafe La Mama, July 13, 1966); *Untitled Play* (Judson Poets' Th., Jan. 26, 1968); *The Gingham Dog* (world premiere, Washington Th. Club, Washington, D.C., Sept. 26, 1968; John Golden Th., N.Y.C., Apr. 23, 1969); *Serenading Louie* (world premiere, Washington Th. Club, Mar. 25, 1970); *Lemon Sky* (world premiere, Buffalo Studio Arena, Buffalo, N.Y., Mar. 26, 1970; Playhouse Th., N.Y.C., May 17, 1970); *One Arm*, adapted from Tennessee Williams (1970); *Sextet (Yes)* (Circle Th. Co., 1971); a program of three one-act plays: *The Great Nebula in Orion*, *The Family Continues*, and *Ikke, Ikke, Nye, Nye, Nye* (Circle Th. Co., May 21, 1972); and *The Hot L Baltimore* (Circle Th. Co., Jan. 27, 1973; Circle in the Square, Mar. 22, 1973).

Mr. Wilson also wrote the libretto for the opera *Summer and Smoke*, based on the Tennessee Williams play (world premiere, St. Paul, Minn., Summer 1971; NY City Opera, State Th., Mar. 20, 1972). He is playwright in residence at Circle Repertory.

Television. Mr. Wilson wrote, with Tennessee Williams, *The Migrants* (Playhouse 90, CBS, 1973), and *The Hot L Baltimore* became the basis for a television series (ABC, 1975).

Awards. Mr. Wilson received Rockefeller grants (1967, 1973); an ABC-Yale Fellowship in motion picture writing (1968); a Guggenheim Fellowship (1972); and an American Institute of Arts and Letters Award (1974). *The Rimers of Eldritch* won the Drama Desk Vernon Rice Award (1967), and *The Hot L Baltimore* was named best American play of the 1972–73 season by the NY Drama Critics Circle and received a *Village Voice* Off-Bway (Obie) Award (1973).

Recreation. Gardening, reading.

WILSON, LOIS. Actress. b. June 28, 1898, Pittsburgh, Pa., to Andrew Kenly and Constance Barbara (Dooling) Wilson. Grad. Alabama Normal Sch., Livingston, Ala., 1914. Studied acting with Francis Robinson Duff, N.Y.C., 1936; under Mary Agnes Doyle at Goodman Theatre, Chicago, Ill., 1937. Member of AEA (fourth vice-pres., 1958–to date; on council, 1950–to date); AFTRA; SAG. Address: 10 Mitchell Place, New York, NY 10017, tel. (212) PL 3-3259.

Miss Wilson was the first Miss Alabama (1915), winning a national beauty contest sponsored by Universal Pictures to inaugurate the opening of Universal City, Calif.

Theatre. She made her debut as the Ingenue in *The Gossipy Sex* (Vine St. Th., Hollywood, Calif., 1928); subsequently appeared in productions with the Henry Duffy Stock Co. (San Francisco, Calif., 1930).

She made her N.Y.C. debut as Keith Stuart in *Farewell, Summer* (Fulton, Mar. 29, 1937); appeared in stock productions (Wharf Th., Provincetown, Mass., Summer 1937); played Mary Haines in the national company of *The Women* (opened Buffalo, N.Y., Sept. 1937; closed Philadelphia, Pa., 1939); and toured as Mrs. Graves in *Junior Miss* (opened Buffalo, N.Y., 1942).

She succeeded (Aug. 1944) Mary Phillips as Emily Blachman in *Chicken Every Sunday* (Henry Miller's Th., N.Y.C., Apr. 5, 1944; tour, 1944–45); played Bertha Corrigan in *The Mermaids Singing* (Empire, Nov. 28, 1945); the Sister-in-Law in the summer tryout of *Red Letter Day* (Warwick Musical Th., R.I., Summer 1959); played the Mother in a summer production of *John Loves Mary* (Summer 1960); and was standby for Lillian Gish in *I Never Sang for My Father* (Longacre, N.Y.C., Jan. 25, 1968).

Films. Miss Wilson has appeared in some one hundred films. Among them are *Miss Lulu Bett* (Par., 1921); *What Every Woman Knows* (Par., 1921); *Manslaughter* (Par., 1922); *The Covered Wagon* (Par., 1923); and *Icebound* (Par., 1924). She starred as Daisy Buchanan in the silent version of *The Great Gatsby* (Par., 1926); appeared in *On Trial* (WB, 1928); *The Show Off* (Par., 1926); *French Dressing* (1st Natl., 1927); *Broadway Nights* (1st Natl., 1927); *The Gamblers* (WB, 1929); *Miss Information* (1929); *Once a Gentleman* (World Wide, 1930); *Seed* (U, 1931); *Law and Order* (U, 1932); *Rider of Death Valley* (U, 1932); *Obey the Law* (Col., 1933); *Laughing at Life* (Mascot, 1933); *The Deluge* (RKO, 1933); *There's Always Tomorrow* (U, 1934); *Bright Eyes* (20th-Fox, 1934); and *School for Girls* (Liberty, 1934).

Also, *Born to Gamble* (Rep., 1935); *Public Opinion* (Chesterfield, 1935); *Wedding Present* (Par., 1936); *Laughing at Trouble* (20th-Fox, 1937); and *For Love or Money* (U, 1939).

Television. Miss Wilson appeared on the Kate Cameron Show (WPIX, N.Y.C., 1947); and was television's first Mrs. Aldrich on The Henry Aldrich Family. She has also appeared on Armstrong Circle Th. (NBC, 1954), Goodyear Playhouse (NBC), Ford Th. (CBS), The Guiding Light (CBS), From These Roots (NBC), Our Five Daughters, and The Secret Storm (CBS).

Recreation. Travel, opera, theatre, ballet, books, horseback riding, cooking.

WILSON, ROBERT M. Artistic director, teacher, architect, painter. b. 1944, Waco, Tex., to D. M. and Loree (Hamilton) Wilson. Father, lawyer. Educ. Univ. of Texas, 1959–62; Pratt Institute, M.F.A. 1965. Studied painting in Paris, France (1962) and was apprentice to Paolo Soleri, Phoenix, Ariz. (1966). Address: (home) 147 Spring St., New York, NY 10012, tel. (212) 966-1365; (bus.) Byrd Hoffman Foundation, 147 Spring St., New York, Ny 10012, tel. (212) 966-1365; (agent) Ninon Karlweis, 250 E. 65th St., New York, NY 10021, tel. (212) PL 5-5845.

Theatre. Mr. Wilson and the Byrd Hoffman School of Byrds, of which he is artistic director, formed the Byrd Hoffman Foundation in 1969. He designed sets and costumes for *Motel* (Cafe La Mama, Apr. 28, 1965); directed and performed in a dance event at the NY World's Fair (1965); gave a solo performance in 1966 at the Byrd Hoffman Studio, N.Y.C.; directed *Theater Activity* (Bleecker St. Cinema, 1967); *BYRDwoMAN* (Byrd Hoffman Studio, 1968); *The King of Spain* (Anderson Th., Jan. 30, 1969); and *The Life and Times of Sigmund Freud* (Brooklyn Acad. of Music, 1969). Mr. Wilson also wrote, directed, and performed in *Deafman Glance* (Univ. Th., Iowa City, Iowa, 1970; Brooklyn Acad. of Music, N.Y.C., Feb. 25, 1971; Grand Th. de la Nancy, France; Teatro Eliseo, Rome, Italy; Th. de la Musique, Paris, France; and Stadsschouwburg Th., Amsterdam, Netherlands, all 1971); *Program Prologue Now, Ouverture for a Deafman* (Espace Pierre Cardin, Paris, 1971; Byrd Hoffman Studio, N.Y.C., 1972; Khaneh-e Zinatolmolk, Shiraz, Iran, 1972; and Musée Galliera and Opéra Comique, Paris, 1972); *KA MOUNTAIN AND GUARDenia TERRACE,* A Story About a Family and Some People Changing (Festival of Arts, Haft Tan Mountain, Shiraz, Iran, 1972); *The Life and Times of Joseph Stalin* (Det Ny Th., Copenhagen, Denmark, 1973; Brooklyn Acad. of Music, N.Y.C., Dec. 15–16, 1973); and *A Letter for Queen Victoria* (Spoleto Festival, Italy, June 1974; ANTA Th., N.Y.C., Mar. 22, 1975).

Other Activities. Mr. Wilson taught body movement and awareness with people of all ages, including children, the elderly, and individuals with physical and mental handicaps. He worked in the Headstart program as a consultant and teacher and has taught in schools in New Jersey and New York.

Awards. Mr. Wilson received the Paris Syndicat de la Critique Dramatique et Musicale award (1970) for *Deafman Glance* as best foreign play; the Vernon Rice Award (1971) for direction of *Deafman Glance;* a Guggenheim Fellowship (1971); and a special citation (1974) from the *Village Voice* off-Bway (Obie) Award committee for *The Life and Times of Joseph Stalin.*

WILSON, SANDY. Playwright, composer, lyricist. b. Alexander Galbraith Wilson, May 19, 1924, Sale, Cheshire, England, to George Walter and Caroline Elsie (Humphrey) Wilson. Father, shipping agent. Grad. Elstree (Hertfordshire, Eng.) Prep. Sch., 1937; Harrow, 1942; Oriel Coll., Oxford, B.A. 1948. Studied for the theatre at the Old Vic School, London, 1948–49. Relatives in theatre: uncle, Frank Vernon, director, producer; aunt, Virginia Vernon, writer, producer. Served British Army, Royal Ordinance Corps, 1943–46; rank, Pvt. Member of ALA; Dramatists Guild; Performing Rights Society; Songwriters Union; The Players. Address: (home) 2 Southwell Gardens, London, S.W.7, England tel. 01-373-6172; (bus.) 122 Chancery Lane, London E.C.1, England tel. 01-242-6021.

Theatre. Mr. Wilson contributed material to the revue, *Oranges and Lemons* (Lyric, Hammersmith, London, Nov. 26, 1948; Globe, Jan. 26, 1949); and *Slings and Arrows* (Comedy, Nov. 17, 1948). He wrote the book, music, and lyrics for *See You Later* (Watergate, Oct. 3, 1951); *See You Again* (Watergate, Feb. 21, 1952); *The Boy Friend* (Players', Apr. 14, 1953; Wyndham's, Jan. 14, 1954); and *The Buccaneer* (New Watergate, Sept. 8, 1953; revived Lyric, Hammersmith, Sept. 8, 1955); *The Boy Friend* (Royale, N.Y.C., Sept. 30, 1954; revived Downtown Th., Jan. 25, 1958), and on tour in the U.S. (opened Shubert, New Haven, Conn., Nov. 28, 1955; closed Shubert, Philadelphia, Pa., Jan. 5, 1957); and his *Valmouth* was presented (Lyric, Hammersmith, London, Oct. 2, 1958; Saville, Jan. 27, 1959; York, N.Y.C., Oct. 6, 1960).

Mr. Wilson contributed material to the revue, *Pieces of Eight* (Apollo, London, Sept. 23, 1959); wrote the music for *Call It Love* (Wyndham's, June 22, 1960); wrote the book, music and lyrics for *Divorce Me, Darling!* (Players' Th., Dec. 9, 1964; Globe Th., Feb. 1, 1965); the music for *As Dorothy Parker Once Said* (Palace, Watford, Eng., Nov. 8, 1966; Fortune Th., July 21, 1969); a revival of *The Boy Friend* (Comedy Th., London, Nov. 29, 1967; Ambassador, N.Y.C., April 14, 1970); wrote and appeared in *Sandy Wilson Thanks the Ladies* (Hampstead Th. Club., Eng., June 9, 1971, and on tour 1971–72); and wrote the book, music and lyrics for *His Monkey Wife* (Hampstead Th. Club, Eng., Dec. 20, 1971).

Published Works. Mr. Wilson wrote and illustrated *This is Sylvia* (1954); *The Boy Friend* (1955); and *The Poodle from Rome* (1962).

Recreation. Painting, cookery, travel, film-going.

WINCELBERG, SHIMON. Writer. b. Sept. 26, 1924, Kiel, Germany, to David and Helen (Herzberg) Wincelberg. Father, fur worker. Attended Hildesheimer Rabbinical Seminary, Berlin, Ger., 1938; grad. H.S. of Music and Art, N.Y.C., 1942. Studied painting at Veterans' Art Ctr., Museum of Modern Art, 1946. Married July 4, 1954, to Anita Marateck, writer; two sons, one daughter. Served US Army, Combat Intelligence, 1943–46; rank, Pfc. Okinawa Campaign (106th Inf., 27th Div.). Member of WGA; West; Dramatists Guild; West Coast Talmudical Seminary (bd. of dir.). Address: 9169 Sunset Blvd., Los Angeles, CA 90069, tel. (213) CR 1-5165.

Pre-Theatre. Newspaperman, writer, educator, diamond-cutter, farmhand, bellhop, commercial artist.

Theatre. Mr. Wincelberg wrote the one-act play, *No One Ever Comes Here Twice* (Benjamin Zemach Workshop, Los Angeles, Calif., 1951); and *The Windows of Heaven* (from a story by R. Bryks; Royal Dramatic Th., Stockholm, Sweden, Oct. 17, 1969); and his one-act play, *The Conqueror,* has been presented at universities in the US (1954–63). He wrote *Kataki* (Ambassador, N.Y.C., Apr. 9, 1959; St. Marks Playhouse, Dec. 15, 1959; Little Th., Helsinki, Finland, 1959; Blanche, Stockholm, Sweden, 1959; Th. der Courage, Vienna, Austria, 1960–61; Thalia, Hamburg, Germany, 1960–63; Powszechny, Lodz, Poland, 1963).

Television. Mr. Wincelberg wrote The Sea Is Boiling Hot (Kraft Television Th., NBC, 1958); and scripts for Have Gun, Will Travel (CBS, 1959–62); Naked City (ABC, 1962–63); GE Th. (CBS), Gunsmoke (CBS), Route 66 (CBS), Medical Center (CBS), Mannix (CBS), Eternal Light (NBC), Hec Ramsey (NBC), and for many others.

Other Activities. Mr. Wincelberg was an instructor of English at Medical Coll., Niigata, Japan (Winter 1954).

Published Works. Mr. Wincelberg's short stories, poetry, and critical reviews have appeared in *The New Yorker, Harpers Bazaar, Punch, Commentary, The New Leader,* and *Story.* His play, *The Windows of Heaven,* was published in *Gambit* (1963); and a condensed version in *Midstream* (1962). His story, *The Conqueror,* was published in *Best American Short Stories of 1953,* and his play, *The Conqueror,* was included in *Best American Short Plays of 1954–55. Kataki* was included in *Best Plays of 1958–59.* .

Awards. A five-time nominee of the Writers Guild of America, he has received their award for the year's best television script for *The Sea Is Boiling Hot* (1957); *The Long, Long Curfew* (1967); and *The Artist in His Own Right* (1969). He is the recipient of the Edgar Allen Poe Special Award of the Mystery Writers of America for *The Crimson Halo* (1972).

WINDHAM, DONALD. Playwright, novelist. b. July 2, 1920, Atlanta, Ga., to Fred L. and Louise (Donaldson) Windham. Father, salesman. Grad. Boys' H.S., Atlanta, 1938. Address: (home) 230 Central Park South, New York, NY 10019; (bus.) c/o Curtis Brown, Ltd., 60 E. 56th St., New York, NY 10022.

Theatre. Mr. Windham wrote, with Tennessee Williams, *You Touched Me!* (Booth Th., N.Y.C., Sept. 5, 1945); wrote *The Starless Air* (Playhouse, Houston, Tex., May 13, 1953); and *The Angelic Avengers* (unproduced), adapted from a novel by Isak Dinesen.

Published Works. Mr. Windham wrote a novel about the theatre, *The Hero Continues* (1960); *The Dog Star* (1950); a collection of short stories, *The Warm Country* (1962); an autobiography, *Emblems of Conduct* (1964); and *Two People* (1965) and *Tanaquil, or The Hardest Thing of All* (1972), two novels.

Awards. He received a Guggenheim Fellowship in creative writing (1960).

Recreation. Studying Italian.

WINDOM, WILLIAM. Actor. b. Sept. 28, 1923, New York City, to Paul and Isobel Wells (Peckham) Windom. Father, architect. Grad. Admiral Billard Acad., New London, Conn., 1942; attended Williams Coll., 1942; The Citadel, 1943; Antioch Coll., 1943; Univ. of Kentucky, 1943–44; Biarritz Amer. Univ. (France), 1945; Fordham Univ., 1946; Columbia Univ., 1946. Married Aug. 10, 1947, to Carol Keyser, dancer (marr. dis. Dec. 1955); married June 30, 1958, to Barbara Joyce, actress (marr. dis. Mar. 1963); married Apr. 12, 1963, to Barbara G. Clare (marr. dis.); two daughters; married Aug. 8, 1969, to Jacquylyne Dean Hopkins; one daughter. Served WW II, US Army, ETO; rank, T/5. Member of AEA; AFTRA; SAG; The Players; Malibu Yacht Club. The Corinthians, Friends of Richard III. Address: 22244 Pacific Coast Highway, Malibu, CA 90265.

Theatre. Mr. Windom first appeared on a stage at age nine in a minstrel show (Camp Overall, Va., 1932); and played the title role in a US Army tour of *Richard III* (ETO camps, 1945–46).

For the Amer. Repertory Th. at the Intl. Th. (N.Y.C.), he played the Earl of Surrey in *Henry VIII* (Nov. 6, 1946), Erhart Borkman in *John Gabriel Borkman* (Nov. 12, 1946), a Townsman in *What Every Woman Knows* (Nov. 18, 1946), Retiarius in *Androcles and the Lion* (Dec. 19, 1946), McClelland in *Yellow Jack* (Feb. 17, 1947), and the White Rabbit and the Gentleman Dressed in White Paper in *Alice in Wonderland* (Apr. 5, 1947).

At the Cape Playhouse (Dennis, Mass.), he played a juvenile in *The Marquise*, the Poet in *Joan of Lorraine*, and appeared in *Dream Girl* (1947); and at the Brookfield (Conn.) Ctr., as the Janitor in *My Sister Eileen*, and Bill Page in *The Voice of the Turtle* (1948).

He appeared as a juvenile in *The Jailor's Wench* (Cape Playhouse, 1949); and at the Southbury (Conn.) Playhouse, appeared in juvenile roles in *The Vinegar Tree, Three-Cornered Moon, It's a Wise Child, Your Uncle Dudley*, and *Meet the Wife*, and played the Doctor in *Blithe Spirit*, the Author in *Light Up the Sky*, and appeared in *Charm* (1950). He toured as Nicky Holroyd in *Bell, Book and Candle* (opened Playhouse, Wilmington, Del., Dec. 21, 1951), also playing the role in summer theatres; played a Telephone Voice and was an understudy in *A Girl Can Tell* (Royale, Oct. 29, 1953); Edouard in *Mademoiselle Colombe* (Longacre, Jan. 6, 1954); and at the Th. in the Round (Glen Falls, N.Y.), appeared in *Private Lives, Affairs of State, I Am a Camera*, and *The Voice of the Turtle* (1954).

Mr. Windom played David in *Claudia*, and the Snake Man in *My Three Angels* (Putnam Playhouse, Conn., 1954); a juvenile in *The Automobile Man* (Bucks County Playhouse, New Hope, Pa., 1954); the Frenchman in *Sabrina Fair* (Sacandaga Garden Th., Sacandaga Park, N.Y., 1954); John Condon Mitchell in *The Grand Prize* (Plymouth, N.Y.C., Jan. 26, 1955); appeared in *The Shoemaker's Children* (Bucks County Playhouse, 1955); *You Never Can Tell* (Olney Th., Md., 1955); played Morris Townsend in *The Heiress* (The Tent, Philadelphia, Pa., 1955); and appeared in *Mrs. Gibbon's Boys* (Bucks County Playhouse, 1955).

He played Frederick Starbuck in *Fallen Angels* (Playhouse, N.Y.C., Jan. 17, 1956); understudied William Redfield as Henry Waterhouse and Laurence Hugo as Mack Daniels in *Double in Hearts*, for which he was also stage manager (John Golden Th., Oct. 16, 1956); worked as a stage hand for the musical *Candide* (Martin Beck Th., Dec. 1, 1956); appeared as a walk-on in *Hotel Paradiso* (Henry Miller's Th., Apr. 11, 1957); was assistant stage manager for *The Greatest Man Alive* (Ethel Barrymore Th., May 8, 1957); and at the NY Shakespeare Festival, played Orsino in *Twelfth Night* (Belvedere Lake Th., Aug. 6, 1958).

He was understudy in *The World of Suzie Wong* (Broadhurst, Oct. 14, 1958); appeared in Dos Passos' *U.S.A.* (Martinique, Oct. 28, 1959); played Jim Leary in *Viva Madison Avenue!* (Longacre, Apr. 6, 1960); Adam Cockney in *Drums Under the Window* (Cherry Lane, Oct. 6, 1960); Guido Venanzi in *The Rules of the Game* (Gramercy Arts, Dec. 19, 1960); and understudied Hal March as Alan Baker in *Come Blow Your Horn* (Brooks Atkinson Th., Feb. 22, 1961).

For the Theatre Group at the Univ. of California at Los Angeles he appeared in Dos Passos' *U.S.A.*, (Spring 1961), *Period of Adjustment* (1961–62), and *The Child Buyer* (1962). He toured the country in his one-man show, as *Thurber* (1975).

Films. Mr. Windom played the District Attorney in *To Kill a Mockingbird* (U, 1962), and has appeared in *For Love or Money* (U, 1963), *Cattle King* (MGM, 1963), as the Rev. Clifford Peale in *One Man's Way—The Norman Vincent Peale Story* (UA, 1964); Capt. Harry Spaulding in *The Americanization of Emily* (MGM, 1964); in *Hour of the Gun* (UA, 1967); as Collin McGiver in *The Detective* (20th-Fox, 1968); in *The Angry Breed* (David Commons Assoc., 1969); as Allen Brandon in *The Gypsy Moths* (MGM, 1969); and as Haskell Weeks in *Brewster McCloud* (MGM, 1970).

Television. He made his debut in the title role of *Richard III* (Philco Television Playhouse, NBC, 1950); and has made more than a hundred appearances on various shows, as well as having been a regular performer on the series The Farmer's Daughter (ABC, premiere Sept. 20, 1963; through Spring 1966); and My World and Welcome to It (NBC, premiere Sept. 15, 1969; through Spring 1970).

Awards. He received the Citation of Merit from the Actors Fund (1958), and the NATAS (Emmy) Award for My World and Welcome to it (1970).

Recreation. Sailing, tennis, chess.

WINGREEN, JASON. Actor, producer. b. Queens, N.Y. Grad. Brooklyn Coll. Served US Army Air Corps. Member of AEA; SAG.

Mr. Wingreen began his theatrical career as a puppeteer with the Berkeley Marionettes. He played several seasons of summer stock with the Maverick Th. (Woodstock, N.Y.) where he met Emilie Stevens, Theodore Mann and Jose Quintero, with whom he organized and founded in 1950 The Loft Players, the original producing company at Circle in the Square (N.Y.C.). There he made his N.Y.C. producing and acting debut as Preacher Haggler in *Dark of the Moon* (Feb. 1951); subsequently co-produced *Amata* (Mar. 16, 1951); *Antigone* (Apr. 26, 1951), in which he appeared; *The Enchanted* (June 9, 1961); *Burning Bright* (Sept. 5, 1951) in which he also appeared; *Bonds of Interest* (Nov. 30, 1951); *Yerma* (Feb. 7, 1952); *Summer and Smoke* (Apr. 24, 1952), in which he played Dr. John Buchanan, Sr.; *The Grass Harp*, in which he appeared (Apr. 27, 1953); *American Gothic* (Nov. 10, 1953); and *The Girl on the Via Flaminia*, in which he played the Police Inspector (Feb. 9, 1954; moved to 48 St. Th., Apr. 1, 1954), and which ended his association with Circle in the Square.

He played Pfc. Snowden in *The Fragile Fox* (Belasco, N.Y.C., Oct. 12, 1954); and, with the Center Th. Group (Mark Taper Forum, Los Angeles), appeared in *Crystal and Fire* (Apr. 9, 1970), and played Rafferty in *A Meeting by the River* (1971–72 season).

Films. His appearances include *Three Brave Men* (20th-Fox, 1956); *The Bravados* (20th-Fox, 1958); *The Slender Thread* (Par., 1965); *A Guide for the Married Man* (20th-Fox, 1967); *The Dunwich Horror* (AI, 1970); *The Cheyenne Social Club* (Natl. Gen., 1970); *The Magnificent Seven Ride!* (UA, 1972); *They Only Kill Their Masters* (MGM, 1972); and *The Terminal Man* (WB, 1974).

WINSHIP, LOREN. Educator, director. b. Frank Loren Winship, May 30, 1904, Denver, Colo., to Frank David and Alice May (Hume) Winship. Father, salesman. Grad. Univ. Place H.S., Lincoln, Neb., 1922; Nebraska Wesleyan Univ., B.A. 1928; Univ. of Nebraska, M.A. 1930; attended Univ. of Michigan, 1935–37; grad. Univ. of Texas, Ed.D., 1953. Married Aug. 9, 1929, to Margaret Reid, librarian; one daughter. Served USAAF, WW II, Special Services, rank, Lt. Col. Member of Texas Educational Th. Assn. (co-fdr., 1950), Southwest Th. Conference (pres., 1956); AETA; NTC; ANTA; Phi Kappa Tau; Theta Alpha Phi. Address: (home) 5601 Exeter Dr., Austin, TX 78723, tel. (512) 926-7140; (bus.) c/o Dept. of Drama, Univ. of Texas, Austin, TX 78712, tel. (512) 471-3353.

Since 1948, Mr. Winship has been chairman of the Dept. of Drama at the Univ. of Texas, where he has been a member of the faculty since 1946 (associate professor of drama, 1946–49), and where he has directed 12 student productions.

Mr. Winship was chairman of the department of drama, Univ. of Texas at Austin, from 1948–68, where he was a faculty member since 1941 (assoc. prof. of drama, 1941–49), prof. of drama, 1949–68), and where he directed twenty-one student productions. He retired in June 1973 as professor of drama, emeritus. He was director of drama activities for the Univ. of Texas Interscholastic League (1938–42); and was a high school principal and drama teacher in three Nebraska schools (1929–38).

He played the Young Boy in *Message from Mars* on the Chautauqua Circuit, as well as minor roles in other plays (Summer 1926); and performed in vaudeville (1929).

He was managing editor of *Educational Theatre Journal* (1949–52); and chancellor of fellows of AETA (1965–71).

Awards. He received the Theta Alpha Phi Award of Merit (1963); an honorary D.Litt. degree from Nebraska Wesleyan Univ. (1967); the AETA Award of Merit (1968); the Founders Award, Secondary School Th. Assn. (1968); and the Excellence Award from the Southwest Th. Conf. (1973).

WINTERS, MARIAN. Actress, playwright. b. Apr. 19, 1924, New York City. Grad. Erasmus Hall H.S., Brooklyn, N.Y.; attended Brooklyn Coll. Married Nov. 18, 1945, to Jay H. Smolin, advertising executive. Member of AEA; AFTRA; SAG. Address: 7 St. Luke's Place, New York, NY 10014, tel. (212) WA 4-5499.

Theatre. Miss Winters made her debut at age 16 in summer stock productions and appeared in productions at Wildwood, N.J., Pocono, Pa., Cedarhurst, N.Y., Sea Island, Ga., and Sea Cliff, N.Y.

She understudied Frances Dee as Susan Beverly in *The Secret Room* (Royale Th., N.Y.C., Nov. 7, 1945); played Lady Constance in *King John* (ELT, May 6, 1949); toured as the Shoplifter in *Detective Story* (Oct. 1949–Jan. 1950), Marion Almond in *The Heiress* (July–Aug. 1950); and played Miriam Allerton Lucas and Arabella in *Dream Girl* (NY City Ctr., May 9, 1951).

For the ANTA Experimental Th. invitational series, she played Cleo, Muse of History, in *E= MC(*- Brander Mathews Th., June 16, 1948), and Artemis in *Hippolytus* (Humphrey-Weidman Th., Nov. 22, 1948). Subsequently she appeared as Natalia Landauer in *I Am a Camera* (Empire, Nov. 28, 1951), also touring in it (opened Cass, Detroit, Mich., Sept. 1, 1952; closed Her Majesty's, Montreal, Can., May 2, 1953); Maddy Hertzog in *Sing Me No Lullaby* (Phoenix, N.Y.C., Oct. 14, 1954); and Gelda in *The Dark Is Light Enough* (ANTA, Feb. 23, 1955). She played the First Woman of Corinth in the ANTA Salute to France production of *Medea* (Sarah Bernhardt Th., Paris, June 1955); Sally Cato MacDougal in *Auntie Mame* (Broadhurst, N.Y.C., Oct. 31, 1956); Myra Solomon in *Tall Story* (Belasco, Jan. 29, 1959); Tracey Lowe in *The 49th Cousin* (Ambassador, Oct. 27, 1960); Madame Ranevsky in *The Cherry Orchard* (Th. Four, Nov. 14, 1962); Marge Weber in *Nobody Loves an Albatross* (Lyceum, Dec. 19, 1963); Senator Lucia Barrett in *Mating Dance* (Eugene O'Neill Th., N.Y.C., Nov. 3, 1965); and, for the NY Shakespeare Festival, Constance in *King John* (Delacorte, July 5, 1967); and wrote *Animal Keepers* (Thirteenth St. Th., Oct. 1966); *A Is for All* (1968); *All Is Bright* (1970); and *Assembly Line* (Neighborhood Playhouse Sch. of the Th., May 12, 1969).

Television. Miss Winters has appeared on the Brighter Day (CBS), Love of Life (CBS), The Guiding Light (CBS), Kitty Foyle (NBC), Camera Three (CBS), The Defenders (CBS), The Nurses (CBS), Armstrong Circle Th. (NBC), Philco Television Playhouse (NBC), Alcoa Premiere (ABC), in *A Very Special Baby* (Play of the Week, WNTA); Girl Talk (ABC); *T. S. Eliot—The Wasteland* (NET); Directions '66 (ABC); Hawk (ABC); and played Claire Bernard in her own work, *Animal Keepers* (CBS).

Awards. For her performance as Natalia Landauer in *I Am a Camera* she received the Antoinette Perry (Tony) Award, Donaldson Award, *Theatre World* Award, and won the *Variety* NY Drama Critics Poll (1952). For her performance as Marge Weber in *Nobody Loves an Albatross*, she was nominated for the *Variety* NY Drama Critics Poll.

WINTERS, ROLAND. Actor. b. Roland Winternitz. Member of AEA; AFTRA; SAG. Address: c/o Smith-Stevens, 1650 Broadway, New York, NY 10019.

Theatre. Mr. Winters played Harry Powell in *Who Was That Lady I Saw You With?* (Martin Beck Th., N.Y.C., Mar. 3, 1958); General Rivers in *A Cook for Mr. General* (Playhouse, Oct. 19, 1961); Malcolm Turnbull in *Calculated Risk* (Ambassador, Oct. 31, 1962); E. E. Albee in *Minnie's Boys* (Imperial, Mar. 26, 1970); and the Producer in *The Country Girl* (Billy Rose Th., Mar. 15, 1972).

Films. He has appeared in *So Big* (WB, 1950); *Guilty of Treason* (Elstree, 1949); *The West Point Story* (WB, 1950); *Top Secret Affair* (WB, 1957); *Blue Hawaii* (Par., 1961); *Raton Pass* (WB, 1951); *Cash McCall* (WB, 1959); *Malaya* (WB, 1962); and starred in six Charlie Chan films (Mono. Int.).

Television. He played General Rivers in *A Cook for Mr. General;* Mr. Bone in the series, Meet Millie; appeared in *The Iceman Cometh* (Play of the Week, WNTA); played Henry J. Schuyler in *The Roaring 20th* (Kraft Television Th., NBC, June 5, 1957); he appeared in the Peter Lind Hayes series (ABC); the *Allan Young Show* (CBS); and *The Smothers Brothers Comedy Hour* (CBS).

WINTERS, SHELLEY. Actress. b. Shirley Schrift, Aug. 18, 1922, East St. Louis, Ill., to Jonas and Rose (Winter) Schrift. Father, designer of men's clothing; mother, singer. Attended Thomas Jefferson H.S., Brooklyn, N.Y. Studied acting at Drama Workshop of the New Sch. for Social Research, N.Y.C.; Actors' Studio, N.Y.C.; with Elia Kazan, N.Y.C.; Michael Chekhov, Hollywood, Calif.; Charles Laughton, Hollywood; singing with Viola Spers. Married Jan. 1, 1943, to Mack Paul Mayer, textile salesman (marr. dis. Oct. 1948); married Apr. 28, 1952, to Vittorio Gassman, actor (marr. dis. June 2, 1954); one daughter; married May 4, 1957, to Anthony Franciosa, actor (marr. dis. Nov. 18, 1960). Member of AEA; SAG; AFTRA; AGVA.

Pre-Theatre. Salesgirl, model.

Theatre. Miss Winters understudied Julie Hayden as Kitty Duval in *The Time of Your Life* (Booth Th., N.Y.C., Oct. 25, 1940); subsequently played Miss Holvaag in the pre-Bway tryout of *Conquest in April,* which closed out of town (opened Locust Th., Philadelphia, Pa., Nov. 11, 1940); Flora in *The Night Before Christmas* (Morosco, N.Y.C., Apr. 10, 1941); toured in the revue *Meet the People* (opened New Haven, Conn., May 22, 1941); played Fifi in *Rosalinda* (44 St. Th., N.Y.C., Oct. 28, 1942); and Clo-Clo in *The Merry Widow* (Municipal Aud., Long Beach, Calif., Oct. 2, 1946).

Miss Winters alternated (1947–48) with Celeste Holm and Vivienne Allen as Ado Annie Carnes in *Oklahoma!* (St. James, N.Y.C., Mar. 31, 1943); played Billie Dawn in a touring company of *Born Yesterday* (Summer 1950); Stella Kowalski in *A Streetcar Named Desire* (Circle Th., Hollywood, Calif., Aug. 9, 1952); Stella in the pre-Bway stock tryout of *Wedding Breakfast* (Triple Cities Playhouse, Binghamton, N.Y., July 4, 1955); Celia Pope in *A Hatful of Rain* (Lyceum, N.Y.C., Nov. 11, 1955); Hilda Brookman in *Girls of Summer* (Longacre, Nov. 19, 1956); Mrs. Topaze in a tryout of *The Saturday Night Kid* (opened Westport Country Playhouse, Conn., Sept. 9, 1957; closed Locust St. Th., Philadelphia, Pa., Sept. 28, 1958); Kay in *A Piece of Blue Sky* (North Jersey Playhouse, Fort Lee, N.J., May 5, 1959); toured as Gittel Mosca in *Two for the Seesaw* (Summer 1960); played Georgie Elgin in *The Country Girl* (Paper Mill Playhouse, Millburn, N.J., Apr. 3, 1961); Beatrice in *A View from the Bridge* (Paper Mill Playhouse, Millburn, N.J., Apr. 19, 1961); and succeeded Bette Davis (1962) as Maxine Faulk in *The Night of the Iguana* (Royale, N.Y.C., Dec. 28, 1961).

She was the Prostitute in *Snowangel* and the Wife in *Epiphany* on the double-bill *Cages* (York Playhouse, June 13, 1963); toured (1965–66) in *Two for the Seesaw;* played Flora Sharkey in *Part I,* Marcella Vankuchen in *Part II,* and Hilda in *Part III,* three one-act plays billed as *Under the Weather* (Cort, Oct. 27, 1966); was Minnie Marx in *Minnie's Boys* (Imperial, Mar. 26, 1970); wrote three one-act plays presented as *One Night Stands of a Noisy Passenger* (Actors Playhouse, Dec. 30, 1970); and toured (1973) as Beatrice in *The Effect of Gamma Rays on Man-in-the-Moon Marigolds.* .

Films. Miss Winters has appeared in *What a Woman!* (Col., 1943); *The Racket Man* (Col., 1944); *Two-Man Submarine* (Col., 1944); *She's a Soldier, Too* (Col., 1944); *Nine Girls* (Col., 1944); *The Gangster* (Allied, 1947); *Cry of the City* (20th-Fox, 1948); *A Double Life* (U, 1948); *Larceny* (U, 1948); *The Great Gatsby* (Par., 1949); *South Sea Sinner* (U, 1950); *Winchester '73* (U, 1950); *Behave Yourself!* (RKO, 1951); *Frenchie* (U, 1950); *He Ran All the Way* (UA, 1951); *A Place in the Sun* (Par., 1951); *The Raging Tide* (U, 1951); *Meet Danny Wilson* (U, 1952); *Untamed Frontier* (U, 1952); *My Man and I* (MGM, 1952); *Phone Call from a Stranger* (20th-Fox, 1952); *Saskatchewan* (U, 1954); *Tennessee Champ* (MGM, 1954); *Executive Suite* (MGM, 1954); *Playgirl* (U, 1954); *Mambo* (Par., 1955); *I Died a Thousand Times* (WB, 1955); *I Am a Camera* (DCA, 1955); *The Night of the Hunter* (UA, 1955); *The Big Knife* (UA, 1955); *The Treasure of Pancho Villa* (RKO, 1955); *Cash on Delivery* (RKO, 1956); *The Diary of Anne Frank* (20th-Fox, 1959); *Odds Against Tomorrow* (UA, 1959); *Let No Man Write My Epitaph* (Col., 1960); *The Young Savages* (UA, 1961); *Lolita* (MGM, 1962); *The Chapman Report* (WB, 1962); *Wives and Lovers* (Par., 1963); *The Balcony* (Continental, 1963); and *A House Is Not a Home* (Par., 1964).

She also appeared in *A Patch of Blue* (MGM, 1965); *Harper* (WB, 1966); *Alfie* (Par., 1966); *Enter Laughing* (Col., 1967); *The Scalp Hunters* (UA, 1968); *Wild in the Streets* (Amer. Internatl., 1968); *The Mad Room* (Col., 1969); *Bloody Mama* (Amer. Inter., 1970); *Arthur, Arthur* (Rank, 1970); *What's the Matter with Helen?* (UA, 1971); *The Poseidon Adventure* (20th-Fox, 1972); *Cleopatra Jones* (WB, 1973); *Blume in Love* (WB, 1973); *Last Stop, Greenwich Village* (20th-Fox, 1976); and *The Tenant* (Par., 1976).

Television. Miss Winters has appeared in *The Women* (Producers Showcase, NBC, Feb. 7, 1955); *A Double Life* (Alcoa Hour, NBC, Jan. 6, 1957); *Beyond This Place* (Dupont Show of the Month, CBS, Nov. 1957); *A Piece of Blue Sky* (Play of the Week, WNTA, May 9, 1960); and *Two Is the Number* (Chrysler Th., NBC, 1963).

She also appeared in episodes of Ben Casey (ABC, 1964); in *Back to Back* (Bob Hope Chrysler Th., NBC, 1965); on Batman (ABC, 1966); That's Life (ABC, 1968); *Death of Innocence* (CBS, 1971); *The Adventures of Nick Carter* (ABC, 1972); *The Vamp* (London TV, England, Oct. 1972); *The Devil's Daughter* (ABC, Jan. 1973); McCloud (NBC, 1974); and in the pilot *Big Rose* (CBS, Apr. 1974).

Night Clubs. She has performed at the La Conga (N.Y.C., 1940); Serenade Club (Los Angeles, Calif.); and The Flamingo (Las Vegas, Nev., Oct. 1953).

Awards. She was nominated for two Academy (Oscar) Awards for her performances in *A Double Life* (1948) and *A Place in the Sun* (1951); received the *Holiday* Magazine Award (1952); the Academy (Oscar) Award for her performances in *The Diary of Anne Frank* (1959) and *A Patch of Blue* (1965); the NATAS (Emmy) Award for her performance in *Two Is the Number* (1964).

Recreation. Reading, tennis, swimming, dancing.

WINWOOD, ESTELLE. Actress. b. Jan. 24, Lee, Kent, England, to George Goodwin and Rosalie (Ellis) Goodwin. Attended Margate Coll., Margate, Kent, England. Studied acting at the Lyric Stage Acad., Eng. Married to Arthur Chesney (marr. dis. 1928); married 1928 to Francis Barlow Bradley (dec. 1929); married June 1, 1944, to Robert Barton Henderson. Member of AEA; SAG; AFTRA. Address: 4050 Wilkinson Ave., Studio City, CA 91604.

Theatre. Miss Winwood made her stage debut as Laura in *School* (Th. Royal, Manchester, England, 1898), which she repeated in London (Globe, Jan. 7, 1899); subsequently toured in Drury Lane dramas for several years; appeared as Flytton in *Heroic Stubbs,* Mollie in *The Younger Generation,* and Rosie Platt in *The New Clown* (Terry's, London, Jan.–Mar. 1906); Lady Millicent Eggington in *When Knights Were Bold* (Wyndham's, Jan. 29, 1907); and Hobson in *Mrs. Skeffington* (Queen's, Oct. 21, 1910).

From 1911–12, she was a member of the Liverpool Repertory Th., where her roles included Lady Mary Lasenby in *The Admirable Crichton,* Litterkin in *Fininella,* Nora Helmer in *A Doll's House,* Polly Eccles in *Caste,* Dolly Compton in *The Right To Die,* Jenny Pargetter in *Nan,* Harriet in *Shock Headed Peter,* Lady Jessica Nepean in *The Liars,* Beryl Burden in *Love—and What Then?,* Stella Warren in *The Kiss Cure,* Mrs. Allonby in *A Woman of No Importance,* Elizabeth Thompson in *Don,* Clare in *The Fugitive,* Effie Pemberton in *The Blindness of Virtue,* and Ethel Borridge in *The Cassilis Engagement.*

She played Cynthia Harrington in *The Cage* (Court, London, June 10, 1913); Dorothy Fullerton in *The Fugitive* (Court, Sept. 16, 1913); Jenny Pargetter in *Nan* (St. James's, Dec. 2, 1913); Stella Warren in *The Kiss Cure* (Gaiety, Manchester, Aug. 10, 1914); Avonia Bunn in *Trelawny of the Wells* (Kingsway, London, May 10, 1915); Mercy Jarland in *A Bit o' Love* (Kingsway, May 25, 1915); appeared in the revue *Hullo! Repertory!* (Coliseum, June 21, 1915); and *Half-Past Eight* (Comedy, Aug. 19, 1916).

Miss Winwood made her N.Y.C. debut as Lucilla in *Hush!* (Little, Oct. 3, 1916); subsequently played Emmie in *A Successful Calamity* (Booth, Feb. 5, 1917); Helen in *Why Marry?* (Astor, Dec. 25, 1917); the title role in *Helen with the High Hand* (Belasco, Washington, D.C., Aug. 1918); Julie Rutherford in *A Little Journey* (Little, N.Y.C., Dec. 26, 1918); Bejart in *Molière* (Liberty, Mar. 17, 1919); Victoria in *Too Many Husbands* (Booth, Oct. 8, 1919); Madame Feriand in *The Tyranny of Love* (Bijou, Mar. 8, 1921); Elizabeth in *The Circle* (Selwyn, Sept. 12, 1921); Charlotte in *Madame Pierre* (Ritz, Feb. 15, 1922); Claire in *The Red Poppy* (Greenwich Village Th., Dec. 20, 1922); Helen Springer in *Anything Might Happen* (Comedy, Feb. 20, 1923); Mona in *Spring Cleaning* (Eltinge, Nov. 9, 1923); Dona Lisa (Lady Elizabeth Neville) in *The Buccaneer* (Plymouth, Oct. 2, 1925); and Katharina in *The Taming of the Shrew* (Klaw, Dec. 18, 1925).

She played Arlette Leterne in *A Weak Woman* (Ritz, Jan. 26, 1926); a Dancer in *The Chief Thing* (Guild, Mar. 22, 1926); Miss Gee in *Beau Strings* (Mansfield, Apr. 26, 1926); succeeded (July 1926) Lynn Fontanne as Laura Pasquale in *At Mrs. Beam's* (Guild, April 26, 1926); played Kitty Tamas and Katie in *Head or Tail* (Waldorf, Nov. 9, 1926); Avonia Bunn in *Trelawny of the Wells* (New Amsterdam, Jan. 31, 1927); Jane Banbury in *Fallen Angels* (49 St. Th., Dec. 1, 1927); Laura Deane in *We Never Learn* (Eltinge, Jan. 23, 1928); Fern Andrews in *The Furies* (Shubert, Mar. 7, 1928); Cinder in *Scarlet Sister Mary* (Ethel Barrymore Th., Nov. 25, 1930); and Tweeny in *The Admirable Crichton* (New Amsterdam, Mar. 9, 1931).

Miss Winwood succeeded Marie Lohr as Margaret Armstrong in *The Love Game* (Prince of Wales's, London, Aug. 7, 1931); appeared in *See Naples and Die* (Playhouse, Liverpool, Oct. 1931); played the title role in *Maya,* and Topsy in *Pleasure Garden* (Gate, London, 1932); the Woman in *Murder* (Gate, Nov. 10, 1933); Mrs. Frobisher (Liz) in *The Distaff Side* (Booth, N.Y.C., Sept. 25, 1934); at Carmel (N.Y., July 1935), played Lady Emily Lyons in *The Bishop Misbehaves,* Molly Larkens in *The Farmer Takes a Wife,* and Florence Lancaster in *The Vortex;* appeared as Stella Kirby in *Eden End* (Masque, N.Y.C., Oct. 21, 1935); Lady Breen in *I Want a Policeman!* (Lyceum, Jan. 14, 1936); Evie Millward in *The Distaff Side* (El Capitan, Los Angeles, Calif., Aug. 1936); Portia in *The Merchant of Venice* (El Capitan, Mar. 1937); toured in *Tonight at 8:30* (1937–38); played Mistress Page in *The Merry Wives of Windsor* (Empire, N.Y.C., Apr. 14, 1938); the Lady in Gray in *On the Rocks* (Daly's, June 15, 1938); Grace Hargreaves in *Good Hunting* (Hudson, Nov. 21, 1938); Lady Bracknell in *The Importance of Being Earnest* (Vanderbilt, Jan. 12, 1939); Annie Parker in *When We Were Married* (Lyceum, Dec. 25, 1939); Louisa Creed in *Ladies in Retirement* (Henry Miller's Th., Mar. 26, 1940), and on tour; and Madame Arcati in the Chicago (Ill.) company of *Blithe Spirit* (Feb. 1942).

She played Ines in *The Pirate* (Martin Beck Th., N.Y.C., Nov. 25, 1942); Agatha in *The Lady and the Clown* (Civic Aud., Chicago, Ill., Mar. 1944); Emily Brent in *Ten Little Indians* (Broadhurst, N.Y.C., June 27, 1944); Judith Bliss in *Hay Fever* (Royal Alexandra Th., Toronto, Ontario, Canada, July 1945); Mrs. Thomas Avery in the pre-Bway tryout of *West of the Moon* (opened National, Washington, D.C., Mar. 25, 1946; closed Wilbur, Boston, Mass., Apr. 13, 1948); the Duchess of Berwick in *Lady Windermere's Fan* (Cort, N.Y.C., Oct. 14, 1946); appeared in a stock production of *The Royal Family* (Summer 1947); played Mme. Constance in *The Madwoman of Chaillot* (Belasco, N.Y.C., Dec. 27, 1948); toured as Lady Bracknell in *The Importance of Being Earnest* (1949); appeared in the title role in *Mrs. Warren's Profession* (Bleecker St. Th., N.Y.C., Oct. 1950); performed in *George and Margaret* and *Door to a Room* (Summer 1951); played Julia Shuttlethwaite in the national tour of *The Cocktail Party* (opened Curran, San Francisco, Calif., Oct. 15, 1951); Mrs. Leo Hunter in *Mr. Pickwick* (Plymouth, N.Y.C., Sept. 17, 1952); Alicia de St. Ephlam in *Gigi* (New, London, May 23, 1956); toured as Miz Annabell Cotton in the pre-Bway tryout of *Crazy October* (opened Shubert, New Haven, Conn., Oct. 8, 1958; closed Geary, San Francisco, Calif., Jan. 3, 1959); played Madame Tsai in *Lute Song* (NY City Ctr., Mar. 12, 1959); appeared in *The Circle* (June 1960); and toured cross-country as Mrs. Windrew in *Here Today* (Sombrero Playhouse, Phoenix, Ariz., Jan. 1963).

Miss Winwood played Julie Clarke in *The Other 23 1/2 Hours* (Ivar Th., Los Angeles, Aug. 3, 1964); Mrs. St. Maugham in *The Chalk Garden* (Cleveland, Ohio, Playhouse, Francis E. Drury Th., Dec. 9, 1964); Eleanor Bonnardon in a stock tryout of *Madame Mousse* (Westport, Conn., Country Playhouse, Aug. 16, 1965); and Mrs. Snow in *Nathan Weinstein, Mystic, Connecticut* (Brooks Atkinson Th., N.Y.C., Feb. 25, 1966).

Films. Miss Winwood appeared in *The Glass Slipper* (MGM, 1955); *Twenty-three Paces to Baker Street* (20th-Fox, 1956); *The Swan* (MGM, 1956); *This Happy Feeling* (U, 1958); *The Misfits* (UA, 1961); *The Magic Sword* (UA, 1962); *The Cabinet of Dr. Caligari* (20th-Fox, 1962); *Alive and Kicking* (England); *Dead Ringer* (WB, 1964); *Cat Ballou* (Col., 1965); and *The Producers* (Embassy, 1968).

Television. She has appeared in *Blithe Spirit; Great Expectations; Miss Mabel;* and has appeared in all major networks, including segments of Th. of the Air; Adventures in Paradise (ABC); Alfred Hitchcock Presents (CBS); Thriller (Ind.); The Donna Reed Show (ABC); Lucille Ball (CBS); The Rogues (NBC); The F.B.I. (ABC); The Mike Douglas Show (Ind.); Perry Mason (CBS); The Man from U.N.C.L.E. (NBC); Bewitched (ABC); Stage 67 (ABC); Batman (ABC); and the Ann Southern Show (ABC).

Awards. Miss Winwood received an award (1940) for her role as Louisa Creed in *Ladies in Retirement.*

Recreation. Riding, tennis, bridge.

WISDOM, NORMAN. Actor, comedian, variety artist. b. Feb. 4, 1920, London, England. Married Freda Simpson; one son, one daughter. Served in British Army.

Theatre. Mr. Wisdom made his stage debut as a comedian in a variety act at Collins Music Hall, Islington, London, England (1946). This was followed by similar appearances at the London Casino (1948), at Scarborough, in Birmingham, and in *Buttons and Bows* (Blackpool). He was in the revue *Sauce Piquante* (Cambridge, Apr. 27, 1950) in the revue *Paris to Piccadilly* (Prince of Wales Th., London, Apr. 1952); in *The 1954 Palladium Show* (Palladium, May 1954); in *Painting the Town* (Palladium, Aug. 1955); and was Aladdin in *The Wonderful Lamp* Palladium, Dec. 1956).

He was Charley Wykeham in *Where's Charley?* (Palace, Feb. 1958); was Dick Whittington in *Turn Again, Whittington* (Palladium, Dec. 1960); was in *Robinson Crusoe* (Hippodrome, Bristol, Dec. 1961; Empire, Liverpool, Dec. 1963); and toured as Cocky in *The Roar of the Grease Paint— The Smell of the Crowd* (Aug. 1964).

Mr. Wisdom made his Bway debut as Will Mossop in *Walking Happy* (Lunt-Fontanne Th., Nov. 26, 1966) and followed this with his portrayal of Arnold Crouch in *Not Now Darling* (Brooks Atkinson Th., Oct. 29, 1970).

Films. Mr. Wisdom's motion pictures include *One Good Turn* (Gen. Film, 1954); *Trouble in Store* (Rep., 1955); *Man of the Moment* (Rank, 1955); *Up in the World* (Rank, 1956); *The Square Peg* (Rank, (1958); *Follow a Star* (Rank, 1959); *A Stitch in Time* (Rank, 1963); *The Night They Raided Minsky's* (UA, 1968); and *There Was a Crooked Man* (WB, 1970).

Television. Mr. Wisdom starred in the British series Norman (ATV, 1970) and Nobody Is Norman Wisdom (ATV, 1973) and has appeared on other television programs both in England and the US,.

WISEMAN, JOSEPH. Actor. b. May 15, 1918, Montreal, Quebec, Canada, to Louis and Pearl (Rubin) Wiseman. Father, merchant; mother, seamstress. Grad. John Adams H.S., Ozone Park, N.Y., 1935; attended City Coll. of New York, 1935. Married Aug. 28, 1943, to Nell Kinard; one son, one daughter. Served US Army, Signal Corps, 1942. Member of AEA; SAG; AFTRA.

Theatre. Mr. Wiseman made his professional debut at the New Barn Th. (Saugerties, N.Y., Summer 1936) as an actor and stage manager in productions of *Three Men on a Horse, The Milky Way,* and *The Warrior's Husband.*

He made his N.Y.C. debut as a Union Soldier in *Abe Lincoln in Illinois* (Plymouth, Oct. 15, 1938), also touring in it as Bab and a Cavalry Captain (1939–40); played Kulygin in *The Three Sisters* and the News Boy in *The Grass Is Always Greener* (Surrey Th., Me., Summer 1939); the Beggar and the Second Money Changer in *Journey to Jerusalem* (Natl., N.Y.C., Oct. 5, 1940); Cpl. Mueller in *Candle in the Wind* (Shubert, Oct. 22, 1941), also touring in it (1942–43); took over Eric Dressler's role as Andrey Prozorov during the run of *The Three Sisters* (Ethel Barrymore Th., Dec. 21, 1942), also touring in it; played the Second German Soldier in *The Barber Had Two Sons* (Playhouse, Feb. 1, 1943); and billed as Carlo Respighi, played Stefano in *Storm Operation* (Belasco, Jan. 11, 1944).

Mr. Wiseman played Champlain (Father Massieu) in *Joan of Lorraine* (Alvin, Nov. 18, 1946); Mardian in *Antony and Cleopatra* (Martin Beck Th., Nov. 26, 1947), also touring in it; Charlie in *Detective Story* (Hudson, Mar. 23, 1949); Juan de Escovedo in *That Lady* (Martin Beck Th., Nov. 22, 1949), also touring in it (Feb.–June 1950); Boris in a summer production of *Within a Glass Bell* (Westport Country Playhouse, Conn., July 1950); Edmund in Louis Calhern's *King Lear* (National, N.Y.C., Dec. 25, 1950); and Eddie Fuseli in *Golden Boy* (ANTA, Mar. 12, 1952).

Also, Oliver Erwenter in a summer production of *The Silver Whistle* (Westchester County Playhouse, Mt. Kisco, N.Y., July 1952); Dick Dudgeon in *The Devil's Disciple* (Playhouse-in-the-Park, Philadelphia, Pa., Sept. 1952); Sergius in *Arms and the Man* (Playhouse-in-the-Park, Philadelphia, Pa., Aug. 1953); played the Inquisitor in *The Lark* (Longacre, N.Y.C., Nov. 17, 1955); and the Stranger in *Susan and the Stranger* (Westchester County Playhouse, July 1956); Ferdinand, Duke of Calabria, in *The Duchess of Malfi* (Phoenix, N.Y.C., Mar. 19, 1957); the Driver in a pre-Bway tryout of *The Saturday Night Kid* (opened Westport Country Playhouse, Sept. 9, 1957; closed Locust, Philadelphia, Sept. 28, 1957); Mr. Frank in *The Diary of Anne Frank* (Coconut Grove Playhouse, Miami, Fla., Nov. 1958); Amos in *The Queen and the Rebels* (Bucks County Playhouse, New Hope, Pa., Aug. 1959); Dr. Rafael Taurez in the pre-Bway tryout of *Sweet Love Remember'd* (opened Shubert, New Haven, Conn., Dec. 28, 1959; closed there Dec. 31, 1959); the Father in *Six Characters in Search of an Author* for the Th. Group at the Univ. of California at Los Angeles (Jan. 17, 1961); Bocadur in a summer production of *Turn on the Night* (Playhouse-in-the-Park, Philadelphia, Aug. 1961); and Nota in *Naked* (Royal Court, London, Eng., Mar. 1963).

As a member of the Lincoln Ctr., Repertory Co., he played Chu Yin in *Marco Millions* (ANTA, Wash. Sq. Th., N.Y.C., Feb. 20, 1964); and Le Duc, a Doctor, in *Incident at Vichy* (ANTA Washington Sq. Th., Dec. 3, 1964; and Huntington Hartford Th., Los Angeles, Oct. 25, 1965).

For the Amer. Shakespeare Fest. (Stratford, Conn.) Mr. Wiseman played Thomas in *Murder in the Cathedral* (1966); subsequently played the title role in *In the Matter of J. Robert Oppenheimer* (Mark Taper Forum, Los Angeles, 1968; and Vivian Beaumont Th. Lincoln Ctr., N.Y.C., Mar. 6, 1969); and played Astrov in *Uncle Vanya* (Mark Taper Forum, Los Angeles, 1969).

Films. Mr. Wiseman has appeared in *With These Hands* (CLC, 1950); *Detective Story* (Par., 1951); *Viva Zapata!* (20th-Fox, 1952); *Les Miserables* (20th-Fox, 1952); *Champ for a Day* (Rep., 1953); *The Silver Chalice* (WB, 1954); *The Prodigal* (MGM, 1955); *The Garment Jungle* (Col., 1957); *The Unforgiven* (UA, 1960); *The Happy Thieves* (UA, 1962); *Dr. No* (UA, 1963); *The Night They Raided Minsky's* (UA, 1968); and *Bye, Bye Braverman* (WB-7 Arts, 1968). He also narrated two documentary films, *Mella* (ORT, 1955), and *Eliahu* (ORT, 1957).

Television. He has appeared in *Macbeth* (CBS, Feb. 21, 1959; Jan. 2, 1960); *Darkness at Noon* (Producers Showcase, NBC, May 2, 1955); on Frontiers of Faith (NBC, 1950–60); *The Lincoln Center Day* special (CBS, 1964); The Loretta Young Show (NBC, 1964); Desilu Playhouse (NBC, 1965); The Untouchables (Ind., 1965); Camera Three (CBS, 1965); The Eternal Light (NBC, 1965); Jesse James (ABC, 1966); The Bob Hope Show (NBC, 1966); Preview Tonight (ABC, 1966); Twilight Zone (ABC, 1966); T.H.E. Cat (NBC, 1966); Coronet Blue (CBS, 1967); and Theatre in America (NET, 1975).

WITCOVER, WALT. Director, actor, teacher of acting. b. Walter Witcover Scheinman, Aug. 24, 1924, New York City, to Louis J. and Juliette T. Scheinman Benton. Father, sculptor; mother, lecturer. Grad. Townsend Harris H.S., N.Y.C., 1940; Cornell Univ., B.A. (Phi Beta Kappa) 1946; M.A. 1947. Studied at Amer. Th. Wing, N.Y.C., 1947–50; acting with Lee Strasberg, N.Y.C., 1950–53; at Actors' Studio, N.Y.C. (director-observer, 1962–74). Served US Army 44th Inf. Div. Field Artillery, ETO, 1943–45; rank, Pvt. Relative in theatre: cousin, James Yaffe, playwright. Member of AEA; AFTRA; SAG; SSD&C (exec. bd., 1965–68). Address: (home) 105 W. 13th St., New York, NY 10011, tel. (212) 691-4367; (bus.) 55 W. 42nd St., New York, NY 10036.

Theatre. Mr. Witcover made his first appearance on a stage as Mischka in a high school production of *The Inspector General* (Mar. 1940); while a student at Cornell Univ., made his professional debut as Ed in *You Can't Take It with You* (Priscilla Beach Th., Plymouth, Mass., July 8, 1942); and was on the production staff of the Univ. Th. at Cornell Univ. (Mar. 1946–Feb. 1947).

He was lighting designer and electrician for *The Great God Brown* (ELT, N.Y.C., Mar. 1947); played Huhu in *Peer Gynt* (Greenwich Mews, Mar. 24, 1947); was stage manager for *There's Always Juliet* (ELT, Apr. 1947); lighting director at the Barter Th. (Abingdon, Va., June–Aug. 1947), and also at this theatre, played Charles Moulton-Barrett in *The Barretts of Wimpole Street.* Curio in *Twelfth Night,* and directed *The Hasty Heart* (Aug. 1947).

He played Berthold in Pirandello's *Henry IV* (Cherry Lane, N.Y.C., Dec. 10, 1947); the Prince of Arragon in *The Merchant of Venice* (Lenox Hill Playhouse, Apr. 11, 1948); and at the Stanford Univ. Th., played Jacques in *The Miser* (Apr. 14, 1948), Mr. Coade in *Dear Brutus* (Apr. 29, 1948), Crocker in *Jason* (June 10, 1948), and David in *The Rivals* (Aug. 12, 1948).

Mr. Witcover directed the following productions for the Manor Club (Pelham, N.Y.): *The Philadelphia Story* (Nov. 11, 1948), *Kind Lady* (Apr. 28, 1949), *Arsenic and Old Lace* (Dec. 2, 1949), and *Light Up the Sky* (Apr. 2, 1950).

He served as lighting director and general stage manager at the Barter Th. (Abingdon, Va., June–Aug. 1949), where he appeared as Fleurant in *The Imaginary Invalid* (Aug. 26, 1949); played the Steward in *Saint Joan* (Lenox Hill Playhouse, N.Y.C., Nov. 5, 1949); and Gunner in *Misalliance* (Lenox Hill Playhouse, Nov. 9, 1950).

At the NY City Ctr., Mr. Witcover played Hassan in *Captain Brassbound's Conversion* (Dec. 27, 1950), and Another Hallboy in *The Royal Family* (Jan. 10, 1951); served as Theatrical Specialist at the Amerikino Theatre (Landsberg, Bavaria), for *Ten Little Indians* (June 13, 1951), *Peter Rabbitt* (July 12, 1951), and *An Airman's Dream* (Aug. 20, 1951).

At the Old Town Th. (Smithtown, N.Y.), he played Ensign Pulver in *Mister Roberts* (June 26, 1953), Rev. Winemiller in *Summer and Smoke* (July 6, 1953), Faker Englund in *Room Service* (July 13, 1953); directed *I Am a Camera* (Aug. 3, 1953), and *John Loves Mary* (Aug. 17, 1953); played Dude Lester in *Tobacco Road* (Aug. 24, 1953); and directed *The Moon Is Blue* (Aug. 31, 1953).

He toured as Muff Potter in a Children's World Th. production of *Tom Sawyer* (1953); at the Lenox Hill Playhouse (N.Y.C.), played Buzz Collins in *Finian's Rainbow* (Feb. 25, 1953), Francis Ignatius in *Shadow and Substance* (Nov. 18, 1953), and directed *The Hasty Heart* (Mar. 3, 1954); directed *The Stages of Love* for an ELT concert-reading touring program (June 1954); a summer stock tour of *The Hasty Heart* (1954); and *The Little Red Shoes* for the Children's World Th. (Oct. 1954).

He directed *Maedchen in Uniform* (Lenox Hill Playhouse, N.Y.C., Apr. 20, 1955); *The Sun-dial* (White Barn, Westport, Conn., June 22, 1955); *Three Times Three* (Chanin Aud., N.Y.C., May 23, 1956); played Starveling in *A Midsummer Night's Dream* (NY State Music-Drama Festival, Ellenville, July 1956); and at the Legion Star Playhouse (Ephrata, Pa.), directed *Tea and Sympathy* (Aug. 7, 1956), *The Solid Gold Cadillac* (Aug. 14, 1956), *The Philadelphia Story* (Aug. 21, 1956), and *Picnic* (Sept. 3, 1956).

He directed *Exiles* (Renata, N.Y.C., Mar. 12, 1957); *Red Roses for Me* (Stella Adler Studio Workshop, Apr. 5, 1957); summer tours of *The Reluctant Debutante* (Lakewood Summer Playhouse, June 24, 1957) and *The Waltz of the Toreadors* (Ogunquit Playhouse, Me., July 7, 1958).

At the Crystal Lake Playhouse (Chestertown, N.Y.), he directed the following productions: *The Glass Menagerie* (July 1, 1959), *Overruled*, and *How He Lied to Her Husband*, a double bill (July 4, 1959), *Rocket to the Moon* (July 10, 1959), *The Marriage* (July 28, 1959), and *Thieves' Carnival* (Sept. 5, 1959).

Mr. Witcover directed *Born Yesterday* (Candlelight Playhouse, Washington, D.C., July 11, 1960); *Three Modern Noh Plays* (White Barn, Westport, Conn., Aug. 20, 1960); *Two Modern Noh Plays* (Th. de Lys, N.Y.C., Nov. 14, 1960); The Brooklyn (N.Y.) Poetry and Drama Ensemble in *An Evening with Brooklyn Authors* (Fall 1960); played Wagner in *Faust* (HB Studio, N.Y.C., Jan. 4, 1961); directed the Brooklyn Poetry and Drama Ensemble in *An Evening with Italian Authors* (Fall 1961); *Signs Along the Cynic Route* (Actors Playhouse, N.Y.C., Dec. 14, 1961); and *Talk to Me* (HB Studio, Mar. 9, 1963).

He directed *The Fantasticks* (Bermuda, Aug. 1964); *The Exhaustion of Our Son's Love* (Sheridan Square Playhouse, N.Y.C., Nov. 1964; Cherry Lane Th., Oct. 18, 1965); *What Color Goes With Brown?* (Theatre 65, Village South Th., Dec. 1964); and, at Actors Studio, *One of Us Has Been Ignited* (Mar. 1965), *La Traviata*, Act 1 (Mar. 1966), *The Rivals* (Mar. 1967), *La Traviata*, Act 2 (Dec. 1967), *La Traviata*, Acts 1 and 2 (May 1968), and *La Traviata*, Acts 3 and 4 (Spring 1969). He also directed *Judas Maccabeus* (Long Island Cultural Festival, Salisbury, L.I., N.Y., Summer 1966); *The Miser* (Syracuse Repertory Th., Feb. 29, 1968); and *Next Year in Jerusalem* (HB Playwrights Foundation, N.Y.C., June 1968).

Mr. Witcover was a co-founder in 1969 and has been artistic director since then of Masterworks Laboratory Th., N.Y.C., for which he has directed, at Theatre-in-the-Courthouse: *Experiments in Lyric Theatre* (Mar. 1970), *From the World of Young Chekhov* (Mar. 1971), and *Boubouroche!* (June 1971); at the Madison Avenue Baptist Ch., N.Y.C., *Marriage* (Feb. 12, 1972); at Lolly's Theatre Club, *Lyric Theatre '72* (May 1972); at Spencer Memorial Ch., *A Serving of Verve* (Feb. and Nov. 1973), *Mozart as Dramatist* (May 1973), *A Door Must Be Open or Shut* and *One Cannot Think of Everything* (Apr. 1974), and *Lovelives* (June 1974).

Films. In 1973–74, Mr. Witcover was co-director, writer, producer, and a performer in a documentary film on the M.L.T. process, *Mozart in Motion*. .

Television. He has appeared on Studio One (CBS, 1948), Search for Tomorrow (CBS, 1949), and Actors' Studio (1950).

Other Activities. Mr. Witcover conducted private acting classes (1954–60); taught acting at the John Mace Studio (N.Y.C., 1957–58); Stella Adler Studio (N.Y.C., 1958–59); Brooklyn Music Sch. (1958–59); HB Studio (N.Y.C., 1960–to date); Roslyn N.Y. Community Th. (1962); is a private coach for performers in the theatre, opera, nightclubs, and motion pictures; and lectures and conducts seminars and workshops on acting and directing.

He spoke at the 21st annual conference of the NY State Community Th. Association, Albany, N.Y., on procedures in directing (Fall 1966); spoke on "The Production of a Play" at the NJ Theatre League Annual conference, Trenton State Coll. (1966); was a finals judge for the 19th annual drama tournament of the NJ Theatre League, Trenton State Coll. (Spring 1967); participated in a ten-day intensive summer session workshop in acting and directing for the Cultural Services Branch, Province of Alberta, Canada (Aug. 1967); and was guest speaker initiating a theatre arts lecture series, "Directors on Directing," Monmouth County (N.J.) Mobile Arts Ctr., Lindcroft, N.J.

WITHERS, IVA. Actress, singer. b. July 7, 1917, Rivers, Manitoba, Canada, to Roy Allan and Edith Elizabeth (Keenan) Withers. Grad. Gordon Bell H.S., Winnipeg, Manitoba, 1934. Studied at Joyce Hague and Grant Muradoff ballet schools, N.Y.C. Married 1943 to Robert G. Strom (marr. dis. 1947); married 1949 to Kazimir Kokich; one son, one daughter, Kim, dancer, model. Member of AEA; AFTRA; SAG. Address: 145 W. 55th St., New York, NY 10010, tel. (212) CI 5-5470.

Pre-Theatre. Restaurant cashier.

Theatre. Miss Withers made her debut as a dancer in vaudeville (Capitol Th., Winnipeg, Can., 1928); subsequently in Canada, played the Rag Doll in *Toymaker's Dream* (1933); Margaret in *Dear Brutus* (1934); Eustasia in *Kempy* (1937); and appeared in *Sock and Buskin*, and *Madam Sherry* (Little Th., Winnipeg, 1938).

She made her N.Y.C. debut in the chorus of *Carousel*, in which she understudied Jan Clayton as Julie Jordan (Majestic, Apr. 19, 1945); succeeded (St. James, Sept. 1945) Evelyn Wyckoff as Laurey in *Oklahoma!* (Majestic, Apr. 19, 1945); succeeded (Majestic, Jan. 1, 1946) Miss Clayton as Julie Jordan in *Carousel*, also touring in this role (1947–49), returned to N.Y.C. in it (NY City Ctr., Jan. 25, 1949), and made her London debut in it (Drury Lane, June 7, 1950). She succeeded (Sept. 1950) Fran Warren as Kathy Robinson in *As the Girls Go* (Winter Garden, N.Y.C., Nov. 13, 1948); was standby for Nanette Fabray in *Make a Wish* (Winter Garden, Apr. 18, 1951); played Magnolia in *Show Boat*, and the title role in *Sally* (St. Louis Municipal Opera, Mo., Summer 1952); succeeded (Sept. 1952) Carol Channing as Lorelei Lee in the touring production of *Gentlemen Prefer Blondes* (opened Palace, Chicago, Ill., Sept. 20, 1951); succeeded (1952) Vivian Blaine as Miss Adelaide in *Guys and Dolls* (46 St. Th., N.Y.C., Nov. 24, 1950); and took over role of Ensign Nellie Forbush during the tour of *South Pacific* (opened Shubert, Chicago, Ill., Nov. 14, 1950).

She played Mae in *Redhead* (46 St. Th., N.Y.C., Feb. 5, 1959); was standby for Tammy Grimes in the title role of *The Unsinkable Molly Brown* (Winter Garden, Nov. 3, 1960), playing the role 17 times during the tryout in Philadelphia, Pa., and 60 times in N.Y.C.; and was standby for Miss Grimes as Cyrenne in *Rattle of a Simple Man* (Booth, Apr. 17, 1963); and Elvira in *High Spirits* (Alvin, Mar. 31, 1964), which she played during Miss Grimes' vacation (July 6–11, 1964). She was standby for Mary Martin during the pre-Bway tour of *I Do! I Do!* (Summer 1966); appeared in *The Happy Time* (Ahmonson, Los Angeles, 1967; and Broadway Th., N.Y.C., Jan. 18, 1968); played Mrs. Adams, understudied and later played the roles of Mrs. Margolin and Mrs. Latham, and, as understudy to Julie Harris, June Allyson and Zsa Zsa Gabor, played the lead role of Anne Stanley in *Forty Carats* (Morosco, N.Y.C., Dec. 26, 1968).

Television. Miss Withers has appeared in *Hit the Deck* (1952); on the Kate Smith Show (NBC, 1953); the Stork Club Show (1953); and Mike Wallace's PM East (WABD, 1960).

Recreation. Sewing, skating.

WITTOP, FREDDY. Costume designer, scenic designer, dancer. b. Fred Wittop Koning, July 26, 1921, Bussum, Holland, to Adriaan Wittop and Anna (Du Moulin) Koning. Father, architect. Educated in France. Served US Army, 1943–46. Member of United Scenic Artists. Address: 7 E. 75th St., New York, NY 10021.

Theatre. Mr. Wittop first performed as a Spanish dancer under the name, Frederico Rey, touring the US as partner to Argentinita (1941–43); made his Bway debut in *Top Notches* (44 St. Th., May 29, 1942); was costume designer for *Beat the Band* (46 St. Th., Oct. 14, 1942); and for the Ballet Theatre productions of *El Amor Brujo*, *Pictures of Goya*, and *Bolero* (Metropolitan Opera House, Apr. 10, 1944); designed the scenery and costumes for *Madeleine Bastille* (Alhambra, Paris, Fr., 1946); and toured the US and Europe with his own dance company (1951–58).

He designed costumes for *Heartbreak House* (Billy Rose Th., N.Y.C., Oct. 18, 1959); *Carnival!* (Imperial, Apr. 19, 1961); *Subways Are for Sleeping* (St. James, Dec. 27, 1961); *Judith* (Her Majesty's London, England, June 20, 1962); *Hello, Dolly!* (St. James, N.Y.C., Jan. 10, 1964; and Th. Royal, Drury Lane, London, Dec. 2, 1965); the NY World's Fair production of *To Broadway with Love* (Texas Pavilion, Apr. 22, 1964); *Bajour* (Shubert, N.Y.C., Nov. 23, 1964); *Kelly* (Broadhurst, Feb. 6, 1965); was one of several designers for the ballet *Vaudeville* (Harkness Ballet, Opera Comique, Paris, Mar. 1965); designed the costumes for the pre-Bway tryout of *Pleasures and Palaces* (opened Fisher Th., Detroit, Mich., Mar. 11, 1965; closed there Apr. 10, 1965); *The Roar of the Greasepaint, The Smell of the Crowd* (Shubert, May 16, 1965); *The Great Waltz* (Music Ctr., Los Angeles, July 27, 1965); and *On a Clear Day You Can See Forever* (Mark Hellinger Th., N.Y.C., Oct. 17, 1965).

He designed costumes for *Three Bags Full* (Henry Miller's Th., N.Y.C., Mar. 6, 1966); *Holly Golightly* (Forrest Th., Philadelphia, Pa., Oct. 1, 1966) which closed during previews under the title *Breakfast at Tiffany's* (Majestic, N.Y.C., closed Dec. 14, 1966); *I Do! I Do!* (46 St. Th., Dec. 5, 1966; and London, 1968); *The Happy Time* (Broadway Th., Jan. 18, 1968); *George M* (Palace, Apr. 10, 1968); *Dear World* (Mark Hellinger Th., Feb. 6, 1969); *A Patriot for Me* (Imperial, Oct. 5, 1969); *Lovely Ladies, Kind Gentlemen* (Majestic, Dec. 28, 1970); *Knickerbocker Holiday* (Curran Th., San Francisco, May 11, 1971); and *Candide* (Curran Th., San Francisco, July 6, 1971).

Night Clubs. Mr. Wittop was costume designer of N.Y.C.'s French Casino production of the *Folies* (Jan. 7, 1937) and the *New Folies Bergère* (1938); the *Plaisirs de Paris* (London Casino, Apr. 29, 1938); the *Folies Bergère* at the San Francisco's World's Fair (Aud., Treasure Island, Calif., 1939); the Latin Quarter Revue (N.Y.C., 1950–60); and for the night club version of *Hello, Dolly* (Riviera, Las Vegas, Nev., Dec. 23, 1965).

Other Activities. He designed costumes for the touring productions of *Ice Capades* (Madison Square Garden, N.Y.C., 1940–41); and *Holiday on Ice* (1959–63; 1966).

Awards. He received the Antoinette Perry (Tony) Award (1964) for his costumes for *Hello, Dolly!*.

WITTSTEIN, ED. Scenic, lighting, and costume designer. b. Edwin Frank Wittstein, Apr. 7, 1929, Mt. Vernon, N.Y., to Nathan Harry and Miriam (Goldman) Wittstein. Father, shoe merchant; mother, secy., welfare worker. Grad. David H.S., Mt. Vernon, 1946; Parson's Sch. of Design, N.Y.C., 1950; New York Univ., B.S. 1951; attended Cooper Union, 1951–52. Studied at Irwin Piscator's Dramatic Workshop, N.Y.C., 1946–47. Relative in theatre: cousin, Ed Wittstein, band leader. Member of United Scenic Artists, local 829. Address: 339 E. 87th St., New York, NY 10028.

Theatre. Mr. Wittstein was first engaged as set designer for *The Inspector General* (Irwin Piscator Dramatic Workshop, N.Y.C., 1947); subsequently was resident designer for the Litchfield (Conn.) Summer Th. (1948); and designed sets for the Guilford (Conn.) Summer Th. productions (1949), including *Lady in the Dark.*

He was set designer for *Yes Is for a Very Young Man* (Cherry Lane, N.Y.C., June 6, 1949); set and costume designer for the opera *Ounga* (Acad. of Music, Philadelphia, Pa., 1950); set designer for the 16th Intl. Music Festival's production of *Jumping Frog of Calaveras County* (La Fenice Th., Venice, Italy, Sept. 23, 1953); designed the sets and costumes for *Dr. Willy Nilly* (Barbizon-Plaza Th., N.Y.C., June 4, 1959); *Legend of Lovers* (41 St. Th., Oct. 27, 1959); *The Fantasticks* (Sullivan St. Playhouse, May 3, 1960); and *The Gondoliers* (NY City Ctr., Jan. 25, 1961).

He designed sets and costumes for *Kean* (Bway Th., Nov. 2, 1961); the costumes for *Bravo Giovanni* (Broadhurst, May 19, 1962); sets and lighting for the pre-Bway tryout of *La Belle* (opened Shubert, Philadelphia, Pa., Aug. 13, 1962; closed there Aug. 25, 1962). As a member of Writers Stage Co., he was a co-producer of *P.S. 193* (Writers Stage Th., N.Y.C., Oct. 30, 1962); and designed the sets for *The Love Nest* (Jan. 25, 1963), which he also co-produced.

He designed the entire production of *Enter Laughing* (Henry Miller's Th., Mar. 13, 1963); supervised the production and was lighting designer for *Chips with Everything* (Plymouth, Oct. 1, 1963); designed sets, costumes, and lights for *A Rainy Day in Newark* (Belasco, Oct. 22, 1963); costumes for *The Ginger Man* (Orpheum, Nov. 21, 1963); sets for *Trumpets of the Lord* (Astor Place Th., Dec. 21, 1963; moved to One Sheridan Square Th., Jan. 22, 1964); sets and costumes for *The White House* (Henry Miller's Th., May 19, 1964); the decor and costumes for the Summer Promenade concerts at Lincoln Ctr. (Philharmonic Hall, May 21, 1964); designed the sets and co-produced *Two by Ionesco* (Writers Stage Th., May 24, 1964); designed The New Th. (N.Y.C.) and its first production, *The Knack* (May 27, 1964); and designed the sets, lights, and costumes for four ballets (Opernhaus, Cologne, Germany, July 9, 1964).

Mr. Wittstein designed sets for *Dr. Faustus* (Phoenix, N.Y.C., Oct. 6, 1964); *The New Pinter Plays* (Writers Stage Th., Dec. 9, 1964), including *A Slight Ache,* and *The Room;* the double-bill of *Sing to Me Through Open Windows* and *The Day the Whores Came Out To Play Tennis* (The Players, Mar. 15, 1965); and *And Things That Go Bump in the Night* (Royale, Apr. 26, 1965); sets and costumes for the NY City Opera Co. productions of *The Marriage of Figaro* (1965) and *The Yearling* (Alvin, Dec. 10, 1965); and sets and lighting for the touring production of *The Amen Corner* (opened Vienna, Austria; played major European cities, 1965).

He was set designer for *Sergeant Musgrave's Dance* (Th. de Lys, N.Y.C., Mar. 8, 1966); designed the entire production of *The Office* (Henry Miller's Th., closed during previews, Apr. 30, 1966); the sets for *The Kitchen* (81 St. Th., June 13, 1966); *Thornton Wilder's Triple Bill* (Cherry Lane Th., Sept. 6, 1966), including *The Long Christmas Dinner, Queens of France,* and *The Happy Journey to Trenton and Camden; The Natural Look* (Longacre, Mar. 11, 1967); the Bway, London, and touring productions of *You Know I Can't Hear You When the Water's Running* (opened Ambassador, N.Y.C., Mar. 13, 1967); the sets for The American Shakespeare Festival (Stratford, Conn.) productions of *The Merchant of Venice* (June 20, 1967) and *Richard II* (June 22, 1968), and sets and costumes for *As You Like It* (June 23, 1968); for the Cincinnati (Ohio) Playhouse in the Park, sets for *The Miser* (Main Th., June 13, 1967), and *Honor and Offer* (Shelter House Th., Nov. 21, 1968); sets for *The Man in the Glass Booth* (Royale, N.Y.C., Sept. 26, 1968); and *The Tea Party* and *The Basement* (Eastside Playhouse, Oct. 15, 1968).

He designed sets for *The Little Murders* (Circle in the Square, N.Y.C., Jan. 5, 1969); sets, lights, and costumes for *Celebration* (Ambassador, Jan. 22, 1969); again at the Cincinnati (Ohio) Playhouse in the Park (Apr.–Sept. 1969), sets for *Volpone* and *The Good Woman of Setzuan;* and, for The American Shakespeare Festival (Stratford, Conn.), sets for *Much Ado About Nothing* (June 18, 1969). He was the set designer for *The Scent of Flowers* (Martinique, N.Y.C., Oct. 20, 1969); *The Last Sweet Days of Isaac* (Eastside Playhouse, Jan. 26, 1970); *I Dreamt I Dwelt in Bloomingdale's* (Provincetown Playhouse, Feb. 12, 1970); *Blood Red Roses* (John Golden Th., Mar. 22, 1970); for the Cincinnati (Ohio) Playhouse in the Park production of *He Who Gets Slapped* (Robert S. Marx Th., Aug. 27, 1970); *Happy Birthday, Wanda June* (Th. de Lys, N.Y.C., Oct. 7, 1970); *Tough to Get Help* (Royale, May 4, 1972); *Ring Round the Bathtub* (Martin Beck Th., Apr. 29, 1972); *The Soft Core Pornographer* (Stage 73, Apr. 11, 1972); *Echoes* (Bijou, Mar. 26, 1973); the American Shakespeare Festival production of *The Country Wife* (Stratford, Conn., June 1, 1973); and *Ulysses in Nighttown* (Winter Garden, N.Y.C., Mar. 10, 1974).

Films. Mr. Wittstein was production designer for *Bananas* (UA, 1971); *Play It Again, Sam* (Par., 1972); and *The Seven-Ups* (20th-Fox, 1973).

Television. Mr. Wittstein was set designer for the Armstrong Circle Th. (NBC, 1961); Experimental TV Design (Milan, Italy, 1952); Anthology of American-Italian Television Films (Italy, 1953); the Tonight show (NBC, 1955); and *La Bohème* (NBC Televison Opera Th., 1957), which toured the US (Nov. 1957).

Also for the NBC Television Opera Th., he designed sets and costumes for *Cosi fan Tutti* (1958), *Cavalleria Rusticana* (1960), *Boris Godunov* (1961), and sets for *The Love of Three Kings* (1962).

He was the set designer for *Camino Real* (NET); *The Confession* (ABC); *The Diary of Anne Frank* (ABC); *Blithe Spirit* (NBC); *Home* (NET); *The Connection* (ABC); *A Memory of Two Mondays* (NET); *The Front Page;* The Woody Allen Special (CBS); Sand Castle (NET); and A Touch of the Poet (NET). In addition, he designed for Esso Repertory Theatre (Ind.), which included the productions of thirteen repertory companies throughout the country; and was production designer for The Adams Chronicles (NET); and the pilot film, *Streets of Gold* (CBS).

Night Clubs. He designed the sets for Julius Monk's revues, *Demi-Dozen, Pieces of Eight,* and *Dressed to the Nines* (Upstairs at the Downstairs, N.Y.C., 1958).

Other Activities. Artist, free-lance photographer. As an interior decorator, he restyled (with Robert Miller) the Palm Court of the Plaza Hotel (N.Y.C. 1963); and designed the Plaza Nine room at the Plaza Hotel (N.Y.C., 1965).

His work has been included in *Contemporary Stage Design USA* at Lincoln Ctr. (1975), and on tour under the auspices of the Smithsonian Institute (Feb. 1, 1976–Mar. 15, 1978); *Stage Design Exhibit* at the Touchstone Gallery (N.Y.C., Sept. 1975); and in one-man and group showings of drawings and paintings at the Adam Gallery (1972, 1973).

Awards. Mr. Wittstein received the Off-Bway (Obie) Award (1965–66) for Distinguished Design for his settings for *Sergeant Musgrave's Dance;* and the Maharam Award (1974) for *Ulysses in Nighttown.*

Recreation. Traveling, drawing, photography.

WOLF, JAY. Casting director, producer. b. Julius Rosenthal Wolf, Mar. 25, 1929, Cincinnati, Ohio, to J. M. and Flora Therese (Rosenthal) Wolf. Father, jewelry manufacturing executive. Grad. Walnut Hills H.S., Cincinnati, 1947; Dartmouth Coll., B.A. 1951. Member of The Players; Chelsea Theater Ctr. (bd. of dir.); Encounter (bd. of sponsors); Great Performers of the Hamptons, Inc. (bd. of dir.). Address: 26 E. 63rd St., New York, NY 10021, tel. (212) TE 2-8954.

Mr. Wolf has been vice-president (1966–68), Equity Dept., of General Artists Corp. (later called Creative Management Assoc.); head of the talent department of Artists Agency Corp. (1964–66); head of the talent department at Frank Cooper Associates Agency, Inc. (1963–64); production associate for Oscar Lewenstein, Ltd. (1961–63); and talent representative with the Ashley-Famous Agency (1958–61); the Milton Goldman Agency (1955–58); and the Jules Ziegler Agency (1953–55).

Theatre. Mr. Wolf, with Jacqueline Babbin, co-produced *Ring Round the Bathtub* (Martin Beck Th., N.Y.C., Apr. 29, 1972); and was casting director for *Cyrano* (Palace, N.Y.C., May 13, 1973).

Films. He was casting director for *Don't Drink the Water* (Avco-Embassy, 1969); *The Telephone Book* (Rosebud Films, 1971); and *The Discovery of America* (Independent, 1972).

Television. He was the daytime casting director (1970–71) for the ABC productions, *A World Apart* and *Best of Everything;* casting director for *A Ceremony of Innocence* (NET); *A Memory of Two Mondays* (NET); *Hogan's Goat* (NET); *The Rimers of Eldritch* (NET); *Pueblo* (ABC); *F. Scott Fitzgerald and the Last of the Belles* (ABC); *June Moon* (NET); Daytime 90 (CBS); The Adams Chronicles (NET); and casting director and assistant to the producers for five Wide World of Entertainment specials (ABC).

Other Activities. Mr. Wolf was associate editor for *Esquire's Apparel Arts* (1951–52); copy researcher and writer for Benton & Bowles, advertising agency (1952–53); and assistant director of The Downtown Gallery (1962–63).

Recreation. Contemporary American art, reading, opera, travel, needlepoint.

WOLFINGTON, IGGIE. Actor. b. Ignatius Wolfington, Oct. 14, 1920, Philadelphia, Pa., to Harry J. and Martha T. (Eustace) Wolfington. Father, automotive executive. Grad. West Philadelphia Catholic Boys H.S., 1938. Studied at Philadelphia Sch. of Th., 1939–40; Amer. Theatre Wing, N.Y.C., 1946–47. Served US Army, Infantry, 1942–46; awarded Bronze Star, Purple Heart with oakleaf cluster; rank 1st Lt. Member of AEA (council, 1959–62, 1964–69); SAG; AFTRA; Catholic Actor's Guild (former chmn. of bd.); The Players.

Theatre. Mr. Wolfington made his debut playing minor roles in a Mercury Th. pre-Bway tryout of *Five Kings* (closed Chestnut St. Opera House, Philadelphia, Pa., Feb. 1939); subsequently played George in a summer production of *Out of the Frying Pan* (Yardley Summer Th., Pa., Sept. 1941); Pinky in the pre-Bway tryout of *Hey Day* (closed Shubert, New Haven, Conn., Mar. 15, 1947); appeared in summer productions at the Red Barn Th. (Westboro, Mass., 1947–48), and the John Drew Th. (East Hampton, N.Y., 1949); played Alexander in *The New Moon* (Hyannis Music Circus, Mass., July 4, 1950); Huck in *Roberto* (Melody Fair, Toronto, Canada, July 1951); and appeared at the Melody Fair (Toronto, Canada, Summers 1951–54).

He made his N.Y.C. debut as Chef (Ellsworth) in *Mrs. McThing* (Martin Beck Th., Feb. 20, 1952), subsequently played Tommy in *The Hasty Heart* (Ann Arbor Dramatic Festival, Mich., May 1953); Throttlebottom in *Of Thee I Sing* (Hyannis Melody Tent; Cohasset Melody Tent, Mass., Aug. 1953); and the Rev. Dr. Moon in *Anything Goes* (Hyannis Melody Tent; Cohasset Melody Tent, July 1954). He played Officer Morrison in *Gramercy Ghost* (Ann Arbor Dramatic Festival, Mich., June 1954); Sheriff Meyers in *One Eye Closed* (Bijou, N.Y.C., Nov. 24, 1954); performed at the Palm Beach (Fla.) Playhouse (Jan.–Mar. 1955); toured summer theatres as

Tommy in *The Hasty Heart* (June 1955); and played Taxi Black in *One Touch of Venus* (Dallas State Fair, Tex., July 1955).

He toured summer theatres as Clifford Snell in *The Solid Gold Cadillac* (1956); played Marcellus in *The Music Man* (Majestic, N.Y.C., Dec. 19, 1957); Jenkins in a summer tour of *The Firefly* (Aug. 1960); Rev. Humphrey in *See How They Run* (Royal Poinciana Playhouse, Palm Beach, Fla., Mar. 1961); Novakovitch in *The Merry Widow* (Los Angeles Civic Light Opera Assn.; San Francisco Civic Light Opera Assn.; Apr.–June 1961); and toured summer theatres as Count Peppi in *Song of Norway* (Aug. 1961).

He played Hercule in *Can-Can* (NY City Ctr., May 16, 1962); at the St. Louis (Mo.) Municipal Opera, appeared as the Cowardly Lion in *The Wizard of Oz*, and Marcellus in *The Music Man* (Aug. 1962); played Mr. MacAfee in *Bye Bye Birdie* (Sheridan-Palace Dinner Th., San Francisco, Calif., Mar. 1963); Captain Andy in *Show Boat* (Starlight Th., Kansas City, Mo., June 1963); toured summer theatres as the Rev. Dr. Moon in *Anything Goes* (July–Aug. 1963); played Jenkins in *The Firefly* (Melodyland, Anaheim, Calif., Sept. 1963); Bozo in *Marathon '33* (ANTA, N.Y.C., Dec. 22, 1963); and appeared in four Eugene Ionesco plays at the Buffalo (N.Y.) Festival of the Arts (Mar. 10–13, 1965).

Films. Mr. Wolfington played Buddy in *Edge of the City* (MGM, 1957).

Television. He has appeared on the Chevrolet Television Th. (NBC, 1949); the Tonight Show (NBC, 1954); *Mayerling* (NBC, 1955); *The Christmas Tie* (Dumont, 1955); *One Touch of Venus* (Hallmark Hall of Fame, NBC, 1955); Novakovitch in *The Merry Widow* (Omnibus, CBS, 1955); the Chef in *Cinderella* (CBS, 1956); appeared on the Life of Riley (1957); played Ellsworth in *Mrs. McThing* (Omnibus, NBC, 1958); appeared on Sgt. Bilko (NBC, 1958); and in *Judgment Eve* (The Defenders, CBS, 1963).

Awards. Mr. Wolfington was nominated for an Antoinette Perry (Tony) Award for his performance as Marcellus in *The Music Man* (1958).

Recreation. Bridge.

WOLFSON, VICTOR. Playwright, novelist. b. Mar. 8, 1910, New York City, to Adolph and Rebecca (Hochstein) Wolfson. Father, newspaper and candy store proprietor boarding house owner and operator; mother, dressmaker. Grad. Experimental Coll. at the Univ. of Wisconsin, A.B. 1931. Married Mar. 21, 1942, to Alice L. Dodge, administrative assistant; four sons. Relative in theatre: brother, Martin Wolfson, actor. Member of Dramatists Guild (on council, 1941–56; secy., 1943–46); ALA (rep. to council, 1947–to date); WGA, East; P.E.N. Club. Address: 549 E. 86th St., New York, NY 10028, tel. (212) RE 4-2157.

Theatre. Mr. Wolfson was assistant stage manager for *Counsellor-at-Law* (Plymouth, N.Y.C., Nov. 6, 1931); subsequently with Victor Trivas adapted *Crime and Punishment* (Biltmore, Jan. 22, 1935); wrote *Bitter Stream* (Civic Repertory Th., Mar. 30, 1936); *Excursion* (Vanderbilt, Apr. 9, 1937); *Pastoral* (Henry Miller's Th., Nov. 1, 1939); *The Family* (Windsor, Mar. 30, 1943); *Love in the City*, (Cleveland Play House, Ohio, Feb. 1947); *Pride's Crossing* (Biltmore, N.Y.C., Nov. 20, 1950); *Murder in the Family* (Berkshire Playhouse, Stockbridge, Mass., July 1952); *American Gothic* (Circle in the Sq., N.Y.C., Nov. 10, 1953); with Stella Unger, wrote the book for the musical, *Seventh Heaven* (ANTA, May 26, 1955); wrote *Boston Love Story* (Bucks County Playhouse, New Hope, Pa., Aug. 1958); and adapted Marc-Gilbert Sauvejon's *All in the Family* (Strand, London, June 17, 1959).

Television. Mr. Wolfson has written for Alfred Hitchcock Presents (CBS), Suspense (CBS), Climax (CBS), The Invisible Man (CBS); Solitaire (CBS); Janet Dean, Registered Nurse; Line-Up (CBS); Five Star Matinee (NBC); the documentary, *Winston Churchill-The Valiant Years* (ABC); The FDR series (ABC); and the Truman series (WNEW-TV).

Other Activities. He taught a course in playwriting at the New York Univ. Sch. of General Studies (1941–42).

Published Works. He wrote the novels, *The Lonely Steeple* (1944); *The Eagle on the Plain* (1946); *Midsummer Madness* (1948); and *My Prince, My King!* (1962); *The Mayerling Murder* (1969); and *Cabral* (1972); and a biography of Harry S. Truman entitled *The Man Who Cared* (1966); and has published short stories in *The New Yorker, Harper's* and *McCall's*.

Awards. Mr. Wolfson received the NATAS (Emmy) Award for *Winston Churchill—the Valiant Years* (1961).

WOOD, AUDREY. Literary representative. b. Feb. 28, 1905, New York City, to William H. and Ida M. Wood. Father, producer, manager. Grad. Washington Irving H.S., N.Y.C., 1925. Married Mar. 24, 1938, to William Liebling, talent representative (dec. Dec. 29, 1969). Member of Amer. Th. Wing; New Dramatists Comm.; Society of Authors' Representatives. Address: c/o International Creative Management, Inc., 40 W. 57 St., New York, NY 10019, tel. (212) 556-5600.

Miss Wood was a play reader for the Century Play Co. (N.Y.C., 1927); a partner in the artists' representatives agency, Liebling-Wood, Inc. (N.Y.C., 1937–54), which she founded with her husband; an associate with Music Corporation of America (MCA) (N.Y.C., 1954–62); and since Aug. 1962 has been with International Creative Management, Inc. (then known as Ashley Famous Agency, Inc.).

She has been literary agent for Tennessee Williams, Robert Anderson, William Inge, Arthur Kopit, Brian Friel, Truman Capote, Jane Bowles, Maurice Valency, and Carson McCullers, among others.

Other Activities. Miss Wood has been an advisor to the Eugene O'Neill Memorial Theater Foundation (Waterford, Conn., 1965); taught a course for new playwrights at Wesleyan College (Conn., 1967); and conducted a playwrights workshop at the Asolo Th. (Sarasota, Fla., Feb. 1968), sponsored by Florida St. Univ.

Awards. Miss Wood received the honorary degree of D.H.L. from Florida St. Univ. (Apr. 22, 1970).

Recreation. Gardening, walking, island hopping, museums, reading, "breathing.".

WOOD, DEEDEE. Choreographer, actress, dancer. b. Audrey Donella Wood, June 7, 1927, Boston, Mass. Grad. Staples High, Westport, Conn., 1945. Married Sept. 11, 1955, to Marc Breaux; one son. Member of AEA; SAG; AFTRA.

Theatre. Miss Wood made her professional debut as a dancer in the national tour of *Guys and Dolls* (opened Curran Th., San Francisco, Calif., June 4, 1951); made her N.Y.C. debut dancing and playing the Jailer in *Can-Can* (Shubert, May 7, 1953).

She danced in, played one of the wives, and was understudy to Tina Louise as Appassionata Von Climax in *Li'l Abner* (St. James, Nov. 15, 1956), succeeding (Aug. 1957) Miss Louise in the role. Miss Wood and Marc Breaux also assisted choreographer Michael Kidd in the musical; restaged, with her husband, the dances for a touring production of *Li'l Abner* (opened Riviera, Las Vegas, Nev., Sept. 1, 1958; closed, Royal Alexandra, Toronto, Canada, Jan. 3, 1959); assisted choreographer Michael Kidd for *Destry Rides Again* (Imperial N.Y.C., Apr. 23, 1959); they choreographed *Do Re Mi* (St. James, Dec. 26, 1960; Prince of Wales Th., London, Oct. 12, 1961), and the national tour (opened O'Keefe Centre, Toronto, Canada, Jan. 16, 1962; closed, Fisher, Detroit, Mich., Mar. 19, 1962).

Films. Miss Wood and Mr. Breaux recreated Michael Kidd's dances for *Li'l Abner* (Par., 1959); choreographed *Mary Poppins* (Buena Vista, 1964) and staged the dances for *The Sound of Music*.

Television. Miss Wood and Mr. Breaux choreographed *Shubert Alley* (Spring 1959); the Bing Crosby Show (NBC Dec. 24, 1962); two Bing Crosby specials (NBC, Nov. 1963, Feb. 1964); the Pat Boone special (ABC, 1962); the Jimmy Durante special (NBC, 1962); the Dick Van Dyke Show (NBC, 1963); and the Jack Benny Show (CBS, 1963).

Recreation. Painting, reading, horseback riding.

WOOD, G. Actor, playwright, composer, lyricist, writer. b. Dec. 31, 1919, Forrest City, Ark. Grad. Carnegie Institute of Technology; NY Univ. Served US Army, Special Services theatrical adviser.

Theatre. Mr. Wood played Carbon de Castel-Jaloux in the NY City Th. Co. production (NY City Ctr.) of *Cyrano de Bergerac* (Nov. 11, 1953), and a Priest in *King Richard III* (Dec. 9, 1953); Ignatz in the pre-Bway tryout of *Reuben Reuben* (opened Shubert, Boston, Oct. 10, 1966); closed there Oct. 22, 1955); the Poet in *Cradle Song* (Circle in the Square, N.Y.C., Dec. 1, 1955); Briggs in *Thunder Rock* (Broadway Congregational Church, Feb. 26, 1956); understudied Martyn Green in *Shangri-La* (Winter Garden, June 13, 1956); at the Broadway Congregational Church, played Cymen in *Thor, with Angels* (Oct. 14, 1956), wrote the book, music, and lyrics for *A Box of Watercolors* (Feb. 7, 1959) in which he appeared as Frank Hedge, played Raquel in *Tobias and the Angel* (Oct. 20, 1957), and Fr. William Callifer in *The Potting Shed* (Nov. 2, 1958); and, off-Bway, appeared as Dr. Hobie Merganser in *Kittiwake Island* (Martinique, Oct. 12, 1960).

As a member of the National Repertory Th. Co., he played Romainville in *Ring 'Round the Moon* (tour, opened Aycock Aud., Greensboro, N.C., Oct. 10, 1963); Yevegny Sergeyevitch Dorn in *The Seagull* (Belasco, N.Y.C., Apr. 5, 1964); Thomas Putnam in *The Crucible* (Belasco, Apr. 6, 1964); on tour (opened American Th., St. Louis, Mo., Oct. 19, 1964; closed Blackstone, Chicago, Mar. 27, 1965) played the Police Captain in *Liliom*, and Mr. Hardcastle in *She Stoops To Conquer*; again toured (opened ANTA, N.Y.C., Nov. 8, 1965; closed Los Angeles, Mar. 26, 1966) playing The President in *Madwoman of Chaillot*, Sir Anthony Absolute in *The Rivals*, and the God Poseidon in *The Trojan Women*; played M. Argon in *The Imaginary Invalid* (ANTA, N.Y.C., May 1, 1967); Jamie in *A Touch of the Poet* (ANTA, May 2, 1967); in a bill entitled *Tonight at 8:30* (ANTA, May 3, 1967), that included *Still Life*, directed *Fumed Oak*, and played Albert in *Ways and Means*; played Robert E. Lee, John Brown and Abraham Lincoln in *John Brown's Body* (Ford's Th., Washington, D.C., Feb. 12, 1968); appeared as Solinus and directed *The Comedy of Errors* (Ford's, Feb. 26, 1968); and played Mr. Hardcastle in *She Stoops To Conquer* (Ford's, Mar. 26, 1968).

With the Amer. Conservatory Th. (San Francisco), he appeared in *The Little Murders* (Jan. 1, 1969); played Exeter in the American Shakespeare Fest. production of *Henry V* (ANTA, N.Y.C., Nov. 10, 1969); returned to ACT to appear in *Hadrian VII* (May 12, 1970; re-opened Nov. 18, 1970), *The Latent Heterosexual* (Jan. 12, 1971), played George Smith in *The Selling of the President* (world premiere, Mar. 30, 1971), and appeared in *Paradise Lost* (Feb. 1, 1972), and *The Contractor* (Mar. 14, 1972).

Mr. Wood appeared with the National Shakespeare Fest. (San Diego, Summer 1972); subsequently appeared with the Milwaukee (Wis.) Repertory Th. Co. in *The Cherry Orchard* (1972–73 season), wrote the music and lyrics for *All Together* (June 8, 1973) in which he played Horace, and appeared in *The Service for Joseph Axminster* (Apr. 25, 1974), and *The Little Foxes* (June 7, 1974); and, returning to Bway, played Gen. Mike O'Henry in *Who's Who in Hell* (Lunt-Fontanne, N.Y.C., Dec. 9, 1974).

In addition to Mr. Wood's original works in which he has appeared, he has written special material for Hermione Gingold, Beatrice Lillie, and Elizabeth Welch; the London revues, *Sweetest and Lowest*, and *Slings and Arrows*; lyrics for *Shoestring '57* (Barbizon-Plaza Th., N.Y.C., Nov. 5, 1956); music and lyrics for *Kaleidoscope* (Provincetown Playhouse, June 13, 1957); material for *Put It in Writing* (Th. de Lys, May 13, 1963); music and lyrics to "The Old Eight-Ten" and "Merry-Go-Round" for Julius Monk's *Baker's Dozen* (Plaza 9, Jan. 9, 1964), music and lyrics to "Three Cheers for the Tired Businessman" for *Happy Medium* (Chicago, Dec. 26, 1963); and the music and lyrics, and with Theodore Mann, the book for *F. Jasmine Adams* (Circle in the Square, N.Y.C., Oct. 27, 1971), a musical adaptation of Member of the Wedding.

WOOD, PEGGY. Actress, writer. b. Margaret Wood, Feb. 9, 1892, Brooklyn, N.Y., to Eugene and Mary (Gardner) Wood. Father, author. Grad. Manual Training H.S., Brooklyn, 1909. Studied voice with Eleanor McLellan, 1919–29; Emma Calvé, Summer 1922. Married Feb. 14, 1924, to John V. A. Weaver, author (dec. June 18, 1938); one son; married Oct. 1, 1946, to William H. Walling, executive. Member of AEA (council, 1919–40; 1958–64; 4th vice-pres., 1934–41); AFTRA; SAG; ALA; Dramatists Guild; ANTA (pres., 1959–65; hon. pres., 1966); Episcopal Actors' Guild (vice-pres., 1950–64). Address: 1022 Sunset Rd., Stamford, CT tel. (203) 322-0154.

Theatre. Miss Wood made her N.Y.C. debut as a member of the chorus in *Naughty Marietta* (New York Th., Nov. 7, 1910); subsequently appeared as Vera Steinway in *The Three Romeos* (Globe, Nov. 13, 1911); Valerie in *The Lady of the Slipper* (Globe, Oct. 28, 1912); Fanchette in *Mlle. Modiste* (Globe, May 26, 1913); Gillette in *The Madcap Duchess* (Globe, Nov. 11, 1913); the title role in a touring production of *Adele* (1914); and Elsie Workingson in *Hello, Broadway* (Astor, N.Y.C., Dec. 25, 1914).

She played Edith Doray in *Young America* (Astor, Aug. 28, 1915); appeared in stock (Waterbury, Conn., 1916); played Peggy in *Love o' Mike* (Shubert, N.Y.C., Jan. 15, 1917); Ottillie in *Maytime* (Shubert, Aug. 16, 1917), and on tour; Julie in *Buddies* (Selwyn, N.Y.C., Oct. 27, 1919); the title role in *Marjolaine* (Broadhurst, Jan. 24, 1922); and Antoinette Allen in *The Clinging Vine* (Knickerbocker, Dec. 25, 1922), and on tour.

She played Marie Duquesne in *The Bride* (39 St. Th., N.Y.C., May 5, 1924); Rose in the pre-Bway tryout of *The Roses* (Stuart Walker Stock Co., Indianapolis, Ind.); the title role in *Candida* (Comedy, N.Y.C., Nov. 9, 1925); Lady Percy in The Players' production of *Henry IV, Part 1* (Knickerbocker, May 31, 1926); Imogen Parrott in a touring production of *Trelawney of the Wells* (1926–27); Clarissa in *A Lady in Love* (Lyceum, N.Y.C., Feb. 21, 1927); Portia in George Arliss' production of *The Merchant of Venice* (Broadhurst, Jan. 16, 1928), and on tour; and Anne Russell in *A Play Without a Name* (Booth, N.Y.C., Nov. 26, 1928).

She made her London debut as the Marchioness of Shayne, Sarah Millick, and Sari Linden in *Bitter Sweet* (His Majesty's, July 18, 1929); subsequently played Shirley Sheridan in *The Cat and the Fiddle* (Palace, Mar. 4, 1932); and the Prima Donna in *Tonight or Never* (Duke of York's, Nov. 10, 1932).

Miss Wood appeared as Marguerite Langdon in *A Saturday Night* (Playhouse, N.Y.C., Feb. 28, 1933); Jacqueline in *Best Sellers* (Morosco, May 3, 1933); Rosalinde in *Champagne Sec* (Morosco, Oct. 14, 1933); Jennifer Lawrence in *Birthday* (49 St. Th., Dec. 26, 1934); Katherine in *The Taming of the Shrew* (Greek Th., Berkeley, Calif., July 1934), in the title role in *The Countess Maritza* (Greek Th., Berkeley, Calif., July 1936); Truth in *Everyman* (Hollywood Bowl, Calif., Summer 1936); Liz Quis in *Miss Quis* (Henry Miller's Th., N.Y.C., Apr. 7, 1937); Charlotte Shaw in the pre-Bway tryout of *Never Trouble Trouble* (Brighton Beach, Brooklyn, Aug., 1937); Rozanne Gray in *Operette* (His Majesty's, London, Mar. 16, 1938); and Julie Cavendish in *Theatre Royal* (*The Royal Family*) (King's, Hammersmith, May 1939).

She played Mrs. Foresight in The Players' production of *Love for Love* (Hudson, N.Y.C., June 3, 1940); Mildred Watson Drake in *Old Acquaintance* (Morosco, Dec. 23, 1940); Ruth in *Blithe Spirit* (Morosco, Nov. 5, 1941), and on a USO tour (France, England, Oct. 12, 1944–June 4, 1945); Clara Graves in *The Happiest Years* (Lyceum, N.Y.C., Apr. 25, 1949); Mrs. George in *Getting Married* (ANTA, May 7, 1951); Mama in a summer-theatre touring production of *Here's Mama* (Summer 1952); Donna Lucia in *Charley's Aunt* (NY City Ctr., Dec. 22, 1953); Mrs. Kittridge in a tryout production of *A Swim in the Sea* (Royal Poinciana Playhouse, Palm Beach, Fla., May 1958); Mrs. St. Maugham in *The Chalk Garden* (Drury Lane, Chicago, Ill., July 1958); Aunt Hettie in *The Girls in 509* (Belasco, N.Y.C., Oct. 15, 1958); Hera in *Rape of the Belt* (Martin Beck Th., Nov. 5, 1960); Fabia in *The Knight from Olmedo* (IASTA Th., Nov. 30, 1962); Fanny Ellis in *Opening Night*, part of a double-bill of one-act plays (East End Th., Oct. 2, 1963); and Amanda in *The Glass Menagerie* (Goodman, Chicago, Ill., Jan. 10, 1964).

Miss Wood has subsequently appeared in *Pictures in the Hallway* (Th. de Lys, N.Y.C., Dec. 16, 1964); *The Golden Warriors* (Dallas, Tex., Th. Ctr., May 10, 1966); *The Chalk Garden* (Playhouse in the Park, Philadelphia, Pa., Aug. 1966); *A Madrigal of Shakespeare* (Th. de Lys, N.Y.C., Feb. 1968); played Mme. Constance in *The Madwoman of Chaillot* (Sokol Th., Mar. 1970); and appeared in *A Passage to E. M. Forster* (Th. de Lys, Oct. 1970).

Films. Miss Wood has appeared in *Jalna* (RKO, 1931); *Handy Andy* (20th-Fox, 1934); *Right to Live* (WB, 1935); *The Bride Wore Boots* (Par., 1946); *Dream Girl* (Par., 1948); and has played Naomi in *The Story of Ruth* (20th-Fox, 1960); and the Mother Abbess in *The Sound of Music* (20th-Fox, 1964).

Television. She played Mama in the series, I Remember Mama (CBS, July 1, 1949–June 1, 1957); and has made numerous appearances on such shows as For the People (CBS); U.S.A.-Theatre (NET); NY Television Theatre (NET); Children Talk To (NBC); Girl Talk (ABC); and the Mike Douglas Show (ABC).

Other Activities. She has lectured at Hamilton Coll.; Boston Coll.; Baylor Univ.; Yale Univ.; Brown Univ.; Columbia Univ.; Univ. of Washington; at The Institute, a symposium under the aegis of the Univ. of the State of New York; and was appointed professor of dramatic art at State Univ. of N.Y. (1966).

She has given a one-woman dramatized program of poetry by her late husband, John V. A. Weaver, entitled *Finders in the Dark* (1960–to date). Miss Wood has also served on the permanent advisory drama panel of the US State Department's cultural presentations program.

Published Works. She wrote *The Flying Prince*, in collaboration with Eugene Wood (1927); wrote *The Splendid Gypsy; John Drew* (1928); *The Star Wagon* (1936); the autobiography, *How Young You Look; Memoirs of a Middle-Sized Actress* (1941); and *Arts and Flowers* (1963).

She has written articles for *Theatre Arts* Magazine, *The Saturday Evening Post*, *Good Housekeeping*, *The Ford Times*, the NY *Sunday Times*, and *This Week*.

Awards. Miss Wood received the Order of St. Olaf from King Haakon VII of Norway (1951) for her performance as Mama in the television series, I Remember Mama; the Kelsey Allen Award (1964).

She received the following honorary degrees: L.H.D. (Lake Erie Coll., 1950); L.H.D. (Hobart Coll., 1959); and D.A.L. (Hamilton Coll., 1964); and the honorary degree of DAL from Mt. Holyoke Coll. (1967). She was named fellow of Timothy Dwight Coll., Yale Univ. (1967); and of Westminster Choir Coll. (1969); and received an ATA Citation (1974) for distinguished service to the theatre.

Recreation. "See my book *Arts and Flowers*".

WOOD, PETER. Director. b. Oct. 8, 1927, Colyton, Devonshire, England, to Frank and Lucy Eleanor (Meeson) Wood. Educated public school, Taunton, Somerset; Downing Coll., Cambridge Univ. Served Royal Air Force, 1946–48.

Theatre. Mr. Wood gained his first experience in amateur productions at Cambridge Univ.; engaged by H. M. Tennent's, he spent nearly three years as assistant stage manager and understudy in *Seagulls Over Sorrento;* made his directorial debut with *The Moment of Truth* (Arts Th. Club, Cambridge, 1954); directed for the Worthing Repertory Th.; was resident director of the Oxford Playhouse (1955–56); next, was appointed resident director of the Arts Th. Club (London, 1956), where he staged the double-bill *The Bald Prima Donna* and *The New Tenant* (Nov. 1956), marking both his West End debut and that of Ionesco in England; there, subsequently directed *No Laughing Matter* (Jan. 1957); and *The Iceman Cometh* (Jan. 1958; transferred to the Winter Garden, Mar. 1958). He directed the original production of *The Birthday Party* (Lyric, Hammersmith, May 1958); for the Old Vic Co., *Mary Stuart* (Edinburgh Fest., Sept. 1958; transferred to Old Vic, London, Sept. 1958); *Who's Your Father* (Cambridge, Dec. 1958); *As You Like It* (Shakespeare Festival, Stratford, Ontario, Canada, June 1959); directed the replacement company of *Five Finger Exercise* (Comedy, London, Sept. 1959), when the original company moved to New York; *The Winter's Tale* (Shakespeare Mem. Th., Stratford-upon-Avon, Aug. 1961); *The Devils* (Aldwych, London, Feb. 2, 1961); and *Hamlet* (Shakespeare Mem. Th., Stratford-upon-Avon, Apr. 11, 1961).

He directed *The Private Ear* and *The Public Eye* (Globe, London, May 10, 1962); The Beggar's Opera (Aldwych, July 16, 1963); made his US debut with *The Private Ear* and *The Public Eye* (Morosco, N.Y.C., Oct. 9, 1963); directed *The Master Builder* (Old Vic, London, June 9, 1964); *Carving a Statue* (Haymarket, Sept. 17, 1964); *Poor Richard* (Helen Hayes Th., N.Y.C., Dec. 2, 1964); a touring production of *Loot* (England, 1965); the National Theatre's production of *Love for Love* (Old Vic, London, Oct. 20, 1965); *Incident at Vichy* (Phoenix, Jan. 26, 1966); again directed *Love for Love* (Expo '67, Montreal; and Toronto, Canada, 1967); the replacement company of *White Liars* and *Black Comedy* (Lyric, London, Feb. 21, 1967); *Design for Living* (Ahmanson, Los Angeles, 1971); for the National Th., *Jumpers* (Old Vic, London, Feb. 2, 1972; Kennedy Ctr., Washington, D.C., Feb. 19, 1974; and Billy Rose Th., N.Y.C., Apr. 22, 1974); *Macbeth* (Ahmanson, Los Angeles, Jan. 28, 1975); and *Travesties* (Aldwych, London, June 10, 1974; and Ethel Barrymore Th., N.Y.C., Oct. 30, 1975).

Films. Mr. Wood directed *In Search of Gregory* (U, 1970).

Television. From 1957–74, Mr. Wood directed over twenty plays on television, including *Hamlet* (NBC, 1970); and *Long Day's Journey into Night* (ABC, 1970), based upon the Old Vic production.

Discography. He has directed for both Caedmon Records and RCA.

Awards. His production of *The Iceman Cometh* received the *Evening Standard* Award (1958); and he received an Arts Council Grant (1958) to study methods of production in France, Germany, and Switzerland.

Recreation. Travel.

WOODBURY, LAEL J. Director, producer, educator. b. July 3, 1927, Fairview, Idaho, to Raymond and Wanda (Dawson) Woodbury. Father, businessman; mother, nurse. Grad. Utah State Univ., B.S. 1952; Brigham Young Univ., M.A. 1953; Univ. of Illinois, Ph.D. 1954. Married July 30, 1944, to Laurabelle Young (dec. Jan. 11, 1949); one daughter; married Dec. 19, 1949, to Margaret Swenson, actress; two sons, one daughter. Served USN, 1942–46; rank, Electrician's Mate 1/c. Member of ATA (chmn., Natl. Comm. on Royalties, 1972–to date); Rocky Mt. Th. Conf.; (pres., 1959); SAA; Western Speech Communications Assn. (chmn., Drama Dir., 1971). Address: 1303 Locust Lane, Provo, UT 84601, tel. (801) 374-5581.

Theatre.

Mr. Woodbury became dean, College of Fine Arts and Communications, Brigham Young Univ. in 1973. He began his academic career as a teaching assistant, Univ. of Illinois (1953); was associate professor, Brigham Young Univ. (1954–61); assistant professor, Bowling Green State Univ. (1961–62); guest professor, Colorado State Coll. (Summer 1962); and associate professor, Univ. of Iowa (1962–65). He became professor of speech and dramatics and chairman of his department, Brigham Young Univ., in 1965 and was associate dean, College of Fine Arts and Communications at Brigham

Young (1965–73).

He first performed as Bezano in *He Who Gets Slapped* (USAC Th., Logan, Utah, 1949); subsequently toured as the Gentleman Caller in *The Glass Menagerie* with The Proscenium Players in Utah (Winter 1952); and directed the Las Vegas (Nev.) Centennial Pageant (Helldorado Stadium, 1955).

Mr. Woodbury was co-producer (1961–63) at the Ledges Playhouse, Lansing, Mich., and producer (1963–65). In 1963 at the Ledges Playhouse, he appeared as Henri in *My Three Angels* (June 18); Beverly Carlton in *The Man Who Came to Dinner* (June 25); Petruchio in *The Taming of the Shrew* (July 2); directed *Arsenic and Old Lace* (July 9); produced *Blithe Spirit* (July 16); directed and appeared as Biff in *Death of a Salesman* (July 23); directed *Charley's Aunt* (July 30); *Golden Fleecing* (Aug. 6); played Mr. Paravicini in, and directed *The Mousetrap* (Aug. 13); and directed *Out of the Frying Pan* (Aug. 20).

Television. Mr. Woodbury was narrator of the series Speaking of Music (ABC).

Published Works. Mr. Woodbury wrote "The American Theatre's First Star: Thomas Abthorpe Cooper." *The Theatre Annual, XV* (1957–58); *Play Production Handbook* (1959); "Director's Foreword," *BYU Studies, II* (1960); "The Externalization of Emotion," *Educational Theatre Journal, XII* (October 1960); "Natural Acting," *Western Speech, XXIV* (Fall 1960); "The Director's Use of Rhythm," *Educational Theatre Journal, XIV* (March 1962); "A Theatre of Involvement!," *The Ohio Speech Journal, I* (1962); "How To Steal a Scene," *Players Magazine, XXXIV* (Feb. 1963); "Death on the Romantic Stage," *The Quarterly Journal of Speech, XLIX* (Feb. 1963); "A New Mormon Theatre," *BYU Studies, X* (Autumn 1969); "Mormonism and the Commercial Theatre," *BYU Studies, XII* (Winter 1972). He also has written numerous reviews of books on theatrical subjects for *Choice, Books for College Libraries,* and he was associate editor of *Mormon Arts,* vol. I (Provo, Utah, 1972).

Awards. Mr. Woodbury received a University Fellowship from the Univ. of Illinois (1953–54), and he received the $3,000 Karl G. Maeser creative arts award from Brigham Young University (1971).

Recreation. "Research into history of American Theatre — especially acting styles.".

WOODMAN, WILLIAM. Artistic director. b. Oct. 1, 1932, New York City, to William E. and Ruth (Cornman) Woodman, Sr. Grad. Deerfield (Mass.) Acad., 1950; Hamilton College, B.A. 1954; Columbia Univ., M.F.A. 1959. Served in US Army, 1954–56. Married June 5, 1971, to Elizabeth Roberts. Member of SSD&C; AGMA; Arts Club of Chicago; Cliff Dwellers of Chicago. Address: (home) 1340 North Astor St., Chicago, IL 60610, tel. (312) 266-2350; (bus.) 200 South Columbus Dr., Chicago, IL 60603, tel. (312) 236-3238.

Theatre. Mr. Woodman became artistic director of the Goodman Theatre Center, Chicago, Ill., in 1973. He had previously directed at several other regional theatres; had been on the drama faculty, Juilliard School, N.Y.C. (1968–73); and had directed the new playwrights program, O'Neill Memorial Center, New London, Conn. (July 1969).

Mr. Woodman made his theatrical debut as a child, playing Sneezy in *Snow White* (Rye Country Day School, Rye, N.Y., Oct. 1939). As an adult, he was assistant stage manager for a touring production of *Much Ado About Nothing* (Dec. 1957); and he directed *Tall Story* (Robin Hood Th., Arden, Del., July 1961); *The Night of the Iguana* (Cleveland Play House, Oct. 1963); *The Imaginary Invalid* (Hartford Stage Co., Hartford, Conn., Oct. 23, 1964); *A Midsummer Night's Dream* (Front St. Th., Memphis, Tenn., Apr. 8, 1965); *Tartuffe* (Cleveland Play House, Cleveland, Ohio, Oct. 6, 1965); *Carved in Snow* (Cleveland Play House, Nov. 10, 1965); *Becket* (Front St. Th., Memphis, Mar. 17, 1966); *Antony and Cleopatra* (Front St. Th., Apr. 4, 1966); *The Bat* (Barter Th., Abingdon, Va., June 21, 1966); *The Miser* (Cleveland Play House, Sept. 28, 1966); *The Skin of Our Teeth* (Cleveland Play House, Nov. 2, 1966); *The Wood Demon* (Master Th., N.Y.C., Mar. 1967); and *The Tavern* (Craft Ave. Th., Pittsburgh, Pa., Sept. 30, 1967), He directed *Night of the Dunce* (Actors Th. of Louisville, Ky., Apr. 4, 1968); was stage director for the Lake Erie Opera production of *Capriccio* (Severance Hall, Cleveland, Ohio, Sept. 1968); directed *Othello* (Loretto-Hilton Repertory Th., St. Louis, Mo., Jan. 1970); *Hamlet* (American Shakespeare Festival, Stratford, Conn., Mar. 1970); and the world premiere of the opera *Huckleberry Finn* (Juilliard Opera Center, N.Y.C., May 1971). He also directed *Marat/Sade* (Loretto-Hilton Repertory, Jan. 1972); *The Rivals* (Walnut St. Th., Philadelphia, Mar. 1972); *Twentieth Century* (Goodman Th., Chicago, Ill., Feb. 18, 1973); was stage director for the opera *La Dafne* (Festival of Two Worlds, Spoleto, Italy, June 1973); directed *The Freedom of the City* (world premiere, Goodman Th., Oct. 9, 1973; Alvin Th., N.Y.C., Feb. 17, 1974); and *Henry IV* (Goodman Th., Mar. 29, 1974).

WOODRUFF, JOHN R. Educator. b. June 14, 1909, Akron, Ohio. Grad. Oberlin College, B.A. 1933; Western Reserve Univ., M.A. 1937; Cornell Univ., Ph.D. 1949. Married 1959; four children. Member of Natl. Th. Conf.; U.S. Institute Th. Technology; AETA. Address: Carleton Arena Theatre, Carleton College, Northfield, MN 55057.

Since 1957, Mr. Woodruff has been professor of drama at Carleton College. Previously he had been professor of drama at Tufts Univ. (1940–57).

He is a member of the board of directors of the Tyrone Guthrie Th., Minneapolis (1970–to date).

WOODS, DONALD. Actor. b. Dec. 2, 1906, Brandon, Manitoba, Canada, to William and Margaret Jane (Hoag) Woods. Father, shoe merchant. Grad. Burbank (California) H.S.; attended Univ. of California at Berkeley. Married Nov. 1, 1927, to Josephine Van der Horck; one son, one daughter. Relative in theatre: brother, Russ Conway, actor. Member of AEA; AFTRA; SAG (bd. of dir., 1937–43); The Lambs; Los Angeles Tennis Club; Racquet Club; Palm Springs (Cal.) bd. of realtors; Phi Delta Theta.

Since 1970, Mr. Woods has been a real estate broker with the Eadie Adams Realty Co., Palm Springs, Calif. 985 La Jolla Rd., Palm Springs, CA 92262.

Pre-Theatre. Theatre usher, factory worker, post office employee.

Theatre. Mr. Woods' first professional work was with a stock company in Salt Lake City, Utah, following his high school graduation. His N.Y.C. debut was in the role of Eric Hope in *Singapore* (48 St. Th., Nov. 14, 1932). Subsequent appearances include his role as Roland Pierce in *Quiet, Please!* (Guild, Nov. 8, 1940); as Johannes Rosmer in *Rosmersholm* (4th St. Th., Apr. 11, 1962); Ben Nichols in the pre-Bway tryout of *There Must Be a Pony* (Summer tour, 1962); Ashley Brewster in "Damn You, Scarlett O'Hara" and Harrison Ross in "All My Pretty Ones," a double bill entitled *Riverside Drive* (Th. de Lys, N.Y.C., Feb. 4, 1964); and Charles Lacey in *One by One* (Belasco, Dec. 1, 1964).

He has played more than 200 roles in stock and on tour, including Chico in *Seventh Heaven,* Simon in *Counsellor-at-Law,* the Father in *Street Scene,* Elyot Chase in *Private Lives,* the Fighter in *All My Sons,* Charlie Marsden in *Strange Interlude,* David Slater in *The Moon Is Blue,* and has appeared in *Point of No Return* (1956); *Dial "M" for Murder* (1957); *Goodbye, Again* (1958); *Holiday for Lovers* (1960); and *For Love or Money* (1964).

Recently, he has made guest appearances in regional repertory theatres, including (at the Goodman Th., Chicago) the part of Bishop of Chichester in *Soldiers* (Oct. 20, 1969), Martin Vanderhof in *You Can't Take it with You* (Dec. 1, 1969), Malvolio in *Twelfth Night* (Nov. 30, 1970), and the Prosecutor in *Assassination, 1865* (Oct. 27, 1971); at the Seattle Rep. Th. (Wash.) he appeared in *Child's Play* (Jan. 3, 1973), portrayed Horace Vandergelder in *The Matchmaker* (Mar. 5, 1975; and on tour in Washington through Apr. 19, 1975).

Films. Since his debut as Stan in *As the Earth Turns* (WB, 1934), Mr. Woods has made approximately sixty films, including *A Tale of Two Cities* (MGM, 1935); *The Story of Louis Pasteur* (1936); *Anthony Adverse* (WB, 1936); *The Girl from Mexico* (RKO, 1939); *Mexican Spitfire* (RKO, 1940); *Mexican Spitfire Out West* (RKO, 1940); *I Was a Prisoner on Devil's Island* (Col., 1941); *The Gay Sisters* (1942); *Corregidor* (1943); *Watch on the Rhine* (WB, 1943); *The Bridge of San Luis Rey* (UA, 1944); *Hollywood Canteen* (1944); *Night and Day* (1946); *Kissin' Cousins* (MGM, 1964); *Moment to Moment* (U, 1966); *Door-to-Door Maniac* (Amer. Int., 1966); *Tammy and the Millionaire* (U, 1967); *A Time to Sing* (MGM, 1968); and *True Grit* (Par., 1969).

Television and Radio. Mr. Woods played Dr. Leslie Foster on the radio series Those We Love (NBC, CBS, 1937–43) and was host of the Woolworth Hour (CBS, 1953–54).

On television he has appeared on Fireside Th. (NBC, 1952–53); Robert Montgomery Presents (NBC); US Steel Hour (ABC); Pulitzer Prize Th. (ABC); Philco Television Playhouse (NBC); Alcoa Presents (ABC); GE Th. (CBS); Bat Masterson (ABC); The Rebel (ABC); Laramie (ABC); The Law and Mr. Jones (ABC); Ben Casey (ABC); Trailmaster (ABC); Wagon Train (NBC); Thriller (NBC); Stoney Burke (ABC); Sam Benedict (NBC); Deputy (ABC); as John Brent (Tammy's father) in the Tammy series (ABC, 1965–66); The Roaring 20's (ABC); Wild, Wild West (CBS); Bonanza (NBC); and Coronet Blue (CBS).

Recreation. Tennis.

WOODWARD, EDWARD. Actor. b. Edward Albert Arthur Woodward, June 1, 1930, Croydon, Surrey, England, to Edward Oliver and Violet (Smith) Woodward. Father, metal worker. Attended Kingston Coll., Hook, Surrey, England, 1944–46; RADA, London (scholarship), 1946–47. Studied acting with Dame Irene Vanburgh at RADA, 1944–46; singing with Ernest Urbach, London, 1950–52. Married July 1952 to Venetia Mary Collett; two sons, one daughter. Member of AEA; British AEA; British Actors' Church Union. Address: c/o Eric Glass, Ltd., 28 Berkeley Square, London W.1, England tel. May 7162-5; c/o Frank Cooper Associates, 680 Fifth Ave., New York, NY tel. (212) PL 7-1100; Hollywood, CA 90028, tel. (213) CR 4-5971.

Pre-Theatre. Clerk.

Theatre. Mr. Woodward made his stage debut in England at age five as a drummer in the back row of a school concert (1935); his professional debut as walk-on in *A Kiss for Cinderella,* for which he was also assistant stage manager (Farnham Repertory Th., Surrey, England, Dec. 1946); appeared (1947–50) with repertory companies (Perth, St. Andrews, Scotland; Guildford, Oxford, England), playing classic and modern roles; toured India and Ceylon as Horatio in *Hamlet* and Cassio in *Othello* (opened in a movie house in Hyderabad, India, Aug. 16, 1951); appeared in many roles with the Guildford Repertory Th. (England, Aug. 4, 1952); and the Croydon Repertory Th., where he played 36 leading roles (Surrey, Apr. 6, 1953). He made his London debut as Ralph Stokes in *Where There's a Will . . !* (Garrick, June 17, 1954); toured Germany and France in a revue *Intimacy at 8:30* (opened Jan. 10, 1955); after which he joined (Feb. 24, 1955) the London production of *Intimacy at 8:30* (Criterion, Apr. 29, 1954), as understudy; appeared in the revue *Happy Returns* (New Watergate, May 19, 1955); as John Brooke in *A Girl Called Jo* (Piccadilly, Dec. 15, 1955); Tim in *Salad Days* (Vaudeville, London, Dec. 15, 1955; Olympia Th., Dublin, Ireland, Dec. 29, 1955); and John Evans in *Doctor in the House* (Victoria Palace, London, July 30, 1956).

Mr. Woodward returned to the Guildford (England) Repertory Th. for a season of stock, appearing in *Jessica* (Mar. 29, 1957), touring England as the Reverend John in *The Telescope* (opened May 3, 1957), and returning to Guildford to finish the season (June 14, 1957); appeared at the Edinburgh (Scotland) Festival as Owen Tudor in *The Queen and the Welshman* (St. Mary's Th., Aug. 20, 1957; Lyric,

Hammersmith, London, Nov. 7, 1957); played for a season at the Shakespeare Memorial Th. (Stratford-upon-Avon) as Mercutio in *Romeo and Juliet* (Apr. 8, 1958), Laertes in *Hamlet* (June 3, 1958), and Claudio in *Much Ado About Nothing* (Aug. 26, 1958); toured USSR with the company as Mercutio in *Romeo and Juliet* and Laertes in *Hamlet* (Palace of Culture, Leningrad, Dec. 12, 1959).

He appeared in London in the revue *The Art of Living* (Criterion, Aug. 18, 1960); played Percy Winthram in a pre-London tryout of *Rattle of a Simple Man* (Richmond Th., Oct. 2, 1961); toured in *Our Little Life* (opened Olympia Th., Dublin, Ireland, Nov. 13, 1961); played Percy in *Rattle of a Simple Man*, which he directed (Alexander Th., Johannesburg, South Africa, Dec. 18, 1961); appeared as Haggis in the musical *Scapa* (Adelphi, London, Mar. 8, 1962); Percy in *Rattle of a Simple Man* (Garrick, Sept. 19, 1962); at the Nottingham Playhouse, England, played Lucio in *Measure for Measure* (Sept. 22, 1965) and Elyot Chase in *Private Lives* (Sept. 29, 1965); appeared as Captain Yule in *The High Bid* (Mermaid, London, Oct. 18, 1967); Sydney Carton in the musical *Two Cities* (Palace, Feb. 1969); and joined (1969) the National Theatre to play Flamineo in *The White Devil* and Cyrano in *Cyrano de Bergerac* (Oct. 27, 1970).

Mr. Woodward made his N.Y.C. debut as Percy Winthram in *Rattle of a Simple Man* (Booth, Apr. 17, 1963); played Charles in *High Spirits* (Alvin, N.Y.C., Apr. 7, 1964); and Jason Beckman in *The Best Laid Plans* (Brooks Atkinson Th., Mar. 25, 1966).

Films. Mr. Woodward played Ralph Stokes in *Where There's a Will . . !* (England, 1954); Clement in *Becket* (Par., 1964); Thompson in *The File on the Golden Goose* (UA, 1969); appeared in *Murders in the Rue Morgue* (Amer. Intl., 1971); *Julius Caesar* (Amer. Intl., 1971); as Captain Haldane in *Young Winston* (Col., 1972); and Inspector Milton in *Sitting Target* (MGM, 1972).

Television. Mr. Woodward made his London debut in a vaudeville show (ITV, Aug. 1955); subsequently appeared on more than two hundred shows, including the Emergency Ward 10 series (ATV); *Fabulous Money Make* (ABC); *Julius Caesar* (BBC); the Sky Port series (Granada); *Major Barbara; A Dream Divided;* in the title role of the Callan series (ABC-TV, Manchester, England, 1967–70); and the Edward Woodward Show (Thames-TV, 1972). In the US, he has appeared on The Defenders series (CBS).

Awards. In England, Mr. Woodward has received the Variety Award for Best Performance in a Musical (for *Two Cities*, 1969); and for his performances in the Callan series, both the Television Actor of the Year Award (1969) and the *Sun* Top Television Actor of the Year Award (1969).

Recreation. Boating, swimming, reading, and acting.

WORK, WILLIAM. Executive, director, educator. b. Aug. 10, 1923, Ithaca, N.Y., to Paul and Grace N. (Nicholas) Work. Parents, educators. Grad. Ithaca (N.Y.) H.S., 1940; Cornell Univ., A.B. 1946; Univ. of Wisconsin, M.A. 1948; Ph.D. 1954. Married Nov. 26, 1960, to Jane Magruder, educator; one son. Member of SCA; AETA (bd. of dir., 1961–63); AAUP; ASAE; SAES; NEA; Central States Speech Assn. (vice-pres., 1962–63); Pi Kappa Phi. Address: (home) 48 Lefurgy Ave., Hastings-on-Hudson, NY 10706, tel. (914) GR 8-0154; (bus.) Speech Association of America, Statler Hilton Hotel, New York, NY 10001, tel. (212) PE 6-6625.

Since 1963, he has been executive secretary of the Speech Communication Association.

During 1946–47, Mr. Work was theatre assistant for the Kalamazoo (Mich.) Civic Players, serving in several technical capacities, as well as acting in six productions. He acted and directed at the Dorset (Vt.) Summer Th. (1947). From 1948–50, he was instructor in speech and associate theatre director at Purdue Univ., where he directed and designed student productions. He was director of Th. at Eastern Michigan Univ. from 1951–63 (instructor, 1951–53; assistant professor, 1953–55; associate professor, 1955–58; professor in speech, 1958–63), where he directed student productions.

He was administrative assistant at the Cragsmoor (N.Y.) Playhouse (Summer 1956); and visiting professor of theatre at Southern Illinois Univ. (Summer 1959).

Published Works. Mr. Work has contributed articles to *Educational Theatre Journal, Quarterly Journal of Speech, Players Magazine;* and was drama editor of *The Speech Teacher*, 1962–63.

Awards. He received the Cornell Univ. Prize for One Act Plays (1946); and the Alex Drier Prize (1962) for a radio script which he wrote, produced, and directed for the American Foundation for the Blind.

Recreation. Travel, music, reading, tennis.

WORLEY, JO ANNE. Actress, singer. b. Sept. 6, 1937, Lowell, Ind., to Joseph L. and Rose I. (Gardner) Worley. Father, farmer, house painter. Grad. Lowell (Ind.) H.S., 1955; attended Midwestern Univ., 1955–57; Los Angeles City Coll., 1957–58. Studied theatre at Pasadena (Calif.) Playhouse, 1958; voice with Vivian Long, Los Angeles, 1959–60; drama with Mike Eagan, N.Y.C., 1961. Married May 11, 1975, to Roger Perry, actor. Member of AEA; AFTRA; SAG; AGMA.

Pre-Theatre. Secretary, switchboard operator.

Theatre. Miss Worley made her professional debut as the "Talking Lady" in the revue, *Laff Capades of 1959* (Le Grande Comedy Th., Hollywood, Calif., Mar. 1959); subsequently joined the *Billy Barnes Revue* (Las Palmas, Hollywood, Calif., June 1959; Fontainebleau Hotel, Miami, Fla., Oct. 1959; Ritz Th., Los Angeles, Calif., Dec. 1959); and appeared in the revue *Billy Barnes People* (Las Palmas, Jan., 1961; Royale, N.Y.C., June 12, 1961).

Miss Worley appeared in stock, playing Dorothy in *Gentlemen Prefer Blondes* (Kenley Players, Warren and Columbus, Ohio, July 1961); also for the Kenley Players, played Lizette in *Naughty Marietta* (July 30, 1961), and Gretchen in *The Student Prince* (Aug. 28, 1961); after understudying Kaye Ballard as The Incomparable Rosalie in *Carnival!* (Imperial, N.Y.C., Apr. 13, 1961), played that role in the national tour (opened Rochester Aud., N.Y., Dec. 7, 1961); appeared in the revue *Put It in Writing* (Happy Medium Cabaret, Chicago, June 28, 1962); stood by for Carol Channing in *Hello, Dolly!* (St. James, N.Y.C., Jan. 16, 1964); appeared in the Lincoln-Mercury industrial show (Sept. 1964); the revue *That Thing at the Cherry Lane (Cherry Lane Th., N.Y.C., May 18, 1965); played Angelique Pinglet in Hotel Passionato* (E. 74 St. Th., Oct. 22, 1965); appeared in the revue *The Mad Show* (New, Jan. 9, 1966; P.J.'s Th., Hollywood, 1966–67); and performed in other stock shows including *Gypsy* (Kenley Players, Summer 1969; Sacramento Music Circus, Summer 1975); and *Goodbye, Charlie!* (Arlington Park Th., Summer 1972).

Films. Miss Worley appeared as a "beatnik" in Moon Pilot (Buena Vista, 1962).

Television. Miss Worley was a regular performer on Rowan and Martin's Laugh-In (NBC, Jan. 1968 through 1970), and has been seen on the On Broadway Tonight series (CBS); the Merv Griffin Show (Ind.; CBS); Girl Talk (ABC); appeared on *American Humor: Sick, Black and Blue* (Wednesday Review, Educ., June 22, 1966); was a regular on the Las Vegas Show series (Ind., 1966–67); appeared on the Dobie Gillis show (ABC); This is Tom Jones (ABC); as well as other talk and variety shows. She appeared in a dramatic role in *The Feminist and the Fuzz* (ABC-TV Movie, Jan. 26, 1971).

Night Clubs. She appeared in *Playgirls of 1960* (Statler Hilton Hotel, N.Y.C.); Bimbo's 365 Club (San Francisco); Upstairs at the Duplex (N.Y.C.); The Americana Hotel (N.Y.C.); the Down Stage Room (Chicago); the Bon Soir (N.Y.C.); the Statler Hilton (Los Angeles); etc.

WORTH, BILLIE. Actress. b. Wilhelmino Rothmund, Oct. 20, 1917, Rome, N.Y. to Otto and Grace (McDermott) Rothmund. Father, haberdasher. Grad. Professional Children's Sch., N.Y.C., 1934. Studied voice with Ole Olsen, 1950–51; dance with Nanette Charisse, 1945. Married Oct. 24, 1935, to Donald Burr, actor, director; one son, one daughter. Relatives in theatre: brother, Coley Worth, actor; sister, Grace Worth, actress, singer; niece, Carol Worth, actress, singer; niece, Penny Worth, actress, singer, dancer. Member of AEA; AFTRA. Address: R.D., Long Valley, NJ tel. (201) 876-4100.

Pre-Theatre. Tennis player.

Theatre. Miss Worth first performed as a dancer in *Good News* (Motion picture houses, June 1932); subsequently danced in *Let 'Em Eat Cake* (Imperial Th., N.Y.C., Oct. 21, 1933), also touring in it; *Thumbs Up* (St. James, Dec. 27, 1934); and on Bobby Sanford's Showboat (Hudson River, N.Y. Summer 1935).

She toured England and Scotland as Bonnie in *Anything Goes* (1936); and Australia and New Zealand in *Swing Along, Over She Goes, Jill Darling, Nice Goin'*, and *No! No! Nanette!* (1937).

She danced in the Aquacade at the N.Y. World's Fair (May 1939); in *Very Warm for May* (Alvin, N.Y.C., Nov. 17, 1939); played Dottie in *Higher and Higher* (Shubert, Apr. 4, 1940); danced in vaudeville (State Lake, Chicago, Ill., Mar. 1941; Loew's State, N.Y.C., May 1941); in a stock production of *Two for the Show* (Maplewood Th., N.J., June 1941); and *Rio Rita* (Paper Mill Playhouse, Millburn, N.J., 1942).

She appeared in *Bright Lights* (Forrest, N.Y.C., Sept. 16, 1943); danced in *Jackpot* (Alvin, Jan. 13, 1944); and at the Paper Mill Playhouse, played Tine in *The Red Mill* (May 1944), Siddonie in *The Prince of Pilsen* (July 1944), appeared in *Sally* (Aug. 1944), and played Susan in *The Desert Song* (Sept. 1944).

Miss Worth appeared in the revue, *The Seven Lively Arts* (Ziegfeld, N.Y.C., Dec. 7, 1944); *Rosalie* (Paper Mill Playhouse, June 1946); *Apple Blossom*, and *The Cat and the Fiddle* (St. Louis Municipal Opera, Mo. July 1947); as Tina in *Rio Rita*, and in *Rose Marie* (Paper Mill Playhouse, Sept. 1947).

She played Winnie in *Annie Get Your Gun* (Dallas State Fair Park Aud., Tex., Oct. 1947), later touring in it as Annie Oakley (opened, Shubert, Chicago, Ill., July 1948; closed Shubert, Detroit, Mich., May 1949); appeared with the Detroit (Mich.) Civic Light Opera Co. (Masonic Temple, Oct. 1949); and was standby (Apr. 1950–Feb. 1951) for Mary Martin as Nellie Forbush in *South Pacific* (Majestic, N.Y.C. Apr. 7, 1949).

She played Araminta in *Courtin' Time* (Natl., June 13, 1951); Adams in *Call Me Madam* (Coliseum, London, Mar. 15, 1952); Liza Elliott in *Lady in the Dark* (Pittsburgh Light Opera Co., Pa., Aug. 1953); Sally Adams in *Call Me Madam* (Kansas City Light Opera Co., Mo., June 1954); Dorothy in *Gentlemen Prefer Blondes* (St. Louis Municipal Opera, June 1954); and Nellie Forbush in *South Pacific* (Guthsville Playhouse, Allentown, Pa., May 1955; Music Circus, Sacramento, Calif., June 1955; Valley Forge Music Fair, Devon, Pa. Aug.–Sept. 1955).

She was the standby for Mary Martin in the title role in *Peter Pan* (Winter Garden, N.Y.C., Oct. 20, 1954), and played this role in stock (Sacramento Light Opera Co., June 1957); played Sally Adams in *Call Me Madam* (Sacramento Light Opera Co., Calif., June 1957; Meadowbrook Dinner Th., Cedar Grove, N.J., Jan. 1958; Oakdale Musical Th., Wallingford, Conn., Aug. 1959; Warwick Musical Th., R.I., Aug. 1959); and Martina in the pre-Bway tryout of *The Carefree Heart* (opened Cass, Detroit, Mich., Sept. 30, 1957; closed Hanna, Cleveland, Ohio, Oct. 26, 1957).

She played Liz in *Happy Hunting* (Lambertville Music Circus, N.J., May 1958; Meadowbrook Dinner Th., Apr. 1959); Ella Peterson in *Bells Are Ringing* (Lambertville Music Circus, June 1959); the title role in *Auntie Mame* (Meadowbrook Dinner Th., May 1960); Annie Oakley in *Annie Get Your Gun* (Charlotte Light Opera Co., N.Y.C., July 1961); and toured England and Scotland as Mary in *Yankee*

Doodle (Dec. 1961).

Now retired from the professional theatre, Miss Worth is a real estate broker and directs musicals for New Jersey amateur theatre groups.

Television. Miss Worth has appeared on the Bert Parks Show (ABC, 1950); in *The Tin Wedding* (US Steel Hour, CBS, 1953); and on the US Steel Hour (ABC, Nov. 1954).

Night Clubs. She performed at the Grosvenor House (London, 1935).

WORTH, IRENE. Actress. b. June 23, 1916, Nebraska. Studied acting with Elsie Fogerty, London, 1944. Grad. Univ. of California at Los Angeles, B.E. 1937. Address: 38 Ladbroke Sq., London W. 11, England.

Pre-Theatre. Teacher.

Theatre. Miss Worth made her professional debut as Fenella in *Escape Me Never* (on tour, 1942); made her N.Y.C. debut as Cecily Hardin in *The Two Mrs. Carrolls* (Booth Th., Aug. 3, 1943). She made her London debut as Elsie in *The Time of Your Life* (Lyric, Hammersmith, Feb. 14, 1946); and succeeded (Apr. 1946) Pamela Alan as Miss Phillipa Forna in *This Way to the Tomb!* (Mercury, Oct. 11, 1945); played Annabelle Jones in *Love Goes to Press* (Embassy, June 18, 1946); and toured the provinces as Ilona Szabo in *The Play's the Thing* (Oct. 1946). She played Donna Pascuala in *Drake's Drum* (Embassy, London, Dec. 18, 1946); repeated her role in *The Play's the Thing* (Lyric, Hammersmith, Apr. 15, 1947); toured the provinces in *Return Journey* (Oct. 1947).

She played Olivia Brown in *Love in Idleness* ("Q," Feb. 1948); Mary Dalton in *Native Son* (Bolton's, Feb. 20, 1948); and the title role in *Lucrece* (Bolton's, Apr. 15, 1948).

She succeeded (July 1948) Leueen McGrath as Eileen Perry in *Edward, My Son* (His Majesty's, May 30, 1947); toured as Lady Fortrose in *Home Is Tomorrow* before appearing in the role in London (Cambridge, Nov. 4, 1948). She appeared as Olivia Raines in *Champagne for Delilah* (New, June 9, 1949); and played Celia Coplestone in *The Cocktail Party* at the Edinburgh (Scotland) Festival (premiere Aug. 1949), in N.Y.C. (Henry Miller's Th., Jan. 21, 1950), and followed (July 1950) Margaret Leighton in the role in the London production (New, May 3, 1950).

With the Old Vic (Old Vic Th.), she played Desdemona in *Othello* (Oct. 31, 1951), Helena in *A Midsummer Night's Dream* (Dec. 26, 1951), and Catherine de Vausselles in *The Other Heart* (Apr. 15, 1952); toured South Africa with the company in these roles and as Lady Macbeth in *Macbeth* (1952). After appearing at the Old Vic Th. as Portia in *The Merchant of Venice* (Jan. 6, 1953), she appeared at the Stratford (Ontario, Canada) Shakespeare Festival as Helena in *All's Well That Ends Well* and Queen Margaret in *Richard III* (1953).

She played Frances Farrar in *A Day by the Sea* (Haymarket, London, Nov. 26, 1953); appeared as Argia in *The Queen and the Rebels* (Midland Th., Coventry, world premiere, Mar. 1955); played Alcestis in *A Life in the Sun* (Edinburgh Festival, Scot., 1955); and repeated her role in *The Queen and the Rebels* (Haymarket, London, Oct. 26, 1955). She played Marcella in *Hotel Paradiso* (Winter Garden, May 2, 1956); the title role in *Mary Stuart* (Phoenix, N.Y.C., Oct. 8, 1957); and Sara Callifer in *The Potting Shed* (Globe, London, Feb. 5, 1958). She repeated her role in *Mary Stuart* (Edinburgh Festival, Scotland, 1958), and at the Old Vic Th. (London, Sept. 17, 1958); at the Stratford (Ont., Can.) Shakespeare Festival, played Rosalind in *As You Like It* (June 1959).

She played Albertine Prine in *Toys in the Attic* (Hudson, N.Y.C., Feb. 25, 1960); and with the Royal Shakespeare Co. (Stratford-upon-Avon), appeared as Goneril in *King Lear* (Nov. 6, 1962), and in London (Aldwych, Dec. 12, 1962); appeared as Dr. Mathilde von Zahnd in *The Physicists* (Aldwych, 1963); Clodia Pulcher in *The Ides of March* (Haymarket, 1963); and played Goneril in *King Lear* with the Royal Shakespeare Co. in N.Y.C. (NY State Th., May 18, 1964).

Miss Worth appeared as Miss Alice in *Tiny Alice* (Billy Rose Th., N.Y.C., Dec. 29, 1964); Hilde Latymer in *A Song at Twilight* (Queen's Th., London, Apr. 14, 1966); Anne Hilgay in *Shadows of the Evening*, and Anna-Mary Conklin in *Come Into the Garden, Maude* in Noel Coward's *Suite in Three Keys* (Queen's Th., London, Apr. 25, 1966); with Sir John Gielgud performed *Men and Women of Shakespeare* in a US and South American university tour (1966–67); appeared in *Prometheus Bound* (Yale Univ., New Haven, Conn., May 1967); played Hesione Hushabye in *Heartbreak House* (Chichester Festival, England, July 1967; and Lyric, London, Nov. 1967); Iocasta in *Oedipus* (Old Vic, London, Mar. 1968); Miss Alice in *Tiny Alice* (Aldwych, London, Jan. 1970); and the title role in *Hedda Gabler* (Stratford, Ontario, Canada, June 1970).

Films. Miss Worth appeared as Leonie in *Orders to Kill* (UMP, 1958); Françoise in *The Scapegoat* (MGM, 1959); and Queen Elizabeth in *King of the Seven Seas* (1961); and appeared in *Nicholas and Alexandra* (Col., 1971).

Television and Radio. Miss Worth has performed on British radio as Eve in *The Tree* and Lady Fortrose in *Home Is Tomorrow* (1949); Celia in *The Cocktail Party* (1951); Cleopatra in *Goddess and God* (1953); Anna Petrovna in *Ivanov*, the title role in *Major Barbara*, Helena in *All's Well That Ends Well*, Argia in *The Queen and the Rebels*, and appeared on The London Forum (1954); played Karen Selby in *The Flashing Stream*, Laurencia in *Fuente Ovejuna*, the Marquise in *A Door Must Be Kept Open or Shut*, Charlotte in *The Golden Bowl*, and Isabella Andreini in *The Great Desire I Had* (1955); appeared on What Goes On and This Is Brittain (1956); played Mrs. Porella in *Man, Beast and Virtue* (1957); Lady Godiva in *Scandal at Coventry*, Baroness Munster in *The Europeans*, Portia in *The Merchant of Venice*, appeared in *Orders to Kill*, and played Rebecca West in *Rosmersholm* (1958); played Argia in *The Queen and the Rebels* (1962); appeared on Woman's Hour: Guest of the Week, and played Dr. von Zahnd in *The Physicists* (1963); and played Lucile in *Duel of Angels* (1964).

On television, she has appeared on BBC, as Hazel Crawford in *Myself a Stranger*, Leslie in *Counsel's Opinion*, and the title roles in *Antigone*, and *The Duchess of Malfi* (1949); appeared in *Dawn, Day and Night* (1951); played Anne in *William's Other Anne*, Stella in *The Lake*, and Ellida Wangel in *The Lady from the Sea* (1953); played the title roles in *Candida*, *Antigone*, and *The Duchess of Malfi* and Nurse Wayland in *The Sacred Flame* (1955); and the White Lady in *Stray Cats and Empty Bottles* (1964). She also appeared on the ATV programs as Mrs. Moon in *Mr. Kettle and Mrs. Moon* (1957), Mrs. Borkman in *John Gabriel Borkman* (1958), and Inez in *Other People's Houses* (1960). In the US, she has appeared on television in *The American* (1950), played Clytemnestra in *Prince Orestes* (1959), and Jocasta in *Oedipus* (1960); and on Canadian television, played Rachel Verney in *The Offshore Island* (CBC, 1961).

Miss Worth has been a guest on Girl Talk (ABC); did readings from *The Poems of Edith Sitwell* for Camera Three (CBS); played Miss Collins in *Portrait of a Madonna* (BBC); and Rose Fish in *Variations on a Theme* (ITV).

Awards. Miss Worth received the *Daily Mail* National Television Award for her performances in *The Lake* (1953) and *Lady from the Sea* (1954). She received the British Film Academy Award (1958) for *Orders to Kill*, and the NY Page One Award (1960) for her performance as Albertine Prince in *Toys in the Attic*.

For her performance in Tiny Alice, Miss Worth tied for first place in The Annual Variety NY Drama Critics Poll (1964–65), and the Antoinette Perry (Tony) Award (1965). She received the (London) Evening Standard Award (1966) for her performance in *Suite in Three Keys*. .

Recreation. Travel, music.

WOUK, HERMAN. Novelist, playwright. b. May 27, 1915, New York City, to Abraham Isaac and Esther (Levine) Wouk. Father, industrialist in power laundry field. Grad. Townsend Harris H.S. 1930; Columbia Coll. A.B. 1934. Married Dec. 9, 1945, to Betty Sarah Brown; three sons. Served USN, PTO, 1942–46; rank, Lt.; received four Campaign Stars; Unit Commendation Ribbon. Member of ALA, Dramatists Guild. Address: c/o Harold Matson Company, Inc., 22 E. 40th Street, New York, NY 10016, tel. (212) 679-4490.

Theatre. Mr. Wouk wrote three plays that have appeared on Bway, *The Traitor* (48 St. Th., Apr. 4, 1949); *The Caine Mutiny Court-Martial* (Plymouth, Jan. 20, 1954); and *Nature's Way* (Coronet, Oct. 15, 1957).

Films. Motion pictures based on Mr. Wouk's novels include *Slattery's Hurricane* (20th-Fox, 1949); *Her First Romance* (Col., 1951), based on *The City Boy; The Caine Mutiny* (Col., 1954); *Marjorie Morningstar* (WB, 1958); and *Youngblood Hawke* (WB, 1964).

Radio. Mr. Wouk was a scriptwriter for Fred Allen (1936–1941); wrote and produced US Treasury radio shows in bond drive as a dollar-a-year man (1941).

Other Activities. Mr. Wouk has served as visiting professor of English at Yeshiva Univ. (1953–58), on the board of trustees at the College of the Virgin Islands (1961–69); and on the board of directors of the Washington National Symphony (1969–71).

Published Works. Mr. Wouk wrote the novels *Aurora Dawn* (1947); *The City Boy* (1948); *The Caine Mutiny* (1951); *Marjorie Morningstar* (1955); *Youngblood Hawke* (1962); *Don't Stop the Carnival* (1965); *The Winds of War* (1971); and a non-fiction work, *This Is My God* (1959).

Awards. He won the Pulitzer Prize for fiction for *The Caine Mutiny* (1952); all of his published books have been major book club choices and along with his plays, have received various literary honors abroad; he received the Columbia Univ. Medal for Excellence (1952); and honorary degrees from Yeshiva Univ. (L.H.D. 1955) and Clark Univ. (Litt.D., 1959).

WRIGHT, BOB. Actor, singer, announcer. b. 1911, Columbia, Mo. Attended Univ. of Missouri. Studied with Oscar Seagle. Married; four children. Member of AEA; AFTRA. Address: (home) Wilton, CT; (bus.) 211 W. 53rd St., New York, NY 10019.

Theatre. Mr. Wright made his debut on the operatic stage as Mephisto in *Faust* (Colony Opera Guild); subsequently appeared as Zuniga in *Carmen* (Colony Opera Guild); and as Friar Lawrence in *Romeo and Juliet* (Colony Opera Guild).

He made his first appearance on Bway in the revue, *Make Mine Manhattan* (Broadhurst, Jan. 15, 1948); succeeded Alfred Drake as Fred Graham in *Kiss Me, Kate* (New Century, Dec. 30, 1948), and toured in the national company (opened Shubert, New Haven, Conn., Sept. 17, 1951), in N.Y.C. (Bway Th., Jan. 8, 1952), and in stock (Cape Cod Melody Tent, Hyannis, Mass., June 30, 1952). He played the Mayor of New York in *Hazel Flagg* (State Fair Music Hall, Dallas, Tex., July 12, 1954); Murph in *Hit the Trail* (Mark Hellinger Th., N.Y.C., Dec. 2, 1954); Fred Graham in *Kiss Me, Kate* (Los Angeles Civic Light Opera, Calif., May 2, 1955); with the San Francisco (Calif.) Civic Light Opera, Count Eisenstein in *Rosalinda* (Curran Th., 1956); Emile de Becque in *South Pacific* (NY City Ctr., Apr. 24, 1957); Harmon Nagel in *Tall Story* (Belasco, Jan. 29, 1959); and, billed as Bob Wright, appeared as Prince Danilo in *The Merry Widow* (NY State Th., Aug. 17, 1964); Fred Graham in *Kiss Me, Kate* (NY City Ctr., Mar. 12, 1965); Capt. von Trapp in *The Sound of Music* (NY City Ctr., Apr. 26, 1967); and assumed (Martin Beck Th., Sept. 22, 1968) the title role in *Man of La Mancha* (ANTA Washington Square Th., Nov. 22, 1965); subsequently touring in it.

Films. *Tall Story* (WB, 1960).

Television and Radio. Mr. Wright performed on

the radio show Voices Down the Wind (NBC) and the serial Road to Life (CBS); made his first television appearance in *The Telephone;* was the announcer for You Are There (CBS, 1956); appeared as Count Eisenstein in *Rosalinda* (July 23, 1956); played in *The Stingiest Man in Town; The Mercer Girls; Green Hills* (Hallmark Hall of Fame, NBC); was a guest on the Today Show (NBC); and played Amadeo in *Top Secret Mission* (Mar. 26, 1958). He also appeared in Kent Cigarette commercials.

WRIGHT, EDWARD A. Educator, lecturer, actor. b. Edward Arlington Wright, Jan. 25, 1906, Mt. Pleasant, Iowa, to Fred David and Clara Ann (Holland) Wright. Father, hardware merchant. Grad. New London H.S., Iowa, 1924; State Univ. of Iowa, B.A. 1928; M.A. 1930; Univ. of London, certificate, Summers 1950 and 1960; Univ. of Calif., Los Angeles, certificate, Summers 1937 and 1938; attended Iowa Wesleyan Col., 1924–27; Univ. of Michigan, Summers 1940 and 1941. Married June 12, 1940, to Louise Wellman. Served WW II, troop entertainer with Amer. Th. Wing. Member of AEA; NTC (bd. of dir., treas., 1958–1967); AETA; ANTA; NCP; Intl. Platform Assn. (pres., 1964–66); Sigma Phi Epsilon (pres., Iowa Gamma Chapter, 1927–28, 1929–30). Address: Parklabrea Towers, 350 So. Fuller Ave., #11-C, Los Angeles, CA 90036.

From 1937–1967, Mr. Wright was chairman and professor of Theatre Arts at Denison Univ., Granville, O., where he was founder and director of the Denison Summer Th. (1947–1953). From 1967–74, he was head of the Acting Area, Dept. of Theatre Arts, at California State Univ., Long Beach, until he retired in the latter year as professor emeritus.

He has given more than 5,000 performances of a program of stories, character sketches, and impersonations throughout the US, Canada, Europe and the Far East (1922–to date); billed as "The Boy Impersonator," he toured the Midwest (1922) and the Chautauqua Summer Circuit and the Lyceum Winter Circuit as a student of Elias Day (1922–32).

From 1933–46, he acted in summer stock productions with The Farragut Players (New Hampshire, 1933, 1934); Berkeley Th. (Hollywood, Calif., 1936); Salisbury-Wright Players (Vermilion, O., 1940); Cain Park Th. (Cleveland, O., 1942–1943); The Valley Players (Holyoke, Mass., 1945, 1946); and Playhouse-on-the-Green (Worthington, O., 1963–1969).

Television and Radio. In 1945–46, while on sabbatical leave, Mr. Wright was heard over ABC, CBS, and NBC radio in Counterspy, Gang Busters, David Harum, Woman's Life, The Eternal Light, Parson Jim, Cimarron Tavern, and others; furnished BBC with a series of sketches entitled Americans You Do Not Read About in the Newspapers, which was based on characters he knew in his youth from New London, Iowa.

He also did a television series for the American Embassy in Tokyo, Japan (1959–60).

Published Works. Mr. Wright wrote the textbooks *Primer for Playgoers* (1957; rev. 1969); and *Understanding Today's Theatre* (1959; 2nd ed. 1972).

Awards. Mr. Wright received citations from the US State Dept. for entertaining troops during WW II and for taking play groups to the Far East twice and to Europe three times (Summers 1953–58); was Fulbright lecturer on theatre of the US and England in Tokyo (Japan, 1959–60); received an honorary D.F.A. degree from Iowa Wesleyan Coll. (1961); and the Edward A. Wright Th. Arts Scholarship was established at Denison Univ. by Mr. Wright's former students (1962). He also received the Certificate of Merit for distinguished service as actor, author, director, and teacher of theatre from the Dictionary of International Biography (London, 1970).

WRIGHT, LOUIS B. Library director, educator. b. Louis Booker Wright, Mar. 1, 1899, Greenwood County, S.C., to Thomas Fleming and Lena (Booker) Wright. Grad. Wofford Coll., B.A. 1920; Univ. of North Carolina, M.A. 1924, Ph.D. 1926. Married 1925, to Frances Black; one son. Served US Army, 1918. Member of MLA; Amer. Historical Assn.; Amer. Antiquarian Soc.; Amer. Philosophical Soc.; The Grolier Club; American Acad. of Arts and Sciences; Colonial Soc. of Mass.; Mass. Historical Soc.; Phi Beta Kappa Senate; History Book Club (member, editorial board); John Harvard Library (member, editorial board); Fellow of the Royal Soc. of Lit.; Royal Soc. of Arts; Royal Hist. Soc.; Guggenheim Memorial Foundation (member, advisory board; chairman, 1950–71); Inst. of Early Amer. History and Culture (member, advisory board, 1938–54); Pacific Coast Comm. for the Humanities (vice-chairman, 1946–48); Council on Library Resources, Inc. (vice-chairman, board of dir., 1956–to date); Henry Francis du Pont Winterthur Museum (board of dir., 1955–to date); Harry S. Truman Library Inst. for Natl. and Intl. Affairs (board of dir., 1956–to date); Amer. Council of Learned Societies (vice-chairman, board of dir., 1958–60). Address: (home) 3702 Leland St., Chevy Chase, MD 20015, tel. (301) 652-5509; (bus.) National Geographic Soc., Washington, DC 20036, tel. (202) 223-3426. been Consultant in History to the National Geographic Soc.

While still a student, he became a newspaper correspondent and city editor for the Greenwood *Index-Journal* (1918–23). After receiving his Ph.D. degree, he became an instructor of English at the Univ. of North Carolina (1926), assistant professor (1927), and associate professor (1930); was also a Johnston Research Scholar at Johns Hopkins Univ. (1927–28); a Guggenheim Fellow in Eng. and on the continent (1928–30); visiting professor at Emory Univ. (1930); and visiting scholar, Huntington Library (1931–32).

From 1932–48, he served as a member of the Permanent Research Group of the Huntington Library and chairman of the Committee of Fellowships and member of the executive committee; during this period he also served as an associate member of the faculty of the California Inst. of Technology. He was appointed visiting professor at the Univ. of Michigan (1935); visiting professor, Univ. of Washington, on a Walker-Ames Foundation (1942); visiting professor of bibliography and research methods on the graduate faculty of the Univ. of California at Los Angeles (1934–48); visiting professor of Amer. civilization at Pomona Coll. (1941–48); visiting professor of history, Univ. of Minnesota (1946); and visiting professor on Patten Foundation, Indiana Univ. (1935).

Published Works. He has published articles in magazines including the *Atlantic, National Geographic,* and various professional journals; short monographs; and books, including *Middle-Class Culture in Elizabethan England* (1935; rev. 1959); *Puritans in the South Seas,* in collaboration with Mary Isabel Fry (1936); *The First Gentlemen of Virginia* (1940); *Religion and Empire: The Alliance Between Piety and Commerce in English Expansion, 1558–1625* (1942); *The First Americans in North Africa,* in collaboration with Julia MacLeod (1945); *The Atlantic Frontier; Colonial American Civilization, 1607–1763* (1947; 1959), entitled in the English edition, *The Colonial Civilization of North America, 1607–1763* (1949); *The Colonial Search for a Southern Eden* (1953); *Culture on the Moving Frontier* (1955); *The Cultural Life of the American Colonies* (1957); *Shakespeare for Everyman* (1964); *American Heritage History of the Thirteen Colonies* (1967); *Gold, Glory, and the Gospel* (1970); *Everyday Life in the New Nation,* in collaboration with Elaine W. Fowler (1972); *Barefoot in Arcadia: Memories of a More Innocent Era* (1974); *Tradition and the Founding Fathers* (1975).

He has edited works, including *Letters of Robert Carter, 1720–1727* (1940); *The Secret Diary of William Byrd of Westover, 1709–1712,* in collaboration with Marion Tinling (1941); *The American Tradition,* in collaboration with H. T. Swedenberg, Jr. (1941); *Quebec to Carolina in 1785–1786,* in collaboration with Marion Tinling (1943); *An Essay upon the Government of the English Plantation on the Continent of America, 1701* (1945); *The History and Present State of Virginia (1705),* by Robert Beverly (1947); *The Historie of Travell into Virginia Britinia (1612),* by William Strachey (1953); *American Heritage, An Anthology and Interpretative Survey of Our Literature,* with Leon Howard and Carl Bode (1955); *William Byrd of Virginia, The London Diary, 1717–1721, and Other Writings,* with Marion Tinling (1958); the Folger Library General Reader's Shakespeare (in collaboration with Virginia A. LaMar; the whole corpus of Shakespeare's works); *English Colonization of North America: Documents of Modern History,* in collaboration with Elaine W. Fowler (1968); *West and By North: North America Seen Through the Eyes of Its Seafaring Discoverers,* in collaboration with Elaine W. Fowler (1971); *The Moving Frontier: North America Seen Through the Eyes of Its Pioneer Discoverers,* in collaboration with Elaine W. Fowler (1972).

Mr. Wright also edited *The Huntington Library Quarterly* (1946–48); and was associate editor of *The Journal of the History of Ideas* (1940–55); *The Pacific Spectator* (1947–48); and *The William and Mary Quarterly* (1944–45, 1958).

Awards. He has received honorary degrees, including D.Litt., Wofford Coll. (1941); D.Litt., Mills Coll. (1947); D.Litt., Princeton Univ. (1948); L.H.D., Northwestern Univ. (1948); D.Litt., Amherst Coll. (1948); D.Litt., Occidental Coll. (1949); LL.D., Tulane Univ. (1950); L.H.D., Univ. of North Carolina (1950); D.Litt., Bucknell Univ. (1951); L.H.D., Rockford Coll. (1956); D.Litt., Franklin and Marshall Coll. (1957); LL.D., George Washington Univ. (1958); LL.D., Univ. of Chattanooga (1959); L.H.D., Coe Coll. (1959); D.Litt., Colby Coll. (1959); L.H.D., Georgetown Univ. (1961); LL.D., Univ. of Akron (1961); LL.D., St. Andrews Univ. (Scot.) (1961); D.Litt., Univ. of British Columbia (Can.) (1961); D.Litt., Univ. of Birmingham (Eng.) (1964); LL.D., Washington & Lee Univ. (1964); Litt.D., Univ. of Leicester (1965); LL.D., Mercer Univ. (1965); L.H.D., Calif. State College (1966); L.H.D., Brown Univ. (1968); L.H.D., Univ. of S.C. (1972); L.H.D., Lander College (1974). He was also awarded the Commonwealth Club of S.F. Gold Medal for Lit. (1947); Benjamin Franklin Gold Medal by Royal Soc. of Arts (1969); Cosmos Club Award (1973); appointed Hon. Officer of the Order of the British Emp. (O.B.E.) (1968).

Recreation. Fishing.

WRIGHT, MARTHA. Actress, singer. b. Martha Lucile Wiederrecht, Mar. 23, Seattle, Wash., to J. F. and Lucile W. (Wright) Wiederrecht. Grad. Franklin H.S., Seattle, 1941; attended Univ. of Washington, 1941–43. Studied voice with Ena Berge Ligne, 1943–63. Married May 27, 1955, to George J. Manuche, restaurateur; one son, two daughters. Member of AEA; AGVA; AFTRA; SAG. Address: (home) Hidden House, Grand Park Ave., Scarsdale, NY; (bus.) c/o Dick Ruben, General Artists Corp., 640 Fifth Ave., New York, NY 10021, tel. (212) CI 7-7543.

Theatre. Miss Wright made her N.Y.C. debut as Desiree Arteau in *Music in My Heart* (Adelphi Th., Oct. 2, 1947); subsequently appeared in *The Three Musketeers,* and *White Eagle* (St. Louis Municipal Opera, Mo., Summer 1948); played Carol in *Great to Be Alive* (Winter Garden, N.Y.C., Mar. 23, 1950); and succeeded (June 4, 1951) Mary Martin as Nellie Forbush in *South Pacific* (Majestic, Apr. 7, 1949), and has played this role at the following summer theatres: (Green Lake Aqua Th., Seattle, Wash., 1955; Sacandaga Garden Th., Sacandaga Park, N.Y., 1956; Starlight Opera Th., Kansas City, Mo., 1957; So. Shore Music Circus, Cohasset, Mass., 1963); also in stock, played Rosabella in *The Most Happy Fella* (Green Lake Th., Seattle, 1958); and Babe in *The Pajama Game* (Oakdale Musical Th., Wallingford, Conn.; Warwick Musical Th., R.I., 1958).

Miss Wright succeeded (Oct. 1961) Mary Martin as Maria von Trapp in *The Sound of Music* (Lunt-Fontanne Th., N.Y.C., Nov. 16, 1959); and repeated the role in summer theatres: (Oakdale Musical Th., Wallingford, Conn.; Carousel Th., Framingham, Mass., 1964).

Television and Radio. She was hostess on her radio program, the Martha Wright Show (WCBS,

1954–62), which was also telecast (ABC, 1954–55). She has appeared on the Bell Telephone Hour (NBC); was occasional hostess and singer on American Musical Theatre (CBS, 1961–64); has appeared on the Candid Camera series (CBS); The Today Show (NBC); and as the Announcer in Douglas Moore's one-act opera *Gallantry* (CBS, Aug. 1962).

Night Clubs. Miss Wright has performed at the Empire Room (Waldorf-Astoria Hotel, N.Y.C.); Cocoanut Grove (Ambassador Hotel, Los Angeles, Calif.); Shoreham Hotel (Washington, D.C.), and others.

WRIGHT, ROBERT. Lyricist, composer. b. Robert Craig Wright, Sept. 25, 1914, Daytona Beach, Fla., to J.A. Scheffel and Mona Long (Leatherman) Wright. Father, manufacturing chemist. Grad. Miami (Fla.) H.S., 1931; attended Univ. of Miami, 1931–33. Studied music with Manna-Zucca and Olive Dungan. Member of ASCAP; AGAC; Dramatists Guild.

Pre-Theatre. Dance orchestra leader and pianist, accompanist, theatre organist.

Theatre. Mr. Wright and George Forrest, who have always collaborated for the musical theatre, composed music and lyrics for *Thank You, Columbus* (Hollywood Playhouse, Calif., Nov. 15, 1940); lyrics for additional music in stock productions of *Naughty Marietta* and *Rio Rita* (Curran, San Francisco, Calif., 1941; Philharmonic Aud., Los Angeles, Calif., 1941); wrote for *Fun for the Money* (Hollywood Playhouse, Aug. 1941); and for 11 Camp Tamiment revues (Tamiment Playhouse, Stroudsburg, Pa., 1942).

They contributed material to the *Ziegfeld Follies* (Winter Garden, N.Y.C., Apr. 1, 1943); wrote music and lyrics for *Song of Norway*, whose score was adapted from the music of Edvard Grieg (Imperial, N.Y.C., Aug. 21, 1944; Palace, London, Mar. 7, 1946); composed music and lyrics for the pre-Bway tryout of *Spring in Brazil* (opened Shubert, Boston, Mass., Oct. 1, 1945; closed Great Northern Th., Chicago, Ill., Jan. 12, 1946). They directed and wrote new lyrics for *Gypsy Lady*, whose score was derived from two Victor Herbert operettas, *The Fortune Teller* and *Serenade* (Century, N.Y.C., Sept. 17, 1946), and for the London production, retitled *Romany Love* (His Majesty's, Mar. 7, 1947); supplied the adaptation and lyrics for Heitor Villa-Lobos music in *Magdalena* (Ziegfeld, N.Y.C., Sept. 20, 1948); provided lyrics for a revised stock production of *The Great Waltz* (Curran, San Francisco, Calif., 1949; Philharmonic Aud., Los Angeles, Calif., 1949), and additional lyrics for a second production (Philharmonic Aud., Los Angeles, 1953; Curran, San Francisco, 1953).

Messrs. Wright and Forrest wrote lyrics, and did the musical adaptation for *Kismet*, which was based on the music of Alexander Borodin (Ziegfeld, N.Y.C., Dec. 3, 1953; Stoll, London, Apr. 20, 1955); wrote the book, music, and lyrics for the pre-Bway tryout of *The Carefree Heart* (opened Cass, Detroit, Mich., Sept. 30, 1957; closed Hanna, Cleveland, Ohio, Oct. 26, 1957); music and lyrics for the pre-Bway tryout of *At the Grand* (opened Philharmonic Aud., Los Angels, Calif., July 7, 1958; closed Curran, San Francisco, Calif., Sept. 13, 1958); composed for a revised London production of *The Carefree Heart*, called *The Love Doctor* (Piccadilly, Oct. 12, 1959); and wrote music and lyrics for *Kean* (Bway Th., N.Y.C., Nov. 2, 1961). Messrs. Wright and Forrest, with Foreman Brown, provided additional musical adaptation and lyrics for a revival of *The Great Waltz* (Music Center, Los Angeles, Calif., July 27, 1965); and Messrs. Wright and Forrest wrote music and lyrics for *Anya* (Ziegfeld Th., N.Y.C., Nov. 29, 1965); and for *Dumas and Son* (Dorothy Chandler Pavilion, Los Angeles, Calif., Aug. 1, 1967).

Films. Messrs. Wright and Forrest's first musical collaboration was for the short subject *New Shoes* (MGM, 1936). They wrote the lyrics or lyrics and music, including musical adaptation, for the films *The Longest Night* (MGM, 1936); *After the Thin Man* (MGM, 1936); *Libeled Lady* (MGM, 1936); *Sinner Take All* (MGM, 1936); *Maytime* (MGM, 1937); *The Firefly* (MGM, 1937); *The Good Old Soak* (MGM, 1937); *London By Night* (MGM, 1937); *Madam "X"* (MGM, 1937); *Mama Steps Out* (MGM, 1937); *Mannequin* (MGM, 1937); *Man of the People* (MGM, 1937); *Navy Blue and Gold* (MGM, 1937); *Parnell* (MGM, 1937); *Saratoga* (MGM, 1937); *Bad Man of Brimstone* (MGM, 1938); *You're Only Young Once* (MGM, 1938); *Boy's Town* (MGM, 1938); *The First Hundred Years* (MGM, 1938); *Lord Jeff* (MGM, 1938); *Marie Antoinette* (MGM, 1938); *Paradise for Three* (MGM, 1938); *Sweethearts* (MGM, 1938); *Three Comrades* (MGM, 1938); *The Toy Wife* (MGM, 1938); *Vacation from Love* (MGM, 1938); the short features *Happily Buried* (MGM, 1938); *The Magician's Daughter* (MGM, 1938); *Nuts and Bolts* (MGM, 1938); *Our Gang Follies* (MGM, 1938); *Snow Gets in Your Eyes* (MGM, 1938); the full-length features *Broadway Serenade* (1939); *The Girl Downstairs* (MGM, 1939); *The Hardys Ride Again* (MGM, 1939); *Honolulu* (MGM, 1939); *Let Freedom Ring* (MGM, 1939); *Balalaika* (MGM, 1939); *These Glamor Girls* (MGM, 1939); *The Women* (MGM, 1939); *Florian* (MGM, 1940); *The New Moon* (MGM, 1940); *Strange Cargo* (MGM, 1940); *Music in My Heart* (Col., 1940); *Dance, Girl, Dance* (RKO, 1940); *South of Pago-Pago* (UA, 1940); *Kit Carson* (UA, 1940); *Blondie Goes Latin* (Col., 1941); the short features *Cubana* and *Fiesta* (Hal Roach, 1941); the full-length feature *I Married an Angel* (MGM, 1942); and the film adaptation of their Bway show, *Kismet* (MGM, 1955).

Television and Radio. Messrs. Wright and Forrest composed music and lyrics for the Vicks Radio Hour (NBC, 1936); Maxwell House Good News (NBC, 1937); Tune-Up Time (NBC, 1940); the US Treasury radio show, Treasury Star Parade (world broadcasting transcriptions played on all networks, 1942–43); and 13 revues for the television program Startime Hour (Dumont, 1950).

Night Clubs. They collaborated on *Folies Bergère Revue* (Edison Hotel, N.Y.C., 1942–43); Vaughn Monroe's *Commodore Hotel Revue* (N.Y.C., 1943); four Copacabana revues (N.Y.C., 1942–43); three Colonial Inn revues (Hollywood, Fla., 1945–48); and created night club acts and special material for Jane Froman (1942 through 1956); Celeste Holm (1943); Anne Jeffreys and Robert Sterling (1952–53).

Awards. Messrs. Wright and Forrest were nominated for an Academy (Oscar) Award in 1937 for the song "Donkey Serenade," from *The Firefly*. They received the Antoinette Perry (Tony) Award (1953) for their music and lyrics in *Kismet*.

Recreation. Theatre, concerts, opera, reading, travel.

WRIGHT, TERESA. Actress. b. Muriel Teresa Wright, Oct. 27, 1918, New York City, to Arthur H. and Martha (Espy) Wright. Father, insurance business. Grad. Columbia H.S., Maplewood, N.J., 1938. Married May 23, 1942, to Niven Busch, novelist (marr. dis. Nov. 1952); one son, one daughter; married Dec. 11, 1959, to Robert Anderson, playwright. Member of AEA; SAG; AFTRA. Address: 1172 Park Ave., New York, NY 10028.

Theatre. Miss Wright made her first appearance on a stage as Grazia in a high school production of *Death Takes a Holiday* (May 1928); her professional debut as the Daughter in *The Vinegar Tree* (July 1938); subsequently appeared as Blossom Trexel in *Susan and God* (Wharf Th., Provincetown, Mass., Aug. 1938); joined (Oct. 1938) the N.Y.C. company of *Our Town* as a walk-on and understudy to Dorothy McGuire as Emily, and toured in it as Rebecca (Jan.–Feb. 1939), and Emily (Spring 1939).

She appeared in stock with the Barnstormers (Tanworth, N.H., Summer 1939); played Mary in *Life with Father* (Empire, N.Y.C., Nov. 8, 1939); in stock appeared in *The King's Maid* (Gloucester, Mass., Aug. 1941); *Bell, Book and Candle* (Sombrero Playhouse, Phoenix, Ariz., Winter 1953); *The Country Girl* (Vancouver, Can., 1953); *The Heiress* (Palm Springs, Calif., 1954); and *The Rainmaker* (La Jolla Playhouse, Calif., Summer 1954).

She played Cora Flood in *The Dark at the Top of the Stairs* (Music Box, N.Y.C., Dec. 5, 1957); toured as Mary in *Mary, Mary* (Santa Barbara, Los Angeles, San Francisco, Calif., 1962); and Mrs. Pew-Pickett in *Tchin-Tchin* (Mineola Playhouse, N.Y.; Westport Country Playhouse, Conn.; Paper Mill Playhouse, Millburn, N.J., June 1963).

Miss Wright played Katherine Butler Hathaway in *The Locksmith* (tour, 1965); Alice in *I Never Sang for My Father* (Longacre, N.Y.C., Jan. 1968); and Mary Hallen in *Who's Happy Now?* (Village South Th., N.Y.C., Nov. 1969); gave a concert reading of *A Passage to E. M. Forster* (Th. de Lys, Oct. 26, 1970); appeared in *A Long Day's Journey into Night* Hartford (Conn.) Stage Co., Oct. 1970); *You Can't Take It with You* (Long Wharf Th., New Haven, Conn., 1971); played Beatrice in *The Effect of Gamma Rays on Man-in-the-Moon Marigolds* (tour, 1972); and Linda in *Death of a Salesman* (Philadelphia Drama Guild, 1973).

Films. Miss Wright made her film debut as Alexandra in *The Little Foxes* (RKO, 1941); subsequently appeared in *Mrs. Miniver* (MGM, 1942); *Pride of the Yankees* (RKO, 1942); *Shadow of a Doubt* (U, 1943); *Casanova Brown* (RKO, 1944); *Best Years of Our Lives* (RKO, 1946); *Pursued* (WB, 1947); *Trouble with Women* (Par. 1947); *Imperfect Lady* (Par., 1947); *Enchantment* (RKO, 1948); *The Capture* (RKO, 1950); *The Men* (UA, 1950); *The Steel Trap* (20th-Fox, 1952); *Count The Hours* (RKO, 1953); *The Actress* (MGM, 1953); and *Escapade in Japan* (U, 1957).

Television. She has appeared on US Steel Hour (CBS), Robert Montgomery Presents (NBC), Lux Video Theatre (NBC), Alcoa Hour (ABC), as Louella Parsons in *The Louella Parsons Story* (Climax, CBS, 1955); *Shadow of Evil* (1956); Annie Sullivan in *The Miracle Worker* (Playhouse 90, CBS, 1957); Miss Bourke-White in *The Margaret Bourke-White Story* (NBC, 1959); in *Big Deal in Laredo* (Dupont Show of the Month, NBC, 1962); on Alfred Hitchcock Presents (CBS, 1964); Suspense (CBS, 1964); The Defenders (CBS, 1965); and played Carrie Ellis in *The Autumn Garden* (NET, 1966).

Awards. Miss Wright received an Academy (Oscar) Award for her performance as Carol in *Mrs. Miniver* (1942); Academy (Oscar) Award nominations for her performances as Alexandra in *The Little Foxes* (1941), and in *Pride of the Yankees* (1942); received the *Look* Award for *Pride of the Yankees* (1942); was nominated for the NATAS (Emmy) Award for her performances as Annie Sullivan in *The Miracle Worker* (1958), and Miss Bourke-White in *The Margaret Bourke-White Story* (1960).

WYATT, JANE. Actress. b. Aug. 12, 1912, Campgaw, N.J., to Christopher Billopp and Euphemia Van Rensselaer (Waddington) Wyatt. Father, investment banker; mother, playwright, drama critic, drama editor. Grad. Miss Chapin's Sch., N.Y.C., 1928; attended Barnard Coll., 1929–30. Studied acting with Frances Robinson Duff, N.Y.C., 1933–34; Lee Strasberg, N.Y.C., 1940; Charles Laughton, Hollywood, Calif., 1949. Married Nov. 9, 1935, to Edgar Bethune Ward, investor; two sons. Member of AEA; SAG; AFTRA; AMPAS; NATAS (governor, Hollywood chapter, 1956–60; trustee, natl. academy, 1957–60). Address: 651 Siena Way, Los Angeles, CA 90024.

Theatre. Miss Wyatt made her debut as an apprentice at the Berkshire Playhouse (Stockbridge, Mass., Summer 1930); subsequently was a walk-on and understudy in the pre-Bway tryout of *Trade Winds* (Philadelphia, 1930); understudy in *The Vinegar Tree* (Playhouse, N.Y.C., Nov. 19, 1930); made her Bway debut as Freda Mannock in *Give Me Yesterday* (Charles Hopkins Th., Mar. 4, 1931); was a member of the Osgood Perkins Rep. Co., which opened the Westport (Conn.) Country Playhouse (Summer 1931); with a production of *The Streets of New York;* played Flora Ackroyd in *The Fatal Alibi* (Booth, N.Y.C., Feb. 8, 1932); Geneva Hope in *The Mad*

Hopes (Broadhurst, Dec. 1, 1932); Pauline Lacey in *Evensong* (Selwyn, Jan. 31, 1933); Eva Locke in *Conquest* (Plymouth, Feb. 17, 1933); Lois Ardsley in *For Services Rendered* (Booth, April 12, 1933); and succeeded (May 1933) Margaret Sullavan as Paula Jordan in *Dinner at Eight* (Music Box, Oct. 22, 1932) in N.Y.C. and on tour.

She played Theresa Farley Battle in *The Joyous Season* (Belasco, N.Y.C., Jan. 29, 1934); Janet Evans in *Lost Horizons* (St. James, Oct. 15, 1934); Hester in *The Bishop Misbehaves* (Cort, Feb. 20, 1935); Princess Claudine in *Save Me the Waltz* (Martin Beck Th., Feb. 28, 1938); Marion Froude in *Biography* (Summer tour, 1938); appeared at Elitch Gardens (Denver, Colo., Summer 1939); played Fay Tucker in *Night Music* (Broadhurst, N.Y.C., Feb. 22, 1940); Carol Adams in *Quiet, Please!* (Guild, Nov. 8, 1940); Lucille Daly in *Hope for the Best* (Fulton, Feb. 7, 1945); Nina Denery in *Autumn Garden* (Coronet, Mar. 7, 1951); Sabina in *The Skin of Our Teeth* (Coronet, Hollywood, Calif., June 11, 1947); Catherine Winslow in *The Winslow Boy* (Las Palmas, Hollywood, Calif., Nov. 6, 1950); the title role in *Candida* (Sombrero Playhouse, Phoenix, Ariz., Jan. 31, 1961); toured as Olivia Brown in *Oh Mistress Mine* (Summer 1961); played Wynn Bonard in *The Strangers* (Westport Country Playhouse, Conn., Nov. 1963); and Laura Haviland in *The Decent Thing* (Pasadena Playhouse, Calif., Nov. 9, 1966).

Miss Wyatt has appeared on the concert stage narrating Edith Sitwell's *Facade* (Evenings on the Roof, Hollywood, Sept. 24, 1951); and Benjamin Britten's *A Young Person's Guide to the Orchestra* (Pasadena Aud., Calif., 1960).

Films. She made her film debut as Dina in *One More River* (U, 1934); subsequently appeared in *Great Expectations* (U, 1934); *The Luckiest Girl in the World* (U, 1936); *Lost Horizon* (Col., 1937); *We're Only Human* (RKO, 1937); *Girl from God's Country* (Rep., 1940); *Kisses for Breakfast* (WB, 1941); *Weekend for Three* (RKO, 1941); *Hurricane Smith* (Rep., 1941), re-released as *Double Identity; Army Surgeon* (RKO, 1942); *The Navy Comes Through* (RKO, 1942); *Buckskin Frontier* (UA, 1943); *The Kansan* (UA, 1943); *None But the Lonely Heart* (RKO, 1944); *The Bachelor's Daughters* (UA, 1946); *Strange Conquest* (U, 1946); *Boomerang* (20th-Fox, 1947); *Gentlemen's Agreement* (20th-Fox, 1947); *The Pitfall* (UA, 1948); *Task Force* (WB, 1949); *No Minor Vices* (MGM, 1949); *Bad Boy* (AA, 1949); *Canadian Pacific* (20th-Fox, 1949); *Our Very Own* (RKO, 1950); *My Blue Heaven* (20th-Fox, 1950); *House by the River* (Rep., 1950); *Criminal Lawyer* (Col., 1951); *The Man Who Cheated Himself* (20th-Fox, 1951); *Interlude* (U, 1952); *Hurricane Smith* (Par., 1952); *The Two Little Bears* (20th-Fox, 1961); and *Never Too Late* (WB, 1965).

Television. She made her debut in *Kitty Foyle* (Robert Montgomery Presents, NBC, Feb. 13, 1950); played Margaret Anderson on the series Father Knows Best (CBS, premiere Oct. 3, 1954, through Spring 1961); and has made guest appearances on major network panel programs, Project 120, Bob Hope Chrysler Th. (NBC), The Virginian (NBC), Ford Th. (CBS), Wagon Train (NBC), Going My Way (ABC), Alcoa Th. (NBC), GE Th. (CBS), Robert Montgomery Presents (NBC), Studio One (CBS), Producers Showcase (NBC), Climax! (CBS), Bell Telephone Hour (Four Christmas Shows, NBC), US Steel Hour (CBS), Story of a Family, the Mike Douglas Show; Alias Smith and Jones (ABC); Trailmaster (ABC); Alfred Hitchcock Presents (NBC); the Christopher Program series (Ind.); and *Ladies of the Corridor* (Hollywood Television Th., PBS, Apr. 21, 1975).

Awards. Miss Wyatt received three NATAS (Emmy) Awards for her performance as Margaret Anderson in Father Knows Best (1958–60); a citation from the Calif. State Assembly, the McElligott Medallion from the Assn. of Marquette Univ. of Women, and the Poverello Medal.

Recreation. Gardening, bird-watching, camping, theatre-going.

WYLER, GRETCHEN. Dancer, actress, singer. b. Gretchen Patricia Wienecke, Feb. 16, 1932, Oklahoma City, Okla., to Louis Gustave and Peggy (Highley) Wienecke. Father, engineer. Grad. Central H.S., Bartlesville, Okla. Studied dancing Bartlesville and Tulsa, Okla., at June Runyon Dance Sch., fourteen years; Caird Leslie Ballet Sch., N.Y.C., three years; modern jazz dance with José Limón, Frank Wagner, Matt Mattox, and Eugene Lewis; acting at Verian Chaney Dramatic Sch., Bartlesville, three years. Married June 18, 1956, to Shepard Coleman, musical director. Member of AEA; AGVA; SAG; AFTRA; Great Dane Club of America; Amer. Vivisection Society; ASPCA (bd. of managers, 1972). Address: (home) R.D. #2, Warwick, NY tel. (914) 986-4195; (bus.) c/o Ray Smith, 1860 Broadway, New York, NY 10019, tel. (212) JU 2-1412.

Pre-Theatre. Had her own dancing school in Bartlesville, Okla.

Theatre. Miss Wyler made her debut as "one of many bumblebees" in a dance recital (Civic Ctr., Bartlesville, Okla., May 1938); and made her professional debut with the Ballet Guild, dancing variations from *Giselle* and *Sleeping Beauty* (Auditorium, Little Rock, Ark., Feb. 10, 1950). In stock, she was a member of the corp de ballet and played Jane Ashton in *Brigadoon* (St. Louis Municipal Opera, Mo., Summer 1950). She made her N.Y.C. debut (Dec. 1950) in the chorus and as understudy to Allyn McLerie as Amy in *Where's Charley?* (Bway Th., Oct. 11, 1948), followed by the national tour; subsequently appeared as a dancer in tent stock musicals (Melody Fair, Toronto, Ont., Can., Summer 1951). Miss Wyler joined (Nov. 16, 1951) the national company of *Guys and Dolls* (opened Curran, San Francisco, Calif., June 4, 1951), to understudy Pamela Britton as Miss Adelaide, and succeeded (Nov. 9, 1953) her in this role; and joined the N.Y.C. company of *Guys and Dolls* (46 St. Th., Nov. 24, 1950), as understudy to Vivian Blaine in the same role.

After another season of stock as resident understudy (St. Louis Municipal Opera, Mo., Summer 1954), she played Janice Dayton in *Silk Stockings* (Imperial, N.Y.C., Feb. 24, 1955), and on tour (opened Curran, San Francisco, Calif., Apr. 23, 1956); succeeded (Nov. 1956) Gwen Verdon as Lola in *Damn Yankees* (46 St. Th., N.Y.C., May 5, 1955), and on tour (St. Louis Municipal Opera, Mo.; Civic Opera, Pittsburgh, Pa.; Theatre-Under-the-Stars, Atlanta, Ga.; Aqua Th., Seattle, Wash.; Starlight, Kansas City, Mo.; Summer 1957). Miss Wyler played Kate Drew in *Rumple* (Alvin, Nov. 6, 1957); succeeded (American Th., St. Louis, Mo., Dec. 1960) Anne Jeffries as Frenchy in the national tour of *Destry Rides Again* (opened Riviera, Las Vegas, Nev., July 31, 1960; closed O'Keefe Ctr., Toronto, Ont., Can., Jan. 28, 1961); succeeded (Shubert, Apr. 9, 1961) Chita Rivera as Rose in *Bye Bye Birdie* (Martin Beck Th., N.Y.C., Apr. 14, 1960), and subsequently toured with this show (opened Shubert, Boston, Mass., Oct. 9, 1961; closed Forrest, Philadelphia, Pa., Mar. 3, 1962); and repeated this role in stock (St. Louis Municipal Opera, Mo., Summer 1962).

She played Irene Lavalle in a stock production of *Say, Darling* (Kenley Players, Warren and Columbus, Ohio, Summer 1962); Rose in *Bye Bye Birdie* (Westchester Dinner Th., Nov. 1962); in stock, played Adelaide in *Guys and Dolls* (Metropolitan Musicals, Baltimore, Md., Oct. 1962); Annie in *Annie Get Your Gun* (Westchester Town House, June 4, 1963); in stock, Essie Whimple in *Redhead* (Aqua, Seattle, Wash., July 8, 1963); appeared in an industrial show version of *Bells Are Ringing* (Mark Hellinger Th., Aug. 11, 1963); in stock, Cherie in *Bus Stop* (Atlanta Winter Th., Ga., Feb. 4, 1964); appeared in Wonder World (NY World's Fair, May 7, 1964); played Lizzie Curry in *110 in the Shade* (St. Louis Municipal Opera, Mo., July 5, 1965); wrote the lyrics for the songs in the play, *Noah* (Pittsburgh Playhouse, Aug. 19, 1965); played Lola in *Damn Yankees* (Salt Lake City Music Th., Utah, Oct. 5, 1965); Rose in *Bye Bye Birdie* (St. Louis Municipal Opera, July 18, 1966); at the Warwick (N.Y.) Playhouse played Cyrenne in *Rattle of a Simple Man* (Sept. 1966) and appeared in *Hatful of Rain* (1966); played Charity in *Sweet Charity* (Westbury Music Fair, N.Y., Sept. 5, 1967; Cocoanut Grove Playhouse, Miami, Sept. 1967; Prince of Wales Th., London, Oct. 11, 1967); Olivia in *Your Own Thing* (Chicago); stood by for Lauren Bacall as Margo Channing in *Applause* (Palace, N.Y.C., Mar. 30, 1970); toured as Anna Reardon in *And Miss Reardon Drinks a Little* (opened Powers Aud., Youngstown, Ohio, Jan. 25, 1973; closed Masonic Aud., Scranton, Pa., Apr. 8, 1973); played Joanne in *Company* (Meadowbrook Dinner Th., Cedar Grove, N.J., Apr. 25, 1973); toured as Margo Channing in *Applause* (Summer 1973); and played Evy Meara in *The Gingerbread Lady* (Univ. of Miami Ring Th., 1974).

Miss Wyler produced *The Ballad of Johnny Pot* (Th. Four, N.Y.C., Apr. 26, 1971).

Films. *The Devil's Brigade* (UA, 1968).

Television. Miss Wyler made her first appearance on the Kate Smith Show (NBC, Sept. 25, 1950), as a member of the John Butler dance group; subsequently appeared on the Colgate Comedy Hour (NBC); Walter Winchell (NBC); Sgt. Bilko (CBS); the Bell Telephone Hour (NBC); I've Got a Secret (CBS); the Tonight Show (NBC); To Tell the Truth (CBS); Stump the Stars (CBS); Naked City (ABC); Password (CBS); Picture This (CBS); the Bob Crosby Show (NBC, 1958); the Perry Como Show (NBC); the Garry Moore Show (CBS); Music '60 (CBS); the Andy Williams Show (NBC); the Ed Sullivan Show (CBS); Match Game (NBC); The Price Is Right (CBS); Get the Message (ABC); Girl Talk (ABC); Call My Bluff (NBC); *An Evening with Gretchen Wyler* (ABC special); the Dean Martin Show (NBC); and various other variety and game shows. She was hostess on the Step This Way series (Ind., 1965–1967); and a continuing character on the serial, Somerset (NBC).

Night Clubs. Miss Wyler has performed her own act at Le Cupidon (N.Y.C.); Royal York Hotel (Toronto, Ont., Can.); Statler Hotel (Houston, Tex.); Roosevelt Hotel (New Orleans, La.); International (N.Y.C.); Diplomat Hotel (Miami, Fla.); Fontainebleau Hotel (Miami, Fla.); Americana Hotel (Miami, Fla.); Ankara (Pittsburgh, Pa.); Adophus Hotel (Dallas, Tex.); Eddy's (Kansas City, Mo.); Shoreham Hotel (Washington, D.C.); Sahara Hotel (Las Vegas, Nev.); Edgewater Beach Hotel (Chicago, Ill.); the Copacabana (N.Y.C.); Holiday House (Pittsburgh, Pa.); and at The Riverboat (N.Y.C.).

Recreation. Raising and showing Great Danes in championship competition.

Y

YANKOWITZ, SUSAN. Playwright, novelist. b. Feb. 20, 1941, Newark, N.J., to Irving N. and Ruth (Katz) Yankowitz. Father, attorney; mother, lecturer, actress. Grad. Sarah Lawrence Coll., Bronxville, N.Y., B.A. 1963; Yale Drama School, M.F.A. 1968; studied at Exeter (England) Univ., 1961–62.

Miss Yankowitz taught at Quinnipiac Coll. (part-time, 1965–67); Noroton (Conn.) School (Summer 1968); Southern Connecticut Coll. (part-time, 1967–68); Harvard Univ. (Summer 1969); and Bronx (N.Y.) Community Coll. (part-time, 1969–71).

Theatre. Miss Yankowitz's first play produced was *The Cage* (Omar Khayyam Cafe, N.Y.C., 1965). Later productions include *Nightmare* (Yale Univ., New Haven, Conn., 1967); *That Old Rock-a-Bye* (Cooper Square Th., N.Y.C., 1968); *Terminal* (American Place Th., 1969; Fortune, 1970; Roundhouse, London, England, 1973); *The Ha-Ha Play* and *The Lamb* (Cubiculo Th., 1970); *Transplant* (Magic Th., Omaha, Neb., 1971); *Sideshow* (National Theatre of the Deaf on tour, 1971); *Slaughter-*

house Play (Public Th., N.Y.C., 1971); *Basics in Tabula Rasa* (Brooklyn Acad. of Music, N.Y.C., 1972); *Positions in Up!* (Westbeth Cabaret, 1972); *Boxes* (Bronx Community Coll., N.Y.C., 1972); monologues in *The Wicked Women Revue* and in *?!* (Th. for the New City; Little Church Around the Corner, 1973); *Acts of Love* (Academy Th., Atlanta, Ga., 1973); *Wooden Nickels* (Th. for the New City, N.Y.C., Feb. 22, 1973). Miss Yankowitz also collaborated on characters for *The America Piece* (Provisional Th., Los Angeles, Calif., 1974).

Films. Miss Yankowitz's film *Danny AWOL* (1969) has been shown at university film festivals.

Radio. Miss Yankowitz wrote the radio play *Rats' Alley* (WGBH 1969).

Published Works. Miss Yankowitz's essays have been published in *African Forum* and *Yale/Theatre;* her screenplay *The Land of Milk and Funny* appeared in *Yale/Theatre* (Fall 1974).

Awards. Miss Yankowitz received a Joseph E. Levine Fellowship in screenwriting (1968–69); a MacDowell Colony Fellowship (1971); a National Endowment for the Arts Creative Writing Fellowship Grant (1972–73); a Rockefeller Foundation Grant in playwriting (1973–74); a C.A.P.S. award in playwriting (1974); and a Guggenheim Fellowship in playwriting.

YEATON, KELLY. Educator, director. b. Charles Kendall Yeaton, Apr. 21, 1911, Portland, Me., to Arthur Charles and Ella (Sylvester) Yeaton. Father, educator; mother, physician. Grad. Edward Little H.S., Auburn, Me., 1928; Tufts Univ., B.A. (English) 1932; Bates Coll., Summer 1932; Univ. of Washington, M.A. (Theatre) 1938; Pennsylvania State Univ., graduate work in psychology, 1951. Studied under Lee Simonson, Lincoln Kirstein, and Rose Bogdanoff at Fordham Univ., Summer 1948; Lee Strasberg, Joseph Kramm, and Ben Kranz at the Amer. Th. Wing, 1950; attended Miami Arena Th. Conf. Married Dec. 21, 1944, to Shirley Coe (marr. dis. 1953); married Apr. 7, 1955, to Ruth Marie Lyne; one son, one daughter. Served USAAF, radio operator and instructor, 1942–45, rank, Sgt. Member of ATA; ANTA (Bd. of dir., 1963–to date); AEA; USITT; SSD & C. Address: (home) 1439 E. Branch Rd., State College, PA 16801, tel. (814) 237-3109; (bus.) 107 Arts II Bldg., University Park, PA 16802.

Mr. Yeaton is a professor (1970–to date) in the Dept. of Theatre and Film at Pennsylvania State Univ. He previously served there as assistant professor (1947–55), and associate professor (1955–70). He also held academic positions at the Univ. of Washington (teacher of acting, 1938–39); The Dramatic Workshop, The New Sch. for Social Research (Dean of professional students, 1946); and Ohio State Univ. (guest director, 1961). He began in the theatre, playing the role of Mansky in a stock production of *The Play's the Thing* with the College Players (Brunswick, Me., 1932); was a supernumerary and technician for Maude Adam's touring production of *Twelfth Night* (Summer 1933); was technical director and assistant stage manager at the Ogunquit (Me.) Playhouse (Summers 1936–37); and technical director for a production of *Rip Van Winkle* (Copley Th., Boston, Mass., Nov. 1937). While a student at the Univ. of Washington he acted in university productions at the Tryout Th., Studio Th., and the Penthouse Th. (Seattle, Wash., 1937–39). For community theatre, he was director of the Mummers of St. Louis (Mo., 1939–41), and stage manager of the St. Louis Civic Th. (Summer 1941); introduced arena staging to St. Louis; and was director of the Little Th. of Lafayette (Ind., 1941–42). While in the army, he designed and was stage manager for an Army Show (Ft. Devens, Mass., 1943).

In stock, Mr. Yeaton was exec. director of the Erie (Pa.) Playhouse (Summer 1946); directed *The Play's the Thing* and *The Male Animal* at the Orangeburg (N.J.) Circle Playhouse (Summer 1950); was a founding member and stage manager of the Green Hills Playhouse (Reading, Pa., Summer 1952); directed *Mr. Roberts* at the Standing Stone Playhouse (Neffs Mills, Pa., 1956); directed *Clutterbuck* and *The Royal Family* at Mateer Playhouse (Neffs Mills, Pa., 1958); and was guest director for *Thieves' Carnival* at the Stadium Th. (Ohio State Univ., Columbus, Summer 1961).

He assisted in designing and forming the policy of two arena theatres, the Millbrook Playhouse (Millhall, Pa.), and the Boal Barn Playhouse (Boalsburg, Pa.).

Other Activities. Mr. Yeaton was editor of the *Pennsylvania Theatre Conference Bulletin* (1955); and associate editor of *Players* Magazine (1950–55). He has written many articles on production methods for arena staging which have been published in *Players* Magazine, *Dramatics, High School Thespian, Educational Theatre Journal, Playshop, N.Y. Community Theatre Bulletin,* the *Wisconsin Idea Theatre Quarterly,* and *Theatre Arts.*

He was consultant, director, and photographer for Project M2121, for the Natl. Inst. for Mental Health (1958–59). His photographs, air-brush paintings, and masks have been exhibited in Maine, New York, Massachusetts, and Pennsylvania.

Published Works. He is the author of *Memorization by Analysis* (1937); *A Plan for Acting* (1947); *The Most Human Art* (1952); the chapter on arena production in *Producing the Play* (1953); the article, "Arena Stages in the United States" for the *Encyclopedia della spettacolo* (1960); and has edited acting editions of the *Alchemist* (1956), and *Oedipus Rex* and *Oedipus at Colonus* (1960). Other articles by Mr. Yeaton have appeared in *The Tulane Drama Review, Co-Evolution Quarterly,* and *The Whole Earth Catalog.* His essay, "Mirror Companies, DNA, and The Reproductive Process," appears in *Actor Training 2.*.

Awards. Mr. Yeaton received research grants from the Central Council on Research for study of arena staging.

Recreation. Travel, crafts, arts, camping, boating.

YELLEN, JACK. Lyricist, playwright. b. Selig Yellen, July 6, 1892, Razcki, Poland, to Abram and Bessie (Wallens) Yellen. Father, merchant. Grad. Univ. of Michigan, B.A. 1913. Married Sept. 13, 1944, to Lucille Hodgeman, ballet dancer. Served WW I, US Army; rank, Pvt. Member of ASCAP (dir., 1951).

Pre-Theatre. News reporter on Buffalo *Courier.*

Theatre. Mr. Yellen first worked as a lyricist in 1913. He collaborated with John Murray Anderson on the book and lyrics for *What's in a Name* (Maxine Elliott's Th., N.Y.C., Mar. 19, 1920); wrote the lyrics for *Rain or Shine* (George M. Cohan Th., Feb. 9, 1928); and for *Follow a Star* (Winter Garden, London, England, Dec. 1, 1930); composed the lyrics, wrote, with Sid Silvers, the book, and produced, with Lew Holtz, *You Said It* (46 St. Th., N.Y.C., Jan. 19, 1931); wrote the lyrics for the *George White Scandals* (New Amsterdam, Dec. 25, 1934; Alvin, Aug. 28, 1939); with Sam E. Fain, wrote songs for *Sons o' Fun* (Winter Garden, Dec. 1, 1941); and, with Ray Henderson, the songs for the *Ziegfeld Follies* (Winter Garden, Apr. 1, 1943).

Films. Mr. Yellen wrote the lyrics for the song, "Happy Days Are Here Again," from the film *Chasing Rainbows* (MGM, 1930); wrote the screenplay for *George White's Scandals* (20th-Fox, 1935); the screenplay and the lyrics for the title song in *Sing, Baby, Sing* (20th-Fox, 1936); the screenplays for *Pigskin Parade* (20th-Fox, 1936); *Wake Up and Live* (20th-Fox, 1937); *Love Is News* (20th-Fox, 1937); *Submarine Patrol* (20th-Fox, 1938); *Hold That Co-Ed* (20th-Fox, 1938); and *Little Miss Broadway* (20th-Fox, 1938).

Published Works. In 1922, Mr. Yellen formed his own musical publishing house, Ager, Yellen & Bornstein, Inc., which published many of the songs for which he wrote the lyrics, such as "Lovin' Sam, the Sheik of Alabam'" (1922); "Louisville Lou," (1923); "I Wonder What's Become of Sally?" (1924). His other songs include "All Aboard for Dixieland" (1913); "Ain't She Sweet?" (1924); "Hard-Hearted Hannah" (1923); "My Yiddisha Momma" (1924); "Are You Havin' Any Fun?" (1939); "Alabama Jubilee" (1915); "Are You from Dixie?"(1913); "Down By the O-H-I-O" (1920); "I'm Waiting for Ships That Never Come In" (1920); "Happy in Love" (1941); "Mama Goes Where Papa Goes" (1923); and "Something I Dreamed Last Night" (1929).

YORDAN, PHILIP. Screenwriter, producer, playwright. b. c. 1914, Chicago, Ill. Attended Roosevelt H.S., Chicago, Ill.; Kent Coll. Member of SWG.

Theatre. Mr. Yordan wrote *Any Day Now* (Studio Th., New Sch. for Social Research, N.Y.C., June 9, 1941); *Anna Lucasta* (NY Public Library, W. 135 St.; American Negro Th., June 8, 1944; Mansfield, Aug. 30, 1944; Natl., Sept. 22, 1947), which was also produced in London (His Majesty's, Oct. 29, 1947).

Films. Mr. Yordan was the screenwriter for *The Devil and Daniel Webster,* released as *All That Money Can Buy* (RKO, 1941); *Syncopation* (RKO, 1942); *Dillinger* (Mono., 1945); *Whistle Stop* (UA, 1946); *Suspense* (Mono., 1946); *The Chase* (1946); *House of Strangers* (1949); *Bad Men of Tombstone* (Mono., 1949); *The Black Book* (Eagle-Lion, 1949); *Edge of Doom* (RKO, 1950); *Detective Story* (Par., 1951); *Mara Maru* (WB, 1952); *Mutiny* (UA, 1952); *Houdini* Par., 1953); *Blowing Wild* (WB, 1953); *Johnny Guitar* (Rep., 1953); *The Naked Jungle* (Par., 1954); *Broken Lance* (20th-Fox, 1954); *The Big Combo* (AA, 1955); *Conquest of Space* (Par., 1955); *The Man from Laramie* (Col., 1955); *The Last Frontier,* released as *Savage Wilderness* (Col., 1956); *Joe MacBeth* (Col., 1956); *Gun Glory* (MGM, 1957); *Street of Sinners* (UA, 1957); *No Down Payment* (20th-Fox, 1957); *Four Boys and a Gun* (UA, 1957); *The Bravados* (20th-Fox, 1958); *Anna Lucasta* (UA, 1958); *The Bramble Bush* (WB, 1960); *El Cid* Allied, 1961), *King of Kings* (MGM, 1961); *55 Days at Peking* (Allied, 1963); *The Fall of the Roman Empire* (Par., 1964); *Circus World* (Par., 1964); and *The Royal Hunt of the Sun* (Natl. Gen., 1969).

He produced his own screen version of his play, *Anna Lucasta* (Col., 1949); and produced and wrote the screenplays for *The Harder They Fall* (released by Col., 1956); *The Fiend Who Walked the West* (20th-Fox, 1958); *Studs Lonigan* (UA, 1960); *The Battle of the Bulge* (WB, 1965); *Crack in the World* (Par., 1965); and *Badman's River* (Philip Yordan Prods., 1972).

Mr. Yordan was founder (1957) and president of Security Pictures, for which he produced and wrote the following screenplays; *Men in War* (released by UA, 1957); *God's Little Acre* (UA, 1958); *The Day of the Triffids* (AA, 1963); and *Custer of the West* (Sec. Pics., 1968).

Published Works. He wrote the novel, *Man of the West* (1954).

Awards. Mr. Yordan received an Academy (Oscar) Award (1954) for best motion picture story for *Broken Lance.*.

YOUNG, EDGAR BERRYHILL. Executive, administrator. b. Apr. 27, 1908, Anderson, Ind., to Earl Edgar and Irene (Berryhill) Young. Father, banker, credit manager. Grad. La Grange (Ill.) H.S., 1925; DePauw Univ., B.A. 1929; attended Univ. of Pennsylvania, 1929–30; London (England) Sch. of Economics, 1930–31; American Univ. (1934–36). Married Aug. 9, 1930, to Jane White; three sons. Member and director of Japan Soc., Inc. (secy., 1952–58; vice-pres., 1973–to date); The Asia Soc. (founding mbr., and secy., 1956–58); Community Arts Council, Inc. (dir., 1947–64); Public Personnel Assn.; Phi Kappa Psi; Univ. Club; Rockefeller Center Luncheon Club; Council on Foreign Relations. Address: 60 Oak Ridge Ave., Summit, NJ 07901.

Mr. Young has been associated with Lincoln Center for the Performing Arts (N.Y.C.) since 1955, when the Exploratory Committee for a Musical Arts Center was formed; was elected secretary of the Center's corporation, 1956, and became director, May 1961; was acting president from Apr. to Dec. 1961; and was executive vice-president, 1962–65; was chairman of the building committee; and is now a member of the board of directors of

Lincoln Center and of the Executive and Education committees.

Other Activities. Mr. Young was an instructor at the Wharton Sch. of Finance and Commerce (Univ. of Pennsylvania, 1930–31); and was a part-time faculty member at the American Univ. and George Washington Univ. (1933–39). In Washington, D.C., he worked with the US Dept. of Labor and with the US Employment Service (1933–39); with the executive office of the President of the US and with the bureau of the budget (1939–45); with the Port of NY Authority (1945–46); and was an associate of John D. Rockefeller 3rd (1946–73) and then a consultant; and in Washington, D.C., with the budget director and budget bureau (1951–52).

YOUNG, HARRY L. Stage manager, actor, director. b. Nov. 6, 1910, Grand Rapids, Mich., to Frank F. and Avice (Blakeslee) Young. Married Oct. 7, 1939, to Mary Farrell, actress. Served USN, 1942–45; rank, Radar Technician 3/c. Member of AEA; SAG; AFTRA; The Players. Address: 50 W. 96th St., New York, NY 10025, tel. (212) 866-7081.

Theatre. Mr. Young made his debut at the Community Little Th. (Grand Rapids, Mich., 1934), appearing in such roles as Gordon in *Dangerous Corner*, and Hildy Johnson in *The Front Page*. He directed and appeared in productions at the Woodstock (N.Y.) Th. (Summer 1938), at Brattleboro (Vt., Summers 1939–42).

He made his N.Y.C. debut as Michael Fenet in *Kindred* (Maxine Elliott's Th., Dec. 26, 1939); played Johnny Boyle in *Juno and the Paycock* (Mansfield, Jan. 16, 1940); and Michael Allen in *At the Stroke of 8:00* (Belasco, May 20, 1940); directed and appeared in productions at Brattleboro (Vt., Summers 1946–52) and Albany (N.Y., 1947–52); appeared as the Rev. Samuel Parris in *The Crucible* (Martin Beck Th., N.Y.C., Jan. 23, 1953); *The Flowering Peach*, for which he was the stage manager (Belasco, Dec. 28, 1954).

He served as stage manager for the Salute to France production of *The Skin of Our Teeth*, in which he played a minor role and understudied George Abbott (Th. Sarah Bernhardt, Paris, France, June 1955); was stage manager for *A View from the Bridge* (Coronet, N.Y.C., Sept. 29, 1955); *Major Barbara* (Martin Beck Th., Oct. 30, 1956); *Copper and Brass* (Martin Beck Th., Oct. 17, 1957); *Sunrise at Campobello* (Cort, Jan. 30, 1958); and *Heartbreak House* (Billy Rose Th., Oct. 18, 1959).

Mr. Young toured Europe as stage manager for *Free and Easy* (Jan. 1–Feb. 15, 1960); stage managed *Face of a Hero* (Eugene O'Neill Th., N.Y.C., Oct. 20, 1960); *The Devil's Advocate* (Billy Rose Th., Mar. 9, 1961); *Something About a Soldier* (Ambassador, Jan. 4, 1962); *Isle of Children* (Cort, Mar. 16, 1962); *Tovarich* (Bway Th., Mar. 18, 1963); Richard Burton's *Hamlet* (Lunt-Fontanne, Apr. 9, 1964); *Do I Hear a Waltz?* (46 St. Th., Mar. 18, 1965); *The Zulu and the Zayda* (Cort, Nov. 13, 1965); *Ivanov* (Shubert, May 3, 1966); *Under the Weather* (Cort, Oct. 27, 1966); *South Pacific* (NY State Th., Lincoln Ctr., June 12, 1967); *The Prime of Miss Jean Brodie* (Helen Hayes Th., Jan. 18, 1968); *Angela* (Music Box, Oct. 30, 1969); *Two by Two* (Imperial, Nov. 10, 1970); *Butley* (Morosco, Oct. 16, 1972); *Freedom of the City* (Alvin, Feb. 9, 1974); and *Of Mice and Men* (Brooks Atkinson Th., Dec. 18, 1974).

YOUNG, HOWARD. Producer. b. Howard Luttrell Young, July 16, 1911, Chicago, Ill., to B. M. and Louella C. Young. Father, designing engineer. Grad. Winter Haven (Fla.) H.S. 1928; Univ. of California, B.A., 1936. Married 1941 to Charlotte Brockway; three daughters. Served US Army, Coast Artillery. Member of Musical Arena Theatres Assn. (bd. of dir., 1963); League of NY Theatres; Council of the Living Theatre. Address: (home) 2810 Ontiveros Rd., Santa Ynez, CA 90210, tel. (213) Santa Ynez 4585; (bus.) 457 N. Canon Dr., Beverly Hills, CA 90210, tel. (213) CR 6-9069.

Theatre. Mr. Young was, at first, production manager for a Univ. of California production of *Yellow Jack* (1935); subsequently served as general and company manager for *The Children's Hour* (Curran, San Francisco, 1936); a West Coast tour of *Reflected Glory* (1936); a tour of *Tovarich* (1937); company manager for *A Story to Be Whispered* (Curran, San Francisco, 1937); general manager for a tour of *Candida* (1938).

Mr. Young joined the Los Angeles and San Francisco Civic Light Opera Associations (1938–42). At the Curran Th., San Francisco, and the Philharmonic Aud., Los Angeles, he served as general manager for such productions as *The Student Prince, The New Moon, Broom for the Bride* (1938); *The Cat and the Fiddle, The Gypsy Baron, The Great American Family* (1939); *Show Boat, H.M.S. Pinafore, The Merry Widow* (1940); *Rio Rita, The Chocolate Soldier* (1941); *Bittersweet* and *Music in the Air* (1942).

Also during this period, he was general manager for *Tonight at 8:30* (El Capitan, Hollywood, Calif., 1940); *Charlot's Revue*, which was presented for the benefit of the British War Relief (El Capitan, Hollywood, 1940); a tour of *Anna Christie* (1941); and a West Coast tour of *Goodnight Ladies* (1941).

Mr. Young began his production partnership with Russell Lewis in 1940. Their first production was the national tour of *Meet the Wife* (opened Lobero, Santa Barbara, Calif., 1940); during 1942 at the Belasco Th., Los Angeles, they produced *Grand Guignol (Horror Tonight), Hey, Rockie*, and *Immortal Girl*.

They produced *Desert Song* (NY City Ctr., Jan. 8, 1946), which subsequently toured; Homer Curran, in association with Messrs. Lewis and Young, presented *Obsession* (Plymouth, Oct. 1, 1946), which also toured; and *Lady Windermere's Fan* (Cort, Oct. 14, 1946), which toured: Mr. Young, with Mr. Lewis, produced *The Story of Mary Surrat* (Henry Miller's Th., Feb. 8, 1947); they, with Mr. Curran, presented *Tonight at 8:30* (National, Feb. 20, 1948); Messrs. Lewis and Young produced *Time for Elizabeth* (Fulton, Sept. 27, 1948); and with the Theatre Guild, presented *The Curious Savage* (Martin Beck Th., Oct. 24, 1950).

Lewis & Young Productions also produced tours of *Silver Whistle* (opened Walnut St. Th., Philadelphia, Pa., Mar. 6, 1950; closed La Jolla Playhouse, Calif.); *The Cocktail Party* (opened Curran, San Francisco, Calif., Oct. 15, 1951; closed Royal Alexandra, Toronto, Canada, May 22, 1952); *The Happy Time* (opened Cass, Detroit, Mich., Oct. 22, 1951; closed Blackstone, Chicago, Ill., Jan. 1, 1952); and others.

Since 1951, Messrs. Young and Lewis have been producers at the Sacramento (Calif.) Music Circus. Their productions include *Show Boat, Brigadoon, The Great Waltz, Annie Get Your Gun, The Red Mill, The Desert Song, Naughty Marietta, Rose Marie, Song of Norway* (1951); *The New Moon, The Chocolate Soldier, The Vagabond King, Bloomer Girl, The Student Prince, The Wizard of Oz, The Firefly, Blossom Time, Roberta, Finian's Rainbow, Die Fledermaus* (1952); *Kiss Me Kate, Anything Goes, High Button Shoes, No! No! Nanette!, Hit the Deck, Gentlemen Prefer Blondes, Carousel, Call Me Madam, Carmen* (1953); *Paint Your Wagon, One Touch of Venus, Wish You Were Here, New Faces of 1952, Where's Charley?, Rio Rita, Oklahoma!* (1954); *On the Town, The Mikado, South Pacific, The Red Mill, Guys and Dolls* (1955); *The King and I, Kismet, Music in the Air, Girl Crazy, Plain and Fancy, Panama Hattie* (1956); *Peter Pan, The Teahouse of the August Moon, The Boy Friend, Silk Stockings* (1957); *Happy Hunting, Pipe Dream, Fanny, Rosalinda, Irene, Wonderful Town, The Most Happy Fella* (1958); *Li'l Abner, Tom Sawyer, Auntie Mame* (1959); *Meet Me in St. Louis, Redhead, West Side Story* (1960); *Destry Rides Again, The Chocolate Soldier, Cinderella, Take Me Along, Pal Joey* (1961); *Gypsy, Fiorello!* (1962); *The Unsinkable Molly Brown, Anything Goes, Irma La Douce*, and *West Side Story* (1963); *The Boys from Syracuse, Flower Drum Song, My Fair Lady, She Loves Me, The Sound of Music*, and *Stop the World* (1964); *Bye Bye Birdie, Camelot, Forum, Music Man*, and *110 in the Shade* (1965); *How To Succeed in Business without Really Trying* and *Oliver* (1966); *The Fantasticks, Funny Girl, Half a Sixpence*, and *On a Clear Day* (1967); *Heydey of Burlesque* (1968); *Mame, George M.*, and *State Fair* (1969); *Cabaret, I Do, I Do*, and *Man of La Mancha* (1970); *Fiddler on the Roof* and *Hello Dolly* (1971); *Promises, Promises* and *1776* (1972); *Applause* and *Godspell* (1973); and *Once Upon a Mattress, Gigi*, and *No, No, Nanette* (1974).

Since 1962, Lewis & Young Productions has produced at the Lewis & Young Dinner Th. (Garden Court, Sheraton Palace, San Francisco, Calif.): *Guys and Dolls, Take Me Along, Damn Yankees, Can-Can, The Bells Are Ringing, The Boy Friend, The Pajama Game* and *The Music Man* (1962); *The Flower Drum Song, The Student Prince, Bye Bye Birdie, Wildcat* and *South Pacific* (1963).

In 1966, under the auspices of the US State Dept., Lewis and Young toured South America playing *Carousel* and *Show Boat* in repertory in Mexico City, Guadalajara, Caracas, and other cities.

Messrs. Lewis and Young also produced the Fresno Music Th. productions of *My Fair Lady* and *The Sound of Music* (1964); *South Pacific, Guys and Dolls, Oklahoma*, and *Forum* (1965); *Oliver, Camelot, How To Succeed in Business without Really Trying, Carousel*, and *Show Boat* (1966).

In 1972, Messrs. Lewis and Young produced *Cabaret* in Las Vegas at the Union Plaza Hotel.

Recreation. Golf, swimming, riding & scuba diving.

YOUNG, JOHN WRAY. Director, writer, educator. b. July 5, 1909, Bloomfield, Iowa, to John Wray and Myra (Colliver) Young. Father, physician. Grad. Iowa Univ., B.A. 1929; graduate study, 1933. Married Oct. 5, 1929, to Margaret Mary Anderson, designer; one son, one daughter. Member of SWTC (co-fdr., 1948, pres., 1952); AETA (pres., 1959); ANTA (bd. of dir., 1952–58); NCTC (vice-pres., 1963–65); ACTA; The Players; Rotary Club; Beta Theta Pi. Address: (home) 704 Huron, Shreveport, LA 71106, tel. (318) 868-4924; (bus.) c/o Shreveport Little Theatre, 812 Margaret Place, Shreveport, LA 71102, tel. (318) 424-4439.

Theatre. Mr. Young's first professional assignment was director of the Sioux City (Iowa) Little Th. (1929–31); subsequently became instructor in theatre at the State Univ. of Iowa (1931–32); was guest director at the Pasadena (Calif.) Playhouse (1933); director of the Duluth (Minn.) Playhouse (1933–36), founder of the Duluth (Minn.) Summer Th. Sch. (1934); director of the Little Th. in Shreveport (La., 1936); and head of the Drama Dept. at Centenary Coll. (1936–45).

He has lectured at Univ. of Alabama, Yale Univ., Texas Christian Univ., Oklahoma Univ., Kansas Univ., and Michigan Univ., and was guest professor at Wisconsin Univ. (1959–61), Univ. of Denver (1958), Louisiana State Univ. (1941), and Texas Woman's Univ. (1963).

Mr. Young and his wife, designer Margaret Mary, have directed the Shreveport (La.) Little Th., staging some 300 major productions as a director-designer team (1936–73).

Mr. Young has played leading roles in *Loyalties, The Swan, The Tailor-Made Man, There's Always Juliet, Libel, The Wind and the Rain, Kind Lady, The Man Who Came to Dinner, On Borrowed Time, Uncle Harry* and *Harvey*.

With Margaret Mary Young he has appeared in *Mr. and Mrs. North, Angel Street, State of the Union, Pygmalion, Candida, Still Life, The Great Sebastians, The Village Wooing* and *Dear Liar*. .

Published Works. He contributed "Community Theatre" to John Gassner's *Producing the Play* (1941); wrote *The Community Theatre and How It Works* (1958); *Directing the Play from Selection to Opening Night* (1959–73); with Margaret Mary Young, wrote *How to Produce the Play* (1961); wrote *Audition Scenes for Students*, volumes I & II (1967; 1973); *Community Theatre—A Manual for Success* (1971); and *Play Direction for the High School Theatre* (1974).

He has written articles in *Theatre Arts, Players* Magazine. *Dramatics* Magazine and *Educational Theatre Journal*. .

Awards. Mr. Young received the Palm Award from *Stage* Magazine (1937, 1939); the Award of Merit from SWTC (1953); from AETA (1959); and an award (1962) from the Advertising Club in Shreveport (La.) for the best advertisement for "advancing favorably the name of Shreveport throughout the region and the Nation." Award from The Theatre of Louisiana (1973). Distinguished Service Award from Southwest Theatre Conference (1974).

YOUNG, MARGARET MARY. Designer, director. b. Margaret Mary Anderson, Apr. 24, 1911, Cedar Rapids, Iowa, to Samuel and Neda (Lacy) Anderson. Father, railroader; mother, school supplies executive. Grad. Mt. Mercy Acad., 1926; Univ. of Iowa, B.A. (theatre) 1930, graduate study, 1933. Married Oct. 5, 1929, to John Wray Young, director, author; one son, one daughter. Member of AETA (bd., 1957–59); ANTA; ACTA (bd., 1962–64); Theta Phi Alpha; Natl. Thespians (hon.); Phi Beta (hon.); Southwest Th. Conf. Address: (home) 704 Huron, Shreveport, LA 71106, tel. (318) 868-4924; (bus.) Shreveport Little Theatre, 812 Margaret Place, Shreveport, LA 71102, tel. (318) 424-4439.

Since 1959, Mrs. Young has been director of the Lagniappe series, which she founded for the Shreveport Little Th., where she has been designer since 1936. With her husband, as director, she has designed about 250 productions for the Shreveport Little Th.

She first worked as designer for the Sioux City (Iowa) Little Th. (1929–31); subsequently founded and directed the Iowa Univ. Children's Th. (1932); and was designer for the Duluth (Minn.) Playhouse (1933–36), where she and her husband founded the Duluth Summer Theatre Sch.

She has taught theatre at the Univ. of Wisconsin, Centenary Coll. and Louisiana State Univ.

Margaret Mary Young has appeared at the Shreveport Little Th. in *But Not Goodby,* and with John Wray Young in *Angel Street, Mr. and Mrs. North, State of the Union, Pygmalion, Candida, Still Life, The Great Sebastians, The Village Wooing,* and *Dear Liar.*.

Published Works. She wrote, with her husband, *How To Produce the Play.*.

Awards. In 1964, she received the first annual Shreveport *Journal* Theatre Award for her direction of the Lagniappe series; an award from The Theatres of Louisiana (1973); and the Distinguished Service Award from the Southwest Th. Conf. (1974).

Recreation. Writing.

YOUNG, NORMA. Theatre administrator, actress, director, educator. b. Norma Young Smith, Aug. 2, 1928, Dallas, Tex., to T. G., Sr., and Helen (Holbrook) Smith. Father, railroad man; mother, government employee. Educ. Dallas, Tex., public schools; Sul Ross State Univ., Alpine, Tex.; Columbia Univ. Professional training with Mrs. Freda G. Powell, Sul Ross; Nina Vance, Alley Th., Houston, Tex. Married July 1, 1961, to William Jac Alder, theatre manager. Member of Alpha Psi Omega. Address: (home) 2704 Routh, Apt. 4, Dallas, TX 75201, tel. (214) 823-4187; (bus.) 2800 Routh (Theatre Three), Dallas, TX 75201, tel. (214) 748-5191.

Pre-Theatre. Receptionist, secretary, and teacher in public secondary schools.

Theatre. Miss Young appeared in productions as a student at Sul Ross State Univ., in the title role of *Laura* (Spring 1948), as Ruth in *Blithe Spirit* (Fall 1950), and as Margaret in *The Hasty Heart* (Spring 1951). She directed *The Innocents, The Home of the Brave, Mrs. McThing,* and *Julius Caesar* at McCamey (Tex.) High School (1951–55); at Galveston Little Th., she played Sabrina in *Sabrina Fair* (Fall 1955), Jennet in *The Lady's Not for Burning* (Spring 1956), and Gladys in *The Pajama Game* (Fall 1956); and at Summer Circle Th., Galveston, directed five productions (Summer 1956).

At the Alley Th., Houston, Tex., she was stage manager (June 1957–Fall 1958); played Calpurnia in *Julius Caesar,* the Daughter in *Middle of the Night* (both Fall 1957); was choral director for *Seventeen* (Spring 1958); and played Minnie Fay in *The Matchmaker* (Fall 1958). She appeared off-Bway in N.Y.C. as Katharine of Aragon and Anne Boleyn in *The Royal Gambit* (Sullivan St. Playhouse, Mar. 4, 1959); was stage manager of thirteen productions at Cherry County (Mich.) Playhouse (Spring 1959); and in N.Y.C. for *The Power of Darkness* (York Playhouse, Sept. 29, 1959).

In 1961, Miss Young founded Theatre Three in Dallas, and she has been its artistic director to date. She directed many of Theatre Three's productions, including the first seven, which were staged in the ballroom of the Sheraton Dallas Hotel (Mar.–Oct. 1961): *The Reluctant Debutante, The Lady's Not for Burning, Home of the Brave, Liliom, Born Yesterday, Sabrina Fair,* and *Waiting for Godot.* From Oct. 1961 to 1969, Theatre Three was located in a theatre that had been converted from a garage; during that period, Miss Young directed *Six Characters in Search of an Author, Mrs. McThing, The Member of the Wedding, The Moon Is Blue,* a revival of *Waiting for Godot, Look Back in Anger, The Little Foxes, The Tavern,* and *Don Juan in Hell* (all 1961–62); *Light Up the Sky, Two for the Seesaw, The Hostage,* and *The New Drunkard* (all 1962–63); *The Caretaker, The Night of the Iguana, Champagne Complex, The Emperor Jones, The American Dream, Zoo Story, Count Dracula,* and she played Mary L. in *The Time of Your Life* (all 1963–64); she played Madame Rosepettle in *Oh Dad, Poor Dad* and directed *The Tender Trap, Tea and Sympathy, Of Mice and Men,* and *Alice in Wonderland* (all 1964–65); directed *Write Me a Murder, In White America, Cat's Eye, The Solid Gold Cadillac,* and *Visit to a Small Planet* (all 1965–66); *The Devil's Disciple,* played Widow Begbick in *A Man's a Man* and directed *The Maids, Miss Julie,* and *The Spare Rib* (all 1966–67); directed *Eh?, The Innocents,* and *Pantagleize* (all 1967–68); played the Queen in *The Cave Dwellers* and directed *The Miracle Worker* (both 1968–69).

In 1969, Theatre Three moved into a new home in Dallas's Quadrangle Center, where Miss Young directed *Tartuffe, Celebration, The Adding Machine,* and played the title role in *Hedda Gabler* (all 1969–70); played the Fortune Teller in *The Skin of Our Teeth* (1970–71); directed *The Rainmaker* and played the title role in *Colette* (1971–72); directed *The School for Wives,* a revival of *The Emperor Jones,* and played Catherine Reardon in *And Miss Reardon Drinks a Little* (1972–73); and played Lady Bracknell in *The Importance of Being Earnest* and Clytemnestra in *Electra* (1973–74).

Awards. Miss Young was named Dallas "Showman of the Year" (1961) and received Titche's (Dallas) Arete Award for excellence (1963).

Recreation. Reading poetry, histories, and mysteries. Miss Young states that she enjoys reading aloud, particularly poetry, and she has done taping for the blind. She also maintains collections of family, theatrical, and literary memorabilia.

YOUNG, STANLEY. Executive, playwright. b. Stanley Preston Young, Feb. 3, 1906, Greencastle, Ind., to Augustus and Martha (Watson) Young. Father, businessman. Grad. Univ. of Chicago, Ph.B. 1929; attended Univ. of Grenoble, France, 1927–28; Univ. of Munich, Germany, 1929–30; grad. Columbia Univ., M.A. 1930. Married Dec. 20, 1929, to Margaret Elneth Linde (marr. dis. 1940); one son, two daughters; married Dec. 20, 1941, to Nancy Wilson Ross. Served USAAF, Foreign Correspondent, ETO, 1944–45. Relative in theatre: nephew, James Young, director. Member of Dramatists Guild; ALA (council, 1941); ALC (bd. of dir., 1946–60); Dramatists Play Service (bd. of dir., 1950–62); The Players (bd. of dir., 1956–58); The Owl and Serpent; Japan Society; The Century Assn. (1964–to date); Sigma Nu. Address: Old Westbury, L.I., NY 11568.

Theatre. Mr. Young was executive director of American National Theatre and Academy (ANTA) (1959–65).

He wrote *Robin Landing* (46 St. Th., N.Y.C., Nov. 18, 1937); *Bright Rebel* (Lyceum, Dec. 27, 1938); *Ask My Friend Sandy* (Biltmore, Feb. 4, 1943); *Mr. Pickwick* (Plymouth, Sept. 16, 1952), which previously had been presented in London (Westminster, Feb. 7, 1951); and the pre-Bway tryout of *Laurette* (opened Shubert, New Haven, Conn., Sept. 26, 1960; closed Philadelphia, Oct. 7, 1960).

He wrote the one-act plays: *Farmer Brown's Pig* (1940), *A Bunyan Yarn* (1945), and *The Sound of Apples* (1957), all included in *The Best One-Act Plays* series; and wrote a revised version of *Laurette* (Dublin Intl. Th. Festival, Ireland, Sept. 22, 1964).

Other Activities. Mr. Young was instructor of English at Polytechnic Inst. of Brooklyn (1930–31); Williams Coll. (1931–34); literary advisor, MacMillan Co., publishers (N.Y.C., 1934–36); literary critic NY *Times* (1936–to date); editor, Harcourt, Brace and Co., N.Y.C. (1937–40); managing director, Bollingen Foundation (1942–47); director, Farrar, Straus & Co., N.Y.C. (1945–to date); partner, Farrar, Straus & Young, N.Y.C., (1950–55); chairman of the exec. committee, National Council on the Arts (1965–67); and professor of drama and special presidential assistant for the arts, Hofstra Univ. (1965–73).

Published Works. Mr. Young wrote the novel *Sons without Anger* (1939); three books for children, *Young Hickory* (1940), *Mayflower Boy* (1944); and *Tippecanoe and Tyler Too* (1959); and has contributed articles and verse to magazines.

Awards. Mr. Young received two Rockefeller Foundation Fellowships (1937, 1938); the John Golden Fellowship for Playwriting (1938); his play *Mr. Pickwick* was chosen for *Theatre '53;* and his one-act play, *The Sound of Apples* received a verse-play prize from the Acad. of Amer. Poets and CBS (1957).

Recreation. Tennis, skiing.

Z

ZANK, RIC. Director, actor. b. Eau Claire, Wisc., to Richard A. and Janis (Rowland) Zank. Attended Univ. of Wisconsin at Eau Claire and Madison; Acad. of Dramatic Art, Rochester, Mich. Address: (home) 331 So. Johnson, Iowa City, IA 52240, tel. (319) 351-0392; (bus.) P.O. Box 1122, Iowa City, IA 52240, tel. (319) 353-3346.

Pre-Theatre. Under the auspices of the Peace Corps, Mr. Zank taught the Nepali language to the Gurung tribe in Nepal (1963–65).

Theatre. Mr. Zank is the artistic director of the Iowa Theatre Lab (Iowa City).

While attending the Univ. of Wisc. (1965–67), Mr. Zank played Nichols in *J. B.;* the King in *Escurial;* Matt Stanton in *Hogan's Goat;* Geoff in *A Taste of Honey;* Oswald in *Ghosts;* and the Director in *No Exit.* In summer stock (Green Ram Th., Baraboo, Wisc., Summer 1966) he played Bob in *Mary, Mary;* the Judge in *The Chalk Garden;* and Ferdinand in *The Italian Straw Hat;* at the F. A. Bower Th. (Flint, Mich., Summer 1968) played Bentley in *Misalliance;* Pantalone in *The Servant of Two Masters;* and the title role in *Tartuffe;* subsequently played Jack in *The Second Coming of Bert,* and Black Circle in *The Imperial Nightingale* (Meadow Brook Th., Rochester, Mich., 1969); for the Champlain Shakespeare Festival (Burlington, Vt., 1969) played the Old Shepherd in *The Winter's Tale,* Catesby in *Richard III,* and Lodovico in *Othello;* with the Milwaukee (Wisc.) Repertory Th. (1969–70), played Puck in *A Midsummer Night's Dream;* and Michael in *The Kitchen;* again with the Champlain Shakespeare Festival (Burlington, Vt., 1970); played Agamemnon in *Troilus and Cressida,* and Sir Andrew Aguecheek in *Twelfth Night.*

With the Iowa Theatre Lab. (Iowa City), Mr. Zank directed *Reflexa* (Jan. 1971); *Othello Variations* (Jan. 1971); *Osiris* (Nov.–Dec. 1971); and *The Naming* (Oct. and Dec. 1972), which was subsequently presented at the Chelsea Theatre Center (Brooklyn, N.Y., April 1973), The Festival Mondial du Theatre (Nancy, France, Apr.–May 1973) and Espace

Pierre Cardin (Paris, May–June 1973); and *Dancer Without Arms* (March–Apr. 1974).

Recreation. Films, collecting classical records, poetry.

ZIMBALIST, EFREM JR. Actor, producer, composer. b. Nov. 30, 1918, New York City to Efrem and Alma (Gluck) Zimbalist. Father, concert violinist; mother, operatic soprano. Grad. St. Paul's H.S., Concord, N.H.; attended Yale Univ., 1935–37; studied acting at Neighborhood Playhouse Sch. of the Th., N.Y.C. Married 1942, to Emily McNair (dec. 1950); one son; one daughter; married Feb. 2, 1956, to Loranda Stephanie Spaulding (marr. dis., Dec. 5, 1961; subsequently remarr.); one daughter. Enlisted (Apr. 2, 1941) US Army; rank, 1st Lt. Member of AEA; SAG; AFTRA. Address: Encino, CA.

Pre-Theatre. NBC page.

Theatre. Mr. Zimbalist made his N.Y.C. debut succeeding (Dec. 1945) Rex Williams as Gil Hartnick in *The Rugged Path* (Plymouth Th., Nov. 10, 1945); subsequently appeared with the American Repertory Th. (Intl. Th.), as the Duke of Suffolk in *Henry VIII* (Nov. 6, 1946), a Butler in *What Every Woman Knows* (Nov. 8, 1946), Secutor in *Androcles and the Lion* (Dec. 19, 1946), and Aristides Agramonte in *Yellow Jack* (Feb. 2, 1947).

With Chandler Cowles and Edyth Lutyens, he produced *The Telephone* and *The Medium* (Ethel Barrymore Th., May 1, 1947); appeared as Eilert Lovborg in the American Repertory Th. production of *Hedda Gabler* (Cort, Feb. 24, 1948); produced, again with Chandler Cowles and Edith Lutyens, *The Consul* (Ethel Barrymore Th., Mar. 15, 1950); played a season of stock at the Bucks County Playhouse (New Hope, Pa., Summer 1955); played Maurice Duclos in *Fallen Angels* (Playhouse, Jan. 17, 1956); and was narrator of Copland's *A Lincoln Portrait* (Acad. of Music, Philadelphia, Pa., Jan. 21, 1961).

Films. Mr. Zimbalist made his debut as Tony in *House of Strangers* (20th-Fox, 1949); played Col. Jim Herlihy in *Bomber B-52* (WB, 1957); Ethan Sears in *Band of Angels* (WB, 1957); Lt. Blanchard in *The Deep Six* (WB, 1958); Jake Diamond in *Home Before Dark* (WB, 1958); in *Violent Road* (WB, 1958); Vincent Bryant in *Too Much, Too Soon* (WB, 1958); Dale Heath in *Crowded Sky* (WB, 1961); Judge Leland Hoffman in *A Fever in the Blood* (WB, 1961); Arthur Winner in *By Love Possessed* (UA, 1961); Paul Radford in *The Chapman Report* (WB, 1962); Frank Bryant in *The Reward* (20th-Fox, 1965); William Mansfield in *Harlow* (Magna, 1965); Sam in *Wait Until Dark* (WB, 1967); and Stacy in *Airport 1975* (U, 1974).

Television. Mr. Zimbalist starred as Stuart Bailey in the series, 77 Sunset Strip (ABC, premiere Oct. 10, 1958, through Spring 1964); and as Inspector Lewis Erskine in the series The FBI (ABC, premiere Sept. 19, 1965, through Spring 1974). He made his debut as a regular on the daytime series Concerning Miss Marlowe (NBC, season 1954–55). He has also performed in *Stopover at Sublimity* (CBS, Aug. 1, 1956); Reporter (CBS), Rawhide (CBS); Hawaiian Eye (Ind.); Alfred Hitchcock Presents (NBC); Insight (Ind.); the Christopher Program series (Ind.); narrated an Apollo 11 Mission documentary (ABC, July 21, 1969); and appeared in *Who Is the Black Dahlia?* (NBC, Feb. 1975).

Other Activities. From 1950–54, he served as an assistant to his father at the Curtis Inst. of Music (Philadelphia, Pa.). His composition, *"Laudate Dominum," a choral setting of the 150th Psalm, was presented in a concert at Town Hall (N.Y.C., 1955).*

Recreation. Music, swimming, tennis.

ZINDEL, PAUL. Playwright, author. b. May 15, 1936, Staten Island, N.Y. Grad. Wagner Coll., N.Y., B.S., M.A. Married 1973 to Bonnie Hildebrand; one son.

Pre-Theatre. Mr. Zindel was a chemistry teacher at Tottenville (N.Y.) H.S. (1960–69) and held other teaching positions.

Theatre. Mr. Zindel's plays include *Dimensions of Peacocks* (prod. N.Y.C., 1959; Eleanor Gould Th., Oct. 21, 1961); *Euthanasia and the Endless Hearts* (N.Y.C., 1960); *A Dream of Swallows* (Jan Hus House, Apr. 14, 1964); *The Effects of Gamma Rays on Man-in-the-Moon Marigolds* (Alley Th., Houston, Tex., May 12, 1965; Mercer-O'Casey Th., N.Y.C., Apr. 7, 1970); *And Miss Reardon Drinks a Little* (Mark Taper Forum, Los Angeles, Calif., 1967; Morosco, N.Y.C., Feb. 25, 1971); *The Secret Affairs of Mildred Wild* (Ambassador, Nov. 14, 1972); and *Ladies at the Alamo* (Actors Studio, May 29, 1975).

Films. Mr. Zindel wrote scripts for *Up the Sandbox* (National, 1972) and *Mame* (WB, 1974).

Published Works. In addition to his plays, Mr. Zindel has written several children's books, including *I Love My Mother* (1975), and is the author of three adult novels: *The Pigman* (1968); *My Darling, My Hamburger* (1969); and *I Never Loved Your Mind* (1970).

Awards. Mr. Zindel was awarded the honorary degree of D.H.L. by Wagner Univ. (1971). *The Effect of Gamma Rays on Man-in-the-Moon Marigolds* received a Pulitzer Prize (1971), a *Village Voice* Off-Bway (Obie) Award (1970) as best play of its season, and a NY Drama Critics Circle Award (1970) as best American play, and Mr. Zindel received a Vernon Rice Drama Desk Award (1970) as most promising playwright.

ZIPPRODT, PATRICIA. Costume designer. b. Feb. 24, 1925, Evanston, Ill., to Herbert Edward and Irene (Turpin) Zipprodt. Grad. Wellesley Coll., A.B. (sociology) 1946. Professional training at Chicago Art Institute, 1935–49; Fashion Institute of Technology, N.Y.C., 1952–53. Address: 45 University Place, New York, NY 10003, tel. (212) 677-3142.

Theatre. Miss Zipprodt was assistant to the costume designer for *The Amazing Adele* (opened Shubert Th., Philadelphia, Pa., Dec. 26, 1955; closed Shubert Th., Boston, Mass., 1956). She designed costumes for *The Potting Shed* (Bijou Th., N.Y.C., Jan. 29, 1957); *A Visit to a Small Planet* (Booth Th., Feb. 7, 1957); for a Jean Giraudoux double bill: *The Virtuous Island* and *The Apollo of Bellac* (Carnegie Hall Playhouse, Apr. 9, 1957); *Miss Lonelyhearts* (Music Box, Oct. 3, 1957); and *The Rope Dancers* (Cort, Nov. 20, 1957).

Also for *The Crucible* (Martinique, Mar. 11, 1958); *Back to Methusaleh* (Ambassador, Mar 26, 1958); *The Night Circus* (John Golden Th., Dec. 2, 1958); *Our Town* (Circle in the Square, Mar. 23, 1959); *The Gang's All Here* (Ambassador, Oct. 1, 1959); *The Balcony* (Circle in the Square, Mar. 3, 1960); and *Camino Real* (St. Mark's Playhouse, May 16, 1960). She designed costumes for *Period of Adjustment* (Helen Hayes Th., Nov. 10, 1960); *The Blacks* (St. Mark's Playhouse, May 4, 1961); *The Garden of Sweets* (ANTA Th., Oct. 31, 1961); *Sunday in New York* (Cort, Nov. 29, 1961); *Madame Aphrodite* (Orpheum Th., Dec. 29, 1961); *Oh Dad, Poor Dad, Mama's Hung You in the Closet and I'm Feeling So Sad* (Phoenix, Feb. 26, 1962); *A Man's a Man* (Masque Th., Sept. 19, 1962); and *Step on a Crack* (Ethel Barrymore Th., Oct. 17, 1962).

Miss Zipprodt also designed costumes for *The Dragon* (Phoenix Th., Apr. 9, 1963); *She Loves Me* (Eugene O'Neill Th., Apr. 23, 1963); *Oh Dad, Poor Dad, Mama's Hung You in the Closet and I'm Feeling So Sad* (Morosco, Aug. 27, 1963); and *Morning Sun* (Phoenix, Oct. 6, 1963). Also for *Too Much Johnson* (Phoenix, Jan. 15, 1964); *Fiddler on the Roof* (Imperial, Sept. 22, 1964); *The Tragical Historie of Dr. Faustus* (Phoenix, Oct. 5, 1964); *Anya* (Ziegfeld Th., Nov. 29, 1965); *Pousse-Café* (46 St. Th., Mar. 18, 1966); *Cabaret* (Broadhurst, Nov. 20, 1966); *The Little Foxes* (Vivian Beaumont Th., Oct. 26, 1967); and *Plaza Suite* (Plymouth, Feb. 14, 1968).

She designed costumes for *Zorba* (Imperial, Nov. 17, 1968); *1776 (46 St. Th., Mar. 16, 1969); Georgy* (Winter Garden Th., Feb. 26, 1970); *Scratch* (St. James Th., May 6, 1971); *Pippin* (Imperial, Oct. 23, 1972); *The Mother of Us All* (Guggenheim Museum, N.Y.C., Nov. 26, 1972); *Dear Nobody* (Cherry Lane Th., Feb. 19, 1974); *Mack & Mabel* (Majestic, Oct. 6, 1974); and *All God's Chillun Got Wings* (Circle in the Square, Mar. 20, 1975).

Miss Zipprodt's work also includes costume designs for American Ballet Theatre's *Les Noces* (1965); National Ballet's *La Sonnambula* (1965); for *The Poppet* (1969); and for other ballets; and she has designed costumes for Boston Opera Co. productions of *Madama Butterfly* and *La Bohème* and for operas produced by the NY City Opera.

Films. Miss Zipprodt designed costumes for *The Graduate* (Embassy, 1967) and *The Last of the Mobile Hotshots* (WB, 1969).

Awards. Miss Zipprodt received Antoinette Perry (Tony) awards for her costumes for *Fiddler on the Roof* (1965) and *Cabaret* (1967) and was a *Variety* poll winner in 1967 for *Cabaret.* She received a Joseph Maharam Award in 1969 for her costumes for *1776.* In 1970, she was a *Variety* poll winner for *1776* and runner-up for *Zorba.* She also received Tony nominations in 1969 for her costumes for *Zorba,* in 1973 for *Pippin,* and in 1975 for *Mack & Mabel.*

ZORINA, VERA. Dancer, actress. b. Eva Brigitta Hartwig, Jan. 2, 1917, Berlin, Germany, to Fritz and Billi (Wimpelmann) Hartwig. Studied dancing with Mme. Edwardova; Tatiana and Victor Gsovsky, Berlin; Anton Dolin and N. Legat, London. Married Dec. 24, 1938, to George Balanchine, choreographer (marr. dis., 1946); married 1946 to Goddard Lieberson; two sons. Member of AEA; SAG; AGMA.

Theatre. Miss Zorina made her first stage appearance as the First Fairy in *A Midsummer Night's Dream* (Berlin, Germany, 1930); subsequently danced in *Tales of Hoffman* (Berlin, 1931); appeared at the Gaiety Th. (London, Oct. 10, 1933); toured with the Ballet Russe de Monte Carlo in *Boutique Fantastique; Bleu Danube;* and *Cotillon* (1934–36); and played Vera Barnova in *On Your Toes* (London, 1936).

She made her N.Y.C. debut as Angel in *I Married an Angel* (Shubert Th., May 11, 1938); subsequently played Marina Van Linden in *Louisiana Purchase* (Imperial, May 28, 1940); with the Ballet Th., danced the title role in *Helen of Troy,* Terpsichore in *Apollo,* and *Petrouchka* (1943). She appeared as Ariel in *The Tempest* (Alvin, N.Y.C., Jan. 25, 1945); and Suzette in *Temporary Island* (Maxine Elliott's Th., Mar. 14, 1948). In concert, she spoke the title role in *Jeanne d'Arc au bûcher* (Carnegie Hall, 1948); and was narrator of *A Parable of Death* (Louisville, Ky., Mar. 1953; Town Hall, N.Y.C., Apr. 1953); and played Vera Barnova in *On Your Toes* (46 St. Th., Oct. 11, 1954). She performed the title role in *Persephone* (Salzburg Festival, Aust., 1955); Venere in *Ballo delle ingrate* (Lyric Th., Chicago, Ill., 1955); and the title role in *Persephone* (Rome Opera House, Italy, Apr. 1956).

Miss Zorina has performed as narrator with all major symphonies (1956–to date) in works by Honegger, Stravinsky, Milhand, Schoenberg, and Walton. For the Santa Fe (N.Mex.) Opera Co. she has directed *La Boheme, Madama Butterfly, Dialogue of the Carmelites, Daphne,* and *Capsiccio;* and, for NY City Opera (N.Y. State Th., Lincoln Ctr., Fall 1967), directed *Pagliacci* and *Cavallaria Rusticana.* In Oslo (Norway), she directed *Cabaret* (Det Nye Th., Oslo, Norway).

Films. Miss Zorina made her debut in *The Goldwyn Follies* (UA, 1938); followed by *On Your Toes* (WB, 1939); *I Was an Adventuress* (20th-Fox, 1940); *Louisiana Purchase* (Par., 1941); *Star Spangled Rhythm* (Par., 1942); *Follow the Boys* (U, 1944); and *Lover Come Back* (U, 1946).

Night Clubs. Miss Zorina has appeared at Ciro's (London, 1934).

ZUNSER, JESSE. Editor, drama and film critic. b. 1898, New York City, to Philip and Bertha Zunser. Grad. Manual Training H.S., Bklyn., 1914; City Coll. of New York, 1918. Married 1920, to Mary Singer, writer; one daughter. Served WW I, US Army, SATC. Member of NY Drama Critics Circle, The Drama Desk, Outer Circle, Overseas Press Club. Address: 303 E. 37th St., New York,

NY 10016.

Mr. Zunser was an editor on staff for the *American Jewish News* (1918–20); and free-lance advertising and feature magazine and newspaper writer (1920–33).

In 1933, he became the first editor of *Cue* Magazine; and has been editor, executive, managing editor, and film critic (1933–to date); drama editor (1940–45), holding all three positions simultaneously. After having reviewed more than 12,000 films and 500 plays, Mr. Zunser retired from *Cue* in 1964. He has since been contributing editor of *Film Bulletin* (Philadelphia, Pa.); *Dimensions Magazine Quarterly;* and a *Motion Picture* consultant.

Recreation. Piano, chess, photography.

ZWERDLING, ALLEN. Newspaper publisher, director, editor, writer. b. Allen Paul Zwerdling, Oct. 11, 1922, Brooklyn, N.Y., to William and Yetta (Nagler) Zwerdling. Father in wholesale produce business. Grad. S. J. Tilden H.S., Brooklyn, N.Y. 1940; City Coll. of New York, B.S. 1946. Studied with June Justice and Frank Nagler, Players Guild of Manhattan, N.Y.C., 1930–41; Dr. Oscar Wertelin, Zurich Schauspielhaus, Switzerland, 1946–47. Served USAF, Special Services, 1942–45; was also physical education instructor. Married Dec. 2, 1946, to Shirley Hoffman; one son, two daughters. Member of the Drama Desk. *Back Stage*, 165 W. 46th St., New York, NY 10036, tel. (212) LT1-1080.

Theatre. Mr.Zwerdling made his debut at age eight at the Players Guild of Manhattan, as actor and stage manager; subsequently was producer-director of the American Players (Zurich, Switzerland, 1946–47); assistant to the director of the Zurich State Th. (1946–47); director of the Kansas City Resident Th. (1947–48); producer-director of 95 servicemen shows for USAF Special Services; director of the City Coll. of New York Th. Workshop; and actor-stage manager of the Players Guild (N.Y.C.). He wrote for and edited a weekly theatrical trade paper, *Show Business*, and eight other theatrical periodicals (1948–60); was editor of the US Army newspaper in Foggia, Italy; wrote three short plays, published by the US Army Special Services; nationally syndicated stories on the theatre that have appeared in more than 350 newspapers; and has been publisher and managing editor of *Back Stage*, a trade paper covering television commercials and industrials, theatre, and other fields, and editor of *Back Stage Television, Film, Tape & Syndication Directory.*